INTERNATIONAL LITERARY MARKET PLACE™

ILMP 2003

International Literary Market Place™
36th Edition

Publisher
Thomas H. Hogan

Managing Director
Owen O'Donnell

Senior Editor
Karen Hallard

Associate Editors
Kevin Araujo, Kathryn Eaton, Mary-Anne Lutter

Tampa Operations:

Manager, Tampa Editorial Operations
Debbie James

Project Coordinator
Carolyn Victor

Associate Project Coordinator
Paula Watts

Data Entry Clerk
John Begg

INTERNATIONAL LITERARY MARKET PLACE™

ILMP 2003

The Directory of the International Book Publishing Industry

OVER 180 COUNTRIES COVERED

Published by

Information Today, Inc.
143 Old Marlton Pike
Medford, NJ 08055-8750
Phone: (609) 654-6266
Fax: (609) 654-4309
E-mail (Orders): custserv@infotoday.com
Web site: http://www.infotoday.com
Copyright 2002, Information Today, Inc. All Rights Reserved

ISSN 0074-6827
ISBN 1-57387-144-3
Library of Congress Catalog Card Number: 77-70295

© COPYRIGHT 2002 INFORMATION TODAY, INC. All rights reserved. No part of this publication may be reproduced, stored in a retrieval system, or transmitted, in any form or by any means, electronic, mechanical, photocopy, recording, or otherwise without the prior written permission of the publisher.

Information Today, Inc. uses reasonable care to obtain accurate and timely information. However, Information Today, Inc. disclaims any liability to any party for any loss or damage caused by errors or omission in *International Literary Market Place*™ whether or not such errors or omissions result from negligence, accident or any other cause.

Printed in the United States of America

CONTENTS

Preface ... vii
Editorial Revision Form ... ix
Copyright Conventions ... xi
The ISBN System ... xiii
Abbreviations ... xxiii

PUBLISHING

Publishers ... 1
   Type of Publication Index ... 771
   Subject Index ... 873
Literary Agents ... 1109
International Publishing Services ... 1123
Translation Agencies & Associations ... 1125

MANUFACTURING

Complete Book Manufacturing ... 1131
   Prepress Services Index ... 1147
Prepress Services ... 1153
   Printing, Binding & Book Finishing Index ... 1169
Printing, Binding & Book Finishing ... 1193
   Manufacturing Materials Index ... 1209
Manufacturing Materials ... 1211
   Manufacturing Services & Equipment Index ... 1219
Manufacturing Services & Equipment ... 1221

BOOK TRADE INFORMATION

Book Clubs ... 1127
Book Trade Organizations ... 1235
Major Book Dealers ... 1271
Book Trade Reference Books & Journals ... 1327

LITERARY ASSOCIATIONS & PRIZES

Literary Associations & Societies ... 1359
Literary Prizes ... 1373

BOOK TRADE CALENDAR

   Alphabetical Index of Sponsors ... 1415
   Alphabetical Index of Events ... 1421
Calendar of Book Trade & Promotional Events ... 1427

LIBRARY RESOURCES

Major Libraries ... 1449
Library Associations ... 1511
Library Reference Books & Journals ... 1527

INDEXES

Industry Yellow Pages ... 1547
Index to Advertisers ... 1739

Preface

Since 1965, *International Literary Market Place (ILMP)* and its companion *Literary Market Place*, have covered the world of book publishing. These directories provide detailed information on the global book publishing industry. This edition of *ILMP* includes 17,000 entries in over 180 countries. Publishers account for 10,537 of these entries.

Organization & Content
The six areas of coverage into which *ILMP* is arranged are as follows: Publishing, Manufacturing, Book Trade Information, Literary Associations & Prizes, Book Trade Calendar and Library Resources. Within most chapters, companies are sorted first by their country, then by key words in the company name. Sorting preference is determined by the entrant.

Pertinent information regarding each country represented - such as capital, language, population, currency, trade and copyright restrictions - can be found at the beginning of that country's listings in the Publishers section. The basic content of company entries includes - but is not limited to - address, telecommunications data, key personnel, a descriptive annotation and assorted statistics.

There are exceptions to this arrangement. International Publishing Services, located within the Publishing chapter, contains U.S. and Canadian companies that do a significant amount of international business and wish to advertise their services to users of *ILMP*. Also, those U.S. and Canadian book manufacturing companies that do 10% or more of their business overseas are included in the appropriate sections within the Manufacturing chapter.

Compilation
ILMP is updated throughout the year via a number of methods. A questionnaire is mailed to every current listing to corroborate and update the information contained on our database. All returned mailers are edited for the next product release. If a reply is not received, public sources are researched to determine the status of the listee.

Information on new listings is gathered using a similar method. ILMP editors identify possible new listings through their daily research or as a result of nominations from the organization itself or from third parties. A questionnaire is then sent to gather the essential listing information. Unless we receive information directly from the organization, the new listing will not be included in the *ILMP* database.

Updated information or suggestions for new listings can also be submitted by using the form that follows this preface.

Simply fill in the information requested and send the form to:

International Literary Market Place
630 Central Avenue
New Providence, NJ 07974
United States of America
Fax: 908-219-0192

An updating method using Internet technology is also available for *ILMP* listings:

- You can use the *Literary Market Place* web site to update an *ILMP* listing. **Literarymarketplace.com** allows you the opportunity to provide new information for a listing by clicking on the option Update or Correct Your Entry. The Feedback option on the home page of the web site can be used to suggest new entries as well.

Once information regarding a suggested new entry or a correction to an existing listing has been submitted, our editors verify the data with the organization to ensure the accuracy of the update.

Related Services
International Literary Market Place, along with its companion volume *Literary Market Place*, is now available through the World Wide Web at **www.literarymarketplace.com**. Designed to give users simple, logical access to the information they require, the site offers the choice of searching for data alphabetically, geographically, by type, or by subject. Continuously updated by Information Today, Inc.'s team of editors, this is a truly enhanced version of the *ILMP* and *LMP* databases, incorporating features that make "must have" information easily available.

Your feedback is important to us. We strongly encourage you to contact us with comments on this 2003 edition of *ILMP*, as well as suggestions and comments for future editions. Our editorial office can be reached at 908-286-1090, or by e-mail at khallard@infotoday.com. Most importantly, thanks are due to those entrants who took the time to respond to our questionnaires.

Return this form to:
International Literary Market Place
630 Central Avenue
New Providence, NJ 07974 USA
Fax: (908) 219-0192

INTERNATIONAL LITERARY MARKET PLACE™
EDITORIAL REVISION FORM

Company Name:_____

The company listing is found on page number:_____

☐ Please check here if you are nominating this organization for a new listing in the directory

General Information

Address:_____

City:_____ State/Country:_____ Postal Code:_____

Phone:_____ Fax:_____

E-mail:_____ Web Site:_____

Brief Description:_____

Personnel

☐ Addition   ☐ Deletion   ☐ Correction

First Name:_____ Last Name:_____ Title:_____

☐ Addition   ☐ Deletion   ☐ Correction

First Name:_____ Last Name:_____ Title:_____

☐ Addition   ☐ Deletion   ☐ Correction

First Name:_____ Last Name:_____ Title:_____

☐ Addition   ☐ Deletion   ☐ Correction

First Name:_____ Last Name:_____ Title:_____

(continued on back)

Other Information

Indicate other information to be added to or corrected in this listing; please be as specific as possible, noting erroneous data to be deleted.

_____
_____
_____
_____
_____
_____
_____

Verification

Data for this listing will not be updated without the following information.

Your First Name: _____ Your Last Name: _____

Organization Name: _____

Address: _____

City: _____ State/Country: _____ Postal Code: _____

Phone: _____ E-mail: _____

Indicate if you are a: ☐ Representative of this organization   ☐ User of this directory   ☐ Other

If other, please specify: _____

Thank you for helping International Literary Market Place maintain the most up-to-date information available. Please return by fax to 908-219-0192, or visit our website at www.literarymarketplace.com and click on the option for Update or Correct Your Entry.

Copyright Conventions

The Universal Copyright Convention was sponsored by Unesco in 1952. It states that 'Each signatory country extends to foreign works covered by UCC the same protection which such country extends to works of its own nationals published within its own borders.'

The Berne Convention is a system of international copyright which is maintained among countries which have become signatories of the International Copyright Union for the Protection of Literary and Artistic Works. This Union plan, which was first agreed upon at Berne, Switzerland, in 1886, has been subject to later revisions.

The basic principle of the agreement is that any work properly copyrighted in its country of origin has protection in every Union country. Any work originating in a non-Union country, if it is simultaneously published in a Union country, has the same standing as it would if it had originated in a Union country. Different countries have different relationships under one or more of the revisions (Berlin, 1908; Rome, 1928; Brussels, 1948; Stockholm, 1968; and Paris, 1971).

The Florence Agreement, also known as the 'free flow of book', is a Unesco-sponsored international agreement aimed at easing the flow of books and other scientific, educational and cultural materials, through the elimination or reduction of tariffs and other barriers.

The Buenos Aires Convention: In most Latin-American countries, compliance with the copyright law of the country of first publication protects the work in other countries of the Buenos Aires Convention (1910). To secure copyright, each work must carry a notice to the effect that any use of the book or article will not be permitted without the consent of the copyright owner, and that copyright is reserved in English or any other language; for complete safety it is advised to add 'All rights reserved'. A later revision of the Buenos Aires Convention was made at the Washington Conference (Pan-American Copyright Convention) of 1946 which goes into greater detail than the Buenos Aires Convention.

See the General Information for each country in the Publishers Section for country specific copyright information.

The ISBN System

Background

The question of the need and feasibility of an international numbering system for books was first discussed at the third International Conference on Book Market Research and Rationalization in the Book Trade held in November 1966 in Berlin. At this time a number of publishers and book distributors in Europe were considering the use of computers in order processing and inventory control; and it was evident that a prerequisite of an efficient automated system was a unique and simple identification number for a published item.

The system which fulfilled this requirement and which became known as the International Standard Book Number (ISBN) System developed out of the book numbering system introduced into the United Kingdom in 1967.

In a report to the British Publishers Association, Professor F.G. Foster of the London School of Economics stated that there was '...a clear need of the introduction into the book trade of standard numbering...and substantial benefits would accrue to all parties therefrom'. After further study and deliberation, a detailed plan for standard numbering was produced. At the same time, the Technical Committee on Documentation of the International Standards Organization (ISO/TC 46) set up a working party (with the British Standards Institution acting as secretariat) to investigate the possibility of adapting the British system for international use. A meeting was held in London in 1968 with representatives from Denmark, France, Federal Republic of Germany, Eire, the Netherlands, Norway, the United Kingdom, the United States of America and an observer from Unesco. Other countries contributed written suggestions and expressions of interest. A report of the meeting was circulated to all countries belonging to the ISO. Comments on this report and subsequent proposals were considered at meetings held in Berlin and Stockholm in 1969.

As a result of these meetings there emerged ISO Recommendations 2108 which sets out the principles and procedures for international standard book numbering. The purpose of the ISO Recommendations is to coordinate and standardize internationally the use of book numbers so that an International Standard Book Number (ISBN) identifies one title or edition of a title from one specific publisher and is unique to that edition.

The ISBN applies in the main to books - for which the system was originally created - but, by extension, it may be used for any item produced by publishers or collected by libraries.

How the International Standard Book Number (ISBN) is Built Up

Every International Standard Book Number (ISBN) consists of ten digits; and whenever it is printed it is preceded by the letters ISBN. (Note: In those countries where the Latin alphabet is not used, an abbreviation in the characters of the local alphabet may be used in addition to the Latin letters ISBN.)

The ten-digit number is divided into four parts of variable length, each part when printed being separated by a hyphen or space. (Note: Experience suggests that the hyphen is preferable to the space.)

The four parts are as follows:

Part 1. Group Identifier
This part identifies the national, geographic or other similar grouping of publishers.

Part 2. Publisher's Prefix
This part identifies a particular publisher within a group.

Part 3. Title Identifier
This part identifies a particular title or edition of a title published by a particular publisher.

Part 4. Check Digit
This is a single digit at the end of the ISBN which provides an automatic check on the correctness of the ISBN.

Group Identifier
Group identifiers are allocated by the International ISBN Agency and a publisher wishing to participate in the ISBN system must belong to a recognized ISBN group. Groups are determined by national, geographic, language or other pertinent considerations. Experience has shown that groups based on national or geographic consideration are the most satisfactory. The following group identifiers are in use at present:

0 and 1	Australia, English-speaking Canada, Gibralter, Ireland, New Zealand, Puerto Rico, South Africa, Swaziland, UK, USA, Zimbabwe
2	France, French-speaking Belgium, French-speaking Canada, Luxembourg, French-speaking Switzerland
3	Austria, Germany, German- speaking Switzerland
4	Japan
5	Armenia (also 99930), Azerbaijan (also 9952), Belarus (also 985), Estonia (also 9949 and 9985), Georgia (also 99928), Kazakhstan (also 9965), Kyrgyzstan (also 9967), Latvia (also 9984), Lithuania (also 9955 and 9986), Moldova (also 9975), Russian Federation, Tajikistan, Turkmenistan, Ukraine (also 966), Uzbekistan
7	People's Republic of China
80	Czech Republic, Slovakia
81	India (also 93)
82	Norway
83	Poland
84	Spain
85	Brazil
86	Bosnia and Herzegovina (also 9958), Croatia (also 953), Macedonia (also 9989), Slovenia (also 961), Yugoslavia
87	Denmark
88	Italy, Italian-speaking Switzerland
89	Republic of Korea
90	Netherlands, Flemish-speaking Belgium
91	Sweden
92	International Publishers (UNESCO, EU); European Community Organizations
93	India (also 81)
950	Argentina (also 987)
951	Finland (also 952)
952	Finland (also 951)
953	Croatia (also 86)
954	Bulgaria
955	Sri Lanka
956	Chile
957	Taiwan, China (also 986)
958	Colombia
959	Cuba
960	Greece
961	Slovenia (also 86)
962	Hong Kong (People's Republic of China) (also 988)
963	Hungary
964	Iran
965	Israel

THE ISBN SYSTEM

966	Ukraine (also 5)	9955	Lithuania (also 5 and 9986)	99904	Netherlands Antilles, Aruba
967	Malaysia (also 983)	9956	Cameroon	99905	Bolivia
968	Mexico (also 970)	9957	Jordan	99906	Kuwait
969	Pakistan	9958	Bosnia and Herzegovina (also 86)	99908	Malawi
970	Mexico (also 968)	9959	Libya	99909	Malta (also 99932)
971	Philippines	9960	Saudi Arabia	99910	Sierra Leone
972	Portugal	9961	Algeria	99911	Lesotho
973	Romania	9962	Panama	99912	Botswana
974	Thailand	9963	Cyprus	99913	Andorra (also 99920)
975	Turkey	9964	Ghana (also 9988)	99914	Suriname
976	Caribbean Community (CARICOM): Antigua, Bahamas, Barbados, Belize, Cayman Islands, Dominica, Grenada, Guyana, Jamaica, Montserrat, Saint Kitts and Nevis, Saint Lucia, Saint Vincent and the Grenadines, Trinidad and Tobago, British Virgin Islands	9965	Kazakhstan (also 5)	99915	Maldives
		9966	Kenya	99916	Namibia
		9967	Kyrgyzstan (also 5)	99917	Brunei Darussalam
		9968	Costa Rica (also 9977)	99918	Faroe Islands
977	Egypt	9970	Uganda	99919	Benin
978	Nigeria	9971	Republic of Singapore (also 981)	99920	Andorra (also 99913)
979	Indonesia	9972	Peru	99921	Qatar
980	Venezuela	9973	Tunisia	99922	Guatemala (also 99939)
981	Republic of Singapore (also 9971)	9974	Uruguay	99923	El Salvador
982	South Pacific: Cook Islands, Fiji, Kiribati, Marshall Islands, Nauru, Niue, Solomon Islands, Tokelau, Tonga, Tuvalu, Vanuatu, Western Samoa	9975	Moldova (also 5)	99924	Nicaragua
		9976	Tanzania (also 9987)	99925	Paraguay
		9977	Costa Rica (also 9968)	99926	Honduras
983	Malaysia (also 967)	9978	Ecuador	99927	Albania
984	Bangladesh	9979	Iceland	99928	Georgia (also 5)
985	Belarus (also 5)	9980	Papua New Guinea	99929	Mongolia
986	Taiwan, China (also 957)	9981	Morocco (also 9954)	99930	Armenia (also 5)
987	Argentina (also 950)	9982	Zambia	99931	Seychelles
988	Hong Kong (also 962)	9983	Gambia	99932	Malta (also 99909)
989	Portugal (also 972)	9984	Latvia (also 5)	99933	Nepal
9948	United Arab Emirates	9985	Estonia (also 5 and 9949)	99934	Dominican Republic
9949	Estonia (also 5 and 9985)	9986	Lithuania (also 5 and 9955)	99935	Haiti
9950	Palestine	9987	Tanzania (also 9976)	99936	Bhutan
9951	Kosovo	9988	Ghana (also 9964)	99937	Macau
9952	Azerbaijan (also 5)	9989	Macedonia (also 86)	99938	Srpska
9953	Lebanon	99901	Bahrain	99939	Guatemala (also 99922)
9954	Morocco (also 9981)	99903	Mauritius		

THE ISBN SYSTEM

Publisher's Prefix

The publisher's prefix designates the publisher of a given book. Publishers with a large output of books are assigned a short publisher's prefix; publishers with a small output of books are assigned a longer publisher's prefix.

Title Identifier

The title identifier is assigned to a particular title or edition of a title by the publisher from within the range of numbers assigned to him and which will depend upon the length of his publisher's prefix. Title identifiers are normally assigned by the publisher himself. Publishers who assign their own title identifiers may use them to identify titles in the publishing house throughout the planning stages.

Check Digit

The 'check digit' is the last digit in an ISBN and is computed as the result of an elaborate calculation on the other nine digits.

This calculation is performed almost instantaneously by an electronic computing device, and is a means of detecting incorrectly transcribed numbers. The check digit is calculated on a modulus 11 with weights 10-2, using X in lieu of 10 where ten would occur as a check digit.

This means that each of the first nine digits on the ISBN - i.e. excluding the check digit itself - is multiplied by a number ranging from 10 to 2; and the sum of the products thus obtained, plus the check digit, must be divisible, without remainder, by 11. For example:

	Group Identifier		Publisher's Prefix	
ISBN	0	8	4	3 6
Weight	10	9	8	7 6
Products	0+	72+	32+	21+ 36+

	Title Number			Check Digit
ISBN	1	0	7	2 7
Weight	5	4	3	2
Products	5+	0+	21+	4+ 7+

Total: 198

As 198 can be divided by 11 without remainder 0 8436 1072 is a valid International Standard Book Number.

The number of digits in each part, and how to recognize them in an ISBN

The number of digits in each of the identifying parts 1, 2 and 3 is variable, though the total number of digits contained in these parts is always 9. These nine digits together with the check digit bring the total number of digits in an ISBN to ten.

The number of digits in the group identifier will vary according to the likely output of books in a group. Thus, groups with an expected large output will get numbers of one or two digits; and publishers with an expected large output will get numbers of two or three digits.

Exceptionally, a one-digit number may be assigned to a publisher, but it will be appreciated that the assignment of one-digit publisher identifiers greatly reduces the range of possible identifiers in the group. For ease of reading, the four parts of the ISBN are divided by spaces or hyphens. These spaces or hyphens, however, are not retained in a computer which depends upon the special distribution of ranges of numbers for the recognition of the parts.

Scope of the ISBN

For the purposes of the ISBN system books and other items to be numbered include:

Printed books and pamphlets

Mixed media publications

Other similar media including educational films/ videos and transparencies

Books on cassettes

Microcomputer software (educational only)

Electronic publications
 – machine-readable tapes (designed to produce readable printout)
 – CD-ROM etc

Micro-form publications

Braille publications

Atlases & Maps

Except:

Ephemeral printed materials such as diaries, calendars, advertising matter and the like

Art prints and art folders without title page and text

Sound recordings

Serial publications

Principles and procedures to be observed by the publisher numbering his own publications

A publisher must ensure that a competent person is responsible for the assignment of ISBN and the application of the pertinent regulations. A publisher will be assigned a publisher identifier (publisher's prefix) by the group agency which will determine the range of title identifiers available to him. The number of title identifiers will depend upon the length of the publisher identifier assigned to him. The publisher should ensure that the group agency has as much information as possible about his back lists of books still available; and present and future publication programmes in order that a suitable publisher identifier can be assigned. A publisher is responsible for assigning title identifiers to the individual items he publishes.

A publisher may wish to incorporate an existing non-classifying identification system into his ISBN allocation. This may be arranged provided that such incorporation does not alter the fundamental characteristics of the ISBN system or reduce the amount of numbers available. For example: the publisher must not incorporate digits other than numerals which cause the resulting ISBN to be longer than or shorter than ten digits, nor must the publisher attempt to build in special meanings or hierarchical order to groups of numbers, if by so doing he reduces the amount of available numbers in the range allocated to him.

Non-participating publishers

If by choice, or for any other reason, a publisher does not accept responsibility for assigning ISBN to his publications, two alternatives are open to the group agency.

1. The group agency can allocate a block of numbers for miscellaneous publishers and number all titles within that block irrespective of the publisher. In such a case the resulting ISBN will not identify the publisher of a specific title. (It is strongly recommended that this procedure should be reserved for publishers who only publish an occasional title and who are never likely to be in a position to assume the responsibility for numbering themselves.)

2. The group agency can assume responsibility for assigning a publisher identifier, a block of ISBNs associated with the publisher identifier and a number to each publication as well as informing the publisher before publication of the number assigned. In such a case, if the publisher agrees to do so, the ISBN can be printed in the book. It is expected that such a publisher will eventually assume full responsibility for assigning his own ISBN.

Application of ISBN

General

A separate ISBN must be assigned to every different edition of a book; but NOT to an unchanged impression or unchanged reprint of the same book in the same format and by the same publisher. Price changes do not need new ISBN.

Facsimile reprints

A separate ISBN must be assigned to a facsimile reprint produced by a different publisher.

Books in different formats

A separate ISBN must be assigned to the different formats in which a particular title is published. For example: a hardback edition and a paperback edition each receives a separate ISBN. On the same principle, a microform edition receives a separate ISBN.

Looseleaf publications

If a publication appears in looseleaf form, an ISBN is allocated to identify an edition at a given time. Individual issues of additions or replacement sheets will likewise be given an ISBN.

Multi-volume works

An ISBN must be assigned to the whole set of volumes of a multi-volume work, as well as to each individual volume in the set.

THE ISBN SYSTEM

Back stock
A publisher is required to number his back stock and publish the ISBN in his catalogues. He must also print the ISBN in the first available reprint of an item from his back stock.

Collaborative publications
A publication issued as a coedition or joint imprint with other publishers is assigned an ISBN by the publisher in charge of distribution.

Books sold or distributed by agents
According to the principles of the ISBN system, a particular edition published by a particular publisher receives only one ISBN; this ISBN must be retained no matter where or by whom the book is distributed or sold.

A book imported by an exclusive distributor or sole agent from an area not yet in the ISBN system and for which, therefore, no ISBN has been assigned may be assigned an ISBN by the exclusive distributor.

A book imported by an exclusive distributor or sole agent to which a new title-page, bearing the imprint of the exclusive distributor, has been added in place of the title page of the original publisher, is to be given a new ISBN by the exclusive distributor or sole agent. The ISBN of the original publisher is also to be given as a related ISBN.

A book imported by several distributors from an area not yet in the ISBN system and for which, therefore, no ISBN has been assigned may be assigned an ISBN by the group agency responsible for those distributors.

Publishers with more than one place of publication
A publisher operating in a number of places which are listed together in the imprint of a book will assign only one ISBN to the book. A publisher operating separate and distinct offices or branches in different places may have a publisher identifier for each office or branch. Nevertheless, each book published is to be assigned only one ISBN, the assignment being made by the office or branch responsible for publication.

Register of ISBNs
Every publisher must keep a register of ISBNs that have been assigned to published and forthcoming books. The register is to be kept in numerical sequence giving ISBN, author, title and edition (where appropriate).

ISBNs are not to be re-used under any circumstances
An ISBN once allocated must not under any circumstances be re-used. This is of the utmost importance to avoid confusion. It is recognized that, owing to clerical errors, numbers will be incorrectly assigned. If this happens, the number must be deleted from the list of usable numbers and must not be assigned to another title. Every publisher will have sufficient numbers in his range for the loss of these numbers to be insignificant. Publishers should advise the group agency of the numbers thus deleted and of the titles to which they were erroneously assigned.

Guidelines for ISBN assignment to software

An ISBN is used to identify a specific software product. If there is more than one version (perhaps versions adapted for different machines, carrier media or language version), each version must have a different ISBN. When a software product is updated, revised or otherwise amended and the changes are sufficiently substantial for the product to be called a new edition (and thus probably the subject of a new launch, or marketing push) then a new ISBN must be allocated. A relaunch of an existing product, even in new packaging, where there is no basic difference in the performance of the new and the old product, does NOT justify a new ISBN, and the original ISBN must be used.

When software is accompanied by a manual, useful only as an adjunct to the software, and the software needs the manual before it can be operated, and the two items are always sold as a package, one ISBN must be used to cover both items. When two or more items in a software package (as above) can be used separately, or are sold separately as well as together, then
(i) the package as a whole must have an ISBN
(ii) each item in the package must have its own ISBN.

ISBNs should be allocated to a software product independent of its physical form, eg, if software is only available from a remote database form whence it is downloaded to the customer.

As well as identifying the product itself, an ISBN identifies the publisher or manufacturer; it should not be used to identify a distributor or wholesaler.

Printing of the ISBN

General
The ISBN must appear on the item itself. This is essential for the efficient running of the system.

Printing of ISBN on books
In the case of books, the ISBN must appear whenever possible:

On the reverse of the title page, or, if this is not possible, on the base of the title page, or, if this too is not possible, at some other conspicuous location in the book.

On the base of the spine.

On the back of the cover in 9-point type or larger.

On the back of the dust jacket, and on the back of any other protective case or wrapper.

The ISBN should always be printed in type large enough to be easily legible (i.e. not smaller than 9 point).

Printing of ISBN on books in machine readable coding
In the last few years there has been much work done on machine-readable representations of the ISBN. The rapid, worldwide extension of bar code scanning has brought into prominence the agreement reached between the International Article Numbering Association (EAN) and the International ISBN Agency, which allows the ISBN to be translated into an EAN bar code.

All EAN bar codes start with a national identifier **except** those on books and periodicals. The agreement replaces the usual national identifier with a special 'Bookland' identifier represented by the digits 978 for books and 977 for periodicals. The 978 Bookland/EAN prefix is followed by the first nine digits of the ISBN. The check digit of the ISBN is dropped and replaced by a check digit calculated according to the EAN rules.

Optional 5-digit add-on code
There is an optional 5-digit add-on code which can be used for additional information. In the publishing industry it can be used for price information which may have the following formats:
a) Five-digit bar code indicating the price with human readable numbers above the bar code or
b) Five-digit bar code indicating the price with no human readable numbers.

Administration of the ISBN System

General
The administration of the ISBN system is carried on at three levels. These are the international, group and publisher levels.

International administration
The international administration of the system is in the hands of the International Standard Book Number Agency which has an Advisory Panel representing the ISO and the publishing and library world. The address of the International Agency is:

International ISBN Agency
Staatsbibliothek zu Berlin
Preussischer Kulturbesitz
10772 Berlin
Germany

The principal functions of the International Agency are:

To supervise the use of the system

To approve the definition and structure of groups

To allocate identifiers to groups

To advise groups on the setting up and functioning of group agencies

THE ISBN SYSTEM

To advise group agencies on the allocation of publisher identifiers

To promote the worldwide use of the system

In addition, the International Agency also offers the following services. It will:

Provide a group agency with lists of ISBNs (with computer-generated check digits) for the use of publishers in the group

Provide international registers of publishers, prefixes and publishers' names

Provide from information supplied by group agencies a computer printout of lists of publishers' prefixes, names and locations

Provide from information supplied by group agencies a computer printout of invalid or duplicate ISBNs

Group administration
Groups are administered by Group Agencies. Within the group there may be several national agencies, eg. group 0/1 has separate agencies in USA, United Kingdom, Canada, Australia, etc, with the main agency for the whole group in the UK.

The functions of a group agency are:

To manage and administer the affairs of the group

To handle relations with the International ISBN Agency on behalf of all the publishers in the group

To decide, in consultation with trade organizations and publishers, the publisher identifier ranges required

To allocate publishers' prefixes to publishers eligible to join the group and to maintain a register of publishers and their prefixes

To decide, in consultation with trade organizations and publishers, which publishers shall assign numbers to their own titles and which publishers shall have numbers assigned to their titles by the group agency

To provide technical advice and assistance to the publishers and to ensure that standards and approved procedures are observed in the group

To make available a manual of instruction for publishers

To make available computer printouts of ISBNs to publishers numbering their own books with check digits already calculated (Such printouts may be obtained from the International Agency on request)

To validate all ISBNs assigned by publishers numbering their own books and keep a register of them

To inform publishers of any invalid or duplicate ISBNs assigned by them

To assign numbers to all publications from those publishers who do not assign their own ISBNs and advise the publishers concerned of ISBNs assigned upon request

To achieve, thereby, total numbering in the group

To arrange with book listing and bibliographic agencies for the publication of ISBNs with the titles to which they refer

To arrange with publishers for the numbering of their back lists and for the publication of these in appropriate trade lists and bibliographies

To maintain liaison with all elements of the book trade and introduce new publishers to the system

To assist the trade in the use of the ISBN in computer systems

The national agencies are:

Albania
Ms. Vjollca Sinoimeri, Republika e Shqiperise, Biblioteka Kombetare, Agjensia Kombetare e ISBN, Tirana

Algeria
Bibliotheque Nationale, Agence ISBN, 1 Av Frantz Fanon, Alger

Andorra
Sr. Pilar Burgues, Andorran Standard Book Numbering Agency, Biblioteca Nacional, Placeta Sant Esteve s/n, Andorra la Vella

Argentina
Sra. Claudia Rodriguez, Camara Argentina del Libro, Agencia Argentina ISBN, Avenida Belgrano 1580 4° Piso, 1093 Buenos Aires

Armenia
Mr. Alvard Bekmezyan, National Book Chamber of Armenia, ISBN Agency, G. Kochar st. 21, 375009 Yerevan-9

Australia
DW Thorpe, ISBN Agency Australia, 18 Salmon St, Port Melbourne, Vic 3207

Austria
Herrn Walter Hess, Hauptverband des Osterreichischen Buchhandels, Grunangergasse 4, 1010 Vienna 1

Azerbaijan
Mr. Ramin N. Aliyev, Khazar University Press, 11 Mehseti St., Baku 370096

Bahrain
Directorate of Publication and Press, Ministry of Cabinet Affairs & Information, ISBN Agency, PO Box 253, Manama

Bangladesh
Mr. Prof. Sharif uddin Ahmed, National Library, ISBN Agency, 32, Justice Syed Mahbub Murshed Sarani, Sher-e-Bangla Nagar (Agargaon), Dhaka 1207

Belarus
Mr. Anatoli I. Voronko, National Book Chamber of Belarus, ISBN Agency, 31a Very Khoruzhey St, 220002 Minsk

Belgium (Flemish-speaking)
Mr. Ben Klomp, Bureau ISBN, Centraal Boekhuis, Postbus 360, 4100 AJ Culemborg

Belgium (French-speaking)
Mr. Bruno Bardin, Electre, AFNIL (Agence Francophone pour la Numerotation Internationale du Livre), 35 rue Gregoire de Tours, 75006 Paris

Benin
Agence Nationale ISBN, Bibliotheque Nationale, BP 401, Porto-Novo

Bhutan
Mr. Sonam Kinga, The Centre for Bhutan Studies, ISBN Agency, Post Box 111, Thimphu

Bolivia
Camara Boliviana del Libro, Agencia ISBN, Calle Capitan, Ravelo, No. 2116, Casilla 682, La Paz

Bosnia and Herzegovina
Mrs. Nevenka Hajdarovic, The National and University Library of Bosnia and Herzegovina, ISBN Centre, Zmaja od Bosne 8b, 71000 Sarajevo

Botswana
Mrs. Vivian Maje, Botswana National Library Service, Private Bag 0036, Gaborone

Brazil
Mr. Elmer C. Barbosa, Biblioteca Nacional, Rua da Impresa, 1611-ander, 20042 Rio de Janeiro, RJ

Brunei Darussalam
Ms. Nellie Dato Paduka Haji Sunny, Dewan Bahasa dan Pustaka Brunei, Lapangan Terbang Lama, Bandar Seri Begawan 2064, Negara

Bulgaria
Ms. Tatjana Dermendzieva, National Library, St Cyril and St Methodius, National ISBN Agency, Boul V Levski 88, 1504 Sofia

Cameroon
Agence ISBN, Bibliotheque Nationale, Yaounde

Canada (English-speaking)
Mrs. Maryse Plouffe, Canadian ISBN Agency, Acquisitions and Bibliographic Services Branch, National Library of Canada, 395, Wellington St, Ottawa, Ontario K1A 0N4

Canada (French-speaking)
Mme. Lucie Martel, ISBN/BNQ, Section du depot legal, Bibliotheque nationale du Quebec, 2275, rue Holt, Montreal, Quebec H2G 3H1

Caribbean Community
Ms. Maureen Newton, Regional ISBN Agency, Caribbean Community Secretariat, Bank of Guyana Bldg, PO Box 10827, Georgetown, Guyana

THE ISBN SYSTEM

Chile
Jaime Pizarro Carrasco, Agencia Chilena ISBN, Camara Chilena del Libro AG, Avda Lib Bernardo O'Higgins 1370, Of 202, Santiago de Chile

People's Republic of China
Mr. Yang Muzhi, China ISBN Agency, 85 Dongsi Nan Dajie 100703, Beijing

Colombia
Sra. Gladys Torres Bazurto, Agencia Colombiana del ISBN, Camara Colombiana del Libro, Carrera 17A No 37-27, Apartado Aereo 8998, Santafe de Bogota

Costa Rica
Elena Alpizar, Agencia Nacional ISBN, Biblioteca Nacional "Miguel Obregon Lizano", Apartado Postal 10008, 1000 San Jose

Croatia
Ms. Daniela Zivkovic, Hrvatski ured za ISBN, Nacionalna i sveucilisna knjizica, Hrvatske bratske zajednice 4, HR-10000 Zagreb

Cuba
Sra. Rosa Amelia Lay Portuondo, Camara Cubana del Libro, Agencia Cubana del ISBN, Calle 15 No 602 esq C, Vedado, Ciudad Havana

Cyprus
Mr. Antonis Maratheftis, Cyprus Centre for the Registration of Books and Serials, The Cyprus Library, Eleftherias Square, 1011 Nicosia

Czech Republic
Mr. Antonin Jerabek, Narodni agentura ISBN v CR, Narodni Knihovna CR, Klementinum 190, 110 01 Prague 1

Denmark
Ms. Randi Diget Hansen, Dansk BiblioteksCenter as, ISBN group agency, Tempovej 7-11, 2750 Ballerup

Dominican Republic
Sr. Stalin Ciprian, Agencia Domenicana de ISBN, Biblioteca Nacional Pedro Henriquez Urena, Calle Cesar Nicolas Penson No 91, Plaza de la Cultura, Santo Domingo

Ecuador
Sr. Patricio Mena, Agencia Ecuatoriana del ISBN, Av Eloy Alfaro N29-61 e Inglanterra, Edificio Eloy Alfaro Piso 9, Quito

Egypt
Ms. Blanche Asaad, National Library and Archives, Corniche El Nil-Boulac, Cairo

El Salvador
Sra. Doris Elizabeth Siliezar Orellana, Biblioteca Nacional, Agencia ISBN, Avenida Mons. Oscar A. Romero y 4a Calle Oriente No 124, San Salvador

Estonia
Ms. Mai Valtna, Eesti Rahvusraamatukogu, National Library of Estonia, Estonian ISBN agency, Tonismagi 2, 15189 Tallinn

European Community Organizations
Mrs. Madeleine Kiss, Office for Official publications for the European Community, Direction A, ISBN Agency, 2 rue Mercier, 2985 Luxembourg, Luxembourg

Faroe Islands
Mr. Erhard Jacobsen, Foroya Landsbokasavn, Faroese ISBN office, J.C. Svabosgotu 16, PO Box 61, FR-110 Torshavn

Finland
Ms. Maarit Huttunen, Finnish ISBN Agency, Helsinki University Library, PO Box 26, (Teollisuuskatu 23), FIN-00014 University of Helsinki

France
Mr. Bruno Bardin, AFNIL (Agence Francophone pour la Numerotation Internationale du Livre), 35, rue Gregoire de Tours, 75006 Paris

Gambia
Mr. Abdou Wally Mbye, Chief Librarian, Gambia National Library, Reg Pye Lane, PMB, Banjul

Georgia
Mr. Nino Simonishvili, Georgian Parliament I. Chavchavadze National Library, ISBN Agency, 5 Gudiashvili St., 380007 Tbilisi

Germany
Ms. Anke Lehr, Buchhandler-Vereinigung GmbH, ISBN-Agentur fur die Bundesrepublik Deutschland, Postfach 10 04 42, 60004 Frankfurt am Main

Ghana
Ms. Sarah Dorothy Kanda, Ghana Library Board, George Padmore, Research Library on African Affairs, PO Box 2970, Accra

Gibraltar
John Mackintosh Hall Library, Knightsfield Holdings Ltd., 308 Main St, PO Box 939, Gibraltar

Greece
Dr. George Zachos, National Library of Greece, National Centre of ISBN, Panepistimiou 32, 10679 Athens

Guatemala
Sra. Silvia Regina De Leon, Agencia ISBN, Gremial de Editores de Guatemala, Ruta 6, 9-21 zona 4, Edificio Camara de Industria 8vo nivel, Ciudad Guatemala

Haiti
Bibliotheque Nationale d'Haiti, 193, rue du centre, Port-au-Prince

Honduras
Sra. Lesly Vazquez, Agencia ISBN de Honduras, Antiguo Local Tipografia Nacional, Barrio El Centro, 1 cuadra al Sur Hotel Prado, Tegucigalpa, MDC

Hong Kong (People's Republic of China)
Yung Chi-shing, Leisure & Cultural Department, Books Registration Office, 805, 8/F, Training School, 19 Lai Wan Rd, Lai Chi Kok, Kowloon

Hungary
Ms. Susanne Berke, Magyar ISBN Iroda, Orszagos Szechenyi Konyvtar, Budavari Palota F epulet, 1827 Budapest

Iceland
Ms. Nanna Bjarnadottir, Landsbokasafn Islands-Haskolabokasafn, National and University Library of Iceland, Acquisitions Department, Legal Deposit, Arngrimsgotu 3, IS-107 Reykjavik

India
Ms. Anurahada S. Chagti, Government of India, Ministry of Human Resource Development, Raja Rammohun Roy, National Agency for ISBN, B.2 W 3, Curzon Road Barracks, Kasturba Gandhi Marg, New Delhi-110001

Indonesia
National ISBN Agency, National Library of Indonesia, Perpustakaan Nasional Indonesia, Jl Salemba Raya 28, PO Box 3624, Jakarta 10002

International Publishers (Unesco, EU)
Ms. Maha Bulos, UNESCO, Division of Arts and Cultural Enterprise, 1 rue Miollis, 75732 Paris Cedex 15, France

Iran
Mr. Vahraz Nowruzpur Deilami, Iran Book House, Iran ISBN Agency, 1178 Palestine Crossroad, Enghelab Ave, PO Box 13145-1483, Tehran 13157

Ireland
United Kingdom agency

Israel
Ms. Anna Sela, Israel ISBN Group Agency, The Israeli Center for Libraries, 18 Baruch Hirsh St, POB 3251, Bnei-Berak 51131

Italy
Dr. Michele Costa, Associazione Italiana Editori, Agenzia ISBN per l'area di lingua italiana, Editrice Bibliografica SpA, Via Bergonzoli, 1/5, 20127 Milan

Japan
Mr. Minoru Kubota, Japan ISBN Agency, c/o Japan Publishers Bldg, 6 Fukuro-machi Shinjuku-ku, Tokyo 162

Jordan
Director General, The Department of the National Library, ISBN agency, P.O. Box (6070), Code No 1118, Amman

Kazakhstan
Ms. K. M. Mukhataeva, Book Chamber of Kazakhstan, ISBN agency, Ulica Puskina 2, Almaty 480016

Kenya
Kenya National Library Services, ISBN Agency, PO Box 30573, Nairobi

THE ISBN SYSTEM

Republic of Korea
Ms. Mi-Hae Kim, The National Library of Korea, Korea ISBN agency, 60-1 Panpo-Dong, Seocho-Gu, Seoul 137-702

Kosovo
Ms. Shukrije Rama, The National and University of Kosova, Sheshi "Hasan Prishtina", National ISBN Agency, Prishtina

Kuwait
Ms. Wafa'a H. Al-Sane, The National Library of Kuwait, ISBN agency, P.O. Box 26182, 13122 Safat

Kyrgyzstan
ISBN Agency, State Book Chamber, Goskonzern Akyl of Kyrgyzstan, Ul Sovetskaja 170, a/ 806, 720000 Bischkek

Latvia
Ms. Laimdota Pruse, Latvijas Bibliografijas Instituts, Anglikanu iela 5 (Bibliotekas iela\), LV 1816 Riga

Lebanon
Ministry of Culture, ISBN Agency, Starco centre-Bloc B - 12th floor, Omar Daouk St, Beirut

Lesotho
Mrs. M. Kotele, Librarian, ISBN Agency, The National University of Lesotho Library, PO Roma 180, Lesotho

Libya
Mr. Saleh M. Najim, National Library of Libya, PO Box 9127, Benghazi

Lithuania
Ms. Dalia Smoriginiene, Martynas Mazvydas, National Library of Lithuania, Gedimino Str 51, 2600 Vilnius

Luxembourg
Hernn Andre-Nicolas Schoup, Bibliotheque nationale Grand-Duche de Luxembourg, 37, blvd F-D Roosevelt, 2450 Luxembourg

Macau
Ms. Tang Mei Lin, Central Library of Macau, Director, Av Cons Ferreira de Almeida, No. 89A-B, Macau

Macedonia
Mme. Zlata Talaganova, Narodna i Univerzitetska Biblioteka, "Sv Kliment Ohridski", ISBN Agencija na Republika Makedonia, Bul "Goce Delev", 6, 1000 Skopje

Malawi
Stanley S. Gondwe, National Archives of Malawi, ISBN agency, PO Box 62, Zomba

Malaysia
Mr. Zulkefli Abdul Samad, National Library of Malaysia, National Depository Centre, ISBN National Centre, 232 Jalan Tun Razak, 50572 Kuala Lumpur

Maldives
Mr. Mohammed Waheed, Research Analyst, Ministry of Education, Ghaazee Bldg, Ameeru Ahmed Magu, Male 20-05

Malta
Mr. Emanuel Debattista, Publishers Enterprises Group (PEG) Ltd, PEG Bldg, UB 7 Industrial Estate, San Gwann SGN 09

Mauritius
Ms. Sadhna Ramalallah, Editions de l'Ocean Indien Ltee, Stanley, Rose Hill

Mexico
Sr. Alfredo Toral Azuela, Instituto Nacional del Derecho de Autor, Agencia Nacional ISBN, Calle Dinamarca N° 84°, Colonia Juarez, Delegacion Cuauhtemoc, 06600 Mexico, DF

Moldova
Chambre Nationale du Livre, Agence ISBN, bd Stefan cel Mare, 180, Office 202, 2004 Chisinau

Mongolia
Mongolian Book Publishers Association, Amar Str., Building #1, Room 306, Central Post Box 5, Ulan Bator

Morocco
Mme. Meryem Moussaid, Agence Marocaine de l'ISBN, Bibliotheque Generale et Archives, Service du depot legal, Av Ibn Battouta, BP 1003, Rabat

Namibia
Mr. Werner Hillebrecht, National Library of Namibia, Private Bag 13349, Windhoek

Nepal
Tribhuvan University, Central Library, ISBN Agency, Kirtipur, Kathmandu

Netherlands
Mr. Ben Klomp, Bureau ISBN, Centraal Boekhuis, Postbus 125, 4100 AC Culemborg

Netherlands Antilles
Mr. J. Sluis, Director, Bureau Intellectual Property, Berg Carmelweg 10-A, POB 3068, Curacao

New Zealand
Ms. Joy Grove, The ISBN Agency, New Zealand National Bibliography, National Library of New Zealand, Cnr Molesworth & Aitken Streets, PO Box 1467, Wellington 6001

Nicaragua
Sra. Maribel Otero, Biblioteca Nacional Ruben Dario, Agencia Nacional ISBN, Apartado Postal 101, Managua

Nigeria
The Director, Nigerian ISBN Agency, National Bibliographic Control Dept, National Library of Nigeria, 4, Wesley St, PMB 12626, Lagos

Norway
Mr. Ingebjorg Rype, ISBN-kontoret Norge, Katalogseksjonen, Bibliografiske tjenester, Nasjonalbiblioteket, avdeling Oslo, Postboks 2674, Solli, 0203 Oslo

Pakistan
Mr. Azmat Hussain Siddiqui, Research Officer, in charge of ISBN, Dept of Libraries, National Library, Constitution Ave, Islamabad-44000

Panama
Guadalupe G. de Rivera, Biblioteca Nacional, "Ernesto J. Castillero R.", Agencia ISBN, Apartado 7906, Zona 9, Panama

Papua New Guinea
Mr. Chris Kelly Meti, Bibliographical Services Librarian, Papua New Guinea ISBN Agency, National Library Service, PO Box 734, Waigani, NCD

Paraguay
Dr. Francisco Perez-Maricevich, Direccion General, de Industrias Culturales, Independencia Nacional 874, c/ Piribebuy-1er. piso-, Asuncion

Peru
Sra. Rosa M. Panizo Uriarte, Agencia Peruana del ISBN, Av Abancay cdra 4 s/n, Lima 1

Philippines
Ms. Leonila Tominez, The National Library of the Philippines, Standard Book Numbering Agency, PO Box 2926, Manila

Poland
Ms. Jadwiga Sadowska, Biblioteka Narodowa, Instytut Bibliograficzny, Krajowe Biuro ISBN, Al Niepodleglosci 213, skr poczt 36, 00-973 Warsaw 22

Portugal
Ms. Conceicao Tome, Associacao Portuguesa de Editores e Livreiros, Agencia Nacional de ISBN, Av Estados Unidos da America, 97-6° Esq, 1050 Lisbon

Puerto Rico
United States agency

Qatar
Mr. Sami Abdel Jawad, National Library, ISBN group agency, PO Box 205, Doha

Romania
Ms. Mihaela Leaua, Biblioteca Nationala, Centrul National de Numerotare Standardizata, (ISBN, ISSN, CIP), Str Ion Ghica 4, cod 79708 Bucharest

Russian Federation
Mr. Boris Lenski, Director-General, Russian Book Chamber, Russian ISBN Agency, Kremlevskaja nab 1/9, 121019 Moscow

Saudi Arabia
Mr. Ali S. Al-Sowaine, General Director, King Fahd National Library, Registration and Book Numbering Dept, PO Box 7572, Riyadh 11472

THE ISBN SYSTEM

Seychelles
Ms. C. Stokes, Ministry of Culture and Information, Seychelles National Library, Seychelles ISBN Agency, Victoria, Mahe

Sierra Leone
Ms. Marina Lisk, Sierra Leone Library Board, ISBN agency, PO Box 326, Freetown

Republic of Singapore
Ms. Annick Wong, National Library Board, No 3 Changi South St 2, Tower B #03-00, Singapore 486548

Slovakia
Ms. Jarmila Majerova, Narodna agentura ISBN v SR, Slovenska narodna kniznica, Nam JC Hronskeho 1, 03601 Martin

Slovenia
Ms. Alenka Kanic, Narodna in univerzitetna knjiznica v Ljubljani, Slovenska agencija za ISBN, Turjaska 1, pp 259, 11001 Ljubljana

South Africa
Ms. Magret Kibido, The National Libray, BibSA-ISN Agency, PO Box 397, Pretoria 0001

South Pacific
Ms. Joan Yee, ISBN Officer, Regional ISBN Centre, The University of the South Pacific Library, PO Box 1168, Suva, Fiji

Spain
Sra. Pilar Gomez Font, Agencia Espanola del ISBN, Santiago Rusinol, 8, 28040 Madrid

Sri Lanka
Mr. M.S.U. Amarasiri, Director, National ISBN Agency, National Library of Sri Lanka, No 14, Independence Ave, Colombo 07

Srpska
National and University Library of Republic of Srpska, ISBN Agency, Jevrejska 30, 78000 Banjaluka

Suriname
Mr. E. Hogenboom, Publishers Association Suriname, Standard Book Numbering Agency, Domineestr 32 boven, PO Box 1841, Paramaribo

Swaziland
Ms. M.R. Mavuso, University Librarian, Uniswa Library, Private Bag 4, Kwaluseni

Sweden
Ms. Katarina Synnermark, Swedish National ISBN Agency, Division of Legal Deposit, Royal Library, Box 5039, 10241 Stockholm 5

Switzerland (French-speaking)
Mr. Bruno Bardin, AFNIL (Agence Francophone pour la Numerotation Internationale du Livre), 35, rue Gregoire de Tours, 75006 Paris, France

Switzerland (German-speaking)
Mrs. Claudia Cammisa, ISBN-Agentur Schweiz, c/o Schweizerischer Buchhandler- und Verleger-Verband, Alderstr 40, Postfach, 8034 Zurich

Switzerland (Italian-speaking)
Dr. Michele Costa, Associazione Italiana Editori, Agenzia ISBN per l'Area di Lingua Italiana, Editrice Bibliografica SpA, Via Bergonzoli, 1/5, 20127 Milan, Italy

Taiwan, China
Ms. Li-chien Lee, ISBN Agency, National Central Library, 20 Chung Shan South Rd, Taipei 10001

Tajikistan
Russian Federation agency

Tanzania
Mr. Felician Ray Katiya, Director General, Tanzania Library Services Board, National Bibliographic Agency, PO Box 9283, Dar es Salaam

Thailand
Mrs. Siriporn Chiruppapa, National Library of Thailand, ISBN Thailand, Samsen Rd., Dusit, Bangkok 10300

Tunisia
Mme. Nabiha Ben Sedrine, National ISBN Agency, Bibliotheque Nationale, Service de la Documentation et de l'Information, 20, Souk El Attarine, BP 42, 1008 Tunis

Turkey
Ms. Gokcin Yalcin, General Director, ISBN Turkiye Ajansi, Kultur Bakanligi, Kutuphaneler Genel Mudurlugu, Necatibey Cad No 55 Sihhiye, 06440 Ankara

Turkmenistan
Russian Federation agency

Uganda
Mr. Martin Okia, Uganda Publishers and Booksellers Association, PO Box 7732 Kampala

Ukraine
Ms. Irina Pogorelovskaya, Knyzkova Palata Ukrainy, National ISBN Agency, 27 Yuri Gagarin Ave, 02094 Kiev

United Arab Emirates
Mr. Khalid Abdullah Al Raboy, Ministry of Information and Culture, Copyright Section, ISBN Agency, PO Box 17, Abu Dhabi

United Kingdom & Ireland
Ms. Stella Griffiths, ISBN Agency, Woolmead House West, Bear Lane, Farnham, Surrey, GU9 7LG

United Nations see *International Publishers*

United States of America
Mr. Don Riseborough, R.R. Bowker LLC, International Standard Book Numbering, United States Agency, 630 Central Ave., New Providence, NJ 07974

Uruguay
Julio Castro, Biblioteca Nacional, Seccion Bibliografia Nacional, Agencia Nacional del ISBN, Casilla de Correo 452, 11200 Montevideo

Uzbekistan
Russian Federation agency

Venezuela
Maria Coromoto Mendez, Agencia Venezolana del ISBN, Biblioteca Nacional, Division de Deposito Legal, Final Avenida Panteon, Esquina Fe a Remedios, Parroquia Altagracia, Apartado de Correos, 6525 Caracas

Yugoslavia
Ms. Emilija Brasic, Jugoslovenski Bibliografsko-Informacijski Institut, Agencija za ISBN, Terazije 26, 11000 Belgrade

Zambia
Dr. H. Mwacalimba, Booksellers and Publishers Association of Zambia, The ISBN Secretariat, c/o University of Zambia Library, PO Box 32379, Lusaka

Zimbabwe
Director, National Archives of Zimbabwe, Causeway, Private Bag 7729, Harare

ISBN and ISSN

In addition to the International Standard Book Number System, a complementary numbering system for serial publications has also been established.

A serial is defined as any publication issued in successive parts, usually bearing numerical or chronological designations and intended to be continued indefinitely.

Serials include periodicals, yearbooks and monographic series.

The International Standard Serial Number system (ISSN) is administered by the ISSN International Centre, whose address is:

ISSN International Centre
20, rue Bachaumont
75002 Paris
France

Publishers of serials should apply to the ISSN International Centre or to their National Serials Data Centre, if there is one, for ISSNs for their serial publications.

Certain publications, such as yearbooks, annuals, monographic series, etc, should be assigned an ISSN for the serial title (which will remain the same for all the parts or individual volumes of the serial) and an ISBN for each individual volume.

Both ISSN and ISBN, when they are assigned, must be given on the publication and clearly identified.

(The preceding information is mainly from the ISBN User's Manual, compiled by the International ISBN Agency, Staatsbibliothek zu Berlin, Preussischer Kulturbesitz, Berlin, Germany.)

Abbreviations

+	Publisher's indication of interest in buying/selling international rights or editions
†	Organizations that are international in scope
∮	Publications that are international in scope
◇	Organizations with publishing activities
‡	United nations agencies with publishing activities
☆	Prizes with no geographical restriction placed upon recipients
AB	aktiebolag (=public limited company)
AE	anonymous etaireia
AG	Aktiengesellschaft (=public limited company)
al	aleja
Apdo	apartado (=post-box)
ApS	anpartsselskab (=private limited company)
A/S	(Norwegian) aksjeselskap. (Swedish) aaktieselskab (=limited company)
AS	anonim sirketi
ASBL	association sans but lucratif (=non-profit-making society)
Ave	(English, French) avenue. (Portuguese, Spanish) avenida
Bldg	Building
Blvd	(Bulgarian, Romanian) bulevard. (English, French) boulevard
BP	boite postale (=post-box)
BV	besloten vennootschap (=private limited company)
C	compagnia (=company)
CA	compania anonima (=public limited company)
CEDEX	Courrier d'enterpise a distribution exceptionnelle
CFA	Communaute financiere africaine
CFP	comptoirs fracais du Pacifique
Cia	companhia, compania (=company)
Cie	compagnie (=company)
Co	(English) company, county. (German) Kompanie
c/o	care of
CP	(Italian) casetta postale. (Portuguese) caixa postal, (=post-box)
CV	commanditaire vennootschap (=limited partnership)
Dept	department
Dir	Director
EE	eterorruthmos etaireia
eV	einetragener Verein (=registered society)
ext	extension
GmbH	Gesellschaft mit beschrankter Haftung (=private limited company)
Inc	incorporated
ISBN	international standard book number
Jl	jalan (=street)
KG	Kommanditgesellschatt (=partnership)
KK	kabushiki kaisha (=public limited company)
Lda	limitida (=limited)
Ltd	limited
Ltda	limitada (=limited)
Man Dir	Managing Director
Nachf	Nachfolger(s) (=successor(s))
nam	namesti (=square)
NV	naamloze vennootschap (=public limited company)
OE	omorruthmos etaireia of oficina (=office)
Off	office
Oy	osakeyhitio (=limited company)
pA	per Adresse (=care of)
Pl	(Bulgarian) ploshtad. (English, French) place. (Polish) plac. (Russian) ploshchad. (Spanish) plaza
PL	postriokero (=post-box)
PLC	public limited company
PMB	private mail bag
PO	Post Office
Prof	Professor
Pty	proprietary
PVBA	personenvennootschap met beperkte aansprakelijkheid (=private limited company)
Pvt	private
Rd	Road
SA	(French) societe anonyyme. (Portuguese) sociedade anonima. (Spanish) sociedad anonima (=public limited company)
Sarl	societe a responsabilite limitee (=private limited company)
SAS	societa in accomandita semplice (=limited partnership)
SCA	sociedad en comandita por acciones (=limited partnership)
S de RL	sociedad de responsabilidad limitada (=private limited company)
Sdn Bhd	sendirian berhad (=private limited company)
SL	sociedad de responsabilidad limitada (=private limited company)
SNC	societa in nome collettivo (=partnership)
SpA	societa per azioni (=public limited company)
SPRL	societe de personnes a responsabilite (=private limited company)
SRL	(Italian) societa a responsabilita limita. (Spanish) sociedad de responsabilida limitada. (=private limited company)
St	Saint, street
STD	subscriber trunk dialing
Str	(Danish) straede. (Dutch) straat. (German) Strasse. (Icelandic) straeti. (Italian) strada. (Romanian) strada (=street)
Sq	square
Tel	telephone number
u	utca (=street)
UCC	Universal Copyright Convention
ul	(Bulgarian) ulitsa. (Czech) ulice. (Polish) ulica. (Romanian) ulita. (Russian) ulitsa. (Serbocroatian, Slovak, Slovene) ulica (=street)
UK	United Kingdom
USA	United States of America
VEB	volkseigener Betrieb (=people's enterprise)
VZW	vereniging zonder winstoogmerk (=non-profit-making society)

A limited company is a corporation owned by shareholders (or stockholders) who may contribute capital to the company but are not otherwise generally liable for its debts.

A public company may invite anyone to become a shareholder, and its shares (or stock) are usually traded on a stock exchange.

A private, or proprietary, company has a restricted number of shareholders and its shares are not traded on a stock exchange.

The owners of a partnership or proprietorship are generally liable for its debts, but a limited partnership has some owners who only contribute capital and are not otherwise liable for debts.

Publishing

Publishers

This section covers book publishers throughout the world, with the exception of U.S. and Canadian publishers, which can be found in the companion publication, *Literary Market Place*. Publishers and their imprints are listed alphabetically within their country of business. General information for each country can be found preceding the entries for that country.

+ following a publisher's name indicates those who are involved in the buying or selling of international rights.

Immediately following this section are indexes that list publishers by type of publication and by subjects.

Afghanistan

General Information

Capital: Kabul
Language: Pushtu and Dari Afghan
Religion: Sunni Muslim with approximately 1 million Shiite Muslim
Population: 16.1 million
Bank Hours: 0800-1200, 1300-1600 Saturday-Wednesday; 0800-1300 Thursday
Shop Hours: 0800-about 1800 Saturday-Thursday
Currency: 100 puls = 2 krans = 1 afghani
Copyright: Florence (see Copyright Conventions, pg xi)

Book Publishing Institute
Herat
Founded: 1970 (by cooperation of Government Press and citizens of Herat)
Subjects: Fiction, History, Religion - Other

Franklin Book Programs Inc
PO Box 332, Kabul

Government Press
Kabul
Tel: 26851
Founded: 1870
Under supervision of Ministry of Information and Culture.
Subjects: Ethnicity, History, Regional Interests

Historical Society of Afghanistan
Kabul
Tel: 30370
Founded: 1931
Publications include: *Afghanistan* (in English, French and German); *Aryana* (in Dari and Pushtu), both quarterly.
Subjects: Ethnicity, History, Regional Interests

Ministry of Education, Department of Educational Publications
Kabul
Tel: 25151

Pushtu Toulana, Afghan Academy
Alikhan St, Kabul
Tel: 20350

Albania

General Information

Capital: Tirane
Language: Albanian
Religion: Islamic, Orthodox, Roman Catholic
Population: 3.3 million
Bank Hours: 0730-2330 Monday-Saturday
Shop Hours: 0900-1200 and 1600-2000; one day per week is holiday
Currency: 100 qintars = 1 lek
Export/Import Information: Importation of books is through State Trading Organization, Nd. Shperndarjes Te (or NST) Librit, Blvd K e Pezes, Tirana. Correspondence should be in English, French, German or Italian. Copies of correspondence to Albanian Legation in Rome. Some import licenses but no strict exchange controls.
Copyright: Berne (see Copyright Conventions, pg xi)

Botimpex Publications Import-Export Agency
P 84, Shk 2, Ap 37, Tirana
Mailing Address: PO Box 140, Tirana
Tel: (042) 34023 *Fax:* (042) 26886
E-mail: botimpex@albaniaonline.org; botimpex@icc-al.org
Web Site: pages.albaniaonline.net/botimpex/
Key Personnel
Dir: Dr Estref Bega
Founded: 1991
Subjects: Biography, Fiction, History, Literature, Literary Criticism, Essays, Poetry
Number of titles published annually: 11 Print

Encyclopaedia Publishing House
Rr Muhamet Gjollesha, Tirana
Tel: (042) 28064 *Fax:* (042) 28064
Key Personnel
Gen Dir: Arben Xoxa
Founded: 1991
Subjects: Labor, Industrial Relations, Regional Interests

Fan Noli Verlag Rexhep Hida+
Rr Bulev, Shqip e Re, P 33/4/8, Tirana
Tel: (042) 61673
E-mail: fannoli2002@yahoo.com
Founded: 1991
Subjects: Fiction, Nonfiction (General)
Total Titles: 670 Print

Ndermarrja e Botimeve Ushtarake
Tirana
Subjects: Military Science, Technology

NL SH+
Rruga Muhamet Gjollesha, Tirana
Tel: (042) 34207 *Fax:* (042) 34207
Key Personnel
Dir: Hilmi Brace
Subjects: Accounting, Advertising, Aeronautics, Aviation, Agriculture, Americana, Regional, Animals, Pets, Anthropology, Antiques, Archaeology, Architecture & Interior Design, Art, Astronomy, Biblical Studies, Biography, Biological Sciences, Business, Career Development, Chemistry, Chemical Engineering, Child Care & Development, Cookery, Crafts, Games, Hobbies, Developing Countries, Drama, Theater, Earth Sciences, Economics, Education, Electronics, Electrical Engineering, Energy, Engineering (General), English as a Second Language, Finance, Foreign Countries, Gardening, Plants, Geography, Geology, Government, Political Science, History, Humor, Labor, Industrial Relations, Language Arts, Linguistics, Law, Library & Information Sciences, Literature, Literary Criticism, Essays, Management, Marketing, Mathematics, Mechanical Engineering, Medicine, Nursing, Dentistry, Microcomputers, Military Science, Music, Dance, Mysteries, Native American Studies, Nonfiction (General), Philosophy, Photography, Physical Sciences, Physics, Poetry, Psychology, Psychiatry, Public Administration, Publishing & Book Trade Reference, Radio, TV, Science (General), Science Fiction, Fantasy, Securities, Self-Help, Social Sciences, Sociology, Sports, Athletics, Technology, Theology, Veterinary Science, Women's Studies
Total Titles: 9,999 Print
Branch Office(s)
Rruga Kavajes, NR 116, Tirana *Tel:* (042) 47129; (042) 47130
Distributed by Zina Bunjaj
Distributor for Klodiana Peci
Showroom(s): Tirana *Tel:* (042) 47130

SHBLSH, *imprint of* State Textbook Publishing House

State Textbook Publishing House+
Rruga e Kavajes, Tirana
Tel: (042) 22331 *Fax:* (042) 22331
E-mail: apullumbi@tbph.gov.al

Key Personnel
Dir: Mati Teuta
Founded: 1967 (STPH was created to prepare all school textbooks for the pre-university system)
Member of IngTeuti Mati. Over 800 textbook titles & wishes to have connections with other publishing houses which specialize for schools.
Subjects: Accounting, Animals, Pets, Art, Biological Sciences, Business, Communications, Earth Sciences, Education, Electronics, Electrical Engineering, Energy, Engineering (General), English as a Second Language, Government, Political Science, History, Literature, Literary Criticism, Essays, Mathematics, Medicine, Nursing, Dentistry, Psychology, Psychiatry, Radio, TV, Science (General), Social Sciences, Sociology, Sports, Athletics, Technology
Total Titles: 700 Print
Imprints: SHBLSH
Branch Office(s)
STPH Sector Computer *Tel:* (042) 26177
Shipping Address: Nderrmarrja e Perhapjes se Librit
Warehouse: Nderrmarrja e Shpernolarjes se Librit Shkollor

Algeria

General Information

Capital: Algiers (El Djazair)
Language: Arabic. French is the language of business and administration
Religion: Islamic
Population: 26.7 million
Bank Hours: 0900-1500 or 1600 Saturday-Wednesday
Shop Hours: 0900-1200, 1500-1900 Monday-Saturday
Currency: 100 centimes = 1 Algerian dinar
Export/Import Information: Books may be imported or exported only by or with permission of SNED State Monopoly, 3 blvd Zirout Yousef, BP 49, Alger Strasbourg. There are also quota restrictions. Permission to import usually entitles holder to obtain necessary foreign exchange; strict controls are in effect. Documentation formalities are rigidly enforced.
Copyright: UCC (see Copyright Conventions, pg xi)

Les Editions Algeriennes En-Nahdha+
2 rue Larbi Ben M'Hidi, Alger 16000
Tel: (021) 737627 *Fax:* (021) 737627
Fax on Demand: (021) 479424
Key Personnel
Chief Executive: Omar Mimouni *Tel:* (213) 61 55 20 62 *E-mail:* omimouni2000@yahoo.com
Founded: 1946
Membership(s): Association of Algerian Editors; Vice President of National Syndicate of Book Business.
Subjects: History
Number of titles published annually: 15 Print
Total Titles: 150 Print
Parent Company: Les Editions Algeriennes En-Nahdha
Associate Companies: Editions Mimouni
Subsidiaries: Mimomultimedia (Canada)
Bookshop(s): Avenue du 1er Novembre, Laghouat *Tel:* (029) 90 40 85
Book Club(s): Association del Editeurs Algeriens
Orders to: 37 rue Amar El Kama, Alger

Chihab, see SARL DAR-Echihab

SARL DAR-Echihab
10, av Brahim Ghoriefo, Bab El-Qued, 16009 Alger
Mailing Address: BP 36, 16009 Alger
Tel: (02) 626727; (02) 626734 *Fax:* (02) 574632
ISBN Prefix(es): 9961-63
Subsidiaries: Chihab 2000
Showroom(s): 11, Ave Brahim, Ghoriefo
Bookshop(s): Ave de l'independance n 10, Batna

Enterprise Nationale du Livre (ENAL)+
23 Nahj al-'Arabi St, Algiers
Tel: (02) 639712; (02) 639643
Telex: 53845 Sneda *Cable:* SNEDA ALGER
Key Personnel
Dir General: Seghir Benamar
Editorial: Abdel Krim Saiighi; Abdel Kader M'Silti
Founded: 1983 (SNED 1966)
Subjects: Biography, Fiction, History, Nonfiction (General), Philosophy, Poetry, Regional Interests, Religion - Other, Science (General), Social Sciences, Sociology, Sports, Athletics, Travel

Angola

General Information

Capital: Luanda
Language: Portuguese (official), several African languages also in common use
Religion: Christian (mainly Roman Catholic)
Population: 8.9 million
Currency: 100 iwei = 1 new kwanza
Export/Import Information: No tariff on books and advertising. Very restricted issuance of import licenses. Advertising matter is currently given considerably lower priority. Exchange controls.

Biblioteca Nacional
Ave Commandante Jika, Luanda
Mailing Address: CP 2915, Luanda
Tel: (02) 322070 *Fax:* (02) 323979

Antigua & Barbuda

General Information

Capital: St John's
Language: English (official) and local dialects
Religion: Predominantly Anglican; other Protestant sects; some Roman Catholic
Population: 64,246
Currency: 2.70 East Caribbean dollars = $1 US

FT Caribbean (BVI) Ltd
PO Box 1037, Saint John's
Tel: 462-3392; 462-3692 *Fax:* 462-3492
E-mail: ftcarib@candw.ag
Key Personnel
Publisher: Edna Fortescue
Founded: 1978
Specialize in Caribbean economic-business & tourism publications.
Total Titles: 1 Print
Branch Office(s)
PO Box 675, Saint George's, Grenada, Yvonne Warren *Tel:* 444-4930 *Fax:* 444-3391
E-mail: warrenp@caribsurf.com (Caribbean South)
19 Mercers Rd, London N19 4PH, United Kingdom, Man Editor: Lindsay Maxwell
Tel: (020) 7281-5746 *Fax:* (020) 7281-7157
E-mail: ftcaribbean@btinternet.com (International)

Argentina

General Information

Capital: Buenos Aires
Language: Spanish
Religion: Roman Catholic
Population: 33 million
Bank Hours: 1000-1500 Monday-Friday
Shop Hours: 0900-1900 Monday-Saturday
Currency: 100 centavos = 1 nuevo peso argentino
Export/Import Information: No import licenses required. Import duties are assessed ad valorem. However, no import duties on books or similar material.
Copyright: UCC, Berne, Buenos Aires (see Copyright Conventions, pg xi)

Editorial Abaco de Rodolfo Depalma SRL+
Viamonte 1336, 6th floor, Capital Federal
Tel: (011) 4371-1675 *Fax:* (011) 43711675
E-mail: info@abacoeditorial.com.ar
Web Site: www.abacoeditorial.com.ar
Key Personnel
Man Dir & Editorial: Rodolfo Depalma
Production: Susana P Garcia de Gigena
Founded: 1975
Subjects: Economics, History, Journalism, Law, Philosophy, Psychology, Psychiatry, Public Administration, Social Sciences, Sociology
ISBN Prefix(es): 950-569
Number of titles published annually: 20 Print
Total Titles: 150 Print

Abeledo-Perrot SAE e I+
Lavalle 1280, 1048 Buenos Aires
Tel: (011) 4124-9750 *Fax:* (011) 4371-5156
E-mail: editorial@abeledo-perrot.com
Key Personnel
Man Dir: Emilio Jose Perrot *E-mail:* eperrot@abeledo-perrot.com
General Manager: Carlos Alberto Pazos *E-mail:* cpazos@abeledo-perrot.com
Founded: 1901
Subjects: Criminology, Law, Philosophy, Public Administration
ISBN Prefix(es): 950-20
Total Titles: 17 CD-ROM

Editorial Abril SA+
Avda Leandro, N Alem, 896, Capital Federal, 1001 Buenos Aires
Tel: (011) 3752450; (011) 3752451
Telex: 22630 Ryela
Key Personnel
Man Dir, Editor, Sales & Publicity: Roberto M Ares
Rights & Permissions: Alberto Cervetto
Founded: 1961
Editorial Huemul SA is the division of the company producing secondary & primary school textbooks.
Subjects: Fiction, Nonfiction (General)
ISBN Prefix(es): 950-10
Parent Company: Bramihuemul

Academia Argentina de Letras (Bulletin of the Argentine Academy of Literature)
Sanchez de Bustamante 2663, C1425DVA Buenos Aires
Tel: (011) 4-8023814; (011) 4-8027509; (011) 4-8025161 *Fax:* (011) 4-8028340
E-mail: aaldespa@fibertel.com.ar; aaladmin@fibertel.com.ar; aalbibl@fibertel.com.ar

Founded: 1931
Specialize in Literature, Philology & Linguistics.
Subjects: Language Arts, Linguistics, Literature, Literary Criticism, Essays
ISBN Prefix(es): 950-585
Number of titles published annually: 4 Print

Editorial Acme SA+
Suipacha 245 Piso 1, 1008 Buenos Aires
Tel: (011) 4328-1508; (011) 4328-1662
 Fax: (011) 4328-9345
E-mail: acme@redynet.com.ar
Key Personnel
Man Dir: Emilio I Gonzalez
Founded: 1949
Subjects: Biography, Fiction, How-to
ISBN Prefix(es): 950-565

Ada Korn Editora SA+
Uruguay 651, floor 8 H, 1015 Buenos Aires
Tel: (011) 4374-6199 *Fax:* (011) 4374-9699
E-mail: adakorn@datamarket.com.ar
Key Personnel
President: Ada Korn
Founded: 1984
Subjects: Drama, Theater, Fiction, Nonfiction (General), Science (General)
ISBN Prefix(es): 950-9540
Number of titles published annually: 3 Print
Total Titles: 50 Print

Aguilar Altea Taurus Alfaguara SA de Ediciones
Beazley 3860, 1437 Buenos Aires
Tel: (011) 4912-7220 *Fax:* (011) 4912-7440
Web Site: www.alfaguara.com.ar
Key Personnel
President & General Manager: Esteban Fernandez Rosado
Editorial Dir: Juan Martini
Founded: 1946
Subjects: Economics, Literature, Literary Criticism, Essays, Philosophy
ISBN Prefix(es): 950-511
Parent Company: Aguilar, Altea, Taurus, Aflaguara SA de Ediciones, Madrid- Espana

Libreria Akadia Editorial+
Paraguay 2078, 1121 Buenos Aires
Tel: (011) 4961-8614; (011) 4961-8595
 Fax: (011) 4961-8614
E-mail: akadia@syb.com.ar
Key Personnel
President: Jose Patlallan
Dir: Daniel Patlallan
Founded: 1967
Specialize in books.
Membership(s): Argentina Book Association.
Subjects: Health, Nutrition, Medicine, Nursing, Dentistry
ISBN Prefix(es): 950-9020

Editorial Albatros SACI+
Torres Las Plazas, J Salguero 2745, Piso 5, Oficina 51, 1425 Buenos Aires
Tel: (011) 4807-2030 *Fax:* (011) 4807-2010
E-mail: info@edalbatros.com.ar
Web Site: www.edalbatros.com.ar
Key Personnel
President: Andrea Ines Canevaro
Vice President, Executive: Gustavo Gabriel Canevaro
Founded: 1945
Subjects: Agriculture, Animals, Pets, Astrology, Occult, Economics, Electronics, Electrical Engineering, Environmental Studies, Gardening, Plants, Health, Nutrition, Medicine, Nursing, Dentistry, Social Sciences, Sociology, Sports, Athletics, Veterinary Science
ISBN Prefix(es): 950-24

Distributed by Artemis Distribuciones (Guatemala); Centro Libros Book Shop (Puerto Rico); Daisy Sel S Kuan Lau (Nicaragua); Distribuidora Lewis (Panama); Distribuidora Luongo SA (Argentina); Edaf (Spain); Edaf y Morales SA (Mexico); Editorial La Celba (El Salvador); La Familia Distribuidora de Libros SA (Peru); Gaierna SRL (Argentina); Lectorum Publications (United States); Libreria Amenguai (Dominicana Republic); Libreria Lehmann SA (Costa Rica); Libreria Libertad (Chile); Libro Shop (Argentina); Libros Sin Fronteras (United States); Litexsa Venezolana (Venezuela); Mr Books (Ecuador); Multicor SRL (Uruguay); Panamericana Libreria y Papeleria (Colombia)
Bookshop(s): Libreria Editorial Albatros S A C 1, J Salguero 2745, 1425 Buenos Aires

Alfagrama SRL ediciones
Bolivar 547, Piso 2A, 1066 Buenos Aires
Tel: (011) 4342-2452; (011) 4345-2299
 Fax: (011) 4345-5411
E-mail: libros@alfagram.com.ar
Web Site: www.alfagrama.com.ar
Key Personnel
Contact: Alfredo Nunez
Subjects: Disability, Special Needs, Gay & Lesbian, Library & Information Sciences, Publishing & Book Trade Reference, Science (General), Technology, Women's Studies
ISBN Prefix(es): 987-95615

Alianza Editorial de Argentina SA+
Av Belgrano 355, Piso 10, 1092 Buenos Aires
Tel: (011) 4342-4426; (011) 4342-9029
 Fax: (011) 4342-4426; (011) 4342-9025
Key Personnel
General Manager: Jorge Laforque
Founded: 1985
Subjects: Anthropology, Fiction, History, Literature, Literary Criticism, Essays, Philosophy, Psychology, Psychiatry, Social Sciences, Sociology
ISBN Prefix(es): 84-206; 950-40
Parent Company: Alianza Editorial SA, Juan Ignacio Luca de Tena 15, 28027 Madrid, Spain
Showroom(s): Av Cordoba 2064, 1120 Buenos Aires
Bookshop(s): Av Cordoba 2064, 1120 Buenos Aires

Amorrortu Editores SA+
Paraguay 1225, Piso 7, 1057 Buenos Aires
Tel: (011) 4816-5812; (011) 4816-5869
 Fax: (011) 4816-3321
E-mail: amorrortueditores@vianetworks.net.ar
Key Personnel
President: Horacio de Amorrortu
Founded: 1967
Subjects: Anthropology, Economics, Education, Philosophy, Psychology, Psychiatry, Regional Interests, Religion - Other, Social Sciences, Sociology
ISBN Prefix(es): 950-518

Editorial Argentina Plaza y Janes SA
Lambare 893, 1185 Buenos Aires
Tel: (011) 4862-6769; (011) 4862-6785
 Fax: (011) 4864-4970
Key Personnel
Man Dir: Jorge Perez
Sales Dir: Ernesto Pena
Subjects: Fiction, Nonfiction (General)
ISBN Prefix(es): 950-644

Argentine Bible Society+
Formerly Bible Society of Argentina
Tucuman 358, 1 Piso, 1049 Buenos Aires
Tel: (011) 4312-3533 *Fax:* (011) 4312-3400
E-mail: socbiblicaarg@biblica.org

Web Site: www.biblesociety.org
Key Personnel
General Secretary: Marcelo Figuero
General Manager: Juan Terranova
Subjects: Biblical Studies
ISBN Prefix(es): 950-711; 950-99044
Branch Office(s)
Centro Regional de las Americas, 1989 NW 88 Court, Miami, FL 33177, United States
Obispo Salguero 141, 5000 Cordoba
Avda Francia 1129, 2000 Rosario

Asociacion Bautista Argentina de Publicaciones+
Av Rivadavia 3474, 1203 Buenos Aires
Tel: (011) 863-6745 *Fax:* (011) 863-6745
Key Personnel
Assistant Manager: Emanuel Benavidez
Founded: 1911
Subjects: Religion - Other
ISBN Prefix(es): 950-841; 950-9074
Branch Office(s)
Tucuman 351, 5000 Cordoba
San Martin 1572, 2000 Rosario, Santa Fe

Asociacion Educacionista Argentina, see Editorial Stella

Editorial Astrea de Alfredo y Ricardo Depalma SRL+
Lavalle 1208, 1048 Buenos Aires
Tel: (011) 4382-1880 *Fax:* (011) 4382-4203
E-mail: info@astrea.com.ar
Web Site: www.astrea.com.ar
Key Personnel
Man Dir: Alfredo Depalma
Sales Dir: Ricardo Depalma
Founded: 1968
Subjects: Economics, Government, Political Science, History, Law, Philosophy, Social Sciences, Sociology
ISBN Prefix(es): 950-508
Number of titles published annually: 60 Print
Total Titles: 800 Print
Bookshop(s): Libreria Astrea, Lavalle 1208, 1048 Buenos Aires

Editorial Atlantida SA+
Azopardo 579, 1307 Buenos Aires
Tel: (011) 4331-4591; (011) 4331-4599
 Fax: (011) 3313341
Web Site: www.atlantida.com.ar
Telex: 21163 *Cable:* EDIATLAN
Key Personnel
Executive Dir: Alfredo Vercelli
Editorial Dir: Jorge Naveiro
Founded: 1918
Subjects: Fiction, Nonfiction (General)
ISBN Prefix(es): 950-08
U.S. Office(s): 31 West 57 St, 6th floor, New York, NY 10019, United States, Contact: Maria Campbell
Bookshop(s): Galerias Pacifico, San Martin 760, Local 5215, 1004 Buenos Aires *Tel:* (011) 3116411; Nuevo Centro Shopping, D Quiros 1400, Local 2241, 5000 Cordoba *Tel:* (051) 891440
Shipping Address: Rio Cuarto 1907, 1292 Buenos Aires
Warehouse: Rio Cuarto 1907, 1292 Buenos Aires

AZ Editora SA+
Paraguay 2351, 1121 Buenos Aires
Tel: (011) 4961-4036; (011) 4961-4037; (011) 4961-4038; (011) 4961-0088 *Fax:* (011) 4961-0089
E-mail: promocion@azeditora.com.ar
Key Personnel
President: Dante Omar Villalba
Vice President: Luis Alberto Villone
Technical Dir: Luis Mendez Davila
Founded: 1976

ARGENTINA

Subjects: Economics, History, Law, Psychology, Psychiatry
ISBN Prefix(es): 950-534

La Azotea Editorial Fotografica SRL
Paraguay 1480, 1061 Buenos Aires
Tel: (011) 4811-0931 *Fax:* (011) 4811-0931
E-mail: azotea@laazotea.com.ar
Web Site: www.laazotea.com

Beas Ediciones SRL+
Inclan 3945, 1258 Buenos Aires
Tel: (011) 4923-4030; (011) 4924-5337
  Fax: (011) 4924-0217
Key Personnel
President: Hugo S Beas
Commercial Dir: Jorge Luis Sanchez
Founded: 1992
Subjects: Fiction, Humor, Nonfiction (General), Self-Help
ISBN Prefix(es): 950-834
Parent Company: Circulo del Buen Lecetor SRL, Argentina
Associate Companies: Circulo del Buen Lector SA de CV, Mexico

Beatriz Viterbo Editora+
Espana 1150, 2000 Rosario
Tel: (041) 4827560 *Fax:* (041) 4261919
E-mail: beatrizviterbo@arnet.com.ar
Key Personnel
Contact: Adriana Astutti; Sandra Contreras
Founded: 1991
Subjects: Drama, Theater, Fiction, Literature, Literary Criticism, Essays, Nonfiction (General), Poetry
ISBN Prefix(es): 950-845; 950-99766
Distributed by Fernando Garcia Cambeiro e Hijos

Fundacion Editorial de Belgrano
Federico Lacroze 1959, Piso 4, 1426 Buenos Aires
Tel: (011) 4772-4014 *Fax:* (011) 4775-8788
Key Personnel
President: Avelino J Porto
Subjects: Architecture & Interior Design, Economics, Government, Political Science, Law, Literature, Literary Criticism, Essays, Psychology, Psychiatry, Radio, TV, Social Sciences, Sociology
ISBN Prefix(es): 950-577; 987-95823

Bible Society of Argentina, see Argentine Bible Society

Revista Biblica, *imprint of* Editorial Guadalupe

Bonum Editorial SACI+
Av Corrientes 6687, 1427 Buenos Aires
Tel: (011) 4554-1414 *Fax:* (011) 4554-1414
  Cable: BONUM
Key Personnel
Dir Commerce: Martin Gremmelmspacher
Founded: 1960
Membership(s): Argentina Book Association, Foreign Trade.
Subjects: Drama, Theater, Education, Literature, Literary Criticism, Essays, Music, Dance, Nonfiction (General), Philosophy, Psychology, Psychiatry, Religion - Catholic, Religion - Other, Securities, Self-Help, Theology
ISBN Prefix(es): 950-507
Bookshop(s): Maipu 869, 1006 Buenos Aires
  Fax: (011) 4314-0888

Bosco Don Ediciones Argentina, see Ediciones Don Bosco Argentina

Ediciones Botella al Mar
Luis Agote 2280, Piso 7, 1425 Buenos Aires
Tel: (011) 4803-8246
ISBN Prefix(es): 950-513

Editorial Cangallo SACl+
Av Belgrano 609, 1092 Buenos Aires
Tel: (011) 4331-0204; (011) 4331-8848
Key Personnel
Man Dir: Norberto del Hoyo
President: Rosa del Valle Cardozo
Founded: 1968
Subjects: Business, Economics, Law
ISBN Prefix(es): 950-543

Editorial Caymi SACl
15 de Noviembre de 1889 N 1149, 1130 Buenos Aires
Tel: (011) 4305-0784 *Fax:* (011) 4304-2474
Founded: 1945
Subjects: Animals, Pets, Astrology, Occult, Automotive, Cookery, Gardening, Plants, Medicine, Nursing, Dentistry, Science Fiction, Fantasy, Self-Help, Sports, Athletics
ISBN Prefix(es): 950-501

Centro Editor de America Latina SA
Tucuman 1736, 1050 Buenos Aires
Tel: (011) 4371-2411 *Cable:* Centroedit
Key Personnel
Man Dir: Jose Boris Spivacow
Sales Dir: Aldo Antonio Sangoi
Founded: 1966
Subjects: Art, Biography, Education, History, How-to, Literature, Literary Criticism, Essays, Psychology, Psychiatry, Science (General), Social Sciences, Sociology
ISBN Prefix(es): 950-25

Cesarini Hermanos+
Sarmiento 3219/31, 1196 Buenos Aires
Tel: (011) 4861-1152
Key Personnel
Associate Manager: Osvaldo Cesarini
Founded: 1940
Member of Argentina Book Association.
Subjects: Environmental Studies, Music, Dance, Nonfiction (General), Technology
ISBN Prefix(es): 950-526

Cientifica Interamericana SACI, Editorial
Marcelo T de Alvear 2147, 1122 Buenos Aires
Tel: (011) 4822-8883 *Fax:* (011) 4827-0486
E-mail: edit@interame.satlink.net
Key Personnel
President: Mauricio Modai
ISBN Prefix(es): 950-9428

Editorial Claretiana+
Lima 1360, 1138 Buenos Aires
Tel: (011) 4305-9510; (011) 4305-9597
  Fax: (011) 4305-6552
E-mail: editorial@editorialclaretiana.com.ar
Web Site: www.editorialclaretiana.com.ar *Cable:* EDITORIAL CLARETIANA
Key Personnel
Man Dir, Editorial, Rights & Permissions: Gustavo Larrazabal
Manager: Eduardo Righetti
Publicity: Jose Luis Perez
Founded: 1956
Subjects: Religion - Catholic, Theology
ISBN Prefix(es): 950-512

Editorial Claridad SA+
Viamonte 1730, Piso 1, 1055 Buenos Aires
Tel: (011) 4371-5546 *Fax:* (011) 4375-1659
E-mail: editorial@heliasta.com
Web Site: www.editorialclaridad.com.ar *Cable:* CLARIDAD BAIRES
Key Personnel
President: Dr Ana Maria Cabanellas
Vice President: Dr Guillermo Cabanellas

Founded: 1922
Subjects: Biography, Government, Political Science, History, Law, Philosophy, Poetry
ISBN Prefix(es): 950-620; 950-9065
Subsidiaries: Editorial Heliasta SRL

Club de Lectores+
Av de Mayo 624, 1084 Buenos Aires
Tel: (011) 4342-6251; (011) 4342-3955
Key Personnel
Man Dir: Mercedes Fontenla
Sales: Carlos A Alvano
Publicity: Cesar Tomas Fontenla
Founded: 1938
Subjects: History, Philosophy, Psychology, Psychiatry, Religion - Other, Social Sciences, Sociology
ISBN Prefix(es): 950-9034
Bookshop(s): Libreria Accion, Av de Mayo 624, 1084 Buenos Aires; Libreria Universitaria Fontis, Av de Mayo 624, 1084 Buenos Aires

Coleccion Juridica Bco de Datos en Computacion, *imprint of* Editorial Zeus SRL

Libreria del Colegio SA+
Humberto 1 531, 1103 Buenos Aires
Tel: (011) 4362-1616; (011) 4362-1222
  Fax: (011) 3627364 *Cable:* LIBRECOL
Key Personnel
Contact: Javier Lopez Llovet
Founded: 1830
Subjects: Education
ISBN Prefix(es): 950-548
Parent Company: Editorial Sudamericana SA

Colmegna SA
San Martin 2546, 3000 Sante Fe
Tel: (042) 523102; (042) 557345 *Fax:* (042) 4557345
Key Personnel
President: Jose Luis Anessi
Manager: Guillermo Goatherd
Founded: 1889
Subjects: Literature, Literary Criticism, Essays, Poetry
ISBN Prefix(es): 950-535

Concilium, *imprint of* Editorial Guadalupe

Ediciones Corregidor SAlCl y E+
Rodriguez Pena 452, 1020 Buenos Aires
Tel: (011) 4374-4959; (011) 4374-5000
  Fax: (011) 4374-5000
Web Site: www.corregidor.com
Key Personnel
Dir: Manuel Pampin
Founded: 1970
Subjects: Drama, Theater, Economics, Literature, Literary Criticism, Essays, Music, Dance, Poetry
ISBN Prefix(es): 950-05
Warehouse: Pasaje Berg 4060, Lanus Oeste, 1826 Buenos Aires

Cosmopolita SRL
Piedras 744, 1070 Buenos Aires
Tel: (011) 4361-8925; (011) 4361-8049
  Fax: (011) 4361-8049; (011) 4361-8925
Key Personnel
Man Dir: Eva Ruth F de Rapp
Founded: 1940
Subjects: Agriculture
ISBN Prefix(es): 950-9069

Critica+
Belgrano 1256 PB, 1093 Buenos Aires
Tel: (011) 3834940; (011) 3837403
E-mail: info@grijalbo.com.ar
Web Site: www.grijalbo.com.ar

PUBLISHERS

ARGENTINA

Key Personnel
Gen Mgr: Felipe Munde *E-mail:* fmunoz@grijalbo.com.ar
Subjects: Fiction, Nonfiction (General)
ISBN Prefix(es): 950-28
Parent Company: Grijalbo Mondadori SA

Studia Croatica
Matienzo 2530, 1426 Buenos Aires
Tel: (011) 4771-4954 *Fax:* (011) 4771-4954
ISBN Prefix(es): 987-95467

Depalma SRL+
Talcahuano 494, 1013 Buenos Aires
Tel: (011) 371-7306 *Fax:* (011) 371-6913
E-mail: info@ed-depalma.com
Web Site: www.ed-depalma.com
Key Personnel
Man Dir, Production: Roberto Suardiaz
General Manager: Alberto Evaristo Baron
International Marketing Manager: Nicolas von der Pahlen
Founded: 1944
Also acts as distributor of Iberiamerican Juridical books.
Subjects: Business, History, Law, Social Sciences, Sociology
ISBN Prefix(es): 950-14
Showroom(s): Lavalle 1302, Buenos Aires

Diana Argentina SA, Editorial
Beauchef 559, 1424 Buenos Aires
Tel: (011) 4922-5035; (011) 4922-5036
 Fax: (011) 4922-5035; (011) 4922-5036
E-mail: todianaarg@sinectis.com.ar
Key Personnel
General: Jorge Baez Arganaraz
ISBN Prefix(es): 987-96980
Parent Company: Casa Amtriz

Diario la Voz del Interior
Tte Gral JD Peron 1628, Piso 2, 1037 Buenos Aires
Tel: (011) 4382-2267 *Fax:* (011) 3822508
E-mail: info@nueva.com.ar
Key Personnel
Dir: Cuesta Carlos Enrique
ISBN Prefix(es): 950-879; 950-884

Editorial Ruy Diaz SAEIC+
Elpidio Gonzalez 5562/66, 1407 Buenos Aires
Tel: (011) 4567-4055; (011) 4567-2865
 Fax: (011) 4567-4918
E-mail: ruydiaz@pinos.com
Web Site: www.ruydiaz.com.ar *Cable:* EDIRUY
Key Personnel
President: Rafael Juan Zucotti
Man Dir: Gustavo H Zuccotti
Founded: 1966
Member of Argentina Book Association.
Subjects: Cookery, Education, Law
ISBN Prefix(es): 950-9023; 987-516
Branch Office(s)
Casilla de Correo 46, Suc 6, 1406 Buenos Aires

Ediciones Don Bosco Argentina+
Don Bosco 4069, 1206 Buenos Aires
Tel: (011) 4981-7314; (011) 4981-1388
 Fax: (011) 4958-1506
Key Personnel
Contact: Roque R Cella
Founded: 1941
Member of Camara del Libro.
Subjects: Accounting, Drama, Theater, Education, History, Journalism, Radio, TV, Religion - Catholic
ISBN Prefix(es): 950-514
Distributed by Centro Salesiano de Estudios
Distributor for Edebe

Bookshop(s): Don Bosco 4069, 1206 Capital Federal
Orders to: Don Bosco 4069, 1206 Capital Federal

ECA (Ediciones Culturales Argentinas)
Ayacucho 1578, 1112 Buenos Aires
Tel: (011) 49232579; (011) 49232658
Key Personnel
Dir: Juan Carlos Manoukian
Founded: 1961
Member of CERLAL.
Subjects: Education, Ethnicity, Regional Interests
ISBN Prefix(es): 950-36
Warehouse: Avda Directorio 1781, Buenos Aires (1406)

Ediciones del Eclipse+
Julian Alvarez 843, 1414 Buenos Aires
Tel: (011) 4771-3583 *Fax:* (011) 4771-3583
E-mail: deleclipse@overnet.com.ar
Web Site: www.deleclipse.com
Key Personnel
President: Maria Del Rosario Charquero
Subjects: Literature, Literary Criticism, Essays, Psychology, Psychiatry
ISBN Prefix(es): 987-9011; 950-99530

Edicial SA+
Rivadavia 739/43, 1002 Buenos Aires
Tel: (011) 342 84 81; (011) 342 84 82; (011) 342 84 83 *Fax:* (011) 343 11 51
E-mail: edicial@ssdnet.com.ar
Web Site: www.ssdnet.com.ar/edicial
Key Personnel
President: Juan A Musset
Founded: 1931
Subjects: Communications, Language Arts, Linguistics, Literature, Literary Criticism, Essays, Philosophy, Regional Interests
ISBN Prefix(es): 950-506
U.S. Office(s): Distribooks, 8220 N Christiana Ave, Skokie, IL 60076-2911, United States
Showroom(s): Palacio del Libro International, Suipacha 1136, 1008 Buenos Aires

Editorial Ciudad Nueva de la Sefoma+
Lezica 4358, 1202 Buenos Aires
Tel: (011) 4981-4885 *Fax:* (011) 4981-3719
Key Personnel
Manager: Alejandro Frere
Editor: Carlos Mana
Founded: 1964
Subjects: Biography, Education, Religion - Catholic, Securities, Theology
ISBN Prefix(es): 950-586
Parent Company: Citta Nuova Editrice (for associate companies), Italy
Distributed by Ciudad Nueva (Chile, Uruguay, Paraguay, Colombia, Mexico)

Editorial Idearium de la Universidad de Mendoza (EDIUM)
S Boulogne Mer 683, 5500 Mendoza
Tel: (0261) 420-2017 *Fax:* (0261) 420-1100
E-mail: umimen@um.edu.ar
Web Site: www.um.edu.ar/um/
Key Personnel
Dir: Dr Juan Carlos Menghini
Manager: Jose Miguel Ciarcia
Founded: 1979
Subjects: Architecture & Interior Design, Electronics, Electrical Engineering, Engineering (General), Environmental Studies, Law, Social Sciences, Sociology, Technology
ISBN Prefix(es): 950-624
Distributed by Abeledo-Perrot

Editorial Kapelusz SA, see Kapelusz Editora SA

Editorial Universitaria de Buenos Aires, see EUDEBA (Editorial Universitaria de Buenos Aires)

EDIUM, see Editorial Idearium de la Universidad de Mendoza (EDIUM)

Emece Editores SA+
Av Independencia 1668, 1100 Buenos Aires
Tel: (011) 4954-0105; (011) 4954-0120
 Fax: (011) 4953-4200
E-mail: editorial@emece.com.ar
Web Site: www.emece.com.ar
Key Personnel
President: Ing Alfredo del Carril *E-mail:* acarril@emece.com.ar
Administration: Marcos I Fantin
Editorial Director: Bonifacio P del Carril
 E-mail: bcarril@emece.com.ar
Editorial: Eduardo Garcia Belsunce
 E-mail: edicion@emece.com.ar
General Director: Francisco F del Carril
 E-mail: fcarril@emece.com.ar
Sales Dir, Export: Carlos A Bustillo
 E-mail: cbustillo@emece.com.ar
Editorial Dept: Stella Maris Rozas
 E-mail: srozas@emece.com.ar
Founded: 1939
Subjects: Art, Biography, Fiction, History, Literature, Literary Criticism, Essays, Mysteries, Nonfiction (General)
ISBN Prefix(es): 950-04
Number of titles published annually: 120 Print
Associate Companies: Emece Editores SA, Mallorca 237 Entlo, 1a, 08008 Barcelona, Spain, Siprid Kraus *Tel:* (03) 215-1199 *Fax:* (03) 215-4636; Emece Mexicana SA, de CV Vito Alessio Robles 140, Col Florida CP, 01030 Mexico, DF, Mexico, Iuan Mozo *Tel:* (05) 661-7590 *Fax:* (05) 661-4110 *E-mail:* emece@podernet.com.ar; Av Uruguay 1579, Montevideo, Uruguay, Reinaldo Rodriguez *Tel:* (02) 42-9358 *Fax:* (02) 42-9359 *E-mail:* pero@adinet.com.uy; Emece/Urano SA, av Francisco Bilbao, 2809 Santiago de Chile, Chile, Ricardo Ulasteliga *Tel:* (02) 341-6731 *Fax:* (02) 225-3896 *E-mail:* emc-uran@entelchile.net
Branch Office(s)
Sanford J Greenburger Associates Inc, 55 Fifth Ave, New York, NY 10003, United States, Carol Frederick *Tel:* 212-206-5600 *Fax:* 212-463-8718; 687-9281

Errepar SA+
Av San Juan 960, 1147 Buenos Aires 1147
Tel: (011) 4300-3942; (011) 4300-0549
 Fax: (011) 4307-9541
E-mail: libros@errepar.com
Web Site: www.errepar.com
Key Personnel
Vice President: Dr Francisco Canada
International Rights Contact: Veronica Parada; Irene Acero
Subjects: Astrology, Occult, Cookery, Economics, Education, Religion - Catholic, Religion - Hindu, Religion - Other, Self-Help
ISBN Prefix(es): 950-739; 950-9524; 950-9088

Espasa-Calpe Argentina SA+
Av Independencea 1668, 1100 Buenos Aires
Tel: (011) 4382-4043; (011) 4382-4045
 Fax: (011) 4383-3793
E-mail: info@eplaneta.com.ar
Key Personnel
Dir General: Guillermo Schavelzon
Founded: 1929
ISBN Prefix(es): 950-852
Parent Company: Grupo Planeta
Subsidiaries: Seix Barral; Destino; Ariel; Deusto; Austral

5

ARGENTINA

Angel Estrada y Cia SA
Bolivar 462, 1066 Buenos Aires
Tel: (011) 4344-5589 *Fax:* (011) 4331-6527
E-mail: editocom@estrada.com.ar
Web Site: www.estrada.com.ar
Telex: 17990 Estra
Key Personnel
President: Zsolt Arardy
Director: Tomas de Estrada
Publishing Manager: Marcela Iraola
Founded: 1869
Subjects: Education, How-to
ISBN Prefix(es): 950-01

EUDEBA (Editorial Universitaria de Buenos Aires)+
Av Rivadavia 1573, 1033 Buenos Aires
Tel: (011) 4383-8025 *Fax:* (011) 4383-2202
E-mail: eudela@eudeba.com
Web Site: www.eudeba.com.ar
Key Personnel
President: Alicia Rosalia Wigdorovitz de Camilloni
Manager of Institutional Relations: Martin Unzue
  E-mail: institucionales@eudeba.com.ar
Publishing Manager: Victor Palaces
  E-mail: geditorial@eudeba.com.ar
Commercial Manager: Gustavo Kogan
  E-mail: ventas@eudeba.com.ar
Founded: 1958
Subjects: Accounting, Archaeology, Architecture & Interior Design, Art, Astrology, Occult, Chemistry, Chemical Engineering, Drama, Theater, Economics, Education, Geography, Geology, History, Law, Literature, Literary Criticism, Essays, Mathematics, Medicine, Nursing, Dentistry, Music, Dance, Philosophy, Physics, Psychology, Psychiatry, Science (General), Theology, Veterinary Science
ISBN Prefix(es): 950-23
Number of titles published annually: 150 Print; 5 CD-ROM
Bookshop(s): Pasaje El Fundador-Loca, 9 Obispo Trejo, 29 Cordoba, 5000 Codigo

Ediciones Librerias Fausto+
Av Corrientes 1316, 1043 Buenos Aires
Tel: (011) 4372-4919 *Fax:* (011) 4372-3914
E-mail: fausto@fausto.com
Web Site: www.fausto.com
Key Personnel
President: Rafael Pedro Zorrilla
Manager: Jose Luis Retes
ISBN Prefix(es): 950-653
Branch Office(s)
Corrientes 1243, Santa Fe 1715
Galerias Pacifico, Santa Fe 1311
Bookshop(s): Libreria Fausto

Ediciones de la Flor SRL+
Gorriti 3695, 1172 Buenos Aires
Tel: (011) 4963-7950 *Fax:* (011) 4963-5616
E-mail: edic-flor@datamarkets.com.ar
Web Site: www.edicionesdelaflor.com.ar
Key Personnel
Dir: Daniel Divinsky *Tel:* (011) 4963-1460
Man Dir: Ana M Miler
Publicity & Advertising Dir, Rights & Permissions: Daniel Borenstein
Founded: 1967
Subjects: Biography, Drama, Theater, Fiction, History, Humor, Literature, Literary Criticism, Essays, Philosophy, Psychology, Psychiatry, Social Sciences, Sociology
ISBN Prefix(es): 950-515
Number of titles published annually: 40 Print
Total Titles: 500 Print

Ediciones de Arte Gaglianone
Chilavert 1146, 1437 Buenos Aires
Tel: (011) 4923-2579; (011) 4923-2658
  Fax: (011) 4923-0150
E-mail: webmaster@gaglianone.com.ar
Web Site: www.gaglianone.com.ar
Key Personnel
President: Jose Horacio Gaglianone
General Manager: Oscar A Aimar
Editor: Patricio Lopez Tobares
Accounting & Finances: Gustavo Portela
Subjects: Music, Dance
ISBN Prefix(es): 950-720; 950-9004

Editorial Galerna SRL+
Lambare 893, 1185 Buenos Aires
Tel: (011) 4867 1661 *Fax:* (011) 4862-5031
E-mail: galerna@overnet.com.ar *Cable:* GALERNA
Key Personnel
Dir: Hugo Benjamin Levin; Juan Jose D'AAbtibua
Founded: 1967
Afiliados a la Camara Argentina del Libro.
Member of Argentina Book Association.
Subjects: Drama, Theater, History, Literature, Literary Criticism, Essays, Social Sciences, Sociology, Theology
ISBN Prefix(es): 950-556
Subsidiaries: Librogal SRL
Bookshop(s): Septimo Rayo, Callao 729, Buenos Aires; Libreria Galerna, Corrientes 1776, Mar del Plata, Buenos Aires; Ramon L Falcon 7115, Loc 305, Buenos Aires; Rivadavia 3050, Loc 21, Mar del Plata, Buenos Aires; Nazarre 3175, Loc 119/20, Buenos Aires; Gueemes 369, Loc 50, Haedo

Gram Editora
Cochabamba 1652, 1148 Buenos Aires
Tel: (011) 4304-4833; (011) 4305-8397
  Fax: (011) 4304-5692
E-mail: grameditora@infovia.com.ar
Web Site: www.grameditora.com.ar
Key Personnel
Dir: Manuel Herrero Montes
Founded: 1925
Subjects: Computer Science, Education, Religion - Catholic, Religion - Other
ISBN Prefix(es): 950-530
Branch Office(s)
Libreria Marista, Av Callao 226, 1148 Buenos Aires *Tel:* (011) 374-3114 *Fax:* (011) 374-3146

Grupo Editorial Planeta, see Editorial Planeta Argentina SAIC

Grupo Editorial Planets, see Seix Barral

Editorial Guadalupe+
Mansilla 3865, 1425 Buenos Aires
Tel: (011) 4826-8587 *Fax:* (011) 4823-6672
E-mail: ventas@editorialguadalupe.com.ar
Web Site: www.editorialguadalupe.com.ar
Key Personnel
Man Dir, Production: Mario V Keiner
Publicity Dir: Osvaldo Lopez
Founded: 1895
Member Argentina Book Association.
Subjects: Anthropology, Education, History, Language Arts, Linguistics, Literature, Literary Criticism, Essays, Music, Dance, Philosophy, Psychology, Psychiatry, Religion - Catholic, Social Sciences, Sociology, Theology
ISBN Prefix(es): 950-500
Imprints: Revista Biblica; Concilium
Branch Office(s)
Libreria Verbo Divino, Velez Sarsfield 76-5000 Cordoba
Bookshop(s): Libreria Guadalupe, Mansilla 3865, 1425 Buenos Aires; Libreria Verbo Divino, Velez Sarsfield 76, 5000 Cordoba

Editorial Heliasta SRL
Viamonte 1730 Piso 1, 1055 Buenos Aires
Tel: (011) 4371-5546 *Fax:* (011) 4375-1659
E-mail: editorial@heliasta.com.ar
Web Site: www.heliasta.com.ar

Editorial Hemisferio Sur SA+
Pasteur 743, 1028 Buenos Aires
Tel: (011) 49529825 *Fax:* (011) 49528454
E-mail: informe@hemisferiosur.com.ar
Web Site: www.hemisferiosur.com.ar
Key Personnel
President & Man Dir, Licensing: Adolfo Julian Pena
Founded: 1966
Subjects: Agriculture, Animals, Pets, Biological Sciences, Gardening, Plants, Science (General), Veterinary Science, Wine & Spirits
ISBN Prefix(es): 950-504

Editorial Huemul SA, see Editorial Abril SA

Libreria Huemul SA+
Ave Santa Fe 2237, 1123 Buenos Aires
Tel: (011) 825-2290 *Fax:* (011) 822-1666
Key Personnel
President & Manager: Antonio Rego
Sales, Publicity, Rights & Permissions: Carlos L Sanchez
Founded: 1941
ISBN Prefix(es): 950-571

INCYTH, see Instituto Nacional de Ciencia y Tecnica Hidrica (INCYTH)

Inter-Medica+
Junin 917, Piso 1 A, 1113 Buenos Aires
Tel: (011) 4961-9234 *Fax:* (011) 4961-5572
E-mail: intervet@satlink.com
Key Personnel
President: Jorge Modyeievsky
Vice President: Sonia M B de Modyeievsky
General Manager: Tatiana Modyeievsky Bakenroth; Eduardo Modyeievsky Bakenroth; Daniel Sergio
Founded: 1959
Subjects: Veterinary Science
ISBN Prefix(es): 950-555
Branch Office(s)
Editorial Intervet SA, Junin 917-1 A, Capital 1113

Juegos & Co SRL+
Av Corrientes 1312, Piso 8, 1043 Buenos Aires
Tel: (011) 4374-7903; (011) 4371-1825
  Fax: (011) 4372-3829
E-mail: comercial@demente.com
Web Site: www.demente.com
Key Personnel
Dir: Jaime Poniachik
Editor: Diego Uribe
Founded: 1980
Member of Argentina Association of Magazine Publishers.
Subjects: Mathematics
ISBN Prefix(es): 950-765
Associate Companies: Zugarto Ediciones, Madrid, Spain

Juris Editorial+
Dorrego 3668 - Moreno 1580, 2000 Rosario-Santa Fe
Tel: (0341) 4267301; (0341) 4267302 *Fax:* (0341) 4267301; (0341) 4267302
E-mail: editorialjuris@arnet.com.ar
Key Personnel
International Contact: Luis Maesano
Founded: 1952
Subjects: Criminology, Law
ISBN Prefix(es): 950-817

Kapelusz Editora SA
San Jose 831, 1076 Buenos Aires

PUBLISHERS

ARGENTINA

Tel: (011) 4382-7400 *Fax:* (011) 4383-8020
E-mail: empresa@kapelusz.com.ar
Web Site: www.kapelusz.com.ar
Telex: 18342 Ekasa *Cable:* Kapelusz
Key Personnel
President: Tomas Castle
Vice President: Juan Silva Baptist
Director: Ivan Dario Pineda
Sales Manager: Hernando S Ferreres
Publicity: Carlos O Otero
Founded: 1905
Subjects: Education, Psychology, Psychiatry
ISBN Prefix(es): 950-13
Subsidiaries: Editorial Kapelusz Colombiana SA; Editorial Kapelusz Mexicana SA; Editorial Cincel SA; Editorial Kapelusz SA; Editorial Kapelusz Venezolana SA
Bookshop(s): Corrientes 999, Buenos Aires

Editorial Kier SACIF1+
Ave Santa Fe 1260, 1059 Buenos Aires
Tel: (011) 4811-0507 *Fax:* (011) 4811-3395
E-mail: ediciones@kier.com.ar
Web Site: www.kier.com.ar
Key Personnel
President: Hector Pibernus
Vice President: Alfonso Sergio Pibernus
Man Dir: Osvaldo Pibernus
Sales Dir: Sergio F Pibernus
Founded: 1907
Specialize in medicine.
Subjects: Anthropology, Astrology, Occult, Health, Nutrition, Parapsychology, Religion - Buddhist, Religion - Hindu, Religion - Islamic, Religion - Jewish, Religion - Other, Self-Help
ISBN Prefix(es): 950-17
Number of titles published annually: 40 Print
Total Titles: 800 Print
Bookshop(s): Libreria Kier, Ave Santa Fe 1260, 1059 Buenos Aires

Laffont Ediciones Electronicas SA
Av Reg Patricios 929, 1265 Buenos Aires
Tel: (011) 4302-8668 *Fax:* (011) 4301-2525
E-mail: cliente@laffont.com.ar
Web Site: www.laffont.com.ar
Key Personnel
Contact: Dr Julio Laffont
Member of Camara del Libro.
Subjects: Art, Education, Geography, Geology, History, Science (General)
ISBN Prefix(es): 987-9220; 987-95410

Ediciones Larousse Argentina SA
Valentin Gomez 3530, 1191 Buenos Aires
Tel: (011) 4865-9581; (011) 4865-9582; (011) 4865-9583
E-mail: editorial@aique.com.ar; comercial@aique.com.ar
Web Site: www.larousse.com.ar
Telex: 0121783 *Cable:* Editlarousse
Key Personnel
President: Dominique Bertin
ISBN Prefix(es): 950-538

Latina SA, see Ediciones Preescolar SA

La Ley SA Editora e Impresora+
Tucuman 1471, 1050 Buenos Aires
Tel: (011) 4378-4841 *Fax:* (011) 4372-0953
E-mail: bausilic@la-ley.com.ar
Web Site: www.la-ley.com.ar
Telex: 17465 Laley
Key Personnel
President: Juan C Milberg
Vice President: Enrique J Algorta
General Dir: Enrique J Algorta Gaona
Commercial Manager: Manuel E Schkolnik
Production: Roberto Pedretti
Founded: 1935

Subjects: Economics, History, Law, Philosophy
ISBN Prefix(es): 950-527

Libres, *imprint of* Ediciones Macchi

Librograf+
Chacabuco 1185, 1069 Buenos Aires
Tel: (011) 4300-5662; (011) 4300-1466
 Fax: (011) 4300-3670
Key Personnel
Contacts: Eduardo Rosales; Adriana Arribas
Founded: 1968
Subjects: Cookery, Education
ISBN Prefix(es): 950-848; 950-99827

Ediciones Lidiun
Patagones 2459, 1282 Buenos Aires
Tel: (011) 4942-9002 *Fax:* (011) 4942-9162
E-mail: info@ateneo.com
Web Site: www.ateneo.com
Founded: 1970
Subjects: Animals, Pets, Health, Nutrition, Outdoor Recreation, Psychology, Psychiatry, Religion - Other, Sports, Athletics
ISBN Prefix(es): 950-524

Lopez Libreros Editores S R L
Av Cordoba 2370, 1120 Buenos Aires
Tel: (011) 4963-9646
Key Personnel
Man Dir: Dr Pablo A Lopez; Josefina A Lopez
Founded: 1927
Subjects: Medicine, Nursing, Dentistry
ISBN Prefix(es): 950-505

Editorial Losada SA+
Moreno 3362, 1209 Buenos Aires
Tel: (011) 4373-4006; (011) 4375-5001
 Fax: (011) 4373-4006; (011) 4375-5001
 Cable: EDILOSADA
Key Personnel
President: Jose Juan Fernandez Reguera
Vice President: Dr Moretti Luis Angel
Secretary & Vice President: Mabel Peremarti
Founded: 1938
Subjects: Biography, Drama, Theater, Education, Fiction, History, Law, Philosophy, Poetry, Psychology, Psychiatry
ISBN Prefix(es): 950-03

Ediciones LR SA+
Sarmiento 835, 1041 Buenos Aires
Tel: (011) 4326-3725; (011) 4326-3826
Telex: 22087 Elerre
Key Personnel
President: Bautista L Tello
Founded: 1981
Member of Camara Argentina de Publicaciones.
ISBN Prefix(es): 950-604
Parent Company: Libreria Rodriguez SA
Associate Companies: LR Distribuidora SA
Distributor for LR Distribuidora SA
Warehouse: Boedo 377, 1206 Buenos Aires

Ediciones Macchi+
Alsina 1535/37, 1088 Buenos Aires
Tel: (011) 4375-1195 *Fax:* (011) 4375-1870; (011) 4374-2506
E-mail: info@macchi.com.ar
Web Site: www.macchi.com
Key Personnel
President: Raul Luis Macchi
Founded: 1947
ISBN Prefix(es): 950-537
Imprints: Libres
Bookshop(s): Cordoba 2015, 1120 Bueno Aires

Macchi Grupo Editors SA, see Ediciones Macchi

Marymar Ediciones SA+
Chile 1432, 1098 Buenos Aires
Tel: (011) 4988-0200
Key Personnel
President: Isay Klasse
Vice President: Saul Chernicoff
Founded: 1960
Also book packager.
Subjects: Architecture & Interior Design, Economics, Education, Environmental Studies, Fiction, Film, Video, Government, Political Science, History, Library & Information Sciences, Music, Dance, Philosophy, Psychology, Psychiatry, Science (General), Social Sciences, Sociology, Technology
ISBN Prefix(es): 950-503

Editorial Medica Panamericana
MT de Alvear 2145, 1122 Buenos Aires
Tel: (091) 4570203 *Fax:* (091) 4570919
E-mail: edmedpan@emp.es
Web Site: www.medicapanamericana.com
Key Personnel
Contact: Patrick Martin
Subjects: Biological Sciences, Medicine, Nursing, Dentistry, Psychology, Psychiatry, Social Sciences, Sociology, Ecology, Pharmacy Veterinary Medicine
ISBN Prefix(es): 84-7903; 84-85320

Editorial Medica, Panamericana SA+
Marcelo T de Alvear 2143/45, 1122 Buenos Aires
Tel: (011) 4821-5520; (011) 4821-0175
 Fax: (011) 4821-1214
E-mail: postmaster@edmedpan.satlink.net
Key Personnel
President: Hugo Brik
Founded: 1953
Subjects: Biological Sciences, Medicine, Nursing, Dentistry, Psychology, Psychiatry
ISBN Prefix(es): 950-06
Branch Office(s)
A Aereo, 076037 Bogota, Colombia
Alberto Alcocer, 24, 28015 Madrid, Spain
Calzada de Tlalpan 5022, Col La Joya, 14090 DF, Mexico
Edificio Polar, Torre Oeste, Piso 7, Oficina 7-A, Plaza Venezuela, Urbanizacion Los Caobos, Parroquia El Recreo, Municipio Libertador, Distrito Federal, Venezuela

Ediciones Medicas SA
Cerrito 512 Piso 2, 1010 Buenos Aires
Tel: (011) 4384-0750 *Fax:* (011) 4384-0750
E-mail: emsa@havasmedimedia.com.ar
Key Personnel
Dir: Juan Jose Vallory
ISBN Prefix(es): 987-97055

Ediciones Minotauro SRL
Humberto I 531, 1103 Buenos Aires
Tel: (011) 4362-1616; (011) 4362-1222
 Fax: (011) 4362-7364
ISBN Prefix(es): 950-547

Instituto Nacional de Ciencia y Tecnica Hidrica (INCYTH)
Empalme Ruta 205 KM 2.5, Lomas de Zamora, 1832 Buenos Aires
Tel: (011) 4295-1503 *Fax:* (011) 4800094
Key Personnel
President: Dr Mario Rodolfo de Marco Naon
Subjects: Computer Science, Earth Sciences, Geography, Geology, Law, Library & Information Sciences, Mathematics, Technology
ISBN Prefix(es): 950-634

Instituto de Publicaciones Navales+
Division of Centro Naval - Argentina
Cordoba 354, 1054 Buenos Aires

Tel: (011) 4311-0042; (011) 4311-0043
 Fax: (011) 4312-8461; (011) 4312-8462; (011) 4312-8463
Key Personnel
President: Julio Degrange
Manager: Jorge Horacio Urroz
Founded: 1961
Specialize in strategy, naval history & international relations.
Member of Argentina Book Association.
Subjects: Maritime, Military Science, Sports, Athletics, International Relations, Narrative, Nautical Sports, Sailing, Strategics
ISBN Prefix(es): 950-899
Number of titles published annually: 7 Print
Total Titles: 155 Print

Editorial Norte SA+
Jose Marmol 2131, 1255 Buenos Aires
Tel: (011) 4921-1440 *Fax:* (011) 4921-1440
Key Personnel
Dir General: Alejandro I Lamarque
Founded: 1961
Specializes in marketing.
Subjects: Education
ISBN Prefix(es): 950-27; 950-598

Ediciones Nueva Vision SAIC+
Tucuman 3748, 1189 Buenos Aires
Tel: (011) 4863-1461; (011) 4863-5980
 Fax: (011) 4863-5980
Key Personnel
Man Dir: Haydee P de Giacone
Sales Manager: Anibal Victor Giacone
Founded: 1954
Subjects: Architecture & Interior Design, Art, Drama, Theater, Psychology, Psychiatry, Social Sciences, Sociology
ISBN Prefix(es): 950-602

Oikos+
Rivadavia 1823, Piso 9, 1033 Buenos Aires
Tel: (011) 4951-9489; (011) 4951-8129
E-mail: postmaster@atlas.edu.ar
Key Personnel
President: Mario C Fuschini Mejia
Founded: 1975
Subjects: Earth Sciences, Geography, Geology, Social Sciences, Sociology
ISBN Prefix(es): 950-601
Bookshop(s): Hipolito Yrigoyen 1970, 1089 Buenos Aires

Editorial Paidos SAICF
Defensa 599 - Piso 1, 1065 Buenos Aires
Tel: (011) 4331-2275; (011) 4331-9399
 Fax: (011) 4331-2275
E-mail: paidos@internet.siscotel.com
Key Personnel
Man Dir, Rights & Permissions: Maria Gottheil
Founded: 1945
Subjects: Child Care & Development, Communications, Education, Environmental Studies, Government, Political Science, Philosophy, Psychology, Psychiatry, Self-Help, Social Sciences, Sociology, Women's Studies
ISBN Prefix(es): 950-12
Subsidiaries: Ediciones Paidos Iberica SA (Mexico & Spain)

Editora Patria Grande
Rivadavia 6369, 1406 Buenos Aires
Tel: (011) 4631-6446
Key Personnel
General Manager and Rights & Permissions: Washington Uranga
Editorial: Carlos J Duran
Sales: Elsa S de Fernandez
Production: Carlos D Arnedillo
Publicity: Duilio Lopez
Founded: 1974
Subjects: Poetry, Religion - Other
ISBN Prefix(es): 950-546
Branch Office(s)
Casilla de Correo 5, Suc 8, 1408 Buenos Aires
Bookshop(s): Libreria Didaje, Jose Cubas 3543, Buenos Aires

Pearson Educacion de Argentina
Avenida Regimiento Patricios 1959, 1266 Buenos Aires
Tel: 011 4 309 6100 *Fax:* 011 4 309 6199
E-mail: firstnamelastintial@pearsoned.com.ar
Key Personnel
President - Southern Cone: Juan Carlos Cavin
Manager, Finance & Administration: Ernesto Merlo
Manager, Argentinean ELT/School: Diane Repetto
Publisher, Manager Professional/Trade: Guillermo Rivas
Publisher, Manager College: Esteban Lo Presti

Editorial Planeta Argentina SAIC+
Av Independencia 1668, 1100 Buenos Aires
Tel: (011) 4382-4045; (011) 4382-4043
 Fax: (011) 4383-3793
E-mail: info@eplaneta.com.ar
Key Personnel
Executive President: Julio Perez Vega
General Director: Guillermo Schavelzon
Editorial Manager: Leandro de Sagastizabal
Edirorial Manager: Ricardo Sabanes
Founded: 1983
Subjects: Biography, Environmental Studies, Fiction, Health, Nutrition, History, How-to, Literature, Literary Criticism, Essays, Nonfiction (General), Parapsychology, Psychology, Psychiatry, Religion - Other
ISBN Prefix(es): 950-742; 950-9216; 950-49
Parent Company: Planeta Internacional SA, Barcelona, Spain
Subsidiaries: Ariel; Destino; Deusto; Espese Calpe; Montiuez Rica; Seix Berral; Teures de Teay

Plaza & Janes, see Editorial Argentina Plaza y Janes SA

Editorial Pleamar
Pena 3161, Piso 7 B, 1425 Buenos Aires
Tel: (011) 485-6597
Key Personnel
Man Dir: Andres Alfonso Bravo
Founded: 1965
Subjects: Government, Political Science, Social Sciences, Sociology
ISBN Prefix(es): 950-583

Editorial Plus Ultra SA
Callao 575, 1022 Buenos Aires
Tel: (011) 4374-2973 *Fax:* (011) 4374-2973
E-mail: plus_ultra@epu.virtual.ar.net *Cable:* Plusultra
Key Personnel
President: Rafael Roman Picon
Man Dir: Lorenzo Marengo
Editorial: Carlos Alberto Loprete; Jose Isaacson
Sales: Ricardo Errea
Production: Renato Gardoni
Publicity: Lily Sosa de Newton
Founded: 1964
Subjects: Economics, Education, Government, Political Science, History, Law, Literature, Literary Criticism, Essays, Philosophy, Psychology, Psychiatry, Social Sciences, Sociology
ISBN Prefix(es): 950-21

Polemos SA+
Moreno 1785 Piso 5, Buenos Aires 1093
Tel: (011) 4383-5291 *Fax:* (011) 4382-4181
E-mail: editorial@polemos.com.ar
Web Site: www.polemus.com.ar
Key Personnel
President: Juan Carlos Stagnaro
Founded: 1990
Subjects: Behavioral Sciences, Medicine, Nursing, Dentistry, Psychology, Psychiatry, Science (General), Social Sciences, Sociology, Psychoanalysis
ISBN Prefix(es): 987-9165; 987-99545

Biblioteca Popular Judia
Larrea 744, 1030 Buenos Aires
Tel: (011) 4961-4534 *Fax:* (011) 4963-7056
E-mail: cjl@mayo.com.ar
Web Site: www.counsnet.com/ojicjl *Cable:* WORLDGRESS BAIRES
Key Personnel
Editorial: Roberto Brzostowski; Pedro Olschansky
ISBN Prefix(es): 987-99868
Parent Company: Congreso Judio Latinoamericano

Ediciones Preescolar SA+
Argerich 1928, 1416 Buenos Aires
Tel: (011) 581-3182 *Fax:* (011) 581-3182
Key Personnel
Editorial: Juan Carlos Orgueira
Founded: 1971 (1984)
Incorporating Latina SA.
Subjects: Cookery, Education, Health, Nutrition, Sports, Athletics
ISBN Prefix(es): 950-9574

Quetzal-Domingo Cortizo+
Barragan 740, 1408 Buenos Aires
Tel: (011) 4641-5639
E-mail: profika@ciudad.com.ar
Founded: 1952
Subjects: Art, Biography, Drama, Theater, Literature, Literary Criticism, Essays, Music, Dance, Poetry
ISBN Prefix(es): 950-590

Ricordi Americana SAEC
Tte Gral J D Peron 1558, 1037 Buenos Aires
Tel: (011) 4373-3405 *Fax:* (011) 4372-3452; (011) 4372 3453
E-mail: ricordi@sminter.com.ar
Telex: 1222580 for Ricordi *Cable:* Ricordamericana
Key Personnel
President, General Manager: Renzo Valcarenghi
Dir & Deputy Manager: Ernesto R Larcade
Marketing: Claudio Firmenich
Founded: 1924
Subjects: Education, Music, Dance
ISBN Prefix(es): 950-22
Associate Companies: Ricordi Brasileira S/A, Rua Conselheiro Nebias 1136, 01203 Sao Paulo SP, Brazil; G e C Ricordi SpA, Italy; G Ricordi & Co, Paseo de la Reforma 481-A, 06500 Mexico DF, Mexico

Ediciones La Rocca+
Talcahuano 467, 1013 Buenos Aires
Tel: (011) 4382-8526 *Fax:* (011) 4384-5774
Web Site: www.dtj.com.ar/ediciones_la_rocca.htm
Key Personnel
Dir: Alfonso La Rocca
Founded: 1985
Subjects: Law
ISBN Prefix(es): 950-9714; 987-517

San Pablo+
Riobamba 230, 1025 Buenos Aires
Tel: (011) 4953-2421; (011) 4953-2737
 Fax: (011) 4953-2737
E-mail: isanpablo@impsat1.com.ar
Key Personnel
Man Dir: P Arcangel Cadenas
Founded: 1931
Subjects: Biblical Studies, Education, Health, Nutrition, Human Relations, Language Arts, Lin-

guistics, Psychology, Psychiatry, Religion - Catholic, Self-Help, Theology
ISBN Prefix(es): 950-861
Distributed by Paulinas (Brazil); San Pablo (Brazil)
Distributor for San Pablo (Columbia, Chile, Spain)

Editorial Santiago Rueda
Bacacav 2647, 1406 Buenos Aires
Tel: (011) 4611-9174
Key Personnel
Man Dir: Enrique S Rueda
Founded: 1940
Subjects: Literature, Literary Criticism, Essays
ISBN Prefix(es): 950-564

Seix Barral+
Av Independencia 1668, 1100 Buenos Aires
Tel: (011) 382-4043; (011) 382-4045; (011) 381-8285 *Fax:* (011) 383-3793
E-mail: planeta@teletel.com.ar
Web Site: www.seix-barral.es
Key Personnel
General Dir: Guillermo Schavelzon
Founded: 1950
Subjects: Literature, Literary Criticism, Essays
ISBN Prefix(es): 950-742; 950-9216

Sigmar, *imprint of* Editorial Sigmar SACl

Editorial Sigmar SACl+
Av Belgrano 1580, 7 Piso, 1089 Buenos Aires
Tel: (011) 4381-4474 *Fax:* (011) 4383-5633
E-mail: editorial@sigmar.com.ar
Web Site: www.sigmar.com.ar *Cable:* SIGMAR
Key Personnel
President & Man Dir: Robert G Chwat
 E-mail: rchwat@sigmar.com.ar
Founded: 1941
Member of Argentina Book Association.
ISBN Prefix(es): 950-11
Number of titles published annually: 100 Print
Total Titles: 1,200 Print
Imprints: Sigmar
Distributor for Albatros (Argentina & Latin America)

Editorial Sopena Argentina SACl e l
Maza 2140, 1240 Buenos Aires
Tel: (011) 4912-2383; (011) 4912-2385; (011) 4912-2386 *Fax:* (011) 4912-2383
E-mail: edsopena@elsitio.net
Key Personnel
President: Roberto Omar Antonio
Dir: Marta A J Olsen; Leopoldo Costa Urruty
Manager: Hipolito Oscar Dhers
Subjects: Ethnicity, Government, Political Science, Health, Nutrition, History, How-to, Language Arts, Linguistics, Literature, Literary Criticism, Essays
ISBN Prefix(es): 950-542

Editorial Stella
Viamonte 1984, 1056 Buenos Aires
Tel: (011) 4374-0346 *Fax:* (011) 4374-8719
Web Site: www.editorialstella.com.ar
Founded: 1941
Asociacion Educacionista Argentina.
Subjects: Nonfiction (General)
ISBN Prefix(es): 950-525

Editorial Sudamericana SA+
Division of Random House-Mondadori
Humberto 1 545, 1103 Buenos Aires
Tel: (011) 4300-5400 *Fax:* (011) 4362-7364
E-mail: admventas@edsudamericana.com.ar
Web Site: www.edsudamericana.com.ar *Cable:* LIBRECOL
Key Personnel
President: Javier Lopez Llovet
Editor: Gloria Lopez Llovet de Rodrigue
Sales Dir: Francisco La Falce
Publicity Dir: Ana Maria Muchnik
Rights & Permissions: Susana Kaluzynski
Founded: 1939
Subjects: Biography, Fiction, History, Literature, Literary Criticism, Essays, Nonfiction (General), Philosophy, Psychology, Psychiatry
ISBN Prefix(es): 950-07; 950-37
Parent Company: Editorial Sudamericana
Associate Companies: Random House-Mondadori, Edificio del Comercio, Momjitas 392, Piso 11 Of. 1101/1102, Comuna de Santiago, Chile *Tel:* (02) 782-8200 *Fax:* (02) 782-8210 *E-mail:* sudchile@edsudamericana.com.ar; Editorial Sudamericana Uraguaya, ConcepcionArenal 1769, 11800 Montevideo, Uruguay *Tel:* (02) 203 3668 *Fax:* (02) 203 3668
Subsidiaries: Editorial Sudamericana Chilena

Theoria SRL Distribuidora y Editora+
Av Rivadavia 1255, Piso 4 "407", 1033 Buenos Aires
Tel: (011) 4381-0131 *Fax:* (011) 4381-0131
Key Personnel
Man Dir: Jorge O Orus
Sales Dir: Jose Luis Menendez
Founded: 1954
Subjects: Anthropology, Biography, Genealogy, Government, Political Science, History, Literature, Literary Criticism, Essays, Military Science, Religion - Catholic
ISBN Prefix(es): 950-99711; 987-9048

Tipografica Editora Argentina
Lavalle 1430, Piso 1, 1048 Buenos Aires
Tel: (011) 4373-2581 *Fax:* (011) 4775-2521
E-mail: bernardosm@sinectis.com.ar
Key Personnel
President: Pedro G San Martin
Founded: 1946
Subjects: Anthropology, Archaeology, History, Law
ISBN Prefix(es): 950-521

Instituto Torcuato Di Tella
Minones 2177, 1428 Buenos Aires
Tel: (011) 4783-8680 *Fax:* (011) 4783-3061
E-mail: postmaster@itdtar.edu.ar
Web Site: www.aaep.org.ar *Cable:* INSTELLA BAIRES
Key Personnel
President: Guido Di Tella
Founded: 1958
Subjects: Economics, Government, Political Science, History, Social Sciences, Sociology
ISBN Prefix(es): 950-621

Ediciones Tres Tiempos SRL
Av Belgrano 225, Piso 3, 1092 Buenos Aires
Tel: (011) 4331-8785 *Fax:* (011) 4331-8785
Key Personnel
Man Dir: Jose C Ibars Orries
Man Dir & Editor: Canio Carmelo Cillo
Assistant Manager: Jose Di Marco
Production Dir: Carmelo Mangiardo
Sales Dir: Veronica Movssesian; Raul Villar
Advertising & Promotion: Florinda Mintz
Rights & Permissions: Teresa Cillo
Imports/Exports: Alejandro Luis Calegari
Founded: 1975
Also book packager.
Subjects: Anthropology, Architecture & Interior Design, Art, Drama, Theater, Economics, Education, Environmental Studies, Fiction, Government, Political Science, Management, Philosophy, Poetry, Psychology, Psychiatry, Science (General), Social Sciences, Sociology, Technology
ISBN Prefix(es): 950-18
Branch Office(s)
Finochietto 1260, Buenos Aires

Editorial Troquel SA+
Pichincha 969, 1219 Buenos Aires
Tel: (011) 4308-3638; (011) 4308-3637
 Fax: (011) 4941-3110
E-mail: troquel@ba.net
Web Site: www.troquel.com.ar *Cable:* TROQUELSA
Key Personnel
President: Gustavo Ressia
Founded: 1954
Subjects: Literature, Literary Criticism, Essays, Psychology, Psychiatry, Religion - Other, Technology
ISBN Prefix(es): 950-16

Editorial Universidad SRL+
Rivadavia 1225, 1003 Buenos Aires
Tel: (011) 4382-9022; (011) 4382-6850
 Fax: (011) 4381-2005
E-mail: univers@nat.com.ar
Web Site: www.nat.com.ar/universidad
Key Personnel
Partner: Raul Caracciolo; Alejandro lo Iacono; Rafael del Buono
Founded: 1970
Member of Camara Argentina del Libro.
Subjects: Economics, Law, Social Sciences, Sociology
ISBN Prefix(es): 950-679; 950-9072
Branch Office(s)
Facultad de Derecho, UBA
Bookshop(s): Talcahuano 487, 1013 Buenos Aires

Universidad Nacional de la Patagonia, see Editoria Universitaria de la Patagonia

Editoria Universitaria de la Patagonia
Ciudad Universitaria Rm 4, Comodoro Rivadavia, Chubut 9000
Tel: (02967) 428834; (02967) 424969
E-mail: rcesar@unpbib.edu.ar
Key Personnel
Dir: Romeo Cesar
Founded: 1993
Subjects: Agriculture, Biological Sciences, Fiction, Geography, Geology, History, Philosophy
ISBN Prefix(es): 950-763

Javier Vergara Editor SA+
Paseo Colon 221, Piso 6, 1399 Buenos Aires
Tel: (011) 4343-7510; (011) 4343-7706
 Fax: (011) 4334-0173
E-mail: ediciones-b-arg@ciudad.com.ar
Key Personnel
President: Javier Vergara
Vice President & Rights: Gabriela Cruz de Vergara
Editorial Dir: Trinidad Vergara
Sales Dir: Ricardo Bianchini
Publicity Manager: Marilen Stengel
Founded: 1975
Subjects: Biography, Business, Fiction, History, Music, Dance, Nonfiction (General), Psychology, Psychiatry, Self-Help
ISBN Prefix(es): 950-15
Branch Office(s)
Rancagua 549, Casilla Postale 10471, Santiago, Chile *Tel:* (02) 2049583 *Fax:* (02) 2096929
Carrera 53 A No 81-24, Bodega Entre Rios, Bogota, Colombia *Tel:* (01) 2507297 *Fax:* (01) 2506005
Ctra Boadilla del Monte, KM 5800, Poligono Industrial Ventorro del Cano, 28925 Alcorcon, Madrid, Spain *Tel:* (01) 6332395 *Fax:* (01) 6332312
Kansas 161, Col Ampliacion Napoles, Delegacion Benito Juarez, CP 03840 Mexico, DF, Mexico *Tel:* (05) 6829636 *Fax:* (05) 6829511
Edificio Yolanda Local Norte, Calle Madrid con Av Trieste, California Sur, Estado Miranda,

Caracas, Venezuela *Tel:* (02) 228854 *Fax:* (02) 228854
Warehouse: Vieytes 1534, 1275 Buenos Aires

Manrique Zago Ediciones SRL
Luis Saenz Rock 232, 1110 Buenos Aires
Tel: (011) 4382-8880; (011) 4382-8881; (011) 4383-2611 *Fax:* (011) 4382-8890
E-mail: mzago@lud.com.ar
Key Personnel
Dir: Manrique Zago
Subjects: Art, Ethnicity
ISBN Prefix(es): 950-9517; 987-509

Victor P de Zavalia SA+
Alberti 835, 1223 Buenos Aires
Tel: (011) 942-1274; (011) 942-3046 *Fax:* (011) 942-5706
Key Personnel
Man Dir: Victor H de Zavalia
Sales Dir: Ricardo L de Zavalia
Founded: 1950
Subjects: Law
ISBN Prefix(es): 950-572

Editorial Zeus SRL+
Balcarce 730, 2000 Rosario, Santa Fe
Tel: (0341) 449-5585 *Fax:* (0341) 425-4259
E-mail: editorialzeus@citynet.net.ar
Web Site: www.editorial-zeus.com.ar
Key Personnel
President & Editor: Gustavo Luis Cauiglia
Founded: 1970
Subjects: Law
ISBN Prefix(es): 950-664
Imprints: Coleccion Juridica Bco de Datos en Computacion

Armenia

General Information

Capital: Yerevan
Language: Armenian (officially) and Kurdish
Religion: Predominantly Christian (Armenian Apostolic Church)
Population: 3.4 million
Bank Hours: Generally open for short hours between 0930-1230 Monday-Friday
Shop Hours: Generally 0900-1800 Monday-Friday; often open weekends
Currency: 100 kopeks = 1 rubl
Export/Import Information: According to Ukrainian quotas and customs duties, companies engaged in trade should register with the Ukraine Ministry of Foreign Economic Relations. Licenses for export and import are also required for trade with Russia.

Ajstan Publishers+
Isaakjana 28, 375009 Erevan
Tel: (02) 528520
Key Personnel
Dir: D M Sarkissian
Editor in Chief: V K Sanbekian
Founded: 1921
Subjects: Agriculture, Government, Political Science, Law, Literature, Literary Criticism, Essays, Military Science, Science (General)
ISBN Prefix(es): 5-540

Arevik
Terjan 91, 375009 Erevan
Tel: (02) 524561
Key Personnel
Marketing Dir: Houhannes David
Founded: 1986
ISBN Prefix(es): 5-8077

Australia

General Information

Capital: Canberra
Language: English
Religion: Predominantly Christian
Population: 17.6 million
Bank Hours: 1000-1500 Monday-Thursday; 1000-1700 Friday
Shop Hours: 0900-1700 Monday-Saturday
Currency: 100 cents = 1 Australian dollar
Export/Import Information: No tariffs on books. Most books, especially of literary or educational nature, free of sales tax. No import licenses for books; no seditious literature permitted.
Copyright: UCC, Berne (see Copyright Conventions, pg xi)

ABC Books (Australian Broadcasting Corporation)+
700 Harris St, Ultimo, NSW 2007
Mailing Address: GPO Box 9994, Sydney, NSW 2001
Tel: (02) 9950 3999 *Fax:* (02) 9950 3888
E-mail: abcbooks@your.abc.net.au
Web Site: abcshop.com.au
Key Personnel
General Manager: Grahame Grassby
Publisher: Stuart Neal *Tel:* (02) 9950 3954
E-mail: neal.stuart@abc.net.au
Subjects: Fiction, Nonfiction (General)
ISBN Prefix(es): 0-7333
Number of titles published annually: 85 Print
Parent Company: ABC Enterprises
Ultimate Parent Company: Australian Broadcasting Corporation
Distributed by Allen & Unwin Pty Ltd
Orders to: Allen & Unwin Pty Ltd, 9 Atchison St, St Leonards, NSW 2065, Liz Bray *Tel:* (02) 99062218 *Fax:* (02) 99062218
E-mail: frontdesk@allen-unwin.net.au

Aboriginal Studies Press+
GPO Box 553, Canberra, ACT 2601
Tel: (02) 6246 1111 *Fax:* (02) 6261 4285
E-mail: sales@aiatsis.gov.au
Web Site: www.aiatsis.gov.au
Key Personnel
Principal: Russell Taylor
Dir, Archives & Production: Dianne Hosking
Publications Manager: Penelope Lee
E-mail: pene@aiatsis.gov.au
Subjects: Anthropology, Archaeology, Art, Biography, Biological Sciences, Education, Ethnicity, History, Language Arts, Linguistics, Music, Dance, Regional Interests
ISBN Prefix(es): 0-85575
Parent Company: Australian Institute of Aboriginal & Torres Strait Islander Studies, Dir, Archives & Production: Dianne Hosking

Academic Press, *imprint of* Harcourt Australia Pty Ltd

Access Press, *imprint of* Access Press

Access Press+
PO Box 446, Bassendean, WA 6054
Tel: (08) 93793188 *Fax:* (08) 93793199
Key Personnel
Man Dir & Managing Editor: Helen Weller
Publicity & Rights & Permission: John Harper-Nelson
Founded: 1978
Standard publishing contract but also specialize in small print runs privately funded.

Subjects: Biography, Genealogy, History, Literature, Literary Criticism, Essays, Nonfiction (General), Poetry
ISBN Prefix(es): 0-949795; 0-86445
Number of titles published annually: 14 Print
Total Titles: 90 Print
Parent Company: Reeve Pty Ltd as trustee for Reeve Unit Trust
Ultimate Parent Company: Reeve Etc
Imprints: Access Press

ACER, see The Australian Council for Educational Research Ltd

ACER Press+
19 Prospect Hill Rd, Camberwell, Victoria 3124
Mailing Address: Private Bag 55, Camberwell, Victoria 3124
Tel: (03) 9277 5555 *Fax:* (03) 9277 5500
E-mail: sales@acer.edu.au
Web Site: www.acer.edu.au
Key Personnel
Publishing Manager & Training Liaison Officer: Deirdre Morris *Tel:* (03) 9277 5557 *Fax:* (03) 9277 5500
Founded: 1930
Subjects: Education, Human Relations, Psychology, Psychiatry
Distributed by Stylus Publishing (USA)

ACHPER Inc (Australian Council for Health, Physical Education & Recreation)
214 Port Rd, Hindmarsh, SA 5007
Mailing Address: PO Box 304, Hindmarsh, SA 5007
Tel: (08) 8340 3388 *Fax:* (08) 8340 3399
E-mail: achper@achper.org.au
Web Site: www.achper.org.au
Key Personnel
Executive Dir: Jeff Emmel
National President: Dr Colvin
National Vice President: Mr Adamson; Ms Sheehan
Contact: Felicity Vanderheul
E-mail: membership@achper.org.au
Founded: 1955
Specialize in Community Fitness & Movement Sciences, Dance, Health Education, Physical Education, Recreation, Sports.
Subjects: Education, Sports, Athletics
Branch Office(s)
73 Wakefield St, 1st floor, Adelaide, SA 5000, Matt Schmidt *E-mail:* info@achpersa.com.au
PO Box 57, Claremont, WA 6010, Denyse Passmore *E-mail:* denyse@achperwa.asn.au
PO Box 84, Croydon, NSW 2132, Julie Percival *E-mail:* achperns@ozemail.com.au
PO Box 789, Jamieson, ACT 2614, Jodie Sindeberry *E-mail:* ihellyer@dynoamite.com.au
C1-117 Canning St, Launceston, Tas 7250, Peter Daniel
GPO BOX 412C, Melbourne, Victoria 3001, Mary Wilson *E-mail:* achvic@unite.com.au
PO Box 8141, Woolloongabba, Qld 4102, Jill Duffield *E-mail:* achqld@ecn.net.au
Bookshop(s): Achper Healthy Lifestyles Bookshop, Emma Price *E-mail:* bookshop@achper.org.au

Acorn Press, *imprint of* Rainbow Book Agencies Pty Ltd

ACP Publishing Pty Ltd+
54-58 Park St, Sydney, NSW 1028
Tel: (02) 9282 8000 *Fax:* (02) 9267 4361
Web Site: www.acp.com.au
Key Personnel
Publisher: Richard Walsh
Subjects: Cookery
ISBN Prefix(es): 0-949892; 1-86396
Parent Company: Australian Consolidated Press

Imprints: The Australian Women's Weekly; Home Library
Branch Office(s)
Arnoul Media Services Pty Ltd, 45 Ward St, North Adelaide, SA 5006 *Tel:* (08) 8361 999 *Fax:* (08) 83619990
Bowengate Office Park, 2nd fl, Cnr Bowen Bridge Rd & Campbell St, Bowen Hills, Qld 4006 *Tel:* (07) 3000 8500 *Fax:* (07) 3000 8555
73 Atherton Rd, Oakleigh, Victoria 3166 *Tel:* (03) 9567 4200 *Fax:* (03) 9563 4554
102-108 Toorak Rd, South Yarra VIC 3141 *Tel:* (03) 9823 6333 *Fax:* (03) 9823 6300
Foreign Rep(s): Melanie Franklin (Asia & the Pacific, Europe, US); Christian Hyland (Asia & the Pacific, Europe, US); Michael Sport (Asia & the Pacific, Europe, US)

Addison Wesley, *imprint of* Pearson Education Australia

The Advancement Centre
9 Brett Ave, Wentworthville 2145
Tel: (02) 9896-2311
Subjects: Education, Psychology, Psychiatry
ISBN Prefix(es): 0-9586212
Distributed by University of NSW

Aeolian Press
PO Box 606, Bridgetown, WA 6255
Tel: (08) 9761 2772 *Fax:* (08) 9761 4151
Founded: 1985
Subjects: Art, Poetry, Australian Art, Italian Classic Text & Illustration
ISBN Prefix(es): 1-875306
Distributor for Edizioni Tallone (Australia); Edizioni Valdonega (Australia)

Aerospace Publications
PO Box 1777, Fyshwick, ACT 2609
Tel: (02) 6280 0111 *Fax:* (02) 6280 0007
Web Site: www.ausaviation.com
Subjects: Aeronautics, Aviation
ISBN Prefix(es): 0-9587978

AHB Publications+
24/14 Lansell Rd, Toorak 3142
Subjects: Foreign Countries
Distributor for Random House (Australia)

AIFS, see Australian Institute of Family Studies (AIFS)

Aletheia Publishing
Box 486, Alderley 4051
Tel: (07) 38552056
E-mail: aletheia@powerup.com.au
Key Personnel
Contact: David Holden
Founded: 1992
Subjects: Biblical Studies, History, Religion - Protestant, Religion - Other, Theology
ISBN Prefix(es): 0-9577; 7-6130
Total Titles: 3 Print

Allen & Unwin Pty Ltd, The Australian Newspaper, Vogel Breads+
83 Alexander St, Crows Nest, Sydney, NSW 2065
Mailing Address: PO Box 8500, St Leonards, Sydney, NSW 1590
Tel: (02) 8425 0100 *Fax:* (02) 9906 2218
E-mail: frontdesk@allenandunwin.com
Web Site: www.allenandunwin.com
Key Personnel
Man & Publishing Dir: Patrick Gallagher
Sales & Marketing Dir: Paul Donovan
Rights & Export Manager: Angela Namoi
Head of Publicity: Andrew Hawkins
Finance & Distribution Dir: Peter Eichorn
National Sales Manager: Lou Johnson
Children's Publishing Dir: Rosalind Price
Academic Publisher: Elizabeth Weiss
Academic & Professional Marketing Manager: Carolyn Crowther
Founded: 1976
Member of Australian Publishers Association (APA), Publish Australia (PA), Australian Multimedia Industry Association (AMIA).
Subjects: Alternative, Art, Asian Studies, Behavioral Sciences, Business, Cookery, Earth Sciences, Economics, Education, Ethnicity, Fiction, Gay & Lesbian, Government, Political Science, Health, Nutrition, History, Labor, Industrial Relations, Literature, Literary Criticism, Essays, Nonfiction (General), Science (General)
ISBN Prefix(es): 1-86448; 1-86508
Subsidiaries: Osborne House
Branch Office(s)
406 Albert St, East Melbourne, Victoria
One John St, Kingswood, Adelaide
One Park Rd, Milton, Brisbane 4064
Distributor for Osborne House
Warehouse: ADS, PO Box 520, 9 Pioneer Ave, Tuggerah, NSW 2259 *Tel:* (02) 43901300 *Fax:* (02) 43901333 (Also Ordering)

AMCS, see Australian Marine Conservation Society Inc (AMCS)

AMPCO, see Australasian Medical Publishing Company Ltd (AMPCO)

Anchor, *imprint of* Random House Australia

Anchor, *imprint of* Transworld Publishers Pty Ltd

Robert Andersen & Associates Pty Ltd+
433 Wellington St, Clifton Hill, Melbourne, Victoria 3068
Tel: (03) 4893968 *Fax:* (03) 4822416
E-mail: 100357.354@compuserve.com
Web Site: www.educationprofile.com.au
Key Personnel
Man Dir: Bob Andersen
Subjects: Education
ISBN Prefix(es): 0-949133

Anderson, *imprint of* Random House Australia

Michelle Anderson Publishing Pty Ltd+
Formerly Hill of Content Publishing Co Pty Ltd
86 Bourke St, Melbourne, Victoria 3000
Tel: (03) 9662 2282 *Fax:* (03) 9662 2527
E-mail: hocpub@collinsbooks.com.au; hillofcontent@bizland.com
Key Personnel
Publisher, Rights & Permissions: Michelle Anderson
Executive Assistant: Adrienne Fanning
Founded: 1965
Member of Australian Publishers Association.
Subjects: Health, Nutrition, Philosophy, Psychology, Psychiatry, Also specialize in bushwalking & cycling
ISBN Prefix(es): 0-85572
Number of titles published annually: 15 Print
Total Titles: 70 Print
Distributed by Bookwise International (Australia); Deep Books U K (UK); Peter Hyde & Associates (South Africa)
Foreign Rep(s): Choicemaker (Korea); Love Fountain (France); Prava: Provida (Russia)
Foreign Rights: Thomas Schluck (Germany); Susan Schulman (US)
Warehouse: 180 Wellington St, Collingwood 3066

Angel Publications
5 Lithgow St, Goulburn, NSW 2580
Tel: (02) 48211463

Key Personnel
Contact: Steven Shackel *E-mail:* shack@goulburn.net.au
Founded: 1982
Subjects: Astrology, Occult, Fiction, Parapsychology, Philosophy, Self-Help
ISBN Prefix(es): 0-9593419

Ansay Pty Ltd+
19-25 Beeson St, Leichhardt, NSW 2040
Tel: (02) 5602044 *Fax:* (02) 5694585
Key Personnel
Man Dir: Philip Lindsay
Editorial, Production & Publicity: H E Lindsay
Sales, Rights & Permissions: P S Lindsay
Founded: 1972
Subjects: Education, Fiction
ISBN Prefix(es): 0-909245
Parent Company: A L Lindsay & Co Pty Ltd
Imprints: Dollar Books

Anzea Publishers Ltd+
17-21 Bellevue St, Surry Hills, NSW 2010
Tel: (02) 7631211 *Fax:* (02) 7643201
Key Personnel
Head of Company: Jeffrey Blair
Subjects: Religion - Other
Imprints: Lancer; Scripture Union
Divisions: Boronia Book Agencies; Emu Book Agencies; Waverley House

APACE, see Appropriate Technology Development Group (Inc) WA

APACE Aid Inc, *imprint of* Appropriate Technology Development Group (Inc) WA

Appropriate Technology Development Group (Inc) WA
One Johannah St, North Fremantle, WA 6159
Tel: (08) 9336 1262 *Fax:* (08) 9430 5729
E-mail: apace@argo.net.au
Web Site: www.argo.net.au/apace
Key Personnel
President: Richard Cooke
Coordinator: Tony Freeman
Founded: 1983
Not for profit community group - environmental.
Subjects: Alternative, Environmental Studies, Technology, Appropriate Technology, Bush Regeneration, Revegetation
ISBN Prefix(es): 0-9590309
Number of titles published annually: 5 Print
Associate Companies: Apace Aid Inc
Imprints: APACE Aid Inc

Aquila Press
PO Box A287, Sydney South, NSW
Tel: (02) 8268 3344 *Fax:* (02) 9283 3987
E-mail: sales@youthworks.asn.au
Key Personnel
Chief Executive Officer: Alan Stewart
Founded: 1994
Subjects: Biblical Studies, Religion - Protestant
ISBN Prefix(es): 1-875861
Parent Company: Anglican Press Australia
Imprints: Christian Education Publications

Arabian Focus Pty Ltd
PO Box 8, Samford 4520
Mailing Address: Kerijo Stud, Samsonvale 4523
Tel: (07) 3425-1766; (07) 851180; (07) 34251180 *Fax:* (07) 34251857
Key Personnel
Contact: Joan Flynn
Founded: 1997
Specialize in magazines.
Subjects: Regional Interests, Arabian Horses

Arcadia, *imprint of* Australian Scholarly Publishing

Archaeological Publications
3 Buxton St, Elsternwick 3185
Mailing Address: PO Box 216, Caulfield South 3162
Tel: (03) 95230549 *Fax:* (03) 95230549
E-mail: auraweb@hotmail.com
Key Personnel
Dir & International Rights: Robert Bednarik
 E-mail: robertbednarik@hotmail.com
Founded: 1983
Books, Periodicals, Academic Textbooks & Conference Proceedings.
Subjects: Anthropology, Archaeology, Art
ISBN Prefix(es): 0-646
Number of titles published annually: 3 Print
Distributed by Piedra Pintada Books (USA); ANH Publications (Australia)

Argyle Pacific, *imprint of* Austed Publishing Co

Armadillo Publishers
11 Dingley Dell Rd, Warrandyte North 3113
Mailing Address: PO Box 12358, Melbourne, Victoria 8006
Tel: (03) 9844-4558 *Fax:* (03) 9489-5576
Key Personnel
Contact: Elaine Howell

Edward Arnold (Australia) Pty Ltd+
12 Strathalbyn St, Kew East, Victoria 3102
Mailing Address: PO Box 885, Kew, Victoria 3101
Tel: (03) 98599011 *Fax:* (03) 98599141
Key Personnel
Man Dir: Malcolm Edwards
General Manager: R Bartlett
Publishing: Anita Ray
Production: Jane Hazell
Marketing: Penny Doust
Tertiary: Louise Cook
Founded: 1966
Member of Australian Book P A and acts as agent for Edward Arnold (UK), Taylor & Francis & Blackie & Sons (Secondary only).
Subjects: Accounting, Asian Studies, Behavioral Sciences, Career Development, Computer Science, Cookery, Geography, Geology, Government, Political Science, Health, Nutrition, Law, Mathematics, Nonfiction (General), Psychology, Psychiatry, Technology
ISBN Prefix(es): 0-7131; 0-7267
Parent Company: Hodder & Stoughton (Australia) Pty Ltd
Ultimate Parent Company: Hodder & Stoughton Ltd, United Kingdom
Warehouse: Hodder & Stoughton Pty Ltd, 10-16 South St, Rydalmere NSW 2116 (Australia)
Orders to: Hodder & Stoughton (Australia) Pty Ltd, PO Box 386, Rydalmere, NSW 2116

Arrow, *imprint of* Random House Australia

Art Gallery of South Australia Bookshop
North Terrace, Adelaide, SA 5000
Tel: (08) 8207 7029 *Fax:* (08) 8207 7069
E-mail: agsa.bookshop@saugov.sa.gov.au
Web Site: www.artgallery.sa.gov.au
Key Personnel
Head of Company: Ron Radford
Bookshop Manager: Letitia Ashworth
 E-mail: ashworth.letitia@saugov.sa.gov.au
Subjects: Art
ISBN Prefix(es): 0-7308

Art Gallery of Western Australia+
47 James St, Perth 6000
Tel: (08) 9492 6600 *Fax:* (08) 9492 6655
E-mail: admin@artgallery.wa.gov.au
Web Site: www.artgallery.wa.gov.au
Key Personnel
Dir: Alan Dodge
Chief Curator: Gary Dufour
Dir, Strategic & Commercial Programs: Keith Lord
Manager Information Services: Joyce Carter
Tel: (08) 9492 6622
Founded: 1895
Exhibition Catalogues.
Subjects: Art
ISBN Prefix(es): 0-7309; 0-7244
Total Titles: 22 Print

Art on the Move
4 Roe St, Perth, WA 6000
Mailing Address: GPO Box M937, Perth, WA 6843
Tel: (08) 9227 7505 *Fax:* (08) 9227 5304
E-mail: artmoves@highwayl.com.an
Web Site: www.imago.com.au/artmoves
Key Personnel
Dir: Mr Paul Thompson
Founded: 1996
Subjects: Architecture & Interior Design, Art, Marketing
ISBN Prefix(es): 0-9585326

Artemis Publishing, *imprint of* Rainbow Book Agencies Pty Ltd

Artemis Publishing Pty Ltd+
PO Box 151, Market Street Post Office, Melbourne, Victoria 8007
Tel: (03) 6143920 *Fax:* (03) 6701252
E-mail: jasart@magnafield.com.au
Web Site: www.magnafield.com.au/~jasart
Key Personnel
Dir: Melanie Young
Editor: J Terry
Distribution: Fiona Skepper
Founded: 1992
Australian Publishers Association, Publish Australia.
Subjects: Behavioral Sciences, Biography, Career Development, Criminology, Education, Ethnicity, Fiction, Gay & Lesbian, Government, Political Science, History, Law, Social Sciences, Sociology, Women's Studies, Autobiography
ISBN Prefix(es): 1-875658
Distributor for McCulloelr Publishing; Women's Redress Press

Artmoves+
Nicholas Bldg, 37 Swanston St, Room 17, 4th floor, Melbourne 3000
Tel: (03) 96500744; (03) 98828116 *Fax:* (03) 98828162; (03) 96506916
E-mail: rastawoman@msn.com
Key Personnel
Contact: Helen Vivian
Founded: 1987
Subjects: Art, History, Women's Studies
ISBN Prefix(es): 0-646

Ashling Books+
26 Hewlett Court Florey, Florey, ACT 2615
Tel: (02) 62591027
Key Personnel
Man Dir & International Rights: Edward J Murtagh
Founded: 1992
Subjects: Fiction, How-to, Poetry, Religion - Catholic, Self-Help
ISBN Prefix(es): 0-9585244

Ashton Egan, *imprint of* Egan Publishing Pty Ltd

Ashwood House, *imprint of* Dellasta Publishing

Ashwood House Medical, *imprint of* Dellasta Publishing

Assert Publishing
4 Colleen St, Gosnells 6110
Tel: (09) 398-8279 *Fax:* (09) 398-8279
Key Personnel
International Rights: Pauline Rayner
Founded: 1994
Self-publisher.
Subjects: Alternative, Genealogy, Health, Nutrition, Literature, Literary Criticism, Essays, Marketing, Nonfiction (General), Poetry
ISBN Prefix(es): 0-9587564

Athena Press+
PO Box 1497, Potts Point, NSW 2011
Tel: (02) 9357-3720 *Fax:* (02) 9357-3720
Key Personnel
Contact: Dr Marlene J Norst
Subjects: Biography, Ethnicity, History
ISBN Prefix(es): 0-9577

Auslib Press Pty Ltd+
PO Box 622, Blackwood, SA 5051
Tel: (08) 8278 4363 *Fax:* (08) 8278 4000
E-mail: info@auslib.com.au
Web Site: www.auslib.com.au
Key Personnel
Man Dir: Judith Bundy
Editorial & Sales Manager: Dr Alan Bundy
Founded: 1984
Specialize in Library & Information Science Titles, Education Directories, Mailing Labels for Australian & New Zealand Libraries.
Subjects: Education, Library & Information Sciences
ISBN Prefix(es): 1-875145; 0-9589895
Total Titles: 43 Print

Ausmed Publications Pty Ltd+
275-277 Mt Alexander Rd, Ascot Vale, Victoria 3032
Mailing Address: PO Box 4086, Parksville, Victoria 3052
Tel: (03) 9375-7311 *Fax:* (03) 9375-7299
E-mail: ausmed@ausmed.com.au
Web Site: www.ausmed.com.au
Key Personnel
Head of Company & Dir: Cynthea Wellings
 E-mail: cwelling@ausmed.com.au
General Manager: Natalie Angove
 E-mail: nangove@ausmed.com.au
Man Editor: Bernadette Keane *E-mail:* bkeane@ausmed.com.au
Founded: 1987
Specialize in books & conferences for nurses & other workers in related health fields.
Subjects: Behavioral Sciences, Ethnicity, Health, Nutrition, Medicine, Nursing, Dentistry, Social Sciences, Sociology, Allied Health, Clinical Issues
ISBN Prefix(es): 0-9577; 0-646; 0-9587171
Total Titles: 24 Print
Online services available through World Wide Web.

Aussie Books
Unit 6, 30 Lensworth St, Coopers Plains, Qld 4108
Mailing Address: PO Box 542, Archerfield, Qld 4108
Tel: (07) 3345 4253 *Fax:* (07) 3344 1582
E-mail: sildale@yahoo.com
Web Site: www.treasureenterprises.com
Key Personnel
Dir: David A Cooper
Founded: 1977
Supplier of Detection & Treasure Hunting Equipment.
Subjects: Earth Sciences, Geography, Geology, History
ISBN Prefix(es): 0-947336
Parent Company: Sildale Pty Ltd
Distributor for Hesperian Press

PUBLISHERS

AUSTRALIA

Aussies Afire Publishing
PO Box 954, Port Macquarie, NSW 2444
Tel: (02) 6581 0654 *Fax:* (02) 6581 0745
Web Site: www.gracechurchpm.org.au
Key Personnel
Head of Company: Kerry Medway
  E-mail: kerrymedway@tsn.cc
Founded: 1989
Subjects: Humor, Regional Interests, Religion - Protestant
ISBN Prefix(es): 0-646
Number of titles published annually: 1 Print
Total Titles: 5 Print

IE Aust Publications, *imprint of* EA Books

Austed Publishing Co+
PO Box 8205, Subiaco East, WA 6008
Tel: (08) 9388 8099 *Fax:* (08) 9245 8247
E-mail: netquery@austed.com.au
Key Personnel
Man Dir: W B R Banks
Head of Company: K Chesson
Founded: 1984
Subjects: Accounting, Animals, Pets, Education, Fiction, Mathematics
ISBN Prefix(es): 1-86307
Imprints: Argyle Pacific; Churchill House

Australasian Medical Publishing Company Ltd (AMPCO)+
26-32 Pyrmont Bridge Rd, Level 2, Pyrmont, NSW 2009
Mailing Address: Locked 3030, Strawberry Hills, NSW 2012
Tel: (02) 9562 6666 *Fax:* (02) 9562 6600
E-mail: ampco@ampco.com.au
Web Site: www.ampco.com.au
Key Personnel
Chief Executive: Dr Martin Van Der Weyden
  Fax: (02) 99548699
Founded: 1913
Member of ABP, Commercial & publishing arm of the Australian Medical Association. Publisher of The Medical Journal of Australia, Medical Directory of Australia & distributor of medical publications.
Subjects: History, Medicine, Nursing, Dentistry
Parent Company: Australian Medical Association Limited

Australasian Textiles Publishers
11 Woodlands Drive, Ocean Grove 3226
Mailing Address: PO Box 286, Belmont, Victoria 3216
Tel: (03) 5255 5500 *Fax:* (03) 5256 1668
Web Site: www.atfmag.com
Key Personnel
Publisher: Rosemary Boston *E-mail:* roseboston@atfmag.com
Dir & Managing Editor: Stan Boston
  E-mail: sboston@atfmag.com
Associate Editor: Jack Finlay *E-mail:* jfinlay@atfmag.com
Marketing Manager: James Boston
  E-mail: jboston@atfmag.com
Subjects: Fashion, Textiles
ISBN Prefix(es): 0-9590875

Australian Academic Press Pty Ltd+
32 Jeays St, Bowen Hills, Qld 4006
Tel: (07) 3257 1176 *Fax:* (07) 3252 5908
E-mail: info@australianacademicpress.com.au
Web Site: www.australianacademicpress.com.au
Key Personnel
Man Dir: Stephen May
Founded: 1987
Specialize in book production; also acts as book packager. Independent publisher for the behavioral sciences.
Subjects: Behavioral Sciences, Psychology, Psychiatry
ISBN Prefix(es): 1-875378

Australian Academy of Science
Ian Potter House, Gordon St, Canberra, ACT 2600
Mailing Address: GPO Box 783, Canberra, ACT 2601
Tel: (02) 6247 5777 *Fax:* (02) 6257 4620
E-mail: aas@science.org.au
Web Site: www.science.org.au
Key Personnel
Publications: Maureen Swanage *E-mail:* maureen.swanage@science.org.au
Founded: 1956
Subjects: Biological Sciences, Chemistry, Chemical Engineering, Environmental Studies, Geography, Geology, Mathematics
ISBN Prefix(es): 0-85847

Australian Association for the Study of Religion, *imprint of* Rainbow Book Agencies Pty Ltd

Australian Broadcasting Authority
Level 15, Darling Park, 201 Sussex St, Sydney, NSW 2000
Mailing Address: Queen Victoria Bldg, Post Office, PO Box Q500, Sydney, NSW 1230
Tel: (02) 9344 7700 *Toll Free Tel:* 800 22 6667
  Fax: (02) 9334 7799; (02) 93447700
E-mail: info@aba.gov.au
Web Site: www.aba.gov.au
Key Personnel
Chairman: Prof David Flint
Publisher: Anne Hewer
Manager Media & Public Relations: Donald Robertson
Founded: 1992
Subjects: Communications, Broadcasting
ISBN Prefix(es): 0-642
Branch Office(s)
Blue Bldg, Benjamin Offices, Chan St, Belconnen, Canberra, ACT 2617 *Tel:* (02) 6256 2800 *Fax:* (02) 6253 3277

Australian Broadcasting Corporation, see ABC Books (Australian Broadcasting Corporation)

Australian Chart Book Pty Ltd
PO Box 148, Turramurra, NSW 2074
Tel: (02) 9489 4786 *Fax:* (02) 9487 2089
E-mail: davidkent@austchartbook.com.au
Web Site: www.austchartbook.com.au
Key Personnel
Contact: David Kent

The Australian Council for Educational Research Ltd+
19 Prospect Hill Rd, Camberwell, Victoria
Mailing Address: Private Bag 55, Camberwell, Victoria 3124
Tel: (03) 9277 5555 *Fax:* (03) 9277 5500
Key Personnel
Man Dir: Dr Geoff Masters
Publishing Manager: Anne Peterson *Tel:* (03) 9277 5557 *E-mail:* peterson@acer.edu.au
Founded: 1930
Subjects: Child Care & Development, Disability, Special Needs, Education, Psychology, Psychiatry, Human Resources, Parent Education
ISBN Prefix(es): 0-86431
Distributor for AGS; CPP; Davies-Black; IPAT; NFER-Nelson; PAR

Australian Film Television & Radio School
Cnr Epping and Balaclava Roads, North Ryde, NSW 2113
Mailing Address: PO Box 126, North Ryde, NSW 1670
Tel: (02) 9805-6611 *Fax:* (02) 9887-1030
E-mail: info_nsw@aftrs.edu.au
Web Site: www.aftrs.edu.au
Key Personnel
Publisher & Training Officer: Meredith Quinn
  E-mail: meredith.quinn@syd.aftrs.edu.au
Founded: 1973
Subjects: Film, Video, Radio, TV
Branch Office(s)
5 Trumpeter St, Battery Point, Tas 7004, Representative: Craig Kirkwood *Tel:* (03) 6223-8703 *Fax:* (03) 6224-6143 *E-mail:* info_tas@aftrs.edu.au
Judith Wright Centre of Contemporary Arts, Cnr Brunswick & Berwick, Level 2, PO Box 1480, Fortitude Valley, Qld 4006, Manager: Alex Daw *Tel:* (07) 3257-7646 *Fax:* (07) 3257-7641 *E-mail:* info_qld@aftrs.edu.au
92 Adelaide St, Fremantle, WA 6160, Tom Lubin *Tel:* (08) 9335-1055 *Fax:* (08) 9335-1283 *E-mail:* info_wa@aftrs.edu.au
SAFS Studios, 3 Butler Dr, Hendon, SA 5014, Representative: Ann Walton *Tel:* (08) 8244-0357 *Fax:* (08) 8244-5608 *E-mail:* info_sa@aftrs.edu.au
144 Moray St, 1st fl, PO Box 1008, South Melbourne, Victoria 3205, Manager: Simon Britton *Tel:* (03) 9690-7111 *Fax:* (03) 9690-1283 *E-mail:* info_vic@aftrs.edu.au
Distributed by Allen & Unwin

Australian Government Publishing Service
GPO Box 84, Canberra, ACT 2601
Tel: (062) 62954031 *Fax:* (062) 62954888
Web Site: www.agps.gov.au
Key Personnel
General Manager: Alan Law
Editorial: L McKerras
Sales: K Blair
Client Services & Marketing: Jane Wolf
Contact: Chris Oman
Founded: 1970
ISBN Prefix(es): 0-642; 0-644
Bookshop(s): Australian Government Bookshops

Australian Institute of Criminology
74 Leichhardt St, Griffith, ACT 2603
Tel: (02) 6260 9200 *Fax:* (02) 6260 9201
E-mail: aicpress@aic.gov.au
Web Site: www.aic.gov.au
Key Personnel
Dir: Dr Adam Graycar *Tel:* (02) 6260 9205
  E-mail: Adam.Graycar@aic.gov.au
Executive Officer, Research: Leanne Huddy
  Tel: (02) 6260 9255 *E-mail:* leanne.huddy@aic.gov.au
Founded: 1976
Subjects: Criminology
ISBN Prefix(es): 0-642
Branch Office(s)
Criminal Justice Press, PO Box 249, Monsey, NY 10952, United States
Orders to: AusInfo, GPO Box 84, Canberra, ACT 2601 *Fax:* (02) 6295 4888

Australian Institute of Family Studies (AIFS)
300 Queen St, Melbourne, Victoria 3000
Tel: (03) 9214 7888 *Fax:* (03) 9214 7839
Web Site: www.aifs.org.au
Key Personnel
Marketing Manager: Catherine Rosenbrock
  Tel: (03) 9214 7804 *E-mail:* cathr@aifs.org.au
Founded: 1980
Undertake research & factors affecting family stability & well-being; Australian government statutory authority.
Subjects: Behavioral Sciences, Criminology, Disability, Special Needs, Economics, Human Relations, Social Sciences, Sociology, Women's Studies
ISBN Prefix(es): 0-642

Number of titles published annually: 3 Print; 1 CD-ROM
Total Titles: 12 Print; 4 CD-ROM

Australian Large Print Audio & Video P/L, see Australian Large Print Pty Ltd

Australian Large Print Pty Ltd+
Formerly Australian Large Print Audio & Video P/L
15 Mohr St, Tullamarine, Victoria 3043
Tel: (03) 3380666 *Fax:* (03) 3380975
E-mail: alpav@tpgl.com.au
Key Personnel
Dir: Philip Walshe
Marketing Manager: Rebecca Walshe
Founded: 1985
Specialize in Large-Print Publishing & unabridged audio books.
Subjects: Disability, Special Needs, Fiction, Nonfiction (General)
ISBN Prefix(es): 0-947072; 1-86340; 1-74030; 1-876584
Imprints: Bolinda; Bolinda Audio; Bolinda Press; Compass Press; Ghost Gum; Goanna; Sagebrush
Divisions: Printalkmedia; Bolinda Audio; Bolinda Press
Distributed by Beeler; Iris
Distributor for Assembled Stories; Beeler; Iris; Mills & Boon; Recorded Books; Spundings; Spoken Arts

Australian Marine Conservation Society Inc (AMCS)
Level 1, 92 Hyde Rd, Yeronga, Qld 4104
Mailing Address: PO Box 3139, Yeronga, Qld 4104
Tel: (07) 3848 5235 *Toll Free Tel:* 800 066 299 *Fax:* (07) 3892 5814
E-mail: amcs@amcs.org.au
Web Site: www.amcs.org.au
Key Personnel
Dir: E J Hegerl
National Coordinator: Kate Davey
Subjects: Biological Sciences, Earth Sciences, Environmental Studies, Geography, Geology, Maritime, Natural History
Branch Office(s)
Adelaide, SA, John Emmett *Tel:* (08) 8353 6614
Bundaberg, Qld, Liz Tanner *Tel:* (07) 4155 6020 *E-mail:* tannerl@mailexcite.com
Hobart, Tas, Christian Bell *Tel:* (03) 6234 3665
Kangaroo Island, SA, John Lavers *Tel:* (08) 8553 1072 *E-mail:* echidna@kin.on.net *Web Site:* www.nexus.edu.au/schools/kingscot/pelican/amcs_kib.htm
Melbourne, Victoria, Michelle Barret-Dean *Tel:* (03) 9508 1820
Morebon Bay, Qld, Diana Patchett *Tel:* (07) 3892 2332 *E-mail:* patchett@powerup.com.au
2 Delhi St, City West Lotteries House, West Perth, WA 6005, Secretary: Dennis Beros *Tel:* (08) 9420 7209 *Fax:* (08) 9486 7833 *E-mail:* amcswa@iinet.net.au
Sydney NSW, Will Jones *Tel:* (02) 9664 6032 *E-mail:* marinediscovery@bigpond.com
Great Oceans Rd, Victoria, Terry Gunn *Tel:* (03) 5263 1392

Australian National University Press, *imprint of* A S Wilson Inc

Australian Scholarly, *imprint of* Australian Scholarly Publishing

Australian Scholarly Publishing+
PO Box 299, Kew, Victoria 3101
Tel: (03) 8175208 *Fax:* (03) 8176431
E-mail: aspic@ozemail.com.au
Key Personnel
Publisher: Nicholas Walker
Senior Editor: Dr Diane Carlyle
Founded: 1991
Subjects: Environmental Studies, Geography, Geology, Government, Political Science, History, Nonfiction (General), Publishing & Book Trade Reference, Social Sciences, Sociology, Wine & Spirits
ISBN Prefix(es): 1-875606
Imprints: Arcadia; Australian Scholarly

The Australian Women's Weekly, *imprint of* ACP Publishing Pty Ltd

Australia's Best Garden Guide Series, *imprint of* Hyland House Publishing Pty Ltd

Autonomous Learning Publications & Specialists, *imprint of* Hawker Brownlow

Avon, *imprint of* Random House Australia

Axiom Publishers & Distributors
108 Rundle St, Kent Town, SA 5071
Tel: (08) 83627052
E-mail: axiompub@camtech.net.au
Key Personnel
Contact: John Gallehawk
ISBN Prefix(es): 0-947338; 0-9594164; 1-86476

Babel Handbooks, *imprint of* Nimrod Publications

Babysitters Club, *imprint of* Scholastic Australia Pty Ltd

Bahloo Publishers Real-Life Education, *imprint of* R J Cleary Publishing

R G Bahnsen
Unit 67, Masonic Village, Ridgehaven, SA 5097
Tel: (08) 2630670
Key Personnel
Head of Company: R G Bahnsen
Founded: 1988
Subjects: Biography
ISBN Prefix(es): 0-9577

Ballantine, *imprint of* Random House Australia

Bandicoot Books
PO Box 50, Margate, Tas 7054
Tel: (03) 6267 1223
Web Site: www.bandicootbooks.com
Key Personnel
Contact: Marion Isham *E-mail:* ishams@ozemail.com.au
Subjects: Animals, Pets, Fiction, Foreign Countries, History, Language Arts, Linguistics, Mysteries, Poetry
ISBN Prefix(es): 0-9586536

Bantam Books, *imprint of* Random House Australia

Bantam, *imprint of* Transworld Publishers Pty Ltd

Bay Books, *imprint of* Murdoch Books

Bayda Books
PO Box 178, East Brunswick 3057
Tel: (0613) 9380-2988 *Fax:* (0613) 9380-2988
E-mail: bayda@ozemail.com.au
Web Site: www.ozemail.com.au/~bayda/
Key Personnel
Marketing Representative: Yuri Tkach
Founded: 1976
Mail order book supplier.
Specialize in books in Russian, Ukrainian, Polish, Czech, Serb & Hungarian; also acts as library supplier.
Total Titles: 11 Print; 3 Audio
Distributor for Lastivka Press

Joycelyn Bayne
2 Lee St, Fulham Gardens 5024
Mailing Address: PO Box 59, Brooklyn Park 5022
Tel: (08) 3561748
Subjects: History
ISBN Prefix(es): 7-316

BBC Worldwide, *imprint of* Random House Australia

Beazer Publishing Company Pty Ltd+
PO Box 150, Paynesville, Victoria 3880
Tel: (03) 5156 0556 *Fax:* (03) 5156 0556
E-mail: beazer@s140.aone.net.au
Web Site: www.beazerpublishing.com
Key Personnel
Contact: Margaret Beazer
Founded: 1994
Subjects: Earth Sciences, Environmental Studies, Law, Science (General)
Total Titles: 8 Print; 1 Audio

BEC Publications, *imprint of* Hawker Brownlow

Barbara Beckett Publishing Pty Ltd
14 Hargrave St, Paddington, NSW 2021
Tel: (02) 3312871 *Fax:* (02) 3603106
Web Site: bbeckett-peg.apc.org
Key Personnel
Publisher: Barbara Beckett
Founded: 1994
Subjects: Art, Cookery
ISBN Prefix(es): 1-875891
Book Club(s): Doubleday Australia

Bellcourt Books
63 Gray St, Hamilton, Victoria 3300
Tel: 055 72 1310 *Fax:* 055 72 1310
Key Personnel
Contact: Roz Greenwood
Subjects: History

Beri Publishing+
36 Alfred Rd, Burwood, Victoria 3125
Tel: (03) 98091434 *Fax:* (03) 98091434
E-mail: beripub@ozemail.com.au
Key Personnel
Head of Company: Nola Schlegel
Founded: 1991
Subjects: Education
ISBN Prefix(es): 0-9577; 0-646

Bernal Publishing+
4 Frank St, Box Hill South, Victoria 3128
Tel: (0613) 9808-3775 *Fax:* (0613) 9888-7572
E-mail: sales@bernalpublishing.com
Web Site: www.bernalpublishing.com
Key Personnel
Man Editor: Robert Martin
Founded: 1991
Subjects: Agriculture, Biography, History, Nonfiction (General), Farming (commercial chick sexing)
ISBN Prefix(es): 0-646

Robert Berthold Photography
15 Wolfe Rd, North Ryde 2113
Tel: (02) 9887-3986 *Fax:* (02) 9887-3986
Key Personnel
Head of Company: Robert Berthold

PUBLISHERS

AUSTRALIA

Subjects: Biological Sciences, Environmental Studies, Maritime, Natural History, Outdoor Recreation, Photography, Physics, Science (General), Sports, Athletics

Better Homes & Gardens, *imprint of* Murdoch Books

Bewitched Books
Philbrooke, Woolrich Rd, Olinda, Victoria 3788
Tel: (03) 9751-1931
Key Personnel
Contact: Jane Brooks

Beyond Bullying Association, *imprint of* Rainbow Book Agencies Pty Ltd

Bible Society in Australia National Headquarters+
Member of United Bible Societies
30 York Rd, Ingleburn, NSW 2565
Tel: (02) 9829 9000 *Fax:* (02) 98294685
E-mail: customer.service@bible.org.au
Web Site: www.biblesociety.com.au
Key Personnel
Marketing Manager: Gregory N Page
 E-mail: greg.page@bbla.org.au
Founded: 1817
Specialize in Bibles & related publications.
Subjects: Biblical Studies, Religion - Catholic, Religion - Protestant, Theology
ISBN Prefix(es): 0-647
Bookshop(s): 2-6 Albert St, Blackburn, Victoria 3130 *Tel:* (03) 9877 9233 *Fax:* (03) 9877 8399; 212 Main St, Lilydale, Victoria 3140 *Tel:* (03) 9735 0410 *Fax:* (03) 9735 2013; Locked Bag 3, Minto, NSW 2566 *Fax:* (02) 9829 4685 *E-mail:* bsdirect@bible.org.au; 95 Bathurst St, Sydney, NSW 2000 *Tel:* (02) 9267 6862 *Fax:* (02) 9267 7415 *E-mail:* shop@biblesociety.com.au

Bio Concepts Publishing
Unit 5/321, Kelvin Grove Rd, Kelvin Grove, Qld 4059
Tel: (07) 33525088 *Fax:* (07) 33566081
E-mail: orthplet@ozemail.com.au
Web Site: www.bioconcepts.com.au
Key Personnel
President: Henry Osiecki
Sales Manager: Mary Waldie
Subjects: Alternative, Health, Nutrition, Self-Help, Sports, Athletics
ISBN Prefix(es): 1-875239

Birchgrove Books
18 Louisa Rd, Birchgrove 2041
Tel: (02) 98105040 *Fax:* (02) 98106053
E-mail: 100406.343@compuserve.com

Black Dog Books+
15 Gertrude St, Fitzroy, Victoria 3065
Tel: (03) 9419 9406 *Fax:* (03) 9419 1214
E-mail: dog@bdb.com.au
Web Site: www.bdb.com.au
Key Personnel
Contact: Andrew Kelly *E-mail:* andrew@bdb.com.au

Black Swan, *imprint of* Random House Australia

Black Swan, *imprint of* Transworld Publishers Pty Ltd

Blackbooks Co-operative for Aborigines Ltd
13 Mansfield St, Glebe, NSW 2037
Tel: (0612) 9660 3444 *Fax:* (0612) 9660 1924
E-mail: Tranby@tranby.com.au
Web Site: www.midcoast.com.au

Key Personnel
Head of Company: Kevin Cook
Founded: 1982
Specialize in Aboriginal & Torres Strait Islands.
Orders to: Allbooks Distribution, 16 Darghan St, Glebe, NSW 2037

Blackhead Ink Publishing+
13 High St, Hallidays Point 2430
Tel: (065) 592981 *Fax:* (065) 510518
Key Personnel
Head of Company: Adrian Emery
Subjects: Cookery, Health, Nutrition, Parapsychology, Self-Help
ISBN Prefix(es): 0-646

Blackstone, *imprint of* Pascoe Publishing

Blackstone Press Pty Ltd
L1/104 Ebley, Bondi Junction, NSW 2022
Tel: (02) 9389 7677
E-mail: c.l.e.@laams.com.au
Subjects: Law
ISBN Prefix(es): 1-875114

Blackwell Science Pty Ltd+
PO Box 378, Carlton South, Victoria 3053
Tel: (03) 93470300 *Fax:* (03) 9347 5001
E-mail: dimi.katsiens@blacksci-asia.com.au
Web Site: www.blacksci.co.uk
Key Personnel
Chief Executive, Man Dir: Mark Robertson
Marketing & Operations Dir: Neil Walsh
Publishing & Finance Dir: Jane Watson
Customer Service: Robert Turner
Founded: 1971
Subjects: Computer Science, Earth Sciences, Engineering (General), Mathematics, Medicine, Nursing, Dentistry, Physical Sciences, Physics, Psychology, Psychiatry, Science (General)
ISBN Prefix(es): 0-86793
Parent Company: Blackwell Science Ltd, United Kingdom
Subsidiaries: Blackwell Science KK
Branch Office(s)
Blackwell Science Inc, Suite 208, 3 Cambridge Center, Cambridge, MA 02142, United States
Distributor for American Society for Microbiology; American Psychiatric Press Inc; Garland Publishers; Jones & Bartlett; Springer Verlag (all Australia and New Zealand only)
Warehouse: 26 Albert St, Brunswick, Victoria 3056

Horst Blaich Pty Ltd
24 John St, Bayswater, Victoria 3153
Tel: (03) 7202658 *Fax:* (03) 7624225
ISBN Prefix(es): 1-86347

Joan Blair
15 Antrim St, Kiama, NSW 2533
Mailing Address: PO Box 432, Kiama, NSW 2533
Tel: (02) 42321642
Key Personnel
Author & Publisher: Joan Blair
Founded: 1986
Subjects: Human Relations, Self-Help
ISBN Prefix(es): 1-86252
Distributed by ROSE Education & Training (Australia)

Bloomings, *imprint of* Bloomings Books

Bloomings Books+
7 Newry St, Richmond, Victoria 3121
Tel: (03) 9427 1234; (03) 9427 1490 *Fax:* (03) 9427 9066

Key Personnel
Man Dir: Warwick Forge *E-mail:* warwick@bloomings.com.au
Founded: 1994
Publish, distribute & wholesale horticulture & natural history books.
Subjects: Gardening, Plants, Natural History
Total Titles: 12 Print
Imprints: Bloomings; Rodale; Timber

Blubber Head Press
PO Box 475, Sandy Bay, Tas 7006
Tel: (03) 6223 8644 *Fax:* (03) 6223 8644
E-mail: books@astrolabebooks.com.au
Key Personnel
Official Delegate: Michael Sprod
 E-mail: michael@astrolabebooks.com.au
Founded: 1978
Subjects: History, Regional Interests, Travel
ISBN Prefix(es): 0-908528
Bookshop(s): Astrolabe Antiquarian Booksellers, 81 Salamanca Place, First Floor, Hobart, Tasmania 7004

Board of Studies
117 Clarence St, Sydney, NSW 2000
Mailing Address: GPO Box 5300, Sydney, NSW 2001
Tel: (02) 9367 8111 *Fax:* (02) 9367 8484
Web Site: www.boardofstudies.nsw.edu.au
Key Personnel
President: Gordon Stanley *Tel:* (02) 9367 8176
General Manager: John Ward *Tel:* (02) 9367 8169
Member of NSW Government Dept.
Subjects: Education
ISBN Prefix(es): 0-7305; 0-7310

Boat Books Group
31 Albany St, Crows Nest, NSW 2065
Tel: (02) 94391133 *Fax:* (02) 94398517
E-mail: boatbook@boatbooks-aus.com.au
Key Personnel
Contact: Philip Brook
Founded: 1973
Subjects: Nautical Titles (Recreational & Professional)
Branch Office(s)
Brisbane *E-mail:* boatbks@bluesky.net.au
Melbourne *E-mail:* boatbks@ozemail.com.au

Boinkie Publishers
PO Box 27, Brighton-Le-Sands, NSW 2216
Tel: (02) 588-7010 *Fax:* (02) 9311-3428
ISBN Prefix(es): 0-9587468

Bolinda, *imprint of* Australian Large Print Pty Ltd

Bolinda Audio, *imprint of* Australian Large Print Pty Ltd

Bolinda Press, *imprint of* Australian Large Print Pty Ltd

Herbert Bolles
130 Warks Hill Rd, Kurrajong Heights 2758
Tel: (02) 45 67 7350
ISBN Prefix(es): 0-646

Boobook Publications
PO Box 163, Tea Gardens, NSW 2324
Tel: (049) 97 0811 *Fax:* (049) 97 1089
Key Personnel
Head of Company: Ian Hoyle; Sally Hoyle
Founded: 1981
Subjects: Sports, Athletics
ISBN Prefix(es): 0-908121

AUSTRALIA

Book Agencies of Tasmania+
PO Box 327, Rosny Park, Tas 7018
Tel: (03) 62 477 405 *Fax:* (03) 62 471 116
E-mail: bookagencies@trump.net.au
Web Site: www.ontas.com.au/book_agencies/contact.htm
Key Personnel
Manager: Graeme Thurlow
Founded: 1982
Subjects: Regional Interests
Number of titles published annually: 2 Print
Total Titles: 15 Print

Book Collectors' Society of Australia
16 Edwin St South, Croydon NSW 2132
Tel: (02) 9798 8984 *Fax:* (02) 9798 8984
E-mail: jeff@bcspl.com.au
Key Personnel
President: Ben Haneman
Secretary: Jeff Bidgood
Founded: 1944
ISBN Prefix(es): 0-646

The Book Company Publishing Pty Ltd
Austlink Corporate Park, One Minna Close, Belrose, Sydney, NSW 2085
Tel: (02) 94863711 *Fax:* (02) 94863722
E-mail: sales@thebookcompany.com.au
Web Site: www.thebookcompany.com.au
Key Personnel
Chief Operating Officer: Andrew G Steele-Smith
  Tel: (0402) 214 218 *E-mail:* andrewss@thebookcompany.com.au
Publisher: Glenn Johnstone
Founded: 1986
Specialize in innovative childrens' novelty books & adult stationery items.
Number of titles published annually: 200 Print

Book Lures Inc, *imprint of* Hawker Brownlow

Bookman Press Pty Ltd
607 Saint Kilda Rd, Level 8, Melbourne, Victoria 3004
Tel: (03) 9521 3250 *Fax:* (03) 9521 3270
E-mail: fayg@bookman.com.au
Web Site: www.bookman.com.au

Books for Our Times+
42 Milan Terrace, Stirling 5152
Tel: (08) 3709990 *Fax:* (08) 3709995
E-mail: creativefax@cobweb.com.au
Key Personnel
Head of Company: Jim Craig
Founded: 1990
Subjects: Advertising, Business, Crafts, Games, Hobbies, How-to, Marketing, Nonfiction (General), Science (General), Technology
ISBN Prefix(es): 0-646

Bookus Fastinandi, *imprint of* Wild & Woolley Pty Ltd

Boolarong Press
35 Hamilton Rd, Moorooka, Qld 4105
Tel: (07) 8541920 *Fax:* (07) 8541705
Key Personnel
Head of Company: Lester Padman
General Manager, Sales & Publicity: R J Keirnan
Editorial: M Weaver
Production: C L Padman
Founded: 1977
Subjects: Art, Biography, Business, History, Management, Nonfiction (General)
ISBN Prefix(es): 0-86439; 0-908175
Parent Company: Artists Associated Pty Ltd

Boombana Publications+
PO Box 118, Mount Nebo 4520
Tel: (07) 3289 8106 *Fax:* (07) 3289 8107
E-mail: J.Lacherez@uq.net.au
Web Site: www.boombanapublications.com
Key Personnel
Contact: Jean-Claude Lacherez
Founded: 1992
Subjects: Language Arts, Linguistics, Literature, Literary Criticism, Essays, Nonfiction (General)

M J Bowen & Pty Ltd
18 Ranfurlie Drive, Glen Waverley, Victoria 3150
Tel: (03) 95613425 *Fax:* (03) 98829405
Key Personnel
Dir: M J Bowen
ISBN Prefix(es): 7-316

Boxtree, *imprint of* Pan Macmillan Australia Pty Ltd

David Boyce Publishing+
44 Regent St, Redfern, NSW 2016
Tel: (02) 6997484
Key Personnel
Owner, Publisher & Sales Dir: David Boyce
  E-mail: david@boyces.com
Founded: 1975
Specialize in Automotive Manuals for workshops & software.
Subjects: Automotive, Technology
ISBN Prefix(es): 0-909682
Distributor for Robert Bosch

Louis Braille Audio
454 Glenferrie Rd, Kooyong, Victoria 3144
Tel: (03) 9864 9645 *Fax:* (03) 9864 9646
E-mail: lba.sales@visionaustralia.org.au
Web Site: www.louisbrailleaudio.com
Key Personnel
Managing Dir: Rose Blustein *E-mail:* rose.blustein@visionaustralia.org.au
Publishing & Rights Manager: Edwina Kenrick
  Tel: (03) 9864 9615 *E-mail:* edwina.kenrick@visionaustralia.org.au
Founded: 1993
Subjects: Biography, Fiction, History, Travel
ISBN Prefix(es): 0-7320; 0-86764
Total Titles: 258 Print; 258 Audio
Parent Company: Vision Australia Foundation Library
Ultimate Parent Company: Vision Australia Foundation
Distributor for Louis Braille Audio

Bridge To Peace Publications+
149 Dartford Rd, Thornleigh, NSW 2120
Tel: (02) 9875 1912
E-mail: books@bridgetopeace.com.au; adesso@bridgetopeace.com.au
Web Site: www.bridgetopeace.com.au
Key Personnel
General Manager: Jim Scarano
Founded: 1997
Specializes in internet e-mail orders for all books published.
Subjects: Alternative, History, How-to, Human Relations, Nonfiction (General), Philosophy, Psychology, Psychiatry, Self-Help, Alexander Technique, Italian culture, yoga, meditation & personal development
ISBN Prefix(es): 0-9587094; 0-9577615
Subsidiaries: Adesso Studio
Branch Office(s)
Paul Laccona, 341 Farleigh Terrace, Marietta, GA 30068, United States

Bridgeway Publications+
12 Christina Pl, Belmont 4153
Mailing Address: GPO Box 2547, Brisbane 4001
Tel: (07) 3390 4323 *Fax:* (07) 3390 4323
E-mail: info@bridgeway.org.au
Web Site: www.bridgeway.org.au
Key Personnel
Executive Dir: Don Fleming
  E-mail: donfleming@bridgeway.org.au
Founded: 1988
Non-profit organization which sends sponsored Christian reference materials to churches & institutions in needy countries.
Subjects: Biblical Studies, Religion - Protestant, Theology
ISBN Prefix(es): 0-947342
Total Titles: 17 Print
Distributed by AMG Publishers (USA); Copperbelt Christian Publications (Zambia); Horizon Publishers (India); Riverside World Inc (USA)
Shipping Address: Harvest Products, PO Box 108, Upper Gravatt, Queensland 4122, Contact: Gordon Cowell *Tel:* (07) 3849 1812 *Fax:* (07) 3849 1820 *E-mail:* harvest@tpgi.com.au
Warehouse: Harvest Products, PO Box 108, Upper Gravatt, Queensland 4122, Contact: Gordon Cowell *Tel:* (07) 3849 1812 *Fax:* (07) 3849 1820 *E-mail:* harvest@tpgi.com.au
Orders to: Harvest Products, PO Box 108, Upper Gravatt, Queensland 4122, Contact: Gordon Cowell *Tel:* (07) 3849 1812 *Fax:* (07) 3849 1820 *E-mail:* harvest@tpgi.com.au

R A Broadberh, *imprint of* Universal Press Pty Ltd

Broadway Books, *imprint of* Random House Australia

Broadway Dela Corte, *imprint of* Transworld Publishers Pty Ltd

Brookfield Press
871 Upper Brookfield Rd, Upper Brookfield 4069
Mailing Address: PO Box 738, Kenmore 4069
Tel: (07) 3374-1053 *Fax:* (07) 3374-2059
Key Personnel
Dir: Frank Stacey *E-mail:* frank.stacey@csiro.au
Subjects: Earth Sciences, Geography, Geology, Physics

Broughton Books, *imprint of* E J Dwyer (Australia) Pty Ltd

Robert Brown & Associates Australia Pty Ltd+
154 Bentinck St, Bathhurst, NSW 2795
Tel: (063) 318577 *Fax:* (063) 321273
Key Personnel
Man Editor: Robert Brown
Subjects: Natural History, Travel
ISBN Prefix(es): 0-949267; 0-909197; 1-86173; 1-86273
Total Titles: 24 Print

Budget Books Pty Ltd
17 Redwood Drive, Dingly, Victoria 3172
Tel: (03) 5516111 *Fax:* (03) 6466925
Key Personnel
Man Dir: Robert Ungar
ISBN Prefix(es): 0-86801; 0-947192; 0-908505; 0-7323

Bureau of Resource Sciences
PO Box E11, Kingston, ACT 2604
Tel: (02) 6272 4282 *Fax:* (02) 6272 4747
Web Site: www.infomine.com/index/suppliers/Bureau_of_Resource_Sciences, Australia.html
Key Personnel
Dir: Ian Lambert *E-mail:* ian@mailpc.brs.gov.au
Subjects: Agriculture, Biological Sciences, Science (General), Veterinary Science
ISBN Prefix(es): 0-642; 0-644

Butterworths Australia Ltd
Member of The Lexis Nexis Group
PeopleSoft House, 475-495 Victoria Ave, Chatswood, NSW 2067
Tel: (02) 9422 2222 *Fax:* (02) 9422 2444

E-mail: orders@butterworths.com.au
Web Site: www.butterworths.com.au
Key Personnel
CEO & Man Dir: Tony Kinnear
Publishing Dir: James Broadfoot
Finance Dir: Philip Cauwood
Sales & Marketing Dir: Catherine Yeomans
Human Resources Manager: Rachel Sutton
Founded: 1910
A division of Reed International Books Australia Pty Ltd (ABN 7000 1002 357).
Subjects: Accounting, Business, Law
ISBN Prefix(es): 0-409
Parent Company: Reed Elsevier Australia Pty Ltd
Ultimate Parent Company: Reed Elsevier plc, 25 Victoria St, London SW1H 0EX, United Kingdom
Associate Companies: Butterworth & Co (Publishers) Ltd UK; Butterworth Publishers (Pty) Ltd, South Africa; Butterworths Canada Ltd; Butterworth & Co (Asia) Pte Ltd, India; Butterworths (Ireland) Ltd; Butterworths Asia, Singapore; Butterworths of New Zealand Ltd; Guiffre Editore SpA, Italy; Editions du Juris-Classeur, France; Malayan Law Journal Sdn Bhd, Malaysia; Wydawnictwa Prawnicze PWN, Poland; Verlag Stampfli, Switzerland; Lexis-Nexis, USA
Branch Office(s)
St George Centre, 60 Marcus Clarke St, Canberra, ACT 2600
Adelaide Chambers, 122 Pirie St, Adelaide, SA 5000
461 Bourke St, Melbourne, Victoria 3000
44 St George's Terrace, Perth, WA 6000
286 Montague Rd, West End, Qld 4101

Cairns Art Society Inc
PO Box 992, Cairns, Qld 4870
Tel: (07) 4039 1122
E-mail: cas@internetnorth.com.au
Key Personnel
President: Mr K Ryan
Founded: 1931
ISBN Prefix(es): 7-316

Cambridge University Press
10 Stamford Rd, Oakleigh, Victoria 3166
Mailing Address: PO Box 85, Oakleigh, Victoria 3166
Tel: (03) 95680322 *Fax:* (03) 95631517
E-mail: info@cambridge.edu.au
Web Site: www.cambridge.edu.au
Key Personnel
Dir: Kim Harris
Subjects: Education
ISBN Prefix(es): 0-521; 0-949168; 1-86360
Parent Company: Cambridge University Press, United Kingdom
U.S. Office(s): Cambridge University Press, 40 W 20 St, New York, New York, NY 10011-4211, United States
Distributor for Currency Press (Australia); Stanford University Press (Australia & New Zealand)

Rod Campbell Books, *imprint of* Pan Macmillan Australia Pty Ltd

Canadian Conference of Catholic Bishops, *imprint of* Rainbow Book Agencies Pty Ltd

Candlelight Trust T/A Candlelight Farm
12 Dryandra Crescent, Darlington 6070
Tel: (08) 92520456 *Fax:* (08) 92520456
Web Site: www.cfpermaculture.com
Key Personnel
Editorial Manager: Ross Mars *E-mail:* rossmars@yahoo.com
Subjects: Agriculture, Education, Environmental Studies, Gardening, Plants

ISBN Prefix(es): 0-9587626
Total Titles: 4 Print

Jonathon Cape, *imprint of* Random House Australia

Captain Jonas Publications
133 Bedford Rd, Andergrove 4740
Tel: (07) 9555230 *Fax:* (07) 4956-2633
Key Personnel
Manager: Anthony G Wheeler

Carter's Publications
Locked Bag 3, Terrey Hills 2084
Tel: (02) 9450 0011 *Fax:* (02) 9450 2532
E-mail: info@carters.com.au
Web Site: www.carters.com.au
Key Personnel
Contact: Alan Carter *E-mail:* alan@carters.com.au
Founded: 1980
Subjects: Antiques, Antiques & Collectibles
Number of titles published annually: 4 Print
Total Titles: 2 Print

Casket Publications
Macquarie University, North Ryde, Sydney NSW 2109
Tel: (02) 98058878; (02) 94819145; (02) 98755382 *Fax:* (02) 98506593; (02) 98755382
Key Personnel
Contact: Prof D B Waterson
Founded: 1992
Self publishing: research tools.
Subjects: Biography, History, Queenland political biographical retailers
ISBN Prefix(es): 0-646
Total Titles: 2 Print
Branch Office(s)
20 Angophora Place, Pennant Hills, Sydney NSW 2120 *Tel:* 9481 9145 *Fax:* 9875 5382

Cassel PLC, *imprint of* Hawker Brownlow

Catchfire Press Inc
PO Box 2101, Dangar, NSW 2309
Tel: (02) 49264029
E-mail: catchfire@idl.com.au
Web Site: cust.idl.com/au/catchfire/hmpage04.html
Key Personnel
President: Lisbet de Castro Lopo

Catholic Institute of Sydney+
99 Albert Rd, Strathfield, NSW 2135
Tel: (02) 9752 9530 *Fax:* (02) 9746 6022
E-mail: cisinfo@cis.catholic.edu.au
Web Site: www.cis.catholic.edu.au
Key Personnel
President: Dr Neil Brown
Subjects: Biblical Studies, History, Philosophy, Religion - Catholic, Theology
ISBN Prefix(es): 0-908224

Cavendish Publishing, *imprint of* Cavendish Publishing Pty Ltd

Cavendish Publishing Pty Ltd+
Malleson Stephen Jaques, Governor Philip Tower, One Farrer Pl, Level 53, Sydney NSW 2000
Tel: (02) 99182199
Web Site: www.cavendishpublishing.com
Key Personnel
Publishing Dir: Mr Sonny Leong *Tel:* (0171) 278 8000 *E-mail:* sonnyleong@cavendishpublishing.com
Subjects: *Specializes in:* Law & Medicine
ISBN Prefix(es): 1-876213
Total Titles: 50 Print

Ultimate Parent Company: Cavendish Publishing Ltd, The Glass House, Wharton St, London WC1X 9PX, United Kingdom
Imprints: Cavendish Publishing

Centenary of Technical Education in Bairnsdale Group
32 Grant St, Bairnsdale, Victoria 3875
Tel: (03) 5152-4556
Key Personnel
Editorial Manager: Lorna Prendergast
Subjects: History
ISBN Prefix(es): 0-9577

Centre for Comparative Literature & Cultural Studies
Monash University, Clayton Campus, Victoria 3800
Tel: (03) 9905 4000; (03) 9905 3059 *Fax:* (03) 9905 4007
Key Personnel
Editorial Manager: C G Worth
Administrative Officer: G P Ward *E-mail:* gail.ward@arts.monash.edu.au
Subjects: Ethnicity, Literature, Literary Criticism, Essays
ISBN Prefix(es): 0-7326; 0-86746

Centre for Creative Learning, *imprint of* Hawker Brownlow

Centre Publications+
226 Moggill Rd, Taringa 4068
Tel: (03) 8700149
Key Personnel
Man Dir: Robert Snow
Founded: 1974
Subjects: Education, Health, Nutrition
ISBN Prefix(es): 0-909698
Associate Companies: THE Foundation; The Yoga Education Centre, 226 Moggill Rd, Taringa 4068

Century, *imprint of* Random House Australia

Chalkface Press Pty Ltd+
PO Box 23, Cottesloe, Perth, WA 6011
Tel: (061) 8 9385 1923 *Fax:* (061) 8 9385 1922
E-mail: info@chalkface.net.au
Web Site: www.chalkface.net.au
Key Personnel
Dir: Stephen Mellor; Bronwyn Mellor
Founded: 1987
Member of Australian Publishers Association.
ISBN Prefix(es): 1-875136
Distributed by English & Media Centre (UK)
Distributor for English & Media Centre (UK)
Foreign Rep(s): Gould Media (US)
Orders to: E-mail: orders@chalkface.net.au

Channel 4, *imprint of* Pan Macmillan Australia Pty Ltd

Chapter & Verse, *imprint of* Wellington Lane Press Pty Ltd

Chase Just Publishing
93 Cobden St, Kew 3101
Tel: (03) 9853-8799
Key Personnel
Contact: C Judge
Subjects: Child Care & Development, Disability, Special Needs, History, Medicine, Nursing, Dentistry, Psychology, Psychiatry

Chatto & Windus, *imprint of* Random House Australia

AUSTRALIA

Childerset Publishers+
1/106 Noosa Parade, Noosavilla, Qld 4566
Mailing Address: PO Box 1107, Noosaville DC 4566
Tel: (07) 5474 0242 *Fax:* (07) 5474 4446
E-mail: tessgsp@ozemail.com.au
Key Personnel
Man Dir: David Ridyard
Founded: 1970
ISBN Prefix(es): 0-909404; 0-947130

China Books
234 Swanston St, 2nd floor, Melbourne, Victoria 3000
Tel: (03) 9663 8822 *Fax:* (03) 9663 8821
E-mail: info@chinabooks.com.au
Web Site: www.chinabooks.com.au
Key Personnel
Man Dir: Ian Fox; Tony McGlinchey
Founded: 1989
Book importer, wholesaler & retailer/specialist.
Subjects: Asian Studies, Language Arts, Linguistics, China, Chinese Studies
ISBN Prefix(es): 0-646
Bookshop(s): 81 Enmore Rd, Enmore, NSW 2042 *Tel:* (02) 9557 2701 *Fax:* (02) 9661 8727 *E-mail:* chinabooks@hotkey.net.au

Chingchic Publishers
77 Boomerang Crescent, Isle of Sorrento, Qld 4217
Tel: (07) 55385945 *Fax:* (07) 55385945
E-mail: chingchic@winshop.com.au
Key Personnel
Proprietor: Judy Eather
Manager, Author & Historian: Charles E Eather
Founded: 1993
Subjects: Aeronautics, Aviation
ISBN Prefix(es): 0-646; 0-9586746; 0-949756
Foreign Rep(s): Pacific Century Ditribution Ltd (Hong Kong)

Chiron Media
PO Box 6069, Mooloolah, Qld 4553
Tel: (074) 947311 *Fax:* (074) 947890
E-mail: chiron@acslink.net.au
Key Personnel
Contact: Helen Penridge
Founded: 1990
Subjects: Animals, Pets, Environmental Studies, Government, Political Science, Public Administration, Veterinary Science
ISBN Prefix(es): 0-9586784
Parent Company: Penridge Information Pty Ltd

CHOICE Magazine+
57 Carrington Rd, Marrickville, NSW 2204
Tel: (02) 9577 3399 *Fax:* (02) 9577 3377
E-mail: ausconsumer@choice.com.au
Web Site: www.choice.com.au
Key Personnel
Publisher: Keren Lavelle
General Manager: Norm Crothers
Founded: 1960
Member of Australian Publishers' Association, Publish Australia.
Subjects: Architecture & Interior Design, Automotive, Health, Nutrition, House & Home, Self-Help, Travel
ISBN Prefix(es): 0-947277; 0-9591120; 0-9596536
Parent Company: Australian Consumers' Association

Christian Education Publications, *imprint of* Aquila Press

Christian Literature Crusade
125 New Rd, West Pennant Hills, NSW 2120
Tel: (02) 8751566 *Fax:* (02) 4818304
Key Personnel
Contact: K T Ridley
ISBN Prefix(es): 0-87508; 0-9595552
Branch Office(s)
Christian Literature Crusade, PO Box 1449, Fort Washington, PA 19034-8449, United States

Christian Research Association, *imprint of* Rainbow Book Agencies Pty Ltd

Church Archivists Press
PO Box 130, Virginia, Qld 4014
Tel: (07) 38650466 *Fax:* (07) 38650458
Key Personnel
Dir: Leo J Ansell *E-mail:* ANSELL@staff.nudgee.com
Founded: 1980 (Known as Church Archives Society Press until 1992)
Subjects: Biography, Computer Science, Genealogy, History, Poetry, Theology
ISBN Prefix(es): 1-876194
Total Titles: 75 Print

Churchill House, *imprint of* Austed Publishing Co

Churchill Livingstone, *imprint of* Harcourt Australia Pty Ltd

CIS Publishers
22 Salmon St, Port Melbourne, Victoria 3027
Tel: (03) 92467131 *Fax:* (03) 3470175
Key Personnel
Managing Dir: Elio Guarnuccio
Subjects: Education
ISBN Prefix(es): 0-949919; 1-875633; 1-86391; 1-74070

Classroom Magazine, *imprint of* Scholastic Australia Pty Ltd

R J Cleary Publishing+
PO Box 939, Darlinghurst, NSW 2010
Tel: (02) 2643750
Key Personnel
Man Dir: R J Cleary
Founded: 1969
Subjects: Film, Video, Regional Interests
ISBN Prefix(es): 0-85567
Imprints: Bahloo Publishers Real-Life Education; Education; Success Education

Clunies Ross Press
Suite 5, 233 Cardigan St, Carlton, Victoria 3053
Tel: (03) 9347-6077 *Fax:* (03) 9347-0605
E-mail: icr@crnet.com.au
Key Personnel
Chief Executive: Dr Boris Grego
Founded: 1958
Subjects: Science (General), Technology

Coconut Productions+
46 Doggett St, Fortitude Valley 4005
Tel: (07) 3854 1350 *Fax:* (07) 3854 1533
E-mail: camquinn@cheerful.com
Key Personnel
Head of Company: Cameron Quinn
Founded: 1987
Subjects: Asian Studies, Nonfiction (General), Philosophy, Real Estate, Self-Help, Sports, Athletics
ISBN Prefix(es): 0-9577

Cole Publications
3 Creswick St, Hawthorne, Victoria 3122
Tel: (03) 815640
Key Personnel
Head of Company: Merron Cullum
Editorial Manager: Cole Turnley
Founded: 1868
Subjects: Humor
ISBN Prefix(es): 0-909900
Parent Company: Alterns Pty Ltd, 5 Cooba St, Canterbury, Victoria 3126

Commonwealth Scientific & Industrial Research Organisation, see CSIRO Publishing (Commonwealth Scientific & Industrial Research Organisation)

Community Quarterly+
Ross House, 4th floor, 247 Finders Lane, Melbourne 3000
Tel: (03) 9654 1595 *Fax:* (03) 9654 1595
E-mail: comm_quar@vicnet.net.au
Key Personnel
Contact: Chris Morris
Founded: 1984
Subjects: Human Relations, Self-Help, Social Sciences, Sociology

Companion Travel Guide Books+
19 Kilmorey St, Busby NSW 2168
Tel: (02) 9608-1169 *Fax:* (02) 9608-1169
E-mail: 6LEI937764@aol.com
Key Personnel
International Rights: G R Leitner
Founded: 1990
Subjects: Travel, Latin America
ISBN Prefix(es): 0-646; 0-9587498
Distributed by Hunter Publishing Inc (USA, Canada, Central America, Caribbean)

Compass Press, *imprint of* Australian Large Print Pty Ltd

Conscious Living Publications
Wholistic Books, C/L Jacobson, Byron Bay 2481
Mailing Address: PO Box 434, Byron Bay 2481
Tel: (02) 66858585
Web Site: www.leonardjacobson.com
Key Personnel
Author & Publisher: Leonard Jacobson *E-mail:* leonard@leonardjacobson.com
Subjects: Psychology, Psychiatry, Spiritual
ISBN Prefix(es): 1-890580
Number of titles published annually: 1 Print
Total Titles: 3 Print

Constitutional Publishing Co Pty Ltd
622 Hay St, Perth, WA 6000
Mailing Address: GPO Box D152, Perth, WA 6001
Tel: (09) 4216216 *Fax:* (09) 2211572
Key Personnel
Customer Service: Roger L Day

Cookery Book
31 Albany St, Crows Nest, NSW 2065
Tel: (02) 9439 3144 *Fax:* (02) 9439 3405
E-mail: answers@cookerybook.com.au
Web Site: www.cookerybook.com.au
Key Personnel
Man Dir: John T Ivimey
Founded: 1985
Australia's only exclusive distributor of cookery books for the professional chef & the home cook.
Subjects: Cookery, Wine & Spirits, Culinary Arts
Total Titles: 3,200 Print
Parent Company: Ivimey & Associates Pty Ltd
Branch Office(s)
9 Axon St, Subiaco, Perth, WA 6008, Contact: Jennie Ivimey *Tel:* (09) 382 2122 *Fax:* (09) 381 3256

Coolabah Publishing
352 Peel St, Tamworth, NSW 2340
Tel: (02) 6766 4420 *Fax:* (02) 6766 1058
E-mail: edubook@mpx.com.au
Web Site: www.narnia.com

Key Personnel
International Rights: Patrick O'Connor
Founded: 1991
Subjects: Education, Aboriginal
ISBN Prefix(es): 0-646

Corgi, *imprint of* Random House Australia

Corgi, *imprint of* Transworld Publishers Pty Ltd

Cornford Press
6 Salisbury Crescent, Launceston, TAS 7250
Tel: (03) 6331 9658 *Fax:* (03) 6331 9685
E-mail: dadaa_tas@vision.net.au; info@cornfordpress.com
Web Site: www.cornfordpress.com
Key Personnel
Managing Editor: Tim Thorne
Founded: 1989
Subjects: Biography, Poetry, Travel
Number of titles published annually: 3 Print
Total Titles: 10 Print
Distributor for CACTI

Cornucopia Press
PO Box 27, Subiaco, WA 6008
Tel: (08) 9388 1965 *Fax:* (08) 9388 1852
E-mail: cornucop@aoi.com.au
Key Personnel
Principal: David Noel
Founded: 1982
Subjects: Agriculture, Gardening, Plants, Trees, Tree Crops, Useful Horticulture
ISBN Prefix(es): 0-9593205
Imprints: R*O*D Books
Subsidiaries: Personal Publishing Press Services
Divisions: R*O*D Books
Showroom(s): Tree Crops Centre, 208 Nicholson Rd, Subiaco WA 6008

Coronet, *imprint of* Hodder Headline Australia

Covenanter Press
PO Box 636, Lithgow, NSW 2790
Tel: (02) 6351 4611 *Fax:* (02) 6351 4611
Web Site: www.covenanterpress.com.au
Key Personnel
Sales Manager: Don Burgess *E-mail:* dlburgess@ozemail.com.au
Founded: 1967
Publisher of Christian books.
Subjects: History, Religion - Protestant, Theology
ISBN Prefix(es): 0-908189
Number of titles published annually: 2 Print
Total Titles: 50 Print
Online services available through World Wide Web.
Parent Company: Presbyterian Reformed Church of Australia

Craftsman House, *imprint of* Fine Arts Press Pty Ltd

Crawford House Publishing+
PO Box 181, Hindmarsh SA 5007
Tel: (08) 8340 1411 *Fax:* (08) 8340 1811
E-mail: frontdesk@chp.com.au
Web Site: www.chp.com.au
Key Personnel
Man Dir: Anthony L Crawford
Editorial Manager: David H Barrett
 E-mail: chpdavid@chp.com.au
Secretary: Jennifer Crawford *E-mail:* frontdesk@chp.com.au
Founded: 1989
Private company specializing in book publishing.
Subjects: Anthropology, Asian Studies, Biography, Government, Political Science, History, Maritime, Natural History, Science Fiction, Fantasy, Self-Help, Social Sciences, Sociology, Travel, Wine & Spirits
ISBN Prefix(es): 1-86333
Number of titles published annually: 15 Print
Total Titles: 82 Print
Imprints: Pants on Fire
Distributed by University of Hawaii Press

Creative Learning Consultants, *imprint of* Hawker Brownlow

Creative Learning Press, *imprint of* Hawker Brownlow

Creative Learning Systems
PO Box 165, Gisborne 3437
Tel: (03) 3700131 *Fax:* (03) 93701102
Key Personnel
Man Dir: Grant Nelson

Crista International+
PO Box 8096, Bundall, Qld 9726
Tel: (07) 5537 2956 *Fax:* (07) 5537 2956
Key Personnel
Principal: Helen Derrington
Founded: 1994
How-To Publishing for Consultants & Sales Professionals.
Subjects: Business, How-to, Marketing, Self-Help
ISBN Prefix(es): 0-9587262

Critical Thinking Press & Software, *imprint of* Hawker Brownlow

Crossroad Distributors Pty Ltd
9 Euston St, Rydalmere, NSW 2116
Tel: (02) 898-0644 *Fax:* (02) 898-0690
E-mail: custserv@crossroad.com.au
Subjects: Biblical Studies, Child Care & Development, Human Relations, Religion - Protestant, Self-Help, Theology

Crown Publishing Group, *imprint of* Random House Australia

Crystal Publishing+
6 Park St, Saint Kilda, Victoria 3182
Tel: (03) 95254549
E-mail: minx@alphalink.com.au
Key Personnel
President: Beryl K Rohan
Founded: 1980
Specialize in Economics & Sociology.
Subjects: Economics, Government, Political Science, Philosophy, Social Sciences, Sociology
ISBN Prefix(es): 0-86819

CSIRO Publishing (Commonwealth Scientific & Industrial Research Organisation)+
150 Oxford St, Collingwood, Victoria 3066
Mailing Address: PO Box 1139, Collingwood, Victoria 3066
Tel: (03) 9662 7500 *Fax:* (03) 9662 7582
E-mail: publishing@csiro.au
Web Site: www.publish.csiro.au
Telex: 30236
Key Personnel
General Manager: Paul Reekie *Tel:* (03) 9662 7650 *Fax:* (03) 9662 7555
Founded: 1926
Subjects: Agriculture, Biological Sciences, Chemistry, Chemical Engineering, Environmental Studies, Natural History, Physical Sciences, Physics, Science (General), Technology
ISBN Prefix(es): 0-643
Number of titles published annually: 50 Print
Distributed by Antipodes Books & Beyond Ltd (USA & Canada); Eurospan (UK, Europe, Middle East & North Africa); Manaaki Whenua Press (New Zealand); Publishers Marketing Services Pte Ltd (Singapore, Malaysia & Brunei)

Currency Press Pty Ltd+
201 Cleveland St, Redfern, NSW 2016
Mailing Address: PO Box 2287, Strawberry Hills, NSW 2012
Tel: (02) 9319 5877 *Fax:* (02) 9319 3649
E-mail: enquiries@currency.com.au
Web Site: www.currency.com.au
Key Personnel
Chairman: Nicholas Parsons
Publisher: Victoria Chance
Sales & Marketing Dir: Deborah Franco
 E-mail: franco@currency.com.au
Founded: 1971
Specialize in Performing Arts.
Subjects: Drama, Theater, Film, Video, Music, Dance
ISBN Prefix(es): 0-86819
Number of titles published annually: 30 Print
Total Titles: 400 Print
Distributor for Nick Hern Books (Australia); Oberon Books (Australia)

Curriculum Associates Inc, *imprint of* Hawker Brownlow

Curriculum Corporation+
Casselden Pl, Level 5, 2 Lonsdale St, Melbourne, Victoria 3000
Mailing Address: PO Box 177, Carlton South, Victoria 3053
Tel: (03) 9207 9600 *Fax:* (03) 9639 1616
E-mail: sales@curriculum.edu.au
Web Site: www.curriculum.edu.au *Cable:* EDUCATION CANBERRA
Key Personnel
Chief Executive Officer: Bruce Wilson
 E-mail: bruce.wilson@curriculum.edu.au
Executive Dir: David Francis
Publishing Manager: Esther Grounds
Sales & Marketing Dir: Sandra Hay
 E-mail: sandra.hay@curriculum.edu.au
Business Development Manager: Martin Murley
 E-mail: martin.murley@curriculum.edu.au
Production Manager: Bernie Handley
 E-mail: bernie.handley@curriculum.edu.au
General Manager, Curriculum Operations: Keith Gove *E-mail:* keith.gove@curriculum.edu.au
General Manager, Curriculum Programs: Pamela Macklin *E-mail:* pamela.macklin@curriculum.edu.au
Founded: 1990
Specialize in curriculum & education support material.
Subjects: Education
ISBN Prefix(es): 1-86366
Parent Company: Australian Ministers for Education
Orders to: PO Box 177, Carlton South, Victoria 3053

Eleanor Curtain Publishing+
906 Malvern Rd, Armadale, Victoria 3143
Tel: (03) 9822 0344 *Fax:* (03) 9824 8851
Key Personnel
Managing Dir: Eleanor Curtain *E-mail:* ecurtain@ozemail.com.au
International Rights: Jane Curtain
Subjects: Education, Literature, Literary Criticism, Essays, Poetry
ISBN Prefix(es): 1-875327
Distributed by Horwitz Martin
Distributor for Heinemann Education (US); Stenhouse

Cygnet Books, *imprint of* University of Western Australia Press

AUSTRALIA

D&B Marketing Pty Ltd
19 Havilah St, Chatswood, NSW 2067
Tel: (02) 9935 2700 *Fax:* (02) 9935 2777
E-mail: csc.austral@dnb.com.au
Web Site: www.dbmarketing.com.au
Key Personnel
Man Dir: Mike Stensland
General Manager: Chris Pellegrinetti
  E-mail: pellegrc@dnb.com
Man Editor: Sue Francis
Founded: 1887
Subjects: Business, Finance
ISBN Prefix(es): 1-875430; 0-9593441
Parent Company: D&B (Australia) Pty Ltd, 24 Alberta Rd, South Melbourne, Victoria 3174
Divisions: Riddell Publishing

Dabill Publications
PO Box 707, Wollongong, NSW 2520
Tel: (02) 4228 8836 *Fax:* (02) 4226 9367
Web Site: www.dabill.com.au
Key Personnel
Author: Tim Cattell *E-mail:* tim@dabill.com.au
Business Manager: Frances Cattell
Founded: 1980
Subjects: Economics, Education, Environmental Studies, Geography, Geology, Social Sciences, Sociology

Dagraja Press+
3 Verco St, Hackett, ACT 2602
Tel: (02) 62470782; (02) 62627533
E-mail: granorab@ozemail.com.au
Key Personnel
Owner: Mr Graeme Barrow
Founded: 1977
Specialize in bushwalking guides & local history.
ISBN Prefix(es): 0-9587552
Number of titles published annually: 1 Print
Total Titles: 5 Print
Distributed by MacStyle Media

Dandy Lion Publications, *imprint of* Hawker Brownlow

Dangaroo Press+
PO Box 93, New Lambton, NSW 2305
Tel: (02) 49545938 *Fax:* (02) 49546531
Key Personnel
Sales Manager: Allan Rich
Founded: 1978
Subjects: Art, Ethnicity, Literature, Literary Criticism, Essays, Nonfiction (General), Poetry, Social Sciences, Sociology, Women's Studies
ISBN Prefix(es): 1-871049; 1-875523

D'Artagnan Publishing+
PO Box 107, Burnside, SA 5066
Tel: (08) 2726718
Key Personnel
Head of Business: Hazel l Barrett
Writer: Elizabeth Whitbread
Founded: 1982
Member of Australian Journalist Association.
Subjects: Animals, Pets, Art, Romance
ISBN Prefix(es): 0-9593142; 1-875201

D'Assis Books+
PO Box 1189, Noosa Heads Qld 4567
Tel: (0754) 482145 *Fax:* (0754) 475200
ISBN Prefix(es): 0-646
Orders to: Gemcraft, 14 Duffy St, Burwood, Melbourne, Vic 3125
Warwick Page Eagle Heights Relaxation Retreat, 168 McDonell Rd, Eagle Heights, Mount Harborite, Qld 4271 *Tel:* (075) 545-3903 *Fax:* (075) 545-2426
Bhudens, PO Box 163, West Burleight, Old Australia *Tel:* (075) 534 9200 *Fax:* (073) 302 2998

Wendy Davies
PO Box 174, Dalby 4405
Tel: (0746) 622-595 *Fax:* (0746) 625-994

Deakin University Press+
Pigdons Rd, Geelong, Victoria 3217
Tel: (03) 5227 1100 *Fax:* (03) 5227 2001
E-mail: lynnew@deakin.edu.au
Web Site: www.deakin.edu.au
Telex: 35625
Key Personnel
Manager, Sales: David Oswell *E-mail:* doswell@deakin.edu.au
Chief Executive: Ed Brumby
Manager: Marie Kelly
Founded: 1979
Member of Australian Book Publishers Association, National Book Council.
Subjects: Anthropology, Business, Environmental Studies, Mathematics, Medicine, Nursing, Dentistry, Women's Studies
ISBN Prefix(es): 0-949823; 0-86828; 0-7300
Total Titles: 356 Print
Parent Company: Learning Resources Services Deakin University

Del Rey, *imprint of* Random House Australia

Dell, *imprint of* Transworld Publishers Pty Ltd

Dell Publishing, *imprint of* Random House Australia

Dellasta Publishing+
10 Worrall St, Burwood, Victoria 3125
Mailing Address: PO Box 777, Mount Waverley, Victoria 3149
Tel: (03) 9888 9188 *Fax:* (03) 9888 7806
E-mail: dellasta@publishaust.net.au
Web Site: www.dellasta.com.au
Key Personnel
Man Dir: Christian Esterhuyse
Customer Service: Irene Horwood
Founded: 1986
Member of Publish Australia.
Subjects: Education, Environmental Studies, Geography, Geology, Language Arts, Linguistics, Mathematics, Science (General)
ISBN Prefix(es): 0-947138; 1-875627; 1-875640
Imprints: Ashwood House; Ashwood House Medical
Divisions: Ashwood Medical; Ashwood House Medical
Distributor for Green Submarine (UK); Learning Resources Inc (USA); Ver Lag An Der Ruhr (Germany)
Orders to: PO Box 777, Mount Waverley, Victoria 3149

Demonvamp Publications
24 Kiah St, Glen Waverley, Victoria 3150
Tel: (03) 98023875
Key Personnel
Publisher: W H Brook
ISBN Prefix(es): 1-86252

Department for Education & Children's Services, South Australia
Darlington Materials Development Centre, Banksia Ave, Seacombe Gardens, SA 5047
Tel: (08) 3770399 *Fax:* (08) 3770341
Key Personnel
Man Editor: Pamela Ball
Founded: 1974
Member of APA.
Subjects: Education
ISBN Prefix(es): 7-243; 7-308

Bookshop(s): The Shop, The Orphanage Teachers Centre, 181 Coodwood Rd, Millswood 5034
Orders to: Curriculum Resources Australia, PO Box 33, Campbelltown, SA 5074 *Tel:* (08) 38736077 *Fax:* (08) 82345086

Department of Energy (NSW)+
29-57 Christie St, Saint Leonards, NSW 2065
Mailing Address: PO Box 536, Saint Leonards, NSW 1590
Tel: (02) 9901 8888 *Fax:* (02) 9901 8777
Web Site: www.doe.nsw.gov.au
Key Personnel
Marketing: Peter Walker
Subjects: Earth Sciences

Department of Mineral Resources (NSW), see Department of Energy (NSW)

Department of Primary Industries, Queensland
Primary Industries Bldg, 1st floor, Publishing Services, 80 Ann St, Brisbane, Qld 4000
Mailing Address: GPO Box 46, Brisbane, Qld 4001
Tel: (07) 32393772 *Fax:* (07) 32396509
E-mail: books@dpi.qld.gov.au
Web Site: www.dpi.qld.gov.au
Subjects: Agriculture, Animals, Pets, Gardening, Plants
ISBN Prefix(es): 0-7242
Orders to: DPI Publications, Primary Industries Bldg, Brisbane, Qld 4000

Desbooks, *imprint of* Rainbow Book Agencies Pty Ltd

Desbooks Pty Ltd
56 Wales St, Thornbury, Victoria 3071
Tel: (03) 94842465 *Fax:* (03) 94843877
E-mail: desb@alphalink.com.au
Key Personnel
Contact: Hugh McGinlay
Founded: 1981
Subjects: Religion - Other, Theology
ISBN Prefix(es): 0-949824
Imprints: Wisdom Press

Desert Pea Press, *imprint of* The Federation Press

Deva Wings Publications+
PO Box 200, Daylesford, Victoria 3460
Tel: (03) 5348 1414 *Fax:* (03) 5348 1414
E-mail: devawings@netconnect.com.au
Web Site: www.spacountry.net.au/devawings/
Key Personnel
Author: Tarajyoti Govinda *E-mail:* govinda@netconnect.com.au
Contact: Artuna Govindamurti
Founded: 1994
Subjects: Human Relations, Nonfiction (General), Psychology, Psychiatry, Self-Help

Dharma Publishing, *imprint of* Windhorse Books

Dollar Books, *imprint of* Ansay Pty Ltd

Doubleday, *imprint of* Random House Australia

Doubleday, *imprint of* Transworld Publishers Pty Ltd

Dragon Press+
PO Box 209, Scarborough, WA 6019
Tel: 09 3412004
Key Personnel
Contact: Bryn Griffiths
Founded: 1989

Subjects: Literature, Literary Criticism, Essays, Maritime, Poetry
ISBN Prefix(es): 1-875662
Parent Company: Dragon International
Imprints: Platypus Press Australia
Showroom(s): 9 The Glebe, Bishopston, Gower, Swansea, United Kingdom

Dryden Press, *imprint of* Harcourt Australia Pty Ltd

Dryden Press
PO Box 46, Darlinghurst, NSW 2010
Tel: (02) 331-4571 *Fax:* (02) 398-9782
Key Personnel
Contact: Ian R Stubbin
Subjects: Business, History, Travel
ISBN Prefix(es): 0-909162

Dubois Publishing
10 Grafton St, Chippendale 2008
Tel: (02) 92111178 *Fax:* (02) 92111868
Key Personnel
Publisher & Author: Bob Wood *Tel:* (02) 65671407
Distributor: Ron Wood *E-mail:* books@elt.com.an
Subjects: Mathematics
Total Titles: 1 Print
Distributed by Melting Pot Press

Dun & Bradstreet Marketing Pty Ltd, see D&B Marketing Pty Ltd

E J Dwyer (Australia) Pty Ltd+
Locked Bag 71, Alexandria, NSW 2015
Tel: (02) 9550 2355 *Fax:* (02) 9519 3218
Key Personnel
Man Dir & Sales: Anthony Dwyer
Publisher (Religious Books): Catherine Hammond
Founded: 1904
Also acts as Australian distributor for Liturgical Press, Regina Press, Catholic Book Publishing, Michael Glazier, Pueblo, SVS Press, Inner Traditions International, Conari Press, Hazelden, Ten Speed Press, Celestial Arts, Tricycle Press, White Cloud Press, Gurze Books, Rutlege Hill Press.
Subjects: Marketing, Religion - Other, Self-Help, Social Sciences, Sociology, Theology
ISBN Prefix(es): 0-85574; 1-86429
Parent Company: E J Dwyer (Holdings) Pty Ltd
Imprints: Millennium Books; Broughton Books
Divisions: Millennium Books
Distributed by Morehouse Publishing (religious books, USA); Novalis (religious books, Canada)

Dynamo House P/L+
4-10 Yorkshire St, Richmond, Victoria 3121
Mailing Address: PO Box 110, Richmond, Victoria 3121
Tel: (03) 9427 0955; (03) 9428 3636 *Fax:* (03) 9429 8036
E-mail: info@dynamoh.com.au
Key Personnel
Publisher: Stefan Mager
Founded: 1979
Subjects: Astrology, Occult, Health, Nutrition, Humor, Aromatherapy, reflexology, alternative therapies & philosophies
ISBN Prefix(es): 0-949266; 1-876100; 0-949383
Subsidiaries: Dynamo Press
Distributed by Aromaland Inc (USA); Asiapac Books (Singapore); Milk & Honey, Inc. (USA)

EA Books
2 Ernest St, Crows Nest, NSW 1585
Mailing Address: PO Box 588, Crows Nest, NSW 1585
Tel: (02) 9438 1533 *Fax:* (02) 9438 5934
E-mail: eabooks@engaust.com
Web Site: www.engaust.com.au
Key Personnel
General Manager: Bruce Roff *E-mail:* broff@engaust.com.au
Editor: Dietrich Georg *E-mail:* dgeorge@engaust.com.au
Editorial: Bob Jackson *E-mail:* bjackson@engaust.com.au; Nathan Menser *E-mail:* nmenser@engaust.com.au; Paul Woolnough *E-mail:* pwoolnough@engaust.com.au
Advertising Manager: Terry Marsden *E-mail:* tmarsden@engaust.com.au
Advertising Sales: Maria Mamone *E-mail:* mmamone@engaust.com.au
Advertising Coordinator: Kristy Ireland *E-mail:* kireland@engaust.com.au
Subscriptions: Pam Chenery *E-mail:* jmcgregor@engaugst.com.au
Founded: 1919 (I E Aust, 1976 E A Books)
Subjects: Chemistry, Chemical Engineering, Civil Engineering, Electronics, Electrical Engineering, Mechanical Engineering
ISBN Prefix(es): 0-85825; 1-86445
Parent Company: Institution of Engineers Australia, 11 National Circuit, Barton ACT 2600
Associate Companies: Engineering World Magazine; Engineers Australia Magazine; Chemical Engineering in Australia Magazine
Imprints: IE Aust Publications
Branch Office(s)
Accents Publications Service Inc, 911 Silver Spring Ave, Silver Spring, MD 20910, United States *Tel:* 301-588-5496 *Fax:* 301-588-5249

Ebury Press, *imprint of* Random House Australia

The Edge of It, *imprint of* Feakle Press

Edubook, *imprint of* Egan Publishing Pty Ltd

Education, *imprint of* R J Cleary Publishing

Educational Advantage+
29 Meninya St, Moama, NSW 2731
Mailing Address: PO Box 1068, Echuca, Vic 3564
Tel: (03) 5480 9466 *Fax:* (03) 5480 9462
E-mail: info@mathsmate.net
Web Site: www.mathsmate.net
Key Personnel
Manager: Joanna Tutos
Contact: Joseph B Wright
Founded: 1995
Subjects: Education, Mathematics
ISBN Prefix(es): 1-876081
Total Titles: 44 Print
Associate Companies: Learning Cycles USA; Math's Mate USA
Foreign Rep(s): Kathy Frick (US); Trish Kidd (New Zealand)

Educational Assessment Service Inc, *imprint of* Hawker Brownlow

Educational Impressions, *imprint of* Hawker Brownlow

Educational Insights, *imprint of* Hawker Brownlow

Educational Supplies Pty Ltd (The Dominie Group)
8 Cross St, Brookvale, NSW 2100
Mailing Address: PO Box 33, Brookvale, NSW 2100
Tel: (02) 99050201 *Fax:* (02) 99055209
Key Personnel
Man Dir: Ross Martin
Founded: 1951
ISBN Prefix(es): 1-86251; 0-909268; 0-949029

Edwina Publishing+
20 Willandra Ave, Canterbury, Victoria 3126
Tel: (03) 9836 3810 *Fax:* (03) 9830 1356
Key Personnel
President: Christopher J Venn
Author: Susan L Venn
Subjects: Art
ISBN Prefix(es): 0-646

Egan Publishing Pty Ltd+
8 Waverley St, East Brighton, Victoria 3187
Mailing Address: PO Box 283, East Brighton, Victoria 3187
Tel: (03) 5923451 *Fax:* (03) 95931026
Key Personnel
Head of Company: Cecilia Egan
Founded: 1986
Subjects: Animals, Pets, Cookery, Crafts, Games, Hobbies, Fiction, Gardening, Plants
ISBN Prefix(es): 0-947272; 0-9593542
Imprints: Edubook; Ashton Egan

Egmont, *imprint of* Random House Australia

EK Press
Midpath, Tumoulin, Ravenshoe 4872
Mailing Address: PO Box 57, Ravenshoe 4872
Tel: (07) 4097 6474 *Fax:* (07) 4097 6474
Key Personnel
Chairman: John Taylor
Editor: David de Vaux *E-mail:* dvaux@iig.com.au
Founded: 1989
Subjects: Drama, Theater, Fiction, Poetry
Distributed by Interactive Publications
Distributor for Interactive Publications

El Kumanand Press, see EK Press

Elephas Books Pty Ltd+
1/18 Mooney St, Bayswater, WA 6053
Tel: (09) 3701461 *Fax:* (09) 3418952
Key Personnel
Head of Company: Rume Karlson; Alan Falkson
Founded: 1989
Specialize in How-to & Informational titles, also acts as importer & distributor of small press titles through Practical Books subsidiary.
Subjects: How-to, Library & Information Sciences
ISBN Prefix(es): 1-875273
Parent Company: The Firs
Imprints: Wilbur

David Ell Press Pty Ltd+
PMB 14, Balmain, NSW 2041
Tel: (02) 5551634 *Fax:* (02) 5557067
Key Personnel
Head of Company: David Ell
Man Editor: Kathryn Lamberton
Founded: 1978
Subjects: Art, Crafts, Games, Hobbies
ISBN Prefix(es): 0-908197
Imprints: Ellsyd Press (Paperbacks & Children's)
Subsidiaries: Ellsyd Press Pty Ltd; Longueville Publications
Orders to: Tower Books, 2 Sydenham Rd, Brookvale, NSW 2100

Ellsyd Press (Paperbacks & Children's), *imprint of* David Ell Press Pty Ltd

Elton Publications+
57 Camden St, Wembly Downs, WA 6019
Tel: (08) 9 446 1328 *Fax:* (08) 9 445 8229
E-mail: elton@iinet.net.au
Web Site: www.elton.iinet.net.au
Key Personnel
Contact: Richard Lyon
Founded: 1994

Blackline Masters books which are used by teachers; educational, internet, Australia, Aborigines.
Member of Copyright Agency Ltd.
Subjects: History, Culture, Wildlife
ISBN Prefix(es): 0-646; 1-876486
Number of titles published annually: 8 Print; 3 E-Book
Total Titles: 42 Print; 6 E-Book
Distributed by A & M Bookshop; Chalkies n Kids Dominie; Holding Educational Aids; Narnia Bookshop; Wooldridges

Emerald City Books+
21 Redmyre Rd, Strathfield, NSW 2135
Mailing Address: PO Box 222, Strathfield NSW 2135
Tel: (02) 7641115 *Fax:* (02) 7641115
E-mail: emeraldcitybooks@hotmail.com
Key Personnel
Dir: Ken Preece
Founded: 1995
Subjects: Biological Sciences, Business, Chemistry, Chemical Engineering, Computer Science, Economics, Mathematics, Physics, Science (General)
ISBN Prefix(es): 1-876133

Emmaus Productions, *imprint of* Rainbow Book Agencies Pty Ltd

Emperor Publishing+
c/o Oxford Property Group, 55 Oxford St, Darlinghurst 2010
Tel: (02) 9261-4055 *Fax:* (02) 9264-9435
E-mail: pa@oxfordsquare.com.au
Key Personnel
Head of Company & Dir: Phil Birnbaum
Founded: 1989
Subjects: Anthropology, Biography, Foreign Countries, Humor, Nonfiction (General), Photography, Travel
ISBN Prefix(es): 7-316
Total Titles: 2 Print

Encyclopaedia Britannica (Australia) Inc
12 Anella Ave, Castle Hill, NSW 2154
Tel: (02) 96805666 *Fax:* (02) 98993231
Telex: 23044 Enbrit
Key Personnel
President: Alan Booth
Vice President, Sales Administration: N Bechler
Vice President, Operations: Danny McCamey
Subjects: Art, Biological Sciences, Geography, Geology, Science (General)
ISBN Prefix(es): 0-909263
Parent Company: Encyclopaedia Britannica Inc, Britannica Centre, 310 South Michigan Ave, Chicago, IL 60604, United States
Associate Companies: Encyclopaedia Britannica International Ltd, UK, United Kingdom (for other associate companies)

Enrich, *imprint of* Hawker Brownlow

Enterprise Publications+
PO Box 16, Goodwood, SA 5034
Tel: (08) 2619528 *Fax:* (08) 2619528
Key Personnel
Sales Manager: Robert Mossel
Founded: 1972
Member of Fellow of Royal Photographic Society (FRPS).
Subjects: History, Maritime, Natural History, Outdoor Recreation, Photography, Regional Interests
ISBN Prefix(es): 0-85913
Distributed by State Mutual Books (USA)

Envirobook+
38 Rose St, Annandale, NSW 2038
Tel: (02) 96606397
E-mail: trekaway@sia.net.au
Telex: 271206
Key Personnel
Man Dir: Patrick Thompson
Subjects: Environmental Studies, Natural History, Outdoor Recreation, Aboriginal Children
ISBN Prefix(es): 0-85881
Number of titles published annually: 15 Print
Total Titles: 30 Print

ERA Picture Books, *imprint of* Era Publications

Era Publications+
220 Grange Rd, Flinders Park, SA 5025
Mailing Address: PO Box 231, Brooklyn Park, SA 5032
Tel: (08) 8352 4122 *Fax:* (08) 8234 0023
E-mail: admin@erapublications.com
Web Site: www.erapublications.com
Key Personnel
Chief Executive Officer & Man Dir: Dr Rodney Martin *E-mail:* rod@erapublications.com
Founded: 1971
Primary school educational materials.
Subjects: Education, Nonfiction (General), Primary/Elementary School Literature
ISBN Prefix(es): 86-374
Total Titles: 250 Print; 1 CD-ROM; 28 Audio
Parent Company: R D Martin Pty Ltd, 220 Grange Rd, Flinders Park, SA
Imprints: ERA Picture Books; Magic Bean
Distributed by Ragged Bears (UK, Picture Books)
Distributor for Gareth Stevens Inc; Moonlight (Australia); Tessloff
Foreign Rep(s): The Choice Maker InterAustralia Co (Korea); Daniel Doglioli (Italy); Martina Oepping (France)

Escutcheon Press
37 Cornelian Rd, Pearl Beach NSW 2256
Tel: (02) 4344-2304 *Fax:* (02) 4341-1248
Key Personnel
Contact: R E Summers
ISBN Prefix(es): 1-875862; 0-9588066

Essien, *imprint of* Hudson Publishing

Experimental Art Foundation
Lion Arts Centre, N Terrace & Morphett St, Adelaide, SA 5000
Mailing Address: PO Box 8091, Station Arcade, SA 5000
Tel: (08) 8211 7505 *Fax:* (08) 8211 7323
E-mail: eaf@eaf.asn.au
Web Site: www.eaf.asn.au
Key Personnel
Head of Company: Richard Grayson
Administrator: Julie Lawton
Founded: 1974
Subjects: Art, Literature, Literary Criticism, Essays, Philosophy
ISBN Prefix(es): 0-949836; 0-9596729
Associate Companies: Otis Rush Magazine & Little Esther Books

Fairfield Press, *imprint of* Rainbow Book Agencies Pty Ltd

Family Circle, *imprint of* Murdoch Books

Family Health Publications+
Suite 1, 88 Broadway, Nedlands, WA 6009
Mailing Address: PO Box 3100, Nedlands, WA 6009
Tel: (08) 9389 8777 *Fax:* (08) 9389 8444
Web Site: www.familyhealth.info/fhp.php
Key Personnel
President: Allan Borushek *E-mail:* allan@calorieking.com
Founded: 1972
Subjects: Health, Nutrition
ISBN Prefix(es): 0-947091
Branch Office(s)
Allan Borushek & Associates Inc, 1760 Monrovia Ave, PO Box 3100, Costa Mesa, CA 92628, United States *Tel:* 949-642-8500 *Fax:* 949-642-8900

Family Reading Publications
B100 Ring Rd, Ballarat, Victoria 3352
Tel: (03) 5334 3244 *Fax:* (03) 5334 3299
E-mail: info@familyreading.com.au
Web Site: www.familyreading.com.au
Key Personnel
Contact: Colin Handreck *E-mail:* colin.handreck@familyreading.com.au; Ian Ruddick
Founded: 1976
Wholesale distributor - Christian books.
Distributor for Baker Book House; Christian Focus Publications (Australia); J Countryman; Harvest House Publishing; Intervarsity Press (Australia); Thomas Nelson; Tommy Nelson; Word Publishing; Zondervan (Australia)

Fawcett, *imprint of* Random House Australia

Feakle Press
126 Lennox St, Newtown 2042
Mailing Address: PO Box 832, Newtown, 2042 Sydney, NSW
Tel: (02) 95573248
Key Personnel
International Rights: Colleen Burke
Founded: 1992
Subjects: Poetry
ISBN Prefix(es): 0-646
Imprints: The Edge of It; Wildlife in Newtown

Fearon Teacher Aids, *imprint of* Hawker Brownlow

The Federation Press+
71 John St, Leichhardt, NSW 2040
Mailing Address: PO Box 45, Annandale, NSW 2038
Tel: (02) 9552-2200 *Fax:* (02) 9552-1681
E-mail: info@federationpress.com.au
Web Site: www.federationpress.com.au
Key Personnel
Dir: Christopher Holt; Diane Young *E-mail:* d.young@federationpress.com.au
Founded: 1988
Legal & social issues publisher.
Subjects: Business, Environmental Studies, Law, Academic Texts
ISBN Prefix(es): 1-86287
Total Titles: 300 Print
Imprints: Desert Pea Press; Hawkins Press
Distributed by Dunmore Press (New Zealand); Willan Publishing UK (Australiasia)
Distributor for Criminal Justice Press US; Dunmore Press (New Zealand)

Fernfawn Publications+
83 Weekes Rd, Moggill, Qld 4070
Tel: (07) 3202 6157 *Fax:* (07) 3202 6157
Key Personnel
Head of Company: Jarvis L Finger
Founded: 1992
Subjects: Education, Humor, Law, Management

Filef Italo-Australian Publications
157 Marion St, Leichhardt 2040
Tel: (02) 9568-3776 *Fax:* (02) 9568-3776
Key Personnel
Contact: Vera Zaccarr

Finch Publishing+
PO Box 120, 1595 Lane Cove
Tel: (02) 9418 6247 *Fax:* (02) 9418 8878
E-mail: info@finch.com.au

Web Site: www.finch.com.au
Key Personnel
Publisher: Rex Finch
Dir: Vicki Finch
Marketing Coordinator: Julian Sheedy
Editor: Sean Doyle
Founded: 1992
Subjects: Child Care & Development, Communications, Education, Human Relations, Non-fiction (General), Psychology, Psychiatry, Self-Help, Social Sciences, Sociology, Women's Studies, Parenting, Relationships, Mens Studies, Social Issues, Children's Health
Number of titles published annually: 10 Print
Total Titles: 17 Print
Distributed by Pearson Education South (South Africa); Simon & Schuster (Australia)

Fine Arts Press Pty Ltd+
42 Chandos St, St Leonards, NSW 2065
Tel: (02) 9966 8400 *Fax:* (02) 9966 0355
E-mail: sacret@gbpub.com.au
Web Site: www.artasiapacific.com *Cable:* IMPRINT SYDNEY
Key Personnel
Publisher: Sam Ure Smith
Editor: Dinah Dysart; Leon Paroissien
Editorial Manager: Hannah Fink
Founded: 1963
Art & Australia, quarterly journal.
Company also produces books for other publishers.
Subjects: Art
ISBN Prefix(es): 0-86917; 90-5703
Associate Companies: G+B Arts International; Gordon 2nd Breach Publishing Group
Imprints: Craftsman House
Divisions: Craftsman House (Book Division)

The Five Mile Press Pty Ltd
22 Summit Rd, Noble Park, Victoria 3174
Mailing Address: PO Box 760, Noble Park, Victoria 3174
Tel: (03) 9790 5000 *Fax:* (03) 9790 6688
E-mail: info@fivemile.com.au
Web Site: www.fivemile.com.au
Key Personnel
Man Dir: David Horgan
Subjects: Regional Interests
ISBN Prefix(es): 0-86788; 1-875971; 1-86503

Flactem
7 Burwood Hwy, Burwood 3125
Tel: (03) 98083444 *Fax:* (03) 98888948
Key Personnel
Contact: Judith Paphazy

Flora Publications International Pty Ltd+
371 Queen St, 8th Floor, Brisbane 4001
Mailing Address: GPOB 2792, Brisbane, Qld 4001
Tel: (07) 3229 6366 *Fax:* (07) 3229 8782
E-mail: info@flora.com.au
Key Personnel
President & International Rights: Paul Niederer
Founded: 1995
Subjects: Gardening, Plants, Outdoor Recreation, Horticulture
ISBN Prefix(es): 1-876060
Associate Companies: Infomedia Publishing Pty Ltd, Brisbane, Qld
Imprints: Infomedia

Florilegium+
PO Box 644, Rozelle, NSW 2039
Tel: (02) 95558589 *Fax:* (02) 98184409
E-mail: florileg@ozemail.com.au
Key Personnel
Manager: Gilbert Teague
Founded: 1989
Member of ABPA, NIAA.
Subjects: Gardening, Plants
ISBN Prefix(es): 0-9586498; 1-876314

Fodor, *imprint of* Random House Australia

Forge, *imprint of* Pan Macmillan Australia Pty Ltd

Fortune Publications
PO Box 1220, Box Hill 3128
Tel: (03) 9890-7731
Key Personnel
Contact: John D Lines
Founded: 1992
Subjects: Geography, Geology
ISBN Prefix(es): 0-646

Foundation for Critical Thinking, *imprint of* Hawker Brownlow

Fraser Publications+
PO Box 215, Rutherglen, Victoria 3685
Tel: (018) 039845 *Fax:* (018) 261775
E-mail: fraspub@albury.net.au
Key Personnel
Manager: Ian C Fraser
Founded: 1987
Subjects: Health, Nutrition, Medicine, Nursing, Dentistry, Self-Help
ISBN Prefix(es): 0-9588384

Free Spirit Publishing Inc, *imprint of* Hawker Brownlow

Oliver Freeman Editions, *imprint of* Prospect Media Pty Ltd

Fremantle Arts Centre Press
25 Quarry St, Fremantle, WA 6160
Mailing Address: PO Box 158, North Fremantle, WA 6159
Tel: (08) 9430 6331 *Fax:* (08) 9430 5242
E-mail: facp@iinet.net.au
Web Site: members.iinet.au/~facp/
Key Personnel
Publisher: Ray Coffey
Rights: Helen Kirkbride
Founded: 1976
Subjects: Art, Biography, Education, Fiction, History, Literature, Literary Criticism, Essays, Poetry
ISBN Prefix(es): 1-86368; 0-949144; 0-909206
Number of titles published annually: 35 Print
Total Titles: 250 Print
Imprints: Sandcastle Books
U.S. Office(s): International Specialized Book Service, 5804 NE Hassalo St, Portland, OR 97213-3644, United States, Contact: Tamma Greenfield *Tel:* 503-287-3093 *Fax:* 503-280-8832 *E-mail:* mail@isbs.com (For distribution in USA only)
Distributed by International Specialized Book Services Inc (North America); Penguin Books Australia Ltd (Australia); Penguin Books (NZ) Ltd (New Zealand)
Foreign Rep(s): International Specialized Book Services (North America)

Freshet Press+
2 Lyttleton Ave, Castlemaine, Victoria 3450
Tel: (03) 53483085
Key Personnel
International Rights: J Richards
Founded: 1982
Subjects: Gardening, Plants, Literature, Literary Criticism, Essays, Philosophy, Poetry, Psychology, Psychiatry, Religion - Other, Social Sciences, Sociology
ISBN Prefix(es): 0-9593361

Full Circle Publications Co-Operative
12 Cornell St, Melbourne, Victoria 3124
Tel: (03) 98304253
ISBN Prefix(es): 0-9577
Distributor for Australian Council for Educational Research
Bookshop(s): Politics & Prose Bookstore, 5015 Connecticut Ave NW, Washington, DC 20008, United States *Tel:* 202-364-1919

Galations Group, *imprint of* Rainbow Book Agencies Pty Ltd

Galley Press Publishing+
50 Arthur St, Surry Hills, NSW 2010
Tel: (02) 9360 5312 *Fax:* (02) 9360 1968
E-mail: galleypr@ozemail.com.au
Key Personnel
Contact: Tony Markidis
Founded: 1992
Also acts as bookshop & infoserver, stop distribution service.
Subjects: Fiction, Poetry, Sports, Athletics
ISBN Prefix(es): 1-875701
Total Titles: 15 Print
Associate Companies: Home Grown Book Distribution Co-op Ltd; Isbin Bookspider

Gamco Industries Inc, *imprint of* Hawker Brownlow

Gangan Publishing+
PO Box 522, Strawberry Hills NSW 2012
Tel: (02) 9280 2120 *Fax:* (02) 9280 2130
E-mail: books@gangan.com
Web Site: www.gangan.com
Key Personnel
Publisher: Gerald Ganglbauer *Tel:* (0411) 156 309 *E-mail:* gerald@gangan.com
Founded: 1984
Subjects: Fiction, Literature, Literary Criticism, Essays, Poetry, Regional Interests, Contemporary literature from Australia & Austria
ISBN Prefix(es): 1-86336; 3-900530
Imprints: Gangaroo
Orders to: Brodtrager & Partner OEG, Rainleiten 62, A-8045 Graz, Austria, Guenter Brodtrager *Tel:* (0316) 670 4090 *Fax:* (0316) 670 4096 *E-mail:* gbrodtrager@greenbrains.com

Gangaroo, *imprint of* Gangan Publishing

Garr Publishing
Palm Court 464 The Entrance Rd, Erina Heights 2260
Tel: (02) 43677223 *Fax:* (02) 43670762
E-mail: garrpub@ozemail.com.au
Web Site: www.ozemail.com.au/~garrpub/
Key Personnel
Contact: R Symington *Tel:* (02) 43677008
Founded: 1994
An all Australian Enterprise, whose aim is to introduce, establish & market Australian works to the national & international markets.
Specialize in fiction based on fact (Australian authors).
Subjects: Fiction
Number of titles published annually: 2 CD-ROM; 4 Online; 4 E-Book
Total Titles: 4 Print; 2 CD-ROM; 8 Online; 6 E-Book; 2 Audio
Subsidiaries: Softmail Computing

Garradunga Press
1/33 Jensen St, Manoora QLD 4870
Tel: (0409) 320 619 (mobile) *Fax:* (07) 4032 5918
E-mail: bolton@iig.com.au
Key Personnel
Contact: Colleen Rowe
Specialize in Travel.

Subjects: Travel
ISBN Prefix(es): 0-646

John Garratt Publishing+
32 Glenvale Crescent, Mulgrave, Victoria 3170
Mailing Address: Private Bag 400, Mulgrave, Victoria 3170
Tel: (03) 9545 3111 *Fax:* (03) 9545 3222
E-mail: sales@johngarratt.com.au
Web Site: www.johngarratt.com.au
Key Personnel
Man Dir: Garry Eastman *E-mail:* garryeastman@johngarratt.com.au
Founded: 1995
Importation & marketing of overseas religious titles.
Membership(s): CBAA.
Subjects: Religion - Other
ISBN Prefix(es): 1-875938
Number of titles published annually: 5 Print
Total Titles: 20 Print
Distributor for Emmas Publications; General Synod of the Anglican Church of Australia
Book Club(s): Sophia Booknet

Gerald Griffin Press+
156 The Avenue, Parkville, Victoria 3052
Tel: (03) 93475723; (03) 93475065 *Fax:* (03) 93494595
Key Personnel
Manager & Contact: K N Mortensen
  E-mail: kgmortensen@sp-cfc.vic.edu.au
Founded: 1959
Calls cannot be returned, if details supplied, will be dealt with by air mail.
Subjects: Asian Studies, Education, History, Military Science, Social Sciences, Sociology
ISBN Prefix(es): 0-85554
Total Titles: 14 Print

Germinal Press
PO Box 345, Toowong 4066

Ghost Gum, *imprint of* Australian Large Print Pty Ltd

Gifted Children Information Centre, *imprint of* Hawker Brownlow

Ginninderra Press
PO Box 53, Charnwood, ACT 2615
Tel: (02) 6258-9060 *Fax:* (02) 6258-9069
Web Site: www.ginninderrapress.com.au
Key Personnel
Publisher: Stephen Matthews *E-mail:* smgp@cyberone.com.au
Founded: 1996
Subjects: Biography, Disability, Special Needs, Education, Fiction, Health, Nutrition, History, Library & Information Sciences, Music, Dance, Poetry
ISBN Prefix(es): 1-876259; 0-9586825; 1-74027
Number of titles published annually: 40 Print
Total Titles: 200 Print
Imprints: Indigo; Mockingbird

Global Business Network, *imprint of* Prospect Media Pty Ltd

Gnostic Editions
12 Miller Gve, Kew 3101
Mailing Address: PO Box 410, Kew, Victoria 3101
Tel: (03) 9853 1401 *Fax:* (03) 9853 1481
E-mail: mail@gnoticeditions.com
Web Site: www.gnosticeditions.com
Key Personnel
Dir: Ian Watchorn *E-mail:* ian@ianwatchorn.com
Contact: Robyn Lambert
Founded: 1992

Associate companies located in Brazil, Portugal, Spain, Thailand & United Kingdom.
Subjects: Alternative, Anthropology, Archaeology, Astrology, Occult, Human Relations, Mysteries, Parapsychology, Philosophy, Psychology, Psychiatry, Religion - Other, Self-Help, Theology
ISBN Prefix(es): 0-646
Number of titles published annually: 2 Print
Total Titles: 10 Print
Parent Company: Nous Editores, Calle Mina N° 209, Col Tetela del Monte, CP 62130, Cuernavaca Morelos DF, Mexico
Associate Companies: Anubis Publishers Int, Canada (Canada)

Goanna, *imprint of* Australian Large Print Pty Ltd

Gould Books
PO Box 126, Gumeracha, SA 5233
Tel: (08) 8389 1611 *Fax:* (08) 8389 1599
E-mail: inquiries@gould.com.au
Web Site: www.gould.com.au
Key Personnel
Contact: Alan Phillips
Founded: 1976
Subjects: Genealogy, History
ISBN Prefix(es): 0-947284

Graffiti Publications+
69 Forest St, Castlemaine, Victoria 3450
Mailing Address: PO Box 232, Castlemaine 3450
Tel: (03) 5472-3653 *Fax:* (03) 5472-3805
E-mail: graffiti@netcon.net.au
Web Site: www.graffitipub.com.au
Key Personnel
Dir: Larry O'Toole
Founded: 1976
Subjects: Automotive, Crafts, Games, Hobbies
Total Titles: 10 Print
Distributed by Celebrity Books (New Zealand); MotorBooks International
Distributor for The Rodder's Journal; Tex Smith Library
Foreign Rep(s): Motorbooks International (North America)

Grainger Museum
University of Melbourne, Melbourne, Victoria 3010
Tel: (03) 9344 5270 *Fax:* (03) 9349 1707
E-mail: grainger@unimelb.edo.au
Web Site: www.lib.unimelb.edu.au/collections/grainger/introduction/intro.html
Telex: AA 35185
Key Personnel
Curator: Rosemary Florrimell
Founded: 1938
Subjects: Music, Dance

Granrott Press
The Old Rectory, Lule Rd, Clarendon SA 5157
Mailing Address: PO Box 6, Clarendon SA 5157
Tel: (08) 8383-6081 *Fax:* (08) 8383 6067
Key Personnel
Dir: N Hjorth
Founded: 1984
Family business that was founded based on the need to cross boundaries of an autobiographical book w/feminine based visual arts.
Subjects: Art, Theology, Women's Studies
Total Titles: 4 Print

Grass Roots, *imprint of* Night Owl Publishers Pty Ltd

Great Western Press Pty Ltd+
22 Ganmain Rd, Pymble, NSW 2073
Mailing Address: PO Box 482, Chatswood, NSW 2067
Tel: (02) 94497929 *Fax:* (02) 91445566

Key Personnel
Man Dir: John Isaacs *E-mail:* jisaacssydney@aol.com
Sales: Anne Isaacs
Rights & Permissions: Robert Elliott
Founded: 1974
Subjects: How-to, Romance, Science (General), Autobiographies, Memoirs
ISBN Prefix(es): 0-86901
Number of titles published annually: 2 Print
Total Titles: 57 Print
Associate Companies: Pymble Trading Pty Ltd
Imprints: GWP
Shipping Address: ACP Customs Services Pty Ltd, PO Box 148, Rosebery, NSW 2018, Geoff Dickson *Tel:* (02) 9669 0966 *Fax:* (02) 9669 0999 *E-mail:* acpcustoms@att.net.au
Warehouse: Unit 3, 809-821 Botany Rd, Rosebery, NSW 2018, Peter Reid

Greater Glider Productions Australia Pty Ltd+
Book Farm, 330 Reesville Rd, 4552 Maleny, Qld
Tel: (07) 5494 3000 *Fax:* (07) 5494 3284
E-mail: greaterglide@publishaust.apc.org
Web Site: www.greaterglider.com
Key Personnel
Publishing Dir: Jill Morris
Manager: Cheryl Wickes
Founded: 1983
Cairns Commission Agent: Belinda Nissen, 13 Jade Crescent, Lake Placid 4875.
Subjects: Education, Health, Nutrition, Natural History, Science (General)
ISBN Prefix(es): 0-947304
Bookshop(s): Peace of Green, Maple St, Maleny 4552
Book Club(s): Scholastic; Choice Magazine; Wilderness Society

Gregory's, *imprint of* Universal Press Pty Ltd

Griffin, *imprint of* Pan Macmillan Australia Pty Ltd

GWP, *imprint of* Great Western Press Pty Ltd

Hahndorf Academy Foundation Inc
68 Main St, Hahndorf, SA 5245
Tel: (08) 3887250
E-mail: info@postcards.sa.com.au
Key Personnel
Secretary: Lyssa Liebelt
Subjects: Art, Genealogy, History, Religion - Other
ISBN Prefix(es): 0-9577

Halbooks Publishing+
30 Elouera Rd, Avalon, NSW 2107
Tel: (02) 9918 7043 *Fax:* (02) 9973 1081
Key Personnel
Contact: Alan Halbish
Also acts as print broker & literary agent.
ISBN Prefix(es): 0-9585807

Hale & Iremonger Pty Ltd+
76-82 Chapel St, Marrickville NSW 2204
Mailing Address: PO Box 205, 2015 Alexandria NSW
Tel: (02) 9560 0470 *Fax:* (02) 9550 0097
E-mail: info@haleiremonger.com
Web Site: www.haleiremonger.com
Key Personnel
Marketing Manager: Matthew Harrigan
  E-mail: matthew@haleiremonger.com
Publisher & General Manager: Sylvia Hale
  E-mail: sylvia@haleiremonger.com
Founded: 1977
Member of Australian Publishers Association, Australian Booksellers Association.
Subjects: Asian Studies, Biography, Business, Career Development, Child Care & Develop-

ment, Genealogy, Government, Political Science, Health, Nutrition, History, Management, Nonfiction (General), Philosophy, Psychology, Psychiatry, Public Administration, Self-Help, Women's Studies
ISBN Prefix(es): 0-86806
Number of titles published annually: 10 Print
Total Titles: 200 Print
Online services available through World Wide Web.
Distributed by Forrester Books 2 (New Zealand); Pacific Island Books (USA); Roundhouse Publishing Group (UK & Western Europe)

F H Halpern+
67 Inkerman St, 1st Floor, Saint Kilda, Victoria 3182
Tel: (03) 9534 6033 *Fax:* (03) 9534 3998
Key Personnel
Contact: F H Halpern
Subjects: History, Travel
ISBN Prefix(es): 7-316
Branch Office(s)
Melbourne

Kerri Hamer+
73 Haig St, Maroubra 2035
Tel: (02) 93495170 *Fax:* (02) 93495170
Key Personnel
Publisher & Author: Kerri Hamer
Subjects: Behavioral Sciences, Communications, Education, How-to, Human Relations, Psychology, Psychiatry, Self-Help, Social Sciences, Sociology

Hamish Hamilton, *imprint of* Penguin Books Australia Ltd

Hamlyn Childrens, *imprint of* Random House Australia

Geoffrey Hamlyn-Harris
5 Garden St, Stanthorpe, Qld 4380
Tel: (0746) 811450; (018) 063662 *Fax:* (018) 063662
Key Personnel
Proprietor & Author: Geoffrey Hamlyn-Harris *Fax:* (076) 811450
Subjects: Drama, Theater, Fiction, Nonfiction (General), Poetry, Science Fiction, Fantasy
ISBN Prefix(es): 0-9592203
Total Titles: 7 Print; 7 Online; 1 Audio

Hampden Press+
51 Hampden Rd, Five Dock, NSW 2046
Mailing Address: PO Box 134, Five Dock, NSW 2046
Tel: (02) 9712 5755 *Fax:* (02) 9712 5756
Key Personnel
Publisher: Saul Kamerman *E-mail:* saulk@bigpond.com
Subjects: Child Care & Development, Medicine, Nursing, Dentistry, Psychology, Psychiatry
ISBN Prefix(es): 1-875648

H&H Publishing
6 Southern Court, Forest Hill 3131
Tel: (03) 6307 624 *Fax:* (03) 9877 4222
E-mail: mvent@iaccess.com.au
Key Personnel
Contact: A K Hosking
Founded: 1981
Subjects: Civil Engineering, Mechanical Engineering
ISBN Prefix(es): 0-646

Harcourt Australia Pty Ltd+
Locked Bag 16, Marrickville, NSW 2204
Tel: (02) 5178999 *Fax:* (02) 5172249

Key Personnel
Man Dir: Brian Brennan *Fax:* (02) 95506007 *E-mail:* bbrennan@harcourt.com.au
Financial Controller & Operations Manager: Jim Robinson *Fax:* (02) 95506007 *E-mail:* jrobinson@harcourt.com.au
General Manager College Division: Paul Barry *Fax:* (02) 95506007 *E-mail:* pbarry@harcourt.com.au
TPC General Manager: Dianne Lissner *Fax:* (02) 95506007 *E-mail:* dlissner@harcourt.com.au
General Manager STM Division: Anneke Baeten *Fax:* (02) 95506007 *E-mail:* abaeten@harcourt.com.au
Founded: 1972
Subjects: Business, Education, Mathematics, Medicine, Nursing, Dentistry, Psychology, Psychiatry, Science (General), Social Sciences, Sociology, Veterinary Science
ISBN Prefix(es): 0-7295
Total Titles: 8,000 Print; 65 CD-ROM
Parent Company: Harcourt Inc, 6277 Sea Harbor Dr, Orlando, FL 32887, United States
Associate Companies: HB & Co/Holt Canada, 55 Horner Ave, Toronto, ON M8Z 4X6, Canada; Harcourt Brace Japan Inc, Ichibancho Central Bldg, 22-1, Ichibancho, Chiyoda-ku, Tokyo 102, Japan; Academic Press Ltd, Harcourt Place, 32 Jamestown Road, London NW1 7BY, United Kingdom; Bailliere Tindall Ltd, Harcourt Place, 32 Jamestown Road, London NW1 7BY, United Kingdom; Harcourt Publishers Ltd, Harcourt Place, 32 Jamestown Road, London NW1 7BY, United Kingdom; Academic Press Inc, 1250 Sixth Ave, San Diego, CA 92101, United States; Harcourt Inc, 6277 Sea Harbor Dr, Orlando, FL 32821, United States; W B Saunders Co, The Curtis Center, Independence Sq, Philadelphia, PA 19106-3399, United States; Holt Rinehart & Winston Inc, 1627 Woodland Ave, Austin, TX 78741, United States; Harcourt College Publishers, 301 Commerce St, Suite 3700, Fort Worth, TX 78741, United States; The Psychological Corporation, 555 Academic Court, San Antonio, TX 78204-0952, United States
Imprints: Academic Press; Churchill Livingstone; Dryden Press; Harcourt Brace; Holt, Rinehart and Winston; Industrial Press; Island Press; Mayfield Publishing; Morgan Kaufmann; Mosby; The Psychological Corporation; W B Saunders/Bailliere Tindall; Saunders College; Singular Press; Technomic Publishing
Divisions: College; Medical; Psychological Testing; Professional/Trade
Branch Office(s)
Level 3, 71 Queens Rd, Melbourne, Victoria 3004
236 Dominion Rd, Mt Eden, Auckland 3, New Zealand
Distributor for Mayfield (Australia & New Zealand); Technomic Publishing (Australia & New Zealand)

Harcourt Brace, *imprint of* Harcourt Australia Pty Ltd

Hargreen Publishing Co
144 Chetwynd St, North Melbourne 3051
Tel: (03) 9329 9714 *Fax:* (03) 3295295
Key Personnel
Chief Executive: Michael Haratsis, Sr
Editorial & Production: Rick Navarro
Founded: 1972
Specialize in Australian History.
Subjects: Education, History, Nonfiction (General)
ISBN Prefix(es): 0-949905
Parent Company: Scotshouse Corp Pty Ltd

Harlequin Books
Unit 2/3 Gibbes St, Chatswood, NSW 2067
Mailing Address: Locked bag 2, Chatswood, NSW 2067

Tel: (02) 9415 9200 *Fax:* (02) 417-5232
E-mail: bhobbs@romance.net.au
Key Personnel
Man Dir: Nancy Peters
Parent Company: Harlequin Enterprises

HarperCollins Publishers (Australia) Pty Limited+
25-31 Ryde Rd, Pymble NSW 2073
Mailing Address: PO Box 321, Pymble, NSW 2073
Tel: (02) 9952 5445 *Fax:* (02) 9952 5544
Web Site: www.harpercollins.com.au
Key Personnel
Man Dir: Brian Murray
Finance Dir: Malcolm Boyd
Commercial Dir: Lil Velis
Publishing Dir: Shona Martyn
Sales Dir: Phil Klink
Publishing Manager: James Herd
Marketing Dir: Jim Demetriou
Publicity Manager: Christine Farmer
Production Manager: Jill Donald
Art Dir: Russell Jeffrey
IT Manager: Richard Beath
Manager, Multimedia & Internet Services: Laura Tricker
Rights Manger: Airlie Lawson
ISBN Prefix(es): 0-7322
Parent Company: HarperCollins Publishers Group
Associate Companies: Bay Books; Angus & Robertson Publishers; Collins Dove; HarperCollins Publishers India (P) Ltd, India; HarperCollins Ltd, Hong Kong; HarperCollins Publishers - Japan, Japan; HarperCollins Publishers, New Zealand; Golden Press, New Zealand; HarperCollins Publishers Asia Pte Ltd, Singapore; HarperCollins Publishers (SA) (Pty) Ltd, South Africa; HarperCollins General Books, United Kingdom; Fontana, United Kingdom; Grafton Books, United Kingdom; Thorsons Times Books, United Kingdom; Marshall Pickering, United Kingdom; Bartholomew, United Kingdom; HarperCollins; Zondervan; Collins Inc; Scott Foresman

Hartys Creek Press
c/o Lois Higgins, PO Box 342, Wauchope 2446
Tel: (02) 65871100
Key Personnel
Contact: Lois Higgins
Subjects: Art, Environmental Studies, Geography, Geology, Humor, Travel
ISBN Prefix(es): 0-646
Publication(s): *Antartica Alphabetically*; *Australia Alphabetically*; *Log Book of an Antarctic Journey*

Roland Harvey Studios+
62 Beach St, Port Melbourne 3207
Tel: (03) 9646 8711 *Fax:* (03) 9646 2245
Key Personnel
Publisher: Roland Harvey
Founded: 1978
Member of ABPA.
ISBN Prefix(es): 0-949714
Imprints: Periscope Press
Warehouse: Unit 1, 13 Downarh St, Braeside, Victoria 3195

Hat Box Press
3 Huntingfield Dr, Hoppers Crossing 3029
Tel: (03) 97492510
Key Personnel
Contact: Bronwen Hickman *E-mail:* bghickman@bigpond.com.au
Subjects: Fiction, History, Literature, Literary Criticism, Essays, Short stories by Mary Gaunt
ISBN Prefix(es): 0-9590422
Number of titles published annually: 1 Print

Hawker Brownlow+
1123a Nepean Highway, Highett, Victoria 3190

AUSTRALIA

Mailing Address: PO Box 580, Cheltenham, Victoria 3192
Tel: (03) 9555-1344 *Fax:* (03) 9553-4538
E-mail: brown@hbe.com.au
Web Site: www.hbe.com.au/custserv.html
Key Personnel
Man Dir: David Brownlow
General Manager: Elaine Brownlow
Founded: 1981
Subjects: Asian Studies, Human Relations, Mathematics, Technology
ISBN Prefix(es): 1-86299; 0-947326
Parent Company: Hawker Brownlow Education
Imprints: Autonomous Learning Publications & Specialists; BEC Publications; Book Lures Inc; Cassel PLC; Centre for Creative Learning; Creative Learning Consultants; Creative Learning Press; Critical Thinking Press & Software; Curriculum Associates Inc; Dandy Lion Publications; Educational Assessment Service Inc; Educational Impressions; Educational Insights; Enrich; Fearon Teacher Aids; Foundation for Critical Thinking; Free Spirit Publishing Inc; Gamco Industries Inc; Gifted Children Information Centre; The Learner's Dimensions; The Learning Works; Michael Grinder & Associates; Modern Learning Press; New Horizons for Learning; Ohio Psychology Press; Perfection Learning Corporation; Personal Power Press International Inc; Prufrock Press; Skylight Publishing Inc; Star Teaching; Sterling Publishing Co Inc; Sundance Inc; Teacher Created Materials; Trillium Press; United Educational Services (DDK); Zephyr Press
Subsidiaries: Learner's World

Hawkins Press, *imprint of* The Federation Press

Hayes Publishing
52 Dewar Terrace, Sherwood, Qld 4075
Tel: (07) 3379 4137 *Fax:* (07) 3379 4137
Key Personnel
Contact: P C Hayes *E-mail:* p.hayes@minmet.uq.edu.au
Subjects: Engineering (General)
Number of titles published annually: 1 Print
Total Titles: 1 Print
Orders to: Koala Books of Canada, 14327-95A Ave, Edmonton, AB T5N 0B6, Canada
Tel: (780) 452 5149

Hayward Books, *imprint of* In-Tune Books

Headline, *imprint of* Hodder Headline Australia

Headline Feature, *imprint of* Hodder Headline Australia

Headline Review, *imprint of* Hodder Headline Australia

Headway, *imprint of* Hodder Headline Australia

Heinemann, *imprint of* Random House Australia

Heinemann, *imprint of* Reed Educational Publishing Australia

Heinemann Library
22 Salmon St, Port Melbourne, Victoria 3207
Tel: (03) 9245 7111
Parent Company: Reed Educational & Professional Publishing
Ultimate Parent Company: Reed Elsevier

Hema Maps Pty Ltd+
25 McKechnie Drive, Eight Mile Plains, Qld 4113
Mailing Address: PO Box 4365, Eight Mile Plains, Qld 4113
Tel: (07) 3340 0000 *Fax:* (07) 3340 0099
E-mail: manager@hemamaps.com.au
Web Site: www.hemamaps.com
Key Personnel
Man Dir: Henry Boegheim
Founded: 1983
Member of IMTA.
Subjects: Travel
ISBN Prefix(es): 1-875610; 1-875992; 1-86500
Distributed by Brettschneider GmbH (Germany); Cartotheque (France); T B Clarke (Overseas) Pty Ltd; Craenen Cartografie (Belgium); Estate Publications (United Kingdom); Freytag & Berndt u Artaria (Austria); Geocentre (Germany); Gordon & Gotch (PNG) Pty Ltd (Papua New Guinea); Hema Maps NZ Ltd (New Zealand); Inteligentni Turisticke Mapy (Czech Republic); ITMB Publishing Ltd (Canada); Jana Seta (Latvia); Kartbutiken (Sweden); Magellan Buchversand (Germany); Map House Co Ltd (Tokyo); Map Link Inc (USA); Map Co Trading (Singapore); Namdo Net (South Korea); Nilsson & Lamm (Holland); OLF (Switzerland); Scanvik Books (Denmark)
Distributor for Ausmap; Australian Geographic; Mapland; Sunmap; Tasmap; Westprint (all Australia)

Henry Holt, *imprint of* Pan Macmillan Australia Pty Ltd

Heresy Press, *imprint of* Prospect Media Pty Ltd

Hihorse Publishing Pty Ltd+
14 Duffy St, Burwood, Victoria 3125
Tel: (03) 9397 3084 *Fax:* (03) 9397 3084
E-mail: hihorse@c031.aone.net.au
Key Personnel
Contact: Patricia Kovac
Founded: 1995
Subjects: Alternative, Astrology, Occult, Parapsychology, Self-Help, Aromatherapy, Meditation, Crystal Healing
ISBN Prefix(es): 0-909223
Associate Companies: Gemcraft Pty Ltd, 14 Duffy St, Burwood 3125

Hill of Content Publishing Co Pty Ltd, see Michelle Anderson Publishing Pty Ltd

Histec Publications
c/o B E Lloyd & Assoc, 13 Connor St, East Brighton, Victoria 3187
Tel: (03) 95923787 *Fax:* (03) 95922823
Key Personnel
Dir: Dr Brian E Lloyd *E-mail:* belloyd@projectx.com.au
Founded: 1987
Subjects: Biography, Engineering (General), History, Labor, Industrial Relations, Regional Interests, Social Sciences, Sociology
ISBN Prefix(es): 0-9587705
Number of titles published annually: 2 Print
Total Titles: 2 Print
Parent Company: B E Lloyd & Associates Histec Nominees Pty Ltd

Hodder, *imprint of* Hodder Headline Australia

Hodder Headline Australia+
Level 22, 201 Kent Street, Sydney, NSW 2000
Tel: (02) 82480800; (02) 43901300 (customer service) *Fax:* (02) 82480810
E-mail: Auspub@hha.com.au (Australian publishing); hsales@alliancedist.com.au; adscs@alliancedist.com.au (customer service)
Web Site: www.hha.com.au; www.hodderheadline.co.us
Key Personnel
Man Dir: Malcolm Edwards
Sales & Marketing Dir: Mary Drum
Publishing Dir: Lisa Highton
Founded: 1958
Distributor of group product agents for Piatkus (UK) & Lion (UK).
ISBN Prefix(es): 0-340; 0-450
Number of titles published annually: 120 Print
Total Titles: 1,500 Print
Parent Company: Hodder Headline UK, United Kingdom
Ultimate Parent Company: W H Smith
Imprints: New English Library; Sceptre; Teach Yourself; Coronet; Headway; Headline; Headline Feature; Headline Review; Hodder
Distributor for Hodder Headline plc UK; Lion

Holt, Rinehart and Winston, *imprint of* Harcourt Australia Pty Ltd

Home Library, *imprint of* ACP Publishing Pty Ltd

Homestead Books
29 Lisbeth Ave, Donvale, Victoria 3111
Tel: (03) 9873 7202 *Fax:* (03) 9873-0542
E-mail: service@theruralstore.com.au
Web Site: www.theruralstore.com.au
Key Personnel
Proprietor: Jim Lowden *E-mail:* jim@theruralstore.com.au

Horan Wall & Walker+
162 Goulburn St, Darlinghurst NSW 2010
Mailing Address: PO Box 996, Darlinghurst NSW 2010
Tel: (02) 8268 8268 *Fax:* (02) 8268 8267
E-mail: info@hww.com.au
Web Site: www.hww.com.au
Key Personnel
Man Dir: Stephen Wall
Founded: 1974
Subjects: Cookery, Crafts, Games, Hobbies, Finance, Real Estate, Travel, Entertainment, Leisure
ISBN Prefix(es): 0-9590027; 0-9599177; 1-875700
Parent Company: HWW Pty Ltd
Associate Companies: Australian Property Monitors

Hospitality Books
7 Regent St, Ryde 2112
Mailing Address: PO Box 3007, Putney NSW 2112
Tel: (02) 9809 5793 *Fax:* (02) 9809 4884
Web Site: www.hospitalitybooks.com.au
Key Personnel
Head of Company & Dir: Maureen Puckeridge *E-mail:* sales@hospitalitybooks.com.au
Founded: 1987
Publish "how-to" books on Professional Bartending, Waiting, the Australian Wine Guide & Hospitality Core Units.
Member of Copyright Agency Ltd.
Subjects: How-to, Wine & Spirits, Food & Beverage Service, Hospitality Industry
ISBN Prefix(es): 0-9577
Total Titles: 4 Print

Hospitality Press Pty Ltd+
Imprint of Pearson Education Australia
38 Riddell Parade, Elsternwick, Victoria 3185
Mailing Address: PO Box 426, Elsternwick, Victoria 3185
Tel: (03) 9528 5021 *Fax:* (03) 9528 2645
E-mail: hosppress@access.net.au
Key Personnel
Man Dir & Rights: David Cunningham
Founded: 1985

Publisher of books for professional training in hospitality & tourism at all levels from High School upwards.
Member of Publish Australia Group Enterprises & Australian Publishers Association.
Subjects: Accounting, Business, Career Development, Communications, Cookery, Management, Marketing, Travel, Wine & Spirits, Specialize in all professional & educational aspects of hospitality & tourism from vocational education in high schools to postgraduate
ISBN Prefix(es): 1-86250
Number of titles published annually: 8 Print
Total Titles: 50 Print; 1 Audio
Distributed by Applied Media (India); Eddington Hook Ltd (UK & Europe); Publishers Marketing Services PtyLtd (Singapore & Malaysia); Virtue Books (New Zealand)
Distributor for Matthaes Verlag GMBH (Australia & New Zealand); Waterbury Press (Australia & New Zealand)
Foreign Rep(s): Applied Media (India); Eddington Hook Ltd (Europe & UK); Virtue Books NZ (New Zealand)
Foreign Rights: Waterbury Press (US)
Warehouse: Matrae Pty Ltd, 568 Geelong Rd, West Footscray Victoria 3012, Barry Fulton *Tel:* (03) 93180100 *E-mail:* matrae@ozemail.com.au
Orders to: Hospitality Press, PO Box 426, Elsternwick Victoria 3185, David Cunningham *Tel:* (03) 95285021 *Fax:* (03) 95282645 *E-mail:* hosppress@access.net.au

Hudson Publishing+
Division of NS Hudson Publishing Services P/L
89 Stevenson St, Kew, Victoria 3101
Mailing Address: PO Box 2088, Kew, Victoria 3101
Tel: (03) 9853 7753 *Fax:* (03) 9853 7290
E-mail: hudson@c031.aone.net.au
Key Personnel
Head of Company, Editorial Dir & Manager: Nick Hudson
Founded: 1985
Member of APA (Australian Publishers Association).
Subjects: Literature, Literary Criticism, Essays, Nonfiction (General)
ISBN Prefix(es): 0-949873
Total Titles: 50 Print
Imprints: Essien
Distributed by Jenny Nagle Addenda Publishing Sales & Marketing Services (New Zealand)
Warehouse: Peribo P/L, 50 Beaumont Rd, Mount Kuring Gai NSW 2080 *Tel:* (02) 9457 0011 *Fax:* (02) 9457 0022 (National Distributor)
Orders to: Peribo P/L, 50 Beaumont Rd, Mount Kuring Gai, NSW 2080 *Tel:* (02) 9457 0011 *Fax:* (02) 9457 0022 (National Distributor)

Hunter Books
PO Box 3362, Weston Creek 2611
Subjects: Fiction

Hunter House Publications+
PO Box 536, Raymond Terrace, NSW 2324
Tel: (02) 4988-6401 *Fax:* (02) 4988-6401
E-mail: wf&mc@hunterlink.net.au
Key Personnel
Author & Publisher: Cynthia Hunter
Founded: 1991
Specialize in history research.
Subjects: History
ISBN Prefix(es): 0-646
Number of titles published annually: 1 Print
Total Titles: 5 Print

Hutchinson, *imprint of* Random House Australia

Hyland House Publishing Pty Ltd+
50 Pin Oak Crescent, Flemington, Victoria 3031
Mailing Address: PO Box 122, Flemington, Victoria 3031
Tel: (03) 9376 4461 *Fax:* (03) 9376 4461
E-mail: hyland3@netspace.net.au
Key Personnel
Man Dir: Michael Schoo
Publicity & Promotions: Ruth Cosgrove
  E-mail: hyland1@netspace.net.au
Administration & Accounts: Anna Schoo
Founded: 1976
Agents: Frederique Porretta, Agence Litteraire, 70 Rue D'Assas, 75006 Paris, France. Tel: (045) 44 88 68 Fax: (045) 44 69 36. Tel: (020) 420 4156 Fax: (020) 420 4156; Kerrigan/Miro/Calonte Literary Agency, Traversa de Gracia (012) 52, 08021 Barcelona, Spain. Tel: (093) 209 3820 Fax: (093) 414 4328.
Subjects: Animals, Pets, Asian Studies, Biography, Cookery, Fiction, Gardening, Plants, History, Literature, Literary Criticism, Essays, Nonfiction (General)
ISBN Prefix(es): 0-908090; 0-947062; 1-875657; 1-86447
Associate Companies: Australian Book Distribution Group
Imprints: Hylanders; Young Hylanders; Australia's Best Garden Guide Series
Branch Office(s)
c/o Seven Hills Book Distributors, 49 Central Ave, Cincinnati, OH 45202, United States
Foreign Rep(s): Kerrigan/Miro/Calonte Literary Agency (Spain); Frederique Porretta (France)
Showroom(s): Gazelle Book Services, Falcon House, Queen Sq, Lancaster LA1 ARN, United Kingdom; Seven Hills Book Distributors, 49 Central Ave, Cincinnati, OH 45202, United States
Warehouse: Australian Book Group, Calway St, Drouin, Victoria 3818 *Tel:* (03) 5625 4290 *Fax:* (03) 5625 4272
Orders to: Australian Book Group, Calway St, Drouin, Victoria 3818 *Tel:* (03) 5625 4290 *Fax:* (03) 5625 4272

Hylanders, *imprint of* Hyland House Publishing Pty Ltd

IAD, see Institute of Aboriginal Development (IAD Press)

Illert Publications+
2/3 Birch Crescent, East Corrimal, NSW 2518
Tel: (0242) 83-3009 (international); (0242) 833009 (within Australia) *Fax:* (0242) 833009 (within Australia)
Key Personnel
Editorial Manager: C Illert
Subjects: Anthropology, Asian Studies, Biological Sciences, Computer Science, Education, Environmental Studies, Genealogy, History, Language Arts, Linguistics, Mathematics, Natural History, Physics, Science (General), Technology
ISBN Prefix(es): 0-949357; 0-9597201

The Images Publishing Group Pty Ltd+
Images House, 6 Bastow Pl, Mulgrave, Victoria 3170
Tel: (03) 9561 5544 *Fax:* (03) 9561 4860
E-mail: books@images.com.au
Web Site: www.imagespublishinggroup.com
Key Personnel
Dir: Alessina Rose Brooks; Paul Alan Latham
Founded: 1983
Subjects: Accounting, Advertising, Architecture & Interior Design, Art, Biography, Civil Engineering, Engineering (General), Fashion
ISBN Prefix(es): 1-875498
Number of titles published annually: 40 Print
Parent Company: Images Australia Pty Ltd
Distributed by ACC UK; ACC US; Antique Collectors' Club (Europe & USA); Bookwise International (Australia); Gingko Bookspan; Nippan IPS (Asia); Anthony Rudkin Associates (Middle East (excluding Israel) Malta, Cypress, Turkey & Iran)

In-Tune Books+
PO Box 193, Avalon, NSW 2107
Tel: (02) 9974 5981 *Fax:* (02) 9974 4552
Key Personnel
Manager: Malcolm Cohan *E-mail:* mcohan@ozemail.com.au
Founded: 1984
Subjects: Alternative, Art, Philosophy, Self-Help
Imprints: Hayward Books
Distributed by Harper Collins; Words Distributing; World Leisure Marketing Grantham Book Services

Incunabula Press
608 Canning St, North Carlton 3054
Tel: (03) 93811559
Key Personnel
Contact: John Ryrie *E-mail:* jryrie@pgrad.unimelb.edu.au
Founded: 1990
Specializes in handmade books in a limited edition of 20 to 30 copies, letterpress & printmaking.
Subjects: Art, Poetry
Total Titles: 10 Print

Indigo, *imprint of* Ginninderra Press

Indra Publishing+
142 Ryans Rd, Eltham, North Victoria 3095
Mailing Address: PO Box 7, Briar Hill, Victoria 3088
Tel: (03) 9439 7555 *Fax:* (03) 9439 7555
Web Site: www.indra.com.au
Key Personnel
Dir: Ian James Fraser *E-mail:* ian@indra.com.au
Founded: 1987
Worldwide (USA & Canada via ISBS Corp, Portland Or).
Member of Australian Publisher's Association.
Subjects: Asian Studies, Biography, Disability, Special Needs, Ethnicity, Fiction, Foreign Countries, Literature, Literary Criticism, Essays, Romance, Women's Studies, Australia, Pacific, Asia
ISBN Prefix(es): 0-9587718; 0-9585805; 0-9578735
Number of titles published annually: 6 Print
Total Titles: 26 Print
Distributed by Australian Book Group P/L (Australia); Horizon Books Pte Ltd (Southeast Asia); International Specialized Book Services (USA & Canada)
Foreign Rep(s): ISBS Corp (Canada, US)
Foreign Rights: Portas Agency (Europe)

Industrial Press, *imprint of* Harcourt Australia Pty Ltd

Infomedia, *imprint of* Flora Publications International Pty Ltd

Inner City Books, *imprint of* Rainbow Book Agencies Pty Ltd

Instauratio Press
St Benedict's Dr, Gladysdale, Victoria 3797
Mailing Address: PO Box 36, Yarra Junction, Victoria 3797
Tel: (03) 59666217 *Fax:* (03) 59666447
E-mail: catholic@scservnet.com
Key Personnel
Head of Company: Andrina McLean
Founded: 1982
Subjects: Religion - Catholic

ISBN Prefix(es): 0-9577; 0-646
Subsidiaries: St Benedict Book Centre
Branch Office(s)
Instauratio Press, Box 1789, Post Falls, ID 83854, United States
Distributor for The Angelus Press (USA); Neumann Books (USA); Tan Books (USA)

Institute of Aboriginal Development (IAD Press)+
3 South Terrace, Alice Springs, NT 0871
Mailing Address: PO Box 2531, Alice Springs, NT 0871
Tel: (089) 8951 1331 *Fax:* (089) 8952 2527
E-mail: press@iad.edu.au
Key Personnel
Dir: Eileen Shaw
Publisher: Josie Douglas
Founded: 1969 (Aboriginal community controlled, publishing arm of Institute for Aboriginal Development)
Indigenous publishing house producing works by Aboriginal & Torres Strait Islander peoples of Australia.
Member of APA (Australian Publishers Association) & Publish Australia.
Subjects: Anthropology, Art, Biography, Education, History, Language Arts, Linguistics, Literature, Literary Criticism, Essays, Natural History, Nonfiction (General), Regional Interests, Dictionaries, Language & Bilingual Books, Literature
ISBN Prefix(es): 0-949659; 1-86465
Number of titles published annually: 10 Print; 1 E-Book; 1 Audio
Total Titles: 55 Print; 1 CD-ROM; 3 E-Book; 3 Audio
Online services available through aboriginalaustralia.com.
Imprints: Jukurrpa Books
U.S. Office(s): ISBS International Specialized Book Services, 5804 NE Massalo St, Portland, OR 97213-3644, United States, Contact: Tamma Greenfield *Tel:* 503-287-3093 *Fax:* 503-280-8882 *E-mail:* tamma@isbs.com

Int Press+
386 Mt Alexander Rd, Ascot Vale, Victoria 3032
Tel: (03) 93262416 *Fax:* (03) 93262413
E-mail: intpress@ozemail.com.au
Web Site: www.intpress.com.au
Key Personnel
International Rights: Luiai Rizzo
Founded: 1981
Subjects: English as a Second Language, Ethnicity
ISBN Prefix(es): 1-86310
Associate Companies: Int Press Distribution Pty Ltd
Bookshop(s): The Lote Int Bookshop

Intext Book Company Pty Ltd
825 Glenferrie Rd, Hawthorn, Victoria 3122
Tel: (03) 9819-4500 *Fax:* (03) 9819-4511
E-mail: customerservice@intextbook.com.au
Web Site: www.intextbook.com.au
Key Personnel
Man Dir: Jillian Taylor *E-mail:* jillian@intextbook.com.au
Founded: 1982
Specialize in foreign languages other than English; distribution & promotion.
Subsidiaries: Language International Bookshop
Distributor for ALC Press (Japan); Alma Edizione (Italy); Bonacci (Italy); Cheng & T sui (USA); Cle International; Duerr Kessler (Germany); Diesterweg (Germany); Difusion (Spain); Duden (Germany); Edelsa (Spain); Ediciones SM (Spain); European School Books (UK); Gallimard (France); Giunti (Italy); Guerra (Italy); Hachette Livre International (France); Hatier/Didier (France); Klett (Germany); Kumon (Japan); Langenscheidt Texts & Dictionaries (Germany); Larousse (France); Menschenkinder (Germany); Nathan (France); Nihongo Journal (Japan); Ravensburger (Germany); Robert (France); SGEL (Spain); Santillana (Spain); Senmon Kyouiku (Japan); Soleil (Canada); The Japan Times (Japan); Vut Caps (Australia)

Inwardpath Publishers
76 McArthur Rd, Ivanhoe East, Victoria 3079
Tel: (03) 9499 3405 *Fax:* (03) 94975656
Key Personnel
Proprietor: Peter Besley
Subjects: Philosophy, Esoteric, New Age
ISBN Prefix(es): 0-9585722
Distributor for Specialist Publications (Australia & Territories)
Foreign Rep(s): Four Corners (England)

Island Press, *imprint of* Harcourt Australia Pty Ltd

Island Press
29 Park Rd, Woodford, NSW 2778
Tel: (02) 98956119 *Fax:* (02) 98957077
Key Personnel
Man Dir: Philip Hammial
Founded: 1970
Subjects: Art, Poetry
ISBN Prefix(es): 0-909771; 0-9596379

Jabiru Press
13 Ferdinand Ave, Balwyn North, Victoria 3104
Tel: (03) 9857-7362 *Fax:* (03) 9857-9110
Key Personnel
Contact: Dick Johnson *E-mail:* djohnson@netspace.net.au
ISBN Prefix(es): 0-908104

James Nicholas Publishers Pty Ltd
PO Box 244, Albert Park 3206
Tel: (03) 9696 5545; (03) 9690 5955 *Fax:* (03) 9699 2040
E-mail: custservice@jamesnicholaspublishers.com.au
Web Site: www.jamesnicholaspublishers.com.au
Key Personnel
Education Editor: Dr Joseph Zajda
Editor: Ms Rea Zajda
Founded: 1978
Subjects: Business, Communications, Education, Government, Political Science, Health, Nutrition, Management, Marketing, Medicine, Nursing, Dentistry, Social Sciences, Sociology
ISBN Prefix(es): 1-875408
Total Titles: 10 Print

Jared Publishing
One Warrock Rd, Donvale, Victoria 3111
Tel: (03) 9874-2415

Jarrah Publications+
42 Chisholm Circle, Heritage Estate, Armadale, WA 6112
Mailing Address: PO Box 1041, Kelmscott 6997
Tel: (09) 4954569 *Fax:* (09) 4954569
Web Site: www.jarpub73.com.au
Key Personnel
Head of Company: W F Vormair
Sales Dir & International Rights: Willy Frank
Author: Jean Vormair
Editor & International Rights: Jan Margaret
Founded: 1987
Partnership.
Subjects: Fiction, Human Relations, Romance, Science Fiction, Fantasy, Specialize in Fantasy; Contemporary issues
ISBN Prefix(es): 0-9577; 0-646
Total Titles: 2 Print

JBCE, *imprint of* Rainbow Book Agencies Pty Ltd

Jenelle Press
PO Box 656, Gladesville, NSW 2111
Tel: (02) 4281531 *Fax:* (02) 4284144
Key Personnel
Head of Company: Mark Robert Mannering
Subjects: Education
ISBN Prefix(es): 1-875734

Jesuit Publications+
Unit of Society of Jesus
300 Victoria St, Richmond, Victoria 3121
Tel: (03) 9427-7311 *Fax:* (03) 9428-4450
E-mail: paul-jp@jespub.jesuit.org.au
Web Site: www.openplanet.com.au
Key Personnel
Publisher: Andrew Hamilton
Editor: Morag Fraser
General Manager: Mark Dowgll
International Rights: Sylvana Scannapiego
Founded: 1988
Subjects: Poetry, Religion - Catholic, Religion - Protestant, Religion - Other, Theology
ISBN Prefix(es): 1-86355
Divisions: Aurora Books; Madonna; Eureka Street; Australian Catholics

Jesuit Publications/Aurora Books, *imprint of* Rainbow Book Agencies Pty Ltd

Jika Publishing+
3 Witney Way, Bundoora 3083
Tel: (03) 9467-3295 *Fax:* (03) 9467-1770
Subjects: Drama, Theater, Poetry
ISBN Prefix(es): 0-9577; 0-646

JL Publications+
Division of Submariner Publication, P/C
26 Highgate Gue, Ashburton, Victoria 3147
Mailing Address: 387, Ashburton, Victoria 3147
Tel: (03) 98860200 *Fax:* (03) 98860200
E-mail: jlpubs@c031.aone.net.au
Key Personnel
Contact: John Lippmann
Subjects: Scuba Diving Safety
Total Titles: 12 Print
Distributed by Aqua Quest Publications (New York)

John Wiley & Sons Australia Ltd+
33 Park Rd, 3rd Floor, Milton, Qld 4064
Mailing Address: PO Box 1226, Milton Qld 4064
Tel: (07) 3859 9755 *Fax:* (07) 3859 9715
E-mail: brisbane@johnwiley.com.au
Web Site: www.johnwiley.com.au
Key Personnel
Man Dir: Peter C Donoughue
Dir Finance & Administration: Quentin Smith
General Manager, School: Peter Van Noorden
General Manager, Tertiary: Lucy Russell
General Manager, Distribution: Jim Dwyer
General Manager, Editorial/Production: David Wilson
Promotions: Stephen Buckley
Rights & Permissions: Julie Barnett
Information Technology: Richard Ciechanowski
Founded: 1954
Member of Australian Publishers Association.
Subjects: Education, Nonfiction (General)
ISBN Prefix(es): 0-471
Parent Company: John Wiley & Sons Inc, 605 Third Ave, New York, NY 10158, United States
Associate Companies: John Wiley & Sons Canada Ltd, Canada; John Wiley & Sons (Asia) Pte Ltd, Singapore; John Wiley & Sons Ltd, United Kingdom
Imprints: John Wiley & Sons; The Jacaranda Press

PUBLISHERS AUSTRALIA

Branch Office(s)
Suite 2, 38-40 Prospect St, Box Hill, Victoria 3128 *Tel:* (03) 9898 0255 *Fax:* (03) 9898 4255
E-mail: melbourne@johnwiley.com.au
Suite 4A, 113 Wicks Rd, North Ryde NSW 2113 *Tel:* (02) 9805 1100 *Fax:* (02) 9805 1597
E-mail: sydney@johnwiley.com.au
Distributor for Houghton Mifflin; W W Norton
Warehouse: Australian Center, 56 Edmonstone Rd, Bowen Hills, Qld 4006

Michael Joseph, *imprint of* Penguin Books Australia Ltd

Journeys, *imprint of* Lonely Planet Publications Pty Ltd

Joval Publications
PO Box 618, Bacchus Marsh, Victoria 3340
Tel: (053) 674593
Key Personnel
Contact: John Reid
Founded: 1986
Subjects: History, Photography, Poetry
ISBN Prefix(es): 0-9588112

Jukurrpa Books, *imprint of* Institute of Aboriginal Development (IAD Press)

Kangaroo Press, *imprint of* Simon & Schuster Australia Pty Ltd

Kangaroo Press+
Imprint of Simon & Schuster Australia
PO Box 6125, Dural Delivery Centre, NSW 2158
Tel: (02) 6541502 *Fax:* (02) 6541338
Key Personnel
Publisher: David Rosenberg
Publicity Manager: Pricilla Rosenberg
Founded: 1981
Subjects: Biography, Crafts, Games, Hobbies, Gardening, Plants, History, Natural History, Nonfiction (General), Regional Interests, Sports, Athletics, Transportation, Travel
ISBN Prefix(es): 0-949924; 0-86417
Imprints: Roo Books

Gregory Kefalas Publishing
5a Byron St, Campsie, NSW 2194
Tel: (02) 9789 6049 *Fax:* (02) 97876181
Subjects: Automotive
ISBN Prefix(es): 0-9586798

Ken Fin, *imprint of* Social Club Books

Killara Press+
MS 660, Proston, Qld 4613
Tel: (07) 5499-7717 *Fax:* (07) 4168-0244
Web Site: www.gippsnet.com.au/sylvia/kettle/kettle.htm
Key Personnel
Contact: Sylvia Seiler *E-mail:* seiler@gippsnet.com.au
Founded: 1991
Writing & publishing.
Subjects: Disability, Special Needs, Fiction, Human Relations
ISBN Prefix(es): 0-646; 0-9585731

Kingfisher Books+
CnR Brixton & Wangara Rds, Cheltenham, Victoria 3192
Key Personnel
Contact: Joyce Walker
Founded: 1989
Subjects: Maritime
ISBN Prefix(es): 0-9593999

Kingsclear Books+
36 Kingsclear Rd, Alexandria, NSW 2015
Mailing Address: PO Box 335, Alexandria, NSW 1435
Tel: (02) 95574367 *Fax:* (02) 95572337
E-mail: kingsclear@wr.com.au
Web Site: www.kingsclearbooks.com.au
Key Personnel
Chief Executive Officer & Dir Sales & Production: Catherine Warne
Founded: 1983
Specialize in local history, alternative health & tourism.
Subjects: Animals, Pets, Criminology, Health, Nutrition, History, Outdoor Recreation, Photography, Religion - Other, Transportation, Travel
ISBN Prefix(es): 0-908272
Number of titles published annually: 6 Print
Total Titles: 30 Print
Imprints: Kingsclear Books Pty Ltd
Subsidiaries: Atrand Pty Ltd
Shipping Address: Tower Books, 9/19 Rodborough Rd, Frenchs Forest 2086, Dale Druikman *Tel:* (02) 9975-5586 *Fax:* (02) 9975-5599
Warehouse: Federation Press, 71 John St, Leichhardt 2040, John Xenos *Tel:* (09552) 2200

Kingsclear Books Pty Ltd, *imprint of* Kingsclear Books

Knopf Publishing, *imprint of* Random House Australia

Kookaburra Technical Publications Pty Ltd
PO Box 648, Dandenong, Victoria 3175
Tel: (03) 9560 0841 *Fax:* (03) 95451121
E-mail: kookaburra@boundy39.com
Key Personnel
Head of Company: Geoff Pentland
Customer Service: Jean Edwards
Sales: Lyn Johannessen
Founded: 1963
Specialize in reference books for modelers & historians.
Subjects: Aeronautics, Aviation
ISBN Prefix(es): 0-85880

Kurlana Publishing
PO Box 481, North Adelaide, SA 5006
Tel: (08) 3886619
Founded: 1988
Subjects: Psychology, Psychiatry
ISBN Prefix(es): 0-9587998

Laams Publications
PO Box 978, Bondi Junction, NSW 1355
Fax: (02) 9369 1812
E-mail: cle@laams.com.au
Web Site: www.laams.com.au
Key Personnel
Editorial Man: Paul K Cooper
Founded: 1986
Subjects: Business, Law
ISBN Prefix(es): 1-86474; 1-86455; 1-875263

Lachlan Publishing+
PO Box 971, Albury 2640
Tel: (060) 216933 *Fax:* (060) 412950
Key Personnel
Head of Company: Kevin Passey
Founded: 1986
Member of Australian Institute of History & Arts, Australian Writers Guild, History-Bushranging; also acts as a script writer.
Subjects: History, Regional Interests

Lancer, *imprint of* Anzea Publishers Ltd

Landarc Publications
46 McIlwraith St, North Carlton, Victoria 3054
Tel: (03) 93801276 *Fax:* (03) 93801276
E-mail: carmar@bigpond.com
Key Personnel
Manager: Carolyn Pike
Founded: 1981
Subjects: Gardening, Plants
ISBN Prefix(es): 0-9587100; 0-9594220
Total Titles: 3 Print

Lansdowne Publishing Pty Ltd+
PO Box 48, Millers Point, NSW 2000
Tel: (02) 9240 9222 *Fax:* (02) 9241 4818
E-mail: sales@lanspub.com.au
Key Personnel
Chief Executive: Steven Morris
Publisher: Deborah Nixon
Publicity & Office Manager: Valerie Sadlier *Tel:* (02) 9240 9201 *E-mail:* valerie@lanspub.com.all
Porduction Manager: Sally Davies
Subjects: Animals, Pets, Cookery, Gardening, Plants, Health, Nutrition, History, Mythology
ISBN Prefix(es): 1-86302; 0-947116; 0-949708
Parent Company: Kirin Publishing Pty Ltd

Laurel Press+
850 Huon Rd, Ferntree, Tas 7054
Mailing Address: PO Box 132, Sandy Bay, Tas 7005
Tel: (03) 62391139 *Fax:* (03) 62391139
Key Personnel
Head of Company: Chris Bell *E-mail:* chrisjen@southcom.com.au
Founded: 1990
Publisher of on-going large-format fine editions.
Subjects: Natural History, Photography
ISBN Prefix(es): 0-646; 0-958
Total Titles: 2 Print

Law Book Co Information Services+
44-50 Waterloo Rd, North Ryde, NSW 2113
Mailing Address: PO Box 24, Toronto Dominion Centre, Toronto, ON M5K 1A1, Canada
Tel: (02) 99366444 *Fax:* (02) 98882229
Telex: 27995 Asbook *Cable:* Asbook
Key Personnel
Publishing Manager: E Costigan; A M O'Neill
National Sales Manager: B Crane
Marketing Manager: C Simmons
Manager, Editorial: Y Stewart
Founded: 1898
Subjects: Accounting, Business, Criminology, Environmental Studies, Finance, Labor, Industrial Relations, Law, Medicine, Nursing, Dentistry, Real Estate
ISBN Prefix(es): 0-455
Parent Company: Thomson Corporation Publishing Ltd, United Kingdom
Ultimate Parent Company: The Thomson Corp, Suite 2706, Toronto Dominion Bank Tower, Toronto, ON M5K 1A1, Canada
Subsidiaries: Centre for Professional Development; Newsletter Information Services
Branch Office(s)
Thomson International Publishing Group, Metro Center, One Station Place, Stamford, CT 06902, United States
Bookshop(s): 4/167 Phillip St, Sydney NSW 2000; 560 Lonsdale St, Melbourne, Victoria 3000; 1/40 Queen St, Brisbane, Qld 4000; 77 St Georges Terr, 13th Floor, Perth 6000, WA
Warehouse: 50 Waterloo Rd, North Ryde NSW 2113
Orders to: 50 Waterloo Rd, North Ryde, NSW 2113

LBC Information Services, see Law Book Co Information Services

Sandra Lee Agencies
23 Arthur St, Brighton 3186
Mailing Address: PO Box 32, Brighton 3186
Tel: (03) 95925235 *Fax:* (03) 95927608

AUSTRALIA

E-mail: winston@ozonline.com.au
Key Personnel
Marketing: Sandra Lewin-Smith
Founded: 1970
Subjects: Cookery
ISBN Prefix(es): 7-316

Legal Books, *imprint of* Prospect Media Pty Ltd

Let's Go, *imprint of* Pan Macmillan Australia Pty Ltd

Levanter Publishing & Associates+
2 Bowlers Ave, Bexley, NSW 2207
Tel: (02) 93717824
Key Personnel
Head of Company: David Ehrlich
Sales Manager: Claudine Auger
Editor: Frank Hariri
Founded: 1991
Subjects: Fiction, Romance
ISBN Prefix(es): 0-646
Showroom(s): Flat 5, No 3 Rockley St, Bondi NSW 2026
Warehouse: Flat 5, No 3 Rockley St, Bondi NSW 2026
Orders to: Flat 5, No 3, Rockley St, Bondi, NSW 2026

Libra Books Pty Ltd
39 Maning Ave, Sandy Bay, Tasmania 7005
Tel: (03) 6225 1479 *Fax:* (03) 6225 0900
Key Personnel
Head of Company: Bert Wicks *E-mail:* bwicks@trump.net.au
Founded: 1972
ISBN Prefix(es): 0-909619

Library of Australian History
17 Mitchell St, North Sydney, NSW 2060
Mailing Address: PO Box 795, North Sydney, NSW 2059
Tel: (02) 9929 5087 *Fax:* (02) 9929 5087
E-mail: grdxxx@ozemail.com.au
Key Personnel
Editorial Manager: Keith Johnson
Founded: 1977
Subjects: Genealogy, History, Regional Interests, Australian history & reference, family history
ISBN Prefix(es): 0-908120; 0-9579524
Subsidiaries: Genealogical Research Directory
Branch Office(s)
John Poole, 130 E Montecito Ave, No. 120, Sierra Madre, CA 91024-1924, United States *Tel:* 626-792-1339 *E-mail:* grdusa@earthlink.net

Life Planning Foundation of Australia, Inc
341 Queen St, Ground floor, Melbourne, Victoria 3000
Tel: (03) 9670 4417 *Fax:* (03) 9640 0094
E-mail: lifeclub@vicnet.net.au
Founded: 1974
Subjects: Finance, Health, Nutrition, Human Relations, Nonfiction (General), Self-Help
ISBN Prefix(es): 0-9590567

Lightbild PTY Ltd+
21 Margate St, Beaumaris 3193
Tel: (03) 95849638 *Fax:* (03) 95849638
E-mail: lightbild@compuserve.com
Key Personnel
Contact: Berthold Daum
Founded: 1994
Subjects: Photography, Poetry, Technology, Travel
ISBN Prefix(es): 0-646

Lineup, *imprint of* Troll Books of Australia

Linking Up Publishing+
99 First Ave, Five Dock 2046
Tel: (02) 9712-5576 *Fax:* (02) 9712-1963
Key Personnel
Contact: Julian Raimundo
Subjects: Psychology, Psychiatry
ISBN Prefix(es): 0-646
Distributor for Castalia Publishing; Chevron Corp; Taylor Publishing

Little Hills Press+
18 Bearing Rd, Unit 3, Seven Hills, NSW (Sydney) 2147
Tel: (02) 9838 4373 *Fax:* (02) 9838 7929
E-mail: lhills@idx.com.au
Web Site: www.littlehills.com
Key Personnel
Chief Executive & Sales: Charles C Burfitt
Founded: 1981
Subjects: Crafts, Games, Hobbies, Fashion, Nonfiction (General), Travel
ISBN Prefix(es): 0-949773; 1-86315
Total Titles: 59 Print
Online services available through World Wide Web.
Imprints: Mount
Distributed by Cimino Publishing (USA); Pelican (USA); Ulysses Books (Canada); World Leisure Marketing (UK)
Distributor for Berndston & Berndston Maps; Camerapix; Firefly; Formac Publishing; Four Courts; Gault Millau; Gracewing; Hunter Publications; John Muir; Kuemmerly & Frey Maps; Marcopolo; Pallas Athena; Penton Overseas Inc; Scepter (USA & UK); Sinag-Tala (Philippines); Ulysses Travel Publishers; World Leisure Marketing
Warehouse: Little Hills Press, 11/37 Alexander St, Crows Nest, NSW 2065
Orders to: Little Hills Press, 11/37 Alexander St, Crows Nest, NSW 2065

Little Red Apple Publishing+
PO Box K152, Haymarket NSW 1240
Tel: (02) 9430 6867 *Fax:* (02) 9440 3771
E-mail: littleredapple@hotmail.com
Key Personnel
Vice President: Jonathan Solomon
Contact: Larissa Solomon; Rosa Melino
Founded: 1988
Also specializing in novels & Aboriginal myths & legends. Network for author, publisher & artists.
Subjects: Biography, Child Care & Development, Disability, Special Needs, Education, Fiction, History, Human Relations, Humor, Nonfiction (General), Poetry, Religion - Catholic, Religion - Other, Romance
ISBN Prefix(es): 0-9577; 1-875329
Number of titles published annually: 10 Print
Total Titles: 18 Print; 12 E-Book
Distributed by Gro-Sett Pty Ltd
Distributor for Acre Books; Gro-Sett Pty Ltd; Ripostes; Il Castello

Living Books, *imprint of* Random House Australia

Local Consumption Publications
42 Forbes St, Newtown, Sydney 2042
Mailing Address: PO Box 116, Wentworth Bldg, Sydney University, Sydney, NSW 2006
Tel: (02) 9519-7503 *Fax:* (02) 95197503
E-mail: s.muecke@hum.uts.edu.au
Web Site: www.hss.uts.edu.au
ISBN Prefix(es): 0-949793

Lonely Planet Publications Pty Ltd+
ABN 36 005 607 983, Locked Bag 1, Footscray, Victoria 3011
Tel: (03) 8379 8000 *Fax:* (03) 8379 8111
E-mail: talk2us@lonelyplanet.com.au
Web Site: www.lonelyplanet.com
Key Personnel
Dir: Tony Wheeler
Publisher: Sue Galley; Rob van Dreisum; Sally Steward; Paul Smitz
Rights & Permissions: Annalisa Guidici
Production: Graham Imeson
Promotions & Publicity: Anna Bolger
Co-General Manager: Steve Hibbard
Dir: Maureen Wheeler
Publisher: Susan Keogh
Founded: 1973
Subjects: Travel, Phrasebooks, Travel Literature, *walking & diving guides & pictorials*
ISBN Prefix(es): 1-55992; 0-908086; 0-86442; 1-86450; 1-876327; 1-876277
Imprints: Journeys; Pisces
Branch Office(s)
Lonely Planet, One rue du Dahomey, 75011 Paris, France *Tel:* (01) 55 25 33 00 *Fax:* (01) 55 25 33 01 *E-mail:* bip@lonelyplanet.fr
Lonely Planet, 10a Spring Pl, London NW5 3BH, United Kingdom *Tel:* (20) 7428 4800 *Fax:* (20) 7428 4828 *E-mail:* go@lonelyplanet.co.uk
Lonely Planet Publications Inc, 150 Linden St, Oakland, CA 94607, United States *Tel:* 510-893-8555 *Fax:* 510-893-8563 *E-mail:* info@lonelyplanet.com

Lonestone Press, *imprint of* Oceans Enterprises

Barry Long Books+
The Council Bldg, Station St, Mullumbimby, NSW 2482
Key Personnel
International Rights: Clive Tempest *E-mail:* clive.tempest@btinternet.com
Founded: 1994
Non-profit educational company.
Specialize in books, audio & video tapes & seminars.
Subjects: Religion - Other, Self-Help, The work of spiritual teacher Barry Long
ISBN Prefix(es): 0-9508050; 1-899324
Number of titles published annually: 2 Print
Total Titles: 20 Print
Parent Company: The Barry Long Foundation International, PO Box 574, Mullumbimby NSW 2482, Sara Koh
Branch Office(s)
Barry Long Books, BCM Box 876, London WC1N 3XX, United Kingdom, Clive Tempest *Tel:* (01823) 430061 *Fax:* (01823) 430062 *E-mail:* contact@barrylongbooks.com *Web Site:* www.barrylongbooks.com
U.S. Office(s): Barry Long Books, 6230 Wilshire Blvd, Suite 251, Los Angeles, CA 90048, United States, Simon Warwick Smith *Tel:* 707-939-9212 *Fax:* 707-938-3515 *Web Site:* www.barrylongbooks.com
Distributed by Associated Publishers Group (US & Canada); Chapter Book Agencies (South Africa); Deep Books (UK & Ireland); Gemcraft Books (Australia); New Leaf Distributing Co (US & Canada); Peaceful Living (New Zealand)
Orders to: Bookworld Services, 1933 Whitfield Park Loop, Sarasota, FL 34243, United States *E-mail:* sales@bookworld.com *Web Site:* www.bookworld.com

Longman, *imprint of* Pearson Education Australia

Lothian Books, see Thomas C Lothian Pty Ltd

Thomas C Lothian Pty Ltd+
Level 5, 132-136 Albert Rd, South Melbourne, Victoria 3205
Tel: (03) 9694 4900 *Fax:* (03) 9645 0705
E-mail: books@lothian.com.au
Web Site: www.lothian.com.au

PUBLISHERS

AUSTRALIA

Key Personnel
Man Dir & Publishing: Peter Lothian
 E-mail: peter_lothian@lothian.com.au
Sales & Marketing Dir: Bruce Hilliard
 E-mail: bruce_hilliard@lothian.com.au
Founded: 1888
Book publisher.
Member of Australian Publishers Association.
Subjects: Astrology, Occult, Business, Health, Nutrition, Nonfiction (General), Self-Help, New Age
ISBN Prefix(es): 0-85091; 0-7344
Number of titles published annually: 100 Print
Total Titles: 800 Print
Distributed by Forrester Books (New Zealand); Star Bright Books USA; STP/Times Publishing Group (Singapore); Ragged Bears (Children); Roundhouse Publishing GRP (Adult); Phambili Agencies CC (South Africa); Vanwell Publishing (Canada)
Distributor for Barron's; Lothian Publishing Co; North South Books

David Lovell Publishing, *imprint of* Rainbow Book Agencies Pty Ltd

Lowden Publishing Co
29 Lisbeth Ave, Donvale, Victoria 3111
Tel: (03) 9873 7202 *Fax:* (03) 9873 0542
E-mail: service@theruralstore.com.au
Web Site: www.theruralstore.com.au *Cable:* LOWDEN KILMORE
Key Personnel
Man Dir: Jim Lowden *E-mail:* jim@theruralstore.com.au
Founded: 1969
Subjects: Biography, History, Religion - Other, Transportation
ISBN Prefix(es): 0-909706
Associate Companies: The Rural Store (Agricultural Booksellers)

Lucasville Press
3 Dalzell Rd, Point Cook 3030
Tel: (03) 93951446
Key Personnel
Head of Company: S Campbell-Wright
Founded: 1987
Specialize in Australian History.
Subjects: Biography, Genealogy, History
ISBN Prefix(es): 0-9577

MacLennan & Petty Pty Ltd+
152 Bunnerong Road, Suite 405, Eastgardens 2036 NSW
Tel: (02) 9349 5811 *Fax:* (02) 9349 5911
E-mail: macpetty@zip.com.au
Web Site: www.maclennanpetty.com.au
Key Personnel
Man Dir & International Rights Contact: Pamela Petty
Special Projects Dir: Rod Mead *E-mail:* rmead@maclennanpetty.com.au
Founded: 1988
Specialize in human services.
Subjects: Disability, Special Needs, Education, Health, Nutrition, Medicine, Nursing, Dentistry
ISBN Prefix(es): 0-86433
Number of titles published annually: 10 Print
Total Titles: 55 Print
Distributed by APAC Publishers (Southeast Asia); Jessica Kingsley Publishing Co; F A Davis (United States); Springer Publishing Co (Europe & UK)
Distributor for Adis Press (New Zealand); Aspen Publishers Inc (US); Brookes Publishing Co (United States); F A Davis; Health Press (United Kingdom); Health Professions Press (United States); Icon Learning Systems (United States); Isis Medical Media (United Kingdom); J & S Publishing (United States); Love Publishing Co; MacLennan & Petty (Australia); Merit Publishing (United Kingdom); Paul H Brookes; Pavilion Publishers (United Kingdom); Quay Books (Div of Mark Allen Publishing) (United Kingdom); Roeher Institute (Canada); Slack Inc (United States); Springhouse Publishing (United States); Springhouse Publishing (United States); Whurr Publishers (United Kingdom); York Press (United States)

Macmillan, *imprint of* Pan Macmillan Australia Pty Ltd

Macmillan Education Australia+
Level 4 & 5, 627 Chapel St, Locked Bag 1400, South Yarra, Victoria 3141
Tel: (03) 9825 1025 *Fax:* (03) 9825 1010
E-mail: mea@macmillan.com.au
Web Site: www.macmillan.com.au
Key Personnel
Man Dir: Shane Armstrong *E-mail:* shane.armstrong@macmillan.com.au
Sales Dir: Peter Huntley *E-mail:* peter.huntley@macmillian.com.au
Marketing Manager: Christine Powers
 E-mail: christine.powers@macmillan.com.au
Senior Sales Coordinator: Vicky Cheong
 E-mail: vicky.cheong@macmillan.com.au
Founded: 1896
Subjects: Accounting, Behavioral Sciences, Economics, Education, Geography, Geology, Government, Political Science, History, Management, Mathematics, Physics, Science (General), Social Sciences, Sociology
ISBN Prefix(es): 0-7329
Parent Company: Macmillan Publishers Australia Pty Ltd
Branch Office(s)
Level 2, St Martins Tower, 31 Market St, Sydney, NSW 2000 *Tel:* (02) 9264 0522 *Fax:* (02) 9264 0770 *E-mail:* measyd@macmillan.com.au
Warehouse: Macmillan Distribution Services Pty Ltd, 56 Parkwest Dr, Derrimut, Victoria 3030, Man Dir: Andy Palmer *Tel:* (03) 9825 1000 *Fax:* (03) 9825 3210 *E-mail:* mds@macmillan.com.au *Web Site:* www.ozemail.com.au/~mds/; www.macmillan.com.au

Macquarie Library, *imprint of* Pan Macmillan Australia Pty Ltd

The Macquarie Library Pty Ltd
Macquarie University, Sydney, NSW 2109
Tel: (02) 98059800 *Fax:* (02) 9888 2984
E-mail: alison@dict.mq.edu
Key Personnel
Publisher: Richard Tardif
Founded: 1980
ISBN Prefix(es): 0-949757
Parent Company: Kirin Publishing Pty Ltd
Orders to: Gary Allen Pty Ltd, 9 Cooper St, Smithfield, Sydney 2164

Magabala Books Aboriginal Corporation+
PO Box 668, Broome, WA 6725
Tel: (091) 921991 *Fax:* (091) 935254
E-mail: info@magabala.com
Key Personnel
Publishing Manager: Bruce Sims
Administration Manager: Jill Walsh
Management Committee Chairperson: Arnhem Hunter
Founded: 1987
Specialize in Indigenous Publishing.
Subjects: Anthropology, Art, Biography, Drama, Theater, Fiction, Human Relations, Literature, Literary Criticism, Essays, Natural History, Nonfiction (General), Philosophy, Religion - Other
ISBN Prefix(es): 1-875641; 0-9588101
Warehouse: Discount Freight Express, PO Box 260, Bentley, WA 6102

Magic Bean, *imprint of* Era Publications

Magpie Books
PO Box 2038, Brighton 3186
Tel: (0613) 9592 9931 *Fax:* (0613) 9592 2045
E-mail: admin01@magpiebooks.com.au
Web Site: www.magpiebooks.com.au
Founded: 1980
Publisher of price guides for the second hand book trade.
Subjects: Publishing & Book Trade Reference

Magpie Publications
PO Box 3427, Weston Creek 2611
Tel: 06 2509442
Key Personnel
Contact: T A Orchard
Specialize in Philatey.
Subjects: Philatey & Postal History
ISBN Prefix(es): 0-9587862; 1-875579

Magpies Magazine
13 Frome St, Grange, Queensland 4051
Mailing Address: PO Box 98, Grange, Queensland 4051
Tel: (07) 3356 4503 *Fax:* (07) 3356 4649
E-mail: james@magpies.net.au
Key Personnel
Editor: Ray Turton
Founded: 1986
Subjects: Library & Information Sciences
ISBN Prefix(es): 1-875249

Mammoth UK, *imprint of* Random House Australia

Maquileadora, *imprint of* Wild & Woolley Pty Ltd

Margaret Hamilton Books+
Imprint of Scholastic Australia
PO Box 579, Lindfield, NSW 2070
Tel: (02) 98162561 *Fax:* (02) 98175144
Web Site: www.scholastic.com.au
Key Personnel
Dir: Margaret Hamilton
Founded: 1988
ISBN Prefix(es): 0-947241; 1-876289
Ultimate Parent Company: Scholastic Inc

Margin Magazines, *imprint of* Mulini Press

Marketing Focus
26 Central Rd, Kalamunda 6076
Tel: (08) 92571777 *Fax:* (08) 92571888
Web Site: www.marketingfocus.net.au
Key Personnel
Head of Company & Man Dir: Barry Ross Urquhart *E-mail:* urquhart@marketingfocus.net.au
Founded: 1978
Marketing & strategic planning consultant.
Subjects: Business, Marketing
ISBN Prefix(es): 0-9586558

Marque Publishing
911 King Georges Rd, Blakehurst, NSW 2221
Mailing Address: PO Box 203, Hurtsville, NSW 2220
Tel: (02) 9546 5521 *Fax:* (02) 9547 2061
E-mail: books@marque.com.au
Web Site: www.marque.com.au
Key Personnel
Editorial Dir: Ewan Kennedy
Business Manager: Alistair Kennedy
Founded: 1987
Specialize in motoring books.
Subjects: Transportation
ISBN Prefix(es): 0-947079
Distributed by Bookworks Pty Ltd

AUSTRALIA

Tracy Marsh Publications Pty Ltd+
2-25 Seaview Rd, West Beach, SA 5024
Mailing Address: PO Box 116, Henley Beach, SA 5022
Tel: (08) 8355 4716 *Fax:* (08) 8355 4916
E-mail: enquires@tracymarsh.com
Web Site: www.tracymarsh.com
Key Personnel
Chief Executive: Tracy Marsh
Co-Editions Manager: Jane Moseley
Founded: 1984
Subjects: Crafts, Games, Hobbies, Travel
ISBN Prefix(es): 1-875899; 0-9590174

Horwitz Martin Education+
Horwitz House, 55 Chandos St, St Leonards, NSW 2065
Tel: (02) 9901 6100 *Fax:* (02) 9901 6155
Key Personnel
General Manager: Stephen Wilson
 E-mail: stephenw@horwitz.com.au
Founded: 1958
Educational publishing company; specialize in elementary textbook and literacy materials.
Subjects: Education, Literature, Literary Criticism, Essays, Literacy
ISBN Prefix(es): 0-7253
Number of titles published annually: 120 Print
Total Titles: 500 Print
Parent Company: Horwitz Publications Pty Ltd

Matthias Media
Suite 1, 42 Gardeners Rd, Kingsford, NSW 2032
Mailing Address: PO Box 225, Kingsford, NSW 2032
Tel: (02) 3100813; (02) 9663-1478 (overseas)
 Toll Free Tel: 800 814 360 *Fax:* (02) 9663-3265; (02) 9663-3265
E-mail: info@matthiasmedia.com.au
Web Site: www.matthiasmedia.com.au
Key Personnel
Man Dir & International Rights: Ian Carmichael
Founded: 1988
Subjects: Education, Religion - Protestant, Christianity, Bible, Evangelicalism, Ministry
ISBN Prefix(es): 1-875245
Parent Company: St Matthias Press

Maxwell Macmillan Publishing (Australia) Pty Ltd+
Member of Maxwell Macmillan International Publishing Group
Level 4, 627 Chapel St, South Yarra, Victoria 3141
Tel: (03) 9825 1000 *Fax:* (03) 9825 1010
Web Site: www.macmillan.co.uk
Key Personnel
Man Dir: Ross Gibb *E-mail:* ross.gibb@macmillan.com.au
Sales/Trade Manager: Laurie Giles
College Sales Manager: Harry Khoury
Customer Service: Younia Jarmam
Founded: 1968
Sales offices in Melbourne & Sydney, Australia.
Subjects: Education, Engineering (General), Literature, Literary Criticism, Essays, Military Science, Psychology, Psychiatry, Science (General), Social Sciences, Sociology
ISBN Prefix(es): 0-02; 0-08
Subsidiaries: Australian National University Press
Warehouse: 2-A Lord St, Botany, NSW 2019

Mayfield Publishing, *imprint of* Harcourt Australia Pty Ltd

Mayne Publishing+
22 William St, Clifton 4361
Tel: (076) 973558
Key Personnel
Contact: C Mayne
Founded: 1993

Subjects: Behavioral Sciences, Cookery, Crafts, Games, Hobbies, Fiction, Government, Political Science, Health, Nutrition, How-to, Self-Help
ISBN Prefix(es): 0-646

Yvonne McBurney
10 South St, Strathfield, NSW 2135
Tel: (02) 7467962
Key Personnel
Dir: Yvonne McBurney
Founded: 1976
Subjects: History, Regional Interests
ISBN Prefix(es): 0-908053
Warehouse: 140L Obley Rd MS3, Dubbo NSW 2830 *Tel:* (068) 873608

McDonald-Kirkwood Pty Ltd+
104 South TCE, Adelaide, SA 5000
Mailing Address: Attn: Ross McDonald, PO Box 6079, Halifax Street PO, SA 5000
Tel: (08) 8221 6111 *Fax:* (08) 8221 6211
Key Personnel
Head of Company: Ross McDonald
Customer Liaison Officer: Karen Dwyer
Founded: 1988
Subjects: Cookery
ISBN Prefix(es): 0-9577
Parent Company: Donco Holdings Pty Ltd

McGraw-Hill Australia Pty Ltd+
Formerly McGraw-Hill Book Company Australia Pty Ltd
4 Barcoo St, Roseville, NSW 2069
Mailing Address: PO Box 239, Roseville NSW 2069
Tel: (02) 9415 9899 *Fax:* (02) 9417 8872
E-mail: cservice_sydney@mcgraw-hill.com.au
Web Site: www.mcgraw-hill.com.au
Key Personnel
Man Dir & Official Delegate: Firgal Adams
General Manager, Higher Education Division: Yasminka Nemet
General Manager, Professional & Education Division: Tony Wong
Rights & Permissions: Natalie Muir *Tel:* (02) 9415 9842 *Fax:* (02) 9417 5687
Executive Assistant: Diane Muchar *Tel:* (02) 9415 9827 *E-mail:* diane_muchar@mcgraw-hill.com
Copy Editor & Permissions Higher Education Division: Leanne Peters *Tel:* (02) 9415 0908 *Fax:* (02) 9417 7773
Founded: 1964
Subjects: Accounting, Advertising, Aeronautics, Aviation, Anthropology, Architecture & Interior Design, Art, Automotive, Behavioral Sciences, Biological Sciences, Chemistry, Chemical Engineering, Child Care & Development, Computer Science, Criminology, Disability, Special Needs, Earth Sciences, Economics, Education, Electronics, Electrical Engineering, Engineering (General), English as a Second Language, Environmental Studies, Film, Video, Geography, Geology, Health, Nutrition, Journalism, Labor, Industrial Relations, Language Arts, Linguistics, Management, Maritime, Marketing, Mathematics, Mechanical Engineering, Medicine, Nursing, Dentistry, Philosophy, Photography, Physical Sciences, Physics, Psychology, Psychiatry, Social Sciences, Sociology, Sports, Athletics
ISBN Prefix(es): 0-07; 0-697; 0-256
Parent Company: McGraw-Hill Inc, 1221 Avenue of the Americas, New York, NY 10020, United States
Associate Companies: McGraw-Hill Book Co N2 Ltd, Westfield Tower, 2nd Floor, Westfield Shopping Centre, Manukau City, Auckland, New Zealand, Contact: Max Loveridge *Tel:* (09) 262 2717 *Fax:* (09) 262 2540; McGraw-Hill Book Co, Lakeside Place, Upper Ground Floor, Bruma Lake Office Park, Ernest Oppenheimer St, Johannesburg, South Africa, General Manager: Lawrence Mulligan *Tel:* (011) 622-7512 *Fax:* (011) 622 9045
Imprints: PressXpress
Branch Office(s)
Melbourne Office, Suite 1, Ground Floor, 407 Canterbury Road, Surrey Hills, 3127 Victoria, PTR State Manager: Nick Dallas *Fax:* (03) 9836 2867
Brisbane Office, 588 Boundary St, Spring Hill Qld 4000, PTR State Manager: Brent Pattison *Tel:* (07) 3835 1166 *Fax:* (07) 3831 7119
Distributed by Amacom (American Mangement); Active Path (Wrox); American Education Publishing; Appleton & Lange; ASQ (American Society of Quality); Barnell Loft Ltd; Benziger Publishing Co; Brown & Benchmark; William C Brown; Business Week Books; Certification Press; Charles E Merrill; Citrix Press; Clearway Exam Questions (HSC); Clearway Textbooks; CommerceNet Press; Computing McGraw-Hill; Contemporary Publications/NTC; Corel Press; Custom Publications; Dushkin Publishing Group; J D Edwards; Fine Arts Press; Friends of Ed; Glencoe/McGraw; Harvard Business School Press; International Marine; Irwin Publishers; Richard D Irwin; James Town Publishers/NTC; Keats Publishing/NTC; Learning Triangle Press; London House; MacMillan/McGraw-Hill School; Mayfield Publishing Co; McGraw-Hill Canada; Tata McGraw-Hill India; McGraw-Hill Italy; McGraw-Hill Microsoft Press; McGraw-Hill Singapore; McGraw-Hill UK; McGraw-Hill USA; Metric Schaum; New Holland Publishers; NTC (National Textbook Co); Oracle Press; Osborne; Platts (USA); Possum Press; Prmis; Quicken Press; Quilt Digest Press/NTC; Ragged Mountain Press; Rebol Press; Republic of Texas Press; RSA Press; Sapphire Books; Schaum; Science Research Associates (SRA); Tab Books; Terrific Science Press; Visual Education Corp (School); Webster Publishing; Windcrest; Wordware Publishing; Wright Group/McGraw-Hill; Wrox Press; Xebec/McGraw-Hill
Distributor for Alfred Waller (UK); Amacom - American Management (USA); Barnell Loft Ltd (USA); Benziger Publishing Co (USA); Brown & Benchmark; William C Brown; Clearway Textbooks; Custom Publications ((USA) part of McGraw); Charles E Merrill (USA); Clearway Exam Questions-HSC; Dushkin Publishing Group; Glencoe/McGraw (USA); Harvard Business School Press (USA); International Marine (USA); Irwin Professional PRO (USA); Irwin Publishers (USA); Richard D Irwin (USA); London House (USA); Webster Publishing; MacMillan/McGraw-Hill School (USA); McGraw-Hill Canada (Canada); McGraw-Hill Italy (Italy); McGraw-Hill Singapore (Singapore); Tata McGraw-Hill India (India); McGraw-Hill (UK); McGraw-Hill USA (USA); Metric Schaum (Singapore); Osborne (USA); Possum Press (Australia); Primis; Ragged Mountain Press ((USA) part of McGraw); Republic of Texas Press (USA); Sapphire Books (Australia); Schaum (USA); Science Research Associates SRA (USA); Tab Books (USA); Wordware Publishing (USA); Wrox Press; Windcrest

McGraw-Hill Book Company Australia Pty Ltd, see McGraw-Hill Australia Pty Ltd

J M McGregor Pty Ltd+
PO Box 40, Double Bay, NSW 2028
Tel: (02) 91351923
Key Personnel
Man Dir: Malcolm McGregor
Founded: 1968
Subjects: Crafts, Games, Hobbies, Education, Photography

ISBN Prefix(es): 0-85921
Subsidiaries: J M McGregor NZ Ltd

Media East Press
PO Box 363, Kingsford, NSW 2032
Tel: (02) 9349-6683 *Fax:* (02) 9349-6683
Key Personnel
Man Dir: Thomas E King
Founded: 1977
Award-winning editorial agency/book publisher specializing in golf venues & travel destinations.
Member of Australian Society of Travel Writers & Australian Society of Authors.
Subjects: Nonfiction (General), Travel
Total Titles: 5 Print
Parent Company: Media East Pty Ltd

Melbourne Institute of Applied Economic & Social Research
6th Floor, University of Melbourne, Parkville, Victoria 3010
Tel: (03) 8344 5330 *Fax:* (03) 8344 5630
E-mail: melb.inst@iaesr.unimelb.edu.au
Web Site: www.melbourneinstitute.com
Key Personnel
Dir & Prof: Peter Dawkins *Tel:* 8344 7915 *E-mail:* p.dawkins@iaesr.unimelb.edu.au
Founded: 1963
Specialize in Economic & Social research.
Subjects: Economics, Social Sciences, Sociology, Working papers, Newsletters, reports
Parent Company: The University of Melbourne, 3010
Distributed by Blackwells Australian Economic Review
Orders to: Blackwell Publishers Journals, PO Box 805, 108 Cowley Rd, Oxford OX4 1FH, United Kingdom *Tel:* (01865) 244083 *Fax:* (01865) 381381 *E-mail:* jnlinfo@blackwellpublishers.co.uk *Web Site:* www.blackwellpublishers.co.uk (Only for Australian Economic Review)

Melbourne University Press+
PO Box 278, Carlton South, Victoria 3053
Tel: (03) 9342 0300 *Fax:* (03) 9342 0399
E-mail: info@mup.unimelb.edu.au
Web Site: www.mup.unimelb.edu.au
Key Personnel
Dir: John Meckan *E-mail:* j.meckan@unimelb.edu.au
Marketing Man: Ms D Clark *E-mail:* d.clark@unimelb.edu.au
Comm Editor (General Nonfiction): Ms T Pitt
Assistant Dir (Head of Production, Editorial, Electronic Publishing): Mr Andrew Watson *Tel:* (03) 9420305 *E-mail:* a.watson@unimelb.edu.au
Founded: 1922
Subjects: Biography, History, Literature, Literary Criticism, Essays, Natural History, Nonfiction (General), Psychology, Psychiatry, Travel
ISBN Prefix(es): 0-522
Number of titles published annually: 50 Print; 2 CD-ROM
Total Titles: 600 Print; 3 CD-ROM
Parent Company: The University of Melbourne
Imprints: Miegunyah Press
Warehouse: Uni Reps, Govett St, Randwick, NSW 2031 (Also orders)

Melting Pot Press+
10 Grafton St, Chippendale, NSW 2008
SAN: 901-1005
Tel: (02) 9211 1660 *Fax:* (02) 9211 1868
E-mail: books@elt.com.au
Web Site: www.elt.com.au
Key Personnel
Dir: Ron Wood *Tel:* (02) 9211 1178; Rita Yip *Tel:* (02) 9212 1882
Founded: 1983
Specialize in distributing & publishing English Language Teaching (ELT) titles.
Subjects: English as a Second Language
ISBN Prefix(es): 0-947103
Total Titles: 3 Print; 3 Audio
Distributor for Academic English Press; Dubois Publishing; Darrell Hilton Productions; Miasico-Piscean Productions

Melway Publishing Pty Ltd
19 High St, Glen Iris, Victoria 3146
Tel: (03) 98859900 *Fax:* (03) 98854254
E-mail: melway@ausway.com
Web Site: www.ausway.com
Key Personnel
Dir: Murray Godfrey *E-mail:* murray@ausway.com
Founded: 1966
Member of IMTA.
Subjects: Publishing & Book Trade Reference
Total Titles: 2 Print; 2 CD-ROM
Online services available through World Wide Web.
Parent Company: Ausway Publishing Pty Ltd
Associate Companies: Sydway Publishing Pty Ltd, PO Box 693, Cooger 2034, Contact: Murray Godfrey *Tel:* (03) 9885 1146 *Fax:* (03) 9885 4254 *E-mail:* murray@ausway.com

Michael Grinder & Associates, *imprint of* Hawker Brownlow

Miegunyah Press, *imprint of* Melbourne University Press

Millenium Books Pty Ltd, see E J Dwyer (Australia) Pty Ltd

Millennium Books, *imprint of* E J Dwyer (Australia) Pty Ltd

Mimosa Publications Pty Ltd+
PO Box 779, Hawthorn, Victoria 3122
Tel: (03) 9819 0511 *Fax:* (03) 9819 0524
E-mail: info@mimosa.pub.com.au
Key Personnel
International Marketing & Publishing Dir: Sue Donovan
Man Dir: John Gilder
Founded: 1980
Subjects: Language Arts, Linguistics, Mathematics, Poetry, Science (General), Reading, ESL
ISBN Prefix(es): 0-7327
Parent Company: Tribune Co
Associate Companies: Mimosa Education Inc, 50 South Steele St, Suite 755, Denver, CO 80209, United States
Subsidiaries: Dragon Media P/L
Divisions: Mimosa Shortland

Minerva, *imprint of* Random House Australia

Mission Publications of Australia
PO Box 21, Lawson, NSW 2783
Tel: (02) 4759 1003 *Fax:* (02) 4759 1101
Founded: 1960
Specialize in Easy English Christian Literature.
Subjects: Religion - Other
ISBN Prefix(es): 0-909448; 1-86288
Associate Companies: Aborigines Inland Mission & United Aborigines Mission

Mockingbird, *imprint of* Ginninderra Press

Modern Learning Press, *imprint of* Hawker Brownlow

Moggy Publications
PO Box 628, South Yarra 3141
Tel: (03) 9867-2347
E-mail: rose-1@rocketmail.com
Key Personnel
Contact: Lesley Sharon Rosenthal
Founded: 1990
Small press & self publisher.
Member of Fellowship of Australian Writers.
Subjects: Fiction, Humor, Novels
ISBN Prefix(es): 0-646
Total Titles: 2 Print

Moon-Ta-Gu Books
POB 444, Oberon, NSW 2787
Tel: (02) 6336 0317 *Fax:* (02) 6336 1319
E-mail: taiji@ozemail.com.au
Key Personnel
Contact: Erle Montaigue
Subjects: Health, Nutrition, Self-Help, Martial Arts

Moonlight Publishing
PO Box 5, Golden Square, Victoria 3555
Tel: 03 5447 8221
E-mail: moonlight@impulse.net.au
Key Personnel
Manager: Chris Spencer *E-mail:* chris_spencer@bssc.edu.au
Founded: 1989
Subjects: Music, Dance
ISBN Prefix(es): 1-876187
Total Titles: 60 Print; 1 Audio
Imprints: Windwood

Morgan Kaufmann, *imprint of* Harcourt Australia Pty Ltd

Mosby, *imprint of* Harcourt Australia Pty Ltd

Mosby Lifeline+
PO Box 431, Artarmon, NSW 2064
Tel: (02) 4383155 *Fax:* (02) 4383284
Telex: 178059
Key Personnel
Man Dir & Rights & Permissions: Geoff Hasler
Marketing Manager: George Ciofuli
Subjects: Business, Health, Nutrition, Medicine, Nursing, Dentistry, Veterinary Science
ISBN Prefix(es): 0-8016; 1-875897

K & Z Mostafanejad+
PO Box 118, Geraldton, WA 651
Tel: (099) 233741 *Fax:* (099) 233741
E-mail: mostak@grton.training.wa.gov.au
Key Personnel
Head of Company: Karola Mostafanejad
Sales Manager: Zaim Mostafanejad
Founded: 1989
Subjects: Mathematics, Science (General), Science Fiction, Fantasy
ISBN Prefix(es): 0-646

Mostly Unsung+
LPO Gardenvale, Box 7020, Brighton, Victoria 3186
Tel: (03) 9555 5401 *Fax:* (03) 9555 5401
E-mail: milhis@alphalink.com.au
Key Personnel
Head of Company: Neil C Smith
Founded: 1990
Subjects: History, Military Science, Regional Interests
ISBN Prefix(es): 1-876179
Total Titles: 35 Print
Branch Office(s)
c/o Anzar Services, Inc, PO Box 274, Lexington, VA 24450, United States

Mount, *imprint of* Little Hills Press

Mountain House Press
370 Wallace Rd, The Channon, NSW 2480

Tel: (02) 66886318 *Fax:* (02) 66886318
Key Personnel
Contact: Margery J Kemp *E-mail:* kkemp@nor.com.au
Subjects: Art, Photography, Poetry
ISBN Prefix(es): 0-9586639

Mouse House Press
343 Cliff Dr, Katoomba, NSW 2780
Tel: (047) 82-2929 *Fax:* (047) 82-5534
E-mail: mouhoupr@pnc.com.au
Key Personnel
Contact: M L Beggs
Subjects: Behavioral Sciences, Health, Nutrition

Mulavon Press Pty Ltd+
131 Ryedale Rd, West Ryde, NSW 2114
Tel: (02) 808 3662 *Fax:* (02) 9552-1608
Key Personnel
Contact: Rebecca Pinchin
Subjects: Environmental Studies, Natural History, Nonfiction (General), Outdoor Recreation, Australia Flora & Fauna
ISBN Prefix(es): 0-85899

Mulini Press+
PO Box 82, Jamison Centre, Canberra 2614
Tel: (02) 6251 2519 *Fax:* (02) 6251 2519
Key Personnel
Dir: Victor Crittenden
Founded: 1965
Also specializes in Early Australian history.
Subjects: Biography, Gardening, Plants, History, Literature, Literary Criticism, Essays, Poetry
ISBN Prefix(es): 0-949910
Number of titles published annually: 10 Print
Total Titles: 80 Print
Imprints: Margin Magazines

Murdoch Books+
213 Miller St N, Sydney, NSW 2060
Tel: (02) 8220 2000 *Fax:* (02) 8220 2558
Web Site: www.mm.com.au
Key Personnel
International Sales Dir: Mark Newman *E-mail:* markn@mm.com.au
Chief Executive Officer & Publisher: Anne Wilson *E-mail:* annew@mm.com.au
Founded: 1989
General nonfiction illustrated publisher.
Subjects: Domestic & decorative arts
ISBN Prefix(es): 0-86411; 0-85835; 1-86256; 1-86378
Total Titles: 800 Print
Parent Company: Murdoch Magazines Pty Ltd
Imprints: Bay Books; Better Homes & Gardens; Family Circle
Warehouse: Unit 2, 8A Ethel Ave, Brookvale NSW 2100

Museum of Victoria
GPO Box 666E, Melbourne, Victoria 3001
Tel: (03) 8341 7777 *Fax:* (03) 9651 6321
Web Site: www.museum.vic.gov.au
Key Personnel
Productions Manager: Teresa Paterson *E-mail:* tpater@mov.vic.gov.au
Subjects: Education, History

Narkaling Inc+
39 Helena St, 6936 Midland, Western Australia
Mailing Address: PO Box 1409, 6936 Midland, Western Australia
Tel: (08) 9274 8022 *Fax:* (08) 9274 8362
E-mail: info@narkaling.com.au
Web Site: www.narkaling.com.au
Key Personnel
Executive Dir: Marion Slany
Administrative Officer: Erika Troy
Founded: 1997 (Our motto: All people have the right to read)
Narkaling reading kits consists of slow speed audio tape, along with a print copy of the book. Provides an educational source to people with reading difficulties: adults, teenagers & children (all audio books).
Independent non-profit organization.
Subjects: Fiction, Nonfiction (General)
Number of titles published annually: 40 Audio
Total Titles: 300 Audio

National Association of Forest Industries Ltd
PO Box E89, Kingston, ACT 2604
Tel: (02) 6285 3833 *Fax:* (02) 6285 3855
E-mail: enquiries@nafi.com.au
Web Site: www.nafi.com.au
ISBN Prefix(es): 1-86346

National Gallery of Australia+
Parkes Pl, Canberra, ACT 2601
Mailing Address: GPO Box 1150, Canberra, ACT 2601
Tel: (02) 6240 6501; (02) 6240 6502 *Fax:* (06) 6240 6427
E-mail: information@nga.gov.au
Web Site: www.nga.gov.au
Telex: 61500 *Cable:* NGA CANBERRA
Key Personnel
Publications Manager: Jane Arms *E-mail:* jane.arms@nga.gov.au
Editorial: Alistair McGhie
Rights & Permissions: Leanne Handreck
Founded: 1982
Subjects: Art
ISBN Prefix(es): 0-642

National Gallery of Victoria
Federation Sq, 180 St Kilda Rd, Melbourne, Victoria 3004
Mailing Address: PO Box 7259, Melbourne, Victoria 8004
Tel: (03) 9208 0222 *Fax:* (03) 9208 0245
E-mail: enquiries@ngv.vic.gov.au
Web Site: www.ngv.vic.gov.au
Key Personnel
Dir: Gerard Vaughan
Merchandise Manager: Philip Jago *Tel:* (03) 9208 0275 *E-mail:* philip.jago@ngv.vic.gov.au
Founded: 1861
Specialize in large collections of art for the state of Victoria, Australia.
Subjects: Art, Fashion
ISBN Prefix(es): 0-7241
Number of titles published annually: 10 Print
Total Titles: 52 Print
Distributed by Arts Bibliographic (UK); Bookwise International (Australia & New Zealand)
Bookshop(s): The Gallery Shop *Tel:* (03) 9208 0310 *Fax:* (03) 9208 0201 *E-mail:* gallery.shop@ngv.vic.gov.au

National Library of Australia
Parkes Pl, Canberra, ACT 2600
Tel: (062) 62 1593 *Fax:* (062) 73 4493
E-mail: nlasales@nla.gov.au
Web Site: www.nla.gov.au
Telex: AA62100
Key Personnel
Publication Dir: Dr Paul Hetherington
Editor: Paul Cliff
Editorial & Production Coordinator: Kathryn Favelle *E-mail:* kfavelle@nla.gov.au
Founded: 1960
ISBN Prefix(es): 0-642

Navarine Publishing
PO Box 1275, Woden, ACT 2606
Tel: (02) 62824602
Key Personnel
Contact: Graeme Broxam *E-mail:* gjbroxam@bigpond.com.au
Founded: 1992
Member of Roebuck Society.
Subjects: Genealogy, History, Maritime, Nonfiction (General), Regional Interests, Transportation
ISBN Prefix(es): 0-9586561
Number of titles published annually: 2 Print
Total Titles: 8 Print
Associate Companies: The Roebuck Society, PO Box 1275, Woden, ACT 2606
Distributor for Roebuck Society

Network Promotions P/L+
107 Carrington St, Adelaide 5000
Tel: (018) 82-1848
Key Personnel
Head of Company: Lucille Orr
Founded: 1968
Member of National Speakers Association; specialize in business/motivation.
Subjects: Business, Women's Studies
Associate Companies: Women in Successful Enterprises P/L Founder & International President
Subsidiaries: Australian Executive Men's Network
Divisions: Australian Executive Women's Network

New Albion Press
GPO Box 252C, Hobart, Tas 7001
Tel: (03) 62202223
Key Personnel
Editorial Manager: John Winter
Founded: 1977
Subjects: Poetry
ISBN Prefix(es): 0-85901

New American Library, *imprint of* Penguin Books Australia Ltd

New Creation Publications Ministries & Resource Centre
Ackland Hill Rd, Coromandel Valley, South Australia 5051
Mailing Address: PO Box 403, Blackwood 5051
Tel: (08) 8270-1497 *Fax:* (08) 8270-1861
E-mail: sales@newcreation.org.au
Web Site: www.newcreation.org.au
Key Personnel
Dir, Ministry: Martin Bleby
General Manager: John David Skewes *E-mail:* john@newcreation.org.au
Founded: 1974
Christian publishing.
Subjects: Biblical Studies, Fiction, Human Relations, Theology
ISBN Prefix(es): 0-86408; 0-949851
Number of titles published annually: 10 Print
Total Titles: 360 Print
Imprints: Troubadour Press

New Endeavour Press+
PO Box 1596, Strawberry Hills, NSW 2012
Tel: (02) 3182384 *Fax:* (02) 3103613
Key Personnel
Head of Company: Philippe Tanguy
Founded: 1989
Specialize in quality Australian Fiction, Poetry & Art Books.
Subjects: Anthropology, Art, Fiction, Humor, Journalism, Language Arts, Linguistics, Poetry
ISBN Prefix(es): 1-875505
Associate Companies: New South Wales Uni Press

New English Library, *imprint of* Hodder Headline Australia

New Era Publications Australia Pty Ltd
Subsidiary of New Era Publications International
Level 1, 61-65 Wentworth Ave, Surry Hills NSW 2010
Tel: (02) 9211-0692 *Fax:* (02) 9211-0686
Web Site: www.newerapublications.com

Key Personnel
Executive Dir: Gabi Lumsden *Tel:* (02) 2110691
Also specialize in L Ron Hubbard books.
Subjects: Fiction, Self-Help
Total Titles: 16 Print; 17 Audio
Distributed by Victorian Wholesalers

New Horizons for Learning, *imprint of* Hawker Brownlow

Newman Centre Publications
Catechist Centre, Marist Pl, Parramatta, NSW 2150
Tel: (02) 9637-9406 *Fax:* (02) 9637-3351
Key Personnel
Contact: Rev Fr B J H Tierney
Founded: 1974
Subjects: Education, Fiction, Philosophy, Religion - Catholic, Catholic Catechism
ISBN Prefix(es): 0-909615; 0-9587535

Night Owl Publishers Pty Ltd
Box 242, Euroa, Victoria 3666
Tel: (057) 947 256 *Fax:* (057) 947 285
Key Personnel
Head of Company: David A Miller
Production: Meg Miller
Founded: 1973
ISBN Prefix(es): 0-9595244; 0-9590152; 0-947065
Imprints: Grass Roots

Nimaroo Publishers
PO Box 2046, Wollongong, NSW 2500
Tel: (042) 292297
Key Personnel
Manager & Publicity: Stephen Standish
Editorial: P Balnaves
Sales: T Balnaves
Production: M Standish
Rights & Permissions: N Standish
Founded: 1978
Subjects: Business, Science (General)
ISBN Prefix(es): 0-9596525
Branch Office(s)
11 Airds Rd, Lower Templestone, Victoria 3107

Nimrod Publications+
c/o Professor Norman Talbot, PO Box 170, New Lambton, NSW 2305
Tel: (02) 4957 5562; (02) 4921 5173 *Fax:* (02) 4950 9658
E-mail: nimrod@hunterlink.com.au
Founded: 1964
Subjects: Language Arts, Linguistics, Literature, Literary Criticism, Essays, Poetry, Science Fiction, Fantasy
ISBN Prefix(es): 0-909242 (Nimrod & Babel)
Imprints: Babel Handbooks
Subsidiaries: Babel Handbooks

NMA Publications
42 Canterbury St, Richmond, Victoria
Mailing Address: PO Box 5034, Burnley, Victoria 3121
Tel: (03) 9428 2405
Web Site: www.rainerlinz.net/NMA/
Key Personnel
Publisher: R G Linz
Founded: 1982
Subjects: Literature, Literary Criticism, Essays, Music, Dance
ISBN Prefix(es): 0-9577; 0-646; 0-9577549
Total Titles: 1 Print
Distributed by Frog Peak Music (USA)

NSW Agriculture
161 Kite St, Orange, NSW 2800
Mailing Address: Locked Bag 21, Orange, NSW 2800
Tel: (02) 6391 3100 *Fax:* (02) 6391 3336
Web Site: www.agric.nsw.gov.au
Key Personnel
Publisher: Geof Murray
ISBN Prefix(es): 7-240; 7-305
Parent Company: Agriculture Department, New South Wales
Branch Office(s)
Florida Science Source Inc, PO Box 927, Lake Alfred, FL 33850-0927, United States

Ocean Press+
546 Queensberry St, Melbourne N Victoria 3051
Mailing Address: GPO Box 3279, Melbourne, Victoria 3001
Tel: (03) 9326 4280 *Fax:* (03) 9329 5040
E-mail: edit@oceanpress.com.au
Web Site: www.oceanbooks.com.au
Key Personnel
President: David Deutschmann
Founded: 1989
Subjects: Biography, Developing Countries, Environmental Studies, Government, Political Science, History, Social Sciences, Sociology, Women's Studies
ISBN Prefix(es): 1-875284; 1-876175
Total Titles: 60 Print
U.S. Office(s): Ocean Press, PO Box 834, Hoboken, NJ 07030, United States *Tel:* 201-617-7247 *Fax:* 201-617-0203 *E-mail:* edit@oceanpress.com.au
Warehouse: LPC Warehouse, 4029 W George St, Chicago, IL 60641, United States *E-mail:* ftg@lpcgroup.com
Orders to: LPC, 1436 W Randolph St, Chicago, IL 60607, United States

Oceans Enterprises+
303 Commercial Rd, Yarram 3971
Tel: (03) 5182 5108 *Fax:* (03) 5182 5823
E-mail: oceans@netspace.net.au
Web Site: www.oceans.com.au
Key Personnel
Contact: Peter Stone
Founded: 1982
Specialize in marine, military & history publications.
Subjects: History, Maritime, Military Science, Sports, Athletics, Travel, Specialize in commercial & sport scuba diving
ISBN Prefix(es): 0-9586657
Imprints: Lonestone Press
Subsidiaries: Lonestone Press
Distributed by Gary Allen PL, Sydney

Anne O'Donovan Pty Ltd+
PO Box 5073, Glenferrie South, Victoria 3122
Tel: (03) 9819 2203 *Fax:* (03) 9818 6849
E-mail: odonovan@netspace.net.au
Key Personnel
Head of Company: Anne O'Donovan
Founded: 1978
Subjects: Cookery, Finance, Health, Nutrition, Music, Dance, Nonfiction (General), Self-Help
ISBN Prefix(es): 1-876026; 0-908476
Distributed by Penguin Books Australia Ltd (Australia)
Warehouse: Penguin Books, 487 Maroondah Hwy, Ringwood 3134
Orders to: Penguin Books, 487 Maroondah Hwy, Ringwood 3134

Off the Shelf Publishing+
9 Silver Strand Circle, Hyams Beach, NSW 2540
Tel: (02) 4443 7555 *Fax:* (02) 4443 7666
E-mail: offshelf@ozemail.com.au
Key Personnel
Publisher: Gillian Souter
Co-Proprietor: John Souter
Founded: 1991
Specialize in illustrated international craft & leisure books.
Subjects: Crafts, Games, Hobbies, Travel

ISBN Prefix(es): 0-646; 0-9586682; 1-876779
Total Titles: 20 Print
Distributed by Australian Book Group in Australia (Australia)

Ohio Psychology Press, *imprint of* Hawker Brownlow

Oidium Books+
PO Box 191, Corio, Victoria 3214
Tel: (052) 757045
E-mail: tecnilab@ozemail.com.au
Key Personnel
Contact: Richard Turner
Founded: 1985
Subjects: Health, Nutrition
ISBN Prefix(es): 0-9589510

Ollif Publishing+
41 Galston Rd, Hornsby, NSW 2077
Mailing Address: PO Box 439, Hornsby, NSW 2077
Tel: (02) 9477-3496
Key Personnel
President: Lorna Ollif
Founded: 1965
Subjects: Biography, Fiction, History
ISBN Prefix(es): 0-9599183
Number of titles published annually: 1 Print
Total Titles: 6 Print
Distributed by NSW Military Historical Society

Omnibus Books+
52 Fullarton Rd, Norwood, SA 5067
Tel: (08) 8363 2333 *Fax:* (08) 8363 1420
Key Personnel
Publisher: Dyan Blacklock
General Manager: Mick Nolan
  E-mail: mick_nolan@scholastic.com.au
Senior Editor: Penny Matthews
Founded: 1980
Subjects: Fiction, Nonfiction (General), Poetry
ISBN Prefix(es): 0-86896; 1-86291
Number of titles published annually: 25 Print
Total Titles: 238 Print
Parent Company: Scholastic Australia Ltd, Railway Terrace, Lisarow, Gosford NSW
Shipping Address: Scholastic Australia Ltd, Railway Terrace, Lisarow, Gosford NSW
Warehouse: Scholastic Australia Ltd, Railway Terrace, Lisarow, Gosford NSW

On The Stone+
32 Campbell St, Ainslie ACT 2602
Tel: (06) 62576267 *Fax:* (06) 2497323
E-mail: thestone@dynamite.com.au
Key Personnel
Man Dir: Marye Prior
Subjects: Asian Studies, Regional Interests

Online Information Resources Pty Ltd
PO Box 476, Doncaster, Victoria 3108
Tel: (03) 98503361 *Fax:* (03) 98503641
Key Personnel
Dir: Sherrey Quinn
Subjects: Library & Information Sciences
ISBN Prefix(es): 0-646

Open Training & Education Network, see OTEN (Open Training & Education Network)

Openbook Publishers+
205 Halifax St, Adelaide, SA 5000
Mailing Address: GPO Box 1368, Adelaide, SA 5001
Tel: (08) 8223 5468 *Fax:* (08) 8223 4552
E-mail: enquiries@openbook.com.au
Web Site: www.openbook.com.au
Key Personnel
General Manager: Warren Schirmer
  E-mail: wschirmer@openbook.com.au

AUSTRALIA

Editorial & Rights & Permission: John Pfitzner
 E-mail: jpfitzner@openbook.com.au
Marketing Man: Wayne Gehling
 E-mail: wgehling@openbook.com.au
Founded: 1913
Subjects: Education, Religion - Protestant, Religion - Other
ISBN Prefix(es): 0-85910
Number of titles published annually: 20 Print
Total Titles: 180 Print
Bookshop(s): The Open Book, 110 Gawler Place, Adelaide, SA 5000; 61B Murray St, Tanunda, SA 5352; 20 McDougall St, Queensland 4064; Australia Arcade, Ruthven St, Toowoomba, Qld 4350; 198 Gray St, Hamilton, Victoria 3300; 703 Station St, Box Hill, Victoria 3128; 538 David St, Albury, NSW 2640

Oriental Publications+
16 Market St, Adelaide, SA 5000
Tel: (08) 8210 0863 Fax: (08) 8410 0863
E-mail: oriental@dove.net.au
Key Personnel
Dir: Tiny Bruzzone
Subjects: Antiques, Art, Asian Studies, Cookery, Language Arts, Linguistics, Religion - Buddhist, Religion - Hindu, Religion - Islamic
ISBN Prefix(es): 0-9577

Orin Books
25 Barkly St, St Kilda, Victoria 3182
Tel: (03) 9534 5680; (03) 9534 4746 Fax: (03) 9527 3308
Key Personnel
Man Dir: S E Shifrin
Member of Australian Publishers Association.
Subjects: Humor
ISBN Prefix(es): 1-875230; 0-9588190; 0-9588648; 0-9592263

OTEN (Open Training & Education Network)+
51 Wentworth Rd, Strathfield, NSW 2135
Tel: (02) 9715 8000; (02) 9715 8222 Fax: (02) 9715 8111; (02) 9715 8174
E-mail: oten.dir@tafensw.edu
Web Site: www.oten.edu.au
Key Personnel
Dir: Greeme Dobbs
Founded: 1994
Member of Australian Publishers Association; specialize in college textbooks & video cassettes.
Subjects: Accounting, Aeronautics, Aviation, Agriculture, Automotive, Business, Child Care & Development, Civil Engineering, Computer Science, Disability, Special Needs, Electronics, Electrical Engineering, English as a Second Language, Fashion, Finance, Management, Maritime, Marketing, Microcomputers, Real Estate
Parent Company: New South Wales Technical & Further Education Commission

Outback Books, imprint of Outback Books - CQU Press

Outback Books - CQU Press
Old Supreme Court, CQU, East Street Mall, Rockhampton, Qld 4702
Mailing Address: PO Box 1615, Rockhampton Mail Centre, Rockhampton, Qld 4700
Tel: (07) 4923 2520 Fax: (07) 4923 2525
E-mail: cqupress@cqu.edu.au
Web Site: www.outbackbooks.com
Key Personnel
Dir: Prof David Myers E-mail: d.myers@cqu.edu.au
Founded: 1993
Specialize in subjects about country heritage, regional history, South Pacific & Australiana.
Subjects: Biography, History, Nonfiction (General), Regional Interests
ISBN Prefix(es): 1-875998
Imprints: Outback Books; South Pacific Books

Outdoor Press Pty Ltd+
PO Box 866, Shepparton 3632
Tel: (03) 57905226 Fax: (03) 57905393
Web Site: www.goldexpeditions.com
Key Personnel
Manager: Douglas M Stone Tel: (0438) 369919
Founded: 1976
Specialize in gold & gemstone guides to Australia.
Subjects: Gold & Gemstones
Total Titles: 4 Print

Owl Books, imprint of Pan Macmillan Australia Pty Ltd

Owl Publishing
22 Rooding St, Brighton, Victoria 3186
Tel: (03) 95966064 Fax: (03) 95966942
Key Personnel
Contact: Helen Nickas
ISBN Prefix(es): 0-9586390

Oxfam Community Aid Abroad
Affiliate of Oxfam International
156 George St, First Floor, Fitzroy, Victoria 3065
Tel: (03) 9289 9444 Fax: (03) 9419 5895
E-mail: enquire@caa.org.au
Web Site: www.caa.org.au
Key Personnel
Publications Coordinator: Sarah Lowe
Specialize in overseas aid & development.
Subjects: Economics, Education, Environmental Studies, Foreign Countries, Genealogy, Government, Political Science, Health, Nutrition, Women's Studies
Associate Companies: Oxfam Great Britain
Distributed by Oxfam Great Britain

Jill Oxton Publications Pty Ltd+
PO Box 283, Park Holme, SA 5043
Tel: (08) 2762722 Fax: (08) 3743494
E-mail: jill@jilloxtonxstitch.com
Web Site: www.jilloxtonxstitch.com
Key Personnel
Contact: Jill Oxton
Founded: 1989
Publishing cross stitch & beading charted designs.
Subjects: Crafts, Games, Hobbies
ISBN Prefix(es): 0-9587576
Number of titles published annually: 4 Print
Total Titles: 50 Print

Oz Publishing Co Pty Ltd+
PO Box 1083, Milton, Qld 4064
Tel: (07) 8922313 Fax: (07) 8462491
Key Personnel
Official Delegate: Bob Raftopoulos
Founded: 1982
Subjects: Art, Natural History, Regional Interests
ISBN Prefix(es): 0-947207

Pacific Publications (Australia) Pty Ltd
GPO Box 3408, Sydney, NSW 2001
Tel: (02) 20231 Fax: (02) 2883322
Key Personnel
Publisher: Geoff Husey
Founded: 1930
Papua New Guinea Handbook.
Subjects: Agriculture, Regional Interests
ISBN Prefix(es): 0-85807
Parent Company: News Ltd
Branch Office(s)
Pacific Publications, Herald & Weekly Times Bldg, 61 Flinders Lane, Melbourne, Victoria
Orders to: Robert Brown & Associates, 7 Atherton St, Buranda, Qld 4102

Pademelon Press+
7/3 Packard Ave, Castle Hill, NSW 2154
Mailing Address: PO Box 6500, Baulkham Hills BC, NSW 2153
Tel: (02) 9634-4655 Fax: (02) 9680-4634
E-mail: info@pademelonpress.com.au
Web Site: www.pademelonpress.com.au
Key Personnel
Dir & International Rights: Rodney Kenner
Founded: 1990
Specialize in early childhood teacher resource & reference books.
Subjects: Child Care & Development
ISBN Prefix(es): 1-876138
Associate Companies: The Book Garden Pty Ltd
Distributor for Child Care Information Exchange; Building Blocks; Gryphon House; High/Scope Press; Humanics Publishing; Parenting Press; Redleaf Press; School-Age Notes; Teacher's College Press; Teaching Strategies; Totline; William Publishing Co (all restricted to Australia & New Zealand)
Bookshop(s): 173 Elizabeth St, Brisbane, Qld 4000

Charles Paine Pty Ltd
8 Ferris St, North Parrmatta, NSW 2151
Tel: (02) 9890-1388 Fax: (02) 9890-1915
ISBN Prefix(es): 0-909687

Pali Text Society, imprint of Windhorse Books

Palm Beach Press
40 Palm Beach Rd, Palm Beach, NSW 2108
Tel: (066) 46-1622 Fax: (02) 9946-1515
Key Personnel
Contact: Nat Young E-mail: nato@hor.com.au
Founded: 1976
Subjects: Surfing
ISBN Prefix(es): 0-9591816

Palms Press
87 Newport Rd, Dora Creek, NSW 2264
Tel: (049) 731236
Key Personnel
Contact: H K Garland
Subjects: Environmental Studies, History, How-to, Humor, Public Administration
ISBN Prefix(es): 0-9593041

Pan, imprint of Pan Macmillan Australia Pty Ltd

Pan Macmillan Australia, see Pan Macmillan Australia Pty Ltd

Pan Macmillan Australia Pty Ltd+
Formerly Pan Macmillan Australia
Level 18, St Martins Tower, 31 Market St, Sydney, NSW 2000
Tel: (02) 9285 9100 Fax: (02) 9285 9100
E-mail: pansyd@macmillan.com.au (General); panpublicity@macmillan.com.au (Publicity)
Web Site: www.panmacmillan.com.au
Key Personnel
Publishing Dir: James Fraser E-mail: james.fraser@macmillan.com.au
Sales Dir, Melbourne Office: Peter Phillips
 Tel: (03) 9825 1000 Fax: (03) 9825 1015
 E-mail: peter.phillips@macmillan.com.au
Product Department Manager, Melbourne Office: Andrew Farrell Tel: (03) 9825 1000 Fax: (03) 9825 1015 E-mail: andrew.farrell@macmillan.com.au
Founded: 1983
Submissions must include a short cover letter (1 or 2 pages), along with a detailed chapter outline for nonfiction or a synopsis of the plot for fiction. See web site for additional submission information. No children's picture books, short story collections or poetry.

Subjects: Biography, Fiction, Health, Nutrition, Humor, Literature, Literary Criticism, Essays, Nonfiction (General), Self-Help, Travel
ISBN Prefix(es): 0-330; 0-7329
Parent Company: Macmillan Ltd, United Kingdom
Imprints: Boxtree; Rod Campbell Books; Channel 4; Forge; Griffin; Henry Holt; Let's Go; Macmillan; Macquarie Library; Owl Books; Pan; Pancake; Papermac; Picador; Priddy & Bicknell; Sidgwick & Jackson; St Martins; Sun; Tor Books
Branch Office(s)
Level 5, 627 Chapel St, South Yarra, Victoria 3141 *Tel:* (03) 9825 1000 *Fax:* (03) 9825 1015 *E-mail:* panmel@macmillan.com.au *Web Site:* www.panmacmillan.com.au
Warehouse: Macmillan Distribution Services Pty Ltd, 56 Parkwest Dr, Derrimut, Victoria 3030, Man Dir: Andy Palmer *Tel:* (03) 9825 1000 *Fax:* (03) 9825 3210 *E-mail:* mds@macmillan.com.au *Web Site:* www.ozemail.com.au/~mds; www.macmillan.com.au

Pan Pacific Publications+
PO Box 250, Moorooka, Qld 4106
Tel: (07) 38480350 *Fax:* (07) 38484945
Key Personnel
Head of Company: Donald Jefferies
Founded: 1982
Subjects: Religion - Other, Theology
ISBN Prefix(es): 0-9596931
Parent Company: Donald Jefferies (Q) Pty Ltd
Subsidiaries: Paramount Books
Orders to: Gary Allen Pty Ltd, 9 Cooper St, Smithfield, NSW 2164

Pancake, *imprint of* Pan Macmillan Australia Pty Ltd

Pandani Press
17 Derwentwater Ave, Sandy Bay, TAS 7005
Tel: (03) 62349925
E-mail: pandani@iprimus.com.au
Key Personnel
Head of Company: Sue Backhouse *Tel:* (03) 6225 1956
Subjects: Art, Natural History
Total Titles: 1 Print

Panorama Books, *imprint of* St George Books

Pantheon, *imprint of* Random House Australia

Pants on Fire, *imprint of* Crawford House Publishing

Papermac, *imprint of* Pan Macmillan Australia Pty Ltd

Papyrus Publishing
c/o Post Office, Scarsdale, Victoria 3351
Tel: (03) 9758 9395 *Fax:* (03) 9752 4032
Web Site: www.papyrus.com
Key Personnel
Contact: Herbert Stein
Founded: 1991
Subjects: Ethnicity, Fiction, Literature, Literary Criticism, Essays, Poetry
ISBN Prefix(es): 1-875934

Parabel Place+
67 Exeter Rd, North Croydon, Victorian 3136
Mailing Address: PO Box 528, North Croydon 3136
Tel: (03) 97271894 *Fax:* (03) 97271857
Key Personnel
Head of Company: Brigitte Lambert
Founded: 1991

Member of Society of Women Writers (Vic Branch) Australia.
Subjects: Cookery, Women's Studies
ISBN Prefix(es): 0-646

Pascal Press+
655 Parramutta Rd, Leiuhhardt, NSW 2040
Mailing Address: PO Box 250, Glebe, NSW 2037
Tel: (02) 8585 4044 *Fax:* (02) 8585 4001
Web Site: www.askblake.com.au
Key Personnel
Man Dir: Matthew B Sandblom *Tel:* (612) 85854024 *Fax:* (612) 85854024
E-mail: matthew@pascalpress.com.au
Primary Publisher: Katy Pike *Tel:* (612) 95186777 *Fax:* (612) 95186888
Founded: 1989
Specialize in school publishing.
Member of Australian Publishers Association.
Subjects: Education
Total Titles: 1,000 Print; 16 CD-ROM; 50 Online; 50 E-Book; 20 Audio
Online services available through World Wide Web.
Parent Company: S D & M Software Pty Ltd
Subsidiaries: Blake Education Pty Ltd; Video Education Australia
Distributed by Nelson Thomes (United Kingdom); Sundance (United States)
Distributor for Wild Daisies (New Zealand)
Shipping Address: TLD Distribution, 15-23 Hellen Ave, Moorebank, NSW 2170, Chris Stasis *Tel:* (0612) 8585 4044 *Fax:* (0612) 8585 4001

Pascoe Publishing+
30 Gambler St, Apollo Bay, Victoria 3233
Mailing Address: PO Box 42, Apollo Bay, Victoria 3233
Tel: (052) 379227 *Fax:* (052) 376559
Web Site: www.bruce-pascoe.pho-online.net
Key Personnel
Dir: Bruce Pascoe *E-mail:* pascoe@vicnet.net.au
Dir & International Rights: Lyn Harwood
Founded: 1983
Subjects: Fiction, History, Literature, Literary Criticism, Essays, Social Sciences, Sociology, Australian Literary Fiction
ISBN Prefix(es): 0-947087
Number of titles published annually: 4 Print
Total Titles: 110 Print
Imprints: Blackstone; Seaglass
Subsidiaries: Koori Tours

Pavillion, *imprint of* Random House Australia

PCE Press
35 Amelia St, Fortitude Valley, Qld 4006
Mailing Address: PO Box 1508, Fortitude Valley, Qld 4006
Tel: (07) 3252 1114 *Fax:* (07) 3852 1564
E-mail: webmaster@pcq.org.au
Web Site: www.pcq.org.au
Key Personnel
Dir: Rev J C Nicol *E-mail:* director@pcq.org.au
Publications Department of the Presbyterian Church of Queensland.
Subjects: Religion - Protestant

Pearson Education Australia+
Unit 4, Level 2, 14 Aquatic Drive, Frenchs Forest NSW 2086
Mailing Address: LMB 507, Frenchs Forest NSW 1640
Tel: (02) 9454 2200 *Fax:* (02) 9453 0089
E-mail: firstname.lastname@pearsoned.com.au
Web Site: www.pearson.com.au
Key Personnel
Man Dir: Pat Evans
Financial Controller: Ted Impey

General Manager, Humanities & Sciences: David Barnett
General Manager, Professional & Vocational Education: Gillian May
General Manager, Business & Economics: Michael Page
General Manager, Computer, Trade & Reference: Paul Summers
Educational Publishers.
Subjects: Accounting, Anthropology, Behavioral Sciences, Biological Sciences, Business, Child Care & Development, Communications, Computer Science, Criminology, Economics, Education, Engineering (General), Fiction, Government, Political Science, Health, Nutrition, History, Journalism, Labor, Industrial Relations, Language Arts, Linguistics, Law, Library & Information Sciences, Management, Mathematics, Medicine, Nursing, Dentistry, Science (General), Social Sciences, Sociology
ISBN Prefix(es): 0-201; 0-582; 0-7015; 0-589; 0-8053; 1-56609; 0-86911
Number of titles published annually: 500 Print
Parent Company: Pearson Plc
Imprints: Prentice Hall; Addison Wesley; Longman
Branch Office(s)
95 Coventry St, South Melbourne, Victoria 3205
Suite B, Level 2, 57 Coronation Drive, Milton, Qld 4000
Unit 29, 3rd floor, 123B Colin St, West Perth, WA 6005
Unit 5, 532 - 542 Station St, Box Hill, Victoria 3128 *Tel:* (03) 9899 9200 (sales); (03) 9899 8699 (editorial)
CWA House, 1174 Hay St, West Perth, WA 6005 *Tel:* (09) 322 6054 *Fax:* (09) 321 0054

Penguin, *imprint of* Penguin Books Australia Ltd

Penguin Books Australia Ltd+
250 Camberwell Rd, Camberwell, Victoria 3124
Mailing Address: PO Box 701, Hawthorn, Victoria 3122
Tel: (03) 9811 2400 *Fax:* (03) 9811 2620
Web Site: www.penguin.com.au
Key Personnel
Chief Executive Officer: P Field
Publishing Dir: Robert Sessions *Tel:* (03) 9811 2468 *Fax:* (03) 9811 2621 *E-mail:* robert-sessions@penguin.com.au
Sales Dir: P Blake
Mgr Rts: Peg McColl
Founded: 1946
Subjects: Biography, Cookery, Fiction, Humor, Literature, Literary Criticism, Essays, Nonfiction (General), Science Fiction, Fantasy, Self-Help, Travel
ISBN Prefix(es): 0-14; 0-670; 1-872031; 0-86914
Parent Company: Pearson Australia Ltd
Ultimate Parent Company: Pearson plc (London)
Associate Companies: Pearson Education; The Penguin Group Ltd Books Canada Ltd, 10 Alcorn Ave, Suite 300, Toronto, ON M4V 3B2, Canada; Penguin Books (NZ) Ltd, New Zealand; Penguin USA, 375 Hudson St, New York, NY 10014-3657, United States; Penguin Books India Pvt Ltd, India; Penguin Books (South Africa) (Pty) Ltd, South Africa
Imprints: Hamish Hamilton; Michael Joseph; New American Library; Penguin; Puffin; Viking; Signet; Frederick Warne
Divisions: Penguin Adult, Penguin Children
Branch Office(s)
Penguin Putnam Inc, 375 Hudson St, New York, NY 10014-3657, United States

Perfection Learning Corporation, *imprint of* Hawker Brownlow

Peribo Pty Ltd
58 Beaumont Rd, Mount Kuring-gai, NSW 2080

Tel: (02) 4457 0011 *Fax:* (02) 9457 0022
E-mail: peribo@bigpond.com
Key Personnel
Chairman: Edward Coffey
Founded: 1981
ISBN Prefix(es): 1-86322

Periscope Press, *imprint of* Roland Harvey Studios

Personal Power Press International Inc, *imprint of* Hawker Brownlow

Phoenix Education Pty Ltd+
1 Nelson Pl, South Melbourne 3205
Tel: (03) 9699 8377; (02) 9809 3579 *Fax:* (03) 9699 9242; (02) 9808 1430
Key Personnel
Dir: Barney Rivers
Founded: 1991
Subjects: Language Arts, Linguistics, Mathematics
ISBN Prefix(es): 1-875695
Orders to: Phoenix Education, PO Box 3141, Putney, NSW 2112

Picador, *imprint of* Pan Macmillan Australia Pty Ltd

Pimlico, *imprint of* Random House Australia

Pinchgut Press
6 Oaks Ave, Cremorne, NSW 2090
Tel: (02) 9908-2402 *Fax:* (02) 9960-4689
Key Personnel
Chief Executive & Dir: Marjorie Pizer
Art Dir: Judy Lane
Founded: 1947
Small independent publisher.
Subjects: Poetry, Self-Help
ISBN Prefix(es): 0-9598913; 0-949625
Total Titles: 17 Print

Pinevale Publications+
Pike Rd, Emerald Creek, Mareeba, Qld 4880
Mailing Address: PO Box 822, Mareeba, Qld 4880
Tel: (07) 93-3169
Key Personnel
Publisher & Editor: Glenville Pike
Founded: 1981
Subjects: Biography, History, Travel
ISBN Prefix(es): 0-9593783; 1-875375
Number of titles published annually: 2 Print
Total Titles: 23 Print
Orders to: 45 Pike Rd, Emerald Creek, Mareeba, Qld *Tel:* (07) 933169

Pioneer Design Studio Pty Ltd+
31 North Rd, Lilydale, Victoria 3140
Tel: (03) 9735 5505
Key Personnel
Head of Company: Derrick I Stone
Sales Manager: Carolyn R Stone
Subjects: Environmental Studies, Gardening, Plants, History
ISBN Prefix(es): 0-909674

Pisces, *imprint of* Lonely Planet Publications Pty Ltd

PJ Publishing
Professional Centre, Taylors Rd, Norfolk Island 2899
Mailing Address: PO Box 410, Norfolk Island 2899
Tel: (06723) 22-368 *Fax:* (06723) 22-218

Plantagenet Press+
PO Box 934, Fremantle, WA 6160
Tel: (09) 4304466 *Fax:* (09) 4305217
E-mail: 100240.3406rogergarwood@compuserve.com
Key Personnel
Dir: Trish Ainslie
Founded: 1989
Also acts as distributor.
Subjects: Fiction, History, Humor, Journalism, Nonfiction (General)
ISBN Prefix(es): 0-646; 1-875968
Book Club(s): Lucky Book Club

Plantain Park
PO Box 142, Creswick, Victoria 3363
Key Personnel
Head of Company: Bridh Hancock
Founded: 1988
Subjects: Drama, Theater, Humor, Poetry, Religion - Other, Theology
ISBN Prefix(es): 1-875347

Platypus Press Australia, *imprint of* Dragon Press

Playbox Theatre Co+
113 Sturt St, Southbank, VIC 3006
Tel: (03) 9685 5100 *Fax:* (03) 9685 5112
E-mail: playbox@netspace.net.au
Key Personnel
General Manager: Jill Smith
Subjects: Drama, Theater
ISBN Prefix(es): 0-7326
Distributed by Currency Press
Distributor for Currency Press

Playlab Press
Level 3, 109 Edward St, Brisbane, Qld 4000
Tel: 3236 1396 *Fax:* 3236 1026
E-mail: cluster@thehub.com.au
Web Site: www.thehub.com.au/~cluster/playlab
Key Personnel
Project Officer: Louise Terry
Founded: 1972
Subjects: Drama, Theater, History, Humor, Literature, Literary Criticism, Essays, Music, Dance, Women's Studies, Australian, Youth, Comedy
ISBN Prefix(es): 0-908156

Jurriaan Plesman
17/54-56 Beach Rd, Bondi Beach, NSW 2026
Tel: (02) 91306202 *Fax:* (02) 91306202
Subjects: Behavioral Sciences, Criminology, Health, Nutrition, How-to, Medicine, Nursing, Dentistry, Psychology, Psychiatry, Self-Help, Social Sciences, Sociology
ISBN Prefix(es): 1-86252

Plum Press+
PO Box 419, Toowong, Qld 4066
Tel: (07) 3870 2964 *Fax:* (07) 3870 2860
Web Site: www.justasktom.com
Key Personnel
Head of Company: Neil Flanagan *E-mail:* neilfl@squirrel.com.au
Founded: 1989
Subjects: Management
ISBN Prefix(es): 0-9577

Pluto Press Australia+
248 Johnston St, Annandale, NSW 2038
Mailing Address: Locked Bag 199, Annandale 2038
Tel: (02) 9692 5111 *Fax:* (02) 9692 5192
E-mail: info@socialchange.net.au
Web Site: www.plutoaustralia.com
Key Personnel
Man Dir: Sean Kidney
Publisher: Tony Moore
Founded: 1984
Subjects: Environmental Studies, Government, Political Science, History, Labor, Industrial Relations, Social Sciences, Sociology, Women's Studies
ISBN Prefix(es): 0-949138; 1-86403
Parent Company: Social Change Media
Associate Companies: Social Change On-Line
Divisions: University of NSW Press
Orders to: University of NSW Press, 45 Beach St, Coogee 2031 *Tel:* (02) 9664 0999 *Fax:* (02) 9664 5420

The Polding Press+
343 Elizabeth St, Melbourne, Victoria 3000
Tel: (03) 675157; (03) 671740 *Fax:* (03) 96390879
Key Personnel
Head of Company: Therese Hilton
Founded: 1968
Subjects: Biography, History, Religion - Other
ISBN Prefix(es): 0-85884
Bookshop(s): Central Catholic Library Bookshop, 322 Lonsdale St, Melbourne, Victoria 3000 *Tel:* (03) 9639 0844

Pollitecon Publications
PO Box 324, Five Dock, NSW 2046
Tel: (02) 9713 7608 *Fax:* (02) 9713 1004
Web Site: members.ozemail.com.au/~pollitec/
Key Personnel
Publisher: Victor Bivell *E-mail:* vbivell@ozemail.com.au
Founded: 1992
Subjects: Anthropology, Ethnicity, Foreign Countries, History, Literature, Literary Criticism, Essays, Regional Interests, Social Sciences, Sociology, Macedonians of Greece, Human Rights
ISBN Prefix(es): 0-9586789
Total Titles: 6 Print

Power Publications+
Power Institute, Mills Bldg, A26, University of Sydney, Sydney, NSW 2006
Tel: (02) 9351 6904 *Fax:* (02) 9351 7323
E-mail: power.publications@arthist.usyd.edu.au
Web Site: metapix.arts.usyd.edu.au/power/institute/Publications
Key Personnel
Dir: Terry Smith
Publisher: Elisabeth Schwaiger *E-mail:* elisabeth.schwaiger@fine.arts.su.edu.au
Executive Editor: Julian Pefanis
Founded: 1987
Subjects: Art, Film, Video
ISBN Prefix(es): 0-909952
Distributed by Indiana University Press (North America & Canada)

Prentice Hall, *imprint of* Pearson Education Australia

Press for Success+
One Ensign Lane, East Perth WA 6004
Mailing Address: Perth Business Centre, PO Box 8142, Perth BC 6849
Tel: (08) 9221 6166 *Fax:* (08) 9221 6166
E-mail: press4@press4success.com.au
Web Site: www.press4success.com.au
Key Personnel
Dir: Jill Yelland
Founded: 1993
Member of International Type Designers Association A Type 1.
Subjects: Architecture & Interior Design, Art, Business, How-to
ISBN Prefix(es): 0-646
Parent Company: Yelland & Associates Pty Ltd
Associate Companies: Yelland INK

PressXpress, *imprint of* McGraw-Hill Australia Pty Ltd

PUBLISHERS

AUSTRALIA

Price Publishing+
5B/5 Girilang Ave, Vaucluse 2030
Tel: (02) 9337-1598 *Fax:* (02) 9337-2158
E-mail: pricesys@localnet.com.au
Founded: 1994
Subjects: Education, Microcomputers, Learning & Training

Priddy & Bicknell, *imprint of* Pan Macmillan Australia Pty Ltd

Priestley Consulting+
PO Box 1003, Buderim, Qld 4556
Tel: (07) 54453968 *Fax:* (07) 54458288
E-mail: priestd@squirrel.com.au
Key Personnel
Contact: Andrew Priestly *E-mail:* adpriestly@ozemail.com.au
Subjects: Advertising, Child Care & Development, Education, Marketing, Self-Help, Social Sciences, Sociology
ISBN Prefix(es): 0-9587298

Primary English Teaching Association
PO Box 3106, Marrickville, NSW 2204
Tel: (02) 9565 1277 *Fax:* (02) 9565 1070
E-mail: info@peta.edu.au
Web Site: www.peta.edu.au
Key Personnel
Executive Dir: Peter O'Brien
ISBN Prefix(es): 0-909955; 1-875622

Prospect, *imprint of* Prospect Media Pty Ltd

Prospect Media Pty Ltd+
Level 1, 7173 Lithgow St, St Leonards, NSW 2065
Tel: (02) 93496077 *Fax:* (02) 94395411
E-mail: prospect@prospectmedia.com.au
Web Site: www.prospectmedia.com.au
Key Personnel
Man Dir & Publisher: Oliver Freeman
Finance Manager: Vicky Mahadeva
Managing Editor: Jenny Berich
Senior Editor: Carolyn Stott
Marketing Manager: Matthew Langman
Sales Manager: Sue Howard
Founded: 1987
Member of Australian Publishers Association; Publish Australia.
Subjects: Accounting, Business, Computer Science, Environmental Studies, Finance, Law
ISBN Prefix(es): 1-86316; 0-947309; 0-949553
Total Titles: 40 Print
Parent Company: Oliver Freeman Pty Ltd
Imprints: Global Business Network; Heresy Press; Legal Books; Oliver Freeman Editions; Prospect
Subsidiaries: Australian Business Network Pty Ltd
Divisions: Legal Books; Prospect; Legal Publications
Bookshop(s): Legal Publications, 121 William St, Melbourne 3000
Book Club(s): ABN Bookclub
Shipping Address: Mezzanine Level, G10 Bldg, 60-70 Elizabeth St, Sydney, NSW 2000
Orders to: Mezzanine Level, G10 Bldg, 60-70 Elizabeth St, Sydney, NSW 2000

Protestant Publications
7 Park St, Peakhurst NSW 2210
Tel: (02) 98684591 *Fax:* (02) 98687953
Key Personnel
Contact: D Shelton
Founded: 1945
Subjects: History, Religion - Catholic, Religion - Protestant

Prufrock Press, *imprint of* Hawker Brownlow

The Psychological Corporation, *imprint of* Harcourt Australia Pty Ltd

Puffin, *imprint of* Penguin Books Australia Ltd

The Pythagorean Press+
27 Power Ave, Alexandria, NSW 2015
Tel: (02) 3193555 *Fax:* (02) 9314 1760
Key Personnel
Publisher: Dr David Phillips
Founded: 1975
Member of NAPRA.
Subjects: Environmental Studies, Health, Nutrition, Parapsychology
ISBN Prefix(es): 0-9587696; 0-9596389; 1-875281
Parent Company: Meridian Promotions Pty Ltd (ACN 051 898 223)

Quakers Hill Press+
6 Caper Pl, Quakers Hill, NSW 2763
Tel: (02) 9626 6112 *Fax:* (02) 6269846
E-mail: dayp@mpx.com.au
Key Personnel
Publisher: Peter Day
Founded: 1993
Subjects: Biography, Fiction, History, Mathematics, Nonfiction (General), Philosophy
ISBN Prefix(es): 1-876192

Queen Victoria Museum & Art Gallery Publications
Division of Launceston City Council
2 Wellington St, Launceston, Tas 7250
Tel: (03) 6323 3777 *Fax:* (03) 6323 3776
E-mail: library@qvmag.tas.gov.au
Web Site: www.qvmag.tas.gov.au
Key Personnel
Editor: Mr Chris B Tassell *E-mail:* chris.tassell@qvmag.tas.gov.au
Publications Coordinator: Kaye Dimmack *E-mail:* kaye.dimmack@qvmag.tas.gov.au
Founded: 1891
Operated as a department of Launceston City Council.
Subjects: Anthropology, Archaeology, Art, Biological Sciences, Earth Sciences, History, Natural History, Physical Sciences
ISBN Prefix(es): 0-7246
Number of titles published annually: 1 Print
Total Titles: 27 Print

Queensland Art Gallery
Melbourne St, South Brisbane, Qld 4101
Mailing Address: PO Box 3686, South Brisbane, Qld 4101
Tel: (07) 3840 7333; (07) 3840 7303 *Fax:* (07) 3844 8865; (07) 3840 7350
E-mail: gallery@qag.qld.gov.au
Web Site: www.gag.gld.gov.au
Key Personnel
Manager Gallery Shop: Linda Mehan *E-mail:* linda.mehan@qag.qld.gov.au
Gallery Dir: Mr Doug Hall
Subjects: Art, Asian Studies
Number of titles published annually: 6 Print
Total Titles: 15 Print
Distributed by Thames & Hudson Australia Pty Ltd
Orders to: Gallery Shop, South Brisbane, Contact: Steve Pearce *Tel:* (07) 38 40 713 2 *Fax:* (07) 38 40 714 9 *E-mail:* steve.pearce@qag.qld.gov.au *Web Site:* www.gallerystore.com.au

R & R Publications Marketing P/L+
12 Edward St, Brunswick, Victoria 3056
Mailing Address: PO Box 254, Carlton North, Victoria 3054
Tel: (03) 9381 2199 *Fax:* (03) 9381 2689

Key Personnel
Publisher & International Rights: Richard Carroll *E-mail:* richardc@bigpond.net.au
Founded: 1989
Book packagers; Specializes in cooking, drinking & lifestyles.
Subjects: Cookery, Crafts, Games, Hobbies, Gardening, Plants, Health, Nutrition, How-to, Sports, Athletics, Wine & Spirits, Lifestyle
ISBN Prefix(es): 1-875655
Number of titles published annually: 60 Print
Total Titles: 140 Print; 4 CD-ROM

R*O*D Books, *imprint of* Cornucopia Press

Radiating Books
6 Sapphire Crescent, Coffs Harbour 2450
Tel: (066) 536280 *Fax:* (066) 514970
Key Personnel
Head of Company: Helen Seccombe
Member of OMCE (Organization for Management of Cultural Endeavour).
ISBN Prefix(es): 0-646

Rainbow Book Agencies Pty Ltd+
303 Arthur St, Fairfield, Victoria 3078
Tel: (03) 9481 6611 *Fax:* (03) 9481 2371
E-mail: rba@rainbowbooks.com.au
Web Site: rainbowbooks.com.au
Key Personnel
Dir: Rob Humphrys *E-mail:* rob.humphrys@rainbowbooks.com.au
Founded: 1985
National distibution to the religious & mind, body & spirit trade in Australia.
Subjects: Religion - Other
ISBN Prefix(es): 1-875138
Imprints: Acorn Press; David Lovell Publishing; Artemis Publishing; Australian Association for the Study of Religion; Beyond Bullying Association; Canadian Conference of Catholic Bishops; Christian Research Association (CRA); Desbooks; Emmaus Productions; Fairfield Press; Galations Group; Inner City Books; JBCE; Jesuit Publications/Aurora Books; Templegate Publishers; Uniting Education; Victorian National Parks Association; Word of Life Distributors Pty Ltd
Distributed by Eclipse Music; Leigh Newton; Random House NY (Religious titles only); Redemptorist Publications; Regina Press-Malhame; Spectrum Publications; St pauls Publications
Distributor for Ateliers et Presses de Taize; Earth Dance Music; Forest of Peace Publishing; Innisfree Press; INTJ Books; Liguori Publication/Triumph Books; Liturgy Training Publications; Merciful Love Music (UK); Orbis Books; Our Sunday Visitor; Paulist Press; Resource Publications; Resurrection Press; St Anthony Messenger Press/Franciscan Communications; St Valdimir's Seminary Press (SVS Press); Weston Priory Productions; World Library Publications

Raincloud Productions
6 Castlereach Cres, Macquarie 2614
Mailing Address: PO Box 451, Albury 2640
Tel: (060) 2511765
Key Personnel
Head of Company: Craig Dent
Founded: 1989
Subjects: Photography, Poetry
ISBN Prefix(es): 7-316
Orders to: PO Box 451, Albury, NSW 2640

Rainforest Publishing+
8 Napier St, Paddington, NSW 2021
Tel: (02) 93313004 *Fax:* (02) 93805729
E-mail: rod.ritchie@sfine.arts.sa.edu.au
Key Personnel
Head of Company: Rod Ritchie
Founded: 1985

Subjects: Environmental Studies, History
ISBN Prefix(es): 0-947134
Distributed by Tower Books

Rams Skull Press
12 Fairyland Rd, Kuranda, Qld 4872
Tel: (07) 4093 7474 *Fax:* (07) 4051 4484
E-mail: ramskull@tpg.com.au
Key Personnel
Contact: Ron Edwards
Subjects: Crafts, Games, Hobbies
Number of titles published annually: 20 Print
Total Titles: 130 Print

Random House, *imprint of* Random House Australia

Random House Australia+
Formerly Random House Australia Pty Ltd
Subsidiary of Bertelsmann AG
20 Alfred St, Milson's Point, NSW 2061
Tel: (02) 9954 9966 *Fax:* (02) 9954 4562; (02) 9954 9008
E-mail: randomhouse@randomhouse.com.au
Key Personnel
Man Dir: Margaret Seale
Head of Publishing, Random House: Jane Palfreyman
Sales & Marketing Dir: Carol Davidson
Deputy Man Dir: Margaret Seale
Publisher, Bantam Doubleday: Fiona Henderson
Children's Publisher: Linsay Knight
Illustrated - Managing Editor: Jude McGee
Head of Publicity: Karen Reid
Rights & Permission: Nerrilee Weir
Business Man: Andrew Leake
Production Man: Lisa Hanrahan
Agencies: Andersen Press; Everyman's Library; TSR; Pavillion; Robinson; Virgin; World Book International, BBC.
APA Australia.
Subjects: Fiction, Nonfiction (General)
ISBN Prefix(es): 0-09
Ultimate Parent Company: Bertelsmann AG
Associate Companies: Random House NZ, 18 Poland Road, Glenfield, Auckland, New Zealand *Tel:* (09) 444 7197 *Fax:* (09) 444 7524; Random House South Africa, Endulini, East Wing, 5A Jubilee Road, Parktown 2193, South Africa *Tel:* (011) 484 3538 *Fax:* (011) 484 6180; Random House UK, 20 Vauxhall Bridge Rd, London SW1V 2SA, United Kingdom *Tel:* (020) 8840 8400 *Fax:* (020) 8840 8408; Random House, Inc, 201 E 50th St, New York, NY 10022, United States *Tel:* (212) 940-7478 *Fax:* (212) 572-6045
Imprints: Arrow; Ballantine; Century; Chatto & Windus; Del Rey; Ebury Press; Fawcett; Fodor; Hutchinson; Jonathon Cape; Random House; Knopf Publishing; Pantheon; Pimlico; Rider; Heinemann; Minerva; Secker & Warburg; Anchor; Anderson; Avon; Bantam Books; BBC Worldwide; Dell Publishing; Black Swan; Broadway Books; Corgi; Crown Publishing Group; Doubleday; Hamlyn Childrens; Living Books; Mammoth UK; Pavillion; Ravette; Red Fox; Robinson; Running Press; Sesame Street; Vermillion; Vintage; Virgin; Egmont
Shipping Address: 16 Dalmore Dr, Scoresby, Victoria 3179 *Tel:* (03) 9753 4511 *Fax:* (03) 9753 3944
Warehouse: 16 Dalmore Dr, Scoresby, Victoria 3179
Orders to: 16 Dalmore Dr, Scoresby, Victoria 3179 *Tel:* (03) 97534511 *Fax:* (03) 94533944

Random House Australia Pty Ltd, see Random House Australia

Rangging Yeshe Publications, *imprint of* Windhorse Books

Rankin Publishers
PO Box 500, Sumner Park 4074
Tel: (07) 3376 9115 *Fax:* (07) 3376 9360
E-mail: info@rankin.com.au
Web Site: www.rankin.com.au
Key Personnel
Proprietor & International Rights: Robert Rankin *E-mail:* info@rankin.com.au
Founded: 1980
Subjects: Outdoor Recreation, Photography, Physics, Science (General), Australiana
ISBN Prefix(es): 0-9592418

Ravette, *imprint of* Random House Australia

Rawlhouse Publishing
PO Box 145, West Perth 6005
Tel: (08) 9321 8951 *Fax:* (08) 9481 1914
E-mail: info@rawlhouse.com
Web Site: www.rawlinsons.com
Key Personnel
Dir & Editor: I A Baillie
Founded: 1983
Construction cost reference books.
Total Titles: 2 Print

RD Press, *imprint of* Reader's Digest (Australia) Pty Ltd

Reader's Digest (Australia) Pty Ltd+
26-32 Waterloo St, Surry Hills, Sydney, NSW 2010
Mailing Address: GPO Box 4353, Sydney, NSW 2001
Tel: (02) 96906935 *Fax:* (02) 96906390
Cable: READIGEST SYDNEY
Key Personnel
Man Dir: William Toohey
Editorial, Condensed Books: Joshua Shrubb
Editorial, General Books: Margaret Fraser
Publisher, Catalog & Trade Books: Robert Sarsfield
Founded: 1946
Subjects: Education
ISBN Prefix(es): 0-86438; 0-909486; 0-949819; 0-86449; 0-9577023
Parent Company: The Reader's Digest Association Inc, PO Box 235, Pleasantville, NY 10570, United States
Imprints: RD Press; Reader's Digest Condensed Books
Book Club(s): Reader's Digest Condensed Books
Orders to: Hodder Headline Australia, PO Box 386, Rydalmere, NSW 2116

Reader's Digest Condensed Books, *imprint of* Reader's Digest (Australia) Pty Ltd

Ready-Ed Publications+
11/17 Foley St, Balcatta WA 6021
Mailing Address: PO Box 276, Greenwood, WA 6024
Tel: (08) 9349 6111 *Fax:* (08) 9349 7222
E-mail: info@readyed.com.au
Key Personnel
International Rights: Tim Lowson *E-mail:* tim@readyed.com.au
Founded: 1984
Subjects: Education
ISBN Prefix(es): 1-83697

The Real Estate Institute of Australia+
16 Thesiger Court, Deakin, West ACT 2600
Mailing Address: PO Box 234, Deakin, West ACT 2600
Tel: (02) 6282 4277 *Fax:* (02 6285 2444
E-mail: reia@reiaustralia.com.au
Web Site: www.reiaustralia.com.au
Key Personnel
Publisher: Sandra Green

Subjects: Accounting, Advertising, Business, Finance, Management, Marketing, Real Estate, Self-Help
ISBN Prefix(es): 0-909784
Imprints: REIA; RIAL
Distributor for Dearborn Trade (Australia & New Zealand)

Red Fox, *imprint of* Random House Australia

Reed Educational Publishing Australia+
Division of Reed Educational & Professional Publishing
22 Salmon St, Port Melbourne, Victoria 3207
Mailing Address: PO Box 460, Port Melbourne, Victoria 3207
Tel: (03) 9245 7188 *Fax:* (03) 9245 7265
E-mail: admin@reededucation.com.au; customerservice@reededucation.com.au
Web Site: www.reededucation.com.au
Key Personnel
Man Dir: David O'Brian *Tel:* (03) 92457103 *Fax:* (03) 92457173 *E-mail:* david.obrian@reededucation.com.au
Founded: 1982
Subjects: Art, Chemistry, Chemical Engineering, Environmental Studies, Geography, Geology, Health, Nutrition, History, Mathematics, Physics
ISBN Prefix(es): 0-7312; 0-85859
Total Titles: 5,000 Print; 50 CD-ROM; 20 Audio
Imprints: Heinemann

Regency Publishing+
Regency Institute of TAFE, Days Rd, Regency Park, SA 5010
Tel: (08) 8348 4599 *Fax:* (08) 8348 4400
E-mail: julie.fuss@regency.tafe.sa.edu.au
Web Site: www.tafe.sa.edu.au/institutes/regency/regency-publishing/main.htm
Key Personnel
Manager: Liz Daniels *E-mail:* danielse@regency.tafe.sa.edu.au
Educational textbooks specifically related to the vocational training sector.
Subjects: Cookery, Engineering (General), Health, Nutrition, Hospitality studies, commercial cookery, food science, food & beverage service, hotel management, butchery, bakery, Chinese & Asian cooking
Total Titles: 120 Print; 2 CD-ROM
Parent Company: Regency Institute TAFE

REIA, *imprint of* The Real Estate Institute of Australia

RIAL, *imprint of* The Real Estate Institute of Australia

RIC Publications Pty Ltd+
4 Bendsten Pl, Balcatta, WA 6021
Mailing Address: PO Box 332, Greenwood, WA 6924
Tel: (09) 9240 1511 *Fax:* (09) 9240 1513
E-mail: mail@ricgroup.com.au
Web Site: www.ricgroup.com.au
Key Personnel
Man Dir: Peter Woods *E-mail:* peter@ricgroup.com.au
Founded: 1986
Subjects: Education
ISBN Prefix(es): 1-86400; 1-86311
Number of titles published annually: 90 Print
Total Titles: 800 Print
Subsidiaries: Prim Ed Publishing PM Ltd
Branch Office(s)
Prim-Ed Publishing Limited, Bosheen New Ross, County Wexford, Ireland
Prim Ed Publishing (UK) Limited, 5A Kelsey Close, Attleborough Field, Nuneaton CV11 6RS, United Kingdom

Rider, *imprint of* Random House Australia

RMIT Publishing+
Level 3, 449 Swanston St, Melbourne, Victoria 3000
Mailing Address: PO Box 12058, A'Beckett St, Melbourne, Victoria 8006
Tel: (03) 9925 8100 *Fax:* (03) 9925 8134
E-mail: info@rmitpublishing.com.au
Web Site: www.rmitpublishing.com.au
Key Personnel
Training Liaison Officer: Judy Benson
Member of Australian Publishers Association National Book Council; also acts as distributor.
Subjects: Accounting, Business, Child Care & Development, Engineering (General), Fashion, Language Arts, Linguistics, Management, Travel
ISBN Prefix(es): 0-7241; 0-7306
Imprints: RMIT Press; TAFE Publications

RMIT Press, *imprint of* RMIT Publishing

Tom Roberts (Pat Roberts)+
241 Richmond Rd, Richmond, SA 5033
Tel: (08) 84437578
Key Personnel
Owner & Dir: Pat Roberts
Founded: 1971
Specialize in Equestrian Control.
Subjects: Animals, Pets, Family History, Horse Training & Educating, War, World War II Diaries
ISBN Prefix(es): 0-646; 0-9599413
Total Titles: 6 Print
Branch Office(s)
Western International Inc, 1875 Oddie Blvd, Sparks, NV 89431-6238, United States
Tel: 775-359-4400 *Fax:* 775-359-4439
Distributed by Rom Kerrigan; Western International Inc (USA)
Orders to: Western International Inc, 1875 Oddie Blvd, Sparks, NV 89431-6238, United States
Tel: 775-359-4400 *Fax:* 775-359-4439

Robinson, *imprint of* Random House Australia

Robinson's, *imprint of* Universal Press Pty Ltd

Rodale, *imprint of* Bloomings Books

Roo Books, *imprint of* Kangaroo Press

Royal Society of New South Wales
PO Box 1525, Macquarie Centre, NSW 2113
Tel: (02) 98874448 *Fax:* (02) 9887 4448
E-mail: p.williams@uws.edu.au
Web Site: www.phys.uts.edu.au/rsnsw/intro.html
Founded: 1821
Subjects: Chemistry, Chemical Engineering, Environmental Studies, Geography, Geology, Mathematics, Medicine, Nursing, Dentistry, Physics, Science (General)
ISBN Prefix(es): 0-9598274

Royal Society of Victoria Inc
9 Victoria St, Melbourne, Victoria 3000
Tel: (03) 9663 5259 *Fax:* (03) 9663 2301
E-mail: sciencevictoria@org.au
Web Site: www.sciencevictoria.org.au
Key Personnel
Executive Officer: Camilla van Megen
Founded: 1854
Learned scientific organization.
Subjects: Science (General)
Number of titles published annually: 1 Print

Rumsby Scientific Publishing
PO Box Q355, QVB Sydney, Nsw 1230
Tel: (02) 98076184 *Fax:* (02) 98076184
Subjects: Mathematics

Running Press, *imprint of* Random House Australia

Ruskin Rowe Press+
28 Ruskin Rowe, Avalon Beach, NSW 2107
Tel: (02) 9918-8810 *Fax:* (02) 9918-8884
Key Personnel
Author & International Rights: Dr Jan Roberts
Founded: 1996
Subjects: Architecture & Interior Design, Art, Biography, Education, History, Nonfiction (General), Regional Interests, Women's Studies
ISBN Prefix(es): 0-9587095

Sagebrush, *imprint of* Australian Large Print Pty Ltd

St Clair Press+
PO Box 287, Rozelle, NSW 2039
Tel: (02) 9818 1942 *Fax:* (02) 9418 1923
E-mail: stclair@australis.net.au
Web Site: www.stclairpress.com.au
Key Personnel
Dir: Bruce Watson
Subjects: Education
ISBN Prefix(es): 0-949898
Total Titles: 63 Print
Distributor for Broadview Press (Restrictions in Australia); Carcanet (Australia); Seren (Australia); University of Hull (Australia); University of Wales (Australia)

St George Books
125 St George's Terrace, Perth, WA 6000
Mailing Address: Box D162, GPO Perth, WA 6840
Tel: (09) 4829051 *Fax:* (09) 4829043
Key Personnel
Publications Manager: Simon Waight *Tel:* 89 4829043 *E-mail:* simon.waight@wanews.com.au
Founded: 1980
Subjects: Nonfiction (General), Regional Interests
ISBN Prefix(es): 0-86778; 0-949864; 0-909699
Total Titles: 40 Print; 1 CD-ROM
Parent Company: West Australian Newspapers Holdings Ltd
Imprints: Panorama Books; WA Newspaper
Distributor for Orin Books (Western Australia)

St Joseph Publications+
PO Box 1508, North Sydney, NSW 2060
Tel: (02) 99297344 *Fax:* (02) 91303678; (02) 99297994
E-mail: sosjelt@internet-australia.com
Key Personnel
Contact: Sister Marie Levey; Sister Bernadette O'Sullivan
Founded: 1981
Subjects: Education, History, Music, Dance, Religion - Catholic
ISBN Prefix(es): 1-875933; 1-959231
Total Titles: 30 Print
Showroom(s): Mary MacKillof Place, 7 Mount St, North Sydney 2060

St Martins, *imprint of* Pan Macmillan Australia Pty Ltd

St Pauls+
60-70 Broughton Rd, Strathfield, NSW 2135
Mailing Address: PO Box 906, Strathfield, NSW 2135
Tel: (02) 9746 2288 *Fax:* (02) 9746 1140
E-mail: sales@stpauls.com.au
Web Site: www.stpauls.com.au
Key Personnel
Head of Company: Bruno Colombari
Founded: 1953
Member of Christian Bookselling Association of Australia (CBAA).
Subjects: Biblical Studies, Biography, Education, Human Relations, Nonfiction (General), Religion - Catholic, Social Sciences, Sociology, Theology
ISBN Prefix(es): 0-949080; 0-909986; 1-875570; 1-876295
Distributed by Alba House (US); Editions Mediaspaul (Canada); St Pauls Distribution (Ireland); St Pauls Publishing (United Kingdom)
Distributor for Alba House (US)

Saltwater Publications
PO Box 160, Mount Martha, Victoria 3934
Tel: (03) 5974 1959 *Fax:* (03) 5974 1959
Key Personnel
Contact: Richard Hawkins
Founded: 1983
Subjects: Maritime, Outdoor Recreation, Boating guides

Sandcastle Books, *imprint of* Fremantle Arts Centre Press

Sandpiper Press
2 Prowse St, West Perth, WA 6005
Tel: (08) 94810375 *Fax:* (08) 94816547
Key Personnel
Head of Company: Richard Woldendorp
ISBN Prefix(es): 0-9589454

W B Saunders/Bailliere Tindall, *imprint of* Harcourt Australia Pty Ltd

Saunders College, *imprint of* Harcourt Australia Pty Ltd

Sceptre, *imprint of* Hodder Headline Australia

Scholastic Australia Pty Ltd
PO Box 579, Gosford, NSW 2250
Tel: (02) 4328 3555 *Fax:* (02) 4323 3827
Web Site: www.scholastic.com.au
Key Personnel
Man Dir: Ken A Jolly
Publishing, Rights & Permissions: David Harris
Corporate Communications Manager: Leanie Sweeney
Founded: 1968
Subjects: Education
ISBN Prefix(es): 1-86896; 1-86388
Parent Company: Scholastic Inc, 555 Broadway, New York, NY 10012-3999, United States
Associate Companies: Margaret Hamilton Books; Omnibus Books
Imprints: Classroom Magazine; Babysitters Club
Branch Office(s)
1091 Toorak Rd, Hartwell, Victoria 3124
2/350 Lytton Rd, Morningside Qld 4170
52 Fullarton Rd, Norwood 5067
Book Club(s): Arrow; Lucky; Star; Teachers Bookshelf; Wombat
Shipping Address: Railway Crescent, Lisarow, via Gosford 2250

Science Press+
54a Fitzroy St, Marrickville, NSW 2204
Tel: (02) 5161122 *Fax:* (02) 5501915
Key Personnel
Man Dir: William Boden
Secretary: Robert Koo
Marketing Manager: Barry Brown
Founded: 1945
Subjects: Education
ISBN Prefix(es): 0-85583

AUSTRALIA

Branch Office(s)
6/96 Camberwell Rd, Hawthorn, Victoria 3122
Distributor for NTC Publishing and The Learning Seed

Scripture Union, *imprint of* Anzea Publishers Ltd

Scroll Publishers
PO Box 112, Oxenford, Qld 4210
Tel: (07) 5573-0835 *Fax:* (07) 5529-5155
Key Personnel
Contact: Shirley Bray
Subjects: Alternative
ISBN Prefix(es): 0-646

Seaglass, *imprint of* Pascoe Publishing

Seanachas Press
PO Box 1284, Queanbeyan, NSW 2620
Key Personnel
Contact: Peter Gibson
Founded: 1993
Subjects: Genealogy, History, Family History

Secker & Warburg, *imprint of* Random House Australia

See Australia Guides P/L+
Valley Farm Rd, Healesville, Victoria 3777
Mailing Address: PO Box 1311, Healesville 3777
Tel: (03) 5962 5723 *Fax:* (03) 5962 4718
E-mail: seeaustralia@iprimus.com.au
Key Personnel
Dir: Greg Dunnett
Founded: 1990
Subjects: Travel
ISBN Prefix(es): 0-9586439

Sesame Street, *imprint of* Random House Australia

Shakespeare Head Press, *imprint of* Shakespeare Head Press Pty Ltd

Shakespeare Head Press Pty Ltd+
46 Egerton St, Silverwater NSW 2141
Tel: (02) 96485488 *Fax:* (03) 8958181
Key Personnel
Man Dir: Garry Eastman
Editorial & Rights & Permissions, Education: Peter Cribb
Editorial & Rights & Permissions, Religion: Kevin Mark
Founded: 1972
Subjects: Education, Government, Political Science, Health, Nutrition, Philosophy, Religion - Catholic, Religion - Other, Self-Help
ISBN Prefix(es): 1-86371; 0-85924; 0-85558
Parent Company: HarperCollins Publishers Pty Limited
Ultimate Parent Company: HarperCollins Publishers Group
Imprints: Shakespeare Head Press
Distributor for Ave Maria Press (Australia); Crossroad (Australia); Gill & Macmillan (Australia, UK & Ireland); HarperCollins San Francisco (Australia); HarperCollins UK Religious (Australia)

David Sharpe
PO Box 10, Carlton North 3054
Tel: (03) 93801503
ISBN Prefix(es): 0-646

Shearwater Press
15 Ratho St, Lenah Valley, Tas 7008
Tel: (02) 282 346

Key Personnel
Contact: Don Norman
Subjects: History

Frank Shepherd+
PO Box 484, Turramurra 2074
Tel: (02) 9482 8104
Key Personnel
Head of Company: Frank Shepherd
  E-mail: frankmsh@ozemail.com.au
Founded: 1993
Subjects: Biological Sciences, Gardening, Plants, History, Outdoor Recreation

The Sheringa Book Committee
Lake Hamilton Station, PMB 73, Port Lincoln, SA 5607
Tel: (086) 878750
Key Personnel
Head of Company: William Nosworthy
Subjects: History
ISBN Prefix(es): 7-316

Sidgwick & Jackson, *imprint of* Pan Macmillan Australia Pty Ltd

Signet, *imprint of* Penguin Books Australia Ltd

Simon & Schuster Australia Pty Ltd+
Division of Simon & Schuster Inc
20 Barcoo St, East Roseville, NSW 2069
Mailing Address: PO Box 507, East Roseville NSW 2069
Tel: (02) 9415 9900 *Fax:* (02) 9417 3188
Key Personnel
Man Dir: Jon Attenborough
Founded: 1987
Subjects: Alternative, Animals, Pets, Anthropology, Child Care & Development, Cookery, Crafts, Games, Hobbies, Health, Nutrition, History, House & Home, How-to, Management, Natural History, Nonfiction (General), Outdoor Recreation, Self-Help
ISBN Prefix(es): 0-7318; 0-86417
Number of titles published annually: 70 Print
Total Titles: 700 Print
Ultimate Parent Company: Viacom Inc, 1515 Broadway, New York, NY 10036, United States
Associate Companies: Simon & Schuster UK Ltd, 64-78 Kingsway, London WC2B 6AH, United Kingdom
Imprints: Kangaroo Press
Distributed by The Search Press (craft only - UK & Europe)

Single X Publications+
195 Sheppard's Hill Rd, Eden Hills 5050
Tel: (08) 8363-4272
Key Personnel
Editor & Author: Michael X Savvas
  E-mail: msavvas@usa.net
Founded: 1994
Subjects: Biography, Self-Help, Sports, Athletics, Travel, Motivational

Singular Press, *imprint of* Harcourt Australia Pty Ltd

Skills Publishing
PO Box 514, Hazelbrook, NSW 2779
Tel: (02) 4759 2844 *Fax:* (02) 4759 3721
E-mail: aww@skillspublish.com.au
Web Site: www.skillspublish.com.au
Key Personnel
Publisher: Art Burrows
Man Dir: Steven Burrows
Founded: 1985
Publisher of books & magazines in woodworking, metalworking, home construction & renovation.

Subjects: Crafts, Games, Hobbies, House & Home, How-to
ISBN Prefix(es): 0-646

Skylight Publishing Inc, *imprint of* Hawker Brownlow

Slouch Hat Publications+
PO Box 174, Rosebud, Victoria 3939
Tel: (03) 5986-6437 *Fax:* (03) 5986-6312
Web Site: www.slouch-hat.com.au
Key Personnel
Contact: Ron Austin
Founded: 1989
Subjects: History, Military Science
ISBN Prefix(es): 0-9585296

Social Club Books
6-10 Keele St, Collingwood, Victoria 3066
Mailing Address: PO Box 2937, Fitzroy, Melbourne, Victoria 3065
Tel: (03) 9473 5555 *Fax:* (03) 9417 5574
Web Site: www.scb.com.au
Key Personnel
Man Dir: Ken Finlayson *E-mail:* kenf@scb.com.au
Founded: 1983
Subjects: Astrology, Occult, Cookery, Gardening, Plants
Imprints: Ken Fin

Social Science Press+
PO Box 624, Katoomba, NSW 2780
Tel: (02) 4782 2909 *Fax:* (02) 4782 5303
E-mail: socsci@ozemail.com.au
Key Personnel
International Rights: David Barlow
Founded: 1980
Subjects: Education
ISBN Prefix(es): 0-949218; 1-876033

Somerset Publications
PO Box 8, Samford, Qld 4520
Tel: (07) 3425 1766 *Fax:* (07) 3425 1857
E-mail: info@crabbetarabian.com
Web Site: www.crabbetarabian.com
Key Personnel
Editor: Joan Flynn; Coralie Gordon
Founded: 1987
Subjects: Aramian Horses, Magazines & Books
ISBN Prefix(es): 0-947256
Parent Company: Limbale Pty Ltd
Distributed by J A Allen & Co; Alexander Heriot; Silver Monarch POB (USA)
Distributor for J A Allen & Co (UK); Alexander Heriot (UK); Borden Publishing (USA); Gordon & Gotch

South Head Press
10 Market Place, Berrima, NSW 2577
Tel: (048) 771421
Key Personnel
Head of Company: John Millett
Founded: 1964
Subjects: Poetry
ISBN Prefix(es): 0-909185; 0-901760

South Pacific Books, *imprint of* Outback Books - CQU Press

Southern Cross PR & Press Services
Arakoon, Via Tenterfield, NSW 2372
Tel: (02) 6737-5436 *Fax:* (02) 6737-5436
Key Personnel
Contact: Joan Starr
ISBN Prefix(es): 0-9588021

Spacevision Publishing+
12 Fry's Track, Newborough 3825
Tel: (03) 51272398
Key Personnel
Head of Company: A E Allison

PUBLISHERS

AUSTRALIA

Founded: 1994
Subjects: Mysteries
ISBN Prefix(es): 0-646

Spaniel Books+
PO Box 167, Paddington, NSW 2021
Tel: (02) 9360 9985 *Fax:* (02) 9331 4653
E-mail: spanielb@matra.com.au
Key Personnel
Contact: Michael Giffin
Founded: 1995
Subjects: Literature, Literary Criticism, Essays, Theology
ISBN Prefix(es): 0-646

Specialist Publications
1-5 Edwin St, Mortlake, NSW 2137
Mailing Address: PO Box 143, Concord, NSW 2137
Tel: (02) 97362191 *Fax:* (02) 97362663
Key Personnel
Contact: John Brooks *E-mail:* john@specialist.com.au
ISBN Prefix(es): 0-9588973

Spectrum Publications+
168 Lennox St, Room 3, Richmond, Victoria 3121
Mailing Address: PO Box 75, Richmond, Victoria 3121
Tel: (03) 9429 1404 *Fax:* (03) 9428 9407
E-mail: spectpub@ozemail.com.au
Key Personnel
Sales Manager: Maria Peters
Founded: 1974
Member of Australian Publishers Association.
Subjects: Biography, Education, History, Music, Dance, Nonfiction (General), Psychology, Psychiatry, Religion - Buddhist, Religion - Catholic, Religion - Hindu, Religion - Islamic, Religion - Jewish, Religion - Protestant, Theology
ISBN Prefix(es): 0-86786; 0-909837

Spellbound Promotions
7 Market St, Woolgoolga 2456
Tel: (02) 66542133 *Fax:* (02) 66541258
E-mail: Jodiadv@oncs.com.au
Key Personnel
Manager: Ron Blackmore
Founded: 1987
Publishing, Promotion, Typesetting, Editing & Cover Design.
Privately owned company.
ISBN Prefix(es): 0-87605
Total Titles: 3 Print; 3 Audio
Distributed by Crown Publishing (Taiwan)
Foreign Rep(s): Crown Publishing (Taiwan)

Spinifex Press+
504 Queensberry St, North Melbourne, Victoria 3051
Mailing Address: PO Box 212, North Melbourne, Victoria 3051
Tel: (03) 9329-6088 *Fax:* (03) 9329-9238
E-mail: world@spinifexpress.com.au
Web Site: www.spinifexpress.com.au
Key Personnel
Dir: Susan Hawthorne *E-mail:* hawsu@spinifexpress.com.qu; Renate Klein
Founded: 1991
Member of APA; specialize in feminist publishing.
Subjects: Art, Asian Studies, Developing Countries, Disability, Special Needs, Education, Environmental Studies, Fiction, Gay & Lesbian, Health, Nutrition, Literature, Literary Criticism, Essays, Nonfiction (General), Poetry, Social Sciences, Sociology, Technology, Travel, Women's Studies, Feminism
ISBN Prefix(es): 1-875559; 1-876756

Branch Office(s)
Spinifex Office
Orders to: Australian Book Group (ABG), PO Box 130, Drouin, Victoria 3818
PGW Canada, 74 Rolark Dr, Toronto, ON M1R 4G2, Canada *Tel:* 416-293-3979 *Fax:* 416-299-3065; 293-5756
Strauss Consultants, 45 Main St, Suite 611, Brooklyn, NY 11201-1021, United States

Stafford Books
2V71 Chandos St, Saint Leonards 2065
Mailing Address: PO Box 60, Saint Leonards, NSW 2065
Tel: (02) 906 4322 *Fax:* (02) 438 3813
Key Personnel
Manager: Gerry Wilson
Proprietor: Tim Stafford
Founded: 1990
Subjects: Agriculture, Animals, Pets, Art, Asian Studies, Behavioral Sciences, Cookery, Crafts, Games, Hobbies, Developing Countries, Disability, Special Needs, Foreign Countries, Geography, Geology, Nonfiction (General)
Distributor for Brash; Carolrhoda; Crabtree; Gem; Heian; Lerner; Millbrook; OWLS; Pema; Quinan; Rosen; Stemmer House; Tundra; Tyron Press; Whitman

Standards Association of Australia
PO Box 458, North Sydney, NSW 2060
Tel: (02) 9634231 *Fax:* (02) 9746 8450
Telex: AA26514
Key Personnel
Chief Executive: Ross Wraight
Founded: 1922
Subjects: Chemistry, Chemical Engineering, Civil Engineering, Communications, Electronics, Electrical Engineering, Engineering (General), Mechanical Engineering, Technology
ISBN Prefix(es): 0-7262

Star Teaching, *imprint of* Hawker Brownlow

State Library of NSW Press+
Macquarie St, Sydney, NSW 2000
Tel: (02) 2301500 *Fax:* (02) 92238807
Web Site: www.s/nsw/press
Key Personnel
Manager: Judith Kelly *E-mail:* jkelly@ilanet.slnsw.gov.au
Founded: 1988
Member of Australian Publishers Association.
Subjects: Art, Biography, Ethnicity, Genealogy, History, Literature, Literary Criticism, Essays, Natural History, Nonfiction (General), Social Sciences, Sociology, Women's Studies
ISBN Prefix(es): 0-7305; 0-7310
Parent Company: Library Council of NSW
Distributed by Peribo Pty Ltd (Australia/NZ/PNG)

State Library of Victoria
328 Swanston St, Melbourne, Vic 3000
Tel: (03) 8664 7000
E-mail: abirkenbeil@slv.vic.gov.au
Web Site: www.slv.vic.gov.au
Key Personnel
Publisher: Rob Blackmore
ISBN Prefix(es): 0-9585959

State Publishing Unit of State Print SA+
282 Richmond Rd, Netley, SA 5037
Mailing Address: PO Box 210, Plympton, SA 5038
Tel: (08) 2264677 *Fax:* (08) 2264726
Key Personnel
General Manager: Tony Fitzsimmons
Founded: 1986
Also acts as Agents.

Subjects: History, Regional Interests
ISBN Prefix(es): 7-243

Sterling Publishing Co Inc, *imprint of* Hawker Brownlow

Ian Stewart Marine Publications
PO Box 5154, Rockingham Beach, WA 6168
Tel: (08) 9593 1331 *Fax:* (08) 9593 1331
Key Personnel
Dir: Ian Graham Stewart
Founded: 1992
UK/Europe.
Subjects: Maritime, Shipping Publications
Total Titles: 2 Print
Distributed by Anthony Cooke (United Kingdom & Europe); Cordillera Press (Canada & US)
Distributor for Carmania Press

Stirling Press
69 Paringa/Pde, Old Noorlonga 5168
Mailing Address: PO Box 39, Old Noorlunga, SA 5168
Tel: (08) 327-1166 *Fax:* (08) 327-1166
E-mail: stirl@ozemail.com.au
Subjects: Business, Health, Nutrition, Self-Help
ISBN Prefix(es): 0-949142
Showroom(s): 100 King William Rd, Hyde Park, South Australia 5034

Strucmech Publishing
1A Southey St, Sandringham, Victoria 3191
Tel: (03) 95989245 *Fax:* (03) 95989245
Key Personnel
Author & Manager: Alan K Hosking
Founded: 1984
Subjects: Civil Engineering, Applied structural design
ISBN Prefix(es): 0-9586580

Success Education, *imprint of* R J Cleary Publishing

Summer Institute of Linguistics, Australian Aborigines Branch
60 Vanderlin Dr, Berrimah, NT 0828
Tel: (08) 8922 5700 *Fax:* (08) 8922 5717
E-mail: sildarwin@taunet.net.au
Founded: 1961
Subjects: Anthropology, Education, Language Arts, Linguistics, Australian Aboriginal & Torres Strait Islander Languages
ISBN Prefix(es): 0-86892
Parent Company: Summer Institute of Linguistics, Attn: Academic Publications, 7500 W Camp Wisdom Rd, Dallas, TX 75326, United States

Sun, *imprint of* Pan Macmillan Australia Pty Ltd

Sundance Inc, *imprint of* Hawker Brownlow

Sydney Studies In English
Division of The University of Sydney
University of Sydney, English Department 420, Sydney, NSW 2006
Tel: (02) 9351 2432 *Fax:* (02) 9351 2434
Web Site: www.arts.usyd.edu.au/dep
Key Personnel
Editor: Prof Margaret Harris *Tel:* (02) 9351 2163 *E-mail:* margaret.harris@english.usyd.edu.au
Founded: 1975
Subjects: Drama, Theater, Literature, Literary Criticism, Essays
ISBN Prefix(es): 0-85587
Total Titles: 27 Print

Systex Pty Ltd
2 Ayres Rd, Saint Ives 2075
Tel: (02) 9944 2668
Key Personnel
Head of Company: Peter Burke

T & A, *imprint of* Turton & Armstrong Publishers Pty Ltd

Tabletop Press+
2 Lambell Cl, Palmerston ACT 2913
Tel: (06) 2420995 *Fax:* (06) 2420674
Key Personnel
Head of Company: Klaus Hueneke
Founded: 1985
Also acts as distributor.
Subjects: Geography, Geology, History, Photography, Regional Interests
ISBN Prefix(es): 0-9590841; 0-9587049
Distributed by Evirobook; Tower Books

TAFE Publications, *imprint of* RMIT Publishing

Tamarind Publications
PO Box 624, Warner's Bay, NSW 2282
Tel: (02) 467934 *Fax:* (02) 659515
E-mail: sigi@hunterlink.net.au
Key Personnel
Principal: Pauline Clare Egan
Founded: 1996
Subjects: Philosophy, Poetry, Religion - Buddhist
ISBN Prefix(es): 0-9586836
Number of titles published annually: 1 Print
Total Titles: 2 Print

Tarka Publishing+
8 William St, North Sydney, NSW 2060
Tel: (02) 9955 2074 *Fax:* (02) 9925 0664
E-mail: howbix@netspace.net.au
Key Personnel
Head of Company & Dir: Ann Howard
 E-mail: lnchoward9@aol.com
Founded: 1990
Subjects: History, Poetry, Women's Studies, Juvenile Migration
Number of titles published annually: 1 Print
Total Titles: 12 Print
Distributed by Bay Books; Lothian; Tower Books
Book Club(s): Doubleday

Teach Yourself, *imprint of* Hodder Headline Australia

Teacher Created Materials, *imprint of* Hawker Brownlow

Technomic Publishing, *imprint of* Harcourt Australia Pty Ltd

Templegate Publishers, *imprint of* Rainbow Book Agencies Pty Ltd

Terania Rainforest Publishing
Terania Creek Rd, The Channon, NSW 2480
Tel: (02) 6688 6204 *Fax:* (02) 6688 6227
E-mail: terania@nrg.com.au
Key Personnel
Contact: Nan J Nicholson
Founded: 1985
Subjects: Environmental Studies, Gardening, Plants, Natural History, Botany, Rainforest
ISBN Prefix(es): 0-9589436
Total Titles: 5 Print
Distributed by Frith & Frith (Australia); Tower Books

Tertiary Press+
12-50 Norton Rd, Croydon, Victoria 3136
Tel: (03) 9213 6766 *Fax:* (03) 9213 6806
Web Site: www.tertiarypress.com.au
Key Personnel
Manager: Cathy Grundy *Tel:* (03) 9213 6774
 E-mail: cgrundy@swin.edu.au
Founded: 1995

Subjects: Accounting, Business, Child Care & Development, Computer Science, Economics, Human Relations, Management, Marketing, Microcomputers, Technology
ISBN Prefix(es): 1-875794; 1-875886; 0-86458
Number of titles published annually: 35 Print; 2 CD-ROM; 1 Audio
Total Titles: 200 Print
Online services available through World Wide Web.
Parent Company: Swinburne University of Technology
Foreign Rep(s): Educational Books Ltd (New Zealand)

Text, *imprint of* The Text Publishing Company Pty Ltd

The Text Publishing Company Pty Ltd+
171 Latrobe St, Melbourne, Victoria 3000
Tel: (03) 9272 4700 *Fax:* (03) 9926 4854
E-mail: books@textmedia.com.au
Web Site: www.textpublishing.com.au
Key Personnel
Publisher: Michael Heyward *Tel:* (03) 9272 4716
Publicist: Emily Booth
Administrative Assistant: Donica Bettanin
 Fax: (03) 9926 4841 *E-mail:* donica.bettanin@textmedia.com.au
Founded: 1990
Subjects: Biography, Fiction, History, Humor, Literature, Literary Criticism, Essays, Nonfiction (General), Political Science
ISBN Prefix(es): 1-875847; 1-876485; 1-877008
Number of titles published annually: 40 Print
Total Titles: 105 Print
Associate Companies: The Text Media Group Pty Ltd
Imprints: Text
Distributed by Archetype Book Agents; Penguin Books Australia
Foreign Rights: Agencia Litterari BMSR (Brazil); Antonella Antonelli Agencia (Italy); Agencia Litteraria Carmen Balcells (Portugal, Spain); Bardon-Chinese Media Agency (China, Taiwan); Eliane Benisti Agency (France); Paul & Peter Fritz (Germany); Caroline van Gelderen (Netherlands); Graal Ltd (Poland); International Copyright Agency (Romania); Katai & Bolza (Hungary); Korea Copyright Centre (Korea); Leonhardt & Hoier (Scandinavia); Lutyens & Rubinstein (UK); Tuttle-Mori Agency (Japan); Andrew Nurnberg Associates (Baltic States); Witherspoon Associates Inc (US)
Warehouse: Peguin Books Australia, 30 Centre Rd, Scoresby, Victoria 3179 *Tel:* (03) 9811 2555 *Fax:* (03) 9811 8309
Orders to: Peguin Books Australia, 30 Centre Rd, Scoresby, Victoria 3179 *Tel:* (03) 9811 2555 *Fax:* (03) 9811 8309

Thames & Hudson (Australia) Pty Ltd
Portside Business Park, 11 Central Blvd, Fishermans Bend, Victoria 3207
Tel: (03) 9646 7788 *Fax:* (03) 9646 8790
E-mail: thaust@thaust.com.au
Key Personnel
Man Dir: Peter Shaw
Customer Service Manager: Elizabeth Ioannidis
Founded: 1968 (Wholly owned subsidiary of Thames & Hudson UK)
Distribute books for Thames & Hudson UK & other publishers.
Subjects: Archaeology, Architecture & Interior Design, Art, Fashion, Foreign Countries, History, Literature, Literary Criticism, Essays, Music, Dance, Natural History, Photography, Travel
ISBN Prefix(es): 0-500
Parent Company: Thames & Hudson
Distributor for AA Gallery of New South Wales; AA Gallery of Queensland; AA Gallery of South Australia; Abrams (Australia); Boothe-Clibborn Editions; British Museum Press (Australia); Craftsman House (Australia); Flammarion (Australia); Lawrence King (Australia); MOMA (Australia); National Gallery of Australia (Australia); Rizzoli/Universe; RotoVision; SCALO (Australia); SKIRA (Australia); Tate Gallery (Australia); Vision On

The Jacaranda Press, *imprint of* John Wiley & Sons Australia Ltd

The Learner's Dimensions, *imprint of* Hawker Brownlow

The Learning Works, *imprint of* Hawker Brownlow

Thin Rich Press+
70 Gairloch St, Applecross 6153
Mailing Address: PO Box 650, Claremont 6010
Tel: (09) 3644799 *Fax:* (09) 3163338
Key Personnel
Head of Company: M Smallbone
Subjects: Human Relations, Humor, Philosophy, Poetry, Religion - Buddhist, Self-Help
ISBN Prefix(es): 0-646

Thornbill Press
4 Thornbill Crescent, Coromandel Valley 5051
Tel: (08) 2705172
Key Personnel
Head of Company: Graeme Webster
Subjects: Law, Literature, Literary Criticism, Essays
ISBN Prefix(es): 0-9586973
Parent Company: Thornbill Professional Services Pty Ltd (ACN 050 019 915)

Caroline Thornton+
18 Doonan Rd, Nedlands 6009
Tel: (08) 9386 1555 *Fax:* (08) 9389 5162
Founded: 1988
Subjects: History

D W Thorpe+
Division of R R Bowker LLC
18 Salmon St, Locked Bag 20, Port Melbourne, Victoria 3207
Tel: (03) 9245 7370 *Fax:* (03) 9245 7395
E-mail: yoursay@thorpe.com.au
Web Site: www.thorpe.com.au
Key Personnel
General Manager: Paulene Morey *Tel:* (03) 9245 7372 *E-mail:* pauline.morey@thorpe.com.au
Founded: 1921
Bibliographic & library reference publisher.
Membership(s): ABA, APA, ALIA.
Subjects: Business, Library & Information Sciences, Publishing & Book Trade Reference
ISBN Prefix(es): 0-909532; 1-875589; 0-909605; 0-949910; 0-7312
Distributor for Bowker; R R Bowker; Whitaker

Three Sisters Publications Pty Ltd
PO Box 104, Winmalee, NSW 2777
Tel: (047) 588138
Key Personnel
Principal Officer: Margaret Baker
Founded: 1983
Subjects: Archaeology, Biological Sciences, Gardening, Plants, Geography, Geology, History, Natural History
ISBN Prefix(es): 0-9590203

Threshold Publishing
PO Box 2030, Kew 3101
Fax: (03) 98534307
Key Personnel
Manager: Adrian Anderson *E-mail:* adrian@alphalink.com.au

Founded: 1992
ISBN Prefix(es): 0-646

Timber, *imprint of* Bloomings Books

Time-Life Australia Pty Ltd
3 Talavera Rd, North Ryde, NSW 2113
Mailing Address: PO Box 3814, Sydney, NSW 2001
Tel: (02) 9856 2212 *Toll Free Tel:* 800-251-616
 Fax: (02) 9856 2255
Web Site: www.timelife.com.au
Key Personnel
Man Dir: Bonita L Boezeman
Founded: 1961
Subjects: Books, Music, Videos & Direct Marketing
ISBN Prefix(es): 0-8094
Parent Company: Time Warner Inc
Subsidiaries: Record Clubs of Australia
Branch Office(s)
5 Ottho Heldringstr, 1066 AZ Amsterdam, Netherlands *Tel:* (020) 48 74 293 *Web Site:* www.timelife.nl
Times Inc, Time & Life Bldg, Rockefeller Plaza, New York, NY 10020, United States
U.S. Office(s): PO Box 85060, Richmond, VA 32285-5060, United States *Tel:* 804-261-1300
 Web Site: www.timelife.com
Distributed by Collins New Zealand; Hodder Headline Australia
Book Club(s): The Softback Preview

Tirian Publications
116 Queenscliffe St, Queenscliffe, NSW 2096
Tel: (02) 9905 0533
E-mail: Tirian@bigpond.com
Subjects: Education
ISBN Prefix(es): 0-9586056

Tom Publications+
153 McDonald St, Yoondanna, WA 6060
Tel: (09) 4444570
Key Personnel
Contact: Radmila Mijatovic
Member of WA Writers.
Subjects: Ethnicity, Fiction, Nonfiction (General), Poetry, Romance, Migrants
ISBN Prefix(es): 1-875715; 1-875715; 1-875715; 0-947221

Tomorrow Publications+
62 Gordon Ave, Hamilton 2303
Mailing Address: PO Box 313, Merewether 2291
Tel: (049) 612115
Key Personnel
Contact: Paula Morrow
Subjects: Alternative, Fiction, Health, Nutrition, How-to, Science Fiction, Fantasy, Self-Help

Tor Books, *imprint of* Pan Macmillan Australia Pty Ltd

Tower Books
9/19 Rodborough Rd, French's Forest, NSW 2086
Tel: (02) 9975-5566 *Fax:* (02) 9975-5599
E-mail: towerbks@zipworld.com.au
Key Personnel
Contact: Dale Druckman

Transpareon Press+
PO Box 4, Hornsby, NSW 2077
Tel: (02) 99874570 *Fax:* (02) 99874570
Key Personnel
Dir: Frances Wheelhouse
Founded: 1970
Member of Australian Book Publishers Association.
Subjects: Agriculture, Anthropology, Biography, History, Regional Interests, Science (General), Women's Studies, Australian History, Biographies, Medicine
ISBN Prefix(es): 0-908021

Transworld Publishers Pty Ltd+
15-25 Helles Ave, Moorebank NSW 2170
Mailing Address: Private Bag 12, Neutral Bay 2089
Tel: (02) 96017122 *Fax:* (02) 98211334
Key Personnel
Man Dir & Chief Executive Officer: Geoff Rumpf
Deputy Man Officer Finance & Operations: Greg Little
Publisher: Shona Martyn
National Sales Manager: Chris Raine
Head Publicity & Promotions: Maggie Hamilton
Founded: 1980
Subjects: Fiction, Health, Nutrition, Humor, Nonfiction (General), Romance, Science Fiction, Fantasy, Self-Help
ISBN Prefix(es): 0-553; 0-440; 0-552; 1-86230; 0-86824
Parent Company: Bertelsmann AG
Associate Companies: Transworld Publishers, United Kingdom; Bantam Doubleday Dell Inc, 1540 Broadway, New York, NY 19936, United States
Imprints: Bantam; Corgi; Doubleday; Dell; Anchor; Broadway Dela Corte; Black Swan
U.S. Office(s): Bantam Doubleday Dell, 1540 Broadway, New York, NY 10036, United States
Distributed by Transworld Publishers (New Zealand)
Distributor for Avon; Potentials Unlimited; Ravette; Running Press; Workman
Book Club(s): Doubleday Book & Music Clubs

Travelog, *imprint of* Universal Press Pty Ltd

Trillium Press, *imprint of* Hawker Brownlow

La Trobe University Press+
La Trobe University, Bundoora, Victoria 3086
Tel: (03) 9479 1111 *Fax:* (03) 94702011
Web Site: www.latrobe.edu.au/bundoora/contact.html
Key Personnel
Man Editor: Danielle Garlick
Founded: 1971
Subjects: Anthropology, Asian Studies, Biological Sciences, Chemistry, Chemical Engineering, Education, History, Law, Medicine, Nursing, Dentistry, Social Sciences, Sociology
ISBN Prefix(es): 1-86324
Distributed by International Special Book Service (USA); Portland Press (UK); UNSW Press (Australia)

Troll Books of Australia+
PO Box 522, Roseville, NSW 2069
Tel: (02) 417 2699 *Fax:* (02) 417 1599
Key Personnel
Chief Executive: Terry T Hughes
Founded: 1997
Subjects: Fiction, Nonfiction (General), Science (General), Activity, Teacher Resources with Specialist Materials on early reading & reading recovery
ISBN Prefix(es): 1-875675
Parent Company: Troll Associates, 100 Corporate Dr, Mahwah, NJ 07430, United States
Imprints: Lineup; Watermill
Branch Office(s)
Auckland, New Zealand

Tropicana Press+
PO Box 385, Padstow 2211
Tel: (02) 9543-7728 *Fax:* (02) 732161344
E-mail: infoeis@ozemail.com.au
Key Personnel
Contact: R B Shaw
Subjects: Fiction

Troubadour Press, *imprint of* New Creation Publications Ministries & Resource Centre

Troubadour Press
PO Box 403, Blackwood, SA 5051
Tel: (08) 2704003 *Fax:* (08) 2704003
Key Personnel
Head of Company: Geoffrey Bingham
ISBN Prefix(es): 1-875653

Tuart House, *imprint of* University of Western Australia Press

Tudor Australia Press
14 Tudor St, Dulwich 5065
Tel: (08) 8332-8884
Key Personnel
Manager: Andrew G Peake *E-mail:* agpeake@senet.com.au
Founded: 1984
Subjects: Geography, Geology, History
ISBN Prefix(es): 958-9177
Number of titles published annually: 2 Print
Total Titles: 3 Print

Turton & Armstrong Publishers Pty Ltd+
21 Lister St, Wahroonga, NSW 2076
Tel: (02) 9489-6719 *Fax:* (02) 9489-6719
E-mail: turtarm@attglobal.net
Key Personnel
Dir: Paul T Armstrong
Founded: 1977
Subjects: Aeronautics, Aviation, Automotive, Biography, Crafts, Games, Hobbies, History, Maritime, Music, Dance, Nonfiction (General), Transportation, Special Interest & Motor Racing
ISBN Prefix(es): 0-908031
Number of titles published annually: 6 Print
Total Titles: 40 Print
Imprints: T & A

UBD, *imprint of* Universal Press Pty Ltd

Unichurch Publishing
PO Box E 178, St James, Sydney, NSW 2000
Tel: (02) 2336399 *Fax:* (02) 9261-5879
E-mail: ucb@nsw.uca.org.au
Key Personnel
Contact: Nabanita Ghosh
ISBN Prefix(es): 0-908525

United Educational Services (DDK), *imprint of* Hawker Brownlow

Uniting Church Press, *imprint of* Uniting Education

Uniting Education, *imprint of* Rainbow Book Agencies Pty Ltd

Uniting Education
PO Box 1245, Collingwood, Victoria 3066
Tel: (03) 9416 4262 *Fax:* (03) 9416 4264
E-mail: contact@unitinged.org.au
Web Site: www.unitinged.org.au
Key Personnel
Dir: John Emmett *E-mail:* john@unitinged.org.au
Books Manager: Hugh McGinlay
Founded: 1914
Specialize in Christian Education Resources.
Subjects: Education, Human Relations, Religion - Protestant, Theology
ISBN Prefix(es): 86-407
Imprints: Uniting Church Press

AUSTRALIA

Distributed by National Christian Education Council (UK)
Orders to: Rainbow Books, 303 Arthur St, Fairfield 3068 *Tel:* (03) 9481 6611 *Fax:* (03) 9481 2371 *E-mail:* rainbowb@axs.com.au

Unity Press
6a Ortana Rd, Lindfield, NSW 2070
Tel: (02) 4671342 *Fax:* (02) 9736-2663
Key Personnel
Dir: Nevill Drury; Anna Voigt
Subjects: Anthropology, Art, Astrology, Occult, Health, Nutrition, Music, Dance, Mysteries, Parapsychology, Philosophy, Poetry, Psychology, Psychiatry, Religion - Buddhist, Religion - Other, Self-Help, Women's Studies
ISBN Prefix(es): 0-9589759
Parent Company: Voigt Drury Publishing Pty Ltd

Universal Business Directories, Australia Pty Ltd
64 Talavera Rd, North Ryde, NSW 2113
Tel: (02) 8881877 *Fax:* (09) 6307505
Key Personnel
General Manager: Allan Parker
Founded: 1932
Subjects: Business
ISBN Prefix(es): 0-7261
Parent Company: Wilson & Horton Ltd
Associate Companies: New Zealand Herald
Subsidiaries: Wises Mapping

Universal Press Pty Ltd+
One Waterloo Rd, Macquarie Park, NSW 2113
Mailing Address: PO Box 1530, Macquarie Centre, NSW 2113
Tel: (02) 9857 3700 *Toll Free Tel:* 800 021 987 *Fax:* (02) 9888 9074 *Toll Free Fax:* 800 636 197
Key Personnel
Sales & Marketing Manager: Kim Mouret
Founded: 1950
Large range of D I Y Service, repair car manuals for popular imported & Australian produced vehicles; also list of automotive technical vehicles & automotive technical publications for trade education.
Subjects: Automotive, Travel, Automotive Publications, Maps, Street Directories & Guides
ISBN Prefix(es): 0-85566; 0-7319; 0-949164
Imprints: R A Broadberh; Gregory's; Robinson's; Travelog; UBD
Distributor for Berlitz; Fielding Worldwide; Geographer's A-Z; Michelin; National Geographic Society (maps only); Rand McNally; Replogle Globes

University of New South Wales Press Ltd+
45 Beach St, Coogee, NSW 2034
Mailing Address: University of New South Wales, Sydney, NSW 2052
Tel: (02) 9664 0900 *Fax:* (02) 9664 5420
E-mail: info.press@unsw.edu.au
Web Site: www.unswpress.com.au
Key Personnel
Man Dir: Dr Robin Derricourt *Tel:* (02) 9664 0905 *E-mail:* r.derricourt@unsw.edu.au
Publishing Manager: John Elliot *E-mail:* john.elliot@unsw.edu.au
Marketing Manager: Brett Haydon *E-mail:* b.haydon@unsw.edu.au
Editorial Coordinator: Nicola Young *Tel:* (02) 9664 0903 *E-mail:* n.young@unsw.edu.au
Founded: 1962
Member of Australian Publishers Association.
Subjects: Architecture & Interior Design, Biography, Biological Sciences, Earth Sciences, Engineering (General), Environmental Studies, Gardening, Plants, Government, Political Science, History, Natural History, Nonfiction (General), Science (General), Social Sciences, Sociology, Technology, Women's Studies
ISBN Prefix(es): 0-86840
Number of titles published annually: 50 Print
Total Titles: 300 Print
Divisions: University & Reference Publishers
Distributed by Addenda Ltd; Apac Publishers Services Pte Ltd; Eurospan (UK); United Publishers Services Ltd; University of British Columbia Press; University of Washington Press
Distributor for Auckland University Press; Bios Scientific; Daphne Brasell & Associates; Broadview; Brookings Institution Press; Canterbury University Press; CSIRO Publishing; Currency Press; Deakin University Press; Edinburgh University Press; Hawksmere; C Hurst & Co; Indiana University Press; Key Porter; McGill-Queen's University Press; Melbourne University Press; Pluto Press Australia; Reaktion Books; Rivers Oram (Pandora); Signal Books; Editions Tom Thompson; University of British Columbia Press; University of Otago Press; University of Washington Press
Bookshop(s): UNSW Bookshop, Sydney, NSW 2052
Warehouse: UNSW Press, Govett St, Randwick, NSW 2031

University of Newcastle
Callaghan Campus, Callaghan, NSW 2308
Tel: (02) 4921 5000
Web Site: www.newcastle.edu.au
ISBN Prefix(es): 0-7259

University of Queensland Press+
Unit of The University of Queensland
University of Queensland, Staff House Rd, St Lucia 4067
Mailing Address: PO Box 6042, St Lucia, Qld 4067
Tel: (07) 3365 2127; (07) 3365 2440 (sales) *Fax:* (07) 3365 7579
Web Site: www.uqp.uq.edu.au
Key Personnel
General Manager: Laurie Muller
Editorial & Marketing: Madonna Duffy *E-mail:* editor@uqp.uq.edu.au
Rights Manager: Dinah Johnson *Tel:* (07) 3365 7244 *E-mail:* dinah@uqp.uq.edu.au
Founded: 1948
Publisher of quality literary works of fiction & nonfiction
Also specialize in Black Australian writings, Aboriginal studies & social & political issues, reference books.
Subjects: Biography, Fiction, History, Literature, Literary Criticism, Essays, Nonfiction (General), Poetry, Sports, Athletics, Travel
ISBN Prefix(es): 0-7022
Number of titles published annually: 60 Print
Imprints: UQP
Branch Office(s)
International Specialised Book Services, Inc, 5804 NE Hassalo St, Portland, OR 97213-3640, United States *Tel:* 503-287-3093 *Fax:* 503-380-8832
Distributed by Penguin Books Australia Ltd
Foreign Rep(s): Literary Agent (France); Lora Fountain (France, Italy, Belgium & Germany)
Foreign Rights: Inter Australia Company (Korea)

University of Western Australia Press+
35 Stirling Highway, Crawley, WA 6009
Tel: (08) 9380 3182 *Fax:* (08) 9380 1027
E-mail: uwap@cyllene.uwa.edu.au
Web Site: www.uwapress.uwa.edu.au
Key Personnel
Dir: Dr Jenny Gregory *Tel:* (08) 9380 3670 *E-mail:* jag@cyllene.uwa.edu.au
Marketing Manager: Anastasia Stachewicz *E-mail:* ana@cyllene.uwa.edu.au
Sales Manager: J Brown *E-mail:* jbrown@cyllene.uwa.edu.au
Founded: 1954
Subjects: Biography, Fiction, History, Literature, Literary Criticism, Essays, Natural History, Nonfiction (General), Regional Interests, Science Fiction, Fantasy, Social Sciences, Sociology, Women's Studies
ISBN Prefix(es): 1-875560; 1-876268
Number of titles published annually: 20 Print
Imprints: Cygnet Books; Tuart House
U.S. Office(s): ISBS, 5824 NE Hassalo St, Portland, OR 97213-3644, United States *Tel:* 503-287-3093 *Fax:* 503-280-8832 *E-mail:* orders@isbn.com *Web Site:* www.isbs.com
Distributed by Addenda Ltd; Eurospan; ISBS Inc; United Publishing Services (UPS) (Japan)
Distributor for Centre for Studies in WA History; Centre for Studies in Australian Literature

UQP, *imprint of* University of Queensland Press

The Useful Publishing Co+
2/795 Beaufort St, Mount Lawley, Perth, WA 6050
Tel: (09) 370-4577 *Fax:* (09) 370-2540
Key Personnel
Contact: Murray Davey
Founded: 1992
Subjects: Career Development, Finance, Nonfiction (General)
ISBN Prefix(es): 1-875693
Associate Companies: Davey Business Accountants Pty Ltd

VCTA Publishing+
33-37 Hotham St, Collingwood, Victoria 3066
Mailing Address: PO Box 361, Abbotsford, Victoria 3067
Tel: (03) 94199622 *Fax:* (03) 94191205
E-mail: vcta@vcta.asn.au
Web Site: www.vcta.asn.au
Key Personnel
Dir: Robert Taylor
Publishing Manager: Susan Watson
Production Editor: Maree Keating
Founded: 1953
Subjects: Accounting, Business, Career Development, Communications, Economics, Finance, Law, Regional Interests
Parent Company: Victorian Commercial Teachers' Association

Veritas Press
PO Box 1653, Bundaberg, Qld 4670
Fax: (071) 529256
E-mail: copytype@interworx.com.au
Key Personnel
President & Author: J West
General Manager & Editor: Rob Giles
Founded: 1987
Subjects: Anthropology, Archaeology, Astrology, Occult, Health, Nutrition, Medicine, Nursing, Dentistry, Poetry, Science (General), Expose books in Science & Medicine
ISBN Prefix(es): 0-9588131
Subsidiaries: Whale Books
Distributed by Lilly Books (USA); Veritas Publishing (Australia); Whales Books (UK)
Distributor for Random House (Australia)

Vermillion, *imprint of* Random House Australia

Victorian Arts Centre Trust
100 Saint Kilda Rd, Melbourne, Victoria 3004
Tel: (03) 9281 8000 *Fax:* (03) 9629 2719
Web Site: www.artscentre.net.au
Telex: Vicart AA 39141
Key Personnel
Chief Exec Officer: Brett Randall

Victorian Commercial Teachers' Association, see VCTA Publishing

Victorian National Parks Association, *imprint of* Rainbow Book Agencies Pty Ltd

Viking, *imprint of* Penguin Books Australia Ltd

Villamonta Publishing Service Inc+
2 Downes, La Geelong, Victoria 3220
Tel: (03) 5229 6251 *Fax:* (03) 5222 5399
E-mail: villapub@ozemail.com.au
Key Personnel
Executive Officer: Charles Lucas
Founded: 1993
Subjects: Disability, Special Needs, Law
ISBN Prefix(es): 0-9587635
Total Titles: 14 Print

Vintage, *imprint of* Random House Australia

Virgin, *imprint of* Random House Australia

Vista Publications+
PO Box 82, Eisternwick, Victoria 3185
Tel: (03) 9523 5623 *Fax:* (03) 9523 5623
E-mail: vistaof@mbox.com.au
Key Personnel
Editorial Dir: Christine Mitchell
International Rights: Eva Fabian
Founded: 1996
Publishing nonfiction books (small company).
Member of Victorian Writers' Centre.
Subjects: Biography, Education, Environmental Studies, Government, Political Science, Health, Nutrition, History, How-to, Nonfiction (General), Poetry, Social Sciences, Sociology, Community Development, Peace
ISBN Prefix(es): 0-9586496; 0-9592816; 1-876370
Total Titles: 18 Print

Vital, *imprint of* Vital Publications

Vital Publications
PO Box 101, North Essendon, Melbourne, Victoria 3041
Tel: (03) 9379-1219 *Fax:* (03) 9379-0015
E-mail: vitalpubs@churchesofchrist.org.au; aceditor@ozemail.com.au
Key Personnel
Marketing Representative: Don Smith
Contact: Nigel Pegram
Religious publications.
Subjects: Biblical Studies, Education, Religion - Other
ISBN Prefix(es): 0-909116; 1-875915
Number of titles published annually: 3 Print
Parent Company: National Council Churches of Christ
Imprints: Vital

WA Newspaper, *imprint of* St George Books

Wakefield Crime Classics, *imprint of* Wakefield Press Pty Ltd

Wakefield Press Pty Ltd+
PO Box 2266, Kent Town, SA 5071
Tel: (08) 8362 8800 *Fax:* (08) 8362 7592
E-mail: info@wakefieldpress.com.au
Web Site: www.wakefieldpress.com.au
Key Personnel
Dir: Michael Bollen; Stephanie Johnston
 E-mail: stephanie@wakefieldpress.com.au
Founded: 1989
Subjects: Asian Studies, Cookery, Environmental Studies, Fiction, History, Literature, Literary Criticism, Essays, Mysteries, Travel, Women's Studies
ISBN Prefix(es): 1-86254; 0-949268
Total Titles: 600 Print

Imprints: Wakefield Crime Classics
Distributor for Arsenal Pulp (Australia & New Zealand); SERIF (Australia, New Zealand); Soft Skull Press (Australia & New Zealand)
Foreign Rep(s): Airlift Book Company (UK, Europe); BHB International (North America)
Orders to: Wakefield Press Distribution, PO Box 130, Drouin, Victoria 3818, Peter de Court
Tel: (061) 5625 4290 *Fax:* (061) 5625 3756

Walker Books Australia Pty Ltd
Locked Bag 22, Newtown 2042
Tel: (02) 9517 9577 *Fax:* (02) 9517 9997
Key Personnel
Man Dir: Sarah Foster
Subjects: Education, Fiction
ISBN Prefix(es): 0-7445
Parent Company: Walker Books Limited
Branch Office(s)
Candlewick Press, 2067 Massachusetts Ave, Cambridge, MA 02140, United States

Frederick Warne, *imprint of* Penguin Books Australia Ltd

The Watermark Press+
3-A Llewellyn St, Balmain, NSW 2041
Mailing Address: PO Box 63, Balmain, NSW 2041
Tel: (02) 9818 5677 *Fax:* (02) 9818 5581
E-mail: books@nsw.bigpond.net.au
Key Personnel
Head of Company: Simon Blackall
Founded: 1983
Subjects: Animals, Pets, Architecture & Interior Design, Cookery, Crafts, Games, Hobbies, Gardening, Plants, Humor, Military Science, Nonfiction (General), Travel, Wine & Spirits
ISBN Prefix(es): 0-949284

Watermill, *imprint of* Troll Books of Australia

Franklin Watts Australia
PO Box 826, Lane Cove, NSW 2066
Tel: (02) 427-4922 *Fax:* (02) 418-6935
Key Personnel
General Manager: Tony Watts
ISBN Prefix(es): 0-86415
Parent Company: Franklin Watts Ltd, United Kingdom
Ultimate Parent Company: The House Grolier Ltd, 387 Park Ave S, New York, NY 10016, United States
Associate Companies: Children's Press; Grolier Educational Inc; Grolier Electronic Publishing Inc; Orchard, United Kingdom; Orchard Books, United Kingdom; Franklin Watts, United Kingdom
Divisions: Grolier Educational Australia

Weather Press+
PO Box 107, Boronia 3155
Tel: (03) 9762-1647
Key Personnel
International Rights: Philip Johns
Subjects: Fiction

Weatherlight Press, *imprint of* Windhorse Books

Webster & Associates Pty Ltd
2/25 Frenchs Forest Rd, Frenchs Forest, NSW 2086
Tel: (02) 9751466 *Fax:* (02) 4523493
E-mail: webpub@websterpublishing.com
ISBN Prefix(es): 1-86398; 0-947302

Wellington Lane Press Pty Ltd+
120 Wycombe Rd, Neutral Bay, NSW 2089
Tel: (02) 99040962 *Fax:* (02) 99040962

Key Personnel
Publisher: Carol Dettmann *E-mail:* dettmann@ozemail.com.au
Founded: 1976
Subjects: Art, Photography, Regional Interests
ISBN Prefix(es): 0-908022; 0-947322
Imprints: Chapter & Verse

Wellness Australia+
PO Box 519, Subiaco WA 6904
Tel: (08) 9387 5111 *Fax:* (08) 9383 7323
E-mail: info@workteams.com
Key Personnel
Head of Company & Dir: Grant Donovan
 E-mail: grant@workteams.com
Founded: 1988
Subjects: Health, Nutrition, Management, Psychology, Psychiatry
ISBN Prefix(es): 1-875139
Subsidiaries: Workplace Global Network

Wilbur, *imprint of* Elephas Books Pty Ltd

Wild & Woolley Pty Ltd+
16 Darghan St, Glebe, NSW 2037
Mailing Address: PO Box 41, Glebe, NSW 2037
Tel: (02) 692-0166 *Fax:* (02) 552-4320
E-mail: pwoolley@mpx.com.au
Key Personnel
President & Man Dir: Pat Woolley
Founded: 1974
Member of APA, Women in Publishing; specialize in prints for self-publishers.
ISBN Prefix(es): 0-909331
Imprints: Bookus Fastinandi; Maquileadora
Divisions: Fast Books In Print

Wild Publications
389 Malvern Rd, South Yarra, Victoria 3141
Mailing Address: PO Box 415, Prahran, Victoria 3181
Tel: (03) 9826-8482 *Fax:* (03) 9826-3787
E-mail: wild@wild.com.au
Web Site: www.wild.com.au
Key Personnel
Man Dir: Chris Baxter
Founded: 1981
Publisher of Wild Magazine and Rock Magazine. Specializing in rockclimbing & hiking magazines & guidebooks to Australia.
Subjects: Sports, Athletics, Canoeing, Caving, Cross-Country Skiing, Hiking, Rock Climbing
Parent Company: Wild Holdings Pty Ltd
Distributed by Macstyle (Australia)

Wildlife in Newtown, *imprint of* Feakle Press

Wildscape Australia
Division of Thunderhead Photographics Pty Ltd
6 Ardmore Park, Kuranda, Qld 4872
Tel: (07) 4093 7171 *Fax:* (07) 4093 8897
Web Site: www.thunder.com.au
Key Personnel
Manager: Debbie Jarver
Contact: Peter Jarver *E-mail:* jarver@ozemail.com.au
Founded: 1979
Specializes in books of photographs taken by Peter Jarver.
Subjects: Photography of landscapes, skyscapes, Top End, Central Australia & Queensland
ISBN Prefix(es): 0-9589067
Total Titles: 5 Print

Wileman Publications+
3 Federation Ave, Broadbeach, Qld 4218
Tel: (07) 559 0969
E-mail: wileman@onthenet.com.au
Key Personnel
International Rights: Bud Wileman
Subjects: Art, Behavioral Sciences, Criminology, Education, English as a Second Language,

How-to, Human Relations, Language Arts, Linguistics, Law, Parapsychology, Psychology, Psychiatry, Self-Help, Social Sciences, Sociology
ISBN Prefix(es): 0-949026
Distributed by Barnes & Noble (North America)

John Wiley & Sons, *imprint of* John Wiley & Sons Australia Ltd

A S Wilson, *imprint of* A S Wilson Inc

A S Wilson Inc+
PO Box 296, Jannali, NSW 2226
Tel: (02) 9528 8977 *Fax:* (02) 5890635
Key Personnel
President: Charles M Lossi
Agent, McMahon Publishers: Brian McMahon
Founded: 1994 (Acquired from Maxwell MacMillan Australia Pty Ltd)
Sixty titles in print. High School study guides, trade & tertiary titles.
ISBN Prefix(es): 0-02; 0-08
Parent Company: A S Wilson Inc, 5585 East Silver Mine Place, Tucson, AZ 85715, United States
Imprints: A S Wilson; Australian National University Press
Shipping Address: Harcourt Brace & Co Australia Pty Ltd, Locked Bag 16, Marrickville, NSW 2204 *Tel:* (02) 517 8999 *Fax:* (02) 517 2249

Windhorse Books+
Rear 139 Wells St, Newtown, NSW 2042
Mailing Address: PO Box 574, Newtown, NSW 2042
Tel: (02) 9519 8826 *Fax:* (02) 9519 8826
E-mail: books@windhorse.com.au
Web Site: www.windhorse.com.au
Key Personnel
Contact: Dh Ratnajyoti
Founded: 1994
Subjects: Asian Studies, Human Relations, Poetry, Psychology, Psychiatry, Religion - Buddhist, Self-Help, Women's Studies, Specialize in Buddhism & Meditation
Imprints: Dharma Publishing; Pali Text Society; Rangging Yeshe Publications; Weatherlight Press; Windhorse Publications

Windhorse Publications, *imprint of* Windhorse Books

Windward Publications+
464 Woodhill Mountain Rd, Via Berry, NSW 2535
Tel: (02) 4464 1977 *Fax:* (02) 4464 1906
E-mail: admin@windward.com.au
Key Personnel
Contact: Mr David Colfelt *E-mail:* dc@windward.com.au
Founded: 1984
Subjects: Maritime, Travel, Great Barrier Reef, Whitsunday Islands
ISBN Prefix(es): 0-9590830

Windwood, *imprint of* Moonlight Publishing

Winetitles
Imprint of Wine Publishers Pty Ltd
97 Carrington St, Adelaide, SA 5000
Mailing Address: PO Box 6015, Halifax St, SA 5000
Tel: (08) 8233 4799 *Fax:* (08) 8233 4790
E-mail: admin@winetitles.com.au
Web Site: www.winetitles.com.au
Key Personnel
Publisher: Paul Clancy *E-mail:* pclancy@winetitles.com.au
Dir: Fran Clancy *E-mail:* fclancy@winetitles.com.au
Publisher of two magazines: *Australian Viticulture* and *The Australian & New Zealand Wine Industry Journal*. Also annual wine industry directory, books on viticulture & oenology, & an annual wine industry yearbook.
Subjects: Agriculture, Wine & Spirits
ISBN Prefix(es): 1-875130
Number of titles published annually: 2 Print
Total Titles: 19 Print

Wisdom Press, *imprint of* Desbooks Pty Ltd

Wizard Books Pty Ltd+
PO Box 304, Ballarat, Victoria 3353
Tel: (03) 53323435 *Fax:* (03) 53311488
E-mail: admin@wizardbooks.com.au
Web Site: www.wizardbooks.com.au
Key Personnel
Dir & International Rights: Richard McRoberts
Dir: Valerie McRoberts
Founded: 1991
APA Australian Publishers Association.
Subjects: Drama, Theater, Education, Literature, Literary Criticism, Essays, Science (General)
ISBN Prefix(es): 1-875739; 1-876367
Distributed by Claire Publications (UK); EPB (Singapore)

Women's Health Advisory Service+
19 Little St, Camden, NSW 2570
Mailing Address: PO Box 689, Camden, NSW 2570
Tel: (02) 4655 8855 *Fax:* (02) 4655 8699
Web Site: www.whas.com.au
Key Personnel
Head of Company: Jacqui Comley
Author: Sandra Cabot *E-mail:* cabot@ozemail.com.au
Founded: 1990
Subjects: Health, Nutrition, Women's Studies, Weight loss
ISBN Prefix(es): 0-646; 0-958
Total Titles: 10 Print
Associate Companies: Health Direction Pty Ltd; SCB International
U.S. Office(s): SCB International Inc *Tel:* 602-860-4299
Distributed by Ten Speed Press

Woodlands Publications
PO Box 646, Toronto, NSW 2283
Tel: (02) 4950 5100 *Fax:* (02) 4950 5240
Web Site: www.woodlandspublications.com
Key Personnel
Contact: A N Bendeich
Founded: 1982
Subjects: Business, Career Development, Communications, Education, Finance, Travel
ISBN Prefix(es): 1-875457; 0-9593057

Word of Life Distributors Pty Ltd, *imprint of* Rainbow Book Agencies Pty Ltd

Workaway Guides
PO Box 248, Bondi Junction, NSW 2022
Tel: (02) 9664 4559
Web Site: www.workaway.org
Key Personnel
Contact: Karen Halliday *E-mail:* karen@workaway.org

Worsley Press+
11 Lintel Court, Hastings 3915
Tel: (03) 5979-1112 *Fax:* (03) 5979-1112
E-mail: info@worsleypress.com
Web Site: www.worsleypress.com
Key Personnel
Owner, Publisher & International Rights: Gordon Woolf *E-mail:* gordon@worsleypress.com
Founded: 1991
Specialize in books on publication production.
Subjects: Business, How-to, Publishing & Book Trade Reference
ISBN Prefix(es): 1-875750
Number of titles published annually: 2 Print
Total Titles: 10 Print
Distributed by Florida Academic Press (North America)

Wrightbooks Pty Ltd+
Imprint of John Wiley & Sons Australia Ltd
PO Box 270, Elsternwick, Victoria 3185
Tel: (03) 9532 7082 *Toll Free Tel:* 800 777 474 *Fax:* (03) 9532 7084 *Toll Free Fax:* 800 802 258
E-mail: wbooks@ozemail.com.au
Web Site: www.wrightbooks.com.au
Key Personnel
Man Dir: Geoff Wright
Publisher: Lesley A Beaumont
Founded: 1988
Member of ABPA.
Subjects: Business, Career Development, Finance, Management, Real Estate, Self-Help
ISBN Prefix(es): 0-947351; 1-875857
Total Titles: 90 Print

Writers World
PO Box 1440, Surfers Paradise, Qld 4217
Tel: (075) 552377 *Fax:* (075) 55922001
Key Personnel
Head of Company: Peter Hall
ISBN Prefix(es): 7-316; 0-9587925; 1-875583

Yanagang Publishing
41 Beaufort Rd, Croydon, Victoria 3136
Tel: (03) 9870-3052 *Fax:* (03) 9876-1853
E-mail: gallerywithoutwalls@hotmail.com
Key Personnel
Contact: Dindy Vaughan
Subjects: Art, Environmental Studies, Music, Dance, Poetry
ISBN Prefix(es): 0-9588046
Number of titles published annually: 2 Print
Orders to: PO Box 668, Ringwood 3134

Young Hylanders, *imprint of* Hyland House Publishing Pty Ltd

Zephyr Press, *imprint of* Hawker Brownlow

Zoe Publishing Pty Ltd+
PO Box 77, Tugun, Qld 4224
Tel: (07) 55341522 *Fax:* (07) 55341502
E-mail: zoemkt@onthenet.com.au
Key Personnel
Contact: Tim McClymont
Founded: 1995
Subjects: Child Care & Development, Health, Nutrition, Parenting & Mother & Child Health Guide
ISBN Prefix(es): 0-9586581

Austria

General Information

Capital: Vienna
Language: German, small Croat & Slovene speaking minorities
Religion: Predominantly Roman Catholic, some Protestant and Muslim
Population: 8.1 million
Bank Hours: 0800-1230, 1330-1500 Monday-Wednesday, Friday; 0800-1230, 1300-1730 Thursday

PUBLISHERS   AUSTRIA

Shop Hours: 0800-1800 Monday-Friday; 0800-1200 or 1300 Saturday
Currency: 100 Eurocents = 1 Euro; 13.7603 schillings = 1 Euro
Export/Import Information: Import licenses not required for books. No exchange controls. 10% VAT on books.
Copyright: UCC, Berne, Florence (see Copyright Conventions, pg xi)

Aarachne Verlag+
Vergengasse 6, RH 14, 1220 Vienna
Tel: (01) 2855353 *Fax:* (01) 2855353
Web Site: www.aarachne.at
Key Personnel
Manager: Ernst Petz
Marketing: Astrid Rossbacher
Founded: 1992
Subjects: Drama, Theater, Ethnicity, Fiction, Human Relations, Journalism, Literature, Literary Criticism, Essays, Mysteries, Science Fiction, Fantasy
ISBN Prefix(es): 3-85255

Abakus Verlag GmbH+
Pezoltgasse 50, 5020 Salzburg
Tel: (0662) 662 24 65 84
Founded: 1979
Subjects: Environmental Studies, Language Arts, Linguistics, Mathematics
ISBN Prefix(es): 3-7044

Aeneas Verlagsgesellschaft GmbH+
Hauptstr 38, 2340 Moedling
Tel: (02236) 25422
Key Personnel
Manager: Johanna Theurer; Hermann Theurer
Founded: 1989
ISBN Prefix(es): 3-85065

Agens-Werk, Geyer & Reisser, Druck und Verlagsgesellschaft mbH
Arbeitergasse 1-7, 1051 Vienna
Tel: (01) 545641 *Fax:* (01) 544564166
Key Personnel
Man Dir: Friedrich Geyer
ISBN Prefix(es): 3-7033; 3-85202

Akademische Druck-u Verlagsanstalt Dr Paul Struzl GmbH+
Auersperggasse 12, 8010 Graz
Mailing Address: Postfach 598, 8011 Graz
Tel: (0316) 3644 *Fax:* (0316) 36 44-24
E-mail: info@adeva.com
Web Site: www.adeva.com *Cable:* ADEVA GRAZ
Key Personnel
General Manager: Dr Ursula Struzl *Tel:* (0316) 36 44-30 *E-mail:* struzl@adeva.com
Editor: Dr Christine Brandstaetter *Tel:* (0316) 36 44-34 *E-mail:* bradstaetter@adeva.com; Gerhard Lechner *Tel:* (0316) 36 44-45 *E-mail:* lechner@adeva.com
Distribution: Michael Pichler *Tel:* (0316) 36 44-43 *E-mail:* pichler@adeva.com
Founded: 1949
Specializes in Facsimile.
Subjects: Anthropology, Archaeology, Art, Biography, Language Arts, Linguistics, Military Science, Music, Dance, Regional Interests
ISBN Prefix(es): 3-201; 3-900144
Number of titles published annually: 10 Print
Total Titles: 2,000 Print
Subsidiaries: Codices Selecti

Alekto Verlag GmbH+
Radetzkystr 10/2, 9020 Klagenfurt
Mailing Address: Postfach 502, 9010 Klagenfurt
Tel: (0463) 515 230; (0463) 593 217 *Fax:* (0463) 503 351
E-mail: bali@bali.co.at
Web Site: bali.co.at
Key Personnel
Man Dir: Stefan Zefferer *E-mail:* stefan.zefferer@bali.co.at
Manager & Marketing Dir: Harry Haberl *E-mail:* harry.haberl@bali.co.at
Founded: 1986
Specialize in Austrian Literature.
Subjects: History, Poetry, Politics
ISBN Prefix(es): 3-900743
Total Titles: 200 Print; 5 CD-ROM; 5 E-Book
Foreign Rep(s): VG Dr Glas

Amalthea-Verlag
Subsidiary of Buchverlage Langen-Mueller/Herbig
Am Heumarkt 19, 1030 Vienna
Tel: (01) 712 35 60 *Fax:* (01) 713 89 95
Web Site: www.amalthea.at
Key Personnel
Greschf: Dr Herbert Fleissner
International Rights: Dorothea Esthermann
Founded: 1917
Member of Buchverlage Ullstein Langen Mueller/Herbig, Germany.
Subjects: Art, Fiction, Music, Dance
ISBN Prefix(es): 3-85002
Associate Companies: Ullstein Langen Mueller

Andreas und Andreas Verlagsbuchhandel+
Hans-Seebachstr 10, 5023 Salzburg
Tel: (0662) 64350008 *Fax:* (0662) 6435002
Cable: ANDREASVERLAG SALZBURG
Key Personnel
Publishers: Wolf-Dietrich Andreas; Ingrid Andreas
Dir: Franz Pemwieser
Founded: 1956
Subjects: Fiction
ISBN Prefix(es): 3-85012
Branch Office(s)
Andreas und Andreas Verlagsbuchhandel Zweigniederlassing, D-8228 Freilassingy, Germany
Andreas und Andreas Verlagsanstal, FL-9490 Vaduz, Liechtenstein
Oskar Andreas Nachfolger Herzog & Co, Reise- und Versandbuchhande, A-1170 Vienna, Parhamerpl 9

Annette Betz, *imprint of* Verlag Carl Ueberreuter GmbH

Verlag der Apfel+
Schottenfeldgasse 51, 1070 Vienna
Tel: (01) 52 661 52 *Fax:* (01) 5228718
Key Personnel
Man Dir: Thomas C Cubasch
Founded: 1984
Subjects: Art, Literature, Literary Criticism, Essays
ISBN Prefix(es): 3-85450

Aritbus et Historiae, Rivista Internationale di arti visive ecinema, Institut IRSA - Verlagsanstatt+
Ruedengasse 6, 1030 Vienna
Tel: (01) 7130136 *Fax:* (01) 7130130
E-mail: irsa@irsa.com.pl
Web Site: www.irsa.com.pl
Key Personnel
Publisher: Dr Jozef Grabski
Founded: 1980
Specialize in History of Art.
Subjects: Architecture & Interior Design, Art, History
ISBN Prefix(es): 3-900731

Astor-Verlag, Willibald Schlager+
Rosentalgasse 5-1, 1140 Vienna
Tel: (01) 9144281 *Fax:* (01) 9144281
Founded: 1975
Subjects: Biography, Fiction, Humor, Literature, Literary Criticism, Essays, Regional Interests
ISBN Prefix(es): 3-900277

Autorensolidaritat - Verlag der Interessengemeinschaft osterreichischer Autorinnen und Autoren
Literaturhaus, Seidengasse 13, A-1070 Vienna
Tel: (01) 526 20 44-13 *Fax:* (01) 526 20 44-55
E-mail: ig@literaturhaus.at
Key Personnel
President: Milo Dor
Man Dir: Gerhard Ruiss
Founded: 1982
Subjects: Publishing & Book Trade Reference
ISBN Prefix(es): 3-419

Verlag Alexander Bernhardt
14 Vomperberg, 6134 Vomp/Tirol
Tel: (05242) 6213149 *Fax:* (05242) 72801
E-mail: bernhardt@grafswerk.org; c.bernhardt@tirol.com
Key Personnel
Contact: Siegfried Bernhardt
Founded: 1945
Subjects: Philosophy
ISBN Prefix(es): 3-87860
Associate Companies: Verlag der Stiftung Gralsbotschaft GmbH, Germany
U.S. Office(s): Grail Foundation of America, 2081 Partridge Lane, Binghamton, NY 13903, United States, Richard H Gehl
Grail Movement of America, 7204 Lucern Court, Charlotte, NC 28277, United States, Emanuel O'Biorah
Orders to: Verlag der Stiftung Gralsbotschaft GmbH, Schuckerstr 8, D-71254 Ditzingen, Germany

Bethania Verlag+
Johann-Gottek-Gasse 26, 1230 Vienna
Tel: (01) 6672216
Key Personnel
Contact: Helene Mirtl
Founded: 1982
Subjects: Biological Sciences, Chemistry, Chemical Engineering, Philosophy, Physical Sciences, Science (General)
ISBN Prefix(es): 3-900085

Annette Betz Verlag im Verlag Carl Ueberreuter+
Alserstr 24, 1091 Vienna
Mailing Address: Postfach 306, 1091 Vienna
Tel: (01) 404440 *Fax:* (01) 404445
Web Site: www.annettebetz.com; www.ueberreuter.at
Telex: 114802 *Cable:* UEBER A
Key Personnel
Man Dir: Dr Fritz Panzer; Dr Richard Starkel
Editorial: Irmgard Harrer
Contact: Dr Susanne Czeitschner *Tel:* (01) 40444165 *E-mail:* czeitschner@ueberreuter.at
Founded: 1962
ISBN Prefix(es): 3-219
Parent Company: Verlag Carl Ueberreuter
Shipping Address: Dr Franz Hain Verlagsauscieferung, Dr Otto-Neurath-Gasse 5, 1220 Vienna *Tel:* (01) 2826565 *Fax:* (01) 2825282
Warehouse: Dr Franz Hain Verlagsauscieferung, Dr Otto-Neurath-Gasse 5, 1220 Vienna

Der Baum Wolfgang Biedermann Verlag+
Apollogasse 14/1, 1070 Vienna
Tel: (01) 9319053
Key Personnel
President & Publisher: Wolfgang Bedermann
Subjects: Literature, Literary Criticism, Essays
ISBN Prefix(es): 3-901133

AUSTRIA

Boehlau Verlag GmbH & Co KG+
Sachsenplatz 4-6, Postfach 87, 1201 Vienna
Tel: (01) 330 24 27 *Fax:* (01) 330 24 32
Web Site: www.boehlau.at
Telex: 114506 Spriw A
Key Personnel
Dir: Dr Peter Rauch
Editorial: Dr Eva Reinhold-Weisz
Press: Elizabeth Dechant *E-mail:* elizabeth.dechant@boehlau.at
Production: Ulrike Dietmayer
Sales, Publicity: Roland Tomrle
Founded: 1947
Subjects: Art, Government, Political Science, History, Language Arts, Linguistics, Law, Science (General), Social Sciences, Sociology, Women's Studies
ISBN Prefix(es): 3-205
Associate Companies: Boehlau-Verlag GmbH & Cie, Cologne, Germany
Orders to: Springer Verlagsauslieferung, Postfach 8, A-1201 Vienna *Tel:* (01) 3302415

Bohmann Druck und Verlag GmbH & Co KG
Leberstr 122, 1110 Vienna
Tel: (01) 740950 *Fax:* (01) 74095 183
Web Site: www.bohmann.co.at
Telex: 132312
Key Personnel
Manager: Dr Rudolf Bohmann
Contact: Prof Heinz Keller
Founded: 1936
Subjects: Automotive, Business, Computer Science, Environmental Studies, Transportation, Travel
ISBN Prefix(es): 3-7002; 3-901983

Braintrust Marketing Services Ges mbH Verlag
Schopenhauerstr 36, 1180 Vienna
Tel: (01) 40416-0 *Fax:* (01) 40416-33
E-mail: braintrust@magnet.at
Web Site: www.braintrust.at
Key Personnel
Man Dir: Thomas Stern *E-mail:* stern@braintrust.at
Dir: Christian Seifert *E-mail:* seifert@braintrust.at
Founded: 1989
Subjects: Career Development, Education, Management
ISBN Prefix(es): 3-901116

Christian Brandstatter Verlagsgesellschaft GmbH+
Schwarzenbergstr 5, 1010 Vienna
Tel: (01) 4083814; (01) 4083815 *Fax:* (01) 4087200
E-mail: books@oebv.co.et
Key Personnel
Publisher: Dr Christian Brandstaetter
Manager: Dr Robert Sedlacek; Mag Walter Amon
Founded: 1982
Subjects: Architecture & Interior Design, Art, Biography, Photography, Regional Interests
ISBN Prefix(es): 3-85447; 3-206; 3-85498
Total Titles: 236 Print
Parent Company: Oesterreichischer Bundesverlag

BSE Verlag Dr Bernhard Schuttengruber+
Klosterwiegasse 52, 8010 Graz
Tel: (0316) 839600; 283170
Founded: 1984
Subjects: History, Poetry
ISBN Prefix(es): 3-900542

Buchhandlung WUV Dolmetsch+
Formerly Service Fachverlag an der Wirtschaftsuniversitae Wien
Philippovichgasse 16, 1190 Vienna
Tel: (01) 3685704 *Fax:* (01) 3109023
E-mail: fachverlag@servicebetriebe.at
Telex: 135720 hwusv
Key Personnel
Publishing Dir: Dr Christin Draexler
Founded: 1981
Subjects: Accounting, Business, Career Development, Economics, Finance, Law, Management, Marketing
ISBN Prefix(es): 3-85428
Bookshop(s): Universitat buchhandlung, Doblinger Hauptstr 7A/12, 1190 Vienna
Orders to: Service Fachverlag, Augasse 2-6, A-1090 Vienna *Tel:* (01) 317916221 *Fax:* (01) 3109904

Buchkultur Verlags GmbH Zeitschrift fuer Literatur & Kunst
Huetteldorferstr 26, 1150 Vienna
Tel: (01) 7863380 *Fax:* (01) 7863380-10
E-mail: office@buchkultur.net
Web Site: www.buchkultur.net
Key Personnel
Geschf: Michael Schnepf
Founded: 1989
Subjects: Communications, Journalism, Literature, Literary Criticism, Essays, Publishing & Book Trade Reference, Regional Interests
ISBN Prefix(es): 3-901052
Branch Office(s)
Birkenstr 7, 85774 Unterfoehring, Germany
Fax: (089) 958216-92

Fachverlag fur Burgerinformation, Eigenvelag+
Grabenstr 117, 8010 Graz
Tel: (0316) 686727 *Fax:* (0316) 673078
Key Personnel
Manager: Alfred Steingruber
Founded: 1986
Subjects: Public Administration
ISBN Prefix(es): 3-85363

Camera Austria+
Sparkassenplaz 2, A-8010 Graz
Tel: (0316) 81 55 50-0 *Fax:* (0316) 81 55 50-9
E-mail: camera.austria@styria.com
Web Site: www.camera-austria.at
Key Personnel
Publisher: Manfred Willmann
Editor: Christine Frisinghelli
Founded: 1980
Subjects: Art, Photography

Carinthia Verlag
Voelkermarkter Ring 25, 9020 Klagenfurt
Tel: (0463) 50 12 20-212 *Fax:* (0463) 50 12 20-214
Web Site: www.verlag.carinthia.com
Key Personnel
Dir: Karin Waldner *Tel:* (0463) 50 12 20-210
Founded: 1893
Subjects: Archaeology, Art, Cookery, History, Religion - Other
ISBN Prefix(es): 3-85378; 3-900184; 3-900686
Number of titles published annually: 20 Print
Total Titles: 120 Print

CEEBA Publications Antenne d'Autriche+
A-2340 Modling, Saint Gabriel
Tel: (02236) 803115 *Fax:* (02236) 8033
E-mail: ceeba@steyler.at
Web Site: www.steyler.at/
Key Personnel
Man Dir, Editorial: Dr Hermann Hochegger
Founded: 1965
Specialize in paperback, rituals. Also a study center for traditional culture of Black Africa & Haiti.
Subjects: Agriculture, Anthropology, Art, Ethnicity, Health, Nutrition, History, Language Arts, Linguistics, Literature, Literary Criticism, Essays, Psychology, Psychiatry, Religion - Other, Social Sciences, Sociology
ISBN Prefix(es): 3-902011
Number of titles published annually: 4 Print
Total Titles: 2 Print
Online services available through World Wide Web.
Parent Company: CEEBA, Bandundu, Kongo
Foreign Rep(s): Antenne d'Antride

Compass-Verlag GmbH
Matznergasse 17, 1141 Vienna
Tel: (01) 981 16-113 *Fax:* (01) 981 16-113
E-mail: hfu@compass.co.at
Web Site: www.plau.al; www.maskt.al; www.compass.at
Key Personnel
Man Dirs: Werner Futter; Horst Dolezal
Sales Dir: Michael Bayer *E-mail:* mba@compass.al
Founded: 1867
Specialize in Internet databases.
Member of OeAVV, EAVV.
Subjects: Business, Economics, Finance
ISBN Prefix(es): 3-85041
Number of titles published annually: 4 Print; 2 CD-ROM
Total Titles: 4 Print
Online services available through World Wide Web.
Subsidiaries: Comp Almanach Kft

Cura Verlag GmbH
Beatrixgasse 32, 1037 Vienna
Mailing Address: Postfach 49, Vienna
Tel: (01) 7136480 *Fax:* (01) 7126258; (01) 7126219
Key Personnel
Man Dir: Brigitte Podoschek
Publicity Manager: Eva M Plattner
Subjects: Education, Regional Interests, Religion - Other
ISBN Prefix(es): 3-7027

Czernin Verlag+
Piaristengasse 1, 1080 Vienna
Tel: (01) 512 01 32 *Fax:* (01) 512 01 32-15
E-mail: office@czernin-verlag.com
Web Site: www.czernin-verlag.com
Key Personnel
Publisher: Hubertus Czernin *E-mail:* hoz@czernin-verlag.com
Production: Andrea Schaller *E-mail:* schaller@czernin-verlag.com
Marketing & Press: Anna Mirfattahi *E-mail:* a.mirfattahi@czernin-verlag.com
Founded: 1999
Subjects: Nonfiction (General), Public Administration, Religion - Jewish, Science (General)
ISBN Prefix(es): 3-7076
Total Titles: 70 Print

Dachs-Verlag GmbH+
Biberhaufenweg 100, Haus 38, 1220 Vienna
Tel: (01) 285 22 05-0 *Fax:* (01) 285 22 05-15
E-mail: office@dachs.at
Web Site: www.dachs.at
Key Personnel
Man Dir: Dr Hubert Hladej *E-mail:* hladej.sen@dachs.at
Founded: 1921
Subjects: Art, Education, Ethnicity, Literature, Literary Criticism, Essays, Music, Dance, Psychology, Psychiatry, Social Sciences, Sociology
ISBN Prefix(es): 3-224; 3-7141; 3-900763; 3-85191; 3-85058

Danubia Werbung und Verlagsservice
Viehmarktgasse 4, 1030 Vienna
Tel: (01) 792666 *Fax:* (01) 792666443
Key Personnel
Man Dir: N Schnabl
Publicity Dir: Dr P Wasservogel
Founded: 1952

Subjects: Art, Fiction, Science (General)
ISBN Prefix(es): 3-7006; 3-85044

dbv-Druck Beratungs-und Verlags GmbH
 Verlag fur die Technische Universitat Graz+
Geidorfguertel 20, 8010 Graz
Tel: (0316) 38 30 33 *Fax:* (0316) 38 30 43
E-mail: office@dbv.at
Web Site: www.dbv.at
Key Personnel
Man Dir: Gerhard E Erker
Founded: 1976
ISBN Prefix(es): 3-7041

Denkmayr GmbH Druck & Verlag+
Reslweg 3, 4020 Linz
Tel: (0732) 654511 *Fax:* (0732) 65612417
Key Personnel
Contact: Ernst Denkmayr
International Rights: Regina Noebauer
Founded: 1989
Subjects: Poetry, Regional Interests, Self-Help
ISBN Prefix(es): 3-901838
Warehouse: Ernst Denkmayr GmbH, Reslweg 3, 4020 Linz
Orders to: Ernst Denkmayr GmbH, Reslweg 3, 4020 Linz

Verlag Harald Denzel, Auto- und Freizeitfuehrer+
Maximilianstr 9, A-6020 Innsbruck
Tel: (0512) 586880 *Fax:* (0512) 586880
Key Personnel
Contact: Harald Denzel
Founded: 1952
Subjects: Geography, Geology, Outdoor Recreation, Travel, Illustrated Guide Books
ISBN Prefix(es): 3-85047

Franz Deuticke Verlagsges mbH+
Hagelgasse 21, 1015 Vienna
Tel: (01) 51405210 *Fax:* (01) 51405289
Web Site: www.deuticke.at
Key Personnel
Manager: Dr Martina Schmidt *Tel:* (01) 512 15 44-300 *Fax:* (01) 51405285 *E-mail:* schmidt@oebv.co.et
Marketing & Selling: Ulla Schwaighofer *Tel:* (01) 512 15 75-288
Marketing & Sales: Silvia Wahrstaetter *Tel:* (01) 512 15 75-274
Press & Public Relations: Valerie Besl *Tel:* (01) 512 15 75-293
Founded: 1878
Specialize in psychology.
Subjects: Literature, Literary Criticism, Essays, Mysteries, Nonfiction (General), Philosophy, Regional Interests, Science (General)
ISBN Prefix(es): 3-7005; 3-216; 3-85223
Total Titles: 629 Print
Bookshop(s): Buchhandlung Franz Deuticke, Antiquariat Franz Deutick, Helferstorferstr 4, A-1011 Vienna 1
Orders to: Osterr Schulbuchzentrum, Postfach 133, A-2355 Wiener Neudorf *Fax:* (2236) 63535243

Development News Ltd
21 Pragerstr 92/4, Vienna
Tel: (01) 3880324
Key Personnel
Man Dir & Publisher: Dr Yemi D Ogunyemi
Editorial Manager: Simon Adewale Ebine
Publications Manager: Willy Bruckner
Publicity Executive: Pius Eyitayo Ogunyemi
Sales Executive: T A Ogunyemi
Founded: 1983
Also promotes Nigerian/African literatures through seminars, lectures, symposia, conferences, book presentations & writing workshops.
Subjects: Agriculture, Animals, Pets, Anthropology, Child Care & Development, Communications, Developing Countries, Education, English as a Second Language, Ethnicity, Fiction, Government, Political Science, History, Journalism, Literature, Literary Criticism, Essays, Nonfiction (General), Poetry, Regional Interests, Religion - Other, Social Sciences, Sociology, Women's Studies
ISBN Prefix(es): 978-2843
U.S. Office(s): Diaspora Press of America, 91 Ames St, Box C340, Boston, MA 02124-3033, United States

Diotima Presse+
Bachgasse 22, 3200 Obergrafendorf
Tel: (043) 2747-8528 *Fax:* (043) 2747-8528
E-mail: diotimapresse@utanet.at
Founded: 2000
Handcrafted books with mainly original illustrations.
Subjects: Philosophy, Poetry
Number of titles published annually: 8 Print
Total Titles: 23 Print

Ludwig Doblinger (Bernhard Herzmansky) Musikverlag KG
Dorotheergasse 10, 1010 Vienna
Tel: (01) 515 03-0 *Fax:* (01) 515 03-51
E-mail: music@doblinger.at
Web Site: www.doblinger.at
Key Personnel
Man Dir: Helmuth Pany
Sales Manager: Peter Pany
Rights & Licensing: Christine Prindl
Advertising Manager: Dr Christian Heindl
Distribution Manager: Franz Kucera
Founded: 1876
Specializes in music-notes & books.
Subjects: Music, Dance
ISBN Prefix(es): 3-900695
Distributor for Musikwissenschaftlicher Verlag Wien (MWV)
Bookshop(s): Musikhaus Doblinger, Vienna

Docker Verlag GmbH & Co KG+
Hintzerstr 11/3, A-1030 Vienna
Tel: (01) 7159200 *Fax:* (01) 715920076
E-mail: vgkritik@ping.at
Key Personnel
Man Dir, Production & Rights & Permissions: Ulrike Doecker
Editorial: Peter Horn
Sales, Publicity: Petra Hartlieb
Founded: 1980
Subjects: Archaeology, Biography, Education, Fiction, Film, Video, History, Journalism, Labor, Industrial Relations, Outdoor Recreation, Women's Studies
ISBN Prefix(es): 3-900351; 3-85115

Literature Verlag Droschl+
Alberstr 18, 8010 Graz
Tel: (0316) 32-64-04 *Fax:* (0316) 32-40-71
E-mail: literaturverlag@droschl.com
Web Site: www.droschl.com
Key Personnel
Contact: Dr Rainer Gotz *E-mail:* rainer@droschl.com
Founded: 1978
Publishing honor for contemporary European literature.
Books & Audio CD's.
Subjects: Art, Drama, Theater, Literature, Literary Criticism, Essays, Poetry
ISBN Prefix(es): 3-85420
Number of titles published annually: 18 Print
Total Titles: 300 Print; 5 Audio
Imprints: Edition Neue Text

Edition Neue Text, *imprint of* Literature Verlag Droschl

Edition S der OSD+
Rennweg 12a, 1037 Vienna
Tel: (01) 79789295 *Fax:* (01) 79789455
Telex: 131 805 *Cable:* OESTAATSDRUCK WIEN
Key Personnel
Man Dir: Dr Manfred A Schmid
Founded: 1985
Subjects: Criminology, Fiction, Film, Video, History, Human Relations, Literature, Literary Criticism, Essays, Maritime, Parapsychology
ISBN Prefix(es): 3-7046
Parent Company: Oesterreichische Staatsdruckerei

Ennsthaler GesmbH & Co KG+
Stadtpl 26, 4400 Steyr
Tel: (07252) 52053 *Fax:* (07252) 52053 3
E-mail: buero@ennsthaler.at
Web Site: www.ennsthaler.at
Founded: 1880
Subjects: Cookery, Health, Nutrition, History, Medicine, Nursing, Dentistry, Poetry, Regional Interests, Religion - Catholic, Theology
ISBN Prefix(es): 3-85068

Evangelischer Presseverband in Osterreich
Ungargasse 9/10, 1030 Vienna
Tel: (01) 712 54 61 *Fax:* (01) 712 54 75
E-mail: epd@evang.at
Key Personnel
Man Dir: Paul Weiland
Founded: 1925
ISBN Prefix(es): 3-85073
Warehouse: Ungargasse 12, 1030 Vienna

Fassbaender Verlag
Lichtgasse 10, 1150 Vienna
Tel: (01) 8923546 *Fax:* (01) 8923546-22
E-mail: mail@fassbaender.com
Web Site: www.fassbaender.com
Key Personnel
Executive: Ernst Becvar *Tel:* (01) 8923546-12 *E-mail:* becvar-senior@aon.at
Founded: 1987
Specialize in Literature, Literary Criticism.
Subjects: History, Language Arts, Linguistics, Science (General)
ISBN Prefix(es): 3-900538
Number of titles published annually: 5 Print
Total Titles: 60 Print

Ferdinand Berger und Sohne
Wienerstr 21-23, A-3580 Horn
Tel: (02982) 4161-332 *Fax:* (02982) 4161-382
E-mail: druckerei.office@berger.at
Web Site: www.berger.at
Telex: 78613 *Cable:* BERGER HORN
Key Personnel
Man Dir: Peter Berger
Founded: 1868
Subjects: Anthropology, Archaeology, Art, Natural History
ISBN Prefix(es): 3-85028
Branch Office(s)
Pulverturmasse 3, 1090 Vienna *Tel:* (01) 313 35-0 *Fax:* (01) 313 35-19

Folio Verlagsgesellschaft mbH+
Gruengasse 9, 1050 Vienna
Tel: (01) 5813708-0 *Fax:* (01) 5813708-20
E-mail: office@folioverlag.com
Web Site: www.folioverlag.com/books.php
Founded: 1992
ISBN Prefix(es): 3-85256
Number of titles published annually: 30 Print
Total Titles: 130 Print
Branch Office(s)
Mitterweg 16a, 39100 Bozen, Italy *Tel:* (0471) 971323 *Fax:* (0471) 971603

AUSTRIA

Freytag-Berndt und Artaria, Kartographische Anstalt+
Brunner Str 69, 1231 Vienna
Tel: (01) 869 90 90 *Fax:* (01) 869 88 55
E-mail: office@freytagberndt.at
Telex: 133526
Key Personnel
Chairman: Bernd Mahr
Man Dir: Christian Halbwachs
Sales Manager: Wolfgang Kaiser
Founded: 1770
Subjects: Geography, Geology
ISBN Prefix(es): 3-85084
Bookshop(s): Schottenfeldgasse 62, Postfach 169, A-1070 Vienna; Kohlmarkt 9, A-1010 Vienna; Wilhelm-Greil Str 15, A-6020 Innsbruck

Georg Fromme und Co
Arbeitergasse 1-7, 1051 Vienna
Tel: (01) 5445641 *Fax:* (01) 544564166
Telex: 111969
Key Personnel
Man Dir: Friedrich Geyer
Founded: 1748
Subjects: Science (General)
ISBN Prefix(es): 3-85086

Edition Dr Heinrich Fuchs
Thimiggasse 82, 1180 Vienna
Tel: (01) 4792381 *Fax:* (01) 4792381
E-mail: edition.h.fuchs@aon.at
Subjects: Art
ISBN Prefix(es): 3-85390

Gangan Verlag+
Rainleiten 62, 8045 Graz
Web Site: www.gangan.com
Key Personnel
Publisher: Gerald Ganglbauer
Founded: 1985
Subjects: Literature, Literary Criticism, Essays
ISBN Prefix(es): 3-900530
Number of titles published annually: 2 E-Book
Total Titles: 24 Print; 12 E-Book
Imprints: GanGAROO (The OZlit Collection)
Subsidiaries: Gangan Books Australia
Branch Office(s)
Janet Wells, 15 Naranja Way, Portola Valley, CA 94028, United States

GanGAROO, *imprint of* Gangan Verlag

Gerold & Co
Weihburggasse 26, 1010 Vienna
Tel: (01) 521 4731 *Fax:* (1) 512 473129
E-mail: buch@gerold.at
Telex: 847136157 Gerol; 76157 *Cable:* Geroldbuch Vienna
Key Personnel
Man Dir: Hans Neusser
Subjects: Language Arts, Linguistics, Philosophy
ISBN Prefix(es): 3-900190

Verlag fuer Geschichte und Politik
Neulinggasse 26, 1030 Vienna
Tel: (01) 712 62 58 0 *Fax:* (01) 712 62 58 19
Key Personnel
Man Dir: Dr Erika Ruedegger
Sales Dir: Gerda Adler
Publicity & Advertising: Dr Ursula Huber
Founded: 1947
Subjects: Economics, Government, Political Science, History, Social Sciences, Sociology
ISBN Prefix(es): 3-7028
Associate Companies: Verlag Oldenbourg

Verlag Lynkeus/H Hakel Gesellschaft+
Traisengasse 17/28, 1200 Vienna
Tel: (01) 7342294
Key Personnel
Man Dir: Emmerich Kolovic

Founded: 1988
Subjects: Biography, Fiction, Humor, Literature, Literary Criticism, Essays, Poetry
ISBN Prefix(es): 3-900924

Globus Buchvertrieb
Seilerstatte 22/1, 1010 Vienna
Tel: (01) 513 96 92 0 *Fax:* (01) 513 96 92 9
Key Personnel
General Manager: Hans Jauker; H Zaslawski
Founded: 1945
Firms are also general representatives & distributors.
Subjects: Government, Political Science
ISBN Prefix(es): 3-85364

Alois Goschl & Co
Trummelhofgasse 12, 1190 Vienna
Tel: (01) 321180 *Fax:* (01) 651899
Key Personnel
Proprietor: Hiltraud Lechner
Founded: 1949
Subjects: Health, Nutrition, Psychology, Psychiatry, Veterinary Science
ISBN Prefix(es): 3-85096

Edition Graphischer Zirkel
Langegasse 14/44, 1080 Vienna
Tel: (01) 0277346615
Subjects: Art, Fiction, Literature, Literary Criticism, Essays, Poetry, Travel
ISBN Prefix(es): 3-900308

Graz Stadtmuseum
Sackstr 18, 8010 Graz
Tel: (0316) 822580 *Fax:* (0316) 822580-6
Web Site: homepage.sime.com
Key Personnel
Dir: Dr Guenther Dienes
Subjects: Art, History, Regional Interests
ISBN Prefix(es): 3-900764
Total Titles: 275 Print

Guthmann & Peterson Liber Libri, Edition+
Elsslergasse 17, 1130 Vienna
Tel: (01) 877 04 26 *Fax:* (01) 876 40 04
E-mail: verlag@guthmann-peterson.at
Web Site: www.guthmann-peterson.de
Key Personnel
Man Dir: W Peterson
Founded: 1988
Subjects: Developing Countries, Government, Political Science, Literature, Literary Criticism, Essays, Science (General), Social Sciences, Sociology
ISBN Prefix(es): 3-900782; 3-85306; 3-85481
Divisions: Edition Garamond

Hand-Presse
Hottingergasse 41, 6020 Innsbruck
Tel: (0512) 87975
Key Personnel
Owner: Hans Augustin
ISBN Prefix(es): 3-900862

Haymon-Verlag GesmbH+
Kochstr 10, 6020 Innsbruck
Tel: (0512) 576300 *Fax:* (0512) 576300-14
E-mail: office@haymonverlag.at
Web Site: www.haymonverlag.at
Key Personnel
Man Dir & Rights & Permissions: Dr Michael Forcher *E-mail:* michael.forcher@haymonverlag.at
Sales & International Rights: Alexandra Peischer *Tel:* (0512) 567300-16 *E-mail:* alexandra.peischer@haymonverlag.at
Sales: Gerhard Roedlach *Tel:* (0512) 576300-11 *E-mail:* gerhard.roedlach@haymonverlag.at
Editorial: Matthias Bauer *Tel:* (0512) 576300-11 *E-mail:* matthias.bauer@haymonverlag.at

Production: Dr Benno Peter *Tel:* (0512) 576300-15 *E-mail:* bennopeter@haymonverlag.at
Founded: 1982
Subjects: Architecture & Interior Design, Art, Biography, Fiction, History, Literature, Literary Criticism, Essays, Mysteries, Philosophy, Social Sciences, Sociology
ISBN Prefix(es): 3-85218
Number of titles published annually: 25 Print
Total Titles: 350 Print

Edition Helbling Verlags-Gesellschaft mbH
Kaplanstr 9, A-6063 Rum
Mailing Address: Postfach 12, A-6063 Rum
Tel: (512) 262333-0 *Fax:* (512) 262333-111
E-mail: office@helbling.co.at
Web Site: www.helbling.com
Key Personnel
President: Markus Spielmann
International Rights: Klaus Mayerl *E-mail:* k.mayerl@helbling.co.at
Subjects: Education, English as a Second Language, Music, Dance, Specialize in choral music books
ISBN Prefix(es): 3-85061; 3-900590

Verlag Herder & Co, see Verlag Kerle im Verlag Herder & Co

Hermagoras/Mohorjeva+
Viktringer-Ring 26, 9020 Klagenfurt
Tel: (0463) 56515 21 *Fax:* (0463) 514189
E-mail: office@mohorjeva.at
Web Site: www.mohorjeva.at
Telex: 422801
Key Personnel
Man Dir: Dr Anton Koren
Sales & Publicity: Karl Boehm; Janko Ferk
Editorial & Production: Franz Kattnig
Founded: 1851
Specializes in Books in Slovenian and German Language.
ISBN Prefix(es): 3-85013
Parent Company: Mohorjeva Druzba/Hermagoras Gesellschaft, Viktringer-Ring 26, 9020 Klagenfurt
Subsidiaries: Korotan Import-Export GmbH

Herold Business Data AG+
Guntramsdorferstr 105, 2340 Moedling
Tel: (02236) 401-133 *Fax:* (02236) 401-8
E-mail: kundendienst@herold.at
Web Site: www.herold.co.at
Telex: 114336 herol a
Key Personnel
Manager: Yon M Martinsen
Founded: 1918
Subjects: Marketing
ISBN Prefix(es): 3-85110

Herold Druck-und Verlagsgesellschaft mbH+
Faraday gasse 6, 1032 Modling
Tel: (01) 795 94-115 *Fax:* (01) 79594115
Telex: 111760 Wspro
Key Personnel
Man Dir: Franz Hoermann; Leopold Kurz
Founded: 1893
Subjects: Art, History, Religion - Catholic
ISBN Prefix(es): 3-7008; 3-9500004; 3-901628

Johannes Heyn, Gert und Volkmar Zechner
Friedensgasse 23, 9020 Klagenfurt
Tel: (0463) 33631 *Fax:* (0463) 33631-33
Telex: 042401; 422401 *Cable:* Heyn Klagenfurt
Key Personnel
Man Dir: Gerd Zechner
Founded: 1868
Subjects: Art, Biography, Fiction, History, How-to, Music, Dance, Poetry, Science (General)
ISBN Prefix(es): 3-85366
Bookshop(s): Buchhandlung Johannes Heyn

PUBLISHERS

Edition E Hilger
Dorotheergasse 5, 1010 Vienna
Tel: (01) 512 53 15 *Fax:* (01) 513 91 26
E-mail: hilger@hilger.at
Key Personnel
Man Dir & Production: Ernst Hilger
Sales & Publicity: Monica Zimmermann
Founded: 1973
Subjects: Art
ISBN Prefix(es): 3-900318

Ferdinand Hirt mbH & Co KG
Widerhofergasse 8/111/11, A-1094 Vienna
Tel: (01) 343558
Telex: 115014
Key Personnel
Manager: Goetz Hirt-Reger; Herwig Seebauer; Sabine Hirt-Reger
Founded: 1965
Subjects: Education, Geography, Geology, Science (General)
ISBN Prefix(es): 3-7019; 3-85112
Orders to: Allmannsolorferstr 154/156, A-1232 Vienna

Verlag Hoelder-Pichler-Tempsky+
Frankgasse 4, 1096 Vienna
Mailing Address: Postfach 127, 1096 Vienna
Tel: (01) 401 36-0 *Fax:* (01) 401 35-85
Key Personnel
Man Dir: Gustav Gloeckler
Founded: 1690
Subjects: Mathematics, Philosophy, Physics
ISBN Prefix(es): 3-209
Subsidiaries: hpt Verlagsges mbH & Co KG
Warehouse: Jochen-Rindt-Str 11, Postfach 107, 1232 Vienna

Dr Verena Hofstaetter
Steinfeldgasse 5, 1190 Vienna
Tel: (01) 370 33 02 *Fax:* (01) 370 59 34
E-mail: verlag@vh-communications.at
Subjects: Communications, Film, Video, Marketing, Social Sciences, Sociology
ISBN Prefix(es): 3-900936

Hollinek Bruder & Co mbH Gesellschaftsdruckerei & Verlagsbuchhandring+
Luisenstr 20, 3002 Purkersdorf
Tel: (02231) 67365 *Fax:* (02231) 67365
E-mail: hollinek@via.at
Key Personnel
Man Dir: R Hollinek
Founded: 1872
Subjects: Law
ISBN Prefix(es): 3-85119

hpt Verlagsges mbH & Co KG, see oebv & hpt Verlagsgesellschaft mbH & Co KG

IAEA - International Atomic Energy Agency
Wagramer Str 5, A-1400 Vienna
Mailing Address: Sales & Promotion, PO Box 100, A-1400 Vienna (Sales & Promotion Unit)
Tel: (01) 2600 0 *Fax:* (01) 2600-29302
E-mail: sales.publications@iaea.org
Web Site: www.iaea.org/worldatom/Books
Telex: 112645 ATOM A
Key Personnel
Dir General: Dr Mohamed ElBaradei
Head, Publishing Section: Manfred F Boemeke
E-mail: m.f.boemeke@iaea.org
Founded: 1957
Serves as the worlds central intergovernmental forum for scientific & technical cooperation in the nuclear field.
International Organization.
Subjects: Agriculture, Biological Sciences, Chemistry, Chemical Engineering, Energy, Environmental Studies, Geography, Geology, Health, Nutrition, Law, Physical Sciences, Physics, Technology, Veterinary Science, Nuclear Science
ISBN Prefix(es): 92-0
Number of titles published annually: 40 Print; 5 CD-ROM
Total Titles: 2,000 Print; 3 CD-ROM

Ibera VerlagsgesmbH+
Schubertring 8/2/7, 1040 Vienna
Tel: (01) 513 19 72 *Fax:* (01) 513 19 72-28
E-mail: strobele@ibera.at
Web Site: www.ibera.at
Key Personnel
Manager: Brigitte Strobele
Press: Simon Hoeller *E-mail:* hoeller@ibera.at
Sales: Matthias Strobele *E-mail:* sales@ibera.at
Subjects: Nonfiction (General)
ISBN Prefix(es): 3-900436
Distributed by Herold Verlagsauslieferung GmbH (Germany); Mohr-Morawa

IG Autorinnen Autoren (Austrian Author's Association)
im Literaturhaus, Seidengasse 13, A-1070 Vienna
Tel: (01) 526 20 44-13 *Fax:* (01) 526 20 44-55
E-mail: ig@literaturhaus.at
Web Site: www.literaturhaus.at/lh/ig
Key Personnel
President: Milo Dor
Vice President: Peter Turrini; Anna Mitgutsch
Man Dir: Gerhard Ruiss *Tel:* (1) 526 20 44-35
Founded: 1971
Subjects: Publishing & Book Trade Reference
ISBN Prefix(es): 3-900419

IIASA, see International Institute for Applied Systems Analysis (IIASA)

Inn-Verlag, DrieBlein & Co KG+
Rossaugasse 5, Postfach 29, A-6023 Innsbruck
Tel: (0512) 34 53 31 *Fax:* (0512) 34 12 90
E-mail: office@innverlag.at; innverlag@tirol.com
Web Site: www.innverlag.at *Cable:* INNVERLAG INNSBRUCK
Key Personnel
Publisher: Kaete Kom.Rat Glotz-Hagleitner
Production: Klaus Hagleitner
Sales: Manfred Hagleitner
Founded: 1947
Subjects: History, Public Administration, Sports, Athletics
ISBN Prefix(es): 3-85123
Bookshop(s): Kommissions-Reise & Versandbuchhandlung, Innsbruck

Interessengemeinschaft oesterreichischer Autorinnen und Autoren, see IG Autorinnen Autoren

International Atomic Energy Agency, see IAEA - International Atomic Energy Agency

International Institute for Applied Systems Analysis (IIASA)
Schlossplatz 1, A-2361 Laxenburg
Tel: (02236) 807 433 *Fax:* (02236) 71313
E-mail: info@iiasa.ac.at; publications@iiasa.ac.at
Web Site: www.iiasa.ac.at
Founded: 1972
Subjects: Computer Science, Energy, Environmental Studies, Management, Mathematics, Science (General)
ISBN Prefix(es): 3-7045

Verlag Jungbrunnen - Wiener Spielzeugschachtel GesellschaftmbH+
Rauhensteingasse 5, 1010 Vienna
Mailing Address: Postfach 583, 1011 Vienna
Tel: (01) 512-1299 *Fax:* (01) 512-1299-75
E-mail: office@jungbrunnen.co.at
Key Personnel
Man Dir, Editorial: Hildegard Gaertner
Rights & Permissions: Christina Krajicek
Founded: 1923
Subjects: Developing Countries, Fiction, Human Relations
ISBN Prefix(es): 3-7026

Junius Verlags- und Vertriebs GmbH
Brunnengasse 3, 1160 Vienna
Tel: (01) 4921272
Key Personnel
President & Publisher: Mat Dillinger
ISBN Prefix(es): 3-900370

Jupiter Verlagsgesellschaft mbH
Robertgasse 2, 1021 Vienna
Tel: (01) 21422940 *Fax:* (01) 2160720
Telex: 111563
Key Personnel
Manager: Dr Hans Georg Zeiner
ISBN Prefix(es): 3-900063

Juridica Verlag GmbH
Kohlmarkt 16, 1014 Vienna
Tel: (01) 533 37 47-398 *Fax:* (01) 533 37 47-399
E-mail: juridica@manz.at
Web Site: www.juridica.at
Key Personnel
Manager: Grete Grill; Werner Sopper
ISBN Prefix(es): 3-85131

Kaerntner Druck- und Verlags-GmbH
Viktringer Ring 28, 9010 Klagenfurt
Tel: (0463) 5866 *Fax:* (0463) 5866-321
E-mail: info@kaerntner-druckerei.at
Web Site: www.kaerntner-druckerei.at
Telex: 422415
Key Personnel
Contact: Wolbert Ebner
Founded: 1949
ISBN Prefix(es): 3-85391
Bookshop(s): Kaerntner Buchhandlung, Neuer Platz 11, A-9020 Klagenfurt; 8-Mai-Platz 3, A-9500 Villach; Joh-Offner-Str 11, A-9400 Wolfsberg

Karolinger Verlag GmbH & Co KG+
Staudgasse 12, 1180 Vienna
Tel: (0222) 4302093 *Fax:* (0222) 4302093
Key Personnel
Man Dir, Sales: Jean-Jacques Langendorf
Editorial: Dr Peter Weiss
Publicity: Cornelia Langendorf
Rights & Permissions: Hans Hofinger
Founded: 1980
Subjects: Fiction, Government, Political Science, History, Literature, Literary Criticism, Essays
ISBN Prefix(es): 3-85418
Number of titles published annually: 6 Print
Total Titles: 82 Print
Distributed by Brockhaus Commission

Verlag Kerle im Verlag Herder & Co+
Wollzeile 33, 1010 Vienna
Tel: (01) 521413; (01) 521414 *Fax:* (01) 28828180 *Cable:* HERDERBUCH VIENNA
Key Personnel
Man Dir: Prof Erich M Wolf
Editorial: Dr Evelyn Kapaun
Sales: Susanne Pratscher
Advertising, Rights: Helga Thiele
Founded: 1886
ISBN Prefix(es): 3-210; 3-85303
Associate Companies: Verlag Herder GmbH & Co KG, Germany; Herder Editrice e Libreria, Italy; Editorial Herder SA, Spain; Herder AG, Switzerland
Subsidiaries: Herder Kiado

AUSTRIA

Bookshop(s): Herder & Co, Wollzeile 33, 1010 Vienna
Warehouse: Herder, Viktor Kaplanstr 9, A-2201 Gerasdorf

Johann Kliment KG Musikverlag
Kolingasse 15, 1090 Vienna
Tel: (01) 317 51 47 *Fax:* (01) 310 08 27
E-mail: office@kliment.at
Web Site: www.kliment.at
Founded: 1928
ISBN Prefix(es): 3-85139
Bookshop(s): Neuer Markt 8, A-39210 Zwettl

Horst Knapp Finanznachrichten
Lisztstr 10, 1037 Vienna
Mailing Address: PO Box 97, 1037 Vienna
Tel: (01) 7154460-0 *Fax:* (01) 7154460-22
Key Personnel
Owner: Horst Knapp
Subjects: Business, Economics, Finance, Government, Political Science
ISBN Prefix(es): 3-900068

Edition Koenigstein+
Anzengrubergasse 50, 3400 Klosterneuburg
Tel: (02243) 26046 *Fax:* (02243) 26046
E-mail: edition.koenigstein@aon.at
Web Site: members.aon.at/edition_koenigstein
Key Personnel
Master of Arts: Georg Koenigstein
Contact: Christine Koenigstein
Founded: 1987
Specialize in fine editions and poetry.
Subjects: Art, Poetry
ISBN Prefix(es): 3-901495
Number of titles published annually: 5 Print
Total Titles: 3 Print

Verlag A F Koska
Esterhazygasse 35, 1060 Vienna
Tel: (0222) 5874344
Key Personnel
Manager: Prof Alfred F Koska
ISBN Prefix(es): 3-85334

Kremayr & Scheriau Verlag+
Unparpasse 45/13, A-1030 Vienna
Tel: (01) 713 8770 *Fax:* (01)713 8770-20
Key Personnel
Man Dir: Dr Maria Seifert *Tel:* (01) 713 8770-12 *Fax:* (01) 713 8770-20 *E-mail:* maria.seifert@bertelsmann.de
Founded: 1950
Subjects: Art, History, Music, Dance, Nonfiction (General)
ISBN Prefix(es): 3-218
Parent Company: Bertelsmann AG, Germany
Bookshop(s): Buchhandlung uend Zeitschriftenvertrieb Kremayr und Scheriau, Niederhofstr 37, A-1121 Vienna
Book Club(s): Buchgemeinschaft Donauland Kremayr & Scheriau
Orders to: Dr Otto-Neurath-Gasse 5, A-1220 Vienna

Kuemmerly und Frey Verlags GmbH
Nikolsdorfergasse 8, 1050 Vienna
Tel: (01) 545 14 45 *Fax:* (01) 545 10 80-83
E-mail: kuemmerly-frey@xpoint.at
Subjects: Travel
ISBN Prefix(es): 3-900382
Associate Companies: J Fink-Kuemmerly und Frey Verlag GmbH, Germany; Kuemmerly und Frey, Switzerland (Geographischer Verlag)

Verlag Lafite+
Hegelgasse 13/22, 1010 Vienna
Tel: (01) 5126869 *Fax:* (01) 51268699
E-mail: redaktion@musikzeit.at
Web Site: www.musikzeit.at

Key Personnel
Contact: Prof Dr Diederichs-Lafite
Founded: 1962
Specialize in music
Publisher of the *Austrian Music Magazine.*
Subjects: Journalism, Music, Dance
ISBN Prefix(es): 3-85151
Associate Companies: Internationale Schonberg Gesellschaft, Vienna

Landesverlag, *imprint of* Niederosterreichisches Pressehaus Druck- und Verlagsgesellschaft mbH

Langenscheidt-Verlag GmbH
Sulzengasse 2, 1232 Vienna
Mailing Address: Postfach 260, 1232 Vienna
Tel: (01) 6887133 *Fax:* (01) 68014140
Telex: 131912
Member of Langenscheidt Group, Germany.
ISBN Prefix(es): 3-208
Parent Company: Langenscheidt KG, Germany

Gerda Leber Buch-Kunst-und Musikverlag Proscenium Edition+
Wallnerstr 4, 1010 Vienna
Tel: (01) 5332858; (01) 6390025
Key Personnel
Contact: Dr Gerda Leber-Hageneau
Founded: 1965
Subjects: Drama, Theater, Music, Dance
ISBN Prefix(es): 3-900217; 3-900297

Leopold Stocker Verlag+
Hofgasse 5, 8011 Graz
Tel: (0316) 82 16 36 *Fax:* (0316) 83 56 12
E-mail: landwirt@stocker-verlag.com
Web Site: www.stocker-verlag.com; www.oezv.or.at *Cable:* STOCKERVERLAG GRAZ
Key Personnel
Publisher: Wolfgang Dvorak-Stocker
Founded: 1917
Subjects: Agriculture, Cookery, Gardening, Plants, Government, Political Science, History, Military Science, Wine & Spirits
ISBN Prefix(es): 3-7020
Associate Companies: Buecherquelle Buchhandlungs GmbH

Leykam Buchverlagsges mbH
Stempfergasse 3, 8010 Graz
Tel: (0316) 80 76-31 *Fax:* (0316) 81 66-39
E-mail: verlag@leykam.com
Web Site: www.leykam.com; www.leykamverlag.at
Telex: 032209 *Cable:* LEYKAM GRAZ
Key Personnel
Man Dir: Klaus Oktabetz
Founded: 1585
Subjects: Art, Fiction
ISBN Prefix(es): 3-7011

Linde Verlag Wien GmbH+
Scheydgasse 24, 1210 Vienna
Mailing Address: PF 351, 1210 Vienna
Tel: (01) 2780526 *Fax:* (01) 2780523
E-mail: office@linde-verlag.at; presse@linde-verlag.at
Web Site: www.linde-verlag.at
Key Personnel
Editor: Dr Eleonore Breitegger *Tel:* (01) 278 05 26-21 *Fax:* (01) 278 05 26-51 *E-mail:* redaktion@lindeverlag.at
Public Relations: Andreas Jentzsch *Tel:* (01) 2780526-30 *Fax:* (01) 2780526-53 *E-mail:* andreas.jentzsch@lindeverlag.at; Reingard Sandner *Tel:* (01) 278 05 26-30 *Fax:* (01) 278 05 26-53 *E-mail:* presse@lindeverlag.at
Founded: 1925

BOOK

Subjects: Accounting, Business, Communications, Economics, How-to, Labor, Industrial Relations, Law, Management, Marketing
ISBN Prefix(es): 3-85122; 3-7073
Number of titles published annually: 120 Print; 3 CD-ROM
Total Titles: 300 Print; 20 CD-ROM

Literas-Verlag GmbH
Berggasse 4, A-1090 Vienna
Tel: (01) 31565925 *Fax:* (01) 34368521
Telex: 116529 lcpfa
Founded: 1981
Subjects: Psychology, Psychiatry
ISBN Prefix(es): 3-85429
Associate Companies: Facultas Verlag

Loecker Verlag+
Annagasse 3A, 1015 Vienna
Mailing Address: Postfach 101, 1015 Vienna
Tel: (01) 512 02 82 *Fax:* (01) 512 02 82-22
E-mail: lverlag@loecker.at
Web Site: www.loecker.at
Key Personnel
General Manager: Erhard Loecker
Rights & Permissions: Dr Alexander Lellek
Founded: 1974
Subjects: Architecture & Interior Design, Art, History, Literature, Literary Criticism, Essays, Photography
ISBN Prefix(es): 3-85409
Bookshop(s): Antiquariat Loecker un Woegenstein, Annagasse 5, 1010 Vienna; Loecker GmbH, Gluckgasse 3, 1010 Vienna

LOG-Internationale Zeitschrift fuer Literatur+
Donaustadtstr 30/16/16, 1220 Vienna
Tel: (01) 2313433 *Fax:* (01) 2313433
Key Personnel
Publisher: Prof Wolfgang Mayer Koenig; Leo Detela
Founded: 1978
Subjects: Art, Language Arts, Linguistics, Literature, Literary Criticism, Essays, Poetry
ISBN Prefix(es): 3-900647
Orders to: Eigenauslieferung

Mangold Verlag GmbH+
Saint Peter Hauptstr 28, A-8042 Graz
Tel: (0316) 47142419 *Fax:* (0316) 47142440
Cable: MANGOLDVERLAG
Key Personnel
Man Dir: Bernhard Lernpeiss
Founded: 1977
ISBN Prefix(es): 3-900301; 3-901282

Manz'sche Verlags- und Universitaetsbuchhandlung
Kohlmarkt 16, 1014 Vienna
Tel: (01) 531 61-0 *Fax:* (01) 531 61-181
E-mail: redaktion@manz.co.at
Web Site: www.manz.at
Telex: 75310631
Key Personnel
Man Dir: Franz Stein; Dr Anton C Hilscher
Founded: 1849
Specialize in law books in Europe.
Subjects: Economics, Law
ISBN Prefix(es): 3-214; 3-901357
Distributor for Amt der Europaeischen Gemeinschaften; Auslieferung fuer Oesterreich
Bookshop(s): Kohlmarkt 16, Postfach 163, A-1014 Vienna; FRIC, Technische Fachbuchhandlung, Wiedner Hauptstr 13, A-1040 Vienna
Warehouse: Siebenbrunnengasse 21, 1050 Vienna
Orders to: Siebenbrunnengasse 21, 1050 Vienna

Verlag Wilhelm Maudrich+
Spitalgasse 21A, 1096 Vienna
Tel: (01) 4024712 *Fax:* (01) 4085080
E-mail: medbook@maudrich.com

Web Site: www.maudrich.com
Telex: 135177 *Cable:* MAUDRICH VERLAG VIENNA
Key Personnel
Man Dir: Dr Heinz Pinker; Prof Gerhard Grois
Founded: 1929
Subjects: Medicine, Nursing, Dentistry, Psychology, Psychiatry
ISBN Prefix(es): 3-85175
Bookshop(s): Buchhandlung Wilhelm Maudrich fuer medizinische Wissenschaften, Spitalgasse 21-21A, 1096 Vienna

Medien & Recht+
Danhausergasse 6, 1040 Vienna
Mailing Address: Postfach 83, 1041 Vienna
Tel: (01) 5052766 *Fax:* (01) 5052766-15
E-mail: verlag@medien-recht.ccom
Web Site: www.medien-recht.com
Key Personnel
University Prof: Dr Heinz Wittman *E-mail:* h.wittmann@medieu-reclid.com
Founded: 1985
Subjects: Communications, Computer Science, Journalism, Law
ISBN Prefix(es): 3-900741
Parent Company: Medien & Recht Verlags GmbH

Merbod Verlag+
Postfach 201, Wiener Neustadt 2700
Tel: (02622) 81724 *Fax:* (02622) 817244
Key Personnel
Contact: Peter Zumpf
Founded: 1989
Specializes in: Local listings & authors.
Subjects: Fiction, History, Humor, Literature, Literary Criticism, Essays, Nonfiction (General), Poetry
ISBN Prefix(es): 3-900844
Total Titles: 45 Print
Orders to: Wiener Neustadt 2700

Metrica Fachverlag u Versandbuchhandlung Ing Bartak+
Neugebaeudestr 18-12-8, 1112 Vienna
Mailing Address: Postfach 55, A-1112 Vienna
Tel: (01) 7695160; (01) 7485448
Key Personnel
Publisher: Ing Werner H Bartak
Founded: 1978
Subjects: Energy, Engineering (General), Technology
ISBN Prefix(es): 3-900368; 3-900329

Milena Verlag+
Formerly Wiener Frauenverlag
Lange Gasse 51, 1080 Vienna
Tel: (01) 402 59 90 *Fax:* (01) 408 88 58
E-mail: frauenverlag@milena-verlag.at
Key Personnel
Contact: Karin Ballauff; Martina Kopf
Founded: 1980
Subjects: Biography, Fiction, Gay & Lesbian, History, Library & Information Sciences, Literature, Literary Criticism, Essays, Nonfiction (General), Philosophy, Social Sciences, Sociology, Women's Studies
ISBN Prefix(es): 3-900399; 3-85286
Total Titles: 160 Print
Orders to: Mohr Z-G, Sulzengasse 2, 1230 Vienna *Tel:* (01) 68014-231 *Fax:* (01) 68014-140 *E-mail:* momo@mohr-morawa.co.at

Thomas Mlakar Verlag
Michlbauerweg 1, 8755 Saint Peter ob Judenburg
Tel: (03579) 2258 *Fax:* (03579) 2258
Founded: 1970
Subjects: Fashion, History, Literature, Literary Criticism, Essays, Natural History
ISBN Prefix(es): 3-900289

Modulverlag+
Mahlerstr 3, A-1010 Vienna
Tel: (01) 5129892 *Fax:* (01) 5129893
Key Personnel
Contact: Dr Berthold Schwanzer
Founded: 1973
Specialize in Architecture-Marketing Research.
Subjects: Architecture & Interior Design, Art, Marketing
ISBN Prefix(es): 3-900507
Distributor for Visual Reference Publications Inc (USA for Austria, retail books)

Moedling, *imprint of* Verlag St Gabriel

Verlag Monte Verita+
Hahngasse 15, 1090 Vienna
Tel: (01) 315222
Web Site: www.anares.org
Key Personnel
Publisher: Peter Stipkovics
Founded: 1982
Subjects: History, Literature, Literary Criticism, Essays, Philosophy
ISBN Prefix(es): 3-900434

Otto Mueller Verlag GesmbH & Co KG
Ernst-Thunstr 11, A-5021 Salzburg
Mailing Address: Postfach 167, 5021 Salzburg
Tel: (0662) 881974; (0662) 881970 *Fax:* (0662) 872387 *Cable:* MULLER VERLAG
Key Personnel
Man Dir, Sales & Publicity: Arno Kleibel
Founded: 1937
Subjects: History, Literature, Literary Criticism, Essays, Poetry, Psychology, Psychiatry, Religion - Other, Theology
ISBN Prefix(es): 3-7013

Mueller-Speiser Wissenschaftlicher Verlag
Mitterweg 6, 5081 Anif/Salzburg
Tel: (06246) 73166 *Fax:* (06246) 73166
E-mail: mueller-speiser@salzburg.co.at
Web Site: salzburg.co.at/mueller-speiser
Key Personnel
Contact: U Mueller-Speiser
Founded: 1989
Subjects: Drama, Theater, Music, Dance, Philosophy, Religion - Other, Theology, General Religion & Musicscience/Musicethnology
ISBN Prefix(es): 3-85145

Paul Neff Verlag KG+
Hackingerstrasse 52, 1140 Vienna
Tel: (01) 94061115 *Fax:* (01) 947641288 *Cable:* Neffverlag
Key Personnel
Man Dir: Dagmar Stecher-Konsalik
Founded: 1829
Subjects: Art, Biography, Fiction, Music, Dance
ISBN Prefix(es): 3-7014
Parent Company: Hestia-Verlag GmbH, Germany

Verlag Neues Leben
Thueringerberg 77, 6721 Thueringerberg
Tel: (05550) 3979
Key Personnel
Man Dir: Dr Rudolf Ingrisch
Founded: 1946
Subjects: Biography, Drama, Theater, Economics, Medicine, Nursing, Dentistry
ISBN Prefix(es): 3-85335

Edition Neues Marchen+
Kloster, 8413 St Georgen a d Stiefing
Tel: (03184) 2417 *Fax:* (03183) 7400
Key Personnel
Owner: Folke Tegetthoff
Founded: 1990
Subjects: Poetry
ISBN Prefix(es): 3-85325

Neufeld-Verlag und Galerie
Schillerstr 7, 6890 Lustenau
Tel: (05577) 4657-0
Telex: 59162 *Cable:* Neufeld
Key Personnel
Man Dir: K G Loepfe
Editorial, Rights & Permissions: Ivo Loepfe
Founded: 1962
ISBN Prefix(es): 3-900651
Parent Company: Loepfe KG, Schillerstr 7, 6890 Lustenau
Associate Companies: Neufeld-Verlag und Galerie, Switzerland
Branch Office(s)
Nordstr 227, CH-8037 Zurich, Switzerland

Wolfgang Neugebauer Verlag GmbH
Kalvarienguertel 62, A-8020 Graz
Mailing Address: Kreuzgasse 6, A-6800 Feldkirch
Tel: (0316) 05522 4770 *Fax:* (0316) 05522 4770
E-mail: wnverlag@utanet.at
Key Personnel
Man Dir: Wolfgang Neugebauer
Founded: 1975
Subjects: History, Language Arts, Linguistics, Literature, Literary Criticism, Essays, Theology
ISBN Prefix(es): 3-85376
Total Titles: 100 Print
Bookshop(s): Buchhandlung Bayer, Inh W Neugebauer Verlag GmbH, Kreuzgasse 6, A 6800 Feldkirch *E-mail:* bayer.buch@utanet.at
Orders to: Kreuzgasse 6, A-6800 Feldkirch *E-mail:* wnvrlag@utanet.at

Dr Waltraud Neuwirth Selbstverlag (Dr Waltraud Neuwirth Self Publishing House)
Weinzingergasse 10, Haus 18, 1190 Vienna
Tel: (01) 3207323 *Fax:* (01) 3200225
E-mail: waltraud.neuwith@eunet.at
Founded: 1976
ISBN Prefix(es): 3-900282

Niederosterreichisches Pressehaus Druck- und Verlagsgesellschaft mbH+
Gutenbergstr 12, 3100 Saint Poelten
Tel: (02742) 802-1412 *Fax:* (02742) 802-1431
E-mail: verlag@np-buch.at
Web Site: www.np-buch.at
Telex: 015512
Key Personnel
Man Dir: Herwig Bitsche *Tel:* (02742) 802-1410 *E-mail:* h.bitsche@np-buch.at
Publicity: Johanna Stromberger
Marketing: Roswitha Wonka
Founded: 1889
Subjects: Biography, Cookery, Health, Nutrition, History, Human Relations, Humor, Nonfiction (General), Outdoor Recreation, Travel, Wine & Spirits
ISBN Prefix(es): 3-85326
Number of titles published annually: 40 Print
Total Titles: 200 Print
Imprints: Landesverlag; NP Buchverlag
Orders to: Mohr Morawa, Buchvertrieb GmbH, Sulzengasse 2, Vienna A-1232 *Tel:* (01) 680 14-0 *Fax:* (01) 688 71-30 *E-mail:* momo@mohr-morawa.co.at

NOI - Verlag
MorresStr 13, 9020 Klagenfurt, Oostenrijk
Tel: (0463) 22474 *Fax:* (0463) 224744
Key Personnel
Owner: Dr Dietfried Schoenemann
Subjects: Education, Environmental Studies, Ethnicity, Health, Nutrition, History, Social Sciences, Sociology
ISBN Prefix(es): 3-900453

NP Buchverlag, *imprint of* Niederosterreichisches Pressehaus Druck- und Verlagsgesellschaft mbH

AUSTRIA

NP Buchverlag, see Niederosterreichisches Pressehaus Druck- und Verlagsgesellschaft mbH

Obelisk-Verlag+
Falkstr 1, 6020 Innsbruck
Tel: (0512) 58 07 33 *Fax:* (0512) 58 07 33 13
E-mail: obelisk-verlag@utanet.at
Web Site: www.obelisk-verlag.at
Key Personnel
Proprietor: Helga Buchroithner
Founded: 1946
ISBN Prefix(es): 3-85197

OEAW, see Verlag der Oesterreichischen Akademie der Wissenschaften (OEAW)

oebv & hpt Verlagsgesellschaft mbH & Co KG+
Formerly hpt Verlagsges mbH & Co KG
Frankgasse 4, 1090 Vienna
Tel: (01) 40136-0 *Fax:* (01) 40136-185
E-mail: office@oebvhpt.at
Web Site: www.oebvhpt.at
Key Personnel
Contact: Werner Brunner
International Rights: Hubert W Krenn
Marketing Manager: Herwig Arlt *Tel:* (01) 400 90-91 *Fax:* (01) 400 90-40 *E-mail:* vertrieb@oebvhpt.at
Advertising: Martina Moosleitner *Tel:* (01) 400 90-11 *Fax:* (01) 400 90-40 *E-mail:* werbung@oebvhpt.at
Founded: 1985
Subjects: Education, Mysteries, Nonfiction (General), Romance
ISBN Prefix(es): 3-87254; 3-7004; 3-209; 3-85128
Divisions: Neuer Breitschopf Verlag; Ed Boesskraut & Bernardi; Kurz & Bundigi, hpt Extra
Orders to: Mohr-Morawa, Sulzeng 2, 1230 Vienna *Tel:* (01) 684614-0

Verlag Oesterreich GmbH+
Kandlgasse 19-21, 1070 Vienna
Tel: (01) 6100771333 *Fax:* (01) 6100771502
E-mail: office@verlagoesterreich.at
Web Site: www.verlagoesterreich.at
Key Personnel
Manager: Peter Wittmann *Tel:* (01) 610771401 *Fax:* (01) 610771419 *E-mail:* wittmann@verlagoesterreich.at
Member of Haupt Verband des Osterr Buchhandels & Deutscher Borsevrerein Frankfurt.
ISBN Prefix(es): 3-7046
Total Titles: 1,000 Print; 20 CD-ROM; 1 Online; 1 E-Book
Bookshop(s): Jurbooks, Wollzeile 16, 1010 Vienna, Contact: Gert Weiss *Tel:* (01) 5124885 *Fax:* (01) 5120663 *E-mail:* buchhandlung@verlagoesterreich.at

Oesterreichische Staatsdruckerei (Austrian State Printing Office)
Rennweg 16, 1037 Vienna
Tel: (01) 206 66-0 *Fax:* (01) 206 66-105
E-mail: office@staatsdruckerei.at
Web Site: www.oesd.co.at
Key Personnel
Dir: Aribert Schwarzmann
ISBN Prefix(es): 3-7046

Oesterreichische Verlagsanstalt GmbH
Arbeitergasse 1-7, 1051 Vienna
Tel: (01) 5445641 *Fax:* (01) 544564166
Key Personnel
Man Dir: Friedrich Geyer
ISBN Prefix(es): 3-85202

Verlag der Oesterreichischen Akademie der Wissenschaften (OEAW) (Austrian Academy of Sciences Press)+
Dr-Ignaz-Seipel-Pl 2, 1010 Vienna
Tel: (01) 51581; (01) 5129050 *Fax:* (01) 515813400
E-mail: verlag@oeaw.ac.at
Web Site: verlag.oeaw.ac.at
Key Personnel
Manager: Mag Herwig Stoeger *Tel:* (01) 515813405 *E-mail:* herwig.stoeger@oeaw.ac.at
Founded: 1973
Publishing House of the Austrian Academy of Sciences.
Subjects: Archaeology, Asian Studies, Biography, Biological Sciences, History, Language Arts, Linguistics, Law, Physical Sciences, Science (General), Social Sciences, Sociology
ISBN Prefix(es): 3-7001
Number of titles published annually: 80 Print; 3 Audio
Total Titles: 20 Audio
Divisions: Vertrieb
Distributed by Rinson Books (Japan); University of Washington Press (US)
Showroom(s): Vertrieb

Verlag des Oesterreichischen Gewerkschaftsbundes GmbH
Altmannsdorfer Str 154-156, 1232 Vienna
Tel: (01) 662 32 96-62 36 *Fax:* (01) 662 32 96-63 85
E-mail: office@verlag-oegb.co.at
Web Site: www.verlag-oegb.co.at
Telex: 1311326
Key Personnel
Man Dir: Friedrich Loew
Editor-in-Chief: Fritz Fadler
Founded: 1947
Subjects: Career Development, Government, Political Science, History, Labor, Industrial Relations, Law
ISBN Prefix(es): 3-7035
Subsidiaries: Elbemuhl GmbH; EDV Gmbh; Printex GmbH; Pichler GmbH
Book Club(s): Buechergilde Gutenberg

Oesterreichischer Agrarverlag, Druck- und Verlags- GmbH+
Achauer Str 49A, 2335 Leopoldsdorf
Tel: (02235) 929-0 *Fax:* (02235) 929-929
E-mail: office@agrarverlag.at
Web Site: www.agrarverlag.at
Telex: 14030 *Cable:* AGRARVERLAG
Key Personnel
Man Dir: Dr Wolfgang Brandstetter
Founded: 1945
Subjects: Agriculture, Environmental Studies, Fiction
ISBN Prefix(es): 3-7040
Subsidiaries: Hugo H Hitschmann Verlag
Warehouse: Hennersdorfer Str 32/6, A-2333 Leopoldsdorf
Orders to: Ing H Fischer/AV Buchhandlung, Linzerstr 32, A-1141 Vienna *Fax:* (01) 951501-289

Oesterreichischer Bundesverlag GmbH+
Str 1, Objekt 34, IZ-Noe-Sued, 2632 Vienna Neudorf
Tel: (01) 51405
Telex: 79246 *Cable:* Bundesverlag Vienna
Key Personnel
Man Dir: Kurt Biak
Founded: 1772
Subjects: Art, Education, Fiction, History, Military Science, Music, Dance, Science (General)
ISBN Prefix(es): 3-215
Subsidiaries: Oesterreichischer Gewerbeverlag GmbH
Orders to: A-2351 Weiener Neudorf

Oesterreichischer Gewerbeverlag GmbH
Herrengasse 10, 1010 Vienna
Tel: (01) 53307680 *Fax:* (01) 5330768030
E-mail: gewerbeverlag@tbxa.telecom.at
Key Personnel
Man Dir, Sales, Publicity: Franz Scharetzer
Editorial, Rights & Permissions: Dr Josef Peter Ortner
Production: Heinz Stuiber
Founded: 1945
Subjects: Career Development, English as a Second Language
ISBN Prefix(es): 3-85207
Parent Company: Oesterreichischer Bundesverlag GmbH

Oesterreichischer Jagd-und Fischerei-Verlag der JFB GmbH
Wickenburggasse 3, Vienna 1080
Tel: (01) 421636 *Fax:* (01) 421636
E-mail: verlag@jagd.at
Web Site: members.ping.at
Key Personnel
Publisher: Dr Peter Lebersorger
ISBN Prefix(es): 3-85208
Parent Company: Jagdwirtschafts—, Foerderungs- und Betriebsges mbH

Oesterreichischer Kunst und Kulturverlag+
Freundgasse 11, 1040 Vienna
Tel: (01) 587 85 51 *Fax:* (01) 587 85 82
Key Personnel
Contact: Dr Michael Martischnig
Founded: 1981
Subjects: Antiques, Architecture & Interior Design, Communications, Engineering (General), History, Nonfiction (General), Regional Interests, Social Sciences, Sociology
ISBN Prefix(es): 3-85437
Total Titles: 350 Print; 3 CD-ROM; 3 Audio

Oesterreichisches Katholisches Bibelwerk
Stiftsplatz 8, 3400 Klosterneuburg
Mailing Address: Postfach 48, Klosterneuburg 3400
Tel: (02243) 2938 *Fax:* (02243) 2939
Telex: (61) 3222523
Key Personnel
Man Dir, Editorial, Rights & Permissions: Dr Norbert Hoeslinger
Sales: Elisabeth Csencsics
Publicity: Erika Pruckmoser
Founded: 1966
Member of AMB & WCBFA (World Catholic Federation for the Biblical Apostolate).
Subjects: Religion - Other
ISBN Prefix(es): 3-85396
Bookshop(s): Singerstr 7, A-1010 Vienna

Verlag Oldenbourg+
Neulinggasse 26/12, 1030 Vienna
Tel: (01) 712 62 58-17 *Fax:* (01) 712 62 58-19
E-mail: gala@oldenbourg.co.at
Key Personnel
Sales: Gerda Adler
Publicity & Advertising: Dr Ursula Huber *E-mail:* ursula.huber@oldenbourg.co.at
Mag: Veronika Weidenholzer *E-mail:* veronika.weidenholzer@oldenbourg.co.at
Founded: 1957
Subjects: Engineering (General), History, Philosophy, Science (General), Social Sciences, Sociology
ISBN Prefix(es): 3-7029
Parent Company: R Oldenbourg Verlag GmbH, Germany
Associate Companies: Verlag fuer Geschichte und Politik

Verlag Orac im Verlag Kremayr & Scheriau+
Unparpasse 45/13, A-1030 Vienna
Tel: (01) 713 8770-11 *Fax:* (01) 713 8770-20

PUBLISHERS
AUSTRIA

Key Personnel
Man Dir & Editor-in-Chief: Prof Maria Seifert
Rights & Permissions: Angelika Straus-Fischer
Founded: 1946
Subjects: Cookery, Economics, Environmental Studies, Government, Political Science, Health, Nutrition, Management, Nonfiction (General)
ISBN Prefix(es): 3-7015
Parent Company: Kremayr & Scheriau
Orders to: Dr Otto Neurath Gasse 5, A-1220 Vienna

Verlag des Osterr Kneippbundes GmbH+
Kunigundenweg 10, 8700 Leoben
Tel: (03842) 21682; (03842) 21718; (03842) 24094 *Fax:* (03842) 2171832
E-mail: office@kneippverlag.com
Web Site: www.kneippverlag.com
Key Personnel
Manager: Waltraud Ruth
Founded: 1985
Specializing in Health & Medicine.
Subjects: Alternative, Child Care & Development, Cookery, Health, Nutrition, Medicine, Nursing, Dentistry, Outdoor Recreation, Philosophy, Psychology, Psychiatry, Sports, Athletics
ISBN Prefix(es): 3-900696; 3-901794
Distributed by B&M Medien Service (Switzerland); Knoe (Germany); Morawa (Austria); Weltbild
Distributor for Kneipp-Verlag Bad Woerishofen

Osterreichischer Alpenverein Sektion Weiner Lehrer
Postfach 33, 2103 Langenzersdorf
Tel: (02244) 3536 *Fax:* (02244) 3536
Telex: 75211689 avw a
Key Personnel
Contact: Peterka Fritz
Founded: 1973
Subjects: Travel
ISBN Prefix(es): 3-900451

Osterreichischer Bundesveilag Ges.mbh
Str 1, Objeht 34, 1Z-NO-Sud, 2355 Weiner Neudorf
Tel: (02236) 635 35-290 *Fax:* (02236) 635 35-243
E-mail: oebz@oebv.co.at
Telex: 79246
Key Personnel
Contact: Dr Othmar Spachinger
International Rights: Wilbirg Stoger
Founded: 1772
Subjects: Biological Sciences, Career Development, Chemistry, Chemical Engineering, Education, English as a Second Language, History, Language Arts, Linguistics, Music, Dance, Nonfiction (General), Philosophy, Sports, Athletics
ISBN Prefix(es): 3-215
Showroom(s): Treffpunkt Schullouch, Hegelg 14, 1010 Vienna
Orders to: OBZ Buchaus Lieferungs GmbH Co KG, IZ-No Sud Str 1, Objekt 133

Osterreichischer Wirtschaftsverlag Druck-und Verlagsgesellschaft mbH
Nikolsdorfer Gasse 7-11, 1051 Vienna
Tel: (01) 54664-336 *Fax:* (01) 54664-360
E-mail: s.drabosenig@oewv.at
Key Personnel
Man Dir: Robert Graf
ISBN Prefix(es): 3-85212

Passagen Verlag GmbH+
Walfischgasse 15-14, A-1010 Vienna
Tel: (01) 513 77 61 *Fax:* (01) 512 63 27
E-mail: office@passagen.at
Web Site: www.passagen.at
Key Personnel
Publisher: Dr Peter Engelmann
 E-mail: engelmann@passagen.at

Founded: 1987
Subjects: Architecture & Interior Design, Art, Economics, Government, Political Science, Literature, Literary Criticism, Essays, Philosophy, Theology
ISBN Prefix(es): 3-900767; 3-85165
Total Titles: 600 Print
Orders to: Bugrim Verlagsauslieferung, Saalburgstr 3, 12099 Berlin, Germany, Contact: Herr Lindemann *Tel:* (030) 6068457 *Fax:* (030) 6063476 *E-mail:* bugrim@t-online.de *Web Site:* www.bugrim.de

E Perlinger Naturprodukte Handelsgesellschaft mbH+
Itter 300, 6300 Woergl
Tel: (05332) 75 654 *Fax:* (05332) 75 656
E-mail: engelberts.naturprodukte@tirol.com
Telex: 051205 Teltaz *Cable:* Perlinger Verlag Woergl
Key Personnel
Man Dir: Engelbert Perlinger
Founded: 1977
Subjects: Astrology, Occult, Ethnicity, Medicine, Nursing, Dentistry
ISBN Prefix(es): 3-85399

Verlag Sankt Peter
Postfach 113, 5010 Salzburg
Tel: (0662) 842166-82 *Fax:* (0662) 842166-80
E-mail: verlag-st.peter@magnet.at
Web Site: www.stift-stpeter.at
Telex: 063094
Key Personnel
Man Dir: Dr R Rinnerthaler
 E-mail: rinnerthaler@hotmail.com
Founded: 1946
Subjects: Art, Regional Interests, Religion - Other
ISBN Prefix(es): 3-900173

Anna Pichler Verlag GmbH+
Berggasse 31, 2391 Kaltenleutgeben
Tel: (0043) 2238-77078 *Fax:* (0043) 2238-77076
E-mail: apverlag@magnet.at
Key Personnel
Owner: Anna Pichler
Owner & International Rights: Heinz Lasta
Founded: 1989
Subjects: Environmental Studies, Fiction, Nonfiction (General), Philosophy, Poetry
ISBN Prefix(es): 3-901087
Distributed by Dessauer; EDIS

Pichler Verlag GmbH & Co KG
Hirschstettner Str 21, 1220 Vienna
Tel: (01) 203 28 28-0 *Fax:* (01) 203 28 28-6875
E-mail: office@pichlerverlag.at
Web Site: www.pichlerverlag.at
Key Personnel
Director: Michael Hlatky *Tel:* (01) 2032828-6870
 E-mail: michael.hlatky@pichlerverlag.at
Public Relations: Dr Barbara Brunner *Tel:* (01) 624673955 *E-mail:* barbara.brunner@utanet.at
Founded: 1793
ISBN Prefix(es): 3-85431
Parent Company: Verlag des OeGB GmbH
Bookshop(s): Wipplingerstr 37, 1010 Vienna; Favoritenstr 42, 1040 Vienna

Richard Pils Publication P+
Grosswolfgers 29, 3970 Weitra
Tel: (02815) 635594 *Fax:* (02815) 635592
Key Personnel
Contact: Richard Pils
Founded: 1989
Subjects: Art, Cookery, Drama, Theater, Fiction, Literature, Literary Criticism, Essays, Photography, Poetry
ISBN Prefix(es): 3-900878; 3-85252

Pinguin-Verlag, Pawlowski GmbH+
Lindenbuehelweg 2, 6020 Innsbruck
Tel: (0512) 281183-0 *Fax:* (0512) 293243
Web Site: www.worldport.at *Cable:* PINGUINVERLAG INNSBRUCK
Key Personnel
Man Dir: Hella Pawlowski; Olaf Pawlowski
Founded: 1945
Subjects: Art, Astrology, Occult, Cookery, Foreign Countries, Geography, Geology, Nonfiction (General), Physical Sciences, Travel
ISBN Prefix(es): 3-7016
Distributor for Readers Digest; Verlag Frankfurt

Georg Prachner KG+
Kaerntner Str 30, 1015 Vienna
Tel: (01) 512 85 49-0 *Fax:* (01) 512-01-58
Web Site: www.indiana.edu
Key Personnel
Man Dir: O G Prachner
Founded: 1931
Subjects: Agriculture, Art, Fiction, History
ISBN Prefix(es): 3-85367
Divisions: Prachner GmbH, Verlag und Grosshandel

Progress-Verlag Dr Micolini's Witwe
Glacisstr 57, 8010 Graz
Tel: (0316) 829508 *Fax:* (0316) 829508
Cable: Micolini Graz
Founded: 1934
ISBN Prefix(es): 3-85237

Promedia Verlagsges mbH+
Wickenburgg 5/12, 1080 Vienna
Tel: (01) 405 27 02 *Fax:* (01) 405 71 59 22
E-mail: promedia@mediashop.at
Web Site: www.mediashop.at
Key Personnel
Contact: Hannes Hofbauer
Founded: 1982
Subjects: Anthropology, Architecture & Interior Design, Biography, Developing Countries, Foreign Countries, Government, Political Science, History, Nonfiction (General), Travel, Women's Studies
ISBN Prefix(es): 3-900478; 3-85371
Number of titles published annually: 20 Print
Total Titles: 200 Print

Prugg Verlag
Haydngasse 10, 7000 Eisenstadt
Tel: (02682) 2114
ISBN Prefix(es): 3-85238

Verlag Anton Pustet+
Bergstr 12, 5020 Salzburg
Tel: (0662) 87350-56 *Fax:* (0662) 87350-58
E-mail: buch@verlog-anton-pustet.es
Key Personnel
Rights & Permissions: M A Mona Muery-Leitner
 Tel: (0662) 873507 ext 54
Contact: Dr Roman Hoellbacher *Tel:* (0662) 873507 ext 53
Founded: 1598
Subjects: Architecture & Interior Design, Art, Cookery, History, Philosophy, Psychology, Psychiatry, Theology, Travel
ISBN Prefix(es): 3-7025
Total Titles: 90 Print
Foreign Rep(s): Christine Gigler (Germany)

Reinhold Schmidt Verlag
Kastanienweg 9, 2362 Biedermannsdorf
Tel: (02236) 72469 *Fax:* (02236) 73784
Key Personnel
Editor-in-Chief: Herbert Schwestka
ISBN Prefix(es): 3-900124

Resch Verlag+
Maria-Eich-Str 77, 82166 Graefelfing
Tel: (089) 8 54 65-0 *Fax:* (089) 54 65-11

E-mail: info@resch-verlag.com
Web Site: www.resch-verlag.com
Key Personnel
Contact: Prof P Andreas Resch, PhD; Mag Priska Kapferer
Founded: 1974
Subjects: Parapsychology, Physics, Science (General), Theology, Ethics
ISBN Prefix(es): 3-85382

Residenz Verlag GmbH+
Gaisbergstr 6, 5025 Salzburg
Tel: (0662) 641986; (0662) 641987; (0662) 642571 *Fax:* (0662) 643548
E-mail: info@residenzverlag.at
Web Site: www.residenzverlag.at
Telex: 632887
Key Personnel
Man Dir, Editorial: Dr Martina Schmidt
 E-mail: martina.schmidt@oebv.co.at
Sales Manager: Christl Sennewald
Rights & Permissions: Dr Bernhard Sandbichler
 E-mail: bernhard.sandbichler@oebv.co.at
Publicity: Astrid Bader *E-mail:* astrid.bader@oebv.co.at
Founded: 1956
Subjects: Architecture & Interior Design, Art, Music, Dance, Poetry
ISBN Prefix(es): 3-7017
Number of titles published annually: 30 Print
Total Titles: 250 Print
Parent Company: Oesterreichischer Bundesverlag, Vienna

Rhombus Verlag
Schottenfeldgasse 65, 1070 Vienna
Tel: (01) 526 61 52 *Fax:* (01) 522 87 18
Key Personnel
Man Dir: Thomas C Cubasch
ISBN Prefix(es): 3-85394

Ritter Verlag+
Hagenstr 3, 9020 Klagenfurt
Tel: (0463) 42631 *Fax:* (0463) 42631-77
E-mail: ritterverlag@magnet.at
Key Personnel
Contact: Karin Ritter
Founded: 1980
Subjects: Architecture & Interior Design, Art, Literature, Literary Criticism, Essays, Music, Dance, Art Theory, Exhibition
ISBN Prefix(es): 3-85415

Verlag Roeschnar+
Beethovenstr 4, 9065 Pfaffendorf
Tel: (0463) 740513 *Fax:* (0463) 740817
E-mail: roesch@EUnet.at
Web Site: www.members.EUnet.at/roesch
Key Personnel
Publishing Manager: Renate Peball
Founded: 1876
Subjects: Poetry
ISBN Prefix(es): 3-900735; 3-85277

Roetzer Druck GmbH & Co KG
Mattersburger-Bundesstr 25, 7001 Eisenstadt
Tel: (02682) 62 494 *Fax:* (02682) 65 008
E-mail: roetzer@bnet.at
Web Site: www.buchwirtschaft.at
Key Personnel
Man Dir: Rainer Roetzer
Founded: 1969
Subjects: Physics
ISBN Prefix(es): 3-85253

Verlag St Gabriel+
Gabrielerstr 171, 2340 Moedling
Tel: (02236) 803-225 *Fax:* (02236) 24483
E-mail: org.sgww@steyler.at
Web Site: www.steyler.at

Key Personnel
Man: Elisabeth Birklhuber *Tel:* (02236) 803163
 E-mail: ltg.verlag@steyler.at
Contact: Gerd Milcke *E-mail:* bur.verlag@steyler.at
Founded: 1901
Subjects: Religion - Catholic, Theology
ISBN Prefix(es): 3-85264
Number of titles published annually: 8 Print
Total Titles: 40 Print
Parent Company: Missionshaus Sankt Gabriel, Gabrielerstr 171, A-2340 Moedling
Ultimate Parent Company: Gesellschaft des Gottlichen Wortes, Provinz Osterreich
Imprints: Moedling
Distributed by Rex-Verlag; Steyler Verlag
Bookshop(s): Missions Buch Handlung St Gabriel, Gabrieler Str, A-2340 Moedling, Contact: Mr Queder *Tel:* (02236) 47834 *Fax:* (02236) 803273; Stephansplatz 6, A-1010 Vienna *Tel:* (01) 5122105 *Fax:* (01) 5122105

Verlag der Salzburger Druckerei
Bergstr 12, 5020 Salzburg
Tel: (0662) 873507 *Fax:* (0662) 873507
ISBN Prefix(es): 3-85338

Salzburger Kulturvereinigung
Waagplatz 1a Trakl-Haus, Postfach 42, 5010 Salzburg
Tel: (0662) 845346 *Fax:* (0662) 842665
E-mail: kulturvereinigung@salzburg.co.at
Web Site: www.salzburg.com/kulturvereinigung
Key Personnel
Manager: Dr Heinz Klier
Classic concerts with orchestras.
Subjects: Music, Dance
ISBN Prefix(es): 3-85259

Verlag fuer Sammler+
St Peter Hauptstr 35e, 8042 Graz
Tel: (0316) 47 22 30 *Fax:* (0316) 67 39 87
Web Site: www.literaturhaus.at/buch/verlagsportraits/sammler.html
Key Personnel
Owner: Uta Gratzl
Founded: 1968
Subjects: Art, History, Natural History, Social Sciences, Sociology
ISBN Prefix(es): 3-85365
Showroom(s): Koeroesistr 17/4, 8010 Graz

Sankt Hermagoras Bruderschaft, see Hermagoras/Mohorjeva

Paul Sappl, Schulbuch- und Lehrmittelverlag
Kaiserbach 43, 6330 Kufstein
Tel: (05372) 643 00 *Fax:* (05372) 64 300-17
Telex: 5119115
Founded: 1953
ISBN Prefix(es): 3-85263
Branch Office(s)
Stolberggasse 31-33, A-1050 Vienna

Dr A Schendl GmbH und Co KG
Geblergasse 95, 1170 Vienna
Tel: (01) 484 17 85-0 *Fax:* (01) 484 17 85-15
E-mail: info@schendl.at
Web Site: www.schendl.at
Key Personnel
Dir: Martin Oegg
Founded: 1965
Also acts as packager, warehouse, promoter.
Subjects: Economics, Ethnicity, Geography, Geology, History, Literature, Literary Criticism, Essays, Music, Dance, Natural History
ISBN Prefix(es): 3-85268

Schmid Verlag GmbH+
Wuerttembergstr 10, 93049 Regensburg
Tel: (0941) 21519 *Fax:* (0941) 28766

E-mail: info@schmid-verlag.de
Web Site: www.schmid-verlag.de
Key Personnel
Publisher: Marion Schmid
ISBN Prefix(es): 3-900284

Andreas Schnider Verlags-Atelier
Peterstalerstr 127, 8042 Graz-St Peter
Tel: (0316) 471302 *Fax:* (0316) 4713024
Key Personnel
Owner: Andreas Schnider
Founded: 1989
Subjects: Archaeology, Architecture & Interior Design, Art, Computer Science, Education, Electronics, Electrical Engineering, Fiction, Government, Political Science, History, Law, Literature, Literary Criticism, Essays, Photography, Poetry, Psychology, Psychiatry, Religion - Catholic, Religion - Other, Theology, Veterinary Science
ISBN Prefix(es): 3-900993
Branch Office(s)
Roy Mittelman, 607 West End Ave, New York, NY 10024, United States *Tel:* 212-769-3323 *Fax:* 212-769-2325
Attila Mudrok, Vak u 6, H-2500 Grztergom
Warehouse: Peterstalstr 127, 8042 Graz

Schubert & Franzke Gesellschaft mbH
Kranzbichlertr 57, 3100 Saint Poelten
Tel: (02742) 78 501-0 *Fax:* (02742) 78 501-15
E-mail: office@schubert-franzke.com
Web Site: www.map2web.cc/schubert-franzke
Key Personnel
Manager: Josef Scheibenreif
ISBN Prefix(es): 3-7056; 3-900938

Verlagsbuero Karl Schwarzer
Ziegelofengasse 27 1/2, 1050 Vienna
Tel: (01) 548 31 15-0 *Fax:* (01) 548 31 15-39
E-mail: verlagsbuero@schwarzer.at
ISBN Prefix(es): 3-900392

Service Fachverlag an der Wirtschaftsuniversitae Wien, see Buchhandlung WUV Dolmetsch

Signum Verlag GmbH & Co KG+
Reisnerstr 40, 1031 Vienna
Tel: (01) 40650330 *Fax:* (01) 406503312
E-mail: contact.us@signum.at
Telex: 131717
Key Personnel
Dir & General Manager: Robert Grossmann
General Manger: Stefan Goetz
Dir: Milan Fruehbauer
Founded: 1978
Subjects: Business, Economics, Government, Political Science, Law, Management, Nonfiction (General)
ISBN Prefix(es): 3-85436
Parent Company: Vereinigung der Oesterreichischen Industrie
Imprints: Signum Business
Subsidiaries: Verlag Austria Press GmbH

Signum Business, *imprint of* Signum Verlag GmbH & Co KG

Verlag Josef Otto Slezak+
Wiedner Hauptstr 40-42, 1040 Vienna
Tel: (01) 587 02 59 *Fax:* (01) 587 02 59
E-mail: verlag.slezak@aon.at
Web Site: www.web4you.at/slezak.titel.htm
Key Personnel
Sales Manager: Ilse Slezak
Contact: Josef Otto Slezak
Founded: 1960
Specialize in railway books.
Member of Oesterreichische Verkehrswissenschaftliche Gesellschaft.

Subjects: Foreign Countries, History, Transportation
ISBN Prefix(es): 3-85416
Number of titles published annually: 4 Print
Total Titles: 50 Print
Distributed by Minirex (Switzerland)

SN-Verlag, Salzburger Nachrichten Verlags GmbH & Co KG
5021 Salzburg
Tel: (0662) 8373-223 *Fax:* (0662) 8373-210
Web Site: www.salzburg.com
Telex: 633383
Subjects: Architecture & Interior Design, Drama, Theater, History, Music, Dance, Regional Interests
ISBN Prefix(es): 3-85304

Springer-Verlag Wien+
Sachsenplatz 4-6, 1200 Vienna
Mailing Address: PO Box 89, 1200 Vienna
Tel: (01) 3302415 *Fax:* (01) 3302426
E-mail: books@springer.at (orders); journals@springer.at (orders)
Web Site: www.springer.at
Key Personnel
Dir, Ed, Art, Cultural Studies: Rudolf Siegle
   E-mail: siegle@springer.at
Founded: 1924
Subjects: Anthropology, Architecture & Interior Design, Art, Biological Sciences, Business, Chemistry, Chemical Engineering, Civil Engineering, Communications, Computer Science, Economics, Education, Electronics, Electrical Engineering, Engineering (General), Environmental Studies, Law, Mathematics, Mechanical Engineering, Medicine, Nursing, Dentistry, Philosophy, Physics, Psychology, Psychiatry, Science (General), Technology
ISBN Prefix(es): 3-211
Associate Companies: Springer-Verlag New York Inc, 175 Fifth Ave, New York, NY 10010, United States
Distributor for Birkhaaeuser; Boehlau; L Mueller; Springer; Steinkopff
Bookshop(s): Minerva Wissenschaftliche Buchhandlung GmbH, Sachsenplatz 4-6, 1200 Vienna

J Steinbrener OHG+
Im Eichbuchl 1, Postfach 3, 4780 Scharding
Tel: (07712) 2038 *Fax:* (07712) 5161
Founded: 1855
Subjects: Religion - Other
ISBN Prefix(es): 3-85296
Associate Companies: J Steinbrener OHG Zweigneiderlassung Neuhaus, Wagnerstr 21, Neuhaus, Germany

Dr Paul Struzl GmbH, see Akademische Druck-u Verlagsanstalt Dr Paul Struzl GmbH

Studien Verlag Gmbh
Amraser Str 118, 6010 Innsbruck
Mailing Address: Postfach 104, 6010 Innsbruck
Tel: (0512) 395045 *Fax:* (0512) 395045-15
E-mail: order@studienverlag.at
Web Site: www.studienverlag.at
Key Personnel
Contact: Martin Kopler
Founded: 1984
Publishing company for scientific books.
Subjects: Communications, Education, History, Journalism, Language Arts, Linguistics, Literature, Literary Criticism, Essays, Music, Dance, Philosophy, Science (General), Women's Studies
ISBN Prefix(es): 3-901160; 3-7065; 3-7066
Number of titles published annually: 80 Print
Total Titles: 300 Print
Online services available through World Wide Web.

Verlag Styria+
Schoenaugasse 64, 8010 Graz
Mailing Address: Postfach 435, 8010 Graz
Tel: (0316) 8063-7002 *Fax:* (0316) 8063-7034
E-mail: verlagstyria@styria.com
Web Site: www.verlagstyria.com *Cable:* STYRIAVERLAG GRAZ
Key Personnel
Man Dir: Michael Hlatky *Tel:* (0316) 8063-7000
   E-mail: michael.hlatky@styria.com
Sales: Isabella Scheuringer *Tel:* (0316) 8063-7601
   E-mail: isabella.scheuringer@styria.com
Production: Helmut Lenhart
Marketing Chief: Sabine Gollmann *Tel:* (0316) 8063-7020 *E-mail:* sabine.gollmann@styria.com
Founded: 1869
Subjects: Biography, Education, History, Journalism, Philosophy, Religion - Other
ISBN Prefix(es): 3-222; 3-7012
Number of titles published annually: 70 Print
Parent Company: Styria Medien AG
Associate Companies: Verlag Corinthion, Volkermarkter Ring 25, A-9020, Ulapenfurt
Branch Office(s)
Verlag Styria Koeen, Rodenberg 18, Kuerten-Bechen
Bookshop(s): Buchhandlung Styria, Albrechtgasse 5, A-8010 Graz; Buchhandlung und Antiquariat Moser, Herrengasse 23, A-8010 Graz

Suedwind - Buchwelt GmbH
Schwaizapanierstr 15, 1090 Vienna
Tel: (01) 405 44 34
E-mail: buchwelt@suedwind.at
Web Site: www.suedwind.at
Key Personnel
Man Dir: Rupert Helm
Founded: 1984
Subjects: Government, Political Science, Nonfiction (General)
ISBN Prefix(es): 3-900592
Total Titles: 25 Print

Edition Tau u Tau Type Druck Verlags-und Handels GmbH+
Biriczweg 1, Postfach 19, 7202 Bad Sauerbrunn
Tel: (02625) 32000 *Fax:* (02625) 320003
Key Personnel
Publisher: Erich Greistorfer
Production Dir: Peter Feigl
Contact: Klaus Kopinitsch
Founded: 1988
Subjects: Biography, Nonfiction (General), Religion - Other
ISBN Prefix(es): 3-900977; 3-901997

Thanhaeuser Edition
Wallseerstr 6, A-4100 Ottensheim
Tel: (07234) 83800 *Fax:* (07234) 83800
E-mail: thanhaeuser@otteusheim.at
Key Personnel
Contact: Christian Thanhaeuser; Irmgard Thanhaeuser
Founded: 1989
Subjects: Poetry
ISBN Prefix(es): 3-900986
Total Titles: 40 Print

Edition Thurnhof KEG
Wiener Str 2, 3580 Horn
Tel: (02982) 3333 *Fax:* (02982) 3333
Web Site: www.thurnhof.at
Key Personnel
Publisher: Toni Kurz *E-mail:* toni.kurz@eunet.at
Founded: 1983
Subjects: Art, Poetry
ISBN Prefix(es): 3-900678
Divisions: Galerie-Thurnhof
Branch Office(s)
Druckerei & Atelier, 3580 Muehlfeld 43

Trauner Verlag
Koeglstr 14, 4021 Linz
Tel: (0732) 778240; (0732) 778241 *Fax:* (0732) 283516
Key Personnel
Man Dir: Rudolf Trauner
Founded: 1946
Subjects: Cookery, Medicine, Nursing, Dentistry, Science (General)
ISBN Prefix(es): 3-85320

Edition Tusch+
Heigerleinstr 36-40, 1160 Vienna
Tel: (01) 484 53 30 *Fax:* (01) 484 53 30
Telex: 116262 Tusch *Cable:* EDITUSCH VIENNA
Key Personnel
Man Dir: Anton Tusch
Editorial: Wolfgang Prager
Founded: 1972
Subjects: Architecture & Interior Design, Art, Ethnicity
ISBN Prefix(es): 3-85063

Tyrolia Verlagsanstalt GmbH
Exlgasse 20, 6020 Innsbruck
Tel: (0512) 2233-0 *Fax:* (0512) 2233-501
E-mail: tyrolia@tyrolia.at
Web Site: www.tyrolia.at
Telex: 053620 *Cable:* TYROLIA VERLAG INNSBRUCK
Key Personnel
Dir: Dr Schiemer
Founded: 1888
Subjects: Nonfiction (General), Religion - Other, Travel
ISBN Prefix(es): 3-7022
Bookshop(s): Tyrolia, Exlgasse 20, Postfach 220, 6020 Innsbruck

Verlag Carl Ueberreuter, see Annette Betz Verlag im Verlag Carl Ueberreuter

Verlag Carl Ueberreuter GmbH+
Alser Str 24, Postfach 306, A-1091 Vienna
Tel: (01) 40 444-0 *Fax:* (01) 40 444-5
E-mail: goeller@ueberreuter.at
Web Site: www.ueberreuter.de
Key Personnel
Holding: Ing Michael Salzer
Editorial: Britta Groiss; Irmgard Harrer; Gudula Jungeblodt; Dr Alfred Schierer; Thomas Zauner
Production: Maria Schuster
Publicity: Iris Seidenstricker
Sales: Petra Thomsen
Rights & Permissions: Dr Sibylle Goeller
   Tel: (01) 40444173 *E-mail:* goeller@ueberreuter.at
Man Dir: Dr Fritz Panzer
Contact: Monika Reisenbauer *Tel:* (01) 40444-171
   E-mail: reisenbauer@ueberreuter.at
Founded: 1548
Subjects: Animals, Pets, Art, Astrology, Occult, Biography, Economics, Fiction, Government, Political Science, Health, Nutrition, History, Music, Dance, Nonfiction (General), Science (General), Science Fiction, Fantasy
ISBN Prefix(es): 3-8000
Number of titles published annually: 140 Print
Total Titles: 800 Print
Imprints: Annette Betz
Subsidiaries: Annette Betz Verlag
Foreign Rights: A C E R; A R T Dialog (Czech Republic); Akcali; Ball & Co; Bettiua & Julia Nibbe; China Consult (China & Taiwan); Ashley Grayson (US); Hercules (China & Taiwan); Imprima Korea (Korea); Iris; Liu Media (China); Onon L J Pren (Japan); Margit Schaleck; Shing-Shang (Taiwan); Tuttle Mori (Japan)

AUSTRIA

Shipping Address: BTG Spedition & Logistik GmbH, Neudorfstr 114, A-2353 Guntramsdorf
Warehouse: BTG Spedition & Logistik GmbH, Neudorfstr 114, A-2353 Guntramsdorf

Universal Edition AG
Boesendorferstr 12, 1010 Vienna
Mailing Address: Postfach 3, 1015 Vienna
Tel: (01) 337 23-0 *Fax:* (01) 337 23-400
E-mail: office@universaledition.com
Web Site: www.universaledition.com *Cable:* MUSIKEDITION VIENNA
Key Personnel
Man Dir: Johann Juranek; Marion von Hartlieb
Sales, Marketing & Public Relations: Ferdinand Walcher *E-mail:* walcher@universaledition.com
Founded: 1901
Subjects: Music, Dance
ISBN Prefix(es): 3-7024
Subsidiaries: Urtext Edition-Musikverlag GmbH KG (jointly owned with B Schott's Soehne, Germany)

Urban und Schwarzenberg GmbH
Frankgasse 4, 1096 Vienna
Tel: (01) 4052731 *Fax:* (01) 405272441
Key Personnel
Manager: Gunter Royer
Founded: 1866
Subjects: Medicine, Nursing, Dentistry, Physics, Psychology, Psychiatry
ISBN Prefix(es): 3-85327
Parent Company: Williams & Wilkins Ltd, 428 East Preston St, Baltimore, MD 21202, United States
Associate Companies: Urban und Schwarzenberg GmbH, Verlag fuer Medizin, Germany

Edition Va Bene+
Max-Kahrer-G 32, 3400 Klosterneuburg
Mailing Address: PO Box 19, Vienna 1196
Tel: (02243) 22 159; (0664) 1616356 (mobile) *Fax:* (02243) 22 159
E-mail: edition@vabene.at
Web Site: www.vabene.at
Key Personnel
Owner: Dr Walter Weiss
Founded: 1991
Subjects: Anthropology, Asian Studies, Communications, Developing Countries, Ethnicity, Foreign Countries, Health, Nutrition, Literature, Literary Criticism, Essays, Philosophy, Physical Sciences, Poetry, Religion - Catholic, Romance, Science (General), Theology, Travel
ISBN Prefix(es): 3-85167
Total Titles: 138 Print; 50 E-Book
Warehouse: Dr Franz Hain, Dr Otto Neurath-Gasse 5, 1220 Vienna *Tel:* (01) 28265650 *Fax:* (01) 2825282

Verband der Wissenschaftlichen Gesellschaften Oesterreichs (VWGOe)
Lindengasse 37, 1070 Vienna
Tel: (01) 932166; (01) 934756 *Fax:* (01) 5262054
Key Personnel
Man Dir: Dr Rainer Zitta
Founded: 1954
Subjects: Archaeology, Business, Education, History, Mathematics, Music, Dance, Philosophy, Physical Sciences
ISBN Prefix(es): 3-85369

Verein Gruppe Wespennest Redaktion, *imprint of* Wespennest - Zeitschrift fuer brauchbare Texte und Bilder

Verlag Veritas Mediengesellschaft mbH+
Hafenstr 1-3, 4020 Linz
Tel: (0732) 776451; (0732) 776450 *Fax:* (0732) 776239

Key Personnel
Man Dir: Christl Manfred
Sales & Publicity: Meraner Manfred
Chief Editor: M Griessner *Tel:* (0732) 776451732
E-mail: mgriessner@veritas.co.at
Founded: 1945
Subjects: Cookery, Education, Health, Nutrition, Outdoor Recreation, Regional Interests
ISBN Prefix(es): 3-85329; 3-7058; 3-85214
Total Titles: 450 Print; 5 CD-ROM; 20 Audio
Parent Company: Cornelsen, Germany
Subsidiaries: Ehrenwirth Verlag; Salzburger Jugend-Verlag
Bookshop(s): Buchhandlung Veritas, Harrachstr 5, A-4020 Linz
Warehouse: Wertpraesent, Boschstr 31, A-4600 Weis *Tel:* (7242) 696-0

Verlag Anton Schroll & Co+
Spengergasse 39, 1051 Vienna
Tel: (01) 5445641-33 *Fax:* (01) 544564166
Cable: Schrollverlag Vienna
Key Personnel
Man Dir: Friedrich Geyer
Founded: 1884
Subjects: Art, History, Travel
ISBN Prefix(es): 3-7031
Branch Office(s)
Anton Schroll & Co GmbH, Germany

Verlag Wilhelm Braumuller Universitats-Verlagsbuchhandlung GmbH
Servitengasse 5, 1092 Vienna
Mailing Address: Postfach 76, 1092 Vienna
Tel: (01) 319 11 59 *Fax:* (01) 310 28 05
E-mail: office@braumueller.at
Web Site: www.braumueller.at
ISBN Prefix(es): 3-7003

Vorarlberger Verlagsanstalt Aktiengesellschaft
Schwefel 81, 6850 Dornbirn
Tel: (05572) 2469778 *Fax:* (05572) 24 6 97-78
E-mail: office@vva.at
Web Site: www.vva.at
Key Personnel
Contact: Marlene Sutter; Karl-Heinz Milz
Founded: 1920
Subjects: Geography, Geology, History, Regional Interests
ISBN Prefix(es): 3-85430

VWGOe, see Verband der Wissenschaftlichen Gesellschaften Oesterreichs (VWGOe)

Universitaetsverlag Wagner GmbH
Andreas-Hoferstr 13, A-6020 Innsbruck
Tel: (0512) 587721 *Fax:* (0512) 582209
E-mail: mail@uvw.at
Cable: UNIVERSITAeTSVERLAG WAGNER INNSBRUCK
Key Personnel
Man Dir: Gottfried Grasl
Contact: Dr Blaas Mercedes *E-mail:* mercedes.blaas@uvw.at
Founded: 1554
Subjects: Archaeology, Automotive, Geography, Geology, History, Language Arts, Linguistics, Science (General)
ISBN Prefix(es): 3-7030

Verlag Mag Wanzenbock+
Landstrasser Hauptstr 88/6, 1030 Vienna
Tel: (01) 7148542 *Fax:* (01) 7135814
Key Personnel
Dir: Hans Wanzenbock *E-mail:* johann.wanzenboeck@chello.at
Founded: 1990
Subjects: English as a Second Language
ISBN Prefix(es): 3-901682
Number of titles published annually: 2 Print

Total Titles: 1 Print
Orders to: Oebz, lz Noe Sued Str 1, OBJ 34, 2355 Wiener Neudorf, Contact: Mrs Prinz *Tel:* (02263) 63535 *Fax:* (02263) 63535243

Waren-Erzeugungs-und Handelsgesellschaft GmbH+
Schwarzstr 15, Postfach 6, 5024 Salzburg
Tel: (0662) 88861011 *Fax:* (0662) 8886202
Telex: 633588 *Cable:* BERGLANDBUCH SALZBURG
Key Personnel
Man Dir: Alfred Schulz
Founded: 1929
Subjects: Fiction, History, Regional Interests, Science (General)
ISBN Prefix(es): 3-7023
Orders to: Morawa & Co, Hackingerstr 52, A-1140

Weilburg Verlag
Pottendorferstr 162, A-2700 Wiener Neustadt
Tel: (02622) 29538 *Fax:* (02622) 2953822
Key Personnel
Owner & Man Dir: Helmut Dresel
Sales: Selbst Liefert
Subjects: Art, Poetry
ISBN Prefix(es): 3-900100; 3-85246

Dr Otfried Weise Verlag Tabula Smaragdina+
Anton-Langer-Gasse 46/2/5, 1130 Vienna
Tel: (01) 804 2974 *Fax:* (01) 961 8287
E-mail: tabula@smaragdina.at
Web Site: smaragdina.at
Key Personnel
Man Dir: Otfried Weise
Founded: 1991
Subjects: Astrology, Occult, Health, Nutrition, Nonfiction (General)
ISBN Prefix(es): 3-9802471; 3-931138
Distributor for Source Publications

Herbert Weishaupt Verlag+
Hauptplatz 27, 8342 Gnas
Tel: (03151) 8487 *Fax:* (03151) 84874
E-mail: verlag@weishaupt.at
Web Site: www.weishaupt.at
Key Personnel
Contact: Herbert Weishaupt; Annemarie Weishaupt
Founded: 1980
Subjects: Aeronautics, Aviation, Maritime, Military Science, Natural History, Nonfiction (General), Regional Interests, Travel
ISBN Prefix(es): 3-7059; 3-900310
Number of titles published annually: 35 Print
Total Titles: 250 Print

Verlag Welsermuehl+
Maria-Theresiastr 41, A-4600 Wels
Tel: (07242) 231-0 *Fax:* (07242) 23118
Telex: 25586 *Cable:* WELSERMUHLDRUCK WELS
Key Personnel
Dir: Karl Pramendorfer
Founded: 1928
Branch office located in Germany.
ISBN Prefix(es): 3-85339

Verlag Galerie Welz Salzburg
Sigmund-Haffner Gasse 16, 5020 Salzburg
Tel: (0662) 841771 *Fax:* (0662) 84177120
E-mail: office@galerie-welz.at
Web Site: www.galerie-welz.at
Key Personnel
Publisher: Franz Eder
Sales: Hannes Lueftenegger
Subjects: Art
ISBN Prefix(es): 3-85349

Wespennest - Zeitschrift fuer brauchbare Texte und Bilder+
Rembrandtstr 31/4, 1020 Vienna
Tel: (043) 1 3326697 *Fax:* (043) 1 3332970
E-mail: office@wespennest.at
Web Site: www.wespennest.at
Key Personnel
Managing Editor: Walter Famler
Contact: Christiane Lerbscher
Founded: 1969
Literary essayistic cultural magazine, quarterly publication.
Subjects: Literature, Literary Criticism, Essays
ISBN Prefix(es): 3-85458
Imprints: Verein Gruppe Wespennest Redaktion
Distributed by Deutsche Verlagsanstalt

Georg Westermann Verlag GmbH+
Loewengasse 47, 1030 Vienna
Tel: (01) 7 14 24 74 *Fax:* (01) 7 18 02 81
E-mail: westermann@plus.at *Cable:* GEWEBUCH
Key Personnel
Man Dir: Hans-Dieter Moeller
Founded: 1838
Subjects: Nonfiction (General)
ISBN Prefix(es): 3-07
Parent Company: Georg Westermann Verlag, Druckerei und Kartographische Anstalt GmbH & Co, Brunswick, Germany (printing & publishing management company)
Orders to: VSB Verlagsservice Braunschweig GmbH, Postfach 3320, 38104 Braunschweig, Germany *Tel:* (0531) 708-0

Wiener Dom-Verlag GmbH
Stephansplatz 5, 1010 Vienna
Mailing Address: Postfach 152, 1014 Vienna
Tel: (01) 512 37 09; (01) 512 77 19 *Fax:* (01) 512 37 09-17
E-mail: stephansplatz@dombuchhandlung.at
Web Site: www.buchwirtschaft.at
Telex: 111760
Key Personnel
Man Dir: Franz Pollhammer
  E-mail: pollhammer@domverlag.at
Founded: 1946
Subjects: Religion - Catholic
ISBN Prefix(es): 3-85351
Divisions: Kunsthandlung
Bookshop(s): Rathausplatz 10, 3390 Melk; Bahnstr 1, 2130 Mistelbach; Stephansplatz 5, 1010 Vienna; Favoritenstr 115, 1100 Vienna; Domgasse 3, 2700 Wiener Neustadt

Wiener Frauenverlag, see Milena Verlag

Wieser Verlag+
Ebentaler Str 34B, 9020 Klagenfurt/Celovec
Tel: (0463) 37036 *Fax:* (0463) 37635
E-mail: office@wieser-verlag.com
Web Site: www.wieser-verlag.com
Key Personnel
Publisher: Lojze Wieser
Founded: 1987
Subjects: Biography, Drama, Theater, Fiction, Government, Political Science, Literature, Literary Criticism, Essays, Poetry
ISBN Prefix(es): 3-85129

Willibald Schlager, see Astor-Verlag, Willibald Schlager

Kunstverlag Wolfrum
Augustinerstr 10, 1010 Vienna
Tel: (01) 512-41-78 *Fax:* (01) 512-15-57
Web Site: www.buchwirtschaft.at
Telex: 75311081 Wolb *Cable:* WITWOLF VIENNA
Key Personnel
Man Dir: Monika Engel

Founded: 1919
Subjects: Art
ISBN Prefix(es): 3-900178

WUV/Facultas Universitaetsverlag
Berggasse 5, 1090 Vienna
Tel: (01) 310 53 56 *Fax:* (01) 319 70 50
E-mail: verlage@facultas.at
Web Site: www.wuv-verlag.at
Telex: 116529 lcpfa
Key Personnel
Publisher: Dr Michael Huter *E-mail:* huter@facultas.at
Manager: Thomas Stauffer *E-mail:* stauffer@facultas.at
Marketing: Christine Bernert *E-mail:* bernert@facultas.at
Founded: 1962
Subjects: Art, Behavioral Sciences, Communications, History, Language Arts, Linguistics, Law, Medicine, Nursing, Dentistry, Nonfiction (General), Philosophy, Psychology, Psychiatry, Science (General), Social Sciences, Sociology, Women's Studies, Specialize in scientific literature
ISBN Prefix(es): 3-85076; 3-85114
Associate Companies: Facultas Universitaetsverlag

Zirkular - Verlag der Dokumentationsstelle fuer neuere oesterreichische Literatur
Seidengasse 13, 1070 Vienna
Tel: (01) 526 20 44-0 *Fax:* (01) 526 20 44-30
E-mail: info@literaturhaus.at
Web Site: www.literaturhaus.at
Key Personnel
President: Dr Uwe Baur
Manager: Dr Heinz Lunzer
Founded: 1979
Subjects: Biography, Literature, Literary Criticism, Essays
ISBN Prefix(es): 3-900467

Paul Zsolnay Verlag GmbH+
Prinz-Eugenstr 30, Postfach 142, A-1041 Vienna
Tel: (01) 50576610 *Fax:* (01) 505766110
E-mail: info@zsolnay.at
Web Site: www.zsolnay.at *Cable:* ZSOLNAYVERLAG WIEN
Key Personnel
Man Dir: Michael Krueger; Stephan Joss
Rights & Permissions: Annette Lechner
Sales Manager: Felicitas Feilhauer
Editorial Dir: Herbert Ohrlinger
Production: Claus Seitz
Contact: Bettina Woergoetter *Tel:* (01) 5057661-14
Founded: 1923
Subjects: Biography, Fiction, History, Nonfiction (General), Poetry
ISBN Prefix(es): 3-552
Number of titles published annually: 40 Print
Total Titles: 500 Print
Parent Company: Carl Hanser GmbH & Co, Vilshofenerstr 10, 81679 Munich, Germany
Orders to: Dr Franz Hain, Dr Otto-Neurath-Gasse 5, A-1220 Vienna *Tel:* (01) 2826565 *Fax:* (01) 2825282
Verlegerdienst Muenchen, Gutenbergstr 1, D-82205 Gilching, Germany, Contact: Evelyne Weindl *Tel:* (08105) 388-122 *Fax:* (08105) 388-100 *E-mail:* weindl@verlegerdienst.de

Azerbaijan

General Information

Capital: Baku
Language: Azerbaijani

Religion: Predominantly Muslim (Shiite and Sunni); also Christian (mainly Russian Orthodox & Armenian Apostolic)
Population: 7.5 million
Bank Hours: Generally open for short hours between 0930-1230 Monday-Friday
Shop Hours: Generally 0900-1800 Monday-Friday; often open weekends
Currency: 1 kopeks = 1 rubl
Export/Import Information: According to Ukrainian quotas & customs duties, companies engaged in trade should register with the Ukraine Ministry of Foreign Economic Relations. Licenses for export & import are also required for trade with Russia.
Copyright: UCC (see Copyright Conventions, pg xi)

AZernesr
41 Gusi Gadzieva 4, 370005 Baku
Tel: (012) 925015
Key Personnel
Dir: A Mustafazade
Editor-in-Chief: A Guseinzade
Founded: 1924
Subjects: Agriculture, Fiction, Government, Political Science, Science (General), Technology
ISBN Prefix(es): 5-552

Sada, Literaturno-Izdatel'skij Centr+
Ul Bol'saja Krepostnaja, 28, 370004 Baku
Tel: (012) 927564 *Fax:* (012) 929843
Key Personnel
Contact: Guliev Tarlan
Subjects: Accounting, Asian Studies, Astrology, Occult, Business, Child Care & Development, Disability, Special Needs, Drama, Theater, Earth Sciences, Economics, Education, English as a Second Language, Finance, History, Humor, Language Arts, Linguistics, Management, Marketing, Music, Dance, Mysteries, Natural History
ISBN Prefix(es): 5-86874
Parent Company: National Peace Fund

Bahrain

General Information

Capital: Manama
Language: Arabic (English also widely spoken)
Religion: Muslims of the Shiite & Sunni sects
Population: 551,000
Bank Hours: 0730-1200 Saturday-Wednesday; 0730-1100 Thursday
Currency: 1000 Fils = 1 Bahrain dinar
Export/Import Information: Generally books dutied at 10%, most schoolbooks free of duty; none on advertising matter. No import license required but no obscene literature permitted & for books (not for advertising) a Chamber of Commerce certificate is mandatory. No exchange controls.

Arab Communicators
PO Box 551, Manama
Tel: (0973) 254 258 *Fax:* (0973) 531 837
Key Personnel
Publisher & Editor-in-Chief: Ahmed A Fakhri
Publisher: Hamed A Abul
Founded: 1981
Parent Company: ArabConsult
Subsidiaries: Arabvision; Arabad

Al Hilal Publications
Government Ave, Manama
Mailing Address: PO Box 224, Manama
Tel: 231122

Telex: 8981 Hilal
Key Personnel
Contact: Mr Silveira Haydn
Bookshop(s): Al Hilal Bookshop

Bangladesh

General Information

Capital: Dhaka
Language: Bengali (English widely used commercially)
Religion: Predominately Muslim with some Hindu
Population: 129.2 million
Bank Hours: 0900-330 Saturday-Wednesday; 0900-1100 Thursday
Shop Hours: 1000-2030 Saturday-Thursday
Currency: 100 pisha = 1 taka (Tk)
Export/Import Information: No tariff on books and advertising matter. Import licenses required for all imports.
Copyright: UCC (see Copyright Conventions, pg xi)

Academic Publishers+
2/7 Nawab-Habibullah Rd, Dhaka 1000
Tel: (02) 507355; (02) 507366 *Fax:* (02) 863060
Key Personnel
Joint Man Dir: Habibur Rahman
Founded: 1982
Subjects: Social Sciences, Sociology
ISBN Prefix(es): 984-08

Adeyle Brothers & Co
60 Patuatuly, Dhaka 1100
Tel: (02) 233508
ISBN Prefix(es): 984-402

Ankur Prakashani+
40/1 Purana Paltan, Dhaka 1000
Tel: (02) 9569121; (02) 9553635 *Fax:* (02) 9567730
E-mail: ankur@bangla.net
Web Site: www.nutra.org/html/ankur.html
Founded: 1986
We are also a library supplier & importer of reference books.
Subjects: Anthropology, Asian Studies, Economics, Education, Fiction, Government, Political Science, Literature, Literary Criticism, Essays, Nonfiction (General)
ISBN Prefix(es): 984-464; 984-8010
Distributor for Narosa (India); Prints India
Orders to: 40/1 Purana Paltan, Dhaka 1000

Bangladesh Publishers+
45 Patuatuli Rd, Dhaka 1100
Tel: (02) 233135
Key Personnel
Dir: Maya Rani Ghosal
Founded: 1952
Member of Book Sellers & Publication Association of Bangladesh, Pranab Math (a philanthropic organization that helps in free education). Also acts as distributor of books & periodicals of both local & foreign countries.
Subjects: Accounting, Drama, Theater, Economics, Physics, Public Administration, Religion - Hindu
ISBN Prefix(es): 984-8012
Associate Companies: Ratan & Sons
Bookshop(s): 38/19/B Banglabazar, 2nd floor, Dhaka 1100

Bangladesh Government Press, Ministry of Establishment, Government of the Peoples Republic of Bangladesh
1-3 Block F, Lalmatia, Dhaka 1207
Tel: (02) 8122845 *Fax:* (02) 8113095
E-mail: adab@bdonline.com
ISBN Prefix(es): 984-01

Boighar
110-286 Bipani Bitan, Chittagong
Tel: (031) 252745
ISBN Prefix(es): 984-423

Chalantika
14 Banglabazar, 1st Floor, Dhaka 1100
Tel: (02) 7123925 *Fax:* (02) 7115691
ISBN Prefix(es): 984-8019

Gatidhara+
38/2-ka Banglabazar, Dhaka 1100
Mailing Address: GPO Box 2723, Dhaka 1000
Tel: (02) 7392077 (press); (02) 7113117 (res); (02) 7115630 (res); (02) 7117515 (showroom); (02) 7118273 (showroom) *Fax:* (02) 9134617; (02) 9566456
E-mail: akter@aitlbd.net; gatidara@bdonline.com
Key Personnel
Publisher & Chief Executive: Sikder Abul Bashar
Founded: 1988
Also acts as distributor & exporter
Member of Publishers Association, Publishers Guild.
Subjects: Behavioral Sciences, Child Care & Development, Drama, Theater, Education, Fiction, Health, Nutrition, Humor, Literature, Literary Criticism, Essays, Poetry, Religion - Islamic
ISBN Prefix(es): 984-461
Parent Company: Gatidhara
Subsidiaries: Gatidhara Computers
Bookshop(s): 38/2 Banglabazar, Dhaka 1100
Book Club(s): National Book Center; National Library
Warehouse: Kumarpatty Rd, Jhalakati 8400
Orders to: 38/4 Banglabazar, Dhaka 1100

Gono Prakashani, Gono Shasthya Kendra+
14/E Dhanmondhi R/A, Dhaka 1205
Tel: (02) 500406; (02) 839366 *Fax:* (02) 863567; (02) 833182
E-mail: gk.mail@drik.bgd.toolnet.org *Cable:* GRAM GORO, DHAKA
Key Personnel
Man Dir: Mr Shafio Khan
Editor: Mr Bazlur Rahim
Chairman & President Editorial Board: Dr Zafrullah Chowdhury
Founded: 1978
Subjects: Child Care & Development, Health, Nutrition, Medicine, Nursing, Dentistry, Self-Help, Social Sciences, Sociology
ISBN Prefix(es): 984-431
Parent Company: Gonoshasthaya Kendra Trust
Associate Companies: Gonoshasthaya Pharmaceutical, Ltd; Gonoshasthya Antibiotic, Ltd
Subsidiaries: Gono Mudran (printing company)
Distributed by Baulman Prakason (Calcutta, India)
Showroom(s): Gono Prakashani Aziz Cooperative Market Shahbagh, Dhaka
Bookshop(s): Gono Prakashani Aziz Cooperative Market Shahbagh, Dhaka
Shipping Address: Gono Prakashani Po Mirzanaga, Nayarhat, 1344 Dhaka
Warehouse: Gono Prakashani Po Mirzanagar, Nayarhat, Dhaka 1344
Orders to: Gono Prakashani Po Mirzanagar, Nayarhat, Dhaka 1344

Mullick Bros
3/1 Bangla Bazar, Dhaka 1100
Tel: (02) 280728

Subjects: Education
ISBN Prefix(es): 984-411

Agamee Prakashani+
36 Banglabazar, Dhaka 1100
Tel: (02) 7111332; (02) 7110021 *Fax:* (02) 9562018; (02) 7123945
E-mail: agamee@bdonline.com *Cable:* AGAMEE
Key Personnel
Chief Executive Officer: Osman Gani *Tel:* (02) 18219024 *Fax:* (02) 9340856 *E-mail:* bfdr@bdonline.com
Founded: 1986
Member of Bangladesh Publishers & Book Sellers Association, Dhaka Chamber of Commerce & Industry, FBCCI, Bangladesh Publishers Council.
Subjects: Fiction, Government, Political Science, Journalism, Literature, Literary Criticism, Essays, Music, Dance, Philosophy, Poetry, Science (General), Social Sciences, Sociology, Women's Studies
ISBN Prefix(es): 984-401
Number of titles published annually: 70 Print
Total Titles: 672 Print
Distributed by Phuthipatra
Distributor for Muktadhara

The University Press Ltd+
Red Crescent Bldg, 114 Motijheel C/A, Dhaka 1000
Mailing Address: GPO Box 2611, Dhaka 1000
Tel: (02) 9565441; (02) 9565444 *Fax:* (02) 9565443
E-mail: upl@bangla.net; upl@bttb.net.bd
Web Site: www.uplbooks.com *Cable:* DUNIPRESS
Key Personnel
Senior Manager Editorial: Badiuddin Nazir
Sales Manager: M A Halim
Production Executive: Abdar Rahman
Man Dir: Mr Mohiuddin Ahmed
Founded: 1975
Specializes in publishing, selling & importing.
Subjects: Agriculture, Anthropology, Archaeology, Architecture & Interior Design, Art, Biography, Economics, Education, Environmental Studies, Finance, Geography, Geology, Government, Political Science, History, Management, Military Science, Public Administration, Publishing & Book Trade Reference, Religion - Islamic, Technology, Travel, Women's Studies
ISBN Prefix(es): 984-05
Number of titles published annually: 70 Print
Total Titles: 500 Print
Branch Office(s)
146 Dampara, Chittagong & 86 K D Ghose Rd, Khulna
Distributed by Paragon Enterprise (India); Manohar Publishers & Distributors (New Delhi, India); Oxford University Press (Pakistan); ZED Books (UK); Intermediate Technology (UK)
Distributor for Oxford University Press (UK, Pakistan & India); Manohar Publishers & Distributors (India); ZED Books (UK); Intermediate Technology (UK)

Barbados

General Information

Capital: Bridgetown
Language: English
Religion: Anglican
Population: 263,000
Bank Hours: 0800-1500 Monday-Thursday; 0800-1750 Friday

Shop Hours: 0800-1600 Monday-Friday; 0800-1200 Saturday
Currency: 100 cents = 1 Barbados dollar
Export/Import Information: No tariff on books. Import license covering exchange required; no obscene literature permitted.
Copyright: Berne, UCC (see Copyright Conventions, pg xi)

Business Tutors
124 Chancery Lane, Christ Church
Mailing Address: PO Box 800 E, Saint Michael, Bridgetown
Tel: (246) 428-5664 *Fax:* (246) 429-4854
E-mail: pchad@caribsurf.com
Subjects: Astrology, Occult, Business, Disability, Special Needs, Management, Microcomputers, Self-Help
ISBN Prefix(es): 976-8084
Subsidiaries: P & R Chad Ltd

Carib Research & Publications Inc
PO Box 556, Bridgetown
Tel: (246) 438-0580
Key Personnel
Chief Executive: Dr Farley Brathwaite
Founded: 1986
Also acts as agent for Antilles Publications.
Subjects: Regional Interests
ISBN Prefix(es): 976-8051
Associate Companies: Antilles Publications

Belarus

General Information

Capital: Minsk
Language: Belarussian
Religion: Predominantly Christian (mostly Roman Catholic & Eastern Orthodox)
Population: 10.4 million
Bank Hours: Generally open for short hours between 0930-1230 Monday-Friday
Shop Hours: Generally 0900-1800 Monday-Friday; often open weekends
Currency: 100 kopeks = 1 rubl
Export/Import Information: According to Ukrainian quotas & customs duties, companies engaged in trade should register with the Ukraine Ministry of Foreign Economic Relations. Licenses for export & import are also required for trade with Russia.
Copyright: UCC (see Copyright Conventions, pg xi)

Belarus (The Belorussia)
Prospect Maserova, 11, 220600 Minsk
Tel: (0172) 238742 *Fax:* (0172) 238731
Key Personnel
Dir: V L Dubovsky
Editor-in-Chief: L N Teterina
Founded: 1921
Subjects: Art, Economics, Government, Political Science, Medicine, Nursing, Dentistry, Music, Dance
ISBN Prefix(es): 5-338

Belaruskaya Encyklapedyya (Byelossian Encyclopaedia)
vul F Skariinii 16a, 220072 Minsk
Tel: (0172) 284 1767; (0172) 284 0600; (0172) 284 0983
Key Personnel
Editor-in-Chief: Genadz P Pashkou
Founded: 1967
Subjects: Archaeology, Architecture & Interior Design, Art, Biography, Biological Sciences, Chemistry, Chemical Engineering, Cookery, Crafts, Games, Hobbies, Education, Fiction, Finance, History, House & Home, Law, Literature, Literary Criticism, Essays, Mathematics, Medicine, Nursing, Dentistry, Natural History, Parapsychology, Physics, Religion - Other, Sports, Athletics
ISBN Prefix(es): 5-85700

Interdigets Publishing House+
Prosp F S Karyny 34, k 25, 172, 220005 Minsk
Mailing Address: 24 Zakharov Ave, Off 20, 172, 220005 Minsk
Tel: (0172) 847888; (0172) 843778 *Fax:* (0172) 133073
Key Personnel
President: Anatoli Kudrjavtsev
Vice President: Vladimir Sivchik
Founded: 1991
Subjects: Animals, Pets, Automotive, Biography, Career Development, Child Care & Development, Criminology, Fiction, Health, Nutrition, Music, Dance, Nonfiction (General), Women's Studies
Total Titles: 25,000 Print
Associate Companies: TOO Echo, Smolensk, Russian Federation; Digest & Kolm, Kaliningrad, Russian Federation
Distributed by TOO Echo (Smolensk, Russia)
Distributor for TOO Echo (Smolensk, Russia)
Showroom(s): 34, Skaryna Ave, Off 25, 220005 Minsk
Bookshop(s): 124, Partizanski Prospect, Minsk
Shipping Address: 3, Ingenernaja, Minsk
Warehouse: 3, Ingenernaja, Minsk

Junactva, Vydavectva
Prasp Masherava 11, 220600 Minsk
Tel: (0172) 23326 *Fax:* (0172) 266616
Founded: 1981
Subjects: Poetry
ISBN Prefix(es): 5-7880; 985-05

Kavaler Publishers+
Member of Belarusian Association of Book Publishers & Book Distribution
7 Ignatenko St, 220035 Minsk
Tel: (0172) 238041; (0172) 548198 *Fax:* (0172) 238041
E-mail: Kavaler@inbox.ru
Key Personnel
Dir & Publisher: Constantine Khotyanovsky
Deputy Dir: Svetlana Morozova
Founded: 1991
Member of Belarusian Association of Book Publishers & Book Distributors, Belarusian Union of Artists; all editions are prize winners of the annual national contests *Art of the Book*.
Subjects: Advertising, Business, English as a Second Language, Fiction, History, Nonfiction (General), Poetry, Wine & Spirits, German as a second language
ISBN Prefix(es): 985-6427
Number of titles published annually: 8 Print
Total Titles: 70 Print
Book Club(s): Minsk Book Exhibition-Sale Club Belakk

Izdatelstvo Mastatskaya Litaratura
Maserava prospect 11, 220617 Minsk
Tel: (0172) 234809 *Fax:* (0172) 269112; (0172) 238363
Key Personnel
Dir: S A Andreyuk
Editor-in-Chief: N S Kusenkov
Founded: 1972
Subjects: Fiction, Literature, Literary Criticism, Essays
ISBN Prefix(es): 5-340

Narodnaya Asveta+
vul Makayonka 12, 220023 Minsk
Tel: (0172) 264-62-68, 264-02-86, 264-64-69, 264-33-97 *Fax:* (0172) 236184
E-mail: ngpna@asveta.belpak.minsk.by.
Key Personnel
Dir: I Laptenok
Founded: 1951
Subjects: Biological Sciences, Economics, Environmental Studies, Geography, Geology, History, Mathematics
ISBN Prefix(es): 5-341

Publishing Center of Belarus State University+
Division of BSU
Krasnoarmejskaja 6, 220030 Minsk
Tel: (0172) 227 18 08 *Fax:* (0172) 226 01 75
E-mail: pubcentre@org.bsu.unibee.by
Key Personnel
Dir: Alexandre Nechaj
Founded: 1997
Subjects: Computer Science, Education, Law, Mathematics, Physics, Science (General)
Total Titles: 20 Print
Parent Company: BSU

Yunatstva
11, Masherova av, 220600 Minsk
Tel: (0172) 2333326 *Fax:* (0172) 266616
Key Personnel
Dir: Valentin A Luksha
Founded: 1981
Subjects: Science Fiction, Fantasy
ISBN Prefix(es): 5-7880

Belgium

General Information

Capital: Brussels
Language: Dutch in the north, French in the south. Brussels is officially bilingual. German in eastern Belgium
Religion: Predominantly Roman Catholic, some Protestant
Population: 10.2 million
Bank Hours: Main towns: 0900-1200/1300 & 1400-1530/1600: Monday-Friday
Shop Hours: 0900-1900 with variations
Currency: 100 Eurocents = 1 Euro; 40.3399 Belgian francs = 1 Euro
Export/Import Information: Member of the European Economic Community. No import license required, just Model A form of notice declaration of payment. No exchange controls. 6% VAT on books.
Copyright: UCC, Berne, Florence (see Copyright Conventions, pg xi)

Abimo+
Beukenlaan 8, 9250 Waasmunster
Tel: (052) 462407 *Fax:* (052) 461962
E-mail: info@abimo-uitgeverij.com
Web Site: www.abimo-uitgeverij.com
Key Personnel
Publisher: K David *E-mail:* k.david@planetinternet.be
Founded: 1993
Member of Vlaamse Uitgevers Vereniging.
Subjects: Drama, Theater, Earth Sciences, Education, Foreign Countries, Specialize in Geography
ISBN Prefix(es): 90-75905; 90-801767; 90-59320

Academia-Bruylant+
Subsidiary of Bruylant
Grand'Place 29, 1348 Louvain-la-Neuve
Tel: (010) 45 23 95 *Fax:* (010) 45 44 80
E-mail: academia-bruylant@skynet.be
Web Site: www.academia-bruylant.be

Key Personnel
President: Jean Vandeveld
Founded: 1987
Member of ADEB.
Subjects: Accounting, Anthropology, Journalism, Law, Physical Sciences, Religion - Islamic, Social Sciences, Sociology
ISBN Prefix(es): 2-87209
Total Titles: 500 Print

Academia Press+
Eekhout 2, 9000 Ghent
Tel: (09) 233.80.88 *Fax:* (09) 233.14.09
E-mail: info@academiapress.be
Web Site: www.academiapress.be
Key Personnel
International Rights: Peter Laroy
Founded: 1989
Scientific Publishers.
Subjects: Business, Economics, Journalism, Psychology, Psychiatry, Science (General), Social Sciences, Sociology
ISBN Prefix(es): 90-382
Parent Company: J Story-Scientia Scientia bvba, Van Duyseplein 8, 9000 Ghent

Acco CV
Tiensestraat 134, 3000 Leuven
Tel: (016) 29 11 00 *Fax:* (016) 20 73 89
Key Personnel
Dir: L Van Gompel
Founded: 1960
Subjects: Criminology, Economics, Education, History, Language Arts, Linguistics, Law, Mathematics, Medicine, Nursing, Dentistry, Philosophy, Psychology, Psychiatry, Religion - Other, Science (General), Social Sciences, Sociology
ISBN Prefix(es): 90-334
Imprints: De Horstink
Subsidiaries: Acco; Broadcast Book Services (UK & Ireland)
Orders to: Acco-Uitgeverij, Tiensestraat 134-136, 3000 Leuven

Actualquarto+
Allee des Bouleaux 20, 6280 Gerpinnes
Tel: (071) 21.61.53 *Fax:* (071) 21.77.13
Key Personnel
Man Dir & Sales, Rights & Permission: Michel Paunet
Editorial: Jean Delahaut
Founded: 1970
Subjects: Education

Centre Aequatoria
Stationsstr 48, 3360 Lovenjoel
Tel: (016) 46 44 84 *Fax:* (016) 46 44 84
Web Site: www.aequatoria.be; www.abbol.com
Key Personnel
Dir: Honore Vinck *E-mail:* vinck.aequatoria@belgacom.net
Documentaliste: Guillaume Essalo
Founded: 1980
Promotes research on Central African humanities preference for Central African authors.
Subjects: Anthropology, Biography, Ethnicity, History, Language Arts, Linguistics, Regional Interests, Social Sciences, Sociology
Branch Office(s)
BP 276, Mbandaka, Congo
U.S. Office(s): The Missionaries of the S Heart (Aequatoria), 305 S Lake St, PO Box 270, Aurora, IL 60507, United States *Fax:* 630-892-3071 *E-mail:* mscusafin@ibm.net (only for payments of subscriptions to Annales Aequatoria)
Distributed by Editions St Paul (Zaire)

Alamire vzw, Music Publishers+
Division of Musica VZW
Toekomstlaan 5B, 3910 Neerpelt
Tel: (011) 610 510 *Fax:* (011) 610 511
E-mail: info@alamire.com
Web Site: www.alamire.com
Key Personnel
Director: Herman Baeten
Sales: Annelies Van Boxel *E-mail:* annelies.vanboxel@alamire.com
Founded: 1978
Specialize in early music facsimiles.
Subjects: Library & Information Sciences, Music, Dance
ISBN Prefix(es): 90-6853

Altina+
Dirk Lippens Vredestraat 34, 8400 Ostende
Tel: (059) 80-16-51 *Fax:* (059) 51-27-17
Key Personnel
President & International Rights: Dirk Lippens *Tel:* (059) 703324
Author: Christiane Beerlandt *Tel:* (059) 70 3324
Administration: Davina Doom *Tel:* (059) 80 1651
Founded: 1996
Publish works of Belgian author Christiane Beerlandt.
Audio.
Subjects: Alternative, Astrology, Occult, Health, Nutrition, Music, Dance, Nonfiction (General), Philosophy, Psychology, Psychiatry, Self-Help, Philosophy of Joyful Life, Original Fairy Tales, Psychological Causes for Disease, Self Knowledge & realization, Physical Immortality, Health & Nutrition
ISBN Prefix(es): 90-75849
Number of titles published annually: 10 Print; 1 Audio
Total Titles: 25 Print; 3 Audio
Online services available through World Wide Web.

Amnesty International VZW
Kerkstraat 156, 2060 Antwerp
Tel: (03) 271.16.16 *Fax:* (03) 235.78.12
E-mail: amnesty@aivl.be
Web Site: www.aivl.be
Telex: 32079
Key Personnel
Contact: Katrien Scholiers *E-mail:* promotie@aivl.be
ISBN Prefix(es): 90-70895

Libraire Ancienne Noel Anselot
18 rue de Transinne, 6890 Redu
Tel: (060) 6165 6091 *Fax:* (060) 6165 6091
Key Personnel
Man Dir: A De Rache
Founded: 1954
Subjects: Art, Biography, Poetry
ISBN Prefix(es): 2-8015

Artel SC
2 Place Baudouin 1 er, 5004 Namur, Bouge
Tel: (081) 21 37 00 *Fax:* (081) 21 23 72
E-mail: erasme@skynet.be
Key Personnel
General Manager: Joseph Ponet
Editorial Dir: Francoise Dury
Subjects: Biological Sciences, Environmental Studies, Government, Political Science, History, Mathematics, Religion - Catholic, Social Sciences, Sociology, Theology
ISBN Prefix(es): 2-87374
Parent Company: Editions Erasme SA
Divisions: Ciaco editeur
Distributed by GM Diffusion (Switzerland); Liber-T (Canada); Presses de Belgique
Distributor for Bit-Ilo; Feuilles familales

SA Artis-Historia+
Postbus 224, 2550 Kontich
Tel: (078) 150.150 *Fax:* (078) 150.150
E-mail: info@artis-historia.be
Web Site: www.artis-historia.bc
Key Personnel
Chief Executive, Editing & Marketing Dir: Christian Kremer
Founded: 1948 (Companies merged to form Artis-Historia in 1976)
Subjects: Art, Cookery, Crafts, Games, Hobbies, Geography, Geology, History, Music, Dance, Natural History, Travel
ISBN Prefix(es): 2-87391; 90-5657
Total Titles: 180 Print
Parent Company: Vicindo
Ultimate Parent Company: Belgian Post Group
Divisions: Artoria

Assimil NV
Rue de Congres 13 Congresstraat, 1000 Brussels 1
Tel: (02) 5114502 *Fax:* (02) 5129138
E-mail: assimilbenelux@wanadoo.be
Web Site: www.assimil.be
Key Personnel
Dir: S Peters
Editorial: E Defraene; R Deblomme
Founded: 1939
Member of VBVB-VUNB and CBL-ADEB.
Subjects: Language Arts, Linguistics, Language study method
ISBN Prefix(es): 90-70077; 90-74996

Aurelia Books PVBA
Museumlaan 17, 9831 Deurne
Tel: (091) 82 55 82 *Fax:* (091) 82 72 47
Key Personnel
Dir: A d'Oosterlynck
Sales & Publicity: L Bullaert
Founded: 1972
Subjects: Medicine, Nursing, Dentistry, Regional Interests, Religion - Other
ISBN Prefix(es): 90-70827

NV Uitgeverij Altiora Averbode+
Abdijstraat 1, 3271 Averbode
Mailing Address: PB 54, 3271 Averbode
Tel: (013) 780141 *Fax:* (013) 773311
E-mail: averbode.publ@verbode.be
Key Personnel
Dir: R Biemans *Tel:* (013) 780102 *Fax:* (013) 776837 *E-mail:* dir@verbode.be
Editor: N C Vranckx *Tel:* (013) 780170 *Fax:* (013) 780179
Production: 1 Willems *Tel:* (013) 780140 *Fax:* (013) 780310
Founded: 1934
Subjects: Education, Religion - Other, Novels
ISBN Prefix(es): 90-317

Averbode Publishers+
Abdijstraat 1, 3271 Scherpenheuvel-Zichem (Averbode)
Tel: (013) 780111 *Fax:* (013) 780183; (013) 780179
E-mail: averbode.publ@verbode.be
Web Site: www.averbode.com
Key Personnel
Commercial Dir: Patrick Hermans
General Manager: Roland Biemans
Founded: 1993
Subjects: Religion - Catholic, Educational youth magazines
ISBN Prefix(es): 90-317
Number of titles published annually: 50 Print
Total Titles: 400 Print
Online services available through World Wide Web.

Maison d'Editions Baha'ies ASBL
rue du Trone, 205, 1050 Brussels
Tel: (02) 647 07 49 *Fax:* (02) 646 21 77
Web Site: www.adeb.irisnet.be

Key Personnel
President, Editor & International Rights: Maurieette Baert-Valee
Founded: 1970
Member of Association of Belgian Publishers.
Subjects: Biography, History, Law, Philosophy, Religion - Other
ISBN Prefix(es): 2-87203

Bakermat NV
Wollemarkt 18, 2800 Mechelen
Tel: (015) 42 05 08 *Fax:* (015) 42 05 73
E-mail: info@bakermat.com
Web Site: www.bakermat.com
Key Personnel
General Dir: Jos Baekens
Founded: 1991
ISBN Prefix(es): 90-5461

Bartleby & Co+
Priesterstraat 15, 1000 Brussels
Tel: (02) 538 10 51
E-mail: bartleby@skynet.be
Key Personnel
Contact: Thorsten Baensch
Founded: 1996
Specialize in artist books.
Subjects: Art, Literature, Literary Criticism, Essays, Artist books & limited edition prints
ISBN Prefix(es): 2-930279
Number of titles published annually: 3 Print
Total Titles: 15 Print

Bibliotheque des Signes, *imprint of* Editions Delta SA

Editions Gerard Blanchart & Cie SA+
Ave Ernest Masoin, 15, 1090 Brussels
Tel: (02) 4783706 *Fax:* (02) 4786429
Key Personnel
President: Charles Blanchart *E-mail:* charles.blanchart@chello.be
Production, Rights & Permissions: Therese Chantrenne
Founded: 1958
Specialize in railways & animals.
Subjects: Animals, Pets, Art, Biblical Studies, Photography, Religion - Catholic, Religion - Protestant, Religion - Other, Transportation
ISBN Prefix(es): 2-87202; 90-74760
Total Titles: 13 Print

Editions Blanco SA+
Tweehuizenweg 61, 1200 Brussels
Tel: (02) 7720320 *Fax:* (02) 7706429
Key Personnel
Administrator & General Dir: Guy Leblanc
Founded: 1987
ISBN Prefix(es): 2-87297; 90-73106

Blitz, *imprint of* De Schaar/Geknipt Papier

De Boeck et Larcier SA+
Fond Jean-Paques, 4, 1348 Louvain-la-Neuve
Tel: (010) 48 25 11 *Fax:* (010) 48 26 50
Web Site: www.larcier.be/larcier.html
Key Personnel
Man Dir: Goerges Hoyos
Editor, School Books: Francoise Goethals
Editor, University Books: Michel Jezierski
Founded: 1918
Subjects: Education, English as a Second Language, Language Arts, Linguistics, Literature, Literary Criticism, Essays
ISBN Prefix(es): 2-8011
Parent Company: Groupe de Boeck SA
Associate Companies: Acces+ SPRL; De Boeck & Larcier SA
Distributed by Editions Belin (France); Editions du Renouveau Pedagogique (Canada); G M Diffusion (Suisse); Litec (France)

Showroom(s): Rue des Minimes 39, B-1000 Brussels *Tel:* (02) 548 07 11 *Fax:* (02) 513 90 09
Orders to: Acces Plus SPRL, Fond Jean-Paques 4, B-1348 Louvain-La-Neuve

Bourdeaux-Capelle SA
32 rue Barre, 5500 Dinant
Tel: (082) 222283; (082) 222277 *Fax:* (082) 226378
Key Personnel
Dir: Michel Bourdeaux
Founded: 1913
Subjects: Language Arts, Linguistics

Brepols, *imprint of* Brepols Publishers NV

Brepols Publishers NV+
Begijnhof 67, 2300 Turnhout
Tel: (014) 448020 *Fax:* (014) 428919
E-mail: info.publishers@brepols.com
Web Site: www.brepols.net
Key Personnel
Chairman: J L de Cartier de Marchienne
General Manager: Paul De Jongh *Tel:* (014) 44.80.21 *E-mail:* paul.dejongh@brepols.com
Commercial Manager: Hans Deraeve *Tel:* (014) 44.80.22 *E-mail:* hans.deraeve@brepols.com
Publishing Manager: Christophe Lebbe *Tel:* (014) 44.80.26 *E-mail:* christophe.lebbe@brepols.com; Johan Van der Beke *Tel:* (207) 794 98 47 *Fax:* (207) 794 99 07 *E-mail:* johan.van.der.beke@brepols.com; Luc Jocque *Tel:* (050) 368820 *Fax:* (050) 371457 *E-mail:* luc.jocque@brepols.com; Simon Forde *Tel:* (020) 7284-4359, (014) 44 80 25 *Fax:* (020) 7267-8764 *E-mail:* simon.forde@brepols.com; Roland Demeulenaere *Tel:* (050) 368822 *Fax:* (050) 371457 *E-mail:* roland.demeulenaere@brepols.com; Roel Vander Plaetse *Tel:* (050) 368821 *Fax:* (050) 371457 *E-mail:* roel.vander.plaetse@brepols.com
Production Manager: Jean Verstraete *Tel:* (014) 44.80.28 *E-mail:* jean.verstraete@brepols.com
Marketing Manager: Patrick Daemen *Tel:* (014) 44.80.31 *E-mail:* patrick.daemen@brepols.com
Administration & IT Manager: Wim Borgers *Tel:* (014) 44.80.39 *E-mail:* wim.borgers@brepols.com
Customer Care Manager: Ann Duchene *Tel:* (014) 44.80.34 *E-mail:* ann.duchene@brepols.com
Publishing Manager: Chris Vanden Borre *Tel:* (014) 44.80.27 *E-mail:* chris.vandenborre@brepols.com
Founded: 1796
International academic publishers.
Subjects: Archaeology, Architecture & Interior Design, Art, Asian Studies, Biblical Studies, History, Language Arts, Linguistics, Literature, Literary Criticism, Essays, Native American Studies, Philosophy, Religion - Other
ISBN Prefix(es): 2-503; 90-5622; 2-85006; 90-72100
Number of titles published annually: 240 Print
Parent Company: Brepols Group NV
Imprints: Brepols; Corpus Christianorum; Harvey Miller

Vanden Broele NV+
Lieven Bauwensstr 33, 8200 Brugge
Tel: (050) 456 177 *Fax:* (050) 456 199
E-mail: graphic.group@vandenbroele.be
Web Site: www.vandenbroele.be
Key Personnel
Dir: E de Jonghe
Founded: 1957
Subjects: Government, Political Science, Law, Public Administration, Social Sciences, Sociology
ISBN Prefix(es): 90-5753; 90-6267

Eteblissements Emile Bruylant SA+
rue de la Regence 67, 1000 Brussels

Tel: (02) 512.98.45 *Fax:* (02) 511.72.02
E-mail: info@bruylant.be
Web Site: www.bruylant.be
Key Personnel
Pres & Dir: Jean Vandeveld *Tel:* (02) 512.98.42 *Fax:* (02) 511.94.77 *E-mail:* vdv@bruylant.be
Founded: 1838
Publisher & bookseller of law books & law periodicals.
Subjects: Government, Political Science, Law
ISBN Prefix(es): 2-8027
Distributor for Carl Heymans Verlag; Nomos Verlag; MANZ'sche Verlag; Editions Yvon Blais; Editions Themis Inc; Editorial ARANZADI; Editions CUJAS; Editions Dalloz Sirey; LGDJ; Editions du JURIS-CLASSEUR; Editions Legislatives; Monsieur Pedone; Blackstone Press Ltd; Butterworths; Cambridge University Press; Lloyd's of London; Oxford University Press; Sweet & Maxwell; Wiley Law; Dott A Giuffre Editore; Kluwer Law Intenational; Editions du Comite international de la Croix-Rouge; Verlag Stampfli & Co

Campinia Media VZW+
Kleinhoefstraat 4, 2440 Geel
Tel: (014) 59 09 59 *Fax:* (014) 59 03 44
E-mail: info@campiniamedia.be
Web Site: www.campiniamedia.be
Key Personnel
Dir: Erik Borgmans *E-mail:* erik.borgmans@campiniamedia.be
Founded: 1983
Subjects: Agriculture, Behavioral Sciences, Biological Sciences, Computer Science, Language Arts, Linguistics, Physics, Science (General), Social Sciences, Sociology
ISBN Prefix(es): 90-356

Caramel, *imprint of* Caramel SA

Caramel SA+
Otto de Mentockplein 19, 1853 Strombeek-Bever
Tel: (02) 2632051 *Fax:* (02) 2632050
E-mail: caramel@skynet.be
Key Personnel
Contact: Yvan Meyers *E-mail:* yvan.meyers@caramel.de
International Rights: Dirk Mennes *Tel:* (02) 263 2046 *E-mail:* production@caramel.de
Founded: 1993
Also acts as packager.
Subjects: Crafts, Games, Hobbies, Fiction
ISBN Prefix(es): 90-5562
Number of titles published annually: 250 Print
Imprints: Caramel

Carmelitana VZW+
Burgstraat 46, 9000 Ghent
Tel: (09) 225.48.36 *Fax:* (09) 224.06.01
E-mail: boekhandel@carmelitana.be
Web Site: www.carmelitana.be
Key Personnel
President: Jos Rymen
Editor: F Lodewijckx
Founded: 1941
Subjects: Religion - Other
ISBN Prefix(es): 90-76671

Carto BVBA
Pagodenlaan 241, 1020 Brussels
Tel: (02) 26803455 *Fax:* (02) 2680345 *Cable:* Cartopress
Key Personnel
Man Dir: Michiel Plaizier
Founded: 1950
Subjects: Education, Geography, Geology, History, Travel
ISBN Prefix(es): 90-74437

Subsidiaries: Carpress, International Press Agency; European Cartographic Institute; Cremers (Schoollandkaarten) PVBA; Cremers Cartographic Institute

Cartoeristiek (Federatie van Belgische Autobus- en Autocarondernemers) (BAAV)+
Motestraat 41, 8800 Roeselare
Tel: (051) 226060 *Fax:* (051) 229273
Key Personnel
Contact: Luc Glorieux
Secretary: Mrs Riet Espeel *E-mail:* riet.espeel@busworld.org
Subjects: Travel
ISBN Prefix(es): 90-71408

Cartoon Creation+
85 rue du Cerf, 1332 Genval
Tel: (02) 6520220 *Fax:* (02) 6520160
Key Personnel
Dir General: Hendrik Coysman
Founded: 1984
ISBN Prefix(es): 2-87345

Editions Casterman SA+
Rue Pasquier Grenier 4, 7500 Tournai
Tel: (032) 22098300 *Fax:* (032) 22098301
Web Site: www.casterman.com
Key Personnel
Man Dir: Robert Vangeneberg
Vice President: Didier Platteau
Vice President, Rights & Permissions: Ivan Noerdinger
Vice President, Editor & Author: Etienne Pollet
Founded: 1780
Also acts as printers, binders.
Subjects: Art, History, Humor
ISBN Prefix(es): 90-303

Editions Casterman SA+
rue Royale, 132-boite 2, 1000 Brussels
Tel: (02) 209 83 00 *Fax:* (02) 209 83 01
Web Site: www.casterman.com
Key Personnel
Man Dir: Frederic Morel
General Manager: Louis Delas
Dir of Production: Moline France
International Dir: Willy Insipidity
Marketing: Simon Casterman
International Rights Manager: Fabiana Angelini
Founded: 1780
ISBN Prefix(es): 2-203
Parent Company: Editions Flammarion
Ultimate Parent Company: RCS Group

CED-Samsom
Kouterveld 14, 1831 Diegem
Tel: (02) 7231111 *Fax:* (02) 7231050
E-mail: customer.cedsamson@wkb.be
Web Site: www.cedsamson.be
Key Personnel
Man Dir: Hans Van Zaaijen
Founded: 1964
Subjects: Accounting, Business, Economics, Labor, Industrial Relations, Law, Social Sciences, Sociology
ISBN Prefix(es): 90-5334; 90-5754
Parent Company: Wolters Kluwer Belgium NV
Ultimate Parent Company: Wolters Kluwer NV, Netherlands

Editions du CEFAL+
Affiliate of UDC Consortium
Blvd Frere-Orban 31, 4000 Liege
Tel: (04) 254 25 20 *Fax:* (04) 254 24 40
E-mail: cefal.celes@skynet.be
Web Site: www.cefal.com
Key Personnel
Dir: Jacques Burlet
Founded: 1993

Member of French Editor UDC Consortium; Editions de l'Universite de Liege.
Subjects: Library & Information Sciences, Specialize in Para-Literary - school books
ISBN Prefix(es): 2-87130
Number of titles published annually: 30 Print
Total Titles: 80 Print
Distributor for Editions de l'Universite de Liege (Belgium)

Centrale d'Impression et d'Achats en Cooperative, see CIACO

Centre d'Action Laique+
av Arnaud Fraiteur, ULB, Bd du Triomphe, Campus de la Plane, CP 236, 1050 Brussels
Tel: (02) 6276860 *Fax:* (02) 6266861
Key Personnel
Collections Dir: Patrice Dartevelle
 E-mail: espace@cal.vlb.ac.be
Founded: 1979
Member of A D E B.
Subjects: Biography, Government, Political Science, History, Philosophy, Religion - Other, Social Sciences, Sociology
ISBN Prefix(es): 2-930001
Imprints: Editions Espace de Libertes

Centre de Recherches Culturelles Africanistes, see Centre Aequatoria

Centre International de Recherches 'Primitifs Flamands' ASBL+
One parc du Cinquantenaire, B-1000 Brussels
Tel: (02) 7396866 *Fax:* (02) 7320105
Key Personnel
President & Rights & Permissions: H Pauwels
Scientific Editor & Sales: H Mund
 E-mail: helene.mund@kikirpa.be; C Stroo
 E-mail: cyriel.stroo@kikirpa.be
Founded: 1950
Specialize in Flemish Painting XV Century.
Subjects: Art
ISBN Prefix(es): 2-87033

Editions de la Chambre de Commerce et d'Industrie SA+
Palais de Congres, Esplanade de l'Europe, 2, 4020 Liege
Tel: (04) 344-50-88 *Fax:* (04) 343-05-53
Web Site: www.ecci.be
Founded: 1998
Subjects: Accounting, Business, Law
ISBN Prefix(es): 2-930287
Number of titles published annually: 10 Print
Total Titles: 30 Print
Distributor for Patrimoine (Belgium); Soficom (France)

Editions Chanlis
52 rue de Lennery, 5650 Walcourt
Tel: (071) 326394
Key Personnel
Man Dir: Pierre Magain
Sales: M Nowak
Founded: 1968
Subjects: Antiques, Archaeology, Art, Crafts, Games, Hobbies, History, Military Science
ISBN Prefix(es): 2-87039

Editions Chantecler+
Vluchtenburgstraat 7, 2630 Aartselaar
Tel: (03) 8 77 14 64 *Fax:* (03) 8 77 21 15
Telex: 31739 Zuidb
Key Personnel
Man Dir: Jan Vande Velden
Editorial: Bart Clinckemalie
Production: Eric Feyten
Rights & Permissions: Wilfried Wuyts
Founded: 1947
Subjects: Fiction, Nonfiction (General)

ISBN Prefix(es): 2-8034
Parent Company: Zuidnederlandse Uitgeverij NV
Imprints: Pre-Ecole

Chanteller, *imprint of* Zuid-Nederlandse Uitgeverij NV/ Central Uitgeverij

La Charte Editions juridiques
rue Guimard 19/2, 1040 Brussels
Tel: (02) 512 29 49 *Fax:* (02) 512 26 93
E-mail: info@lacharte.be
Web Site: www.lacharte.be
Key Personnel
Dir Editor-Legal: Rik Carton
Dir Editor-Educational: Jean-Paul Steevens
Founded: 1948
Subjects: Government, Political Science, Language Arts, Linguistics, Law, Social Sciences, Sociology
ISBN Prefix(es): 2-87403

CIACO+
Chez Erasme 2, pl Baudoin-ler, 5004 Bouge-Namur
Tel: (018) 213700 *Fax:* (018) 212372
Key Personnel
Dir: Gerard Lambert
Founded: 1983
ISBN Prefix(es): 2-87085
Subsidiaries: Artel SC

CIEFR (Centre International d'Etudes de la Formation Religieuse), see Editions Lumen Vitae ASBL

De Clauwaert VZW+
Blijde Inkomststraat 79-81, 3000 Leuven
Tel: (016) 310-660 *Fax:* (016) 310-608
E-mail: uitgeverij@davidsfonds.be
Key Personnel
General Dir: J Rens
Founded: 1945
Subjects: Literature, Literary Criticism, Essays
ISBN Prefix(es): 90-6306
Imprints: Leuven

Uitgeverij Clavis+
Vooruitzichtstr 42, 3500 Hasselt
Tel: (011) 28 68 68 *Fax:* (011) 28 68 69
E-mail: info@clavis.be
Web Site: www.clavis.be
Key Personnel
Man Dir, Editorial: Philippe Werck
Commercial Dir, Editorial: Sigrid Werck
Rights & Permissions: Ingrid Vandekerekhove
Production: Lisette Aerts
Promotion: Tanja Appeltants *E-mail:* tanja@clavis.be
Financial Dir: Jos Rens
Editorial: Mark Lens; Hilde Vanmechelen
Founded: 1981
Subjects: Fiction, Nonfiction (General)
ISBN Prefix(es): 90-6822; 90-5933; 90-77106; 90-448; 90-77060
Total Titles: 560 Print
Imprints: Mozaiek
Bookshop(s): Poespas, Kapelstr 38, B-3500 Hasselt

Coach & Bus Federation, see Cartoeristiek (Federatie van Belgische Autobus- en Autocarondernemers) (BAAV)

Coalition of the Flemish North South Movement, see Koepel van de Vlaamse Noord - Zuidbeweging 11.11.11

Coda+
Dubbelrij 50, 3920 Lommel
Tel: (011) 540403 *Fax:* (011) 540403

Key Personnel
President: Bert Vinken
Vice President: Roger Ulburghs; Jef Geboers
Editor: Guy Brugmans
Founded: 1988
Subjects: Aeronautics, Aviation, Architecture & Interior Design, Biography, Business, Cookery, Health, Nutrition, House & Home, Publishing & Book Trade Reference
ISBN Prefix(es): 90-5232
Parent Company: Media Marketing Communications

Concraid+
Parc de la Sablonniere Bte 707, 7000 Mons
Tel: (065) 34-72-34 *Fax:* (065) 34-72-34
Key Personnel
General Dir: E Preud'homme
Founded: 1983
Member of ADEB; Specialize in Finance, Stockmarket & Health.
ISBN Prefix(es): 2-87189

Conservart SA+
Chee Alsemberg 965, 1180 Brussels
Tel: (02) 3322538 *Fax:* (02) 3754040
Key Personnel
General Dir: Jean-Claude Echement
Subjects: Architecture & Interior Design, Art, Chemistry, Chemical Engineering, Literature, Literary Criticism, Essays, Photography
ISBN Prefix(es): 2-930022

Contact NV
Elsbos 33, 2650 Edegem
Tel: (03) 4572024 *Fax:* (03) 4581327
Key Personnel
Dir: A J H Binneweg
Founded: 1946
Subjects: Art, Crafts, Games, Hobbies, Education, Literature, Literary Criticism, Essays, Sports, Athletics
ISBN Prefix(es): 90-73185

Corpus Christianorum, *imprint of* Brepols Publishers NV

Creadif
52 ave de Tervueren, 1040 Brussels
Tel: (02) 7360630 *Fax:* (02) 7348747
Key Personnel
Dir: N Servais
Founded: 1974
Subjects: Business, Economics, Ethnicity, Geography, Geology, History, Law, Travel
ISBN Prefix(es): 2-8022

Credit Communal, see Dexia Bank

Cremers (Schoollandkaarten) PVBA
Pagodenlaan 241, 1020 Brussels
Tel: (02) 2680345 *Fax:* (02) 2680345 *Cable:* Cartopress
Key Personnel
Dir: Michiel Plazier
Founded: 1950
Subjects: Ethnicity, Geography, Geology, History, Travel
ISBN Prefix(es): 90-74437
Parent Company: Carto BVBA

Le Cri Editions+
43 rue Guilaume Stocq, 1050 Brussels
Tel: (02) 6466533 *Fax:* (02) 6466607
E-mail: lecri@shynet.be
Key Personnel
Dir: Lutz Christian
Founded: 1981
Subjects: Biography, History, Literature, Literary Criticism, Essays
ISBN Prefix(es): 2-87106

Cultura
Hoenderstraat 22, 9200 Wetteren
Tel: (09) 9 369 15 95 *Fax:* (09) 3695925
E-mail: cultura@cultura-net.com
Key Personnel
President: Rene De Meester, Sr
Vice President: Jan De Meester, Jr
Specialize in numismatic publications.
ISBN Prefix(es): 90-74623

Le Daily-Bul
rue Daily Bul 29, 7100 La Louviere
Tel: (064) 222973 *Fax:* (064) 222973
Key Personnel
Man Dir: Andre Balthazar
Founded: 1957
Subjects: Art, Literature, Literary Criticism, Essays, Poetry
ISBN Prefix(es): 2-930136

Daphne Diffusion SA
Poortakkerstraat, 29, 9051 Ghent
Tel: (09) 221 45 91 *Fax:* (09) 220 16 12
E-mail: info@daphne.be
Telex: 11659
Key Personnel
General Manager: Francois Dubrulle
Administrator & Sales Manager: Pierre Dubrulle
Subjects: Travel
ISBN Prefix(es): 2-504

Davidsfonds - Infodok NV+
Blijde-Inkomststraat 79-81, 3000 Leuven
Tel: (016) 310-600 *Fax:* (016) 310-608
E-mail: informatie@davidsfonds.be
Web Site: www.davidsfonds.be
Key Personnel
Dir: J Rens
Subjects: Child Care & Development, Fiction, Poetry
ISBN Prefix(es): 90-6152; 90-6565
Distributor for NBCC (Netherlands)
Bookshop(s): Blijde-Inkomststraat 79-81, 3000 Leuven
Warehouse: Distributiecentrum AGORA, De Vunt 5, 3220 Holsbeek

Davidsfonds VZW+
Blijde Inkomststraat 79-81, 3000 Leuven
Tel: (016) 310-600 *Fax:* (016) 310-608
E-mail: informatie@davidsfonds.be
Web Site: www.davidsfonds.be
Key Personnel
Dir: N D'Hulst
Editorial: M Vanvaeck
Founded: 1875
Subjects: Art, Education, Government, Political Science, Law, Literature, Literary Criticism, Essays, Philosophy, Religion - Other, Social Sciences, Sociology
ISBN Prefix(es): 90-6152; 90-6565

Editions De Boeck-Larcier SA+
rue des Minimes 39, Brussels 1000
Mailing Address: Fond Jean-Paques 4, B-1348 Louvain La Neuve
Tel: (02) 482511 *Fax:* (02) 482650
Web Site: www.deboeck.be
Key Personnel
General Dir, Editorial & Production: Christian De Boeck
Dir: Georges Hoyos
University Publications: Michel Jezierski
School Book Publications: Francoise Goethals
Publicity: Nora Ramakers
Law: Patricia Wilhelm
R/D: Genevieve Dieu
Founded: 1883
Subjects: Accounting, Anthropology, Art, Behavioral Sciences, Biological Sciences, Business, Chemistry, Chemical Engineering, Communications, Economics, Education, English as a Second Language, Environmental Studies, Finance, Geography, Geology, Government, Political Science, Health, Nutrition, Human Relations, Language Arts, Linguistics, Law, Management, Marketing, Mathematics, Medicine, Nursing, Dentistry, Philosophy, Physical Sciences, Psychology, Psychiatry, Science (General), Social Sciences, Sociology
ISBN Prefix(es): 2-8041
Parent Company: Groupe De Boeck SA
Associate Companies: Acces Plus SPRL
Divisions: De Boeck Universite; De Boeck-Wesmael, Larcier; Dessain; Duculot; Didacta
Showroom(s): Acces Plus SPRL, Fond Jean-Paques 4, B-1348 Louvain-la-Neuve *Tel:* (010) 482500 *Fax:* (010) 482519
Bookshop(s): Acces Plus SPRL, Fond Jean-Paques 4, B-1348 Louvain-la-Neuve *Tel:* (010) 482500 *Fax:* (010) 482519
Shipping Address: Acces Plus SPRL, Fond Jean-Paques 4, B-1348 Louvain-la-Neuve *Tel:* (010) 482500 *Fax:* (010) 482519
Warehouse: Acces Plus SPRL, Fond Jean-Paques 4, B-1348 Louvain-la-Neuve *Tel:* (010) 482500 *Fax:* (010) 482519
Orders to: Acces Plus SPRL, Fond Jean-Paques 4, B-1348 Louvain-la-Neuve *Tel:* (010) 482500 *Fax:* (010) 482519

De Horstink, *imprint of* Acco CV

DEF (De Blauwe Vogel) NV/SA+
Jan Carlierstraat, 1, Bus, 3800 Sint-Truiden
Tel: (011) 68-57-51 *Fax:* (011) 67-21-70
Telex: 39810
Key Personnel
Contact: Willy-Paul Carlier
Founded: 1929
Subjects: Travel
ISBN Prefix(es): 90-72432
Parent Company: G O Bluebird

Maison d'Editions Cl Dejaie+
1154 chaussee de Dinant, 5100 Namur-Wepian
Tel: (081) 460748
Key Personnel
Dir: M Cl M Dejaie
Founded: 1972
Subjects: Art, Literature, Literary Criticism, Essays, Philosophy
ISBN Prefix(es): 2-87157

Editions Delta SA+
55 rue Scailquin, 1210 Brussels
Tel: (02) 217 55 55 *Fax:* (02) 217 93 93
E-mail: editions.delta@skynet.be
Key Personnel
Man Dir: Georges-Francis Seingry
Founded: 1976
Specialize in European public affairs, hotel & restaurant guides.
Subjects: Art, Biography, Cookery, Public Administration, Regional Interests
ISBN Prefix(es): 2-8029
Number of titles published annually: 8 Print
Parent Company: Guides Delta Euro-references
Imprints: Bibliotheque des Signes; Euro-references; Guides Delta
Divisions: Guides Delta Euro-references
Distributed by Bernan (USA); Cedar Media House; LGDJ-Montchrestien
Foreign Rep(s): Bernan; Cegar Tree House; LGDJ Montchretien

Deltas, *imprint of* Zuid-Nederlandse Uitgeverij NV/ Central Uitgeverij

Dessain - Departement de De Boeck & Larcier SA+
rue Des Minimes, 39, 1000 Brussels
Tel: (02) 48 25 11 *Fax:* (02) 48 26 50
E-mail: dbw@deboeck.be
Web Site: www.adeb.irisnet.be
Key Personnel
General Dir: Christia De Boeck
Dir: Georges Hoyos
Editor, Scholarly Books: Francoise Goethals
Founded: 1719
Subjects: Education, Geography, Geology, Mathematics, Natural History, Physics, Religion - Catholic, Science (General)
ISBN Prefix(es): 2-8041; 2-502
Parent Company: Groupe De Boeck SA
Associate Companies: De Boeck & Larcier SA - Acces Plus Sprl
Warehouse: Acces Plus SPRL, Fond Jean-Paques 4, B-1348 Louvain-la-Neuve *Tel:* (010) 482500 *Fax:* (010) 482519
Orders to: Access Plus SPRL, Fond Jean-Paques 4, B-1348 Louvain *Tel:* (010) 482500 *Fax:* (010) 482519

Dexia Bank+
Formerly Credit Communal
Blvd Pacheco 44, 1000 Brussels
Tel: (02) 222 54 89 *Fax:* (02) 222 57 52
Key Personnel
Contact: Renaud Gahide
Subjects: Art, Genealogy, Geography, Geology, History, Music, Dance, Photography
ISBN Prefix(es): 90-5066; 2-87193
Number of titles published annually: 10 Print
Distributed by Exhibitions International

Diligentia-Uitgeverij
Schrijnwerkerstr 11, 9240 Zele
Tel: (052) 44 45 11 *Fax:* (052) 44 45 22
E-mail: diligentia.book@planetinternet.be
Key Personnel
Contact: C Van den broeck
Founded: 1908
ISBN Prefix(es): 90-70978

Documenta CV
August Reyerslaan 80, 1020 Brussels
Tel: (02) 7068181 *Fax:* (02) 7068170
Key Personnel
President: Philippe de Buck van Overstraeten
Manager: Christian Franzen
Founded: 1986
Subjects: Business, Economics, Electronics, Electrical Engineering, Management, Technology
ISBN Prefix(es): 2-930096; 90-75062
Distributed by Academia
Distributor for Academia; Mim

Duculot, see De Boeck et Larcier SA

Editions Dupuis SA+
Rue Destree 52, 6001 Marcinelle
Tel: (071) 600 500 *Fax:* (071) 600 519
Web Site: www.dupuis-entertainment.com
Key Personnel
Dir General: Jean Deneumostier
Editorial Dir: Philippe Vandooren
Sales Dir: Philippe Buck
Finance: Stephane Desmet
Rights & Permissions: Jean-Philippe Doutrelugne
Dir Audiovisual & Development: Leon Perahia
Founded: 1898
Subjects: Humor
ISBN Prefix(es): 90-314; 2-8001; 90-6574
Parent Company: Groupe Jean Dupuis SA
Associate Companies: Editions Dupuis France SA; Mediatoon SA

Easy Computing NV
Horzelstraat 100, 1180 Brussels
Tel: (02) 346 52 52 *Fax:* (02) 346 01 20
E-mail: info@easycomputing.com
Key Personnel
Contact: F Wiener *Tel:* (02) 3401521
E-mail: fwiener@easycomputing.com
Founded: 1989
Subjects: Computer Science, Electronics, Electrical Engineering, Microcomputers
ISBN Prefix(es): 90-5167
Total Titles: 100 Print; 70 CD-ROM
Subsidiaries: Easy Computing bv
Distributor for Micro Application

Ecobooks
Heerbaan 132, 1840 Steenhuffel
Tel: (052) 37 11 38 *Fax:* (052) 37 11 51
E-mail: ecobooks@ping.be
Key Personnel
Contact: Mevr M Muylaert
International Rights: Hugo Vanderstadt
Subjects: Ecology, Sustainability
ISBN Prefix(es): 90-75855

Ediblanchart sprl+
Ave Ernest Masoin, 15, 1090 Brussels
Tel: (02) 4783706 *Fax:* (02) 4786429
Key Personnel
President & Administrator: Charles Blanchart
E-mail: charles.blanchart@chello.be
Founded: 1962
Subjects: Animals, Pets, Transportation, Railways, Flowers
ISBN Prefix(es): 2-87202
Number of titles published annually: 2 Print
Total Titles: 9 Print

Editest, SPRL+
16 rue de Chambery, 1040 Brussels
Tel: (02) 6476284 *Fax:* (02) 7325629
Key Personnel
Dir: B Evrard
Specialize in Psychological Tests.
ISBN Prefix(es): 2-8000

Eenhoorn BVBA+
Vlasstraat 17, 8710 Wielsbeke
Tel: (056) 605460 *Fax:* (056) 616981
E-mail: info@eenhoorn.be
Web Site: users.skynet.be/eenhoorn
Key Personnel
Man Dir & International Rights: Bart Desmyter
E-mail: bart.desmyter@eenhoorn.be
Founded: 1990
Subjects: Fiction, Health, Nutrition
ISBN Prefix(es): 90-73913; 90-5838
Number of titles published annually: 30 Print
Imprints: Medaillon

EMPC, see Editions Medicales et Paramedicales de Charleroi (EMPC)

Editions les eperonniers
rue Picard 7, 1000 Brussels
Tel: (02) 4283033 *Fax:* (02) 4283525
Key Personnel
President: Lysiane D'Haeyere-Antoine
Subjects: Literature, Literary Criticism, Essays, Philosophy, Science (General)
ISBN Prefix(es): 2-87132; 2-87015; 2-87159

EPO Publishers, Printers, Booksellers+
Lange Pastoorstr 25-27, 2600 Berchem-Antwerp
Tel: (03) 2396874 *Fax:* (03) 2184604
E-mail: vitgevery@epo.be
Web Site: www.epo.be
Key Personnel
Man Dir: Jos Hennes
Publisher: Hugo Franssen
Sales: Kris Van Kersschaever
Founded: 1978
Subjects: Anthropology, Biography, Communications, Developing Countries, Fiction, History, Journalism, Literature, Literary Criticism, Essays, Nonfiction (General), Psychology, Psychiatry, Social Sciences, Sociology
ISBN Prefix(es): 90-6445; 2-87262
Branch Office(s)
Chaussee de Haecht L55, 1030 Brussels
Tel: (02) 215 6651 *Fax:* (02) 215 6604
E-mail: editions@epo.be
Distributed by De Geus (The Netherlands)
Distributor for De Geus (The Netherlands); Coutinho (The Netherlands)
Bookshop(s): Groene Waterman, Wolstr 7, B-2000 Antwerp; Librairie Internationale, Ave LeMonnier 171, B-1000 Brussels
Book Club(s): Komma's en Punten

Esco BVBA
Venusstraat 31, 2000 Antwerp 1
Tel: (03) 2223800 *Fax:* (03) 2223838
Key Personnel
Contact: Jan Fremeijer
ISBN Prefix(es): 90-6415

Editions Espace de Libertes, *imprint of* Centre d'Action Laique

Euro-references, *imprint of* Editions Delta SA

EVO, see Les Editions Vie ouvriere ASBL

Facet NV+
Willem Linnigstr 13, 2060 Antwerp
Tel: (03) 227 40 28 *Fax:* (03) 227 37 92
E-mail: Facet@village.uunet.be
Key Personnel
Publisher: Walter A P Soethoudt
Founded: 1986
Specialize in children's books.
ISBN Prefix(es): 90-5016

Uitgevery Gelbis NV+
Cockerillaai 30, 2000 Antwerp
Tel: (03) 2410202 *Fax:* (03) 2410200
E-mail: gelbis.boeken@lequana.com
Key Personnel
Contact: Leo van der Linden
Founded: 1982
Subjects: Automotive, Travel
ISBN Prefix(es): 90-71288
Divisions: GelbiStudio; Gelbis Boekhandel

Geocart Uitg Cartogr AG Claus BVBA+
Breedstraat 94, 9100 Sint-Niklaas
Tel: (03) 760 14 60 *Fax:* (03) 760 15 28
E-mail: site@geocart.be
Web Site: www.geocart.be
Key Personnel
Algemene Dir: Egide Van Eyck
Founded: 1972
Specialize in Cartography.
ISBN Prefix(es): 90-6736
Subsidiaries: Girault Gilbert, BVBA
Divisions: Geocart Information System
Warehouse: Libricart, Breedstraat 94, 9100 Sint-Niklaas

Georeto-Geogidsen
Rozenstr 11, 3723 Kortessem
Tel: (011) 37 52 54 *Fax:* (011) 37 52 54
E-mail: georeto@pandora.be
Web Site: www.geogidsen.be
Key Personnel
Contact: P Diriken
Founded: 1991
Subjects: Geography, Geology, History, Outdoor Recreation
ISBN Prefix(es): 90-75229
Number of titles published annually: 4 Print
Total Titles: 45 Print

PUBLISHERS   BELGIUM

Girault Gilbert bvba+
Zuidstr 19, 1000 Brussels
Tel: (02) 2171430; (02) 2175880 *Fax:* (02) 2173375
Key Personnel
President: Egide Van Eyck
Founded: 1928 (Reconstituted: 1956)
ISBN Prefix(es): 2-87273
Warehouse: Libricart, Breedstr 94, 9100 Sint-Niklaas

Glenat Benelux SA+
131 rue Saint-Lambert, 1200 Brussels
Tel: (02) 7612640 *Fax:* (02) 7612645
E-mail: glenat@glenat.be
Key Personnel
Dir, Editor & International Rights: Paul Herman
Administrative Delegate: Dominique Leblan
Founded: 1985
Subjects: Antiques, Art, Automotive, Crafts, Games, Hobbies, Humor, Regional Interests, Wine & Spirits, Comics
ISBN Prefix(es): 2-87174
Subsidiaries: Glenat France
Distributor for Vent D'Ouest
Bookshop(s): Slumberland, 20 rue des sables, 1000 Brussels; Slumberland, 131 rue Saint-Lambert, 1200 Brussels; Slumberland, 3 Louvain-la-Neuve

Globe, *imprint of* Roularta Books NV

Globe, *imprint of* Uitgevery Scoop Infotex NV

Graton Editeur SA+
Onze-Lieve-Heersbeestjesln 70, 1170 Watermaal-Bosvoorde, Brussels
Tel: (02) 6756 666 *Fax:* (02) 6756 363
E-mail: graton.sa@skynet.be
Key Personnel
Executive: Ph Graton
Founded: 1981
Subjects: Film, Video, Journalism, Photography, Sports, Athletics, Motorracing, Comic Strips
ISBN Prefix(es): 90-70816; 2-87098
Divisions: Kurz & Bundigi, hpt Extra
Distributed by Diffulivre (Switzerland); Hachette (France); Dupuis (Belgium); Mediavision (USA); Seven Island (Germany)

Groeninghe NV
Lange Steenstr 2, 8500 Kortrijk
Tel: (056) 22-22-62 *Fax:* (056) 22-82-86
Web Site: www.groeningbe.com
Key Personnel
General Director: Robert Timperman
Founded: 1924
Subjects: Archaeology, Art, History
ISBN Prefix(es): 90-71868
Parent Company: Groeninghe Printers
Associate Companies: Groeninghe Bookbinders
Showroom(s): Budastr 64, 8500 Kortrijk

Guides Delta, *imprint of* Editions Delta SA

Imprimerie Hayez SPRL
Rue Fernand Brunfaut 19, 1080 Brussels
Tel: (02) 413 02 00 *Fax:* (02) 411 23 78
E-mail: com@hayez.be
Web Site: www.hayez.be
Telex: 63467 Hayez
Key Personnel
Man Dir: Serge Hayez
Sales Dir: Frederic Hayez
Founded: 1780
Subjects: History, Medicine, Nursing, Dentistry, Philosophy, Poetry, Religion - Other, Science (General), Sports, Athletics
ISBN Prefix(es): 2-87126

Heideland-Orbis NV
Santvoortbeeklaan 21-23, 2100 Deurne
Tel: (03) 3247890 *Fax:* (03) 3600212
Telex: 3600212 *Cable:* 33649
Key Personnel
Dir: C van Baelen
Editorial Manager: R Fransen
Production: H Leduc
Founded: 1969
ISBN Prefix(es): 90-291

Uitgeverij Helios
Kapelsestr 222, 2080 Kapellen
Tel: (03) 6645320
Telex: 32242 Anvers Dnb
Key Personnel
Man Dir: J Pelckmans
Founded: 1976
ISBN Prefix(es): 90-333
Associate Companies: Uitgeverij De Nederlandsche Boekhandel

Helyode Editions (SA-ADN)+
Sint-Pieterstr 58, 1000 Brussels
Tel: (02) 2112733 *Fax:* (01) 2112762
Key Personnel
General Dir: Patrice le Hodey
Dir: Marie Vernofstede
Assistant: Yolande Pierrared; Marie-Eve Van Mechelen
Founded: 1991
Specialize in Cartoons.
Subjects: Fiction, History, Humor
ISBN Prefix(es): 2-87353; 90-5415
Subsidiaries: Memoire D'Europe

Van Hemeldonck NV+
Van Hemeldonckstr, 5, 2350 Vosselaar
Tel: (014) 611034 *Fax:* (014) 620288
E-mail: booksell@innet.be
Key Personnel
President: Johan Van Hemeldonck
Vice President: Georges Aerts
Founded: 1932
Specialize in large prints.
ISBN Prefix(es): 90-6933; 90-5274
Associate Companies: Grootdruk-Uitgevery Eindhoven BV, Netherlands
Orders to: Van Hemeldonckstr, 5, 2350 Vosselaar

Editions Hemma+
106, rue de Chevron, 4987 Chevron
Tel: (086) 43 01 01 *Fax:* (086) 43 36 40
Web Site: www.hemma.be
Telex: 41507 *Cable:* HEMMAB
Key Personnel
Dir: Albert Hemmerlin
Founded: 1952
ISBN Prefix(es): 2-8006; 90-6804; 90-380; 90-412
Subsidiaries: Editions Diffusion Hemma; Hemma Verlag GmbH; Hemma Joven SA
Distributed by Dar Almoufid (Lebanon); Diffusion Transat SA (Switzerland); Impato (Switzerland); Les Presses D-Or (Canada) Inc (Canada); Messageries du Livre (Luxembourg); Socadis Inc (Canada)

Huis Van Het Boek
Hof ter Schriecklaan 17, B-2600 Berchem, Antwerp
Tel: (03) 230 89 23 *Fax:* (03) 281 22 40
E-mail: info@boek.be
Web Site: www.boek.be
Key Personnel
Dir: Dorian Van Der Brempt *E-mail:* dorian.van.der.brempt@vbvb.be
Founded: 1929
Professional organization for booksellers, distributors & editors.
Subjects: Literature, Literary Criticism, Essays, Publishing & Book Trade Reference

Infoboek NV
Lil 51, 2450 Meerhout
Tel: (014) 30 04 77 *Fax:* (014) 30 32 43
E-mail: info@infoboek.be
Key Personnel
Dir: W Verhaert
Founded: 1971
Subjects: Crafts, Games, Hobbies, Education, Language Arts, Linguistics, Literature, Literary Criticism, Essays, Music, Dance, Philosophy, Religion - Other, Sports, Athletics
ISBN Prefix(es): 90-5535

Centre National Infor Jeunes
Rue Jean Volders 10, 1060 Brussels
Tel: (02) 537 64 63 *Fax:* (081) 228264
Key Personnel
Dir: Georges Vallee
Member of ERYICA (European Youth Information & Counselling Agency).
ISBN Prefix(es): 2-8091

Institut Royal des Relations Internationales
(Royal Institute for International Relations)
59 rue de Namur, 1000 Brussels
Tel: (02) 2234114 *Fax:* (02) 2234116
E-mail: info@irri-kiib.be
Web Site: www.irri-kiib.be
Key Personnel
President: Vte E Davignon
Dir General: Francois de Kerchove d'Exaerde
Librarian: Alexandre Buchet *E-mail:* a.buchet@irri-kiib.be
Founded: 1947
Research institute.
Subjects: Developing Countries, Economics, Foreign Countries, Government, Political Science, Law
Number of titles published annually: 5 Print
Total Titles: 2 Print

International Peace Information Service (Ipis VZW), see Ipis VZW (International Peace Information Service)

Intersentia Uitgevers NV
Churchilllaan 108, 2900 Schoten-Antwerp
Tel: (03) 680 15 50 *Fax:* (03) 658 71 21
E-mail: mail@intersentia.be
Web Site: www.intersentia.com
Key Personnel
Sales: Kenny Janssens *E-mail:* k.janssens@intersentia.be
Founded: 1996
Academic publishing house specializing in international law & economics.
Subjects: Accounting, Finance, Law, Human Rights, European Law
ISBN Prefix(es): 90-5095
Distributed by Hart (UK); Schulthess (Switzerland); Transnational (USA & Canada); Verlag Osterreich (Austria)
Distributor for Transnational Publishing (Benelux)

Invader, *imprint of* Zuid-Nederlandse Uitgeverij NV/ Central Uitgeverij

Ipis VZW (International Peace Information Service)+
Italielei 98A, 2000 Antwerp 1
Tel: (03) 225-0022 *Fax:* (03) 231-01-51
E-mail: ipis@skynet.be
Web Site: www.skynet.be/ipis/
Key Personnel
Executive Dir: Johan Peleman
Research: Dr Ann Vrankx
Founded: 1981
Member of ngo; Specialize in World Security & Human Rights, Conflict Areas, Arms Trade & International Relations.

Subjects: Developing Countries, Foreign Countries, Government, Political Science, Military Science, Nonfiction (General)
ISBN Prefix(es): 90-70316; 90-71247

IRRI-KIIB, see Institut Royal des Relations Internationales

Uitgeverij J van In+
Grote Markt 38, 2500 Lier
Tel: (03) 4805511 *Fax:* (03) 4807664
Key Personnel
Man Dir & Rights & Permissions: Dr Laurent Woestenburg
Editorial: Ludo Camps
Production: Danielle Brabants
Publicity: Fred Caluwe
Founded: 1833
Firm is part of Educational Book Publishing division of V N U BV, Netherlands.
Subjects: Education, Language Arts, Linguistics, Law
ISBN Prefix(es): 90-306
Subsidiaries: Van In J Editions
Divisions:

Die Keure+
Oude Gentweg 108, 8000 Brugge
Tel: (050) 47 12 72 *Fax:* (050) 33 51 54
E-mail: die.keure@pophost.eunet.be
Web Site: www.diekeure.be
Key Personnel
Dir: Jean Paul Steevens
Founded: 1948
Subjects: Education
ISBN Prefix(es): 90-6200
Parent Company: Die Keure, Oude Gentweg 108, Brugge

King Baudouin Foundation
Rue Brederodestr 21, 1000 Brussels
Tel: (02) 511 18 40 *Fax:* (02) 511 52 21
E-mail: publi@kbs-frb.be
Web Site: www.kbs-frb.be
Key Personnel
Program Officer & Contact: Bridgitte Kessel *Tel:* (032-2) 549 0238 *E-mail:* kessel.b@kbs-frb.be
Contact: Paule Tits *Tel:* (02) 549 0212 *E-mail:* paule.tits@kbs-fbs.be
Improve living conditions for the population taking economic, social, scientific & cultural factors into account.
Subjects: Agriculture, Architecture & Interior Design, Economics, Labor, Industrial Relations, Social Sciences, Sociology
ISBN Prefix(es): 90-5130; 2-87212

Kluwer Rechtswetenschappen Belgie, see Editions Juridiques Kluwer a Deurne Anvers

Editions Juridiques Kluwer a Deurne Anvers
Kouterveld, 2, 1831 Diegem
Tel: (02) 300 3000 *Fax:* (03) 360-04
E-mail: custumer.kejb@wkb.be
Web Site: www.editionskluwer.be
Telex: 33649
Key Personnel
Dir: B Houdmont
Manager: B Houdmont; G VanPeel
Publisher: A Knops; D Lefebvre; D Vanhove
Logistic Manager: A Geladi
Founded: 1977
Subjects: Economics, Law
ISBN Prefix(es): 90-6321; 2-87377
Parent Company: Wolters Kluwer Belgie NV
Ultimate Parent Company: Wolters Kluwer NV, Netherlands
Imprints: E Story-Scientia; Service

KnackBibliotheek/Radio 1, *imprint of* Roularta Books NV

Koepel van de Vlaamse Noord - Zuidbeweging 11.11.11 (Coalition of the Flemish North South Movement)+
Formerly NCOS (Nationaal Centrum voor Ontwikkelingssamenwerking) VZW
Vlasfabriekstraat 11, 1060 Brussels
Tel: (02) 536-11-13 *Fax:* (02) 536-19-10
E-mail: info@11.be
Web Site: www.11.be
Key Personnel
Education Coordinator: Bart Demedts *Tel:* (02) 536-11-14 *Fax:* (02) 536-19-02 *E-mail:* bart.demedts@11.be
Founded: 1966
Specialize in Third World affairs.
Subjects: Anthropology, Child Care & Development, Cookery, Developing Countries, Economics, Geography, Geology, Government, Political Science, Health, Nutrition, Journalism, Labor, Industrial Relations, Literature, Literary Criticism, Essays, Travel
ISBN Prefix(es): 90-71665
Distributed by Jan Van Arkel (Holland); Van Haelewyck-Uitgeverij (Belgium)
Distributor for Kit (Holland); Jan Mets (Holland); Novib (Holland)
Orders to: Eric Vander Borght *Tel:* (02) 536 1122 *E-mail:* eric.vanderborght@ncos.ngonet.be

Koninklijke Vlaamse Academie van Belgie voor Wetenschappen en Kunsten
Paleis der Academien, Hertogsstr 1, B-1000 Brussels
Tel: (02) 550 23 23 *Fax:* (02) 550 23 25
E-mail: info@kvab.be
Web Site: www.kvab.be
Key Personnel
Permanent Secretary: Niceas Schamp *E-mail:* niceas.schamp@kvab.be
Publications: Gilbert Reynders *Tel:* (02) 550 23 32 *E-mail:* gilbert.reynders@kvab.be
Founded: 1938
Dutch-speaking Royal Belgian Academy of Sciences, Letters & Fine Arts.
Member of International Academic Association.
Subjects: Art, Music, Dance, Philosophy, Science (General)
ISBN Prefix(es): 90-6569
Orders to: Brepols Publishers IGP, Steenweg op Tielen 68, B-2300 Turnhout *Tel:* (079) 99 80 20 *Fax:* (079) 99 89 79 *E-mail:* info.publishers@brepols.com *Web Site:* www.brepols.com/publishers

De Krijger+
Dorpsstraat, 144, 9420 Erpe-Mere
Tel: (053) 808449 *Fax:* (053) 808453
E-mail: de.krijger@primemedia.be
Key Personnel
Owner: Vammabost Koem
Founded: 1987
Subjects: Military Science
ISBN Prefix(es): 90-72547; 90-5868
Number of titles published annually: 15 Print
Total Titles: 68 Print

Kritak Uitgeverij+
Diestsestraat 249, 3000 Leuven
Tel: (016) 231264 *Fax:* (016) 223310
Key Personnel
Man Dir: Andre Van Halewijck
Founded: 1976
Subjects: Government, Political Science, Humor, Literature, Literary Criticism, Essays, Social Sciences, Sociology
ISBN Prefix(es): 90-6303
Parent Company: J M Meulenhoff, Amsterdam, Netherlands

Editions Labor
Quai du Commerce 29, 1000 Brussels
Tel: (02) 250-06-70 *Fax:* (02) 217-71-97
E-mail: labor@labor.be
Web Site: www.labor.be
Telex: 25532 Labor
Key Personnel
President: Th Vanderworst
Administrator: Fabienne Herc
General Services: Jean-Pierre Van Mullem *E-mail:* vanmullen@labor.be
Founded: 1927
Subjects: Biography, Economics, Education, History, Philosophy, Poetry, Psychology, Psychiatry, Science (General), Social Sciences, Sociology
ISBN Prefix(es): 2-8040

Editions Lampe d'Or ASBL+
Subsidiary of Scripture Union
Ave Giele, 23, 1090 Brussels
Tel: (02) 427-92-77 *Fax:* (02) 428-82-06
E-mail: llb_ibb@freegates.be
Key Personnel
Man Dir: J Makkink
Founded: 1955
Subjects: Religion - Other
ISBN Prefix(es): 2-87001
Number of titles published annually: 3 Print
Distributed by Lique pour la Lecture de la Bible France; Lique pour la Lecture de la Bible Quebec, Canada; Maison de la Bible Suisse
Distributor for Ligue pour la Lecture de la Bible France; Ligue pour la Lecture de la Bible Suisse

Uitgeverij Lannoo NV+
Kasteelstr 97, B-8700 Tielt
Tel: (051) 42 42 11 *Fax:* (051) 40 11 52
E-mail: lannoo@lannoo.be
Web Site: www.lannoo.be
Key Personnel
President: Matthias Lannoo
Man Dir: Luc Demeester
Editorial Dir: Lieven Sercu
Executive Assistant: Heidi Dhondt *E-mail:* heidi.dhondt@lannoo.be
Founded: 1909
Subjects: Architecture & Interior Design, Art, Biography, Cookery, Economics, Gardening, Plants, Government, Political Science, Health, Nutrition, History, House & Home, Management, Nonfiction (General), Photography, Poetry, Religion - Other, Self-Help, Travel, Greeting cards & staty, and specialize in interior design
ISPN Prefix(es): 90-209
Associate Companies: Bakermat NV, Meghelen
Subsidiaries: Editions Racine; DistriMedia nv
Divisions: Lannoo Publishers; Lannoo Graphics
Branch Office(s)
Lannoo Nederland, Gorinchem, Netherlands
Uitgevery Terra Zutphen, Warnsveld, Netherlands
Distributed by OLF (Switzerland); Terra (Netherlands); Vilo (France & Canada)
Distributor for A A (UK); ANWB (Netherlands); Averbode (Belgium); Bakermat; Dakota; Kuemmerly & Frey (Switzerland); Lonely Planet (Australia); Scriptum; Terra
Showroom(s): Trade Mart Utrecht, Utrecht
Warehouse: DistriMedia nv, Meulebeeksesteenweg 20, 8700 Tielt

Lansman Editeur+
63-65, rue Royale, B-7141 Carnieres-Morlanwelz
Tel: (064) 23-78-40 *Fax:* (064) 44-31-02; (064) 23-78-49
E-mail: lansman.editeur@freeworld.be
Web Site: www.lansman.org
Key Personnel
Dir: Emile Lansman
Press, Bookshop: Caroline Cullus
Founded: 1989

Specialize in theatre in French language (plays & research books).
Subjects: Art, Drama, Theater, Education, Literature, Literary Criticism, Essays
ISBN Prefix(es): 2-87282
Number of titles published annually: 35 Print
Total Titles: 360 Print
Distributed by Alterdis/Nemodiffusion (France); Dimedia (Canada)
Distributor for Cahiers de Theatre Jeu (Europe); Solitaires Intempestifs (outside France)

Larcier-Department of De Boeck & Larcier SA
Minimenstr 39, 1000 Brussels
Mailing Address: Fond Jean-Pacques 4, 1348 Louvain-la-Neuve
Tel: (02) 548 07 11 *Fax:* (02) 513 90 09
E-mail: deboeck.larcier@deboeck.be
Web Site: www.larcier.be
Key Personnel
Man Dir: Christian de Boeck *Tel:* (010) 10-48 26 21 *Fax:* (010) 10-48 26 50 *E-mail:* christian.deboeck@deboeck.be
Editor: Patricia Wilhelm
Administrator: Georges Hoyos *Tel:* (010) 10-48 26 04 *Fax:* (010) 10-48 26 50 *E-mail:* georges.hoyos@deboeck.be
Press: Nora Jezierski-Ramakers *Tel:* (010) 10-48 26 22 *Fax:* (010) 10-48 26 50 *E-mail:* nora.jezierski@deboeck.be
Communication Dir: Catherine Ullens de Schooten *Tel:* (010) 10-48 26 04 *Fax:* (010) 10-48 26 50 *E-mail:* catherine.ullens@deboeck.be
Information Technology Dir: Pierre-Yves Thomas *Tel:* (010) 10-48 26 28 *Fax:* (010) 10-48 25 58 *E-mail:* pierreyves.thomas@deboeck.be
Founded: 1839
Subjects: Law
ISBN Prefix(es): 2-8044
Parent Company: Groupe De Boeck SA
Associate Companies: De Boeck & Larcier SA-Acces Plus SPRL
Distributed by LITEC (France Only)
Orders to: Acces Plus SPRL, Fond Jean-Paques 4, 1348 Louvain-La-Neuve

Claude Lefrancq Editeur+
Alsembergse Steenweg 386, 1180 Brussels
Tel: (02) 344-49-34 *Fax:* (02) 347-55-34
E-mail: claude.lefrancq@skynet.be
Key Personnel
Chairman & Man Dir: R Demartin
Editor: Claude Lefrancq
Founded: 1995
Subjects: Anthropology, Biography, Film, Video, Humor, Literature, Literary Criticism, Essays, Mysteries, Romance
ISBN Prefix(es): 2-87153; 90-71987; 90-75388

Editions Lessius ASBL+
Division of South Belgian Area of the Company of Jesus
Blvd Saint-Michel, 24, 1040 Brussels
Tel: (02) 739 34 90 *Fax:* (02) 739 34 91
E-mail: info@editions-lessius.be
Key Personnel
Dir: Daniel Dideberg *Tel:* (02) 739 34 92 *E-mail:* d.dideberg@iet.be
Director of Collection: Rene Lafontaine; Benoit Malvaux; Jacques Scheuer; Jean-Pierre Sonnet
Communication Manager: Nathalie Dubois *Tel:* (02) 739 34 93 *E-mail:* nath.dubois@skynet.be
Founded: 1997
Specialize in exegetic Biblical commentaries; essays (language, philosophy, theology, psychology, art, law); meditation & pray; biography; & meeting between religions.
Subjects: Art, Biblical Studies, Biography, Language Arts, Linguistics, Law, Literature, Literary Criticism, Essays, Philosophy, Religion - Catholic, Religion - Hindu, Religion - Jewish, Social Sciences, Sociology, Theology
ISBN Prefix(es): 2-87299
Number of titles published annually: 12 Print
Total Titles: 120 Print
Distributed by Editions du Cerf

Leuven, *imprint of* De Clauwaert VZW

Leuven University Press+
Blijde Inkomststr 5, 3000 Leuven
Tel: (016) 32 53 45 *Fax:* (016) 32 53 52
E-mail: university.press@upers.kuleuven.ac.be; universitaire.pers@upers.kuleuven.ac.be
Web Site: www.lup.be
Key Personnel
Dir & Publisher: Mrs Hilde Lens *E-mail:* hilde.glelis@upers.kuleuven.ac.be
Public Relations & Marketing: Ineke Deckers *E-mail:* ineke.deckers@upers.kuleuven.ac.be
Founded: 1971
Member of International Association of Scholarly Publishers.
Subjects: Agriculture, Archaeology, Biological Sciences, Criminology, Economics, Education, Environmental Studies, Geography, Geology, Government, Political Science, History, Language Arts, Linguistics, Law, Literature, Literary Criticism, Essays, Mathematics, Medicine, Nursing, Dentistry, Music, Dance, Philosophy, Physical Sciences, Physics, Psychology, Psychiatry, Science (General), Social Sciences, Sociology, Theology
ISBN Prefix(es): 90-6186; 90-5867
Number of titles published annually: 100 Print; 1 Audio
Total Titles: 1,400 Print; 1 CD-ROM; 3 Audio

Liberica, *imprint of* Zuid-Nederlandse Uitgeverij NV/ Central Uitgeverij

Licap CVBA
Guimardstraat 1, 1040 Brussels
Tel: (02) 509 97 03 *Fax:* (02) 509 97 04
Key Personnel
Contact: R Wellens
Subjects: Education, Religion - Catholic, Theology
ISBN Prefix(es): 90-6858

Editeurs de Litterature Biblique+
Chaussee de Tubize, 479, 1420 Braine-l'Alleud
Tel: (02) 384-54-02; (02) 384-52-12 *Fax:* (02) 384-98-66
E-mail: elb@elbeurope.org
Web Site: www.elbeurope.org
Key Personnel
Dir: Joel Rousseau
Founded: 1959
Subjects: Crafts, Games, Hobbies, Education, Music, Dance, Philosophy, Religion - Other, Sports, Athletics
ISBN Prefix(es): 2-8045
Branch Office(s)
Biblical Publications, 22 W 569 Winthrop, Glen Ellyn, IL 60139, United States

Uitgeverij Loempia+
Mechelsestraatweg, 123, 2018 Antwerp
Tel: (03) 2184292
Key Personnel
Man Dir: Jef Meert
Founded: 1983
ISBN Prefix(es): 90-6771

Les Editions du Lombard SA+
Subsidiary of Sofidar
7 av Paul-Henri-Spaak, 1060 Brussels
Tel: (02) 5266811 *Fax:* (02) 5204405
E-mail: info@lombard.be
Web Site: www.lelombard.com
Telex: 23097 *Cable:* LOMBARBEL BRUSSELS
Key Personnel
General Manager: Francois Pernot
Editorial Manager: Yves Sente
Public Relations: Anne-Marie De Coster *E-mail:* annemarie.decoster@lelombard.be
Licensing, Rights, Press: Jean-Philippe Buysschaert *E-mail:* jeanphilippe.buysschaert@edlbm.be
Rights & Permissions: Sophie Castille
Founded: 1946
Subjects: Fiction, History, Humor, Science Fiction, Fantasy
ISBN Prefix(es): 2-8036; 2-87389
Subsidiaries: Citel & Dargaud; Dargaud Benelux; Dargaud Marina; Dargaud Suisse
Branch Office(s)
15-27 rue Moussorgski, 75018 Paris, France
Tel: (01) 53 26 32 32 *Fax:* (01) 53 26 32 40
Orders to: MDS, ZI de la Gaudree, 91417 Cedex, Dourdan, France *Tel:* (01) 60818700 *Fax:* (01) 64593063

La Longue Vue+
Division of RVJ Editions
Dreve Pittoresque 92, 1640 Rhode Saint-Genese
Tel: (02) 3582012 *Fax:* (02) 3581737
E-mail: longuevue@skynet.be
Key Personnel
Dir, Editions: Charles de Trazegnies *Tel:* (02) 3582393
Founded: 1984
Specialize in Belgian literature & translation; also acts as a translation agency.
Subjects: Biblical Studies, Fiction, Literature, Literary Criticism, Essays, Philosophy, Poetry
ISBN Prefix(es): 2-87121
Total Titles: 100 Print
Distributed by Nord-Sud Diffusion (Belgium); Casteilla-Chiron (France)

Editions Lumen Vitae ASBL+
Division of CIEFR Centre Lumen Vitae
184-186 rue Washington, 1050 Brussels
Tel: (02) 3490399; (02) 3490370 *Fax:* (02) 3490385
E-mail: lumen.vitae.editions@euronet.be
Web Site: www.catho.be/lumen
Key Personnel
Man Dir, Sales: Henri Derroitte
International Rights: Gabriella Tihon-Gyorffy *E-mail:* gabriella.tihon@euronet.be
Founded: 1937
Subjects: Biblical Studies, Education, Religion - Catholic, Theology
ISBN Prefix(es): 2-87324
Number of titles published annually: 20 Print
Total Titles: 100 Print
Distributed by Cerf (France & Switzerland); Novalis (Canada & USA)

LW Press, see Wouters Import PVBA

Maklu+
Somersstraat 13-15, B-2018 Antwerp 1
Tel: (03) 231-29-00 *Fax:* (03) 233-26-59
E-mail: info@maklu.be
Web Site: www.maklu.be
Key Personnel
Dir: Bert Boerwinkel; Huug Van Gompel *E-mail:* huug.vangompel@maklu.be
Publisher: Stephan Svacina
Promotion: Frederic Van der Planken
Founded: 1972
Also acts as wholesaler (Dutch books); specialize in law books & dictionaries.
Subjects: Economics, Government, Political Science, Law, Management, Social Sciences, Sociology
ISBN Prefix(es): 90-6215
Number of titles published annually: 60 Print
Total Titles: 600 Print

Associate Companies: Garant Publishers (Sweden)
Subsidiaries: Maklu bv
Distributed by Bayliss (London); Gaunt & Sons (USA); Juridik & Samhaelle (Sweden); Nomos Verlag (Germany); Schulthess Verlag (Switzerland)

Manteau, *imprint of* Standaard Uitgeverij

Marabout+
Ave de l'Energie, 30, 4432 Alleur
Tel: (04) 246 3863; (04) 4146 3815 *Fax:* (04) 246 3635
Key Personnel
President: Jacques Firmin
Financial Dir: Andre Palmans
Dir: Jean Arache
Foreign Rights: Michele Boschis
Founded: 1949
Subjects: Animals, Pets, Astrology, Occult, Behavioral Sciences, Career Development, Child Care & Development, Computer Science, Cookery, Crafts, Games, Hobbies, English as a Second Language, Gardening, Plants, Genealogy, Health, Nutrition, History, Human Relations, Humor, Medicine, Nursing, Dentistry, Self-Help
ISBN Prefix(es): 2-501
Parent Company: Hachette
Distributed by Diffulivre Suisse; Hachette Canada; Hachette Livre France; Tous Pays

Mardaga, Pierre 12
Hayen 11, B-4140 Sprimont
Tel: (04) 3684242 *Fax:* (04) 3684240
Key Personnel
Dir & Rights & Permissions: Pierre Mardaga
Founded: 1938
1600 titles on catalogue.
Subjects: Architecture & Interior Design, Education, Human Relations, Language Arts, Linguistics, Music, Dance, Philosophy, Psychology, Psychiatry
ISBN Prefix(es): 2-87009
Number of titles published annually: 45 Print

Medaillon, *imprint of* Eenhoorn BVBA

Editions Medicales et Paramedicales de Charleroi (EMPC)
rue Saint-Charles, 9, 6061 Charleroi
Tel: (071) 324689 *Fax:* (071) 324689
Key Personnel
General Director: Chantal Zanella
ISBN Prefix(es): 2-87133

Editions Memor
Rue Gustave Biot 23-25, 1050 Brussels
Tel: (02) 644-04-43 *Fax:* (02) 644-04-43
Web Site: www.memor.cjb.net
Key Personnel
Dir: John F Ellyton *E-mail:* john.ellyton@skynet.be
Founded: 1995
Specialize in general Collection Couleurs Teenagers, Transparences Adults.
Subjects: Fiction, Literature, Literary Criticism, Essays
ISBN Prefix(es): 2-930133
Number of titles published annually: 8 Print
Total Titles: 3 Print
Foreign Rep(s): Alterdis (France)

Mercatorfonds NV+
Meir 85, 2000 Antwerp
Tel: (03) 2027260 *Fax:* (03) 2311319
E-mail: artbooks@mercatorfonds.be
Web Site: www.mercatorfonds.be
Key Personnel
Publisher: Jan Martens *E-mail:* jm@mercatorfonds.be
Founded: 1965
Publisher of fine art books & illustrated historical studies.
Subjects: Architecture & Interior Design, Art, History
ISBN Prefix(es): 90-6153
Number of titles published annually: 10 Print

Michelin Editions des Voyages
33 quai de Willebroek, B1000 Brussels
Tel: (02) 274 45 03 *Fax:* (02) 274 43 62
E-mail: kontakt@viamichelin.com
Web Site: www.viamichelin.com *Cable:* PNEUMICLIN
Key Personnel
Dir: Robert Van Keerberghen *E-mail:* robert-vankeerberghen@be.michelin.com
Founded: 1913
Subjects: Travel, Tourist Guides
Parent Company: Michelin Editions Des Voyages
Ultimate Parent Company: Manufacture Francaise Des Pneumatiques Michelin
Branch Office(s)
Michelin Travel Publications & Michelin Tire Corporation, One Parkway S, Greenville, SC 29615, United States

Harvey Miller, *imprint of* Brepols Publishers NV

Mozaiek, *imprint of* Uitgeverij Clavis

Nauwelaerts Edition SA+
rue de l'Eglise Saint-Sulpice 16, 1320 Beauvechain
Tel: (010) 861655 *Fax:* (010) 7517408
Key Personnel
Man Dir: Stephane Rouget
Founded: 1934
Subjects: Economics, History, Literature, Literary Criticism, Essays, Medicine, Nursing, Dentistry, Philosophy, Psychology, Psychiatry, Social Sciences, Sociology, Theology
ISBN Prefix(es): 2-8038
Associate Companies: Vander Publishing

NCOS (Nationaal Centrum voor Ontwikkelingssamenwerking) VZW, *see* Koepel van de Vlaamse Noord - Zuidbeweging 11.11.11

Les Nouvelles Editions Marabout SA, *see* Marabout

Pandora+
Indiestr 21, 2000 Antwerp
Tel: (03) 475730978 *Fax:* (03) 32333399
Founded: 1988
Subjects: Art, Catalogues, Monographs, Catalogue Raisonne
ISBN Prefix(es): 90-5325
Number of titles published annually: 30 Print
Total Titles: 180 Print

Paradox Express - Manuscripten, *imprint of* Paradox Pers vzw

Paradox Pers vzw+
Leopoldstraat 55/1, 2000 Antwerp
Tel: (03) 2322313 *Fax:* (03) 2322313
E-mail: paradox@glo.be; paradoxpers@belgacom.be
Key Personnel
Dir: Dirk Claus
Founded: 1960
Subjects: Fiction, Philosophy, Poetry
ISBN Prefix(es): 90-72533
Number of titles published annually: 10 Print
Imprints: Paradox Express - Manuscripten
Distributed by EPO

Parasol NV+
Mechelse Steenweg 434, 2650 Edegem
Tel: (03) 460 1880 *Fax:* (03) 460 1881
E-mail: info@parasol.be
Key Personnel
Man Dir: Wilfried Wuyts *Tel:* (03) 4601880 *Fax:* (03) 460 1888 *E-mail:* ww@parasol.be
Founded: 1994
Specialize in sticker books & children's activities; publish in Dutch & French.
ISBN Prefix(es): 90-5593; 90-5888
Number of titles published annually: 60 Print
Total Titles: 300 Print

Parsifal BVBA
Gulden Vlieslaan 67, 8000 Brugge
Tel: (050) 339516 *Fax:* (050) 333386
E-mail: info@parsifal.be
Web Site: www.parsifal.be
Key Personnel
Chief Executive, Rights & Permissions: Christian Vandekerkhove
Production: Erna Droesbeke
Founded: 1979
Subjects: Astrology, Occult, Parapsychology, Philosophy
ISBN Prefix(es): 90-6458; 2-87259
Associate Companies: Editions Verrycken
Branch Office(s)
Steenhouwersvest, 2000 Antwerp *Tel:* (03) 2316039
Bookshop(s): Librairie Verrycken, Weigstr 30, 2000 Antwerp (jointly owned with Editions Verrycsen); Occult Bookshop, Hoogstr 68, B-2000 Antwerp

La Part de L'Oeil+
Rue du Midi, 144, 1000 Brussels
Tel: (02) 514 18 41 *Fax:* (02) 514 18 41
E-mail: lapartdeloeil@brunette.brucity.be
Web Site: aca-bxl.be/intro/index.htm
Key Personnel
Contact: Lucien Massaert
International Rights Contact: Karine Barbareau
Founded: 1985
La Part de L'Oeil, our review of Aesthetics, is currently the only theoretical arts review published in French. Since 1985, La Part de L'Oeil has kept up with the latest research & investigation concerning the essence of the creative process, with the objective being to fill in the outlines while delineating the features of contemporary Aesthetics. Specifically, to deal with the theoretical vacuum which has surrounded art for years, by testing the discourse through its relationship to the art work which is the base of aesthetic thought. For seventeen years La Part de L'Oeil has stood out as one of the main authorities in the field of aesthetics. The most important critics, philosophers, artists, academics, writers...contribute every year to the review. A section of each issue is dedicated to approaching the major questions of art from a contemporary prospective.
Subjects: Art, Language Arts, Linguistics, Literature, Literary Criticism, Essays, Philosophy, Poetry, Psychology, Psychiatry
ISBN Prefix(es): 2-930174
Number of titles published annually: 4 Print
Total Titles: 28 Print
Distributed by Alterdis (France & Switzerland); Diffusion NEMO

Uitgeverij Peeters Leuven (Belgie)+
Bondgenotenlaan 153, 3000 Leuven
Tel: (016) 23 51 70 *Fax:* (016) 22 85 00
E-mail: peeters@peeters-leuven.be
Web Site: www.peeters-leuven.be
Key Personnel
Dir: Mr P Peeters

Product Manager: Liesbeth Verloove *Tel:* (16) 235170 *E-mail:* lverloove@peeters-leuven.be
Founded: 1857
Specialize in canon law & patristics.
Publish Oriental & foreign-language books.
Subjects: Archaeology, Asian Studies, Biblical Studies, History, Language Arts, Linguistics, Philosophy, Religion - Other, Theology
ISBN Prefix(es): 90-6831; 90-429; 2-8017
Subsidiaries: Peeters
U.S. Office(s): Books International, PO Box 605, Herndon, VA 20172-0605, United States, Contact: K Hughes *E-mail:* intpubmkt@aol.com
Distributed by VRIN

Pelckmans NV, De Nederlandsche Boekhandel+
Kapelsestraat 222, 2080 Kapellen
Tel: (03) 664-53-20 *Fax:* (03) 664-70-80
Key Personnel
General Director: Jan en Rudi Pelckmans
Founded: 1892
Subjects: Geography, Geology, History, Language Arts, Linguistics, Literature, Literary Criticism, Essays, Mathematics, Philosophy, Religion - Catholic
ISBN Prefix(es): 90-289

Uitgeverij Pelckmans N V
Kapelsestraat 222, 2950 Kapellen
Tel: (03) 660 27 00 *Fax:* (03) 660 27 00
E-mail: uitgeverij@pelckmans.be
Web Site: www.pelckmans.be
Telex: 32242 Anvers Dnb
Key Personnel
Man Dir: J Pelckmans; R Pelckmans
Founded: 1892
Subjects: History, Philosophy, Religion - Other, Social Sciences, Sociology
ISBN Prefix(es): 90-289
Associate Companies: Uitgeverij Helios; Uitgeverij Patmos
Bookshop(s): Sint Jacobsmarkt 7, B-2000 Antwerp

Poeziecentrum+
Hoornstraat 11, B-9000 Ghent
Tel: (09) 225 22 25 *Fax:* (09) 225 90 54
E-mail: info@poeziecentrum.be
Web Site: www.poeziecentrum.be
Key Personnel
Man Dir: Willy Tibergien
Founded: 1980
Subjects: Poetry
ISBN Prefix(es): 90-5655; 90-70968

Le Pole Nord ASBL
Rue du Nord, 66, 1000 Brussels
Tel: (02) 2184576 *Fax:* (02) 2184576
E-mail: pole.nord@skynet.be
Key Personnel
President: Anny Frenay
Secretary: Charlotte Goetz
Founded: 1983
Also acts as Scientific Research Association.
Subjects: History, French Revolution, Jean-Paul Marat
ISBN Prefix(es): 2-930040
Distributed by Pole Nord Asbl

Pre-Ecole, *imprint of* Editions Chantecler

Preschool, *imprint of* Zuid-Nederlandse Uitgeverij NV/ Central Uitgeverij

Presses agronomiques de Gembloux ASBL+
2, Passage des Deportes, 5030 Gembloux
Tel: (081) 62 22 42 *Fax:* (081) 62 22 42
E-mail: pressesagro@fsagx.ac.be
Web Site: www.bib.fsagx.ac.be/presses/
Key Personnel
Dir: Mr B Pochet
Founded: 1964
Specialize also in chemistry & the food industry.
Subjects: Agriculture, Biological Sciences, Environmental Studies, Mathematics, Technology
ISBN Prefix(es): 2-87016
Number of titles published annually: 3 Print

Presses Universitaires de Namur ASBL
Rempart de la Vierge 13, 5000 Namur
Tel: (081) 72 48 84 *Fax:* (081) 72 49 12
E-mail: pun@fundp.ac.be
Web Site: www.pun.be
Key Personnel
Dir: Rene Robaye
Editor: Myriam Despineux *Tel:* (081) 72 48 86 *E-mail:* myriam.despineux@fundp.ac.be
Public Relations: Stephanie Herfurth *Tel:* (081) 72 48 85 *E-mail:* stephanie.herfurth@fundp.ac.be
Founded: 1977
Membership(s): ADEB (Association des Editeurs Belges).
ISBN Prefix(es): 2-87037
Number of titles published annually: 15 Print

Presses Universitaires de Bruxelles ASBL
42 av Paul Heger, CP 149, 1000 Brussels
Tel: (02) 641 14 46 *Fax:* (02) 647 79 62
Key Personnel
President: Thierry Lambrecht
Man Dir: Jeannine De Backer *E-mail:* jdbacker@ulb.ac.be
Sales: Henri De Smet
Founded: 1958
Subjects: Architecture & Interior Design, Economics, Engineering (General), Medicine, Nursing, Dentistry, Philosophy, Science (General)
ISBN Prefix(es): 2-500

Presses Universitaires de Liege
Domaine Universi du Sart-Tilman, Batiment 87, bte 27, 4000 Liege
Tel: (041) 562218
Founded: 1969
Subjects: Government, Political Science, Law, Medicine, Nursing, Dentistry, Social Sciences, Sociology
ISBN Prefix(es): 2-87014
Branch Office(s)
7, Place du 20-Aout Bat A1, 04000 Leige
Tel: (041) 420080

Prodim SPRL+
Blvd General Jacques 184, 1050 Brussels
Tel: (02) 640.59.70 *Fax:* (02) 640.59.91
E-mail: prodim.books@prodim
Web Site: www.prodim.be
Key Personnel
President: Mdme Nile Patrick
Founded: 1968
Physiotherapy.
Member of ADEB.
Subjects: Medicine, Nursing, Dentistry
ISBN Prefix(es): 2-87017
Subsidiaries: de Visscher
Distributor for Jibena (Belgium); Similia (Belgium)
Foreign Rep(s): Nile Pa

Production et Diffusion de Medias SPRL, see Prodim SPRL

Henri Proost & Co, Pvba
Everdongenlaan 23, 2300 Turnhout
Tel: (014) 40 08 11 *Fax:* (014) 42 87 94
Web Site: www.proost.be
Telex: 33185
Key Personnel
Man Dir: Herman Peeters *E-mail:* herman.peeters@proost.be
Sales Dir: Jan Jacobs
Subjects: Cookery, Gardening, Plants, History, Religion - Other, Travel
ISBN Prefix(es): 90-6150
Subsidiaries: Bedford Editions Ltd; Salamander Books Ltd

Publications des Facultes Universitaires Saint Louis+
Blvd du Jardin Botanique 43, 1000 Brussels
Tel: (02) 211 78 94 *Fax:* (02) 211 79 97
E-mail: mfthoua@fusl.ac.be
Web Site: www.fusl.ac.be/files/general/publications.html
Key Personnel
Man Dir: Francois Ost
Sales, Publicity: Marie-Francoise Thoua
Founded: 1973
Member of Association des coliteuver belges.
Subjects: Economics, History, Law, Mathematics, Philosophy, Psychology, Psychiatry, Social Sciences, Sociology, Theology
ISBN Prefix(es): 2-8028

Editions Racine+
Rue du Chatelain 49, 1050 Brussels
Tel: (02) 646 44 44 *Fax:* (02) 646 55 70
Web Site: www.lannoo.be
Key Personnel
Dir: Emmanuel Brutsaert
Founded: 1993
Specialize also in nature.
Subjects: Architecture & Interior Design, Art, History, Nonfiction (General)
ISBN Prefix(es): 2-87386
Total Titles: 160 Print
Parent Company: Lannoo
Ultimate Parent Company: Lannoo
Distributed by Lannoo (Belgium); Vilo (France); Altera Diffusion (Begium)
Orders to: Editions Racine, Rue Du Chatelain, 49, B-1050 Brussels *Tel:* (02) 6464444 *Fax:* (02) 6465570

Rainbow Grafics Intl - Baronian Books SC+
63 rue Charles Legrelle, 1040 Brussels
Tel: (02) 7348114 *Fax:* (02) 7325764
Key Personnel
Man Dir: Mdme Anne Lous Baronian
Editorial Dir: Jehn Baptiste Lous Baronian
Specialize in International Co-Production.

Reader's Digest SA
blvd Paepsem 20, 1070 Brussels
Tel: (02) 5268111 *Fax:* (02) 5268112
Telex: 21876
Key Personnel
Man Dir: J H Beauduin
Founded: 1947
Subjects: Education, Geography, Geology, History, Sports, Athletics, Travel
ISBN Prefix(es): 90-70818; 2-87101

La Renaissance du Livre+
52 Chaussee de Roubaix, 7500 Tournai
Mailing Address: Fond Jean-Paques, Louvain la Neuve
Tel: (069) 89.15.55 *Fax:* (069) 89.15.50
Web Site: www.larenaissancedulivre.com
Founded: 1923
Subjects: Art, History
ISBN Prefix(es): 2-8041; 2-87148

Roularta Books NV+
Research Park De Haak, 1731 Zellik
Tel: (0475) 63 46 23
E-mail: info@roularta.be
Web Site: www.roulartabooks.be
Key Personnel
President: Rik De Nolf
Business Mgr: Piet Bulteel
Founded: 1988

Subjects: Architecture & Interior Design, Art, Business, Economics, Gardening, Plants, Literature, Literary Criticism, Essays, Management, Marketing, Nonfiction (General), Sports, Athletics, Travel
ISBN Prefix(es): 90-5466; 90-72411
Imprints: Globe; KnackBibliotheek/Radio 1

Samson (CED), see CED-Samsom

Editions Scaillet, SA+
Rue de Marchienne 203, 6110 Montigny-le-Tilleul
Tel: (071) 516335 *Fax:* (071) 511795
Key Personnel
Administrative Delegate: Andre Scaillet
Founded: 1984
Also acts as a printing office.
Subjects: History
ISBN Prefix(es): 2-930002

Schaar, *imprint of* De Schaar/Geknipt Papier

Schaar, *imprint of* Scissors Books

De Schaar/Geknipt Papier+
Penitentenstr 24, 9000 Ghent
Tel: (09) 2255414 *Fax:* (09) 2259724
E-mail: geknipt@skynet.be
Web Site: users.skynet.be
Key Personnel
International Rights: Carla Wauben
Contact: Paul D'Haene
Founded: 1989
Subjects: Comics
ISBN Prefix(es): 90-5775; 90-73619
Imprints: Blitz; Schaar; Scissors

Paul Schiltz
3 Place Rotenberg, 4700 Eupen
Tel: (087) 553271
Key Personnel
Man Dir: Paul Schiltz
Founded: 1963
Subjects: Medicine, Nursing, Dentistry
ISBN Prefix(es): 2-87058

Schott Freres SA (Editeurs de Musique)
30 rue Saint-Jean, 1000 Brussels
Tel: (02) 5123980 *Fax:* (02) 5142845
Key Personnel
Man Dir: Jean-Jacques Junne
Founded: 1823
Subjects: Music, Dance
Associate Companies: Schott Freres Sarl, France

Scissors, *imprint of* De Schaar/Geknipt Papier

Scissors Books+
Penitentenstr 24, 9000 Ghent
Tel: (09) 2255414 *Fax:* (09) 2259724
E-mail: geknipt@skynet.be
Key Personnel
General Dir: Paul D'haene
International Rights: Carla Wauben
Founded: 1989
Editor & distributor of comic books in Flemish, English, French & Dutch, USA & UK; postcards & t-shirts.
Subjects: Fiction, Human Relations, Humor, Mysteries, Science Fiction, Fantasy
ISBN Prefix(es): 90-5775; 90-73619
Parent Company: Geknipt Papier CV
Imprints: Schaar
Bookshop(s): De Schaar, Serpentstr 28, 9000 Ghent; De Schaar, Fontainasplein 24, 1000 Brussels

Service, *imprint of* Editions Juridiques Kluwer a Deurne Anvers

Uitgeverij De Sikkel NV+
Nijverheidstr 8, 2390 Oostmalle
Tel: (03) 312 86 30 *Fax:* (03) 311 77 39
E-mail: info@desikkel.be
Web Site: www.desikkel.be
Key Personnel
Man Dir: Bart Hye *Tel:* (03) 3128643
E-mail: bhye@desikkel.be
Contact: Bieke Berhaers *E-mail:* bberhaers@desikkel.be; Patrick Vandevelde *Tel:* (03) 3128644 *E-mail:* pvandevelde@desikkel.be
Founded: 1919
Member of Flemish Publishers Association.
Subjects: Education, English as a Second Language
ISBN Prefix(es): 90-260
Parent Company: De Pioen, Oostmalle
Distributor for Dijkstra (Groningen); Ediciones SM (Madrid); Panta Rhei; Spruyt; Verpleegkundig fonds (Leiden); Von Mantgem en de Does; UBS (Oegstgeest); De Vey-Mestdagh (Middelburg); Westermann Lernspiel (Braunschweig)
Bookshop(s): De Pioen, Oostmalle

Snoeck-Ducaju en Zoon NV
Begijnhoflaan 464, 9000 Ghent
Tel: (09) 267.04.11 *Fax:* (09) 267.04.60
E-mail: sdz@sdz.be
Web Site: www.sdz.be
Telex: 12765
Key Personnel
Algemene Dir: S Snoeck
Founded: 1782
Subjects: Literature, Literary Criticism, Essays
ISBN Prefix(es): 90-70481; 90-5349

Sonneville Press (Uitgeverij) VTW
Karel De Stoutelaan 142, 8000 Brugge
Tel: (050) 321112
Key Personnel
Dir: J Sonneville
Founded: 1987
Subjects: Art, Education, Ethnicity, Geography, Geology, Government, Political Science, History, Language Arts, Linguistics, Law, Literature, Literary Criticism, Essays, Music, Dance, Philosophy, Religion - Other, Social Sciences, Sociology, Sports, Athletics, Travel
ISBN Prefix(es): 90-5149

Stafeto, *imprint of* Vlaamse Esperantobond VZW

Standaard Uitgeverij+
Belgielei 147a, 2018 Antwerp
Tel: (03) 285 72 00 *Fax:* (03) 285 72 99
E-mail: info@standaard.com
Web Site: www.standaard.com
Key Personnel
Man Dir: Eric Willems
Editorial Dir: Johan de Koning; Diane Devriendt
Publisher: Wim Verheije
Editorial Dir: Herman Cauwels
Founded: 1919
Subjects: Biography, Fiction, Humor, Poetry
ISBN Prefix(es): 90-02
Parent Company: PCM Algemene Boeken bv, Nieuwekade 1, NL-3511 R V Utrecht, Netherlands
Imprints: Manteau
Warehouse: Libridis-Bulkmagazijn Temse, Schoenstr 6, 9140 Temse
Orders to: Libridis-Bulkmagazijn Temse, Schoenstr 6, 9140 Temse

Stichting Kunstboek bvba+
Blankenberge Steenweg 14, 8000 Brugge
Tel: (050) 312352 *Fax:* (050) 313173

Key Personnel
Contact: Jaak van Damme; Karel Puype
Founded: 1992
Subjects: Architecture & Interior Design, Art, Crafts, Games, Hobbies, Gardening, Plants, History, Music, Dance
ISBN Prefix(es): 90-74377

Stichting Ons Erfdeel VZW
Murissonstr 260, B-8930 Rekkem
Tel: (056) 41 12 01 *Fax:* (056) 41 47 07
E-mail: info@onserfdeel.be
Web Site: www.onserfdeel.be
Key Personnel
Man Dir & Chief Editor: Luc Devoldere
Head, Administration: Bernard Viaene
E-mail: adm@onserfdeel.be
Founded: 1970
Specialize in promoting cultural cooperation among all speakers of the Dutch language & increase awareness of Flemish & Dutch culture abroad. Publish & distribute a range of periodicals & other publications, both in Dutch & other languages.
Subjects: Art, Ethnicity, Language Arts, Linguistics, Literature, Literary Criticism, Essays, Regional Interests
ISBN Prefix(es): 90-70831; 90-75862

E Story-Scientia, *imprint of* Editions Juridiques Kluwer a Deurne Anvers

Editions Techniques et Scientifiques SPRL
37 rue Borrens, 1050 Brussels
Tel: (02) 6401040 *Fax:* (02) 6400739
Key Personnel
Man Dir: A Louis
Founded: 1919
Subjects: Ethnicity, Geography, Geology, History, Law, Mathematics, Science (General), Technology, Travel
ISBN Prefix(es): 2-87004

Toneelfonds J Janssens BVBA+
Te Boelaerlei 107, 2140 Borgerhout-Antwerp
Tel: (03) 366 44 00 *Fax:* (03) 366 45 01
E-mail: info@toneelfonds.be
Web Site: www.toneelfonds.be
Key Personnel
Dir: Jessica Janssens *E-mail:* jessica.janssens@toneelfonds.be
Founded: 1880
Publisher of plays & brochures. Also acts as literary agent for playwrights.
Subjects: Drama, Theater
ISBN Prefix(es): 90-385
Number of titles published annually: 100 Print

Toulon Uitgeverij
Sportstr 35, 8400 Oostende
Tel: (059) 800927
Key Personnel
Dir: P A Toulon
Subjects: Education
ISBN Prefix(es): 90-70270

UCL, see Presses Universitaires de Louvain-UCL

UGA Editions (Uitgeverij)
Stijn Streuvelslaan 73, Heule 8501
Tel: (056) 363200 *Fax:* (056) 356096
E-mail: publ@uga.be
Web Site: www.uga.be *Cable:* UGA
Key Personnel
Dir: L Deschildre
Editorial, Sales: Patrick van Assche *E-mail:* pva@uga.be
Founded: 1948
Also acts as packager.
Subjects: History, Language Arts, Linguistics, Law, Public Administration, Social Sciences, Sociology

ISBN Prefix(es): 90-6768
Branch Office(s)
19 rue Guimard Bte 2, 1040 Brussels *Tel:* (02) 512-09-75 *Fax:* (02) 512-26-93

Uitgeverij De Garve
Groene Poortdreef 27, 8200 Brugge
Tel: (050) 400050 *Fax:* (050) 388099
E-mail: info@degarve.be
Web Site: www.degarve.be
Key Personnel
Dir: G Barbiaux
Founded: 1909
Subjects: Biography, Government, Political Science, Language Arts, Linguistics, Law, Mathematics, Music, Dance, Physics, Social Sciences, Sociology
ISBN Prefix(es): 90-5148
Parent Company: Drukkerij PVBA G Barbiaux

Uitgevery Scoop Infotex NV+
Subsidiary of VUM Group
Forelstr 22, 9000 Ghent
Tel: (02) 4672495 *Fax:* (02) 4669351
E-mail: scoop@infotex.be
Key Personnel
Delegate Dir: Johan De Koning
Editor: Leen Van Troys *E-mail:* leen.vantroys@infotex.be
Founded: 1991
Subjects: Biography, Business, Career Development, Economics, Government, Political Science, History, Journalism, Literature, Literary Criticism, Essays, Management, Marketing, Travel
ISBN Prefix(es): 90-5312
Number of titles published annually: 30 Print; 1 CD-ROM
Online services available through AZUR.BE.
Imprints: Globe

Unistad Verspreiding CV+
Jan Moorkensstr 46, 2600 Berchem
Tel: (03) 2307725 *Fax:* (03) 2307725
Key Personnel
Dir: Rob Claes
Editorial: Bennie Callebaut
Founded: 1984
Subjects: Religion - Other
ISBN Prefix(es): 90-70276
Parent Company: Citta Nuova Editrice, Italy

Universitaire Pers Leuven, see Leuven University Press

Presses Universitaires de Louvain-UCL
Place de l'Universite, 1, 1348 Louvain-la-Neuve
Tel: (010) 478935 *Fax:* (010) 472531
Web Site: www.ucl.ac.ba
Telex: UCL AC 59516
Key Personnel
Dir: Jacqueline Tulkens
Member of ADEB.
Subjects: Science (General)
ISBN Prefix(es): 2-87200

Editions de l'Universite de Bruxelles+
26, ave Paul-Heger, CP 163, 1000 Brussels
Tel: (02) 650 37 99 *Fax:* (02) 650 37 94
E-mail: editions@admin.ulb.ac.be
Web Site: www.editions-universite-bruxelles.be
Key Personnel
President: Robert Tollet
Editorial Manager: Michele Mat *Tel:* (02) 650 37 97 *E-mail:* mmat@admin.ulb.ac.be
Founded: 1972
Subjects: Economics, Government, Political Science, History, Law, Mathematics, Medicine, Nursing, Dentistry, Philosophy, Social Sciences, Sociology
ISBN Prefix(es): 2-8004

Number of titles published annually: 20 Print
Total Titles: 260 Print
Distributed by Somabec (Canada)

Imprimeur - Editeur Vaillant-Carmanne SA
20 Zevenputtenstr, 3690 Zutendaal
Tel: (011) 612452 *Fax:* (011) 612451
Key Personnel
Man Dir: G Dengis
Founded: 1838
Subjects: Education, Government, Political Science, History, Law, Medicine, Nursing, Dentistry, Religion - Other, Science (General)
ISBN Prefix(es): 2-87021

Marc Van de Wiele bvba+
Jakobinessenstr 5, 8000 Brugge
Tel: (050) 333805 *Fax:* (050) 346457
Key Personnel
Contact: M van de Wiele
Founded: 1979
Subjects: Art, History
ISBN Prefix(es): 90-6966
Bookshop(s): Antiquariaat Marc Van de Wiele, St Salvator Keru Hof 7, B-8000 Brugge; Zeewindstr 4, B-8300 Knouue-Heist

Vander Editions, SA
321 Ave des Volontaires, 1150 Brussels
Tel: (02) 761 12 12 *Fax:* (02) 761 12 13
Web Site: www.adeb.irisnet.be
Key Personnel
Man Dir: Willy Vandermeulen
Editorial Dir: Stephane Rouget,
Founded: 1880
Subjects: Economics, Government, Political Science, Law, Psychology, Psychiatry, Science (General), Social Sciences, Sociology
ISBN Prefix(es): 2-8008
Associate Companies: Nauwelaerts Edition SA

VBVB, see Huis Van Het Boek

Les Editions Vie ouvriere ASBL
rue Anderlecht 4, 1000 Brussels
Tel: (02) 5125090 *Fax:* (02) 5145231
Key Personnel
Chief Executive: Andre Samain
Founded: 1958
Subjects: Economics, History, Photography, Psychology, Psychiatry, Religion - Other, Social Sciences, Sociology
ISBN Prefix(es): 2-87003

Vita+
Speelstraat 14, 9750 Zingem
Tel: (09) 3842114 *Fax:* (09) 3842114
Key Personnel
Contact: Eric De Preester
Founded: 1964
Subjects: Alternative, Crafts, Games, Hobbies, Health, Nutrition, Literature, Literary Criticism, Essays, Philosophy, Poetry, Theology
ISBN Prefix(es): 90-73323
Number of titles published annually: 3 Print
Total Titles: 22 Print

Vlaamse Esperantobond VZW+
Frankrijklei 140, 2000 Anvers
Tel: (03) 2343400 *Fax:* (03) 2335433
E-mail: esperanto@agoranet.be
Web Site: bold.belnet.be
Key Personnel
General Dir: Paul Peeraerts *E-mail:* pp@fel.agoranet.be
Founded: 1979
Subjects: Education, Fiction, Language Arts, Linguistics, Poetry
ISBN Prefix(es): 90-71205
Total Titles: 10 Print

Imprints: Stafeto
U.S. Office(s): Esperanto League of North America, PO Box 1129, El Cerrito, CA 94530-1129, United States

Volk NV, Boekandel het
Forelstr 22, 9000 Ghent
Tel: (091) 265 67 20 *Fax:* (091) 225 20 71
Telex: 11228
Key Personnel
Man Dir: J van Haverbeke
ISBN Prefix(es): 90-6334
Bookshop(s): Boekhandel Het Volk

C De Vries Brouwers BVBA
Haantjeslei 80, 2018 Antwerp
Tel: (03) 2374180 *Fax:* (03) 2377001
Key Personnel
Dir: I de Vries
Founded: 1946
Subjects: History
ISBN Prefix(es): 90-6174

VUB University Press+
Waverse Steenweg 1077, 1160 Brussels
Tel: (02) 6293590 *Fax:* (02) 6292694
E-mail: vubpress@vnet3.vub.ac.be
Web Site: www.vubpress.org
Key Personnel
General Manager: Kris Van Scharen *E-mail:* kvschare@vub.ac.be
Founded: 1988
Specialize in scientific publications.
Subjects: Communications, Environmental Studies, Government, Political Science, History, Philosophy, Science (General), Social Sciences, Sociology, Women's Studies
ISBN Prefix(es): 90-5487
Orders to: Paul & Co, PO Box 442, Concord, MA 01792, United States *Tel:* 508-369 3049 *Fax:* 508-369 2385 *E-mail:* pauline@tiac.net
Gazelle Book, Falcon House, Queensquare, Lancaster LA1 1RN, United Kingdom *Tel:* (01524) 68765 *Fax:* (01524) 68232 *E-mail:* gazelle4go@aol.com

Wereldwijd Vzw+
Hoogstr 139, 1000 Brussels
Tel: (02) 513 12 70 *Fax:* (02) 513 12 71
E-mail: wereldwijd@wereldwijd.ngonet.be
Web Site: www.educa.be
Key Personnel
Dir: Agnes Van Speybroeck
Founded: 1970
Member of VBVB.
Subjects: Developing Countries
ISBN Prefix(es): 90-76421

Editions Luce Wilquin+
rue d'Atrive 48, 4280 Avin/Hannut
Tel: (019) 69 98 13 *Fax:* (019) 69 98 13
E-mail: wilquin.bouquin@skynet.be
Web Site: www.wilquin.com
Founded: 1992
Subjects: Art, Fiction, History, Literature, Literary Criticism, Essays, Romance
ISBN Prefix(es): 2-88253
Number of titles published annually: 20 Print
Total Titles: 170 Print

Wolters Plantyn Educatieve Uitgevers
Santvoortbeeklaan 21-25, 2100 Deurne
Tel: (03) 360 03 11 *Fax:* (03) 360 03 30
E-mail: klantendienst@woltersplantyn.be
Web Site: www.woltersplantyn.be
Founded: 1959
Educational publishers.
Subjects: Computer Science, Economics, Education, Language Arts, Linguistics, Mathematics, Physics, Psychology, Psychiatry, Science (General)

ISBN Prefix(es): 90-309; 90-301
Parent Company: Wolters Kluwer Belgie NV
Ultimate Parent Company: Wolters Kluwer NV, Netherlands
Orders to: Zeutestraat 5, B-2800 Mechelen

Wouters Import PVBA
Groenstr 178, 3001 Heverlee
Tel: (016) 232481 *Fax:* (016) 229841
Key Personnel
Contact: Paul Verplancke
Also acts as distributor of computer books.
ISBN Prefix(es): 90-5497
Parent Company: Wouters BVBA, Naamsestraat 48, 3000 Leuven

Zuid En Noord VZW
Hanebergstr 75, 3581 Beringen
Tel: (011) 34 4991
Web Site: www.schrijversnet.nl
Key Personnel
Algemene directie: Edith Oeyen
Subjects: Biography, Literature, Literary Criticism, Essays, Poetry, Romance
ISBN Prefix(es): 90-72087; 90-5684

Zuid-Nederlandse Uitgeverij NV/ Central Uitgeverij+
Vluchtenburgstr 7, 2630 Aartselaar
Tel: (03) 8771464 *Fax:* (03) 8772115
Telex: 31739 Zuidb
Key Personnel
Man Dir: Jan Vande Velden
Publisher: Bart Clinckemalie
Production: Eric Feyten
Sales Dir: Wilfried Wuyts
Founded: 1946
Subjects: Animals, Pets, Child Care & Development, Crafts, Games, Hobbies, English as a Second Language, Gardening, Plants, Humor
ISBN Prefix(es): 90-243
Imprints: Deltas; Preschool; Chanteller; Invader; Liberica
Subsidiaries: Editions Chantecler (Belgium); Editions Chantecler (France); Centrale Uitgeverij; Invader Ltd; Liberica

Benin

General Information

Capital: Porto-Novo
Language: French
Religion: About 15% Christian (mostly Roman Catholic), 13% Islamic, remainder traditional beliefs
Population: 4.5 million
Bank Hours: 0800-1000, 1500-1600 Monday-Friday
Shop Hours: 0800-1300, 1500-1900 Monday-Saturday. Larger ones close Monday, some open for a few hours Sunday morning
Currency: 100 centimes = CFA franc
Export/Import Information: Import license required but issued automatically for imports from EEC countries. Exchange controls for non-franc zone.
Copyright: Berne (see Copyright Conventions, pg xi)

Les Editions du Flamboyant
Carre 236, BP 08-271, Cotonou
Tel: 312517
E-mail: IPEC@leland.bj
Key Personnel
Contact: Oscar De Souza
Founded: 1997
ISBN Prefix(es): 2-909130

Logos de l'Office, *imprint of* Office National d'Edition de Presse et d'Imprimerie (ONEPI)

Office National d'Edition de Presse et d'Imprimerie (ONEPI)
BP 1210, Cotonou
Tel: 300299; 301152 *Fax:* 303463
Key Personnel
Administrator: Innocent Adjaho
Founded: 1975
Imprints: Logos de l'Office

ONEPI, see Office National d'Edition de Presse et d'Imprimerie (ONEPI)

Bermuda

General Information

Capital: Hamilton
Language: English & some Portuguese
Religion: Predominantly Anglican
Population: 60,213
Bank Hours: 0930-1500 Monday-Thursday; 0930-1500, 1630-1800 Friday
Shop Hours: 0900-1700 Monday-Saturday
Currency: 100 cents = 1 Bermuda dollar. US currency circulates
Export/Import Information: No tariff on books and advertising matter. No import license. Exchange controls on imports valued over $100.
Copyright: Berne (see Copyright Conventions, pg xi)

Bermudian Publishing Co
PO Box HM283, Hamilton HM AX
Tel: (441) 295-0695 *Fax:* (441) 295-8616
E-mail: berpub@ibl.bm
Web Site: www.bermuda.bm *Cable:* BERPUBLISH
Key Personnel
Publisher: Tina Stevenson
Publish magazines.
Subjects: Business, Fiction, Social Sciences, Sociology, Sports, Athletics, Specializes in Bermuda
ISBN Prefix(es): 976-8143
Warehouse: Addendum Lane, Pitts Bay Rd, Pembroke

Bolivia

General Information

Capital: Sucre
Religion: Predominantly Roman Catholic
Population: 7.3 million
Bank Hours: 0900-1200, 1400-1630 Monday-Friday
Shop Hours: 0900-1200, 1400-1800 Monday-Friday; 0900-1200 Saturday
Currency: 100 centavos = 1 Boliviano
Export/Import Information: Member of the Latin American Free Trade Association. No tariffs on books, except for 10% luxury bindings. No import licenses, except for textbooks, but no pornography allowed. No advertising that includes imitation money, stamps, etc, allowed. No exchange controls.
Copyright: UCC, Berne, Buenos Aires (see Copyright Conventions, pg xi)

Los Amigos del Libro Ediciones+
Member of Distripress

Casilla 450, Cochabamba
Mailing Address: Av Ayacucho S-0156, Cochabamba Casilla 450
Tel: (04) 4504150; (04) 4504151 *Fax:* (04) 4115128
Web Site: www.librosbolivia.com
Key Personnel
President & Man Dir: Werner Guttentag
Sales Dir: Ingrid Guttentag *E-mail:* gutten@amigol.bo.net
Foreign Sales Manager: Eva Guttentag
Production: Norma de Rivero; Rita Arze
Founded: 1945
Member of Distripress.
Subjects: Regional Interests, All aspects of Bolivia
ISBN Prefix(es): 84-8370
Number of titles published annually: 1,250 Print
Total Titles: 600 Print
Parent Company: Los Amigos del Libro, Cochabamba
Subsidiaries: Bio Bibliografia Boliviana
Branch Office(s)
La Paz
Santa Cruz
Distributed by Fondo de Cultura Economica (Argentina & Chile)
Distributor for Time; Newsweek; Fondo de Cultura Economica; Serres
Bookshop(s): Libreria los Amigos del Libro, Casilla 450 Avenida Ayacucho, S-0156 Cochabamba

Editorial Don Bosco
Av 16 de Julio 1899, Casilla de Correo 4458, La Paz
Tel: (02) 357755; (02) 371149 *Fax:* (02) 362822
Cable: EDEBE-LA PAZ
Key Personnel
Dir: Gramaglia Magliano; R P Giorgio
Subjects: Chemistry, Chemical Engineering, History, Literature, Literary Criticism, Essays, Mathematics, Philosophy, Physics, Religion - Catholic, Science (General)

Gisbert y Cia SA
Calle Comercio 1270, Plaza Murillo La Paz, La Paz
Mailing Address: Casilla Postal 195, La Paz
Tel: (02) 20 26 26 *Fax:* (02) 20 29 11
E-mail: libgis@ceibo.entelnet.bo
Web Site: www.sonnegocios.com *Cable:* GISBERCIA
Key Personnel
President: Javier Gisbert
Manager: Antonio Schulczewski; Maria del Carmen Schulczewski
Founded: 1907
Subjects: History, Law
Number of titles published annually: 2 Print
Distributor for Pearson Education

Universidad Autonoma Tomas Frias, Div de Extension Universitaria
Casilla 36, Avda del Maestro, Potosi
Tel: (062) 273-28; (062) 273-00 *Fax:* (062) 266-63; (062) 231-96
E-mail: rector@rect.nrp.edu.bo
Web Site: www.unam.mx/udal/afiliacion/frias.htm
Subjects: History, Literature, Literary Criticism, Essays

Universidad Mayor de San Andres, Editorial Universitaria
Casilla 4787, La Paz
Tel: (02) 359490 *Fax:* (02) 359491
Key Personnel
Contact: David Barrientos Zapata

Bosnia and Herzegovina

General Information

Capital: Sarajevo
Language: Bosnian, Servian, Croatian
Religion: Predominantly Sunni Muslim, also Serbian Orthodox and Roman Catholic
Population: 4.4 million
Currency: 100 convertible pfenniga = 1 convertible marka (KM)
Copyright: UCC, Berne (see Copyright Conventions, pg xi)

Bemust doo Novinsko-Izdavacko stamparsko i trgovacko preduzece (Bemust Printing House, Publishing & Trade Company)
Put Famosa 38, 71000 Sarajevo
Tel: (033) 414-050; (033) 414-051 *Fax:* (033) 414-050; (033) 414-051
E-mail: bemust@bih.net.ba
Subjects: Education, Geography, Geology, History, Law, Philosophy, Poetry, Regional Interests, Religion - Islamic, Technology

IP Oslobodenje
Dzemala Bijedica 185, 71000 Sarajevo
Tel: (071) 205-488 *Fax:* (071) 442-500
E-mail: redaction@oslobodjenje.com.ba
Web Site: www.oslobodjenje.com.ba//
Telex: 41148; 41136
Key Personnel
Dir: Ivica Lovric
ISBN Prefix(es): 86-319

Veselin Maslesa
Obla Vojvode, Stepe 4, PF 237, 71000 Sarajevo
Tel: (071) 214633; (071) 218636 *Fax:* (071) 41154
Telex: 41154 Yu Vesmas *Cable:* Vesmas Maslesa
Key Personnel
Man Dir, Editorial, Rights & Permissions: Alija Velic
Founded: 1950
Subjects: Fiction, Government, Political Science, Philosophy, Science (General)
ISBN Prefix(es): 86-21
Branch Office(s)
Belgrade
Skopje
Zagreb

Sarajevo Publishing, see Veselin Maslesa

Svjetlost
Muhameda Kantardzica 3, 71000 Sarajevo
Tel: (071) 200-840
Telex: 41326 Yu Ikpres *Cable:* Svjetlost Sarajevo
Key Personnel
Man Dir: Abdulah Jesenkovic
Sales Dir: Rizvanbegovic Enver
Editorial: Miodrag Bogicvic
Subjects: Business, Science (General)
ISBN Prefix(es): 86-81903
Branch Office(s)
Subiceva 65, Zagreb, Croatia
Obilicev venac 10, Belgrade, Yugoslavia

Botswana

General Information

Capital: Gaborone
Language: English (official) & Setswana (national)
Religion: Traditional African
Population: 1.3 million
Bank Hours: 0830-1300 Monday-Friday; 0830-1100 Saturday
Shop Hours: 0800-1300, 1400-1700 or 1800 Monday-Saturday
Currency: 100 thebe = 1 pula
Export/Import Information: No import license required; no obscene literature. Exchange controls.

The Botswana Society
PO Box 71, Gaborone
Tel: 351500 *Fax:* 359321
E-mail: botsoc@info.bw
Web Site: ubh.tripod.com/bsoc/botsoc.htm
Key Personnel
Editor: Rev D Jones
Executive Secretary: Trevor Burnett
Founded: 1968
Subjects: Archaeology, Art, Earth Sciences, Environmental Studies, Government, Political Science, History, Language Arts, Linguistics, Law, Music, Dance, Natural History, Regional Interests
ISBN Prefix(es): 99912-60

Heinemann Educational Botswana
PO Box 10103, Village Post Office, Gaborone
Tel: 372305 *Fax:* 371832
Key Personnel
Man Dir: Lesedi Seitei
ISBN Prefix(es): 99912-63
Parent Company: Heinemann Publishers Ltd, Oxford, United Kingdom
Ultimate Parent Company: Reed Elsevier plc, 25 Victoria St, London SW1H 0EX, United Kingdom

Maskew Miller Longman
Plot 14386, New Labatse Rd, West Industrial Site, Gaborone
Mailing Address: PO Box 1083, Gaborone
Tel: 322969 *Fax:* 322682
E-mail: firstname@longman.info.bw
Key Personnel
Man Dir: Joe Chalashika
Sales & Marketing Manager: Carlson Moilwa
Publishing Manager: Michelle Aarons
Subjects: English as a Second Language, Fiction, Geography, Geology, History, Language Arts, Linguistics, Literature, Literary Criticism, Essays, Poetry, Travel
ISBN Prefix(es): 99912-66
Parent Company: Pearson Education
Ultimate Parent Company: Pearson Plc, United Kingdom

Morula Press, Business School of Botswana
PO Box 402492, Gaborone
Tel: 353499 *Fax:* 304809
Key Personnel
Contact: Mr A Briscoe
Founded: 1994
Subjects: Business, Law
ISBN Prefix(es): 99912-902

National Library Service
Private Bag 0036, Gaborone
Tel: 352288; 352397 *Fax:* 301149
ISBN Prefix(es): 99912-0

Sygma Publishing
PO Box 753, Gaborone
Tel: 351371 *Fax:* 372531
E-mail: sygma@info.bw
Key Personnel
International Rights: Mary-Anne Lovera

Brazil

General Information

Capital: Brasilia
Language: Portuguese
Religion: Predominantly Roman Catholic
Population: 157 million
Bank Hours: Generally 1000-1500 Monday-Friday
Shop Hours: 0900-1700 Monday-Friday (many open much later); 0900-1400 Saturday
Currency: 100 centavos = 1 real
Export/Import Information: Member of the Latin American Free Trade Association. No tariffs on books & advertising, but luxury bindings & children's picture books are dutied. Import licenses & deposits required; exchange controls operate.
Copyright: UCC, Berne, Buenos Aires, Florence (see Copyright Conventions, pg xi)

A & A & A Edicoes e Promocoes Internacionais Ltda+
Rua Jose Lemos, 82 Bonsucesso, 25725-020 Petropolis RJ
Tel: (024) 221-1467 *Fax:* (024) 221-3669
Key Personnel
President: Gianvittore Calvi
General Dir: Lucilla Martinez
Founded: 1977
Member of National Syndication of Book Publishers.
Subjects: Child Care & Development, Cookery, Education, Library & Information Sciences, Public Administration, Science Fiction, Fantasy
ISBN Prefix(es): 85-7210
Subsidiaries: IPE Amarelo Criacao Multimidia Ltda
Branch Office(s)
Gian Calvi & Asun Balzola & Assn, Calle de Clara del Rey, 39 Ofic 708, 28002 Madrid, Spain
Showroom(s): Livraria Amais, Rua Real Grandeza, 314 Botafogo

A Laser, *imprint of* Centro de Estudos Juridicosdo Para (CEJUP)

Abril SA
Av Otaviano Alves de Lima, 4400, 02909-900 San Paulo SP
Tel: (011) 3990-1322 *Fax:* (011) 3990-2100
Web Site: pp.uol.com/br
Telex: 21-34716
Key Personnel
Contact: Sir Roberto Civita
Founded: 1983
Subjects: Cookery, Science (General)
ISBN Prefix(es): 85-86476
Parent Company: Editora Abril SA Sao Paulo
Associate Companies: Time-Life Inc, Alexandria, VA, United States

Action Editora Ltda+
Avenida das Americas 3333, sala 807, 22631-003 Rio de Janeiro RJ
Tel: (021) 3325-7229 *Fax:* (021) 3325-7229
Web Site: editora.com.br
Key Personnel
Dir: Carlos Lorch

BRAZIL

Business Manager: Raimundo Carlos Bezerra
Founded: 1986
Member of SNEL (Sindicato Nacional de Editores de Livros); specialize in military history, natural history, aviation.
Subjects: Aeronautics, Aviation, History, Military Science, Sports, Athletics
ISBN Prefix(es): 85-85654
Distributed by Howell Press (USA)

Addison Wesley, *imprint of* Pearson Education Do Brasil

Affonso & Reichmann Editores Associados+
Ruado Ouvidor 161/1302, 20040-030 Rio de Janeiro
Tel: (021) 507-1270 *Fax:* (021) 507-1270
Key Personnel
Dir: Renato Reichmann *E-mail:* rrre@lb.com
Contact: Aluisia Affonso *E-mail:* aaff@ar.inf
Subjects: STM
Number of titles published annually: 18 Print

Agalma Psicanalise Editora Ltda+
Rua Agnelo de Brito 187, Centro Odontomedico Henri Dunant, sala 309, 40170-100 Salvador
Tel: (071) 332-8776 *Fax:* (071) 245-7883
E-mail: agalma@agalma.com.br
Web Site: www.agalma.com.br
Key Personnel
Contact: Marcus Do Rio Teixeira
Founded: 1991
Member of National Syndicate of Book Publishers of Brazil (SNEL).
Subjects: Anthropology, Child Care & Development, Nonfiction (General), Philosophy, Psychology, Psychiatry, Romance
ISBN Prefix(es): 85-85458
Distributor for Editions De L'Association Freudienne

AGIR S/A Editora+
Rua dos Invalidos 198, 20231-020 Rio de Janeiro
Mailing Address: Caixa Postal 3291, 2001-970 Rio de Janeiro
Tel: (021) 509-6424; (021) 252-8261 *Fax:* (021) 509-0410
E-mail: info@agireditora.com.br
Web Site: www.visualnet.com.br/cmaya/cm-ft-01.htm *Cable:* AGIRSA
Key Personnel
President: Jose de Paula Machado
Editorial: Regina Lemos
Founded: 1944
Subjects: Architecture & Interior Design, Art, Biography, Communications, Cookery, Drama, Theater, Education, Fiction, History, Literature, Literary Criticism, Essays, Philosophy, Social Sciences, Sociology
ISBN Prefix(es): 85-220; 85-85076
Distributor for Armand Collin; Ed Nathan; Ed Seuil; HarperCollins; Random House
Bookshop(s): Livraria Agir, Rua Mexico, 98-B, 20031-141
Book Club(s): Circulo do Livro

Editora Agora Ltda+
Rua Itapicuru 613 cj 72, 05006-000 Perdizes-Sao Paulo
Tel: (011) 38723322 *Fax:* (011) 38727476
E-mail: agora@editoraagora.com.br
Web Site: www.editoraagora.com.br
Key Personnel
Editor: Edith M Elek
Founded: 1979
Subjects: Astrology, Occult, Health, Nutrition, Psychology, Psychiatry, Self-Help
ISBN Prefix(es): 85-7183

Aide Editora e Comercio de Livros Ltda
Rua Bela, 740, 20930-380 Rio de Janeiro RJ
Tel: (021) 2589-9926 *Fax:* (021) 2589-9926
E-mail: aideeditora@radnet.com.br
Web Site: www.radnet.com.br/aideditora
Key Personnel
President: Ruy de Castro
Editor: Joao Virgilio de Castro *Tel:* (0371) 5724958
Founded: 1976
Member of SNEL.
Subjects: Law
ISBN Prefix(es): 85-321
Total Titles: 5 Print

Livraria Alema+
Rua Dr Amadeu da Luz, 260 Center, 89010-160 Blumenau SC
Tel: (0473) 3264558 *Fax:* (0473) 3263062
Key Personnel
Executive: Juergen Konig
Founded: 1989
ISBN Prefix(es): 85-85415
Subsidiaries: Editora EKO/Disbribuidora Alema

Editora Alfa Omega Ltda+
Rua Lisboa, 489, 05413-000 Sao Paulo SP
Tel: (011) 3062-6400; (011) 3062-6690 *Fax:* (011) 3083-0746
E-mail: alfaomega@alfaomega.com.br
Web Site: www.alfaomega.com.br
Telex: 011 22888 XPSPBR
Key Personnel
Editorial Dir: Fernando Celso De C Mangarielo
Founded: 1973
Subjects: Anthropology, Behavioral Sciences, Biography, Economics, History, Law, Management, Philosophy, Social Sciences, Sociology
ISBN Prefix(es): 85-295
Divisions: Estudio Alfa Omega; Alfa Omega Data; Distribuidora Alfa Omega e Disque Livros

Livraria Francisco Alves Editora SA+
Rua Urguaiana, 94-13 Andar-Centro, 20050-091 Rio de Janeiro
Tel: (021) 221-3198 *Fax:* (021) 242-8215
Founded: 1854
Member of Sindicato Nacional de Editores de Livros.
Subjects: Astrology, Occult, Criminology, Fiction, Literature, Literary Criticism, Essays, Nonfiction (General), Science (General), Science Fiction, Fantasy
ISBN Prefix(es): 85-265
Warehouse: Rua Luis de Camoes 100, Centro rio de Janeiro Janeiro RJ

Antenna Edicoes Tecnicas Ltda+
Ave Marechal Floriano, 143 S/204, 20080-005 Rio de Janeiro RJ
Mailing Address: Caixa Postal 1131, 20001-970 Rio de Janeiro RJ
Tel: (021) 223-2442 *Fax:* (021) 263-8840
E-mail: antenna@unisys.com.br
Key Personnel
Man Dir: Maria Beatriz Affonso Penna
Publicity: Sergio Porto
Founded: 1926
Subjects: Computer Science, Electronics, Electrical Engineering, Microcomputers, Technology
ISBN Prefix(es): 85-7036
Number of titles published annually: 5 Print
Total Titles: 60 Print
Associate Companies: Selecoes Eletronicas Editora Ltda
Bookshop(s): Lojas do Livro Electronico, Ave Mal Floriano 167, 20080-005 Rio de Janeiro RJ
Book Club(s): SNEL-Sind Nac Editors Livros, Ave Rio Branco 37, 20090-003 Rio de Janeiro, RJ *Tel:* (021) 233-6481 *Fax:* (021) 253-8502 *E-mail:* snel@snel.org.br

Editora Antroposofica Ltda+
Rua da Fraternidade, 174, 04738-020 Sao Paulo SP
Tel: (011) 2464550 *Fax:* (011) 2479714
E-mail: editora@antroposofica.com.br
Web Site: www.sab.org.br/edit; www.antroposofica.com.br
Key Personnel
General Manager & International Rights: Jacira S Cardoso *E-mail:* jacira.c@zaz.com.br
Founded: 1981
Member of Brazilian House of Books.
Subjects: Agriculture, Child Care & Development, Cookery, Disability, Special Needs, Economics, Education, Health, Nutrition, Medicine, Nursing, Dentistry, Philosophy, Psychology, Psychiatry, *Also specializes in Therapy & Anthroposophy.*
ISBN Prefix(es): 85-7122
Number of titles published annually: 15 Print
Total Titles: 140 Print
Parent Company: Livraria Antroposofica
Ultimate Parent Company: Sociedade Antroposofica no Brasil

Ao Livro Tecnico Industria e Comercio Ltda+
Rua Sa Freire, 36/40, 20930-430 Rio de Janeiro RJ
Tel: (021) 580-6230; (021) 580-1168 *Fax:* (021) 580-9955
Web Site: www.editoraaolivrotecnico.com.br
Cable: LITECNICO
Key Personnel
Man Dir: Reynaldo Max Paul Bluhm
Editorial, Production, Sales, Rights & Permissions, Publicity: Gisela Bluhm
Founded: 1933
Member of IPA.
Subjects: Education, Language Arts, Linguistics, Sports, Athletics
ISBN Prefix(es): 85-215
Associate Companies: Sociedade Distribuidora de Livros Ltda (Sodilivro)
Subsidiaries: DISAL (Distribuidores Associados de Livros Ltda); SODILIVRO (Sociedade Distribuidora de Livros Ltda)
Warehouse: Rua Sa Freire, 40

Editora Aquariana Ltda+
Rua Lacedemonia, 68, 04634-020 Sao Paulo SP
Tel: (11) 5031 1500 *Fax:* (11) 5031 3462
E-mail: aquariana@ground.com.br
Key Personnel
Executive Director: Jose Carlos Rolo Venancio *E-mail:* jcvenancio@ground.com.br
Founded: 1988
Member of the Brazilian Association of Publishers.
Subjects: Alternative, Environmental Studies, Management, Marketing, Self-Help, Occult, Health & New Science
ISBN Prefix(es): 85-7217
Parent Company: Editora Ground Ltda
Associate Companies: Editora Ground Ltda, R Lacedomonia, 68, Sao Paulo, Contact: Jose Carlos Venancio *Tel:* (011) 5031 1500 *Fax:* (011) 5031 3462 *E-mail:* editora@ground.com.br

M J Bezerra de Araujo Editora Ltda
Rua Haddoc Lobo, 72, Sala 507 e-508, 20260-132 Rio de Janeiro RJ
Tel: (021) 5024435 *Fax:* (021) 5024435
Key Personnel
Dir & President: Maria Jose Bezerra de Araujo
ISBN Prefix(es): 85-85767
Branch Office(s)
Alameda Santos 734, Apt 02, Jardim Paulista, Sao Paulo, SP CEP 01418-100
Warehouse: Rua Haddock Lobo 17B, Estacio, RJ, Bradesco AG 2013-3, Conta 9958-9

PUBLISHERS

Arquivo Nacional
Rua Azeredo Coutinho, 77 3 Andar, 7th floor,
  20230-170 Rio de Janeiro
Tel: (021) 252 2617 *Fax:* (021) 252 9821
E-mail: arqnacdg@rio.com.br
ISBN Prefix(es): 85-7009

Ars Poetica Editora Ltda+
Av Irai, 79, Cj 114-B, 04082-001 Sao Paulo
Tel: (011) 2405598 *Fax:* (011) 5312648
Key Personnel
Contact: Ubiratan Ramos-Mascarenhas
Founded: 1991
Subjects: Anthropology, Archaeology, Biography, Language Arts, Linguistics, Poetry, Psychology, Psychiatry, Religion - Protestant, Sports, Athletics, Theology
ISBN Prefix(es): 85-85470

Artes e Oficios Editora Ltda+
Rua Henrique Dias, 201, 90035-100 Porto Alegre
Tel: (051) 311 0832; (051) 311 5442 *Fax:* (051) 311 0832
E-mail: artesofi@pro.via-rs.com.br
Key Personnel
Contact: Sergio Boeck-Ludtke
Founded: 1991
Subjects: Biography, Fiction, Human Relations, Humor, Journalism, Psychology, Psychiatry, Romance, Travel
ISBN Prefix(es): 85-85418; 85-7421

ARTMED+
Av Jeronimo de Ornellas 670, 90040-340 Porto Alegre RS
Tel: (051) 3303444; (051) 3318244 *Fax:* (051) 3302378
E-mail: artmed@artmed.com.br
Web Site: www.artmed.com.br
Key Personnel
President: Henrique L Kiperman
Vice President: Celso Kiperman
International Rights Manager & Permissions: Angelo I Castrogiovanni *E-mail:* angelo@artmed.com.br
Founded: 1973
Member of Brazilian Book Association & Publishers Club of Southern Rio Grande 1.
Subjects: Architecture & Interior Design, Behavioral Sciences, Biological Sciences, Child Care & Development, Civil Engineering, Computer Science, Economics, Education, Health, Nutrition, Management, Marketing, Medicine, Nursing, Dentistry, Psychology, Psychiatry, Science (General), Sports, Athletics, Technology, Veterinary Science
ISBN Prefix(es): 85-7307
Number of titles published annually: 90 Print; 3 CD-ROM
Total Titles: 893 Print; 11 CD-ROM
Associate Companies: Bookman Companhia Editora Ltda, Patio Revista Pedagogica
Branch Office(s)
Av Reboucas, 1073, 05414-020 Sao Paulo, SP
Bookshop(s): Rua General Vitorino 277, 90020 Porto Alegre RS, Dir: Celso Kiperman
Tel: (051) 32251579

Associacao Arvore da Vida
Rua Tuiuti, 1372, 03081-000 Tatuape-Sao Paulo
Tel: (011) 2185399 *Fax:* (011) 2181401
E-mail: editora@eavida.com.br
Key Personnel
Dir: Ildeu R Dos Santos
Contact: Andre Dong
Founded: 1981
Member of Camara Brasileira de Livros.
Subjects: Biblical Studies
ISBN Prefix(es): 85-7304
Divisions: Jornal Arvore Da Vida
Book Club(s): Sindicato Nacional de Editores (SNEL)

Associacao Brasileira de Liverivos Antiquarios
Rua do Rosario 155, Loja E 1 ll5 Andares, 20041-005 Rio de Janeiro
Tel: (021) 224-8616 *Fax:* (021) 221-4582 *Cable:* EIKOS
Key Personnel
Man Dir: Stefan Geyerhahn; Luiz C Poppi
Founded: 1935
Subjects: Engineering (General), History, Language Arts, Linguistics, Music, Dance, Travel
ISBN Prefix(es): 85-7096

Associacao Palas Athena do Brasil+
Rua Serra de Paracaina, 240, 01522-020 Cambuci-Sao Paulo SP
Tel: (011) 3209-6288 *Fax:* (011) 3277-8137
E-mail: grafica@palasathena.org; editora@palasathena.org
Web Site: www.palasathena.org
Key Personnel
Contact: Basilio Pawlowicz
Founded: 1972
Subjects: Anthropology, Philosophy, Psychology, Psychiatry, Religion - Other
ISBN Prefix(es): 85-7242
Orders to: R Jose Bento 384, 01523-030 Sao Paulo SP

Editora Atheneu Ltda+
Rua Jesuino Pascoal, 30, 01224-050 San Paulo
Tel: (011) 220-9186 *Fax:* (011) 221-3389
E-mail: atheneau@nutecnet.com.br
Web Site: www.atheneu.com.br *Cable:* ZIGADAG
Key Personnel
Man Dir & Editorial Dir: Paulo Rezinski
Sales Dir: Alexandre Massa
Production Dir: Prado Orimar
Founded: 1928
Subjects: Medicine, Nursing, Dentistry, Psychology, Psychiatry
ISBN Prefix(es): 85-7379
Subsidiaries: Editora Atheneu Cultura
Branch Office(s)
Rua Domingos Vieira 319 Conj 1.104, Santa Efigenia, Belo Horizonte 30150-240
E-mail: atheneu@u-net.com.br

Editora Atica SA
Rua Barao de Iguape 110, 01507-900 Sao Paulo SP
Tel: (011) 278 93 22 *Fax:* (011) 277 41 46
Telex: 32969 Edat *Cable:* BOMLIVRO
Key Personnel
Edit Dir: Sr Renato Jose Laporta Filho Pimazzoni *E-mail:* rpimazzoni@atica.com.br
Publicity Dir: Vera Elena Hoexter Esau
Founded: 1965
Subjects: Literature, Literary Criticism, Essays, Regional Interests
ISBN Prefix(es): 85-08
Branch Office(s)
Rua Barao de Uba 173, Praca da Bandeira, 20260 Rio de Janeiro RJ

Editora Atlas SA+
Rue Conselheiro Nebias, 1384, Campos Elisios, 01203-904 Sao Paulo SP
Tel: (011) 221 9144 *Fax:* (011) 220 7830
E-mail: edatlas@editora-atlas.com.br
Web Site: www.edatlas.com.br *Cable:* ATLASEDITA
Key Personnel
Vice President: Luiz Herrmann, Jr
Editorial & Marketing Dir: A B Brandao
Production: S Gerencer
Founded: 1944
Subjects: Accounting, Business, Economics, Finance, Law, Management, Marketing
ISBN Prefix(es): 85-224
Branch Office(s)
Brazilia
Rio de Janeiro
Amazonas
Bahia
Goias
Minas Gerais
Parana
Pernambuco
Santa Catarina
Ceara
Rio Grande do Sul
Bookshop(s): Livraria Atlas Ltda, Rua Pedroso Alvarenga, 1285 - Itaim, 04531-012 Sao Paulo
Tel: (011) 881-8799

BCD Uniao de Editoras SA, see Editora Bertrand Brasil Ltda

Berkeley Brasil Editora Ltda+
AV Raimundo Pereira De Magalhaes, 3305, 3 Andar, 05145-200 Sao Paulo
Tel: (011) 3649-4663 *Fax:* (011) 261-1342
E-mail: berkeley@siciliano.com.br
Web Site: berkeley.com.br
Key Personnel
President: Osvaldo Siciliano, Jr
Executive Vice President: Ricardo Reinprecht
Founded: 1986
Specialize in computer & business books.
Subjects: Business, Computer Science, Microcomputers, Technology
ISBN Prefix(es): 85-7251

Bertrand Brasil, *imprint of* Editora Bertrand Brasil Ltda

Editora Bertrand Brasil Ltda+
Formerly BCD Uniao de Editoras SA
R Argentina, 171, S20 Cristoras, 20921-380 Rio de Janeiro RJ
Tel: (021) 2585 2070 *Fax:* (021) 2585 2087
E-mail: professor@bertrandbrasil.com.br
Web Site: www.bertrandbrasil.com.br
Key Personnel
President: Sergio Abreu Da Cruz Machado *E-mail:* sacm@record.com.br
Rights & Permissions: Rosemary Alves *E-mail:* rosemary@bertrandbrasil.com.br
Founded: 1951 (as Difusao Editorial SA (DIFEL))
Subjects: Anthropology, Astrology, Occult, Behavioral Sciences, Biography, Cookery, Drama, Theater, Education, Fiction, Geography, Geology, Government, Political Science, Literature, Literary Criticism, Essays, Nonfiction (General), Poetry, Religion - Buddhist, Religion - Hindu, Religion - Jewish, Romance, Self-Help, Women's Studies
ISBN Prefix(es): 85-286
Number of titles published annually: 80 Print
Total Titles: 1,000 Print
Parent Company: Distribuidora Record De Serv IMP SA
Imprints: Bertrand Brasil; Difel
Branch Office(s)
Sao Paulo, R. do Paraiso 139, 7º audar, CEP 04103-000 San Paulo *Tel:* (011) 3171-1540 *Fax:* (011) 285-0251

Editora Betania S/C+
Rua Padre Pinto, 2435 Venda Nova, 31510-000 Belo Horizonte
Tel: (031) 4511122 *Fax:* (031) 4476088
E-mail: betania@prover.com.br
Key Personnel
Dir: Kleber Castro de Faria, Sr
Founded: 1967
Subjects: Religion - Other
Imprints: Temos Grafica Propria

Bloch Editores SA
22210-010 Rio de Janeiro

Tel: (021) 205-8682 *Fax:* (021) 205-8682
E-mail: blocheditores@ieq.com.br
Web Site: www.blocheditores.hpg.ig.com.br
Key Personnel
Contact: Anna Maria de O. Renhack
Publicity: Expedito Jose Chaves Grossi
ISBN Prefix(es): 85-258

Editora Edgard Blucher Ltda
Rua Pedroso Alvarenga 1245, 2 Andar, Conj 22, 04531-012 Sao Paulo
Tel: (011) 3078-5366 *Fax:* (011) 3079-2707
E-mail: eblucher@uol.com.br *Cable:* BLUCHERLIVRO
Key Personnel
Man Dir: Edgard Blucher
Founded: 1966
Subjects: Biological Sciences, Earth Sciences, Electronics, Electrical Engineering, Engineering (General), Management, Mathematics, Physics, Science (General), Technology
ISBN Prefix(es): 85-212

Editora do Brasil SA+
Rua Conselheiro Nebias, 887, 01203-001 Sao Paulo
Tel: (011) 222 0211 *Fax:* (011) 222 5583 *Cable:* EDITABRAS
Key Personnel
President: Dr Carlos Costa
Superintendent: Luis Roberto Netto
Founded: 1943
Subjects: Education, History, Psychology, Psychiatry, Social Sciences, Sociology
ISBN Prefix(es): 85-10
Branch Office(s)
Rua do Resende 89, 20231 Rio de Janeiro RJ
Tel: (021) 224-8123

Instituto Brasileiro de Edicoes Pedagogicas (IBEP)
Rua Joli 294, 03016-020 Sao Paulo
Mailing Address: Caixa Postal 285, 03016-020 Sao Paulo
Tel: (011) 6099-7799 *Fax:* (011) 6694-5338
Web Site: www.ibep-nacional.com.br
Key Personnel
Contact: Jorge Junes
ISBN Prefix(es): 85-342
Branch Office(s)
Ave Lobo Junior 1011, Penha, 21020 Rio de Janeiro RJ

Instituto Brasileiro de Informacao em Ciencia e Tecnologia
SAB Quadra 5 Lote 6 Bloco H, 70070-914 Brasilia, DF
Tel: (061) 217-6360; (061) 217-6350 *Fax:* (061) 226-2677
E-mail: webmaster@ibick.br
Web Site: www.ibict.br
Telex: (061) 2481
ISBN Prefix(es): 85-7013

Editora Brasiliense SA+
Rua Airi, 22, Tatuape, 03310-010 Sao Paulo
Tel: (011) 6671-2016 *Fax:* (011) 6671-5946
E-mail: brasilienseedit@uol.com.br
Web Site: www.editorabrasiliense.com.br
Cable: EDIBRASA
Key Personnel
Man Dir & Editor: Yolanda Prado
Sales: C C Guerrato
Production: Antonio Orzari
Founded: 1943
Seven bookshops in Sao Paulo.
Subjects: Education, Literature, Literary Criticism, Essays, Social Sciences, Sociology
ISBN Prefix(es): 85-11; 85-206
Bookshop(s): Livraria Brasiliense Editora SA, Sao Paulo

Brasilivros Editora e Distribuidora Ltda
Rua Conselheiro Ramalho 701, Matriz Loja 22, 01325-001 Sao Paolo
Tel: (011) 3284-8155 *Fax:* (011) 2850305; (011) 2856406
Key Personnel
Executive: Juarez Cordeiro de Oliveira

Brinque Book Editora de Livros Ltda+
Av Dr Guilherme Dumot Villares, 2352 1 andar, 05640-004 Sao Paulo SP
Tel: (011) 37428142 *Fax:* (011) 37432235
E-mail: brinquebook@infantil.net
Key Personnel
President: Suzana Taves de Sanson
Founded: 1990
Specialize in Children's Literature; Member of SNEL, FNLIJ & CBL.
Subjects: Cookery, Music, Dance
ISBN Prefix(es): 85-7412

Cadence Publicacoes Internacionais Ltda+
Rua Visconde Inhauma 134, Sala 1532, 20091-000 Rio de Janeiro RJ
Tel: (021) 2637885 *Fax:* (021) 2830812
E-mail: cadence@mtecnet.com.br
Key Personnel
Associate Manager: Reinaldo C Palmeira
Executive Secretary: Geni Celia Miranda
Founded: 1980
Subjects: Science (General), Technology
Parent Company: Cadence

Callis Editora Ltda+
Rua Afonso Bras 203, 04511-010 Sao Paulo SP
Tel: (011) 3842-2066 *Fax:* (011) 3849-5882
E-mail: callis@sanet.com.br
Web Site: www.callis.com.br
Key Personnel
President: Miriam Gabbai
Founded: 1987
Subjects: Art, Computer Science, Cookery, Microcomputers, Military Science, Nonfiction (General)
ISBN Prefix(es): 85-85642; 85-7416

Camara Dos Deputados Coordenacao De Publicacoes (Chamber of Deputies, Coordination of Publications)
Division of Chamber of Deputies
Praca dos Tres Poderes, Brasilia 70160-900
Tel: (061) 318-5151 *Fax:* (061) 318-2190
E-mail: publicacoes.cedi@camara.gov.br
Web Site: www.camara.gov.br
Key Personnel
Coordination of Publications Dir: Nelda Raulino
Librarian: Andrea Perna *Tel:* (061) 318-6864
 E-mail: andrea.perna@camara.gov.br
Founded: 1971
Produces & distributes Chamber of Deputies printed publications. Created primarily to satisfy the printing needs of Chamber of Deputies, today has contributed to disseminate Brazilian legislative information around the country & the world.
Subjects: Government, Political Science, Public Administration
ISBN Prefix(es): 85-7365
Number of titles published annually: 60 Print
Total Titles: 781 Print

Editora Caminho Suave Ltda
rua Fagundes 157, 01508-030 Sao Paulo SP
Tel: (011) 2783377 *Fax:* (011) 2783537
Key Personnel
Contact: Branca Alves de Lima
ISBN Prefix(es): 85-473

Instituto Campineiro de Ensino Agricola Ltda
Rua Romoaldo Andreazzi, 425, 13036-100 Campinas SP

Tel: (019) 3272-2280; (019) 3272-2677
 Fax: (019) 3272-6004
E-mail: icea@icea.com.br
Web Site: www.icea.com.br
Key Personnel
Contact: Gervasio de Souza Cavalcanti
Founded: 1955
Subjects: Agriculture
ISBN Prefix(es): 85-7121

Editora Campus Ltda+
Rua Sete de Setembro, 111, 16 Andar, 20050-002 Centro Rio de Janeiro RJ
Tel: (021) 509 5340 *Fax:* (021) 507 1991
E-mail: info@campus.com.br
Web Site: www.campus.com.br
Key Personnel
Publishing Manager: Ricardo Redisch
 E-mail: ricardo@campus.com.br
Production Dir: Daniel Sant'Anna
Rights & Permissions: Emilia Fernandez
Founded: 1976
Subjects: Art, Civil Engineering, Communications, Computer Science, Economics, Electronics, Electrical Engineering, Engineering (General), Environmental Studies, Government, Political Science, Health, Nutrition, History, Microcomputers, Nonfiction (General), Physics, Psychology, Psychiatry, Science (General), Social Sciences, Sociology, Travel
ISBN Prefix(es): 85-7001; 85-352
Number of titles published annually: 190 Print
Parent Company: Elsevier Science
Ultimate Parent Company: Reed Elsevier plc
Branch Office(s)
Rua da Consolacao 348/10, Andar-Conj 102, Sao Paulo SP 01302-000 *Fax:* (011) 259 9944

Alzira Chagas Carpigiani+
Av Gethsemani, 85, 05625-090 Sao Paulo
Mailing Address: Caixa Postal 3702, Cep 01060-970, Sao Paulo SP
Tel: (011) 849-0189 *Fax:* (011) 227-3384
E-mail: kerredit@uol.com.br
Key Personnel
Executive: Alzira Chagas Carpigiani
Founded: 1997
Subjects: Literature, Literary Criticism, Essays, Religion - Protestant, Romance
Parent Company: Sao Paulo, SP, Cep 01028-000
Subsidiaries: Kerr Editorial Ltda
Divisions: Rua Maua 960-Casa 10

Centro de Estudos Juridicosdo Para (CEJUP)+
Travessa Rui Barbosa 726, 66053-260 Belem PA
Tel: (091) 225-0355 *Fax:* (091) 241-3184
Key Personnel
Contact: Gengis Freire de Souza
Founded: 1979
Member of Associacao Nacional de Livrarias (ANL) & Sindicato Nacional de Livrarias (SNL).
Subjects: Biological Sciences, Criminology, Drama, Theater, Education, Fiction, Law, Science Fiction, Fantasy, Social Sciences, Sociology
ISBN Prefix(es): 85-338
Imprints: Off Set; A Laser
Branch Office(s)
Av Rio Branco, 37 Sala 601, CEP 20040-004 Rio de Janeiro, RJ
Bookshop(s): Assis de Vasconcelos, N 498, CEP 66017-070 Belem PA

Centro Editor de Psicologia Aplicada Ltda, see CEPA - Centro Editor de Psicologia Aplicada Ltda

CEPA - Centro Editor de Psicologia Aplicada Ltda
Rua Senador Dantas 118, GR 910/920, 20031-201 Rio de Janeiro RJ
Tel: (021) 2220-6545 *Fax:* (021) 2510-3468
Web Site: www.psicocepa.com.br *Cable:* EDICEPA
Key Personnel
Man Dir: Antonio Rodrigues, Jr
Founded: 1952
Subjects: Psychology, Psychiatry
ISBN Prefix(es): 85-7043

Codice Comercio Distriduicao e Casa Editorial Ltda+
Rua Simoes Pinto, 120, 04356-100 Sao Paulo
Tel: (011) 2408033
E-mail: codice@codicenet.com.br
Key Personnel
Contact: Eduardo Augusto-Serverino
Founded: 1991

Comissao Nacional de Energia Nuclear
Rua General Severiano, 90 Terreo, Botafogo, 22294-900 Rio de Janeiro
Tel: (021) 2546 2481 *Fax:* (021) 2546 2447
E-mail: macedo@cnen.gov.br
Web Site: www.cnen.gov.br
Founded: 1970
Acts as the Brazilian national center for the International Nuclear Information System (INIS) & for the Energy Technology Data Exchange (ETDE).
Subjects: Energy, Engineering (General), Environmental Studies, Nuclear Energy
ISBN Prefix(es): 85-334

Companhia das Letras, see Editora Companhia das Letras/Editora Schwarcz Ltda

Companhia Editora Naciona, see Cia Editora Nacional

Companhia Melhoramentos de Sao Paulo, see Editora Melhoramentos Ltda

Concordia Editora Ltda
Av Sao Pedro 633, Bairro Sao Geraldo, 90230-120 Porto Alegre RS
Tel: (051) 342 2699 *Fax:* (051) 343 5254
E-mail: pedido@editoraconcordia.com.br; ediluter@zaz.com.br
Web Site: www.editoraconcordia.com.br
Cable: CONCORDIA
Key Personnel
Man Dir: Martinho Krebs
Sales & Publicity: Walter Eidam
Founded: 1923
Subjects: Music, Dance, Religion - Other, Theology
Parent Company: Igreja Evangelica Luterana do Brasil
Branch Office(s)
Ave Getulio Vargas 4388, Sao Leopoldo RS
Bookshop(s): Livraria Concordia, Av Sao Pedro 639, 90000 Porto Alegre RS

Conquista, Empresa de Publicacoes Ltda
Av 28 de Setembro, 174, Vila Isabel, 20551-031 Rio de Janeiro RJ
Tel: (021) 569-6752
Key Personnel
Dir: Nilde Hersen Aragao da Fonseca; Leonardo Hersen da Costa
Sales Dir: Antonio da Silva Aragao da Fonseca
Founded: 1951
Subjects: Art, Cookery, Literature, Literary Criticism, Essays
ISBN Prefix(es): 85-7066
Bookshop(s): Livraria Conquista, Ave 28 de Setembro 174, Vila Isabel,, 20551-031 Rio de Janeiro RJ

Consultor Assessoria de Planejamento Ltda
General Gurjao, 479, 20931-040 Rio De Janeiro RJ
Tel: (021) 5893030 *Fax:* (021) 580-2163
Key Personnel
Contact: Sra Andreia Niskier Chelman; Selmado Amaral
Founded: 1988
Subjects: Education, Literature, Literary Criticism, Essays
ISBN Prefix(es): 85-85206; 85-7434

Editora Contexto (Editora Pinsky Ltda)+
Rua Acopiara 199, 05083-110 Sao Paulo SP
Tel: (011) 3832-5838 *Fax:* (011) 3832-1043
E-mail: contexto@editoracontexto.com.br
Web Site: www.editoracontexto.com.br
Key Personnel
Executive: Jaime Pinsky *E-mail:* pinsky@editoracontexto.com.br
Founded: 1987
Member of Camara Brasileina do Livro.
Subjects: Economics, Education, Health, Nutrition, History
ISBN Prefix(es): 85-7244; 85-85134
Number of titles published annually: 30 Print
Total Titles: 20 Print

Editora Crescer Ltda+
Rua Do Ouro 104, Conj 501-Serra, 30220-000 Belo Horizonte MG
Tel: (031) 221-9235 *Fax:* (031) 221-7482
E-mail: crescer@crescer.com.br
Web Site: www.crescer.com.br
Key Personnel
Executive: Clara Feldman
Founded: 1983
Subjects: Human Relations, Self-Help

Editora Cultura Medica Ltda+
Rua Sao Francisco Xavier 111, 20550-010 Rio de Janeiro RJ
Tel: (021) 2567-3888 *Fax:* (021) 2569-5443
E-mail: cultmed@terra.com.br
Web Site: www.culturamedica.com.br
Key Personnel
Man Dir: Ezequiel Feldman
Founded: 1966
Subjects: Medicine, Nursing, Dentistry, Biomedicine
ISBN Prefix(es): 85-7006
Orders to: Rua Lucio de Mendonca, 37, Apt 401, Cep 20, 470-040 Rio de Janeiro

Difel, *imprint of* Editora Bertrand Brasil Ltda

Editorial Dimensao Ltda+
Rua Santo Cristo, 201, 20220-301 Rio de Janeiro MG
Tel: (021) 2263-3077 *Fax:* (021) 2263-3123
E-mail: memoria@ig.com.br
Key Personnel
Contact: Gilberto Gusmao Andrade
Founded: 1985
Member of the Brazilian House of Books.
Subjects: Law, Psychology, Psychiatry
ISBN Prefix(es): 85-86163

Editora e Distribuidora Irradiacao Cultural Ltda
Rua Visconde de Santa Isabel 46-Fundos, 20560-120 Rio de Janeiro RJ
Tel: (021) 5773522 *Fax:* (021) 5771249
Key Personnel
Dir, President: Stelio De Andrade Soares
Founded: 1980
ISBN Prefix(es): 85-85677

Livraria Duas Cidades Ltda
Rua Bento de Freitas 158, 01220-000 Sao Paulo
Tel: (011) 220-5134 *Fax:* (011) 220-5813
Key Personnel
Man Dir: Jose Petronillo de Santa Cruz
Sales Dir: Mitsuro Nagata
Publicity Dir: Mara Valles
Founded: 1956
Subjects: Literature, Literary Criticism, Essays, Philosophy, Psychology, Psychiatry, Religion - Other, Social Sciences, Sociology
ISBN Prefix(es): 85-235
Branch Office(s)
Ave Rio Branco 9, Sala 116, Centro, 20090 Rio de Janeiro RJ

Dumara Distribuidora de Publicacoes Ltda+
Rua Barata Ribeiro 17/202, 22011-000 Rio de Janeiro RJ
Tel: (021) 5420248 *Fax:* (021) 2750294
Key Personnel
Contact: Alberto Jak Schprejer; Ari Roitman
Founded: 1989
Subjects: Anthropology, Drama, Theater, Fiction, Social Sciences, Sociology
ISBN Prefix(es): 85-7316

E P U Editora Pedagogica e Universitaria Ltd
Rua Joaquim Floriano, 72 6 andar Conjuntos 65/68, 04534-000 Sao Paulo
Tel: (011) 3168-6077 *Fax:* (011) 3078-5803
E-mail: vendas@epu.com.br
Web Site: www.epu.com.br
Key Personnel
Executive: Wolfgang Knapp *E-mail:* knapp@epu.com.br
Founded: 1952
Subjects: Education, Medicine, Nursing, Dentistry, Philosophy, Psychology, Psychiatry
ISBN Prefix(es): 85-12

EBAL, see Editora Brasil-America (EBAL) SA

Edicon Editora e Consultorial Ltda
Rua Herculano de Freitas, 181, Cerqueira Cesar, 01308-020 Sao Paulo SP
Tel: (011) 3255-1002 *Fax:* (011) 2559828
E-mail: edicon@edicon.com.br
Web Site: www.edicon.com.br
Key Personnel
Executive: Valentina Ljubschenko
Founded: 1981
Subjects: Antiques, Art, Astrology, Occult, Drama, Theater, Earth Sciences, Education, Gay & Lesbian, Mathematics, Philosophy, Physics, Poetry, Romance, Science Fiction, Fantasy
ISBN Prefix(es): 85-290

Ediouro Publicacoes, SA+
Rua Nova Jerusalem, 345, 21042-230 Rio de Janeiro RJ
Tel: (021) 5606122 *Fax:* (011) 55893300
E-mail: ediourolivrosp@openlink.com.br; livros@ediouro.com.br
Web Site: www.ediouro.com.br
Key Personnel
President: Jorge Carneiro
Editor: Paul Christoph, Jr
Subjects: Animals, Pets, Biography, How-to, Journalism, Literature, Literary Criticism, Essays, Mysteries, Science Fiction, Fantasy
ISBN Prefix(es): 85-00

Edipro-Edicoes Profissionais Ltda+
Rua 1 de Agosto, 2-51, 17010-011 Bauru
Tel: (014) 232-3375 *Fax:* (014) 232-4684
Key Personnel
Contact: Jair Lot-Viera
Subjects: Law
ISBN Prefix(es): 85-7283

BRAZIL

Editora Artes Medicas Ltda+
R Dr Cesario Motta Jr, 63, Sao Paulo SP 01221-020
Tel: (011) 221-9033 *Fax:* (011) 223-6635
E-mail: artesmedicas@artesmedicas.com.br
Web Site: www.artesmedicas.com.br *Cable:* LEAM
Key Personnel
Man Dir: Henrique Hecht
Editorial, Production: M Hecht
Sales: C dos Santos
Publicity: J Hecht
Founded: 1964
Subjects: Medicine, Nursing, Dentistry
ISBN Prefix(es): 85-7404

Editora Brasil-America (EBAL) SA+
Rua General Almerio de Moura 302/320, 20921-060 Rio de Janeiro RJ
Tel: (021) 5800303 *Fax:* (021) 5801637
Key Personnel
Man Dir: Luba Aizen
Editorial: Naumim Aizen
Dir: Paulo Adolfo Aizen
Production: Fernando Albagli
Founded: 1945
Subjects: Film, Video, Children & Young People's Books
ISBN Prefix(es): 85-272

Editora Cidade Nova Socieda de Movimentodos Focolari+
Rua Jose Ernesto Tozzi, 198, 06730-000 Vargen Grande Paulista SP
Tel: (011) 7960 2252 *Fax:* (011) 7960 2252
E-mail: editoria@cidadenova.org.br
Web Site: www.cidadenova.org.br
Key Personnel
Man Dir: Olavo de Freitas
Editor & Publicity: Klaus Brueschke
Superintendent Dir: Ekkehard Andreas Schneider
Founded: 1960
Subjects: Biblical Studies, Religion - Catholic, Social Sciences, Sociology, Theology
ISBN Prefix(es): 85-7112
Parent Company: Citta Nuova Editrice, Italy
Branch Office(s)
Av Serzedelo Correa 89, Sala 2, 66025-240 Belem PA
Av Do Contorno, 2905, Loja 1007, 30110-080 Belo Horizonte MG
Rua Arthus da Silva Bernardes, 769, Loja 34, 80320-300 Curitiba PR
Av Assis Brasil, 115, Sala 308, 50020-036 Recife PE
City New Press, 206 Skillman Ave, Brooklyn, NY 11211, United States
Living City, PO Box 837, New York, NY, United States
Showroom(s): Av Arthur da Silva Bernardes 769, Loja 34, 80320-300 Curitiba PR; Av Assis Brasil, 115, Sala 308, 50010-036 Recife PE; Rua Said Aiach, 131, 04008-020 523 Paulo SP

Editora Companhia das Letras/Editora Schwarcz Ltda+
Formerly Editora Schwarcz Ltda/Companhia das Letras
Rua Bandeira Paulista, 702, cj 32, 04532-002 Sao Paulo SP
Tel: (011) 3846-0801 *Fax:* (011) 3846-0814
E-mail: editora@companhiadasletras.com.br
Web Site: www.companhiadasletras.com.br
Key Personnel
Editor: Luiz Schwarcz
Foreign Rights Manager: Ruth Lanna
 E-mail: ruth.lanna@companhiadasletras.com.br
Foreign Rights Assistant: Ana Paula Hisayama *E-mail:* ana.paula.hisayama@companhiadasletras.com.br
Founded: 1986

Subjects: Anthropology, Biblical Studies, Biography, Cookery, Fiction, History, Humor, Literature, Literary Criticism, Essays, Philosophy, Photography, Poetry
ISBN Prefix(es): 85-7164; 85-85095; 85-85466
Number of titles published annually: 150 Print
Online services available through World Wide Web.
Distributed by Jorge Zahar (Rio de Janeiro)
Distributor for Jorge Zahar (Sao Paulo)
Foreign Rights: Carmen Balcells for Rubem Fonseca (Europe); Melanie Jackson for Rubem Fonseca & Patricia Melo (US); Ray-Guede Mertin (Europe); Anne Marie Vallat for Milton Hatoum (Spain)

Editora Elevacao+
Affiliate of Brazilian Book Chamber
Rua Doraci 2A, Bom Retiro, 01134-050 Sao Paulo SP
Tel: (011) 3225-4800; (011) 3225-4780; (011) 3225-4778 *Fax:* (011) 220-5803
E-mail: info@elevacao.com.br
Web Site: www.elevacao.com.br
Key Personnel
Contact: Marcus Alexandre Pineze
 E-mail: mpineze@uol.com.br
Founded: 1998
Subjects: Biblical Studies, Biography, Business, Communications, Education, Health, Nutrition, Human Relations, Parapsychology, Philosophy, Poetry, Religion - Other, Romance, Self-Help, Sports, Athletics, Theology
Number of titles published annually: 84 Print; 2 Audio
Total Titles: 35 Print; 2 Audio
Distributed by Distribooks Inc

Companhia Editora Forense+
Av Erasmo Braga, 299-2, 20020-000 Rio de Janeiro RJ
Tel: (021) 2533-5537 *Fax:* (021) 2533-4752
E-mail: forense@forense.com.br; gryphus@gryphus.com.br
Web Site: www.forense.com.br; www.gryphus.com.br
Key Personnel
President: Regina Bilac Pinto
Vice President: Francisco Bilac Pinto
Founded: 1904
Subjects: Biography, Cookery, Education, History, Law, Music, Dance, Nonfiction (General), Philosophy, Psychology, Psychiatry, Religion - Buddhist, Romance, Self-Help, Sports, Athletics, Travel, Women's Studies
ISBN Prefix(es): 85-309
Number of titles published annually: 360 Print
Imprints: Gryphus Editora (Book Editor)
Subsidiaries: Companhia Forense de Artes Graficas (Printing Plant)
Bookshop(s): Livraria Forense, Av Erasmo Braga, 227 loja, Rio de Janeiro, Contact: Guilherme Zingoni *Tel:* (021) 2533-5537 *Fax:* (021) 253-4931 *E-mail:* guilherme@forense.com.br
Orders to: Av Erasmo Braga, 299 2° andar, Rio de Janeiro 20020-000, Contact: Guilherme Zingoni *Tel:* (021) 2533-5537 *Fax:* (021) 2533-4931 *E-mail:* guilherme@forense.com.br

Editora Koinonia Ltda, see Koinonia Comunidade Edicoes Ltda (Editora Koinonia Ltda)

Cia Editora Nacional
Rua Joli 294, 03016-020 Sao Paulo SP
Tel: (011) 2912355 *Fax:* (011) 2918614
Cable: EDITORA
Key Personnel
Man Dir, Rights & Permissions: Jorge Antonio Miguel Yunes
Editorial: Paulo Marti
Founded: 1925

Subjects: Business, Education, Fiction, History, Philosophy, Psychology, Psychiatry, Science (General), Social Sciences, Sociology, Technology
ISBN Prefix(es): 85-04
Branch Office(s)
Aracatuba
Bauru
Belem
Belo Horizonte
Edificio Venancio VI - DS bloco 0 - lojas 13 e 17, Brasilia
Campo Grande
Caruaru
Cuiaba
Curitiba
Fortaleza
Goiania
Manaus
Natal
Porto Alegre
Presidente Prudente
Recife
Ribeirao Preto
Rio de Janeiro, Ave Lobo Junior 1011, Bairro Penha, Rio de Janeiro
Sa Luis
Salvador
Sao Jose do Rio Preto
Teresina
Vila Velho

Editora Schwarcz Ltda/Companhia das Letras, see Editora Companhia das Letras/Editora Schwarcz Ltda

Editora 34, see 34 Literatura S/C Ltda

EDUC - Editora da PUC-SP+
Rua Ministro Godoi, 1213, 05015-001 Sao Paulo SP
Tel: (011) 38733359 *Fax:* (011) 38733359
E-mail: educsp@puc001.pucsp.ansp.br
Key Personnel
Dir: Maria do Carmo Guedes
Vice Dir: Maria Eliza Mazzilli Pereira
Founded: 1984
Member of C B L, ABEU, ABEC.
Subjects: Anthropology, Biological Sciences, Communications, Disability, Special Needs, Economics, Education, English as a Second Language, Geography, Geology, Government, Political Science, History, Humor, Language Arts, Linguistics, Law, Literature, Literary Criticism, Essays, Mathematics, Medicine, Nursing, Dentistry, Music, Dance, Philosophy, Psychology, Psychiatry, Social Sciences, Sociology, Theology
ISBN Prefix(es): 85-283
Total Titles: 230 Print; 1 Audio
Online services available through World Wide Web.
Parent Company: Pontificia Universidade Catolica de Sao Paulo
Ultimate Parent Company: Funda cao Cultural Sao Paulo
Bookshop(s): Espaco EDUC, Rua Monte Alegre, 984 *Tel:* (011) 36708297 *Fax:* (011) 38733359
Orders to: Livraria Cultura, Avenida Paulista, 2073, Conj Nacional Cerqueira Cesar, Sao Paulo SP 01310-300, Contact: Ana Regina *Tel:* (011) 2854033 *Fax:* (011) 2854457 *E-mail:* livro@livcultura.com.br

EDUSC - Editora da Universidade do Sagrado Coracao (Sacred Heart University Press)+
Rua Irma Arminda 10-50, 17011-160 Bauru SP
Tel: (014) 235 7111 *Fax:* (014) 235 7219
E-mail: edusc@usc.br
Web Site: www.usc.br/edusc
Key Personnel
President: Sr Jacinta Turolo Garcia

Publisher: Dr Luiz Eugenio Vescio
 E-mail: lpelegrin@usc.br
Founded: 1996
Subjects: Biological Sciences, Child Care & Development, Education, Health, Nutrition, History, Journalism, Law, Literature, Literary Criticism, Essays, Philosophy, Psychology, Psychiatry, Religion - Catholic, Science (General), Social Sciences, Sociology, Brazilian originals
ISBN Prefix(es): 85-7460
Number of titles published annually: 80 Print

EFE Tres D-Pub Juridicas Ltda
Rua Torres Galvao, 35, 1 andar, 59032-160 Natal RN
Tel: (084) 2233394 *Fax:* (084) 2232263
E-mail: f3dsat@truenetrn.com.br
Key Personnel
Contact: Manoel Digesio de Costa

Selecoes Eletronicas Editora Ltda+
Ladeira Do Faria 23-2 andar pt, 20221-380 Rio de Janeiro RJ
Tel: (021) 2539268 *Fax:* (021) 2638840
Key Personnel
Man Dir: Maria B A Penna
Editorial: Gilberto A Penna Jr
Publicity: Helio N Santos
Founded: 1960
Subjects: Computer Science, Electronics, Electrical Engineering, Microcomputers, Technology
ISBN Prefix(es): 85-7037
Associate Companies: Antenna Edicoes Tecnicas Ltda

Emporio de Promocao Artistica Cultural e Editora Ltda+
Rua Ceara 184, 01243-010 Sao Paulo SP
Tel: (011) 8262992 *Fax:* (011) 661135
Key Personnel
Contact: Luiz Bueno D'Horta
Founded: 1989
Member of C B L.
ISBN Prefix(es): 85-85431

Empresa Brasileira de Pesquisa Agropecaria+
Park Station Biologica-PqEB S/N, 70770-901 Brasilia DF
Tel: (061) 448-4433 *Fax:* (061) 347-1041
E-mail: web@spi.embrapa.br
Web Site: www.embrapa.br
Subjects: Agriculture, Biological Sciences, Earth Sciences, Economics, Journalism, Social Sciences, Sociology, Technology, Veterinary Science
ISBN Prefix(es): 85-7383

Escrituras Editora e Distribuidora de Livros Ltda+
Rua Maestro Callia, 123, Vila Mariana, 04012-100 Sao Paulo/SP
Tel: (011) 5082-4190 *Fax:* (011) 5082-4190
E-mail: vendas@escrituras.com.br
Web Site: www.escrituras.com.br
Key Personnel
Executive: Raimundo Nonato Rocha Gadelha

Editora Expressao e Cultura Exped Ltda
Est dos Bandeirantes, 1700, 22710-113 Rio de Janeiro RJ
Tel: (021) 2444 0650 *Fax:* (021) 2444 0651
Telex: 33280
Key Personnel
Dir & Editor: Ferdinando Bastos de Souza
Publisher: Gilberto Huber
Editorial Manager: Paulo Schvinger
Founded: 1967
Subjects: Education, Literature, Literary Criticism, Essays
ISBN Prefix(es): 85-208
Parent Company: Grupo Gilberto Huber

Associate Companies: Ebid-Editora Paginas Amarelas SA
Orders to: CP 20030, Rio de Janeiro RJ

FAE, see Fundacao de Assistencia ao Estudante

Editora FCO Ltda+
Av do Conturno, 2205, 30110-070 Belo Horizonte MG
Tel: (031) 2131288 *Fax:* (031) 2243825
E-mail: ottomi@fco.org.br
Key Personnel
Contact: Sr Lucio Fernando Borges
Founded: 1994
Subjects: Civil Engineering, Education, Engineering (General), Management

FEI, *imprint of* Editora Gaia Ltda

Livraria Martins Fontes Editora Ltda+
Rua Conselheiro Ramalho 330, 01325-000 Sao Paulo SP
Tel: (011) 3241 3677 *Fax:* (0800) 11 3619
E-mail: info@martinsfontes.com.br
Web Site: www.martinsfontes.com.br *Cable:* CABOGRAMA
Key Personnel
Contact: Waldir Martins Fontes
Founded: 1960
Subjects: Art, Education, English as a Second Language, History, Law, Nonfiction (General), Philosophy, Psychology, Psychiatry, Social Sciences, Sociology
ISBN Prefix(es): 85-336

Editora Forense+
Av Erasmo Braga, 227 B e 299, 20020-000 Rio de Janeiro RJ
Tel: (021) 2533-5537 *Fax:* (021) 5334931
E-mail: forense@forense.com.br
Web Site: www.forense.com
Key Personnel
Manager, Gryphus: Gisela Zingoni
 E-mail: gisela@gryphus.com.br
Contact: Regina Bilac Pinto
Founded: 1904
Subjects: Biography, Criminology, Health, Nutrition, Law, Music, Dance, Psychology, Psychiatry, Social Sciences, Sociology, Travel
ISBN Prefix(es): 85-309
Subsidiaries: Livraria Forense, Sao Paulo; Livraria Forense, Belo Horizonte
Divisions: Editora Gryphus
Branch Office(s)
Belo Horizonte
Sao Paulo
Bookshop(s): Rua Senador Feijo, 137 Centro, 01006-001 Sao Paulo; Rua Guajajaras, 1.934, Barro Preto 30180-101

Forense Universitaria Editora+
Rua do Rosario, 100, 20041-002 Rio de Janeiro RJ
Tel: (011) 580-0776 *Fax:* (011) 589-2084
E-mail: foruniv@unisys.com.br
Key Personnel
Dir: Regina Bilac Pinto
Founded: 1973
Member of National Book Publishers of Rio de Janeiro, Brasil.
Subjects: Economics, Government, Political Science, Language Arts, Linguistics, Law, Philosophy, Psychology, Psychiatry, Social Sciences, Sociology
ISBN Prefix(es): 85-218
Bookshop(s): Livraria Forense Universitaria Lg Sao Francisco, Lg. Sao Francisco, 20, 01005-010 Sao Paulo SP, Paulo Abrantes *Tel:* (011) 31040396
Warehouse: Rua Sa Freire, 25, 20930-430 Rio De Janeiro RJ

Scott Foresman, *imprint of* Pearson Education Do Brasil

Formato Editorial ltda+
Rua Alipio de Melo 151, Bairro Jardim Montanhes, 30750 Belo Horizonte-MG
Tel: (031) 4211588 *Fax:* (031) 4211803
E-mail: editorial@formatoeditoral.com.br
Web Site: www.formatoeditorial.com.br
Key Personnel
Dir: Jose de Alencar Mayrink *E-mail:* alencar@formatoeditorial.com.br
Editor: Sonia Marta Junqueira *Tel:* (031) 4218544
 E-mail: soniajunqueira@formatoeditorial.com.br
Dir: Claudia Pereira-Rezende *Tel:* (031) 4211777
 E-mail: claudia@graficaformato.com.br
Founded: 1986
Member of Camara Brasileira do Livro & Fundacao Nacional do Livro Infantil e Juvenil.
Subjects: Education, Literature, Literary Criticism, Essays
ISBN Prefix(es): 85-7208
Number of titles published annually: 35 Print
Total Titles: 268 Print

Livraria Freitas Bastos Editora SA+
Avenida Londre, 381 Bonsucesso, 21041-030 Rio de Janeiro RJ
Tel: (021) 2573-8949 *Fax:* (021) 2573-8949
E-mail: fbastos@netfly.com.br; freitasbastos@freitasbastos.com.br *Cable:* ETIEL
Key Personnel
President: Isaac Delgado Abulafia *E-mail:* isaac@netfly.com.br
Founded: 1917
Member of the Association of Brazilian Publishers.
Subjects: Accounting, Law
ISBN Prefix(es): 85-353

Editora FTD SA
Rua Manoel Dutra, 225, Bairro Bela Vista, 01328-010 Sao Paulo SP
Tel: (011) 3284-8500 *Fax:* (011) 3283-5011
E-mail: ftd@dial&ta.com.br
Web Site: www.ftd.com.br
Key Personnel
Man Dir: Joao Tissi
Contact: Romeu Rossi
Founded: 1897
ISBN Prefix(es): 85-322
Branch Office(s)
Rua Agenor Meira 4/67, Bauru, Sao Paulo
Rua Lavras 235, Carmo Sion, Belo Horizonte MG
Ave Goias 1146, Goiania GO
Ave Tiradentes 963, Maringa
Rua Andre Cavalcanti 78, Rio de Janeiro GB
Ave Joana Angelica 963, Salvador BA
Rua Mal Deodoro 887, Curitiba PR
Ave do Imperador 1203, Fortaleza CE
Ave Rio Branco 185, Londrina PR
Rua Martins Junior 39, Recife PE
Rua Prof Baltazar 12, Vitoria ES

Fundacao Cultural Avatar
R Pereira Nunes, 141, 24210-430 Niteroi
Tel: (021) 621-0217 *Fax:* (021) 2719-1574
E-mail: fcavatar@nitnet.com.br
Web Site: www.nitnet.com.br/~fcavatar
Subjects: Asian Studies, Astrology, Occult, Biography, Education, Philosophy, Psychology, Psychiatry, Religion - Other
ISBN Prefix(es): 85-7104

Fundacao de Assistencia ao Estudante
SAS Quadra 1- B1/A-9 andar, 70729-900 Brasilia
Tel: (061) 212-4150; (061) 225-6603 *Fax:* (061) 226-7712

Key Personnel
Man Dir: Rubens Jose de Castro Albuquerque
Editorial Dir: Luiz Pasquale Filho
Sales Dir: Avari de Campos
Production Manager: Maria Aparecida de Oliveira
Publicity Manager: Geni Hirata
Rights & Permissions: Jose Ribeiro de Castro Neto
Founded: 1967
276 bookshops throughout Brazil.
ISBN Prefix(es): 85-222

Fundacao Instituto Brasileiro de Geografia e Estatistica (IBGE - CDDI/DECOP)
Rua General Canabarro, 706, Bairro Maracana, 20271-201 Rio de Janeiro
Tel: (021) 2514-4732 *Fax:* (021) 2234-8400
Web Site: www.ibge.gov.br
Telex: (021) 2139128
Key Personnel
President: Sergio Besserman Vionna *Fax:* 021 220-5943
Senior Technician: Raul Aloysio Telles Ribeiro *Tel:* (021) 569-2043 *E-mail:* raultri@ibge.gov.br
Founded: 1936
Subjects: Economics, Geography, Geology, Mathematics
ISBN Prefix(es): 85-240
Bookshop(s): Av Franklin Roosevet, 146 lj.A, 20021 Castelo RJ
Orders to: IBGE - CDDI/DECOP/DICOM, Rua General Canabarro 666, Bloco B - 2/Andar, 20271-200 Rio de Janerio RJ, Contact: Carlos Lessa *Tel:* (021) 569-2043 *Fax:* (021) 234-8480 *E-mail:* atandicddi@ibge.gov.br

Fundacao Joaquim Nabuco Editora+
R Dois Irmaos, 92, 52071-440 Apipucos
Tel: (081) 4415900 R298 *Fax:* (081) 4414201
E-mail: joanildo@fundaj.gov.br
Web Site: www.fundaj.gov.br
Telex: 081 1180
Key Personnel
Dir General: Leonardo Dantas Silva
Founded: 1978
Subjects: Anthropology, Economics, Education, History, Social Sciences, Sociology
ISBN Prefix(es): 85-7019
Bookshop(s): Av Dezessete de agosto, 2187 Casa Forte CEP 52061-540

Editora Gaia Ltda+
Rua Pirapitingui, 111A, 01508-020 Sao Paulo
Tel: (011) 32777999 *Fax:* (011) 32778141
E-mail: gaia@dialdata.com.dr
Key Personnel
Prof: Carlos Alberto Pereira de Oliveira
Founded: 1989
Subjects: Cookery, Environmental Studies, Health, Nutrition, Self-Help
ISBN Prefix(es): 85-85351
Parent Company: Global Editora E Distribuidora Ltda
Associate Companies: Editora Ground Ltda
Imprints: FEI

Editora Gente Livraria e Editora Ltda+
Rua Pedro Soares de Almeida 114, 05029-030 Sao Paulo SP
Tel: (011) 3675 2505 *Fax:* (011) 36750430
E-mail: gentedit@mandic.com.br
Key Personnel
Editor: Rosely Boschini
Founded: 1976
Subjects: Philosophy, Psychology, Psychiatry
ISBN Prefix(es): 85-7312

Global Editora e Distribuidora Ltda+
Rua Pirapitingui, 111, 01508-020 Sao Paulo SP
Tel: (011) 32777999 *Fax:* (011) 32778141
E-mail: global@dialdata.com.br
Key Personnel
Man Dir, Sales: Luis Alves, Jr
Editorial, Production, Rights & Permissions: Jose Venancio
Founded: 1973
Subjects: Anthropology, Biography, Education, Fashion, Health, Nutrition, History, Music, Dance, Poetry, Romance, Social Sciences, Sociology
ISBN Prefix(es): 85-260
Associate Companies: Editora Ground Ltda; Editora Gaia Ltda
Imprints: Parma; Prol; Sao Paulo Editora
Subsidiaries: Centro Editorial Latino Americano Ltda

Editora Globo SA+
Av. Jaguare, 1485, 05346-902 Sao Paulo SP
Tel: (011) 37677890 *Fax:* (011) 37677870
E-mail: wcarelli@edglobo.com.br
Web Site: www.editoraglobo.com.br
Telex: 81574
Key Personnel
General Dir: Ricardo Alberto Fischer
Editorial Dir: Flavio Barros Pinto
Sales Dir: Fernando Alberto Costa
Founded: 1954
Subjects: Biography, Business, Cookery, Drama, Theater, Economics, Education, Environmental Studies, Fiction, History, How-to, Humor, Journalism, Language Arts, Linguistics, Law, Literature, Literary Criticism, Essays, Medicine, Nursing, Dentistry, Music, Dance, Mysteries, Poetry, Science (General), Self-Help, Sports, Athletics, Travel
ISBN Prefix(es): 85-250; 85-217
Branch Office(s)
Rua Itapiru, 1209, 20251 Rio de Janeiro
Warehouse: Alameda Tocantins, 679 Alphaville Barueri, Sao Paulo

Edicoes Graal Ltda+
CP 128, 06801-970 Embau RJ
Tel: (011) 7961-0006 *Fax:* (011) 7961-0006
Key Personnel
Man Dir, Editorial & Publicity Dir & Rights & Permissions: Fernando Gasparian
Sales & Production Dir: Marcus F Gasparian
Founded: 1977
Subjects: Economics, Education, History, Medicine, Nursing, Dentistry, Philosophy, Psychology, Psychiatry, Social Sciences, Sociology
ISBN Prefix(es): 85-7038
Associate Companies: Editora Paz e Terra

Ordem do Graal na Terra
CP 128, Embu, SP 06801-970
Tel: (011) 4781-0006 *Fax:* (011) 4781-0006 ext 217
E-mail: graal@graal.org.br
Web Site: www.graal.org.br
Key Personnel
President: Harald Schuler
Distribution Mgr: Paulo Nobre *Tel:* (011) 4781 1671 *Fax:* (011) 4781 1671 *E-mail:* nobrebooks@graal.org.br
Founded: 1947
Subjects: Philosophy, Religion - Other, Self-Help, New-Age, Spiritualism
ISBN Prefix(es): 85-7279
Number of titles published annually: 3 Print
Total Titles: 52 Print
U.S. Office(s): Nobre Books Distributor, 5117 Black Diamond Court, Raleigh, NC 27604, United States *Tel:* 919-255-1775
Bookshop(s): Av Sao Luiz, 192-lj14, Sao Paulo, SP 01046-000 *Tel:* (011) 259-7646
Shipping Address: Biblio Distribution, 15200 NBN Way, Blue Ridge Summit, PA 17214, United States
Warehouse: Biblio Distribution, 15200 NBN Way, Blue Ridge Summit, PA 17214, United States
Orders to: Biblio Distribution, 15200 NBN Way, Blue Ridge Summit, PA 17214, United States

Editora e Grafica Carisio Ltda+
Av Batalhao Maua, 1055, 38440-000 Araguari
Tel: (034) 2413557 *Fax:* (034) 2413310
Key Personnel
Contact: Publio Carisode Paula
Founded: 1984
Subjects: Fiction, Religion - Other, Self-Help

Grafica Editora Primor Ltda+
Rua Presidente Dutra 2611, 21535-500 Rio de Janeiro
Tel: (021) 4744966
Key Personnel
Man Dir: Sergio Jacques Waissman; Simao Waissman
Sales & Publicity: Miguel Paixao
Production: Paulo Duante
Founded: 1969
Subjects: Art, Education
ISBN Prefix(es): 85-7024
Parent Company: Editora Primor Ltda

Editora Ground Ltda+
Rua Lacedemonia, 68, 04634-020 Sao Paulo SP
Tel: (011) 5031 1500 *Fax:* (011) 5031 3462
E-mail: editora@ground.com.br
Web Site: www.ground.com.br
Key Personnel
Executive & Publisher: Jose Carlos Rolo Venancio *E-mail:* jcvenancio@ground.com.br
Founded: 1973
Subjects: Asian Studies, Astrology, Occult, Environmental Studies, Health, Nutrition, Philosophy
ISBN Prefix(es): 85-7187
Associate Companies: Editora Aquariana Ltda, Rua Lacedemonia, 68, Sao Paulo, Contact: Jose Carlos Venancio *Tel:* (011) 5031 1500 *Fax:* (011) 5031 3462 *E-mail:* aquariana@ground.com.br
Subsidiaries: Merlin Comicstore

Gryphus Editora, *imprint of* Companhia Editora Forense

Editora Guanabara Koogan SA+
Travessa do Ouvidor 11, 1º AO 8º Andares, 20040-040 Rio de Janeiro RJ
Tel: (021) 2217106 *Fax:* (021) 2215744
E-mail: norengbk@unisys.com.br
Key Personnel
Dir: Joao Pedro Lorch; Mauro Koogan Lorch
Rights & Permissions: Christina Noren
Founded: 1930
Subjects: Biological Sciences, Environmental Studies, Medicine, Nursing, Dentistry, Veterinary Science
ISBN Prefix(es): 85-277

Enio Matheus Guazzelli e Cia Ltd, see Livraria Pioneira Editora/Enio Matheus Guazzelli e Cia Ltd

Editora Harbra Ltda+
Rua Joaquim Tavora, 779, Vila Mariana, 04015-001 Sao Paulo
Tel: (011) 5084-2403; (011) 5084-2482; (011) 5571-1122; (011) 5549-2244; (011) 5571-0276 *Fax:* (011) 5575-6876; (011) 5571-9777
E-mail: editorial@harbra.com.br
Web Site: www.harbra.com.br
Key Personnel
Dir: Julio Esteban Emod-Eghy *Tel:* (011) 50842482 *E-mail:* emod@harbra.com.br
Founded: 1986

Subjects: Behavioral Sciences, Biography, Biological Sciences, Computer Science, Earth Sciences, Management, Physical Sciences, Science (General), Self-Help, Social Sciences, Sociology
Total Titles: 250 Print; 1 CD-ROM; 1 Audio
Online services available through World Wide Web.
Branch Office(s)
Rua Joaquim Tavora, 629, 04015-001 Sao Paulo
 E-mail: editorial@harbra.com.br
Rua 70, No 687 Qd 127 Lt 05, 74055-120 Goiania *Tel:* (062) 212-9875; (062) 225-8632 *Fax:* (062) 212-9874
Rua do Riachuelo 453, Loja 7, 50050-400 Recife *Tel:* (081) 3221-0700; (081) 3222-2808 *Fax:* (081) 3221-3655
Rua Conde de Bomfim 944-A (Tijuca), 20520-000 Rio de Janeiro *Tel:* (021) 572-4668; (021) 238-4670 *Fax:* (021) 572-8576
Rua Guajajaras 1148, 30180-100 Belo Horizonte *Fax:* (031) 3275-4016
Distributor for editora Edgard Blucher; editora Universidade de Brasilia
Warehouse: Rua Joaquim Tavora, 779, Vila Mariana, 04015-001 Sao Paulo

Hemus Editora Ltda+
Rua da Gloria 312, Caixa Postal 9686, Sao Paulo, SP CEP 01065-970
Tel: (011) 2799911 *Fax:* (011) 2799721
Telex: 32005 Edil *Cable:* HETEC
Key Personnel
President: Rachel Behar
Man Dir: Maxim Behar
Founded: 1965
Subjects: Archaeology, Architecture & Interior Design, Astrology, Occult, Career Development, Civil Engineering, Electronics, Electrical Engineering, Law, Philosophy
ISBN Prefix(es): 85-289

Horus Editora Ltda+
Rua dos Ingleses, 222 cj 121, 01329-902 Sao Paulo-SP
Tel: (011) 288-7681 *Fax:* (011) 288-7681
E-mail: horus@horuseditora.com.br
Web Site: www.horuseditora.com.br
Key Personnel
President: Juan Ferre' Serrano
Manager: Roberto Ferre' Serrano
Founded: 1977
Also acts as distributor.
Subjects: Astrology, Occult, Music, Dance, Psychology, Psychiatry, Religion - Buddhist, Religion - Catholic, Religion - Hindu, Religion - Islamic, Religion - Jewish, Religion - Other, Theology
ISBN Prefix(es): 85-86204

IBEP, see Instituto Brasileiro de Edicoes Pedagogicas (IBEP)

Livro Ibero-Americano Ltda
Hermenegildo de Barros, 40-Gloria, 20241-040 Rio de Janeiro RJ
Tel: (021) 221-2026 *Fax:* (021) 2252-8814
Web Site: www.livroiberoamericano.hpg.ig.com.br
 Cable: NEBRIJA
Key Personnel
Man Dir: Sir Joao Francisco J Gomes
Founded: 1946
Subjects: Agriculture, Art, Electronics, Electrical Engineering, History, Language Arts, Linguistics, Philosophy, Photography, Psychology, Psychiatry, Religion - Other
ISBN Prefix(es): 85-7032
Branch Office(s)
Rua Conselheiro Crispiniano 29 - 1 pav, Sao Paulo SP

IBICT, see Instituto Brasileiro de Informacao em Ciencia e Tecnologia

IBRASA (Instituicao Brasileira de Difusao Cultural Ltda)+
Rua Treze De Maio, 365/367, 01327-000 Sao Paulo SP
Tel: (011) 3107 41 00 *Fax:* (011) 3107 35 13
E-mail: editora.ibrasa@uol.com.br
Web Site: www.ibrasa.com.br
Key Personnel
Man Dir: Jorge Leite
Founded: 1958
Subjects: Economics, Education, Government, Political Science, Health, Nutrition, History, Literature, Literary Criticism, Essays, Medicine, Nursing, Dentistry, Parapsychology, Philosophy, Psychology, Psychiatry, Science (General), Social Sciences, Sociology, Sports, Athletics, Physical education
ISBN Prefix(es): 85-348
Bookshop(s): IBREX - Distribuidora de Livros e Material de Escritorio Ltda
Orders to: IBREX Ltda, Rua Treze de Maio 361, 01327-000 Sao Paulo

Icone Editora Ltda+
Rua das Palmeiras, 213-Sta Cecilia, 01226-010 Sao Paulo SP
Tel: (011) 826-7074; (021) 826-9510 *Fax:* (011) 826-9510
Key Personnel
President: Luiz Carlos Fanelli
Vice President: Tatiana Fanelli
Founded: 1985
Member of Brazilian House of Books, National Syndication of Books, Brazilian Association of Books & Collections; also acts as distributor.
Subjects: Agriculture, Astrology, Occult, Biography, Crafts, Games, Hobbies, Law, Medicine, Nursing, Dentistry, Science (General), Sports, Athletics, Technology
ISBN Prefix(es): 85-274; 85-85503
Divisions: Editorial, Production, Publication & Distribution Departments

Iglu Editora Ltda
Rua Duilio 386, Lapa, 05043-020 Sao Paulo SP
Tel: (011) 3873-0227 *Fax:* (011) 872-9907
Key Personnel
Contact: Julio Igliori Netto
Founded: 1987
Subjects: Education, Health, Nutrition, Law
ISBN Prefix(es): 85-85631

Iluminuras - Projetos e Producoes Editoriais Ltda+
Rua Oscar Freire 1233, 01426-001 Sao Paulo SP
Tel: (011) 3068-9433 *Fax:* (011) 2825317
Key Personnel
Contact: Beatriz Costa; Sir Samuel Leon
Founded: 1987
ISBN Prefix(es): 85-85219

Imago Editora Importacao e Exportacao Ltda+
Rua Santos Rodrigues, 201 A, Estacio, 20250-430 Rio de Janeiro RJ
Tel: (021) 5029092 *Fax:* (021) 5025435
E-mail: imago@imagoeditora.com.br
Key Personnel
President: Jayme Salomao
Executive Dir: Eduardo Salomao
Founded: 1967
Member of SNEL, CBL.
Subjects: Biblical Studies, Biography, Fiction, History, Literature, Literary Criticism, Essays, Nonfiction (General), Philosophy, Psychology, Psychiatry, Science Fiction, Fantasy, Self-Help
ISBN Prefix(es): 85-312

Editora Index Ltda+
Av Rio Branco 45, Centro, 20090-003 Rio de Janeiro RJ
Tel: (021) 5162336 *Fax:* (021) 2533507
E-mail: editoraindex@ax.ibase.org.br
Key Personnel
President: Jose Paulo M Soares; Christina Ferrao
Founded: 1982
Member of Chealsea Arts Club (London).
Subjects: Art, Environmental Studies, History
ISBN Prefix(es): 85-7083
Associate Companies: Editora Libris
Warehouse: Rua Sacadura Cabral 81 gr 804, Rio de Janeiro 20221

Instituicao Brasileira de Difusao Cultural Ltda (IBRASA), see IBRASA (Instituicao Brasileira de Difusao Cultural Ltda)

Fundacao Instituto Brasileiro de Geografia e Estatistica (IBGE - CDDI/DECOP), see Fundacao Instituto Brasileiro de Geografia e Estatistica (IBGE - CDDI/DECOP)

Editora Interciencia Ltda
Rua Verna Magalhaes, 66, 20710-290 Engenho Novo RJ
Tel: (021) 2241-6916 *Fax:* (021) 2501-4760
Key Personnel
Man Dir & Rights & Permissions: Edson G S Nascimento
Publicity: Nize Nascimento
Founded: 1969 (1975 as publisher)
Subjects: Science (General)
ISBN Prefix(es): 85-7193

Interlivros Edicoes Ltda
Rua Comandante Coelho 1085, 21250-510 Rio de Janeiro RJ
Tel: (021) 3913134 *Fax:* (021) 3521005
E-mail: interlivros@ibm.net
Key Personnel
Executive: Abel Simoes de Morais
Subjects: Biological Sciences, Health, Nutrition, Medicine, Nursing, Dentistry, Psychology, Psychiatry
ISBN Prefix(es): 85-7236; 85-85891

Irmaos Vitale S/A Industria e Comercio
Rua Franca Pinto, 42, vila Mariana, 04704-000 Sao Paulo SP
Tel: (011) 5574-7001 *Fax:* (011) 5574-7388
E-mail: irmaos@vitale.com.br
Web Site: www.vitale.com.br
ISBN Prefix(es): 85-7407; 85-85188
Parent Company: Irmaos Vitale S/A Ind. E Comercio
Subsidiaries: Casa Vitale
Divisions: Edicoes musicais e Instrumentos musicais (Nacionais e importados)

ISAEC, see Editora Sinodal

JUERP, see Junta de Educacao Religiosa e Publicacoes da Convencao Batista Brasileira (JUERP)

Junta de Educacao Religiosa e Publicacoes da Convencao Batista Brasileira (JUERP)+
Rua Silva Vale, 781, 21370 Rio de Janeiro RJ
Mailing Address: Caixa Postal 320, 20001 Rio de Janeiro RJ
Tel: (021) 2690772 *Fax:* (021) 2690296
E-mail: juerp@openlink.com.br
Web Site: www.juerp.org.br *Cable:* BATISTAS
Key Personnel
General Superintendent: Dr Claudio Mazzoni
Editorial & Rights & Permissions: Prof Joelcio Barreto
Marketing: Dr Oswaldo Paiao Jr
Production: Dr Samuel Justino
Founded: 1907

BRAZIL

Member of Association of Brazilian Christian Publishers, Association of Brazilian Baptist Publishers.
Subjects: Religion - Other
ISBN Prefix(es): 85-350
Branch Office(s)
Filial Juerp, Ave Sao Joao 816/820, 01036-100 Sao Paulo SP
SDS B1 G - loja 17 - Conj Baracat, 70302 Brasilia DF
Rua Barao de Itapemirim 208, 29000 Vitoria ES
Trav Padre Prudencio 61, 66000 Belem PA
Rua do Hospicio 187, 50000 Reclife PE
Rua Bahia 360 - Sobre loja, 30000 Belo Horizonte MG
Rua Treze de Maio 2659, 79100 Camop Grande MS
Juerp Suese, Rua Silva Vale, 781 - Cavalcante, 21370-360 Rio de Janeiro RJ
Av Sao Pantaleao 195, LJS A E B, Centro, 65015 Sao Kyis MA
Rua Rui Barbosa 139, 69007 Manaus AM
Abba Press Editora, Rua do Mar, 20 Interlagos, 04654-060 Sao Paulo SP
Bookshop(s): Rua fo Rosario 141/216, Centro, 20041 Rio de Janeiro RJ; Rua Mariz e Barris 39, Praca da Bandeira, 20270 Rio de Janeiro RJ; Ave Nil Pecanha 411, 25000 Caxais RJ; Rua Otavio Tarquinio 178, 26000 Nova Iguacu RJ; Rua XV de Novembro 49, 24000 Niteroi RJ; Rua Cel Vicente 614, 90000 Porto Alegre RS; Ave Viscondede Sao Lourenco 6, 40000 Salvador BA

Koinonia Comunidade Edicoes Ltda (Editora Koinonia Ltda)
SCLN 203 - BL/A N/24, 1 Andar A Norte (P Piloto), 70833-510 Brasilia
Tel: (061) 223 3070 *Fax:* (061) 3228377
Key Personnel
Contact: Divino Soares da Silva
Founded: 1992
Subjects: Biblical Studies, Religion - Protestant
ISBN Prefix(es): 85-85810
Divisions: Gravadora Koinonia Music
Bookshop(s): Praca Carlos Gomes, 104 CEP 01501-040, Liberdide-Sao Paulo SP *Tel:* (011) 606-2644; Rua 4 N 906-Sector Central CEP, 74025-020 Gioania-Go

Editora Kuarup Ltda+
rua Diamantina, 381, Caixa Postal 3093, 91040-460 Porto Alegre, RS
Tel: (051) 361-6044 *Fax:* (051) 3613550
E-mail: kuarup@conex.com.br
Key Personnel
Director: Adalberto Felix Souto
Editor: Vera Miranda Ritter-Souto
Founded: 1983
Subjects: Astrology, Occult, Education, Religion - Other
ISBN Prefix(es): 85-269

Francisco J Laissue Livraria
Prace Olavo Bilac 28, Mezzanine 201, 20041-010 Rio de Janeiro
Tel: (021) 509-7298
Founded: 1947
Bookshop specializing in Portuguese, Spanish, French & English.
Subjects: African American Studies, Anthropology, Archaeology, Asian Studies, Astrology, Occult, Religion - Buddhist, Religion - Hindu, Religion - Islamic, Religion - Jewish
Foreign Rep(s): Editorial Kier (Argentina)

Lake-Livraria Allan Kardec Editora+
Rua Assuncao, 45, Bras, Sao Paulo SP 03005-020
Tel: (011) 229-0526; (011) 229-1227; (011) 227-1396; (011) 229-0937; (011) 229-4592; (011) 229-0514 *Fax:* (011) 229-0935; (011) 227-5714
E-mail: lake@lake.com.br
Web Site: www.lakelivraria.com.br
Key Personnel
Contact: Roberto Francisco-Ferrero
Founded: 1937
ISBN Prefix(es): 85-7360

LDA Editores Ltda+
Rua Teixeira Mendes, 280, 82520-410 Curitiba PR
Tel: (041) 362-9173 *Fax:* (041) 262-3439
E-mail: lda.editores@uol.com.br
Key Personnel
Executive: Lionel de Almeida
Founded: 1991
Subjects: Architecture & Interior Design, Biography, Cookery, History, Journalism, Literature, Literary Criticism, Essays, Philosophy, Travel
Imprints: Peninsula

Editora Leitura Ltda
Rua Pedra Bonita, 870, Belo Horizonte MG 30430-390
Tel: (031) 3371-4902 *Fax:* (031) 3714902
E-mail: leitura@editoraleitura.com.br
Web Site: www.editoraleitura.com.br/
Subjects: Education
ISBN Prefix(es): 85-7358

Libreria Editora Ltda+
Rua Taquaritinga, 137 - Mooca, 03170-010 Sao Paulo SP 03170-010
Tel: (011) 6085411 *Fax:* (011) 6085411
E-mail: libreria@libreria.com.br
Web Site: www.libreria.com.br
Key Personnel
Dir Coml: Fiorentino S Mario
Founded: 1974
Member of the Association of Brazilian Publishers, Association of Brazilian Distributors.
Subjects: Cookery, English as a Second Language, Geography, Geology, Language Arts, Linguistics, Natural History, Globes

Editora Lidador Ltda+
Rua Hilario Ribeiro 154, Praca da Bandeira, 20270-180 Rio de Janeiro
Tel: (021) 25690594 *Fax:* (021) 22040684
E-mail: lidador@terra.com.br
Key Personnel
Publicity Manager: Ruy Carvalho
Founded: 1960
Subjects: Astrology, Occult, Astronomy, Communications, Economics, Education, Erotica, Fiction, Human Relations, Music, Dance, Parapsychology, Social Sciences, Sociology
ISBN Prefix(es): 85-7003
Number of titles published annually: 9 Print
Distributed by Topbook

Waldyr Lima Editora
Rue 24 de Maio, 347, Rio de Janeiro RJ 20950-090
Tel: (05521) 501-5000 *Fax:* (05521) 581-8900
E-mail: geapo@ccaa.com.br
Web Site: www.ccaa.com.br
Key Personnel
Dir-General, Rights & Permissions: Waldyr Lima
Editorial, Research & Planning Dir: Rosane Roale
Sales, Production & Publicity Dir: Rogerio Gama
Founded: 1967
Specialize in English, Portuguese & Spanish language instruction.
Subjects: Education, English as a Second Language, Language Arts, Linguistics
ISBN Prefix(es): 85-341
Total Titles: 2,000,000 Print
Branch Office(s)
CCLS Publishing House, 3181 Coral Way, Miami, FL 33145, United States
Showroom(s): Publishing House, 3181 Coral Way, Miami, FL 33145, United States
Orders to: Publishing House, 3181 Coral Way, Miami, FL 33145, United States

LISA (Livros Irradiantes SA)
Rua Major Sertorio, 671 - 5º And, Sao Paulo SP 01222-001
Tel: (011) 32563755 *Fax:* (011) 32575776
E-mail: lerlisalivros@ig.com.br
Key Personnel
Man Dir: Leonidio Balbino da Silva
Sales Dir: Francisco de Paula Oliveira Filho
Founded: 1965
Subjects: Education
ISBN Prefix(es): 85-257

Livraria Dos Advogados Editora Ltda
Rua Riachuelo, 201, 3º andar, 01007-905 Sao Paulo
Tel: (011) 3107-3979 *Fax:* (011) 3107-6878
E-mail: lael@lael.com.br
Web Site: www.lael.com.br
Subjects: Law

Livraria Editora Infobook SA+
Rua do Mercado 34 Sala 1501, 20010-120 Rio de Janeiro RJ
Tel: (021) 2633807 *Fax:* (021) 2633807
Key Personnel
Contact: Virginia Maria Reeve Andrea
Founded: 1993
Subjects: Computer Science, Management
ISBN Prefix(es): 85-85588

Livraria Nobel S/A+
Rua da Balsa, 559, Freguesia do O, 02910-000 Sao Paulo SP
Tel: (011) 3933 2822; (011) 3933 2811
Fax: (011) 3931 3988
E-mail: ednobel@livrarianobel.com.br
Web Site: www.livrarianobel.com.br
Founded: 1943
Subjects: Advertising, Agriculture, Architecture & Interior Design, Biography, Business, Cookery, Gardening, Plants, Romance, Self-Help, Sports, Athletics, Technology, Travel
Imprints: Marco Zero; Studio Nobel
Subsidiaries: Editora Marco Zero; Editora Studio Nobel
Distributor for Heinemann; Harper Collins

Livros Irradiantes SA, see LISA (Livros Irradiantes SA)

Oficina de Livros Ltda+
Rua Tupinambas, 360, 30120-070 Belo Horizonte
Tel: (031) 2221577 *Fax:* (031) 2244473
Key Personnel
President: Bernardino Jose Monteiro Moniz
Commercial Dir: Geraldo Alberto Alvares
Editor: Antonio Roberto Bertelli
Founded: 1987
Subjects: Literature, Literary Criticism, Essays, Social Sciences, Sociology
ISBN Prefix(es): 85-85170
Branch Office(s)
Rua Genebra, 135-9 andar, 01316 Sao Paulo SP
Tel: (011) 379872

Editora Logosofica
Rua Coronel Oscar Porto, 818, Paraiso, 04003-004 Sao Paulo SP
Tel: (011) 8851476; (011) 8856574 *Fax:* (011) 8879480
Key Personnel
Man Dir, Editorial: Jose Antonio Antonini
Author: Carlos Bernardo Gonzalez Pecotche
Sales: Alayde Thereza Melloni
Production: Darcio Giavoni
Founded: 1964

PUBLISHERS

BRAZIL

Member of Brazilian Book Association.
Subjects: Behavioral Sciences, Education, Philosophy
ISBN Prefix(es): 85-7097
Branch Office(s)
Centro de Estudos Logosoficos, 50 Woodfall Rd, Belmont, MA 02178, United States
Bookshop(s): SHCG - Norte, Area de Escolas Q704, 70000 Brasilia DF; Rua Piaui 74 2, 30000 Belo Horizonte MG; Rua General Polidoro 36, 22280 Rio de Janeiro RJ; others in Argentina, Mexico & Uruguay

Longman, *imprint of* Pearson Education Do Brasil

Edicoes Loyola SA+
Rua 1822 No 347, 04216-000 Sao Paulo SP
Tel: (011) 69141922 *Fax:* (011) 61634275
E-mail: editorial@loyola.com.br
Web Site: www.loyola.com.br
Key Personnel
Dir: Fidel Garcia Rodriguez
Editorial & Rights & Permissions: Marcos Marcionilo
Founded: 1965
Also acts as book packager.
Subjects: Art, Biblical Studies, Communications, Computer Science, Drama, Theater, Economics, Education, History, Law, Literature, Literary Criticism, Essays, Management, Philosophy, Psychology, Psychiatry, Religion - Other, Self-Help, Social Sciences, Sociology
ISBN Prefix(es): 85-15
Parent Company: Seas Edicoes Loyola
Divisions: Loyola Multimidia

LTC-Livros Tecnicos e Cientificos Editora S/A+
Travessa do Ouvidor, 11, 6th Andar-Parte, 20040-040 Rio de Janeiro RJ
Tel: (021) 2221-7106 *Fax:* (021) 2252-2732; (021) 2221-5744
Key Personnel
Dir: Joao Pedro Lorch; Mauro Koogan Lorch
Rights & Permissions: Christina Noren
E-mail: norenltc@unisys.com.br
Founded: 1968
Subjects: Chemistry, Chemical Engineering, Computer Science, Economics, Engineering (General), Management, Mathematics, Physics, Technology
ISBN Prefix(es): 85-216

LTR Editora Ltda
Rua Jaguaribe, 571, 01224-001 Sao Paulo SP
Mailing Address: CP 2112, 01224-001 Sao Paulo
Tel: (011) 8262788; (011) 663289; (011) 675499 *Fax:* (011) 3667-7172
E-mail: livtr@mandic.com.br
Web Site: www.ltr.com.br/web/home.htm
Key Personnel
Man Dir: Vbiratan de Freitas Mesquita
Sales: Vbiratan de Freitas Mesquita
Founded: 1937
Subjects: Law
ISBN Prefix(es): 85-7322
Branch Office(s)
Rua Anfilofio de Carvalho 29 - salas 607/8, Castelo, 20030-000 Rio de Janeiro RJ

Editora Lucre Comercio e Representacoes+
Av. Paulista, 1159-Cj 507, 01311-200 San Paulo SP
Tel: (019) 287-8593 *Fax:* (019) 287 8593
E-mail: lucre@mute.net.br
Key Personnel
Contact: Eduardo Montalban
Founded: 1996
Subjects: Career Development, Economics, Finance, Management

Madras Editora+
Rua Paulo Goncalves, 88, 02403-020 Sao Paulo SP
Tel: (011) 6959-1127 *Fax:* (011) 6959-3090
E-mail: editor@madras.com.br
Web Site: www.madras.com.br
Key Personnel
Pres: Wagner Veneziani Costa
Founded: 1991
Books for University students, professional people esoteric ones, self-help, mysticism, freemasonry. Distribute for self & 30 publishing houses throughout Brazil.
Subjects: Astrology, Occult, Self-Help
ISBN Prefix(es): 85-7374
Total Titles: 300 Print
Imprints: WVC
Foreign Rights: H Katia Schumer (Brazil)

Makron Books do Brasil Editora Ltda+
Rua Tabapua 1348, 04533-004 Sao Paulo-SP
Tel: (011) 829-1518 *Fax:* (011) 829-4970
E-mail: makron@books.com.br
Web Site: www.makron.com.br
Key Personnel
President: Milton Assumplao *Fax:* (011) 8294970
E-mail: milton@makron.com.be
Founded: 1985
Subjects: Business, Computer Science
ISBN Prefix(es): 85-346

Editora Manole Ltda+
Avenida Ceci, 672, 06460-120 Barueri SP
Tel: (011) 4196-6000 *Fax:* (011) 2872853
E-mail: manole@virtual-net.com.br
Web Site: www.linux.manole.com.br
Key Personnel
Editorial, Production, Rights & Permissions: Dinu Manole
Sales: Carlos Telles
Publicity: Ilma Manole
Production: Amarylis Manle
Founded: 1969
Subjects: Cookery, Crafts, Games, Hobbies, Health, Nutrition, Medicine, Nursing, Dentistry, Sports, Athletics, Veterinary Science
ISBN Prefix(es): 85-204
Total Titles: 120 Print
Distributed by Dina Livros

Editora Mantiqueira de Ciencia e Arte+
Av Eduardo Moreira da Cruz 295, 04010-970 Campos do Jordao
Tel: (0122) 621832 *Fax:* (0122) 622126
Key Personnel
Executive: Antonio Fernando Costella
Subjects: Animals, Pets, Art, Communications, Fiction, History, Journalism, Poetry, Travel
ISBN Prefix(es): 85-85681

Editora Manuais Tecnicos de Seguros Ltda
Rua Brigadeiro Galvao 288, 01151-00 Sao Paulo SP
Tel: (011) 8260844 *Fax:* (011) 8250833
Key Personnel
Contact: Christina Roncarati
Founded: 1970
Subjects: Securities
ISBN Prefix(es): 85-85549

Marco Zero, *imprint of* Livraria Nobel S/A

Editora Marco Zero Ltda+
Rua da Balsa, 559, 02910-000 Sao Paulo
Tel: (011) 876-2822 *Fax:* (011) 257-2744
E-mail: marcozero@mutecnet.com.br
Key Personnel
International Rights: Maria Jose Silveria
Founded: 1980

Subjects: Biography, Child Care & Development, Cookery, How-to, Literature, Literary Criticism, Essays, Mysteries, Nonfiction (General), Travel
ISBN Prefix(es): 85-279
Parent Company: Nobel
Associate Companies: Studio Nobel

McKids, *imprint of* Editora Mundo Cristao

Editora Meca Ltda
Rua Araujo 81, 01220-020 Sao Paulo SP
Tel: (011) 2599049; (011) 2599034; (011) 2575346 *Fax:* (011) 2570312 *Cable:* CABOGRAMA
Key Personnel
Man Dir & Editor: Cosmo Juvela
Sales: Anna Maria Santos Brasil
Publicity: Marcos Juvela
Rights & Permissions: Guarany Gallo
Founded: 1970
Subjects: English as a Second Language, Parapsychology
Imprints: Jogos Pedagogicos
Warehouse: Rio de Janeiro, 51 Campos Eliseos, Sao Paulo SP

Medicina Panamericana Editora Do Brasil Ltda+
Rua Santa Isabel 265, 012221-010 Sao Paulo SP
Tel: (011) 222-0366 *Fax:* (011) 222-0542
Key Personnel
Executive: Nivacir Carlos Emmerick
Founded: 1950
Subjects: Medicine, Nursing, Dentistry
ISBN Prefix(es): 85-303
Parent Company: Editorial Medica Panamericana SA, Buenos Aires, Argentina
Subsidiaries: RJ/MG/RS

Medsi - Editora Medica e Cientifica Ltda
Rua Visconde de Cairu, 165, 20270-050 Rio de Janeiro RJ
Tel: (021) 5694342 *Fax:* (021) 2646392
Key Personnel
Dir: Jackson Alves de Oliveira
Founded: 1981
Subjects: Medicine, Nursing, Dentistry
ISBN Prefix(es): 85-7199; 85-85019
Branch Office(s)
Rua Dr Cesario Motta Jr, 179, CEP 01221-020 Sao Paulo, SP

Editora Melhoramentos Ltda+
Formerly Companhia Melhoramentos de Sao Paulo
Subsidiary of Companhia Melhoramentos de Sao Paulo
Rua Tito, 479, Sao Paulo 05051-000
Tel: (011) 3874 0854 *Fax:* (011) 3874 0855
E-mail: blerner@melhoramentos.com.br
Web Site: melhoramentos.com.br
Key Personnel
Publishing Dir: Breno Lerner *E-mail:* blerner@melhoramentos.com.br
Contact: Alfredo Weiszflog *E-mail:* aweiszfl@melhoramentos.com.br
Founded: 1915
Specialize in reference books.
Subjects: Archaeology, Art, Cookery, English as a Second Language, History, Literature, Literary Criticism, Essays
ISBN Prefix(es): 85-06
Total Titles: 1,200 Print; 20 CD-ROM; 8 Audio
Online services available through Melhoramentos.
Distributed by ACME; Atlantida; Capeletti; Emece; L Rodrigues; SEP; Sigmar; Volcano Press
Distributor for Disney

BRAZIL

Memorias Futuras Edicoes Ltda+
Rua Pereira da Silva 322, 22221-010 Rio de Janeiro RJ
Tel: (021) 205-3549 *Fax:* (021) 2252518
E-mail: memorias@br.homeshopping.com.br
Key Personnel
Contact: Hedy Costa de Oliveira
Founded: 1982
Subjects: Fiction
ISBN Prefix(es): 85-287

Editora Mercado Aberto Ltda+
Rua Dona Margarida, 894, Bairro Navegantes, 90240-610 Porto Alegre RS
Tel: (051) 3337-4833 *Fax:* (051) 3337-4905
E-mail: mercado@mercadoaberto.com.br
Web Site: www.mercadoaberto.com.br
Key Personnel
Executive: Roque Jacoby
Founded: 1977
Subjects: Anthropology, Education, Fiction, Health, Nutrition, History, Literature, Literary Criticism, Essays, Romance
ISBN Prefix(es): 85-280

Mercuryo Jovem, *imprint of* Editora Mercuryo Ltda

Editora Mercuryo Ltda+
Alameda dos Guaramomis, 1267, 04076-012 Sao Paulo SP SP
Tel: (011) 5531-8222 *Fax:* (011) 5093-3265
E-mail: diretoraeditorial@mercuryo.com.br
Web Site: www.mercuryo.com.br/
Key Personnel
Editor: Julia Barany
Founded: 1987
Subjects: Art, Biblical Studies, Biography, Fiction, History, Human Relations, Mysteries, Nonfiction (General), Parapsychology, Psychology, Psychiatry, Religion - Other, Science Fiction, Fantasy, Self-Help
ISBN Prefix(es): 85-7272
Number of titles published annually: 10 Print
Total Titles: 143 Print
Imprints: Unicornio Azul; Mercuryo Jovem
Divisions: Unicornio Azul

MG Editores Associados Ltda
Rua Primavera, 261, 01435-050 Sao Paulo SP
Tel: (011) 8890861 *Fax:* (011) 8858646
Key Personnel
Contact: Flavio Gikovate
Subjects: Behavioral Sciences, Education
ISBN Prefix(es): 85-7255

Ministerio da Marinha Diretoria de Hidrografia Navegacao
Rua Barao de Jaceguai, s/n Ponta da Areia, 24048-900 Niteroi RJ
Tel: (021) 613 8001; (021) 719 4824 *Fax:* (021) 6138063; (021) 719 4824
E-mail: 01@dhm.mar.mil.sr
Telex: 2133858/213220
Key Personnel
Bilingual Asst: Jose Mauro F Lopes
 E-mail: 122@bhm.mar.mil.sr

Editora Moderna Ltda+
Rua Padre Adelino, 758, Sao Paulo SP 03303-904
Tel: (011) 6090-1500 *Fax:* (011) 6090-1501
E-mail: moderna@moderna.com.br
Web Site: www.moderna.com.br
Key Personnel
President & Man Dir: Ricardo Arissa Feltre
 Tel: (011) 60901369 *E-mail:* ricardo@moderna.com.br
Man Editor: Geraldo Fernandes
Founded: 1968
Subjects: Education, Fiction, History, Literature, Literary Criticism, Essays, Mathematics, Social Sciences, Sociology
ISBN Prefix(es): 85-16
Total Titles: 1,515 Print; 12 CD-ROM
Online services available through Moderna.com.br.
Subsidiaries: R Senador Furtado 31; R Santos Dumond 721; Ave Farrapos 2840; R Eptacio Pessoa 163; R Dona Eufrosina 65; Rua do Sossego, 102; R Machado Sidney, 55; R Oswaldo Aranha; R Visconde de Itaborai; Rio Grande Do Sul
Branch Office(s)
Rua Sen Furtado 31, 20270 Rio de Janeiro RJ

Modulo Editora e Desenvolvimento Educacional Ltda
Rua Albano Reis, 1093, 80520-530 Curitiba
Tel: (041) 2530077 *Fax:* (041) 2530103
E-mail: moduloed@moduloeditora.com.br
Key Personnel
Contact: Fausto Luiz Charneski
Founded: 1991
Subjects: Education, Geography, Geology, History, Mathematics, Science (General), Sports, Athletics
ISBN Prefix(es): 85-7397; 85-85764

Editora Mundo Cristao+
Rua Antonio Carlos Tacconi 79, Caixa Postal 21357, 04698-970 Sao Paulo, Spain
Tel: (011) 566-64829 *Fax:* (011) 566-65011
E-mail: editora@mundocristao.com.br
Key Personnel
President: Mark L Carpenter
Founded: 1965
Subjects: Biblical Studies, Biography, Child Care & Development, Fiction, Religion - Protestant, Theology
ISBN Prefix(es): 85-7325
Imprints: Nexo; McKids

Musa Editora Ltda
Rua Monte Alegre, 1276, 05014-001 Perdizes SP
Tel: (011) 62-2586 *Fax:* (011) 62-2586
E-mail: musaeditora@vol.com.br
Key Personnel
Executive: Ana Candida Costa
ISBN Prefix(es): 85-85653

Musimed Edicoes Musicais Importacao E Exportacao Ltda+
SDS ED Venancio IV, Terreo, Loja 14 - Parte A, 70393-900 Brasilia - Distrito Federal
Mailing Address: Cx Postal 09693, Ag Central, 70001-970 Brasilia DF
Tel: (061) 226-0478 *Fax:* (061) 226-0478
E-mail: cartas@musimed.com.br
Web Site: www.musimed.com.br
Key Personnel
Purchasing Manager: Joselita Soares
Dir: Bohumil Med *E-mail:* bohumil@brnet.com.br
Founded: 1984
Subjects: Music, Dance, Sheet music & music books
Total Titles: 23 Print
Showroom(s): SDS Ed Venaneio IV, Sobreloja, loja-14 Brasilia
Orders to: MusiMed Ediciões Musicias, SDS Edicioes Vanancio IV, Sobreloja, loja 14 Brasilia, Purchasing Managaer: Joselita Soares

Nexo, *imprint of* Editora Mundo Cristao

Editora Nova Aguilar SA+
Rua Dona Mariana, 205-Casa 01, Botafogo, 22280-020 Rio de Janeiro RJ
Tel: (021) 537-7189 *Fax:* (021) 537-8275
Telex: 34695 Enfs *Cable:* AGUILAR
Key Personnel
President: Sebastiao Lacerda
Man Dir: Carlos Augusto Lacerda
Founded: 1958
ISBN Prefix(es): 85-210
Parent Company: Editora Nova Fronteira SA
Branch Office(s)
Ave Pedro Bueno 1509-1511, Jabaquara, 04342 Sao Paulo SP

Editora Nova Alexandria Ltda+
Rua Dionisio da Costa, 141, 04117-110 Sao Paulo
Tel: (011) 5571-5637 *Fax:* (011) 5571-5637
E-mail: novaalexandria@novaalexandria.com.br
Web Site: www.novaalexandria.com.br
Key Personnel
Associate: Luiz Baggio-Neto *E-mail:* lbaggio@novaalexandria.com.br
Founded: 1992
Subjects: Biography, Cookery, Education, Fiction, History, Literature, Literary Criticism, Essays, Philosophy, Poetry, Romance, Sports, Athletics
ISBN Prefix(es): 85-7492
Number of titles published annually: 18 Print
Total Titles: 136 Print

Editora Nova Era, *imprint of* Distribuidora Record de Servicos de Imprensa SA

Editora Nova Fronteira SA+
Rua Bambina, 25, 22251-050 Rio de Janeiro RJ
Tel: (021) 25 37 87 70; (021) 22 66 51 84
 Fax: (021) 22 86 67 55
Web Site: www.novafronteira.com.br
Key Personnel
General Dir: Carlos Augusto Lacerda
 E-mail: caml@novafronteira.com.br
Foreign Rights Dir: Carlos Barbosa
Sales: Elson M da Rocha
International Rights: Carlos Augusto Lacerda; Carlos Barbosa
Founded: 1965
Subjects: Art, Astrology, Occult, Astronomy, Biography, Biological Sciences, Business, Education, Fiction, Health, Nutrition, History, Language Arts, Linguistics, Literature, Literary Criticism, Essays, Mysteries, Natural History, Nonfiction (General), Philosophy, Poetry, Psychology, Psychiatry, Publishing & Book Trade Reference, Regional Interests, Romance, Science (General), Self-Help, Social Sciences, Sociology, Theology
ISBN Prefix(es): 85-209
Number of titles published annually: 90 Print
Total Titles: 1,200 Print
Associate Companies: Lexikon Informatica Ltd

Editora Objetiva Ltda+
Rua Cosme Velho, 103, 22241-090 Rio de Janeiro RJ
Tel: (021) 2556-7824 *Fax:* (021) 2556-3322
Web Site: www.objetiva.com.br
Key Personnel
Publisher: Roberto Feith
Foreign Rights Acquisitions Manager: Alessandra Blocker *E-mail:* aless.blocker@ibm.net
Subjects: Behavioral Sciences, Biography, Fiction, Human Relations, Humor, Nonfiction (General), Science (General), Self-Help
Number of titles published annually: 60 Print
Online services available through World Wide Web.

Off Set, *imprint of* Centro de Estudos Juridicosdo Para (CEJUP)

Olho D'Agua Comercio e Servicos Editoriais Ltda+
Rua Dr Homem de Melo, 1036, 05007-002 Sao Paulo SP

PUBLISHERS	BRAZIL

Tel: (011) 2631287 *Fax:* (011) 2631287
E-mail: editora@olhodaguo.com.br
Web Site: www.olhodaguo.com.br
Key Personnel
Executive: Jorge Claudio Noel Ribeiro, Jr
Founded: 1991
Subjects: Behavioral Sciences, Education, Journalism, Literature, Literary Criticism, Essays, Psychology, Psychiatry, Social Sciences, Sociology, Theology
ISBN Prefix(es): 85-85428
Distributed by Distribuidora Loyola

Oliveira Rocha-Comercio e Servics Ltda+
Av Bernardino de Campos, 327, cj 24, 04004-050 Sao Paulo
Tel: (011) 2845527; (011) 2886440 *Fax:* (011) 2845362; (011) 2842096
E-mail: dialetic@virtual.net.com.br
Key Personnel
Contact: Valdir Oliveira Rocha
Founded: 1995
Subjects: Law
ISBN Prefix(es): 85-86208

Organizacao Andrei Editora Ltda+
Rua Conselheiro Nebias, 1071, 01203-002 Sao Paulo SP
Tel: (011) 223-5111 *Fax:* (011) 221-0246
E-mail: andrei@cepa.com.br
Web Site: www.editora-andrei.com.br
Key Personnel
Executive: Edmundo Andrei
Founded: 1955
Subjects: Medicine, Nursing, Dentistry, Veterinary Science, Homeopathy & Acupuncture
Total Titles: 4 Print; 3 CD-ROM

Editora Ortiz SA
Av Julio de Castilhos, 159, 8 andar, 90030-131 Porto Alegre RS
Tel: (051) 225-3026 *Fax:* (051) 225-3026
Key Personnel
President: Airton Ortiz
Founded: 1982
Subjects: Accounting, Agriculture, Business, Economics, Finance, Management, Marketing, Public Administration
ISBN Prefix(es): 85-85279

Edit Palavra Magica+
Rua Americo Brasiliense, 1205/1, Centro, Ribeirao Preto SP 14015-050
Tel: (016) 6100074 *Fax:* (016) 610-0204
E-mail: editora@palavramagica.com.br
Web Site: www.palavramagica.com.br
Key Personnel
Contact: Galeno de Amorim
Founded: 1995
Subjects: Behavioral Sciences, Earth Sciences, Human Relations, Regional Interests, Religion - Catholic, Religion - Other, Romance, Social Sciences, Sociology
ISBN Prefix(es): 85-85997

Pallas Editora e Distribuidora Ltda+
Rua Frederico de Albuquerque, 44 Higienopolis, 21050-840 Rio de Janeiro RJ
Tel: (021) 270-0186 *Fax:* (021) 590-6996; (21) 5618007
E-mail: pallas@alternex.com.br
Web Site: www.pallaseditora.com.br/
Key Personnel
Man Dir: Antonio Carlos Fernandes
Editorial, Rights & Permissions: Cristina Fernandes Warth
Sales: Antonio Carlos Fernandes
Founded: 1975
SNEL - Sindicets Notional des Editores de Livros.

Subjects: African American Studies, Anthropology, Art, Biography, Ethnicity, Human Relations, Music, Dance, Philosophy, Religion - Catholic, Religion - Other, Self-Help, Social Sciences, Sociology, Theology, Afro-Brasilian religions, culture, history, social sciences
ISBN Prefix(es): 85-347
Number of titles published annually: 30 Print
Total Titles: 200 Print

Parma, *imprint of* Global Editora e Distribuidora Ltda

Paulinas Editorial+
Rua Pedro de Toledo, 164, 04039-000 Sao Paulo SP
Tel: (011) 50855199 *Fax:* (011) 50855198
E-mail: editora@paulinas.org.br
Subjects: Biblical Studies, Biography, Child Care & Development, Communications, Education, Human Relations, Psychology, Psychiatry, Religion - Catholic, Self-Help, Social Sciences, Sociology, Theology
ISBN Prefix(es): 85-356; 85-7311

Paulus Editora+
Rua Francisco Cruz, 229, 04117-091 Sao Paulo SP
Tel: (011) 50843066; (011) 5757362 *Fax:* (011) 5703627
E-mail: dir.editorial@paulus.org.br
Web Site: www.paulus.org.br
Telex: 1139464 Pssp *Cable:* PAULINOS
Key Personnel
Man Dir, Publicity & Production: Arno Brustolin
Editorial & Rights & Permissions: Zolferino Tonon
Sales: A C D'Elboux
Founded: 1931
Bookshops throughout Brazil.
Subjects: Biblical Studies, Education, Philosophy, Psychology, Psychiatry, Religion - Catholic, Self-Help, Social Sciences, Sociology, Theology
ISBN Prefix(es): 85-05; 85-349
Bookshop(s): Praca da Se 180, Sao Paulo; Rua Mexico 111-B, Rio de Janeiro

Editora Paz e Terra+
Rua do Triunfo, 177, Sta Ifigenia, 01212-010 Sao Paulo
Tel: (011) 3337-8399 *Fax:* (011) 223-6290
E-mail: vendas@pazeterra.com.br
Web Site: www.pazeterra.com.br
Key Personnel
General Manager, Sales & Editorial: Fernando Gasparian
Production, Publicity & Rights & Permissions: Marcus F Gasparian
Founded: 1966
Subjects: Drama, Theater, Government, Political Science, Literature, Literary Criticism, Essays, Philosophy, Regional Interests, Social Sciences, Sociology
ISBN Prefix(es): 85-219
Subsidiaries:
Bookshop(s): Livraria Argumento, Rua Oscar Freire 608, San Paulo; Rua Dias Ferreira 199, Rio de Janeiro; Livraria e Editora Livre, Rua Armando Penteado 44, Sao Paulo

Pearson Education Do Brasil
Rua Emilio Goeldi, 747 Lapa, Sao Paulo 05065-110
Tel: (011) 3611 0740 *Fax:* (011) 3611 0444
E-mail: firstname.lastname@pearsoned.com.br
Telex: 2121799
Key Personnel
Interim General Manager/Commercial Dir: Jaime Carneiro
Finance Dir: Solange Beletatti

Promotion Manager ELT: Marco Malossi
Marketing Manager ELT: Helena Nagano
Administrative Assistant: Claudia Fisher
Representative, Higher Education: Luiz Henrique
Founded: 1996
Subjects: Accounting, Behavioral Sciences, Biological Sciences, Business, Economics, Engineering (General), Marketing, Technology
ISBN Prefix(es): 85-7054; 85-87675
Number of titles published annually: 20 Print
Parent Company: Pearson Plc
Imprints: Addison Wesley; Longman; Scott Foresman; Prentice Hall
Branch Office(s)
Belo Horizonte, Rua Silva Jardim 235, Sao Paulo 30150-010
Foreign Rights: Roger Trimer

Jogos Pedagogicos, *imprint of* Editora Meca Ltda

Peninsula, *imprint of* LDA Editores Ltda

Editora Perspectiva
Ave Brigadeiro Luis Antonio, 3025/3035, 01401-000 Sao Paulo SP
Tel: (011) 8858388 *Fax:* (011) 3885-8388
E-mail: editora@editoraperspectiva.com.br
Web Site: www.editoraperspectiva.com.br/
Key Personnel
Man Dir: Jaco Guinsburg
Founded: 1965
Subjects: Drama, Theater, Economics, Education, History, Human Relations, Music, Dance, Philosophy, Psychology, Psychiatry, Religion - Other, Social Sciences, Sociology
ISBN Prefix(es): 85-273

Petit Editora e Distribuidora Ltda+
Rua Atuai, 383 5 V Esperanca, Sao Paulo SP 03646-000
Tel: (011) 6684 6000; (011) 6917 165 *Fax:* (011) 2924616
E-mail: petit@dialdata.com.br
Web Site: www.petit.com.br
Key Personnel
Contact: Flavio Machado
Founded: 1982
Subjects: Religion - Other
ISBN Prefix(es): 85-7253

Pia Sociedade Filhas De Sao Paulo, see Paulinas Editorial

Editora Pini Ltda
Rua Anhaia, 964, Sao Paulo SP 01130-900
Tel: (011) 224-8811 *Fax:* (011) 224-0314; (011) 224-8541
E-mail: construcao@pini.com.br
Web Site: www.piniweb.com.br
Telex: 11-37803
Key Personnel
Contact: Ricardo Bertagnon
Founded: 1948
ISBN Prefix(es): 85-7266
Bookshop(s): R Vitoria, 486/496, 01210 Sao Paulo SP; Rua Gentil de Moura, 128, 04278 San Paulo SP

Livraria Pioneira Editora/Enio Matheus Guazzelli e Cia Ltd+
Praca Dirceu de Lima 313, Casa Verde, 02515-050 Sao Paulo, SP SP
Tel: (011) 8583199 *Fax:* (011) 8580443
E-mail: pioneira@virtual-net.com.br
Key Personnel
Editor & Rights & Permissions: Liliana Guazzelli
Dir of Finance: Roberto Guazzelli
Founded: 1960
Subjects: Accounting, Advertising, Agriculture, Architecture & Interior Design, Astrology, Occult, Behavioral Sciences, Business, Computer

BRAZIL
BOOK

Science, Economics, Education, History, Language Arts, Linguistics, Management, Mysteries, Photography, Psychology, Psychiatry, Social Sciences, Sociology
ISBN Prefix(es): 85-221
Associate Companies: Disal, Distribuidores Associados de Livros Ltda

Pool Editorial Ltda
Rau Manoel Caetano 135, Berbe, 52010-170 Recife PE
Tel: (081) 2215355; (081) 2215150; (081) 2215096
Telex: 2273 Alpp *Cable:* Poolne
Key Personnel
Man Dir, Editorial: Marco Aurelio de Alcantara
Sales: Maristela Oliveira
Production: Marcos Lyra
Publicity: Hilton Cunha
Subjects: Economics, Government, Political Science, History, Poetry
ISBN Prefix(es): 85-7010
Parent Company: Alcantara Promocoes e Publicidade Ltda, Rau Manoel Caetano 135, Berbe, 52010-170 Recife, PE
Subsidiaries: ANE - Agencia Nordestina de Noticias
Branch Office(s)
Ave Franklin Roosevelt 23 - sala 605, 20000 Rio de Janeiro RJ
Bookshop(s): Livraria do Estacionamento Periferico da Ilha Joana Bezerra, Recife

Prentice Hall, *imprint of* Pearson Education Do Brasil

Casa Editora Presbiteriana S.C.+
Rua Miguel Telles Junior, 382-394, Cambuci, 01540-040 Sao Paulo SP
Mailing Address: Cx Postal 15136, 01599-970 Sao Paulo SP
Tel: (011) 270-7099 *Fax:* (011) 279-1255
E-mail: cep@cep.org.br
Web Site: www.cep.org.br
Key Personnel
Editor: Claudio A B Marra
Founded: 1948
Subjects: History, Religion - Other
ISBN Prefix(es): 85-86886

Primor Editora Ltda, see Grafica Editora Primor Ltda

Editora Primor Ltda+
Rua Presidente Dutra 2611, 21535-500 Rio de Janeiro
Tel: (021) 4744966
Telex: 22150 *Cable:* Primor
Subjects: Fiction, Humor, Nonfiction (General)
ISBN Prefix(es): 85-7024
Subsidiaries: Grafica Editora Primor SA

Prol, *imprint of* Global Editora e Distribuidora Ltda

Proton Editora Ltda
Ave Reboucas 3819, 05401-450 Sao Paulo SP
Tel: (011) 2103616; (011) 8147922; (011) 8159708 *Fax:* (011) 8159920
Key Personnel
President: Norberto R Keppe
Man Dir: Claudia S Pacheco
Founded: 1976
Subjects: Medicine, Nursing, Dentistry, Psychology, Psychiatry, Science (General)
ISBN Prefix(es): 85-7072

Editora de Publicacoes Medicas Ltda
Rua do Russel, 404-grs 901/2-parte, 22210 Rio de Janeiro

Tel: (021) 2654047; (021) 2253516 *Fax:* (021) 2613749
Key Personnel
Man Dir: Jose Maria de Sousa e Melo
Editorial: Dr Almir Lourenco da Fonseca
Sales & Publicity: Jose Ayrton de Souza Avila
Production: Edson de Oliveira Vilar
Founded: 1959
Subjects: Medicine, Nursing, Dentistry
Associate Companies: Editora de Publicacoes Medicas Ltda (EPUME), Rua do Russel, 404-grs 901/2-parte, 22210 Rio de Janeiro
Branch Office(s)
Rua Borges Lagoa 426, Sao Paulo
Book Club(s): Club do Livro Cientifico

Qualitymark Editora Ltda+
R Teixeira Junior, 441, Sao Cristovao, Rio de Janeiro RJ 20921-400
Tel: (021) 3860-8422 *Fax:* (021) 3860-8424
E-mail: quality@unisys.com.br
Web Site: www.qualitymark.com.br/
Key Personnel
Contact: Saidual Rahman Mahomed
Founded: 1991
Promote events dealing with seminars & lectures.
Subjects: Career Development, Economics, Education, Environmental Studies, Finance, Labor, Industrial Relations, Management, Medicine, Nursing, Dentistry, Nonfiction (General), Public Administration, Self-Help
ISBN Prefix(es): 85-7303; 85-85360

Raboni Editora Ltda+
CP 17000, 13001-970 Campinas SP
Tel: (019) 32428433 *Fax:* (019) 32428505
E-mail: raboni@raboni.com.br
Web Site: www.raboni.com.br
Key Personnel
Contact: Regis Castro
Dir: Stella Castro *E-mail:* stella@raboni.com.br
Founded: 1991
Subjects: Religion - Catholic
ISBN Prefix(es): 85-85592

Editora Record, *imprint of* Distribuidora Record de Servicos de Imprensa SA

Distribuidora Record de Servicos de Imprensa SA+
Rua Argentina 171, Sao Cristovao, 20921-380 Rio de Janeiro RJ
Mailing Address: Caixa Postal 884, 20001-97 Rio de Janeiro RJ
Tel: (021) 2585-2000 *Fax:* (021) 2585-2085
E-mail: record@record.com.br
Web Site: www.record.com.br
Key Personnel
Chairman, President & General Manager: Sergio C Machado *Tel:* (021) 5852030
Vice President Operations: Sonia M Sardim, Jr *Tel:* (021) 5852040
Editorial Dir: Luciano Villas Boas
Founded: 1942
Subjects: Biography, Business, Fiction, History, Nonfiction (General), Philosophy
ISBN Prefix(es): 85-01
Number of titles published annually: 250 Print
Total Titles: 2,000 Print
Imprints: Editora Nova Era; Editora Rosa dos Tempos; Editora Record
Subsidiaries: BCD-Uniao de Editoras SA
Divisions: Bertrand Brasil, Difel, Civilizacao Brasileira
Branch Office(s)
Paraiso 139, 7 audar, Sao Paulo SP, Contact: Francinete Zerbetto *Tel:* (011) 286-0802 *Fax:* (011) 0800-212380

Rede Das Artes (Boccato Editores Collector's)+
Rua Graham Bell 355, 04737-030 Sao Paulo SP

Tel: (011) 246-5556 *Fax:* (011) 246-5556
Key Personnel
Executive: Andre Boccato
Founded: 1993
Subjects: Art, Cookery, Gardening, Plants, Health, Nutrition, Photography, Sports, Athletics, Travel, Wine & Spirits
ISBN Prefix(es): 85-85657

Editora Resenha Tributaria Ltda
Rua Quatinga, 12, 04140-020 Sao Paulo SP
Tel: (011) 5772822 *Fax:* (011) 5772526
Key Personnel
Man Dir: Vaner Bicego
Editorial Dir: Valdyr Rezende Xavier
Commercial Dir: Jose Figueira da Cruz
Subjects: Education, Law
ISBN Prefix(es): 85-236

Editora Revan Ltda+
Av Paulo de Frontin, 163, Casa 2, 20260-010 Rio de Janeiro
Tel: (021) 25027495 *Fax:* (021) 2736873
E-mail: editor@revan.com.br
Web Site: www.revan.com.br
Key Personnel
Contact: Dr Ing Renato Guimaraes-Cupertino
Founded: 1983
Subjects: Anthropology, Art, Behavioral Sciences, Biography, Computer Science, Criminology, Fiction, Military Science, Science (General), Self-Help, Social Sciences, Sociology
ISBN Prefix(es): 85-7106
Number of titles published annually: 40 Print
Total Titles: 300 Print

Livraria Editora Revinter Ltda+
Rua do Matoso 170, Tijuca, Rio de Janeiro RJ 20270-000
Tel: (021) 563-9700 *Fax:* (021) 502-6830
E-mail: livraria@revinter.com.br
Web Site: www.revinter.com.br/
Key Personnel
Contact: Sergio Duarte Dortas
Subjects: Medicine, Nursing, Dentistry
ISBN Prefix(es): 85-7309
Distributor for Lippincott; Churchill Livingstone; Mosby; W B Saunders; Georg Thieme

RHJ Livros Ltda+
Rua Cuiaba, 415, Prado, Belo Horizonte CEP 30410-140
Tel: (031) 1334-1566 *Fax:* (031) 332-5823
E-mail: rhjbooks@terra.com.br
Key Personnel
Dir: Rafael Borges de Andrade
Founded: 1974
Member of SNEL-457.
Subjects: Literature, Literary Criticism, Essays
ISBN Prefix(es): 85-7153

Editora Rideel Ltda+
Alameda Afonso Schmidt No 879, Santa Terezinha, Sao Paulo SP CEP 02450-001
Tel: (011) 6977-8344 *Fax:* (011) 6976-7415
E-mail: rideel@virtual-net.com.br
Web Site: www.rideel.com.br
Key Personnel
Man Dir, Editorial: Italo Amadio
Production: Roberto Amadio
Founded: 1970
Subjects: Cookery, History, Language Arts, Linguistics, Medicine, Nursing, Dentistry, Religion - Other
ISBN Prefix(es): 85-339
Bookshop(s): Al Afonso Schmidt, No 877, Sta Terezinha, SP

Livraria Roca Ltda+
Rua Dr Cesario Mota Jr 73, 01221-020 Sao Paulo SP

Tel: (011) 221-8609; (011) 221-6814 *Fax:* (011) 3331-8653
E-mail: editoraroca@editoraroca.com.br
Web Site: www.editoraroca.com.br
Key Personnel
Contact: Casimiro Paya Piqueres
Founded: 1973
Subjects: Medicine, Nursing, Dentistry, Veterinary Science
ISBN Prefix(es): 85-7241
Associate Companies: Livraria Paya Ltda

Editora Rocco Ltda+
Rua Rodrigo Silva 26-5 andar, Rio de Janeiro RJ 20011-040
Tel: (021) 507-2000 *Fax:* (021) 507-2244
E-mail: rocco@rocco.com.br
Web Site: www.rocco.com.br
Key Personnel
Contact: Paulo Roberto Rocco
Founded: 1975
Subjects: Anthropology, Biography, Communications, Management, Science (General), Self-Help, Social Sciences, Sociology, Women's Studies
ISBN Prefix(es): 85-325
Warehouse: Av Brasil, 10-600, Rio de Janeiro 21012-351

Editora Rosa dos Tempos, *imprint of* Distribuidora Record de Servicos de Imprensa SA

Salamandra Consultoria Editorial SA+
Ave Nilo Pecanha 155, Grupo 301, 20020-100 Rio de Janeiro RJ
Tel: (021) 2406306 *Fax:* (021) 5331622; (021) 2404775
E-mail: salprod@openlink.com.br
Key Personnel
Contact: Sir Geraldo Jordao Pereira
Founded: 1982
Subjects: Art
ISBN Prefix(es): 85-281

Livraria Santos Editora Comercio e Importacao Ltda+
Rua Dona Brigida, 701, 04111-081 Sao Paulo SP SP
Tel: (011) 55741200 *Fax:* (011) 55738774
E-mail: editorasantos@terra.com.br
Key Personnel
Contact: Rui Santos
Founded: 1974
Subjects: Medicine, Nursing, Dentistry, Veterinary Science
ISBN Prefix(es): 85-7288
Number of titles published annually: 60 Print
Total Titles: 510 Print

Editora Santuario+
Rua Padre Claro Monteiro 342, 12570-000 Sao Paulo SP
Tel: (012) 565 2140 *Fax:* (012) 565 2141
E-mail: vendas@redemptor.com.br
Web Site: www.redemptor.com.br
Key Personnel
Administrative Manager: Padre Luis Rodrigues Batista
Founded: 1900
Specialize in graphics.
Subjects: Literature, Literary Criticism, Essays, Religion - Catholic
ISBN Prefix(es): 85-7200; 85-7265
Parent Company: Congregacao do Santissimo Redentor
Bookshop(s): Praca Nossa Senhora Aparecida 292, Aparecida SP

Sao Paulo Editora, *imprint of* Global Editora e Distribuidora Ltda

Saraiva SA, Livreiros Editores+
Ave Marques de Sao Vicente 1697, 01139-904 Sao Paulo SP
Tel: (011) 36133000 *Fax:* (011) 36113308
E-mail: diretoria.editora@editorasaraiva.com.br
Web Site: www.editorasaraiva.com.br
Telex: 1126789 *Cable:* ACADEMICA
Key Personnel
President: Jorge Eduardo Saraiva
Man Dir: Ruy Mendes Gonolalves; Jose Luiz M A Prosper; Wander Soares
Editorial Dir, Education: Antonio Alexandre Faccioli
Editorial Dir, Law: Juarez de Oliveira
Sales Dir: Nilson Lepera
Founded: 1914
17 Branches in Sao Paulo.
Subjects: Accounting, Business, Economics, Education, Finance, Law, Management, Marketing, Mathematics, Philosophy, Psychology, Psychiatry, Securities
ISBN Prefix(es): 85-02
Subsidiaries: Saraiva Data-Informatica
Branch Office(s)
Ave Marechal Rondon 2231, Rio de Janeiro
Rua Celia de Souza 571, Belo Horizonte
Ave Princesa Isabel 1555, Curitiba
Ave Chicago 307, Porto Alegre

Sarvier - Editora de Livros Medicos Ltda
Rua Dr Amancio de Carvalho 459, 04012-090 Sao Paulo SP
Tel: (011) 571-3439
Key Personnel
Man Dir: Fernando Silva Xavier
Founded: 1965
Subjects: Medicine, Nursing, Dentistry
ISBN Prefix(es): 85-7378

Karin Schindler Representante de Direitos Autorais
CP 19051, 04505-970 Sao Paulo SP
Tel: (011) 241-9177 *Fax:* (011) 241-9077
Key Personnel
Executive: Karin Schindler *E-mail:* kschind@terra.com.br

Editora Scipione Ltda+
Praca Carlos Gomes, 46, 01501-040 Sao Paulo SP
Tel: (011) 2392255 *Fax:* (011) 2391700
E-mail: marketing@scipione.com.br
Web Site: www.scipione.com.br
Key Personnel
General Dir: Luis Esteves Sallum
General Marketing: Maria Jose Rosolino
General Editorial: Aurelio Goncalves Filho
Founded: 1983
Member of Brazilian Book Association, National Book Foundation for Children & Juveniles. Specialize in books pre-school to second grade & also in technical & professional books.
Subjects: Astronomy, Biological Sciences, Chemistry, Chemical Engineering, Education, Environmental Studies, Fiction, Geography, Geology, History, Literature, Literary Criticism, Essays, Mathematics, Mysteries, Nonfiction (General), Physics, Religion - Other, Romance, Science (General)
ISBN Prefix(es): 85-262
Branch Office(s)
S P R Teodoro da Silva, 1004 Rio de Janeiro
Av Visconde de Suassuna, 634 Recife PE
Rua da Independecia, 21/13, Salvador BA
Rua Gago Coutinho, 238, Lapa, Sao Paulo
Distributor for Allca XX/Scipione Culture - Collection Archivos (South America)
Showroom(s): Rua Fagundes, 121 Sao Paulo SP 01508-030
Warehouse: Via BR 116, 84 - km 291, 6 - Itapecerica da Serra, Sao Paulo SP

Seculo XXI Editora e Comercio de Livros
Rua Marcos Moreira, 119, Sala 201, 91350-040 Porto Alegre
Tel: (051) 3614459 *Fax:* (051) 3614459
E-mail: sewloxxi@poa-online.com.br
Key Personnel
Contact: Carlos Mauricio Igreja do Prado
Founded: 1993

Selecoes Eletronicas Editora Ltda, see Selecoes Eletronicas Editora Ltda

Selinunte Editora Ltda+
Ave Miguel Stefano 183 Cj 01, 04301-010 Sao Paulo SP
Tel: (011) 2760318
Key Personnel
Editorial Dir: Roberto Wilson
Administrative Dir, Financial: Arnaldo Majer
Founded: 1987
Member of The Brazilian House of Books.
Subjects: Literature, Literary Criticism, Essays
ISBN Prefix(es): 85-85538

SELTRON, see Selecoes Eletronicas Editora Ltda

Agencia Siciliano de Livros Jornais e Rivistas Ltda+
Ave Raimundo Pereira de Magalhaes 3305, 05145-200 Sao Paulo SP
Tel: (011) 8395500; (011) 8319911 *Fax:* (011) 8328616
Telex: 1180677
Key Personnel
Contact: Oswaldo Siciliano
Founded: 1952
Subjects: Literature, Literary Criticism, Essays
ISBN Prefix(es): 85-267
Divisions: Editorial, Livraria, Distribuidora de revistas

Editora Sinodal+
Rua Amadeo Rossi 467, 93001-970 Sao Leopoldo RS
Mailing Address: Caixa Postal 11, 93001-970 Sao Leopoldo RS
Tel: (051) 590-2366 *Fax:* (051) 590-2664
Web Site: www.editorasinodal.com.br
Telex: 511219 Xpsl *Cable:* SINODAL
Key Personnel
General Dir: Eloy Teckemeier *E-mail:* diretor@editorasinodal.com.br
Publishing Manager: Joao Artur M da Silva *E-mail:* editor@editorasinodal.com.br
Manager of Production: Silvio J dos Santos *E-mail:* grafica@editorasinodal.com.br
Manager of Vendas: Asciepiades Pomme *E-mail:* gerentedevendas@editorasinodal.com.br
Founded: 1949
Subjects: Education, Music, Dance, Religion - Other, Social Sciences, Sociology, Theology
ISBN Prefix(es): 85-233
Parent Company: Instituicao Sinodal de Assistencia, Educacao e Cultura (ISAEC), Rua Amadeo Rossi 467, 93030-220 Sao Leopoldo, RS
Associate Companies: Colegio Sinodal, Rua Amadeo Rossi 467, 93030-220 Sao Leopoldo, RS
Subsidiaries: Escola Superior de Teologia
Showroom(s): Rua Buenos Aires, 123 Sao Paulo SP
Bookshop(s): Editora Sinodal-Livraria, Rua Amadeo Rossi 467, 93030-220 Sao Leopoldo RS; Livraria Volante, Rua Amadeo Rossi 467, 93030-220 Sao Leopoldo RS

Sobrindes Linha Grafica E Editora Ltda+
Sig Sul Quadra 2 Lote 460, 70610-400 Brasilia DF

Tel: (061) 2247778; (061) 2247706; (061) 2247756 Fax: (061) 2241895
E-mail: linhagrafica@conectanet.com.br
Subjects: Fiction, History, Journalism, Religion - Other
ISBN Prefix(es): 85-7238

Sociedade Distribuidora de Livros Ltda (Sodilivro)+
Rua Sa Freire 36/40, Parte, Sao Cristovao, 20930-430 Rio de Janeiro RJ
Tel: (021) 580-1168; (021) 580-6230 Fax: (021) 580-5868
Key Personnel
Executive: Reynaldo Max Paul Bluhm
ISBN Prefix(es): 85-215
Parent Company: Ao Livro Tecnico Ind e Com Ltda

Spala Editora Ltda
Lauro Muller, 116-31 Andar 51 3101, 22290-160 Rio de Janeiro
Tel: (021) 542-9995 Fax: (021) 542-4738
Telex: (021) 2664093
Key Personnel
Contact: Luis Fernando Freire
Founded: 1974
Subjects: Architecture & Interior Design, Art, Biography
ISBN Prefix(es): 85-7048
Subsidiaries: Spala Publicidade; Spala Comunicacoes

Studio Nobel, *imprint of* Livraria Nobel S/A

Livraria Sulina Editora+
Rua Cel Genuino 290, 90010-350 Porto Alegre RS
Mailing Address: CP 357, 90000 Porto Alegre
Tel: (051) 228 1966 Fax: (051) 228 1966
E-mail: sulina@sulina.com.bm Cable: ZIPASUL
Key Personnel
President: Vilson Nailon Noen
Editor: Luis Gomes
Founded: 1946
Subjects: Law, Psychology, Psychiatry, Science (General)
ISBN Prefix(es): 85-205
Parent Company: Organizacao Sulina de Representacoes SARua Cel Gennino, 290, 90010-350 Porto Alegre, RS
Subsidiaries: Editora Sulina
Showroom(s): Rua Deuetrio Ribeiro, 990 202 Porta Alegre
Bookshop(s): Livraria Sulina, Rua Riachuelo, 1218 Porta Alegre

Summus Editorial Ltda+
Rua Itapicuru 613 cj 72, 05006-000 Perdizes SP
Tel: (011) 38723322 Fax: (011) 38727476
E-mail: summus@summus.com.br
Web Site: www.summus.com.br
Key Personnel
Dir: Raul Wassermann
Founded: 1974
Subjects: Advertising, Behavioral Sciences, Business, Communications, Education, Film, Video, Human Relations, Journalism, Marketing, Music, Dance, Psychology, Psychiatry, Radio, TV, Self-Help, Sports, Athletics, Women's Studies
ISBN Prefix(es): 85-323

Edicoes Tabajara
Rua dos Andradas 1774, 90000 Porto Alegre RS
Tel: (0512) 241073; (0512) 247724
Key Personnel
Assistant Manager: Maria Azambuja

Subjects: Drama, Theater, Education, Language Arts, Linguistics, Mathematics, Science (General), Social Sciences, Sociology
Branch Office(s)
Rua Santa Ifigenia 72, Sao Paulo

Talento Publicacoes Editora e Grafica Ltda
rua Augusta 2529, 01413-100 Sao Paulo SP
Tel: (011) 8835400 Fax: (011) 2823752
E-mail: talento@talento.com.br
Web Site: www.talento.com.br
Key Personnel
Contact: Robert Henry Lennard Seadon
Subjects: Advertising, Communications
ISBN Prefix(es): 85-85062

Livros Tecnicos e Cientificos Editora Ltda, see LTC-Livros Tecnicos e Cientificos Editora S/A

Temos Grafica Propria, *imprint of* Editora Betania S/C

Tempus Editores
Rua Viana do Castelo, 8 r/c Dir, Bairro Sao Joao, 2775 Caravelos
Tel: (01) 4535000 Fax: (01) 4426482
Key Personnel
Contact: Paula Santos
Founded: 1994
Subjects: Law, Literature, Literary Criticism, Essays, Romance
ISBN Prefix(es): 972-8198

Thex Editora e Distribuidora Ltda+
Rua da Lapa 180, S1/804/805, 20021-180 Rio de Janeiro
Tel: (021) 252-9338; (021) 221-4458; (021) 221-4079 Fax: (021) 252-9338
Fax on Demand: (021) 252-9338
E-mail: thexedit@domain.com.br
Web Site: www.thexeditora.com.br
Key Personnel
International Rights: Thex Correa da Silva
E-mail: thex@domain.com.br
Founded: 1992
Subjects: Earth Sciences, Economics, Education, Fiction, Human Relations, Literature, Literary Criticism, Essays, Marketing, Mysteries, Poetry, Self-Help, Social Sciences, Sociology
ISBN Prefix(es): 85-85575
Number of titles published annually: 10 Print
Total Titles: 50 Print

34 Literatura S/C Ltda+
Rua Hungria 592, 01455-000 Rio de Janeiro RJ
Tel: (021) 816-6777 Fax: (021) 816-0078
Key Personnel
Contact: Beatriz Bracher
Founded: 1992
Subjects: Anthropology, Drama, Theater, Fiction, Literature, Literary Criticism, Essays, Music, Dance, Philosophy, Poetry, Romance, Science Fiction, Fantasy, Technology
ISBN Prefix(es): 85-85490; 85-7326
Branch Office(s)
Rua Massaca, 276 Alto de Pinheiros, 05465-050 Sao Paulo Tel: (011) 2609738 Fax: (011) 8321041

Totalidade Editora Ltda+
Rua Eng Alcides Barbosa 29, 01430-010 Sao Paulo SP
Tel: (011) 3064 3688 Fax: (011) 3081 9503
E-mail: totail@terra.com.br
Web Site: www.totalidade.com.br
Key Personnel
Contact: Elisa Guerra Malta Campos
Founded: 1989
Member of Brazilian House of Books, National Syndication of Book Publishers, Astrological-Psychological Institute, English Huber School of Astrology, Seven Ray Institute & University of the Seven Rays & Meditation Mount.
Subjects: Art, Astrology, Occult, Psychology, Psychiatry, Self-Help
ISBN Prefix(es): 85-85293

Triom Centro de Estudos Marina e Martin Hawey Editorial e Comercial Ltda+
Rua Aracari, 208, 01453-020 Sao Paulo
Tel: (011) 3168-8380 Fax: (011) 3845-0966
E-mail: info@triom.com.br
Web Site: www.triom.com.br
Key Personnel
Contact: Ruth Cunha-Cintra
Founded: 1991
Bookstore, publishing house.
Subjects: Alternative, Astrology, Occult, Music, Dance, Women's Studies
ISBN Prefix(es): 85-85464
Number of titles published annually: 5 Print
Total Titles: 40 Print; 2 Audio

Editora UNESP+
Praca Da Se, 108, Sao Paulo, SP CEP 01001-900
Tel: (011) 3242-7171 Fax: (011) 3242-7172
E-mail: feu@editora.unesp.br
Web Site: www.editora.unesp.br
Key Personnel
Dir: Jose Castilho Marques E-mail: castilho@editora.unesp.br
Executive Editor: Jezio H B Gutierre
E-mail: jezio@editora.unesp.br
Founded: 1987
Member of Camara Brasileira do Livro; Associacao Brasileira das Editoras Universitarias; Associacao Brasileira de Direitos Reprograficos; Asociacion de Editoriales de America Latina y el Caribe.
Subjects: Anthropology, Education, Government, Political Science, History, Philosophy, Psychology, Psychiatry, Social Sciences, Sociology
ISBN Prefix(es): 85-7139
Number of titles published annually: 100 Print
Parent Company: State University of Sao Paulo
Bookshop(s): Alameda Santos, 647, CEP 01419-901 Sao Paulo SP, Contact: Sandra Pedro
Tel: (011) 252 0630 Fax: (011) 252 0631
E-mail: livraria@editora.unesp.br

Unicornio Azul, *imprint of* Editora Mercuryo Ltda

Editora Universidade de Brasilia
SCS Quadra 2, Bloco C, No 78, 2o andar, Ed OK, 70300-500 Brasilia DF
Tel: (061) 226 6874 Fax: (061) 225 5611
E-mail: editora@unb.br
Web Site: www.editora.unb.br
Telex: 611083 Unbs Cable: UNIVERBRASILIA EDITORA
Key Personnel
Chairman: Antonio A Briquet de Lemos
Editorial Dir & Rights & Permissions: Airton Lugarinho
President: Alexandre Lima
Production: Elmano Rodrigues Pinheiro
Founded: 1962
Subjects: Government, Political Science, Human Relations, Physical Sciences, Social Sciences, Sociology
ISBN Prefix(es): 85-230
Branch Office(s)
Escritorio de Representacao da Universidade de Brasilia, Ave Presidente Vargas 542 - 1309, 20210 Rio de Janeiro RJ Tel: (021) 2636959
Rua Joao Adolfo 118 - 6 andar - sala 608, 01050 Sao Paulo SP Tel: (011) 321413
Bookshop(s): SCS, Ed Anapolis, 70300 Brasilia
Book Club(s): Clube do Livro da Universidade de Brasilia
Warehouse: Subsolo ICC-SUL, Caixa Postal 04551, 70919 Brasilia

Editora da Universidade de Sao Paulo+
Ave Prof Luciano Gualberto Travessau 374, 6 andar, 05655-010 Sao Paulo SP
Tel: (011) 8184160; (011) 8138837 *Fax:* (011) 2116988
Telex: 36950 *Cable:* RUSPAULO
Key Personnel
President: Sergio Miceli Pessoa De Barros
Chairman: Heitor Ferraz
Publishing Dir: Plinio Martins Filho
Founded: 1962
Specializes in Academic Text.
Subjects: Anthropology, Art, Literature, Literary Criticism, Essays, Medicine, Nursing, Dentistry, Philosophy, Science (General), Social Sciences, Sociology
ISBN Prefix(es): 85-314
Bookshop(s): Antigo Predio da Reitoria, Avenida Prof Luciano Gualberto, Travessa J, n 374, Cidade Universitaria, 05508 Sao Paulo SP; Centro de Convivencia da Reitoria, Rua da Reitoria, 74, Cidade Universitaria, 05508 Sao Paulo SP; Faculdade de Educacao, Avenida da Universidade, Travessa 11, n 251, Cidade Universitaria, 05508 Sao Paulo; FFLCH, Departamento de Historia e Geografia, Avenida Prof Lineu Prestes, n 338, Cidade Universitaria, 05508 Sao Paulo SP; Instituto de Ciencias Biomedicas, Avenida Prof Lineu Prestes, 1524. Cidade Universitaria, 05508 Sao Paulo SP; Instituto de Biociencias, Rua do Matao, 277; Escola Politecnica Avenida Prof Almeida Prado, Travessa 2, n 128, 05508 Sao Paulo; Faculdade de Medicina de Ribeirao Preto Predio da Biblioteca, Avenida Bandeirantes, n 3900, 14049 Ribeirao Preto SP; Escola Superior de Agricultura "Luis de Queiroz", Avenida Padua Dias, n 11, 13400 Piracicaba SP

Editora Universidade Federal do Rio de Janeiro+
Forum de Ciencia e Cultura Avenida Pasteur, 250-Urca, 1o andar, 22295-900 Rio de Janeiro
Tel: (021) 2957096 *Fax:* (021) 5423899
E-mail: editora@ufrj.br
Web Site: www.editora.ufrj.br; www.ufrj.br *Cable:* 22924
Key Personnel
Contact: Heloisa Buarque de Hollanda
Founded: 1986
Subjects: Anthropology, Architecture & Interior Design, Art, Economics, Education, History, Language Arts, Linguistics, Library & Information Sciences, Management, Physical Sciences, Social Sciences, Sociology
ISBN Prefix(es): 85-7108

Livraria e Editora Universitaria de Direito Ltda
Rua Constant Youngest child, 171, 01005 Sao Paulo
Tel: (011) 605-6374 *Fax:* (011) 3140-0317
Key Personnel
Man Dir, Production: Armando Luiz Almeida Martins
Editorial Dir: Pedro Gellindo Sommavilla
Sales Dir: Armando des Santos Mesquita Martins
Founded: 1968
Subjects: Law
ISBN Prefix(es): 85-7456

Fundacao Getulio Vargas+
Praia de Botafogo, 190-Botafogo, 22253-900 Rio de Janeiro
Tel: (021) 2559 6000 *Fax:* (021) 2553 6372
Web Site: www.fgv.br
Telex: 36811 *Cable:* FUGEVAR
Key Personnel
Man Dir: Francisco de Castro Azevedo
Sales Dir: Juarez Nery de Souza
Subjects: Accounting, Business, Economics, Education, Marketing, Psychology, Psychiatry, Public Administration, Social Sciences, Sociology
ISBN Prefix(es): 85-225

Editora Vecchi SA
Rua do Resende 144, Esplanda do Senado, 20234 Rio de Janeiro RJ
Tel: (021) 2444522
Telex: 32756 *Cable:* Vekieditora
Key Personnel
Dir-Superintendent: Delman Bonatto
Founded: 1913
Subjects: Astrology, Occult, Biography, Cookery, Philosophy, Religion - Other

Editora Verbo Ltda
Rua Campinas 98, 96835-070 Sao Paulo
Tel: (051) 715-1565 *Fax:* (051) 715-1565
E-mail: verbo@virtual-net.com.br
Web Site: www.editorialverbo.pt *Cable:* Verbo
Founded: 1966
Subjects: Art, Education, Geography, Geology, History, Psychology, Psychiatry, Religion - Other, Social Sciences, Sociology
ISBN Prefix(es): 85-7230

Editora Vida Crista Ltda+
Rua Carlos Meira 396, 03605-010 Sao Paulo SP
Tel: (011) 217-0522 *Fax:* (011) 217-0522
E-mail: editora@vidacristi.com.br
Web Site: www.vidacrista.com.br
Key Personnel
Executive: Alan Leite
Founded: 1977
Subjects: Religion - Protestant
ISBN Prefix(es): 85-7163

Editora Vigilia Ltda
Rua Felipe dos Santos 508, Lourdes, 30180-160 Belo Horizonte MG
Tel: (031) 3372744; (031) 3372363 *Fax:* (031) 3372834
Founded: 1960
Subjects: Education, Philosophy
ISBN Prefix(es): 85-259

Vozes Editora Ltda
Rua Frei Luis, 100, 25689-900 Petropolis RJ
Tel: (024) 2375112 *Fax:* (024) 2314676
Cable: VOZES
Key Personnel
Man Dir: Stephan Ottenbreit
Founded: 1901
Subjects: Communications, Language Arts, Linguistics, Philosophy, Psychology, Psychiatry, Public Administration, Religion - Other, Social Sciences, Sociology
ISBN Prefix(es): 85-326
Branch Office(s)
Rua Sergope, 120 Bairro Funcionarios, Belo Horizonte
Rua Tupis, 114, Belo Horizonte
SCLR/Norte, Q-704, bl A, N 16, Brasilia
Rua Barao de Jaguara, 1164, Campinas
Rua Dr Faivre, 1271, Curitiba
Rua Voluntarios da Patria, 41, Curitiba
Av Osmar Cunha, 183 Loja 15, Florianopolis
Rua Major Facundo, 730, Fortaleza
Rua 3, n 291, Goiania
Rua Espirito Santo, 963, Juiz de Fora
Rua Piaui, 72 Loja 1, Londrina
Rua Ramiro Barcelos, 386, Porto Alegre
Rua Riachuelo, 1280, Porto Alegre
Rua do Principe, 482, Recife
Rua Benedito Hipolito 1, Rio de Janeiro
Rua Senador Dantos, 118-l, Rio de Janeiro
Rua Carlos Gomes, 698-A, Salvador
Rua Luis Coelho, 295, Sao Paulo
Rua Senador Feijo, 168, Sao Paulo
Haddock Lobo, 360, Sao Paulo

WVC, *imprint of* Madras Editora

Jorge Zahar Editor+
Rua Mexico 31, S/203 Centro, 20031-144 Rio de Janeiro RJ
Tel: (021) 2400226 *Fax:* (021) 2625123
E-mail: jze@zahar.com.br
Web Site: www.zahar.com.br
Key Personnel
General Manager: Jorge Zahar, Jr; Ana Cristina Zahar
Editorial: Mariana Zahar Ribeiro
 E-mail: mzahar@zahar.com.br
Founded: 1957
Subjects: Anthropology, Art, Behavioral Sciences, Biography, Economics, Education, Finance, History, Human Relations, Literature, Literary Criticism, Essays, Management, Marketing, Music, Dance, Philosophy, Psychology, Psychiatry, Science (General), Social Sciences, Sociology
ISBN Prefix(es): 85-7110; 85-85061
Number of titles published annually: 40 Print
Total Titles: 600 Print
Online services available through Home Page.
Warehouse: Rua Cotia 35 (Rocha), 20960 Rio de Janeiro RJ *E-mail:* comercial@zahar.com.br

Zip Editora Ltda
Rua Filomena Nunes 162, Olaria, 21021 Rio de Janeiro RJ
Mailing Address: CP 20095, 21021 Rio de Janeiro
Tel: (021) 2807272
Key Personnel
Man Dir: Jan Rais
Marketing: Paul Margittai
Founded: 1978

Brunei Darussalam

General Information

Capital: Bandar Seri Begawan
Language: Malay, English & Chinese
Religion: Predominantly Sunni Muslim
Population: 369,000
Bank Hours: 0900-1200, 1400-1500 Monday-Friday; 0900-1100 Saturday
Shop Hours: 0730-1930 or 2000 Monday-Saturday in Bandar Seri Begawan, Tuesday-Sunday in Seria, Wednesday-Monday in Kuala Belait
Currency: 100 sen = 1 Brunei dollar
Export/Import Information: No tariff on books. No obscene literature allowed. Import licenses not required. No exchange controls.

Leong Brothers
52 Jl Bunga Kuning, Seria
Mailing Address: PO Box 167, Seria 7001
Tel: (03) 225193 *Fax:* (03) 222223
Telex: BU 3338 *Cable:* Leong

Bulgaria

General Information

Capital: Sofia
Language: Bulgarian
Religion: Bulgarian Orthodox & Islamic
Population: 8.9 million
Bank Hours: 0800-1200 Monday-Friday

BULGARIA

Shop Hours: 0900-1230, 1300-1800 Monday-Saturday
Currency: 100 stotinki = 1 lev
Export/Import Information: Books imported by the foreign trade organization 'Hemus', pl Slavejkov 11, Sofia. Exchange controls. 18% VAT on books.
Copyright: UCC, Berne (see Copyright Conventions, pg xi)

Abagar Pablioing+
ul Golas 18, 1111 Sofia
Tel: (02) 702826 *Fax:* (02) 702926
Key Personnel
Contact: Maria Arabadjieva
Founded: 1990
Subjects: Art, Fiction, History, Mathematics, Mysteries, Physical Sciences, Publishing & Book Trade Reference, Science (General), Science Fiction, Fantasy
ISBN Prefix(es): 954-584; 954-8004
Divisions: Abanas Ltd; Abhadon Ltd
Showroom(s): 55 Neofit Rilsui Str, Sofia 1000
Bookshop(s): Rousse Str, Rostislav Bluskov 1; Kjustendil Str, Tzar Osvoboditel 1; 55 Neofit Rilsui Str

Abagar, Veliko Tarnovo+
98 Nikola Gabrovski St, 5000 Veliko Tarnovo
Tel: (062) 43936; (062) 47814 *Fax:* (062) 46993
Key Personnel
General Manager: Marian Kenarov
Founded: 1991
Member of Bulgarian Book Publishers Association.
Subjects: Art, Education, Fiction, Health, Nutrition, History, Science (General)
ISBN Prefix(es): 954-427
Distributed by Damian Jacob (Sofia); Hermes (Plovdiv)
Showroom(s): 47N Tzarigradsko shose Str, Sofia

AECD, *imprint of* Agencija Za Ikonomicesko Programirane i Razvitie

Agencija Za Ikonomicesko Programirane i Razvitie+
ul Aksakov 31, Sofia 1000
Tel: (02) 9816597 *Fax:* (02) 466110
E-mail: aecd@sf.cit.bg
Key Personnel
Vice President: Ms Mariel Nenova
International Rights: Ana-Maria Yankova
Head of Publications: Mr Ventsislav Voikov
Founded: 1991
Subjects: Economics
ISBN Prefix(es): 954-567
Imprints: AECD

Agency for Economic Coordination & Development, see Agencija Za Ikonomicesko Programirane i Razvitie

Aleks Print Publishing House+
ul Kavala 22, et 1, ap 1, 9000 Varna
Tel: (052) 823147 *Fax:* (052) 823147
Key Personnel
Contact: Anelia Stankova
Founded: 1992
Subjects: Romance, Science (General), Science Fiction, Fantasy, Travel
ISBN Prefix(es): 954-8261
Parent Company: Aleks Print & Tourism, Krali Marko 3, Varna
Bookshop(s): Alex Print & Tourism, Krali Marko 3, Varna 9000

Aleks Soft+
ul Ekzarh Josif 10, Kjustendil 2500
Tel: (078) 46136 *Fax:* (078) 46136

Key Personnel
General Manager: Alexander Alexandrov
Founded: 1994
Subjects: Computer Science, Microcomputers
ISBN Prefix(es): 954-656
Parent Company: Aleks Soft

Andina Publishing House
ul G S Rokovski 18, 9002 Varna
Tel: (052) 257002
Key Personnel
Contact: Panko Anchev
ISBN Prefix(es): 954-432
Distributor for Longman (UK); Pengiun (UK)

Antroposofsko Izdatelstvo Dimo R Daskalov OOD
ul M Stanev 61-A, 6000 Stara Zagora
Mailing Address: PO Box 255, 6000 Stara Zagora
Tel: (042) 54481
Key Personnel
Contact: Dr Dimitar Dimchev
Founded: 1991
Subjects: Astrology, Occult, Biblical Studies, Education, Philosophy, Science (General), Social Sciences, Sociology
ISBN Prefix(es): 954-495

Aratron, IK+
PO Box 1587, Sofia 1000
Tel: (02) 980-74-55 *Fax:* (02) 958-19-31
E-mail: aratron@techno-link.com
Key Personnel
President: Dobrin Vassilev
Founded: 1993
Specialize in New Age Books.
Subjects: Astrology, Occult, Business, Health, Nutrition, How-to, Nonfiction (General), Parapsychology, Self-Help
ISBN Prefix(es): 954-626

Izdatelstvo na Balgarskata Akademija na Naukite
ul Akad Georgi Boncev - bl 3, 1113 Sofia
Tel: (02) 720922; (02) 722466 *Fax:* (02) 700204
Telex: 32123 Izdban
Key Personnel
Editor-in-Chief: Todor Rangelov
Sales & Publicity Manager: Maria Arabadjieva
Production Manager: Peter Tsanev
Founded: 1869
Publishing House of the Bulgarian Academy of Sciences.
Subjects: Science (General)
ISBN Prefix(es): 954-430
Bookshop(s): ul Rakovski 135, 1000 Sofia; ul V Kolarov 19, 4000 Plovdiv

Bilblioteka Nov den - Sajuz na Svobodnite Demokrati (Union of Free Democrats)+
Zk Mladost 4, bl 468, ent 2, et 5, ap 41, 1000 Sofia 1715
Mailing Address: 5 Lege St, Sofia 1000
Tel: (02) 773-982 *Fax:* (02) 327972
Key Personnel
President & Editor: Prof Ivan Kaltchev
 E-mail: ivan_kaltchev@yahoo.com
Founded: 1991
Specialize in theoretical books only.
Member of Union of Bulgarian Foundations.
Subjects: Ethnicity, History, Philosophy, Religion - Other
ISBN Prefix(es): 954-8575
Number of titles published annually: 4 Print
Total Titles: 24 Print
Parent Company: Research Center for Direct Democracy
Imprints: Dimiter Blagoev; L1K
Subsidiaries: Bulgarian Philosophical Association
Distributed by Filvest; Dimiter Blagoev
Distributor for L1K

Bookshop(s): 15, Tzar Osvoboditel Blvd, Sofia 1000, Sacho Savov *Tel:* (02) 85-81, code 003592
Book Club(s): Abagar, 47, Tzar Osvoboditel Blvd, Sofia 1000, Stefan Vlakhov *Tel:* (02) 46-31, code 003592

Bojko Kacarmazov+
ul Vasil Levski 50, Sofia 1000
Mailing Address: 50 Levski Blvd, Sofia 1000
Tel: (02) 654969 *Fax:* (02) 654969
E-mail: eto@einet.bg
Subjects: Education, Language Arts, Linguistics, Literature, Literary Criticism, Essays, Poetry, Social Sciences, Sociology
ISBN Prefix(es): 954-603

Bulgarski Houdozhnik Publishers+
6 Shipka Str, et 1, 1504 Sofia
Tel: (02) 467285 *Fax:* (02) 946 0212
Key Personnel
Dir: Bouyan Filchev *E-mail:* filchev@bulnet.bg
Founded: 1952 (reformation 1991)
ISBN Prefix(es): 954-406
Subsidiaries: Union of Bulgarian Artists

Bulgarski Pissatel+
6 Septemvri 35, 1000 Sofia
Tel: (02) 875873; (02) 873454; (02) 874527
 Fax: (02) 872495
Key Personnel
Dir: Gertcho Atanasov
Publishing House of the Union of Bulgarian Writers.
Subjects: Fiction
ISBN Prefix(es): 954-443

Bulvest 2000 Ltd+
13 Serdika St, 1000 Sofia
Tel: (02) 9833286; (02) 9833169 *Fax:* (02) 9815464
E-mail: bulvest@internet-bg.net
Key Personnel
President: Vladimir Topencharov
Founded: 1990
Subjects: Education
ISBN Prefix(es): 954-18

CHRIKER+
Banichora, 17-A, vh b, et 5 ap 65, Sofia 1233
Tel: (02) 319-217
Key Personnel
Contact: Ms Nevena Konstantinova Keremedchieva
Founded: 1994
Subjects: Art, Ethnicity, Literature, Literary Criticism, Essays, Philosophy, Poetry
ISBN Prefix(es): 954-8498
Number of titles published annually: 12 Print
Total Titles: 61 Print
Book Club(s): Club of Modern Bulgarian Poetry

Ciela Publishing House+
Member of Wolters Kluwer Group
80-A Patriarh Evtimii Blvd, 1463 Sofia
Tel: (02) 9516376; (02) 9549397; (02) 9516697
 Fax: (02) 9549397
E-mail: ciela@bulnet.bg
Web Site: www.ciela.net
Telex: 24 611
Key Personnel
Dir: Vesselin Todorov
Editor-in-Chief & International Rights: Stefka Angelova
Marketing & Promotion: Borislav Gyurov
Founded: 1990
Member of Bulgarian Book Publishers Association.
Subjects: Accounting, Business, Economics, Education, Fiction, Finance, Law, Medicine, Nursing, Dentistry, Nonfiction (General), Psychol-

ogy, Psychiatry, Publishing & Book Trade Reference, Technology
ISBN Prefix(es): 954-649
Number of titles published annually: 39 Print
Total Titles: 487 Print
Associate Companies: Ciela Consultancy, Ciela Printing House
Distributed by New Star; Sofi-R

DA-Izdatelstvo Publishers+
ul Patriarh Evtimij 26, Sofia 1000
Tel: (02) 988 1208 *Fax:* (02) 986 6290
Key Personnel
Dir: Aleko Djankov *E-mail:* alekoda@aster.net
Founded: 1996
Subjects: Fiction, History, Medicine, Nursing, Dentistry, Psychology, Psychiatry, Transportation

Hristo G Danov State Publishing House+
ul Stojan Calakov 1, 4025 Plovdiv
Tel: (032) 231201; (032) 265421 *Fax:* (032) 260560
Key Personnel
Dir: Nacho Hristoskov
Editorial: Dimitur Stoilov
Founded: 1855
Subjects: Fiction, Poetry
ISBN Prefix(es): 954-442

Darzavno Izdatelstvo Narodna Kultura
ul Angel Kanchev 1, 1000 Sofia
Mailing Address: PO Box 421, 1000 Sofia
Tel: (02) 9872722; (02) 9878063 *Fax:* (02) 894946
Key Personnel
Dir: Alexander Donev
Founded: 1944
Subjects: Social Sciences, Sociology
ISBN Prefix(es): 954-04

Darzhavno Izdatelstvo Zemizdat
Obul Carigradsko Sose 47, 1504 Sofia
Tel: (02) 441829 *Fax:* (02) 442319
Key Personnel
Dir: Petar Angelov
Chief Editor: Emil Krustev
Founded: 1949
State Agricultural Publishing House.
Subjects: Agriculture, Cookery, Crafts, Games, Hobbies, Environmental Studies, Nonfiction (General), Science (General)
ISBN Prefix(es): 954-05

DATAMAP - Europe+
22 Shandor Petiofi St, Sofia 1606
Tel: (02) 510090 *Fax:* (02) 510090
E-mail: datamap@mail.techno-linek.com
Web Site: www.datamap.dir.bg
Key Personnel
President: Chaudor Dinev
Founded: 1991
Specialize in digital & printed maps, atlases & catalogues.
ISBN Prefix(es): 87-17
Total Titles: 25 Print; 2 CD-ROM
Associate Companies: Datamap Review Ltd, Sofia, Contact: Christo Assenor *Tel:* (02) 510090 *Fax:* (02) 510090

Dimiter Blagoev, *imprint of* Bilblioteka Nov den - Sajuz na Svobodnite Demokrati (Union of Free Democrats)

Dolphin Press Group Ltd+
PO Box 296, Bourgas 8000
Tel: (056) 844044 *Fax:* (056) 844077
Web Site: www.dolphin-press.com
Key Personnel
Chairman: Valentin Fortunov *Tel:* (088) 206 530
E-mail: valentin.fortunov@unacs.bg

Founded: 1990
Subjects: Business, Career Development, Economics, Finance, Law, Management, Marketing, Public Administration
ISBN Prefix(es): 954-721
Subsidiaries: AB-Direct, Ltd; Eurobook, Ltd
Bookshop(s): 17 Botev St, Bourgas 8000
Book Club(s): The Golden Dolphin

EA Publishing House+
43 San Stefano St, 5800 Pleven
Mailing Address: PO Box 151, 5800 Pleven
Tel: (064) 800974 *Fax:* (064) 22528
E-mail: ea@famahold.com
Key Personnel
President: V Velikova
Editor-in-Chief: M Phillipova
Sales Manager: Y Raikova
Founded: 1991
Member of the Bulgarian Publishers Association.
Subjects: Behavioral Sciences, Biography, Fiction, Literature, Literary Criticism, Essays, Philosophy, Poetry, Psychology, Psychiatry, Romance
ISBN Prefix(es): 954-450
Bookshop(s): Pleven, V Levski St 161

EnEffect, Center for Energy Efficiency
One, Christo Smirnensky Blvd, 3rd floor, Sofia 1421
Mailing Address: PO Box 85, Sofia 1606
Tel: (02) 963 1714; (02) 9630723; (02) 9632169 *Fax:* (02) 9632574
E-mail: eneffect@mail.orbitel.bg
Web Site: www.eneffect.bg
Key Personnel
Executive Dir: Dr Zdravko Genchev *Fax:* (02) 9632574
Founded: 1992
Subjects: Energy, Environmental Studies

Eurasia Academic Publishers+
Lyulin 331 A-1, Sofia 1336
Mailing Address: Lyulin 332 B-25, 1336 Sofia
Tel: (02) 252547
E-mail: eurasia@realsci.com
Web Site: www.biblio.hit.bg
Key Personnel
President: Plamen Gradinarov
Founded: 1990
Subjects: Asian Studies, Education, History, Natural History, Philosophy, Psychology, Psychiatry, Religion - Buddhist, Religion - Hindu
ISBN Prefix(es): 954-628

Evrazija, see Eurasia Academic Publishers

Factor-Alias+
Zk Mladost 1, bl 62, vh 1, ap 27, Sofia 1784
Tel: (02) 747-891
E-mail: factoral@omega.bg
Key Personnel
President: Bakalova Rossitza
Founded: 1997
Subjects: Education, English as a Second Language, Fiction, Western Fiction
Orders to: 12-14 Demkogly St, Rm 508, Sofia 1000

Fama+
ul Aksakov 10, Sofia 1000
Tel: (02) 881175
Key Personnel
Editor: Maria Koeva; Igor Shemtov
Founded: 1992
Subjects: Literature, Literary Criticism, Essays
ISBN Prefix(es): 954-597

Foi-Commerce+
PO Box 775, 1000 Sofia
Tel: (02) 227116 *Fax:* (02) 227116
E-mail: foi@nlcv.net

Key Personnel
President: Markov Krassimir
Founded: 1990
Subjects: Accounting, Business, Computer Science, Library & Information Sciences, Mathematics, Science (General)
ISBN Prefix(es): 954-16

Fondacija Zlatno Kljuce+
Zk Mladost 1A, bl 523, vh 5, ap 115, Sofia 1729
Tel: (02) 760-671; (02) 623517 *Fax:* (02) 623517
E-mail: ynfirst@mat.bg
Key Personnel
President & International Rights: Mr M Tsvetanov
Founded: 1991
Promotion & subsidizing of miscellaneous pieces of art-created by & addressed to children; puppet theatre.
Member of ASIFA.
Subjects: Art, Child Care & Development, Drama, Theater, Education
ISBN Prefix(es): 954-90237

Galaktika Publishing House+
Nezavisimost Sq 6, 9000 Varna
Tel: (052) 225077; (052) 241132; (052) 241156 *Fax:* (052) 234750
Key Personnel
General Dir: Assya Kadreva
Publicity Manager: Dimitrichka Telezarova
Founded: 1960
Subjects: Economics, Literature, Literary Criticism, Essays, Science Fiction, Fantasy
ISBN Prefix(es): 954-418

Gea-Libris Publishing House+
16 B Alexander Batenberg St, 1000 Sofia
Mailing Address: PO Box 365, 1000 Sofia
Tel: (02) 986-31-71; (02) 986-46-04 *Fax:* (02) 986-69-00
E-mail: emilgea@techno-link.com
Web Site: www.gea-libris.search.bg
Key Personnel
Editor-in-Chief: Svetla Evstatieva
Dir: Emil Krastev
Computer & Design: Galina Krasteva
International Rights Contact: Milena Kardeleva
Founded: 1990
Subjects: Animals, Pets, Biological Sciences, Chemistry, Chemical Engineering, Economics, Environmental Studies, Gardening, Plants, Geography, Geology, Health, Nutrition, Mathematics, Physical Sciences, Science (General)
Total Titles: 500 Print
Branch Office(s)
Gea-Libris-Varna, Boucher Str No 5, Anton Apostolov *Tel:* 052-250452/824369

Global Kontakts Balgarija
34 Vladajska St, 1606 Sofia 1606
Tel: (02) 540636 *Fax:* (02) 528790
Web Site: www.m3.bulgaria.com
Key Personnel
Man Dir: Maxim Behar *E-mail:* max@mbox.cit.bg
Founded: 1997
Subjects: Advertising
ISBN Prefix(es): 954-90246

Heliopol
zk Bakstan, bl 15, vh A, ap 1, 1784 Sofia 1618
Tel: (02) 746-850; (02) 718513
ISBN Prefix(es): 954-578

Hermes Publishing House+
16 Dobry Voynikov St, 4000 Plovdiv
Tel: (032) 630630 *Fax:* (032) 634095
E-mail: hermes@plovdiv.techno-link.com
Key Personnel
President: Stoyo Vartolomeev

International Rights: Victoria Petrova
Founded: 1991
Member of Bulgarian Bookpublishers Association.
Subjects: Education, Fiction, Health, Nutrition, Nonfiction (General), Romance
ISBN Prefix(es): 954-459
Subsidiaries: Hermes Publishers
Book Club(s): Friends of Hermes; Connoisseurs of the Book

Heron Press Publishing House+
18 Oboriste St, 1504 Sofia
Tel: (02) 443368 Fax: (02) 443368
E-mail: heron_press@attglobal.net
Key Personnel
Contact: Ilia Petrov
Founded: 1993
Subjects: Fiction, Geography, Geology, History, Mathematics, Medicine, Nursing, Dentistry, Natural History, Nonfiction (General), Physical Sciences, Physics, Science (General)
ISBN Prefix(es): 954-580
Book Club(s): Association of Bulgarian Publishers

Publishing House Hristo Botev+
ul Slavjanska vh Aet, 1000 Sofia
Tel: (02) 441408; (02) 443503 Fax: 441490
Key Personnel
Dir: Ivan Dinkov
Founded: 1944
Subjects: Biography, Fiction, Government, Political Science, History, Literature, Literary Criticism, Essays, Philosophy, Social Sciences, Sociology
ISBN Prefix(es): 954-445

Interpres+
1343, Ljulin-2 bl 214-d-102, 1343 Sofia
Mailing Address: PO Box 18, 1582 Sofia
Tel: (02) 517915 Fax: (02) 517915
E-mail: interpres@bis.bg; intrpres@usa.net
Key Personnel
President: Mariana Evlogieva
Founded: 1992
Subjects: Advertising, Business, Crafts, Games, Hobbies, Education, Human Relations, Humor, Language Arts, Linguistics, Literature, Literary Criticism, Essays
ISBN Prefix(es): 954-664

Izdatelska kasta JA
ul Preslav 19, Jambol 8600
Tel: (046) 26166; (046) 20077
ISBN Prefix(es): 954-615

Izdatelstvo Prosveta as, see Prosveta Publishers as

Kibea Publishing Co+
Mailing Address: PO Box 70, 1336 Sofia
Tel: (02) 24 10 20; (02) 925 01 52 Fax: (02) 925 07 48
E-mail: kibea@internet-bg.net; office@kibea.net
Web Site: www.kibea.net
Key Personnel
Publisher: Dimitar Zlatarev
Founded: 1991
Subjects: Alternative, Anthropology, Art, Astrology, Occult, Biography, Cookery, Fiction, Foreign Countries, Health, Nutrition, History, How-to, Human Relations, Nonfiction (General), Parapsychology, Philosophy, Poetry, Psychology, Psychiatry, Religion - Buddhist, Religion - Other, Self-Help
ISBN Prefix(es): 954-474
Total Titles: 300 Print
Bookshop(s): Kibea Books & Health Centre
Book Club(s): Friends of Kibea Club

Kolibri Publishing Group
Ul Solunska 40, Sofia 1000
Tel: (02) 814728; (02) 813625 Fax: (02) 814728
Key Personnel
President: Raymond Wagenstein
Editor: Zhechka Georgieva
Founded: 1990
Subjects: Fiction, Literature, Literary Criticism, Essays, Nonfiction (General)
ISBN Prefix(es): 954-529
Distributor for Abrams, Thames & Hudson; Larousse; Robert; Taschen; etc; Random House Group
Bookshop(s): 2 Levski St, Sofia 1000

Kralica MAB (Queen Mab)+
Mladost 1, bl 29A, vh 2 ap 21, Sofia 1750
Tel: (02) 767357 Fax: (02) 767357
Web Site: www.mab.hit.bg
Key Personnel
President: Mariana Aretova
Senior Editor: Nikolay Aretov E-mail: naretov@yahoo.com
Founded: 1992
Subjects: Astrology, Occult, Cookery, Literature, Literary Criticism, Essays, Mysteries, Parapsychology, Philosophy, Psychology, Psychiatry, Theology
ISBN Prefix(es): 954-533
Number of titles published annually: 20 Print
Total Titles: 110 Print

Lettera+
62 Rhodope Str, 4000 Plovdiv
Tel: (032) 600 930 Fax: (032) 600 940
E-mail: lettera@plovdiv.techno-link.com
Web Site: www.lettera.bg
Key Personnel
President: Nadja Furnadjieva
Founded: 1991
Subjects: Education, English as a Second Language, Fiction, Humor, Language Arts, Linguistics, Mathematics
ISBN Prefix(es): 954-516
Distributed by Damian Yakov

LIK, imprint of Bilblioteka Nov den - Sajuz na Svobodnite Demokrati (Union of Free Democrats)

LIK IZDANIJA+
ul Ivan Basov 3, Bozuriste, Sofjsko 2227
Mailing Address: Sofia, Sejnovo No 15, Sofia 1504
Tel: (02) 444121 Fax: (02) 444 121
E-mail: lik@ttm.bg
Key Personnel
President: Liuben Kosarev
Founded: 1993
Subjects: Anthropology, Education, Health, Nutrition, History, Literature, Literary Criticism, Essays, Mathematics, Philosophy, Psychology, Psychiatry, Social Sciences, Sociology
ISBN Prefix(es): 954-607

Litera Prima+
Drouzhba-2, Bl 418, Entr 2, App 46, 1582 Sofia
Mailing Address: PO Box 38, 1528 Sofia
Tel: (02) 423698
E-mail: mmihales@vmei.acad.bg
Key Personnel
Contact: Marin Naydenov Tel: (02) 9731698 Fax: (02) 9731698 E-mail: mmihalev@vmei.acad.bg
Founded: 1993
Subjects: Anthropology, Archaeology, Astronomy, Mysteries, Natural History, Parapsychology, Physical Sciences, Science (General)
ISBN Prefix(es): 954-8163; 954-738

Makros 2000 - Plovdiv+
Bul Nezavisimost 119, zk Izgrev, 4019 Plovdiv
Tel: (032) 828391
Key Personnel
President & Owner: Georgi Stanchev Nikolov
Founded: 1991
Subjects: Art, Astronomy, Biography, Biological Sciences, Business, Chemistry, Chemical Engineering, Computer Science, Economics, Education, Electronics, Electrical Engineering, Geography, Geology, History, Literature, Literary Criticism, Essays, Management, Mathematics, Medicine, Nursing, Dentistry, Microcomputers, Music, Dance, Philosophy, Physical Sciences, Physics, Psychology, Psychiatry, Science (General), Social Sciences, Sociology
ISBN Prefix(es): 954-561
Bookshop(s): Makros 2000, Tsar Assen 16, Plovdiv 4000

Mateks, see MATEX

MATEX+
ul Han Omurtag 10, Sofia 1000
Tel: (02) 430177
E-mail: mmk_fte@uacg.acad.bg
Key Personnel
President: Mihail Konstantinov
Manager: Emil Enchev
Founded: 1991
Subjects: Cookery, Education, Electronics, Electrical Engineering, Fiction, Health, Nutrition, Mathematics, Nonfiction (General), Science Fiction, Fantasy
ISBN Prefix(es): 954-508
Associate Companies: ELMA Publishing House, Sofia
Subsidiaries: BIAR

Medicina i Fizkultura EOOD
pl Slavejkov 11, Sofia 1000
Tel: (02) 871308; (02) 884068 Fax: (02) 897165
Subjects: Biological Sciences, Geography, Geology, Health, Nutrition, Medicine, Nursing, Dentistry, Sports, Athletics
ISBN Prefix(es): 954-420

Izdatelstvo na Ministerstvoto na Otbranata
ul Ivan Vazov 12, Sofia 1000
Tel: (02) 878188; (02) 9885570 Fax: (02) 881568
Subjects: History, Military Science, Social Sciences, Sociology
ISBN Prefix(es): 954-509

Mladezh+
ul Car Kalojan 10, 1000 Sofia
Tel: (02) 882137 Fax: (02) 876135
Key Personnel
Dir: Stanimir Ilchev
Founded: 1945
Youth Publishing House.
Subjects: Fiction, Government, Political Science, Philosophy, Social Sciences, Sociology
ISBN Prefix(es): 954-413

Musica EOOD, see Musica Publishing House Ltd

Musica Publishing House Ltd+
11 Slavejkov Sq, 1000 Sofia
Tel: (02) 9877963; (02) 9802256 Fax: (02) 9877965
E-mail: mphsofia@hotmail.com
Web Site: www.geocities.com/musicapublishinghouse
Key Personnel
Man Dir: Nelly Koulaksazova
Founded: 1975
Member of Bulgarian Book Publishing Association.

Subjects: Art, Biography, Child Care & Development, Education, Music, Dance, Poetry, Publishing & Book Trade Reference
ISBN Prefix(es): 954-405

Naouka i Izkoustvo, Ltd+
11 Slavejkov, 1000 Sofia
Tel: (02) 9874790; (02) 9872496 *Fax:* (02) 9872496
E-mail: nauk_izk@sigma-bg.com
Key Personnel
Dir: Loreta Poushkarova
Founded: 1948
bulgarian & foreign scientific literature in the fields of philosophy, psychology, linguistics, history, dictionaries & language learning materials.
Subjects: Art, Business, Economics, History, Law, Mathematics, Philosophy, Physics, Psychology, Psychiatry, Science (General), Social Sciences, Sociology
ISBN Prefix(es): 954-02

Narodna Kultura+
One Angel Kunchev, 1000 Sofia
Tel: (02) 981 4739 *Fax:* (02) 987 2722
E-mail: peepcult@internet-bg.net
Web Site: web.narodnakultura.hit.bg
Key Personnel
Dir: Petar Manolov
Founded: 1944
Subjects: Literature, Literary Criticism, Essays, Poetry
ISBN Prefix(es): 954-04

Publishing House Narodno delo OOD+
Bul Hristo Botev 3, PO Box 59, Varna 9000
Tel: (052) 230241; (052) 288516
Key Personnel
Contact: Mr Konstantin Paskalev
Founded: 1990
Subjects: Advertising, Maritime, Regional Interests, Travel
ISBN Prefix(es): 954-627
Branch Office(s)
Bourgas
Dobritch
Rouse
Shoumen
Sofia
Orders to: Festival & Congress Centre, Varna

Nauka i Izkustovo EOOD, see Naouka i Izkoustvo, Ltd

New Man Publishers, *imprint of* Nov Covek Publishing House

Nov Covek Publishing House+
28 Antim I St, 1303 Sofia
Tel: (02) 9863766 *Fax:* (02) 9863772
E-mail: newman@mbox.cit.bg
Key Personnel
President: Rumen Papratilov
Founded: 1990
Produces & distributes theological, reference & sociological literature.
Member of International Literature Associates, Bulgarian Book Publishers Association.
Subjects: Biblical Studies, Child Care & Development, History, Human Relations, Philosophy, Psychology, Psychiatry, Social Sciences, Sociology, Theology
ISBN Prefix(es): 954-407
Imprints: New Man Publishers

Universitetsko Izdatelstvo 'Kliment Ochridski'
Blvd Carigradsko Sose 125, bl 4, 1113 Sofia
Tel: (02) 71288; (02) 71265; (02) 704271; (02) 71151 *Fax:* (02) 704271
E-mail: gzisha@ns.sclg.uni-sofia.bg

Key Personnel
Dir: Dimitaz Tomov
Subjects: Science (General)
ISBN Prefix(es): 954-07

Pensoft Publishers+
Akad G Bonchevstr, Bldg 6, 1113 Sofia
Tel: (02) 716451 *Fax:* (02) 704508
E-mail: pensoft@mbox.infotel.bg
Web Site: www.pensoft.net
Key Personnel
Managing Dir: Dr Lyubomir D Penev, PhD
Publisher-in-Chief: Sergei I Golovatch
Founded: 1993
Also acts as book supplier for East European books.
Subjects: Agriculture, Archaeology, Biological Sciences, Business, Earth Sciences, Environmental Studies, Finance, History, Language Arts, Linguistics, Mathematics, Natural History, Physics, Religion - Other, Science (General), Zoology, Botany
ISBN Prefix(es): 954-642
Number of titles published annually: 60 Print
Total Titles: 160 Print
Online services available through World Wide Web.
Divisions: Pensoft-Moscow
Branch Office(s)
Institute for Problems of Ecology & Education, Leninsky pr 33, V-71 Moscow, Russian Federation, Dr Sergei Golovatch *E-mail:* spol@orc.ru *Web Site:* www.pensoft.net
Distributed by Coronet Books Inc (USA); DA Information Services; Goecke & Evers Antiquariat (Germany); Kabourek; NHBS-Natural History Book Service
Distributor for Academic Publishing House-Sofia; Heron Press
Orders to: Coronet Books Inc, 311 Bainbridge St, Philadelphia, PA 19147, United States *Tel:* 215-925-2762 *Fax:* 215-925-1912 *E-mail:* jeffgolds@aol.com *Web Site:* www.coronetbooks.com

Pet Plus+
142 Rakovski St, 1000 Sofia
Tel: (02) 9874188 *Fax:* (02) 9809726
E-mail: fiveplus@bulgaria.net; petplus@bnc.bg
Key Personnel
President: Petyo Hristov
Founded: 1990
Specialize in books with cassette.
Member of Association of the Bulgarian Editors.
Subjects: Biography, Literature, Literary Criticism, Essays, Poetry, Religion - Other
ISBN Prefix(es): 954-462
Total Titles: 2 Print
Book Club(s): Association of Book Publications

Prosveta Publishers as+
Formerly Izdatelstvo Prosveta as
117, Tzarigradsko Shousse Blvd, 1184 Sofia
Tel: (02) 760651; (02) 9743696; (02) 761182 *Fax:* (02) 764451
E-mail: prosveta@intech.bg
Key Personnel
President: Joana Tomova
Founded: 1945
Specialize in school textbooks.
Subjects: Education
ISBN Prefix(es): 954-01
Bookshop(s): 39 Ivan Assen II Str, Sofia

Prozoretz, see Prozoretz Ltd Publishing House

Prozoretz Ltd Publishing House (Izdatelsica Kushta Prozoretz)+
117, Tzarigradsko Shousse Blvd, 1784 Sofia
Tel: (02) 765171; (02) 746053 *Fax:* (02) 746053
E-mail: prozor@tea.bg

Key Personnel
Man Dir: Joana Tomova
Subjects: English as a Second Language, Fiction, Health, Nutrition, Philosophy, Poetry, Religion - Other, Self-Help
ISBN Prefix(es): 954-733
Bookshop(s): 39 Ivan Assen II Str, Sofia

Rakla+
Zk Borovo, bl 222 A, vh D, et 6, ap 112, Sofia 1680
Tel: (02) 580-569
E-mail: grigorit@yahoo.com
Key Personnel
Senior Manager: Velichka Bojinova *E-mail:* rakla.net@usa.net
Founded: 1993
Member of Union of Bulgarian Journalists.
Subjects: Cookery, Gardening, Plants, History
ISBN Prefix(es): 954-90251

Regalia 6 Publishing House+
PO Box 172, 1700 Sofia
Tel: (02) 754111 *Fax:* (02) 566573
E-mail: vpruu@dir.bg
Key Personnel
Contact: Raicho Ushatov
Founded: 1991
Publication of school aids & supplementary materials for all levels of education, compiled by the specialists in the corresponding areas.
Subjects: Career Development, Computer Science, Crafts, Games, Hobbies, Education, English as a Second Language, Mathematics, Science (General)
ISBN Prefix(es): 954-8147

Reporter+
113 Tsarigradsko chausse, 1784 Sofia
Tel: (02) 760834 *Fax:* (02) 718377
E-mail: reporter@techno-link.com
Key Personnel
Manager: Krum Blagov *Tel:* (02) 76 08 34 *E-mail:* reporter@mail.techno-link.com
Founded: 1990 (Ltd)
Non-fiction & fiction Bulgarian & foreign literature, planners & calendars.
Subjects: Advertising, Biography, Child Care & Development, Fiction, Health, Nutrition, Nonfiction (General)
ISBN Prefix(es): 954-8102
Number of titles published annually: 12 Print
Total Titles: 30 Print

Sanra Book Trust
zk Javorov, bl54 vhA et2, Sofia 1111
Tel: (02) 721927 *Fax:* (02) 721927
Key Personnel
Contact: Sasho Ranguelov
Founded: 1993
Subjects: English as a Second Language
ISBN Prefix(es): 954-662

Seven Hills Publishers+
ul Veliko Tarnovo 13, Plovdiv 4000
Mailing Address: PO Box 976, Plovdiv 4000
Tel: (032) 262235 *Fax:* (032) 262235
Key Personnel
President: Valeri Nichevski
Vice President: Evelina Proeva
Founded: 1993
Subjects: Art, Business, English as a Second Language, Language Arts, Linguistics, Law, Medicine, Nursing, Dentistry, Psychology, Psychiatry
ISBN Prefix(es): 954-669

Sibi+
4 Slavejkov Sq, 1000 Sofia
Tel: (02) 9870141 *Fax:* (02) 9875709
E-mail: sibi@sibi.bg

BULGARIA

Key Personnel
President: Mr Vassil Tashev
Vice President & International Rights: Mrs Natalia Goudjeva
Founded: 1990
Sibi has own bookshops in major Bugarian cities.
Subjects: Labor, Industrial Relations, Law
ISBN Prefix(es): 954-8150; 954-730
Bookshop(s): City Court of Plovdiv, 6 Septemvri St 168, 4000 Plovdiv; Sibi Specialize Bookshop, Supreme Administrative Court Building, Stambolijski Blvd 18, 1000 Sofia
Shipping Address: 1799 Sofia, Mladost-2, bl 227, vh 5, et 2, ap 96
Warehouse: Mladost-2, bl 227, vh 5, et 2, ap 96, 1799 Sofia
Orders to: Mladost-2, bl 227, vh 5, et 2, ap 96, 1799 Sofia

Sila & Zivot
ul Dimitar Blagoev St, vh. 3, 8001 Burgas
Mailing Address: PO Box 609, 8001 Burgas
Tel: (056) 20965
E-mail: silajivot@bse.bg
Key Personnel
Publisher: Milka Kraleva
Founded: 1992
Specialize in books & music of Peter Deunov (1864-1944).
Subjects: Astrology, Occult, Biblical Studies, Child Care & Development, Education, Music, Dance, Parapsychology, Philosophy, Self-Help, Theology
ISBN Prefix(es): 954-8146

Sinodalno Izdatelstvo
ul Oboriste 4, 1000 Sofia
Tel: (02) 875611; (02) 875237
Synodal Publishing House.
Subjects: Religion - Other
ISBN Prefix(es): 954-8398

Sita-MB+
ul Vasil Drumev 47, vhA ap21, Varna 9002
Tel: (092) 872285
Founded: 1992
Subjects: Communications, Human Relations, Labor, Industrial Relations, Management
ISBN Prefix(es): 954-518

Slance, see Sluntse Publishing House

Slavena+
ul Radko Dimitriev No 59A, 9000 Varna
Tel: (052) 602 465 *Fax:* (052) 225 935
E-mail: slavena@triada.bg
Web Site: www.slavena.net
Key Personnel
Contact: Nasko Yakimov
Founded: 1990
Subjects: Art, Crafts, Games, Hobbies, Economics, Education, History, Law, Literature, Literary Criticism, Essays, Science (General)
ISBN Prefix(es): 954-579

Sluntse Publishing House+
11 Slaveykov Sq, 1000 Sofia
Tel: (02) 9883797 *Fax:* (02) 9871405
E-mail: sluntse@dlr.bg
Key Personnel
President: Nadia Kabakchieva
Founded: 1937
Subjects: Astrology, Occult, Biography, Child Care & Development, Education, Fiction, Foreign Countries, Gardening, Plants, Health, Nutrition, House & Home, Human Relations, Marketing, Native American Studies, Nonfiction (General), Publishing & Book Trade Reference, Autobiography/Memoirs/Letter & Beauty
ISBN Prefix(es): 954-742

Srebaren lav+
ul Plovdivsko pole, bl2 vhA ap3, 1756 Sofia
Tel: (02) 752298
Founded: 1991
Subjects: Literature, Literary Criticism, Essays
ISBN Prefix(es): 954-571

Svetra Publishing House+
Major Thompson St, Bl 12, entr 2, 1407 Sofia
Tel: (02) 62 27 39; (02) 983 45 41 *Fax:* (02) 234966
E-mail: svetlev@cybernet.bg
Key Personnel
President: Nickolay Svetlev
Founded: 1993
Subjects: Advertising, Art, Biblical Studies, Fiction, Literature, Literary Criticism, Essays, Poetry, Science Fiction, Fantasy
ISBN Prefix(es): 954-8430
Warehouse: 83A Simeon St, 1000 Sofia *Tel:* (02) 834541

Sviat Publishers
11 Slaveikov Sq, 1000 Sofia
Tel: (02) 892202 *Fax:* (02) 800704; (02) 822851
Key Personnel
Dir: Bela Lazarova
ISBN Prefix(es): 954-415

Svjat EOOD, see Sviat Publishers

Technica+
One Slaveikov Sq, 1000 Sofia
Tel: (02) 987 1283 *Fax:* (02) 987 4906
Key Personnel
Manager: Ms Nina Deneva *Tel:* (02) 987 1283 *Fax:* (02) 987 4906
Editorial Manager: Ms Evelina Kachakova
Founded: 1958
Subjects: Science (General)
ISBN Prefix(es): 954-03

Tehnika EOOD, see Technica

TEMTO
Bul Gen Skobelev 35, Sofia 1463
Tel: (02) 524-924
E-mail: temto@sf.icn.bg
Key Personnel
President: Temenouga Todorova
Programmer: Kiril Voykov
Artist: Monika Voykova
Founded: 1991
Subjects: Advertising, Agriculture, Architecture & Interior Design, Computer Science, Health, Nutrition, Mathematics, Microcomputers, Poetry, Psychology, Psychiatry, Advertising, Programming
ISBN Prefix(es): 954-9566

Trud - Izd kasta+
15 Dunav Str, 1000 Sofia 1000
Tel: (02) 9814110 *Fax:* (02) 467565
E-mail: kktrud@netel.bg
Web Site: www.trud.bg
Key Personnel
President: Nikola Kitsevski *Tel:* (02) 9214157
Founded: 1994
Subjects: Biography, Fiction, History, Humor, Mysteries, Western Fiction
ISBN Prefix(es): 954-528
Number of titles published annually: 40 Print
Total Titles: 500 Print
Parent Company: Media Holding, 119 Ekzarh Joseph, 1000 Sofia
Ultimate Parent Company: WAZ- Germany
Branch Office(s)
Trud Publishing House, Contact: Krasimir Mirchev *Tel:* (02) 987-29-24

Ivan Vazov Publishing House
ul. Georgi Benkovski 14, Sofia 1000
Tel: (02) 878481; (02) 871572 *Fax:* (02) 878416
Founded: 1948
Subjects: Biography, Fiction, Government, Political Science, History, Humor, Literature, Literary Criticism, Essays, Nonfiction (General), Poetry, Science (General)
ISBN Prefix(es): 954-604

WTU Todor Kableskov+
158 Geo Milev St, Sofia 1574
Tel: (2) 717 104 *Fax:* (2) 706 342
E-mail: office@vtu.acad.bg
Web Site: www.vtu.acad.bg
Key Personnel
Rector of VVTU: Michael Karamarinov
Associate Prof: Nencho Nenov
Founded: 1922
Subjects: Advertising, Behavioral Sciences, Business, Civil Engineering, Communications, Economics, Electronics, Electrical Engineering, Engineering (General), Mechanical Engineering, Transportation
ISBN Prefix(es): 954-12
Number of titles published annually: 45 Print
Parent Company: Ministry of Transport

Peyo K Yavorov Publishing House+
52 Dondukov Blvd, 1000 Sofia
Tel: (02) 875201; (02) 880137; (02) 876765 *Fax:* (02) 875592
Key Personnel
Man Dir: Julia Bouchkova
Founded: 1945
State owned publisher.
Subjects: Cookery, Fiction, History, Humor, Nonfiction (General), Poetry
ISBN Prefix(es): 954-525

Zunica+
Zk Bakston, bl 10, et 11, ap 48, Sofia 1618
Tel: (02) 551-977
Subjects: Art, Drama, Theater, Fiction, Humor, Mysteries, Poetry, Romance, Science Fiction, Fantasy
ISBN Prefix(es): 954-9604

Burundi

General Information

Capital: Bujumbura
Language: French & Kirundi (Swahili & French commercially)
Religion: About half Roman Catholic; others follow traditional animist beliefs
Population: 6.0 million
Bank Hours: Normally closed for cash transactions in afternoon but open for all other business morning & afteroon
Shop Hours: 0800-1200, 1400-1630 Monday-Friday; 0800-1200 Saturday
Currency: 100 centimes = 1 Burundi franc
Export/Import Information: Import license required over value of 20,000 Burundi francs.

Government Printer (INABU)
BP 991, Bujumbura
Tel: (02) 22214; (02) 24046

Editions Intore+
5 Av de France, Bujumbura
Mailing Address: BP 2524, Bujumbura
Tel: (02) 225167
Key Personnel
Edition Dir: Dr Andre Birabuza

Founded: 1992
Subjects: Developing Countries, Ethnicity, History, Journalism, Literature, Literary Criticism, Essays, Philosophy, Social Sciences, Sociology
ISBN Prefix(es): 2-9506222
Divisions: Binensuel Intore; Librairie Papeterie Intore

Les Presses Lavigerie
5 Av de l'Uprona, BP 1640 Bujumbura
Tel: (02) 22368 *Fax:* (02) 220318
E-mail: lpl~bujumbura@cbinf.com
Key Personnel
Contact: Geiss Anton *Tel:* (22) 8508

Cameroon

General Information

Capital: Yaounde
Language: French & English (officially bilingual)
Religion: Christian, Islamic, traditional
Population: 12.7 million
Bank Hours: East: 0800-1130, 1430-1630 Monday-Friday; West: 0800-1330 Monday-Friday
Shop Hours: 0800-1200, 1430-1730 (earlier closing in West) Monday-Friday; 0800-1200 Saturday
Currency: 100 centimes = 1 CFA franc
Export/Import Information: Member of Customs & Economic Union of Central Africa. Import license, entitling holder to provision for necessary foreign exchange, required if value of import is over 500,000 CFA francs.
Copyright: UCC, Berne, Florence (see Copyright Conventions, pg xi)

Editions Buma Kor+
BP 727, Yaounde
Tel: (023) 7 23 07 68 *Fax:* (023) 23 29 03
Telex: 8438 KN
Key Personnel
Man Dir, Rights & Permissions: B D Buma Kor
Founded: 1977
Also act as representatives for Oxford University Press, Oxford, England.
Subjects: Drama, Theater, Economics, Fiction, Mathematics, Nonfiction (General), Poetry, Religion - Protestant, Self-Help
Parent Company: Buma Kor & Co (Sarl)
Associate Companies: Speedymint Centres
Imprints: CAW Series
Bookshop(s): Librairie Bilingue/The Bilingual Bookshop

CAW Series, *imprint of* Editions Buma Kor

Centre d'Edition et de Production pour l'Enseignement et la Recherche (CEPER)+
BP 808, Yaounde
Tel: (023) 7 23 12 93
Telex: 838 KN *Cable:* Cepmae Yaounde
Key Personnel
Dir General: Jean Claude Fouth
Sales Manager: Thomas Victor Mang Ngouni
Production Manager: Sonny Ekono
Contact: Theophile Maurice
Founded: 1967
Subjects: History, Nonfiction (General), Science (General), Social Sciences, Sociology, Technology
ISBN Prefix(es): 2-7405

CEPER, see Centre d'Edition et de Production pour l'Enseignement et la Recherche (CEPER)

Editions CLE+
BP 1501, Ave Marechal Foch, Yaounde
Tel: (023) 7-22-35-54 *Fax:* (023) 7-23-27-09
E-mail: edition@iccnet.cm *Cable:* CLE YAOUNDE
Key Personnel
Dir: Mr Comlan Prosper
Founded: 1963
Subjects: Drama, Theater, Fiction, How-to, Literature, Literary Criticism, Essays, Poetry, Religion - Protestant, Social Sciences, Sociology
ISBN Prefix(es): 2-7235
Distributed by CEC (Brussels); Editions ZOE (Geneva); L'Harmattan (Paris); Presence Africaine (Paris)
Distributor for CEDA (Ivory Coast); Editions Reynald Goulet (Quebec, Canada); Modulo Editeur (Quebec, Canada)
Bookshop(s): Librairie CLE, BP 1501, Yaounde

Presses Universitaires d'Afrique+
BP 8106, Yaounde
Tel: (023) 22 23 25 *Fax:* (023) 22 23 25
Founded: 1986
Member of Cameroon Publisher Association.
Subjects: Economics, Education, Finance, Law, Literature, Literary Criticism, Essays, Public Administration, Social Sciences, Sociology, Theology
ISBN Prefix(es): 2-912086
Parent Company: L'Africaine D'Edition et de Services (AES)
Distributed by Editions CLE (West Africa); Librarie de France

Editions Semences Africaines+
BP 5329, Yaounde Nlongkak
Tel: (023) 224058
Key Personnel
Man Dir, Production: Philippe-Louis Ombede
Editorial, Rights & Permissions: Martin King Mbida
Sales: Lea Ombede
Founded: 1974
Subjects: Drama, Theater, Fiction, History, Poetry, Regional Interests, Religion - Other
ISBN Prefix(es): 2-907553

Cape Verde

General Information

Capital: Praia
Language: Portuguese (official), French & English are also widely spoken
Religion: Predominantly Roman Catholic
Population: 398,000
Currency: 100 centavos = 1 Cape Verde escudo = $0.82 US
Export/Import Information: Member of the Economic Community of the West African States (ECWAS); Member of the ACP.

Centro de Documentacao e Informao para o Desenvolvimento
CP 120, Praia
Tel: 613969 *Fax:* 1527
Telex: 6037 CV

Chad

General Information

Capital: N'Djamena
Language: French & Arabic
Religion: Islamic in north, traditional and some Christian in south
Population: 5.2 million
Bank Hours: 0700-1200 Monday-Saturday
Shop Hours: 0700 or 0800-1200 or 1230. 1600-1900 Monday-Saturday; some close Monday
Currency: 100 centimes = 1 CFA franc
Export/Import Information: No tariff on books. Consumption tax on children's picture-books & advertising. Import licenses required except for imports from the European Econimic Community & the Franc Zone.
Copyright: Berne (see Copyright Conventions, pg xi)

Government Printer (Imprimerie National Du Tchad)
BP 453, N'Djamena

Chile

General Information

Capital: Santiago
Language: Spanish
Religion: Roman Catholic
Population: 14 million
Bank Hours: 0900-1400 Monday-Friday
Shop Hours: 1000-1900 Monday-Friday; 1000-1800 Saturday-Sunday
Currency: 100 centavos = 1 Chilean peso
Export/Import Information: Member of Latin American Integration Association (ALADI). 19% VAT on books, 11% tariff.
Copyright: UCC, Berne, Buenos Aires (see Copyright Conventions, pg xi)

Alfabeta Impresores Ltda
Lira 140, Santiago
Tel: (02) 6397765 *Fax:* (02) 6391752
Key Personnel
Contact: Jaime Vicente Martinez

Arrayan Editores
Bernarda Morin 435, Providencia, Santiago
Tel: (02) 4314200 *Fax:* (02) 2741041
E-mail: web@arrayan.cl
Web Site: www.arrayan.cl
Key Personnel
President: Ramon Luis Undurraga Laso
Manager: Pablo Marinkovic
Editor: Juan Andres Pina Riquelme
Founded: 1982
Subjects: Accounting, Anthropology, Archaeology, Art, Astronomy, Biography, Biological Sciences, Chemistry, Chemical Engineering, Communications, Computer Science, Drama, Theater, Economics, Education, Engineering (General), Environmental Studies, Ethnicity, Geography, Geology, History, Journalism, Language Arts, Linguistics, Literature, Literary Criticism, Essays, Marketing, Mathematics, Medicine, Nursing, Dentistry, Music, Dance, Mythology, Philosophy, Physical Sciences, Psychology, Psychiatry, Radio, TV, Regional Interests, Self-Help, Social Sciences, Sociology, Sports, Athletics, Technology, Travel, Veterinary Science, Customs, Design, Folklore, Religion, Zoology
ISBN Prefix(es): 956-240

Ediciones Bat+
Silvina Hurtado 1841-C, Providencia, Santiago
Tel: (02) 2743171 *Fax:* (02) 2250261
Key Personnel
Manager: Jose Cayuela Arzac
Founded: 1988

Subjects: Biography, History, Literature, Literary Criticism, Essays
ISBN Prefix(es): 956-7022

Editorial Andres Bello/Editorial Juridica de Chile+
Avda Ricardo Lyon 946, Providencia, Santiago
Tel: (02) 2049900; (02) 4619500 *Fax:* (02) 2253600
Web Site: www.editorialandresbello.com
Telex: 240901 Edjur *Cable:* EDIBEL
Key Personnel
General Manager: Julio Serrano Lamas
 E-mail: julio_serrano@entelchile.net
Dir: Ana Maria Garcia B
Publisher: Pilar de Iruarrizaga B; Karem Duffoo C
Founded: 1947
Subjects: Art, Education, History, Law, Literature, Literary Criticism, Essays, Medicine, Nursing, Dentistry
ISBN Prefix(es): 85-613
Bookshop(s): Libreria Andres Bello (under Major Booksellers)
Book Club(s): Clubs de Lectores 'Andres Bello'

Bibliografica Internacional SA
Monjitas 308, Santiago
Tel: (02) 6394057 *Fax:* (02) 6397693
Key Personnel
Manager: Ramon Trepat-Pinilla
ISBN Prefix(es): 956-7240

Cesoc Ltda+
Esmeralda 636, Santiago
Tel: (02) 6391081; (02) 6336992 *Fax:* (02) 6325382
E-mail: cesoc@bellsouth.cl
Key Personnel
Manager: Julio Silva Solar
Founded: 1984
ISBN Prefix(es): 956-211
Branch Office(s)
Para Textor, 6 Avery St, Saratoga Springs, NY 12866, United States *Tel:* (0518) 587-3774 *Fax:* (0518) 581-1859

Cetal Ediciones
Abtao 576, Cerro Concepcion, Valparaiso
Tel: (032) 213360 *Fax:* (032) 214851
Key Personnel
Manager: Pedro Berho Arteagotia
Founded: 1984
Services in technology.
Subjects: Environmental Studies
ISBN Prefix(es): 956-209

Ediciones Cieplan
Francisco Noguera 217, piso 4, depto 40, Providencia, Santiago
Tel: (02) 2323212; (02) 2324558 *Fax:* (02) 3340312
E-mail: cieplan@ctcreuna.cl
Web Site: www.cieplan.cl
Key Personnel
President: Pablo Pinera
Subjects: Developing Countries, Economics, Public Administration, Technology
ISBN Prefix(es): 956-204

Congregacion Paulinas - Hijas de San Pablo
Vicuna Mackenna 6299, Santiago
Tel: (02) 221 2832 *Fax:* (02) 294 3426
E-mail: paulinasedit@entelchile.net
Key Personnel
Sister Superior: Hortensia Lizama
Dir: Veronica Pinto Pasten
Subjects: Religion - Catholic, Theology
ISBN Prefix(es): 956-7433

Bookshop(s): Libreria San Pablo (under Major Booksellers); Centro Catequistico, Cienfuegos 60, Casilla, 3429 Santiago
Orders to: Centro Catequistico Cienfuegos 60, Casilla, 3429 Santiago *Tel:* (02) 6964650 *Fax:* (02) 6990327

Corporacion de Promocion Universitaria
Av Miguel Claro No 1460, Providencia, Codigo Postal 664 1209 Casilla 11 Correo 28, Santiago
Tel: (02) 2749022 *Fax:* (02) 2741828
ISBN Prefix(es): 956-229

Editorial Cuarto Propio
Keller 1175, Providencia, Santiago
Tel: (02) 204 7645 *Fax:* (02) 204 7622
E-mail: clic@netup.cl
Web Site: www.cuartopropio.cl
Key Personnel
General Manager: Marisol Vera
Founded: 1987
Member of Chilean Chamber of the Book.
Subjects: Fiction, Nonfiction (General), Poetry, Women's Studies
Distributed by Paratextos (USA)
Distributor for Editorial Biblos (Argentina); Editorial La Marca (Argentina)
Bookshop(s): Libros sin Frontera, PO Box 2085, Olympia, WA 98507-2085, United States
Orders to: Paratextos, 6 Avery St, Saratoga Springs, NY 12866, United States

Editora Cuatro Vientos (Cuatro Vientos Publishing House)+
Av Jaime Guzman Errazuriz 3293, Santiago
Mailing Address: PO Box 131, Santiago 29
Tel: (02) 2258381 *Fax:* (02) 3413107
E-mail: 4vientos@netline.cl
Web Site: http//www.cuatrovientos.net
Key Personnel
Manager: Dr Francisco Huneeus *Tel:* (02) 2258381
Commercial Manager: Renato Valenzuela
Founded: 1980
Member of the Chilean Association of Publishers.
Subjects: Nonfiction (General), Psychology, Psychiatry
ISBN Prefix(es): 956-242
Number of titles published annually: 12 Print
Total Titles: 120 Print
Distributed by Editorial Universitaria (Chile); Editorial Andres Bello (Chile); Edin (Argentina)
Distributor for Be-Uve-Drais (Chile); Editorial Troquel (Argentina); Editorial Nuevo Extremo (Argentina); Luz De Luna (Argentina)

Dolmen Ediciones SA+
Cirujano Guzman 194, Providencia, Casilla 43 D - Correo Central, Santiago
Tel: (02) 235 8295 *Fax:* (02) 235 8812
Key Personnel
General Manager: Juan Carlos Saez Contreras
 E-mail: jcsaez@netup.cl
Commercial Manager: Jaime Valenzuela S
International Rights: Cristobal Santa Cruz
Founded: 1920
Subjects: Education, Literature, Literary Criticism, Essays
ISBN Prefix(es): 956-201
Subsidiaries: Libreria Europea SA
Divisions: Librairie Francaise

Edeval (Universidad de Valparaiso)
Errazuriz 2190, mesa central: 56-32-507000, Valparaiso
Tel: (02) 250792 *Fax:* (02) 252125
E-mail: rrpp@uv.cl
Web Site: www.uv.cl
Key Personnel
International Rights: Arturo Salas Caceres
Founded: 1961

Subjects: Criminology, Economics, Government, Political Science, History, Human Relations, Labor, Industrial Relations, Law, Maritime, Philosophy, Publishing & Book Trade Reference, Social Sciences, Sociology
ISBN Prefix(es): 956-200
Bookshop(s): Libreria Andres Bello, Huerfanos, 1158 Santiago

Instituto Geografico Militar
Dieciocho N° 369, Santiago
Tel: (02) 4606800 *Fax:* (02) 4608294
E-mail: ventas@igm.cl; informaciones@igm.cl
Web Site: www.igm.cl
Telex: 441677 16M C2
Key Personnel
Brig General: Enrique Gillmore Callejas
Contact: Mercedes Lucar
Founded: 1992
Specialized in: Cartography & topography of national territory.
Subjects: Earth Sciences, Geography, Geology
ISBN Prefix(es): 956-202
Total Titles: 30 Print; 2 CD-ROM

Grijalbo y Cia Ltda
Almirante Barroso 27, Santiago
Tel: (02) 696-5152; (02) 696-1154 *Fax:* (02) 672-1850
E-mail: ramiro@senderos.cl
Web Site: www.senderos.cl
Key Personnel
Contact: Gian Carlo Corte Truffello
ISBN Prefix(es): 956-258
Parent Company: Ediciones Grijalbo SA, Spain

Ediciones Mil Hojas Ltda
Av Antonio Varas 1480, Providencia, Santiago
Tel: (02) 2743172 *Fax:* (02) 2250261
Key Personnel
Dir: David R Turkieltaub
Founded: 1991
Subjects: Anthropology, Art, Astrology, Occult, Education, Self-Help, Sports, Athletics, Travel
ISBN Prefix(es): 956-7741
Subsidiaries: Abanico Libros Ltda

Editorial Juridica de Chile, see Editorial Andres Bello/Editorial Juridica de Chile

Libreria Libertad SA
Rosas No 1281, Santiago
Tel: (02) 695 7777 *Fax:* (02) 672 6314
Key Personnel
Manager: Alejandro Melo
Founded: 1967
ISBN Prefix(es): 956-7348

Ediciones y Publicidad Melquiades
Bandera 341 of 352, Casilla 144/12, Santiago
Tel: (02) 2731545 *Fax:* (02) 2266602 *Cable:* 240984
Key Personnel
Editor: Arturo Navarro
Founded: 1987
Subjects: Government, Political Science, Literature, Literary Criticism, Essays, Social Sciences, Sociology
ISBN Prefix(es): 956-231

Museo Chileno de Arte Precolombino
Bandera 361, Santiago
Tel: (02) 6953851; (02) 6953627 *Fax:* (02) 6972779
E-mail: lcb.mchap@huelen.renna.cl
Web Site: www.precolombino.cl
Specialize in Pre-Colombian Art.
Subjects: Archaeology, Art
ISBN Prefix(es): 84-89332; 956-243

PUBLISHERS

CHILE

Norma de Chile
Av Costanera Andres Bello 1531, Providencia, Santiago
Tel: (02) 236 3355 *Fax:* (02) 236 3362
Web Site: www.norma.com
Key Personnel
Publishing Manager: Juliana Gutierrez
 E-mail: jgutierrez@carvajal.cl
Contact: Octavio Alvarez Piedrahita
Subjects: Art, Literature, Literary Criticism, Essays, Management, Marketing, Science Fiction, Fantasy, Self-Help
ISBN Prefix(es): 956-7250

Editora Nueva Generacion+
Casilla 22, Covero 30 Santiago
Tel: (02) 2183974 *Fax:* (02) 2182281
Key Personnel
Manager: Pablo Huneeus
Founded: 1982
Also acts as TV commentator & sociologist.
Subjects: Cookery, Human Relations, Humor, Social Sciences, Sociology
ISBN Prefix(es): 956-226

Editorial Patris SA+
Jose Miguel Infante 132, Providencia, Santiago
Tel: (02) 2351343 *Fax:* (02) 2351343
E-mail: edit.patris@entelchile.net
Web Site: www.patris.cl
Key Personnel
Contact: German B Pumpin
Founded: 1974
Subjects: Religion - Other
ISBN Prefix(es): 956-246
Distributor for Edit Patris (Argentina)
Bookshop(s): Libreria Patris, Providencia, 1001 Santiago

Pehuen Editores Ltda+
Avda Antonio Varas 2043, Santiago
Tel: (02) 204 93 99 *Fax:* (02) 204 93 99
E-mail: pehuen@cmet.net
Key Personnel
Dir: Jorge T Barros
General Manager: Alicia Z Cerda
Sales Manager: J Sebastian Barros
Founded: 1983
Subjects: Biography, Literature, Literary Criticism, Essays, Philosophy, Poetry, Social Sciences, Sociology
ISBN Prefix(es): 956-16
Subsidiaries: Temuco

Planeta SA+
Santa Lucia 360, Piso 7, Santiago
Mailing Address: PO Box 14422, Correo 21, Santiago
Tel: (02) 6962374 *Fax:* (02) 6957260
Telex: 242514 EPCMl
Key Personnel
General Manager: Bartolo Ortiz Henriquez
ISBN Prefix(es): 956-247
Parent Company: Planeta Internacional SA
Subsidiaries: Inversiones Planeta SA

Editorial Planeta Chilena, see Planeta SA

Pontificia Universidad Catolica de Chile+
Av Libertador Bernardo O'Higgins 340 of 311, Santiago
Mailing Address: Casilla 114-D, Santiago 6513677
Tel: (02) 2224516 (ext 2417) *Fax:* (02) 2225515
Web Site: www.puc.cl
Telex: 240395
Key Personnel
Dir & Editor: Gabriela Echeverria-Duco *Tel:* (02) 6862424 *E-mail:* gechever@vra.puc.cl
Founded: 1981
50% University textbooks & 50% all reader.

Subjects: Art, Biological Sciences, Economics, Education, Engineering (General), History, Literature, Literary Criticism, Essays, Philosophy, Psychology, Psychiatry, Religion - Other, Agronomy
ISBN Prefix(es): 956-14
Total Titles: 15 Print
Online services available through World Wide Web.
Foreign Rep(s): Alfaomega Grupo Editor SA de CV (Argentina, Colombia, Mexico); Alfaomega Grupo Editor, S A de C V (Argentina, Colombia, Mexico)

Proa S.A.+
Mac Iver 140, Casilla 9935 Dir Postal, Santiago
Tel: (02) 633 65 34; (02) 633 98 54 *Fax:* (02) 634 02 60
E-mail: proa@eutelchile.net
Key Personnel
Manager: Jose Luis Benavente; Guillermo Varas Valdes
Founded: 1954
Specialize in importing Reproductive Art.
Subsidiaries: Libreria Noray

Publicaciones Lo Castillo SA
Perez Valenzuela No 1620, Providencia, Santiago
Tel: (02) 235 2606 *Fax:* (02) 235 2007
Key Personnel
General Manager: Alvaro Perez
Editor: Bartolome Yankovic
Founded: 1982
Subjects: Education, House & Home, Journalism, Travel
ISBN Prefix(es): 956-237
Imprints: Revista DATO

Publicaciones Nuevo Extremo
Bombero Adolfo Ossa 1067, Santiago
Tel: (02) 698 1523; (02) 697 2337 *Fax:* (02) 697 2545
E-mail: nexxtremo@entelchile.net
Key Personnel
Managing Dir: Eduardo G Castillo
ISBN Prefix(es): 956-7063

Red Internacional Del Libro+
El Vergel 2882, of 11, Providencia, Santiago
Tel: (02) 2238100 *Fax:* (02) 2254269
E-mail: ril@rileditores.com
Web Site: www.rileditores.com
Key Personnel
Legal Representative: Ricardo Diaz Ramirez
Publisher: Daniel Calabrese; Eleonora Finkelstein
Sales: Emilio Campos
Founded: 1991
Subjects: Education, Literature, Literary Criticism, Essays, Poetry
ISBN Prefix(es): 956-284; 956-7159

Ediciones Rehue Ltda
Argomedo 40, Santiago
Tel: (02) 6344653; (02) 6341804 *Fax:* (02) 6351096
Key Personnel
Dir: Anibal Pastor Ninez
ISBN Prefix(es): 956-228

Revista DATO, *imprint of* Publicaciones Lo Castillo SA

Publicaciones Tecnicas Mediterraneo+
Elidoro Yanez 2541, Santiago
Tel: (02) 251 62 57; (02) 233 82 72 *Fax:* (02) 231 06 94
E-mail: msalinero@entelchile.net
Key Personnel
Manager: Ramon Alvarez Minder
Founded: 1981
Member of Chilean Book Association.

Subjects: Medicine, Nursing, Dentistry
ISBN Prefix(es): 956-220

Texido Ltda, see Editorial Texido Ltda

Editorial Texido Ltda+
Av Einstein 921, Recoleta, Santiago
Tel: (02) 6224652 *Fax:* (02) 6224660
Founded: 1969
Subjects: Gardening, Plants, Human Relations, Nonfiction (General)
ISBN Prefix(es): 956-273
Associate Companies: Comercial Distribuidora Librimundi Ltda; Altima Ltda

Ediciones de la Universidad de la Frontera
Av Francisco Salazar 01145, Temuco
Mailing Address: Casilla 54-D, Temuco
Tel: (045) 325000 *Fax:* (045) 325950
ISBN Prefix(es): 956-236

Universidad de Valparaiso, see Edeval (Universidad de Valparaiso)

Editorial Universitaria SA+
Maria Luisa Santander 0447, Providencia, Santiago
Tel: (02) 2234555; (02) 2233628 *Fax:* (02) 2099455; (02) 2237982
E-mail: achamorrom@hotmail.com
Web Site: www.universitaria.cl.index.pl *Cable:* EDUNSA
Key Personnel
Man Dir: Rodrigo Castro
Editor: Braulio Fernandez
Founded: 1947
Subjects: Literature, Literary Criticism, Essays, Science (General), Social Sciences, Sociology
ISBN Prefix(es): 84-8340; 956-11
Subsidiaries: Talleres Graficos; Texto Libro
Distributed by Axius (Argentina); Contemporanea de Ediciones (Venezuela); Ediciones Coliguee (Argentina); Ericiencia (Ecuador); Maria Ester Garcia (Paraguay); Librerias Faustos (Argentina); Zulema Medina (Uruguay)
Showroom(s): Sala Matte, Av Libertador B O'Higgins, 1050 Santiago *Fax:* (02) 6956387
Bookshop(s): Av Libertador Bernardo O'Higgins 1050, Santiago *Tel:* (02) 6951529 *Fax:* (02) 6956387; Agustinas 1138, Santiago *Tel:* (02) 6994666; Av Dag Hammarskjold S/N, Santiago *Tel:* (02) 2085051; Orrego Luco 040, Providencia, Santiago *Fax:* (02) 2319023; Latorre 2515, Antofagasta *Fax:* (02) 222175; 18 de Septiembre 727, Chillan *Fax:* (042) 216443; Barros Arana 741, Local 3, Galeria Martinez, Concepcion *Fax:* (041) 224113; Cordovez 470, La Serena *Fax:* (051) 224685; Cochrane 545, Osornor *Fax:* (064) 232613; Diego Portales 861, Temuco *Fax:* (045) 215330; Maipu 168, Valdivia *Fax:* (063) 212645; Esmeralda 1132, Valparaiso *Fax:* (032) 257573
Shipping Address: Ricardo Matte Perez 04310, Casilla 10220, Providencia, Santiago *Tel:* (02) 2233765 *Fax:* (02) 2099455/2049058
Orders to: Ricardo Matte Perez 04310, Casilla, 10220 Providencia, Santiago *Tel:* (02) 2233765 *Fax:* (02) 2049058

Ediciones Universitarias de Valparaiso+
12 De Febrero 187, Valparaiso
Tel: (032) 273087; (02) 6332230 *Fax:* (032) 273429
Telex: 230389 Ucval Cl
Key Personnel
Manager: Karlheinz H Laage
Founded: 1970
Subjects: Art, Education, Engineering (General), History, Law, Literature, Literary Criticism, Essays, Music, Dance, Philosophy, Science (General), Social Sciences, Sociology, Technology
ISBN Prefix(es): 956-17

Parent Company: Universidad Catolica de Valparaiso, 12 De Febrero 187, Valparaiso
Branch Office(s)
Moneda 673 - 8 piso, Santiago *Tel:* (02) 633233

Zig-Zag SA+
Los Conquistadores 1700, piso 17 of 17B, Providencia, Santiago
Tel: (02) 335 7447 *Fax:* (02) 335 7545
Web Site: www.zigzag.cl
Key Personnel
General Manager: Francisco Perez Frugone
Publishing Manager: Jose Manuel Zanartu
Founded: 1934
Distribuidor en Chile de otros sellos editoriales.
Subjects: Literature, Literary Criticism, Essays
ISBN Prefix(es): 956-12
Distributor for Editorial Atlantida (Argentina); Editorial Voluntad (Colombia)
Showroom(s): Compania 2752, Santiago
Orders to: Compania 2752, Santiago

China

General Information

Capital: Beijing
Language: Principally Northern Chinese (Mandarin). Local dialects spoken in the south & southeast
Religion: Confucianism, Buddhism & Daoism with small Muslim & Christian minorities
Population: 1.2 billion
Shop Hours: Generally 0900-1900 every day
Currency: 100 fen = 10 jiao = 1 yuan
Export/Import Information: Foreign trade is a state monopoly. The foreign distributor for Chinese publications is Guoji Shudian, PO Box 399, Beijing. The importing organization is Waiwen Shudian, PO Box 88, Beijing.
Copyright: UCC, Berne (see Copyright Conventions, pg xi)

Agricultural Publishing House, see China Agriculture Press

Anhui People's Publishing House+
283 Jinzhailu, Anhui Providence, Hefei 230063
Tel: (0551) 257134; (0551) 253673 *Cable:* 1344
Key Personnel
Dir: Mr Guo Minggang
Founded: 1952
Subjects: Accounting, Advertising, Behavioral Sciences, Economics, Government, Political Science, History, Law, Philosophy, Social Sciences, Sociology
ISBN Prefix(es): 7-212

Asia 2000 Ltd+
Seabird House, Rm 1101, 22-28 Wyndham St Central, Hong Kong
Tel: (02) 530 1409 *Fax:* (02) 526 1107
E-mail: info@asia2000.com.hk
Key Personnel
Man Dir: Michael Morrow
Editor: Alan Sargent
Marketing, Distribution Manager: Edowan Bersma
Founded: 1980
Independent publisher of English language books. Distributor for overseas publishers.
Subjects: Art, Asian Studies, Fiction, Government, Political Science, Photography, Regional Interests
ISBN Prefix(es): 962-7160
Parent Company: Asia 2000 Group
Associate Companies: Manager Media
Subsidiaries: Asia Inc
Distributor for St Martens Press; World Bank; World Trade Press

Aviation Industry Press+
14 Xiaoguan Dongli, Hepingli, Beijing 100029
Mailing Address: PO Box 9817, Beijing 100029
Tel: (010) 4221690 *Fax:* (010) 4221696
Key Personnel
Dir General Editorial Dept: Tiejun Zhang
Founded: 1985
Subjects: Aeronautics, Aviation, Computer Science, Economics, English as a Second Language, Mechanical Engineering
ISBN Prefix(es): 7-80046

Beijing Ancient Books Publishing House+
6 Beisanhuan Zhonglu, Beijing 100011
Tel: (010) 2016699 313; (010) 2013122 *Fax:* (010) 2012339
E-mail: geo@bph.com.cn *Cable:* 8909
Key Personnel
Rights Dir: Ms Jackie Huang
Founded: 1979
ISBN Prefix(es): 7-5300
Parent Company: Beijing Publishing House

Beijing Arts & Crafts Publishing House
30 Shatan Houjie, Beijing 100009
Tel: (010) 4035477; (010) 4031811
Key Personnel
President: Wang Zhen
Vice President: Wu Peng
Subjects: Art
ISBN Prefix(es): 7-80526
Subsidiaries: Beijing Stars Advertisement Co

Beijing Education Publishing House+
6 Beisanhuan Zhonglu, Beijing 100011
Tel: (010) 2016699-268; (010) 62013122 *Fax:* (010) 2012339
E-mail: geo@bph.com.cn *Cable:* 8909
Key Personnel
Rights Dir: Ms Jackie Huang
Founded: 1983
Subjects: Education
ISBN Prefix(es): 7-5303
Parent Company: Beijing Publishing House

Beijing Fine Arts & Photography Publishing House+
6 Beisanhuan Zhonglu, Beijing 100011
Tel: (010) 2016699; (010) 62016699-315 *Fax:* (010) 2012339
E-mail: geo@bph.com.cn *Cable:* 8909
Key Personnel
Rights Dir: Ms Jackie Huang
Founded: 1983
ISBN Prefix(es): 7-80501
Parent Company: Beijing Publishing House

Beijing Juvenile & Children's Books Publishing House+
6 Beisanhuan Zhonglu, Beijing 100011
Tel: (010) 2016699-350; (010) 62013122 *Fax:* (010) 2012339
E-mail: geo@bph.com.cn *Cable:* 8909
Key Personnel
Rights Dir: Ms Jackie Huang
Founded: 1983
Subjects: Child Care & Development, Education, Self-Help
ISBN Prefix(es): 7-5301
Parent Company: Beijing Publishing House

Beijing Medical Univ Press+
Beijing Medical University, 38 Xue Yuan Rd, Haidian, Beijing 100083
Tel: (010) 62092249 *Fax:* (010) 62029848
E-mail: bmupress@public.fhnet.cn.net
Web Site: www.bjmu.edu.cn
Key Personnel
Dir: Dr Lin An *Tel:* (010) 62092249
E-mail: cbi@mail.bjmu.edu.cn
Contacts: Dipl Ing Zheng-bao Lu *Tel:* (010) 62092405; Yin-dao Lu
Founded: 1989
Subjects: Biological Sciences, Environmental Studies, Health, Nutrition, Medicine, Nursing, Dentistry, Psychology, Psychiatry
ISBN Prefix(es): 7-81034
Number of titles published annually: 180 Print; 4 CD-ROM
Total Titles: 950 Print; 2 CD-ROM

Beijing Publishing House+
6 Beisanhuan Zhonglu, Beijing 100011
Tel: (010) 62012335 *Fax:* (010) 62012339
E-mail: geo@bph.com.cn
Web Site: www.bph.com.cn *Cable:* 8909
Founded: 1956
Subjects: Agriculture, Antiques, Architecture & Interior Design, Art, Behavioral Sciences, Biography, Business, Child Care & Development, Computer Science, Cookery, Drama, Theater, Economics, Education, Engineering (General), English as a Second Language, Fiction, Finance, History, How-to, Human Relations, Language Arts, Linguistics, Law, Literature, Literary Criticism, Essays, Management, Marketing, Medicine, Nursing, Dentistry, Nonfiction (General), Philosophy, Physics, Poetry, Science (General), Self-Help, Social Sciences, Sociology, Western Fiction, Women's Studies
ISBN Prefix(es): 7-200

Beijing University Press+
Haidianqu, Beijing 100871
Tel: (010) 2561166-3672 *Fax:* (010) 2564095
E-mail: psj@pup.pku.edu.cn
Key Personnel
President: Peng Songjian
Founded: 1979
Subjects: Biological Sciences, Chemistry, Chemical Engineering, Computer Science, Economics, Education, English as a Second Language, Finance
ISBN Prefix(es): 7-301

Book Marketing Ltd+
North Point Industrial Bldg, 499 King's Rd, 17F, Flat A, Hong Kong, SAR
Tel: (02) 5620121 *Fax:* (02) 5650187
Key Personnel
Man Dir: Bernard King Sum Chiu
Founded: 1973
Wholesaler.
Subjects: English as a Second Language, Self-Help
ISBN Prefix(es): 962-211
Associate Companies: Leo Publications Ltd, 499 King's Rd, 17F, Flat A, Hong Kong, SAR

Chemical Industry Press+
Huixinli No 3, Chaoyang District, Beijing 100029
Tel: (010) 64918054 *Fax:* (010) 64918054
E-mail: liangh@cip.com.cn
Web Site: www.cip.com.cn
Key Personnel
President: Feng Peizong
Rights Manager: Liang Hong *E-mail:* liangh@cip.com.cn
Founded: 1953
Subjects: Agriculture, Biological Sciences, Chemistry, Chemical Engineering, Civil Engineering, Communications, Education, Electronics, Electrical Engineering, Energy, Engineering (General), Environmental Studies, Health, Nutrition, Mechanical Engineering, Medicine, Nursing, Dentistry, Technology, Transportation
ISBN Prefix(es): 7-5025
Number of titles published annually: 1,000 Print
Total Titles: 10,000 Print

Divisions: The Applied Chemistry & Agricultural Reader Publishing Center; Beijing Progress Periodical; The Environmental Science & Engineering Publishing Center; The Fine Chemical Publishing Center; The Industrial Equipment & Information Engineering Publishing Center; The Material Science & Engineering Publishing Center; The Modern Biotech & Medical Sci-Tech Publishing Center; The Multi-Media Publishing Center; The Textbook Publishing Center
Bookshop(s): Chemical Bookstore

Chengdu Maps Publishing House+
Longquanyi, Chengdu 610100 Sichuan Province
Tel: (028) 442512-493 *Fax:* (028) 4852529
E-mail: ccph@public.cd.sc.cn *Cable:* 9570
Key Personnel
President: Yao Rusong
Founded: 1985
Member of Sichuan Surveying & Mapping Bureau & Sichuan News Publishing Bureau.
Subjects: Advertising, Communications, Computer Science, Earth Sciences, Education, Foreign Countries, Geography, Geology, Travel
ISBN Prefix(es): 7-80544
Divisions: Mapping Dept, Printing Factory
Distributor for China Cartography Publishing House
Shipping Address: Chengdu Cartography Publishing House, 29 Yikuan N Rd, 3rd Section, Wholesale Dept., Chengdu, Sichuan, PR China

China Agriculture Press+
2 Nongzhanguan North Rd, Chaoyang Dist, Beijing 100026
Tel: (010) 5005665 *Fax:* (010) 5005894
E-mail: fcap@bj.col.com.cn
Key Personnel
President: Cai Shenglin
International Rights: Hui Xu
Founded: 1958
Specialize in agricultural, scientific & technological books.
Subjects: Agriculture, Animals, Pets, Biological Sciences, Gardening, Plants, Technology, Veterinary Science
ISBN Prefix(es): 7-109
Subsidiaries: Rural Readings Press

China Braille Press
39 Chengnei St, Lu Gou Qiao, Fengtaiqu District, Beijing 100071
Tel: (010) 6383 3585 *Fax:* (010) 6383 3585
Key Personnel
President: Song Jianmin
Founded: 1953
Production of books & magazines in braille & tapes for the blind.
Member of Press & Publication Administration; specialize in braille books; also acts as China Library for the Blind.
Subjects: Animals, Pets, Art, Child Care & Development, Crafts, Games, Hobbies, Disability, Special Needs, Economics, Education, English as a Second Language
ISBN Prefix(es): 7-5002
Subsidiaries: Beijing Hengji Co
Book Club(s): China Library for the Blind; Reading Club

China Cartographic Publishing House+
3 Baizhifang Xijie, Xuanwu Dist, Beijing 100054
Tel: (010) 6356 4947 *Fax:* (010) 6352 9403
E-mail: fanyi@chinamap.com *Cable:* 1955
Key Personnel
President: Wang Jixian
International Rights: Fan Yi
Founded: 1954
Subjects: Earth Sciences, Geography, Geology, Transportation, Travel
ISBN Prefix(es): 7-5031

China Film Press+
22 Beisanhuan Donglu, Beijing 100013
Tel: (010) 4216761; (010) 4219977 *Fax:* (010) 4219489
Telex: 222669 CFP CN *Cable:* 8468 BEIJING
Key Personnel
Editor in Chief: Cui Junyan
Founded: 1956
Member of International Film Exchange; specialize in film.
Subjects: Advertising, Art, Biography, Career Development, Crafts, Games, Hobbies, Drama, Theater, Fashion, Fiction, Film, Video, History, Law, Literature, Literary Criticism, Essays, Marketing, Outdoor Recreation, Photography
ISBN Prefix(es): 7-106
Subsidiaries: Beijing Film Book; Shanghai Film Services Co
Bookshop(s): China film Bookshop

China Foreign Economic Relations & Trade Publishing House+
28 Donghouxiang, Andingmenwai Dajie, Beijing 100710
Tel: (010) 64263813; (010) 64219742 *Fax:* (010) 64219392
Web Site: www.cfertph.com
Key Personnel
President: Yan Weijing *E-mail:* yanweijing@263.net
Vice President: Song Dongjin
Founded: 1980
Business Books & Magazines.
Subjects: Accounting, Business, Economics, English as a Second Language, Finance, Government, Political Science, Management, Marketing
ISBN Prefix(es): 7-80004

China Forestry Publishing House+
7 Liuhai Hutong, Xichengqu District, Beijing 100009
Tel: (010) 6013117; (010) 661884477-2038 *Fax:* (010) 66180373
E-mail: cfph@public3.bta.net.cn *Cable:* 1010
Key Personnel
Vice Editor-in-Chief: Chen Li
Subjects: Agriculture, Animals, Pets, Biological Sciences, Chemistry, Chemical Engineering, Economics, Gardening, Plants
ISBN Prefix(es): 7-5038
Distributed by University of British Columbia Press (UBC Press) (North America)

China Labour Publishing House+
Niuwangmiao Chaoyangqu, Beijing 100716
Tel: (010) 4910448
Key Personnel
President: Yunqi Tang
Editor-in-Chief: Wang Jianxin
Deputy Editor-in-Chief: Mengxin Zhang
Sales Dir: Hongrui Li
Production Dir: Yongguang Xie
Publicity Dir: Zhang Jiasheng
Rights & Permissions: Chao Zhou
Founded: 1980
Subjects: Business, Labor, Industrial Relations
ISBN Prefix(es): 7-5045

China Light Industry Press+
6 Dongchanganjie St, Beijing 100740
Tel: (010) 5121122-565 *Fax:* (010) 65121371
Cable: 1508
Key Personnel
President: Zhao Ti-Qing
Founded: 1954
Subjects: Art, Cookery, Fashion, Film, Video, House & Home, Language Arts, Linguistics, Wine & Spirits
ISBN Prefix(es): 7-5019

China Machine Press (CMP)+
22 Baiwanzhuang Rd, Beijing 100037
Tel: (010) 68326677 (trunk line); (010) 68320405 *Fax:* (010) 68320405
E-mail: cjhui@mail.machineinfo.gov.cn
Web Site: www.cmpbooks.com
Telex: 222557 STIP CN
Key Personnel
Chief Executive: Wang Wenbin
Editorial: Li Ai
Sales: Tang Xiaoming
Production: Cheng Jingning
Publicity: Chen Jianhui
Rights & Permissions: Chen Jianhui
I D D Dir: Lu Naiyao
Founded: 1952
Subjects: Automotive, Business, Computer Science, Electronics, Electrical Engineering, Management, Mechanical Engineering, Microcomputers, Technology
ISBN Prefix(es): 7-111
Number of titles published annually: 1,500 Print
Associate Companies: The Printing Company of China Machine Press, 4 Ganjiakou, Haidian District, Beijing 100037; Jingfeng Printing Company of China Machine Press, 88 Liuzhuangzi, Fengtai District, Beijing 100071
Bookshop(s): Jigong Bookstore, 22 Baiwanzhuang St, Bejing 100037
Warehouse: Dianchangxiang, Beijing 100071
Orders to: International Development Dept, No 22 Baiwanzhuang Rd, Xicheng District, Beijing 100037

China Materials Management Publishing House+
25 Yuetan Beijie, Xichengqu District, Beijing 100834
Tel: (010) 8392745 *Fax:* (010) 8392911
Cable: 1444
Key Personnel
President: Fan Xiyi
General Editor: Zhang Lizhong
Founded: 1981
Subjects: Automotive, Behavioral Sciences, Business, Economics, Human Relations, Management, Marketing
ISBN Prefix(es): 7-5047
Book Club(s): China Copyright Association

China Ocean Press+
Subsidiary of State Oceanic Administration
8 Dar Hui Si Rd, Haidian District, Beijing 100081
Tel: (010) 62173322 (ext 212) *Fax:* (010) 62173569
E-mail: oceanpress@china.com
Web Site: www.oceanpress.com.cn
Key Personnel
President: Gai Guangsheng
Editor-in-Chief: Yang Suihua
Dir, International Dept: Yang Qing *Tel:* (010) 62173322 Ext 212
Founded: 1978
Publish mainly in English, other languages available; specialize in marine science & technology.
Subjects: Biography, Biological Sciences, Chemistry, Chemical Engineering, Civil Engineering, Computer Science, Earth Sciences, Environmental Studies, Geography, Geology, Management, Maritime, Mechanical Engineering, Physical Sciences, Physics, Real Estate, Religion - Buddhist, Religion - Islamic, Religion - Jewish, Science (General), Social Sciences, Sociology, Technology
ISBN Prefix(es): 7-5027
Number of titles published annually: 10 Print
Total Titles: 300 Print

CHINA

China Oil & Gas Periodical Office+
One Lou, 2 Qu Anhuali, Andingmenwai, Beijing 100011
Tel: (010) 4219111
Key Personnel
Editor-in-Chief: Zhaoren Li
Distribution Manager: Baoguo Wu
Founded: 1994
Subjects: Energy
ISBN Prefix(es): 7-5021

China Pictorial Publishing House
33 Chegongzhuang West Rd, Haidian District, Beijing 100044
Tel: (010) 68412392; (010) 68414896; (010) 68412665 *Fax:* (010) 68413023
Web Site: www.china-pictorial.com *Cable:* CHINAPIC 3973
Key Personnel
Contact: Li Lian
Founded: 1985
ISBN Prefix(es): 7-80024

China Social Sciences Publishing House+
Jia 158 Hao, Gulou Xidajie, Beijing 100724
Tel: (010) 64074509 *Fax:* (010) 64074509
Key Personnel
Dir, Social Sciences: Wang Baochun
Dir, Reader Services: Wana Shan
Dir: Cui Yaqin
Founded: 1978
Specialize in the task of editing & publishing monographs, reference books, teaching materials & basic reading materials in the fields of Philosophy & Social Sciences as well as Chinese translations of major foreign works; also acts as publisher for Social Sciences in China (Journal of Cass) & periodicals for several Research Institutes.
Subjects: Social Sciences, Sociology
ISBN Prefix(es): 7-5004
Bookshop(s): A62 Jianguomennei Dajie, Benjing 100005; No 31 Book-Town Haidian Dajie, Beijing 10080

China Theatre Publishing House+
A81 Dazhongsi Nancun, Haidianqu District, Beijing 100086
Tel: (010) 2550255
Key Personnel
President: Li Haichuan
Founded: 1957
Subjects: Crafts, Games, Hobbies, Drama, Theater, Education, Fiction, History, Literature, Literary Criticism, Essays, Nonfiction (General)
ISBN Prefix(es): 7-104

China Tibetology Publishing House+
PO Box 9704, Yayuncun, Beijing 100101
Tel: (010) 4910088-213 *Fax:* (010) 4917619
Key Personnel
Dir: Tendzin Sr
Editor-in-Chief: Liao Zugui
Specialize in Tibetan studies.
Subjects: Anthropology, Archaeology, Asian Studies, Economics, Education, Religion - Buddhist, Social Sciences, Sociology
ISBN Prefix(es): 7-80057
Orders to: China International Book Trading Corporation, PO Box 399, Beijing 100080

China Translation & Publishing Corp+
4 Taipingqiao Dajie, Xichengqu District, Beijing 100810
Tel: (010) 6022134 *Fax:* (010) 6022734
E-mail: ctpc@public.bta.net.cn
Key Personnel
Contact: Xu Jihong
International Rights & Deputy General Manager: Hsuan-chin Chou
Subjects: Economics, Education, Management
ISBN Prefix(es): 7-5001

China Youth Publishing House, see Youth Publishing House

China Youth Publishing House+
21 Dongsi Shiertiao, Beijing 100708
Tel: (010) 4032266-328 *Fax:* (010) 4031803
Cable: 4357
Key Personnel
President: Cai Yun
Editor: Kan Daolong
Contact: Mr Bingbin Bi
Founded: 1950
Subjects: Education, Language Arts, Linguistics, Literature, Literary Criticism, Essays, Science (General), Social Sciences, Sociology
ISBN Prefix(es): 7-5006

Chinese Literature Press+
24 Baiwanzhuang Rd, Beijing 100037
Tel: (010) 68326678 *Fax:* (010) 68326678
E-mail: chinalit@public.east.cn.net
Key Personnel
Commissioning Editor: Zhang Shaoning
Contact: Shen Jieying
Founded: 1951 (English; 1964 French)
Subjects: Art, Fiction, Poetry
ISBN Prefix(es): 7-5071
Parent Company: China International Publishing Group
Orders to: China International Book Trading Corp, PO Box 399, Beijing 100044

Chinese Pedagogics Publishing House+
24 Baiwanzhuanglu Rd, Beijing 100037
Mailing Address: PO Box 399, Beijing 10004
Tel: (010) 8315599-602 *Fax:* (010) 8317390
Telex: 222475 FLP CN *Cable:* FOLAPRESS BEIJING
Key Personnel
President & Chief Executive: Shan Ying
Tel: (010) 68994599
Editor-in-chief: Jia Yinhuai
Sales (Overseas Dept Sinolingua) & Publicity: Hui Han
Rights & Permissions: Ling Yu
Founded: 1985
Specialize in: Teaching Chinese as a foreign language.
Member of China International Publishing Group.
Subjects: Education, Language Arts, Linguistics
ISBN Prefix(es): 7-80052
Total Titles: 300 Print; 30 Audio
Parent Company: Foreign Languages Press
Associate Companies: China International Book Trading Corporation, 35 Chegong-zhuang Xilu, Beijing 100044 *Fax:* (010) 68412023
E-mail: om@mail.cibtc.com.cn
Branch Office(s)
CBT China Book Trading GmbH, Max-Planck Str 6-A, 63322 Rodermark, Germany *Fax:* (0674) 95271 *E-mail:* chinabook@aol.com
Cypress Book Co Ltd, 10 Swinton St, London WC1X 9NX, United Kingdom *Fax:* (020) 7833 0220
U.S. Office(s): Cypress Books (US) Co Inc, 450 Third St, Unit 4B, San Francisco, CA 94124, United States
Distributed by China Books & Periodicals
Shipping Address: China International Book Trading Corporation, 35 Chegong-zhuang Xilu, Beijing 100044 *Fax:* (010) 68412023 *E-mail:* om@mail.cibtc.com.cn; CBT China Book Trading GmbH, Max-Planck Str 6-A, 63322 Rodermark, Germany *Fax:* (0674) 95271 *E-mail:* chinabook@aol.com
Warehouse: China International Book Trading Corporation, 35 Chegong-zhuang Xilu, Beijing 100044 *Fax:* (010) 68412023 *E-mail:* om@mail.cibtc.com.cn
CBT China Book Trading GmbH, Max-Planck Str 6-A, 63322 Rodermark, Germany *Fax:* (0674) 95271 *E-mail:* chinabook@aol.com
Orders to: Cypress Book Co (UK) Ltd, 10 Swinton St, London WC1X 9NX, United Kingdom *Fax:* (020) 7837 7768
CBT China Book Trading GmbH, Max-Planck Str 6-A, 63322 Rodermark, Germany *Tel:* (0674) 95271 *E-mail:* chinabook@aol.com
Cypress Books (US) Co Inc, 450 Third St, Unit 4B, San Francisco, CA 94124, United States

Chongqing University Press+
174 Shapingba St, Chongqing 400044
Tel: (023) 6511 1125 *Fax:* (023) 6510 6789
E-mail: office@cqup.com.cn
Web Site: www.cqup.com.cn
Key Personnel
Dir: Zhang Gesheng
Founded: 1985
Subjects: Language Arts, Linguistics, Management, Science (General), Social Sciences, Sociology, Technology
ISBN Prefix(es): 7-5624
Number of titles published annually: 500 Print
Total Titles: 4,000 Print

CITIC Publishing House+
Capital Mansion No 6, Xinyuan Nanlu, Chaoyangqu District, Beijing 100004
Tel: (010) 64661098 *Fax:* (010) 64661098
E-mail: citicph@mx.cei.gov.cn
Web Site: www.citic.com.cn
Telex: 210026 CITIC CN
Key Personnel
President: Wang Minghui
Assistant President: Luo Weiyao
Chief Editor: Li Debao
Senior Revisor: Gong Yuang
Senior Editor: He Peihui
CITIC Executive Dir: Wang Jun
Founded: 1988
Specialize in both copyright transactions & co-publication of books with foreign publishers, bookdealers or any other relevant groups or individuals, & launching joint ventures on business in publication & distribution.
Subjects: Accounting, Business, Economics, Finance, How-to, Law, Management, Marketing, Nonfiction (General)
ISBN Prefix(es): 7-80073
Parent Company: China International Trust & Investment Corporation (Holdings)
Associate Companies: CITIC Representative Office in Tokyo, 3/F, The Landic Third Akasaka Buildings, 203002, Akasaka, Minato-Ku, Tokyo 107, Japan; CITIC Representative Office in New York, 2 World Trade Center, Suite 2250, New York, NY 10048, United States; CITIC Representative Office in Europe, Bockenheimer Landstra 51-53, 60323 Frankfurt am Main, Germany

CMP, see China Machine Press (CMP)

Commercial Press (Hong Kong) Ltd+
36 Wangfujing Dajie, Beijing 100710
Tel: (010) 65241547 *Fax:* (010) 65135899
E-mail: comprs@public.gb.com.cn
Web Site: www.cp.com.cn
Telex: 86564 Cmprs HX *Cable:* COMPRESS
Key Personnel
Man Dir & Chief Editor: Chan Man Hung
Deputy General Manager: Chan Kwok Fai
Assistant General Manager: Leung Chung Ho; Tseng Kwok Tai
Marketing Manager & Copyright Controller: Charlemagne Choi
Production Manager: Yam Kin Wah
Founded: 1897

Subjects: Art, Education, Ethnicity, How-to, Medicine, Nursing, Dentistry
ISBN Prefix(es): 962-07
Subsidiaries: Hong Kong Educational Publishing Co
Branch Office(s)
KL Commercial Book Malaysia Sdn. Bhd Co, Malaysia
Commercial Press Ltd, Republic of Singapore, Singapore
Bookshop(s): Book Centre, 9-15 Yee Wo St, Causeway Bay *Tel:* (05) 8908028 *Fax:* (05) 8951027; Central Branch & Stamp Centre, 28 Wellington St, Central *Tel:* (05) 5250315 *Fax:* (05) 8450035; Shatin Book Plaza, 165 Level 1 & 266-270 Level 2, Phase 1, Shatin; North Point Branch, 395 King's Rd, North Point *Tel:* (05) 5620266 *Fax:* (05) 5656763; Mongkok Branch, 608 Nathan Rd, Kowloon *Tel:* (05) 3848228 *Fax:* (05) 7703861; Tuen Mun Branch, G/F, Yaohan Stores, Tuen Mun Town Plaza, NT, Tuen Mun, NT *Tel:* (05) 4589332 *Fax:* (05) 4591925; Kornhill Branch, 3/F, Jusco Stores, Quarry Bay *Tel:* (05) 5600238 *Fax:* (05) 5679801; Tai Po Branch, 212-215, 1/F Tai Wo Shopping Mall, Tai Po, NT *Tel:* (05) 6502628; New Town Plaza, Shatin *Tel:* (05) 6931933 *Fax:* (05) 6912064
Orders to: 2/F, Heng Ngai Jewelry Centre, 4 Hok Yuen St E, Hunghom, Kowloon, Hong Kong

Cultural Relics Publishing House+
Affiliate of Chinese Administration For Cultural Heritage
29 Wusi Dajie, Beijing 100009
Tel: (010) 64048057 *Fax:* (010) 64010698
E-mail: web@wenwu.com
Web Site: www.wenwu.com
Key Personnel
International Division: Mr Zhao Lihua *Tel:* (010) 64048057
Founded: 1957
Subjects: Anthropology, Antiques, Archaeology, Art, Asian Studies, History
ISBN Prefix(es): 7-5010
Divisions: International Division
Orders to: International Division, 29 Wusi Dajie, Beijing 100009

CWPP, see Water Resources and Electric Power Press (CWPP)

Dalian Maritime University Press+
Lingshuiqiao, Ganjingziqu, Dalian, Liaoning 116024
Tel: (0411) 4729605 *Fax:* (0411) 4727996
E-mail: dmup@dmupress.com; cbs@dmupress.com
Web Site: www.dmupress.com
Key Personnel
Dir: Yuan Linxin
Founded: 1987
Subjects: Communications, Computer Science, Economics, Electronics, Electrical Engineering, English as a Second Language, Management, Maritime, Science (General)
ISBN Prefix(es): 7-5632

Dolphin Books+
24 Baiwanzhuanglu, Beijing 100037
Tel: (010) 8315599-353 *Fax:* (010) 8317390
Telex: 222475 Flp *Cable:* FOLAPRESS BEIJING
Key Personnel
Dir: Jiang Cheng'an
Publicity & Production: Zhangyun He
Founded: 1986
Specialize in illustrated children's books.
ISBN Prefix(es): 7-80051
Parent Company: Foreign Languages Press
U.S. Office(s): Cypress Book (US) Co Inc, 3450 Third St, Unit 4B, San Francisco, CA 94124, United States *Tel:* (415) 821-3582

Shipping Address: China International Book Trading Corporation, 35 Chegong-zhuang Zilu, Beijing 100044
Warehouse: China International Book Trading Corporation, 35 Chegong-zhuang Zilu, Beijing 100044
Orders to: Cypress Book Co (UK) Ltd, 10 Swinton St, London WC1X 9NX, United Kingdom
Cypress Book (US) Co Inc, 3450 Third St, Unit 4B, San Francisco, CA 94124, United States *Tel:* 415-821-3582

East China Normal University Press+
3663 Zhongshan Beilu, Shanghai 200062
Tel: (021) 62863896 *Fax:* (021) 62864922
E-mail: lxb@ecnu.edu.cn
Web Site: www.ecnu.edu.cn
Key Personnel
President: Hong Ben Jian
Vice President: Fan Jian Hua
Editor: Jin Qin Xiang
Author: Kuan Guang Ye
Founded: 1957
ISBN Prefix(es): 7-5617
Subsidiaries: Da Hua Industry & Trade Company

East China University of Science & Technology Press
130 Meilonglu, Shanghai 200237
Tel: (021) 64252769 *Fax:* (021) 64250735
Web Site: www.ecust.edu.cn *Cable:* 9006
Key Personnel
President: Zhu Xuecun
Founded: 1986
Subjects: Agriculture, Computer Science, Education, Engineering (General), English as a Second Language, Environmental Studies, Finance, Technology
ISBN Prefix(es): 7-5628

Education Science Publishing House
Education Science Press, 46 Beisanhuan Zhonglu, Beijing 100088
Tel: (010) 2011177-365 *Fax:* (010) 62012454
E-mail: esph@public.net.china.com.cn
Key Personnel
International Rights: Ms Li Bin *Tel:* (010) 62003353
Founded: 1980
Subjects: Education, English as a Second Language, Human Relations, Military Science, Natural History, Science Fiction, Fantasy
ISBN Prefix(es): 7-5041
Total Titles: 1,866 Print; 12 Audio
Parent Company: Yan-Li Gin
Ultimate Parent Company: Xu-Chang Fa

Electronics Industry Publishing House
PO Box 173, Wanshoulu, Beijing 100036
Tel: (010) 8212233-3462 *Fax:* (010) 86106821-4062
Key Personnel
President: Mr Liang Xiang Feng
International Rights: Mr Huang Zhi Yu
Subjects: Communications, Computer Science, Electronics, Electrical Engineering, Microcomputers, Radio, TV
ISBN Prefix(es): 7-5053

Encyclopedia of China Publishing House+
17 Fuchengmen Bei Dajie, Beijing 100037
Tel: (010) 68345014 *Fax:* (010) 68316510
E-mail: ygh@bj.col.com.cn *Cable:* ECPH
Key Personnel
President: Shan Jifu
Founded: 1978
Subjects: Art, Education, Fiction, Technology
ISBN Prefix(es): 7-5000
Subsidiaries: Knowledge Publishing House

First Edition, *imprint of* Jinan Publishing House

Foreign Language Teaching & Research Press+
No 19, Xisanhuabeilu, Beijing 100081
Tel: (010) 6891 7641 *Fax:* (010) 6842 0956
Key Personnel
President: Li Pengyi
Vice President, Sales & Publishing Manager: Zhao Wenyan
Assistant President & Head of the Inter-area & International Cooperation Dept: Yu Chunchi
Chief of the General Editorial Office: Lei Hang
Chief of the First Editorial Section: Wang Weiguo
Chief of the Second Editorial Section: Cai Jianfeng
Chief of the Third Editorial Section: Xu Jianzhong
Chief of the Fourth Editorial Section: Xu Chunjian
Editorial Manager, Publicity & Rights & Permissions: Zheng Jiande
Head, Inter-Area & International Cooperation Dept: Yu Chanchi
Chief of the Finance Section: Ge Jusheng
Founded: 1979
Subjects: English as a Second Language, Foreign Countries, History, Language Arts, Linguistics, Literature, Literary Criticism, Essays, Social Sciences, Sociology, Western Fiction
ISBN Prefix(es): 7-5600

Foreign Languages Press+
24 Baiwanzhuang Rd, Beijing 100037
Tel: (010) 8320579 *Fax:* (010) 8317390
E-mail: flpcn@public3.bta.net.cn
Web Site: www.flp.com.cn
Telex: 222475 FLP CN *Cable:* FOLAPRESS BEIJING
Key Personnel
President: Xu Mingqiang
Vice President: Li Zhengno
Over Seas Dept Dir & Rights & Permissions: Sun Haiyu
Founded: 1952
Published Languages (in addition to Chinese): Arabic, Bengali, English, French, German, Hindi, Indonesian, Italian, Japanese, Korean, Myanmar, Portuguese, Russian, Spanish, Swahili, Urdu, & Vietnamese.
Subjects: Anthropology, Archaeology, Art, Biography, Cookery, Drama, Theater, Economics, Geography, Geology, Government, Political Science, History, Law, Literature, Literary Criticism, Essays, Medicine, Nursing, Dentistry, Philosophy, Science (General), Sports, Athletics, Travel
ISBN Prefix(es): 0-8351; 7-119
Total Titles: 1,500 Print; 40 Audio
Online services available through World Wide Web.
Parent Company: China International Publishing Group
Imprints: Phoenix
Subsidiaries: Dolphin Books; Sinolingua
U.S. Office(s): Cypress Book Co Inc, 3450 Third St, Unit 4B, San Francisco, CA, United States *Tel:* 415-821-3582
Orders to: Cypress Book (US) Co Inc, 3450 Third St, Suite 4B, San Francisco, CA 94124, United States
Cypress Book Co (UK) Ltd, 10 Swinton St, London WC1X 9NX, United Kingdom

Fudan University Press+
579 Guoquanlu, Shanghai 200433
Tel: (021) 5484906-2842 *Fax:* (021) 65104812; (021) 65642840
E-mail: fupirc@fudan.edu.cn
Key Personnel
President: Zhiwei Xu
Dir: Xianghua Lin
Founded: 1981
Subjects: Accounting, Advertising, Art, Asian Studies, Behavioral Sciences, Biography, Bio-

logical Sciences, Business, Chemistry, Chemical Engineering, Communications, Computer Science, Economics, Education, Electronics, Electrical Engineering, English as a Second Language, Finance, Genealogy, Geography, Geology, Government, Political Science, Health, Nutrition, History, How-to, Human Relations, Language Arts, Linguistics, Law, Library & Information Sciences, Literature, Literary Criticism, Essays, Management, Marketing, Mathematics, Microcomputers, Natural History, Philosophy, Photography, Physical Sciences, Physics, Poetry, Psychology, Psychiatry, Public Administration, Regional Interests, Religion - Buddhist, Science (General), Securities, Social Sciences, Sociology, Technology, Women's Studies, Comprehensive
ISBN Prefix(es): 7-309

Fujian Children's Publishing House+
76, Dongshui Rd, Fuzhou, Fujian Province 350001
Fax: (0591) 7606554
E-mail: fcph@163.net
Subjects: Art, Education, Humor, Literature, Literary Criticism, Essays
ISBN Prefix(es): 7-5395
Total Titles: 320 Print

Fujian Science & Technology Publishing House+
15F, Fujian Publishing Center Blg, 76 Dongshui Rd, Fuzhou 350001
Tel: (0591) 7538472 *Fax:* (0591) 7538472
Web Site: www.fjbook.com
Founded: 1979
Subjects: Agriculture, Communications, Computer Science, Electronics, Electrical Engineering, Health, Nutrition, Medicine, Nursing, Dentistry, Science (General), Technology, Transportation
ISBN Prefix(es): 7-5335
Total Titles: 300 Print
Parent Company: Fujian General Publishing House

Geological Publishing House+
10 Lou, 7 Qu, Hepingli, Beijing 100013
Tel: (010) 4219994-268; (010) 4221120
Fax: (010) 6024523
Telex: 22531 MGMRC
Key Personnel
Man Dir & Rights & Permissions: Ma Qingyang
Editor-in-Chief: Shen Shurong
Sales Manager: Xu Yixiao
Production Manager: Wei Hongzhen
Founded: 1954
Subjects: Geography, Geology
ISBN Prefix(es): 7-116
Bookshop(s): Geological Bookshop, Xisi, Beijing

Guangdong Science & Technology Press+
13-14F/11 Shuiyin Rd, Huangshidong Rd, Guangzhou 510075
Tel: (020) 87768688; (020) 87618870 (Directorial Office); (020) 87769412 (Foreign Cooperation Editorial Office) *Fax:* (020) 87764169
E-mail: gdkjwb@ns.guangzhou.gb.com.cn
Web Site: www.gdpress.gov.cn *Cable:* 3934
Key Personnel
President: Ouyang Lian
International Rights: Yunfei (Violet) Ding
Founded: 1979
Subjects: Agriculture, Architecture & Interior Design, Computer Science, Cookery, English as a Second Language, Gardening, Plants, Mathematics, Medicine, Nursing, Dentistry
ISBN Prefix(es): 7-5359

Guizhou Education Publishing House
289 Zhonghua Beilu, Guiyang, Guizhou Province 550001

Tel: (0851) 627904; (0851) 524211
Key Personnel
President: Jize Zhang
Founded: 1990
Subjects: Art, Chemistry, Chemical Engineering, Child Care & Development, Economics, Education, Gardening, Plants, History, Human Relations
ISBN Prefix(es): 7-80583

Heilongjiang Science & Technology Press+
35 Jianshejie Nangangqu, Harbin, 150001 Heilongjiang Province
Tel: (0451) 332486 *Fax:* (0451) 3642127
Key Personnel
President: Xiao Erbin
International Rights: Liu Zhong
Founded: 1979
Subjects: Advertising, Agriculture, Architecture & Interior Design, Business, Communications, Economics, Electronics, Electrical Engineering, Health, Nutrition, How-to, Management, Marketing, Medicine, Nursing, Dentistry, Photography, Physical Sciences, Science (General), Technology, Transportation, Veterinary Science
ISBN Prefix(es): 7-5388

Wissenschaft und Technik Verlag Henan Henan Scientific & Technological Publishing House+
73 Nongye Rd, Zhengzhou, 450002 Henan Province
Tel: (0371) 551756-565 *Fax:* (0371) 5720158
E-mail: hnkj565@public2.22.ha.cn *Cable:* 5171
Key Personnel
President & Rights Contact: Kong Dongyao
Editor-in-Chief: Liu Zhenjie *Tel:* (0371) 5724958
Founded: 1980
Specialize in scientific & technological subjects.
Subjects: Architecture & Interior Design, Biological Sciences, Chemistry, Chemical Engineering, Gardening, Plants, Mechanical Engineering, Medicine, Nursing, Dentistry, Physical Sciences
ISBN Prefix(es): 7-5349
Total Titles: 300 Print
Parent Company: News & Publishing Bureau of Henan Province, Hong Kong
Ultimate Parent Company: News & Publicity Bureau of China

HEP, *imprint of* Higher Education Press

Higher Education Press+
55 Shatan Houjie, Beijing 100009
Tel: (10) 64014043 *Fax:* (10) 64054602
Web Site: www.hep.edu.cn; www.hep.com.cn
Cable: 7559
Key Personnel
President: Liu Zhipeng
Vice President & Editor in Chief: Zhang Zengshun
Dir International Cooperation Division: Lin Mei
E-mail: linm@public.bta.net.cn
Founded: 1954
Publications for textbooks & references in higher education, vocational & adult educational.
Subjects: Agriculture, Architecture & Interior Design, Biological Sciences, Civil Engineering, Computer Science, Cookery, Education, Engineering (General), English as a Second Language, Finance, Gardening, Plants, Geography, Geology, History, Language Arts, Linguistics, Management, Psychology, Psychiatry, Science (General), Social Sciences, Sociology, Technology, Travel, Women's Studies
ISBN Prefix(es): 7-04
Number of titles published annually: 4,000 Print
Total Titles: 12,000 Print
Parent Company: Ministry of Education
Imprints: HEP
Subsidiaries: Beijing Kewen Higher Education Co Ltd

Divisions: Shanghai Office
U.S. Office(s): Science Press New York Ltd, 84-04 58 Ave, Elmhurst, NY 11373, United States
Tel: 718-476-0238 *Fax:* 718-476-0273

Inner Mongolia Science & Technology Publishing House+
4 Lunan Yidun, Hadajie, Chifengshi 024000
Tel: (0476) 22942 *Cable:* 5536
Key Personnel
President: Edensanbu
Founded: 1982
Subjects: Agriculture, Astronomy, Electronics, Electrical Engineering, Mathematics, Microcomputers, Physics, Publishing & Book Trade Reference, Science (General), Veterinary Science
ISBN Prefix(es): 7-5380

International Academic Publishers
Xizhimenwai Dajie, Beijing Exhibition Centre, Beijing 100044
Tel: (010) 8316677-530 *Fax:* (010) 4015664
Telex: 22313 CPC CN
Key Personnel
Dir: Lu Bohua
Founded: 1988
Subjects: Agriculture, Biological Sciences, Chemistry, Chemical Engineering, Computer Science, Electronics, Electrical Engineering, Engineering (General), Medicine, Nursing, Dentistry, Technology
ISBN Prefix(es): 7-80003

International Culture Publishing Corp+
40 Andingmennei Dajie, Beijing 100009
Tel: (010) 4013415; (010) 4010830 *Fax:* (010) 4013437
Founded: 1984
ISBN Prefix(es): 7-80049

Jiangsu People's Publishing House
165 Nanjing Central Rd, Jiangsu, Nanjing 210009
Tel: (025) 6634309 *Fax:* (025) 3379766
Web Site: www.book-wind.com
Telex: 0512
ISBN Prefix(es): 7-214

Jiangsu Science & Technology Publishing House+
47 Hunan Rd, Nanjing 210009
Tel: (025) 6633121; (025) 3273012; (025) 3273033 *Fax:* (025) 3273111
E-mail: cnjsstph@public1.ptt.js.cn
Key Personnel
President: Ms Hu Mingxiu
International Rights: Ms Deng Haiyun; Mr Sun Lianmin
Founded: 1978
Subjects: Chemistry, Chemical Engineering, Computer Science, Earth Sciences, Engineering (General), Environmental Studies, Geography, Geology, Health, Nutrition, Physical Sciences, Science (General), Technology
ISBN Prefix(es): 7-5345

Jilin Science & Technology Publishing House+
22A Tongzhijie, Changchun, Jilin 130021
Tel: (431) 845184; (431) 845175 *Fax:* (431) 5635185
E-mail: jlkjcbs@public.ec.jl.cn
Key Personnel
Rights Director: Frank Young
E-mail: frankyoung@sina.com
Founded: 1984
Publishing house.
Subjects: Accounting, Advertising, Agriculture, Animals, Pets, Anthropology, Architecture & Interior Design, Astronomy, Automotive, Biography, Biological Sciences, Business, Career Development, Chemistry, Chemical Engineering, Child Care & Development, Civil Engi-

neering, Computer Science, Cookery, Electronics, Electrical Engineering, Engineering (General), English as a Second Language, Environmental Studies, Health, Nutrition, House & Home, How-to, Management, Marketing, Mathematics, Mechanical Engineering, Medicine, Nursing, Dentistry, Microcomputers, Outdoor Recreation, Photography, Physical Sciences, Physics, Science (General), Science Fiction, Fantasy, Sports, Athletics, Technology, Travel, Veterinary Science
ISBN Prefix(es): 7-5384
Number of titles published annually: 200 Print
Total Titles: 500 Print

Jinan Publishing House+
251 Jingqilu, Jinan, Shandong 250001
Tel: (0531) 613006
Key Personnel
President: Weng Cheng
Founded: 1988
Subjects: Agriculture, Cookery, Economics, Education, Medicine, Nursing, Dentistry, Nonfiction (General), Social Sciences, Sociology
ISBN Prefix(es): 7-80572
Imprints: First Edition

Juvenile & Childrens Books Publishing House
1538 Yan'an Xilu, Shanghai 200052
Tel: (021) 2512851 *Fax:* (021) 2512851
ISBN Prefix(es): 7-5324

Knowledge Press+
17 Fuchengmen Beidajie, Beijing 100037
Tel: (010) 8315533 *Fax:* (010) 8316510
E-mail: ecphtdb@public3.bta.net.cn *Cable:* ECPH
Key Personnel
President: Zhai Defang
Subjects: Civil Engineering, Health, Nutrition, Human Relations, Science (General), Social Sciences, Sociology
ISBN Prefix(es): 7-5015

Kunlun Publishing House+
3A Maowu Hutong Xishiku, Beijing 100034
Tel: (010) 6732721 *Fax:* (010) 62183683; (010) 66847703
Key Personnel
President: Cheng Bu-tao
Vice President: Zhu Ya-nan; Fan Chuan-xin
Founded: 1951
Subjects: Biography, Literature, Literary Criticism, Essays, Military Science, Nonfiction (General), Social Sciences, Sociology
ISBN Prefix(es): 7-80040
Parent Company: The Cultural Dept of the General Political Dep
Bookshop(s): 36 Middle North Sanhuan Rd, Beijing 100084

Language Publishing House+
51 Nanxiaojie Chaonei, Beijing 100010
Tel: (010) 550075
Key Personnel
President: Li Xingjian
Founded: 1980
Subjects: Communications
ISBN Prefix(es): 7-80006

Lanzhou University Press+
216 Tianshuilu, Lanzhou, Gansu 730000
Mailing Address: General Edition Office, 308 Tianshui Rd, Lanzhou, Gansu 730000
Tel: (0931) 22991-272 *Fax:* (0931) 8615095
E-mail: press@lzu.edu.cn
Key Personnel
Chairman: Prof Li Ji-Jun *Tel:* (0931) 891-1282 *Fax:* (0931) 891-1282 *E-mail:* lijj@lzu.edu.cn
President: Mr Yu Zejun
Vice President: Mrs Rao Hui; Mr Lei Hongchang
General Editor: Mr Zhang Kefei

Founded: 1985
Subjects: Behavioral Sciences, Economics, Education, Government, Political Science, History, Law, Philosophy, Physics, Psychology, Psychiatry, Social Sciences, Sociology
ISBN Prefix(es): 7-311
Bookshop(s): 268 Tianshui Rd, Lanzhou University, Lanzhou, Gansu 730000

The Law Publishing House
17 Denglai Hutong, Guangneidajie, Xuanwugu, Beijing 100053
Tel: (010) 3266792
Key Personnel
Executive Dir, Editorial: Lan Ming-Liang
Sales: Wang Jia-jing
Production, Publicity: Ling Yu-jie
Rights & Permissions: Jiang Xou Yuan
Founded: 1980
Also book packager.
Subjects: Law
ISBN Prefix(es): 7-5036

Liaoning People's Publishing House+
108 Beiyi Malu, Hepingqu, Liaoning Shenyang 110001
Tel: (024) 363316; (024) 363541 *Fax:* (024) 371472 *Cable:* 3652
Key Personnel
Chief Executive: Ren Huiying
Editorial Dir: Li Fan
Sales: Li Wenshan
Founded: 1951
Subjects: Economics, History
ISBN Prefix(es): 7-205
Subsidiaries: Liao-Shen Publishing House

Metallurgical Industry Press (MIP)+
39 Songzhuyuan Beixiang, Beiheyan Dajie, Beijing 100009
Tel: (010) 64013877; (010) 4015599 *Fax:* (010) 64013877
Telex: 222753 CMMI CN *Cable:* 3658
Key Personnel
President: Qing Qiyun
Sales: Yang Jin
Editors-in-Chief: Yang Chuanfu; Liu Shan
Founded: 1953
Subjects: Chemistry, Chemical Engineering, Computer Science, Earth Sciences, Electronics, Electrical Engineering, Engineering (General), Environmental Studies, Geography, Geology, Management, Mathematics, Mechanical Engineering, Technology
ISBN Prefix(es): 7-5024

MIP, see Metallurgical Industry Press (MIP)

Modern Press
504 Anhuali, Andingmenwai, Beijing 100011
Tel: (010) 4215031-383 *Fax:* (010) 4214540 *Cable:* 1200
Key Personnel
President: Lou Ming
ISBN Prefix(es): 7-80028

Morning Glory Publishers+
35 Chegongzhuang Xilu, Beijing 100044
Tel: (010) 68411973; (010) 68433187 *Fax:* (010) 68412023; (010) 68485739
E-mail: zh@mail.cibtc.com.cn; zh1@mail.cibtc.com.cn *Cable:* CIBTC BEIJING
Key Personnel
Contact: Ms Zheng Wenlei
Founded: 1982
Copyright transfer; purchase of entire editions.
Subjects: Art, Cookery, History, Photography
ISBN Prefix(es): 7-5054
Parent Company: China International Book Trading Corporation

Nanjing University Press+
22 Hankoulu Rd, Nanjing University, Nanjing, Jiangsu 210008
Tel: (025) 302695; (025) 3593642
Key Personnel
President: Shi Huirong
Founded: 1984
Subjects: Biography, Biological Sciences, Chemistry, Chemical Engineering, Computer Science, Earth Sciences, Economics, English as a Second Language, Environmental Studies
ISBN Prefix(es): 7-305

National Defence Industry Press+
7 Laohumiao, Chegongzhuang Xilu, Beijing 100044
Tel: (010) 8412244-214 *Fax:* (010) 68413125; (010) 68427707
E-mail: ndip@public3.bta.net.cn
Web Site: www.ndip.com.cn
Key Personnel
President: Zeng Duo
Foreign Rights: Chen Bin *E-mail:* chenbin@public3.bta.net.cn
Founded: 1954
Subjects: Aeronautics, Aviation, Automotive, Computer Science, Electronics, Electrical Engineering, Microcomputers, Military Science, Science (General), Technology
ISBN Prefix(es): 7-118

The Nationalities Publishing House+
5 Hepingli Beijie, Beijing 100013
Tel: (010) 4212794; (010) 4212031
Founded: 1953
ISBN Prefix(es): 7-105
Bookshop(s): The Nationalities Culture Bookshop, 5 Hepingli Beijie, Beijing 100013

New Times Press+
7 Laohumiao, Chegongzhuang Xilu, Beijing 100044
Tel: (010) 8412244 *Fax:* (010) 68413125
Key Personnel
Foreign Rights: Chen Bin *E-mail:* chenbin@public3.bta.net.ca
Founded: 1980
Subjects: Education, Electronics, Electrical Engineering, English as a Second Language, Science (General), Technology
ISBN Prefix(es): 7-5042

Patent Documentation Publishing House
Xueyuanlukou Beisanhuan Xilu, Beijing 100088
Tel: (010) 2013103; (010) 2026893 *Fax:* (010) 2019307
Subjects: Law, Science (General), Technology
ISBN Prefix(es): 7-80011

Peking Union Medical Col and Beijing Medical Univ Press, see Beijing Medical Univ Press

The People's Communications Publishing House+
10 Hepingli St (E), Beijing 100013
Tel: (010) 4214479 *Fax:* (010) 4213713 *Cable:* 3652
Key Personnel
Contact: Gao Zhendu
Founded: 1952
Subjects: Automotive, Civil Engineering, Communications, Film, Video, Transportation, Ship building & repairing
ISBN Prefix(es): 7-114

People's Education Press+
55 Sha Tan Hou St, Beijing 100009
Tel: (010) 6402 4555 *Fax:* (010) 6401 0370
E-mail: yaod@pep.com.cn (English); dongyj@pep.com.cn (Japanese)

Key Personnel
Editor-in-Chief: Wei Guodong
Dir: Han Shaoxiang
Founded: 1950
Subjects: Disability, Special Needs
ISBN Prefix(es): 7-107
Number of titles published annually: 300 Print
Total Titles: 1,400 Print

People's Fine Arts Publishing House+
32 Beizongbu Hutong, Beijing 100735
Tel: (010) 5122371 *Fax:* (010) 5122370
Key Personnel
President: Yunhe Chen
Vice President: Youyuan Zhang
Founded: 1951
Member of China Publishing Association.
Subjects: Art, Biography, History, Photography
ISBN Prefix(es): 7-102
Book Club(s): Art Books Research Association

People's Health Publishing House, see People's Medical Publishing House (PMPH)

People's Literature Publishing House
166 Chaonei Dajie, Beijing 100705
Tel: (010) 65138394 *Fax:* (010) 65138394
Founded: 1951
Subjects: Literature, Literary Criticism, Essays, Nonfiction (General), Poetry, Cultural history & studies; current events
ISBN Prefix(es): 7-02
Branch Office(s)
Shanghai

People's Medical Publishing House (PMPH)+
10 Tian Tanxili, Congwen District, Beijing 100050
Tel: (010) 67015802 *Fax:* (010) 67025429 *Cable:* 0427
Key Personnel
President: Dong Mianguo
Deputy Editor-in-Chief: Zhang Yuankang
Sales Dir: Yao Lingi
Production: Wang Duzhong
Head, Centre: Mr Liu Yiqing
Founded: 1953
Division of Ministry of Public Health.
Subjects: Health, Nutrition, Medicine, Nursing, Dentistry
ISBN Prefix(es): 7-117
Bookshop(s): 92 Dongdan Beidajie, Beijing

The People's Posts & Telecommunication Publishing House
27 Dongchanganjie, Beijing 100740
Tel: (010) 5138139; (010) 5138129 *Fax:* (010) 5138139
Key Personnel
President: Niu Tianjia
Founded: 1953
Subjects: Communications, Computer Science, Crafts, Games, Hobbies, Electronics, Electrical Engineering
ISBN Prefix(es): 7-115

People's Sports Publishing House+
8 Tiyuguanlu, Beijing 100061
Tel: (010) 754525 *Fax:* (010) 67116129
Key Personnel
Chief Executive: Pei Jiarong
Rights & Permissions: He Yang
Founded: 1954
Subjects: Crafts, Games, Hobbies, Sports, Athletics
ISBN Prefix(es): 7-5009
Number of titles published annually: 440 Print; 70 Audio
Total Titles: 3,800,000 Print; 70,000 Audio
Bookshop(s): Wu Huan Bookshops, 8 Tiyuguanlu Rd, Beijing 100061

Petroleum Industry Publishing House, see China Oil & Gas Periodical Office

Phoenix, *imprint of* Foreign Languages Press

Popular Science Press
32 Baishiqiao Lu, Haidianqu, Beijing 100081
Tel: (010) 8023226; (010) 8318877
Telex: 5198
Key Personnel
President: Wen Zuning
Vice President: Wu Zhijing; Gu Lizhi
Editor-in-Chief: Jin Tao
ISBN Prefix(es): 7-110

Printing Industry Publishing House+
2 Cuiweilu Fuxingmenwai, Beijing 100036
Tel: (010) 8219966 *Fax:* (010) 8214683
E-mail: capt@public3.bta.net.cn
Key Personnel
President: Shen Haixiang
Founded: 1981
Subjects: Chemistry, Chemical Engineering, Electronics, Electrical Engineering, Engineering (General), Management, Mechanical Engineering, Photography, Technology
ISBN Prefix(es): 7-80000

The Publishing House of Shanghai University of Traditional Chinese Medicine+
530 Lingling Rd, Shanghai 200032
Tel: (021) 64175039 *Fax:* (021) 64175039
Key Personnel
President: Hong Jiahe
Founded: 1985
Subjects: Asian Studies, Behavioral Sciences, Health, Nutrition, Science (General)
ISBN Prefix(es): 7-81010

Qi Lu Press
39 Shengli Dajie, Jingjiulu, Jinan, Shandong 250001
Tel: (0531) 610055-313 *Fax:* (0531) 2906811 *Cable:* 0427
Key Personnel
Dir: Meng Fan-Hai; Li Xin
Editorial: Zhao Bing-Nan; Sun Yan-Cheng
Founded: 1979
ISBN Prefix(es): 7-5333
Branch Office(s)
76 Jing-Shi Rd, Jinan

Qingdao Publishing House+
77 Xuzhoulu Qingdao, Shandong 266071
Tel: (0532) 514611; (0532) 362524 *Fax:* (0532) 515240
Key Personnel
President: Xu Cheng
Subjects: Accounting, Advertising, Aeronautics, Aviation, Agriculture, Alternative, Animals, Pets, Anthropology, Antiques, Archaeology, Architecture & Interior Design, Art, Asian Studies, Astrology, Occult, Astronomy, Automotive, Behavioral Sciences, Biblical Studies, Biography, Biological Sciences, Business
ISBN Prefix(es): 7-5436
Showroom(s): Cui Zifan Art Gallery

Science Press+
16 Donghuangchenggen N St, Beijing 100717
Tel: (010) 64010642; (010) 64034205 *Fax:* (010) 64010642
Key Personnel
President: Mr Wang Jixiang
Dir, International Sales & Marketing: Shi Xiong Zhao
Founded: 1954
Subjects: Animals, Pets, Archaeology, Biological Sciences, Chemistry, Chemical Engineering, Computer Science, Earth Sciences, Electronics, Electrical Engineering, Environmental Studies, Gardening, Plants, Law, Mathematics, Medicine, Nursing, Dentistry, Natural History, Physics, Science (General), Technology
ISBN Prefix(es): 7-03
Number of titles published annually: 500 Print; 20 Audio
Total Titles: 5,000 Print
Subsidiaries: Science Press New York Ltd
U.S. Office(s): 84-04 58 Ave, Elmhurst, NY 11373, United States, Contact: Mr Zhang Ju
Tel: 718-476-0238 *Fax:* 718-476-0273

SDX (Shenghuo-Dushu-Xinzhi) Joint Publishing Co
166 Chaoyangmennei Dajie, Beijing 100706
Tel: (010) 555159 *Fax:* (010) 5138378 *Cable:* 1003
Key Personnel
President: Shen Changwen
Vice President: Dong Xiuyu
Rights & Permissions: Ze Wei; Yang Jin
Founded: 1932
Subjects: Biography, Economics, Government, Political Science, History, Literature, Literary Criticism, Essays, Management, Philosophy, Psychology, Psychiatry, Social Sciences, Sociology
ISBN Prefix(es): 7-108

Shandong Education Publishing House+
321 Weiyilu, Jinan, Shandong Province 250001
Tel: (0531) 2050801 *Fax:* (0531) 2061455
E-mail: sdjys@jn-public.sd.cninfo.net
Web Site: www.sjs.com.cn *Cable:* 0427
Key Personnel
Vice President: Yang Wen Hui *Tel:* (0531) 2016904
Dir: Wang Hongxin
Chief Editor: Xie Rongdai
Editor-in-Chief: Sun Yong Da *Tel:* (0531) 2907274
Founded: 1982
Subjects: Child Care & Development, Education, Fiction
ISBN Prefix(es): 7-5328
Parent Company: Shandong General Publication Bureau, 39 Shengli Dajie, Jingjiulu Shandong, Jinan 250001
Orders to: 39 Shengli St, Jinan, Shandong

Shandong Fine Arts Publishing House+
227 Jingsilu Rd, Jinan, Shandong 250001
Tel: (021) 6911563 *Fax:* (021) 6911563 *Cable:* 0427
Key Personnel
Dir & Editor-in-Chief: Liu Zhenqing
Deputy Dir: Jingchun Wang
Deputy General Editorial: Ying Wang; Yarbo Jiang
Founded: 1984
Books, commercial printing, engineering & architectural services, newspapers.
ISBN Prefix(es): 7-5330
Parent Company: Shandong General Publication Bureau, 227 Jingsilu, Jinan, Shandong 250001
Bookshop(s): Fine Arts Bookshop, Bldg No 1, Shunhe Commercial St, Jinan

Shandong Friendship Press+
39 Shengli Dajie, Jinan, Shandong 250001
Tel: (0531) 2063686 *Fax:* (0531) 2909354 *Cable:* 0427
Key Personnel
Dir & Editor-in-Chief: Xu Shidian
Deputy Dir: Han Chun
Deputy Editor-in-Chief: Yang Qizhang; Zhao Zhiping
Founded: 1986
Subjects: Fashion, Fiction, Travel, Comics/cartoons, lifestyle

ISBN Prefix(es): 7-209
Parent Company: Shandong General Publication House, 39 Shengli Dajie, Jinan, Shandong 250001

Shandong Literature & Art Publishing House+
39 Shengli Dajie, Jinan, Shandong 250001
Tel: (0531) 610051 (ext 239) *Fax:* (0531) 613584
Cable: 0427
Key Personnel
Dir: Guo Zhenming
Editor-in-Chief: Wang Shuguo
Founded: 1984
Subjects: Drama, Theater, Literature, Literary Criticism, Essays, Music, Dance
ISBN Prefix(es): 7-209
Parent Company: Shandong General Publications Bureau, 39 Shengli Dajie, Shandong, Jinan 250001
Showroom(s): 85 Culture Market, 46 Maarshan Rd, Jinan, Shandong PC 25001 *Tel:* (0531) 6915710
Warehouse: 85 Culture Market, 46 Maarshan Rd, Jinan, Shandong PC 25001 *Tel:* (0531) 6915710
Orders to: 85 Culture Market, 46 Maarshan Rd, Jinan, Shandong PC 25001 *Tel:* (0531) 6915710

Shandong People's Publishing House+
39 Shengli Daljie, Jingjiulu, Jinan, Shandong 250001
Tel: (0531) 610051 *Fax:* (0531) 613584
Cable: 0427
Key Personnel
Dir: Lui Tongshun
Deputy Dir: Tin Mingshan
Editor-in-Chief: Liu Dejiu
Deputy Editor-in-Chief: Yin Ming
Dir, General Editorial Affairs: Wang Xiaolin
Founded: 1951
Subjects: Economics, Government, Political Science, History, Law, Philosophy, Social Sciences, Sociology
ISBN Prefix(es): 7-209
Parent Company: Shandong General Publication Bureau, 39 Shengli Daljie, Shandong, Jinan 250001
Associate Companies: Shangdong East Book Co

Shandong Science & Technology Press+
16 Yuhan Rd, Jinan, Shandong Province 250002
Tel: (0531) 2065109 *Fax:* (0531) 2023898
E-mail: li_yujn@sina.com
Web Site: www.ikj.com.cn *Cable:* 0067
Key Personnel
President: Xie Rongdai
Dir of International Cooperation: Li Yu
Founded: 1978
Subjects: Agriculture, Architecture & Interior Design, Business, Earth Sciences, Economics, Education, Electronics, Electrical Engineering, Energy, Engineering (General), English as a Second Language, Environmental Studies, Mechanical Engineering, Medicine, Nursing, Dentistry, Technology, Computers, Foreign Language Study
ISBN Prefix(es): 7-5331
Parent Company: Shandong General Publishing House, 39 Shengli Dajie St, Jinan, Shandong 250001

Shandong University Press+
Shanda Nanlu, Jinan, Shandong 250100
Tel: (027) 642602; (027) 642600
E-mail: hustpub@blue.hust.edu.cn
Key Personnel
Vice President: Li Qiuping
Founded: 1980
Subjects: Accounting, Architecture & Interior Design, Behavioral Sciences, Business, Chemistry, Chemical Engineering, Communications, Computer Science, Economics, Electronics, Electrical Engineering, Energy, Engineering (General), English as a Second Language, Environmental Studies, Finance, Geography, Geology, History, Human Relations, Library & Information Sciences, Management, Mathematics, Mechanical Engineering, Microcomputers, Philosophy, Physical Sciences, Physics, Public Administration, Science (General), Technology
ISBN Prefix(es): 7-5607

Shanghai Educational Publishing House+
123 Yong Fu Rd, Shanghai 200031
Tel: (021) 64 37 71 65 *Fax:* (021) 64 33 99 95
E-mail: wuyiyang@public2.sta.net.cn *Cable:* 3413
Key Personnel
Chief Executive, Production & International Rights: Chen He
Editorial: Bao Nan Ling
Adjoint Dir Editorial: M Zhang Wen-Jie
Founded: 1958
Subjects: Child Care & Development, Education, English as a Second Language, History, Microcomputers, Physics, Science (General), Social Sciences, Sociology
ISBN Prefix(es): 7-5320
Distributor for Xin Hua Book Store (Peoples Republic of China)

Shanghai Fine Arts Publishers+
81 Qinzhou South Lu, Shanghai 200235
Tel: (021) 64519016 *Fax:* (021) 64519015 *Cable:* 5600
Key Personnel
President: Zhu Junbo
Founded: 1960
Subjects: Antiques, Art, Biography, Fashion, Photography, Culural Studies, Lifestyles
ISBN Prefix(es): 7-80635
Bookshop(s): Shanghai

Shanghai Foreign Language Education Press+
One Road 295, Zhongshan, North Shanghai 200083
Tel: (021) 5425300 *Fax:* (021) 5422956
Web Site: www.sflep.com
Key Personnel
President: Zhuang Zhixiang
International Rights: Zhang (John) Hong
  E-mail: johnhzhang@sflep.com
Founded: 1979
Subjects: Business, Education, English as a Second Language, Language Arts, Linguistics, Literature, Literary Criticism, Essays
ISBN Prefix(es): 7-81009
Bookshop(s): 564 Dalian Xi Rd, Changhai 200083

Shanghai Science & Technology Publishers+
450 Ruijin Erlu, South Shanghai 200020
Tel: (021) 64184881; (021) 64174349 *Fax:* (021) 64730679
Web Site: www.sstp.com.cn
Telex: 33384 Cpts
Key Personnel
President: Gorg Gang
Editorial: Ye Lu; Wang Pei-lin
Dir International Division: Hu Da-wei
Sales: Wang Feng-ying
Founded: 1956
Subjects: Agriculture, Engineering (General), Medicine, Nursing, Dentistry, Science (General), Technology
ISBN Prefix(es): 7-5323
Bookshop(s): SSTP Bookshop, 50 Ruijin Erlu, Shanghai 200020

Shanghai Scientific & Technological Literature Publishing House
2 Wukanglu, Shanghai 200031
Tel: (020) 4373312; (020) 4370782 *Fax:* (020) 0028621; (020) 4335311 *Cable:* 2115
Key Personnel
Chief Executive: Shu Feng Xiang
Editorial: Wen Jun Chi
Sales: Yi Liang Zhao
Production & Publicity: Cheng Qing Qu
Rights & Permissions: Jian Yue Sun
Founded: 1978
Subjects: Agriculture, Engineering (General), Medicine, Nursing, Dentistry, Science (General)
ISBN Prefix(es): 7-5439; 7-80513
Parent Company: Science & Technology Commission of Shanghai Municipality, 30 Fu Zhou Rd, Shanghai

Sichuan Science & Technology Publishing House+
3 Yandaojie, Chengdu, Sichuan 610012
Tel: (028) 664982 *Fax:* (028) 6654063 *Cable:* CHENGDU 1555
Key Personnel
President: Li Guangwei
International Rights: Luo Xiaoyan
Subjects: Agriculture, Crafts, Games, Hobbies, Fashion, Health, Nutrition, Medicine, Nursing, Dentistry, Science (General), Technology
ISBN Prefix(es): 7-5364

Sichuan University Press+
29 Wangjianglu, Chengdu, Sichuan 610064
Tel: (028) 583875-2529
Key Personnel
President: Wang Jintrou
Founded: 1985
Subjects: Accounting, Antiques, Computer Science, Economics, History, Marketing, Mathematics
ISBN Prefix(es): 7-5614

South China University of Science and Technology Press+
South China University of Science and Technology Press, Wushan Guangzhou, Guangdong 510641
Tel: (020) 5516863; (020) 5511311-2802 *Cable:* 7003
Key Personnel
President: Zhou Shaohua
Founded: 1985
Subjects: Agriculture, Biological Sciences, Chemistry, Chemical Engineering, Civil Engineering, Computer Science, Economics, Education, Electronics, Electrical Engineering
ISBN Prefix(es): 7-5623

Southwest China Jiaotong University Press+
Jiulidi, Chengdu, Sichuan 610031
Tel: (028) 784160-763 *Fax:* (028) 24377
E-mail: swju@swjtu.edu.cn
Telex: 600072 SWJUCN *Cable:* 6445
Key Personnel
President: Fan Ziliang
Vice President: Zhang Xue
Editor-in-Chief: Zhu Yonglin
Founded: 1985
Member of Sichuan Publishers Association.
Subjects: Civil Engineering, Computer Science, Electronics, Electrical Engineering, Engineering (General), Management, Mathematics, Mechanical Engineering, Publishing & Book Trade Reference, Science (General), Transportation
ISBN Prefix(es): 7-81022
Divisions: Division of Audiovisual Publication, SWJU Press
Bookshop(s): SWJUP Readers Service, Chengdu, Sichuan

Tianjin Science & Technology Publishing House+
Unit of Bureau of Publications

189 Zhangzizhong Rd, Heping District, Tianjin 300020
Tel: (022) 27312755; (022) 700919 *Fax:* (022) 27312755
E-mail: tjstp@public.tpt.tj.on
Key Personnel
Dir: Wang Shu-Ze *Tel:* (022) 27301162
Editor-in-Chief: Kou Xiu-Rong *Tel:* (022) 27306821
Editor: Wu Chun-Li
Founded: 1979
Subjects: Agriculture, Architecture & Interior Design, Biological Sciences, Chemistry, Chemical Engineering, Child Care & Development, Computer Science, Cookery, Electronics, Electrical Engineering, Engineering (General), English as a Second Language, Gardening, Plants, Health, Nutrition, Mathematics, Medicine, Nursing, Dentistry, Microcomputers, Physical Sciences, Science (General), Technology
ISBN Prefix(es): 7-5308
Number of titles published annually: 300 Print
Total Titles: 1,000,000 Print

Tomorrow Publishing House+
39 Shengli Dajie, Jingjiu Rd, Jinan 250001
Tel: (0531) 201 0055 ext 4716, 4622, 4270
  Fax: (0531) 290 2094
E-mail: tomorrow@sd.cei.gov.cn *Cable:* 0427
Key Personnel
President & Editor-in-Chief: Liu Haiqi
Dir, Rights Section: David Fu
Founded: 1984
ISBN Prefix(es): 7-5332
Parent Company: Shandong General Press
Associate Companies: Shandong Xinhua Book Store

Tsinghua University Press+
Tsinghua University Haidiangu District, Beijing 100084
Tel: (010) 62783132 *Fax:* (010) 62770278
E-mail: right-tup@mail.tsinghua.edu.cn
Telex: 22617 QHTSC CN *Cable:* 1331 BEIJING
Key Personnel
President: Wang Minfu
Editor-in-Chief: Zhang Zhaoqi
Founded: 1980
Also diskettes & eBooks.
Subjects: Architecture & Interior Design, Chemistry, Chemical Engineering, Civil Engineering, Computer Science, Education, Electronics, Electrical Engineering, Engineering (General), English as a Second Language, Mathematics, Technology, Computers: Educational Software, Operating Systems, Programming Languages & Software
ISBN Prefix(es): 7-302
Number of titles published annually: 250 Print
Total Titles: 700 Print

Water Resources and Electric Power Press (CWPP)+
6 Sanlihelu, Fuxingmenwai, Beijing 100044
Tel: (010) 898031 *Fax:* (010) 68353010
  Cable: BEIJING 81605
Key Personnel
President: Mr Tang Xinhua
Vice President: Mr Liu Fengtong
Editor-in-Chief: Mr Jin Yan
International Cooperation Office & Project Manager: Ms Fang Ping
Founded: 1956
Subjects: Civil Engineering, Electronics, Electrical Engineering, Energy, Engineering (General), Environmental Studies
ISBN Prefix(es): 7-120
Bookshop(s): CWPP Retail Dept, 6 Sanlihe Rd, Bejing 100044
Orders to: International Cooperation Div, 6 Sanlihe Rd, Beijing 100044

World Affairs Press+
A31 Waijiaobujie, Dongcheng, Beijing 100005
Tel: (010) 5125544 *Fax:* (010) 65265961; (010) 5133181
E-mail: wap@bj.col.com.cn
Key Personnel
President: Mr An Guozheng
Founded: 1934
Subjects: Biography, Developing Countries, Fiction, Foreign Countries, Government, Political Science, History, Journalism, Social Sciences, Sociology
ISBN Prefix(es): 7-5012
Imprints: World Affairs Printing House

World Affairs Printing House, *imprint of* World Affairs Press

World Books Publishing Corporation+
137 Chaonei Dajie, Beijing 100704
Tel: (010) 4016320 *Fax:* (010) 4016320
E-mail: wpc@china.kw.co.cn
ISBN Prefix(es): 7-5062
Branch Office(s)
Beijing World Publishing Corp

Writers' Publishing House+
10 Nongzhanguan Nanli, Chaoyang Dist, Beijing 100026
Tel: (010) 65004079 *Fax:* (010) 65930761
E-mail: wrtspub@public.bta.net.cn
Web Site: www.zuojiachubanshe.com
Founded: 1953
A state enterprise publishing reprints of Chinese literature.
Subjects: Fiction, Poetry, Romance, Essay
ISBN Prefix(es): 7-5063
Number of titles published annually: 200 Print

Wuhan University Press+
Luojiashan, Wuhan, Hubei 430072
Tel: (027) 812712-427 *Fax:* (027) 712661
Telex: 5678
Key Personnel
President: Xiong Yulian
Vice President: Li Haojie; Wang Wen-Hao
Founded: 1981
Subjects: Biological Sciences, Chemistry, Chemical Engineering, Computer Science, Economics, English as a Second Language, Government, Political Science, History, Law, Library & Information Sciences, Mathematics, Social Sciences, Sociology
ISBN Prefix(es): 7-307
Subsidiaries: Edit Computer Company; Wuhan University

Xiamen University Press
Xiamen University, Xiamen, Fujian 361005
Tel: (0592) 227128
E-mail: chbanshe@jingxian.xmu.edu.cn; xmdx@fjbook.com
Founded: 1985
ISBN Prefix(es): 7-5615

Xi'an Cartography Publishing House+
124 Youyi Donglu, Xi'an, Shaanxi 710054
Tel: (029) 52831
Key Personnel
President: Xu Guohua
International Rights: Huang Meihua
Founded: 1985
Subjects: Earth Sciences, Environmental Studies, Geography, Geology, Nonfiction (General)
ISBN Prefix(es): 7-80545
Distributor for China Cartography Publishing House

Xi'an Maps Publishing House, see Xi'an Cartography Publishing House

Xinhua Publishing House+
Division of Xinhua News Agency
57 Xuanwumen Xidajie, Beijing 100803
Tel: (010) 63073765; (010) 63073787 *Fax:* (010) 3073880
E-mail: nianzh@xinhuanet.com
Web Site: www.xinhua.2699.com
Telex: 22316 Xnabj *Cable:* 1631
Key Personnel
Dir: Qiu Yongsheng
Editor-in-Chief & Deputy Dir: Zhang Shoudi
Deputy Dir: Juo Bomin
Founded: 1979
Subjects: Biography, Economics, Ethnicity, Government, Political Science, Journalism, Social Sciences, Sociology, People's Republic of China Year Book
ISBN Prefix(es): 7-5011
Bookshop(s): China Journalism Bookstore

Youth Publishing House
21 Dongsi Shiertiao, Beijing 100708
Tel: (010) 4032266-328 *Fax:* (010) 4031803
ISBN Prefix(es): 7-5006

Zhejiang Education Publishing House+
347 Stadium Rd, Hangzhou, Zhejiang 310006
Tel: (0571) 576944; (0571) 5170300 *Fax:* (0571) 5176944
E-mail: cheny@zjcb.com; zjjy@zjcb.com
Web Site: www.jys.zjcb.com *Cable:* 2403
Key Personnel
President: Luo Dan
Founded: 1983
Education publishing house.
Subjects: Education, English as a Second Language
ISBN Prefix(es): 7-5338
Parent Company: Zhejiang General Publishing House

Zhejiang University Press+
20 Yugu Rd, Hangzhou, Zhejiang 310027
Tel: (0571) 87984670 *Fax:* (0571) 87952331
E-mail: zupress@mail.hz.zj.cn
Web Site: www.zjupress.com
Key Personnel
President: Han Zhaoxiong
International Rights: You Jianzhong
Founded: 1984
Main publications include almost all fields of Natural & Social Sciences & Medicine.
Subjects: Accounting, Agriculture, Art, Biological Sciences, Business, Chemistry, Chemical Engineering, Civil Engineering, Computer Science, Education, History, How-to, Science (General), Technology, Computers, Teaching Methods & Materials & Electronic Media
ISBN Prefix(es): 7-308

Zhong Hua Book Co
36 Wangfujing Dajie St, Beijing 100710
Tel: (010) 555161; (010) 554504
Founded: 1912
ISBN Prefix(es): 7-101

Colombia

General Information

Capital: Bogota
Language: Spanish (English widely used in business)
Religion: Roman Catholic
Population: 34.3 million
Bank Hours: 0900-1500 Monday-Friday
Shop Hours: 0900-1230, 1430-1830 Monday-Saturday

Currency: 100 centavos = 1 Colombian peso
Export/Import Information: Member of Latin American Free Trade Association. Value added taxes on all imports; no sales tax on books. Ad valorem: none generally on books except on books bound in leather or similar materials, on photonovels of thrillers, detective stories, etc, on horoscopes, children's picture books, atlases & advertising catalogues. No import license for books. Exchange license from Banco de la Republica required.
Copyright: UCC, Berne, Buenos Aires (see Copyright Conventions, pg xi)

ACPO, see Dosmil Editora

Amazonas Editores Ltda
Carrera 11 No 94-02 Ofc 121, Santafe de Bogota, 47009 Cundinamarca, Bogota DC
Mailing Address: AA 140 472 Santafe de Bogota, Chia, Cundinamarca
Tel: (091) 8621443; (091) 6762596; (091) 6760616; (091) 6760656; (091) 6180256; (091) 2182760 *Fax:* (091) 8620081; (091) 2762596; (091) 6180326
Key Personnel
Legal Representative: Ferrer Lucia Montano
Founded: 1991
Distribuidor de libros de otras Editoriales Colombianas.
Subjects: Archaeology, Architecture & Interior Design, Art, Environmental Studies, Government, Political Science, History, Poetry
ISBN Prefix(es): 958-95493
Distributor for Cridtina Uribe Editores; El Sello Editorial; Fondo FEN Colombia
Book Club(s): Camara Colombiana del Libro

El Ancora Editores+
Av 25C, No 3-99, AA 56882 Santa Fe de Bogota
Tel: (01) 283 9040; (01) 342 6224; (01) 283 9235 *Fax:* (01) 283 9235
E-mail: ancoraed@interred.net.co
Key Personnel
Man Dir: Patricia Hoher
Editorial, Rights & Permissions: Felipe Escobar Uribe
Founded: 1980
Subjects: Art, Economics, History, Humor, Journalism, Literature, Literary Criticism, Essays, Poetry, Social Sciences, Sociology
ISBN Prefix(es): 958-36; 958-96577

Asociacion Instituto Linguistico de Verano
Calle 13 No 8-38 Ofc 409, 27744 Apdo Aereo Santa Fe de Bogota Cundinamarca
Tel: 2829886; 2821047; 3416185 *Fax:* 2860358
E-mail: langaffairs_cob@sil.org
Founded: 1962
Subjects: Language Arts, Linguistics
ISBN Prefix(es): 958-21

Bedout Editores SA+
Calle 61 No 51-04, Apdo Aereo 760, Medellin, Antioquia
Tel: (04) 5112900 *Fax:* (04) 2517946 *Cable:* BEDOUT
Key Personnel
President: Campuzano R Ilbgnacio
Manager: Mario Gutierrez
Founded: 1889
Subjects: Education, Literature, Literary Criticism, Essays, Social Sciences, Sociology
ISBN Prefix(es): 84-8274; 958-03
Divisions: Editora Beta SA
Branch Office(s)
Calle 13 No 21-51, Local 5, Bucaramanga *Tel:* (076) 352171
Calle 25N No 3 bis-35, 200 piso, Cali *Tel:* (02) 672367
Calle 39 No 233-25, Santa Fe de Bogota DC *Tel:* (01) 2445232

Cekit SA+
Calle 22, No 8-22 Piso 2, Adpo Aereo 194, Pereira, Risaralda
Tel: (01) 333535; (01) 345075; (01) 352575 *Fax:* (01) 342615
Web Site: www.cekit.com.co
Key Personnel
Contact: William Rojas
Founded: 1985
Specialize in learning material for the study of electronics.
Subjects: Electronics, Electrical Engineering
ISBN Prefix(es): 958-9108
Branch Office(s)
Cekits Carrera 17 No 53-48, Piso 2, Bogota DC

Centro Regional para el Fomento del Libro en America Latina y el Caribe
Calle 70 N° 9-52, Apdo Aereo 57348, Santafe de Bogota Cundinamarca
Tel: (01) 2126056; (01) 2495141; (01) 3125690; (01) 3217501; (01) 5402071 *Fax:* (01) 2554614; (01) 3217503
E-mail: cerlalc@impsat.net.co; info@cerlalc.org
Web Site: www.cerlalc.com
Key Personnel
Dir: Carmen Bravo
Founded: 1971
Subjects: Law, Literature, Literary Criticism, Essays, Editing, lecture promotion, production & circulation
ISBN Prefix(es): 92-9057; 958-671

CERLALC, see Centro Regional para el Fomento del Libro en America Latina y el Caribe

CIAT - Centro Internacional de Agricultura Tropical
Kilometro 167 Via Cali-Palmira, Palmira
Tel: (02) 675050; (02) 4450000 *Fax:* (02) 4550073
E-mail: ciat@cgnet.com; ciat@cgiar.org
Web Site: www.ciat.cgiar.org
Telex: 05769CIAT CO
Key Personnel
Dir General: Grant M Scobie
Specializes in Investigation of Tropical Agriculture.
ISBN Prefix(es): 84-89206; 958-9183

Consejo Episcopal Latinoamericano Celam+
Race ae No 118-31, AA 51086 Santafe de Bogota Cundinamarca
Mailing Address: Apartado aereo 253353, Santafe de Bogota Cundinamarca
Tel: (01) 6714789; (01) 6578330 *Fax:* (01) 2158990; (01) 6121929
E-mail: editora@celam.org; celam@celam.org; itepal@celam.org
Web Site: www.celam.org
Key Personnel
President: Eduardo Pena Vanegas
Founded: 1970
Subjects: Biblical Studies, Child Care & Development, Education, Nonfiction (General), Philosophy, Regional Interests, Religion - Catholic, Theology
ISBN Prefix(es): 958-625

Ediciones Cultural Colombiana Ltda
Calle 72, No 16-15, Apdo Aereo 6307, Santafe de Bogota Cundinamarca
SAN: 001-6462
Tel: (01) 2176529; (01) 2116090 *Fax:* (01) 2176570 *Cable:* CULBIANA
Key Personnel
Man Dir: Jose Porto
Editorial: Jose Porto Vazquez
Sales Dir: Hernando Salazar
Production: Maximilian Nicolas
Founded: 1951
ISBN Prefix(es): 84-8273; 958-9013
Bookshop(s): Libreria Cultural Colombian

Ediciones Culturales Ver Ltda+
Calle 37 No 16-64, Apdo Aereo 51095, Santafe de Bogota Cundinamarca
Tel: (01) 2859362; (01) 2859204 *Fax:* (01) 2859362
Telex: 45805
Key Personnel
Manager: Gaspar Alfonso Bacca
Founded: 1989
Member of The House of Books.
Subjects: Education
ISBN Prefix(es): 958-9204

Derecho Penal y Criminologia, *imprint of* Universidad Externado de Colombia

Dosmil Editora
Carrera 39A, No 15-11, Santafe de Bogota Cundinamarca
Tel: (01) 2699698; (01) 2694800
Telex: 45623 Accpo *Cable:* Radiofonicas Bogota
Key Personnel
Man Dir: Hernando Bernal A
Editorial: Javier Martinez Naranjo
Sales & Rights & Permissions: Luis Felipe Delgado; Manuel Hoyos
Founded: 1947 (ACPO - Editora Dosmil 1964)
Formerly Accion Cultural Popular ACPO - Editora Dosmil.
Subjects: Art, Literature, Literary Criticism, Essays, Regional Interests, Social Sciences, Sociology
ISBN Prefix(es): 84-8275

Ecoe Ediciones Ltda
Calle 32 bis No 17-22, Santafe de Bogota Cundinamarca
Tel: (01) 2882556; (01) 2433949; (01) 2889821; (01) 2889871 *Fax:* (01) 3201377
E-mail: ecoe@col1.telecom.com.co
Web Site: www.ecoeediciones.com
ISBN Prefix(es): 958-648

Editorial Educativo Ltda, see Fondo Educativo Interamericano SA

Escala Ltda
Calle 30 No 17-70, Santafe de Bogota Cundinamarca
Tel: (01) 2878200 *Fax:* (01) 2325148
Key Personnel
Contact: Ana Medina De Serna
Founded: 1962
Subjects: Architecture & Interior Design, Art, Engineering (General)
ISBN Prefix(es): 958-9082
Branch Office(s)
Ave San Antonio No 79 Of 101 Napoles, Mexico, DF, Mexico *Tel:* 5633672
Edif Tacagua piso 19 Apdo 19Q, Parque Central Ave Lecuna, Caracas, Venezuela
Apoquinto 4900 of 147-148 las Condes, Santiago de Chile *Tel:* 2466111

Eurolibros Ltda+
Affiliate of Camara de Comercio de Bogota
Calle 40 N° 20-27, Apdo 6125, Santafe de Bogota Cundinamarca
Tel: (01) 2886400; (01) 3401837 *Fax:* (01) 2450291; (01) 2886400
Telex: 3 40 18 11; 3 40 18 37
Key Personnel
Legal Representative: Carlos Roberto Jimenez
E-mail: carlosji@latino.net.co
Founded: 1983

COLOMBIA

Member of Camara Colombiana de la Industria Editorial.
Subjects: Education, Outdoor Recreation, Religion - Catholic
ISBN Prefix(es): 958-99925; 958-9417; 958-95525
Number of titles published annually: 2 Print
Total Titles: 12 Print
Associate Companies: Libros Leo Ltda
Distributed by Oriente (Argentina)

Universidad Externado de Colombia+
Calle 12 No 1-17 Este, Santafe de Bogota
Mailing Address: PO Box 034141, 034141, Bogota, DC
Tel: (01) 3419900; (01) 3420288; (01) 3452500 (ext 3151); (01) 2826066 *Fax:* (01) 2843769
E-mail: publicaciones@uexternado.edu.co; sitioweb@uexternado.edu.co
Web Site: www.uexternado.edu.co
Key Personnel
Dir: Rafael Antonio Milla
Founded: 1886
Subjects: Criminology, Education, Finance, Government, Political Science, Law, Management, Mathematics, Social Sciences, Sociology
ISBN Prefix(es): 958-616
Imprints: Derecho Penal y Criminologia; Informativo; Juridica
Distributor for Siglo del Hombre Editores

Fondo Educativo Interamericano SA+
Calle 36 No 22-33, Apdo Aereo 29696, Santafe de Bogota Cundinamarca
Tel: (01) 2459279; (01) 2852773; (01) 2852542; (01) 2859180; (01) 3382877 *Fax:* (01) 2852891
E-mail: eeducativa@multi.net.co
Telex: 45581 *Cable:* ADIWES BOGOTA
Key Personnel
Man Dir: Alvaro Toledo
Founded: 1970
ISBN Prefix(es): 958-9188

Fundacion Centro de Investigacion y Educacion Popular (CINEP)+
Carrera 5a Nº 33A-08, Santafe de Bogota, DC
Tel: (01) 2858977 *Fax:* (01) 2879089
E-mail: info@cinep.org.co
Web Site: www.cinep.org.co
Key Personnel
Man Dir & Rights & Permissions: Francisco de Roux
Production, Publicity & Publications Manager: Helena Gardeazabal
Founded: 1959
Specialize in Social Science.
Subjects: Economics, Regional Interests, Social Sciences, Sociology
ISBN Prefix(es): 958-644; 958-9027

Fundacion Universidad de la Sabana Ediciones Udes+
Calle 70 No 12-08, Apdo Aereo 53753, Santafe de Bogota Cundinamarca
Tel: (01) 6760867
E-mail: susabana@col1.telcom.com.co
Founded: 1987
Subjects: Biological Sciences, Economics, Management, Philosophy, Religion - Catholic
ISBN Prefix(es): 958-12
Bookshop(s): Sede del Puente del Comon-Chiacundina-marca

Ediciones Gamma+
Carrera 10 No 64-65, Apdo Aereo 7818, Santafe de Bogota Cundinamarca
Tel: (01) 2122873; (01) 2128966; (01) 3460800 *Fax:* (01) 2128931
E-mail: r-diners@colomsat.net.co
Key Personnel
Contact: Gustavo Casadiego

Founded: 1978
Subjects: Travel
ISBN Prefix(es): 958-95108; 958-95237
Parent Company: Diners Club of Colombia

Editora Guadalupe Ltda
Carrera 42 No 10-57, Santafe de Bogota Cundinamarca
Tel: (01) 2690788; (01) 2690211 *Fax:* (01) 2685308
Key Personnel
Man Dir & Editorial: Marco A Moreno H
Sales: Mario E Joya Hernandez
Production: Jose Adel Lopez Q
Founded: 1969
Member of the Columbian Booksellers Association.
Subjects: Literature, Literary Criticism, Essays, Science (General), Technology
ISBN Prefix(es): 958-608

Editorial Hispanoamerica+
Carrera 56 B, No 45-27, Apdo Aero, 15652 Santafe de Bogota Cunidinamarca
Tel: (01) 2492929; (01) 2489682; (01) 2216694 *Fax:* (01) 2213020
Key Personnel
Contact: Alvaro Pinzon
ISBN Prefix(es): 958-9104; 958-658

Imprenta de la Universidad Nacional
Ciudad Universitaria Edif 561, Apdo Aereo 37855, Santafe de Bogota Cundinamarca
Tel: (01) 2686965; (01) 2699111 (ext 860) *Fax:* (01) 2441035
ISBN Prefix(es): 958-628

Informativo, *imprint of* Universidad Externado de Colombia

Instituto Caro y Cuervo+
Calle 10 Nº 4-69, Apdo Aereo 51502, Santafe de Bogota, DC
Tel: (01) 255-82-89; (01) 248-84-66 *Fax:* (01) 217-02-43; (01) 342-21-21
E-mail: carocuer@gaitana.interred.net.co
Web Site: www.caroycuervo.gov.co; www.caroycuervo.edu.co
Key Personnel
Man Dir: Ignacio Chaves Cuevas
Founded: 1942
Subjects: Education, Language Arts, Linguistics
ISBN Prefix(es): 84-8271; 958-611
Bookshop(s): Libreria Yerbabuena, Carrera 11 Nº 64-37, Apdo Aero 51502, Santafe de Bogota; Libreria Cuervo

Juridica, *imprint of* Universidad Externado de Colombia

Editorial Juventud Colombiana Ltda
Calle 58 Nº 19-41, Apdo Aereo 53694, Santafe de Bogota Cundinamarca
Tel: (01) 2557485; (01) 2490543; (01) 2557416 *Fax:* (01) 2557416
Key Personnel
Man Dir: Cecilia De Huidobro
ISBN Prefix(es): 958-23
Parent Company: Editorial Juventud SA, Spain

Kapelusz Ltda Editorial+
Calle 37 Nº 25-10, Bogota Cundinamarca
Tel: (01) 2482235; (01) 2359291; (01) 2442035; (01) 3350031 *Fax:* (01) 3350042
Telex: 3350042 *Cable:* Kapelusz
Key Personnel
Man Dir, Sales & Rights & Permissions: Diego Tenorio
Founded: 1964

Subjects: Education, Physics, Psychology, Psychiatry
ISBN Prefix(es): 958-9010

LEGIS - Editores SA+
Avda Eldorado 81-10, AA 98888 Santafe de Bogota
Tel: (01) 2634100; (01) 2957387 *Fax:* (01) 2952650
Telex: 43300 Legis *Cable:* LEGISLACION
Key Personnel
Man Dir: Mauricio Serna Melendez
Founded: 1952
Subjects: Economics, Law, Management, Marketing
ISBN Prefix(es): 958-9042; 958-653
Subsidiaries: Legislacion Economica Srl; URB Industrial la Urbina
Orders to: CRA 16, No 98-62, Bogota

Lerner Limitada
Street 8B, No 6A-41, Apdo Aereo 8304 Bogota Cundinamarca
Mailing Address: PO Box 8304, Santafe de Bogota Cundinamarca
Tel: (01) 2628200; (01) 2624224 *Fax:* (01) 2624459
Telex: 43195 *Cable:* Edilerner
Key Personnel
Man Dir: Jack A Grimberg Possin
Editorial: Juan Francisco di Domenico
Sales: Diego Jaramillo
Founded: 1959
Subjects: History, Literature, Literary Criticism, Essays, Medicine, Nursing, Dentistry
ISBN Prefix(es): 958-95013; 958-9135
Bookshop(s): Libreria y Distribuidora Lerner Ltda

Libiosy Libres, Editorial+
Av Americas No 64A-39, Apdo Aereo 006642, Bogota DC, Cundinamarca
Tel: (01) 2907145; (01) 2907862; (01) 2886188 *Fax:* (01) 2696830
Key Personnel
Man Dir, Sales, Publicity: Alberto Umana Carrizosa
Editorial: M C Jimero
Production: Jose B Restreps
ISBN Prefix(es): 958-9008

Libros, *imprint of* RAM Editores

Editorial Libros y Libres SA+
Av Americus No 64A-39, Apdo Aero 006642, Santafe de Bogota, Cundinamarca
Tel: (01) 2907145; (01) 2907862; (01) 2886188 *Fax:* (01) 2696830
E-mail: edilibro@colomsat.net.co
Key Personnel
General: Rivero Samuel Diaz
Founded: 1985
Subjects: Behavioral Sciences, Biological Sciences, Earth Sciences, Education, Science (General), Social Sciences, Sociology
ISBN Prefix(es): 958-9253; 958-9008

Lito Technion Ltda
Calle 21 No 43A-23, Apdo Aereo 80085, Bogota DC, Cundinamarca
Tel: (01) 2443502; (01) 2443177; (01) 2441538
Telex: 41456 Trnf
Key Personnel
Man Dir: Benjamin Bursztyn V
Editorial: Samuel Bursztyn V
Sales: Ricardo Herrera G
Production: German Arias G
Publicity: Yonatan Bursztyn V
Founded: 1980
ISBN Prefix(es): 958-9007

PUBLISHERS

COLOMBIA

McGraw-Hill InterAmericana SA+
Av de Las Americas, No. 46-41, Santafe' de Bogota, DC Cundinamarca
Tel: (01) 3682700 *Fax:* (01) 3687484; (01) 3686460
Telex: 43306 MNLACO
Key Personnel
Dir General: Carlos G Marquez H
 E-mail: cmarquez@attmail.com
Professional Division Manager: Martha Edna Suarez
College Division Manager: Luis Fernando Pinzon
Education Division Manager: Hector Zulauga
Controller: Luis Fernando Garavito
Production Manager: Consuelo Ruiz
Founded: 1974
Colombia, Venezuela, Ecuador, Peru & Bolivia.
Subjects: Accounting, Biological Sciences, Business, Chemistry, Chemical Engineering, Economics, Engineering (General), Physics, Psychology, Psychiatry, Social Sciences, Sociology, Technology
ISBN Prefix(es): 958-600
Parent Company: McGraw-Hill Inc, 1221 Avenue of the Americas, New York, NY 10020, United States
Associate Companies: McGraw-Hill/Interamericana de Venezuela CA, Caracas, Venezuela
Subsidiaries: McGraw-Hill Interamericana de Venezuela
Distributor for Houghton Mifflin; Microsoft Press; Harvard Business
Warehouse: Calle 22 No 90-27

Migema Ediciones Ltda
Calle 32 No 19-22, Bogota DC, Cundinamarca
Tel: (01) 2873158; (01) 2858538 *Fax:* (01) 2858538; (01) 2858224
E-mail: emigema@cc-net.net
Key Personnel
Legal Representative: Miguel Angel Torres Campos
ISBN Prefix(es): 958-681; 958-9212
Orders to: Calle 33A N 18-2D, Santafe de Bogota

Instituto Misionerao Hijas De San Pablo+
Carrera 9A No 13 27, Santafe de Bogota DC, Cundinamarca
Tel: (01) 2435885; (01) 6 71 89 74 *Fax:* (01) 670 6378
Key Personnel
Editorial Dir: Lucero Patino
Superior Provincial: Yermy Castano
Founded: 1948
Subjects: Communications, Education, Philosophy, Women's Studies
ISBN Prefix(es): 958-9335
Branch Office(s)
Barranquilla (two)
Bogota
Cali
Cucuta
Manizales
Medellin
Bookshop(s): Carrera No 32A 161A 04, Apdo Aereo 6291, Santafe de Bogota Cundinamarca; Carrera 13 No 72-41, Bogota

Ediciones Monserrate+
Calle 122 Nº 53A-29, Santafe de Bogota Cundinamarca
Tel: (01) 2531347; (01) 6130343; (01) 2713049 *Fax:* (01) 2534300; (01) 2534300
E-mail: edimonse@cable.net.co
Web Site: www.edimonserrate.com
Key Personnel
Man Dir & Editorial: P Enrique Fajardo
Sales: Maria Consuelo de Fajardo
Founded: 1977
Subjects: Law
ISBN Prefix(es): 958-95014

Editorial Norma SA
Av Eldorado No 90-10, Apdo Aereo 53550, Santafe de Bogota, Cundinamarca
Tel: (01) 410 6355 ext 1754; (01) 2853297 *Fax:* (01) 410 5414
Telex: 45584 NORMA *Cable:* Edinorma
Key Personnel
President: Francisco Piedrahita
General Manager: Fernando Gomez
Editorial Dir, Trade Division: Maria del Mar Ravassa
Editorial Dir, Textbook Division: Bernardo Pena
Editorial Dir, Periodicals Division: Maria C Posada
Editorial Dir, International Division: Gustavo Adolfo Carvajal
ISBN Prefix(es): 84-8276; 958-04
Parent Company: Carvajal SA
Branch Office(s)
Barranquilla
Bogota
Bucaramanga
Cartagena
Cucuta
Ibaque
Manizales
Medellin
Neiva

Editorial Oveja Negra+
Carrera 14 Nº 79-17, Santafe de Bogota, Cundinamarca
Tel: (01) 2577900; (01) 2368198 *Fax:* (01) 6100931
Key Personnel
Editor: Jose Vicente Katarain
Commercial Manager: Leyla Bibiana Cangrejo
Founded: 1977
Subjects: Biography, Humor, Literature, Literary Criticism, Essays, Social Sciences, Sociology
ISBN Prefix(es): 958-06; 84-8280

Editorial Panamericana
Calle 12 No 34-20, Apartado Aereo No 6210, Santafe de Bogota DC
Tel: (01) 277 46 13; (01) 360 30 77 *Fax:* (01) 2774991
Web Site: www.panamericanaeditorial.com
Key Personnel
Marketing Manager: Fernando Rojas
 E-mail: frojas@panamericanaeditorial.com
ISBN Prefix(es): 958-30

Pearson Educacion de Colombia LTDA+
Imprint of Prentice Hall - Pearson
Carrera 68A No 22-25, Santa Fe de Bogota
Tel: (01) 405 9300 *Fax:* (01) 405 9330
E-mail: firstname.lastname@pearsoned.com
Web Site: www.pearsoned.com.mx
Key Personnel
President: Mauricio Mikan *E-mail:* mauricio.mikan@pearsoned.com
Man Dir, Columbia: Antonio Ballesteros
Manager, Operations: Hector Franco
Publisher & Manager, Escolar Division: Oscar E Rodriguez
Publisher & Manager, College Division: Carlos E Bermudez
Publisher & Manager, Professional/Trade: Liliana Gonzalez
Founded: 1999
Educational texts in Spanish language.
Subjects: Computer Science, Education
ISBN Prefix(es): 958-9498
Number of titles published annually: 40 Print
Parent Company: Pearson Plc

Procultura SA
Av 25C No 3-97, Apdo Aereo 044700, Bogota DC, Cundinamarca
Tel: (01) 2818154 *Fax:* (01) 2815913

Key Personnel
Manager: Ana Cristina Mejia
General Secretary: Lelia Arango
Founded: 1980
Nueva Biblioteca Colombiana de Cultura.
Subjects: Economics, History, Literature, Literary Criticism, Essays, Poetry
ISBN Prefix(es): 958-9043

RAM Editores+
Calle 20 Sur No 60-24, Bogota DC, Cundinamarca
Tel: (01) 2623067
Key Personnel
Man Dir: Jaime Ramirez Palmar
Sales: Luz Helena S de Ramirez
Production: Bernarda Sabogal Rodriguez
Founded: 1983
Also acts as book packager.
Subjects: Astrology, Occult, Crafts, Games, Hobbies, Fashion, Health, Nutrition, Regional Interests, Self-Help
ISBN Prefix(es): 958-9063
Imprints: Libros

Editorial Santillana SA+
Calle 80, No 10-23, Santafe de Bogota
Tel: (01) 635 12 00; (01) 2189795; (01) 2189935; (01) 2482897; 01 2496350 *Fax:* (01) 236 93 82; (01) 2360311; (01) 2351655; (01) 6351200
Web Site: www.santillana.com.co
Key Personnel
President: Gonzalo Arboleda
General Manager: Francisco Abbad
Founded: 1988
Member of Colombia Book Association; Also acts as distributor.
Subjects: Animals, Pets, Antiques, Art, Cookery, Management, Science Fiction, Fantasy, Self-Help
ISBN Prefix(es): 958-24

Siglo XXI Editores de Colombia Ltda
Carrera 14 No 80-44, Bogota DC, Cundinamarca
Tel: (01) 6110787 *Fax:* (01) 6110757
Key Personnel
Man Dir: Santiago Pombo Vejarano
Contact: Lina Maria Perez Gaviria
Founded: 1976
Subjects: Anthropology, Architecture & Interior Design, Art, Fiction, Government, Political Science, History, Language Arts, Linguistics, Philosophy, Psychology, Psychiatry, Social Sciences, Sociology
ISBN Prefix(es): 958-606
Parent Company: Siglo XXI de Espana Editores SA, Spain
Associate Companies: Siglo XXI Editores SA de CV, Mexico

Susaeta Ediciones
Street 50 S No 46-06, Envigado
Tel: (01) 288 44 22 *Fax:* (01) 288 14 72
E-mail: mdsusaet@medellin.impsat.net.co
Key Personnel
Contact: William Armando Rodriguez
ISBN Prefix(es): 958-07

Tercer Mundo Editores S A, *imprint of* Tercer Mundo Editores SA

Tercer Mundo Editores SA+
Transversal 2A No 67-27, Santafe de Bogota, Cundinamarca
Tel: (01) 2551539; (01) 2550737; (01) 2556691; (01) 2551695 *Fax:* (01) 2125976
E-mail: tmunoded@polcola.com.co
Telex: 42192 *Cable:* TERCER MUNDO
Key Personnel
President: Santiago V Pombo
Editorial Dir: Maria Teresa Barajas
Founded: 1961

Editing, printing & distribution of book, mainly in Colombia & Latino America, with or without the company's name. Administration, management & city's studies.
Member of Tercer Mundo Distribuidores S A.
Subjects: Anthropology, Astrology, Occult, Economics, Education, Environmental Studies, Government, Political Science, History, Literature, Literary Criticism, Essays, Psychology, Psychiatry, Science Fiction, Fantasy, Self-Help, Social Sciences, Sociology, Technology, Women's Studies
ISBN Prefix(es): 958-601
Number of titles published annually: 60 Print
Total Titles: 500 Print
Imprints: Tercer Mundo Editores S A
Divisions: Tercer Mundo Editores, Grafica
Distributed by Alfaomega Grupo Editor SA de CV (Mexico & Central America); Centro de Investigacion Para el Desarrollo Cid; Dolmen Ediciones SA (Chile); Edisa, Ediciones Y Disribuciones Del Istmo SA (Costa Rica); La Familia (Peru); Latin American Book Source Inc (United States); Libri Mundi (Equador); Presa Peyran Editores CA (Venezuela)
Distributor for Tercer Mundo Distribuidores SA
Bookshop(s): Libreria Tercer Mundo, Carrera 7 No 16-91, Bogota, Clara Cortes
Tel: (01) 3340504 Fax: (01) 2125976
E-mail: tmundolib@polcola.com.co (Bolivia)
Book Club(s): Libreria Tercer Mundo, CRA 13 No 44-70, Sandra Guerrero
E-mail: tmundolib@polcola.com.co
Shipping Address: Calle 69 No 6-46, Bogota

Unidad Universitaria del Sur (UNISUR)
Calle 53 No 14-39, Apdo Aereo 42891, Santafe de Bogota Cuninamarca
Tel: (01) 255 3216; (01) 212 0159; (01) 346 0088 Fax: (01) 255 3497
E-mail: unisur12@gaitana.interred.net.co
Key Personnel
Contact: Jesus Emilio Martinez Henao
Founded: 1981
Subjects: Accounting, Agriculture, Biological Sciences, Business, Chemistry, Chemical Engineering, Communications, Computer Science, Economics, Environmental Studies, Film, Video, Finance, Management, Mathematics, Philosophy, Physics, Science (General), Social Sciences, Sociology
ISBN Prefix(es): 958-651
Bookshop(s): Cread Jose Acevedo y Gomex, Autopista Sur No 16-38, Santafe de Bogota

UNISUR, see Unidad Universitaria del Sur (UNISUR)

Universidad de Antioquia, Division Publicaciones+
Calle 67 No 53-108, Ciudad Universitaria, Bloque 28, oficina 233, Apdo 1226, Medellin
Tel: (0574) 210 50 10 Fax: (0574) 210 50 12
E-mail: direccion@editorialudea.com; comunicaciones@editorialudea.com
Web Site: www.editorialudea.com
Key Personnel
Dir & Professor: Luis Fernando Macias Zuluaga
E-mail: macias25@hotmail.com
Founded: 1984
Specializes in publishing of the most remarkable scientific & cultural texts, not only from the institution, but also from other intellectual & academic environments. This helps in contributing to the Latin American advance in the social & cultural fields.
Member of the University Editorial Association of Columbia - ASEUC & the Asociancion of Editorials.
Subjects: Art, Drama, Theater, Education, History, Journalism, Literature, Literary Criticism, Essays, Medicine, Nursing, Dentistry, Music, Dance, Philosophy, Poetry, Social Sciences, Sociology
ISBN Prefix(es): 958-9021; 958-655
Number of titles published annually: 80 Print
Total Titles: 79 Print

Universidad de los Andes Editorial
Apdo Aereo 34383, Bogota DC
SAN: 005-2027
Tel: (01) 2824066 (ext 2717-2713) Fax: (01) 2841890; (01) 2815771
Telex: 42343 Cable: UNAND
Key Personnel
Dir: Jose Leibovich
Founded: 1958
Subjects: Economics
ISBN Prefix(es): 84-89202; 958-695; 958-9057
Distributed by Libreria Uniandes (Colombia)

Universidad Nacional Centro Editorial
Ciudad Universitaria, Torre Activa 602, Apdo Aereo 14490, Santafe de Bogota DC, Cundinamarca
Tel: (01) 2448640
Key Personnel
Editor: Santiago Mutis Duran
ISBN Prefix(es): 958-17

Editorial Universitaria de America Ltda
Calle 41 No 20-39, Bogota DC
Tel: (01) 2566948; (01) 3201097; (01) 2572679 Fax: (01) 3201097; (01) 2480367
ISBN Prefix(es): 958-613

Carlos Valencia Editores+
Av 25C No 3-99, Santafe de Bogota DC, Cundinamarca
Tel: (01) 2839040; (01) 3426224; (01) 2114928 Fax: (01) 2839235
Key Personnel
Man Dir: Patricia Hoher
Editorial, Rights & Permissions: Felipe Escobar Uribe
Founded: 1976
Specialize in literature for children & juveniles.
Subjects: Art, Economics, Government, Political Science, Regional Interests, Social Sciences, Sociology
ISBN Prefix(es): 958-9044; 84-8277; 958-8048

Vertice Ltda
Apdo Aereo 71137, Bogota
Tel: (01) 2437113
Key Personnel
General Manager: Jesus Antonio Villa Posse
Founded: 1980
ISBN Prefix(es): 84-8281

Villegas Editores Ltda
Ave 82 No 11-50, Int 3, Santafe de Bogota
Tel: (01) 6161788 Fax: (01) 6160020; (01) 6160073
E-mail: villegas@colomsat.net.co; villedi@cable.net
Web Site: www.villegaseditores.com
Key Personnel
President & Editor: Benjamin Villegas
Subjects: Art, Cookery, Photography
ISBN Prefix(es): 958-9138

Editorial Voluntad SA+
Carrera 7 No 24-89 Pisos 20, 21 & 24, Santafe de Bogota DC
Tel: (01) 241 04 44 Fax: (01) 241 04 39
E-mail: secsai@voluntad.com.co
Web Site: www.voluntad.com.co
Key Personnel
Man Dir: Gaston de Bedout-Arbelaez
Editorial Dir: William Gomez
Administration Dir: Hector Hurtado
Sales & Publicity Dir: Jairo Roldan
Founded: 1930
Subjects: Art, Communications, Cookery, Crafts, Games, Hobbies, Journalism, Language Arts, Linguistics, Music, Dance, Sports, Athletics
ISBN Prefix(es): 958-02
Branch Office(s)
Barranquilla
Bogota
Cali
Cartagena
Cucuta
Florenica
Ibague
Medellin
Neiva
Pasto
Pereira
Santa Marta
Sincelejo
Tunja
Valledupar

Ediciones Alfred y Cia Wild Ltda
Calle 82 N° 12-35 floor 2, Santafe de Bogota Cundinamarca
Tel: (01) 6218000; (01) 2566731 Fax: (01) 6114338
E-mail: info@galeriaalfredwild.com
Web Site: www.galeriaalfredwild.com
Key Personnel
Legal Representative: Alfred Wild Toro
ISBN Prefix(es): 958-95327; 958-96323
Subsidiaries: Casa Poblana (3 almacenes)

The Democratic Republic of the Congo

General Information

Capital: Kinshasa
Language: Officially French
Religion: Most follow traditional African beliefs; some Catholic and Protestant
Population: 39 million
Shop Hours: 0800-1200, 1500-1800 Monday-Friday; 0800-1200 Saturday
Currency: 100 makutu = 1 zaire
Export/Import Information: No tariff, but for books not of educational, scientific or cultural use there is a revenue tax; children's picture books and atlases are also taxed. Small quantities of advertising matter free. Statistical Tax on all imports. Goods subject to duty also subject to Turnover Tax of percentage of CIF value and customs and statistical tax. No import licences for books. Exchange controls.
Copyright: Berne, Florence (see Copyright Conventions, pg xi)

CDPZ, see Connaissance et Pratique du Droit Zairos (CDPZ)

Centre de Recherche, et Pedagogie Appliquee
BP 8815, Kinshasa 1
Key Personnel
Dir: P Detienne Tel: (012) 22248
Adminstration: J Vannuffelen
Founded: 1959
Subjects: Accounting, Education, Geography, Geology, Language Arts, Linguistics, Mathe-

matics, Medicine, Nursing, Dentistry, Physical Sciences
Distributor for L'Epiphamie
Shipping Address: 1142 11e Rue, Limete, Kinshasa
Warehouse: 1142 11e Rue, Limete, Kinshasa
Orders to: 1142 11e Rue, Limete, Kinshasa

Centre de Vulgarisation Agricole
BP 4008, Kinshasa 2
Tel: (012) 71165 *Fax:* (012) 21351
Key Personnel
Dir General: Kimpianga Mahaniah
Publications: Ntanama Kamba
Subjects: Agriculture, Environmental Studies, Gardening, Plants, Health, Nutrition
Branch Office(s)
1920 Roosevelt Dr, Apt 52, Northfield, MN, United States
Distributed by Inades Formation (Zaire)

Centre Protestant d'Editions et de Diffusion (CEDI)+
PO Box 11398, Kinshasa 1
Tel: 02 22202
Key Personnel
Man Dir: Henry Dirks
Founded: 1935
Subjects: Biography, Fiction, Poetry, Religion - Other
Bookshop(s): CEDI Bookshop

Connaissance et Pratique du Droit Zairos (CDPZ)+
BP 5502, Kinshasa, Gombe
Key Personnel
Editor: Dibunda Kabuinji
Founded: 1987
Subjects: Law
Total Titles: 6 Print; 6 Online
Associate Companies: Societe d'Etudes Juridiques du Congo (SEJC)
Imprints: Reper Toire General be Jurisprubence be la Cour Supreme be Justice; Revue Analytiqu ebe Jurisprubencebu Congo; Revue Juritique bu Congo
Bookshop(s): One rue Limete, Kinshasa/Masina-Petro Congo, Republique Democratique du Congo
Warehouse: One, Rue Limete, Kinshasa-Masina/Petro Congo

Facultes catholiques de Kinshasa c/o Prof Dr L Bertsch S J
Ave de l'Universite 2, BP 1534, Kinshasa-Limete
Tel: (0243) 88 46 965 *Fax:* (0243) 88 46 965
E-mail: facakin@yahoo.fr

Facultes Catoliques de Kinshasa
BP 1534, Kinshasa-Limete
Tel: (012) 78476 *Fax:* (012) 46965
Key Personnel
Dir: Prof Abbe Waswandi Kakule
Editorial: Prof Abbe Mukuna Wa Mutanda; Prof Abbe Atal; Prof Pere Leon de Saint Moulin; Prof Mweze
Founded: 1957
Subjects: Anthropology, Art, Biblical Studies, Communications, Computer Science, Economics, Government, Political Science, History
Bookshop(s): Librarie Saint Paul, Kinshasa-Limete
Orders to: SEDIP (Service de Diffusion des Publications), Kinshasa-Limete

Presses Universitaires du Zaire (PUZ)
Blvd du 30 Juin 4113, Kinshasa 1
Mailing Address: BP 1682, Kinshasa 1
Tel: (012) 30652
Telex: 21394 Bce Es *Cable:* PUZ Enseignement
Key Personnel
Man Dir, Rights & Permissions: Mumbanza mwa Bawele
Editorial: Kabongo Kabongo
Sales: Nsolo Abeyingi
Production: Kawumbu Kabemba
Publicity: Bisimwa Nabintu
Founded: 1972
Subjects: Biography, Economics, Education, Ethnicity, Foreign Countries, History, Law, Literature, Literary Criticism, Essays, Medicine, Nursing, Dentistry, Philosophy, Poetry, Psychology, Psychiatry, Religion - Other, Science (General), Social Sciences, Sociology, Technology
Parent Company: Enseignement Superieu, Universitaire et Recherche Scientifique, BP 1682, Kinshasa-Gombe
Imprints: PUZ
Branch Office(s)
Lubumbashi
Bookshop(s): Librairie des Presses Universitaires; Librairie Universitaire de l'ISP/Kawanga; Librairie du 'Groupe du Mukuba', Lubumbashi

PUZ, *imprint of* Presses Universitaires du Zaiire (PUZ)

Reper Toire General be Jurisprubence be la Cour Supreme be Justice, *imprint of* Connaissance et Pratique du Droit Zairos (CDPZ)

Revue Analytiqu ebe Jurisprubencebu Congo, *imprint of* Connaissance et Pratique du Droit Zairos (CDPZ)

Revue Juritique bu Congo, *imprint of* Connaissance et Pratique du Droit Zairos (CDPZ)

Saint-Paul+
10, rue Limete, Kinshasa
Mailing Address: BP 127, Limete, Kinshasa
Key Personnel
President: Charles Djunju-Simba
International Rights: M Claude Lechat
Founded: 1989
Subjects: Communications, Drama, Theater, Fiction, Literature, Literary Criticism, Essays
ISBN Prefix(es): 2-7414
Distributed by Mediaspaul

Editions Saint Paul-Afrique
BP 8505, Kinshasa
Tel: (012) 77726
Key Personnel
Dir: Sister Franka Perona
Subjects: Fiction, Nonfiction (General), Poetry, Religion - Other

Costa Rica

General Information
Capital: San Jose
Language: Spanish
Religion: Roman Catholic
Population: 3.2 million
Bank Hours: 0900-1500 Monday-Friday
Shop Hours: 0800-1200, 1400-1800 Monday-Saturday (some close Saturday afternoon)
Currency: 100 centimos = 1 Costa Rican colon
Export/Import Information: No import licenses, but statistical recording prior to importation necessary. Imports over a certain value must be registered with Banco Central to be eligible for foreign exchange allocation.
Copyright: Berne, UCC, Buenos Aires (see Copyright Conventions, pg xi)

Academia de Centro America+
Apdo 6347, 1000 San Jose
Tel: 224-6644; 227520 *Fax:* 2246642
E-mail: academia@sol.racsa.co.cr
Key Personnel
President: Eduardo Lizano
Subjects: Agriculture, Business, Economics, Environmental Studies, Finance, Health, Nutrition, Labor, Industrial Relations
ISBN Prefix(es): 9977-21

Asamblea Legislativa, Biblioteca Monsenor Sanabria
Apdo 1013, 1000 San Jose
Tel: 223-2396; 243-2397 *Fax:* 243-2400
E-mail: jvolio@congreso.aleg.go.cr; vvargas@congreso.aleg.go.cr; epaniagu@congreso.aleg.go.cr
Subjects: Economics, Education, Social Sciences, Sociology
ISBN Prefix(es): 9977-916

CATIE, see Centro Agronomico Tropical de Investigacion y Ensenanza (CATIE)

Centro Agronomico Tropical de Investigacion y Ensenanza (CATIE)
Apdo 7170, 7170 Turrialba
Tel: 5560501 *Fax:* 5560858; 5560176; 5568464
Web Site: www.catie.ac.cr
Telex: 8005 CATIE CR *Cable:* CATIE TURRIALBA
Key Personnel
Editor: Eli Rodriguez *E-mail:* erodrigu@catie.ac.cr
Founded: 1942
Research & Higher Educational Center.
Specialize in scientific investigation & techniques of Tropical America, Research & Training of Tropical Agriculture & Natural Resouces.
Subjects: Agriculture, Biological Sciences, Developing Countries, Economics, Education, Engineering (General), Environmental Studies, Gardening, Plants, How-to, Natural History, Social Sciences, Sociology, Technology
ISBN Prefix(es): 9977-57; 9977-951

Confederacion de Cooperativas del Caribe y Centro America+
400 mts este, del Edificio el ICE en Tibas, San Jose
Tel: 506-240-4641; 506-240-4592 *Fax:* 506-240-4284; 233-3122
E-mail: ccocca@sol.racsa.co.cr
Key Personnel
Executive Director: Felix J Cristia
Subjects: Finance, Public Administration
ISBN Prefix(es): 9977-82
Subsidiaries: Sistema de Informacion Cooperativa (REDI-COOP)
Branch Office(s)
CCC-CA/Oficina Subregional, PO Box 360707, San Juan 00936-0707, Puerto Rico

Editorial Costa Rica
Apdo 10010, 1000 San Jose
Tel: 253-5354 *Fax:* 253-5091
E-mail: editocr@racsa.co.cr
Key Personnel
General Manager: Ana Patricia Cartin
Sales: Enilda Campos Barrantes
Production: Dennis Mesen Segura
Publicity Manager: Gustavo Adolfo Gonazalez Mederas
Founded: 1959
Subjects: Regional Interests
ISBN Prefix(es): 84-8361; 9977-23

COSTA RICA

Editorial DEI (Departamento Ecumenico de Investigaciones)+
Section 389-2070, Sabanilla, San Jose
Tel: 2530229; 2539124; 2533713; 2539142
   Fax: 2531541
E-mail: asodei@sol.racsaco.cr
Web Site: www.dei-cr.org
Telex: 3472 ADEI
Key Personnel
General Manager: Alcides Hernandez Chavez
Founded: 1977
Subjects: Economics, Government, Political Science, History, Theology, Women's Studies
ISBN Prefix(es): 9977-904; 9977-83
Imprints: Revista Pasos
Bookshop(s): Libreria Horizonte, Apartado 447-2070, San Jose

Fundacion Omar Dengo
Apdo 1032-2050, San Jose
Tel: 257 6263 *Fax:* 2221654
E-mail: info@fod.ac.cr
Web Site: www.fod.ac.cr
Key Personnel
President: Alfonso Gutierrez Cerdas
Founded: 1987
ISBN Prefix(es): 9977-11

Departamento Ecumenico de Investigaciones, see Editorial DEI (Departamento Ecumenico de Investigaciones)

Asocicion Escuela Para Todos+
Apdo 4757, 1000 San Jose
Tel: 2255438; 2255338; 2340530; 2341339
   Fax: 2243014
Key Personnel
President: Manuela Tattenbach
Founded: 1963
ISBN Prefix(es): 9977-51

EUNA, see Editorial Universidad Nacional (EUNA)

Ediciones FLACSO Costa Rica
Del Automercado los Yoses, 400 mts al sur y 200 al oeste, 1000 San Jose
Mailing Address: Apdo 11747, 1000 San Jose
Tel: 2346890; 2248059 *Fax:* 2256779
ISBN Prefix(es): 9977-68; 84-89401

Garcia Hermanos Imprentay Litografia
De la Contraloria General de la Republica, 200 mts Oeste y 500 mts Sur, Sabana Sur
Tel: 2202003 *Fax:* 2310675
E-mail: garcia@sol.racsa.co.cr
Web Site: www.novanet.co.cr/garcia/main.html
ISBN Prefix(es): 9977-38

IICA, see Instituto Interamericano de Cooperacion para la Agricultura (IICA)

Imprenta y Litografia Trejos SA
Apdo 10-096, 1000 San Jose
Tel: 2242411 *Fax:* 2241528
Key Personnel
President: Alvaro Trejos
ISBN Prefix(es): 9977-54

INCAE, see Insituto Centroamericano de Administracion de Empresas (INCAE)

Insituto Centroamericano de Administracion de Empresas (INCAE)
Apdo 960-4050, Campus de Alajuela, Alajuela
Tel: 506-433-9908; 433-9961; 433-9269; 443-0506 *Fax:* 506-433-9955; 433-9983; 433-9101
Web Site: www.incae.ac.cr

Key Personnel
Chief Marketing: Sonia Jimenez
   E-mail: jimenezs@mail.incae.ac.cr
Contact: Brizio Biondi Morra
ISBN Prefix(es): 9977-71

Instituto Interamericano de Cooperacion para la Agricultura (IICA)
PO Box 55-2200, San Isidro de Coronado, San Jose
Tel: (02) 2443680 *Fax:* (02) 2469175
E-mail: iicahq@iica.ac.cr
Web Site: www.iica.int
Subjects: Agriculture, Computer Science, Developing Countries, Earth Sciences, Environmental Studies, Marketing, Technology, Veterinary Science, Women's Studies
ISBN Prefix(es): 956-212

Jose Alfonso Sandoval Nunez+
100 mts este de la Municipalidad, Residencia El Carmen San Pedro, Montes de Oca
Tel: 2252331
E-mail: asandova@alpha.emate.ucr.ac.cr; k_sanny@hotmail.com
Subjects: Education, Mathematics
ISBN Prefix(es): 9968-9882
Total Titles: 5 Print

Juricom+
De la Pops Curridabat, 100 mts sur, Apdo 4387, AA 11270-1000, San Jose
Tel: 2836942 *Fax:* 2253800
E-mail: juricom@sol.racsa.co.cr
Key Personnel
Contact: Alejandra Linner de Silva
Founded: 1996
Subjects: Law
ISBN Prefix(es): 9968-769

Libreria Imprenta y Litografia Lehmann SA
Apdo 10011, San Jose
Tel: 2231212
Telex: 2540 Lill Eh
Key Personnel
Man Dir: Antonio Lehmann Struve
Publicity: Orlando Mora
Founded: 1894
Subjects: Fiction, Nonfiction (General)
ISBN Prefix(es): 9977-949

Litografia Artex, SA+
Apdo 7111, 1000 Heredia
Tel: 2373144 *Fax:* 2379568
Key Personnel
Contact: Gilbert Campos Gamboa
Founded: 1971
Subjects: Advertising, Medicine, Nursing, Dentistry, Poetry, Religion - Catholic
ISBN Prefix(es): 9977-86

Litografia e Imprenta LIL SA
Apdo 75 - 1100, Tibas
Tel: 2350011; 2213622 *Fax:* 2407814
Key Personnel
Contact: Mario Salazar Fonseca
Founded: 1974
ISBN Prefix(es): 9977-47

Museo Historico Cultural Juan Santamaria
Apdo 785, 4050 Alajuela
Tel: 441-4775; 442-1838 *Fax:* 441-6926
E-mail: mhcjscr@racsa.co.cr
Web Site: www.museojuansantamaria.go.cr
Key Personnel
Dir: Raul Aguilar
Founded: 1980
Subjects: Genealogy, History
ISBN Prefix(es): 9977-953

Editorial Nacional de Salud y Seguridad Social Ednass
Apdo 101-105, San Jose
Tel: 2905744 *Fax:* 2327451
E-mail: cendeiss@info.ccss.sa.cr
Web Site: www.ccss.sa.cr
Key Personnel
Contact: Gerardo Campos Gamboa
Founded: 1988
Subjects: Behavioral Sciences, Biological Sciences, Health, Nutrition, Medicine, Nursing, Dentistry, Public Administration, Social Sciences, Sociology
ISBN Prefix(es): 9977-984
Number of titles published annually: 10 Print
Total Titles: 2 Print

Revista Pasos, *imprint of* Editorial DEI (Departamento Ecumenico de Investigaciones)

Editorial Porvenir
300 sur y 50 este, rotulo CECADE, San Pedro de Monte, San Pedro
Mailing Address: Apdo 447-2050, San Pedro
Tel: 224-8119; 224-1052; 225-3115 *Fax:* 283-8893; 224-8119
E-mail: porvenir@racsa.co.cr
Telex: 3220 CECADE CR
Key Personnel
President: William Reuben
Dir: Victoria Paris
Founded: 1979
Subjects: Economics, History, Law, Psychology, Psychiatry, Social Sciences, Sociology
ISBN Prefix(es): 9977-944

Promesa, Ediciones+
Division of Electronic Engineering
Contiguo a Taco Bell, Barrio Dent, Apdo 4300, San Jose
Tel: 253-3759; 225-1511; 283-3033 *Fax:* 225-1286
E-mail: edicionespromesa@hotmail.com
Key Personnel
President: Helena Ospina *E-mail:* helenaospina@hotmail.com
Manager: Erika Chinchilla
Founded: 1982
Publishing, video, CD & documentation cultural center.
Is a cultural project interrelating the arts. Member of Camara Costarricense del Libro.
Subjects: Anthropology, Art, Behavioral Sciences, Biography, Child Care & Development, Drama, Theater, Education, Fashion, Film, Video, History, Human Relations, Language Arts, Linguistics, Literature, Literary Criticism, Essays, Music, Dance, Philosophy, Poetry, Psychology, Psychiatry, Religion - Catholic, Self-Help, Social Sciences, Sociology, Theology, Women's Studies
ISBN Prefix(es): 9977-947
Number of titles published annually: 24 Print; 6 Audio
Total Titles: 85 Print; 2 E-Book; 20 Audio
Parent Company: Promotora de Medios de Comunicacion, SA
Associate Companies: Electronic Engineering, PO Box 4300-1000, San Jose, Contact: Helena Maria Fonseca
U.S. Office(s): Ma Rosa Noda, 9022 SW 123rd Court 0-109, Miami, FL 33186, United States, Contact: Maria Rosa Noda *Tel:* 305-279-9997 *E-mail:* mrnoda@un.int
Showroom(s): Edificio Electronic Engineering, Frente a Rectoria, Universidad de Costa Rica, Carretera a Sabanilla, San Jose 1000, Contact: Helena Maria Fonseca *Tel:* (305) 283-3033 *Fax:* (305) 225-1286 *E-mail:* hf@eecrica.com
Web Site: www.eecrica.com
Bookshop(s): Libreria Universal, Libreria Lehmann, San Jose

Scout Interamericana+
Apdo 2067, 1000 San Jose
Tel: 2292121 *Fax:* 2685332
Key Personnel
Contact: Daniel Oscar Tagata
Founded: 1955
Subjects: Career Development, Crafts, Games, Hobbies, Education, Environmental Studies, Health, Nutrition, Maritime, Outdoor Recreation, Religion - Catholic, Religion - Protestant, Self-Help, Sports, Athletics
ISBN Prefix(es): 9977-56

Editorial Tecnologica de Costa Rica+
Apdo 159, 7050 Cartago
Tel: 552-5333 ext 2297 *Fax:* 552-5354; 551-5348
E-mail: editec@itcr.ac.cr
Web Site: www.itcr.ac.cr
Key Personnel
Dir: Mario Castillo-Mendez
Founded: 1978
Member of EULAC (Association of University Publishers of Latin American & the Caribbean).
Subjects: Science (General), Technology
ISBN Prefix(es): 9977-66; 84-89400

Editorial Texto Ltda+
Apdo 2988, 1000 San Jose
Tel: 2316643 *Fax:* 2962429
Key Personnel
President: Frank Thomas Gallardo
  E-mail: gallardo@sol.racsa.co.cr
Vice President: Renee Echeverria Rodriguez de Luz
Founded: 1963
Private Company.
Online translating from Spanish to English & vice versa.
Subjects: Animals, Pets, Real Estate, Regional Interests
ISBN Prefix(es): 9977-29
Total Titles: 8 Print

UICN, see Union Mundial para la Naturaleza (UICN), Oficina Regional para Mesoamerica

Union Mundial para la Naturaleza (UICN), Oficina Regional para Mesoamerica
Apdo 1161-2150, Moravia
Tel: 356-568; 355-788; 362-733 *Fax:* 409 934
E-mail: uicnorma@nicarao.apc.org
Key Personnel
Contact: Dr Enrique J Lahmann
Founded: 1988
Subjects: Biological Sciences, Developing Countries, Environmental Studies, Coastal Zone Management, Wetlands, Gender & Development, Nature Conservation, Sustainable Development, Wildlife Management, Forest Management
ISBN Prefix(es): 9968-743
U.S. Office(s): IUCN-US, Suite 502, 1400 16th St NW, Washington, DC 20036, United States
Tel: 202-797-5454 *Fax:* 202-797-5461

Editorial de la Universidad de Costa Rica+
Imprint of University of Costa Rica
2060 Ciudad Universitaria Rodrigo Facio, San Jose
Mailing Address: Apartado Postal 75, San Jose
Tel: 207-5853 *Fax:* 207-5257
Web Site: www.vinv.ucr.ac.cr
Telex: 2544 Unicori
Key Personnel
President, Editorial Commission: Mario Murillo Rodriguez *Fax:* 2075257
Administrative Chief: Gilbert Carazo Gutierrez
  Tel: 2075849
Founded: 1975
Subjects: Agriculture, Anthropology, Archaeology, Architecture & Interior Design, Art, Behavioral Sciences, Biological Sciences, Career Development, Civil Engineering, Computer Science, Cookery, Earth Sciences, Economics, Education, Energy, Engineering (General), English as a Second Language, Environmental Studies, Government, Political Science, Health, Nutrition, History, Language Arts, Linguistics, Law, Management, Natural History, Physical Sciences, Poetry, Public Administration, Science (General), Social Sciences, Sociology, Sports, Athletics
ISBN Prefix(es): 9977-67
Total Titles: 40 Print; 1 CD-ROM

Editorial Universidad Estatal a Distancia (EUNED)
Apdo 474-2050, San Pedro de Montes De Oca
Tel: 234-7954; 253-2121 ext 2440 *Fax:* 234-9138
E-mail: editoria@uned.ac.cr
Web Site: www.uned.ac.cr
Telex: 3003 *Cable:* UNED
Key Personnel
President, Rights & Permissions: Dr Alberto Canas Escalante
Editorial Dir: Carlos F Zamora Murillo
Sales Dir: Hernan Mora Gonzalez
Production: Mario J Sibaja Bustamante
Publicity: Annie Umana Campos
Founded: 1977
Subjects: Agriculture, Economics, Education, Government, Political Science, History, Medicine, Nursing, Dentistry, Philosophy
ISBN Prefix(es): 9977-64; 84-8362
Showroom(s): Calle 11, Ave 12-14, San Jose
  Fax: 331601
Bookshop(s): Libreria UNED, Apdo 474-2050, Montes De Oca; Calle 11, Ave 12-14, San Jose

Editorial Universidad Nacional (EUNA)
Apdo 86, 3000 Heredia
Tel: 277-3204; 277-3825 *Fax:* 277-3204
E-mail: editoria@una.ac.cr
Key Personnel
Contact: Sr Francisco Carballo
Founded: 1978
Member of EULAC-CERLAC.
Subjects: Education, History, Literature, Literary Criticism, Essays, Poetry
ISBN Prefix(es): 9977-65
Number of titles published annually: 45 Print
Total Titles: 250 Print
Distributed by ACAL

Universidad para la Paz
Apdo 138, 6100 Ciudad Colon
Mailing Address: 225 Oeste Pali Curridabat, San Jose
Tel: 249-1072; 249-1511 ext 20 *Fax:* 249-1929
E-mail: upazrena@sol.racsa.co.cr
ISBN Prefix(es): 9977-925

Editorial Universitaria Centroamericana (EDUCA), see Editorial Universitaria Centroamericana (EDUCA)

Editorial Universitaria Centroamericana (EDUCA)+
Calle 41, Av 0 y 2, Apdo 64, 2060 Los Yoses, San Jose
Tel: 2243727; 2258740 *Fax:* 2539141; 2340071
E-mail: educacr@sol.racsa.co.cr
Web Site: www.csuca.ac.cr
Telex: 3011 COSUCA
Key Personnel
Dir: Sebastian Vaquerano
Sales: Anita de Formoso
Founded: 1969
Subjects: History, Poetry, Regional Interests, Romance, Social Sciences, Sociology
ISBN Prefix(es): 9977-30; 84-8360

Cote d'Ivoire

General Information

Capital: Yamoussoukro
Language: French (officially) and several African languages
Religion: Traditional, 20% Islamic, 20% Christian (mostly Roman Catholic)
Population: 13.5 million
Bank Hours: 0800-1200, 1500-1900 Monday-Friday
Shop Hours: 0800-1200, 1530-1830 or 1900 Monday-Friday; 0800-1200, 1430-1730 Saturday
Currency: 100 centimes = 1 CFA franc
Export/Import Information: Member of West African Economic Community. No tariff on books; single copies free but most advertising subject to customs duty, fiscal duty and VAT. No import licenses required for imports from EEC or Franc Zone.
Copyright: Berne, Florence (see Copyright Conventions, pg xi)

Akohi Editions
13 BP 585, Abidjan 13
Tel: 24 39 54 79 *Fax:* 24 39 75 58
Key Personnel
President: Bosson Brou Evariste *Tel:* 24 39 58 01; 05 99 25 52
Founded: 1995
Subjects: Drama, Theater, Human Relations, Literature, Literary Criticism, Essays, Music, Dance, Poetry
ISBN Prefix(es): 2-9507542; 2-910569
Total Titles: 10 Print
Parent Company: Editions Akohi
Ultimate Parent Company: Editions Akohi
Associate Companies: Biennale Internationale des Arts Lettres et du Tourisme, 13 BP, 585 Abidjan, Contact: Bosson Brou Evariste *Tel:* 24 39 54 79; 24 39 58 01; 24 99 25 52; 24 39 40 37 *Fax:* 39 75 58
Subsidiaries: Imprimerie Akohi
Divisions: Akohi Diffusion
Distributed by Ed Passerelle Abidjan
Distributor for Ed Baudhouat Abidjan; Ed Passerelle Abidjan
Showroom(s): Librairie Akohi *Tel:* 05 992552
Book Club(s): Association des Editeurs-Ivoiriens, Contact: Mariam Sy Diawara *Tel:* 35 35 35 *Fax:* 39 75 58; Association des Ecrivains, Josetti Abondio *Tel:* 24 39 10 37 *Fax:* 39 75 58
Shipping Address: Abobo, 2e Arret Sotra, 500M apres Brigade Gendarmerie Route, Anyama, Contact: Bosson Brou Evariste Kowouka *Tel:* 24 39 54 79 *Fax:* 24 39 75 58

CEDA, see Centre d'Edition et de Diffusion Africaines

Centre de Publications Evangeliques
BP 900, Abidjan 08
Tel: 444805 *Fax:* 445817
Key Personnel
Dir: Jules Ouoba
Founded: 1970
Subjects: Biblical Studies, Nonfiction (General), Religion - Protestant, Religion - Other
ISBN Prefix(es): 2-910307

Centre d'Edition et de Diffusion Africaines
04 BP 541, Abidjan 04
Tel: 22 20 55; 21 72 62 *Fax:* 21 72 62
E-mail: infos@ceda-ci.com
Web Site: www.ceda-ci.com

COTE D'IVOIRE

Key Personnel
Editorial Dir: Marie Agathe Amoikon
Man Dir: Venance Kacou
Founded: 1961
Distributors on behalf of INADES, the National University of the Ivory Coast & the Bibliotheque nationale.
Subjects: Biography, History, Law, Nonfiction (General), Philosophy, Regional Interests, Science (General), Social Sciences, Sociology
ISBN Prefix(es): 2-86394

Universite d' Abidjan+
BP V 34, Abidjan 01
Tel: 441285 *Fax:* 434254
E-mail: puci@africaonline.co.ci
Telex: 3469
Key Personnel
Publications Dir: Alain Poiri
Founded: 1964
Subjects: Biography, Communications, Developing Countries, Economics, Environmental Studies, Law, Microcomputers, Public Administration, Social Sciences, Sociology
ISBN Prefix(es): 2-7166
Number of titles published annually: 50 Print

Heritage Publishing Co+
BP 54, Cidex 3 Abidjan-Riviera
Tel: 433056 *Fax:* 433056
Key Personnel
Contact: Tah Asongwed
Founded: 1993
Subjects: Biography, Developing Countries, Fiction, Government, Political Science, Language Arts, Linguistics, Nonfiction (General)
ISBN Prefix(es): 2-910021
Imprints: HP
U.S. Office(s): Heritage Publshing Company, 1015 Stirling Rd, Silver Spring, MD 20901, United States *Tel:* 301-593-6450
Distributed by Waterville Publishing House (Ghana)
Distributor for Three Dimensional Publishing (USA)

HP, *imprint of* Heritage Publishing Co

NEI, see Les Nouvelles Editions Ivoiriennes (NEI)

Les Nouvelles Editions Africaines+
One blvd de Marseille, 01 Abidjan
Mailing Address: BP 3525, 01 Abidjan
Tel: 32-12-51; 32-16-22; 32-60-09
Telex: 22564 Nea Cl
Key Personnel
Dir General: Mrs K L Liguer-Laubhouet
Founded: 1972
Subjects: Art, Drama, Theater, History, Literature, Literary Criticism, Essays, Religion - Other
ISBN Prefix(es): 2-7236
Parent Company: Les Nouvelles Editions Africaines, Senegal
Associate Companies: Les Nouvelles Editions Africaines, Togo

Les Nouvelles Editions Ivoiriennes (NEI)+
One blvd de Marseille, 01 BP 1818, 01 Abidjan
Mailing Address: BP 1818, Abidjan 01
Tel: (021) 240766; (021) 240825 *Fax:* (021) 242456
Key Personnel
Dir General: Guy Lambin
Founded: 1992
Subjects: Art, Literature, Literary Criticism, Essays, Poetry
ISBN Prefix(es): 2-910190; 2-911725; 2-84487
Distributed by Edicef (France)
Distributor for Classiques Hachette sur Cote d'Ivoire; Hachette Livres

PUCI, see Universite d' Abidjan

Croatia

General Information
Capital: Zagreb
Language: Croatian
Religion: Predominantly Roman Catholic & Eastern Orthodox
Population: 4.8 million
Bank Hours: 0700-1900 Monday-Friday; 0700-1200 Saturday; 0800-1600 in the small towns
Shop Hours: 0800-1900 Monday-Friday & 0800-1300 Saturday
Currency: kuna, divisible into 100 lipa
Export/Import Information: Firms trade freely with foreign partners in accordance with international agreements & treaties, and with measures which are in line with the principles & demands of the World Trade Organization.
Copyright: UCC, Berne (see Copyright Conventions, page xi)

AGM doo+
Mihanoviceva 28, 10000 Zagreb
Tel: (01) 4856309; (01) 4856307 *Fax:* (01) 4856316
E-mail: agm@agm.hr
Web Site: www.agm.hr
Subjects: Art, Drama, Theater, History, Literature, Literary Criticism, Essays, Nonfiction (General), Philosophy, Social Sciences, Sociology

ALFA dd za izdavacke, graficke i trgovacke poslove+
Nova Ves 23/a, 10000 Zagreb
Tel: (01) 4666 066; (01) 4666 077 *Fax:* (01) 4666 258
E-mail: alfa-zg@zg.tel.hr
Key Personnel
Manager: Miro Petric
Editor: Bozidar Petrac
Public Relations & Marketing: Ana Maria Bogisic
Founded: 1971
Subjects: Cookery, Education, Fiction, Gardening, Plants, Government, Political Science, Literature, Literary Criticism, Essays, Poetry, Religion - Catholic
Bookshop(s): Krjizara (bookshop), ALFA, Importanne Centar, 1000 Zagreb
Shipping Address: Platana bb, 10000 Zagreb
Warehouse: Platana bb, 10000 Zagreb

ArTresor naklada+
Amruseva, 9, 10000 Zagreb
Tel: (01) 4846 791 *Fax:* (01) 4846 916
E-mail: artresor@zg.tel.hr
Key Personnel
Manager: Silva Tomanic Kis
Founded: 1996
Subjects: History, Language Arts, Linguistics, Literature, Literary Criticism, Essays, Philosophy, Poetry
ISBN Prefix(es): 953-6522

Drzavna Uprava za Zastitu Prirode i Okolisa (State Directorate for the Protection of Nature & Environment)
Ulica Grada Vukovara 78, HR-10000 Zagreb
Tel: (01) 610 6555; (01) 610 6556; (01) 610 6578 *Fax:* (01) 6118 388; (01) 611 2073
E-mail: duzo@ring.net
Web Site: www.mzopu.hr
Key Personnel
Dir: Ante Kutle, MD
Founded: 1991
Subjects: Environmental Studies
ISBN Prefix(es): 953-97087

Durieux d o o+
Smodekova 2, 10000 Zagreb
Tel: (01) 23 00 337; (01) 23 21 178 *Fax:* (01) 23 00 337
E-mail: durieux@zg.tel.hr
Web Site: www.durieux.hr
Key Personnel
President: Drazen Toncic
Editor: Nenad Popovic
Founded: 1990
Subjects: Drama, Theater, Fiction, History, Literature, Literary Criticism, Essays, Philosophy, Poetry

Faust Vrani+
Kersovanijev Trg 1, 10000 Zagreb
Tel: (01) 213646; (01) 2332 302 *Fax:* (01) 213646; (01) 2332 302
E-mail: faust.vrancic@zg.tel.hr
Web Site: www.pontes.com; www.nomad.hr
Key Personnel
Dir: Valerij Juresi *E-mail:* valerij.juresic@pontes.hr
Editor: Katarina Mazuran *E-mail:* katarina.mazuran@pontes.hr
Founded: 1995
Specialize in new literature, promotion of Croatian literature & new authors from abroad
Membership: Croatian Independent Publishers.
Subjects: Fiction, Journalism, Literature, Literary Criticism, Essays, Music, Dance, Philosophy, Poetry, Science Fiction, Fantasy
ISBN Prefix(es): 953-6804
Number of titles published annually: 8 Print
Total Titles: 5 Print

Filozofski Fakultet Sveucilista u Zagrebu
Ivana Lucica 3, 10000 Zagreb
Tel: (01) 6120 111 *Fax:* (01) 6156 879
Web Site: www.ffzg.hr
Key Personnel
Editor & Author: Ms Jadranka Brncic *E-mail:* jbrncic@mudrac.ftzg.hr
Subjects: History, Language Arts, Linguistics, Literature, Literary Criticism, Essays, Social Sciences, Sociology
ISBN Prefix(es): 86-80279; 953-175

Globus-Nakladni zavod
Vlaska 109, 10000 Zagreb
Tel: (01) 4628 400 *Fax:* (01) 4551 146 *Cable:* GLOBUS ZAGREB
Key Personnel
President & Editor: Tomislav Pusek
Founded: 1969
Subjects: Art, Fiction, Government, Political Science, History, Philosophy, Social Sciences, Sociology
ISBN Prefix(es): 86-343; 953-167

Graficki zavod Hrvatske
Radnicka Cesta 210, 10000 Zagreb
Tel: (01) 240-4444; (01) 240-7166 *Fax:* (041) 430331
Telex: 21606 Yu Gzh *Cable:* GZH ZAGREB
Key Personnel
Man Dir: Zdravko Zidovec
Editor: Branko Matan
Sales: Vilma Lopuh
Rights & Permissions: Maja Kotur
Production: Boro Brekalo
Founded: 1874
Subjects: Art, Biography, Fiction
ISBN Prefix(es): 86-399; 953-6009

Izdavacka Delatnost Hrvatske Akademije Znanosti I Umjetnosti
Zrinski trg 11, 10000 Zagreb

Tel: (01) 49 22 373; (01) 48 72 902 *Fax:* (01) 48 19 979
E-mail: izddjel@hazu.hr
Key Personnel
Man Dir: Gordana Poletto Ruzic
Founded: 1861
Subjects: Education, Government, Political Science, History, Medicine, Nursing, Dentistry, Philosophy, Science (General)
ISBN Prefix(es): 3-85154

Hrvatsko filozofsko drustvo (Croatian Philosophy Society)+
Ivana Lucica 3 (FF), 10000 Zagreb
Tel: (01) 6111808 *Fax:* (01) 6170682
E-mail: filozofska-istrazivanja@zg.tel.hr
Key Personnel
President: Milan Polio
Vice President: Dubravka Kuzina
Founded: 1957
Subjects: Ethnicity, Philosophy, Psychology, Psychiatry, Social Sciences, Sociology
ISBN Prefix(es): 86-81173; 953-164
Divisions: Journal Filozofska Istrazivanja/Synthesis Philosophica
Warehouse: Krcka 1, 10000 Zagreb

Informator dd+
Zelinska 3, 10000 Zagreb
Tel: (01) 6111-500 *Fax:* (01) 6111-446
E-mail: info@informator.hr
Web Site: www.informator.hr
Telex: 21264 *Cable:* YU INF
Key Personnel
Manager: Dr Ivo Buric
Editor-in-Chief: Jasna Vukoja
Sales Manager: Milan Jerbic
Subjects: Economics, Finance, Government, Political Science, Law, Marketing, Social Sciences, Sociology
ISBN Prefix(es): 86-301; 953-170
Bookshop(s): Ilica 24, 41000 Zagreb; M Visnsic, 7800 Banja Luka, Bosnia and Herzegovina; Kej M Pijade 8, 21000 Novi Sad; Trg Lava Mirskog 3, 54000 Osijek; Dj Djakovica 30, 51000 Rijeka; Vojv, Putnika 16B, 71000 Sarajevo, Bosnia and Herzegovina
Warehouse: Janka Gredelja 3, 41000 Zagreb
Orders to: Odjel Prodaje Knjiga, Ilica 24, 41000 Zagreb *Tel:* (041) 433666

Krscanska sadasnjost
Marulicev trg 14, 10 000 Zagreb
Tel: (01) 48 28 219; (01) 48 28 222 *Fax:* (01) 48 28 227
E-mail: ks@zg.tel.hr
Web Site: www.ks.hr
Company also acts as a press agency.
Subjects: Art, Biblical Studies, Religion - Other, Theology
ISBN Prefix(es): 86-397; 953-151

Knjizevni Krug Split
Boananska 4/1, 21000 Split
Tel: (021) 342 226; (021) 361 081 *Fax:* (021) 342 226
E-mail: bratislav.lucin@public.srce.hr
Key Personnel
President: Prof Nenad Cambi, PhD
Vice President: Prof Ivo Petrinovic, PhD
Editor: Prof Bratislav Lucin
Founded: 1979
Subjects: Archaeology, Drama, Theater, History, Language Arts, Linguistics, Law, Literature, Literary Criticism, Essays, Maritime, Poetry
ISBN Prefix(es): 86-7397; 953-163

Leksikografski Zavod Miroslav Krleza
Frankopanska 26, 10000 Zagreb
Tel: (01) 4800 492; (01) 4800 300 *Fax:* (01) 4800 399
E-mail: lzmk@hlz.hr
Web Site: www.hlz.hr
Key Personnel
Dir: Vlaho Bogisic *Tel:* (01) 4800 398; Dalibor Brozovic *Tel:* (01) 4800 379 *E-mail:* brozovic@hlz.hr; Tomislav Ladan *Tel:* (01) 4800 398; Vladimir Pezo *Tel:* (01) 4800 377 *E-mail:* vpezo@hlz.hr
Assistant Dir: Damir Boras *Tel:* (01) 4800 424 *E-mail:* dboras@hlz.hr; Igor Gostl *Tel:* (01) 4800 384 *E-mail:* igostl@hlz.hr; Nenad Prelog *Tel:* (01) 4800 383 *E-mail:* nprelog@hlz.hr
Contact: Lidija Zrnic *Tel:* (01) 4800 91 *E-mail:* lzrnic@hlz.hr
Founded: 1950
ISBN Prefix(es): 953-6036
Total Titles: 4 Print

Masmedia+
Ulica baruna Trenka 13, 10000 Zagreb
Tel: (01) 45.77.400 *Fax:* (01) 45.77.769
E-mail: masmedia@zg.tel.hr
Web Site: www.masmedia.hr
Key Personnel
President: Stjepan Andrasic *E-mail:* stjepan.andrasic@zg.tel.hr
Contact: Romina Belak
Founded: 1990
Subjects: Business, Economics, Finance, Management, Marketing
ISBN Prefix(es): 953-157
Associate Companies: Andratom; Creditreform; GBMA; Rimedia
Subsidiaries: Masmedia-Split
Branch Office(s)
Associated Book Publishers, Inc, PO Box 5657, Scottsdale, AZ 85261-5657, United States
Distributed by Associated Book Publishers
Distributor for Braun Verlag; Euredit (Europages) BDI; Gentner Verlag; Herold
Bookshop(s): Masmedia Rijeka, Dolac 9A, 51000 Rijeka
Book Club(s): Croatian Book Clubs

Matica hrvatska+
Matice hrvatske 2, Strossmayerov trg 4, 10000 Zagreb
Tel: (01) 4819-310; (01) 4819-325; (01) 4819-313; (01) 4819-321 *Fax:* (01) 4819-319
E-mail: matica@matica.hr
Web Site: www.matica.hr
Key Personnel
President: Vlado Gotovac
International Rights: Vera Cicin-Sain
Founded: 1842
Publisher of Biweekly Newspaper Vijenac.
Subjects: Agriculture, Archaeology, Art, Drama, Theater, History, Language Arts, Linguistics, Literature, Literary Criticism, Essays, Medicine, Nursing, Dentistry, Natural History, Nonfiction (General), Philosophy, Poetry, Regional Interests, Science (General), Social Sciences, Sociology
ISBN Prefix(es): 86-401; 86-7807
Bookshop(s): Maticina 2, 10000 Zagreb

Mladost d d Izdavacku graficku i informaticku djelatnost
Borongajska 69, 10000 Zagreb
Tel: (01) 215-853; (01) 229-811 *Fax:* (01) 239-5336
Telex: 21263 yu mladzg *Cable:* IRO ZAGREB
Key Personnel
Man Dir: Branko Juricevic
Import-Export Dir: Branko Vukovic
Publisher: Josip Fruk
Production Manager: Stipan Medak
Marketing Manager: Eduard Osredecki
Founded: 1948
Subjects: Art, Crafts, Games, Hobbies, Fiction, History, How-to, Music, Dance, Philosophy, Poetry, Science (General), Social Sciences, Sociology, Sports, Athletics
ISBN Prefix(es): 86-05; 953-152
Book Club(s): Mladost's Book Fans Club

Muzicka Naklada
Nikole Tesle 10/I, 41000 Zagreb
Tel: (01) 424099
Telex: 22430
Key Personnel
Dir: Rajko Latinovic
Founded: 1952
Publish music editions & scores.
Subjects: Music, Dance
ISBN Prefix(es): 86-80637

Nakladni zavod Matice hrvatske+
Ulica Matice hrvatske 2, 41000 Zagreb
Mailing Address: PO Box 515, 41000 Zagreb
Tel: (01) 272143 *Fax:* (01) 432430
E-mail: nzmh@zg.tel.hr
Key Personnel
Man Dir, Rights & Permissions: Mr Hrvoje Bozicevic
Editorial: Ms Jadranka Pintaric
Sales: Ms Kovacic Bozica
Production: Boris Kreber
Founded: 1960
Subjects: Art, Biography, Economics, Fiction, Government, Political Science, History, Literature, Literary Criticism, Essays, Science (General), Social Sciences, Sociology
ISBN Prefix(es): 86-401; 86-7807; 953-150
Bookshop(s): Poljana Paska Milicevica 7 052, 20000 Dubrovnik; Ilica 62, 10000 Zagreb
Warehouse: Cazmanska BB, 10000 Zagreb

Naprijed d d Naklada
Palmoticeva 30/I, 10000 Zagreb, Hrvatska
Tel: (01) 4873-296 *Fax:* (01) 4873-313
E-mail: info@croatian-book.com; naklada-naprijed@zg.tel.hr
Web Site: www.naklada-ljevak.hr
Telex: 21449 Yu lkpnzg *Cable:* Izdavacko Naprijed
Key Personnel
Man Dir: Autun Zvan
Subjects: Art, Economics, Fiction, Government, Political Science, History, Philosophy, Psychology, Psychiatry, Science (General), Social Sciences, Sociology
ISBN Prefix(es): 86-349; 953-178

Narodne Novine
Trg hrvatskih velikana 7/II, 10000 Zagreb
Tel: (01) 416-404 *Fax:* (01) 449-629
Web Site: www.nn.hr
Key Personnel
Dir: Ilija Dautovic
Subjects: Career Development, Law, Science (General)
ISBN Prefix(es): 86-337; 953-6053

Nasa Djeca Publishing+
Gajeva 7, 41000 Zagreb
Tel: (01) 423550 *Fax:* (01) 423550
Key Personnel
Dir: Prof Drago Kozina
Secretary of Editorial Office: Verica Ozimec
Founded: 1951
Also publish children's periodical *Radost*.
Subjects: Literature, Literary Criticism, Essays, Poetry
ISBN Prefix(es): 953-171
Number of titles published annually: 30 Print

Edit Niro (Novinska-izdavacka radna organizacija)
Ulica kralja Zvonimira 20a, 51 000 Rijeka
Tel: (051) 672 107; (051) 672 119 *Fax:* (051) 672 112

CROATIA

E-mail: niro-edit@ri.tel.hr
Telex: 24247
Key Personnel
Dir: Ennio Machin
ISBN Prefix(es): 86-7127; 953-6150
Bookshop(s): Korzo Narodne Revolucije 37, 51000 Rijeka

Otokar Kersovani
Janeza Trdine 2, 51000 Rijeka
Tel: (051) 338 558; (051) 338 016 *Fax:* (051) 331 690
E-mail: otokar-kersovani@ri.tel.hr *Cable:* Otokar Kersovani
Key Personnel
Man Dir & Editor-in-Chief: Tomislav Pilepic
Founded: 1954
Subjects: Biography, Fiction
ISBN Prefix(es): 86-385; 953-153
Branch Office(s)
Mehmed-pase Soholovica 24, Sarajevo, Bosnia and Herzegovina
Slavise Vajiera-Cice 3, Rijeka
Biankinijeva, 11 Zagreb
Zrmanjska 2/a, Belgrade, Yugoslavia
Nade Tomic 15, Nis, Yugoslavia

Prosvjeta
Berislaviceva 10, 10000 Zagreb
Tel: (01) 4872 477 *Fax:* (01) 434017 *Cable:* Prosvjeta Zagreb
Key Personnel
Dir: Branislav Celap
Subjects: Business, Journalism
ISBN Prefix(es): 86-353; 953-6279
Bookshop(s): trg Bratstva i Jedinstva 5, Zagreb

Prosvjeta (Novinsko-izdavacko i Stamparsko)
Vladimira Nazora 25, 43000 Bjelovar
Tel: (043) 245 222; (043) 245 223 *Fax:* (043) 245 220 *Cable:* Nisp Prosvjeta Bjelovar
Key Personnel
Dir: Branimir Premuzic *Tel:* (043) 245 224
Production: Ivan Ninic
ISBN Prefix(es): 86-80823; 953-6340
Branch Office(s)
Mose Pijade 31, Zagreb

Skolska Knjiga
Masarykova 28, 10000 Zagreb
Mailing Address: POB 1039, 10000 Zagreb
Tel: (01) 48 30 511 *Fax:* (01) 48 30 506
E-mail: skolska@skolskaknjiga.hr
Web Site: www.skolskaknjiga.hr
Telex: 21894 *Cable:* SKOLSKA KNJIGA ZAGREB
Key Personnel
General Manager: Dr Dragomir Maderic, PhD
Marketing Manager: Dr Jozo Marevic
Publishing Manager: Prof Antun Zibar
Founded: 1950
Subjects: Art, Biography, Education, Engineering (General), History, How-to, Medicine, Nursing, Dentistry, Music, Dance, Philosophy, Poetry, Psychology, Psychiatry, Science (General), Social Sciences, Sociology
ISBN Prefix(es): 86-03; 953-0
Bookshop(s): Knjizara Skolske knjige, Bogoviceva 1/a, 41000 Zagreb; Knjizara Skolska knjiga, Masarykova 28, 41000 Zagreb; Knjizara Studentski trg, Studentski trg 6, 11000 Belgrade, Yugoslavia

Privlacica Slavonska Naklada+
Genschera 2, 32100 Vinkovci
Tel: (032) 332 587; (032) 20716; (032) 331610 *Fax:* (032) 331735
Key Personnel
Contact: Martin Grgurovac
ISBN Prefix(es): 953-156

Sveucilisna tiskara doo
Trg marsala Tita 14, 10000 Zagreb
Tel: (01) 4564430; (01) 4564428 *Fax:* (01) 4564427
Key Personnel
Editor: Vera C Sain; Nikola Petrak
Publishing service of Zagreb University.
Subjects: Ethnicity, Language Arts, Linguistics, Literature, Literary Criticism, Essays, Science (General)
ISBN Prefix(es): 86-7819; 86-329; 953-6231

Tehnicka Knjiga
Jurisiceva 10, 41000 Zagreb
Tel: (01) 248172 *Fax:* (01) 423611 *Cable:* Tehnoknjiga
Key Personnel
Man Dir, Chief Editor: Zvonimir Vistricka
Founded: 1947
Subjects: Engineering (General), Literature, Literary Criticism, Essays, Science (General)
ISBN Prefix(es): 86-7059; 953-172
Bookshop(s): Knjizara Tehnicka Knjiga, Masarykova 17; Antikvarijat, Zagreb; Gunduliceva 19, Zagreb

Vitagraf+
Slogin kula 12, HR-51000 Rijeka
Tel: (051) 215087; (051) 338489
Toll Free *Tel:* (051) 322880 *Fax:* (051) 212622
E-mail: vitagraf@ri.hinet.hr
Key Personnel
President: Prof Boze Mimica
Author: Ivan Sokolic; Jeurem Brkovic; Lujo Margetic; Zjonimie Dusper
Founded: 1990
Specialize in Numismatic, History, Vine Books, Gastronomy Guide.
Subjects: Cookery, Crafts, Games, Hobbies, History, Radio, TV, Wine & Spirits
ISBN Prefix(es): 953-6059

Znaci Vremena, Institut Za Istrazivanje Biblije
Klaiceva 40, 10000 Zagreb
Tel: (01) 3774 283 *Fax:* (01) 174861
Key Personnel
Dir: Karlo Lenart
Subjects: Archaeology, Biblical Studies, Health, Nutrition, Human Relations, Religion - Protestant, Theology
ISBN Prefix(es): 86-425; 953-183

Znanje d d+
Zvonimira 17, Ulica Kralja 10000 Zagreb 1000
Tel: (01) 4551500 *Fax:* (01) 4553-652
E-mail: znanje@zg.tel.hr *Cable:* ZNANJE ZAGREB
Key Personnel
President: Zarko Sepetavc
Vice President: Branko Jazbec
Founded: 1946
Subjects: Textbooks
ISBN Prefix(es): 86-313; 953-195; 953-6124; 953-6473
Divisions: Printing House
Branch Office(s)
Riva 8, Rijeka
Osijek, Vukovarska 71, 31000 Osijeck
Znanje d o o Mostar, Stjepana Radica 76E, 88000 Mostar, Bosnia and Herzegovina
Showroom(s): Vojnoviceva, 42 Zagreb
Bookshop(s): AG Matos stationary & bookstore, Frankopanska 5; 1 G Kovacic stationary & bookstore, Marticeva 12; Miroslav Krleza bookstore, Trg bana J Jelacica 17; Tin Ujevic second-hand bookstore, Zrinjevac 16; Znanje stationary & book store, Llica 17; Znanje stationary & bookstore, Ozaljska 102; Znanje stationary/paper shop, Gajeva 2

Cuba

General Information

Capital: Havana
Language: Spanish
Religion: Predominantly Roman Catholic
Population: 10.8 million
Bank Hours: 0800-1200, 1415-1615 Monday-Friday; 0800-1200 Saturday
Currency: 100 centavos = 1 Cuban peso
Export/Import Information: Control of all import & export by Ministry of Foreign Trade; books imported & exported by Ediciones Cubanas, Apdo 605, Havana. No commercial advertising permitted in Cuba; brochures etc must be sent to the appropriate foreign trade organization. Exchange controlled by National Bank of Cuba.
Copyright: UCC, Florence (see Copyright Conventions, pg xi)

Apocalipis Digital+
Calle 47 No 869, 3er Piso, Apto 6 entre 26 y Sta Ana, Plaza de la Revolucion, Havana
Tel: (07) 816625
E-mail: adigital@tinored.cu; adigital@colombus.cu
Key Personnel
President: Pedro E Garcia
Founded: 1987
Member of Comicion Nacional de Proteccion de Datos.
Subjects: Computer Science, Microcomputers
ISBN Prefix(es): 959-231

Editorial Capitan San Luis+
Av 25 No 3406 entre 34 y 36, La Habana, Playa
Tel: (07) 234475; (07) 307397 *Fax:* (07) 332070
Key Personnel
Dir: Carlos Morales Quevedo
Founded: 1989
Subjects: Government, Political Science, Literature, Literary Criticism, Essays
Warehouse: Ave 41 No 1410 entre 14 y 18, Playa, La Havana

Casa de las Americas
Calle 3 3/4 y G, Vedado CP 10400, Plaza de la Revolucion, Havana
Tel: (07) 327271; (07) 323588 *Fax:* (07) 327272
Telex: 511019
Key Personnel
Dir: Abel Martinez
Founded: 1960
Subjects: Art, Ethnicity, Social Sciences, Sociology
ISBN Prefix(es): 959-04

Casa Editora Abril+
Prado 553 esq a Tte Rey, CP 10200 Habana Vieja, Havana
Tel: (07) 624330
E-mail: eabril@jcce.org.cu
Web Site: www.almamater.cu
Key Personnel
Dir: Fernando Rojas
Sub-Dir: Silvio Gutierrez Perez
Founded: 1980
Subjects: Advertising, Film, Video, History, Humor, Journalism, Literature, Literary Criticism, Essays, Microcomputers, Philosophy, Poetry, Science Fiction, Fantasy
ISBN Prefix(es): 959-210

CDICT, see Universidad Central de la Villas, Centro Documentacion e Informacion Cientifica Tecnica

PUBLISHERS

Editorial de Ciencias Sociales
Calle 14, No 4104, entre 41 y 43, Playa, Ciudad de la Havana
Tel: (07) 23 3959; (07) 23 6090; (07) 23 4801
Fax: (07) 2304801
Key Personnel
Dir: Ricardo Garcia Pampin
Founded: 1967
Subjects: Social Sciences, Sociology
Orders to: Ediciones Cubanas, Obispo y Bernaza, La Habana Vieja

Editorial Cientifico Tecnica+
Calle 14 No 4104 entre 41 y 43, Playa, Havana 10400
Tel: (07) 236090; (07) 234801 *Fax:* (07) 333441
Key Personnel
Dir: Isidro Fernandez Rodriguez
Founded: 1965
Subjects: Engineering (General), Science (General)
ISBN Prefix(es): 959-05

Editora Cultura Popular, *imprint of* Editora Politica

Union Escritores y Artistas de Cuba, see Ediciones Union

Editorial Gente Nueva+
O'Reilly No 4 esq a Tacon, CP 10100 Havana
Tel: (07) 624753 *Fax:* (07) 338187
Key Personnel
Dir: Elenia Rodriguez Oliva
Founded: 1967
ISBN Prefix(es): 959-08

Holguin, Ediciones
Arias No 144, esq a Fomento, CP 80100, Holguin
Tel: (24) 424974
E-mail: cpllhlg@tauronet.cult.cu
Founded: 1986
Subjects: Art, Biography, Drama, Theater, History, Literature, Literary Criticism, Essays, Poetry
ISBN Prefix(es): 959-221
Book Club(s): SCAL (Sociedad Cabana de Amigos del Libro)

Instituto de Informacion Cientifica y Tecnologica (IDICT)+
Prado y San Jose, CP 10200 La Habana, Habana Vieja
Tel: (07) 626501 *Fax:* (07) 338237
E-mail: decoreli@ceniai.inf.cu; garriga@ceniai.inf.cu
Web Site: www.idict.cu
Subjects: Career Development, Library & Information Sciences, Technology

ISCAH Fructuoso Rodriguez
Carretera de Tapaste y Autopista Nacional, San Jose de las Lajas, Havana 32700
Tel: (07) 62936 *Fax:* (07) 330942
E-mail: athena.isch.cu
Key Personnel
Contact: Julian Garcia Gomex *E-mail:* julian@reduniv.edu.cu
Subjects: Agriculture, Alternative, Economics, Education, Environmental Studies, Management, Sports, Athletics, Veterinary Science
ISBN Prefix(es): 959-232

Editorial Letras Cubanas+
Member of Instituto Cubano del Libro
O'Reilly No 4 esq Tacon, La Habana, Havana 10100
Tel: (07) 626864 *Fax:* (07) 338187
E-mail: elc@icl.cult.cu
Telex: 511881

Key Personnel
Dir: Juan Nicolas Padron Barquin; Daniel Garcia Santos
Sub-Dir: Basilia Papastamatiu; Esther Acosta Testa
Founded: 1977
Subjects: Art, Drama, Theater, Fiction, Literature, Literary Criticism, Essays, Poetry, Romance, Science Fiction, Fantasy
ISBN Prefix(es): 959-10
Number of titles published annually: 70 Print
Total Titles: 70 Print

Editorial Oriente+
Santa Lucia No 356, Santiago de Cuba CP 90100
Tel: (0226) 22496; (0226) 28096 *Fax:* (0226) 86111
E-mail: edoriente@cultstgo.cult.cu
Web Site: www.amafra.com.ar/oriente/
Telex: 061170
Key Personnel
President: Aida Bahr
Editorial: Consuel Muniz
Production: Sergio Daquin
Publicity: Ana Maria Rodriguez
Rights & Permissions: Omar Betancourt
Founded: 1971
Subjects: African American Studies, Cookery, Crafts, Games, Hobbies, Fiction, Health, Nutrition, History, House & Home, Literature, Literary Criticism, Essays, Poetry, Self-Help, Sports, Athletics
ISBN Prefix(es): 959-11
Total Titles: 821 Print
Parent Company: Vicepresidencia Editorial
Ultimate Parent Company: Instituto Cubano del Libro

Editora Politica+
Calle Belascoain No 864, esq a Desaguee, Municipio Centro Habana, Havana CP 10300
Tel: (07) 79 8553-59 *Fax:* (07) 811024
Web Site: www.cuba.cu/politica/webpcc/editora.htm
Telex: 1380
Key Personnel
Dir: Santiago Dorquez Perez
Chief Editor: Anolan Aguila
Founded: 1963
Subjects: Biography, Economics, Education, Government, Political Science, Health, Nutrition, History, Human Relations, Law, Philosophy, Poetry, Psychology, Psychiatry, Religion - Catholic, Religion - Other, Science (General), Social Sciences, Sociology
ISBN Prefix(es): 959-01
Associate Companies: Editora Cultura Popular
Imprints: Editora Cultura Popular
Showroom(s): Pabelloo Medios de Difusion EXPOCUBA, Tienda 11 y Paseo
Bookshop(s): Centro Internacional de Prensa, Calle 23 esq O Vedado

Pueblo y Educacion Editorial (PE)+
Ave 3ra No 4601 e/ 46 y 60, Playa, Havana 11300
Tel: (07) 22-1490; (07) 29-4688 *Fax:* (07) 24-0844
E-mail: epe@ceniai.inf.cu
Key Personnel
Dir: Catalina Lajud Herrero
Sub-Dir: Juan Alberto Andino
Founded: 1971
Subjects: Computer Science, Education, Literature, Literary Criticism, Essays, Psychology, Psychiatry, Science (General), Social Sciences, Sociology, Sports, Athletics, Technology
ISBN Prefix(es): 959-13
Number of titles published annually: 138 Print
Total Titles: 75 Print
Distributed by Ediciones Cubanas Empresa de Comercio Exterior de Publicaciones (Pueblo y Educacion also distributes & exports its books)

Ediciones Union+
Calle 17 No 354,e/ G y H, Vedado, Plaza de la Revolucion, Havana CP 10400
Tel: (07) 324551; (07) 324252; (07) 324553; (07) 324571 *Fax:* (07) 333158
Telex: 051156364
Key Personnel
Dir: Daniel Garcia Santos
Production: Jose Raul Garrido
Publicity: Emilio Comas Paret
Founded: 1961
Rights & Permissions, National Center of Author Rights, Linea y G, Vedado.
Subjects: Art, Literature, Literary Criticism, Essays, Regional Interests

Universidad Central de la Villas, Centro Documentacion e Informacion Cientifica Tecnica
Carretera a Camajuani, Km 5.5, 54830 Santa Clara, Las Villas
Tel: (07) 81419
Subjects: Agriculture, Economics, Engineering (General), Law, Social Sciences, Sociology
ISBN Prefix(es): 959-216

Cyprus

General Information

Capital: Nicosia
Language: Greek & Turkish (English widely spoken)
Religion: Greek Orthodox & Islamic (among Turks)
Population: 716,000
Bank Hours: 0830-1200 Monday-Saturday
Shop Hours: Winter: 0800-1300, 1430-1700 Monday-Friday; 0730-1300 Saturday. Summer: 0730-1300, 1600-1830 Monday-Friday. Closed Wednesday afternoon (both winter & summer)
Currency: 100 cents = 1 Cyprus pound
Export/Import Information: No tariffs on books or advertising matter. No import license specially required. Exchange control administered by Central Bank of Cyprus.
Copyright: UCC, Berne, Florence (see Copyright Conventions, pg xi)

Action Publications
PO Box 4676, Nicosia
Tel: (02) 444104 *Fax:* (02) 450048
Telex: 4455
Key Personnel
President: Tony Christodoulou
Vice President: Mickey Christodoulou
Production Dir: Dina Wilde
Editor: Steve Myles; Marios Solomou
Founded: 1971
Subjects: Travel
ISBN Prefix(es): 9963-7587
Parent Company: Action Public Relations & Publishing Ltd
Subsidiaries: Action Media
Orders to: 35 Ayiou Nicolaou St, Engomi, Nicosia

Air Larko Panorama, ALP
11 Nicos Antonlades, Paphos
Tel: (06) 236181 *Fax:* (06) 245046
ISBN Prefix(es): 9963-574

ALITHIA Publishing Co
Pindarou & Androkleous, Nicosia 1060

CYPRUS

Tel: (02) 463040 *Fax:* (02) 463945 *Cable:* ALITHIA
ISBN Prefix(es): 9963-586

AndreouChr- Publishers
64A Regenis, Nicosia
Tel: (02) 666877 *Fax:* (02) 666878
E-mail: andzeou2@cytanet.com.cy
Founded: 1979
Specialize in Cypress History, Literature, Biography & Bibliographies.
Subjects: Biography, History, Literature, Literary Criticism, Essays, Regional Interests
ISBN Prefix(es): 9963-563
Associate Companies: Practorion Vivliou; Chr. Andreou Co Ltd
Bookshop(s): Rigenis 64a, Nicosia; Rigenis 67A, Nicosia *Fax:* (02) 666563

James Bendon Ltd
PO Box 56484, 3307 Limassol
Tel: (05) 323047 *Fax:* (05) 2563 2352
E-mail: books@jamesbendon.com
Web Site: www.jamesbendon.com
Key Personnel
President: James Bendon
Vice President: Rida Bendon
Founded: 1988
Subjects: Crafts, Games, Hobbies, History
ISBN Prefix(es): 9963-579; 9963-7624
Distributor for Christie's Robson Lowe

Chrysopolitissa Publishers
27 Al Papadiamanti, 2400 Nicosia
Tel: (02) 2353929 *Fax:* (02) 2353929
Key Personnel
Dir: Rina Catselli *E-mail:* rina@spidernet.com.cy
Founded: 1973
Subjects: Drama, Theater, Literature, Literary Criticism, Essays
ISBN Prefix(es): 9963-559
Number of titles published annually: 4 Print
Showroom(s): 9 Othello's St, 2018 Nicosia; MAM, C Paleologos St, No 10, Nicosia
Bookshop(s): Kypriaka Themata, PO Box 3835, Nicosia; MAM, PO Box 21722, Nicosia

Cyprus Telecommunications Authority (CYTA)
Telecommunications Str, Strobolos, OE 24929, CY-1396 Nicosia
Tel: (02) 22701000 *Fax:* (02) 497155
E-mail: enquiries@cyta.com.cy
Web Site: www.cyta.com.cy
Telex: 2288 CYTA ENAC CY
Key Personnel
Chairman: Mr Stathis Papadakis
Vice-Chairman: Mr Markos Drakos
General Manager: Mr Nicos M Timotheou
Deputy General Manager: Mr Photios Savvides
Assistant General Manager - Operations: Mr Christos C Chappas
Assistant General Manager - Administration: Mr Michael I Economides,
ISBN Prefix(es): 9963-43

CYTA, see Cyprus Telecommunications Authority (CYTA)

Kenek Ltd
PO Box 4611, Nicosia
Tel: (02) 365842 *Fax:* (02) 475150
ISBN Prefix(es): 9963-596

KY KE M+
PO Box 4108, Nicosia
Tel: (02) 450302 *Fax:* (02) 463624
Telex: 4022
Key Personnel
President: Nicos Koutsou
Vice President: Soula Zavou

Founded: 1983
ISBN Prefix(es): 9963-562

Kyrenia Municipality+
PO Box 5182, Nicosia
Tel: (02) 351460
Key Personnel
Editor: Rina Catselli
ISBN Prefix(es): 9963-559
Associate Companies: Chrysopolitissa Publishers
Showroom(s): 9 Othello's St, Nicosia
Bookshop(s): Kypriaka Themata, PO Box 3835, Nicosia

A G Leventis Foundation
1 Vassileos Constantinou, 10674 Nicosia
Tel: (01) 729 3015-18 *Fax:* (01) 725 1951
E-mail: leventcy@zenon.logos.cy.net
Web Site: www.leventisfoundation.org
Subjects: Archaeology, Art, History
ISBN Prefix(es): 9963-560

MAM (The House of the Cyprus & Cyprological Publications)
46 Faneromenes, 1011 Nicosia
Mailing Address: PO Box 21722, 1512 Nicosia
Tel: (02) 464698; (02) 472744 *Fax:* (02) 465411
E-mail: mam@mam.cy.net
Web Site: www.mam.cy.net
Key Personnel
Gen Mgr: Mr Mikis A Michaelides
Founded: 1965
Authorized distributors of Cyprus Government publications & works about Cyprus, & of publications by United Nations agencies & major international organizations.
Subjects: Ethnicity
Bookshop(s): Laiki Yltonia, 13 Aristokypros St *Tel:* (2) 472744
Book Club(s): Cyprus Bibliophiles Association

The Moufflon Book & Art Centre, see Romantic Cyprus Publications

Nikoklis Publishers+
PO Box 3697, Nicosia
Tel: (02) 456544 *Fax:* (02) 360668
Key Personnel
Editor: Ellada Sophocleous
Founded: 1978
Subjects: Ethnicity, Travel
ISBN Prefix(es): 9963-566

Omilos Pnevmatikis Ananeoseos
29 Ionon, Nicosia 1096
Tel: (02) 775854 *Fax:* (02) 311931
Subjects: Literature, Literary Criticism, Essays
ISBN Prefix(es): 9963-552
Orders to: Omerou 1, Egomi, Nicosia 2407

Pierides Foundation
4, Zennonos Kitieos, 6023 Larnaka
Mailing Address: PO Box 25, Larnaca
Tel: (02) 444486 *Fax:* (02) 466412
Telex: 4498
Key Personnel
Administration: M Polyvia
ISBN Prefix(es): 9963-560

POLTE (Pancyprian Organization of Tertiary Education)
c/o Higher Technical Institute, Nicosia
Tel: (02) 305030 *Fax:* (02) 494953
Key Personnel
President: Costas Neocleous
ISBN Prefix(es): 9963-564

Romantic Cyprus Publications
PO Box 2375, Nicosia
Fax: (02) 445155

ISBN Prefix(es): 9963-571
Bookshop(s): One Bophoulis St, PO Box 2375, Nicosia

Czech Republic

General Information

Capital: Prague
Language: Czech (official)
Religion: Predominantly Christian (mostly Roman Catholic)
Population: 10.4 million
Currency: 100 halerue = 1 koruna
Export/Import Information: 5% VAT on books.
Copyright: UCC, Berne (see Copyright Conventions, pg xi)

Academia
Legerova 61, 120 00 Prague 2
Tel: (02) 2494 1976 *Fax:* (02) 24212582
Web Site: www.academia.cz *Cable:* ACADEMY BOOKS PRAGUE
Key Personnel
Man Dir: Vaclav Zverina
Editor-in-Chief: Jitka Zykanova *Tel:* (02) 2494 2583 *E-mail:* zykanova@academia.cz
Export Manager: Mrs Milena Buzkova
Publicity & Advertising: Mrs Jirina Klasterska
Founded: 1953
Subjects: Archaeology, Chemistry, Chemical Engineering, Economics, Engineering (General), Geography, Geology, History, Language Arts, Linguistics, Mathematics, Philosophy, Physics
ISBN Prefix(es): 80-200

Albatros Publishing House, Co Ltd+
Member of Bonton Group
Truhlarska 9, 11000 Prague 1
Tel: (02) 24810704; (02) 2311156; (02) 2314289 *Fax:* (02) 24810850
E-mail: albatros@bonton.cz
Web Site: www.albatros.cz *Cable:* ALBATROS PRAHA
Key Personnel
Man Dir: Martin Slavik
Editorial Dir: Ondrej Muller *Tel:* (02) 24810850
Rights Dir: Stanislava Zabrodska *Tel:* (02) 24811061
Founded: 1949
ISBN Prefix(es): 80-00
Total Titles: 8,700 Print; 2 CD-ROM
Bookshop(s): Krizikova, Thamova 22, Prama 8 *Tel:* (02) 248 14 725
Book Club(s): KMC (Young Readers' Club), Truhlarska 9, Prama 1, Contact: Mrs Ludmila Hobova *Tel:* (02) 2319739 *Fax:* (02) 2311178
Warehouse: 252 16 Nucice, Contact: Mrs Dekastelova *Tel:* (0311) 670609 *Fax:* (0311) 670525
Orders to: Truhlarska 9, Contact: Lenka Prochazkova *Tel:* (02) 24811061 *Fax:* (02) 24810850 *E-mail:* albatros@bonton.cz

Aleko, Nakladatelska Divize+
Ohradni 61, 140 00 Prague 4
Tel: (02) 6921024; (02) 6921025 *Fax:* (02) 6921025
Key Personnel
Man Dir: Stanislav Kansky
Editorial: Dr V Sestak
Rights & Permissions: Dr A Vacek
Founded: 1895
Subjects: Economics, Engineering (General), Science (General)
ISBN Prefix(es): 80-03; 80-85341

PUBLISHERS

CZECH REPUBLIC

Bookshop(s): Stredisko technicke literatury, Ohradni 61, 14000 Prague (Centre of Technical Literature)
Book Club(s): Klub ctenaru technicke Literatury (Club for Readers of Technical Literature

AMA nakladatelstvi+
Gen Svobody 636, 674 01 Trebic
Tel: (0618) 265 84 *Fax:* (0618) 228 31
E-mail: rstudio@login.cz
Key Personnel
Contact: Karel Karmasin
Founded: 1990
Specialize in Desk Top Publishing & Pre-Press Technology.
Subjects: Radio, TV
ISBN Prefix(es): 80-900232
Associate Companies: Ar Nakladatelstvi
Orders to: Eliscina 24, 67401 Trebic

Atlantis sro+
Jakubska 7, 602 00 Brno
Tel: (05) 42213552 *Fax:* (05) 42214425
Key Personnel
Publisher & International Rights: Jitka Uhdeova
Founded: 1989
Subjects: Biography, History, Literature, Literary Criticism, Essays
ISBN Prefix(es): 80-7108

AULOS sro
Kosarkovo nabrezi 1, 118 00 Prague 1
Tel: (02) 536863 *Fax:* (02) 90004536
E-mail: aulos@volny.cz
Key Personnel
Editor: Zdenek Krenek
Founded: 1992
Subjects: Fiction, Literature, Literary Criticism, Essays, Philosophy, Poetry
ISBN Prefix(es): 80-901261; 80-901895; 80-86184
Showroom(s): Michalska 21, 110 00 Prague 1
Bookshop(s): Michalska 21, 110 00 Prague 1
Shipping Address: Michalska 21, 110 00 Prague 1, Czech Republic
Warehouse: Michalska 21, Prague 1, 110 00 Czech Republic

Aurora
Opletalova 8, 110 00 Prague 1
Tel: (02) 24 21 43 26 *Fax:* (02) 24 21 43 26
E-mail: aurora@aurora-books.cz
Web Site: www.aurora-books.cz
Key Personnel
Owner: Eva Michalkova
Editor: Katerina Zavadova *E-mail:* zavadova@aurora-books.cz
Founded: 1993
Subjects: Art, Fiction, Humor, Military Science, Nonfiction (General), Outdoor Recreation, Philosophy, Poetry
ISBN Prefix(es): 80-85974; 80-901603
Total Titles: 75 Print

Aventinum Nakladatelstvi+
Nikoly Vapcarova 3274, 14300 Prague, Modrany 4
Tel: (02) 4021907; (02) 4019069; (02) 40193056 *Fax:* (02) 4018534
Web Site: www.piscia.comp.cz/knihy/kni-aq09_cz.htm
Key Personnel
Man Dir: Zdenek Pavlik
Founded: 1990
Specialize in illustrated books.
Subjects: Animals, Pets, Art, Astrology, Occult, Biological Sciences, Gardening, Plants, Natural History
ISBN Prefix(es): 80-7151; 80-85277

Babtext Nakladatelska Spolecnost+
Zirovnicka 2, 106 00 Prague 10
Tel: (02) 435 992 *Fax:* (02) 768992; (02) 61221868
Key Personnel
Contact: Hilar Baburek
Founded: 1990
Subjects: Economics, Law
ISBN Prefix(es): 80-900178; 80-901444; 80-85816

Bakalar spol sro+
Rusna 417, 321 03 Plzen
Tel: (019) 523197
Key Personnel
Dir & President: Katerina Rubasova
Founded: 1991
Bachelor Ltd.
ISBN Prefix(es): 80-901213

Barollet Publishers Inc, see Baronet

Baronet+
Siroka 22, 110 00 Prague 1
Tel: (02) 74 77 18 06 (ext 31) *Fax:* (02) 74 77 38 70
E-mail: baronet.odbyt@volny.cz
Web Site: www.baronet-knihy.cz; www.baronet.cz; www.knihy.de
Key Personnel
Publishing Dir: Mr Milan Soska, PhD
Founded: 1993
Subjects: Fiction, Military Science, Nonfiction (General), Romance, Science Fiction, Fantasy, *Specializes in:* Historical romances, horoscopes & English/American fiction
ISBN Prefix(es): 80-7214

Barrister & Principal+
Martinkova 7, 602 00 Brno
Tel: (05) 45211015 *Fax:* (05) 45210607
E-mail: barrister@barrister.cz
Key Personnel
Manager: Ivo Lukas *Tel:* (05) 45211015 *E-mail:* lukas@barrister.cz
Founded: 1994
Subjects: Archaeology, Economics, Education, Government, Political Science, History, Journalism, Language Arts, Linguistics, Philosophy, Poetry, Psychology, Psychiatry, Religion - Catholic, Social Sciences, Sociology, Theology
ISBN Prefix(es): 80-85947; 80-86598
Number of titles published annually: 20 Print
Total Titles: 5 Print

Nakladatelstvi Blok
Rooseveltova 4, 657 00 Brno
Tel: (05) 42321245 *Fax:* (05) 42321245
Key Personnel
Dir: Jaroslav Novak
Subjects: Art, Ethnicity, Fiction, History, Literature, Literary Criticism, Essays, Poetry, Regional Interests
ISBN Prefix(es): 80-7029

Brody+
Nakladatelství krásných knih, Spanelska 6, 120 00 Prague 2
Tel: (02) 22252077; (02) 376630
E-mail: brody@draha.czcom.cz
Web Site: www.brody.cz
Key Personnel
Contact: Dita Horakova
Founded: 1995
Subjects: Art, Fiction, Literature, Literary Criticism, Essays, Nonfiction (General), Philosophy, Specialize in publishing books on the Far East & Russian Avant-Garde for reference markets in all areas of humanities
ISBN Prefix(es): 80-86112; 80-902113

Canis Vydavatelstvi a Nakladatelstvi+
Korunni 9, 120 00 Prague 2
Tel: (02) 251096
Key Personnel
Editor & Publisher: Dr M Cisarovsky
Founded: 1990
ISBN Prefix(es): 80-900820
Associate Companies: Canis centrum, Vrsovicka 7/27, Prague 10
Divisions: Manesova 48

Ceska Biblicka Spolecnost (Czech Bible Society)
Nahorni 12, 180 00 Prague 8
Tel: (02) 20181412 *Fax:* (02) 24315723
E-mail: cbs@biblenet.cz
Key Personnel
Contact: Jiri Lukl
Founded: 1990
Member of United Bible Societies.
ISBN Prefix(es): 80-85810; 80-900881

Ceska Expedice+
Jihozapadni III, 14, 141 00 Prague 4
Tel: (02) 727 612 04
Key Personnel
Contact: Jaromir Horec
Founded: 1989
Subjects: History, Literature, Literary Criticism, Essays, Poetry, Russie Subcarpatig
ISBN Prefix(es): 80-85281

Cesky Filmovy ustav+
Malesicka 12, 130 00 Prague 3
Mailing Address: Bartolomejeska 11, 110 00 Prague 1 *Tel:* (02) 24231988
Tel: (02) 894300; (02) 894686-9 *Fax:* (02) 894501
Key Personnel
President: Jaroslav Bocek
Founded: 1970
Subjects: Film, Video
ISBN Prefix(es): 80-7004

Cesky spisovatel
Pod Nuselskymi schody 3, 120 00 Prague 2
Tel: (02) 6911902; (02) 6911909; (02) 6911897 *Fax:* (02) 6911902
Telex: 122645 *Cable:* Spisovatel Prague
Key Personnel
Dir: Zdenek Pochop
Founded: 1949
Subjects: Biography, Fiction, Philosophy, Poetry
ISBN Prefix(es): 80-202
Bookshop(s): Ceska 7, Brno
Book Club(s): Klub pratel poezie (Club of the Friends of Poetry)

Jiri Chvojka
Smilovskeho 3, 120 00 Prague 2
Mailing Address: Machova 22, 101 00 Prague 10 *Tel:* (02) 717 430 23
Tel: (02) 225 169 65 *Fax:* (02) 225 169 65
Key Personnel
Contact: Jiri Chvojka
Subjects: Alternative, Astrology, Occult, History, Parapsychology, Psychology, Psychiatry
ISBN Prefix(es): 80-900239; 80-901270; 80-901622; 80-86183

Cinema+
Seifertova 47, 130 00 Prague 3
Tel: (02) 627 83 95-6 *Fax:* (02) 627 72 39
E-mail: schur@comp.cz
Key Personnel
International Rights: Roland Schuer
Founded: 1991
Subjects: Film, Video
ISBN Prefix(es): 80-85933; 80-901675

Columbus+
Nad Kolcavkov 8, 190 00 Prague 9

Tel: (02) 683 10 17 *Fax:* (02) 683 10 17
E-mail: columbus@alpha-net.cz
Key Personnel
Contact: Ivo Smoldas
Founded: 1991
Subjects: Biography, Geography, Geology, History, Parapsychology
ISBN Prefix(es): 80-85928; 80-901578; 80-901696; 80-901727; 80-7249

Concordia+
Belohorska 99, 169 00 Prague 6
Tel: (02) 3413751 *Fax:* (02) 7929747
Key Personnel
Executive: Ales Pech
Founded: 1990
Subjects: Literature, Literary Criticism, Essays
ISBN Prefix(es): 80-900124; 80-901389; 80-85997

Diderot sro
Ceskomoravska 31, CZ 19000 Prague 9
Tel: (02) 66035757; (02) 21841004 *Fax:* (02) 66035381; (02) 21841001
E-mail: fialkovam@bp.diderot.cz
Web Site: www.diderot.cz
Key Personnel
Contact: Martina Fialkova *E-mail:* obchool@diderot.ez
Founded: 1988
Private publishing organization.
Total Titles: 2 Print; 1 CD-ROM
Branch Office(s)
Moravian Branch, Sevcovska 1156, Ziln 76001
Tel: (067) 34156 *Fax:* (067) 779493

Dimenze 2 Plus 2 Praha+
Soukenicka 21, 110 00 Prague 1
Tel: (02) 231 11 41 *Fax:* (02) 231 11 41
Key Personnel
President: Tomas Pfeiffer
Founded: 1990
Subjects: Health, Nutrition, Philosophy
ISBN Prefix(es): 80-85238

Divadelni Ustav (Theatre Institute Prague)+
Subsidiary of Ministry of Culture, Czech Republic
Celetna 17, 110 00 Prague 1
Tel: (02) 24809141 *Fax:* (02) 24811452
E-mail: info@theatre.cz
Web Site: institute.theatre.cz
Key Personnel
Dir: Ondrej Cerny *Tel:* (02) 24809138
Contact: Paula Kucharova *Tel:* (02) 24809192
E-mail: pavla.kucharova@theatre.cz
Founded: 1960
Subjects: Drama, Theater, Theatre plays
ISBN Prefix(es): 80-7008
Number of titles published annually: 10 Print
Bookshop(s): Prospero Bookshop, Celetna St 17, Prague 1 110 00 *E-mail:* prospero@theatre.cz
Web Site: www.divadlo.cz/prospero (Also distribution)

Doplnek+
Bratislavská 48/50, 602 00 Brno
Mailing Address: Kallabova 29, 616 00 Brno
Tel: (05) 452-424-55 *Fax:* (05) 546346
E-mail: doplnek.brno@quick.cz
Web Site: www.sky.cz; www.doplnek.cz
Key Personnel
Contact: Jan Sabata *E-mail:* sabata@sky.cz
Founded: 1991 (Founded in Bruo, Czech Republic)
Specialize in publishing of books with subject specialties.
Member of The Association of Czech Booksellers & Publishers.
Subjects: Biography, Economics, Education, Environmental Studies, History, Humor, Journalism, Law, Literature, Literary Criticism, Essays, Psychology, Psychiatry, Science Fiction, Fantasy, Social Sciences, Sociology
ISBN Prefix(es): 1-898218
Number of titles published annually: 35 Print
Total Titles: 200 Print
Subsidiaries: Jan Sabata
Distributor for Jan Sabata
Foreign Rep(s): Andrew Nurberg Associate (Czech Republic); Thomas Perry (US)
Bookshop(s): Zerotinovo nam 9, 60200 Brno
Tel: 05 42128382

Erika+
Jarnikova 1894, 148 00 Prague 4
Mailing Address: PO Box 27, 148 00 Prague 4
Tel: (02) 7950452 *Fax:* (02) 7929351
Key Personnel
Contact: Jan Suchl
Founded: 1990
Subjects: Health, Nutrition, Nonfiction (General)
ISBN Prefix(es): 80-900091; 80-85612; 80-7190
Orders to: Spira, Horska 10, 46014 Liberec

Exemplare, *imprint of* Granit SRO

Galaxie, vydavatelelstvi a nakladatelstvi+
Petrska 29, 110 00 Prague 1
Tel: (02) 2317801; (02) 2317875 *Fax:* (02) 2311351
Key Personnel
Man Partner, Editor-in-Chief: Milan Pavek
Subjects: Education, Ethnicity, Fiction, Literature, Literary Criticism, Essays
ISBN Prefix(es): 80-85204

Geodeticky a kartograficky podnik v Praha, sp
Frantiska Krizkal 1, 170 30 Prague 7
Mailing Address: Kostelni 42, 170 30 Prague 7
Tel: (02) 204 121 11; (02) 204 121 51; (02) 204 121 50 *Fax:* (02) 204 121 17; (02) 333 747 25
E-mail: digiteam@kartografie.cz
Telex: 121471 guvs c *Cable:* GEOKART
Key Personnel
Man Dir: Miroslav Miksovsky
Editor-in-Chief: Ales Hasek
Founded: 1954
Geodetic & Cartographic Enterprise in Prague.
ISBN Prefix(es): 80-7011
Orders to: Artia, Foreign Trade Corporation, Ve Smeckach 30, 11127 Prague 1

Grada Publishing sro+
U Pruhonu 22, 170 00 Prague 7
Tel: (02) 20386401; (02) 20386402 *Fax:* (02) 20386400
E-mail: info@gradapublishing.cz
Web Site: www.grandpublishing.cz
Founded: 1993
Subjects: Computer Science, Economics, Law, Technology, Medicine
ISBN Prefix(es): 80-7169; 80-85424; 80-85623; 80-900250
Total Titles: 850 Print

Granit SRO+
Drtinova 10, 150 00 Prague 5
Tel: (00420) 57018357; (00420) 57018356; (00420) 57018361 *Fax:* (00420) 57018361
E-mail: info@granit-publishing.cz
Web Site: www.granit-publishing.cz
Key Personnel
Dir: Lubomir Mlcoch
International Rights: Hilda Novakova
Founded: 1992
Subjects: Animals, Pets, Biological Sciences, Crafts, Games, Hobbies, Education, Gardening, Plants, Geography, Geology, Health, Nutrition, Natural History, Science (General)
ISBN Prefix(es): 80-85805
Number of titles published annually: 12 Print
Total Titles: 80 Print
Imprints: Exemplare

Historicky ustav Akademie ved Ceske republiky
Prosecka 76, 190 00 Prague 9
Tel: (02) 884190 *Fax:* (02) 887513
Key Personnel
Dir Productions: Dr Pavla Vosahlikova
Founded: 1921
Subjects: History
ISBN Prefix(es): 80-85268

Galerie Hlavniho Mesta Prahy
Mickiewiczova 3, 160 00 Prague 6
Tel: (02) 3332 1200 *Fax:* (02) 3332 3664
Web Site: www.citygalleryprague.cz
Key Personnel
Dir: Jaroslav Fatka
ISBN Prefix(es): 80-7010

Nakladatelstvi Josef Hribal+
Na Vaclavce 10/1202, 150 21 Prague 5
Mailing Address: PO Box 210, 150 21 Prague 5
Tel: (02) 542731
Key Personnel
Contact: Zdenek Hribal
Founded: 1893
Subjects: Economics, Law, Nonfiction (General)
ISBN Prefix(es): 80-900132; 80-900892; 80-901381

Infoa+
Nova 141, 789 72 Dubicko
Tel: (0648) 449-091 *Fax:* (0648) 449-091
E-mail: infoa@ova.pvtnet.cz
Web Site: www.infoa.cz
Key Personnel
Contact: Stanislav Sojak
Founded: 1992
Has own distribution network in the Czech Republic, Slovakia & Poland.
Private Company.
Subjects: *Specializes in:* Foreign languages
ISBN Prefix(es): 80-7240
Total Titles: 250 Print
Online services available through World Wide Web.
Branch Office(s)
Potocna 103, 90901 Skalica, Slovakia, Contact: Pavol Rehus *Tel:* (0801) 646172 *Fax:* (0801) 646172
Distributor for Express Publishing (Distribution rights for the Czech Republic & Slovakia)

Inspirace+
Volsinach 11, 100 00 Prague 10
Tel: (02) 7356615
Key Personnel
Contact: Alois Myslik
Founded: 1990
Subjects: Philosophy, Religion - Other
ISBN Prefix(es): 80-900119

Iuventus+
Nedvezska 6, 100 00 Prague 10
Tel: (02) 7817314
Key Personnel
President: Dr Josef Smolka, CSC
Founded: 1990
Subjects: Government, Political Science
ISBN Prefix(es): 80-7123

Jan Vasut Publishing+
Vitkova 10, 18621 Prague 8
Tel: (02) 2319318; (02) 2319319 *Fax:* (02) 2481 1059
E-mail: vasut@mbox.vol.cz
Web Site: www.vasut.cz
Key Personnel
Publisher: Jan Vasut *Tel:* (02) 22 31 87 07
E-mail: jan.vasut@vasut.cz

Foreign Rights: Milena Taralezkovova
Founded: 1990
Subjects: Cookery, Crafts, Games, Hobbies, Humor, Sports, Athletics
ISBN Prefix(es): 80-7236
Warehouse: Grada Bohemia sro, Luzna 591, Prague 6 *Tel:* (02) 20121360

Karel Janak Amosium Servis
Hladnovska 119 b, 712 00 Ostrava
Tel: (069) 624 55 01
Key Personnel
Dir: Karel Janak
Founded: 1990
ISBN Prefix(es): 80-85498

Jednota Ceskych Matematiku A Fysiku
Zitna 25, 117 10 Prague 1
Tel: (02) 24230877; (02) 242139
ISBN Prefix(es): 80-7015

Jota+
Krenova 19, 602 00 Brno
Tel: (05) 4353 0210; (05) 4353 0203 *Fax:* (05) 4353 0203
E-mail: jota@netbrno.cz; books@bm.cesnet.cz
Web Site: www.jota.cz
Key Personnel
Contact: Marcel Nekvinda
Founded: 1990
Subjects: Alternative, Biography, Crafts, Games, Hobbies, Health, Nutrition, History, Military Science, Outdoor Recreation, Science Fiction, Fantasy
ISBN Prefix(es): 80-85617; 80-900281; 80-7217

Kalich SRO
Jungmannova 9, 111 21 Prague 1
Mailing Address: PO Box 220
Tel: (02) 24947505; (02) 24220296 *Fax:* (02) 24947504; (02) 24220296
Key Personnel
Dir: Ema Snelia
Manager: Juan Vasin
Founded: 1922
Subjects: History, Philosophy, Religion - Catholic, Religion - Jewish, Religion - Protestant, Religion - Other, Social Sciences, Sociology, Theology
ISBN Prefix(es): 80-7017; 80-7072

Jan Kanzelsberger
Jana Masaryka 56, 120 00 Prague 2
Tel: (02) 22 51 42 40; (02) 22 52 02 64 *Fax:* (02) 22 51 15 73
E-mail: masarykova@volny.cz
Founded: 1990
Subjects: Biography, Language Arts, Linguistics
ISBN Prefix(es): 80-900095; 80-85387; 80-900184
Branch Office(s)
Vaclavske nam 42, 110 00 Prague *Tel:* (02) 24217335 *Fax:* (02) 24221243
Bookshop(s): Knihkupectvi Orbis, Scobarova 5, 130 00 Prague

Karmelitanske Nakladatelstvi+
Kostelni Vydri 58, 380 01 Dacia
Tel: (0332) 420295 *Fax:* (0332) 420295
E-mail: karmelnakl@da.bohem-net.cz
Web Site: www.karmelitanske-nakladatelstvi.cz
Key Personnel
Dir: Jan Fatka *Tel:* (02) 20 181 350
Founded: 1991
Subjects: Biblical Studies, Biography, History, Poetry, Religion - Catholic, Theology
ISBN Prefix(es): 80-7192; 80-7195; 80-85527
Total Titles: 530 Print; 150 Audio

Branch Office(s)
Thakurova 3, 160 00 Prague 6 *Tel:* (02) 20181350 *Fax:* (02) 20181390
Bookshop(s): Knihkvpectvt SV VTT, Hradcenske, N9MESTT 16 *Tel:* (02) 20392185

Karolinum, nakladatelstvi+
Ovocny trh 3, 116 36 Prague 1
Tel: (02) 24491276 *Fax:* (02) 24212041
E-mail: cupress@ruk.cuni.cz
Web Site: www.cupress.cuni.cz
Key Personnel
Dir: Jaroslav Jirsa *E-mail:* jaroslav.jirsa@ruk.cuni.cz
International Rights: Adela Sorfova
Editor: Renata Camska *Tel:* (02) 24 491 266 *E-mail:* renata.camska@ruk.cuni.cz
Production: Nadezda Lemochova *Tel:* (02) 24 491 271 *E-mail:* nadezda.lemochova@ruk.cuni.cz; Kamila Schullerova *Tel:* (02) 24 491 272 *E-mail:* kamila.schullerova@ruk.cuni.cz
Distribution: Jaroslava Stribrska *Tel:* (02) 24491275 *E-mail:* jaroslava.stribrska@ruk.cuni.cz
Editor: Marie Bernardova *Tel:* (02) 24 491 631 *E-mail:* marie.bernardova@ruk.cuni.cz; Zdenka Lubenova *Tel:* (02) 24 491 273; Milada Motlova *Tel:* (02) 24 491 266 *E-mail:* milada.motlova@ruk.cuni.cz; Lenka Seerbanieova *Tel:* (02) 24 491 482; Petr Valo *Tel:* (02) 24 491 268 *E-mail:* petr.valo@ruk.cuni.cz; Jana Velova *Tel:* (02) 24 491 274 *E-mail:* jana.velova@ruk.cuni.cz
Foreign Rights: Martin Janecek *Tel:* (02) 24 491 269 *E-mail:* martin.janecek@ruk.cuni.cz
Promotion: Milan Susta *Tel:* (02) 24 491 265 *E-mail:* milan.susta@ruk.cuni.cz
Founded: 1990
Publishing House of Charles University, Prague.
Subjects: Architecture & Interior Design, Art, Business, Economics, Education, Fiction, Foreign Countries, History, Language Arts, Linguistics, Law, Mathematics, Medicine, Nursing, Dentistry, Philosophy, Physical Sciences, Religion - Other, Science (General), Social Sciences, Sociology
ISBN Prefix(es): 80-7066; 80-7184
Bookshop(s): Celetna 18, 11636 Prague 1

Knihovna A Tiskarna Pro Nevidome
Ve Smeckach 15, 115 17 Prague 1
Tel: (02) 22 21 04 92; (02) 22 21 15 23 *Fax:* (02) 22 21 04 94
Web Site: www.ktn.cz
Key Personnel
Dir: Dr Josef Doksansky
Subjects: Biography, Fiction, Humor, Mysteries, Poetry, Psychology, Psychiatry, Religion - Other, Science Fiction, Fantasy
ISBN Prefix(es): 80-7061

Konias+
Waltrova 26, 32334 Plzen
Mailing Address: PO Box 35, 31800 Plzen
Tel: (019) 738 06 90 *Fax:* (019) 285879
Key Personnel
Contact: Miroslav Moravek
Founded: 1990
Subjects: Travel
ISBN Prefix(es): 80-900167; 80-901379

Konsultace+
Bilkova 8, 110 00 Prague 1
Tel: (02) 2310363 *Fax:* (02) 2310363
Key Personnel
Publisher (Oberengstringen): Antonin Pasek
Publisher (Zurich): Sarka Pasek
Director: Antonin Seda
Founded: 1990
Subjects: Government, Political Science, History, Humor, Philosophy, Poetry
ISBN Prefix(es): 80-7124

Associate Companies: Consultation Verlag, Oberengstringen, Switzerland
Orders to: S Pasek, Consultation, Regensdorfestr 175, 8049 Zurich, Switzerland

Kosik
Hajecka 184, Chyne, 253 01 Hostivice
Tel: (02) 670929 *Fax:* (02) 2359403
Key Personnel
Contact: Jiri Kosik
ISBN Prefix(es): 80-900248; 80-902007

Svet Kridel+
PO Box 147, 350 02 Cheb
Tel: (0166) 430371 *Fax:* (0166) 23395
Key Personnel
Contact: Arnost Moucha
Subjects: Aeronautics, Aviation
ISBN Prefix(es): 80-85280

Labyrint+
Sokolovska 74, Karlin, Prague 8
Mailing Address: Box 52, Jablonecka 715, 190 00 Prague 9
Tel: (02) 2321934 *Fax:* (02) 2321934
E-mail: labyrint@wo.cz
Web Site: labyrint.net
Key Personnel
Contact: Joachim Dvorak
Founded: 1992
Subjects: Art, Fiction, Library & Information Sciences, Poetry
ISBN Prefix(es): 80-85935; 80-901289
Number of titles published annually: 8 Print; 1 E-Book
Total Titles: 60 Print; 2 E-Book
Subsidiaries: Via Vestra

Libri s r o+
Na Hutmance 7, 158 00 Prague 5
Tel: (02) 5161 3113 *Fax:* (02) 5161 1013
E-mail: libri@libri.cz
Web Site: www.libri.cz
Key Personnel
Manager: Marie Honzakova
Founded: 1992
Original Czech encyclopedia, popularization.
Member of Federation of Czech Publishers & Booksellers.
Subjects: Archaeology, Architecture & Interior Design, Economics, Geography, Geology, History, Social Sciences, Sociology
ISBN Prefix(es): 80-901579; 80-85983; 80-7277
Number of titles published annually: 50 Print
Total Titles: 189 Print; 3 CD-ROM; 2 E-Book

Lidove noviny Nakladatelstvi
Jana Masaryka 56, 120 00 Prague 2
Tel: (02) 225 140 12; (02) 225 223 50 *Fax:* (02) 225 120 79
E-mail: nlnpress@iol.cz *Cable:* Lidove nakladatelstvi Prague
Key Personnel
Editor-in-Chief: Eva Pleskova
Founded: 1948 (formerly Svet Sovetu)
Subjects: Fiction, Nonfiction (General), Poetry, Social Sciences, Sociology
ISBN Prefix(es): 80-7106

Josef Lukasik A Spol+
Ortenovo nam 6, 170 00 Prague 7
Tel: (02) 80 31 05
Key Personnel
Contact: Marie Lukasikova
Founded: 1939
Subjects: Humor, Mysteries, Nonfiction (General), Romance
ISBN Prefix(es): 80-900303; 80-901763; 80-902508

CZECH REPUBLIC

Luxpress VOS+
Maliiska 6, 170 00 Prague 7
Tel: (02) 203 972 60 *Fax:* (02) 203 972 60
E-mail: ibs.czech@iol.cz
Founded: 1990
Subjects: Health, Nutrition, Human Relations, Religion - Other
ISBN Prefix(es): 80-7130

Mariadan+
Kloboucnicka 7, 140 00 Prague 4
Tel: (02) 41 40 83 91
Key Personnel
Contact: Marie Jehlickova-Gucklerova
Founded: 1990
Subjects: Archaeology, Art, Earth Sciences, Fiction, Foreign Countries, History, Science Fiction, Fantasy
ISBN Prefix(es): 80-900304
Imprints: Tesinska

Maxdorf Ltd+
Na Sejdru 247, Libus, Prague 4
Tel: (02) 4171 0243; (02) 4171 0244 *Fax:* (02) 4171 0245
E-mail: maxdorf@maxdorf.cz
Web Site: www.maxdorf.cz
Key Personnel
Editor-in-Chief: Jan Hugo *E-mail:* hugo@maxdorf.cz
Founded: 1993
Publishing house of scientific & professional literature.
Subjects: Art, Health, Nutrition, History, Medicine, Nursing, Dentistry, Science (General), Specialize in medicine, monograhies & handbooks
ISBN Prefix(es): 80-85800; 80-85912
Number of titles published annually: 40 Print
Total Titles: 105 Print; 1 E-Book

Melantrich
Vaclavske nam 36, 112 12 Prague 1
Tel: (02) 24227258 *Fax:* (02) 24213176
Telex: 121422 *Cable:* Melantrich
Key Personnel
Man Dir: Petr Zantovsky
Sales Dir: K Volesky
Editorial: Dr K Houba
Production: M Nevole
Founded: 1898
Subjects: Biography, Philosophy, Poetry
ISBN Prefix(es): 80-7023
Bookshop(s): Na prikope 3, Prague 1; Jilska 9, Prague 1

Mendelova zemedelska a lesnicka univerzita v Brne (Mendel University of Agriculture & Forestry Brno)
Zemedelska 1, 613 00 Brno
Tel: (05) 4513 1111; (05) 4513 2678 *Fax:* (05) 4513 5008
Web Site: www.mendelu.cz
Key Personnel
Contact: Dr Jiri Potacek *E-mail:* potacek@mendelu.cz
Founded: 1992
Subjects: Agriculture, Animals, Pets, Biological Sciences, Earth Sciences, Economics, Physical Sciences
ISBN Prefix(es): 80-7157
Number of titles published annually: 70 Print; 30 Audio
Total Titles: 400 Print; 2,000 Audio

MF, *imprint of* Mlada fronta

Mlada fronta+
Division of Mlada fronta a s
Radlicka 61, 150 00 Prague 5
Tel: (02) 2527 6120
Telex: 00245 *Cable:* MF PRAGUE
Key Personnel
Dir: Martina Hartova *E-mail:* hartova@mf.cz
Editor-in-Chief: Vlastimil Fiala
Founded: 1945
Subjects: Art, Astronomy, Biography, Fiction, History, Nonfiction (General), Philosophy, Poetry, Science Fiction, Fantasy, Travel, Fairytales
ISBN Prefix(es): 80-204
Number of titles published annually: 120 Print
Total Titles: 6,500 Print
Imprints: MF

Pavla Momcilova+
V Zahradach 146, Cestlice, 251 70 Dobrejovice
Tel: (02) 677 101 28 *Fax:* (02) 677 101 28
Key Personnel
Publisher: Pavla Momcilova
Founded: 1990
Subjects: Child Care & Development, Cookery, Education, Health, Nutrition, Medicine, Nursing, Dentistry, Poetry, Self-Help
ISBN Prefix(es): 80-900140; 80-901137; 80-85936
Total Titles: 52 Print
Imprints: Nakladatelstvi Momcilova
Warehouse: PEMIC, Ostrava 71900, Vratimovska 101, Contact: Mr Petr Michalek *Tel:* (02) 95683169
Orders to: Momcilova Publishing, 25170 Cestlice, Vzahradach 146, Ljuben Momcilov *Tel:* (02) 67710128 *Fax:* (02) 67710128

Editio Moravia-Moravske hudebni vydavatelstvi+
Sosnova 18, 637 00 Brno
Tel: (05) 41220025
E-mail: emdl@vtx.cz *Cable:* CS-61300 BRNO 13
Key Personnel
Publishing Dir: Dr Jaromir Dlouhy
Marketing Manager: Mag Martin Dlouhy
Founded: 1990
Specialize in music literature for schools.
Subjects: Education, Music, Dance
ISBN Prefix(es): 80-85322

Moravska Galerie v Brne
Husova 18, 66226 Brno
Tel: (05) 42 215 753; (05) 32 169 111 *Fax:* (05) 32 169 180
E-mail: m-gal@moravska-galerie.cz
Web Site: www.moravska-galerie.cz
Key Personnel
Dir: Mrs Kaliopi Chamonikola, PhD *Tel:* (05) 32 169 132
Founded: 1873
Exhibition Catalogues; Bulletin of Moravian Gallery.
Subjects: Architecture & Interior Design, Art, Photography, Applied Art
ISBN Prefix(es): 80-7027
Total Titles: 30 Print

Nadace Lyry Pragensis
Karlova 2, 110 00 Prague 1
Tel: (02) 222 202 89 *Fax:* (02) 222 212 67
Founded: 1967
Subjects: Drama, Theater, Fiction, Music, Dance, Philosophy, Poetry, Religion - Buddhist
ISBN Prefix(es): 80-7059
Subsidiaries: Spolecnost pratel kultury slova

Nakladatelstvi Momcilova, *imprint of* Pavla Momcilova

Nakladatelstvi Svoboda+
Jungmannova 12, 113 03 Prague 1
Mailing Address: K Safine 145, 149 00 Prague 4
Tel: (02) 24 22 98
Tel: (02) 449 132 58; (02) 23 06 14 *Fax:* (02) 449 132 58
Key Personnel
Dir: Stefan Szerynski
Rights & Permissions: Michal Bencok
Founded: 1970
Publishing house in state ownership.
Subjects: Finance, History, Management, Marketing, Mysteries, Nonfiction (General)
ISBN Prefix(es): 80-205
Book Club(s): Friends of Antiquity; Readers Club of Svoboda

Narodni Knihovna CR (The National Library of the Czech Republic)+
Klementinum 190, 110 01 Prague 1
Tel: (02) 81013316 *Fax:* (02) 81013333
E-mail: mirosovsky.ivo@cdh.nkp.cz
Web Site: www.nkp.cz
Key Personnel
Head, Publishing Department: Milena Redinova, PhD *E-mail:* redinova.milena@cdh.nkp.cz
The publishing department manages & coordinates publishing activities of the National Library in the areas of librarianship, bibliography & scientific information.
Publishing department is responsible for editorial planning, production, sales & shipping
Memberships: Conference of European National Librarians (CENL), Czech Association of Booksellers & Publishers, Czech Association of Librarian & Information Professionals, International Federation of Library Associations & Institutions (IFLA), Lique des Bibliotheques Europeennes de Recherche (LIBER)
Subjects: Library & Informational Sciences
ISBN Prefix(es): 80-7050
Number of titles published annually: 32 Print; 2 CD-ROM; 1 Online
Total Titles: 94 Print; 2 CD-ROM; 1 Online
Online services available through www.nkp.cz.
Imprints: National Library of the Czech Republic
Distributed by National Library of the Czech Republic (Address same as Returns & Shipping)
Orders to: National Library of the Czech Republic, Publishing Department, Central Depository Hostivar, Sterboholska 55, 10200 Prague 15 (Address same as Returns & Shipping)

Narodni Muzeum
Vaclavske Nam 68, 115 79 Prague 1
Tel: (02) 24497111; (02) 24226488 *Fax:* (02) 264919
E-mail: ais@nm.anet.cz
Web Site: www.nm.cz/
Key Personnel
Dir: Dipl Ing Milan Plaeek *Tel:* (02) 24497235 *Fax:* (02) 24224940 *E-mail:* milan.placek@nm.cz
Manager: Lukas Viktora *Tel:* (02) 24497350 *Fax:* (02) 264919 *E-mail:* lukas.viktora@nm.cz
Dir: Dr Milan Stloukal
Founded: 1818
Subjects: Animals, Pets, Anthropology, Archaeology, Art, Asian Studies, Biological Sciences, Drama, Theater, Earth Sciences, History, Music, Dance, Natural History, Science (General), Sports, Athletics
ISBN Prefix(es): 80-7036

Nase vojsko, nakladatelstvi a knizni obchod+
Vitezne nam 4, 16000 Prague 6
Tel: (02) 24915288; (02) 24917147 *Fax:* (02) 24915288
Key Personnel
Dir: Jakub Cisar
Editorial: Dr Zdenka Alanova
Sales: Miroslav Ambros
Rights & Permissions: Marie Kutilkkova
Founded: 1945
Subjects: History, Humor, Maritime, Military Science, Mysteries, Nonfiction (General), Philosophy
ISBN Prefix(es): 80-206
Warehouse: Ostrovni 32, Prague 1

PUBLISHERS — CZECH REPUBLIC

National Library of the Czech Republic, *imprint of* Narodni Knihovna CR

Nava+
Hankova 6, 301 33 Plzen
Tel: (019) 7235633; (019) 7235721; (019) 7223294; (019) 7223251; (019) 7235509 *Fax:* (019) 223143
Key Personnel
Contact: Ota Rubner
Founded: 1990
Specializes in Children's Books.
Subjects: Fiction, History, Humor
ISBN Prefix(es): 80-85254; 80-7211

NLN, Ltd The Lidove noviny Publishing House+
Jana Masaryka 56, CZ-12000 Prague
Tel: (02) 22510843 *Fax:* (02) 22514012
E-mail: nlnpress@iol.cz; nln@iol.cz
Key Personnel
Man Dir: Dr Eva Pleskova *E-mail:* pleskovi@iol.cz
Founded: 1995
Subjects: Archaeology, Art, Biography, History, Language Arts, Linguistics, Nonfiction (General), Science (General), Travel
ISBN Prefix(es): 80-4106
Number of titles published annually: 70 Print
Total Titles: 750 Print

Cesky normalizacni institut
Biskupsky dvur 5, 110 02 Prague 1
Tel: (02) 21 80 21 11 *Fax:* (02) 21 80 23 10
E-mail: u30-csni@login.cz *Cable:* NORMALIZACE PRAHA
Key Personnel
Contacts: Otakar Kunc; Jan Jelinek; Ms Buresova Zdenka
Founded: 1922
Member of CEN, CENELEC, ETSi, IEC & ISO.
Subjects: Automotive, Chemistry, Chemical Engineering, Electronics, Electrical Engineering, Engineering (General), Environmental Studies, Mechanical Engineering, Medicine, Nursing, Dentistry
ISBN Prefix(es): 80-85111

Odeon, nakladatelstvi krasne literatury a umeni+
V Jamw 1, 111 21 Prague 1
Tel: (02) 241 625 21-6 *Fax:* (02) 241 623 28
E-mail: odeon@comp.cz *Cable:* ODEON PRAHA
Key Personnel
Man Dir: Ing Jiri Havlik
Editorial Rights & Permissions: Dr Jiri (Fiction) Nasinec; Dr Milada (Art) Motlova
Publicity: Eva Svobodova
Production: Zdenek Suska
Founded: 1953
Publishing House of Literature & Art.
Subjects: Art, Biography, Fiction, Poetry
ISBN Prefix(es): 80-207
Bookshop(s): Na Florenci 3, 11586 Prague 1
Book Club(s): Odeon Book Club (Klub Ctenaru)

Nakladatelstvi Olympia AS+
Klimenstka 1, 110 00 Prague 1
Tel: (02) 24810146 *Fax:* (02) 2312137; (02) 2315136
E-mail: olympia@mbox.vo.cz
Web Site: olympia.gcomp.cz
Telex: 121717 *Cable:* OLYMPIA PRAGUE
Key Personnel
Man Dir: Karel Zelnicek
Dir: Alexander Zurman
Sales Dir: Zdenek Pobuda
Publicity & Advertising: Monika Charvatova
Editor: Josef Smatlak
Founded: 1954
Publishing House of Sports & Tourism.
Subjects: Sports, Athletics, Travel
ISBN Prefix(es): 80-7033
Bookshop(s): Opletalova 59, Prague 1

Omnipress Praha+
Na Sypcine 9, 147 00 Prague 4
Mailing Address: PO Box 106, 14000 Prague
Tel: (02) 61211406 *Fax:* (02) 61211856
E-mail: dcf.clock@omnipress.cz
Web Site: www.omnipress.cz
Key Personnel
Contact: Dr Metodej K Chytil
Founded: 1990
Subjects: Communications, Medicine, Nursing, Dentistry, Philosophy, Science (General)
ISBN Prefix(es): 80-900153
Associate Companies: Omikron Desk-Top Publishing
Orders to: PO Box 106, 14000 Prague

P R Centrum, *imprint of* Pop Plus Rock Centrum

Nakladatelstvi a vydavatelstvi Panorama+
Halkova 1, 120 72 Prague 2
Tel: (02) 24222509; (02) 24222762; (02) 2422392630 *Fax:* (02) 22422474
Telex: 122657 *Cable:* PANORAMA PRAGUE 2
Key Personnel
Man Dir: Vladimir Voznicka
Founded: 1978
Subjects: Archaeology, Asian Studies, Biography, Biological Sciences, Film, Video, Health, Nutrition, History
ISBN Prefix(es): 80-7038
Bookshop(s): V Tunich 11, 12072 Prague

Panton+
Radlicka 99, 150 00 Prague 5
Tel: (02) 515 539 52; (02) 515 545 11 *Fax:* (02) 515 559 94
E-mail: panton@panton.cz
Web Site: www.panton.cz *Cable:* PANTON
Key Personnel
Dir: Tomas Bartak
Business Dir: Dr Zdenek Veselka
Chief Editor: Dr Martinkova Alena
Founded: 1958
Publishers of the Czech Music Fund - Prague
Also publisher of music records & cassettes.
Specialize in the training & instruction for musical instruments.
Subjects: Education, Music, Dance
ISBN Prefix(es): 80-7039
Bookshop(s): Kaprova 23, 11000 Prague 1
Warehouse: U Luzickeho seminare 42, 110 00 Prague 1

Paseka
Chopinova 4, 120 00 Prague 2
Tel: (02) 22710752; (02) 22718887 *Fax:* (02) 22718886
E-mail: paseka@mbox.vol.cz
Web Site: www.paseka.cz
Key Personnel
Dir: Vladimir Pistorius
Publisher: Ladislav Horacek
Founded: 1989
Subjects: Art, Biography, Fiction, History, Literature, Literary Criticism, Essays, Poetry
ISBN Prefix(es): 80-85192; 80-7185

Pop Plus Rock Centrum
Pod Barvirkou 14, 150 00 Prague 5
Tel: (02) 51555598 *Fax:* (02) 51554485
E-mail: olda@katapult.cz
Key Personnel
Publisher: Milan Nestaval
Founded: 1990
Also a music agency.
Subjects: Language Arts, Linguistics, Literature, Literary Criticism, Essays, Music, Dance
ISBN Prefix(es): 80-85333
Imprints: P R Centrum
Divisions: Zborovska 60
Bookshop(s): Belgicka 36, 120 00 Prague 2

Portal, *imprint of* Portal Ltd

Portal Ltd+
Klapkova 2, 182 00 Prague 8
Tel: (02) 83028111 *Fax:* (02) 83028112
E-mail: naklad@portal.cz
Web Site: www.portal.cz
Key Personnel
Dir: Jaroslav Kuchar
Rights: Dominik Dvorak *Tel:* (02) 83028111 (602) *E-mail:* dvorak@portal.cz
Founded: 1990
Member of Association of Catholic Publishers & Booksellers.
Subjects: Child Care & Development, Communications, Disability, Special Needs, Education, Human Relations, Psychology, Psychiatry, Religion - Catholic
ISBN Prefix(es): 80-7178
Number of titles published annually: 90 Print
Total Titles: 450 Print
Imprints: Portal
Foreign Rep(s): Artforum s.r.o., Kozin, Bratislava, 81 103 (Slovak Republic)
Bookshop(s): Jindrisska 30, 11000 Prague 1 *Tel:* (02) 24213415; Dominikanske nam 3, Brno 601 00 *Tel:* (05) 42213140; Klapkova 2, 182 00 Prague 8 *Tel:* (02) 83028111

Prace
Vaclavske nam 17, 11258 Prague 1
Tel: (02) 378315; (02) 373507; (02) 377346 *Fax:* (02) 20103376
E-mail: prace@terminal.cz
Key Personnel
Dir: Juraj Himal
Founded: 1945
Publishing House of the Czech Trade Union Movement.
Subjects: Engineering (General), Fiction, Government, Political Science, How-to, Law, Nonfiction (General)
ISBN Prefix(es): 80-208
Book Club(s): ERB; Kamarad

Pragma 4+
Vezenska 3, 110 00 Prague 1
Tel: (02) 231 58 28; (02) 231 07 76; (02) 231 07 74; (02) 231 65 90 *Fax:* (02) 231 07 76; (02) 231 65 90
Key Personnel
Business Manager: Ivan Marinec
Contact: Robert Nemec
Founded: 1989
Subjects: Business, Health, Nutrition, Philosophy, Self-Help, Specialize in US publishers
ISBN Prefix(es): 80-7205; 80-85213
Total Titles: 480 Print; 20 Audio
Parent Company: Pragma
Distributed by Kanzelsberger

Prazske nakladatelstvi Pluto
Kremencova 1, 110 00 Prague 1
Tel: (02) 249 301 89; (02) 43 25 05 *Fax:* (02) 249 301 89
Key Personnel
Owner: Jiri Polacek; Leontina Polackova
Founded: 1990
Subjects: Art, History, Travel
ISBN Prefix(es): 80-900192; 80-901224; 80-901544; 80-86435; 80-902183

Press Art+
Aloisina vyhlidka 628/100, 460 05 Liberec
Tel: (048) 29377 *Fax:* (048) 27958

Key Personnel
President: Jiri Oplt
Vice President: Petr Bartos
Founded: 1990
Subjects: Advertising, Business, Drama, Theater
ISBN Prefix(es): 80-900367
Parent Company: PressART
Associate Companies: Bohemia Union
Subsidiaries: M-Print; Eurotip
Divisions: Exportabt, Innlandabt

Pressfoto Vydavatelstvi Ceske Tiskove Kancelare
Zirovnicka 2389, 106 00 Prague 10
Tel: (02) 727 700 10 *Fax:* (02) 727 700 10
Telex: 122908 ctKC
Founded: 1963
Subjects: History, Regional Interests
ISBN Prefix(es): 80-7046

Prostor, Ltd+
Tynska 21, 110 00 Prague 1
Tel: (02) 224826688 *Fax:* (02) 224827722
E-mail: prostor@ini.cz
Web Site: www.prostor-nakladatelstvi.cz
Key Personnel
International Rights: Sylva Kurdiovska
Foreign Rights Agent: Kristin Olson
  Tel: (02) 222580048 *Fax:* (02) 222582042
  E-mail: kolson@vol.cz
Founded: 1990
Specializes in Czech & German history.
Member of Svaz ceskych knihkupcu a nakladatelu.
Subjects: Biography, Fiction, Government, Political Science, History, Nonfiction (General), Philosophy, Photography
ISBN Prefix(es): 80-7260
Number of titles published annually: 20 Print
Total Titles: 175 Print

Psychoanalyticke Nakladatelstvi+
Vinohradska 71, 120 00 Prague 2
Tel: (02) 33340305 *Fax:* (02) 33340305
E-mail: georg.phe@worldonline.cz
Key Personnel
Assistant Professor: Jiri Kocourek, PhD
Founded: 1992
Subjects: Education, Medicine, Nursing, Dentistry, Psychology, Psychiatry, Psychoanalysis, Psychotherapy, Scientific & Popular
ISBN Prefix(es): 80-901601
Number of titles published annually: 10 Print
Total Titles: 40 Print
Branch Office(s)
Vitezne nam 10, 16000 Prague 6
Distributed by Grada, Mata, Kolporter

Verlag Harry Putz+
PO Box 89, 460 31 Liberec
Tel: (048) 515 21 20 *Fax:* (048) 510 32 75
E-mail: harrputz@mbox.vol.cz
Subjects: Language Arts, Linguistics
ISBN Prefix(es): 80-901119; 80-902165

Simon Rysavy
Ceska 31, 602 00 Brno
Tel: (05) 42212052; (05) 42213849; (05) 42219703 *Fax:* (05) 42216633
E-mail: info@rysavy.cz
Web Site: www.itn.cz/rysavy-books
ISBN Prefix(es): 80-86137; 80-902143

SEVT, see Statisticke a evidencni vydavatelstvi tiskopisu (SEVT)

Slon Sociologicke Nakladatelstvi+
Jilska 1, 110 00 Prague 1
Mailing Address: P O Box 36, 156 80 Prague 5
Tel: (02) 24220979 *Fax:* (02) 24220979-82

Key Personnel
Contact: Alena Miltova
Founded: 1991
Subjects: Anthropology, Government, Political Science, History, Philosophy, Psychology, Psychiatry, Social Sciences, Sociology
ISBN Prefix(es): 80-85850; 80-901059; 80-901424

Sofiprin+
PO Box 1006, 111 21 Prague 1
Tel: (02) 291044 *Fax:* (02) 758280
Key Personnel
Dir: Jiri Horak
Foreign Relations Officer: Jan Spousta
Founded: 1991
ISBN Prefix(es): 80-85391

Statisticke a evidencni vydavatelstvi tiskopisu (SEVT)
Pekoiova 4, 181 06 Prague 8
Tel: (02) 855 17 11 *Fax:* (02) 855 34 22
E-mail: vydavatel@sevt.cz
Publishing House of Statistics & Data.
ISBN Prefix(es): 80-7049

Statni Vedecka Knihovna Usti Nad Labem
PO Box 134, CZ-401 34 Usti Nad Labem
Tel: (047) 5200045; (047) 5209126; (047) 5200172; (047) 5209669 *Fax:* (047) 5200045
E-mail: library@svkul.cz
Web Site: www.svkul.cz
Key Personnel
Library Dir: Mr Brozek Ales *E-mail:* brozeka@svkul.cz
Founded: 1945
Subjects: Library & Information Sciences
ISBN Prefix(es): 80-7055

Institut Pro Stredoevropskou Kulturu A Politiku
Vyserhradskae 4, 128 00 Prague 2
Tel: (02) 29 51 10 *Fax:* (02) 295 110
ISBN Prefix(es): 80-85241; 80-86130

Studio Dobre Nalady Spol SRO+
Kupeckeho 847, 140 00 Prague 4
Tel: (02) 67910482; (02) 67910486; (02) 67910488
Subjects: Publishing & Book Trade Reference
ISBN Prefix(es): 80-85279; 80-7171

Supraphon
Palackeho 1/740, 120 00 Prague 2
Tel: (02) 24 94 87 22 *Fax:* (02) 24 94 87 25
E-mail: supraphon@bonton.cz
Web Site: www.supraphon.cz
Telex: 121218 Sunp *Cable:* SUPRAPHON PRAHA
Key Personnel
Man Dir: Zdenek Cejka
Foreign Connections & Rights & Permissions: Lubos Cmuchar
Editorial: Vaclav Matatko
Founded: 1946
Publishing House of Music, Recordings, Sheet Music & Musicological Literature. Rental library of orchestral materials.
Subjects: Music, Dance
ISBN Prefix(es): 80-7058

Svepomoc
Senovazne nam 10, 113 28 Prague 1
Tel: (02) 24223446; (02) 24223450 *Fax:* (02) 24223439
Publishing House of the Central Cooperative Council.
ISBN Prefix(es): 80-7063

Svoboda Servis GmbH+
Politickych veznu 9, 110 00 Prague 1
Tel: (02) 449 132 58 *Fax:* (02) 449 132 58
E-mail: svobserv@volny.cz
Key Personnel
Foreign Rights Representative: Michal Bencok
  Tel: (02) 24009277 *Fax:* (02) 22247383
  E-mail: ak.bencok@cmail.cz
Dir: Stefan Szerynski
Founded: 1994
Subjects: Business, Management, Mysteries, Philosophy, Science Fiction, Fantasy
ISBN Prefix(es): 80-205
Number of titles published annually: 4 Print
Total Titles: 30 Print

Svojtka & Co+
Sobeslavska 32, 130 00 Prague 3
Tel: (02) 71 73 41 43; (02) 71 73 66 10 *Fax:* (02) 72 73 14 13
E-mail: svojtka@mbox.vol.cz
Web Site: www.svojtka.cz
Key Personnel
Editor: V Svojtka
Rights Manager & Manager Eastern Europe Programme: Patricia Pasqualini
Founded: 1990
One of the leading publishers on Czech market of illustrated books, also organizes local co-printings with Eastern Europe partners.
Subjects: Animals, Pets, Cookery, Crafts, Games, Hobbies, Gardening, Plants, Health, Nutrition, How-to, Music, Dance, Sports, Athletics, Travel
ISBN Prefix(es): 80-900259; 80-900258; 80-85521; 80-7180
Number of titles published annually: 150 Print
Total Titles: 250 Print
Subsidiaries: S V Records

SystemConsult+
Bartonova 675, 530 12 Pardubice
Tel: (040) 650 1585; (040) 466 501 585 *Fax:* (040) 5165 85; (040) 650 1585
E-mail: system.consult@worldonline.cz
Web Site: www.systemconsult.cz
Key Personnel
Contact: Ivo Machacka
Founded: 1990
Specialize in Computer Dictionaries (German-Czech, English-Czech), Road-Transport Techniques & Automotive Industry Dictionaries (German-English-Czech), Travel Dictionaries (English & German) & Road Transport, traffic signs in Europe.
Subjects: Business, Computer Science, History, Transportation, Travel
ISBN Prefix(es): 80-900344; 80-85629
Number of titles published annually: 5 Print
Total Titles: 50 Print

Tesinska, *imprint of* Mariadan

Touzimsky & Moravec
Pod Lazni 12, 140 00 Prague 4
Tel: (02) 612 13 631; (02) 612 12 458 *Fax:* (02) 612 12 458
Key Personnel
Contact: Michal Moravec
Subjects: Science Fiction, Fantasy, Western Fiction
ISBN Prefix(es): 80-900955; 80-900137; 80-85773; 80-7264

Trizonia
Archeologicka 2256, 155 00 Prague 5
Tel: (02) 6515016 *Fax:* (02) 6515016
Telex: Trizonia Prag 2
Key Personnel
President: Dr Jindrich Jirka
Founded: 1990

Subjects: Economics, Law
ISBN Prefix(es): 80-900953; 80-900117; 80-85573

Evzen Uher, Musikverlag UHER+
Kollarova 404, 686 01 Uherske Hradiste
Tel: (0632) 40376
Key Personnel
Contact: Evzen Uher
Founded: 1990
Subjects: Music, Dance
ISBN Prefix(es): 80-900136; 80-901386

Univerzity Karlovy, see Karolinum, nakladatelstvi

Ladislav Vasicek+
Pellicova 17, 602 00 Brno
Key Personnel
Contact: Ladislav Vasicek
Founded: 1990
Subjects: Poetry
ISBN Prefix(es): 80-900164
Bookshop(s): Ing Vasicek, Kr Pole Berkova 46, 61200 Brno
Orders to: Kvetinarska 1, 600 00 Brno

Vitalis SRO+
U Zelezne lavky 568/10, 118 00 Prague 1
Tel: (02) 57530732 *Fax:* (02) 57531974
E-mail: info@vitalis-verlag.com
Web Site: vitalis-verlag.com
Key Personnel
Publisher: Dr Harald Salfellner
Sales Manager: Marion Klompken
Founded: 1992
Specialize in Bohemica.
Subjects: Biography, Cookery, Fiction, Foreign Countries, Poetry
ISBN Prefix(es): 80-85938; 80-901621; 80-901370; 80-7253
Total Titles: 60 Print
Warehouse: LKG Potzschauer Weg, D-04579 Espenhain
Orders to: LKG, Potzschauer Weg, D-04579 Espenhain, Germany

Vodnar
Radlicka 2, 150 00 Prague 5
Tel: (02) 51563603 *Fax:* (02) 51563603
E-mail: naklvodnar@volny.cz
Web Site: www.volny.cz/naklvodnar
Key Personnel
Contact: Vladimir Kvasnicka
Founded: 1990
Subjects: Astrology, Occult, Philosophy
ISBN Prefix(es): 80-85255; 80-86226
Number of titles published annually: 10 Print

Volvox Globator
1 Pluku 7, 186 00 Prague 8
Tel: (02) 242 177 21
Key Personnel
Contact: Vit Houska
ISBN Prefix(es): 80-7207; 80-85769; 80-900906; 80-901226

Votobia sro+
Lazecka 70a, 771 00 Olomouc
Mailing Address: PO Box 214, 771 00 Olomouc
Tel: (068) 523 18 90 *Fax:* (068) 522 46 21
E-mail: votobia@mbox.vol.cz
Key Personnel
Contact: Tomas Koudela
Founded: 1991
Subjects: Alternative, Art, Astrology, Occult, Biography, Computer Science, Cookery, History, Literature, Literary Criticism, Essays, Music, Dance, Philosophy, Poetry, Religion - Buddhist

ISBN Prefix(es): 80-7198; 80-85619; 80-85885; 80-900614
Bookshop(s): Riegrova 33, 77100 Olomouc

Vydavatelstvi Ceskeho Geologickeho Ustavu
Klarov 3, 118 00 Prague 1
Tel: (02) 24002576 *Fax:* (02) 57320438
Founded: 1919
Subjects: Chemistry, Chemical Engineering, Earth Sciences, Geography, Geology, Physical Sciences
ISBN Prefix(es): 80-7075

Vysehrad+
Bartolomejska 9, 110 00 Prague 1
Mailing Address: PO Box 85, 128 00 Prague
Tel: (02) 2326 851; (02) 24 22 17 03 *Fax:* (02) 24 22 17 03
E-mail: info@ivysehrad.cz
Web Site: www.ivysehrad.cz
Founded: 1934
Specialize in Christian-Oriented Books.
Subjects: Ethnicity, Philosophy, Poetry, Public Administration, Religion - Other, Science (General)
ISBN Prefix(es): 80-7021

Zvon+
Thakurova 3, 160 00 Prague 6
Tel: (02) 20181773 *Fax:* (02) 24315153
Key Personnel
Manager of Publishing: Dr Jaroslava Trckova'
International Rights: Eliska Ruzickova'
Founded: 1990
Specialize in Religious Literature.
Subjects: History, Human Relations, Philosophy, Psychology, Psychiatry, Religion - Catholic, Religion - Jewish, Religion - Other, Theology
ISBN Prefix(es): 80-7113
Divisions: Katolicky tydenik
Bookshop(s): Jindrisska 23, 110 00 Prague 1; Dominikanske Namesti 8, 602 00 Brno
Warehouse: Sklad nakladatelstvi Zvon, Jindrisska 23, 110 00 Prague 1 *Tel:* (02) 24212376

Denmark

General Information

Capital: Copenhagen
Language: Danish (English and German widely spoken). Faeroese in the Faroes. Greenlandic in Greenland
Religion: Evangelical Lutheran
Population: 5.2 million
Bank Hours: 0930-1600 Monday-Friday; open until 1800 Thursday
Shop Hours: 0800 or 0900-1700 or 1730 Monday-Thursday; open until 1900 Friday; open until 1300 or 1700 Saturday
Currency: 100 ore = 1 krone
Export/Import Information: Denmark is a member of the European Union, Faroes and Greenland are not. No tariff on books except children's picture-books from non-EU. No import licenses required. Importers must use longest of alternative credit terms in contract, otherwise no exchange controls. 25% VAT on books.
Copyright: UCC, Berne, Florence (see Copyright Conventions, pg xi)

Aarhus Universitetsforlag (Aarhus University Press)+
Langelandsegade 177, 8200 Aarhus N
Tel: 89425370 *Fax:* 89425380
E-mail: unipress@au.dk
Web Site: www.unipress.dk

Key Personnel
Man Dir: Claes Hvidbak *E-mail:* ch@unipress.au.dk
Sales Manager: Sanne Lind Hansen *Tel:* (45) 89425376 *E-mail:* slh@unipress.au.dk
Founded: 1985
Member of International Association of Scholarly Publishers.
Subjects: Anthropology, Archaeology, Asian Studies, Biblical Studies, Drama, Theater, Language Arts, Linguistics, Literature, Literary Criticism, Essays, Philosophy, Psychology, Psychiatry, Religion - Other, Social Sciences, Sociology, Theology
ISBN Prefix(es): 87-7288
Total Titles: 650 Print
Distributed by David Brown Book Co (USA & Canada); Lavis Marketing (UK & Eire)
Distributor for Aalborg University Press; Jutland Archaeological Society
Warehouse: Katrinebjergvej 89B, 8200 Aarhus N

Academic Press, see Akademisk Forlag

Agertofts Forlag A/S+
Egedal 1C, 2690 Karlsunde
Tel: 046151248 *Fax:* 046151248
Key Personnel
Man Dir: Ejnar Agertoft
Founded: 1986
ISBN Prefix(es): 87-88014; 87-89970; 87-7878
Bookshop(s): The Children's Bookshop, Kobmagergade 50, DK-1150 Copenhagen K

Akademisk Forlag+
PO Box 54, 1002 Copenhagen K
Tel: 33 43 40 80 *Fax:* 33 43 40 99
E-mail: info@akademisk.dk
Web Site: www.akademisk.dk
Key Personnel
Man Dir: Helle Lehrmann Madsen
Marketing: Gitte Kolbaek Jensen
Founded: 1962
Subjects: Economics, Education, Engineering (General), History, Language Arts, Linguistics, Law, Medicine, Nursing, Dentistry, Philosophy, Psychology, Psychiatry, Science (General), Social Sciences, Sociology
ISBN Prefix(es): 87-500
Subsidiaries:

Alinea A/S+
PO Box 2159, 1016 Copenhagen
Tel: 33694666 *Fax:* 33694660
E-mail: alinea@alinea.dk; skoleservice@alinea.dk
Web Site: www.alinea.dk
Key Personnel
Man Dir: Jan B Thomsen
Founded: 1996
ISBN Prefix(es): 87-23
Parent Company: Munksgaard

Alma+
Kaalundsvej 13, 3400 Hillerod
Tel: 48 25 54 41 *Fax:* 48 25 20 41
Key Personnel
Chief Executive: Susanne Vebel
Founded: 1984
Specialize in picture books.
Subjects: Fiction
ISBN Prefix(es): 87-7243; 87-985145
Shipping Address: Stabrand Spedition, Billedvej 8, Frihavnen, DK-2100 Copenhagen O
Warehouse: Jernholmen 29, DK-2650 Hvidovre
Orders to: DBK, Siljangade 2-8, Box 1731, DK-2300 Copenhagen S

Forlaget alokke AS+
Porskaervej 15, Nim, 8700 Horsens
Tel: 75671119 *Fax:* 75671074
E-mail: alokke@get2net.dk

Key Personnel
President: Bertil Toft Hansen
Founded: 1977
Member of Danish Publishers Association.
Subjects: Advertising, English as a Second Language
ISBN Prefix(es): 87-592; 87-87777

Amanda
Rathsacksvej 7, 1862 Frederiksberg C
Tel: 33790110 *Fax:* 33790011
E-mail: forlag@dansklf.dk
Key Personnel
Editorial Dir: Emborg Uhd Gert
ISBN Prefix(es): 87-89537

Forlaget Apostrof ApS+
Berggreensgade 24, Postboks 2580, 2100 Copenhagen O
Tel: 3920 8420 *Fax:* 3920 8453
E-mail: info@apostrof.dk
Web Site: www.apostrof.dk
Key Personnel
Publisher: Mia Thestrup; Ole Thestrup
 E-mail: ot@apostrof.dk
Founded: 1980
Specialize in Psychology books.
ISBN Prefix(es): 87-591; 87-88002
Number of titles published annually: 30 Print
Total Titles: 400 Print
Warehouse: Dbks Forlagsekspedition, Siljangade 2-8, 2300 Copenhagen S

Arkitektens Forlag
Strandgade 27 A, 1401 Copenhagen K
Tel: 32836900 *Fax:* 32836940
E-mail: eksp@arkfo.dk
Web Site: www.arkitektens-forlag.dk
Key Personnel
Dir: Kim Dirckinck-Holmfeld
Founded: 1949
Subjects: Architecture & Interior Design
ISBN Prefix(es): 87-7407

Arnkrone Forlaget A/S
Fuglebaekvej 4, 2770 Kastrup
Tel: 32507000 *Fax:* 32522652
Key Personnel
Man Dir: J Juul Rasmussen
Founded: 1941
Subjects: Art, Ethnicity, Medicine, Nursing, Dentistry
ISBN Prefix(es): 87-87007

Aschehoug Dansk Forlag A/S+
8 Landemaerket, 1017 Copenhagen K
Mailing Address: PO Box 2179, 1017 Copenhagen K
Tel: 33305522 *Fax:* 33305822
E-mail: info@ash.egmont.com
Web Site: www.ascheoug.dk
Key Personnel
Man Dir, Rights & Permissions: Anette Wad
Production: Finn Larsen
Publicity: Bente Reinvaldt
Founded: 1977
Subjects: Biography, Cookery, Fiction, Health, Nutrition, How-to, Maritime
Total Titles: 900 Print
Parent Company: Egmont
Imprints: Sesan

Atuakkiorfik A/S Det Greenland Publishers+
Hans Egedesvej a, Postboks 840, 3900 Nuuk (Greenland)
Tel: 322122 *Fax:* 322500
E-mail: henri@atuakkiorfik.gl
Web Site: www.atuakkiorfik.gl
Key Personnel
Man Dir: Nukaaraq Eugenius
Manager: Ove-Karl Berthelsen

Founded: 1956
The Greenlandic Publishing House.
Also acts as Educational book publisher, public relations.
Subjects: Art, Education, Fiction, Nonfiction (General)
ISBN Prefix(es): 87-588
Number of titles published annually: 35 Print

Bibelselskabets Forlag og Vajsenhusets Forlag+
Det danske Bibelselskab, 50 Frederiksborggade, DK-1360 Copenhagen K
Tel: 33127835 *Fax:* 33932150
E-mail: bibelselskabet@bibelselskabet.dk
Web Site: www.bibelselskabet.dk
Key Personnel
General Secretary: Rev Morten Aagaard
Publishing Secretary International Rights: Maiann Uhrlund-Wille *E-mail:* mariann@bibelselskab.dk
Founded: 1814
ISBN Prefix(es): 87-7523

Bierman og Bierman I/S
Vestergade 126, 7200 Grindsted
Tel: 75320288 *Fax:* 75321548
E-mail: mail@bierman.dk
Web Site: www.bierman.dk
Key Personnel
Man Dir: Bo Lorentzen; Tom Selmer-Petersen
Founded: 1968
Subjects: Management

Blackwell Munksgaaard
Formerly Munksgaard International Publishers Ltd
Norre Sogade 35, 1370 Copenhagen K
Mailing Address: PO Box 2148, 1016 Copenhagen K
Tel: 77333333 *Fax:* 77333377
E-mail: headoffice@munksgaard.dk
Web Site: www.blackwellmunksgaard.com
Key Personnel
Chairman of the Board: Rene Olivieri
Man Dir: Lise Baltzer *E-mail:* lba@munksgaard.dk
Medical Sales Manager: Eric Rozario
 E-mail: er@munksgaard.dk
Manager, Online Journals: Katrine Flindt Christensen *E-mail:* kfc@munksgaard.dk
Founded: 1917
ISBN Prefix(es): 87-16
Parent Company: Blackwell Publishing Ltd, United Kingdom
Orders to: Blackwell Science Ltd, Journal Customer Services, PO Box 88, Oxford OX2 0EL, United Kingdom *Tel:* (01865) 206126 *Fax:* (01865) 206219 *E-mail:* journals.cs@blacksci.co.uk

Bogan's Forlag+
Kastaniebakken 8, 3540 Lynge
Tel: 48188055 *Fax:* 48188769
Key Personnel
Owner & Publisher: Evan Bogan
Founded: 1974
Subjects: Astrology, Occult, Health, Nutrition, Humor, Nonfiction (General), Science (General)
ISBN Prefix(es): 87-87533; 87-7466; 87-7525
Number of titles published annually: 30 Print
Total Titles: 250 Print
Imprints: My Best Book
Warehouse: DBK, Siljangade 6, DK-2300 Copenhagen S *Tel:* (45) 32697788 *Fax:* (45) 32697789

Bogfabrikken Fakta ApS
Jacob Dannefaerds Vej 6, 1973 Frederiksberg C
Tel: 35373533 *Fax:* 35373299

Subjects: Crafts, Games, Hobbies, Environmental Studies, Fashion, Nonfiction (General), Science (General), Transportation
ISBN Prefix(es): 87-7771
Parent Company: K D - Consult A/S

Bonnier Publications AS+
Amager Strandvej 26, DK - 2300 Copenhagen S
Tel: 32833100 *Fax:* 32833123
Web Site: www.bonnierpublications.com
Key Personnel
Man Dir: Michael Cordsen
Founded: 1966
Subjects: Criminology, Fiction, Military Science, Western Fiction
ISBN Prefix(es): 82-535; 82-92001
Parent Company: Bonnier AB
Branch Office(s)
Nils Hansens Vei 13, N - 0604 Oslo, Norway

Bonniers Specialmagasiner A/S Bogdivisionen+
Strandboulevarden 130, 2100 Copenhagen 0
Tel: 39 17 20 00 *Fax:* 39 17 23 00
Telex: 15712 bonmag dk
Key Personnel
Publisher: Jette Juliusson
Founded: 1989
Subjects: Fiction, Nonfiction (General)
ISBN Prefix(es): 87-7741
Parent Company: Bonnier Publication A/S
Subsidiaries: Autour Du Fil, Editions Bonnier; Bonniers Blade OG Boker
Book Club(s): Bogklubben 12 Boger A/S (jointly owned with Lindhardt Ringhof) & Munksgaard
Warehouse: Bonniers Boger, Islevdalvej 148, 2610 Rodovre

Borgens Forlag A/S+
Valbygardsvej 33, DK-2500 Valby
Tel: 36 15 36 15 *Fax:* 36 15 36 16
E-mail: post@borgen.dk
Web Site: www.borgen.dk
Key Personnel
Chairman: Jarl Borgen
Man Dir: Niels Borgen
Editorial Dir: Helle Borgen
Production: Dennis Stovring
Sales: Jan Wass
Rights & Permissions Manager: Mette Nymark
 E-mail: mnymark@borgen.dk
Founded: 1948
Subjects: Alternative, Animals, Pets, Art, Astrology, Occult, Behavioral Sciences, Child Care & Development, Crafts, Games, Hobbies, Education, Environmental Studies, Fiction, Health, Nutrition, How-to, Human Relations, Humor, Literature, Literary Criticism, Essays, Music, Dance, Nonfiction (General), Philosophy, Poetry, Psychology, Psychiatry, Regional Interests, Religion - Other, Self-Help
ISBN Prefix(es): 87-418; 87-21
Number of titles published annually: 250 Print; 5 Audio
Total Titles: 2,000 Print; 10 Audio
Subsidiaries: Hekla; Sommer & Sorensen; Forlaget Vindrose A/S
Book Club(s): Borgens Bogklub
Orders to: DBK-bogdistribution, Siljangade 2-8, DK-2300 Copenhagen S

Bornegudstjeneste-Forlaget+
25 Korskaervej, 7000 Fredericia
Tel: 75934455 *Fax:* 75924275
E-mail: lohse@imh.dk
Key Personnel
Dir: Finn Andersen
Founded: 1868
ISBN Prefix(es): 87-87828; 87-89682

Borsens Forlag
Montergade 19, 1140 Cophenhagen K
Tel: 33320102 *Fax:* 33935422
E-mail: borsens.forlag@borsen.dk

Key Personnel
Publishing Manager, Editorial: Flemming Cumberland
Sales Manager: Bjarne Birch
Production: Svend Erik Larsen
Subjects: Management
ISBN Prefix(es): 87-7553; 87-7664; 87-7901; 87-88184

Ca Luna Forlaget+
Herningvej 74 1st, 8600 Silkeborg
Tel: 86828688 *Fax:* 86828664
E-mail: caluna@caluna.dk
Web Site: www.caluna.dk
Founded: 1995
Subjects: *Special in:* New age books
Total Titles: 10 Print

Carit Andersens Forlag A/S
Affiliate of Mercantila Publishers A/S
18 Upsalagade, 2100 Copenhagen O27
Tel: 436222 *Fax:* 435151
E-mail: info@caritandersens.dk
Web Site: www.caritandersen.dk
Key Personnel
Publisher: Erik Albrechtsen
Founded: 1982
Subjects: Fiction, Nonfiction (General)
ISBN Prefix(es): 87-424

Forlaget Carlsen A/S+
Krogshojvej 32, 2880 Bagsvaerd
Tel: 44443233 *Fax:* 44443633
E-mail: carlsen@carlsen.dk
Web Site: www.carlsen.dk
Key Personnel
Man Dir: Jesper Holm
Founded: 1942
Subjects: Humor
ISBN Prefix(es): 87-562
Number of titles published annually: 300 Print; 3 CD-ROM; 75 Audio
Total Titles: 2,000 Print; 8 CD-ROM; 120 Audio
Online services available through www.carlsen.dk.
Parent Company: Bonniers Forlagene A/S
Ultimate Parent Company: Bonnier Media ATS
Imprints: Carlsen Comics
Subsidiaries: Carlsen Book Production
Book Club(s): Bogklubben Rasmus & Den Faktyrlige Boklub
Warehouse: Holme Forlags Service, Lise Lundvej 4, DK-4791 Borre *Tel:* 55812252 *Fax:* 55 812078
Holme Forlag Service APS
Semil Forlag NE A/S

Carlsen Comics, *imprint of* Forlaget Carlsen A/S

Forlaget Centrum (Central Publishers)+
Imprint of Bonnier
Store Kongensgade 92, 3tv, 1264 Copenhagen K
Tel: 33 32 12 06 *Fax:* 33 32 12 07
E-mail: info@forlaget-centrum.dk
Key Personnel
Publisher: Lisbeth Moller-Madsen
Founded: 1979
Subjects: Fiction, Nonfiction (General)
ISBN Prefix(es): 87-583

Cicero-Chr Erichsens
Vester Voldgade 83, 1552 Copenhagen V
Tel: 33160308 *Fax:* 33160307
E-mail: info@cicero.dk
Web Site: www.cicero.dk *Cable:* BOGERICH
Key Personnel
Dir: Niels Gudbergsen; Alis Caspersen
Ed: Carsten Berthelsen; Anders Mejlbjerg
Founded: 1902
Subjects: Fiction, How-to, Mysteries
ISBN Prefix(es): 87-7714; 87-555

Copenhagen, *imprint of* Spektrum Forlagsaktieselskab

Copenhagen Business School Press
Solbjergvej 3, 2000 Copenhagen F
Tel: (45) 38153960 *Fax:* (45) 38153962
E-mail: cbspress@cbs.dk
Web Site: www.cbspress.dk

Dafolo Forlag+
Division of Dafolo A/S
Dafolo A/S, Suderbovej 22-24, DK-9900 Frederikshavn
Tel: 96206666 *Fax:* 98431388
E-mail: dafolo@dafolo.dk
Web Site: www.dafolo.dk
Key Personnel
Man Dir: Michael Schelde *E-mail:* ms@dafolo.dk
Founded: 1960
Subjects: Education, Foreign Countries, History, Specialize in Elementary Textbooks
ISBN Prefix(es): 87-7794

The Danish Literature Centre
Kongens Nytorv 3, 3, 1021 Copenhagen
Mailing Address: Postboks 3012, 1021 Copenhagen
Tel: 33744500 *Fax:* 33911545
E-mail: danlit@danlit.dk
Web Site: www.danlit.dk; www.literaturenet.dk
Key Personnel
Chief Sub-Editor: Annette Bach
Founded: 1990
Promotion of Danish literature abroad & foundation for translation grants.
Subjects: Drama, Theater, Fiction, Literature, Literary Criticism, Essays, Poetry

Danish National Library Authority+
Tempovej 7-11, 2750 Ballerup
Tel: 44867777 *Fax:* 44867891
E-mail: dbc@dbc.dk
Web Site: www.dbc.dk
Key Personnel
Man Dir: Mogens Brabrand Jensen
Editor: Kirsten Waneck
Founded: 1991
Subjects: Library & Information Sciences
ISBN Prefix(es): 87-552

Danmarks Forvaltningshojskole Forlaget
6 Lindevangs Alle, 2000 Frederiksberg
Tel: 38 14 52 00 *Fax:* 38 14 53 45
E-mail: le@dkdfh.dk
Key Personnel
Dir: Peter Mehlbye
ISBN Prefix(es): 87-7392

Dansk Historisk Handbogsforlag ApS
Buddingevej 87 A, DK-2800 Lyngby
Tel: 45 93 48 00 *Fax:* 45 93 47 47
E-mail: genos@worldonline.dk
Key Personnel
Owner, Man Dir: Henning Jensen
Founded: 1976
Subjects: Biography, Ethnicity, Genealogy, History, Law, Regional Interests
ISBN Prefix(es): 87-85207; 87-88742; 87-90222
Parent Company: Tordenskjold Forlag ApS
Subsidiaries: Juridisk Forlag

Dansk Psykologisk Forlag
Stockholmsgade 29, 2100 Copenhagen 0
Tel: 35381655 *Fax:* 35381655
E-mail: dk-psych@dpf.dk
Web Site: www.dpf.dk
Key Personnel
Man Dir: Hans Gerhardt
Chief Editor: Lone Berg Jensen
Member of European Test Publishers Group.
Subjects: Psychology, Psychiatry
ISBN Prefix(es): 87-7706; 87-87580

Dansk Teknologisk Institut, Forlaget
Postboks 141, 2630 Taastrup
Tel: 72 20 20 00 *Fax:* 72 20 20 19
E-mail: info@teknologisk.dk
Web Site: www.teknologisk.dk
Telex: 33416 ti dk *Cable:* TEKNOLOGISK
Key Personnel
Information Dept Manager: Leif Pjetursson
Subjects: Crafts, Games, Hobbies, Labor, Industrial Relations
ISBN Prefix(es): 87-7511; 87-7756

Djof Publishing Jurist-og Okonomforbundets Forlag
17, Lyngbyvej, 2100 Copenhagen O
Mailing Address: Postboks 2702, 2100 Copenhagen O
Tel: 39 13 55 00 *Fax:* 39 13 55 55
E-mail: fl@djoef.dk
Web Site: www.djoef-forlag.dk
Key Personnel
President: Rolf Tvedt
Founded: 1959
Member of IUS-Nordica, Nordic Legal Publishers Group.
Subjects: Economics, Finance, Law, Social Sciences, Sociology
ISBN Prefix(es): 87-574; 87-7318; 87-986304
Subsidiaries: Handelshojskolens Forlag; Nyt Juridisk Forlag

Egmont-Easy Readers+
8 Landemaerket, 1119 Copenhagen K
Tel: 33305830
E-mail: um@ash.egmont.com
Web Site: www.easyreader.dk
Subjects: Language Arts, Linguistics
Number of titles published annually: 10 Print
Total Titles: 200 Print

Egmont Group
Vognmagergade 11, 1148 Copenhagen K
Tel: 33305550 *Fax:* 33321902
E-mail: egmont@egmont.com; info@egt.egmont.com
Web Site: www.egmont.com
Key Personnel
Vice President, Communications: Lene Balleby
ISBN Prefix(es): 87-982380

Egmont Lademann A/S+
Gerdasgade 37, DK-2500 Valby
Tel: 36 15 66 00 *Fax:* 36 44 11 62
Web Site: www.egmont.com; www.egmontbogklub.dk (Book Club)
Founded: 1954
Specialize in general illustrated nonfiction, CD-ROM, commercial fiction, children book upmarket fiction & true stories.
ISBN Prefix(es): 87-15; 87-632
Parent Company: Egmont Group

Egmont Serieforlaget A/S
Vognmagergade 9, 1148 Copenhagen K
Tel: 33305000 *Fax:* 33305510
Web Site: www.serieforlaget.dk
Key Personnel
Marketing Dir: Jesper Christiansen
ISBN Prefix(es): 87-89601

Christian Ejlers' Forlag aps+
Brolaeggerstraede 4, 1711 Copenhagen K
Mailing Address: Postboks 2228, 1018 Copenhagen K
Tel: 33122114 *Fax:* 33122884
E-mail: liber@ce-publishers.dk
Web Site: www.ejlers.dk
Key Personnel
Publisher: Christian Ejlers

Clerk: Rie Molgaard
Founded: 1967
Subjects: Architecture & Interior Design, Art, Biography, Cookery, Education, History, Law, Nonfiction (General)
ISBN Prefix(es): 87-7241
Number of titles published annually: 20 Print; 1 CD-ROM; 1 Audio
Total Titles: 100 Print; 3 CD-ROM; 3 Audio

FADL's Forlag A/S (Foreningen af danske Laegestuderendes Forlag)+
Blegdamsvej 30, DK-2200 Copenhagen N
Tel: 35356287 *Fax:* 35366229
E-mail: forlag@fadl.dk
Web Site: forlag.fadl.dk
Key Personnel
Man Dir: Hans Jespersen
Founded: 1962
Member of STM.
Subjects: Biological Sciences, Medicine, Nursing, Dentistry
ISBN Prefix(es): 87-7437; 87-7749

Forlaget for Faglitteratur A/S
Vandkunsten 6, 1467 Copenhagen K
Tel: 33137900 *Fax:* 33145156
Subjects: Medicine, Nursing, Dentistry, Technology
ISBN Prefix(es): 87-573

Faktor Funf, *imprint of* Kaleidoscope Publishers Ltd

Ficcion Espanola, *imprint of* Kaleidoscope Publishers Ltd

Fiction Factory, *imprint of* Kaleidoscope Publishers Ltd

Fiction Francaise, *imprint of* Kaleidoscope Publishers Ltd

Forum Publishers
Kobmagergade 62, 1, 1019 Copenhagen K
Tel: 33411830 *Fax:* 33411831
E-mail: gyldendal@gyldendal.dk
Web Site: www.gyldendal.dk *Cable:* FORUMBOOKS COPENHAGEN
Key Personnel
Man Dir: Werner Svendsen
Editor, Juvenile & Children: Lotte Nyholm
Founded: 1940
Subjects: Fiction, History, Humor, Mysteries
ISBN Prefix(es): 87-553
Parent Company: Gyldendalske Boghandel - Nordisk Forlag A/S
Divisions: Spektrum Publishers (at above address)

Fremad A/S
Kobmagergade 62, 1019 Copenhagen K
Mailing Address: Kobmagergade 62, 1019 Copenhagen K
Tel: 33411810 *Fax:* 33411811
Web Site: www.fremad.dk *Cable:* Bogfremad
Key Personnel
Man Dir: Niels Kolle *E-mail:* niels_koelle@gyldendal.dk
Founded: 1912
Subjects: Business, Child Care & Development, Economics, Fiction, Health, Nutrition, History, Language Arts, Linguistics, Mathematics, Science (General), Social Sciences, Sociology
ISBN Prefix(es): 87-557
Bookshop(s): Boghandelen Fremad, Frederikssundsvej 168, Bronshoj, DK-2700 Copenhagen

J Frimodts Forlag+
Korskaervej 25, 7000 Fredericia
Tel: 75334455 *Fax:* 75924275
E-mail: lohse@imh.dk
Key Personnel
Man Dir: Finn Andersen
Subjects: Fiction, Religion - Protestant
ISBN Prefix(es): 87-7446
Associate Companies: Lohses Forlag

Forlaget FSR A/S (1T1D A/S)+
Nytorv 5, 1405 Copenhagen K
Tel: 33740700 *Fax:* 33933077
E-mail: thomson@thi.dk
Key Personnel
Man Dir: Vibeke Christiansen
Subjects: Accounting, Business, Education, Law
ISBN Prefix(es): 87-7747; 87-88109; 87-980953
Parent Company: The Thomson Corporation

GEC Gads Forlag Aktieselskab af 1994
Klosterstraede 9, 1157 Copenhagen K
Tel: 33150558 *Fax:* 33110800
E-mail: marketing@gads-forlag.dk
Web Site: www.gads-forlag.dk *Cable:* BOGGAD
Key Personnel
Man Dir: Axel Kielland
International Rights: Lars Boesgaard
Founded: 1855
Subjects: Biological Sciences, Cookery, Crafts, Games, Hobbies, Economics, Education, English as a Second Language, Environmental Studies, Gardening, Plants, History, Mathematics, Natural History, Nonfiction (General), Physics, Travel
ISBN Prefix(es): 87-12; 87-13; 87-577
Associate Companies: Alinea A/S; Systime A/S
Bookshop(s): G E C Gads Boglader A/S GADs, Antikuariat Fiolstr 31-33, Copenhagen

Forlaget GMT+
Havet 66 A, 8585 Glaesborg
Tel: 86386095
Key Personnel
Publishers: Hans Jorn Christensen; Erik Bjorn Olsen
Founded: 1971
Subjects: Education, Fiction, Government, Political Science, History, Philosophy, Psychology, Psychiatry, Social Sciences, Sociology
ISBN Prefix(es): 87-7330

Greenland Publishers, see Atuakkiorfik A/S Det Greenland Publishers

Grevas Forlag
Auningvej 33, Sdr Kastrup, 8544 Morke
Tel: 86997065
Key Personnel
Sales & Man Dir: Luise Hemmer Pihl
Founded: 1966
Subjects: Art, Biography, Fiction, Poetry
ISBN Prefix(es): 87-7235

Gyldendalske Boghandel - Nordisk Forlag A/S
Klareboderne 3, 1001 Copenhagen K
Tel: 33755555 *Fax:* 33755556
E-mail: gyldendal@gyldendal.dk
Web Site: www.gyldendal.dk
Telex: 15887 Gyldaldk *Cable:* GYLDENDALSKE
Key Personnel
Dir: Per Hedeman; Jorn Lund
Man Dir: Stig Andersen; Johannes Riis
Juveniles: Flemming Moldrup
Nonfiction: Lars Boesgaard
Dictionaries: Liisa Theilgaard
Audiovisual: Ken Barnewitz
Marketing Dir: Tine Smedegaard Andersen
Rights & Permissions, Juveniles: Eyvind Thorsen
Rights & Permissions, Adult Fiction & Nonfiction: Esthi Kunz
Rights & Permissions, Nonfiction: Louise Englyst
Founded: 1770
Subjects: Art, Biography, Education, Fiction, History, How-to, Medicine, Nursing, Dentistry, Music, Dance, Philosophy, Poetry, Psychology, Psychiatry, Science (General), Social Sciences, Sociology
ISBN Prefix(es): 87-01; 87-00
Subsidiaries: Forlaget Forum A/S; Samlerens Forlag A/S; Forlaget Fremad A/S; Tiderne Skifter; Spektrum A/S; Rosinante Forlag A/S; Hans Reitzels Forlag A/S; Host & Sons Forlag A/S; Hans Reitzels Forlag A/S; Rosinante Forlag A/S
Book Club(s): Gyldendals Bogklub; Gyldendals Bornebogklub; Samlerens Bogklub

P Haase & Sons Forlag A/S+
Loevstraede 8, 2 tv, 1152 Copenhagen K
Tel: 33144175 *Fax:* 33115959
E-mail: haase@haase.dk
Web Site: www.haase.dk
Key Personnel
Man Dir: Michael Haase
Foreign Rights: Nina Jensen *E-mail:* nj@haase.dk
Founded: 1877
Subjects: Education, Fiction, Health, Nutrition, Humor, Maritime, Nonfiction (General)
ISBN Prefix(es): 87-559
Imprints: Rasmus Naver

Edition Wilhelm Hansen AS
Bornholmsgade 1, 1266 Copenhagen K
Tel: 33117888 *Fax:* 33148178
E-mail: ewh@ewh.dk
Web Site: www.ewh.dk; www.wilhelm-hansen.dk
Cable: MUSIKHANSEN
Key Personnel
Man Dir: Tine Birger Christensen
Founded: 1857
Subjects: Art, Education, Music, Dance
ISBN Prefix(es): 87-7455
Parent Company: Music Sales Ltd, 8/9 Frith St, London W1V 5TZ, United Kingdom

Hekla Forlag+
Valbygaardsvej 33, DK-2500 Valby
Tel: 36 15 36 15 *Fax:* 36 15 36 16
Key Personnel
Publisher: Helle Borgen
Founded: 1979
Subjects: Fiction, Nonfiction (General)
ISBN Prefix(es): 87-7474
Number of titles published annually: 5 Print
Total Titles: 20 Print
Parent Company: Borgens Forlag A/S
Orders to: DBK-bogdistribution, Siljangade 2-8, DK-2300 Copenhagen 0

Hernovs Forlag+
Siljangade 6, 4, 2300 Copenhagen S
Tel: 32963314 *Fax:* 32960446
E-mail: admin@hernov.dk
Web Site: www.hernov.dk
Key Personnel
Man Editor: Else Hernov
Founded: 1941
Subjects: Fiction, Nonfiction (General)
ISBN Prefix(es): 87-7215; 87-590
Subsidiaries: Vinimport ApS
Warehouse: DBK-Dansk Boghandleres Kommissionsanstalt, Siljangade 6, 2300 Copenhagen S

Forlaget Hjulet
Bakkegardsalle 9 kld, 1804 Frederiksberg C
Tel: 31310900 *Fax:* 31310900
E-mail: aloa@gte2net.dk
Key Personnel
Contact: Vagn Plenge
Founded: 1976
Subjects: Cookery, Developing Countries, Fiction, Literature, Literary Criticism, Essays, Travel

ISBN Prefix(es): 87-87403; 87-89213
Subsidiaries: Foerlaget Hjule

Holkenfeldt 3
Fuglevadsvej 71, 2800 Lyngby
Tel: 93 12 21 *Fax:* 93 82 41
Key Personnel
Man Dir: Kay Holkenfeldt
Subjects: Nonfiction (General)
ISBN Prefix(es): 87-90368; 87-7720; 87-89906

Host & Son Publishers Ltd+
Kobmagergade 62, 1018 Copenhagen
Mailing Address: PO Box 2212, 1018 Copenhagen K
Tel: 33382888 *Fax:* 33382898
E-mail: host@euroconnect.dk *Cable:* BOOKHOST
Key Personnel
Man Dir: Erik C Lindgren
Editorial, Reference Books: Kirsten Fasmer; Hans Kristian Harbo
Editorial, Juvenile Books: Christel Amundsen
Editorial, Young Adults: Anne Morch-Hansen; Nanna Gyldenkaerne
Founded: 1836
Subjects: Crafts, Games, Hobbies, Environmental Studies, Fiction, History, Regional Interests
ISBN Prefix(es): 87-14
Parent Company: Gyldendalske Boghandel, Nordisk Forlag A/S
Warehouse: NBC, Bokvej 10-12, 4690 Haslev

Forlaget Hovedland+
21 Stenvej, 8270 Hojbjerg
Tel: 86276500 *Fax:* 86276537
E-mail: mail@hovedland.dk
Web Site: www.hovedland.dk
Key Personnel
Publisher: Steen Piper
Founded: 1984
Subjects: Biography, Crafts, Games, Hobbies, Economics, Environmental Studies, Fiction, History, Humor, Literature, Literary Criticism, Essays, Mysteries, Nonfiction (General), Philosophy, Self-Help, Social Sciences, Sociology, Sports, Athletics, Theology
ISBN Prefix(es): 87-7739; 87-88589

IBIS
Norrebrogade 68B, 2200 Copenhagen N
Tel: 35358788 *Fax:* 35350696
E-mail: ibis@ibis.dk
Web Site: www.ibis.dk
Telex: 1585 0 wus dk
Key Personnel
Editorial Dir, Rights & Permissions: Virginia Allen Jensen
Founded: 1972
ISBN Prefix(es): 87-87804
Parent Company: International Children's Book Service (ICBS)

Ingenioeren/Boger (Ingineering Books Danish Technical Press)+
Skelbaekgade 4, 1503 Copenhagen V
Tel: 33265300 *Fax:* 33265390
E-mail: bogservice@ing.dk
Web Site: www.bog.ing.dk
Key Personnel
Man Dir: Per Westergaard
Manager Book Dept: Henrik Larsen *E-mail:* hla@ing.dk
Founded: 1948
Subjects: Business, Computer Science, Engineering (General)
ISBN Prefix(es): 87-571
Number of titles published annually: 80 Print; 4 CD-ROM; 3 E-Book
Parent Company: Ingenioeren A/S
Book Club(s): Ingenioeren/Bogklubben

Interpresse A/S+
Krogshoejvej 32, 2880 Bagsvaerd
Tel: 33337535 *Fax:* 33337505
Key Personnel
Man Dir: Haahon W Isachsen
Founded: 1954
Subjects: Fiction, Film, Video, Humor
ISBN Prefix(es): 87-456; 87-7529; 87-90008
Parent Company: Semic International AB, Sweden
Shipping Address: Bent Bagger Speditsion, Peder Skrams Gade 11, DK-1054 Copenhagen K

Jespersen og Pio, see Lindhardt og Ringhof

Kaleidoscope Publishers Ltd+
3 Klareboderne, 1001 Copenhagen K
Tel: 33755555 *Fax:* 33755544
E-mail: gujbt@gyldendal.dk
Web Site: www.kaleidoscope.publishers.dk; www.gyldendal.dk *Cable:* GYLDENDALSKE
Key Personnel
Publisher: Jens Bendtsen *Tel:* 33755509
E-mail: jens_bendtsen@gyldendal.dk
Founded: 1983
Subjects: Education, English as a Second Language, Film, Video, Language Arts, Linguistics, Literature, Literary Criticism, Essays
ISBN Prefix(es): 87-7565; 87-431; 87-00
Parent Company: Gyldendal
Imprints: Faktor Funf; Ficcion Espanola; Fiction Factory; Fiction Francaise
Subsidiaries: Fiction Factory International Ltd/APS
Warehouse: Baekvej
Gyldendal
Haslev

KD - Consult A/S
Jakob Dannefaerds Vej 6, 1973 Frederiksberg C
Tel: 35373533 *Fax:* 35373299
Subsidiaries: Bogfabrikken Fakta ApS

Forlaget Klematis A/S+
One Ostre Skovvej, 8240 Risskov
Tel: 86175455 *Fax:* 86175959
E-mail: klematis@klematis.dk; production@klematis.dk
Web Site: www.klematis.dk
Key Personnel
President: Claus Dalby
Editor: Mette Jorgensen
Founded: 1987
Children's Craft, Fiction, Nonfiction.
Subjects: Crafts, Games, Hobbies, Fiction, Nonfiction (General)
ISBN Prefix(es): 87-7721; 87-7905
Shipping Address: JEURO Danmark, Baggeskaervej 6, DK-7400 Herning, M Stausholm
Warehouse: D B K, Siljangade 6-8, DK-2300 Kobenhavn S

Kraks Forlag AS
Virumgardsvej 21, 2830 Virum
Tel: 956500 *Fax:* 956565
E-mail: krak@krak.dk
Web Site: www.krak.dk
Key Personnel
Chief Executive & Rights & Permissions: Ib Topholm
Production, Editorial: Jorgen Pedersen
Publisher, Sales: Carsten Engsig
Founded: 1770
Subjects: Regional Interests
ISBN Prefix(es): 87-7225

Lindhardt og Ringhof+
Frederiksborggade 1, 1360 Copenhagen K
Tel: 33695000 *Fax:* 33695001
E-mail: lr@lrforlag.dk

Web Site: www.logr.dk *Cable:* ELETEREDIT
Key Personnel
Man Dir: Lars Ringhof
Editor-in-Chief: Hans Henrick Schwab
Publisher: Liv Bentsen
Founded: 1971
Subjects: Fiction, Nonfiction (General)
ISBN Prefix(es): 87-595; 87-7560
Parent Company: Bonniers & Stockholm
Divisions: Jespersen og Pio
U.S. Office(s): Maria B Campbell Associates, United States
Book Club(s): Bogklubben 12 Boger (part owner)

Lohses Forlag+
Korskaervej 25, 7000 Fredericia
Tel: 75934455 *Fax:* 75924275
E-mail: lohse@imh.dk
Web Site: www.lohse.dk
Key Personnel
Dir: Finn Andersen
Founded: 1868
Subjects: Biblical Studies, Fiction, Religion - Other
ISBN Prefix(es): 87-564
Associate Companies: J Frimodts Forlag

Mallings ApS
Forlaget Carlsen A/S, Krogshujvej 32, 2880 Bagsvaerd
Tel: 44443233 *Fax:* 44443633
E-mail: carlsen@carlsen.dk
Web Site: www.carlsen.dk
Telex: 15817 Jmco *Cable:* Mallingbook
Key Personnel
Man Dir, Editorial, Rights & Permissions: Joachim Malling
Owner: Hannah Malling
Production: Michael Malling
Publicity: Dorthe Malling
Founded: 1975
Subjects: Education
ISBN Prefix(es): 87-7333

Mellemfolkeligt Samvirke+
Borgergade 14, 1300 Copenhagen K
Tel: 77310000 *Fax:* 77310101
E-mail: ms@ms-dan.dk
Web Site: www.ms.dk
Subjects: Asian Studies, Developing Countries, Economics, Energy, Environmental Studies, Ethnicity, Foreign Countries, Government, Political Science
ISBN Prefix(es): 87-7028; 87-7907
Bookshop(s): Verdenshjornet

Mercantila Publishers A/S
18 Upsalagade, 2100 Copenhagen
Tel: 35436222 *Fax:* 35435151
E-mail: info@mercantila.dk
Web Site: www.mercantila.dk
Key Personnel
Man Dir: Erik Albrechtsen
Founded: 1986
The guides to food transport are reference books with basic information about transporting perishables.
Subjects: Transportation, Specialize in food & food transport
ISBN Prefix(es): 87-89010
Associate Companies: Carit Andersens Forlag A/S

Mikro, *imprint of* Wisby & Wilkens

Forlaget Modtryk AMBA+
Anholtsgade 4-6, 8000 Aarhus C
Tel: 87317600 *Fax:* 87317601
E-mail: forlaget@modtryk.dk
Web Site: www.modtryk.dk
Telex: Mod

DENMARK

Key Personnel
Man Dir, Rights & Permissions: Preben Bach
Man Dir, Rights & Permissions (Textbooks): Ilse Noer
Sales: Niels Jorgen Jensen
Production: Henning Morch Jensen
Founded: 1972
Subjects: Fiction, Mysteries, Nonfiction (General)
ISBN Prefix(es): 87-87458; 87-7394; 87-87620; 87-87817; 87-88135

Munksgaard International Publishers Ltd, *see* Blackwell Munksgaaard

Museum Tusculanum Press+
University of Copenhagen, Njalsgade 92, 2300 Copenhagen S
Tel: 35329109 *Fax:* 35329113
E-mail: mtp@mtp.dk
Web Site: www.mtp.dk
Key Personnel
Dir: Marianne Alenius *Tel:* 35329110
  E-mail: alenius@mtp.dk
Marketing: Marius Hansteen *E-mail:* marius@mtp.dk
Marketing & Promotion Manager: Nana Klitgaard
  Tel: (045) 35 32 9110 *E-mail:* nana@mtp.dk
Founded: 1975
Subjects: Anthropology, Antiques, Archaeology, Art, Asian Studies, Foreign Countries, History, Language Arts, Linguistics, Literature, Literary Criticism, Essays, Philosophy, Religion - Other, Social Sciences, Sociology, Women's Studies
ISBN Prefix(es): 87-980131; 87-88073; 87-7289
Number of titles published annually: 100 Print
Total Titles: 600 Print
Distributed by Gazelle Book Service Ltd (Europe, excluding Scandinavia & Germany); ISBS International Specialized Bookservices (USA & Canada)

My Best Book, *imprint of* Bogan's Forlag

Rasmus Naver, *imprint of* P Haase & Sons Forlag A/S

New Era Publications International ApS+
Subsidiary of New Era Publications Private Ltd
Store Kongensgade 53, 1264 Copenhagen K
Tel: (045) 33736666 *Fax:* (045) 33736633
E-mail: books@newerapublications.com
Web Site: www.newerapublications.com
Key Personnel
Man Dir: Ruth Lanciai
Senior Vice President: Thomas Bucher; Christiane Dumas
Publicity Dir & Foreign Rights Dir: Stephen Shinn
Founded: 1969
Subjects: Art, Education, Management, Philosophy, Science Fiction, Fantasy, Self-Help
ISBN Prefix(es): 87-7336; 87-87347; 87-7816; 87-7968
Subsidiaries: New Era Publications Australia Pty Ltd; New Era Publications Deutschland GmbH; New Era Publications Italia Srl; New Era Publications Japan Inc; New Era Publications Group; Continental Publications Pty Ltd; New Era Publications UK Ltd

Nyt Nordisk Forlag Arnold Busck A/S+
Kobmagergade 49, DK-1150 Copenhagen K
Tel: (045) 33733575 *Fax:* (045) 33733576
E-mail: nnf@nytnordiskforlag.dk
Web Site: www.nytnordiskforlag.dk
Key Personnel
Man Dir: Ole Arnold Busck
Dir: Jesper Toft Fensrig
Founded: 1896
Subjects: Art, Biography, Fiction, History, How-to, Medicine, Nursing, Dentistry, Music, Dance, Philosophy, Psychology, Psychiatry, Religion - Other, Science (General), Social Sciences, Sociology
ISBN Prefix(es): 87-17
Subsidiaries: Det Schonbergske Forlag A/S; Haandbog for Bygningsindustrien, HFB
Bookshop(s): Arnold Busck International Boghandel A/S, Kobmagergade 49, DK-1150 Copenhagen K *Tel:* (045) 33733500 *Fax:* (045) 33733535; Birkerod Boghandel & Kontorforsyning Arnold Busck A/S, Hovedgaden 37, DK-3460 Birkerod; Arnold Busck Antiquarian A/S, Fiolstraede 24, DK-1171 Copenhagen K *Tel:* (045) 33733545 *Fax:* (045) 33733587; Arnold Busck Boghandel A/S, Ballerup Centret, PO Box 604, DK-2750 Ballerup *Tel:* (045) 44979009 *Fax:* (045) 44682327; Arnold Busck Boghandel A/S, Stengade 51, PO Box 167, DK-3000 Helsingor *Tel:* (045) 49210128 *Fax:* (045) 49210111; Arnold Busck Boghandel A/S, Bredgade 18, DK-7400 Herning *Tel:* (045) 97120299 *Fax:* (045) 97120521; Arnold Busck Boghandel A/S, Ostergade 17, DK-7500 Holstebro *Tel:* (045) 97423433 *Fax:* (045) 97427722; Arnold Busck Boghandel A/S, Norregade 5, DK-4600 Koge *Tel:* (045) 56650254 *Fax:* (045) 56636005; Arnold Busck Boghandel A/S, Vestergade 82, DK-5000 Odense C *Tel:* (045) 66126803 *Fax:* (045) 66114670; Arnold Busck Boghandel A/S, Perlegade 8, DK-6400 Sonderborg *Tel:* (045) 74423800 *Fax:* (045) 74432240; Arnold Busck Boghandel A/S, Haderslev, Apotekergade 4, DK-6100 Haderslev *Tel:* (045) 74522703 *Fax:* (045) 74530582; Arnold Busck Boghandel, Nakskov, Sondergade 24, DK-4900 Nakskov *Tel:* (045) 54923246; Arnold Busck Boghandel, Nykobing F, Lilletorv, DK-4800 Nykobing F *Tel:* (045) 54850255; Arnold Busck Boghandel, Randers, Radhusstraede 2, DK-8900 Randers *Tel:* (045) 86420113 *Fax:* (045) 86409113; Bornenes Boghandel ApS, Kobmagergade 50, DK-1150 Copenhagen K *Tel:* (045) 33154466 *Fax:* (045) 33931460; Arnold Busck Boghandel, Maribo, Ostergade 5, DK-4930 Maribo *Tel:* (045) 53881244 *Fax:* (045) 53881525
Orders to: Nordisk Bog Center, Baekvej 2, DK-4690 Haslev *Tel:* (045) 56364010 *Fax:* (045) 56364038

Odense Universitetsbibliotek, *see* Syddansk Universitetsforlag

Olivia - det gronne forlag+
Frederiksholms Kanal 2/2, DK-1220 Copenhagen K
Tel: 33 15 67 44 *Fax:* 33 15 67 45
E-mail: books@olivia.dk
Web Site: www.olivia.dk
Key Personnel
President & Publisher: Kirsten Skaarup
Founded: 1986
Subjects: Alternative, Cookery, Crafts, Games, Hobbies, Health, Nutrition, Psychology, Psychiatry, Self-Help
ISBN Prefix(es): 87-89019; 87-90181; 87-7963
Warehouse: D B K Bogdistribution, Siljangade 2-8, 2300 Copenhagen S

Padagogisk Bogklub, *imprint of* Hans Reitzel Publishers Ltd

Palle Fogtdal A/S
22 Ostergade, 1100 Copenhagen K
Tel: 33153915 *Fax:* 33933505
Key Personnel
Man Dir: Palle Fogtdal
ISBN Prefix(es): 87-7248

Joergen Paludans Forlag ApS
Fiolstraede 16, 1171 Copenhagen K
Tel: 49751556 *Fax:* 49751537
Key Personnel
Man Dir: Joergen Paludan
Subjects: Economics, Education, Government, Political Science, History, Nonfiction (General), Psychology, Psychiatry
ISBN Prefix(es): 87-7230
Associate Companies: Erik Paludan International Booksellers

Politisk Revy+
Nansensgade 70/st, DK-1366 Copenhagen K
Tel: 33 91 41 41 *Fax:* 33 91 51 15
E-mail: politiskrevy@forlagene.dk
Web Site: www.forlagene.dk/politiskrevy
Key Personnel
Publisher: Johannes Sohlman *E-mail:* sohlman@danbbs.dk
Founded: 1963
Small press, Independent publisher.
Subjects: Fiction, Government, Political Science, Literature, Literary Criticism, Essays, Nonfiction (General), Philosophy, Photography, Poetry, Psychology, Psychiatry, Social Sciences, Sociology
ISBN Prefix(es): 87-7378; 87-85186
Total Titles: 250 Print
Warehouse: Nordisk Bogcenter A/S, Baekvej 2, Haslev DK-4690

Polyteknisk Forlag+
Anker Engelundsvej 1, DTU, Bygn 101 A, 2800 Lyngby
Tel: 77424344 *Fax:* 77424354
E-mail: poly@poly.dtu.dk
Web Site: www.polyteknisk.dk
Key Personnel
Man Dir: Peter Langford
Senior Editor: Ole Jorgensen
Founded: 1962
Subjects: Engineering (General), Science (General)
ISBN Prefix(es): 87-502

C A Reitzel A/S+
Norregade 20, 1165 Copenhagen K
Mailing Address: Postboks 1073, 1008 Copenhagen K
Tel: 33122400 *Fax:* 33140270
E-mail: info@careitzel.dk
Web Site: www.careitzel.dk
Key Personnel
Man Dir: Svend Olufsen
Founded: 1819
Subjects: Human Relations, Literature, Literary Criticism, Essays, Nonfiction (General), Philosophy, Science (General)
ISBN Prefix(es): 87-412

Hans Reitzel Publishers Ltd+
Kobmagergade 62, 1008 Copenhagen K
Mailing Address: PO Box 1073, 1008 Copenhagen K
Tel: 33382800 *Fax:* 33382808
E-mail: hrf@hansreitzel.dk
Web Site: www.hansreitzel.dk *Cable:* REITZELBOOKS
Key Personnel
Man Dir: Erik C Lindgren *E-mail:* lindgren@hansreitzel.dk
Editorial, Rights & Permissions: Ole Gammeltoft
  Tel: 3338 2813 *E-mail:* og@hansreitzel.dk; Andreas Bonnevie *Tel:* 3338 2812 *E-mail:* ab@hansreitzel.dk; Dorte Ipsen *Tel:* 3338 2815
  E-mail: di@hansreitzel.dk
Founded: 1949
Subjects: Education, Philosophy, Psychology, Psychiatry, Social Sciences, Sociology
ISBN Prefix(es): 87-412
Total Titles: 350 Print
Parent Company: Gyldendalske Boghandel
Ultimate Parent Company: Nordisk Forlag Ltd, United Kingdom

Imprints: Padagogisk Bogklub
Book Club(s): Padagogisk Bogklub (Educational Bookclub)
Warehouse: Nordisk Bog Center, Bcekvej 10-12, DK-4690 Haslev

Rhodos, International Science & Art Publishers
Strandgade 36, 1041 Copenhagen K
Tel: 32543020 *Fax:* 32543022
E-mail: rhodos@rhodos.com
Web Site: www.rhodos.dk *Cable:* SCIENCEBOOKS
Key Personnel
Man Dir: Niels Blaedel
ISBN Prefix(es): 87-7245; 87-7496

Rosenkilde & Bagger
Kronprinsensgade 3, Copenhagen K
Mailing Address: PO Box 111, DK - 2920 Charlottenlund
Tel: 33157044 *Fax:* 33937007
E-mail: r-b@rosenkilde-bagger.dk
Web Site: www.rosenkilde-bagger.dk
Key Personnel
Proprietor: Hans & Soren Bagger
Founded: 1941
Rare book department at above address.
Subjects: Science (General)
ISBN Prefix(es): 87-423

Samfundslitteratur+
Rosenorns Alle 11, 1970 Frederiksberg C
Tel: 35356366 *Fax:* 35357822
E-mail: slforlag@sl.cbs.dk
Web Site: www.samfundslitteratur.dk
Key Personnel
Man Dir: Mogens Eliasson *Tel:* 35356399
 E-mail: me@sl.cbs.dk
Editorial Dir, Rights & Permissions: Birgit Vra *Tel:* 35356399 *E-mail:* bv@sl.cbs.dk
Founded: 1967
Publishers at Copenhagen Business School.
Subjects: Accounting, Advertising, Business, Communications, Developing Countries, Economics, Education, English as a Second Language, Environmental Studies, Finance, History, Journalism, Language Arts, Linguistics, Management, Marketing, Public Administration, Religion - Protestant, Social Sciences, Sociology
ISBN Prefix(es): 87-593; 87-7313; 87-87322
Total Titles: 600 Print; 3 CD-ROM
Parent Company: Samfundslitterator
Distributor for The World Bank (Denmark)
Bookshop(s): Dalgas Have 15, DK-2000 Frederiksberg C; RUC, Bygn 01, Marbjergvej 35, 4000 Roskilde; Rosenorns Alle 11, 1970 Frederiksberg, C
Book Club(s): Erhverislitteratur

Samlerens Forlag A/S+
Kobmagergade 62, 1, DK-1018 Copenhagen K
Tel: 33411800 *Fax:* 33411801
Key Personnel
Man Dir: Peter Holst
Founded: 1942
Subjects: Fiction, Government, Political Science, History, Literature, Literary Criticism, Essays
ISBN Prefix(es): 87-568
Total Titles: 150 Print
Parent Company: Gyldendalske Boghandel - Nordisk Forlag A/S

Samtid, *imprint of* Tiderne Skifter Forlag A/S

Scan-Globe A/S
Ulvevej 25, 4622 Havdrup
Tel: 46185400 *Fax:* 46185270
E-mail: info@scanglobe.dk
Web Site: www.scanglobe.dk

Telex: 40275
Key Personnel
Man Dir: Mr Per Lund-Hansen
Founded: 1963
Subjects: Geography, Geology
ISBN Prefix(es): 87-87343; 87-90468

Scandinavia Publishing House+
Drejervej 11-21, 2400 Copenhagen NV DK
Tel: 35 31 03 30 *Fax:* 35 31 03 34
Web Site: www.scanpublishing.dk
Key Personnel
President & Publisher: Jorgen Vium Olesen
 E-mail: jvo@scanpublishing.dk
Editor & Secretary: Jytte Larsen *Tel:* 35 31 03 31
 E-mail: jytte@scanpublishing.dk
Sales & Marketing: Anthony Hoglind
Founded: 1979
Specialize in education & religion.
Subjects: Biblical Studies, Biography, Education, Theology
Total Titles: 323 Print
Book Club(s): Den Kristne Bogklub, Contact: Bo Nielsen *Tel:* 35 31 03 36

Det Schonbergske Forlag+
Landemaerket 5, 1119 Copenhagen K
Tel: 33733585 *Fax:* 33733586
E-mail: Schoenberg@nytnordiskforlag.dk
Web Site: www.nytnordiskforlag.dk *Cable:* SCHOENBOOK
Key Personnel
Dir: Joakim Werner
Production Manager: Arvid Honore
Sales Manager: Max-Erik Reinhold
Founded: 1857
Subjects: Art, Biography, Career Development, Fiction, History, Humor, Philosophy, Poetry, Psychology, Psychiatry, Travel
ISBN Prefix(es): 87-570
Parent Company: Nyt Nordisk Forlag Arnold Busck A/S
Divisions: Woeldike

J H Schultz Information A/S+
Herstedvang 12, 2620 Albertslund
Tel: 43632300 *Fax:* 43631969
E-mail: schultz@schultz.dk
Web Site: www.schultz.dk
Key Personnel
Man Dir: Henrik Christiansen
Division Manager: Gert Eriksen *E-mail:* ge@schultz.dk
Contact: Anette Klubien
Founded: 1661
Specialize in law information.
Subjects: Business, Environmental Studies, Law, Nonfiction (General)
ISBN Prefix(es): 87-569; 87-609
Online services available through World Wide Web.
Parent Company: J H Schultz Holding A/S
Ultimate Parent Company: J H Schultz-Fondeu
Associate Companies: J H Schultz Grafisk A/S; Synergi Data A/S; Schultz Interactive Information A/S
Bookshop(s): Schultz Boghandel, Vognmagergade 7, DK 1220 Copenhagen K *Tel:* 043 632300 *Fax:* 043 155772

Forlaget Sesam
Aschehoug Dansk Forlag A/S, Vognmagergade 7, 1120 Copenhagen K
Tel: 33305044; 33305522 *Fax:* 33305824
E-mail: aschehoug@ash.egmont.com
Key Personnel
Publishing Dir: Per Kolle *Tel:* 33305044
 Fax: 33305824
ISBN Prefix(es): 87-7258; 87-7324; 87-7801
Divisions: Aschehoug, Egmont

Sesan, *imprint of* Aschehoug Dansk Forlag A/S

A/S Skattekartoteket
Palaegade 4, 1022 Copenhagen K
Mailing Address: Postboks 9026, 1022 Copenhagen K
Tel: 33117874 *Fax:* 33938025
E-mail: magnus@cddk.dk
Key Personnel
Man Dir: Peter Taarnhoj
Subjects: Public Administration
ISBN Prefix(es): 87-87451; 87-7762
Parent Company: CD-Danmark A/S

Sommer og Soerensen Forlag ApS
Valbygaardsvej 33, DK-2500 Valby
Tel: 36153615 *Fax:* 36153616
Key Personnel
Dir: Niels Borgen
Editorial Dir: Jens Christiansen
Contact: Mette Nymark
Subjects: Fiction
ISBN Prefix(es): 87-7499
Number of titles published annually: 5 Print
Total Titles: 10 Print
Parent Company: Borgens Forlag A/S

Spektrum Forlagsaktieselskab+
4 Snaregade, 1205 Copenhagen K
Tel: 33147714 *Fax:* 33147791
Key Personnel
Man Dir: Werner Svendsen
Founded: 1990
Subjects: Nonfiction (General)
ISBN Prefix(es): 87-7763
Imprints: Copenhagen

Square Dance Partners Forlag+
Hasselvej 18, 2830 Virum
Tel: 45 83 99 83
Key Personnel
President & International Rights Contact: Margot Gunzenhauser *E-mail:* mgunz@worldonline.dk
US Representative: Dorothy Gunzenhauser *Tel:* (215) 579-2298 *E-mail:* deg@tradenet.net
Founded: 1987
Specialize in the publishing of books, tapes & CD's dealing with traditional style American square & contra dancing, related dance forms & their music.
Subjects: Crafts, Games, Hobbies, How-to, Music, Dance
ISBN Prefix(es): 87-982674
Total Titles: 4 Print
U.S. Office(s): K-113 Pennswood Village, 1382 Newtown-Langhorne Rd, Newton, PA 18940, United States, Dorothy Gunzenhauser *Tel:* (215) 579-2298
Distributed by Barn Dance Publications LTD (UK)

Statens Information (Danish State Information Service)
Postboks 1300, 2300 Copenhagen S
Tel: 33379228 *Fax:* 33379299
E-mail: si@si.dk
Web Site: www.denmark.dk; www.si.dk
Key Personnel
Manager: Simon Hansen
Also acts as agent for official government publications.
Subjects: Environmental Studies, Government, Political Science, Library & Information Sciences, Public Administration
ISBN Prefix(es): 87-503; 87-601

Strandbergs Forlag+
Vedbaek Strandvej 475, 2950 Vedbaek
Tel: 45894760 *Fax:* 45894701
E-mail: strandberg.publishing@get2net.dk
Key Personnel
Publisher: Hans Joergen Strandberg

DENMARK

Founded: 1861
Also book packager.
Subjects: Ethnicity, Humor
ISBN Prefix(es): 87-7717; 87-87200
Parent Company: Strandberg

Strubes Forlag og Boghandel ApS
65 Damhus Blvd, 2610 Rodovre
Tel: 36721750 *Fax:* 36721752 *Cable:* STRABEBOOKS
Key Personnel
Man Dir: Jonna Strube

Syddansk Universitetsforlag (University Press of Southern Denmark)+
Formerly Odense Universitetsbibliotek
Campusvej 55, DK-5230 Odense M
Tel: 66 15 79 99 *Fax:* 66 15 81 26
E-mail: press@forlag.sdu.dk
Web Site: www.universitypress.dk
Key Personnel
Man Dir: Thomas Kaarsted *E-mail:* thk@forlag.sdu.dk
Founded: 1966
Subjects: Archaeology, Fiction, History, Literature, Literary Criticism, Essays, Medicine, Nursing, Dentistry, Philosophy, Technology
ISBN Prefix(es): 87-7492; 87-7838

Systime+
Skt Pauls Gade 25, 8000 Aarhus C
Tel: 70 12 11 00 *Fax:* 70 12 11 05
E-mail: systime@systime.dk
Web Site: www.systime.dk
Key Personnel
Man Dir: P H Mikkelsen
Editor: Anja Riis Madsew; Stefan Emkjaer; Bitte Annette Noerregaard; Claes Soenderriis
Rights & Permissions: Inga-Lill Amini
Founded: 1980
Specialize in educational materials.
Subjects: Accounting, Chemistry, Chemical Engineering, Computer Science, Economics, English as a Second Language, Film, Video, Geography, Geology, History, Mathematics, Philosophy, Physics, Religion - Other, Technology, Reference books
ISBN Prefix(es): 87-616; 87-7351; 87-7783; 87-87454
Total Titles: 100 Print
Parent Company: GEC Gad

Teaterforlaget Drama
Kobmagergade 5/3, 1150 Copenhagen K
Tel: 33321519 *Fax:* 33329818
E-mail: drama@drama.dk
Web Site: www.drama.dk
Key Personnel
Man Dir: Erling Barkholt *Tel:* 33222247 *Fax:* 33225847 *E-mail:* eb@drama-kbh.dk
Founded: 1977
Specialize in drama & theatre, books & manuscripts.
Subjects: Drama, Theater
Associate Companies: Teater Hjornet; International Teater Boghandel, Vesterbrogade 175, DK-1800 Frederisberg *Tel:* 33222247 *Fax:* 33225847 *E-mail:* drama@dats.dk

Tiderne Skifter Forlag A/S
Kobmagergade 62, 1, 1019 Copenhagen K
Tel: 33411820 *Fax:* 33411821
E-mail: tiderneskifter@tiderneskifter.dk
Web Site: www.tiderneskifter.dk
Key Personnel
Man Dir: Claus Clausen
Founded: 1973
Subjects: Behavioral Sciences, Ethnicity, Fiction, Literature, Literary Criticism, Essays, Photography
ISBN Prefix(es): 87-7445

Number of titles published annually: 35 Print
Parent Company: Gyldendalske Boghandel - Nordisk Forlag A/S
Imprints: Samtid
Orders to: Gyldendal, Lindgreens Alle 12, DK-2300 Copenhagen S *Tel:* (31) 547175

Unitas Forlag+
Valby Langgade 19, 2500 Valby
Tel: 36166481 *Fax:* 36160818
E-mail: forlag@unitas.dk
Web Site: www.unitas.dk
Key Personnel
Publisher: Peder Gundersen
Founded: 1914
Subjects: Biblical Studies, Biography, Fiction, Religion - Protestant, Theology
ISBN Prefix(es): 87-7517
Parent Company: YMCA/YWCA

Vandrer mod Lysets Forlag ApS
108 Adelgade, 1304 Copenhagen K
Tel: 33157815 *Fax:* 33157815
Web Site: www.vandrer-mod-lyset.dk
Key Personnel
Dir: Borge Bronnum
Publisher: Mrs Konny Falck
ISBN Prefix(es): 87-87871; 87-980350

Forlaget Vindrose A/S+
Valbygardsvej 33, DK-2500 Valby
Tel: 36153615 *Fax:* 36153616
Key Personnel
Man Dir: Niels Borgen
Rights & Permissions Manager: Mette Nymark *E-mail:* mnymark@borgen.dk
Production: Dennis Stovring
Sales: Jan Wass
Publisher: Jens Christiansen
Founded: 1980
Subjects: Fiction, Poetry, Science (General), Social Sciences, Sociology
ISBN Prefix(es): 87-7456
Number of titles published annually: 20 Print
Total Titles: 200 Print
Parent Company: Borgens Forlag A/S
Orders to: D B K-bogdistribution, Siljangade 2-8, DK-2300 Copenhagen S

Wisby & Wilkens+
Vestergade 6, DK-8464 Galten
Mailing Address: Box 98, DK-8464 Galten
Tel: 7023 4622 *Fax:* 7043 4722
E-mail: mail@wisby-wilkens.com
Web Site: www.wisby-wilkens.com
Key Personnel
Dir: Jacob Wisby
Founded: 1986
Member of Danish Publishers Association.
Subjects: Crafts, Games, Hobbies, Fiction, Humor, Literature, Literary Criticism, Essays, Nonfiction (General), Outdoor Recreation, Science Fiction, Fantasy
ISBN Prefix(es): 87-89190; 87-89191; 87-7046
Number of titles published annually: 24 Print
Total Titles: 200 Print
Imprints: Mikro
Subsidiaries: MIKRO
Distributor for Grandview USA (Scandinavia)
Warehouse: DBK, Siljangade 2, DK-2300 Copenhagen S

Forlaget Woldike K/S
5 Landemaerket, c/o Det Schonbergske Forlag, 1119 Copenhagen K
Tel: 33 73 35 85
Founded: 1969
Subjects: Fiction, Nonfiction (General)
ISBN Prefix(es): 87-7233

Dominican Republic

General Information

Capital: Santo Domingo
Language: Spanish
Religion: Predominantly Roman Catholic
Population: 7.5 million
Bank Hours: 0830-1230 Monday-Friday; some open 0830-1130 Saturday
Shop Hours: 0800-1200, 1400 or 1500-1800 Monday-Friday; some open Saturday
Currency: 100 centavos = 1 Dominican Republic peso. US currency is widely used
Export/Import Information: No import licenses required for books. Exchange license and approval from Central Bank required.
Copyright: UCC, Berne, Buenos Aires (see Copyright Conventions, pg xi)

Editorama SA
St Eugene Contreras No 54, Santo Domingo
Mailing Address: TheTrinitarios, PO Box 2074, Santo Domingo
Tel: (809) 5966669 (ext 4274) *Fax:* (809) 5941421
E-mail: editorama@codetel.net.do
Web Site: www.editorama.com
Key Personnel
Dir: Juan R Quinones
Founded: 1970
ISBN Prefix(es): 9977-88

Editora Listin Diario
Paseo de los Periodistas 52, Santo Domingo
Tel: (809) 6866688; (809) 6897171 *Fax:* (809) 6866595
Telex: (809) 346-0206 *Cable:* LISTIN
Key Personnel
President: Eduardo Pellerano

Pontificia Universidad Catolica Madre y Maestra+
Departamento de Puplicaciones, Autopista Duparte, km 1, 1/2, Santiago de los Caballeros
SAN: 004-5527
Tel: (809) 5801962; (809) 5350111 *Fax:* (809) 5824549; (809) 5350053
Telex: 3461032 PUCMM
Key Personnel
Editorial: Carmen Perez de Cabral
Founded: 1962
Member of University Editorial Association of Latin America & the Caribbean.
Subjects: Accounting, Agriculture, Archaeology, Architecture & Interior Design, Biblical Studies, Biography, Biological Sciences, Business, Career Development, Chemistry, Chemical Engineering, Civil Engineering, Communications, Developing Countries, Drama, Theater, Economics, Education, Electronics, Electrical Engineering, Energy, Engineering (General), English as a Second Language, Environmental Studies, Geography, Geology, Government, Political Science, Health, Nutrition, History, Language Arts, Linguistics, Law, Library & Information Sciences, Literature, Literary Criticism, Essays, Management, Marketing, Mathematics, Mechanical Engineering, Medicine, Nursing, Dentistry, Philosophy, Physical Sciences, Physics, Poetry, Regional Interests, Religion - Catholic, Social Sciences, Sociology, Technology, Theology
ISBN Prefix(es): 84-89548
Warehouse: Economato Universitario, PUCMM

Sociedad Editorial Dominicana SA+
Apdo 559, Calle Ramon Santana 2B, qazcue, Santo Domingo
Tel: (809) 6875775; (809) 6889378 *Fax:* (809) 6889378 *Cable:* FRANKLIN FRANCO
Key Personnel
President: Franklin Franco *Tel:* (809) 6897813
Founded: 1975
Subjects: Economics, History, Law, Literature, Literary Criticism, Essays, Philosophy, Social Sciences, Sociology
Total Titles: 2 CD-ROM
Parent Company: Credilibros, Apdo 559, Calle Ramon Santana 2B, Santo Domingo

Editora Taller+
Calle Juan vallenilla esq Jauncio Dolores, Zona Industrial de Herrera, 2190 Santo Domingo
SAN: 002-2136
Tel: (809) 531-7975 *Fax:* (809) 531-7979
E-mail: editora.taller@codetel.net.do
Key Personnel
Contact: Lourdes Cuello
Founded: 1971
Subjects: Economics, History, Literature, Literary Criticism, Essays
ISBN Prefix(es): 84-8400
Distributor for Editora Vicens Vives
Orders to: Vicente Celestino Duarte, No 2

Ecuador

General Information

Capital: Quito
Language: Spanish
Religion: Predominantly Roman Catholic
Population: 10.9 million
Bank Hours: 0900-1330 Monday-Friday
Shop Hours: 0930-1300, 1500-1900 Monday-Friday; 0930-1300 Saturday
Currency: 100 centavos = 1 sucre
Export/Import Information: Member of the Latin American Free Trade Association. Books and most advertising catalogues not dutiable. No import licenses or exchange controls for books.
Copyright: UCC, Buenos Aires (see Copyright Conventions, pg xi)

Ediciones Abya-Yala+
Ave 12 de Octubre 1430 y Wilson, Casilla 17-12-719 Quito
Tel: (02) 562633; (02) 506247 *Fax:* (02) 506255
E-mail: admin-info@abyayala.org; editorial@abyayala.org; enlace@abyayala.org
Web Site: www.abyayala.org
Key Personnel
Dir: Padre Juan Bottasso
Administrative Dir: Carmen Ochoa
Founded: 1975
Member of Quito Book Association.
Subjects: Anthropology, Environmental Studies, Language Arts, Linguistics, Theology
ISBN Prefix(es): 9978-04
Total Titles: 1,060 Print; 2 CD-ROM; 900 E-Book

Biblioteca Ecuatoriana 'Aurelio Espinosa Polit'
Jose Nogales 220 y Francisco Arcos, 17-01-160 Quito
Tel: (02) 492190 *Fax:* (02) 493928
E-mail: beaep@isio.satnet.net
Web Site: www.cultura.com.ec
Key Personnel
Dir: Rev Julian G Bravo *E-mail:* beap@uio.satnet.net
Founded: 1929
Subjects: Specialize in all publications by Ecuadorians and/or about Ecuador.
ISBN Prefix(es): 9978-971

Centro De Educacion Popular
Ave America 3584, Apdo 17-08-8604, Quito
Tel: (02) 525521 *Fax:* (02) 542818
E-mail: cedep@fmlaluna.com
Web Site: www.jacomenet.com/laluna/cedep.html
Key Personnel
Dir: Diego Landazuri
Founded: 1978
Subjects: Communications, Economics
ISBN Prefix(es): 9978-00

CEPLAES
Av 6 de Diciembre 2912 y Alpallana, Casilla 17-11-61277, Quito
Tel: (02) 232261; (02) 547854 *Fax:* (02) 566207
E-mail: ceplaes@ceplaes.ec
Key Personnel
Executive Dir: Alexandra Ayala Marin
Founded: 1978
Subjects: Agriculture, Anthropology, Child Care & Development, Education, Health, Nutrition, Social Sciences, Sociology, Women's Studies
ISBN Prefix(es): 9978-93

CIDAP
Calle Hno Miguel 3-23, La Escalinata, Apdo 01-01-1943, Cuenca
Tel: (07) 829451; (07) 828878 *Fax:* (07) 831450
E-mail: cidap1@cidap.org.ec
Web Site: www.uazuay.edu.ec/cidap/home.htm
Key Personnel
Dir: Claudio Malo Gonzalez
Subjects: Art, Crafts, Games, Hobbies
ISBN Prefix(es): 84-89420; 9978-85

CIESPAL (Centro Internacional de Estudios Superiores de Comunicacion para America Latina)
Av Diego de Almagro N32-133 y Andrade Marin, Apdo 17-01-484, Quito
Tel: (02) 2548011 *Fax:* (02) 2502487
E-mail: info@ciespal.net
Web Site: www.ciespal.net
Telex: 2474 Ciespl *Cable:* Ciespal
Key Personnel
Dir: Dr Edgar Jaramillo
Dir, Orders: Jorge Jarrin
Founded: 1959
Subjects: Biography, Communications, Journalism, Publishing & Book Trade Reference, Radio, TV, Technology
ISBN Prefix(es): 9978-55

Corporacion de Estudios y Publicaciones
Acuna 168 y Agama, 17-21-00186 Quito, Casilla
Tel: (02) 221-711 *Fax:* (02) 226-256
E-mail: cep@accessinter.net
Founded: 1963
Subjects: Law, Public Administration
ISBN Prefix(es): 9978-86

Corporacion Editora Nacional
Roca E9-59 y Tamayo, Casilla 17-12-886, Quito
Mailing Address: P O Box 17-12-886, Quito
Tel: (02) 554358; (02) 554558; (02) 554658 *Fax:* (02) 566340
E-mail: cen@accessinter.net
Key Personnel
President: Ernesto Alban Gomez
Founded: 1978
Editorial corporation with non-profits.
Subjects: Archaeology, Biography, Economics, Education, Geography, Geology, Government, Political Science, History, Law, Literature, Literary Criticism, Essays, Philosophy, Social Sciences, Sociology

ISBN Prefix(es): 9978-84; 9978-958
Total Titles: 332 Print

Ediciones Legales SA
Unit of Corporacion Myl
Psje Donoso 131 y Whimper, Casilla 17-03-186-A, Quito
Tel: (02) 548422 *Fax:* (02) 554954
Key Personnel
President: Manuel Mejia Dalmau
General Manager: Ernesto Alban Gomez
Founded: 1989
Subjects: Law
ISBN Prefix(es): 9978-81
Total Titles: 28 Print; 2 CD-ROM

Libresa S A+
Murgeon 364 y Ulloa, Casilla 356, entre Jorge Juan y Ulloa, Quito
Tel: (02) 230925 *Fax:* (02) 502992
Key Personnel
President: Fausto Coba Estrella
General: Jaime Pena Novoa
Founded: 1979
Subjects: Education, Literature, Literary Criticism, Essays, Philosophy
ISBN Prefix(es): 9978-80; 9978-952
Associate Companies: Delibresa, Librerias Espanolas

Pontificia Universidad Catolica de Ecuador, Centro de Publicaciones
Ave 12 de Octubre y Carron, Apdo 17-01-2184, Quito
Tel: (02) 529240 *Fax:* (02) 567117
Key Personnel
Dir: Dr Marco Vinicio Rueda
Founded: 1946
Subjects: Anthropology, Archaeology, Art, Economics, Government, Political Science, History, Law, Literature, Literary Criticism, Essays, Philosophy, Science (General), Social Sciences, Sociology, Theology
ISBN Prefix(es): 9978-77

Pudeleco/Publicaciones de Legislacion
Reina Victoria 477 y Roca, Casilla 17-15-00164-B, Quito
Tel: (02) 543273 *Fax:* (02) 543607
ISBN Prefix(es): 9978-966

SECAP
Jose Arizaga entre Londres y Jorge Drom, Casilla 2221, Quito
Tel: (02) 446248 *Fax:* (02) 448644
Subjects: Agriculture, Automotive, Education, Library & Information Sciences, Public Administration
ISBN Prefix(es): 9978-64

Universidad Central del Ecuador, Departamento de Publicaciones
Avda America y A Perez Guerrero, Quito
Mailing Address: PO Box 3291, Quito
Tel: (02) 226080 *Fax:* (02) 501207

Egypt (Arab Republic of Egypt)

General Information

Capital: Cairo
Language: Arabic (English and French widely used)

EGYPT (ARAB REPUBLIC OF EGYPT)

Religion: Predominantly Muslim (of the Sunni sect)
Population: 56.4 million
Bank Hours: Generally 0830-1230 Monday-Thursday; 1000-1200 Saturday
Shop Hours: 0830-1330, 1630-1900 Monday-Saturday
Currency: 1,000 milliemes = 100 piastres = 5 tallaris = 1 Egyptian pound
Export/Import Information: Exchange rate set by individual banks. No longer government monopoly but some book importing done by Foreign Trade Company, Misr Import & Export Co, 6 Adly St, Cairo.
Copyright: Berne, Florence (see Copyright Conventions, pg xi)

Al Ahram Establishment
6 Al-Galaa' St, Cairo
Tel: (02) 748248 *Fax:* (02) 745888
Telex: 20185-92544
Key Personnel
Editor-in-Chief: Ibrahim Nafei
Sales: Hany Tolba
Production: Fathi Al Charkawi
Rights & Permissions: Mrs Nawal El Mahallawi
Founded: 1875
Also translation agency, printer, distributor, importer, exporter; member of Distripreso STM.
Subjects: Human Relations, Science (General)
ISBN Prefix(es): 977-13
Associate Companies: Al Ahram Commercial Press; Al Ahram Agency for Distribution
Subsidiaries: Al Ahram Center for Strategic & Political Studies; Al Ahram Center for Scientific Translation & Publishing; Al Ahram Center for Microfilm & Organization; Al Ahram Center for Computer & Management; Al Ahram Advertising Agency; Al Ahram Org 8 Information Technology Center; Al Ahram Commercial Press; Al Ahram Press Agency
Bookshop(s): Al Ahram Bookshop, 165 Mohamed Faird St, Cairo
Book Club(s): Al Ahram Book Club; ARL (Al-Ahram Research Library)

American University in Cairo Press+
113 Sharia Kasr el Ainy, Cairo
Tel: (02) 3542964 *Fax:* (02) 3557565
Telex: 92224 Aucai un *Cable:* VICTORIOUS
Key Personnel
Dir: Mark Linz
Asst Dir: Aleya Serour
Man Editor: Neil Hewison
Marketing Manager: Atef El-Hoteiby
Distribution Supervisor: Tahany Shamaa
Founded: 1960
Member of AAUP.
Subjects: Anthropology, Architecture & Interior Design, Art, Earth Sciences, History, Language Arts, Linguistics, Literature, Literary Criticism, Essays, Social Sciences, Sociology
ISBN Prefix(es): 977-424
Distributed by Columbia University Press

Al Arab Publishing House+
23 Faggalah St, Cairo
Tel: (02) 908027
Key Personnel
Man Dir: Prof Saladin Boustany, PhD
Sales Manager: George G Edde
Founded: 1900
Specialize in Modern, Contemporary & Out-of-Print Arabic Monographs & Periodicals.
Subjects: Developing Countries, Economics, Fiction, Government, Political Science, History, Journalism, Language Arts, Linguistics, Law, Literature, Literary Criticism, Essays, Philosophy, Poetry, Psychology, Psychiatry, Religion - Islamic, Religion - Other, Social Sciences, Sociology

Cairo University Press
Al-Giza, Cairo
Tel: (02) 846144
ISBN Prefix(es): 977-223

Centre d'Etudes et Documentation Economique Juridique et Sociale (CEDEJ)
Ambassade de France en Egypte - BP 494 Dokki, Cairo
Tel: (02) 704641
Key Personnel
Dir: Philippe Fargues
Founded: 1970
ISBN Prefix(es): 2-905838

Dar Al-Kitab Al-Masri+
33 Kasr El-Nile St, 11511 Cairo
Mailing Address: PO Box 156 Atabah, 11511 Cairo
Tel: (02) 3922168; (02) 3934301; (02) 3924614 *Fax:* (02) 3924657
E-mail: hlelzein@datum.com.eg
Key Personnel
President & Man Dir: El-Zein Hassan
Founded: 1929
Also distributor & printer.
Member of Time Life Time Warner.
Subjects: Education, Regional Interests
ISBN Prefix(es): 977-238
Parent Company: Dar Al-Kitab Al-Lubnani, 33 Kasr El-Nile St, PO Box 156 Atabah, 11511 Cairo
Associate Companies: Dar Al-Kitab Allubnani, Madame Kuri St in front of Hotel Bristol, PO Box 11-8330, Beirut, Lebanon *Tel:* (01) 735731, (01) 735732 *Fax:* (01) 351433
Branch Office(s)
Cairo
Paris, France
Beirut, Lebanon
Casablanca, Morocco
Madrid, Spain
Geneva, Switzerland

Dar Al-Matbo at Al-Gadidah
5 Saint Mark St, Alexandria
Tel: (03) 4825508 *Fax:* (03) 4833819
Subjects: Agriculture, Animals, Pets, Library & Information Sciences, Social Sciences, Sociology
ISBN Prefix(es): 977-207

Dar al-Nahda al Arabia
32 Abdel Khalik Tharwat St, Cairo
Founded: 1960
Also distributor.
Subjects: Law, Literature, Literary Criticism, Essays
ISBN Prefix(es): 977-04

Dar Al-Thakafah Al-Gadidah+
32 Sabry Abou Alam St, Cairo
Tel: (02) 42718
Key Personnel
President: Mohamed Youssef Elguindi
Founded: 1968
ISBN Prefix(es): 977-221

Dar El Shorouk+
8 Sebaweh El Masry St, Nasr City, Cairo
Tel: (02) 4023399; (02) 4037567 *Fax:* (02) 3934814
E-mail: dar@sharouk.com
Web Site: www.sharouk.com
Telex: 93091 Shrok *Cable:* SHOROUK
Key Personnel
Chief Executive, Editorial, Rights & Permissions: Ibrahim El Moallem
Sales: Ahmad El Sawy
Production: Ahmed El Zayadi
Children's Books: Amira Aboulmadg
Founded: 1976
Subjects: Behavioral Sciences, Biography, Business, Computer Science, Education, English as a Second Language, Fiction, History, Law, Literature, Literary Criticism, Essays, Management, Mysteries, Nonfiction (General), Poetry, Psychology, Psychiatry, Religion - Islamic
ISBN Prefix(es): 977-09
Associate Companies: Shorouk Press
Subsidiaries: Shorouk Bookshop
Bookshop(s): The First Mall, 25 Giza St, Giza; One Soliman Pasha Sq, Cairo

Dar El Shorouk Publishing & Distributing House+
7-8 Sebaweh El Masry St, 11371 Nasr City, Cairo
Tel: (02) 4023399 *Fax:* (02) 4037567
E-mail: dar@shorouk.com
Web Site: www.shorouk.com
Key Personnel
Owner & Chairman: Ibrahim El-Moallem
E-mail: imoallem@shorouk.com
Founded: 1968
Specialize in publishing, printing, bookstores, distributing children's books, political religious, modern Arabic thoughts, literature, encyclopedias & art books.
Subjects: Archaeology, Art, Biography, Child Care & Development, Developing Countries, Drama, Theater, Education, Energy, Engineering (General), English as a Second Language, Fiction, Foreign Countries, Geography, Geology, Government, Political Science, History, Language Arts, Linguistics, Law, Library & Information Sciences, Literature, Literary Criticism, Essays, Mechanical Engineering, Music, Dance, Mysteries, Nonfiction (General), Philosophy, Poetry, Psychology, Psychiatry, Religion - Islamic, Science (General), Science Fiction, Fantasy, Social Sciences, Sociology, Sports, Athletics, Theology
Number of titles published annually: 120 Print
Distributor for Thames & Hudson - BBC English
Bookshop(s): One Talaat Harb St, Cairo *Tel:* (02) 3912480

The Egyptian Society for the Dissemination of Universal Culture and Knowledge (ESDUCK)
1081 Corniche El Nil St, Garden City, Cairo
Mailing Address: PO Box 21, Cairo
Tel: (02) 35425079; (02) 35420295 *Fax:* (02) 3540295 *Cable:* ESDUCK
Key Personnel
Executive Manager: Dr Amin El-Gamal
Production: Amal Kilany
Rights & Permissions: Inas Effat
Founded: 1953
Co-publisher with local and American firms. Also translation agency.

Elias Modern Publishing House+
One Al-Rum, Al-Kathulik, Al Zaher, Cairo
Mailing Address: PO Box 954, Cairo
Tel: (02) 903756 B *Fax:* (02) 2490736; (02) 938003 *Cable:* DICTIONARY-CAIRO
Key Personnel
Contact: Nadim Edward Elias
Founded: 1913
Subjects: Language Arts, Linguistics, Literature, Literary Criticism, Essays, Poetry
ISBN Prefix(es): 977-5028
Subsidiaries: Elias Modern Press
Distributor for Oxford University Press

ESDUCK, see The Egyptian Society for the Dissemination of Universal Culture and Knowledge (ESDUCK)

General Egyptian Book Organization+
Corniche El-Nil-Boulaq, Cairo
Mailing Address: PO Box 1660, Cairo

Tel: (02) 775371; (02) 775649; (02) 5775109
 Fax: (02) 754213
Telex: 93932bookun *Cable:* GEBO
Key Personnel
Chairman: Samir Sarhan
Commercial Sector & Fairs: Mr Samir Saad Khalil *E-mail:* s.s.khalil@usa.net
Founded: 1961
26 Branches throughout Egypt.
ISBN Prefix(es): 977-01
Bookshop(s): International Book Centre, Cairo

Dar Al Hilap Publishing Institution
16 Mohammed Ezz El - Araab St 'Al-Mubtadian, Cairo
Tel: (02) 20610
Telex: 92703 Hilal *Cable:* Al Mussawar Cairo
Key Personnel
Chief Executive: Makram Mohamed Ahmed
Subjects: Fiction, Nonfiction (General)
ISBN Prefix(es): 977-07

Lehnert & Landrock Bookshop
44 Sherif St, Cairo 11511
Mailing Address: PO Box 1013, Cairo 11511
Tel: (02) 3927606 *Fax:* (02) 3934421
Key Personnel
Manager: Dr E Lambelet
Founded: 1924
Subjects: Archaeology, History, Travel
ISBN Prefix(es): 977-243
Number of titles published annually: 2 Print

Dar Al Maaref+
1119 Corniche El Nil St, Cairo
Tel: (02) 759411; (02) 759552 *Fax:* (02) 5744999
Telex: 92199 Marefun *Cable:* Damaref
Key Personnel
Chairman & Man Dir: Ragab Al-Banna
Founded: 1890
Also co-publishers, importers and exporters.
Subjects: Education, Regional Interests, Science (General)
ISBN Prefix(es): 977-02
Subsidiaries: Dar Al-Maaref Liban Sarl
Bookshop(s): Alexandria; El Arish; Assiut; Asswan; Cairo; Ismailia; Mansoura; Qena; Shebin El kom; Sohage; Suez; Tanta; Zagazig

Middle East Book Centre
45 Kasr Al-Nil St, Cairo
Tel: (02) 910980
Key Personnel
Man Dir: Dr A M Mosharrafa
Sales Manager: A Ismail
Founded: 1954
Subjects: Biography, Fiction, History, Language Arts, Linguistics, Literature, Literary Criticism, Essays, Philosophy, Poetry, Regional Interests, Religion - Other, Science (General), Social Sciences, Sociology

Senouhy Publishers
54 Sharia Abdel-Khalek, Tharwat, Cairo
Key Personnel
Man Dir: Leila A Fadel
Founded: 1956
Subjects: History, Nonfiction (General), Poetry, Regional Interests, Religion - Other

Sphinx Publishing Co
3 Shawarby St, 3rd fl, Cairo
Tel: (02) 392 4616 *Fax:* (02) 391 8802
E-mail: sphinx@intouch.com
Telex: 93927
Key Personnel
Man Dir: Habib Sayegh
Founded: 1958
Part of Librairie du Liban Group, Lebanon.
Subjects: Education
Parent Company: Pearson Plc

Ummah Press for Translation & Publishing+
24 Deglah St from Shehab St, Al-Muhandesin, Giza
Tel: (03) 378556 *Fax:* (03) 378556
Key Personnel
President: Ahmad El Shazly
Subjects: Economics, Government, Political Science, Journalism, Regional Interests, Religion - Islamic

El Salvador

General Information

Capital: San Salvador
Language: Spanish
Religion: Predominantly Roman Catholic
Population: 5.6 million
Bank Hours: 0900-1200, 1345-1530 Monday-Friday
Shop Hours: 0800-1200, 1400-1800 Monday-Friday; 0800-1200 Saturday
Currency: 100 centavos = 1 Salvadorean colon
Export/Import Information: Member of the Central American Common Market. No import licenses but exchange license from Exchange Control Department of Central Reserve Bank required, if goods coming from outside Central America. Commercial banks authorize certain import payments.
Copyright: UCC, Berne, Buenos Aires, Florence (see Copyright Conventions, pg xi)

Clasicos Roxsil Editorial SA de CV+
Cuarta Avenida Sur 2-3, La Libertad, Santa Tecla
Tel: 228-1832; 288-2646; 229-6742 *Fax:* 228-1212
Key Personnel
Manager: Rosa Serrano de Lopez
Chief Editorial Department: Roxana Beatriz Lopez *Tel:* 228-2646 *E-mail:* roxanabe@havegaute.com.sv
Founded: 1976
Subjects: Biography, Literature, Literary Criticism, Essays, Poetry
ISBN Prefix(es): 84-89541; 84-89899; 99923-24
Number of titles published annually: 10 Print
Total Titles: 130 Print
Distributor for Fondo Editorial UNESCO (El Salvador)
Book Club(s): Club de Lectores de Clasicos Roxsil, 4a Av Sur No 2-3, Santa Tecla, Marco Antonio Barraza *Tel:* 2281832; 2296742 *Fax:* 2281212

UCA Editores+
Universidad Centroamericana Jose Simeon Canas, Apdo 01-575 Autopista Sur, Jardinesde Guadalupe, San Salvador
Tel: 234491 *Fax:* 733556
Key Personnel
Dir: Rodolfo Cardenal SJ
Editorial: Rafael Rodriguez; Jon Sobrino
Production: Rogelio Pedraz
Founded: 1975
Subjects: Philosophy, Religion - Other, Social Sciences, Sociology, Theology
ISBN Prefix(es): 84-8405
Bookshop(s): Libreria UCA (under Major Booksellers)
Orders to: Distribuidora de Publicaciones de la Universidad Centroamericana, Universidad Centroamericana Jose Simeon Canas, Apdo 01-575, Autopista Sur, Jardinesde Guadalupe, San Salvador

Editorial Universitaria de la Universidad de El Salvador
Ciudad Universitaria, Apdo de Correos 3110, San Salvador
Tel: 2558826 *Fax:* 254208
Key Personnel
Dir: Armando Herrara
Contact: Francisco Guzman Argueta
Founded: 1923
Subjects: Gardening, Plants, Government, Political Science, Literature, Literary Criticism, Essays, Philosophy, Poetry, Regional Interests, Social Sciences, Sociology
ISBN Prefix(es): 84-89540

Estonia

General Information

Capital: Tallinn
Language: Estonian, Russian, Finnish & English
Religion: Evangelical Lutheran
Population: 1.5 million
Currency: 100 cents = 1 kroon (eek); 8 eek = 1 dem
Export/Import Information: No export/import duties. 18% VAT on books (except educational & medical).
Copyright: Berne (see Copyright Conventions, pg xi)

Oue Eesti Raamat
Laki tn 26, Tallinn 12915
Tel: (02) 6587885; (02) 6587886; (02) 6587887; (02) 6587889 *Fax:* (02) 6587889
Key Personnel
Dir: Anne Kask
Rights & Contract Manager: Georg Grunberg *E-mail:* georg.grynberg@mail.ee
Founded: 1964
Book publishing.
Subjects: Biography, Fiction, Poetry
ISBN Prefix(es): 9985-65
Number of titles published annually: 50 Print

Estonian Academic Library
Ravala 10, Tallinn 15042
Tel: (02) 6659401; (02) 6659402 *Fax:* (02) 6659400
E-mail: ear@ear.ee
Web Site: www.ear.ee
Key Personnel
Head Librarian: Anne Valmas *E-mail:* anne.valmas@ear.ee
Learned Secretary: Aita Kraut *Tel:* (372) 6659404 *E-mail:* aita.kraut@ear.ee
Founded: 1946
Subjects: Biological Sciences, Ethnicity, Geography, Geology, History, Library & Information Sciences, yearbooks, exhibition catalogues
ISBN Prefix(es): 9985-50
Number of titles published annually: 7 Print
Parent Company: Ministry of Education, Munga 18, 50088 Tartu

Estonian Academy Publishers
Unit of Estonian Academy of Sciences
Mailing Address: Estonia Blvd 7, 10143 Tallinn
Tel: (02) 6454504 *Fax:* (02) 6466026
Web Site: www.kirj.ee/
Key Personnel
Dir: Ylo Niine *E-mail:* niine@kirj.ee
Deputy Editor-in-Chief: Virve Kurnitski *Tel:* (02) 6454156 *E-mail:* virve@kirj.ee
Marketing Manager: Asta Tikerpae *E-mail:* asta@kirj.ee
Founded: 1994
Subjects: Science (General)
ISBN Prefix(es): 9985-50

ESTONIA

Number of titles published annually: 30 Print
Total Titles: 360 Print

Estonian Bible Society+
Member of United Bible Societies
Kaarli pst 9, Tallinn 10119
Tel: (02) 6311671 *Fax:* (02) 6311438
E-mail: eps@eps.ee
Key Personnel
Head of Publications: Sra Tarmo Lilleoja
  E-mail: tarmo@eps.ee
Founded: 1813
Subjects: Biblical Studies, History, Estonian bibles, new testaments and portions, bible related literature
ISBN Prefix(es): 9985-889; 9985-9627
Number of titles published annually: 4 Print; 1 CD-ROM
Total Titles: 2 Print

Estonian Encyclopaedia Publishers Ltd+
Mustamae tee 5, 10616 Tallinn
Tel: (02) 6259413 *Fax:* (02) 6566542
E-mail: encyclo@online.ee
Key Personnel
Dir: Tonu Koger
International Rights: Mari Ets
Chief Editor: Ulo Kaevats
Founded: 1991 (as the successor of former Encyclopedia Editorial Board, founded 1963)
Member of the Estonian Publishers Association.
Subjects: Agriculture, Art, Biography, History, Nonfiction (General), Science (General)
ISBN Prefix(es): 5-89900; 9985-70

Estonian ISBN Agency
Tonismaegi 2, 15189 Tallinn
Tel: (02) 6307372 *Fax:* (02) 6311200
E-mail: eraamat@nlib.ee
Key Personnel
Contact: Mai Valtna
Parent Company: National Library of Estonia

Ilmamaa+
Vanemuise 19, 51014 Tartu
Tel: (07) 427320; (07) 427290 *Fax:* (07) 427320
E-mail: ilmamaa@ilmamaa.ee
Web Site: www.ilmamaa.ee
Key Personnel
Chairman: Hando Runnel
Dir: Mart Jagomaegi
Founded: 1992
Subjects: Fiction, History, Literature, Literary Criticism, Essays, Nonfiction (General), Philosophy, Poetry
ISBN Prefix(es): 9985-821; 9985-878; 9985-77
Number of titles published annually: 30 Print; 6 Online
Total Titles: 105 Print; 23 Online

Koolibri+
Parnu Mnt 10, 10148 Tallinn
Tel: (02) 445223; (02) 441975 *Fax:* (02) 446813
Key Personnel
Publicity Manager: Maire Tanna *Fax:* (02) 2446813 *E-mail:* maire@koolibri.ee
ISBN Prefix(es): 9985-0
Total Titles: 300 Print

Kunst Publishers Ltd+
Lai St 34, Tallinn 10133
Mailing Address: PO Box 105, Tallinn 10502
Tel: (02) 6411764 *Fax:* (02) 6411762
E-mail: helme@skkke.ee
Key Personnel
Editorial Dir: Katre Oim
Marketing: Asta Pajumaee
Design: Tiiu Allikvee
Finance: Marika Kirbits
Foreign Rights Manager: Eve Kork *Tel:* (02) 6411363
Founded: 1957
Specialize in Art.
Subjects: Architecture & Interior Design, Art, Biography, Fiction, History
ISBN Prefix(es): 5-89920
Number of titles published annually: 40 Print
Total Titles: 8 Print

Kupar Publishers+
Paernu mnt 67A, 10134 Tallinn
Tel: (02) 6286173 *Fax:* (02) 6462076
E-mail: kupar@netexpress.ee
Key Personnel
Chairman: Mihkel Mutt
Man Dir: Ivo Sandre
Editor-in-Chief: Marilin Lips
Founded: 1987
Subjects: Fiction, Human Relations, Parapsychology, Social Sciences, Sociology, Western Fiction
ISBN Prefix(es): 9985-61
Bookshop(s): Kupar, Lossi 9, Poltsamaa; Kupar, Harju 1, EE0001 Tallinn

Mats Publishers Ltd+
Laki 15, EE 12915 Tallinn
Tel: (O2) 6563589
Key Personnel
President & Man Dir: Heido Ots
Founded: 1991
Subjects: Automotive, History, House & Home, Transportation
ISBN Prefix(es): 9985-51
Number of titles published annually: 10 Print
Total Titles: 30 Print
Imprints: Mats Tallinn

Mats Tallinn, *imprint of* Mats Publishers Ltd

AS Medicina+
Gonsiori 29, 10147 Tallinn
Tel: (02) 42 1474 *Fax:* (02) 42 5098
Key Personnel
Man Dir: Kaja Uska
Founded: 1993
Member of the Estonian Book Publishers Association.
Subjects: Medicine, Nursing, Dentistry
ISBN Prefix(es): 9985-829
Parent Company: Kustannus Oy Duodecim, Finland, Finland

National Library of Estonia
Tonismaegi 2, 15189 Tallinn
Tel: (02) 6307500; (06) 307501 *Fax:* (02) 6311410
E-mail: nlib@nlib.ee
Web Site: www.nlib.ee
Key Personnel
Dir General: Tiiu Valm *E-mail:* valm@nlib.ee
Marketing Manager: Triin Soone *E-mail:* triin@nlib.ee
Founded: 1918
Information services on humanities & social sciences; exhibition and conference service; book binding and conservation; photocopying; publishing.
Member of CDNL, CENL, EIA, IALL, IAML, IFLA, International Council of Archives, International Paper Conservation Institute & LIBER.
Subjects: Art, History, Law, Library & Information Sciences, Music, Dance, Specialize in information services, exhibition & conference services, preservation, publishing for Parliament & other libraries. Specialize in dictionaries & reference books
ISBN Prefix(es): 9985-803
Number of titles published annually: 50 Print; 2 CD-ROM; 2 E-Book; 1 Audio
Total Titles: 2 CD-ROM; 8 E-Book; 1 Audio

Olion Publishers+
POB 18, Tallinn 110502
Mailing Address: Pikk 2, 10502 Talliun
Tel: (02) 6445403 *Fax:* (02) 6443488
E-mail: olin@eol.ee
Key Personnel
Dir: Hulle Unt
Editor-in-Chief: Veiko Talts *Tel:* (02) 644 43 47
Founded: 1989
Subjects: Biography, Business, Economics, Education, Fiction, History, Law, Nonfiction (General), Philosophy, Social Sciences, Sociology, Western Fiction
ISBN Prefix(es): 9985-66
Number of titles published annually: 40 Print

Perioodika+
Voorimehe 9, PO Box 3648, Tallinn 10507
Tel: (02) 644 3158 *Fax:* (02) 644 2484
Key Personnel
Manager, Editorial Board: Ivar Sinimets
Dir: Uuno Sillajoe *Tel:* (02) 644 1262
Founded: 1973
Subjects: Astrology, Occult, Cookery, Romance, Women's Studies
ISBN Prefix(es): 5-7979
Number of titles published annually: 30 Print
Total Titles: 90 Print

Sinisukk+
Tueri 9, Tallinn 11314
Tel: (02) 555748; (02) 65618721 *Fax:* (02) 6561872
E-mail: sinisukk@sinisukk.ee
Key Personnel
President & International Rights: Marie Edala
  E-mail: marie@sinisukk.ee
Founded: 1992
Subjects: Animals, Pets, Astrology, Occult, Biography, Child Care & Development, Cookery, Crafts, Games, Hobbies, Fiction, Film, Video, Gardening, Plants, House & Home, How-to, Nonfiction (General), Psychology, Psychiatry, Self-Help
Number of titles published annually: 180 Print
Total Titles: 212 Print

Tael Ltd
Rueuetli 6, Tallinn EE0001
Tel: (02) 6314162 *Fax:* (02) 6314162
E-mail: tael@teleport.ee
Key Personnel
Publisher: Vladimir Sokolovski
Founded: 1991
Subjects: Archaeology
Total Titles: 1 Print

TEA Publishers+
28 Liivalaia St, 10118 Tallinn
Tel: (02) 6459206 *Fax:* (02) 6459208
E-mail: tea@tea.ee
Web Site: www.tea.ee
Key Personnel
Pres: Mrs Silva Tomingas
General Manager: Mr Olavi Valner *Fax:* (02) 6459207
International Rights Manager: Kersti Neiman
  E-mail: kersti.neiman@tea.ee
Founded: 1992
Publishing & design of books & dictionaries on diskettes. Subject specialties include textbooks, practice books & grammar books.
ISBN Prefix(es): 9985-71; 9985-843; 9985-9003; 9985-9029
Number of titles published annually: 50 Print; 1 CD-ROM; 3 Audio
Total Titles: 130 Print; 1 CD-ROM; 10 Audio
Branch Office(s)
Parnu, Sirje Manna *Tel:* (02) 4476303
TARTU, Botooni 9 *Tel:* (02) 7307959 *Fax:* (02) 7307970
Bookshop(s): 27 Narva Mnt, Tallinn, Contact: Mrs Ene Tiidelepp *Tel:* (02) 6426019

Tuum+
Harju 1, 10146 Tallinn
Tel: (02) 442272; (02) 6313374 *Fax:* (02) 446832
Key Personnel
Contact: Piret Viires
Founded: 1992
Subjects: Human Relations, Literature, Literary Criticism, Essays, Natural History, Philosophy, Poetry, Psychology, Psychiatry, Science Fiction, Fantasy
ISBN Prefix(es): 9985-802

Valgus Publishers+
Tulika 19, Tallinn 410613
Tel: (02) 6505026 *Fax:* (02) 6505104
Key Personnel
Dir: Ants Sild
Founded: 1965
Subjects: Agriculture, Animals, Pets, Archaeology, Architecture & Interior Design, Biological Sciences, Child Care & Development, Cookery, Crafts, Games, Hobbies, Electronics, Electrical Engineering, Engineering (General), English as a Second Language, Geography, Geology, Health, Nutrition, Medicine, Nursing, Dentistry, Science (General)
ISBN Prefix(es): 5-440

Ethiopia

General Information

Capital: Addis Ababa
Language: Amharic (official), English also widely used
Religion: Ethiopian Orthodox
Population: 51.1 million
Bank Hours: 0830-1230, 1430-1730 Monday-Friday; 0830-1230 Saturday
Shop Hours: Addis Ababa: 0900-1300, 1500-2000 Monday-Saturday. Asmara: 0800-1300, 1600-2000 Monday-Friday
Currency: 100 cents = 1 birr
Export/Import Information: No tarriff on books, but additional taxes. Advertising subject to customs and same taxes. No import license required but Exchange Payment License necessary.
Copyright: No copyright conventions signed

Addis Ababa University Press
PO Box 1176, Addis Ababa
Tel: (01) 119418; (01) 550844 (ext 227) *Fax:* (01) 550655 *Cable:* AA UNIV
Key Personnel
General Editor & Dir: Prof Taddesse Tamrat *Fax:* (01) 550655
Assistant General Dir: Messelech Habte
Founded: 1968
Publishing House of the Addis Ababa University.
Member of Ethiopian Publishers Association, African Association of Science Editors, AP-NET & ABC.
Subjects: Geography, Geology, Health, Nutrition, History, Language Arts, Linguistics, Literature, Literary Criticism, Essays, Science (General), Technology, Academic, Scholarly & Books for general readers: Also, Botany, Chemistry, Climatology, Public Health, & Hydrology
Total Titles: 12 Print
Parent Company: Addis Ababa University
Associate Companies: James Currey Publishers, United Kingdom; Illinois University Press, IL, United States; Lund University Press, Sweden; Norwegian University of Science and Technology, Norway

Ethiopian Nutrition Institute (ENI)
PO Box 5654, Addis Ababa
Tel: (01) 151600 *Fax:* (01) 754744 *Cable:* NUTRITION
Key Personnel
Dir: Dr Zewdie Wolde-Gebriel
Parent Company: Ministry of Health
Divisions: Medical, Laboratory, Training, Food Science & Technology

Government Printer
Government Printing Press, Addis Ababa
Mailing Address: PO Box 1241, Addis Ababa

Fiji

General Information

Capital: Suva
Language: Fijian & Hindi. English widely spoken
Religion: Christian (mainly Methodist) with large minority of Hindus
Population: 800,000
Bank Hours: 1000-1500 Monday-Thursday; 1000-1600 Friday
Shop Hours: 0800-1630 or later Monday-Friday; early closing Wednesday or Saturday
Currency: 100 cents = 1 Fiji dollar
Export/Import Information: No tariffs on books and advertising. No import licenses. Exchange control by Reserve Bank of Fiji; no specific Exchange license required and authorized banks perform transaction upon application.
Copyright: Berne, UCC (see Copyright Conventions, pg xi)

Islands Business International Ltd
GPO Box 12718, Suva
Tel: 303108; 303616 *Fax:* 301423
E-mail: editor@ibi.com.fj
Telex: 2350

Library Service of Fiji
Government Bldgs, Suva
Mailing Address: PO Box 2526, Suva
Tel: 315303; 315344 *Fax:* 314994
Key Personnel
Chief Librarian: Humesh Prasad *Tel:* 315303
Founded: 1964
Listing & information service.
Branch Office(s)
Nausori Library, Nausori *Tel:* 476387 *Fax:* 400048
Northern Regional Library, Ministry of Education, Labasa *Tel:* 812894 *Fax:* 814770
Western Regional Library, PO Box 150, Lautokia *Tel:* 660091 *Fax:* 668195
Raki Raki Branch Library, PO Box 1, Raki Raki *Tel:* 694153 *Fax:* 694855
Savu Savu Branch Library, Savu Savu *Tel:* 850154 *Fax:* 850154
Tavua Branch Library, Tauna *Tel:* 694153 *Fax:* 681390

Lotu Pacifika Productions
Government Bldgs, Suva
Mailing Address: PO Box 2401, Suva
Tel: 301314 *Fax:* 301183 *Cable:* LOTUPAK
Key Personnel
Manager: Seru L Verebalavu
Founded: 1973
Subjects: Cookery, Education, Ethnicity, Poetry, Religion - Other

University of the South Pacific+
University Media Centre, Suva
Mailing Address: PO Box 1168, Suva

Tel: 313900 *Fax:* 301305
E-mail: farkas_g@nsp.ac.fj
Telex: 2276 usp fj *Cable:* UNIVERSITY SUVA
Founded: 1986
Subjects: Education, Environmental Studies, Natural History, Regional Interests

Finland

General Information

Capital: Helsinki
Language: Finnish and Swedish (officially bilingual); English and German spoken widely
Religion: Predominantly Evangelical Lutheran
Population: 5.2 million
Bank Hours: 0915-1615 Monday-Friday
Shop Hours: 0900-1700 or later Monday-Friday; 0900-1600 (1400 in summer) Saturday
Currency: 100 Eurocents = 1 Euro; 5.94573 markkas = 1 Euro
Export/Import Information: Member of the European Union. 12% VAT on books. No import licenses required on books. No exchange controls.
Copyright: UCC, Berne, Florence (see Copyright Conventions, pg xi)

AB Svenska Laromedel-Editum+
Rusthaellargatan 1, 02270 Esbo
Tel: (09) 8043188 *Fax:* (09) 8043257
Key Personnel
Chief Executive: Jan-Peter Kullberg
Founded: 1971
Subjects: Education, Fiction, Nonfiction (General)
ISBN Prefix(es): 951-553
Showroom(s): Kyruoesplanaden 9, 65100 Vasa

Abo Akademis forlag - Abo Akademi University Press
Tavastgatan 30-C, FIN-20700 Abo
Tel: (02) 2153292 *Fax:* (02) 2154490
E-mail: forlaget@abo.fi
Web Site: www.abo.fi/instut/forlag
Key Personnel
Secretary: Inger Hassel *E-mail:* ihassel@abo.fi; inger.hassel@abo.fi
Founded: 1987
Subjects: Science (General)
ISBN Prefix(es): 951-9498; 952-9616; 951-765
Number of titles published annually: 20 Print
Distributed by Oy Tibo-Trading
Orders to: Oy Tibo-Trading Ab, PO Box 33, FIN-21601 Pargas *Tel:* (02) 4589355 *Fax:* (02) 4589164 *E-mail:* tibo@tibo.net

Aika Oy Kristilliset Kirjat (Aika Oy Christian Books)
Heiggilanti 177, 42701 Keuruu
Mailing Address: PO Box 99, Keuruu 42701
Tel: (014) 7514751 *Fax:* (014) 7514757
E-mail: aika@aikaoy.fi
Web Site: www.aikaoy.fi
Key Personnel
Man Dir: Onni Haapala
Secretary: Merja Lamsa
Founded: 1926
Subjects: Religion - Protestant
ISBN Prefix(es): 951-605; 951-606
Imprints: Hengellinen Laulukirja; Raamatun Tietokirja

Akateeminen Kustannusliike Oy+
Arkadiankatu 12, 00100 Helsinki
Tel: (09) 434 2320
Key Personnel
Manager: Tapani Mattila
Sales: Ulla-Riitta Tuulenmaki
Founded: 1927

Subjects: History, Language Arts, Linguistics, Religion - Protestant
ISBN Prefix(es): 951-9023

Art House Group
Bulevardi 19 C, 00120 Helsinki
Tel: (09) 6933725 *Fax:* (09) 6933762
ISBN Prefix(es): 951-884; 951-96086; 951-96135

Atena Kustannus Oy+
PL 436, 40101 Jyvaskyla
Tel: (014) 620192 *Fax:* (014) 620190
Key Personnel
Contact: Pekka Maekelae
Founded: 1986
Subjects: History, Nonfiction (General)
ISBN Prefix(es): 951-9362

Basam Books Oy+
Bulevardi 14, 00120 Helsinki
Mailing Address: PO Box 354, 00121 Helsinki
Tel: (09) 605391 *Fax:* (09) 4521261
Key Personnel
Man Dir & International Rights: Batu Samaletdin
Founded: 1993
Subjects: Fiction, Literature, Literary Criticism, Essays, Philosophy, Poetry, Psychology, Psychiatry
ISBN Prefix(es): 952-9842

Book Studio
Hameenkatu 39, 05800 Hyvinkaa
Tel: (0914) 451441 *Fax:* (0914) 419142
E-mail: books@bookstudio.fi
Web Site: www.bookstudio.fi
Key Personnel
Man Dir: Kari Lindgren
ISBN Prefix(es): 951-611; 951-9247; 951-9298

Ekenas Tryckeri AB
PB 26, 10601 Ekenaes
Tel: (09) 222800 *Fax:* (09) 222813
E-mail: leif.rex@eta.fi
Key Personnel
Man Dir: Sven Sundstroem
Founded: 1881
Subjects: Government, Political Science, History
ISBN Prefix(es): 951-9000; 951-9001

Fenix-Kustannus Oy+
PL 11, 02211 Espoo
Tel: (09) 420 8190 *Fax:* (09) 420 8045
Key Personnel
Chief Executive, Rights & Permissions: Reima T A Luoto
Editorial: Kalevi Viljanen
Sales: Tapio Vaekevaeinen
Production: Matti Saarinen
Founded: 1993
Subjects: Nonfiction (General)
ISBN Prefix(es): 951-862

Finnish Building Centre Ltd
Runeberginkatu 5, FIN-00100 Helsinki
Mailing Address: PO Box 1004, FIN 00101 Helsinki
Tel: (09) 5495570
Web Site: www.rakennustieto
Key Personnel
Marketing Manager: Mr Heimo Salo *Tel:* (09) 54955390 *E-mail:* heimo.salo@rakennstieto.fi
Marketing Assistant: Laana Lapatto *Tel:* (09) 54955397 *E-mail:* laana.lapatto@rakennustieto.fi
Total Titles: 5 CD-ROM; 1 Online; 1 E-Book
Parent Company: The Building Information Institute, Helsinki
Ultimate Parent Company: The Building Information Group
Associate Companies: Helsinki Building Centre, Runeberginkatu 5, 2nd floor, PO Box 1004, FIN 00101 Helsinki *Tel:* (09) 5495 5426 *Fax:* (09) 5495 5420; Lappeenranta Building Centre, Kauppakatu 29-31, FIN 53100 Lappeenranta *Tel:* (05) 415 0990 *Fax:* (05) 415 2600; Kuopio Building Centre, Kauppakatu 40-42, FIN 70110 Kuopio *Tel:* (017) 261 6109 *Fax:* (017) 261 8666; Oulu Building Centre, Uusikatu 32, FIN 90100 Oulu *Tel:* (08) 311 6122 *Fax:* (08) 377 334; Tampere Building Centre, Tuomiokirkonkatu 7, FIN 33100 Tampere *Tel:* (03) 212 6961 *Fax:* (03) 212 6989; World Trade Center, Aleksanterinkatu 17, PO Box 800, FIN 00101 Helsinki, Editor-in-Chief: Mr Markku Lappalainen *Tel:* (09) 6969163 *Fax:* (09) 2126989 (International Services)
Foreign Rep(s): Latvian Building Centre Ltd (LBC) (Latvia); Estonian Building Centre (Estonia); Moscow Construction Centre ZAO (Russia); St Petersburg Construction Centre Ltd (Russia)
Bookshop(s): Helsinki *Tel:* (09) 54955400 *Fax:* (09) 54955340

Finnish Lawyers' Publishing Co, see Kauppakaari Oyj Lakimiesliiton Kustannus, Yrityksen Tietokirjat

Foersamlingsfoerbundets Foerlags AB+
Bangatan 29, 00120 Helsingfors
Mailing Address: POB 285, 00121 Helsingfors
Tel: (09) 6126150; (09) 61261535 *Fax:* (09) 603963
Key Personnel
Man Dir: Leif Westerling *E-mail:* leif.westerling@ff-forlag.fi
Sales: Asa Nordstrom
Founded: 1920
Subjects: Biblical Studies, Psychology, Psychiatry, Religion - Protestant
ISBN Prefix(es): 951-550
Distributor for Verbum-Sweden

Forlagsaktiebolaget Scriptum
Handelsesplanaden 23 A, 65100 Vasa
Tel: (06) 3242228 *Fax:* (06) 3242210
E-mail: scriptum@svof.fi
Web Site: www.syh.fi/scriptum/
Key Personnel
Chairman: Vivan Lygdbaeck
Founded: 1987
Subjects: Archaeology, Fiction, Poetry, Essays
ISBN Prefix(es): 951-8902
Number of titles published annually: 9 Print
Total Titles: 100 Print

Frenckell Printing Work Ltd
Niittyrinne 4, 02270 Espoo
Tel: (09) 8036044 *Fax:* (09) 8036090
Key Personnel
Man Dir: Berndt von Frenckell
Founded: 1642
ISBN Prefix(es): 951-9417; 951-95311

Gummerus Publishers+
Arkadiankatu 23 B, FIN-00100 Helsinki
Mailing Address: PO Box 749, FIN-00101 Helsinki
Tel: (09) 584 301 *Fax:* (09) 5843 0200
Web Site: www.gummerus.fi/kustannus
Key Personnel
Man Dir: Ilkka Kylmala
Publishing Manager, Nonfiction: Risto Vaisanen
Publishing Manager, Foreign Fiction & Nonfiction: Anna Baijars
Publishing Manager, Dictionaries: Virpi Kalliokuusi
Publishing Manager, Educational Materials: Jaana Jokiniemi
Rights & Permissions: Paula Peltola
Founded: 1872
Subjects: Fiction, Nonfiction (General)
ISBN Prefix(es): 951-20
Parent Company: Gummerus Oy
Associate Companies: Ajatus Kirjat, Publishing Manager: Juhani Aromaeki *Tel:* (09) 5843 0229 *Fax:* (09) 5843 0299 *E-mail:* juhani.aromaki@ajatuskustannus.fi *Web Site:* www.ajatuskustannus.fi; Book Studio, Publishing Manager: Kari Lindgren *Tel:* (09) 5843 0235 *Fax:* (09) 5843 0232 *E-mail:* kari.lindgren@bookstudio.fi *Web Site:* www.bookstudio.fi

Hengellinen Laulukirja, *imprint of* Aika Oy Kristilliset Kirjat

Herattaja-yhdistys Ry
PL 21, 62101 Lapuan
Tel: (06) 438 8911 *Fax:* (06) 438 7430
Key Personnel
Executive Dir: Jouko Kuusinen
Founded: 1892
Subjects: Biblical Studies, History, Literature, Literary Criticism, Essays, Poetry, Religion - Protestant, Theology
ISBN Prefix(es): 951-878

Kaantopiiri Oy+
Meritullinkatu 21, 00170 Helsinki
Tel: (09) 1351385 *Fax:* (09) 1351372
Key Personnel
Man Dir: Hannu Paloviita
Editor: Paivi Paappanen *Tel:* (09) 1351395 *E-mail:* paivi.paappanen@likekustannus.fi
Founded: 1987
Specialize in Literature by Women in Third World.
Subjects: Fiction, Foreign Countries, Literature, Literary Criticism, Essays, Nonfiction (General), Women's Studies
ISBN Prefix(es): 951-8989
Parent Company: Like Publishing Oy

Karas-Sana Oy+
Kaisaniemenk 8 A, 4 krs, 00100 Helsinki
Tel: (09) 68155640 *Fax:* (09) 68155611
E-mail: kirjat@karas-sana.fi
Key Personnel
Man Dir: Hans Krause *E-mail:* hans.krause@karas-sana.fi
Publishing Manager: Paivi Karri *E-mail:* paivi.karri@karas-sana.fi
Founded: 1974
Subjects: Human Relations, Religion - Protestant, Self-Help
ISBN Prefix(es): 951-655
Number of titles published annually: 15 Print
Total Titles: 172 Print; 1 Audio
Parent Company: Kansan Raamattuseuran Saeaetioe, PO Box 48, Vivamo SF-08101 Lohja

Karisto Oy+
Paroistentie 2, SF-13100 Haemeenlinna
Mailing Address: PO Box 102, SF-13101 Haemeenlinna
Tel: (03) 6161 551 *Fax:* (03) 6161 565
Key Personnel
Man Dir: Simo Moisio
Publishing Dir: Hannu Sarrala
Editorial & Foreign Rights: Pirkko Mikkola
Founded: 1900
Subjects: Fiction, Nonfiction (General)
ISBN Prefix(es): 951-23
Warehouse: Libri-Logistiikka Oy, Hakakalliontie 10, SF-05800 Hyvinkaeae

Kauppakaari Oyj Lakimiesliiton Kustannus, Yrityksen Tietokirjat
Uudenmaankatu 4-6A, 00120 Helsinki
Tel: (09) 647 101 *Fax:* (09) 602 127
E-mail: kustannus@kauppakaari.fi
Web Site: www.kauppakaari.fi
Key Personnel
Publishing Dir: Mr Tuomo Rasanen

PUBLISHERS

FINLAND

Sales Secretary: Ms Taija Haapaniemi
Founded: 1958
Subjects: Business, Law
ISBN Prefix(es): 951-640; 952-14
Bookshop(s): Lakipiste, Uudenmaankatu 4-6A, 00120 Helsinki *Tel:* (09) 54212230 *Fax:* (09) 54212223

Kirja-Leitzinger+
Keinutie 9 A 7, 00940 Helsinki
Tel: (09) 3493850 *Fax:* (09) 3421853
Key Personnel
Man Dir: Antero Leitzinger
Founded: 1993
Subjects: Asian Studies, Ethnicity, Foreign Countries, Genealogy, Government, Political Science, History, Music, Dance, Travel
ISBN Prefix(es): 952-9752
Total Titles: 15 Print

Kirjatoimi+
Ketarantie 4, 33680 Tampere
Mailing Address: PL 94, 33101 Tampere
Tel: (03) 3611200 *Fax:* (03) 3600454
E-mail: kirjatoimi@sdafin.org *Cable:* KIRJATOIMI
Key Personnel
Man Dir & Chief Editor: Kalliokoski Klaus
Office Manager: Kallman Maarit
 E-mail: wellwoma@sdafin.org
Founded: 1897
Subjects: Health, Nutrition, Religion - Protestant
ISBN Prefix(es): 951-629
Parent Company: Seventh-Day Adventist Church in Finland

Kirjayhtymae Oy
Urho Kekkosen Katu 4-6E, 00100 Helsinki
Tel: (09) 6937641 *Fax:* (09) 69376366
E-mail: oppikirjat@kirjayhtyma.fi
Web Site: www.kirjayhtyma.fi *Cable:* KIRJAYHTYMAe
Key Personnel
Man Dir: Olli Arrakoski
Publishing Dir, Textbooks: Tuija Nurmiranta
Publishing Dir, Fiction, Non-fiction: Jaakko Tapaninen
Contact: Haarala Paeivi
Founded: 1958
Subjects: Fiction, Nonfiction (General)
ISBN Prefix(es): 951-26
Parent Company: Tammi Publishers
Bookshop(s): Kirjava Satama, Urho Kekkosen Katu 4-6E, 00100 Helsinki
Warehouse: Libri-Logistiikka Oy, Hakakalliontie 10, 05800 Hyvinkaa
Orders to: Libri-Logistiikka Oy, Hakakalliontie 10, 05800 Hyvinkaa

Koala-Kustannus/Oy Greenbay House Publishing Ltd+
Vahaniityntie 19 A 1, 00570 Helsinki
Tel: (09) 4111 7177 *Fax:* (09) 684 5034
E-mail: info@koalakustannus.fi
Web Site: www.koalakustannus.fi
Key Personnel
Man Dir & International Rights: Lassi Eskola
 E-mail: lassi.eskola@koalakustannus.fi
Founded: 1997
Member of Finnish Book Publishers Association.
Subjects: Aeronautics, Aviation, Film, Video, History, Maritime, Military Science, Music, Dance, Nonfiction (General), Sports, Athletics
ISBN Prefix(es): 952-5186
Number of titles published annually: 20 Print; 1 CD-ROM
Total Titles: 40 Print

Kustannus Oy Duodecim (Duodecim Medical Publications Ltd)+
Kalevankatu 11 A, 00100 Helsinki
Mailing Address: PO Box 713, 00101 Helsinki
Tel: (09) 618 851 *Fax:* (09) 6188 5400
Web Site: www.duodecim.fi
Key Personnel
Secretary: Raija Orndahl *E-mail:* raija.orndahl@duodecim.ti
Man Dir: Pekka Mustongn *E-mail:* pekka.mustongn@duodecim.ti
Founded: 1984
Member of the Finnish Book Publishers Association.
Subjects: Medicine, Nursing, Dentistry, Psychology, Psychiatry
ISBN Prefix(es): 951-656; 951-8917
Number of titles published annually: 15 Print
Associate Companies: AS Medicina, Gonsiori 29, Tallinn, Estonia *Tel:* (06) 484 679

Kustannus Oy Kolibri+
Office Center, Lautatarhankatu 6 A, 00580 Helsinki
Mailing Address: PL45, 00581 Helsinki
Tel: (09) 7019443 *Fax:* (09) 7019351
Key Personnel
Man Dir: Rauno Malmstrom
Founded: 1989
Subjects: Nonfiction (General), Wine & Spirits
ISBN Prefix(es): 951-576

Rakentajain Kustannus Oy (Building Publications Ltd)+
Rahakamarinportti 3A, 00240 Helsinki
Tel: (09) 142855 *Fax:* (09) 5032542
Key Personnel
Chief Executive Officer: Pertti Sarmala
Publishing Dir: Eeva Kalin
Founded: 1916
Specialize in books on all fields & levels of construction.
Subjects: Architecture & Interior Design, How-to
ISBN Prefix(es): 951-676
Bookshop(s): Fredrikinkatu 53, 00100 Helsinki

Kustannus Oy Semic
Paasikiventie 16C, 33101 Tampere
Mailing Address: PL 317, 33101, Tampere
Tel: (031) 2738700 *Fax:* (031) 2438287
E-mail: jaana.huttunen@semic.fi
Telex: Semic
Key Personnel
Chief Executive & Publicity: Pentti Molander
Editorial, Production: Marjaana Tulosmaa
Founded: 1971
ISBN Prefix(es): 951-9112; 951-876; 951-95793; 951-95794; 951-95231; 951-95232
Parent Company: Semic International AB, Sweden

Kustannus Oy Uusi Tie+
Ohikulkutie 198, 12310 Ryttyla
Tel: (01) 977820 *Fax:* (01) 9757055
E-mail: uusitie@sci.fi
Key Personnel
Editor-at-Large: Vuokko Vanska
Sales: Raimo Raukko
Founded: 1965
Subjects: Fiction, Religion - Other, Theology
ISBN Prefix(es): 951-619

Kustannuskiila Oy
Vuorikatu 21, 70100 Kuopio
Tel: (017) 303551 *Fax:* (017) 303243
Telex: 42111 Sasan
Key Personnel
President, Editorial, Production, Publicity & Sales: Juhani Pitkaenen *E-mail:* juhani.pitkaenen@savonsanomat.fi
Founded: 1964
Subjects: History
ISBN Prefix(es): 951-657
Parent Company: Savon Sanomat, Vuorikatu 21-23, 70100 Kuopio

Kuva ja Sana+
Pajuniityntie 1, 00320 Helsinki
Tel: (09) 4774920 *Fax:* (09) 550892
Key Personnel
CEO, President, Editor in Chief, Rights & Permissions: Leo Meller
Production, Publicity: Olli Palen
Founded: 1942
Subjects: Government, Political Science, Religion - Other, Social Sciences, Sociology
ISBN Prefix(es): 951-9024; 951-9072; 951-9073; 951-9203; 951-585
Associate Companies: Patmos International, PL 86, 00381 Helsinki
Subsidiaries: Ideakustannus
Bookshop(s): Christian Center, Harjukatu 2, SF-00500 Helsinki

Lasten Keskus Oy
Saerkiniementie 7A, 00210 Helsinki
Tel: (09) 6926344 *Fax:* (09) 6926393 *Cable:* LASTEN KESKUS
Key Personnel
Man Dir: Pertti Rosenholm
Manager Children's Books & Juveniles: Arja Kanerva
Manager: Maisa Tonteri
Founded: 1974
Subjects: Biblical Studies, Child Care & Development, Crafts, Games, Hobbies, Education, Human Relations, Religion - Protestant
ISBN Prefix(es): 951-627; 951-626
Associate Companies: Suomen Kirkko-Mediat Oy
Subsidiaries: Pentella Oy
Bookshop(s): Lasten Kirjakauppa, Fredrikinkatu 61, SF-00100 Helsinki (Children's Bookstore)

Otava Publishing Co Ltd+
Affiliate of Otava Books & Magazines Group Ltd
Uudenmaankatu 8-12, FIN-00120 Helsinki
Mailing Address: PO Box 134, FIN-00121 Helsinki
Tel: 19961 *Fax:* 643136
E-mail: otava@otava.fi
Web Site: www.otava.fi *Cable:* OTAVA HELSINKI
Key Personnel
Chairman: Olli Reenpaa
Man Dir: Antti Reenpaa
Publishing Dir, General Books: Leena Majander
Publishing Dir, Educational Books: Jukka Vahtola
Publishing Manager, General Nonfiction: Liisa Steffa
Publishing Manager, Translated Fiction: Minna Castren
Publishing Manager, Children's Books: Katriina Kauppila
Publishing Manager, Special Books: Eva Reenpaa
Publishing Manager, Otava Education/Humanities & Arts Dept: Helena Ruuska
Publishing Manager, Otava Education/Modern Languages Dept: Laura Paivanen
Publishing Manager, Otava Education/Science Dept: Teuvo Sankila
Publishing Manager, Otava Education/Basic Education: Juha Vuorinen
Publishing Manager, Reference Books: Jrja Hamalainen
Publishing Manager, Handbooks: Heli Hottinen
Foreign Rights Manager, Selling: Eila Mellin
Founded: 1890
Subjects: Fiction, How-to, Nonfiction (General)
ISBN Prefix(es): 951-1
Book Club(s): Suuri Suomalainen Kirjakerho Oy - The Great Finnish Book Club

Oy Edita AB+
Siltasaarenkata 14, 00530 Helsinki
Mailing Address: PL 700, 200043 Edita (Helsinki)
Tel: (09) 56601 *Fax:* (00) 5660396
Telex: 123458 Vapk

FINLAND

Key Personnel
Dir-General: Mikko Suotsalo
Dir, Publication: Leo Eskola
Editorial Dir: Lauri Veijola; Lepisto Timo
Marketing Manager & Rights & Permissions: Pauli Niemi-Jaskari
Founded: 1859
ISBN Prefix(es): 951-37; 951-859; 951-860; 951-861
Bookshop(s): Annankatu 44, 00100 Helsinki; Etelaeesplanadi 4

Oy LIKE Kustannus Ltd+
Meritullinkatu 21, 00170 Helsinki
Tel: (09) 1351385 *Fax:* (09) 1351372
Web Site: www.likekustannus.fi
Key Personnel
Man Dir: Hannu Paloviita *E-mail:* hannu.paloviita@likekustannus.fi
Founded: 1987
The leading independent publishing house in Finland. Publishes a cultural magazine, circulation 700,000 copies.
Subjects: Fiction, Nonfiction (General), Science Fiction, Fantasy
ISBN Prefix(es): 951-578
Number of titles published annually: 100 Print
Total Titles: 600 Print
Bookshop(s): Like Kirjokauppe, Vuorikatz 5, 00700 Helsinki, Otto Salkinen *Tel:* (09) 2600288

Paiva Osakeyhtio+
Lukiokatu 15, 13100 Hameenlinna
Mailing Address: PL 10, 13101 Haemeenlinna
Tel: (01) 976446113 *Fax:* (09) 176122109
E-mail: paivaoy@svk.fi
Web Site: www.svk.fi/paivaoy/
Key Personnel
Executive Dir: Olavi Rintala
Founded: 1962
Subjects: Religion - Protestant, Religion - Other
ISBN Prefix(es): 951-622

Pohjoinen
Ahjotiel, 90100 Oulu
Mailing Address: PL 70, 90151 Oulu
Tel: (09) 815377570 *Fax:* (09) 815377572
E-mail: annariitta.lankela@kaleva.fi
Key Personnel
Publishing Manager: Peerit Taehtinen
Founded: 1964
ISBN Prefix(es): 951-749; 951-9099; 951-9152
Parent Company: Kirjapaino Osakeyhito Kaleva

Raamatun Tietokirja, *imprint of* Aika Oy Kristilliset Kirjat

Rakennusalan Kustantajat Rak+
Kaupintie 13, 00440 Helsinki
Tel: (09) 5032541 *Fax:* (09) 5032542
E-mail: rak@sarmala.pp.fi
Key Personnel
Publisher: Pertti Sarmala
Founded: 1991
ISBN Prefix(es): 952-9687; 951-664

Rakennustieto Oy - Building Information Ltd
Runeberginkatu 5, 00100 Helsinki
Mailing Address: PL 1004, 00101 Helsinki
Tel: (09) 5495570 *Fax:* (09) 54955390
E-mail: firstname.familyname@rakennustieto.fi
Web Site: www.rakennustieto.fi
Key Personnel
Man Dir: Markku Salmi
Assistant Man Dir: Heimo Salo
Founded: 1974
Subjects: Architecture & Interior Design
ISBN Prefix(es): 951-682
Parent Company: Rakennustietosaeaetio - Building Information Foundation RTS

Recallmed Oy+
Valkjarventie 45, 01800 Klaukkala
Tel: (09) 8797177 *Fax:* (09) 8797088
Key Personnel
Publishing Dir: Timo Saarinen
Chairman of the Board: Dr Bruno Taajamaa
Subjects: Biography, Medicine, Nursing, Dentistry, Music, Dance, Sports, Athletics
ISBN Prefix(es): 951-9221; 951-847

Sairaanhoitajien Koulutussaatio+
Sitratori 5, 00420 Helsinki
Tel: (09) 5666788 *Fax:* (09) 531504
Key Personnel
Executive Dir: Paivi Huopalahti
Financial Manager: Raija Jarvio
Chief Editor: Maija Tupala
Founded: 1944
Subjects: Medicine, Nursing, Dentistry
ISBN Prefix(es): 951-8963; 951-9105

Schildts Foerlagsaktiebolag+
Rusthallargatan 1, 02270 Esbo 1
Mailing Address: PO Box 86, 02271 Esbo
Tel: (00) 8870400 *Fax:* (00) 8043257
E-mail: schildts@schildts.fi
Web Site: www.schildts.fi *Cable:* BOKSCHILDT
Key Personnel
Man Dir: Mr Johan Johnson *E-mail:* jjohnson@schildts.fi
Rights & Permissions: Helen Svensson *E-mail:* helen@schildts.fi
Marketing Dir: Elisabeth Jansson *E-mail:* bettan@schildts.fi
Founded: 1913
Subjects: Art, Biography, Fiction, History, Music, Dance, Philosophy, Poetry
ISBN Prefix(es): 951-50
Associate Companies: Pagina

Soederstroem et Co Foerlagsaktiebolag
Wavulinsvaegen 4, 00210 Helsingfors
Mailing Address: PB 97, 00211 Helsingfors
Tel: (09) 6922010 *Fax:* (09) 6926346; (09) 6822425 *Cable:* SOeDERSTROeMS
Key Personnel
Man Dir: Carl Appelberg
Founded: 1891
Subjects: Art, Biography, Fiction, History, Howto, Philosophy, Poetry, Psychology, Psychiatry, Religion - Other, Science (General)
ISBN Prefix(es): 951-52

Suomalaisen Kirjallisuuden Seura (Finnish Literature Society)
Hallituskatu 1, 00170 Helsinki
Mailing Address: PO Box 259, 00171 Helsinki
Tel: (09) 131231 *Fax:* (09) 13123220
E-mail: firstname.familyname@finlit.fi
Key Personnel
Secretary-General-Dir: Jussi Nuorteva
Publisher: Paivi Vallisaari *Tel:* (09) 131 23 210 *E-mail:* paivi.vallisaari@finlit.fi
Founded: 1831
Subjects: Anthropology, History, Language Arts, Linguistics, Literature, Literary Criticism, Essays
ISBN Prefix(es): 951-717; 951-746
Number of titles published annually: 100 Print
Total Titles: 1,500 Print

Suomen Matkailuliitto ry (The Finish Travel Association)
Atomitie 5C, 00370 Helsinki
Tel: (09) 6226280 *Fax:* (09) 654358
E-mail: matkailuliitto@matkailuliitto.org
Web Site: www.tunturioppaat.org
Founded: 1887
Subjects: Travel
ISBN Prefix(es): 951-838

Suomen pipliaseura RY+
Kauppiaankatu 7A, 00160 Helsinki
Mailing Address: PL 173, 00161 Helsinki
Tel: (09) 625925 *Fax:* (09) 625719
E-mail: info@bible.fi
Founded: 1812
Specialize in Bibles, fund raising for Bible Society & development of teaching methods of the Bible.
Subjects: Biblical Studies
ISBN Prefix(es): 951-9010; 951-577

SV-Kauppiaskanava Oy+
Kanavakatu 3B, 00160 Helsinki
Fax: (09) 175 426
E-mail: kaija.tynkkynen@kesko.fi
Key Personnel
Man Dir: Rinta Perttu
Publishing Manager: Tommi Tanhuanpaa
Founded: 1912
Publishing House of the Finnish Retailers Association.
Subjects: Cookery, Crafts, Games, Hobbies, House & Home
ISBN Prefix(es): 951-635

Svenska Oesterbottens Litteraturfoerening
Stagnas Vagen 85, 66640 Maxmo
Tel: (06) 3450286
Key Personnel
Contact: Gun Anderssen
Subjects: Poetry
ISBN Prefix(es): 951-95007

Tammi Publishers
Urho Kekkosen katu 4-6 E, 00100 Helsinki
Mailing Address: PO Box 410, 00101 Helsinki
Tel: (09) 6937 621 *Fax:* (09) 6937 6266
E-mail: firstname.familyname@tammi.net
Web Site: tammi.net *Cable:* TAMMI
Key Personnel
Man Dir, Publisher: Olli Arrakoski
Managers, Children's & Juvenile: Terttu Toiviainen
Literary Dir: Jaakko Tapaninen
Founded: 1943
Subjects: Fiction, Nonfiction (General)
ISBN Prefix(es): 951-30; 951-31
Parent Company: Bonnier Media AB, Sweden
Associate Companies: Libri-Logistiikka Oy
Subsidiaries: Kirjayhtymae Oy; Kirjasuomi Oy; Kustannus Oy Kolibri; Oy Opifer Ltd; Oy Satusiivet-Sagovingar AB
Bookshop(s): Kirjava Satama, Urho Kekkosen katu 4-6 E, 00100 Helsinki
Book Club(s): ExLibris; Lasten Parhaat Kirjat
Warehouse: Libri-Logistiikka Oy, Hakakalliontie 10, 05800 Hvyinkaa
Orders to: Libri-Logistiikka Oy, Hakakalliontie 10, 05800 Hvyinkaa

Teknolit Oy+
Asemakatu 4 C, 40100 Jyvaskyla
Tel: (014) 3100555 *Fax:* (014) 3100566
E-mail: teknolit@teknoli.pp.fi
Web Site: www.teknolit.fi
Key Personnel
Man Dir: Sahlman Mika
Founded: 1990
Subjects: Civil Engineering, Computer Science, Engineering (General), Microcomputers
ISBN Prefix(es): 952-9823; 952-5159; 951-96321
Parent Company: Werner Soderstrom Oy

Tietoteos Publishing Co
Oikkalantie 31, 02880 Veikkola
Mailing Address: PL 22, 02881 Veikkola
Tel: (09) 264475 *Fax:* (09) 264575
E-mail: jyrki.talvitie@att.inet.fi
Web Site: www.jkttietoteos.fi

Key Personnel
Man Dir: Jyrki K Talvitie *E-mail:* jyrki.talvitie@tt.inet.fi
Founded: 1948
Subjects: Economics, Travel
ISBN Prefix(es): 951-9035; 951-8919

Ursa ry+
Raatimiehenkatu 3A2, 00140 Helsinki
Tel: (09) 684 0400 *Fax:* (09) 6840 4040
E-mail: markku.sarimaa@ursa.fi
Web Site: www.ursa.fi
Key Personnel
Publications Dir: Markku Sarimaa *Tel:* (09) 6840 4060 *E-mail:* markku.sarimaa@ursa.fi
Founded: 1921
Subjects: Earth Sciences, Physical Sciences, Science (General)
ISBN Prefix(es): 951-9269

Osuuskunta Vastapaino+
Yliopistonkatu 60 A, 33100 Tampere
Tel: (03) 2146246; (03) 2146245; (03) 2146248 *Fax:* (03) 2146646
E-mail: vastapaino@vastapaino.fi
Key Personnel
Man Dir: Teijo Makkonen
Founded: 1981
Subjects: Behavioral Sciences, Education, History, Journalism, Literature, Literary Criticism, Essays, Philosophy, Social Sciences, Sociology, Women's Studies
ISBN Prefix(es): 951-9066; 951-768
Number of titles published annually: 25 Print
Total Titles: 180 Print

Watti-Kustannus Oy
Meritullinkatu 11 C, 00170 Helsinki
Tel: (09) 1356878 *Fax:* (09) 1356437
ISBN Prefix(es): 951-95945

Weilin & Goeoes Oy+
Ahertajantie 5, 02100 Espoo
Mailing Address: PO Box 27, 02101 Espoo
Tel: (00) 43771 *Fax:* (00) 4377270
E-mail: firstname.familyname@wgoy.fi
Key Personnel
President: Koskinen Olle
Publishing Dir: Juhani Mikola
Editorial Manager, Nonfiction: Kuosmanen Riitta-Liisa
Information Officer: Irmeli Kotkavuori
Founded: 1872
Subjects: Animals, Pets, Art, Health, Nutrition, History, Nonfiction (General)
ISBN Prefix(es): 951-35
Parent Company: WSOY Group
Subsidiaries: Bertmark Media AB

Werner Soederstroem Osakeyhtioe (WSOY)+
Bulevardi 12, 00120 Helsinki
Mailing Address: PO Box 222, 00121 Helsinki
Tel: (00) 61681 *Fax:* (00) 61683566
Telex: 122644 Wsoy *Cable:* WSOY HELSINKI
Key Personnel
Man Dir: Jorma Kaimio
Rights & Permissions: Sirkku Klemola
Literary Dir: Touko Siltala *E-mail:* jkai@cc.wsoy.ti
Translated Fiction: Kiti Kattelus
Nonfiction (How-to & Reference): Kaarina Joutsenniemi; Micttinen Kaarina
General Nonfiction: Aleksi Siltala
Founded: 1878
Subjects: Education, Fiction, Nonfiction (General)
ISBN Prefix(es): 951-0
Associate Companies: Rautakirja Oy, Koivuvaarankuja 2, 01640 Vantaa *Tel:* (00) 85281 *Fax:* (00) 8533281; WS Bookwell, Teollisuustie 4, 06100 Porvoo *Tel:* (019) 21941 *Fax:* (019) 219 4802
Subsidiaries: Bertmark A/S; Bertmark Media AB; Bertmark Norge AS; Bertmarks Forlag AB; AB Foerlagsinkasso; Ajasto Osakeyhtio; Weilin & Goos Oy; Werner Soderstrom GmbH
Book Club(s): Uudet Kirjat

WSOY, see Werner Soedstroem Osakeyhtioe (WSOY)

Yliopistopaino/Helsinki University Press+
PL 4/ Vuorikatu 3 A, FIN-00014 Helsingin Yliopisto
Tel: (09) 70102360 *Fax:* (09) 70102374
E-mail: rki@yopaino.helsinki.fi
Founded: 1987
Subjects: Behavioral Sciences, Biological Sciences, Communications, Drama, Theater, Education, Environmental Studies, Gay & Lesbian, Health, Nutrition, History, Journalism, Language Arts, Linguistics, Literature, Literary Criticism, Essays, Mathematics, Medicine, Nursing, Dentistry, Music, Dance, Psychology, Psychiatry, Social Sciences, Sociology, Theology, Travel, Women's Studies
ISBN Prefix(es): 951-570
Parent Company: Helsinki University

Yritystieto Oy - Foretagsdata AB
PO Box 148, 00181 Helsinki
Tel: (00) 648292 *Fax:* (00) 648250
Key Personnel
Publisher: Boerje Thilman
Founded: 1972
Subjects: Business
ISBN Prefix(es): 951-9102

France

General Information

Capital: Paris
Language: French (regional dialects), Basque in the Basque country of the southwest, Breton in Brittany, Catalan in Roussillon, Corsican in Corsica, Dutch along parts of border with Belgium, German in Alsace, Occitan in south; most people in these minority linguistic groups also speak French
Religion: Predominantly Roman Catholic
Population: 59.3 million
Bank Hours: 0900-1200, 1400-1600 Monday-Friday. Some closed Monday.
Shop Hours: 0900-1930 Monday-Saturday. Many closed Monday
Currency: 100 Eurocents = 1 Euro; 6.55957 French francs = 1 Euro
Export/Import Information: Member of the European Economic Community. 5.5% VAT on books. Import licenses not required. There is a control of the book trade based on a number of legal and regulating provisions applying to the import of pirated publications, articles and writings that offend against morality and public order, publications harmful to youth, writings forbidden by the Minister for the Interior; the customs official must submit articles subject to control for examination by the General Information Service of the Ministry of the Interior.
Copyright: UCC, Berne, Buenos Aires, Florence (see Copyright Conventions, pg xi)

Editions A M Metailie+
5 rue de Savoie, 75006 Paris
Tel: (01) 55 42 83 00 *Fax:* (01) 55428304
E-mail: presse@metailie.info
Web Site: www.metailie.info
Key Personnel
Man Dir & Editor: Anne Marie Metailie *E-mail:* editions.metailie@worldnet.fr
Literary Dir: P Dibie; P Leglise-Costa
Founded: 1979
Subjects: Anthropology, Fiction, Literature, Literary Criticism, Essays, Mysteries, Social Sciences, Sociology
ISBN Prefix(es): 2-86424
Total Titles: 400 Print
Warehouse: Seuil, 13 ave du General Leclere, 91120 L Ballainvilliers, Longjumeau
Orders to: Seuil, 27 rue Jacob, 75261 Parid Cedex 06

ABC Editions+
One rue de Rome, 93561 Rosny-sous-Bois cedex
Tel: (01) 48122222 *Fax:* (01) 48122239
Key Personnel
Man Dir: Jean-Michel Zunquin
Founded: 1982
Subjects: Communications, Education, Language Arts, Linguistics, Literature, Literary Criticism, Essays, Marketing, Philosophy
ISBN Prefix(es): 2-86769
Associate Companies: Breal
Imprints: Les Cahiers du BAC; Les Cahiers du College
Bookshop(s): Librairie des Prepas, 34 rue Serpente, F-75006 Paris
Shipping Address: Bat N 9, 20 rue Escoffier, 94671 Charenton
Orders to: Breal, rue de Rome, 1, 93561 Rosny-sous-Bois Cedex

Academie Nationale de Reims
7 rue des Ecoles, 51100 Reims
Tel: (0326) 910449 *Fax:* (0326) 910449
Key Personnel
Secretary General: Patrick Demouy *Tel:* (0326) 479819 *E-mail:* patrick.demouy@laposte.net
Administrative Secretary: Philippe Petit-Stervinou
Founded: 1841 (Founded by Cardinal Gousset, archeveque de Reims)
Subjects: Biography, Communications, History
Total Titles: 500 Print
Foreign Rep(s): Champagne

Editions Accarias, see L'Originel - Editions Accarias

ACLA, see EPLS - ACLA Edition

ACR Edition Internationale (Art Creation Realisation)+
20 ter, rue de Bezons, Les Poissons 1196, 92400 Courbevoie, Paris
Tel: (01) 47 88 14 92 *Fax:* (01) 43 33 38 81
E-mail: acredition@acr-edition.com
Web Site: www.acr-edition.com
Key Personnel
Man Dir, Rights & Permissions: A Rafif
Editorial: Mrs M P Kerbrat
Founded: 1983
Member of Syndicat de L'Edition Groupe Art.
Subjects: Art
ISBN Prefix(es): 2-86770
Foreign Rep(s): Artbook International (London)

Actes Graphiques+
29 Pl Bobby Sands BP 81, 42010 Saint-Etienne Cedex 2
Tel: (04) 77 59 28 95; (06) 09 42 21 13 *Fax:* (04) 77592903
Web Site: www.actes-graphiques.com
Key Personnel
Dir: Georges Callet *E-mail:* georges.callet@free.fr
Founded: 1994
Subjects: Geography, Geology, Government, Political Science, Humor, Literature, Literary Criticism, Essays, Mysteries, Photography, Re-

FRANCE

gional Interests, Religion - Catholic, Religion - Other
ISBN Prefix(es): 2-910868
Subsidiaries: Le Henaff-Action Graphique
Distributor for Action Graphique; Le Henaff

Editions Actes Sud+
Pl Nina-berberova, 13200 Arles
Tel: (04) 90 49 86 91 *Fax:* (04) 90 96 95 25
E-mail: contact@actes-sud.fr
Web Site: www.actes-sud.fr
Key Personnel
President: Hubert Nyssen
Man Dir: Francoise Nyssen
Editorial: Bertrand Py
Rights: Franck Benalloul
Foreign Rights: Elisabeth Beyer *Tel:* 490495666
  E-mail: e.beyer@actes-sud.fr
Financial Dir: Jean Paul Capitani
Founded: 1978
Subjects: Biography, Drama, Theater, Literature, Literary Criticism, Essays, Poetry
ISBN Prefix(es): 2-7427; 2-86869; 2-86943
Number of titles published annually: 300 Print
Imprints: Babel (paperback); Solin (nonfiction: essays, biographies & foreign literature); Travel Aventure; Cactus
Subsidiaries: Actes Sud Junior (Children books & literature); Babel (paperback); Sinbad (Arabv literatures & Islam); Solin (nonfiction: essays, biographies & foreign literature)
Branch Office(s)
18 rue de Seguier, 75006 Paris *Tel:* (033) 155426300 *Fax:* (033) 155426301
Distributor for Andre Dimanche; Lemeac; Paris-Musees
Bookshop(s): Le Mejan, 13200 Arles
Orders to: U D Union Distributors Flammarion, 2A Delta, 29-31 ave Guynemer, BP 403, Chevilly Lorue, 94152 Rungis Cedex

Action Artistique de la Ville de Paris
25 rue Saint-Louis-en-l lle, 75004 Paris
Tel: (01) 43 25 30 30 *Fax:* (01) 43 25 17 69
E-mail: aavp@club-internet.fr
Also specializes in Urbanism.
Subjects: Architecture & Interior Design, Art, History
ISBN Prefix(es): 2-905118; 2-913246
Total Titles: 70 Print
Distributor for CiD

ADEC, see Art Price Annual ADEC

ADPF Publications
6, rue Ferrus, 75683 Paris, Cedex 14
Tel: (01) 43 13 11 00 *Fax:* (01) 43 13 11 25
Web Site: www.france.diplomatie.fr; www.adpf.asso.fr
Key Personnel
International Rights: Anne Parian
Service Communication: Anne du Parquet
Founded: 1996
Subjects: Art, Biography, Literature, Literary Criticism, Essays, Philosophy, Photography, Poetry
ISBN Prefix(es): 2-911127

Adrian+
12 rue bachaumont, 75002 Paris
Tel: (01) 42364429 *Fax:* (01) 42364429
Key Personnel
Publisher: Paul Adrian
Specializes in spectacles & cinema.
ISBN Prefix(es): 2-900107

Adverbum SARL+
La Fresquiere, 04340 Meolans-Revel
Tel: (04) 92812881 *Fax:* (04) 92813711
E-mail: info@adverbum.fr
Web Site: www.adverbum.fr

Key Personnel
Manager: Michel Mirale
Founded: 1989
Subjects: Anthropology, Behavioral Sciences, Biblical Studies, Health, Nutrition, How-to, Medicine, Nursing, Dentistry, Religion - Catholic
ISBN Prefix(es): 2-907653; 2-911328; 2-914338
Number of titles published annually: 12 Print
Total Titles: 80 Print
Imprints: Editions Desiris; Editions Gregoriennes; Editions le Sureau

Agence Bibliographique de L'Enseignement Superieur
Unit of French Ministry for Higher Education
25, rue Guillaume-Dupuytren, BP 4367, 34196 Montpellier Cedex 5
Tel: (04) 67 54 84 10 *Fax:* (04) 67 54 84 14
E-mail: nom@abes.fr
Web Site: www.abes.fr
Key Personnel
Dir: Sabine Barral *E-mail:* barral@abes.fr
Librarian: Anne Brigant *E-mail:* brigant@abes.fr
Founded: 1994
Member of GFII, ADBS, IFLA, EUSIDIC & AFUGI.
Subjects: Library & Information Sciences
ISBN Prefix(es): 2-912292
Total Titles: 2 CD-ROM
Imprints: CCNPS
Branch Office(s)
Repertoire des bibliotheque
Distributed by Bibliopolis

Editions Al Liamm
2 banell Poulbriken, 29200 Brest
Tel: 0298021084
Key Personnel
Man Dir: Ronan Huon
Founded: 1949
This is a non-commercial organization specializing in the Breton Language.
Subjects: Drama, Theater, Education, Fiction, Literature, Literary Criticism, Essays, Poetry
ISBN Prefix(es): 2-7368
Parent Company: Association Al Liamm, 2 Venelle Poulbriquen, 29200 Brest
U.S. Office(s): Schoenhof's Foreign Books, Catalogue Dept, 76A Mount Auburn St, Cambridge, MA 02138, United States *Tel:* 617-5478855 *Fax:* 617-5478551
Stephen Griffin, 9 Irvington Rd, Medford, MA, United States
Orders to: R Huon L Vennelle Poulbriquen, 29200 Brest

Editions Albatros, see Copernic

Editions Albin Michel+
22, rue Huyghens, 75014 Paris
Tel: (01) 42 79 10 00 *Fax:* (01) 43 27 21 58
Web Site: www.albin-michel.fr
Key Personnel
President: Francis Esmenard
Vice President: Richard Ducousset
General Secretary: Agnes Fruman
  E-mail: afrumen@aldin-michel.pr; Thierry Pfister
Man Dir: Alexis Esmenard; Henri Esmenard; Patrice Gueriy
Sales Dir: Jean-Yves Bry
Dir, Advertising & Promotion: Sylvie Hoare
Foreign Rights: Jacqueline Favero
Subsidiary Rights: Marie Dormann
Dir, Foreign Dept: Tony Cartano
Public Relations: Regine Billot; Florence Godfernaux
Children's Books: Marion Jablonski
Foreign Rights (Children's books): Aurelie Lapautre
Founded: 1902

BOOK

Subjects: Art, Biography, Child Care & Development, Cookery, Fiction, History, How-to, Humor, Literature, Literary Criticism, Essays, Music, Dance, Nonfiction (General), Philosophy, Religion - Other, Social Sciences, Sociology
ISBN Prefix(es): 2-226

Alliance Biblique Universelle, *imprint of* Societe Biblique Francaise

Alsatia SA
4 pl de la Reunion, 68100 Mulhouse Cedex
Mailing Address: BP 66, 68051 Mulhouse
Tel: (03) 89 45 21 53 *Fax:* (03) 89 45 18 98
Key Personnel
Man Dir: Eric de Valence
Sales, Publicity, Advertising, Rights & Permissions: Virginie Poussier
Founded: 1896
Subjects: Biography, Education, History, How-to, Medicine, Nursing, Dentistry, Poetry, Religion - Other
ISBN Prefix(es): 2-7032
Bookshop(s): Librairie Alsatia, 31 pl de la Cathedrale, F-67000 Strasbourg; Librairie Union, 28 rue des Tetes, F-68000 Colmar; 26 rue Charles de Gaulle, F-68130 Altkirch; 108 ruede la Republique, F-68500 Guebwiller

Editions Alternatives+
5 rue de Pontoise, 75005 Paris
Tel: (01) 43 26 26 82 *Fax:* (01) 43290270
E-mail: ealterna@club-internet.fr
Key Personnel
President: Gerard Aime *Tel:* (01) 46334922
Founded: 1975
Subjects: Alternative, Architecture & Interior Design, Art, House & Home, How-to, Music, Dance, Photography
ISBN Prefix(es): 2-86227; 2-86738
Orders to: CDE, 17 rue de Tournon, 75006 Paris

ALTESS Editions Argel+
4 rue des Petits Hotels, 75010 Paris
Tel: (01) 64403589 *Fax:* (01) 64402757
E-mail: eliaur@club-internet.fr
Web Site: www.ifrance.com/3eMillenaire/altess/index.htm
Key Personnel
Contact: Alain-Rene Gelineau
Founded: 1990
Subjects: Biography, Health, Nutrition, Poetry, Psychology, Psychiatry, Religion - Other, Spirituality; personal development
ISBN Prefix(es): 2-84243
Number of titles published annually: 15 Print
Total Titles: 160 Print
Distributed by LAVAL Distribution (Quebec Canada)
Distributor for Editions Voici la Clef (Here's the Key) (France)
Showroom(s): Espace Harmonie, 4 rue des Petits Hotels, 75010 Paris *Tel:* (01) 47707879 *Fax:* (01) 47707877
Warehouse: ALTESS-AR Gelineau, 95 Residence Vincennes, 77330 Ozoir-la-Ferriere *Tel:* (01) 64403589 *Fax:* (01) 64402757
Orders to: ALTESS-AR Gelineau, 95 Residence Vincennes, 77330 Ozoir-la-Ferriere *Tel:* (01) 64403589 *Fax:* (01) 64402757

Alzieu Editions+
19, rue Chenoise, 38816 Grenoble Cedex 1
Mailing Address: BP 3045, 38816 Grenoble Cedex 1
Tel: (04) 76 51 09 51 *Fax:* (04) 76 51 09 51
E-mail: editions-alzieu@wanadoo.fr
Key Personnel
Dir: Claude Alzieu
Founded: 1991
ISBN Prefix(es): 2-910717
Distributed by Brepols

Editions de l'Amateur+
25 rue Ginoux, 75015 Paris
Tel: (01) 45 77 08 05 *Fax:* (01) 45799715
Key Personnel
President-Dir General: Nuria Boussac
Subjects: Art
ISBN Prefix(es): 2-85917

Editions d'Amerique et d'Orient, Adrien Maisonneuve+
11 rue St-Sulpice, 75006 Paris
Tel: (01) 43 26 86 35 *Fax:* (01) 43 54 59 54
E-mail: maisonneuve@maisonneuve-adrien.com
Key Personnel
Man Dir: Jean Maisonneuve
Founded: 1926
Subjects: Art, Ethnicity, History, Philosophy, Religion - Other, Social Sciences, Sociology
ISBN Prefix(es): 2-7200
Imprints: Librairie D'Amerique Et D'Orient

Editions Amez+
One Sq de l'Aiguillage, 67100 Strasbourg
Tel: (03) 88845656 *Fax:* (03) 88845684
Key Personnel
Associate Editor: Christine Vanet
Founded: 1991
Subjects: Art
ISBN Prefix(es): 2-909242

L'Amitie par le Livre+
13 ave du 60 Ri, 25001 Cedex, Besancon
Mailing Address: BP 1031, 25001 Cedex, Besancon
Tel: (03) 81820894 *Fax:* (03) 81820894
Key Personnel
Dir General: Gerard Varin
Founded: 1930
Subjects: Biography, Education, Humor, Literature, Literary Criticism, Essays, Natural History, Photography, Poetry
ISBN Prefix(es): 2-7121

Editions Amphora SA+
14 rue de l'Odeon, 75006 Paris
Mailing Address: 27 rue Saint Andre des Arts, 75006 Paris
Tel: (01) 43 29 03 04; (01) 43 26 10 87 *Fax:* (01) 43 29 49 49; (01) 40 46 85 76
Web Site: www.ed-amphora.fr
Key Personnel
Man Dir & Publicity: Bernard Dubois
Founded: 1954
Subjects: Crafts, Games, Hobbies, Sports, Athletics
ISBN Prefix(es): 2-85180
Distributed by Dimedia (Canada); OLF Diffusion (Switzerland); Presses De Belgique (Belgium)

Editions Amrita SA+
Les Cheyroux, 24580 Plazac
Tel: (05) 53507954 *Fax:* (05) 53508020
E-mail: amrita.editions@perigord.com
Key Personnel
PDG: Anne Meurois-Givaudan
Founded: 1984
Subjects: Art, Astrology, Occult, Health, Nutrition, How-to, Parapsychology, Philosophy, Religion - Other
ISBN Prefix(es): 2-904616; 2-911022

L'Anabase+
284 rue de Croisades, 34280 La Grande Motte
Tel: (01) 30410747 *Fax:* (01) 34858073
Key Personnel
Contact: Christian Molinier
Founded: 1991
Subjects: Literature, Literary Criticism, Essays, Philosophy, Psychology, Psychiatry, Social Sciences, Sociology

ISBN Prefix(es): 2-909535
Bookshop(s): Librairie Roudil, 53, rue Saint Jacques, F-75005 Paris

Anako Editions+
236 Ave Victor Hugo, 94120 Fontenay-Sous-Bois
Tel: (01) 43 94 92 88 *Fax:* (01) 43 94 02 45
E-mail: anako.editions@anako.com
Web Site: www.anako.com
Key Personnel
Dir: Patrick Bernard
Sales & Administration: Jean-Marie Gehin
Founded: 1988
Subjects: Anthropology, Photography, Travel
ISBN Prefix(es): 2-907754

Editions l'Ancre de Marine+
4 rue Porcon-de-la-Barbinais, 35400 Saint-Malo
Tel: 99 56 78 43 *Fax:* 99 40 00 77
Key Personnel
Dir: Bertrand de Queretain
Founded: 1985
Subjects: History, Maritime, Regional Interests
ISBN Prefix(es): 2-905970; 2-84141
Number of titles published annually: 20 Print
Total Titles: 200 Print
Parent Company: Syndicat National de l'edition
Imprints: Cifonit Figle
Distributed by Edilarge Ouest France

Editions d'Annabelle+
8 rue d'Anjou, 75008 Paris
Mailing Address: 11, rue Tronchet, 75008 Paris
Tel: (01) 47420161 *Fax:* (01) 47424214
Key Personnel
Manager: Lydia Rolland
Founded: 1991
Subjects: Animals, Pets
ISBN Prefix(es): 2-909660
Branch Office(s)
93 rue du Fg St, Monore, 75008 Paris
Bookshop(s): Sofedis, 29 rue St, Sulpice 6e, Paris
Warehouse: Sodis

Annales de l'Est, *imprint of* Presses Universitaires de Nancy

Annales du Bac, *imprint of* Librairie Vuibert

Annales de la Recherche Urbaine+
Division of Plan Urbanisme Contruction Architecture
Puca-Metl-Arche Nord, 92055 Paris la Defense Cedex
Tel: (01) 40816371 *Fax:* (01) 40816378
Web Site: www.equipement.gouv.fr
Key Personnel
Editor: Pierre Lassave *Tel:* (01) 40816370 *E-mail:* pierre.lassave@equipement.gouv.fr; Anne Querrien *Fax:* (01) 40812446 *E-mail:* anne.querrien@equipement.gouv.fr
Founded: 1979
Subjects: Developing Countries, Environmental Studies, Ethnicity, Government, Political Science, Public Administration, Regional Interests, Social Sciences, Sociology, Transportation, Urban Research
Number of titles published annually: 3 Print; 3 Online
Total Titles: 1 Print
Online services available through World Wide Web.
Distributed by Lavoisier Abonnements

Edition Anthese+
30 ave Jean-Jaures, 94117 Arcueil Cedex
Tel: (01) 46 56 06 67 *Fax:* (01) 49 85 09 92
Telex: 202382 F
Key Personnel
Man Dir: Claude Draeger
Sales: Fransoise Benoit-Latour

Press: Cristina Campodonico
Founded: 1983
Subjects: Architecture & Interior Design, Art, Biography
ISBN Prefix(es): 2-904420; 2-912257
Orders to: Generale du Livre, 13 rue Ernest Cressou, 75014 Paris

Editions Anthropos Sarl+
49 rue Hericarte, 75015 Paris
Tel: (01) 45781292 *Fax:* (01) 45750567
Key Personnel
Man Dir: Maurice Guini
Manager: Pierre Guini
Founded: 1964
Subjects: Anthropology, Economics, Government, Political Science, History, Military Science, Philosophy, Social Sciences, Sociology
ISBN Prefix(es): 2-7157
Orders to: Editions Anthropos, Librairie des Sciences de l'Homme, 15 rue Lacepede, Paris 75005 *Tel:* (01) 45352247

APRD - Association pour la Recherche et l'Information demographiques
Universite de Paris-Sorbonne, 191 rue Saint-Jacques, 75005 Paris
Tel: (01) 44321400 *Fax:* (01) 40462588
Key Personnel
Chairman & President: Gerard-Francois Dumont *E-mail:* Gerard-Francois.Dumont@paris4.sorbonne.fr
Founded: 1976
Subjects: Social Sciences, Sociology
ISBN Prefix(es): 2-86419
Total Titles: 27 Print

Editions Arabes, *imprint of* Naufal Group Sarl

L'Arbalete
8 rue Paul-Bert, 69150 Decines
Tel: (04) 72933434 *Fax:* (04) 72933400
Subjects: Art, Literature, Literary Criticism, Essays
ISBN Prefix(es): 2-902375

Editions Arcam
40 rue de Bretagne, 75003 Paris
Tel: (01) 42729312
E-mail: phreatiq@multimania.com
Key Personnel
Man Dir: Lorris Murail
Editorial, Sales, Production & Publicity: Gerard Murail
Founded: 1971
Subjects: Art, Poetry
ISBN Prefix(es): 2-86476

L'Arche Editeur
86, rue Bonaparte, F-75006 Paris
Tel: (01) 46334645 *Fax:* (01) 46335640
E-mail: contact@arche-editeur.com
Web Site: www.arche-editeur.com
Key Personnel
Dir: Rachel Rudolf
Stage Rights: Katharina Bismarck *Tel:* (01) 46336326
Bookstore Dept: Laurence Dorveaux *Tel:* (01) 46335747 *E-mail:* commande@arche-editeur.com
Founded: 1947
Publishes some of the most famous dramatic authors of the 19th & 20th centuries, but also contemporary texts. Essays on art, music, cinema and philosophy.
Membership: SNE (Syndicate National de L'Edition.
Subjects: Art, Biography, Drama, Theater, Literature, Literary Criticism, Essays, Music, Dance, Philosophy, Psychology, Psychiatry, Social Sciences, Sociology

FRANCE

ISBN Prefix(es): 2-85181
Number of titles published annually: 15 Print
Total Titles: 436 Print
Foreign Rep(s): Claude M Diffusion (Canada)

L'Archipel+
34 rue des Bourdonnais, 75001 Paris
Tel: (01) 55807740 *Fax:* (01) 55807741
E-mail: ecricom@wanadoo.fr
Key Personnel
Dir: Jean-Daniel Belfond
Founded: 1991
Subjects: Biography, Fiction, Literature, Literary Criticism, Essays
ISBN Prefix(es): 2-84187
Number of titles published annually: 80 Print
Total Titles: 300 Print
Divisions: Editions Ecriture; Presses du Chatelet
Foreign Rep(s): Chloe Ataroff (US); Michel Claeys Bouuaert (China); Young-Sun Choi (Korea); Arabella Cruse (Netherlands & Scandinavia); Anna Droumeva (Bulgaria, Serbia); Catherine Fragou-Rassinier (Greece); Efrat Goller (Israel); Laura Grandi (Italy); Judit Hermann (Croatia, Hungary); Asli Karasuil (Turkey); Eva Koralnik (Germany); Corinne Quentin (Japan); Ingrida Sniedze (Baltic States); Maria Strarz-Kanska (Poland); Ludmilla Sushkova (Russia); Corina Tat (Romania); Petra Tobiskova (Czech Republic, Slovenia); Anne-Marie Vallat (Spain)

Architecture-Modelisme, *imprint of* Editions l'Instant Durable (Soprep)

Publications Aredit+
357 blvd Gambetta, 59200 Tourcoing
Tel: 20267981
Telex: 130372 F
Key Personnel
Editor: Emile Keirsbilk
Editorial, Publicity: Yves Catteloin
Subjects: Fiction, Military Science, Romance, Science Fiction, Fantasy, Western Fiction
ISBN Prefix(es): 2-7346; 2-7311

Editions de l'Argus, *imprint of* Groupe Moniteur -L'Argus

L'Argus, *imprint of* Groupe Moniteur -L'Argus

Editions de l'Armancon+
24, rue de l'Hotel-de-Ville BP 14, 21390 Precy-sous-Thil
Tel: (03) 80 64 41 87 *Fax:* (03) 80 64 46 96
Web Site: www.editions-armancon.fr/presentation.htm
Key Personnel
Dir: Gerard Gautier
Founded: 1987
Subjects: Art, Biography, Cookery, History, Literature, Literary Criticism, Essays, Photography, Regional Interests, Wine & Spirits
ISBN Prefix(es): 2-906594; 2-84479
Number of titles published annually: 10 Print
Total Titles: 110 Print

Armand Colin Drott, *imprint of* Editions Dalloz Sirey

Arnette-Blackwell+
224, blvd Saint-Germain, 75007 Paris
Tel: (01) 45496500 *Fax:* (01) 45491288
Telex: 270150F TXFRA 690
Key Personnel
General Dir: Gil Raveux
Founded: 1915
Subjects: Medicine, Nursing, Dentistry
ISBN Prefix(es): 2-7184

Parent Company: Blackwell Scientific Publications, United Kingdom
U.S. Office(s): Blackwell Scientific Publication, Boston, MA, United States
Orders to: One rue d Lille, 75007 Paris *Tel:* (01) 44860770 *Fax:* (01) 44860766

Art & Metiers Du Livre/Editions+
110, ave de Villiers, 75017 Paris
Tel: (01) 42 27 32 36 *Fax:* (01) 47 63 25 52
E-mail: infos@faton.fr
Web Site: www.art-metiers-du-livre.com/revue.html
Key Personnel
Dir: Louis Faton
Publicity: Marie Garrigue
Founded: 1994
Subjects: Art, *Presse-edition*
ISBN Prefix(es): 2-911071
Total Titles: 3 Print

Art Creation Realisation, see ACR Edition Internationale (Art Creation Realisation)

Art Price Annual ADEC+
BP 69, 69270 Saint-Romain-au-Mont-d'Or
Tel: (01) 478 220 000 *Fax:* (01) 478 220 606
Key Personnel
Dir General: Jacques Madina
ISBN Prefix(es): 2-909711
U.S. Office(s): Immagini Inc, 47 Indian Hill Rd, Bedford, NY 10056, United States

Arthaud, *imprint of* Flammarion SA

Compagnie Francaise des Arts Graphiques SA+
47 rue des Murs, 45300 Ecrennes
Tel: (01) 46243925
Key Personnel
President: V P Victor-Michel
Founded: 1939
Subjects: Art, Drama, Theater, Music, Dance
ISBN Prefix(es): 2-85001
Imprints: CFAG
Orders to: 129 Ave Achille Peretti, 92200 Neuilly sur Seine

Asa Editions
5, rue Laffitte, 75009 Paris
Tel: (01) 47704290 *Fax:* (01) 47704298
Web Site: www.asaeditions.com
Key Personnel
Administrative & Sales Manager: Marc Wiltz
Dir Commercial/Export: Catherine Sas
ISBN Prefix(es): 2-911589

L'Asiatheque, see Langues & Mondes/L'Asiatheque

Editions Assimil SA
13 rue Gay-Lussac, 94431 Chennevieres-sur-Marne Cedex cedex
Tel: (01) 45768737 *Fax:* (01) 45940655
E-mail: contact@assimil.com
Web Site: www.assimil.com
Key Personnel
Dir & Editorial: J L Cherel
Sales, Advertising: J P Vandenhende
Production: A Blanquet
Founded: 1929
Subjects: Language Arts, Linguistics
ISBN Prefix(es): 2-7005

L'Association
16 rue de la Pierre-Levee, 75011 Paris
Tel: (01) 43558587 *Fax:* (01) 43558621
E-mail: lassocia@club-internet.fr
Key Personnel
President: Jean-Christophe Menu

BOOK

Founded: 1990
ISBN Prefix(es): 2-909020; 2-84414

Association Francaise de Normalisation+
11, ave Francis de Pressense, 93571 Saint-Denis La Plaine Cedex
Tel: (01) 41 62 80 00 *Fax:* (01) 49 17 90 00
Web Site: www.afnor.fr
Key Personnel
Dir of Publication & General Manager: Alan Bryden
Administrator & International Rights: Gildas Bourdais
Subjects: Management
ISBN Prefix(es): 2-12

Association pour la Recherche et l'Information demographiques, see APRD - Association pour la Recherche et l'Information demographiques

Les Editions de l'Atelier SA+
12 ave Soeur Rosalie, 75013 Paris
Tel: (01) 44089515 *Fax:* (01) 44089500
Key Personnel
President: Daniel Prin
Editor: Bernard Stephan
Foreign Rights: Valerie Francois
Sales Manager: Patrick Merrant
Founded: 1939
Subjects: Biblical Studies, Biography, Economics, Government, Political Science, History, Religion - Catholic, Social Sciences, Sociology
ISBN Prefix(es): 2-7082

Atelier National de Reproduction des Theses
Universite Lille III, 9 rue Auguste-Angellier, 59046 Lille Cedex
Tel: (03) 20 30 86 73 *Fax:* (03) 20 54 21 95
E-mail: anrt@univ-lille3.fr
Key Personnel
Dir: Elisabeth Fichez
Founded: 1971
Reproduction sur micro-fiches et numerisation de theses universitaires soutenues en France.
Subjects: Art, Geography, Geology, History, Language Arts, Linguistics, Law, Literature, Literary Criticism, Essays, Philosophy, Psychology, Psychiatry, Social Sciences, Sociology
ISBN Prefix(es): 2-284; 2-7295
Distributed by Presses du Septentrion (Universite Lille III at Villeneuve d'Ascq)

Les Ateliers d'Orion+
21 rue Notre Dame, 30000 Nimes
Tel: (04) 66 21 87 02 *Fax:* (04) 66 21 85 39
Key Personnel
Contact: Jean-Pierre Auvy
Founded: 1997
Specializing in graphic illustrations.
Subjects: Animals, Pets, Education, Law, Public Administration, Religion - Catholic, Religion - Jewish
ISBN Prefix(es): 2-910032

Ateliers et Presses de Taize+
71250 Taize-Communaute
Tel: 3 85 50 30 30 *Fax:* 3 85 50 30 15
E-mail: rencontres@taize.fr
Web Site: www.taize.fr
Key Personnel
Contact: Reynold Gallusser
Founded: 1959
Subjects: Religion - Other
ISBN Prefix(es): 2-85040
Imprints: Les Presses de Taize
Orders to: Ateliers et Presses de Taize, 71250 Taize-Communaute

Editions Atlas
89 rue de la Boetie, 75008 Paris
Tel: (01) 40 74 38 38 *Fax:* (01) 49 53 07 25

E-mail: contact@editionsatlas.fr
Web Site: www.editionsatlas.fr
Telex: 642481F
Key Personnel
Contact: Patrick Lemarchand
ISBN Prefix(es): 2-7312

ATP - Packager+
ZA les Vignettes, BP 75, 63405 Chamalieres cedex
Tel: (0473) 19 58 80 *Fax:* (0473) 195899
E-mail: atp.chamalieres@wanadoo.fr
Key Personnel
Dir: Herve Chaumeton
International Rights: Isabelle Leyris-Chambon
Tel: 473195896
Founded: 1984
Subjects: Aeronautics, Aviation, Animals, Pets, Archaeology, Automotive, Cookery, Earth Sciences, Gardening, Plants, Health, Nutrition, History, House & Home, Natural History, Outdoor Recreation, Wine & Spirits
Number of titles published annually: 100 Print

Aubanel SA+
2, rue Christine, 75006 Paris
Tel: (01) 40515200; (01) 40515205
Key Personnel
Man Dir: Laurent Theodore-Aubanel
Founded: 1744
Subjects: Fiction, Psychology, Psychiatry, Regional Interests, Travel
ISBN Prefix(es): 2-7006
Branch Office(s)
4, rue Pedro Meylan, 1208 Geneva, Switzerland
Tel: (022) 7365110 *Fax:* (022) 7352402

Editions de l'Aube+
Le Moulin du Chateau, 84240 La-Tour-d'Aigues
Tel: (04) 90 07 46 60 *Fax:* (04) 90 07 53 02
Key Personnel
Man Dir: Jean Viard
Literary Dir: Marion Hennebert
Founded: 1987
Subjects: Cookery, Economics, Environmental Studies, Foreign Countries, Literature, Literary Criticism, Essays, Mysteries, Philosophy, Social Sciences, Sociology
ISBN Prefix(es): 2-87678
Distributed by Editions Zoe (Switzerland)

Aubie, *imprint of* Flammarion SA

Editions Aubier-Montaigne SA
26, rue Racine, 75278 Paris Cedex 06
Tel: (01) 40 51 31 00 *Fax:* (01) 43 29 21 48
Key Personnel
Man Dir: Mrs M Aubier-Gabail
Sales Manager, Rights & Permissions: Patrice Mentha
Founded: 1924
Subjects: Education, History, Language Arts, Linguistics, Philosophy, Poetry, Psychology, Psychiatry, Religion - Other, Social Sciences, Sociology
ISBN Prefix(es): 2-7007
Parent Company: Flammarion et Cie

Etudes Augustiniennes, see Institut d'Etudes Augustiniennes

Editions d'Aujourd'hui (Les Introuvables)
c/o L'Harmattan, 5-7 rue de l'Ecole-Polytechnique, 75005 Paris
Tel: (01) 43547910 *Fax:* (01) 43298620
Key Personnel
Man Dir: Odette Charriere
Founded: 1974
Subjects: Drama, Theater, Ethnicity, Fiction, Film, Video, Human Relations, Literature, Literary Criticism, Essays, Music, Dance, Poetry

ISBN Prefix(es): 2-7307; 2-85775
Distributed by UNIVERS (Canada)
Bookshop(s): 16 rue des ecoles, 75005 Paris
Tel: (01) 40 46 79 11; (01) 40 46 79 20

Aurore Editions D'Art, *imprint of* Editions Cercle d'Art SA

Autrement Editions
77 rue du Faubourg Saint-Antoine, 75011 Paris
Tel: (01) 40260606 *Fax:* (01) 40260026
E-mail: contact@autrement.com
Web Site: www.autrement.com
Key Personnel
President, Chief Executive Officer & Dir Publication: Henry Dougier *E-mail:* henry.dougier@autrement.com
Sales & Transfer of Rights: Anne-Marie Bellard *E-mail:* commercial@autrement.com; Chloe Pathe *E-mail:* commercial@autrement.com
Founded: 1975
Subjects: Anthropology, Behavioral Sciences, Fiction, Foreign Countries, History, Literature, Literary Criticism, Essays, Natural History, Nonfiction (General), Philosophy, Psychology, Psychiatry, Regional Interests, Social Sciences, Sociology, Travel
ISBN Prefix(es): 2-86260
Total Titles: 700 Print
Distributed by Editions du le Seuil

Autres Temps+
97, ave de la Gouffonne, 13009 Marseille
Tel: (0491) 26 80 33 *Fax:* (0491) 41 11 01
Key Personnel
Contact: Gerard Blua
Founded: 1990
Subjects: Literature, Literary Criticism, Essays
ISBN Prefix(es): 2-908805; 2-911873; 2-84521
Total Titles: 200 Print
Imprints: Litterature Generale

Editions Philippe Auzou+
24-32 rue des Amandiers, 75020 Paris
Tel: (01) 40338400 *Fax:* (01) 47972008
Telex: Auzou Sofradif 220686 F
Key Personnel
Man Dir: M Philippe Auzou
Dir: M van Gendt; J Gerlag
Founded: 1978
Subjects: Art
ISBN Prefix(es): 2-7338
Subsidiaries: A Diffusion-Sofradif

Editions l'Avant-Scene de Prette Technique+
6 rue Git-le-Coeur, 75006 Paris
Tel: (01) 46342820 *Fax:* (01) 43545014
Key Personnel
Man Dir: Jacques Leclere
Founded: 1949
Subjects: Drama, Theater, Film, Video, Music, Dance
ISBN Prefix(es): 2-907468
Warehouse: 6 Mail Nord, 5350 Boynes

Babel, *imprint of* Editions Actes Sud

Bac en Poche, *imprint of* Librairie Vuibert

Editions J B Bailliere
2 cite de paradis, 75010 Paris
Tel: (01) 55 33 69 00 *Fax:* (01) 55 33 68 07
Telex: Livrcom 201326 F
Key Personnel
Dir General: Dr Philippe Le Due
Rights & Permissions: Arlette Hertig
Advertising: Marika Papageoriou
Founded: 1802

Subjects: Agriculture, Labor, Industrial Relations, Medicine, Nursing, Dentistry, Technology
ISBN Prefix(es): 2-7008

La Baleine, *imprint of* Editions du Seuil

Editions Baleine+
14, rue Paul Bert, 75011 Paris
Tel: (01) 43724960 *Fax:* (01) 43728760
Key Personnel
Manager: Antoine De Kerverseau
Editor: Helene Bihery
Assistant Editor: Alexandra Semon
Founded: 1995
Subjects: Fiction, Mysteries, Science Fiction, Fantasy
ISBN Prefix(es): 2-84219

Editions Balland+
33 rue St-Andre-des-Arts, 75006 Paris
Tel: (01) 43 25 74 40 *Fax:* (01) 46 33 56 21
Key Personnel
Publisher: Jean-Jacque Auj-ier
Sales: Jean-Paul Hirsch
Founded: 1966
Subjects: Biography, Fiction, Film, Video, Humor
ISBN Prefix(es): 2-7158

La Bartavelle
39, rue Jean-Jaures, 42190 Charlieu
Tel: 37821450 *Fax:* 37821463
Key Personnel
Publications Dir: Eric Ballandras
Subjects: Literature, Literary Criticism, Essays, Photography
ISBN Prefix(es): 2-87744

Editions A Barthelemy+
Domaine de Fontvert, 84132 Le Pontet Cedex
Mailing Address: BP 50, 84132 Le Pontet Cedex
Tel: (04) 90036000 *Fax:* (04) 90036009
E-mail: infos@editions-barthelemy.com
Web Site: www.editions-barthelemy.com
Key Personnel
Editor: Alain Barthelemy; Odile Barthelemy
Founded: 1978
Subjects: Cookery, Health, Nutrition, Regional Interests, Travel
ISBN Prefix(es): 2-903044; 2-87923

Societe Nouvelle Rene Baudouin+
10, rue de Nesle, 75006 Paris
Tel: (01) 43290050 *Fax:* (01) 43257241
Key Personnel
President: Alain Levy *E-mail:* al.levy@wanadoo.fr
Founded: 1974
Remainder dealer.
Subjects: Antiques, Art, Cookery
ISBN Prefix(es): 2-86396
Total Titles: 4 Print
Divisions: Le Dernier Terrain Vague; Levy; Editions Charles Moreau

Bayard Editions, *imprint of* Bayard Presse - Department Livre

Bayard Presse - Department Livre+
3, rue Bayard, 75008 Paris
Tel: (01) 44 35 60 60 *Fax:* (01) 44 35 61 61
Web Site: www.bayardpresse.com
Key Personnel
President: Alain Cordier
Dir: Frederic Boyer
Sales & Marketing Dir: Anne Duchemin
Dir Communication: Didier Robiliard *Tel:* (01) 44 35 65 73
Founded: 1873
Specialize in Essays, Adult Books.
Subjects: Art, Education, Religion - Other
ISBN Prefix(es): 2-227
Number of titles published annually: 60 Print

Imprints: Bayard Editions; Centurion
Orders to: Sofedis, The Soufflot, F-75005 Paris

Editions des Beatitudes, Pneumatheque+
Burtin, 41600 Nouan le Fuzelier
Tel: (02) 54 88 21 18 *Fax:* (02) 54 88 97 73
E-mail: edd.etrangers@wandadoo.com
Web Site: www.editions-beatitudes.fr
Key Personnel
Foreign Rights Manager: Laurence de Feydean
Founded: 1984
Subjects: Religion - Catholic
ISBN Prefix(es): 2-905480; 2-84024

Beauchesne Editeur+
7, rue du Lemoine Cardinal, 75005 Paris
Tel: (01) 53 10 08 18 *Fax:* (01) 53 10 85 19
Key Personnel
Contact: Mr Jean Pierre Druaud
Editorial: Mdme Francoise Druaud
Founded: 1851
Subjects: Biography, Government, Political Science, History, Human Relations, Journalism, Literature, Literary Criticism, Essays, Religion - Other, Social Sciences, Sociology, Theology
ISBN Prefix(es): 2-7010
Total Titles: 800 Print; 1 CD-ROM; 1 Audio
Distributed by O L F S A (Suisse)
Distributor for Anne Sigier France (Belgique & Luxembourg); Anne Sigier (Canada)

Editions Belfond+
12, ave d'Italie, 75013 Paris
Tel: (01) 45-44-38-23 *Fax:* (01) 45 44 98 04
Key Personnel
Chairman: Jerome Talamon
Vice President: Jean Manuel Bourgois
Dir General Adjoint: Fabienne Delmote
Rights & Permissions: Frederique Polet
Founded: 1963
Subjects: Art, Biography, Fiction, Health, Nutrition, History, How-to, Human Relations, Literature, Literary Criticism, Essays, Music, Dance, Mysteries, Nonfiction (General), Poetry, Romance
ISBN Prefix(es): 2-7144; 2-84228
Parent Company: Masson

Editions Belin+
8, rue Ferou, 75278 Paris Cedex 06
Tel: (01) 55 42 84 00 *Fax:* (01) 43 25 18 29
E-mail: contact@edition-belin.fr
Web Site: www.editions-belin.com
Key Personnel
President: Marie Claude Brossollet
Man Dir: Olivier Brossollet *Tel:* (01) 55 42 84 20
  E-mail: olivier.brossollet@editions-belin.com
Documentation: Soraya Eghbal-Dupouey
Marketing: Stephane Montouchet
Rights & Permissions: Sandra Dutortre
Founded: 1777
Subjects: Art, Education, Gardening, Plants, Literature, Literary Criticism, Essays, Poetry, Science (General)
ISBN Prefix(es): 2-7011
Number of titles published annually: 150 Print; 5 CD-ROM; 10 Audio
Total Titles: 2,000 Print; 40 Audio
Subsidiaries: Editions Herscher; Pour la Science SARL
Shipping Address: Editions Belin, 4 rue Ferdinand de Lesseps, 91420 Morangis
Warehouse: Editions Belin, 4 rue Ferdinand de Lesseps, 91420 Morangis *Tel:* (01) 69090097 *Fax:* (01) 69348198

Societe d'Edition Les Belles Lettres+
95 Blvd Raspail, 75006 Paris
Tel: (01) 44398420 *Fax:* (01) 45449288
Web Site: www.lesbelleslettres.com

Key Personnel
President, Man Dir: Michel Desgranges
International Rights: Marie Jose D'Hoop
Founded: 1919
Subjects: Education, Fiction, History, Language Arts, Linguistics, Literature, Literary Criticism, Essays, Philosophy, Religion - Other, Classical studies
ISBN Prefix(es): 2-251
Imprints: Manitoba; Sortileges
Bookshop(s): Librairie Guillaume Bude, Paris

Berg International Editeurs+
129 blvd Saint-Michel, 75005 Paris
Tel: (01) 43267273 *Fax:* (01) 46339499
  Cable: BERGEDIT PARIS
Key Personnel
Man Dir: Georges Nataf
Contact: Marie Gougaud
Founded: 1969
Subjects: Anthropology, History, Literature, Literary Criticism, Essays, Philosophy, Religion - Islamic, Religion - Jewish, Religion - Other
ISBN Prefix(es): 2-900269
Orders to: Press Universitairs de France, 14 Ave du Boisdel', Epi F-91003 Evry

Berger-Levrault SA
5, Rue Andre Ampere - BP 79, 54250 Champigneulles
Tel: (03) 83 38 83 83 *Fax:* (03) 83 38 86 10; (03) 83 38 37 12
E-mail: blc@berger-levrault.fr
Web Site: www.berger-levrault.fr
Telex: 270797 F
Key Personnel
Man Dir: Bernard Ajac
Editorial: Frederic Toncieu
Production: Christine Frohly
Rights & Permissions: Cecile Gateff
Founded: 1676
Subjects: Architecture & Interior Design, Art, Ethnicity, History, Social Sciences, Sociology
ISBN Prefix(es): 2-7013
Parent Company: Berger-Levrault Imprimerie, Nancy
Branch Office(s)
5 rue Auguste-Compte, 75000 Paris *Tel:* (01) 40467031
Bookshop(s): Librairie Berger-Levrault, 23 pl Broglie, F-67000 Strasbourg

Editions Bertout
2, st Gutenberg, 76810 Luneray
Tel: (02) 35 04 69 68 *Fax:* (02) 35846327
Key Personnel
Responsable Diffusion: Florence Levasseur-Bertout
Founded: 1934
Subjects: Cookery, Genealogy, History, Regional Interests
ISBN Prefix(es): 2-86743
Imprints: La Memoire Normande

Editions Bertrandl-Lacoste
36 rue St-Germain-l'Auxerrois, 75041 Paris Cedex 01
Tel: (01) 53 40 53 53 *Fax:* (01) 42 33 82 47
E-mail: contact@bertrand-lacoste.fr
Web Site: www.bertrand-lacoste.fr
Key Personnel
Publicity: Marie-Laurence Deslogis
Founded: 1980
Subjects: Accounting, Computer Science, Economics, Law
ISBN Prefix(es): 2-7352

Bibliotheque des Arts+
78, rue Bonaparte, 75006 Paris
Tel: (01) 40467590

Key Personnel
Chairman: Francois Daulte
Founded: 1954
Subjects: Architecture & Interior Design, Art, Literature, Literary Criticism, Essays, Poetry, Travel
ISBN Prefix(es): 2-85047
Distributor for Ides & Calendes

Bibliotheque Nationale de France+
11 quai Francois Mauriac, 75706 Paris Cedex 13
Mailing Address: BNF Service Editorial et Commercial, 58, rue de Richelieu, 75084 Paris Cedex 02
Tel: (01) 53 79 88 98; (01) 53 79 81 75 *Fax:* (01) 53 79 81 72
E-mail: commercial@bnf.fr
Web Site: editionsl.bnf.fr
Key Personnel
President: Jean-Noel Jeanneney
Head, Publications & Sales: Christopher Beslon
  Tel: (01) 53 79 88 01 *Fax:* (01) 53 79 81 72
  E-mail: christopher.beslon@bnf.fr
Publishing department of the French National Library.
Subjects: History, Library & Information Sciences, Literature, Literary Criticism, Essays
ISBN Prefix(es): 2-7177
Number of titles published annually: 30 Print
Total Titles: 500 Print
Foreign Rep(s): Sevil (World)

Societe Biblique Francaise+
5 Ave des Erables, 95400 Villiers-le-Bel
Mailing Address: BP 47, 95400 Villiers-le-Bel
Tel: (01) 39945051 *Fax:* (01) 39905351
E-mail: contacts@alliance-biblique-fr.org
Web Site: www.la-bible.net
Key Personnel
Editorial: Elsbeth Scherrer
  E-mail: elsbethscherrer@wanadoo.fr
Sales & Production: Pascal Dubs
Founded: 1818
Member of United Bible Societies/Alliance Biblique Universelle.
Subjects: Religion - Catholic, Religion - Protestant
ISBN Prefix(es): 2-85300
Total Titles: 140 Print
Imprints: Alliance Biblique Universelle
Branch Office(s)
American Bible Society, 1865 Broadway, New York, NY 10023-9980, United States
Distributed by CERF; Excelsis; Oberlin
Distributor for Brepols; CERF; CLC; Desclee de Brower; Farel; Vie et Sante

Societe Nouvelle Adam Biro+
28, rue de Sevigne, 75004 Paris
Tel: (01) 44 59 84 59 *Fax:* (01) 44 59 87 17
Key Personnel
Editor: Adam Biro
Editor & Publicity: Laurence Golstennel
Authors: Daniel Arasse; Bernard Comment; Tzvetan Todorov; Ernst Gombrich; Georges Didi-Huberman
Founded: 1987
Subjects: Antiques, Architecture & Interior Design, Art, Fashion, Photography
ISBN Prefix(es): 2-87660
Number of titles published annually: 20 Print
Total Titles: 285 Print
Distributor for Office du Livre (Switzerland); Presse de Belgique (Beligum)
Warehouse: Vilo, 21 Leval 11 ave Arago, Morangis
Orders to: Vilo, 25 rue Ginoux, 75015 Paris

William Blake & Co+
BP 4, F 33037 Bordeaux cedex
Tel: (05) 56 31 42 20 *Fax:* (05) 56 31 45 47
Web Site: www.editions-william-blake-and-co.com

Key Personnel
Publications Dir: Jean-Paul Michel
Founded: 1976
Subjects: Architecture & Interior Design, Art, Literature, Literary Criticism, Essays, Philosophy, Photography, Poetry
ISBN Prefix(es): 2-84103; 2-905810
Imprints: L'Invention du Lecteur; La Pharmacie de Platon
Distributor for Arts & Arts

Librairie Scientifique et Technique Albert Blanchard, see Librairie Scientifique et Technique Albert Blanchard

Blay-Foldex
Formerly Recta Foldex
40-48 rue des Meuniers, 93108 Montreuil
Tel: (01) 49889210 *Fax:* (01) 49889209
Web Site: 195.11.148.32:8055
Founded: 1934
Subjects: How-to

Blondel La Rougery SARL
268, rue de Brement, 93561 Rosny-Sous-Bois Cedex
Tel: (01) 48949452 *Fax:* (01) 48949438
Key Personnel
Chairman: J Barbotte
Founded: 1902
Subjects: Advertising, Foreign Countries, Geography, Geology, How-to, Public Administration, Transportation
ISBN Prefix(es): 2-903862

De Boccard Edition-Diffusion
11, rue de Medicis, 75006 Paris
Tel: (01) 43 26 00 37 *Fax:* (01) 43 54 85 83
Key Personnel
Man Dir: Dominique Chaulet
Manager: Jean-Bernard Chaulet
Founded: 1866
Subjects: Archaeology, Art, Asian Studies, History, Religion - Other
ISBN Prefix(es): 2-7018

Editions Andre Bonne+
29 rue Marceau, 94200 Ivry-sur-Seine
Tel: (01) 45150061 *Fax:* (01) 45218175
Key Personnel
Dir General: Annet-Georges Aupois
Dir Literature: Alain Armand-Villoy
Subjects: Art, Biography, Crafts, Games, Hobbies, History, Literature, Literary Criticism, Essays, Poetry, Travel
ISBN Prefix(es): 2-7019

Bookmaker+
12, rue Servandoni, 75006 Paris
Tel: (01) 43548434 *Fax:* (01) 43547102
E-mail: bookmake@club-internet.fr
Key Personnel
Editor: Jean-Loup Chiflet
Founded: 1985
Specialize in packaging.
Subjects: Art, Astronomy, Gardening, Plants
ISBN Prefix(es): 2-906986

Bordas, *imprint of* Editions Bordas

Editions Bordas+
89, blvd Auguste Blanqui, 75013 Paris
Tel: (01) 44395445 *Fax:* (01) 44394350
Key Personnel
General Manager: Jean Lissarrague
Man Dir: Dominique Desmottes; Didier Tetaud
Editorial, Trade: Philippe Fournier-Bourdier
Editorial, School: Alain Cardona
Sales, France: Jean-Michel Angenault
Sales, Export: Alain Guilermin
Production: Francoise Barbera
Publicity, Trade: Dominique de Romanet
Publicity, School: Isabelle Brunelin
Rights & Permissions: Mireille Debenne
Founded: 1946
Subjects: Education, Nonfiction (General)
ISBN Prefix(es): 2-04; 2-7294; 2-7109
Parent Company: Groupe de la Cite, 20 ave Hoche, F-75008 Paris
Imprints: Bordas; Pedagogie Modern; Technique et Vulgarisation
Subsidiaries: Societe Gauthier-Villars; Privat SA; Dunod Editeur SA (all France); Bordas-Dunod Bruxelles
Bookshop(s): Librairie Dunod, 30 rue St-Sulpice, F-75006 Paris; Librairie Beranger, Liege, Belgium
Warehouse: Route d'Etampes, F-45330 Malesherbes *Tel:* (01) 38349249 *Fax:* (01) 38347385
Orders to: 11 rue Gossin, F-92543 Montrouge Cedex *Tel:* (01) 46565266 *Fax:* (01) 46560476

Pierre Bordas et Fils
PO Box 46, 75261 Paris Cedex 06
Tel: (01) 43 25 04 51 *Fax:* (01) 43 25 47 84
E-mail: pierre.bordas.filsd@wanadoo.fr
Key Personnel
Man Dir: Nicole Bordas
Editorial, Rights & Permissions: Pierre Bordas
Founded: 1978
Subjects: Art, Cookery, Crafts, Games, Hobbies, Education, Environmental Studies, Literature, Literary Criticism, Essays, Poetry, Travel
ISBN Prefix(es): 2-86311

Presses Universitaires de Bordeaux (PUB)+
Universite Michel de Montaigne Bordeaux 3, Domaine Universitaire, 33607 Pessac cedex
Tel: (05) 57 12 44 22 *Fax:* (05) 57 12 45 34
E-mail: pub@montaigne.u-bordeaux.fr
Web Site: www.montaigne.u-bordeaux.fr
Key Personnel
Dir General: Bernard Gilbert *Tel:* (05) 5712 4421
Dir Commercial: Antoine Poli *Tel:* (05) 5712 4634
Founded: 1983
Subjects: Anthropology, Education, Environmental Studies, Geography, Geology, History, Law, Literature, Literary Criticism, Essays, Philosophy, Wine & Spirits
ISBN Prefix(es): 2-86781
Orders to: CID, 131 blvd Saint-Michel, 75005 Paris *Tel:* (01) 43 54 47 15 *Fax:* (01) 43 54 80 73 *E-mail:* cid@msh-paris.fr
Nord-Sud, 150, rue Berthelot, 1190 Brussels, Belgium *Tel:* 022 343 10 13 *Fax:* 022 343 42 91
University of Exeter Press, Reed Hall, Streatham Drive, Exeter EX4 4QR, United Kingdom *Tel:* (01392) 263066 *Fax:* (01392) 263064 *E-mail:* uep@exeter.ac.uk *Web Site:* www.ex.ac.uk/uep/

Bornemann, *imprint of* Editions Sang de la Terre

Editions Bornemann
62, rue Blanche, 75009 Paris
Tel: (01) 42 82 74 44 *Fax:* (01) 48 74 14 88
Key Personnel
Manager: Pierre C Lahaye
Founded: 1829
Subjects: Animals, Pets, Art, Environmental Studies, How-to, Sports, Athletics
ISBN Prefix(es): 2-85182

Bottin SA
4, rue Andre Boulle, 94961 Creteil Cedex 9
Tel: (01) 49 81 56 56 *Fax:* (01) 49 81 56 76
Telex: 262 407
Key Personnel
President: Jean Paul Devai
Founded: 1796
Subjects: Agriculture, Business, Finance, Human Relations, Medicine, Nursing, Dentistry, Sports, Athletics
ISBN Prefix(es): 2-7039
Parent Company: Editions du Juris-Classeur
Ultimate Parent Company: Reed Elsevier plc

Christian Bourgois, see Presses de la Cite

Editions Colin Bourrelier, see Armand Colin, Editeur

Bragelonne+
15 rue Girard, 93100 Montreuil
Tel: (01) 4818 1970 *Fax:* (01) 4818 0247
E-mail: info@bragelonne.fr
Web Site: www.bragelonne.fr
Key Personnel
Senior Editor: Stephane Marsan *E-mail:* s.marsan@bragelonne.fr; Alain Nevant *Tel:* (01) 4818 1971 *E-mail:* a.nevant@bragelonne.fr
Founded: 2000
Subjects: Crafts, Games, Hobbies, Fiction, Film, Video, History, Humor, Literature, Literary Criticism, Essays, Mysteries, Radio, TV, Science Fiction, Fantasy
ISBN Prefix(es): 2-914370
Number of titles published annually: 16 Print
Total Titles: 8 Print
Foreign Rights: L'Agebce de l'Est (Bulgaria, Croatia, Czech Republic, Estonia, Germany, Latvia, Lithuania, Poland, Slovak Republic, Slovenia)

Breal
One rue de Rome, 93561 Rosny-sous-Bois Cedex
Tel: (01) 48122222 *Fax:* (01) 48122239
Web Site: www.editions-breal.fr/contacts/default_main.asp
Key Personnel
Man Dir: Jean-Michel Zunquin
Founded: 1969
Subjects: Accounting, Advertising, Biological Sciences, Communications, Computer Science, Economics, Electronics, Electrical Engineering, History, Language Arts, Linguistics, Law, Management, Marketing, Mathematics, Philosophy, Physical Sciences, Physics
ISBN Prefix(es): 2-85394; 2-84291
Associate Companies: ABC Editions
Bookshop(s): Librairie Des Prepas, 34 rue Serpente, F-75006 Paris
Orders to: Breal Diffusion, Bat No 9, 20 rue Escoffier, 94671 Charenton Cedex

Emgleo Breiz+
10 rue de Quimper, 29200 Brest
Tel: (02) 98026817 *Fax:* (02) 98026817
E-mail: emgleobreiz@hotmail.com
Web Site: emgleo-breiz.online.fr/
Key Personnel
Man Dir, Rights & Permissions: M le Mercier
Sales: Miss Allain
Production: M le Gall
Publicity: M Keravel
Founded: 1954
ISBN Prefix(es): 2-900828; 2-911210

Editions Jacques Bremond+
Le Clos de la Cournilhe, 30210 Remoulins-sur-Gardon
Tel: (04) 66 37 27 40 *Fax:* (04) 66 37 27 40
Key Personnel
Chairman: Jacques Bremond
Founded: 1975
Subjects: Drama, Theater, Literature, Literary Criticism, Essays, Poetry
ISBN Prefix(es): 2-910063; 2-903108
Orders to: Le Livreatermain, F-30260 Cannes et Clairan *Tel:* (04) 66 80 50 17

Alain Brethe Editions+
142 rue de Rivoli, 75001 Paris
Mailing Address: 3, rue de la Liberte Le Parc, 78280 Guyancourt
Tel: (01) 30609862; (01) 42039570
Key Personnel
Editor: Alain Brethes
Subjects: Astrology, Occult, Health, Nutrition, Human Relations, Philosophy, Psychology, Psychiatry
ISBN Prefix(es): 2-906803

Editions BRGM+
3 Ave Claude-Guillemin, 45060 Orleans Cedex 02
Mailing Address: BP 6009, 45060 Orleans Cedex 02
Tel: (02) 38643028 *Fax:* (02) 38643682
E-mail: infoterreve@brgm.fr
Web Site: www.infoterre.brgm.fr
Key Personnel
Dir: Florence Jaudin *Tel:* (02) 38643161
  E-mail: f.jaudin@brgm.fr
Founded: 1962
BRGM is the Office of Geological & Mineral Research in France & French Geological Survey.
Subjects: Earth Sciences, Environmental Studies, Geography, Geology
ISBN Prefix(es): 2-7159; 2-901709
Number of titles published annually: 20 Print
Total Titles: 800 Print; 80 E-Book; 3 Audio
Parent Company: BRGM, 39-43 quai Andre Citroen, 75739 Paris Cedex 15

Michele Broutta Oeuvres Graphiques Contemporaines
31 rue des Bergers, 75015 Paris
Tel: (01) 45779379 *Fax:* (01) 40590432
Key Personnel
Man Dir: Michele Broutta
Founded: 1970
Subjects: Art, Library & Information Sciences
ISBN Prefix(es): 2-900332; 2-902886

Brud Nevez
6 sraed Beaumarchais, 29200 Brest
Tel: (02) 98449842 *Fax:* (02) 98804970
Key Personnel
Man Dir: M Le Mercier
Subjects: Education, Fiction, Geography, Geology, Language Arts, Linguistics, Literature, Literary Criticism, Essays, Maritime, Poetry, Travel
ISBN Prefix(es): 2-86775
Divisions: Ar Skol Vrezoneg, Engelo Breiz, Liogam

BSI - ELOR Editions Jeunesse
10 rue du Chandelier, 56350 Saint-Vincent-sur-Oust
Tel: (02) 99912280 *Fax:* (02) 99913445
Key Personnel
Dir: Jacqueline Frain
Founded: 1976
Subjects: Crafts, Games, Hobbies, Religion - Catholic
ISBN Prefix(es): 2-907524; 2-912214
Imprints: Editions de Iorme Rond; Editions ELOR
Distributed by Duquesne Diffusion

Editions Buchet/Chastel
18 rue de Conde, 75006 Paris
Tel: (01) 44320560; (01) 44320563 (sales)
  Fax: (01) 44320561
E-mail: buchet.chastel@wanadoo.fr
Web Site: www.theatre-contemporain.net/editions/buchet/buchet.htm
Key Personnel
Rights & Permissions, Editorial Dir: Guy Buchet
Sales Dir: Aubouin
Editor: Pierre Zech
Founded: 1930
Subjects: Biography, Fiction, History, Medicine, Nursing, Dentistry, Music, Dance, Philosophy, Religion - Other, Social Sciences, Sociology
ISBN Prefix(es): 2-7020; 2-283

Editions du Buot
212, rue Saint-Maur, chez Acte 3, 75010 Paris
Tel: (01) 53388110 *Fax:* (01) 53388119
Founded: 1975
Subjects: Art, Travel
ISBN Prefix(es): 2-908480

Bureau des Longitudes de France
3 rue Mazarine, 75006 Paris
Tel: (01) 43265902 *Fax:* (01) 43268090
E-mail: contact@bureau-des-longitudes.fr
Web Site: www.bureau-des-longitudes.fr/
Key Personnel
Dir: Jean-Eudes Arlot
President: Nicole Captaine
Vice President: Jean-Paul Poirier
Founded: 1795
Subjects: Earth Sciences, Science (General)
ISBN Prefix(es): 2-910015

Cactus, *imprint of* Editions Actes Sud

Le Cadratin+
Division of MCP Sarl
16 rue Jean Baptiste Pigalle, 75009 Paris
Tel: (01) 42821701 *Fax:* (01) 42821701
Key Personnel
Editor: Marie-Claude Dufourneaud
Founded: 1979
Subjects: Art, History, Literature, Literary Criticism, Essays
ISBN Prefix(es): 2-86549

Editions des Cahiers Bourbonnais+
Rue de l'Horloge, 03140 Charroux
Tel: (04) 70568061 *Fax:* (04) 70568080
E-mail: ecb@cahiers-bourbonnais.com
Web Site: www.cahiers-bourbonnais.com/barre_liens.htm
Key Personnel
Dir: Jean-Pierre Petit
Founded: 1957
Subjects: Agriculture, Archaeology, Art, Business, History, Literature, Literary Criticism, Essays, Poetry, Publishing & Book Trade Reference
ISBN Prefix(es): 2-85370

Editions Cahiers d'Art
14 rue du Dragon, 75006 Paris
Tel: (01) 45487673 *Fax:* (01) 45449850
E-mail: cahiersart@aol.com
Key Personnel
Man Dir: Yves de Fontbrune
Founded: 1926
Subjects: Art
ISBN Prefix(es): 2-85117

Les Cahiers du BAC, *imprint of* ABC Editions

Cahiers du Cinema, *see* L'Etoile/Cahiers du Cinema

Les Cahiers du College, *imprint of* ABC Editions

Les Cahiers Fiscaux Europeens Sarl+
51 ave Reine-Victoria, 06000 Nice
Tel: (04) 93538939 *Fax:* (04) 93536628
E-mail: auteurs@fontaneau.com
Web Site: www.fontaneau.com/cfe99.htm
Key Personnel
Man Dir: Simone Branca
Founded: 1968
Subjects: Economics
ISBN Prefix(es): 2-85444
Parent Company: Societe d'Etudes Juridiques Internationales et Fiscales, Nice
Subsidiaries: CFE Belgique

Cahiers Rouges, *imprint of* Societe des Editions Grasset et Fasquelle

Editions Calmann-Levy SA+
3 rue Auber, 75009 Paris
Tel: (01) 47 42 38 33 *Fax:* (01) 47 42 77 81
Key Personnel
President & Man Dir: Denis Bourgeois
  E-mail: dbourgeois@calmann_levy.fr
Sales Dir: Marc Grinsztajn
Rights & Permissions: Heidi Warneke
  E-mail: hwarneke@calmann_levy.fr
Founded: 1836
Subjects: Biography, Economics, Fiction, History, Humor, Philosophy, Psychology, Psychiatry, Science Fiction, Fantasy, Social Sciences, Sociology, Sports, Athletics
ISBN Prefix(es): 2-7021
Orders to: Hachette Distribution, ZA de Coignieres, One Avenue Gutenberg, 78316 Maurepas Cedex

Editions Canal+
8 av du Maine, 75015 Paris
Tel: (01) 42222730 *Fax:* (01) 42223025
Key Personnel
Man Dir: Richard Ducousset
Editorial Dir: Herve Desinge
Public Relations: Soraya Devisscher
Rights & Permissions: Joschi Guitton
Founded: 1991
Subjects: Humor, Nonfiction (General), Sports, Athletics
ISBN Prefix(es): 2-911493

Canal+ Editions, see Editions Canal

Editions Canope+
20 Bd Gambetta, 63400 Chamalieres
Tel: (04) 73-93-82-90 *Fax:* (04) 73-39-33-00
E-mail: editions.canope@wanadoo.fr
Web Site: editionscanope.com
Key Personnel
Dir: Marcel Antonio
Founded: 1984
Subjects: Art, Biography, History, Regional Interests
ISBN Prefix(es): 2-906320
Number of titles published annually: 2 CD-ROM
Total Titles: 30 Print

La Capitelle, *imprint of* Editions Casteilla

Editions Caracteres+
7 rue de l'Arbalete, 75005 Paris
Tel: (01) 43379698 *Fax:* (01) 43372610
E-mail: caracteres2000@aol.com
Web Site: www.editions-caracteres.fr/contact.htm
Key Personnel
Contact: Bruno Durocher
Founded: 1950
Subjects: Philosophy, Poetry
ISBN Prefix(es): 2-85446
Distributed by Alterna

Editions Didier Carpentier
7 street Saint-Lazare, 75009 Paris
Tel: (01) 48780072 *Fax:* (01) 42829199
Key Personnel
Manager: Didier Carpentier
Founded: 1982
Subjects: Crafts, Games, Hobbies, House & Home
ISBN Prefix(es): 2-84167; 2-906962

PUBLISHERS   FRANCE

Editions Casteilla+
25 rue Monge, 75005 Paris
Tel: (01) 30141930 *Fax:* (01) 34603132
E-mail: info@casteilla.fr
Web Site: www.casteilla.fr/contact/princ_contact.htm
Key Personnel
Manager: Marinus Visser *Tel:* (01) 30141945
   E-mail: visser@chiron.as
Founded: 1950
Specialize in textbooks, vocational training.
Subjects: Art, Economics, Law, Vocational Training
ISBN Prefix(es): 2-7135
Number of titles published annually: 100 Print
Total Titles: 800 Print
Parent Company: VisLand SA
Imprints: Educalivre; Desforges; La Capitelle; Techniplus

Editions Casterman+
36, rue du Chemin-Vert, 75011 Paris
Tel: (01) 55 28 12 00 *Fax:* (01) 55 28 12 60
Web Site: www.casterman.com
Telex: 200001 F Edicast
Key Personnel
President: Didier Platteau
Dir: Jacques Simon
Sales Dir: Simon Casterman
Publicity, Advertising Dir: Odile Mardon
Rights & Permissions: Ivan Noerdinger
Founded: 1780 (Tournai; 1857 Paris)
Subjects: Antiques, Archaeology, Architecture & Interior Design, Art, Cookery, Fiction, History, How-to
ISBN Prefix(es): 90-303
Subsidiaries: Districast

Le Castor Astral+
52 rue des Grilles, 93500 Pantin
Mailing Address: BP 11, 33038 Bordeaux Cedex
Tel: (01) 48401490 *Fax:* (01) 48401973
E-mail: swproduction@magic.fr
Web Site: perso.magic.fr/swproduction/castocau.html
Key Personnel
Man Editor: Marc Torralba
Founded: 1975
Subjects: Literature, Literary Criticism, Essays
ISBN Prefix(es): 2-85920

CCNPS, *imprint of* Agence Bibliographique de L'Enseignement Superieur

CELSE (Compagnie d'Editions Libres, Sociales et Economiques SA)
10 rue Leon Coqniet BP106, 75821 Paris Cedex 17
Tel: (01) 42674123 *Fax:* (01) 42274020
E-mail: celse@celsedit.com
Web Site: www.celsedit.com
Founded: 1957
Subjects: Transportation
ISBN Prefix(es): 2-85009
Total Titles: 72 Print

Cemagref Editions+
Parc de Tourvoie, BP22, 92163 Antony Cedex
Tel: (01) 4096 62 85 *Fax:* (01) 4096 61 64
E-mail: info@cemagref.fr
Web Site: www.cemagref.fr
Key Personnel
Dir: Nicolas de Menthiere
Chief of Service: Odile Hologne
Subjects: Agriculture, Earth Sciences, Engineering (General), Environmental Studies, Mechanical Engineering
ISBN Prefix(es): 2-85362

Editions Cenomane+
33-39 rue des Ponts Neufs, 72000 Le Mans
Tel: (02) 43242157 *Fax:* (02) 43771916
Key Personnel
Dir General: Alain Mala
Founded: 1986
Member of SNE.
Subjects: Art, History, Literature, Literary Criticism, Essays, Military Science, Regional Interests, Transportation
ISBN Prefix(es): 2-905596

Cent Pages
27 rue Nicolas - Chorier, BP 291, 38009 Grenoble Cedex
Tel: (02) 38121620 *Fax:* (04) 38121629
E-mail: editions@editions-centpages.fr
Web Site: www.editions-centpages.fr/contact/contact.htm
Key Personnel
Literary Dir: Olivier Gadet
ISBN Prefix(es): 2-906724
Distributed by Les Belles Lettres

Center Technique des Industries de la Fonderie, see CTIF (Center Technique des Industries de la Fonderie)

Centre de Formation et de Perfectionnement des Journalistes, see Les Editions du CFPJ (Centre de Formation et de Perfectionnement des Journalistes) - Sarl Presse et Formation

Centre de Librairie et d'Editions Techniques (CLET)
c/o Dunod, 15 rue Gossin, 92543 Montrouge cedex
Tel: (01) 40926500 *Fax:* (01) 40926550
Telex: 634916
Key Personnel
Man Dir: Binnen Dyke
Editorial & Sales: Philippe Gualino
Founded: 1975
Subjects: Accounting, Economics, Finance, Law, Management
ISBN Prefix(es): 2-85354
Bookshop(s): Librairie CLET, 15 rue Gossin, 92543 Montrouge

Centre de Recherche d'Etude et de Documentation en Economie de la Sante, see CREDES - Centre de Recherche d'Etude et de Documentation en Economie de la Sante

Centre National de Documentation Pedagogique (CNDP)+
29 rue d'Ulm, 75230 Paris Cedex 05
Tel: (01) 55436000 *Fax:* (01) 55436001
Web Site: www.cndp.fr/cndp_reseau/enregion/ulm.htm
Key Personnel
Dir: Claude Mollard
Publisher of multimedia works under direction of the Minister of Education.
Subjects: Education
ISBN Prefix(es): 2-240
Orders to: 13-15 bd d'Italie ZA Paris-Zud, 77127 Lieusaint

Centre national de la recherche scientifique editions, see CNRS Editions

Centre Technique National d'Etudes et de Recherches sur les Handicaps et les Inadaptations, see CTNERHI - Centre Technique National d'Etudes et de Recherches sur les Handicaps et les Inadaptations

Centurion, *imprint of* Bayard Presse - Department Livre

CEP Editions
17 rue d'Uzes, 75002 Paris
Tel: (01) 42961550 *Fax:* (01) 48243489
Telex: 680 876 f
Key Personnel
President: Christian Bregou
Subjects: Architecture & Interior Design, Technology
ISBN Prefix(es): 2-281
Associate Companies: Editions du Moniteur
Subsidiaries: Librairie Larousse
Branch Office(s)
rue d'Uzes, F-75002 Paris *Tel:* (01) 42961550

Cepadues Editions SA+
111, rue Nicolas Vauquelin, 31100 Toulouse
Tel: (05) 61 40 57 36 *Fax:* (05) 61 41 79 89
E-mail: cepadues@cepadues.com
Web Site: www.cepadues.com
Key Personnel
President: Jean-Claude Joly
Dir: Annie Joly
Sales Manager & International Rights: Jean-Pierre Marson
Founded: 1969
Specialize in scientific & technical books.
Subjects: Aeronautics, Aviation, Computer Science, Education, Mathematics, Mechanical Engineering, Science (General), Technology, Transportation
ISBN Prefix(es): 2-85428
Total Titles: 200 Print

Editions Cercle d'Art SA+
10 rue Sainte-Anastase, 75003 Paris
Tel: (01) 48879212 *Fax:* (01) 48874779
E-mail: info@officieldesarts.com
Web Site: www.officieldesarts.com/cercledart/
Telex: 206685 Cerdart
Key Personnel
Man Dir: Philippe Monsel
Founded: 1950
Subjects: Art
ISBN Prefix(es): 2-7022
Imprints: Diagonales; Aurore Editions D'Art

CERDIC-Publications+
11 Rue Jean Sturm, 67520 Nordheim
Tel: (0388) 877107 *Fax:* (0388) 877125
Key Personnel
Man Dir: Marie Zimmerman
Founded: 1968
Subjects: History, Law, Religion - Catholic, Religion - Islamic, Religion - Jewish, Religion - Protestant, Religion - Other, Social Sciences, Sociology, Women's Studies
ISBN Prefix(es): 2-85097
Total Titles: 1 Print

Editions du Cerf
29 bd La Tour-Maubourg, 75340 Paris Cedex 07
Mailing Address: 20 rue Escoffier, Bat 4,5,6, 94671 Charenton-le-Pont Cedex
Tel: (01) 44181212 *Fax:* (01) 45560427
Web Site: www.editionsducerf.fr/html/contact/contact.htm
Key Personnel
General Dir: P Moity
Editorial Dirs: D Barrios-Delgado; F D Boespflug; B Lauret; N J Sed
Sales Dir, Publicity & Advertising: P Marion
Rights & Permissions: Mrs F de Chassey
Founded: 1929
Subjects: Biblical Studies, History, Philosophy, Religion - Other, Social Sciences, Sociology
ISBN Prefix(es): 2-204
Distributed by Fides; Labor & Fides Medialogue; Novalis; Saint Paul
Warehouse: 3 Chemin de Prunais, 94350 Villiers sp Marne

CF, *imprint of* References cf

CF, see References cf

CFAG, *imprint of* Compagnie Francaise des Arts Graphiques SA

Les Editions du CFPJ (Centre de Formation et de Perfectionnement des Journalistes) - Sarl Presse et Formation+
Affiliate of CFPJ
35 rue du Louvre, 75002 Paris
Tel: (01) 44822000 *Fax:* (01) 44822001
Web Site: www.cfpj.com
Key Personnel
General Dir: Marc Ladefroux *Tel:* (01) 44822065 *Fax:* (01) 44822004
Founded: 1988
Subjects: Communications, Journalism
ISBN Prefix(es): 2-85900
Imprints: Presse et Formation

Chadwyck-Healey France+
50 rue de Paradis, 75010 Paris
Tel: (01) 44838181 *Fax:* (01) 44838183
Key Personnel
Man Dir: Jean-Pierre Sakoun
Sales: Charles Myara
Founded: 1985
Publisher of CD-ROMs.
ISBN Prefix(es): 2-86976
Parent Company: Chadwyck-Healey Ltd, United Kingdom
Associate Companies: Chadwyck-Healey, Spain
U.S. Office(s): Chadwyck-Healey Inc, 1101 King St, Alexandria, VA 22314, United States

Editions du Chalet+
11 rue Duguay-Trouin, 75006 Paris
Tel: (01) 45443834 *Fax:* (01) 45499392
Telex: 202036 F (Begedis SA)
Key Personnel
Publishing Manager: Bernard Le Bras
Founded: 1946
Subjects: Biblical Studies, Religion - Catholic, Religion - Other, Theology
ISBN Prefix(es): 2-7023
Associate Companies: Editions Desclee et Cie; Editions Gamma; Nouvelles Editions Mame; Editions Universitaires
Orders to: Begedis, 11 rue Duguay-Trouin, 75006 Paris
Arc-en-Ciel International, Z1 Tournai Ouest, B-7713 Marquain, Belgium (Foreign)

Jacqueline Chambon+
3 place d'Assas, 30900 Nimes
Tel: (04) 66676396 *Fax:* (04) 666739 74
Founded: 1988
Subjects: Art, Literature, Literary Criticism, Essays, Philosophy, Photography
ISBN Prefix(es): 2-87711
Total Titles: 150 Print
Shipping Address: Harmonia Mundi, BP 150, F-13631 Arles Cedex *E-mail:* webmaster@harmoniamundi.com
Orders to: Harmonia Mundi, BP 150, F-13631 Arles Cedex

Champ Libre, *imprint of* Editions Ivrea

Editions Champ Vallon+
01420 Seyssel
Tel: (04) 50561551 *Fax:* (04) 50561564
E-mail: info@champ-vallon.com
Web Site: www.champ-vallon.com
Key Personnel
Editor: Patrick Beaune
International Rights: Myriam Monteiro-Braz *E-mail:* myriam.monteiro@wanadoo.fr
Founded: 1980
Subjects: Biography, Fiction, History, Literature, Literary Criticism, Essays, Philosophy, Poetry, Psychology, Psychiatry, Social Sciences, Sociology
ISBN Prefix(es): 2-87673; 2-903528
Total Titles: 380 Print
Distributed by Presses Universitaires de France (diffusion); Union Diffusion (distribution)

Editions Honore Champion
7 quai Malaquais, 75006 Paris
Mailing Address: 13 Chemin du Levant, Immeuble J-B Say/C1B, 01210 Fernay-Voltaire
Tel: (01) 46340729 *Fax:* (01) 46346406
E-mail: champion@honorechampion.com
Web Site: www.honorechampion.com
Key Personnel
Man Dir: Michel Slatkine
Subjects: History, Comparative Literature, Freemasonry, French Literature, Grammar, Jewish Studies, Lexicography, Linguistics, Music
ISBN Prefix(es): 2-85203; 2-7453

Champs Dominos, *imprint of* Flammarion SA

Librairie des Champs-Elysees SA+
43 Quai De Grenelle, 75015 Paris Cedex 15
Tel: (01) 45759602 *Fax:* (01) 43923573
Key Personnel
Man Dir: Michel Averlant; Didier Imbot
Founded: 1927
Subjects: Criminology
ISBN Prefix(es): 2-7024
Imprints: Le Masque; Club des Masques; Editions du Masque

Philippe Chancerel Editeur
17, route de Meulan, 78480 Verneuil-sur-Seine
Tel: (01) 39656918
Telex: 314235 F
Key Personnel
Chairman: Philippe Chancerel
Founded: 1960
Subjects: Crafts, Games, Hobbies, Humor, Sports, Athletics
ISBN Prefix(es): 2-907390
Associate Companies: Chancerel Publishers Ltd, United Kingdom

Chardon Bleu+
29 rue Charton, 69600 Oullins
Tel: (016) 72390213 *Fax:* (016) 72390403
E-mail: chardonbleued@aol.com
Web Site: www.chardonbleu.com/presentation/presentation.html
Key Personnel
Responsible: Dominique Isnard; Claude Four
Founded: 1983
ISBN Prefix(es): 2-86833
Orders to: BP 3050, 14018 Caen Cedex

Le Chariot+
BP 14, 28190 Saint Georges S/Eure
Tel: (02) 37258989 *Fax:* (02) 37258900
E-mail: edchariot@aol.com
Web Site: www.editions-du-chariot.com
Key Personnel
Publisher & Editor: Liliane Genin-Muchery *Tel:* (02) 37258662
Founded: 1927
Subjects: Astrology, Occult, Parapsychology
ISBN Prefix(es): 2-85371

Editions Charles-Lavauzelle SA+
Le Prouet, BP 8, 87350 Panazol
Tel: (05) 55584545 *Fax:* (05) 55584525
Key Personnel
Man Dir: Jean Claude Mazaud
Publicity & Production: Henri Chabrier
Founded: 1830
Subjects: Law, Military Science, Sports, Athletics
ISBN Prefix(es): 2-7025
Branch Office(s)
20 rue de Saint Petersbourg, 75008 Paris Cedex
Tel: (01) 43874230

Chasse Maree-Armen
Le Port-Rhu, Boulevard General De Gaulle, 29177 Douarnenez Cedex
Tel: (02) 98920919 *Fax:* (02) 98928001
E-mail: chasse-maree.armen@wanadoo.fr
Web Site: www.chasse-maree.com
Key Personnel
Publisher & Contact: Gilles Cadoret
Export Manager: Junien Bayle *E-mail:* junien.bayle@wanadoo.fr
Founded: 1981
Subjects: Art, Crafts, Games, Hobbies, History, How-to, Maritime, Music, Dance
ISBN Prefix(es): 2-903708; 2-914208

Editions du Chene+
Quai de Grenelle, 75905 Paris Cedex 15
Tel: (01) 43 92 30 00 *Fax:* (01) 43 92 33 81
Key Personnel
Man Dir: Isabelle Jendron
Rights & Co-Editions Manager: Sherri Aldis
Editorial Dir: Philippe Pierrelee
Founded: 1941
Specializes in illustrated books.
Subjects: Architecture & Interior Design, Art, Cookery, Travel
ISBN Prefix(es): 2-85108
Number of titles published annually: 65 Print
Parent Company: Hachette Livre SA
Imprints: Editions du Chene, EPA
Orders to: Hachette Livre SA, 43, Quai de Grenelle, 75905 Paris Cedex 15

Le Cherche Midi Editeur+
23 rue du Cherche-Midi, 75006 Paris
Tel: (01) 42227120 *Fax:* (01) 45440838
E-mail: infos@cherche-midi.com
Web Site: www.cherche-midi.com/scripts
Key Personnel
Man Dir: Philippe Heracles; Jean Orizet
Founded: 1978
Subjects: How-to, Humor, Literature, Literary Criticism, Essays, Mysteries, Poetry, Transportation
ISBN Prefix(es): 2-86274
Distributed by Serviois

Editions Chiron+
10 rue Leon-Foucault, 78180 Montigny-le-Bretonneux
Tel: (01) 30141930 *Fax:* (01) 34603132
E-mail: chiron@wanadoo.fr
Key Personnel
Chairman: Denys Ferrando-Durfort
Promotion & Foreign Rights: Chantal Ferrando-Durfort
Founded: 1906
Subjects: Aeronautics, Aviation, Automotive, Health, Nutrition, How-to, Music, Dance, Outdoor Recreation, Psychology, Psychiatry, Sports, Athletics
ISBN Prefix(es): 2-7027

Chotard et Associes Editeurs
One av Edouard-Belin, 92856 Rueil-Malmaison
Tel: (01) 41299605 *Fax:* (01) 41299815
Key Personnel
Man Dir: Nicole Boinet
Founded: 1969
Subjects: Economics, Engineering (General), Management, Marketing, Psychology, Psychiatry, Social Sciences, Sociology
ISBN Prefix(es): 2-7127
Orders to: Sofedis, 29 rue St Sulpice, F-75006 Paris

PUBLISHERS   FRANCE

Christian Bourgois Editeur
116 rue du bac, Paris 75007
Tel: (01) 45 44 09 13 *Fax:* (01) 45 44 87 86
E-mail: bourgois-editeur@wanadoo.fr
Web Site: www.christianbourgois-editeur.fr
Key Personnel
Contact: Dominique Bourgois *E-mail:* dominique.bourgois2@wanadoo.fr
Subjects: Fiction, Essays, Music
ISBN Prefix(es): 2-267

Chronique Sociale+
7 rue du Plat, 69288 Lyon Cedex 02
Tel: (04) 78372212 *Fax:* (04) 78420318
Key Personnel
Commercial Dir: Andre Soutrenon
Founded: 1920
Subjects: Human Relations, Philosophy, Psychology, Psychiatry, Religion - Other, Self-Help, Social Sciences, Sociology
ISBN Prefix(es): 2-85008
Distributor for Beauchemin (Canada); Vie Ouriere (EVO) (Brussles)

Cicero Editeurs+
6, rue de la Sorbonne, 75005 Paris
Tel: (01) 43544757 *Fax:* (01) 40517385
Founded: 1989
Subjects: Art, Drama, Theater, Literature, Literary Criticism, Essays, Music, Dance
ISBN Prefix(es): 2-908369
Orders to: Klincksieck, 18 rue de Lille, 75007 Paris

Cifonit Figle, *imprint of* Editions l'Ancre de Marine

CILF, see Counseil International de la Langue Francaise

Cimaise sarl
95 rue Vieille du Temple, 75003 Paris
Tel: (01) 45437045 *Fax:* (01) 45437045
Key Personnel
Publication Dir: Nartine Arnault-tran
Founded: 1953
Art magazine (contemporary art).

Cirad+
Avenue Agropolis, 34398 Montpellier Cedex 5
Mailing Address: TA 483/05, 34398 Montpellier Cedex 5
Tel: (0467) 61 55 23 *Fax:* (0467) 61 55 13
Web Site: www.cirad.fr
Key Personnel
Head, Publication Unit: Martine Sequier-Guis *Tel:* (0467) 61 44 86 *E-mail:* seguier@cirad.fr
Promotion & Export: Florence Bessette *E-mail:* bessette@cirad.fr
Founded: 1985
Subjects: Agriculture, Veterinary Science, Tropical Agronomy, Scientific & Technical Books
ISBN Prefix(es): 2-87614
Total Titles: 250 Print
Online services available through World Wide Web.
U.S. Office(s): PO Box 699, May St, Enfield, NH 03748, United States *Tel:* 603-632-7377 *Fax:* 603-632-5611 *E-mail:* enfield@connriver.net

Circe+
20 rue de l'Arcade, 75008 Paris
Tel: (01) 48249676
Key Personnel
Dir: Claude Lutz
Founded: 1988
Subjects: Drama, Theater, Fiction, Literature, Literary Criticism, Essays, Nonfiction (General), Philosophy, Poetry

ISBN Prefix(es): 2-9505426
Orders to: Harmonia Mundi, Le Mas de Vert, 13200 Arles

Circonflexe+
12 rue de la Montagne Sainte Genevieve, 75005 Paris
Tel: (01) 46347777 *Fax:* (01) 43253467
E-mail: info@circonflexe.fr
Web Site: www.circonflexe.fr/nous/centre.php
Telex: 200128
Key Personnel
Dir: Paul Fustier
Commercial Dir: Benoit Rouillard
Founded: 1989
Subjects: Art, Education, Fiction, History, Humor, Language Arts, Linguistics
ISBN Prefix(es): 2-87833
Parent Company: Info Media Communication
Orders to: Dilisco, 122 rue Marcel Hartmann, 92400 Ivry sur Seine

Editions Citadelles & Mazenod+
33 rue de Naples, 75008 Paris
Tel: (01) 53043060 *Fax:* (01) 45220427
E-mail: info@citadelles-mazenod.com
Web Site: www.citadelles-mazenod.com
Key Personnel
Chairman: Francois de Waresquiel
Editorial Manager: Agnes de Gorter *Tel:* (01) 53043064 *E-mail:* a.degorter@citadelles-mazenod.com
Commercial Manager: Martine Dumond *Tel:* (01) 53043066 *E-mail:* m.dumond@citadelles-mazenod.com
Foreign Rights: Clair Morizet *Tel:* (01) 53043070 *E-mail:* c.morizet@citadelles-mazenod.com
Founded: 1936
Specialize in architecture & art.
Subjects: Architecture & Interior Design, Art
ISBN Prefix(es): 2-85088
Number of titles published annually: 7 Print
Total Titles: 80 Print
Distributed by Diffulivre (Switzerland); Hatchet Canada Inc (Canada); Hachette livre/CDL (France); Marabout (Belgium)

Editions de la Cite, *imprint of* Editions Ouest-France

CLD+
42 avenue des Platanes BP 203, 37172 Chambray-les-Tours cedex
Tel: (02) 47282068 *Fax:* (02) 47288548
Key Personnel
Man Dir, Editorial: Michel Magat
Sales & Rights & Permissions: Michel Jacquet
Production: Emmanuel Magat
Founded: 1961
Subjects: Architecture & Interior Design, Ethnicity, History, Regional Interests, Religion - Other, Travel
ISBN Prefix(es): 2-85443
Total Titles: 300 Print

Cle International+
27 rue de la Glaciere, 75013 Paris
Tel: (01) 45874400 *Fax:* (01) 45874410
Key Personnel
Dir: Jean-Luc Wollensack
Sales Dir: Dominique Richard
Editorial Dir: Michele Grandmangin
Founded: 1973
Subjects: Education, Language Arts, Linguistics
ISBN Prefix(es): 2-19; 2-09
Showroom(s): Espace Luxembourg, 103 Boulevard Saint-Michel, 75005 Paris *Tel:* (01) 53104120 *Fax:* (01) 45874425

CLET, *imprint of* Dunod Editeur

Climapoche, *imprint of* Sedit

Climats+
470 chemin des Pins, 34170 Castelnau-le-Lez
Tel: (04) 99583091; (04) 67453790 *Fax:* (04) 99583092
E-mail: climats.editions@wanadoo.fr
Web Site: www.editions-climats.com/
Key Personnel
Man Editor: Alain Martin
Founded: 1988
Subjects: Film, Video, Literature, Literary Criticism, Essays, Music, Dance, Mysteries
ISBN Prefix(es): 2-84158; 2-907563
Shipping Address: Harmonia Mundi, BP 150, 13631 Arles Cedex
Warehouse: Harmonia Mundi, BP 150, 13631 Arles Cedex
Orders to: Harmonia Mundi, BP 150, 13631 Arles Cedex

Club des Masques, *imprint of* Librairie des Champs-Elysees SA

Club J G, *imprint of* Sarl Editions Jean Grassin

CNDP, see Centre National de Documentation Pedagogique (CNDP)

CNE, see Comite National d'Evaluation (CNE)

CNRS Editions+
15 rue Malebranche, 75005 Paris
Tel: (01) 53102700 *Fax:* (01) 53102727
Web Site: www.cnrseditions.fr
Key Personnel
Man Dir: Danielle Saffar *Tel:* (01) 53 10 27 15
Publicity & Advertising Manager: Liliane Bruneau *Tel:* (01) 53 10 27 11 *E-mail:* liliane.bruneau@cnrseditions.fr
Editorial: Pascal Rouleau
Founded: 1986
Subjects: Archaeology, Art, Astrology, Occult, Biological Sciences, Chemistry, Chemical Engineering, Communications, Economics, Education, Environmental Studies, Ethnicity, Geography, Geology, History, Language Arts, Linguistics, Law, Literature, Literary Criticism, Essays, Mathematics, Music, Dance, Philosophy, Physics, Psychology, Psychiatry, Religion - Other, Science (General), Social Sciences, Sociology, Specializes in Scientific books
ISBN Prefix(es): 2-222; 2-271
Number of titles published annually: 100 Print
Total Titles: 2 CD-ROM
Parent Company: Centre national de la recherche scientifique

Codes Rousseau
BP 93, 85103 Les Sables d'Olonne Cedex
Mailing Address: BP 93, 85103 Les-Sables-d'Olonne
Tel: (02) 51231100 *Fax:* (02) 51213102
E-mail: info@codes-rousseau.fr
Web Site: www.codesrousseau.fr
Key Personnel
President: Mr C Czajka
Dir General: M Goepp
Subjects: Education, Electronics, Electrical Engineering, Law, Transportation
ISBN Prefix(es): 2-7095
Parent Company: Bertelsmann A G
Subsidiaries: Les Editions du Bateau, Les Editions; La Baule; Rousseau Diffusion, Sables d'Olonne

Armand Colin, Editeur
21, rue Montparnasse, 75298 Paris cedex 6
Tel: (01) 44395447 *Fax:* (01) 44394343
E-mail: infos@armand-colin.com
Web Site: www.armand-colin.com/pr/infosf.html

Telex: Acolin 201269 F
Key Personnel
Man Dir: Jean-Max Leclerc
Sales Dir: Remy Bourrelier
Publicity & Advertising: Yvette Dardenne
Rights & Permissions: Antoine Bonfait
  E-mail: abonfait@her.fr
Editor: Armand Colin
General Manager: Alain Cardona
  E-mail: acardona@vuef.fr
Founded: 1870
Incorporates publications of former separate Company, Editions Armand Colin Bourrelier.
Subjects: Education, Geography, Geology, History, Literature, Literary Criticism, Essays, Philosophy, Psychology, Psychiatry, Social Sciences, Sociology
ISBN Prefix(es): 2-200
Orders to: BP 107, F-75663 Paris Cedex 14

College de Philosophie, *imprint of* Societe des Editions Grasset et Fasquelle

Editions du Comite des Travaux Historiques et Scientifiques (CTHS)+
One rue Descartes, 75231 Paris Cedex 05
Tel: (01) 46 34 47 76 *Fax:* (01) 46 34 47 60
Key Personnel
Administrative Secretary: Martine Francois
Founded: 1834
Subjects: Archaeology, Art, Ethnicity, Geography, Geology, History
ISBN Prefix(es): 2-7355
Shipping Address: Distique, 5 rue du Marechal Leclerc, 28600 Luisant

Comite National d'Evaluation (CNE)
43 rue de la Procession, 75015 Paris
Tel: (01) 55 55 63 63 *Fax:* (01) 55 55 63 94
E-mail: j-c.martin@cne-evaluation.fr
Web Site: www.cne-evaluation.fr
Key Personnel
Publisher: Francine Sarrazin *Tel:* (01) 55556363
  E-mail: francine.sarrazin@cne-evaluation.fr
President: Gilles Bertrand *Tel:* (01) 55556980
  E-mail: pdtcne@cne-evaluation.fr
Deputy General: Jolivet Jean-Wolf
  E-mail: sgcne@cne-evaluation.fr
Founded: 1986
Subjects: Education
ISBN Prefix(es): 0-9838740
Number of titles published annually: 20 Print; 20 E-Book
Total Titles: 187 Print; 101 E-Book
Divisions: Service Publications

COMP'ACT+
157, Carre Curial, 73000 Chambery
Tel: (04) 79 85 27 85 *Fax:* (04) 79 85 29 34
E-mail: editionscomp.act@wanadoo.fr
Web Site: www.theatre-contemporain.net/editions/compact/compact.htm
Key Personnel
Literary Dir: Henri Poncet
Founded: 1986
Subjects: Literature, Literary Criticism, Essays, Photography, Poetry
ISBN Prefix(es): 2-87661
Number of titles published annually: 30 Print

Compagnie d'Editions Libres, Sociales et Economiques, see CELSE (Compagnie d'Editions Libres, Sociales et Economiques SA)

Compagnie Europeenne de Publication, see CEP Editions

Compagnie 12+
210 rue du Faubourg-Saint-Antoine, 75012 Paris
Tel: (01) 43709900 *Fax:* (01) 43708088
Founded: 1981
ISBN Prefix(es): 2-903866; 2-221
U.S. Office(s): Company 12 Inc, 190 E 56 St, New York, NY 10017, United States

Editions Complexe SPRL+
16 rue Seguier, 75006 Paris
Mailing Address: 16, rue Seguier, 75006, Paris
Tel: (01) 4634 6040 *Fax:* (01) 4329 9433
Telex: 64507 Patica
Key Personnel
Man Dir, Publicity: Danielle Vincken
Man Dir, Editorial: Andre Versaille
Founded: 1971
Subjects: History, Literature, Literary Criticism, Essays, Science (General)
ISBN Prefix(es): 2-87027
Associate Companies: Nouvelle Diffusion SPRL DP1, 24 rue de Bosnie, 1060 Brussels, Belgium
  Tel: (02) 538 8846 *Fax:* (02) 538 8842

Editions de Compostelle+
BP 7, 77890 Beaumont-du-Gatinais
Tel: (01) 64299404
Key Personnel
Contact: Francois-Xavier Chaboche
Founded: 1988
Subjects: Human Relations, Parapsychology, Philosophy, Religion - Other, Theology
ISBN Prefix(es): 2-907449
Total Titles: 10 Print

Le Conseiller Juridique Pour Tous, *imprint of* Editions du Puits Fleuri

Continent Europe, *imprint of* Hermes Science Publications

Cooperative Regionale de l'Enseignement Religieux (CRER)
22 blvd Jacques-Millot BP 848, 49008 Angers Cedex 01
Tel: (02) 41689140 *Fax:* (02) 41689141
E-mail: crer49@wanadoo.fr
Key Personnel
Man Dir: Michel Pourrias
Founded: 1968
Subjects: Religion - Other
ISBN Prefix(es): 2-85733

Copernic
25 rue Barque, 75015 Paris
Tel: (01) 40619767 *Fax:* (01) 40619633
Key Personnel
Man Dir: Bertrand Sorlot
Sales, Production, Rights & Permissions, Publicity: Jeanne Bordeau
Founded: 1976
Subjects: Film, Video, History, Philosophy, Religion - Other, Science Fiction, Fantasy
ISBN Prefix(es): 2-85984
Associate Companies: Editions Albatross, Publeditec

Editions Coprur+
34 rue du Wacken, 67913 Strasbourg Cedex 9
Tel: (0388) 147241 *Fax:* (0388) 147239
E-mail: coprur@editions-coprur.fr
Key Personnel
Dir: Bernard Sadoun
Founded: 1871
Subjects: History, Natural History, Regional Interests
ISBN Prefix(es): 2-84208; 2-903297
Number of titles published annually: 25 Print
Total Titles: 300 Print

Corsaire Editions+
rue Royole, 45000 Orleans
Tel: (02) 38 53 1500 *Fax:* (02) 38 54 0892
E-mail: corsaire.editions@wanadoo.fr
Key Personnel
President: Gilbert Trompas
Founded: 1994
Subjects: Biography, Biological Sciences, Earth Sciences, History, Humor, Literature, Literary Criticism, Essays, Poetry, Social Sciences, Sociology
ISBN Prefix(es): 2-901475
Distributed by Diffusion Transat (Switzerland)
Distributor for Castor & Pollux

Librairie Jose Corti+
11 rue de Medicis, 75006 Paris
Tel: (01) 43266300; (01) 43268048 *Fax:* (01) 40468924
E-mail: corti@noos.fr
Web Site: www.jose-corti.fr
Key Personnel
Man Dir: Bertrand Fillaudeau
Editorial: Fabienne Raphoz-Fillaudeau
Publicity, Rights & Permissions: Isabelle Dibie
Founded: 1938
Subjects: Fiction, Literature, Literary Criticism, Essays, Poetry
ISBN Prefix(es): 2-7143
Total Titles: 799 Print
Orders to: Edition du Seuil, 27 rue Jacob, 75006 Paris

Council of Europe Publishing+
Division of Council of Europe
Palais de l'Europe, 67075 Strasbourg Cedex
Tel: (0388) 412581 *Fax:* (0388) 413910
E-mail: publishing@coe.int
Web Site: book.coe.int
Telex: 870943F
Key Personnel
Commercial Manager: Sophie Lobey
  Tel: 0388412263 *E-mail:* sophie.lobey@coe.int
Rights & Permissions Manager: Charalambos Papadopoulos *Tel:* 0388412952
  E-mail: charalambos.papadopoulos@coe.int
Editorial Manager: Francine Raveney
  Tel: 0388415114 *E-mail:* francine.raveney@coe.int
Founded: 1949
Official publisher of the Council of Europe & reflects many different aspects of the Council's work, addressing the main challenges facing European society & the world today. Our catalogue of over 1500 titles in French & English includes topics ranging from international law, human rights, ethical & moral issues, society, environment, health, education & culture.
Subjects: Law, Social Sciences, Sociology, Human Rights, Criminology, Sociology, Nature, Consumer Protection, Education, Sports, Culture, Social Security, Youth, Local Authorities
ISBN Prefix(es): 92-871
Number of titles published annually: 120 Print
Total Titles: 1,500 Print
Distributed by Manhattan Publishing Co
Foreign Rep(s): Akademika A/S Universitetsbokhandel; Akateeminen Asta Liimen (Finland); Bersy (Switzerland); Bookshop Jean de Lannoy (Belgium); De Lindeboom Int Publikaties/Inor (Netherlands); Euro Information Service (Hungary); European Bookshop SA (Belgium); Glowna Ksiegarnia Naukowa im. B Prusa (Poland); Hunter Publications (Australia); Kauffmann Bookshop (Greece); Libreria Commissionaria Sansoni (Italy); Livraria Portugal (Portugal); Manhattan Publishing Co (US); Mundi-Prensa Libros SA (Spain); Munksgaard Book & Subscription Service (Denmark); Renouf Publishing Co Ltd (Canada); TSO (UK); UNO Verlag (Austria, Germany)
Shipping Address: T S O, 51 Nine Elms Lane, London SW8 5DR, United Kingdom *Tel:* (020) 7873 8200

PUBLISHERS

FRANCE

Counseil International de la Langue Francaise
11 rue de Navarin, 75009 Paris
Tel: (01) 48787395 *Fax:* (01) 48784928
E-mail: cilf@cilf.org
Web Site: www.cilf.org
Key Personnel
Secretary-General: Hubert Joly
Founded: 1968
Specialize in multilingual scientific dictionaries.
Subjects: Agriculture, Architecture & Interior Design, Language Arts, Linguistics, Medicine, Nursing, Dentistry, Public Administration
ISBN Prefix(es): 2-85319

Courrier du Livre Sarl
65 rue Claude Bernard, 75005 Paris
Tel: (01) 43364105 *Fax:* (01) 43310745
E-mail: info@tredaniel-courrier.com
Web Site: www.tredaniel.com/
Subjects: Environmental Studies, Gardening, Plants, Health, Nutrition, Philosophy, Religion - Other, Sports, Athletics
ISBN Prefix(es): 2-7029

CPL- La Communication Par le Livre
3, square du Croisic, 75015 Paris
Mailing Address: 28 rue Vaneau, 75007 Paris
Tel: (01) 42733047 *Fax:* (01) 42733047
Key Personnel
General Dir: Philippe Leclerc
Founded: 1989
Subjects: Advertising, Architecture & Interior Design, Art, History, Real Estate
ISBN Prefix(es): 2-908867

CREDES - Centre de Recherche d'Etude et de Documentation en Economie de la Sante
One rue Paul-Cezanne, 75008 Paris
Tel: (01) 53934300 *Fax:* (01) 53934350
Web Site: www.credes.fr
Key Personnel
Chair: Francois Joliclerc
Dir: Domenica Polton
Founded: 1985
ISBN Prefix(es): 2-87812

Editeurs Crepin-Leblond
Editions Crepin Leblond, 14 rue du Patronage Laique, B P 2057, 52902 Chaumont Cedex 9
Tel: (032) 5038748 *Fax:* (032) 5038740
Web Site: www.graphycom.com
Key Personnel
Man Dir: Jean Bletner
Publicity: Laurent Picart *Tel:* (032) 5038749; Francoise Pelletier *Tel:* (032) 5038749; Christophe Inoux *Tel:* (032) 5038645 *Fax:* (032) 5038652
Founded: 1952
Subjects: Animals, Pets, Environmental Studies, Sports, Athletics
ISBN Prefix(es): 2-7030

CRER, see Cooperative Regionale de l'Enseignement Religieux (CRER)

Editions Criterion+
11 rue Duguay-Trouin, 75006 Paris
Tel: (01) 45443834 *Fax:* (01) 45499392
Key Personnel
Dir General: Pierre-Marie Dumont
Founded: 1990
Subjects: Biography, History, Literature, Literary Criticism, Essays, Social Sciences, Sociology
ISBN Prefix(es): 2-903702; 2-7413; 2-903701; 2-902105

CTHS, see Editions du Comite des Travaux Historiques et Scientifiques (CTHS)

CTIF (Center Technique des Industries de la Fonderie)
Formerly ETIF (Ed Technique des Industries de la Fonderie)
44 ave de la Division Leclerc, 92318 Cedex, Sevres
Tel: (01) 41146300 *Fax:* (01) 45341434
Web Site: www.ctif.com
Key Personnel
Contact: Michel Guiny *E-mail:* guiny_mi@ctif.com
Subjects: Technology
ISBN Prefix(es): 2-7119

CTNERHI - Centre Technique National d'Etudes et de Recherches sur les Handicaps et les Inadaptations
236 Bis rue de Tolbiac, 75013 Paris
Tel: (01) 45655900 *Fax:* (01) 45654494
E-mail: ctnerhi@club-internet.fr
Web Site: www.perso.club-internet.fr/ctnerhi
Key Personnel
Dir: Marc Maudinet
President: Elisabeth Aubourg
Subjects: Disability, Special Needs, Psychology, Psychiatry, Social Sciences, Sociology
ISBN Prefix(es): 2-87710; 2-902402
Distributed by Presses Universitaires de France

Editions Cujas+
4-8 rue de la Maison Blanche, 75006 Paris Cedex 13
Mailing Address: BP 417, 75013 Paris Cedex 13
Tel: (01) 44242436; (01) 44242437 *Fax:* (01) 44242438
Telex: 200513
Key Personnel
Man Dir: Pierre Joly
Founded: 1946
Subjects: Economics, Education, Government, Political Science, History, Law, Social Sciences, Sociology
ISBN Prefix(es): 2-254
Bookshop(s): Cujjas Librairie, 2 rue de Rouen, 92000 Nanterre

Culture et Bibliotheque pour Tous
Formerly Notes Bibliographiques-Culture et Bibliotheques pour Tous
212, rue Lecourbe, 75015 Paris
Tel: (01) 45 33 07 07 *Fax:* (01) 45 33 45 76
E-mail: uncbpt.services@wanadoo.fr
Key Personnel
Publication Dir: Marie-Francoise Cathala
Founded: 1943
Monthly periodicals.
Subjects: Biography, Fiction, History, Human Relations, Literature, Literary Criticism, Essays, Mysteries, Publishing & Book Trade Reference, Romance

Les Editions Roger Dacosta+
19 blvd Raspail, 75007 Paris
Tel: 45441491
Key Personnel
Man Dir: Marie-Madeleine Dacosta
Sales Dir: Isabelle Dacosta
Founded: 1912
Subjects: Medicine, Nursing, Dentistry
ISBN Prefix(es): 2-85128

DAFSA
117 quai de Valmy, 75010 Paris
Tel: (01) 44372600 *Fax:* (01) 44372635
E-mail: dorra.medjani@dri-wefa.com
Web Site: www.dafsa.fr/contact/contact.cfm
Telex: 640472 Daf Doc
Key Personnel
Chairman: Pierre Cabon
Man Dir: Yves Wilmors
Subjects: Economics, Finance
ISBN Prefix(es): 2-270

Dalloz, *imprint of* Editions Dalloz Sirey

Editions Dalloz Sirey+
31-35 rue Froidevaux, 75685 Paris Cedex 14
Tel: (01) 40645454 *Fax:* (01) 40645460
E-mail: ventes@dalloz.fr
Web Site: www.dalloz.fr
Telex: 206446 F
Key Personnel
President: Charles Vallee *Tel:* (01) 40655436
CEO: Philippe Chagnon *Tel:* (01) 40645434
Marketing: Nathalie Thouny *Tel:* (01) 40645438
Foreign Rights: Muriel Funel *Tel:* (01) 40645420
Founded: 1845 (Sirey, 1845 Dalloz)
Administration Office: 35 rue Tournefort, F-75240 Paris, Cedex 05. Tel: (01) 40515454.
On-line Publishing.
Subjects: Advertising, Economics, Finance, Law, Marketing
ISBN Prefix(es): 2-247
Total Titles: 2,000 Print; 50 CD-ROM; 10 E-Book
Parent Company: Havas Vivendi
Imprints: Armand Colin Drott; Dalloz; Delmas; Sirey
Distributor for Groupe Revue Fiduciaire
Bookshop(s): 14 rue Soufflot, 75005 Paris; 22 rue Soufflot, 75005 Paris

Librairie D'Amerique Et D'Orient, *imprint of* Editions d'Amerique et d'Orient, Adrien Maisonneuve

Editions Dangles SA+
18 rue Lavoisier, BP 30 039, 45801 Saint Jean-de-Braye
Tel: (02) 38864180 *Fax:* (02) 38837234
E-mail: dangles@wanadoo.fr
Web Site: www.editions-dangles.com
Key Personnel
Man Dir, Rights & Permissions: J Y Anstet Dangles
Sales: Alain Queant
Contact: Berangere Lemaiitre
Founded: 1926
Subjects: Medicine, Nursing, Dentistry, Parapsychology, Psychology, Psychiatry
ISBN Prefix(es): 2-7033
Branch Office(s)
30 rue des Freres Lumiere, 94260 Fresnes

Dargaud+
15/27 rue Moussorgski, 75018 Paris
Tel: (01) 53 26 32 32 *Fax:* (01) 53 26 32 00
E-mail: contact@dargaud.fr
Web Site: www.dargaud.fr
Key Personnel
President & Publisher: Claude de Saint Vincent
Editorial: Guy Vidal
Rights & Permissions: Sophie Castille *E-mail:* castille@dargaud.fr
Dir, Commercial & International: Eric de Moutlivault
Founded: 1943
Subjects: Fiction, Humor, Mysteries, Science Fiction, Fantasy, Western Fiction, Comics
ISBN Prefix(es): 2-205
Parent Company: Sofidar
Subsidiaries: Citel Video; Dargaud Benelux; Dargaud Publishing International; Dargard Suisse; Delta Verlag; Editions Blake et mortimer; Editions du Lombard; Grijalbo-Dargaud; Hodder-Dargaud; Marina Productions; Millesime Productions
Distributor for Blake et Mortimer; Lombard
Orders to: MDS, ZI de la Gaudree, 91417 Dourdan Cedex *Tel:* (01) 60818700 *Fax:* (01) 64593063

FRANCE

Editions du Dauphin+
43 rue Tombe-Issoire, 75014 Paris
Tel: (01) 43277631
Key Personnel
Publishing Manager: Anne Tromelin
Founded: 1935
Subjects: Fiction, How-to, Psychology, Psychiatry
ISBN Prefix(es): 2-7163
Subsidiaries: Editions Jacqueline Renard

Michel De Maule Editions+
5 rue du Sommerard, 75005 Paris
Tel: (01) 56249874
Key Personnel
President: Hubert de Bouville
Founded: 1997
Specialize in Latin & Greek publications.
ISBN Prefix(es): 2-87623
Parent Company: Editions Tum

De Vecchi Editions SA
20 rue de la Tremoille, 75008 Paris
Mailing Address: 29 rue Gustave-Eiffel, Zlle Val, 91420 Morangis
Tel: (01) 47204041 *Fax:* (01) 40701336
Key Personnel
Dir: J M Gosselin
Founded: 1971
Subjects: Animals, Pets, Astrology, Occult, Business, Health, Nutrition, How-to, Outdoor Recreation, Parapsychology, Sports, Athletics
ISBN Prefix(es): 2-7328; 2-85177

Nouvelles Editions Debresse
17 rue Duguay-Trouin, 75006 Paris
Tel: (01) 45481047
Key Personnel
Man Dir: Pierre Moulin
Editorial, Sales & Publicity: Vincent Moulin
Founded: 1933
Subjects: Astrology, Occult, Fiction, History, Poetry, Religion - Other, Social Sciences, Sociology
ISBN Prefix(es): 2-7164
Bookshop(s): 17 rue Duguay-Trouin, 75006 Paris *Tel:* (01) 45481047

Decanord
30 rue de Verlinghem, 59130 Lambersart Cedex
Mailing Address: BP 139, 59832 Lambersart
Tel: (03) 20 09 90 60 *Fax:* (03) 20 09 92 75
Key Personnel
General Dir: Luc Jonghmans
Founded: 1948
Subjects: Religion - Catholic
ISBN Prefix(es): 2-903898

La Decouverte et Syros+
9 bis, rue Abel-Hovelacque, 75013 Paris
Tel: (01) 44 08 84 00 *Fax:* (01) 44 08 84 19
E-mail: ladecouverte@ladecouverte-syros.com
Key Personnel
Man Dir: Francois Geze
Foreign Rights Manager: Delphime Ribouchon
Founded: 1959
Member of SNE.
Subjects: Communications, Developing Countries, Economics, Fiction, Foreign Countries, History, Philosophy, Social Sciences, Sociology
ISBN Prefix(es): 2-7071
Subsidiaries: Le Monde-Editions

Delagrave Edition SA
15 rue Soufflot, 75254 Paris Cedex 05
Tel: (01) 44 41 89 30 *Fax:* (01) 44 41 89 39
E-mail: delagrave@delagrave-editions.fr
Web Site: www.delagrave-edition.fr
Telex: Limodel 204252 F *Cable:* DELAGRAVE PARIS
Key Personnel
Man Dir: Patrick Baradean

Founded: 1865
Subjects: Education, Science (General), Technology
ISBN Prefix(es): 2-206
Parent Company: Flammarion

Guy Delcourt Productions+
54, rue d'Hauteville, 75010 Paris
Tel: (01) 56-03-92-20 *Fax:* (01) 56-03-92-30
Web Site: www.editions-delcourt.fr
Key Personnel
Dir: Guy Delcourt
International Rights: Catherine Cropsal
Founded: 1986
ISBN Prefix(es): 2-906187; 2-84055
Distributed by Diffulivre (Switzerland); Evadix Logistics (Benelux); Flammarion; Flammarion-Casterman (Benelux); Flammarion Export (Switzerland); OLF (Switzerland); Union-Distribution; Vertige Graphic

La Delirante
112, rue Rambuteau, 75001 Paris
Tel: (01) 45 08 86 65 *Fax:* (01) 55 42 12 67
Key Personnel
President: Patrick Genevaz
Founded: 1967
Subjects: Drama, Theater, Literature, Literary Criticism, Essays, Poetry
ISBN Prefix(es): 2-85745

Delmas, *imprint of* Editions Dalloz Sirey

Editions Delmas
31-35 rue Froidevaux, 75685 Paris Cedex 14
Tel: (08) 20 80 00 17 *Fax:* (01) 40 64 89 90
E-mail: delmas@dalloz.fr
Web Site: www.editions-delmas.com
Key Personnel
Man Dir: Charles Vallee
Dir Sales: Philippe Nani
Publicity: Monique Remillieux
International Rights: Christian Roblin
Founded: 1947
Subjects: Accounting, Economics, Law, Public Administration, Real Estate, Securities
ISBN Prefix(es): 2-247; 2-7034
Parent Company: Editions Dalloz Sirey

Editions Delville+
40, rue du Cherche Midi, 75006 Paris
Tel: (01) 42 22 72 90 *Fax:* (01) 42 22 65 62
E-mail: editions.delville@wanadoo.fr
Key Personnel
Man Dir: Jean-Pierre Delville
Founded: 1976
Subjects: Aeronautics, Aviation, Automotive, Cookery, History, How-to
ISBN Prefix(es): 2-85922

Georges-Charles Demay+
10, Residence de Beauregard, 91330 Yerres
Tel: (01) 69 48 92 54 *Fax:* (01) 69 49 56 08
Key Personnel
Owner, Author & Self-publisher: Georges Charles Demay
Founded: 1983
Member of Association of Self-Edited Authors & Association l'Image et la Lettre; Probationary Member of Society of French Men of Letters, Union des Ecrivains.
Subjects: Drama, Theater, Fashion, Fiction, History, How-to, Humor, Literature, Literary Criticism, Essays, Mysteries, Poetry, Romance, Science Fiction, Fantasy, Specializes in last World War histories (Forced labour in Germany 1943/1945)
ISBN Prefix(es): 2-904561
Number of titles published annually: 2 Print
Total Titles: 35 Print

Showroom(s): Dokumente Verlag, Postfach 1340, D-7600 Offenburg, Germany
Bookshop(s): Calligrammes, 8 rue Collegiale, Paris 75005 (theater); Le Coupe Papier, 19 rue de l'Odeon, Paris 75006 *Tel:* (01) 43 54 65 95 *Fax:* (01) 40 51 79 46 (theater); Lib Bonaparte, 31 rue Bonaparte, 6e, Paris 75006 *Tel:* (01) 43 29 44 65; Librairie Marivaux, 3 rue Marivaux, Paris 75002 *Tel:* (01) 42 21 46 55 (theater)
Shipping Address: CELF, 9 rue de Toul, 75012 Paris
Orders to: CELF, 9 rue de Toul, 75012 Paris, A Cordebard *Tel:* (01) 44 67 83 83 *Fax:* (01) 43 47 59 43 *E-mail:* celf@celf.fr

Editions du Demi-Cercle+
29 rue Jean-Jacques-Rousseau, 75001 Paris
Tel: (01) 42330685 *Fax:* (01) 42330862
Key Personnel
Manager: Veronique Hartmann
Founded: 1987
Subjects: Archaeology, Architecture & Interior Design, Environmental Studies
ISBN Prefix(es): 2-907757

Editions Denoel Sarl+
9 rue du Cherche-Midi, 75006 Paris
Tel: (01) 44 39 73 72 *Fax:* (01) 44397390 *Cable:* Edepege
Key Personnel
Man Dir: Olivier Rubinstein
Rights & Permissions: Juliette Moreau; Marie-Fransoise Bothorel
Foreign Rights: Marie Ledereg
Founded: 1932
Subjects: Art, Economics, Fiction, Government, Political Science, History, Philosophy, Psychology, Psychiatry, Science Fiction, Fantasy
ISBN Prefix(es): 2-207
Parent Company: Editions Gallimard, 5 rue Sebastien-Bottin, 75328 Paris Cedex 07
Associate Companies: Mercure de France

Dervy, *imprint of* Dervy-Livres

Dervy-Livres+
34 blvd Edgar-Quinet, 75014 Paris
Tel: (01) 42 79 10 89 *Fax:* (01) 42 79 19 37
Key Personnel
Dir General: Pierre Madelpuech
Man Editor: Henri Norel
Manager: Stephanie Magnard
Founded: 1946
Subjects: History, Human Relations, Psychology, Psychiatry, Religion - Other, Social Sciences, Sociology
ISBN Prefix(es): 2-85076
Parent Company: SFP1
Imprints: Dervy
Subsidiaries: CQFDL
Bookshop(s): Librarie des Sciences Traditionelles, 6 rue de Savoie, 75006 Paris
Warehouse: Comptoir de Vente Paris, 46 rue Saint-Antoine, 75004 Paris

Desclee de Brouwer SA+
76 bis rue des Sts-Peres, 75007 Paris
Tel: (01) 45 49 61 92 *Fax:* (01) 42 22 61 41
E-mail: direction@descleedebrouwer.com
Web Site: www.descleedebrouwer.com
Key Personnel
President: Marc Leboucher
General Manager: Etienne Leroy
Editorial: Charles Chauvin; Jacques Deschanel
Sales, Rights & Permissions: Anna-Marie Coquier
Promotion & Publicity: Corine Hannequin
Founded: 1877
Subjects: History, Literature, Literary Criticism, Essays, Religion - Other, Social Sciences, Sociology, Theology
ISBN Prefix(es): 2-220; 2-7045
Divisions: (Social Sciences) Epi

PUBLISHERS — FRANCE

Desclee et Cie, Editeurs
11, rue Duguay-Trouin, 75006 Paris
Tel: (01) 45443834 *Fax:* (01) 45499392
 Cable: Desclee Marquain
Key Personnel
Literary Dir: A Paul
Founded: 1872
Subjects: Literature, Literary Criticism, Essays, Philosophy, Religion - Other
ISBN Prefix(es): 2-7189
Associate Companies: Editions Gamma; Editions Desclee; Mame; Droquet & Ardant; Editions Gamma, Belgium
Divisions: Groupe Mame

Desforges, *imprint of* Editions Casteilla

Editions Desiris, *imprint of* Adverbum SARL

Deslogish-Lacoste
c/o Editions Bertrand-Lacoste, 36, rue Saint-Germain-l'Auxerrois, 75041 Paris Cedex 01
Tel: (01) 53 40 53 53 *Fax:* (01) 42 33 82 47
Web Site: www.bertrand-lacoste.fr
ISBN Prefix(es): 2-7399; 2-7352

Dessain et Tolra SA+
21 rue du Montparnasse, 75283 Paris Cedex 06
Tel: (01) 44 39 44 00 *Fax:* (01) 44 39 43 43
Telex: 260776F
Key Personnel
Director: Marie-Pierre Levallois
General Manager: Philippe Fournier-Bourdier
Editorial Manager: Jean Gueret
Founded: 1964
Subjects: Architecture & Interior Design, Art, Crafts, Games, Hobbies, How-to
ISBN Prefix(es): 2-249; 2-04
Bookshop(s): Diff-edi, 96 BD DU Montparnasse, 75680 Paris Cedex 14

Editions Desvigne
10 rue Leon Foucault, 78184 Saint-Quentin Yvelines Cedex
Tel: (01) 30 14 19 30 *Fax:* (01) 34 60 31 32
E-mail: info@casteilla.fr
Web Site: www.casteilla.fr
Key Personnel
President: Visser Marinus *Tel:* (01) 30141945 *Fax:* (01) 30141946
Subjects: Education
ISBN Prefix(es): 2-7037
Total Titles: 800 Print
Ultimate Parent Company: Editions Casteilla

Les Editions des Deux Coqs d'Or+
43 Quai de Grenelle, 75905 Cedex 15
Tel: (01) 43923334 *Fax:* (01) 43923338
Telex: 650780 Deucodo *Cable:* Deucodo Paris
Key Personnel
Man Dir: Frederique de Buron
Editor: Christine Foulquies
Art Manager: Maryvonne Denizet
Rights & Permissions: Monique Lantelme
Founded: 1949
Member of the Syndicat National de L'Edition Francaise.
Subjects: Animals, Pets, Fiction, History, Religion - Catholic, Religion - Other
ISBN Prefix(es): 2-01; 2-7192; 2-906017
Parent Company: Hachette Livre SA
Warehouse: Centre de Distribution du Livre, Z A de Coignieres-Maurepas, 1 avenue Gutenberg, 78316 Maurepas Cedex
Orders to: Hachette Livre, 43 Quai de Grenelle, 75905 Paris Cedex 15

Deux Coqs d'Or, *imprint of* Hachette Jeunesse Image

Institut pour le Developpement Forestier
 (Institute for Forestry Development)
23 ave Bosquet, 75007 Paris
Tel: (01) 40622280 *Fax:* (01) 45559854
E-mail: paris@association-idf.com
Key Personnel
President: Roland Martin
Founded: 1960
Subjects: Agriculture, Environmental Studies
ISBN Prefix(es): 2-904740

Devenirs Visuels SA+
65 rue du Faubourg Poissonniere, 75010 Paris
Tel: (01) 47 70 60 02 *Fax:* (01) 47 70 60 03
Key Personnel
Contact: Claive Rius
Founded: 1987
Specialize in packaging.
Subjects: Economics, Geography, Geology, Physical Sciences
ISBN Prefix(es): 2-910745

Diagonales, *imprint of* Editions Cercle d'Art SA

Dictionnaires Le Robert
27 rue de la Glaciere, 75640 Paris Cedex 13
Tel: (01) 45 87 43 20 *Fax:* (01) 45 87 32 33
Web Site: www.lerobert.com.fr
Telex: Dicorob 240763 F
Key Personnel
President, Man Dir: Bertrand Eveno
Publicity: Denis A Fasse
Technical Manager: Jacques Pierre
Export Manager: Michel Terrier
Founded: 1951
ISBN Prefix(es): 2-85036

Editions de la Difference+
Formerly La Difference
47 rue de la Villette, 75019 Paris
Tel: (01) 53 38 85 38 *Fax:* (01) 42 45 34 94
E-mail: editions-de-la-difference@wanadoo.fr
Web Site: www.ladifference.fr
Key Personnel
Dir: Colette Lambrichs; Joaquim Vital
Press: Frederique Martinie
Administration: Parcidio Gonclaves
Founded: 1976
Subjects: Art, Literature, Literary Criticism, Essays, Poetry
ISBN Prefix(es): 2-7291

Le Dilettante+
9-11 rue du Champ-de-l'Alouette, 75013 Paris 13e
Tel: (01) 43-37-98-98 *Fax:* (01) 43-37-06-10
E-mail: info@ledilettante.com
Web Site: www.ledilettante.com
Key Personnel
President: Dominique Gaultier
Founded: 1985
Subjects: Literature, Literary Criticism, Essays, Science (General)
ISBN Prefix(es): 2-84263; 2-905344
Branch Office(s)
Impasse du Ferradou, 11170 Montolieu

Dilicom
20, rue des Grands-Augustins, 75006 Paris
Tel: (01) 43254335 *Fax:* (01) 43297688
E-mail: dilicom@edilectre.fr
Web Site: www.dilicom.net
Key Personnel
President: Dominique Maillotte

Direction du Patrimoine
8 rue Vivienne, 75002 Paris
Tel: (01) 40-15-80-00 *Fax:* (01) 42606673
Web Site: www.culture.gouv.fr

Key Personnel
Director: Wanda Diebolt
ISBN Prefix(es): 2-911200

Editions Dis Voir+
3 rue Beautreillis, 75004 Paris
Tel: (01) 48 87 07 09 *Fax:* (01) 48 87 07 14
E-mail: disvoir@aol.com
Web Site: www.disvoir.com
Key Personnel
Dir General & Editor: Daniele Riviere
 E-mail: daniele.riviere@free.fr
Founded: 1986
Subjects: Architecture & Interior Design, Art, Fiction, Film, Video, Literature, Literary Criticism, Essays, Music, Dance, Philosophy
ISBN Prefix(es): 2-906571; 2-914563
Total Titles: 100 Print; 55 Online
U.S. Office(s): DAP, 636 Broadway, 12th fl, New York, NY, United States *Tel:* 212-473-5119 *Fax:* 212-673-2887
Distributed by Dimedia (Canada); CELF (South America, Italy, Spain, Japan, Germany, Greece, Portugal); Central Books (UK); Exhibitions International (Netherlands); DAP (USA); Manic Ex-Poseur/BAM (Australia); NORD-SUD (Belgium); Onslow Books (Scandinavia); Sevil (France)

Disney Hachette Edition+
10 rue du Colisee, 75008 Paris
Tel: (01) 53898500 *Fax:* (01) 45632201
Key Personnel
President: Pierre Sissmann
Director: Catherine Teissandier
Founded: 1992
Subjects: Child Care & Development
ISBN Prefix(es): 2-230
Parent Company: The Walt Disney Company France/Hachette Groupe Livre
Shipping Address: Centre de distribution du Livre, One ave Gutenberg, 78316 Maurepas
Warehouse: Centre de distribution du Livre, One ave Gutenberg, 78316 Maurepas
Orders to: Hachette - Service Commercial, 79 blvd St Germain, 75006 Paris

Societe de Documentation et d'Analyses Financieres, see DAFSA

La Documentation Francaise+
29-31 Quai Voltaire, 75007 Paris Cedex 07
Tel: (01) 40157000 *Fax:* (01) 40 15 68 00
E-mail: postmaster@ladocfrancaise.gouv.fr
Web Site: www.ladocfrancaise.gouv.fr
Telex: 204826 Docfran Paris
Key Personnel
Man Dir: Sophie Moati *E-mail:* s-moati@ladocfrancaise.gouv.fr
Sales, Promotion: Alain-Marie Bassy *Tel:* (01) 40157080 *Fax:* (01) 40157230 *E-mail:* ambassy@ladocfrancaise.gouv.fr; Sophie Seyer *E-mail:* s-seyer@ladocfrancaise.gouv.fr
Publicity: Laura Esterhazy
Foreign Rights: Francoise Bacnus *E-mail:* f-bacnus@ladocfrancaise.gouv.fr; Bernard Meunier *E-mail:* b-meunier@ladocfrancaise.gouv.fr
Founded: 1945
Mail Order & Documentation Requests to 124 rue Henri Barbusse, 93308 Aubervilliers Cedex, Publications of the General Secretary's Office of the French Government.
Member of Syndicat National de l'Edition.
Subjects: Art, Economics, Environmental Studies, Government, Political Science, Law, Management, Technology
ISBN Prefix(es): 2-11
Number of titles published annually: 500 Print; 3 CD-ROM; 200 E-Book
Total Titles: 6,000 Print; 5 CD-ROM; 500 E-Book

FRANCE

Foreign Rep(s): Distribudora Bertrand (Portugal); DPLU Inc (Canada); Jean de Lannoy (Belgium, Luxembourg); Librairie Kauffmann SA (Greece); Licosa (Italy); Maruzen Co (Japan); Mundi Prensa Libros SA (Spain); Servidis SA (Switzerland)
Bookshop(s): 165 rue Garibaldi, 69401 Lyon Cedex 03 Tel: (01) 78 63 23 02 Fax: (01) 78 63 32 24 E-mail: docfr@easynet.fr; 29 quai Voltaire, 75007 Paris Tel: (01) 40 15 71 10 Fax: (01) 40 15 72 30 E-mail: libparis@ladocumentationfrancaise.fr
Orders to: 124 rue Henri Barbusse, 93308 Aubervilliers Cedex, Charles Mbanda Tel: (01) 40 15 68 74 Fax: (01) 40 15 68 01 E-mail: libauber@ladocumentationfrancaise.fr

Doin Editeurs+
1, av Edovard-Belin, 92500 Ruel Malmaison
Tel: (01) 34633333 Fax: (01) 34653985
Key Personnel
President: M Thierry Verret; M Jean-Francois Roure
Founded: 1874
Subjects: Biological Sciences, Chemistry, Chemical Engineering, Earth Sciences, Education, Health, Nutrition, How-to, Medicine, Nursing, Dentistry, Psychology, Psychiatry, Science (General), Social Sciences, Sociology
ISBN Prefix(es): 2-7040
Parent Company: Groupe Lamarre
Warehouse: Editions Maisonneuve, 386 route de Paris, Sainte-Ruffine, 57162 Moulins-les-Metz
Orders to: Tothemes, 47 rue Saint-Andre-des-Arts, 75006 Paris

Les Dossiers d'Aquitaine
5, impasse Bardos, 33800 Bordeaux
Tel: (05) 56 91 84 98 Fax: (05) 56916492
E-mail: ddabx@wanadoo.fr
Key Personnel
President: Andre Desforges
Founded: 1978
Publisher.
Subjects: Biography, History, How-to, Literature, Literary Criticism, Essays, Poetry, Publishing & Book Trade Reference
ISBN Prefix(es): 2-905212
Number of titles published annually: 10 Print
Total Titles: 50 Print
U.S. Office(s): Ayral-Clause, 300 Ferrini, San Luis Obispo, CA 93405, United States

Draeger Editeur, see Edition Anthese

Dreamland Editeur+
60, rue Blanche, 75009 Paris
Tel: (01) 53204666 Fax: (01) 53204667
E-mail: dreamland@nous.fr
Subjects: Art, Film, Video, Radio, TV
ISBN Prefix(es): 2-910027
Total Titles: 70 Print; 33 E-Book

Droguet et Ardant
11 rue Duguay-Trouin, 75006 Paris
Tel: (01) 45443834 Fax: (01) 45499392
Telex: 580934
Key Personnel
Man Dir: Robert Ardant
Publicity Dir: Suzanne Ardant
Subjects: Religion - Catholic
ISBN Prefix(es): 2-7041

Librairie Generale de Droit et de Jurisprudence (LGDJ) - Montchrestien+
14 rue Pierre et Marie Curie, 75005 Paris
Tel: (01) 56541600 Fax: (01) 56541649
Key Personnel
Man Dir: Lionel Guerin
Man Dir & Sales Manager, Rights & Permissions: Nathalie Jouven

Sales Manager: Piene Coustols
Founded: 1836
Subjects: Economics, Law, Social Sciences, Sociology
ISBN Prefix(es): 2-275
Parent Company: Petites Affiches
Imprints: Jupiter; Navarre
Distributed by CELF
Distributor for Bruylant; Georg; GLN JOLY; Imprimerie Nationale
Bookshop(s): 20 rue Soufflot, 75005 Paris
Orders to: 160 rue Saint-Jacques, 75005 Paris

B Drouaud Editions, see Editions J H Paillet et B Drouaud

Du May+
20, rue de la Saussiere, 92100 Boulogne-Billancourt
Tel: (01) 46992424 Fax: (01) 48255692
Key Personnel
Dir General: Jacques Peron
Founded: 1986
ISBN Prefix(es): 2-84102

Dunod Editeur+
5 rue Laromiguiere, 75005 Paris
Tel: (01) 40 46 35 00 Fax: (01) 40 46 49 95
E-mail: infos@dunod.com
Web Site: www.dunod.com
Key Personnel
President: Charles Vallee
General Manager: Philippe Gualino
Assistant General Manager: Pierre-Andre Michel
Editorial: Pierre-Andre (Sciences & Letters) Michel
Editorial, Information & Electronics: Jean-Luc Sensi
Editorial, Reference: Eileen Lignot
Marketing: Marc Laforge
Rights & Permissions: Maryvonne Vitry
Technical Education: Francoise Menasce
Founded: 1800
Subjects: Computer Science, Economics, Education, Electronics, Electrical Engineering, Film, Video, Language Arts, Linguistics, Literature, Literary Criticism, Essays, Management, Microcomputers, Photography, Psychology, Psychiatry, Science (General)
ISBN Prefix(es): 2-10; 2-7370; 2-04
Parent Company: Editions Bordas, 17 rue Remy Dumoncel, BP 50, F-75661 Paris Cedex 14
Imprints: CLET; Gauthier-Villars; Privat-Garnier; PSI; Radio
Subsidiaries: Classiques Garnier
Branch Office(s)
Gauthier-Villars North America Inc, 875-81 Massachusetts Ave, Cambridge, MA 02139, United States
Showroom(s): 5 rue Mabillon, 75006 Paris
Bookshop(s): Librairie Saint-Sulpice, 30 rue St Sulpice, F-75006 Paris; Librairie des Arts et Metiers, 33 rue Reaumur, F-75003 Paris; Librairie Dauphine, Place du Marechal de Lattre de Tasigny, F-75016 Paris
Warehouse: Route d'Etampes, 45330 Malesherbes
Orders to: 11 rue Gossin, 92543 Montrouge Cedex

Duo, Harlequin, imprint of Harlequin SA

Editions J Dupuis+
57, blvd de la Villette, 75010 Paris
Tel: (01) 44 84 40 80 Fax: (01) 44 84 40 99
Web Site: www.dupuis-entertainment.com
Key Personnel
President & General Manager: Jean-Manuel Bourgois
Founded: 1898
Subjects: Humor

BOOK

ISBN Prefix(es): 90-314; 2-8001
Parent Company: Editions Dupuis SA, Belgium

Editions de l'Eclat+
BP 61337, Nimes
Tel: (04) 66 21 17 50 Fax: (04) 66 21 03 42
E-mail: eclat@lyber-eclat.net
Web Site: www.lyber-eclat.net
Key Personnel
General Dir: Michel Valensi
Founded: 1985
Subjects: Philosophy, Religion - Islamic, Religion - Jewish
ISBN Prefix(es): 2-84162
Total Titles: 160 Print
Online services available through World Wide Web.
Distributed by Caravelle (Belgium); Dimedia (Canada); Harmonia Mundi; Zoe (Switzerland)

Editions de l'Ecole des Hautes Etudes en Sciences Sociales (EHESS)+
Unit of E HESS
131 blvd Saint Michel, 75005 Paris
Tel: (01) 40 46 70 80 Fax: (01) 44 07 08 89
E-mail: editions@ehess.fr
Web Site: www.ehess.fr
Key Personnel
Man Dir: Jean C Lebreton Tel: (01) 40467081
Founded: 1959
Subjects: Anthropology, Asian Studies, Economics, History, Social Sciences, Sociology
ISBN Prefix(es): 2-7132
Number of titles published annually: 15 Print
Total Titles: 650 Print
Orders to: CID, 131 blvd St Michel, 75005 Paris

L'Ecole/L'Ecole des Loisirs Sarl
11 rue de Sevres, 75006 Paris Cedex 06
Tel: (01) 42 22 94 10 Fax: (01) 45 48 04 99
Web Site: www.ecoledesloisirs.fr
Telex: Ecolois 205735 F Cable: LIBRECOLE
Key Personnel
Man Dir: Jean Fabre
Export Sales Manager, Rights & Permissions: S Sevray
Publicity & Advertising: Jean Delas
Subjects: Education
Divisions: Pastel A (Christiane Lapp, Man Dir)

Ecole Nationale Superieure des Beaux-Arts+
14, rue Bonaparte, 75006 Paris
Tel: (01) 47035055 Fax: (01) 47035086
E-mail: info@ensba.fr
Web Site: www.ensba.fr
Key Personnel
Dean: Alfred Pacquement
Editor: Pascale Le Thorel-Daviot E-mail: pascale.lethoreldaviot@ensba.fr
Subjects: Art
ISBN Prefix(es): 2-84056
Number of titles published annually: 15 Print; 1 CD-ROM
Total Titles: 100 Print
Online services available through ensba.fr.
Parent Company: Ministry of Culture
Bookshop(s): 13, quai Malaquais, 75006 Paris

Presses de l'Ecole Normale Superieure
45 rue d'Ulm, 75230 Paris Cedex 05
Tel: (01) 44 32 30 00 Fax: (01) 44 32 20 99
Web Site: www.ens.fr
Key Personnel
Man Dir: Etienne Guyon
Editorial: Frederique Matonti
Sales: Angustinee Belsoeur
Production: Pascale Lehec
Founded: 1975
Subjects: Archaeology, Economics, History, Literature, Literary Criticism, Essays, Philosophy, Science (General), Social Sciences, Sociology
ISBN Prefix(es): 2-7288
Orders to: Regie des Pens, Paris

EDHIS, see Editions d'Histoire Sociale (EDHIS)

Edicef - Editions Classiques d'Expression Francaise
58 rue Jean Bleuzen, 92178 Vanves Cedex
Tel: (01) 46 62 10 10 *Fax:* (01) 40 95 10 74
E-mail: infos@foliesdencre.com
Web Site: www.foliesdencre.com/afr/edicef.html
Key Personnel
Dir General: Laurent Loric
Subjects: Economics, Education, English as a Second Language, Environmental Studies, Law, Literature, Literary Criticism, Essays, Mathematics, Physics
ISBN Prefix(es): 2-84129; 2-85069
Parent Company: Hachette Livre SA
Subsidiaries: NEI (Nouvelles Editions Ivoiviennes)

Edisud+
La Calade, 3120 Route d'Avignon, 13090 Aix-en-Provence
Tel: (04) 42 21 61 44 *Fax:* (04) 42 21 56 20
E-mail: info@edisud.com
Web Site: www.edisud.com
Key Personnel
Man Dir, Sales, Production: Charly-Yves Chaudoreille
Editorial: Anne-Marie Lapillonne
Rights & Permissions: Marie-Noelle Boudon
Founded: 1971
Subjects: Agriculture, Anthropology, Archaeology, Architecture & Interior Design, Art, Cookery, Energy, Environmental Studies, Ethnicity, Gardening, Plants, Geography, Geology, History, How-to, Music, Dance, Outdoor Recreation, Regional Interests, Sports, Athletics, Wine & Spirits
ISBN Prefix(es): 2-85744; 2-7449

Les Editeurs Reunis+
11 rue de la Montagne-Ste-Genevieve, 75005 Paris
Tel: (01) 43 54 74 46; (01) 43 54 43 81 *Fax:* (01) 43 25 34 79
Founded: 1932
The company acts as sole agent for YMCA Press in publishing a comprehensive list of Russian books in the original Russian.
Subjects: Literature, Literary Criticism, Essays, Religion - Other
ISBN Prefix(es): 2-85065

Edition1+
43 Quai de Grenelle, 75905 Paris Cedex 15
Tel: (01) 43923587 *Fax:* (01) 43923585
Key Personnel
Publisher, Editor, Man Dir & Right & Permissions: Rene Guitton
Editor: Isabelle Brossard
Founded: 1979
Subjects: Biography, Literature, Literary Criticism, Essays, Nonfiction (General), Self-Help, Sports, Athletics
ISBN Prefix(es): 2-86391
Parent Company: Hachette Group

Editions d'Organisation+
One rue Thenard, 75005 Paris Cedex 05
Tel: (01) 44 41 46 41 *Fax:* (01) 44 41 46 00
E-mail: service-lecteurs@editions-organisation.com
Web Site: www.editions-organisation.com
Key Personnel
President: Serge Eyrolles
General Manager: Jean Pierre Tissier
Founded: 1952
Subjects: Business, Computer Science, Electronics, Electrical Engineering, Engineering (General), House & Home, How-to, Law, Management, Social Sciences, Sociology

ISBN Prefix(es): 2-7081
Number of titles published annually: 550 Print
Parent Company: Groupe Eyrolles SA, 55 blvd Saint Germain, Paris
Bookshop(s): Librairie Eyrolles, Paris *Tel:* (01) 44411179; Librairie Des Entreprises, 79 ave de la Republique, ESCP Hall Blondeau, 75543 Paris, Cedex 11 *Tel:* (01) 43382671; Librairie De Provence, 31 Cours Mirabeau, 13100 Aix-en-Provence *Tel:* (042) 42260723; Librairie Des Entreprises, One rue de la Liberation, Centre HEC-ISA, Jouy-en-Josas *Tel:* (01) 39679459; Librarie Des Entreprises, Av Bernard Hirsch, BP 105, 95021 Cergy Pontoise Cedex *Tel:* (01) 30381452

Editions du Chene, EPA, *imprint of* Editions du Chene

Editions du Conseil de l'Europe, see Council of Europe Publishing

Editions du Masque, *imprint of* Librairie des Champs-Elysees SA

Les Editions ESF+
17 rue Viete, 75017 Paris
Tel: (01) 44691500 *Fax:* (01) 44692107
Web Site: www.pratique.fr/prat/
Key Personnel
President: Dominique Prat
Man Dir: Vincent Wackenheim
Founded: 1947
Subjects: Business, Communications, Economics, Education, Finance, Law, Management, Marketing, Microcomputers, Psychology, Psychiatry, Technology
ISBN Prefix(es): 2-7101
Parent Company: Le Groupe PRAT
Warehouse: PRAT, Zi de Comhre, 28481 Thiron
Orders to: Dimedia, Canada
Servidis, Switzerland
Presses de Belgique, Belgium
CDE, 17 rue de Tournon, 75006 Paris

Editions Grund+
60 rue Mazarine, 75006 Paris
Tel: (01) 53103600 *Fax:* (01) 43294986
E-mail: grund@grund.fr
Web Site: www.grund.fr *Cable:* GRUND PARIS
Key Personnel
President: Alain Grund
Sales: Yannick Lemonnier
Chief Editor: Monique Souchon
Public Relations: Chantal Janisson *Tel:* (01) 53103612 *E-mail:* chantal.janisson@grund.fr
Founded: 1880
Subjects: Animals, Pets, Art, Environmental Studies, How-to, Travel
ISBN Prefix(es): 2-7000; 2-85205
Number of titles published annually: 180 Print
Associate Companies: Editions Alpina; Editions Guy Le Prat

Editions Litteraires et Linguistiques de l'Universite de Grenoble III, see ELLUG (Editions Litteraires et Linguistiques de l'Universite de Grenoble III)

Editions Recherche sur les Civilisations (ERC)
Unit of ADPF
6, rue Ferrus, 75683 Paris, Cedex 14
Tel: (01) 43 13 11 00 *Fax:* (01) 43 13 11 25
Web Site: www.france.diplomatie.fr; www.adpf.asso.fr
Key Personnel
Editorial Dir: Hina Descat
Contact: Guillaume Desanges
Founded: 1980
Subjects: Anthropology, Archaeology, Ethnicity, History, Social Sciences, Sociology

ISBN Prefix(es): 2-86538
Total Titles: 268 Print

Editions Tarmeye+
Roudon, 43520 Mazet Saint Voy
Tel: (0471) 650153; (0477) 435814 *Fax:* (0471) 650154; (0477) 435899
Key Personnel
Publisher: Jacqueline Tartar; Jean-Marc Tartar
Founded: 1986
Subjects: Humor
ISBN Prefix(es): 2-906029

Editions Verticales, *imprint of* Editions du Seuil

EDJA, *imprint of* Editions Juridiques Africaines

EDP Sciences+
Subsidiary of Societe Francaise de Physique
7 ave du Hoggar, Parc d'Activities de Courtaboeuf, 91944 Les Ulis Cedex A
Tel: (01) 69 18 75 75 *Fax:* (01) 69 28 84 91
E-mail: edps@edpsciences.org
Web Site: www.edpsciences.org
Key Personnel
Man Dir & Publications Manager: Jean-Marc Quilbe *E-mail:* quilbe@edpsciences.org
Founded: 1920
Services for electronic publications, web site development & printing.
Subjects: Astronomy, Engineering (General), Mathematics, Mechanical Engineering, Physics, Science (General), Social Sciences, Sociology, Technology
ISBN Prefix(es): 2-86883; 2-902731
Number of titles published annually: 15 Print
Total Titles: 120 Print; 28 E-Book
Online services available through World Wide Web.
U.S. Office(s): 875-81 Massachusetts Ave, Cambridge, MA 02139, United States, Contact: Doug Wright *Tel:* 617-354-7275 *Fax:* 617-354-6875

Educalivre, *imprint of* Editions Casteilla

EHESS, see Editions de l'Ecole des Hautes Etudes en Sciences Sociales (EHESS)

Electre Editions du Cercle de la Librairie
35 rue Gregoire-de-Tours, 75279 Paris Cedex 06
Tel: (01) 44 41 28 00 *Fax:* (01) 44 41 28 65
Web Site: www.imaginet.fr/electre
Key Personnel
Man Dir: Jean-Marie Doublet
Sales: Pascal Fouche
Founded: 1983
Subjects: Library & Information Sciences
ISBN Prefix(es): 2-7654

Elf Exploration Production+
Ave Larribau, 64018 Pau Cedex
Tel: (05) 59 83 65 80 *Fax:* (05) 59 83 57 88
Web Site: www.cgt-totalfina-elf.org
Key Personnel
Editor: Jean-Francois Raynaud
Founded: 1967
Subjects: Earth Sciences, Geography, Geology
ISBN Prefix(es): 2-901026; 2-85843
Book Club(s): France Edition; Syndicate National de L'Edition; Unipresse

Ellebore
5 Impasse Mousset, 75012 Paris Cedex 12
Mailing Address: BP 01, 75560 Paris Cedex 12
Tel: (01) 40 01 09 49 *Fax:* (01) 40 01 09 94
E-mail: ellebore@wfi.fr
Web Site: www.wfi.fr/ellebore
Telex: 213907 Parac
Key Personnel
Manager: Jean-Paul Barriolade

Founded: 1980
Subjects: Health, Nutrition, Psychology, Psychiatry
ISBN Prefix(es): 2-86898

Ellipses - Edition Marketing SA
8-10 rue de la Quintinie, 75740 Paris Cedex 15
Mailing Address: 32 rue Bargue, 75740 Paris Cedex 15
Tel: (01) 56 56 64 10 *Fax:* (01) 45 31 07 67
E-mail: infos@editions-ellipses.com
Web Site: www.editions-ellipses.com
Key Personnel
Man Dir: Jean-Pierre Benezet
Founded: 1973
Subjects: Medicine, Nursing, Dentistry, Science (General)
ISBN Prefix(es): 2-7298

ELLUG (Editions Litteraires et Linguistiques de l'Universite de Grenoble III)+
Universite Stendhal, BP 25, 38040 Cedex 9, Grenoble
Tel: (04) 76 82 43 72; (04) 76 82 77 74 *Fax:* (04) 76 82 41 12
E-mail: ellug@u-grenoble3.fr
Web Site: www-ellug.u-grenoble3.fr
Key Personnel
Editor: Elisabeth Greslou
Founded: 1978
Member of International Association of Scholarly Publishers.
Subjects: Antiques, Communications, Language Arts, Linguistics, Literature, Literary Criticism, Essays
ISBN Prefix(es): 2-902709; 2-84310
Number of titles published annually: 10 Print
Total Titles: 120 Print

Editions ELOR, *imprint of* BSl - ELOR Editions Jeunesse

Encres Vives
31 Sq de Montgeoffroy, 49300 Cholet
Tel: (05) 62740787
E-mail: encres@mygale.org
Key Personnel
Dir: Michel Cosem
Founded: 1960
Subjects: Poetry
ISBN Prefix(es): 2-85550

Encyclopedia Universalis France SA+
18 rue de Tilsitt, 75809 Paris Cedex 17
Tel: (01) 45 72 72 72 *Fax:* (01) 45 72 03 43
E-mail: communication@universalis.fr
Web Site: www.universalis.fr
Key Personnel
President: Giuseppe Annoscia
Editorial: Bernard Couvelaire
Financial Manager: Herve Rouanet
Export Manager: Speranta Gallage *Tel:* (01) 45 72 72 52 *E-mail:* sgallage@universalis.fr
Production Manager: Dominique Reyren
Founded: 1967
ISBN Prefix(es): 2-85229

L'encyclopedie Poetique, *imprint of* Sarl Editions Jean Grassin

Editions Entente+
12 rue Honore-Chevalier, 75006 Paris
Tel: (01) 42 22 80 70 *Fax:* (01) 40 49 01 02
Key Personnel
Man Dir: Edouard Esmerian
Founded: 1975
Publish *La Gazette du Livre* (La Tribune des Petits Editeurs).
Member of Association des Petits Editeurs Francophones.
Subjects: Cookery, Developing Countries, Economics, Education, Energy, Environmental Studies, Human Relations, Literature, Literary Criticism, Essays, Poetry, Science (General), Technology
ISBN Prefix(es): 2-7266
Total Titles: 102 Print; 1 Audio
Distributor for l'Athanor; Editions d'En-Bas; Jacques Laget; Robert Jauze; Lierre & Coudrier; Mamamelis; Le Nid; La Pleine Lune; Le Signet
Bookshop(s): Librairie Entente 12 rue Honore-Chevalier, 75006 Paris

Histoire D'Entreprises, *imprint of* Institute

EPA SA (Editions Presse Audiovisuel)+
Imprint of Editions du Chene
43 quai de Grenelle, 75905 Paris Cedex 15
Tel: (01) 43 92 30 00 *Fax:* (01) 43 92 33 81
Key Personnel
President: Fatine Layt
Man Dir: Isabelle Jendron
Editorial Dir: Philippe Pierrelee
Editor: Denis Jacob
Automobile Editor: Gilles Blanchet
Publicity, Mail Order, Sales: Anne-Francoise d'Angerville
Production: Pascale Ragot
Rights Manager: Sherri Aldis
Founded: 1972
Subjects: Aeronautics, Aviation, Architecture & Interior Design, Automotive, Cookery, History, Maritime, Military Science, Sports, Athletics, Transportation, Wine & Spirits
ISBN Prefix(es): 2-85120
Parent Company: Hachette Livre

Epanouissement, *imprint of* Editions Trois Fontaines

Les Editions de l'Epargne+
5 rue Masseran, 75341 Paris Cedex 07
Tel: (01) 44169580 *Fax:* (01) 44169590
Key Personnel
Man Dir: Dominique Therond
Founded: 1957
Subjects: Architecture & Interior Design, Art, Economics, Finance, History, How-to, Law
ISBN Prefix(es): 2-85015

EPEL+
29 rue Madame, 75006 Paris
Tel: (06) 81 06 02 52 *Fax:* (01) 45 44 22 85
Web Site: www.ecole-lacanienne.net/popup-epel.html
Key Personnel
Dir: Jean Allouch *E-mail:* jallouch@noos.fr
Founded: 1990
Subjects: Philosophy, Psychology, Psychiatry
ISBN Prefix(es): 2-908855

EPLS - ACLA Edition+
5 bis, rue Saint Paul, 75004 Paris
Tel: (01) 48040075 *Fax:* (01) 42777298
Telex: 613814
Key Personnel
Man Dir: Thierry Schimpff
Founded: 1980
Subjects: Sports, Athletics
ISBN Prefix(es): 2-86519

ERC, see Editions Recherche sur les Civilisations (ERC)

Ere Nouvelle+
BP 171, 06407 Cannes Cedex
Tel: (0493) 99-30-13
E-mail: lerenouvelle@wanadoo.fr
Web Site: assoc.wanadoo/fr/lerenouvelle/pub
Key Personnel
Dir: Pierre Lance *E-mail:* pierre.lance@wanadoo.fr
Founded: 1980
Subjects: Energy, Health, Nutrition, Philosophy, Psychology, Psychiatry, Social Sciences, Sociology
ISBN Prefix(es): 2-905825

Editions Eres+
11 rue des Alouettes, 31520 Ramonville
Tel: (05) 61 75 15 76 *Fax:* (05) 61 73 52 89
E-mail: eres@edition-eres.com
Web Site: www.edition-eres.com
Key Personnel
President & Dir General: Jean Sacrispeyre
Founded: 1980
Subjects: Criminology, Law, Philosophy, Psychology, Psychiatry, Social Sciences, Sociology
ISBN Prefix(es): 2-86586
Number of titles published annually: 60 Print

Editions Errance
7 rue Jean du Bellay, 75004 Paris
Tel: (01) 43 26 40 41 *Fax:* (01) 43 29 34 88
Key Personnel
Editor: Frederic Lontcho
Founded: 1982
Subjects: Archaeology, History
ISBN Prefix(es): 2-87772; 2-903442

Editions Eska
12, rue du Quatre Septembre, 75002 Paris
Tel: (01) 42 86 56 00 *Fax:* (01) 42 86 55 95
E-mail: eska@multimediart.fr
Web Site: www.sybex.fr
Key Personnel
Sales Dir: Patricia Fousweray
Subjects: Aeronautics, Aviation, Economics, Engineering (General), Labor, Industrial Relations, Law, Management, Medicine, Nursing, Dentistry
ISBN Prefix(es): 2-86911
Distributor for Presses Universitaires du Quebec (Canada)

Editions Espaces 34
BP 2080, 34025 Montpellier Cedex
Tel: (04) 67 84 11 23 *Fax:* (04) 67 84 00 74
E-mail: chesp34@club-internet.fr
Key Personnel
President: Laurent Chevallier
Subjects: Biological Sciences, Drama, Theater, Literature, Literary Criticism, Essays, Mathematics, Medicine, Nursing, Dentistry, Social Sciences, Sociology
ISBN Prefix(es): 2-907293; 2-84705

L'Esprit Du Temps+
88 av Leon-Blum, 33491 Cedex, Le Bouscat
Mailing Address: BP 107, 33491 Le Bouscat, Cedex
Tel: (056) 02 84 19 *Fax:* (056) 02 91 31
Key Personnel
Manager: Beatrice Bessieres
Literary Dir: Philippe Brenot
Founded: 1989
Subjects: Drama, Theater, Literature, Literary Criticism, Essays, Medicine, Nursing, Dentistry
ISBN Prefix(es): 2-908206; 2-913062
Orders to: PUF, 14 ave du Bois de l'Epiue, BP 90, 91003 Evry Cedex

Editions de L'Est+
Rue Gabriel Faure, Zila California BP 50, 54140 Jarville-la-Malgrange
Tel: (016) 83567677 *Fax:* (016) 83533456
Telex: 961749F
Key Personnel
President: Pascal Chipot
Dir General: Gerard Gabriel
ISBN Prefix(es): 2-86955

Institut d'Ethnologie du Museum National d'Histoire Naturelle
Museum National d'Histoire Naturelle, Service des Publications Scientifiques, 57, rue Cuvier, 75231 Paris Cedex 05
Tel: (01) 4079 48 38 *Fax:* (01) 4079 38 58
E-mail: diff.pub@mnhn.fr
Web Site: www.mnhn.fr/publication
Founded: 1925
Subjects: Archaeology, Ethnicity, Language Arts, Linguistics
ISBN Prefix(es): 2-85653; 2-85265
Number of titles published annually: 1 Print
Total Titles: 125 Print

ETIF (Ed Technique des Industries de la Fonderie), see CTIF (Center Technique des Industries de la Fonderie)

L'Etoile/Cahiers du Cinema+
9 passage de la Boule-Blanche, 75012 Paris
Tel: (01) 53 44 75 75 *Fax:* (01) 43 43 95 04
Key Personnel
Dir: Serge Toubiana
Editor: Claudine Paquot
Contact: Pierre Zins
Founded: 1951
Subjects: Drama, Theater
ISBN Prefix(es): 2-86642

ETSF, see Editions Techniques et Scientifiques Francaises

Institut d'Etudes Augustiniennes
3 rue de l'Abbaye, 75006 Paris
Tel: (01) 43-54-80-25 *Fax:* (01) 43 54 39 55
E-mail: iea@wanadoo.fr
Key Personnel
Man Dir: Jean-Claude Fredouille
Contact: Claudine Croyere
Founded: 1954
Subjects: Antiques, Archaeology, History, Philosophy, Religion - Catholic, Theology
ISBN Prefix(es): 2-85121
Shipping Address: Brepols Steen Weg op Tielen 68, B-2300 Turnhout, Belgium
  Tel: (032) 14 40 27 00 *Fax:* (032) 14 42 89 19 *E-mail:* publishers@brepols.com
Warehouse: Brepols Steen Weg op Tielen 68, B-2300 Turnhout, Belgium *Tel:* (032) 14 40 27 00 *Fax:* (032) 14 42 89 19 *E-mail:* publishers@brepols.com
Orders to: Brepols Steen Weg op Tielen 68, B-2300 Turnhout, Belgium *Tel:* (032) 14 40 27 00 *Fax:* (032) 14 42 89 19 *E-mail:* publishers@brepols.com

Institut d'Etudes Slaves+
9, rue Michelet, 75006 Paris
Tel: (01) 43 26 50 89; (01) 43 26 79 18 *Fax:* (01) 43 26 16 23
E-mail: etudes.slaves@paris4.sorbonne.fr
Key Personnel
President: Michel Aucouturier
Sales, Publicity: Katarzyna Gornicka-Knoch
Production, Rights & Permissions: Serge Aslanoff
Founded: 1920
Subjects: History, Language Arts, Linguistics, Literature, Literary Criticism, Essays, Slavic Studies
ISBN Prefix(es): 2-7204

l'Europeenne, *imprint of* Editions de Septembre

L'Expansion Scientifique Francaise
15, rue Saint-Benoit, 75006 Paris
Tel: (01) 45 48 42 60 *Fax:* (01) 45 44 81 55
E-mail: expansionscientifiquefrancaise@wanadoo.fr
Web Site: www.expansionscientifique.com

Key Personnel
Man Dir: Pierre Bergeaud
Founded: 1925
Subjects: Biological Sciences, Medicine, Nursing, Dentistry
ISBN Prefix(es): 2-7046
Bookshop(s): Librairie des Facultes de Medecine et de Pharmacie, 174 blvd St-Germain, F-75297 Paris Cedex 06 *Tel:* (01) 45485448

Editions Eyrolles+
61 blvd Saint-Germain, 75240 Paris Cedex 05
Tel: (01) 44 41 11 11 *Fax:* (01) 44 41 11 85
E-mail: service-lecteurs@editions-eyrolles.com
Web Site: www.editions-eyrolles.com
Telex: Eyrotp 203385 F
Key Personnel
Man Dir: Jean-Pierre Tissier
Editorials: Eric Sulpice; Jean-Jacques Brisebarre
Foreign Rights: Marlyne Tolentino *Tel:* (01) 44 41 11 16 *Fax:* (01) 44 41 46 00 *E-mail:* foreignrights@eyrolles.com
Contact: Miguel Tejedor
Founded: 1918
Subjects: Architecture & Interior Design, Computer Science, Crafts, Games, Hobbies, Earth Sciences, Electronics, Electrical Engineering, Management, Mechanical Engineering, Physical Sciences
ISBN Prefix(es): 2-212
Parent Company: Ecole Speciale des Travaux Publics
Associate Companies: Editions d'Organisation
Distributor for Microsoft Press France

FAB
37, rue des Murlins, 45000 Orleans-France
Tel: (0238) 70 84 44 *Fax:* (0238) 70 56 76
E-mail: fab45.paradigme@wanadoo.fr
Web Site: pradigme.com
Key Personnel
Editorial Assistant: Olivier Grolleau
ISBN Prefix(es): 2-86878

Fac Editions
30, rue Madame, 75006 Paris
Tel: (01) 45487651 *Fax:* (01) 42222231
Key Personnel
General Dir: Max Huot De Longchamp
Subjects: Philosophy, Religion - Catholic, Theology
ISBN Prefix(es): 2-903422
Imprints: Paroisse & Famille
Distributor for CLD

Falguiere 36, see Galerie Esther Woerdehoff

Bernard de Fallois
22 rue La Boetie, 75008 Paris
Tel: (01) 42669195 *Fax:* (01) 49240637
Founded: 1987
Subjects: Literature, Literary Criticism, Essays
ISBN Prefix(es): 2-87706
Orders to: Hachette Export, 58 rue Jean Bleuzen, 92178 Vanves Cedex
22 rue La Boetie, 75008

Editions Fanlac+
12 Rue du Professeur-Peyrot, BP 2043, 24002 Perigueux Cedex
Tel: (05) 53-53-41-90 *Fax:* (05) 53-08-05-85
E-mail: fanlac-edition@aquinet.tm.fr
Web Site: www.fanlac.com
Key Personnel
Dir General: Bernard Tardien
Founded: 1943
Subjects: Art, Cookery, Literature, Literary Criticism, Essays, Photography, Poetry, Regional Interests, Travel
ISBN Prefix(es): 2-86577

Number of titles published annually: 10 Print
Branch Office(s)
31, rue Faidherbe, 75011 Paris *Tel:* (01) 43-67-51-32 *Fax:* (01) 40-09-94-00

Editions Farel+
BP 20, 77421 Marne-la-Vallee Cedex 2
Tel: (01) 64 68 46 44 *Fax:* (01) 64 68 39 90
E-mail: lire@editionsfarel.com
Web Site: www.editionsfarel.com
Key Personnel
Dir: D Steven Dixon
Founded: 1978
Subjects: Religion - Protestant
ISBN Prefix(es): 2-86314
Number of titles published annually: 20 Print
Total Titles: 165 Print
Distributed by Diffusion Emmaues (Switzerland); Inter-Books LLB (Canada); Le Bon Livre (Belgium)
Distributor for G-Lu Publishing House; Janz Team/Peniel

Fata Morgana+
Fontfroide-le Haut, 34980 Saint-Clement
Tel: (04) 67 54 40 40 *Fax:* (04) 67 04 14 91
E-mail: fatamorgan@wanadoo.fr
Key Personnel
President: Roy Bruno
International Rights: David Massabuau
Founded: 1966
Subjects: Art, Asian Studies, Literature, Literary Criticism, Essays, Philosophy, Religion - Catholic, Religion - Hindu, Religion - Islamic, Religion - Jewish, Religion - Other
ISBN Prefix(es): 2-85194
Subsidiaries: Fakir Press; Bibliotheque Artistique & Litteraire
Distributed by DPLU (Canada); L'Age-D'Homme (Switzerland); Nouvelle Diffusion (Belgium)
Bookshop(s): Librairie Freecyb, 41 rue Basfroi, Paris, Jean-Francois Poupelin *E-mail:* yanndortin@freecyb.com *Web Site:* freecyb.com
Orders to: Les Belles Lettres, 95 Bd Raspail, 75006 Paris *Tel:* (01) 44-39-84-20 *Fax:* (01) 45-48-92-88

Librairie Artheme Fayard+
75, rue des Saints-Peres, 75006 Paris Cedex 6
Tel: (01) 45498200 *Fax:* (01) 42224017
Web Site: www.editions-fayard.fr
Telex: 264918 trace
Key Personnel
President & Man Dir: Claude Durand
Publicity: Caroline Gutmann
Advertising Dir: Frederique Larvor
Rights & Permissions: Martine Bertea
Founded: 1854
Subjects: Biography, Fiction, History, Music, Dance, Philosophy, Religion - Other, Science (General), Social Sciences, Sociology, Technology
ISBN Prefix(es): 2-213
Parent Company: Hachette
Subsidiaries: Editions Le Sarment

FBT de R Editions/Editions des Limbes d'Or
31, quai de la Tournelle, 75005 Paris
Tel: (01) 41151969; (06) 07683371 *Fax:* (01) 41151969
Key Personnel
President: Francoise Thiam
Founded: 1995
Subjects: Art, Criminology, Economics, Fiction, Foreign Countries, Government, Political Science, Human Relations, Literature, Literary Criticism, Essays, Travel
ISBN Prefix(es): 2-911064

FRANCE

Federation Francaise de la Randonnee Pedestre+
14, rue Riquet, 75019 Paris
Tel: (01) 44 89 93 93 *Fax:* (01) 40 35 85 67
E-mail: info@ffrp.asso.fr
Web Site: asp.ffrp.asso.fr
Key Personnel
President: Maurice Bruzek
Founded: 1947
Subjects: Outdoor Recreation, Sports, Athletics
ISBN Prefix(es): 2-85699
Shipping Address: IGN, lamp des Landes, 41200 Villefranche s/cher
Warehouse: IGN, lamp des Landes, 41200 Villefranche s/cher
Orders to: IGN, lamp des Landes, 41200 Villefranche s/cher

Des Femmes+
6 rue de Mezieres, 75006 Paris Cedex 6e
Tel: (01) 4548 8380 *Fax:* (01) 40358548
E-mail: adfemmes@iway.fr
Key Personnel
Proprietor & Man Dir: Antoinette Fouque
General Manager: Marie-Claude Grumbach
Founded: 1974
Subjects: Art, Biography, Drama, Theater, Fiction, History, Literature, Literary Criticism, Essays, Photography, Poetry
ISBN Prefix(es): 2-7210
Number of titles published annually: 5 Print; 2 Audio
Total Titles: 450 Print; 100 Audio
Online services available through des-femmes.com.
Distributor for Sonjis

Editions du Feu Nouveau+
DCI-TIM 01/BP, 93351 Le Bourget Cedex
Tel: (01) 44844797
Key Personnel
Man Dir: Henri Caffarel
Founded: 1946
Subjects: Literature, Literary Criticism, Essays, Religion - Catholic, Religion - Other
ISBN Prefix(es): 2-85017
Shipping Address: SOFEDIS (Diffuseur), 29 rue Saint-Sulpice, 75006 Paris

Figures, *imprint of* Societe des Editions Grasset et Fasquelle

Editions Filipacchi-Sonodip+
151 rue Anatole-France, 92598 Levallois-Perret Cedex
Tel: (01) 41349069; (01) 41349055 *Fax:* (01) 41349070
Key Personnel
Manager, Editorial: Marie-Francoise Acdouard
Founded: 1970
Subjects: Cookery, House & Home, Photography, Travel
ISBN Prefix(es): 2-85018

Librairie Fischbacher, International Art Book Distribution (import-export)
33, rue de Seine, 75006 Paris
Tel: (01) 43 26 84 87 *Fax:* (01) 43 26 48 87
Key Personnel
Dir, Production, Publicity, Rights & Permissions: Marie-Colette Galand
Sales: P Diani-Garel
Founded: 1850
Member of the Library of Fine Arts; specialize in original art.
Subjects: Art, History, Music, Dance, Philosophy, Religion - Protestant, Social Sciences, Sociology, Theology
ISBN Prefix(es): 2-7179
Parent Company: Librairie Fischbacher SA

Editions Fivedit
96 rue du Faubourg-Poissonniere, 75010 Paris
Mailing Address: BP 146 Annecy Le Vieux, 74941 Cedex
Tel: (0450) 663378 *Fax:* (0450) 233308
Key Personnel
Man Dir: Rene Fivel-Demoret
Founded: 1976
Subjects: How-to, Travel
ISBN Prefix(es): 2-904394; 2-913140
Total Titles: 30 Print
Branch Office(s)
Distribution Ulysse, 4176 Saint Denis, Montreal, PQ, Canada
Distributed by Vivendi Universal Publishing Services
Distributor for APCA Bienvenue a la Ferme; Gites de France; Logis de Belgique; Logis de France; Logis D' Italia; Tables et Auberges de France

Fixot+
24 av Marceau, 75008 Paris
Tel: (01) 53 67 15 22 *Fax:* (01) 53 67 14 14
Telex: 260 808
Key Personnel
Dir: Agnes Hirtz
Founded: 1987
Subjects: Fiction
ISBN Prefix(es): 2-221; 2-87645
Associate Companies: Bellitz Fixot

Flammarion SA+
26 rue Racine, 75278 Paris, Cedex 06
Tel: (01) 40513008 *Fax:* (01) 43250118
Telex: flamedit 205641 *Cable:* 205146
Key Personnel
Chairman: Charles-Henri Flammarion
Man Dir: Danielle Nees
Sales Manager: Alain Flammarion
Publicity, Advertising: Catherine Bachelez
Rights & Permissions: Renata Morteo
Press: Francine Brobeil *Fax:* (01) 40 51 31 29
E-mail: fbr@flammarion.fr
Founded: 1875
Subjects: Architecture & Interior Design, Art, Fiction, Gardening, Plants, House & Home, Literature, Literary Criticism, Essays, Medicine, Nursing, Dentistry, Nonfiction (General), Wine & Spirits
ISBN Prefix(es): 2-257
Associate Companies: Pygnalion
Imprints: Arthaud; Aubie; Champs Dominos; GF; Glacial; Fluide; J'ailu; Librio; Medecine-Sciences; Pere Castor
Subsidiaries: Aubie; Beau Arts SA; Delagrave; Editions Aubier, Flammarion Canada; Flammarion 4; Flammarion Presse; Flammarion 2; Flammarion Switzerland; Flammarion USA Inc; J'ai Lu; Union-Distribution
Branch Office(s)
Flammarion USA Inc, 200 Park Ave S, Suite 1406, New York, NY 10003, United States
Tel: 212-777-6888 *Fax:* 212-777-3438
Distributed by Abbeville (USA); Thames & Hudson (UK)
Distributor for Abbeville; Actes Sud; Assouline; Bibliotheque de l'Image; CNAC; Delcourt; Flohic; Hoebeke; Horay; Le Petit Fute; Pygnalion; Revue du Vin de France; Zulma
Bookshop(s): Flammarion 4, 19 Rue Visconti, 75006 Paris
Warehouse: UD-Union Distribution, 06 rue Petit le roy, Chevilly-Larue, F-94152 Rungis Cedex
Tel: (01) 41802020 *Fax:* (01) 46875104
Orders to: UD-Union Distribution, 106 rue Petit le roy, Chevilly-Larue, F-94152 Rungis Cedex
Tel: (01) 41802020 *Fax:* (01) 46875180

FLE, see Hachette francais langue etrangere - FLE

Groupe Fleurus-Mame+
15-27 rue Moussorgski, 75895 Paris Cedex 18
Tel: (01) 53 26 33 35 *Fax:* (01) 53 26 33 36
Telex: 201650 F
Key Personnel
Man Dir: Pierre-Marie Dumont
Dir: Christopher Savoure
Editorial: Janine Boudineau
Sales Dir: Dominique Delage
Foreign Rights: Euriel Donval; Chantal Hourcade
Founded: 1944
Subjects: Architecture & Interior Design, Art, Crafts, Games, Hobbies, Fiction, Psychology, Psychiatry, Religion - Other, Social Sciences, Sociology
ISBN Prefix(es): 2-215

Fleuve No ite Editions, see Presses de la Cite

Fluide, *imprint of* Flammarion SA

Folklore Comtois
Musee de Plein Air des Maisons Comtoises, Rue du Musee, 25360 Nancray
Tel: 81552977 *Fax:* 81552397
Key Personnel
President: Jean Louis Clade
Vice President: Pierre Bourgin
Subjects: Agriculture, Architecture & Interior Design, History, House & Home

Presses de la Fondation Nationale des Sciences Politiques+
44 rue du Four, 75006 Paris
Tel: (01) 44 39 39 60 *Fax:* (01) 45 48 04 41
Web Site: www.sciences.po.fr
Telex: Scipol 201002 F
Key Personnel
Man Dir, Sales: Louis Bodin
Editorial, Rights & Permissions: Mireille Perche
Periodicals: Josee Cabillon
Public Relations: Christelle Michel-Flandin
Founded: 1975
Subjects: Economics, Government, Political Science, History, Social Sciences, Sociology
ISBN Prefix(es): 2-7246

Les Editions Foucher SA
Subsidiary of Hachette
31, rue de Fleurus, 75278 Paris Cedex 06
Tel: (01) 49 54 35 35 *Fax:* (01) 49 54 35 00
E-mail: contact@foucher.fr
Web Site: www.ecodroit.editions-foucher.fr
Key Personnel
President: Christine Breiteinstein
General Manager: Daniel Segala
Founded: 1936
Subjects: Accounting, Economics, Education, Medicine, Nursing, Dentistry, Public Administration
ISBN Prefix(es): 2-216
Total Titles: 1,000 Print

Editions Fragments
5 rue de Charonne, 75011 Paris
Tel: (01) 47 00 76 48 *Fax:* (01) 47 00 22 04
E-mail: art@fragmentseditions.com
Web Site: www.fragmentseditions.com
Key Personnel
Dir: Francois de Villandry
Publishing Coordinator: Helene Joubert
Press & Public Relations: Sophie Godard
Founded: 1990
Specialize in contemporary art.
Subjects: Art, Photography
ISBN Prefix(es): 2-908066
Number of titles published annually: 7 Print
Total Titles: 80 Print
Distributed by Goutal-Darly (Europe); Vilo (China, Europe, Japan, Korea, North America, South America)

Warehouse: Zone Industrielle Leval, 11 ave Arago, 91420 Morangis
Orders to: Vilo Diffusion, 25 rue Ginoux, 75015 Paris

Institut Francais de Recherche pour l'Exploitation de la Mer (IFREMER)
155, rue Jean-Jacques Rousseau, 92138 Issy-les-Moulineaux Cedex
Mailing Address: BP 70, 29280 Plouzane
Tel: (02) 98 22 40 13 *Fax:* (02) 98 22 45 86
E-mail: editions@ifremer.fr
Web Site: www.ifremer.fr
Key Personnel
Chief Executive Officer: Jean-Francois Minster
Contact: Patrick Phliponeau *Tel:* (02) 98 22 43 13 *Fax:* (02) 98 22 45 86 *E-mail:* patrick.phliponeau@ifremer.fr
Editorial & Promotion: Courtay Nelly *Tel:* (02) 98 22 40 13 *E-mail:* nelly.courtay@ifremer.fr
Founded: 1985
On line catalogue.
Subjects: Environmental Studies, Maritime, Outdoor Recreation, Technology, Transportation, Scientific & technical publications
ISBN Prefix(es): 2-905434; 2-84433
Total Titles: 4 CD-ROM; 40 Audio
Orders to: ALT Brest Service Logistique, 3, rue Edouard Belin BP 23, 29801 Brest Cedex 9 *Tel:* (02) 98024234 *Fax:* (02) 98020584 *E-mail:* alt.belin@wanadoo.fr

France-Caraiibes, *imprint of* Editions Louis Soulanges Le Livrer Ouvert

France Edition Office de Promotion Internationale
Association d'editeurs, 115, Boulevard Saint-Germain, 75006 Paris
Tel: (01) 44 41 13 13 *Fax:* (01) 46 34 63 83
E-mail: info@franceedition.com
Web Site: www.franceedition.com
Key Personnel
President: Liana Levi
General Secretary: Marc Franconie *E-mail:* franconie@franceedition.com
Managing Dir: Jean-Guy Boin *E-mail:* jgboin@franceedition.com
Specialize in all subjects.
Branch Office(s)
France Edition Vietnam, Mlle Ho Thi Ngoc Lan, 30 rue Dinh Ngaug, Hanoi, Viet Nam *Tel:* (04) 826 48 62 *Fax:* (04) 825 34 11 *E-mail:* lanfevn@hn.vnn.vn
U.S. Office(s): France Edition Inc, 853 Broadway, New York, NY 10003-4703, United States, Lucinda Karter *Tel:* 212-254-4540 *Fax:* 212-979-6229 *Web Site:* www.frenchpubagency.com
Foreign Rights: France Edition Inc

France-Empire+
13, rue Le Sueur, 75116 Paris
Tel: (01) 45 00 33 00 *Fax:* (01) 45 00 20 77
E-mail: france-empire@france-empire.fr
Web Site: www.france-empire.fr
Key Personnel
Contact: Jean-Louis Giral
Founded: 1945
ISBN Prefix(es): 2-7048
Parent Company: Desquenne et Giral
Bookshop(s): Librairie France-Empire, 30 rue Washington, 75008 Paris

France-Loisirs
123 blvd de Grenelle, 75015 Paris
Tel: (01) 45 68 60 00 *Fax:* (01) 42 73 14 38
Web Site: www.franceloisirs.com
Telex: 202 459 f
Key Personnel
Publicity: A Cinar

Subjects: Art, Literature, Literary Criticism, Essays
ISBN Prefix(es): 2-7242

Les Editions Franciscaines SA
9, rue Marie-Rose, 75014 Paris
Tel: (01) 45407351 *Fax:* (01) 40447504
E-mail: editofm@club-internet.fr
Key Personnel
President: Fr Gerard Guitton, OFM
Founded: 1935
Specialize in books.
Subjects: Religion - Catholic, Theology, Franciscan Spirituality
ISBN Prefix(es): 2-85020
Number of titles published annually: 3 Print
Total Titles: 105 Print
Distributed by Alliances Service (Belgium); Univers (Canada)
Distributor for Franciscan Printing Press

Association Frank+
c/o Frank Books, 32 rue Eeouard Vaillant, 93100 Montreuil
Tel: (01) 43656405 *Fax:* (01) 48596668
Key Personnel
President: David Applefield *E-mail:* david@paris-anglo.com
Founded: 1990
A special group called Lawyers for Literature functions as honorary publishers for Frank, The Literary Journal.
Subjects: Drama, Theater, Fashion, Fiction, How-to, Labor, Industrial Relations, Literature, Literary Criticism, Essays, Poetry
ISBN Prefix(es): 2-908171
Associate Companies: Anglophone SA
U.S. Office(s): Mosaic Press, 85 River Rock Drive, No 202, Buffalo, NY, United States *Tel:* 800-387-8992
Distributed by Houghton-Mifflin (UK)

Futuribles SARL+
55, rue de Varenne, 75341 Paris Cedex 07
Tel: (01) 53633770 *Fax:* (01) 42226554
E-mail: revue@futuribles.com
Web Site: www.futuribles.com
Key Personnel
General Dir: Hugues de Jouvenel *Tel:* (01) 53633773 *E-mail:* hjouvenel@futuribles.com
International Rights & General Secretary: Corinne Roels *Tel:* (01) 53633771
Founded: 1975
Publish a monthly independent transdisciplinary policy oriented journal.
Subjects: Developing Countries, Economics, Environmental Studies, Government, Political Science, Labor, Industrial Relations, Management, Social Sciences, Sociology, Technology
ISBN Prefix(es): 2-84387
Number of titles published annually: 11 Print
Online services available through World Wide Web.
Associate Companies: Association Futuribles International

J Gabalda et Cie (Librairie Lecoffre) SA
18, rue Pierre et Marie Curie, 75005 Paris
Tel: (01) 43 26 53 55 *Fax:* (01) 43 25 04 71
E-mail: editions@gabalda.com
Web Site: www.gabalda.com
Key Personnel
Proprietor: J Gabalda
Founded: 1845
Subjects: Religion - Other, Theology
ISBN Prefix(es): 2-85021
Parent Company: Librarie Lecoffre, 18 rue Pierre-et-Marie-Curie, 75005 Paris

Editions Jacques Gabay+
151 bis, rue Saint-Jacques, 75005 Paris
Tel: (01) 43 54 64 64 *Fax:* (01) 43 54 87 00
E-mail: infos@gabay.com
Web Site: www.gabay.com
Key Personnel
Man Dir: Jacques Gabay
Founded: 1987
Subjects: Astronomy, Chemistry, Chemical Engineering, Economics, Mathematics, Philosophy, Physical Sciences, Physics, Science (General)
ISBN Prefix(es): 2-87647
Total Titles: 190 Print
Imprints: Oblong

Edition Galilee+
9, rue de Linne, 75005 Paris
Tel: (01) 43 31 23 84 *Fax:* (01) 45 35 53 68
E-mail: editions.galilee@free.fr
Key Personnel
Man Dir: Michel Delorme
Founded: 1971
Subjects: Art, History, Literature, Literary Criticism, Essays, Philosophy, Poetry, Psychology, Psychiatry, Social Sciences, Sociology
ISBN Prefix(es): 2-7186
Shipping Address: 128 ave du Marechalde Laltre-de-Tattiguy, 77400 Lagny
Warehouse: 128 ave du Marechalde Laltre-de-Tattiguy, 77400 Lagny (also Shipping)
Orders to: Sodis, BP 142, F-77403 Lagny sur Marne *Tel:* (01) 45311606

Editions Gallimard
5, rue Sebastien-Bottin, 75328 Paris, Cedex 07
Tel: (01) 49 54 42 00 *Fax:* (01) 45 44 94 03
Web Site: www.gallimard.fr *Cable:* Enerefene Paris 044
Key Personnel
President: Antoine Gallimard
Editorial Dir: Teresa Cremisi
Sales Dir: Bruno Caillet
Rights & Permissions: Prune Berge; Anne Solange Noble
Editor: Jean-Loup Champion; Francoise Cibiel; Colline Faure-Poiree; Yvon Girard; Gustavo Guerrero; Veronique Jacob; Christine Jordis; Bernard Lortholary; Jean Mattern; Patrick Raynal; Eric Vigne
Art Dir: Jacques Maillot
Export: Jean-Charles Grunstein
Founded: 1911
Subjects: Art, Biography, Fiction, History, Music, Dance, Philosophy, Poetry
ISBN Prefix(es): 2-07
Subsidiaries: Editions Denoel; Editions Gallimard Jeunesse; Editions Gallimard Images (Canada); Editions Mercure de France; Schoenhof's Foreign Books (USA); Les Editions de la Table Ronde
Distributed by Centre de Diffusion de l'Edition; Centre de Diffusion de l'Edition; France Export Diffusion; La SODIS
Bookshop(s): Le Divan, Paris; Librairie Delamain, Paris; Librairie des Facultes, Strasbourg; Librairie Gallimard, 15 blvd Raspail, 75007 Paris; Librairie Kleber, Strasbourg; Librairie de Paris, Paris

Editions Gamma
Les Comptoirs de Bonneuil, 60120 Bonneui-les-Eaux
Tel: (03) 44806868 *Fax:* (03) 44806860
Telex: 202036 (Begedis SA)
Key Personnel
President: Bernard Ramspaxher
Editor: Jean Nicolas Moreau
Founded: 1963
Subjects: Social Sciences, Sociology
ISBN Prefix(es): 2-7130
Parent Company: Gedit SA Tournai
Associate Companies: Editions Desclee et Cie, Paris; Editions du Chalet, Paris; Nouvelles Editions Mame, Paris; Editions Universitaires,

FRANCE

Paris; Desclee Editeurs, Belgium; Editions Gamma, Belgium
Orders to: Begedis, 11 rue Duquay-Trouin, 75006 Paris
Arc-en-Ciel International, 2 1 Tournai Ouest, B-7713 Marquain, Belgium (Foreign)

Editions Gammaprim+
78, rue de Dunkerque, 75009 Paris
Tel: (01) 49959492 *Fax:* (01) 40230134
E-mail: fgosselin@gammaprim.fr
Key Personnel
Editor: Franck Gosselin
Founded: 1982
Subjects: Biological Sciences, Chemistry, Chemical Engineering, Economics, Geography, Geology, History, Literature, Literary Criticism, Essays, Mathematics, Philosophy, Physics
ISBN Prefix(es): 2-903908; 2-84391
Distributed by Sodis; Sofedis
Warehouse: Sodis, 128 ave du Mal de lattre de Tassigny, 77400 Lagny Sur Marne
Orders to: Sodis, 128 ave du Mal de Lattre de Tassigny, 77400 Lagny sur Marne

Ganymede+
BP 12, 77220 Presles-en-Brie
Tel: (01) 48945232 *Fax:* (02) 64 42 86 68
Web Site: www.hatem.com
Key Personnel
Dir & International Rights: Frank Hatem
Founded: 1973
Subjects: Philosophy, Physics, Psychology, Psychiatry, Science (General)
ISBN Prefix(es): 2-9500999; 2-85824

Editions du Garde-Temps+
106, rue Vieille-du-Temple, 75003 Paris
Tel: (01) 44788477 *Fax:* (01) 44788479
E-mail: studio-magnet@calva.net
Key Personnel
Contact: Michel Le Louarn
Founded: 1995
Subjects: Travel
ISBN Prefix(es): 2-9509273
Warehouse: Vilo, 25 rue Gihoux, 75737 Paris, Cedex 15, Sophie Praquin *Tel:* (01) 45770805 *Fax:* (01) 45799715

Imprimerie Librairie Gardet
Unit of Edimontagne
Le Bouchet, 74310 Servor
Tel: (04) 50 47 58 10 *Fax:* (04) 50 47 58 11
E-mail: edimontagne@wanadoo.fr
Key Personnel
Editor: Jacques Gendrault
Founded: 1836
Subjects: Art, Crafts, Games, Hobbies, Education, History, Regional Interests
ISBN Prefix(es): 2-7049
Total Titles: 70 Print

Gauthier-Villars, *imprint of* Dunod Editeur

Gautier Languereau, *imprint of* Hachette Jeunesse Image

Librairie Generale Francaise SA
43, Quai de Grenelle, 75905 Paris, Cedex 15
Tel: (01) 43 92 30 00 *Fax:* (01) 43 92 35 90
The above is the Head Office. Editorial and Production are run from Le Livre de Poche.
ISBN Prefix(es): 2-253

Editions Generales First+
33 Ave de la Republique, 75011 Paris
Tel: (01) 40 21 46 46 *Fax:* (01) 40 21 46 20
E-mail: firstinfo@efirst.com
Web Site: www.efirst.com

Key Personnel
Editorial Dir: Henri Bovet
Production & Administration: Jean Fontanieu
Rights: Stephanie Koch
Founded: 1985
Subjects: Computer Science, Health, Nutrition, Humor, Marketing
ISBN Prefix(es): 2-87691

Editions Gerard de Villiers
43 quai de Grenelle, 75905 Paris, Cedex 15
Tel: (01) 43 92 30 00 *Fax:* (01) 43 92 30 30
Web Site: www.editionsgerarddevilliers.com
Telex: 204434
Key Personnel
President, Dir-Gen: M Gerard de Villiers
Editorial Dir: Christine de Grandmaison
Founded: 1988
Subjects: Fiction, Mysteries
ISBN Prefix(es): 2-7386

Paul Geuthner Librairie Orientaliste+
12, rue Vavin, 75006 Paris
Tel: (01) 43297564 *Fax:* (01) 46347130
E-mail: geuthner@geuthner.com
Web Site: www.geuthner.com *Cable:* LIBORIENT PARIS
Key Personnel
Man Dir: Marc F Seidl-Geuthner
Founded: 1901
Subjects: Anthropology, Antiques, Art, Biblical Studies, Biography, Foreign Countries, Geography, Geology, History, Law, Music, Dance, Philosophy, Religion - Buddhist, Religion - Catholic, Religion - Hindu, Religion - Islamic, Religion - Jewish, Religion - Protestant, Social Sciences, Sociology
ISBN Prefix(es): 2-7053

GF, *imprint of* Flammarion SA

Gippe-Les Amoureux des Livres, *imprint of* Gippe-Marche Du Livre Ancien

Gippe-Marche Du Livre Ancien (Gippe Antiquarian Book Market)
49-51, rue Santos-Dumont, 75015 Paris
Tel: (01) 45 32 12 75 *Fax:* (01) 45 32 12 75
E-mail: gippe@free.fr
Key Personnel
General Secretary: Rene Froment
Founded: 1987
Subjects: Literature, Literary Criticism, Essays
ISBN Prefix(es): 2-9508635
Parent Company: Les Amoureux des Livres-Gippe (Publisher)
Imprints: Gippe-Les Amoureux des Livres

Editions Jean Paul Gisserot+
10, rue Gracieuse, 75005 Paris
Tel: (01) 43 31 88 25 *Fax:* (01) 43 31 88 15
E-mail: editions@editions-gisserot.com
Key Personnel
Dir: Thibault Chattard *E-mail:* thibault.chattard@editions-gisserot.com
Founded: 1988
Subjects: Aeronautics, Aviation, Animals, Pets, Anthropology, Archaeology, Architecture & Interior Design, Art, Astronomy, Biography, Cookery, Education, English as a Second Language, Foreign Countries, Gardening, Plants, Genealogy, History, How-to, Humor, Maritime, Music, Dance, Natural History, Regional Interests, Religion - Catholic, Religion - Protestant, Travel, Wine & Spirits
ISBN Prefix(es): 2-87747
Number of titles published annually: 50 Print
Total Titles: 560 Print
Subsidiaries: Telegiss Distribution (France)

Shipping Address: TeleGiss Distribution, Z 1 de Saint Eloi, 29800 Plouedern *Tel:* (02) 9821 3663 *Fax:* (02) 9821 5631
Orders to: TeleGiss Distribution, Z 1 de Saint Eloi, 29800 Plouedern *Tel:* (02) 9821 3663 *Fax:* (02) 9821 5631

Glacial, *imprint of* Flammarion SA

Editions J Glenat SA+
6, rue Lieutenant-Chanaron, 38008 Grenoble
Tel: (04) 76 88 75 75 *Fax:* (04) 76 88 75 70
Web Site: www.glenat.com
Telex: 320030 glenat
Key Personnel
President & Joint Man Dir: Jacques Glenat
Editorial: Dominique Burdot; Jean-Claude Camano
Sales (Export): Christine Glenat
Production: Francis Bernard
Rights & Permissions: Jean-Brice Roux
Founded: 1974
Subjects: Cookery, Fiction, Humor, Science Fiction, Fantasy, Sports, Athletics, Travel, Comic Books
ISBN Prefix(es): 2-7234
Subsidiaries: Glenat-Images; Glenat-Benelux; Glenat Espagne
Bookshop(s): Glenat-Librairie, 16 Lafayette, F-75009 Paris *Tel:* (01) 42469881

Editions Grancher+
98, rue de Vaugirard, 75006 Paris
Tel: (01) 42 22 64 80 *Fax:* (01) 45 48 25 03
E-mail: info@grancher.com
Web Site: www.grancher.com *Cable:* SCE DE VENTE/LIBRAIRIES 5480317
Key Personnel
Man Dir: Jacques Grancher
Editor: Michel Grancher *E-mail:* m.grancher@worldonline.fr; Philippe Grancher *E-mail:* grancher@worldonline.fr
Founded: 1952
Sales of books.
Subjects: Astrology, Occult, Cookery, Health, Nutrition, How-to, Humor, Military Science, Nonfiction (General), Parapsychology, Psychology, Psychiatry, Religion - Catholic, Religion - Islamic, Religion - Jewish, Religion - Protestant, Religion - Other, Travel
ISBN Prefix(es): 2-7339
Number of titles published annually: 40 Print
Total Titles: 400 Print
Distributed by Hachette

Grand Angle, *imprint of* Editions l'Instant Durable (Soprep)

Les Grandes Anthologies, *imprint of* Sarl Editions Jean Grassin

Editions Grandir (To Grow)+
Rue des 3 Ponts, 30000 Nimes
Tel: (04) 66 84 01 19; (04) 66 84 01 79 (showroom) *Fax:* (04) 66 26 14 50; (04) 66 26 14 50 (showroom)
Key Personnel
Manager: Rene Turc
Founded: 1978
Subjects: Art, Fiction, Physical Sciences
ISBN Prefix(es): 2-84166; 2-904292
Total Titles: 250 Print

Granit
24, rue de Varize, 75017 Paris
Tel: (01) 40 71 98 75 *Fax:* (01) 46 51 30 06
Key Personnel
Dir: Francois Xavier Jaujard
ISBN Prefix(es): 2-86281
Orders to: Distique, 5 rue du Marechal Leclerc, 28600 Luisant

PUBLISHERS

FRANCE

Sarl Editions Jean Grassin
Pl de Port-en-Dro, 56342 Carnac-Plage
Mailing Address: BP 75, 56342 Carnac, Cedex
Tel: (02) 97 52 93 63 *Fax:* (02) 97 52 83 90
E-mail: j.grassin@wanadoo.fr
Web Site: perso.wanadoo.fr/j.grassin/contact.htm
Key Personnel
Man Dir: Jean Grassin
Founded: 1957
Subjects: History, Literature, Literary Criticism, Essays, Poetry
ISBN Prefix(es): 2-7055
Imprints: Club J G; L'encyclopedie Poetique; Les Grandes Anthologies; Sequences
Book Club(s): Poetes Presents

Editions Gregoriennes, *imprint of* Adverbum SARL

Groupe de Recherche et d'Echanges Technologiques (GRET)
211-213 rue la Fayette, 75010 Paris
Tel: (01) 40 05 61 61 *Fax:* (01) 40 05 61 10
E-mail: gret@gret.org; librairie@gret.org
Web Site: www.gret.org
Key Personnel
President: Herve Bichat
Dir: Didier Pillot
Founded: 1976
Subjects: Agriculture, Anthropology, Developing Countries, Finance, Journalism, Technology
ISBN Prefix(es): 2-86844
Total Titles: 60 Print

Groupe de Recherche et d'Echanges Technologiques, see Groupe de Recherche et d'Echanges Technologiques (GRET)

Groupe des Editions du Rocher
6, pl St-Sulpice, 75279 Paris Cedex 06
Tel: (01) 40 46 54 00 *Fax:* (01) 40 46 91 36
E-mail: jpb@post.club-internet.fr
Key Personnel
President: Jean-Paul Bertrand

Groupe Expansion
25 rue Leblanc, 75842 Paris Cedex 15
Tel: (01) 40604060 *Fax:* (01) 40604116
Telex: 205581 f
Key Personnel
President & Man Dir: Jean-Louis Servan-Schreiber
General Manager: Damien Dufour *Tel:* (01) 4060 4412 *Fax:* (01) 4060 4129
Publicity, International Advertising Dirs: Vincent Perrote
Subjects: Architecture & Interior Design, Economics, Education, Government, Political Science, Law, Literature, Literary Criticism, Essays, Science (General), Social Sciences, Sociology, Technology
ISBN Prefix(es): 2-904833

Groupe Hatier International+
31 rue de Fleurus, 75006 Paris
Tel: (01) 44-39-28-84 *Fax:* (01) 42-84-03-19
E-mail: hatier@intl.com
Key Personnel
Man Dir: Patrick C Dubs *Fax:* (01) 44-39-28-16
E-mail: pdubs@hatier.intl.com
Promotion: Nathalie Hernandez *Tel:* (01) 44-39-28-14 *Fax:* (01) 42-84-03-19
E-mail: nhernandez@hatier-intl.com
Specialize in Export & Textbook publishing for French & Arabic speaking countries. Educational materials, maps.
Number of titles published annually: 60 Print
Total Titles: 300 Print
Parent Company: Groupe Alexandre Hatier
Ultimate Parent Company: Hachette SA
Distributor for Editions Didier

Groupe Moniteur -L'Argus+
17 rue d'Uzes, 75108 Paris Cedex 02
Tel: (01) 40-13-30-30 *Fax:* (01) 40-13-51-06
E-mail: infos@collectiviteslocales.com
Telex: UPRESSE 680876F
Key Personnel
President & Dir General: Marc Noel Vigier
Assistant & Man Dir: Marc Auburtin
Editor: Frank Audonnet; Xavier Castaing
Founded: 1877
Subjects: Economics, Finance, Law
ISBN Prefix(es): 2-7097
Parent Company: Havas Publications Editions
Imprints: L'Argus; Editions de l'Argus

Librairie Guenegaud Sarl
Subsidiary of P M C
10, rue de l'Odeon, 75006 Paris
Tel: (01) 43260791 *Fax:* (01) 40468872
E-mail: libraire.guenegaud@wanadoo.fr
Web Site: www.guenegaud.com
Key Personnel
Man Dir: Philippe Barrault
Founded: 1910
Subjects: Biography, Genealogy, History, Outdoor Recreation, Regional Interests, Romance
ISBN Prefix(es): 2-85023
Number of titles published annually: 10 Print
Total Titles: 95 Print
Associate Companies: La Societe et le High Life

Guide Franck, *imprint of* Editions Franck Mercier

Guide Pratique, *imprint of* Les Presses du Management

Guides Gallimard, *imprint of* Societe Nouveaux Loisirs

Editions d'Art Albert Guillot
4 rue de Seze, 69006 Lyon
Tel: (04) 78521026
Subjects: Art
ISBN Prefix(es): 2-85096

Hachette Education+
43 Quai de Grenelle, 75905 Paris, Cedex 15
Tel: (01) 43923000; (01) 43923516 *Fax:* (01) 43923501
Telex: 204145 Haclass *Cable:* HACHECI-PARIS 25
Key Personnel
Deputy Dir: Marie-Agnes Bousquet
Dir: Christian Travers
Foreign Rights: Rebecca Byers
Founded: 1826
CD-ROM & reference books.
Subjects: Education, French as a second language
ISBN Prefix(es): 2-01
Total Titles: 3,000 Print
Online services available through World Wide Web.
Parent Company: Hachette Livre
Ultimate Parent Company: Lagardere Groupe
Subsidiaries: Edicef; CEC; Sylemma-Andrieu; Hachette Diffusion Internationale
Showroom(s): Espace Enseignant, 106 blvd Saint-Gerrain, 75006 Paris

Hachette francais langue etrangere - FLE+
58, rue Jean-Bleuzen, 92178 Vanves
Tel: (01) 46 62 10 10 *Fax:* (01) 40 95 10 39
E-mail: fle@hachette-livre.fr
Web Site: www.fle.hachette.livre.fr
Key Personnel
Publishing Dir: Anne Reberioux *Tel:* (01) 46621058 *E-mail:* anneberioux@hachette.lane.fr
Number of titles published annually: 50 Print; 4 Audio
Total Titles: 50 Print
Online services available through World Wide Web.
Parent Company: Hachette Livre SA, Paris

Hachette Jeunesse, *imprint of* Hachette Jeunesse Image

Hachette Jeunesse Image+
43 quai de Grenelle, 75905 Paris Cedex 15
Tel: (01) 43923000 *Fax:* (01) 43923030
Key Personnel
Dir: Frederique de Buron
Editor: Christine Foulquies; Emmamelle Massonaud
International Rights Manager: Monique Lantelme
Founded: 1885
Subjects: Nonfiction (General), Picture & Character Books
ISBN Prefix(es): 2-01; 2-217
Parent Company: Hachette Livre SA
Imprints: Hachette Jeunesse; Gautier Languereau; Deux Coqs d'Or
Warehouse: Centre de Distribution du Livre, ,Z A Coignieres-Maurepas, One ave Gutenberg, 78316 Maurepas Cedex

Hachette JeunesseRoman+
43 Quai de Grenelle, 75905 Paris Cedex 15
Tel: (01) 43923000 *Fax:* (01) 43923222
Cable: HACHECI-PARIS 25
Key Personnel
Dir: Catherine Tessandier
International Rights Manager: Monique Lantelme
Founded: 1856
Parent Company: Hachette

Hachette Livre
43 Quai de Grenelle, 75905 Paris Cedex 15
Tel: (01) 43923000; (01) 43923587 *Fax:* (01) 43923030; (01) 43923585
Key Personnel
CEO: Jean-Louis Lisimachio
Founded: 1826
Bookshops throughout the world.
Subjects: Architecture & Interior Design, Art, Economics, Education, Engineering (General), Fiction, Government, Political Science, History, Language Arts, Linguistics, Nonfiction (General), Philosophy, Science (General), Self-Help, Social Sciences, Sociology, Sports, Athletics, Travel
ISBN Prefix(es): 2-01
Subsidiaries: Hachette Pratique (General Interest); Hachette Litteratures (General Interest); Editions du Chene (General Interest)

Hachette Pratiques+
43 Quai de Grenelle, 75905 Paris Cedex 15
Tel: (01) 43923238 *Fax:* (01) 43923030
Key Personnel
Dir: Jean Arcache *E-mail:* jarcache@hachette-livre.fr
Editorial: Pierre Baron
Publicity: Cecile Boyer
Foreign Rights: Monique Lanthelme
Coeditions & Foreign Rights: David Inman
Founded: 1826
Subjects: Animals, Pets, Astrology, Occult, Biography, Cookery, Crafts, Games, Hobbies, Fashion, Gardening, Plants, Health, Nutrition, Management, Sports, Athletics, Wine & Spirits
ISBN Prefix(es): 2-01
Warehouse: Hachette Distribution, ZA Coignietires, One avenue Gutenberg, 78316 Maurepas Cedex

Harlequin SA
83-85 blvd Vincent-Auriol, 75013 Paris
Tel: (01) 42166363 *Fax:* (01) 45828694

Key Personnel
Man Dir: Frederique Sarfati
Editorial Manager: Anne Coquet
Founded: 1978
Subjects: Astrology, Occult, Romance
ISBN Prefix(es): 2-280; 2-86259
Parent Company: Hachette SA
Imprints: Duo, Harlequin

L'Harmattan+
5-7 rue de l'Ecole-Polytechnique, 75005 Paris
Tel: (01) 40 46 79 11; (01) 40 46 79 20 *Fax:* (01) 43 25 82 03
E-mail: harmat@worldnet.fr
Web Site: www.editions-harmattan.fr
Key Personnel
Man Editor: Denis Pryen
Foreign Relations: Armelle Riche
Founded: 1975
Subjects: Developing Countries, Foreign Countries, Language Arts, Linguistics, Literature, Literary Criticism, Essays, Science (General), Social Sciences, Sociology
ISBN Prefix(es): 2-7384; 2-85802
Total Titles: 1,400 Print
Subsidiaries: Diffusion Nord-Sud (Belgium); L'Harmattan Hongrie; L'Harmattan Inc (Canada); L'Harmattan Italia SRL; L'Age d'Homme
Distributed by Distribution de Livres Univers (Canada)
Bookshop(s): 16 rue des Ecoles, 75005 Paris
Tel: (01) 40467911 *Fax:* (01) 43298620

Editions Hatier SA+
8, rue d'Assas, 75278 Paris, Cedex 06
Tel: (01) 49 54 49 54 *Fax:* (01) 40 49 00 45
Web Site: www.editions-hatier.fr
Telex: 202732 F
Key Personnel
Man Dir: Bernard Foulon
Sales Dir: Andre Cazaux
Sales, Distribution: Fabienne Fera *Tel:* (01) 49 54 48 04 *Fax:* (01) 49 54 49 71 *E-mail:* ffera@editions-hatier.fr
Foreign Rights: Anne Risaliti *Tel:* (01) 49 54 48 99 *Fax:* (01) 49 54 47 30 *E-mail:* arisaliti@editions-hatier.fr
Human Resources Dir: Alain Bergdoll *Fax:* (01) 49 54 49 51 *E-mail:* drh@editions-hatier.fr
Founded: 1880
Subjects: Architecture & Interior Design, Biological Sciences, Economics, Education, English as a Second Language, Environmental Studies, Self-Help
ISBN Prefix(es): 2-11
Imprints: Rageot Editeur
Bookshop(s): 59 blvd Raspail, 75006 Paris, Christian Reynaud *E-mail:* creynaud@editions-hatier.fr

Pierre Hautot SA
36, rue du Bac, 75007 Paris
Tel: (01) 42 61 10 15 *Fax:* (01) 49 27 00 06
Telex: 214293
Founded: 1952
Subjects: Art

Fernand Hazan Editeur SA+
64 Quai Marcel Cachin, 94290 Villeneuve le Roi
Tel: (01) 44 41 17 00 *Fax:* (01) 44 41 17 09
Telex: 250769
Key Personnel
Chairman: Eric Hazan
Rights Manager: Martina Cubiles
Founded: 1945
Subjects: Architecture & Interior Design, Art
ISBN Prefix(es): 2-85025; 2-7198
Bookshop(s): Editions Fernand Hazan, 35-37 rue de Seine, 75006 Paris

Hemma Joven, SA+
8 rue Florian, 93500 Pantin
Tel: 01 48 10 34 86
E-mail: hemma@libronet.es
Telex: 235 569 f
Key Personnel
General Manager: Julian Ocana Carreno
Founded: 1954
Subjects: Crafts, Games, Hobbies, Fiction, Mysteries, Science Fiction, Fantasy
ISBN Prefix(es): 2-8006
Imprints: Petit Marteau
Distributor for FLSA; Nathan (Games)
Warehouse: c/o Santa Mariadel Paramo 5-7-9, 28940 Fuenlabrada-Madrid, Spain

Editions Herault
BP 14, 49360 Maulevrier
Tel: (02) 41554590 *Fax:* (02) 41586228
Key Personnel
General Manager: Andre Hubert Herault
Founded: 1971
Subjects: Biography, Genealogy, History, Regional Interests
ISBN Prefix(es): 2-7407; 2-903851
Parent Company: Farre, BP 345, 49305 Cholet Cedex

Hermann editeurs des Sciences et des Arts SA+
293 rue Lecourbe, 75015 Paris
Tel: (01) 45 57 45 40 *Fax:* (01) 40 60 12 93
E-mail: hermann.sa@wanadoo.fr
Key Personnel
Man Dir: Pierre Beres
Foreign Rights: Nissa Bernard
Founded: 1870
Subjects: Art, Chemistry, Chemical Engineering, Mathematics, Medicine, Nursing, Dentistry, Physics, Science (General), Technology
ISBN Prefix(es): 2-7056
Number of titles published annually: 50 Print
Total Titles: 1,000 Print
Subsidiaries: La Palme; Pierre Beres; Richard Masse (music)
Showroom(s): 6 rue de la Sorbonne, 75005 Paris
Bookshop(s): 6 rue de la Sorbonne, 75005 Paris

Hermes Science Publications+
8, Quai du Marche-neuf, 75004 Paris
Tel: (01) 53 10 15 20 *Fax:* (01) 53 10 15 21
E-mail: hermes@iway.fr
Web Site: www.hermes-science.com; www.editions-hermes.fr
Key Personnel
Man Dir: M Menasce
Marketing Dir: M Philippe
Founded: 1981
Member of French Publishers Association.
Subjects: Chemistry, Chemical Engineering, Civil Engineering, Electronics, Electrical Engineering, Engineering (General), Geography, Geology, Health, Nutrition, Language Arts, Linguistics, Law
ISBN Prefix(es): 2-86601; 2-7462; 2-84176
Number of titles published annually: 300 Print; 150 Online; 150 E-Book
Total Titles: 1,200 Print; 1 CD-ROM; 15 Online; 15 E-Book
Online services available through World Wide Web.
Associate Companies: Hermes Science Publishing Ltd, 120 Pentonville Rd, N1 9JN Oxford, United Kingdom, Sami Menasce *Tel:* (020) 78 431920 *Fax:* (020) 78 376348 *E-mail:* hermes_science@BTinternet.com
Imprints: Continent Europe
Distributed by Editions Continent Europe

Editions de l'Herne
41, rue de Verneuil, 75007 Paris
Tel: (01) 42 61 25 06 *Fax:* (01) 42 60 10 00
E-mail: lherne@freesurf.fr
Key Personnel
Chairman, Rights & Permissions: Constantin Tacou
Director: Laurence Tacou
Editorial, Press Agent: Alexandre Tacou
Founded: 1964
Subjects: Art, Fiction, Government, Political Science, Philosophy, Poetry, Social Sciences, Sociology
ISBN Prefix(es): 2-85197

Herscher+
8 rue Ferou, 75006 Paris, Cedex 06
Tel: (01) 55 42 84 00 *Fax:* (01) 43 25 18 29
Web Site: www.editions-belin.fr
Key Personnel
President: Marie Claude Brossollet
Subjects: Art
ISBN Prefix(es): 2-7335
Total Titles: 1,200 Print; 50 Audio
Online services available through World Wide Web.
Parent Company: Editions Belin, 8, rue Ferou, 75278 Paris
Bookshop(s): *Tel:* (01) 55 42 84 55 *Fax:* (01) 55 42 84 58
Shipping Address: 4 rue Ferdinand de Lesseps, 91420 Morangis
Warehouse: 4 rue Ferdinand de Lesseps, 91420 Morangis

Hervas
123, ave Philippe-Auguste, 75011 Paris
Tel: (01) 43 79 12 54 *Fax:* (01) 43797710
ISBN Prefix(es): 2-903118; 2-84334

Editions d'Histoire Sociale (EDHIS)
23 rue de Valois, 75001 Paris
Tel: (01) 42614778
Key Personnel
Man Dir: Anne Centner
Founded: 1967
Subjects: Economics, Foreign Countries, History, Social Sciences, Sociology
ISBN Prefix(es): 2-7156
Bookshop(s): 144 Galerie de Valois, Paris

Editions Hoebeke+
12 rue du Dragon, 75006 Paris
Tel: (01) 42 22 83 81 *Fax:* (01) 45 44 04 96
Key Personnel
Dir: Lionel Hoebeke
Dir, Commercial/Export: Mdme Aline Goujon
Subjects: Art, Fiction, Humor, Photography
ISBN Prefix(es): 2-905292; 2-84230

Pierre Horay Editeur
22 bis, passage Dauphine, 75006 Paris
Tel: (01) 43 54 53 90 *Fax:* (01) 43 54 63 50
E-mail: editions@horay-editeur.fr
Web Site: www.horay-editeur.fr
Key Personnel
Man Dir & Rights & Permissions: Sophie Horay
Founded: 1946
Subjects: Art, Biography, Fiction, History, How-to, Music, Dance
ISBN Prefix(es): 2-7058
Orders to: Flammarion, 26 rue Racine, F-75006 Paris

Editions Hors Collection+
12 ave d'Italie, 75627 Paris Cedex 13
Tel: (01) 44 16 05 00 *Fax:* (01) 44 16 05 05
Key Personnel
Man Dir: Georges Leser
Dir Literature: Jean-Louis Festjens
International Rights: Florence De Bourgues
Founded: 1993
Subjects: Humor
ISBN Prefix(es): 2-258; 2-285
Parent Company: Presses/Solar

PUBLISHERS

FRANCE

Editions Humblot, *imprint of* Presses Universitaires de Nancy

IBE, *imprint of* UNESCO Publishing

Ici et Ailleurs-Vents des Iles
4, allee des Argelas-la-Gavotte, 13790 Chateauneuf-le-Rouge
Tel: (04) 42533087 *Fax:* (04) 42533097
E-mail: mail@kaona.com
Web Site: www.kaona.com
Key Personnel
General Dir: Gilles Colleu *E-mail:* gcolleu@kaona.com
International Rights: Jutta Hepka
 E-mail: jhepka@kaona.com
Assistant: David Barrel *E-mail:* dbarrel@kaona.com; Sebastian Mengin *E-mail:* smengin@kaona.com
Founded: 1995
Publisher of multimedia & Caribbean literature.
Subjects: Literature, Literary Criticism, Essays

Editions Ifremer, see Institut Francais de Recherche pour l'Exploitation de la Mer (IFREMER)

IGN (Institut Geographique National)
136 bis, rue de Grenelle, 75700 Paris O7 SP
Tel: (01) 43988000 *Fax:* (01) 43988400
Web Site: www.ign.fr/fr/pi/adresse
Key Personnel
Man Dir: J F Carrez
Sales: J P Grelot
Production: J Moschetti
Publicity: A C Ferrari
Rights & Permissions: C Dupre
Founded: 1940
ISBN Prefix(es): 2-85595

IIEP, *imprint of* UNESCO Publishing

Image/Magie+
4, rue Diderot, 92150 Suresnes
Tel: (01) 66803402 *Fax:* (01) 66803456
Key Personnel
Editor: Jean-Paul Menges
Subjects: Art, Photography, Travel
ISBN Prefix(es): 2-907059

Editions Imago+
7, rue Suger, 75006 Paris
Tel: (01) 46-33-15-33 *Fax:* (01) 60-23-87-51
E-mail: info@editions-imago.fr
Web Site: www.editions-imago.fr
Key Personnel
Dir General: Thierry Auzas
Subjects: Anthropology, History, Literature, Literary Criticism, Essays, Philosophy, Psychology, Psychiatry, Social Sciences, Sociology, Ethnology, Romance, Fine Arts, Religions
ISBN Prefix(es): 2-902702; 2-911416
Number of titles published annually: 20 Print
Total Titles: 200 Print
Distributed by Diffusion Dimedia Inc (Canada); Nouvelle Diffusion (Belgium); Office du Livre (Switzerland); Presses Universitaires de France

IMEC+
9 rue Bleue, 75009 Paris
Tel: (01) 53 34 23 23 *Fax:* (01) 53 34 23 00
E-mail: bibliotheque@imec-archives.com
Web Site: www.imec-archives.com
Key Personnel
General Manager: Olivier Corpet *E-mail:* olivier.corpet@imec-archives.com
Founded: 1989
Preserves & manages archives & studies linked to the writing & book world of the 20th century allowing academic researches in intellectual, artistic & literary domains.
Subjects: History of literature & publications
ISBN Prefix(es): 2-908295
Number of titles published annually: 4 Print
Total Titles: 30 Print
Branch Office(s)
l'abbaye d'Ardenne, St Germain-La-Blanche-Herbe, F-14280 Caen, Catherine Girerd
 Tel: (02) 31 29 37 37 *Fax:* (02) 31 29 36 36
 E-mail: ardenne@imec-archives.com

Indigo & Cote-Femmes Editions+
4 rue de la Petite Pierre, 75011 Paris
Tel: (1) 43797479 *Fax:* (1) 43794687
E-mail: indigo.cote-femmes.edition@wanadoo.fr
Web Site: www.indigo-cf.com
Key Personnel
Dir: Milagros Palma
Founded: 1989
Subjects: Anthropology, Art, Biography, Literature, Literary Criticism, Essays, Women's Studies
Number of titles published annually: 20 Print

Editions Infrarouge+
8 rue du Delta, 75009 Paris
Tel: (01) 49950874 *Fax:* (01) 49950874
E-mail: editions.infrarouge@libertysurf.fr; editions.infrarouge@caramail.com
Web Site: www.chez.com/editinfrarouge
Key Personnel
President: Isabelle Soubrillard
Vice President: Yves Soubrillard *E-mail:* yves.soubrillard@libertysurf.fr
Founded: 1996
Subjects: Drama, Theater, Fiction, Humor, Literature, Literary Criticism, Essays, Religion - Catholic, Science Fiction, Fantasy, Social Sciences, Sociology
ISBN Prefix(es): 2-908614
Number of titles published annually: 6 Print
Total Titles: 50 Print

INRA Editions, see INRA Editions (Institut National de la Recherche Agronomique)

INRA Editions (Institut National de la Recherche Agronomique)+
RD10, Route de St Cyr, 78026 Versailles Cedex
Tel: (01) 30833406 *Fax:* (01) 30833449
E-mail: inra_editions@versailles.inra.fr
Web Site: www.inra.fr/editions
Key Personnel
Service Dir: Claudine Geynet
International Rights: Christiane Colon
Founded: 1946
Subjects: Agriculture, Biological Sciences, Earth Sciences, Economics, Environmental Studies, Geography, Geology, Health, Nutrition, Social Sciences, Sociology, Veterinary Science
ISBN Prefix(es): 2-7380; 2-85340
Number of titles published annually: 25 Print
Distributed by Backhuys Publishers (Germany, Netherlands, Scandinavia); De Lannoy (Benelux); Dokumente Verlag (Germany); DPLU (Canada); Estem (France); Interscientia (Italy); Librairie Albert le Brand (Switzerland); Librairie Antoine (Lebanon); Librairie Internationale (Morocco); Librairie le Point (Lebanon); Mundi-Prensa Libros (Spain); Patri Moine (Benelux); Le Triangle Universitaire (Morocco)

Editions INSERM+
Member of STM Group
101 rue de Tolbiac, 75654 Paris, Cedex 13
Tel: (01) 44 23 60 82 *Fax:* (01) 44 23 60 99
Web Site: www.inserm.fr
Telex: inserm 270532 F
Key Personnel
Man Dir, Editorial, Rights & Permissions: Claudine Geynet *E-mail:* geynet@tolbiac.inserm.fr
Contact: Brigitte Durrande *E-mail:* durrande@tolbiac.inserm.fr
Founded: 1970
Subjects: Biological Sciences, Health, Nutrition, Medicine, Nursing, Dentistry, Social Sciences, Sociology, Biomedical Research, Public Health
ISBN Prefix(es): 2-85598
Total Titles: 2 Print
Online services available through World Wide Web.
Parent Company: Institut National de la Sante et de la Recherche Medicale, 101 rue de Tolbiac, F-75654 Paris Cedex 13
Distributed by Estem (France)
Orders to: CELF International Inc, 799 Broadway, Suite 416, New York *Tel:* 212-529-7798

Editions l'Instant Durable (Soprep)+
BP 234, 63007 Clermont-Ferrand Cedex 1
Tel: (04) 73 92 07 89 *Fax:* (04) 73 91 13 87
E-mail: art@instantdurable.com
Web Site: www.instantdurable.com
Key Personnel
Publisher: Alain de Bussac
Founded: 1983
Member of SNE (Syndicat National de L'Edition - Paris).
Subjects: Architecture & Interior Design, Art
ISBN Prefix(es): 2-86404
Imprints: Architecture-Modelisme; Grand Angle

Institut Francais de Recherche Scientifique Pour Le Developpement en Cooperation, see IRD Editions

Institut Geographique National, see IGN (Institut Geographique National)

Institut national de la recherche agronomique, see INRA Editions (Institut National de la Recherche Agronomique)

Institute
63, rue Edouard-Vaillant, 92300 Levallois-Perret
Tel: (01) 0871717 *Fax:* (01) 40871718
E-mail: graphite@wandadoo.fr
Key Personnel
Dir: Claudine Muller
Founded: 1989
Subjects: Advertising, Architecture & Interior Design, Electronics, Electrical Engineering, History, Management
ISBN Prefix(es): 2-907904
Imprints: Histoire D'Entreprises

InterEditions Paris+
5, rue Laromiguiere, 75005 Paris
Tel: (01) 40463500 *Fax:* (01) 40466111
Key Personnel
Man Dir: Lidy Arslan
Rights & Permissions: Valere Talamon
Publicity: Veronique Bernier
Founded: 1976
Subjects: Biological Sciences, Business, Chemistry, Chemical Engineering, Computer Science, Management, Mathematics, Medicine, Nursing, Dentistry, Physics, Psychology, Psychiatry
ISBN Prefix(es): 2-7296

Editions Interferences
4 rue Cesar Franck, 75015 Paris
Tel: (01) 45 67 33 56
E-mail: interferences@editions-interferences.com
Web Site: www.editions-interferences.com
Key Personnel
Translator: Sophie Benech
Publisher-Bookseller: Alain Benech
Founded: 1992

Subjects: Literature, Literary Criticism, Essays
ISBN Prefix(es): 2-909589

International Art Books Distribution, see Librairie Fischbacher, International Art Book Distribution (import-export)

Institut International de la Marionnette
7 pl Winston Churchill, 08000 Charleville-Mezieres
Tel: (03) 24337250 *Fax:* (03) 24337269
E-mail: inst.marionnette@ardennes.com
Web Site: perso.wanadoo.fr/institut; www.marionnette.com
Key Personnel
Dir: Roman Paska
Founded: 1981
Subjects: Art, Drama, Theater
ISBN Prefix(es): 2-9505282

Interpublications+
85 rue Gabriel-Peri, 92120 Montrouge
Tel: (01) 40921221 *Fax:* (01) 42310729
Key Personnel
President: Thomas Jallaud
Founded: 1987
Subjects: Literature, Literary Criticism, Essays
ISBN Prefix(es): 2-87658

Les Introuvables-Editions L'Harmattan+
5-7 rue de l'Ecole Polytechnique, 75005 Paris
Tel: (01) 40467910 *Fax:* (01) 43298620
E-mail: harmat@worldnet.fr
Web Site: www.editions-harmattan.fr
Key Personnel
Editor: Jean-Philippe Bouillouol; Thierry Paquot
Founded: 1975
Subjects: African American Studies, Asian Studies, Developing Countries, Foreign Countries, History, Human Relations, Social Sciences, Sociology
ISBN Prefix(es): 2-7384; 2-85802
Number of titles published annually: 10 Print; 1 CD-ROM
Total Titles: 10 Print; 1 CD-ROM
Parent Company: L Hartmattan SARL
Foreign Rep(s): Harmattan Hungary; Harmaltan Canada; Harmattan Italia
Foreign Rights: Perrine Fourgeald
Bookshop(s): 16 rue des Ecoles, 75005 Paris
  Tel: (01) 40 46 79 11 *Fax:* (01) 40 46 79 20

L'Invention du Lecteur, *imprint of* William Blake & Co

Editions de lorme Rond, *imprint of* BSI - ELOR Editions Jeunesse

IRD Editions
209-213 rue La Fayette, 75480 Paris, Cedex 10
Tel: (01) 48037602 *Fax:* (01) 48037612
E-mail: editions@paris.ird.fr
Web Site: www.ird.fr *Cable:* ORSTOM PARIS
Key Personnel
Dir: T Mourier *E-mail:* mourier@paris.ird.fr
Founded: 1962
Subjects: Developing Countries, Earth Sciences, Environmental Studies, Geography, Geology, Health, Nutrition, Science (General), Social Sciences, Sociology, Technology
ISBN Prefix(es): 2-7099
Number of titles published annually: 15 Print; 2 CD-ROM
Total Titles: 800 Print; 5 CD-ROM
Shipping Address: IRD Editions-Diffusion, 32 ave Henri Varagnat, F-93143 Bondy Cedex, Alain Morliere *Tel:* (01) 48025500 *Fax:* (01) 48473088 *E-mail:* direction-centre@bondy.ird.fr *Web Site:* www.bondy.ird.fr

Isoete
123 rue Emile Zola, 50100 Cherbourg
Tel: (0233) 533409 *Fax:* (0233) 534731
Key Personnel
Dir: Alain Fleury
Founded: 1984
Subjects: History, Literature, Literary Criticism, Essays, Photography, Regional Interests
ISBN Prefix(es): 2-905385
Distributor for Distique

Editions Ivrea+
One Place Paul Painleve, 75005 Paris
Tel: (01) 43260621 *Fax:* (01) 43261168
Key Personnel
Contact: Valentin Lorenzo
International Rights: Dodart Jacques
  E-mail: jacques.dodart@liane.net
Founded: 1970
Subjects: History, Literature, Literary Criticism, Essays, Military Science, Poetry, Social Sciences, Sociology
ISBN Prefix(es): 2-85184
Imprints: Champ Libre
Bookshop(s): 27 rue du Sommerard, 75005 Paris
Warehouse: SODIS, 128 ave du Marechal de Lattre de Tassigny, BP 142, 77400 Lagny
Orders to: CDE, 17 rue de Tounon, 75006 Paris

Editions Selection J Jacobs SA, see Editions Selection J Jacobs SA

Editions du Jaguar
57 bis rue d'Auteuil, 75016 Paris
Tel: (01) 44301970 *Fax:* (01) 44301979
Telex: 651 105F
Key Personnel
General Manager & Foreign Rights: Danielle Ben Yahmed
Vice President: Jany Lecreux-Cournot
Press: Arlette Gelbert
Founded: 1985
Subjects: Art, Cookery, Geography, Geology, Government, Political Science, Health, Nutrition, History, How-to, Human Relations, Regional Interests, Religion - Islamic, Social Sciences, Sociology, Travel
ISBN Prefix(es): 2-86950; 2-85258

Editions J'ai Lu
Subsidiary of Flammarion et Cie
84 rue de Grenelle, 75007 Paris
Tel: (01) 44393470 *Fax:* (01) 44393260
Web Site: www.flammarion.com
Telex: Jailu 202765
Founded: 1958
Subjects: Fiction, Science Fiction, Fantasy
ISBN Prefix(es): 2-277; 2-290; 2-293

J'ailu, *imprint of* Flammarion SA

Editions Jannink
127 rue de la Galciere, 750013 Paris
Tel: (01) 45 89 14 02 *Fax:* (01) 45 89 14 02
E-mail: jannink@cybercable.fr
Web Site: www.parissimo.com/pages/jannink.htm
Key Personnel
Dir: Baudouin Jannink
Literary Dir: Maire Caroline Aubert
Commercial Dir: Jocelyn Mame
Production: Didier Chapelot
Founded: 1977
Subjects: Art, History, Adult books; contemporary art
ISBN Prefix(es): 2-902462
Associate Companies: SIPEL, 127 rue de la Galciere, 750013 Paris

Editions Jean-Claude Lattes+
17 rue Jacob, F-75006 Paris
Tel: (01) 44417400 *Fax:* (01) 43253047
E-mail: jpeguillam@editions-jclattes.fr
Key Personnel
Man Dir: Isabelle Laffont *Fax:* (01) 43 26 91 04
Editorial: Laurent Laffont *Fax:* (01) 43 26 91 04;
  Jean Francois Colosimo *Fax:* (01) 43 26 91 04
Foreign Rights: Sabine Fontaine *Tel:* (01) 44 41 74 34 *Fax:* (01) 43 26 91 04
  E-mail: sfontaine@edition-jclattes.fr
Founded: 1968
General trade publisher.
Subjects: Criminology, Fiction, Nonfiction (General)
ISBN Prefix(es): 2-7096
Number of titles published annually: 100 Print
Total Titles: 1,250 Print
Parent Company: Hachette Livre
Ultimate Parent Company: Hachette/Lagardere

Editions du Jeu de Paume
One Place de la Concorde, Jardin des Tuileries, 75001 Paris
Tel: (01) 47 03 12 50 *Fax:* (01) 42 61 26 10
Key Personnel
Dir General: Daniel Abadie
Editor & International Rights: Francoise Bonnefoy *E-mail:* francoise.bonnefoy@jeudepaume.org
Founded: 1991
Specialize in exhibitions catalogues.
Subjects: Art, Film, Video
ISBN Prefix(es): 2-908901
Number of titles published annually: 5 Print
Total Titles: 60 Print

Joly Editions+
31 rue Falguiere, 41 Paris, Cedex 15
Tel: (01) 56 54 16 29 *Fax:* (01) 56 54 16 49
E-mail: sandrine.jacques@editions-joly.com
Web Site: www.editions-joly.com
Key Personnel
Manager: Nathalic Jouven
Subjects: Law, Securities
ISBN Prefix(es): 2-907512
Parent Company: EJA
Distributed by EJA

Le Jour, Editeur+
Division of Sogides
Immeuble Paryseine 3, alle de la Seine, 94854 Ivry Cedex
Tel: (01) 49591189 *Fax:* (01) 49591196
Web Site: www.edjour.com
Key Personnel
Contact: H Laurent *E-mail:* hlaurent@sogides.com
Subjects: Animals, Pets, Astrology, Occult, Career Development, Health, Nutrition, How-to, Medicine, Nursing, Dentistry, Psychology, Psychiatry, Women's Studies
ISBN Prefix(es): 2-89044
Branch Office(s)
955 rue Amherst, Montreal, PQ H2L 3K4, Canada, Contact: Pierre Lesperance
  Tel: 514-523-1182 *Fax:* 514-597-0370
  E-mail: edhomme@sogides.com
Foreign Rights: Chantal Galtier-Roussel

Jupiter, *imprint of* Librairie Generale de Droit et de Jurisprudence (LGDJ) - Montchrestien

Editions Juridiques Associees - LGDJ/Montchrestien+
Affiliate of Petites Appiches
31 rue Falguiere, 75015 Paris, Cedex 15
Tel: (01) 56 54 16 00 *Fax:* (01) 56 54 16 47
Key Personnel
President: Lionel Guerin
Dir General: Nathalie Jouven
Founded: 1836
Subjects: Economics, Government, Political Science, History, Law, Public Administration

ISBN Prefix(es): 2-275
Bookshop(s): 20 rue Soupplot, 75005 Paris

Editions Juridiques Africaines
44 rue Poliveau, 75005 Paris
Tel: (01) 43370401 *Fax:* (01) 43370401
Founded: 1987
Subjects: Foreign Countries, Law
ISBN Prefix(es): 2-87838
Imprints: EDJA
Divisions:

Editions Juridiques et Techniques Lamy SA
Quai de Valmy, 75490 Paris Cedex 10
Tel: (01) 44721200 *Fax:* (01) 44721389
Telex: 214398
Key Personnel
President: Jean-Marc Detailleur
Sales: Jean-Luc Cretal; Eric Forein
Publicity: Jean-Pierre Benedi
Founded: 1949
Subjects: Law, Social Sciences, Sociology
ISBN Prefix(es): 2-7212
Parent Company: Wolters Kluwer NV, Netherlands

Jurif (Societe d' Etudes Juridiques Internationales et Fiscales), see Les Cahiers Fiscaux Europeens Sarl

Editions du Juris-Classeur
141 rue de Javel, 75747 Paris, Cedex 15
Tel: (01) 45 58 93 79 *Fax:* (01) 45 58 94 00
E-mail: editorial@juris-classeur.com
Web Site: www.ed-juris-classeur.fr
Key Personnel
President: Martin Desprez
Editorial Dir: Bernard Bonjean; Christophe Veyrin Forrer
Marketing: Bruno DecLementi
Subjects: Law
ISBN Prefix(es): 2-7110
Parent Company: Lexis-Nexis Group
Ultimate Parent Company: Reed Elsevier plc
Warehouse: 14 rue de la Passerelle, 31200 Toulouse Cedex

Editions Juris Service
12 Quai Andre-Lassagne, 69001 Lyon
Tel: (04) 72 10 10 03 *Fax:* (04) 78 28 93 83
E-mail: info@editionsjuris.com
Web Site: www.editionsjuris.com
Key Personnel
Pres: Philippe Chagnon
Founded: 1983
Subjects: Communications, Law, Management, Real Estate, Specialize in tourism & law, non-profit sector, real-estate joint ownership, liberal professions
ISBN Prefix(es): 2-907648
Number of titles published annually: 5 Print
Total Titles: 70 Print; 2 CD-ROM

Kailash Editions+
69 rue Saint-Jacques, 75005 Paris
Tel: (01) 43.29.52.52 *Fax:* (01) 46.34.03.29
E-mail: kailash@imaginet.fr
Key Personnel
Dir: Raj de Condappa
Founded: 1991
Subjects: Anthropology, Archaeology, Art, Asian Studies, Biography, History, Literature, Literary Criticism, Essays, Travel, Specialize in Asia & Indian continent
ISBN Prefix(es): 2-909052; 2-84268
Distributor for Kwokon
Bookshop(s): Librairie Kailash, 69 rue Saint-Jacques, 75005 Paris

Kaleidoscope+
11 Rue de Sevres, 75006 Paris
Tel: (01) 45440708 *Fax:* (01) 45445371
E-mail: infos@editions-kaleidoscope.com
Web Site: www.editions-kaleidoscope.com
Key Personnel
President: Isabel Finkenstaedt
Founded: 1988
ISBN Prefix(es): 2-87767
Warehouse: Ecole des loisirs, Lotissment de la Butte, 11 rue Gutenberg, 91620 Nozay
Orders to: L'Ecole des Loisirs, 11 rue de Sevres, 75006 Paris

Karger, *imprint of* Librairie Luginbuhl

Karthala Editions-Diffusion+
22-24 Blvd Arago, 75013 Paris
Tel: (01) 43 31 15 59 *Fax:* (01) 45 35 27 05
E-mail: karthala@wanadoo.fr
Telex: 250303 Public Paris
Key Personnel
Man Dir, Editorial, Rights & Permissions, & Production: Robert Ageneau
Publicity: Farida Benbelaid
Founded: 1980
Subjects: Anthropology, Asian Studies, Developing Countries, Economics, Education, Geography, Geology, Literature, Literary Criticism, Essays, Religion - Catholic, Religion - Islamic, Religion - Protestant, Social Sciences, Sociology, Travel
ISBN Prefix(es): 2-86537
Branch Office(s)
Editions Hurthbise, 7360 Blvd Newtian, La Salle, PQ H8N 1X2, Canada
Distributor for Codesria; CRA; Haho; Hurthbise; Inades; Institut Royal des Tropiques; Jasor

Editions Klincksieck
8 rue de la Sorbonne, 75005 Paris
Tel: (01) 43.54.59.53 *Fax:* (01) 43.25.25.53
Key Personnel
Joint Man Dir: Alain Baudry
Founded: 1842
Subjects: Archaeology, Art, History, Language Arts, Linguistics, Literature, Literary Criticism, Essays, Music, Dance, Science (General), Social Sciences, Sociology
ISBN Prefix(es): 2-252
Associate Companies: Aux Amateurs De Livres

Eric Koehler+
6 rue du Mail, 75002 Paris
Tel: (01) 49270637 *Fax:* (01) 47033986
Founded: 1987
Subjects: Photography
ISBN Prefix(es): 2-7107; 2-907220

La Difference, see Editions de la Difference

Lacour-Olle+
25 Bd Am Courbet, 30000 Nimes
Tel: (04) 66 67 33 06 *Fax:* (04) 66 21 11 23
Key Personnel
Contact: Christian Lacour
Founded: 1791
Subjects: Astrology, Occult, Cookery, Parapsychology, Regional Interests, Religion - Catholic, Religion - Protestant, Religion - Other
ISBN Prefix(es): 2-86971; 2-84149; 2-84406

L'Adret editions+
Route de Soueiche, Encausse-les-Thermes, 31160 Aspet
Key Personnel
Man Dir: Jean Mandion
Founded: 1983
Subjects: History, Regional Interests
ISBN Prefix(es): 2-904458

Laffitte Reprint, *imprint of* Laffitte Reprints

Laffitte Reprints
25, cours d'Estienne d'Orves, 13225 Marseille cedex 01
Mailing Address: BP 1903, Cedex 1 Marseille
Tel: (0491) 59 80 43 *Fax:* (0491) 54 25 64
Web Site: www.jeanne-laffitte.com
Key Personnel
President: Jeanne Laffitte *E-mail:* editions@jeanne-laffitte.com
Founded: 1980
Subjects: Ethnicity, History, Regional Interests
ISBN Prefix(es): 2-86276; 2-7348; 2-86604
Imprints: Laffitte Reprint
Distributed by CELF; Editions Jeanne Laffitte (France)

Editions Jacques Lafitte - Who's Who in France
16, rue Camille Pelletan, 92300 Levallois-Perret
Tel: (0141) 272 830 *Fax:* (0141) 272 840
E-mail: whoswho@whoswho.fr
Web Site: www.whoswho.fr
Key Personnel
President: Antoine Hebrard *E-mail:* antoine.hebrard@whoswho.fr
Dir General: Eleonore de Dampierre *E-mail:* eleonore.de.dampierre@whoswho.fr
Publicity: Carole Nehme *E-mail:* carole.nehme@whoswho.fr
ISBN Prefix(es): 2-85784

Editions Michel Lafon SA+
103 Blvd Murat, 75016 Paris
Tel: (01) 40 71 11 11 *Fax:* (01) 46 51 01 31
Key Personnel
Publisher: Michel Lafon
General Manager: Nicole Gruyer
Editor: Huguette Maure
Publicity: Nathalie Ladurantie
Rights & Permissions: Gerald Gauthier
Founded: 1983
Subjects: Biography, Cookery, Drama, Theater, Fiction, Film, Video, History, Sports, Athletics
ISBN Prefix(es): 2-84098

Librairie Leonce Laget
88, rue Bonaparte, 75006 Paris
Tel: (01) 43 29 90 04 *Fax:* (01) 43 26 89 68
E-mail: liblaget@wanadoo.fr
Web Site: www.franceantiq.fr/slam/laget/uk.htm
Cable: LIBLAGET PARIS 110
Key Personnel
President: Veronique Delvaux
Founded: 1955
Subjects: Architecture & Interior Design, Art, Career Development, Crafts, Games, Hobbies, History
ISBN Prefix(es): 2-85204

Editions Lamarre SA
One, ave Edouard Belin, 92856 Rueil-Malmaison Cedex
Tel: (01) 41.29.97.27; (01) 41.29.97.34 *Fax:* (01) 41.29.77.35
E-mail: vpc@espaceinfirmier.com
Key Personnel
Dir: Marie-Laure Dechatre *Tel:* (01) 41 29 76 76 *E-mail:* mldechatre@groupeliaisons.fr
Sales Manager: Thierry de Puniet de Parry
Marketing: Nelly Couret *Tel:* (01) 41 29 77 03 *E-mail:* ncouret@groupeliaisons.fr
Commercial: Philippe Hamel *Tel:* (01) 41 29 96 89 *E-mail:* phamel@groupeliaisons.fr
Founded: 1957
Subjects: Medicine, Nursing, Dentistry
ISBN Prefix(es): 2-85030

Langues & Mondes/L'Asiatheque+
Cite Veron 11, 75018 Paris
Tel: (01) 42620400 *Fax:* (01) 42621234

E-mail: info@asiatheque.com
Web Site: www.asiatheque.com
Key Personnel
General & Editorial Dir: Mdme Christiane Thiollier
Editorial Dir: Alain Thiollier
Editorial Assistant: Elizabeth Eldin
Founded: 1973
Specialize in material for learning of foreign languages & books about cultures & civilizations of the whole world.
Subjects: Asian Studies, Cookery, Education, Foreign Countries, Language Arts, Linguistics, Literature, Literary Criticism, Essays, Religion - Buddhist, Religion - Hindu, Self-Help
ISBN Prefix(es): 2-911053
Total Titles: 100 Print; 1 CD-ROM; 23 Audio
Distributor for Presses Universitaires de France (PUF); Union Distribution Flammarion (UD)

Editions Fernand Lanore Sarl+
One rue Palatine, 75006 Paris
Tel: (01) 43256661 *Fax:* (01) 43296981
Key Personnel
Dir: Francois Sorlot
Founded: 1920
Subjects: Education, History, Language Arts, Linguistics, Outdoor Recreation, Philosophy, Religion - Other, Travel
ISBN Prefix(es): 2-85157

LT Editions-J Lanore-H Laurens+
131, rue Paul-Vaillant-Couturier, 92240 Malakoff
Tel: (01) 55580540 *Fax:* (01) 46542193
Key Personnel
Contact: A M Tabaste
Subjects: Architecture & Interior Design, Career Development, Child Care & Development, Cookery, Health, Nutrition, House & Home, Law, Technology, Travel
ISBN Prefix(es): 2-86268; 2-85158
Associate Companies: Librairie-Editions J Lanore, 4 rue de Tournon, F-75006 Paris *Tel:* (01) 43294350

Editions du Laquet+
Rue Droite, 46600 Martel
Tel: (05) 65 37 43 54 *Fax:* (05) 65 37 43 55
E-mail: contact@editions-dulaquet.fr
Web Site: editions-dulaquet.fr
Key Personnel
Sales Manager: Dominique Barbier
Founded: 1990
Subjects: Art, Cookery, Drama, Theater, Fiction, Literature, Literary Criticism, Essays, Travel
ISBN Prefix(es): 2-910333; 2-84523
Number of titles published annually: 25 Print
Total Titles: 170 Print

L'Argus Editions, see Groupe Moniteur -L'Argus

Librairie Larousse+
21 rue du Montparnasse, 75006 Paris
Tel: (01) 44394343 *Fax:* (01) 44394107
Telex: 250828 *Cable:* Liblarous 43 Paris
Key Personnel
Chairman & Man Dir: Christian Bregou
Foreign Trade Dir: Gilbert F Mitry
Rights & Permissions: H Deveaux
Founded: 1852
Subjects: Animals, Pets, Art, Child Care & Development, Cookery, Gardening, Plants, History, Language Arts, Linguistics, Medicine, Nursing, Dentistry, Music, Dance, Psychology, Psychiatry, Regional Interests, Science (General), Self-Help, Social Sciences, Sociology, Sports, Athletics, Technology
ISBN Prefix(es): 2-03
Parent Company: CEP Editions
Subsidiaries: Ediciones Larousse Argentina SA; Ediciones Larousse Colombiana Ltda; Ediciones Larousse SA; Editions Francaises Inc; Editora Larousse do Brazil; Larousse-Belgique; Larousse (Suisse) SA

Larousse Nathan International
27 rue de la Glacie're, 75013 Paris Cedex 06
Tel: (01) 45874300 *Fax:* (01) 45870553
Telex: 201426
ISBN Prefix(es): 2-288

Editions Henri Laurens Successeurs Sarl, see LT Editions-J Lanore-H Laurens

Le Laurier
19, Passage Jean-Nicot, 75007 Paris
Tel: (01) 45.51.55.08 *Fax:* (01) 45.51.81.83
E-mail: web@lelaurier.fr
Web Site: www.lelaurier.fr
Key Personnel
Manager: Nicolas Macarez
Founded: 1981
Subjects: Religion - Catholic
ISBN Prefix(es): 2-86495; 2-910095

Lavoisier, *imprint of* Lavoisier

Lavoisier+
Formerly Technique et Documentation Lavoisier
11 rue Lavoisier, 75008 Paris
Tel: (01) 42 65 39 95 *Fax:* (01) 42 65 02 46
E-mail: editions@lavoisier.fr
Web Site: www.lavoisier.fr
Key Personnel
Man Dir: Patrick Fenouil
Import Manager: Romuald Verrier
Editorial: Jean-Marc Bocabeille; Philippe Zawieja
Marketing & Publicity: Christine Cardinal
E-mail: cardinal@lavoisier.fr
Founded: 1947
Subjects: Agriculture, Biological Sciences, Chemistry, Chemical Engineering, Cookery, Electronics, Electrical Engineering, Engineering (General), Environmental Studies, Geography, Geology, Labor, Industrial Relations, Maritime, Medicine, Nursing, Dentistry, Technology
ISBN Prefix(es): 2-85206; 2-7430
Number of titles published annually: 100 Print
Imprints: Lavoisier; TEC & DOC
Branch Office(s)
Intercept Ltd, PO Box 716, Andover, Hants SP10 1YG, United Kingdom *Tel:* (01264) 334748 *Fax:* (01264) 334058 *E-mail:* intercept@andover.co.uk
Lavoisier Publishing Inc, Springer Verlag Customer Services, PO Box 2485, Secaucus, NJ 07096-2485, United States *Tel:* 201-348-4505 *E-mail:* orders@springer-ny.com
Shipping Address: 14 rue de Provigny, 94236 Cachan Cedex *Tel:* (01) 47406700 *Fax:* (01) 47406702

Editions Universitaires LCF
18, rue Edmond-Michelet, BP 717, 33006 Bordeaux, cedex
Tel: (0556) 81.89.82
Key Personnel
Dir: Alain Yagues
Founded: 1989
Subjects: Health, Nutrition, History, Law, Wine & Spirits
ISBN Prefix(es): 2-908193

Librairie Lecoffre, see J Gabalda et Cie (Librairie Lecoffre) SA

Editions Francis Lefebvre
42 rue de Villiers, 92532 Levallois, Cedex
Tel: (01) 41 05 22 00 *Fax:* (01) 41 05 22 30
Key Personnel
Dir: J Icart
Contact: Y Chareton
Subjects: Law
ISBN Prefix(es): 2-85115; 2-85786

Editions Legislatives+
80 ave de la Marne, 92546 Montrouge, Cedex
Tel: (01) 40 92 36 36 *Fax:* (01) 46 56 00 15
E-mail: info@editions-legislatives.fr
Web Site: www.editions-legislatives.fr
Telex: 632855F
Key Personnel
General Dir: Pierre-Paul Richard
Dir, Foreign Relations: Michel Blanc
Founded: 1947
Subjects: Agriculture, Business, Career Development, Economics, Environmental Studies, Labor, Industrial Relations, Law, Library & Information Sciences, Medicine, Nursing, Dentistry, Real Estate
ISBN Prefix(es): 2-85086

Editions Dominique Leroy+
22, rue de l'Odeon, 75006 Paris
Tel: (01) 44 41 68 40 *Fax:* (01) 44 41 68 42
E-mail: curiosa@enfer.com
Web Site: www.enfer.com
Key Personnel
Man Dir: Dominique Leroy
Founded: 1970
Subjects: Art, Erotica, Fiction, Humor, Literature, Literary Criticism, Essays
ISBN Prefix(es): 2-86688
Total Titles: 110 Print
Imprints: Librairie Curiosa; Vertiges Bulles
Bookshop(s): Librairie Curiosa, 7 rue Crebillon, 75006 Paris, Contact: Daniele Masson *Tel:* (01) 40 46 01 15 *Fax:* (01) 44 44 68 42 *E-mail:* curiosa@enfer.com

Lethielleux, *imprint of* Pierre Zech Editeur

P Lethielleux Editions+
18 rue de Conde, 75006 Paris
Tel: (01) 44 32 05 60 *Fax:* (01) 44 32 05 61
Telex: ELITA 283155 F
Key Personnel
Dir: M Pierre Zech
International Rights: Sophie Zech
Subjects: Biblical Studies, Religion - Catholic, Theology
ISBN Prefix(es): 2-249
Parent Company: Pierre Zech Editeur

Letouzey et Ane Sarl
87, blvd Raspail, 75006 Paris
Tel: (01) 45 48 80 14 *Fax:* (01) 45 49 03 43
Key Personnel
General Dir: Mrs Florence Letouzey-Dumont
Founded: 1885
Subjects: Biblical Studies, Biography, History, Religion - Catholic, Religion - Islamic, Religion - Other
ISBN Prefix(es): 2-7063
Distributor for CIF; L'Annee Canonique

Lettres Modernes
10 rue de Valence, 75005 Paris
Tel: (01) 43362583
E-mail: editorat.lettresmodernes@wanadoo.fr
Key Personnel
Contact: Dominique Alice Minard
Founded: 1954
Subjects: Film, Video, Literature, Literary Criticism, Essays
ISBN Prefix(es): 2-256
Number of titles published annually: 20 Print
Shipping Address: Minard Distribution, 45 rue de Saint Andre, F-14123 Fleury Sur Orne
Tel: (02) 31844706 *Fax:* (02) 31844809
E-mail: minard.lettresmodernes@wanadoo.fr
Warehouse: Minard Distribution, 45 rue de Saint Andre, F-14123 Fleury Sur Orne *Tel:* (02)

PUBLISHERS

FRANCE

31844706 *Fax:* (02) 31844809 *E-mail:* minard.lettresmodernes@wanadoo.fr
Orders to: Minard Distribution, 45 rue de Saint Andre, F-14123 Fleury Sur Orne *Tel:* (02) 31844706 *Fax:* (02) 31844809 *E-mail:* minard.lettresmodernes@wanadoo.fr

Lettres Vives+
4, rue Beautreillis, 75004 Paris
Tel: (01) 42781379 *Fax:* (01) 42783761
E-mail: lettresvives@mic.fr
Key Personnel
Editor: Claire Tievant *Tel:* (04) 95364096 *Fax:* (04) 95365992
International Rights: Michel Camus *E-mail:* michelca@club-internet.fr
Founded: 1981
Subjects: Literature, Literary Criticism, Essays, Poetry
ISBN Prefix(es): 2-903721
Imprints: Ulysse Diffusion

Editions Liana Levi Sarl+
One Paul Painleve Pl, 75005 Paris
Tel: (01) 43262961 *Fax:* (01) 46336956
Key Personnel
Man Dir: Liana Levi *E-mail:* llevi@club-internet.fr
Rights & Permissions: Colette Fradin
Foreign Rights: Sylvie Mouches
Editor: Stephanie Neumayer
Founded: 1983
Subjects: Art, Fiction, History, Nonfiction (General)
ISBN Prefix(es): 2-86746

LGDJ, *see* Librairie Generale de Droit et de Jurisprudence (LGDJ) - Montchrestien

L'Harmattan Paris, *imprint of* Revue Espaces et Societes

John Libbey Eurotext+
Subsidiary of John Libbey Co Ltd
127 ave de la Republique, 92120 Montrouge
Tel: (01) 46 73 06 60 *Fax:* (01) 40 84 09 99
E-mail: contact@jle.com
Web Site: www.john-libbey-eurotext.fr
Key Personnel
Dir of Publications: Gilles Cahn *Tel:* (01) 463 06 79 *E-mail:* gilles.cahn@jle.com
Dir of Marketing: Valerie Parroco *Tel:* (01) 46 73 01 32 *E-mail:* valerie.parroco@john-libbey-eurotext.fr
Dir of Publicity: Anne Coche *Tel:* (01) 46 73 06 77 *E-mail:* anne.coche@jle.com
Founded: 1986
Subjects: Agriculture, Economics, Environmental Studies, Medicine, Nursing, Dentistry, Life Sciences
ISBN Prefix(es): 2-7420

Librairie Curiosa, *imprint of* Editions Dominique Leroy

Librairie des Champs-Elysees, Groupe Hachette+
43, Quai de Grenelle, 75905 Paris Cedex 15
Tel: (01) 43923577 *Fax:* (01) 43923573
Key Personnel
Dir: Michel Averlant
Adjoint Dir: Didier Imbot
Responsable de Collections: Helene Amalric
Founded: 1927
Subjects: Mysteries
ISBN Prefix(es): 2-7024

Librairie Generale de Droit et de Jurisprudence, *see* Librairie Generale de Droit et de Jurisprudence (LGDJ) - Montchrestien

Librairie Luginbuhl
36 blvd de Latour-Maubourg, 75007 Paris
Tel: (01) 45 51 42 58 *Fax:* (01) 45 56 07 80
E-mail: liblug@club-internet.fr
Key Personnel
Contact: Jean Luginbuhl
Subjects: Medicine, Nursing, Dentistry
Imprints: Karger

Librairie Scientifique et Technique Albert Blanchard
9, Rue de Medicis, 75006 Paris
Tel: (01) 43 26 90 34 *Fax:* (01) 43 29 97 31
E-mail: librairie.blanchard@wanadoo.fr
Web Site: www.blanchard75.fr
Key Personnel
Contact: Laurent Debruyne
Subjects: Astronomy, Chemistry, Chemical Engineering, Earth Sciences, Mathematics, Natural History, Philosophy, Physics, Science (General)
ISBN Prefix(es): 2-85367
Number of titles published annually: 3 Print
Total Titles: 1,721 Print

Libraries Techniques SA, *see* LiTec (Librairies Techniques SA)

Librio, *imprint of* Flammarion SA

Lierre et Coudrier+
83, rue Lamarck, 75018 Paris
Mailing Address: PO Box 54, 75861 Paris cedex 18
Tel: (01) 42550027 *Fax:* (01) 42570497
ISBN Prefix(es): 2-907975; 2-9502146
Associate Companies: La Lonave-vue, 363 b, Chaunic de Waterloo, B10 1060 Bruyelle, Belgium

Lignes De Vie, *imprint of* Editions de Septembre

Ligue pour la Lecture de la Bible, *see* LLB France (Ligue pour la Lecture de la Bible)

Editions des Limbes d'Or/FBT de R Editions
31, quai de la Tournelle, 75005 Paris
Tel: (01) 41151969; (06) 07683371 *Fax:* (01) 41151969
Key Personnel
President: Francoise Thiam
Founded: 1995
Subjects: Art, Criminology, Economics, Fiction, Foreign Countries, Government, Political Science, Human Relations, Literature, Literary Criticism, Essays, Travel
ISBN Prefix(es): 2-911064

LiTec (Librairies Techniques SA)+
141, rue de Javel, 75015 Paris
Tel: (01) 43 26 60 90 *Fax:* (01) 46 34 22 98
Key Personnel
Dir: Alexandre Guegan
Sales Manager: Marie Oneissi
Founded: 1927
Subjects: Accounting, Government, Political Science, Labor, Industrial Relations, Law
ISBN Prefix(es): 2-7111
Parent Company: Editions du Juris-Classeur
Ultimate Parent Company: Reed Elsevier plc/Lexis Nexis
Branch Office(s)
26 rue Soufflot, 75005 Paris *Tel:* (01) 43 29 07 71 *Fax:* (01) 40 51 83 72
Warehouse: Zone Artisanale-Route de Niort, 85205 Fontenay le Comte Cedex

Editions Lito
41, rue de Verdun, 94503 Champigny-sur-Marne, Cedex
Mailing Address: BP 363, 94503 Champigny-sur-Marne, Cedex
Tel: (01) 45161700 *Fax:* (01) 48820085
E-mail: annick.cabrelli@editionslito.com
Key Personnel
Man Dir, Editorial, Rights & Permissions: Pierre Rosdahl
Founded: 1958
Subjects: Crafts, Games, Hobbies, Nonfiction (General)
ISBN Prefix(es): 2-244
Subsidiaries: Lito Editrice

Litterature Generale, *imprint of* Autres Temps

Le Livre de Paris+
58, rue Jean Bleuzen, 92178 Vanves, Cedex
Tel: (01) 41 23 60 00 *Fax:* (01) 41 45 34 42
Web Site: www.livre-de-paris.com; www.livredeparis.com
Key Personnel
General Director: Patrice Burckel de Tell
International Rights Contact: Monica Mondardini
Founded: 1935
Member of the Syndicat National de L'Edition.
Subjects: Art, How-to
ISBN Prefix(es): 2-245
Imprints: Livres de Paris; Quillet; Tout L'Univers

Le Livre de Poche-L G F (Librairie Generale Francaise)+
43, Quai de Grenelle, 75905 Paris Cedex 15
Tel: (01) 43923555 *Fax:* (01) 43923590
Key Personnel
Man Dir & Dir, Foreign Rights & International Development: Dominique Goust
Founded: 1953
Subjects: Biography, Drama, Theater, Environmental Studies, Fiction, Government, Political Science, History, Language Arts, Linguistics, Literature, Literary Criticism, Essays, Philosophy, Poetry, Science (General), Science Fiction, Fantasy, Social Sciences, Sociology
ISBN Prefix(es): 2-253
Parent Company: Hachette

Livre des Vacances, *imprint of* Librairie Vuibert

Livres de Paris, *imprint of* Le Livre de Paris

Les Livres du Dragon d'Or+
60 Rue Mazazine, 75006 Paris 02
Tel: (01) 53 10 36 37 *Fax:* (01) 53 10 36 39
E-mail: dragondor@gruend.fr
Key Personnel
Man Dir: Nathalie Perrin
Founded: 1989
Specialize in license publishing & book packaging for the international market.
ISBN Prefix(es): 2-87881
Number of titles published annually: 10 Print
Total Titles: 100 Print
Parent Company: Editions Gruend
Orders to: Editions Gruend, 60 Rue Mazazine, Paris 75006 *Tel:* (01) 53 10 36 00 *Fax:* (01) 43 29 49 86 *Web Site:* www.grund.fr

LLB France (Ligue pour la Lecture de la Bible)+
51 Blvd Gustave-Andre, 26007 Valence, Cedex
Mailing Address: BP 728, 26007 Valence, Cedex
Tel: (04) 75 56 02 68 *Fax:* (04) 75 56 02 97
E-mail: contact@llbfrance.com
Web Site: www.llbfrance.com
Key Personnel
President: Pierre Berthoud
General Dir: Marc Deroeux
Editor: Eric Denimal *E-mail:* eric.denimal@llbfrance.com
Founded: 1946

FRANCE   BOOK

Subjects: Archaeology, How-to, Religion - Protestant, Theology
ISBN Prefix(es): 2-85031
Branch Office(s)
Scripture Union, Suite 115, 150 Shafford Ave, Wayne, PA 19087, United States
Distributed by Cedis; CLC; Vida (France)

Lonely Planet
One rue du Dahomey, 75011 Paris
Tel: (01) 55 25 33 00 *Fax:* (01) 55 25 33 01
E-mail: 100560.415@compuserve.com
Web Site: www.lonelyplanet.fr
Key Personnel
General Dir: Zahia Hafs
Founded: 1992
Subjects: Travel
ISBN Prefix(es): 2-84070
Parent Company: Lonely Planet Publications, Australia
U.S. Office(s): Autre Filiale de Lonely Planet-Aux E-U Cette Fois, 155 Filbert St, Suite 251, Oakland, CA 94607, United States
Orders to: Vilo Diffusion, 25 rue Ginoux, 75015 Paris

Editions Loubatieres+
10 bis rue de l'Europe, 31190 Portet-sur Garonne Cedex
Tel: (05) 61 72 83 53 *Fax:* (05) 61 72 83 50
Key Personnel
Dir: Francis Loubatieres
Founded: 1970
Subjects: Art, Geography, Geology, History, Regional Interests, Travel
ISBN Prefix(es): 2-86266
Divisions: Librairie Loubatieres

LT Editors, *see* LT Editions-J Lanore-H Laurens

Lumiere Biblique series, *imprint of* Les Editions de la Source Sarl

Editions Josette Lyon+
11 bis rue Georges-Sache, 75014 Paris
Tel: (01) 40 44 81 60 *Fax:* (01) 45 42 30 99
E-mail: editions.josette.lyon@wanadoo.fr
Web Site: www.editions-josette-lyon.com
Key Personnel
Man Dir: Josette Lyon
Founded: 1986
Subjects: Health, Nutrition
ISBN Prefix(es): 2-906757; 2-84319

Editions Lyonnaises d'Art et d'Histoire
3, Quai Claude-Bernard, 69 007 Lyon
Tel: (04) 78 72 49 00 *Fax:* (04) 78 69 00 48
E-mail: editions.lyonnaises@wanadoo.fr
Web Site: www.perso.wandoo.fr/editions. lyonnaises
Key Personnel
General Dir: Corinne Poirieux
Founded: 1995
Subjects: Archaeology, Biography, Genealogy, History, How-to, Literature, Literary Criticism, Essays
ISBN Prefix(es): 2-84147; 2-905230
Distributor for Ed Nichel Chomarer; Ed Nichel Repnier

Macdonald, *imprint of* Naufal Group Sarl

Macula+
6, rue Coetlogon, 75006 Paris
Tel: (01) 45 48 58 70 *Fax:* (01) 45 44 45 89
Key Personnel
Dir: Jean Clay
Founded: 1980

Subjects: Antiques, Art, Film, Video, History, Literature, Literary Criticism, Essays, Photography, Psychology, Psychiatry
ISBN Prefix(es): 2-86589
Total Titles: 58 Print

Magnard SA
20 rue Berbier-du-Mets, 75647 Paris Cedex 13
Tel: (01) 44088585 *Fax:* (01) 44084979
Telex: 202294 F
Key Personnel
Contact: Jean-Manuel Bourgois
Founded: 1933
Subjects: Education
ISBN Prefix(es): 2-210
Subsidiaries: Dilisco (Diffusion du Livre Scolaire)

Maison de la Revelation+
46 av de la Liberation, 33740 Aves
Mailing Address: BP 16, 33740 Aves
Tel: (05) 56602477 *Fax:* (05) 56931631
Key Personnel
President: Dominique Mottas
Author: Michel Potay
Founded: 1974
Subjects: Philosophy, Religion - Other
ISBN Prefix(es): 2-901821

La Maison des Instituteurs, *see* Editions MDI (La Maison des Instituteurs)

Editions de la Maison des Sciences de l'Homme, Paris
54, blvd Raspail, 75270 Paris Cedex 06
Tel: (01) 49 54 20 30; (01) 49 54 20 31 *Fax:* (01) 49 54 21 33
Web Site: www1.msh-paris.fr
Telex: 203104 F
Key Personnel
Dir: Maurice Aymard
Head of Services: F Kahn *E-mail:* kahn@msh-paris.fr
Production: R Arcier; S Farraut; Jacky Thowmine
Founded: 1975
Specializes in French-German Programs.
Subjects: Anthropology, Archaeology, Economics, History, Music, Dance, Psychology, Psychiatry, Social Sciences, Sociology
ISBN Prefix(es): 2-7351; 2-901725
Orders to: CID, 131 blvd St-Michel, F-75005 Paris

La Maison du Dictionnaire+
98 Bd du Montparnasse, 75014 Paris
Tel: (01) 43 22 12 93 *Fax:* (01) 43 22 01 77
E-mail: lamaison@artinternet.fr
Web Site: www.lmdd.com
Key Personnel
Man Dir: Michel Feutry
Founded: 1976
Specialize in Software Aides, Electronic Dictionaries, CD-ROM.
ISBN Prefix(es): 2-85608
Branch Office(s)
DPLU, 5165 Ouest Rue Sherbrooke, Montreal, PQ H4A 1T6, Canada
U.S. Office(s): International Book Distributor Ltd, 24 Hudson St, Kinderhook, NY 12106, United States

Adrien Maisonneuve, *see* Editions d'Amerique et d'Orient, Adrien Maisonneuve

Maisonneuve
c/o Initiatives Sante, 26, Av de l'Europe, 78141 Velizy cedex
Mailing Address: BP 60, 78141 Velizy cedex
Tel: (03) 34 63 33 80 *Fax:* (03) 34 65 93 08
Key Personnel
Man Dir: Andre G Maisonneuve
Founded: 1959

Subjects: Health, Nutrition, Medicine, Nursing, Dentistry
ISBN Prefix(es): 2-7160

Editions Maisonneuve
Librairie d'Amerique et d'Orient, 11 rue Saint Sulpice, 75006 Paris
Tel: (01) 43 26 86 35 *Fax:* (01) 43 54 59 54
E-mail: maisonneuve@maisonneuve-adrien.com
Key Personnel
Dir General: Jean Maisonneuve
ISBN Prefix(es): 2-7200

Editions G P Maisonneuve et Larose+
15 rue Victor-Cousin, 75005 Paris
Tel: (01) 44414930 *Fax:* (01) 43257741
Key Personnel
President: Ms France Roque
Man Dir: Alain Jauson
Founded: 1835 (& 1860 respectively, merged 1961)
Subjects: Agriculture, Animals, Pets, Astrology, Occult, Language Arts, Linguistics, Regional Interests, Religion - Jewish
ISBN Prefix(es): 2-7068
Distributed by Belles Lettres; Servedit
Distributor for Ecole Francais d'Extreme Orient

Editions Maloine+
23, rue de l'Ecole de Medecine, 75006 Paris
Tel: (01) 43 25 60 45; (01) 43 29 54 50 *Fax:* (03) 44 23 02 27
E-mail: vpc@vigot.fr
Web Site: www.vigotmaloine.fr
Telex: 203215 F
Key Personnel
President, Man Dir, Rights & Permissions: Daniel Vigot
Dir: Christian Vigot
Sales, Publicity & Advertising: Thierry de Puniet
Production, Publicity & Advertising: Jean Phillipart
Founded: 1881
Subjects: Medicine, Nursing, Dentistry, Veterinary Science
ISBN Prefix(es): 2-224

Editions Mango+
36 rue Fontaine, 75009 Paris
Mailing Address: PO Box 24, 75013 Paris
Tel: (01) 49 70 15 55 *Fax:* (01) 49 70 15 49
Key Personnel
Dir General: Hugues de Saint Vincent
International Rights: Sophie Thunierelle
Founded: 1990
Subjects: Art, Child Care & Development, Crafts, Games, Hobbies, Gardening, Plants, Health, Nutrition, House & Home, How-to, Microcomputers, Outdoor Recreation, Sports, Athletics, Wine & Spirits
ISBN Prefix(es): 2-7404; 2-84270
Parent Company: Editions Fontaine
Divisions: Editions du Sport

Manitoba, *imprint of* Societe d'Edition Les Belles Lettres

Editions Marcus
25, rue Ginoux, 75015 Paris
Tel: (01) 45770404 *Fax:* (01) 45759251
Telex: 643841
Key Personnel
Man Dir: Patrick Arfi
Sales: Mrs Gaubert
Founded: 1963
Subjects: Travel
ISBN Prefix(es): 2-7131

La Marge+
4 rue Emmanuel Arene, 20000 Ajaccio
Tel: (04) 95215301 *Fax:* (04) 95215721

Key Personnel
Dir: Jean Jacques Colonna d'Istria
Founded: 1986
ISBN Prefix(es): 2-86523

Editions Marie-Noelle+
7, rue de la Liberte, 39700 Orchamps
Tel: (03) 81877500; (03) 84812891 *Fax:* (03) 81875669
Key Personnel
General Dir: Michel Siegwart
Founded: 1993
Subjects: Fiction, Literature, Literary Criticism, Essays, Science Fiction, Fantasy
ISBN Prefix(es): 2-910186

Editions Maritimes et d'Outre-Mer SA
17 rue Jacob, 75006 Paris
Tel: (04) 91 54 79 40 *Fax:* (04) 91 54 79 49
E-mail: webmaster@librairie-outremer.com
Web Site: www.librairie-outremer.com
Telex: 205652 JCLates
Key Personnel
Man Editor: Pierre Gutelle
Rights & Permissions: Emilie Levi
Founded: 1839
Subjects: Maritime, Sports, Athletics
ISBN Prefix(es): 2-7070
Parent Company: Editions Jean-Claude Lattes

Editions Maritimes et D'Outremer, *imprint of* Editions Ouest-France

Martelle
3, rue des Vergeaux, 80005 Amiens, Cedex 1
Tel: (03) 22715454 *Fax:* (03) 22928933
Telex: 145306
Key Personnel
Contact: M Cochard
Founded: 1990
Subjects: Regional Interests
ISBN Prefix(es): 2-87890
Bookshop(s): Centre Amiens, 2 le Fleure, 94 rue St Lazare, Paris

Editions de la Martiniere
2, rue Christine, 75006 Paris
Tel: (01) 40515200 *Fax:* (01) 40515205
Key Personnel
President: Herve De La Martiniere
General Dir: Olivier d' Arrouzat
Editorial: Philippe Gadesaude
Foreign Rights: Marianne Lassandro
ISBN Prefix(es): 2-7324

Marval+
7, pl St-Sulpice, 75006 Paris
Tel: (01) 43 25 33 33 *Fax:* (01) 43 25 88 88
E-mail: info@marval.com
Web Site: www.marval.com
Key Personnel
Manager: Yves-Marie Marchand
 E-mail: ymarval@noos.fr
Founded: 1942 (New company 1999)
Subjects: Art, Photography
ISBN Prefix(es): 2-86234
Total Titles: 180 Print
Online services available through World Wide Web.
Ultimate Parent Company: Vilo

Le Masque, *imprint of* Librairie des Champs-Elysees SA

Editions Charles Massin et Cie
16-18 rue de l'Amiral Mouchez, 75686 Paris, cedex 14
Tel: (01) 45 65 48 48 *Fax:* (01) 45 65 47 00
E-mail: info@massin.fr
Web Site: www.massin.fr

Telex: 4264918 Trace
Founded: 1910
Subjects: Architecture & Interior Design, Art, House & Home
ISBN Prefix(es): 2-7072

Masson SA+
Division of Havas
120 blvd St-Germain, 75280 Paris, Cedex 06
Tel: (01) 40 46 60 00 *Fax:* (01) 40 46 60 01
E-mail: infos@masson.fr
Web Site: www.masson.fr; www.e2med.com
Telex: Massoned 260946 *Cable:* GEMAS PARIS 025
Key Personnel
Chairman & Dir of Publication: Pierre Dutilleul
Foreign Rights Mgr: Gail Markham
 Tel: (01) 4409 6858 *Fax:* (01) 4409 5856
 E-mail: gmarkham@mmi.tm.fr
Founded: 1804
Publish medicine & health care-related subjects & 50 journals in paper & on-line versions; dictionaries.
Subjects: Medicine, Nursing, Dentistry, Psychology, Psychiatry, Veterinary Science
ISBN Prefix(es): 2-225; 2-294
Number of titles published annually: 200 Print
Total Titles: 3,000 Print
Online services available through World Wide Web.
Ultimate Parent Company: Vivendi Universal, 33 rue de Colisee, Paris 75008
Subsidiaries: Masson SpA; Masson SA
Distributed by Havas Diffusion International; Havas Services Suisse; Livredis; O L F; Presses de Belgique; Somabec

Masson-Williams et Wilkins+
Formerly Editions Pradel
3-5, rue Laromiguiere, 75005 Paris
Tel: (01) 40466000 *Fax:* (01) 40466126
E-mail: pradel@lsicom.fr
Key Personnel
Contact: Mariette Guena; Ray Pitt
Founded: 1988
Subjects: Biological Sciences, Medicine, Nursing, Dentistry
ISBN Prefix(es): 2-907516; 2-84360
Parent Company: Waverly Inc

Matrice
71, rue des Camelias, 91270 Vigneux
Tel: (01) 69 42 13 02 *Fax:* (01) 69 40 21 57
Key Personnel
President: Jacques Pain
Founded: 1984
Subjects: Human Relations
ISBN Prefix(es): 2-905642
Showroom(s): Le Scarabee, 3 rue de la Montagne Sainte Genevieve, 75005 Paris

Maxima Laurent du Mesnil Editeur+
192, bd Saint-Germain, 75007 Paris
Tel: (01) 44397400 *Fax:* (01) 45484688
Web Site: www.maxima.fr
Key Personnel
President & General Dir: Laurent du Mesnil du Buisson
Dir: Stephane Derville *E-mail:* sderville@maxima.fr
Founded: 1990
Subjects: Business, Career Development, Economics, Finance, Human Relations, Law, Management, Marketing
ISBN Prefix(es): 2-84001
Number of titles published annually: 20 Print
Total Titles: 200 Print
Associate Companies: Editions Francis Lefebvre
Distributed by Vivendi Universal Publishing Services

Editions MDI (La Maison des Instituteurs)
Service Clients, 75704 Paris, Cedex 13
Tel: (01) 45 87 58 20 *Fax:* (01) 43 31 39 60
E-mail: serviceclient@mdi-editions.com
Web Site: www.mdi-editions.com
Telex: MDI Edit 698094 F
Key Personnel
Man Dir: Marc Baudry
Export Dir: Daniel Beaudat
Founded: 1954
Subjects: Education, Geography, Geology, History, Science (General)
ISBN Prefix(es): 2-223
Parent Company: Editions Bordas

Medecine-Sciences, *imprint of* Flammarion SA

Editions Medianes+
72 rue d'Amiens, 76000 Rouen
Tel: (02) 35 88 85 71 *Fax:* (02) 35 15 28 44
E-mail: medianesconseil@wanadoo.fr
Key Personnel
Dir General: Jean-Marie Tiercelin
Contact: Christian de Chanteloup
Founded: 1989
Member of SNE.
Subjects: Art, Biography, Drama, Theater, History, Literature, Literary Criticism, Essays, Photography, Regional Interests
ISBN Prefix(es): 2-908345

Editions Mediaspaul+
48, rue du Four, 75006 Paris
Tel: (01) 64 90 88 07
Key Personnel
Editorial: Mr Leone
Founded: 1981
Subjects: Biblical Studies, Religion - Catholic, Theology
ISBN Prefix(es): 2-7122
Bookshop(s): 16 rue de la Visitation, 71600 Paray Le Monial
Warehouse: BP 26, 91291 Arpajon Cedex

Editions Memo+
4 rue Premion, 44000 Nantes
Tel: (02) 40 47 98 19 *Fax:* (02) 40 47 98 21
Key Personnel
General Dir: Christine Morault
Founded: 1993
Subjects: Art
ISBN Prefix(es): 2-910391

Editions Memoire des Arts+
7, rue Neuveg, 69002 Lyon
Mailing Address: PO Box 4553, 69244 Lyon, Cedex 04
Tel: (04) 78 83 22 62 *Fax:* (04) 72 19 48 74
Web Site: www.editions-memory-of-arts.fr
Key Personnel
General Dir: Alain Vollerin *E-mail:* alain.vollerin@wanadoo.fr
Founded: 1991
Subjects: Art
ISBN Prefix(es): 2-912544

La Memoire Normande, *imprint of* Editions Bertout

Societe des Editions Menges
6, rue du Mail, 75002 Paris
Tel: (01) 44 55 37 50 *Fax:* (01) 40 20 99 74
Telex: Cflglm 630385
Key Personnel
Man Dir: Gerard Mareuil
General Manager: Jean Paul Menges
Production: Michel Geneau
Marketing: Laurence Martin
Founded: 1975
Subjects: Cookery, Gardening, Plants, Health, Nutrition, Sports, Athletics
ISBN Prefix(es): 2-85620

FRANCE

Editions Franck Mercier+
One bis rue du Forum, BP 404, 74013 Annecy, cedex
Tel: (04) 50 57 16 50 *Fax:* (01) 450579301
E-mail: franck@mercier.com.ch
Key Personnel
Contact: Franck Mercier
Founded: 1985
Subjects: Geography, Geology, How-to, Outdoor Recreation, Sports, Athletics, Travel
ISBN Prefix(es): 2-86868
Total Titles: 120 Print
Imprints: Guide Franck

Mercure de France SA
26, rue de Conde, 75006 Paris
Tel: (01) 55 42 61 90 *Fax:* (01) 43 54 49 91
E-mail: mercure@mercure.fr
Web Site: www.gallimard.fr
Key Personnel
Production Dir: Brigitte Duverger
Foreign Rights & Permissions: Nicole Boyer
Editor: Nicolas Brehal; Jean-Marc Roberts
Founded: 1891
Subjects: Astrology, Occult, Biography, Fiction, History, Literature, Literary Criticism, Essays, Philosophy, Poetry
ISBN Prefix(es): 2-7152
Parent Company: Editions Gallimard
Associate Companies: Editions Denoel Sarl

Michelin et Cie (Services de Tourisme)
46, ave de Breteuil, 75324 Paris
Tel: (01) 45661234 *Fax:* (01) 45661163
Telex: 270 789 F
Key Personnel
Contact: M Alain Arnaud
Founded: 1900
Subjects: Travel
ISBN Prefix(es): 2-06
Associate Companies: Elastika Michelin, Greece; Michelin Asia Co PTE Ltd, Singapore; Michelin Asia Ltd, Hong Kong; Michelin Companhia Luso Pneu LDA Portugal; Michelin Reifenwerke, Austria; Michelin Reifenwerke, Germany; Michelin Travel Publications; Michelin Tyre PLC, United Kingdom; Nihon Michelin Tire KK, Japan; S A Belge du Pneumatique Michelin, Belgium; SA des Pneumatiques Michelin, Switzerland; SAFE de Neumaticos Michelin, Spain; S P A Michelin Italiana, Italy; Ste Canadienne des Pneus Michelin

Microsoft Press France
18 ave du Quebec, 91957 Courtaboeuf, Cedex
Tel: (0825) 827 8291 *Fax:* (01) 69 86 47 55
E-mail: msfrance@microsoft.com
Web Site: www.microsoft.com/france
Founded: 1992
Subjects: Computer Science
ISBN Prefix(es): 2-84082

Mille et Une Nuits+
37, rue du Four, 75006 Paris
Tel: (01) 45 4982 00 *Fax:* (01) 45 4979 96
Key Personnel
President: Monsieur Maurizio Medico
International Rights: Monsieur Olivier Rubinstein
Founded: 1993
Subjects: Literature, Literary Criticism, Essays
ISBN Prefix(es): 2-84205; 2-910233

Librairie Minard
45 rue de St-Andre, 14 123 Fleury/Orne
Tel: (02) 31844706 *Fax:* (02) 31844809
Key Personnel
Man Dir: Michel J Minard
Contact: Daniele Minard
Founded: 1978
Subjects: Film, Video, Literature, Literary Criticism, Essays

ISBN Prefix(es): 2-85210
Distributor for Lettres Modernes

Minerva
Subsidiary of La Martiniere Groupe
2, rue Christine, 75006 Paris
Tel: (01) 40 51 52 00 *Fax:* (01) 40 51 52 05
Web Site: www.lamartiniere.net
Key Personnel
President: Herve De La Martiniere
ISBN Prefix(es): 2-7324

Les Editions de Minuit SA+
7, rue Bernard-Palissy, 75006 Paris
Tel: (01) 44 39 39 20 *Fax:* (01) 45 44 82 36
Web Site: www.leseditionsdeminuit.fr
Key Personnel
Pres Dir Gen: Jerome Lindon *Tel:* (01) 66 39 39 22
Gen Dir: Irene Lindon *Tel:* (01) 66 39 39 27 *Fax:* (01) 66 39 39 23
Founded: 1942
Subjects: Fiction, Literature, Literary Criticism, Essays, Philosophy, Social Sciences, Sociology
ISBN Prefix(es): 2-7073
Number of titles published annually: 20 Print
Total Titles: 600 Print
Distributed by La Cite - L'Age d'Homme (Switzerland); Dimedia Inc (Canada)
Bookshop(s): Compagnie, 58 rue des Ecoles, 75005 Paris
Orders to: Le Seuil, 27 rue Jacob, F-75006 Paris
Tel: (01) 43547486

Presses Universitaires du Mirail+
Universite Toulouse-Le Mirail, 5 allees Antonio Machado, 31058 Toulouse, cedex 1
Tel: (0561) 503808 *Fax:* (0561) 503800
E-mail: pum@univ-tlse2.fr
Web Site: www.crlmidipyrenees.asso.fr/editeurs/pum.htm
Key Personnel
Dir Science: Wilfrid Rotge *Tel:* 561503805
Founded: 1987
University press that publishes books written mainly by academics.
Subjects: Geography, Geology, History, Language Arts, Linguistics, Literature, Literary Criticism, Essays, Philosophy, Psychology, Psychiatry, Social Sciences, Sociology, Women's Studies
ISBN Prefix(es): 2-85816
Number of titles published annually: 30 Print
Total Titles: 600 Print; 1 CD-ROM; 1 E-Book
Imprints: PUM Toulouse

Miroir Sprint Publications, see Les Editions Vaillant-Miroir-Sprint Publications

Editions Modernes Media+
21 Rue du Cardinal Lemoine, 75005 Paris
Tel: (01) 43268384 *Fax:* (01) 42333535
Key Personnel
Literary Dir: AM Marina Mediavilla
Founded: 1972
Subjects: Education, Language Arts, Linguistics, Literature, Literary Criticism, Essays, Philosophy
ISBN Prefix(es): 2-85398

Gerard Monfort Editeur Sarl+
68, rue St-Antoine, 75004 Paris
Tel: (01) 40 27 95 54 *Fax:* (01) 40 27 95 60
E-mail: contact@gerard-monfort.com
Web Site: www.gerard-monfort.com
Founded: 1960
Subjects: Art, History, Literature, Literary Criticism, Essays, Specialize in Art History
ISBN Prefix(es): 2-85226

Editions du Moniteur+
Division of HAVAS

17, rue d'Uzes, 75108 Paris, Cedex 02
Tel: (01) 40 13 33 72 *Fax:* (01) 40 41 08 87
E-mail: clients@editionsdumoniteur.com
Web Site: www.editionsdumoniteur.com
Telex: 680876 F
Key Personnel
President: Marc N Vigier *Tel:* (01) 40133201
Man Dir: Frederic Lenne *Tel:* (01) 40133434
Commercial Manager: Frederique Jeske *Tel:* (01) 40133110
Founded: 1981
Subjects: Architecture & Interior Design, Economics, Law, Technology
ISBN Prefix(es): 2-281; 2-7327; 2-902302
Ultimate Parent Company: Vivendi
Associate Companies: CEP Edition
Bookshop(s): Librairies du Moniteur, 15 rue d'Uzes, F-75002 Paris; 7 pl de l'Odeon, F-75006 Paris

Editions Paul Montel
11, rue Gossin, 92543 Montrouge Cedex
Tel: (01) 46565266
Key Personnel
Man Dir: Marc Vigier
Dir: Guy de Dampierre
Sales: Yves-Louis Walle
Subjects: Film, Video, Photography
ISBN Prefix(es): 2-7075

Gabriel Mony+
Mas St-Louis - Rte de Lorgues, 83300 Draguignan
Tel: (04) 94472832 *Fax:* (04) 94472832
Telex: 409 000 f
Founded: 1954
Subjects: Fiction, Literature, Literary Criticism, Essays, Philosophy, Poetry, Science (General)
ISBN Prefix(es): 2-905667

Muller Edition+
BP 122, 92134 Issy-les-moulineaux, Cedex
Tel: (01) 40 90 0965 *Fax:* (01) 47 76 3397
E-mail: courrier@muller-edition.com
Web Site: www.muller-edition.com
Key Personnel
President: Joseph Muller *E-mail:* courrier@muller-edition.com
Founded: 1990
Subjects: Archaeology, History, How-to, Military Science
ISBN Prefix(es): 2-904255
Total Titles: 500 Print; 300 E-Book
Distributed by Editions Picard; Goutiere diffusioer; Histoire et documents
Distributor for Editions Bertout; Editions Jean Curutchet; Editions des Ecrivains Associes; Editions Domens; Editions Etoile De La Pensee; Editions L' Harmattan; Editions Charles Lavauzelle; Martelle; Ouest-France

Editions de la Reunion des Musees Nationaux+
49, rue Etienne Marcel, 75001 Paris
Tel: (01) 40 13 48 37 *Fax:* (01) 40 13 48 61
E-mail: communication@rmn.fr
Web Site: www.rmn.fr
Key Personnel
Dir: J J Lugbull
Founded: 1931
Subjects: Antiques, Archaeology, Architecture & Interior Design, Art, Ethnicity, History
ISBN Prefix(es): 2-7118
Branch Office(s)
Reumusnat Paris *Fax:* (01) 42225073 (Telex: Rm 200115 F)
Distributed by Editions du Seuie
Bookshop(s): Grand Louvre, 75001 Paris; Librairie du Musee d'Orsay, 60ter rue de Lille, 75001 Paris
Warehouse: Centre de Distribution de la R M N, 1-31, allee du 12 fevrier 1934, 77186 Noisiel

Editions Maurice Nadeau, Les Lettres Nouvelles+
135 rue, St-Martin, 75194 Paris
Tel: (01) 48 87 48 58 *Fax:* (01) 48 87 13 01
Key Personnel
President: Bernard Coutaz
Manager: Maurice Nadeau
Subjects: Literature, Literary Criticism, Essays
ISBN Prefix(es): 2-86231
Parent Company: Societe D'Editions Litteraires et Scientifiques (SELIS)
Orders to: Harmonia Mundi, 13200 Arles

Nanga
1 a rue Daubigny, 14113 Villerville
Tel: (06) 11 19 47 53 *Fax:* (02) 31 87 05 92
E-mail: nanga@nanga.fr
Web Site: nanga.fr; feugereux.com
Key Personnel
Publisher: Jerome Feugereux *E-mail:* jerome@feugereux.com
Founded: 1991
Subjects: Art, Earth Sciences, Literature, Literary Criticism, Essays, Poetry
ISBN Prefix(es): 2-909152
Number of titles published annually: 4 Print; 2 E-Book
Total Titles: 20 Print; 3 E-Book

Fernand Nathan
9 rue Mechain, 75014 Paris
Tel: (01) 45 87 50 00 *Fax:* (01) 45 87 57 57
Web Site: www.nathan.fr
Telex: Nataned 204525 F *Cable:* NATHANED PARIS
Key Personnel
Chairman: Bertrand Eveno
Executive Vice President: Jean-Paul Baudouin
Elementary Dir: Arnaud Langlois-Meurinne
Educational Dir: Michel Legrain
Educational Aids & University Dir: Philippe Merlet
Dir, Children's Books: Marc Baudry
Languages Dir: Marc Gudimard
Sales Dirs: Alain Carita; Patrick de Porcaro
Marketing Dir: Emilie Carelli
Finance Dir: Serge Grand
Rights & Permissions: Evelyne Mathiaud
Founded: 1881
Subjects: Education, History, Philosophy, Psychology, Psychiatry, Science (General), Social Sciences, Sociology, Specialize in Children & Pedagogy
ISBN Prefix(es): 2-09
Parent Company: Groupe de la Cite
Subsidiaries: CLE; Retz; Le Robert

Centre National de la Photographie+
11 rue Berryer, Hoetel Salomon de Rothschild, 75008 Paris
Tel: (01) 53 76 12 31 *Fax:* (01) 53 76 12 33
E-mail: centre.national.de.la.photographie@wanadoo.fr
Web Site: www.cnp-photographie.com/cnp_version_fr/lieux/page_liste.html
Key Personnel
Dir: Robert Delpire
Commercial Dir: Benoit Rivero
Founded: 1982
Subjects: Photography
ISBN Prefix(es): 2-86754
Showroom(s): Hoetel Salomon de Rotschild, 11 rue Berryer, 75008 Paris

Centre National de la Recherche Scientifique
Formerly Institut National de la Langue Francaise
44 Ave de La Liberation, Universite de Nancy 2, 54063 Nancy, Cedex
Mailing Address: BP 30687, 54063 Nancy Cedex
Tel: (03) 83 96 21 76 *Fax:* (03) 83 97 24 56
Web Site: www.inalf.fr

Key Personnel
Dir: Bernard Combettes *E-mail:* bernard.combettes@inalf.fr
Director: Jean-Marie Pierrel *E-mail:* jean-marie.pierrel@inalf.fr
Deputy Dir: Gerard Gorcy
Secretary-General: Nicole Nicoli
Founded: 1977
ISBN Prefix(es): 2-86484

Institut National de Recherche Pedagogique
29 rue d'Ulm, 75230 Paris, Cedex 05
Tel: (01) 46 34 90 00 *Fax:* (01) 43 54 32 01
Web Site: www.inrp.fr *Cable:* INATREP
Key Personnel
Dir: Aydre Hussenet
Founded: 1879
Subjects: Education
ISBN Prefix(es): 2-7342
Parent Company: Ministere de l'Education Nationle, 110 rue de Grenelle, 75357 Paris

Institut National de la Langue Francaise, see Centre National de la Recherche Scientifique

Naufal, *imprint of* Naufal Group Sarl

Naufal Group Sarl+
6 rue Quentin Bauchart, 75008 Paris
Mailing Address: PO Box 11-2161, Beirut, Lebanon
Tel: (01) 40701280 *Fax:* (01) 40701298
Key Personnel
Man Dir, Editorial & Rights & Permissions: Tony P Naufal
Editorial: Kamal Khauli
Sales, Production: Khaled Shamaa
General Manager (Paris): Sami Naufal
Founded: 1970
Subjects: Fiction, History, Law, Literature, Literary Criticism, Essays
ISBN Prefix(es): 2-906958
Imprints: Naufal; Macdonald; Editions Arabes
Subsidiaries: Macdonald Middle East Sarl; Les Editions Arabes SA
Bookshop(s): Librairies Antoine, Hamra, PO Box 656, Beirut, Lebanon (five shops)

Navarre, *imprint of* Librairie Generale de Droit et de Jurisprudence (LGDJ) - Montchrestien

NEF, see Nouvelles Editions Francaises

NEL, *imprint of* Nouvelles Editions Latines

Nil Editions+
24, Ave Marceau, 75008 Paris
Tel: (01) 53 67 14 00 *Fax:* (01) 53 67 14 90
Web Site: www.laffont.fr
Key Personnel
President: Nicole Lattes
International Rights: Celine Chiflet
Contact: Olga Begin *E-mail:* obegin@robert-laffont.fr; Renata de La Chapelle *E-mail:* rdelachapelle@robert-laffont.fr; Gwenael Gouiffes *E-mail:* ggouiffes@robert-laffont.fr; Benita Edzard *E-mail:* bedzard@robert-laffont.fr; Camille Schyrr *E-mail:* cschyrr@robert-laffont.fr
Founded: 1993
Subjects: Biography, Fiction, Literature, Literary Criticism, Essays, Philosophy, French literature, Spirituality
ISBN Prefix(es): 2-84111
Orders to: Edition du Sevil, BP 281, 911621 Longjumeau Cedex *Tel:* (01) 64 48 49 63

Librairie A-G Nizet Sarl+
41 rue de l'Auberdiere, F-37510 Saint Genouph
Tel: (02) 47455041 *Fax:* (02) 47455015

E-mail: librairie-a.g-nizet@wanadoo.fr
Key Personnel
Man Dir & General Manager: Daniel Nizet
Founded: 1945
Member of Edition Syndication, Group "Scholarship".
Subjects: Drama, Theater, Education, Literature, Literary Criticism, Essays
ISBN Prefix(es): 2-7078
Number of titles published annually: 6 Print
Total Titles: 740 Print
Distributed by D P L U (North America); L'Age d'homme (Switzerland); Nord-Sud (Benelux)
Distributor for France Tosho

F De Nobele
35 rue Bonaparte, 75006 Paris 6e
Tel: (01) 43 26 08 62 *Fax:* (01) 40 46 85 96
Cable: Denobelef Paris 110
Key Personnel
Man Dir: F de Nobele
Founded: 1885
Subjects: Art
ISBN Prefix(es): 2-85189

Noir Sur Blanc+
5 rue Moliere, 75001 Paris
Tel: (01) 42 86 07 10 *Fax:* (01) 42 86 08 90
E-mail: noirsurblanc@noirsurblanc.com
Web Site: www.noirsurblanc.com
Key Personnel
Literary Dir: Jan Michalski
Dir: Vera Michalski
Founded: 1990
Subjects: Biography, Cookery, Drama, Theater, Fiction, Literature, Literary Criticism, Essays
ISBN Prefix(es): 2-88250
Parent Company: Editions Noir sur Blanc

Editions Nord-Sud (North-South Editions)
Imprint of Nord-Sud Verlag
2, rue Racine, 78100 St Germain-en-Laye
Tel: (01) 39 21 90 40 *Fax:* (01) 39 21 90 42
E-mail: nord-sug@editions-nord-sud.com
Web Site: www.ldj.tm.fr
Key Personnel
President: Davy Sidjanski
Dir: Didier Teyras
Founded: 1981
Parent Company: Nord-Sud Verlag

Editions Norma+
86 rue Castagnary, 75015 Paris
Tel: (01) 40430498 *Fax:* (01) 40439875
Key Personnel
Manager: Maiite Hudry
Founded: 1991
Subjects: Architecture & Interior Design, Art, Drama, Theater, Foreign Countries, History, House & Home, Regional Interests, 20th Century Decorative Arts
ISBN Prefix(es): 2-909283
Warehouse: ETAI, 20 rue de la Saussiere, 92100 Boulogne *Tel:* (01) 46992424

Mare Nostrum
6 rue Edmond Bartissol, 66000 Perpignan
Tel: (04) 68511750 *Fax:* (05) 61411543
Telex: 34421415
Key Personnel
President: Philippe Salus
Treasurer: Henri Taverner
Founded: 1990
Subjects: Literature, Literary Criticism, Essays, Philosophy, Poetry, Religion - Jewish
ISBN Prefix(es): 2-908476
Warehouse: Taye, 28110 Luce
Orders to: Taye, 28110 Luce

Notes Bibliographiques-Culture et Bibliotheques pour Tous, see Culture et Bibliotheque pour Tous

FRANCE

Nouvelle Cite+
37, Ave de la Marne, 92120 Montrouge
Tel: (01) 40927085 *Fax:* (01) 40921168
Web Site: www.perso.wanadoo.fr/nouvelle.
cite/commcpe.html
Key Personnel
Man Dir, Rights & Permissions: Henri-Louis Roche
Sales: Christian Charnay
Founded: 1963
Subjects: Education, Literature, Literary Criticism, Essays, Religion - Other
ISBN Prefix(es): 2-85313

Nouvelle Diffusion SPRL DPI, see Editions Complexe SPRL

Nouvelles Editions Fiduciaires
2 bis, rue de Villiers, 92 300 Levallois-Perret
Tel: (01) 46 39 47 13; (01) 46 39 47 00 *Fax:* (01) 47 58 00 63
Key Personnel
Dir: Sophie Robert
Founded: 1980
Subjects: Economics, Law, Management
ISBN Prefix(es): 2-86544

Nouvelles Editions Francaises+
152, rue de Picpus, 75583 Paris, Cedex 12
Tel: (01) 44 74 16 00 *Fax:* (01) 44 04 98 03
Key Personnel
Man Dir: Eliane Allegret
Founded: 1843
Subjects: Art, History, House & Home
ISBN Prefix(es): 2-7079

Nouvelles Editions Latines+
One, rue Palatine, 75006 Paris
Tel: (01) 43 54 77 42 *Fax:* (01) 43 29 69 81
Key Personnel
Man Dir: Jean Sorlot
Founded: 1928
Subjects: Fiction, History, Poetry, Religion - Other, Travel
ISBN Prefix(es): 2-7233; 2-85147
Imprints: NEL

La Nuee Bleue - Dernieres Nouvelles d'Alsace
3 rue St-Pierre-le-Jeune, 67000 Strasbourg
Tel: (03) 88 15 77 27 *Fax:* (03) 88 75 16 21
Web Site: www.sdv.fr/nuee-bleue/
ISBN Prefix(es): 2-7165

Oblong, *imprint of* Editions Jacques Gabay

Editions Obsidiane+
11 rue Andre Gateau, 89100 Sens
Tel: (01) 86965218 *Fax:* (01) 86870112
E-mail: genevieve.bigant@wanadoo.fr
Key Personnel
Manager: Francois Boddaert
Founded: 1985
Subjects: Literature, Literary Criticism, Essays, Poetry
ISBN Prefix(es): 2-904469; 2-911914
Number of titles published annually: 10 Print
Distributed by Les Belles-Lettres

Editions Odile Jacob+
15, rue Soufflot, 75005 Paris
Tel: (01) 44 41 64 84 *Fax:* (01) 44 41 64 99; (01) 43 29 88 77
Web Site: www.odilejacob.fr
Key Personnel
President: Odile Jacob
Rights & Permissions: Claire Teeuwissen
 Tel: (01) 44 41 64 80
Founded: 1985
Subjects: Biography, Economics, Fiction, Government, Political Science, History, How-to, Law, Philosophy, Psychology, Psychiatry, Science (General), Social Sciences, Sociology
ISBN Prefix(es): 2-7381
Number of titles published annually: 120 Print
Imprints: Poches Odile Jacob

OECD
2, rue Andre Pascal, 75775 Paris, Cedex 16
Tel: (01) 45 24 82 00 *Fax:* (01) 45 24 83 00
Web Site: www.oecd.org; www.oecd.org/bookshop
Key Personnel
Sales Manager: Toby Green *Tel:* (01) 45 24 94 15 *Fax:* (01) 45 24 94 53 *E-mail:* toby.green@oecd.org
International Rights: Laurence Gerrer *Tel:* (01) 45 24 13 90 *Fax:* (01) 45 10 42 15
 E-mail: laurence.gerrer@oecd.org
Founded: 1960
Specialize in economic co-operation & development.
Subjects: Economics
ISBN Prefix(es): 92-64; 92-821
Number of titles published annually: 250 Print; 100 CD-ROM; 250 Online
Branch Office(s)
OECD Bonn Centre, August-Bebel-Allee-6, 53175 Bonn, Germany *Tel:* (0228) 959 1215 *Fax:* (0228) 959 1278 *E-mail:* bonn.contact@oecd.org *Web Site:* www.oecd.org/bonn (Austria, Germany & Switzerland)
OECD Mexiko Centre, av. Presidente Mazaryk 526, Polanco 11560, Mexico *Tel:* (0525) 281 3810 *Fax:* (0525) 280 0480 *E-mail:* mexico.contact@oecd.org *Web Site:* www.rtn.net/mx/ocde/ (Latin America)
OECD Tokyo Centre, Nippon Press Center Bldg, 2-2-1, 3rd fl, Uchisaiwaicho, Chiyoda-ku, Tokyo 100-0011, Japan *Tel:* (03) 5532 0021 *Fax:* (03) 5532 0036 *E-mail:* centre@oecdtokyo.org *Web Site:* www.oecdtokyo.org (Asia)
U.S. Office(s): OECD Washington Center, 2001 "L" St NW, Suite 650, Washington, DC 20036-4922, United States *Tel:* 202-785-6323 *Fax:* 202-785-0350 *E-mail:* washington.contact@oecd.org *Web Site:* www.oecdwash.org (United States)
Distributor for International Energy Agency; Nuclear Energy Agency

L' Olivier, *imprint of* Editions du Seuil

Editions Ophrys+
6 ave J Jaures, 05000 Gap
Tel: (04) 92 53 85 72 *Fax:* (04) 92 53 35 60
E-mail: edition.ophrys@wanadoo.fr
Web Site: www.ophrys-editions.com
Key Personnel
Man Dir, Publicity & Advertising: Mrs B Monnier
Founded: 1934
Subjects: Earth Sciences, Education, English as a Second Language, Genealogy, Geography, Geology, History, Language Arts, Linguistics, Regional Interests, Self-Help, Social Sciences, Sociology, Travel
ISBN Prefix(es): 2-7080
Bookshop(s): Succursale de Paris, 10 rue de Nesle, 75006 Paris *Tel:* (01) 44 41 63 75 *Fax:* (01) 46 33 15 97
Orders to: 10 rue de Nesle, 75006 Paris *Tel:* (01) 44 41 63 75 *Fax:* (01) 46 31 15 97

Opsys Operating System
3, rue Paul-Valerien-Perrin, Seyssinet-Pariset 38172
Tel: (04) 76 84 34 20 *Fax:* (04) 76 84 34 21
E-mail: opsys@opsys.fr
Web Site: www.opsys.fr
Key Personnel
President: Alain Gagne *E-mail:* agagne@opsys.fr

BOOK

Commercial Director: Thierry Ponset
 E-mail: tponset@opsys.fr
Operations Director: Jean-Pierre Schmitt
 E-mail: jpschmit@opsys.fr
Development Director: Joseph Ramblas
 E-mail: jramblas@opsys.fr
Research Director: Jacques Kergomard
 E-mail: jkergomard@opsys.fr
Subjects: Library & Information Sciences

Editions de l'Orante+
6 rue du General-Bertrand, 75007 Paris
Tel: (01) 47 83 55 02 *Fax:* (01) 45 66 00 16
Key Personnel
Man Dir: Jacques Lafarge
Founded: 1940
Member of Syndicat National de l'Edition.
Subjects: History, Philosophy, Poetry, Religion - Other
ISBN Prefix(es): 2-7031
Total Titles: 80 Print

Librairie Orientaliste, see Paul Geuthner Librairie Orientaliste

L'Originel - Editions Accarias+
18 cite Industrielle, 75011 Paris
Mailing Address: 5, passage de la Folie-Regnault, 75011 Paris
Tel: (01) 43 48 73 07 *Fax:* (01) 43 48 73 07
E-mail: originel-accarias@club-internet.fr
Key Personnel
Dir: Jean-Louis Accarias
Founded: 1980
Subjects: Philosophy, Religion - Buddhist, Religion - Hindu, Religion - Other, Social Sciences, Sociology
ISBN Prefix(es): 2-86316
Shipping Address: Dilisco, 122 rue Rarcel Martmann, 94200 Ivny sur Seine
Orders to: Dilisco, 122 rue Rarcel Martmann, 94200 Ivny sur Seine

Ouest Editions
Presses Academiques, One, rue de la Noe, 44321 Nantes Cedex 3
Mailing Address: BP 52106, Nantes Cedex
Tel: (02) 40 14 34 34 *Fax:* (02) 40 14 36 36
Key Personnel
Dir General: Yves Suaudeau
Founded: 1989
Subjects: Accounting, Biological Sciences, Chemistry, Chemical Engineering, Civil Engineering, Earth Sciences, Economics, Geography, Geology, History, Regional Interests
ISBN Prefix(es): 2-908261
Distributed by Alena Libert Inc (Canada); Boinemouth (UK); Chinon Diffusion (Europe); Continental Books

Editions Ouest-France+
13 rue du Breil, 35063 Rennes Cedex
Mailing Address: BP 6339, 35063 Rennes Cedex
Tel: (016) 99 32 58 27 *Fax:* (016) 99 32 58 30
Web Site: www.edilarge.com
Key Personnel
Dir General: Antoine de Tarle
Founded: 1975
Subjects: History, Science (General), Travel
ISBN Prefix(es): 2-7373; 2-85882
Imprints: Editions de la Cite; Editions Maritimes et D'Outremer

Editions J H Paillet et B Drouaud+
73 rue de La Varenne, 41120 Cellettes
Tel: 54704303
Key Personnel
Editor: Jean-Hubert Paillet; Brigitte Drouaud
Founded: 1989
Subjects: Literature, Literary Criticism, Essays
ISBN Prefix(es): 2-9504241; 2-909565

PUBLISHERS

FRANCE

Editions du Papyrus
17, blvd Rouget de Lisle, 93189 Montreuil cedex
Tel: (01) 4 85 27 05 *Fax:* (01) 48 57 26 79
E-mail: papyrus@netfly.fr
Web Site: www.editions-papyrus.com
Founded: 1986
Subjects: Law
ISBN Prefix(es): 2-86541

Editions Paradigme
37, rue des Murlins, 45000 Orleans
Tel: (02) 38 70 84 44 *Fax:* (02) 38 70 56 76
E-mail: fab45.paradigme@wanadoo.fr
Web Site: paradigme.com
Key Personnel
President & Editor: Bernard Legrand
  E-mail: blegrand@wanadoo.fr
Founded: 1983
Specialize in Erudition.
Subjects: Energy, Geography, Geology, History, Literature, Literary Criticism, Essays, Maritime, Philosophy
ISBN Prefix(es): 2-86878
Total Titles: 170 Print
Parent Company: FAB

Pardes+
9 rue Jules Dumesnil, 45390 Puisseaux
Mailing Address: BP 47, 45390 Puisseau
Tel: (02) 38 33 53 28 *Fax:* (02) 38 33 58 99
Web Site: perso.wanadoo.fr/mackadam/livre/
  Editeurs/pardes.htm
Key Personnel
Man Editor: Georges Gondinet
Founded: 1982
Subjects: Archaeology, Astrology, Occult, Health, Nutrition, History, Religion - Buddhist, Religion - Hindu, Social Sciences, Sociology
ISBN Prefix(es): 2-86714

Editions Parentheses
72, cours Julien, 13006 Marseille
Tel: (0496) 08 18 20 *Fax:* (0495) 08 18 24
Key Personnel
General Dir: Varoujan Arzoumanian
Dir: Patrick Bardon
Founded: 1978
Subjects: Anthropology, Architecture & Interior Design, Art, Ethnicity, Music, Dance
ISBN Prefix(es): 2-86364
Total Titles: 150 Print

Paris Musees+
28, rue Notre Dame des Victoires, 75002 Paris
Tel: (01) 44 58 99 41 *Fax:* (01) 47 03 36 44
Key Personnel
Publisher: Arnauld Pontier
Distribution: Virginie Perreau
Founded: 1985
Specialize in Art-Exhibition's Catalogues.
Subjects: Architecture & Interior Design, Art, Fashion, History, Photography
ISBN Prefix(es): 2-87900

Paroisse & Famille, *imprint of* Fac Editions

Le Parvis des Arts, *imprint of* Presses Universitaires de Nancy

Editions Payot & Rivages+
106, Blvd Saint-Germain, 75006 Paris
Tel: (01) 44 41 39 90 *Fax:* (01) 44 41 39 69
E-mail: payotrivages@wanadoo.fr
Key Personnel
Man Dir: Jean-Francois Lamuniere
Founded: 1984
Subjects: Anthropology, Biography, Cookery, Fiction, History, Humor, Language Arts, Linguistics, Literature, Literary Criticism, Essays, Mysteries, Nonfiction (General), Philosophy, Religion - Other, Science Fiction, Fantasy, Social Sciences, Sociology, Technology, Transportation, Travel, Contemporary History, Cultural Studies, Ethnology, Fantasy, Modern History, Political Science, Sexuality Short Stories, Thriller
ISBN Prefix(es): 2-7436; 2-903059; 2-86930
Parent Company: Eol Rivagei
Orders to: Le Seuil, 27 rue Jacod, 75006 Paris

Pearson Education/CampusPress, *imprint of* Pearson Education France

Pearson Education France+
19 rue Michael le Comte, 75003 Paris
Tel: (01) 4454 5110 *Fax:* (01) 4804 5361 (sales); (01) 4887 7130 (finance)
E-mail: firstname.lastname@pearson.fr
Web Site: www.pearsoned.fr
Key Personnel
President: Helene Dennery
Vice President, Finance & Operations: Patricia Gasquet
Editor, CampusPress Man Dir: Patrick Ussunet
Editor, Village Mondail Man Dir: Geoff Staines
Founded: 1995
Publisher of computer books.
Subjects: Business, Computer Science, Education, Finance, Microcomputers
ISBN Prefix(es): 2-7440
Total Titles: 300 Print
Parent Company: Pearson Education
Ultimate Parent Company: Pearson Plc
Imprints: Pearson Education/CampusPress; Pearson Education/Les Echos; Pearson Education/Les Echos.fr Press

Pearson Education/Les Echos, *imprint of* Pearson Education France

Pearson Education/Les Echos.fr Press, *imprint of* Pearson Education France

Pedagogie Modern, *imprint of* Editions Bordas

Editions Pedone+
13 rue Soufflot, 75005 Paris
Tel: (01) 43 54 05 97 *Fax:* (01) 46 34 07 60
E-mail: editions-pedone@wanadoo.fr
Web Site: www.franceedition.org/Pedone
Key Personnel
Man Dir: Denis Pedone
Founded: 1837
Subjects: Agriculture, Earth Sciences, Economics, Engineering (General), Law, Management, Maritime, Air Law, Criminal Philosophy, Diplomatic History, International Law, International Relations, Penal Sciences, Philosophy of the Right, Right European, Right of the Sea
ISBN Prefix(es): 2-233

Peeters-France
52 Blvd Michaelmas, 75006 Paris
Tel: (016) 244000 *Fax:* (016) 228500
Web Site: www.peeters-leuven.be
Key Personnel
Editor: Vladimir Randa
Subjects: Anthropology, Archaeology, Biblical Studies, History, Language Arts, Linguistics, Literature, Literary Criticism, Essays, Philosophy, Theology, Specialize in Classical Studies, Eastern Studies, Egyptology, History of Art, Medicine, Oriental Studies & Ethics, Patriotics
ISBN Prefix(es): 2-87723; 90-6831; 90-429
Number of titles published annually: 120 Print; 2 CD-ROM
Parent Company: Peeters, Bondgenoten Laan 153, B-3000 Leuven, Belgium
U.S. Office(s): Peeters Academic Publishers, Inc, 6 Ash Lane, Dudley, MA 07517, United States, Contact: Catherine Cocnille *Fax:* 508-949-0557 *E-mail:* peeters@charter.net
Distributed by BR&D
Bookshop(s): Bondgenotenlaan 153, 3000 Leuven, Belgium, I Huenaerts *Tel:* (016) 23 51 70 *Fax:* (016) 22 85 00 *E-mail:* peeters@peeters-leuven.be; Grand rue 56, B-1348 Louvain-la-Neuve, Belgium
Shipping Address: Kolonel Begaultlaan 61, B-3000 Leuven, Belgium *Tel:* (016) 24 40 00 *Fax:* (016) 22 85 00 *E-mail:* peeters@peeters-leuven.be
Warehouse: Kolonel Begaultlaan 61, B-3000 Leuven, Belgium
Orders to: Bondgenotenlaan 153, 3000 Leuven, Belgium, I Huenaerts *Tel:* (016) 23 51 70 *Fax:* (016) 22 85 00

PEMF, see Editions Publications de l'Ecole Moderne Francaise sa (PEMF)

Pere Castor, *imprint of* Flammarion SA

Petit Marteau, *imprint of* Hemma Joven, SA

La Pharmacie de Platon, *imprint of* William Blake & Co

Editions Phebus
12 rue Gregoire de Tours, 75006 Paris
Tel: (01) 46332929 *Fax:* (01) 43256769
Key Personnel
Man Dir: Jean-Pierre Sicre
Founded: 1976
Subjects: Art, Literature, Literary Criticism, Essays
ISBN Prefix(es): 2-85940
Orders to: SEUIL Diffusion, 27 rue Jacob, 75006 Paris

Editions A et J Picard SA
82, rue Bonaparte, 75006 Paris
Tel: (01) 43 26 96 73 *Fax:* (01) 43 26 42 64
E-mail: livres@librairie-picard.com
Web Site: www.abebooks.com/home/libpicard
Telex: Bsc Picaredit 305551 F
Key Personnel
Man Dir: Chantal Pasini-Picard
Founded: 1869
Subjects: Antiques, Archaeology, Architecture & Interior Design, Art, Education, Ethnicity, History, Language Arts, Linguistics, Literature, Literary Criticism, Essays, Music, Dance, Religion - Other
ISBN Prefix(es): 2-7084

Editions Jean Picollec+
47 rue Auguste Lancon, 75013 Paris
Tel: (01) 45 89 73 04 *Fax:* (01) 45 89 40 72
E-mail: jean.picollec@noos.fr
Key Personnel
Publisher & Man Dir: Jean Picollec
Publishing Consultant: Helene Simon
Public Relations & Sales: Corinne Saulneron
Founded: 1979
Specialize in reference books & documents - Celtic World.
Subjects: Biography, Ethnicity, Fiction, Government, Political Science, History, Literature, Literary Criticism, Essays, Nonfiction (General), Regional Interests, Travel
ISBN Prefix(es): 2-86477
Number of titles published annually: 12 Print
Total Titles: 25 Print
Distributed by Age d'Homme (Switzerland); Nouvelle Diffusion (Belgium)
Foreign Rep(s): L'age d'Homme (Switzerland); Nouvelle Diffusion (Belgium)
Foreign Rights: Arabella Cruse (Scandinavia); Laura Dail (North America); Catherine Fragou

(Greece); Patricia Pasqualini (Central & Eastern Europe)
Orders to: CED, 73 quai Auguste Deshaies, 94200 Ivry-Sur-Seine *Tel:* (01) 46 58 38 40 *Fax:* (01) 46 71 25 59

Editions Philippe Picquier+
Le Mas de Vert BP 150, 13631 Arles
Tel: (04) 90496156 *Fax:* (04) 90499614
Key Personnel
Dir: Philippe Picquier
Founded: 1986
Subjects: Literature, Literary Criticism, Essays
ISBN Prefix(es): 2-87730
Orders to: Harmonia Mundi Diffusion Livres, Le Mas de Vert BP 150, 13631 Arles Cedex

Editions Pierron+
2, rue Gutenberg, 57206 Sarreguemines Cedex
Tel: (03) 87951089 *Fax:* (03) 87956095
Telex: 860495 F
Key Personnel
Dir: Jeannie Jung-Pierron
Subjects: Education, History
ISBN Prefix(es): 2-7085
Parent Company: Pierron Entreprise SA

Editions Christian Pirot+
13 rue Maurice-Adrien, 37540 Saint-Cyr-Sur-Loire
Tel: (02) 47 54 54 20 *Fax:* (02) 47 51 57 96
Web Site: www.friendship-first.com
Key Personnel
Dir: Christian Pirot
Founded: 1979
Subjects: Biography, Cookery, Fiction, Literature, Literary Criticism, Essays, Music, Dance, Poetry, Travel
ISBN Prefix(es): 2-86808
Number of titles published annually: 12 Print
Total Titles: 160 Print
Branch Office(s)
Diffusion Canada, Diffusion DIMEDIA, 539 Blvd Libeau, Ville Saint Laurent, Quebec, ON H4N 1S2, Canada *Tel:* 514-336-3941 *Fax:* 514-331-3916 *E-mail:* dimedia@infopuq.uquebec.ca
Diffusion USA, University Press of the South, 5500 Prytania St, Suite 421, New Orleans, LA 70115, United States *Tel:* 504-866-2791 *Fax:* 504-866-2750 *E-mail:* unprsouth@aol.com; punmonde@aol.com
Distributed by Harmonia Mundi Diffusion; University Press of the South (USA)
Orders to: Harmonia Mundi Diffusion, BP 150, 13631 Arles Cedex *Tel:* (04) 90499049 *Fax:* (04) 90499614

Jean-Michel Place+
3, rue Lhomond, 75005 Paris
Tel: (01) 44 32 05 90 *Fax:* (01) 44 32 05 91
E-mail: place@jmplace.com
Web Site: www.jmplace.com
Founded: 1973
Subjects: Anthropology, Art, Literature, Literary Criticism, Essays, Philosophy, Photography, Publishing & Book Trade Reference
ISBN Prefix(es): 2-85893

Librairie Plon SA
76, rue Bonaparte, 75006 Paris 06
Tel: (01) 44 41 35 00 *Fax:* (01) 44 41 35 02
Key Personnel
Man Dir: Xavier de Bartillat
ISBN Prefix(es): 2-259

Editions Plume+
51 rue de Turenne, 75003 Paris
Tel: (01) 40 29 96 09 *Fax:* (01) 40 29 96 11
Key Personnel
Director: Nathalie Peillard
Editor & Publicity: Catherine Laulhere-Vigneau
Chief of Manufacturing: Julie Rouart
Authors: Michel Boujut; Frederic Mitterand; Isabel Munoz
Founded: 1989
Subjects: Drama, Theater, Fashion, Film, Video, Music, Dance, Photography
ISBN Prefix(es): 2-84110; 2-908034
Orders to: Harmonia Mundi, Petite Route de Saint Gilles, Mas de Vert, 13200 Arles

Poches Odile Jacob, *imprint of* Editions Odile Jacob

POF, see Publications Orientalistes de France (POF)

Point Hors Ligne
28, rue Barbet de Jouy, 75007 Paris
Tel: (01) 43544964 *Fax:* (01) 43253032
Subjects: Psychology, Psychiatry
ISBN Prefix(es): 2-904821

Editions du Point Veterinaire+
9, rue Alexandre, 94702 Maisons-Alfort cedex
Tel: (01) 45 17 02 25 *Fax:* (01) 42 07 93 88
Web Site: www.pointveterinaire.com
Key Personnel
President: Patrick Join-Lambert
International Rights: Christine Graffard-Lenormand
Subjects: Animals, Pets, Veterinary Science
ISBN Prefix(es): 2-86326

POL Editeur+
33, rue Saint-Andre-des-Arts, 75006 Paris
Tel: (01) 43 54 21 20 *Fax:* (01) 43 54 11 31
Web Site: www.pol-editeur.fr
Key Personnel
President: Paul Otchakovsky-Laurens
Founded: 1983
Subjects: Drama, Theater, Fiction, Literature, Literary Criticism, Essays, Poetry
ISBN Prefix(es): 2-86744
Foreign Rep(s): Gallimard/La Caravelle (Belgium); Gallimard Limitee (Canada); Gallimard/Office du Livre (Switzerland); SODIS (France)
Orders to: Sodis, BP 142, 77403 Lagny sur Maine Cedex

Polytechnica+
15, rue Lacepede, 75005 Paris
Tel: (01) 47074079 *Fax:* (01) 45350619
Key Personnel
President: Daniel Loizeau
Promotion & International Rights: Isabelle Doal
Founded: 1992
Subjects: Agriculture, Biological Sciences, Chemistry, Chemical Engineering, Electronics, Electrical Engineering, Energy, Engineering (General), Health, Nutrition, Mechanical Engineering, Physical Sciences, Physics, Science (General), Technology
ISBN Prefix(es): 2-84054
Distributor for AIA; CIIA; INA

Editions du Centre Pompidou+
75191 Paris Cedex 04
Tel: (01) 44 78 12 33 *Fax:* (01) 44 78 12 05
Web Site: www.centrepompidou.fr
Key Personnel
President: Jean-Jacques Aillagon
Head of Publications & Sales: Martin Bethenod
Deputy Manager: Philippe Bidaine
Sales Manager & Foreign Rights: Benoit Collier
Founded: 1977
Subjects: Architecture & Interior Design, Art, Film, Video, Gay & Lesbian
ISBN Prefix(es): 2-85850; 2-84426
Distributed by Art Data (Great Britain); Flammarion (Canada); Flammarion Export (Greece, Turkey, Syria); Idea Books (Holland); Union Distribution (France, Belgium & Switzerland); Yohan (Japan)
Distributor for BPI
Foreign Rep(s): Richard Bowen (Denmark, Finland, Norway, Sweden); Phillip Galgiani (US)
Orders to: Service Commercial, 75191 Paris Cedex 04

Editions Pradel, see Masson-Williams et Wilkins

Pratique Sante, *imprint of* Editions Trois Fontaines

Presence Africaine Editions+
25 bis, rue des Ecoles, 75005 Paris
Tel: (01) 43 54 13 74; (01) 43 54 15 88 *Fax:* (01) 43 25 96 67
Web Site: www.letissue.com
Telex: 200891 F *Cable:* PRESAFRIC PARIS
Key Personnel
Director: Mrs Alioune Diop
Publicity, Rights & Permissions: Simone Howlett
Press Relations: R J Agonse
Manufacturing: W Alliot
Founded: 1947
Subjects: Fiction, History, Philosophy, Poetry, Religion - Other
ISBN Prefix(es): 2-7087
Distributed by Hurtubise (Canada); Nord-Sud (Benelux); Zoe (Switzerland)

Editions Presse Audiovisuel, see EPA SA (Editions Presse Audiovisuel)

Presse et Formation, *imprint of* Les Editions du CFPJ (Centre de Formation et de Perfectionnement des Journalistes) - Sarl Presse et Formation

Presses, *imprint of* Presses de la Cite

Presses de la Cite+
Imprint of Belfond
12 Ave d'Italie, 75627 Paris Cedex 13
Tel: (01) 44160500 *Fax:* (01) 44160505
Web Site: www.pressesdelacite.com
Telex: preci 204 807 f *Cable:* SVENNIL PARIS
Key Personnel
Man Dir: Georges Leser
General Dir: Pierre Dutilleul
Founded: 1947
Subjects: Biography, Fiction, History, Mysteries, Nonfiction (General), Romance, Science Fiction, Fantasy, Family Saga, Horror, Humor, Mystery & Detective, Thriller
ISBN Prefix(es): 2-258
Total Titles: 300 Print
Online services available through BOL.
Parent Company: Havas
Ultimate Parent Company: Vivendi
Imprints: Presses; Solar

Presses de la Renaissance+
Subsidiary of Havas
12, Ave de Italie, 75627 Paris Cedex 13
Tel: (01) 44 16 05 86 *Fax:* (01) 44 16 05 13
Web Site: www.presses-renaissance.com
Key Personnel
Man Dir: Pierre Dutilleul
Literary Manager: Alain Noel *Tel:* (01) 44 16 05 96 *E-mail:* alainoel@aol.com
Rights Manager: Delphina Ribouchon *Tel:* (01) 44 08 84 35 *Fax:* (01) 44 08 84 05
Founded: 1997
Subjects: Biography, Philosophy, Spirituality, Novels, Documents & Testimonials
ISBN Prefix(es): 2-85616
Total Titles: 40 Print
Ultimate Parent Company: Vivendi

PUBLISHERS — FRANCE

Presses de la Sorbonne Nouvelle/PSN
Universite Paris III, 13, rue Santeuil, 75231 Paris Cedex 05
Tel: (01) 45874027; (01) 45874168 *Fax:* (01) 45877854; (01) 45874175
E-mail: n.carbon@univ-paris3.fr
Web Site: www.univ-paris3.fr/p.sn
Key Personnel
General Dir: Pierre Vilar
Founded: 1982
Subjects: Drama, Theater, History, Language Arts, Linguistics, Literature, Literary Criticism, Essays
ISBN Prefix(es): 2-87854
Number of titles published annually: 20 Print
Total Titles: 20 Print
Distributor for Cid (France)
Bookshop(s): CID, 131 Blvd St Michel, 75005 Paris, Michel Zumkir *Tel:* (01) 43544745 *Fax:* (01) 43548073 *E-mail:* cid@msh-paris.fr

Presses de l'Ecole Nationale des Ponts et Chaussees+
Unit of Ponts Formation Edition SA
28, rue des Saints-Peres, 75343 Paris Cedex 07
Tel: (01) 44582740 *Fax:* (01) 44582744
Web Site: www.enpc.fr
Key Personnel
Dir: Guy Coronio *Tel:* (01) 44582460
   E-mail: coronio@enpc.fr
Assistant Dir: Dominique Ogier *Tel:* (01) 44582742 *E-mail:* ogier@mail.enpc.fr
Founded: 1977
Specialize in scientific, technical and professional subjects.
Member of Syndicat National de l'Edition.
Subjects: Civil Engineering, Computer Science, Earth Sciences, Real Estate, Transportation
ISBN Prefix(es): 2-85978
Total Titles: 200 Print; 2 CD-ROM
Distributed by Geodif

Les Presses de Taize, *imprint of* Ateliers et Presses de Taize

Les Presses d'Ile-de-France Sarl+
54 Ave Jean-Jaures, 75940 Paris Cedex 19
Tel: (01) 44 52 37 37 *Fax:* (01) 42 38 09 87
E-mail: scouts@scouts-france.fr
Web Site: www.scouts-france.fr
Key Personnel
Man Dir: Pierre Tremeau
Manager: Bernard Le Roux
Founded: 1929
Subjects: Crafts, Games, Hobbies, Music, Dance, Outdoor Recreation, Religion - Catholic
ISBN Prefix(es): 2-7088

Les Presses du Management+
103, Blvd Murat, 75016 Paris
Tel: (01) 40 71 11 11 *Fax:* (01) 46 51 45 35
Key Personnel
Contact: Jacques Descubes Marie
Founded: 1989
Subjects: Business, Career Development, Economics, How-to, Management, Marketing, Psychology, Psychiatry, Self-Help
ISBN Prefix(es): 2-87845
Parent Company: Editions Michel Lafon
Imprints: Guide Pratique; Turbo
Orders to: 7, rue de Malte, 75011 Paris

Presses-Pocket, see Presses de la Cite

Presses Universitaires de Caen
14032 Caen Cedex
Tel: (02) 31 56 62 20 *Fax:* (02) 31 56 62 25
Web Site: www.unicaen.fr
Key Personnel
Dir, University Press: Michel Zuinghedau
Founded: 1984
Subjects: Accounting, Antiques, Biological Sciences, Geography, Geology, History, Language Arts, Linguistics, Literature, Literary Criticism, Essays, Philosophy, Social Sciences, Sociology
ISBN Prefix(es): 2-84133; 2-904461

Presses Universitaires de France (PUF)+
6, Ave Reille, 75685 Paris Cedex 14
Tel: (01) 58 10 31 00 *Fax:* (01) 58 10 31 82
E-mail: puf.com@puf.com
Web Site: www.puf.com
Key Personnel
President & Director General: Michel Prigent *Tel:* (01) 53 10 00 07 *Fax:* (01) 53 10 41 79
Dir: Eric Amaudry *Tel:* (01) 43 26 7741 *Fax:* (01) 46 33 21 94; Bruno Clerc *Tel:* (01) 44 41 17 20 *Fax:* (01) 46 33 61 21
Sales Dir: Jean-Pierre Giband *Tel:* (01) 60 87 30 00 *Fax:* (01) 60 79 20 45
Technical Dir: Bruno Clerc
Dir of Development: Dominique Morel *Tel:* (01) 55 02 20 61
Publicity, Advertising: Alain Papillaud *Tel:* (01) 44 41 39 39 *Fax:* (01) 43 54 78 87
Foreign Rights: Marion Colns *E-mail:* colas@puf.com
Press: Dominique Reymond *Tel:* (01) 58 10 31 80
Editorial: Jean-Christophe Brochier
Founded: 1921
Administration & Editorial offices are located at the above main address; Public Relations & Publicity departments are at 90 Blvd St-Germain, 75005 Paris.
Subjects: Art, Biography, Engineering (General), Geography, Geology, Government, Political Science, History, Human Relations, Law, Medicine, Nursing, Dentistry, Music, Dance, Philosophy, Psychology, Psychiatry, Religion - Other, Social Sciences, Sociology
ISBN Prefix(es): 2-13
Bookshop(s): Librairie generale des PUF, 49, Blvd Saint Michel, 75005 Paris, Dominique Morel *Tel:* (01) 44 41 81 20 *Fax:* (01) 43 54 64 81 (Under Major Booksellers); La Pochotheque, 17 rue Soufflot, F-75005 Paris *Tel:* (01) 43267741 *Fax:* (01) 46332196
Orders to: 14 Ave du Bois de l'Epine, BP 90, 91003 Evry Cedex, Jean-Pierre Giband *Tel:* (01) 60 87 30 00 *Fax:* (01) 60 79 20 45

Presses Universitaires de Grenoble+
1041, rue de Residences, 38040 Grenoble Cedex 9
Mailing Address: BP 47, 38040 Grenoble Cedex 09
Tel: (04) 76 82 56 51; (04) 76 82 56 52 *Fax:* (04) 76 82 78 35
E-mail: pug@pug.fr
Web Site: www.pug.fr
Telex: Unisog 980910
Key Personnel
General Manager: Bernard Wirbel
   E-mail: bernard.wirbel@pug.fr
Editorial Manager: Rene Bourgeois
   Fax: rene.bourgeois@pug.fr
Finance Manager: Corine Desbenoit
   E-mail: corine.desbenoit@pug.fr
Sales Manager: Barbara Muller *E-mail:* barbara.muller@pug.fr
Manufacturing: Muriel Girard *E-mail:* muriel.girard@pug.fr
Founded: 1972
Subjects: Accounting, Chemistry, Chemical Engineering, Communications, Economics, History, Language Arts, Law, Literature, Literary Criticism, Essays, Management, Marketing, Mathematics, Psychology, Psychiatry, Social Sciences, Sociology, Sports, Athletics, Economics, Europe, French Language, Political Science
ISBN Prefix(es): 2-7061
Number of titles published annually: 45 Print
Total Titles: 1,000 Print
Imprints: PUG
Orders to: Sofedis, 11 rue Soufflot, 75005 Paris
Tel: 01 53102526

Presses Universitaires de Lyon+
Member of Syndicat National de l"Edition
86, Blvd de la Croix Rousse, 69242 Lyon Cedex 07
Tel: (04) 78 29 39 39 *Fax:* (04) 78 29 39 41
Web Site: www.univ-lyon2.fr
Key Personnel
Man Dir: Andre Pelletier
Founded: 1976
Subjects: Economics, Government, Political Science, History, Human Relations, Language Arts, Linguistics, Law, Literature, Literary Criticism, Essays, Management
ISBN Prefix(es): 2-7297
Distributor for Editions W a Macon; Editions Lyonnaises d'Art et d'Histoire a'Lyon

Presses Universitaires de Nancy+
42-44 Ave de la Liberation, 54014 Nancy Cedex
Mailing Address: BP 3347, 54014 Nancy, Cedex
Tel: (016) 83 96 84 30 *Fax:* (016) 83 96 84 39
Web Site: www.univ-nancy2.fr
Key Personnel
Chairman: Jean-Marie Bonnet
Man Dir: Alain Trognon
General Manager: Jeanne Weill
Editorial Manager: Daniele Silvy-Leligois
Sales: Sophie Izorche
Publicity, Rights & Permissions: Daniele Silvy-Leligois
Founded: 1976
Subjects: Communications, Drama, Theater, Economics, Education, Geography, Geology, Government, Political Science, History, Language Arts, Linguistics, Law, Literature, Literary Criticism, Essays, Philosophy, Psychology, Psychiatry, Religion - Other, Social Sciences, Sociology
ISBN Prefix(es): 2-86480
Associate Companies: Editions Serpenoise, BP 89, F-57140 Metz-Woippy
Imprints: Annales de l'Est; Editions Humblot; Le Parvis des Arts
Warehouse: Sodis-128, ave de Lattre de Tassigny, 77400 Lagny-Sur-Marne
Orders to: Sofedis, 29 rue Saint-Sulpice, 75006 Paris

Presses Universitaires de Strasbourg
Palais Universitaire, 9, place de l'Universite, 67084 Strasbourg Cedex
Tel: (03) 88 25 97 21 *Fax:* (03) 88 35 65 23
Web Site: www.pu-strasbourg.com
Key Personnel
President: Lucien Braun
Founded: 1920
Subjects: Art, History, Literature, Literary Criticism, Essays, Philosophy, Social Sciences, Sociology
ISBN Prefix(es): 2-86820

Presses Universitaires du Septentrion+
Rue du Barreau, 59650 Villeneuve d'Asq, Cedex
Tel: (03) 20 41 66 80 *Fax:* (03) 20 41 66 90
E-mail: septentrion@septentrion.com
Web Site: www.sepentrion.com
Key Personnel
Editorial & Production: Jerome Vaillant
Sales, Publicity, Rights & Permissions: Jean-Gabriel Caby
Founded: 1971
Subjects: History, Language Arts, Linguistics, Law, Literature, Literary Criticism, Essays, Philosophy, Psychology, Psychiatry, Social Sciences, Sociology
ISBN Prefix(es): 2-284; 2-85939; 2-86531; 2-907170

Privat-Garnier, *imprint of* Dunod Editeur

PRODIG UMR 8586 CNRS-Paris 1,4,7 ephe+
191, rue St-Jacques, 75005 Paris
Tel: (01) 44 32 14 81; (01) 42 34 56 21 *Fax:* (01) 43 29 63 83
E-mail: prodig@univ-paris1.fr
Web Site: www.univ-paris1.fr/PRODIG
Key Personnel
Dir: Marie-Francoise Courel *Tel:* (01) 42 34 56 24 *E-mail:* courel@univ-paris1.fr
Contact: Beatrice Velard *E-mail:* bvelard@univ-paris1.fr
Founded: 1947
Subjects: Geography, Geology, Library & Information Sciences
ISBN Prefix(es): 2-901560
Parent Company: Centre national de la recherche scientifique (CNRS)
Associate Companies: Universite de Paris One; Universite de Paris Four; Universite de Paris Seven

Propos de Campagne+
Allee de Provence, 04100 Manosque
Tel: (04) 92 77 03 51 *Fax:* (04) 92 73 08 94
E-mail: ProposdeC@aol.com
Web Site: www.lisez.com/propos/contact.html
Key Personnel
Publications Dir: Michel Foissier
Founded: 1993
Revue d art et de Poesie.
Subjects: Art, Poetry

Editions Prosveta SA
BP 12, 83601 Frejus Cedex
Tel: (04) 94408241 *Fax:* (04) 94408005
E-mail: international@prosvesta.com
Web Site: www.prosveta.com
Telex: 970809F
Key Personnel
President: Marcel Cieutat
Author: Mikhael Aivanhov
Founded: 1976
Subjects: Education, Philosophy, Religion - Other
ISBN Prefix(es): 2-85566
U.S. Office(s): Prosveta USA, PO Box 49614, Los Angeles, CA 90049, United States

PSI, *imprint of* Dunod Editeur

PUB, see Presses Universitaires de Bordeaux (PUB)

Publi-Fusion+
Village Artisanal de Regourd, 46000 Cahors
Tel: (05) 65220303 *Fax:* (05) 65220322
Key Personnel
Contact: Jean-Claude Delmas
Founded: 1987
Subjects: Automotive, Literature, Literary Criticism, Essays
ISBN Prefix(es): 2-907265

Publi Union, *imprint of* Editions Village Mondial

Editions Publications de l'Ecole Moderne Francaise sa (PEMF)+
06370 Mouans Sartoux, Cedex
Tel: (04) 92921757 *Fax:* (04) 92921804
Key Personnel
Man Dir & Editorial: Robert Poitrenaud
Man Dir: Norbert Jouve
Founded: 1986
ISBN Prefix(es): 2-87785; 2-84526

Publications de l'Universite de Rouen
One, rue Lavoisier, 76821 Mont-Saint-Aignan Cedex
Tel: (02) 35 14 63 43 *Fax:* (02) 35 14 65 38

Key Personnel
Man Dir: Henry Decaens
Communications: Patricia Lanoe
Founded: 1968
Subjects: Geography, Geology, History, Law, Literature, Literary Criticism, Essays, Psychology, Psychiatry
ISBN Prefix(es): 2-87775
Orders to: CID, 131 Blvd St-Michel, 75005 Paris

Publications Orientalistes de France (POF)+
14, Ave du Garric, 15000 Aurillac
Tel: (04) 71 43 23 78 *Fax:* (04) 71 43 23 78
E-mail: sieffert@pofjapon.com
Web Site: www.pofjapon.com
Key Personnel
Dir: Simone Sieffert
Founded: 1973
Subjects: Drama, Theater, History, Language Arts, Linguistics, Literature, Literary Criticism, Essays, Music, Dance, Poetry, Social Sciences, Sociology
ISBN Prefix(es): 2-7169
Orders to: Distique, 5, rue du Mal Leclerc, 28600 Luisant

Publisud+
15 rue des Cinq-Diamants, 75013 Paris
Tel: (01) 45 80 78 50 *Fax:* (01) 45 89 94 15
Key Personnel
Managing Editor: Marybel Boix
Founded: 1980
ISBN Prefix(es): 2-86600

PUF, see Presses Universitaires de France (PUF)

PUG, *imprint of* Presses Universitaires de Grenoble

Editions du Puits Fleuri+
22 Ave de Fontainebleau, 77850 Hericy
Tel: (01) 64 23 61 46 *Fax:* (01) 64 23 69 42
Key Personnel
Literary Dir: Emile Guchet
Founded: 1981
Subjects: How-to, Law
ISBN Prefix(es): 2-86739
Imprints: Le Conseiller Juridique Pour Tous
Showroom(s): Amphora, 14 rue de l'Odeon, 75006 Paris

PUM Toulouse, *imprint of* Presses Universitaires du Mirail

PUS, see Presses Universitaires du Septentrion

PYC Edition+
16-18 Place de la Chapelle, 75018 Paris
Tel: (01) 53 26 48 00 *Fax:* (01) 53 26 48 01
E-mail: info@pyc.fr
Web Site: www.pyc.fr
Key Personnel
Man Dir: Pierre Benichou
Founded: 1934
Subjects: Energy, Mechanical Engineering
ISBN Prefix(es): 2-85330; 2-911008

Editions Pygmalion - Gerard Watelet+
70 Ave de Breteuil, 75007 Paris
Tel: (01) 45674077 *Fax:* (01) 47345152
E-mail: Pygmalio@easynet.fr
Key Personnel
Man Dir, Editorial: Gerard Watelet
Sales, Rights & Permissions: Sylvie Goguel
Founded: 1974
Subjects: Archaeology, Art, Biography, Fiction, History, Literature, Literary Criticism, Essays, Parapsychology
ISBN Prefix(es): 2-85704

Total Titles: 500 Print
Warehouse: Union Distribution, 106 rue Petit Leroy, Cherilly-La rue, 94152 Rungis Cedex

Quillet, *imprint of* Le Livre de Paris

Radio, *imprint of* Dunod Editeur

Rageot Editeur, *imprint of* Editions Hatier SA

Rageot Editeur+
6, rue Cassette, 75006 Paris
Tel: (01) 45 48 07 31 *Fax:* (01) 42 22 68 01
Key Personnel
Man Dir: Caroline Westberg
Founded: 1941
ISBN Prefix(es): 2-7002
Orders to: Librairie Hatier SA, 8 rue d'Assas, F-75006 Paris

Editions Ramsay
60, rue Saint Andres des Arts, 75006 Paris
Tel: (01) 53 10 02 80 *Fax:* (01) 53 10 02 88
Key Personnel
Man Dir: Jean-Claude Gawsewitch
Rights & Permissions: Zeline Guena
Founded: 1976
Subjects: Drama, Theater, Fiction, History, Literature, Literary Criticism, Essays, Nonfiction (General)
ISBN Prefix(es): 2-84114

Realisations pour l'Enseignement Multilingue International (REMI)
70, rue du Theatre, 75015 Paris
Tel: (01) 44 37 00 80 *Fax:* (01) 45 79 06 66
Key Personnel
Man Dir: Mrs D Holtzer
Founded: 1966
ISBN Prefix(es): 2-85134

Recta Foldex, see Blay-Foldex

Refclim, *imprint of* Sedit

References cf
F-26340 Saint Nazaire le Desert
Tel: (04) 75-27-52-59 *Fax:* (04) 75275259
E-mail: refercf@incident.net
Web Site: www.incident.net/refercf
Key Personnel
Publisher: Bernard Dermineur
Founded: 1984
Subjects: Art, Genealogy, History, Library & Information Sciences, Publishing & Book Trade Reference
ISBN Prefix(es): 2-908302
Total Titles: 20 Print; 3 CD-ROM; 2 E-Book
Imprints: CF
Bookshop(s): Librairie la Stravaganza, 32 rue Traversiere, 75012 Paris *Tel:* (01) 43458083 *Fax:* (01) 43455096

REMI, see Realisations pour l'Enseignement Multilingue International (REMI)

Les Editions Albert Rene+
26, Ave Victor Hugo, 75116 Paris
Tel: (01) 45 00 41 41 *Fax:* (01) 40 67 95 12
E-mail: rene.cominfo@editions-albert-rene.com
Web Site: www.editions-albert-rene.com
Telex: 613160 F
Key Personnel
Dir: Sylvie Uderz
Founded: 1979
Subjects: Humor
ISBN Prefix(es): 2-86497
Distributed by Hachette
Orders to: Les Presses de la Cite, 8 rue Garanciere, F-75006 Paris

PUBLISHERS — FRANCE

Editions Revue EPS+
11, Ave of Tremblay, 75012 Paris
Tel: (01) 41 74 82 82 *Fax:* (01) 43 98 37 38
E-mail: revue@revue-eps.com
Web Site: www.revue-eps.com
Key Personnel
President: Jean Eisenbeis
Subjects: Education, Sports, Athletics
ISBN Prefix(es): 2-86713

Revue Espaces et Societes+
Université de Toulouse-Le-Mirail, 5, allee A Machado, 31058 Toulouse Cedex
Tel: (0551) 60 35 70 *Fax:* (0551) 60 49 58
E-mail: jjaquin@espacesetsocietes.com
Web Site: www.espacesetsocietes.com
Key Personnel
Dir: Jean Remy
Head Writer: Maurice White
Editorial: Joelle Jacquin
Founded: 1968
2 or 3 installments/year in 16 x 24 cm format (about 600 pages/year).
Subjects: Anthropology, Environmental Studies, Social Sciences, Sociology
ISBN Prefix(es): 2-7384
Imprints: L'Harmattan Paris
Distributed by L' Harmattan

Revue Noire
8 rue Cels, 75014 Paris
Tel: (01) 43 20 92 00 *Fax:* (01) 43 22 92 60
E-mail: redaction@revuenoire.com
Web Site: www.revuenoire.com
Key Personnel
President: Michelle Rakotoson
Dir of Publications & Editor: Jeau Loup Pivin *Tel:* (01) 43 20 78 38
Editor: Simon Njami *Tel:* (01) 43 20 79 56
Distribution & Web Dir: N'Gone Fall *Tel:* (01) 43 20 82 34
Art Dir: Pascal Martin St Leon *Tel:* (01) 43 20 83 02
Editor Member: Bruno Tilliette
Administration Dir: Gwendal Vaillant *Tel:* (01) 43 20 80 07 *E-mail:* order@revuenoire.com
Founded: 1991
Subjects: African American Studies, Architecture & Interior Design, Art, Fashion, Literature, Literary Criticism, Essays, Music, Dance, Photography, Poetry
ISBN Prefix(es): 2-909571
Parent Company: Revue Noire Sarl
Distributed by Editions Hazan Distribution (France, Belgium, Switzerland, Canada)
Distributor for DAP

Rivages, see Editions Payot & Rivages

Yves Riviere Editeur+
117 rue Vieille-du-Temple, 75003 Paris
Tel: (01) 42747784 *Fax:* (01) 42781265
E-mail: yvesrivi@mail.club.internet.fr
Founded: 1971
Specialize in catalogues & reference books, art posters & prints signed & numbered.
Subjects: Art
ISBN Prefix(es): 2-85666
Total Titles: 75 Print

Editions Robert Laffont, Nil, Fixot, Seghers, Julliard+
Division of Havas
24 Ave Marceau, 75008 Paris Cedex 08
Tel: (01) 53671400 *Fax:* (01) 53671414
Web Site: www.laffont.fr
Key Personnel
President: Leonello Brandolini
Vice President: Nicole Lattes
Acquisitions Dir: Maggie Doyle
Foreign Rights Dir: Benita Edzard
Contract Manager: Olga Begin
Foreign Rights: Dorothie Cureo; Gwenael Gouiffes; Beatrix Vernet
Foreign Rights, Eastern Europe: Renata de la Chapelle
Founded: 1941
Subjects: Fiction, Literature, Literary Criticism, Essays, Nonfiction (General), Philosophy, Poetry, Psychology, Psychiatry, Science (General), Science Fiction, Fantasy, Self-Help, Social Sciences, Sociology
ISBN Prefix(es): 2-221
Ultimate Parent Company: Vivendi
Associate Companies: Fixot, Seghers, Julliard, NIL

Editions Rombaldi SA
58 rue Jean-Bleuzen, 92178 Vanves Cedex
Tel: (01) 41236500 *Fax:* (01) 46453442
Telex: rombald 641253 F
Key Personnel
President: Etienne Vendroux
Commercial Dir & Production Manager: Henri Kaufman
Commercial Dir: Francis Petit
Founded: 1920
Subjects: Cookery, Crafts, Games, Hobbies, Humor
ISBN Prefix(es): 2-231

Guide Rosenwald
10 rue Vineuse, 75784 Paris Cedex 16
Tel: (01) 44 30 81 00 *Fax:* (01) 44 30 81 11
E-mail: rosenwald@wanadoo.fr
Web Site: www.rosenwald.com
Key Personnel
Editor: Afif Ben Yedder *E-mail:* benyedder@wanadoo.fr
Founded: 1887
Subjects: Health, Nutrition, How-to, Medicine, Nursing, Dentistry
ISBN Prefix(es): 2-907749
Parent Company: 1 C Publications

Editions Roudil
53 rue Saint Jacques, 75005 Paris
Tel: 01 43544797
Key Personnel
Man Dir: Henry Roudil
Founded: 1954
Subjects: Fiction, History, Philosophy
ISBN Prefix(es): 2-85044

Editions du Rouergue+
Parc Saint-Joseph, BP 3522, 12035 Rodez Cedex 9
Tel: (05) 65.77.73.70 *Fax:* (05) 65.77.73.71
E-mail: info@lerouergue.com
Web Site: www.lerouergue.com
Key Personnel
Contact: Danielle Dastugue; Anne Marcy
Founded: 1986
Subjects: Cookery, Fiction, Gardening, Plants, Health, Nutrition, How-to, Romance, Wine & Spirits
ISBN Prefix(es): 2-84156; 2-905209

Les Editions du Sagittaire
61 rue des Saints-Peres, 75006 Paris
Tel: (01) 44392200 *Fax:* (01) 42226418
Key Personnel
Dir: Jean-Claude Fasquelle
Founded: 1929
Subjects: Biography, Fiction, History, Literature, Literary Criticism, Essays
ISBN Prefix(es): 2-7275

Editions Saint-Germain-des-Pres SA+
23 rue Racine, 75006 Paris
Tel: (01) 43269724 *Fax:* (01) 43269724
Key Personnel
Editorial: Jean Breton
Publicity: Philippe Heracles
Founded: 1969
Subjects: Poetry
ISBN Prefix(es): 2-243; 2-84328

Editions Saint-Michel SA+
Fougerolles, La Reserve de Gamillon Saint-Michel-de-Boulogne, 07200 Saint-Michel-de-Boulogne
Tel: (04) 7587-1050 *Fax:* (04) 7587-1061
Key Personnel
Contact: Guy Dupuis
Subjects: Astrology, Occult, Behavioral Sciences, Medicine, Nursing, Dentistry, Parapsychology
ISBN Prefix(es): 2-902450

Editions Saint-Paul SA+
3 rue de la Porte-de-Buc, 78006 Versailles Cedex
Tel: (01) 39 67 16 00 *Fax:* (01) 30 21 41 95
Key Personnel
Man Dir: M Lerozier
Dir of Religous Edition: M Larive
Founded: 1879
Subjects: Philosophy, Religion - Other, Theology
ISBN Prefix(es): 2-85049
Total Titles: 150 Print
Subsidiaries: Editions Saint-Paul SA
Distributed by CERF

Editions Salvator Sarl+
103 rue Notre-Dame-des-Champs, 75006 Paris
Tel: (01) 53 10 38 38 *Fax:* (01) 53 10 38 39
Founded: 1924
Subjects: Human Relations, Religion - Other
ISBN Prefix(es): 2-7067

Salvy Editeur+
33 rue Saint Andre des Arts, 75006 Paris
Tel: (01) 43257440 *Fax:* (01) 46335621
Key Personnel
President: Gerard-Julien Salvy
Founded: 1989
Subjects: Literature, Literary Criticism, Essays
ISBN Prefix(es): 2-905899

Editions Sand et Tchou SA
6 rue Mail, 75002 Paris
Tel: (01) 44.55.37.50 *Fax:* (01) 40.20.99.74
Key Personnel
Man Dir: Carl van Eiszner
Rights & Permissions: Agnes de Gorter
Founded: 1979
Subjects: Astrology, Occult, Biography, Fiction, Health, Nutrition, How-to, Music, Dance, Psychology, Psychiatry, Social Sciences, Sociology
ISBN Prefix(es): 2-7107
Subsidiaries: Editions Menges

Editions Sang de la Terre+
62 rue Blanche, 75009 Paris
Tel: (01) 42 82 08 16 *Fax:* (01) 48 74 14 88
E-mail: editeur@sangdelaterre.com
Web Site: www.sangdelaterre.com
Key Personnel
Publications Dir: Dominique Bigourdan
Editor: Karine Reysset
Founded: 1986
Subjects: Agriculture, Animals, Pets, Cookery, Crafts, Games, Hobbies, Environmental Studies, Gardening, Plants, Health, Nutrition, How-to
ISBN Prefix(es): 2-86985
Imprints: Bornemann
Subsidiaries: 670 Bornemann

Sante Spiritualite, *imprint of* Editions Trois Fontaines

FRANCE BOOK

Editions Le Sarment+
75 rue des Saints-Peres, 75006 Paris
Tel: (01) 45.49.82.00 *Fax:* (01) 45.48.82.36
E-mail: cremond@editions-fayard.fr
Key Personnel
Man Dir: Jean-Claude Didelot
Assistant Editor: Odile Level
Responsable Commercial: Christophe Remond
    E-mail: cremond@editions-fayard.fr
Founded: 1980
Subjects: Religion - Catholic
ISBN Prefix(es): 2-86679
Number of titles published annually: 30 Print
Parent Company: Librairie Artheme Fayard

Sauramps Medical+
11 blvd Henri IV, 34000 Montpellier
Tel: (04) 67636880 *Fax:* (04) 67525905
E-mail: sauramps.medical@livres-medicaux.com
Web Site: www.livres-medicaux.com
Key Personnel
Man Dir: Dominique Torreilles
Founded: 1985
Subjects: Medicine, Nursing, Dentistry, Gynecology-Obstetrics, Orthopaedic Surgery, Radiology
ISBN Prefix(es): 2-905030; 2-84023
Number of titles published annually: 35 Print
Total Titles: 500 Print
Distributed by Lidel (Portugal); SODIS (France); Somabec (Canada); Vivendi (Belgium)
Bookshop(s): Librairie Sauramps Medical (under Major Booksellers); 30, rue Godefroy Cavaignac, 75011 Paris, George Lauret *Tel:* (01) 40092771 *Fax:* (01) 40038071

Editions Scala+
26 rue de Charonne Passage Lhomme, 75011 Paris
Tel: (01) 49 29 42 25 *Fax:* (01) 49 29 99 33
E-mail: editions.scala@wanadoo.fr
Web Site: www.ldj.tm.fr/editeurs/editeurs/scala.htm
Key Personnel
Contact: Chantal Desmazieres
Founded: 1980
Subjects: Antiques, Art
ISBN Prefix(es): 2-86656
Total Titles: 110 Print

Editions du Scarabee
3 rue de la Montagne-Ste-Genevieve, 75005 Paris
Tel: (01) 43 26 23 94 *Fax:* (01) 43 26 23 94
Key Personnel
Man Dir, Editorial, Production, Publicity, Rights & Permissions: Jacqueline Copfermann
Sales: Nelly Bourgeois
Founded: 1982
Subjects: Education, Physical Sciences, Psychology, Psychiatry
ISBN Prefix(es): 2-7145
Bookshop(s): Librairie du Scarabee
Book Club(s): Amis du Scarabee

Editions Scientifiques et Medicales Elsevier
2, rue Linois, 75724 Paris Cedex 15
Tel: (01) 45589110 *Fax:* (01) 45589425
Web Site: www.elsevier.fr
Key Personnel
President Dir-General: Catherine Lucet
Finance Dir: Patrick Regnier
Founded: 1984
Subjects: Mathematics, Medicine, Nursing, Dentistry, Physics
ISBN Prefix(es): 2-84299

Sedit
Domaine de Saint-Paul BP 66, 78470 Saint-Remy-les-Chevreuse
Tel: (01) 30852010 *Fax:* (01) 30852038
E-mail: costic-sr@costic.asso.fr
Web Site: www.costic.asso.fr
Key Personnel
Contact: Armel Jegou; C Lheraud
ISBN Prefix(es): 2-236
Imprints: Refclim; Climapoche

Seghers
Imprint of Editions Robert Laffont
24 rue ave Marceau, 75008 Paris Cedex 08
Tel: (01) 53.67.14.00 *Fax:* (01) 53.67.14.14
Key Personnel
President & Man Dir: Leonello Brandolini
Literary Manager: Alain Beiastein
Rights & Permissions: Beatrix Vernet *Tel:* (01) 53671489 *E-mail:* bvernet@robert.laffont.fr
Founded: 1944
Subjects: Poetry
ISBN Prefix(es): 2-232
Associate Companies: Editions Robert Laffont
Orders to: Inter Forum, 46 route de Sermaires, BP 11, 45337 Nalesherbes Cedex *Tel:* (02) 38327100

Nouvelles Editions Seguier+
3 rue Seguier, 75005 Paris
Tel: (01) 55 42 61 40 *Fax:* (01) 55 42 61 41
Web Site: php.atlantica.fr
Key Personnel
Literary Dir: Jean-Paul Morel
Founded: 1992
Subjects: Art, Biography, Fiction, Literature, Literary Criticism, Essays
ISBN Prefix(es): 2-84049

Selection du Reader's Digest SA
212 blvd Saint Germain, 75007 Paris
Mailing Address: BP 101, 92225 Bagneux Cedex
Tel: (01) 45480426 *Fax:* (01) 46748582
Cable: Readigest Paris
Key Personnel
Man Dir: Henri Capdeville
Marketing Dir: Daniele Franck
Editorial: Denise Freidin
Publicity: Daniel Hubert
Founded: 1947
Subjects: Architecture & Interior Design, Art, Economics, Environmental Studies, Fiction, History, How-to, Medicine, Nursing, Dentistry, Science (General), Social Sciences, Sociology, Technology, Travel
ISBN Prefix(es): 2-7098
Branch Office(s)
1-7 av Louis-Pasteur, 92200 Bagneux *Tel:* (01) 46748484 *Fax:* (01) 46748582

Editions Selection J Jacobs SA+
66 rue Falguiere, 75015 Paris
Subjects: Art, How-to, Technology
ISBN Prefix(es): 2-7174

Maren Sell+
3 rue Auber, 75009 Paris
Tel: (01) 47423833 *Fax:* (01) 47427781
Web Site: www.editions-calmann-levy.com
Founded: 1987
Subjects: Fiction, History, Literature, Literary Criticism, Essays, Nonfiction (General), Philosophy, Psychology, Psychiatry, Religion - Other, Science (General), Social Sciences, Sociology, Theology
ISBN Prefix(es): 2-87604
Orders to: SODIS, 128 ave du Marechal-de-Laftie de Tassiguy, BP 142, 77400 Laguy

Le Seneve, *imprint of* Pierre Zech Editeur

Editions du Seneve+
18 rue de Conde, 75006 Paris
Tel: (01) 44 32 05 60 *Fax:* (01) 44 32 05 61
Telex: ELITA 283155 F
Key Personnel
Dir: M Pierre Zech
Subjects: Education, Religion - Catholic, Theology
ISBN Prefix(es): 2-283
Parent Company: Pierre Zech Editeur

Sepia
6 Ave du Gouverneur General Binger, 94100 Saint-Maur
Tel: (01) 43 97 22 14 *Fax:* (01) 43 97 32 62
E-mail: sepia@club-internet.fr
Key Personnel
Dir: Patrick Merand
Founded: 1987
Specialize in Africa.
Subjects: Archaeology, Art, Ethnicity, Fiction, Foreign Countries, Social Sciences, Sociology
ISBN Prefix(es): 2-84280; 2-907888

Editions de Septembre+
34 rue de l'Abbe-Groult, 75015 Paris
Tel: (01) 53689620 *Fax:* (01) 53689621
Key Personnel
Dir: Christophe Roux; Jean-Luc Simonin
Editor: Alain Vuyet; Rodolphe Fouano
Founded: 1990
Member of SNE.
Subjects: Biography, Fiction, Humor, Journalism, Literature, Literary Criticism, Essays, Science (General), Social Sciences, Sociology
ISBN Prefix(es): 2-87914
Imprints: l'Europeenne; Lignes De Vie
Divisions: Atelier Graphique des Editions de Septembre; Septembre Communication

Sequences, *imprint of* Sarl Editions Jean Grassin

Le Serpent a Plumes
20 rue des Petits Champs, 75002 Paris
Tel: (01) 55 35 95 85 *Fax:* (01) 42 61 17 46
E-mail: contact@serpentaplumes.com
Web Site: www.serpentaplumes.com
Key Personnel
Dir: Pierre Astier
Sales: Xavier Belrose
Production: Franck Remy
Rights: Laure Pecher
Founded: 1988
Subjects: Fiction, Foreign Countries, Literature, Literary Criticism, Essays
ISBN Prefix(es): 2-908957; 2-84261
Distributed by CDE; Foliade-La Caravelle; Gallimard Export; Gallimard Ltee; Office du Livre; SODIS

Servedit+
15, rue Victor-Cousin, 75005 Paris
Tel: (01) 44 41 49 30 *Fax:* (01) 43 25 77 41
E-mail: servedit@free.fr
Key Personnel
President: Alain Jauson
ISBN Prefix(es): 2-86877

Service des Publications Scientifiques du Museum National d'Histoire Naturelle
57 rue Cuvier, 75231 Paris Cedex 05
Tel: (01) 40 79 48 38 *Fax:* (01) 40 79 38 58
E-mail: diff.pub@mnhn.fr
Web Site: www.mnhn.fr/publication
Key Personnel
Dir: Philippe Bouchet
Head of Publications: J D Moreno
Founded: 1802
Subjects: Earth Sciences, Environmental Studies, Natural History, Also bilingual
ISBN Prefix(es): 2-85653; 2-86515
Number of titles published annually: 314 Print
Warehouse: Bibliotheque Centrale du Museum National d, 38 rue Geoffroy, Saint Hilaire, 75005 Paris

Orders to: Universal Book Services, Dr Backhuys, PO Box 321, 2300 AH Leiden, Netherlands (Only for the memoires collection/series, except Geology)

Service Hydrographique et Oceanographique de la Marine (SHOM)
3 avenue Octave Greard, BP 5, 00307 Armees
Mailing Address: BP 426, 29275 Cedex Brest
Tel: (01) 44 38 41 16
Web Site: www.shom.fr
Key Personnel
Off Manager: Ica Bessero
ISBN Prefix(es): 2-11

Service Technique pour l'Education
19 blvd Poissonniere, 75002 Paris
Tel: (01) 45084756
Key Personnel
Man Dir: Mrs Gradvohl
Founded: 1962
Subjects: Art, Biography, Education, Fiction, History, Music, Dance, Philosophy, Poetry, Religion - Jewish, Religion - Other
ISBN Prefix(es): 2-901041

Editions du Seuil+
27 rue Jacob, 75006 Paris
Tel: (01) 40 46 50 50 *Fax:* (01) 40 46 43 00
E-mail: contact@seuil.com
Web Site: www.seuil.com *Cable:* EDISEUIL
Key Personnel
Chairman: Claude Cherki
General Manager: Pascal Flamand
Chairman Editorial Advisor: Olivier Cohen
Chairman Advisor: Francoise Peyrot
Marketing Manager: Remi Amar
Executive Dir: Marie-France Fontaine
Publicity: Nathalie Cordier
Production: Daniel Glorel
Rights & Permissions Manager: Mireille Reissoulet *Tel:* (01) 40465103 *E-mail:* mreissou@sevil.com
Editorial: Vincent Bardet; Jacques Binsztok; Evelyne Cazade; Rene de Ceccatty; Richard Figuier; Anne Freyer; Louis Gardel; Martine van Geertruyden; Jean-Luc Giribone; Jean-Claude Guillebaud; Claude Henard; Jean-Marc Levy-Leblond; Thierry Marchaisse; Annie Morvan; Maurice Olender; Christelle Paris; Robert Pepin; Denis Roche; Jean-Louis Schlegel; Michel Winock
Founded: 1935
Subjects: Art, Biography, Fiction, Government, Political Science, History, How-to, Literature, Literary Criticism, Essays, Music, Dance, Philosophy, Photography, Poetry, Psychology, Psychiatry, Religion - Other, Science (General), Social Sciences, Sociology
ISBN Prefix(es): 2-02
Parent Company: Editions de l'Olivier
Imprints: La Baleine; L' Olivier; Editions Verticales
Subsidiaries: Societe d'Editions Scientifiques; Boreal (Montreal, Canada); College de France
Distributor for Alliage; L'Ane; Arlea; Autrement; Baleine; Belin; Bibliotheque Nationale de France; Boreal; Bourgois; Cahiers Cinema du; Callicephale; Cause Freudienne; Corti; Esprit; Genre Humain; Hoebeke; Les 400 coups; L'Homme; Liana Levi; O Jacob; A M Metailie; Maison des Roches; Milan; Minuit; Mollat; Montparnasse Editions Video; Navarin; Noir sur Blanc; Olivier; Panoramiques; Payot-Rivages; Phebus; Raisons d'Agir; RMN; Regard; Sept Video Arte; Taize; Textuel; Thames & Hudson; Verticales
Orders to: 13 rue du General Leclerc, Ballainvilliers, 91160 Longjumeau

SHOM, see Service Hydrographique et Oceanographique de la Marine (SHOM)

Siloe - Kerdore+
BP 319, 53003 Laval Cedex
Tel: (02) 43532601 *Fax:* (02) 43535601
E-mail: siloe-kerdore@wanadoo.fr
Key Personnel
Man Dir: Michel Thierry
Founded: 1982
Subjects: Geography, Geology, History, How-to, Literature, Literary Criticism, Essays, Photography, Regional Interests, Religion - Catholic, Travel, Wine & Spirits
ISBN Prefix(es): 2-905259; 2-84231
Total Titles: 250 Print
Branch Office(s)
18 rue des Carmelites, 44000 Nantes *Tel:* (0240) 98 61 10
La Rinjardiene, 44370 Varades, Yves Brien
Tel: (0240) 98 61 10 *Fax:* (0240) 98 61 10

Editions Andre Silvaire Sarl+
20 rue Domat, 75005 Paris
Tel: (01) 43.26.72.34 *Fax:* (01) 55.42.16.69
Founded: 1944
Subjects: Drama, Theater, Fiction, Literature, Literary Criticism, Essays, Philosophy, Poetry, Social Sciences, Sociology
ISBN Prefix(es): 2-85055

Sirey, *imprint of* Editions Dalloz Sirey

Slavonic, see Institut d'Etudes Slaves

Societe des Editions Grasset et Fasquelle+
61 rue des Sts-Peres, 75006 Paris
Tel: (01) 44392200 *Fax:* (01) 42226418
E-mail: editorial@edition-grasset.fr
Web Site: www.grasset.fr
Telex: 615887
Key Personnel
Chairman: Jean-Claude Fasquelle
Man Dir: Yves Berger; Manuel Carcassonne; Jean-Paul Enthoven
Sales: Jean-Pierre Pigeard
General Manager, Publicity & Advertising: Denis Bourgeois
Production: Jean-Pierre Decaens
Administrative Dir: Denis Lepeu
Rights & Permissions: Marie-Helene d'Ovidio
Public Relations: Claude Dalla-Torre; Joelle Faure; Martine Savary
Founded: 1907
Subjects: Fiction, Literature, Literary Criticism, Essays, Nonfiction (General), Philosophy
ISBN Prefix(es): 2-246
Imprints: Figures; College de Philosophie; Cahiers Rouges
U.S. Office(s): c/o Sanford & Greenburger Associates, 55 Fifth Ave, 15th fl, New York, NY 10003, United States

Societe des Editions Privat SA+
10 rue des Arts, 31080 Toulouse Cedex
Mailing Address: BP 828, 31080 Toulouse, Cedex 6
Tel: (0534) 31 81 81 *Fax:* (0534) 31 64 44
E-mail: editionsprivat@wanadoo.fr
Key Personnel
Dir: Dominique Porte
Publicity & Press Relations: Anne-Marie Bagieu
Permissions & Commercial: Marie-Helene Devesa
Editor: Veronique Sucere
Foreign Rights: Elisabeth Knebelmann
Founded: 1839
Subjects: Regional Interests, Patrimony, Health, National & International, Southern History
ISBN Prefix(es): 2-7089
Number of titles published annually: 70 Print
Parent Company: Laboratoires Pierre Fabre, Le Carla-Burlats, 81106 Castres Cedex

Societe d'Etudes Juridiques Internationales et Fiscales, see Les Cahiers Fiscaux Europeens Sarl

Societe Francaise des Imprimeries Administratives Centrales, see Sofiac (Societe Francaise des Imprimeries Administratives Centrales)

Societe Mathematique de France - Institut Henri Poincare
11 rue Pierre-et-Marie-Curie, 75005 Paris Cedex 05
Tel: (01) 44276796 *Fax:* (01) 40469096
E-mail: smf@dma.ens.fr
Web Site: smf.emath.fr
Key Personnel
President: M Waldschmidt
Secretary General: Claire Ropartz
Founded: 1872
Subjects: Mathematics
Number of titles published annually: 20 Print
Bookshop(s): Maison de la SMF, BP 67, 13276 Marseille Cedex 9, C Munusami *Tel:* (0491) 833025 *Fax:* (0491) 411751 *E-mail:* smf@smf.univ-mrs.fr

Societe Nouveaux Loisirs+
5 rue Sebastien Bottin, 75007 Paris Cedex 07
Tel: (01) 49 54 42 00 *Fax:* (01) 45 44 39 45
Web Site: www.gallimard.fr
Key Personnel
Dir of Development: Ghislain de Compreignac
International Rights: Hedwige Pasquet
Founded: 1992
Subjects: Architecture & Interior Design, Art, Environmental Studies, Geography, Geology, History, How-to, Regional Interests
ISBN Prefix(es): 2-7424
Parent Company: Editions Gallimard
Associate Companies: Gallimard Jeunesse
Imprints: Guides Gallimard
Distributed by Dohosna (Japan); Dumont (Germany); Everytian (UK); Knopf (USA); Owl Publishing (China, Taiwan); SM-Acento (Spain); Standard (Netherlands); TCI (Italy)

Sofiac (Societe Francaise des Imprimeries Administratives Centrales)+
17 rue Remy-Dumoncel, 75014 Paris Cedex 06
Tel: (01) 40-64-42-42 *Fax:* (01) 40-64-42-40
Key Personnel
President: Bruno Declementi
Publisher: Veronique Fastrez
Subjects: Accounting, Business, Law, Public Administration
ISBN Prefix(es): 2-85130
Orders to: BP 44, 54250 Champigneulles

Sofradif Editions Philippe Auzou+
24-32 rue des Amandiers, 75020 Paris
Tel: (01) 40.33.84.00 *Fax:* (01) 47.97.20.08
Key Personnel
Publisher: Philippe Auzou
Sales Manager: Fred Frangeul
Subjects: Animals, Pets, Architecture & Interior Design, Art, Biography, Biological Sciences, Career Development, Cookery, Crafts, Games, Hobbies, English as a Second Language, Film, Video, Foreign Countries, Gardening, Plants, Geography, Geology, Health, Nutrition, History, House & Home, How-to, Language Arts, Linguistics, Law, Mathematics, Medicine, Nursing, Dentistry, Natural History, Nonfiction (General), Outdoor Recreation, Psychology, Psychiatry, Science (General), Self-Help
ISBN Prefix(es): 2-7338

Solar, *imprint of* Presses de la Cite

Solin, *imprint of* Editions Actes Sud

FRANCE

Soline+
10 blvd de la Paix, 92400 Courbevoie
Tel: (01) 43 33 74 24 *Fax:* (01) 43 33 67 37
E-mail: edsoline@wanadoo.fr
Web Site: perso.wanadoo.fr/soline
Key Personnel
Manager: Nicole Pialet
Founded: 1988
Subjects: Automotive, Fashion, Gardening, Plants, House & Home, Wine & Spirits
ISBN Prefix(es): 2-87677
Total Titles: 90 Print
Distributed by VILO
Warehouse: 23 rue Pierre Curie, 92400 Courbevoie

Somogy editions d'art+
57 rue de la Roquette, 75011 Paris
Tel: (01) 48 05 70 10 *Fax:* (01) 48 05 71 70
Key Personnel
Man Dir: Nicolas Neumann
Editorial: Veronique le Dosseur
International Rights: Jana Navratil-Nanent
Founded: 1937
Subjects: Antiques, Archaeology, Architecture & Interior Design, Art, Biography, Photography
ISBN Prefix(es): 2-85056

Publications de la Sorbonne
One rue Victor Cousin, 75231 Paris Cedex 05
Tel: (01) 40 46 28 48 *Fax:* (01) 40 46 28 49
E-mail: publisor@univ-paris1.fr
Key Personnel
Dir: Martine Tabeaud
Founded: 1971
Subjects: Archaeology, Art, Economics, Geography, Geology, Government, Political Science, History, Law, Literature, Literary Criticism, Essays, Philosophy, Social Sciences, Sociology
ISBN Prefix(es): 2-85944
Number of titles published annually: 25 Print
Total Titles: 25 Print
Orders to: Diffusion CID, 131 Bd Saint Michel, 75005 Paris *Tel:* (01) 43 54 47 15 *Fax:* (01) 43 54 80 73

Association d'Editions Sorg
54 rue de l'Est, 92100 Boulogne
Tel: (01) 48252524 *Fax:* (01) 46052563
Key Personnel
Chairman & International Rights: Jacques Sorg
Founded: 1986
Subjects: Aeronautics, Aviation, Fiction, History, Humor, Philosophy
ISBN Prefix(es): 2-906794

Sortileges, *imprint of* Societe d'Edition Les Belles Lettres

Editions SOS (Editions du Secours Catholique)
11, rue de Cambrai Batiment 28, 2E Etage, 75007 Paris
Tel: (01) 40354465 *Fax:* (01) 40354273
Key Personnel
Man Dir: Maurice Herr
Publicity & Advertising: Georges Fanucchi
Founded: 1949
Subjects: History, Philosophy, Religion - Other, Social Sciences, Sociology
ISBN Prefix(es): 2-7185

Editions Louis Soulanges Le Livrer Ouvert
BP 442, 75769 Paris Cedex 16
Tel: (01) 43262538; (01) 43256782
Key Personnel
Man Dir, Sales Dir & Publicity: Louis Drouot Soulanges
Founded: 1960
Subjects: Fiction, Philosophy, Religion - Other
Associate Companies: Paris-Caraiibes

Imprints: France-Caraiibes
Branch Office(s)
5-7 rue Abel Ferry, 75016 Paris *Tel:* (01) 5240609

Les Editions de la Source Sarl
5 rue de la Source, 75016 Paris
Tel: (01) 45253007
Key Personnel
Man Dir: Rev Father Dom Gozier
All Other Offices: Rev Father Dom Balladur
Founded: 1927
Subjects: Biblical Studies, Religion - Other, Theology
ISBN Prefix(es): 2-900005
Imprints: Lumiere Biblique series
Bookshop(s): Librairie Sainte Marie, 5 rue de la Source, 75016 Paris
Orders to: Office General du Livre, 14 bis rue Jean-Ferrandi, 75006 Paris *Tel:* (01) 45483828

Spectres Familiers
29, rue Barthelemy, 13001 Marseille
Tel: (0491) 912645 *Fax:* (0491) 909951
Key Personnel
Literature Dir: Emmanuel Ponsart
Subjects: Literature, Literary Criticism, Essays, Poetry
ISBN Prefix(es): 2-909097

Spengler Editeur+
130 blvd Saint Germain, 75006 Paris
Tel: (01) 49701555 *Fax:* (01) 49701550
Founded: 1992
Subjects: Fiction, Literature, Literary Criticism, Essays
ISBN Prefix(es): 2-909997
Distributed by Prologue (Canada)

Editions Spratbrow+
BP 1, 59301 Valenciennes Cedex
Tel: (03) 27 33 62 58 *Fax:* (03) 27 45 29 99
E-mail: sjbv.cdi@wanadoo.fr
Key Personnel
President: Francoise Begrand
Founded: 1990
Subjects: Education, English as a Second Language, Language Arts, Linguistics, Self-Help
ISBN Prefix(es): 2-903891
Distributed by Groupe Deboeck a Louvin (Belgium)
Distributor for Santillana (France)
Warehouse: 27 rue Weil, 59770 Marly

Editions Springer France+
10 rue Vercingetorix, 75014 Paris
Tel: (01) 56541313; (01) 56541300 *Fax:* (01) 56541317
Web Site: www.springer.de
Founded: 1986
Subjects: Astronomy, Chemistry, Chemical Engineering, Civil Engineering, Computer Science, Earth Sciences, Economics, Electronics, Electrical Engineering, Engineering (General), Mathematics, Mechanical Engineering, Medicine, Nursing, Dentistry, Physics, Psychology, Psychiatry
ISBN Prefix(es): 2-287; 3-540
Parent Company: Springer-Verlag GmbH & Co KG, Heidelberger Platz 3, 14197 Berlin, Germany

Stil
5 rue de Charonne, 75011 Paris
Tel: (01) 48 06 28 19 *Fax:* (01) 47 00 41 89
Key Personnel
Editor: Alain Villain
Founded: 1971
Subjects: Art, Literature, Literary Criticism, Essays, Music, Dance
ISBN Prefix(es): 2-85254

BOOK

Editions Stock+
27 rue Cassette, 75006 Paris
Tel: (01) 42848700 *Fax:* (01) 42848709
Key Personnel
President: Claude Durand
Editor in Chief: Monique Nemer
Secretary General, Editorial: Philippe Rey
Rights & Permissions: Fabienne Roussel
Founded: 1708
Subjects: Biography, Child Care & Development, Fiction, Film, Video, Literature, Literary Criticism, Essays, Nonfiction (General), Poetry, Social Sciences, Sociology
ISBN Prefix(es): 2-234
Parent Company: Librairie Hachette
Branch Office(s)
US Office: Bureau du Livre Francais, 583 Broadway, New York, New York, NY 10003, United States

Subervie Editions
Parc des Moutiers, 12032 Rodez Cedex 09
Tel: (05) 65 67 20 17 *Fax:* (05) 65 67 36 38
E-mail: contact@subervie.com
Key Personnel
Contact: Jo Subevio
ISBN Prefix(es): 2-85644; 2-911381

SUD+
62 rue Sainte, BP 38, 13484 Marseille Cedex 20
Tel: (0491) 336068 *Fax:* (0491) 336068
Key Personnel
Man Dir: Yves Broussard
Founded: 1970
Subjects: Literature, Literary Criticism, Essays, Poetry
ISBN Prefix(es): 2-86446

Editions Sud Ouest
6 rue de la Merci BP 130, 33036 Bordeaux Cedex
Tel: (0556) 446821 *Fax:* (0556) 444083
E-mail: editions-gso@groupesudouest.com
Web Site: www.gso.enfrance.com
Key Personnel
Contact: Catherine Dubourg *Tel:* (0556) 003508
E-mail: c.dubourg@sudouest.com
Founded: 1988
Subjects: Cookery, History, How-to, Outdoor Recreation, Regional Interests
ISBN Prefix(es): 2-87901
Number of titles published annually: 60 Print
Total Titles: 500 Print
Parent Company: Groupe Sud-Ouest, 33000 Bordeaux
Distributor for Editions Jean Paul Gisserot
Warehouse: Raudo SA, Queeynes, 33000 Bordeaux

Editions le Sureau, *imprint of* Adverbum SARL

Sybex+
Immeuble Polaris, 76 ave Pierre Brossolette, 92247 Malakoff Cedex
Tel: (01) 55 58 40 00 *Fax:* (01) 49 65 04 10
E-mail: contact@sybex.fr
Web Site: www.sybex.fr
Key Personnel
President: Francois-Xavier Chaussonniere
Founded: 1976
Subjects: Microcomputers
ISBN Prefix(es): 2-7361; 2-902414
Parent Company: Sybex Inc, 1151 Marina Village Parkway, Alameda, CA 94501, United States
Foreign Rep(s): Woodslane Pty Limited (Australia & New Zealand); Acorn Publishing Co (Korea); BPB Publications (Bangladesh, India, Pakistan); Express Trains Distributors Computer (Caribbean & Latin America); Firefly Books Ltd (Canada); International Sybex (UK, Europe & Middle East, North Africa); Intersoft (South Africa); Lidel Edicoes Tecnicas Lda

PUBLISHERS — FRANCE

(Portugal); Livraria Cultura (Brazil); Sulcor Investindo (Indonesia); TransQuest Publishers Pte Ltd (Hong Kong, Singapore & Malaysia, Thailand)

Les Editions de la Table Ronde
7 rue Corneille, 75006 Paris
Tel: (01) 40467070 *Fax:* (01) 40467101
Key Personnel
President & Dir General: Denis Tillinac
Publisher: Olivier Frebourg
Rights & Permissions: Marie-Therese Caloni
Founded: 1944
Subjects: Biography, Fiction, History, Nonfiction (General), Psychology, Psychiatry, Religion - Other
ISBN Prefix(es): 2-7103
Associate Companies: Editione la Palatine

Tacor International
13 rue Saint-Honore, 78000 Versailles
Mailing Address: BP 1, 78170 La Celle-Saint Cloud
Tel: (01) 39182939 *Fax:* (01) 30824390
Key Personnel
Man Dir: Annette Riis-Zahrai
Founded: 1988
Subjects: Human Relations, Religion - Other, Social Sciences, Sociology
ISBN Prefix(es): 2-907308

Editions Tallandier+
74, Ave du Maine, 75014 Paris
Tel: (01) 44 10 10 10 *Fax:* (01) 44 10 10 32
Founded: 1865
Subjects: Art, Fiction, Geography, Geology, History
ISBN Prefix(es): 2-235
Warehouse: Editions Tallandier, BP 65, 45390 Puiseaux
Orders to: Editions Tallandier, BP 65, 45390 Puiseaux

Editions Tardy SA+
30 rue de la Passerelle, 93164 Noisy-Le-Grand
Tel: (01) 45443834 *Fax:* (01) 42841091
Telex: 205781
Key Personnel
Man Dir, Rights & Permissions: Pierre Penet
Dir: Pierre-Marie Dumont
Founded: 1938
Subjects: Religion - Catholic, Religion - Other
ISBN Prefix(es): 2-7105
Warehouse: 48 rue Galande, 75005 Paris

Cartes Taride+
2 Bis Place du Puits de l'Ermite, 75005 Paris
Tel: (01) 433 640 40 *Fax:* (01) 470 727 16
Key Personnel
Man Editor: Gerard Boulanger
Founded: 1852
Subjects: Cook books, travel guides
ISBN Prefix(es): 2-7106

Taride Editions+
Division of ULISSE Edition
15 rue Mansart, 75009 Paris
Tel: (01) 48 78 40 74 *Fax:* (01) 48 78 40 77
Key Personnel
Man Dir: Pierre-Alain Imhof
General Manager: Frederique Imhof
Founded: 1852
Subjects: Cookery, Geography, Geology, Travel
ISBN Prefix(es): 2-7106

TEC & DOC, *imprint of* Lavoisier

Editions Technip SA+
27 rue Ginoux, 75737 Paris Cedex 15
Tel: (01) 45 78 33 80 *Fax:* (01) 45 75 37 11
E-mail: commerce@editionstechnip.com
Web Site: www.editionstechnip.com
Key Personnel
President & Dir General: Sylvie Haxaire
Sales Manager: Corinne Herran
Founded: 1956
Specialize in the publishing of scientific & technical books on the oil & gas industry.
Subjects: Automotive, Chemistry, Chemical Engineering, Computer Science, Earth Sciences, Electronics, Electrical Engineering, Energy, Engineering (General), Mathematics, Technology
ISBN Prefix(es): 2-7108
Number of titles published annually: 20 Print
Parent Company: Institut Francais du Petrole
Distributed by Hikari Book Trading Co Ltd; Kaigai Publications Ltd; PF Book; Progressive International Agencies (Pvt) Limited
Bookshop(s): Australian Mineral Foundation, 63 Conyngham St, Glenside, South 5065, Australia *Tel:* (08) 8379-0444 *Fax:* (08) 8379-4634 *E-mail:* bookshop@amf.com.au; Brown Book Shop, 1517 San Jacinto, Houston, TX 77002, United States *Tel:* 713-652-3937 *Fax:* 713-652-1911 *E-mail:* info@brownbookshop.com; DeMille Technical Books, 815 Eighth Ave SW, Calgary, AB T2P 3P2, Canada *Tel:* (403) 264 7411 *Fax:* (403) 262 1445 *E-mail:* sales@demilletech.com; Gulf Publishing Co, Book Publishing Division, 3301 Allen Parkway, Houston, TX 77019-1896, United States *Tel:* 713-529-4301 *Fax:* 713-520-4438 *E-mail:* ezorder@gulfpub.com; J A Majors Co, 9464 Kirby Dr, Houston, TX 77054-2518, United States *Tel:* 713-662-3984 *Fax:* 713-662-9627 *E-mail:* houston@majors.com

Techniplus, *imprint of* Editions Casteilla

Technique et Documentation Lavoisier, see Lavoisier

Technique et Vulgarisation, *imprint of* Editions Bordas

Editions Techniques et Scientifiques Francaises
120 blvd Saint-Germain SESJM, 75006 Paris
Tel: (01) 463500 *Fax:* (01) 466100
Telex: pgv230472f
Key Personnel
Man Dir: Jean-Pierre Ventillard
Editorial, Sales, Production & Publicity: Christian Cheneau
ISBN Prefix(es): 2-85535

Le Temps apprivoise, *imprint of* Pierre Zech Editeur

10/18+
Imprint of Havas Poche
12 avenue d'Italie, 75627 Paris Cedex 13
Tel: (01) 44 16 05 00
Telex: 204807F
Key Personnel
Publisher: Jean-Claude Dubost
Editor: Jean-Claude Zylberstein
Founded: 1961
Quality paperbacks.
Subjects: Fiction, Government, Political Science, Literature, Literary Criticism, Essays, Mysteries, International fiction & mysteries (mostly historical crime)
ISBN Prefix(es): 2-264
Membership(s): Vivendi Universal Publishing Group

Librairie Pierre Tequi et Editions Tequi
82 Le Roc Saint-Michel, 53150 Saint-Cenere
Tel: (02) 43.01.01.81 *Fax:* (02) 43.02.25.52
E-mail: pierre.tequi@wanadoo.fr
Web Site: www.librairietequi.com
Key Personnel
General Manager: Pierre Lemaire
Literary Manager: G Cerbelaud Salagnac
Founded: 1845
Subjects: Education, Philosophy, Religion - Catholic, Social Sciences, Sociology, Theology
ISBN Prefix(es): 2-7403; 2-85244
Bookshop(s): S A Vander (Belgium); Iris Diffusion (Canada); Editions Saint-Augustin (Switzerland)

Editions Pierre Terrail/Finest SA
3 rue Bayard, 75008 Paris
Tel: (01) 44 35 59 13
Web Site: www.bayardpresse.com/fr/groupe/contacts.asp
Key Personnel
Dir Editorial: Jean-Francois Gonthier
Dir Ventes & Marketing: Erik Boursier
Specialize in Art Books.
Subjects: Archaeology, Architecture & Interior Design, Art
ISBN Prefix(es): 2-87939
Parent Company: Groupe Bayard Presse

Terre Vivante+
Domaine de Raud, 38710 Mens
Mailing Address: BP 20, 38711 Mens Cedex
Tel: (04) 76 34 80 80 *Fax:* (04) 76 34 84 02
E-mail: infos@terrevivante.org
Web Site: www.terrevivante.org
Key Personnel
Man Dir: Claude Aubert
Founded: 1980
Subjects: Agriculture, Cookery, Energy, Gardening, Plants, Health, Nutrition, House & Home, Technology
ISBN Prefix(es): 2-904082
Total Titles: 2 Print; 60 Audio

TF 1 Editions+
24 Ave Marceau, 75381 Paris Cedex 08
Tel: (01) 41413151 *Fax:* (01) 41413153
Web Site: www.laffont.fr
Telex: 260 808
Key Personnel
Man Dir: Adelaide Barbey
Founded: 1987
Subjects: Fiction

Thames & Hudson+
4 Impasse des Peintres, 75002 Paris
Tel: (01) 42219515 *Fax:* (01) 42213336
Key Personnel
Dir: Thomas Neurath
Editor: Helene Borraz; Frederique Popet
Founded: 1989
Subjects: Archaeology, Architecture & Interior Design, Art, Fashion, Photography, Religion - Jewish
ISBN Prefix(es): 2-87811
Parent Company: Thames & Hudson Londres, 30/36 Bloomsbury St, WC1 B3QP Londres, Graude, Bretagne
Orders to: Hazan *Tel:* (01) 49619207 *Fax:* (01) 45978347

Editions Theatrales+
38, st of the suburb St Jacques, 75014 Paris
Tel: (01) 53102300 *Fax:* (01) 53102301
E-mail: info@editionstheatrales.fr
Web Site: www.theatre-contemporain.net
Key Personnel
Dir: J P Engelbach
Founded: 1990
Subjects: Drama, Theater
ISBN Prefix(es): 2-907810; 2-84260
Distributed by Distique
Distributor for CNDP collection Theatre Aujourd-hui; Theatre du Soleil

FRANCE

Alain Thomas Editeur+
18 passage Foubert, 75013 Paris
Tel: (01) 45 88 28 03 *Fax:* (01) 45 88 49 24
Web Site: alainthomasimages.com
Key Personnel
Editor: Alain Thomas *E-mail:* alain-thomas@wanadoo.fr
Founded: 1991
Subjects: Photography, Travel, Western Fiction
ISBN Prefix(es): 2-9503864
Total Titles: 3 Print
Distributed by Centre Cartographique (in Belgium only)

Editions Tiresias Michel Reynaud+
BP 249, 75866 Paris Cedex 18
Tel: (01) 42 23 47 27 *Fax:* (01) 42 23 73 27
E-mail: firesias@club-internet.fr
Key Personnel
Contact: Michel Reynaud
Founded: 1990
Subjects: Biography, History, Literature, Literary Criticism, Essays
ISBN Prefix(es): 2-908527

Top Editions+
Member of Casteilla
10 rue Leon Foucault, 78184 Saint-Quentin Yvelines Cedex
Tel: (01) 30 14 19 30 *Fax:* (01) 34 60 31 32
E-mail: info@casteilla.fr
Key Personnel
Dir General: Marinus Visser
Founded: 1982
Subjects: Accounting, Career Development, Communications, Finance, How-to, Management, Marketing, Securities
ISBN Prefix(es): 2-87731
Number of titles published annually: 25 Print
Total Titles: 75 Print

Tout L'Univers, *imprint of* Le Livre de Paris

Transedition ASBL
11 rue d'odessa, 75014 Paris
Tel: (01) 43211080 *Fax:* (01) 43211079
Key Personnel
Man Dir, Editorial: Marc Dachy
Sales: Anne Barres
Production: Paule Pousseele
Publicity: Stephanie Gregoire
Rights & Permissions: Jacques Bekaert
Founded: 1972
Subjects: Art, Literature, Literary Criticism, Essays
ISBN Prefix(es): 2-8025
Associate Companies: Montfaucon Research Center, 8 rue d'Anjou, 75008 Paris
Subsidiaries: Editions Luna-Park

Transeuropeennes/RCE+
51, rue de Maubeuge, 75009 Paris
Tel: (01) 55 07 88 90 *Fax:* (01) 55 07 97 38
E-mail: te.revue@wanadoo.fr
Web Site: www.transeuropeennes.org
Key Personnel
Editor-in-Chief: Ghislaine Glasson Deschaumes
Man Dir: Gaele de la Brosse
Distribution Manager: Yacine Saadi
Founded: 1993
Comprehensive & interdisciplinary review.
Subjects: Art, Drama, Theater, Foreign Countries, History, Literature, Literary Criticism, Essays, Philosophy, Photography, Social Sciences, Sociology
ISBN Prefix(es): 2-912002
Number of titles published annually: 3 Print
Total Titles: 14 Print

Travel Aventure, *imprint of* Editions Actes Sud

Editions Trois Fontaines+
613, av Charles-de-Gaulle, 01330 Villars-les-Dombes
Tel: (04) 74981754 *Fax:* (04) 74981812
Key Personnel
Manager & International Rights: Nelly Irniger
Founded: 1991
Subjects: Earth Sciences, Health, Nutrition, How-to, Human Relations, Medicine, Nursing, Dentistry, Philosophy, Psychology, Psychiatry, Self-Help, Sports, Athletics
ISBN Prefix(es): 2-909206
Imprints: Pratique Sante; Epanouissement; Sante Spiritualite
Distributor for Carthame editions

Turbo, *imprint of* Les Presses du Management

Ulisse Edition+
15 rue Mansart, 75009 Paris
Tel: (01) 48 78 40 74 *Fax:* (01) 48 78 40 77
Key Personnel
Man Editor: Gerard Boulanger
Founded: 1990
Subjects: Architecture & Interior Design, Art, Crafts, Games, Hobbies, House & Home, Sports, Athletics, Travel
ISBN Prefix(es): 2-907601; 2-84415; 2-921403

Ulysse Diffusion, *imprint of* Lettres Vives

Editions Unes+
BP 205, 83006 Draguignan Cedex
Tel: (016) 94673158 *Fax:* (016) 94673175
Key Personnel
Contact: Jean-Pierre Sintive
Founded: 1981
Subjects: Library & Information Sciences, Literature, Literary Criticism, Essays, Poetry
ISBN Prefix(es): 2-87704
Branch Office(s)
Raphaille Dedourge, 15 rue ar Maire, 75003 Cedex Paris *Tel:* (01) 42 77 25 82
E-mail: raphaellededourge2@compuses.com

UNESCO Publishing+
Imprint of UNESCO Publishing
7 place de Fontenoy, 75352 Paris 07-SP
Tel: (01) 45 68 10 00 *Fax:* (01) 45 67 16 90
Web Site: www.unesco.org/general/eng/about/address.shtml
Telex: 204461; 270602
Key Personnel
Chief, Promotion & Sales: Chandran Nair
Chief Publisher: Michiko Tanaka
Promotion: Cristina Laje
Founded: 1946
Subjects: Art, Communications, Education, Human Relations, Science (General), Social Sciences, Sociology
ISBN Prefix(es): 92-3
Imprints: IBE; IIEP
Distributed by Bernan Associate (USA); Stationery Office Books (UK)

Union Generale d'Editions
12 av d'Italie, 75627 Paris Cedex 13
Tel: (01) 44160500 *Fax:* (01) 44160511
Key Personnel
Literary Dir: J C Zyberstein
Founded: 1962
Subjects: Fiction, Mysteries
ISBN Prefix(es): 2-264

Universitas
Subsidiary of Buchverlage Langen-Mueller/Herbig
62 ave de Suffren, 75015 Paris
Tel: (01) 45.67.18.38 *Fax:* (01) 45.66.50.70
Key Personnel
Dir: Andrew Brown

Founded: 1989
Subjects: History, Language Arts, Linguistics, Literature, Literary Criticism, Essays, Philosophy
ISBN Prefix(es): 2-7400

Publications de l'Universite de Pau
Av de l'Universite, 64000 Pau
Tel: (05) 59923347 *Fax:* (05) 59923275
Key Personnel
Dir: Bertrand Rouge
Man Dir: Alain Andreucci
Founded: 1992
Subjects: Art, Geography, Geology, Language Arts, Linguistics, Law, Literature, Literary Criticism, Essays, Photography, Poetry, Social Sciences, Sociology
ISBN Prefix(es): 2-908930

La Vague a l'ame+
BP 22, 38701 La Tronche Cedex
Tel: 76470784
Key Personnel
President: Georges Elisee
Founded: 1980
Subjects: Cookery, Drama, Theater, Humor, Photography, Poetry, Religion - Catholic, Travel
ISBN Prefix(es): 2-84063

La Vague Verte+
271 rue d'en Haut, 80460 Woignarue
Tel: (03) 22.30.72.50 *Fax:* (03) 22.26.58.73
E-mail: edlavagueverte@wanadoo.fr
Key Personnel
Dir: Jimmy Grandsire
Founded: 1989
Subjects: Art, Biography, Earth Sciences, Environmental Studies, History, Literature, Literary Criticism, Essays, Mysteries, Natural History, Poetry, Regional Interests, Travel
ISBN Prefix(es): 2-908227
Number of titles published annually: 25 Print

Les Editions Vaillant-Miroir-Sprint Publications
146 rue du Faubourg Poissoniere, 75010 Paris
Tel: (01) 42819103
Telex: f 281353
Key Personnel
International Sales Manager: Alain Lesaint
Subjects: Humor, Sports, Athletics
ISBN Prefix(es): 2-7325

Editions Van de Velde+
La Haute Limougere, 37230 Fondettes
Tel: (02) 47 49 43 43 *Fax:* (02) 47 49 43 49
E-mail: vandereede.musique@wanadoo.fr
Web Site: www.yacht-in-books.com
Key Personnel
Dir: Francis Van de Velde
Copyrights: Ursula Van De Velde *Tel:* (02) 47 49 43 40 *E-mail:* vandervelde.musique@wanadoo.fr
Founded: 1898
Subjects: Music, Dance, Classic yachting
ISBN Prefix(es): 2-85868
Number of titles published annually: 20 Print
Total Titles: 197 Print
Online services available through World Wide Web.
Distributor for Konemann Music Budapest

Editions Van Wilder
91 bis Rue Truffaut, 75017 Paris
Tel: (01) 53069212 *Fax:* (01) 53069213
Key Personnel
Man Dir: F Van Wilder *E-mail:* fwilder@aetprice.com;
Founded: 1962
Subjects: Art
ISBN Prefix(es): 2-85299
Number of titles published annually: 5 Print

Total Titles: 50 Print
Online services available through Artdata.com.

Gerard Varin, see L'Amitie par le Livre

Vents d'Ouest+
31-33 Rue Ernest-Renan, 92130 Issy-les-
 Moulineaux
Tel: (01) 41 46 11 11 *Fax:* (01) 41 46 11 13
Web Site: www.glenat.com
Key Personnel
Contact: Estelle Revelant *E-mail:* estelle.
 revelant@glenat.com
International Rights: Laetitue Denier
Subjects: Humor, Science Fiction, Fantasy
ISBN Prefix(es): 2-86967

Editions Verdier
11220 Lagrasse
Tel: (04) 68 24 05 75 *Fax:* (04) 68 24 00 89
E-mail: contact@editions_verdier.fr
Web Site: www.editions-verdier.fr
Key Personnel
Dir Literature: Gerard Bobillier
Founded: 1979
Subjects: Literature, Literary Criticism, Essays,
 Philosophy, Religion - Islamic, Religion - Jew-
 ish
ISBN Prefix(es): 2-86432
Number of titles published annually: 25 Print
Total Titles: 400 Print
Branch Office(s)
Bureau Parisien, 234 rue du Faubourg-Saint-
 Antoine, Paris 75012 *Tel:* (01) 43 79 20 45
 Fax: (01) 43 79 84 20
Distributed by SODIS

Editions de Vergeures+
23 ave Villemain, 75014 Paris
Tel: (01) 4543 8260 *Fax:* (01) 4543 8140
Key Personnel
Manager: Robert Cauchuix
Founded: 1979
Subjects: Art, How-to
ISBN Prefix(es): 2-7309; 2-909175

Vertiges Bulles, *imprint of* Editions Dominique
 Leroy

Editions Vigot Freres
23 rue de l'Ecole de Medecine, 75006 Paris
Tel: (01) 4329 5450 *Fax:* (01) 4634 0589
Telex: 201708 F
Key Personnel
Man Dir: Daniel Vigot
Founded: 1890
Subjects: Medicine, Nursing, Dentistry, Sports,
 Athletics, Veterinary Science
ISBN Prefix(es): 2-7114
Bookshop(s): Librairie Vigot

Editions Village Mondial+
13 rue de la Grand-Chaumiere, 75006 Paris
Tel: (01) 44.32.08.00 *Fax:* (01) 43.25.43.37
E-mail: vilmon@easynet.fr
Web Site: www.village-mondial.com
Key Personnel
President: Geoffrey Staines
Founded: 1995
Specialize in higher education textbooks.
Subjects: Economics, Finance, Human Relations,
 Management, Marketing
ISBN Prefix(es): 2-84211
Total Titles: 100 Print
Online services available through www.village-
 mondial.com.
Imprints: Publi Union
Shipping Address: Publi Union
Warehouse: Publi Union
Orders to: Publi Union

La Villeguerin+
102 rue Lafayette, 75010 Paris
Tel: (01) 45232132 *Fax:* (01) 47701484
Key Personnel
Dir General: Yves-Robert De la Villeguerin
ISBN Prefix(es): 2-86521
Associate Companies: Societe Europeenne de
 Presse Fiscale, Juridique
Orders to: 45 rue Victor Hugo, 93507 Pantin
 Tel: (01) 48 40 01 11

Editions Vilo SA
25 rue Ginoux, 75015 Paris
Tel: (01) 45 77 08 05 *Fax:* (01) 45 79 97 15
Telex: 200305 F *Cable:* Edivilo Paris
Key Personnel
Man Dir: Mme Larfillon
Subjects: Architecture & Interior Design, Art, Au-
 tomotive, History, Language Arts, Linguistics,
 Literature, Literary Criticism, Essays, Nonfic-
 tion (General), Religion - Other, Sports, Athlet-
 ics, Travel
ISBN Prefix(es): 2-7191

Editions Viviane Hamy+
89 rue du Faubourg Saint Antoine, 75011 Paris
Tel: (01) 53171600 *Fax:* (01) 53171609
E-mail: information@viviane-hamy.fr
Web Site: www.viviane-hamy.fr
Key Personnel
Contact: Viviane Harny; Frederic Martin
 E-mail: frederic.martin@viviane-hamy.fr
Founded: 1990
Subjects: Literature, Literary Criticism, Essays
ISBN Prefix(es): 2-87858
Number of titles published annually: 12 Print
Total Titles: 120 Print
Distributed by Flammarion

Editions VM+
44, av George V, 75008 Paris
Tel: (01) 49 52 14 53; (01) 49 52 14 00 *Fax:* (01)
 49 52 14 41
Founded: 1965
Subjects: Photography
ISBN Prefix(es): 2-86258
Bookshop(s): La Photo Librairie, 49 Ave de Vil-
 liers, 75017 Paris

La Voix du Regard
11 rue Henri Martin, 94200 Ivy-sur-Seine
Tel: (01) 46.70.88.69 *Fax:* (01) 46.70.88.69
E-mail: jnelva@club-internet.fr
Key Personnel
President: Jocelyn Maixent
Editor: Ghislain Deslandes
International Rights: Pauline Jacquey
Founded: 1991
Subjects: Art, Drama, Theater, Fiction, Film,
 Video, Literature, Literary Criticism, Essays,
 Photography, Poetry, Radio, TV

Librairie Philosophique J Vrin+
6 place de la Sorbonne, 75005 Paris
Tel: (01) 43 54 03 47 *Fax:* (01) 43 54 48 18
E-mail: contact@vrin.fr
Web Site: www.vrin.fr
Key Personnel
Man Dir: Anne-Marie Arnaud
Founded: 1920
Publisher & Bookseller of New Books, Book-
 seller of Secondhand Books.
Subjects: History, Philosophy, Psychology, Psy-
 chiatry, Religion - Other, *Specializes in philos-
 ophy*
ISBN Prefix(es): 2-7116
Number of titles published annually: 50 Print; 1
 CD-ROM
Total Titles: 1,500 Print
Bookshop(s): Philosophy, Law, Religion, Litera-
 ture, Art & History, 75005 Paris

Librairie Vuibert+
20 rue Berbier-du-Mets, 75647 Paris Cedex 13
Tel: (01) 44 08 49 00 *Fax:* (01) 44 08 49 39
Web Site: www.vuibert.com
Telex: 201005 F Vuibpar *Cable:* VUIBERT
 PARIS
Key Personnel
President: Philippe Sylvestre
Founded: 1877
Subjects: Biological Sciences, Chemistry, Chem-
 ical Engineering, Earth Sciences, Economics,
 Law, Mathematics, Physics
ISBN Prefix(es): 2-7117
Imprints: Annales du Bac; Bac en Poche; Livre
 des Vacances

Gerard Watelet, see Editions Pygmalion -
 Gerard Watelet

Galerie Lucie Weill-Seligmann
6 rue Bonaparte, 75006 Paris
Tel: (01) 4354 7195 *Fax:* (01) 4051 8288
Key Personnel
President: France Faure-Seligmann
Founded: 1930
Book Club(s): Nouveau Cercle Parisien du Livre

Editions Weka
249 rue de Crimea, 75935 Paris Cedex 19
Tel: (01) 53 35 16 16; (01) 53 35 17 17 *Fax:* (01)
 53 35 17 01
Web Site: www.weka.fr
Telex: 210 504 f
Key Personnel
General Man: Robert Christian
Editorial: Philippe Dorenlot
Commercial (Sales Direct Marketing): Jean-Pierre
 Chauvet
Founded: 1979
Subjects: Computer Science, Electronics, Elec-
 trical Engineering, Labor, Industrial Relations,
 Law, Management, Social Sciences, Sociology
ISBN Prefix(es): 2-7337
Parent Company: Weka-Verlag, Postfach 1180,
 8901 Kissing, Germany
Associate Companies: Weka Presse, 82 rue Cu-
 rial, 75935 Paris
Branch Office(s)
50 Main St, Suite 1000, White Plains, NY 10606,
 United States
U.S. Office(s): Weka Publishing Inc, 97 Indian
 Field Rd, Greenwich, CT 06830, United States

Galerie Esther Woerdehoff
36 rue Falguiere, 75015 Paris
Tel: (01) 43 2144 83 *Fax:* (01) 43 2145 03
E-mail: galerie@falguiere36.org
Web Site: www.falguiere36.org

YMCA-Press
11 rue de la Montagne Sainte-Genevieve, 75005
 Paris
Tel: (01) 4354 7446 *Fax:* (01) 4325 3479
See also Les Editeurs Reunis.
Subjects: Literature, Literary Criticism, Essays,
 Religion - Other
ISBN Prefix(es): 2-85065

Editions Philateliques Yvert et Tellier
37 rue des Jacobins, 80036 Amiens Cedex 1
Tel: (03) 22.71.71.71 *Fax:* (03) 22.71.71.89
Telex: 145010f
Subjects: Sports, Athletics
ISBN Prefix(es): 2-86814

Pierre Zech Editeur+
18 rue de Conde, 75006 Paris
Tel: (01) 44 32 05 60 *Fax:* (01) 44 32 05 61
Key Personnel
Dir: Pierre Zech

Founded: 1986
Subjects: Art, Biblical Studies, Crafts, Games, Hobbies, Education, Photography, Religion - Catholic, Theology
ISBN Prefix(es): 2-7020; 2-283
Imprints: Le Seneve; Le Temps apprivoise; Lethielleux
Subsidiaries: Marque le Temps Apprivoise

Zodiaque+
Abbaye de la Pierre Qui Vire, 89630 St Leger Vauban
Tel: (03) 86 33 19 24 *Fax:* (03) 86 33 19 25
E-mail: info@editions-zodiaque.fr
Web Site: www.editions-zodiaque.fr; www.zodiaque.com *Cable:* ZODIAQUE-89630 ST LEGER
Key Personnel
Man Dir: Jacques Collin
Founded: 1951
Specialize essentially in architecture & mediaeval art; periodicals.
Subjects: Architecture & Interior Design, Art, History, Travel
ISBN Prefix(es): 2-7369
Number of titles published annually: 5 Print
Total Titles: 170 Print
Distributed by Desclee de Brouwer

French Guiana

General Information

Capital: Cayenne
Language: French and Creole
Religion: Roman Catholic
Population: 133,000
Bank Hours: 0700-1130, 1400-1600 Monday-Friday
Shop Hours: 0800-1300, 1500-1800 Monday-Friday
Currency: 100 centimes = 1 French franc
Export/Import Information: Overseas department of France, which is a member of the European Economic Community. Tariff as for France. See France for domiciliation of documents. No import licenses required. Same exchange restrictions as France.
Copyright: Berne, UCC (see Copyright Conventions, pg xi)

Guy Delabergerie Editions Sarl
PO Box 682, 97303 Cayenne
Tel: 311162 *Fax:* 311759
ISBN Prefix(es): 2-906262
Warehouse: Zl du Larivot Lot, Dalmuzin Haugar Briot, 97351 Matoury

French Polynesia

General Information

Capital: Papeete
Language: French (official) & Polynesian languages
Religion: Mainly Protestant & Roman Catholic
Population: 199,031
Bank Hours: 0730-1530 Monday-Friday; some 0730-1130 Saturday
Shop Hours: 0730-1100, 1400-1700 Monday-Friday; 0730-1130 Saturday
Currency: 100 centimes = 1 CFA franc

Export/Import Information: No tariff on books other than children's picture books; advertising matter subject to customs duty, import duty, although catalogues generally considered printed books. Advertising subject to Statistical Tax. Miscellaneous tax of 2% of customs value on books and advertising. No import license required. Exchange controls.

Ancre de Polynesie, *imprint of* Simone Sanchez

Scoop/Au Vent des Iles+
BP 5670, 98716 Pirae, Tahiti
Tel: (689) 43 54 56 *Fax:* (689) 42 61 74
E-mail: contact@tahiti-books.com
Web Site: www.tahiti-books.com
Key Personnel
Manager: Robert Christian
Founded: 1992
Member of Ligne Editoriale Rattachee au Pacifique Sud, Pacific Islands Book Council.
Subjects: Biography, Cookery, Fiction, Geography, Geology, History, How-to, Literature, Literary Criticism, Essays, Mysteries, South Pacific
ISBN Prefix(es): 2-909790
Imprints: Nouvelles du Pacifique

Collection Moemoea, *imprint of* Simone Sanchez

Haere Po No Tahiti+
BP 1958, 8713 Papeete Tahiti
Tel: 582636 *Fax:* 582333
Key Personnel
Man Dir: L Shan
Founded: 1981
Subjects: Anthropology, Earth Sciences, Ethnicity, History, Language Arts, Linguistics, Natural History, Travel
ISBN Prefix(es): 2-904171

Nouvelles du Pacifique, *imprint of* Scoop/Au Vent des Iles

Simone Sanchez
BP 13973, Punaauia, Tahiti
Tel: 533260
Key Personnel
Contact: Simone Sanchez
Founded: 1993
Subjects: Fiction, History, Regional Interests
ISBN Prefix(es): 2-910256
Imprints: Collection Moemoea; Ancre de Polynesie
Branch Office(s)
Art in Fact, PO Box 6217, Thousand Oaks, CA 91359-6217, United States

Scoop, see Scoop/Au Vent des Iles

Gambia

General Information

Capital: Banjul
Language: English
Religion: Predominantly Islamic
Population: 1,026,000
Bank Hours: 0800-1300 Monday-Thursday; 0800-1000 Friday-Saturday
Shop Hours: 0800 or 0900-1200, 1400-1700 Monday-Thursday; 0800 or 0900-1200, 1500-1700 Friday; 0800 or 0900-1200 Saturday
Currency: 100 butut = 1 dalasi
Export/Import Information: No tariff on books. Import tax on all. No import license required.

National Trading Corporation has no monopoly. Exchange controls.
Copyright: Berne (see Copyright Conventions, pg xi)

Government Printer
PO Box 898, Banjul
Tel: 227399
Telex: 2204
ISBN Prefix(es): 9983-86

Georgia

General Information

Capital: Tbilisi
Language: Georgian
Religion: Predominantly Georgian Orthodox
Population: 5.6 million
Currency: 100 tetri = 1 lari; 1 dollar = 2.23 lari
Export/Import Information: Customs duty for import, 12% to 20% of VAT.

Georgian Encyclopedia Main Science Editorial Board
52 Rustaveli Ave, Tbilisi 8
Tel: (0995) 32-998891 *Fax:* (0995) 32-998823
E-mail: frg@gas.acnet.ge
Web Site: www.acnet.ge/index.html
ISBN Prefix(es): 5-89500

Merani Publishing House
prosp Rustaveli 42, 380008 Tbilissi
Tel: (099532) 996492 *Fax:* (099532) 935514; (099532) 934675
Key Personnel
President & Dir: G E Gvertfsiteli
Editor in Chief: G I Alhazishvili
Commercial Manager: E G Gamezardashvili
Founded: 1925
Subjects: Regional Interests
ISBN Prefix(es): 5-515
Bookshop(s): prosp Rustaveli 42, 380008 Tbilissi

Izdatelstvo Sabtchota Sakartvelo
ul. Mar djanishvili, 380002 Tbilisi
Tel: (08832) 954201
Key Personnel
Dir: D A Tcharkviani
Chief Editor: V R Djavakhadze
Founded: 1921
Subjects: Agriculture, Government, Political Science, Science (General), Social Sciences, Sociology
ISBN Prefix(es): 5-529

Germany

General Information

Capital: Berlin
Language: German. Sorbian speaking minority. Danish spoken by a Danish minority in South Schleswig, North Frisian in North Frisian Islands
Religion: Predominately Protestant and Roman Catholic
Population: 82.7 million
Bank Hours: 0900-1300, 1430-1600 Monday-Friday
Shop Hours: 0900-1830 Monday-Friday; 0900-1400 Saturday
Currency: 100 Eurocents = 1 Euro; 1.95583 Deutsche marks = 1 Euro

Export/Import Information: Member of the European Economic Community. No tariff on books except children's picture books from non-EEC. None on advertising to be distributed free, if exporter's country grants reciprocal treatment, otherwise charged. Import turnover tax on books and advertising. Also, 7% VAT on books. No import license required. No exchange controls.
Copyright: UCC, Berne, Florence (see Copyright Conventions, pg ix)

A Francke Verlag (Tubingen und Basel)+
PO Box 25 60, Dischingerweg 5, D-72070 Tuebingen
Mailing Address: Postfach 2560, 72015 Tubingen
Tel: (07071) 97970 *Fax:* (07071) 75288
E-mail: foolfrancke@tonline.de
Web Site: www.geist.de/francke/info-D.html
Key Personnel
Publisher: Gunter Narr
Manufacturing: Horst Schmid
Founded: 1831
Subjects: Drama, Theater, Economics, Government, Political Science, Literature, Literary Criticism, Essays, Philosophy, Psychology, Psychiatry, Social Sciences, Sociology, Theology
ISBN Prefix(es): 3-7720
Associate Companies: Gunter Narr Verlag
Branch Office(s)
A Francke Verlag (Tubingen und Basel), Gerbergasse 48, CH-4001 Basel, Switzerland

Abakus Musik Barbara Fietz
Haversbach 1, 35753 Greifenstein
Tel: (06478) 2250 *Fax:* (06478) 1355
E-mail: hotline@abakus-musik.de
Web Site: www.abakus-musik.de
Key Personnel
Man Dir: Barbara Fietz *Tel:* (06478) 911060
 E-mail: hotline@abakus-musik.de
Man Dir, Production: Siegfried Fietz
Founded: 1974
Member of JFPI, Borsenverein & DMV.
Subjects: Music, Dance, Religion - Other, Musical & notebook publications
ISBN Prefix(es): 3-88124
Total Titles: 100 E-Book; 150 Audio
Distributed by BMK Verlagsauslieferung Wien (Austria); Brunnen Verlag Basel (Switzerland); Universal (Germany/Switzerland/Austria)

ABC der Deutschen Wirtschaft, Verlagsgesellschaft mbH
Berliner Allee 8, D-64295 Darmstadt
Mailing Address: Postfach 100262, 64202 Darmstadt
Tel: (06151) 38920 *Fax:* (06151) 33164; (06151) 389280
E-mail: info@abconline.de
Web Site: www.abconline.de
Key Personnel
Man Dir: Margit Selka
Publisher of industrial reference directories.
ISBN Prefix(es): 3-87000
Number of titles published annually: 3 Print
Total Titles: 5 Print
Associate Companies: ABC Europe Production; Industrischow Verlags GmbH

Acbrecht Kraus Verlag GmbH
Possartstr 20, 81679 Munich
Tel: (089) 99 84 01-0 *Fax:* (089) 4372-2440
E-mail: vertrieb.verlagsgruppe@bertelsmann.de
Telex: 529965
Key Personnel
Publisher: Eck Klaus
Production: Peter Sturm
Sales: Volker Neumann
Publicity: Margrid Schoeberger
Foreign Rights: Angelika Straus-Fischer
 Tel: (089) 43 72-25 33 *Fax:* (089) 43 72-27 19
 E-mail: foreignrights@bertelsmann.de
Personnel: Helga Nirschl *Tel:* (089) 43 72-24 70
 Fax: (089) 43 72-24 85 *E-mail:* personal.random.house@bertelsmann.de
Founded: 1978
Subjects: Fiction
ISBN Prefix(es): 3-8135
Parent Company: Verlagsgrueppe Bertelsmann
Orders to: VVA Bertelsmann Distribution, Postfach 7777, 33310 Gutersloh

Accedo Verlagsgesellschaft mbH+
Gnesenerstr 1, 81929 Munich
Tel: (089) 935714 *Fax:* (089) 9294109
E-mail: accedoverlag@web.de
Web Site: www.accedoverlag.de
Key Personnel
Manager: Dr Manfred Holler *E-mail:* holler@econ.uni-hamburg.de
Founded: 1988
Subjects: Art, Economics, Government, Political Science, Management, Philosophy, Science (General), Social Sciences, Sociology, Art history, Medicine
ISBN Prefix(es): 3-89265
Total Titles: 50 Print
Associate Companies: Verlag Holler
Imprints: Homo Oeconomicus
Distributor for Verlag Holler

Achterbahn AG Buch+
Achterbahn AG, Werftbahnstr 8, D-24143 Kiel
Mailing Address: Postfach 6128, 24122 Kiel
Tel: (0431) 702-800 *Fax:* (0431) 7028-228
E-mail: 100424.1232@compuserve.com
Key Personnel
Sole Member of Board: Jens Nieswand
Chairman of Supervisory Board: Hans Kettwig
Founded: 1991
Subjects: Humor
ISBN Prefix(es): 3-928950; 3-89719
Warehouse: KVA Verlagsauslieferung, Speckenbeker Weg 116, 24113 Kiel

Joh van Acken GmbH & Co KG
Magdeburgerstr 5, D-47800 Krefeld
Mailing Address: Postfach 105, 47701 Krefeld
Tel: (02151) 44 00-0 *Fax:* (02151) 44 00-11
E-mail: verlag@vanacken.de
Web Site: www.spendengrusskarten.de/willkommen.html
Key Personnel
Publisher & International Rights: Ulrich Kaltenmeier
Founded: 1890
Subjects: Regional Interests
ISBN Prefix(es): 3-923140

R van Acken GmbH Druckerei und Verlag
Josefstr 35, 49809 Lingen, Ems
Mailing Address: Postfach 1124, 49781 Lingen
Tel: (0591) 97312-0 *Fax:* (0591) 74631
Key Personnel
Manager: Werner Marquardt
Founded: 1868
Subjects: Cookery, Literature, Literary Criticism, Essays, Regional Interests
ISBN Prefix(es): 3-87001
Parent Company: Verlag Heinz Heise, Helstorferstr 7, Postfach 610407, 30625 Hannover
Divisions: Hochdruck; Offset; DTP; Buchbinderei

F A Ackermanns Kunstverlag GmbH
PO Box 71 01 08, Meglinger Rd 60, 81451 Munich
Tel: (089) 78580826 *Fax:* (089) 7858028
E-mail: info@ackermannkalender.de
Web Site: www.ackermannkalender.de *Cable:* KUNSTACKERMANN MUNICH
Key Personnel
Man Dir: Michael G Kathan
Founded: 1874
Specialize in Calendars.
Subjects: Art, Photography
ISBN Prefix(es): 3-8173; 3-87002
Parent Company: Busche Unternehmensgrugge, Dortmund
Branch Office(s)
Ackermann Kunstverlag, Attn: Frau Uta Gadeke, 32-62 37 St, Astoria, Astoria, NY 11103, United States

ADAC Verlag GmBH+
Auf der Krautweide 24, 65812 Bad Soden/Taunus
Tel: (06196) 6096-0 *Fax:* (06196) 27450
E-mail: info@cartotravel.de
Web Site: www.cartotravel.de *Cable:* ADACVERLAG
Key Personnel
Manager, Rights & Permissions: Manfred M Angele
Editorial: Michael Dultz
Sales & Advertising: Herbert Edbauer
Production: Eberhard Wagner
Website Technologist: Michael Ritz
 E-mail: mritz@gmx.de
Founded: 1958
Also carry magazines & travel guides.
Subjects: Automotive, Travel
ISBN Prefix(es): 3-87003; 3-8264

Addison Wesley Verlag, see Pearson Education Deutschland GmbH

Adyar Edition, *imprint of* Aquamarin Verlag

Adyar Verlag, *imprint of* Aquamarin Verlag

Adyar-Verlag+
Birkelbacherstr 4, 74589 Sattelorf
Tel: (07950) 925010 *Fax:* (07950) 925029
Key Personnel
Dir: Hank Troemel
Founded: 1947
Theosophical literature.
Subjects: Religion - Buddhist, Religion - Hindu, Theology
ISBN Prefix(es): 3-927837
Total Titles: 25 Print

Aerogie-Verlag+
Fliessstr 20, 12526 Berlin
Tel: (030) 6 76 32 00 *Fax:* (030) 6 76 32 00
Key Personnel
Man Dir: Gerd Otto
Founded: 1990
Specialize in Environmental Energy.
Subjects: Energy, Engineering (General), Environmental Studies, Science (General), Transportation
ISBN Prefix(es): 3-910142
Associate Companies: Ingenieurbuero fuer Windenergie und Schadstofffreie Energetik

Aethera, *imprint of* Verlag Freies Geistesleben

The African Literature Club+
Formerly Books on African Studies
Ladenburgerstr 50, 69120 Heidelberg
Mailing Address: Postfach 1320, 69193 Schriesheim
Tel: (06221) 411861 *Fax:* (06221) 411861
Key Personnel
Man Dir: Jerry Bedu-Addo *E-mail:* jbeduaddo@aol.com
Founded: 1982
Book publication & distribution.
Subjects: Africa
ISBN Prefix(es): 3-927198

Associate Companies: Timbuktu, Ladenburgerstr 50, 69120 Heidelberg
Branch Office(s)
Books on African Studies, PO Box BT, 328, Tema, Ghana *Tel:* (022) 206135 *Fax:* (022) 206134 *E-mail:* beaddo@ghana.com
Book Club(s): African Literature Club, Ladenburgerstr 50, Heidelberg 69120, Eva Groppenbaecher *Tel:* (06221) 411861 *Fax:* (06221) 473946 *E-mail:* evagroppe@aol.com

Agentur des Rauhen Hauses Hamburg GmbH
Beim Bruederhof 8, 22844 Norderstedt
Mailing Address: Postfach 1260, 22802 Norderstedt
Tel: (040) 53 53 88-0 *Fax:* (040) 53 53 88-43
E-mail: kundenservice@agentur-rauhes-haus.de
Web Site: www.agentur-rauhes-haus.de
Key Personnel
Man Dir: Willi Kohlmann
Rights & Permissions: Hans-Heinrich Holm
Cataloging: Ms Schrom
Founded: 1842
Subjects: Religion - Protestant, Religion - Other, Theology
ISBN Prefix(es): 3-7600
Divisions: Reise-und Versandbuchhandlung des Rauhen Hauses

Agis Verlag GmbH
Ooser Luisenstr 23, 76532 Baden-Baden
Mailing Address: Postfach 22 20, 76492 Baden-Baden
Tel: (07221) 95 75-0 *Fax:* (07221) 6 68 10
E-mail: info@agis-verlag.de *Cable:* AGIS BADEN BADEN
Key Personnel
Man Dir: Karl G Fischer; Karin Grochowiak
Media consulting.
Subjects: Art, Philosophy, Science (General)
ISBN Prefix(es): 3-87007

Ahriman-Verlag GmbH+
Stuebeweg 60, 79108 Freiburg
Mailing Address: Postfach 6569, 79041 Freiburg
Tel: (0761) 502303 *Fax:* (0761) 502247
E-mail: ahriman@t-online.de
Web Site: www.ahriman.com
Key Personnel
Man Dir: Edeltraud Rudow *E-mail:* thanilo@t-online.de
Founded: 1983
Subjects: Government, Political Science, Psychology, Psychiatry, Science (General)
ISBN Prefix(es): 3-922774; 3-89484
Total Titles: 1 Print; 1 CD-ROM; 70 Online; 70 E-Book; 20 Audio
Online services available through World Wide Web.

aid infodienst - Verbraucherdienst, Ernaehrung, Landwirtschaft eV
Friedrich-Ebert-Str 3, 53177 Bonn - Bad Godesberg
Tel: (0228) 8499-0 *Fax:* (0228) 9526952; (0228) 8499-177
E-mail: aid@aid.de
Web Site: www.aid.de

Air Gallery Edition, Helmut Kreuzer
Goethestr 8, 85425 Erding
Mailing Address: Postfach 1526, 85425 Erding
Tel: (08122) 84487 *Fax:* (08122) 84487
Key Personnel
President: Helmut Kreuzer
Founded: 1988
Subjects: Aeronautics, Aviation
ISBN Prefix(es): 3-9802101; 3-9805934

Aisthesis Verlag Dr Detlev Kopp und Dr Michael Vogt+
Oberntorwall 21, D-33602 Bielefeld
Mailing Address: Postfach 100427, 33504 Bielefeld
Tel: (0521) 172604; (0521) 172812 *Fax:* (0521) 172812
E-mail: aisthesis@bitel.net
Web Site: www.fechenbach.de
Key Personnel
Man Dir, Rights & Permissions: Dr Detlev Kopp; Dr Michael Vogt
Founded: 1985
Subjects: Art, History, Literature, Literary Criticism, Essays, Philosophy, Science (General)
ISBN Prefix(es): 3-925670; 3-89528

Akademie Verlag GmbH+
Palisadenstr 40, D-10243 Berlin
Tel: (030) 422006-05 *Fax:* (030) 422006-57
E-mail: mktg@akademie-verlag.de
Web Site: www.akademie-verlag.de
Key Personnel
Man Dir: Dr Gerd Giesler *E-mail:* giesler@akademieverlag.de
Professor of History: Manfred Karras *Tel:* (030) 4 22 00 630 *E-mail:* karras@akademieverlag.de
Professor of Philosophy & Editorship German Magazine: Dr Mischka Dammaschke *Tel:* (030) 4 22 00 650 *E-mail:* dammaschke@akademieverlag.de
Professor of Editions: Peter Heyl *Tel:* (030) 4 22 00 645 *E-mail:* heyl@akademieverlg.de
Magazines: Christina Gericke *Tel:* (030) 4 22 00 640 *E-mail:* gericke@akademicverlag.de
Founded: 1946
Member of the Association of German Booksellers.
Subjects: History, Language Arts, Linguistics, Literature, Literary Criticism, Essays, Philosophy, Social Sciences, Sociology
ISBN Prefix(es): 3-05
Parent Company: R Oldenbourg Verlag Muenchen, Rosenheimerstr 145, D-81671 Munich
Orders to: Verlegerdienst Muenchen, Gutenbergstr 1, 82205 Gilching

M Akselrad+
Hauptstr 190, 69117 Heidelberg
Tel: (06221) 183030 *Fax:* (06221) 181223
E-mail: m_akselrad@compuserve.com
Key Personnel
Dir: Michael Akselrad
Founded: 1972
Subjects: Literature, Literary Criticism, Essays, Nonfiction (General)
ISBN Prefix(es): 3-921265

Alba Fachverlag GmbH und Co KG+
Willstaetterstr 9, 40549 Duesseldorf
Mailing Address: Postfach 11 01 50, 40501 Duesseldorf
Tel: (0211) 52013-51 *Fax:* (0211) 52013-18
Web Site: www.alba-verlag.de
Telex: 8585536
Key Personnel
Publishing Dir: Robert Braun
Man Dir, Rights & Permissions: Alf Teloeken *E-mail:* at@albaverlag.de
Manager: Tim Teloeken *E-mail:* teloeken@albaverlga.de
Sales, Publicity: Willi Lennartz; Cornelia Honekamp
Production: P Gerens
Founded: 1951
Subjects: Crafts, Games, Hobbies, Film, Video, Outdoor Recreation
ISBN Prefix(es): 3-87094
Associate Companies: Alba Publikation Alf Teloeken GmbH und Co KG; Schwesterngesellschaft: Alba Fachverlag GmbH & Co KG

Albarello Verlag GmbH+
Domaperstr 23, 42327 Wuppertal
Tel: (0202) 2058 8279 *Fax:* (0202) 2058 80534
Founded: 2001

Albatros, *imprint of* Verlag an der Ruhr GmbH

Verlag Karl Alber GmbH+
Postfach, D-79080 Freiburg
Tel: (0761) 27 17-365 *Fax:* (0761) 27 17-212
E-mail: alber-buch@alber.freinet.de
Web Site: www.alber.freinet.de
Key Personnel
Man Dir: Dr Jurgen A Bach
Founded: 1939
Subjects: Communications, Government, Political Science, History, Journalism, Law, Philosophy, Science (General)
ISBN Prefix(es): 3-495
Total Titles: 50 Print
Parent Company: Verlag Herder
Orders to: Verlagsauslieferung Koch, Neff & Oetinger, Schockenriedstr 39, Postfach 800620, 70565 Stuttgart

Albert Nauck & Co
Luxemburgerstr 449, 50939 Cologne
Tel: (0221) 94373-0 *Fax:* (0221) 94373-901
Key Personnel
Contact: B Gallus; J Kuth
ISBN Prefix(es): 3-87574

Albert Propster Verlag und Buchhandlung
Schillerstr 46, 87435 Kempten im Allgaeu
Mailing Address: Postfach 2149, 8711 Kempten im Allgaeu
Tel: (0831) 22797 *Fax:* (0831) 201732
Key Personnel
Man Dir, Rights & Permissions: Rosa Proepster
Founded: 1945
Subjects: Cookery
ISBN Prefix(es): 3-87647

Albino Verlag, *imprint of* Bruno Gmuender Verlag GmbH

E Albrecht Verlags-Kommanditgesellschaft+
Freihamestr 2, 82166 Graefelfing
Mailing Address: Postfach 11 20, 82153 Graefelfing
Tel: (089) 85 85 31 00 *Fax:* (089) 85 85 31 99
E-mail: av@albrecht.de
Key Personnel
Man Dir & Publisher: Hansgeorg Albrecht
Publisher: Oliver Albrecht
Founded: 1927
Subjects: Career Development, Sports, Athletics
ISBN Prefix(es): 3-87014

Verlag und Antiquariat Frank Albrecht
Panoramastr 4, 69198 Schriesheim
Tel: (06203) 65713 *Fax:* (06203) 65311
E-mail: albrecht@antiquariat.com
Web Site: www.antiquariat.com
Key Personnel
Publisher: Frank Albrecht
Founded: 1985
Member of PEN International & German Antiques.
Subjects: Government, Political Science, History, Literature, Literary Criticism, Essays
ISBN Prefix(es): 3-926360
Total Titles: 1 Print

Alexander Verlag Berlin+
Fredericiastr 12, D-14050 Berlin
Mailing Address: Postfach 191824, 14008 Berlin
Tel: (030) 3021826 *Fax:* (030) 3029408
E-mail: info@alexander-verlag.com
Web Site: www.alexander-verlag.com

Key Personnel
Owner: Alexander Wewerka *E-mail:* alex@alexander-verlag.com
Founded: 1983
Subjects: Drama, Theater, Film, Video, Literature, Literary Criticism, Essays, Music, Dance
ISBN Prefix(es): 3-923854; 3-89581
Total Titles: 85 Print; 8 CD-ROM; 3 Audio
Distributed by AVA-Buch 2000 (Switzerland); AS Verlagsservice Holler (Austria)
Orders to: Sova, Friesstr 20-24, 60388 Frankfurt am Main, Contact: Brigitte Platteel *Tel:* (069) 410211 *Fax:* (069) 410280 *E-mail:* sovaffm@t-online.de

Alibaba Verlag GmbH+
Nordendstr 20, 60318 Frankfurt
Tel: (069) 590097 *Fax:* (069) 559855
Web Site: www.alibaba-verlag.de
Key Personnel
International Rights: Anne Teuter
Contact: Abraham Teuter
Founded: 1980
Subjects: Literature & art
ISBN Prefix(es): 3-922723; 3-927926; 3-86042
Imprints: Krimi-Reihe
Distributed by Sova

Alkor-Edition Kassel GmbH+
Heinrich-Schuetz-Allee 35, 34131 Kassel-Wilhelmshoehe
Tel: (0561) 3105-280 *Fax:* (0561) 37755
E-mail: alkor-edition@baerenreiter.com
Web Site: www.alkor-edition.com
Key Personnel
Man Dir: Barbara Scheuch-Voetterle
Subjects: Music, Dance
ISBN Prefix(es): 3-920018
Subsidiaries: Barenreiter Verlag Basel AG
Distributed by Baerenreiter Ltd (Great Britain, Ireland, New Zealand & Australia); Baerenreiter Music Corporation (Canada & US); Editio Baerenreiter Praha (Slovakian & Czech Republic); Baerenreiter Verlag Basel AG (Switzerland); Casa Musicale Sonzogno (Italy); Faber Music Distribution (Great Britain, Ireland, New Zealand & Australia); Hartai Music Agency (Hungary); Israel Music Institute (Israel); Muziekhandel Albersen & Co (Netherlands); SEEMSA (Spain & Portugal); Zamp (Croatia & Slovenia)
Distributor for Editio Baerenreiter Praha (Germany, Austria & Switzerland); Baerenreiter Verlag Kassel (Basel, London, New York, Prag) (Worldwide); Gustav Boss Verlag Kassel (Worldwide); Dilla Prag (Germany, Austria, Switerland, Benelux countries, Scandinavia); Faber Music London (Germany, Austria & Switzerland); Henie Verlag Muenchen (Worldwide); Henschel Verlag fuer Musik Berlin (Worldwide); Editions Henry Lemoine Paris (Germany, Austria & Switzerland); Musikwissenschaftlicher Verlag Wien (Worldwide with the exception of Austria); Slowakischer Musikfonds Bratislava (Germany, Austria, Switerland, Benelux countries); Strauss Edition Wien (Worldwide); Sueddeutscher Musikverlag Heidelberg (Worldwide); Tschechischer Musikfonds Praha (Germany, Austria, Switzerland, Benelux countries, Scandinavia, Spain & Portugal)

Alouette Verlag+
Uferstr 41, 2113 Oststeinbek
Tel: (040) 712 23 53 *Fax:* (040) 713 41 88
E-mail: webmaster@alouette-verlag.de
Web Site: www.alouette-verlag.de
Key Personnel
President & Publisher: Juergen F Boden
 E-mail: juergen.boden@alouette-verlag.de
Editor: Elke Emshoff
Art Dir: Petra Horn
Founded: 1983
Book & film publishers.
Specialize in nature-oriented picture & text books (pictorials with profound text matter) mainly about North America, the Arctic & Siberia, TV documentaries & cultural books.
Subjects: Natural History, Travel, Foreign Cultures
ISBN Prefix(es): 3-924324
Number of titles published annually: 2 Print; 2 Audio
Total Titles: 20 Print; 4 Audio
Online services available through T-Online.

Alpha Literatur Verlag/Alpha Presse
August-Siebertstr 9, 60323 Frankfurt
Tel: (069) 555325 *Fax:* (069) 558361
Key Personnel
Man Dir: Dr Gisela Philipps
Founded: 1969
Subjects: Drama, Theater, Poetry
ISBN Prefix(es): 3-924510

ALS-Verlag GmbH+
Voltastr 3, Jurgen Hills, 63128 Dietzenbach
Mailing Address: Postfach 1440, 63114 Dietzenbach
Tel: (06074) 82160 *Fax:* (06074) 27322
E-mail: info@als-verlag.de
Web Site: www.als-verlag.de
Key Personnel
Publisher: Ingrid Kreide-Michels
International Rights: Ingrid Enger
Founded: 1977
Subjects: Art, Crafts, Games, Hobbies, Education, Environmental Studies, How-to, Outdoor Recreation
ISBN Prefix(es): 3-89135; 3-921366
Imprints: Dietzenbach

Altberliner Verlag GmbH+
Neue Schoenhauserstr 8, 10178 Berlin (Mitte)
Tel: (030) 284 992-0 *Fax:* (030) 284 992-20
E-mail: presse@altberliner.de
Web Site: www.altberliner.de
Key Personnel
Owner: Dr Stephan Schmidt
Owner & Dir: Renate Nickl
Founded: 1945
Subjects: Developing Countries, Fiction, Literature, Literary Criticism, Essays, Mysteries
ISBN Prefix(es): 3-357
Branch Office(s)
Zentuerstr 19, 80798 Munich *Tel:* (089) 1 23 62-59 *Fax:* (089) 12 779 954 *E-mail:* vertrieb@altberliner.de

Anneliese Althoff, see Asso Verlag

Aluminium-Verlag Marketing & Kommunikation GmbH
Aachenerstr 172, 40474 Duesseldorf
Mailing Address: Postfach 101262, 40003 Duesseldorf
Tel: (0211) 4796227 *Fax:* (0211) 4796412
Web Site: www.alu-verlag.com
Key Personnel
Man Dir: Werner Lenzen *Tel:* (0211) 15 91-370
 E-mail: w.lenzen@alu-verlag.com
Sales Manager: Anne Tappen *Tel:* (0211) 15 91-371 *E-mail:* a.tappen@alu-verlag.com
Seminar & Advertising Manager: Christiane Czech *Tel:* (0211) 15 91-372 *E-mail:* c.czech@alu-verlag.de
Library: Eva Kammerling *Tel:* (0211) 47 96-276 *E-mail:* eva.kaemmerling@aluinfo.de
Founded: 1953
Subjects: Earth Sciences
ISBN Prefix(es): 3-87017
Total Titles: 9 Print
Parent Company: Aluminium-Zentrale eV, Am Bonneshof 5, 40474 Duesseldorf
Associate Companies: Cambridge Scientific Abstracts *Web Site:* www.csa.com/journals; Deutsche Verlage technisch-wissenschaftlicher Vereine *Web Site:* www.dvt-verlag.de

Anabas-Verlag Guenter Kaempf GmbH & Co KG+
Friesstr 20-24, 60388 Frankfurt
Tel: (069) 94 21 98 71 *Fax:* (069) 94 21 98 72
E-mail: info@anabas-verlag.com
Key Personnel
Man Dir: Guenter Kaempf
Founded: 1966
Member of Borsenverein des Deutschen Buchandles, Hessischen Buchhandler- und Verlegerverband.
Subjects: Art, History, Poetry, Travel
ISBN Prefix(es): 3-87038
Number of titles published annually: 12 Print
Total Titles: 275 Print
Foreign Rep(s): Pierre Bachofner (Switzerland); Burkard Steinmetz (Germany); Gabriela Wachter (Switzerland)
Orders to: Sozialistische Verlagsauslieferung GmbH, Friesstr 20-22, 60388 Frankfurt am Main *Tel:* (069) 410211 *Fax:* (069) 410280 *E-mail:* sovaffm@t-online.de

Andernach Atelier Verlag (AVA)
Einsteinstr 10, 53757 St Augustin
Mailing Address: Postfach 1465, 53732 St Augustin
Tel: (02241) 31640 *Fax:* (02241) 316436
Key Personnel
Manager: Dr Werner Hippe
Founded: 1947
Subjects: Government, Political Science, Health, Nutrition, Medicine, Nursing, Dentistry, Public Administration, Social Sciences, Sociology
ISBN Prefix(es): 3-537
Subsidiaries: Siegler & Co Verlag fur Zeitarchive GmbH

Angel, *imprint of* Egmont vgs verlagsgesellschaft mbH

Angelika und Lothar Binding
Gaisbergstr 68, 69115 Heidelberg
Tel: (06221) 20955 *Fax:* (06221) 181846
Web Site: www.binding-singles.de
Key Personnel
Owner: Angelika Binding *E-mail:* angelika.binding@gmx.net; Lothar Binding
Founded: 1984
Subjects: Music, Dance
ISBN Prefix(es): 3-9804710
Total Titles: 2 Print

Anrich Verlag GmbH+
Postfach 10 01 54, D-69441 Weinheim
Tel: (06201) 6007-0; (06201) 6007-358
 Fax: (06201) 6007-92
E-mail: g.anrich@beltz.de
Key Personnel
Man Dir: Gerold Anrich
Founded: 1970
Member of Arbeitsgemeinschaft von Jugend Buchverlegern in Der Brd eV.
ISBN Prefix(es): 3-920110; 3-89106

Antex Verlag-Hans Joachin Schuhmacher+
Am Gabelsee, 15306 Falkenhagen
Tel: (033603) 40410 *Fax:* (033603) 40400
Key Personnel
Publisher: Hajo Schuhmacher
Sales: Heidi Schuhmacher
Author: Tina Rau
Founded: 1988
ISBN Prefix(es): 3-9801871

GERMANY

Antiqua-Verlag GmbH
Dorneckstr 3a, 79793 Wutoeschingen-Horheim
Tel: (07746) 2273 *Fax:* (07746) 2260
Key Personnel
Manager: Ottfried Ludwig
Founded: 1977
Subjects: Geography, Geology, Medicine, Nursing, Dentistry
ISBN Prefix(es): 3-88210

Antiquariat und Verlag Auvermann Keip GmbH+
Bayernstr 9, D-63773 Goldbach
Tel: (06021) 59 05 0 *Fax:* (06021) 59 05 42
E-mail: info@keip.net
Web Site: www.keip.net
Key Personnel
Publisher: Dominik Anvemam; Ulrich Keip
Manager, Office Chief: Dr Michael Simon
Founded: 1967
Member of ILAB; Also acts as antiquarian bookseller.
Subjects: Economics, History, Law, Social Sciences, Sociology
ISBN Prefix(es): 3-8051

Antiquariats-Union Vertriebs GmbH & Co KG
Luener Rennbahn 14, 21339 Lueneburg
Tel: (04131) 983504
Web Site: www.restauflagen.de
Key Personnel
Contact: Jens Harelberg *E-mail:* harelberg@antiquariats-union.de
Number of titles published annually: 15 Print
Total Titles: 70 Print

Anzeigenverwaltung & Herstellung, *imprint of* Johann Wolfgang Goethe Universitat

AOL-Verlag Frohmut Menze
Waldstr 18, 77839 Lichtenau-Scherzheim
Tel: (07227) 95 88-0 *Fax:* (07227) 95 88-95
E-mail: info@aol-verlag.de; bestellung@aol-verlag.de
Web Site: www.aol-verlag.de
Key Personnel
Man Dir: Frohmut Menze *Fax:* (07227) 95 88-22 *E-mail:* frohmut.menze@aol-verlag.de
Order Department: Doris Futterer *Fax:* (07227) 95 88-16; Andrea Hansel *Fax:* (07227) 95 88-12; Carmen Herberth *Fax:* (07227) 95 88-25; Barbel Stenftenagel *Fax:* (07227) 95 88-11
Web Editorship: Kai Mailitis *Fax:* (06772) 96 97 08 *E-mail:* aolverlag@mailitis.de
Graphics: Bibo Mayer *Fax:* (07227) 95 88-18 *E-mail:* bibo@aol-verlag.de
Advertising: Ute Hettel *Fax:* (07227) 95 88-21 *E-mail:* ute.hettel@aol-verlag.de
Subjects: Advertising, Art, Biological Sciences, Career Development, Chemistry, Chemical Engineering, Child Care & Development, Computer Science, Drama, Theater, Education, Energy, English as a Second Language, Environmental Studies, Fiction, Film, Video, Foreign Countries, Government, Political Science, Health, Nutrition, History, Literature, Literary Criticism, Essays, Management, Mathematics, Natural History, Nonfiction (General), Outdoor Recreation, Physical Sciences, Physics, Science (General), Sports, Athletics, Transportation
ISBN Prefix(es): 3-89111

Verlag APHAIA Svea Haske, Sonja Schumann GbR
Radickestr 44, 12489 Berlin-Treptow
Tel: (030) 813 39 98 *Fax:* (030) 813 39 98
E-mail: info@aphaia-verlag.de
Web Site: www.aphaia-verlag.de
Key Personnel
Contact: Svea Haske; Sonja Schumann
Founded: 1986
Subjects: Art, Literature, Literary Criticism, Essays, Music, Dance, Poetry, Bookart, Literature, Lyrics, Music
ISBN Prefix(es): 3-926677
Number of titles published annually: 5 Print
Total Titles: 125 Print
Distributor for Friedrich Nolte Verlag; Paian Verlag
Orders to: Aphaia Verlag, Berlin-Treptow

Apollo-Verlag Paul Lincke GmbH
Weihergarten 5, 55116 Mainz
Mailing Address: Postfach 3640, 55026 Mainz
Tel: (06131) 246300 *Fax:* (06131) 246861
E-mail: apollo@schott-musik.de
Key Personnel
Contact: Dr Christian Sprang
Subjects: Music, Dance
ISBN Prefix(es): 3-920030
Sales Office(s): SMD Schott Music Distribution GmbH, Carl Zeissstr 1, 55129 Mainz

Aquamarin Verlag+
Muehlenstr 43, 85567 Grafing
Tel: (08092) 9444 *Fax:* (08092) 1614
E-mail: aquamarin-verlag@t-online.de
Key Personnel
Man Dir: Dr Peter Michel
Founded: 1980
Subjects: Art, Astrology, Occult, Parapsychology, Philosophy, Religion - Buddhist, Religion - Hindu, Science (General)
ISBN Prefix(es): 3-922936; 3-89427
Imprints: Adyar Edition; Adyar Verlag; Sulamith Wulfing Edition; Sulamith Wulfing Verlag
U.S. Office(s): Bluestar, 160 Camino Don Miguel, Orinda, CA 94563, United States, Petra Michel *Tel:* 925-386-0440 *Fax:* 925-386-0386 *Web Site:* www.bluestar.com
Foreign Rep(s): Dr. Fiuliana Bernardi (Italy)
Foreign Rights: Katia Schume (Portugal, South America, Spain)
Shipping Address: Muehlenstr 43, 85567 Grafing

arani-Verlag GmbH+
Gneisenaustr 23, 10961 Berlin
Mailing Address: Postfach 19 16 28, D-10730 Berlin
Tel: (030) 691-7073 *Fax:* (030) 691-4067
Key Personnel
Man Dir: Volker Spiess
Founded: 1947
Subjects: History, Regional Interests, Religion - Jewish, Judaica
ISBN Prefix(es): 3-7605
Associate Companies: Haude und Spenersche Verlagsbuchhandlung; Wissenschaftsverlag Volker Spiess GmbH
Orders to: VAH-Jager Verlagsauslieferungen, Miraustr 54, 13509 Berlin

Arbeiterpresse Verlag GmbH+
Postfach 500105, 45055 Essen
Tel: (0201) 6462106 *Fax:* (0201) 6462108
E-mail: vertrieb@arbeiterpresse.de
Web Site: www.arbeiterpresse.de
Key Personnel
Contact: Wolfgang Zimmermann *E-mail:* wz@arbeiterpresse.de
Founded: 1979
Subjects: Government, Political Science, History, Labor, Industrial Relations, Social Sciences, Sociology
ISBN Prefix(es): 3-88634
Number of titles published annually: 4 Print
Total Titles: 32 Print
U.S. Office(s): Mehring Books, PO Box 48377, Oak Park, MI 48237, United States *Tel:* 967-2924 *Fax:* 967-3023 *E-mail:* inquiries@mehring.com

Arbeitsgruppe LOK Report eV
Sigmaringerstr 26, D-10713 Berlin
Tel: (030) 86 40 92 62 *Fax:* (030) 86 40 92 64
E-mail: redaktion@lok-report.de
Web Site: www.lok-report.de
Key Personnel
Chief Editor: Martin Stertz
Founded: 1972
Specialize in transport, railways, locomotive, German & Eastern European railways; monthly railway magazine 'Lok Report'.
ISBN Prefix(es): 3-927980
Number of titles published annually: 2 Print
Total Titles: 6 Print

Arcadia Verlag GmbH+
Heimhuderstr 36, 20148 Hamburg
Mailing Address: Postfach 130848, 20108 Hamburg
Tel: (040) 4141000 *Fax:* (040) 41410041
E-mail: contact@sikorski.de
Web Site: www.sikorski.de
Key Personnel
Man Dir: Prof Hans-Wilfred Sikorski; Dagmar Sikorski
Rights & Permissions: Karl-Hermann Adrio
Founded: 1935
Subjects: Drama, Theater, Music, Dance
ISBN Prefix(es): 3-920033
Parent Company: Buehnen-und Musikverlage Dr Sikorski KG, Heimhuderstr 36, 20148 Hamburg

ARCult Media+
Dahlmannstr 26, 53113 Bonn
Tel: (0228) 211059 *Fax:* (0228) 217493
E-mail: info@arcultmedia.de
Web Site: www.arcultmedia.de
Key Personnel
Contact: Dr Andreas Joh Wiesand
Founded: 1969
Publications and research documents in all fields of the arts & culture industries.
Subjects: Art, Developing Countries, Drama, Theater, Journalism, Management, Music, Dance, Outdoor Recreation, Publishing & Book Trade Reference, Radio, TV, Social Sciences, Sociology, Women's Studies
ISBN Prefix(es): 3-930395
Total Titles: 50 Print; 1 CD-ROM
Branch Office(s)
Berlin
Vienna
Distributed by C H Beck (Munich); Leske & Budrich (Opladen); Nomos (Baden-Baden)

Arcus-Medien Wolfgang Steinhardt+
Clayallee 74a, 14195 Berlin
Tel: (030) 8 32 50 41 *Fax:* (030) 8 32 73 23
Key Personnel
Owner: Wolfgang Steinhardt
Founded: 1984
Subjects: Cookery, How-to, Nonfiction (General), Travel, Wine & Spirits
ISBN Prefix(es): 3-924720

Ardey-Verlag GmbH
An den Speichern 6, 48157 Muenster
Tel: (0251) 4132-0 *Fax:* (0251) 4132-20
Web Site: www.ardey-verlag.de
Key Personnel
Man Dir: Dr Walter Bakenecker; Friedhelm Nolte
Founded: 1951
Subjects: Architecture & Interior Design, Art, Geography, Geology, History, Literature, Literary Criticism, Essays, Nonfiction (General), Regional Interests, Religion - Other
ISBN Prefix(es): 3-87023
Orders to: CVK, Kammeratsheide 66, 33609 Bielefeld

Arena Verlag GmbH+
Rottendorferstr 16, 97074 Wuerzburg

Mailing Address: Postfach 5169, PLZ 97001 Wuerzburg
Tel: (0931) 79 644-0 *Fax:* (0931) 79 644-13
Key Personnel
Man Dir: Juergen Weidenbach
Publicity: Dirk Meyer
Sales Dir: Albrecht Oldenbourg
Production: Winfried Popp
Foreign Rights: Monika Obrist *Tel:* (0931) 73644-62 *E-mail:* monika.obrist@arena-verlag.de
Founded: 1949
Subjects: Fiction, Nonfiction (General)
ISBN Prefix(es): 3-401
Number of titles published annually: 500 Print
Total Titles: 2,000 Print
Parent Company: Georg Westermann GmbH & Co, Georg-Westermann-Allee 66, 38104 Braunschweig
Imprints: Edition Buecherbar im Arena Verlag; Ensslin Verlag im Arena Verlag
Warehouse: VSB Verlagsservice Braunschweig GmbH, Georg-Westermann-Allee 66, 38104 Braunschweig

Argon Verlag GmbH+
Unit of S Fischer Verlag
Neuenburger Str 17, 10969 Berlin
Tel: (030) 25 37 38-0; (030) 25 37 38-301 (ISDN) *Fax:* (030) 25 37 38-99
E-mail: info@argon-verlag.de
Web Site: www.argon-verlag.de
Key Personnel
Editor-in-Chief: Hans Christian Rohr *Tel:* (030) 253738-24 *E-mail:* christian.rohr@argon-verlag.de
Founded: 1952
Subjects: Fiction, Nonfiction (General), General fiction
ISBN Prefix(es): 3-87024
Orders to: S Fischer Verlag, 60591 Frankfurt/Main *Tel:* (069) 60620 *Fax:* (069) 6062214 *E-mail:* verkauf@s.fischer.de

Argument-Verlag+
Eppendorfer Weg 95a, 20259 Hamburg
Tel: (040) 401800-0 *Fax:* (040) 401800-20
E-mail: verlag@argument.de
Web Site: www.argument.de
Key Personnel
Contact: Bettina Fischer; Wolfgang Fritz Haug; Frigga Haug
Founded: 1959
Subjects: Fiction, Gay & Lesbian, Government, Political Science, Philosophy, Science Fiction, Fantasy, Social Sciences, Sociology, Women's Studies
ISBN Prefix(es): 3-88619; 3-920037
Divisions: Redaktion

Aries-Verlag Paul Johannes Muller+
Ringstr 32a, D-83355 Grabenstaett
Mailing Address: Postfach 166, 83355 Grabenstaett
Tel: (08661) 8209 *Fax:* (08661) 985 980
E-mail: pjm@aries-verlag.de
Key Personnel
Owner: Paul J Mueller
Founded: 1965
Subjects: Architecture & Interior Design, Art
ISBN Prefix(es): 3-920041

Ariston, *imprint of* Heinrich Hugendubel Verlag GmbH

Arkana Verlag Tete Bottger Rainer Wunderlich GmbH+
Hainbundstr 17, 37085 Goettingen
Mailing Address: Postfach 1140, 37085 Goettingen
Tel: (0551) 41709 *Fax:* (0551) 43868
Key Personnel
Owner: Mr Boettger *E-mail:* aboettg@gwdg.de
Founded: 1981
Subjects: Art, History, Science (General), History of Science
ISBN Prefix(es): 3-923257

Arnoldsche Verlagsanstalt GmbH (Arnoldsche Art Publishers)+
Liststr 9, 70180 Stuttgart
Tel: (0711) 645618-0 *Fax:* (0711) 645618-79
E-mail: art@arnoldsche.com
Web Site: www.arnoldsche.com
Key Personnel
International Rights: Dieter Zuehlsdorff
Marketing, Distribution & Public Relations: Dirk Allgaier *Tel:* (0711) 645618-20 *E-mail:* allgaier@arnoldsche.com
Founded: 1988
Subjects: Antiques, Architecture & Interior Design, Art, Fashion, Photography, Specialize in jewelry, glass, porcelain, Asian art & Non-European Art
ISBN Prefix(es): 3-925369; 3-89790
Number of titles published annually: 15 Print
Total Titles: 80 Print
Associate Companies: Forum fuer Europaeische Kunst und Kultur, Stuttgart
U.S. Office(s): Antique Collectors' Club Ltd, 51 Market St, Industrial Park, Wappings Falls, NY 12590, United States *Tel:* 845-297-0003 *Fax:* 845-297-0068

Ars Edition GmbH+
Friedrichstr 9, 80801 Munich
Mailing Address: Postfach 430151, 80731 Munich
Tel: (089) 381006-77 *Fax:* (089) 381006-58
Key Personnel
Man Dir: Marcel Nauer
Man Dir, Rights & Permissions: Sabine Lippert
Production: Gregor Schulze
Public Relations: Birgit Welzel
Founded: 1896
Subjects: Art, Child Care & Development, Cookery, Crafts, Games, Hobbies, Fiction, House & Home, Nonfiction (General), Romance
ISBN Prefix(es): 3-7607
Subsidiaries: Ars Edition

Ars Vivendi Verlag+
Bauhof 1, D-90556 Cadolzburg
Mailing Address: Postfach 9, 90553 Cadolzburg
Tel: (091) 03-719 29 0 *Fax:* (091) 03 719 59 19
E-mail: ars@arsvivendi.com
Web Site: www.arsvivendi.com
Key Personnel
Owner: Norbert Treuheit
Founded: 1988
Subjects: Cookery, Nonfiction (General), Travel
ISBN Prefix(es): 3-927482; 3-931043

Art Directors Club Verlag GmbH
Leibnizstr 65, 10629 Berlin/Charlottenburg
Tel: (030) 59 00 31 0 *Fax:* (030) 59 00 31 0
E-mail: adc@adc.de
Web Site: www.adc.de
Key Personnel
Manager: Elly Koszytorz; Susann Schronen *Tel:* (030) 59 22 31 0-21 *Fax:* (030) 59 22 31 0-21 *E-mail:* susann.schronen@adc.de
Project Manager: Astrid Hegenauer *Tel:* (030) 59 00 31 0-21 *Fax:* (030) 59 00 31 0-21 *E-mail:* astrid.hegenauer@adc.de
Project Management Events/Seminars: Katrin Puelacher *Tel:* (030) 59 00 31 0-21 *Fax:* (030) 59 00 31 0-21 *E-mail:* katrin.puelacher@adc.de
Founded: 1964
Art Directors Club is only licenser.
Subjects: Advertising, Communications
ISBN Prefix(es): 3-87439

Orders to: Universitaetsdruckerei und Verlag Hermann Schmidt Mainz, Robert-Koch-St 8, 55214 Mainz *Tel:* (06131) 506030 *Fax:* (06131) 506080

ARTC/OLOR+
Ostenallee 78, 59071 Hamm
Mailing Address: Postfach 1149, 59001 Hamm
Tel: (02381) 980190 *Fax:* (02381) 9801999
Key Personnel
Rights & Permissions: Christof Kaplanek
Contact: Wilhelm Spindelndreier
Founded: 1987
Specialize in postcards, books, travel & pictures.
Subjects: Art, Cookery, Photography, Regional Interests, Travel
ISBN Prefix(es): 3-89743; 3-923166
Associate Companies: Eggenkamp Verlageu
Distributed by Buchzentrum (Switzerland); Olten (Switzerland); Schweizer (Switzerland)
Warehouse: Verlagsservice Braunschweig, Westermannallee 66, 38104 Braunschweig *Tel:* (0531) 708646

Arts & Antiques Edition Munich Verlag, Buch & Kunsthandel GmbH
Germaniastr 14, D-80802 Munich
Mailing Address: Postfach 400128, 80701 Munich
Tel: (089) 349830 *Fax:* (089) 349834
E-mail: wine-price@wine-auction-world.com
Key Personnel
Manager: Harry Blattel
Founded: 1990
Subjects: Art, Wine & Spirits
ISBN Prefix(es): 3-928263

Arun-Verlag+
Ortsstr 28, D-07407 Engerda
Tel: (036743) 233-0 *Fax:* (036743) 233-17
E-mail: info@arun-verlag.de
Web Site: www.arun-verlag.de
Key Personnel
Publisher: Stefan Ulbrich
Founded: 1989
Subjects: Astrology, Occult, Native American Studies, Philosophy, Religion - Other
ISBN Prefix(es): 3-927940
Total Titles: 50 Print

Roland Asanger Verlag GmbH
Boedldorf 3, 84178 Kroening
Tel: (08744) 7262 *Fax:* (08744) 967755
E-mail: verlag@asanger.de
Web Site: www.asanger.de
Key Personnel
Publisher: Dr Gerd Wenninger
Founded: 1987
Subjects: Environmental Studies, Health, Nutrition, Psychology, Psychiatry, Social Sciences, Sociology
ISBN Prefix(es): 3-89334
Distributed by Herder AG Basel
Orders to: Verlagsservice Suedwest, Boschstr 2, 68753 Waghaeusel *Tel:* (07254) 507 13 *Fax:* (07254) 507 24 *E-mail:* verlagsservice-sw@t-online.de

Aschendorffsche Verlagsbuchhandlung GmbH & Co KG+
Soesterstr 13, 48155 Muenster
Tel: (0251) 690133 *Fax:* (0251) 690143
E-mail: buchverlag@aschendorff.de
Web Site: www.aschendorff.de/buch
Telex: 892555
Key Personnel
Contact: Dr Jurgeu Beuedikt Huffer; Dr Eduard Huffer
Founded: 1720
Member of VGS - Verlagsgesellschaft mbH & Co KG.

Subjects: History, Language Arts, Linguistics, Philosophy, Psychology, Psychiatry, Regional Interests, Religion - Other, Theology
ISBN Prefix(es): 3-402
Number of titles published annually: 80 Print; 2 CD-ROM

Asclepios Edition Lothar Baus+
Zum Lappentascher Hof 65, 66424 Homburg/Saar
Tel: (06841) 71863
E-mail: lotharbaus@web.de
Web Site: www.asclepiosedition.de
Key Personnel
Contact: Lothar Baus
Founded: 1985
Specialize in Goethe-Studies & Friedrich Nietzsche.
Subjects: Biography, Literature, Literary Criticism, Essays, Philosophy
ISBN Prefix(es): 3-925101; 3-935288

Assimil GmbH
Hinterden Hagen 1, 52388 Noervenich
Mailing Address: Postfach 47, 752386 Noervenich
Tel: (02426) 9400 *Fax:* (02426) 4862
E-mail: kontakt@assimil.com
Web Site: www.assimil.com
Founded: 1988
Specialize in textbooks-foreign languages.
Subjects: Language Arts, Linguistics
ISBN Prefix(es): 3-89625

Asso Verlag+
Martin-Heix-Platz 3, 46045 Oberhausen
Tel: (0208) 802356 *Fax:* (0208) 809882
Key Personnel
Contact: Anneliese Althoff
Founded: 1970
Subjects: Labor, Industrial Relations, Poetry, Regional Interests, Social Sciences, Sociology
ISBN Prefix(es): 3-921541
Warehouse: Lothringerstr 64, 46045 Oberhausen

Verlag Atelier im Bauernhaus+
In der Bredenau 6, 28870 Ottersberg-Fischerhude
Tel: (04293) 491; (04293) 493 *Fax:* (04293) 1238
Key Personnel
Publisher: Wolf-Dietmar Stock
Rights & Permissions: Hans-Guenther Pawelzik
Founded: 1976
Subjects: Art, Fiction, Regional Interests
ISBN Prefix(es): 3-88132
Orders to: VVA, An der Autobahn, 33310 Guetersloh

Atelier Verlag Andernach (AVA)+
Antel 74, 56626 Andernach
Tel: (02632) 44432 *Fax:* (02632) 31383
Key Personnel
Man Dir, Rights & Permissions: Fritz Werf
Founded: 1966
Subjects: Art, Poetry
ISBN Prefix(es): 3-921042

Atlantis Musikbuch+
Imprint of Schott Musik International
Weihergarten 5, 55116 Mainz
Tel: (06131) 246-0 *Fax:* (06131) 246-211
Founded: 1976
Subjects: Music, Dance
ISBN Prefix(es): 3-254

AUE-Verlag GmbH+
Korberstr 20, 74219 Moeckmuehl
Mailing Address: Postfach 1108, 74215 Moeckmuehl
Tel: (06298) 1328 *Fax:* (06298) 4298
E-mail: aue-verlag@web.de
Web Site: www.aue-verlag.com

Key Personnel
Manager: Thomas Gauger
Founded: 1919
Subjects: Crafts, Games, Hobbies, Education, Religion - Protestant, Religion - Other
ISBN Prefix(es): 3-87029
Divisions: Redaktion

Auer Verlag GmbH+
Heilig-Kreuzstr 16, 86609 Donauwoerth
Mailing Address: Postfach 1152, 86601 Donauwoerth
Tel: (0906) 730 *Fax:* (0906) 73177; (0906) 73178
E-mail: info@auer-verlag.de
Web Site: www.auer-verlag.de *Cable:* AUER DONAUWORTH
Key Personnel
Man Dir: Herr Buechler *Tel:* (0906) 73242
Contact: Tanja Auernhamer *Tel:* (0906) 73152
E-mail: auernhamer@auer-verlag.de
Founded: 1875
Member of TR-Verlagsunion GmbH.
Subjects: Education, History, Psychology, Psychiatry, Religion - Catholic
ISBN Prefix(es): 3-403
Number of titles published annually: 100 Print; 20 CD-ROM; 5 Audio
Total Titles: 1,000 Print; 60 CD-ROM; 20 Audio
Branch Office(s)
Westenhellweg 126, 44137 Dortmund *Tel:* (0231) 5844830 *Fax:* (0231) 58448320
August-Bebelstr 43, 04275 Leipzig *Tel:* (0341) 3026270 *Fax:* (0341) 3026271

Aufbau Taschenbuch Verlag GmbH
Neue Promenade 6, 10178 Berlin
Mailing Address: Postfach 193, 10105 Berlin
Tel: (030) 283 94-0 *Fax:* (030) 283 94 100
E-mail: info@aufbau-verlag.de
Web Site: www.aufbau-verlag.de
Key Personnel
Program Manager: Rene Strien
Manager: Peter Dempewolf
International Rights: Astrid Poppenhusen
Tel: (030) 283 94 212 *E-mail:* poppenhusen@aufbau-verlag.de
Contact: Barbara Stang
Rights & Permissions: Kathrin Schulz
Founded: 1994
Subjects: Fiction, Film, Video, Government, Political Science, Literature, Literary Criticism, Essays, Poetry, Romance
ISBN Prefix(es): 3-7466
Number of titles published annually: 150 Print
Total Titles: 500 Print
Shipping Address: Mohr Morawa, Buchvertrieb Gesellschaft mbH, Postfach 260, A-1101 Vienna, Austria; Buecher Balmer Verlagsauslieferung, Neugasse 12, CH-6301 Zurich, Switzerland
Warehouse: Libri-Distributions GmbH, August-Schanzstr 33, 60433 Frankfurt
Orders to: Libri-Distributions GmbH, August-Schanz Str 33, 60433 Frankfurt

Aufbau-Verlag GmbH+
Neue Promenade 6, 10178 Berlin
Mailing Address: Postfach 193, 10105 Berlin
Tel: (030) 28 394-0 *Fax:* (030) 28 394-100
E-mail: info@aufbauverlag.de
Web Site: www2.aufbauverlag.de
Key Personnel
Program Manager: Rene Strien
Manager: Peter Dempewolf
International Rights: Astrid Poppenhusen
Tel: (030) 28394212 *E-mail:* poppenhussen@aufbau-verlag.de
Contact: Barbara Stang
Rights & Permissions: Kathrin Schulz
Founded: 1945

Subjects: Fiction, Film, Video, Government, Political Science, Literature, Literary Criticism, Essays, Mysteries, Poetry, Romance
ISBN Prefix(es): 3-351
Number of titles published annually: 80 Print; 20 Audio
Total Titles: 400 Print
Shipping Address: Mohr Morawa, Buchvertrieb Gesellschaft mbH, Postfach 260, 1101 Vienna, Austria; Buecher Balmer Verlagsauslieferung, Neugasse 12, 6301 Zurich, Switzerland
Warehouse: Libri-Distributions-GmbH, August-Schanz-Str 33, 60433 Frankfurt
Orders to: Libri-Distributions-GmbH, August-Schanz-Str 33, 60433 Frankfurt

Aufstieg-Verlag GmbH
Isarweg 37, 84028 Landshut
Tel: (0871) 54112 *Fax:* (0871) 54112
Web Site: www.aufstieg-verlag.de
Key Personnel
Man Dir & International Rights: Gisela Werner
Founded: 1947
Subjects: Cookery, Fiction, Foreign Countries, History, Humor
ISBN Prefix(es): 3-7612; 3-920235

August Guse Verlag GmbH
Hauptstr 103, 61184 Karben
Tel: (06039) 480110 *Fax:* (06039) 480148
E-mail: info@guese.de
Web Site: www.guese.de
Key Personnel
Man Dir: Johannes Guese
Founded: 1954
Subjects: Gardening, Plants
ISBN Prefix(es): 3-87278

J J Augustin GmbH Verlag
Am Fleth 36-37, 25348 Glueckstadt
Mailing Address: Postfach 1106, 25342 Glueckstadt
Tel: (04124) 20442046 *Fax:* (04124) 4709
Key Personnel
President & International Rights: Walter Pruess
Founded: 1920
Subjects: Asian Studies, Literature, Literary Criticism, Essays, Religion - Islamic, Science (General)
ISBN Prefix(es): 3-87030

Augustinus-Verlag Wurzburg Inh Augustinerprovinz
Grabenberg 2, 97070 Wuerzburg
Mailing Address: Postfach 110252, 97029 Wuerzburg
Tel: (0931) 3097400 *Fax:* (0931) 3097401
Web Site: www.augustiner.de
Key Personnel
Publishing Dir: Eric Englert
Contact: Jrina Nebel
Founded: 1922
Subjects: Religion - Other
ISBN Prefix(es): 3-7613
Bookshop(s): Buch und Kumst, Dominikanerplarz 4, 97070 Wuerzburg

Augustus Verlag+
Hilblestrasse 54, 80636 Munich
Tel: (0821) 7004-700 *Fax:* (0821) 7004-179
Web Site: www.droemer-weltbild.de
Key Personnel
Sales Manager: Juergen Wohltmann
Publishing Dir: Jutta Hamberger
Rights & Permissions: Barry Sandoval
E-mail: barry.sandoval@droemer-weltbild.de
Founded: 1989
Subjects: Animals, Pets, Architecture & Interior Design, Crafts, Games, Hobbies, Gardening, Plants, Photography
ISBN Prefix(es): 3-8043

PUBLISHERS

GERMANY

Parent Company: Verlagsgruppe Droemer Weltbild
Orders to: VVA-Bertelsmann Distribution GmbH, Postfach 7600, 33310 Guetersloh

Aulis Verlag Deubner & Co KG+
Antwerpenerstr 6-12, 50672 Cologne
Tel: (0221) 9514540 *Fax:* (0221) 518443
Key Personnel
Publisher: Wolfgang Deubner
Founded: 1950
Subjects: Biological Sciences, Chemistry, Chemical Engineering, Geography, Geology, History, Mathematics, Nonfiction (General), Physics, Science (General)
ISBN Prefix(es): 3-7614

Aurum Verlag GmbH+
Georg-Westermann-Allee 66, 38104 Braunschweig
Tel: (0531) 708790 *Fax:* (0531) 708706
E-mail: westermann_wsv@bs.magicvillage.de
Telex: 952841
Key Personnel
Editorial: Dr Juliane Molitor
Founded: 1974
Subjects: Health, Nutrition, Psychology, Psychiatry, Religion - Other
ISBN Prefix(es): 3-591
Orders to: VSB-Verlagsservice Braunschweig GmbH, Georg-Westermann-Allee 66, 38104 Braunschweig *Tel:* (0531) 708625

Aussaat Verlag+
Andreas Braemstr 18/20, 47506 Neukirchen-Vluyn
Mailing Address: Postfach 101265, 47497 Neukirchen-Vluyn
Tel: (02845) 392234 *Fax:* (02845) 392250
E-mail: info@neukirchener-verlag.de
Web Site: www.aussaat-verlag.de
Key Personnel
Man Dir: Klaus Guenther
Sales Representative: Christoph Siepermann
E-mail: vertrieb@neukirchener-verlag.de
Founded: 1978
Subjects: Biblical Studies, Education, Fiction, Religion - Protestant, Religion - Other, Theology
ISBN Prefix(es): 3-7615
Number of titles published annually: 50 Print
Total Titles: 400 Print
Online services available through World Wide Web.
Parent Company: Verlagsgesellschaft des Erziehungsvereins mbH, Andreas-Braem-Str 18-20, 47506 Neukirchen-Uluyn
Divisions: Edition Sonnenweg, Friedrich Bahn Verlag

Verlag der Autoren GmbH & Co KG+
Schleusenstr 15, 60327 Frankfurt
Mailing Address: Postfach 111963, 60054 Frankfurt
Tel: (069) 2385740 *Fax:* (069) 24277644
E-mail: buch@verlag-der-autoren.de
Web Site: www.verlag-der-autoren.de *Cable:* AUTORENVERLAG FRANKFURT
Key Personnel
Man Dir: Dr Victor Marion; Ingo Flie *Tel:* (069) 33857933 *E-mail:* film@verlag-der-autoren.de
Founded: 1969
One of Germany's leading theatre & film agencies, publishing a growing line of important titles on theatre & film.
Subjects: Drama, Theater, Film, Video
ISBN Prefix(es): 3-920983; 3-88661
Number of titles published annually: 15 Print
Total Titles: 160 Print
Foreign Rep(s): International Editors (Argentina, South America, Spain); Marton Agency of New York (US); Orion Library Agency of Tokyo (Japan); Rosica Colin Ltd (Canada, London)

Orders to: Edition Text und Kritik, Levelingstr 6a, 81673 Munich, Mrs Forman *Tel:* (089) 432929 *Fax:* (089) 433997 *E-mail:* etk.muenchen@t-online.de

Autovision Verlag Guther Co+
Kronprinzenstr 54, 22587 Hamburg
Tel: (040) 810327 *Fax:* (040) 87932995
Key Personnel
Publisher: Dieter Guenther
Founded: 1992
Subjects: Automotive, Technology
ISBN Prefix(es): 3-9802766
Orders to: VAL, Luener Dennbahn 16, 21339 Luneburg

AVA, see Atelier Verlag Andernach (AVA)

Aviatic Verlag GmbH+
Kolpingring 16, 82041 Oberhaching
Tel: (089) 613890-0 *Fax:* (089) 613890-10
E-mail: aviatic@t-online.de
Web Site: www.aviatic.de
Key Personnel
Manager: Peter Pletschacher
Founded: 1985
Specialize in aeronautics.
Subjects: Aeronautics, Aviation
ISBN Prefix(es): 3-925505
Total Titles: 35 Print
Distributed by Airlife Publishing (UK); Schiffer Publishing (USA)

AvivA Britta Jurgs GmbH
Emdenerstr 33, 10551 Berlin
Tel: (030) 39731372 *Fax:* (030) 39731371
E-mail: aviva@txt.de
Web Site: www.aviva-verlag.de
Key Personnel
Publisher: Jurgs Britta
Founded: 1997
Subjects: Art, Literature, Literary Criticism, Essays, Women's Studies
ISBN Prefix(es): 3-932338

Axel Juncker Verlag Jacobi KG
Mies-van-der-Rohe-Str 1, 80807 Munich
Mailing Address: Postfach 401120, 80711 Munich
Tel: (089) 360960 *Fax:* (089) 36096222
Telex: 5215379 lkgmd
Key Personnel
Man Dir: Karl Ernst Tielebier-Langenscheidt; Andreas Langenscheidt
Founded: 1902
Sales & Promotion through Langenscheidt KG.
Member of the Langenscheidt Group.
ISBN Prefix(es): 3-558
Orders to: Langenscheidt KG, Neusser Str 3, 80807 Munich

AZ Bertelsmann Direct GmbH
Formerly AZ Direct Marketing Bertelsmann GmbH
Division of Bertelsmann Services Group
Unit of Avarto AG
Carl-Bertelsmann-Str 161S, D-33311 Guetersloh
Tel: (05241) 805046 *Fax:* (05241) 809336
E-mail: az@bertelsmann.de
Web Site: www.az.bertelsmann.de
Founded: 1966
International full-service direct marketing.
Subjects: Business, Marketing
ISBN Prefix(es): 3-573

AZ Direct Marketing Bertelsmann GmbH, see AZ Bertelsmann Direct GmbH

B & B Verlag Anita und Klaus Buscher+
Erika-Koth-Str 56, 67435 Neustadt-Konigsbach

Tel: (06321) 968485 *Fax:* (06321) 968486
Key Personnel
Man Dir: Anita Buscher
Founded: 1988
ISBN Prefix(es): 3-927419

Babel Verlag Kevin Perryman+
Lorenz Paul Str 4, 86920 Denklingen
Mailing Address: PO Box 1, 86920 Denklingen
Tel: (08243) 961691 *Fax:* (08243) 961614
E-mail: info@babel-verlag.de
Web Site: www.babel-verlag.de
Key Personnel
Publisher: Kevin Perryman
Founded: 1983
Specializes in poetry, bilingual poetry & translations.
Subjects: Poetry
ISBN Prefix(es): 3-931798
Number of titles published annually: 2 Print
Total Titles: 39 Print

J P Bachem Verlag GmbH+
Ursulaplatz 1, 50668 Cologne
Mailing Address: Postfach 100352, 50443 Cologne
Tel: (0221) 1619-0 *Fax:* (0221) 1619159; (0221) 1619231 (Vertrieb)
E-mail: info@bachem-verlag.de
Web Site: www.bachem-verlag.de
Telex: 8881128 *Cable:* BACHEMHAUS COLOGNE
Key Personnel
Dir: Dipl Kfm Lambert Bachem
Publisher: Reinhard Metz
Founded: 1818
Subjects: Regional Interests
ISBN Prefix(es): 3-7616
Parent Company: Bachem Publishing Group

Dr Bachmaier Verlag GmbH+
Kagerstr 8B, 81669 Munich
Tel: (089) 685120; (089) 68008255 *Fax:* (089) 685120; (089) 68008255
E-mail: contact@verlag-drbachmaier.de
Web Site: www.verlag-drbachmaier.de
Key Personnel
Man Dir: Dr Peter Bachmaier
Contact: Barbara Bachmaier
Also acts as Bookseller.
Subjects: History, Literature, Literary Criticism, Essays, Poetry, Science (General), Science Fiction, Fantasy
ISBN Prefix(es): 3-931680
Number of titles published annually: 7 Print
Total Titles: 34 Print
Foreign Rights: Dr Doglioli (Italy)

Badenia Verlag und Druckerei GmbH+
Rudolf-Freytagstr, 76189 Karlsruhe
Mailing Address: Postfach 210248, 76152 Karlsruhe
Tel: (0721) 95450 *Fax:* (0721) 9545125
E-mail: verlag@badeniaverlag.de
Web Site: www.badeniaverlag.badeniaonline.de
Key Personnel
Man Dir: Dr Helmut Walter
Founded: 1874
Subjects: Regional Interests, Travel
ISBN Prefix(es): 3-7617

Badischer Landwirtschafts-Verlag GmbH
Friedrichstr 43, 79098 Freiburg
Mailing Address: Postfach 209, 79098 Freiburg
Tel: (0761) 2713342 *Fax:* (0761) 2021887
E-mail: redaktion@blv-freiburg.de *Cable:* BBZ FRBG
Key Personnel
Assistant Editor-in-Chief: Richard Briskowski
Rights: Manfred Zimper
Founded: 1947

Subjects: Agriculture
ISBN Prefix(es): 3-9801818

Baedeker, *imprint of* Mairs Geographischer Verlag

Hans A Baensch, *see* Mergus Verlag GmbH Hans A Baensch

Baerenreiter-Spieltexte, *imprint of* Otto Teich

Baha'i Verlag GmbH+
Eppsteinerstr 89, 65719 Hofheim
Tel: (06192) 22921 *Fax:* (06192) 22936
E-mail: info@bahai-verlag.de
Web Site: www.bahaipublishers.org
Key Personnel
Man Dir, Rights & Permissions: F Ardalan
Founded: 1925
Subjects: Religion - Other
ISBN Prefix(es): 3-87037

Bahnsport Aktuell Verlag GmbH
Birkenweiherstr 14, 63505 Langenselbold
Tel: (06184) 923330; (06184) 923350
Founded: 1971

Baken-Verlag Walter Schnoor+
Kastanienallee 16, 25548 Kellinghusen
Tel: (04822) 1671; (04192) 1784 *Cable:* BAKEN
Key Personnel
Owner: Uwe Jens Schnoor
Founded: 1951
Subjects: Environmental Studies, History, Regional Interests
ISBN Prefix(es): 3-7622
Bookshop(s): Buecherstube, Maienbeeck 4, 24576 Bad Bramstedt

Edition Balance Marion Gunther Bonsack+
Brunnenstr 12, 99867 Gotha
Tel: (03621) 750061 *Fax:* (0721) 151315156
E-mail: info@edition-balance.de
Key Personnel
International Rights: Henry Guenther
Founded: 1990
Subjects: Art
ISBN Prefix(es): 3-928440
Associate Companies: Atelier Buchkunst, Brunenstr 12, 99867 Gotha

C Bange GmbH & Co KG+
Marienplatz 12, 96142 Hollfeld
Mailing Address: Postfach 1160, 96139 Hollfeld
Tel: (09274) 94130 *Fax:* (09274) 94132
E-mail: service@bange-verlag.de
Web Site: www.bange-verlag.de
Key Personnel
Manager: Thomas Appel
Assistant Manager: Kerstin Lange
Founded: 1871
Subjects: Education, Fiction
ISBN Prefix(es): 3-8044
Number of titles published annually: 20 Print
Total Titles: 850 Print
Imprints: Bange Lernhilfen; Koenigs Erlaeuterungen; Koenigs Lektueren; Kon & Bundig

Bange Lernhilfen, *imprint of* C Bange GmbH & Co KG

Bank-Verlag GmbH+
Wendelinstr 1, 50933 Cologne
Mailing Address: Postfach 450209, 50877 Cologne
Tel: (0221) 54900 *Fax:* (0221) 5490120
E-mail: bank-verlag@bank-verlag.de
Web Site: www.bank-verlag.de

Key Personnel
Manager: Helmut Gsanger
Founded: 1961
Subjects: Business, Economics, Finance, Law, Management, Securities

Barenreiter-Verlag Karl-Votterle GmbH & Co KG+
Heinrich-Schuetz-Allee 35, 34131 Kassel- Wilhelmshohe
Mailing Address: Postfach 100329, 34003 Kassel
Tel: (0561) 31050 *Fax:* (0561) 3105176
E-mail: info@baerenreiter.com
Web Site: www.baerenreiter.com
Key Personnel
Man Dir: Leonhard Scheuch *E-mail:* lscheuch@baerenreiter.com; Barbara Scheuch-Voetterle
E-mail: bscheuch@baerenreiter.com
Dir of Finances: Anne Schaefer
E-mail: schaefer@baerenreiter.com
Publishing Dir: Dr Wendelin Goebel
E-mail: goebel@baerenreiter.com
Dir of Sales & Marketing: Dr Juergen Wulf
E-mail: wulf@baerenreiter.com
Sales Manager: Uta Dangelmaier
E-mail: dangelmaier@baerenreiter.com; Dr Christiane Loskant *E-mail:* loskant@baerenreiter.com; Corinne Votteler
E-mail: votteler@baerenreiter.com; Petra Woodfull-Harris *E-mail:* pwoodfull-harris@baerenreiter.com
Product Information: Ilse-Lore Krummel-Laartz
E-mail: krummel-laartz@baerenreiter.com
International Rights: Thomas Tietze
Founded: 1923
Subjects: Music, Dance
ISBN Prefix(es): 3-7618
Associate Companies: Baerenreiter Verlag Basel
Subsidiaries: Gustav Bosse Verlag; Sueddeutscher Musikverlag, Alkor-Edition, Henschel Verlag Fuer Musik; KGA, Verlags-Service GmbH (at above main address)
Branch Office(s)
Basel, Switzerland
Prague, Czech Republic
London, United Kingdom
Music Associates of America, 224 King St, Englewood, NJ 07631, United States, George Strum *Tel:* 201-569-2898 *Fax:* 201-569-7023
New York, NY, United States
Distributed by Barenreiter Ltd (UK); Baerenreiter Verlag Basel AG (Switzerland)
Bookshop(s): Neuwerk-Buch-und Musikalienhandlung, Heinrich-Schuetz-Allee 35, 34131 Kassel
Shipping Address: KGA-technischer Betrieb, Brandaustr 10, 34127 Kassel
Warehouse: KGA-technischer Betrieb, Brandaustr 10, 34127 Kassel
Orders to: KGA, Postfach 102180, 34021 Kassel

Verlag Dr Albert Bartens KG
Luckhoffstr 16, 14129 Berlin
Mailing Address: Postfach 380250, 14112 Berlin
Tel: (030) 8035678 *Fax:* (030) 8032049
Key Personnel
Contact: Dr Juergen Bruhns
Founded: 1876
Subjects: Agriculture, Economics, Energy, Technology
ISBN Prefix(es): 3-87040

Johann Ambrosius Barth GmbH+
Fritz-Frey Str 21, 69121 Heidelberg
Tel: (0341) 9929200 *Fax:* (0341) 9929209
Key Personnel
Man Dir: Holger Huethig
Marketing: Josef Weisbrod
Founded: 1780
Subjects: Chemistry, Chemical Engineering, Mathematics, Medicine, Nursing, Dentistry, Physical Sciences, Physics, Psychology, Psychiatry
ISBN Prefix(es): 3-335
Parent Company: Huethig GmbH
Shipping Address: Verlagsservice Suedwest,, Boschstr 2, 68753 Waghaeusel - Kirrlach
Warehouse: Verlagsservice Suedwest, Boschstr 2, 68753 Waghaeusel- Kirrlach
Orders to: Heidelberger Verlagsservice, Im Weiher 10, 16928 Heidelberg

Otto Wilhelm Barth-Verlag KG
Hilblestr 54, 80638 Munich
Mailing Address: Postfach 190862, 80608 Munich
Tel: (089) 92170 *Fax:* (089) 9217168
Key Personnel
Man Dir: Peter Lohmann; Andreas Wiedmann
Sales: Wolfgang Radaj
Editor: Graf Eckhard
Rights & Permissions: Barbara Fankhauser
Founded: 1924
Subjects: Astrology, Occult, Philosophy, Religion - Other
ISBN Prefix(es): 3-502
Parent Company: Scherz Verlag AG, Marktgasse 25 Postf 66, 3000 Bern, Switzerland
Associate Companies: Scherz Verlag GmbH, Munich

Bartkowiaks Forum Book Art
Koernerstr 24, 22301 Hamburg
Tel: (040) 2793674 *Fax:* (040) 2704397
E-mail: 0402793674-1@t-online.de
Web Site: www.forumbookart.com
Key Personnel
Man Dir: Heinz Stefan Bartkowiak
Founded: 1988
Subjects: Art
ISBN Prefix(es): 3-9802935
Branch Office(s)
Joanne Cotter, 526 Bredford Dr, Brandon MS 39042 *Tel:* 601-992-1018 *Fax:* 601-992-1018

Basilisken-Presse+
Hirschberg 5, 35037 Marburg
Mailing Address: Postfach 561, 35017 Marburg
Tel: 06421 15188
Key Personnel
Owner, Rights & Permissions: Armin Geus
Founded: 1976
Subjects: Art, History, Specialize in medicine, nursing & history of science
ISBN Prefix(es): 3-925347

BasisDruck Verlag GmbH
Schliemannstr 23, 10437 Berlin
Tel: (030) 4457680 *Fax:* (030) 4459599
E-mail: basisdruck@planet-interkom.de
Web Site: www.basisdruck.de
Key Personnel
Man Dir: Michael Kukutz
Founded: 1990
Subjects: Government, Political Science, History
ISBN Prefix(es): 3-86163

Bassermann Verlag+
Neumarkter Str 18, 81673 Munich
Tel: (089) 43 72-0
E-mail: vertrieb.verlagsgruppe@bertelsmann.de
Web Site: www.randomhouse.de/bassermann
Key Personnel
Publisher: Stefan Ewald *E-mail:* stefan.ewald@bertelsmann.de
Foreign Rights: Silke Bruenink *Tel:* (089) 43 72-26 48 *Fax:* (089) 43 72-27 47 *E-mail:* silke.bruenink@bertelsmann.de
Founded: 1843
Subjects: Cookery, Crafts, Games, Hobbies, Gardening, Plants, Nonfiction (General), Outdoor Recreation
ISBN Prefix(es): 3-8094

Bastei Luebbe Taschenbuecher, *imprint of* Verlagsgruppe Luebbe GmbH & Co KG

Bastei Luebbe Taschenbuecher+
Imprint of Verlagsgruppe Luebbe GmbH & Co KG
Scheidtbachstr 23-31, 51469 Bergisch Gladbach
Mailing Address: Postfach 200180, 51431 Bergisch Gladbach
Tel: (02202) 121-0 *Fax:* (02202) 121-933
E-mail: info@luebbe.de
Web Site: www.luebbe.de
Founded: 1963
Subjects: Fiction, Nonfiction (General)
ISBN Prefix(es): 3-404
Total Titles: 500 Print

Bastei Verlag, *imprint of* Verlagsgruppe Luebbe GmbH & Co KG

Bastei Verlag+
Imprint of Verlagsgruppe Luebbe GmbH & Co KG
Scheidtbachstr 23-31, 51469 Bergisch Gladbach
Mailing Address: Postfach 200180, 51431 Bergisch Gladbach
Tel: (02202) 121-0 *Fax:* (02202) 121-936
E-mail: info@bastei.de
Web Site: www.bastei.de *Cable:* SCHEIDTBACHSTR 23-31
Key Personnel
Man Dir: Horst Scholz
Editorial: H P Ditges
Sales: Werner Kraus
Production (Juveniles): Dieter Deichmann; Johannes Dittmann
Publicity: Barbara Fischer
Rights & Permissions: Manfred Koelzer
Founded: 1949
Subjects: Fiction, Science Fiction, Fantasy, Western Fiction
ISBN Prefix(es): 3-404
Number of titles published annually: 80 Print
Associate Companies: Gustav Luebbe Verlag

Battenberg Verlag+
Hilblestr 54, 80636 Munich
Tel: (089) 9271280 *Fax:* (089) 9271236
Key Personnel
Editorial Dir: Michael Schoenberger
  E-mail: michael.schoenberger@droemer-weltbilt.de
Rights & Permissions: Renate Abrasch
Foreign Rights: Barry Sandoval
Founded: 1956
Subjects: Antiques, Numismatics, Collectors' Guides, Cultural History
ISBN Prefix(es): 3-89441
Number of titles published annually: 20 Print
Parent Company: Verlagsgruppe Droemer-Weltbild
Foreign Rights: Barry Sandoval
Orders to: VVA, PF 7600, 33310 Guetersloh, Jennifer Strebinger *Tel:* (05241) 801754 *Fax:* (05241) 8041862

Verlag Hermann Bauer KG+
Kronenstr 2-4, 79100 Freiburg
Mailing Address: Postfach 167, 79001 Freiburg
Tel: (0761) 70820 *Fax:* (0761) 701811
E-mail: info@hermann-bauer.de
Web Site: www.hermann-bauer.de
Telex: 772821
Key Personnel
Man Dir: Friedrich Kirner
Rights & Permissions: Petra Danner
Sales Manager: Wilfried Hille
Editorial: Katin Vial
Founded: 1937
Subjects: Astrology, Occult, Health, Nutrition, Parapsychology, Philosophy
ISBN Prefix(es): 3-7626
Imprints: Kutz und praktisch; Esotere Taschenbuch
Subsidiaries: Ebertin-Verlag

Baumann GmbH & Co KG+
E-C-Baumannstr 5, 95326 Kulmbach
Mailing Address: Postfach 1149, 95301 Kulmbach
Tel: (09221) 949401; (09221) 949382; (09221) 949360 *Fax:* (09221) 84434
E-mail: service@baumann-online.de
Key Personnel
Dir: Helmut Korndoerfer
Sales: Walter Ruisinger
Founded: 1902
ISBN Prefix(es): 3-922091
Subsidiaries: Coburger Tageblatt; Filialbetrieb Naila

Dr Wolfgang Baur Verlag Kunst & Alltag+
Poignring 24c, 82515 Wolfratshausen
Tel: (089) 217514 *Fax:* (089) 217515
E-mail: mail@kunstalltag.de
Web Site: www.kunstalltag.de
Key Personnel
Owner: Dr Wolfgang Baur
Founded: 1977
Subjects: Art, Environmental Studies, Ethnicity, Humor, Philosophy, Poetry, Science (General)
ISBN Prefix(es): 3-88410
Imprints: Edition Jonas; Edition U
Bookshop(s): Balanstr 35, 81669 Munich

Institut fuer Baustoffe, Massivbau und Brandschutz/Bibliothek (Institute for Building Materials, Reinforced Concrete Construction & Fire Protection Library)+
Beethovenstr 52, 38106 Braunschweig
Tel: (0531) 391 5454 *Fax:* (0531) 391 5900
E-mail: ibmb@tu-bs.de
Web Site: www.ibmb.tu-bs.de
Key Personnel
Librarian: Oliver Dienelt *E-mail:* o.dienelt@tu-bs.de
Founded: 1963
Subjects: Civil Engineering, Proceedings, Reports, Theses
ISBN Prefix(es): 3-89288
Total Titles: 8 Print

Bautz Traugott
Eisenacherstr 15, 37412 Herzberg
Tel: (05521) 5700; (05521) 5588 *Fax:* (05521) 5780
Web Site: www.bautz.de
Key Personnel
Contact: Traugott Bautz
Founded: 1971
Subjects: Regional Interests, Theology
ISBN Prefix(es): 3-88309

Bauverlag GmbH+
Am Klingenweg 4a, 65396 Walluf
Tel: (06123) 7000 *Fax:* (06123) 700122
  Cable: BAUVERLAG WALL&U14FF
Key Personnel
Dir: Derek Carter; Reiner Grochowski
Sales, Publicity & Advertising: Hans-Joachim Kopp
Founded: 1929
Subjects: Architecture & Interior Design, Civil Engineering, Energy, Environmental Studies
ISBN Prefix(es): 3-7625
Parent Company: Emap
Imprints: LBO-Dienst
Branch Office(s)
Nikolsburger Str 11, 10717 Berlin

Bayerische Akademie der Wissenschaften (Bavarian Academy of Sciences)
Marstallplatz 8, 80539 Munich
Tel: (089) 230310 *Fax:* (089) 23031100
Web Site: www.badw.de
Key Personnel
President: Noeth Heinrich
Secretary General: Monika Stoermer
Librarian: Heldegard Glaser *Tel:* (089) 23037746
  E-mail: glaser@bsb.badw-muencher.de
Founded: 1759
Subjects: Science (General)
ISBN Prefix(es): 3-7696
Number of titles published annually: 130 Print
Orders to: CH Beck'sche Verlags Buchhandlung, Postfach 400340, D-80703 Munich, Oscar Beck *Tel:* (089) 381890 *Fax:* (089) 38189/381398

Bayerische Verlagsanstalt GmbH+
Laubanger 23, 96052 Bamberg
Mailing Address: Postfach 2709, 96018 Bamberg
Tel: (0951) 967120 *Fax:* (0951) 96712235
Key Personnel
Man Dir: Helmut Treml
Founded: 1949
Subjects: Economics, Literature, Literary Criticism, Essays, Regional Interests
ISBN Prefix(es): 3-87052
Parent Company: Sankt Otto-Verlag GmbH
Bookshop(s): Goerres Buchhandlung, Lange Str 24, 96047 Bamberg

Bayerischer Schulbuch-Verlag GmbH
Rosenheimerstr 145, 81671 Munich
Mailing Address: Postfach 801360, 81613 Munich
Tel: (089) 450510 *Fax:* (089) 45051200
Key Personnel
Dir: Hartmut Koeppelmann; Roland Mayr
Subjects: Biological Sciences, Business, Chemistry, Chemical Engineering, English as a Second Language, Environmental Studies, Geography, Geology, History, Literature, Literary Criticism, Essays, Mathematics, Music, Dance, Philosophy, Physics
ISBN Prefix(es): 3-7627
Warehouse: Bayerischer Schulbuch-Verlag, Ohmstr 10, 85757 Karlsfeld

BdWi, see Bund demokratischer Wissenschaftlerinnen und Wissenschafler eV (BdWi)

be.bra verlag GmbH+
Kulturbraverei Havs S, Schonhauser Allee36, 10435 Berlin
Tel: (030) 44023810 *Fax:* (030) 44023819
E-mail: info@bebraverlag.de
Web Site: www.bebraverlag.de
Key Personnel
Publisher: Ulrich Hopp
Press Manager: Antje Struve *Tel:* (030) 44023812
Sales Managers: Antje Steinriede *Tel:* (030) 44023813
Founded: 1994
Member of Borsenverein des Deutschen Buchhandels.
Subjects: Architecture & Interior Design, Government, Political Science, Regional Interests
ISBN Prefix(es): 3-930863
Number of titles published annually: 20 Print
Total Titles: 46 Print

Beacon Verlag Koerber OHG
Birkenthal 13, 67098 Bad Duerkheim
Mailing Address: Postfach 1161, 67085 Bad Duerkheim
Tel: (06322) 2056 *Fax:* (06322) 2056 *Cable:* BEACON-DUERKHEIM
Key Personnel
Editor: Mrs Ortrun Scheumann

Founded: 1949
Subjects: Language Arts, Linguistics
ISBN Prefix(es): 3-920075

Ludwig Bechauf Verlag
Friedrichstr 48, 33615 Bielefeld
Tel: (0521) 130648 *Fax:* (0521) 139347
Key Personnel
Owner: Wilfried Carlmeyer
Founded: 1893
Subjects: Theology
ISBN Prefix(es): 3-8076

Bechtermunz Verlag
Steinerne Furt, 86167 Augsburg
Mailing Address: Postfach 1143, 65331 Eltville
Tel: (06123) 2312 *Fax:* (06123) 62559
Tel: (0821) 70040 *Fax:* (0821) 7004-179
ISBN Prefix(es): 3-86047
Parent Company: Weltbild Verlag GmbH, Steinerne Furt 68-72, 86167 Augsburg

Bechtle Graphische Betriebe und Verlagsgesellschaft mbH und Co KG
Zeppelinstr 116, 73730 Esslingen
Mailing Address: Postfach 100209, 73702 Esslingen am Neckar
Tel: (0711) 29088-0 *Fax:* (0711) 29088-154
Key Personnel
Manager, International Rights: Otto W Bechtle; Dr Christine Bechtle-Koberg
Manager: Ulrich Gottlieb
Founded: 1868
Subjects: Biography
ISBN Prefix(es): 3-7628
Subsidiaries: Rotenberg Verlag GmbH

Beck & Gluckler Verlag GmbH & Co KG+
Maximilianstr 30, 79100 Freiburg im Breisgau
Tel: (0761) 701530 *Fax:* (0761) 701580
Key Personnel
Man Dir, Rights & Permissions: Jutta Beck
Founded: 1985
ISBN Prefix(es): 3-89470
Shipping Address: Prolit Verlagsauslieferung, Siemensstr 16, 35463 Fernwald-Annerod
Warehouse: Prolit Verlagsauslieferung, Siemensstr 16, 35463 Fernwald-Annerod
Orders to: Prolit Verlagsauslieferung, Siemensstr 16, 35463 Fernwald-Annerod *Tel:* (0641) 943930 *Fax:* (0641) 9439393

Verlag C H Beck (OHG)+
Wilhelmstr 9, 80801 Munich
Mailing Address: Postfach 400340, 80703 Munich
Tel: (089) 381890 *Fax:* (089) 38189402 (Sales); (089) 38189398 (Editorial)
E-mail: bestellung@beck.de
Web Site: www.beck.de
Telex: 5215085 beck d
Key Personnel
Dir: Dr Hans D Beck; Wolfgang Beck
Editorial, Fiction, Humanities: Dr Detlef Felueu
Rights & Permission: Susanne Hauptmann
Rights & Permissions: Susanne Simor
Editorial Law & Taxation Economy: Burkail Schulz
Founded: 1763
Subjects: Anthropology, Archaeology, Art, Economics, History, Language Arts, Linguistics, Law, Literature, Literary Criticism, Essays, Management, Music, Dance, Nonfiction (General), Philosophy, Social Sciences, Sociology, Theology
ISBN Prefix(es): 3-406
Associate Companies: Verlag Franz Vahlen GmbH
Branch Office(s)
Palmengartenstr 14, 60325 Frankfurt am Main

Beerenverlag
Morfelder Landstr 109, 60598 Frankfurt
Tel: (0611) 376316 *Fax:* (0611) 376316
Key Personnel
Manager: Bernard Rensinghoff
Art Dir: Thomas Majevszky
Editorial: Andreas Golm
Founded: 1992
Subjects: Fiction, Humor, Poetry, Travel
ISBN Prefix(es): 3-929198
Imprints: Kleine Reike; Rudi der Bar ist las
Distributed by Harrassourk Verlag

M P Belaieff, *imprint of* C F Peters Musikverlag GmbH & Co KG

Beleke KG Verlag+
Kronprinzenstr 13, 45128 Essen
Mailing Address: Postfach 103952, 45039 Essen
Tel: (0201) 81300 *Fax:* (0201) 8130108
E-mail: info@beleke.de
Web Site: www.beleke.edu
Key Personnel
Owner & Man Dir: Norbert Beleke
Man Dir: Heike Bogott
International Rights: Dr Michael Platzkoester *Tel:* (0201) 8130-118 *E-mail:* mplatzkoester@beleke.de
Founded: 1964
Member of Verband Deutscher Auskunfts und Verzeichnismedien eV, European Association of Directory & Database Publishers & Boersenverein des Deutschen Buchhandels eV.
Subjects: Biography, Business, Criminology, Medicine, Nursing, Dentistry, Nonfiction (General), Regional Interests
ISBN Prefix(es): 3-7950; 3-8215
Associate Companies: ELVIKOM Film-Verlag GmbH, Essen; Hansisches Verlagskontor, Postfach 2051, 23508 Luebeck *Tel:* (0451) 703101 *Fax:* (0451) 7031281; NOBEL-Verlag GmbH, Postfach 103952, 45039 Essen *Tel:* (0201) 81300 *Fax:* (0201) 8130108; ntv neue television FILM-TV-PRODUKTION GmbH, Essen; Das Rathaus Verlagsgesellschaft mbH & Co KG, Kronprinzenstr 13, 45128 Essen *Tel:* (0201) 81300; Verlag Schmidt-Roemhild, Luebeck; Schmidt-Roemhild Verlagsgesellschaft mbH, Brandenburg
Showroom(s): Verlag Beleke KG, Hohe Str 56, 44139 Dortmund 1; Verlag Beleke KG, Redaktionsbuero Duesseldorf, Berliner Allee 30, 40212 Duesseldorf; Verlag Beleke KG, Drei-Lilien-Platz 1, 65183 Wiesbaden; Verlag Schmidt-Roemhild, Prinzregentenstr 42, 10715 Berlin; Verlag Schmidt-Roemhild, Mengstr 16, 23552 Luebeck; Schmidt-Roemhild Verlagsgesellschaft mbH Brandenburg, August-Bebel-Str 23-27, 14770 Brandenburg

Belser Wissenschaftlicher Dienst+
Gartenstr 1, 72218 Wildberg
Mailing Address: PO Box 126, 72215 Wildberg
Tel: (07054) 2475 *Fax:* (07054) 2639
E-mail: 101553.3467@compuserve.com
Web Site: www.belser.com
Key Personnel
General Manager: Dr Rolf D Schmid *Tel:* (079) 63763 *Fax:* (079) 63764 *E-mail:* rolf.schmid@belser.com
Founded: 1989
Subjects: Drama, Theater, Labor, Industrial Relations, Library & Information Sciences, Poetry, Psychology, Psychiatry, Religion - Catholic, Social Sciences, Sociology, Women's Studies, Microform Publisher, Electronic Publications
ISBN Prefix(es): 3-628
Total Titles: 100 CD-ROM; 15,000 E-Book
Associate Companies: Belser Wissenschaftlicher Dienst Ltd, Maple Dr, Boyle, Co Roscommon, Ireland *Tel:* (079) 63763 *Fax:* (079) 63764

Julius Beltz GmbH & Co KG+
Werderstr 10, 69469 Weinheim
Mailing Address: Postfach 100154, 69441 Weinheim
Tel: (06201) 60070 *Fax:* (06201) 6007-310
E-mail: info@beltz.de
Web Site: www.beltz.de
Key Personnel
Man Dir: Joachim Radmer; Dr Manfred Beltz Ruebelmann
Marketing: Eckhard Mueller
Rights: Charlotte Larat
Marketing: Rosemarie Bornholt *Tel:* (06201) 6007-433 *Fax:* (06201) 6007-493 *E-mail:* r.bornholt@beltz.de
Founded: 1841
Member of VGS - Verlagsgesellschaft mbH & Co KG.
Subjects: Science (General)
ISBN Prefix(es): 3-407
Subsidiaries: Beltz Athenaeum Verlag, Anrich Verlag; Deutscher Studien Verlag; PsychologieVerlagsUnion
Warehouse: Koch, Neff & Oetinger Verlagsauslieferung, 70551 Stuttgart *Tel:* (0711) 7899 20 30 *Fax:* (0711) 7899 10 10 *E-mail:* order@kno-va.de

Petra Bornhauber Benleo Verlag+
Bahnstr 16, 50126 Bergheim
Tel: (02271) 4782-0 *Fax:* (02271) 4782-20
Web Site: www.benleo.de
Key Personnel
International Rights: Petra Bornhauber
Founded: 1996
ISBN Prefix(es): 3-9805061

Bergmoser & Holler Verlag GmbH
Karl-Friedrichstr 76, 52072 Aachen
Mailing Address: Postfach 50 04 04, Aachen 52088
Tel: (0241) 93888123 *Fax:* (0241) 93888188
E-mail: kontakt@buhv.de
Web Site: www.buhv.de
Key Personnel
Man Dir: Josef Bergmoser
Founded: 1971
ISBN Prefix(es): 3-88997
U.S. Office(s): ci Publishing Inc, 230 Fifth Ave NE, Hickory, NC 28601, United States

Bergstadtverlag Wilhelm Gottlieb Korn GmbH Wuerzburg+
Karlstr 10, 72488 Sigmaringen
Tel: (07571) 728170 *Fax:* (07571) 728280
Key Personnel
Dir: Dr Joachim Bensch
Founded: 1732
Subjects: Art, Biography, History, Literature, Literary Criticism, Essays, Poetry, Regional Interests, Travel
ISBN Prefix(es): 3-87057

Bergverlag Rudolf Rother GmbH+
Haidgraben 3, 85521 Ottobrunn
Tel: (089) 6086690 *Fax:* (089) 60866969
E-mail: bergverlag@rother.de
Web Site: www.rother.de
Key Personnel
Publisher: Walter Theil; Richard Gerin
Founded: 1920
Specialize in Alpine Literature, Documents & Guidebooks.
Subjects: Nonfiction (General), Outdoor Recreation, Sports, Athletics
ISBN Prefix(es): 3-7633
Parent Company: Freytag-Berndt u Artaria KG, Postfach 169, A-1071 Vienna, Austria

Berlin Verlag Arno Spitz GmbH+
Axel-Springer-Str 54b, 10117 Berlin
Tel: (030) 8417700 *Fax:* (030) 84177021

PUBLISHERS — GERMANY

E-mail: berlin-verlag.spitz@t-online.de
Web Site: www.berlin-verlag.de
Key Personnel
Man Dir: Dr Volker Schwarz
Manager: Brigitta Weiss
Founded: 1962
Subjects: Business, Economics, Environmental Studies, Government, Political Science, History, Law, Library & Information Sciences, Management, Marketing, Mathematics, Medicine, Nursing, Dentistry, Music, Dance, Philosophy, Public Administration, Publishing & Book Trade Reference, Real Estate, Theology
ISBN Prefix(es): 3-87061
Parent Company: Nomos Verlagsgesellschaft GmbH, Waidseestr 3-5, 76530 Baden-Baden, Baden Baden
Imprints: Ostrecht
Warehouse: Nomos Verlagsgesellschaft, Waldseestr 3-5, 75630 Baden-Baden
Orders to: Nomos Verlagsgesellschaft, Waldseestr 3-5, 76530 Baden-Baden

Berliner Debatte Wissenschafts Verlag, GSFP-Gesellschaft fur Sozialwissen-schaftliche Forschung und Publizistik mbH &Co KG
Erich-Weinertstr 19, D-10439 Berlin
Mailing Address: Postfach 580275, 10412 Berlin
Tel: (030) 44651355 *Fax:* (030) 44651358
E-mail: web@berlinerdebatte.de
Web Site: www.berlinerdebatte.de
Key Personnel
Manager: Dr Rainer Land; Dr Erhard Crome
Founded: 1992
Subjects: Government, Political Science, History, Philosophy, Social Sciences, Sociology
ISBN Prefix(es): 3-929666; 3-931703
Orders to: Bugrim, Saalburgstr 3, 12099 Berlin

Berliner Handpresse Wolfgang Joerg und Erich Schonig
Prinzessinenstr 20, 10969 Berlin
Tel: (030) 6148728; (030) 6142605
Key Personnel
Publisher: Wolfgang Joerg
Founded: 1961
Subjects: Art, Fiction

Berliner Zeitung
Karl Liebknecht-Str 29, 10178 Berlin
Tel: (030) 2327-9 *Fax:* (030) 2327-5681
E-mail: berlinerzeitung@berlinonline.de
Web Site: www.berlinzeitung.de
Founded: 1945
Specialize in newspapers.
Parent Company: Gruner & Jahr, Hamburg
Ultimate Parent Company: Bertelsmann AG

Bernard und Graefe Verlag+
Heilsbachstr 26, 53123 Bonn
Mailing Address: Postfach 140261, 53057 Bonn
Tel: (0228) 64830 *Fax:* (0228) 6483106
E-mail: 101336.245@compuserve.com
Key Personnel
Man Dir: Manfred Sadlowski
Rights & Permissions (Sales): Jung Horst
Founded: 1918
Subjects: Military Science
ISBN Prefix(es): 3-7637

Berndtson & Berndtson GmbH Verlag-Publishing+
Dachauerstr 6, 82256 Furstenfeldbruck
Tel: (08141) 32410 *Fax:* (08141) 324120
E-mail: redaktion@berndtson.de
Web Site: www.mapmyway.com
Key Personnel
Publisher: Kaj Berndtson *Tel:* (08141) 324116
 E-mail: kaj@berndtson.de
Man Dir: Sepp Habersetzer *Tel:* (08141) 324118
 E-mail: habersetzer@berndtson.de
International Sales Manager: Kerstin Borch
 E-mail: borch@berndtson.de
Founded: 1989
Produces a wide range of cartography-related marketing products.
Specialize in laminated road & city maps
Member of Borsenverein des Deutschen Buchhandels, Verkehrsnummer: 10404.
Subjects: Geography, Geology, Travel
ISBN Prefix(es): 3-928855; 3-929811; 3-89707
Total Titles: 180 Print
Associate Companies: Frog Map Co, 14031 80 Ave, Seminole, FL 33776, United States, Contact: Lisa Bohart

A Bernecker Verlag GmbH
Unter dem Schoeneberg 1, 34212 Melsungen
Mailing Address: Postfach 1163, 34201 Melsungen
Tel: (05661) 731-0 *Fax:* (05661) 731111
Web Site: www.bernecker.de
Key Personnel
Manager: Conrad Fischer *E-mail:* fischer@bernecker.de
Assistant Editor-in-Chief: Mr Roennfranz
Founded: 1869
ISBN Prefix(es): 3-87064
Subsidiaries: A Bernecker GmbH & Co Druckerei KG; Agentur Bernecker Media Ware GmbH

C Bertelsmann Verlag GmbH
Neumarkter Str 18, 81673 Munich 80
Mailing Address: Postfach 800360, 81603 Munich
Tel: (089) 4372-0 *Fax:* (089) 4372-2812
E-mail: vertrieb.verlagsgruppe@bertelsmann.de
Web Site: www.randomhouse.de
Telex: 523259 vbm ve d
Founded: 1835
Member of TR- Verlagsunion GmbH.
Subjects: Art, Biography, Fiction, Government, Political Science, Nonfiction (General)
ISBN Prefix(es): 3-570
Parent Company: Verlagsgruppe Bertelsmann GmbH
Associate Companies: Verlagsgruppe Bertelsmann GmbH
U.S. Office(s): Bettina Schrewe Literary Scouting, 101 Fifth Ave, Suite 11B, New York, NY 10003, United States (US Scout)

Bertelsmann Fachinformation, see BertelsmannSpringer Science & Business Media GmbH

Bertelsmann Lexikon Verlag GmbH
Avenwedder Str 55, D-33311 Gutersloh
Mailing Address: Postfach 800360, 81603 Munich
Tel: (05241) 800 *Fax:* (05241) 73075
E-mail: vertrieb.verlagsgruppe@bertelsmann.de
Web Site: www.lexiconverlag.de/lexiconverlag.html
Telex: 933646 *Cable:* BERTELSMANN GUTERSLOH
Key Personnel
President & Chief Executive Officer: Dr Mark Woessner
Division President, Bertelsmann Publishing Group International: Bernhard von Minckwitz
Division President: Frank Woessner
Division President, Electronic Media: Manfred Lahnstein
Division President, Printing & Manufacturing: Dr Gunter Thielen
Vice Chairman & Chief Executive Officer, Gruner & Jahr AG: Gerd Schulte-Hillen
Chairman & Chief Executive Officer, Bertelsmann Music Group (BMG), New York: Dr Michael Dornemann
Subjects: Anthropology, Art, Biography, Business, Career Development, Communications, Economics, Fiction, Film, Video, Foreign Countries, History, How-to, Law, Management, Marketing, Medicine, Nursing, Dentistry, Radio, TV, Technology, Travel
ISBN Prefix(es): 3-570
Parent Company: Bertelsmann HG
Associate Companies: Bertelsmann Inc, 1540 Broadway, New York, NY 10036, United States
Divisions: International Book & Record Clubs; Book Germany; Bertelsmann Publishing Group International Printing & Manufacturing; Bertelsmann Music Group, Electronic Media; Gruner + Jahr; Book Germany
U.S. Office(s): Bettina Schrewe Literary Scouting, 101 Fifth Ave, Suite 11B, NY 10003, United States (US Scout)
Book Club(s): Bertelsmann Club; Bertelsmann Club Vertrieb; Buchgemeinschaft Donauland, Kremayr & Scheriau; Buch-und Schallplattenfreunde; Deutsche Buch-Gemeinschaft; Deutscher Buecherbund; EBG Buch & Musik; Hallo RTL; Ring der Musikfreunde; Club Top 13; Doubleday Australia, Australia; ECl voor Boeken en Platen, Belgium; France Loisirs Belgique, Belgium; Doubleday Book & Music Clubs; Quebec Loisirs; France Loisirs, France; Librarie Papeterie Marigny et Joly, France; Setradis, France; SGED, France; Bookclub of Ireland; Euroclub Italia, Italy; Librum, Italy; ECl voor Boeken en Platen, Netherlands; Eurobook, Netherlands; Grambo BV, Netherlands; Nederlandse Lezerskring Boek en Plaat, Netherlands; Doubleday New Zealand, New Zealand; Circulo de Leitores, Portugal; Circulo de Lectores, Spain; France Loisirs Suisse, Switzerland; Book Club Associates, United Kingdom; Doubleday Book & Music Club, New York, NY, United States; Magyar Konyvklub, Budapest, Hungary; Magyar Konyvklub, Budapest, Hungary

Verlag Bertelsmann Stiftung (Bertelsmann Foundation Publishers)+
Carl-Bertelsmannstr 256, Postfach 103, 33311 Gutersloh
Tel: (05241) 8181197 *Fax:* (05241) 8181931
E-mail: sabine.klemm@bertelsmann.de
Web Site: www.bertelsmann-stiftung.de/verlag
Subjects: Education, Government, Political Science
ISBN Prefix(es): 3-89204
Number of titles published annually: 50 Print
Total Titles: 308 Print
Orders to: Brooking Institution Press, 1775 Massachusetts Ave NW, Washington, DC 20036, United States *Fax:* 202-797-2960

W Bertelsmann Verlag GmbH & Co KG
Auf dem Esch 4, 33619 Bielefeld
Mailing Address: Postfach 100633, 33506 Bielefeld
Tel: (0521) 911-01-0 *Fax:* (0521) 911 01-79
E-mail: wbv@wbv.de
Web Site: www.wbv.de; www.berufsbildung.de; www.berufe.net
Key Personnel
Dir: Thomas Kellersohn *Tel:* (0521) 91101-38
 E-mail: thomas.kellersohn@wbv.de
Founded: 1864
Subjects: Career Development, Education, Foreign Countries, Labor, Industrial Relations, Law, Management, Public Administration, Science (General), Social Sciences, Sociology, Vocational Training
ISBN Prefix(es): 3-7639
Distributor for Bundesanstalt fuer Arbeit; Bundesinstitut fuer Berufsbildung; Deutsches Institute fuer Erwachsenenbildung

GERMANY

BertelsmannSpringer Science & Business Media GmbH+
Formerly Bertelsmann Fachinformation
Heidelberger Platz 3, 17197 Berlin
Mailing Address: Postfach 140207, 14302 Berlin
Tel: (030) 82787-0 *Fax:* (030) 8274091
Web Site: www.bertelsmannspringer.de
Key Personnel
Pres & CEO: Dr Jurgen Richter
Man Dir, ScienceTechnology & Medicine: Dr Dietrich Sotze
Man Dir, Central Administration: Dr Ultich Vest
Founded: 1953
Subjects: Architecture & Interior Design, Economics, Engineering (General), Medicine, Nursing, Dentistry, Science (General), Transportation
Parent Company: Bertelsmann AG, Gutersloh
Branch Office(s)
ABI Building Data Ltd, United Kingdom
ArchiPoint, Belgium
ARZTE WOCHE Zeitungsverlagsgesellschaft mbH, Austria
Artze Zeitung Verlagsgesellschaft mbH, Austria
Auto Business Verlag GmbH & Co KG
Autohaus Online
Bau-Data Osterreich GmbH, Austria
BauDatenbank GmbH
BauNetz Online-Dienst GmbH & Co KG
Bauverlag GmbH
Bertelsmann Fachzeitschriften GmbH
Bertelsmann Information Professionnelle, France
BertelsmannSpringer Benelux, Belgium
BertelsmannSpringer B2B (Schweiz) AG, Switzerland
BertelsmannSpringer CZ, s r o, Czech Republic
BertelsmannSrpinger Magyarorszag Kft, Hungary
BertelsmannSpringer Medizin Online GmbH (BSMO)
Betriebswirtschaftlicher Verlag Dr Th Gabler GmbH
Birkhauser Verlag AG, Switzerland
Birkhauser Verlag Boston, United States
CoboSystems, Belgium
Codes Rosseau SAS, France
Dutscher Universitats-Verlag
Dr Hans Fuchs GmbH Verlag FUCHSBRIEFE
ETRASA Editorial Trafico Vial SA, Spain
Eurosoft, Spain
Friedr Vieweg & Sohn Verlagsgesellschaft mbH
Forum Press AG, Switzerland
Garage Fachverlag AG, Switzerland
Groupe Impact Medecin SA, France
Grupa Image Sp z o o, Poland
GWV Fachverlage GmbH
Heinze GmbH
ibau Informationsdienst fur den Baumarkt GmbH
ICW Publications Ltd, United Kingdom
IMS Investitions Media Service Werbe- & Public Relations GmbH, Austria
INFO-BUILD SA, Belgium
InfoChem Gesellschaft fur chemische Information mbH
Key Curriculum Press, United States
Media-Daten AG, Switzerland
Media-Daten Verlag
Media Office SA, Belgium
MMV Medien & Medizin Verlag AG, Switzerland
Physica-Verlag
PlusPointMarketing, Belgium
Princeton Architectural Press, United States
Schuck AG, Switzerland
Springer-Verlag Berlin/Heidelberg
Springer-Verlag France S A R L, France
Springer-Verlag Hong Kong Ltd, Hong Kong
Springer-Verlag Iberica SA, Spain
Springer-Verlag GmbH & Co KG Indian Liaison Office, India
Springer-Verlag Italia Srl, Italy
Springer-Verlag London Ltd, United Kingdom
Springer-Verlag New York Inc, United States
Springer-Verlag Tokyo Inc, Japan
Springer-VDI-Verlag GmbH & Co KG
Springer-Verlag KG Wien New York, Austria
Steinkopff-Verlag
technopress Fachzeitschriftenverlags-Ges m b H, Austria
B G Teubner GmbH
TransportWeb
Universitatsdruckerei H Sturz AG
Urban & Vogel Medien und Medizin Verlagsgesellschaft mbH
Verlag Aktuelle Information GmbH DER PLATOW BRIEF
Verlag Dieter Zimpel
Verlag Heinrich Vogel GmbH Fachverlag
Wendel-Verlag GmbH
Westduetscher Verlag GmbH
Zimpel Online

Verlag Beruf + Schule Belz KG+
Albert-Schweitzer-Ring 45, 25524 Itzehoe
Mailing Address: Postfach 2008, 25510 Itzehoe
Tel: (04821) 40140 *Fax:* (04821) 4941
E-mail: info@verlag-beruf-schule.de
Web Site: www.verlag-beruf-schule.de
Key Personnel
Contact: Renate Golpon
Founded: 1970
Subjects: Career Development, Chemistry, Chemical Engineering, Computer Science, Humor, Mathematics, Poetry, Publishing & Book Trade Reference
ISBN Prefix(es): 3-88013
Imprints: Edition Heitere Poetik
Divisions: Edition Heitere Poetik; Buchdienst B & S
Orders to: VVA Bertelsmann Distribution GmbH, Postfach 7777, 33310 Guetersloh

Verlag Das Beste GmbH
Augustenstr 1, 70178 Stuttgart
Mailing Address: Postfach 106020, 70049 Stuttgart
Tel: (0711) 66020 *Fax:* (0711) 6602858
E-mail: verlag@readersdigest.de
Web Site: www.dasbeste.de; www.readersdigest.de
Cable: READIGEST STUTTGART
Key Personnel
Man Dir: Gerhard Faisst
Founded: 1948
Publisher of periodicals, books, music & video editions.
ISBN Prefix(es): 3-87070
Parent Company: The Reader's Digest Association Inc, PO Box 235, Pleasantville, NY 10570, United States
Subsidiaries: Pegasus Buch- und Zeischriften-Vertriebs-GmbH; Optimail Direktwerbeservice GmbH

Bettendorf'sche Verlagsanstalt GmbH+
Thomas-Wimmer-Ring, 80539 Munich
Tel: (089) 29088-0 *Fax:* (089) 356384-20
Key Personnel
Man Dir: Gert Scheurmann; Johannes von Buttlar
Founded: 1994
Subjects: Aeronautics, Aviation, Archaeology, Astronomy, Environmental Studies, Genealogy, History, Medicine, Nursing, Dentistry, Nonfiction (General), Religion - Other
ISBN Prefix(es): 3-88498
Branch Office(s)
Bettendorf'sche Verlagsanstalt, Kortumstr 50, 45130 Essen

Betzel Verlag GmbH+
Weberstr 70, 60318 Frankfurt
Mailing Address: Postfach 1905, 31569 Nienburg
Tel: (050) 21914869 *Fax:* (050) 21914868
E-mail: betzelverlag@proximedia.de
Web Site: www.proximedia.com/local/20000099001
Key Personnel
Man Dir, Rights & Permissions: Anita Kubicek

BOOK

Formerly Gruppe Hinterhaus.
Subjects: Art, Drama, Theater, Fiction, Philosophy, Poetry
ISBN Prefix(es): 3-921818; 3-929017

Beust Verlag GmbH+
Fraunhoferstr 13, 80469 Munich
Tel: (089) 230895-0 *Fax:* (089) 266471
E-mail: mail@beustverlag.de
Founded: 1994
Subjects: Child Care & Development, Psychology, Psychiatry
ISBN Prefix(es): 3-89530
Subsidiaries: Gaia Text Publishing

Beuth Verlag GmbH
Burggrafenstr 6, 10787 Berlin
Tel: (030) 26010 *Fax:* (030) 26011260
E-mail: info@beuth.de
Web Site: www.beuth.de; www.mybeuth.de
Telex: 183622 bvb d; 185730 bvb d *Cable:* DEUTSCHNORMEN BERLIN
Key Personnel
Man Dir: Rudiger Marquardt
Publicity Dir: Dr Guntiam Platter
Sales Dir: Claudia Michalski
Founded: 1924
One of the largest tecnical & scientific publishing houses in Europe.
Standards, tecnical rules, standardization literature.
Subjects: Architecture & Interior Design, Chemistry, Chemical Engineering, Communications, Electronics, Electrical Engineering, Energy, Engineering (General), Environmental Studies, Health, Nutrition, Management, Mathematics, Mechanical Engineering, Physics, Securities, Technology, Theology, Transportation
ISBN Prefix(es): 3-410
Parent Company: DIN Deutsches Institut fuer Normung eV
Orders to: Osterreichisches Normungsinstitut, Heinestr 38, A-1021 Wein 2, Austria (in austria)
Schweizerische Normenvereinigung, Muehlebachstr 54, CH-8008 Zuerich, Switzerland (in Switzerland)

Bewnsster leben, *imprint of* Koenigsfurt Verlag, Evelin Burger et Johannes Fiebig

Joachim Beyer Verlag+
Langgasse 25, 96142 Hollfeld
Tel: (09274) 95051 *Fax:* (09274) 95053
E-mail: Beyer.Verlag@t-online.de
Web Site: www.derschachladen.de
Key Personnel
Owner: Joachim Beyer
Founded: 1972
Subjects: Crafts, Games, Hobbies
ISBN Prefix(es): 3-88805; 3-921202; 3-89168

Bezugsbedingungen, *imprint of* Johann Wolfgang Goethe Universitat

BBT Bhaktivedanta Book Trust
Boeckingstr 8, 55767 Abentheuer
Tel: (06782) 2214
E-mail: p.huy@t-online.de
Subjects: Cookery, Music, Dance, Philosophy, Religion - Hindu, Religion - Other
ISBN Prefix(es): 91-7149; 91-85580
Branch Office(s)
BBT, Watseka Ave, Los Angeles, CA 90034, United States

Biblio-Zeller Verlag
Postfach 1949, 49009 Osnabrueck
Tel: (0541) 404590 *Fax:* (0541) 41255
E-mail: zeller@zeller.os.emnet.de
Web Site: www.militaria-biblio.de

Subjects: Archaeology, Art, History, Language Arts, Linguistics, Law, Military Science, Philosophy, Religion - Other
ISBN Prefix(es): 3-7648

Bibliographisches Institut & F A Brockhaus AG+
Duden Route 6, 68167 Mannheim
Mailing Address: Postfach 10 03 11, 68003 Mannheim
Tel: (0621) 3901-01 *Fax:* (0621) 3901-3 91
Web Site: www.brockhaus.de *Cable:* BIFAB
Key Personnel
Man Dir: Dr Karl-Josef Schmidt; Albrecht Kiel; Andreas Langenscheidt; Dr Florian Langenscheidt; Dr Michael Wegner
Sales: Rosita Throm
Publicity Manager: Hans Gareis
Sales Dir, Rights & Permissions: Claus Greuner
Public Relations: Anja zum Hingst
Product Informations: Michaela Thuerling
 Tel: (0621) 3901-650 *Fax:* (0621) 3901-633
Pressing & Public Work: Klaus Holoch
 Tel: (0621) 3901-385 *Fax:* (0621) 3901-395
Personnel: Wolf of Zobeltitz *Tel:* (0621) 3901-267
Founded: 1805
Publishers of the Duden Series of Dictionaries, Brockhaus and Meyer Series of Encyclopedias.
Subjects: Engineering (General), Geography, Geology, Language Arts, Linguistics, Medicine, Nursing, Dentistry, Science (General)
ISBN Prefix(es): 3-411
Associate Companies: Thueringer Verlagsauslieferung Langenscheidt KG, Langenscheidtstr 10, 99867 Gotha; Mohr MORAWA, Sulzengasse 2, A-1232 Vienna, Austria; Schweizer Buchzentrum, Postfach 522, CH-4600 Olten, Switzerland
Subsidiaries: Bibliographisches Institut & F A Brockhaus AG, Zug, Suedbuch Vertrieb AG, Zuerich (both in Switzerland); Bibliographisches Institut GmbH; Foreign Daughter Companies: VBH-Verlagsbuchhandelsgesellschaft mbH, Salzburg, (both in Austria); Thueringer Verlagsauslieferung Langenscheidt KG (all three in Mannheim)

Bibliographisches Institut GmbH+
Subsidiary of Bibliographisches Institut und F A Brockhaus AG
Querstr 18, 04103 Leipzig
Mailing Address: Postfach 100130, 04001 Leipzig
Tel: (0341) 97 86-30 *Fax:* (0341) 97 86-5 60
Key Personnel
Man Dir: Dieter Baer
Dir, Rights & Permissions: Dr Karl-Josef Schmidt; Dr Michael Wegner
Founded: 1826

Bibliomed - Medizinische Verlagsgesellschaft mbH
Stadtwaldpark 10, 34212 Melsungen
Mailing Address: Postfach 1150, 34201 Melsungen
Tel: (05661) 73440 *Fax:* (05661) 8360
E-mail: info@bibliomed.de
Web Site: www.bibliomed.de
Key Personnel
Man Dir: Uta Meurer
Dir: Dr Annette Beller
Editorial: Markus Boucsein
Sales, Rights & Permissions: Harald Horchler
Founded: 1977
Subjects: Medicine, Nursing, Dentistry
ISBN Prefix(es): 3-89556
Total Titles: 8 CD-ROM
Imprints: Krankenpflegeforschung; Melsunger Medizinische Mitteilungen

Bibliothek Klassischer Texte, *imprint of* Wissenschaftliche Buchgesellschaft

Bibliothek Natur & Wissenschaft, *imprint of* Verlag Natur & Wissenschaft Harro Hieronimus & Dr Jurgen Schmidt

Edition Bielefelden Kunstverein, *imprint of* Pendragon Verlag

Bielefelder Verlagsanstalt GmbH & Co KG Richard Kaselowsky+
Ravensbergerstr 10 F, 33602 Bielefeld
Mailing Address: Postfach 100653, 33506 Bielefeld
Tel: (0521) 595 0 *Fax:* (0521) 595 518
E-mail: kontakt@bva-bielefeld.de
Web Site: www.bva-bielefeld.de
Key Personnel
Publishing Dir: Hans-Joerg Kaiser *Tel:* (0521) 510-514
Books & Maps: Ralph Plum *Tel:* (0521) 521-510
Public Services: Barbara Poltrock *Tel:* (0521) 595542 *E-mail:* poltrock@bva-bielefeld.de
Founded: 1946
Member of Borsenverein.
Subjects: How-to, Outdoor Recreation, Travel, Books & maps for cyclists (travel guides) and in Germany bicycle report books
ISBN Prefix(es): 3-87073
Total Titles: 170 Print
Parent Company: E Gundlach GmbH & Co KG
Distributed by Mairs Geographischer Verlag

Biermann Verlag GmbH
Otto-Hahn-Str 7, 50997 Cologne
Tel: (02236) 376-0 *Fax:* (02236) 376-999
E-mail: info@biermann.net
Web Site: www.biermann-online.de
Key Personnel
Contact: Dr Hans Biermann
Man Dir: Ernst-Uwe Kopperf
Leader: Christoph Dusse *Tel:* (02236) 376-202 *Fax:* (02236) 376-203 *E-mail:* du@biermann-verlag.de
Editor: Bernd Schunk *Tel:* (02236) 376-400 *Fax:* (02236) 376-401 *E-mail:* sk@biermann-verlag.de
CVD Print: Axel Viola *Tel:* (02236) 376-402 *Fax:* (02236) 376-403 *E-mail:* av@biermann-verlag.de
Graphics: Heike Dargel *Tel:* (02236) 376-151 *E-mail:* hd@biermann-verlag.de
Marketing: Uwe Koppert *Tel:* (02236) 376-300 *Fax:* (02236) 376-301 *E-mail:* ko@biermann-verlag.de
EDP: Thomas Narres *Tel:* (02236) 376-260 *Fax:* (02236) 376-261 *E-mail:* it@biermann-verlag.de
Founded: 1989
Subjects: Medicine, Nursing, Dentistry
ISBN Prefix(es): 3-924469

Bild und Heimat Verlagsgesellschaft GmbH
Zwickauerstr 68, 08468 Reichenbach
Mailing Address: Postfach 43, 08461 Reichenbach
Tel: (03765) 78 15-0 *Fax:* (03765) 1 22 45
Key Personnel
Man Dir & Owner: Harald Guenther; Stephan Treuleben
Man Dir: Sven Hoefgen
Founded: 1964
ISBN Prefix(es): 3-7310
Parent Company: Treuleben & Bischof Beteiligungsgesellschaft, Planegg

Bild und Text, *imprint of* Wilhelm Fink GmbH & Co Verlags-KG

Bildarchiv Preussischer Kulturbesitz bpk+
Maerkisches Ufer 16-18, 10179 Berlin
Mailing Address: Postfach 610317, 10925 Berlin
Tel: (030) 278 792 0
E-mail: bildarchiv@bpk.spk-berlin.de
Web Site: www.bildarchiv-bpk.de
Key Personnel
Man Dir, Rights & Permissions: Dr Karl H Puetz
Founded: 1965
Subjects: Photography, Prussian picture archives
Parent Company: Stiftung Preussischer Kulturbesitz

BW Bildung und Wissen Verlag und Software GmbH+
Suedwestpark 82, 90449 Nuremberg
Mailing Address: Postfach 820150, 90252 Nuremberg
Tel: (0911) 96 76-179 *Fax:* (0911) 96 76-189
E-mail: info@bwverlag.de
Web Site: www.bwverlag.de
Key Personnel
Man Dir & International Rights Contact: L Lodter; U Sippel
Contact: Silke Radzuweit *Tel:* (0911) 9676158 *E-mail:* silke.radzuweit@bwverlag.de
Founded: 1975
Specialist publishers for initial & further training, occupation & employment.
Member of Stock Exchange of German Booksellers, Bavarian Booksellers & Publishers Association.
Subjects: Career Development, Education
ISBN Prefix(es): 3-8214
Orders to: Contact: Thomas Preuss *Tel:* (0911) 9676175 *Fax:* (0911) 9676189 *E-mail:* thomas.preuss@bwverlag.de

Bindernagelsche Buchhandlung
Kaiserstr 72, 61169 Friedberg
Tel: (06031) 55 64 *Fax:* (06031) 6 48 40
Key Personnel
Owner: Karl C Herrmann
Founded: 1834
Subjects: Regional Interests
ISBN Prefix(es): 3-87076

Birkner & Co Zweigniederlassung Mecklenburg-Vorpommern
Winsbergring 38, 22525 Hamburg
Mailing Address: Postfach 540750, 22507 Hamburg
Tel: (040) 85308502 *Fax:* (040) 85308381
Key Personnel
Man Dir: Dr Christoph Dunnrath
Contact: Stefan Otto
Founded: 1904
Also acts as Internationale Zellstoff- und Papierindustrie.
ISBN Prefix(es): 3-923543
Parent Company: Dumrath & Fassnacht Komm Gesellschaft

BKV-Brasilienkunde Verlag GmbH
Sunderstr 15, 49497 Mettingen
Tel: (05452) 4598 *Fax:* (05452) 4357
E-mail: brasilien@T-Online.de
Web Site: www.brasilienkunde.de; home.t-online.de/home/Brasilien
Key Personnel
Man Dir, Rights & Permissions: P O Gogolok
Founded: 1979
Subjects: Ethnicity, Foreign Countries, Regional Interests, Religion - Other, Social Sciences, Sociology
ISBN Prefix(es): 3-88559
Imprints: Aspekter der Brasilienkunde; BTB

Blackwell Wissenschafts-Verlag GmbH+
Kurfuerstendamm 57, 10707 Berlin
Tel: (030) 32 79 06-0 *Fax:* (030) 32 79 06-10
E-mail: verlag@blackwis.de; rights@blackwis.de
Web Site: www.blackwis.de
Key Personnel
Manager: Dr Axel Beduerftig; Leonard Korff
International Rights: Katrin Blanke

Founded: 1989
Integration in 1994 of the Scientific Program of Paul Parey Publishers (Berlin/Hamburg) & 1996 Integration of the Professional List of Paul Parey Publishers (Berlin/Hamburg).
Subjects: Agriculture, Animals, Pets, Biological Sciences, Environmental Studies, Gardening, Plants, Medicine, Nursing, Dentistry, Natural History, Nonfiction (General), Physical Sciences, Veterinary Science
ISBN Prefix(es): 3-89412; 3-8263
Parent Company: Blackwell Science, Ltd, Osney Mead, Oxford OX2 OEL
Imprints: Parey Buchverlag
Subsidiaries: Blackwell Wissenschafts-Verlag
U.S. Office(s): Blackwell Science Inc, Commerce Place, 350 Main St, Malden, MA 02148, United States
Orders to: Koch, Neff & Oetinger, Schockenriedstr 39, 70565 Stuttgart

Blanvalet VerlagGmbH+
Neumarkter Str 18, 81673 Munich
Mailing Address: Postfach 800360, 81603 Munich
Tel: (089) 4372-0 *Fax:* (089) 4372-2812
E-mail: vertrieb.verlagsgruppe@bertelsmann.de
Telex: 529965 wg vmn d *Cable:* Bertelsmann Muenchen
Founded: 1935
Subjects: Biography
ISBN Prefix(es): 3-7645
Parent Company: Verlagsgruppe Bertelsmann GmbH
U.S. Office(s): Bettina Schrewe Literary Scouting, 101 Fifth Ave, Suite 11B, New York, NY 10003, United States (US Scout)

Verlag Die Blaue Eule
Annastr 74, 45130 Essen
Tel: (0201) 8 77 69 63 *Fax:* (0201) 8 7769 64
E-mail: info@die-blaue-eule.de
Web Site: www.die-blaue-eule.de
Key Personnel
Publisher: Dr W L Hohmann
Contact: Eva Wunsch
Founded: 1983
Galeria.
Subjects: Art, Education, History, Language Arts, Linguistics, Music, Dance, Mythology, Philosophy, Psychology, Psychiatry, Science (General), Social Sciences, Sociology, Theology
ISBN Prefix(es): 3-924368; 3-89206; 3-89924
Total Titles: 1,000 Print
Distributed by Engros Buchhandlung Dessauer; Freihofer AG Verlagsauslieferung Wissenschaft

Blaukreuz-Verlag Wuppertal+
Freiligrathstr 27, 42289 Wuppertal
Mailing Address: Postfach 200252, 42202 Wuppertal
Tel: (0202) 6200361 *Fax:* (0202) 6200381
E-mail: bkv@blaukreuz.de
Web Site: www.blaukreuz.de
Key Personnel
Publisher: Horst Westmeier *E-mail:* westmeier@blaukreuz.de
Founded: 1892
Subjects: Health, Nutrition, Human Relations, Literature, Literary Criticism, Essays, Poetry, Self-Help, Addiction & Assistance
ISBN Prefix(es): 3-920106; 3-89175
Number of titles published annually: 7 Print
Total Titles: 100 Audio
Parent Company: Blaues Kreuz in Deutschland eV, Wuppertal
Distributed by Blaukreuz-Verlag Bern (Switzerland); BMK Vienna (Austria)
Distributor for Blaukreuz-Verlag Bern (Switzerland); Jordan-Verlag (Switzerland); Nicol-Verlag Kassel

Bleicher Verlag GmbH+
Weilimdorfestr 76, 70839 Gerlingen
Mailing Address: Postfach 10 01 23, 70826 Gerlingen
Tel: (07156) 43 08-20 *Fax:* (07156) 43 08-40
E-mail: info@bleicher_verlag.de
Web Site: www.bleicher-verlag.de
Key Personnel
Director: Rainer Abel
Publisher, Editorial: Ev Marie Bartolitius
Publisher, Editorial, Rights & Permissions: Thomas Bleicher
Sales: Klaus Vahlbruch
Press Relations: Edda Bournot
Founded: 1968
Subjects: Fiction, Government, Political Science, History, Social Sciences, Sociology
ISBN Prefix(es): 3-88350
Number of titles published annually: 20 Print
Subsidiaries: Hoffmann Verlag GmbH

Verlag Wolfgang Bleiweis
Postfach 4013, 97408 Schweinfurt
Tel: (09721) 26721 *Fax:* (09721) 26751
Founded: 1990
Subjects: Automotive, Biography, Engineering (General), History, Transportation
ISBN Prefix(es): 3-928786

BLISTA, see Deutsche Blinden-Bibliothek

Eberhargd Blottner Verlag+
Silberbachstr 9, 65232 Taunusstein
Mailing Address: Postfach 1104, 65219 Taunusstein
Tel: (06128) 2 36 00 *Fax:* (06128) 21180
E-mail: blottner@blottner.de
Web Site: www.blottner.de *Cable:* BLOTTNERTAUNUSSTEIN
Key Personnel
Publisher, Rights & Permissions: Eberhard Blottner
Marketing: Britta Blottner
Founded: 1988
Subjects: Architecture & Interior Design, Crafts, Games, Hobbies, Earth Sciences, Environmental Studies, House & Home
ISBN Prefix(es): 3-89367
Total Titles: 28 Print
Associate Companies: Blottner Fachverlag GmbH & Co KG

BLT, *imprint of* Verlagsgruppe Luebbe GmbH & Co KG

Brigitte Blume
Goerlitzerstr 33, 80993 Munich
Tel: (089) 1418639 *Fax:* (089) 1418639
ISBN Prefix(es): 3-9800464

BLV Verlagsgesellschaft mbH+
Lothstr 29, 80797 Munich
Mailing Address: Postfach 400320, 80703 Munich
Tel: (089) 127050 *Fax:* (089) 12705354
E-mail: blv.verlag@blu.de
Web Site: www.blv.de *Cable:* BLV VERLAG
Key Personnel
Man Dir, Book Division: Hartwig Schneider
Man Dir, Journal Division: Peter Kliemann
Marketing & Distribution Manager: Michael Wellbrock
Editorial, Nature: Wilhelm Eisenreich
Editorial, Sports: Juergen Kemmler
Foreign Rights: Undine Hoegl *Tel:* (089) 12705-417 *Fax:* (089) 12705-415 *E-mail:* undine.hoegl@blv.de; Hannelore Koenig *Tel:* (089) 12705-416 *Fax:* (089) 12705-415 *E-mail:* hannelore.koenig@blv.de
Book Trade: Karin Herbschleb *E-mail:* karin.herbschleb@blv.de
Warehouse & Specialty Shop: Helga Weingartner *E-mail:* helga.weingartner@blv.de
Delivery Trade: Eva Bednarek *E-mail:* eva.bednarek@blv.de
Founded: 1946
Member of TR-Verlagsunion GmbH.
Subjects: Agriculture, Animals, Pets, Astronomy, Gardening, Plants, Natural History, Outdoor Recreation, Sports, Athletics, Travel
ISBN Prefix(es): 3-405
Number of titles published annually: 80 Print
Total Titles: 600 Print
Imprints: VUA (agricultural titles)
Subsidiaries: DLV Deutscher Landwirtschafts-Verlag Berlin
Branch Office(s)
BLV Verlagsgesellschaft mbH, Verlagsbuero Berlin, Gurtelstr 29a-30, D-10247 Berlin
Distributed by Athesia Buch GmbH (Italy)
Distributor for Ceres Verlag
Warehouse: BLV Auslieferung, Rotwandweg 2, 82024 Taufkirchen

Verlag Erwin Bochinsky GmbH & Co KG+
Muenchenerstr 45, 60329 Frankfurt am Main
Tel: (069) 2 71 37 89-0 *Fax:* (069) 2 71 37 89-94
Web Site: www.das-musikinstrument.de
Key Personnel
General Manager: Winfried Kumetat
Founded: 1952
Member of Europiano; Specialize in musical instruments (acoustic & electronic).
Subjects: Electronics, Electrical Engineering, Music, Dance, Nonfiction (General)
ISBN Prefix(es): 3-920112; 3-923639
Parent Company: PPV-Verlag, Dachauerstr 376, 85232 Feldgeding

Bock und Herchen Verlag
Reichenbergerstr 11e, 53604 Bad Honnef
Mailing Address: Postfach 11 45, 53581 Bad Honnef
Tel: (02224) 57 75 *Fax:* (02224) 7 83 10
E-mail: buh@bock-net.de
Web Site: www.b-u-b.de
Key Personnel
Man Dir, Rights & Permissions: Karl Heinrich Bock
Founded: 1977
Subjects: Library & Information Sciences, Science (General)
ISBN Prefix(es): 3-88347

Boehlau-Verlag GmbH & Cie+
Ursulaplatz 1, 50668 Cologne
Tel: (0221) 91 39 0-0 *Fax:* (0221) 91 39 0-11
E-mail: vertrieb@boehlau.de
Web Site: www.boehlau.de *Cable:* BOHLAU, COLOGNE
Key Personnel
Man Dir: Dr Peter Rauch *E-mail:* vertrieb@boehlau.de
Sales & Distribution: Joachim Bischofs *Tel:* (0221) 91390-16
Founded: 1951
Subjects: Anthropology, Archaeology, Art, Education, History, Journalism, Language Arts, Linguistics, Social Sciences, Sociology, Women's Studies
ISBN Prefix(es): 3-412
Number of titles published annually: 180 Print
Total Titles: 1,800 Print
Online services available through World Wide Web.
Associate Companies: Boehlau Verlag GmbH, Sachsenplatz 4-6, 1201 Vienna, Austria *Tel:* (01) 33024270 *Fax:* (01) 3302432 *E-mail:* boehlau@boehlau.at *Web Site:* www.boehlau.at

PUBLISHERS

GERMANY

Branch Office(s)
Boehlau Verlag GmbH & Cie, Eisfeld 5, 99423 Weimar
Orders to: Koch, Neff und Oetinger & Co, Postfach 800620, 70506 Stuttgart

Verlag Hermann Boehlaus Nachfolger Weimar GmbH & Co+
Prellerstr 2a, 99423 Weimar
Mailing Address: Postfach 2260, 99403 Weimar
Tel: (03643) 8508-90 *Fax:* (03643) 8508-92
Key Personnel
Editor & International Rights: Gunter Lauterbach
Founded: 1624
Subjects: Architecture & Interior Design, Art, Foreign Countries, History, Law, Literature, Literary Criticism, Essays, Poetry, Science (General), Theology
ISBN Prefix(es): 3-7400
Orders to: Verlagsaurlieferung Karlstr 10, Postfach 546, 72488 Sigmaringen

Klaus Boer Verlag+
Vokartstr 30, 80634 Munich
Tel: (089) 13938099 *Fax:* (089) 13989098
E-mail: boerv@online.de
Web Site: www.boerverlag.de
Key Personnel
Owner: Klaus Boer
Founded: 1984
Subjects: Art, History, Literature, Literary Criticism, Essays, Philosophy
ISBN Prefix(es): 3-924963
Orders to: Buchvertrieb Grimmstr, Saalburgstr 3, 12099 Berlin

Edition Boiselle+
Wormsestr 30, 67346 Speyer
Tel: (06232) 629662 *Fax:* (06232) 629664
E-mail: info@edition-boiselle.de
Web Site: www.edition-boiselle.de
Key Personnel
Man Dir: Gabriele Boiselle
Founded: 1990
Subjects: Calendars, Equestrian
ISBN Prefix(es): 3-927589
Sales Office(s): Kraemer Pferdesportversandhaus, 68764 Hockenheim *Tel:* (0180) 5949400 *Fax:* (06205) 949488 *E-mail:* info@kraemer-pferdesport.de *Web Site:* www.kraemer-pferdesport.de
Distributed by Buecher Zentrum (Austria); Edition Boiselle (UK, US, France & Spain); Islandpferdehof Plarenga (Switzerland); Mias Ridsport (Sweden)

Bolanz Verlag fur Alle
Friedrichstr, Moltkestr 11/1, 88046 Friedrichshafen
Tel: (07541) 33 6 99 *Fax:* (07541) 32467
Specialize in calendars.
ISBN Prefix(es): 3-927744
Bookshop(s): Christliche Buchhandlung Buecherecke, Ailingerstr 11, 88046 Friedrichshafen; Christliche Buchhandlung Buecherecke, Zeppelinstr 2, 88212 Ravensburg; Christliche Buchhandlung Buecherecke, Ambrosius-Blaresstr 3, 78532 Tuttlingen

CB-Verlag Carl Boldt
Baselerstr 80, 12205 Berlin
Mailing Address: Postfach 45 02 07, 12172 Berlin
Tel: (030) 833 70 87 *Fax:* (030) 833 91 25
E-mail: cb-verlag@t-online.de
Key Personnel
Contact: Wolf P Gesellius

Bollmann-Bildkarten-Verlag GmbH & Co KG
Lilienthalplatz 1, 38108 Braunschweig
Tel: (0531) 332069 *Fax:* (0531) 353064
E-mail: info@bollmann-bildkarten.de
Web Site: www.bollmann-bildkarten.de
Key Personnel
Man Dir, Rights & Permissions: Friedrich Bollmann
Founded: 1948

Dr Bolte KG, see Polyglott-Verlag

Verlag Aurel Bongers
Johann-Sebastian-Bachstr 19, 45657 Recklinghausen
Mailing Address: Postfach 100264, 45602 Recklinghausen
Tel: (02361) 27000 *Fax:* (02361) 27007
Cable: BONGERS RECKLINGHAUSEN
Key Personnel
Proprietor, Publishing Dir, Rights & Permissions: Aurel Bongers, Jr
Founded: 1931
ISBN Prefix(es): 3-7647

Bonifatius GmbH Druck-Buch-Verlag+
Karl-Schurzstr 26, 33100 Paderborn
Mailing Address: Postfach 1280, 33042 Paderborn
Tel: (05251) 153 171 *Fax:* (05251) 153 104
Web Site: www.bonifatius.de
Key Personnel
Manager: Rainer Beseler
Founded: 1869
Subjects: Art, Literature, Literary Criticism, Essays, Music, Dance, Theology
ISBN Prefix(es): 3-87088
Imprints: Kontur; Creator

Bonsai-Centrum
Mannheimerstr 401, 69123 Heidelberg-Weiblingen
Tel: (06221) 8491-0 *Fax:* (06221) 849130
E-mail: info@bonsai-centrum.de
Web Site: www.bonsai-centrum.de
Key Personnel
President, Publisher & Author: Paul Lesniewicz
Subjects: Gardening, Plants
ISBN Prefix(es): 3-924982; 3-9800345

Adolf Bonz Verlag GmbH+
Rottenkamp 6A, 38239 Salzgitter
Tel: (05300) 901053 *Fax:* (0503) 901053
Key Personnel
Manager: Wilma Gaupe
Founded: 1867
Subjects: Education, Psychology, Psychiatry
ISBN Prefix(es): 3-87089

Books on African Studies, see The African Literature Club

Richard Boorberg Verlag GmbH & Co
Scharrstr 2, 70563 Stuttgart
Mailing Address: Postfach 800260, 70502 Stuttgart
Tel: (0711) 73 85-0 *Fax:* (0711) 73 85-100
Web Site: www.boorberg.de
Key Personnel
Manager: Dr Berndt Oesterhelt
Administration: Markus Ott
Production: Werner Frasch
Sales: Hermann Ruckdeschel
International Rights: Roderich Dohse
Founded: 1927
Subjects: Law
ISBN Prefix(es): 3-415
Subsidiaries: Josef Moll Verlag GmbH & Co
Branch Office(s)
Berlin
Hanover
Levelingstr a, 81673 Munich *Tel:* (089) 43 60 00-0 *Fax:* (089) 4 36 15 64
Weimar

Boosey & Hawkes Music Publishers LTD, London+
Luetzowufer 26, 10787 Berlin
Tel: (030) 25001300 *Fax:* (030) 25001399
E-mail: musikverlag@boosey.com
Web Site: www.boosey.com/publishing
Key Personnel
Chief Executive: Richard Holland
Manager: W Jacobs
Founded: 1838
Subjects: Music, Dance
ISBN Prefix(es): 3-7931
Parent Company: Boosey & Hawkes Music Publishers Ltd, London
Branch Office(s)
Boosey & Hawkes Pty Ltd, Unit 12/6 Campbell St, Artarmon, NSW 2076, Australia *Tel:* (02) 9439 4144 *Fax:* (02) 9439 2912 *E-mail:* info@boosey.au.com
Buffet Crampon Limited, 8-17, Toyo-4, Koto-ku, Tokyo 135-0016, Japan *Tel:* (05632) 5511 *Fax:* (05632) 5527 *E-mail:* tokyo@boosey.com
Boosey & Hawkes Music Publishers LTD, 295 Regent St, London W1B 2JH, United Kingdom *Tel:* (020) 7580 2060 *Fax:* (020) 7637 7109 *E-mail:* composers@boosey.com
U.S. Office(s): Boosey & Hawkes New York Inc, 35 East 21 St, New York, NY 10010-6216, United States *Tel:* 212-358-5300 *Fax:* 212-358-5301 *E-mail:* info.ny@boosey.com
Bookshop(s): 10623 Berlin *Tel:* (030) 31100310

Born-Verlag+
Leuschnerstr 72-74, 34134 Kassel
Mailing Address: Postfach 420220, 34071 Kassel
Tel: (0561) 40950 *Fax:* (0561) 4095112
E-mail: info.born@ec-jugend.de
Web Site: www.born-buch.de
Key Personnel
Publishing Manager: Claudia Siebert *Tel:* (0561) 4095107 *E-mail:* siebert.born@ec-jugend.de
Founded: 1898
Subjects: Religion - Catholic, Religion - Protestant
ISBN Prefix(es): 3-87092

Borntraeger Verlagsbuchhandlung, *imprint of* Gebrueder Borntraeger Science Publishers

C Bosendahl
Klosterstr 32/33, 3260 Rinteln
Mailing Address: Postfach 1240, 31722 Rinteln
Tel: (05751) 40000 *Fax:* (05751) 400077
Key Personnel
Publisher: Hans Niemeyer; Guenther Niemeyer; Ewald Schienke
Editor: Al Ackeron; Tom Saunders; Carl Wiehelm Niemeyer
Founded: 1621
Subjects: Fiction, Regional Interests
ISBN Prefix(es): 3-87085
Parent Company: C W Niemeyer GmbH & Co KG, Hameln
Associate Companies: Generalanzeiger Schaumburg GmbH, Stadthagen
Branch Office(s)
Grimmesche Hofbuchdruckerei, Buecheburg

Gustav Bosse GmbH & Co KG+
Heinrich-Schutz-Allee 35, 34131 Kassel
Mailing Address: Postfach 101420, 34014 Kassel
Tel: (0561) 31 05-0 *Fax:* (0561) 31 05-2 40
E-mail: info@bosse-verlag.de
Web Site: www.bosse-verlag.de
Key Personnel
Man Dir: Barbara Scheuch-Voetterle; Leonhard Scheuch
Rights & Permissions: Thomas Tietze
Editor: Berthold Kloss
Founded: 1912
Subjects: Education, Music, Dance

ISBN Prefix(es): 3-7649
Parent Company: Verlag Baerenreiter, Kassel
Distributed by Barenreiter Ltd (UK); Barenreiter Verlag Basel AG (Switzerland)
Warehouse: KGA-Technischer Betrieb, Brandaustr 10, 34127 Kassel
Orders to: KGA, Postfach 102180, 34021 Kassel

Bote & Bock Musikalienhandelsgesellschaft mbH+
Lutzowufer 26, 10787 Berlin
Tel: (030) 2500-1300 *Fax:* (030) 2500-1399
E-mail: musikverlag@boosey.com
Key Personnel
Contact: Regina Steinhauber *Tel:* (030) 3110013-14
Founded: 1838
Primarily a music store.
Subjects: Music, Dance
ISBN Prefix(es): 3-7931

Bouvier Verlag+
Am Hof 28, 53113 Bonn
Mailing Address: Postfach 1268, 53002 Bonn
Tel: (0228) 729010 *Fax:* (0228) 637909
E-mail: verlag@books.de
Key Personnel
Publishing Dir & International Rights: Peter Parusel
Sales, Press: Elisabeth Keuthen-Nuechel
Sales, President: Sabine Taeffner
Manager & Publishing Dir: Thomas Grundmonn
Founded: 1828
Subjects: Government, Political Science, Regional Interests, Science (General)
ISBN Prefix(es): 3-416
Orders to: Koch, Neff, Oetinger & Co, Schockenriedstr 39, 70565 Stuttgart *Tel:* (0711) 78991120 *Fax:* (0711) 78991155

Verlag Brandenburger Tor GmbH
Luisenstr 39, 10117 Berlin
Tel: (030) 2834171 *Fax:* (030) 2834916
Key Personnel
Publisher: Klaus-Juergen Holzapfel; Andreas Holzapfel
Founded: 1973
Subjects: Government, Political Science
ISBN Prefix(es): 3-921226
Subsidiaries: Verlag Brandenburger Tor
Orders to: NDV Neue Darmstaedter Verlagsanstalt, Postfach 1560, 53585 Bad Honnef *Tel:* (022241) 3232 *Fax:* (022241) 78639
E-mail: ndv@ndvverlag.de

Brandenburgisches Verlagshaus, *imprint of* Verlagsgruppe Dornier

Brandenburgisches Verlagshaus in der Dornier Medienholding GmbH+
Dircksenstr 48, 10178 Berlin
Tel: (030) 28447-112; (030) 28447-113 *Fax:* (030) 28447-123
E-mail: info@dornier-verlage.de
Web Site: www.dornier-verlage.de
Key Personnel
Man Dir: Dr Juergen A Bach; Peter Gutsch
Founded: 1956
Subjects: Biography, Engineering (General), Foreign Countries, History, Management, Maritime, Military Science, Nonfiction (General), Regional Interests, Travel
ISBN Prefix(es): 3-89488
Parent Company: Dormier Medienholding GmbH

Brandes & Apsel Verlag GmbH+
Scheidswaldstr 33, 60385 Frankfurt am Main
Tel: (069) 957 301 86 *Fax:* (069) 957 301 87
E-mail: brandes-apsel@t-online.de
Web Site: www.brandes-apsel-verlag.de
Founded: 1986

Subjects: Anthropology, Developing Countries, Education, Ethnicity, Fiction, Government, Political Science, Human Relations, Literature, Literary Criticism, Essays, Poetry, Psychology, Psychiatry, Social Sciences, Sociology, Dance, Psychoanalysis, Theater, Self Psychology
ISBN Prefix(es): 3-925798; 3-86099
Number of titles published annually: 40 Print
Total Titles: 300 Print
Orders to: Prolit Verlagsauslieferung, Siemensstr 16, 35463 Fernwald-Annerod *Tel:* (0641) 94393-22, 23 *Fax:* (0641) 94393-29

Oscar Brandstetter Verlag GmbH & Co KG+
Wilhelminenstr 1a, 65193 Wiesbaden
Mailing Address: Postfach 1708, 65007 Wiesbaden
Tel: (0611) 9 91 20-0 *Fax:* (0611) 3 08 37 85
E-mail: brandstetter-verlag@t-online.de
Web Site: www.brandstetter-verlag.de
Key Personnel
Man Dir: Guenther H Froehlen
Founded: 1862
Subjects: Chemistry, Chemical Engineering, Communications, Computer Science, Economics, Electronics, Electrical Engineering, Engineering (General), Language Arts, Linguistics, Law, Medicine, Nursing, Dentistry, Physical Sciences, Technology
ISBN Prefix(es): 3-87097
Shipping Address: Koch, Neff & Oetinger & Co, Verlagsauslieferung Smlt, Stuttgart, Contact: Mr Kirchknopf *Tel:* (0711) 78992112 *Fax:* (0711) 78991010
Warehouse: Koch, Neff & Oetinger & Co, Verlagsauslieferung Smlt, 70551 Stuttgart, Contact: Mr Kirchknopf *Tel:* (0711) 78992112 *Fax:* (0711) 78991010
Orders to: Koch, Neff & Oetinger & Co, Verlagsauslieferung Smlt, 70551 Stuttgart, Contact: Mr Kirchknopf *Tel:* (0711) 78992112 *Fax:* (0711) 78991010

Aspekter der Brasilienkunde, *imprint of* BKV-Brasilienkunde Verlag GmbH

Brasilienkunde Verlag GmbH, *see* BKV-Brasilienkunde Verlag GmbH

Breitkopf & Hartel+
Walkmuehlstr 52, 65195 Wiesbaden
Mailing Address: Postfach 1707, 65007 Wiesbaden
Tel: (0611) 450080 *Fax:* (0611) 4500859; (0611) 4500860; (0611) 4500861
E-mail: info@breitkopf.com
Web Site: www.breitkopf.com; www.breitkopf.de
Cable: BREITKOPFS WIESBADEN
Key Personnel
Man Dir: Gottfried Moeckel; Lieselotte Sievers
International Rights: Vivian Rehman *Tel:* (0611) 45008 36 *Fax:* (0611) 45008 60 *E-mail:* rehman@breitkopf.de
UK Sales Representative: Robin Winter *Tel:* (01263) 768732 *Fax:* (01263) 768733 *E-mail:* sales@breitkopf.com
Founded: 1719
Music publisher.
Subjects: Music, Dance
ISBN Prefix(es): 3-7651
Branch Office(s)
22 rue Chauchat, 75009 Paris, France, Contact: Mr Farid Aiech *Tel:* (01) 48 01 01 33 *Fax:* (01) 48 01 01 66 *E-mail:* breitkopf.aich@wanadoo.fr
Deutscher Verlag fuer Musik, Bauhofstr 3-5, 04103 Leipzig *Tel:* (0341) 997190 *Fax:* (0341) 9971930 *E-mail:* leipzig@breitkopf.com
Obere Waldstr 30, 65232 Taunusstein *Tel:* (06128) 9663 0 *Fax:* (06128) 9663 50; (06128) 966360 *E-mail:* sales@breitkopf.com

Broome Cottage, The Street, Suffield Norwich NR 11 7EQ, United Kingdom, Contact: Robin Winter *Tel:* (01263) 768732 *Fax:* (01263) 768733 *E-mail:* sales@breitkopf.com

Breitner, Chirurgische Operationslehte, *imprint of* Urban und Fischer Verlag fur Medizin

Breklumer Buchhandlung und Verlag
Church Rd 1, 25821 Breklum
Tel: (04671) 910020 *Fax:* (04671) 910030
E-mail: verlag@breklumer.de
Web Site: www.breklumer.de *Cable:* BREKLUMER VERLAG BREKLUM
Key Personnel
Publisher: Manfred Siegel
Founded: 1875
Subjects: Religion - Other
ISBN Prefix(es): 3-7793

Joh & Sohn Brendow Verlag GmbH+
Gutenbergstr 1, 47443 Moers
Tel: (02841) 97761-21 *Fax:* (02841) 97761-30
E-mail: brendow.verlag@brendow.de
Web Site: www.brendow.de
Key Personnel
Dir: Armin Schmidt
Sales: Thomas von der Heyde *Tel:* (02841) 9776126 *E-mail:* vdheyde@biendow.de
Rts & Perms: Hildegard Bernert
Founded: 1849
Subjects: Religion - Other
ISBN Prefix(es): 3-87067

BrennGlas Verlag Assenheim Juergen Seuss+
Niederwoellstaedterstr 18, 61194 Niddatal
Tel: (06034) 3663 *Fax:* (06034) 3663
Web Site: www.minipresse.de
Founded: 1981
Subjects: Art, Literature, Literary Criticism, Essays

Brigg Verlag Franz-Joset Buchler KG
Zusamstr 9, 86165 Augsburg
Tel: (0821) 711347 *Fax:* (0821) 711347
Key Personnel
Man Dir: Franz-Josef Buechler
Founded: 1950
Subjects: Poetry, Regional Interests
ISBN Prefix(es): 3-87101

Verlag Ekkehard & Ulrich Brockhaus GmbH & Co KG
An den Eichen 3a, 42699 Solingen
Tel: (0212) 65 87-29; (0172) 2 55 59 61 *Fax:* (0202) 42 82 82; (0212) 65 87-99
E-mail: mail@verlag-brockhaus.de
Web Site: www.verlag-brockhaus.de
Subjects: Genealogy, Cultural History
ISBN Prefix(es): 3-930132

Brockhaus/Kommission GmbH
Kreidlerstr 9, 70806 Kornwestheim
Tel: (07154) 1327-0 *Fax:* (07154) 1327-13
Key Personnel
Man Dir: Dr Wolfgang Berg; Steffen Goehler
Founded: 1805
Subjects: Geography, Geology
ISBN Prefix(es): 3-87103

R Brockhaus Verlag+
Member of Stiftung Christliche Medien
Champagne 7, 42781 Haan
Mailing Address: Postfach 2220, 42766 Haan
Tel: (02104) 968600; (02104) 968620 (sales) *Fax:* (02104) 968601
E-mail: edit@brockhaus-verlag.de
Web Site: www.brockhaus-verlag.de
Key Personnel
Publisher: Thomas Lardon
Editorial: Hans-Werner Durau
International Rights: Christina Bradel

Founded: 1853
Subjects: Biography, Fiction, Music, Dance, Psychology, Psychiatry, Religion - Other, Theology
ISBN Prefix(es): 3-417
Associate Companies: Oncken Verlag KG
Subsidiaries: R Brockhaus Verlag AG

Die Brucke - Neumunster ev Abt Verlag, see Paranus Verlag - Bruecke Neumuenster GmbH

Bruecke-Verlag Kurt Schmersow
Arnekenstr 22-25, 31134 Hildesheim
Tel: (05121) 91 92 0 *Fax:* (05121) 91 92 20
Web Site: www.bruecke-verlag.de
Key Personnel
Owner: Gerda Niemz
Founded: 1920
ISBN Prefix(es): 3-87105

Bruehlsche Uni-Druckerei Verlag, der Giessener Anzeiger GmbH & Co KG
Am Urnenfeld 12, 35396 Giessen
Mailing Address: Postfach 100451, 35334 Giessen
Tel: (0641) 95040 *Fax:* (0641) 9504100
Telex: 482859 bruel
Key Personnel
Manager & International Rights: Dr Wolfgang Maass
ISBN Prefix(es): 3-922300

BRUEN-Verlag, Gorenflo
Weserstr 22, 65428 Ruesselsheim
Mailing Address: Postfach 1356, 65403 Ruesselsheim
Tel: (06142) 61434 *Fax:* (06142) 61259
E-mail: 0614261434-1@t-online.de
Key Personnel
Man Dir: R Gorenflo
Founded: 1987
Subjects: Art, Fiction, History, Nonfiction (General), Poetry, Regional Interests
ISBN Prefix(es): 3-926759

Brunnen-Verlag GmbH+
Gottlieb-Daimler Str 22, 35398 Giessen
Tel: (0641) 6059-0 *Fax:* (0641) 6059-100
E-mail: brunnen.gi@t-online.de
Web Site: www.brunnen-verlag.de
Key Personnel
Man Dir: Wilfried Jerke
Editorial: Eva-Maria Busch; Renate Huebsch; Hartmut Schweitzer; Ralf Tibusek
Rights & Permissions: Irmgard Barth
Sales Manager: Reinhard Engeln
Founded: 1919
Subjects: Religion - Other, Theology
ISBN Prefix(es): 3-7655
Associate Companies: Brunnen Verlag, Basel, Switzerland

BTB, *imprint of* BKV-Brasilienkunde Verlag GmbH

Buch- und Kunstverlag Kleinheinrich+
Koenigsstr 42, D-48143 Muenster
Tel: (06071) 55572 *Fax:* (06071) 55572
Key Personnel
International Rights: Dr Josef Kleinheinrich
Founded: 1986
Subjects: Art, Literature, Literary Criticism, Essays
ISBN Prefix(es): 3-926608; 3-930754

Bucharchiv, see Deutsches Bucharchiv Muenchen, Institut fur Buchwissenschaften

Verlag C J Bucher GmbH+
Paul-Heysestr 28, 80336 Munich
Tel: (089) 51480-20 *Fax:* (089) 5148-2233
Key Personnel
Man Dir: Axel Schenck
Sales & Publicity: Alexander Herrmann
Production: Angelika Kerscher
Publisher: Christian Strasser
Rights & Permissions: Bettina Breitling
Publicity: Michael Then
Founded: 1956
Subjects: Art, Nonfiction (General), Photography, Travel
ISBN Prefix(es): 3-7658
Associate Companies: Paul List Verlag; Suedwest Verlag; W Ludwig Verlag
Orders to: Koch, Neff, Oetinger & Co Verlagsauslieferung GmbH, Schockenriedstr 39, D-70506 Stuttgart

Buchhaendler-Vereinigung GmbH
Grosser Hirschgraben 17/21, 60311 Frankfurt
Mailing Address: Postfach 10 04 42, 60004 Frankfurt
Tel: (069) 1306-0; (069) 1306-339 (Boersenblatt); (069) 1306-340 (Boersenblatt) *Fax:* (069) 1306-201
E-mail: info@buchhaendler-vereinigung.de
Web Site: www.buchhaendler-vereinigung.de
Key Personnel
Prof: Peter Schuck *Tel:* (069) 1306-232 *Fax:* (069) 1306-269
Advertising Manager: Lilli Fleck *Tel:* (069) 1306-243 *E-mail:* fleck@buchhaendler-vereinigung.de
Founded: 1947
Subjects: Publishing & Book Trade Reference
ISBN Prefix(es): 3-7657
Total Titles: 200 Print; 15 CD-ROM
Parent Company: Boevenrserein des Deutschen Buchhandels ev

Buchheim-Verlag
Biersackstr 23, 82340 Feldafing
Tel: (08157) 1221 *Fax:* (08157) 3143
Key Personnel
Owner & International Rights: Lothar-Guenther Buchheim
Founded: 1951
Subjects: Art
ISBN Prefix(es): 3-7659

BuchMarkt Verlag K Werner GmbH
(Bookmarket)
Sperberweg 4a, 40668 Meerbusch
Tel: (02150) 9191-0 *Fax:* (02150) 919191
E-mail: redaktion@buchmarkt.de
Web Site: buchmarkt.de
Key Personnel
Dir, International Rights: Christian Von Zittwitz
Founded: 1966
Publishers of the trade magazine Buchmart for the booktrade.
Subjects: Publishing & Book Trade Reference
ISBN Prefix(es): 3-920518

C C Buchners Verlag
Laubanger 8, 96052 Bamberg
Mailing Address: Postfach 1269, 96003 Bamberg
Tel: (0951) 96 501-0 *Fax:* (0951) 61-774
E-mail: service@ccbuchner.de
Web Site: www.ccbuchner.de
Key Personnel
Dir, Rights & Permissions: Gunnar Gruenke
Founded: 1832
Subjects: Earth Sciences, Government, Political Science, History, Regional Interests
ISBN Prefix(es): 3-7661

Buchverlag Junge Welt GmbH
Oranienburger Str 65, 10117 Berlin
Tel: (030) 231079 0 *Fax:* (030) 2826989
E-mail: bvjw.berlin@t-online.de
Web Site: www.buchverlagjw.com

Key Personnel
Manager: Liesl Richter; Eberhard Tackenberg
Founded: 1991
Subjects: Education, Science (General), Technology
ISBN Prefix(es): 3-7302

Buchverlage Langen-Mueller/Herbig+
Thomas-Wimmer-Ring 11, 80539 Munich
Tel: (089) 2 90 88-0 *Fax:* (089) 29088-144; (089) 29088-155; (089) 29088-178
Web Site: www.herbig.net
Key Personnel
Man Dir: Dr Herbert Fleissner
International Rights: Frauke Hoppen *E-mail:* f.hoppenaherbig@net
Subjects: Cookery, Economics, Fiction, Health, Nutrition, Parapsychology, Self-Help
ISBN Prefix(es): 3-7766; 3-7844
Subsidiaries: Amalthea; Bechtle; F A Herbig Verlagsbuchhandlung GmbH; Langen Mueller; Mary Hahn; Nymphenburger; Signum; Terra Magica; Universitas; Wirtschaftsverlag
Warehouse: Vereinigte Verlagsauslieferung, Guetersloh

Buecher und Zeitschriften, *imprint of* Landbuch-Verlagsgesellschaft mbH

Edition Buecherbar im Arena Verlag, *imprint of* Arena Verlag GmbH

Buchergilde Gutenberg Verlagsgesellschaft mbH
Untermainkai 66, 60329 Frankfurt am Main
Mailing Address: Postfach 160165, 60064 Frankfurt am Main
Tel: (069) 27 39 08-0 *Fax:* (069) 27 39 08-26; (069) 27 39 08-25
Web Site: www.buechergilde.de
Key Personnel
Man Dir, Editorial, Rights & Permsissions: Mario Frueh
Sales & Publicity: Carol Mueller
Production: Grit Fischer
Founded: 1924
Primarily a Book Club, but also a publisher.
Subjects: Art, Government, Political Science, History, Literature, Literary Criticism, Essays
ISBN Prefix(es): 3-7632
Book Club(s): Buechergilde Gutenberg

Buechse der Pandora Verlags-GmbH+
Schulstr 20, 35579 Wetzlar, OT Steindorf
Mailing Address: Postfach 2820, 35538 Wetzlar OT Steindorf
Tel: (06441) 911312 *Fax:* (06441) 911314 *Cable:* 35579 WETZLAR-STEINDORF
Key Personnel
Man Dir: Peter Grosshaus
Founded: 1977
Subjects: Art, Education, Literature, Literary Criticism, Essays, Philosophy
ISBN Prefix(es): 3-88178
Orders to: Rotation Verlagsauslieferung, Mehringdamm 51, D-10961 Berlin

Buffy, *imprint of* Egmont vgs verlagsgesellschaft mbH

Bund demokratischer Wissenschaftlerinnen und Wissenschafler eV (BdWi)+
Gisselberger Str 7, 35037 Marburg
Tel: (06421) 2 13 95 *Fax:* (06421) 2 46 54
E-mail: verlag@bdwi.de
Web Site: www.bdwi.de
Key Personnel
Manager: Dr Rainer Rilling
Founded: 1993
Subjects: Government, Political Science, Psychology, Psychiatry, Social Sciences, Sociology, Women's Studies

ISBN Prefix(es): 3-924684
Associate Companies: Informationsstelle Wissenschaft und Frieden (IWIF), D-53113 Bonn *Tel:* (0228) 210744 *Fax:* (0228) 214924; Informationsdienst Wissenschaft und Frieden ev, Reuterstr 44, D- 5300 Bonn 1 *Tel:* (0228) 213334 *Fax:* (0228) 214924
Imprints: Forum Wissenschaft Studien; Internationale Studien zen Fatigkeititleone; Sammlung; Schriftenfeibe Wissenschaft und Frieden
Branch Office(s)
BdWi Bonn ev, Reuterstr 44, 53115 Bonn 1 *Tel:* (0228) 219946 *Fax:* (0228) 214924
Orders to: Bugtiur-Verlagsanslieferung, Sodelburgstr 3, 12099 Berlin

Bund Deutscher Schriftsteller (German Writers Association)
Romerstr 2, 63128 Dietzenbach
Tel: (06074) 47566 *Fax:* (06074) 47540
Web Site: www.bund-deutscher-schriftsteller.de
Founded: 1997
Member of World Writers Association, London
Also acts as Literary Agent.
ISBN Prefix(es): 3-00
Total Titles: 2 Print
Publication(s): Authors Yearbook; Register of German Authors

Bund fuer deutsche Schrift und Sprache
Postfach 1110, 26189 Ahlhorn
Tel: (04435) 1313 *Fax:* (04435) 3623
Web Site: www.bfds.de
Key Personnel
Man Dir: Helmut Delbanco
Founded: 1918
ISBN Prefix(es): 3-930540

Bund-Verlag GmbH+
Theodor-Heuss-Allee 90-98, 60486 Frankfurt
Mailing Address: Postfach 90 10 68, 60441 Frankfurt am Main
Tel: (069) 79 50 10 0 *Fax:* (069) 79 50 10 10
E-mail: kontakt@bund-verlag.de
Web Site: www.bund-verlag.de
Key Personnel
Man Dir: Dr Wolf-Dieter Klingelhoefer; Hubert Leiting
Sales: Thomas Weie
Production: Heinz Biermann
Publicity: Waldemar Block
Rights & Permissions: Dr Angermund Schroeder
Founded: 1947
Subjects: Economics, Fiction, Finance, Government, Political Science, Law, Poetry
ISBN Prefix(es): 3-7663

Bundes-Verlag GmbH
Soil fount 43, 58452 Witten
Mailing Address: Postfach 40 65, 58426 Witten
Tel: (02302) 930 93-0 *Fax:* (02302) 930 93-10
E-mail: info@bundesverlag.de
Web Site: www.bundes-verlag.de
Key Personnel
Man Dir: Erhard Diehl
Founded: 1887
Subjects: Religion - Catholic
ISBN Prefix(es): 3-926417

Bundesanzeiger Verlagsgesellschaft
Amsterdamerstr 192, 50735 Cologne
Mailing Address: Postfach 10 05 34, 50445 Cologne
Tel: (0221) 9 76 68-0 *Fax:* (0221) 9 76 68-278
E-mail: vcotiicb@bundesanzeiger.de
Web Site: www.bundesanzeiger.de
Key Personnel
Contact: Birgit Drehsen
Founded: 1948
Subjects: Government, Political Science, History, Law, Regional Interests

ISBN Prefix(es): 3-88784
Subsidiaries: Deutscher Bundesverlag

Burckhardthaus-Laetare Verlag GmbH+
Schumannstr 161, 63069 Offenbach am Main
Tel: (069) 8400030 *Fax:* (069) 84000333
Key Personnel
Publisher & Manager: Andre Juenger
Rights & Permissions: Alexandra Cordes
Founded: 1918
Subjects: Education, Psychology, Psychiatry, Religion - Other
ISBN Prefix(es): 3-7664

Aenne Burda Verlag
Am Kestendamm 1, 77652 Offenburg
Mailing Address: Postfach 1160, 77601 Offenburg
Tel: (0781) 8402 *Fax:* (0781) 3386
Telex: 752804 *Cable:* BURDAMODEN OFFENBURG
Founded: 1949
Subjects: Cookery, Crafts, Games, Hobbies
ISBN Prefix(es): 3-920158; 3-88978
Subsidiaries: Burda Patterns Inc; Dipa SA; ZVB Zeitschriften Vertriebs AB

Ulrich Burgdorf/Homeopathic Publishing House+
Tegeler Weg 8, 37085 Goettingen
Tel: (0551) 796050 *Fax:* (0551) 796955
E-mail: Burgdorf-Verlag@t-online.de
Web Site: www.burgdorf-verlag.de
Key Personnel
Contact: Dons Scheleper
Founded: 1979
Subjects: Philosophy, Photography, Psychology, Psychiatry
ISBN Prefix(es): 3-922345

Kartographischer Verlag Busche GmbH
Schleefstr 1, 44287 Dortmund
Tel: (0231) 4 44 77-0 *Fax:* (0231) 4 44 77-77
E-mail: info@kvbusche.de
Web Site: www.kvbusche.de
Key Personnel
Man Dir, Publicity: Juergen Ruediger Klaffka
Editorial: Barbara Roemer
Marketing Management: Ulrike Rudolph
 Tel: (05221) 775-275
Founded: 1972
Subjects: Travel
ISBN Prefix(es): 3-88584; 3-921143
Parent Company: Busche KG

Helmut Buske Verlag GmbH+
Richardstr 47, 22081 Hamburg
Mailing Address: Postfach 760244, 22052 Hamburg
Tel: (040) 2999580 *Fax:* (040) 29995820
E-mail: info@buske.de
Web Site: buske.de
Key Personnel
Man Dir: Manfred Meiner
Publishing Dir: Michael Hechinger *Tel:* (040) 29 99 58-25
Rights, Marketing: Johannes Kambylis *Tel:* (040) 29 99 58-23 *E-mail:* kambylis@buske.de
Founded: 1959
Subjects: Language Arts, Linguistics
ISBN Prefix(es): 3-87118; 3-87548
Ultimate Parent Company: Felix Meiner Verlag GmbH

Verlag Busse und Seewald GmbH+
Ahmserstr 190, 32052 Herford
Mailing Address: Postfach 1344, 32003 Herford
Tel: (05221) 77 5-0 *Fax:* (05221) 77 52 04
E-mail: info@busse-seewald.de
Web Site: www.busse-seewald.de

Key Personnel
Manager: Harald Busse
Sales & Advertising: Regina Benecke
Rights & Permissions: Ulrike Rudolph
 Tel: (05221) 775-275
Founded: 1947
Subjects: Architecture & Interior Design, Maritime, Nonfiction (General), Outdoor Recreation, Regional Interests, Travel, Wine & Spirits
ISBN Prefix(es): 3-512; 3-87120
Associate Companies: Buchdruckerei und Verlag Busse, Ahmerstr 190, 32052 Herford; Westdeutsche Verlagsanstalt GmbH, Ahmserstr 190, 32052 Herford
Distributor for DSV-Verlag (Germany, Austria, Switzerland)

Butzon & Bercker GmbH+
Hoogeweg 71, 47623 Kevelaer
Mailing Address: Postfach 215, 47613 Kevelaer
Tel: (02832) 929-0 *Fax:* (02832) 929-211
E-mail: service@butzonbercker.de
Web Site: www.butzonbercker.de *Cable:* BUTZONBERCKER
Key Personnel
Dir: Dr Edmund J Bercker; Klaus Bercker
Editorial: Pit Stenmans
Sales: Helga Behr
Publicity: Helmut Kaiser
Rights & Permissions: Anne Moore
Founded: 1870
Subjects: Religion - Catholic, Theology
ISBN Prefix(es): 3-7666
Distributor for Lahn (Limburg); Styria (Graz/Koln)

BVB, see Bayerische Verlagsanstalt GmbH

Caann Verlag, Klaus Wagner
Am Anger 11, 85570 Ottenhofen
Tel: (08121) 9 32 71 *Fax:* (08121) 9 32 78
E-mail: webmaster@caann-verlag.de
Web Site: www.caann-verlag.de
Key Personnel
Man Dir: Klaus Wagner *E-mail:* klaus@t-online.de
Founded: 1969
Subjects: Nonfiction (General), Philosophy, Social Sciences, Sociology
ISBN Prefix(es): 3-87121

Cadmos Verlag GmbH+
Luener Rennbahn 14, 21339 Lueneburg
Tel: (04131) 981 666 *Fax:* (04131) 981 668
E-mail: info@cadmos.de
Web Site: www.cadmos.de
Key Personnel
Publisher: Hans J Schmidtke
Founded: 1986
Subjects: Dogs, Equestrian, Horses
ISBN Prefix(es): 3-925760; 3-86127
Number of titles published annually: 50 Print; 2 Audio
Total Titles: 150 Print; 8 Audio
Foreign Rep(s): Hans Schmidtke

Verlag Georg D W Callwey GmbH & Co+
Streitfeldstr 35, 81673 Munich
Mailing Address: Postfach 800409, 81604 Munich
Tel: (089) 4360050 *Fax:* (089) 436005113
Web Site: www.callwey.de *Cable:* CALLWEYVERLAG
Key Personnel
Man Dir: Amos Kotte
Editorial: Dr Stefan Granzow
Rights & Permissions, Publicity & Sales: Jens-Peter Arndt
Rights & Permissions: Dorothea Montigel
Publicity: Andreas Hagenkord
Advertising: Matthias Weichhaus
Founded: 1884

Subjects: Architecture & Interior Design, Crafts, Games, Hobbies, Gardening, Plants, House & Home, How-to, Photography
ISBN Prefix(es): 3-7667
Subsidiaries: Laterna magica

Calwer Verlag Stuttgart eV+
Balinger Str 31, 70567 Stuttgart
Tel: (0711) 167 22-0 *Fax:* (0711) 167 22 77
E-mail: info@calwer.com
Web Site: www.calwer.com
Key Personnel
Dir: Berthold Brohm; Joachim Hinderer
Marketing: Beatrice Basgier
Production: Karin Klopfer
Rights: Susanne Hien
Founded: 1836
Subjects: Education, Religion - Other, Theology
ISBN Prefix(es): 3-7668
Orders to: Brockhans Kommission, Kreidlestr 9, 70806 Kornwestheim *Fax:* (07154) 13 27 13

Campus Verlag GmbH+
49 Kurfuerstenstr, 60486 Frankfurt am Main
Tel: (069) 976 516-0 *Fax:* (069) 976 516-78
E-mail: info@campus.de
Web Site: www.campus.de
Key Personnel
Executive Dir & Publisher: Thomas Carl Schwoerer *Tel:* (069) 976 516-43 *E-mail:* schwoerer@campus.de
Rights & Permissions: Thomas Carl Schwoeser *Tel:* (069) 976 516-33 *E-mail:* schwoeser@campus.de
Foreign Rights: Franziska Stadler *Tel:* (069) 976 516-15 *E-mail:* stadler@campus.de
Editor-in-Chief: Britta Kroker *Tel:* (069) 976 516-56 *E-mail:* kroker@campus.de
Editor: Adalbert Hepp *Tel:* (069) 976 516-52 *E-mail:* hepp@campus.de
Sales Dir: Gabriele Rubner *Tel:* (069) 976 516-14 *E-mail:* rubner@campus.de
Production: Klaus Schoeffner *Tel:* (069) 976 516-14; Ulrich Begemeier *Tel:* (069) 976 516-14
Advertising: Markus J Karsten *Tel:* (069) 976 516-32
Publicity: Margit Knauer *Tel:* (069) 976 516-21
Founded: 1975
Specialize also in cultural studies.
Subjects: Business, Economics, Government, Political Science, History, Philosophy, Social Sciences, Sociology, Women's Studies
ISBN Prefix(es): 3-593
Number of titles published annually: 240 Print; 4 Audio
Imprints: Edition Pandora; Edition Qumran
Orders to: Campus Verlag c/o Brockhaus Commission, Postfach 1220, 70803 Kornwestheim

campusbooks Medien AG+
Bonner Platz 4, 80803 Munich
Tel: (089) 18921730 *Fax:* (089) 18921731
E-mail: partner@campusbooks.de
Web Site: www.campusbooks.de
Key Personnel
Dir Business Development: Juergen Reuter
Founded: 2000
Bookseller for corporate customers & publishing house for theses & magazines.
Number of titles published annually: 10 Print

Dr Cantz'sche, Druckerei GmbH & Co, Cantz Verlag+
Senefelderstr 12, 73760 Ostfildern-Ruit
Tel: (0711) 4405-0 *Fax:* (0711) 4405-220
E-mail: bklein@jfink.de
Key Personnel
Publisher & International Rights: Annette Kulenkanpff
Publisher: Bernd Barde
Man Dir & Sales Dir: Markus Hartmann
Founded: 1980

Distributor of Art Books.
Subjects: Architecture & Interior Design, Art, Photography
ISBN Prefix(es): 3-89322
Branch Office(s)
DAP (Distributed Art Publishers), 636 Broadway, Rm 1200, New York, NY 10012, United States *Tel:* 212-627-1999 *Fax:* 212-627-9484
Distributed by Thames & Hudson Ltd (London)
Distributor for Guggenheim Museum; Skira Editore (Milano)
Orders to: Cantz Verlag, Senefelderstr 12, 73760 Ostfildern-Ruit
Koch, Neff, Oetinger & Co, Postfach 800620, D-70565 Stuttgart

Carl-Auer-Systeme Verlag+
Weberstr 2, 69120 Heidelberg
Tel: (06221) 64 38 0 *Fax:* (06221) 64 38 22
E-mail: info@carl-auer.de
Web Site: www.carl-auer.de
Key Personnel
Program & Production: Beate Ch Ulrich *Tel:* (06221) 64 38-15 *E-mail:* ulrich@carl-auer.de
Publishing: Klaus W Muller *Tel:* (06221) 64 38-16 *E-mail:* mueller@carl-auer.de
Sales: Johannes Altrock *Tel:* (06221) 64 38-20 *E-mail:* altrock@carl-auer.de
Publicity: Francoise Jaouiche *Tel:* (06221) 64 38-17 *E-mail:* jaouiche@carl-auer.de
Founded: 1989
Subjects: Child Care & Development, Human Relations, Management, Philosophy, Psychology, Psychiatry
ISBN Prefix(es): 3-927809; 3-931574; 3-89670
Total Titles: 110 Print; 90 Audio

Fachverlag Hans Carl GmbH+
Andernacher Str 33a, 90411 Nuermberg
Mailing Address: Postfach 990153, 90268 Nuremberg
Tel: (0911) 95285-0 *Fax:* (0911) 95285-48; (0911) 9528571; (0911) 9528561
E-mail: info@hanscarl.com
Web Site: www.hanscarl.com
Key Personnel
Man Dir, Editorial: Dr Karl-Ullrich Heyse *Tel:* (0911) 9528522 *Fax:* (0911) 9528560 *E-mail:* heyse@hanscarl.com
Man Dir: Wolfgang Illguth *Tel:* (0911) 9528540 *Fax:* (0911) 9528578 *E-mail:* illguth@hanscarl.com
Board: Michael Schmitt *Tel:* (0911) 9528562 *E-mail:* schmitt@hanscarl.com
Founded: 1861
Subjects: Art, Chemistry, Chemical Engineering, Fiction, History, Outdoor Recreation, Philosophy, Poetry, Regional Interests, Science (General), Wine & Spirits
ISBN Prefix(es): 3-418
Bookshop(s): Fachbuchhandlung Hans Carl, Christina Semmler *Tel:* (0911) 9528531 *E-mail:* fachbuchhandlung@hanscarl.com

Carl Link Verlag-Gesellschaft mbH Fachverlag fur Verwaltungsrecht
Kolpingstr 10, 96317 Kronach
Mailing Address: Postfach 1552, 96305 Kronach
Tel: (09261) 969-0 *Fax:* (09261) 969-699
E-mail: info@carllink.de
Web Site: www.carllink.de
Key Personnel
Man Dir & International Rights: Folker O Link-Wiesend
Founded: 1884
Subjects: Law
ISBN Prefix(es): 3-556
Parent Company: Carl Link
Associate Companies: Carl Link Druck GmbH, Kronach; Bueromarkt, Kronach

Bookshop(s): Buchdienst, Gueterstr 7, 96317 Kronach
Warehouse: Carl Link Bueromarkt, Gueterstr 7, 96317 Kronach

Carlsen Verlag GmbH+
Voelckersstr 14-20, 22765 Hamburg
Mailing Address: Postfach 500380, 22703 Hamburg
Tel: (040) 39 804 0 *Fax:* (040) 39 804 390
Key Personnel
Dir: Klaus Humann; Klaus Kaempfe-Burghardt
Editorial: Anne Bender; Ruth Gellersen; Frank Kuehne; Ulrike Schuldes; Katja Schultze
Sales: Ann Hotzapfel
Production: Hartmut Zierau
Advertising: Marianne Ohmann
Public Relations: Cornelia Berger
Press Manager: Katrin Hogrebe *E-mail:* katrin.hogrebe@carlsens.de
Foreign Rights: Erdmut Gross
Founded: 1953
Specialize in picture books & comics.
Subjects: Fiction, Humor
ISBN Prefix(es): 3-551
Parent Company: Bonnier Media Holding GmbH, Hamburg
Associate Companies: ARS Edition; Piper Verlag; Thienemann Verlag

Catia Monser Eggcup-Verlag
Werstener Feld 235, 40591 Duesseldorf
Tel: (0211) 215122 *Fax:* (0211) 215122
E-mail: cmonserev@aol.com
Web Site: members.aol.com/CMonserEV
Key Personnel
Contact: Catia Monser
Founded: 1992
Subjects: Disability, Special Needs, Health, Nutrition, Human Relations, Medicine, Nursing, Dentistry, Mysteries
ISBN Prefix(es): 3-930004

CEC-Cosmic Energy Connections+
Maria - Theresiastr 15, 79102 Freiburg
Tel: (0761) 7059 632 *Fax:* (0761) 7059 633
Founded: 1985
Subjects: Education, Human Relations, Philosophy, Psychology, Psychiatry, Self-Help, Sports, Athletics
ISBN Prefix(es): 3-905276
Warehouse: Bailey Distribution Ltd, Lea Royd Rd, Mountfield Industrial Estate, New Romney, Kent TN28 8XU, United Kingdom *Tel:* (0679) 66905 *Fax:* (0679) 66638
Orders to: Bailey Distribution Ltd, Lea Royd Rd, Mountfield Industrial Estate, New Romney, Kent TN28 8XU, United Kingdom *Tel:* (0679) 66905 *Fax:* (0679) 66638

Centaurus-Verlagsgesellschaft GmbH
Bugstr 7-9, 79336 Herbolzheim
Tel: (07643) 93 39-0 *Fax:* (07643) 93 39-11
E-mail: info@centaurus-verlag.de
Web Site: www.centaurus-verlag.de
Key Personnel
Manager: Petra Sanft; Britta Schulz
Founded: 1983
Member of the Stock Exchange of German Booksellers.
Subjects: Criminology, Education, History, Law, Psychology, Psychiatry, Religion - Other, Social Sciences, Sociology, Women's Studies
ISBN Prefix(es): 3-89085; 3-8255

Charmed, *imprint of* Egmont vgs verlagsgesellschaft mbH

Verlag fur chemische Industrie H Ziolkowsky GmbH
Postfach 10 25 65, 86015 Augsburg
Tel: (0821) 325-830 *Fax:* (0821) 325-8323

GERMANY

Key Personnel
Contact: Bernd Ziolkowsky
ISBN Prefix(es): 3-87846

Chiron-Verlag Reinhardt Stiehle+
Staeudach 6/1, 72074 Tuebingen
Mailing Address: Postfach 1250, 72002 Tuebingen
Tel: (07071) 8884150 *Fax:* (07071) 8884151
E-mail: info@chironverlag.de
Web Site: www.chironverlag.com
Key Personnel
President & Publisher: Reinhardt Stiehle
Founded: 1985
Member of the Stock Exchange of German Booksellers.
Subjects: Astrology, Occult
ISBN Prefix(es): 3-925100
Orders to: Brockhaus Commission, Kreidlerstrasse 9, 70806 Kornwestheim

Chmielorz GmbH Verlag
Marktplatz 13, 65183 Wiesbaden
Mailing Address: Postfach 22 29, 65183 Wiesbaden
Tel: (0611) 360980 *Fax:* (0611) 301303
Key Personnel
Dir, Rights & Permissions: Werner Augsburger
Dir: Juergen Wamser
Founded: 1949
Subjects: Cookery, Earth Sciences, Film, Video, Health, Nutrition, Social Sciences, Sociology, Sports, Athletics
ISBN Prefix(es): 3-87124
Branch Office(s)
Druck-und Verlagshaus Chmielorz, Ostring 13, 65205 Wiesbaden-Nordenstadt

Chorus-Verlag
Wichernweg 22 A, 81737 Munich
Tel: (089) 634 999 60 *Fax:* (089) 634 999 61
Web Site: www.chorus-verlag.de
Key Personnel
Dir: Martin van der Koelen *Tel:* (089) 63499960
Founded: 1995
Subjects: Art, Specialize in museum catalogues & catalog raisonnes
ISBN Prefix(es): 3-931876; 3-926663
Total Titles: 60 Print
Distributed by Arteko Galeria de Arte (Spain); AVA-Buch 2000 Verlagsauslieferung (Switzerland); Bugrim Verlagsauslieferung (Germany & Austria); Continent Books (Benelux); Joker Art Diffusion (France); Hurtado de Ediciones (Spain)

Chr Belser AG fur Verlagsgeschaefte und Co KG+
Pfizerstr 5-7, 70184 Stuttgart
Mailing Address: Postfach 100561, 70004 Stuttgart
Tel: (0711) 2191-0 *Fax:* (0711) 2191-355 *Cable:* BELSERVERLAG
Key Personnel
Publisher: Dr Herbert Fleissner
Manager: Axel Meffert
Rights & Permissions: Andrea Ahlers
Publicity: Renate Palmer
Production: Ulrich Dotzauer
Founded: 1835
Subjects: Art, History, Music, Dance, Nonfiction (General), Religion - Other, Theology, Travel
ISBN Prefix(es): 3-7630
Parent Company: Chr Belser AG Zuerich
Subsidiaries: Amalthea; Bechtle; Kronos; Langen Mueller; Lentz; Mahnert-Lueg; Mary Hahn; Meyster; Nymphenburger; Reich; Universitas; USM Soft Media; Wirtschaftsverlag
Warehouse: VVA, An der Autobahn, 33310 Gutersloh

Christian Verlag GmbH+
Amalienstr 62, 80799 Munich
Tel: (089) 381803-17 *Fax:* (089) 38180381
E-mail: info@christian-verlag.de
Web Site: www.christian-verlag.de
Key Personnel
Manager: Martin Dort; Johannes Heyne
Chief Editor: Florentine Schwabbauer
Sales & Advertising: Ev Friz *Tel:* (089) 38 18 03-30 *Fax:* (089) 38 18 03-81; Dr Ingeborg Klunge *Tel:* (089) 38 18 03-17; Susanne Pietsch *Tel:* (089) 38 18 03-31
Editorial Rights: Margot Bogner; Alexandra Michelis; Andrrea Leskovec
Public Relations: Gudrun Schroeder *Tel:* (089) 2 01 40 10 *Fax:* (089) 2 01 40 11 *E-mail:* gschroeder.muc@t-online.de
Founded: 1979
Subjects: Architecture & Interior Design, Cookery, Gardening, Plants, Nonfiction (General), Photography, Wine & Spirits
ISBN Prefix(es): 3-88472

Hans Christians Druckerei und Verlag GmbH & Co+
Behringstr 28 a, 22765 Hamburg
Tel: (040) 35 60 06-0 *Fax:* (040) 35 60 06-26
E-mail: vertag@christians.de
Web Site: www.christians.de *Cable:* CHRISTIANS DRUCK
Key Personnel
Man Dir: Susanne Liebelt *Tel:* (040) 35 60 06-11 *E-mail:* susanne.liebelt@christians.de
Rights & Permissions: Dagmar Gutsmann
Manager: Martin Lind *Tel:* (040) 35 60 06-27 *E-mail:* martin.lind@christians.de
Public Relations: Sabine Bayer *Tel:* (040) 35 60 06-15 *E-mail:* sabine.bayer@christians.de
Sales: Petra Jehnichen *Tel:* (040) 35 60 06-35 *E-mail:* petra.jehnichen@christians.de
Founded: 1740
Subjects: Architecture & Interior Design, Art, Biography, Communications, Cookery, Crafts, Games, Hobbies, Education, Ethnicity, Gardening, Plants, Geography, Geology, History, Music, Dance, Natural History, Nonfiction (General), Outdoor Recreation, Photography, Regional Interests, Religion - Jewish, Social Sciences, Sociology, Travel
ISBN Prefix(es): 3-7672
Parent Company: Christians Verwaltungs GmbH
Distributor for Boyens; Eylers; Verlag fuer Medienliteratur
Warehouse: Auslieferung, Neumann-Reichardt-Str 31, Haus 12, Hamburg 22041

Christliche Verlagsgesellschaft mbH+
Molkestr 1, 35683 Dillenburg
Tel: (02771) 8302-0 *Fax:* (02771) 8302-30
E-mail: 101741.2264@compuserve.com
Web Site: www.cv-dillenburg.de
Key Personnel
Editorial, Publicity, Production: Siegfrid Lambeck
Sales: Rudi Joas
Rights & Permissions: Guenther Kausemann
Founded: 1957
Subjects: Religion - Other
ISBN Prefix(es): 3-89436; 3-921292
Subsidiaries: Christliche Buecherstuben GmbH
Branch Office(s)
Garather Weg 63, 40789 Monheim (Production & Sales Office)
Distributed by Brunnenverlag (Switzerland); Hansler-Verlag (Germany)
Distributor for CLV
Bookshop(s): Molkestr 1, 35683 Dillenburg; Marburger Tor 22, 57072 Siegen 1; Alte Linner Str 124, 47799 Krefeld 1; Muensterstr 27, D-4670 Luenen; Lindauerstr 8, 87700 Memmingen; Im Kobbenrod 3, 58840 Plettenberg; Harschbacherstr 12, 56316 Raubach; Poststr 24, D-4780 Lippstadt; Am Koenigshof 43, 40822 Mettman; Neustadtstr 12, 58791 Werdohl; Lennestr 25, 58762 Altena; Kirchstr 19, 52531 Uebach-Palenberg; Freitagsgasse 11, 74889 Sinsheim; Schwelmerstr 48, 42389 Wuppertal 22; Hofgarten 4, 52249 Neunkirchen; Duerenerstr 21, 52249 Eschweiler; Koenigstr 20, Rendsburg; Friedrichsstr 10, Duesseldorf

Christliches Verlagshaus GmbH+
Postfach 311141, 70471 Stuttgart
Tel: (0711) 830000 *Fax:* (0711) 830003
Key Personnel
Man Dir: Armin Jetter
Founded: 1872
Subjects: Literature, Literary Criticism, Essays, Religion - Other
ISBN Prefix(es): 3-7675
Subsidiaries: Anker Buch und Medien GmbH; Druckhaus West GmbH

Christophorus-Verlag GmbH+
Subsidiary of Verlag Herder GmbH & Co KG
Hermann-Herderstr 4, 79104 Freiburg im Breisgau
Tel: (0761) 27170 *Fax:* (0761) 2717352
Key Personnel
Man Dir: Dr Klaus-Christoph Scheffels
International Rights: Norbert Landa
Founded: 1935
Subjects: Crafts, Games, Hobbies, How-to, Outdoor Recreation
ISBN Prefix(es): 3-419
Book Club(s): Bertelsmann; Weltbild
Shipping Address: Koch, Neff & Oetinger, Schockenriedstr 39, 70565 Stuttgart
Warehouse: Koch, Neff & Oetinger, Schockenriedstr 39, 70565 Stuttgart
Orders to: Koch, Neff & Oetinger, Schockenriedstr 39, 70565 Stuttgart

Christusbruderschaft Selbitz ev, Abt Verlag
Wildenberg 23, 95152 Selbitz
Mailing Address: Postfach 1260, 95147 Selbitz
Tel: (09280) 68-34 *Fax:* (09280) 68-68
E-mail: info@verlag-christusbruderschaft.de
Web Site: www.verlag-christusbruderschaft.de
Key Personnel
International Rights: Sr Baerbel Quarg
Founded: 1953
Subjects: Art, Poetry, Religion - Protestant, Theology
ISBN Prefix(es): 3-928745

Cicero Presse Verlag & Antiquariat
D25980 Morsum/Sylt
Tel: (04651) 89 03 05 *Fax:* (04651) 89 08 85
E-mail: ciceropresse@t-online.de
Founded: 1965
Member of International League of Antiquarian Booksellers (ILAB) & Verband Deutscher Antiquare (VDA).
ISBN Prefix(es): 8-9120
Total Titles: 20 Print

Marianne Cieslik+
Theodor-Heuss-Str 185, 52428 Juelich
Tel: (02461) 51222; (02461) 57661 *Fax:* (02461) 52772
Key Personnel
Owner: Marianne Cieslik
E-mail: verlagmariannecieslik@t-online.de
Manager: Jurgen Cieslik
Founded: 1975
Publishers for collector books & magazines (dolls, toys, teddy bears).
Subjects: Crafts, Games, Hobbies, Price guides
ISBN Prefix(es): 3-921844

Claassen Verlag GmbH+
Paul-Heysstr 28, 80336 Munich
Tel: (089) 5148-0; (089) 5148 20 *Fax:* (089) 5148-2229; (089) 5148 2233
E-mail: info@ullstein-heyne-list.de

Web Site: www.claassen-verlag.de
Telex: 927108
Key Personnel
Manager: Dr Bruno Gerstenberg; Edmund Jacoby
Production Manager: Friedrich Weskott
Marketing: Wolfgang J Dietrich
International Rights: Ulrike Bastong
Founded: 1934
Subjects: Biography, Fiction, Literature, Literary Criticism, Essays, Nonfiction (General)
ISBN Prefix(es): 3-546
Parent Company: Gebrueder Gerstenberg GmbH & Co

Claudius Verlag+
Birkerstr 22, 80636 Munich
Tel: (089) 121 72-0 *Fax:* (089) 121 72-138
E-mail: claudius@csi.com
Web Site: www.claudius.de
Key Personnel
Dir: Hartmut Joisten *Tel:* (089) 12172112
Publisher: Dr Manuel Zelger *Tel:* (089) 12172136 *E-mail:* mzelger@epv.de
International Rights: Antje Fritsch-Brown *Tel:* (089) 12172132 *E-mail:* afritsch@epv.de
Founded: 1954
Subjects: Developing Countries, Humor, Religion - Protestant, Religion - Other, Self-Help, Theology
ISBN Prefix(es): 3-532
Number of titles published annually: 30 Print
Total Titles: 300 Print
Parent Company: Evangelischer Presseverband fuer Bayern eV
Bookshop(s): Claudius Versandbuchhandlung, Contact: Regine Zendrek *Tel:* (089) 12172119 *Fax:* (089) 12172138 *E-mail:* vsb@epv.de

CMA Edition+
Roter Brach Weg 54b, 93049 Regensburg
Tel: (0941) 23939; (0941) 34003; (08458) 8960 *Fax:* (0941) 8960; (0941) 34003
Key Personnel
Contacts: Dietrich Leisching; Christine Adlhoch
Founded: 1984
Subjects: Biography, Poetry
ISBN Prefix(es): 3-9801025

Charles Coleman Verlag GmbH & Co KG
Wahmstr 56, 23552 Luebeck
Mailing Address: Postfach 21 34, 23509 Luebeck
Tel: (0451) 7 99 33-0 *Fax:* (0451) 7 99 33-99
E-mail: coleman@rudolf.mueller.de
Web Site: www.coleman-verlag.de; www.rudolf-mueller.de
Founded: 1894
Subjects: Career Development, Engineering (General), Mechanical Engineering
ISBN Prefix(es): 3-87128
Parent Company: Verlagsgesellschaft Rudolf Mueller GmbH, Stolbergerstr 84, 50933 Cologne

Collection b, *imprint of* Deutsche Bibelgesellschaft

Columbus Verlag Paul Oestergaard GmbH+
Am Bahnhof 2, 72505 Krauchenwies
Mailing Address: Krauchenwies 72502
Tel: (07576) 96 03-0 *Fax:* (07576) 96 03-29
E-mail: info@columbus-verlag.de
Web Site: www.columbus-verlag.de *Cable:* COLUMBUS-VERLAG
Key Personnel
Publisher: Torsten Oestergaard
Founded: 1909
Subjects: Astronomy, Geography, Geology, House & Home, Globes
ISBN Prefix(es): 3-87129
Subsidiaries: Leipziger Globusmanufaktur
Orders to: Columbus Haus, an der Station 2, 72505 Krauchenwies

ComMedia & Arte Verlag Bernd Mayer+
Am Hang 27, 74622 Bretzfeld
Mailing Address: Postfach 1117, 74622 Bretzfeld
Tel: (07945) 950719 *Fax:* (07945) 950718
Key Personnel
Owner: Bernd Mayer
Founded: 1982
Subjects: Fiction, Gay & Lesbian
ISBN Prefix(es): 3-924244
Orders to: Rotation, Mehringdamm 51, W-10000 Berlin *Tel:* (030) 6927934 *Fax:* (030) 6942006

Compact Verlag GmbH+
Zuerichstr 29, 81476 Munich
Tel: (089) 7451610 *Fax:* (089) 756095; (089) 7593922
E-mail: info@compactverlag.de
Web Site: www.compactverlag.de
Key Personnel
Publisher, Manager & International Rights: Friedrich Niendieck
Man Dir: Bernd Steier
Foreign Rights: Sandra Brack *Tel:* (089) 74516183 *E-mail:* sandra.brack@compactverlag.de
Founded: 1976
Specialize in nonfiction books.
Subjects: Business, Cookery, Crafts, Games, Hobbies, Education, English as a Second Language, Gardening, Plants, Health, Nutrition, History, House & Home, How-to, Law, Nonfiction (General), Real Estate, Travel
ISBN Prefix(es): 3-8174
Number of titles published annually: 180 Print
Total Titles: 1,000 Print
Warehouse: CDC GmbH, Rotwandweg 1, 82024 Taufkirchen-Potzham

Concordia-Buchhandlung & Verlag+
Bahnhofstr 8, 08056 Zwickau
Tel: (0375) 21 28 50 *Fax:* (0375) 29 80 80; (0375) 21 28 50
E-mail: concordia@t-online.de
Web Site: www.concordiabuch.de
Key Personnel
Business Associate: Dr Gottfried Herrmann
Founded: 1990
Subjects: Religion - Other, Theology
ISBN Prefix(es): 3-910153

Connection Medien GmbH+
Hauptstr 5, 84494 Niedertaufkirchen
Tel: (08639) 98 34-0 *Fax:* (08639) 1219
E-mail: seminare@connection-medien.de
Web Site: www.connection-medien.de; www.seminar-connection.de
Key Personnel
Contact: Wolf Schneider *E-mail:* schneider@connection-medien.de
Founded: 1985
Subjects: Astrology, Occult, Human Relations, Parapsychology, Religion - Buddhist, Religion - Other, Self-Help
ISBN Prefix(es): 3-928248
Parent Company: Connection Medien GmbH
Divisions: Satzstudio, Seminar-und organisation, Vertrieb

Copernicus, *imprint of* Springer-Verlag GmbH & Co KG

Coppenrath Verlag+
Subsidiary of Verlag Wolfgang Hoelker
Hafenweg 30, 48155 Muenster
Mailing Address: Postfach 3820, 48021 Muenster Westf
Tel: (0251) 4 14 11-0 *Fax:* (0251) 4 14 11 20
E-mail: info@coppenrath.de
Web Site: www.coppenrath.de
Key Personnel
Man Dir: Wolfgang Hoelker
Production: Wolfgang Foerster
Publicity: Tomas Rensing
Sales: Hubert Bergmoser
Rights & Permissions: Anette Riedel
Founded: 1768
Subjects: Architecture & Interior Design, Art, Nonfiction (General)
ISBN Prefix(es): 3-88547; 3-8157
Divisions: Edition Spiegelburg
Warehouse: Coppenrath-Hoelker Distribution, 48612 Horstmar *Tel:* (02558) 98818 *Fax:* (02558) 98819

Copress Verlag+
Imprint of Stiebner Verlag GmbH
Nymphenburgerstr 86, 80636 Munich
Tel: (089) 1 25 74 14 *Fax:* (089) 12 16 22 82
E-mail: info@stiebner.com
Web Site: www.stiebner.com *Cable:* COPRESS MUNCHEN
Subjects: Health, Nutrition, History, Outdoor Recreation, Sports, Athletics
ISBN Prefix(es): 3-7679

Corian-Verlag Heinrich Wimmer
Bernhard-Monath-Str 28, 86405 Meitingen
Tel: (08271) 5951 *Fax:* (08271) 6931
E-mail: 082716941-0001@t-online.de; 101374.1022@compuserve.com
Key Personnel
Man Dir: Heinrich Wimmer
Founded: 1983
Subjects: Film, Video, Science Fiction, Fantasy
ISBN Prefix(es): 3-89048

Cornelsen und Oxford University Press GmbH & Co
Johannisbergerstr 74, 14197 Berlin
Tel: (030) 827936-0 *Fax:* (030) 827936-36
Web Site: www.cornelsen.de
Telex: 184968 cvk b
Key Personnel
Dir: Jesus Lezcano; Alfred Predhumean
Founded: 1971
Subjects: Education
ISBN Prefix(es): 3-8109
Subsidiaries: Cornelsen Verlag GmbH & Co

Cornelsen Verlag GmbH & Co OHG+
Mecklenburgischestr 53, 14197 Berlin
Tel: (030) 897 85-0 *Fax:* (030) 897 85-299
E-mail: c-mail@cornelsen.de
Web Site: www.cornelsen.com
Key Personnel
Man Dir: Fritz von Bernuth; Hans-Joerg Duellmann; Wolf-Rudiger Feldmann; Alfred Gruener; Martin Hueppe; Dr Hans Weymar
International Relations & Foreign Rights: Holger Behm *Tel:* (030) 897 85-341 *E-mail:* holger.behm@cornelsen.de
Founded: 1946
Textbook publisher in all areas of learning.
Member of European Educational Publishers Group (EEPG); Association of German Booksellers.
Subjects: Accounting, Advertising, Biological Sciences, Career Development, Chemistry, Chemical Engineering, Communications, Economics, Education, English as a Second Language, Geography, Geology, History, Management, Marketing, Mathematics, Physical Sciences, Physics, Technology
ISBN Prefix(es): 3-464
Total Titles: 7,000 Print; 70 CD-ROM; 150 Audio
Associate Companies: ALL-Group, Bucharest, Romania; Cornelsen Experimenta, Berlin; Cornelsen Verlagskontor GmbH Co KG; CS Druck Cornelsen Stuertt, Berlin; Nakladatelstri Fraus, Plzen, Czech Republic; Kamp Schulbuchverlag Due sseldorf, PZV Berlin; Lernland GmbH &

Co KG, Berlin; VERITAS, Linz, Austria; Volk und Wissen Verlag, Berlin
Subsidiaries: Cornelsen Verlag Scriptor; Cornelsen und Oxford University Press GmbH
Orders to: CVK Cornelsen Verlagskontor, Kammerratsheide 66, 33609 Bielefeld

Cornelsen Verlag Scriptor GmbH & Co KG+
Subsidiary of Cornelsen Verlag
Krampasplatz 1, 14199 Berlin
Tel: (030) 897 77 4-0 *Fax:* (030) 897 77 4-44
E-mail: c-mail@cornelsen.de
Web Site: www.cornelsen.de
Key Personnel
General Manager: Alfred Gruener; Horst Linder
Founded: 1973
Subjects: Education
ISBN Prefix(es): 3-589
Orders to: CVK Cornelsen Verlagskontor, Kammerratsheide 66, 33598 Bielefeld

Corona Verlag+
Bramfelder Chaussee 330, 22175 Hamburg
Tel: (040) 6424144 *Fax:* (040) 64221023
Key Personnel
Editor: Joachim Stiller
Publisher: Halina Kamm
Founded: 1990
Subjects: Esoteric books, psychology, natural science, music & meditation
ISBN Prefix(es): 3-928084
Total Titles: 100 Print; 100 CD-ROM; 100 Audio

Cosmic Energy Connections-CEC, see CEC-Cosmic Energy Connections

J G Cotta'sche Buchhandlung Nachfolger GmbH+
Rotebuehlstr 77, 70178 Stuttgart
Mailing Address: Postfach 106016, 70049 Stuttgart
Tel: (0711) 6672-0 *Fax:* (0711) 6672-2000
E-mail: info@klett-cotta.de
Web Site: www.klett-cotta.de
Telex: 7222232 klet d
Key Personnel
Publisher: Michael Klett
Man Dir: Rainer Just
Foreign Relations: Derrik Jenkins
Foreign Rights: Roland Knappe
Founded: 1659
Subjects: Child Care & Development, Education, Fiction, History, Human Relations, Literature, Literary Criticism, Essays, Management, Nonfiction (General), Philosophy, Poetry, Psychology, Psychiatry, Science (General)
ISBN Prefix(es): 3-12; 3-7681; 3-608; 3-7885; 3-7835
Total Titles: 3,000 Print
Parent Company: Ernst Klett AG
Imprints: Pfeiffer bei Klett-Cotta
Warehouse: BDK Bucherdienst GmbH, Kolnerstr 248, Cologne

Creator, *imprint of* Bonifatius GmbH Druck-Buch-Verlag

Verlag CSA Rosemarie Schneider+
Limesstr 16, 61389 Schmitten-Oberreifenberg
Tel: (06082) 970116 *Fax:* (06082) 970123
E-mail: csa-europa@csa-activ.de
Web Site: www.csa-activ.de
Key Personnel
Owner: Rosemarie Schneider
Senior Partner: Brigitte K Schneider
Founded: 1978
Subjects: Education, Psychology, Psychiatry, Religion - Other, Self-Help
ISBN Prefix(es): 3-922779
U.S. Office(s): Rosemarie Schneider, 66 Indian Springs, 49305 Highway 74, Palm Desert, CA 92260, United States

CTL-Presse Clemens-Tobias Lange
Borselstr 9-11, 22765 Hamburg
Tel: (040) 39902223 *Fax:* (040) 39902224
E-mail: mail@ctl-presse.de
Web Site: www.ctl-presse.de
Founded: 1989
Subjects: Art, Photography, Poetry, Artist's Books, Literature
Number of titles published annually: 2 Print
Total Titles: 12 Print

D & D Kommunikation Verlug Dirk Nishen Gmbh & Co KG+
Buelowstr 66, 10783 Berlin
Tel: (030) 2173830 *Fax:* (030) 21738393
Key Personnel
Publisher, Rights & Permissions: Dirk Nishen
Founded: 1982
Subjects: Art, History, Photography, Regional Interests
ISBN Prefix(es): 3-88940
Associate Companies: D & D Kemmunikationsdesign GmbH Verlag & Grafik, Buelowstr 66, 10783 Berlin
Orders to: VAH Jager Verlagsauslieferungen GmbH, Postfach 3248, 10779 Berlin *Tel:* (030) 2611641-44 *Fax:* (030) 2628941

Daco Verlag Guenter Blase oHG+
Christophstr 40-42, 70180 Stuttgart
Tel: (0711) 96421-0 *Fax:* (0711) 96421-10
E-mail: info@daco-verlag.de
Web Site: www.daco-verlag.de
Key Personnel
Publishing Dir, Rights & Permissions: Stephan Goetz
Founded: 1943
Subjects: Art
ISBN Prefix(es): 3-87135
Imprints: Hanfstaengl-Verlag; Nadif

Daedalus Verlag+
Oderstr 25, 48145 Muenster
Tel: (0251) 231 355 *Fax:* (0251) 232 631
E-mail: info@daedalus-verlag.de
Web Site: www.daedalus-verlag.com
Key Personnel
Publisher, Rights & Permissions: Joachim Herbst
Founded: 1984
Subjects: Communications, Government, Political Science, Nonfiction (General), Psychology, Psychiatry, Social Sciences, Sociology
ISBN Prefix(es): 3-89126

Dagmar Dreves Verlag+
Hamburgstr 14, 21224 Rosengarten
Tel: (04108) 6866
Key Personnel
Manager: Horst Ernst
Founded: 1989
Subjects: Mysteries, Nonfiction (General), Parapsychology
ISBN Prefix(es): 3-924532
Bookshop(s): Dagmar Dreves Verlag, Knoopstr 8, Hamburg 21073
Warehouse: Dagmar Dreves Verlag, Knoopstr 8, 21073 Hamburg
Orders to: Dagmar Dreves Verlag, Knoopstr 8, 21073 Hamburg

Dana Verlag
Campemoorweg 8, 49565 Bram
Tel: (05468) 1813 *Fax:* (05468) 239
Key Personnel
Contact: Wolfgang Sewald; Gonda Sewald
Founded: 1988
Subjects: Science Fiction, Fantasy
ISBN Prefix(es): 3-9801976; 3-931335

Beate Danker-Verlag+
Kohlhaeuserstr 8, 61200 Woelfersheim-Berstadt
Tel: (06036) 9430 *Fax:* (06036) 6270
Key Personnel
Publisher: Beate Danker
Founded: 1989
Subjects: Animals, Pets, Sports, Athletics
ISBN Prefix(es): 3-927456

Verlag Darmstaedter Blaetter Schwarz und Co
Haubachweg 5, 64285 Darmstadt
Tel: (06151) 48196
Key Personnel
Man Dir: Dr Guenther Schwarz
Founded: 1967
Subjects: Language Arts, Linguistics, Philosophy, Psychology, Psychiatry, Religion - Jewish, Social Sciences, Sociology
ISBN Prefix(es): 3-87139

Das Arsenal, Verlag fuer Kultur und Politik GmbH+
Tegeler Weg 97, 1000 Berlin 10
Tel: (030) 3441827; (030) 34651360 *Fax:* (030) 3441827
Key Personnel
Man Dir: Dr Peter Moses-Krause
Publisher: Jutta Siegert
Founded: 1977
Member of Stock Exchange of German Booksellers.
Subjects: Art, Drama, Theater, Fiction, History, Philosophy
ISBN Prefix(es): 3-921810; 3-931109
Orders to: Bugrim, Saalburgstr 3, 12099 Berlin

Das Grosse, Technothek, *imprint of* Heel Verlag GmbH

Das Original, *imprint of* Heel Verlag GmbH

Data Becker GmbH & Co KG+
Merowingerstr 30, 40223 Duesseldorf
Mailing Address: Postfach 102044, 40011 Duesseldorf
Tel: (0211) 9331 800; (0211) 9334 900 (orders) *Fax:* (0211) 9331 444; (0211) 9334 999 (orders)
E-mail: info@databecker.de
Web Site: www.databecker.de
Key Personnel
President: Harald Becker
President & Marketing: Dr Achim Becker
Founded: 1981
Subjects: Computer Science, Microcomputers
ISBN Prefix(es): 3-8158

Datacom Buchverlag GmbH+
Zum Biotop 15, 50127 Bergheim
Tel: (02271) 6080 *Fax:* (02271) 608290
Key Personnel
International Rights: Klaus Lipinski
Founded: 1984
Subjects: Communications
ISBN Prefix(es): 3-89238
Associate Companies: Datacom Zeidschriften-Verlag GmbH

Verlag Werner Dausien+
Burgallee 67, 63454 Hanau
Tel: (06181) 92810; (06181) 259052 (orders) *Fax:* (06181) 257387
Key Personnel
Man Dir, Rights & Permissions: Werner Dausien
Founded: 1949
Subjects: Art, How-to, Music, Dance
ISBN Prefix(es): 3-7684

Associate Companies: Verlag Mueller und Kiepenheuer
Divisions: Verlag Fuer Zahnmedizin

Dawson's Creek, *imprint of* Egmont vgs verlagsgesellschaft mbH

DBV, *imprint of* Don Bosco Verlag

R v Decker's Verlag, G Schenck GmbH, see Huthig GmbH & Co KG

Degener & Co, Manfred Dreiss Verlag+
Nuernbergerstr 27, 91413 Neustadt an der Aisch
Tel: (09161) 886039 *Fax:* (09161) 1378
E-mail: degener@degener-verlag.com
Web Site: www.degener-verlag.com
Key Personnel
Contact: Manfred Dreiss
Founded: 1910
Subjects: Genealogy, History, Military Science, Regional Interests
ISBN Prefix(es): 3-7686; 3-87947
Associate Companies: Verlag Bauer & Raspe; Heinz Reise-Verlag
Distributor for Bauer & Raspe; Heinz-Reise-Verlag
Orders to: Verlag Degener & Co, Nurnbergerstr 27, 91413 Neustadt

Verlag Horst Deike KG+
Robert-Bosch-Str 18, 78467 Konstanz
Mailing Address: Postfach 100452, 78404 Konstanz
Tel: (07531) 81550 *Fax:* (07531) 815581
E-mail: deike@deike-verlag.de
Web Site: www.deike-verlag.de
Key Personnel
President: Wolfgang Deike
Founded: 1923
Subjects: Art, Literature, Literary Criticism, Essays, Music, Dance
ISBN Prefix(es): 3-87142
Subsidiaries: Deike AG
Branch Office(s)
Horst Deike KG Verlag, 463 State St, Santa Barbara, CA, United States

Delius, Klasing und Co+
Siekerwall 21, 33602 Bielefeld
Tel: (0521) 55 90 *Fax:* (0521) 55 91 13
E-mail: info@delius-klasing.de
Web Site: www.delius-klasing.de
Telex: 0932934 Dekla *Cable:* BUCHKLASING BIELEFELD
Key Personnel
Dir: Konrad-Wilhelm Delius; Kurt Delius
Production: Hermann Ludewig
Publicity: Susanne Lange
Rights & Permissions: Petra Trueltzsch
Founded: 1911
Subjects: Automotive, Maritime, Outdoor Recreation
ISBN Prefix(es): 3-7688
Associate Companies: Edition Maritim Hamburg; Moby Dick Kiel
Distributed by Ermatingen; Lechner & Sohn (Austria); Neptun Verlag; Schweiz
Orders to: Delius Klasing Verlag GmbH, Siekerwall 21, 33602 Bielefeld

Delius Klasing Verlag+
Siekerwall 21, 33602 Bielefeld
Tel: (0521) 55 90 *Fax:* (0521) 55 91 13
E-mail: info@delius-klasing.de
Web Site: www.delius-klasing.de *Cable:* BUCHKLASING BIELEFELD
Key Personnel
Librarian: Baerbel Schubel
Publisher: Kurt Delius
Sales & Publicity Manager: Susanne Lange
Rights & Permissions: Petra Trueltzsch
Producer: Hermann Ludewig
Founded: 1911
Subjects: Maritime
ISBN Prefix(es): 3-87412
Parent Company: Delius, Klasing und Co
Associate Companies: Edition Maritim Hamburg; Moby Dick Verlag Uiel
Distributed by Ermatingeni; Lechner & Sohn (Austria); Neptun Verlag; Schweiz

Delphin Verlag GmbH+
Emil-Hoffmannstr 1, 50996 Cologne
Tel: (02236) 39990 *Fax:* (02236) 399997
Telex: 8886642/2236364kvg
Key Personnel
Man Dir: Guenter Goebel; Juergen Naumann
Founded: 1962
ISBN Prefix(es): 3-7735
Parent Company: Naumann & Goebel Verlagsgesellschaft mbH
Associate Companies: Verlag 'Das persoenliche Geburtstagsbuch' GmbH; VEMAG Verlags- und Medien AG; Daumueller Werbeges mbH; Tigris Verlag GmbH; V & M Verlags & Medienges Koeln mbH; Naturalis Verlags und Vertriebsgesellschaft mbH; Delphin AG; Neuer Pawlak Verlag GmbH

Delp'sche Verlagsbuchhandlung
Kegetstr 11, 91438 Bad Windsheim
Tel: (09841) 9030 *Fax:* (09841) 90315
Telex: 61524
Key Personnel
Man Dir: Heinrich Delp
Founded: 1961
Subjects: Art, Regional Interests
ISBN Prefix(es): 3-7689

Delta, *imprint of* Egmont EHAPA Verlag GmbH

Engelbert Dessart Verlag KG, see Siebert und Engelbert Dessart Verlag GmbH

Verlag fuer Deutsch GmbH+
Max-Hueber-Str 4, 85737 Ismaning
Mailing Address: Postfach 1142, 85729 Ismaning
Tel: (089) 9602-0 *Fax:* (089) 9602-358
Telex: 523613 hueb d
Key Personnel
Man Dirs: Michaela Hueber; Renate Luscher
Production: Peer Koop
Founded: 1979
Subjects: Education
ISBN Prefix(es): 3-88532
Parent Company: Max Hueber Verlag
Branch Office(s)
Adler's Foreign Books, 8220 N Christiana Ave, Skokie, IL 60076-2911, United States *Tel:* 708-676-9944 *Fax:* 708-676-9909

Verlag Harri Deutsch+
Graefstr 47/51, 60486 Frankfurt am Main
Tel: (069) 77015860 *Fax:* (069) 77015869
E-mail: verlag@harri-deutsch.de
Web Site: www.harri-deutsch.de
Key Personnel
Dir, Rights & Permissions: Harri Deutsch
Editor: Bernd Mueller
Production: Torsten Hellbusch
Founded: 1960
Subjects: Biological Sciences, Chemistry, Chemical Engineering, Earth Sciences, Economics, Electronics, Electrical Engineering, Engineering (General), Mathematics, Natural History, Physical Sciences, Physics, Sports, Athletics
ISBN Prefix(es): 3-87144; 3-8171
Subsidiaries: Verlag Harri Deutsch AG
Bookshop(s): Naturwissenschaftliche Fachbuchhandlung Harri Deutsch, Graefstr 47/51, 60486 Frankfurt am Main

Deutsche Bibelgesellschaft+
Balingerstr 31, 70567 Stuttgart
Tel: (0711) 7181-0 *Fax:* (0711) 7181-250
E-mail: infoabt@dbg.de
Web Site: www.dbg.de
Telex: 7255299 Bibl d *Cable:* BIBELHAUS STUTTGART
Key Personnel
Dir & International Rights: Dr Volkmar J Loebel
Dir: Rev Jan A Buehner, PhD
Founded: 1812 (1981)
German Bible Society.
Subjects: Biblical Studies
ISBN Prefix(es): 3-438
Imprints: Collection b
Branch Office(s)
American Bible Society, New York, NY, United States *Fax:* 212-408-1456 *Web Site:* www.americanbible.org

Deutsche Bibliothek der Wissenschaften/German Library of Sciences, *imprint of* Dr Haensel-Hohenhausen AG

Die Deutsche Bibliothek/Deutsche Buecherei Leipzig
Adickesallee 1, 60322 Frankfurt am Main
Tel: (069) 15250 *Fax:* (069) 15251010
E-mail: info@dbf.ddb.de
Web Site: www.ddb.de
Key Personnel
Dir: Dr Elisabeth Niggemann
Contact: Kathrin Ansorge *Tel:* (069) 15251004 *E-mail:* ansorge@dbf.ddb.de
Founded: 1912
Deutsches Buch-und Schriftmuseum.
Subjects: Literature, Literary Criticism, Essays
ISBN Prefix(es): 3-922051; 3-933641
Branch Office(s)
Deutsche Buecherei Leipzig, Deutscher Platz 1, 04103 Leipzig *Tel:* (0341) 22710 *Fax:* (0341) 2271444
Distributed by Buchhaendler-Vereinigung GmbH

Deutsche Blinden-Bibliothek+
Am Schlag 8, 35037 Marburg
Mailing Address: Postfach 1160, 35001 Marburg
Tel: (06421) 6060 *Fax:* (06421) 606229
E-mail: info@blista.de
Web Site: www.blista.de
Key Personnel
Man Dir: Juergen Hertlein *Tel:* (06421) 606101 *E-mail:* hertlein@blista.de
Library Dir, Publishing Manager & International Rights: Rainer F V Witte *Tel:* (06421) 606103 *Fax:* (06421) 606269 *E-mail:* witte@blista.de
Founded: 1916
German Library for the Blind.
ISBN Prefix(es): 3-89642
Parent Company: Deutsche Blindenstudienanstalt eV (DBSTA)
Divisions: Archiv und Internat Dokumentation zzuum Blinden-und Sehbehindertenwesen; Bibliographic Centre; Deutsche Blindenhoerbuecherei (aufgesprochene Literatur/talking books); Emil-Krueckmann-Bibliothek (Blindenschift/Braille)

Deutsche Gesellschaft fuer Eisenbahngeschichte eV
Kleinsorgenring 14, 59457 Werl
Tel: (02922) 84970 *Fax:* (02922) 84927
E-mail: gs@dgeg.de
Web Site: www.dgeg.de
Founded: 1967
Subjects: Transportation
ISBN Prefix(es): 3-921700

Deutsche Gesellschaft fuer Luft-und Raumfahrt Lilienthal Oberth eV
Godesberger Allee 70, 53175 Bonn

Tel: (0228) 30 80 5-0 Fax: (0228) 30 80 5-24
E-mail: geschaeftsstelle@dglr.de
Web Site: www.dglr.de
ISBN Prefix(es): 3-922010; 3-932182

Deutsche Hochschulschriften/German University Studies, imprint of Dr Haensel-Hohenhausen AG

Deutsche Landwirtschaft-Gesellschaft VerlagsgesGmbH+
Eschborner Landstr 122, 60489 Frankfurt
Tel: (069) 24788-0 Fax: (069) 24788-480
E-mail: dlg-verlag@dlg-frankfurt.de
Web Site: www.dlg-verlag.de
Telex: veber 413185 dig.ffm
Key Personnel
President & International Rights: Dr Klaus Schroeter
Marketing Manager: Stefan Pierre-Louis
  Tel: (069) 24788466 E-mail: s.pierrelouis@dlg-frankfurt.de
Founded: 1952
Subjects: Agriculture
ISBN Prefix(es): 3-7690
Number of titles published annually: 20 Print
Total Titles: 500 Print
Parent Company: DLG eV
Distributed by Verlagsunion Agrar

Verlag Deutsche Unitarier+
Birkenstr 4, 88214 Ravensburg
Tel: (0751) 6 25 96 Fax: (0751) 6 72 01
E-mail: verlag@unitarier.de
Web Site: www.unitarier.de
Key Personnel
Publisher: Micha Ramm
Founded: 1950
Member of International Association for Religious Freedom (IARF) & International Council of Unitarians & Universalists (ICUU)
Subjects: Philosophy, Religion - Other
ISBN Prefix(es): 3-922483
Total Titles: 14 Print
Parent Company: Deutsche Unitarier Religionsgemeinschaft eV, Hamburg
Divisions: Zeitschriftenverlag; Buchverlag; Versandbuchhandlung

Deutsche Verlags-Anstalt GmbH (DVA)+
Neckarstr 121, 70190 Stuttgart
Mailing Address: Postfach 106012, 70049 Stuttgart
Tel: (0711) 2631-0 Fax: (0711) 2631-292
E-mail: info@dva.de
Web Site: www.dva.de
Telex: 7111193DVA d Cable: DEVA STUTTGART
Key Personnel
President: Juergen Horbach
Editorial Dir, Architecture: Renate Jostmann
Editorial Dir, Nonfiction: Ulrich Volz
Editorial Dir, Fiction, Belles Lettres & Poetry: Werner Loecher-Lawrence
Publisher: Dr Franz-Heinrich Hackel
Publicity: Sabine Ilfrich
Sales & Marketing: Heiko Windfelder
Subsidiary Rights: Ursula Michelfelder
Foreign Rights: Heide Radkowitz Tel: (0711) 26 31 261 E-mail: Heide.Radkowitz@dva.de
Production: Rudolf Wolf
Founded: 1831
Subjects: Architecture & Interior Design, Astronomy, Biography, Earth Sciences, Fiction, Government, Political Science, History, Literature, Literary Criticism, Essays, Music, Dance, Philosophy, Poetry, Psychology, Psychiatry, Science (General)
ISBN Prefix(es): 3-421
Parent Company: Verlagsgruppe, Frankfurter Allgemeine Zeitung GmbH, Frankfurt am Main

Subsidiaries: Engelhorn Verlag GmbH; Julius Hoffmann Verlag GmbH; Manesse Verlag GmbH
U.S. Office(s): Del Commune Enterprises, Inc, 285 W Broadway, Suite 310, New York, NY 10013, United States Tel: 212-226-6664 Fax: 212-965-9294
Bookshop(s): Buchversand Herbert Krebs GmbH, Neckarstr 121, 70179 Stuttgart
Warehouse: Vereinigte Verlagsauslieferung VVA, Postfach 7777, 33310 Guetersloh

Deutscher Adressbuch-Verlag fuer Wirtschaft und Verkehr GmbH
Arheilger Weg 17, 64380 Rossdorf
Mailing Address: PO Box 1262, 64204 Darmstadt
Tel: (06154) 699500 Fax: (06154) 6995480; (06154) 6995490
E-mail: info@businessdeutschland.de
Web Site: www.businessdeutschland.de
Key Personnel
Man Dir & Publisher: Klaus Boller
Editorial: Helmut Kolb
Production & Publicity: Hans Zimmer
Founded: 1923
The German Directory Publishing Company for Industry & Commerce.
Member of German & European Book Publishers Association.
Subjects: Business
ISBN Prefix(es): 3-87148
Parent Company: De Te Medien GmbH/alle Gelbe Seiten Verlage

Deutscher Aerzte-Verlag GmbH+
Dieselstr 2, 50859 Cologne
Tel: (02234) 7011-0 Fax: (02234) 7011-398; (02234) 7011-475
E-mail: zielinka@aerzteverlag.de
Web Site: www.aerzteverlag.de
Key Personnel
Man Dir: Hermann Dinse
Man Dir & International Rights: Dieter Weber
Founded: 1949
Subjects: Medicine, Nursing, Dentistry
ISBN Prefix(es): 3-7961
Subsidiaries: CEDIP Verlags GmbH; J F Lehmanns Med Buchhandlung GmbH; Otto Spatz GmbH & Co KG; Schwarzeck-Verlag GmbH

Deutscher Apotheker Verlag+
Birkenwaldstr 44, 70191 Stuttgart
Mailing Address: Postfach 101061, 70009 Stuttgart
Tel: (0711) 2582-0 Fax: (0711) 2582-290
E-mail: service@deutscher-pharmacist-verlag.de
Web Site: www.deutscher-apotheker-verlag.de
Key Personnel
Man Dir: Dr Klaus Brauer; Reinhold Hack; Dr Christian Rotta; Dr Thomas Schaber
International Rights: Sabine Koerner
Contact: Siegmar Bauer
Founded: 1861
Subjects: Medicine, Nursing, Dentistry, Pharmacy
ISBN Prefix(es): 3-7692
Subsidiaries: S Hirzel Verlag GmbH & Co; Medpharm Scientific Publishers; Franz Steiner Verlag Wiesbaden GmbH; Wissenschaftliche Verlagsgesellschaft mbH
Distributor for American Society of Hospital Pharmacists; Drug Intelligence Publications (Europe); Pharmaceutical Press (London, UK); United States Pharmacopeial Convention Inc (USA)
Shipping Address: Deutscher Apotheker Verlag

Deutscher Betriebswirte-Verlag GmbH+
Bleichstr 20-22, 76593 Gernsbach
Mailing Address: Postfach 1332, 76586 Gernsbach
Tel: (07224) 9397-151 Fax: (07224) 9397-251

E-mail: info@betriebswirte-verlag.de
Web Site: www.betriebswirte-verlag.de
Telex: 78915 dbv d Cable: DBV GERNSBACH
Key Personnel
Man Dir: Dr Casimir Katz; Christel Katz
Editor, Rights & Permissions, Publicity: Regina Meier
Founded: 1926
Subjects: Business, Economics, Public Administration
ISBN Prefix(es): 3-921099; 3-88640

Deutscher Drucker Verlagsgesellschaft (German Printer Publishing House)
Riedstr 25, 73760 Ostfildern
Tel: (0711) 448170 Fax: (0711) 442099
E-mail: info@publish.de
Web Site: www.publish.de
Key Personnel
Contact: Martin Metzger E-mail: m.metzger@publish.de
Information for professionals, dealing with all aspects of digital workflow. Print communication, colour publishing & packaging.
ISBN Prefix(es): 3-10226
Parent Company: Ebner Verlag
Foreign Rep(s): Babel Marketing (UK); Ebner Publishing (US); Andrew Karning (Scotland)

Deutscher EC-Verband
Leuschnerstr 72-74, 34134 Kassel
Tel: (0561) 40950 Fax: (0561) 4095112
E-mail: info.dv@ec-jugend.de
Web Site: www.ec-jugend.de
Subjects: Religion - Catholic, Religion - Protestant

Deutscher Fachverlag GmbH
Mainzer Landstr 251, 60326 Frankfurt am Main
Tel: (069) 7595-01 Fax: (069) 75952999
E-mail: zilling@dfu.de
Web Site: www.dfv.de
Key Personnel
Man Dir: Klaus Kottmeier; Peter Russ; Eva Lorch
Manager: Joerg Hintz
Founded: 1946
Sportswear International New York.
Subjects: Advertising, Agriculture, Business, Communications, Engineering (General), Fashion, Marketing, Nonfiction (General)
ISBN Prefix(es): 3-87150
Associate Companies: Manstein Zeitschnfton Verlag, Perchtoldsdorf B Wein, Austria; Edizioni Ecomarket SpA, 1-20121 Milan
Subsidiaries: Verlag Alfred Strothe GmbH & Co

Deutscher Gemeindeverlag GmbH
Max-Planck-Str 12, 50858 Cologne
Tel: (02234) 1060 Fax: (02234) 106284
Founded: 1925
Subjects: Government, Political Science
ISBN Prefix(es): 3-555
Parent Company: Verlag W Kohlhammer GmbH
Branch Office(s)
Postfach 1865, 24017 Kiel Tel: (0431) 554857 Fax: (0431) 554944
Postfach 261134/55057, Mainz Tel: (06131) 891540 Fax: (06131) 891624
Postfach 040204, 19026 Schwerin Tel: (0385) 616105 Fax: (0385) 616146
Rudolf-Leonhardstr 28, 01097 Dresden Tel: (0351) 5022685 Fax: (0351) 5670664
Gustav-Freytag Str 59, 99096 Erfurt Tel: (0361) 3735379 Fax: (0361) 3460537
Postfach 1465, 30014 Hannover Tel: (0511) 327029 Fax: (0511) 320143
Schleinufes 14, 39104 Magdeburg Tel: (0391) 597080 Fax: (0391) 5970813
Sellostr 19, 14471 Potsdam Tel: (0331) 964670 Fax: (0331) 964672 (German Municipality Publishing Company)
Warehouse: Verlagsvertrieb Stuttgart GmbH, Hepbruehlstr 69, 76565 Stuttgart

Deutscher Instituts-Verlag GmbH+
Subsidiary of Koelner Universitaetsverlag GmbH
Gustav-Heinemann Ufer 84-88, 50968 Cologne
Mailing Address: Postfach 510670, 50942 Cologne
Tel: (0221) 49 81-0 *Fax:* (0221) 49 81
E-mail: div@iwkoeln.de
Web Site: www.divkoeln.de
Key Personnel
Man Dir, Rights & Permissions: Dr Franz Josef Link *Tel:* (0221) 49 81-410 *Fax:* (0221) 49 81-501; Ulrich Brodersen *Tel:* (0221) 49 81-420 *Fax:* (0221) 49 81-501
Marketing: Michael Opferkuch *Tel:* (0221) 49 81-285 *Fax:* (0221) 49 81-286
Man Dir, Rights & Permissions: Axel Rhein *Tel:* (0221) 49 81-510 *Fax:* (0221) 49 81-533 *E-mail:* geisler@iwkoeln.de
Founded: 1951
Subjects: Developing Countries, Economics, Labor, Industrial Relations
ISBN Prefix(es): 3-602
Number of titles published annually: 100 Print
Total Titles: 148 Print
Parent Company: Institut der deutschen Wirtschaft, Cologne (German Economics Institute)
Subsidiaries: Alpha Omega GmbH; Berolino.pr GmbH; Edition Agrippa GmbH; Rheinsitemedia GmbH

Deutscher Klassiker Verlag
Lindenstr 29-35, 60325 Frankfurt am Main
Mailing Address: Postfach 101945, 66019 Frankfurt am Main
Tel: (069) 75601-0 *Fax:* (069) 75601-522
Web Site: www.suhrkamp.de
Key Personnel
Publisher: Dr Siegfried Unseld
Rights & Permissions: Dr Petra Hardt
Man Dir: Philip Roeder *Tel:* (069) 75 601 500 *E-mail:* roeder@suhrkamp.de
Founded: 1981
ISBN Prefix(es): 3-618
Parent Company: Insel Verlag
Associate Companies: Suhrkamp Verlag; Suhrkamp Verlag AG, Switzerland

Deutscher Kunstverlag GmbH
Nymphenburgerstr 84, 80636 Munich
Mailing Address: Postfach 190354, 80603 Munich
Tel: (089) 121516-0; (089) 12516-22; (089) 12516-24 *Fax:* (089) 121516-10; (089) 121516-16
E-mail: vertrieb@deutscher-kunstverlag.ccn.de
Key Personnel
Man Dir: Albert Hirmer; Juergen Kleidt
Rights & Permissions: Elisabeth Motz
Founded: 1921
Subjects: Art
ISBN Prefix(es): 3-422
Orders to: Koch, Neff, Oetinger & Co, Schockenriedstr 39, Postfach 800620, 70565 Stuttgart
Buch 2000, Affoltesn CH 8910, Switzerland

Deutscher Literatur-Verlag
Muehlenstieg 16-22, 22041 Hamburg
Mailing Address: Postfach 701009, 22010 Hamburg
Tel: (040) 6 28 95-0 *Fax:* (040) 68 28 95 50
E-mail: info@kelter.de
Web Site: www.kelter.de
Telex: 213126
Key Personnel
Man Dir: Gerhard Melchert; Otto Melchert
Sales: Richard de Vries
Founded: 1905
ISBN Prefix(es): 3-87152
Associate Companies: Martin Kelter Verlag GmbH & Co, Muehlenstieg 16-22, 22041 Hamburg; Mero-Druck GmbH & Co KG
Orders to: Martin Kelter Verlag GmbH & Co

Deutscher Psychologen Verlag GmbH (DPV)
Oberer Lindweg 2, 53129 Bonn
Tel: (0228) 987310 *Fax:* (0228) 641023
E-mail: service@bdp-verband.org
Web Site: www.bdp-verband.org
Key Personnel
Man Dir: Petra Walkenbach *Tel:* (0228) 19873118 *Fax:* (0228) 641023 *E-mail:* dpv@bdp-verband.org
Founded: 1984
Subjects: Psychology, Psychiatry
ISBN Prefix(es): 3-925559; 3-931589
Number of titles published annually: 5 Print
Total Titles: 65 Print
Parent Company: Berufsverband Deutscher Psychologinnen und Psychologen eV
Warehouse: Deutscher Psychologen Verlag, Verlagsauslieferung, Holzwiesenstr 2, 72127 Kusterdingen, Petra Wallenbach

Deutscher Sparkassenverlag GmbH
Am Wallgraben 115, 70565 Stuttgart
Tel: (0711) 782-21 02 *Fax:* (0711) 782-16 35
Web Site: www.dsv-gruppe.de
Key Personnel
Man Dir: Bernd Kobarg
Founded: 1947
Member of Boersenverein des Deutschen Buchhandels; Suedwestdeutsches Zeitschriftenverleger-Verband; Verband der Verlage und Buchhandlungen; Specialize in Literature on Banking Business Management.
ISBN Prefix(es): 3-09
Associate Companies: Deutsche Sparkassen-Datendienste GmbH; AM-Werbegesellschaft mbH

Deutscher Studien Verlag+
Werderstr 10, 69469 Weinheim
Mailing Address: Postfach 100154, 69441 Weinheim
Tel: (06201) 60070 *Fax:* (06201) 6007-310
E-mail: info@beltz.de
Web Site: www.beltz.de
Key Personnel
Man Dir: Dr Manfred Beltz Ruebelmann; Joachim Radmer
Contact: Rosemarie Bornholt *Tel:* (06201) 6007 433 *E-mail:* r.bornholt@beltz.de
Rights: Peter E Kalb
Subjects: Psychology, Psychiatry, Social Sciences, Sociology
ISBN Prefix(es): 3-89271
Parent Company: Julius Beltz GmbH
Warehouse: Koch, Neff & Detringer, Verlagsauslieferung, 70551 Stuttgart *Tel:* (0711) 7899 20 30 *Fax:* (0711) 7899 10 10

Deutscher Taschenbuch Verlag GmbH & Co KG (dtv)+
Friedrichstr 1a, 80801 Munich
Mailing Address: Postfach 400422, 80704 Munich
Tel: (089) 38167-0 *Fax:* (089) 346428
E-mail: info@dtv.de
Web Site: www.dtv.de
Key Personnel
Man Dir: Wolfgang Balk
Finance Dir: Markus Angst
Editor: Winfried Groth; Maria Schedl-Jokl; Anne Schieckel; Dr Andrea Woerle; Dr Lutz-Werner Wolff
Distribution: Elke Gerhart
Sales Manager: Norbert Beyss
Advertising: Gabriele Fischer
Rights & Permissions: Constance Chory
Manager: Fritz Steinle
Marketing Manager: Rudolf Frankl
Founded: 1961
Subjects: Art, Astronomy, Behavioral Sciences, Biography, Child Care & Development, Computer Science, Cookery, Education, Fiction, Government, Political Science, History, How-to, Humor, Literature, Literary Criticism, Essays, Medicine, Nursing, Dentistry, Music, Dance, Nonfiction (General), Philosophy, Poetry, Psychology, Psychiatry, Religion - Other, Social Sciences, Sociology, Travel
ISBN Prefix(es): 3-423
Orders to: Koch, Neff, Oetinger & Co, Schockenriedstr 39, 70506 Stuttgart *Tel:* (0711) 78603322

Deutscher Universitats-Verlag
Abraham-Lincoln-Str 46, 65189 Wiesbaden
Mailing Address: Postfach 1546, 65173 Wiesbaden
Tel: (0611) 7878-239 *Fax:* (0611) 7878-411
Web Site: www.duv.de
Key Personnel
General Manager: Dr Hans-Dieter Haenel
Man Dir: Dr Heinz Weinheimer
Editorial: Ute Wrasmann *E-mail:* ute.wrasmann@bertelsman.de
Subjects: Economics, Science (General), Social Sciences, Sociology
ISBN Prefix(es): 3-8244
Parent Company: BertelsmannSpringer Science & Business Media

Deutscher Verlag fur Grundstoffindustrie GmbH+
Ruedigerstr 14, 70469 Stuttgart
Mailing Address: Postfach 301120, 70451 Stuttgart
Tel: (0711) 8931-0 *Fax:* (0711) 8931-410
E-mail: custserv@thieme.de
Web Site: www.thieme.de
Key Personnel
Editor: Christoph Iven *E-mail:* christoph.iven@thieme.de
Foreign Rights: Barbara Pfeifer *Tel:* (0711) 8931184 *E-mail:* barbara.pfeifer@thieme.de
Contact: Martin Spencker
Founded: 1960
Subjects: Chemistry, Chemical Engineering, Earth Sciences, Energy, Engineering (General), Environmental Studies, Geography, Geology, Mechanical Engineering, Nonfiction (General), Technology
ISBN Prefix(es): 3-342
Number of titles published annually: 3 Print
Total Titles: 90 Print
Parent Company: Georg Thieme Verlag

Deutscher Verlag fur Kunstwissenschaft GmbH+
Charlottenstr 13, 10969 Berlin
Tel: (030) 25913864; (030) 25913865 *Fax:* (030) 25913537
Key Personnel
Man Dir: Holger Beer
Publishing Dir: Andreas A Catsch
Founded: 1964
Subjects: Art
ISBN Prefix(es): 3-87157
Parent Company: Springer-Verlag
Associate Companies: Gebr Mann Verlag, Charlottenstr 13, 10969 Berlin
Orders to: Koch, Neff, Oetinger & Co Verlagsauslieferung GmbH, Schockenriedstr 39, Postfach 800620, 70565 Stuttgart

Deutscher Wanderverlag Dr Mair & Schnabel & Co+
Zeppelinstr 44-1, 73760 Ostfildern-Kemnat
Tel: (0711) 455005 *Fax:* (0711) 4569952
Key Personnel
Publisher: Rudolf K Fr Schnabel
Founded: 1978
Subjects: Outdoor Recreation, Travel
ISBN Prefix(es): 3-8134

GERMANY

Deutscher Wirtschaftsdienst John von Freyend GmbH+
Marienburger Str 22, 50968 Cologne
Tel: (0221) 93763-0 *Fax:* (0221) 93763-99
E-mail: box@dwd-verlag.de
Web Site: www.dwd-verlag.de
Key Personnel
Sales, Rights & Permissions Dir: Peter John von Freyend
Editorial & Publicity: Michael Rieck
Editorial: Dr Reinhardt Spindler
Founded: 1949
Member of the Stock Market.
Subjects: Business, Career Development, Communications, Energy, Environmental Studies, Finance, Management, Technology
ISBN Prefix(es): 3-87156
Subsidiaries: VWV Verlag fuer Wirtschaft und Verwaltung GmbH; Weltforum Verlag fuer Politik und Auslandskunde GmbH; Kontaplan Werbegesellschaft mbH

Deutsches Bucharchiv Muenchen, Institut fur Buchwissenschaften
Salvatorplatz 1, 80333 Munich
Tel: (089) 291951-0 *Fax:* (089) 291951-95
E-mail: kontakt@bucharchiv.de
Web Site: www.bucharchiv.de
Key Personnel
Doctor of Law: Prof Ludwig Delp *Tel:* (089) 7901190
Founded: 1948
Member of Borsenverein des Deutschen Buchhandels eV; Verband BayerischerVerlage und Buchandlungen eV.
Subjects: Communications, Journalism, Library & Information Sciences, Publishing & Book Trade Reference
ISBN Prefix(es): 3-447; 3-920145
Total Titles: 3 Print
Distributed by Otto Harrassowitz Verlag

Deutsches Jugendinstitut (DJI)
Nockherstr 2, 81541 Munich
Tel: (089) 62306-241 *Fax:* (089) 62306-265
Web Site: www.dji.de
Key Personnel
Man Dir: Prof Ingo Richter, PhD
Editorial, Publicity, Rights & Permissions, Sales & Production: Hans-Hermann Schwarzer
Sales & Production: Maria-Anne Weber
Sales: Kartrin Metzmacher *E-mail:* metzmacher@dji.de
Founded: 1963
Subjects: Education, Social Sciences, Sociology
ISBN Prefix(es): 3-87966
Associate Companies: Juventa Verlag GmbH
Orders to: Juventa Verlag, Ehretstr 3, 69469 Weinheim

Dharma Edition, Tibetisches Zentrum+
Hermann Balkstr 106, 22147 Hamburg
Tel: (040) 6443585 *Fax:* (040) 6443515
E-mail: tz@tibet.de
Web Site: www.tibet.de
Key Personnel
President: Gabriele Kistermann
Publisher: Rolf Kraemer
Founded: 1989
Subjects: Religion - Buddhist
ISBN Prefix(es): 3-927862
Bookshop(s): Tsongkang Buddhistische Buecher *Tel:* (040) 6449828 *E-mail:* tk@tibet.de

di animali V
Kopernikusplatz 36, 90459 Nurnberg
Tel: (0911) 951 9490 *Fax:* (0911) 951 9489
E-mail: di.animali@web.de

Edition Dia+
Fidicinstr 9, 10965 Berlin
Tel: (030) 6235021; (030) 6235022 *Fax:* (030) 6235023
E-mail: info@editiondia.de
Web Site: www.editiondia.de
Key Personnel
Man Dir: Helmut Lotz *E-mail:* lotz@editiondia.de
Man Dir, International Rights: Kai Precht
Founded: 1984
Subjects: Biography, Cookery, Gay & Lesbian, Nonfiction (General)
ISBN Prefix(es): 3-86034

Diagonal-Verlag GbR Rink-Schweer+
Alte Kasselerstr 43, 35039 Marburg
Mailing Address: Postfach 1248, 35002 Marburg
Tel: (06421) 681936 *Fax:* (06421) 681944
E-mail: info@diagonal-verlag.de
Web Site: www.diagonal-verlag.de
Key Personnel
Publisher: Steffen Rink *E-mail:* rink@diagonal-verlag.de; Thomas Schweer *E-mail:* schweer@diagonal-verlag.de
Founded: 1988
Specialize in science of religion.
Subjects: Literature, Literary Criticism, Essays, Poetry, Religion - Other, Science (General)
ISBN Prefix(es): 3-927165
Total Titles: 35 Print

Dialog-Verlag GmbH
Haidkoppelweg 24a, 21465 Reinbek
Tel: (040) 7111424 *Fax:* (040) 7101267
Founded: 1982
Subjects: Regional Interests, Travel
ISBN Prefix(es): 3-923707

Die Andere Bibliothek, *imprint of* Eichborn AG

Die Blauen Buecher (The Blue Book), *imprint of* Karl Robert Langewiesche Nachfolger Hans Koester KG

Die Verlag H Schafer GmbH+
Industriestr 16, 61381 Friedrichsdorf
Mailing Address: Postfach 2243, 61292 Bad Homburg
Tel: (06172) 95830 *Fax:* (06172) 71288
E-mail: dieverlag@t-online.de
Key Personnel
Man Dir: Peter Vollrath-Kuhne
Founded: 1923
Subjects: Economics, Government, Political Science, Law, Management, Radio, TV
ISBN Prefix(es): 3-920826
Associate Companies: Menschund Leben Verlagsgesellschaft, Postfach 2243, 61292 Bad Homburg

Diederichs, *imprint of* Heinrich Hugendubel Verlag GmbH

Eugen Diederichs Verlag GmbH & Co KG+
Postfach 151027, 80048 Munich
Tel: (089) 51480 *Fax:* (089) 5148111
Key Personnel
Owner: Heinrich Hugendubel
Publishing Manager, Man Dir: Thomas Kniffler
Editorial: Dr Michael Guenther
Advertising: Tina Steenbuck
Press: Michael Then
Rights & Permissions: Brigitte Hugendubel
Founded: 1896
Subjects: Architecture & Interior Design, Biography, Ethnicity, History, Literature, Literary Criticism, Essays, Philosophy, Religion - Buddhist, Religion - Hindu, Religion - Other, Social Sciences, Sociology
ISBN Prefix(es): 3-424
Orders to: Koch, Neff, Oetinger & Co Verlagsauslieferung GmbH, Schockenriedstr 39, 70565 Stuttgart

BOOK

Diesterweg, Moritz Verlag+
Heddrichstr 108-110, 60596 Frankfurt am Main
Mailing Address: Postfach 701161, 60561 Franfurt am Main
Tel: (069) 42081-0 *Fax:* (069) 42081-200
Web Site: www.diesterweg.de
Key Personnel
Man Dir: Ralf Meier; Karl Slipek
Founded: 1860
Subjects: Education, Language Arts, Linguistics, Social Sciences, Sociology
ISBN Prefix(es): 3-425
Distributed by European Book Co (USA); IBIS (USA)
Warehouse: Sigloch GmbH, Zeppelinstr 35, D-74653 Kuenzelsau
Orders to: Schroedel Verlag, Hildesheimerstr 202-206, D-30517 Hannover

Sammlung Dietrich Verlagsgesellschaft mbH
Gerichtsweg 28, 04103 Leipzig
Mailing Address: Postfach 101563, 04015 Leipzig
Tel: (0341) 9954600 *Fax:* (0341) 9954620
E-mail: info@aufbau-verlag.de
Web Site: www.aufbau-verlag.de
Key Personnel
Man Dir: Peter Dempewolf; Birgit Peter
Founded: 1991
Subjects: Literature, Literary Criticism, Essays, Philosophy
ISBN Prefix(es): 3-7350
Parent Company: Leipziger Verlags- und Vertriebsgesellschaft mbH
Associate Companies: Gustav Kiepenheuer Verlag Leipzig und Weimar GmbH
Shipping Address: Mohr-Morava Buchrertrieb Gesellschatt mbH, Sulzengasse 2, A-1101 Vienna, Austria; Pegasus-Stichting, Uitgeverijen-Boekhandel, Rhijuvis Feithstr 28, PO Box 59687, NL-1054 PZ Amsterdam, Netherlands; Verlaapauslieferung Balmer, Bosch 41, Huenenberg, CH-6331 Olten, Switzerland

Dieterichsche Verlagsbuchhandlung Mainz+
Beuthenerstr 17, 55131 Mainz
Tel: (06131) 573276 *Fax:* (06131) 571061
E-mail: DVB~mainz@t-online.de
Key Personnel
Publisher: Prof Alfred Klemm, PhD
Founded: 1766
Subjects: Art, Asian Studies, History, Literature, Literary Criticism, Essays, Philosophy, Poetry, Religion - Other
ISBN Prefix(es): 3-87162
Number of titles published annually: 3 Print
Orders to: A Eipper, Kirchensteig 12, 71126 Gaeufelden
GVA Postfach 2021, D-37010 Gottingen
Tel: (0551) 487177 *Fax:* (0551) 41392

Maximilian Dietrich Verlag+
Postfach 1636, 87686 Memmingen
Tel: (08331) 2853 *Fax:* (08331) 490364
Telex: ueber 54524 mzdruk d
Key Personnel
Man Dir: Curt Visel
Sales: Jurgen Schweitzer
Founded: 1946
Subjects: Biography, Human Relations, Regional Interests
ISBN Prefix(es): 3-87164
Subsidiaries: Edition Curt Visel

Dietrich zu Klampen Verlag+
Barckhausenstr 36, 21335 Lueneburg
Mailing Address: Postfach 1963, 21309 Lueneburg
Tel: (04131) 733030 *Fax:* (04131) 733033
E-mail: info@zuklampen.de
Web Site: www.dan4u.de/zuklampen

Key Personnel
Owner: Dietrich zu Klampen
Publisher: Dr Rolf Johannes
Founded: 1983
Subjects: Government, Political Science, Philosophy, Poetry, Psychology, Psychiatry, Science (General), Social Sciences, Sociology
ISBN Prefix(es): 3-924245; 3-933156

Verlag J H W Dietz Nachf GmbH+
In der Raste 2, 53129 Bonn
Tel: (0228) 23 80 83 *Fax:* (0228) 23 41 04
E-mail: info@dietz-verlag.de
Web Site: www.dietz-verlag.de
Key Personnel
Manager: Dr Gerhard Fischer
Dir, Sales: Hilde Holthamp *E-mail:* hilde.holtkamp@dietz-verlag.de
Editorial, Rights & Permissions: Susanna Weineck *E-mail:* susanna.weineck@dietz-verlag.de
Founded: 1881
Subjects: Developing Countries, Environmental Studies, Government, Political Science, History, Nonfiction (General), Social Sciences, Sociology
ISBN Prefix(es): 3-8012
Foreign Rep(s): Elisabeth Anintah-Hirt (Austria)

Dietz Verlag Berlin GmbH+
Weydingerstr 14-16, 10178 Berlin
Mailing Address: Postfach 273, 10124 Berlin
Tel: (030) 248409290 *Fax:* (030) 28409590
Key Personnel
Man Dir: Dr Reinhard Semmelmann
Sales Dir: Hartmut Goetze
Editorial, Rights & Permissions: Christine Krauss
Founded: 1945
Subjects: Biography, Government, Political Science, History, Social Sciences, Sociology
ISBN Prefix(es): 3-320
Shipping Address: Bugrim Verlagsauslieferung, Saalburgstr 3, 12099 Berlin
Warehouse: Bugrim Verlagsauslieferung, Saalburgstr 3, 12099 Berlin
Orders to: Bugrim Verlagsauslieferung, Saalburgstr 3, 12099 Berlin

Dietzenbach, *imprint of* ALS-Verlag GmbH

Digital Publishing+
Tumblingerstr 32, 80337 Munich
Tel: (089) 747482-0 *Fax:* (089) 74792308
E-mail: info@digitalpublishing.de
Web Site: www.digitalpublishing.de
Key Personnel
Content & Technology, Chief Executive Officer: Jorg Koberling *E-mail:* j.koberling@digitalpublishing.de
Marketing & Communications, Chief Executive Officer: Armin Hopp *E-mail:* a.hopp@digitalpublishing.de
Public Relations Manager: Heike Eiber *E-mail:* h.eiber@digitalpublishing.de
Founded: 1994
Independent publisher.
ISBN Prefix(es): 3-89477; 3-930947
Total Titles: 65 CD-ROM
Online services available through World Wide Web.
Distributor for M8 das medieu team (Bookstores/Germany)

Dingfelder-Verlag Inh Gerd Gmelin+
Erlinger Hoehe 9, 82346 Andechs
Tel: (08152) 6671 *Fax:* (08152) 5120
Web Site: www.gmelin-verlag.de
Key Personnel
Owner, Rights & Permissions: Gerd E Gmelin
Founded: 1949
Subjects: Fiction, Health, Nutrition, Literature, Literary Criticism, Essays, Medicine, Nursing, Dentistry, Nonfiction (General), Philosophy, Physical Sciences, Science (General)
ISBN Prefix(es): 3-926253

Dipa-Verlag GmbH+
Friesstr 20-24, 60388 Frankfurt
Tel: (069) 95732044 *Fax:* (069) 576128
Key Personnel
Man Dir, Rights & Permissions: Gerd Hofmann
Founded: 1948
Subjects: Education, Fiction, Government, Political Science, History, Nonfiction (General)
ISBN Prefix(es): 3-7638

Discordia Verlagsgesellschaft mbH
Wiehlerstr 5, 51545 Waldbroel
Tel: (02291) 911024 *Fax:* (02291) 911925
Founded: 1978
ISBN Prefix(es): 3-922733

Edition Diskord
Schwaerzlocherstr 104/b, 72070 Tuebingen
Tel: (07071) 40102 *Fax:* (07071) 44710
E-mail: ed.diskord@t-online.de
Web Site: www.edition-diskord.de
Key Personnel
Man Dir: Gerd Kimmerle
Founded: 1985
Subjects: Biography, History, Philosophy, Psychology, Psychiatry, Social Sciences, Sociology, Women's Studies
ISBN Prefix(es): 3-89295

Divyanand Verlags GmbH+
Saegestr 37, 79737 Herrischried
Tel: (07764) 93 97-0 *Fax:* (07764) 93 97-39
E-mail: sandila@t-online.de
Web Site: www.sandila.de
Founded: 1987
Specialize in Spirituality.
Subjects: Parapsychology, Philosophy, Religion - Other, Self-Help
ISBN Prefix(es): 3-926696
Number of titles published annually: 2 Print
Total Titles: 23 Print
U.S. Office(s): 129 Juneberry Court, San Jose, CA 95136, United States

DJI, see Deutsches Jugendinstitut (DJI)

DLV Deutscher Landwirtschaftsverlag Berlin
Kabelkamp 6, 30179 Hanover
Mailing Address: Postfach 14 40, 30014 Hanover
Tel: (0511) 678 06-0 *Fax:* (0511) 678 06-200
E-mail: dlv-berlin@t-online.de
Web Site: www.dlv.de
Key Personnel
Man Dir: Hans Peter Kliemann; Bernd Kuhrmeier; Hans's Mueller
Founded: 1960
Subjects: Agriculture, Animals, Pets, Environmental Studies, Gardening, Plants, Fishing, Forestry, Hunting
ISBN Prefix(es): 3-331
Parent Company: BLV Verlagsgesellschaft Muenchen GmbH
Branch Office(s)
Guertelstr 29A-30, 10247 Berlin *Tel:* (030) 29 39 74-50 *Fax:* (030) 29 39 74-59
Lothstr 29, 80797 Munich *Tel:* (089) 12 70 50 *Fax:* (089) 1 27 05-354

Christoph Dohr
Kasselberger Weg 120, 50769 Cologne
Tel: (0221) 70 70 02 *Fax:* (0221) 70 43 95
E-mail: info@dohr.de
Web Site: www.dohr.de
Key Personnel
Contact: Christoph Dohr
Founded: 1990
Music publisher.
Subjects: Music, Dance
ISBN Prefix(es): 3-925366; 3-936655
Number of titles published annually: 80 Print
Total Titles: 900 Print

Dolling und Galitz Verlag GmbH+
Ehrenbergstr 62, 22767 Hamburg
Tel: (040) 3893515 *Fax:* (040) 388587
E-mail: doellingundgalitzverlag@compuserve.com
Key Personnel
Editor: Dr Peter Dolling; Dr Robert Galitz
Press: Brita Reimers
Manager: Sabine Niemann
Founded: 1986
Subjects: Architecture & Interior Design, Art, History, Literature, Literary Criticism, Essays, Music, Dance, Photography, Religion - Jewish, Religion - Other
ISBN Prefix(es): 3-926174; 3-930802; 3-933374
Warehouse: Siemensstrasse 16, 35463 Fernwald (Annerod) *Fax:* 06419439329
Orders to: PROLIT Verlagsauslieferung

agenda Verlag Thomas Dominikowski+
Hammerstr 223, 48153 Muenster
Tel: (0251) 79 96 10 *Fax:* (0251) 79 95 19
E-mail: info@agenda.de
Key Personnel
Publisher: Thomas Dominikowski
International Rights: Michael Alfs
Founded: 1992
Subjects: Developing Countries, Environmental Studies, Government, Political Science, History, Journalism, Regional Interests, Social Sciences, Sociology, Women's Studies
ISBN Prefix(es): 3-929440; 3-89688

Domino Verlag, Guenther Brinek GmbH
Menzingerstr 13, 80638 Munich
Tel: (089) 17 91 30 *Fax:* (089) 17 91 34 13
Web Site: www.domino-verlag.de
Key Personnel
Manager: Guenther Brinek
Founded: 1964
Subjects: Drama, Theater
ISBN Prefix(es): 3-926123

Domowina Verlag GmbH
Tuchmacherstr/Sukelnska 27, 02625 Bautzen
Tel: (03591) 5770 *Fax:* (03591) 577243
E-mail: DomowinaVerlag@t-online.de
Web Site: www.buchhandel.de/domowinaverlag
Key Personnel
Man Dir: Ludmila Budar *Tel:* ()3591) 577 241
Marketing & Management: Manja Bujnowska *Tel:* (03591) 577 262
Press: Mirana Mieth *Tel:* (03591) 577 256 *E-mail:* Werbung.LND@t-online.de
Publications & Bookshop: Dr Ruth Thiemann *Tel:* (03591) 422 32
Founded: 1958
Subjects: Ethnicity, Scientific, Technical Literature
ISBN Prefix(es): 3-7420

Don Bosco Verlag+
Saint Wolfgangsplatz 10, 81669 Munich
Tel: (089) 48008300 *Fax:* (089) 48008309
Key Personnel
Dir: Alfons Friedrich
Editorial: Reinhold Storkenmaier
Sales: Gerhard Sacher
Founded: 1948
Subjects: Education, Religion - Other
ISBN Prefix(es): 3-7698
Imprints: DBV
Branch Office(s)
Rixdorferstr 15, 51063 Cologne
Kaulbachstr 63a, 805369 Munich

Donat Verlag+
Borgfelder Heerstr 29, 28357 Bremen

Tel: (0421) 274886 *Fax:* (0421) 275106
E-mail: donatverlag@excite.de
Key Personnel
Publisher: Helmut Donat
Founded: 1988
Member of Bvrsenverein des Deutschen Buchhandels.
Subjects: Art, Government, Political Science, History, Regional Interests, Religion - Jewish
ISBN Prefix(es): 3-924444; 3-931737
Number of titles published annually: 35 Print
Total Titles: 220 Print

Verlagsgruppe Dornier (Publishing Group Dornier)+
Formerly Dornier Medienholding
Dircksenstr 48, 10178 Berlin
Mailing Address: Postfach 021108, 10122 Berlin
Tel: (030) 28447-101 *Fax:* (030) 28447-103
E-mail: info@dornier-verlage.de
Web Site: www.dornier-verlage.de *Cable:* EDILEIP
Key Personnel
Man Dir: Sabine Schubert *E-mail:* s.schubert@dornier-verlage.de
Parent Company: Verlagsgruppe Dornier, Dircksenstr 48, 10178 Berlin, Sabine Schubert
Associate Companies: Cross Publishing House, Postfach 80 06 69, 70506 Stuttgart *Tel:* (0711) 788 03-0; Kreuz Verlag, Breitwiesenstr 30, 70565 Stuttgart *Tel:* (0711) 78803-91 *Fax:* (0711) 78803-10 *E-mail:* info@kreuzverlag.de *Web Site:* www.kreuzverlag.de (Books on religion, self-help, spiritual giftbooks); Theseus Verlag, Dircksenstr 48, 10178 Berlin, Contact: Ursula Richard *Tel:* (030) 28447-100 *Fax:* (030) 28447-103 *E-mail:* theseus@dornier-verlage.de *Web Site:* www.theseus-verlage.de (Buddhist publisher); Urania Verlag, Berlin (Germany; Books on parenting, home improvement, arts & crafts)
Imprints: Brandenburgisches Verlagshaus (Germany; Military history); EA Seemann Verlag (Germany; Books on art, photography); Edition Leipzig (Germany; Publisher of regional art, architecture and history books (Saxonia); official publisher of books on Meissen porcelaine); Henschel Verlag (Germany; Books on performing arts (theater, cinema, music, ballet)); Alf Luechow Verlag (Germany; Books on advaita, spiritual health, self-help)
Orders to: Leipziger Kommissions und Grossbuchhandelsgesellschaft mbH, Poetzschauer Weg, 04579 Espenhain

DPV, see Deutscher Psychologen Verlag GmbH (DPV)

Dr Oetker Verlag KG+
Lutterstr 14, 33617 Bielefeld
Tel: (0521) 521 155-0 *Fax:* (0521) 521 155-2995
E-mail: presse@oetker.de
Web Site: www.oetker-gruppe.de
Key Personnel
Man Dir: Annelore Strullkoetter *Tel:* (0521) 520643 *E-mail:* strullkoetter@oetker-verlag.de
Founded: 1951
Subjects: Cookery
ISBN Prefix(es): 3-7670
Parent Company: August Oetker, Bielefeld

Drei Brunnen Verlag GmbH & Co
Heusee 19, 73655 Pluederhausen
Tel: (0711) 86020 *Fax:* (0711) 860229
E-mail: mail@drei-brunnen-verlag.de
Web Site: www.drei-brunnen-verlag.de
Key Personnel
Man Publisher: Emmerich Mueller
Publisher: Dieter Rath
Contact: Thomas Mueller
Founded: 1950
Subjects: Outdoor Recreation, Travel

ISBN Prefix(es): 3-7956
Number of titles published annually: 10 Print
Total Titles: 60 Print
Shipping Address: Geo Center, Schockenriedstr 44, 70565 Stuttgart
Orders to: Geo Center, Schockenriedstr 44, 70565 Stuttgart

Drei Eichen Verlag Manuel Kissener+
Rote Kreuzstr 30, 97762 Hammelburg
Mailing Address: Postfach 1147, 97754 Hammelburg
Tel: (09732) 9142-0 *Fax:* (09732) 9142-20
E-mail: info@drei-eichen.de
Web Site: www.drei-eichen.de
Key Personnel
President & International Rights: Manuel Kissener
Founded: 1931
Subjects: Philosophy, Science Fiction, Fantasy, Self-Help
ISBN Prefix(es): 3-7699
Number of titles published annually: 10 Print
Total Titles: 200 Print
Imprints: Edition Kima; Politik und Spiritualitaet

Drei Ulmen Verlag GmbH+
Schleissheimerstr 274, 80809 Munich
Tel: (089) 3087911; (089) 3088343 (orders)
Key Personnel
Publisher: Dr Hermann Schreiber
Founded: 1985
Member of Small Publishers Study Group.
Subjects: Biography, Literature, Literary Criticism, Essays, Travel
ISBN Prefix(es): 3-926087
Associate Companies: AVA-GmbH, Seeblickstr 46, 82211 Herrsching

Dreisam Ratgeber in der Rutsker Verlag GmbH+
Schreberstr 2, 51105 Cologne
Tel: (0221) 921635-0 *Fax:* (0221) 921635-24
E-mail: kontakt@hayit.com
Web Site: www.hayit.com
Key Personnel
International Rights: Ertay Hayit *E-mail:* hayit@hayit.com
Editorial: Cornelia Auschra *Tel:* (0221) 921635-13 *E-mail:* cornelia.auschra@hayit.com; Mike Gahn *E-mail:* mike@hayit.com; Ute Hayit *Tel:* (0221) 921635-11 *E-mail:* ute.hayit@hayit.com; Simone Kruger-Naujoks *Tel:* (0221) 921635-22 *E-mail:* simone-naujoks@hayit.com
Founded: 1988
Subjects: Biological Sciences, Career Development, Cookery, Economics, Education, Environmental Studies, Health, Nutrition, Human Relations, Law, Medicine, Nursing, Dentistry, Psychology, Psychiatry, Religion - Islamic
ISBN Prefix(es): 3-89607

Cecilie Dressler Verlag+
Poppenbuetteler Chaussee 53, 22397 Hamburg
Mailing Address: Postfach 658230, 22374 Hamburg
Tel: (040) 607909-03 *Fax:* (040) 6072326
Web Site: www.cecilie-dressler.de
Key Personnel
Man Dir & Sales: Thomas Huggle
Man Dir, Rights & Permissions: Silke Weitendorf
Editorial: Ursula Heckel
Publicity: Heike Bovensmann
International Rights: Renate Reichstein
Tel: (040) 607909-13 *Fax:* (040) 607909-51
E-mail: lizenzen@vsg.hamburg.de
Press: Judith Richter *Tel:* (040) 607909-65 *Fax:* (040) 607909-40 *E-mail:* presse@vsg-hamburg.de; Frauke Wedler *Tel:* (040) 607909-23 *Fax:* (040) 607909-40 *E-mail:* presse@vsg-hamburg.de

Internet Editor: Ilon Materna *Tel:* (040) 607909-47 *Fax:* (040) 607909-51
E-mail: internetredaktion@vsg-hamburg.de
Marketing: Dr Juergen Huebner *Tel:* (040) 607909-55 *Fax:* (040) 607909-50
E-mail: vertrieb@vsg-hamburg.de
Founded: 1928
Subjects: Fiction
ISBN Prefix(es): 3-7915
Associate Companies: Atrium Verlag
Warehouse: Runge Verlagsauslieferung, Bergstr 2, 33803 Steinhagen

Droemer Knaur Verlag, see Droemersche Verlagsanstalt Th Knaur Nachfolger GmbH & Co

Droemersche Verlagsanstalt Th Knaur Nachfolger GmbH & Co+
Hilblestr 54, 80636 Munich
Mailing Address: Postfach 7600, 33310 Guetersloh
Tel: (089) 92710 *Fax:* (089) 9271168
E-mail: info@dioemer-weltbild.de
Web Site: www.dioemer-weltbilt.de *Cable:* DROEMERVERLAG
Key Personnel
Publisher: Hans Peter Uebleis
Publishing Dir: Beate Kuckertz
Program Dir: Klaus Fricke; Carolin Graehl; Christine Steffen-Reimann; Annette Weber
Rights & Permissions: Renate Abrasch
Founded: 1901
Also known as Droemer Knaur Verlag.
Subjects: Biography, Business, Cookery, Erotica, Fiction, How-to, Humor, Mysteries, Nonfiction (General), Science (General), Self-Help, Wine & Spirits, Anthology, Fairy Tales, Family Saga, Fantasy, Food/Drink, Horror, Movie or Television, Thriller
ISBN Prefix(es): 3-426
Parent Company: Verlagsgruppe Dioemer Weltbild GmbH & Co KG
Associate Companies: Knaur Taschenbuchverlag; Schneekluth Verlag GmbH
Imprints: MenSana
Shipping Address: VVA Bertelsmann Distribution

Droste Verlag GmbH
Postfach 10 11 35, 40196 Duesseldorf
Tel: (0211) 5050 *Fax:* (0211) 5052671
Telex: 8582495 dv d *Cable:* DROSTEVERLAG DUSSELDORF
Key Personnel
Chairman & Man Dir: Clemens Bauer
Man Dir: Dieter Reichel
Publishing Dir: Dr Manfred Lotsch
Editorial: Heidemarie Alertz
Production, Publicity: Helmut Schwanen
Founded: 1711
Subjects: Art, Economics, Government, Political Science, History, Humor, Social Sciences, Sociology
ISBN Prefix(es): 3-7700
Subsidiaries: Wilhelm Knapp Verlag
Warehouse: Xantheuerstr 3a, 41460 Neuss

Karl Elser Druck GmbH
Formerly Karl Elser GmbH Buch-und Zeitungsverlag
Kisslingweg 35, 75417 Muehlacker
Tel: (07041) 805-41 *Fax:* (07041) 805-50
E-mail: info@elserdruck.de
Web Site: www.elserdruck.de
Key Personnel
Man Dir & International Rights: Brigitte Wetzel-Haendle
Man Dir: Else Haendle
Founded: 1890
Also acts as newspaper & printing office.
Subjects: Biography, Fiction, Regional Interests
ISBN Prefix(es): 3-7987

Associate Companies: Karl Elser Druck GmbH
Bookshop(s): Buch-Elser, Bahnhofstr 62, 75417 Muehlacker

Druckerei u Verlagsanstalt Bayerland GmbH
Konrad-Adenauerstr 19, 85221 Dachau
Mailing Address: Postfach 1868, 85208 Dachau
Tel: (08131) 7 20 66 *Fax:* (08131) 73 53 99
E-mail: zentrale@bayerland-amperbote.de
Web Site: www.bayerland.de
ISBN Prefix(es): 3-89251; 3-922394; 3-9800040
Number of titles published annually: 20 Print
Total Titles: 250 Print

Druffel-Verlag+
Kreuzanger 8, 82335 Berg
Tel: (08151) 50024 *Fax:* (08151) 51856
Key Personnel
Publisher: Dr Gert Suedholt
Founded: 1952
Subjects: Government, Political Science, History
ISBN Prefix(es): 3-8061

DRW-Verlag Weinbrenner-GmbH & Co+
Fasanenweg 18, 70771 Leinfelden-Echterdingen
Tel: (0711) 75 91-0 *Fax:* (0711) 75 91-333
Web Site: www.drw-verlag.de; www.weinbrenner.de
Key Personnel
Dir: Karl-Heinz Weinbrenner
Business Manager: Bernhard Driehaus
Founded: 1874
Subjects: Nonfiction (General), Physical Sciences, Regional Interests
ISBN Prefix(es): 3-87181; 3-87422
Subsidiaries: BIT-Verlag Weinbrenner; Verlagsanstalt Alexander Koch GmbH
Divisions: Fachbuch Service
Orders to: Koch, Neff & Oetinger Verlagsauslieferung, Schockenriedstr 39, 70565 Stuttgart

DSI Data Service & Information
Kaiserstege 4, 47495 Rheinberg
Mailing Address: Postfach 1127, 47476 Rheinberg
Tel: 2843 3220 *Fax:* 2843 3230
E-mail: dsi@dsidata.com
Web Site: www.dsidata.com
Key Personnel
Contact: Konrad Wilms *E-mail:* konrad.wilms@dsidata.com
Founded: 1985
Electronic preparation & publishing of national & international statistical information (numerical databases) on CD-ROM & on the internet.
Subjects: Economics, Social Sciences, Sociology
Distributor for Asia 2000; Bernan; Enerdata SA; European Union; International Bank for Reconstruction & Development; Organization for Economic Co-Operation & Development; Smartal Solutions Ltd; TRADE Inc
Foreign Rep(s): ABE Marketing (Poland); Albertina Data SRO (Slovak Republic); Albertina Data SRO (Czech Republic); Albertina Incone Praha (Czech Republic); BH Sistemas de Informacao (Portugal); CD Publishing Worshop Ltd (Hong Kong); CD Rom International (Chile); Cd-Rom International Ed c Com LtdA (Brazil); Cosmo Info & Technology Service (Korea); Diaz de Santos SA (Spain); Edutech (United Arab Emirates); Euro Info Service (Hungary); Family Art Co Ltd (Taiwan); Far Eastern Booksellers (Kyokuto Shoten) (Japan); Greendata (Spain); IBS Buke SDN BHD (Malaysia); Info Access & Distribution Pte Ltd (Singapore); Info Technology Supply Ltd (UK); IPS International Publishing Service (Poland); Kaiga Kyozai Center (Japan); Kinokuniya Co Ltd (Japan); Kyobo Book Centre (Korea); Leader Books SA (Greece); Licosa SpA (Italy); Lics Pvt Ltd (Botswana, Zimbabwe); LICS Pvt Ltd; Logiser SA (Portugal); LSYS-M (Bulgaria); LUSODOC (Portugal); Maruzen Co, IRN Import (Books) (Japan); Mediamorphose (Turkey); Microinfo Ltd (UK); Micromedia Ltd (Canada); Mladinska Knjiga Trgovina (Slovenia); Mundi-Prensa Libros SA (Spain); Munkgaard Direct (Denmark); Oasis Official (New Zealand); OCD Office Central de Documentation (France); Paradox Libros (Spain); Prio Info AB (Sweden); Publiworld (Colombia); Quantec Research Pty Ltd (South Africa); RoweCom Espana (Spain); Sedona (Romania); Sistemas Documentales SL (Spain); Stratus (Poland); Trade Inc (UK); Transmission Books & Microinfo Co Ltd (Taiwan); Wennergren-Williams Info AB (Sweden); Worldwide Target Corp SDN BHD (Malaysia)

dtv, see Deutscher Taschenbuch Verlag GmbH & Co KG (dtv)

Verlag Duerr & Kessler GmbH+
Haidplatz 2, 93047 Regensburg
Tel: (0941) 568940 *Fax:* (0941) 568999
E-mail: info@wolfverlag.de
Web Site: www.wolfverlag.de
Key Personnel
Publisher: Wilmar Diepgrond
Marketing Dir: Rita Lenzen
Founded: 1953
Subjects: Education, Language Arts, Linguistics
ISBN Prefix(es): 3-8181

Archibook Verlag Martina Duettmann+
Westendallee 97e, 14052 Berlin
Tel: (030) 3046578 *Fax:* (030) 3049902
Founded: 1979
Subjects: Architecture & Interior Design
ISBN Prefix(es): 3-88531
Orders to: Springer Verlag c/o Birkhaeuser-Auftragsbear Beitung, Heidelberger Platz 3, 14197 Berlin 33 *Tel:* (030) 8207423 *Fax:* (030) 8207448

Dumjahn Verlag
Immenhof 12, 55128 Mainz
Mailing Address: Postfach 1746, 55007 Mainz
Tel: (06131) 330810 *Fax:* (06131) 330811
E-mail: railway@dumjahn.de
Web Site: www.dumjahn.de
Founded: 1974
Specialize in railway
Member of Borsenverein des Deutschen Buchhandels.
Subjects: Publishing & Book Trade Reference, Transportation, Travel
ISBN Prefix(es): 3-921426; 3-88992
Number of titles published annually: 2 Print; 2 E-Book
Total Titles: 18 Print
Bookshop(s): Versandbuchhandlung und Antiquariat Horst-Werner Dumjahn, Immenhof 12, 55128 Mainz

DuMont Buchverlag GmbH & Co KG+
Amsterdanerstr 192, 50735 Cologne
Tel: (0221) 2 24 18-0 *Fax:* (0221) 2 24 18-12
E-mail: info@dumontverlag.de
Web Site: www.dumontverlag.de/dumont
Telex: 8882 975 dbeb d
Key Personnel
Publisher: Ernst Bruecher
Publisher, Rights & Permissions: Daniel Bruecher
Founded: 1956
Subjects: Archaeology, Art, Cookery, Gardening, Plants, Travel
ISBN Prefix(es): 3-8320
Orders to: BDK Buecherdienst, Koelner 87 248, 50859 Cologne

DuMont Monte+
Neven DuMont Haus, Amsterdamerstr 192, 50735 Cologne
Tel: (0221) 224-180 *Fax:* (0221) 224-1828
E-mail: info@dumontverlag.de
Web Site: www.dumontverlag.de/monte
Telex: 8882975 dbeb d
Key Personnel
Man Dir: Helena Bommersheim
Foreign Rights: Julia Schulli *Tel:* (0221) 224-1896 *E-mail:* schuelli@dumontmonte.de
Founded: 1998
Subjects: Architecture & Interior Design, Art, Cookery, Crafts, Games, Hobbies, Gardening, Plants, House & Home, How-to
ISBN Prefix(es): 3-8320
Total Titles: 75 Print
Parent Company: Dumont

Duncker und Humblot GmbH+
Carl Heinrich Becker Weg 9, 12165 Berlin
Mailing Address: Postfach 410329, 12113 Berlin
Tel: (030) 79 00 06-0 *Fax:* (030) 79 00 06-31
E-mail: info@duncker-humblot.de
Web Site: www.duncker-humblot.de
Key Personnel
Publisher & International Rights: Prof H C Norbert Simon, PhD *Tel:* (030) 790006-19 *Fax:* (030) 790006-43 *E-mail:* verlag@duncker-humbolt.de
Marketing: Ingrid Buehrig *Tel:* (030) 790006-30 *Fax:* (030) 790006-53 *E-mail:* buehrig@duncker-humblot.de
Founded: 1798
Subjects: Asian Studies, Biography, Criminology, Developing Countries, Economics, Environmental Studies, Finance, Government, Political Science, History, Law, Literature, Literary Criticism, Essays, Marketing, Military Science, Philosophy, Science (General), Social Sciences, Sociology, Theology
ISBN Prefix(es): 3-428
Number of titles published annually: 350 Print
Total Titles: 9,300 Print
Subsidiaries: Speyer & Peters GmbH; Berliner Buchdruckerei Union Gmb

Dustri-Verlag Dr Karl Feistle+
Bajuwarenring 4, 82041 Oberhaching
Mailing Address: Postfach 1351, 82032 Deisenhofen
Tel: (089) 61 38 61-0 *Fax:* (089) 613 54 12
E-mail: info@dustri.de
Web Site: www.dustri.de
Key Personnel
Dir: Frank Feistle; Joerg Feistle *Tel:* (089) 61 38 61-30 *E-mail:* joerg.feistle@dustri.de
Founded: 1965
Subjects: Medicine, Nursing, Dentistry
ISBN Prefix(es): 3-87185

Klaus D Dutz+
Postfach 5725, 48031 Muenster
Tel: (0251) 65514 *Fax:* (0251) 66 16 92
E-mail: dutz.nodus@t-online.de
Key Personnel
Contact: Klaus D Dutz
Founded: 1987
Subjects: Film, Video, Language Arts, Linguistics, Philosophy, Science (General)
ISBN Prefix(es): 3-89323
Subsidiaries: Stichting Neerlandistiek VU; Stichting Uitgeverij De Keltische Draak

DVA, see Deutsche Verlags-Anstalt GmbH (DVA)

DVG-Deutsche Verlagsgesellschaft mbH+
Brueckenstr 1, 83022 Rosenheim
Mailing Address: Postfach 1180, 32352 Preussisch Oldendorf
Tel: (08031) 15643 *Fax:* (08031) 380662

GERMANY

Key Personnel
Contact: Waldemar Schuetz
Founded: 1969
Subjects: Government, Political Science, History, Military Science
ISBN Prefix(es): 3-920722
Associate Companies: Verlag fuer Aussergewoehnliche Perspektiven
Orders to: VAP Verlagsauslieferung, Mindenerstr 34, 32361 Preussisch Oldendorf

DVS-Verlag GmbH, see Verlag fur Schweissen und Verwandte Verfahren

E Schweizerbart'sche Verlagsbuchhandlung (Nagele und Obermiller)+
Affiliate of Gebrueder Borntraeger Verlagsbuchhandlung
Johannesstr 3A, 70176 Stuttgart
Tel: (0711) 625001 *Fax:* (0711) 625005
E-mail: mail@schweizerbart.de
Web Site: www.schweizerbart.de
Key Personnel
Man Dir, Production: Dr Erhard Naegele
Man Dir, Sales: Dr Walter Obermiller
Exhibition Manager: Martina Ihringer
Founded: 1826
Subjects: Anthropology, Archaeology, Biological Sciences, Earth Sciences, Environmental Studies, Geography, Geology, Maritime, Science (General)
ISBN Prefix(es): 3-510 (Schweizerbart); 3-443 (Borntraeger)
U.S. Office(s): Balogh Scientific Books, 1911 N Duncan Rd, Champaign, IL 61822, United States, Contact: Pamela Burns-Balogh *Tel:* 217-355-9331 *Fax:* 217-355-9413 *E-mail:* balogh@balogh.com *Web Site:* www.balogh.com
Distributor for Bundesanstaltfuer Geowissenschaften und Rohstoffe; Senckenbergische Naturforschende Gesellschaft

EA Seemann Verlag, *imprint of* Verlagsgruppe Dornier

Ebenhausen bei Muenchen, *imprint of* Verlag Langewiesche-Brandt KG

Ebersberg, *imprint of* Eironeia-Verlag

Echo Verlag+
Postfach 1704, 37007 Goettingen
Tel: (0551) 796824 *Fax:* (0551) 74035
E-mail: clages.echoverlag@t-online.de
Web Site: www.echoverlag.de
Key Personnel
Man Dir, Rights & Permissions: Andrea Clages
Founded: 1985
Member of the Stock Exchange of German Booksellers; Land Association Lower Saxony.
Subjects: Animals, Pets, Environmental Studies
ISBN Prefix(es): 3-9801216; 3-926914

Echter Wurzburg Frankische Gesellschaftsdruckerei und Verlag GmbH+
Domini Kanerplatz 8, 97070 Wuerzburg
Mailing Address: Postfach 5560, 97005 Wuerzburg
Tel: (0931) 66068-0; (0931) 6671252; (0931) 6671253 *Fax:* (0931) 66068-23
E-mail: info@echter-verlag.de
Web Site: www.echter-verlag.de *Cable:* ECHTERVERLAG
Key Personnel
Dir: Gerhard Schaefer *Tel:* (0931) 6671-220 *Fax:* (0931) 6671-295 *E-mail:* g.schaefer@echter.de; Albrecht Siedler *Tel:* (0931) 6671-216 *Fax:* (0931) 6671-295 *E-mail:* a.siedler@echter.de

Publisher: Thomas Haeussner *Tel:* (0931) 6671-158 *Fax:* (0931) 6671-151 *E-mail:* th.haeussner@echter.de
Founded: 1900
Subjects: Art, Biblical Studies, Fiction, History, Regional Interests, Religion - Catholic, Religion - Other, Theology, Wine & Spirits
ISBN Prefix(es): 3-429
Total Titles: 600 Print

Eckardt & Messtorff GmbH
Roedingsmarkt 16, 20459 Hamburg
Tel: (040) 374842-0 *Fax:* (040) 37500768
E-mail: e&m-sales@eum.hh.eunet.de
Web Site: www.em-seacharts.de
Founded: 1882
Subjects: Maritime
ISBN Prefix(es): 3-7702

Ecomed Verlagsgesellschaft AG & Co KG+
Justus-Von-Liebig Str 1, 86899 Landsberg
Mailing Address: Postfach 1752, 86887 Landsberg
Tel: (08191) 125 0 *Fax:* (08191) 125 492
E-mail: medicine@ecomed.de
Web Site: www.ecomed.de
Telex: 527114 moind
Key Personnel
Publishing Manager: Harald Heim *Tel:* (08191) 125208
Foreign Rights Manager: Gerlinde Stanglmeier *Tel:* (08191) 125571 *E-mail:* g.stanglmeier@ecomed.de
Marketing: Gerhard Heinzman *Tel:* (08191) 125399
Product Management: Manuela Czech *Tel:* (08191) 125420; Ursula Jahn *Tel:* (08191) 125488; Karin Preussner *Tel:* (08191) 125486; Isabella de la Rosee *Tel:* (08191) 255191; Dr Nrobert Schueller *Tel:* (08191) 255804
Sales: Stefanie Braeuer *Tel:* (08191) 255541; Nina Karlsdorfer *Tel:* (08191) 255800; Silke Matschiner *Tel:* (08191) 255609
Customer Service: Gabriele Honzu *Tel:* (08191) 255152
Founded: 1979
Subjects: Biological Sciences, Chemistry, Chemical Engineering, Engineering (General), Environmental Studies, Gardening, Plants, Labor, Industrial Relations, Medicine, Nursing, Dentistry, Technology, Transportation
ISBN Prefix(es): 3-609
Total Titles: 520 Print
Parent Company: moderne industrie AG

Econ Taschenbuchverlag+
Kaiserswertherstr 282, 40474 Duesseldorf
Tel: (0211) 43596
Key Personnel
Chief Executive Officer & Publisher: Dr Dietrich Oppenberg
Marketing & Sales: Felicitas Wendt
Rights & Permissions: Herbert Borgartz
Founded: 1951
Publishing group comprised of: Econ-Verlag GmbH; Econ Taschenbuch Verlag GmbH. The group forms part of the newspaper publishing concern Rheinisch-Westfaelische Verlagsgesellschaft mbH, Pressehaus NRZ, Sachsenstr 30, 45128 Essen
Representative: Christina McInerney International Ltd, 730 Fifth Ave, Suite 402, New York, NY 10019, USA.
Subjects: Career Development, Computer Science, Economics, Health, Nutrition, Mysteries, Nonfiction (General), Self-Help
Parent Company: Econ Verlagsgruppe
Associate Companies: Groethe str 43, 80336 Munich
Warehouse: VVA, Guetersloh

BOOK

Econ Verlag GmbH+
Paul-Heysestr 28, 80336 Munich
Tel: (089) 5148-0 *Fax:* (089) 5148-2229
Web Site: www.econ-verlag.de *Cable:* ECON-VERLAG
Key Personnel
Chief Executive Officers & Publishers: Heinrich Meyer; Christian Strasser
Marketing: Herbert Borgartz
Rights & Permissions: Felicitas Wendt
Founded: 1950
Subjects: Economics, Fiction, Nonfiction (General), Science (General)
ISBN Prefix(es): 3-430
Subsidiaries: Econ Taschenbuch Verlag GmbH; Marion von Schroeder Verlag GmbH
U.S. Office(s): Jane Starr, Planetarium Station, PO Box 907, New York, NY 10024, United States
Distributor for Stiftung Warentest GmbH (Berlin/Germany)
Warehouse: VVA, An der Autobahn, 33310 Guetersloh

Ede Vau Verlag GmbH
Halskestr 3-5, 47877 Willich
Tel: (02154) 490080 *Fax:* (02154) 490081
E-mail: evvgmbh@tonline.de
Key Personnel
Manager: Horst Stuhlweissenburg
Founded: 1989
ISBN Prefix(es): 3-89428

Edition Aragon-Verlagsgesellschaft mbH+
Neumarkt 7-9, 47441 Moers
Tel: (02841) 16561 *Fax:* (02841) 24336
Key Personnel
President & Publisher: Willi Klauke
Founded: 1984
Subjects: Art, Drama, Theater, Travel
ISBN Prefix(es): 3-89535
Distributed by AVA b+i (Switzerland)
Orders to: Prolit, Siemensstr 18a, 35463 Fernwald/Annerod

Edition Belletriste, *imprint of* Weidler Buchverlag Berlin

Edition Buecherbaer im Arena Verlag, see Arena Verlag GmbH

Edition Heitere Poetik, *imprint of* Verlag Beruf + Schule Belz KG

Edition Jonas, *imprint of* Dr Wolfgang Baur Verlag Kunst & Alltag

Edition Klaus Blahak Dr Fredric Kroll+
Hasburgerstr 78, 79104 Freiburg
Tel: (049) 761-244-73 *Fax:* (049) 761-244-73
Key Personnel
Contact: Stefan Blahak; Dr Fredric Kroll *Tel:* (049) 761-243-77
Founded: 1976
Subjects: Biography, Literature, Literary Criticism, Essays
Total Titles: 10 Print
Publication(s): Biography of Klaus Mann; German Literature in Exile, 1933-1949
Distributed by MaennerschwarmSkript Verlag

Edition Leipzig, *imprint of* Verlagsgruppe Dornier

Edition Mariannepresse
Riesbulldeich 2, 25889 Witzort
Tel: (04864) 660
E-mail: quehilie@onlinehome.de

Edition Markt, *imprint of* Heel Verlag GmbH

edition q Berlin Edition in der Quintessenz Verlags-GmbH+
Ifenpfad 2-4, 12107 Berlin
Mailing Address: Postfach 42 04 52, 12064 Berlin
Tel: (030) 7 61 80-5 *Fax:* (030) 7 61 80-693
E-mail: info@quintessenz.de
Web Site: www.quintessenz.de
Telex: 500/183815
Key Personnel
Publisher: Horst-Wolfgang Haase *Tel:* (030) 761 80-622 *Fax:* (030) 761 80-691
Publishing Director: Johannes W Wolters *Tel:* (030) 761 80-670 *Fax:* (030) 761 80-692
Editor Edition Q: Dr Juergen Schebera *Tel:* (030) 761 80-641
Editor Berlin Edition: Bernhard Thieme *Tel:* (030) 761 80-640
Online Editor: Joachim Liebers *Tel:* (030) 761 80-604 *Fax:* (030) 761 80-693
International Rights: Gerhard Kirsten *Tel:* (030) 761 80-611 *Fax:* (030) 761 80-693
Sales Manager: Helga Schebera *Tel:* (030) 761 80-611 *Fax:* (030) 761 80-692
Marketing: Uwe Janssen *Tel:* (030) 761 80-614 *Fax:* (030) 761 80-680
Commercial Manager: Thomas Fritz *Tel:* (030) 761 80-658 *Fax:* (030) 761 80-692
Manager Electronic Publishing: Andreas Mueller *E-mail:* mueller@quintessenz.de
Advertising: Gudrun Matthes *Tel:* (030) 761 80-629 *Fax:* (030) 761 80-691 *E-mail:* anzeigen@quintessenz.de
Product Manager Offline-Media: Martin Hecklinger *Tel:* (030) 761 80-677 *E-mail:* hecklinger@quintessenz.de
Assistant Manager: Christian Haase *Tel:* (030) 761 80-605
Subscriptions: Angela Koethe *E-mail:* abo@quintessenz.de
Book Orders: Leo Korff *E-mail:* buch@quintessenz.de
Graphics: Ines Bluemel *Tel:* (030) 761 80-608 *Fax:* (030) 761 80-680
Founded: 1990
Member of Boersenverein des Deutschen Buchhandels e.V.
Subjects: Art, History, Literature, Literary Criticism, Essays, Special series on Japanese Literature-Japan Edition. Arts & Culture, Contemporary History, History, Literature
ISBN Prefix(es): 3-86124; 3-928024
Total Titles: 200 Print
Imprints: Quintessenz Verlags GmbH
U.S. Office(s): Quintessence Publishing Co Inc/Édition q Inc, 551 N Kimberly Dr, Carol Stream, IL 60188-1881, United States *Tel:* 630-682-3223 *Fax:* 630-682-3288 *E-mail:* quintpub@aol.com
Foreign Rep(s): Edition q Inc (US); Quintessence Publishing Co Inc (US)
Foreign Rights: Quintessence Publishing Co Ltd (UK)
Shipping Address: LKG Leipziger Kommissions und GroBbuchhandels GmbH, Potzschauer Weg, D-04579 Espenhain, Contact: Ms Angelika Bock *Tel:* (034206) 65220 *Fax:* (034206) 65130
Warehouse: LKG Leipziger Kommissions und Grossbuchhandels GmbH, Potzschauer Weg, D-04579 Espenhain, Contact: Ms Angelika Bock *Tel:* (034206) 65220 *Fax:* (034206) 65130
Orders to: Edition Guides, Quintessenz Verlags GmbH, Berlin, Contact: Ms Helga Schebera *Tel:* (030) 761 80-635 *Fax:* (030) 761 80-692

Edition Solitude - Akademie Schloss Solitude
Solitude 3, 70197 Stuttgart
Tel: (0711) 996190 *Fax:* (0711) 99619-50
E-mail: mail@akademie-solitude.de
Web Site: www.akademie-solitude.de
Key Personnel
Akademie Dir: Jean-Baptiste Joly
Founded: 1989
Publishes literary books, artists' books & catalogs by the Akademie Schloss Solitude fellows only.
Subjects: Architecture & Interior Design, Art, Drama, Theater, Fiction, Music, Dance, Photography
ISBN Prefix(es): 3-929085
Number of titles published annually: 12 Print
Total Titles: 110 Print

Edition Sternenprinz, *imprint of* Hans-Nietsch-Verlag

Edition Tranvia, see Verlag Walter Frey

Edition U, *imprint of* Dr Wolfgang Baur Verlag Kunst & Alltag

editionLuebbe, *imprint of* Verlagsgruppe Luebbe GmbH & Co KG

Egmont EHAPA Verlag GmbH+
Wallstr 59, 10179 Berlin
Mailing Address: Postfach 040740, 10064 Berlin
Tel: (030) 24008-0 *Fax:* (030) 24008-599
Key Personnel
Man Dir: Frank Knau
International Rights: Klaus M Mrositzki
Public Relations Manager: Marion Egenberger *Tel:* (0711) 7971 203 *E-mail:* kontakt@ehapa.de
Founded: 1951
Childrens magazines.
Subjects: Humor, Comics
ISBN Prefix(es): 3-7704
Number of titles published annually: 200 Print
Total Titles: 1,000 Print
Parent Company: Egmont Holding GmbH
Imprints: Delta; Feest
Subsidiaries: Cultfish Entertainment GmbH (Cultfish)
Divisions: OU Character Kids (Comic Magazine & Juvenile Journals); OU Disney Kids (Disney Publication); Egmont Manga @ Anime Europe (Manga)

Egmont Franz Schneider Verlag GmbH+
Schleissheimerstr 267, 80809 Munich
Tel: (089) 3 58 11-6 *Fax:* (089) 3 58 11-7 55
E-mail: postmaster@schneiderbuch.de
Web Site: schneiderbuch.funonline.de
Telex: 05215804
Key Personnel
Publisher: Rehue Heriq
Foreign Rights: Michaela Hauauer
Marketing: Hans-Juergen Schneider
Account: Sabine Sommer
Production: Alfred Lahner
Publicity: Dr Birgit Schumacher
Founded: 1913
Subjects: Fiction, Film, Video, History, Nonfiction (General), Science Fiction, Fantasy, Specialize in Disney books, Television/Film related books
ISBN Prefix(es): 3-505
Parent Company: Egmont

Egmont Pestalozzi-Verlag+
Schleissheimer Str 267, 80809 Munich
Tel: (089) 3 58 11-8 62 *Fax:* (089) 58 11-8 69
E-mail: postmaster@pestalozzi-verlag.de
Web Site: pestalozzi-verlag.funonline.de
Telex: 629766 Pevau *Cable:* PESTALOZZI ERLANGEN
Key Personnel
Man Dir: Dr Reinhold Weigand; Norbert Franke
Editorial, Rights & Permissions: Wolfgang Kaiser
Founded: 1844
Subjects: Crafts, Games, Hobbies
ISBN Prefix(es): 3-614; 3-87624
Subsidiaries: Boje-Verlag
Distributed by Groupe de la Cite (France); Gutenberghus (Scandinavia); Arnoldo Mondadori (Italy); Simon & Schuster (USA)

Egmont vgs verlagsgesellschaft mbH+
Gertrudenstr 30-36, 50667 Cologne
Mailing Address: Postfach 101251, 50452 Cologne
Tel: (0221) 20811-0 *Fax:* (0221) 20811-66
E-mail: info@vgs.de
Web Site: www.vgs.de
Key Personnel
Man Dir: Dr Bernward Malaka *E-mail:* b.malaka@vgs.de
Man Dir & Publisher: Michael Schweins
Communications: Dr Juergen Puetz
Sales: Andrea Rueller
Advertising: Ingrid Reisner
Editorial Dir: Kurt-Juergen Heering; Stefanie Koch
Press Man: Johanna Noelle *E-mail:* j.noelle@vgs.de
Founded: 1970
Market-leading TV tie-in publisher in the German-speaking territory; popular nonfiction on health subjects, illustrated books.
Subjects: Animals, Pets, Art, Asian Studies, Biography, Crafts, Games, Hobbies, Fiction, Film, Video, Foreign Countries, Gardening, Plants, Health, Nutrition, History, House & Home, Music, Dance, Mysteries, Natural History, Nonfiction (General), Outdoor Recreation, Radio, TV, Science Fiction, Fantasy, Travel
ISBN Prefix(es): 3-8025
Number of titles published annually: 120 Print
Total Titles: 500 Print
Parent Company: Egmont Holding GmbH (Berlin)
Imprints: Angel; Buffy; Charmed; Dawson's Creek; Milka; Roswell High; Star Wars; The Stay-at-homes
Warehouse: Cornelsen Verlagskontor, Kammerratsheide 66, 33609 Bielefeld
Orders to: Cornelsen Verlagskontor, Kammerratsheide 66, 33609 Bielefeld

Ehrenwirth Verlag, *imprint of* Verlagsgruppe Luebbe GmbH & Co KG

Ehrenwirth Verlag+
Imprint of Verlagsgruppe Luebbe GmbH & Co KG
Scheidtbachstr 23-31, 51469 Bergisch Gladbach
Mailing Address: Postfach 200180, 51431 Bergisch Gladbach
Tel: (02202) 121-0 *Fax:* (02202) 121-920
E-mail: info@luebbe.de
Web Site: www.luebbe.de
Founded: 1945
Subjects: Fiction, How-to, Nonfiction (General)
ISBN Prefix(es): 3-431
Number of titles published annually: 25 Print

Ehrenwirth Verlag GmbH+
Schwanthalerstr 91, 80336 Munich
Tel: (089) 54 43 35-0 *Fax:* (089) 534739
Web Site: www.ehrenwirth.de
Key Personnel
Man Dir: Eveline Pupeter
Editorial, Rights & Permissions: Dr Rainer Schoettle
Sales, Publicity & Advertising Dir: Ellen Weiss
Press: Elfriede John
Founded: 1945
Member of TR-Verlagsunion GmbH.
Subjects: Biography, Crafts, Games, Hobbies, Fiction, History, How-to, Poetry, Psychology, Psychiatry, Social Sciences, Sociology
ISBN Prefix(es): 3-431

Parent Company: Veritas-Verlag und Handelsgesellschaft mbH, Linz, Austria
Orders to: Verlegerdienst Muenchen, Postfach 1280, 82205 Gilching

Eichborn AG+
Kaiserstr 66, 60329 Frankfurt am Main
Tel: (069) 2560030 *Fax:* (069) 25600330
E-mail: rights@eichborn.de
Web Site: www.eichborn.de
Key Personnel
Chief Executive: Matthias Kierzek
Sales & Publicity: Andreas Horn
Production: Ulrike Bettermann
Publishing Dir: Dr Wolfgang Ferchl
Founded: 1980
Subjects: Fiction, History, Humor, Literature, Literary Criticism, Essays, Mysteries, Nonfiction (General)
ISBN Prefix(es): 3-8218
Imprints: Die Andere Bibliothek

Eiland-Verlag Sylt Frank Roseman
Friesiechestr 53, 25980 Westerland
Tel: (04651) 936212 *Fax:* (04651) 936214
E-mail: info@eiland-verlag.de
Web Site: www.eiland-verlag.de
Founded: 1975
ISBN Prefix(es): 2-922753

Ein Fach-Verlag+
Monheimsallee 21, 52062 Aachen
Tel: (0241) 405501 *Fax:* (0241) 400 96 67
E-mail: einfachverlag@gmx.de
Web Site: www.philosophinnen.de/verlag/index.htm
Founded: 1989
Member of Boersenverein.
Subjects: Language Arts, Linguistics, Philosophy, Religion - Hindu, Science (General), Women's Studies, Feminist Philosophy
ISBN Prefix(es): 3-928089
Total Titles: 26 Print
Orders to: GVA - Gemeinsame Verlagsauslierung, Postfach 20 21, D-37010 Gottingen *Tel:* (0551) 487177 *Fax:* (0551) 41392 *E-mail:* rabe@gva-verlage.de

EinfallsReich Verlagsgesellschaft MbH+
Breitenkamp 43, 37619 Kirchbrak
Tel: (05533) 2017 *Fax:* (0531) 791507
Founded: 1987
Subjects: Art, Environmental Studies, Fiction, Humor, Literature, Literary Criticism, Essays, Music, Dance, Nonfiction (General), Travel
ISBN Prefix(es): 3-926207

Einfuehrungen, *imprint of* Wissenschaftliche Buchgesellschaft

Eironeia-Verlag
Sonnhalde 37, 79194 Gundelfingen
Tel: (0761) 581617 *Fax:* (0761) 581617
Key Personnel
Man Dir: Thomas Ebersberg
Founded: 1987
Subjects: History, Human Relations, Literature, Literary Criticism, Essays, Philosophy
ISBN Prefix(es): 3-926607
Imprints: Ebersberg; Th Kirchbaum, K

Eisenbahn-Kurier Verlag, see EK-Verlag GmbH

EK-Verlag GmbH+
H-V Stephanstr 15, 79100 Freiburg
Mailing Address: Postfach 55 60, 79022 Freiburg
Tel: (0761) 70310-0 *Fax:* (0761) 70310-50
Key Personnel
Man Dir: Rudolf Wesemann
Man Dir & Production: Wolfgang Schumacher
Editorial & Publicity: Klaus Eckert
Editorial: Ingo Seifert
Sales: Karin Klemm
Rights & Permissions: Hansjuergen Wenzel
Founded: 1966
Subjects: Film, Video, Transportation
ISBN Prefix(es): 3-88255

Elefanten Press Verlag GmbH+
Neumarkterstr 18, 81673 Munich
Tel: (01805) 99 05 05
Web Site: www.randomouse.de/elefantenpress/
Key Personnel
Manager: Maruta Schmidt
Sales Manager: Martina Hayo
Public Relations & Rights: Claudia Schulz
Founded: 1977
Subjects: Art, Developing Countries, Government, Political Science, History, Humor, Literature, Literary Criticism, Essays, Mysteries, Photography, Social Sciences, Sociology, Women's Studies
ISBN Prefix(es): 3-88520
Total Titles: 200 Print

Elektor-Verlag, *imprint of* Elektor-Verlag GmbH

Elektor-Verlag GmbH+
Susterfeldstr 25, 52072 Aachen
Tel: (0241) 889090 *Fax:* (0241) 8890988
E-mail: redaktion@elektor.de
Web Site: www.elektor.de
Key Personnel
Man Dir: M M F Landman
Publications Man: A Schommers
Marketing Man: G Klein
Founded: 1972
Member of German Association of Book Distributors.
Subjects: Electronics, Electrical Engineering, Engineering (General), Environmental Studies, Microcomputers, Nonfiction (General), Physical Sciences, Technology, Travel
ISBN Prefix(es): 3-921608; 3-928051
Parent Company: Elektuur BV
Imprints: Elektor-Verlag

Verlag Heinrich Ellermann GmbH & Co KG+
Poppenbuetteler Chaussee 53, 22397 Hamburg
Tel: (040) 60790901 *Fax:* (040) 6072326
E-mail: ellermann@vsg-hamburg.de
Web Site: www.ellermann.de
Key Personnel
Publishing Manager: Gerd Rumler
Founded: 1934
ISBN Prefix(es): 3-7707
Parent Company: Koesel-Verlag GmbH & Co
Orders to: Moderne Industrie Verlagsservice, Landsberg

Ellert & Richter Verlag GmbH+
Grosse Brunnenstr 116, 22763 Hamburg
Tel: (040) 39 84 77-0 *Fax:* (040) 39 84 77-23
E-mail: info@ellert-richter.de
Web Site: www.ellert-richter.de
Key Personnel
International Rights: Marita Ellert-Richter
Founded: 1979
Subjects: Architecture & Interior Design, Art, Foreign Countries, Gardening, Plants, Nonfiction (General), Travel
ISBN Prefix(es): 3-89234
Warehouse: Runge GmbH, Bergstr 2, 4803 Steinhagen

Elpis Verlag GmbH+
Rohrbacherstr 20, 69115 Heidelberg
Tel: (06221) 165789
Key Personnel
Dir: Lothar Faas; Dr Manfred Thiel
Founded: 1977
Subjects: Philosophy, Poetry
ISBN Prefix(es): 3-921806

Karl Elser GmbH Buch-und Zeitungsverlag, see Karl Elser Druck GmbH

N G Elwert Verlag+
Reitgasse 7-9, Pilgrimstein 30, 35037 Marburg
Tel: (06421) 17090 *Fax:* (06421) 15487
E-mail: elwertmail@elwert.de
Web Site: www.elwert.de *Cable:* ELWERT MARBURG
Key Personnel
Man Dir: Rudolph Braun-Elwert
Founded: 1726
Subjects: History, Law, Literature, Literary Criticism, Essays, Religion - Other, Social Sciences, Sociology
ISBN Prefix(es): 3-7708
Bookshop(s): N G Elwert Universitaetsbuchhandlung GmbH & Co KG, Reitgasse 7-9, Pilgrimstein 30, 35037 Marburg/Lahn

Gholam EMAMI
Fritz-von-Rothstr 25, 90249 Nurnberg
Mailing Address: Postfach 810451, 90249 Nurnberg
Tel: (0911) 288356 *Fax:* (0911) 288356
ISBN Prefix(es): 3-9801145

Emons Verlag+
Lutticherstr 38, 50674 Cologne
Tel: (0221) 569 77-0 *Fax:* (0221) 52 49 37
E-mail: info@emons-verlag.de
Web Site: www.emons-verlag.de
Key Personnel
Contact: Hejo Emons; Dr Christel Steinmetz
Founded: 1984
Subjects: Film, Video, Mysteries
ISBN Prefix(es): 3-924491
Total Titles: 120 Print

Encyclopedia Britannica
Rosenstr 12/13, 48143 Munster
Tel: (0251) 48 227-0 *Fax:* (0251) 48 227-27
E-mail: lexikadienst@aol.com
Web Site: www.britannica.de
Key Personnel
Contact: Hans-Dieter Blatter

Engel & Bengel Verlag+
Haardtweg 3, 67273 Bobenheim
Tel: (06353) 8107 *Fax:* (06353) 507057
E-mail: verlag@engelundbengel.de
Web Site: www.engelundbengel.de
Founded: 1990
Subjects: Animals, Pets, Disability, Special Needs, Fiction, How-to, Human Relations
ISBN Prefix(es): 3-928129
Orders to: Verlag Koch, Neff & Oetinger, Stuttgart
Koehler & Volckmar, Cologne

Engelhorn Verlag+
Neckarstr 121, 70190 Stuttgart
Tel: (0711) 2631-0 *Fax:* (0711) 2631-292 *Cable:* uber 71 11193-DVA
Key Personnel
Publisher: Jurgen Horbach
Founded: 1860
Subjects: Biography
ISBN Prefix(es): 3-87203
Parent Company: Deutsche Verlags-Anstalt GmbH

Englisch Verlag GmbH+
Topferstr 14, D-65191 Wiesbaden
Mailing Address: Postfach 2309, 65013 Wiesbaden
Tel: (0611) 9 427 2-0 *Fax:* (0611) 9 42 72-40
E-mail: englisch@englisch-verlag.de

PUBLISHERS

GERMANY

Web Site: www.englisch-verlag.de
Key Personnel
Publisher: Tring T Englisch *Tel:* (0611) 9 42 72-18 *E-mail:* fe@englischverlag.de
Program Management: Britta Sopp *Tel:* (0611) 9 42 72-15 *E-mail:* programm@englischverlag.de
Sales: Carmen Gildemeister *Tel:* (0611) 9 42 72-12 *E-mail:* verkauf1@englischverlag.de
Lektorat: Tina Heuser *Tel:* (0611) 9 42 72-14 *E-mail:* lektorat1@englischverlag.de
Press: Sandra Wants *Tel:* (0611) 9 42 72-16 *E-mail:* presse@englischverlag.de
Founded: 1973
Boresenverein des Deutschen Buchhandels.
Subjects: Art, Crafts, Games, Hobbies, How-to
ISBN Prefix(es): 3-8241
Number of titles published annually: 80 Print
Total Titles: 300 Print
Foreign Rep(s): Schweizer Buchzentrum (Switzerland); Dr Franz Hain (Austria)
Warehouse: VVA Vereinigle Verlagsausheferung, 33310 Guetersloh, Ms Muller *Tel:* (05241) 803893 *Fax:* (05241) 46750
Orders to: VVA Bertelsmann Distribution, Postfach 7777, 33310 Guetersloh

Verlag Peter Engstler
Oberwaldbehrungen 10, 97645 Ostheim
Tel: (09774) 858490 *Fax:* (09774) 858491
E-mail: engstler-verlag@t-online.de
Web Site: www.engstler-verlag.de
Key Personnel
Contact: Peter Engstler
Founded: 1988
Subjects: Art, Fiction, Government, Political Science, Literature, Literary Criticism, Essays, Poetry
ISBN Prefix(es): 3-929375; 3-9801770; 3-9802826

Enke, *imprint of* Georg Thieme Verlag KG

Ensslin Jugendbuchverlag, see Ensslin und Laiblin Verlag GmbH & Co KG

Ensslin und Laiblin Verlag GmbH & Co KG+
Harretstr 6, 72800 Eningen
Tel: (01721) 98 98 0 *Fax:* (01721) 98 98 44
E-mail: ensslin-verlag@t-online.de
Web Site: www.ensslin-verlag.de *Cable:* BUCHHAUS REUTLINGEN
Key Personnel
Man Dir, Rights & Permissions: Ariane Hanfstein *Tel:* (07121) 989822
Sales Dir: Joachim Hanfstein *Tel:* (01721) 989825
Production: Birgit Weber *Tel:* (07121) 989831
Public Relations, Advertising: Friederike Tiemann *Tel:* (07121) 989829
Founded: 1818
Specialize in children's & juvenile literature & in highly qualified teaching materials for pre-school & elementary school children. A special focus of the program is on "playing & learning" educational aids like the "Ensslin-Lernpuck®" or the "New learning games" (NELS) which enable children to exercise topics of various subjects at their very own pace. A new kind of educational aid are the "Duesenberg-Kids" - funny comics combined with detailed information & activity-tips which encourage children to have self-confidence & sense of responsibility.
Member of Association of Children's Books.
Subjects: Education, Fiction, Literature, Literary Criticism, Essays, Nonfiction (General), Science Fiction, Fantasy
ISBN Prefix(es): 3-7709
Total Titles: 180 Print
Warehouse: Libri Distributions GmbH, August-Schanz-Str 33, 60433 Frankfurt *Tel:* 069 95422219 *Fax:* 069 542013

Ensslin Verlag im Arena Verlag, *imprint of* Arena Verlag GmbH

EOS Verlag der Benefiktiner der Erzabtel St. Ottilien+
Formerly EOS Verlag, Erzabtei Sankt Ottilien+
86941 St Ottilien
Tel: (08193) 71261 *Fax:* (08193) 6844
E-mail: mail@eos-verlag.de
Web Site: www.eos-verlag.de
Key Personnel
Man Dir: P Walter Sedlmeier
Founded: 1885
Subjects: Art, Fiction, History, Religion - Other, Theology
ISBN Prefix(es): 3-88096; 3-920289
Subsidiaries: Druckerei
Divisions: Satz, Repro, Druckerei, Buchbiudeve
Bookshop(s): Klosterladen, Erzabtei St Ottilien, 86941 Sankt Ottilien

EOS Verlag, Erzabtei Sankt Ottilien+, see EOS Verlag der Benefiktiner der Erzabtei St. Ottilien

Eppinger-Verlag OHG
Stauffenbergstr 18-10, 74523 Schwaebisch Hall
Tel: (0791) 95061-0 *Fax:* (0791) 95061-40
E-mail: info@eppinger-verlag.de *Cable:* EPPINGER-VERLAG SCHWAEBISCH HALL
Key Personnel
Man Dir: Hans Paul Eppinger
Founded: 1970
Subjects: Business, Career Development, Developing Countries, Economics, Foreign Countries, Management, Regional Interests, Technology
ISBN Prefix(es): 3-87176

Erasmus Grasser-Verlag GmbH
Bachtal 6, 86978 Hohenfurch
Tel: (08861) 241900 *Fax:* (08861) 241901
Key Personnel
Manager: Wolfgang Vogelsgesang
Founded: 1974
ISBN Prefix(es): 3-925967

Verlag Peter Erd GmbH+
Gaissacherstr 18, 81371 Munich
Tel: (089) 725 30 04 *Fax:* (089) 725 01 41
Key Personnel
Man Dir & Other Offices: Peter Erd
Customer Service: Sabina Ferhatbegovic *Tel:* (08015) 388-306
Accounts Receivable: Ingrid Nottensteiner *Tel:* (08105) 388-327
Founded: 1975
Subjects: Health, Nutrition, Human Relations, Parapsychology
ISBN Prefix(es): 3-8138

Edition Erdmann, *imprint of* K Thienemanns Verlag

Eremiten-Presse und Verlag GmbH
Fortunastr 11, 40235 Duesseldorf
Mailing Address: Postfach 170143, 40082 Duesseldorf
Tel: (0211) 66 05 90 *Fax:* (0211) 698 94 70
Key Personnel
Man Dir: Friedolin Reske; Jens D Olsson
Founded: 1949
Subjects: Art, Fiction, Poetry
ISBN Prefix(es): 3-87365

Eres Editions-Horst Schubert Musikverlag
Haupstr 35, 28865 Lilienthal
Mailing Address: Postfach 1220, 28859 Lilienthal
Tel: (04298) 1676 *Fax:* (04298) 5312
E-mail: info@eres-musik.de
Web Site: www.eres-musik.de

Key Personnel
Man Dir: Horst Schubert
Founded: 1946
Subjects: Music, Dance
ISBN Prefix(es): 3-87204

ERF-Verlag GmbH+
Berliner Ring 62, 35576 Wetzlar
Mailing Address: c/o Bundes-Verlag, Postfach 40 86, 58246 Witten
Tel: (06441) 9570 *Fax:* (06441) 957120
E-mail: info@erf.de
Web Site: www.erf.de
Key Personnel
Chairman: Ulrich Ruesch; Juergen Werth
Man Dir: Thomas Quast
Head Sales & Distribution: Lars Kissner
Founded: 1978
Specialize in audio & video.
Subjects: Music, Dance, Religion - Other
ISBN Prefix(es): 3-89562
Parent Company: Evangeliums-Rundfunk eV
Branch Office(s)
Vienna, Austria
Zurich, Switzerland
U.S. Office(s): Trans World Radio, Cary, NC, United States

Ergebnisse Verlag GmbH+
Abendrothsweg 58, 20251 Hamburg
Tel: (040) 4801027 *Fax:* (040) 4801592
Key Personnel
Editor: Dietrich Lueders; Wolfgang Schwibbe; Michael Wildt
Sales, Rights & Permissions: Dr Thomas Neumann
Sales, Advertising & Publicity: Inge Busch
Founded: 1978
Subjects: Health, Nutrition, History, Medicine, Nursing, Dentistry, Psychology, Psychiatry, Regional Interests
ISBN Prefix(es): 3-87916
Orders to: PNV Petersen und Nieswand Vertriebsservice GmbH, Werftbahnstr 8, 24143 Kiel

Ergon Verlag Dr H J Dietrich+
Grombuehlstr 7, 97080 Wurzburg
Tel: (0931) 280084 *Fax:* (0931) 282872
E-mail: service@ergon-verlag.de
Web Site: www.ergon-verlag.de
Key Personnel
Press: Brigitte Miebach-Schrader
E-mail: miebach-schrader@ergon-verlag.de
Contact: Dr Hans-Juergen Dietrich *E-mail:* dr.dietrich@ergon-verlag.de
ISBN Prefix(es): 3-928034; 3-932004; 3-933563

Erlanger Verlag Fuer Mission und Okumene
(Erlanger Publishing House for Missions & Ecumerics)+
Hauptstr 2, 91564 Neuendettelsau
Mailing Address: Postfach 68, 91561 Neuendettelsau
Tel: (09131) 33064 *Fax:* (09131) 39481
E-mail: erlanger.verlag@gmx.de
Key Personnel
Director: Dr Johannes Triebel
Founded: 1897
Subjects: Asian Studies, Developing Countries, Religion - Islamic, Religion - Other, Theology, Specialize in African studies
ISBN Prefix(es): 3-87214
Total Titles: 106 Print
Parent Company: Evang Luth Church in Bavaria, Germany

Ernst Kabel Verlag GmbH+
Imprint of Piper Verlag Gmbh
Georgeustr 4, 80799 Munich
Tel: (089) 381801-0 *Fax:* (089) 338704
E-mail: info@piper.de
Web Site: www.kabel-verlag.de

GERMANY

Key Personnel
Publisher: Victor Niemann
Man Dir: Hartmyt Jedicke
Editorial: Bettiva Feldweg
Founded: 1977
Specialize in gift books.
Subjects: Biography, Fiction, Nonfiction (General), Psychology, Psychiatry, Self-Help
ISBN Prefix(es): 3-8225
Number of titles published annually: 25 Print
Ultimate Parent Company: Bounier Media Holding GmbH
Orders to: Koch Neff Ogtinger & Co, Schockenriedstr 39, 7055A Stuttgart

Ernst, Wilhelm & Sohn, Verlag Architektur und technische Wissenschaft GmbH & Co+
Buhringstr 10, 13086 Berlin
Tel: (030) 47031-200 *Fax:* (030) 47031-270
E-mail: info@ernst-und-sohn.de
Web Site: www.ernst-und-sohn.de
Key Personnel
Dir: Dagmar Stehle
Editorial, Rights & Permissions: Monika Herr
Founded: 1851
Subjects: Architecture & Interior Design, Civil Engineering, Technology
ISBN Prefix(es): 3-433
Parent Company: Wiley-VCH Verlag GmbH, Boschstr 12, 69469 Weinheim
Shipping Address: VSW GmbH, Postfach 1355, 68745 Waghaeusel
Warehouse: Wiley-VCH Verlag GmbH, Boschstr 12, 69469 Weinheim

Ertraege der Forschung zur Forschung-, *imprint of* Wissenschaftliche Buchgesellschaft

Verlagsgesellschaft des Erziehungsvereins GmbH+
Andreas-Braemstr 18-20, 47506 Neukirchen-Vluyn
Tel: (02845) 392-222 *Fax:* (02845) 33689
E-mail: info@neukirchener-verlag.de
Web Site: www.neukirchener-verlag.de *Cable:* VERLAGSHAUS NEUKIRCHEN VLUYN
Key Personnel
Man Dir: Jochen Boeckler; Dr Rudolf Weth
Publishing Manager: Dr Volker Hampel
 E-mail: verlagsleitung@neukirchener-verlag.de
Sales Representative: Stefan Schubert
 E-mail: vertrieb@neukirchener-verlag.de
Lecturer: Ekkehard Starke *E-mail:* letkorat@neukirchener-verlag.de
Production: Hans Hegner *E-mail:* herstellung@neukirchener-verlag.de; Karin Jacobs *E-mail:* herstellung@neukirchener-verlag.de; Volker Kuschnik *E-mail:* herstellung@neukirchener-verlag.de
Advertising: Christoph Siepermann
 E-mail: vertrieb@neukirchener-verlag.de
Dispatch Bookshop: Angelika Boos *Tel:* (02845) 392-218 *E-mail:* vsb@neukirchener-verlag.de
Subjects: Religion - Protestant, Theology
ISBN Prefix(es): 3-7615; 3-7887; 3-920524
Online services available through World Wide Web.
Associate Companies: Aussaat Verlag; Kalenderverlag des Erziehungsvereins; Neukirchener Verlag

Verlag am Eschbach GmbH+
lm Alten Rathaus, Haupstr 37, 79427 Eschbach/Markgraeflerland
Tel: (07634) 1088 *Fax:* (07634) 3796
E-mail: e-mail@verlag-am-eschbach.de
Web Site: www.verlag-am-eschbach.de
Key Personnel
Gesellschafter-Geschaeftsfuehrers: Heribert Mohr; Martin Schmeisser; Juergen Schwarz
Founded: 1979

Subjects: Art, Religion - Catholic, Religion - Protestant
ISBN Prefix(es): 3-88671

Esogetics GmbH+
Hildastr 8, 76646 Bruchsal
Mailing Address: Postfach 2060, 76610 Bruchsal
Tel: (07251) 8001-30 *Fax:* (07251) 8001-55
E-mail: info-de@esogetics.com
Web Site: www.esogetics.com
Key Personnel
Man Dir: Sophocles Amanatidis *E-mail:* sa@esogetics.com; Markus Wunderlich
Founded: 1988
Subjects: Health, Nutrition, Medicine, Nursing, Dentistry, Science (General)
ISBN Prefix(es): 3-925806
Total Titles: 2 Print
Foreign Rep(s): Techiche Nuove, Hay
Foreign Rights: Techiche Nuove, Hay (Spain)

Esotere Taschenbuch, *imprint of* Verlag Hermann Bauer KG

Verlag Esoterische Philosophie GmbH
Goedekeweg 8, 30419 Hannover
Tel: (0511) 755331 *Fax:* (0511) 755334
E-mail: info@esoterische-philosophie.de
Web Site: www.esoterische-philosophie.de
Key Personnel
Art Dir: Matthias Winter
Contact: Baerbel Ackermann
Founded: 1984
Specializes in: Translations of English literature.
Subjects: Anthropology, Astrology, Occult, Parapsychology, Philosophy, Religion - Buddhist, Religion - Other, Science (General), Cosmology, Science of Religions
ISBN Prefix(es): 3-924849

Esslinger Verlag J F Schreiber GmbH+
Marktplatz 19, 73728 Esslingen
Mailing Address: Postfach 10 03 25, 73703 Esslingen
Tel: (0711) 310594-6 *Fax:* (0711) 310594-77
E-mail: esslinger@klett-mail.de
Key Personnel
Man Dir: Franz Scharetzer
Man Dir & Publishing Dir: Mathias Berg
Editor, Publicity: Sabine Frankholz
Editor: Urte Fiutak
Founded: 1831
ISBN Prefix(es): 3-480
Parent Company: Ernst Klett Information, Oesterreichischer Bundesverlag

Eulen Verlag+
Hebelstr 11, 79104 Freiburg im Breisgau
Tel: (0761) 2 62 67 *Fax:* (0761) 2 58 61
E-mail: info@eulenverlag.de
Web Site: www.eulen-verlag.de
Key Personnel
Owner & Publisher: Harald Glaeser
Founded: 1983
Subjects: Art, Crafts, Games, Hobbies, Outdoor Recreation, Photography, Regional Interests, Travel
ISBN Prefix(es): 3-89102
Total Titles: 125 Print
Warehouse: Libri Distributions Gmbh, August-Schanzstr 33, 60433 Frankfurt am Main

Eulenhof-Verlag Wolfgang Ehrhardt Heinold+
Iris Wolf, Appener Weg 3b, 20251 Hamburg
Tel: (040) 49 00 05-0 *Fax:* (040) 49 00 05-15
E-mail: eulenwolf@compuserve.com
Web Site: www.eulenhof.de
Key Personnel
Man Dir: Iris Wolf *Tel:* (0171) 4181248
Founded: 1981

Membership(s): Borsenverein Des Deutschen Buchhandels & Arbetskreis Fur Jugendliteratur E.V. Specialize in information on children's media, also online.
Subjects: Library & Information Sciences
ISBN Prefix(es): 3-88710
Number of titles published annually: 1 Print
Total Titles: 3 Print
Online services available through World Wide Web.
Associate Companies: Eulenhof Institut, WE Heinold Beratungs Gesellschaft mbH, Contact: Wolfgang Ehrhardt Heinold *Tel:* (040) 4900050 *Fax:* (040) 49000515 *E-mail:* eulenwolf@compuserve.com
Branch Office(s)
Nuernbergerstr 25, 86609 Donauwoerth
Tel: (0906) 24 61-17 *Fax:* (0906) 24 61-16
E-mail: m.j.bock@eulenhof.de

Europ Export Edition GmbH
Berliner Allee 8, 64295 Darmstadt
Mailing Address: Postfach 10 02 62, 64202 Darmstadt
Tel: (06151) 51-38 92 0 *Fax:* (06151) 51-3 31 64; (06151) 38 92 80
E-mail: info@abconline.de
Web Site: www.abconline.de
Key Personnel
Publisher: Margit Selka
Founded: 1958
ISBN Prefix(es): 3-87208
Foreign Rep(s): Export Edition SA (France, Italy, Switzerland)

Verlag Europa-Lehrmittel, Nourney, Vollmer GmbH & Co+
Duesselbergerstr 23, 42781 Haan-Gruiten
Mailing Address: Postfach 21 60, 42781 Haan-Gruiten
Tel: (02104) 6916-0 *Fax:* (02104) 6916-27
Web Site: www.europa-lehrmittel.de
Key Personnel
General Manager, Rights & Permissions: Joachim Nourney
Editor: Armin Steinmueller
Sales: Wolfgang Baldauf
Founded: 1947
Subjects: Automotive, Computer Science, Economics, Electronics, Electrical Engineering, Geography, Geology, Physics
ISBN Prefix(es): 3-8085

Europa Union Verlag GmbH+
Bachstr 32, 53115 Bonn
Mailing Address: Postfach 1529, 53005 Bonn
Tel: (0228) 7 29 00 10 *Fax:* (0228) 7 29 00 13
E-mail: Service@euverlag.de
Web Site: www.europa-union-verlag.de
Key Personnel
Man Dir, Rights & Permissions: Gerhard Eickhorn
Sales: Rainer Mertens; Rothe Ulrike
Founded: 1959
Subjects: Government, Political Science
ISBN Prefix(es): 3-7713
Subsidiaries: Verlag fur Internationale Politik GmbH
Warehouse: VVA, Postfach 7777, 33310 Guetersloh

Europa Verlag GmbH+
Neuer Wall 10, 20354 Hamburg
Tel: (040) 355434-0 *Fax:* (040) 355434-66
E-mail: info@europaverlag.de
Web Site: www.europaverlag.de *Cable:* EUROPAVERLAG
Key Personnel
Manager: Vito von Eichborn
Editorial Dir, Sales & International Rights: Gisela Anna Stuempel

International Rights: Peter Hahn
 E-mail: lizenzen@europaverlag.de
Publisher Reader: Dr Edgar Bracht; Afra Margaretha
Press: Eva Betzwieser *E-mail:* presse@europaverlag.de
Programmer: Aenne Glienke
Production: Frank Wagner *E-mail:* herstellung@europaverlag.de
Founded: 1933
Subjects: Biography, Fiction, Government, Political Science, Literature, Literary Criticism, Essays, Mysteries, Nonfiction (General), Philosophy
ISBN Prefix(es): 3-203
Parent Company: Europaverlag GmbH Muenich
Subsidiaries: Europaverlag GmbH
Foreign Rep(s): Tom Franke (Germany); Gabriele Funcke (Germany); Barbara Haab (Switzerland); Mareile Handrich (Germany); Peter Handrich (Germany); Juergen Niemeier (Germany); Guenther Poelking-Henkel (Germany); Achim Reigel (Germany); Raimund Thomas (Germany); Guenter Weber (Germany); Okkar Wuthe (Austria)

Europaeische Verlagsanstalt GmbH & Rotbuch Verlag GmbH & Co KG+
Bei den Muehren 70, 20457 Hamburg
Tel: (040) 45 01 94-0 *Fax:* (040) 45 01 94 55
E-mail: info@rotbuch.de
Web Site: www.rotbuch.de; www.europaeische-verlagsanstalt.de
Key Personnel
Publisher: Dr Sabine Groenewold
Editor: Irlen Kauser
International Rights: Helge Juergens *Tel:* (040) 45 01 94-31
Lektorat - Literature: Olaf Irlenkaeuser *Fax:* (040) 45 01 94-50 *E-mail:* irlenkaeuser@rotbuch.de
Lektorat - Special Book: Knuellig Christina *Fax:* (040) 45 01 94-50 *E-mail:* knuellig@rotbuch.de
Film: Gabriele Dietze *Tel:* (030) 240 09-626 *Fax:* (030) 240 09-626 *E-mail:* krimi@rotbuch.de; Lisa Kuppler *Tel:* (030) 240 09-626 *Fax:* (030) 240 09-626 *E-mail:* krimi@rotbuch.de
Founded: 1946
Subjects: Anthropology, Architecture & Interior Design, Biography, Criminology, Government, Political Science, History, Literature, Literary Criticism, Essays, Philosophy
ISBN Prefix(es): 3-434; 3-88022
Total Titles: 600 Print; 2 CD-ROM
Subsidiaries: Rotbuch Verlag; Syndikat Autoren und Verlagsgesellschaft
Foreign Rep(s): Rolf-Peter Baacke (Germany); Richard Bhend (Switzerland); Fina Bothur (Germany); Fritz Denke (Germany); Karlheinz Flessenkemper (Germany); Edwin Gantert (Germany); Stefan Moedritscher (Austria); Guenther Raunjak (Austria); Juergen Stelling (Germany); Verena Suery (Switzerland)

Verlag Europaeische Wehrkunde+
Steintorwall 17, 32052 Herford
Tel: (0228) 340884 *Fax:* (040) 79713304
Key Personnel
Publisher: Peter Tamm
Manager: Lothar Lichtenheldt
Associate Companies: Verlagsgruppe Koehler/Mittler, Steintorwall 17, 32052 Herford
Branch Office(s)
Austr 19, 53179 Bonn *Tel:* (0228) 530962-64 *Fax:* (0228) 230102

Evangelische Haupt-Bibelgesellschaft und von Cansteinsche Bibelanstalt+
Ziegelstr 30, 10117 Berlin
Tel: (030) 2827573 *Fax:* (030) 2824266
E-mail: kontakt@ehbg.de
Web Site: www.bibelgesellschaftberlin.de
Key Personnel
Church President: Helge Klasson
Man Dir & Pastor: Friedrich Delius *Tel:* (030) 288788500 *E-mail:* delius@ehbg.de
Founded: 1814
Subjects: Literature, Literary Criticism, Essays
ISBN Prefix(es): 3-7461

Evangelische Verlagsanstalt GmbH+
Blumenstr 76, 04155 Leipzig
Mailing Address: Postfach 221561, 04135 Leipzig
Tel: (0341) 7 11 41-0 *Fax:* (0341) 7 11 41 40
E-mail: info@eva-leipzig.de
Web Site: www.eva-leipzig.de *Cable:* EVAVERLAG LEIPZIG
Key Personnel
Dir: Ulrich Roebbelen
Founded: 1946
Subjects: Biblical Studies, Biography, Fiction, Religion - Protestant, Religion - Other, Theology
ISBN Prefix(es): 3-374
Total Titles: 270 Print
Bookshop(s): Buchhandlung an der Thomaskirche, Burgstr 1, 04109 Leipzig; C L Ungelenk Kreuzstr 7, 01067 Dresden *Tel:* (0351) 4969804
Warehouse: Leipziger Kommissions- und Grosbuchhandelsgesellschaft, Potzschauer Weg, 04579 Espenhain
Orders to: Leipziger Kommissions- und Grossbuchhandelsgesellschaft, Potzchauer Weg, 04579 Espenhain

Evangelischer Presseverband fur Bayern eV+
Birkerstr 22, 80636 Munich
Tel: (089) 121 72-111; (089) 121 72-110; (089) 121 72-0 *Fax:* (089) 121 72-138
E-mail: verlag@epv.de
Web Site: www.epv.de
Telex: 523718
Key Personnel
Dir: Hartmut Joisten
Publisher: Dr Manuel Zelger
International Rights: Antje Fritsch-Brown *Tel:* (089) 12172132 *E-mail:* afritsch@epv.de
Founded: 1932
Bavarian Evangelical Press Union.
Subjects: Philosophy, Theology
ISBN Prefix(es): 3-583
Total Titles: 60 Print

Evangelischer Presseverband STET Baden eVerlag
Vorholzstr 7, 76137 Karlsruhe
Mailing Address: Postfach 2280, 76010 Karlsruhe
Tel: (0721) 932750 *Fax:* (0721) 9175950
Key Personnel
Manager: Herwig Schelling
Subjects: Religion - Protestant
ISBN Prefix(es): 3-87210
Subsidiaries: Hans Thoma Verlag

EVT Energy Video Training & Verlag GmbH
Waldschmidstr 113, 60314 Frankfurt am Main
Tel: (069) 431575 *Fax:* (069) 2169852
Key Personnel
Author: Marianne Uhl
International Rights: Karsten Schloberg
 E-mail: kschloberg@aol.com
Founded: 1991
Subjects: Alternative, Astrology, Occult, Medicine, Nursing, Dentistry, Music, Dance, Parapsychology, Psychology, Psychiatry, Self-Help, Esoteric, Healing, Meditation
ISBN Prefix(es): 3-930255

Exil Verlag+
Rheinstr 20, 60325 Frankfurt
Mailing Address: PO Box 170234, 60076 Frankfurt 1M
Tel: (069) 751102 *Fax:* (069) 751547
E-mail: fs7a020@uni-hamburg.de
Key Personnel
Publisher: Edita Koch *Tel:* (069) 751102
Founded: 1981
A journal about literature, arts, theater, film & science of Germans in exile 1933-1945. Books about German theater in exile 1933-1945.
Subjects: Specialize in books & magazines about German writers, artists, scientists in Exile 1933-1945
Total Titles: 36 Print
Distributed by Otto Harrassowitz

expert verlag GmbH, Fachverlag fur Wirtschaft & Technik+
Wankelstr 13, 71272 Renningen
Tel: (07159) 92 65-0 *Fax:* (07159) 92 65-20
E-mail: expert@expertverlag.de
Web Site: www.expertverlag.de
Key Personnel
Publisher: Elmar Wippler
Editor: Dr Arnulf Krais *Tel:* (07159) 92 65-12 *E-mail:* krais@expertverlag.de
Advertising: Rainer Paulsen *Tel:* (07159) 92 65-16 *E-mail:* paulsen@expertverlag.de
Press: Christa Beran *Tel:* (07159) 92 65-16 *E-mail:* presse@expertverlag.de
Founded: 1979
Subjects: Electronics, Electrical Engineering, Energy, Environmental Studies, Management, Mechanical Engineering
ISBN Prefix(es): 3-8169
Number of titles published annually: 100 Print
Total Titles: 800 Print
Online services available through World Wide Web.
Distributed by Baufachverlag (Switzerland); Lindeverlag (Austria); Schweizer Baudokumentation (Switzerland)

Expolibri GmbH
Buchwebung & Austellungen Gerichtsweg 26, 0-7010 Leipzig
Tel: (0341) 2113 231 *Fax:* (0341) 2115 996
Key Personnel
Man Dir: Marion Renker
Founded: 1991

Extent Verlag und Service Wolfgang M Flamm+
Pestalozzistr 64, 10627 Berlin-Charlottenburg
Tel: (030) 3279805-11 *Fax:* (030) 3279805-35
E-mail: extent@t-online.de
Key Personnel
International Rights: Flamm Wolfgang-Martin
Founded: 1987
Subjects: Art, Astrology, Occult, Communications, Fashion, Human Relations, Literature, Literary Criticism, Essays, Music, Dance
ISBN Prefix(es): 3-926671
Imprints: Pixel Transfer Design Studio

F A Brockhaus, GmbH
Dudenstr 6, 68167 Mannheim
Tel: (0341) 9786-30 *Fax:* (0341) 9786-560
Web Site: www.brockhaus.de
Key Personnel
Contact: Dieter Baer; Dr Karl-Josef Schmidt; Dr Michael Wegner
Founded: 1805
Parent Company: Bibliographisches Institut & F A Brockhaus AG, Mannheim

F Bruckmann Munchen Verlag & Druck GmbH & Co Produkt KG+
Innsbrucker Ring 15, 81637 Munich
Mailing Address: Postfach 80 02 40, 81602 Munich
Tel: (089) 13 06 99 11 *Fax:* (089) 13 06 99 10
E-mail: info@bruckmann.de
Web Site: www.bruckmann-verlag.de *Cable:* BRUCKMANNKOGE MUNICH

Key Personnel
Editor & Publishing Manager: Dr Joerg D Stiebner
Editor: Michael Wellbrock
Sales Manager: Dr Klaus Beckschulte *Tel:* (089) 13 06 99 48 *E-mail:* klaus.beckschulte@bruckmann.de; Andreas von Bleichert *Tel:* (089) 13 06 99 49 *E-mail:* andreas.vonbleichert@bruckmann.de
Marketing Manager: Thilo Heller *Tel:* (089) 89 13 06 99 45 *E-mail:* thilo.heller@bruckmann.de
Manager, Magazines & Periodicals: Dr Regine Hahn *Tel:* (089) 13 06 99 17 *E-mail:* regine.hahn@bruckmann.de
Sales: Maria Elisabeth Jantzer
Publicity: Barbara Aschenberner
Production: Helmut Huber
Sales & Trade Service: Nina Baier *Tel:* (089) 13 06 99 14 *E-mail:* nina.baier@bruckmann.de; Angelika Maerz *Tel:* (089) 13 06 99 15 *E-mail:* angelika.maerz@bruckmann.de
Customer Service: Sabine Korb *Tel:* (089) 13 06 99 15 *E-mail:* sabine.korb@bruckmann.de
Press: Carola Schindler *Tel:* (089) 13 06 99 27 *E-mail:* carola.schindler@bruckmann.de
Product Management: Renate Dernedde *E-mail:* renate.dernedde@bruckmann.de; Robert Rischer *E-mail:* robert.fischer@bruckmann.de; Diana Thaler *E-mail:* diana.thaler@bruckmann.de
Founded: 1858
Member of TR - Verlagsunion GmbH.
Subjects: Art, Film, Video, Gardening, Plants, History, Humor, Outdoor Recreation, Regional Interests, Science (General), Travel
ISBN Prefix(es): 3-7654

FAB-Verlag+
Uhlandstr 179/180, 10623 Berlin
Tel: (030) 88 92 16 42 *Fax:* (030) 88 92 16 50
E-mail: e-mail@fab-berlin.de
Web Site: www.fab-berlin.de
Key Personnel
Man Dir: Guenther Fannei; Klaus Siebenhaar
International Rights: Sibulle Soering
Founded: 1987
Subjects: Architecture & Interior Design, Communications, History, Marketing, Music, Dance, Nonfiction (General), Regional Interests
ISBN Prefix(es): 3-927551
Orders to: Buchvertrieb Grimmstra, Saalburgstr 3, 12099 Berlin

Fabel-Verlag Gudrun Liebchen+
Kirchenstr 6, 97657 Sandberg
Tel: (09701) 1463 *Fax:* (09701) 1463
Key Personnel
Dir: Gudrun Liebchen
Founded: 1989
Subjects: Drama, Theater, Environmental Studies, Literature, Literary Criticism, Essays, Nonfiction (General), Poetry
ISBN Prefix(es): 3-9802142

Fabylon-Verlag+
Forststr 10-12, 80997 Munich
Tel: (089) 8110881 *Fax:* (089) 8110882
Key Personnel
Publisher, Editor, Rights & Permissions: Gerald Jambor
Publisher & Authoress: Uschi Zietsch-Jambor
Founded: 1987
Member of the Stock Exchange of German Booksellers.
Subjects: Mysteries, Science Fiction, Fantasy
ISBN Prefix(es): 3-927071

Fachbuchverlag Pfanneberg & Co
Duesselbergstr 23, 42781 Haan-Gruiten
Mailing Address: Postfach 21 60, 42765 Haan-Gruiten
Tel: (02104) 6916-0 *Fax:* (02104) 6916-27
E-mail: gero.pfanneberg@giessen.netsurf.de
Web Site: www.pfanneberg.de
Key Personnel
Man Dir, Rights & Permissions: Dr Guenther Pfanneberg
Production: Gerhard Duske
Founded: 1949
Subjects: Business, Career Development, Cookery, Health, Nutrition
ISBN Prefix(es): 3-8057

Fachbuchverlag Leipzig im Carl Hanser Verlag+
Kolbergerstr 22, 81679 Munich
Mailing Address: Postfach 86 04 20, 81631 Munich
Tel: (089) 9 98 30 0 *Fax:* (089) 98 48 09
E-mail: info@hanser.de
Web Site: www.hanser.de *Cable:* FACHBUCH LEIPZIG
Key Personnel
Man Dir, Publisher, Rights & Permissions: Wolfgang Beisler
Sales: Barbara Kothe
International Rights: Evelyn Waizenegger
Editorial: Christine Fritzsch; Erika Hotho; Lochen Horn
Technical Book - Press: Barbara Elias
Tel: (089) 99830 313 *Fax:* (089) 99830 269 *E-mail:* elias@hanser.de
Literary Press: Christina Knecht *E-mail:* knecht@hanser.de
Special Book - Press: Kirsten Vogelsang *E-mail:* vogelsang@hanser.de
Webmaster: Martin Schweizer *Tel:* (089) 99 830-258 *E-mail:* schweizer@hanser.de
Technical Computer: Fernando Schneider *Tel:* (089) 998 30-315 *E-mail:* fernando.schneider@hanser.de
Founded: 1949
Subjects: Chemistry, Chemical Engineering, Computer Science, Crafts, Games, Hobbies, Electronics, Electrical Engineering, Engineering (General), Environmental Studies, Mathematics, Mechanical Engineering, Microcomputers, Physical Sciences, Physics, Technology
ISBN Prefix(es): 3-446
Parent Company: Carl Hanser Verlag, Kolbergerstr 22, Munich 81679
Shipping Address: Verlegerdienst Munich GmbH & Co KG, Gutenbergstr 1, D-82429 Gilching *Tel:* (8105) 388128 *Fax:* (8105) 388100
Warehouse: Verlegerdienst Munich GmbH & Co KG, Gutenbergstr 1, D-82429 Gilching *Tel:* (8105) 388128 *Fax:* (8105) 388100
Orders to: Verlegerdienst Munich GmbH & Co KG, Gutenbergstr 1, D-82429 Gilching *Tel:* (8105) 388128 *Fax:* (8105) 388100

Fachmedien Verlag Winfried Ruf (FMV)+
Parsevalstr 20, 86415 Mering
Tel: (08233) 4924 *Fax:* (08233) 4789
Key Personnel
Contact: Winfried Ruf
Founded: 1990
ISBN Prefix(es): 3-928752

Fachverlag fur das graphische Gewerbe GmbH
Friedrichstr 22, 80801 Munich
Mailing Address: Postfach 401929, 80719 Munich
Tel: (089) 332568; (089) 399061 *Fax:* (089) 3401396
Key Personnel
Man Dir & International Rights: Dr Klaus Beichel
Founded: 1955
Subjects: Business
ISBN Prefix(es): 3-87218
Imprints: Mitteilungsblatt der Verbandes deds bayerischen Druckincleestrie eV

Fachverlag Schiele & Schoen GmbH+
Markgrafenstr 11, 10969 Berlin
Mailing Address: Postfach 610280, Berlin 10924
Tel: (030) 253 75 20 *Fax:* (030) 251 72 48
E-mail: service@schiele-schoen.de
Web Site: www.schiele-schoen.de
Key Personnel
Man Dir, Rights & Permissions: Peter Schoen *Fax:* (030) 25 37 52 37 *E-mail:* peter.schoen@schiele-schoen.de
Sales: Ingrid Bade
Production: Lutz Stehr
Founded: 1946
Publishers of technical & scientific publications.
Subjects: Biological Sciences, Communications, Crafts, Games, Hobbies, Engineering (General), Medicine, Nursing, Dentistry, Technology
ISBN Prefix(es): 3-7949
Foreign Rep(s): Norwin A Merens Ltd (North America)

Fackeltrager-Verlag GmbH+
Wurzburger Str 14, 26121 Oldenburg
Mailing Address: Postfach 3407, 26024 Oldenburg
Tel: (0441) 980 66-0 *Fax:* (0441) 980 66-34
E-mail: info@lappan.de
Web Site: www.lappan.de
Key Personnel
Editorial Dir: Peter Baumann; Dieter Schwalm
Marketing: Bianca Wintzek *E-mail:* vertrieb@lappan.de
International Rights: Heidtun Viampl
Publicity: Elke Horstmann
Rights: Nicola Heinrichs
Advertising: Andrea Groteluschen *E-mail:* presse@lappan.de
Founded: 1949
Subjects: Art, History, Humor
ISBN Prefix(es): 3-89082; 3-8303
Parent Company: Lappan Verlag GmbH

Fahrner & Fahrner
Bergerstr 278, 60385 Frankfurt am Main
Tel: (069) 584777
Key Personnel
Proprietor: Barbara Fahrner
International Rights: Markus Fahrner
Founded: 1982
Specialize in Unique Books & Small Editions.
Subjects: Art, Fiction, Literature, Literary Criticism, Essays
Branch Office(s)
28 Fendyke Rd, Belvedere, Kent DA 175 DP, United Kingdom, Contact: Markus M Fahrner

Christa Falk-Verlag+
Ischl 11, 83370 Seeon
Tel: (08667) 14 13 *Fax:* (08667) 14 17
E-mail: email@chfalk-verlag.de
Web Site: www.chfalk-verlag.de
Key Personnel
Publisher: Christa Falk
Founded: 1982
Specialize in esoteric books.
ISBN Prefix(es): 3-924161; 3-89568
Number of titles published annually: 10 Print; 1 Audio
Total Titles: 180 Print; 196 Online; 16 Audio
Online services available through Home Page.
Foreign Rep(s): AS Batsch Holler (Austria)

Falk Verlag AG
Marco Polo Zentrum, 73760 Ostfildern
Tel: (089) 431890; (089) 43146; (089) 43256 *Fax:* (089) 43189-160; (089) 43189-783
Key Personnel
CEO: Hans J Moock
Editorial: Dr Helge Lintzhoeft
Technical: Christopm Riess
Sales & Marketing: Michael Staehler
Founded: 1945

Specialize in, cartography (city maps & atlases, road maps & road atlases).
ISBN Prefix(es): 3-88445; 3-8279; 3-920317
Subsidiaries: GeoData, GmbH & Co KG
Branch Office(s)
Berlin
Hamburg
Lepzig
Stuttgart
Distributor for Berlitz; DCC; Gruner & Jahr; Iwanowski; Ravenstein

Falken-Verlag GmbH+
Schoene Aussicht 21, 65527 Niedernhausen
Mailing Address: Postfach 1120, 65521 Niedernhausen
Tel: (06127) 702-0 *Fax:* (06127) 702-133
E-mail: vertrieb.verlagsgruppe@bertelsmann.de
Web Site: www.randomhouse.de/falken
Key Personnel
Man Dir: Frank Sicker
Publishing Manager: Manfred Abrahamsberg
Production: Josef Jung
Publicity: Stefan Becht *Tel:* (06127) 702-190 *Fax:* (06127) 702-248 *E-mail:* presse@falken.de
Foreign Rights: Silke Bruenink *Tel:* (06127) 702-178 *Fax:* (06127) 702-277
Founded: 1923
Subjects: Cookery, Crafts, Games, Hobbies, Education, Gardening, Plants, Health, Nutrition, History, How-to, Humor, Photography, Sports, Athletics
ISBN Prefix(es): 3-8068
Associate Companies: Moeller Verlag
Subsidiaries: Falken Taschenbuch Verlag; Friedrich Bassermann'sche Verlagsbuchhandlung
Orders to: KNO, Schockenriedstr 39, 70565 Stuttgart 80

Fannei & Walz Verlag+
Uhlandstr 179/180, 10623 Berlin
Tel: (030) 88 92 16 42 *Fax:* (030) 88 92 16 50
E-mail: mail@fab-berlin.de
Web Site: www.fab-berlin.de/Verlage
Key Personnel
Man Dir: Guenther Fannei; Klaus Siebenhaar
Founded: 1989
Subjects: Fiction, Literature, Literary Criticism, Essays, Regional Interests
ISBN Prefix(es): 3-927574
Orders to: Buchvertrieb Grimmstr, Saalburgstr 3, 12099 Berlin

Ekkehard Faude Verlag
Postfach 100524, 78405 Konstanz
Tel: (0041) 6883555 *Fax:* (0041) 6883565

Favorit-Verlag Huntemann und Markus & Co GmbH+
Stettiner Str 16, 76437 Rastatt
Mailing Address: Postfach 1645, 76406 Rastatt
Tel: (07222) 2 22 54 *Fax:* (07222) 2 98 38
E-mail: info@favorit-verlag.de
Web Site: www.favorit-verlag.de
Telex: 786630 *Cable:* FAVORITVERLAG
Founded: 1965
ISBN Prefix(es): 3-921102; 3-8227

Feest, *imprint of* Egmont EHAPA Verlag GmbH

Feinschmecker, *imprint of* Graefe und Unzer Verlag GmbH

Dr Karl Feistle, see Dustri-Verlag Dr Karl Feistle

Felicitas Huebner Verlag, see Huebner Felicitas Verlag

Feltron-Elektronik Zeissler & Co GmbH
Auf dem Schellerod 22, 53842 Troisdorf
Mailing Address: Postfach 1263, 53822 Troisdorf
Tel: (02241) 48670 *Fax:* (02241) 404241
Key Personnel
Owner: M Zeissler
Founded: 1947
Subjects: Communications, Computer Science, Electronics, Electrical Engineering, Microcomputers
ISBN Prefix(es): 3-88050

Ferd Dummler's Verlag+
Kaiserstr 31-37, 53113 Bonn
Mailing Address: Postfach 1480, 53004 Bonn
Tel: (0228) 91340 *Fax:* (0228) 213040
Key Personnel
Man Dir: Helmut Lehmann
Founded: 1808
Member of VGS - Verlagsgesellschaft mbH & Co KG.
Subjects: Chemistry, Chemical Engineering, Civil Engineering, Computer Science, Crafts, Games, Hobbies, Earth Sciences, Government, Political Science, History, Language Arts, Linguistics, Mathematics, Mechanical Engineering, Physical Sciences, Physics, Sports, Athletics
ISBN Prefix(es): 3-427

Ferdinand Enke Verlag+
Rosensteinstr 24, 70191 Stuttgart
Mailing Address: Postfach 300366, 70443 Stuttgart
Tel: (0711) 8931-0 *Fax:* (0711) 8931-706
Web Site: www.enke.de
Telex: 07252275 *Cable:* ENKEBUCH STUTTGART
Key Personnel
Man Dir: Fr Marlis Kuhlmann, PhD; Albrecht Hauff
Sales Dir, Rights & Permissions: Martin Spencker
Publicity: Marcus Boeggemann
Founded: 1837
Subjects: Art, Geography, Geology, Medicine, Nursing, Dentistry, Psychology, Psychiatry, Science (General), Social Sciences, Sociology, Veterinary Science
ISBN Prefix(es): 3-432
Associate Companies: Georg Thieme Verlag KG
Subsidiaries: Deutscher Verlag fur Grundstoffindustrie

Franz Ferzak World & Space Publications+
Am Bachl 1, 93336 Altmannstein
Tel: (09446) 1403 *Fax:* (089) 7293 9737
Key Personnel
Owner: Franz Ferzak *Tel:* (089) 182089393
Founded: 1987
Subjects: Astronomy, Electronics, Electrical Engineering, Energy, Engineering (General), Physical Sciences, Physics, Science (General), Technology
ISBN Prefix(es): 3-9801465; 3-9805835
Number of titles published annually: 2 Print
Total Titles: 11 Print
Orders to: Michaels Verlag, 86971 Peiting *Tel:* (08861) 59018 *Fax:* (08861) 67091 *E-mail:* mvv@michaelsverlag.de

Festland Verlag GmbH
Basteistr 88, 53173 Bonn
Mailing Address: Postfach 200561, 53135 Bonn
Tel: (0228) 36 20 21 *Fax:* (0228) 35 17 71
E-mail: festland@t-online.de
Key Personnel
International Rights: Heinz H Hey
Founded: 1950
Subjects: Communications, Economics, Education, Government, Political Science, Social Sciences, Sociology

ISBN Prefix(es): 3-87224
Parent Company: C W Niemeyer GmbH & Co KG, 31784 Hameln

Festo Didactic GmbH & Co
Rechbergstr 3, 73770 Denkendorf
Mailing Address: Postfach 100710, 73707 Esslingen
Tel: (0711) 3467-0 *Fax:* (0711) 3467-1318
E-mail: did@festo.com
Web Site: www.festo.com
Key Personnel
Man Dir: Dr Theodor Niehaus; Dr Wilfried Stoll
Founded: 1980
Member of Association of German Publishing Companies.
Subjects: Career Development, Education, Electronics, Electrical Engineering, Engineering (General)
ISBN Prefix(es): 3-8127
U.S. Office(s): Festo Corporation, 395 Moreland Rd, Hauppauge, NY 11788, United States
Tel: 516-435-0800 *Fax:* 516-435-8026

Fibre Verlag
Martinistr 37, 49080 Osnabrueck
Tel: (0541) 431838 *Fax:* (0541) 432786
E-mail: info@fibre-verlag.de
Web Site: www.fibre-verlag.de

Wolfgang Fietkau Verlag+
Ernst-Thaelmann Str 152, 14532 Kleinmachnow
Tel: (033203) 71 105 *Fax:* (033203) 71 109
E-mail: fietkau@fietkau.de
Web Site: www.fietkau.de
Key Personnel
Publisher, Rights & Permissions: Wolfgang Fietkau
Founded: 1959
Acts as booktrader on German Stockmarket.
Subjects: Poetry
ISBN Prefix(es): 3-87352

Barbara Fietz, see Abakus Musik Barbara Fietz

Filmfaust Verlag - Internationale Filmzeitschrift
Schumannstr 64, 60325 Frankfurt
Tel: (069) 748305 *Fax:* (069) 564321
Key Personnel
Man Dir: Bion Steinborn
Rights & Permissions: Dr Christine V Eichel-Streiber
Founded: 1976
Divisions: Redaktion in Berlin; Filmfaust Redaktion

Emil Fink Verlag
Siemensstr 52, 70469 Stuttgart
Tel: (0711) 814646 *Fax:* (0711) 8106070
E-mail: info@fink-verlag.de
Key Personnel
Publisher, Rights & Permissions: Stefan Scheibel
Founded: 1919
Specialize in calendars, greeting cards & postcards.
Subjects: Art
ISBN Prefix(es): 3-7717
Foreign Rep(s): Arcaldion (Austria, Netherlands, France, Switzerland); Art Bula; Calandars-Cards; Edition Classic Art; Verlagsauslieferung R & B

Fink - Kummerly und Frey Verlag GmbH+
Zeppelinstr 29-32, 73760 Ostfildern
Tel: (0711) 4506400 *Fax:* (0711) 4506456
Telex: 723737 fkf d *Cable:* Buch-Fink
Key Personnel
Man Dir: Bodo Neiss; Wolfgang Titze
Man Dir, Rights & Permissions: Sigmund Zipperle
Rights & Permissions: Beatrice Weber

Public Relations: Helmut Braun
Founded: 1935
Firm has developed from an association between the German company J Fink (founded 1894) & the Swiss cartographic company Kuemmerly und Frey (founded 1852). The latter firm also continues as an independent company in Switzerland.
Subjects: Health, Nutrition, Nonfiction (General), Outdoor Recreation, Sports, Athletics
ISBN Prefix(es): 3-7718
Parent Company: Kuemmerly und Frey Verlag, Bern, Switzerland

Wilhelm Fink GmbH & Co Verlags-KG+
Juehenplatz am Rathans, 33098 Paderborn
Tel: (089) 348017; (089) 348018 *Fax:* (089) 341378
E-mail: kontakt@fink.de
Web Site: www.fink.de *Cable:* FINK MUNCHEN
Key Personnel
Publisher: Ferdinand Schoeningh *Tel:* 0 52 51/1 27-777 *Fax:* 0 52 52/1 27-670 *E-mail:* info@schoeningh.de
Editor & Man Dir: Dr Raimar Zons
Founded: 1962
Subjects: Archaeology, Art, History, Language Arts, Linguistics, Literature, Literary Criticism, Essays, Music, Dance, Philosophy, Psychology, Psychiatry, Social Sciences, Sociology
ISBN Prefix(es): 3-7705
Imprints: Poetik und Hermeneutik; Bild und Text
Orders to: Ferdinand Schoeningh Verlag, Juehenplatz 1-3, 33098 Paderborn *Tel:* (05251) 1 27-777 *Fax:* (05251) 1 27-670 *E-mail:* info@schoeningh.de

Finken Junior, *imprint of* Finken Verlag GmbH

Finken-Verlag, see Finken Verlag GmbH

Finken Verlag GmbH+
Postfach 1546, 61440 Oberursel
Tel: (06171) 6388-18 *Fax:* (06171) 6388-44
E-mail: info@finken.de
Web Site: www.finken.de *Cable:* NEUER FINKENVERLAG OBERURSEL
Key Personnel
Dir: Manfred Krick
International Rights: Karoline Jockel
   E-mail: karoline.jockel@finken.de
Founded: 1985
Specialize in learning & teaching material for children from 3 to 12 years-old at school & at home, LOGICO™-the new learning system with selfchecking; also reading skills & early learning.
Member of Deutscher Didacta Verband-Germany, Worlddidac Association, Boersenverein des deutschen Buchhandels Germany.
Subjects: Education, English as a Second Language, Mathematics, Natural History
ISBN Prefix(es): 3-8084
Imprints: Finken Junior

Harald Fischer Verlag GmbH+
Theaterplatz 31, 91054 Erlangen
Mailing Address: Postfach 1565, 91005 Erlangen
Tel: (09131) 205620 *Fax:* (09131) 206028
E-mail: info@haraldfischerverlag.de
Web Site: www.haraldfischerverlag.de
Key Personnel
Contact: Dr Claudia Schorcht
Founded: 1984
Microfiche Editions.
Member of Boersenverein des dt Buchhandels.
Subjects: Disability, Special Needs, Engineering (General), History, Language Arts, Linguistics, Library & Information Sciences, Medicine, Nursing, Dentistry, Philosophy, Publishing & Book Trade Reference, Religion - Jewish, Science (General), Women's Studies
ISBN Prefix(es): 3-89131
Total Titles: 350 Print; 2 CD-ROM
Online services available through World Wide Web.

Verkehrs-Verlag J Fischer GmbH & Co KG
Paulusstr 1, 40237 Duesseldorf
Mailing Address: Postfach 140265, 40072 Duesseldorf
Tel: (0211) 99193-0 *Fax:* (0211) 6801544
E-mail: vvf@verkehrsverlag-fischer.de
Web Site: www.verkehrsverlag-fischer.de
Key Personnel
Publisher: Paul Urban *Tel:* (0211) 9919311
   E-mail: paul.urban@verkehrsverlag-fischer.de
Founded: 1904
Subjects: Transportation
ISBN Prefix(es): 3-87841

Karin Fischer Verlag GmbH+
Wallstr 50, 52064 Aachen
Mailing Address: Postfach 1987, 52021 Aachen
Tel: (0241) 960 90 90 *Fax:* (0241) 960 90 99
Web Site: www.karin-fischer-verlag.de
Key Personnel
President & Editor: Karin Fischer
Reader: Dr Manfred S Fischer
Founded: 1989
Subjects: Fiction, Literature, Literary Criticism, Essays, Nonfiction (General), Philosophy, Poetry, Social Sciences, Sociology
ISBN Prefix(es): 3-927854; 3-89514

Verlag Reinhard Fischer
Weltistr 34, 81477 Munich
Tel: (089) 791 88 92 *Fax:* (089) 791 83 10
E-mail: verlagfischer@compuserve.de
Web Site: www.verlag-reinhard-fischer.de
Key Personnel
Owner: Reinhard Fischer
Founded: 1982
Subjects: Communications, Journalism, Marketing, Radio, TV
ISBN Prefix(es): 3-88927

Rita G Fischer Verlag+
Orberstr 30, 60386 Frankfurt
Tel: (069) 941942-0 *Fax:* (069) 941942-99; (069) 941942-98
E-mail: r.g.fischer.verlag@t-online.de
Web Site: www.buchhandel.de/r.g.fischer/
Key Personnel
Man Dir: Rita G Fischer *E-mail:* r.g.fisher.verlag@t-online.de
Founded: 1977
Subjects: Engineering (General), Fiction, Government, Political Science, How-to, Medicine, Nursing, Dentistry, Poetry, Psychology, Psychiatry, Social Sciences, Sociology
ISBN Prefix(es): 3-88323; 3-89406; 3-89501

S Fischer Verlag GmbH+
Hedderichstr 114, 60596 Frankfurt am Main
Mailing Address: Postfach 700355, 60553 Frankfurt am Main
Tel: (069) 6062-0 *Fax:* (069) 6062-214
Web Site: www.s-fischer.de *Cable:* BUCHFISCHER
Key Personnel
Man Dir: Lothar Kleiner; Monika Schoeller
Founded: 1886
Subjects: Fiction, Literature, Literary Criticism, Essays, Nonfiction (General)
ISBN Prefix(es): 3-10
Subsidiaries: Wolfgang Krueger Verlag; Fischer Taschenbuch Verlag

Fischer Taschenbuch Verlag GmbH+
Subsidiary of S Fischer Verlag GmbH
Hedderichstr 114, 60596 Frankfurt am Main
Tel: (069) 60620 *Fax:* (069) 606214
Web Site: www.s-fischer.de
Key Personnel
Man Dir: Monika Schoeller; Dr Hubertus Schenkel
Man Dir, Rights & Permissions: Wolfgang Mertz
Sales: Ralf Alkenbrecher
Publicity: Margarete Schwind
Production: Wilfried Meiner
Editorial: Martin Bauer; Dr Ursula Koehler
Founded: 1952
Subjects: Biography, History, Literature, Literary Criticism, Essays, Nonfiction (General), Psychology, Psychiatry, Women's Studies
ISBN Prefix(es): 3-596

Fit fuers Leben Verlag, *imprint of* NaturaViva Verlags GmbH

Flaschenpost, *imprint of* Keysersche Verlagsbuchhandlung GmbH

Flechsig Buchvertrieb
Imprint of Verlagshaus Wurzburg
Beethovenstr 5, 97080 Wurzburg
Tel: (0931) 385235 *Fax:* (0931) 385305
E-mail: info@verlagshaus.com
Web Site: www.verlagshaus.com
Key Personnel
Publishing Dir: Dieter Krause
Dir of Production: Juergen Roth
Sales Dir: Johannes Glesius
Subjects: Travel

Erich Fleischer Verlag
Postfach 1264, 28818 Achim
Tel: (04202) 517-0 *Fax:* (04202) 517-41
E-mail: info@efv-online.de
Web Site: www.efv-online.de
Key Personnel
Contact: Gerhard Schroeter *Tel:* (04202) 51729
   E-mail: schroeter@efv-online.de
Founded: 1954
Subjects: Law
ISBN Prefix(es): 3-8168

Fleischhauer & Spohn GmbH & Co
Mundelsheimer Str 3, 74321 Bietigsheim-Bissingen
Mailing Address: Postfach 1764, 74307 Bietigsheim-Bissingen
Tel: (07142) 596161 *Fax:* (07142) 596280
E-mail: verlag-fleischhauer@t-online.de
Web Site: www.verlag-fleischhauer.de
Telex: 724237 umco d
Key Personnel
Marketing: Dieter Keilbach
Man Dir: Dr Max Bez; Thomas Bez; Simone Roth; Martin Roth
Founded: 1830
Subjects: History, Regional Interests, Travel
ISBN Prefix(es): 3-87230
Associate Companies: Barsortiment G Umbreit GmbH & Co (book wholesaler)

Flensburger Hefte Verlag GmbH+
Holm 64, 24937 Flensburg
Tel: (0461) 2 63 63; (0461) 2 14 72 *Fax:* (0461) 2 69 12
E-mail: flensburgerhefte@t-online.de
Web Site: www.flensburgerhefte.de
Key Personnel
Man Dir: Wolfgang Weirauch
Founded: 1987
Subjects: Education, Health, Nutrition, History, Human Relations, Philosophy, Religion - Other, Social Sciences, Sociology
ISBN Prefix(es): 3-926841
Warehouse: Helemenallee 4, 24937 Flensburg

PUBLISHERS

Flugzeug Publikations GmbH+
Thomas Mann Str 3, 89257 Illertissen
Mailing Address: Postfach 3055, 89253 Illertissen
Tel: (07303) 964220 *Fax:* (07303) 964141
E-mail: online@flugzeug-publikation.de
Web Site: www.flugzeug-publikation.de
Key Personnel
Sales: Manfred Franzke; Werner Richter
Founded: 1985
Subjects: Aeronautics, Aviation, History
ISBN Prefix(es): 3-927132
Total Titles: 4 Print

FN-Verlag der Deutschen Reiterlichen Vereinigung GmbH+
Freiherr-von-Langen-Str 8a, 48231 Warendorf
Mailing Address: Postfach 110363, 48205 Warendorf
Tel: (02581) 63 62-115 *Fax:* (02581) 63 31 46
E-mail: fnverlag@fn-dokr.de
Web Site: www.fnverlag.de
Telex: 258113 FENGER
Key Personnel
Manager: Siegmund Friedrich; Rainer Reisloh
Tel: (02581) 63 62-205
Marketing: Heike Ourajini *Tel:* (02581) 63 62-221
E-mail: hourajini@fn-dokr.de
Sales: Tamara Erkelenz *Tel:* (02581) 63 62-154
E-mail: terkelenz@fn-dokr.de; Tanja Kneupper
Tel: (02851) 63 62-254 *E-mail:* tkneupper@fn-dokr.de
Founded: 1977
Subjects: Film, Video
ISBN Prefix(es): 3-88542

Focus-Verlag Gesellschaft mbH+
Lonystr 19a, 35398 Giessen
Tel: (0641) 76031 *Fax:* (0641) 76031
E-mail: info@focus-verlag.de
Web Site: www.focus-verlag.de
Key Personnel
Man Dir, Sales, Rights & Permissions: Mr Schmid
Publicity, Advertising Dir: Mr Neuhofer
Founded: 1970
Subjects: Environmental Studies, History, Psychology, Psychiatry, Social Sciences, Sociology
ISBN Prefix(es): 3-920352; 3-88349
Orders to: Unterer Hardthof 29, 35398 Giessen
Tel: (0641) 68225 *Fax:* (0641) 68331

Forum, *imprint of* Wissenschaftliche Buchgesellschaft

Forum Verlag GmbH & Co
Schrempfstr 8, 70597 Stuttgart
Tel: (0711) 76727-0 *Fax:* (0711) 76727-28
E-mail: info@forumverlag.de
Web Site: www.forumverlag.de
Founded: 1964
Our journal *Deutsches Architektenblatt* is sent to every architect who is a member of the German Architektenkammer, approximately 110,000 monthly.
Subjects: Architecture & Interior Design
ISBN Prefix(es): 3-8091

Forum Verlag Leipzig Buch-Gesellschaft+
Gottschedstr 30, 04109 Leipzig
Tel: (0341) 980 50 08 *Fax:* (0341) 980 50 07
Web Site: www.leipzig-plus.de
Key Personnel
Manager: Helen Jannsen
Founded: 1995
Member of Leipzig Topsellers; Specialize in GDR History.
Subjects: Government, Political Science, History, Humor, Nonfiction (General), Regional Interests
ISBN Prefix(es): 3-931801

Total Titles: 1 Audio
Orders to: L K G mbH, Poetzschauer Weg, 04579 Espenhain *Fax:* (0342) 0665110

Forum Wissenschaft Studien, *imprint of* Bund demokratischer Wissenschaftlerinnen und Wissenschafler eV (BdWi)

Fouque-Literaturverlag, *imprint of* Dr Haensel-Hohenhausen AG

Fouque-Publishers Inc, *imprint of* Dr Haensel-Hohenhausen AG

Verlag der Francke Buchhandlung GmbH+
Am Schwanhof 19, 35037 Marburg
Mailing Address: Postfach 200640, 35018 Marburg
Tel: (06421) 17 25-0 *Fax:* (06421) 17 25-30
E-mail: info@francke-buch.de
Web Site: www.francke-buch.de
Key Personnel
Man Dir, Editorial & Publicity: Uwe Schmidt
Sales: Margot Agel
Founded: 1934
Firm is contributor to the Telos series of evangelical paperbacks.
Subjects: Theology
ISBN Prefix(es): 3-88224; 3-86122
Bookshop(s): Gunzenhausen; Velbert; Lemfoerde; Oberursel; Elbingerode; Neustadt

Frankfurter Societaets-Druckerei GmbH, see Societaets-Verlag

Verlag Frankfurter Buecher, *imprint of* Societaets-Verlag

FVA-Frankfurter Verlagsanstalt GmbH+
Danneckerstr 39A, 60594 Frankfurt am Main
Tel: (069) 96220610 *Fax:* (069) 96220630
E-mail: info@frankfurter-verlagsanstalt.de
Web Site: www.frankfurter-verlagsanstalt.de
Key Personnel
Publisher: Dr Joachim Unseld
Manager: Dagmar Fretter *E-mail:* fretter@frankfurter-verlagsanstalt.de
Foreign Rights: Meike Breitkreutz *Tel:* (069) 962206 15
Founded: 1986
Subjects: Biography
ISBN Prefix(es): 3-627
Parent Company: Unseld
Associate Companies: Sophienbuchhandlung
Orders to: Libri Distribution, August-Schanz-Str 33, 60433 Frankfurt am Main

Franz-Sales-Verlag+
Rosental 1, 85072 Eichstaett
Tel: (08421) 93 489-31 *Fax:* (08421) 934 89-35
E-mail: info@franz-sales-verlag.de
Web Site: www.franz-sales-verlag.de
Key Personnel
President & Editor: P Herbert Winklehner
E-mail: herbert.winklehner@franz-sales-verlag.de
Founded: 1931
Disseminate the work of St Francis de Soles (1567-1622) into the modern world.
Member of VKB, AKB, Borsenverein Des Deutschen Buchhandels & Verband Bayrischer Verleger Und Buchhandler.
Subjects: Art, Biography, Religion - Catholic, Theology
ISBN Prefix(es): 3-7721
Total Titles: 100 Print

Verlag Franz Vahlen GmbH+
Wilhelmstr 9, 80801 Munich
Tel: (089) 38189-0 *Fax:* (089) 38189-402

GERMANY

E-mail: info@vahlen.de
Web Site: www.vahlen.de
Key Personnel
Manager: Dr Hans D Beck
Founded: 1870
Subjects: Economics, Finance, Law, Management, Marketing
ISBN Prefix(es): 3-8006
Associate Companies: Verlag C H Beck (OHG)

Franzis-Verlag GmbH+
Gruber Str 46a, 85586 Poing
Tel: (08121) 95 14 44 *Fax:* (08121) 95 16 96
Web Site: www.franzis.de
Key Personnel
Man Dirs: Helmuth Schmitz; Michael Boos
Editorial Dir, Rights & Permissions: Thomas Kaesbohrer
Sales, Publicity Manager: Volker Schmitt
Founded: 1924
Subjects: Communications, Computer Science, Electronics, Electrical Engineering
ISBN Prefix(es): 3-7723
Parent Company: WEKA Firmengruppe GmbH & Co KG

Frauenoffensive Verlagsgesellschaft MbH+
Metzstr 14, 81667 Munich
Tel: (089) 489500-48 *Fax:* (089) 489500-49
Key Personnel
Dir, Rights & Permissions: Gerlinde Kowitzke
Editorial: H Schlaeger
Sales: S Kohlstadt
Founded: 1974
Subjects: Women's Studies
ISBN Prefix(es): 3-88104

Fraunhofer IRB Verlag Fraunhofer Informationszentrum Raum und Bau+
Division of Fraunhofer-Gesellschaft
Nobelstr 12, 70569 Stuttgart
Tel: (0711) 9 70-25 00 *Fax:* (0711) 9 70-25 08
E-mail: info@irb.fhg.de
Web Site: www.irbdirekt.de
Key Personnel
Man Dir: Dr Wilhelm Wissmann
Sales Manager: Barbara Scherer
Founded: 1947
Specialize in literature on building construction, building damages & regional planning.
Subjects: Architecture & Interior Design, Civil Engineering, Earth Sciences, Environmental Studies, House & Home, Outdoor Recreation, Regional Interests
ISBN Prefix(es): 3-8167
Number of titles published annually: 100 Print; 6 CD-ROM
Total Titles: 20 Print; 6 CD-ROM

Frech-Verlag GmbH und Co Druck KG+
Turbinenstr 7, 70499 Stuttgart
Mailing Address: Postfach 311253, 70472 Stuttgart
Tel: (0711) 83086-0 *Fax:* (0711) 8 30 86-56
Web Site: www.frech.de
Key Personnel
Man Dir: Gerhard Schierbling; Gerhard Striegl
Business Manager & Sales: Berud Leuz
Founded: 1955
Specialize in Hobby & Leisure Activities.
Subjects: Crafts, Games, Hobbies, Electronics, Electrical Engineering
ISBN Prefix(es): 3-7724

Fredebeul und Koenen GmbH
Ruhrtalstr 52-60, 45239 Essen
Mailing Address: Postfach 164180, 45221 Essen
Tel: (0201) 49821 *Fax:* (0201) 8492415
Key Personnel
Man Dir: Dr Albert E Fischer
ISBN Prefix(es): 3-87236

Frederking & Thaler Verlag GmbH+
Infanteriestr 19, Haus 2, 80797 Munich
Tel: (089) 12113 0 *Fax:* (089) 12113 14
Key Personnel
Owner, Publisher & International Rights:
 Monika Thaler *Tel:* (089) 12113 11
 E-mail: monikathaler@frederking-thaler.de
Founded: 1988 (1988 as independent publisher,
 1998-2001 Bertelsmann/Random House Publishing Group, in 2002 independent publisher)
Specialize in high quality illustrated books in the
 realm of wonders of nature, foreign cultures &
 their spiritual worlds. Also nonfiction narrative
 reports (culture, nature & travel).
Subjects: Archaeology, Art, Foreign Countries,
 Photography, Travel, World Religions
ISBN Prefix(es): 3-89405
Number of titles published annually: 30 Print
Total Titles: 120 Print; 120 E-Book
Online services available through Bertelsmann,
 Media Mount.
Imprints: Villa Arceno; Sierra
Warehouse: VVA Bertelsmann Distribution,
 33310 Gutersloh

Erika G Freese Verlag+
Potsdamerstr 16, 12205 Berlin
Tel: (030) 8333077 *Fax:* (030) 8333077
Key Personnel
Man Dir, Rights & Permissions: Erika Freese
Founded: 1982
Member of the Stock Market of German Booksellers.
ISBN Prefix(es): 3-88942
Orders to: Buchvertrieb Grimmstrasse, Grimmstrasse 27, 12305 Berlin 16

Verlag Freies Geistesleben+
Division of Verlag Freies Geistesleben & Urachhaus GmbH
Postfach 131122, 70069 Stuttgart
Tel: (0711) 28532 00 *Fax:* (0711) 28532 10
E-mail: info@geistesleben.com
Web Site: www.geistesleben.com
Key Personnel
Publishing Dir: Jean-Claude Lin *Tel:* (0711)
 2853221 *E-mail:* lin@geistesleben.com; Andreas Neider *E-mail:* a.neider@geistesleben.com
Sales: Reinhardt Stiehle *Tel:* (0711) 2853232
 E-mail: r.steihle@geistesleben.com
Founded: 1947
Member of Community of Youth Book Publishers.
Subjects: Art, Biography, Education, History,
 How-to, Medicine, Nursing, Dentistry, Music, Dance, Philosophy, Psychology, Psychiatry,
 Religion - Other, Science (General), Social Sciences, Sociology, Picture books
ISBN Prefix(es): 3-7725
Number of titles published annually: 60 Print
Total Titles: 800 Print
Imprints: Aethera
Orders to: Koch, Neff & Oetinger, Schockenriedstr 39, Postfach 800620, Stuttgart *Tel:* (0711)
 78992140 *Fax:* (0711) 78991010

Freiherr von Stein Gedaechtnisausgabe, *imprint of* Wissenschaftliche Buchgesellschaft

Freimund-Verlag der Gesellschaft fur Innere und Aeussere Mission im Sinne der Lutherischen Kirche eV
Ringstr 15, 91564 Neuendettelsau
Mailing Address: Postfach 48, 91561 Neuendettelsau
Tel: (09874) 6 89 39 80 *Fax:* (09874) 6 89 39 99
E-mail: info@freimund-verlag.de
Web Site: www.freimund-buchhandlung.de/verlag
Key Personnel
Man Dir: Dr Martin Kobler; Hildegard Wickert
Founded: 1933
Subjects: Religion - Other
ISBN Prefix(es): 3-7726
Bookshop(s): Freimund-Buchhandlung, Hauptstr
 2, 91564 Neuendettelsau

Margarethe Freudenberger - selbstverlag fur jedermann+
Gartenstr 22, 97906 Faulbach
Tel: (09392) 8449
Founded: 1979
Subjects: Art, Fiction, How-to, Human Relations,
 Humor, Poetry
ISBN Prefix(es): 3-924711

Verlag Walter Frey+
Postfach 30 36 26, 10727 Berlin
Tel: (030) 883 25 61 *Fax:* (030) 883 25 61
E-mail: tranvia@aol.com
Key Personnel
Man Dir: Walter Frey
Founded: 1985
Subjects: Literature of and about Spain, Portugal,
 and Latin America
ISBN Prefix(es): 3-925867
Number of titles published annually: 10 Print

FRICK Verlag-GmbH+
Postfach 447, 75104, Pforzheim
Tel: (07231) 102842 *Fax:* (07231) 357744
E-mail: info@frickverlag.de
Web Site: www.frickverlag.de
Key Personnel
Contact: Jim Rosemergy
Founded: 1970
Specialize in Religion, Metaphysics, Esoteric.
Member of Deutschief Bosenverlise.
ISBN Prefix(es): 3-920780
Number of titles published annually: 3 Print
Total Titles: 3 Print
Branch Office(s)
Haupt, Str 279, Rosrath, Thele Jung *Tel:* (02205)
 3308 *Fax:* (02205) 53308
Witere Weinberg, Str 11-1, Eisengen, Peter
 D'Orazio *Tel:* (07232) 383083 *Fax:* (07232)
 383084

Friedemann von Engel Verlag
Friedbergstr 5, 14057 Berlin
Tel: (030) 3233145
Key Personnel
Man Dir: F V Engel
Subjects: Travel
ISBN Prefix(es): 3-921676
Imprints: Tips fuer Trips
Subsidiaries: Tips fur Trips

Erhard Friedrich Verlag
Im Brande 17, 30926 Seelze
Mailing Address: Postfach 10 01 50, 30917
 Seelze
Tel: (0511) 400040 *Fax:* (0511) 40004-119
Web Site: www.friedrich-verlagsgruppe.de
Telex: 0922923 *Cable:* FRIEDRICH
Key Personnel
International Rights: Uwe Brinkmann
Founded: 1960
Subjects: Art, Drama, Theater, Education
ISBN Prefix(es): 3-617

Friedrich Kiehl Verlag GmbH+
Postfach 140108, 67021 Ludwigshafen
Tel: (0621) 6 35 02-0 *Fax:* (0621) 6 35 02-22
E-mail: hotline@kiehl.de
Web Site: www.kiehl.de
Telex: 464810 Kiehl d
Key Personnel
Dir: Ernst-Otto Kleyboldt; Dr Karl-Friedrich Peter
Sales Manager: Klaus Bissinger
Rights & Permissions, International Rights: Adolf
 Schmidt
Founded: 1932
Subjects: Advertising, Business, Career Development, Computer Science, Economics, Education, Finance, Law, Marketing, Medicine,
 Nursing, Dentistry
ISBN Prefix(es): 3-470
Parent Company: Verlag Neue Wirtschafts-Briefe
 GmbH
Distributed by Linde-Verlag
Distributor for Linde-Verlag Ostereicli
Warehouse: Schuechtermannstr 180, 44628 Herne

Frieling & Partner GmbH
Huenefeldzeile 18, 12247 Berlin-Steglitz
Tel: (030) 7 66 99 90 *Fax:* (030) 7 74 41 03
Web Site: www.frieling.de *Cable:* FRIELING
 BERLIN
Key Personnel
Publisher: Wilhelm Ruprecht Frieling
Founded: 1871
ISBN Prefix(es): 3-89009

Verlag A Fromm im Druck- u Verlagshaus Fromm GmbH & Co KG+
Breiter Gang 10, 49074 Osnabrueck
Tel: (0541) 3100 *Fax:* (0541) 310315; (0541)
 310440
Telex: 94916 fromm d
Key Personnel
Publisher: Leo V Fromm
Chief Executive Officer & International Rights:
 Annette Harms-Hunold
Sales Manager: Annegret Busch
Public Relations: Ursula Malzahn
Founded: 1868 (Parent Company)
Subjects: Economics, Education, Environmental Studies, Ethnicity, Government, Political
 Science, History, Science (General), Social Sciences, Sociology
ISBN Prefix(es): 3-7729
Parent Company: Druck- und Verlagshaus Fromm
 GmbH & Co KG
Associate Companies: Fromm International Publishing Corp, 560 Lexington Ave, New York,
 NY 10022, United States
Imprints: Osnabrueck
Branch Office(s)
Edition Interfrom AG, Postfach 5005, Zurich,
 Switzerland *Tel:* (0041) 1 202 0900

Friedrich Frommann Verlag+
Koenig-Karl-Str 27, 70372 Stuttgart
Tel: (0711) 955969-0 *Fax:* (0711) 955969-1
E-mail: info@frommann-holzboog.de
Web Site: www.frommann-holzboog.de
Key Personnel
Man Dir, Editorial, Rights & Permissions: Guenther Holzboog
Man Dir: Eckhart Holzboog
Editor: H Tina Strauch *E-mail:* lectorat@
 frommann-holzboog.de
Press & Promotion Manager: Sybille Wittmann
 E-mail: presse@frommann-holzboog.de
Production Manager: Charles Paczkowski
 E-mail: herstellung@frommann-holzboog.de
Sales Manager: H Tobias Schmid
 E-mail: vertrieb@frommann-holzboog.de
Marketing Assistant: Ulrike Doerr
Founded: 1727
Specialize in CD-ROM, fine editions, textbooks.
 An independent publisher of arts & humanities.
 Titles with a focus in philosophy, psychoanalysis & theology.
Subjects: Language Arts, Linguistics, Law, Library & Information Sciences, Literature, Literary Criticism, Essays, Philosophy, Psychology,
 Psychiatry, Religion - Protestant, Social Sciences, Sociology, Theology
ISBN Prefix(es): 3-7728
Number of titles published annually: 50 Print; 1
 CD-ROM
Total Titles: 1,800 Print; 2 CD-ROM

PUBLISHERS

GERMANY

Fuldaer Verlagsanstalt GmbH
Rangstr 3-7, 36037 Fulda
Tel: (0661) 295-0 *Fax:* (0661) 295-71
E-mail: info@fva.de
Web Site: www.fva.de
Telex: 49739-FVAD
Subsidiaries: Vito von Eichborn GmbH & Co, Verlag KG

FVA, see FVA-Frankfurter Verlagsanstalt GmbH

FVerlag Anke Schaefer
Luxemburgstr 2, 65185 Wiesbaden
Mailing Address: Postfach 5266, 65042 Wiesbaden
Tel: (0611) 371515 *Fax:* (0611) 371913
Key Personnel
Owner: Anke Schaefer
Manager: Ines Schaefer
Founded: 1978
Subjects: Gay & Lesbian, Women's Studies
ISBN Prefix(es): 3-922229
Divisions: Feministischer Buchverlag (at above address)
Bookshop(s): Frauenbuchversand, Luxemburgstr 2, 65185 Wiesbaden

G Braun (vormals G Braun'sche Hofbuchdruckerei und Verlag) Gmbh+
Karl-Friedrich-Str 14-18, 76133 Karlsruhe
Tel: (0721) 165-195 *Fax:* (0721) 165-855
E-mail: buchverlag@gbraun.de
Web Site: www.gbraun.de
Telex: 7826904
Key Personnel
Publisher: Klaus Kapp
Dir: Georg van Griesheim; Peter Scheuble
Founded: 1813
Subjects: Art, History, Regional Interests, Travel
ISBN Prefix(es): 3-7650

Gabal-Verlag GmbH+
Schumannstr 161, 63069 Offenbach
Tel: (069) 84 000 3-0 *Fax:* (069) 84 000 3-33
E-mail: info@juenger.de
Web Site: www.juenger.de/gabal.htm
Key Personnel
Man Editor: Helmut Juergen
Founded: 1979 (Vorlaufer)
Subjects: How-to, Literature, Literary Criticism, Essays, Management
ISBN Prefix(es): 3-923984; 3-89444; 3-930799
Parent Company: Juergen Verlag GmbH
Associate Companies: PLS Sprachen, 176 Solothurn, Switzerland
Subsidiaries: Rot Gelb Grain Verlag
Divisions: Verlag

Franz-J Gaber, see Verlagsbuchhandlung Megapress, Franz-J Gaber

Verlagsbuchhandlung Megapress, Franz-J Gaber+
Bahnhofstr 56, 63263 Neu Isenburg
Tel: (0610) 225951; (0610) 2327044 *Fax:* (0610) 231018
Key Personnel
Publisher: F J Gaber
Founded: 1977
Subjects: Government, Political Science
ISBN Prefix(es): 3-87979

Betriebswirtschaftlicher Verlag Dr Th Gabler GmbH+
Abraham-Lincoln-Str 46, D-65189 Weisbaden
Mailing Address: Postfach 1546, 65173 Wiesbaden
Tel: (0611) 7878615 *Fax:* (0611) 7878470
Web Site: www.gabler.de
Key Personnel
General Manager: Dr Hans-Dieter Haenel
Man Dir: Dr Heinz Weinheimer
Editorial: Claudia Splittgerber; Ulrike Vetter
Sales & Marketing Manager: Rolf-Guenther Hobbeling; Ramona Rockel
Rights & Permissions: Angelika Bolisega
Founded: 1929
Professional information for managers, personal assistants; textbooks for students, encyclopedias.
Subjects: Accounting, Business, Economics, Finance, Management, Marketing
ISBN Prefix(es): 3-409
Total Titles: 1,500 Print
Parent Company: Bertelsmann Springer Science & Business Media

Gabriel Verlag, *imprint of* K Thienemanns Verlag

Galerie der Klassiker, *imprint of* Heel Verlag GmbH

Galerie Der Spiegel-Dr E Stunke Nachfolge GmbH
Richartzstr 10, 50667 Koeln
Tel: (0221) 25 55 52 *Fax:* (0221) 25 55 53
E-mail: thatspiegel@galerie.de
Web Site: www.galerie.de/der-spiegel
Founded: 1945
Specialize in international art editions & book catalogue portfolios.
Member of Bundesverband Deutscher Galerie & Boisenvereln Des Deutschen Buchhandels.
Subjects: Art
ISBN Prefix(es): 3-87285

Galrev Druck-und Verlagsgesellschaft Hesse & Partner OHG+
Lychener Str 73, 10437 Berlin
Tel: (030) 44 65 01 83 *Fax:* (030) 44 65 01 84
E-mail: galrev@galrev.com
Web Site: www.galrev.com
Key Personnel
Manager: Egmont Hesse; Rainer Schedlinski
Founded: 1989
Subjects: Poetry
ISBN Prefix(es): 3-910161

Garbe Verlag Ellen Vogt+
Kinkel-Str 15, 90482 Nuernberg
Tel: (0911) 5430983 *Fax:* (0911) 5430983
Key Personnel
Contact: Ellen Vogt
Founded: 1994
Subjects: Environmental Studies, Humor, Philosophy, Poetry
ISBN Prefix(es): 3-930143

Gatzanis Verlags GmbH
Alte Weinsteige 28, 70180 Stuttgart
Tel: (0711) 9640570 *Fax:* (0711) 9640572
E-mail: info@gatzanis.de
Web Site: www.gatzanis.de
Key Personnel
Owner: Jolanta Gatzanis
Founded: 1995
Subjects: Art, Biography, Child Care & Development, Gay & Lesbian, Human Relations, Humor, Self-Help
ISBN Prefix(es): 3-932855; 3-9803897
Number of titles published annually: 2 Print
Total Titles: 13 Print

Gebrueder Borntraeger Science Publishers+
Affiliate of E Schweizerbart'sche Verlagsbuchhandlung
Johannesstr 3 A, 70176 Stuttgart
Tel: (0711) 3514560 *Fax:* (0711) 35145699
E-mail: mail@schweizerbart.de
Web Site: www.schweizerbart.de
Key Personnel
Man Dir, Sales: Dr Walter Obermiller
Man Dir, Production: Dr Erhard Naegele
Exhibition Manager: Martina Ihringer
Founded: 1790
Subjects: Biological Sciences, Earth Sciences, Geography, Geology, Maritime
ISBN Prefix(es): 3-443
Imprints: Borntraeger Verlagsbuchhandlung

Konkursbuch Verlag Claudia Gehrke+
Hechingerstr 203, im Sudhaus, 72072 Tuebingen
Tel: (07071) 66551; (07071) 78779 *Fax:* (07071) 63539; (07071) 763780
E-mail: gehrke@konkursbuch.com
Web Site: www.konkursbuch.com
Key Personnel
International Rights: Claudia Gehrke
Founded: 1978
Subjects: Literature, Literary Criticism, Essays, Travel, Women's Studies
ISBN Prefix(es): 3-88769

Verlag Junge Gemeinde E Schwinghammer GmbH & Co KG+
Max-Eyth-Str 13, 70771 Leinfelden-Echterdingen
Tel: (0711) 7978994 *Fax:* (0711) 7970660 *Cable:* JUNGEGEMEINDEVERLAG
Key Personnel
Manager: Siegfried Krumrey
Founded: 1928
Specialize in books for Sunday school.
Subjects: Education, Religion - Protestant
ISBN Prefix(es): 3-7797

Genius Verlag (Genius Publishing House)+
Aach 34, 87534 Oberstaufen
Tel: (08386) 960401 *Fax:* (08386) 960402
E-mail: contact@genius-verlag.de
Web Site: www.genius-verlag.de
Key Personnel
Contact: Dagmar Neubronner
Founded: 1997
Publish spiritual books.
Subjects: Biblical Studies, Biography, Career Development, Human Relations, Music, Dance, Philosophy, Science (General), Self-Help, Theology
ISBN Prefix(es): 3-9806106; 3-934719
Number of titles published annually: 3 Print
Total Titles: 12 Print

Alfons W Gentner Verlag GmbH & Co KG+
Forststr 131, 70193 Stuttgart
Tel: (0711) 63672-0 *Fax:* (0711) 63672747
E-mail: gentner@gentnerverlag.de
Web Site: www.gentnerverlag.de
Key Personnel
Publisher: E F Reisch
Founded: 1927
Subjects: Automotive, Business, Career Development, Engineering (General), Environmental Studies, Medicine, Nursing, Dentistry
ISBN Prefix(es): 3-87247
Subsidiaries: Technischer Fachverlag GmbH; GEMA Strucna Naklada; Europska Strucna Naklada; CNTL spool sra; EUROMEDIA; B & V Kiado Kft; Magyar Mediprint Szakkiado Kft; EUROMEDIA; Instalator Polski zoo; Verbatim Publishers (Pvt) Ltd

GeoCenter Touristik Medienservice GmbH
Schockenriedstr 44, 70565 Stuttgart
Mailing Address: Postfach 800830, 70508 Stuttgart
Tel: (0711) 781946 10 *Fax:* (0711) 781946 54
E-mail: geocenterilh@t-online.de
Key Personnel
Man Dir: Dr Klaus Hohne *Tel:* (0711) 78 946 41; Hans Jurgen Pfister *Tel:* (0711) 78 946 41
Wholesaler in all kinds of maps, guides & geoscientific publications. Publisher of: Geokatalog; Touristic & Geokatalog; Geosciences.

Subjects: Geography, Geology
ISBN Prefix(es): 3-920137
Associate Companies: Touristik & Medien, Beimerstetten

Georgi GmbH+
Landsberger Str 77, 82205 Gilching
Tel: (08105) 3763-0 *Fax:* (08105) 3763-772
Web Site: www.korsch-verlag.de
Key Personnel
Man Dir: Manfred Georgi; Werner Georgi
Rights & Permissions: Adriane Georgi
Sales: Josef Brauers
Founded: 1928
Subjects: History, How-to, Music, Dance, Science (General)
ISBN Prefix(es): 3-87248
Subsidiaries: Georgi Publishers

Carl Gerber Verlag, see Schwaneberger Verlag GmbH

Gerhard Wolf Janus-Press GmbH+
Amalienpark 7, 13187 Berlin
Tel: (030) 47535220 *Fax:* (030) 47533790
Founded: 1990
ISBN Prefix(es): 3-928942

Germanisches Nationalmuseum
Postfach 11 95 80, 90105 Nuernberg
Tel: (0911) 13310; (0911) 1331 165 (orders)
Fax: (0911) 1331 200
E-mail: verlag@gnm.de; j.hofmann@gnm.de (orders)
Web Site: www.gnm.de
Key Personnel
Chief of Publishing Dept: Dr Hermann Maue
Assistant in Publishing Dept: Christine Kupper *Tel:* (0911) 1331165 *E-mail:* c.kupper@gnm.de
Founded: 1853
Books & catalogues about artistic & cultural history from German speaking regions from prehistoric times to present, related to the museum's collections.
Subjects: Archaeology, Art, History, Musical instruments
ISBN Prefix(es): 3-926982
Number of titles published annually: 10 Print
Total Titles: 180 Print; 2 CD-ROM

Gerstenberg Verlag+
Rathausstr 18-20, 31134 Hildesheim
Mailing Address: Postfach 100555, 31105 Hildesheim
Tel: (05121) 1060 *Fax:* (05121) 106498; (05121) 106499
E-mail: verlag@gerstenberg-verlag.de
Web Site: www.gerstenberg-verlag.de
Telex: 927108 gberg d
Key Personnel
Man Dir: Dr Edmund Jacoby *Tel:* (05121) 106 451 *E-mail:* dr.edmund.jacoby@gerstenbergverlag.de
Editorial: Petra Albers *Tel:* (05121) 106 460 *E-mail:* petra.albers@gerstenbergverlag.de
Publisher: Dr Bruno Gerstenberg
Manager, Sales & Advertising: Wolfgang J Dietrich *Tel:* (05121) 106 470 *E-mail:* wolfgang.dietrich@gerstenbergverlag.de
Production: Friedrich Weskott *Tel:* (05121) 106 465 *E-mail:* friedrich.weskott@gerstenbergverlag.de
Rights & Permissions: Ina Feist *Tel:* (05121) 106 454 *E-mail:* ina.feist@gerstenbergverlag.de
Publicity: Andrea Deyerling-Baier *Tel:* (05121) 106 456 *E-mail:* andrea.deyerlingbaier@gerstenbergverlag.de
Founded: 1792
Subjects: Architecture & Interior Design, Gardening, Plants, Nonfiction (General)
ISBN Prefix(es): 3-8067

Gerth, Klaus, Verlag GmbH+
Dillerberg 2, 35614 Asslar
Tel: (06443) 68-0 *Fax:* (06443) 6849
E-mail: info@gerth.de
Web Site: www.gerth.de
Key Personnel
Man Dir & International Rights: Klaus Gerth *Tel:* (06443) 6811 *Fax:* (06443) 6813 *E-mail:* gerth@gerth.de
Man Dir: Dieter Spahn
Founded: 1949
Subjects: Music, Dance, Religion - Other, Theology
ISBN Prefix(es): 3-89615
Distributor for Ganzteam Music

Verlag fuer Geschichte der Naturwissenschaften und der Technik+
Schlossstr 1, 49356 Diepholz
Tel: (05441) 92 71 29 *Fax:* (05441) 92 71 27
E-mail: service@gnt-verlag.de
Web Site: www.gnt-verlag.de
Key Personnel
Publisher: Reinald Schroeder
Founded: 1990
Specialize in Scientific Publications.
Subjects: History, History of Science & Technology
ISBN Prefix(es): 3-928186
Shipping Address: LKG, Bestellannahme, Potzschauer Weg, 04579 Espenhain
Warehouse: LKG, Bestellannahme, Potzschauer Weg, 04579 Espenhain
Orders to: LKG Bestellannahme, Poetzschauer Weg, 04579 Espenhain

Gesellschaft, *imprint of* Anton Hiersemann, Verlag

Gesellschaft fur Organisationswissenschaft e V+
Haus No 18 A, 95490 Mistelgau-Truppach
Tel: (9206) 480 *Fax:* (9206) 628
Key Personnel
Chairman: Mr Rudiger W Monz
Vice Chairman: Theodor Konig
Founded: 1956
Spreading of Organization Science according to (& authorized by) the late Dr.techn. Kurt V Wieser, Vienna, by instruction & books. Sell rights of non-English translations.
Subjects: Social Sciences, Sociology
ISBN Prefix(es): 3-926980
Number of titles published annually: 0 Print
Total Titles: 24 Print

Gesundheits-Dialog Verlag GmbH+
Postfach 14 53, 82033 Oberhaching
Tel: (089) 6 13 40 24 *Fax:* (089) 6 13 37 87
E-mail: dialog.top@t-online.de
Web Site: www.gesundheit-naturheilkunde.de
Key Personnel
Publisher: Franz Woellzenmueller
Subjects: Child Care & Development, Health, Nutrition, Medicine, Nursing, Dentistry, Sports, Athletics
ISBN Prefix(es): 3-929732

Gieck Reiner v Ursel Gieck+
Nimrodstr 26, 82110 Germering
Tel: (089) 8415906 *Fax:* (089) 8403310
Key Personnel
Contact: R Gieck
Founded: 1931
Subjects: Engineering (General), Mechanical Engineering
ISBN Prefix(es): 3-920379
Orders to: Dunod, 5, rue Laromiguiere, F-75241 Paris Cedex 05, France
Delta Press, Endseweg 3 NL, 3959 AT Amerougen, Overberg, Netherlands
McGraw Hill Inc, 1221 Avenue of the Americas, New York, NY 10020, United States
Brockhaus Commission, Postfach 1220, D-70806 Kornwestheim
Alfaomega Grupo Editor, SA, Pitagoras 1139, Col Del Valle 03100, Mexico

Verlag Ernst und Werner Gieseking GmbH
Deckertstr 30, 33617 Bielefield
Mailing Address: Postfach 13 01 20, 33544 Bielefeld
Tel: (0521) 1 46 74 *Fax:* (0521) 14 37 15
Web Site: www.gieseking.de
Key Personnel
Man Dir & Publisher: Dr Klaus Schleicher
Founded: 1937
Subjects: Law, Music, Dance
ISBN Prefix(es): 3-7694
Orders to: VVA

H Gietl Verlag & Publikationsservice GmbH+
Pfaelzer Str 11, 93128 Regenstauf
Mailing Address: Postfach 166, 93122 Regenstauf
Tel: (09402) 93 37-0 *Fax:* (09402) 93 37-24
E-mail: gietl-verlag@t-online.de
Web Site: www.gietl-verlag.de
Key Personnel
Man Dir: Heinrich Gietl *Tel:* (09402) 93 37-15 *E-mail:* heinrich.gietl@gietl-verlag.de; Josef Roidl *Tel:* (09402) 93 37-13 *E-mail:* josef.roidl@gietl-verlag.de
Advertising Manager: Kurt Fischer *Tel:* (09402) 93 37-14 *E-mail:* kurt.fischer@gietl-verlag.de
Special publishing house for numismatic literature.
Subjects: Crafts, Games, Hobbies, History

Gildefachverlag GmbH & Co KG+
Foehrster Str 8, 31061 Alfeld
Tel: (05181) 8004-0 *Fax:* (05181) 800490
Key Personnel
Man Dir: Wilhelm Schlame
Founded: 1949
Specialize in Gastronomy & Crafts.
Subjects: Cookery, Crafts, Games, Hobbies, Health, Nutrition
ISBN Prefix(es): 3-7734
Imprints: IWT Magazine Publishing House GmbH
Subsidiaries: Gildebuchverlag

Gilles und Francke Verlag+
Blumenstr 67-69, 47057 Duisburg
Tel: (0203) 362787 *Fax:* (0203) 355520
E-mail: gilles-francke@t-online.de
Web Site: www.gilles-francke.de
Key Personnel
Publisher & Proprietor: Werner Francke
Sales: Barbara Francke
Founded: 1900
Subjects: Fiction, Literature, Literary Criticism, Essays, Poetry
ISBN Prefix(es): 3-921104; 3-925348
Number of titles published annually: 4 Print
Total Titles: 3 Print
Bookshop(s): G & F Buch und Zeitschriftenhandlung *E-mail:* buchversand@gilles-francke.de
Web Site: www.gilles-francke.de

GLB Parkland Verlags-und Vertriebs GmbH+
Zollstockguertel 5, 50969 Cologne
Mailing Address: Postfach 510604, 50942 Cologne
Tel: (0221) 9364380 *Fax:* (0221) 9364383
Telex: 721907
Key Personnel
Man Dir: Heiner Taubert; Gerd Fiegweil
Founded: 1974
Subjects: Antiques, Architecture & Interior Design, Art, Gardening, Plants, Poetry, Travel
ISBN Prefix(es): 3-88059

Warehouse: VSB Verlagsservice Braunschweig GmbH, Georg-Westermann-Allee 66, 38104 Braunschweig, Postfach 4738, 38037 Braunschweig
Orders to: VSB Verlagsservice Braunschweig GmbH, Georg-Westermann-Allee 66, 38104 Braunschweig

Gloatz, Hille GmbH & Co KG fur Mehrfarben und Zellglasdruck
Poleigrund 14-20, 12307 Berlin
Mailing Address: Postfach 490108, 12281 Berlin
Tel: (030) 721 99 12; (030) 723 254 93
Fax: (030) 721 95 65
E-mail: gloatz.hille.gmbh@gmx.de; info@gloatz-hille.de
Web Site: www.gloatz-hille.de *Cable:* GEHACO D
Key Personnel
Manager: Hans-Peter Gloatz
Founded: 1936
Subjects: Engineering (General), Geography, Geology, Medicine, Nursing, Dentistry

Verlagsgesellschaft R Gloess & Co+
Notkestr 11, 22607 Hamburg
Mailing Address: Postfach 520362, 22593 Hamburg
Tel: (040) 890 5202 *Fax:* (040) 890 5193
Key Personnel
Owner, Publisher, Rights & Permissions: Wolfgang Gloess
Founded: 1932
Also book packager.
Subjects: Biography, Government, Political Science, Health, Nutrition, Science (General), Travel
ISBN Prefix(es): 3-87261
Subsidiaries: Hanseatic Buch- und Presse Erzeugnisse GmbH; MCS MedienCreativService GmbH

Verlag Glueckauf GmbH+
Montebruchstr 2, 45219 Essen
Mailing Address: Postfach 185620, 45206 Essen
Tel: (02054) 924121 *Fax:* (02054) 924129
E-mail: vge-vertrieb@t-online.de
Web Site: www.vge.de
Key Personnel
Man Dir, Editorial, Rights & Permissions: Bernd Litke
Sales, Publicity: H Schwab
Founded: 1918
Member of German Society for Geotechnical Engineering (DGGT) & Austrian Society for Geomechanics (OEGG).
Subjects: Earth Sciences, Energy, Environmental Studies
ISBN Prefix(es): 3-7739

Bruno Gmuender Verlag GmbH+
Leuschnerdamm 31, 10999 Berlin
Mailing Address: Postfach 610104, 10921 Berlin
Tel: (030) 6150030 *Fax:* (030) 6159007
E-mail: info@brunogmuender.com
Web Site: www.brunogmuender.com
Key Personnel
Man Dir: B Gmuender
Founded: 1981
Subjects: Gay & Lesbian
ISBN Prefix(es): 3-86187
Imprints: Albino Verlag
Bookshop(s): Bruno's in Berlin, Nuernbergerstr 53, 10789 Berlin; Bruno's in Cologne, Friesenwall 24, 50672 Cologne

GNT-Verlag, see Verlag fuer Geschichte der Naturwissenschaften und der Technik

Cornelia Goethe Literaturverlag
Hanauer Landstr 334, 60314 Frankfurt am Main
Tel: (069) 40894-0 *Fax:* (069) 40894-194
E-mail: literatur@fouque-verlag.de
Web Site: www.cornelia-goethe.de; www.fouque-verlag.de
Founded: 1987
ISBN Prefix(es): 3-8267
Branch Office(s)
1402 John F Kennedy Crwy, PM 3113, North Bay Village, Miami, FL 33141, United States

Wilhelm Goldmann Verlag GmbH
Neumarkterstr 18, 81673 Munich
Mailing Address: Postfach 800709, 81607 Munich
Tel: (089) 4372-0 *Fax:* (089) 43722812
E-mail: vertrieb.verlagsgruppe@bertelsmann.de
Telex: 529965 wgvmn d
Key Personnel
Man Dir: Klaus Eck
Editorial: Dr Georg Reuchlein-Diehl
Sales: Volker Neumann
Publicity: Brigitte Nunner
Founded: 1922
Subjects: Art, Astrology, Occult, Biography, Criminology, Education, Fiction, Film, Video, History, How-to, Law, Medicine, Nursing, Dentistry, Psychology, Psychiatry, Science (General), Science Fiction, Fantasy, Social Sciences, Sociology
ISBN Prefix(es): 3-442
Parent Company: Verlagsgruppe Bertelsmann GmbH
U.S. Office(s): Bettina Schrewe Literary Scouting, 101 Fifth Ave, Suite 11B, NY 10003, United States (US Scout)
Foreign Rep(s): Angelika Straus-Fischer

Goldschneck Verlag+
Burghaldenstr 57, 71384 Weinstadt
Mailing Address: Postfach 1265, 71399 Korb
Tel: (07151) 66 01 19 *Fax:* (07151) 66 07 78
E-mail: goldschneck@t-online.de
Web Site: www.goldschneck.de
Key Personnel
Owner: Werner Weidert
Founded: 1983
Specialize in Paleontology.
Subjects: Geography, Geology
ISBN Prefix(es): 3-926129
Number of titles published annually: 2 Print
Total Titles: 1 Print

Goll Bruno Verlag fur Aussergewoehnliche Perspektiven (VAP)+
Postfach 1180, 32352 Preussisch Oldendorf
Tel: (05742) 93 04 44 *Fax:* (05742) 93 04 55
Web Site: www.vap-buch.de
Founded: 1972
Subjects: Government, Political Science
ISBN Prefix(es): 3-922367
Divisions: Edition ScienTerra; Edition Freie Energie; Edition Life Energie
Shipping Address: VAP-Verlagsauslieferung, Postfach 1180, 32352 PreuBisch Oldendorf & Mindenerstr 34, PreuBisch Oldendorf

Gondrom Verlag GmbH & Co KG+
Buehlstr 4, 95463 Bindlach
Mailing Address: Postfach 1, 95463 Bindlach
Tel: (09208) 51-0 *Fax:* (09208) 51-21
E-mail: service@gondrom.de
Web Site: www.gondrom.de
Telex: 920882
Key Personnel
President: Volker Gondrom
Man Dir: Jens Brase
Editorial, Rights & Permissions: Reinhard Fabian
Founded: 1974
Subjects: Art, History, Literature, Literary Criticism, Essays, Nonfiction (General)
ISBN Prefix(es): 3-8112
Associate Companies: Loewe Verlag, Buehlstr 4, 95461 Bindlach

Govi-Verlag Pharmazeutischer Verlag GmbH+
Carl Mannich Str 26, 65760 Eschborn
Mailing Address: Postfach 5360, 65728 Eschborn
Tel: (06196) 928 250 *Fax:* (06196) 928 259
E-mail: service@govi.de
Web Site: www.govi.de
Key Personnel
Man Dir: Peter J Egenolf *Tel:* (06196) 928 201 *Fax:* (06196) 928 203
Founded: 1949
Subjects: Specialized in Pharmaceuticals & Medicine
ISBN Prefix(es): 3-7741
Total Titles: 140 Print; 20 CD-ROM
Online services available through World Wide Web.
Parent Company: Bundesvereinigung Deutscher Apothekerverbaende, Ginnheimer Str 26, 65760 Echborn Tannus
Associate Companies: Werbe-und Vertriebsgesellschaft Deutscher Apotheker mbH; Zentrallaboratorium Deutscher Apotheker; Marketing-Gesellschaft Deutscher Apotheker mbH
Distributor for WHO World-Health-Organization
Bookshop(s): Versandbuchhandlung, 65760 Eschborn Taunus *E-mail:* service@govi.de
Warehouse: Industriestr 1, Eschborn

Grabert-Verlag+
Am Apfelberg 18, 72076 Tuebingen
Mailing Address: Postfach 1629, 72006 Tuebingen
Tel: (07071) 40700 *Fax:* (07071) 407026 *Cable:* GRABERT-TUBINGEN
Key Personnel
Man Dir & Owner: Wigbert Grabert
Founded: 1953
Subjects: Art, Biography, History
ISBN Prefix(es): 3-87847
Number of titles published annually: 10 Print
Total Titles: 200 Print
Book Club(s): Deutscher Buchkreis

Brigitte Grabitz - ikoo Buchverlag+
Schindellohe 25, Pullenreuth 95704
Tel: (09234) 1295 *Fax on Demand:* (09234) 8468
Founded: 1980
Subjects: Biography, Fiction, Human Relations, Photography, Regional Interests
ISBN Prefix(es): 3-88677

Graefe und Unzer Verlag GmbH+
Grillparzerstr 12, 81675 Munich
Mailing Address: Postfach 86 03 66, 81630 Munich
Tel: (089) 4 19 81-0 *Fax:* (089) 4 19 81-113
Web Site: www.graefe-und-unzer.de
Key Personnel
Publisher & Man Dir: Georg Kessler *Tel:* (089) 41981404 *E-mail:* kessler@graefe-und-unzer.de
Man Dir, Distribution & Sales: Guenter Kopietz *Tel:* (089) 41981307 *E-mail:* kopietz@graefe-und-unzer.de
Man Dir, Finances: Stefan Hoyer *Tel:* (089) 41981300 *E-mail:* hoyer@graefe-und-unzer.de
Rights Dir: Annette Beetz *Tel:* (089) 41981150 *E-mail:* beetz@graefe-und-unzer.de
Foreign Rights Manager (US, UK, Latin America, Spain & Portugal): Manuela Kerkhoff *Tel:* (089) 41981153 *E-mail:* kerkhoff@graefe-und-unzer.de
Foreign Rights Manager (France, Italy, Eastern EU, Asia): Gabriella Hoffman *Tel:* (089) 41981419 *E-mail:* hoffmann@graefe-und-unzer.de
Foreign Rights Manager (Germany & Northern Europe): Ingrid Puchner *Tel:* (089) 41981412 *E-mail:* puchner@graefe-und-unzer.de

Man Editor GU: Doris Birk *Tel:* (089) 41981409
 E-mail: birk@graefe-und-unzer.de
Editorial Dir, Cookery: Birgit Rademacker
 Tel: (089) 41981401 *E-mail:* rademacker@
 graefe-und-unzer.de
Editorial Dir, Gardening: Anne Hahnstein
 Tel: (089) 41981319 *E-mail:* hahnstein@
 graefe-und-unzer.de
Editorial Dir, Pets: Anita Zellner *Tel:* (089)
 41981215 *E-mail:* zellner@graefe-und-unzer.de
Editorial Dir, Health: Ulrich Ehrlenspiel
 Tel: (089) 41981118 *E-mail:* ehrlenspiel@
 graefe-und-unzer.de
Editorial Dir, Travel: Veronica Reisenegger
 Tel: (089) 41981426 *E-mail:* reisenegger@
 graefe-und-unzer.de
Editorial Dir, Business: Steffen Haselbach
 Tel: (089) 41981486 *E-mail:* haselbach@
 graefe-und-unzer.de
Distribution & Sales, Trade: Jan Wiesemann
 Tel: (089) 41981305 *E-mail:* wiesemann@
 graefe-und-unzer.de
Distribution & Sales, Non-Trade: Erik Vogel
 Tel: (089) 41981302 *E-mail:* vogel@graefe-
 und-unzer.de
Marketing Dir: Kerstin Moskon *Tel:* (089)
 41981205 *E-mail:* moskon@graefe-und-unzer.
 de
Production Manager: Thomas Narr *Tel:* (089)
 41981402 *E-mail:* narr@graefe-und-unzer.de
Founded: 1722
Subjects: Animals, Pets, Business, Cookery, Gardening, Plants, Health, Nutrition, Natural History, Self-Help, Travel
ISBN Prefix(es): 3-7742
Number of titles published annually: 120 Print
Total Titles: 1,050 Print
Imprints: Feinschmecker (Gourmet Cookery); Hallwag (Wine); Merian (Travel Guide Series); Teubner Edition (Cookery)
Warehouse: Verlegerdienst Munchen, Gutenbergstr 1, 82205 Gilching

Graf Editions
Elisabethstr 29, 80796 Munich
Tel: (089) 27 159 57 *Fax:* (089) 27 159 97
Web Site: www.grafeditions.de
Key Personnel
Contact: Dieter Graf
Founded: 1993
Subjects: Language Arts, Linguistics, Travel, Hiking
ISBN Prefix(es): 3-9803130
Total Titles: 3 Print
Distributed by Baseline Book Co (UK); Fotofolio (USA); Map Link (USA); Museum of Contemporary Art (USA); OLF SA Centre de Distribution (Switzerland); R&B Verlagsauslieferung (Austria); Umbreit Verlagsauslieferung; Willems Adventure (Netherlands)
Foreign Rep(s): Baseline Book Company (UK); Cordee Distributors (UK); Fotofolio (US); Hellenic Distribution Agency (Greece); MapLink (US); Scanmaps (Denmark); Willems Adventure (Netherlands)
Bookshop(s): Museum of Contemporary Art Bookstore, 250 S Grand Ave, Los Angeles, CA 90012, United States

Grafit Verlag GmbH+
Chemnitzerstr 31, 44139 Dortmund
Tel: (0231) 7 21 46 50 *Fax:* (0231) 7 21 46 77
E-mail: info@grafit.de
Web Site: www.grafit.de
Key Personnel
Manager: Rutger Booss
Founded: 1989
Member of Boersenverein des deutschen Buchhandels.
Subjects: Fiction, Mysteries, Modern detective stories, crime fiction
ISBN Prefix(es): 3-89425
Number of titles published annually: 20 Print

Total Titles: 150 Print
Orders to: CVK Cornelsen, Postfach 100271, 33502 Bielefeld

Verlag der Stiftung Gralsbotschaft GmbH+
Lenzhalde 15, 70192 Stuttgart
Tel: (07156) 5096 *Fax:* (07156) 18663
E-mail: info@gral.de
Web Site: www.gral.de
Key Personnel
Man Dir, Editor: Juergen Sprick
Founded: 1928
Subjects: Health, Nutrition, Human Relations, Nonfiction (General), Parapsychology, Philosophy, Religion - Other, Self-Help
ISBN Prefix(es): 3-87860
U.S. Office(s): Grail Foundation Press, PO Box 45, Gambier, OH 43022, United States

Grand Prix Stars, *imprint of* Heel Verlag GmbH

Grass-Verlag
Bleerstr 107, 40789 Monheim
Mailing Address: Postfach 100219, 40766 Monheim
Tel: (02173) 51305 *Fax:* (02224) 79671
Key Personnel
Publisher: Aloys Grass
Founded: 1984
Subjects: Religion - Protestant
ISBN Prefix(es): 3-924974

Greuthof Verlag und Vertrieb GmbH+
Herrenweg 2, 79261 Gutach i Br
Tel: (07681) 6025 *Fax:* (07681) 6027
ISBN Prefix(es): 3-923662

Greven Verlag Koeln GmbH+
Neue Weyerstr 1-3, 50676 Cologne
Mailing Address: Postfach 101644, 50478 Cologne
Tel: (0221) 20 33-161 *Fax:* (0221) 20 33-162
E-mail: greven.verlag@greven.de
Web Site: www.greven-verlag.de
Telex: 8882249 grev d *Cable:* GREVENVERLAG KOLN
Key Personnel
Man Dir, Rights & Permissions: Irene Greven
Publishing Managers: Dr Diethelm Schmidt; Manfred vom Stein
Founded: 1827
Subjects: Art, Regional Interests
ISBN Prefix(es): 3-7743

Griese Ingolf Wipe Griese+
Franz-Hitzestr 15, 44263 Dortmund
Mailing Address: Postfach 300247, 44232 Dortmund
Tel: (0231) 417412 *Fax:* (0231) 418461; (0231) 417418
Key Personnel
President & Publisher: Ingo Griese Privat-Dozent
Subjects: Economics, Sports, Athletics
ISBN Prefix(es): 3-9801985; 3-928594

Grote'sche Verlagsbuchhandlung GmbH & Co KG
Max-Planckstr 12, 50858 Cologne
Mailing Address: Postfach 400263, 50832 Cologne
Tel: (02234) 1060 *Fax:* (02234) 106284
Cable: GROTEVERLAG
Key Personnel
Publisher: Dr Juergen Gutbrod
Founded: 1661
Subjects: History
ISBN Prefix(es): 3-7745
Parent Company: W Kohlhammer GmbH, Hessbruehlstr 69, 70565 Stuttgart

Warehouse: Verlagsvertrieb Stuttgart GmbH, 70549 Stuttgart
Orders to: W Kohlhammer GmbH, 70549 Stuttgart

Verlag Grundlagen und Praxis GmbH & Co+
Bergmannstr 20, 26789 Leer
Tel: (0491) 6 18 86 *Fax:* (0491) 36 34
E-mail: grundlagen-praxis@t-online.de
Web Site: www.grundlagen-praxis.de
Key Personnel
Man Dir, Rights & Permissions: Margarete Harms
Manager: Dr Carsten Brandt
Founded: 1972
Subjects: Language Arts, Linguistics, Medicine, Nursing, Dentistry
ISBN Prefix(es): 3-921229

Gruner + Jahr AG & Co
Am Baumwall 11, 20459 Hamburg
Mailing Address: Postfach 110011, 20459 Hamburg
Tel: (040) 37030 *Fax:* (040) 37036000
E-mail: oeffentlichkeiharbeit@guj.de
Key Personnel
Chief Executive Officer: Gerd Schulte-Hillen
Subjects: Human Relations, Photography
ISBN Prefix(es): 3-570

Gruppe 21 GmbH+
Landsberger Str 101, 45219 Essen
Tel: (02054) 1048-90 *Fax:* (02054) 1048-929
E-mail: marketing@gruppe21.de
Web Site: www.gruppe21.de
Key Personnel
Manager: Gerhard Klaes
Founded: 1986
Specialize in Database & Electronic Publishing Services.
ISBN Prefix(es): 3-928930
Orders to: Siehe Zeile 010

Verlag Gruppenpaedagogischer Literatur+
Rudolf-Diesel-Str 8, 61273 Wehrheim
Mailing Address: Postfach 1252, 61269 Wehrheim
Tel: (06081) 5 67 40 *Fax:* (06081) 5 74 38
E-mail: info@vglw.de
Web Site: vglw.de
Founded: 1976
Boersenverein des deutschen Buchhandels.
Subjects: Career Development, Child Care & Development, Crafts, Games, Hobbies, Education, Music, Dance, Outdoor Recreation, Sports, Athletics
ISBN Prefix(es): 3-921496; 3-89544

Walter de Gruyter GmbH & Co KG+
Genthinerstr 13, 10785 Berlin
Tel: (030) 260 05-0 *Fax:* (030) 260 05-222
E-mail: wdg-info@degruyter.de
Web Site: www.degruyter.de
Telex: 184027 *Cable:* WISSENSCHAFT BERLIN 0184027
Key Personnel
Man Dir: Dr Hans-Robert Cram; Reinhold Tokar
Sales: Harald Hoffmann
Marketing: Matern von Marschall
Marketing Dir: Dorothea Kern *E-mail:* kern@degruyter.de
Advertising: Dietlind Makswitat *E-mail:* ad@degruyter.de
Public Relations: Ulrike Lippe *E-mail:* ulrike.lippe@degruyter.com
Founded: 1919
Subjects: Archaeology, Biological Sciences, Business, Earth Sciences, Geography, Geology, Government, Political Science, History, Journalism, Language Arts, Linguistics, Law, Literature, Literary Criticism, Essays, Management, Marketing, Mathematics, Medicine, Nurs-

ing, Dentistry, Philosophy, Physical Sciences, Physics, Science (General), Social Sciences, Sociology, Theology
ISBN Prefix(es): 0-202; 3-11
Total Titles: 12,000 Print
Subsidiaries: Aldine de Gruyter; Mouton de Gruyter
U.S. Office(s): Walter de Gruyter, Inc, 200 Saw Mill River Rd, Hawthorne, NY 10532, United States *Tel:* 914-747-0110 *Fax:* 914-747-1326

Arthur L Sellier & Co-Walter de Gruyter & Co, see Dr Arthur L Sellier & Co-Walter de Gruyter GmbH & Co KG OHG

GTB Guetersloher Taschenbuecher (pocketbooks), *imprint of* Guetersloher Verlagshaus Gerd Mohn

Gunter Olzog Verlag GmbH+
Fuerstenriederstr 250, 81377 Munich
Tel: (089) 71 04 66 60 *Fax:* (089) 71 04 66 61
E-mail: olzog.verlag@t-online.de
Web Site: www.olzog.de
Key Personnel
Publisher: Dr Reinhard Moestl *Tel:* (089) 71 04 66 64 *E-mail:* moestl@olzog.de
Man Dir, Rights & Permissions: Dr Dirk F Passmann
Sales: Stefan Keim *Tel:* (089) 71 04 66 65 *E-mail:* keim@olzog.de
Rights & Permissions: Gerlinde Stanglmeier
Advertising: Martina Gesierich
Publicity: Claudia Franz *E-mail:* franz@olzog.de
Founded: 1949
Member of TR- Verlagsunion GmbH.
Subjects: Economics, Film, Video, Foreign Countries, Government, Political Science, History, Journalism, Management, Marketing, Publishing & Book Trade Reference, Social Sciences, Sociology
ISBN Prefix(es): 3-7892
Parent Company: Verlag Moderne Industrie AG

Guenther Butkus+
Stapenhorststr 15, 33615 Bielefeld
Tel: (0521) 69689 *Fax:* (0521) 174470
E-mail: pendragon.verlag@t-online.de
Web Site: www.pendragon.de
Key Personnel
Publisher: Gunther Butkus
Founded: 1981
Subjects: Art, Fiction, Poetry, Novels, poems & music
ISBN Prefix(es): 3-929096
Total Titles: 200 Print; 4 Audio
Distributed by Prolit

Guetersloher Verlagshaus Gerd Mohn+
Carl-Bertelsmann-Str 270, Guetersloh 33311
Mailing Address: Postfach 450, 33311 Guetersloh
Tel: (05241) 74050 *Fax:* (05241) 740548
E-mail: info@guetersloher-vh.de
Web Site: www.guetersloher-vh.de
Telex: 933868 bert d *Cable:* BERTELSMANN GUTERSLOH
Key Personnel
Man Dir, Rights & Permissions: Hans Juergen Meurer
International Rights Contact: Heike Daut-Ruenger
Founded: 1835 (1959)
Subjects: Anthropology, Biblical Studies, Biography, Government, Political Science, Philosophy, Religion - Protestant, Religion - Other, Theology
ISBN Prefix(es): 3-579
Parent Company: Verlagsgruppe Bertelsmann International GmbH
Imprints: GTB Guetersloher Taschenbuecher (pocketbooks); K T Kaiser Taschenbuecher (pocketbooks)
Subsidiaries: Kaiser Christian/Guetersloher Verlaghaus
Shipping Address: VVA Bertelsmann Distribution, Postfach 7777, Guetersloh
Warehouse: VVA Bertelsmann Distribution, Postfach 7777, Guetersloh
Orders to: VVA Bertelsmann Distribution, Postfach 7777, Guetersloh

Verlag Klaus Guhl
Knobelsdorffstr 8, 14059 Berlin
Mailing Address: Postfach 191532, 14005 Berlin
Tel: (030) 3213062 *Fax:* (030) 3215549
Key Personnel
Man Dir: Dr Klaus-Dieter Guhl
Editorial: Fabian Carlos Guhl
Sales: Florian Robert Guhl
Production: Hans Paul Guhl
Publicity: Dr Kurt Kreiler
Rights & Permissions: Dr Thomas Bark
Founded: 1974
Subjects: Art, Government, Political Science, Literature, Literary Criticism, Essays
ISBN Prefix(es): 3-88220
Subsidiaries: Fanel GmbH; Buchladen Bunter Baer GmbH
Bookshop(s): Bunter Baer-Guhl, Knobelsdorffstr 8, 14059 Berlin

Verlag des Gustav-Adolf-Werks
Pistorisstr 6, 04229 Leipzig
Tel: (0341) 490 62 18 *Fax:* (0341) 49 62 66
E-mail: gaw-verlag@t-online.de
Key Personnel
Publishing Manager: Evelin Hoehne
Founded: 1968
Subjects: Developing Countries, Religion - Protestant, Theology
ISBN Prefix(es): 3-87593

Gustav Mesmer Stiftung, *imprint of* Silberburg-Verlag Titus Haeussermann GmbH

Gutenberg-Gesellschaft eV
Liebfrauenplatz 5, D-55116 Mainz
Tel: (06131) 22 64 20 *Fax:* (06131) 23 35 30
E-mail: gutenberg-gesellschaft@freenet.de
Web Site: www.gutenberg-gesellschaft.uni-mainz.de
Key Personnel
President: Jens Beutel
Vice President: Senator Hannetraud Schultheiss
Editor-in-Chief: Dr Stephan Fuessel
Secretary General: Karl Delorme
Founded: 1900
Subjects: Publishing & Book Trade Reference
ISBN Prefix(es): 3-7755

Gutersloher Verlaghaus GmbH /Chr Kaiser/Kiefel/Quell+
Carl-Miele-Str 214, 33311 Guetersloh
Mailing Address: Postfach 450, 33311 Guetersloh
Tel: (05241) 74050 *Fax:* (05241) 740550
E-mail: info@guetersloher-vh.de
Web Site: www.gtv.de
Telex: 933868 bert d
Key Personnel
Man Dir, Rights & Permissions: Hans Juergen Meurer
International Rights Contact: Heike Daut-Ruenger
Founded: 1845
Subjects: Religion - Other, Theology
ISBN Prefix(es): 3-579

H B Verlags und Vertriebs-Gesellschaft mbH
Alsterufer 4, 20354 Hamburg
Tel: (040) 4151-04 *Fax:* (040) 41513231
Key Personnel
Dir: Dr Joachim Dreyer; Eike Schmidt; Kurt Bortz
Founded: 1979
ISBN Prefix(es): 3-616; 3-922822

H L Schlapp Buch- und Antiquariatshandlung GmbH und Co KG Abt Verlag
Ludwigsplatz 3, 64283 Darmstadt
Tel: (06151) 17 90-0 *Fax:* (06151) 17 90 40
E-mail: hlschlapp@aol.com
Web Site: www.schlapp.de
Key Personnel
Owner: Karl-Eugen Schlapp; Eckart Schlapp
Founded: 1836
Subjects: Regional Interests
ISBN Prefix(es): 3-87704

Verlag H M Hauschild GmbH
Hans-Bredow-Str 7, 28307 Bremen
Tel: (0421) 1785-0; (0421) 407040 *Fax:* (0421) 1785-285
E-mail: info@hauschild-werbedruck.de
Web Site: www.hauschild.werbedruck.de
Key Personnel
Dir: Friedrich Steinmeyer; Andreas Nagel
Rights & Permissions: Ernst-August Echtermann
Founded: 1854
Subjects: Art, Regional Interests
ISBN Prefix(es): 3-920699; 3-926598; 3-929902; 3-89757; 3-931785
Parent Company: Werbedruck Bremen Grafischer Betrieb GmbH

Haack, *imprint of* Justus Perthes Verlag Gotha GmbH

Haag und Herchen Verlag GmbH+
Fichardstr 30, 60322 Frankfurt am Main
Tel: (069) 550911-13 *Fax:* (069) 552601; (069) 554922
E-mail: verlag@haagundherchen.de
Web Site: www.haagundherchen.de
Key Personnel
Man Dir, Rights & Permissions: Hans-Alfred Herchen
Founded: 1975
Subjects: Engineering (General), Government, Political Science, How-to, Medicine, Nursing, Dentistry, Psychology, Psychiatry, Science (General), Social Sciences, Sociology
ISBN Prefix(es): 3-88129; 3-86137; 3-89228

C W Haarfeld GmbH & Co
Annastr 32-36, 45130 Essen
Mailing Address: Postfach 101562, 45015 Essen
Tel: (0201) 720950 *Fax:* (0201) 7209533
Key Personnel
Man Dir: Wolfgang Otto
Founded: 1867
ISBN Prefix(es): 3-7747
Parent Company: Wolters Kluwer NV, Netherlands

Wolfgang G Haas - Musikverlag Koeln ek+
Rheinbergstr 92, 51143 Cologne
Tel: (02203) 98 88 3-0 *Fax:* (02203) 98 88 3-50
E-mail: info@haas-koeln.de
Web Site: www.haas-koeln.de
Key Personnel
Contact: Wolfgang G Haas
Founded: 1985
Member of International Trumpet Guild & German Society of Music Publishers.
Subjects: Music, Dance
ISBN Prefix(es): 3-928453

Dr Rudolf Habelt GmbH
Am Buchenhang 1, 53115 Bonn
Mailing Address: Postfach 150104, 53040 Bonn
Tel: (0228) 9 23 83-22 *Fax:* (0228) 9 23 83-23
E-mail: info@habelt.de *Web Site:* www.habelt.de
Tel: (0228) 9 23 83-0 *Fax:* (0228) 9 23 83-6

GERMANY

E-mail: info@habelt.de
Web Site: www.habelt.de
Key Personnel
Man Dir: Wolfgang Habelt
Editorial, Production: Renate Schreiber
Founded: 1954
Subjects: Archaeology, History, Regional Interests
ISBN Prefix(es): 3-7749
Number of titles published annually: 30 Print
Bookshop(s): Antiquarian Bookshop, Am Buchenhang 1, 53115 Bonn, Wolfgang Habelt *Tel:* (0228) 9 23 83-33 *Fax:* (0228) 9 23 83-6

Hachmeister Verlag+
Klosterstr 12, 48143 Munster
Tel: (0251) 51210 *Fax:* (0251) 57217
E-mail: hachmeister.galerie@t-online.de
Web Site: www.hachmeister-galerie.de
Key Personnel
Dir: Dr Heiner Hachmeister
Founded: 1979
Catalogues & books.
Subjects: Art
ISBN Prefix(es): 3-88829
Total Titles: 35 Print
Parent Company: Hachmeister Galerie

Walter Haedecke Verlag+
Lukas-Moser-Weg 2, 71263 Weil der Stadt
Mailing Address: Postfach 1203, 71256 Weil der Stadt
Tel: (07033) 13 80 80 *Fax:* (07033) 13 80 813
E-mail: haedecke_vlg@t-online.de
Key Personnel
Owner & Publisher: Joachim Graff
Founded: 1919
Subjects: Cookery, Health, Nutrition, Self-Help, Wine & Spirits
ISBN Prefix(es): 3-7750
Number of titles published annually: 16 Print
Total Titles: 112 Print
Distributor for NaturaViva Verlags GmbH

Dr Curt Haefner-Verlag GmbH+
Bachstr 14-16, 69121 Heidelberg
Mailing Address: Postfach 106060, 69050 Heidelberg
Tel: (06221) 64 46-0 *Fax:* (06221) 64 46-40
E-mail: info@haefner-verlag.de
Web Site: www.haefner-verlag.de
Key Personnel
President: Wolfram Poeschel
Founded: 1956
Medicine, Nursing & Social Sciences.
Subjects: Business, Child Care & Development, Education, Health, Nutrition, Human Relations, Medicine, Nursing, Dentistry, Public Administration, Science (General), Social Sciences, Sociology, Safety on Work & Occupational Health
ISBN Prefix(es): 3-87284
Total Titles: 22 Print
Subsidiaries: Werkschriften Verlag GmbH

Dr Haensel-Hohenhausen AG+
German Library of Sciences, Hanauer Landstr 338, 60314 Frankfurt
Tel: (069) 40894-0 *Fax:* (069) 40894-194
E-mail: info@haensel-hohenhausen.de
Web Site: www.german-library.com
Key Personnel
Publishing Manager: Dr Rafael Huentelmann
 Tel: (069) 40894-151 *E-mail:* huentelmann@haensel-hohenhausen.de
Founded: 1986
Member of AAP, ABA & World Union of Publishers.
Subjects: Philosophy, Theology, Humane Sciences
ISBN Prefix(es): 3-8267
Number of titles published annually: 5 Print
Total Titles: 8 Print

Imprints: Deutsche Bibliothek der Wissenschaften/German Library of Sciences; Deutsche Hochschulschriften/German University Studies; Fouque-Literaturverlag; Fouque-Publishers Inc
Foreign Rep(s): EuroBooks Inc

Haenssler Verlag GmbH+
Max-Eyth-Str 41, 71088 Holzgerlingen
Tel: (07158) 1770 *Fax:* (07158) 177119; (07158) 177100
E-mail: info@haenssler.de
Web Site: www.haenssler.de
Key Personnel
Man Dir: Dr Raimund Utsch
Founded: 1919
Member of the Telos Group; Publishes all publications of the American Institute of Musicology.
Subjects: Art, Film, Video, Literature, Literary Criticism, Essays, Music, Dance, Religion - Other
ISBN Prefix(es): 3-7751
Bookshop(s): Hanssler Verlag-Buchhandlung

Haering, Siegfried, Literaten-Verlag Ulm+
Weichselstr 21, 89231 Neu-Ulm
Tel: (0731) 9806040 *Fax:* (0731) 9806042
E-mail: ratart.edition@t-online.de
Key Personnel
Man Dir: Siegfried Haering
Founded: 1986
Subjects: Drama, Theater
ISBN Prefix(es): 3-926217

Heinz-Jurgen Hausser+
Frankfurterstr 64, 64293 Darmstadt
Tel: (06151) 22824 *Fax:* (06151) 26854
Founded: 1989
Subjects: Architecture & Interior Design, Art, Literature, Literary Criticism, Essays
ISBN Prefix(es): 3-927902; 3-89552
Orders to: Lamuv, Nikolaikirchhof 7, 37073 Goettingen

Lehrmittelverlag Wilhelm Hagemann GmbH+
Karlstr 20, 40210 Duesseldorf
Tel: (0211) 17 92 70-0 *Fax:* (0211) 17 92 70-70
E-mail: aktuell@hagemann.de
Web Site: www.hagemann.de *Cable:* HAGEMANNVERLAG DUSSELDORF
Key Personnel
General Manager: Maria Schuette-Hagemann
Sales: Walter Kils-Huetten
Founded: 1929
Member of VGS (Verlagsgesellschaft mbH & Co KG); Association of School Book Publishers; German Didactic Associations; Worlddidac.
Subjects: Biological Sciences, Environmental Studies, Health, Nutrition, Physical Sciences
ISBN Prefix(es): 3-544
Subsidiaries: Hagemann & Partner; Bildungsmedien Verlagsges mbH
Warehouse: Karlstr 16, 40210 Duesseldorf

Hahner Verlagsgesellschaft mbH+
Heidchenberg 11, 52076 Aachen-Hahn
Tel: (02408) 55 05 *Fax:* (02408) 58081
E-mail: office@hvg.de
Key Personnel
Manager: Peter Brand
Founded: 1986
Subjects: Science (General)
ISBN Prefix(es): 3-89294
Parent Company: IZOP-Institut zur Objektivierung von Lern-und Pruefungsverfahren GmbH

Mary Hahn's Kochbuchverlag+
Subsidiary of Buchverlage Langen-Mueller/Herbig

Thomas-Wimmer-Ring 11, 80539 Munich
Tel: (089) 2 90 88-0 *Fax:* (089) 29088154
E-mail: l.eggs@herbig.net
Web Site: www.herbig.net
Key Personnel
Sales, Publicity Manager: Gerhard Koralus
Subjects: Cookery, House & Home
ISBN Prefix(es): 3-87287
Orders to: VVA, An der Autobahn, 33310 Guetersloh

Hahnsche Buchhandlung
Leinstr 32, 30159 Hannover
Mailing Address: Postfach 2460, 30024 Hannover
Tel: (0511) 80 71 80 40 *Fax:* (0511) 36 36 98
E-mail: verlag-hahnsche-buchhandlung@t-online.de
Key Personnel
Manager, Rights & Permissions: Dr Horst Zimmerhackl
Founded: 1792
Specialize in German History.
Member of the Stock Exchange of German Booksellers & Association of German Magazine Publishers.
Subjects: Education, History, Regional Interests
ISBN Prefix(es): 3-7752
Bookshop(s): Abt Verlag, Leinstr 32, 30159 Hannover; Kirchroeder Str 107, 30625 Hannover

Hallwag, *imprint of* Graefe und Unzer Verlag GmbH

Hallwag Verlag GmbH+
Brunnwiesenstr 23, 73760 Ostfildern
Mailing Address: Postfach 4266, 73745 Ostfildern
Tel: (0711) 449840 *Fax:* (0711) 4498460
Key Personnel
Dir: Juerg Burri
Manager: Dr Beat Koellinker
Sales: Frau Guenther
Advertising: Petra Friedlein
Subjects: Cookery, Physical Sciences, Wine & Spirits
ISBN Prefix(es): 3-444; 3-8283

Hamburger Lesehefte Verlag Iselt & Co Nfl mbH+
Nordbahnhofstr 2, 25813 Husum
Mailing Address: Postfach 1480, 25804 Husum
Tel: (04841) 8352-0 *Fax:* (04841) 8352-10
E-mail: verlagsgruppe.husum@t-online.de
Web Site: www.verlagsgruppe.de
Key Personnel
Man Dir, Editorial, Rights & Permissions: Ingwert Paulsen
Founded: 1953
ISBN Prefix(es): 3-87291
Parent Company: Husum Druck- und Verlagsgesellschaft mbH & Co KG
Associate Companies: Hansa Verlag Ingwert Paulsen Jr; Matthiesen Verlag Ingwert Paulsen Jr; Verlag der Nation

Liselotte Hamecher
Goethestr 18, 34119 Kassel
Tel: (0561) 16611 *Fax:* (0561) 775262
Key Personnel
Owner: Liselotte Hamecher
Founded: 1947
Subjects: History, Maritime, Military Science
ISBN Prefix(es): 3-920307
Shipping Address: Goethestr 74, 34119 Kassel
Warehouse: Goethestr 74, 34119 Kassel

Alfred Hammer+
EJARM Publishing House, Curtigasse 4, 64823 Gross-Umstadt
Tel: (06078) 71622 *Fax:* (06078) 71655
Key Personnel
Man Dir: Freddy Hammer
Founded: 1996

Subjects: Aeronautics, Aviation, Law, Management, European Joint Aviation Requirements
ISBN Prefix(es): 3-9805586

Peter Hammer Verlag GmbH+
Foehrenstr 33-35, 42283 Wuppertal
Mailing Address: Postfach 200963, 42209 Wuppertal
Tel: (0202) 505066; (0202) 505067 *Fax:* (0202) 509252
E-mail: peter-hammer-verlag@t-online.de
Web Site: www.peter-hammer-verlag.de
Key Personnel
Dir: Hermann Schulz
International Rights: Monika Bilstein
Advertising, Press: Dr Claudia Putz
Founded: 1966
Subjects: Developing Countries, Foreign Countries, Literature, Literary Criticism, Essays
ISBN Prefix(es): 3-87294
Associate Companies: Jugenddienst Verlag, Foehrenstr 33-35, 42283 Wuppertal
Distributed by Prolit Verlagsauslieferung GmbH

Hammonia-Verlag GmbH Fachverlag der Wohnungswirtschaft+
Tangstedter Landstr 83, 22415 Hamburg
Mailing Address: Postfach 620228, 22402 Hamburg
Tel: (040) 520 103-0 *Fax:* (040) 520 103-30
E-mail: info@hammonia.de
Web Site: www.hvh.de
Key Personnel
Man Dir, Publisher & International Rights: Egon Koschel
Sales Manager: Rolf Roemer *Tel:* (040) 52 01 03-35 *E-mail:* rolf.roemer@hammonia.de
Founded: 1946
Subjects: House & Home
ISBN Prefix(es): 3-87292

Verlag Handwerk und Technik GmbH+
Lademannbogen 135, 22339 Hamburg
Mailing Address: Postfach 630500, 22331 Hamburg
Tel: (040) 5 38 08-0 *Fax:* (040) 5 38 08-101
Web Site: www.handwerk-technik-shop.de
Key Personnel
Dir, Rights & Permissions: Johann Carl Buechner
Dir: Oskar Kummer
Founded: 1949
Subjects: Career Development, Education, Labor, Industrial Relations
ISBN Prefix(es): 3-582
Subsidiaries: Holland & Josenhans Gmbh & Co
Showroom(s): Informationsbuero Leipzig mit Verlagsausstellung, August- Bebel-Str 65, 04275 Leipzig; Informationsbuero Stuttgart mit Verlagsausstellung, Feuerseeplatz 2, 70176 Stuttgart
Orders to: Techn Fachbuch - Vertrieb AG M Studer, Spitalstr 12, Postfach 119, 2501 Biel, Switzerland *Tel:* (032) 322 61 41 *Fax:* (032) 322 61 30 *E-mail:* info@tfv.ch (Switzerland)
Veritas - Verlags und Handelsgessellschaft mbH & Co OHG, Hafenstra 1-3, 4010 Linz, Austria *Tel:* (0732) 776451-280 *Fax:* (0732) 776451-239 *E-mail:* veritas@veritas.at *Web Site:* www.veritas.at (Austria)

Hanfstaengl-Verlag, *imprint of* Daco Verlag Guenter Blase oHG

Edition Hannemann, *imprint of* Verlag Stephanie Naglschmid

Hannibal-Verlag+
Lochhamerstr 9, 82152 Planegg
Tel: (089) 857 95-0 *Fax:* (089) 857 95 294
E-mail: info@hannibal-verlag.de
Web Site: www.hannibal-verlag.de

Key Personnel
Man Dir & Publisher: Francoise Degrave
Tel: (089) 857 95 415 *E-mail:* francoise.degrave@kochbooks.com
Founded: 1986
Subjects: Literature, Literary Criticism, Essays, Musical Biographies
ISBN Prefix(es): 3-85445
Number of titles published annually: 72 Print
Total Titles: 740 Print
Parent Company: Verlagsgruppe Koch
Warehouse: b & i buch und information ag, Centralweg 16, CH-8910 Affoltern, Switzerland
Prolit Verlagsauslieferung, Siemensstr 16, 35463 Fernwald-Annerod

Hansa Verlag Ingwert Paulsen Jr
Nordbahnhofstr 2, 25813 Husum
Mailing Address: Postfach 1480, 25804 Husum
Tel: (04841) 8352-0 *Fax:* (04841) 8352-10
E-mail: verlagsgruppe.husum@t-online.de
Web Site: www.verlagsgruppe.de
Key Personnel
International Rights: J Paulsen,
Founded: 1954
Subjects: Literature, Literary Criticism, Essays
ISBN Prefix(es): 3-920421
Parent Company: Husum Druck-und Verlagsgesellschaft
Associate Companies: Hamburger Lesehefte Verlag Iselt & Co Nfl mbH; Husum Druck- und Verlagsgesellschaft mbH & Co KG; Matthiesen Verlag Ingwert Paulsen Jr; Verlag der Nation

Carl Hanser Verlag+
Kolbergerstr 22, 81679 Munich
Mailing Address: Postfach 860420, 81631 Munich
Tel: (089) 9 98 30 0 *Fax:* (089) 98 48 09
E-mail: info@hanser.de
Web Site: www.hanser.de/verlag/
Key Personnel
Man Dir & Publisher, Technical & Science: Wolfgang Beisler *E-mail:* beisler@hanser.de
Man Dir, Financial: Stephan D Joss *E-mail:* joss@hanser.de
Publisher, Fiction & Non-Fiction: Michael Krueger *E-mail:* krueger@hanser.de
Editorial, Plastics: Dr Wolfgang Glenz
Editorial, Technical & Science: Dr Hermann Riedel *E-mail:* riedel@hanser.de
Sales Dir, Fiction & Nonfiction: Felicitas Feilhauer *E-mail:* feilhauer@hanser.de
Sales Dir, Technical & Science: Barbara Kothe *E-mail:* kothe@hanser.de
Advertising Dir, Technical & Science: Guenter Scheffel *E-mail:* scheffel@hanser.de
Publicity, Fiction & Nonfiction: Christina Knecht *E-mail:* knecht@hanser.de
Foreign Rights, Fiction & Nonfiction: Susanne Bauknecht *E-mail:* bauknecht@hanser.de
Foreign Rights, Technical & Science: Evelyn Waizenegger
Founded: 1928
Subjects: Computer Science, Economics, Electronics, Electrical Engineering, Engineering (General), Environmental Studies, Fiction, Management, Mathematics, Mechanical Engineering, Microcomputers, Nonfiction (General), Philosophy, Physics, Poetry
ISBN Prefix(es): 3-446
Imprints: Zsolnay
U.S. Office(s): Hanser Publishers, 6915 Valley Ave, Cincinnati, OH 45244, United States
Hanser/Gardner Publishers Inc, 6915 Valley Ave, Cincinnati, OH 45244, United States

Happy Mental Buch- und Musik Verlag
Am Hoehenberg 21, 82327 Tutzing
Tel: (08158) 993303 *Fax:* (08158) 993305
Subjects: Health, Nutrition, Music, Dance, Religion - Buddhist, Religion - Hindu

ISBN Prefix(es): 3-9805692
Book Club(s): Bertelsmann; Weltbild

Hardt und Worner Marketing fur das Buch+
Saalburgstr 20, 61381 Friedrichsdorf
Tel: (06172) 7005-0 *Fax:* (01672) 71547
E-mail: hardt.woerner@t-online.de
Founded: 1993
Subjects: Publishing & Book Trade Reference
ISBN Prefix(es): 3-930120
Total Titles: 12 Print
Distributor for Blueprint (Germany)
Orders to: LKG, Potsahower Weg, 04579 Espenhain

Harenberg Kommunikation Verlags- und Medien GmbH & Co KG+
Koenigswall 21, 44137 Dortmund
Tel: (0231) 9056-0 *Fax:* (0231) 9056-110
E-mail: post@harenberg.de
Web Site: www.harenberg.de
Key Personnel
Man Dir: Bodo Harenberg
Founded: 1973
Subjects: Architecture & Interior Design, Art, History, Music, Dance, Travel
ISBN Prefix(es): 3-88379; 3-611; 3-921846

Harrassowitz Verlag+
Taunusstr 14, 65183 Wiesbaden
Tel: (0611) 530-0 *Fax:* (0611) 530-570; (0611) 530-560 (orders)
E-mail: verlag@harrassowitz.de; service@harrassowitz.de
Web Site: www.harrassowitz.de *Cable:* HARRASSOWITZ VERLAG WIESBADEN
Key Personnel
Man Dir & International Rights: Michael Langfeld *Tel:* (0611) 530-550 *E-mail:* mlangfeld@harrassowitz.unet.de
Publicity Dir: Robert Gietz *Tel:* (0611) 530-551 *E-mail:* rgietz@harrassowitz.de
Founded: 1872
Specialize in Slavic Studies & Eastern European Research.
Subjects: Asian Studies, Language Arts, Linguistics, Library & Information Sciences, Dictionaries, Linguistics, Eastern European Research & Civic Studies
ISBN Prefix(es): 3-447
Total Titles: 2,600 Print

Harth Musik Verlag-Pro musica Verlag GmbH
Frankenforsterstr 40, 51427 Bergisch Gladbach
Tel: (02204) 2003-0 *Fax:* (02204) 2003-33 *Cable:* Musica Leipzig
Key Personnel
Manager: Rita Preiss
Founded: 1946
Subjects: Music, Dance
ISBN Prefix(es): 3-7334

Litteraturverlag Karlheinz Hartmann
Rodheimerstr 17, 61381 Friedrichsdorf
Tel: (06007) 7622 *Fax:* (069) 614606
Key Personnel
Man Dir: M A Karlheinz Hartmann
Founded: 1976
Subjects: Film, Video, Literature, Literary Criticism, Essays, Poetry
ISBN Prefix(es): 3-87293
Branch Office(s)
Schneckenhofstr 17, 60596 Frankfurt am Main
Tel: (069) 6032191

Haschemi Edition Cologne Kunstverlag+
Mechternstr 44, 50823 Cologne
Tel: (0221) 561007; (0221) 561008 *Fax:* (0221) 529282
E-mail: info@haschemi.de
Web Site: www.haschemi.de

GERMANY

Key Personnel
Contact: Baback Haschemi
International Rights: Mario Hayenga
Founded: 1983
Subjects: Photography, Travel
ISBN Prefix(es): 3-924169; 3-931282
Subsidiaries: Haschemi Edition California

von Hase & Koehler Verlag KG+
Bahnhofstr 6, 55116 Mainz
Tel: (06131) 232334 *Fax:* (06131) 227952
Key Personnel
Publisher, Rights & Permissions: Volker Hansen
Founded: 1964
Subjects: Biography, Communications, Education, Finance, Literature, Literary Criticism, Essays, Poetry, Radio, TV
ISBN Prefix(es): 3-7758
Subsidiaries: Niederlassung Munchen

Hatje Cantz Verlag (Hatje Cantz Publishers)+
Senefelderstr 12, 73760 Ostfildern
Mailing Address: PO Box 4259, 73745 Ostfildern
Tel: (0711) 44 05-0 *Fax:* (0711) 44 05-220
E-mail: contact@hatjecantz.de
Web Site: www.hatjecantz.de
Key Personnel
Senior Publisher: Gerd Hatje *Tel:* (0711) 44 05-200
Man Dir & Publisher: Annette Kulenkampff *Tel:* (0711) 44 05-200
International Sales Dir & Foreign Rights: Markus Hartmann *Tel:* (0711) 44 05-203 *E-mail:* m.hartmann@hatjecantz.de
International Sales Manager & Foreign Rights: Evelin Georgi *Tel:* (0711) 44 05-218 *E-mail:* e.georgi@hatjecantz.de
Promotion: Stefanie Gommel *Tel:* (0711) 44 05-208 *E-mail:* s.gommel@hatjecantz.de; Martina Reitz *Tel:* (0711) 44 05-213 *E-mail:* m.reitz@hatjecantz.de
Press: Meike Gatermann *Tel:* (0711) 6 57 32 95 *Fax:* (0711) 65 02 12 *E-mail:* press@hatjecantz.de
Founded: 1945
Publisher of art books, books on architecture, design & photography, exhibition catalogues.
Subjects: Architecture & Interior Design, Art, Photography
ISBN Prefix(es): 3-7757
Number of titles published annually: 150 Print
Total Titles: 1,000 Print
Parent Company: Dr Cantz'sche Druckerei
Associate Companies: belser kunst quartal *Tel:* (0711) 4405226/-227 *Fax:* (0711) 4405228 *E-mail:* belser@hatjecantz.de
Warehouse: Koch, Neff & Oetinger
Orders to: Koch, Neff & Oetinger, Schockenriedstr 39, 70565 Stuttgart *Tel:* (0711) 78992031 *Fax:* (0711) 78991010

Haude und Spenersche Verlagsbuchhandlung+
Gneisenaustr 33, 10961 Berlin
Mailing Address: Postfach 610494, 10928 Berlin
Tel: (030) 6917073 *Fax:* (030) 6914067
Cable: HAUDE
Key Personnel
Owner, Manager, Rights & Permissions: Volker Spiess
Founded: 1614
Subjects: History, Nonfiction (General), Regional Interests, Religion - Jewish, Travel
ISBN Prefix(es): 3-7759
Associate Companies: Wissenschaftsverlag Volker Spiess GmbH; Arani-Verlag GmbH
Orders to: VAH-Jager Verlagsauslieferungen, Miraustr 54, 1350? ?rlin

Haufe Mediengruppe
Hindenburgstr 64, 79102 Freiburg
Mailing Address: Postfach 740, 79007 Freiburg
Tel: (0761) 3683-0 *Fax:* (0761) 3683-195
E-mail: online@information-verlag.de
Web Site: www.haufe.de
Key Personnel
Executive Board: Helmuth Hopfner; Martin Laqua
Chairman: Uwe Renald Mueller
Founded: 1934 (by Rudolf Haufe in Berlin)
Subjects: Business, Education, Law, Information Management, Taxation
Number of titles published annually: 150 Print
Associate Companies: Haufe Akademie, Freiburg; Haufe + Kisling Verlag AG, Zurich, Switzerland; Haufe Publishing, Planegg; Rudolf Haufe Verlag, Freiburg; Haufe Service Center, Freiburg; Intuit Inc (US); LEGIOS, Frankfurt; Lexware, Freiburg; Memento Verlag AG, Freiburg; Mobilecom AG; Openshop AG, Munich; Max Schimmel Verlag, Wuerzburg; SoftUse, Freiburg; WRS Verlag, Planegg

Rudolf Haufe Verlag GmbH & Co KG+
Hindenburgstr 64, 79102 Freiburg
Mailing Address: Postfach 740, 79007 Freiburg
Tel: (0761) 3683-0 *Fax:* (0761) 3683-195
E-mail: online@haufe.de
Web Site: www.haufe.de *Cable:* HAUFEVERLAG
Key Personnel
Man Dir: Helmuth Hopfner; Martin Laqua; Uwe Renald Mueller
Founded: 1934
Subjects: Accounting, Business, Computer Science, Economics, Finance, Law, Management, Marketing, Real Estate
ISBN Prefix(es): 3-448
Subsidiaries: Lexware Gesellschaft fur Softwareentwicklung der rechts- und steuerberatenden Berufe mbH; WRS Verlag Wirtschaft, Recht und Steuern GmbH & Co
Branch Office(s)
Haufe Berlin, Albrechtstr 146, 10117 Berlin

Haug, *imprint of* Georg Thieme Verlag KG

Karl F Haug Verlag GmbH & Co+
Steiermaerkerstr 3-5, 70469 Stuttgart
Mailing Address: Postfach 10 28 69, 69121 Heidelberg
Tel: (00711) 8931-0 *Fax:* (0711) 8931-706
Web Site: www.haug-verlag.de/ *Cable:* HAUGVERLAG
Key Personnel
Man Dir: Florian Fischer; Jens Steinle
Advertising: Gisela Werner
Production: Dietmar Sieber
Sales: Alfred Fuchs
Publicity: Lucie Trauner
International Rights: Rolf Lenzen
Founded: 1903
Subjects: Health, Nutrition, Medicine, Nursing, Dentistry
ISBN Prefix(es): 3-7760
Parent Company: Huethig Verlag, Im Weiher 10, 69121 Heidelberg
Associate Companies: Arkana Verlag; Verlag fuer Medizin Dr Ewald Fischer GmbH
Subsidiaries: Editions Haug International

Dr Ernst Hauswedell & Co Verlag+
Haldenstr 30, 70376 Stuttgart
Mailing Address: Postfach 140155, 70071 Stuttgart
Tel: (0711) 54 99 71-0; (0711) 54 99 71-11 *Fax:* (0711) 54 99 71-21
Key Personnel
President: Charles Gerd Hiersemann *E-mail:* hiersemann.hauswedell.verlage@t-online.de
Vice President: Dr Reimar W Fuchs
Founded: 1927
Subjects: Antiques, Library & Information Sciences, Publishing & Book Trade Reference, Science (General), Literature, Nature, Typography

ISBN Prefix(es): 3-7762
Total Titles: 200 Print; 3 CD-ROM
Distributor for Staats-Und Universitaets-Bibliothek
Book Club(s): Maximilian Gesellschaft

Hayit Reisefuhrer in der Rutsker Verlag GmbH+
c/o Mundo Media GmbH, Schreberstr 2, 51105 Cologne
Tel: (0221) 921635-0 *Fax:* (0221) 921635-24
E-mail: kontakt@hayit.com
Web Site: www.hayit.com
Key Personnel
Man Dir, Publicity, Rights & Permissions & Sales: Ertay Hayit *E-mail:* ertay.hayit@hayit.com
Editorial: Cornelia Auschra *Tel:* (0221) 921635-13 *E-mail:* cornelia.auschra@hayit.com; Mike Gahn *E-mail:* mike@hayit.com; Ute Hayit *Tel:* (0221) 921635-11 *E-mail:* ute.hayit@hayit.com
Founded: 1988
Subjects: Travel
ISBN Prefix(es): 3-89607; 3-88676; 3-89210; 3-922145; 3-925727
Associate Companies: Adl Hayit, Amsterdam, Netherlands
U.S. Office(s): County Route 9, PO Box 357, Chatham, NY 12037, United States *Tel:* 518-392-4526 *Fax:* 518-392-4557
Hayit Publishing USA Inc, c/o Pratley International, 30 East 81St, New York, NY 10028, United States *Tel:* 212-772-2267 *Fax:* 212-772-3692 (Telex: 277258)

Heckners Verlag
Harzstr 22/23, 38300 Wolfenbuettel
Mailing Address: Postfach 1559, 38285 Wolfenbuettel
Tel: (05331) 8008-0 *Fax:* (05331) 8008-58
Key Personnel
Dir, Rights & Permissions: Siegfried Mathea
Founded: 1895
Subjects: Career Development, Economics
ISBN Prefix(es): 3-449
Parent Company: Kieser Verlag GmbH, Neusaess
Distributed by Orell Fuessli (Switzerland)

Heel Verlag GmbH+
Gut Pottscheidt, 53639 Koenigswinter
Mailing Address: Postfach 1220, 53622 Konigswinter
Tel: (02223) 92 30-0 *Fax:* (02223) 92 30-13; (02223) 92-30-26
E-mail: info@heel-verlag.de
Web Site: www.heel-verlag.de
Key Personnel
Man Dir & International Rights: Franz-Christoph Heel
Foreign Rights Manager: Karin Michelberger *Tel:* (02223) 923046 *E-mail:* k.michelberger@heel-verlag.de
Founded: 1980
Subjects: Aeronautics, Aviation, Automotive, Cookery, Crafts, Games, Hobbies, Film, Video, Gardening, Plants, Humor, Maritime, Music, Dance, Nonfiction (General), Outdoor Recreation, Photography, Science Fiction, Fantasy, Sports, Athletics, Transportation, Travel
ISBN Prefix(es): 3-922858; 3-89365
Number of titles published annually: 80 Print
Total Titles: 250 Print
Imprints: Das Grosse, Technothek; Das Original; Edition Markt; Galerie der Klassiker; Grand Prix Stars; Motion Books
Distributor for Edition Fuchs; Highlights Verlag; Johansens; Editions J R Piccard; Serag AG
Bookshop(s): Buchhandlung Heel, Hauptstr 354, 53639 Konigswinter *Tel:* (02223) 26667
Shipping Address: VSB Lager/Wareneingang, Helmstedter Str 99, 38126 Braunschweig

Warehouse: VSB Verlagsservice, Georg-Westermann-Allee 66, 38104 Braunschweig, Contact: Herr Wandert *Tel:* (0531) 708650 *Fax:* (0531) 708608

Joh Heider Verlag GmbH
Paffratherstr 102-116, 51465 Bergisch Gladbach
Tel: (02202) 95 40-35 *Fax:* (02202) 2 15 31
E-mail: 101447.1712@compuserve.com
Web Site: www.heider-verlag.de/mb/mediadaten/
Key Personnel
Man Dir: Hans Heider
Publisher: Dr Dieter Boeck; Dr Dieter Mitrenga
Editorial: Anna von Borstell; Barbara Huennighausen; Dr Lutz Retzlaff; Angelika Steimer-Schmid
Founded: 1889
Subjects: Economics, Law, Social Sciences, Sociology
ISBN Prefix(es): 3-87314
Sales Office(s): Burgstr 122, 51427 Bergisch Gladbach, Contact: Christine Kaffka *Tel:* (02204) 96 18 18 *Fax:* (02204) 96 29 50 *E-mail:* anzeigen@marburger-bund.de

Heigl Verlag, Horst Edition+
Oberhaslach 6, 88633 Heiligenberg
Tel: (07554) 283 *Fax:* (07552) 4280
Key Personnel
Manager: Horst Heigl
Author: Horst Lozynski
Founded: 1987
Subjects: Art, Astrology, Occult, Physical Sciences, Religion - Other
ISBN Prefix(es): 3-89316

Verlag Otto Heinevetter Lehrmittel GmbH
Papenstr 41, 22089 Hamburg
Tel: (040) 25 90 19 *Fax:* (040) 251 2128
E-mail: info@heinevetter-verlag.de
Web Site: www.heinevetter-verlag.de
Key Personnel
Manager: Werner Klopfer
Founded: 1947
ISBN Prefix(es): 3-87474

Wolfgang Heinold, see Eulenhof-Verlag Wolfgang Ehrhardt Heinold

Heinrichshofen's Verlag GmbH & Co KG+
Liebigstr 16, 26389 Wilhelmshaven
Mailing Address: Postfach 1655, 26356 Wilhelmshaven
Tel: (04421) 92 67 0 *Fax:* (04421) 20 20 07
E-mail: info@heinrichshofen.de; heinrichshofen@t-online.de
Web Site: www.heinrichshofen.de *Cable:* HEINRICHSHOFEN WILHELMSHAVEN
Key Personnel
President: Eva Noetzel
Production, Printing: Peter Hensel *Tel:* (04421) 92 67 11
Marketing: Jutta Hegner *Tel:* (04421) 92 67 20 *Fax:* (04421) 20 22 66
Founded: 1797
Also publish music, printing shop & bindery.
Subjects: Music
Associate Companies: Heinrichshofen Edition New York, United States; Otto Heinrich Noetzel Verlag; C F Peters Corporation, 70-30 80 St, Glendale, NY 11385, United States
Distributed by CPEA; C F Peters Corporation (New York); Peters Edition (London)

Heinz-Theo Gremme Verlag+
Tobiaspark 2, 44534 Lunen
Mailing Address: Postfach 1428, 44504 Lunen
Tel: (02592) 984200
E-mail: theo.gremme@epost.de
Web Site: www.gremme-verlag.de
Founded: 1991

Subjects: Fiction, Human Relations, Poetry, Science Fiction, Fantasy, Self-Help
ISBN Prefix(es): 3-9802679

Heinze GmbH
Bremer Weg 184, 29219 Celle
Mailing Address: Postfach 1505, 29219 Celle
Tel: (05141) 500 *Fax:* (05141) 50104
E-mail: info@heinze.de
Web Site: www.heinze.de/
Telex: 925202
Key Personnel
President: Guenter Caro
Founded: 1964
Subjects: Advertising
ISBN Prefix(es): 3-921724
Parent Company: Bertelsmann Fachinformationen Munich

Heitz Librarie, *imprint of* Verlag Valentin Koerner GmbH

HelfRecht Verlag und Druck
Markgrafenstr 32, 95680 Bad Alexandersbad
Tel: (09232) 6010 *Fax:* (09232) 601280
E-mail: info@helfrecht.de
Web Site: www.helfrecht.de
Key Personnel
Man Dir: Manfred Helfrecht; Gottfried Haberkorn; Werner Bayer
Public Relations & International Rights: Christoph Beck
Public Relations Assistant: Theresa Kraupner
Founded: 1975
Subjects: Career Development, Economics
ISBN Prefix(es): 3-920400
Parent Company: Firmengruppe HelfRecht GmbH & Co-Holding KG, Markgrafenstr 32, 95680 Bad Alexandersbad
Branch Office(s)
Rittet-von-Eitzeuberger-Strasse 25, 95448 Bayreuth *Tel:* (0921) 9088 *Fax:* (0921) 9088

Heliopolis-Verlag+
Schellingstr 41, 72072 Tuebingen
Mailing Address: PO Box 1827, 72008 Tuebingen
Tel: (07473) 5427 *Fax:* (07473) 5427
Key Personnel
Manager: Dr Volker Katzmann
Founded: 1949
ISBN Prefix(es): 3-87324
Associate Companies: Katzmann-Verlag KG, Schellingstr 41, 72072 Tuebingen

Hellerau-Verlag Dresden GmbH
Koenigstr 12, 01097 Dresden
Tel: (0351) 803 5293 *Fax:* (0351) 826 0130
E-mail: info@hellerau-verlag.de
Web Site: www.hellerau-verlag.de/
Key Personnel
Publisher: Lothar Dunsch
Founded: 1990
Subjects: Fiction, History, Regional Interests
ISBN Prefix(es): 3-910184

G Henle Verlag
Forstenrieder Allee 122, 81476 Munich
Mailing Address: PO Box 710466, 81454 Munich
Tel: (089) 759820 *Fax:* (089) 7598240
E-mail: info@henle.de
Web Site: www.henle.de
Key Personnel
Chief Executive Officer & President: Dr Wolf-Dieter Seiffert *Tel:* (089) 75982-21 *E-mail:* seiffert@henle.de
Head of Manufacturing: Gerhard Fischl *E-mail:* fischl@henle.de
Manager of Advertising: Johannes Raber *E-mail:* raber@henle.de
Dir, Distribution: Michael Ingendaay *E-mail:* ingendaay@henle.de

Sales: Ulrike Lucht Lorenz *E-mail:* luchtlorenz@henle.de
Marketing: Juliane Dutertre *E-mail:* dutertre@henle.de
Founded: 1948
Subjects: Music, Dance
ISBN Prefix(es): 3-87328
Subsidiaries: G Henle USA Inc

Henschel Verlag, *imprint of* Verlagsgruppe Dornier

Edition Hentrich Druck & Verlag Gebr Hentrich und Tank GmbH & Co KG+
Albrechtstr 111/112, 12167 Berlin
Tel: (030) 7927011 *Fax:* (030) 7929428
Key Personnel
Publisher & Manager: Werner Buchwald
Founded: 1982
Subjects: Art, Biography, Drama, Theater, Government, Political Science, History, Nonfiction (General), Religion - Jewish, Social Sciences, Sociology
ISBN Prefix(es): 3-89468

Herausgeber, *imprint of* Johann Wolfgang Goethe Universitat

F A Herbig Verlagsbuchhandlung GmbH+
Subsidiary of Buchverlage Langen-Mueller/Herbig
Thomas-Wimmer-Ring 11, 80539 Munich
Tel: (089) 290880 *Fax:* (089) 29088144
E-mail: l.eggs@herbig.net *Cable:* LANGENMULLER
Key Personnel
Man Dir & Publisher: Dr Herbert Fleissner
Man Dir: Dr Brigitte Sinhuber
Sales: Sissi Klauser *E-mail:* s.klauser@herbig.net
Publicity: Heidrun Gebhardt
Rights & Permissions: Dorothea Estermann; Frauke Hoppen *Tel:* (089) 29088156 *Fax:* (089) 29088178 *E-mail:* f.hoppen@herbig.net
Editorial: Dr Bernhard Struckmeyer
Founded: 1821
Subjects: Art, Astronomy, Biography, Cookery, Health, Nutrition, History, Nonfiction (General), Physical Sciences, Travel
ISBN Prefix(es): 3-7766
Orders to: VVA, An der Autobahn, 33310 Guetersloh

Hans-Alfred Herchen & Co Verlag KG
Fichardstr 30, 60322 Frankfurt am Main
Tel: (069) 550911 *Fax:* (069) 552601; (069) 554922
Key Personnel
Contact: Hans-Alfred Herchen
Founded: 1984
Subjects: Government, Political Science, Social Sciences, Sociology
ISBN Prefix(es): 3-89184

Verlag Herder GmbH & Co KG+
Hermann-Herder-Str 4, 79104 Freiburg
Tel: (0761) 2717440 *Fax:* (0761) 2717360
E-mail: kundenservice@herder.de
Web Site: www.herder.de/ *Cable:* HERDER FREIBURGBREISGAU
Key Personnel
Man Dir: Dr Hermann Herder; Manuel-Gregor Herder; Ulrich Peters; Dr Klaus-Christoph Scheffels
Rights & Permissions: Franziska Komm
Sales Dir: Rainer Lege
Export: Peter Pagendarm
Founded: 1801
Subjects: Biblical Studies, Education, Government, Political Science, History, Nonfiction (General), Religion - Buddhist, Religion - Catholic, Religion - Islamic, Religion - Other, Self-Help, Theology

ISBN Prefix(es): 3-451
Associate Companies: Herder Editrice e Libreria, Italy; Editorial Herder SA, Spain; Herder Ag, Switzerland
Imprints: Herderbuecherei; Herder/Spektrum; Uerle Verlag; Verlag Ploetz
Subsidiaries: Verlag Karl Alber GmbH; Christophorus-Verlag GmbH
Divisions: Kerle-Verlag; Ploetz
Bookshop(s): Carolus Buchhandlung Herder, Frankfurt am Main
Book Club(s): Herder Buchgemeinde
Shipping Address: Koch, Neff & Oetinger, Schockenriedstr 39, 70565 Stuttgart
Warehouse: Koch, Neff & Oetinger, Schockenriedstr 39, 70565 Stuttgart

Herder/Spektrum, *imprint of* Verlag Herder GmbH & Co KG

Herderbuecherei, *imprint of* Verlag Herder GmbH & Co KG

Helmut Hermann
Untere Muhle, 71706 Markgroningen
Tel: (07145) 8278 *Fax:* (07145) 26736
Key Personnel
Contact: H Hermann
Founded: 1986
Subjects: Photography, Travel
ISBN Prefix(es): 3-929920; 3-9800975; 3-9803296
Orders to: Prolit, Postfach 9, 35463 Fernwald

Hermetische Truhe Buchhandlung fuer Esoterische Literatur Barbara Dethlefsen
Kurfuerstenstr 45, 80801 Munich
Tel: (089) 2710650 *Fax:* (089) 2724627
Key Personnel
Owner: Barbara Dethlefsen
Founded: 1983
ISBN Prefix(es): 3-927183

Herold Verlag Dr Wetzel+
Kirchbachweg 16, 81479 Munich
Tel: (089) 7915774
Web Site: www.herold-verlag.de
Key Personnel
Man Dir & Publisher: Hans Meisinger
Rights & Publicity: Christiane Schneider
Founded: 1871
ISBN Prefix(es): 3-7767
Orders to: MVS Meisinger Verlagsservice GmbH, Am Steinfeld 4, 94065 Waldkirchen *Tel:* (08581) 9605-0 *Fax:* (08581) 754

Hertenstein, Axel, Hernstein-Presse
Mathystr 36, 75173 Pforzheim
Tel: (07231) 27084 *Fax:* (07231) 27084
Key Personnel
Publicity Manager: Ulrike Hertenstein
Founded: 1967
Specializes in Library Books & Maps.
Subjects: Poetry

Hessisches Ministerium fuer Umwelt, Landwirtschaft und Forsten
Mainzerstr 80, 65189 Wiesbaden
Tel: (0611) 8150 *Fax:* (0611) 8151941
E-mail: poststelle@mulf.hessen.de
Web Site: www.mulf.hessen.de
Telex: 4182011 HMUE D
Key Personnel
Referent: Michael Korwisi
Subjects: Agriculture, Energy, Environmental Studies, Specialize in Ecology
Total Titles: 120 Print; 3 CD-ROM

Hestra-Verlag Hernichel & Dr Strauss GmbH & Co KG+
Holzhofallee 33, 64295 Darmstadt
Mailing Address: Postfach 100751, 64207 Darmstadt
Tel: (06151) 390700 *Fax:* (06151) 390777
Key Personnel
Man Dir & International Rights: Holger Musset *Tel:* (06151) 390731 *E-mail:* musset@hestra.de
Editor: Gerda Gunkel *Tel:* (06151) 390738 *E-mail:* info@hestra.de
Marketing: Inga-Doris Langer *Tel:* (040) 23714267 *Fax:* (040) 23714243 *E-mail:* langer@etp.net
Sales: Marijana Mikulic *Tel:* (040) 23714266 *Fax:* (040) 23714243 *E-mail:* mikulic@etp.net
Founded: 1948
Subjects: Civil Engineering, Engineering (General), Law, Transportation
ISBN Prefix(es): 3-7771

Hexaglot Holding GmbH+
Sportallee 41, 22335 Hamburg
Tel: (040) 514560 *Fax:* (040) 51456991
E-mail: info@hexaglot.de
Web Site: www.hexaglot.de/ *Cable:* HEXAGER
Key Personnel
Manager: Dr Hans-Werner Scholz
Founded: 1989
ISBN Prefix(es): 3-928824
Parent Company: Langenscheidt KG
Subsidiaries: Sita Daten-und Kommunikations GmbH

Erika Heydick Sax-Verlag Beucha
Unit of Erika Heydick
An der Halde 12, 04824 Beucha
Tel: (034292) 75210 *Fax:* (034292) 75220
E-mail: info@sax-verlag.de
Web Site: www.sax-verlag.de
Key Personnel
Contact: Erika Heydick
Founded: 1992
Subjects: Biography, Education, History, Nonfiction (General), Regional Interests, Science (General), Social Sciences, Sociology
ISBN Prefix(es): 3-930076; 3-934544
Number of titles published annually: 15 Print
Total Titles: 100 Print

Friedrich W Heye Verlag GmbH+
Oberweg 8, 82008 Unterhaching
Tel: (089) 66532101 *Fax:* (089) 66532210
E-mail: verlag@heye.de
Web Site: www.heye-verlag.de
Key Personnel
Man Dir: Peter Keil; Claudia Knauss; Juergen Knauss
ISBN Prefix(es): 3-88141; 3-89400
Associate Companies: Heye Top Present GmbH
Warehouse: Kapellenstr 13, 85622 Feldkirchen

Carl Heymanns Verlag KG+
Luxemburgerstr 449, 50939 Cologne
Mailing Address: Postfach 410446, 50864 Cologne
Tel: (0221) 94373-0 *Fax:* (0221) 94373-901
E-mail: welb@heymanns.com; bestellung@heymanns.com; service@heymanns.com
Web Site: www.heymanns.com
Key Personnel
Man Dir, Rights & Permissions: Bertram Gallus *Tel:* (0221) 94373-101 *Fax:* (0221) 94373-105 *E-mail:* gallus@heymanns.com
Editorial: K Endlich *Tel:* (089) 224811 *E-mail:* endlich@heymanns.com; P Halter *Tel:* (0221) 94373-160 *E-mail:* halter@heymanns.com; H Kruppa *Tel:* (0221) 94373-134 *E-mail:* kruppa@heymanns.com; K Pompe *Tel:* (0221) 94373-600 *E-mail:* pompe@heymanns.com; M Sauerwald *Tel:* (0221) 94373-138 *E-mail:* sauerwald@heymanns.com
Production: B Simon *Tel:* (0221) 94373-200 *E-mail:* simon@heymanns.com
Editorial: K-L Steinhaeuser *Tel:* (0221) 94373-132 *E-mail:* steinhaeuser@heymanns.com
Marketing Manager: Gerd Welb *Tel:* (0221) 94373-300 *Fax:* (0221) 94373-310 *E-mail:* welb@heymanns.com
Contact: Mrs Habers *Tel:* (0221) 94373-501 *Fax:* (0221) 94373-502 *E-mail:* habers@heymanns.com
Founded: 1815
Subjects: Economics, Engineering (General), Government, Political Science, Law, Management, Public Administration
ISBN Prefix(es): 3-452
Total Titles: 2,000 Print; 70 CD-ROM
Online services available through World Wide Web.
Subsidiaries: Euroliber Verlags- und Vertriebs- GmbH; Gallus Druckerei KG; Albert Nauck & Co
Branch Office(s)
Baunscheidtstr 6, 53113 Bonn *Tel:* (0228) 9108705
Steinsdorfstr 10, Postfach 26, 80538 Munich 26 *Tel:* (089) 224811
Gutenbergstr 3-4, Berlin *Tel:* (030) 3914081 *Fax:* (030) 3912861

Wilhelm Heyne Verlag+
Paul-Heyse-Str 28, 80336 Munich
Tel: (089) 51480 *Fax:* (089) 51482103
E-mail: verlag@heyne.de
Web Site: www.heyne.de/ *Cable:* HEYNEVERLAG MUNCHEN
Key Personnel
Publisher: Rolf Heyne
Editorial Dir: Lothar Menne
Editorial: Ulrich Genzler; Dr Theda Krohm-Linke; Wolfgang Jeschke; Bernhard Matt; Ria Lottermoser; Ingeborg Meier
Sales Dir: Christian Tesch
Advertising Manager: David Hauptmann
Rights & Permissions: Traudel Eckardt
Founded: 1934
Subjects: Astrology, Occult, Biography, Cookery, Fiction, Film, Video, History, How-to, Humor, Mysteries, Psychology, Psychiatry, Romance, Science Fiction, Fantasy
ISBN Prefix(es): 3-453
Subsidiaries: Collection Rolf Heyne, Diana Verlag; Zabert Sandmann
U.S. Office(s): Franklin & Siegel Assoc, 386 Park Ave S, Suite 1102, New York, NY 10016, United States
Orders to: Schleissheimerstr 106, 85748 Garching-Hochbrueck

Max Hieber KG+
Liebfrauenstr 1, 80331 Munich
Mailing Address: Postfach 330429, 80064 Munich
Tel: (089) 29008023; (089) 227045 *Fax:* (089) 229782
E-mail: info@eminent-orgeln.de
Web Site: www.eminent-orgeln.de/kontakte.htm
Key Personnel
Contact: Daniel Stieb
Founded: 1884
Subjects: Music, Dance
ISBN Prefix(es): 3-920456
Branch Office(s)
Max Hieber Musikverlag, Verlagsauslieferung Einkauf, Musikalien-Versand Loewengrube 10, 80331 Munich 2
Distributed by Musikverlag Preissler

Anton Hiersemann, Verlag+
Haldenstr 30, 70376 Stuttgart
Mailing Address: Postfach 140155, 70071 Stuttgart

Tel: (0711) 5499710; (0711) 5499711 *Fax:* (0711) 54997121
E-mail: hiersemann.hauswedell.verlage@t-online.de
Web Site: www.hiersemann.de/hiersemann.html
Cable: HIERSEMANN
Key Personnel
President & Dir, Rights & Permissions: Gerd Hiersemann
Founded: 1884
Also specialize in monographs, publishing & booktrade reference.
Subjects: Art, Astronomy, Biography, Drama, Theater, Genealogy, History, Library & Information Sciences, Literature, Literary Criticism, Essays, Religion - Buddhist, Religion - Catholic, Religion - Hindu, Religion - Islamic, Religion - Jewish, Religion - Protestant, Religion - Other, Science (General), Theology
ISBN Prefix(es): 3-7772
Total Titles: 1,200 Print; 3 CD-ROM
Associate Companies: Dr Ernst Hauswedell & Co, Verlag
Imprints: Maximilian; Gesellschaft
Subsidiaries: Leipzig, Goldschmidtstr 29; Karl W Hiersemann
Book Club(s): Geschaeftsstelle von: Literarischer Verein in Stuttgart eV

AIG I Hilbinger Verlag GmbH+
Zum Dornbachtal, 65321 Heidenrod-Springen
Tel: (06124) 77704 *Fax:* (06124) 77704
Key Personnel
Man Dir, Rights & Permissions: Immo A Hilbinger
Founded: 1989
Subjects: Astrology, Occult, Parapsychology, Self-Help
ISBN Prefix(es): 3-927110
Associate Companies: Agentur fuer Informationsgestaltung, Zum Dornhachtal, 65321 Heidenrod

Himmelsturmer Verlag+
Hochallee 114, 20149 Hamburg
Tel: (040) 48061717 *Fax:* (040) 48061799
E-mail: himmelstuermer@gmx.de
Founded: 1998
Specialize in gay novels & documentaries.
Subjects: Gay & Lesbian
ISBN Prefix(es): 3-934825; 3-9806249
Number of titles published annually: 6 Print
Total Titles: 25 Print

Verlag Hinder und Deelmann+
Postfach 1206, 35068 Gladenbach
Tel: (06462) 1301 *Fax:* (06462) 3307
Web Site: www.hinderunddeelmann.de/
Key Personnel
Publisher: Johannes Deelmann; Dr Rolf Hinder
Founded: 1953
Subjects: History, Philosophy, Religion - Other, Social Sciences, Sociology
ISBN Prefix(es): 3-87348
Distributor for Pondicherry (India); Sabda (India)

Hinstorff Verlag GmbH+
Lagerstr 7, 18055 Rostock
Tel: (0381) 49690 *Fax:* (0381) 4969103
E-mail: sekretariat@hinstorff.de
Web Site: www.hinstorff.de/
Key Personnel
Manager: Birgit Heinze
Contact: Birgit Kruggel
Founded: 1831
Subjects: Literature, Literary Criticism, Essays
ISBN Prefix(es): 3-356
Parent Company: Heinz Heise Verlag GmbH & Co KG, Hannover
Warehouse: VSB Verlagsservice Braunschweig GmbH, Helmstedtstr 99, 38126 Braunschweig
Orders to: VSB Verlagsservice Braunschweig GmbH, Postfach 4738, D-38037 Braunschweig
Georg Westermann Allee 66, 38104 Braunschweig

Hippokrates-Verlag GmbH+
Steiermaerkerstr 3-5, 70469 Stuttgart
Mailing Address: Postfach 300504, 70445 Stuttgart
Tel: (0711) 89310 *Fax:* (0711) 8931706
Web Site: www.hippokrates.de/
Telex: 7252275 gtvd
Cable: HIPPOKRATESVERLAG
Key Personnel
Man Dir: A Charo
Publicity: Hans-Guenter Zimnik
Sales: Sabine Zenecker
Rights & Permissions (Thieme Verlag KG): Merit Schuett
Founded: 1925
Subjects: Medicine, Nursing, Dentistry
ISBN Prefix(es): 3-7773
Parent Company: Georg Thieme Verlag KG
Subsidiaries: Sonntag Verlag
Shipping Address: Koch, Neff & Oetinger & Co Verlagsauslieferung Hipporkrates, Postfach 210, D-7000 Stuttgart 1
Warehouse: Koch, Neff & Oetinger & Co, Verlagsauslieferung Hippokrates, Postfach 210, D-7000 Stuttgart 1
Orders to: Koch, Neff, Oetinger & Co Verlagsauslieferung Hippokrates, Postfach 210, D-7000 Stuttgart 1

Hirmer Verlag GmbH+
Nymphenburgerstr 84, 80636 Munich
Mailing Address: Postfach 190454, 80604 Munich
Tel: (089) 1215160 *Fax:* (089) 12151610; (089) 12151616 (distribution)
E-mail: vertrieb@hirmer-verlag.ccn.de
Key Personnel
Man Dir & Editorial: Albert Hirmer
Man Dir: Juergen Kleidt
Editorial: Dr Veronika Birbaumer; Margret Haase
Founded: 1948
Subjects: Archaeology, Art
ISBN Prefix(es): 3-7774
Parent Company: Axel-Springer-Verlag

Harro V Hirschheydt
Neue Wiesen 6, 30900 Wedemark-Elze
Tel: (05130) 36758 *Fax:* (05130) 36799
E-mail: hirschheydt.antiquariatverlag@t-online.de
Key Personnel
Owner, Rights & Permissions: Harro V Hirschheydt
Founded: 1950
Subjects: Regional Interests
ISBN Prefix(es): 3-7777

F Hirthammer Verlag GmbH+
Frankfurter Ring 247, 80807 Munich
Tel: (089) 3233360 *Fax:* (089) 3241728
E-mail: hirthammerverlag@t-online.de
Key Personnel
Manager: Franz Hirthammer
Founded: 1965
Subjects: Animals, Pets, Astrology, Occult, Environmental Studies, Health, Nutrition, Medicine, Nursing, Dentistry, Parapsychology, Philosophy, Religion - Buddhist, Religion - Hindu, Religion - Other, Theosophy
ISBN Prefix(es): 3-88721
Number of titles published annually: 15 Print
Total Titles: 200 Print

S Hirzel Verlag GmbH und Co+
Birkenwaldstr 44, 70191 Stuttgart
Mailing Address: Postfach 101061, 70009 Stuttgart
Tel: (0711) 2582206 *Fax:* (0711) 2582290
E-mail: service@hirzel.de
Web Site: www.hirzel.de *Cable:* HIRZELVERLAG, STUTTGART
Key Personnel
Man Dir: Dr Klaus Brauer; R Hack; Dr Christian Rotta; Dr Thomas Schaber
Rights: Sabine Koerner
Contact: Siegmar Bauer
Sales: Siegmar Bauer
Founded: 1853
Subjects: Chemistry, Chemical Engineering, Engineering (General), Language Arts, Linguistics, Philosophy, Psychology, Psychiatry, Regional Interests, Science (General)
ISBN Prefix(es): 3-7776
Parent Company: Deutscher Apotheker Verlag, Postfach 101061, 70009 Stuttgart
Associate Companies: Medpharm Scientific Publishers; Franz Steiner Verlag Wiesbaden GmbH; Wissenschaftliche Verlagagsellschaft mbH

Verlag Wolfgang Hoelker+
Hafenweg 30, 48155 Muenster
Mailing Address: Postfach 3820, 48021 Muenster
Tel: (0251) 414110 *Fax:* (0251) 4141120
E-mail: info@coppenrath.de *Cable:* HAFENWEG3
Key Personnel
Man Dir: Wolfgang Hoelker
Sales: Hubert Bergmoser
Production: Wolfgang Foerster
Publicity: Tomas Rensiny
International Rights: Christiane Leesker
Founded: 1973
Subjects: Cookery
ISBN Prefix(es): 3-88117; 3-9800058
Subsidiaries: Coppenrath Verlag
Warehouse: Coppenrath-Hoelker Distribution, Textilstrasse, 48612 Horstmar *Tel:* (02558) 98818 *Fax:* (02558) 98819

Verlag Peter Hoell+
Darmstaedterstr 14 b, 64397 Modautal
Tel: (06167) 912220 *Fax:* (06167) 912221
E-mail: hoell.verlag@t-online.de
Founded: 1987
Subjects: Anthropology, Astrology, Occult, Human Relations, Literature, Literary Criticism, Essays
ISBN Prefix(es): 3-9801439; 3-928564
Total Titles: 5 Print

Ing W Hofacker GmbH Verlag+
Tegernseerstr 15, 83607 Holzkirchen
Tel: (08024) 7331 *Fax:* (08024) 7580
E-mail: hofacker@t-online.de
Web Site: www.hofacker.de/
Telex: 526983
Key Personnel
Man Dir: Winfried Hofacker
Founded: 1968
Subjects: Computer Science, Electronics, Electrical Engineering, Microcomputers
ISBN Prefix(es): 3-921682; 3-88963
U.S. Office(s): EICOMP Publishing Inc, 4650 Arrow Hwy E-6, Montclair, CA 91763, United States *Tel:* 909-626-4070 *Fax:* 909-624-9574

Hofbauer, Christoph und Trojanow Ilia, Akademischer Verlag Muenchen+
Paul-Heysestr 3la, 80336 Munich
Tel: (089) 51616151 *Fax:* (089) 51616199
E-mail: avm@druckmedien.de
Key Personnel
Contact: Christoph Hofbauer; Ilija Trojanow
Founded: 1991
Subjects: Anthropology, Business, Economics, Literature, Literary Criticism, Essays, Physical Sciences
ISBN Prefix(es): 3-929115; 3-932965; 3-89003

Associate Companies: Marino Verlag, c/o Frederking & Thaler, Neumarkter Str 18, Munich Distributor for GBI-Verlag; Faktum

Edgar Hoff Verlag, see Reise Know-How

Edition Hoffmann & Co
Roemerstr 47, Goerbelheimer Muehle, 61169 Friedberg
Tel: (06031) 2443 *Fax:* (06031) 62965
Founded: 1967
Subjects: Architecture & Interior Design, Art
ISBN Prefix(es): 3-926026

Dieter Hoffmann Verlag
Senefelderstr 75, 55129 Mainz
Tel: (06136) 95100 *Fax:* (06136) 951037
Key Personnel
Man Dir, Rights & Permissions: Dieter Hoffman
Founded: 1960
Subjects: History, Outdoor Recreation
ISBN Prefix(es): 3-87341

H Hoffmann GmbH
An der Stammbahn 53, 14532 Kleinmachnow
Tel: (033203) 305810 *Fax:* (033203) 305820
E-mail: hhvberlin@t-online.de
ISBN Prefix(es): 3-87344

Hoffmann und Campe Verlag GmbH+
Harvestehuder Weg 42, 20149 Hamburg
Mailing Address: Postfach 130444, 20139 Hamburg
Tel: (040) 441880 *Fax:* (040) 44188202
E-mail: email@hoca.de
Web Site: www.hoffmann-und-campe.de/
Telex: 0214259 HoCa
Key Personnel
Man Dir: Dr Rainer Moritz; Dr Ralf Birkelbach; Ulrich Meier
Editorial: Hubertus Rabe; Tania Schlie
Marketing Dir: Margrit Osterwold
Production: Roland Kraft
Publicity Dir: Dr Joachim Koehler
Rights & Permissions: Ingeborg Rose; Sibylle Chory
Rights: Nadja Kossack
Founded: 1781
Subjects: Art, Biography, Fiction, History, Music, Dance, Nonfiction (General), Philosophy, Poetry, Psychology, Psychiatry, Science (General), Social Sciences, Sociology
ISBN Prefix(es): 3-455
Foreign Rep(s): Dagmar Bhend (Switzerland); Helga Riegler (Austria); Herbert Pamminger (Austria)

Verlag Karl Hofmann GmbH & Co+
Steinwasenstr 6-8, 73614 Schorndorf
Mailing Address: Postfach 1360, 73603 Schorndorf
Tel: (07181) 4020 *Fax:* (07181) 402111
E-mail: info@hofmann-verlag.de
Web Site: www.hofmann-verlag.de
Key Personnel
Man Dir, Rights & Permissions: Ottmar Hecht
Man Dir, Sales: Thomas Hecht
Founded: 1904
Subjects: Sports, Athletics
ISBN Prefix(es): 3-7780

Friedrich Hofmeister Musikverlag GmbH+
Karlstr 10, 04103 Leipzig
Tel: (0341) 9600750 *Fax:* (0341) 9603055
E-mail: f.hofmeister.musikverlag@t-online.de
Web Site: www.friedrich-hofmeister.de/
Key Personnel
Manager: Karl Heinz Schwarze
Founded: 1807
Subjects: Music, Dance
ISBN Prefix(es): 3-7331

Hogrefe Verlag GmbH & Co Kg+
Rohnsweg 25, 37085 Goettingen
Mailing Address: Postfach 3751, 37027 Goettingen
Tel: (0551) 496090 *Fax:* (0551) 4960988
E-mail: verlag@hogrefe.de
Web Site: www.hogrefe.de/
Key Personnel
Proprietor: Dr Dr G-Juergen Hogrefe
 E-mail: hogrefe@hogrefe.de
Man Dir: Dr Michael Vogtmeier *Tel:* (0551) 4960921 *E-mail:* vogtmeier@hogrefe.de
Sales Dir: Reinhard Dornieden
Production: B Otto
Promotion: S Otto
Founded: 1949
Subjects: Medicine, Nursing, Dentistry, Psychology, Psychiatry
ISBN Prefix(es): 3-8017
Subsidiaries: Verlag fur Angewandte Psychologie
U.S. Office(s): Hogrefe & Huber Publishing, Seattle Regional Headquarters, Box 2487, Kirkland, WA 98083-2487, United States
Bookshop(s): Oettinger & Hogrefe GmbH, Buchhandlung fuer Medizin und Psychologie, Robert-Bosch-Breite 25, 37079 Goettingen
Warehouse: Robert-Bosch-Breite 25, 37079 Goettingen
Orders to: Brockhaus Commission, Kreidlerstr 9, D-70806 Kornwestheim

Hohenrain-Verlag GmbH+
Am Apfelberg 18, 72076 Tuebingen
Mailing Address: Postfach 1611, 72006 Tuebingen
Tel: (07071) 40700 *Fax:* (07071) 407026
Telex: 17 7071902
Key Personnel
Man Dir: Wigbert Grabert
Founded: 1985
Subjects: Art, Biography, Fiction, Government, Political Science, History
ISBN Prefix(es): 3-89180
Number of titles published annually: 3 Print
Total Titles: 70 Print

Matth Hohner AG Verlag
Andreas-Kochstr 9, 78647 Trossingen
Tel: (07425) 200 *Fax:* (07425) 249
E-mail: info@hohner.de
Web Site: www.matth-hohner-ag.de/
Telex: 760727 hohnd
Key Personnel
Manager: Marcel Kop; Wolfgang Triebs
Founded: 1857
ISBN Prefix(es): 3-920468
Warehouse: Hohnerstr 8, 78647 Trossingen

Holland & Josenhans GmbH & Co+
Subsidiary of Verlag Handwerk und Technik GmbH
Feuerseeplatz 2, 70176 Stuttgart
Tel: (0711) 614390 *Fax:* (0711) 6143922
Web Site: www.holland-josenhans.de/
Key Personnel
Ordering: Ulla Knapp *Tel:* (0711) 6143920 *Fax:* (0711) 6143922 *E-mail:* verlag@huj.03.net
Marketing: Heidi Scheurle *Tel:* (0711) 6143925 *Fax:* (0711) 6143955 *E-mail:* marketing@huj.03.net
Founded: 1861
Subjects: Education
ISBN Prefix(es): 3-7782
Foreign Rep(s): Technischer Fachbuchvertrieb AG (Switzerland)

Holos Verlag+
Ermekeilstr 15, 53113 Bonn
Tel: (0228) 263020; (0228) 262332 *Fax:* (0228) 212435

Key Personnel
Manager: Wolfgang Guting
Founded: 1987
Specialize in Humanities.
Subjects: Anthropology, Archaeology, Fiction, Gay & Lesbian, Geography, Geology, History, Language Arts, Linguistics, Philosophy, Psychology, Psychiatry, Social Sciences, Sociology
ISBN Prefix(es): 3-926216; 3-86097

Guenther Holzboog, see Friedrich Frommann Verlag

Hans Holzmann Verlag GmbH und Co KG
Gewerbestr 2, 86825 Bad Woerishofen
Mailing Address: Postfach 1342, 86816 Bad Woerishofen
Tel: (08247) 35401 *Fax:* (08247) 354170
Web Site: www.holzmannverlag.de
Telex: 539331 *Cable:* HOLZMANN VERLAG
Key Personnel
Man Dir: Alexander Holzmann
Production Dir: Helmut Mauritz
Publishing Dir: Harald Bos
Finances: Arthur Fostmaier
Founded: 1936
Subjects: Business, Education, Law, Marketing
ISBN Prefix(es): 3-7783; 3-920416
Subsidiaries: Druck und Werbung Holzmann GmbH
Divisions: Abt Buchverlag; Abt Fach-Zeitschriften; Abt Anzeigen

Homo Oeconomicus, *imprint of* Accedo Verlagsgesellschaft mbH

Verlag Hoppenstedt GmbH
Havelstr 9, 64295 Darmstadt
Mailing Address: Postfach 100139, 64201 Darmstadt
Tel: (06151) 380100 *Fax:* (06151) 380101
E-mail: info@hopp.de
Web Site: www.hoppenstedt.de
Key Personnel
Man Dir: Werner Reiber; Roland Repp
Contact: Silve Braun *Tel:* (06151) 380 261 *E-mail:* braun@hopp.de
Founded: 1926
Subjects: Finance, Marketing, Securities
ISBN Prefix(es): 3-8203
Associate Companies: ABC voor Handel en Industrie CV, Haarlem, Netherlands *Tel:* (023) 5533533 *Fax:* (023) 5327033 *E-mail:* info@abc-de.nl; Belgisch ABC voor Handel en Industrie Bv, Asse, Belgium *Tel:* (021) 4630213 *Fax:* (021) 4630885 *E-mail:* info@abc-de.be; ComHouse AG, Wuerzburg *Tel:* (0931) 3561-0 *Fax:* (0931) 3561-140 *E-mail:* mail@comhouse.com; Druckhaus Darmstadt GmbH, Darmstadt *Tel:* (06151) 80550 *Fax:* (06151) 8055200; HBI SpA Bassano del Grappa, Bassano del Grappa, Italy *Tel:* (0424) 529088 *Fax:* (0424) 529191 *E-mail:* info@hbiitaly.it; HBI sro, Prague, Czech Republic *Tel:* (02) 6316624 *Fax:* (02) 6516616 *E-mail:* hoppenstedt@televom.cz; Hoppenstedt Bonnier Information GmbH, Darmstadt *Tel:* (06151) 380367 *Fax:* (06151) 380488 *E-mail:* info@catalogic.de; Hoppenstedt Bonnier Information Plock, Polska SP 20-0, Poland *Tel:* (024) 2644120 *Fax:* (024) 2644100 *E-mail:* hbi@indyk.plocman.pl; Hoppenstedt Bonnier & Tarsa Informacios Kft, Budapest, Hungary *Tel:* (01) 2761333 *Fax:* (01) 2760933 *E-mail:* mail@hoppbonn.hu
Subsidiaries: Seibt Verlag GmbH; Verlag Hoppenstedt & Co Wirtschaftsverlag Ges mbH; Hoppenstedt France SNC Compiegne; Hoppenstedt Nederland BV; Hoppenstedt AG Kilchberg

PUBLISHERS

GERMANY

Horlemann Verlag+
Postfach 1307, 53583 Bad Honnef
Tel: (02224) 5984; (02224) 5589 *Fax:* (02224) 5429
E-mail: horlemann@aol.com
Web Site: www.horlemann-verlag.de/
Key Personnel
Owner & International Rights: Beate Horlemann
Founded: 1990
Member of the Stock Exchange of German Booksellers.
Subjects: Asian Studies, Developing Countries, Education, Environmental Studies, Fiction, Foreign Countries, Government, Political Science, Literature, Literary Criticism, Essays, Nonfiction (General), Philosophy, Poetry, Religion - Islamic, Social Sciences, Sociology
ISBN Prefix(es): 3-927905; 3-89502

Hans Huber+
Laenggass-Str 76, 3000 Bern 9
Tel: (031) 3004500 *Fax:* (031) 3004590
E-mail: verlag@hanshuber.com
Web Site: www.hanshuber.com *Cable:* HUBERVERLAG BERN
Key Personnel
Man Dir: Dr G-Juergen Hogrefe
Editorial Dir: Juerg Flury
Marketing: Christian Liengme
Advertising: Anina Burkhalter
Sales: Astrid Iffland
Founded: 1927
Subjects: Education, Medicine, Nursing, Dentistry, Psychology, Psychiatry
ISBN Prefix(es): 3-456
Subsidiaries: Hogrefe & Huber Publishers Inc, Seattle/Toronto; Psychodiagnostika, Brno/Czechia & Bratislava/Slovakia; Testzentrale der Schweizer Psychologen AG
U.S. Office(s): Hogrefe & Huber Publishers Inc, PO Box 2487, Kirkland, WA 98083-2487, United States
Bookshop(s): Schanzenstr 1, 3000 Bern 9, Switzerland *Tel:* (031) 3004646 *Fax:* (031) 3004656 *E-mail:* contactbern@huberlang.com; Zeltweg 6, 8032 Zurich, Switzerland *Tel:* (01) 2683939 *Fax:* (01) 2683920 *E-mail:* contactzurich@huberlang.com

Volker Huber Edition & Galerie+
Berlinerstr 218, 63067 Offenbach am Main
Mailing Address: Postfach 101153, 63011 Offenbach
Tel: (069) 814523 *Fax:* (069) 880155
E-mail: edition-huber@t-online.de
Key Personnel
Owner: Volker Huber
Founded: 1965
Subjects: Art
ISBN Prefix(es): 3-921785

Max Hueber Verlag GmbH & Co KG+
Max-Hueberstr 4, 85737 Ismaning
Mailing Address: Postfach 1142, 85729 Ismaning
Tel: (089) 96020 *Fax:* (089) 9602358
Web Site: www.hueber.de/
Telex: 523613 hueb d
Key Personnel
Dir: Michaela Hueber
Rights: Anneliese Brausse
Founded: 1921
Subjects: Career Development, Literature, Literary Criticism, Essays, Adult Education in Foreign Languages, German as a Foreign Language
ISBN Prefix(es): 3-19
Associate Companies: Sound of People Verlag GmbH; Verlag fue Deutsch GmbH
U.S. Office(s): Buch-Bruecke, 96 Sweet St, Ballstone Lake, NY 12019, United States

Schoenhof's Foreign Books, Inc, 76A Mount Auburn St, Cambridge, MA 02138-5051, United States
Continental Book Company Inc, 625E 70 Ave, Suite 5, Denver, CO 80229, United States
Alder's Foreign Books Inc, 915 Foster St, Evanston, IL, United States
International Book Import Service Inc, 2995 Wall Triana Highway, Huntsville, AL 35824-1532, United States
German Book Center, NA Inc, PO Box 99, Mountaindale, NY 12763-0099, United States
Distributed by Editorial Idiomas (Spain); Hueber-Hellas (Greece); Pre-szt (Hungary)

Huebner Felicitas Verlag+
Warolderstr 1, 34513 Waldeck
Tel: (05695) 1028 *Fax:* (05695) 1027
Key Personnel
Publisher: Felicitas Huebner
Founded: 1981
Subjects: Film, Video, Health, Nutrition, Sports, Athletics
ISBN Prefix(es): 3-927359
Orders to: Bugrim Verlagsauslieferung Dr Laube & Partner, Saalburgstrasse 3, 12099 Berlin

Verlag Uta Huelsey
Postfach 34, 46461 Wesel
Tel: (0281) 27227 *Fax:* (0281) 24682
E-mail: uta.hulsey@t-online.de
ISBN Prefix(es): 3-923185

Huethig, *imprint of* Georg Thieme Verlag KG

Heinrich Hugendubel Verlag GmbH+
Nymphenburger Str 25, 80335 Munich
Tel: (089) 23 55 86-0 *Fax:* (089) 23 55 86-111
Key Personnel
Managing Partner: Heinrich Hugendubel; Dr Monika Roell
Publishing Dir: Stephanie Ehrenschwendner
Rights & Permissions: Brigitte Hugendubel; Susanna Schoeni
Subjects: Astrology, Occult, Health, Nutrition, Human Relations, Management, Nonfiction (General), Psychology, Psychiatry, Religion - Other, Science (General), Self-Help
ISBN Prefix(es): 3-7205; 3-424; 3-88034
Imprints: Ariston; Diederichs; Jrsiiana; Kailash
Orders to: VVA-Vereinigte Verlagsanslieferung, An der Antobahn, Postfach 1111, 33310 Guetersloh *Fax:* (05241) 460367

Human Wissenschaftlicher Verlag+
Bahnhofstr 41, 65185 Wiesbaden
Tel: (0611) 3082096 *Fax:* (0611) 3082096
Key Personnel
International Rights: Beatrix Siebel
Founded: 1988
Subjects: Anthropology, Biological Sciences, Medicine, Nursing, Dentistry, Psychology, Psychiatry, Religion - Catholic, Religion - Protestant, Social Sciences, Sociology, Women's Studies
ISBN Prefix(es): 3-89379; 3-9801744

Edition Humanistische Psychologie (EHP)+
Johannesstr 22, 51465 Bergisch Gladbach
Mailing Address: PO Box 200 222, 51432 Bergisch Gladbach
Tel: (02202) 981236 *Fax:* (02202) 981237
E-mail: info@ehp-koeln.com
Web Site: www.ehp-koeln.com; www.ehp.biz
Key Personnel
Vice President & Manager: Michels Kohlhage *Tel:* (0221) 5303817 *E-mail:* mmk@ehp-koeln.com
Editor: Andreas Kohlhage *E-mail:* andrea.kohlhage@ehp-koeln.com
Founded: 1986

Subjects: Human Relations, Literature, Literary Criticism, Essays, Management, Nonfiction (General), Psychology, Psychiatry, Science (General), Social Sciences, Sociology
ISBN Prefix(es): 3-926176; 3-9804784; 3-89797
Number of titles published annually: 5 Print
Total Titles: 60 Print
Orders to: Brockhaus Commission, Kreidlerstr 9, 70806 Kornwestheim, Mrs Schlayh *Tel:* (07154) 13270 *Fax:* (07154) 132713 *E-mail:* bestell@brocom.de
Hans Huber AG, Langgasstr 76, CH-3012 Bern, Switzerland, Mrs Keller *Tel:* (031) 3004-500 *Fax:* (031) 3004-590 *E-mail:* verlag@huberag.com

Humanistischer Verband Deutschlands, Landesverband Berlin eV
Wallstr 61-65, 10179 Berlin
Tel: (030) 613904-0 *Fax:* (030) 61390450
E-mail: hvd@humanismus.de
Web Site: www.humanismus.de/
Key Personnel
Contact: Christian John *Tel:* (030) 613904-31
Number of titles published annually: 4 Print
Total Titles: 55 Print

Humboldt-Taschenbuchverlag Jacobi KG+
Neusserstr 3, 80807 Munich
Mailing Address: Postfach 401120, 80711 Munich
Tel: (089) 360960 *Fax:* (089) 36096-222 (general); (089) 36096-258 (orders)
E-mail: redaktion@humboldt.de
Key Personnel
Man Dir: Karl Ernst Tielebier-Langenscheidt *E-mail:* redaktion@humboldt.de; Andreas Langenscheidt
Publishing Dir: Rolf Muller
Chief Editor: Claus-Ulrich Schmidt
Sales Dir: Dr Matti Schusseler
Advertising: Brigitte Pasch
Sales & Promotion: through Langenscheidt KG
Founded: 1953
Member of the Langenscheidt Group.
Subjects: Nonfiction (General), Travel
ISBN Prefix(es): 3-581
Orders to: Langenscheidt KG, Neusser Str 3, 80807 Munich

Edition Hundertmark
Bruesselerstr 29, 50674 Cologne
Tel: (0221) 237944 *Fax:* (0221) 249146
E-mail: info@hundertmark-gallery.com
Web Site: www.hundertmark-gallery.com
Key Personnel
Man Dir: Armin Hundertmark
Founded: 1970
Subjects: Art, Literature, Literary Criticism, Essays
Showroom(s): Galerie und Edition Hundertmark, Brusseler Str 29, 50674 Cologne

Huss-Medien GmbH
Am Friedrichshain 22, 10407 Berlin
Tel: (030) 42151438 *Fax:* (030) 42151300
E-mail: huss.medien@hussberlin.de *Cable:* TECHNIKVERLAG BERLIN
Key Personnel
Dir: Guenther Schwarz *Tel:* (030) 42151203 *E-mail:* guenther.schwarz@hussberlin.de
Secretary: Monika Ebert *Tel:* (030) 42151302 *E-mail:* monika.ebert@hussberlin.de
Founded: 1946
Subjects: Career Development, Electronics, Electrical Engineering, Mechanical Engineering, Radio, TV, Technology
ISBN Prefix(es): 3-341
Parent Company: Huss Verlag GmbH, Munich
Orders to: Libri Distribution, August-Schanzstr 33, 60433 Frankfurt
Zeitschrifleuvertrieb, Am Friedrichshain 22, 10400 Berlin

GERMANY

Huss-Verlag GmbH+
Joseph-Dollinger-Bogen 5, 80912 Munich
Tel: (089) 323910 *Fax:* (089) 32391416
E-mail: 101742.3244@compuserve.com
Web Site: www.huss-verlag.de/
Key Personnel
President: Wolfgang Huss
Public Relations: Monica-Ines Oppel
Founded: 1975
Subjects: Automotive, Business, Electronics, Electrical Engineering, Engineering (General), Transportation
ISBN Prefix(es): 3-921455
Associate Companies: Huss GmbH, Friedrichshain 22, 10407 Berlin
Subsidiaries: Verlag Technik GmbH; Verlag Die Wirtschaft GmbH; Verlag fuer Bauwesen GmbH
Orders to: Huss-GmbH, Am Friedrichshain 22, 10407 Berlin

Husum Druck- und Verlagsgesellschaft mbH Co KG+
Nordbahnhofstr 2, 25813 Husum
Mailing Address: Postfach 1480, 25804 Husum
Tel: (04841) 83520 *Fax:* (04841) 835210
E-mail: verlagsgruppe.husum@t-online.de
Web Site: www.verlagsgruppe.de/
Key Personnel
Man Dir, Editorial, Production, Rights & Permissions: Ingwert Paulsen,
Founded: 1973
Subjects: Regional Interests
ISBN Prefix(es): 3-88042; 3-89876
Associate Companies: Hansa Verlag Ingwert Paulsen Jr; Matthiesen Verlag Ingwert Paulsen Jr; Verlag der Nation
Subsidiaries: Hamburger Lesehefte Verlag Iselt & Co Nfl mbH

Huthig GmbH & Co KG+
Im Weiher 10, 69121 Heidelberg
Mailing Address: Postfach 102869, 69121 Heidelberg
Tel: (06221) 4890 *Fax:* (06221) 489279
Web Site: www.huethig.de/
Key Personnel
Man Dir: Huethig Holger; Dr Hans Windsheimer; Bernhard Kessler; Hans-Joern Hoffmann
Marketing: Joseph Weisbrod
Founded: 1925
Subjects: Architecture & Interior Design, Business, Chemistry, Chemical Engineering, Civil Engineering, Communications, Computer Science, Criminology, Earth Sciences, Electronics, Electrical Engineering, Energy, Film, Video, Health, Nutrition, Law, Medicine, Nursing, Dentistry, Science (General), Technology
ISBN Prefix(es): 3-929471
Subsidiaries: C F Mue Verlag; Rv Decker's Verlag, G Schenck; dpunkt Verlag; tuer digitale Technologie; Economica Verlag; Forkel Verlag; Barth Verlag; Heidelberg, Wichmann Verlag; Haug Verlagstuppe
U.S. Office(s): Hennig Wriedt, 29 MacIntosh Dr, Oxford, CT 06478, United States *Tel:* 203-881-2467 *Fax:* 203-881-2795
Warehouse: Verlagsservice Suedwest, Boschstr 2, 68753 Waghaeusel, Kirrlach
Orders to: Heidelberger Verlagsservice GmbH, Im Weiher 10, 69121 Heidelberg

Hyperion - Verlag (Hyperion Publishing House)
Gutenbergstr 25, D - 85748 Garching
Tel: (089) 32954165 *Fax:* (089) 32954175
E-mail: mail@hyperion-verlag.de
Web Site: www.hyperion-verlag.de
Key Personnel
President & International Rights: Martin Wartelsteiner
Founded: 1906

Subjects: Erotica, Fiction, Literature, Literary Criticism, Essays, Philosophy
ISBN Prefix(es): 3-89914
Number of titles published annually: 8 Print
Total Titles: 1 Print
Associate Companies: Miniaturbuchverlag Leipzig, Gutenbergstr 25, D-85748 Garching

Edition ID-Archiv/ID-Verlag+
Gneisenaustr 2a, 10961 Berlin
Mailing Address: Postfach 360205, 10972 Berlin
Tel: (030) 6947703 *Fax:* (030) 6947808
E-mail: id-verlag@mail.nadir.org
Web Site: www.txt.de/id-verlag/
Key Personnel
Contact: Andreas Fanizadeh; Wolfgang Tawereit
Founded: 1988
Subjects: Communications, Developing Countries, Government, Political Science, History, Literature, Literary Criticism, Essays, Publishing & Book Trade Reference
ISBN Prefix(es): 3-89408
Foreign Rep(s): Sebastian Count (Switzerland); Seth Meyer Bruhns (Austria)
Orders to: Sova, Friesstr 20-24, 60388 Frankfurt am Main

Idea Verlag GmbH+
Ringstr 40, 82223 Eichenau
Mailing Address: Postfach 1361, 82169 Puchheim
Tel: (08141) 80939 *Fax:* (08141) 80939
E-mail: idea-verlag@freepage.de
Web Site: www.idea-verlag.de
Key Personnel
Man Dir, Rights & Permissions, Sales, Publicity: Hariet Paschke
Founded: 1980
Subjects: Crafts, Games, Hobbies, Literature, Literary Criticism, Essays, Science (General), Sports, Athletics, Technology
ISBN Prefix(es): 3-88793

IDW-Verlag GmbH+
Tersteegenstr 14, 40474 Duesseldorf
Tel: (0211) 45610 *Fax:* (0211) 4541206
Web Site: www.idw-verlag.de *Cable:* IDEWEVERLAG
Key Personnel
Man Dir: Rainer von Buechau
Founded: 1950
Subjects: Accounting, Business, Finance
ISBN Prefix(es): 3-8021
Subsidiaries: WPA- Wirtschaftsakademie

Igel Verlag Literatur Michael Matthias Schardt
Rauheforst 77, 26127 Oldenburg
Tel: (0441) 6640262 *Fax:* (0441) 6640263
Key Personnel
Contact: Michael Schardt

Ikarus - Buchverlag+
Schuhgasse 6, 36142 Tann Rhoen
Tel: (06682) 919383 *Fax:* (06682) 919385
E-mail: ikarus-verlag@t-online.de
Web Site: www.ikarus-verlag.de
Key Personnel
Man Dir: Dr Wolfgang Hautumm
Founded: 1982
Subjects: Archaeology, History, Literature, Literary Criticism, Essays, Travel
ISBN Prefix(es): 3-9802064; 3-9800471
Number of titles published annually: 2 Print
Total Titles: 25 Print

IKO Verlag fur Interkulturelle Kommunikation+
Postfach 900, 421, 60444 Frankfurt/Main
Tel: (069) 784808 *Fax:* (069) 7896575
E-mail: ikoverlag@t-online.de
Web Site: www.iko-verlag.de

BOOK

Key Personnel
Man Dir: Walter Suelberg
Founded: 1982
Subjects: Alternative, Anthropology, Asian Studies, Business, Developing Countries, Education, Environmental Studies, Ethnicity, Labor, Industrial Relations, Science (General), Women's Studies
ISBN Prefix(es): 3-88939
Associate Companies: Holger Ehluig Publishers at Tho-Verlag fur Tutor-Kultaelle Kouieriko-hou, 4T Leroy House, 436 Essex Rd, London N1 3QP, United Kingdom *Tel:* (020) 76881688 *Fax:* (020) 76881699

ILS, see Institut fuer Landes- und Stadtentwicklungsforschung, ILS Nordrhein-Westfalen

Impuls-Theater-Verlag+
Postfach 1147, 82141 Planegg
Tel: (089) 8597577 *Fax:* (089) 8593044
E-mail: info@buschfunk.de
Web Site: www.buschfunk.de
Key Personnel
Contact: Florian Laber
Founded: 1932
Subjects: Drama, Theater, Film, Video, Music, Dance, Theatre: plays & books
ISBN Prefix(es): 3-7660
Distributed by Teaterverlag elgg (Switzerland)
Distributor for Stutz-Velag (Germany & Austria)

IMSF, see Institut fuer Marxistische Studien und Forschungen eV (IMSF)

Industria-Verlagsbuchhandlung GmbH
Eschstr 22, 44629 Herne
Mailing Address: Postfach 101849, 44621 Herne
Tel: (02323) 1410 *Fax:* (02323) 141123
Telex: 8229870
Key Personnel
Manager: Ernst-Otto Kleyboldt
Subjects: Accounting, Law
ISBN Prefix(es): 3-87373

Industrie- und Handelsverlag GmbH & Co KG
Goettinger Chaussee 76, 30453 Hannover
Tel: (0511) 98489957 *Fax:* (0511) 98489952
E-mail: info@fhb-online.de
Web Site: www.fhb-online.de/
Key Personnel
Man Dir: Heiko Dorn
Procurer: Angelika Lindeberg-Geers
Founded: 1923
Member of the Stock Exchange of German Booksellers.
ISBN Prefix(es): 3-7788
Associate Companies: Verlagsbetriebe Walter Dorn GmbH & Co KG
Branch Office(s)
Berlin
Bremen
Duesseldorf
Filderstadt
Frankfurt
Leipzig
Munich

Industrieschau Verlagsgesellschaft mbH
Berliner Allee 8, 64295 Darmstadt
Mailing Address: Postfach 100262, 64202 Darmstadt
Tel: (06151) 38920 *Fax:* (06151) 33164
E-mail: info@abconline.de
Web Site: www.abconline.de
Key Personnel
Man Dir: Margit Selka
Reference & product directories about German industrial groups.
ISBN Prefix(es): 3-7790

PUBLISHERS   GERMANY

Parent Company: ABC der Deutschen Wirtschaft Verlagsgesellschaft mbH
Branch Office(s)
PO Box 75, 1095 Vienna, Austria *Tel:* (0222) 4053327
U.S. Office(s): Western Hemisphere Publishing Corp, PO Box 847, Hillsboro, OR 97123-0847, United States *Tel:* 503-640-3736 *Fax:* 503-640-2748

Mediteg-Gesellschaft fuer Informatik Technik und Systeme Verlag+
Limesstr 5, 61273 Wehrheim
Tel: (06081) 5171 *Fax:* (06081) 56017
Key Personnel
Manager: Rudolf Putz
Founded: 1984
Subjects: Medicine, Nursing, Dentistry
ISBN Prefix(es): 3-924373

Informationsstelle Suedliches Afrika eV (ISSA)
Koenigswintererstr 116, 53227 Bonn
Tel: (0228) 464369 *Fax:* (0228) 468177
E-mail: issa@comlink.org
Web Site: www.issa-bonn.org
Key Personnel
Man Dir: Hein Moellers
Founded: 1971
Subjects: Developing Countries, Literature, Literary Criticism, Essays
ISBN Prefix(es): 3-921614

Infostelle Industrieverband Deutscher Schmieden e V
Goldene Pforte 1, 58093 Hagen
Tel: (02331) 95 88 28 *Fax:* (02331) 95 87 28
E-mail: oders@metalform.de
Web Site: www.metalform.de
Key Personnel
Marketing: Heinrich Benneker *Tel:* (02331) 958821
Management: Dr Theodore L Tutmann *Tel:* (02331) 958812

Inno Vatio Verlags AG
Kurt Schumacherstr 1, 53113 Bonn
Tel: (0228) 2433180 *Fax:* (0228) 319471
E-mail: medien-tenor@innovatio.de
Web Site: www.innovatio.de; www.medien-tenor.de
Founded: 1985
Subjects: Business, History, Specialize in monthly & quarterly newsletters on media content analysis
Total Titles: 25 Print

Insel Verlag+
Lindenstr 29-35, 60325 Frankfurt
Mailing Address: Postfach 101945, 60019 Frankfurt
Tel: (069) 756010 *Fax:* (069) 75601522
Web Site: www.suhrkamp.de *Cable:* INSELVERLAG
Key Personnel
Publisher: Dr Siegfried Unseld
Dir: Guenter Berg
Man Dir: Philip Roeder *Tel:* (069) 75 601 500
  E-mail: roeder@suhrkamp.de
Rights & Permissions: Dr Petra Hardt
Founded: 1899
Subjects: Art, Ethnicity, Literature, Literary Criticism, Essays
ISBN Prefix(es): 3-458
Associate Companies: Deutscher Klassiker Verlag; Suhrkamp Verlag; Suhrkamp Verlag AG, Switzerland
Branch Office(s)
Jahnallee 27, D-04109 Leipzig *Tel:* (0341) 9804765 *Fax:* (0341) 9804501
Foreign Rep(s): Claudia Brandes (Europe, Japan, Scandinavia & Netherlands); Ulrich Breth (Asia, Greece, Turkey); Christiane Schaefer (Africa, France, Israel, South & Central America, Spain & Portugal); Petra Hardt (Australia, China & Taiwan, France, Italy, Netherlands & Scandinavia, US)
Foreign Rights: Agenzia (Italy); Balla & Co Literary Agents (Hungary); Bardon Chinese Media Agency (Taiwan); Hercules Business (China); Internationaal Literatuur Bureau (Netherlands); International Editors (Brazil, South America, Spain); Leonhardt & Hoier Literary (Scandinavia); Sakai Agency (Japan)

Interconnections Reisen und Arbeiten Georg Beckmann+
Schilerstr 44, 79104 Freiburg
Tel: (0761) 2000 *Fax:* (0761) 200572
Key Personnel
Owner: Georg Beckmann
Founded: 1985
Subjects: Travel
ISBN Prefix(es): 3-924586; 3-86040
Orders to: Internationaler Land Kartenhaus, Schockenreidstr 44a, 705655 Stuttgart

International Thomson Publishing (ITP)+
Koenigswintererstr 418, 53227 Bonn
Tel: (0228) 970240 *Fax:* (0228) 441342
E-mail: mitp@mitp.de
Web Site: www.mitp.de
Key Personnel
President: Hartmut Gante
International Rights: H J Beese
Sales Dir: Markus Kanderer
Founded: 1992
Subjects: Computer Science
ISBN Prefix(es): 3-8266
Subsidiaries: Datacom; ITP - IWT; Wolframs
Warehouse: VVA Bertelsmann, Postfach 7777, 33310 Guetersloh

Verlag fuer Internationale Politik GmbH+
Postfach 1529, 53005 Bonn
Mailing Address: Postfach 1529, 53005 Bonn
Tel: (0228) 7290010 *Fax:* (0228) 695734
Key Personnel
Partner: Alfred Frhr von Oppenheim; Otto Wolff von Amerongen
Man Dir: Gerhard Eickhorn
Man Dir Assistant: Ulrike Rothe
Sales: Rainer Mertens
Founded: 1971
Subjects: Government, Political Science
ISBN Prefix(es): 3-921011
Parent Company: Europa Union Verlag GmbH

Internationale Studien zen Fatigkeititleone, *imprint of* Bund demokratischer Wissenschaftlerinnen und Wissenschafler eV (BdWi)

Internationale Vereinigung fuer Geschichte und Gegenwart der Druckkunst eV, see Gutenberg-Gesellschaft eV

Intertrans-Verlag GmbH+
Neckarstr 37, 63071 Offenbach am Main
Tel: (069) 871500 *Fax:* (069) 852894
Telex: 1631btx(069871500-0001)
Key Personnel
Manager & International Rights: Bernhard Mueller
Founded: 1982
Subjects: Language Arts, Linguistics
ISBN Prefix(es): 3-8223; 3-922718
Distributor for Edition-Disque Omnivox
Orders to: Kurfuenstenstr 7, 67061 Ludwigshafen

Klaus Isele+
Heidelstr 9, 79805 Eggingen
Tel: (07746) 91116 *Fax:* (07746) 91117
E-mail: klaus.isele@t-online.de
Key Personnel
Owner: Klaus Isele
Editorial Dir: Eva Taubert
Founded: 1984
Subjects: Art, Fiction, Literature, Literary Criticism, Essays, Poetry, Religion - Buddhist, Travel
ISBN Prefix(es): 3-925016; 3-86142
Number of titles published annually: 18 Print; 6 Audio
Total Titles: 200 Print; 20 Audio
Orders to: Kock, Neff & Oetinger & Co Verlagsauslieferung GmbH, Schockenriedstrabe 59, 70565 Stuttgart *Tel:* (0711) 78990

Iselt und Co Nfl mbH, see Hamburger Lesehefte Verlag Iselt & Co Nfl mbH

Verlag der Islam+
Babenhaeuser Landstr 25, 60599 Frankfurt
Tel: (069) 681485; (069) 681062 *Fax:* (069) 686504
Telex: 416187 Islam d *Cable:* ISLAM FRANKFURT MAIN
Key Personnel
Editor: Hadayatullah Huebsch *Tel:* (069) 314596
Founded: 1949
Masjid Baitur Rahman, 15000 Good Hope Rd, Silver Spring, MD 20905, USA.
Subjects: Nonfiction (General), Religion - Islamic
ISBN Prefix(es): 3-921458; 3-932244
Total Titles: 110 Print
Warehouse: Hanauer Landstr 50, 60314 Frankfurt, Contact: Mr Munir *Tel:* (069) 43059519

ISSA, see Informationsstelle Suedliches Afrika eV (ISSA)

ITP, see International Thomson Publishing (ITP)

ITpress Verlag+
Mozartweg 24, 76646 Bruchsal
Mailing Address: Postfach 1744, 76607 Bruchsal
Tel: (07251) 300575 *Fax:* (07251) 14823
E-mail: itpress@acm.org
Web Site: www.itpress.com
Key Personnel
Prof: Dr Reiner Hartenstein *Tel:* (0631) 2052606
Founded: 1994
Subjects: Computer Science, Electronics, Electrical Engineering, Microcomputers, Nonfiction (General), Public Administration
ISBN Prefix(es): 3-929814; 0-9639887
Number of titles published annually: 10 Print
Total Titles: 10 Print
Subsidiaries: ITpressHartenstein

Iudicium Verlag GmbH+
Hans-Graessel-Weg 13, 81375 Munich
Mailing Address: Postfach 701067, 81310 Munich
Tel: (089) 718747 *Fax:* (089) 7142039
E-mail: info@iudicium.de
Web Site: www.iudicium.de
Key Personnel
Manager: Dr Peter Kapitza
Contact: Dominique Colmont-Freisinger; Kiyoko Kapitza; Elisabeth Schaidhammer; Dr Lucia Schwellinger
Founded: 1983
Subjects: Anthropology, Art, Asian Studies, Biography, Communications, Drama, Theater, Education, Fiction, Foreign Countries, History, Language Arts, Linguistics, Library & Information Sciences, Literature, Literary Criticism, Essays, Music, Dance, Philosophy, Poetry, Religion - Catholic, Social Sciences, Sociology, Theology, Women's Studies
ISBN Prefix(es): 3-89129

GERMANY

Reisebuchverlag Iwanowski GmbH
Buchnerstr 11, 41540 Dormagen
Tel: (02133) 26030 *Fax:* (02133) 260333
E-mail: info@iwanowski.de
Web Site: www.iwonowski.de
Founded: 1984
Subjects: Travel
ISBN Prefix(es): 3-933041; 3-923975
Number of titles published annually: 5 Print
Total Titles: 70 Print

IWT Magazine Publishing House GmbH, *imprint of* Gildefachverlag GmbH & Co KG

J Ch Mellinger Verlag GmbH+
Burgholzstr 25, 70376 Stuttgart
Tel: (0711) 543787 *Fax:* (0711) 556889
E-mail: mellinger@sambo.de
Key Personnel
Manager: Wolfgang Militz; Tobias Sambo; Gudrun Emmert
Founded: 1926
Subjects: Biography, Education, Fiction
ISBN Prefix(es): 3-88069

Verlag J P Peter, Gebr Holstein GmbH & Co KG
Erlbacher Str 104, 91541 Rothenburg
Mailing Address: Postfach 1262, 91534 Rothenburg
Tel: (09861) 4 00 384 *Fax:* (09861) 4 00 79
E-mail: peter-verlag@rotabene.de
Web Site: www.peter-verlag.de
Key Personnel
Man Dir: Dr Gerhard Prinz; Wolfgang Schneider
Publisher: Dekan Christoph Schmerl
Founded: 1884
Subjects: Poetry, Religion - Other
ISBN Prefix(es): 3-87625; 3-87311
Bookshop(s): Evangel Bucherdrenst Rothenburg

Jaeger & Waldmann, see Telex-Verlag Jaeger & Waldmann GmbH

Jahreszeiten-Verlag GmbH+
Possmoorweg 5, 22301 Hamburg
Mailing Address: Postfach 601220, 22212 Hamburg
Tel: (040) 2717-0; (040) 2493; (040) 2412
Fax: (040) 2063; (040) 2717
E-mail: press@jalag.de
Web Site: www.jalag.de *Cable:* JALAG
Key Personnel
Publisher: Thomas Ganske
Man Dir: Juergen Knop; Klaus Teichmann; Herrmann Schmidt
Founded: 1948
Subjects: Architecture & Interior Design, Automotive, Cookery, Crafts, Games, Hobbies, Fashion, Foreign Countries, Gardening, Plants, Health, Nutrition, House & Home, How-to, Journalism, Travel, Wine & Spirits, Women's Studies
ISBN Prefix(es): 3-87383
Parent Company: Verlagsgruppe Ganske
Associate Companies: Hoffmann & Campe; Prinz Kommunikations GmbH; DLS GmbH; Die Woche; Graefe & Onzer
U.S. Office(s): Publicitas Globe Media, 261 Madison Ave, 19th fl, New York, NY 10016, United States, John Moncure *Tel:* 212-599-5057 *Fax:* 212-599-8298
Bookshop(s): Buchhaus Campe, Karolinenstr 13, 90402 Nuremberg; Schrobsdorff sche Buchhandlung, Koenigsallee 22, 40212 Dusseldorf; Medienhaus Prinz, T11-3, 68161 Mannheim

Jan Thorbecke Verlag GmbH & Co+
Senefelderstr 12, 73760 Ostifildern
Mailing Address: Postfach 42 01, 73745 Ostifildern
Tel: (07571) 728100 *Fax:* (07571) 728280; 728287 (distribution)
Web Site: www.thorbecke.de *Cable:* THORBECKE
Key Personnel
Dir, Editorial, Rights & Permissions: Dr Georg Bensch; Dr Joachim Bensch
Production: Norbert Brey
Publishing Manager & Publicity: Dr Iris Schulz
Dir: Nathalie Donie
Editor: Dr Peter Donie; Dr Peter Nittmann
Founded: 1946
Subjects: Archaeology, Art, Foreign Countries, History, Literature, Literary Criticism, Essays, Regional Interests, Theology, Travel
ISBN Prefix(es): 3-7995
Associate Companies: Bergstadtverlag Wilhelm Gottlieb Korn GmbH, Wuerzburg (Correspondence & Distribution: Karlstr 10, Postfach 546, 72488 Sigmaringen)

Janus Verlagsgesellschaft, Dr Norbert Meder & Co+
Simon-Meister-Str 42, 50733 Cologne
Tel: (0221) 5996035 *Fax:* (0221) 9725519
Founded: 1980
Subjects: History, Language Arts, Linguistics, Science (General), Social Sciences, Sociology
ISBN Prefix(es): 3-922607; 3-922977
Orders to: Prolit Buchvertrieb GmbH, Siemensstr 16, 35463 Fernwald

Verlag Winfried Jenior
Lassallestr 15, 34119 Kassel
Tel: (0561) 7391621 *Fax:* (0561) 774148
E-mail: jenior@aol.com
Web Site: www.jenior.de
Publish book series of Kassel University, travel books on Spain, Spanish cookery books, yearbook & books on Kassel & region.
ISBN Prefix(es): 3-9801438; 3-928172; 3-934377
Distributor for Moll Verlag

JKL Publikationen GmbH+
Klausenpas 14, 12107 Berlin
Tel: (030) 74104625 *Fax:* (030) 74104626
E-mail: info@zeitgut.com
Web Site: www.zeitgut.com
Key Personnel
Contact: Juergen Kleindienst *E-mail:* j.kleindienst@zeitgut.com
Member of Boersenverlin des Deutschen Buchhandels.
Subjects: Biography, History
ISBN Prefix(es): 3-933336

Wolfgang Joerg und Ingrid Joerg, see Berliner Handpresse Wolfgang Joerg und Erich Schonig

Johann Wolfgang Goethe Universitat
Senckenberganlage 31, 60054 Frankfurt am Main
Mailing Address: Graefstr 38, Postfach 11 19 32, 60325 Frankfurt
Tel: (069) 798-23590 *Fax:* (069) 798-28313
E-mail: hrz@rz.uni-frankfurt.de
Web Site: www.rz.uni-frankfurt.de
Key Personnel
President: Prof Werner MeiBhes, PhD
Contact: Ulrike Jaspers
Founded: 1983
Subjects: Science (General)
Imprints: Anzeigenverwaltung & Herstellung; Bezugsbedingungen; Herausgeber; Redaktion & Gestaltung

Johannes Berchmans Verlagsbuchhandlung GmbH
Kaulbachstr 33, 80539 Munich
Tel: (089) 38185-244 *Fax:* (089) 2386-2342

Key Personnel
Manager: Manfred Hanke
ISBN Prefix(es): 3-87056

Johannes Verlag Einsiedeln, Freiburg+
Lindenmattenstr 29, 79117 Freiburg
Tel: (0761) 640168 *Fax:* (0761) 640169
E-mail: johverlag@aol.com
Key Personnel
Contact: Susanne Greiner; Cornelia Capol
Founded: 1947
Subjects: Philosophy, Religion - Catholic, Theology
ISBN Prefix(es): 3-89411
Number of titles published annually: 10 Print
Total Titles: 340 Print

Johannis+
Heiligenstr 24, 77933 Lahr/Schwarzw
Tel: (07821) 5810 *Fax:* (07821) 581-26
E-mail: johannis-druck@t-online.de
Web Site: www.johannis-verlag.de
Key Personnel
Owner: Reinhold Fels
Publisher: Karlheinz Kern
Founded: 1896
Also publish gift books, booklets, stationery & greeting cards.
Subjects: Biblical Studies, Photography, Religion - Protestant, Theology
ISBN Prefix(es): 3-501
Total Titles: 1,100 Print

Jonas Verlag fuer Kunst und Literatur GmbH
Weidenhaeuserstr 88, 35037 Marburg
Tel: (06421) 25132 *Fax:* (06421) 210572
E-mail: jonas@jonas-verlag.de
Key Personnel
Manager: Dieter Mayer-Guerr
Founded: 1978
Subjects: Art, History
ISBN Prefix(es): 3-89445
Orders to: Prolit *Fax:* (0641) 9439389

Dr Werner Jopp Verlag+
Danzigerstr 58, 65191 Wiesbaden
Tel: (0611) 547116 *Fax:* (0611) 542762
Key Personnel
Publisher: Dr Werner Jopp
Founded: 1987
Specialize in Health Advice.
Subjects: Health, Nutrition
ISBN Prefix(es): 3-926955

Verlag Josef Knecht-Carolusdruckerei GmbH, see VJK Verlag Josef Knecht

Jovis Verlag GmbH+
Kurfuerstenstr 15/16, 10785 Berlin
Tel: (030) 261 12 07 *Fax:* (030) 261 15 42
E-mail: jovis@jovis.de
Web Site: www.jovis.de
Key Personnel
Publisher: Jochen Visscher *E-mail:* visscher@jovis.de
Sales & Marketing Manager: Jutta Bornholdt-Cassetti *E-mail:* bornholdt@jovis.de
Founded: 1994
Subjects: Art, Film, Video, History, Nonfiction (General), Photography, Architecture, History of Art
ISBN Prefix(es): 3-931321; 9-936314
Number of titles published annually: 18 Print
Total Titles: 91 Print
Orders to: Distributed Art Publishers (DAP), 155 Sixth Ave, New York, NY 10013-1507, United States *Tel:* 212-627-1999 *Fax:* 212-627-9484
E-mail: dwingate@dapinc.com

Jowi-Verlag+
Muehlbacherstr 5, 97752 Karlstadt-Laudenbach

Tel: (09353) 2921
Founded: 1991
ISBN Prefix(es): 3-9802897

Joy Verlag GmbH+
Am Fichtelholz 5, 87477 Sulzberg
Tel: (08376) 8922 *Fax:* (08376) 8845
E-mail: joy_verlag@compuserve.com
Key Personnel
Manager: Thomas Kettenring
Founded: 1989
Subjects: Health, Nutrition, Religion - Buddhist, Self-Help
ISBN Prefix(es): 3-928554

Jrisiana, *imprint of* Heinrich Hugendubel Verlag GmbH

Juedischer Verlag GmbH+
Lindenstr 29-35, 60325 Frankfurt am Main
Mailing Address: Postfach 101945, 60019 Frankfurt am Main
Tel: (069) 75601-0 *Fax:* (069) 75601-522
Web Site: www.suhrkamp.de
Key Personnel
Publisher: Dr Siegfried Unseld
Man Dir: Philip Roeder *Tel:* (069) 75 601 500
  E-mail: roeder@suhrkamp.de
Editorial Dir: Dr Rainer Weiss
Rights & Permissions: Dr Petra Hardt
Founded: 1902
Subjects: Religion - Jewish
ISBN Prefix(es): 3-633
Parent Company: Suhrkamp Verlag

Jugenddienst-Verlag, see Peter Hammer Verlag GmbH

Julius Klinkhardt Verlagsbuchhandlung+
Ramsauer Weg 5, 83670 Bad Heilbrunn
Tel: (08046) 9304; (08046) 9305 *Fax:* (08046) 9306
E-mail: info@klinkhardt.de
Key Personnel
Contact: Andreus Klinkhardt; Rudiger Hartmann
Founded: 1834
Member of the Stock Exchange of German Booksellers & Association of School Book Publishers.
Subjects: Education, Psychology, Psychiatry
ISBN Prefix(es): 3-7815

Junfermann-Verlag+
Imadstr 40, 33102 Paderborn
Mailing Address: Postf 1840, 33048 Paderborn
Tel: (05251) 1 34 40 *Fax:* (05251) 13 44 44
E-mail: ju@junfermann.de
Web Site: www.junfermann.de
Key Personnel
Contact: Heike Carstensen *Tel:* (05251) 13 44 18
  E-mail: carstensen@junfermann.de
Founded: 1659
Specialize in psychology & psychotherapy.
Subjects: Management, Psychology, Psychiatry, Self-Help
ISBN Prefix(es): 3-87387
Number of titles published annually: 30 Print
Total Titles: 250 Print

Junius Verlag GmbH+
Stresemannstr 375, 22761 Hamburg
Mailing Address: Postfach 500727, 22707 Hamburg
Tel: (040) 89 25 99 *Fax:* (040) 89 12 24
E-mail: junius-verlag@t-online.de
Web Site: www.junius-verlag.de
Key Personnel
Man Dir: Karl Olaf Petters *E-mail:* petters@junius-verlag.de
Founded: 1979
Subjects: Architecture & Interior Design, Government, Political Science, Philosophy, Social Sciences, Sociology
ISBN Prefix(es): 3-88506
Number of titles published annually: 30 Print
Total Titles: 200 Print
Distributed by AVA Book 2000 (Switzerland)
Foreign Rep(s): Idea Books, Amsterdam (Worldwide)
Orders to: LKG, Poetzschauer Weg, 04529 Esperhain *Tel:* (034206) 65720 *Fax:* (034206) 65770

Justus-Liebig-Universitat Giessen
Ludwigstr 23, 35390 Giessen
Tel: (0641) 99-0 *Fax:* (0641) 99-12259
E-mail: michael.kost@admin.uni-giessen.de
Web Site: www.uni-giessen.de
Key Personnel
President: Dr Stefan Hormuth *Tel:* (0641) 99-12000 *Fax:* (0641) 99-12009
Research institution (international economic & social development & environment).
Subjects: Agriculture, Environmental Studies
ISBN Prefix(es): 3-924840

Jutta Pohl Verlag+
Im Buckeberg 11a, 76307 Karlsbad
Tel: (07202) 2239 *Fax:* (07202) 3879
E-mail: jutta@pohlverlag.de
Web Site: www.pohl-verlag.de *Cable:* POHL, CELLE
Key Personnel
Dir: Udo Meyer *Tel:* (05141) 9889-15
Subjects: Health, Nutrition, Music, Dance, Outdoor Recreation, Sports, Athletics
ISBN Prefix(es): 3-7911
Total Titles: 60 Print; 2 Audio
Parent Company: Cellesche Zeitung Schweiger & Pick Verlag, Pfingsten GmbH & Co KG
Foreign Rep(s): As Bartsch-Holler Gmbh (Austria); Schweizer Buchzentruun (Switzerland); Uitgeverij de Vraseborch (Netherlands)

Juventa Verlag GmbH+
Ehretstr 3, 69469 Weinheim
Tel: (06201) 9020-0 *Fax:* (06201) 9020-13
E-mail: juventa@juventa.de
Web Site: www.juventa.de
Key Personnel
Man Dir: Lothar Schweim *Tel:* (06201) 9020-10
  E-mail: schweim@juventa.de
Publicity & International Rights: Margareta Graeber *Tel:* (06201) 9020-11 *E-mail:* graeber@juventa.de
Advertising: Andrea Biernatzki *Tel:* (06201) 9020-15 *E-mail:* biernatzki@juventa.de
Founded: 1953
Subjects: Criminology, Education, Health, Nutrition, History, Psychology, Psychiatry, Social Sciences, Sociology
ISBN Prefix(es): 3-7799
Number of titles published annually: 50 Print
Total Titles: 500 Print
Warehouse: Justus-von-Liebigstr 1, 86899 Landsberg/Lech *Tel:* (08191) 125 243 *Fax:* (08191) 125 198
Orders to: Mi Verlags Service *Tel:* (08191) 125 243 *Fax:* (08191) 125 198

K + G Verlagsgesellschaft, see Karto + Grafik Verlagsgesellschaft (K & G Verlagsgesellschaft)

K L V Konkret Literatur Verlag GmbH+
Hoheluftchaussee 74, 20253 Hamburg
Tel: (040) 47 52 34 *Fax:* (040) 47 84 15
E-mail: info@konkret-literatur-verlag.de
Web Site: www.konkret-verlage.de
Key Personnel
Man Dir, Rights & Permissions: Dr Dorothee Gremliza
Founded: 1978
Subjects: Developing Countries, Government, Political Science, Health, Nutrition, History, Medicine, Nursing, Dentistry, Nonfiction (General), Poetry, Social Sciences, Sociology, Women's Studies
ISBN Prefix(es): 3-922144; 3-89458
Distributed by B&I (Switzerland); Herder & Co (Austria)
Shipping Address: Bertelsmann Distribution/VVA, Postfach 7777, 33310 Guetersloh *Tel:* (05241) 801499 *Fax:* (05241) 809352
Warehouse: Bertelsmann Distribution/VVA, Postfach 7777, 33310 Guetersloh *Tel:* (05241) 801499 *Fax:* (05241) 809352
Orders to: Bertelsmann Distribution/VVA, Postfach 7777, 33310 Guetersloh *Tel:* (05241) 801499 *Fax:* (05241) 809352

K T Kaiser Taschenbuecher (pocketbooks), *imprint of* Guetersloher Verlagshaus Gerd Mohn

Kabel Verlag, *imprint of* Piper Verlag GmbH

Kailash, *imprint of* Heinrich Hugendubel Verlag GmbH

KaJo Verlag+
Imprint of Verlagshaus Wurzburg
Beethovenstr 5, 97080 Wurzburg
Tel: (0931) 385235 *Fax:* (0931) 385305
E-mail: info@verlagshaus.com
Web Site: www.verlagshaus.com
Key Personnel
Publishing Dir: Dieter Krause
Dir of Production: Juergen Roth
Sales Dir: Johannes Glesius
Founded: 1985
Subjects: Travel
ISBN Prefix(es): 3-925544

Kallmeyer'sche Verlagsbuchhandlung GmbH+
Im Brande 19, 30926 Seelze
Mailing Address: Postfach 10 01 34, 30917 Seelze
Tel: (0511) 4 00 04-1 75 *Fax:* (0511) 4 00 04-1 76
E-mail: info@kallmeyer.de
Web Site: www.kallmeyer.de
Key Personnel
Man Dir: Imue Junack *Tel:* (0511) 40004150
  E-mail: junack@kallmeyer.de
Publishinghouse Dir: Hubertus Rollfing
  Tel: (0511) 40004150 *E-mail:* rollfing@kallmeyer.de
Founded: 1986
Specialize in Elementary Drawings, Rhythm & Teaching Goods.
Subjects: Career Development, Crafts, Games, Hobbies, Education, Engineering (General), Environmental Studies, Music, Dance, Nonfiction (General), Sports, Athletics
ISBN Prefix(es): 3-7800

S Karger GmbH Verlag fuer Medizin und Naturwissenschaften+
Loerracherstr 16A, 79115 Freiburg
Tel: (0761) 45 20 70 *Fax:* (0761) 45 20 714
E-mail: karger@karger.de *Cable:* KARGERMEDBOOKS
Key Personnel
Man Dir, International Rights: S Karger
Founded: 1890
Subjects: Medicine, Nursing, Dentistry, Psychology, Psychiatry, Science (General)
ISBN Prefix(es): 3-8055
Parent Company: S Karger AG, Allschwilerstr 10, CH-4009 Basel, Switzerland
U.S. Office(s): S Karger Publishers Inc, 26 W Avon Rd, PO Box 529, Farmington, CT 06085, United States

GERMANY

Bookshop(s): Karger-Buchhandlung Ausstellung und Vertrieb internationaler medizinischer Fachliteratur, Loerracher Str 16a, 79115 Freiburg

Verlag Karl Baedeker GmbH
Marco-Polo-Zentrum, 73760 Ostfildern
Mailing Address: Postfach 3162, 73751 Ostfildern
Tel: (0711) 4502262 *Fax:* (0711) 4502343
E-mail: baedeker@mairs.de
Key Personnel
Man Dir: Dr Volkmar Mair
Chief Editor: Ranier Eisenschmid
Founded: 1827
Member of the Mair Group.
Subjects: Travel
ISBN Prefix(es): 3-87504; 3-89525; 3-8297

Karl-May-Verlag Lothar Schmid GmbH+
Schuetzenstr 30, 96047 Bamberg
Tel: (0951) 98 20 60 *Fax:* (0951) 2 43 67
E-mail: info@karl-may.de
Web Site: www.karl-may.de
Key Personnel
Man Dir, Publicity, Rights & Permissions: Lothar Schmid
Man Dir & Publicity: Bernhard Schmid
Founded: 1913
Subjects: Fiction, Western Fiction
ISBN Prefix(es): 3-7802
Number of titles published annually: 7 Print
Total Titles: 200 Print
Imprints: Edition Ustad
Subsidiaries: Karl May Verwaltungs-und Vertriebs-GmbH

Karto + Grafik Verlagsgesellschaft (K & G Verlagsgesellschaft)+
Schoenberger Weg 15, 60488 Frankfurt
Tel: (069) 76 20 31 *Fax:* (069) 76 91 06
E-mail: kugverlag@aol.com
Web Site: www.hildebrands.de
Key Personnel
Publisher: Volker Hildebrand
Man Dir: Hr Stefan Beyer
Founded: 1980
Subjects: Travel
ISBN Prefix(es): 3-88989
Total Titles: 100 Print
Distributed by Map Link; Librairie Ulysse Inc; ITMB Publishing Ltd; World Leisure Marketing

Kartographischer Verlag Reinhard Ryborsch+
Member of Boersenverein des Deutschen Buchhandels
Laubenstr 3, 63179 Obertshausen
Mailing Address: Postfach 2105, 63170 Obertshausen
Tel: (06104) 79039 *Fax:* (06104) 75356
Key Personnel
Dir: Reinhard Ryborsch
Founded: 1987
Member of Boersenverein des Deutschen Buchhandels & Deutsche Gesellschaft fuer Kartographie.
Subjects: Aeronautics, Aviation, Geography, Geology, Travel
ISBN Prefix(es): 3-920339; 3-927549

Kastell Verlag GmbH+
Postfach 440 312, 80752 Munich
Tel: (089) 33 21 75 *Fax:* (089) 340 11 78
E-mail: kastell-verlag@t-online.de
Key Personnel
Man Dir, Rights & Permissions: Christoph Burgauner
Founded: 1984
Subjects: History, Music, Dance
ISBN Prefix(es): 3-924592

Verlag Katholisches Bibelwerk GmbH+
Silberburgstr 121, 70176 Stuttgart
Tel: (0711) 61920-0 *Fax:* (0711) 61920-44
E-mail: verlag@bibelwerk.de
Web Site: www.bibelwerk.de
Key Personnel
Editor, Rights & Permissions: Herbert Wilfart *Tel:* (0711) 6192027 *E-mail:* wilfart@bibelwerk.de
Man Dir: Jurgen M Schymura MA *Tel:* (0711) 6192020 *E-mail:* schymura@bibelwerk.de
Editor: Wolfgang Hein *Tel:* (0711) 619028 *E-mail:* hein@bibelwerk.de
Founded: 1937
Member of KMV.
Subjects: Biblical Studies, Religion - Catholic
ISBN Prefix(es): 3-460

Katzmann Verlag KG+
Postfach 1827, 72008 Tuebingen
Tel: (07473) 5427 *Fax:* (07473) 5427 *Cable:* KATZMANN VERLAG
Key Personnel
Man Dir, Production, Publicity, Rights & Permissions: Dr Volker Katzmann
Sales Dir: Sibylle Katzmann
Founded: 1945
Specialize in scientific literature.
Subjects: Art, Education, Religion - Other, Social Sciences, Sociology, Theology
ISBN Prefix(es): 3-7805
Associate Companies: Heliopolis-Verlag Ewald Katzmann, Schellingstr 41, 72072 Tuebingen

Verlag Ernst Kaufmann GmbH+
Alleestr 2, 77933 Lahr
Tel: (07821) 93 90-0 *Fax:* (07821) 9390-11
Web Site: www.kaufmann-verlag.de
Key Personnel
Man Dir: Michael Jacob
Chief Editor: Renate Schupp
Founded: 1816
Member of Verlagsring Religionsunterricht (VRU), ATV, AVJ.
Subjects: Religion - Protestant, Religion - Other
ISBN Prefix(es): 3-7806

KBV-Verlags-und Mediengesellschaft mbH+
Wildenburgstr 28, 50935 Cologne
Tel: (0221) 28 26 92 0 *Fax:* (0221) 28 26 91 9
E-mail: info@kbv-verlag.de
Web Site: www.kbv-verlag.de
Key Personnel
Man Dir: Herbert Klein
Founded: 1989
Subjects: Criminology, Fiction, Government, Political Science, Mysteries, Nonfiction (General)
ISBN Prefix(es): 3-927658
Warehouse: LKG Leipziges Komissions- und Grosbuchhandels Gesellschaft mbH, Plotzschauer Wey, 04579 Espenhain
Orders to: LKG Leipziges Kommissions- und Grossbuchhandels Gesellschaft mbH, Plotzschauer Wey, 04579 Espenhain

SachBuchVerlag Kellner (Kellner Publishing House)+
Member of Boersenverein
St-Pauli-Deich 3, 28199 Bremen
Tel: (421) 77866 *Fax:* (421) 704058
E-mail: kellner-verlag@t-online.de
Web Site: kellner-verlag.de
Key Personnel
Editor: Klaus Kellner
Founded: 1988
Also acts as shipping house.
Subjects: Government, Political Science, Labor, Industrial Relations, Law, Nonfiction (General), Outdoor Recreation, Public Administration, Travel
ISBN Prefix(es): 3-927155
Number of titles published annually: 6 Print

Martin Kelter Verlag GmbH u Co
Postfach 70 10 09, 22010 Hamburg
Tel: (040) 68 28 95-0 *Fax:* (040) 68 28 95 50
Web Site: www.kelter.de
Telex: 213126
Key Personnel
Man Dir: Gerhard Melchert
Founded: 1938
ISBN Prefix(es): 3-88832
Associate Companies: Mero-Druck Otto Melchert GmbH & Co KG

P Keppler Verlag GmbH & Co KG
Industriestr 2, 63150 Heusenstamm
Mailing Address: Postfach 1353, 63151 Heusenstamm
Tel: (06104) 606 0 *Fax:* (06104) 606 121
E-mail: info@kepplermediengruppe.de
Key Personnel
Man Dir: Heinz Egon Schmitt
ISBN Prefix(es): 3-87398

Kerber Christof Verlag
Windelsbleicherstr 166-170, 33659 Bielefeld
Tel: (0521) 95008-10 *Fax:* (0521) 95008-88
E-mail: info@kerber-verlag.de
Web Site: www.kerber-verlag.de
Specialize in Paintings & Art.
Subjects: Architecture & Interior Design, Art, History
ISBN Prefix(es): 3-924639; 3-933040
Foreign Rep(s): DAP

Verlag Kerle im Verlag Herder+
Hermann-Herder-Str 4, 79104 Freiburg
Tel: (0761) 2717-0 *Fax:* (0761) 2717-352
E-mail: info@kerle.de
Web Site: www.kerle.de
Key Personnel
Man Dir: Dr Klaus-Christoph Scheffel
Editorial: C Soltau; B Wurster
Sales: W Reisterer
Press, Rights: Helga Theile
Founded: 1886
ISBN Prefix(es): 3-210; 3-85303
Associate Companies: Verlag Herder GmbH & Co KG; Verlag A G Ploetz GmbH & Co KG; Herder Editrice e Libreria, Italy; Editorial Herder SA, Spain; Libraria Herder, Spain; Herder AG
Bookshop(s): Herder Verlag

Keysersche Verlagsbuchhandlung GmbH+
Geibelstr 6, 81679 Munich
Tel: (089) 4554-0 *Fax:* (089) 4554-111
Key Personnel
Publisher, Rights & Permissions: Hermann Farnung
Publisher: Klaus Rudloff
Advertising: Michaela Beck
Sales: Gudrun Shutzenberger
Founded: 1777
Subjects: Science (General)
ISBN Prefix(es): 3-87405
Parent Company: Frankfurter Allgemeine Zeitung GmbH
Associate Companies: BVU Buchverlage Union GmbH; Koehler & Amelang Verlagsgesellschaft mbH
Imprints: Flaschenpost

Kidemus Verlag GmbH+
Ruenderotherstr 15, 51109 Cologne
Mailing Address: Postfach 940225, 51090 Cologne
Tel: (0221) 84 20 97 *Fax:* (0221) 84 20 98
E-mail: info@kidemus.de
Web Site: www.kidemus.de
Founded: 1995
ISBN Prefix(es): 3-9804821; 3-9806910

Number of titles published annually: 3 Print
Total Titles: 17 Print

Gustav Kiepenheuer Verlag GmbH+
Gerichtsweg 28, 04103 Leipzig
Mailing Address: Postfach 193, 10105 Berlin
Tel: (0341) 99 54 60 0 *Fax:* (0341) 9954 620
E-mail: info@aufbau-verlag.de
Web Site: www.aufbau-verlag.de
Key Personnel
Program Manager: Peter Birgit
Foreign Rights & Permissions: Astrid Poppenhusen *E-mail:* poppenhusen@aufbau-verlag.de
German Rights & Permissions: Martin Lorento
 Tel: (30) 28394-118 *E-mail:* lorentz@aufbau-verlag.de
Founded: 1909
Subjects: Biography, Nonfiction (General), Regional Interests
ISBN Prefix(es): 3-378
Parent Company: Leipziger Verlags- und Vertriebsgesellschaft mbH
Associate Companies: Sammlung Dieterich Verlagsgesellschaft mbH, Leipzig
Shipping Address: Mohr-Morava Buchvertrieb Gesellschaft mbH, Postfach 260, A-1101 Vienna, Austria; Pegasus-Stichting, Uitgeverijen-Boekhandel, Rhijuvis Feithstr 28, PO Box 59687, NL-1054 PZ Amsterdam, Netherlands; Verlagsauslieferung Balmer, Boesch 41, Huenenberg
Orders to: Hans Heinrich Petersen GmbH, Bredowstrafe 20, 22113 Hamburg

Verlag Kiepenheuer und Witsch GmbH & Co KG+
Rondorferstr 5, 50968 Cologne
Tel: (0221) 376 85-0 *Fax:* (0221) 376 85-70
E-mail: verlag@kiwi-koeln.de
Web Site: www.kiwi-koelu.de *Cable:* KIEPENBUCHER COLOGNE
Key Personnel
Man Dir: Dr Reinhold Neven Du Mont
Editorial: Helge Malchow; Baerbel Flad; Lutz Dursthoff; Dr Martin Hielscher
Marketing: Dr Raimund Herder
Foreign Rights & Permissions: Traudel Jansen
Finance, Administration, Production & Personnel: Peter Roik
Founded: 1949
Subjects: Biography, Fiction, History, Nonfiction (General), Social Sciences, Sociology
ISBN Prefix(es): 3-462
Imprints: Kiwi-Reihe
U.S. Office(s): Mrs Alison M Bond, 171 W 79 St, New York, NY 10024, United States (Scout)
Joan Daves Agency, 21 W 26 St, New York, NY 10010, United States (Agent), Mrs Jennifer Lyons

Kierdorf Ute Verlag+
Gut Dohrgaul, 51688 Wipperfuerth
Tel: (02267) 4495 *Fax:* (02267) 4458
E-mail: Kierdorfverlag@t-online.de
Web Site: www.kierdorfverlag.de
Key Personnel
Owner: Ute Kierdorf
International Rights: Wolfgang Kierdorf
Founded: 1978
Subjects: Equestrian & Fung Shui
ISBN Prefix(es): 3-89118
Orders to: Grossohaus Wehling, Friedr Hajewann-Str 5560, 33719 Bielefeld

Kilda Verlag
Muensterstr 71, 48268 Greven
Tel: (02571) 52115 *Fax:* (02571) 97098
 Cable: KILDAGREVEN
Key Personnel
Man Dir: Fritz Poelking

ISBN Prefix(es): 3-921427; 3-88949
Orders to: VVA Bertelsmann Distribution, Postfach 7777, 33310 Guetersloh

Verlag im Kilian GmbH+
Schuhmarkt 4, 35037 Marburg
Tel: (06421) 2 93 30 *Fax:* (06421) 16 38 94
Web Site: www.kilian-verlag.de
Telex: 482381
Key Personnel
Man Dir: Barbara von Stackelberg
Founded: 1994
Specialize in health information & advice to professionals & the general public.
Subjects: Child Care & Development, Health, Nutrition, Medicine, Nursing, Dentistry
ISBN Prefix(es): 3-932091
Parent Company: Deutsches Gruenes Kreuz

Edition Kima, *imprint of* Drei Eichen Verlag Manuel Kissener

Der Kinderbuch Verlag GmbH+
Katharinenstr 8, 10711 Berlin
Tel: (030) 89 38 84-0 *Fax:* (030) 89 38 84-20; (030) 885722
Key Personnel
Man Dir & Publisher: Hans Meisinger
Rights & Publicity: Christiane Schneider
Founded: 1949
Subjects: Nonfiction (General)
ISBN Prefix(es): 3-358
Orders to: MVS Meisinger Verlagsservice, Am Steinfeld 4, 94065 Waldkirchen *Tel:* (08581) 9605-0 *Fax:* (08581) 754

Kindler Verlag GmbH+
Hamburgerstr 17, 21465 Reinbek
Tel: (089) 92710 *Fax:* (089) 9271168
E-mail: presse@rowohlt.de
Key Personnel
Man Dir: Helmut Daehne; Alexander Fest; Lutz Kettmann
Editorial Dir: Ulrike Kloepfer
Founded: 1951
Subjects: Biography, Fiction, Government, Political Science, History, Nonfiction (General), Psychology, Psychiatry, Religion - Other, Science (General), Social Sciences, Sociology
ISBN Prefix(es): 3-463
Parent Company: Verlagsgruppe Georg von Holtzbrinck GmbH, Gaenseheidestr 26, 70184 Stuttgart 1
Shipping Address: Sigloch Distribution GmbH, Am Buchberg, 74572 Blaufelden

Kino Verlag GmbH
Milchstr 1, 20148 Hamburg
Tel: (040) 4131-1455 *Fax:* (040) 4131-2045
Web Site: www.vgm.de
Key Personnel
Communications: Yvonne von Stempel
 Tel: (040) 41 31-10 20 *Fax:* (040) 41 31-20 20
 E-mail: ystempel@milchstrasse.de
Founded: 1975
Subjects: Film, Video
ISBN Prefix(es): 3-89324

Th Kirchbaum, K, *imprint of* Eironeia-Verlag

Peter Kirchheim Verlag+
Postfach 14 04 32, 80454 Munich
Tel: (089) 267474 *Fax:* (089) 2605528
Web Site: www.kirchheimverlag.de
Founded: 1977
Subjects: Literature, Literary Criticism, Essays
ISBN Prefix(es): 3-87410
Warehouse: SoVa Sozialistische Verlagsauslieferung Franziusstr 44, 60314 Frankfurt/M

Kirschbaum Verlag GmbH+
Siegfriedstr 28, 53179 Bonn
Mailing Address: Postfach 210209, 53157 Bonn
Tel: (0228) 9 54 53-0 *Fax:* (0228) 9 54 53-27
E-mail: info@kirschbaum.de
Web Site: www.kirschbaum.de
Key Personnel
Man Dir: Bernhard Kirschbaum *E-mail:* b.kirschbaum@kirschbaum.de
Founded: 1949
Subjects: Automotive, Civil Engineering, Geography, Geology, Law, Transportation
ISBN Prefix(es): 3-7812
Total Titles: 195 Print

Kiwi-Reihe, *imprint of* Verlag Kiepenheuer und Witsch GmbH & Co KG

Klages-Verlag
Eckermannstr 8, 30625 Hannover
Tel: (0511) 5358936 *Fax:* (0511) 5358928
E-mail: kv@lsz.de
Key Personnel
Contact: August-Wilhelm Klages
Founded: 1917
Member of German Electronic Book Committee.
Subjects: Economics, Law, Public Administration
ISBN Prefix(es): 3-7813

Klartext Verlagsgesellschaft mbH+
Dickmannstr 2-4, 45143 Essen
Tel: (0201) 86 206-0 *Fax:* (0201) 86 206-22
E-mail: info@klartext-verlag.de
Key Personnel
Man Dir, Rights & Permissions & Editorial: Ludger Classen
Man Dir & Editorial: Ulrich Homann
Man Dir, Production: Stephan Bartjes
Sales & Publicity: Felicitas Bartyes; Kerstin Schoeffel
Founded: 1982
Subjects: Government, Political Science, History, Nonfiction (General), Regional Interests, Self-Help, Social Sciences, Sociology, Sports, Athletics
ISBN Prefix(es): 3-88474
Distributed by Prolit Verlagsauslieferung GmbH (Germany & Austria); Schweizer Buchzentrum (Switzerland)
Foreign Rep(s): Jutta Leitner (Austria)
Warehouse: Postfach 9, 6301 Fernwald (Annerod) *Tel:* (0641) 43071 *Fax:* (0641) 42773
Orders to: Prolit Buchvertrieb, Siemensstr 16

Ingrid Klein Verlag GmbH+
Georgenstr 4, 80799 Munich
Mailing Address: Postfach 430861, 80738 Munich
Tel: (089) 3818010 *Fax:* (089) 338704
E-mail: info@piper.de
Web Site: www.piper.de
Key Personnel
Man Dirs, Editorial: Joachim Jessen; Ingrid Klein
Man Dir: Detlef Lerch
Sales: Heike Latendorf-Janzen
Founded: 1993
Subjects: Fiction, Nonfiction (General), Psychology, Psychiatry, Women's Studies
ISBN Prefix(es): 3-89521
Orders to: VVA Bertelsmann Distribution A: Klein Verlag, Postfach 7777, 33310 Guetersloh

Kleine Reike, *imprint of* Beerenverlag

Verlag Kleine Schritte Ursula Dahm & Co (Little Steps Publisher)+
Medardstr 105, 54294 Trier
Mailing Address: Postfach 3903, 5500 Trier
Tel: (0651) 300 698 *Fax:* (0651) 300 699
E-mail: mail@kleine-schritte.de
Web Site: www.kleine-schritte.de

GERMANY

Key Personnel
Man Dir: Ursula Dahm
Founded: 1980
Subjects: Astrology, Occult, Biography, Fiction, Gay & Lesbian, Human Relations, Nonfiction (General), Poetry, Psychology, Psychiatry, Self-Help, Women's Studies
ISBN Prefix(es): 3-923261

Kleiner Bachmann Verlag fur Kinder und Umwelt+
Berliner Ring 163b, 64625 Bensheim
Tel: (06251) 78 98 22 *Fax:* (06251) 78 98 24
E-mail: mail@kleinerbachmann.de
Web Site: www.kleinerbachmann.de
Key Personnel
Editor: Helmut Bachmann
Publishing Editor: Felicitas Jung
Founded: 1997
Specialize in picture books, Scandinavian authors, travel books for children, young authors under 18 years of age. The picture books try to awake sensitivity for environmental issues in a playful & uncomplicated manner; Member of AVJ (Arbeitsgemeinschaft von Jugendbuchverlagen).
Subjects: Environmental Studies, Fiction, Human Relations, Travel
ISBN Prefix(es): 3-933160
Number of titles published annually: 6 Print
Total Titles: 10 Print; 2 Audio

Unterwegs Verlag, Manfred Klemann+
Dr Andlerstr 28, 78224 Singen
Tel: (07731) 63544 *Fax:* (07731) 62401
E-mail: uv@reisefuehrer.com
Key Personnel
President & Rights: Manfred Klemann
Founded: 1983
ISBN Prefix(es): 3-924334; 3-86112
Subsidiaries: Hohentwiel-Verlag GmbH
Warehouse: VVA-Bertelsmann Distribution GmbH, An der Autonbahn, 33310 Guetersloh

Klens Verlag GmbH+
Carl-Mosterts-Platz 1, 40477 Duesseldorf
Tel: (0211) 4499251 *Fax:* (0211) 4499277
Key Personnel
Publisher: Dr Edmund Bercker; August Gordz
Founded: 1916
Subjects: Education, Religion - Other
ISBN Prefix(es): 3-87309
Bookshop(s): Buecher & Kunst Klens Verlag, Carl-Mosterts-Platz 1, 40477 Dusseldorf

Verlag Klett-Cotta, see J G Cotta'sche Buchhandlung Nachfolger GmbH

Ernst Klett Verlag GmbH+
Rotebuehlstr 77, 70178 Stuttgart
Tel: (0711) 66 72-13 33 *Fax:* (0711) 66 72-20 00
E-mail: klett-kundenservice@klett-mail.de
Web Site: www.klett-verlag.de
Telex: 722232 kletd
Key Personnel
Publisher: Michael Klett
Rights & Export Sales, Klett International: Derrick Jenkins
Founded: 1897
Subjects: Education, Geography, Geology, Educational software
ISBN Prefix(es): 3-12
Associate Companies: Klett International GmbH

Klett-Cotta+
Rotebuehlstr 77, 70178 Stuttgart
Tel: (0711) 66721256 *Fax:* (0711) 66722031
E-mail: info@klett-cotta.de
Web Site: www.klett-cotta.de
Telex: 722225 klet d

Kley, Werner, Beteiligungs GmbH+
Werlerstr 304, 59069 Hamm
Tel: (02381) 95040-0 *Fax:* (02381) 9504019
Key Personnel
Publisher, Rights & Permissions: Kley Werner
Author: Wilhelm Sohlote
ISBN Prefix(es): 3-924607

Klinik der Frauenheilkunde und Geburtshilfe, *imprint of* Urban und Fischer Verlag fur Medizin

Klinik der Gegenwart, *imprint of* Urban und Fischer Verlag fur Medizin

Klink, Vincent, Edition, Stecknadel
Ludwigstr 57, 70176 Stuttgart
Mailing Address: Postfach 150165, 70075 Stuttgart
Tel: (0711) 65863-51 *Fax:* (0711) 65863-53
Founded: 1988
Subjects: Fiction, Music, Dance, Poetry, Religion - Buddhist
ISBN Prefix(es): 3-927350

Klinkhardt & Biermann Verlagsbuchhandlung GmbH+
Mandlstr 26, 80802 Munich
Tel: (089) 38 17 9-0 *Fax:* (089) 38 17 09-35
E-mail: info@prestel.de
Web Site: www.prestel.de
Key Personnel
Manager, Rights & Permissions: Dr Michael Siebler
Publicity: Michaela Beck
Sales Manager: Gudrun Strutzenberger
Founded: 1907
Subjects: Antiques, Art
ISBN Prefix(es): 3-7814
Parent Company: Frankfurter Allgemeine Zeitung GmbH
Associate Companies: BVU Buchverlag Union GmbH; Koehe & Amelang Verlagsgesellschaft mbH

Erika Klopp Verlag GmbH+
Member of Oetinger Group
Poppenbuetteler Chaussee 53, 22397 Hamburg
Tel: (040) 607 90 902 *Fax:* (040) 607 20 326
E-mail: klopp@vsg.hamburg.de
Web Site: www.erika-klopp.de
Key Personnel
Publisher, Rights & Permissions: Jan Weitendorf
Founded: 1925
ISBN Prefix(es): 3-7817
Total Titles: 150 Print
Parent Company: VSG Verlags-Service Gesellschaft MGH
Warehouse: Ruerge Verlagsauslieferung/Steinhagen *Tel:* (05204) 9181-0 *Fax:* (05204) 9181-91

Klosterhaus-Verlagsbuchhandlung Dr Grimm KG
Klosterhaus, 37194 Wahlsburg
Mailing Address: Postfach 1151, 37195 Wahlsburg-Lippoldsberg
Tel: (05572) 7310 *Fax:* (05572) 999823
Key Personnel
President: Dr Holle Grimm
Founded: 1951
Subjects: History
ISBN Prefix(es): 3-87418

Vittorio Klostermann GmbH+
Frauenlobstr 22, 60487 Frankfurt am Main
Mailing Address: Postfach 900601, 60446 Frankfurt am Main
Tel: (069) 97 08 16-0 *Fax:* (069) 70 80 38
E-mail: verlag@klostermann.de
Web Site: www.klostermann.de

Key Personnel
Man Dir & Publisher: Vittorio E Klostermann
International Rights: Anastasia Urban
Contact: Dr Sabine Baumann *Tel:* (069) 97081617 *E-mail:* s.baumann@klostermann.de
Marketing: Mr Martin Warny *E-mail:* m.warny@klostermann.de
Publicity: Ms Friedrike Haertling *E-mail:* f.haertling@klostermann.de
Founded: 1930
Subjects: Genealogy, History, Law, Library & Information Sciences, Literature, Literary Criticism, Essays, Philosophy, Publishing & Book Trade Reference, Science (General)
ISBN Prefix(es): 3-465

Verlag Fritz Knapp GmbH+
Aschaffenburger Str 19, 60599 Frankfurt am Main
Mailing Address: Postfach 11 11 51, 60046 Frankfurt
Tel: (069) 97 08 33-0 *Fax:* (069) 7 07 84 00
E-mail: kreditwesen@t-online.de
Web Site: www.kreditwesen.de
Telex: 411397 Knapp d *Cable:* SCHAUINSLAND
Key Personnel
Man Dir: Klaus-Friedrich Otto
Marketing, Sales, Publicity: Werner Scholz
Production, Rights & Permissions: Claus Wonneberger
Founded: 1949
Subjects: Economics, Finance
ISBN Prefix(es): 3-7819
Associate Companies: Verlag Helmut Richardi GmbH, Theodor-Heuss-Allee 106, 60486 Frankfurt am Main
Subsidiaries: Kreditwesen Service GmbH
Orders to: Koch, Neff & Oetinger, Schockenriedstr 39, Stuttgart

Albrecht Knaus Verlag GmbH+
Neumarkterstr 18, 81673 Munich
Mailing Address: Postfach 800360, 81603 Munich
Tel: (089) 4372-0 *Fax:* (089) 4372-2790
Telex: 529965
Key Personnel
Publisher: Klaus Eck
Production: Peter Sturm
Sales: Verlagsgruppe Bertelsmann GmbH
Publicity: Margit Schoenberger
Founded: 1978
Subjects: Art, Biography, Fiction, History, Nonfiction (General)
ISBN Prefix(es): 3-8135
Parent Company: Verlagsgruppe Bertelsmann GmbH
Orders to: VVA Bertelsmann Distribution, Postfach 7777, 33310 Guetersloh 100

Knesebeck Verlag+
Holzstr 26, 80469 Munich
Mailing Address: Postfach 14 05 60, 80455 Munich
Tel: (089) 264059 *Fax:* (089) 269258
E-mail: vertrieb@knesebeck-verlag.de; presse@knesebeck-verlag.de
Web Site: www.knesebeck-verlag.de
Key Personnel
Publisher & International Rights: Dr Rosemarie von dem Knesebeck *E-mail:* rknesebeck@knesebeck-verlag.de
Publisher: Herneid von dem Knesebeck
Founded: 1987
Subjects: Architecture & Interior Design, Biography, Photography
ISBN Prefix(es): 3-926901; 3-89660
Number of titles published annually: 20 Print
Total Titles: 70 Print

Karl Knoll Verlag Alte Uni
Brettenastr 30, 75031 Eppingen

Tel: (07262) 4417 *Fax:* (07262) 7942
E-mail: alteuni@aol.com
Key Personnel
Contact: Karl Knoll
Founded: 1986
Subjects: Language Arts, Linguistics, Regional Interests
ISBN Prefix(es): 3-926315

Doris Knop-Verlag+
Herbststr 13, 28215 Bremen
Tel: (0421) 451743 *Fax:* (0421) 455406
Founded: 1985
Specialize in Guidebooks.
Subjects: Travel
ISBN Prefix(es): 3-9801077; 3-928760

Druckerei & Verlag Ernst Knoth GmbH
Postfach 226, 49303 Melle
Tel: (05422) 94320 *Fax:* (05422) 9432-20
Key Personnel
Owners, Man Dirs: Ernst-Hermann Knoth; Ernst-Heinrich Knoth
Subjects: Government, Political Science
ISBN Prefix(es): 3-87085; 3-88368

Knowledge Media International+
Leuchtenbergring 20, 81677 Munich
Tel: (089) 4136-8433 *Fax:* (089) 4136-8411
Web Site: www.k-m-i.com
Key Personnel
International Rights Dir: Vanessa Nowak
 E-mail: vanessa.nowak@bertelsmann.de
International Rights Manager: Katharina Wandinger *E-mail:* katharina.wandinger@bertelsmann.de
In addition to the licensing of books & multimedia products to international publishers, we also offer IT services & solutions.
Subjects: Animals, Pets, Architecture & Interior Design, Child Care & Development, Foreign Countries, Gardening, Plants, Geography, Geology, Health, Nutrition, History, Mysteries, Natural History, Nonfiction (General), Religion - Buddhist, Religion - Catholic, Religion - Protestant, Religion - Other, Sports, Athletics, Travel
Parent Company: wissen media Verlag GmbH

Verlag Knut Reim, Jugendpresseverlag
Dammtorstr 30, 20354 Hamburg
Mailing Address: Postfach 302824, 20310 Hamburg
Tel: (040) 34 26 41 *Fax:* (040) 34 46 87
Key Personnel
General Manager: Jens Christians; Knut Reim
Founded: 1958
Subjects: Economics, Fiction, Law
ISBN Prefix(es): 3-87950
Parent Company: Jung end presseverlag, Dammtorstr 30, 20354 Hamburg

Verlagsanstalt Alexander Koch GmbH+
Fasanenweg 18, 70771 Leinfelden-Echterdingen
Tel: (0711) 7591-0 *Fax:* (0711) 7591-380
Key Personnel
Man Dir: Karl-Heinz Weinbrenner; Liselotte Drabarczyk
Founded: 1890
Subjects: Architecture & Interior Design
ISBN Prefix(es): 3-87422
Associate Companies: DRW-Verlag Weinbrenner GmbH & Co; Bit-Verlag Weinbrenner GmbH & Co KG

Kochbuch Verlag Olga Leeb+
Landsbergerstr 238, 80687 Munich
Mailing Address: Postfach 210628, Munich 80676
Tel: (089) 171690; (089) 58998303 *Fax:* (089) 560208; (089) 71690
Telex: 5212486
Key Personnel
Man Dir: Olli Leeb
Founded: 1976
Subjects: Cookery
ISBN Prefix(es): 3-921799

K F Koehler Verlag
Am Wallgraben 110, 70565 Stuttgart
Mailing Address: Postfach 800569, 70553 Stuttgart
Tel: (0711) 7892 130; (0711) 7892 149
 Fax: (0711) 7892 132
E-mail: info@kfk.de; sabine.haegele@kfk.de
Web Site: www.buchkatalog.de
Telex: ueber 7255344 kno d
Key Personnel
Man Dir: Joachim Herkert
Founded: 1789
Subjects: Biography, Geography, Geology, Government, Political Science, History, Law, Publishing & Book Trade Reference, Social Sciences, Sociology
ISBN Prefix(es): 3-87425

Verlagsgruppe Koehler/Mittler+
Striepenweg 31, 21147 Hamburg
Tel: (040) 7971303 *Fax:* (040) 79713324
Web Site: www.koehler-mittler.de/
Key Personnel
Publisher: Peter Tamm
Production: Hans-Peter Herfs-George
Manager: Thomas Bantle
Sales & Publicity: Hans-Focko Koehler
Group Members: Verlag E S Mittler und Sohn GmbH, Koehlers Verlagsgesellschaft mbH, Verlag Offene Worte, Verlag Europaeische Wehrkunde.
Subjects: Aeronautics, Aviation, Film, Video, History, Law, Maritime, Military Science, Philosophy, Public Administration, Social Sciences, Sociology
ISBN Prefix(es): 3-8132; 3-7822
Branch Office(s)
Godesberger Allee 91, 53175 Bonn *Tel:* (0228) 30789-0 *Fax:* (0228) 30789-15 (for all members of group)

Koehler und Amelang Verlagsgesellschaft mbH+
Geibelstr 6, 81679 Munich
Mailing Address: Postfach 22 13 53, 80503 Munich
Tel: (089) 45554-0 *Fax:* (089) 45554110
E-mail: info@dva.de
Web Site: www.dva.de
Founded: 1925
Subjects: Architecture & Interior Design, Art, Biography, History, Regional Interests
ISBN Prefix(es): 3-7338

Koehlers Verlagsgesellschaft mbH+
Striepenweg 31, 21147 Hamburg
Tel: (040) 7 97 13-03 *Fax:* (040) 79713324
Web Site: www.koehler-mittler.de/ *Cable:* KOEHLERS VLG D-21447 HAMBURG
Key Personnel
Publisher: Peter Tamm
Manager: Lothar Lichtenheldt
Sales: Hans-Focko Koehler
Subjects: Fiction, Maritime, Nonfiction (General)
ISBN Prefix(es): 3-7822
Associate Companies: Maximilian-Verlag; E S Mittler und Sohn GmbH; Verlag Offene Worte Verlag Europaeische Wehrkunde (all members of Verlagsgruppe Koehler/Mittler)
Branch Office(s)
Aust 19, 53179 Bonn *Tel:* (0228) 530962-64
 Fax: (0228) 230102

Koelner Universitaets-Verlag GmbH+
Subsidiary of Deutscher Instituts-Verlag
Gustav-Heinemann-Ufer 84-88, 50968 Cologne
Mailing Address: Postfach 51 06 70, 50942 Cologne
Tel: (0221) 48 81 452 *Fax:* (0221) 49 81 445
E-mail: div@iwkoeln.de
Web Site: www.iwkoeln.de/
Telex: 8882071
Key Personnel
Man Dir & International Rights: Mr Lassalle
Founded: 1953
Subjects: Business, Economics, Education, Government, Political Science, Social Sciences, Sociology
ISBN Prefix(es): 3-87427; 3-931206
Parent Company: Aktiv-informedia verlag GmbH

Koenemann Verlagsgesellschaft mbH+
Bonnerstr 126, 50968 Cologne
Tel: (01149) 221-3799-0 *Fax:* (01149) 3799-288
Key Personnel
Publisher: Ludwig Koenemann
Sales Dir: Lutz Billstein
Founded: 1993
Subjects: Architecture & Interior Design, Art, Cookery, History, Literature, Literary Criticism, Essays, Music, Dance, Photography, Transportation
ISBN Prefix(es): 3-89508; 3-8290
Total Titles: 1,200 Print
Branch Office(s)
Koenemann Inc, 137 W 19 St, New York, NY 10011, United States, CEO: Ralf Daab *Tel:* 212-367-8855 *Fax:* 212-367-8866 *E-mail:* rdaab@konemann.com (Contact: Brian Brash, National Sales Manager, bbrash@konemann.com)

R Koenig GmbH
Floessergasse 7, 81369 Munich
Tel: (089) 724970 *Fax:* (089) 7238813
E-mail: info@koenig-specials.com
Web Site: www.koenig-specials.com
Key Personnel
Manager: Rosy Koenig
Founded: 1986
ISBN Prefix(es): 3-8126

Koenigs Erlaeuterungen, *imprint of* C Bange GmbH & Co KG

Koenigs Lektueren, *imprint of* C Bange GmbH & Co KG

Koenigsfurt Verlag, Evelin Burger et Johannes Fiebig+
Koenigsfurt 6, Klein Koenigsfoerde am Nord-Ostsee-Kanal, 24796 Krummwisch
Tel: (04334) 18 99 02; (04334) 18 22 010
 Fax: (04334) 18 22 011
E-mail: info@koenigsfurt.com
Web Site: www.koenigsfurt.com
Key Personnel
Contact: Evelin Buerger
Founded: 1989
Nonfiction; Tarot & Co. Non-books, German market leader on Tarot & Co.
Subjects: Astrology, Occult, Nonfiction (General), Psychology, Psychiatry, Self-Help
ISBN Prefix(es): 3-927808; 3-933939
Number of titles published annually: 100 Print
Total Titles: 500 Print
Imprints: Bewnsster leben
Distributor for Iris Bucher & Welr

Verlag Koenigshausen und Neumann GmbH+
Theodor Koemerstr 3a, 97072 Wuerzburg
Mailing Address: Postfach 6007, 97010 Wuerzburg
Tel: (0931) 78 40-7 00 *Fax:* (0931) 8 36 20
E-mail: info@koenigshausen-neumann.de
Web Site: www.koenigshausen-neumann.de/

Key Personnel
Man Dir: Dr Johannes Koenigshausen; Dr Thomas Neumann
Founded: 1979
Subjects: Archaeology, Economics, Education, Ethnicity, Law, Literature, Literary Criticism, Essays, Philosophy, Psychology, Psychiatry, Social Sciences, Sociology
ISBN Prefix(es): 3-88479; 3-8260

Lucy Koerner Verlag+
Bahnhofstr 49, 70734 Fellbach
Mailing Address: Postfach 1106, 70701 Fellbach
Tel: (0711) 588472 *Fax:* (0711) 5789634
Key Personnel
Man Dir: Lucy Koerner
Subjects: Fiction
ISBN Prefix(es): 3-922028

Verlag Valentin Koerner GmbH
Postfach 100164, 76482 Baden-Baden
Tel: (07221) 22423 *Fax:* (07221) 38697
E-mail: info@koernerverlag.de
Web Site: www.koernerverlag.de/ *Cable:* KOERNERVERLAG
Key Personnel
Publisher: Valentin Koerner
Founded: 1954
Subjects: Art, History, Music, Dance, Theology
ISBN Prefix(es): 3-87320
Number of titles published annually: 20 Print
Total Titles: 500 Print
Imprints: Heitz Librarie

Koesel-Verlag GmbH & Co+
Flueggenstr 2, 80639 Munich
Tel: (089) 17801-0 *Fax:* (089) 17801-111
E-mail: leserservice@koesel.de
Web Site: www.koesel.de/ *Cable:* KOESELVERLAG MUNICH
Key Personnel
Man Dir: Dr Christoph Wild; Felix Opphard-Gewitsch
Production: Friedhelm Jochems
Sales: Dieter Amman
Rights & Permissions: Ingrid Fink
Advertising: Alexander Ludolph
Founded: 1593
Member of TR-Verlagsunion GmbH & Gesellschafter of Deutscher Taschenbuch Verlag (dtv).
Subjects: Education, Philosophy, Psychology, Psychiatry, Religion - Other
ISBN Prefix(es): 3-466
Subsidiaries: Ellermann Verlag
Distributed by Verlagsauslieferung Balmer (Switzerland); WMI Verlagsservice GmbH & Co KG (Germany)
Bookshop(s): Koeselsche Buchhandlung, Roncalliplatz 2, 50667 Cologne 1
Orders to: Moderne Industrie Verlagsservice, Landsberg

Koesler Verlag GmbH+
Brandenburgerstr 19, 51766 Engelskirchen
Mailing Address: Postfach 2263, 51759 Engelskirchen
Tel: (02263) 951650-51 *Fax:* (02263) 951691
Cable: KOSLER VERLAG
Key Personnel
Man Dir, Rights & Permissions: Wolfgang Koesler
Founded: 1970
Specializes in Stock Exchange.
Subjects: Nonfiction (General), Sports, Athletics
ISBN Prefix(es): 3-924208

W Kohlhammer GmbH, abt Haussortiment+
Hessbruhlstr 69, 70565 Stuttgart
Tel: (0711) 7863-7261 *Fax:* (0711) 7863-8204
E-mail: redaktion@kohlhammer.de
Web Site: www.kohlhammer.de *Cable:* KOHLHAMMER STUTTGART
Key Personnel
Man Dir: Dr Juergen Gutbrod; Hans-Joachim Nagel
Sales Dir: Joerg Neumann
Editorial Dir, Rights & Permissions: Dr Alexander Schweickert
Contact: Gerda Schmid
Founded: 1866
Subjects: Architecture & Interior Design, Business, Economics, Education, Engineering (General), Government, Political Science, History, Language Arts, Linguistics, Law, Management, Marketing, Medicine, Nursing, Dentistry, Philosophy, Psychology, Psychiatry, Public Administration, Religion - Catholic, Religion - Islamic, Religion - Jewish, Religion - Protestant, Religion - Other, Social Sciences, Sociology, Theology
ISBN Prefix(es): 3-17
Total Titles: 3,400 Print
Subsidiaries: Deutscher Gemeindeverlag GmbH; Grote'sche Verlagsbuchhandlung GmbH & Co KG; Kohlhammer und Wallishauser GmbH; W Kohlhammer Druckerei GmbH & Co; W Kohlhammer Communication GmbH; Bruellmann GmbH & Co Repro-und Systemtechnik; Data Images Audiovisuelle Kommunikation; Verlagsvertrieb Stuttgart GmbH; Dienst am Buch GmbH
Divisions: W Kohlhammer Intermedia GmbH
Branch Office(s)
Cologne
Rudolf-Leonhard-Str 28, 01097 Dresden *Tel:* (0351) 8022685 *Fax:* (0351) 8020664
Gustav-Freytag-Str 59, 99096 Erfurt *Tel:* (0361) 3735379 *Fax:* (0361) 3460537
Alexanderstr 3, 30159 Hannover *Tel:* (0511) 327029 *Fax:* (0511) 320143
Jagersberg 17, 24103 Kiel *Tel:* (0431) 554857 *Fax:* (0431) 554944
Schleinufer 14, 39104 Magdeburg *Tel:* (0391) 597080 *Fax:* (0391) 5970813
Alexander-Diehl-Str 10, 55130 Mainz *Tel:* (06131) 891540 *Fax:* (06131) 891624
Ernst-Reuter-Haus, Strasse des 17, Juni 110-114, 10623 Berlin
Werkstr 209, 19061 Schwerin *Tel:* (0385) 616105 *Fax:* (0385) 616146
Warehouse: Verlagsvertrieb Stuttgart GmbH, Hessbruhlstr 69, 70565 Stuttgart

Kolibri-Verlags GmbH+
Bartholomaeusstr 57B, 22083 Hamburg
Tel: (040) 2202258 *Fax:* (040) 2276368
E-mail: daomagazin@aol.com
Key Personnel
International Rights: Gabriele Foerster
Founded: 1990
Subjects: Asian Studies, Health, Nutrition, Nonfiction (General), Philosophy, Religion - Buddhist, Sports, Athletics
ISBN Prefix(es): 3-928288
Associate Companies: DAO Zeitschriftenverlag
Subsidiaries: Kolibri Seminare

Kommentator, *imprint of* Hermann Luchterhand Verlag GmbH

Kon & Bundig, *imprint of* C Bange GmbH & Co KG

Konkordia Verlag GmbH
Eisenbahnstr 31, 77815 Buehl
Tel: (07223) 98 89-0 *Fax:* (07223) 98 89-45
E-mail: verlag@konkordia.de
Founded: 1881
Subjects: Education, Mathematics, Regional Interests
ISBN Prefix(es): 3-7826

Anton H Konrad Verlag
Schulstr 5, 89264 Weissenhorn
Mailing Address: Postfach 1206, 89259 Weissenhorn
Tel: (07309) 26 57 *Fax:* (07309) 60 69
E-mail: info@konrad-verlag.de
Web Site: www.konrad-verlag.de/
Key Personnel
Man Dir, Rights & Permissions: Anton H Konrad
Founded: 1961
Subjects: Art, Biography, Geography, Geology, History, Philosophy, Regional Interests
ISBN Prefix(es): 3-87437

Konradin-Verlagsgruppe+
Ernst Meystr 8, 70771 Leinfelden-Echterdingen
Tel: (0711) 7594-0 *Fax:* (0711) 7594-390
E-mail: info@konradin.de
Web Site: www.konradin.de/
Key Personnel
Manager: Konrad Kohlhammer; Dr Bernd Kroeger
Founded: 1929
Subjects: Technology
ISBN Prefix(es): 3-920560
U.S. Office(s): Trade Media International Corp, 1328 Broadway, New York, NY 10001, United States *Tel:* 212-564-3380
Shipping Address: PVS, Sonnengasse 2, 74172 Neckarsulm

KONTEXTverlag+
Lindenhoekweg 2, 10409 Berlin
Tel: (030) 94415444 *Fax:* (030) 94415445
E-mail: service@kontextverlag.de
Web Site: www.kontextverlag.de
Key Personnel
Owner: Torsten Metelka *E-mail:* metelka@kontextverlag.de
Founded: 1990
Subjects: Art, Government, Political Science, Literature, Literary Criticism, Essays, Philosophy
ISBN Prefix(es): 3-86161; 3-931337

Kontur, *imprint of* Bonifatius GmbH Druck-Buch-Verlag

kopaed verlagsgmbh
Pfaelzer-Wald-Str 64, 81539 Munich
Tel: (089) 68890098 *Fax:* (089) 6891912
E-mail: info@kopaed.de
Web Site: www.kopaed.de
Key Personnel
Contact: Dr Ludwig Schlump
Subjects: Education, Film, Video, Nonfiction (General), Radio, TV
ISBN Prefix(es): 3-935686; 3-929061; 3-934079
Number of titles published annually: 20 Print
Total Titles: 150 Print

Koptisch-Orthodoxes Zentrum
St Antonius-Kloster, Pater Michael Hauptstr 10, 35647 Waldsolms-Kroeffelbach
Tel: (06085) 23 17 *Fax:* (06085) 26 66
Web Site: www.kopten.de
Key Personnel
Contact: St Antonius Kloster
Subjects: Nonfiction (General), Religion - Other

Kosmos-Verlag, see Franckh-Kosmos Verlags-GmbH & Co

Franckh-Kosmos Verlags-GmbH & Co+
Pfizerstr 5-7, 70184 Stuttgart
Mailing Address: Postfach 10 60 11, 70049 Stuttgart
Tel: (0711) 2191-0 *Fax:* (0711) 2191-422
E-mail: info@kosmos.de
Web Site: www.kosmos.de
Telex: 721669 Kosm d *Cable:* KOSMOS VERLAG STUTTGART

Key Personnel
President: Axel Meffert *Tel:* (0711) 2191341
Publicity Dir: Bettina Schaub *Tel:* (0711) 2191341 *Fax:* (0711) 2191141 *E-mail:* b.schaub@kosmos.de
Production Dir: Juergen Bischoff *Tel:* (0711) 2191221 *Fax:* (0711) 2191121 *E-mail:* J.bischoff@kosmos.de
Foreign Rights Dir: Andrea D Ahlers *Tel:* (0711) 2191254 *Fax:* (0711) 2191154 *E-mail:* a.ahlers@kosmos.de
Marketing Dir: Manfred Haarer *Tel:* (0711) 2191401 *Fax:* (0711) 2191101 *E-mail:* m.haarer@kosmos.de; Heiko Windfelder *Tel:* (0711) 2191322 *Fax:* (0711) 2191122; Birgit Carlsen *Tel:* (0711) 21911205 *Fax:* (0711) 21911205 *E-mail:* b.carlsen@kosmos.de
Founded: 1822
Specialize in fishing & hunting.
Subjects: Animals, Pets, Astronomy, Biological Sciences, Chemistry, Chemical Engineering, Crafts, Games, Hobbies, Electronics, Electrical Engineering, Engineering (General), Environmental Studies, Fiction, Gardening, Plants, Geography, Geology, House & Home, Natural History, Nonfiction (General), Outdoor Recreation, Physics, Science (General), Technology
ISBN Prefix(es): 3-440
Number of titles published annually: 120 Print
Total Titles: 600 Print
Parent Company: Buchverlage Langen Mueller Herbig
Associate Companies: F A Herbig, Muenchen; Klee-Spiele GmbH, Fuerth
Warehouse: VVA, An der Autobahn, 33310 Guetersloh

Dr Anton Kovac Slavica Verlag+
Elizabethstr 22, 80796 Munich
Tel: (089) 2725612 *Fax:* (089) 2716594
E-mail: 101566.2450@compuserve.com
Key Personnel
Owner: Anton Kovac
Founded: 1987
Subjects: Anthropology, Ethnicity, Fiction, Foreign Countries, Government, Political Science, History, Language Arts, Linguistics, Literature, Literary Criticism, Essays, Philosophy, Poetry, Religion - Other
ISBN Prefix(es): 3-927077
Distributor for Bosnia; Croatia; Slovenia

Roman Kovar Verlag+
Hauptstr 13, 86492 Egling (Paar)
Tel: (08206) 961977 *Fax:* (08206) 961978
E-mail: romankovar@gmx.net
Web Site: www.kovar-verlag.com
Key Personnel
Publisher: Roman Kovar
Founded: 1986
Subjects: Art, Library & Information Sciences, Literature, Literary Criticism, Essays, Religion - Jewish
ISBN Prefix(es): 3-925845

Karl Kraemer Verlag GmbH und Co+
Schulze-Delitzsch-Str 15, 70565 Stuttgart
Mailing Address: Postfach 80 06 50, 70506 Stuttgart
Tel: (0711) 7 84 96-0 *Fax:* (0711) 7 84 96-20
E-mail: info@kraemerverlag.com
Web Site: www.kraemerverlag.de
Key Personnel
President: Karl H Kraemer *E-mail:* karl.kraemer-verlag@kraemerverlag.com
Dir: Gudrun Kraemer *E-mail:* gudrun.kraemer@kraemerverlag.com; Lutz Kraemer *E-mail:* lutz.kraemer@kraemerverlag.com
Founded: 1930
Subjects: Architecture & Interior Design
ISBN Prefix(es): 3-7828
Total Titles: 118 Print

Associate Companies: Verlag Karl Kraemer & Co, Postfach 1209, CH-8034, Switzerland
Bookshop(s): Fachbuchhandlung Karl Kraemer, Rotebuehlstr 40, Postfach 102842, 701784 Stuttgart *Tel:* (0711) 669930 *Fax:* (0711) 628955 *Web Site:* www.karl.kraemer.de
Orders to: Koch, Neff, Oetinger & Co, Postfach 800620, D-70506 Stuttgart

Reinhold Kraemer Verlag+
Rothenbaumchaussee 103F, 20148 Hamburg
Mailing Address: Postfach 13 05 84, 20105 Hamburg
Tel: (040) 4101429 *Fax:* (040) 455770
E-mail: info@kraemer-verlag.de
Web Site: www.kraemer-verlag.de
Key Personnel
Man Dir: Dr Reinhold Kraemer
Founded: 1988
Subjects: Science (General)
ISBN Prefix(es): 3-926952

Adam Kraft Verlag+
Imprint of Verlagshaus Wurzburg
Beethovenstr 5, 97080 Wurzburg
Tel: (0931) 385235 *Fax:* (0931) 385305
E-mail: info@verlagshaus.com
Web Site: www.verlagshaus.com
Key Personnel
Publishing Dir: Dieter Krause
Dir of Production: Juergen Roth
Sales Dir: Johannes Glesius
Founded: 1927
Subjects: Foreign Countries, Regional Interests, Travel
ISBN Prefix(es): 3-8083

Krafthand Verlag Walter Schultz GmbH
Gottlieb-Daimlerstr 10, 86825 Bad Woerishofen
Mailing Address: Postfach 1462, 86817 Bad Woerishofen
Tel: (08247) 30070 *Fax:* (08247) 300770
Web Site: www.krafthand.de
Key Personnel
President, Man Dir, Public Relation: Gottfried Karpstein
Man Dir, Editorial Chief: Walter G Schweizer
Founded: 1927
Subjects: Civil Engineering
ISBN Prefix(es): 3-87441

Edition Kraftpunkt Toni Fedrigotti+
Steinerne Furt 78, 86167 Augsburg
Tel: (0821) 705011 *Fax:* (0821) 705008
Key Personnel
Owner: Toni Fedrigotti
Founded: 1982
ISBN Prefix(es): 3-925557; 3-928086
U.S. Office(s): Dr Eldon Taylor, 816 W Big Bear Blvd, Big Bear City, CA 92314, United States *Tel:* 909-585-6065 *Fax:* 909-585-6365

Karin Kramer Verlag+
Niemetzstr 19, 12055 Berlin
Mailing Address: Postfach 440417, 12004 Berlin
Tel: (030) 6845055; (030) 6842598 *Fax:* (030) 6858577
E-mail: kramer@virtualitas.com
Web Site: www.anares.org/kramer/
Key Personnel
Editorial & Publicity: Bernd Kramer *Tel:* (030) 6842598
Founded: 1970
Subjects: Alternative, Art, Biography, Government, Political Science, History, Literature, Literary Criticism, Essays, Nonfiction (General), Philosophy, Poetry, Science Fiction, Fantasy, Social Sciences, Sociology
ISBN Prefix(es): 3-87956
Online services available through World Wide Web.

Verlag Waldemar Kramer+
Orberstr 38, 60386 Frankfurt am Main
Mailing Address: Postfach 600445, 60334 Frankfurt am Main
Tel: (069) 449045 *Fax:* (069) 449064
E-mail: kramerverlag@frankfurtbuecher.de
Key Personnel
Publisher: Dr Henriette Kramer
Founded: 1939
Subjects: Art, Biological Sciences, Education, Environmental Studies, Geography, Geology, History, Natural History, Science (General)
ISBN Prefix(es): 3-7829
Total Titles: 200 Print

Krankenpflegeforschung, *imprint of* Bibliomed - Medizinische Verlagsgesellschaft mbH

Nara Verlag Josef Krauthaeuser+
Akazienring 6a, 85391 Allershausen
Mailing Address: Postfach 1241, 85388 Allershausen
Tel: (08166) 8530; (08166) 8531 *Fax:* (08166) 8530
E-mail: j.krauthaeuser@nara-verlag.de
Web Site: www.nara-international.de
Key Personnel
Manager, Rights & Permissions: Josef Krauthaeuser
Founded: 1982
Subjects: Aeronautics, Aviation
ISBN Prefix(es): 3-925671

Kretschmar Hubert Leipziger Verlagsgesellschaft+
Pragerstr 163, 04299 Leipzig
Tel: (0341) 8789644 *Fax:* (0341) 8789644
Key Personnel
Proprietor, Rights & Permissions: Hubert Kretschmar
Founded: 1990
Specialize in high quality catalogs & art books.
Subjects: Art, History, Literature, Literary Criticism, Essays, Regional Interests
ISBN Prefix(es): 3-910143

Verlag Hubert Kretschmer+
Nymphenburgerstr 34, 80335 Munich
Mailing Address: Postfach 260117, 80058 Munich
Tel: (089) 1234530 *Fax:* (089) 1238638
E-mail: hubert.kretschmer@t-online.de
Founded: 1980
Subjects: Art, Photography
ISBN Prefix(es): 3-923205
Total Titles: 40 Print

Kriebel Verlag GmbH
Auf der Hoehe 14, 86923 Finning
Tel: (08806) 9360 *Fax:* (08806) 9361
E-mail: info@kriebel-sat.de
Web Site: www.kriebel-sat.de
Key Personnel
Manager: Henning Kriebel
Founded: 1986
Subjects: Communications
ISBN Prefix(es): 3-927617
Parent Company: Kriebel Verlag GmbH
Divisions: Media Service

Krimi-Reihe, *imprint of* Alibaba Verlag GmbH

Alfred Kroner Verlag+
Reinsburgstr 56, 70178 Stuttgart
Mailing Address: Postfach 102862, 70024 Stuttgart
Tel: (0711) 6155363 *Fax:* (0711) 61553646
E-mail: a.kroner@z.zgv.de
Web Site: www.kroener-verlag.de

GERMANY

Key Personnel
Man Dir: Arno Klemm; Dr Imma Klemm; Walter Kohrs
Founded: 1904
Subjects: Art, Drama, Theater, History, Language Arts, Linguistics, Literature, Literary Criticism, Essays, Music, Dance, Philosophy, Religion - Other
ISBN Prefix(es): 3-520
Total Titles: 180 Print
Orders to: VA/KNO Stuttgart

Wolfgang Krueger Verlag GmbH+
Hedderichstr 114, 60596 Frankfurt
Mailing Address: Postfach 700355, 60553 Frankfurt
Tel: (069) 60620 *Fax:* (069) 6062352
Web Site: www.krugschadenberg.de
Key Personnel
Man Dir: Monika Schoeller; Dr Hubertus Schenkel
Man Dir, Rights & Permissions: Wolfgang Mertz
Sales: Joerg Alkenbrecher
Publicity: Margarete Schwind
Production: Wilfried Meiner
Editorial: Peter Wilfert
Subjects: Fiction, Humor, Nonfiction (General)
ISBN Prefix(es): 3-8105
Parent Company: S Fischer Verlag GmbH

Krug & Schadenberg+
Heimstr 19, 10965 Berlin
Tel: (030) 6941243; (030) 61625750 *Fax:* (030) 6941231
E-mail: info@krugschadenberg.de
Web Site: www.krugschadenberg.de
Key Personnel
International Rights: Andrea Krug
Founded: 1993
Member of Women in Publishing.
Subjects: Fiction, Gay & Lesbian, Human Relations, Self-Help, Women's Studies
ISBN Prefix(es): 3-930041

Kubon & Sagner Buchexport-Import GmbH+
Hessstr 39/41, 80798 Munich
Mailing Address: Postfach 340108, 80328 Munich
Tel: (089) 542180 *Fax:* (089) 54218218
E-mail: postmaster@kubon-sagner.de
Web Site: www.kubon-sagner.de
Key Personnel
Manager: Otto Sagner; Sabine Sagner-Weigl
Founded: 1947
Specialize in publications from East & Southeast Europe.
Wholesaler, Distributor, Importer & Independent Bookseller.
Subjects: Regional Interests, Slavic Studies, Hungarian, Romanian, Albanian
ISBN Prefix(es): 3-87690
Subsidiaries: Verlag Otto Sagner

Kubon Und Sagner
Formerly Verlag Otto Sagner
Hesstr 39/41, 80798 Munich
Mailing Address: 80398 Munich
Tel: (089) 54 218-0 *Fax:* (089) 54 218-218
E-mail: postmaster@kubon-sagner.de
Web Site: www.kubon-sagner.de
Key Personnel
Man Dir: Petrols Sagner; Sabine Sagner Weigl *E-mail:* sabine.sagnerweigl@kubon-sagner.de
Publisher: Otto Sagner
Editorial: Prof Peter Rehder, PhD
Founded: 1947
Book export import publishing company.
Subjects: Language Arts, Linguistics, Literature, Literary Criticism, Essays
ISBN Prefix(es): 3-87690
Parent Company: Kubon & Sagner, Munich

Kuemmerley und Frey, see Fink - Kummerly und Frey Verlag GmbH

Verlag Ernst Kuhn+
Mendelssohnstr 7, 10405 Berlin
Mailing Address: PO Box 080147, 10001 Berlin
Tel: (030) 44342230 *Fax:* (030) 4424732
E-mail: ernst-kuhn-verlag@t-online.de
Web Site: www.vek.de
Key Personnel
Publisher: Ernst Kuhn *E-mail:* kuhn@vek.de
Man Dir: Baerbel Bruder *E-mail:* bruder@vek.de
Founded: 1991
Specialize in books on Russian music; also online-bookshop (books on music, sheet music, scores).
Subjects: Biography, History, Music, Dance
ISBN Prefix(es): 3-928864
Orders to: LKG mbH, Potzschauer Weg, 04579 Espenhain bei Leipzig

Kulturbuch-Verlag GmbH
Sprosserweg 3, 12351 Berlin
Mailing Address: Postfach 470449, 12313 Berlin
Tel: (030) 6618484; (030) 6614002 *Fax:* (030) 6617828; (030) 6614002
E-mail: kbvinfo@kulturbuch-verlag.de
Web Site: www.kulturbuch-verlag.de
Key Personnel
Manager: Lothar Seikrit
Founded: 1949
Subjects: Environmental Studies, Law, Regional Interests
ISBN Prefix(es): 3-88961

Kulturstiftung der deutschen Vertriebenen
Kaiserstr 113, 53113 Bonn
Tel: (0228) 915120 *Fax:* (0228) 218397
E-mail: kulturstiftung@t-online.de
Web Site: www.kulturstiftung-der-deutschen-vertriebenen.de/home.html
Key Personnel
Chairperson: Dr Reinold Schleifenbaum
Man Dir: Dr Hans-Jakob Tebarth
Founded: 1974
Subjects: Art, Government, Political Science, History, Law, Literature, Literary Criticism, Essays
ISBN Prefix(es): 3-88557
Number of titles published annually: 12 Print
Total Titles: 200 Print

Archiv fur Kunst & Geschichte Bilderdienst & Verlagsgesellschaft mbH+
Teutonenstr 22, 14129 Berlin
Tel: (030) 804850 *Fax:* (030) 80485500
E-mail: info@akg.de
Web Site: www.akg.de
Key Personnel
Contact: Justus Goepel
Founded: 1945
Subjects: Art, History
ISBN Prefix(es): 3-88912

Verlag der Kunst/G+B Fine Arts Verlag GmbH+
Rosa-Menzerstr 12, 01309 Dresden
Mailing Address: Postfach 190154, 01281 Dresden
Tel: (0351) 3360742; (0351) 3100052 *Fax:* (0351) 3105245
E-mail: verlag-der-kunst@t-online.de
Web Site: www.verlag-der-kunst.de
Key Personnel
Editor: Martina Buder
Marketing Manager: Dr Barbara Schmidt
Founded: 1952
Specialize in architecture.
Subjects: Art, Photography, Regional Interests
ISBN Prefix(es): 3-364; 90-5701; 90-5705
Total Titles: 120 Print
Associate Companies: G+B Arts International

Distributed by IPD
Warehouse: SOVA, Friesstr 20-24, D-60388 Frankfurt

Kunst und Wohnen Verlag GmbH, see Dr Wolfgang Schwarze Verlag

Verlag Antje Kunstmann GmbH+
Georgenstr 123, 80743 Munich
Mailing Address: Postfach 431351, Munich 80743
Tel: (089) 121193-0 *Fax:* (089) 12193-20
E-mail: info@kunstmann.de
Web Site: www.kunstmann.de
Key Personnel
Man Dir, Editorial: Antje Kunstmann
Sales: Ulrich Deurer
Founded: 1970
Subjects: Drama, Theater, Education, Fiction, Government, Political Science, Humor, Literature, Literary Criticism, Essays, Nonfiction (General)
ISBN Prefix(es): 3-921040; 3-88897
Orders to: LKG, Potzschaues Weg, 04579 Espenhain
B & I, Obfelderstr 35, CH-8910 Affoltern a A, Switzerland
Mohr-Morawa, Sulzengasse 2, A-1230 Vienna, Austria

Kunstverlag Maria Laach
Postfach, 56653 Maria Laach
Tel: (0751) 561290 *Fax:* (0751) 5612920
E-mail: kunstverlag@weingarten-verlag.de
Web Site: www.maria-laach.de/verlag/
Key Personnel
Dir: P Cremer *Tel:* (02652) 59360

Kunstverlag Weingarten GmbH+
Laegelerstr 31, 88250 Weingarten
Mailing Address: Postfach 1341, 88242 Weingarten
Tel: (0751) 561290 *Fax:* (0751) 5612920
E-mail: kunstverlag@kv-weingarten.de
Web Site: www.kv-weingarten.de
Key Personnel
President: Rainer Berger
Publisher & International Rights: Hero Schiefer *Tel:* (0751) 5612940 *E-mail:* hschiefer@weingarten-verlag.de
Founded: 1976
Publishers of art & photo calendars.
Subjects: Animals, Pets, Antiques, Architecture & Interior Design, Art, Cookery, Health, Nutrition, Literature, Literary Criticism, Essays, Music, Dance, Photography
ISBN Prefix(es): 3-8170; 3-921617
Total Titles: 180 Print

Deutscher Verlag fuer Kunstwissenschaft, see Deutscher Verlag fur Kunstwissenschaft GmbH

Kupfergraben Verlagsgesellschaft mbH+
Luetzowstr 105, 10785 Berlin
Tel: (030) 2622097 *Fax:* (030) 2621990
Key Personnel
Man Dir: Wolfgang Stapp
Founded: 1984
Subjects: Art, Literature, Literary Criticism, Essays
ISBN Prefix(es): 3-89181

Kutz und praktisch, *imprint of* Verlag Hermann Bauer KG

Kynos Verlag Dr Dieter Fleig GmbH+
Am Remelsbach 30, 54570 Muerlenbach/Eifel
Tel: (06) 594-653 *Fax:* (06) 594-452
E-mail: info@kynos-verlag.de
Web Site: www.kynos-verlag.de

Key Personnel
Dir: Herbert Wolter
Foreign Rights: Gisela Ran
Founded: 1980
Subjects: Animals, Pets
ISBN Prefix(es): 3-929545; 3-924008; 3-933228
Total Titles: 210 Print

Laaber-Verlag+
Regenburgerstr 19, 93164 Laaber
Tel: (09498) 2307 *Fax:* (09498) 2543
E-mail: info@laaber-verlag.de
Web Site: www.laaber.de
Founded: 1977
In 1994, Laaber-Verlag bought the publisher of books on music, Frits Knuf, Buren.
Subjects: Music, Dance
ISBN Prefix(es): 3-89007; 90-6027
Total Titles: 1,000 Print

Labyrinth Verlag Gisela Ottmer
Yorckstr 3, 38102 Braunschweig
Tel: (0531) 64259 *Fax:* (0531) 681358
E-mail: labyrinthbraunschweig@t-online.de
Web Site: www.frauenart.
de/labyrinthbraunschweig

Ambro Lacus, Buch- und Bildverlag Walter Kremnitz
Frieding-Hurtenstr 25, 82346 Andechs
Tel: (8152) 1332 *Fax:* (8152) 40186 *Cable:* KREMNITZ-FRIEDING
Key Personnel
Man Dir, Rights & Permissions: Walter Kremnitz
Bookkeeping: P Kremnitz
Founded: 1974
Subjects: Earth Sciences, Gardening, Plants, Law, Nonfiction (General), Science (General), Travel
ISBN Prefix(es): 3-921445
Number of titles published annually: 2 Print

Lahn-Verlag GmbH+
Jahnstr 2a, 65550 Limburg-Linter
Mailing Address: Postfach 1562, 65535 Limburg
Tel: (06431) 9474-10 *Fax:* (06431) 9474-11
E-mail: lahn-verlag@lahnverlag.de
Web Site: www.lahn-verlag.de *Cable:* LAHN-VERLAG
Key Personnel
Publisher: Engelbert Tauscher
Editorial: Dr Stefan Ohnesorge; Anne Voorhoeve
Founded: 1900
Subjects: Poetry, Religion - Catholic, Theology
ISBN Prefix(es): 3-7840
Total Titles: 200 Print; 50 Audio
Orders to: Butzon & Bercker GmbH, Hoogeweg 71, 47623 Kevelaer *Tel:* (02832) 9290 *Fax:* (02832) 929 211 *E-mail:* service@butzonbercker.de

Johannis Lahr, see Verlag der Sankt-Johannis-Druckerei C Schweickhardt

Lambda Edition GmbH+
Clemens-Schultzstr 77, 20359 Hamburg
Mailing Address: Postfach 304171, 20324 Hamburg
Tel: (040) 312836 *Fax:* (040) 3192096
Key Personnel
Publisher: Michael P Hartleben
Founded: 1980
Member of the Stock Exchange of German Booksellers.
Subjects: Fiction
ISBN Prefix(es): 3-925495

Lambertus Verlag GmbH+
Mitscherlichstr 8, 79108 Freiburg
Mailing Address: Postfach 1026, 79010 Freiburg
Tel: (0761) 368250 *Fax:* (0761) 3682533
E-mail: info@lambertus.de
Web Site: www.lambertus.de
Key Personnel
Man Dir: Fritz Boll; Gerhild Neugart
Founded: 1898
ISBN Prefix(es): 3-7841
Subsidiaries: Freiburge Buchedienst (verlagsbuchhandlung)
Bookshop(s): Freiburger Buecherdienst, Wolfinstr 4, 79104 Freiburg

Lamuv Verlag GmbH+
Gromerstr 20, 37073 Goettingen
Mailing Address: Postfach 2605, 37016 Goettingen
Tel: (0551) 44024 *Fax:* (0551) 41392
E-mail: rabe@lamuv.de
Web Site: www.lamuv.de
Key Personnel
Man Dir, Editorial: Karl-Klaus Rabe
Sales: Leonore Frester
Founded: 1976
Subjects: Developing Countries, Government, Political Science, Literature, Literary Criticism, Essays, Regional Interests
ISBN Prefix(es): 3-921521; 3-88977

Landbuch-Verlagsgesellschaft mbH+
Kabelkamp 6, 30179 Hannover
Mailing Address: Postfach 160, 30001 Hannover
Tel: (0511) 27046230 *Fax:* (0511) 27046220
E-mail: info@landbuch.de
Web Site: www.landbuch.de *Cable:* LANDBUCH HANOVER
Key Personnel
Man Dir, Production, Rights & Permissions: Kuhrmeier Bernd
Sales: Willi Ludwig Kroeck
Founded: 1945
Subjects: Agriculture, Animals, Pets, Asian Studies, Behavioral Sciences, Biological Sciences, Career Development, Cookery, Crafts, Games, Hobbies, Earth Sciences, Environmental Studies, Fiction, Foreign Countries, Gardening, Plants, Genealogy, Geography, Geology, Health, Nutrition, History, House & Home, Humor, Natural History, Nonfiction (General), Outdoor Recreation, Physical Sciences, Regional Interests, Travel, Veterinary Science
ISBN Prefix(es): 3-7842
Imprints: Buecher und Zeitschriften
Divisions: Versandbuchhandlung Orni-Book

Institut fuer Landes- und Stadtentwicklungsforschung, ILS Nordrhein-Westfalen+
Deutschestr 5, 44339 Dortmund
Mailing Address: Postfach 101764, 44017 Dortmund
Tel: (0231) 90510 *Fax:* (0231) 90515155
E-mail: ils@ils.nrw.de
Web Site: www.ils.nrw.de
Key Personnel
Dir: Sierau Ullrich
Founded: 1971
Subjects: Architecture & Interior Design, Energy, Environmental Studies, Law, Outdoor Recreation, Physical Sciences, Public Administration, Regional Interests, Social Sciences, Sociology, Technology, Transportation, Women's Studies
ISBN Prefix(es): 3-8176
Distributed by WAZ-Vertrieb Bitte streichen

Peter Lang GmbH Europaeischer Verlag der Wissenschaften+
Eschborner Landstr 42-50, 60489 Frankfurt am Main
Mailing Address: Postfach 940225, 60460 Frankfurt am Main
Tel: (069) 7807050 *Fax:* (069) 780705-50
E-mail: zentrale.frankfurt@peterlang.com
Web Site: www.peterlang.de
Key Personnel
Man Dir: Juergen-Matthias Springer; Ruprecht Sickel
Licenses: Ruediger Brunsch *Tel:* (069) 78070520 *E-mail:* r.brunsch@peterlang.com
Founded: 1971
Subjects: Education, Government, Political Science, History, Language Arts, Linguistics, Law, Literature, Literary Criticism, Essays, Philosophy, Science (General), Theology
ISBN Prefix(es): 3-631
Parent Company: Verlag Peter Lang AG, Switzerland
Associate Companies: Peter Lang Publishing Inc, 275 Seventh Ave, 28th fl, New York, NY 10001-6708, United States *Tel:* 212-647-7706 *Fax:* 212-647-7707 *E-mail:* customerservice@plang.com *Web Site:* www.peterlang.com
Orders to: Peter Lang AG, Jupiterstr 15, CH-3000 Bern 15, Switzerland *Tel:* (031) 9402121 *Fax:* (031) 9402131 *E-mail:* customerservice@peterlang.com *Web Site:* www.peterlang.ch

Langenscheidt Fachverlag GmbH+
Mies-van-der-Rohestr 1, 80807 Munich
Tel: (089) 36096-476 *Fax:* (089) 36096-479
E-mail: fachverlag@langenscheidt.de
Key Personnel
Manager: Marie-Jeanne Derouin *Tel:* (089) 36096 475 *E-mail:* marie-jeanne.derouin@langenscheidt.de
Assistant: Maria Kaldewey
Founded: 1991
Subjects: Specialized bilingual & multilingual print & electronic versions
ISBN Prefix(es): 3-86117
Parent Company: Langenscheidt KG
Warehouse: TVA Gotha, Langenscheidtstr 70, 99867 Gotha
Orders to: Langenscheidt Fachverlag, Postfach 401120, 80711 Munich

The Langenscheidt Group+
Mies-van-der-Rohestr, 80807 Munich
Mailing Address: Postfach 401120, 80711 Munich
Tel: (089) 36096-0; (089) 36096-258 (Orders) *Fax:* (089) 36096-376; (089) 36096-258
E-mail: mail@langenscheidt.de
Web Site: www.langenscheidt.de
Key Personnel
General Partner: Andreas Langenscheidt; Nare Ernst Tidebier-Langenscheidt
Publishing Dir: Rolf Mueller
Sales Dir & Marketing: Dr Matt Schuesseler
Financial Dir: Dr Eugene Saller
Founded: 1856
The Group consists of: Bibliographisches Institut und F A Brockhaus AG; Axel Juncker Verlag; Langenscheidt KG; Langenscheidt-Hachette GmbH; Langenscheidt-Longman GmbH; Mentor-Verlag; Polyglott Verlag GmbH; Langenscheidt Fachverlag GmbH (all in Germany); Langenscheidt-Verlag GmbH, Austria; Apa Publications; GmbH & Co Verlag KG; Langenscheidt AG, Switzerland; Langenscheidt Publishers, Inc; Creative Sales Corp; American Map Corp; ADC; Trakker Maps Inc Nationwide; Arrow Map Inc; Hagstrom Map Co Inc; The Map Store Inc; Ha ADC Map & Travel Center; Berlitz Publishing; Hammond: Blay Folder SAS France; Langenscheidt Polska; Geo Center International UK.
ISBN Prefix(es): 3-468; 3-86117; 3-595; 3-526; 3-493; 3-5881; 3-82681

Langenscheidt-Hachette+
Neusserstr 3, 80807 Munich
Mailing Address: Postfach 401120, 80711 Munich
Tel: (089) 360960 *Fax:* (089) 36096-222; (089) 36096-472 (general); (089) 36096-258 (orders)

Key Personnel
Man Dir: Karl Ernst Tielebier-Langenscheidt; Marc Moingeon
Editorial: Dr Herbert Bornebusch
Founded: 1977
Sales & Promotion through Langenscheidt KG.
Member of the Langenscheidt Group.
Subjects: Education, Language Arts, Linguistics
ISBN Prefix(es): 3-595

Langenscheidt KG+
Neusser Str 3, 80807 Munich
Mailing Address: Postfach 401120, 80711 Munich
Tel: (089) 36096-0; (089) 36096-258 (Orders) *Fax:* (089) 36096-222
Telex: Munich 5215379 lkgmd *Cable:* LANGENSCHEIDT MUNICH
Key Personnel
Man Dir: Karl Ernst Tielebier-Langenscheidt; Andreas Langenscheidt
Program Manager: Dr Wolfgang Wieter
Chief Editor, English language: Wolfgang Kaul
Chief Editor, Slavonic languages: Dr Paul Ruehl
Chief Editor, German as a Foreign language: Dr Herbert Bornebusch
Chief Editor, Roman languages: Dieter Meier
Production: Helmut Wahl
Sales Dir: Michael Staehler
Advertising: Brigitte Pasch
Publicity: Margrit Philipp
Export: Alan Francis Roberts
Electronic Publishing: Dr Hans Werner Scholz
Rights & Permissions: Walburga Hallet-Wolters
Legal Dept: Dr Martin Wagner
Founded: 1856
Member of the Langenscheidt Group and a member of TR- Verlagsunion GmbH.
ISBN Prefix(es): 3-526
Subsidiaries: Langenscheidt-Longman GmbH; Langenscheidt-Hachette GmbH; Polyglott-Verlag Dr Bolte KG; Humboldt-Taschenbuchverlag Jacobi KG; Mentor Verlag Dr Ramdohu KG; Karl Baedeker GmbH; Bibliographisches Institut und F L Brockhaus AG; Verlag Enzyklopaedie; Langenscheidt-Verlag GmbH; Langenscheidt AG; Trakker Maps Inc; Arrow Map Inc; Creative Sales Corp; Langenscheidt Publishers Inc; American Map Corp; Hagstrom Map Co; ADC; Apa Publications (HK) Ltd

Verlag Langewiesche-Brandt KG+
Lechnerstr 27, 82067 Ebenhausen (Isartal)
Tel: (08178) 4857 *Fax:* (08178) 7388
E-mail: textura@langewiesche-brandt.de
Web Site: www.langewiesche-brandt.de
Key Personnel
Man Dir: Kristof Wachinger *E-mail:* wachinger@langewiesche-brandt.de
Founded: 1906
Subjects: Poetry
ISBN Prefix(es): 3-7846
Number of titles published annually: 4 Print
Total Titles: 60 Print
Imprints: Ebenhausen bei Muenchen

Karl Robert Langewiesche Nachfolger Hans Koester KG+
Member of Motovun Group Association
Gruener Weg 6, 61462 Koenigstein
Mailing Address: Postfach 1327, 61453 Koenigstein
Tel: (06174) 7333 *Fax:* (06174) 933-039
E-mail: info@langewiesche-verlag.de
Web Site: www.langewiesche-verlag.de *Cable:* LANGEWIESCHE KOENIGSTEINTAUNUS
Key Personnel
Publisher & Man Dir, Production: Hans-Curt Koester *E-mail:* koester@langewiesche-verlag.de
Editorial: Gabriele Klempert

Founded: 1902
Specialize in books, journals & calendars
Member of Motovun Group Association, Lucerne.
Subjects: Antiques, Archaeology, Architecture & Interior Design, Art, History, How-to, Photography
ISBN Prefix(es): 3-7845
Number of titles published annually: 5 Print
Total Titles: 120 Print
Imprints: Die Blauen Buecher (The Blue Book)
Distributed by Abaris Books (US)
Orders to: Koch, Neff, Oetinger & Co Verlagsauslieferung, Postfach D-70551 Stuttgart, Mr Heckl *Tel:* (0711) 7899-2120 *Fax:* (0711) 7899-1010

Ingrid Langner
Buchentwiete 24 A, 25355 Barmstedt
Mailing Address: Postfach 1125, 25349 Barmstedt
Tel: (04123) 7780 *Fax:* (04123) 7885
Key Personnel
Owner: Manfred Langner
Founded: 1985
Subjects: Fiction, Language Arts, Linguistics, Literature, Literary Criticism, Essays
ISBN Prefix(es): 3-9801131

Lappan Verlag GmbH+
Wuerzburger Str 14, 26121 Oldenburg
Mailing Address: Postfach 3407, 26024 Oldenburg
Tel: (0441) 980660 *Fax:* (0441) 9806622; (0441) 9806624; (0441) 9806634
Web Site: www.lappan.de
Key Personnel
Man Dir: Dieter Schwalm
Editorial Dir: Peter Baumann
Sales: Bianca Wiemken
International Rights: Heidrun Kaempf
Founded: 1983
Publisher of books for children & adults.
Subjects: Cartoon Books of Uli Stein, Humor
ISBN Prefix(es): 3-89082; 3-8303
Number of titles published annually: 80 Print
Total Titles: 470 Print
Distributor for Edition C (Switzerland)

Michael Lassleben Verlag
Lange Gasse 19, 93183 Kallmuenz
Mailing Address: Postfach 20, 93183 Kallmunz
Tel: (09473) 205 *Fax:* (09473) 8357
E-mail: druckerei@oberpfalzverlag-lassleben.de
Web Site: www.oberpfalzverlag-lassleben.de
Key Personnel
Owner: Erich Lassleben, Sr
Founded: 1907
Subjects: Archaeology, Geography, Geology, History, Literature, Literary Criticism, Essays
ISBN Prefix(es): 3-7847
Number of titles published annually: 20 Print

Verlag Laterna magica GmbH & Co KG+
Streitfeldstr 35, 81673 Munich
Mailing Address: Postfach 800409, 81604 Munich
Tel: (089) 43 6005 162 *Fax:* (089) 43 6005 113
E-mail: info@laterna-magica.de
Web Site: www.laterna-magica.de
Key Personnel
Publisher: Joachim F Richter
Rights & Permissions, Publisher, all other offices: Michael T Robertson
Founded: 1966
Also acts as CD-ROM producer.
Subjects: Computer Science, Film, Video, Photography
ISBN Prefix(es): 3-87467
Orders to: Wolfratshauser Str 278, 81479 Munich

J Latka Verlag GmbH+
Heilsbachstr 32, 53123 Bonn

Tel: (0228) 919320 *Fax:* (0228) 9193217
E-mail: info@latka.de
Web Site: www.latka.de
Key Personnel
President, Rights & Permissions: Joachim Latka
Founded: 1984
Subjects: History, Travel
ISBN Prefix(es): 3-925068
Total Titles: 30 Print
Online services available through World Wide Web.
U.S. Office(s): Cosmedia Inc, 560 Sutter St, Suite 300, San Francisco, CA 94102, United States, Contact: Ms E A Olesen *Tel:* 415-677-9700 *Fax:* 415-677-9300 *E-mail:* cosmedia@sirius.com
Foreign Rep(s): Elizabeth A Olesen (North America)
Orders to: Herold, Kolpingring 4, 82041 Oberhaching, Ms Stanglmeier *Tel:* (089) 6138710 *Fax:* (089) 61387120

H Lauppsche Buchhandlung, *imprint of* Mohr Siebeck

LBO-Dienst, *imprint of* Bauverlag GmbH

Lebensbaum Verlags-GmbH+
Joellenbeckerstr 29, 33613 Bielefeld
Mailing Address: Postfach 101849, 33518 Bielefeld
Tel: (0521) 172875 *Fax:* (0521) 68771
Key Personnel
Contact: Joachim Kamphausen
Founded: 1989
Subjects: Health, Nutrition, Medicine, Nursing, Dentistry
ISBN Prefix(es): 3-928430
Orders to: J Kamphausen Verlag & Distribution GmbH, Jollenbeckerstr 29, 33613 Bielefeld

Lebenshilfe-Verlag Marburg, Verlag der Bundesvereinigung Lebenshilfe fuer Menschen mit geistiger Behinderung eV+
Raiffeisenstr 18, 35043 Marburg
Mailing Address: Postfach 701163, 35020 Marburg
Tel: (06421) 491150; (06421) 491153 *Fax:* (06421) 491167
E-mail: bvlh-verlag@t-online.de
Web Site: www.lebenshilfe.de
Key Personnel
Publishing Dir: Hans-Volker Wagner
Founded: 1958
Subjects: Disability, Special Needs, Health, Nutrition, Law, Medicine, Nursing, Dentistry, Nonfiction (General), Self-Help, Social Sciences, Sociology
ISBN Prefix(es): 3-88617

Verlag fuer Lehrmittel Poessneck GmbH+
Neustaedterstr 63, 07381 Poessneck
Mailing Address: Postfach 1465, 07374 Poessneck
Tel: 03647 425020 *Fax:* (03647) 425020
Key Personnel
Manager: Lothar Stein
Founded: 1947
ISBN Prefix(es): 3-7493

Leibniz Verlag+
Auf dem Haehnchen 34, 56329 St Goar
Tel: (06741) 1720 *Fax:* (06741) 1749
E-mail: reichl-verlag@telda.net
Key Personnel
Man Dir: Matthias Draeger
Founded: 1994
Subjects: Human Relations, Language Arts, Linguistics, Philosophy, Science (General)
ISBN Prefix(es): 3-931155

Leibniz-Buecherwarte+
Robert-Kochstr 12, Bad Muender, Hameln-Pyrmont 31848
Mailing Address: Postfach 1214, Bad Muender 31842
Tel: (05042) 1528 *Fax:* (05042) 1528
E-mail: leibniz-buecherwarte@t-online.de
Web Site: www.leibniz-buecherwarte.de/.com
Key Personnel
Contact: Gabrielle Spaeth
Founded: 1985
Specialize in philosophy with children.
Subjects: Literature, Literary Criticism, Essays, Philosophy, Religion - Other
ISBN Prefix(es): 3-925237

Leipziger Universitaetsverlag GmbH+
c/o Universitaet Leipzig, Augustusplatz 10/11, 04109 Leipzig
Mailing Address: Oststr 41, 04317 Leipzig
Tel: (0341) 9900440 *Fax:* (0341) 9900440
E-mail: info@univerlag-leipzig.de
Key Personnel
International Rights: Dr Gerald Diesener
Founded: 1992
Subjects: Communications, History, Law, Medicine, Nursing, Dentistry, Philosophy, Science (General), Women's Studies
ISBN Prefix(es): 3-929031; 3-931922

Leitfadenverlag Verlag Dieter Sudholt+
Kreuzanger 8, 82335 Berg
Tel: (08151) 51045 *Fax:* (08151) 50357
Key Personnel
Publisher: Dipl Kfm Volker Sudholt
Founded: 1957
Subjects: Business, Economics, Law
ISBN Prefix(es): 3-543
Associate Companies: Leitfadenverlag Gesellschaft mbH, Innsbruck, Austria

Anton G Leitner Verlag (AGLV)+
Buchenweg 3 b, 82234 Wessling
Mailing Address: PO Box 1203, 82231 Wessling
Tel: (08153) 9525-22 *Fax:* (08153) 9525-24
E-mail: info@aglv.com
Web Site: www.dasgedicht.de
Key Personnel
Author: Anton G Leitner
Founded: 1992
Subjects: Education, Literature, Literary Criticism, Essays, Mathematics, Poetry
ISBN Prefix(es): 3-929433
Distributor for Initiative Junger Autoren eV
Foreign Rep(s): Manford Chobot (Austria); Dr Margit Ohuhumma; Markus Hedigo; Jean Portank

Verlag Otto Lembeck+
Gaertnerweg 16, 60322 Frankfurt am Main
Tel: (069) 5970988 *Fax:* (069) 5975742
E-mail: verlag@lembeck.de
Web Site: www.lembeck.de *Cable:* LEMBECKDRUCK FRANKFURTMAIN
Key Personnel
Contact: Dr Wolfgang Neumann
Founded: 1945
Subjects: Religion - Protestant, Religion - Other
ISBN Prefix(es): 3-87476
Warehouse: Stuttgarter Verlagskontor, Expedition Westrampe, Fritz-Klett-Str 61-65, 71404 Korb
Orders to: Stuttgarter Verlagskontor, Rotebuehlstr 77, 70178 Stuttgart, Ingelborg Hoepner *Tel:* (0711) 66721604 *Fax:* (0711) 66724974 *E-mail:* lhoepner@svk.de

Lentz Verlag+
Subsidiary of Buchverlage Langen-Mueller/Herbig
Thomas-Wimmer-Ring 11, 80539 Munich
Tel: (089) 290880 *Fax:* (089) 29088-144
E-mail: l.eggs@herbig.net
Web Site: www.herbig.net
Key Personnel
Man Dir & Publisher: Brigitte Fleissner-Mikorey
Rights & Permissions: Frauke Hoppen *Fax:* (089) 29088178; Dorothea Estermann *Fax:* (089) 29088154
Founded: 1953
Buchverlage Langen Mueller Herbig.
Subjects: Fiction, Nonfiction (General)
ISBN Prefix(es): 3-88010
Total Titles: 10 Print
Distributed by Mohr Morawa Buchvertrieb; Schweizer Buchzentrum
Warehouse: VVA-Bertelsmann Distribution GmbH, Warenannahme 100, An der Autobahn, 33310 Guetersloh
Orders to: VVA-Vereinigte, Postfach 7600, 33310 Guetersloh, Mr Borgartz *Tel:* (05241) 805403 *Fax:* (05241) 806643

Dr Gisela Lermann+
Am Heiligenhaus 18, 55122 Mainz
Tel: (06131) 31149 *Fax:* (06131) 387945
Web Site: www.lermann-verlag.de
Key Personnel
Owner & Dir: Dr Gisela Lermann *E-mail:* dr-gisela-lermann@lermann-verlag.de
Founded: 1988
Subjects: Biography, Fiction, Government, Political Science, Human Relations, Literature, Literary Criticism, Essays, Mysteries, Nonfiction (General), Philosophy, Poetry, Psychology, Psychiatry, Romance, Women's Studies
ISBN Prefix(es): 3-927223
Shipping Address: Herold Verlagsauslieferung, Kolpringring 4, 82041 Oberhaching *Tel:* (089) 6138710 *Fax:* (089) 61387120 *E-mail:* herold-oberhaching@t-online.de
Warehouse: Herold Verlagsauslieferung, Kolpringring 4, 82041 Oberhaching *Tel:* (089) 6138710 *Fax:* (089) 61387120 *E-mail:* herold-oberhaching@t-online.de
Orders to: Herold Verlagsauslieferung, Kolpringring 4, 82041 Oberhaching *Tel:* (089) 6138710 *Fax:* (089) 61387120 *E-mail:* herold-oberhaching@t-online.de

Verlag Leske plus Budrich GmbH+
Gerhart-Hauptmannstr 27, 51379 Leverkusen
Mailing Address: Postfach 300551, 51334 Leverkusen
Tel: (02171) 4907-0 *Fax:* (02171) 4907-11
E-mail: leske-budrich@t-online.de
Web Site: www.leske-budrich.de
Key Personnel
Man Dir: Edmund Budrich
Founded: 1974
Subjects: Career Development, Education, Environmental Studies, Government, Political Science, Philosophy, Psychology, Psychiatry, Social Sciences, Sociology, Women's Studies
ISBN Prefix(es): 3-8100
Number of titles published annually: 300 Print; 300 E-Book
Total Titles: 2,200 CD-ROM; 2,200 E-Book
Associate Companies: UTB
Shipping Address: Brockhaus Commission, Kreidlerstr 9, D-70806 Kornwestheim
Warehouse: Brockhaus Commission, Kreidlerstr 9, 70806 Kornwestheim
Orders to: Brockhaus Commission, Kreidlerstr 9, 70806 Kornwestheim

Lettre International Kulturzeitung+
Rosenthalerstr 13, 10119 Berlin
Tel: (030) 30870440; (030) 30870462 *Fax:* (030) 2833128
E-mail: lettre@lettre.de
Web Site: www.lettre.de
Key Personnel
Editor-in-Chief: Frank Berberich
Founded: 1988
Subjects: Ethnicity, Government, Political Science, Literature, Literary Criticism, Essays

LEU-VERLAG Wolfgang Leupelt+
Herweg 34, 51429 Bergisch Gladbach
Tel: (02204) 981141 *Fax:* (02204) 981143
E-mail: info@leu-verlag.net; leuverlag@aol.com
Web Site: www.leu-verlag.net
Key Personnel
Publisher: Wolfgang Leupelt
Founded: 1990
Specialize in music play along books with CD.
Subjects: Education, Music, Dance, Sheet Music, Music Education Books with CD
ISBN Prefix(es): 3-928825; 3-89775
Number of titles published annually: 10 Print; 5 Audio
Total Titles: 100 Print; 20 Audio

Leuchter-Verlag EG+
Industriestr 6-8, 64390 Erzhausen
Mailing Address: Postfach 1161, 64386 Erzhausen
Tel: (06150) 97 36 20 *Fax:* (06150) 6155
Key Personnel
Man Dir, Sales, Rights & Permissions: Karl-Heinz Neumann
Founded: 1946
Subjects: Religion - Other
ISBN Prefix(es): 3-87482

Verlag Gerald Leue+
Kanzlerweg 24, 12101 Berlin
Tel: (030) 7865020 *Fax:* (030) 78913876
E-mail: vertrieb@leue-verlag.de
Web Site: www.leue.purespace.de
Key Personnel
Publisher: Gerald Leue
Founded: 1982
Subjects: How-to, Humor
ISBN Prefix(es): 3-923421

Libertas- Europaeisches Institut GmbH+
Untere Vorstadt 11, 71063 Sindelfingen
Mailing Address: Postfach 5 67, 71047 Sindelfingen
Tel: (07031) 6186-80 *Fax:* (07031) 6186-86
E-mail: info@libertas-institut.com
Web Site: www.libertas-institut.com
Key Personnel
President: Hans-Juergen Zahorka *E-mail:* hj.zahorka@libertas-institut.com
Man Dir: Ute Hirschburger *E-mail:* ute.hirschburger@libertas-institut.com
Founded: 1976
Think-tank on European & international economy & politics with publication division.
Subjects: Business, Developing Countries, Economics, Environmental Studies, Fiction, Finance, Government, Political Science, History, Law, Management, Nonfiction (General), Philosophy, Regional Interests, Social Sciences, Sociology, Transportation
ISBN Prefix(es): 3-921929
Number of titles published annually: 20 Print; 5 CD-ROM; 5 Audio
Total Titles: 50 Print; 2 CD-ROM

Edition Libri Illustri GmbH+
Neissestr 31, 71638 Ludwigsburg
Tel: (07141) 84720 *Fax:* (07141) 875117
E-mail: libri.illustri@t-online.de
Web Site: www.edition-libri-illustri.de
Key Personnel
Publisher: Peter Teicher
Founded: 1987
Subjects: History, Religion - Other, Nuremberg Chronicle, Aesopus, Apocalypsis
ISBN Prefix(es): 3-927506
Number of titles published annually: 1 Print
Total Titles: 8 Print; 1 Audio

Online services available through Mondia.
U.S. Office(s): Peter KeLehnert, 510 W Forest Dr, Houston, TX, United States

Edition Lidiarte
Knesebeckstr 13/14, 10623 Berlin
Tel: (030) 3137420 *Fax:* (030) 3127117
E-mail: edition@lidiarte.de
Web Site: www.lidiarte.de
Key Personnel
President: Dieter Marx
Founded: 1980
Specialize in architectural posters & postcards.
Subjects: Architecture & Interior Design
Number of titles published annually: 10 Print
Total Titles: 200 Print

Hildegard Liebaug-Dartmann+
J Sebastian Bach Weg 15, 53340 Meckenheim
Tel: (02225) 909343 *Fax:* (02225) 909345
E-mail: liebaug-dartmann@t-online.de
Web Site: www.liebaug-dartmann.de
Key Personnel
Owner: Hildegard Liebaug-Dartmann
Founded: 1982
Member of Boersenveriene des Deutschen Buchhandels.
Subjects: Physics, German as a Foreign Language
ISBN Prefix(es): 3-922989

Liebenzeller Mission, GmbH, Abt. Verlag+
Liobastr 8, 75378 Bad Liebenzell
Mailing Address: Postfach 1265, 75375 Bad Liebenzell
Tel: (07052) 17-163 *Fax:* (07052) 17-170
Key Personnel
Publishing Dir: Arthur Klenk
Founded: 1906
Member of the Telos paperback series publishing group; also produce Games & Radio Games for Children.
Subjects: Biography, Fiction, Theology
ISBN Prefix(es): 3-88002
Orders to: Ausl Edition VLM, Postfach 5, 7630 Lahr, Johannis Lahr *Tel:* (07821) 581-32 *Fax:* (07821) 581-26

Robert Lienau GmbH & Co KG
Strubbergstr 80, 60489 Frankfurt
Tel: (069) 9782866 *Fax:* (069) 97828689
E-mail: info@lienau-frankfurt.de
Web Site: www.lienau-frankfurt.de
Key Personnel
Manager: Cornelia Grossmann; Michael Voily
Founded: 1810
Music publisher.
Subjects: Drama, Theater, Music, Dance
ISBN Prefix(es): 3-87484

Lienhard Pallast Verlag
Stoeckerfeld 7, 53773 Hennef
Tel: (02244) 5863
Web Site: www.pallast-publisher.com
Subjects: Literature, Literary Criticism, Essays, Poetry

Limpert Verlag+
Industriepark 3, 56291 Wiebelsheim
Tel: (06766) 903160 *Fax:* (06766) 903320
E-mail: vertrieb@limpert.de
Telex: 0418135 limp
Key Personnel
Man Dir, Rights & Permissions: Dr Irmgard Meissl *Tel:* (06766) 903242 *Fax:* (06766) 903360 *E-mail:* meissl@aula-verlag.de
Founded: 1921
Subjects: Sports, Athletics
ISBN Prefix(es): 3-7853
Bookshop(s): Humanitas Buchversand

J Lindauer Verlag+
Kaunfingerstr 16, 80331 Munich
Mailing Address: Postfach 626, 80066 Munich
Tel: (089) 223041 *Fax:* (089) 224315
E-mail: lindauerverlag@t-online.de
Web Site: www.lindauer-verlag.de
Key Personnel
Owner, Rights & Permissions: Renate Schaefer
ISBN Prefix(es): 3-87488

Lindemann, H, Buchhandlung
Nadlerstr 4, 70173 Stuttgart
Mailing Address: Postfach 103051, 70027 Stuttgart
Tel: (0711) 24899977 *Fax:* (0711) 2369672
Web Site: www.lindemanns-buchhandlung.de

Linden-Verlag+
Kasseler Str 25, 04155 Leipzig
Tel: (0341) 5902024 *Fax:* (0341) 5904436
E-mail: lindenbuch@aol.com
Web Site: www.linden-buch.de
Key Personnel
International Rights: Thomas Loest
Founded: 1989
Specialize in books by Buecher von Erich Loest.
ISBN Prefix(es): 3-9802139; 3-86152

Martha Lindner Verlags-GmbH+
Jahnstr 22, 76133 Karlsruhe
Tel: (0721) 843965 *Fax:* (0721) 843965
Key Personnel
Manager: Martha Lindner
Founded: 1975
Subjects: Music, Dance, Science (General), Theology
ISBN Prefix(es): 3-921653

Christoph Links Verlag - LinksDruck GmbH+
KulturBrauerei, Schonhauser Allee 36, 10435 Berlin
Tel: (030) 440232-0 *Fax:* (030) 44023229
E-mail: mail@linksverlag.de
Web Site: www.linksverlag.de
Key Personnel
Publisher: Christopher Links
Founded: 1990
Subjects: Biography, Government, Political Science, History
ISBN Prefix(es): 3-86153
Orders to: Cornelsen Verlags Kontor CVK, Kammerratsheide 66, 33609 Bielefeld 1

Siegbert Linnemann Verlag+
Ohlbrocksweg 61, 33330 Guetersloh
Tel: (05241) 14061 *Fax:* (05241) 26439
E-mail: info@linnemann-verlag.com; slinnem477@aol.com; sl@linnemann-verlag.com
Web Site: www.linnemann-verlag.com
Founded: 1986
Specialize in travel picture wall calendars.
Subjects: Geography, Geology, Travel
ISBN Prefix(es): 3-926466; 3-89523
Number of titles published annually: 90 Print
U.S. Office(s): Sormani Calendars, Box 6059, Chelsea, MA, United States *Tel:* 617-387-7300 *Fax:* 617-387-6379

LIT Verlag+
Grevenerstr 179, 48159 Muenster
Tel: (0251) 235091 *Fax:* (0251) 231972
E-mail: lit@lit-verlag.de
Web Site: www.lit-verlag.de
Key Personnel
Man Dir & International Rights: Dr Wilhelm Hopf
Founded: 1981
Subjects: Art, Asian Studies, Economics, Ethnicity, Fashion, Public Administration, Science (General), Social Sciences, Sociology

ISBN Prefix(es): 3-88660; 3-89473; 3-8258
Subsidiaries: Lll Verlag Muenster-Hamburg
U.S. Office(s): c/o J. Bach, 610 W 115 St, No 53B, New York, NY 10025, United States
Tel: (212) 666-7674 *Fax:* (212) 666-7674

Henry Litolff's Verlag, *imprint of* C F Peters Musikverlag GmbH & Co KG

Rainer Loessl Verlag
Johann-Fichtestr 11, 80805 Munich
Tel: (089) 362646
ISBN Prefix(es): 3-9800376

Loewe Verlag GmbH & Co KG+
Buehlstr 4, 95463 Bindlach
Mailing Address: Postfach 1101, 95461 Bindlach
Tel: (0920) 8510 *Fax:* (0920) 8309
Web Site: www.loewe-verlag.de
Telex: 920882
Key Personnel
Publisher & Man Dir: Volker Gondrom
Editorial: Alexandra Borisch; Christiane Duering
Publicity, Sales Dir: Hajo Schwabe
Foreign Rights Manager: Jeannette Hammerschmidt *Tel:* (09208) 51202
Founded: 1863
ISBN Prefix(es): 3-7855

Logophon Lehrmittelverlag GmbH+
Affiliate of Euro-Schulen-Organisation
Alte Gaertnerei 2, 55128 Mainz
Tel: (06131) 71645 *Fax:* (06131) 72596
E-mail: verlag@logophon.de
Web Site: www.logophon.de
Founded: 1979
Subjects: Business, English as a Second Language, Human Relations, Language Arts, Linguistics
ISBN Prefix(es): 3-922514
Number of titles published annually: 8 Print
Total Titles: 80 Print; 2 CD-ROM

Logos Verlag GmbH+
Ehlenbrucherstr 96, 32791 Lage
Tel: (05232) 960120 *Fax:* (05232) 960121
Key Personnel
Manager: Johannes Reimer
Purchasing, Sales Manager: Andreas Bergen
Founded: 1989
Christian books in German and Russian.
Subjects: History, Religion - Protestant, Theology, Autobiography, Memoirs, Letters, Bibliography
ISBN Prefix(es): 3-927767; 3-933828

Logos-Verlag Literatur & Layout GmbH+
Auf der Adt 14 Villa Fledermaus, 66130 Saarbruecken
Tel: (06893) 986096 *Fax:* (06893) 986095; (06893) 374443
Key Personnel
Publisher: Friedhelm Schneidecrond
Founded: 1983
Subjects: Biological Sciences, Fiction, Geography, Geology, Literature, Literary Criticism, Essays, Mysteries, Nonfiction (General), Poetry, Regional Interests, Science Fiction, Fantasy, Social Sciences, Sociology
ISBN Prefix(es): 3-928598

Lokrundschau Verlag GmbH
Geesthachterstr 28a, 21483 Gulzow
Mailing Address: Postfach 80 01 07, 21001 Hamburg
Tel: (04151) 8 28 89 *Fax:* (04151) 8 28 89
E-mail: verlag@lokrundschau.de
Web Site: www.lokrundschau.de
Founded: 1995
Subjects: Specialize in books about German Railway & journals
ISBN Prefix(es): 3-931647

PUBLISHERS   GERMANY

Stefan Loose Verlag+
Zossenerstr 55/2, 10961 Berlin
Tel: (030) 6 91 37 89 *Fax:* (030) 6 93 01 71
E-mail: info@loose-verlag.de
Web Site: www.loose-verlag.de
Key Personnel
President: Renate Ramb
Publisher: Stefan Loose
Founded: 1978
Subjects: Travel
ISBN Prefix(es): 3-922025

Lorber-Verlag & Turm-Verlag Otto Zluhan
Hindenburgstr 5, 74321 Bietigheim
Mailing Address: Postfach 1851, 74308 Bietigheim-Bissingen
Tel: (07142) 940843 *Fax:* (07142) 940844 *Cable:* LORBER, BIETIGHEIM
Key Personnel
Man Dir, Publisher, Rights & Permissions: Friedrich Zluhan
Founded: 1854
Subjects: Parapsychology, Religion - Other
ISBN Prefix(es): 3-87495

Johannes Loriz Verlag der Kooperative Duernau
Im Winkel 11, 88422 Duernau
Tel: (07582) 93000 *Fax:* (07582) 930020
E-mail: kooperative-duernau.rt@eunet.de
Web Site: www.kooperative.de
Key Personnel
Owner: Johannes Loriz
Subjects: Natural History
ISBN Prefix(es): 3-88861

Verlag an der Lottbek+
Susterfedlstr 83, 52072 Aachen
Tel: (0241) 873434 *Fax:* (0241) 875577
Key Personnel
Editor: Peter Jensen
Founded: 1988
Member of the Stock Exchange of German Booksellers.
Subjects: Science (General)
ISBN Prefix(es): 3-926987; 3-86130
Subsidiaries: Edition Hathor
Divisions: Belletriotik
Showroom(s): Bundes Str 74, 2000 Hamburg 13
Warehouse: Bundes Str 74, 2000 Hamburg 13

Antiquariat Oskar Loewe
Subsidiary of Latvijas Nacionala Biblioteka, LV-Riga
Sauerbruchstr 8d, 45661 Recklinghausen-Sued
Tel: (02361) 960813 *Fax:* (02361) 960815
E-mail: loewe.bochum@t-online.de
Web Site: www.antiquariat.net/loewe
Founded: 1876
Subjects: News, Old Books
Distributed by Zentralverzeichnis Antiquarischer Buecher (ZVAB)

Hermann Luchterhand Verlag GmbH
Heddesdorfer Str 31, 56564 Neuwied
Mailing Address: Postfach 2352, 56513 Neuwied
Tel: (02631) 8010 *Fax:* (02631) 801210
E-mail: info@luchterhand.de
Web Site: www.luchterhand.de
Key Personnel
Man Dir: Juergen M Luczak *Tel:* (02631) 801-330 *Fax:* (02631) 801-225 *E-mail:* juergen.luczak@luchterhand.de
Pubn Man: Elke Richter-Weiland *Tel:* (02631) 801-264 *Fax:* (02631) 801-353 *E-mail:* elke.richter-weiland@luchterhand.de; Stefan Wiemuth *Tel:* (06192) 408-229 *Fax:* (06192) 408-248 *E-mail:* 100537.357@compuserve.com; Rainer Joede *Tel:* (06192) 408-200 *Fax:* (06192) 408-248 *E-mail:* rainer.joede@dwd-verlag.de; Rainer Winkler *Tel:* (02631)

801-232 *Fax:* (02631) 801-204; Walter Kastor *Tel:* (02631) 801-239 *Fax:* (02631) 801-415 *E-mail:* walter.kastor@luchterhand.de
Sales Man: Erminold Malzbender *Tel:* (02631) 801-318 *Fax:* (02631) 801-381
Contact: Evelin Gerlach *Tel:* (02631) 801 275 *Fax:* (02631) 801 225 *E-mail:* evelin.gerlach@luchterhand.de
Founded: 1924
Subjects: Business, Education, Law, Management
ISBN Prefix(es): 3-472
Parent Company: Wolters Kluwer Deutschland GmbH
Ultimate Parent Company: Wolters Kluwer NV, Netherlands
Imprints: Kommentator; Alfred Metzner
Subsidiaries: Werner Verlag GmbH & Co KG
Divisions: Fachverlag Deutscher Wirtschaftsdienst GmbH, Koeln
Branch Office(s)
Pestalozzistr 5-8 13187, Berlin *Tel:* (030) 48839011 *Fax:* (030) 48839020
Gutenbergstr 8, Kriftel *Tel:* (06192) 4080 *Fax:* (06192) 408248

Luchterhand Literaturverlag GmbH/Verlag Volk & Welt GmbH+
Langerstr 2, 81673 Munich
Tel: (089) 4372-2751 *Fax:* (089) 21215250
E-mail: info@luchterhand.com
Key Personnel
Owner: Dietrich von Boetticher
Publisher: Gerald J Trageiser
Founded: 1924
Subjects: Fiction, Literature, Literary Criticism, Essays, Nonfiction (General)
ISBN Prefix(es): 3-630; 3-8090
Number of titles published annually: 50 Print
Total Titles: 500 Print
Parent Company: Verlagsgruppe Random House GmbH
Ultimate Parent Company: Bertelsmann AG
Distributor for Gerhard Wolf Janus Press
Orders to: Vereinigte Verlagsauslieferung, An der Autobahn, 33310 Guetersloh

Lucius & Lucius Verlagsgesellschaft mbH+
Gerokstr 51, 70184 Stuttgart
Tel: (0711) 242060 *Fax:* (0711) 242088
E-mail: lucius@luciusverlag.com
Web Site: www.luciusverlag.com
Key Personnel
Publisher: Dr Wulf D von Lucius
Founded: 1996
Specialize in academic books & journals in economics, social sciences & sociology; research monographs & proceedings.
Privately owned; Member of Borsenverein & STM.
Subjects: Economics, Social Sciences, Sociology
ISBN Prefix(es): 3-8282
Number of titles published annually: 35 Print
Total Titles: 420 Print
Warehouse: Brockhaus/Commission, Kreidlerstr 9, 70803 Kornwestheim, Contact: Mrs Rother *Tel:* (07154) 132737 *Fax:* (07154) 132713 *E-mail:* bro@brockhaus-commission.de (Orders)

Luebbe Audio, *imprint of* Verlagsgruppe Luebbe GmbH & Co KG

Gustav Luebbe Verlag, *imprint of* Verlagsgruppe Luebbe GmbH & Co KG

Gustav Luebbe Verlag+
Scheidtbachstr 23-31, 51469 Bergisch Gladbach
Mailing Address: Postfach 200180, 51431 Bergisch Gladbach
Tel: (02202) 121-0 *Fax:* (02202) 121-920
E-mail: info@luebbe.de

Web Site: www.luebbe.de
Key Personnel
Man Dir: Peter E Molden; Dr Peter Roggen
Editor-in-Chief, Paperback Books: Anja Kleinlein
Editorial: Daniela Bentele-Hendricks; Elmar Klupsch; Helmut Feller; Dr Helmut Pesch
Sales: Hans-Jochen Mundt
Advertising: Schmidt Udo
Press & Publicity: Barbara Fischer
Rights & Permissions: Christian Stuewe
Editor: Rolf Schmitz
Founded: 1963
Subjects: Archaeology, Biography, Fiction, History, How-to, Nonfiction (General)
ISBN Prefix(es): 3-404; 3-7857
Ultimate Parent Company: Verlagsgruppe Luebbe GmbH & Co KG
Associate Companies: Bastei Verlag

Verlagsgruppe Luebbe GmbH & Co KG+
Scheidtbachstr 23-31, 51469 Bergisch Gladbach
Mailing Address: Postfach 200180, 51431 Bergisch Gladbach
Tel: (02202) 121-0 *Fax:* (02202) 121-920; (02202) 121-933
E-mail: info@luebbe.de; info@bastei.de
Web Site: www.luebbe.de; www.bastei.de
Founded: 1953
Subjects: Biography, Fiction, Nonfiction (General), Romance
ISBN Prefix(es): 3-404; 3-431; 3-7857
Imprints: Bastei Luebbe Taschenbuecher; Bastei Verlag; BLT; editionLuebbe; Ehrenwirth Verlag; Luebbe Audio; Gustav Luebbe Verlag

Alf Luechow Verlag, *imprint of* Verlagsgruppe Dornier

Lukas Verlag fur Kunst- und Geistesgeschichte
Kollwitzstr 57, 10405 Berlin
Tel: (030) 44049220 *Fax:* (030) 4428177
E-mail: lukas.verlag@t-online.de
Web Site: www.lueasverlag.com
Key Personnel
Contact: Dr Frank Bottcher
Founded: 1995
Subjects: Archaeology, History, Philosophy, Social Sciences, Sociology, Specialize in art history, cistercians, medieval art & GDR
Total Titles: 30 Print

Lusatia Verlag-Dr Stuebner & Co KG+
Toepferstr 35, 02625 Bautzen
Tel: (049) 532400; (049) 532401 *Fax:* (049) 532400
E-mail: lusatiaverlag@t-online.de
Founded: 1992
Member of the Association of German Booksellers.
Subjects: Art, Fiction, Regional Interests, Travel
ISBN Prefix(es): 3-929091
Number of titles published annually: 10 Print
Total Titles: 100 Print
Distributor for Domowina-Verlag

Luther-Verlag GmbH+
Cansteinstr 1, 33647 Bielefeld
Mailing Address: Postfach 140380, 33623 Bielefeld
Tel: (0521) 94 40-137 *Fax:* (0521) 94 40-136
E-mail: vertrieb@luther-verlag.de
Web Site: www.ekvw.de/pressehaus/lv/
Telex: 937325 epdgi
Key Personnel
Man Dir, Rights & Permissions: Wolfgang Riewe
Founded: 1911
Subjects: Religion - Protestant
ISBN Prefix(es): 3-7858

Lutherische Verlagsgesellschaft mbH
Fleethoern 32, 24103 Kiel
Tel: (0431) 51970 *Fax:* (0431) 5197292

259

Key Personnel
Manager: Rainer Thun
Founded: 1956
Subjects: Regional Interests, Theology
ISBN Prefix(es): 3-87503
Parent Company: Evangelischer Presseverband Nord ev, Postfach 3466, 24033 Kiel

Lutherisches Verlagshaus GmbH+
Knochenhauerstr 38-40, 30159 Hannover
Mailing Address: Postfach 3849, 30038 Hannover
Tel: (0511) 1241-716 *Fax:* (0511) 1241-705
E-mail: lvh@lvh.de
Web Site: www.lvh.de
Telex: 922686
Key Personnel
Man Dir, Rights & Permissions: Klaus Woehleke
General Manager: Werner Sass
Management: Dr Hasko von Bassi *Tel:* (0511) 1241 720 *Fax:* (0511) 3681098
Marketing: Carsten Krabbes *Tel:* (0511) 1241-726 *Fax:* (0511) 3681098; (0511) 3 68 10 98
Sales: Andrea Roecher *Fax:* (0511) 3 68 10 98
Advertising: Hannelore Splitt *Tel:* (0511) 1241 710 *Fax:* (0511) 3681098
Founded: 1948
Subjects: Religion - Other, Theology
ISBN Prefix(es): 3-7859
Distributed by CVK Cornelsen Verlagskontor Gmbh & Co KG (Germany); Felix A Gaugler (Switzerland)
Orders to: Cornelsen Verlagskontor, Kammeratsheide 66, 4800 Bielefeld 1

Verlag Waldemar Lutz
Baslerstr 130, 79540 Loerrach
Tel: (07621) 8812 *Fax:* (07621) 12599
E-mail: wlutz@lutz-die-buchhandlung.de
Web Site: www.verlag-lutz.de
Key Personnel
Man Dir, Rights & Permissions: Waldemar Lutz
Founded: 1978
Subjects: Literature, Literary Criticism, Essays, Regional Interests
ISBN Prefix(es): 3-922107
Bookshop(s): Lutz-Die Buchhandlung, Tumringer Str 179, D-79540 Loerrach

Karin Mader
Mittelsmoorerstr 80, 28879 Grasberg
Tel: (04208) 556 *Fax:* (04208) 3429
E-mail: mader@mader-verlag.de
Web Site: www.mader-verlag.de
Founded: 1978
Subjects: Travel
ISBN Prefix(es): 3-921957
Distributed by VAH Jager Verlagsauslieferung
Orders to: VAH Jager Varlagsauslieferung, Postfach 3248, 10729 Berlin

Maeander Verlag GmbH+
Diepoltsberg 2, 84326 Falkenberg
Tel: (08727) 1657 *Fax:* (08727) 1569
Key Personnel
Man Dir, Rights & Permissions: Dr Renate Piel
Founded: 1977
Specialize in monographs & art history in general.
Subjects: Archaeology, Art, Philosophy
ISBN Prefix(es): 3-88219
Total Titles: 78 Print
Orders to: Koch, Neff und Oetinger & Co GmbH, Schockenriedstr 39, 80807 Stuttgart

Annemarie Maeger+
Ebertallee 6, 22607 Hamburg
Tel: (040) 8992480 *Fax:* (040) 8904475
E-mail: re@a-maeger-verlag.de
Web Site: www.a-maeger-verlag.de
Key Personnel
Contact: A Maeger

Founded: 1993
Subjects: Drama, Theater, History, Mathematics, Philosophy, Science (General), Theology, Women's Studies
ISBN Prefix(es): 3-929805

Magdalenen-Verlag GmbH
Gewerbering 14a, 83607 Holzkirchen
Mailing Address: Postfach 1154, 83601 Holzkirchen
Tel: (08024) 5051 *Fax:* (08024) 7064
E-mail: info@magdalenen-verlag.de
Web Site: www.magdalenen-verlag.de
Key Personnel
Manager: Clemens Kopp
ISBN Prefix(es): 3-930350; 3-9800186

Magnus Verlag+
Im Teelbruch 60-62, 45219 Essen
Mailing Address: Postfach 185528, 45205 Essen
Tel: (02054) 5080; (02054) 5094; (02327) 292 0 *Fax:* (02054) 83762
Key Personnel
Man Dir: Walter Stender
Rights & Permissions: Michael Salzwedel
ISBN Prefix(es): 3-88400; 3-920617

Karl Mahnke, Dierk Mahnke+
Grobestr 108, 27283 Verden
Mailing Address: Postfach 1507, 27265 Verden
Tel: (04231) 3011-0 *Fax:* (04231) 3011-11
E-mail: info@mahnke-verlag.de
Web Site: www.mahnke-verlag.de
Key Personnel
Owner: Dierk Mahnke
Founded: 1841
Specialize in Amateur Theater Publishing.
ISBN Prefix(es): 3-920613

Otto Maier Verlag, see Ravensburger Buchverlag Otto Maier GmbH

Mairs Geographischer Verlag+
Marco-Polo-Zentrum, 73760 Ostfildern
Mailing Address: Postfach 3151, 73760 Ostfildern
Tel: (0711) 45020 *Fax:* (0711) 4502340
E-mail: info@mairs.de
Web Site: www.mairs.de
Telex: 721796 *Cable:* MAIRVERLAG
Key Personnel
Man Dir: Dr Volkmar Mair
Sales Dir: Claus Benath
Founded: 1948
Subjects: Regional Interests, Travel
ISBN Prefix(es): 3-87504
Imprints: Baedeker; Marco Polo
Distributed by Fleischmann (Austria); Hallwag AG (Switzerland)
Distributor for ADAC Verlag

Mais Verlag GmbH und Reisefuehrer+
Quellenweg 10, 63303 Dreieich-Buchschlag
Tel: (06103) 62933 *Fax:* (06103) 64885
Key Personnel
Man & Sales Dir: Ingo Schmidt di Simoni; Marie-Luise Schmidt di Simoni
Founded: 1951
Member of Stock Exchange of German Booksellers.
Subjects: Travel
ISBN Prefix(es): 3-87936
Warehouse: VVA Bertelsmann Distribution, 33310 Guetersloh
Orders to: Geo Center Verlagsvertrieb, Neumarkterstr 18, 81673 Munich

Malik Verlag, *imprint of* Piper Verlag GmbH

Manholt Verlag+
Fedelhoeren 88, 28203 Bremen

Tel: (0421) 32 35 94 *Fax:* (0421) 3 36 54 63
E-mail: manholtverlag@t-online.de
Web Site: www.manholt.de
Key Personnel
Editor, Rights & Permissions: Dr Dirk Hemjeoltmanns
Founded: 1985
Publishes French Literature in German.
ISBN Prefix(es): 3-924903

Gebr Mann Verlag GmbH & Co+
Zimmerstr 26-27, Berlin 10969
Mailing Address: Postfach 11 03 03, 10833 Berlin
Tel: (030) 25913864; (030) 25913865 *Fax:* (030) 25913537
E-mail: vertrieb-kunstverlage@reimer-verlag.de
Key Personnel
Man Dir, Rights & Permissions: Holger Beer
Publishing Dir: Andreas A Catsch
Founded: 1917
Subjects: Archaeology, Architecture & Interior Design, Art, Crafts, Games, Hobbies, History
ISBN Prefix(es): 3-7861
Associate Companies: Deutscher Verlag fuer Kunstwissenschaft
Orders to: Koch, Neff & Oetinger & Co Verlagsauslieferung GmbH, Schockenriedstr 39, Postfach 800620, 70565 Stuttgart

Wolfgang Mann-Verlag GmbH+
Meinekestr 4, 10719 Berlin
Tel: (030) 8857210 *Fax:* (030) 89388420
Key Personnel
Manager: Hans Meisinger
Rights & Publicity: Christiane Schneider
Founded: 1986
Subjects: Nonfiction (General)
ISBN Prefix(es): 3-9267410
Orders to: MVS Meisinger Verlagsservice, Am Steinfeld 4, 94065 Waldkirchen *Tel:* (08581) 9605-0 *Fax:* (08581) 754

Mannerschwarm Skript Verlag Bartholomae & Co OHG+
Neuer Pferdemarkt 32, 20359 Hamburg
Tel: (040) 4302650 *Fax:* (040) 4302932
E-mail: verlag@maennerschwarm.de
Web Site: www.maennerschwarm.de
Key Personnel
Publisher: Joachim Bartholomae
Contact: Hans-Jurgen Koster
Founded: 1992
Subjects: Gay & Lesbian
ISBN Prefix(es): 3-928983
Imprints: Schwul Lesbische Studien Universitat Bremen
Shipping Address: So Va, Friesstr 20-24, D-60388 Frankfurt *Tel:* (069) 410 211 *Fax:* (069) 410 280
Warehouse: So Va, Friesstr 20-24, 60388 Frankfurt
Orders to: So Va, Friesstr 20-24, 60388 Frankfurt

Mansterschwarzacher Studien, *imprint of* Vier Tuerme GmbH Verlag Klosterbetriebe

Manutius Verlag+
Eselspfad 1, 69117 Heidelberg
Tel: (06221) 16 32 90 *Fax:* (06221) 16 71 43
E-mail: order@manutius-verlag.de
Web Site: www.manutius-verlag.de
Key Personnel
Publisher: Frank Wuerker
Founded: 1978
Subjects: Art, History, Literature, Literary Criticism, Essays, Music, Dance, Philosophy, Humanist, Jurisprudence, Political Science
ISBN Prefix(es): 3-925678; 3-934877
Total Titles: 80 Print

Manz G J Verlag und Druckerei+
Hermannstr 16, 70178 Stuttgart
Mailing Address: Postfach 103152, 70027 Stuttgart
Tel: (0711) 6151790 *Fax:* (0711) 6151791
Key Personnel
Dir, Publisher & Editorial: Lydia Franzelius
Founded: 1830
Subjects: Education
ISBN Prefix(es): 3-7863
Subsidiaries: Verlag J Pfeiffer; Erich Wewel Verlag
Orders to: Verlagsgruppe MANZ, AG, Anzingerstr 15, 81671 Munich

Marco Polo, *imprint of* Mairs Geographischer Verlag

Margraf Verlag
Laudenbacherstr 9, 97990 Weikersheim
Mailing Address: Postfach 1205, 97990 Weikersheim
Tel: (07934) 3071 *Fax:* (07934) 8156
E-mail: info@margraf-verlag.de
Web Site: www.margraf-verlag.de
Key Personnel
Contact: Dirk Hangstein *E-mail:* hangstein@margraf-verlag.de
Founded: 1985
Subjects: Agriculture, Biological Sciences, Developing Countries, Environmental Studies, Geography, Geology
ISBN Prefix(es): 3-8236; 3-924333
Associate Companies: Backhuys Publishers, PO Box 321, NL-2300 AH Leiden, Holland, Netherlands, Contact: Mike Ruijsenaars *Web Site:* www.backhuys.com
Distributed by DA Books & Journals

Edition Marhold
Gneisenaustr 33, 10961 Berlin
Mailing Address: Postfach 610494, 10928 Berlin
Tel: (030) 6917073 *Fax:* (030) 6914067
Key Personnel
Contact: Volker Spiess
Subjects: Disability, Special Needs
ISBN Prefix(es): 3-89166
Associate Companies: arani-verlag GmbH; Haude und Spenersche Verlagsbuchhandlung; Wissenschaftsverlag Volker Spiess GmbH

Edition Maritim GmbH+
Raboisen 8, 20095 Hamburg
Tel: (040) 3396670; (040) 339667-10 *Fax:* (040) 33966777
E-mail: edmaritim@aol.com
Key Personnel
Dir, Rights & Permissions: Frank Grube
Dir: Konrad Delius *Tel:* (0521) 559-210 *Fax:* (0521) 559-116 *E-mail:* info@delius-klasing.de
Founded: 1978
Subjects: Crafts, Games, Hobbies, Fiction, Maritime, Sports, Athletics, Transportation, Travel
ISBN Prefix(es): 3-922117; 3-89225
Online services available through www.delius-klasing.de.
Parent Company: Delius Klasing Verlag, Siekerwall 21, 33602 Bielefeld

Marketing & Wirtschaft Verlagsges, Flade & Partner mbH+
Elisabethstr 34, 80796 Munich
Tel: (089) 2713021; (089) 278134-0 *Fax:* (089) 2710156
Key Personnel
Publisher: Frido Flade
Chief Editor: Fabian Flade
Founded: 1979
Subjects: Economics, Energy
ISBN Prefix(es): 3-922804

Subsidiaries: Edition Wissen & Literatur
Warehouse: Revilak Verlags-Service, Gutenbergstr 5, 822056 Gilching

Markt & Technik, see Pearson Education Deutschland GmbH

Maro Verlag und Druck, Benno Kasmayr+
Riedingerstr 24, 86153 Augsburg
Tel: (0821) 416034 *Fax:* (0821) 416036
E-mail: maro.augsburg@gmx.de
Web Site: www.maroverlag.de
Key Personnel
Proprietor: Benno Kaesmayr
Founded: 1969
Subjects: Fiction, Poetry
ISBN Prefix(es): 3-87512
Number of titles published annually: 10 Print
Total Titles: 120 Print

Institut fuer Marxistische Studien und Forschungen eV (IMSF)
Koelnerstr 66, 60327 Frankfurt
Tel: (069) 7392934
Key Personnel
Honorary President: Juergen Reusch
Founded: 1968
ISBN Prefix(es): 3-88807

Mattes Verlag GmbH
Steigerweg 69, 69115 Heidelberg
Mailing Address: Postfach 103866, 69028 Heidelberg
Tel: (06221) 459321 *Fax:* (06221) 459322
E-mail: mattes@mattes.de
Web Site: www.mattes.de
Key Personnel
Publisher: Kurt Mattes *E-mail:* info@mattes.de
Founded: 1990
Subjects: Literature, Literary Criticism, Essays, Medicine, Nursing, Dentistry, Psychology, Psychiatry
ISBN Prefix(es): 3-9802440; 3-930978

Hugo Matthaes Druckerei und Verlag GmbH & Co KG
Olgastr 87, 70180 Stuttgart
Mailing Address: Postfach 103144, 70027 Stuttgart
Tel: (0711) 21 33 2 00 *Fax:* (0711) 2133 4 44
Web Site: www.matthaesdruck.de *Cable:* MATTHAESVERLAG
Key Personnel
Sales: Albert Pfeffer *Tel:* (0711) 2133 3 02 *E-mail:* a.pfeffer@matthaes.de; Karl-Heinz Suelzle *Tel:* (0711) 2133 3 24 *E-mail:* k.h.suelzle@matthaes.de
Customer Service: Bernd Decker *Tel:* (0711) 2133 2 83 *E-mail:* b.decker@matthaes.de; Rudolf Freudenberg *Tel:* (0711) 2133 2 93 *E-mail:* r.freudenberg@matthaes.de; Herbert Gollhofer *Tel:* (0711) 2133 3 01 *E-mail:* h.gollhofer@matthaes.de
Founded: 1905
Subjects: Cookery
Branch Office(s)
Frankfurt
Hamburg
Munich

Matthes und Seitz Verlag GmbH+
Huebnerstr 11, 80637 Munich
Mailing Address: Postfach 190624, 80606 Munich
Tel: (089) 1232510 *Fax:* (089) 187534
Key Personnel
Man Dir, Rights & Permissions: Axel Matthes
Founded: 1977
Subjects: Art, Fiction, History, Literature, Literary Criticism, Essays, Music, Dance, Philosophy, Poetry, Theology, autobiography, memoirs, letters
ISBN Prefix(es): 3-88221
Orders to: Koch, Neff & Oetinger, Postfach 800620, 70506 Stuttgart

Matthias-Gruenewald-Verlag GmbH
Member of Verlagsgruppe Engagement
Max Hufschmidtstr 4a, 55130 Mainz
Mailing Address: Postfach 3080, 55020 Mainz
Tel: (06131) 92860 *Fax:* (06131) 928626
E-mail: mail@gruenewaldverlag.de
Web Site: members.aol.com/matthgruen/
Key Personnel
Publisher: Josef Wagner
Publisher Editorial: Hiltraud Laubach
Man Dir: Josef Wagner
Sales Dir: Janine Glaesser
Production: Ellen Schneider
Publicity: Antje Weber
Founded: 1918
Subjects: Biography, Psychology, Psychiatry, Religion - Other, Theology
ISBN Prefix(es): 3-7867

Matthiesen Verlag Ingwert Paulsen Jr+
Nordbahnhofstr 2, 25813 Husum
Mailing Address: Postfach 1480, 25804 Husum
Tel: (04841) 83520 *Fax:* (04841) 835210
E-mail: info@verlagsgruppe.de
Web Site: www.verlagsgruppe.de
Key Personnel
Man Dir, Editorial, Rights & Permissions: Ingwert Paulsen,
Founded: 1892
Subjects: Science (General)
ISBN Prefix(es): 3-7868
Associate Companies: Hamburger Lesehefte Verlag Iselt & Co Nfl mbH; Hansa Verlag Ingwert Paulsen Jr; Husum Druck- und Verlagsgesellschaft mbH & Co KG; Verlag der Naticom

Hans K Matussek Buchhandlung & Antiquariat+
Marktstr 13, 41334 Nettetal
Tel: (02153) 91 64 30 *Fax:* (02153) 1 33 63
Web Site: www.buchkatalog.de/matussek
Key Personnel
Contact: Hans K Matussek; Fabian Matussek *E-mail:* fabian.matussek@t-online.de
Founded: 1961
ISBN Prefix(es): 3-920743

Matzker Verlag DiA
Konigstr 38A, 14109 Berlin
Mailing Address: Postfach 130193, 13601 Berlin
Tel: (030) 80604797
Key Personnel
Contact: Dr Reiner Matzker
Founded: 1985
Subjects: Art, Education, Fiction, Poetry
ISBN Prefix(es): 3-925789

Max Schimmel Verlag
lm Kreuz 9, 97076 Wurzburg
Mailing Address: Postfach 9444, 97094 Wurzburg
Tel: (0931) 27 91 400 *Fax:* (0931) 27 91 444
E-mail: info@schimmelverlag.de
Web Site: www.schimmelverlag.de
Subjects: Marketing
ISBN Prefix(es): 3-920834

Maximilian, *imprint of* Anton Hiersemann, Verlag

J A Mayersche Buchhandlung GmbH & Co KG Abt Verlag
Matthiashofstr 28-30, 52064 Aachen
Mailing Address: Postfach 467, 52005 Aachen
Tel: (0241) 4777 499 *Fax:* (0241) 4777 467
E-mail: info@mayersche.de

GERMANY

Web Site: www.mayersche.de *Cable:* MAYER AACHEN
Key Personnel
Man Dir, Publicity: Helmut Falter
Member of AWS-JASV.
Subjects: Regional Interests
ISBN Prefix(es): 3-87519
Branch Office(s)
Anlage, D-5100 Aachen
Bookshop(s): Ursulinerstr 17-19, 52062 Aachen *Tel:* (0241) 4777 0 *Fax:* (0241) 4777 167 *E-mail:* aachenurs@mayersche.de; Neumarkt 1B, 50667 Cologne; Hohe Str 68-82, 50667 Cologne; Kuhstr 33, 47051 Duisburg; Hindenburgstr 75, 41061 Moenchengladbach 1; Stresemannstr 43, 41236 Moenchengladbach 2; Bahnhofstr 55-65, 45879 Gelsenkirchen; Pontstr 131, 52062 Aachen *Tel:* (0241) 47494 0 *Fax:* (0241) 47494 1 *E-mail:* aachenth@mayersche.de

Mayr Miesbach Druckerei und Verlag GmbH
Am Windfeld 15, 83714 Miesbach
Mailing Address: Postfach 120, 83711 Miesbach
Tel: (08025) 294-0 *Fax:* (08025) 294-235
E-mail: gl@mayrmiesbach.de
Web Site: www.mayrmiesbach.de
Key Personnel
Man Dir, Sales & International Rights: Dieter Bergemann
Man Dir: Wilhelm Friedrich Mayr
Sales & International Rights: Oskar Amann
Parent Company: Schattauer GmbH - Verlag fuer Medizin und Naturwissenschaften, Hoelderlinstr 3, 70174 Stuttgart
Subsidiaries: Verlag Freizeit & Wassersport GmbH

Dr Norbert Meder & Co, see Janus Verlagsgesellschaft, Dr Norbert Meder & Co

Mediapress GmbH+
Hubertusstr 68, 47798 Krefeld
Tel: (02151) 79553334
Telex: 781217
Key Personnel
Man Dir, Rights & Permissions: Dieter Brinzer
Founded: 1982

Medico International eV
Obermainanlage 7, 60314 Frankfurt/Main
Tel: (069) 94438-0 *Fax:* (069) 436002
E-mail: info@medico.de
Web Site: www.medico.de
Telex: 416153 merco d
Key Personnel
Publishing: Juegen Waelthers
Founded: 1968
Subjects: Human Relations
ISBN Prefix(es): 3-923363

Medien-Verlag Bernhard Gregor GmbH+
Rosengasse 7, 36272 Niederaula
Tel: (06625) 5011; (0171) 7723972 *Fax:* (06625) 919743
E-mail: gregor-medien@t-online.de; mail@gregor-medien.de
Web Site: www.gregor-medien.de
Key Personnel
Man Dir: Bernhard Gregor
Founded: 1982
Subjects: Biography, Religion - Catholic, Theology
ISBN Prefix(es): 3-89150; 3-87391; 3-922770
Number of titles published annually: 3 Print
Total Titles: 60 Print
Distributed by Christiana (Switzerland)
Distributor for Verlag Johann Wilhelm Naumann GmbH (Germany)

Dornier Medienholding, see Verlagsgruppe Dornier

Medium-Buchmarkt+
Rosenstr 5-6, D-48143 Munster
Tel: (0251) 46 000 *Fax:* (0251) 46 745
E-mail: info@mediumbooks.com
Web Site: www.mediumbooks.com
Key Personnel
International Rights: Friedrich W Bitzhenner
Editorial: Carsten Schulte
Specialize in books on pop music.
Subjects: Music, Dance
ISBN Prefix(es): 3-933642

Medizinisch-Literarische Verlagsgesellschaft mbH+
Postfach 1151/1152, 29501 Uelzen
Tel: (0581) 808-150 *Fax:* (0581) 808-158
E-mail: ml.verlag.uelzen@t-online.de
Web Site: www.mlverlag.de *Cable:* ML-VERLAG 29525 UELZEN
Key Personnel
Chief: Heike Lodahl *E-mail:* h.lodahl@mlverlag.de
Man Dir, Rights & Permissions: Georg Graetz
Sales: Brigitte Burandt *Tel:* (0581) 80 81 51 *E-mail:* vertrieb@mlverlag.de
Publicity: Marlis Zipser-Jess *Tel:* (0581) 808-152
Administration: Anja Kueker *Tel:* (0581) 80 81 52 *E-mail:* anzeiger@mlverlag.de
Founded: 1957
Subjects: Alternative, Cookery, Health, Nutrition, Medicine, Nursing, Dentistry, Sports, Athletics
ISBN Prefix(es): 3-88136; 3-87522
Parent Company: C Beckers Buchdruckerei, 29525 Uelzen

Medpharm Scientific Publishers+
Birkenwaldstr 44, 70191 Stuttgart
Mailing Address: Postfach 101061, 70009 Stuttgart
Tel: (0711) 2582-0 *Fax:* (0711) 2582-290
E-mail: service@medpharm.de
Web Site: www.dav-buchhandlung.de
Key Personnel
Man Dir: Dr Klaus Brauer; R Hack; Dr Christian Rotta; Dr Thomas Schaber
Rights: Sabine Koerner
Contact: Siegmar Baver
Founded: 1981
Subjects: Medicine, Nursing, Dentistry, Pharmacy
ISBN Prefix(es): 3-88763
Parent Company: Deutscher Apotheker Verlag
Subsidiaries: S Hirzel Verlag GmbH & Co; Franz Steiner Verlag Wiesbaden GmbH; Wissenschaftliche Verlagsgesellschaft mbH

Felix Meiner Verlag GmbH+
Richardstr 47, 22081 Hamburg
Mailing Address: Postfach 760742, 22057 Hamburg
Tel: (040) 29 87 56-0 *Fax:* (040) 29 93 61-4
E-mail: info@meiner.de
Web Site: meiner.de
Key Personnel
Man Dir: Manfred Meiner *E-mail:* meiner@meiner.de
Rights, Marketing: Johannes Kambylis *Tel:* (040) 29 87 56-23 *E-mail:* kambylis@meiner.de
Founded: 1911
Member of the German Book Trade Association.
Subjects: Philosophy
ISBN Prefix(es): 3-7873
Subsidiaries: Helmut Buske Verlag GmbH

Meisenbach Verlag GmbH
Franz-Ludwig Str 7a, 96047 Bamberg
Tel: (0951) 861-0 *Fax:* (0951) 861-158
Web Site: www.meisenbach.de

BOOK

Key Personnel
Man Dir: Hans Limmer *E-mail:* geschltg@meisenbach.de
Founded: 1922
Subjects: Technology
ISBN Prefix(es): 3-87525

Otto Meissner Verlag+
Bingerstr 29, 14197 Berlin
Tel: (030) 8249558 *Fax:* (030) 8233338
Key Personnel
Dir, Rights & Permissions: Dieter Beuermann
Founded: 1848
Subjects: Crafts, Games, Hobbies, Human Relations, Nonfiction (General)
ISBN Prefix(es): 3-87527

Melsunger Medizinische Mitteilungen, *imprint of* Bibliomed - Medizinische Verlagsgesellschaft mbH

Idime Verlag Inge Melzer
Kienestr 37/1, 88045 Friedrichshafen
Tel: (07541) 55220 *Fax:* (07541) 55201
E-mail: idime@t-online.de
Key Personnel
Man Dir: Inge Melzer
Founded: 1983
Subjects: Anthropology, Foreign Countries
ISBN Prefix(es): 3-924026

Edition Axel Menges
Esslingerstr 24, 70736 Fellbach
Tel: (0711) 574759 *Fax:* (0711) 574784
Key Personnel
International Rights: Axel Menges *Tel:* (0711) 574753 *E-mail:* axelmenges@aol.com; Dorothea Dune *Tel:* (0711) 514753 *E-mail:* ddune@aol.com
Founded: 1994
Subjects: Architecture & Interior Design, Art, Film, Video, Photography, Travel
ISBN Prefix(es): 3-930698
Number of titles published annually: 20 Print
Total Titles: 10 Print
Associate Companies: Michal Robinson, 125 Stamford Court, Goldhawk Rd, London W6 OXE, United Kingdom *Tel:* (020) 8995 8340 *Fax:* (020) 8995 0113 *E-mail:* mrrobinson@compuserve.com

MenSana, *imprint of* Droemersche Verlagsanstalt Th Knaur Nachfolger GmbH & Co

Menschenkinder Verlag und Vertrieb GmbH+
An der Kleimannbruecke 97, 48157 Muenster
Tel: (0251) 9 32 52-0 *Fax:* (0251) 32 84 37
E-mail: info@menschenkinder.de
Web Site: www.menschenkinder.de
Key Personnel
Vice President: Wilm Weppelmann
Subjects: Music, Dance
ISBN Prefix(es): 3-927497

mentis Verlag GmbH
Schulze-Delitzschstr 19, 33100 Paderborn
Tel: (05251) 687902; (05251) 6879004 *Fax:* (05251) 687905
E-mail: info@mentis.de
Web Site: www.mentis.de
Founded: 1998
Subjects: Language Arts, Linguistics, Literature, Literary Criticism, Essays, Philosophy
ISBN Prefix(es): 3-89785
Number of titles published annually: 25 Print
Total Titles: 140 Print

Mentor-Verlag Dr Ramdohr KG+
Member of The Langenscheidt Group
Neusserstr 3, 80807 Munich

Mailing Address: Postfach 401120, 80711 Munich
Tel: (089) 360960 *Fax:* (089) 36096-222 (general); (089) 36096-258 (orders)
E-mail: mentor@langenscheidt.de
Key Personnel
Man Dirs: Karl Ernst Tielebier-Langenscheidt; Andreas Langenscheidt
Chief Editor: Dr Brigitte Abel
Sales Dir: Dr Matti Schusseler
Advertising: Brigitte Pasch
Founded: 1904
Sales & Promotion through Langenscheidt KG.
ISBN Prefix(es): 3-580

Mercator-Verlag, *imprint of* Gert Wohlfarth GmbH Verlag Fachtechnik & Mercator Verlag, Verlag Puppen & Spielzeug

Mergus Verlag GmbH Hans A Baensch+
Im Wiele 27, 49328 Melle
Mailing Address: Postfach 86, 49302 Melle
Tel: (05422) 3636 *Fax:* (05422) 1404
E-mail: mergus@t-online.de
Web Site: www.mergus.com *Cable:* MERGUS MELLE
Key Personnel
Man Dir, Rights & Permissions: Hans A Baensch
Founded: 1977
Subjects: Animals, Pets, Natural History
ISBN Prefix(es): 3-88244
Distributed by Rolf C Hagen Inc (Canada); Rolf C Hagen (UK) Ltd; ICA SA (Canary Islands, Spain); IMAZO OFF (Sweden); Microcosm Ltd (USA); Tetra Sales (Warner Lamber Co) (USA); Pet Pacific Pty Ltd (Australia); Primaris, Edizioni d'Accuariofilia (Italy); SAVAC Sa; Taikong Trading Corp (Taiwan)

Merian, *imprint of* Graefe und Unzer Verlag GmbH

Merit, *imprint of* Xenos Verlagsgesellschaft mbH

Merlin Verlag Andreas Meyer Verlags GmbH und Co KG+
Gifkendorf Nr 38, 21397 Vastorf
Tel: (04137) 7207 *Fax:* (04137) 7948
E-mail: info@merlin-verlag.de
Web Site: www.merlin-verlag.de
Key Personnel
Publisher: Andreas J Meyer
Sales Manager: Ilse K Meyer
Manager, Theater Dept: Lilli Nitsche
Junior Publisher, License & Press: Dr Katharina E Meyer
Founded: 1957
Subjects: Anthropology, Art, Biography, Drama, Theater, Fiction, Gay & Lesbian, Government, Political Science, Literature, Literary Criticism, Essays, Parapsychology, Philosophy, Poetry
ISBN Prefix(es): 3-87536; 3-926112
Number of titles published annually: 12 Print
Total Titles: 200 Print; 3 Audio
Associate Companies: Little Tiger Verlag GmbH, Poppenbuetteler Chausee 53, 22397 Hamburg

Verlag Merseburger Berlin GmbH+
Motzstr 9, 34117 Kassel
Mailing Address: Postfach 103880, 34038 Kassel
Tel: (0561) 789809-0 *Fax:* (0561) 789809-16
E-mail: info@merseburger.de; order@merseburger.de
Web Site: www.merseburger.de
Key Personnel
Contact: Corinne Votteler *Tel:* (0561) 78980311
 E-mail: corinne.votteler@merseburger.de
Founded: 1849
Specializes in sheet music & books.
Subjects: Music

ISBN Prefix(es): 3-87537
Online services available through World Wide Web.

Merve Verlag
Crellestr 22, 10827 Berlin
Tel: (030) 784 8433 *Fax:* (030) 788 1074
E-mail: merve@compuserve.com
Web Site: www.merve.de
Key Personnel
Man Dir, Rights & Permissions: Hans-Peter Gente; Heidi Paris
Founded: 1970
ISBN Prefix(es): 3-88396; 3-920986

Verlag fuer Messepublikationen, see Verlag fuer Messepublikationen Thomas Neureuter KG

Metropolis- Verlag fur Okonomie, Gesellschaft und Politik GmbH
Bahnhofstr 16a, 35037 Marburg
Tel: (06421) 67377 *Fax:* (06471) 681918
E-mail: info@metropolis-verlag.de
Web Site: www.metropolis-verlag.de
Key Personnel
Man Dir: Hubert Hoffmann *E-mail:* hoffman@metropolis-verlag.de
Founded: 1987
Subjects: Business, Economics, Environmental Studies, Government, Political Science, Philosophy, Social Sciences, Sociology
ISBN Prefix(es): 3-89518; 3-926570

Metropolitan Verlag+
Haus an der Eisemen Bruecke, 93042 Regensburg
Tel: (0941) 5684132 *Fax:* (0941) 5684111
E-mail: metropolitan@walhalla.de
Web Site: www.metropolitan.de
Key Personnel
Publisher: Eva-Maria Steckenleiter
 E-mail: walhalla@walhalla.de
Founded: 1995
Also specializing in rights.
Subjects: Economics
ISBN Prefix(es): 3-89623
Total Titles: 180 Print; 1 CD-ROM; 1 Online; 1 E-Book; 1 Audio

Karl-Heinz Metz
Josef-Hollerbachstr 14, 76571 Gaggenau
Tel: (07225) 74098 *Fax:* (07225) 74098
E-mail: metzverlag@aol.com
Web Site: www.metz-verlag.de
Key Personnel
Owner: Karl-Heinz Metz
Subjects: Animals, Pets, History, Mysteries, Social Sciences, Sociology, Children's (ages 1-7), Juvenile Fiction (ages 8-12), Young Adult/Teenager Fiction (ages 13-19)
ISBN Prefix(es): 3-927655

J B Metzler'sche Verlagsbuchhandlung+
Werastr 21-23, 70182 Stuttgart
Mailing Address: Postfach 103241, 70028 Stuttgart
Tel: (0711) 2194 0 *Fax:* (0711) 21942 49
E-mail: info@metzlerverlag.de
Web Site: www.metzlerverlag.de *Cable:* METZLERVERLAG STUTTGART
Key Personnel
Publisher: Dr Bernd Lutz *Tel:* (0711) 2194220
 E-mail: lutz@metzlerverlag.de; Ralf Mueller
 E-mail: mueller@metzlerverlag.de
Marketing & Sales Manager: Gerd Hexelschneider *Tel:* (0711) 2194 131
 E-mail: hexelschneider@metzlerveralg.de
Sales: Cornelia Kuehner *Tel:* (0711) 2194 136
 E-mail: kuehner@metzlerverlag.de
Advertising: Katia Tenholt *Tel:* (0711) 2194 132
 E-mail: tenholt@metzlerverlag.de

Adversting: Peter Then *Tel:* (0711) 2194 138
 E-mail: then@metzelerverlag.de
Licensing & Rights: Andrea Rupp *Tel:* (0711) 2194 225 *E-mail:* rupp@metzlerverlag.de
Press: Sabine Mattes *Tel:* (0711) 2194 227
 E-mail: matthes@metzerverlag.de
Electronic Publishing: Monika Johannsen
 Tel: (0711) 2194 228 *E-mail:* johannsen@metzlerverlag.de
Founded: 1682
Member of T R- Verlagsunion GmbH.
Subjects: Antiques, Art, Film, Video, History, Language Arts, Linguistics, Literature, Literary Criticism, Essays, Music, Dance, Philosophy
ISBN Prefix(es): 3-476
Number of titles published annually: 80 Print; 2 CD-ROM
Parent Company: Georg von Holtzbrinck GmbH & Co
Distributor for SFG - Servicecenter Fachverlage GmbH

Alfred Metzner, *imprint of* Hermann Luchterhand Verlag GmbH

Preubmpassling Verlag Gisela Meussling+
Dixstr 29, 53225 Bonn
Tel: (0228) 466347 *Fax:* (0228) 466347
Key Personnel
Man Dir, Rights & Permissions: Gisela Meussling
Founded: 1978
Subjects: Anthropology, History, Philosophy, Physical Sciences, Women's Studies, Esoterics/New Age, Ethnology
ISBN Prefix(es): 3-922129
Warehouse: Stiftsstr 39, 53225 Bonn

Meyer & Meyer Fachverlag und Buchhandel GmbH+
Von-Coels Str 390, 52080 Aachen
Tel: (0241) 95810-0 *Fax:* (0241) 95810-10
E-mail: verlag@m-m-sports.com
Web Site: www.m-m-sports.com
Key Personnel
Manager: Hans Juergen Meyer
Founded: 1984
Also acts as President of WSA (World Sportpublisher Association).
Subjects: Disability, Special Needs, Drama, Theater, Health, Nutrition, Music, Dance, Nonfiction (General), Sports, Athletics, Travel
ISBN Prefix(es): 3-89124; 1-84126
Number of titles published annually: 120 Print
Total Titles: 960 Print
Divisions: Aachener Buch Service
U.S. Office(s): Lewis International, 2201 NW 102 Pl, No 1, PO Box 5076, Miami, FL 33172, United States
Foreign Rep(s): Continental Sales (US)
Warehouse: Aachener Buch Service, Tempelhofer Str 21, 52068 Aachen

Edition Meyster, *imprint of* nymphenburger

MICHEL/Schwaneberger Verlag, see Schwaneberger Verlag GmbH

Gertraud Middelhauve Verlag GmbH & Co KG+
Lucile-Grahn Str 39, 81675 Munich
Tel: (089) 41 94 02-0 *Fax:* (089) 47 01 08-1
Key Personnel
Man Dir: Hans Meisinger
Rights & Publicity: Christiane Schneider
Founded: 1947
ISBN Prefix(es): 3-7876
Parent Company: Meisinger Verlagsgruppe
Orders to: MVS Meisinger Verlagsservice GmbH, Am Steinfeld 4, 94065 Waldkirchen
 Tel: (08581) 9605-0 *Fax:* (08581) 754

GERMANY

Midena Verlag+
Imprint of Weltbild Verlag GmbH
Steinerne Furt 67, 86167 Augsburg
Tel: (0821) 70040 *Fax:* (0821) 700479
Web Site: www.droemer.de
Key Personnel
Editorial Dir: Erhard Held
Rights & Permissions: Silke Breitlaender
Founded: 1981
Subjects: Child Care & Development, Cookery, Education, Health, Nutrition, Human Relations, Medicine, Nursing, Dentistry, Psychology, Psychiatry, Self-Help

Militzke Verlag+
Huttenstr 5, 04249 Leipzig
Tel: (0341) 42643-0 *Fax:* (0341) 42643-99
E-mail: info@militzke.de
Web Site: www.militzke.de
Key Personnel
Editorial: Dr Siegfried Kaetzel *E-mail:* lektorat@militzke.de
Public Relations, Press & Licensing: Christiane Voelkel *Tel:* (0341) 42643-20 *Fax:* (0341) 42643-26 *E-mail:* presse@militzke.de
Contact for Orders: Melitta Siebert *Tel:* (0341) 42643-12
Founded: 1990 (First privately founded publisher on former GDR territory since 1989)
National & international rights bought & sold, publication of textbooks & special interest hardcovers.
Independent Publisher & membership(s): German Publishers & Booksellers Association & Association of Publishers & Bookshops.
Subjects: Biography, Government, Political Science, Special Interest Hardcover, Authentic Criminal Cases, Historical & Political Popular Science & Detective Novels
ISBN Prefix(es): 3-86189
Number of titles published annually: 50 Print
Total Titles: 637 Print; 1 Audio

Milka, *imprint of* Egmont vgs verlagsgesellschaft mbH

Miranda-Verlag Stefan Ehlert+
Humboldtstr 145, 28203 Bremen
Mailing Address: PO Box 101021, 28010 Bremen
Tel: (0421) 7943226 *Fax:* (0421) 7943226
E-mail: miranda-verlag@t-online.de
Founded: 1997
Subjects: Biography, Literature, Literary Criticism, Essays
ISBN Prefix(es): 3-934790
Number of titles published annually: 2 Print
Total Titles: 6 Print

Missio eV Aachen+
Goethestr 43, 52064 Aachen
Mailing Address: Postfach 101248, 52012 Aachen
Tel: (0241) 75 07-00 *Fax:* (0241) 75 07-335
E-mail: info@missio-aachen.de
Web Site: www.missio-aachen.de
Telex: 832719 mira d
Subjects: Developing Countries, Religion - Catholic, Religion - Other
ISBN Prefix(es): 3-930556
Showroom(s): Missio, Goethestr 43, 52064 Aachen
Bookshop(s): Missio am Dom, Muensterplatz, 52064 Aachen
Warehouse: missio eV, Industriestr 12, 52146 Wuerselen

Missionshandlung
Harmsstr 6, 29320 Hermannsburg
Tel: (05052) 471 *Fax:* (05052) 30 82
E-mail: m-druckerei@t-online.de
Key Personnel
Contact: Hans Peter Schiebe; Wilfried Schulte

Founded: 1856
Subjects: Regional Interests
ISBN Prefix(es): 3-87546
Parent Company: Ev.luth Missionswerk in Niedersachsen (ELM)

Mitteilungsblatt der Verbandes deds bayerischen Druckincleestrie eV, *imprint of* Fachverlag fur das graphische Gewerbe GmbH

Mitteldeutscher Verlag GmbH+
Grosse Brauhausstr 18, 06108 Halle
Tel: (0345) 2 33 22-0 *Fax:* (0345) 2 33 22-66
E-mail: mitteldeutscher.verlag@t-online.de
Web Site: www.buecherkisten.de
Key Personnel
Man Dir: Veronika Schneides
Founded: 1946
Subjects: Art, Fiction, History, Literature, Literary Criticism, Essays, Nonfiction (General), Photography, Poetry, Regional Interests, Travel
ISBN Prefix(es): 3-354; 3-932776

E S Mittler und Sohn GmbH+
Striepenweg 31, 21147 Hamburg
Tel: (040) 7 97 13-03 *Fax:* (040) 79713324
Cable: MITTLER & SOHN, HERFORD/WESTF
Key Personnel
Publisher: Peter Tamm
Sales: Hans-Focko Koehler
Manager: Lothar Lichtenheldt
Founded: 1789
Subjects: Aeronautics, Aviation, Government, Political Science, Maritime, Military Science
ISBN Prefix(es): 3-87547; 3-8132
Associate Companies: Koehlers Verlagsgesellschaft; Maximilian-Verlag; Verlag Offene Worte; Verlag Europaeische Wehrkunde (all members of Verlagsgruppe Koehler/Mittler)
Branch Office(s)
Friedrichstr 95, 10117 Berlin *Tel:* (030) 2096-2124 *Fax:* (030) 2096-2126
Austr 19, 53179 Bonn *Tel:* (0228) 530962-64 *Fax:* (0228) 230102

MM-Verlagsgesellschaft mbH+
Zabergaeustr 3, 73765 Neuhausen
Tel: (07158) 940 800 *Fax:* (07158) 940 802
E-mail: mm@ebb.de
Key Personnel
Manager: Matthias Mueller
License & Press Service.
ISBN Prefix(es): 3-88590

MMV Medizin Verlag GmbH Munich
Neumarkterstr 43, 81673 Munich
Tel: (089) 4372-1300 *Fax:* (089) 4372-1399
Web Site: www.urban-vogel.de
Telex: 524631 vervo d
Key Personnel
Manager: Dr Jochen Aumiller
Manager & International Rights: Dr Ruediger Hennigs
International Rights: G Kraus-Nitsch
Founded: 1972
Subjects: Medicine, Nursing, Dentistry
ISBN Prefix(es): 3-8208
Parent Company: Verlagsgruppe Bertelsmann International GmbH
Distributed by Vleweg Verlag (Germany)

Moby Dick Verlag+
Rendsburger Landstr 181, 24113 Kiel
Tel: (0431) 640110 *Fax:* (0431) 6401112
E-mail: mobybook@aol.com
Key Personnel
Publisher: Konrad Delius
Contact: Klaus Bartelt

BOOK

Subjects: Automotive, Crafts, Games, Hobbies, Mysteries, Outdoor Recreation, Sports, Athletics, Technology, Transportation, Travel
ISBN Prefix(es): 3-922843; 3-930392

mode information Heinz Kramer GmbH
Pilgerstr 20, 51491 Overath
Tel: (02206) 60070 *Fax:* (02206) 600717
E-mail: info@modeinfo.com
Web Site: www.modeinfo.com
Subjects: Architecture & Interior Design, Fashion, Management, Marketing

Modellsport Verlag GmbH+
Schulstra 12, 76532 Baden-Baden
Tel: (07221) 95210 *Fax:* (07221) 9521-45
E-mail: mfiredaktion@modellsport.de
Web Site: www.modellsport.de
Key Personnel
Manager: Heinz Ongsieck
Founded: 1977
ISBN Prefix(es): 3-923142

modo verlag GmbH
Runzstr 62, 79102 Freiburg
Tel: (0761) 2022875 *Fax:* (0761) 2022876
E-mail: info@modoverlag.de
Web Site: www.modoverlag.de
Subjects: Architecture & Interior Design, Art, Contemporary Art, Late 20th Century Art
Number of titles published annually: 8 Print
Total Titles: 45 Print

Moeck Verlag und Musikinstrumentenwerk, Inhaber Dr Hermann Moeck
Lueckenweg 4, 29227 Celle
Mailing Address: Postfach 3131, 29231 Celle
Tel: (05141) 88 53-0 *Fax:* (05141) 88 53-42
E-mail: info@moeck-music.de
Web Site: www.moeck-music.de
Key Personnel
Owner: Dr Hermann Moeck
ISBN Prefix(es): 3-87549

Moench Verlagsgesellschaft mbH+
Heilsbachstr 26, 53123 Bonn
Mailing Address: Postfach 140261, 53057 Bonn
Tel: (0228) 64830 *Fax:* (0228) 6483109
E-mail: 101336.245@compuserve.com
Key Personnel
Executive Dir: Manfred Sadlowski
Sales Promotion: Toni Wierer
Subjects: Engineering (General), History, How-to, Science (General)
ISBN Prefix(es): 3-921528
Associate Companies: Bernard & Graefe Verlag GmbH & Co KG; Wehr & Wissen Verlagsgesellschaft mbH; Jules Perel's Publishing Co, 1180 AX Amstelveen, PO Box 913, Matterhorn 35 1180E, Netherlands; Zettel
Imprints: World Defense Almanach

Karl Heinrich Moeseler Verlag+
Hoffmann-von-Fallerslebenstr 8, 38304 Wolfenbuettel
Mailing Address: Postfach 1661, 38286 Wolfenbuettel
Tel: (05331) 95970 *Fax:* (05331) 9597-20
Key Personnel
President & International Rights: Dietrich Moeseler
Founded: 1949
Subjects: Music, Dance
ISBN Prefix(es): 3-7877

Moewig, *imprint of* Pabel-Moewig Verlag KG

Mohr Siebeck+
Wilhelmstr 18, 72074 Tuebingen

Mailing Address: Postfach 2040, 72010 Tuebingen
Tel: (07071) 923-0 *Fax:* (07071) 5 11 04
E-mail: info@mohr.de
Web Site: www.mohr.de *Cable:* SIEBECK TUBINGEN
Key Personnel
Owner & Publisher: Georg Siebeck *Tel:* (07071) 923 32 *Fax:* (07071) 923 67 *E-mail:* siebeck@mohr.de
Sales & Marketing Dir: Sabine Stehle *Tel:* (07071) 923 56 *E-mail:* sabine.stehle@mohr.de
Production: Matthias Spitzner *Tel:* (07071) 923 43 *E-mail:* matthias.spitzner@mohr.de
Rights & Permissions: Jill Sopper *Tel:* (07071) 923 61 *E-mail:* jill.sopper@mohr.de
Editorial Dir Law: Dr Franz-Peter Gillig *Tel:* (07071) 923 50 *Fax:* (07071) 923 67 *E-mail:* franz-peter.gillig@mohr.de
Editorial Dir Theology: Dr Henning Ziebritzki *Tel:* (07071) 923 59 *Fax:* (07071) 511 04 *E-mail:* henning.ziebritzki@mohr.de
Founded: 1801
Academic Books & Journals. Encyclopedias, Historical-critical Editions & Monographs.
Subjects: Economics, History, Law, Philosophy, Religion - Protestant, Religion - Other, Social Sciences, Sociology, Theology, Judaism
ISBN Prefix(es): 3-16
Number of titles published annually: 180 Print
Total Titles: 3,210 Print
Online services available through World Wide Web.
Imprints: H Lauppsche Buchhandlung
Warehouse: Christophstr 32, 72072 Tuebingen

Monastica, *imprint of* Verein der Benediktiner zu Beuron- Beuroner Kunstverlag

Monia Verlag+
Postfach 2120, 66929 Pirmasens
Tel: (6331) 41425 *Fax:* (6331) 41425
Key Personnel
Contact: Elisabeth Dillenburger
Founded: 1971
Novels & bilingual poetry for adults.
Subjects: Biography, Fiction, Literature, Literary Criticism, Essays, Poetry
ISBN Prefix(es): 3-926753; 3-9800383
Branch Office(s)
Strobelallee 62, 66953 Pirmasens

Edition Monika+
Schwedenhof/Am Roemermuseum, 66424 Homburg/Saar
Tel: (06848) 7 21 52 *Fax:* (06848) 7 21 59
E-mail: edmb@mathbeck.de; jphilippi@mathbeck.de
Web Site: www.mathbeck.de/edmb/
Key Personnel
Man Dir & Proprietor: Mathias Beck *E-mail:* mathiasbeck@mathbeck.de
Editorial & Publicity Dir: Julia Beck
Founded: 1967
Edition for Contemporary Art.
Member of BDK (Buntesverband Deutscher Kunstverleger).
ISBN Prefix(es): 3-924360
Number of titles published annually: 8 Print
Total Titles: 248 Print

Moritz Verlag+
Kantstr 12, 60316 Frankfurt am Main
Tel: (069) 4305084 *Fax:* (069) 4305083
E-mail: MoritzVerlag@t-online.de
Key Personnel
Contact: Markus Weber
Founded: 1994
ISBN Prefix(es): 3-89565
Parent Company: l'ecole des loisirs, Paris, France

Warehouse: Koch, Neff & Oetinger, 70551 Stuttgart
Orders to: Koch, Neff & Oetinger, 70551 Stuttgart *Tel:* (0711) 78 99 10 10
E-mail: order@kno-va.de

Morsak Verlag+
Wittelsbacherstr 2-8, 94481 Grafenau
Mailing Address: Postfach 1262, 94476 Grafenau
Tel: (08552) 4200 *Fax:* (08552) 42050
E-mail: info@morsak.de
Web Site: www.morsak.de
Key Personnel
Man Dir, Production: Erich Stecher
Sales: Rosa Zarham
Founded: 1884
Subjects: Regional Interests
ISBN Prefix(es): 3-87553

Morus-Verlag GmbH
Goetzstr 65, 12099 Berlin
Tel: (030) 89 79 37-0 *Fax:* (030) 75 70 81 12
E-mail: mail@morusverlag.de
Web Site: www.morusverlag.de
Key Personnel
Dir: Elmar Bachmann; Ursula Buchner
Founded: 1945
Subjects: Religion - Other
ISBN Prefix(es): 3-87554

Mosaik Verlag GmbH
Neumarkter Str 18, 81673 Munich
Mailing Address: Postfach 800360, 81673 Munich
Tel: (089) 4372-0 *Fax:* (089) 4372-2812
Telex: 523259 vbmue d
Key Personnel
Man Dir: Georg Kessler; Lothar Beyer
Publicity: Helga Mahmoud-Treimer
Rights & Permissions: Angelika Straus-Fischer
Subjects: Animals, Pets, Antiques, Architecture & Interior Design, Career Development, Child Care & Development, Cookery, Crafts, Games, Hobbies, Economics, Film, Video, Finance, Gardening, Plants, Health, Nutrition, House & Home, Human Relations, Self-Help, Sports, Athletics, Wine & Spirits, Women's Studies
ISBN Prefix(es): 3-576
Parent Company: Verlagsgruppe Bertelsmann GmbH
U.S. Office(s): Bettina Schrewe Literary Scouting, 101 Fifth Ave, Suite 11B, New York, NY 10003, United States (US Scout)

Motion Books, *imprint of* Heel Verlag GmbH

Motorbuch-Verlag+
Division of Paul Pietsch Verlage GmbH & Co
Olgastr 86, 70180 Stuttgart
Mailing Address: Postfach 103743, 70032 Stuttgart
Tel: (0711) 210 80 65 *Fax:* (0711) 210 80 70
E-mail: versand@motorbuch.de
Web Site: www.motorbuch-versand.de *Cable:* PICO D
Key Personnel
Man Dir: Paul Pietsch; Dr Patricia Scholten
Sales, Publicity: Thomas Guenther
Rights & Permissions: Patricia Hofmann
Editorial: Martin Benz; Claus-Guergen Jacobson; Joachim Kuch; Oliver Schwarz
Marketing: Jarg Ebert
Founded: 1962
Subjects: Aeronautics, Aviation, Automotive, History, Military Science, Nonfiction (General)
ISBN Prefix(es): 3-87943
Orders to: Koch, Neff, Oetinger & Co Verlagsauslieferung GmbH, Postfach 800620, 70506 Stuttgart

Verlag Mueller und Kiepenheuer+
Burgallee 67, 63452 Hanau
Mailing Address: Postfach 1355, 63403 Hanau
Tel: (0618) 92810 *Fax:* (06181) 257387
Telex: 4184879
Key Personnel
Publisher, Rights & Permissions: Werner Dausien
Founded: 1919
Subjects: Art, Fiction
ISBN Prefix(es): 3-7833
Associate Companies: Werner Dausien

Mueller & Schindler Verlag
Sonnenbergstr 55, 70184 Stuttgart
Tel: (0711) 233204 *Fax:* (0711) 2369977
Key Personnel
Owner: Rolf Mueller
Founded: 1965
Subjects: Art, History, Religion - Other
ISBN Prefix(es): 3-87560

C F Mueller Verlag, Huethig Gmb H & Co+
Im Weiher 10, 69121 Heidelberg
Mailing Address: Postfach 10 28 69, 69121 Heidelberg
Tel: (06221) 489 395 *Fax:* (06221) 489623
E-mail: cfmueller@huethig.de
Web Site: www.huethig.de
Key Personnel
Manager: Anja Freiberger *E-mail:* a.freiberger@huethig.de
Founded: 1797
Subjects: Architecture & Interior Design, Energy, Engineering (General), Technology, Technical books
ISBN Prefix(es): 3-7880
Number of titles published annually: 16 Print
Parent Company: Huethig GmbH & Co KG

Norbert Mueller AG & Co KG Verlag+
Ingolstaedter Str 20, 80807 Munich
Mailing Address: Postfach 450632, 80906 Munich
Tel: (089) 350 93-02 *Fax:* (089) 350 93-218
E-mail: info@vnm.de
Web Site: www.vnm.de
Key Personnel
Publications Manager: Traude Wuest *Tel:* (089) 35093213 *E-mail:* t.west@vnm.de
Advertising Manager: Gabriele David *Tel:* (089) 35093204 *E-mail:* g.david@vnm.de
Rights Director, Foreign Affairs: Maria Pinto-Peuckmann *Tel:* (089) 548 52-84 26 *Fax:* (089) 548 52-84 21
Founded: 1968
Publisher of newsletters.
Subjects: Finance, Management, Marketing, Real Estate
ISBN Prefix(es): 3-920663; 3-89486
Online services available through World Wide Web.
Parent Company: Verlag Moderne Industrie, Justus-Von-Liebig Str 1, 86899 Landsberg am Lech
U.S. Office(s): Verlag Norbert Mueller, 15775 Hillcrest, Suite 508, Dallas, TX 75248-4106, United States
Shipping Address: Verlag Moderne Industrie, Justus-Von-Liebig Str 1, 86899 Landsberg am Lech
Warehouse: Verlag Moderne Industrie, Justus-Von-Liebig Str 1, 86899 Landsberg am Lech

Verlagsgesellschaft Rudolf Mueller GmbH & Co KG+
Stolbergerstr 84, 50933 Cologne
Tel: (0221) 5497-0 *Fax:* (0221) 5497-326
E-mail: service@rudolf-mueller.de
Web Site: www.rudolf-mueller.de
Key Personnel
Dir: Dr Christoph Mueller; Rudolf M Bleser; Dr J F Huffman

Founded: 1840
Subjects: Civil Engineering
ISBN Prefix(es): 3-481
Parent Company: VBV Verlagsbeteiligungen-Verwaltungsgesellschaft mbH & Co KG
Subsidiaries: Charles Coleman Verlag GmbH & Co KG; Edial SARL Paris; Bruderverlag Albert Bruder GmbH & Co KG; SDK Systemdruck Koeln GmbH & Co KG; SSB Spezial Seminare Bau GmbH; Verlag Siegfried Rohn GmbH & Co KG; Technik & Wirtschaft Publications GmbH; Immobilien Informationsverlag Rudolf Mueller GmbH & Co KG

Mueller und Steinicke Verlag
Aidenbachstra 78, 81379 Munich
Tel: (089) 74 99 156 *Fax:* (089) 74 99 157
E-mail: info@mueller-und-steinicke.de
Web Site: www.mueller-und-steinicke.de
Key Personnel
Manager: Werner Gissler
Founded: 1903
Subjects: Medicine, Nursing, Dentistry
ISBN Prefix(es): 3-87569

Karl Muller Verlag+
Danzigerstr 6, 91052 Erlangen
Tel: (09131) 30040 *Fax:* (09131) 300466
Key Personnel
Manager: Mr Doerfler
Founded: 1980
ISBN Prefix(es): 3-86070

Multi Media Kunst Verlag Dresden+
Sarrasanistr 13-0503, 01097 Dresden
Tel: (0351) 8041291 *Fax:* (0351) 8041291
Key Personnel
Author, Publisher: Hans Kromer
Founded: 1990
Subjects: Art, Literature, Literary Criticism, Essays
ISBN Prefix(es): 3-9700002

Mundo Verlag GmbH
Schreberstr 2, 51105 Cologne
Tel: (0180) 9216350 *Fax:* (0180) 921635-24
E-mail: info@mundo-media.de
Web Site: www.mundo-text.de
Key Personnel
Man Dir: Ertay Hayit *E-mail:* ertay.hayit@mundo-media.de
Editorial: Cornelia Auschra *Tel:* (0221) 921635-13 *E-mail:* auschra@mundo-media.de; Mike Gahn *E-mail:* gahn@mundo-media.de; Ute Hayit *Tel:* (0221) 921635-11 *E-mail:* ute.hayit@mundo-media.de
Founded: 1982
Subjects: Travel
ISBN Prefix(es): 3-89607; 3-87322

Munsterschwarzacher Kleinschafter, *imprint of* Vier Tuerme GmbH Verlag Klosterbetriebe

Munzinger-Archiv GmbH Archiv fuer publizistische Arbeit+
Albersfelderstr 34, 88213 Ravensburg
Tel: (0751) 76931-0 *Fax:* (0751) 65 24 24
E-mail: box@munzinger.de
Web Site: www.munzinger.de
Key Personnel
Manager: Dr L Munzinger; Ernst Munzinger
Founded: 1913
Subjects: Biography, Economics, Foreign Countries, Government, Political Science, History, Music, Dance, Sports, Athletics

Musikantiquariat und Dr Hans Schneider Verlag GmbH+
Mozartstr 6, 82323 Tutzing
Tel: (08158) 3050; (08158) 6967 *Fax:* (08158) 7636
E-mail: musikbuch@aol.com; musikantiquar@aol.com *Cable:* MUSIKANTIQUAR
Key Personnel
Manager: Dr Hans Schneider
Founded: 1949
Subjects: Antiques, Biography, History, Music, Dance, Science (General)
ISBN Prefix(es): 3-7952

Musikverlag Zimmermann+
Strubbergstr 80, 60489 Frankfurt am Main
Mailing Address: Postfach 940183, 60459 Frankfurt am Main
Tel: (069) 978286-6 *Fax:* (069) 978286-89
E-mail: info@musikverlag-zimmerman.de; info@lienau-frankfurt.de
Web Site: www.zimmermann-frankfurt.de
Key Personnel
Man Dirs: Cornelia Grossmann *Tel:* (069) 978 286-79 *E-mail:* grossmann@zimmermann-frankfurt.de; Michael Kary *Fax:* (069) 978 286-79 *E-mail:* kary@zimmermann-frankfurt.de
International Rights: Saskia Herchenroeder
Sales & Distribution: Aynalem Gebremedhim *Tel:* (069) 978 286-86 *E-mail:* infor@zimmermann-frankfurt.de; Michael Henne *Tel:* (069) 978 826-86 *E-mail:* henne@zimmermann-frankfurt.de
Rights & Licensing: Saskia Bieber *Tel:* (069) 978 286-72 *Fax:* (069) 978 286-79 *E-mail:* bieber@zimmermann-frankfurt.de
Advertising, Public Relations: Ulrike Osterhage *Tel:* (069) 978 286-75 *Fax:* (069) 978 286-79 *E-mail:* osterhage@zimmermann-frankfurt.de
Editorial & Production: Friedhelm Neubert *Tel:* (069) 978 286-79 *E-mail:* neubert@zimmermann-frankfurt.de; Judith Picard *Tel:* (069) 978 286-76 *Fax:* (069) 978 286-79 *E-mail:* picard@lienau-frankfurt.de; Peter Ruecker *Tel:* (069) 978 286-73 *Fax:* (069) 978 286-79 *E-mail:* ruecker@zimmermann-frankfurt.de
Subjects: Music, Dance
ISBN Prefix(es): 3-921729
Associate Companies: Robert Lienau Musikverlag, Frankfurt

Muster-Schmidt Verlag+
Brauweg 40, 37073 Goettingen
Mailing Address: Postfach 2741, 37017 Gottingen
Tel: (551) 71741; (551) 597690 *Fax:* (551) 7702774
E-mail: info@muster-schmidt.de
Web Site: www.muster-schmidt.de *Cable:* MUSTERSCHMIDT
Key Personnel
Dir: Eva Marie Gerhardy-Loecken
E-mail: muster-schmidt@t-online.de
Founded: 1905
Subjects: Biography, History, Color
ISBN Prefix(es): 3-7881
Branch Office(s)
Vogelsangstr 7, 8033 Zurich, Switzerland
Tel: (01) 251 75 71 *Fax:* (01) 252 44 68
E-mail: info@muster-schmidt.de

MUT Verlag+
Bahnhofstr 1, 27330 Asendorf
Mailing Address: Postfach 1, 27328 Asendorf
Tel: (04253) 566; (04253) 672 *Fax:* (04253) 16 03
Key Personnel
Man Dir, Rights & Permissions: Bernhard C Wintzek
Founded: 1972
Subjects: Government, Political Science, History, Culture
ISBN Prefix(es): 3-89182

Nadif, *imprint of* Daco Verlag Guenter Blase oHG

Verlag Stephanie Naglschmid+
Senefelderstr 10, 70178 Stuttgart
Tel: (0711) 62 68 78 *Fax:* (0711) 61 23 23
E-mail: naglschmid.vsn@t-online.de
Web Site: www.naglschmid.de
Key Personnel
Contact: Dr Friedrich Naglschmid; Stephanie Naglschmid
Founded: 1984
Also acts as book dealer for Diving Literature.
Subjects: Biological Sciences, Environmental Studies, Film, Video, Natural History, Outdoor Recreation, Photography, Physical Sciences, Sports, Athletics, Travel
ISBN Prefix(es): 3-927913; 3-89594; 3-925342
Associate Companies: JLVA Internationale Lizenzvewertungs-Agentur; MTI (Medien - und Touristik Informations Services); Divemaster (Touchmagatin)
Imprints: Edition Hannemann; Edition Schwab

Gunter Narr Verlag+
Dischingerweg 5, 72070 Tuebingen
Mailing Address: Postfach 2567, 72015 Tuebingen
Tel: (07071) 97970 *Fax:* (07071) 75288
E-mail: narr-francke@t-online.de
Web Site: www.geist.de
Key Personnel
Publisher: Gunter Narr
Manufacturing: Horst Schmid
Publicity Dir: Ingo Neubert
Founded: 1969
Subjects: Communications, Drama, Theater, Language Arts, Linguistics, Literature, Literary Criticism, Essays, Mysteries, Psychology, Psychiatry, Social Sciences, Sociology, Classical Philology, Cultural Science
ISBN Prefix(es): 3-87808; 3-8233
Associate Companies: A Francke Verlag

Verlag Natur & Wissenschaft Harro Hieronimus & Dr Jurgen Schmidt (Nature & Science Publishing)+
Postfach 170209, 42624 Solingen
Tel: (0212) 819878 *Fax:* (0212) 816216
E-mail: info@verlagnw.de
Key Personnel
Contact: Harro Hieronimus
Founded: 1989
Member of the Stock Exchange of German Booksellers.
Subjects: Animals, Pets, Biological Sciences, Earth Sciences, Environmental Studies, Gardening, Plants, Geography, Geology, Natural History
ISBN Prefix(es): 3-927889; 3-936616
Imprints: Bibliothek Natur & Wissenschaft
Distributor for ACS-Verlag

NaturaViva Verlags GmbH+
Formerly Waldthausen Verlag GmbH & Co KG Abt Verlag
Lukas-Moser-Weg 4, 71263 Weil der Stadt
Mailing Address: Postfach 1203, 71256 Weil der Stadt
Tel: (07033) 13 80 816 *Fax:* (07033) 13 80 817
E-mail: naturaviva@t-online.de
Key Personnel
Man Dir: Simone Graff
Founded: 1999
Member of Borsenverein des Deutschen Buchhandels eV.
Subjects: Health, Nutrition
ISBN Prefix(es): 3-926453; 3-89525; 3-89881; 3-935407
Number of titles published annually: 6 Print
Total Titles: 80 Print
Online services available through World Wide Web.

Imprints: Fit fuers Leben Verlag; Waldthausen Verlag
Distributed by Walter Haedecke Verlag

Naumann & Goebel Verlagsgesellschaft mbH
Emil-Hoffmann Str 1, 50996 Cologne
Mailing Address: Postfach 501863, 50978 Cologne
Tel: (02236) 39990 *Fax:* (02236) 399999
E-mail: einstieg@aol.com; fdvemag@netcologne.de
Telex: 8886642
Key Personnel
Manager: Guenter Goebel; Juergen Naumann; Juergen Krause
Subjects: Animals, Pets, Art, Biblical Studies, Computer Science, Cookery, Crafts, Games, Hobbies, Education, Fashion, Fiction, Gardening, Plants, Health, Nutrition, History, House & Home, How-to, Mathematics, Medicine, Nursing, Dentistry, Science (General), Travel, Family & Relationships, Foreign Language Study, Nature
ISBN Prefix(es): 3-625
Associate Companies: Delphin AG; Delphin Verlag GmbH; Tigris Verlag GmbH; Naturalis Verlags- u Vertriebsges mbH; Daumueller Werbeges mbH; Reichenbach Verlag GmbH; Verlag Das persoenliche Geburtstagsbuch GmbH; V & M Verlags & Mediengesellschaft Koeln mbH; Neuer Pawlak Verlag GmbH; MZ Medien Zentrum GmbH

Edition Nautilus Verlag+
Alte Hostenstr 22, 21031 Hamburg
Tel: (040) 7213536 *Fax:* (040) 7218399
E-mail: edition-nautilus@t-online.de
Web Site: www.edition-nautilus.de
Key Personnel
Owner: Lutz Schulenburg
Rights & Permissions: Hanna Mittelstaedt
Editiorial & Press: Katharina Leunig
Production: Klaus Voss
Founded: 1974
Subjects: Art, Biography, Government, Political Science, Literature, Literary Criticism, Essays
ISBN Prefix(es): 3-89401; 3-921523
Distributed by B & I Buch und Information AG (Switzerland); Mohr/Morawa (Austria); SoVa Gmbh

NDV Neue Darmstadter Verlagsanstalt
Hauptstr 74, 53619 Rheinbreitbach
Mailing Address: Postfach 1560, 53585 Bad Honnef
Tel: (02224) 3232 *Fax:* (02224) 78639
E-mail: info@ndv-verlag.de
Web Site: www.ndv-verlag.de
Key Personnel
Publisher, Rights & Permissions: Klaus J Holzapfel; Andreas Holzapfel
Editor: Susanne Dirkwinkel
Sales: Eva-Maria Schueller
Marketing, Sales: Markus Fleischer
Founded: 1949
Subjects: Government, Political Science
ISBN Prefix(es): 3-87576
Branch Office(s)
Wittestr 30 K, 13509 Berlin *Tel:* (030) 8557511 *Fax:* (030) 85605332

Nebel Verlag GmbH
Danzigerstr 6, 91052 Erlangen
Tel: (09131) 34042 *Fax:* (09131) 300466
Key Personnel
Contact: Pirmin Nebel
Founded: 1989
Subjects: Cookery, Gardening, Plants, History, Literature, Literary Criticism, Essays, Romance, Travel
ISBN Prefix(es): 3-89555

Neckar Verlag GmbH+
Klosterring 1, 78050 Villingen-Schwenningen
Mailing Address: Postfach 1820, 78008 Villingen-Schwenningen
Tel: (07721) 89 87-0 *Fax:* (07721) 89 87-50
E-mail: service@neckar-verlag.de
Web Site: www.neckar-verlag.de
Key Personnel
Man Dir: Inge Holtzhauer; Dr Heinz Loercher
Marketing: Peter Walter *Tel:* (07721) 87 87-45
E-mail: anzeigen@neckar-verlag.de
Founded: 1945
Subjects: Aeronautics, Aviation, Literature, Literary Criticism, Essays, Literature & Plans for RC-Model Aircraft & RC-Model Ship
ISBN Prefix(es): 3-7883

Neff, *imprint of* Pabel-Moewig Verlag KG

Nelles Verlag GmbH+
Schleissheimerstr 371b, 80935 Munich
Tel: (089) 357 194-0 *Fax:* (089) 357 194-30
E-mail: info@nelles-verlag.de
Web Site: www.nelles-verlag.de
Key Personnel
Man Dir, Rights & Permissions: Guenter Nelles
Founded: 1975
Subjects: Travel
ISBN Prefix(es): 3-88618
Orders to: Geocenter/ILH, Postfach 800830, 70508 Stuttgart

Neue Darmstadter Verlagsanstalt, see NDV Neue Darmstadter Verlagsanstalt

Neue Dimension Buch-und Musik-Verlag+
Ronhofer Hauptstr 201, In der Lohe 13-15, 90765 Fuerth
Tel: (0911) 97987-25 *Fax:* (0171) 7906310
E-mail: mail@neue-dimension.com
Key Personnel
Owner, Rights & Permissions: Hans Peter Neuber
Founded: 1987
Subjects: Health, Nutrition, Music, Dance, Religion - Other
ISBN Prefix(es): 3-9802129; 3-928091
Divisions: H P Neuber
Orders to: Silenzio GmbH, Hainbrunnerstr 8, 91391 Forchheim

Neue Erde Verlags GmbH+
Cecilienstr 29, 66111 Saarbruecken
Tel: (0681) 372313 *Fax:* (0681) 3904102
E-mail: info@neueerde.de
Key Personnel
Publisher: Andreas Lentz
Founded: 1984
Subjects: Environmental Studies, Parapsychology, Self-Help
ISBN Prefix(es): 3-89060
Imprints: Ryvellus
Orders to: VSB Verlagsservice, Postfach 4738, 38037 Braunschweig

Verlag Neue Kritik KG+
Kettenhofweg 53, 60325 Frankfurt
Tel: (069) 727576 *Fax:* (069) 726585
E-mail: neuekritik@compuserve.com
Key Personnel
Man Dir: Dorothea Rein
Founded: 1965
Subjects: Art, Fiction, Philosophy, Poetry, Women's Studies, Judaica
ISBN Prefix(es): 3-8015
Orders to: Sozialistische Verlagsauslieferung GmbH, Franziusstr 44, 60314 Frankfurt am Main

Verlag Neue Musik GmbH
Grabbeallee 15, 13156 Berlin
Tel: (030) 616981-0 *Fax:* (030) 616981-21
E-mail: vnm@verlag-neue-musik.de
Web Site: www.verlag-neue-musik.de
Key Personnel
Manager: Axel Muetze-Kern
Founded: 1957
Subjects: Music, Dance
ISBN Prefix(es): 3-7333
Subsidiaries: Edition Margaux

Verlag Neue Musikzeitung GmbH
Brunnstr 23, 93053 Regensburg
Tel: (0941) 94 59 30 *Fax:* (0941) 94 59 350
E-mail: nmz@nmz.de
Web Site: www.nmz.de
Key Personnel
Publisher & Chief Editor: Theo Geissler
Editor-in-Chief: Gerhard Rohde
Editorial Manager: Andreas Kolb
Founded: 1993
Subjects: Art, Ethnicity, Music, Dance
Parent Company: Con Brio Verlagsgesellschaft mbH, Postfach 100245, Brunnstr 23, 93053 Regensburg

Verlag Neue Stadt GmbH+
Mangfallstr 29, 81547 Munich
Tel: (08093) 2091 *Fax:* (08093) 2096 *Cable:* NEUE STADT
Key Personnel
Man Dir: Wolfgang Bader
Sales, Publicity & Advertising: Gabriele Hartl
Rights: Stefan Liesenfeld
Founded: 1961
Subjects: Biblical Studies, Biography, Fiction, How-to, Music, Dance, Religion - Other, Theology, Autobiography, Family & Relationships
ISBN Prefix(es): 3-87996
Parent Company: Citta Nuova Editrice, Italy
Branch Office(s)
Trostr 116, A-1100 Vienna, Austria
Seestr 426, Postfach 435, CH-8038 Zurich, Switzerland

Verlag Neue Wirtschafts-Briefe GmbH & Co+
Eschstr 22, 44629 Herne
Tel: (02323) 141-900; (02361) 9142-0 (edtorial staff) *Fax:* (02323) 141-123
E-mail: info@nwb.de
Web Site: www.nwb.de *Cable:* STEUERBRIEFE HERNE
Key Personnel
Publisher: Dr Karl-Friedrich Peter
Man Dir: E O Kleyboldt
Sales & Advertising Dir: J Mueller-Grote
Founded: 1947
Subjects: Accounting, Business, Career Development, Law
ISBN Prefix(es): 3-482
Associate Companies: Verlag fuer die Rechts- und Anwaltspraxis GmbH & Co KG
Subsidiaries: Friedrich Kiehl Verlag GmbH
Shipping Address: Schuechtermannstr 180, 44628 Herne
Warehouse: Schuechtermannstr 180, 44628 Herne
Orders to: Postfach 101849, 44621 Herne

Neuer Honos Verlag GmbH+
Emil-Hoffmann- Str 1, 50996 Cologne
Tel: (0221) 3 36 20-0 *Fax:* (0221) 3 36 20-99
E-mail: nhonos@netcologne.de
Key Personnel
Chief Executive Officer: Stefan Sommer *Tel:* (0221) 336200
Founded: 1998
Subjects: Animals, Pets, Biblical Studies, Computer Science, Cookery, Fiction, Health, Nutrition, How-to, Language Arts, Linguistics, Nonfiction (General), Travel, Health & Fitness, Foreign Language Study, Nature
ISBN Prefix(es): 3-8299

Warehouse: GVA, Gesellschaft fur Verlagsauslieferung & Logistik mbH, Heideweg 8a, 36160 Bad-Bwischenahn *Tel:* (0441) 969412 *Fax:* (0441) 969415

Neuer ISP Verlag GmbH
Marienstr 15, 76137 Karlsruhe
Tel: (0721) 31 183 *Fax:* (0721) 31 250
E-mail: alive@sterneck.net
Web Site: www.sterneck.net/alive/isp
Key Personnel
Manager, Rights & Permissions: Wolfgang Feikert
Subjects: Economics, Government, Political Science, History, Philosophy, Social Sciences, Sociology
ISBN Prefix(es): 3-88332; 3-929008
Orders to: Buro Frankfurt lm, Kassler Str 1 a, 60486 Frankfurt

Neuer Jugendschriften-Verlag, see A Weichert Verlag GmbH & Co KG

Neuer Weg Verlag und Druck GmbH+
Alte Bottroper Str 42, 45356 Essen
Tel: (0201) 2 59 15 *Fax:* (0201) 6 14 44 62
E-mail: neuerweg@neuerweg.de
Web Site: www.neuerweg.de
Key Personnel
Rights & Permissions: Gert Bierikoven
Dir: Christoph Klug
Founded: 1971
Subjects: Developing Countries, Education, Environmental Studies, Government, Political Science, Health, Nutrition, History, Physical Sciences, Women's Studies
ISBN Prefix(es): 3-88021
Bookshop(s): Buchladen NeuerWeg, Reuterstr 15, 12053 Berlin; Ernst-Thaelmann-Buchhandlung, Hauptstaetter Str 39, 70173 Stuttgart

Verlag Neues Leben GmbH+
Rosenthaler Str 36, 10178 Berlin
Tel: (030) 284630 *Fax:* (030) 28388075
Cable: NEUESLEBEN BERLIN
Key Personnel
Man Dir, Rights & Permissions: Rudolf Chowanetz
Production: Hannelore Lange
Sales: Walter Toelg
Founded: 1946
Subjects: Biography, Cookery, Fiction, Gay & Lesbian, History, Human Relations, Nonfiction (General), Religion - Jewish
ISBN Prefix(es): 3-355
Warehouse: Moor Morawa Buchvertriebsges mbH, Sulzengasse 2, A-1232 Vienna, Austria Schweizer Bucherzentrum, Postfach, CH-4601 Olten, Switzerland
Orders to: LKG-Verlagsauslieferung, Poetzschauer Weg, 04579 Espenhain

Neues Literaturkontor+
Goldstr 15, 48147 Muenster
Mailing Address: Postfach 101847, 33518 Bielefeld
Fax: (0251) 4 05 65
E-mail: neues-literaturkontor@t-online.de
Web Site: www.neues-literaturkontor.de
Key Personnel
Contact: Dr Hans D Mummendey
International Rights: Dorothea Potthoff
Founded: 1990
Specialize in novels, short stories.
Subjects: Poetry
ISBN Prefix(es): 3-920591
Number of titles published annually: 5 Print
Total Titles: 60 Print

Neuland-Verlagsgesellschaft mbH+
Markt 24-26, 21502 Geesthacht
Mailing Address: Postfach 1422, 21496 Geesthacht
Tel: (04152) 8 13 42 *Fax:* (04152) 8 13 43
E-mail: vertrieb@neuland.com
Web Site: www.neuland.com
Key Personnel
Manager: Jens Burmester *E-mail:* gf@neuland.com
Founded: 1889
Specialize in the area of addictions.
Subjects: Health, Nutrition, Medicine, Nursing, Dentistry, Psychology, Psychiatry, Self-Help, Social Sciences, Sociology
ISBN Prefix(es): 3-87581

Neumann Verlag+
Wollgrasweg 41, 70599 Stuttgart
Mailing Address: Postfach 700561, 70574 Stuttgart
Tel: (0711) 4507-0 *Fax:* (0711) 4507-120
E-mail: info@ulmer.de
Web Site: www.ulmer.de
Founded: 1990
Subjects: Animals, Pets, Biological Sciences, Environmental Studies, Gardening, Plants, House & Home, Natural History, Science (General), Travel
ISBN Prefix(es): 3-7402
Orders to: Eugen Ulmer Verlag Stuttgart, Wollgrasweg 41, 70599 Stuttgart *Tel:* (0711) 4507 124 *Fax:* (0711) 4507 120 *E-mail:* vertrieb@ulmer.de *Web Site:* www.ulmer.de

Verlag J Neumann-Neudamm GmbH & Co KG+
Schwalbenweg 1, 34212 Melsungen
Tel: (05661) 52222 *Fax:* (05661) 6008
E-mail: info@neumann-neudamm.de
Web Site: www.neumann-neudamm.de
Key Personnel
Dir: Walter Schwartz
Foreign Rights: Rolf Roosen
Founded: 1872
Subjects: Outdoor Recreation, Science (General), Sports, Athletics
ISBN Prefix(es): 3-7888
Subsidiaries: JANA (Gesellschaft fur Jagd und Natur GmbH)

Verlag fuer Messepublikationen Thomas Neureuter KG
Sueskindstr 4, 81929 Munich
Mailing Address: Postfach 811060, 81910 Munich
Tel: (089) 99 30 91-0 *Fax:* (089) 93 78 96
E-mail: info@neureuter.de
Web Site: www.neureuter.de
Telex: 522918 mesu d
Key Personnel
Publisher: Thomas Neureuter
Founded: 1948
ISBN Prefix(es): 3-921362
Branch Office(s)
Leipziger Messe Verlag und Vertriebsgesellschaft mbH, Messe-Allee 1, 04358 Leipzig *Tel:* (0341) 67 877-0 *Fax:* (0341) 67 877-12 *E-mail:* info@leipziger-messeverlag.de *Web Site:* www.leipziger-messeverlag.de
Chuang's Enterprises Building, Room 1003, 10/F, 382 Lockhart Rd, Wanchai, Hong Kong *Tel:* 2519 3581 *Fax:* 2519 6941 *E-mail:* info@neureuter.com.hk *Web Site:* www.neureuter.com.hk
Binterimstr 13, Duesseldorf *Tel:* (0211) 34 20 26 *Fax:* (0211) 33 34 85

Neuthor - Verlag+
Obere Pfarrgasse 31, 64720 Michelstadt
Tel: (06061) 40 79 *Fax:* (06061) 26 46
Web Site: www.neuthor-verlag.de
Key Personnel
Publisher: Peter-Jochen Bosse *E-mail:* bosse@neuthor-verlag.de
Founded: 1980
Subjects: Architecture & Interior Design, Biography, Fiction, Foreign Countries, History, Mysteries, Travel
ISBN Prefix(es): 3-88758

New Era Publications Deutschland GmbH
Hittfelder Kirchweg 5a, 21220 Seevetal-Maschen
Tel: (04105) 68330 *Fax:* (04150) 683322
E-mail: buch@newerapublications.de
Web Site: www.newerapublications.com
Key Personnel
Manager: Thomas Goeldenitz
Founded: 1985
Subjects: Religion - Other, Science Fiction, Fantasy, Self-Help
ISBN Prefix(es): 3-929284
Parent Company: New Era Publications Int Aps, Stove Kangensgade 55, DK-1264 Copenhagen, Denmark

Nicolaische Verlagsbuchhandlung Beuermann GmbH+
Neuenburger Str 17, 10969 Berlin
Tel: (030) 253738-0 *Fax:* (030) 253738-39
E-mail: info@nicolai-verlag.de
Web Site: www.nicolai-verlag.de
Key Personnel
Publisher: Dr Hans von Trotha
Marketing: Susanne Boger *Tel:* (030) 253738-12 *Fax:* (030) 253738-40 *E-mail:* susanne.boger@nicolai-verlag.de
Rights & Licenses: Irene von Trotha *Tel:* (030) 253738-33 *Fax:* (030) 253738-39 *E-mail:* irene.trotha@nicolai-verlag.de
Subjects: Architecture & Interior Design, Art, Biography, Photography, Regional Interests
ISBN Prefix(es): 3-87584
Orders to: S Fischer Velope, 60591 Frankfurt/Main *Tel:* (069) 6062-0 *Fax:* (069) 6062-21X

Nie/Nie/Sagen-Verlag+
Silvanerweg 17, 78464 Konstanz
Tel: (07531) 5 35 70 *Fax:* (07531) 6 44 96
E-mail: haberkern-imz@t-online.de
Web Site: www.nie-nie-sagen-verlag.de
Key Personnel
Contact: Dr Joschi Wolfrum
Founded: 1977
Subjects: Literature, Literary Criticism, Essays, Poetry, Religion - Buddhist, Religion - Other, Self-Help
ISBN Prefix(es): 3-921778

Niederland-Verlag Helmut Michel
Winnendestr 20, 71522 Backnang
Mailing Address: Postfach 1480, 71504 Backnang
Tel: (07191) 3277-200 *Fax:* (07191) 3277-15
E-mail: micheldruck@t-online.de
Key Personnel
Owner: Helmut Michel
Subjects: History, Regional Interests
ISBN Prefix(es): 3-923947

Nielsen Frederic W, see Toleranz Verlag, Nielsen Frederic W

C W Niemeyer Buchverlage GmbH+
Osterstr 19, 31785 Hameln
Tel: (05151) 200-312 *Fax:* (05151) 200-319
E-mail: info@niemeyer-buch.de; telefonbuch@niemeyer.buch.de
Web Site: www.niemeyer-buch.de
Key Personnel
Publisher: Hans Freiwald
Founded: 1797

Member of Borsenverein des Deutschen Buchhandels.
Subjects: Architecture & Interior Design, Art, Fiction, History, Humor, Library & Information Sciences, Literature, Literary Criticism, Essays, Mysteries
ISBN Prefix(es): 3-8271
Subsidiaries: Adolf Sponholtz Verlag
Orders to: VSB - Verlagsservice Braunschweig GmbH, Postfach 4738, 38037 Braunschweig *Tel:* (0531) 708650 *Fax:* (0531) 708608

Max Niemeyer Verlag GmbH+
Pfrondorfer Str 6, 72074 Tuebingen
Mailing Address: Postfach 2140, 72074 Tuebingen
Tel: (07071) 98 94 0 *Fax:* (07071) 98 94 50
E-mail: max@niemeyer.de; info@niemeyer.de
Web Site: www.niemeyer.de *Cable:* NIEMEYER TUBINGEN
Key Personnel
Man Dir: Robert Harsch-Niemeyer; Nikolaus Steinberg
Publicity & Marketing: Karin Wenzel *Tel:* (07071) 989413 *E-mail:* wenzel@niemeyer.de
Editorial Dir: Birgitta Zeller *E-mail:* zeller@niemeyer.de
International Rights: Marlene Kirton *Tel:* (07071) 989427 *E-mail:* kirton@niemeyer.de
Marketing: Barbara Opel *E-mail:* opel@niemeyer.de
Sales: Nikolaus Steinberg
Founded: 1870
Subjects: History, Language Arts, Linguistics, Literature, Literary Criticism, Essays, Philosophy
ISBN Prefix(es): 3-484
Number of titles published annually: 160 Print

Nieswand-Verlag GmbH+
Werftbahnstr 8, 24143 Kiel
Tel: (0431) 7028 200 *Fax:* (0431) 7028 228
E-mail: vertrieb@nieswandverlag.de
Web Site: www.nieswand-verlag.de
Key Personnel
Manager: Jens Nieswand
Co-Editor: Ingo Wulff
Marketing: Ines Heinrich
Rights & Permissions: Melanie Voss
Sales: Carola Dreller *Tel:* (0431) 7028 218
Founded: 1986
Member of the Stock Exchange of German Booksellers.
Subjects: Art, Music, Dance, Photography
ISBN Prefix(es): 3-926048
Orders to: Coen Sligting Bookimport, Paulus Potterstraat 20, NL-1071 DA Amsterdam, Netherlands (International Distributor)
PNV Vertriebsservice GmbH, Werftbahnstr 8, 24143 Kiel
DAP Distributed Art Publishers, 155 Avenue of the Americas, 2nd fl, New York, NY 10013-1507, United States *Tel:* 212-627-1999

Hans-Nietsch-Verlag+
Poststr 3, 79098 Freiburg
Mailing Address: PO Box 228, 79002 Freiburg
Tel: (0761) 2966930 *Fax:* (0761) 2966966
E-mail: info@nietsch.de
Web Site: www.nietsch.de
Key Personnel
Contact: Hans Nietsch
Subjects: Religion - Other, Health, Occult
ISBN Prefix(es): 3-934647; 3-929345; 3-929475
Number of titles published annually: 10 Print
Total Titles: 100 Print
Imprints: Edition Sternenprinz
Distributor for Verlag Hans-Juergen Maurer; Edition Synthese

Rainar Nitzsche Verlag+
Gasstr 34, 67655 Kaiserslautern
Tel: (0631) 61305 *Fax:* (0631) 61305
E-mail: rainar.nitzscheverlag@t-online.de
Web Site: home.t-online.de/home/Rainar.NitzscheVerlag/nitzscheb.htm
Key Personnel
Contact: Dr Rainar Nitzsche
Founded: 1989
Subjects: Behavioral Sciences, Biological Sciences, Science Fiction, Fantasy
ISBN Prefix(es): 3-9802102; 3-930304

Nobel-Verlag GmbH Vertrieb Neue Medien
Kronprinzenstr 13, 45128 Essen
Tel: (0201) 81300 *Fax:* (0201) 8130288
E-mail: mplatzkoester@beleke.de
Web Site: www.gewusst-wo.de; www.nobel.de

Florian Noetzel Verlag+
Postfach 1443, 26353 Wilhelmshaven
Tel: (04421) 4 30 03 *Fax:* (04421) 4 29 85
E-mail: florian.noetzel@t-online.de
Key Personnel
Contact: Florian Noetzel
Founded: 1986
Subjects: Music, Dance
ISBN Prefix(es): 3-7959

Nomos Verlagsgesellschaft mbH und Co KG
Waldseestr 3-5, 76530 Baden-Baden
Tel: (07221) 2104-0 *Fax:* (07221) 210427
E-mail: nomos@nomos.de
Web Site: www.nomos.de
Telex: 051-933524
Key Personnel
Man Dir: Volker Schwarz
Publicity: Annette Saeger-Kuehler
Founded: 1936
Subjects: Business, Economics, Government, Political Science, Law
ISBN Prefix(es): 3-7890
Associate Companies: Insel Verlag; Deutscher Klassiker Verlag; Suhrkamp Verlag

Nusser Verlag+
Kaufbeurerstr 3, 80997 Munich
Mailing Address: Postfach 500411, 80974 Munich
Tel: (089) 146788 *Fax:* (089) 1493206
Web Site: www.nusserverlag.de
Key Personnel
Man Dir: Dr Horst Nusser *E-mail:* dr.nusser@nusserverlag.de
Sales: Sibylle Nusser-Festner *Tel:* (089) 1406750 *E-mail:* sibylee_nusser@web.de
Founded: 1972
Print books & publishing on demand.
Subjects: Agriculture, Art, Asian Studies, Biological Sciences, Developing Countries, Economics, Education, Environmental Studies, Foreign Countries, Geography, Geology, Government, Political Science, History, Labor, Industrial Relations, Medicine, Nursing, Dentistry, Military Science, Religion - Buddhist, Religion - Catholic, Religion - Hindu, Religion - Islamic, Religion - Jewish, Religion - Protestant, Science (General)
ISBN Prefix(es): 3-88091; 3-86120
Number of titles published annually: 20 Print
Total Titles: 1,000 Print
Subsidiaries: Nusser Verlag; International Picture- & Press-agency

nymphenburger+
Subsidiary of Buchverlage Langen-Mueller/Herbig
Thomas-Wimmer-Ring 11, 80539 Munich
Tel: (089) 290880 *Fax:* (089) 29088144
E-mail: nymphenburger@herbig.net
Web Site: www.herbig.net
Key Personnel
Man Dir & Publisher: Brigitte Fleissner-Mikorey
Rights & Permissions: Frauke Hoppen *Fax:* (089) 29088178
Assistant: Anne Jaeschke *Tel:* (089) 23088144 *E-mail:* a.jaeschke@herbig.net
Founded: 1946
Buchverlage Langen Mueller Herbig.
Subjects: Art, Biography, Child Care & Development, Crafts, Games, Hobbies, Fiction, Health, Nutrition, Nonfiction (General), Outdoor Recreation, Philosophy, Photography, Religion - Buddhist, Self-Help, Sports, Athletics, True life stories
ISBN Prefix(es): 3-485
Total Titles: 25 Print
Parent Company: F A Herbig Verlagsbuchhandlung GmbH (Germany)
Associate Companies: Langen Mueller Herbig, Thomas-Wimmer-Ring 11, 80539 Munich, Contact: Lydia Eggs *Tel:* (089) 290880 *Fax:* (089) 29088155
Imprints: Edition Meyster
Distributed by Mohr Morawa Buchvertrieb; Schweizer Buchzentrum
Warehouse: VVA-Bertelsmann Distribution GmbH, Warenannahme 100, An der Autobahn, 33310 Gutersloh
Orders to: VVA-Vereinigte Verlagsauslieferung, Postfach 7600, 33310 Gutersloh, Contact: Renate Fechtelhoff *Tel:* (05209) 805403 *Fax:* (05209) 806643

Oberbaum Verlag GmbH+
Friedelstr 6, 12047 Berlin
Tel: (030) 624 69 21 *Fax:* (030) 624 69 21
Key Personnel
Man Dir: Siegfried Heinrichs
Founded: 1966
Subjects: Government, Political Science, History, Literature, Literary Criticism, Essays, Regional Interests
ISBN Prefix(es): 3-926409; 3-928254; 3-933314

Edition Octopus & Okeanos Presse+
Himmeroder Wall 1, 53359 Rheinbach
Tel: 02226 915168 *Fax:* (02226) 915165; (040) 3603561585
E-mail: octopusokeanos@aol.com
Web Site: www.hometown.aol.delanveshaka/homepage/firma.html
Key Personnel
Man Dir: H G Kestel
Founded: 1987
Subjects: Art, Astrology, Occult, Drama, Theater, Literature, Literary Criticism, Essays, Photography, Poetry, Religion - Other
ISBN Prefix(es): 3-926850

Oeko-Test Verlag GmbH & Co KG Betriebsgesellschaft
Kasslerstr 1A, 60486 Frankfurt am Main
Mailing Address: Postfach 90 07 66, 60447 Frankfurt am Main
Tel: (069) 9 77 77-0 *Fax:* (069) 9 77 77-139
E-mail: oet.verlag@oekotest.de
Key Personnel
Man Dir: Bernd Waeltz; Albrecht Martin
Editor: Juergen Stellpflug
Publicity & Marketing: Anette Elnain *Tel:* (069) 9 77 77-133 *E-mail:* anette.elnain@oekotest.de; Friederike Elnain *Tel:* (069) 9 77 77-138 *E-mail:* friederike.elnain@oekotest.de
Founded: 1985
Subjects: Environmental Studies, Health, Nutrition
ISBN Prefix(es): 3-929530

Oekobuch Verlag & Versand GmbH+
Postfach 1126, 79216 Staufen
Tel: (07633) 50613 *Fax:* (07633) 50870
E-mail: oekobuch@t-online.de
Web Site: www.oekobuch.de
Key Personnel
Man Dir: Claudia Ladener

Contact: Heinz Ladener
Founded: 1979
Subjects: Architecture & Interior Design, Civil Engineering, Crafts, Games, Hobbies, Energy, Environmental Studies, House & Home
ISBN Prefix(es): 3-922964
Total Titles: 42 Print

Oekotopia Verlag, Wolfgang Hoffman+
Hafenweg 26, 48155 Muenster
Tel: (0251) 661035 *Fax:* (0251) 48198-0
E-mail: info@oekotopia-verlag.de
Web Site: www.oekotopia-verlag.de
Key Personnel
Owner: Wolfgang Hoffmann
Founded: 1983
Specializes in Environmental/Education.
Subjects: Drama, Theater, Education, Environmental Studies, Fiction, History, Human Relations, Humor, Music, Dance, Nonfiction (General), Outdoor Recreation, Psychology, Psychiatry
ISBN Prefix(es): 3-925169; 3-931902
Foreign Rights: Ule Koether (Brazil, Latin America, Portugal, Spain)

Oekumenischer Verlag Dr R-F Edel
Rathmecker Weg 13, 58513 Luedenscheid
Tel: (02351) 21319 *Fax:* (02351) 568908
Key Personnel
Manager: Klaus Busenius
Founded: 1976
Subjects: Art, Biblical Studies, Ethnicity, History, Language Arts, Linguistics, Philosophy, Religion - Other, Theology
ISBN Prefix(es): 3-87598
Orders to: Verlagsauslieferung Klaus Busenius, Rathmecker Weg 13, 58513 Lundenscheid

Oertel & Sporer GmbH & Co+
Burgstr 1-7, 72764 Reutlingen
Mailing Address: PO Box 1642, D-72706 Reutlingen
Tel: (07121) 302 555; (07121) 302 553
Fax: (07121) 302 558
Telex: 729634
Key Personnel
Member of General Management: Mr Ermo Lehari *Tel:* (07121) 302 122 *Fax:* (07121) 302 123 *E-mail:* lehari@compuserve.com
Founded: 1888
Publishing & printing company.
Books & Periodicals.
Subjects: Animals, Pets, Cookery, Crafts, Games, Hobbies, Nonfiction (General)
ISBN Prefix(es): 3-921017; 3-88627
Total Titles: 140 Print

Paul Oestergaard GmbH, see Columbus Verlag Paul Oestergaard GmbH

Verlag Friedrich Oetinger GmbH+
Subsidiary of Verlag Friedrich Oetinger GmbH
Poppenbuetteler Chaussee 53, 22397 Hamburg
Mailing Address: Postfach 658230, 22374 Hamburg
Tel: (040) 607909-03 *Fax:* (040) 60723-26
E-mail: oetinger@vsg-hamburg.de
Web Site: www.oetinger.de *Cable:* OETINGERBUCH
Key Personnel
Man Dir & Editorial: Silke Weitendorf
Man Dir & Sales: Thomas Huggle
Editorial: Angelika Kutsch
Publicity: Judith Richter *Tel:* (040) 607909-65; Frauke Wedler *Tel:* (040) 607909-23
Rights: Renate Reichstein *Tel:* (040) 607909-13 *Fax:* (040) 607909-51 *E-mail:* lizenzen@vsg-hamburg.de
Sales & Marketing: Dr Juergen Huebner *Tel:* (040) 607909-55 *Fax:* (040) 607909-50 *E-mail:* vertrieb@vsg-hamburg.de

Founded: 1946
Subjects: Fiction
ISBN Prefix(es): 3-7891
Subsidiaries: Cecilie Dressler Verlag

Verlag Offene Worte+
Striepenweg 31, 21147 Hamburg
Tel: (040) 7 97 13-03 *Fax:* (040) 7 97 13-304
Web Site: www.koehler-mittler.de *Cable:* VLG OFFENE WORTE, HAMBURG/W
Key Personnel
Publisher: Peter Tamm
Manager: Lothar Lichtenheldt
Sales: Hans-Focko Koehler
Subjects: Government, Political Science, Military Science
ISBN Prefix(es): 3-87599
Associate Companies: Koehlers Verlagsgesellschaft
Branch Office(s)
Austr 19, 53179 Bonn *Tel:* (0228) 530962-64 *Fax:* (0228) 230102

Oktagon Verlagsgesellschaft mbH+
Albertusstr 1, 50667 Cologne
Tel: (0221) 2059654 *Fax:* (0221) 2059660
E-mail: oktagon@buchhandlung-walterkoenig.de
Web Site: www.oktagon.de
Key Personnel
Manager: Paul Johannes Mueller
Founded: 1989
Subjects: Architecture & Interior Design, Art
ISBN Prefix(es): 3-927789
Bookshop(s): Ehrenstr 4, 50672 Cologne *Tel:* (0221) 20 59 6-0 *Fax:* (0221) 20 59 6-40 *E-mail:* order@buchhandlung-walther-koenig.de

Georg Olms Verlag AG+
Hagentorwall 7, 31134 Hildesheim
Tel: (05121) 15010 *Fax:* (05121) 150150; (05121) 32007
E-mail: info@olms.de
Web Site: www.olms.de *Cable:* HILDESHEIM
Key Personnel
Publisher: Dr Walter Georg Olms; Dietrich Olms *E-mail:* dietrich.olms@olms.de
Editorial: Dr Peter Guyot *E-mail:* guyot@olms.de; Doris Wendt *E-mail:* wendt@olms.de
Production: Andreas Maybaum
Advertising Manager: Michael Haasche
Rights & Permissions: Christiane Busch
Marketing, Editorial (Equestrian Titles): Danielle Schons *E-mail:* marketing@olms.de
Founded: 1945
Subjects: Antiques, Biography, Drama, Theater, Economics, Education, Gardening, Plants, Geography, Geology, Government, Political Science, History, Language Arts, Linguistics, Law, Library & Information Sciences, Literature, Literary Criticism, Essays, Music, Dance, Philosophy, Religion - Islamic, Religion - Jewish, Religion - Protestant, Romance, Science (General), Social Sciences, Sociology, Theology, Travel, Classical Studies, History of Art
ISBN Prefix(es): 3-487
Number of titles published annually: 250 Print; 3 CD-ROM
Total Titles: 5,000 Print
Parent Company: Georg Olms AG, Zurich, Switzerland
Associate Companies: Weidmannsche Verlagsbuchhandlung
Imprints: Olms New Media; Olms Presse
Subsidiaries: Edition Olms AG
U.S. Office(s): Georg Olms Verlag, Empire State Bldg, 350 Fifth Ave, Suite 3304, New York, NY 10118-0069, United States
Warehouse: VVA, Bertelsmann Distribution, 33399 Verl, Contact: Monika Hermesmeier *Tel:* (05241) 803844 *Fax:* (05241) 8060220

Olms New Media, *imprint of* Georg Olms Verlag AG

Olms Presse, *imprint of* Georg Olms Verlag AG

Oncken Verlag KG+
Member of Stiftung Christliche Medien
Champagne 7, 42781 Haan
Mailing Address: Postfach 2220, 42766 Haan
Tel: (02104) 968600; (02104) 968620 (sales) *Fax:* (02104) 968601
E-mail: edit@brockhaus-verlag.de; info@brockhaus-verlag.de
Web Site: www.brockhaus-verlag.de
Key Personnel
Publisher: Thomas Lardon
Editor & Publicity Manager: Hans-Werner Durau
International Rights: Christina Bradel
Founded: 1828
Subjects: Fiction, Religion - Other
ISBN Prefix(es): 3-7893
Associate Companies: R Brockhaus Verlag
Distributed by BMU (Austria); Brunnen (Switzerland)

One Way Medien OHG+
Brillerstr 18, 42105 Wuppertal
Tel: (0202) 309 9946 *Fax:* (0202) 314113
E-mail: one_way@t-online.de
Key Personnel
Publisher: Wolfgang Neuemeister
Editor: H Ralenkotter
Founded: 2000
Member of Evangelical Christian Publishers Association & Boersenverein des Deutschen Buchhandels
Subjects: Biblical Studies, Fiction, Human Relations, Nonfiction (General), Religion - Protestant, Theology
ISBN Prefix(es): 3-927772; 3-931822; 3-89895; 3-89800

Orbis Verlag fur Publizistik GmbH+
Neumarkter Str 18, 81673 Munich
Mailing Address: Postfach 800360, 81603 Munich
Tel: (089) 431890 *Fax:* (089) 43189113
Key Personnel
Man Dirs: Ortner Werner; Wolfgang Kunth
Rights & Permissions: Ms Strauss-Fischer
Founded: 1987
Subjects: Animals, Pets, Archaeology, Cookery, English as a Second Language, Gardening, Plants, Health, Nutrition, History, Language Arts, Linguistics
ISBN Prefix(es): 3-572
Parent Company: Verlagsgruppe Bertelsmann GmbH

Oreos Verlag GmbH+
Krottenthal 9, 83666 Waakirchen
Tel: (08021) 86 68 *Fax:* (08021) 17 50
E-mail: info@oreos.de
Web Site: www.oreos.de
Key Personnel
Publisher: Walter Lachenmann *E-mail:* lachenmann@oreos.de
Founded: 1982
Subjects: Biography, Music, Dance, Regional Interests
ISBN Prefix(es): 3-923657

Orlanda Frauenverlag+
Zossener Str 55-58, 10961 Berlin
Tel: (030) 216-3566; (030) 216-2960 *Fax:* (030) 2153958
E-mail: post@orlanda.de
Web Site: www.orlanda.de
Key Personnel
Manager, Rights & Permissions: Prof Dagmar Schultz, PhD
Contact: Ekpenyong Aui

Founded: 1974
Subjects: Developing Countries, Ethnicity, Gay & Lesbian, Health, Nutrition, Literature, Literary Criticism, Essays, Psychology, Psychiatry, Self-Help, Social Sciences, Sociology
ISBN Prefix(es): 3-922166

Oros Verlag+
Postfach 11 45, 4417 Altenberge
Tel: (02505) 3534 *Fax:* (02505) 3534
Key Personnel
Manager: Prof Adel Th Khoury, PhD
Founded: 1988
Subjects: Literature, Literary Criticism, Essays, Philosophy, Theology
ISBN Prefix(es): 3-89375

Osho Verlag GmbH
Lutticherstr 40, 50674 Cologne
Tel: (0221) 278 04-0 *Fax:* (0221) 278 04-66
E-mail: info@oshoverlag.de
Web Site: www.oshoverlag.de
Key Personnel
Manager: Dr Hansjoerg Sieberer; Joachim Spoh
Founded: 1988
Subjects: Behavioral Sciences, Human Relations, Philosophy, Psychology, Psychiatry, Religion - Buddhist, Religion - Catholic, Religion - Hindu, Religion - Islamic, Religion - Jewish, Religion - Protestant, Religion - Other, Self-Help
ISBN Prefix(es): 3-925205; 3-933556; 3-9800883
Divisions: Osho Times International, Deutsche Ausgabe

Osnabrueck, *imprint of* Verlag A Fromm im Druck- u Verlagshaus Fromm GmbH & Co KG

Ostfalia-Verlag Jurgen Schierer+
Kornbergweg 13, 31224 Peine
Tel: (05171) 41763 *Fax:* (05171) 41769
E-mail: 0517141763-001@t-online.de
Web Site: www.ostfalia-verlag.de
Key Personnel
Manager: Juergen Schierer *E-mail:* juergen.schierer@t-online.de
Founded: 1980
Subjects: Fiction, Poetry, Regional Interests
ISBN Prefix(es): 3-926560
Total Titles: 28 Print

Ostrecht, *imprint of* Berlin Verlag Arno Spitz GmbH

Erzabtei Sankt Ottilien, see EOS Verlag der Benefiktiner der Erzabtei St. Ottilien

Otto-Friedrich Universitat Bamberg
Kapuzinerstr 20, Room 221-223, 96045 Bamberg
Tel: (0951) 863-1020; (0951) 863-1021
Fax: (0951) 863-1005
E-mail: pressestelle@zuv.uni-bamberg.de
Web Site: www.uni-bamberg.de/zuv/presse/mitarbeiter

Outdoor Handbuch Stein KG, see ReiseHandbuch Stein KG & Outdoor Handbuch Stein KG

Pabel-Moewig Verlag KG+
Postfach 23 52, 76413 Rastatt
Tel: (07222) 13 0 *Fax:* (07222) 13 218
E-mail: kontakt@moewig.de
Web Site: www.vpm-online.de
Key Personnel
Book Manager: Eckhard Schwettmann *E-mail:* esch@pobox.com
ISBN Prefix(es): 3-8118
Number of titles published annually: 120 Print
Total Titles: 350 Print

Parent Company: Heinrich Bauer Verlag
Imprints: Moewig; Neff
Subsidiaries: Hestia Verlag; Paul Neff Verlag

Pahl-Rugenstein Verlag Nachfolger-GmbH+
Breite Str 47, 53111 Bonn
Tel: (0228) 632306 *Fax:* (0228) 634968
E-mail: prv@che-chandler.com
Key Personnel
Manager & International Rights: Arnold Bruns
Founded: 1990
Subjects: Biography, Developing Countries, Government, Political Science, History, Philosophy, Religion - Protestant, Social Sciences, Sociology, Theology
ISBN Prefix(es): 3-89144

Pal Verlagsgesellschaft mbH+
Am Oberen Luisenpark 33, 68165 Mannheim
Tel: (0621) 415741 *Fax:* (0621) 415101
E-mail: palverlag@aol.com
Web Site: www.pal-verlag.de
Key Personnel
Manager: Dr Rolf Merkle
Founded: 1986
Subjects: Biography, Psychology, Psychiatry
ISBN Prefix(es): 3-923614

Pala-Verlag GmbH+
Rheinstr 37, 64283 Darmstadt
Tel: (06151) 23028 *Fax:* (06151) 292713
E-mail: info@pala-verlag.de
Web Site: www.pala-verlag.de
Key Personnel
Man Dir: Wolfgang Hertling *E-mail:* w.hertling@pala-verlag.de
Editorial: Barbara Reis *E-mail:* b.reis@pala-verlag.de
Sales: Katrin Kolb *E-mail:* k.kolb@pala-verlag.de
Founded: 1980
Subjects: Cookery, Environmental Studies, Gardening, Plants, Health, Nutrition, Medicine, Nursing, Dentistry, Sports, Athletics
ISBN Prefix(es): 3-923176; 3-89566

Palazzi Verlag GmbH+
Ostertorsteinweg 36, 28195 Bremen
Tel: (0421) 321100 *Fax:* (0421) 321300
Key Personnel
Manager: Voller Hedwig
Founded: 1989
Subjects: Aeronautics, Aviation, Earth Sciences, Environmental Studies, Foreign Countries, Geography, Geology, Natural History, Physical Sciences, Travel
ISBN Prefix(es): 3-927956

Palmyra Verlag+
Haupstr 64, 69117 Heidelberg
Tel: (06221) 165409 *Fax:* (06221) 167310
E-mail: palmyra-verlag@t-online.de
Web Site: www.palmyra-verlag.de
Key Personnel
President: Georg Stein
Founded: 1989
Subjects: Anthropology, Foreign Countries, Government, Political Science, Music, Dance, Nonfiction (General)
ISBN Prefix(es): 3-9802298; 3-930378

Pandion-Verlag, Ulrike Schmoll+
Gartenstr 10, 55469 Simmern
Tel: (06761) 7142 *Fax:* (06761) 77172
E-mail: pandion@t-online.de; info@pandion-verlag.de
Web Site: www.pandion-verlag.de
Founded: 1954
Subjects: Art, Fiction, Poetry, Regional Interests, Religion - Other
ISBN Prefix(es): 3-922929

Edition Pandora, *imprint of* Campus Verlag GmbH

PapyRossa Verlags GmbH & Co Kommanditgesellschaft KG+
Luxemburger Str 202, 50937 Cologne
Tel: (0221) 44 85 45 *Fax:* (0221) 44 43 05
E-mail: mail@papyrossa.de
Web Site: www.papyrossa.de
Key Personnel
Manager: Dr Jurgen Harrer
Founded: 1990
Subjects: Developing Countries, Government, Political Science, History, Human Relations, Social Sciences, Sociology, Women's Studies
ISBN Prefix(es): 3-89438
Orders to: SOVA, Friesstr 20-24, 60388 Frankfurt

Edition Parabolis
Member of European Migration Centre
Schliemannstr 23, 10437 Berlin
Tel: (030) 44 65 10 65 *Fax:* (030) 444 10 85
E-mail: info@emz-berlin.de
Web Site: www.emz-berlin.de
Publishing section of the Berlin Institute for Comparative Social Research (BIVS).
Subjects: Anthropology, Ethnicity, Nonfiction (General), Social Sciences, Sociology, Migration
ISBN Prefix(es): 3-88402
Number of titles published annually: 20 Print

Paranus Verlag - Bruecke Neumuenster GmbH
Formerly Die Brucke - Neumunster ev Abt Verlag
Ehndorfer Str 13-17, 24537 Neumuenster
Mailing Address: Postfach 1264, 24502 Neumuenster
Tel: (04321) 2004-500 *Fax:* (04321) 2004-411
E-mail: verlag@paranus.de
Web Site: www.paranus.de
Key Personnel
International Rights: Fritz Bremer
Founded: 1989
Publishing project which involves mentally ill persons in the editing, producing, printing & distribution of books & periodicals.
Subjects: Art, Literature, Literary Criticism, Essays, Psychology, Psychiatry
ISBN Prefix(es): 3-926200

Parey Buchverlag, *imprint of* Blackwell Wissenschafts-Verlag GmbH

Verlag Parzeller GmbH & Co KG+
Frankfurter Str 8, 36043 Fulda
Tel: (0661) 280-663 *Fax:* (0661) 280-285
E-mail: verlag@parzeller.de
Web Site: www.buchkatalog.de/parzeller
Telex: 49838
Key Personnel
Contact: Rainer Klitsch *Tel:* (0661) 280361 *E-mail:* rainer.klitsch@parzeller.de
Founded: 1874
Subjects: Regional Interests, Religion - Catholic, Religion - Protestant, Religion - Other
ISBN Prefix(es): 3-7900
Subsidiaries: Druckerei Parzeller GmbH & Co KG

Passavia Druckerei GmbH, Verlag
Medienstr 5b, 94036 Passau
Tel: (0851) 802670 *Fax:* (0851) 802680
Web Site: www.passavia.de
Key Personnel
Man Dir: Rudolf Ramelsberger *E-mail:* rudolf.ramelsberger@passavia.de
Publishing Dir, Rights & Permissions: Bernd Kammerer
Sales: Gabi Dietl
Founded: 1888
Subjects: Fiction, House & Home, Humor, Travel

GERMANY

ISBN Prefix(es): 3-87616
Subsidiaries: Passavia Universitaetsverlag und-Druck GmbH

Passavia Universitaetsverlag und -Druck GmbH
Vornholzstr 40, 94036 Passau
Mailing Address: Postfach 2147, 94011 Passau
Tel: (0851) 700226 *Fax:* (0851) 700277
Key Personnel
Publishing Dir, Rights & Permissions: Bernd Kammerer
Subjects: Science (General)
ISBN Prefix(es): 3-922016; 3-86036
Parent Company: Passavia Druckerei GmbH, St Englmarstr 11, 94034 Passau

Patio, Galerie und Druckwerkstatt+
Laubestr 24H, 60594 Frankfurt
Tel: (06150) 84566
Key Personnel
Man Dir: Klaus Muenchschwander
Editorial: David Ward
Sales: Regine Behrends; Franz Gaber
Production: Volker Mueller; Walter Zimbrich
Publicity: Yves Daniel Zimbrich
Rights & Permissions: Manfred Linke; Renate Kafitz-Pfeuffer
Founded: 1963

Patmos Verlag GmbH & Co KG+
Am Wehrhahn 100, 40211 Duesseldorf
Tel: (0211) 16795-0 *Fax:* (0211) 16795-75
E-mail: service@patmos.de
Web Site: www.patmos.de *Cable:* PATMOS VERLAG
Key Personnel
Dir: Dr Tullio Aurelio *Tel:* (0211) 1679569
    E-mail: fauth@patmos.de
Publicity: Ralf Pollmann
Founded: 1910
Subjects: Antiques, Art, History, Literature, Literary Criticism, Essays, Religion - Other, Theology
ISBN Prefix(es): 3-491
Subsidiaries: Walter Verlag AG; Artemis & Winkler Verlag AG; Benziger Verlag AG

Pattloch Verlag GmbH & Co KG+
Hilblestr 54, 80636 Munich
Tel: (089) 9271-0 *Fax:* (089) 9271-168
Web Site: www.droemer-weltbild.de
Key Personnel
Man Dir: Bernhard Meuser
Rights & Permissions: Renate Abrasch
Founded: 1965
Subjects: Nonfiction (General)
ISBN Prefix(es): 3-629
Parent Company: Verlagsgruppe Droemer Weltbild GmbH & Co KG
Orders to: VVA Bertelsmann Distribution, Postfach 7600, 33310 Guetersloh, Jennifer Strebinger *Tel:* (05241) 801754 *Fax:* (05241) 8060260 *E-mail:* jennifer.strebinger@bertelsmann.de

Paulinus Verlag GmbH+
Maximineracht 1c, 54295 Trier
Mailing Address: Postfach 3040, 54220 Trier
Tel: (0651) 4608-100 *Fax:* (0651) 4608-221
E-mail: verlag@paulinus.de
Web Site: www.paulinus.de
Key Personnel
Publisher: Siegfried Faeth
Rights & Permissions: Dr Harald Baulig
Founded: 1875
Subjects: Religion - Other, Theology
ISBN Prefix(es): 3-7902; 3-87760
Parent Company: Paulinus Druckerei GmbH, Fleichstr 62-65, 54290 Trier
Associate Companies: Spee Buchverlag GmbH

Ingwert Paulsen Jr, see Hansa Verlag Ingwert Paulsen Jr

Pawel Panpresse+
Zum Seemenbach Nr 1, 63654 Budingen
Tel: (06041) 5822
Key Personnel
Man Dir, Production, Rights: Sascha Juritz
Founded: 1972
Subjects: Art, Literature, Literary Criticism, Essays, Poetry
ISBN Prefix(es): 3-921454
Associate Companies: Edition Druckhuette No 2
Orders to: Siehe Pawel Panpresse

Pearson Education Deutschland GmbH+
Martin-Kollar-Str 10-12, 81829 Munich
Tel: (089) 46003-0 *Fax:* (089) 46003-120
E-mail: firstinitiallastname@pearson.de
Key Personnel
President: Axel Nehen *Tel:* (089) 46003 401
    Fax: (089) 46003 410
VP, Finance & Operations: Rudolf Nertinger
    Tel: (089) 46003 123
Foreign Rights: Ines Killat *Tel:* (089) 46003 124
Assistant to the President: Britta Tiedtke-Heimers
    Tel: (089) 46003 405
Editorial Dir, M & T: Catherine Magdolen
    Tel: (089) 46003 336 *Fax:* (089) 46003 330
Editorial Dir, Addison Wesley: Christian
    Rauscher *Tel:* (089) 46003 331 *Fax:* (089) 46003 330
Human Resources Manager: Uschi Jacob
    Tel: (089) 46003 122
Founded: 1993
Subjects: Computer Science
ISBN Prefix(es): 3-89090; 3-87791; 3-922120
Imprints: Que; SAMS; Prentice Hall; X-Games
Distributor for Macmillan Computer Publishing USA; Prentice Hall
Warehouse: Adelmannstr 5, 81827 Munich

Pelikan Vertriebsgesellschaft mbH & Co KG+
Podbielskistr 141, 30177 Hannover
Tel: (0511) 6969-0 *Fax:* (0511) 6969-212
Web Site: www.pelikan.de
Telex: 175118481 Pelikan
Key Personnel
Man Dir & Marketing Manager: Terry Edwards
Marketing: Michael Fey *E-mail:* m.fey@pelikan.de
Founded: 1978
Subjects: Fiction
ISBN Prefix(es): 3-8144
Parent Company: Pelikan Holding, Switzerland
Associate Companies: Franz-Buttner, AG/Pelikan-Vertrieb, Wollerau, Switzerland
Distributor for Diverse

Pendragon Verlag+
Stapenhorststr 15, 33615 Bielefeld
Tel: (0521) 69689 *Fax:* (0521) 174470
E-mail: pendragon.verlag@t-online.de
Web Site: www.pendragon.de
Key Personnel
Man Dir, Sales, Rights & Permissions: Andrea Schiffer
Editorial: Gunther Butkus
Production & Publicity: Michael Baltus
Founded: 1981
Subjects: Art, Criminology, Fiction, History, Literature, Literary Criticism, Essays, Poetry
ISBN Prefix(es): 3-923306; 3-929096
Imprints: Edition Bielefelden Kunstverein

Perryman, see Babel Verlag Kevin Perryman

Verlag Sigrid Persen
Postfach 260, 21637 Horneburg
Tel: (04163) 81 40 0 *Fax:* (04163) 8140 50
Web Site: www.persen.de

Founded: 1976
Subjects: English as a Second Language, Language Arts, Linguistics, Mathematics, Music, Dance
ISBN Prefix(es): 3-921809; 2-89358

Justus Perthes Verlag Gotha GmbH+
Justus-Perthes-Str 1-5, 99867 Gotha
Mailing Address: Postfach 274, 99854 Gotha
Tel: (03621) 385-0 *Fax:* (03621) 385-102
E-mail: perthes@klett-mail.de
Web Site: www.klett-verlag.de/klett-perthes *Cable:* PERTHES GOTHA
Key Personnel
Dir: Volker Streibel
Founded: 1785
Subjects: Geography, Geology, History, Cartography
ISBN Prefix(es): 3-7301; 3-623
Parent Company: Ernst Klett Verlag GmbH, Stuttgart
Imprints: Haack; Schreiber-Naturtafeln

Klett Perthes, see Justus Perthes Verlag Gotha GmbH

C F Peters Musikverlag GmbH & Co KG
Kennedyallee 101, 60596 Frankfurt am Main
Mailing Address: Postfach 700851, 60558 Frankfurt am Main
Tel: (069) 6300990 *Fax:* (069) 635401
E-mail: info@musia.de
Web Site: www.musia.de *Cable:* PETERSEDIT
Key Personnel
Partner: Dr Johannes Petschull; Roland Schied
Founded: 1800
Subjects: Music, Dance
ISBN Prefix(es): 3-87626
Associate Companies: C F Peters Corporation, NY, United States; Hinrichsen Edition Ltd, London, United Kingdom
Imprints: M P Belaieff; Henry Litolff's Verlag; Edition Peters; Edition Schwann

Edition Peters, *imprint of* C F Peters Musikverlag GmbH & Co KG

Jens Peters Publikationen+
Gotenstr 65, 10829 Berlin
Tel: (030) 7847265 *Fax:* (030) 7883127
Web Site: www.jenspeters.com
Key Personnel
President, Rights & Permissions: Jens Peters
Founded: 1977
Subjects: Travel
ISBN Prefix(es): 3-923821; 3-9800154
Orders to: Osterholzer Dorfstr 45, 28307 Bremen
Tel: (0421) 451743 *Fax:* (0421) 455406

Pfaffenweiler Presse+
MittlereStr 23, 79292 Pfaffenweiler
Tel: (07664) 8999 *Fax:* (07664) 8999
E-mail: info@pfaffenweiler-presse.de
Web Site: www.pfaffenweiler-presse.de
Key Personnel
Owner: Herta Flicker
Founded: 1974
ISBN Prefix(es): 3-921365; 3-927702

Pfalzische Verlagsanstalt GmbH
Industriestr 15, 76829 Landau
Mailing Address: Postfach 1950, 76809 Landau
Tel: (06341) 142-0 *Fax:* (06341) 142-265
Key Personnel
Publisher: Herr Karl-Friedrich Geissler
Manager: Rolf Schaefer; Horst K Neubauer
Founded: 1892
Subjects: Art, Biography, Fiction, Foreign Countries, Wine & Spirits

ISBN Prefix(es): 3-87629
Orders to: VSB-Braunschweig, Postfach 4738, 3300 Braunschweig

Pfeiffer bei Klett-Cotta, *imprint of* J G Cotta'sche Buchhandlung Nachfolger GmbH

J Pfeiffer Verlag+
Anzingerstr 15, 81671 Munich
Tel: (089) 4130010 *Fax:* (089) 41300138
Key Personnel
Publisher & Editorial: Lydia Franzelius
Editor: Dr Christine Treml
Production: Siegbert Seitz
Founded: 1882
Subjects: Psychology, Psychiatry, Religion - Other
ISBN Prefix(es): 3-7904
Parent Company: Manz Verlag
Shipping Address: mi-Verlags Service GmbH, Justus-von-Liebig-Str 1, 8689 Landsberg-Lech
Warehouse: mi-Verlags Service GmbH, Justus-von-Liebig-Str 1, 86898 Landsberg-Lech
Orders to: Verlagsgruppe Manz

Verlag Dr Friedrich Pfeil
Wolfratshauser Str 27, 81379 Munich
Tel: (089) 7428270 *Fax:* (089) 7242772
E-mail: 100417.1722@compuserve.com
Web Site: www.pfeil-verlag.de
Key Personnel
Editor: Dr Friedrich Pfeil
Founded: 1981
Subjects: Biological Sciences, Philosophy
ISBN Prefix(es): 3-923871; 3-931516
Branch Office(s)
Falkweg 37, 81243 Munich

Richard Pflaum Verlag GmbH & Co KG+
Postfach 190737, 80607 Munich
Tel: (089) 12607-0 *Fax:* (089) 12607-202
E-mail: hoefer-heyne@pflaum.de
Web Site: www.pflaum.de
Key Personnel
Manager: Beda Bohinger
Head Book Dept: Helmut Brackebusch
Founded: 1919
Subjects: Communications, Electronics, Electrical Engineering, Medicine, Nursing, Dentistry
ISBN Prefix(es): 3-7905
Subsidiaries: Gastgewerbe Verlag GmbH & Co KG; Huethig und Pflaum Verlag GmbH & Co KG Laenderdienst Verlag GmbH
Branch Office(s)
Bad Kissingen
Berlin
Dusseldorf
Heidelberg

Philipp Reclam Jun Verlag GmbH+
Siemensstr 32, 71254 Ditzingen
Mailing Address: Postfach 1349, 71252 Ditzingen
Tel: (07156) 163 0 *Fax:* (07156) 163 197
E-mail: info@reclam.de
Web Site: www.reclam.de *Cable:* RECLAM DITZINGEN
Key Personnel
Publisher: Dr Frank R Max
Publicity Dir: Dr Karl-Heinz Fallbacher
Sales Manager: Juergen Bernardi; Anja Krauss
Rights & Permissions: Dr Stephan Koranyi
Founded: 1828
Subjects: Art, Fiction, Film, Video, Music, Dance, Philosophy, Poetry, Religion - Other
ISBN Prefix(es): 3-15
Parent Company: Philipp Reclam jun GmbH & Co, Stuttgart
Distributor for Reclam Verlag Leipzig

Philippka-Sportverlag+
Rektoratsweg 36, 48159 Muenster
Mailing Address: Postfach 150105, 48061 Muenster
Tel: (0251) 230050 *Fax:* (0251) 2300599
E-mail: info@philippka.de
Web Site: www.philippka.de
Key Personnel
Publisher: Konrad Honig *Tel:* (0251) 23005 25
Publicity: Gudrun Quilling *Tel:* (0251) 23005 22
E-mail: quilling@philippka.de
Founded: 1978
Subjects: Sports, Athletics
ISBN Prefix(es): 3-922067
Number of titles published annually: 3 Print
Total Titles: 50 Print

Philipps-Universitaet Marburg
Biegenstr 10, 35032 Marburg
Tel: (06421) 28-20 *Fax:* (06421) 28-22500
E-mail: verwaltung@ub.uni.marburg.de
Web Site: www.uni-marburg.de
Telex: 482-372
Key Personnel
President: Prof Dr Kern,
Public Relations: Klaus Walter
Librarian: Heino Krueger
Subjects: Anthropology, Archaeology, History, Library & Information Sciences, Psychology, Psychiatry, Science (General)
ISBN Prefix(es): 3-8185

Philosophia Verlag GmbH+
Gundelindenstr 4, 80805 Munich
Mailing Address: Postfach 221362, 80503 Munich
Tel: (089) 299975 *Fax:* (089) 299975
E-mail: info@philosophiaverlag.com
Web Site: www.philosophiaverlag.com
Key Personnel
Man Dir & Publisher: Ulrich Staudinger
Editorial Board: Hans Burkhardt; Barry Smith; Ignacio Angelelli; Christian Thiel
Sales & Marketing: Thomas Kiesebrink
Founded: 1966
Publishers for philosophy & economics.
Membership(s): Stock Exchange of German Booksellers; Association of Bavarian Publishers & Booksellers.
Subjects: Economics, Philosophy
ISBN Prefix(es): 3-88405
Number of titles published annually: 3 Print
Total Titles: 70 Print
Orders to: Herold Verlagsauslieferung, Kolpingring 4, 82041 Oberhaching/Munich *Tel:* (089) 613871-0 *Fax:* (089) 61387120 *E-mail:* herold-oberhaching@t-online.de *Web Site:* www.herold-va.de

Physica, *imprint of* Springer-Verlag GmbH & Co KG

Physica-Verlag+
Imprint of Springer-Verlag
Tiergartenstr 17, 69121 Heidelberg
Mailing Address: PO Box 105280, 69042 Heidelberg
Tel: (06221) 4878-0 *Fax:* (06221) 4878-177
E-mail: physica@springer.de
Web Site: www.springer.de
Key Personnel
Man Dir: Dr Werner A Mueller *Tel:* (06221) 4878-345 *E-mail:* w.a.mueller@springer.de
Dir, Division Sales/Marketing & Corporate Development: Arnoud de Kemp *Tel:* (06221) 487-397 *Fax:* (06221) 487-288 *E-mail:* dekemp@springer.de
Journals/LINK Dir: Gertraud Griepke *Tel:* (06221) 487-457 *Fax:* (06221) 487-288 *E-mail:* griepke@springer.de
Territory Manager (Middle East, Africa, Greece, Turkey): Franziska Sachsse *Tel:* (06221) 487-628 *Fax:* (06221) 487-620 *E-mail:* sachsse@springer.de
Marketing Communications Dir: Michael Lechler *Tel:* (06221) 487-515 *Fax:* (06221) 487-156 *E-mail:* lechler@springer.de
Sales & Marketing Manager, Client Presses: Sandra Cortes-Hemmerich *Tel:* (06221) 487-289 *Fax:* (06221) 487-620 *E-mail:* cortes@springer.de
Territory Manager (Scandinavia): Bettina Schies *Tel:* (06221) 487-309 *Fax:* (06221) 487-620 *E-mail:* schies@springer.de
Territory Manager (Belgium, The Netherlands): Marc Puma *Tel:* (01) 53 93 37 79 *Fax:* (01) 53 93 36 83 *E-mail:* puma@springer-paris.fr
Specializes in Statistics & Information Systems.
Subjects: Business, Economics, Finance, Regional Interests, Science (General), Econometrics, Information Systems
ISBN Prefix(es): 3-7908
Number of titles published annually: 100 Print
Total Titles: 500 Print
Branch Office(s)
Springer-Verlag Wien New York, Sachsenplatz 4-6, A-1201 Vienna, Austria *Tel:* (01) 330 24 15 *Fax:* (01) 330 24 26
Foreign Rep(s): Academic Marketing Services (Pty) Ltd (South Africa); Eastern Book Service Inc (Japan); Michael Lechler (Austria, Germany, Luxembourg, Switzerland); Behruz Neirami (Iran); Springer-Verlag (Australia, Africa, Baltic States, Bangladesh, Eastern Europe, Egypt, India, Israel, Middle East, New Zealand, Nepal, Pakistan, Russia & CIS, Sri Lanka, Turkey); Springer-Verlag France (France, Morocco, Tunisia, Algeria); Springer-Verlag Hong Kong Ltd (China, Hong Kong, Indonesia, Malaysia, Myanmar, Philippines, South Korea, Singapore, Thailand, Vietnam, Macao); Springer-Verlag Iberica SAI (Portugal, Spain); Springer-Verlag Italia Srl (Greece, Italy); Springer-Verlag Liaison Office (Bangladesh, India, Nepal, Pakistan, Sri Lanka); Springer-Verlag London Ltd (Belgium, UK, Netherlands, Ireland, Scandinavia); Springer-Verlag New York Inc (North America, South America); Springer-Verlag Singapore Pte Ltd (Malaysia, SE Asia, Singapore, Thailand); Springer-Verlag Taipei (Taiwan)
Shipping Address: Springer Shipping Centre, Hatschekstr 8, 69126 Heidelberg
Orders to: Customer Service, Haberstr 7, 69126 Heidelberg *Tel:* (06221) 345221 *Fax:* (06221) 345229

PIAG, see PIAG Presse Informations AG

Heinz Pier+
Carl-Schurz-Str 98, 50374 Erftstadt
Mailing Address: Postfach 2305, Erftstadt 50357
Tel: (02235) 3998 *Fax:* (02235) 41654
Key Personnel
Owner: Heinz Pier *Tel:* (02235) 44808
Founded: 1922
ISBN Prefix(es): 3-924576
Branch Office(s)
Bonnerstr 26, Lechenich, 50374 Erftstadt, Contact: Hedwig Pier *Tel:* (02235) 71959 *Fax:* (02235) 953753

Paul Pietsch Verlage GmbH & Co+
Olgastr 86, 70180 Stuttgart
Mailing Address: Postfach 103743, 70032 Stuttgart
Tel: (0711) 2 10 80-0 *Fax:* (0711) 2 10 80-82; (0711) 2 36 04-15
E-mail: ppv@motorbuch.de
Key Personnel
Man Dir: Paul Pietsch
Man Dir & Editorial: Dr Patricia Scholten-Pietsch
Rights & Permissions: Patricia Hofmann
Founded: 1962
Subjects: Aeronautics, Aviation, Automotive, How-to, Maritime, Military Science, Travel
ISBN Prefix(es): 3-87943; 3-613; 3-344

Associate Companies: Verlag Mueller-Rueschlikon
Divisions: Motorbuch-Verlag; Pietsch-Verlag; Schrader-Verlag; Transpress
Distributed by Bucheli-Verlag (Switzerland); Mueller-Rueschlikon (Switzerland)
Warehouse: Koch, Neff & Oetinger & Co, Schockenriedstr 39, 70565 Stuttgart

Piper Verlag GmbH+
Georgenstr 4, 80799 Munich
Tel: (089) 381801-0 *Fax:* (089) 338704
E-mail: info@piper.de
Web Site: www.piper.de
Key Personnel
Publisher: Viktor Niemann
Man Dir: Hartmut Jedicke
Editorial: Ulrike Buergel-Goodwin; Bettina Feldweg; Tanja Graf; Thomas Tebbe; Dr Klaus Stadler; Ulrich Wank
Foreign Rights: Ingrid Fuehrer
Contracts & Rights: Annette Sabelus
Sales Manager: Christa Beiling
Press Manager: Eva Brenndorfer
Adverstising Manager: Ingrid Ullrich
Founded: 1904
Specialize in music.
Subjects: Biography, Fiction, History, Music, Dance, Philosophy, Psychology, Psychiatry, Science (General), Theology
ISBN Prefix(es): 3-492
Number of titles published annually: 300 Print
Parent Company: Bonnier Media Holding GmbH
Imprints: Kabel Verlag; Malik Verlag
Orders to: Koch, Neff, Oetinger & Co, Schockenriedstr 39, 70551 Stuttgart

Pixel Transfer Design Studio, *imprint of* Extent Verlag und Service Wolfgang M Flamm

Verlag Ploetz, *imprint of* Verlag Herder GmbH & Co KG

pmi Verlag+
August-Schanz-Str 8, 60433 Frankfurt am Main
Tel: (069) 54 80 00-0 *Fax:* (069) 54 80 00 66
E-mail: pmiverlag@aol.com
Web Site: www.pmi-verlag.de
Key Personnel
Editor & Director: Peter Hoffmann
Manager & International Rights: Karin Hoffmann
Founded: 1975
Subjects: Biological Sciences, Finance, Health, Nutrition, Law, Medicine, Nursing, Dentistry
ISBN Prefix(es): 3-89119; 3-89143; 3-921721; 3-922357; 3-926681; 3-9802599; 3-86007; 3-932765; 3-9804734; 3-89786
Subsidiaries: Universimed; Universimed AG
Warehouse: Koch, Neff & Oettinger & Co, Schockenriedstr 3, 70565 Stuttgart *Fax:* (0711) 78991010 (books only)

Verlag Walter Podszun Burobedarf-Bucher Abt+
Elisabethstr 23-25, 59929 Brilon
Mailing Address: Postfach 1525, 59918 Brilon
Tel: (02961) 53213 *Fax:* (02961) 2508
E-mail: verlag.podszun@t-online.de
Web Site: podszun.com
Key Personnel
Editor: Walter Podszun
International Rights: Brigitte Podszun
Founded: 1969
Subjects: Automotive, Engineering (General), Humor, Transportation
ISBN Prefix(es): 3-86133; 3-923448
Bookshop(s): Buchhandlung Podszun, Bahnhofstr 9, 59929 Brilon

Podzun-Pallas Verlag GmbH+
Kohlhaeuserstr 8, 61200 Woelfersheim
Tel: (06036) 9436 *Fax:* (06036) 6270
Web Site: www.podzun-pallas.de
Key Personnel
Man Dir, Rights & Permissions: Beate Danker
Editorial & Sales: Mrs Karin Kuenzel
Founded: 1979
Subjects: Military Science
ISBN Prefix(es): 3-7909

Poetik und Hermeneutik, *imprint of* Wilhelm Fink GmbH & Co Verlags-KG

Politik und Spiritualitaet, *imprint of* Drei Eichen Verlag Manuel Kissener

Galerie Eva Poll
Luetzowplatz 7, 10785 Berlin
Tel: (030) 261 70 91 *Fax:* (030) 261 70 92
E-mail: galerie@poll-berlin.de
Web Site: www.germangalleries.com/poll
Key Personnel
International Rights: Lothar C Poll
Founded: 1968
Subjects: Art

POLLeditionen Verlag, see Galerie Eva Poll

Pollner Verlag+
Rotdornstr 7, 85764 Oberschleissheim
Tel: (089) 3151890 *Fax:* (089) 3151890
E-mail: info@pollner-verlag.de
Web Site: www.pollner-verlag.de
Key Personnel
Contact: Max Pollner
Schwerpunkt Kanuliteratur Outdoor Sports.
Subjects: Environmental Studies, Humor, Outdoor Recreation, Travel, Sport, Kanu, Kajak
ISBN Prefix(es): 3-925660

Polyband Gesellschaft fur Bild Tontraeger mbH & Co Betriebs KG
Am Moosfeld 37, 81829 Munich
Tel: (089) 420 03-0 *Fax:* (089) 420 03-42
E-mail: contact@polyband.de
Web Site: www.polyband.de
Telex: 522636 pdy d
Key Personnel
Man Dir: Swetlana Winkel
Marketing: Marco Koesling *E-mail:* marco.koesling@polyband.de
Publicity: Marita Heyne *E-mail:* presse@polyband.de
Founded: 1963
Subjects: Film, Video
ISBN Prefix(es): 3-89276

Polyglott-Verlag+
Member of The Langenscheidt Group
Neusserstr 3, 80807 Munich
Mailing Address: Postfach 401120, 80711 Munich
Tel: (089) 360960 *Fax:* (089) 36096-222 (general); (089) 36096-258 (orders)
Key Personnel
Man Dir: Karl Ernst Tielebier-Langenscheidt *E-mail:* redaktion@polyglott.de; Andreas Langenscheidt
Publishing Dir: Rolf Muller
Advertising: Brigitte Pasch
Editorial: Barbara Lennartz
Founded: 1902
Sales & promotion through Langenscheidt KG.
Subjects: Travel
ISBN Prefix(es): 3-493
Orders to: Langenscheidt KG, Neusserstr 3, 80807 Munich

Polygraph Verlag GmbH+
Schaumainkai 85, 60596 Frankfurt
Tel: (069) 630086-0 *Fax:* (069) 630086-50 *Cable:* POLYGRAPHVERLAG FRANKFURT MAIN
Key Personnel
Man Dir, Rights & Permissions: Mrs Ulrike Schulz
Sales Dir & International Rights: Kristian Senn
Production: Dieter Borniger
Editorial-Staff Dir: Walter Mikolasch
Founded: 1947
Subjects: Career Development, Publishing & Book Trade Reference, Technology
ISBN Prefix(es): 3-87641
U.S. Office(s): Fred E Noemer, 50 Sherwood Rd, Norwood, NJ 07648-2320, United States
Tel: 201-784-1666 *Fax:* 201-784-2666

Portikus
Schoene Aussicht 2, 60311 Frankfurt am Main
Tel: (069) 219 987-60; (069) 219 987-59 *Fax:* (069) 219 987-61
E-mail: portikus@pop.stadt-frankfurt.de
Web Site: www.portikus.de
Key Personnel
Dir: Dr Daniel Birnbaum
Curator: Jochen Volz
Founded: 1987
Specialize in exhibition catalogues.
Subjects: Art
ISBN Prefix(es): 3-928071
Number of titles published annually: 8 Print
Total Titles: 90 Print
Parent Company: Staedelschule

Possev-Verlag GmbH+
Flurscheideweg 15, 65936 Frankfurt
Tel: (069) 34-12-65 *Fax:* (069) 34-38-41
E-mail: possev-ffm@t-online.de
Key Personnel
Manager: Leonid Mueller
Founded: 1945
Also runs a translation agency.
ISBN Prefix(es): 3-7912
Branch Office(s)
Redaktion Possev, Postfach 325, 117602 Moscow, Russian Federation *Tel:* (095) 2831090

Postreiter-Verlag GmbH+
Lucile-Grahn-Str 39, 81675 Munich
Tel: (030) 8938840 *Fax:* (030) 89388420
Key Personnel
Man Dir & Publisher: Hans Meisinger
Rights & Publicity: Christiane Schneider
Founded: 1947
ISBN Prefix(es): 3-7421
Shipping Address: MVS Meisinger Verlagsservice, Am Steinfeld 4, 94065 Waldkirchen
Warehouse: MVS Meisinger Verlagsservice, Am Steinfeld 4, 94065 Waldkirchen
Orders to: MVS Meisinger Verlagsservice, Am Steinfeld 4, 94065 Waldkirchen

W Poth GbR, see Verlagsbuchhandlung Megapress, Franz-J Gaber

Potsdamer Verlagbuchhandlung GmbH
Platz der Einheit 14, 14467 Potsdam
Mailing Address: Postfach 601261, 14412 Potsdam
Tel: (030) 253738-0 *Fax:* (030) 253738-39
Key Personnel
Contact: Hubertus Schenkel
ISBN Prefix(es): 3-910196

Prasenz Verlag der Jesus Bruderschaft eV+
Gnadenthal, 65597 Huenfelden
Tel: (06438) 81300 *Fax:* (06438) 81310
Web Site: www.uni-giessen.de/~gfl002/vdbiol/homepage/jesus.htm
Key Personnel
Dir: Jens Oertel
Founded: 1962

Subjects: Art, Poetry, Religion - Jewish
ISBN Prefix(es): 3-87630

Praxis der Zahnheilkunde, *imprint of* Urban und Fischer Verlag fur Medizin

Premop Verlag GmbH+
Kuechelstr 12, 81375 Munich
Mailing Address: Joergstr 86, 80689 Munich
Tel: (089) 562257 *Fax:* (089) 5803214
E-mail: premop@aol.com
Key Personnel
Manager: Bernard Schenkel
Founded: 1988
Subjects: Music, Dance
ISBN Prefix(es): 3-927724
Subsidiaries: Edition Premop

Prentice Hall, *imprint of* Pearson Education Deutschland GmbH

PIAG Presse Informations AG+
Landstr 67a, 76547 Sinzheim Baden
Tel: (07221) 301 7560 *Fax:* (07221) 301 7570
E-mail: office@piag.de; piag.visuell@t-online.de; bestellung@piag.de
Web Site: www.piag.de; www.pictureexchange.de
Key Personnel
Man Dir: Dieter Brinzer
Publicity Dir: Thea Gutzeit *Tel:* (0721) 301 7561
 E-mail: order@piag.de
Sales & Advertising Dir: Sven Kadow
 Tel: (07721) 301 7563 *E-mail:* s.kadow@piag.de
Editorial Services: Dr Stefan Hartmann
 Tel: (07221) 301 7564 *E-mail:* s.hartmann@piag.de
Administration: Christiane Kist *Tel:* (07221) 301 7562 *E-mail:* office@piag.de
Founded: 1963
Publisher of specialized books & magazines for the trade of published photography.
Subjects: Law, Photo law & photo prices in Europe
ISBN Prefix(es): 3-921864; 3-922725

Presse Verlagsgesellschaft mbH+
Ludwigstr 37, 60327 Frankfurt am Main
Tel: (069) 296875 *Fax:* (069) 97460-400
E-mail: journal@mmg.de
Web Site: www.journal-frankfurt.de
Key Personnel
Man Dir, International Rights: Dr Carsten Brandt
 Tel: (01) 61886 *E-mail:* grundlagen-praxis@t-online.de; Carsten Lienemann
Founded: 1980
Subjects: Regional Interests, Homeopathy
ISBN Prefix(es): 3-928789
Number of titles published annually: 2 Print
Total Titles: 7 Print
Parent Company: MMG - Medieu Marketing Gruppe
Subsidiaries: K/C/E Marketing GmbH

Guido Pressler Verlag+
Auf dem Strifft, 52393 Huertgenwald
Tel: (02429) 1385; (02408) 929692 *Fax:* (02408) 955931
E-mail: info@pressler-verlag.com
Web Site: www.pressler-verlag.com
Key Personnel
Owner: Guido Pressler
Founded: 1957
Subjects: Art, History, Literature, Literary Criticism, Essays, Philosophy, Psychology, Psychiatry
ISBN Prefix(es): 3-87646

Prestel Verlag+
Mandlstr 26, 80802 Munich
Tel: (089) 38 17 09 0 *Fax:* (089) 33 51 75
E-mail: presse@prestel.de
Web Site: www.prestel.de *Cable:* PRESTELVERLAG
Key Personnel
Executive Publisher: Urban Meister
Publisher: Juergen Tesch
Sales Dir: Gerhard Grubbe
Advertising Dir: James Gibbs
Publicity Dir: Petra Gut
Financial Dir: Thomas Zuhr
Founded: 1924
Subjects: Architecture & Interior Design, Art, Photography, Travel
ISBN Prefix(es): 3-7913
Branch Office(s)
Prestel Publishing Ltd, 4 Bloomsbury Place, London WC1A 2QA, United Kingdom, Contact: James Attlee *Tel:* (020) 7323 5004 *Fax:* (020) 7636 8004 *E-mail:* sales@prestel-uk.co.uk
U.S. Office(s): Prestel Publishing, 175 Fifth Ave, New York, NY 10010, United States, Contact: Stephen Hulburt *Tel:* 212-995-2720 *Fax:* 212-995-2733 *E-mail:* sales@prestel-usa.com
Distributor for Kehayoff Verlag

Preussische Koepfe, *imprint of* Stapp Verlag Wolfgang Stapp

Helmut Preussler Verlag+
Dagmarstr 8, 90482 Nuremberg
Tel: (0911) 95478 18 *Fax:* (0911) 542486
E-mail: preussler_verlag@t_online.de *Cable:* PREUSSLER-VERLAG
Key Personnel
Man Dir, Editorial, Production & Rights & Permissions: Achin Raak
Sales, Publicity: Annemarie Seeberger
Founded: 1973
ISBN Prefix(es): 3-921332; 3-925362
Associate Companies: Preussler Druck & Versand GmbH
Subsidiaries: Versandbuchhandlung Gebhart; Polizei Verlag Heinz Krause
Bookshop(s): Ernst Gebhard, Dagmarstr 8, 90482 Nuremberg

Pro Natur Verlag GmbH+
Ziegelhuettenweg 43A, 60598 Frankfurt am Main
Tel: (069) 9688610 *Fax:* (069) 96886124
Key Personnel
Manager: Rudolf L Schreiber
Founded: 1979
Subjects: Environmental Studies
ISBN Prefix(es): 3-88582
Parent Company: Pro Natur Gesellschaft zur Foerderung des Umweltschutzes mbH

Projektion J Buch- und Musikverlag GmbH+
Dillerberg 2, 35614 Asslar-Berghausen
Mailing Address: Postfach 1149, 35607 Asslar
Tel: (06443) 680 *Fax:* (06443) 6834
E-mail: info@gerth.de
Web Site: www.gerth.de
Key Personnel
International Rights: Christian Goelker
Founded: 1989
Subjects: Fiction, How-to, Human Relations, Management, Music, Dance, Nonfiction (General), Religion - Other, Self-Help, Theology, Western Fiction, study aids
ISBN Prefix(es): 3-89490; 3-925352; 3-9800258
Showroom(s): Rheingaustr 85A, 65203 Wiesbaden
Bookshop(s): Rheingauster 85A, 65203 Wiesbaden
Shipping Address: Rheingauster 85A, 65203 Wiesbaden
Warehouse: Rheingaustr 85A, 65203 Wiesbaden
Orders to: Rheingaustr 85A, 65203 Wiesbaden

Propylaeen Verlag, Zweigniederlassung Berlin der Ullstein Buchverlage GmbH+
Charlottenstr 13, 10969 Berlin
Mailing Address: Postfach 8030, 10888 Berlin
Tel: (0302) 5913500 *Fax:* (030) 25913533 *Cable:* ULLSTEINBUCH BERLIN
Key Personnel
Man Dir: Dr Wolfram Goebel
Sales Dir: Karl-Heinz Reimann
Chief Editor (Hardcover): Dr Uwe Heldt
Chief Editor (Paperbacks): Dr Juergen Mueller
Rights: Heidi Walitza
Founded: 1903
Subjects: Architecture & Interior Design, Art, Biography, Education, Ethnicity, Fiction, Film, Video, Geography, Geology, Government, Political Science, Health, Nutrition, History, How-to, Humor, Literature, Literary Criticism, Essays, Maritime, Military Science, Music, Dance, Mysteries, Nonfiction (General), Poetry, Romance, Science (General), Social Sciences, Sociology, Travel
ISBN Prefix(es): 3-549; 3-550; 3-548; 3-333
Parent Company: Ullstein Buchverlage GmbH & Co KG
Associate Companies: SVB Sportverlag Berlin
Subsidiaries: Propylaeen Verlag; Ullstein Taschenbuchverlag; Verlag Gesundheit
U.S. Office(s): 439 Ninth St, No 2, New York, NY 10009, United States, Contact: Liz Fried *Tel:* 212-533-2296
Warehouse: VVA Bertelsmann Distribution GmbH, An der Autobahn, 33310 Gutersloh

Psychiatrie-Verlag GmbH+
Thomas-Mannstr 49a, 53111 Bonn
Tel: (0228) 725340 *Fax:* (0228) 7253420
E-mail: verlag@psychiatrie.de
Web Site: www.psychiatrie.de/verlag
Key Personnel
Publishing Manager: York Bieger
 E-mail: bieger@psychiatre.de; Ute Hueper
Founded: 1978
Subjects: Health, Nutrition, Psychology, Psychiatry
ISBN Prefix(es): 3-88414
Orders to: VVA, Fr Bienne, Postfach 7777, 33310 Gutersloh

Psychologie Verlags Union GmbH+
Werderstr 10, 69469 Weinheim
Mailing Address: Postfach 100154, 69441 Weinheim
Tel: (06201) 60070 *Fax:* (06201) 17464
E-mail: info@beltz.de
Web Site: www.beltz.de
Key Personnel
Man Dir: Dr Manfred Beltz Ruebelmann
Publishing Manager: Dr Heike Berger
 Tel: (06201) 6007370 *Fax:* (06201) 6007395
 E-mail: h.berger@beltz.de
Contact: Michaela Frommherz *E-mail:* m.frommherz@beltz.de
Founded: 1986
Subjects: Behavioral Sciences, Biological Sciences, Business, Child Care & Development, Communications, Education, Environmental Studies, Psychology, Psychiatry, Social Sciences, Sociology
ISBN Prefix(es): 3-621
Parent Company: Beltz Verlag, Werderstr 10, 69469 Weinheim

Psychosozial-Verlag+
Goethestr 29, 35390 Giessen
Tel: (0641) 77819 *Fax:* (0641) 77742
E-mail: info@psychosozial-verlag.de; bestellung@psychosozial-verlag.de
Web Site: www.psychosozial-verlag.de
Key Personnel
Publisher: Dr Hans-Jurgen Wirth
Founded: 1991
Specialize in psychoanalysis.
Subjects: History, Psychology, Psychiatry, Social Sciences, Sociology

ISBN Prefix(es): 3-932133; 3-930096; 3-89806
Total Titles: 210 Print

Publik-Forum-Verlagsgesellschaft mbH
Krebsmuehle, 61440 Oberursel, Taunus
Mailing Address: Postfach 2010, 61410 Oberursel
Tel: (06171) 70030 *Fax:* (06171) 700340
Key Personnel
Manager: Dieter Grohmann
ISBN Prefix(es): 3-88095; 3-921807

Pulp Master Frank Nowatzki Verlag+
Imprint of Maas Verlag
Kirchgasse 2, 12043 Berlin
Tel: (030) 6868292 *Fax:* (030) 6868292
E-mail: master@txt.de
Key Personnel
Man Dir, Rights & Permissions: Frank Nowatzki
Founded: 1989
Subjects: Fiction, Mysteries
ISBN Prefix(es): 3-927734
Orders to: Bugrim, Saalburgstr 3, 12099 Berlin

Verlag Friedrich Pustet GmbH & Co Kg+
Gutenbergstr 8, 93051 Regensburg
Mailing Address: Postfach 100862, 93008 Regensburg
Tel: (0941) 9 20 22-0 *Fax:* (0941) 94 86 52
E-mail: pustetverlag@donan.de
Web Site: www.pustetverlag.de *Cable:* PUSTET
Key Personnel
Man Dir: Elisabeth Pustet
Editorial: Fritz Pustet
Founded: 1826
Subjects: Archaeology, Art, Biography, History, Religion - Catholic, Theology
ISBN Prefix(es): 3-7917
Bookshop(s): Buchhandlung Friedrich Pustet, Gesandtenstr 6, Regensburg; Kleiner Exerzierplatz 4, Passau; Karolinenstr 12, Augsburg, Thereseuplatz 41, Straubing; Altstadt 28, Landshut, Residentstr 2-6, 91522 Ausbach

Que, *imprint of* Pearson Education Deutschland GmbH

Quell Verlag+
Augustenstr 124, 70197 Stuttgart
Tel: (0711) 601000 *Fax:* (0711) 6010076
Key Personnel
Dir, Editorial, Publicity, Rights & Permissions: Walter Waldbauer
Founded: 1830
Subjects: Biography, Fiction, History, Philosophy, Religion - Other
ISBN Prefix(es): 3-7918
Parent Company: Evangelische Gesellschaft, Postfach 103852, 70033 Stuttgart
Subsidiaries: Evangelische Gemeindepresse GmbH; Wartburg Verlag GmbH iG
Bookshop(s): Buchhandlung der Evangelischen Gesellschaft in Heidenheim, Heilbronn Ludwigsburg, Schaebisch Hall, Stuttgart

Quelle und Meyer Verlag GmbH & Co+
Industriepark 3, 56291 Wiebelsheim
Tel: (06766) 903140 *Fax:* (06766) 903341
E-mail: vertrieb@quelle-meyer.de
Web Site: www.quelle-meyer.de
Key Personnel
Man Dir: Gerhard Stahl
Sales: Ralf Simolka
Rights & Permissions: Dr Jrmgard Meissl
Founded: 1906
Subjects: Biological Sciences, Education, History, Language Arts, Linguistics, Literature, Literary Criticism, Essays, Philosophy, Psychology, Psychiatry, Religion - Other, Social Sciences, Sociology
ISBN Prefix(es): 3-494

Associate Companies: AULA-Verlag GmbH, Industrie Park 3, Wiebelsheim 56291
Tel: (06766) 903141 *Fax:* (06766) 903320
E-mail: vertrieb@aula-verlag.de; Limpert Verlag GmbH, Industrie Park 3, 56291 Wiebelsheim *Tel:* (06766) 903160 *Fax:* (06766) 903360 *E-mail:* vertrieb@limpert.de

Querverlag GmbH
Akazienstr 25, 10823 Berlin
Tel: (030) 78 70 23 39; (030) 78702340
Fax: (030) 788 49 50
E-mail: mail@querverlag.de
Web Site: www.querverlag.de
Key Personnel
Publisher: Jim Baker *E-mail:* jim@querverlag.de; Ilona Bubeck *Tel:* (030) 78702339 *E-mail:* ilona@querverlag.de
Founded: 1995
Germany's first & only gay & lesbian book publisher.
Member of Borsenverein des Deutschen Buchhandels.
Subjects: Fiction, Gay & Lesbian, Nonfiction (General), Homosexuality, Queer Studies, Gay & Lesbian Fiction & Nonfiction
ISBN Prefix(es): 3-89656
Shipping Address: SOVA, Friesstr 20-24, 60388 Frankfurt *Tel:* (069) 410211 *Fax:* (069) 410280

Quintessenz Verlags GmbH, *imprint of* edition q Berlin Edition in der Quintessenz Verlags-GmbH

Quintessenz Verlags-GmbH+
Ifenpfad 2-4, 12107 Berlin
Mailing Address: Postfach 420452, 12064 Berlin
Tel: (030) 761805 *Fax:* (030) 76180680
E-mail: info@quintessenz.de
Web Site: www.quintessenz.de
Telex: 183815 quint d
Key Personnel
Publisher: H W Haase
International Rights: Gerhard Kirsten *E-mail:* kirsten@quintessenz.de
Founded: 1949
Subjects: Biography, Career Development, Communications, Fiction, Film, Video, Health, Nutrition, Literature, Literary Criticism, Essays, Management, Medicine, Nursing, Dentistry, Mysteries
ISBN Prefix(es): 0-86715; 3-86124; 3-928024; 3-8148; 3-87652
Subsidiaries: Edition Q
U.S. Office(s): Quintessence Publishing Co Inc, 551 N Kimberly Dr, Carol Stream, IL 60188, United States

Edition Qumran, *imprint of* Campus Verlag GmbH

R Oldenbourg Verlag GmbH+
Rosenheimerstr 145, 81671 Munich
Mailing Address: Postfach 801360, 81613 Munich
Tel: (089) 45 05 10 *Fax:* (089) 45051333 (Zeitschriften); (089) 4505200 (Schulbuch); (089) 4505333 (Fachbach)
Key Personnel
Dir: Dr Thomas von Cornides; Wolfgang Dick; Johannes Oldenbourg; Dr Dieter Hohm
Founded: 1858
Member of TR-Verlagsunion GmbH.
Subjects: Education, Electronics, Electrical Engineering, Engineering (General), History, Psychology, Psychiatry, Science (General), Social Sciences, Sociology, Technology
ISBN Prefix(es): 3-486
Subsidiaries: Verlag Oldenbourg; Michael Proegel Verlag; Vulkan Verlag Essen

Showroom(s): Oldenbourg Verlag Informationszentrum, Kaufingerstr 29, 80331 Munich
Orders to: Verlegerdienst Muenchen, Auslieferung R Oldenbourg Verlag, Gutenbergstr 1, Postfach 1280, 82205 Gilching *Tel:* (08105) 3880 *Fax:* (08105) 388100

R V Reise- und Verkehrsverlag GmbH+
Neumarkter Str 43, 81673 Munich
Mailing Address: Postfach 800360, 81603 Munich
Tel: (089) 431890; (030) 254098-0 (Berlin) *Fax:* (089) 43189458; (030) 2629115 (Berlin)
Telex: 523259
Key Personnel
Dir: Wolfgang Kunth; Klaus Juergens
Editorial Dir: Dieter Meinhardt
Sales Manager: Michael Maap
Foreign Rights: Konrad Weinstock-Adorno
ISBN Prefix(es): 3-920317
Parent Company: Verlagsgruppe Bertelsmann GmbH, 81664 Munich
Subsidiaries: Guetersloh; Potsdam/Werder
Orders to: Geo Center Verlagsvertrieb GmbH, Neumarkter Str 18, 81603 Munich

Dr Josef Raabe-Verlags GmbH
Rotebuehlstr 77, 70178 Stuttgart
Mailing Address: Postfach 103922, 70034 Stuttgart
Tel: (0711) 629000 *Fax:* (0711) 6290010
E-mail: info@raabe.de
Web Site: www.raabe.de
Key Personnel
Man Dir: Wolfgang Schulz; Dr Reinhard Sander
Founded: 1985
Specialize in loose leaf editions, universities, school management.
Subjects: Education, Environmental Studies, Management, Public Administration, Science (General)
ISBN Prefix(es): 3-88649; 3-8183
Parent Company: Ernst Klett Information GmbH, Rotebuehlstr 77, 70178 Stuttgart
Ultimate Parent Company: Ernst Klett AG
Subsidiaries: RAABE Bulgarien; Dr Josef Raabe Spolka Wydawnicza; Nakladatelstvi RAABE; RAABE Fachverlag fur Bildungsmanagement; RAABE Fachverlag fur Oeffentliche Verwaltung Duesseldorf; RAABE Fachverlag fur Wissenschaftsinformation; RAABE Fachverlag fur die Schule; RAABE Koenyvkiado
Warehouse: BDK Buecherdienst Koeln, Koelner Str 248, 51149 Koeln
Orders to: Dr Josef Raabe Verlags-GmbH, Kundenservice, Postfach 103922, 70034 Stuttgart *Tel:* (0711) 62900-0 *Fax:* (0711) 62900-10 *E-mail:* info@raabe.de

Raben Verlag von Wittern KG+
Frohschammerstr 14, 80807 Munich
Tel: (089) 3594879 *Fax:* (089) 3596622
Key Personnel
Contact: York von Wittern
Founded: 1980
ISBN Prefix(es): 3-922696

Radius-Verlag GmbH+
Olgastr 114, 70180 Stuttgart
Tel: (0711) 6076666; (0172) 7126573 *Fax:* (0711) 6075555
Key Personnel
Man Dir: Wolfgang Erk
Founded: 1962
Subjects: Fiction, Philosophy, Psychology, Psychiatry, Religion - Other
ISBN Prefix(es): 3-87173

Raethgloben Verlagsgesellschaft mbH
Fraunhoferstr 8, 04430 Boehlitz-Ehrenberg
Tel: (0341) 4511212 *Fax:* (0341) 4427537
E-mail: raethgloben1917@gmx.de *Cable:* RAETHGLOBUS

PUBLISHERS GERMANY

Key Personnel
Manager: Heinz Goeschel; Hans Joachim Niemeyer
Founded: 1917
Subjects: Education, Geography, Geology, Science (General)
ISBN Prefix(es): 3-7491

Rake Verlag GmbH+
Koenigsweg 20, 24103 Kiel
Tel: (0431) 6611515 *Fax:* (0431) 6611517
E-mail: info@rake.de
Web Site: www.rake.de
Key Personnel
Publisher: Michael Rau *E-mail:* rau@rake.de
Sales: Peter Keune *E-mail:* keune@rake.de
Founded: 1994
Subjects: Fiction, Humor, Self-Help, Specialize in publishing contemporary German authors
ISBN Prefix(es): 3-931476
Number of titles published annually: 20 Print
Total Titles: 35 Print; 1 Audio
Branch Office(s)
MediaPartner, Hofackerstr 13, CH-8032 Zurich, Switzerland *Tel:* (01) 385 55 10 *Fax:* (01) 385 55 19 *E-mail:* mediapartner@access.ch
Distributed by PNV Vertriebs Service

Dr Mohan Krischke Ramaswamy Edition RE+
RE Wolfgang-Doringstr 4, 37077 Goettingen
Tel: (0700) 724 836 638 *Fax:* (0700) 724 836 638
E-mail: edition.re@epost.de
Key Personnel
Owner: Dr Mohan Krischke Ramaswamy *E-mail:* ramaswamy@epost.de
Founded: 1979
Subjects: Ethnicity, Music, Dance, Social Sciences, Sociology
ISBN Prefix(es): 3-927636

Dr Ramdohr KG, see Mentor-Verlag Dr Ramdohr KG

Rationalisierungs-Kuratorium der Deutschen Wirtschaft eV (RKW)
Sohnstr 70, 40237 Duesseldorf
Tel: (0211) 680010 *Fax:* (0211) 68001 68; (0211) 68001 69
E-mail: info@rkw-nrw.de
Web Site: www.rkw-nrw.de
Telex: 4072755 rkw d *Cable:* ERKAWE
Key Personnel
Manager: Dr Gerhard Schrick; Dr H Mueller
Publicity Manager: H Degenhard
Publications, Rights: Dr Natascha Breme
Founded: 1921
Registered Society of the German Industrial Rationalization Board.
Subjects: Business, Economics, Engineering (General), Labor, Industrial Relations, Management, Technology
ISBN Prefix(es): 3-926984; 3-921451; 3-929796

Walter Rau Verlag GmbH & Co KG+
Benderstr 164a, 40625 Dusseldorf
Mailing Address: Postfach 120407, 40604 Dusseldorf
Tel: (0211) 92 80 40 *Fax:* (0211) 28 38 27
Web Site: www.rau.de
Telex: 08586682
Key Personnel
Man Dir: Gisela W Rau; Beatrix Rau-Siegert
Founded: 1930
Subjects: Cookery, Sports, Athletics
ISBN Prefix(es): 3-7919
Associate Companies: Verlag Heim und Werk; Asper Verlag; Walter Rau Versandbuchhandlung (Schach)
Showroom(s): Manfred Maedler, Lilienthalstr 52, 40474 Dusseldorf

Werner Rau Verlag+
Feldbergstr 54 D, 70569 Stuttgart
Tel: (0711) 687 21 43 *Fax:* (0711) 68 22 47
E-mail: info@rau_verlag.de
Web Site: www.rau-verlag.de
Founded: 1986
Subjects: Travel
ISBN Prefix(es): 3-926145
Orders to: Bertelsmann Distribution GmbH, Postfach 7777, 33310 Gutersloh 100

Gerhard Rautenberg Druckerei und Verlag GmbH & Co KG
Imprint of Verlagshaus Wurzburg
Beethovenstr 5, 97080 Wurzburg
Tel: (0931) 385235 *Fax:* (0931) 385305
E-mail: info@verlagshaus.com
Web Site: www.verlagshaus.com
Key Personnel
Publishing Dir: Dieter Krause
Dir of Production: Juergen Roth
Sales Dir: Johannes Glesius
Founded: 1825
Subjects: Drama, Theater, Fiction, Humor, Regional Interests
ISBN Prefix(es): 3-7921
Bookshop(s): Rautenbergsche Buchhandlung, Blinke 8, 26767 Leer

Ravensburger Buchverlag Otto Maier GmbH+
Marktstr 22-26, 88212 Ravensburg
Mailing Address: Postfach 1860, 88188 Ravensburg
Tel: (0751) 86 0 *Fax:* (0751) 861155; (0751) 861289; (0751) 86 13 11
E-mail: buchverlag@ravensburger.de
Web Site: www.ravensburger.de *Cable:* MAIERVERLAG
Key Personnel
President: Otto Julius Maier; Dorothee Hess-Maier
Man Dir: Claus Runge
Editorial: Michael Kohlhammer; Cornelius Retting; Valeska Schneider-Finke
Production: Max Weishaupt
International Sales: Michael Bartl
Marketing: Michael Pfleiderer
Publicity: Anja Fahs
Rights & Permissions: Michael Ramm; Florence Roux
Founded: 1883
Subjects: Art, Crafts, Games, Hobbies, Education, Fiction, Nonfiction (General)
ISBN Prefix(es): 3-473
Parent Company: Ravensburger AG
Associate Companies: Ravensburger Verlag GmbH; Ravensburger GmbH, Vienna, Austria; Editions Ravensburger SA, Attenschwiller, France; Ravensburger SpA, Milan, Italy; Ravensburger BV, Amersfoort, Netherlands; Carlit und Ravensburger AG, Wueenlos, Switzerland; Ravensburger Ltd, Bicester, United Kingdom
Divisions: Ravensburger SpieleVerlag GmbH; Ravensburger Interactive Media GmbH; Ravensburger Freizeit & Promotion Service GmbH; Ravensburger Film & TV GmbH

Ravenstein Verlag GmbH+
Auf der Krautweide 24, 65812 Bad Soden
Mailing Address: Postfach 1349, 65800 Bad Soden
Tel: (06196) 609630 *Fax:* (06196) 63619
E-mail: g.koenig@ravenstein-verlag.de
Telex: 4072538 haco d *Cable:* RAVENSTEINVERLAG
Key Personnel
Man Dir: Ruediger Bosse
Founded: 1830
ISBN Prefix(es): 3-87660
U.S. Office(s): Seven Hills Book Div, 49 Central Ave, Cincinnati, OH 45202, United States

Verlag Recht und Wirtschaft GmbH+
Hausserstr 14, 69115 Heidelberg
Mailing Address: Postfach 10 59 60, 69049 Heidelberg
Tel: (06221) 906 0 *Fax:* (06221) 906 259
E-mail: verlag@ruw.de
Web Site: www.ruw-ruw.de *Cable:* RECHTWIRTSCHAFT HEIDELBERG
Key Personnel
Man Dir: Michael Giesecke
Publisher: Angelika Sauer
Founded: 1946
Subjects: Economics, Law, Social Sciences, Sociology
ISBN Prefix(es): 3-8005
Subsidiaries: I H Sauer Verlag GmbH

Reclam Verlag Leipzig+
Inselstr 26, 04103 Leipzig
Tel: (0341) 997170 *Fax:* (0341) 9971730
E-mail: info@reclam-leipzig.de
Web Site: www.reclam.de *Cable:* RECLAM LEIPZIG
Key Personnel
Man Dir: Dr Frank Rainer Max; Franz Schaefer
International Rights: Dr Stephan Koranyi
Founded: 1828
Subjects: Biography, History, Literature, Literary Criticism, Essays, Philosophy
ISBN Prefix(es): 3-379
Parent Company: Philipp Reclam jun GmbH & Co, Stuttgart
Orders to: Philipp Reclam Jun, 71252 Ditzingen

Redaktion & Gestaltung, imprint of Johann Wolfgang Goethe Universitat

Reed Elsevier Deutschland GmbH+
Hans-Cornelius-Str 4, 82166 Grafelfing, Munich
Mailing Address: Postfach 1220, 82154 Grafelfing
Tel: (089) 898170 *Fax:* (089) 85817-102
Key Personnel
Man Dir: Burkhard Bierschenck
Editor: Wolfram Haase
Founded: 1938
Subjects: Environmental Studies, Medicine, Nursing, Dentistry
ISBN Prefix(es): 3-8040
Parent Company: Reed Elsevier, Netherlands
Subsidiaries: ipc magazin verlag GmbH

REGENSBERG Druck & Verlag GmbH & Co
Harkortstr 25, 48163 Muenster
Tel: (0251) 749800 *Fax:* (0251) 7498040
Key Personnel
Manager: Bernhard Lucas
Founded: 1591
Subjects: Regional Interests
ISBN Prefix(es): 3-7923

Verlag fur Regionalgeschichte+
Windelsbleicher Str 13, 33335 Gutersloh
Mailing Address: Postfach 120423, 33653 Bielefeld
Tel: (05209) 6714; (05209) 980266 *Fax:* (05209) 6519; (05209) 980277
E-mail: regionalgeschichte@t-online.de
Web Site: www.regionalgeschichte.de
Key Personnel
Publisher: Olaf Eimer
Assistant Publisher: Gunda Gaus
Founded: 1987
Subjects: Art, History, Regional Interests, Social Sciences, Sociology
ISBN Prefix(es): 3-927085; 3-89534
Number of titles published annually: 40 Print
Total Titles: 350 Print

Regura Verlag
Falkertstr 71, 70176 Stuttgart

Tel: (0711) 2269835 Fax: (0711) 2238829
E-mail: info@regura.de
Web Site: www.regura.de
Key Personnel
Contact: Mr Weipert
Founded: 1997
Digital publications, internet solutions & services for publishers.
International cultural exchange, priority: Orient, Persia & Germany.
Subjects: Art, Cookery, Fiction
ISBN Prefix(es): 3-932814

Konrad Reich Verlag GmbH+
Kaeppen-Pott-Weg 6, 18055 Rostock Brinckmansdorf
Tel: (0381) 693020; (0381) 4922603 Fax: (0381) 693021
Key Personnel
Man Dir, Rights & Permissions: Konrad Reich
Founded: 1990
Subjects: Art, Ethnicity, Fiction, Geography, Geology, Travel
ISBN Prefix(es): 3-86167

Dr Ludwig Reichert Verlag+
Tauernstr 11, 65199 Wiesbaden
Tel: (0611) 461851 Fax: (0611) 468613
E-mail: reichert.verlag@t-online.de
Web Site: www.reichert-verlag.de
Key Personnel
Publisher: Ursula Reichert
Founded: 1970
Worldwide distribution.
Subjects: Archaeology, Art, Asian Studies, Geography, Geology, History, Language Arts, Linguistics, Library & Information Sciences, Music, Dance, Religion - Jewish, Science (General)
ISBN Prefix(es): 3-920153; 3-88226; 3-89500
Warehouse: Brockhaus Commission, Kreidlerstr 9, 70806 Kornwestheim, Contact: Mrs Wunderlich Tel: (07154) 132726 Fax: (07154) 132713 E-mail: reichert@brocom.de
Orders to: Brockhaus Commission, Kreidlerstr 9, 70806 Kornwestheim, Contact: Mrs Wunderlich Tel: (07154) 132726 Fax: (07154) 132713 E-mail: reichert@brocom.de

Reichl Verlag Der Leuchter+
Rheingoldstr 80, 5632 St Goar
Tel: (06741) 1720 Fax: (06741) 1749
Key Personnel
Man Dir: Matthias Draeger
Founded: 1909
Subjects: Astrology, Occult, Medicine, Nursing, Dentistry, Parapsychology, Religion - Other, Self-Help
ISBN Prefix(es): 3-87667
Subsidiaries: Leibniz Verlag
Divisions: Edition Asklepios

Dietrich Reimer Verlag GmbH+
Zimmerstr 26-27, 10969 Berlin
Tel: (030) 259 17 1570 Fax: (030) 259 17 1577
E-mail: vertrieb-kunstverlage@reimer-verlag.de
Key Personnel
Publisher, Rights & Permissions: Dr Friedrich Kaufmann
Editorial & International Rights: Beate Behrens
Sales & Publicity: Gabriele Dornemann
Production: Dieter Eckert; Nicola Willam
Secretary: Brigitte Struck
Founded: 1845
Subjects: Anthropology, Art, Ethnicity, Cartography, Customs & Traditions, Dance, Television, Theatre
ISBN Prefix(es): 3-496
Bookshop(s): Nautische Buchhandlung Dietrich Reimer, Unter den Eichen 57, 12203 Berlin, Contact: Fr Haberey Tel: (030) 8312341 Fax: (030) 8313873; Dietrich Reimer Wissenschaftliche Fachbuchhandlung, 12203 Berlin, Contact: Mrs Carina Ebert Tel: (030) 8314082 Fax: (030) 8313873
Orders to: Koch, Neff, Oetinger & Co Verlagsauslieferung GmbH, Schockenriedstr 39, 70506 Stuttgart

Ernst Reinhardt GmbH & Co KG Verlag+
Kemnatenstr 46, 80639 Munich
Mailing Address: Postfach 380280, 80615 Munich
Tel: (089) 17 80 16 0 Fax: (089) 17 80 16 30
E-mail: contact@reinhardt-verlag.de
Web Site: www.reinhardt-verlag.de
Key Personnel
Man Dir: Hildegard Wehler E-mail: wehler@reinhardt-verlag.de
Production: Dorothea Roll Tel: (089) 17 80 16 20 E-mail: roll@reinhardt-verlag.de
Finance: Ulrike Fochler Tel: (089) 17 80 16 21 E-mail: fochler@reinhardt-verlag.de
Sales: Daniela Postleb Tel: (089) 17 80 16 20 E-mail: postleb@reinhardt-verlag.de
Founded: 1899
Subjects: Child Care & Development, Education, Management, Medicine, Nursing, Dentistry, Music, Dance, Philosophy, Psychology, Psychiatry, Religion - Other, Science (General), Social Sciences, Sociology, Medicine, Nursing
ISBN Prefix(es): 3-497
Distributed by Buch und Medienvertriebs AG (Switzerland); Koch, Neff & Oetinger & Co (Germany); Mohr Morawa Wien (Australia)
Orders to: Koch, Neff, Oetinger & Co Verlagsauslieferung GmbH, Schockenriedstr 39, 70565 Stuttgart

E Reinhold Verlag (E Reinhold Publishing)
Hillgasse 15, 04600 Altenburg
Tel: (03447) 311889 Fax: (03447) 375611
E-mail: erv@querstand.de
Web Site: www.querstand.de
Key Personnel
Publisher: Klaus-Juergen Kamprad
Founded: 1990
Subjects: Biography, History, Photography, Regional Interests, Travel, All subjects specified on regional interests of East Germany
ISBN Prefix(es): 3-910166

Reise Know-How, imprint of Reise Know-How Verlag Peter Rump GmbH

Reise Know-How+
Zwalbacher Str 3, 66709 Rappweiler
Tel: (06872) 91737 Fax: (06872) 91738
E-mail: hoff-verlag@reise-know-how
Web Site: www.reise-know-how.com
Key Personnel
Man Dir: Edgar P Hoff E-mail: edgarhoff@aol.com
Founded: 1981
Publisher of travel guides.
Subjects: Travel, Travel Guides
ISBN Prefix(es): 3-923716
Total Titles: 13 Print
Subsidiaries: Backpacker Information Service

Reise-Know-How Verlag-Daerr GmbH+
Im Grund 12, 83104 Tuntenhausen-Hohenthann
Tel: (08065) 9172 Fax: (08065) 9173
E-mail: rkh.daerr@t-online.de
Web Site: www.reise-know-how.de
Key Personnel
Man Dir: Erika Daerr
Founded: 1987
Subjects: Travel
ISBN Prefix(es): 3-921497; 3-89662
Associate Companies: Reise-Know-How, Rump-Verlag, Haupt Str 198, 33647 Bielefeld Tel: (0521) 440835; Reise-Know-How Verlag Tondok, Nadistr 18, 808009 Munich; Reise-Know-Verlag, Dr HR Grundmann, Heinrich-Schwarz-Weg 36, 27777 Ganderkesee Tel: (04222) 8799; Reise-Know-How-Verlag Hermann, Untere Muehle, 71706 Markgroeningen Tel: (07145) 8278
Shipping Address: Prolit, Postfach 9, 35461 Fernwald Tel: (0641) 43071 Fax: (0641) 42773
Warehouse: Prolit, Postfach 9, 35461 Fernwald Tel: (0641) 43071 Fax: (0641) 42773
Orders to: Prolit, Postfach 9, 35461 Fernwald Tel: (0641) 43071 Fax: (0641) 42773

Reise Know-How Verlag Dr Hans-R Grundmann GmbH
Am Hamjebusch 29, 26655 Westerstede
Tel: (04488) 761994 Fax: (04488) 761030
E-mail: reisebuch@aol.net
Founded: 1988
Specialize in North America travel publications.
ISBN Prefix(es): 3-927554; 3-9800151

Reise Know-How Verlag Peter Rump GmbH+
Osnabrueckerstr 79, 33649 Bielefeld
Tel: (0521) 946 490; (0521) 4329186 Fax: (0521) 441047
E-mail: info@reise-know-how.de
Web Site: www.reise-know-how.de
Key Personnel
Man Dir: Peter Rump
Founded: 1981
Subjects: Foreign Countries, Geography, Geology, Language Arts, Linguistics, Travel
ISBN Prefix(es): 3-922376; 3-89416
Imprints: Reise Know-How
U.S. Office(s): SCB Distributors, PO Box 5446, Carson, CA 90749-5446, United States
Orders to: Prolit GmbH, Siemensstr 16, Postfach 9, 35463 Fernwald (Annerod)

Reise Know-How Verlag Tondok
Nadistr 18, 80809 Munich
Tel: (089) 3514857 Fax: (089) 3518485
E-mail: rkh@tondok-verlag.de
Web Site: www.tondok-verlag.de
Key Personnel
Contact: Wil Tondok
Subjects: Travel
ISBN Prefix(es): 3-921838

Verlagsgruppe Reise-Know-How+
c/o Peter Rump Gmbh, Osnabrueckerstr 79, 33649 Bielefeld
Tel: (521) 946490 Fax: (521) 441047
E-mail: info@reise-know-how.de
Web Site: www.reise-know-how.de
Key Personnel
Rights & Permissions: Peter Rump
Founded: 1981
Subjects: Language Arts, Linguistics, Travel
ISBN Prefix(es): 3-922376; 3-89416; 3-8317
Associate Companies: Reise-Know-How/Daerr-Verlag GmbH, Im Grund 72, Hohenthann E-mail: rkh.daerr@t-online.de; Reise-Know-How Verlag/Hans Grundmann GmbH, Am Hamjebusch 29, Westerstede Tel: (0448) 761994 E-mail: reisebuch@aol.com
Orders to: Prolit Verlagsauslieferung, Siemensstr 16, 35463 Fernwald (Annerod)

Peter Meyer Reisefuhrer+
Schopenhauerstr 11, 60316 Frankfurt am Main
Tel: (069) 49 44 49 Fax: (069) 44 51 35
E-mail: info@PeterMeyerVerlag.de
Web Site: www.meyer-reisefuehrer.de
Key Personnel
International Rights & Man Dir: Peter Meyer
Man Dir: Annette Sievers
Founded: 1976
Subjects: Language Arts, Linguistics, Travel
ISBN Prefix(es): 3-922057

Total Titles: 40 Print
Orders to: GeoCenter, Postfach 800830, 70508 Stuttgart *Tel:* (0711) 78194610 *Fax:* (0711) 78194654 *E-mail:* geocenterilh@t-online.de

ReiseHandbuch Stein KG & Outdoor Handbuch Stein KG+
In der Muehle, 25821 Struckum
Tel: (04671) 93 13 14 *Fax:* (04671) 93 13 15
E-mail: outdoor@tng.de
Web Site: outdoor.tng.de
Subsidiaries: Outdoor Handbuch Stein KG
Distributed by Prolit (Germany); Freytag & Berndt und Artaria (Austria); Buch 2000 (Switzerland)
Foreign Rep(s): Freytag, Berndt & Artaria KG (Austria); Giovanni Ravasio (Switzerland)

Verlag Norman Rentrop+
Rüngsdorfer Straße 2e, 53173 Bonn
Tel: (0228) 36 88 40 *Fax:* (0228) 36 58 75
E-mail: tt@rentrop.com; NR@rentrop.com
Web Site: www.normanrentrop.de
Key Personnel
Man Dir: Norman Rentrop
Editorial, Publicity: Michael Jansen
Production: Monika Graf
Rights & Permissions: Helmut Graf
Founded: 1975
Specialize in looseleaf services.
Subjects: Business, Finance, Public Administration, Real Estate
ISBN Prefix(es): 3-8125
Branch Office(s)
Arenbergstr 33, A-5020 Salzburg, Austria
Sagestr 14, CH-5600 Lenzburg/Zurich, Switzerland
One Place du Lycee, F-68005 Colmar, France
27A Old Gloucester St, London WC1N 3XX, United Kingdom
U.S. Office(s): Georgetown Publishing House, 1101 30 St NW, Washington, DC 20007, United States *Tel:* 202-337-5960 *Fax:* 202-337-1512
117 W Harrison, Suite R-246, Chicago, IL 60605, United States
Orders to: Buchhandel Deutschland an Buecherdienst Cologne, 51169 Cologne

Report-Verlag GmbH, *imprint of* Umschau Buchverlag Breidenstein GmbH

Respublica Verlag
Kaiserstr 99-101, 53721 Siegburg
Mailing Address: Postfach 1831, 53708 Siegburg
Tel: (02241) 62925; (02241) 64039 *Fax:* (02241) 53891
Key Personnel
President, International Rights: Franz Schmitt
Founded: 1932
Subjects: Music, Dance, Regional Interests
ISBN Prefix(es): 3-87710

Verlagsgruppe Rhein Main GmbH & Co KG
Erich Dombrowskistr 2, 55127 Mainz-Marienborn
Tel: (06131) 48-30
Web Site: www.main-rheiner.de
Key Personnel
Contact: Karlheinz Rothemeier
Manager: Holger Albaum *Tel:* (06131) 48 41 80 *Fax:* (06131) 48 41 73 *E-mail:* halbaum@vrm.de; Hubertus Michalczyk
Sales Consultant: Nina Eckes *Tel:* (06131) 48 41 76 *Fax:* (06131) 48 41 73 *E-mail:* neckes@vrm.de
ISBN Prefix(es): 3-920615

Verlag Rheinischer Merkur GmbH
Godesberger Allee 91, 53175 Bonn
Mailing Address: Postfach 201164, 53141 Bonn
Tel: (0228) 88 42 22; (0228) 88 42 25 *Fax:* (0228) 88 41 70
E-mail: abo@merkur.de
Web Site: www.merkur.de
Key Personnel
Man Dir: Bert G Wegener; Helmut Dippel
ISBN Prefix(es): 3-9801913

RVBG Rheinland-Verlag-und Betriebsgesellschaft des Landschaftsverbandes Rheinland mbH+
Abbey Brauweiler, 50259 Pulheim
Mailing Address: Postfach 2140, 50250 Pulheim
Tel: (02234) 805 265 *Fax:* (02234) 82503
Telex: uber 8873335 Lvrkd
Key Personnel
Man Dir: Christian Buepel
Founded: 1958
Subjects: Archaeology, History, Regional Interests
ISBN Prefix(es): 3-7927
Subsidiaries: Rhein Eifel Mosel Verlag
Bookshop(s): Versandbuchhandlung, Abtei Brauweiler, 50259 Pulheim
Shipping Address: Dr Rudolf Habelt Verlag, Am Buchenhang 2, 53315 Bonn

Richardi Helmut Verlag GmbH+
Theodor-Heuss-Allee 106, 60486 Frankfurt am Main
Mailing Address: Postfach 111151, 60486 Frankfurt am Main
Tel: (069) 9708330 *Fax:* (069) 7078400
E-mail: kreditwesen@t-online.de
Key Personnel
Owner: Klaus-Friedrich Otto
Publisher: Claus Wonneberger; Werner Scholz
Founded: 1955
Subjects: Finance, Real Estate
ISBN Prefix(es): 3-921722
Associate Companies: Friz Knapp Verlag

Edition Riesenrad, *imprint of* Xenos Verlagsgesellschaft mbH

Rigodon-Verlag Norbert Wehr+
Nieberdingstr 18, 45147 Essen
Tel: (0201) 77 81 11; (0221) 360 21 92 *Fax:* (0201) 77 51 74; (0221) 360 21 92
E-mail: Schreibheft@NetCologne.de
Web Site: www.schreibheft.de
Key Personnel
Manager: Norbert Wehr
Founded: 1977
Subjects: Literature, Literary Criticism, Essays
ISBN Prefix(es): 3-924071

Rimbaud Verlagsgesellschaft mbH+
Oppenhoffalle 20, 52066 Aachen
Mailing Address: Postfach 10 01 44, 52001 Aachen
Tel: (0241) 54 25 32; (0241) 9019583 *Fax:* (0241) 514117
E-mail: info@rimbaud.de
Web Site: www.rimbaud.de
Key Personnel
Man Dir, Sales, Publicity: Walter Hoerner
Editorial: Dr Reinhard Kiefer
International Rights: Dr Bernard Albers
Founded: 1983
Subjects: Literature, Literary Criticism, Essays, Music, Dance, Photography, Poetry
ISBN Prefix(es): 3-89086
Distributed by Pegasus Verlagsauslieferung (Switzerland); Hora-Verlag (Austria)

Ritterbach Verlag GmbH
Rudolf-Dieselstr 5-7, 50226 Frechen
Mailing Address: Postfach 1820, 50208 Frechen
Tel: (02234) 18 66 0 *Fax:* (02234) 18 66 90
E-mail: service@ritterbach.de; coeln.ml@ritterbach.de
Web Site: www.ritterbach.de
Founded: 1987
Subjects: Architecture & Interior Design, Art, Career Development, Crafts, Games, Hobbies, Education
ISBN Prefix(es): 3-89314

Ritzau KG Verlag Zeit und Eisenbahn+
Landsbergerstr 24, 86932 Puergen
Tel: (08196) 252 *Fax:* (08196) 1240
E-mail: mail@ritzau.kg.de
Web Site: www.ritzau-kg.de
Founded: 1968
Subjects: History, Transportation
ISBN Prefix(es): 3-921304; 3-935101

RKW, *see* Rationalisierungs-Kuratorium der Deutschen Wirtschaft eV (RKW)

Roehrig Universitaets Verlag Gmbh
Eichendorffstr 37, 66386 Sankt Ingbert
Mailing Address: Postfach 1806, 66368 Sankt Ingbert
Tel: (06894) 8 79 57 *Fax:* (06894) 87 03 30
E-mail: info@roehrig-verlag.de
Web Site: www.roehrig-verlag.de
Key Personnel
Publisher: Werner J Roehrig
Editor: Thomas Sick
Founded: 1984
Subjects: Government, Political Science, History, Language Arts, Linguistics, Literature, Literary Criticism, Essays, Science (General)
ISBN Prefix(es): 3-924555; 3-86110
Number of titles published annually: 40 Print
Total Titles: 350 Print
Membership(s): Provincial Federation of Booksellers & Publishers

Erich Roeth-Verlag+
Kastanienweg 4, 39343 Rottmersleben
Tel: (039206) 90103 *Fax:* (039206) 90103 *Cable:* ROTHVERLAG
Key Personnel
Man Dir, Rights & Permissions: Manfred Kaiser
Founded: 1921
Specialize in fairytales.
Subjects: Art, Music, Dance
ISBN Prefix(es): 3-87680
Number of titles published annually: 3 Print; 1 CD-ROM; 1 Audio

Heidi Rogner+
Zum Bosselbach 18, 52393 Huertgenwald
Tel: (02429) 2561
Key Personnel
Contact: Heidi Rogner
Founded: 1995
Subjects: Animals, Pets
ISBN Prefix(es): 3-9804403

Rogner und Bernhard GmbH & Co Verlags KG+
Fettstr 6, 20357 Hamburg
Mailing Address: Postfach 306 243, 20328 Hamburg
Tel: (040) 430 2110 *Fax:* (040) 430 2716
E-mail: robe@on-line.de
Web Site: www.zweitausendeins.de
Key Personnel
Manager: Jarchow Klaas *E-mail:* Jarchow@rogner-bernhard.de; Antje Landshoff *E-mail:* Jarchow@rogner-bernhard.de
Assistant to the Editor: Marlies Hebler
Founded: 1968
Specialize in popular culture.
Subjects: Art, Fiction, Photography
ISBN Prefix(es): 3-8077; 3-920802
Total Titles: 100 Print
Orders to: Zweitausendeins Versand *Tel:* (069) 4208000 *Fax:* (069) 420800198 *E-mail:* service@zweitausendeins.de

GERMANY

Verlag und Buchversand Wolfgang Roller
Goethestr 15, 63225 Langen
Tel: (06103) 71886 *Fax:* (06103) 929501
E-mail: greif@12move.de
Web Site: www.verlag-roller.de
ISBN Prefix(es): 3-923620

Rombach GmbH Druck und Verlagshaus & Co+
Unterwerkstr 5, 79115 Freiburg
Mailing Address: Postfach 5109, 79013 Freiburg
Tel: (0761) 4500 0 *Fax:* (0761) 4500 2125
E-mail: info@buchverlag.rombach.de
Web Site: www.rombach.de
Key Personnel
Man Dirs: Dr Christian H Hodeige; Andreas Hodeige
Dir: Willi Mandery
International Rights: Dr Edelgard Spaude
E-mail: spaude@buchverlag.rombach.de
Sales: Melanie Panzer *Tel:* (0761) 4500 2135
E-mail: panzer@buchverlag.rombach.de
Founded: 1936
Subjects: Art, Government, Political Science, History, Literature, Literary Criticism, Essays, Regional Interests, Social Sciences, Sociology
ISBN Prefix(es): 3-7930
Associate Companies: Rombach Druckhaus KG, Bertoldstr 10, 79098 Freiburg; Rombach Handelshaus KG, Bertoldstr 10, 79098 Freiburg; Rombach Medienhaus KG, Bertoldstr 10, 79098 Freiburg
Bookshop(s): Rombach Buchhandlung, Bertoldstr 10, 79098 Freiburg
Orders to: Waltesverlagsauslieferung, Blochmattastr 11, 7843 Herkesheim

Romiosini Verlag+
Venolerstr 30, 50672 Cologne
Mailing Address: Cologne
Tel: (0221) 5101288 *Fax:* (0221) 5101288
E-mail: romiosini@unisolo.de
Web Site: www.unisolo.de/pls/romiosini/griechische_literatur
Key Personnel
Publisher: Niki Eideneier
Founded: 1982
Specialize in Greek literature in German translation.
Spezialisiert auf Griechische Literatur in deutscher Ubersetzung.
Subjects: Cookery, Fiction, History, Literature, Literary Criticism, Essays, Music, Dance, Poetry, Travel
ISBN Prefix(es): 3-923728; 3-929889
Distributed by PHOIBOS Verlag (Austria); MAM (Cypress); Athener Bookshop AG (Greece); Greek Books Elyki (Switzerland)
Orders to: Unisolo/Despina Kazantzidou, Nordohr 11, 38106 Braunschweig *Tel:* (0531) 336050 *Fax:* (0531) 336049 *E-mail:* despina.kazantzidou@unisolo.de *Web Site:* www.unisolo.de/romiosini.htm

Rosenheimer Verlagshaus GmbH & Co KG+
Am Stocket 12, 83022 Rosenheim
Mailing Address: Postfach 100663, 83006 Rosenheim
Tel: (08031) 2838 0 *Fax:* (08031) 2838 44
E-mail: info@rosenheimer.com
Web Site: www.rosenheimer.com *Cable:* ROSENHEIMER VERLAGSHAUS ROSENHEIM
Key Personnel
Man Dir: Klaus G Foerg
Sales, Rights, Permissions & Publicity: Bernhard Edlmann
Marketing Manager: Uta Lamp *Tel:* (08031) 2838 60
Sales: Regina Rogger *Tel:* (08031) 2838 61; Angelika Krichbaumer *Tel:* (08031) 2838 61
Bookkeeper: Katharina Schuster *Tel:* (08031) 2838 21
Founded: 1949
Subjects: Art, Crafts, Games, Hobbies, Fiction, History, Regional Interests
ISBN Prefix(es): 3-475

ROSPO Verlag+
Colonnaden 43, 20354 Hamburg
Tel: (040) 351603; (040) 351604 *Fax:* (040) 351605
E-mail: rospoverlag@t-online.de
Key Personnel
Editor: Margot Saak-Bitterling
Editor & International Rights: Dr Marianne Schwarz-Scherer
Founded: 1993
Member of Borsenverein des deutschen Buchhandels ev.
Subjects: Literature, Literary Criticism, Essays, Poetry, Specialize in Lyrics, Poetry & Short Stories of Eastern Europe in German Editions
ISBN Prefix(es): 0-930325
Number of titles published annually: 5 Print
Total Titles: 32 Print
Orders to: GVA, Anna-Vandenhoeck, Ring 36, 37081 Gottingen *Tel:* (0551) 487177 *Fax:* (0551) 41392

Rossipaul Kommunikation GmbH+
Menzingerstr 37, 80638 Munich
Mailing Address: Postfach 38 0164, 80614 Munich
Tel: (089) 17 91 06 0 *Fax:* (089) 17 91 06 22
E-mail: info@rossipaul.de
Web Site: www.rossipaul.de
Key Personnel
Man Dir, Rights & Permissions: Rainer Rossipaul
Publicity: Ingo Neubert
Founded: 1952
Subjects: Advertising, Career Development, Computer Science, Finance, Health, Nutrition, Language Arts, Linguistics, Law, Management, Nonfiction (General), Outdoor Recreation
ISBN Prefix(es): 3-87686

Roswell High, *imprint of* Egmont vgs verlagsgesellschaft mbH

Rot-Gelb-Gruen Lehrmittel GmbH & Co Verlagsgesellschaft
Theodor-Heusstr 3, 38122 Braunschweig
Mailing Address: Postfach 3922, 38029 Braunschweig
Tel: (0531) 809070 *Fax:* (0531) 8090721
Key Personnel
Publisher: Gerd J Holtzmeyer
Founded: 1958
Subjects: Education
ISBN Prefix(es): 3-88589

Verlag Roter Morgen
Postfach 401051, 70410 Stuttgart
Tel: (0711) 870 2209 *Fax:* (0711) 870 2445
E-mail: kpd-roter-morgen@t-online.de
Key Personnel
Publisher: Moeller Diethard
Subjects: Developing Countries, Government, Political Science, History, Labor, Industrial Relations, Philosophy
ISBN Prefix(es): 3-928666
Distributor for Red Star Press (London)
Orders to: Literatur Vertrieb RM, Postfach 1942, 61289 Bad Homburg

Rowohlt Berlin Verlag GmbH+
Subsidiary of Rowohlt Verlag GmbH
c/o Rowohlt Verlag GmbH, Hamburgerstr 17, 21465 Reinbek
Tel: (040) 72 72 0 *Fax:* (040) 72 72 342
E-mail: Rowohlt.Berlin@T-online.de
Web Site: www.rowohlt.de
Key Personnel
Man Dir: Dr Helmut Daehne; Lutz Kettmann; Peter Wilfert
Editorial Dir: Dr Siv Bublitz *E-mail:* siv.bublitz@rowohlt.de
Rights & Permissions: Ursula Steffens
Founded: 1990
Specialize in fiction from East and Central Europe; political nonfiction.
Subjects: Fiction, Nonfiction (General)
ISBN Prefix(es): 3-87134
Number of titles published annually: 30 Print
Total Titles: 160 Print

Rowohlt Taschenbuch Verlag GmbH+
Hamburgerstr 17, 21465 Reinbek
Mailing Address: Postfach 1349, 21462 Reinbek
Tel: (040) 72720 *Fax:* (040) 7272319
E-mail: info@rowohlt.de
Web Site: www.rowohlt.de *Cable:* ROWOHLTVERLAG REINBEK
Key Personnel
Dir: Dr Helmut-Daehne
Dir & Editorial: Nikolaus Hansen; Peter Wilfert
Production: Elke Enns
Rights & Permissions: Marianne Sparr
Sales: Lutz Kettmann
Publicity Manager: Frank Scheffter
Dir: Dr Rudige Salat
Founded: 1953
Subjects: Archaeology, Art, Computer Science, Crafts, Games, Hobbies, Education, Fiction, Government, Political Science, History, Literature, Literary Criticism, Essays, Nonfiction (General), Philosophy, Psychology, Psychiatry, Religion - Other, Science (General), Social Sciences, Sociology
ISBN Prefix(es): 3-498; 3-499; 3-8052
Number of titles published annually: 550 Print
Total Titles: 3,500 Print
Online services available through World Wide Web.
Parent Company: Rowohlt Verlag GmbH, Hamburgerstr 17, 21465 Reinbek
Foreign Rep(s): Dessauer Ch

Rowohlt Verlag GmbH+
Hamburgerstr 17, 21465 Reinbek
Mailing Address: Postfach 1349, 21462 Reinbek
Tel: (040) 72720 *Fax:* (040) 7272319; (040) 7272213 (Advertising); (040) 7272391 (Production); (040) 7272395 (Press); (040) 7272342 (Sales)
E-mail: presse@rowohlt.de
Web Site: www.rowohlt.de
Key Personnel
Man Dir: Dr Helmut Daehne; Alexander Fest
Rights & Permissions: Kristina Krombholz
Contact: Eckhard Kloos *Tel:* (040) 7272214
E-mail: eckhard.kloos@rowohlt.de
Founded: 1908
Subjects: Nonfiction (General)
ISBN Prefix(es): 3-498; 3-499; 3-8052
Imprints: Wunderlich Taschenbuch (Pocket Book)
Subsidiaries: Rowohlt Taschenbuch Verlag; Rowohlt Berlin Verlags GmbH
U.S. Office(s): Greenburger New York, 55 Fifth Ave, New York, NY 10003, United States

Rudi der Bar ist las, *imprint of* Beerenverlag

Dieter Ruggeberg Verlagsbuchhandlung+
Wuppermannstr 28, 42275 Wuppertal
Mailing Address: Postfach 13 08 44, 42035 Wuppertal
Tel: (0202) 592811 *Fax:* (0202) 592811
Web Site: www.vbdr.de
Key Personnel
Man Dir, Rights & Permissions: Dieter Rueggeberg *E-mail:* vrggeberg@aol.com
Founded: 1968

PUBLISHERS
GERMANY

Subjects: Astrology, Occult, Government, Political Science, Religion - Other
ISBN Prefix(es): 3-921338

Ruetten & Loening Berlin GmbH+
Neue Promenade 6, 10178 Berlin
Mailing Address: Postfach 193, 10105 Berlin
Tel: (030) 283 94 0 *Fax:* (030) 283 94 100
E-mail: info@aufbau-verlag.de
Web Site: www.aufbau-verlag.de
Key Personnel
Program Manager: Rene Strien
Manager: Peter Dempewolf
International Rights: Astrid Poppenhusen
 Tel: (030) 283 94 212 *E-mail:* poppenhusen@aufbau-verlag.de
Contact: Barbara Stang
Rights & Permissions: Kathrin Schulz
Founded: 1844
Subjects: Fiction, Government, Political Science, History, Literature, Literary Criticism, Essays, Mysteries, Poetry, Romance
ISBN Prefix(es): 3-352
Number of titles published annually: 30 Print
Total Titles: 100 Print
Shipping Address: Mohr Morawa, Buchvertrieb Gesellschaft mbH, Postfach 260, A-1101 Vienna, Austria; Buecher Balmer, Verlagsauslieferung, Neugasse 12, CH-6301 Zurich, Switzerland
Warehouse: Libri-Distributions GmbH, August-Schanzstr 33, 60433 Frankfurt
Orders to: Libri-Distributions GmbH, August-Schanzstr 33, 60433 Frankfurt

Winfried Ruf, see Fachmedien Verlag Winfried Ruf (FMV)

Ruhland Verlag Gimblt
Hermann-Steinhaeuserstr 2, 63065 Offenbach Am Main
Tel: (069) 811768 *Fax:* (069) 811769
Key Personnel
Man Dir, Publicity, Rights & Permissions: Margitta Kieltsch-weidl
Founded: 1968
Subjects: Business, Management
ISBN Prefix(es): 3-88509; 3-920793

Verlag an der Ruhr GmbH+
Alexanderstr 54, 45472 Muelheim an der Ruhr
Mailing Address: Postfach 102251, 45422 Muelheim
Tel: (0208) 4395454 *Fax:* (0208) 4395439
E-mail: info@verlagruhr.de
Web Site: www.verlagruhr.de
Key Personnel
Man Dir & Publisher: Wilfried Stascheit
Man Dir: Annelie Loeber-Stascheit
Founded: 1981
Books & worksheets for pedagogical & educational work in school & extracurricular work. Unconventional methods, innovative contents & topical themes.
Member of German Booksellers Association.
Subjects: Art, Communications, Developing Countries, Education, English as a Second Language, Environmental Studies, Geography, Geology, History, Human Relations, Literature, Literary Criticism, Essays, Mathematics, Philosophy, Physical Sciences, Religion - Other
ISBN Prefix(es): 3-86072; 3-927279; 3-924884
Total Titles: 450 Print
Imprints: Albatros
Distributed by BLMV Berner Lehrmitted-und Medienverlag; Veritas
Orders to: Paedexpress GmbH & Co KG
 Tel: (0208) 495040 *Fax:* (0208) 4950495
 E-mail: info@paedexpress.de

RV, see R V Reise- und Verkehrsverlag GmbH

RVBG, see RVBG Rheinland-Verlag-und Betriebsgesellschaft des Landschaftsverbandes Rheinland mbH

Reinhard Ryborsch, see Kartographischer Verlag Reinhard Ryborsch

Ryvellus, *imprint of* Neue Erde Verlags GmbH

Ryvellus Medienagentur Dopfer+
Lindenallee 1, 82402 Seeshaupt
Tel: (08801) 12391 *Fax:* (08801) 912323
Key Personnel
Manager: Manfred Dopfer
Founded: 1989
Subjects: Environmental Studies, Health, Nutrition, Nonfiction (General), Psychology, Psychiatry, Body, Mind & Spirit, Esoterics/New Age
ISBN Prefix(es): 3-89453

Saarbrucker Druckerei und Verlag GmbH (SDV)
Halbergstr 3, 66121 Saarbruecken
Mailing Address: Postfach 102745, Saarbruecken 66027
Tel: (0681) 6650135 *Fax:* (0681) 6650110
Web Site: www.sdv-saar.de
Key Personnel
Man Dir & Editorial: Olanfred Wagner
Sales Manager: Corinne Wuest *E-mail:* cwuest@sdv-saar.de
Founded: 1922
Subjects: Antiques, Archaeology, Art, History, Language Arts, Linguistics, Literature
ISBN Prefix(es): 3-921646; 3-925036; 3-930843

Saatkorn-Verlag GmbH
Luener Rennbahn 16, 21339 Lueneburg
Tel: (04131) 98 35-02 *Fax:* (04131) 98 35 505
E-mail: info@saatkornverlag.de
Web Site: wwww.saatkorn-verlag.de
Key Personnel
Man Dir: Eckhard Boettge
Editorial, Rights & Permissions Secretary: Eli Diez
Sales: Erhard Knirr
Printing Works: Peter Streit
Founded: 1895
Subjects: Health, Nutrition, Theology
ISBN Prefix(es): 3-8150; 3-87689
Subsidiaries: Grindeldruck GmbH
Warehouse: Auf dem Salzstock 11, 21217 Seevetal-Meckelfeld

Verlag Werner Sachon GmbH & Co
Schloss Mindelburg, 87714 Mindelheim
Tel: (08261) 999-0 *Fax:* (08261) 999 391
E-mail: info@sachon.de
Web Site: www.sachon.de
Telex: 539624
Key Personnel
Contact: Wolfgang Burkart; Werner Sachon
Subjects: Engineering (General), Health, Nutrition, Management, Marketing, Mechanical Engineering, Wine & Spirits
ISBN Prefix(es): 3-920819; 3-929032; 3-929032

Sachsenbuch Verlagsgesellschaft Mbh
Burgstr 12, 04109 Leipzig
Tel: (0341) 9602373 *Fax:* (0341) 9784259
Key Personnel
Manager: Wolf-Diethelm Zastrutzki
Editor: Klaus Hoerhold
Public Relations: W U Schuette
Founded: 1990
Member of the Stock Exchange of German Booksellers.
Subjects: Art, Regional Interests
ISBN Prefix(es): 3-910148; 3-910155; 3-89664

Branch Office(s)
Neuer Sachsenverlag Leipzig, Coppistr 36, 04157 Leipzig
Bookshop(s): Buchhandlung, Neue Leipzigerstr 16, 04205 Leipzig; Buchhandlung, Schwarzackerstr, 04229 Leipzig
Shipping Address: Buchhandlung Sachsenbuch, Bruhl 76, Postfach 461, 04109 Leipzig

Verlag Otto Sagner, see Kubon Und Sagner

Eugen Salzer-Verlag GmbH & Co KG+
Titotstr 5, 74072 Heilbronn
Tel: (07131) 68294 *Fax:* (07131) 171331
Key Personnel
Man Dir: Sibylle Salzer
Procurer, Sales Dir, Rights & Permissions: Monika Nissen
Founded: 1891
Subjects: Biography, Fiction, How-to
ISBN Prefix(es): 3-7936

Sammlung, *imprint of* Bund demokratischer Wissenschaftlerinnen und Wissenschafler eV (BdWi)

SAMS, *imprint of* Pearson Education Deutschland GmbH

Verlag der Sankt-Johannis-Druckerei C Schweickhardt+
Heiligenstr 24, 77933 Lahr
Mailing Address: Postfach 5, 77922 Lahr
Tel: (07821) 5810 *Fax:* (07821) 58126
E-mail: johannis-Druck@t-online.de *Cable:* VERITAS LAHR SCHWARZWALD
Key Personnel
Man Dir: Walter Guthmann
Editorial, Publicity, Rights & Permissions: Dr Thomas Baumann
Sales: Karl-Heinz Kern
Production: Helmut Schlegel
Founded: 1896
Member of the Telos Group Publishing Evangelical Paperbacks.
Subjects: Art, Biography, Fiction, Religion - Protestant
ISBN Prefix(es): 3-501
Associate Companies: Edition VLM; SKV-Edition
Distributed by BMK Verlagsauslieferung (Austria); Brunnen Verlag (Switzerland)

Sankt Otto Verlag GmbH+
Laubanger 23, 96052 Bamberg
Mailing Address: Postfach 2709, 96018 Bamberg
Tel: (0951) 967120 *Fax:* (0951) 96712235
Key Personnel
Man Dir: Helmut Treml
Founded: 1922
Subjects: Religion - Catholic
ISBN Prefix(es): 3-87693
Subsidiaries: Bayerische Verlagsanstalt
Bookshop(s): Goerres Buchhandlung, Lange Str 24, 96047 Bamberg

Sassafras Verlag
Dreikoenigenstr 146, 47799 Krefeld
Tel: (02151) 787770 *Fax:* (02151) 771302
Key Personnel
Man Dir, International Rights: Klaus Ulrich Duesselberg
Founded: 1975
Subjects: Literature, Literary Criticism, Essays, Poetry
ISBN Prefix(es): 3-922690

Sattva Kunst Verlag+
Rechenau 1, 83730 Fischbachau
Tel: (08028) 90 68-0 *Fax:* (08028) 90 68-10; (08028) 90 68-20
Subjects: Music, Dance

ISBN Prefix(es): 3-925035
Divisions: Sattva Music & Sattva Art Design

I H Sauer Verlag GmbH+
Hausserstr 14, 69115 Heidelberg
Mailing Address: Postfach 10 59 60, 69049 Heidelberg
Tel: (06221) 906-0 *Fax:* (06221) 906 259
E-mail: sauerverlag@ruw.de
Web Site: www.ruw-ruw.de
Telex: 461665rewhihd
Key Personnel
Man Dir: Michael Giesecke
Publisher: Angelika Sauer
Contact: Norbert Konda
Founded: 1964
Subjects: Career Development, Communications, Economics, Labor, Industrial Relations, Management, Marketing, Psychology, Psychiatry
ISBN Prefix(es): 3-7938
Associate Companies: Verlag Recht und Wirtschaft GmbH

Verlag Sauerlaender GmbH+
Waechtersbacherstr 89, 60386 Frankfurt
Mailing Address: Postfach 630247, 60352 Frankfurt
Tel: (069) 942118-0 *Fax:* (069) 412099
Key Personnel
Publisher: Hans C Sauerlaender
Founded: 1807
Subjects: Fiction, Science (General)
ISBN Prefix(es): 3-7941
Parent Company: Sauerlaender AG, CH-5001 Aarau, Switzerland
Associate Companies: Verlag Sauerlaender, Muenzgasse 1, A-5020 Salzburg, Austria
Showroom(s): Infortiationsstelle Schlilbuch, CH-5001 Aarau, Laurentenvorstadt 85
Orders to: Sauerlander AG, Laurentenvorstadt 89, CH-5001 Karan, Switzerland *Tel:* (062) 836 8686 *Fax:* (062) 836 8620

J D Sauerlaender's Verlag+
Finkenhofstr 21, 60322 Frankfurt
Tel: (069) 555217 *Fax:* (069) 5964344
E-mail: j.d.sauerlaenders.verlag@t-online.de
Key Personnel
Publisher: Helmut A Baetz
Chief Assistant: Stephanie Aulbach
Founded: 1816
Subjects: Agriculture, Language Arts, Linguistics, Specialize in forest genetics
ISBN Prefix(es): 3-7939
Number of titles published annually: 6 Print

K G Saur Verlag GmbH, A Gale/Thomson Learning Company+
Unit of Thomson Learning
Ortlerstr 8, 81373 Munich
Mailing Address: Postfach 70 16 20, 81316 Munich
Tel: (089) 76902-0 *Fax:* (089) 76902-150
E-mail: info@saur.de
Web Site: www.saur.de
Key Personnel
Man Dir: Prof Dr h c mult Klaus G Saur *E-mail:* K.Saur@saur.de
Sales Dir: Paul Fertl *E-mail:* P.Fertl@saur.de
Promotion & Press Service: Petra Huetter *E-mail:* P.Huetter@saur.de
Production Dir: Manfred Link *E-mail:* M.Link@saur.de
Publishing Dir: Clara Waldrich *E-mail:* C.Waldrich@saur.de
Commercial Dir: Christoph Hahne *E-mail:* C.Hahne@saur.de
Rights & Permissions: Christina Hofmann *E-mail:* C.Hofmann@saur.de
Editorial Dir: Barbara Fischer *E-mail:* b.fischer@saur.de
Founded: 1949
Subjects: Art, Biography, Communications, History, Library & Information Sciences, Literature, Literary Criticism, Essays, Music, Dance, Philosophy, Publishing & Book Trade Reference, Social Sciences, Sociology
ISBN Prefix(es): 3-598; 3-7940; 3-907820; 3-908255
Total Titles: 2,500 Print; 100 CD-ROM; 6 E-Book
Parent Company: Gale
Ultimate Parent Company: The Thomson Corporation

scaneg Verlag
Heiglhofstr 24, 81377 Munich
Tel: (089) 759 33 36 *Fax:* (089) 759 39 14
E-mail: verlag@scaneg.de
Web Site: www.scaneg.de
Founded: 1983
Subjects: Art, History, Literature, Literary Criticism, Essays, Poetry, Art History
ISBN Prefix(es): 3-89235

Verlag Th Schaefer im Vicentz Verlag KG
Schiffgraben 43, 30175 Hannover
Mailing Address: Postfach 6247, 30062 Hannover
Tel: (0511) 9910-012 *Fax:* (0511) 9910-013
Key Personnel
Publisher: Werner Geisselbrecht
Founded: 1980
Specialize in reprints of professional books.
Subjects: Architecture & Interior Design, Art, Crafts, Games, Hobbies, House & Home
ISBN Prefix(es): 3-88746
Parent Company: Th Schaefer Verlag im Vincentz Verlag KG
Orders to: Vincentz Verlag KG, Postfach 6247, 30062 Hannover *Tel:* (0511) 9910-012 *Fax:* (0511) 9910-013 *Web Site:* www.libri_rari.de

Schaeffer-Poeschel Verlag fuer Wirtschaft Steuern Recht+
Werastr 21-23, 70182 Stuttgart
Mailing Address: Postfach 10 32 41, 70028 Stuttgart
Tel: (0711) 2194-0 *Fax:* (0711) 2194-119
E-mail: info@schaeffer-poeschel.de
Web Site: www.schaeffer-poeschel.de
Key Personnel
Man Dir: Michael Justus *E-mail:* justus@schaeffer-poeschel.de
General Manager: Volker Dabelstein; Marita Rollnik Mollenhauer
Sales Dir: Michael Schmid
Marketing Manager: Michael Schmid
Advertising: Sabine Zobeley
Press: Joachim Bader
Electronic Publishing: Ursula Chwalisz
Accounting: Harald Dauber; Ruth Kuonath
Founded: 1902
Subjects: Accounting, Business, Economics, Finance, Management, Marketing
ISBN Prefix(es): 3-7910; 3-8202; 3-7992
Number of titles published annually: 250 Print
Total Titles: 800 Print
Parent Company: Verlagsgruppe Handelsblatt
Ultimate Parent Company: Verlagsgruppe Georg Von Holtzbrinck

Schangrila Verlags und Vertriebs GmbH+
Lindenstr 45, 87648 Aitrang
Tel: (08343) 581 *Fax:* (08343) 657
Web Site: www.schangrila.com
Founded: 1984
Subjects: Cookery, Medicine, Nursing, Dentistry, Philosophy
ISBN Prefix(es): 3-924624

Schapen Edition, H W Louis+
Gartenweg 6b, 38104 Braunschweig
Tel: (04953) 1360921
E-mail: schapen.edition@t-online.de
Key Personnel
International Rights: Dr Hans Walter Louis
Founded: 1990
Subjects: Environmental Studies, Law
ISBN Prefix(es): 3-927942

M & H Schaper GmbH & Co KG+
Borsigstr 5, 31061 Alfeld-Leine
Mailing Address: Postfach 1642, 31046 Alfeld-Leine
Tel: (05181) 8009-0 *Fax:* (05181) 8009-33
E-mail: info@shaper-verlag.de
Web Site: www.schaper-verlag.de
Key Personnel
International Rights: Wolfgang Habeck
Marketing Manager: Dieter Meyer *Tel:* (05181) 8009-40 *E-mail:* mored.meyer@schaper-verlag.de; Rainer Paland *Tel:* (05181) 8009-40 *E-mail:* info@schaper-verlag.de
Sales Manager: Carsten Sadlau *Tel:* (05181) 8009-16 *E-mail:* c.sadlau@schaper-verlag.de
Founded: 1897
Subjects: Animals, Pets, Crafts, Games, Hobbies, Veterinary Science
ISBN Prefix(es): 3-7944

F K Schattauer Verlagsgesellschaft mbH+
Hoelderlinstr 3, 70174 Stuttgart
Tel: (0711) 229870 *Fax:* (0711) 2298750
Web Site: www.schattauer.de
Key Personnel
Publisher, Rights & Permissions: Dieter Bergemann
Founded: 1949
Publishing house for medicine & natural sciences.
Subjects: Medicine, Nursing, Dentistry, Science (General)
ISBN Prefix(es): 3-7945
Shipping Address: Koch, Neff & Oetinger & Co Verlagsauslieferungen, Schockenriedstr 39, 70565 Stuttgart *Tel:* (0711) 78603365
Warehouse: Koch, Neff & Oetinger & Co Verlagsauslieferungen, Schockenriedstr 39, 70565 Stuttgart *Tel:* (0711) 78603365
Orders to: D A Book Depot Pty Ltd, 648 Whitehorse Rd, Mitcham, Vic 3132, Australia *Tel:* (03) 873 4411 *Fax:* (03) 873 5679
Mohr-Morawa Gesellschaft mbH, Sulzengasse 2, A-1210 Vienna, Austria *Tel:* (0222) 684614 *Fax:* (0222) 687130
Allied Publishers Pvt Ltd, 13/14 Asaf Ali Rd, PO Box 155, New Delhi 110002, India *Tel:* 2750001
Verlag Hans Huber AG, Langgassstr 76, CH-3000 Bern 9, Switzerland *Tel:* (031) 262533 *Fax:* (031) 43380
John Wiley & Sons Inc, Wiley-Liss Division, 605 Third Ave, New York, NY 10158-0012, United States *Tel:* 212-850-8800 *Fax:* 212-850-8888

Moritz Schauenburg Verlag+
Kreuzstr 9, 77933 Lahr
Tel: (07821) 90596-0 *Fax:* (07821) 9059666
E-mail: schauenburg_verlag@t-online.de
Key Personnel
Chairman: Dr Thomas Seng *Tel:* (0911) 39906-14
Manager: Margret Sterneck *Tel:* (07821) 90596-61
Founded: 1794
Subjects: Cookery, Health, Nutrition, History, Humor, Travel, Wine & Spirits
ISBN Prefix(es): 3-7946
Total Titles: 100 Print; 6 Audio

Verlag Heinrich Scheffler, *imprint of* Societaets-Verlag

Scheffler-Verlag+
Postfach 1449, 58313, Herdecke
Tel: (02330) 1743 *Fax:* (02330) 2281

PUBLISHERS

GERMANY

Key Personnel
President: Lothor Scheffler
Vice President: Barbel Scheffler
Founded: 1989
ISBN Prefix(es): 3-89029; 3-89704; 3-929880
Total Titles: 15 Print

Schelzky & Jeep, Verlag fuer Reisen und Wissen+
Fidicinstr 29, 10965 Berlin
Tel: (030) 6939495 *Fax:* (030) 6914697
Founded: 1981
Subjects: Architecture & Interior Design, Regional Interests, Social Sciences, Sociology, Travel
ISBN Prefix(es): 3-89541; 3-923024

Renate Schenk Verlag+
Heinkstr 10, 04347 Leipzig
Tel: (0341) 2300825 *Fax:* (0341) 2300826
E-mail: schenk-verlag@t-online.de
Web Site: www.schenk-verlag.de
Founded: 1984
Member of Australian Book Publishers Association (ABPA). Specialize in books about Australia, Australian Books, Antiquariat Aboroginal Art.
Subjects: Anthropology, Earth Sciences, Natural History, Travel
Divisions: Winjeel Shop Alice Springs Australia
Distributor for Magabala (Lansdown); Reader's Digest (Australia); Reed Books (Australia)
Bookshop(s): Koala Trade
Orders to: Geo Center Touristik Medien Service GmbH, Schockenriedstr 44, 70565 Stuttgart, Cornelia Braun *Tel:* (0711) 781946-41143 *Fax:* (0711) 781946-56

Richard Scherpe Verlag GmbH
Glockenspitz 140, 47800 Krefeld
Mailing Address: Postfach 2630, 47726 Krefeld
Tel: (02151) 539-0 *Fax:* (02151) 505390
Key Personnel
Owner: Richard Scherpe
International Rights: Mrs Wendt
Subjects: Education, Fiction, Government, Political Science
ISBN Prefix(es): 3-7948

Schiffahrts-Verlag
Striepenweg 31, 21147 Hamburg
Tel: (040) 79713-02 *Fax:* (040) 79713-324; (040) 79713-208; (040) 79713-214
E-mail: r_spieckermann@hansa-online.de
Subjects: Specializes in Shipping, Ship Technology & Building
ISBN Prefix(es): 3-87700
Number of titles published annually: 2 Print
Total Titles: 20 Print

Schild-Verlag GmbH+
Henschelstr 7, 81249 Munich
Tel: (089) 8 64 1189 *Fax:* (089) 8 63 2310
Key Personnel
Man Dir: Gunther Damerau
Founded: 1951
Subjects: Antiques, History, Literature, Literary Criticism, Essays, Military Science
ISBN Prefix(es): 3-88014
Total Titles: 35 Print

Verlag der Schillerbuchhandlung Hans Banger OHG
Guldenbachstr 1, 50935 Cologne
Tel: (0221) 46014-0 *Fax:* (0221) 46014-25; (0221) 46014-26
E-mail: banger@banger.de
Web Site: www.banger.de
Key Personnel
Man Dir: Ruth Jepsen; Elisabeth Mueller

Founded: 1950
ISBN Prefix(es): 3-87856

Schillinger Verlag GmbH+
Wallstr 14, 79089 Freiburg
Tel: (0761) 33233 *Fax:* (0762) 39055
E-mail: schillingerverlag@t-online.de
Web Site: schillingerverlag.de
Key Personnel
Man Dir: Helga Schillinger; Wolfgang Schillinger
Founded: 1984
Member of the Stock Exchange of German Booksellers.
Subjects: Art, Asian Studies, Environmental Studies, Fiction, Foreign Countries, History, Regional Interests, Travel
ISBN Prefix(es): 3-89155
Number of titles published annually: 15 Print
Total Titles: 214 Print

Schirmer/Mosel Verlag GmbH+
Widenmayerstr 16, 80538 Munich
Mailing Address: Postfach 221641, 80506 Munich
Tel: (089) 2126700 *Fax:* (089) 338695
E-mail: mail@schirmer-mosel.com
Web Site: www.schirmer-mosel.com
Key Personnel
Man Dir, Sales & Publicity: Lothar Schirmer
Production: Roland Hepp
International Rights: Dr Franz Ringel
Founded: 1975
Specialize in Collector's Editions.
Subjects: Art, Photography
ISBN Prefix(es): 3-88814
Branch Office(s)
PO Box 457, New York, NY 10012, United States, US Representative: Phillip Galgiani

Schirner Verlag+
Zerninstr 7, 64297 Darmstadt
Tel: (06151) 29 39 59 *Fax:* (06151) 29 39 87
E-mail: schirner.verlag@t-online.de
Web Site: www.schirner.com
Key Personnel
Man Dir: Kirsten Glueck *Tel:* (06151) 29 39 52
Bookkeeper: Erika Furbush *Tel:* (06151) 29 33 98
Contact: Gabriele Olschok; Uta Wagner
Founded: 1994
Subjects: Ethno-dictionaries, Mandala painting books, Painting books, Practical Workbooks & Spiritual Self-help literature
ISBN Prefix(es): 3-930944; 3-89767
Total Titles: 94 Print; 10 Audio
Foreign Rep(s): AS Bartsch-Hoeller Gmbh Verlagservile (Austria); Engros Buchhandlung Dessauer (Switzerland); Hartmut Ginder Verlagsvertretur (Germany); Verlagsvertretung Klaus-Dieter Guhl (Germany); Mareile & Peter Handrich (Germany); Marting & Detief Jessen (Germany); Verlagsagentur Reinhard Lieber (Germany); Hannelore Lindemann (Germany); Herbert Pamminger (Austria); Walter Stolte Verlagsvertretung (Germany)
Foreign Rights: Daniel Doglioli (Italy); Peter Schmidt Media Service International (France, Spain)

Agora Verlag Manfred Schlosser+
Galvanistr 4, 10857 Berlin
Tel: (030) 3424824 *Fax:* (030) 8545372
E-mail: agora2@gmx.net *Cable:* AGORA BERLIN
Key Personnel
Man Dir, Production: Manfred Schloesser
Sales & Publicity: Monika Schloesser-Fischer
Founded: 1960
Subjects: Fiction, Literature, Literary Criticism, Essays, Music, Dance, Poetry, Religion - Jewish
ISBN Prefix(es): 3-87008
Total Titles: 140 Print

Subsidiaries: Erato-Presse
Orders to: Bugrim Saalburgstr 3, 712099 Berlin

Schmetterling Verlag Jorg Hunger und Paul Sander+
Lindenspuerstr 38B, 70176 Stuttgart
Tel: (0711) 62 67 79 *Fax:* (0711) 62 69 92
E-mail: info@schmetterling-verlag.de
Web Site: www.schmetterling-verlag.de
Key Personnel
Production: Paul Sander
Public Speaker: Joerg Hunger
Contact: Joerg Exner
Subjects: Culture, Politics
ISBN Prefix(es): 3-926369; 3-89657

Schmid Verlag GmbH
Wuerttembergstr 10, 93049 Regensburg
Tel: (0941) 21519; (0941) 26629 *Fax:* (0941) 28766
Web Site: www.schmid-verlag.de
Key Personnel
Owner: Irmigard Schmid
Founded: 1949
Subjects: Travel
ISBN Prefix(es): 3-930572; 3-921657
Branch Office(s)
Karl-Wurmbstr 3, 5020 Salzburg, Austria

Schmidmusic, *imprint of* Silberburg-Verlag Titus Haeussermann GmbH

Verlag Dr Otto Schmidt KG+
Unter den Ulmen 96-98, 50968 Cologne (Marienburg)
Tel: (0221) 9 37 38-01 *Fax:* (0221) 9 37 38-09
E-mail: info@ottoschmidt.de; verlag@ottoschmidt.de
Web Site: www.otto-schmidt.de
Telex: 8883381 osvd *Cable:* SCHMIDTVERLAG
Key Personnel
Man Dir: K P Winters
Editorial: Dr Katherine Knauth
Sales, Publicity & Advertising: Michael Rieck
Organization, Financial: Arno Harms
Founded: 1905
Subjects: Business, Finance, Law
ISBN Prefix(es): 3-504
Associate Companies: Centrale fur GmbH Dr Otto Schmidt
Subsidiaries: Anwalt-Suchservice GmbH; Centrale fur Verbaende und Vereine Verlag Dr Otto Schmidt GmbH
Branch Office(s)
Haus Bayenthalguertel, Bayenthalguertel 13, 50968 Cologne (Marienburg)
Buerocenter Bonnerstr 484-486, 50968 Cologne (Marienburg)
Bookshop(s): Friedrich-Verlegerstr 7, 33602 Bielefeld; Am Yustizzentrum 3, 50939 Cologne 47; Buchhandlung Hermann Sack, Klosterstr 22, 40211 Duesseldorf; Buchhandlung Hermann Sack, Guenthersburgallee 1, 60316 Frankfurt am Main; Harkortstr 7, 04107 Leipzig; Struppe u Winckler, Postfach 10 24 91, 33527 Bielefeld

Erich Schmidt Verlag GmbH & Co+
Genthinerstr 30G, 10785 Berlin
Tel: (030) 25 00 85-0 *Fax:* (030) 25 00 85-21
E-mail: ESV@esvmedien.de
Web Site: www.erich-schmidt-verlag.de *Cable:* ESVERLAG BERLIN
Key Personnel
Man Dir: Claus-Michael Rast
Production: Siegfried Horstmann
Advertising: Winfried Plochl
Administration: Wolfgang Schlueter
Distribution: Sibylle Boehlei
Founded: 1924
Subjects: Economics, Environmental Studies, Language Arts, Linguistics, Law, Management
ISBN Prefix(es): 3-503

Branch Office(s)
Paosostr 6-7, 81234 Munich *Tel:* (089) 8299600
  Fax: (089) 82996010
Viktoriastr 44a, Postfach 1024, 33602 Bielefeld
  Tel: (0521) 583080 *Fax:* (0521) 5830829

Erich Schmidt Verlag GmbH & Co
Formerly S + W Steuer- und Wirtschaftsverlag GmbH
Genthiner Str 30 G, 10785 Berlin
Mailing Address: Postfach 304240, 10724 Berlin
Tel: (030) 25 00 85-0 *Fax:* (030) 25 00 85 11
E-mail: vertrieb@esvmedien.de
Web Site: www.erich-schmidt-verlag.de
Key Personnel
Man Dir: Claus-Michael Rast; Dr Joachim Schmidt
Sales Manager: Sibylle Boehler *Tel:* (030) 25 00 85 80
Founded: 1924
Subjects: Accounting, Business, Finance, Law, Philological Topics
ISBN Prefix(es): 3-503
Number of titles published annually: 220 Print

Verlag Hermann Schmidt Universitatsdruckerei GmbH & Co+
Robert Kochstr 8, 55129 Mainz-Hechtsheim (Gewerbegebiet)
Tel: (06131) 506030 *Fax:* (06131) 506080
E-mail: info@typografie.de
Web Site: www.typografie.de
Key Personnel
International Rights: Karin Schmidt-Friderichs
Founded: 1950
Specialize in typography & design.
Subjects: Art
ISBN Prefix(es): 3-87439
Orders to: Verlag Hermann Schmidt Mainz, Luisenstr 6, 55124 Mainz

Schmidt Periodicals GmbH
Dettendorf, 83075 Bad Feilnbach
Tel: (08064) 221 *Fax:* (08064) 557
E-mail: schmidt@backsets.com
Web Site: www.backsets.com
Key Personnel
Dir: Gerhard Schmidt
Sales & Marketing: Victoria Smith *Tel:* (0034) 921 412194 *Fax:* (0034) 921 412625
  E-mail: vsmith@backsets.com
Founded: 1962
Specialize in back sets, volumes & issues of periodicals, serials & reference works in all subjects & languages.
Subjects: Science (General), Medical, Technical
Total Titles: 9,999 Print
U.S. Office(s): Periodicals Service Company, 11 Main St, Germantown, NY 12526, United States, Contact: James Curran *Tel:* 518-537-4700 *Fax:* 518-537-5899 *E-mail:* psc@backsets.com

Max Schmidt-Roemhild Verlag+
Mengstr 16, 23552 Luebeck
Tel: (0451) 70 31-01 *Fax:* (0451) 70 31-253
  Fax on Demand: (0451) 7031-253
E-mail: msr-luebeck@t-online.de
Web Site: www.schmidt-roemhild.de
Key Personnel
Publisher: Norbert Beleke
Man Dir, Rights & Permissions: Hans-Juergen Sperling
Editorship: Dr Edwin Kube *Tel:* (0228) 28044-40 *Fax:* (0228) 28044-41 *E-mail:* kube@forum-kriminalpraevention.de
Layout: Peter Koesling *Tel:* (0201) 8130-200 *Fax:* (0201) 8130-196
Contact: Dr M Platzkoester
Founded: 1579
Subjects: Criminology, History, Law, Medicine, Nursing, Dentistry, Regional Interests, Social Sciences, Sociology, Sports, Athletics
ISBN Prefix(es): 3-7950; 3-8016
Associate Companies: Schmidt-Roemhild Verlagsgesellschaft mbH Brandenburg, August-Bebelstr 23-27, 14470 Brandenburg *Tel:* (03381) 3693-0
Subsidiaries: Hansisches Verlags Kontor
Branch Office(s)
Schmidt-Roemhild Verlagsgesellschaft mbH Leipzig, Coppistr 2, 04129 Leipzig *Tel:* (0341) 90 48 50
Schmidt-Roemhild verlagsgesellschaft mbH Rostock, Platz der Freundschaft 1, 18059 Rostock *Tel:* (0381) 44 84 55
Schmidt-Romhild Verlagsgesellschaft mbH Schwerin, Graf-Schack-Allee 6, 19053 Schwerin *Tel:* (0385) 5 91 88-0
Verlag fur Polizeiliches Fachschrifttum Georg Schmidt- Roemhild, Mengstr 16, 23552 Luebeck

Buchverlag Andrea Schmitz
Hauptstr 17, 21442 Toppenstedt
Tel: (04173) 512612 *Fax:* (04173) 512612
E-mail: buchverlag@aol.com
Founded: 1988
Subjects: Fiction, Humor, Medicine, Nursing, Dentistry, Mysteries, Nonfiction (General), Outdoor Recreation, Poetry, Publishing & Book Trade Reference, Science Fiction, Fantasy
ISBN Prefix(es): 3-927442

Wilhelm Schmitz Verlag+
Staufenberger Weg 22, 35457 Lollar
Tel: (06406) 23 24
Web Site: www.wilhelm-schmitz-verlag.de
Key Personnel
Man Dir, Rights & Permissions: Siegfried Schmitz
Founded: 1847
Subjects: Art, Ethnicity, Foreign Countries, Language Arts, Linguistics, Literature, Literary Criticism, Essays, Medicine, Nursing, Dentistry
ISBN Prefix(es): 3-87711

Schneekluth Verlag+
Hilblestr 54, 80636 Munich
Tel: (089) 92710 *Fax:* (089) 9271261
Web Site: www.schneekluth.de
Key Personnel
Man Dir: Ralf Mueller; Christian Tesch; Dr Hans-Peter Uebleis
Founded: 1949
ISBN Prefix(es): 3-7951
Number of titles published annually: 30 Print
Parent Company: Verlagsgruppe Droemer Weltbild, Hilblestr 54, 80636 Munich

Rudolf Schneider Verlag+
Freseniusstr 59, 81247 Munich
Tel: (089) 8113466 *Fax:* (089) 8110619
Key Personnel
Publisher & Man Dir: Karl-Heinz Biebl
Founded: 1926
ISBN Prefix(es): 3-7955
Divisions: Edition Hohenstaufen

Verlag Schnell und Steiner GmbH+
Leibnizstr 13, 93055 Regensburg
Tel: (0941) 787850 *Fax:* (0941) 7878516
E-mail: susvertrieb@t-online.de *Cable:* SCHNELLSTEINER REGENSBURG
Key Personnel
Publisher: conrad Lienhardt
Sales & Marketing: Rainer Boos; Christian Pflug
Founded: 1934
Subjects: Archaeology, Art, Biblical Studies, Biography, History, Music, Dance, Religion - Catholic, Religion - Protestant, Theology, Travel
ISBN Prefix(es): 3-7954
Number of titles published annually: 45 Print
Total Titles: 3,500 Print
Imprints: Zodiaque
Distributed by Rex Verlag (Switzerland)

Schnitzer GmbH & Co KG+
Feldbergstr 11, 78112 St Georgen
Tel: (07724) 9432-0 *Fax:* (07724) 9432-20
Web Site: www.medizin.li
Founded: 1966
Subjects: Health, Nutrition
ISBN Prefix(es): 3-922894; 3-921123

Schoeffling & Co+
Kaiserstr 79, 60329 Frankfurt am Main
Tel: (069) 92 07 87-0 *Fax:* (069) 92 07 87-20
E-mail: ida.schoeffling@schoeffling.de
Web Site: www.schoeffling.de
Key Personnel
Publisher: Klaus Schoeffling
Publicity, Editorial: Ida Schoeffling
Rights & Permissions, International Rights: Kathrin Scheel
Founded: 1993
Subjects: Biography, Fiction, Literature, Literary Criticism, Essays, Travel
ISBN Prefix(es): 3-89561

Verlag Hans Schoener GmbH+
Walther-Rathenaustr 13, 75203 Koenigsbach-Stein
Mailing Address: Postfach 69, 75197 Koenigsbach-Stein
Tel: (07232) 4007-0 *Fax:* (07232) 4007-99
E-mail: info@verlag-schoener.de
Web Site: www.verlag-schoener.de
Key Personnel
Man Dir: Elke Schoener *Tel:* (07232) 40 07-20 *E-mail:* es@verlag-schoener.de; Jourg Schoener *Tel:* (07232) 40 07-11 *E-mail:* js@verlag-schoener.de
Editorial: Michael Franz *Tel:* (07232) 40 07-22 *E-mail:* wimo@verlag-schoener.de; Wilfried Morlock *Tel:* (07232) 40 07-23 *E-mail:* mic@verlag-schoener.de
Founded: 1971
Subjects: Fashion, Music, Dance, Photography
ISBN Prefix(es): 3-923765

Ferdinand Schoeningh Verlag GmbH+
Juehenplatz 1, 33098 Paderborn
Mailing Address: Postfach 2540, 33055 Paderborn
Tel: (05251) 1275 *Fax:* (05251) 127860; (05251) 127670
E-mail: info@schoeningh.de
Web Site: www.schoeningh.de
Key Personnel
Man Dir: Ferdinand Schoeningh
Press: Hansgeorg Enzian
Production: Friedhelm Meyer
Editor, Scholarly Books: Dr Hans Jacobs; Dr Diatlund Sawicki; Michael Werner
Founded: 1847
Specialize in scholarly books.
Subjects: Biography, Government, Political Science, History, Language Arts, Linguistics, Literature, Literary Criticism, Essays, Philosophy, Religion - Catholic, Theology
ISBN Prefix(es): 3-506
Number of titles published annually: 100 Print
Total Titles: 1,500 Print
Warehouse: F Schoeningh GmbH, Otto-Stadler-Str 6, 33100 Paderborn

Schott Musik International GmbH & Co KG+
Weihergarten 5, 55116 Mainz
Tel: (06131) 246-0; (06131) 5050 (Auslief)
Fax: (06131) 2462-11; (06131) 505115 (Auslief)

Web Site: www.schott-online.com *Cable:* SCOTSON
Key Personnel
Man Dir: Dr Peter Hansen-Strecker; Rolf Reisinger; Dr Christian Sprang
Editorial: Dr Rainer Mohrs
Production & Printing: Herwig Suess
Sales: Helmut Fischer
Rights & Permissions: Volker Landtag
Founded: 1770
Subjects: Biography, Education, Music, Dance
ISBN Prefix(es): 3-7957
Associate Companies: Wiener Urtext Edition-Musikverlag GmbH & Co KG, Australia (jointly owned with Universal Edition AG, Austria)
Subsidiaries: Ars-Viva-Verlag GmbH; Atlantis Musikbuch-Verlag AG; Cranz GmbH; Ernst Eulenburg & Co GmbH; Eulenburg AG; Fuerstner Musikverlag GmbH; Arnold Schoenberg Gesamtausgabe GmbH; Music Factory GmbH; Musikverlag Kompositor International GmbH; Panton International GmbH; Schotta Wergo Music Media GmbH; SMD Schott Music Distribution GmbH; Wega Verlag GmbH
Branch Office(s)
Espanola de Ediciones Musicales Schott SL, Alcala 70, 28009 Madrid, Spain
Schott & Co Ltd, 48 Great Marlborough St, London W1V 2BN, United Kingdom
Schott Japan Co Ltd, Toyko, Japan
Schott Paris SARL, 40 rue Blomet, 75015 Paris, France
U.S. Office(s): European American Music Distributors Corp, Valley Forge, PA, United States
Bookshop(s): Mainzer Musikalienzentrum, Weihergarten 9, Mainz
Orders to: SMD Schott Music Distribution GmbH, Postfach 3640, 55026 Mainz
Tel: (06131) 5050 *Fax:* (06131) 505115

Schrader Verlag Paul Pietsch Verlage GmbH & Co KG
Olgastr 86, 70180 Stuttgart
Mailing Address: Postfach 103743, 73032 Stuttgart
Tel: (0711) 21080-0 *Fax:* (0711) 2360415

Schreiber-Naturtafeln, *imprint of* Justus Perthes Verlag Gotha GmbH

Verlag Silke Schreiber+
Agnesstr 12, 80798 Munich
Mailing Address: Postfach 431161, 80741 Munich
Tel: (089) 2710180 *Fax:* (089) 2716957
E-mail: metzel@verlagSilkeschreiber.de
Web Site: www.verlag-silke-schreiber.de
Key Personnel
Manager, Rights & Permissions: Dr Luise Metzel
E-mail: metzel@t.online.de
Founded: 1982
Subjects: Art, Modern Art
ISBN Prefix(es): 3-88960
U.S. Office(s): Chris Pichler, Fulfillment Services, 1355 West Grand Rd, Suite 230, Tucson, AZ 85745, United States
Orders to: Vice Versa, Waldemarstr 81, 10997 Berlin, Contact: Gabriela Wachter *Tel:* (030) 61609237 *Fax:* (030) 61609238

Schriftenfeibe Wissenschaft und Frieden, *imprint of* Bund demokratischer Wissenschaftlerinnen und Wissenschafler eV (BdWi)

Verlag und Schriftenmission der Evangelischen Gesellschaft Wuppertal+
Kaiserstr 78, 42329 Wuppertal
Tel: (0202) 278500 *Fax:* (0202) 2785040

Key Personnel
Man Dir: Hans Mohr
Sales, Production: Herbert Becker
Founded: 1954
Member of the Telos group publishing evangelical paperbacks. Publishing House & Scriptural Mission of the German Evangelical Society.
Subjects: Literature, Literary Criticism, Essays, Religion - Other
ISBN Prefix(es): 3-87857

Schrifter zur Kontemplation, *imprint of* Vier Tuerme GmbH Verlag Klosterbetriebe

Schroedel Schulbuchverlag GmbH
Hildesheimerstr 202-206, 30519 Hannover
Tel: (0511) 8388205 *Fax:* (0511) 8388280
Web Site: www.schroedel.de
Key Personnel
Manager: Alfons Rutishauser
ISBN Prefix(es): 3-285

Ferdinand Schroll, see Titania-Verlag Ferdinand Schroll

Carl Ed Schuenemann KG
Zweite Schlachtpforte 7, 28195 Bremen
Mailing Address: Postfach 10 60 67, 28060 Bremen
Tel: (0421) 369 03 71 *Fax:* (0421) 369 03 63
E-mail: kontakt@kunstverlag.de
Web Site: www2.schuenemann-verlag.de
Key Personnel
Man Dir, Sales & Publicity: Klaus Kirchner
Founded: 1810
Subjects: Art, Regional Interests
ISBN Prefix(es): 3-7961

Schueren Verlag GmbH+
Universitaetsstr 55, 35037 Marburg
Tel: (06421) 6 30 84; (06421) 6 30 85
Fax: (06421) 68 11 90
E-mail: schueren.verlag@t-online.de
Web Site: www.schueren-verlag.de
Key Personnel
Manager: Dr Annette Schueren
Founded: 1985
Subjects: Biography, Communications, Economics, Film, Video, Government, Political Science, Labor, Industrial Relations, Nonfiction (General), Radio, TV, Regional Interests, Science (General), Self-Help, Social Sciences, Sociology
ISBN Prefix(es): 3-89472
Total Titles: 150 Print

Verlag Karl Waldemar Schuetz+
Postfach 2554, 96414 Coburg
Tel: (09561) 80780 *Fax:* (09561) 807820
Key Personnel
Man Dir, Rights & Permissions: Peter Dehoust
Editorial: Karl Richter
Founded: 1948
Subjects: History, Military Science
ISBN Prefix(es): 3-87725
Parent Company: Nation Europa Verlags GmbH, Bahnhofstr 25, 96450 Coburg

Verlag Schulte und Gerth GmbH & Co KG+
Dillerberg 2, 35614 Asslar-Berghausen
Mailing Address: Postfach 1148, 35607 Asslar-Berghausen
Tel: (06443) 680 *Fax:* (06443) 6890
Key Personnel
Dir, Rights & Permissions: Klaus Gerth
Sales Dir: Rolf Fischer
Marketing Dir: Stefanie Goemmer
Founded: 1949
Subjects: Biography, Fiction, Music, Dance, Nonfiction (General), Religion - Other
ISBN Prefix(es): 3-89437

Schulz-Kirchner Verlag GmbH+
Mollweg 2, 65510 Idstein
Mailing Address: Postfach 9, 65505 Idstein
Tel: (06126) 93200 *Fax:* (06126) 9320-50
E-mail: info@schulz-kirchner.de
Web Site: www.schulz-kirchner.de
Key Personnel
Manager: Pia Neutzler
Founded: 1984
Subjects: Business, Economics, Energy, Film, Video, Finance, Health, Nutrition, History, Labor, Industrial Relations, Language Arts, Linguistics, Marketing, Medicine, Nursing, Dentistry, Philosophy, Science (General), Social Sciences, Sociology
ISBN Prefix(es): 3-8248; 3-925196

R S Schulz Verlag GmbH+
Bergerstr 8-10, 82319 Starnberg
Tel: (08151) 9144-0 *Fax:* (08151) 9144-190
Web Site: www.rss.de
Key Personnel
Publisher: Dr Rolf Simon Schulz
Subjects: Architecture & Interior Design, Fiction, Health, Nutrition, Law, Social Sciences, Sociology, Veterinary Science
ISBN Prefix(es): 3-7962

H O Schulze KG
V-v-Scheffel-Str 29, 96215 Lichtenfels
Tel: (09571) 78026 *Fax:* (09571) 78058
E-mail: verkauf@schulze-kg.de
Web Site: www.schulze-kg.de
Key Personnel
Publisher: Heinrich Schulze
Founded: 1865
Subjects: Art, Fiction, Geography, Geology, History, Nonfiction (General), Travel
ISBN Prefix(es): 3-87735
Distributed by Colloquium Historicum Wirsbergense; Verlag des Historischen Vereins Bamberg

Theodor Schuster
Muehlenstr 15/17, 26789 Leer
Mailing Address: Postfach 1944, 26769 Leer
Tel: (0491) 925900 *Fax:* (0491) 9259059
E-mail: buchhandlung-Schuster@t-online.de
Key Personnel
Contact: Theo Schuster
Subjects: Fiction, Humor, Nonfiction (General), Poetry
Number of titles published annually: 5 Print; 1 CD-ROM; 2 Audio

Edition Schwab, *imprint of* Verlag Stephanie Naglschmid

Heinrich Schwab Verlag
Eglofstal 42, 88260 Argenbuehl
Mailing Address: Gschwend 77, 6932 Langen bei Bregent
Tel: (0043) 5575-20101 *Fax:* (0043) 5575-4745
E-mail: heinrich.schwab@vol.at
Web Site: www.heinrichschwabverlag.de
Key Personnel
Manager: Verena Brocksieper
Founded: 1926
Subjects: Environmental Studies, Gardening, Plants, Health, Nutrition, Human Relations, Nonfiction (General), Parapsychology, Philosophy, Poetry, Psychology, Psychiatry, Religion - Other, Self-Help, Alternative Medicine, Biological Horticulture, Breathe Therapies, Border Sciences, Esoteric Works & Meditation, Life Assistance, Life-Wise, Medicine, Mental Healing, Naturopathy, Positive Thinking, Religion Science, Yoga
ISBN Prefix(es): 3-7964

Schwabenverlag Aktiengesellschaft+
Senefelderstr 12, 73760 Ostfildern

Tel: (0711) 4406-0 *Fax:* (0711) 4406-177
E-mail: buchverlag@schwabenverlag.de
Key Personnel
President: Udo Vogt
International Rights: Martin Guenther
Founded: 1848
Subjects: Art, Regional Interests, Religion - Catholic, Religion - Other, Theology
ISBN Prefix(es): 3-7966
Subsidiaries: Rottenburger Druckerei; Schwabenverlag AG Ellwangen; Sueddeutsche Verlagsgesellschaft mbH Ulm
Distributed by Auslieferung (Austria & Germany); Auslieferung Schweiz Herder; Brockhaus/Commission; Osterreichisches Katholisches Bibelwerk
Bookshop(s): Schwabenverlag Buchhandlung, Bahnhofstr 21, 73430 Aalen; Spitalstr 17, 73479 Ellwangen; Sueddeutsche Verlagsgesellschaft Ulm, Bahnhofstr 20, 89073 Ulm

Schwaneberger Verlag GmbH
Muthmannstr 4, 80939 Munich
Tel: (089) 3239302 *Fax:* (089) 32393379
E-mail: webmaster@michel.de
Web Site: www.michel.de
Key Personnel
Man Dir, Rights & Permissions: Hans Hohenester
Editorial: Jochen Stenzke
Sales: Joachim Stolz
Publicity: Werner Maier
Founded: 1910
Subjects: Crafts, Games, Hobbies
ISBN Prefix(es): 3-87858
Associate Companies: Carl Gerber Verlag GmbH

Edition Schwann, *imprint of* C F Peters Musikverlag GmbH & Co KG

Otto Schwartz Fachbochhandlung GmbH+
Barfuesserstr 7, 37073 Goettingen
Tel: (0551) 50 85 978 *Fax:* (0551) 50 85 983
E-mail: Schwartz.Stadt@t-online.de
Key Personnel
Man Dir: Dr Herbert Weisser
Man Dir, Rights & Permissions: Konrad Weisser
Rights & Permissions: Ernst Leopold
Branch Manager: Marlis Potthast *Tel:* (0551) 50 85 978
Sales: Mrs Barke *Tel:* (0551) 50 85 978; Mrs Beuermann *Tel:* (0551) 50 85 978; Ms Willgerodt *Tel:* (0551) 50 85 978
Founded: 1871
Subjects: Ethnicity, Law, Public Administration, Social Sciences, Sociology
ISBN Prefix(es): 3-509
Bookshop(s): Fachbuchhandlung Otto Schwartz & Co, Annastr 7, 37075 Goettingen

Dr Wolfgang Schwarze Verlag+
Richard Strauss Allee 35, 42289 Wuppertal
Mailing Address: Postfach 201744, 42217 Wuppertal
Tel: (0202) 622005; (0202) 622006 *Fax:* (0202) 63631
Key Personnel
Man Dir, Rights & Permissions: Dr Wolfgang Schwarze
Sales, Office Chief: Ursula Schwarze
Founded: 1968
Subjects: Antiques, Architecture & Interior Design, Art, House & Home
ISBN Prefix(es): 3-87741

Schweers + Wall GmbH Verlag+
Postfach 1586, 52016 Aachen
Tel: (0241) 87 22 51 *Fax:* (0241) 8 52 06
E-mail: schweers-wall@t-online.de
Web Site: home.t-online.de/home/schweers.wall
Founded: 1986

Subjects: Transportation, Travel
ISBN Prefix(es): 3-921679; 3-89494

Schwul Lesbische Studien Universitat Bremen, *imprint of* Mannerschwarm Skript Verlag Bartholomae & Co OHG

Scientia Verlag und Antiquariat
Adlerstr 65, 73434 Aalen
Mailing Address: Postfach 1660, 73434 Aalen
Tel: (07361) 41700 *Fax:* (07361) 45620
Cable: SCIENTIA AALENWUERTT
Key Personnel
Man Dir: Guenter Schilling
Founded: 1953
Subjects: Archaeology, Economics, Education, History, Law, Philosophy, Religion - Other, Social Sciences, Sociology, Theology
ISBN Prefix(es): 3-511

SDV, see Saarbrucker Druckerei und Verlag GmbH (SDV)

Seibt Verlag GmbH
Leopoldstr 208, 80804 Munich
Tel: (089) 6 09 03-0 *Fax:* (089) 6 43 17
E-mail: info@seibt.com
Web Site: www.seibt.de
Key Personnel
Man Dir: Alfred Augustine; Werner Reiber; Roland Repp
Advertising Dir: Brita Graef
Founded: 1921
Member of VDAV (Verband Deutscher Adressbuchveleger) & EADP (European Association of Directory Publishers).
Subjects: Environmental Studies, Mechanical Engineering, Medicine, Nursing, Dentistry
ISBN Prefix(es): 3-922948; 3-931336
Parent Company: Hoppenstedt GmbH & Co, Havelstr 9, 64295 Darmstadt

Dr Arthur L Sellier & Co-Walter de Gruyter GmbH & Co KG OHG+
Genthinerstr 13, 10785 Berlin
Mailing Address: PO Box 303421, 10728 Berlin
Tel: (030) 26005-0 *Fax:* (030) 260 05-251
Web Site: www.degruyter.de
Telex: 184027 *Cable:* WISSENSCHAFT BERLIN
Key Personnel
Contact: Georg Broeckelmann
Founded: 1990
Subjects: Law
ISBN Prefix(es): 3-11; 3-8059
U.S. Office(s): 200 Saw Mill River Rd, Hawthorne, NY 10532, United States *Tel:* 914-747-0110 *Fax:* 914-747-1326

Sellier Verlag GmbH+
Prinzregentenstr 126, 81677 Munich
Tel: (089) 4705050 *Fax:* (089) 4701081
Key Personnel
Man Dir & Publisher: Hans Meisinger
Rights & Publicity: Christiane Schneider
Founded: 1702
ISBN Prefix(es): 3-8221; 3-87137
Orders to: MVS Meisinger Verlagsservice GmbH, Am Steinfeld 4, 94065 Waldkirchen *Tel:* (08581) 9605-0 *Fax:* (08581) 754

Siebeck, see Mohr Siebeck

Siebenberg-Verlag+
Warolderstr 1, 34513 Waldeck
Tel: (05695) 1028 *Fax:* (05695) 1027
E-mail: fh@huebnerbooks.de
Web Site: www.huebnerbooks.de
Key Personnel
Publisher: Felicitas Huebner
Founded: 1936

Subjects: Art, Asian Studies, Poetry
ISBN Prefix(es): 3-87747
Orders to: Bugrim Verlagsauslieferung Dr Laube & Partner, Saalburgstr 3, 12099 Berlin

Siebert und Engelbert Dessart Verlag GmbH+
Lucille-Grahnstr 39, 81675 Munich
Tel: (089) 4194020 *Fax:* (089) 4701081
Key Personnel
Man Dir & Publisher: Hans Meisinger
Rights & Publicity: Christiane Schneider
Founded: 1967
Subjects: Crafts, Games, Hobbies
ISBN Prefix(es): 3-8089; 3-920215
Orders to: MVS Meisinger Verlagsservice GmbH, Am Steinfeld 4, 94065 Waldkirchen *Tel:* (08581) 9605-0 *Fax:* (08581) 754

Siedler Verlag+
Griefswalderstr 207, 10405 Berlin
Tel: (030) 44 38 45-0 *Fax:* (030) 44384555; (030) 44384546
E-mail: bettine.vonborries@bertelsmann.de
Key Personnel
Contact: Gisela Nicklaus
Foreign Rights: Sabine Oswald *Tel:* (030) 44 38 45-15 *Fax:* (030) 44 38 45-46 *E-mail:* sabine.oswald@bertelsmann.de
Press: Gisela Maria Nicklaus *Tel:* (030) 44 38 45-28 *Fax:* (030) 44 38 45-55 *E-mail:* giselamaria.nicklaus@bertelsmann.de
Founded: 1982
Subjects: Biography, Government, Political Science, History, Journalism, Nonfiction (General)
ISBN Prefix(es): 3-88680
Parent Company: Bertelsmann Verlagsgruppe GmbH, Postfach 800360, 81603 Munich
Orders to: Siedler Verlag Vertiel, Neumarkterstr 18, 81673 Munich

Siegler & Co Verlag fuer Zeitarchive GmbH+
Hauptstr 354, 53639 Koenigswinter
Tel: (02223) 2 10 28 *Fax:* (02223) 2 30 28
Key Personnel
Manager & International Rights: Dr Werner Hippe
Publishing Dir: Gerd Meiser
Founded: 1931
Subjects: Government, Political Science, History
ISBN Prefix(es): 3-87748
Parent Company: Asgard Verlag Dr Werner Hippe KG, Einsteinstr 10, 53757 St Augustin

Siegmund Publishing+
Buxtehuderstr 31B, 21647 Moisburg
Tel: (04) 1656609 *Fax:* (04) 1656011
Key Personnel
Publisher: W Siegmund
Founded: 1981
Subjects: Advertising, Architecture & Interior Design
ISBN Prefix(es): 3-930463

Georg Siemens Verlagsbuchhandlung
Boothstr 11, 12207 Berlin
Mailing Address: Postfach 450169, 12171 Berlin
Tel: (030) 769904-0 *Fax:* (030) 769904-18
E-mail: gsiemensv@t-online.de
Key Personnel
Contact: Hans Klessinger *Tel:* (030) 76990412
Founded: 1891
Subjects: Specializes in Railway transportation & Craft Sanitary facilities & heating
ISBN Prefix(es): 3-87749

Sierra, *imprint of* Frederking & Thaler Verlag GmbH

Sigloch Edition Helmut Sigloch GmbH & Co KG+
Am Buchberg 8, 74572 Blaufelden

Mailing Address: Postfach 1201, Blaufelden 74568
Tel: (07953) 883-138 *Fax:* (07953) 883-130
E-mail: edition@sigloch.de
Web Site: www.sigloch.de
Telex: 74 161
Key Personnel
President: Helmut Sigloch
Production Manager: Michael Sanny
Founded: 1972
Subjects: Cookery, Technology
ISBN Prefix(es): 3-89393
Warehouse: Sigloch Distribution GmbH, Am Buchberg 8, 74572 Blaufelden

Edition Sigma e.Kfm+
Karl-Marxstr 17, 12043 Berlin
Tel: (030) 623 23 63 *Fax:* (030) 623 93 93
E-mail: verlag@edition-sigma.de
Web Site: www.edition-sigma.de
Key Personnel
Editor-in-Chief: Titus Haeussermann
Sales & Advertising: Christel Werner
Contact: Mr R Bohn
Founded: 1984
Subjects: Social Sciences, Sociology
ISBN Prefix(es): 3-924859; 3-89404

Silberburg-Verlag Titus Haeussermann GmbH+
Schoenbuchstr 48, 72074 Tuebingen-Bebenhausen
Tel: (07071) 6885-0 *Fax:* (07071) 6885-20
E-mail: info@silberburg.de
Web Site: www.silberburg.com
Key Personnel
Editor-in-Chief: Titus Haeussermann
Sales & Advertising: Christel Werner
Founded: 1985
Member of Stock Exchange of German Booksellers & Association of Publishers & Booksellers in Baden-Wuerttemberg.
Subjects: Regional Interests
ISBN Prefix(es): 3-925344; 3-87407
Number of titles published annually: 50 Print; 20 Audio
Total Titles: 300 Print; 50 Audio
Imprints: Gustav Mesmer Stiftung; Schmidmusic
Distributed by Maule & Gosch Tontragervertrieb
Distributor for JS Film-Produktion GmbH; Maeule & Gosch Tontragervertrieb; Musekater Musikverlag; Schwoissfuass GmbH
Warehouse: Silberburg-Verlag, c/o Koch, Neff & Oetinger & Co, Verlagsauslieferung GmbH, Schockenriedstr 39, 70565 Stuttgart-Vaihingen
Tel: (0711) 78600

Die Silberschnur Verlag GmbH+
Steinstr 1, 56593 Guellesheim
Tel: (02687) 929068 *Fax:* (02687) 929524
Key Personnel
Man Dir: Tom Hockemeyer; Manfred Huber
Publisher's Reader: N Kugberg *Tel:* (02687) 929089 *E-mail:* info@silberschaur.de
Founded: 1982
Subjects: Alternative, Astrology, Occult, Parapsychology, Alternative healing, Esoteric Teachings & Life After Death
ISBN Prefix(es): 3-923781; 3-931652; 3-89845
Number of titles published annually: 20 Print
Total Titles: 300 Print
Distributor for Adwaita; Arun; Corona; Coudris; Devas Edition; Dude; EVT; Genius; Grasmuck; Heindel; Hubner; ICH; Kopp; 1 au 1; Larimar; Lichtring; Medicum Keg; Naam; Nietsch; NLS; Omega; Ostergaard; PAN; Quadropol; Riechel; Rocke; Sequoyah; Silberschnur; Simeunovic; Sternentor; Subtilis; Weltenhuter

Gerd Simon & Claudia Magiera, Verlagsbuero+
Triftstr 13, 80538 Munich

Mailing Address: Postfach 431062, 80740 Munich
Tel: (089) 21939012 *Fax:* (089) 21939014
Key Personnel
Man Dir: Claudia Magiera; Gerd Simon
Founded: 1979
Subjects: Asian Studies, Fiction, Foreign Countries, Travel
ISBN Prefix(es): 3-88676
Subsidiaries: Tutto Mondo

Rudolf G Smend+
Mainzerstr 31, 50678 Cologne
Tel: (0221) 312047 *Fax:* (0221) 9 32 07 18
E-mail: smend@smend.de
Web Site: www.smend.de
Key Personnel
Contact: Rudolf G Smend
Founded: 1973
Art gallery & publisher of catalogues.
Subjects: Art, Asian Studies, Indonesian art, textile art
ISBN Prefix(es): 3-926779
Number of titles published annually: 1 Print
Total Titles: 10 Print
Orders to: Mainzerstr 33, Cologne *Fax:* (0221) 325134

SMG Stiebner Medien gmbh+
Nymphenburger Str 86, 80636 Munich
Tel: (089) 1257378 *Fax:* (089) 162282
Founded: 1998
Specialize in reproductions.
Subjects: Art, Sports, Athletics
ISBN Prefix(es): 3-7679; 3-8302; 3-8259

Snayder Verlag Gunter VOB & Jurgen Schroder OHG
Josef-Schroderstr 45, 33098 Panderborn
Tel: (05251) 760208 *Fax:* (05251) 74398
Founded: 1993
Subjects: Fiction, Nonfiction (General), Poetry
ISBN Prefix(es): 3-930302; 3-932319; 3-933976

Societaets-Verlag+
Frankenallee 71-81, 60327 Frankfurt am Main
Tel: (069) 75010 *Fax:* (069) 75014398
Telex: 0411655 *Cable:* Zeitung Frankfurtmain
Key Personnel
Publisher: Volker Grams; Dr Peter Kluthe
Publisher, Publicity & Rights: Dr Roland Gerschermann
Publicity: Joerg Emich
Founded: 1921
Subjects: Art, Business, Economics, History, Literature, Literary Criticism, Essays
ISBN Prefix(es): 3-7973
Imprints: Verlag Frankfurter Buecher; Verlag Heinrich Scheffler

Soldi-Verlag im Drockzentrum Harburg
Steinbeckerstr 97, 21244 Buchholz id Nordheide
Tel: (04181) 29 16 22 *Fax:* (04181) 29 16 23
Web Site: www.karismaverlag.de
Key Personnel
Man Dir: Horst Ernst
Founded: 1977
ISBN Prefix(es): 3-928028; 3-923744; 3-931877

Sonnentanz-Verlag Roland Kron+
25, 86165 Augsburg
Tel: (0821) 311070 *Fax:* (0821) 158979
E-mail: sonnentanz@t-online.de
Key Personnel
Contact: Roland Kron
Founded: 1988
Specialize in rock literature & rock biographies.
Subjects: Biography, Music, Dance
ISBN Prefix(es): 3-926794

Sonntag, *imprint of* Georg Thieme Verlag KG

Johannes Sonntag Verlagsbuchhandlung GmbH+
Steiermarkerstr 3-5, 70469 Stuttgart
Tel: (0711) 8931-0 *Fax:* (0711) 8931-133
Web Site: www.sonntag-verlag.com
Key Personnel
President: Andre Caro *Tel:* (0711) 18931-700
Founded: 1927
Specialize in books, magazines, medicine, complementary medicine.
ISBN Prefix(es): 3-87758
Number of titles published annually: 25 Print
Total Titles: 150 Print
Parent Company: Hippokrates Verlag

Spee Buchverlag GmbH+
Fleischstr 62-65, 54290 Trier
Mailing Address: Postfach 3040, 54220 Trier
Tel: (0651) 979900; (0651) 9799162; (0651) 9799160 *Fax:* (0651) 9799165
Key Personnel
Publisher: Siegfried Faeth; Dr Harold Boulig
Founded: 1967
Subjects: Art, History
ISBN Prefix(es): 3-7902; 3-87760
Parent Company: Paulinus GmbH Verlag, Fleischstr 62-65, 54290 Trier
Associate Companies: Paulinus Verlag

Spektrum der Wissenschaft Verlagsgesellschaft mbH
Slevogtstr 3-5, 69126 Heidelberg
Mailing Address: PO Box 10 59 80, 69049 Heidelberg
Tel: (06221) 91 26 600 *Fax:* (06221) 91 26 751
E-mail: marketing@spektrum.com
Web Site: www.spektrum.de
Key Personnel
Man Dir: Dean Sanderson
Publicity: Barbara Kuhn
Founded: 1978
Subjects: Science (General), Technology
Parent Company: Scientific American Inc, 415 Madison Ave, New York, NY 10017, United States

Spiegel-Verlag Rudolf Augstein GmbH & Co KG+
Brandstwiete 19, 20457 Hamburg
Tel: (040) 30 07-26 87 *Fax:* (040) 30 07-29 66
E-mail: spiegel@spiegel.de
Telex: 2161221
Key Personnel
Man Dir: Rudolf Augstein; Karl-Dietrich Seikel
International Rights: Dietrich Krause
Leitung Controlling: Rainer Buss *Tel:* (040) 30072560 *E-mail:* rainer_buss@spiegel.de
Founded: 1946
ISBN Prefix(es): 3-87763
Subsidiaries: Spiegel TV GmbH; Manager Magazine; A 1 Art & Information GmbH & Co
Orders to: Postfach 105840, 20039 Hamburg

Spiess Volker Wissenschaftsverlag GmbH+
Gneisenaustr 33, 10961 Berlin
Mailing Address: Postfach 610494, 10928 Berlin
Tel: (030) 6917073-74 *Fax:* (030) 6914067
Cable: SPIESSVERLAG
Key Personnel
Publisher: Volker Spiess
Founded: 1967
Subjects: Communications, Film, Video, History, Journalism, Language Arts, Linguistics, Social Sciences, Sociology
ISBN Prefix(es): 3-89166; 3-89776
Associate Companies: Haude und Spenersche VerlagsBuchhandlung, Postfach 303046, 10928 Berlin *Tel:* (030) 2165061 *Fax:* (030) 2165064
Subsidiaries: Edition Marhold; Edition colloquium

GERMANY

Spieth-Verlag Verlag fuer Symbolforschung+
Postfach 31 13 08, 10643 Berlin
Tel: (030) 68302041 *Fax:* (030) 683-02042
Key Personnel
Owner: Rudolf Arnold Spieth
Founded: 1969
Subjects: Anthropology, Astrology, Occult, Parapsychology, Philosophy, Psychology, Psychiatry, Religion - Other, Self-Help
ISBN Prefix(es): 3-88093
Subsidiaries: Bund der Runenforscher Deutschlands (BRD)/Internationaler Zentralverband Germanischer Runenforscher (IZGR)

Spiridon-Verlags GmbH+
PO Box 10 45 27, 40036 Duesseldorf
Tel: (0211) 726364 *Fax:* (0211) 786823
Key Personnel
Publisher: Manfred Steffny
Founded: 1974
Subjects: Health, Nutrition, Sports, Athletics
ISBN Prefix(es): 3-922011
Bookshop(s): Steffnys Laufladen, Linienstr 12, 40227 Dusseldorf

Adolf Sponholtz Verlag+
Subsidiary of C W Niemeyer Buchverlage GmbH
Osterstr 19, 31785 Hameln
Mailing Address: Postfach 100752, 31763 Hameln
Tel: (05151) 200312 *Fax:* (05151) 200319
Key Personnel
Dir: Hans Freiwald
Founded: 1894
Subjects: Animals, Pets, Energy, Environmental Studies, Fiction, History, Literature, Literary Criticism, Essays, Nonfiction (General), Outdoor Recreation
ISBN Prefix(es): 3-87766
Orders to: VSB Verlagsservice Braunschweig GmbH, Westerman- Allee 66, 38104 Braunschweig *Tel:* (0531) 708650 *Fax:* (0531) 708608

Sportverlag Berlin GmbH SVB+
Markgrafenstr 11, 10969 Berlin
Tel: (030) 2591-3550 *Fax:* (030) 2591-3516
E-mail: marketing@sportverlag-berlin.de
Web Site: www.sportverlag-berlin.de *Cable:* UND SPORTVERLAG BERLIN
Key Personnel
Man Dir: Dr Wolfram Goeibel
Sales, Rights & Permissions: Brigitte Kummer
Marketing Manager: Helmut Krueger
Editor-in-Chief: Raymund Stolze
Founded: 1947
Subjects: How-to, Sports, Athletics
ISBN Prefix(es): 3-328; 3-333
Warehouse: VVA, A64 DFB/F An der Autobahn, 33370 Gutersloh

Axel Springer Verlag AG
Axel-Springer-Platz 1, Hamburg 20350
Tel: (040) 347-00 *Fax:* (040) 345811
E-mail: info@asv.de
Web Site: www.asv.de
Telex: 2170010; 402255
Key Personnel
Contact: Edda Fels
ISBN Prefix(es): 3-921305; 3-926949

Springer-Verlag GmbH & Co KG+
Tiergartenstr 17, 69121 Heidelberg
Mailing Address: Postfach 105280, 69042 Heidelberg
Tel: (06221) 487-0 *Fax:* (06221) 487-8366
E-mail: orders@springer.de
Web Site: www.springer.de
Key Personnel
Chairman, Supervisory Board of the Springer Group: Dr Jurgen Richter
Man Dir: Dr Dietrich Goetze, PhD; Dr Hans-Dieter Haenel; Dr Ulrich Vest; Rudy Gebauer
Founded: 1842
Member of TR- Verlagsunion GmbH.
Subjects: Agriculture, Architecture & Interior Design, Art, Astronomy, Behavioral Sciences, Biography, Biological Sciences, Business, Chemistry, Chemical Engineering, Child Care & Development, Civil Engineering, Computer Science, Cookery, Criminology, Earth Sciences, Economics, Electronics, Electrical Engineering, Energy, Engineering (General), Environmental Studies, Finance, Geography, Geology, Government, Political Science, Health, Nutrition, History, Law, Management, Marketing, Mathematics, Mechanical Engineering, Medicine, Nursing, Dentistry, Nonfiction (General), Philosophy, Physical Sciences, Physics, Psychology, Psychiatry, Science (General), Social Sciences, Sociology, Technology
ISBN Prefix(es): 0-8194; 0-387; 3-7643; 3-7985; 2-287; 3-540; 3-211; 4-431; 3-7908; 84-07; 1-85233; 3-18; 88-470; 3-88537; 0-8716; 0-907259; 981-3083
Parent Company: BertelsmannSpringer Science & Business Media GmbH, Berlin
Associate Companies: Springer-Verlag New York Inc, 175 Fifth Ave, New York, NY 10010, United States *Tel:* 212-460-1500 *Fax:* 212-473-6272; Springer-Verlag London Ltd, Sweetapple House, Cateshall Rd, Surrey, Godalming GU7 3DJ, United Kingdom *Tel:* (01483) 418822 *Fax:* (01483) 415151; Springer-Verlag France, One rue Paul Cezanne, 75375 Paris, France *Tel:* (01) 5393-3644 *Fax:* (01) 5393-3683; Springer-Verlag Tokyo Inc, 3-13, Hougo 3-chome, Bunkyo-ku, Tokyo, Japan *Tel:* (03) 38120337 *Fax:* (03) 38187454; Eastern Book Service Inc, 3-13, Hongo 3-chome, Bunkyo-ku, Tokyo 113, Japan *Tel:* (03) 38180861 *Fax:* (03) 38180864; Springer-Verlag Hong Kong Ltd, Unit 1702 Tower 1, Enterprise Square, 9 Sheung Yuet Rd, Kowloon Bay, Hong Kong *Tel:* 27239698 *Fax:* 27242366; Springer-Verlag Iberica SA, Corcega 505, entlo 3, 08025 Barcelona, Spain; Springer-VDI-Verlag GmbH & Co KG, Heintichstr, 40239 Dusseldorf, Hungary *Tel:* (0211) 6103-222 *Fax:* (0211) 6103-113; Springer-Verlag Wien, Sachsenpl 4-6, 1201 Vienna, Austria *Tel:* (01) 3302415 *Fax:* (01) 3302426; Springer Italia, Via Podgora 14, 20122 Mailand, Italy *Tel:* (02) 54259721 *Fax:* (02) 55193360; Springer-Verlag GmbH & Co KG, Indian Liaison Office, 906-907, Akash Deep Bldg, Barakhamba Rd, 110001 New Delhi, India *Tel:* (011) 3358590 *Fax:* (011) 3358716; Urban und Vogel, Munich; Springer PWN Ltd, Warsaw, Poland
Imprints: Copernicus; Physica; TELOS
Branch Office(s)
Tiergartenstr 17, 69121 Heidelberg *Tel:* (06621) 487-0 *Fax:* (06221) 487-8366
Distributor for AIP Press (American Institute of Physics)
Bookshop(s): Minerva Wisenschaftliche Buchhandlung GmbH, Sachsenplatz 4-6, 7207 Vienna, Austria *Tel:* (01) 330 2433 *Fax:* (01) 330 2439
Warehouse: Springer GmbH & Co Auslieferungs-Gesellschaft, Haberstr 7, 69126 Heidelberg *Tel:* (06221) 345-112 *Fax:* (06221) 345-182
E-mail: orders@springer.de

L Staackmann Verlag KG+
Lochenerstr 6, 83623 Dietramszell
Tel: (08027) 337 *Fax:* (08027) 816
Key Personnel
Man Dir: Dr Friedrich Vogel
Founded: 1869
Second Address: Verlagsbuero Dr Vogel, Lochener Str 6, 83623 Linden/Obb.
Subjects: Fiction
ISBN Prefix(es): 3-920897; 3-88675

Staatliche Museen Kassel
Schloss Wilhelmshoehe, 34131 Kassel
Mailing Address: Postfach 410420, 34066 Kassel
Tel: (0561) 93 77-7 *Fax:* (0561) 93 77-6 66
E-mail: info@museum-kassel.de
Web Site: www.museum-kassel.de
Key Personnel
Contact: S Naumer *E-mail:* bibliothek@museum-kussel.de
Subjects: Antiques, Architecture & Interior Design, Art, History
ISBN Prefix(es): 3-931787
Divisions: Museums Bibliothek

Staatsbibliothek zu Berlin - Preussischer Kulturbesitz (Berlin State Library - Prussian Cultural Foundation)
unter den Linden 8, 10117 Berlin
Tel: (030) 266-0 *Fax:* (030) 266-1721
E-mail: fragen@sbb.spk-berlin.de; webserveradmin@sbb.spk-berlin.de
Web Site: www.sbb.spk-berlin.de
Telex: 183160 staab d
Key Personnel
General Dir, Rights & Permissions: Dr Antonius Jammers
Founded: 1661
Subjects: Library & Information Sciences
ISBN Prefix(es): 3-88053; 3-7361
Parent Company: Stiftung Preussischer Kulturbesitz

Stadler Verlagsgesellschaft mbH+
Max-Stromeyerstr 172, 78462 Konstanz
Tel: (07531) 898-0 *Fax:* (07531) 898-101
E-mail: info@verlag-stadler.de
Web Site: www.verlag-stadler.de
Founded: 1815
Member of Berscuvevcin des Deutschen Buchhandels ev.
Subjects: Art, Geography, Geology, History, Maritime, Music, Dance, Nonfiction (General), Outdoor Recreation, Regional Interests
ISBN Prefix(es): 3-7977

Stadt Duisburg - Amt Fuer Statistik, Stadtforschung und Europaangelegenheiten
Bismarckstr 150-158, 47049 Duisburg
Tel: (0203) 283 3085 *Fax:* (0203) 288 4404
E-mail: amt12@stadt-duisburg.de
Web Site: uni-duisburg.de/duisburg/statistik.htm
Key Personnel
Dir: German Bensch
Administrator: Anita Rauser *E-mail:* a.rauser@stadt-duisburg.de
Periodicals & irregulars.
Subjects: Education, Education-school organization and administration, public administration-abstracting, statistics and bibliographies
Total Titles: 15 Print
Online services available through World Wide Web.
Parent Company: Municipality, Duisburg

Staedte-Verlag, E v Wagner und J Mitterhuber GmbH+
Steinbeisstr 9, 70736 Fellbach b Stuttgart
Mailing Address: Postfach 2080, 70710 Fellbach b Stuttgart
Tel: (0711) 576201 *Fax:* (0711) 5762243
E-mail: info@staedte-verlag.de
Web Site: www.staedte-verlag.de *Cable:* STAEDTEVERLAG
Key Personnel
Man Dir: Meinhard Mitterhuber; Michael Mitterhuber; Manfred von Wagner
Publicity Dir: Rolf Mueller
Rights Dir: Ulrich Groh
Founded: 1951
Subjects: Geography, Geology, Outdoor Recreation
ISBN Prefix(es): 3-8164

Number of titles published annually: 500 Print
Subsidiaries: NovoPrint Verlags GmbH

Verlag Stahleisen GmbH+
Sohnstr 65, 40237 Duesseldorf
Mailing Address: Postfach 105164, 40042 Duesseldorf
Tel: (0211) 6707-0 *Fax:* (0211) 6707-555
E-mail: stahleisen@stahleisen.de
Web Site: www.stahleisen.de *Cable:* STAHLEISEN DUSSELDORF
Key Personnel
Man Dir, Rights Permissions: Dipl Ing A Schommers *E-mail:* adrian.schommers@stahleisen.de
Founded: 1908
Specialize in Steel, Casting-Practice.
Subjects: Chemistry, Chemical Engineering, Civil Engineering, Engineering (General), Mechanical Engineering, Technology
ISBN Prefix(es): 3-514
Associate Companies: Giesserei-Verlag GmbH, Postfach 102532, 40026 Dusseldorf *Tel:* (0211) 67070 *Fax:* (0211) 6707517 *E-mail:* giesserei@stahleisen.de
Subsidiaries: Montan- und Wirtschaftsverlag GmbH

Verlag H Stam GmbH+
Fuggerstr 7, 51149 Cologne
Mailing Address: Postfach 900629, 51116 Cologne
Tel: (02203) 30290 *Fax:* (02203) 302940
Telex: 887708
Founded: 1959
Subjects: Economics, Technology
ISBN Prefix(es): 3-8018; 3-8181; 3-87183; 3-87772; 3-8237
Branch Office(s)
Lindenstr 54a, 10969 Berlin
Karl-Liebknecht Str 143, 04227 Leipzig
Frauenstr 32, 80469 Munich

Verlag fuer Standesamtswesen GmbH
Hanauer Landstr 197, 60314 Frankfurt am Main
Tel: (069) 40 58 94 0 *Fax:* (069) 40 58 94 99
E-mail: info@vfst.de
Web Site: www.vfst.de
Key Personnel
Manager: Klaudia Metzner
Founded: 1929
Subjects: Law
ISBN Prefix(es): 3-8019

Stapp Verlag Wolfgang Stapp+
Luetzowstr 105, 10785 Berlin
Tel: (030) 2622097 *Fax:* (030) 2621990
Key Personnel
Owner, Rights & Permissions: Wolfgang Stapp
Founded: 1953
Subjects: Biography, Geography, Geology, History, Literature, Literary Criticism, Essays, Music, Dance, Natural History, Nonfiction (General), Outdoor Recreation, Regional Interests, Travel
ISBN Prefix(es): 3-87776
Associate Companies: Kupfergraben Verlags Gesellschaft mBH, Lutzowstr 105, 10785 Berlin *Tel:* (030) 2621990 *Fax:* (030) 2621990
Imprints: Preussische Koepfe
Distributed by Neue Buecher (Switzerland)
Distributor for Kupfergraben Verlag

Star Wars, *imprint of* Egmont vgs verlagsgesellschaft mbH

C A Starke Verlag+
Frankfurterstr 51-53, 65549 Limburg
Tel: (06431) 96 15-0 *Fax:* (06431) 96 15 15
E-mail: starkeverlag@t-online.de
Web Site: www.starkeverlag.de
Key Personnel
Manager Dipl Kfm: Rasched Salem
Founded: 1847
Subjects: Biography, Genealogy, History, Nonfiction (General), Heraldry, Family
ISBN Prefix(es): 3-7980

Stattbuch Verlag GmbH+
Gneisenaustr 2a, 10961 Berlin
Tel: (030) 6913094; (030) 6913095 *Fax:* (030) 6943354
Key Personnel
Contact: Klaus Esche
Founded: 1978
Subjects: Literature, Literary Criticism, Essays, Travel
ISBN Prefix(es): 3-922778
Orders to: Rotation, Mehringdamm 51, 10961 Berlin

Stauffenburg Verlag Brigitte Narr GmbH+
Stauffenbergstr 42, 72074 Tuebingen
Mailing Address: Julius Groos Verlag, Postfach 2525, 72015 Tuebingen
Tel: (07071) 9730-0 *Fax:* (07071) 973030
Web Site: www.stauffenburg.de
Key Personnel
Man Dir & Publisher: Brigitte Narr *Tel:* (07071) 973097 *E-mail:* narr@stauffenburg.de
Founded: 1982
Subjects: Communications, English as a Second Language, Language Arts, Linguistics, Literature, Literary Criticism, Essays, Women's Studies
ISBN Prefix(es): 3-923721; 3-86057
Number of titles published annually: 70 Print
Total Titles: 800 Print
Associate Companies: Julius Groos Verlag, Postfach 2525, 72015 Tuebingen

The Stay-at-homes, *imprint of* Egmont vgs verlagsgesellschaft mbH

Steidl Verlag+
Duestere Str 4, 37073 Goettingen
Tel: (0551) 49 60 60 *Fax:* (0551) 49 60 649
E-mail: mail@steidl.de
Web Site: www.steidl.de
Key Personnel
Marketing & International Rights: Jan Menkens *Tel:* (0551) 49 60 618 *Fax:* (0551) 49 60 617 *E-mail:* jmenkens@steidl.de
Public Relations: Claudia Glenewinkel *Tel:* (0551) 49 60 650 *Fax:* (0551) 49 60 644 *E-mail:* cglenewinkel@steidl.de
Sales: Friederike Sprenger *Tel:* (0551) 49 60 616 *E-mail:* fsprenger@steidl.de
Founded: 1968
Hauseigene Druckerei.
Specializes in marketing.
Subjects: Art, Biography, Fiction, History, Literature, Literary Criticism, Essays, Marketing, Nonfiction (General), Philosophy, Photography, Poetry, Psychology, Psychiatry
ISBN Prefix(es): 3-88243
Distributed by DAP Book Distribution Center (USA); Gemeinsame Verlagsauslieferung Goettingen (GVA) (Germany, Switzerland & Austria); Thames & Hudson Ltd; VILO DIFFUSION (France)

Steiger Verlag+
Steinerne Furt 63-72, 86167 Augsburg
Tel: (0821) 70040 *Fax:* (0821) 7004179
Key Personnel
Man Dir: Dr Petra Altmann
Editor: Frank Heins
Rights & Permissions: Silke Breitlaender
Founded: 1979
Subjects: Astronomy, Earth Sciences, Foreign Countries, Geography, Geology, Outdoor Recreation, Regional Interests, Sports, Athletics, Travel
ISBN Prefix(es): 3-89652
Parent Company: Weltbild Verlag GmbH, Otto Lindenmeyerstr 28, 86153 Augsburg
Book Club(s): Weltbild-Versandhandel

Conrad Stein Verlag+
Inder Muhle, 25821 Struckum
Tel: (04671) 93 13 14 *Fax:* (04671) 93 13 15
E-mail: outdoor@tng.de
Web Site: outdoor.tng.de
Key Personnel
Rights & Permissions: Conrad Stein
Founded: 1980
Subjects: Outdoor Recreation, Travel
ISBN Prefix(es): 3-922965; 3-89392
Total Titles: 150 Print
Online services available through World Wide Web.

Franz Steiner Verlag Wiesbaden GmbH+
Birkenwaldstr 44, 70191 Stuttgart
Mailing Address: Postfach 101061, 70009 Stuttgart
Tel: (0711) 2582 0 *Fax:* (0711) 2582 390
E-mail: service@steiner-verlag.de
Web Site: www.steiner-verlag.de
Key Personnel
Publishing Dir: Dr Thomas Schaber
Man Dir: Dr Klaus Brauer *Tel:* (0711) 2582 226 *Fax:* (0711) 2582 296 *E-mail:* Service@Deutscher-Apotheker-Verlag.de; Reinhold Hack *Tel:* (0711) 2582 364 *Fax:* (0711) 2582 296 *E-mail:* Service@Deutscher-Apotheker-Verlag.de; Dr Christian Rotta *Tel:* (0711) 2582 225 *Fax:* (0711) 2582 290 *E-mail:* Service@Wissenschaftliche-Verlagsgesellschaft.de
Publicity: Susanne Szoradi *Tel:* (0711) 2582 321 *E-mail:* sszoradi@steiner-verlag.de
Distribution: Siegmar Bauer *Tel:* (0711) 2582 219 *E-mail:* Service@Deutscher-Apotheker-Verlag.de
Production: Gregor Hoppen *Tel:* (0711) 2582 305 *E-mail:* ghoppen@steiner-verlag.de
Founded: 1949
Member of Borsenverein des Deutschen Buchhandels.
Subjects: African American Studies, Archaeology, Art, Asian Studies, Developing Countries, Earth Sciences, Education, Foreign Countries, Geography, Geology, History, Language Arts, Linguistics, Law, Music, Dance, Philosophy, Religion - Buddhist, Religion - Hindu, Religion - Islamic, Classical Studies, Science History
ISBN Prefix(es): 3-515
Number of titles published annually: 180 Print
Total Titles: 4,800 Print
Parent Company: Deutscher Apotheker Verlag
Associate Companies: S Hirzel Verlag GmbH & Co *E-mail:* service@hirzel.de; Wissenschaftliche Verlagsgesellschaft mbH *E-mail:* service@wissenschaftliche-Verlagegesellschaft.de
Subsidiaries: Medpharm Scientific Publishers
Warehouse: Brockhaus/Commission, Kornwestheim *Tel:* (07154) 1327-0 *Fax:* (07154) 132713 *E-mail:* bestell@brocom.de

J F Steinkopf Verlag GmbH+
Uhlandstr 24, 70182 Stuttgart
Key Personnel
Man Dir: Rainer Thun
International Rights: Johannes Keussen
Founded: 1792
Subjects: Art, Biblical Studies, History, How-to, Literature, Literary Criticism, Essays, Religion - Other, Social Sciences, Sociology
ISBN Prefix(es): 3-7984

Dr Dietrich Steinkopff Verlag GmbH & Co+
Poststr 9, 64293 Darmstadt

Mailing Address: Postfach 100462, 64204 Darmstadt
Tel: (06151) 82899-0 (bestellungen) *Fax:* (06151) 82899-40
E-mail: info.steinkopff@springer.de
Web Site: www.steinkopff.springer.de *Cable:* STEINKOPFF
Key Personnel
Chief Executive Officer: Dr Thomas Thiekoetter *E-mail:* thiekoetter.steinkopff@springer.de
Marketing & Product Manager: Sabine Scheffler *E-mail:* scheffler.steinkopff@springer.de
Founded: 1908
Advertising through Springer-Verlag.
Subjects: Health, Nutrition, Medicine, Nursing, Dentistry, Psychology, Psychiatry
ISBN Prefix(es): 3-7985
Total Titles: 850 Print; 2 CD-ROM
Online services available through World Wide Web.
Parent Company: Springer-Verlag GmbH & Co KG, Tiesgenstr 17, Heidelberg 69121
U.S. Office(s): Springer Verlag New York Inc, 175 Fifth Avenue, New York, NY 10010, United States *Tel:* 212-493-6272
Distributed by Springer-Verlag
Warehouse: Springer GmbH & Co, Auslieferungs-Gesellschaft, Haberstr 7, 69126 Heidelberg *Tel:* (06221) 345-0 *E-mail:* orders@springer.de

Steintor Verlag, Rudolf Juedes
Postfach 3248, 23581 Luebeck
Tel: (05535) 8851
E-mail: info@steintor-verlag.de
Key Personnel
Owner: Rudolf Juedes
Founded: 1969
Subjects: Art
Bookshop(s): Gallerie Meiborssen, 37647 Meiborssen *Tel:* (05535) 8851

Steinweg-Verlag, Jurgen romHoff+
Fasanenstr 6, 38102 Braunschweig
Tel: (0531) 2339197 *Fax:* (0531) 2336649
Key Personnel
Contact: Juergen Vom Hoff
Founded: 1986
Subjects: Art, History, Photography, Regional Interests, Social Sciences, Sociology
ISBN Prefix(es): 3-925151

Verlag Stendel+
Untere Sackgasse 9, 71332 Waiblingen
Mailing Address: Postfach 1713, 71307 Waiblingen
Tel: (07151) 956603 *Fax:* (07151) 956605
E-mail: info@stendel-verlag.de; verlag.stendel@t-online.de
Web Site: www.verlag-stendel.de
Key Personnel
Manager: Dagmar Kuebler
Founded: 1987
Subjects: Fiction, Literature, Literary Criticism, Essays, Psychology, Psychiatry, Science Fiction, Fantasy
ISBN Prefix(es): 3-926789

Stephanus Edition Verlags GmbH+
Tuefinger Str 3-5, Uhldingen-Muehlofen
Mailing Address: Postfach 1160, 88683 Uhldingen-Muehlofen
Tel: (07556) 921150 *Fax:* (07556) 921130
E-mail: 0755692110@tonline.de
Key Personnel
Man Dir: Sabastian Braun
Editorial: Hans Braun
Founded: 1978
Subjects: Religion - Other
ISBN Prefix(es): 3-921213; 3-922816

Annemarie Stern, see Asso Verlag

Stern-Verlag Janssen & Co+
Friedrichstr 24-26, 40001 Dusseldorf
Mailing Address: Postfach 101053, 40001 Duesseldorf
Tel: (0211) 3881-0 *Fax:* (0211) 3881-280
E-mail: buchhaus-sternverlag@t-online.de
Web Site: www.buchsv.de
Key Personnel
Man Partner: Horst Janssen; Klaus Janssen
Founded: 1900
Subjects: Biography, History, Language Arts, Linguistics, Nonfiction (General), Philosophy
ISBN Prefix(es): 3-87784
Associate Companies: Artibus et Literis
Bookshop(s): Universitaetsbuchhandlung, Universitaetstr 1, 40225 Duesseldorf

Sternberg-Verlag bei Ernst Franz+
Industriestr 8, 72585 Riederich
Mailing Address: Postfach 1262, 72543 Metzingen
Tel: (07123) 938922 *Fax:* (07123) 938920
Key Personnel
Manager: Gerhard Heinzelmann
Founded: 1950
Subjects: Biblical Studies, Biography, History, Religion - Protestant, Theology
ISBN Prefix(es): 3-87785; 3-7722
Parent Company: Ernst Franz Verlag
Distributed by Haenssler; KNO; K&V; Libri; Umbreit (D)

S + W Steuer- und Wirtschaftsverlag GmbH, see Erich Schmidt Verlag GmbH & Co

Steyler Verlag+
Postfach 2460, 41311 Nettetal
Tel: (02157) 120220 *Fax:* (02157) 120222
E-mail: steyler.net@t-online.de
Web Site: www.steyler.de
Key Personnel
Man Dir: Andreas Heider; Albert Buck; Paul Langer
Founded: 1927
Subjects: Anthropology, Biography, Developing Countries, Language Arts, Linguistics, Religion - Catholic, Science (General)
ISBN Prefix(es): 3-87787; 3-8050
Parent Company: Steyler Verlagsbuchhandlung GmbH, Bahnofstr 9, 41334 Nettetal

Stiefel GmbH Wandkarten Verlag+
Felix-Wankel-Ring 1a, 85101 Lenting
Tel: (08456) 924100 *Fax:* (08456) 924134
E-mail: stiefel.gmbH@stiefel_eurocart.de
Web Site: www.stiefel-eurocart.de
Key Personnel
Manager: Heinrich Stiefel
International Rights: Sandra Stiefel
Founded: 1982
Member of World Didac Borsezvenez.
Subjects: Biological Sciences, English as a Second Language, Environmental Studies, History, Language Arts, Linguistics, Mathematics, Religion - Other
ISBN Prefix(es): 3-929627
Subsidiaries: Stiefel Verlag
Branch Office(s)
Stiefel Wandkarten Verlag, Annaburg 7, 8630 Mariazell, Austria
Verlag Stiefel AG, Haretenweg 1, 4413 Bueren, Switzerland
Carto Stiefel KFT, Kolozsvar 13, 1155 Budapest, Hungary
Stiefel Wandkarten Verlag, Verdiplatz 43, 39100 Bozen, Italy
Stiefel sro, Drienova 3, Bratislava, Slovakia
Stiefel Kartografia sro, Komenskeho 66, Novy Jicin, Czech Republic
Stiefel Meridian Sp 200, ul Broniewskiego 14, Szczecin, Poland

Stiftung Buchkunst (Book Art Foundation)
Adickesallee 1, 60322 Frankfurt am Main
Tel: (069) 1525-1800 *Fax:* (069) 1525-1805
E-mail: buchkunst@dbf.ddb.de
Web Site: www.stiftung-buchkunst.de
Key Personnel
Man Dir: Uta Schneider
Founded: 1966
Branch Office(s)
Buero Leipzig, Gerichtsweg 26, Leipzig *Tel:* (0341) 9954-210 *Fax:* (0341) 9954-211

Edition Gunter Stoberlein
Niethamerstr 15, 80997 Munich
Tel: (089) 8115289
Key Personnel
Owner: Gunter Stoberlein
Founded: 1972
Member of Boirsenverein Des Deutschen Buchhandels.
Subjects: Art, Literature, Literary Criticism, Essays, Poetry
ISBN Prefix(es): 3-88045; 3-921430

Stoeppel Verlag-Buchvertrieb KG+
Poertnerstr 1, 82362 Weilheim
Tel: (0881) 9224-0 *Fax:* (0881) 2553
E-mail: stoeppel@oberland.net
Web Site: www.stoeppel.de
Key Personnel
Man Dir: Erich Stoeppel *E-mail:* stoeppel@oberland.net; Robert Stoeppel
Press Manager: Gertraud Rauili
Founded: 1981
Subjects: Outdoor Recreation, Travel
ISBN Prefix(es): 3-924012; 3-89306
Orders to: GeoLenter, Neumarkter Str 18, 81673 Munich

Stollfuss Verlag Bonn GmbH & Co KG+
Dechenstr 7, 53115 Bonn
Tel: (0228) 7 24-0 *Fax:* (0228) 7 24-92 23; (0228) 7 24-92 95
Web Site: www.stollfuss.de *Cable:* STOLLFUSSVERLAG
Key Personnel
Man Dir: Wolfgang Stollfuss; Michael Stollfuss
Editorial: Hans-Josef Metz
Rights & Permissions, Production: Reinhard Just
Founded: 1913
Specialize in Tax & Fiscal Law.
Subjects: Accounting, Economics, Finance, Law, Public Administration
ISBN Prefix(es): 3-08
Distributor for Schriften des BMF und BMA
Warehouse: Justus-von Liebig Str 6, 53121 Bonn

Straelener Manuskripte Verlag+
Venloerstr 45, 47638 Straelen
Mailing Address: Postfach 1324, 47630 Straelen
Tel: (02834) 6588 *Fax:* (02834) 6588
Web Site: www.straelener-manuskripte.de
Key Personnel
Manager: Renate Birkenhauer, PhD *E-mail:* r.birkenhauer@straelener-manuskripte.de
Founded: 1983
Subjects: Literature, Literary Criticism, Essays, Poetry
ISBN Prefix(es): 3-89107
Number of titles published annually: 2 Print
Total Titles: 33 Print

Stroemfeld/Nexus, *imprint of* Stroemfeld Verlag

Stroemfeld/Roter Stern, *imprint of* Stroemfeld Verlag

Stroemfeld Verlag+
Holzhausenstr 4, 60322 Frankfurt

Tel: (069) 955 226-0 *Fax:* (069) 955 226-22
E-mail: info@stroemfeld.de
Web Site: www.stroemfeld.de
Key Personnel
Publisher: Karl D Wolff
International Rights: Doris Kern
Founded: 1981 (Nexus)
Subjects: Literature, Literary Criticism, Essays, Psychology, Psychiatry
ISBN Prefix(es): 3-87877; 3-86109
Parent Company: Stroemfeld Verlag AG, Basel, Switzerland
Imprints: Stroemfeld/Roter Stern; Stroemfeld/Nexus
Branch Office(s)
Basel, Switzerland
Orders to: SOVA, Friesstr 20-24, 60388 Frankfurt

STS Standard Tabellen und Software Verlag GmbH
Subsidiary of Rudolf Haufe Verlag GmbH & Co KG
Fraunhoferstr 5, 80469 Munich
Tel: (089) 89517-200 *Fax:* (089) 89517250
Key Personnel
Dir: Martin Lagua; Helmuth Hopfner; Uwe Renald Muller
Founded: 1939
ISBN Prefix(es): 3-86027

Sturtz Verlag GmbH
Imprint of Verlagshaus Wurzburg
Beethovenstr 5, 97080 Wurzburg
Tel: (0931) 385235 *Fax:* (0931) 385305
E-mail: info@verlagshaus.com
Web Site: www.verlagshaus.com
Key Personnel
Publishing Dir: Dieter Krause
Dir of Production: Juergen Roth
Sales Dir: Johannes Glesius
Founded: 1830
Subjects: Travel
ISBN Prefix(es): 3-8003

Sueddeutsche Verlagsgesellschaft mbH+
Sendlinger Str 8, 80331 Munich
Tel: (089) 2183-0 *Fax:* (089) 2183-8315
E-mail: verlag@sueddeutsche.de
Web Site: www.sueddeutsche.de
Key Personnel
Man Dir, Rights & Permissions: Udo Vogt
Contact: Mr Reinhard Keller
Founded: 1898
Subjects: Art, History, Nonfiction (General), Regional Interests, Religion - Catholic
ISBN Prefix(es): 3-88294; 3-920921
Parent Company: Schwabenverlag AG, Senefelderstr 12, Ostfildern
Branch Office(s)
Schwabenverlag AG, Abt Buchhandlung, Bahnhofstr 21, Aalen
Bookshop(s): Sueddeutsche Verlagsges mbH, Sedelhofgasse, 89073 Ulm/Donau; Schwabenverlag AG, Abt Buchhandlung, Spital Str 19, 73479 Ellwangen

Suedverlag GmbH+
Schuetzenstr 24, 78462 Konstanz
Mailing Address: Postfach 10 20 51, 78420 Konstanz
Tel: (07531) 9053-0 *Fax:* (07531) 9053-98
E-mail: willkommen@uvk.de
Web Site: www.suedverlag.de
Key Personnel
Publishing Manager: Walter Engstle *Tel:* (07531) 905312 *E-mail:* walter.engstle@uvk.de
Founded: 1945
Subjects: Biography, Humor, Regional Interests
ISBN Prefix(es): 3-87800
Associate Companies: UVK Verlagsgesellschaft mbH
Orders to: Brockhaus Commission Verlagsauslieferung, Kreidlerstr 9, 70806 Kornwestheim

Suedwest Verlag GmbH & Co KG+
Paul-Heysestr 28, 80336 Munich
Tel: (089) 5148-0 *Fax:* (089) 5148-2229
Web Site: www.suedwest-verlag.de
Key Personnel
Man Partner: Christian Strasser
Publicity & Co-production: Bettina Breitling
Founded: 1945
Subjects: Cookery, Health, Nutrition, Nonfiction (General), Travel
ISBN Prefix(es): 3-517; 3-7991
Associate Companies: Paul List Verlag GmbH; W Ludwig Verlag GmbH; C J Bucher Verlag GmbH

Suhrkamp Verlag+
Lindenstr 29-35, 60325 Frankfurt am Main
Mailing Address: Postfach 101945, 60019 Frankfurt am Main
Tel: (069) 75601-0 *Fax:* (069) 75601-522; (069) 75601-314
Web Site: www.suhrkamp.de *Cable:* SUHRKAMPVERLAG
Key Personnel
Publisher: Dr Siegfried Unseld
Dir: Guenter Berg
Man Dir: Philip Roeder *Tel:* (069) 75 601 500 *E-mail:* roeder@suhrkamp.de
Rights & Permissions: Dr Petra Hardt
Founded: 1950
Subjects: Biography, Fiction, Philosophy, Poetry, Psychology, Psychiatry, Science (General)
ISBN Prefix(es): 3-518
Associate Companies: Deutscher Klassiker Verlag; Insel Verlag; Juedischer Verlag; Suhrkamp Verlag AG, Switzerland
Foreign Rep(s): Agenzia Letteraria Internazionale (Italy); Balla & Co Literary Agents (Hungary); Bardon Chinese Media Agency (Taiwan); Christiane Scafer (Africa, France, Israel, South America, Spain & Portugal); Claudia Brandes (Netherlands, Eastern Europe, Japan, Southern Europe, Scandinavia); Hercules Business (China); International Editors (Brazil, South America, Spain); International Literature Bureau (Netherlands); Leohardt & Hoier Literary Agency (Scandinavia); Petra Christina Hardt (Australia, British Commonwealth & UK, China, Netherlands, France, Italy, Scandinavia, US); Sakai Agency (Japan); Ulrich Breth (Asia, Greece, Turkey)

Suin Buch-Verlag
Kappstr 29, 64678 Lindenfels Odenw
Tel: (06255) 2657 *Fax:* (06255) 2657
Key Personnel
Owner: Dr Bernhard Suin de Boutemard
Founded: 1975
Subjects: Alternative, Anthropology, Civil Engineering, Education, History, Human Relations, Philosophy, Religion - Catholic, Religion - Protestant, Religion - Other, Self-Help, Social Sciences, Sociology, Theology
ISBN Prefix(es): 3-921559

Sulamith Wulfing Edition, *imprint of* Aquamarin Verlag

Sulamith Wulfing Verlag, *imprint of* Aquamarin Verlag

Svato Zapletal+
Missunderstr 18, 22769 Hamburg
Tel: (040) 4390004; (040) 4300484 *Fax:* (040) 4390004
Key Personnel
Contact: Svato Zapletal
Founded: 1976
Subjects: Art, Fiction, Poetry
ISBN Prefix(es): 3-924283

Sybex Verlag GmbH+
Postfach 150361, 40080 Dusseldorf
Tel: (0211) 9739-0 *Fax:* (0211) 9739-199
E-mail: verkauf@sybex.de
Web Site: www.sybex.de
Key Personnel
President: Dr Rodnay Zaks
Man Dir: Hans Nolden
Sales: Aulich Juergen
Foreign Rights: Daniela Adrian
Founded: 1981
Subjects: Computer Science
ISBN Prefix(es): 3-88745; 3-8155
Associate Companies: Sybex Uitgeverij BV, Birkstr 95, 3768 HD Soest, Netherlands *Tel:* (031) 3560 27625 *Fax:* (031) 3560 26556 *E-mail:* sybex@sybex.nl; Sybex Inc, 1151 Marine Village Parkway, Alameda, CA 94501, United States *Tel:* 510-523-8233 *Fax:* 510-523-2373 *E-mail:* info@sybex.com; Sybex SARL, 76 Ave Pierre Brossolette, 92247 Malakoff Paris Cedex 14, France *Tel:* (01) 55 58 4000 *Fax:* (01) 49 65 0410 *Web Site:* www.sybex.fr
Orders to: VVA, Postfach 7777, 33310 Gutersloh *Tel:* (05) 2410805906 *Fax:* (05) 2410460130

Synthesis Verlag+
Postfach 14 32 06, 45262 Essen
Tel: (0201) 51 01 88 *Fax:* (0201) 51 10 49
E-mail: synthesis@synthesis-verlag.com
Web Site: www.synthesis-verlag.com
Founded: 1979
Subjects: Health, Nutrition, Science (General)
ISBN Prefix(es): 3-922026
Orders to: VSB-Verlagsservice Braunschweig GmbH, Georg-Westermann-Allee 66, 38104 Braunschweig *Tel:* (0531) 7080708277 *Fax:* (0531) 708 619

Systhema Verlag GmbH+
Thomas-Wimmer-Ring 11, 80539 Munich
Tel: (089) 290 88 175 *Fax:* (089) 290 88 160
E-mail: info@usm.de
Web Site: www.systhema.de; www.navigo.de
Key Personnel
Publisher: Heltiar Hipp *Tel:* (089) 3473-0 *E-mail:* helmar.hipp@systhema.de
Founded: 1988
Specialize in film, literature, languages & encyclopedia.
Subjects: Art, Computer Science, History, Language Arts, Linguistics, Natural History, Multimedia
ISBN Prefix(es): 1-898218; 3-89390; 3-634
Total Titles: 180 CD-ROM
Parent Company: United Soft Media GmbH
Bookshop(s): HMH, Sportallee 41, 22335 Hamburg *Tel:* (040) 51456-0
Shipping Address: HMH, Sportallee 41, 22335 Hamburg *Fax:* (040) 51456-990
Warehouse: HMH, Sportallee 41, 22335 Hamburg
Orders to: NVG Neue Verlagsges, Am Ziegelplatz 12, 77746 Schutlerwald *Tel:* (0781) 6396894 *Fax:* (0781) 846145

Tangens Systemverlag GmbH+
Donnerstr 5-7, 22763 Hamburg
Tel: (040) 39901307 *Fax:* (040) 395118
Key Personnel
Contact: Thomas E Panzer
Founded: 1987 (Originally founded under the name Verlagsgnindung)
Subjects: Computer Science, Fiction, Marketing, Nonfiction (General), Poetry
ISBN Prefix(es): 3-926622

Taoasis Verlag, Birgit Meyer+
Bismarckstr 23, 32657 Lemgo
Tel: (05261) 2321 *Fax:* (05261) 9383-21
E-mail: info@taoasis.de
Web Site: www.taoasis.de
Key Personnel
Contact: Axel Luye

TASCHEN GmbH
Hohenzollernring 53, 50672 Cologne
Tel: (0221) 201 80 0 *Fax:* (0221) 25 49 19
E-mail: contact@taschen.com
Web Site: www.taschen.com
Key Personnel
Dir: Benedikt Taschen
Chief Editor: Dr Angelika Taschen
Founded: 1980
Subjects: Architecture & Interior Design, Art, Erotica, Photography
ISBN Prefix(es): 3-8228
Subsidiaries: TASCHEN America; TASCHEN Deutschland; TASCHEN Espana; TASCHEN France; TASCHEN Japan; TASCHEN UK
Bookshop(s): Buchhandlung TASCHEN, Hohenzollernring 28, 50672 Cologne *Tel:* (221) 2573304 *Fax:* (221) 254968 *E-mail:* store@taschen.com; Librairie TASCHEN, 2 rue de Buci, 75006 Paris, France *Tel:* (01) 40517922 *E-mail:* store@taschen-france.com

Te-Wi Verlag Unternehmensbereich Buch der Ziff Verlag GmbH+
Riesstr 25, Haus D, 80992 Munich 50
Tel: (089) 14312470 *Fax:* (089) 14312469
Key Personnel
Man Dir: Gunther Frank
Founded: 1977
Subjects: Computer Science
ISBN Prefix(es): 3-89362
Parent Company: Ziff Verlag GmbH, Riesstr 25, Haus D, 80992 Munich
U.S. Office(s): Ziff Davis Press, 5903 Christie Ave, Emeryville, CA, United States *Tel:* 510-601-2005
Orders to: Revilak Verlagsservice, Gutenbergstr 5, 8031 Gilching, Munich *Tel:* (08105) 5051 *Fax:* (08105) 5408

Verlag fuer Technik und Wirtschaft GmbH & Co KG, see Vereinigte Fachverlage GmbH

Hochschule fur Technik Wirtschaft und Kultur Leipzig (FH)
Karl Liebknechtstr 132, 04277 Leipzig
Mailing Address: PO Box 30 00 66, 04251 Leipzig
Tel: (03841) 3076-0 *Fax:* (03841) 3076-6456
E-mail: studinf@k.htwk.leipzig.de
Web Site: www.htwk-leipzig.de
Key Personnel
Contact: Prof Torsten Seela
Founded: 1992

Otto Teich+
Hilpertstr 9, 64295 Darmstadt
Mailing Address: Postfach 200144, 64300 Darmstadt
Tel: (06151) 824120 *Fax:* (06151) 895656
Key Personnel
Man Dir & International Rights: Christine Otto
Founded: 1889
Specialize in humorous performances.
Subjects: Drama, Theater, Humor
ISBN Prefix(es): 3-8069
Associate Companies: Eduard Bloch Verlag, Hilpertstr 9, 64295 Darmstadt; Bergwald Verlag, Hilpertstr 9, 64295 Darmstadt
Imprints: Baerenreiter-Spieltexte

Telex-Verlag Jaeger & Waldmann GmbH
Birkenweg 8-10, 64295 Darmstadt
Mailing Address: Postfach 111454, 64229 Darmstadt
Tel: (06151) 33020 *Fax:* (06151) 330250
E-mail: jwemail@aol.com
Web Site: www.jwonline.de
Telex: 419389 jwtlx d
Key Personnel
General Manager: Wolfgang Lich *Tel:* (06151) 3302-12 *Fax:* (06151) 3302-70
Contact: D Ashimolowo *Tel:* (06151) 330222
Founded: 1953
Telecommunication company with representation worldwide.
Subjects: Business, Communications
ISBN Prefix(es): 3-87810

Alf Teloeken Verlag KG, see Alba Fachverlag GmbH und Co KG

TELOS, *imprint of* Springer-Verlag GmbH & Co KG

Edition Temmen+
Hohenlohestr 21, 28209 Bremen
Tel: (0421) 34843-0 *Fax:* (0421) 348094
E-mail: info@edition-temmen.de
Web Site: www.edition-temmen.com
Key Personnel
Owner: Horst Temmen
Founded: 1983
Subjects: Government, Political Science, History, Literature, Literary Criticism, Essays, Maritime, Military Science, Nonfiction (General), Social Sciences, Sociology, Travel
ISBN Prefix(es): 3-926958; 3-86108

teNeues Verlag GmbH & Co KG+
Am Selder 37, 47906 Kempen
Tel: (02152) 916-0 *Fax:* (02152) 916-111
E-mail: verlag@teneues.de
Web Site: www.teneues.com
Key Personnel
Publisher & Man Dir: Hendrik te Neues *Tel:* (02152) 916210 *E-mail:* hteneues@aol.com
Man Dir, Marketing: Hartmut Rau *Tel:* (02152) 916126 *E-mail:* hrau@teneues.de
Man Dir, International Division: Marcus Herfort *Tel:* (02152) 916117 *E-mail:* mherfort@teneues.de
Dir Sales & Marketing Book Trade: Ralf Daab *Tel:* (02152) 916120
Man Dir Product Development: Sebastian te Neues
Dir Editorial Dept: Sabine Wurfel *Tel:* (02152) 916245; Kristina Kruger
Man Dir, Chief Financial Officer/Administration: Dieter Schepers
Founded: 1950
International publishing group with offices in Kempen, New York & London, world wide distribution in over 60 countries.
Calendars, art merchandise & internet reference guides.
Subjects: Architecture & Interior Design, Art, Fashion, Photography, Travel
ISBN Prefix(es): 3-8238; 3-87580
Total Titles: 20 E-Book
Online services available through World Wide Web.
Parent Company: te Neues Publishing Co, c/o Macmillan Canada, 29 Birch Ave, Toronto, ON M4V 1E2, Canada
Associate Companies: te Neues Publishing UK, Aldwych House, 71-91 Aldwych, London WC2B 4HN, United Kingdom *Tel:* (020) 8283 6426 *Fax:* (020) 8283 6426; te Neues France, 140 rue de la Croix Nivert, 75015 Paris, France *Tel:* (01) 55-766205 *Fax:* (01) 55-766419 *E-mail:* teneuesfrance@wanadoo.fr
Divisions: te Neues Publishing Canada
U.S. Office(s): te Neues Publishing Company, 16 West 22 St, New York, NY 10010, United States, Dir Sales & Marketing: Stephen Hulburt *Tel:* 212-627-9090 *Fax:* 212-627-9534
Orders to: te Neus Publishing Co New York, 16 W 22 St, New York, NY 10010, United States *Tel:* 212-627-9090 *Fax:* 212-627-9511 *E-mail:* tnp@teneues-usa.com (USA orders)

Terra-Verlag GmbH
Neuhauserstr 21, 78464 Konstanz
Mailing Address: Postfach 102144, 78421 Konstanz
Tel: (07531) 81220 *Fax:* (07531) 812299
E-mail: info@terra-verlag.de
Web Site: www.terra-verlag.de
Key Personnel
Publisher: Eberhard Heizmann
Founded: 1946
ISBN Prefix(es): 3-920942
Subsidiaries: Terra Media Kft

Tessloff Verlag Ragnar Tessloff GmbH & Co KG
Burgschmietstr 2-4, 90419 Nuremberg
Tel: (0911) 39906-0 *Fax:* (0911) 39906-39
E-mail: tessloff@osn.de
Web Site: www.tessloff.com
ISBN Prefix(es): 3-7886

Tetra Verlag GmbH+
Friedensweg 15, 49143 Bissendorf
Tel: (05402) 8889 *Fax:* (05402) 8811
E-mail: info@tetra-verlag.de
Web Site: www.tetra-verlag.de
Key Personnel
Publisher: Dr Hans-Joachim Herrmann
Founded: 1972
Publish calendars
Member of Boersenverein des Deutsche Buchhandels.
Subjects: Animals, Pets, Maritime, Popular Scientific & Lobbyist Literature
ISBN Prefix(es): 3-89745
Number of titles published annually: 8 Print
Total Titles: 93 Print

Tetzlaff Verlag
Nordkanalstr 36, 20097 Hamburg
Mailing Address: Postfach 101607, 20010 Hamburg
Tel: (040) 237 14-03 *Fax:* (040) 237 14-233
Web Site: www.eurailpress.com
Key Personnel
Man Dir: Detlev K Suchanek *Tel:* (040) 237 14-228 *Fax:* (040) 237 14-236 *E-mail:* suchanek@etp.net
Editor: Christoph Mueller *Tel:* (040) 237 14-152 *Fax:* (040) 237 14-205 *E-mail:* mueller@eurailpress.com
Sales: Riccardo di Stefano *Tel:* (040) 237 14-101 *Fax:* (040) 237 14-233 *E-mail:* belsen@eurailpress.com; Sophie Elfendahl *Tel:* (040) 237 14-220 *Fax:* (040) 237 14-236 *E-mail:* elfendahl@eurailpress.com
Founded: 1900
Subjects: Transportation
ISBN Prefix(es): 3-87814

B G Teubner GmbH+
Abraham-Lincoln-Str 46, 65179 Wiesbaden
Mailing Address: Postfach 1546, 65173 Wiesbaden
Tel: (0611) 7878361 *Fax:* (0611) 7878470
Web Site: www.gwv-fachverlage.de
Key Personnel
Man Dir: Dr Heinz Weinheimer
Rights & Permissions Manager: Mrs Angelika Bolisega *E-mail:* angelika.bolisega@bertelsmann.de
General Manager: Hans-Dieter Haenel
Editorial: Ulrike Schmickler-Hirzebruch; Ewald Schmitt

Founded: 1811
Subjects: Chemistry, Chemical Engineering, Civil Engineering, Computer Science, Electronics, Electrical Engineering, Mathematics, Mechanical Engineering, Physics, Technology
ISBN Prefix(es): 3-519; 3-8154
Total Titles: 1,500 Print; 14 Online
Parent Company: BertelsmannSpringer Science & Business Media
Orders to: VVA Bertelsmann Distribution, Postfach 7777, 33310 Guetersloh

Teubner Edition, *imprint of* Graefe und Unzer Verlag GmbH

edition Text & Kritik im Richard Boorberg Verlag GmbH & Co+
Levelingstr 6a, 81673 Munich
Mailing Address: Postfach 800529, 81605 Munich
Tel: (089) 432929 *Fax:* (089) 433997
E-mail: etk.muenchen@t-online.de
Web Site: etk-muenchen.de
Key Personnel
Man Dir: Dr Berndt Oesterhelt
International Rights: Dr Monika Bopp *E-mail:* m.bopp-edition-text+kritik@boorberg.de
Founded: 1975
Subjects: Film, Video, Literature, Literary Criticism, Essays, Music, Dance
ISBN Prefix(es): 3-921402; 3-88377
Divisions: Auslieferung von Verlag der Autoren

TF Fachverlag Gmbh+
Werastr 21-23, 70182 Stuttgart
Mailing Address: Postfach 103241, 700028 Stuttgart
Tel: (0711) 2194-0 *Fax:* (0711) 2194-111
Key Personnel
Man Dir: Georg Haensel
Circulation Manager: Joachim Bader
International Rights: Joern Baumbusch
Editor: Norbert Leuz
Subjects: Accounting, Business, Computer Science, Economics, Law
ISBN Prefix(es): 3-7992
Parent Company: Taylorix AG, Zazenhaeuserstr 106, 70437 Stuttgart

Thalacker Medien GmbH Co KG+
Member of Horti Media Europe (HME)
PO Box 83 64, 38133 Braunschweig
Tel: (0531) 38004 0 *Fax:* (0531) 38004 25
E-mail: info@thalackermedien.de
Web Site: www.thalackermedien.de
Key Personnel
Dipl Oec Troph: Brigitte Mayr *Tel:* (0531) 3800447 *Fax:* (0531) 3800463
E-mail: b_mayr@thalackermedien.de
Founded: 1867
Member of Boersenverein des Deutschen Buchandels & Verband Deutscher Zeitschnfter Verlager.
Subjects: Agriculture, Gardening, Plants, Specialize in floral design, newspapers, magazines, technical books & reference books
ISBN Prefix(es): 3-87815
Number of titles published annually: 10 Print
Total Titles: 100 Print

Thauros Verlag GmbH
Jakob-Huberstr 9, 88171 Weiler-Simmerberg
Mailing Address: Postfach 1141, 88168 Weiler im Allgau
Tel: (08387) 2510 *Fax:* (08387) 3731
E-mail: thaurosverlag@t-online.de
Key Personnel
Editor: Christian Schneider
Founded: 1978
Subjects: Astrology, Occult, Biblical Studies, Biography, Religion - Jewish, Religion - Other
ISBN Prefix(es): 3-88411

Konrad Theiss Verlag GmbH+
Monchaldenstr 28, 70191 Stuttgart
Tel: (0711) 255 27-0 *Fax:* (0711) 255 27-17
E-mail: service@theiss.de
Web Site: www.theiss.de *Cable:* THEISSVERLAG STUTTGART
Key Personnel
Man Dir: Andreas Auth *Tel:* (0711) 125527-11 *E-mail:* auth@theiss.de
Sales: Ruth Geisler
Production: Karin Dechow *Tel:* (0711) 125527-18 *E-mail:* dechow@theiss.de
Program Manager: Jurgen Beckedorf *Tel:* (0711) 125527-16 *E-mail:* beckedorf@theiss.de
Founded: 1997
Subjects: Archaeology, Art, History, Nonfiction (General)
ISBN Prefix(es): 3-8062
Total Titles: 2 CD-ROM
Online services available through World Wide Web.
Distributed by Wissenschoftliche Buchjesellschoft

Therapiehandbuch, *imprint of* Urban und Fischer Verlag fur Medizin

Druck-und Verlagshans Thiele & Schwarz GmbH+
Werner-Heisenbergstr 7, 34123 Kassel
Tel: (0561) 9 59 25-0 *Fax:* (0561) 9 59 25-68
E-mail: info@thiele-schwarz.de
Web Site: www.thiele-schwarz.de *Cable:* THIELE & SCHWARZ KASSEL-WALDAU
Key Personnel
Proprietor: Rolf Schwarz
Founded: 1879
ISBN Prefix(es): 3-87816
Associate Companies: Verlag Schule und Elternhaus
Bookshop(s): Buch und Musik Center Wilhelmshoehe, Wilhelmshoeheer Allee 256, 34119 Kassel; Buchhandlung Am Markt, Markstr 10, 99310 Armkstadt

Georg Thieme Verlag KG+
Ruedigerstr 14, 70469 Stuttgart
Mailing Address: Postfach 301120, 70451 Stuttgart
Tel: (0711) 8931-0 *Fax:* (0711) 8931-298
E-mail: kunden.service@thieme.de
Web Site: www.thieme.de; www.thieme.com *Cable:* THIEMEBUCH
Key Personnel
Publisher: Albrecht Hauff
Man Dir: Dr Wolfgang Knueppe
Press: Anne-Katrin Doebler
Division Head Marketing & Sales: Juergen Seidel
International Rights Manager: Barbara Pfeifer *Tel:* (0711) 8931184 *Fax:* (0711) 8931143 *E-mail:* barbara.pfeifer@thieme.de
Dir, International Marketing & Sales: Malik Lechelt *E-mail:* malik.lechelt@thieme.de
Founded: 1886
Subjects: Biological Sciences, Chemistry, Chemical Engineering, Health, Nutrition, Medicine, Nursing, Dentistry, Psychology, Psychiatry
ISBN Prefix(es): 0-86577; 3-432; 3-13; 3-7773; 3-8304; 3-90503
Number of titles published annually: 600 Print; 20 CD-ROM; 10 Audio
Total Titles: 5,100 Print; 100 CD-ROM; 50 Audio
Online services available through World Wide Web.
Associate Companies: MVS Medizinverlage Stuttgart, Steiermaerker Str 3-5, 70469 Stuttgart
Imprints: Enke; Haug; Huethig; Sonntag; TRIAS
U.S. Office(s): Thieme Medical Publishers, 333 Seventh Ave, 5th floor, New York, NY 10001, United States
Distributed by Academi-text (US); Baker & Taylor (US); Miguel Concha SA (Chile); Coutts Library Services (US); DA Information Services Pty Ltd (Australia & New Zealand - books & journals); Distribuna Libreria Medica Digital (Columbia); Editorial Cientifica Interamericana (Argentina); Hwa Eng Trading Co (Taiwan - books only); Jaypee Brothers Medical Publishers (P) Ltd (India - medicine & dentistry only); Liberia Internacional SA de CV (Mexico); Lidel Edicoes Tecnicas LDA (Portugal, Angola, Mozambique, Guine-Bissau, Cabo-Verde, Sao Tome - books & journals); Login Brothers Canada (Canada); J A Majors Co (US); Matthews Medical Books (US); Medical Books in Print (US); Midwest Library Services (US); Nobel Tip Kitabevleri (Turkey); PF Book Importer (Indonesia - books only); Promociones Editorales (Mexico); Redwing Book Co (US); Ernesto Reichmann Distribuidora de Livros Ltda (Brazil); Rittenhouse Book Distributors (US); Sandi SA Bookstore (Mexico); Seoul Medical Scientific Books Co (South Korea - books only); Wexford Hall (US); Yankee Book Pedler Inc (US)
Distributor for AANS; North Atlantic Books
Foreign Rep(s): Academic Marketing Services (Pty) Ltd (Botswana, Namibia, South Africa); Amin Al-Abini (North Africa, Middle East exc Iran); Michael Goh (Brunei, Burma, Cambodia, China, Indonesia, Korea, Laos, Philippines, Singapore & Malaysia, Taiwan, Thailand, Vietnam); Laszlo Horvath (Eastern Europe, Russia); Akio Hosoya (Japan); Momenta Publishing Ltd (Belgium, Netherlands, UK & Ireland); S Savitzki (Israel); David Towle International (Scandinavia); Trinidad Lopez Gonzalez (Spain); Katia Zevelekakis (Greece)
Bookshop(s): Thieme und Frohberg, Neue Str 15, 72070 Tuebingen *Tel:* (07071) 50110; Thieme und Frohberg, Hindenburgdamm 95b, 12203 Berlin *Tel:* (030) 8390030
Warehouse: Koch, Neff & Oetinger & Co, Verlagsauslieferung, Schockenried Str 39, Postfach 800620, 70506 Stuttgart

Thien, Hans-Gunter, u Hanns Wienold
Verlag Westfalisches Dampfboot, Dorotheenstr 2a, 48145 Munster
Tel: (0251) 608 60 80 *Fax:* (0251) 608 60 20
E-mail: info@dampfboot-verlag.de
Web Site: www.dampfboot-verlag.de
Founded: 1984
ISBN Prefix(es): 3-89691
Number of titles published annually: 40 Print
Distributor for Prolit Verlagaushieferung

K Thienemanns Verlag+
Blumenstr 36, 70182 Stuttgart
Tel: (0711) 210 55-0 *Fax:* (0711) 210 55 39
E-mail: info@thienemann.de
Web Site: www.theinemann.de
Key Personnel
Man Dir: Hansjoerg Weitbrecht; Gunter Ehni
Publicity: Jochen Kraeft
Rights & Permissions: Doris Keller-Riehm
Founded: 1849
Subjects: Fiction, Nonfiction (General)
ISBN Prefix(es): 3-522
Number of titles published annually: 100 Print
Total Titles: 800 Print
Imprints: Edition Erdmann (travel descriptions); Gabriel Verlag (religious children's books); Weitbrecht Verlag (literature & nonfiction)

Verlag Theodor Thoben
Langestr 77-79, 49610 Quakenbrueck
Tel: (05431) 3486 *Fax:* (05431) 3584
E-mail: info@buecher-thoben.de
Web Site: www.buecher-thoben.de
Key Personnel
Publisher: Theodor Thoben
Founded: 1903
Subjects: Regional Interests

ISBN Prefix(es): 3-921176
Bookshop(s): Buecher-Thoben, Lange Str 77-79, 49610 Quakenbrueck

Hans Thoma Verlag GmbH Kunst und Buchverlag
Vorholzstr 7, 76137 Karlsruhe
Tel: (0721) 932 750 *Fax:* (0721) 932 7520
Key Personnel
Manager: Herwig Schelling
Subjects: Art
ISBN Prefix(es): 3-87297
Parent Company: Evangelischer Presseverband

Tiessen, Wolfgang, Moderne
Meisenstr 9, 63263 Neu-Isenburg
Mailing Address: Postfach 2179, 63243 Neu-Isenburg
Tel: (06102) 53335 *Fax:* (06102) 53335
Founded: 1977
Specialize in Limited Editions finely printed with illustrations in original graphic.
ISBN Prefix(es): 3-920947; 3-928395

Tipp Creative, *imprint of* Xenos Verlagsgesellschaft mbH

Tipress Deutschland, *imprint of* Tipress Dienstleistungen fur das Verlagswesen GmbH

Tipress Dienstleistungen fur das Verlagswesen GmbH+
Johannes-Fechtstr 2, 79295 Sulzburg
Tel: (07634) 591193 *Fax:* (07634) 591192
E-mail: tipress@tipress.com
Web Site: www.tipress.com
Key Personnel
President: Roberto Toso
Literary agency & services for publishers in four languages; projects of series of books, realization of books & consultants.
Subjects: Cookery, Crafts, Games, Hobbies, Health, Nutrition
Imprints: Tipress Deutschland
Branch Office(s)
Via Cernaia 34, I-10122 Torino, Italy, Contact: Ms Claudia Robert *Tel:* (011) 533487 *Fax:* (011) 535283 *E-mail:* tipress@fileita.it

Tips fuer Trips, *imprint of* Friedemann von Engel Verlag

Titania-Verlag Ferdinand Schroll+
Forststr 104B, 70193 Stuttgart
Tel: (0711) 63 81 25 *Fax:* (0711) 63 69 872
Cable: TITANIAVERLAG STUTTGART
Key Personnel
Publisher, International Rights: Wolfgang Schroll
Publisher: Gerdi Schroll
Founded: 1949
Subjects: Fiction
ISBN Prefix(es): 3-7996

S Toeche-Mittler Verlag GmbH
Hindenburgstr 33, 64295 Darmstadt
Tel: (06151) 33665 *Fax:* (06151) 314048
E-mail: info@net-library.de
Web Site: www.net-library.de
Key Personnel
Sales Manager: Albrecht Lueft
Founded: 1789
Subjects: Economics, Law, Nonfiction (General), Sports, Athletics
ISBN Prefix(es): 3-87820
Divisions: TRIOPS, Tropical Scientific Books

Toleranz Verlag, Nielsen Frederic W
Sundgauallee 19, 79114 Freiburg im Breisgau
Tel: (0761) 81415
Founded: 1971
Subjects: Biography, Government, Political Science, History, Poetry
ISBN Prefix(es): 3-925745; 3-9800069

Tomus Verlag GmbH+
Einsteinstr 167, 81675 Munich
Tel: (089) 47 07 77-44 *Fax:* (089) 47 07 77-42
E-mail: main@tomus.com
Web Site: www.tomus.de
Key Personnel
Publisher: Claus-Juergen Frank
Dir: Oliver A Frank
Founded: 1962
Member of Stockmarket Association.
Subjects: Animals, Pets, Cookery, Crafts, Games, Hobbies, Humor, Science (General), Travel
ISBN Prefix(es): 3-8231
Associate Companies: Telelit Verlag AG/Fakt Verlag AG
Branch Office(s)
Dr Wernerstr 5, 82194 Groebenzell
Warehouse: VVA, An der Autobahn, 33310 Gutersloh

P J Tonger Musikverlag GmbH & Co
Auf dem Brand 10, 50996 Cologne
Tel: (0221) 935564-0 *Fax:* (0221) 935564-11
E-mail: musikverlag@tonger.de
Web Site: www.tonger.de
Key Personnel
Man Dir & Publicity: Peter Tonger
Sales Dir: Monika Hermans-Krueger
Founded: 1822
Subjects: Sheet Music books
ISBN Prefix(es): 3-920950
Subsidiaries: Carl Engels Musikverlag; Musikverlage Gerhard Rabe; Fritz Spies GmbH

TR - Verlagsunion GmbH+
Thierschstr 11, 80538 Munich
Mailing Address: Postfach 260202, 80059 Munich
Tel: (089) 2121 390 *Fax:* (089) 296129; (089) 296357
E-mail: vertrieb@tr-verlag.de
Web Site: www.tr-verlag.de
Key Personnel
Man Dir, Rights & Permissions: Andreas Keiser *E-mail:* andreaskeiser@tr-verlag.de
Editorial: Gabriele Rieth-Winterherbst *Tel:* (089) 212139-13 *E-mail:* rieth@tr-verlag.de; Inga Dopatka *Tel:* (089) 212139-29 *E-mail:* dopatka@tr-verlag.de
Publicity: Cornelia Wiedemann *Tel:* (089) 212139-18 *E-mail:* wiedemann@tr-verlag.de; Helke Funke *Tel:* (089) 212139-25
Sales: Imogen Fries *Tel:* (089) 212139-17 *E-mail:* fries@tr-verlag.de; Elisabeth Kroier *Tel:* (089) 212139-20 *E-mail:* kroier@tr.verlag.de
Founded: 1968
The Union publishes & distributes books, audio- & videocassette, software, sets of lessons etc to link up with TV & radio programs.
The TR (Television & Radio) Publishing Union comprises two broadcasting companies (Bayerischer Rundfunk & Suedwest und Funk) & the following publishing companies: Ludwig Auer GmbH; BLV Verlagsgesellschaft mbH; Verlag C H Beck; C Bertelsmann Verlag GmbH; Verlag Bruckmann Muenchen; Ernst Klett Verlag; Koesel-Verlag GmbH & Co; Langenscheidt KG; Suddeutscher Verlag, Buchverlag GmbH; JB Metzler Poeschel; R Oldenbourg Verlag GmbH; Guenter Olzog Verlag; K G Saur Verlag; Springer Verlag.
Subjects: Architecture & Interior Design, Education, English as a Second Language, Film, Video, Health, Nutrition, Radio, TV, Religion - Other, Travel
ISBN Prefix(es): 3-8058
Total Titles: 150 Print; 5 CD-ROM; 50 Audio
Online services available through World Wide Web.
Branch Office(s)
TR-Verlagsunion Buero Potsdam, August-Bebel-Str 16, Potsdam, Contact: Harald Smeja *Tel:* (0331) 7312815 *Fax:* (0331) 7312815
Orders to: Moderne Industrie Verlagsservice, Justus-von-Liebig-Str 1, 86899 Landsberg

Traditionell Bogenschiessen Verlag Angelika Hornig
Siebenpfeifferstr 16, 67071 Ludwigshafen
Mailing Address: Postfach 250245, 67034 Ludwigshafen
Tel: (0621) 68 94 41 *Fax:* (0621) 68 94 42
E-mail: info@bogenschiessen.de
Web Site: www.bogenschiessen.de
Key Personnel
Editor: Angelika Hoernig *E-mail:* ah@bogenschiessen.de
Subjects: Archaeology, History, How-to, Outdoor Recreation, Sports, Athletics

Trans Tech Publications+
Freibergerstr 1, 38678 Clausthal-Zellerfeld
Mailing Address: Postfach 1254, 38670 Clausthal-Zellerfeld
Tel: (05323) 96970 *Fax:* (05323) 969796
E-mail: ttp@bulkonline.com
Web Site: www.bulk-online.de
Key Personnel
Publisher: Dr R H Wohlbier
Founded: 1972
Subjects: Chemistry, Chemical Engineering, Civil Engineering, Earth Sciences, Mechanical Engineering
ISBN Prefix(es): 0-87849

Transpress Verlagsgesellschaft mbH+
Olgastr 86, 70180 Stuttgart
Mailing Address: Postfach 103743, 70032 Stuttgart
Tel: (0711) 210 80 65 *Fax:* (0711) 210 80 70
E-mail: versand@motorbuch.de
Web Site: www.motorbuch-versand.de *Cable:* TRANSPRESS STUTTGART
Key Personnel
Publishing Dir: Klaus Hikschhe
Founded: 1990
Subjects: Automotive, Transportation
ISBN Prefix(es): 3-344
Parent Company: Paul Pietsch Verlage GmbH & Co, Olgastr 86, Postfach 103743, 70032 Stuttgart
Bookshop(s): Transpress Buchhandlung, Hauptbahnhof, Mittelbau-Ladenstr, 04103 Leipzig
Shipping Address: Koch, Neff & Oetinger & Co, Postfach 800620, 70506 Stuttgart
Warehouse: Koch, Neff & Oetinger & Co, Postfach 800620, 70506 Stuttgart

Trautvetter & Fischer Nachf
Gladenbacher Way 57, 35037 Marburg
Tel: (06421) 33309 *Fax:* (06421) 34959
E-mail: bestell@trautvetterfischerverlag.de
Web Site: www.trautvetterfischerverlag.de
Key Personnel
Publisher: Dr Wilhelm A Eckhardt *E-mail:* eckhardt@trautvetterfischerverlag.de
Founded: 1941
Specialize in history of Hessen.
Member of Borsenverein Des Deutschen Buchhandels.
Subjects: History, Regional Interests
ISBN Prefix(es): 3-87822
Number of titles published annually: 2 Print
Total Titles: 50 Print

Trees Wolfgang Triangel Verlag+
Fuchserde 44, 52066 Aachen, Permony
Tel: (0241) 6 99 00 *Fax:* (0241) 6 99 15
E-mail: info@triangelverlag.de

Web Site: www.triangel-verlag.de
Key Personnel
Owner: Wolfgang Trees
Founded: 1981
Member of Borsenverein de deutschen Buchhandels.
Subjects: History, Military Science, Regional Interests, Travel, Books about the history & tourism in Euregio Meuse-Rhine, ie Aachen (D), Maastricht (NL) & Liege (B). Especially: WWII 1933-1945, Rhineland, Huertpen Forest & smugglings 1545-1953
ISBN Prefix(es): 3-922974
Number of titles published annually: 2 Print
Total Titles: 12 Print

Trescher Verlag GmbH
Reinhardtstr 9, 10117 Berlin
Tel: (030) 2 83 24 96 *Fax:* (030) 2 81 59 94
Web Site: www.trescherverlag.de
Founded: 1993
Subjects: Film, Video, Nonfiction (General), Outdoor Recreation, Travel
ISBN Prefix(es): 3-928409; 3-89794

Treves Editions Verein Zur Foerderung der Kuenstlerischen Taetigkeiten (Club for the Promotion of Artistic Work)+
Medardstr 105, 54294 Trier
Mailing Address: Postfach 1550, 54205 Trier
Tel: (0651) 309 010 *Fax:* (0651) 300 699
E-mail: mail@treves.de
Web Site: www.treves.de
Key Personnel
Man Dir: Rainer Breuer
Man Dir, Rights & Permissions: Ursula Dahm
Founded: 1974
Subjects: Art, Erotica, Fiction, Health, Nutrition, History, Literature, Literary Criticism, Essays, Music, Dance, Mysteries, Nonfiction (General), Poetry, Travel
ISBN Prefix(es): 3-88081

TRIAS, *imprint of* Georg Thieme Verlag KG

Trias-Thieme, Hippokrates Enke+
Ruedigerstr 14, 70469 Stuttgart
Tel: (0711) 8931-0 *Fax:* (0711) 8931-28
Web Site: www.thieme.de
Telex: 7252275gtud
Key Personnel
Contact: Martin Kegel
Founded: 1989
Subjects: Health, Nutrition, Medicine, Nursing, Dentistry, Nonfiction (General)
ISBN Prefix(es): 3-89373
Parent Company: Georg Thieme Verlag

Trotzdem-Verlags Genossenschaft eG+
Postfach 1159, 71117 Grafenau
Tel: (07033) 44273 *Fax:* (07033) 45264
E-mail: trotzdemusf@t-online.e
Web Site: www.txt.de/trotzdem
Key Personnel
Contact: Wolfgang Haug *E-mail:* wolfganghaug@aol.com
Founded: 1978
Publishing of books & magazines from a libertarian viewpoint.
Subjects: Alternative, Biography, Drama, Theater, Education, Government, Political Science, History, Photography, Social Sciences, Sociology
ISBN Prefix(es): 3-922209; 3-931786
Divisions: Redaktion Schwarzer Faden
Distributor for Anares; Anarchijtische Buchhandlung

Mario Truant Verlag+
Frauenlobstr 95, 55118 Mainz
Tel: (06131) 961660 *Fax:* (06131) 961670
E-mail: viva@truant.com
Web Site: www.truant.com
Key Personnel
Publisher: Mario Truant
Founded: 1990
Subjects: Crafts, Games, Hobbies, Fiction, Parapsychology, Science Fiction, Fantasy
ISBN Prefix(es): 3-926801

Tuduv Verlagsgesellschaft mbH+
Fuerstenstr 15, 80333 Munich
Mailing Address: Postfach 340163, 80098 Munich
Tel: (089) 280 90 95 *Fax:* (089) 280 95 28
E-mail: vvf-verlag@t-online.de; tuduv@t-online.de
Web Site: www.tuduv.de
Key Personnel
Manager: Franz Frank
Founded: 1974
Subjects: Art, Biography, Communications, Ethnicity, Government, Political Science, History, Language Arts, Linguistics, Literature, Literary Criticism, Essays, Medicine, Nursing, Dentistry, Social Sciences, Sociology, Technology
ISBN Prefix(es): 3-88073
Associate Companies: Verlag V Florentz GmbH (WF)

Tuebinger Vereinigung fur Volkskunde eV (TVV)
Ludwig-Uhland-Institut Schloss, 72070 Tuebingen
Tel: (07071) 295449; (07071) 2972374 (Orders) *Fax:* (07071) 295330
E-mail: info@tvv-verlag.de
Web Site: www.tvv-verlag.de
Key Personnel
Man Dir, Editorial, Production & Sales: Bernd Juergen Warneken
Editorial, Production & Sales: Utz Jeggle; Hermann Bausinger; Ute Bechdolf; Gottfried Korff
Founded: 1963
Subjects: Ethnicity, Film, Video, History, Language Arts, Linguistics, Regional Interests, Social Sciences, Sociology, Women's Studies
ISBN Prefix(es): 3-925340; 3-932512

TUeV-Verlag GmbH
Am Grauen Stein, 51105 Cologne
Tel: (0221) 806-3535 *Fax:* (0221) 806-3510
E-mail: tuev-verlag@de.tuv.com
Web Site: www.tuev-verlag.de; www.qm-aktuell.de
Key Personnel
Manager: Dr Anton Reiter
Founded: 1971
Subjects: Energy, Environmental Studies, Regional Interests, Technology, Transportation
ISBN Prefix(es): 3-8249; 3-88585; 3-921059
Parent Company: TUeV Rheinland Holding AG

Turkischer Schulbuchverlag Onel Cengiz+
Silchesto 13, 50827 Cologne
Tel: (0221) 5879084; (0221) 5879085 *Fax:* (0221) 488093; (0221) 5879004
Key Personnel
Vice President: Ibrahim Ilbasi
Publisher: C Hayati Oenel
Founded: 1981
Subjects: Travel
ISBN Prefix(es): 3-924542; 3-929490; 3-933348

Turm-Verlag Lorber-Verlag Otto Zluhan OHG+
Hindenburgstr 3-5, 74321 Bietigheim-Bissingen
Tel: (07142) 940843 *Fax:* (07142) 940844 *Cable:* TURM, BIETIGHEIM
Key Personnel
Man Dir: Friedrich Zluhan
Subjects: Health, Nutrition, Parapsychology, Religion - Other
ISBN Prefix(es): 3-87495
Parent Company: Verlagsgemeinschaft Friedrich Zluhan, Hindenburgstr 3-5, 74321 Bietigheim-Bissingen
Associate Companies: Lorber-Verlag, Hindenburgstr 3-5, 74321 Bietigheim-Bissingen; Rohm-Verlag, Hindenburgstr 3-5, 74321 Bietigheim-Bissingen

Wirtschaftsverlag Carl Ueberreuter+
Lurgialle 6-8, 60439 Frankfurt am Main
Tel: (069) 58 09 05-0 *Fax:* (069) 58 09 05-10
E-mail: info@ueberreuter.de
Web Site: www.redline-wirtschaft.de
Key Personnel
Manager: Hans-Joachim Hartmann
Publisher: Juergen Diessl
Rights Director, Foreign Affairs: Maria Pinto-Peuckmann *Tel:* (089) 548 52-84 26 *Fax:* (089) 548 52-84 21
Founded: 1988
Subjects: Accounting, Business, Law, Management
ISBN Prefix(es): 3-220

Uerle Verlag, *imprint of* Verlag Herder GmbH & Co KG

Verlag Dr Alfons Uhl+
Mittlere Gerbergasse 1, 86720 Noerdlingen
Tel: (09081) 87248 *Fax:* (09081) 23710
Key Personnel
Dir, Rights & Permissions: Dr Alfons Uhl
Subjects: Architecture & Interior Design, Art, Geography, Geology
ISBN Prefix(es): 3-921503

Ullstein Heyne List GmbH & Co KG+
Paul-Heyse-Str 28, 80336 Munich
Tel: (089) 5148-0 *Fax:* (089) 5148-2229
Web Site: www.ullstein.de
Key Personnel
Managing Partner: Bettina Breitling; Christian Strasser
Publicity: Claus Martin Carlsberg
Founded: 1894
Member of TR-Verlagsunion GmbH.
Subjects: Art, Biography, Fiction, History, Literature, Literary Criticism, Essays, Philosophy, Psychology, Psychiatry, Religion - Other, Science (General), Social Sciences, Sociology
ISBN Prefix(es): 3-471
Associate Companies: Bucher Verlag GmbH; W Ludwig Verlag GmbH; Suedwest Verlag

Guenter Albert Ulmer Verlag
Hauptstr 16, 78609 Tuningen
Tel: (07464) 98740 *Fax:* (07464) 3054
E-mail: info@umlertuningen.de
Web Site: www.ulmertuningern.de
Key Personnel
Man Dir: Guenter Albert Ulmer
Founded: 1983
Subjects: Earth Sciences, Environmental Studies, Gardening, Plants, Health, Nutrition, Human Relations, Natural History, Nonfiction (General), Poetry, Regional Interests, Religion - Protestant, Theology, Meditation
ISBN Prefix(es): 3-924191; 3-932346

Verlag Eugen Ulmer GmbH & Co (Eugen Ulmer Publishers)+
Wollgrasweg 41, 70599 Stuttgart, BRD
Mailing Address: Postfach 70 05 61, D-70574 Stuttgart
Tel: (0711) 4507-0 *Fax:* (0711) 4507-120; (0711) 4507-185; (0711) 4507-214; (0711) 4507-207
E-mail: info@ulmer.de
Web Site: www.ulmer.de
Telex: 723634
Key Personnel
Man Dir: Roland Ulmer

Deputy Dir: Matthias Ulmer *E-mail:* mulmer@ulmer.de
Production: Dieter Kleinschrot
Reader: Dr Nadja Kneissler *E-mail:* lektorat@ulmer.de
Sales Dir: Michael Kurzer
Rights & Permissions Man: Sigrun Wagner *E-mail:* wagner@ulmer.de
Founded: 1868
Member of VGS - Verlagsgesellschaft mbH & Co KG.
Subjects: Agriculture, Animals, Pets, Environmental Studies, Gardening, Plants, How-to, Science (General), Veterinary Science
ISBN Prefix(es): 3-8001
Total Titles: 900 Print
Online services available through World Wide Web.
Subsidiaries: Editions Eugen Ulmer; Neumann Verlag, Radebeul

Ulrich Schiefer bahnVerlag+
Hartliebstr 2, 80637 Munich
Mailing Address: Postfach 431154, 80741 Munich
Tel: (089) 89020999 *Fax:* (089) 89020087
Key Personnel
Owner: Ulrich Schiefer
Founded: 1985
Subjects: Crafts, Games, Hobbies, Film, Video, Transportation
ISBN Prefix(es): 3-924969

Ulrike Helmer Verlag+
Altkoenigstr 6a, 61462 Koenigstein
Tel: (06174) 93 60 60; (06174) 93 60 61 *Fax:* (06174) 93 60 65; (06174) 93 60 61
E-mail: info@ulrike-helmer-verlag.de
Web Site: www.ulrike-helmer-verlag.de
Key Personnel
Man Dir: Ulrike Helmer
Founded: 1988
Subjects: Fiction, Gay & Lesbian, History, Literature, Literary Criticism, Essays, Philosophy, Social Sciences, Sociology, Women's Studies
ISBN Prefix(es): 3-927164; 3-89741
Warehouse: SOVA, Friesstr 20-24, 60388 Frankfurt/M

Umschau Buchverlag Breidenstein GmbH+
Stuttgarterstr 18-24, 60329 Frankfurt am Main
Mailing Address: Postfach 110262, 60037 Frankfurt am Main
Tel: (069) 2600550 *Fax:* (069) 2600559
E-mail: umschau-braus@t-online.de *Cable:* UMSCHAU FRANKFURTMAIN
Key Personnel
Publisher: Hans-Juergen Breidenstein
Man Dir: Katharina Toebben
Sales: Till Zander
Founded: 1850
Member of Boersenverein; also acts as distributor.
Subjects: Health, Nutrition, Nonfiction (General), Science (General)
ISBN Prefix(es): 3-524
Associate Companies: Broenners Druckerei Breidenstein GmbH; Broenner Verlag Breidenstein GmbH; Umschau Zeitschriftenverlag Breidenstein GmbH
Imprints: Report-Verlag GmbH

Uni-Taschenbuecher UTB Fuer Wissenschaft CmbH, see UTB fuer Wissenschaft Uni-Taschenbuecher GmbH

Union-Verlag GmbH+
Lucile-Grahn-Str 39, 81675 Munich
Tel: (089) 4701071 *Fax:* (089) 4701081
Key Personnel
Man Dir & Publisher: Hans Meisinger
Rights & Publicity: Christiane Schneider
Founded: 1880
Subjects: Nonfiction (General)
ISBN Prefix: 3-8139
Orders to: MVS Meisinger Verlagsservice GmbH, Am Steinfeld 4, 94065 Waldkirchen *Tel:* (08581) 9605-0 *Fax:* (08581) 754

Universitaetsverlag C Winter Heidelberg GmbH+
Hans-Bunte-Str 18, 69123 Heidelberg
Mailing Address: Postfach 106140, 69051 Heidelberg
Tel: (06221) 77 02-60 *Fax:* (06221) 77 02-69
E-mail: info@winter-hd.de
Web Site: www.winter-verlag-hd.de
Key Personnel
Publisher: Ruprecht Schulze; Eilert Erfling *E-mail:* e.erfling@sinter-verlag-hd.de
Marketing: Mrs Rotraud Hohlbein *E-mail:* r.hohlbein@winter-verlag-hd.de
Founded: 1993
Subjects: Language Arts, Linguistics, Literature, Literary Criticism, Essays
ISBN Prefix(es): 3-8253
Associate Companies: Heidelberger Verlagsanstalt (HVA) & Edition

Universitatsverlag Ulm GmbH
Bahnhofstr 20, 89073 Ulm
Mailing Address: Postfach 4204, 89032 Ulm
Tel: (0731) 15 28 60 *Fax:* (0731) 15 28 62
E-mail: info@uni-verlag-ulm.de
Web Site: www.uni-verlag-ulm.de
Key Personnel
Manager: Meimberg Reinhold; Alexander Schraut
Contact: Siglinde Maichel
Founded: 1988
Specialize in neurology, psychiatry & brain research.
Subjects: Medicine, Nursing, Dentistry, Physical Sciences
ISBN Prefix(es): 3-927402; 3-89559
Parent Company: Schwaebischer Verlag KG, 7970 Leutkirch
Shipping Address: Dalnheph 20, 89073 Ulm

UNO-Verlag mbH, Vertriebs und Verlagsgesellschaft
Am Hofgarten 10, 53113 Bonn
Tel: (0228) 94 90 2-0 *Fax:* (0228) 94 90 2-22
E-mail: info@uno-verlag.de
Web Site: www.uno-verlag.de
Key Personnel
Dir: Wolfgang Fischer *E-mail:* fischer@ono-verlag.de
Subjects: Agriculture, Developing Countries, Economics, Education, Energy, Environmental Studies, Government, Political Science, Health, Nutrition, Labor, Industrial Relations, Social Sciences, Sociology
ISBN Prefix(es): 3-923904
Distributor for Council of Europe; FAO; Inter-American Development Bank; International Monetary Fund (IMF); Nordic Council of Ministers Publications; OECD; UNDP; UNESCO; UNIDO; United Nations Publications; WHO; Worldbank

Unrast Verlag e V+
Postfach 8020, 48043 Munster
Tel: (0251) 666293 *Fax:* (0251) 666120
E-mail: unrast-verlag@gmx.de
Web Site: www.unrast-verlag.de
Key Personnel
International Rights: Martin Schuering
Founded: 1989
Subjects: Developing Countries, Fiction, Government, Political Science, Women's Studies

Urania Verlag mit Ravensburger Ratgebern+
Dircksenstr 48, 10178 Berlin
Tel: (030) 28447-112; (030) 28447-113 *Fax:* (030) 28447-123
E-mail: urania.ravensburger@dornier-verlage.de
Web Site: www.urania-ravensburger.de *Cable:* URANIA LElPZIG
Key Personnel
Manager: Dr Juergen A Bach
Publishing Manager: Bernd Scheiba
Publicity: Ulrike Baak *Tel:* (030) 28447-137 *E-mail:* baak@dornier-verlage.de
Sales Manager: Yvonne de Andres *Tel:* (030) 28447-111 *E-mail:* deandres@dornier-verlage.de
Founded: 1924
Subjects: Biological Sciences, Nonfiction (General)
ISBN Prefix(es): 3-332
Parent Company: Dornier Medienholding
Shipping Address: Leipziger Kommissions- und Grosbuchhandelsgesellschaft mbH, Polzschauer Weg, 04579 Espenhain
Orders to: Leipziger Kommissions- und Grosbuchhandelsgesellschaft mbH, Polzchauer Weg, 04579 Espenhain

Urban & Fischer Verlag GmbH & Co KG Niederlassung Jena+
Loebderbgraben 14a, 07743 Jena
Mailing Address: Postfach 100537, 07705 Jena
Tel: (03641) 62 64 30 *Fax:* (03641) 62 64 21
E-mail: journals@urbanfischer.de
Web Site: www.urbanfischer.de/journals
Key Personnel
Man Dir: Bernd Rolle
Sales Manager & International Rights: Martin Huber *E-mail:* m.huber@urbanfischer.de
Founded: 1878
Subjects: Biological Sciences, Medicine, Nursing, Dentistry, Science (General), Technology, Medical
ISBN Prefix(es): 3-437
Parent Company: Verlagsgruppe Georg von Holtzbrinck, Stuttgart
Orders to: Urban & Fischer Verlag, Abo-Service und Vertrieb, Loebdergraben 14a, 07743 Jena *E-mail:* k.ernst@urbanfischer.de

Urban und Fischer Verlag fur Medizin+
Formerly Urban und Schwarzenberg Verlag fur Medizin
Karlstr 45, 80333 Munich
Mailing Address: Postfach 201930, 80019 Munich
Tel: (089) 5383-0 *Fax:* (089) 5383-939
E-mail: info@urbanfischer.de
Web Site: www.urban.de; www.urbanfischer.de
Key Personnel
Man Dir: Dr Burkhard Scheele; Dr Michael Urban
Rights & Permissions: Susanne Engelhardt
Founded: 1866
Subjects: Medicine, Nursing, Dentistry
ISBN Prefix(es): 3-541
Parent Company: Waverly Inc, 351 West Camden St, Baltimore, MD 21202-2436, United States
Imprints: Breitner, Chirurgische Operationslehte; Klinik der Frauenheilkunde und Geburtshilfe; Klinik der Gegenwart; Praxis der Zahnheilkunde; Therapiehandbuch
Branch Office(s)
Urban & Partner Wydawnictno Medyene nl, Curie-Skldowskiei 55/61, Instytut Elektrotechniki 50, 950 Wroclaw, Poland
Urban & Schwarzenberg GesmbH, Frankgasse 4, A-1096 Vienna, Austria
U.S. Office(s): Waverly, 351 West Camden St, Baltimore, MD 21201-2436, United States
Bookshop(s): Oscar Rothacker Versandbuchhandlung GmbH, Fraunhoferstr 10, 82152 Martinsried

PUBLISHERS — GERMANY

Shipping Address: Verlegerdienst Munich, Gutenbergstr 1, 82197 Gilching
Warehouse: Verlegerdienst Munich, Gutenbergstr 1, 82197 Gilching

Urban und Schwarzenberg Verlag fur Medizin, see Urban und Fischer Verlag fur Medizin

Edition Ustad, *imprint of* Karl-May-Verlag Lothar Schmid GmbH

UTAS-Verlag fur Moderne Lernmethoden Uta Stechl+
Kellerstr 15, 84577 Tussling
Mailing Address: Postfach 62, 84577 Tussling
Tel: (08633) 1450 *Fax:* (08633) 7805
Key Personnel
Owner: Uta Stechl
Founded: 1981
ISBN Prefix(es): 3-925220

UTB fuer Wissenschaft Uni-Taschenbuecher GmbH
Breitwiesenstr 9, 70565 Stuttgart
Tel: (0711) 7 82 95 55 0 *Fax:* (0711) 7 80 13 76
E-mail: utb@utb-stuttgart.de
Web Site: www.utb.de
Key Personnel
Man Dir: Volkmar Kalki
Manager: Ferdinand Schoeningh; Georg Siebeck
Founded: 1970
The company represents a group of 13 publishers (shareholders) producing paperbacks of a general academic/technical/scientific nature.
Subjects: Agriculture, Biological Sciences, Business, Chemistry, Chemical Engineering, Computer Science, Economics, Electronics, Electrical Engineering, Engineering (General), Government, Political Science, Health, Nutrition, History, Language Arts, Linguistics, Library & Information Sciences, Literature, Literary Criticism, Essays, Medicine, Nursing, Dentistry, Philosophy, Physics, Psychology, Psychiatry, Religion - Other, Social Sciences, Sociology, Veterinary Science
ISBN Prefix(es): 3-8252; 3-920971
Distributed by Mohr Morawa (Austria); Reinhardt Media-Service (Switzerland)
Warehouse: Brockhaus Commission, Postfach 1220, 70803 Kornwestheim, Kreidlerstr 9, 708016 Kornwestheim

UVK Universitatsverlag Konstanz GmbH+
Protecting Route 24, 78462 Konstanz
Mailing Address: PO Box 10 20 51, 78420 Konstanz
Tel: (07531) 90 53 0 *Fax:* (07531) 90 53 98
E-mail: willkommen@uvk.de
Web Site: www.uvk.de
Key Personnel
Publishing Manager & International Rights Contact: Walter Engstle *Tel:* (07531) 90 53 12
E-mail: walter.engstle@uvk.de
Founded: 1963
Subjects: Archaeology, History, Literature, Literary Criticism, Essays, Philosophy, Science (General)
ISBN Prefix(es): 3-87940
Number of titles published annually: 10 Print
Total Titles: 700 Print
Associate Companies: Suedverlag GmbH/uvk Verlagsgesellschaft mbH
Orders to: Brockhaus Commission Verlagsauslieferung, Kreidlerstr 9, 70806 Kornwestheim

UVK Verlagsgesellschaft mbH+
Protecting Route 24, D-78462 Konstanz
Mailing Address: PO Box 10 20 51, 78420 Konstanz
Tel: (07531) 90 53 0 *Fax:* (07531) 90 53 98
E-mail: willkrommen@uvk.de
Web Site: www.uvk.de
Key Personnel
Publishing Manager & International Rights: Walter Engstle *Tel:* (07531) 90 53 12
E-mail: walter.engstle@uvk.de
Founded: 1995
Subjects: Communications, History, Journalism, Radio, TV, Social Sciences, Sociology
ISBN Prefix(es): 3-89669; 3-88295
Number of titles published annually: 100 Print
Total Titles: 350 Print
Associate Companies: UVK Universitaetsverlag Konstanz GmbH (University Press)
Orders to: Brockhaus Commission Verlagsauslieferung, Kreidlerstr 9, 70806 Kornwestheim bei Stuttgart

Dorothea van der Koelen
Hinter der Kapelle 54, 55128 Mainz
Tel: (06131) 346 64 *Fax:* (06131) 36 90 76
E-mail: dvanderkoelen@xterna-net.de
Founded: 1986
Art publisher & art gallery.
Subjects: Art, Science (General), Art History
ISBN Prefix(es): 3-926663
Parent Company: Vander Koelen Verlag

Vandenhoeck & Ruprecht+
Robert Bosch-Breite 6, 37079 Gottingen
Tel: (0551) 5084-40 *Fax:* (0551) 5084-422
E-mail: info@vandenhoeck-ruprecht.de
Web Site: www.vandenhoeck-ruprecht.de
Key Personnel
Man Dir, Rights & Permissions: Dr Arndt Ruprecht
Man Dir: Dr Dietrich Ruprecht
Man Dir, International Rights & Permissions, Editorial Theology & Religion: Reinhilde Ruprecht, PhD
Editorial Psychology: Dr Bernd Rachel
Sales: Ursula Nahrgang
Publicity: Regina Lange
Editorial German Literature, Classics/Antiquity, Philosophy: Dr Ulrike Giessmann
Editorial History & Economics: Martin Rethmeier
Marketing Director: Carola Mueller *Tel:* (0551) 5084-420 *E-mail:* c.mueller@vandenhoeck-ruprecht.de
Founded: 1735
Subjects: Economics, Education, History, Language Arts, Linguistics, Philosophy, Psychology, Psychiatry, Religion - Other, Theology
ISBN Prefix(es): 3-525
Associate Companies: Buchhandlung Deuerlich
Subsidiaries: Druckerei Hubert & Company
Distributor for Wallstein Verlag; Weidle Verlag

VAP-Verlag, see Goll Bruno Verlag fur Aussergewoehnliche Perspektiven (VAP)

VAS-Verlag fuer Akademische Schriften, Vas Karl-Heinz Balon+
Kurfuerstenstr 18, 60486 Main
Tel: (069) 77 93 66 *Fax:* (069) 70 73 967
E-mail: info@vas.de
Web Site: www.vas-verlag.de
Key Personnel
International Rights: Karl-Heinz Balon
Founded: 1982
Subjects: Education, Environmental Studies, Government, Political Science, History, Human Relations, Language Arts, Linguistics, Psychology, Psychiatry, Social Sciences, Sociology, Women's Studies
ISBN Prefix(es): 3-88864

VDE-Verlag GmbH+
Bismarckstr 33, 10625 Berlin
Mailing Address: PO Box 120143, Berlin
Tel: (030) 34 80 01 0 *Fax:* (030) 341 70 93
E-mail: voss@vde-verlag.de
Web Site: www.vde-verlag.de
Telex: 181683 vde d
Key Personnel
Manager: Dr Ing A Gruetz
Founded: 1929
Subjects: Communications, Electronics, Electrical Engineering
ISBN Prefix(es): 3-8007
U.S. Office(s): Hallenbook, County Route 9, PO Box 357, Chatham, NY 12037, United States

VDI-Verlag GmbH+
Heinrichstr 24, 40239 Dusseldorf
Mailing Address: Postfach 101054, 40001 Dusseldorf
Tel: (0211) 6188 0 *Fax:* (0211) 6188 112
Web Site: www.vdi-nachrichten.com *Cable:* INGENIEURVERLAG DUSSELDORF
Key Personnel
Man Dir: Raymond Johnson-Obla
Founded: 1923
Subjects: Engineering (General), Science (General), Technology
ISBN Prefix(es): 3-18

Verein der Benediktiner zu Beuron- Beuroner Kunstverlag+
Abteistr 2, 88631 Beuron
Tel: (07466) 17-228 *Fax:* (07466) 17-209
E-mail: kunstverlag@erzabtrei-beuron.de
Web Site: www.erzabtei-beuron.de *Cable:* BEURONER KUNSTVERLAG
Key Personnel
Dir: Gabriel Gawletta
Publicity Manager: Siegfried Studer
Founded: 1898
Subjects: Art, Biblical Studies, Humor, Religion - Catholic, Religion - Protestant, Religion - Other
ISBN Prefix(es): 3-87071
Imprints: Monastica

Vereinigte Fachverlage GmbH
Lise-Meitner-Str 2, 55129 Mainz
Tel: (06131) 992-01 *Fax:* (06131) 992-100
Key Personnel
Manager: Manfred Grunenberg
Founded: 1937
ISBN Prefix(es): 3-7830
Subsidiaries: VF Verlagsgesellschaft GmbH

Vereinte Evangelische Mission, Abt Verlag
Rudolfstr 137, 42285 Wuppertal
Mailing Address: Postfach 201963, 42219 Wuppertal
Tel: (0202) 89004 134 *Fax:* (0202) 89004 179
E-mail: info@vemission.org
Web Site: www.vemission.org
Key Personnel
Editor-in-chief: Thomas Sandner
Founded: 1828
Communion of churches in 3 continents.
Subjects: Theology
ISBN Prefix(es): 3-87855; 3-921900

Verkehrs-Verlag J Fischer, see Verkehrs-Verlag J Fischer GmbH & Co KG

Verlag Beltz & Gelberg+
Werderstr 10, 69469 Weinheim
Mailing Address: Postfach 100154, 69441 Weinheim
Tel: (06201) 60070 *Fax:* (06201) 6007338
E-mail: info@beltz.de
Web Site: www.beltz.de
ISBN Prefix(es): 3-407
Parent Company: Beltz Publishing Group

Verlag fur die Frau GmbH
Kuratorium "Haus des Buches" eV Leipzig, Gerichtsweg 28, 04103 Leipzig
Tel: (0341) 99540 *Fax:* (0341) 9954367

E-mail: kuratorium.hdb@t-online.de
Web Site: www.uni-leipzip.de/leipzig/hdbuches.htm
Telex: 311419
Key Personnel
Manager: Brunhilde Laumann; Adolf Silbermann
Founded: 1946
Subjects: Fashion, Science (General)
ISBN Prefix(es): 3-7304
Parent Company: Gong Verlagsgruppe

Verlag fur die Rechts- und Anwaltspraxis GmbH & Co+
Postfach 10 19 53, 45619 Recklinghausen
Tel: (0 23 61) 91 42-0 *Fax:* (0 23 61) 91 42-35
Web Site: www.zap-verlag.de
Key Personnel
Publisher: Dr Karl-Friedrich Peter
Man Dir: Hermann Boger
Founded: 1989
Subjects: Law
ISBN Prefix(es): 3-927935; 3-89655
Shipping Address: Schuechtermannstr 180, 44628 Herne
Warehouse: Schuechtermannstr 180, 44628 Herne
Orders to: Postfach 101849, 44621 Herne

Verlag fur Schweissen und Verwandte Verfahren (Publishing House for Welding)+
Subsidiary of Deutscher Verband fur Schweissen und verwandte Verfahren eV
Aachener Str 172, 40223 Duesseldorf
Mailing Address: Postfach 101965, 40010 Duesseldorf
Tel: (0211) 15910 *Fax:* (0211) 1591150
E-mail: verlag@dvs-hg.de
Web Site: www.dvs-verlag.de
Key Personnel
Manager: M Stumpf; Dr Ing D von Hofe
Founded: 1955
Subjects: Engineering (General), Mechanical Engineering, Technology, Welding & Allied Processes
ISBN Prefix(es): 3-87155
Number of titles published annually: 15 Print; 3 CD-ROM
Total Titles: 419 Print; 10 CD-ROM
Parent Company: German Welding Society

Verlag Moderne Industrie AG & Co KG+
Emmy-Noetherstr 2, 80992 Munich
Tel: (089) 54852-02 *Fax:* (089) 54852-8428
E-mail: info@mi-verlag.de
Web Site: www.mi-verlag.de
Telex: 527114 moin d
Key Personnel
President: Klaus Hengster *Fax:* (08191) 125-542
Publisher: Evelyn Boos *E-mail:* e.boos@mvg-verlag.de
Rights Director, Foreign Affairs: Maria Pinto-Peuckmann *Tel:* (089) 548 52-84 26 *Fax:* (089) 548 52-84 21 *E-mail:* m.pinto-p@redline-wirtschaft.de
Marketing & Sales: Martin Brueninghaus *E-mail:* m.brueninghaus@mvg-verlag.de
Founded: 1952
Also publishes loose-leaf editions.
Member of EBP-Network.
Subjects: Advertising, Business, Career Development, Communications, Computer Science, Economics, Management, Marketing, Technology, Investment, Money, Success Stories
ISBN Prefix(es): 3-478
Associate Companies: mvg Verlag *Fax:* (089) 548 52-84 21 *E-mail:* info@mvg-verlag.de (career development, communications, motivation & self-help; ISBN 3-478); Verlag Moderne Industrie Buch AG & Co KG, Koenigswintererstr 418, 53227 Bonn *Tel:* (0228) 97024 41 *Fax:* (0228) 97024 21 *E-mail:* info@vmi-buch.de (computer books for beginners & users; coaching, programming, application & data banks; ISBN 3-8266)

Verlag Puppen & Spielzeug, *imprint of* Gert Wohlfarth GmbH Verlag Fachtechnik & Mercator Verlag, Verlag Puppen & Spielzeug

Verlag und Druckkontor Kamp GmbH
Kurfuerstenstr 4a, 44791 Bochum
Tel: (02 34) 5 16 17-0 *Fax:* (02 34) 5 16 17-18
E-mail: verlag@kamp-verlag.de
Web Site: www.kamp-verlag.de
Key Personnel
Owner: Dr Ferdinand Kamp
Founded: 1996
Subjects: Education
ISBN Prefix(es): 3-89709

Verlag und Studio fuer Hoerbuchproduktionen+
Kirchweg 2, 35085 Beltershausen
Tel: (06424) 9439-0 *Fax:* (06424) 9439-29
E-mail: verlag@hoerbuch.de; info@hoerbuch.de
Web Site: www.hoerbuch.de; www.hoerbuch.com
Key Personnel
Publisher: Hans Eckardt; Heidemarie Eckardt
Founded: 1987
Subjects: Biblical Studies, Career Development, Management, Marketing, Mysteries, Poetry
ISBN Prefix(es): 3-89614

Verlag Volk & Welt GmbH, see Luchterhand Literaturverlag GmbH/Verlag Volk & Welt GmbH

Verlagsgruppe Jehle-Rehm GmbH
Emmy-Noether-Str 2, 80992 Munich
Tel: (089) 54 8 52-06 *Fax:* (089) 54 8 52-82 30
E-mail: verlagsgruppe@jehle-rehm.de
Web Site: www.jehle-rehm.de
Key Personnel
Manager: Wolfgang Quadflieg
Publisher: Peter Habit
Founded: 1988
Subjects: Business, Economics, Law
ISBN Prefix(es): 3-8073; 3-7825; 3-87253
Parent Company: Sueddeutscher Verlag, Munich
Divisions: Fachbuchhandlung Kova
Branch Office(s)
Friedrichstr 130a, 10117 Berlin *Tel:* (030) 28 30 98-0 *Fax:* (030) 28 30 98-10 *E-mail:* verlagsgruppe@jehle-rehm.de
Bookshop(s): Kova & Rau, Einsteinstr 172, 81675 Munich

Vervuert Verlagsgesellschaft
Wielandstr 40, 60318 Frankfurt am Main
Tel: (069) 5974617 *Fax:* (069) 5978743
E-mail: info@iberoamericanalibros.com
Web Site: www.ibero-americana.net
Key Personnel
Manager: Klaus Dieter Vervuert
Founded: 1988
Subjects: Developing Countries, Drama, Theater, Ethnicity, Foreign Countries, Language Arts, Linguistics, Literature, Literary Criticism, Essays
ISBN Prefix(es): 3-89354
Distributor for Iberoamericana (Madrid, Spain); Latin American Bookstore (USA)

Vice Versa Verlag+
Dorotheenstr 4, 12557 Berlin
Tel: (030) 61 60 92 37 *Fax:* (030) 61609238
E-mail: viceversa@comp.de
Key Personnel
Publisher: Gabriela Wachter
Founded: 1992
Subjects: Architecture & Interior Design, Art
ISBN Prefix(es): 3-9803212
Associate Companies: Vice Versa Vertrieb; Vice Versa Vertretung

Vier Tuerme GmbH Verlag Klosterbetriebe+
Schweinfurter Str 40, 97359 Muensterschwarzach Abtei
Tel: (9324) 20 292 (Verlag); (9324) 20 214 (Druckerei); (9324) 20 213 (Buchhandlung)
Fax: (9324) 20 495
E-mail: info@vier-tuerme.de
Web Site: www.vier-tuerme.de
Key Personnel
Publisher: Winfried Duenninger
Man Dir: P Anselm Gruen
Founded: 1955
Subjects: Religion - Other, Theology
ISBN Prefix(es): 3-87868
Imprints: Munsterschwarzacher Kleinschafter; Schrifter zur Kontemplation; Mansterschwarzacher Studien
Divisions: Druckerei & Buchhandlung

Friedr Vieweg & Sohn Verlagsgesellschaft mbH+
Abraham-Lincoln Str 46, 65189 Wiesbaden
Mailing Address: Postfach 1546, 65173 Wiesbaden
Tel: (0611) 7878361 *Fax:* (0611) 7878470
Web Site: www.vieweg.de
Key Personnel
General Manager: Dr Hans-Dieter Haenel
Man Dir: Dr Heinz Weinheimer
Editorial: Dr Reinald Klockenbusch; Ulrike Schmickler-Hirzebruch; Ewald Schmitt
Sales Marketing Manager: Rolf-Guenther Hobbeling
Rights & Permissions: Angelika Bolisega *E-mail:* angelika.bolisega@bertelsmann.de
Founded: 1786
Professional information for engineers & technicians; textbooks for students in technology & mathematics.
Subjects: Civil Engineering, Computer Science, Electronics, Electrical Engineering, Mathematics, Mechanical Engineering, Technology
ISBN Prefix(es): 3-528
Number of titles published annually: 5 CD-ROM
Total Titles: 1,500 Print; 25 CD-ROM
Parent Company: BertelsmannSpringer Science+Business Media
Orders to: VVA Bertelsmann Distribution, Postfach 7777, D-33310 Guetersloh

Villa Arceno, *imprint of* Frederking & Thaler Verlag GmbH

Curt R Vincentz Verlag+
Schiffgraben 43, 30175 Hannover
Mailing Address: Postfach 6247, 30062 Hannover
Tel: (05 11) 9910000 *Fax:* (05 11) 9910099
E-mail: info@vincentz.de
Web Site: www.vincentz.de *Cable:* VINHA
Key Personnel
Man Dir, Rights & Permissions: Dr Lothar Vincentz
Commercial Dir: Helmut Fitting
Sales: Ina Baatz
Founded: 1893
Subjects: Chemistry, Chemical Engineering, Medicine, Nursing, Dentistry
ISBN Prefix(es): 3-87870
Warehouse: Emil-Meyer-Str 22, 30165 Hannover

Edition Curt Visel+
Weberstr 36, 87700 Memmingen
Tel: (08331) 2853 *Fax:* (08331) 490364
E-mail: info@editon-curt-visel.de
Web Site: www.edition-curt-visel.de
Key Personnel
Man Dir, Editorial, Production, Publicity, Rights & Permissions: Curt Visel

Sales: Jurgen Schweitzer
Founded: 1963
Subjects: Art, Biography
ISBN Prefix(es): 3-922406
Parent Company: Maximilian Dietrich Verlag

Vista Point Verlag GmbH+
Haendelstr 25-29, 50674 Cologne
Mailing Address: Postfach 270572, 50511 Cologne
Tel: (0221) 921613-0 *Fax:* (0221) 921613-14
E-mail: info@vistapoint.de
Web Site: www.vista-point.net
Key Personnel
Manager: Dr Horst Schmidt-Bruemmer *E-mail:* h.schmidt-bruemmer@vistapoint.de; Andreas Schulz
Founded: 1977
Subjects: Travel
ISBN Prefix(es): 3-88973

VJK Verlag Josef Knecht+
Formerly Verlag Josef Knecht-Carolusdruckerei GmbH
Liebfrauenberg 37, 60313 Frankfurt
Tel: (069) 281767; (069) 281768 *Fax:* (069) 296653
Key Personnel
Man Dir: Dr Hermann Herder; Dr Marianne Regnier
Rights & Permissions: Dieter Naveau
Founded: 1946
Specialize in Religion, Philosphy, Social Problems, Human Sciences (Special interest: the situation of mankind in (post modern times).
Subjects: Philosophy, Religion - Other, Science (General), Social Sciences, Sociology
ISBN Prefix(es): 3-7820

Vogel Medien GmbH & Co KG+
Max-Planck-Str 7/9, 97064 Wuerzburg
Tel: (0931) 418-2028 *Fax:* (0931) 418-2860
E-mail: info@vogel-medien.de
Web Site: www.vogel-medien.de *Cable:* VOGELVERLAG WURZBURG
Key Personnel
Man Dir: Dietmar Salein; Karl-Michael Mehnert
Public Relations Manager: York Seewald
Tel: (0931) 418 2590 *E-mail:* york_seewald@vogel-medien.de
Founded: 1891
Subjects: Automotive, Chemistry, Chemical Engineering, Civil Engineering, Communications, Computer Science, Electronics, Electrical Engineering, Environmental Studies, Management, Mechanical Engineering
ISBN Prefix(es): 3-8023
U.S. Office(s): Vogel Europublishing, 632 Sunflower Court, San Ramon, CA 94583, United States, Contact: Mark Hauser *Tel:* 510-648-1170 *Fax:* 510-648-1171

Voggenreiter-Verlag+
Viktoriastr 25, 53173 Bonn-Bad Godesberg
Tel: (0228) 93 575-0 *Fax:* (0228) 35 50 53
E-mail: info@voggenreiter.de
Web Site: www.voggenreiter.de
Key Personnel
Proprietor: Charles Voggenreiter; Ralph Voggenreiter
Founded: 1919
Music publisher of Rock & Pop; also specialize in full tutorials, reference books, sheet music & videos.
Member of NAMM, RPMDA, DMV.
Subjects: Music, Dance
ISBN Prefix(es): 3-8024
Total Titles: 200 Print; 5 CD-ROM; 15 Audio
U.S. Office(s): MTC, 495 Lorimer St, Brooklyn, NY 11211, United States, Contact: Marcus Demuth *Tel:* 718-963-2777 *Fax:* 718-302-4890 *E-mail:* mtc@inditec.com

Volk und Wissen Verlag GmbH & Co+
Axel-Springer-Str 54b, 10117 Berlin
Mailing Address: Postfach 27, 10107 Berlin
Tel: (030) 201 83-500 *Fax:* (030) 2041846
E-mail: mail@vwv.de
Web Site: www.vwv.de
Telex: 112181 vowiv dd *Cable:* VOLKWISSEN BERLIN
Key Personnel
Man Dir: Walter Funken
Program Dir: Dr Jochen Becher
Business Manager: Dr Roland Tischer
Rights & Permissions: Ortrud Liebau
Sales: Michael Lochner
Editor: Marjus Bente; Dr Sigfrid Motschmann; Dr Gerhild Schenk
Founded: 1945
Subjects: Biological Sciences, Chemistry, Chemical Engineering, Education, Geography, Geology, Mathematics, Physical Sciences, Physics
ISBN Prefix(es): 3-06
Parent Company: Franz-Cornelsen-Stiftung, Berlin
Subsidiaries: Paedagogischer Zeitschriftenverlag GmbH & Co

Verlag Deutsches Volksheimstaettenwerk GmbH+
Neefestr 2a, 53115 Bonn
Tel: (0228) 7259930; (0228) 7259931 *Fax:* (0228) 7259919
Key Personnel
Contact: I Hilderbrand
Founded: 1982
Subjects: House & Home, Law
ISBN Prefix(es): 3-87941

Verlagsgruppe Georg von Holtzbrinck GmbH
Gaensheidestr 26, 70184 Stuttgart
Tel: (0711) 21500 *Fax:* (0711) 2150269
Web Site: www.holtzbrink.com
Key Personnel
Contact: Dieter von Holtzbrinck
Subjects: Education, Fiction, Nonfiction (General), Science (General)

Dokument und Analyse Verlag Bogislaw von Randow
Barer Str 43, 80799 Munich
Tel: (089) 2720100 *Fax:* (089) 2720311
Key Personnel
Publisher: Bogislaw von Randow
Founded: 1972
Subjects: Economics, Government, Political Science, Law, Science (General), Social Sciences, Sociology

von Stengel oHG Verlag+
Gertigstr 10A, 22303 Hamburg
Tel: (040) 2791485 *Fax:* (089) 6099783
Key Personnel
Man Partner: Christian Freiherr von Stengel
Manager: Stefan Freiherr von Stengel
Founded: 1990
Subjects: Sports, Athletics
ISBN Prefix(es): 3-928176

Verlag Philipp von Zabern
Philipp-von-Zabern Platz 1-3, 55116 Mainz
Mailing Address: Postfach 4065, 55030 Mainz
Tel: (06131) 287470 *Fax:* (06131) 223710
E-mail: zabern@zabern.de
Web Site: www.zabern.de
Key Personnel
Man Dir: Franz Rutzen
Management: Dr Annette Nuennerich Asmus
Sales: Daniela Sessner *Tel:* (089) 121516 61 *Fax:* (089) 12151616 *E-mail:* vertrieb@zabern verlag.ccn.de; Christine Vorhoelzer *Tel:* (089) 121516 26 *Fax:* (089) 12151616 *E-mail:* vertrieb@zabern.ccn.de

Advertising: Ms Manuela Dressen *Tel:* (06131) 28747 11 *Fax:* (06131) 28747 44 *E-mail:* m.dressen@zabern.de
Management: Juergen Kleidt
Founded: 1785
Subjects: Archaeology, Art, History, Regional Interests
ISBN Prefix(es): 3-8053
Orders to: PO Box 190930, 80689 Munich, Sales: Christine Vorhoelzer *Tel:* (089) 1215166-26 *Fax:* (089) 12151616 *E-mail:* vertmib@zaberu-verlag.ccn.de

Votum Verlag GmbH+
Grevener Str 89-91, 48159 Muenster
Tel: (0251) 26514-0 *Fax:* (0251) 26514-20
E-mail: info@votum-verlag.de
Web Site: www.votum-verlag.de
Key Personnel
Manager: Ullrich Gintzel
Founded: 1986
Subjects: Law, Psychology, Psychiatry, Social Sciences, Sociology, Women's Studies
ISBN Prefix(es): 3-926549; 3-930405; 3-933158

VS Verlagshaus Stuttgart GmbH+
Wolframstr 36, 70191 Stuttgart
Tel: (0711) 25800 *Fax:* (0711) 2580685
E-mail: vstuttgart@aol.com
Key Personnel
Manager: Manfred Denneler
International Rights: Wolfgang Kellner
Founded: 1992
Specialize in Direct Mail; also acts as packager.
Subjects: Art, Biological Sciences, Cookery, Crafts, Games, Hobbies, Ethnicity, Foreign Countries, Gardening, Plants, History, Music, Dance, Natural History, Nonfiction (General), Outdoor Recreation, Science Fiction, Fantasy, Travel
Parent Company: Reinhard Mohn GmbH, Guetersloh
U.S. Office(s): Tanenbaum International Publishing Services, 27 E 61 St, New York, NY 10021, United States *Tel:* 212-371-4120
Book Club(s): Alle Bertelsmann Club

VUA (agricultural titles), *imprint of* BLV Verlagsgesellschaft mbH

Vulkan-Verlag GmbH+
Huyssenalle 52-56, 45128 Essen
Mailing Address: Postfach 10 39 62, 45039 Essen
Tel: (0201) 82002-14 *Fax:* (0201) 82002-34
Web Site: www.oldenbourg.de/vulkan-verlag
Key Personnel
Manager, Rights & Permissions: Dr Dieter Hohm
Manager: Dr Thomas Cornides
Founded: 1928
Subjects: Chemistry, Chemical Engineering, Energy, Engineering (General), Environmental Studies, Mechanical Engineering
ISBN Prefix(es): 3-8027
Parent Company: R Oldenbourg Verlag, Rosenheimer Str 145, 81671 Munich

VVF Verlag V Florentz GmbH+
Gabelsbergerstr 15, 80333 Munich
Mailing Address: Postfach 34 01 63, 80098 Munich
Tel: (089) 285503 *Fax:* (089) 2809528
Key Personnel
Manager: Franz Frank
Rights & Permissions: Hans Frank
Founded: 1975
Subjects: Government, Political Science, Labor, Industrial Relations, Law, Regional Interests
ISBN Prefix(es): 3-88259; 3-89481; 3-921491
Associate Companies: Tuduv Verlagsgesellschaft mbH

VWB-Verlag fur Wissenschaft & Bildung, Amand Aglaster
Postfach 11 03 68, 10833 Berlin
Tel: (030) 251 04 15 *Fax:* (030) 251 11 36
E-mail: 100615.1565@compuserve.com
Web Site: www.vwb-verlag.com
Key Personnel
Owner: Amand Aglaster
Founded: 1988
Subjects: Anthropology, Art, Biological Sciences, Education, Ethnicity, Geography, Geology, Medicine, Nursing, Dentistry, Music, Dance, Psychology, Psychiatry, Science (General), Social Sciences, Sociology, Women's Studies
ISBN Prefix(es): 3-927408; 3-86135

W Ludwig Verlag GmbH+
Paul Heyse-Str 28, 80336 Munich
Tel: (089) 51 48 0 *Fax:* (089) 51 48 229
E-mail: ludwig-verlag.de@econ-ullstein-list.de
Web Site: www.ludwig-verlag.de
Telex: 151329
Key Personnel
Managing Partner: Bettina Breitling; Christian Strasser
Founded: 1945
Subjects: Art, Fiction, History, Nonfiction (General), Travel
ISBN Prefix(es): 3-7787
Associate Companies: C J Bucher Verlag GmbH; Paul List Verlag GmbH; Suedwest Verlag GmbH & Co KG

Wachholtz Verlag GmbH
Rungestr 4, 24537 Neumuenster
Tel: (04321) 906-276 *Fax:* (04321) 906-275
E-mail: info@wachholtz.de
Web Site: www.wachholtz.de
Key Personnel
Man Dir & Permissions: Gabriele Wachholtz; Dr Gisela Wachholtz
Production: Renate Braus; Henner Wachholtz
Founded: 1871
Subjects: Archaeology, Art, History, Language Arts, Linguistics, Social Sciences, Sociology
ISBN Prefix(es): 3-529

Verlag Klaus Wagenbach GmbH+
Emser Str 40/41, 10719 Berlin
Tel: (030) 23 51 51-0 *Fax:* (030) 2 11 61 40
E-mail: mail@wagenbach.de
Web Site: www.wagenbach.de
Key Personnel
Man Dir, Editorial: Dr Klaus Wagenbach
Sales Dir: Nina Wagenbach
Rights Dir: Dr Susanne Schuessler
Public Relations: Annette Wassermann
Publicity: Per Rumberg
Founded: 1964
Subjects: Fiction, Government, Political Science, History, Literature, Literary Criticism, Essays, Poetry, Social Sciences, Sociology
ISBN Prefix(es): 3-8031
Number of titles published annually: 60 Print; 4 Audio
Total Titles: 10 Audio
Orders to: Koch, Neff & Oetinger, Postfach 800220, 70506 Stuttgart

Friedenauer Presse Katharina Wagenbach-Wolff+
Carmerstr 10, 10623 Berlin
Tel: (030) 312 99 23 *Fax:* (030) 312 99 02
Web Site: www.friedenauer-press.de
Key Personnel
Man Dir & International Rights: Katharina Wagenbach-Wolff
Founded: 1963
Subjects: Literature, Literary Criticism, Essays
ISBN Prefix(es): 3-921592; 3-932109

Waldthausen Verlag, *imprint of* NaturaViva Verlags GmbH

Waldthausen Verlag GmbH & Co KG Abt Verlag, see NaturaViva Verlags GmbH

Walhalla Fachverlag GmbH & Co KG Praetoria+
Haus an der Eisernen Bruecke, 93042 Regensburg
Mailing Address: Postfach 10 10 53, 93010 Regensburg
Tel: (0941) 5684-0 *Fax:* (0941) 5684-111
E-mail: walhalla@walhalla.de
Web Site: www.walhassa.de
Key Personnel
Manager: Bernhard Roloff
Founded: 1949
Subjects: Business, Career Development, Law, Public Administration
ISBN Prefix(es): 3-8029

Uwe Warnke Verlag+
Sonntagstr 22, 10245 Berlin
Tel: (030) 29049903
E-mail: warnke@snafu.de
Key Personnel
Publisher/Author: Uwe Warnke *E-mail:* warnke@snafu.de
Founded: 1982
Subjects: Art, Literature, Literary Criticism, Essays, Photography, Poetry
ISBN Prefix(es): 3-910165
Total Titles: 100 Print; 1 CD-ROM

Wartburg Verlag GmbH+
Lisztstr 2 A, 99423 Weimar
Tel: (03643) 24 61-11 *Fax:* (03643) 24 61-18
E-mail: buch@warbburgverlag.de
Web Site: www.glaube-und-heimat.de
Key Personnel
Man Dir: Torsten Bolduan; Barbara Harnisch
Founded: 1990
Subjects: Art, Literature, Literary Criticism, Essays, Regional Interests
ISBN Prefix(es): 3-86160

Ernst Wasmuth Verlag GmbH & Co+
Fuerststr 133, 72072 Tuebingen
Mailing Address: Postfach 27 28, 72017 Tuebingen
Tel: (07071) 3 36 58; (07071) 3 50 71 *Fax:* (07071) 3 57 76
E-mail: wasmuth.publish@supra-net.net
Web Site: www.wasmuth-verlag.de
Key Personnel
Man Dir: Ernst-Juergen Wasmuth
Sales: Petra Praeg
Rights & Permissions: Beatrix Schomberg-Stickl
Editorial Dir: Dr Sigrid Hauser
Production: Rosa Wagner
Founded: 1872
Subjects: Archaeology, Architecture & Interior Design, Art
ISBN Prefix(es): 3-8030
Distributor for L'Arcaedizioni; Waanders
Bookshop(s): Wasmuth Buchhandlung & Antiquariat GmbH & Co, Pfalzburger Str 43-44, 10717 Berlin *Tel:* (030) 8 63 09 90 *Fax:* (030) 86 30 99 99

Waxmann Verlag GmbH+
Steinfurterstr 555, 48159 Muenster
Mailing Address: Postfach 8603, 48046 Muenster
Tel: (0251) 26504-0 *Fax:* (0251) 26504-26
Web Site: www.waxmann.com
Key Personnel
Man Dir: Dr Ursula Heckel *E-mail:* heckel@waxmann.com
Contact: Beate Plugge *E-mail:* plugge@waxmann.com
Founded: 1987
Subjects: Education, Ethnicity, History, Literature, Literary Criticism, Essays, Psychology, Psychiatry, Science (General), Social Sciences, Sociology, Theology, Women's Studies
ISBN Prefix(es): 3-89325; 3-8309
Total Titles: 1,000 Print
Branch Office(s)
Torstr 195, 10115 Berlin *Tel:* (030) 283900-49 *Fax:* (030) 283900-59 *E-mail:* berlin@waxmann.com
U.S. Office(s): Waxmann Publishing Co, PO Box 1318, New York, NY 10028, United States

WB Verlag+
Nymphenburger Str 84, 80636 Munich
Mailing Address: Postfach 190918, 80609 Munich
Tel: (089) 1269900 *Fax:* (089) 126990-11
E-mail: wb-druck@online-service.de
Web Site: www.wb-druck.de
Key Personnel
Manager: Jurgen Kleidt
Founded: 1988
Subjects: Art
ISBN Prefix(es): 3-927140
Parent Company: Axel-Springer-Verlag

WDV Wirtschaftsdienst Gesellschaft fur Medien & Kommunikation mbH & Co OHG+
Siemensstr 6, 61352 Bad Homburg
Mailing Address: Postfach 2551, 61295 Bad Homburg
Tel: (06172) 670-0 *Fax:* (01672) 670144
Web Site: www.wdv.de
Telex: 414452 widi d
Key Personnel
Managers: Bernhard Frisch; Diether Kuhn; Rolf M Laufer
Founded: 1948
Subjects: Health, Nutrition, Travel
ISBN Prefix(es): 3-926181
Parent Company: Zeitschriften VVG Verlags- und Verwaltungsgesellschaft mbH & Co KG
Subsidiaries: Analyse & Concept Kommunikationsberatung GmbH; Montan-Wirtschaftsverlag GmbH
U.S. Office(s): Conover Brown, International Media, 21 E 40 St, Suite 901, New York, NY 10016, United States
Warehouse: Hertzweg 4, 63071 Offenbach am Main

Weber Zucht & Co+
Steinbruchweg 14, 34123 Kassel
Tel: (0561) 519194; (0561) 515953 *Fax:* (0561) 5102514
E-mail: wezuco@t-online.de
Key Personnel
International Rights: Helga Weber
Contact: Wolfgang Zucht
Founded: 1980
Subjects: Alternative, Biography, Education, Environmental Studies, Government, Political Science, History, Military Science, Nonfiction (General), Philosophy, Science (General), Self-Help, Social Sciences, Sociology
ISBN Prefix(es): 3-88713

Wege der Forschung, *imprint of* Wissenschaftliche Buchgesellschaft

Wehr & Wissen Verlagsgesellschaft mbH+
Heilsbachstr 26, 5300 Bonn 1
Mailing Address: PO Box 1, 5300 Bonn 1
Tel: (0228) 64830 *Fax:* (0228) 6483109
E-mail: 101336.245@compuserve.com
Key Personnel
Man Dir: Manfred Sadlowski
Man Dir, Publicity: Joachim Knoche
Sales Promotion: Toni Wierer
Marketing, Intern: Juergen Hensel
Marketing, National: Hans Werner Steinhoff

Subjects: History, How-to
ISBN Prefix(es): 3-921528

A Weichert Verlag GmbH & Co KG+
Tiestestr 14, 30171 Hannover
Tel: (0511) 813068; (0511) 813069 *Fax:* (0511) 814841
Key Personnel
Man Dir: Alfred Trippo
Sales: Hans H Droste
Rights & Permissions: Renate Gruetzemacher
Founded: 1872
Subjects: Fiction
ISBN Prefix(es): 3-483; 3-8034
Associate Companies: Neuer Jugendschriften-Verlag, Tiestestr 14, 30171 Hannover

Weidler Buchverlag Berlin+
Luebecker Str 8, 10559 Berlin
Mailing Address: Postfach 21 03 15, 10503 Berlin
Tel: (030) 394 86 68 *Fax:* (030) 394 86 98
E-mail: weidler_verlag@yahoo.de
Web Site: www.weidler-verlag.de
Key Personnel
Man Dir: Joachim Weidler
Founded: 1985
Member of Boersenverein des Deutschen Buchhandels.
Subjects: Drama, Theater, Earth Sciences, Education, Fiction, Geography, Geology, Language Arts, Linguistics, Literature, Literary Criticism, Essays, Management, Marketing, Nonfiction (General), Philosophy, Poetry, Psychology, Psychiatry, Regional Interests, Science (General), Social Sciences, Sociology
ISBN Prefix(es): 3-925191; 3-89693
Number of titles published annually: 30 Print
Total Titles: 215 Print
Imprints: Edition Belletriste

Weidlich Verlag+
Imprint of Verlagshaus Wurzburg
Beethovenstr 5, 97080 Wurzburg
Tel: (0931) 385235 *Fax:* (0931) 385305
E-mail: info@verlagshaus.com
Web Site: www.verlagshaus.com
Key Personnel
Publishing Dir: Dieter Krause
Dir of Production: Juergen Roth
Sales Dir: Johannes Glesius
Subjects: Foreign Countries, Travel
ISBN Prefix(es): 3-8035

Weidmannsche Verlagsbuchhandlung GmbH+
Hagentorwall 7, 31134 Hildesheim
Tel: (05121) 15010 *Fax:* (05121) 150150
E-mail: info@olms.de
Web Site: www.olms.de
Key Personnel
Publisher: Dr Walter Georg Olms
Publishing Dir: Dietrich Olms
Founded: 1680
Subjects: Antiques, History, Language Arts, Linguistics, Philosophy, Romance, Classical Studies, Medieval Studies
ISBN Prefix(es): 3-615
Number of titles published annually: 20 Print
Total Titles: 450 Print
U.S. Office(s): Empire State Bldg, 350 Fifth Ave, Suite 3304, New York, NY 10118-0069, United States
Warehouse: VVA, PO Box 1254, 33399 Verl, Contact: Herr Stronz *Tel:* (05241) 803844 *Fax:* (05241) 8060220

Verlag W Weinmann+
Beckerstr 7, 12157 Berlin
Tel: (030) 855 48 95 *Fax:* (030) 8 55 94 64
E-mail: info@weinmann-verlag.de
Web Site: www.weinmann-verlag.de

Key Personnel
Man Dir: Dr Weinmann
Founded: 1961
Member of Boersenverein.
Subjects: Humor, Sports, Athletics, Martial Arts
ISBN Prefix(es): 3-87892
Total Titles: 70 Print
Online services available through World Wide Web.
Foreign Rep(s): Dessauer CH; Ennsthaler A

Weisser Ring, Gemeinnutzige Verlagsgesellschaft mbH
Bundesgeschaeftsstelle, Weberstr 16, 55130 Mainz
Tel: (06131) 83 03 51 *Fax:* (06131) 83 03 45
E-mail: info@weisser_ring.de
Web Site: www.weisser-ring.de
Key Personnel
Editor: Dieter Eppenstein
Founded: 1989
Specializing in the production of books (Mainzer Schriften) relating to issues concerning victims of crime.
Total Titles: 20 Print
Parent Company: Weisser Ring eV

Weitbrecht Verlag, *imprint of* K Thienemanns Verlag

WEKA Firmengruppe GmbH & Co KG+
Roemerstr 4-16, 86438 Kissing
Mailing Address: Postfach 1209, 86425 Kissing
Tel: (08233) 23-0 *Fax:* (08233) 23-7266
E-mail: pr@weka.de
Web Site: www.weka.de; www.weka-group.de; www.weka-group.com
Telex: 533287
Key Personnel
Chairman: Werner Muetzel; Rainer B Wozny
Man Dir: Robert Boss; Wolfgang Materna; Taap Mulder; Gerhard Schierbling
Founded: 1973
Subjects: Architecture & Interior Design, Behavioral Sciences, Business, Career Development, Civil Engineering, Communications, Electronics, Electrical Engineering, Energy, Engineering (General), Environmental Studies, How-to, Law, Management, Mechanical Engineering, Medicine, Nursing, Dentistry, Outdoor Recreation, Real Estate, Technology
ISBN Prefix(es): 3-8111
Subsidiaries: Demeter Verlag GmbH & Co KG, Batinger; DMV Daten-und Medien-Verlag GmbH & Co KG; ECPA; Editions WEKA SA; Editions WEKA SARL; Edizioni WEKA SpA; Franzis-Verlag GmbH & Co KG; Interest-Verlag GmbH; Nidderau und Busborn; Spitta Verlag GmbH; Turnus GmbH; Uitgeverij BV; Verlag Recht & Praxis GmbH; Verwaltungs-Verlag GmbH; WAGO-Curadata Steuerberatungs-Systeme GmbH; WEKA Baufach-Software GmbH; WEKA Baufachverlage GmbH; WEKA Fachverlag fuer Behoerden und Institutionen; WEKA Fachverlag fur technische Fuhrungskrafte GmbH; WEKA Handels-GmbH; WEKA Informationsschriften-und Werbefachverlage GmbH; WEKA Management Fachverlag GmbH; WEKA Publishing Inc; WEKA-Verlag AG; WEKA Verlag Ges mbH; WEKA Verlagsgesellschaft fuer aktuelle Publikationen mbH; WEKA Verlagsservice GmbH
U.S. Office(s): WEKA Publishing Inc, Huntington Point, 1077 Bridgeport Ave, Sheldon, CT 06484, United States *Tel:* 203-925-1711

Weltbild Verlag GmbH, see Verlagsgruppe Weltbild GmbH

Verlagsgruppe Weltbild GmbH (Publishing Group Weltbild GmbH)+
Formerly Weltbild Verlag GmbH
Steinerne Furt, 86167 Augsburg
Tel: (0821) 70 04-70 00 *Fax:* (0821) 70 04-17 90
E-mail: info@weltbild.com
Web Site: www.weltbild.com
Key Personnel
President: Carel Halff
Man Dir: Dr Klaus Driever; Werner Ortner; Herbert Zoch
Founded: 1949
Subjects: Animals, Pets, Art, Cookery, Crafts, Games, Hobbies, Environmental Studies, Ethnicity, Fashion, Fiction, Gardening, Plants, Health, Nutrition, History, Nonfiction (General), Philosophy
ISBN Prefix(es): 3-8289; 3-89604
Associate Companies: Verlagsgruppe Droemer Weltbild GmbH & Co KG, Hilblestr 54, 80636 Munich *Tel:* (0821) 92 71-0 *Fax:* (0821) 92 71-168 *E-mail:* info@droemer-weltbild.org *Web Site:* www.droemer-weltbild.de; Bechtermuenz Verlag; Weltbild Verlag
Subsidiaries: Andreas & Dr Mueller Verlagsbuchhandel GmbH; Bauer-Weltbild Media Spzoo, SpK; Booxtra GmbH & Co Kg; DMC Direkt Marketing Consulting GmbH; Olzog Verlag GmbH; Publica-Data-Service GmbH; Sailer Verlag GmbH & Co KG; Weltbildplus Medienvertriebs GmbH & Co KG; Weltbild Verlag Schweiz GmbH
Shipping Address: VVA-Bertelsmann Distribution GmbH, Postfach 7600, 33310 Gutersloh
Warehouse: VVA-Bertelsmann Distribution GmbH, Postfach 7600, 33310 Gutersloh

Weltforum Verlag GmbH+
Subsidiary of Deutscher Wirtschaftsdienst John von Freyend GmbH
Hohenzollernplatz 3, 53173 Bonn
Tel: (0228) 36842430 *Fax:* (0228) 3682439
E-mail: wfv@internationsafrikaforum.de
Cable: DWD
Key Personnel
Dir, Sales, Rights & Permissions: Peter John von Freyend
Publicity: Deonika Langer
Founded: 1963
Subjects: Developing Countries
ISBN Prefix(es): 3-8039

Weltkunst Verlag GmbH+
Nymphenburgerstr 84, 80636 Munich
Tel: (089) 1269900 *Fax:* (089) 12699011
E-mail: info@weltkunstverlag.de
Web Site: www.weltkunstverlag.de
Key Personnel
Contact: Juergen Kleidt
Founded: 1930
Subjects: Art
Parent Company: Axel Springer Verlag AG, Hamburg
Subsidiaries: Antiquitaeten-Zeitung Verlag; Hirmer Verlag GmbH; W B Verlag
Branch Office(s)
Axel Springer Group Inc, 500 Fifth Ave, Suite 2800, New York, NY 10110, United States *Tel:* 212-972-1720 *Fax:* 212-972-1724 *E-mail:* asg-usa@msn.com

Wer liefert was? GmbH (Who Supplies What?)
Normannenweg, 16-20, 20537 Hamburg
Mailing Address: Postfach 100549, 20004 Hamburg
Tel: (040) 25440 0 *Fax:* (040) 25440 100
E-mail: info@wlw.de
Web Site: www.wlw.de
Key Personnel
Man Dir: Andrew Pylyp; Peter Schulze
Marketing Assistant: Gemma Clarke *Tel:* (040) 25440-232 *E-mail:* gemma.clarke@wlw.de

Founded: 1948
Member of Informationsgemeinschaft zur Feststel ung der Verbreitung von Wer bertraegern eV; Verband Deutscher Andressbuchverleger eV; Europaeischen Andressbuchverleger-Verband; Verband Deutscher Wirtschaftsnachschlagewerke eV.
Subjects: Business, Marketing
ISBN Prefix(es): 3-923878
Total Titles: 1 Print; 5 CD-ROM; 1 Online; 1 E-Book
Online services available through F1Z Technik, GBl, Genios, Lexis-Nexis, T-Online.
Parent Company: Eniro AB, Stockholm, Sweden
Branch Office(s)
Wer liefert was? Ges mBH, Inkustr 1-7/6/1 OG, A-3400 Klosterneuburg, Austria *Tel:* (02243) 33765 *Fax:* (02243) 33765-88 *E-mail:* info@wlw.at *Web Site:* www.wlw.at
Wer liefert was? GmbH, succ belge, Louizalaan 65/11, B-1050 Brussels, Belgium *Tel:* (02) 2452228 *Fax:* (02) 2456213 *E-mail:* info@wlw.be *Web Site:* www.wlw.be
Wer liefert was? spol s r o, Sokolska 52, Cz-120 00 Prague-2, Czech Republic *Tel:* (02) 96330-200 *Fax:* (02) 96330-201 *E-mail:* info@wlw.cz *Web Site:* www.wlw.cz
Wer liefert was? doo, Fallerovo setaliste 22, Hr-10000 Zagreb, Croatia *Tel:* (1) 3030500 *Fax:* (1) 3030501 *E-mail:* info@wlw.hr *Web Site:* www.wlw.hr
Wer liefert was? Nederlandse Vestiging, Hoogorddreef 9, Nl-1101 BA Amsterdam, Netherlands *Tel:* (020) 6960706 *Fax:* (020) 6968866 *E-mail:* info@wlw.nl *Web Site:* www.wlw.nl
Wer liefert was? Doo, Gregorciceva ulica 7, SL-3000 Celje, Slovenia *Tel:* (03) 42508 00 *Fax:* (03) 42508 01 *E-mail:* info@wlw.si *Web Site:* www.wlw.si
Wer liefert was AG, Blegistr 15, Ch-6340 Baar-Walterswil, Switzerland *Tel:* (041) 7603438 *Fax:* (041) 7603430 *E-mail:* info@wlw.ch *Web Site:* www.wlw.ch

Werner Verlag GmbH & Co KG+
Karl-Rudolf-Str 172, 40215 Duesseldorf
Mailing Address: Postfach 10 53 54, 40044 Duesseldorf
Tel: (0211) 3 87 98-0 *Fax:* (0211) 3 87 98-11
E-mail: info@werner-verlag.de
Web Site: www.werner.verlag.de
Key Personnel
Publishing Dir: Klaus-Juergen Schneider
Founded: 1945
Subjects: Economics, Engineering (General), Law
ISBN Prefix(es): 3-8041
Parent Company: Wolters Kluwer

Westdeutscher Verlag GmbH+
Abraham-Lincoln-Str 46, 65189 Wiesbaden
Tel: (0611) 78780 *Fax:* (0611) 7878470
Web Site: www.westdeutschervlg.de
Key Personnel
General Manager: Dr Hans-Dieter Haenel
Man Dir: Dr Heinz Weinheimer
Editorial: Annette Kirsch
Rights & Permissions: Angelika Bolisega *E-mail:* angelika.bolisega@bertelsmann.de
Founded: 1947
Books & periodicals which cover all important topics in the social sciences.
Subjects: Communications, Social Sciences, Sociology
ISBN Prefix(es): 3-531
Total Titles: 1,100 Print
Online services available through www.westdeutschervlg.de.
Parent Company: BertelsmannSpringer Science+Business Media
Orders to: VVA Bertelsmann Distribution, Postfach 7777, D-33311 Guetersloh

Westermann Schulbuchverlag GmbH
Georg-Westermann-Allee 66, 38104 Braunschweig
Tel: (0531) 7 08-0 *Fax:* (0531) 70 82 09
E-mail: schulservice@westermann.de
Web Site: www.westermann.de
Telex: 0952841 wbuch d *Cable:* GEWEBUCH
Key Personnel
Editorial, Production: Juergen Grimm
Sales, Publicity: Hartmut Becker
Subjects: Education, History
ISBN Prefix(es): 3-14
Parent Company: Georg Westermann Verlag, Druckerei und Kartographische Anstalt GmbH & Co, (Printing & Publishing Management Co), Brunswick

Verlag Westfaelisches Dampfboot+
Dorotheenstr 26a, 48145 Muenster
Tel: (0251) 608 60 80 *Fax:* (0251) 608 60 20
E-mail: info@dampfboot-verlag.de
Web Site: www.dampfboot-verlag.de
Key Personnel
Editor: Prof H G Thien, PhD; Prof H Wienold, PhD
Founded: 1984
Subjects: Labor, Industrial Relations, Law, Social Sciences, Sociology, Women's Studies
ISBN Prefix(es): 3-924550; 3-929586; 3-89691
Orders to: Prolit Verlagsauslieferung, Siemensstr 13, 35463 Fernwald *Tel:* (0641) 943 93 33 *Fax:* (0641) 943 93 39 *Web Site:* www.prolit.de

Westholsteinische Verlagsanstalt und Verlagsdruckerei Boyens & Co+
Wulf-Isebrand-Platz, 25746 Heide
Tel: (0481) 6886-151; (0481) 6886-152 *Fax:* (0481) 688467
E-mail: buchhandlung@sh-nordsee.de
Web Site: www.sh-nordsee.de
Telex: 28833 boyens d
Key Personnel
Dir: Dipl Kfm Boyens Uwe
Man Dir: Bernd Rachuth
Sales Dir: Reinhard Lipinski
Technical Dir: Heinz Fuhrberg
Founded: 1869
Subjects: Cookery, Literature, Literary Criticism, Essays, Regional Interests
ISBN Prefix(es): 3-8042
Subsidiaries: Brunsbuetteler Zeitung GmbH
Branch Office(s)
Albersdorf
Busum
Marne
Meldorf Wesselburen
St Michaelisdorn

Erich Wewel Verlag+
Heilig-Kreuz Str 16, 86609 Donauwoerth
Tel: (0906) 73-0 *Fax:* (0906) 73-1 77
Web Site: www.klett.de/geschaeftsbereiche/sachbuch_e.html
Key Personnel
Dir & Editorial: Lydia Franzelius
Founded: 1936
Subjects: Philosophy, Religion - Other, Theology
ISBN Prefix(es): 3-87904
Parent Company: Manz Verlag
Orders to: Verlagsgruppe MANZ, Anzingerstr 15, 81671 Munich

Wichern Verlag+
Georgenkirohstra 69-70, 10249 Berlin
Tel: (030) 28 87 48 10 *Fax:* (030) 28 87 48 12
E-mail: info@wichern.de
Web Site: www.wichern.de
Key Personnel
Contact: Dr Elke Rutzenhofer
Founded: 1880
Member of the Stock Exchange of German Booksellers & the Association of Publishers & Bookstores in Berlin-Brandenburg; Specialize in Christian Literature.
Subjects: Biography, History, Religion - Other, Theology
Distributed by BMK Buchauslieferung (Austria); Evangelische Verlagsauslieferung

Wichern-Verlag GmbH+
Bachstr 1-2, 10555 Berlin
Mailing Address: Postfach 210124, 10501 Berlin
Tel: (030) 3915075 *Fax:* (030) 3936047
E-mail: 101711.1207@compuserve.com
Key Personnel
Publisher: Wolfgang Fietkau
Founded: 1982
Member of the Stock Exchange of German Booksellers & the Association of Publishers & Bookstores in Berlin-Brandenburg.
Subjects: History, Religion - Other
ISBN Prefix(es): 3-88981
Divisions: CZV-Verlag
Distributed by BMK Buchauslieferung (Austria); Evangelische Verlagsauslieferung (Switzerland)
Warehouse: Mehringdamm 32-34, 10961 Berlin

Herbert Wichmann Verlag+
Im Weiher 10, 69121 Heidelberg
Mailing Address: Postfach 102869, 69018 Heidelberg
Tel: (06221) 489395 *Fax:* (06221) 489623
E-mail: wichmann@huethig.de
Web Site: www.huethig.de
Key Personnel
Marketing Manager: Anja Freiberger *E-mail:* a.freiberger@huethig.de
Founded: 1889
Subjects: Aeronautics, Aviation, Communications, Earth Sciences, Geography, Geology
ISBN Prefix(es): 3-87907
Number of titles published annually: 11 Print
Parent Company: Huethig GmbH & Co KG

Wiechmann-Verlag Betriebs GmbH
Haupstr 15, 82237 Worthsee
Tel: (08151) 883-0 *Fax:* (08151) 883-48
Key Personnel
Manager: Heidi Wiechmann; Carsta Korhammer
Founded: 1893
ISBN Prefix(es): 3-87908

Wiley-VCH Verlag GmbH+
Pappelallee 3, 69469 Weinheim
Mailing Address: Postfach 101161, 69451 Weinham
Tel: (06201) 606 0 *Fax:* (06201) 606 328
E-mail: info@wiley-vch.de
Web Site: www.wiley-vch.de
Key Personnel
Man Dir: Dr Manfred Antoni *Tel:* (030) 6201-606213 *Fax:* (030) 6201-606206 *E-mail:* mantoni@wiley-vch.de
Personnel: Sven Kroeger *Tel:* (030) 6201-606159 *Fax:* (030) 6201-606192 *E-mail:* skroeger@wiley-vch.de
Production: Axel Eberhard *Tel:* (030) 6201-606260 *Fax:* (030) 6201-606226 *E-mail:* aeberhard@wiley-vch.de
Publisher: Dr Eva E Wille *Tel:* (030) 6201-606272 *Fax:* (030) 6201-606205 *E-mail:* ewille@wiley-vch.de
EDP, Organization & Distribution: Guenther Kloss *Tel:* (030) 6201-606160 *Fax:* (030) 6201-606479 *E-mail:* gkloss@wiley-vch.de
Public Relations: Susan Sills *Tel:* (030) 6201-606222 *Fax:* (030) 6201-606100 *E-mail:* ssills@wiley-vch.de
Marketing & Sales: Juergen Boos *Tel:* (030) 6201-606401 *Fax:* (030) 6201-606223 *E-mail:* jboos@wiley-vch.de
Founded: 1921
Subjects: Biological Sciences, Chemistry, Chemical Engineering, Law, Physical Sciences, Physics, Science (General)

ISBN Prefix(es): 3-527
Total Titles: 1,580 Print
Parent Company: John Wiley & Sons Inc, 605 Third Ave, New York, NY 10158, United States
Subsidiaries: Wilhelm Ernst & Sohn Verlag fuer Architekur und technische Wissenschaft; Chemical Concepts; Verlagsservice Suedwest; Verlag Helvetica Chimica Actc AG

Windmuehle GmbH Verlag und Vertrieb von Medien+
Gosslerstr 22/24, 22587 Hamburg
Mailing Address: Postfach 551080, 22570 Hamburg
Tel: (040) 86 83 07 *Fax:* (040) 866 31 23
E-mail: info@windmuehle-verlag.de
Web Site: www.windmuehle-verlag.de
Key Personnel
Manager: Rita Bolte
Founded: 1981
Further Education in Organization & Management.
Subjects: Education, Management
ISBN Prefix(es): 3-922789
Warehouse: Metzler-Poeschel, Hermann Leins Auslieferungsdienst, Postfach 7, 7408 Kusterdingen *Tel:* (07071) 93530 *Fax:* (07071) 93530

Windpferd Verlagsgesellschaft mbH+
Friesenriederstr 45, 87648 Aitrang
Mailing Address: Postfach 87648, Aitrang
Tel: (08343) 1404 *Fax:* (08343) 1403
E-mail: service@windpferd.de
Web Site: www.windpferd.com
Key Personnel
Manager: Monika Junemann
Founded: 1987
Subjects: Psychology, Psychiatry
ISBN Prefix(es): 3-89385

Rosa Winkel Verlag GmbH+
Kufsteinerstr 12, 10825 Berlin
Mailing Address: Postfach 302949, 10730 Berlin
Tel: (030) 85729295 *Fax:* (030) 85729296
E-mail: rosawinkel@t-online.de
Web Site: www.rosawinkel.de
Key Personnel
Publisher: Egmont Fassbinder
Subjects: Gay & Lesbian, Nonfiction (General)
ISBN Prefix(es): 3-921495; 3-86149

Dr Dieter Winkler+
Katharinastr 37, 44793 Bochum
Mailing Address: Postfach 102665, 44726 Bochum
Tel: (0234) 9650200 *Fax:* (0234) 9650201
E-mail: winkler-verlag.bochum@tonline.de
Web Site: www.winklerverlag.de
Key Personnel
Owner: Dr Dieter Winkler
Founded: 1984
Member of Boersenverein des Dt Buchhandels.
Subjects: Education, History, Nonfiction (General), Regional Interests, Science (General), Social Sciences, Sociology
ISBN Prefix(es): 3-924517; 3-930083; 3-89911
Number of titles published annually: 10 Print
Total Titles: 115 Print

Winklers Verlag Gebrueder Grimm
Alsfelder Str 7, 64289 Darmstadt
Mailing Address: Postfach 111552, 64230 Darmstadt
Tel: (06151) 87 68-0 *Fax:* (06151) 87 68-61
E-mail: service@winklers.de
Web Site: www.winklers.de
Key Personnel
Manager: Heinz Grimm; Ruediger Grimm
Manager, Rights & Permissions: Walter Grimm
Founded: 1902

Subjects: Career Development
ISBN Prefix(es): 3-8045
Shipping Address: Elisabethenstr 34, 64283 Darmstadt

Verlag fuer Wirtschaft & Verwaltung Hubert Wingen GmbH & Co KG+
Alfredistr 32, 45127 Essen
Mailing Address: Postfach 103824, 45038 Essen
Tel: (0201) 22 25 41; (0201) 22 25 42
Fax: (0201) 229660
Key Personnel
Manager: Martha Wingen; Rainer Wingen
Founded: 1958
Subjects: Architecture & Interior Design, Civil Engineering, Law, Public Administration, Real Estate, Religion - Catholic
ISBN Prefix(es): 3-8028; 3-87497
Subsidiaries: Lugerus Verlag GmbH & Co KG

Wirtschaft, Recht & Steuern, see WRS Verlag Wirtschaft, Recht und Steuern GmbH & Co KG

Wison Verlag GmbH
Weyertal 59, 50475 Cologne 41
Tel: (0221) 9440900 *Fax:* (0221) 448911
Telex: 2214310
Key Personnel
Publicity: Michael Wienand
Founded: 1976
Subjects: Economics, Engineering (General)
ISBN Prefix(es): 3-87951

Verlag fuer Wissenschaft & Bildung, see VWB-Verlag fur Wissenschaft & Bildung, Amand Aglaster

Verlag Wissenschaft und Politik, see Verlag Wissenschaft und Politik/Helker Pflug

Verlag Wissenschaft und Politik/Helker Pflug+
Huhnsgasse 39-41, 50676 Cologne
Mailing Address: Postfach 250150, 50517 Cologne
Tel: (221) 219 64 90 *Fax:* (221) 219 64 91
Web Site: www/oei.fu-berlin.de
Key Personnel
Owner & Man Dir: Helker Pflug *E-mail:* helker.pflug@t-online.de
Founded: 1961
Specialize in regional books on Central and Eastern Europe.
Subjects: Asian Studies, Biography, Economics, Ethnicity, Government, Political Science, History, Language Arts, Linguistics, Law, Social Sciences, Sociology
ISBN Prefix(es): 3-8046
Number of titles published annually: 20 Print
Total Titles: 200 Print
Associate Companies: Publishing House Book Shop "MARE BALTICUM"

Wissenschaftliche Buchgesellschaft+
Hindenburgstr 40, 64295 Darmstadt
Mailing Address: Postfach 100110, 64201 Darmstadt
Tel: (06151) 33080 *Fax:* (06151) 3308208
E-mail: service@wbg-darmstadt.de
Web Site: www.wbg-darmstadt.de
Key Personnel
Man Dir: Herbert Lindauer
Chief Reader: Martin Bredol
Rights & Permissions: Friedericke Ludolph
Press: Barbara Gese *Tel:* (06151) 3308-161 *E-mail:* gese@wbg-darmstadt.de
Founded: 1949
Subjects: Archaeology, Art, Economics, Education, History, Language Arts, Linguistics, Law, Literature, Literary Criticism, Essays, Mathematics, Medicine, Nursing, Dentistry, Music, Dance, Philosophy, Psychology, Psychiatry, Religion - Other, Science (General), Social Sciences, Sociology
ISBN Prefix(es): 3-534
Imprints: Forum; Bibliothek Klassischer Texte; Einfuehrungen; Ertraege der Forschung zur Forschung-; Wege der Forschung; Freiherr von Stein Gedaechtnisausgabe
Distributor for AVA B&I (Switzerland); Dr Franz Hain Verlagsauslieferung (Austria)
Book Club(s): Wissenschaftliche Buchgesellschaft

Wissenschaftliche Verlagsgesellschaft mbH+
Birkenwaldstr 44, 70191 Stuttgart
Mailing Address: Postfach 101061, 70009 Stuttgart
Tel: (0711) 2582-0 *Fax:* (0711) 2582-290
E-mail: service@wissenschaftliche-verlagsgesellschaft.de
Web Site: www.dav-buchhandlung.de
Key Personnel
Man Dir: Dr Klaus Brauer; R Hack; Dr Christian Rotta; Dr Thomas Schaber
Rights: Sabine Koerner
Contact: Siegmar Bauer
Founded: 1921
Subjects: Biological Sciences, Medicine, Nursing, Dentistry, Science (General), Pharmacy
ISBN Prefix(es): 3-8047
Parent Company: Deutscher Apotheker Verlag
Subsidiaries: S Hirzel Verlag GmbH & Co; Medpharm Scientific Publishers; Franz Steiner Verlag Wiesbaden GmbH

Wissenschaftlicher Autoren Verlag KG, see Verlag Grundlagen und Praxis GmbH & Co

Wissenschaftsrat
Brohler Str 11, 50968 Cologne
Tel: (0221) 3776-0 *Fax:* (0221) 38 84 40
E-mail: post@wissenschaftsrat.de
Web Site: www.wissenschaftsrat.de/wr
Founded: 1957
ISBN Prefix(es): 3-923203

Verlag Claus Wittal
Fliednerstr 27, 65191 Wiesbaden
Tel: (0611) 502907 *Fax:* (0611) 503021
E-mail: cw@exlibrisart.com
Web Site: www.exlibrisart.com
Founded: 1979
Subjects: Art
ISBN Prefix(es): 3-922835

Friedrich Wittig Verlag GmbH+
Fleethoern 32, 24103 Kiel
Mailing Address: Postfach 3169, 24030 Kiel
Tel: (0431) 5197206 *Fax:* (0431) 5197292 *Cable:* WITTIGVERLAG
Key Personnel
Man Dir: Rainer Thun
Sales: Wolfgang Steinmeier
International Rights: Johannes Keussen
Founded: 1946
Subjects: Art, Biblical Studies, History, Religion - Other
ISBN Prefix(es): 3-8048
Associate Companies: J F Steinkopf Verlag GmbH

Verlag Konrad Wittwer GmbH+
Postfach 105343, 70046 Stuttgart
Tel: (0711) 25 07 0 *Fax:* (0711) 25 07 145
E-mail: wittwer@wittwer.de
Web Site: www.wittwer.de
Key Personnel
Man Dir: Dr Konrad M Wittwer; Konrad P Wittwer; Michael Wittwer
Editorial, Sales: Mr Zwiauer
Founded: 1867
Subjects: Earth Sciences, Mathematics, Nonfiction (General), Science (General)

ISBN Prefix(es): 3-87919
Bookshop(s): Koenigstr 30, 70173 Stuttgart

WLW, see Wer liefert was? GmbH

Wochenschau, *imprint of* Wochenschau Verlag, Dr Kurt Debus GmbH

Wochenschau Verlag, Dr Kurt Debus GmbH+
Adolf-Damaschke Str 103, 65824 Schwalbach-Taunus
Tel: (06196) 8 60 65 *Fax:* (06196) 8 60 60
E-mail: info@wochenschau-verlag.de
Web Site: info@wochenschau-verlag.de
Key Personnel
Publishing Dir: Bernward Debus
Manager & Editor-in-Chief: Ursula Buch
Founded: 1949
Subjects: Education, Geography, Geology, Government, Political Science, History
ISBN Prefix(es): 3-87920
Imprints: Wochenschau

Edition Woetzel Medizinische und Naturwissenschaftliche Verlags und Vertiebsgesellschaft mbH+
Otto-Hahn-Str 49, 63303 Dreieich-Sprendlingen
Tel: (06103) 3 78 95-50 *Fax:* (06103) 3 78 95-80
E-mail: woetzel-buch@t-online.de
Web Site: www.woetzel.de
Key Personnel
Pres: Mrs Irene Woetzel *Tel:* (06103) 3789511
Founded: 1987
STM - Books, health, psychology.
ISBN Prefix(es): 3-925831
Total Titles: 30 Print; 1 CD-ROM; 3 Audio
Bookshop(s): Akademische Buchhandlung Woetzel, Kirchheimer Str 60, 67269 Gruenstadt-Pfalz *Tel:* (0700) 96389352 *Fax:* (0700) 96389353

Gert Wohlfarth GmbH Verlag Fachtechnik & Mercator Verlag, Verlag Puppen & Spielzeug+
Stresemannstr 20-22, 47051 Duisburg
Tel: (0203) 3 05 27-0 *Fax:* (0203) 3 05 27-820
E-mail: info@wohlfarth.de
Web Site: www.wohlfarth.de
Key Personnel
Manager: Uwe Hennig; Frank Wohlfarth
Book Sales Manager: Lothar Koopmann
E-mail: l.koopmann@wohlfarth.de
Contact: Stephen Hasselbach *E-mail:* s.hasselbach@wohlfarth.de
Founded: 1953
Member of Borsenverein des Deutschen Buchhandels.
Subjects: Architecture & Interior Design, Crafts, Games, Hobbies, House & Home, Regional Interests
ISBN Prefix(es): 3-87463
Total Titles: 5 Print
Imprints: Mercator-Verlag; Verlag Puppen & Spielzeug

Wolfgang Arlt u Ute Schiller
Thurneysserstr 2A, 13357 Berlin
Mailing Address: Postfach 650648, 13306 Berlin
Tel: (030) 4622008 *Fax:* (030) 4624936; (030) 4622008
Key Personnel
Owner: Ute Schiller; Wolfgang Arlt
Founded: 1984
Subjects: Asian Studies, History, Sports, Athletics, Travel
ISBN Prefix(es): 3-925067; 3-929772
Divisions: Verlag Ute Schiller
Distributed by Herder (Austria)

Wolf's-Verlag Berlin+
Bergedorferstr 180, 12623 Berlin
Tel: (030) 5675190
Key Personnel
Publishing Manager: Evelyn Wolf
Founded: 1990
Subjects: Fiction, Literature, Literary Criticism, Essays, Travel
ISBN Prefix(es): 3-86164

Wolgang Fietkau
Ernst-Thaelmann Str 152, 14532 Kleinmachnow
Tel: (033203) 71 105 *Fax:* (033203) 71 109
E-mail: fietkau@fietkau.de
Web Site: www.fietkau.de
Founded: 1959
Subjects: Literature, Literary Criticism, Essays, Poetry, Theology
ISBN Prefix(es): 3-87352

Wolke Verlags GmbH+
Niederholfheimer St 45 a-c, 65719 Hofheim
Tel: (06192) 7243 *Fax:* (06192) 952939
E-mail: wolke-verlag@t-online.de
Web Site: www.wolke-verlag.de
Key Personnel
Man Dir: Peter Mischung
Subjects: Music, Dance
ISBN Prefix(es): 3-923997; 3-936000

World Defense Almanach, *imprint of* Moench Verlagsgesellschaft mbH

The World of Books Literaturverlag+
Friedrich-Ebert Str 80, Worms 67549
Tel: (06241) 205352 *Fax:* (06241) 205352
E-mail: info@twobl-online.de
Web Site: www.twobl-online.de
Key Personnel
Contact: Reinhard Becker
Founded: 1981
ISBN Prefix(es): 3-88325

The World Society of Victimology eV+
c/o Prof Dr Kirchhoff, Richard-Wagner Str 101, 41065 Moenchengladbach
Tel: (02161) 186 609 *Fax:* (02161) 186 633
Web Site: www.world-society-victimology.de/
Key Personnel
Professor: Dr Gerd Ferdinand Kirchhoff
Fax: (02161) 186633 *E-mail:* kirchhoff@bigfoot.com
Founded: 1992
Publishing department of World Society of Victimology.
ISBN Prefix(es): 3-929441
Number of titles published annually: 1 Print; 4 Audio

Verlag DAS WORT GmbH
Max-Braun Str 2, 97828 Martheidenfeld-Altfeld
Tel: (09391) 504135 *Fax:* (09391) 504133
E-mail: info@das-wort.com
Web Site: www.das-wort.com; www.universal.spirit.cc
Key Personnel
General Manager: Christine Schulte *Tel:* (09391) 504132
Member of Borsenverein.
Subjects: Health, Nutrition, Human Relations, Philosophy, Religion - Other, Self-Help
ISBN Prefix(es): 3-89201
Total Titles: 68 Print
Branch Office(s)
Universal Life, The Inner Religion, PO Box 651, Gilford, CT 06437, United States *Fax:* 203-457-9693 *Web Site:* www.universal-life.com

WRS Verlag Wirtschaft, Recht und Steuern GmbH & Co KG
Subsidiary of Rudolf Haufe Verlag GmbH & Co KG
Fraunhoferstr 5, 82152 Planegg
Mailing Address: Postfach 1363, 82142 Planegg
Tel: (089) 89 517-0 *Fax:* (089) 89 517-250
Web Site: www.wrs.de *Cable:* WRS VERLAG
Key Personnel
Dir: Martin Laqua; Helmuth Hopfner; Mueller Uwe Renald
Founded: 1973
Subjects: Accounting, Advertising, Business, Computer Science, Economics, House & Home, Law, Management, Marketing, Non-fiction (General)
ISBN Prefix(es): 3-8092
Subsidiaries: STS Standard Tabellen-und Software Verlag

Das Wunderhorn Verlag GmbH
Bergstr 21, 69120 Heidelberg
Tel: (06221) 402428 *Fax:* (06221) 402483
E-mail: info@wunderhorn.de
Web Site: www.wunderhorn.de
Key Personnel
Publisher: Manfred Metzner
Founded: 1978
Subjects: Art, Biography, Fiction, Film, Video, History, Literature, Literary Criticism, Essays, Poetry, Public Administration, Science (General), Women's Studies
ISBN Prefix(es): 3-88423
Distributed by B & Buch und Information AG (Switzerland); Rudi Deuble; Leitner Verlagsvertretungen (Austria); Prolit Buchvertrieb GmbH (Austria & Germany)

Wunderlich Verlag+
Hamburger Str 17, 21453 Reinbek
Mailing Address: Postfach 1349, 21465 Reinbek
Tel: (040) 72 72 0 *Fax:* (040) 72 72 319
Web Site: www.rowohlt.de *Cable:* WUNDERLICHVERLAG
Key Personnel
Man Dir: Helmut Daehne; Alexander Fest; Lutz Kettmann
Editorial Dir: Eva Marie von Hippec
Contact: Eckhard Kloos
Subjects: Art, Biography, Fiction, History, Nonfiction (General)
Parent Company: Rowohlt Verlag GmbH, Postfach 1349, 21453 Reinbek

Wunderlich Taschenbuch (Pocket Book), *imprint of* Rowohlt Verlag GmbH

Fachbuchverlag Armin W Wuth+
Elisabeth-Sebertstr 9, 44534 Luenen
Mailing Address: Postfach 2127, 44511 Luenen
Tel: (02306) 55686; (02306) 18089 *Fax:* (02306) 55686
Key Personnel
President, Rights & Permissions: Armin W Wuth
Vice President: Susanne L Schenk-Wuth
Founded: 1982
Specializes in Stock Exchange.
Subjects: Business, Computer Science, Economics, Medicine, Nursing, Dentistry
ISBN Prefix(es): 3-924018; 3-87082
Parent Company: Wuth-Verlag, Luenen
Subsidiaries: Wuth-Publishing

X-Games, *imprint of* Pearson Education Deutschland GmbH

Xenos Verlagsgesellschaft mbH (Xenos Publishing)+
Affiliate of Lies & Spiel Publishing Co
Am Hehsel 40, 22339 Hamburg
Tel: (040) 538 093-0 *Fax:* (040) 538 60 00; (040) 538 78 63
E-mail: xenos.verlag@t-online.de
Key Personnel
Man Dirs: Erwin Heimberger *Tel:* (040)

PUBLISHERS

GERMANY

53809320; Bjoern Heimberger *Tel:* (040) 53809329
Sales, Germany: Wolfgang Steigner
Sales Manager, Germany: Oliver Draeger *Tel:* (040) 53809344
Production: Meino Dorbandt *Tel:* (040) 53809340 *Fax:* (040) 5387863
Founded: 1975
Children's Book Publishers. Specialize in wall charts, colony & activity books, atlases.
Member of Borsenverein Chamber of Commerce. Also acts as book packager.
Subjects: Nonfiction (General)
ISBN Prefix(es): 3-8212
Number of titles published annually: 180 Print
Parent Company: Frankfurter Allgemeine Zeitung, Hellerhofstr 2-4, Frankfurt am Main
Imprints: Edition Riesenrad; Merit; Tipp Creative
Subsidiaries: Lies & Spiel Hausparty GmbH
Shipping Address: Spedition Rapid, Wilhelm-Iwan-Ring 5, 21035 Hamburg *Tel:* (040) 734130
Warehouse: PVS Fulfillment Service, Werner-Hass-Str 5, 74172 Neckarsulm, Contact: Mr Jurgens *Tel:* (07132) 9690 *Fax:* (07132) 969170

Zambon Verlag+
Leipzigerstr Str 24, 60487 Frankfurt
Tel: (069) 779223 *Fax:* (069) 773054
E-mail: zambon@online.de
Web Site: www.zambonverlag.de
Key Personnel
Publisher: Dr Giuseppe Zambon
Founded: 1974
Subjects: Cookery, Developing Countries, Government, Political Science, History, Poetry, Regional Interests, Travel
ISBN Prefix(es): 3-88975
Bookshop(s): Internationale Buchhandlung, Kaiserstr 55, 60329 Frankfurt *Fax:* (069) 23 02 77

Zebulon Verlag GmbH & Co KG+
Wormserstr 37, 50677 Cologne
Mailing Address: Postfach 250 369, 50519 Cologne
Tel: (0221) 3405620 *Fax:* (0221) 3405622
E-mail: zebulon-koeln@t-online.de
Key Personnel
Man Dir & Publishing Dir: Hajo Leib
Founded: 1992
Subjects: Criminology, Environmental Studies, Government, Political Science, Health, Nutrition, Nonfiction (General), Women's Studies
ISBN Prefix(es): 3-928679
Warehouse: Prolit Verlagsauslifrung GmbH, Siemensstr 16, 35463 Fernwald (Annerod)

Zeitgeist Media GmbH+
Duesseldorfer Str 60, 40545 Duesseldorf
Mailing Address: Postfach 111335, 40513 Duesseldorf
Tel: (0211) 55 62 55 *Fax:* (0211) 57 51 67
E-mail: info@zeitgeistmedia.de
Web Site: www.zeitgeistverlag.de
Key Personnel
Man Dir, Rights & Permissions: Hubert Buecken
E-mail: hb@zeitgeistmedia.de
Founded: 1989
Subjects: Human Relations, Humor, Outdoor Recreation, Travel
ISBN Prefix(es): 3-926224

Verlag Zeitschrift fur Naturforschung
Uhlandstr 11, 72072 Tuebingen
Mailing Address: Postfach 2645, 72016 Tuebingen
Tel: (07071) 31555 *Fax:* (07071) 360571
E-mail: znaturforsch.redaktion@t-online.de
Web Site: www.znaturforsch.com

Key Personnel
Contact: Tamina Greifeld *Tel:* (089) 3541485
E-mail: greifeld@t-online.de
Founded: 1946
Publisher of scientific periodicals.
Subjects: Biological Sciences, Chemistry, Chemical Engineering, Physical Sciences
ISBN Prefix(es): 3-921015
Total Titles: 3 Print
Branch Office(s)
Beuthener Str 17, 55131 Mainz *Tel:* (6131) 573276 *Fax:* (6131) 571061

Zeller Verlag GmbH & Co
Postfach 1949, 49009 Osnabrueck
Tel: (0541) 404590 *Fax:* (0541) 41255
E-mail: zeller@zeller.os.eunet.de
Web Site: www.militaria-biblio.de
Key Personnel
Manager: Wolfram Zeller; Thorsten Zeller
Founded: 1964
Subjects: Archaeology, Art, History, Language Arts, Linguistics, Law, Military Science, Philosophy, Religion - Other
ISBN Prefix(es): 3-7648; 3-535; 3-920240
Subsidiaries: BiblioVerlag

Zentralantiquariat Leipzig GmbH Buchhandlung
Talstr 29, 04103 Leipzig
Tel: (0341) 2161717 *Fax:* (0341) 9602819
E-mail: info@zvab.com
Web Site: www.zvab.com
Key Personnel
Manager: Dr Georg Thaler *Tel:* (03471) 2761717; Hans-Rainer Arnold
Specialize in antiquarian books.
Subjects: Mathematics, Philosophy
Associate Companies: Antiquariat Talstr/Biuderstr, 04103 Leipzig *Tel:* (0341) 2155851 *Fax:* (0341) 2155852; Dresdener Antiquariat, Bautzener Str 11, 01099 Dresden; Dresdener Buecherfundus, Augsburgerstr 79-81, 01277 Dresden *Tel:* (0351) 3105759; Musik-Antiquariat, Thomaskirchhof 15, 04109 Leipzig *Tel:* (0341) 9604863

Verlag Clemens Zerling+
Graefestr 26a, 10967 Berlin
Tel: (030) 6929278 *Fax:* (030) 6929278
Key Personnel
Man Dir, Editorial: Clemens Zerling
Sales: Daniela Moeser
Founded: 1979
Subjects: Anthropology, Astrology, Occult, Biography, History, Religion - Other
ISBN Prefix(es): 3-88468
Associate Companies: Edition Weber, Berlin

Verlag Andreas Zettner KG+
Hofweg 12, 97209 Veitshoechheim
Tel: (0931) 91970 *Fax:* (0931) 960 097 *Cable:* ZETTNER WURZBURG
Key Personnel
Man Dir: Andreas Zettner
Rights: Dr Doris Sitting
Founded: 1955
Subjects: Fiction
ISBN Prefix(es): 3-87931

ZfKf-Zentrum fur Kulturforschung, see ARCult Media

Verlag im Ziegelhaus Ulrich Gohl+
Pflasteraeckerstr 20, 70186 Stuttgart
Tel: (0711) 46 63 63 *Fax:* (0711) 46 13 41
E-mail: redaktiousbuero.stuttgart.gohl@n.zgs.de
Key Personnel
Owner: Ulrich Gohl
Founded: 1984
Subjects: History

ISBN Prefix(es): 3-925440
Number of titles published annually: 3 Print

Ziethen-Panorama Verlag GmbH+
Flurweg 15, 53902 Bad Mueusterzfel
Tel: (02253) 6047 *Fax:* (02253) 6746
E-mail: mail@ziethen-panoramaverlag.de
Web Site: www.ziethen-panoramaverlag.de
Key Personnel
Owner: Horst Ziethen
Founded: 1992
Subjects: Foreign Countries, Regional Interests, Travel
ISBN Prefix(es): 3-921268; 3-929932
Parent Company: Ziethen Farbdruckmedien GmbH
Warehouse: Ziethen-Panorama Verlag GmbH, Unter Buschweg 17, 50999 Cologne

Zodiaque, *imprint of* Verlag Schnell und Steiner GmbH

ZS Verlag Zabert Sandmann GmbH+
Barerstr 9, 80333 Munich
Tel: (089) 548 25 15-0 *Fax:* (089) 550 18 19
Web Site: www.zsverlag.de; www.zabertsandmann.de
Telex: 114 Jekret
Key Personnel
Man Dir: Dr Friedrich-Karl Sandmann; Dr Hans-Peter Uebleis
International Rights: Petra Schwarz
Licensing Manager: Dr Katrin Bernhard
Licensing: Dr Ulrike Prechtl-Froehlich
Editorial Manager: Kathrin Ullerich
Editorial: Ute Kern; Angelika Schulz
Sales Manager: Markus Klose
Press: Claudia Limmer
Founded: 1983
Subjects: Cookery, Health, Nutrition
ISBN Prefix(es): 3-924678; 3-932023
Parent Company: Rolf Heyne
Warehouse: Schleissheimer Str 106, 85748 Garching-Hochbrueck
Orders to: Schleissheimer Str 106, 85748 Garching-Hochbrueck

Zsolnay, *imprint of* Carl Hanser Verlag

Zweiburgen-Verlag GmbH
Mallaustr 74, 68199 Mannheim *Tel:* (0621) 8769432 *Fax:* (0621) 8769433
Mailing Address: Postfach 100954, 69449 Weinheim
Tel: (06201) 87694-32 *Fax:* (06201) 87694-33
Key Personnel
Manager: Herr Apfel
Founded: 1951
ISBN Prefix(es): 3-921209

Zweimuehlen Verlag GmbH+
Kufsteinerstr 8, 81679 Munich
Tel: (089) 982031 *Fax:* (089) 9827104 *Cable:* FUEI MUHLEN VERLAG
Key Personnel
Dir, Editorial, Rights & Permissions: Karl Pramendorfer
Publicity: Friederike Weiss-Fuereder
Founded: 1928
Subjects: History, Nonfiction (General), Travel
ISBN Prefix(es): 3-85339
Subsidiaries: Welsermuehl Verlag GmbH
Branch Office(s)
Verlag Welsermueh, Austria
Distributor for Neptun Verlag

Zweipunkt Verlag K Kaiser KG+
Gestuet Rossbacher Hof, 64711 Erbach
Tel: (06102) 61108 *Fax:* (06102) 63422
Key Personnel
Partner, Rights & Permissions: Kurt Kaiser

Subjects: Crafts, Games, Hobbies
ISBN Prefix(es): 3-88168

Ghana

General Information

Capital: Accra
Language: English
Religion: About 42% Christian, remainder follow traditional beliefs
Population: 16.2 million
Bank Hours: 0830-1400 Monday-Thursday; 0830-1500 Friday
Shop Hours: 0830-1230, 1330-1730 Monday, Tuesday, Thursday, Friday; 0830-1330 Wednesday & Saturday
Currency: 100 pesawas = 1 new cedi
Export/Import Information: No tariffs on books; advertising matter over 1 kg gross weight 50 percent. Import license required, but single copies of books under Open General License. Levy charged on import lecenses required. Credit terms not permitted.
Copyright: UCC, Berne, Florence (see Copyright Conventions, pg xi)

Adaex Educational Publications Ltd+
No PLT 1 BLK A, Oforikrom, AK 188 Kumasi
Tel: (024) 367145
E-mail: epublication@yahoo.com
Key Personnel
Publisher: Asare Konadu Yamoah
 E-mail: asareyamoah@onebox.com
Founded: 1995
Member of Ghana Book Publishers Association
Also acts as printer, book & literary agent.
Subjects: Cookery, Fiction, Health, Nutrition, History, How-to
ISBN Prefix(es): 9988-573
Number of titles published annually: 5 Print
Total Titles: 37 Print

The Advent Press+
PO Box 0102, Osu Post Office, Osu, Osu-Accra
Tel: (021) 777861; (021) 775327 *Fax:* (021) 774338; (021) 2119
Telex: 2119 *Cable:* ADVENT GH
Key Personnel
General Manager: E C Tetteh
Founded: 1937
Subjects: Religion - Other
ISBN Prefix(es): 9964-962

Adwinsa Publications (Ghana) Ltd+
PO Box M 18, Accra
Tel: (021) 221654; (021) 21577
Key Personnel
Man Dir, Rights & Permissions: Kwabena Amponsah
General Manager & Production: Kofi Kyere-Amponsah
Accountant & Sales: Kwadwo Oppong-Kyeremeh
Editorial & Personnel: Grace Amponsah
Founded: 1977
Member of Ghana Book Publishers Association.
ISBN Prefix(es): 9964-955; 9964-975
Branch Office(s)
Adwinsa Bookstand (Eredec Hotel), PO Box 845, Koforidua
Bookshop(s): Adwinsa Distribution Agency Ltd, Adwinsa House (North Legon), PO Box 92, Legon
Orders to: Adwinsa Distribution Agency Ltd, PO Box M18, Accra

Afram Publications, *imprint of* Afram Publications (Ghana) Ltd

Afram Publications (Ghana) Ltd+
PO Box M18, Accra
Tel: (021) 412561; (021) 024 278844; (021) 024 278855
E-mail: aframpub@punchgh.com
Telex: 217 sic accra *Cable:* AFRAMBOOKS
Key Personnel
Man Dir, Rights & Permissions: Eric Ofei
 E-mail: ericofei@yahoo.co.uk
Marketing Manager: Emmanuel A Manful
Editorial Manager: John Oppong-Mensah
Founded: 1974
Member of Ghana Book Publishers Association & Afro-Asian Book Council.
Subjects: Fiction, Nonfiction (General)
ISBN Prefix(es): 9964-70
Imprints: Afram Publications
Distributed by African Books Collective

Africa Christian Press+
PO Box 30, Achimota
Tel: (021) 244147; (021) 244148 *Fax:* (021) 220271; (021) 668115
E-mail: acpbooks@ghana.com
Key Personnel
General Manager: Richard Crabbe
Deputy General Manager: Mork Eiwuley
Founded: 1964
Member of Ghana Publishers Association; Specialize in Christian literature & children's books.
Subjects: Biography, Fiction, Nonfiction (General), Religion - Other
ISBN Prefix(es): 9964-87
Number of titles published annually: 12 Print
Total Titles: 110 Print
Imprints: Children's Activity Series; Student's Series
Branch Office(s)
50 Loxwood Ave, Worthing, Sussex BN14 7RA UK, United Kingdom
U.S. Office(s): 130 N Bloomingdale Rd, Suite 101, Bloomingdale, IL 60108, United States

Anowuo Educational Publications+
PO Box 3918, Accra
Tel: (021) 669961 *Cable:* ANOWUO PUBS, ACCRA
Key Personnel
Publisher: S A Konadu
Sales Manager: Yamoah Konadu
Founded: 1966
Member of Ghana Publishers Association; also acts as copyright brokers.
Subjects: Fiction, History, How-to, Poetry, Regional Interests, Science (General)
ISBN Prefix(es): 9964-79
Branch Office(s)
PO Box 1, Asamang Ashanti Region
Showroom(s): 2R McCarthy Hill, PO Box 3918, Accra

Asempa Publishers+
PO Box GP919, Accra
Tel: (021) 221706; (021) 233084 *Fax:* (021) 776725; (021) 233130; (021) 235140
E-mail: asempa@ghana.com
Key Personnel
General Manager: Rev Emmanuel Borlabi Bortey
Production: Sarah Apronti
Finance: Stephen K Darku
International Rights: E B Bortey; S Apronti
Founded: 1970
Member of Ghana Book Publishers Association.
Subjects: Biblical Studies, Biography, Fiction, Music, Dance, Nonfiction (General), Poetry, Religion - Protestant, Religion - Other, Social Sciences, Sociology, Theology
ISBN Prefix(es): 9964-78
Number of titles published annually: 20 Print
Total Titles: 112 Print

Parent Company: Christian Council of Ghana
Imprints: IBRA (Ghana)

Beginners Publishers+
PO Box C785, Cantonments, Accra
Tel: (021) 503040 *Fax:* (051) 772642 Attn: Beginners Publishers
Telex: 3047 Attn: Beginners Publishers
Key Personnel
President & Editor: Nana Opoku Ankama-Fofie
Publisher & Author: Akosua Gyamfuaa-Fofie
Vice President: Kwabena Owusu-Peprah
Founded: 1988
Subjects: English as a Second Language, Fiction, Language Arts, Linguistics, Mathematics, Romance
ISBN Prefix(es): 9964-90; 9964-995
Associate Companies: Hope & Faith Agencies, Box C 1096, Cantonments, Accra
Branch Office(s)
Cape Coast
Sunyani
Tamale
Tema
Distributed by Makna Publications
Distributor for Makna Publications; Speedy Variety Publications
Showroom(s): House No 020, North Suntresu, Kumasi; House No Wab-34 TI; New Ashaley Botwe, Madina, Accra
Bookshop(s): Adwen Pa, Madina, Winners & Nsempii-Kumasi; Afram, Box N18, Accra; Catholic Bookshop, Kumasi; Dorilad Bookshop, Abeka, Accra; Gyawu Bookshop, Tamale; Legon Bookshop, Box 1, Legon, Accra; Makna, Box 9820 Airport, Accra; Methodist Bookshops, Accra, Kumasi, Cape-Coast; Obrapa Bookshop, Tema; Omari Bookshop, Labone, Accra; Presbyterian Bookshops, Accra, Kumasi, Cape-Coast, Swedru; Speedy Variety Agencies Ltd, Box 5337, Accra; Topman Book Center, Accra
Warehouse: Box BP 313, Bohyen-Kumasi

Black Mask Ltd+
PO Box 252, Fante New Town, Kumasi
Tel: (021) 234577 *Fax:* (021) 231431 *Cable:* BML
Key Personnel
Man Dir: Yaw Owusu Asante
Publicity: Kwasi Asante
Rights & Permissions: Opia-Mensah Kumah
Founded: 1979
Subjects: Cookery, Drama, Theater, Economics, Education, Social Sciences, Sociology
ISBN Prefix(es): 9964-960
Branch Office(s)
Accra
Freetown, Sierra Leone

BP, see Beginners Publishers

BRRI, see Building & Road Research Institute (BRRI)

Building & Road Research Institute (BRRI)
PO Box 40, Kumasi
Tel: (051) 60064; (051) 60065 *Fax:* (051) 60080
E-mail: brri@ghana.com
Web Site: www.csir.org.gh/brri.html
Key Personnel
Dir: Dr K Amoah-Mensah
Founded: 1952
Subjects: Architecture & Interior Design, Civil Engineering, Computer Science, Earth Sciences, Real Estate, Technology, Transportation
ISBN Prefix(es): 9964-86; 9964-977
Parent Company: Council for Scientific & Industrial Research (CSIR)

Bureau of Ghana Languages
PO Box 1851, Accra

Tel: (021) 64130; (021) 65194
Key Personnel
Dir, Rights & Permissions: J N Nanor
Sales Manager: J C Abbey
Founded: 1951
Also acts as a Translation Agency/Association.
Subjects: Biography, Drama, Theater, Fiction, Poetry, Science (General)
ISBN Prefix(es): 9964-2
Branch Office(s)
PO Box 177, Tamale, Northern Region

Children's Activity Series, *imprint of* Africa Christian Press

Educational Press & Manufacturers Ltd+
PO Box 4434, Kumasi
Tel: (051) 5003; (051) 5845 *Fax:* (051) 227572
Telex: 2236 gh
Key Personnel
International Rights: George Koduah
Founded: 1979
Subjects: Fiction
ISBN Prefix(es): 9964-89
Subsidiaries: Knowledge Publishing & Trading Ltd

Educational Publishers Ltd
PO Box 9184, Accra-KIA
Tel: (021) 220395 *Fax:* (021) 227572
Telex: 2236GH *Cable:* EDU PRESS
ISBN Prefix(es): 9964-953
Parent Company: Halko Book & Educational Assories Ltd

Ekab Business Ltd+
PO Box 6262, Accra-North
Tel: (021) 225318 *Cable:* Emmapus Accra
Key Personnel
Dir: Emmanuel K Nsiah
Founded: 1978
Company has reprint arrangements in Ghana for Oxford University Press publications.
Subjects: Education
ISBN Prefix(es): 9964-91; 9964-73
Bookshop(s): Mayan Book Centre, PO Box 6173, Accra

EPP Books Services+
PMB TUC Post Office, La Education Centre Bldg, Behind Ghana Trade Fair Centre, La, Accra
Mailing Address: PO Box TF 490, La, Accra
Tel: (021) 778853; (021) 778347 *Fax:* (021) 779099
E-mail: epp@africaonline.com.gh
Web Site: www.eppbooks.com
Key Personnel
Executive Dir: Gibrine Adam
Founded: 1991
Also acts as bookseller & stationery distributor.
Subjects: Accounting, Mathematics, Social Sciences, Sociology
ISBN Prefix(es): 9964-997
Associate Companies: Excellent Publishing & Printing; Staples Systems Ghana Ltd
Foreign Rep(s): Epp Books Services (Nigeria)
Foreign Rights: Sterling Publishers Pvt (India)
Bookshop(s): EPP Bookshop, Accra-Nsawam Rd, Achimota-Accra, Mutawakilu Adam *Tel:* (021) 408885 *Fax:* (021) 779099 *E-mail:* epp@africaonline.com.gh *Web Site:* www.eppbooks.com; EPP Bookshop, PO Box TF 490, La, Accra, Koforidua *Tel:* (021) 779099 *E-mail:* epp@africaonline.com.gh *Web Site:* www.eppbooks.com; EPP Bookshop, Behind Kumasi Polytechnic, Amakom-Kumasi, Kumasi, Constance Nuamah *Tel:* (051) 23367 *Fax:* (021) 779099 *E-mail:* epp@africaonline.com.gh *Web Site:* www.eppbooks.com

Frank Publishing Ltd+
PO Box M414, Ministry Branch Post Office, Accra
Tel: (21) 240711 *Cable:* KNOWLEDGE
Key Personnel
Man Dir, Editorial, Production: Francis K Dzokoto
Sales, Public Relations: Moses K Dzokoto
Founded: 1976
Specialize in school textbooks & typesetting for other publishing houses. Member of Ghana Publishers Association & Ghana Association of Book Editors.
Subjects: Economics, English as a Second Language, Government, Political Science, Religion - Catholic, Religion - Protestant, Religion - Other
ISBN Prefix(es): 9964-959

Ghana Academy of Arts & Sciences+
PO Box M32, Accra
Tel: (021) 772002; (021) 772032 *Fax:* (021) 777655
E-mail: gaas@ghastinet.gn.apc.org
Key Personnel
President: D A Bekoe
Founded: 1959
Subjects: Art, Literature, Literary Criticism, Essays, Music, Dance, Science (General)
ISBN Prefix(es): 9964-90; 9964-969; 9964-950

Ghana Institute of Linguistics Literacy & Bible Translation (GILLBT)
PO Box 7271, Accra North
Tel: (021) 777525
Founded: 1962
Subjects: Anthropology, Biblical Studies, English as a Second Language, Environmental Studies, Health, Nutrition, Language Arts, Linguistics, Religion - Protestant, Women's Studies
ISBN Prefix(es): 9964-92; 9988-7525

Ghana Publishing Corporation
PO Box 124, Accra
Tel: (021) 664338 *Fax:* (021) 664330
E-mail: asspcom@africaonline.com.gh
Web Site: www.africaonline.com/assembly/intro.html
Telex: Publishing Tema
Key Personnel
Man Dir: F K Nyarko
General Manager (Publishing Division): K B Arkorful
Editor-in-Chief: J K Fuachie-Sobreh
Rights & Permissions: Miss O Agbenyega
Sales Manager: W D Opare
Production: Fred Odametey
Publicity: Fidelis D Adzakey
Founded: 1965
Subjects: Biography, Ethnicity, Fiction, History, Language Arts, Linguistics, Nonfiction (General), Poetry, Science (General), Social Sciences, Sociology, Technology
ISBN Prefix(es): 9964-1
Parent Company: Ghana Publishing Corporation, Head Office, PO Box 4348, Accra
Branch Office(s)
Accra
Bolgatanga
Cape Coast
Ho
Hohoe
Koforidua
Sunyani
Swedru
Tamale
Wa
Sales Office(s): PO Box 3632, Accra

Ghana Standards Board, see GSB (Ghana Standards Board)

Ghana Universities Press (GUP)+
PO Box 2419, Accra
Tel: (021) 22532
Telex: Univpress Accra
Key Personnel
Dir & Senior Editor: K M Ganu
Business Manger: J K Bosomtwe
Founded: 1962
Member of Ghana Book Publishers Association, International Association of Scholarly Publishers, African Books Collective.
Subjects: Agriculture, Biological Sciences, Communications, Government, Political Science, History, Language Arts, Linguistics, Medicine, Nursing, Dentistry, Social Sciences, Sociology
ISBN Prefix(es): 9964-3
Associate Companies: African Books Collective Ltd, Oxford

GILLBT, see Ghana Institute of Linguistics Literacy & Bible Translation (GILLBT)

Goodbooks Publishing Co+
PO Box 10416, Accra North
Tel: (021) 665629 *Fax:* (021) 302993
E-mail: allgoodbooks@hotmail.com
Key Personnel
Contact: Alberta Asirifi; Mary Asirifi
Founded: 1992
ISBN Prefix(es): 9964-88
Bookshop(s): D803/4 Granville Ave, Okaishie, Accra

GSB (Ghana Standards Board)
PO Box M245, Accra
Tel: (021) 500065; (021) 500066 *Fax:* (021) 500092; (021) 500231
Telex: 2545 MINCOM Attn GSB
ISBN Prefix(es): 9964-990

IBRA (Ghana), *imprint of* Asempa Publishers

Kwamfori Publishing Enterprise+
Dansoman-Estates, Accra
Mailing Address: PO Box 1325, Accra
Key Personnel
Proprietor: Ofori Akuamoah
Founded: 1991
Subjects: Economics, English as a Second Language, Humor
ISBN Prefix(es): 9964-987

Manhil Publications, *imprint of* Paul Ntem Maanoh

Moxon Paperbacks
PO Box M 160, Osu
Tel: (021) 665397
Key Personnel
Man Dir: James Moxon
Founded: 1967
Subjects: Ethnicity, Fiction, History, Nonfiction (General), Poetry, Travel
ISBN Prefix(es): 9964-954
Branch Office(s)
28 Corve St, Dudlow, Shropshire SY8 IDA, United Kingdom
Bookshop(s): The Atlas Bookshop

Osimpam Educational Books
PO Box 1851, Accra
Key Personnel
Man Editor: Armah Asiedu
Founded: 1991
ISBN Prefix(es): 9964-994

Paul Ntem Maanoh+
PO Box 548, Madina-Accra
Tel: (021) 508251 *Fax:* (021) 669078

GHANA

Key Personnel
President & Author: Paul N Maanoh
Vice President: Hilda Maanoh
Editor & Author: Asuma Karikari
Author: Ferkah Ahenkorah; George Amable; Chris Darkwaa
Founded: 1986
Member of Ghana Bible Society & also a distributor of its wares. Dealers in printing materials.
Subjects: English as a Second Language, Fiction, Literature, Literary Criticism, Essays
ISBN Prefix(es): 9964-91; 9964-999
Parent Company: Manhil Publications
Associate Companies: Manhil Enterprise
Imprints: Manhil Publications
Branch Office(s)
Sunyani
Kumasi
Accra
Distributed by Gospel Tracts Information (USA)
Bookshop(s): Manhil Publications, PO Box 1075, Madina-Accra
Orders to: Manhil Publications, PO Box 1075, Madina-Accra

Quick Service Books Ltd+
PO Box 15403, Accra North
Tel: (021) 224236
Key Personnel
Man Dir: Isaac Mensah Dankyi
Editor: D A Addo
Marketing Manager: Kwasi Saka-Dankyi
Founded: 1986
Subjects: Education
ISBN Prefix(es): 9964-90; 9964-970; 9964-985

Sam Woode Ltd+
House No 274/3, Dr Nanka Bruce Rd off Link Rd, Laterbiokorshie
Mailing Address: PO Box 12719, Accra North
Tel: (021) 220257 *Fax:* (021) 662210
Telex: 2687 *Cable:* SAM WOODE ACCRA
Key Personnel
Executive Chairman: Kwesi Sam-Woode
Marketing Coordinator: Vincent Owusu-Ansah
Production Manager: Kweku Esaah Sam-Woode
Pre-Press Editor: Pamela Woode
Founded: 1986
Member of Ghana Book Publishers Association.
Subjects: Agriculture, Career Development, English as a Second Language, Mathematics, Physical Sciences, Science (General)
ISBN Prefix(es): 9964-979
Imprints: SWL Books
Distributed by West African Book Publishers Ltd (Nigeria)
Distributor for Annick Press Ltd (Canada, West African Countries only)
Bookshop(s): No F768 Kaneshie Market, Accra

Sedco, *imprint of* Sedco Publishing Ltd

Sedco Publishing Ltd+
Sedco House, Labon St, Off Ring Rd Central North Ridge, Accra
Mailing Address: PO Box 2051, Accra
Tel: (021) 221332 *Fax:* (021) 220107
E-mail: sedco@africaonline.com.gh
Telex: 2456
Key Personnel
Man Dir: Courage Kwami Segbawu
Marketing Dir: Frank Segbawu
Founded: 1975
Educational materials for all levels.
Subjects: Agriculture, Biological Sciences, Chemistry, Chemical Engineering, Education, English as a Second Language, Fiction, History, Law, Mathematics, Physics, Science (General)
ISBN Prefix(es): 9964-72
Number of titles published annually: 5 Print
Total Titles: 145 Print

Parent Company: Pearson Plc
Imprints: Sedco

Student's Series, *imprint of* Africa Christian Press

Sub-Saharan Publishers+
9 Goodwill Rd, Accra
Mailing Address: PO Box 358, Legon-Accra
Tel: (021) 233371 *Fax:* (021) 233371
E-mail: sub-saharan@ighmail.com
Key Personnel
Man Dir: Akoss Ofori-Mensah
Founded: 1992
Member of Ghana Publishers Association.
Subjects: Education, Environmental Studies, African Literature
Total Titles: 30 Print
Distributed by African Books Collective
Orders to: Sub-Saharan Publishers, PO Box 1176, Cantonments, Accra

SWL Books, *imprint of* Sam Woode Ltd

Unimax Macmillan Ltd
42 Ring Rd South, Industrial Area, Accra North
Mailing Address: PO Box 10722, Accra North
Tel: (021) 227 443; (021) 223 709 *Fax:* (021) 225 215
E-mail: info@unimacmillan.com
Web Site: www.macmillan-africa.com; www.unimacmillan.com
Key Personnel
Man Dir: Edward Addo
Marketing Manager: Abubakari Wumbei
Founded: 1985
International education division of Macmillan Publishers Ltd.
Subjects: Agriculture, Environmental Studies, Mathematics, Science (General)
ISBN Prefix(es): 9988-553
Parent Company: Macmillan Publishers Ltd
Branch Office(s)
Unicorn House, Prempah 11 St, PO Box KS, 1169 Kumasi, Manager: Edward Udzu *Tel:* (051) 39284; (051) 39286 *Fax:* (051) 39285
Showroom(s): Unicorn House, Prempah 11 St, PO Box KS, 1169 Kumasi, Manager: Edward Udzu *Tel:* (051) 39284; (051) 39286 *Fax:* (051) 39285
Warehouse: Unicorn House, Prempah 11 St, PO Box KS, 1169 Kumasi, Manager: Edward Udzu *Tel:* (051) 39284; (051) 39286 *Fax:* (051) 39285

Waterville Publishing House+
Thorpe Rd, Accra
Mailing Address: PO Box 195, Accra
Tel: (021) 663124; (021) 662415 *Fax:* (021) 665594; (021) 662415 *Cable:* BOOKS ACCRA
Key Personnel
Man Dir: H W O Okai
Founded: 1963
Subjects: Biography, Ethnicity, Fiction, History, Nonfiction (General), Poetry, Religion - Other, Science (General), Social Sciences, Sociology
ISBN Prefix(es): 9964-5
Parent Company: Presbyterian Book Depot Ltd
Divisions: Presbyterian Press

Woeli Publishing Services
PO Box K601, Accra-New Town
Tel: (021) 227182; (021) 229294 *Fax:* (021) 777098; (021) 229294
E-mail: woeli@libr.ug.edu.gh; asempa@ghana.com
Key Personnel
Publisher: Mr Woeli Dekutsey
Founded: 1984

BOOK

Member of the Ghana Book Publishers Association.
Subjects: Drama, Theater, Fiction, Poetry, Women's Studies
ISBN Prefix(es): 9964-90; 9964-970; 9964-978
Total Titles: 6 Print
Orders to: African Books Collective, 27 Park End St, Oxford OX1 1HU, United Kingdom

World Literature Project
PO Box 290, Legon
Tel: (022) 2119 *Fax:* (022) 2119
Key Personnel
Publisher: Friedolin Ankrama-Afarie
Founded: 1991
Specialize in dissemination of vital information on better health, welfare, new books, literature, etc.
Subjects: Advertising, Biblical Studies, Child Care & Development, Cookery, Developing Countries, Film, Video, Health, Nutrition, How-to, Human Relations, Humor, Marketing, Medicine, Nursing, Dentistry, Mysteries, Outdoor Recreation, Psychology, Psychiatry, Publishing & Book Trade Reference, Religion - Other, Securities, Self-Help, Women's Studies
ISBN Prefix(es): 9964-986

Greece

General Information

Capital: Athens
Language: Greek (official), English, French
Religion: Predominately Greek Orthodox
Population: 10.6 million
Bank Hours: 0800-1400 Monday-Friday
Shop Hours: Vary. Generally 0800-1500 Monday, Wednesday, Saturday; 0800-1400, 1730-2030 Tuesday, Thursday, Friday
Currency: 100 Eurocents = 1 Euro; 340.750 Greek drachmas = 1 Euro
Export/Import Information: Member of the European Economic Community. No tariff on non-Greek books except children's picture books (free from EEC). Foreign-language advertising catalogues & other advertising matter free from EEC. Children's picture books & advertising matter subject to stamp duty, and books & advertising subject to small additional taxes, University Tax & Bank Fee, Contribution for Farmer's Social Assistance. Only books printed in Greek need import license; all advertising matter other than price lists require license. No special exchange controls. 4% VAT on books.
Copyright: UCC, Berne, Florence (see Copyright Conventions, pg xi)

Akritas+
24 Efessou, 17121 N Smyrni, Athens
Tel: (01) 9334685 *Fax:* (01) 9311436
Key Personnel
Contact: Maria Kokkinou
Founded: 1979
Subjects: Art, Child Care & Development, Cookery, History, Human Relations, Psychology, Psychiatry, Religion - Other, Theology
ISBN Prefix(es): 960-7006; 960-328

Alamo Hellas+
6, Sarantaporou St, 111 44 Athens
Tel: (01) 2280027 *Fax:* (01) 2280027
Key Personnel
President: Dr Ath I Delikastopoulos
Subjects: Biblical Studies, Cookery, English as a Second Language, Gardening, Plants, Law, Philosophy, Religion - Catholic, Religion - Is-

lamic, Religion - Jewish, Religion - Protestant, Theology, Travel
Associate Companies: Alpha Delta

Alexiadou Vefa Editions+
Leoniodu 4, 14452 Metmorphosis, Athens
Tel: (01) 2848086; (031) 245151 *Fax:* (01) 2849689; (01) 2846984
E-mail: vefaeditions@ath.forthnet.gr
Web Site: www.addgr.com/comp/vefa
Key Personnel
Marketing & Sales Dir: Alexia Alexiadou
Founded: 1979
Member of IACP.
Subjects: Cookery
ISBN Prefix(es): 960-85018
Associate Companies: Vefa's House, Alba Editions
Branch Office(s)
16, Nevrokopiou Str, 55226 Thessaloniui
Distributed by Howell Press (USA & Canada); Tower Books (Australia)
Distributor for Sterling Editions (USA)
Bookshop(s): 1, Kresnas St, 14123 Ly Kovrisi, Athens

Anemonylos, *imprint of* Ilias Kambanas Publishing Organization, SA

Anixis Publications+
23 Viltanioti Str, Kifisia, 145 64 Athens
Tel: (01) 6205436 *Fax:* (01) 8079357
Key Personnel
International Rights: Mr Aristotelis Papadimitriou
E-mail: apapa@hol.gr
Founded: 1993
Subjects: Child Care & Development, Geography, Geology, History
Total Titles: 105 Print

Apostoliki Diakonia tis Ekklisias tis Hellados
One Iassiou St, 115 21 Athens
Tel: (010) 7272331 *Fax:* (010) 7238149
E-mail: apostoliki-diakonia@ath.forthnet.gr
Web Site: www.apostoliki-diakonia.gr
Key Personnel
Chief Executive: Archim Agathaggelos Charamantidis
Editorial Manager, Rights & Permissions: Evangelos Lekkos
Production: Socrates Mavrogonatos
Founded: 1936
Subjects: Biblical Studies, Film, Video, History, Music, Dance, Religion - Other, Social Sciences, Sociology, Theology
ISBN Prefix(es): 960-315
Bookshop(s): 2 Dragatsaniou St, 10559 Athens *Tel:* (010) 3228637; (010) 3310977 *Fax:* (010) 3228637; 9-A Ethnikis Aminis & Tsimiski Str, 54621 Thessaloniki *Tel:* (0310) 275126 *Fax:* (0310) 278559; 143 Riga Ferreou Str, Filopimenos, Patra *Tel:* (0610) 223 110 *Fax:* (0610) 223 110

Aquarius
One Notara, 10683 Athens
Tel: (361) 7360
ISBN Prefix(es): 960-7002

D I Arsenidis Publications
57, Akademias Str, 10679 Athens
Tel: (01) 36-29-538; (01) 36-33923 *Fax:* (01) 36-18-707
Web Site: www.arsenidis.gr/NavFrame_en.htm
Key Personnel
Man Dir: John Arsenides
Subjects: Biography, History, Philosophy, Social Sciences, Sociology
ISBN Prefix(es): 960-253

Athina, Mary Mavrogiannis+
43 Emm Benaki St, 106 81 Athens
Tel: (01) 3821308; (01) 3807220 *Fax:* (01) 3838228
Key Personnel
Contact: Mary G Mavrogianni
Founded: 1982
Subjects: Biological Sciences, Education, Mathematics, Poetry
ISBN Prefix(es): 960-7319
Total Titles: 100 Print
Orders to: Mesologiou 5, 106 81 Athens

Atlantis M Pechlivanides & Co SA+
23 Leontiou Str, 117 45 Athens
Tel: (01) 9220071 *Fax:* (01) 9247341
Founded: 1927
Subjects: Art, Education, Fiction, Nonfiction (General)
ISBN Prefix(es): 960-07
Bookshop(s): Korai 8, 105 64 Athens *Tel:* (01) 323-1624

Atlas
6 Tzavella St, 10681 Athens
Tel: (01) 3627342 *Fax:* (01) 3300257

Axiotelis G+
66 Acadimias St & Char Trikoupi, 10679 Athens
Tel: (01) 3610091; (01) 3618247 *Fax:* (01) 3610887
Key Personnel
Contact: George Axiotelis
Founded: 1974
Member of European Educational Publishers Group.
Subjects: Education, Government, Political Science
ISBN Prefix(es): 960-7053; 960-7807

Bell Best-Seller, *imprint of* Harlenic Hellas Publishing SA

Bell Literature, *imprint of* Harlenic Hellas Publishing SA

Bergadis
Mavromichali 4, 106 79 Athens
Tel: (01) 3614263
Subjects: History, Social Sciences, Sociology
Branch Office(s)
Doryleou 22, Athens *Tel:* (01) 3614263

Beta Medical Publishers+
3 Adrianiou St, Psychico, Athens 115 25
Tel: (010) 6714340; (010) 6714371 *Fax:* (010) 6715015
E-mail: betamedarts@hol.gr
Web Site: www.betamedarts.gr
Key Personnel
General Manager: Anastasia Vassilakou
Founded: 1976
Subjects: Medicine, Nursing, Dentistry, Veterinary Science
ISBN Prefix(es): 960-7308
Total Titles: 106 Print

Blaze, *imprint of* Harlenic Hellas Publishing SA

Boukoumanis' Editions+
One Mavromichalistr, 10679 Athens
Tel: (01) 3618502; (01) 3637436 *Fax:* (01) 3630669
E-mail: info@boukoumanis.gr
Web Site: www.boukoumanis.gr *Cable:* 214422 RC GR
Key Personnel
Man Dir: Elias Boukoumanis
Rights & Permissions: Mrs Trisevgeni Vourgarides

Founded: 1968
Subjects: Education, Environmental Studies, Government, Political Science, History, Philosophy, Psychology, Psychiatry, Social Sciences, Sociology
ISBN Prefix(es): 960-7458

Chrysi Penna - Golden Pen Books+
16, Zoodohou Pigis Str, 10681 Athens
Tel: (01) 03805672 *Fax:* (01) 03825205
E-mail: xpenna@acci.gr; info@chrissipenna.com
Web Site: www.chrissipenna.com
Key Personnel
Man Dir: Anne Hood; K Papachrysanthou
Founded: 1964
Specializes in cookbooks & paperback books.
Subjects: Animals, Pets, Astrology, Occult, Child Care & Development, Cookery, Education, Fiction, Health, Nutrition, Nonfiction (General), Technology
ISBN Prefix(es): 960-245
Number of titles published annually: 18 Print
Total Titles: 120 Print
Warehouse: H Trikoupi Str 157, 11472 Athens

Chryssos Typos AE Ekodeis
7 Z Pigis St, 10678 Athens
Tel: (01) 3637945 *Fax:* (01) 3824417
Subjects: Art, History, Medicine, Nursing, Dentistry, Photography, Science (General)

Diachronikes Ekdoseis+
77 Vas Sofias St, 115 21 Athens
Tel: (01) 7213225 *Fax:* (01) 7246180
Key Personnel
President: Costas Sioras
ISBN Prefix(es): 960-85630
Parent Company: ASCENT Ltd - Public Relations-Publications, Athens

Diavlos+
10 Valtetsiou St, 106 80 Athens
Tel: (01) 3631169 *Fax:* (01) 3617473
E-mail: info@diavlos-books.gr
Web Site: www.diavlos-books.gr
Key Personnel
Man Dir: Emmanuel Deligiannakis
Founded: 1988
Subjects: Astronomy, Computer Science, How-to, Humor, Mathematics, Nonfiction (General), Physical Sciences, Physics, Science (General), Science Fiction, Fantasy
ISBN Prefix(es): 960-7140; 960-531
Bookshop(s): 5 Pezmazoglou St, Athens 10564, Contact: Mr D Gongos *Tel:* (01) 3312413

Difros Publications
57 Akadimias St, 106 79 Athens
Tel: (01) 3610811
Subjects: Literature, Literary Criticism, Essays
ISBN Prefix(es): 960-314

Dionysis Noti Karavias
35 Asklipiou, 10680 Athens
Tel: (01) 3620465 *Fax:* (01) 3620465
Subjects: History
ISBN Prefix(es): 960-258

Dioptra Publishing
9 Zalongou str, 10678 Athens
Tel: (01) 33 02 828 *Fax:* (01) 3302882
E-mail: info@dioptra.gov
Web Site: www.dioptra.gr/english/main.htm
Key Personnel
Manager: George Papadopoulos *E-mail:* george@dioptra.gr
Rights Manager: Costas Papadopoulos
E-mail: costas@dioptra.gr
Sales Manager: Helen Papadopoulos
E-mail: helen@dioptra.gr
Founded: 1985

Specialize in alternative therapies, metaphysics & esotericism.
Subjects: Literature, Literary Criticism, Essays, Psychology, Psychiatry
ISBN Prefix(es): 960-364
Total Titles: 100 Print

Dodoni Publications
3 Asklipiou St, 10679 Athens
Tel: (01) 3637973; (01) 3630312; (01) 3641787 *Fax:* (01) 36 37 067
Subjects: Fiction, History, Nonfiction (General)
ISBN Prefix(es): 960-248

Ekdoseis Domi AE+
67 Ippokratous St, 10680 Athens
Tel: (01) 3637389; (01) 3672056; (01) 03646014 *Fax:* (01) 3601782; (01) 3601786
Key Personnel
President: Elias Maniateas
Marketing Manager: George Dimitropoulos
International Rights: Aris Petropoulos
Subjects: Cookery, Geography, Geology

Dorikos Publishing House+
9-11 Charalabou Sotiriou St, 106 80 Athens
Tel: (01) 6854726 *Fax:* (01) 3301866
Key Personnel
Man Dir, Rights & Permissions: Aristides Klados
Editor: Roussos Vranas
Founded: 1958
Subjects: Biography, Crafts, Games, Hobbies, Drama, Theater, Fiction, Government, Political Science, History, Literature, Literary Criticism, Essays, Philosophy, Poetry, Psychology, Psychiatry
ISBN Prefix(es): 960-279
Associate Companies: Aposperitis Editions, Eressou 9, 106 80 Athens *Tel:* (01) 3604161

Ecole francaise d'Athenes+
Didotou 6, 10680 Athens
Tel: (010) 36 79 900 *Fax:* (010) 36 32 101
E-mail: efa@efa.gr
Web Site: www.efa.gr *Cable:* ECOFRANCE
Key Personnel
Man Dir, Editorial: Dominique Mulliez
Publications: Gilles Touchais *Tel:* (01) 36 79 921 *E-mail:* gilles.touchais@efa.gr
Founded: 1846
Subjects: Archaeology, Architecture & Interior Design, Art, History, Social Sciences, Sociology, Ancient History, Ancient Religions, Greek Archaeology & History, Mythology, Sculpture, Town Planning
ISBN Prefix(es): 2-86958
Number of titles published annually: 6 Print
Total Titles: 200 Print; 2 CD-ROM
Distributed by De Boccard Edition-Diffusion
Orders to: Diffusion de Boccard, 11 rue de Medicis, F-75006 Paris, France, Contact: Mr J B Chaulet *Tel:* (01) 43260037 *Fax:* (01) 43548583 *E-mail:* deboccard@deboccard.com
Web Site: www.deboccard.com

Ekdoseis Kazantzaki (Kazantzakis Publications)+
116 Charilaou Trikoupi St, 11472 Athens
Tel: (01) 3642829 *Fax:* (01) 3642829
Key Personnel
Owner & Editor: Mr Patroklos Stavrou
Publish only works by Nickos Kazantzakis & his wife Helen.
Subjects: Drama, Theater, Fiction, Literature, Literary Criticism, Essays, Philosophy, Poetry, Travel
ISBN Prefix(es): 960-7948

Ekdotike Athenon SA+
11 Omirou St, 10672 Athens
Tel: (01) 360-8911; (01) 3606666 *Fax:* (01) 3606157
Web Site: www.addgr.com/comp/ekdotiki/index.html
Key Personnel
President: George A Christopoulos
Man Dir: John C Bastias
Founded: 1961
Specialize in books on Greek history & culture.
Subjects: Archaeology, Art, History, Travel
ISBN Prefix(es): 960-213
Associate Companies: Ekdotike Hellados SA, Philadelphias 8, Athens (Printer)

Elafaki
14 Niriidon St, 11634 Athens
Tel: (01) 7239476 *Fax:* (01) 7239483
Key Personnel
President & Man Dir: John Drossos
Founded: 1963
ISBN Prefix(es): 960-7351; 960-7972
Parent Company: Educational Books & Records SA

Eleftheroudakis, GCSA International Bookstore
4 Nikis Str, 10563 Athens
Tel: (01) 322 63 23 *Fax:* (01) 325 48 89
E-mail: elebooks@netor.gr
Key Personnel
Man Dir: Virginia Eleftheroudakis-Gregos
Founded: 1915
Subjects: Fiction
ISBN Prefix(es): 960-200

Elliniki Leschi Tou Vivliou
3, A Tsocha St, 115 21 Athens
Tel: (01) 6463888 *Fax:* (01) 6463263
E-mail: elli@gezmanosnet.gz
Subjects: Fiction, History, Human Relations, Nonfiction (General), Philosophy, Poetry, Romance, Science Fiction, Fantasy

Epikerotita+
60 Mavromichali St, 10680 Athens
Tel: (01) 3636083
Key Personnel
Contact: Michalis Mpakirtzis
Founded: 1980
Subjects: Computer Science
ISBN Prefix(es): 960-205

Etaireia Spoudon Neoellinikou Politismou Kai Genikis Paideias (The Moraitis Foundation for Literary & Cultural Studies)+
A Papanastasiou & A Dimitriou St, 15452 Athens
Tel: (01) 06795 000 *Fax:* (01) 06795 090
E-mail: admin@moraitis.edu.gr
Web Site: www.moraitis.edu.gr
Key Personnel
President: Prof N Hourmouziadis
Founded: 1972
Subjects: Drama, Theater, Education, History, Literature, Literary Criticism, Essays, Poetry, Social Sciences, Sociology
ISBN Prefix(es): 960-259

Eurotyp, *imprint of* Stochastis

Evrodiastasi
49 Kallifrona St, 113 64 Athens
Tel: (01) 8611303
Founded: 1992
Folios with collection of engravings & texts. Ideal for libraries, museums, universities, schools & collections.
Subjects: Archaeology, Art, History, Travel
ISBN Prefix(es): 960-85724; 960-86262

Exandas Publishers
Didotou, 57, 106 81 Athens
Tel: (01) 3822064; (01) 3084885 *Fax:* (01) 3813065
E-mail: exandas@otenet.gr
Web Site: www.exandasbooks.gr
Key Personnel
President: Magda N Kotzia
Vice President: Lena Philippou
Editor: Manuela Berki; Alexander Panoussis
Founded: 1975
Subjects: Art, Cookery, Economics, Environmental Studies, Erotica, Fiction, Government, Political Science, History, Literature, Literary Criticism, Essays, Mysteries, Psychology, Psychiatry, Public Administration, Romance, Science Fiction, Fantasy, Social Sciences, Sociology, Fairy Tales, Horror
ISBN Prefix(es): 960-256

F & D Stephanides OE, see Sigma

Ekdoseis Filon (Friends' Publications)
10 Panepistimiou St, 10671 Athens
Tel: (01) 3618705 *Fax:* (01) 3618705
Key Personnel
Publisher: Antonios Tsakiris; Kostas Tsiropoulos
Founded: 1961
Subjects: Literature, Literary Criticism, Essays, Philosophy, Poetry
ISBN Prefix(es): 960-289 (Filon); 960-8150 (Eythini Publications)
Number of titles published annually: 20 Print
Total Titles: 915 Print
Parent Company: Eythini

Forma Publications Ltd+
3 Klimenis & Ionias St, 10445 Athens
Tel: (01) 8327008 *Fax:* (01) 8325650
Key Personnel
President: Peter Cottis
Vice President: Themis Sfaellos
Editor: Aristidis Liakouras; Zaphiria Cotti MSc
Founded: 1980
Member of Cooperative of Greek Publishers.
Subjects: Architecture & Interior Design, Economics, History, Literature, Literary Criticism, Essays, Poetry
ISBN Prefix(es): 960-271

Gartaganis D
3 Kon Melenikou St, 540 06 Thessaloniki
Tel: (031) 209680 *Fax:* (031) 209680
Founded: 1934
Subjects: Agriculture, Veterinary Science, Food Technology
ISBN Prefix(es): 960-7013

Giourdas Moschos+
4 Sergiou Patriarchou St, 114 72 Athens
Tel: (01) 3624947
E-mail: mgiurdas@acci.gr
Web Site: www.mgiurdas.gr
Key Personnel
Foreign Rights & Sales Manager: Panagiotis Assonitis *E-mail:* notisass@hotmail.com
Founded: 1967
Translations from USA & German titles.
Self ruling publishing company.
Subjects: Architecture & Interior Design, Computer Science, Engineering (General)
ISBN Prefix(es): 960-512
Total Titles: 500 Print; 18 Online; 25 E-Book
Online services available through World Wide Web.

Giovanis Publications, Pangosmios Ekdotikos Organismos
Zoodochou Pigis 7, 10678 Athens
Tel: (01) 3825798; (01) 3301511 *Fax:* (01) 3824417
E-mail: giovani1@otenet.gr

Web Site: www.geocities.com/giovanis_pub/en_main1.htm
Subjects: Geography, Geology, History, Medicine, Nursing, Dentistry, Photography, Religion - Other, Science (General)

Govostis Publishing SA+
21 Zoodohou Pigis, 106 81 Athens
Tel: (010) 3816661
Key Personnel
President: Costas Govostis *E-mail:* cotsos@gorostis.gr
Founded: 1926
Subjects: Art, Astrology, Occult, Biography, Child Care & Development, Computer Science, Drama, Theater, Fiction, Government, Political Science, History, Nonfiction (General), Physics, Poetry
ISBN Prefix(es): 960-270
Warehouse: 58-60 Laskareos, 114 72 Athens

Gutenberg Dardanos, see Gutenberg Publications

Gutenberg Publications+
99 Char Trikoupi, 11472 Athens
Tel: (01) 3808334 *Fax:* (01) 3642030
E-mail: gut_ub@otenet.gr
Key Personnel
Man Dir, Editorial & Sales in Bookshops: George Dardanos
Production: Christos Stavropoulos
Retail Sales: Karakatsanis Haralambos
Founded: 1963
Specialize in books for education at all degrees.
Member of POEV, SEVA, PFPB.
Subjects: Art, Economics, Education, Government, Political Science, History, Literature, Literary Criticism, Essays, Philosophy, Psychology, Psychiatry, Social Sciences, Sociology
ISBN Prefix(es): 960-01
Associate Companies: Spoudi; Typothito
Distributor for Litera
Bookshop(s): Solonos 103, 106 79 Athens

Harlenic Hellas Publishing SA+
57 Ippokratous St, 10680 Athens
Tel: (01) 3609438 *Fax:* (01) 3614846
E-mail: harlenic@otenet.gr
Web Site: www.harlenic.gr
Key Personnel
Man Dir: Constantine N Ordolis *Tel:* (010) 3610 218 *E-mail:* c.n.ordolis@harlenic.gr
Financial Manager: Eleftheria Chrissicopoulou
Marketing Manager: Evily Sakkalis
Sales Manager: Costas Apostolakis
Editorial Manager: Marina Kouloumoundra
Production Manager: Charalambos Rigas
Founded: 1979
Subjects: Fiction, Literature, Literary Criticism, Essays, Romance
ISBN Prefix(es): 960-450
Number of titles published annually: 450 Print
Parent Company: Harlequin Enterprises Ltd, 225 Duncan Mill Rd, Don Mills, ON M3B 3K9, Canada
Associate Companies: Cora Verlag, Germany; Forlaget Harlequin AB, Sweden; Harlequin SA, France; Harlequin Iberica SA, Spain; Harlequin Holland; Harlequin Japan; Harlequin Mills & Boon (London); Harlequin Mondadori
Imprints: Bell Best-Seller; Bell Literature; Mira; Harlequin; Red Dress Ink; Blaze

Harlequin, *imprint of* Harlenic Hellas Publishing SA

Harmi-Press Publications, Haroula D Papadimitriou G P+
85 Kifisou Ave, 12241 Athens
Tel: (01) 3456734 *Fax:* (01) 3474732
Telex: 210804 aste gr
Key Personnel
Man Dir: Haroula Papadimitriou
Editorial Dir: Anastasia Papadimitriou
Founded: 1980
Parent Company: D A Papadimitrion S A, Agyra Publishing House

Denise Harvey
Katounia, 340 05 Limni, Evia
Tel: (02270) 31154 *Fax:* (02270) 31154
Key Personnel
Man Dir: Denise Harvey *E-mail:* denise@teledomenet.gr
Man Dir, Athens Office: Dimitri Mavropoulos
Founded: 1972
Subjects: Biography, Ethnicity, Literature, Literary Criticism, Essays, Philosophy, Poetry, Theology
ISBN Prefix(es): 960-7120
Total Titles: 50 Print
Imprints: Romiosyni (series)
Distributed by Cosmos Publishing Co Inc (United States); Orthodox Christian Books Ltd (UK & Europe)

Hestia-I D Hestia-Kollaros & Co Corporation+
Odos Solonos 60, 10672 Athens
Tel: (01) 3635970; (01) 3615077; (01) 360574 *Fax:* (01) 3606758; (01) 3606759
Key Personnel
Publicity Manager: Eva Karaitidi
President: Marina Karaitidi
Founded: 1885
Subjects: Animals, Pets, Anthropology, Archaeology, Architecture & Interior Design, Art, Astrology, Occult, Behavioral Sciences, Biblical Studies, Biography, Business, Career Development, Child Care & Development, Communications, Drama, Theater, Education, Energy, Fiction, Geography, Geology, History, Human Relations, Journalism, Language Arts, Linguistics, Law, Library & Information Sciences, Literature, Literary Criticism, Essays, Management, Music, Dance, Mysteries, Natural History, Philosophy, Photography, Poetry, Psychology, Psychiatry, Public Administration, Romance, Science Fiction, Fantasy, Social Sciences, Sociology, Travel, Veterinary Science, Women's Studies
ISBN Prefix(es): 960-05
Divisions: Hestia
Bookshop(s): Hestia Bookstore, 60 Solonos St, 10672 Athens
Warehouse: 85, Evripidou Str, Athens

Hiotellis P+
17, Ippokratous St, 106 79 Athens
Tel: (01) 3638066; (01) 3611159 *Fax:* (01) 2113112
E-mail: panos-x@otenet.gr
Founded: 1949
Bookshop & publishing.
Subjects: Electronics, Electrical Engineering, History, Literature, Literary Criticism, Essays, Poetry
Total Titles: 150 Print

I Prooptiki+
3 Karyatidon, 17455 Alimos, Athina
Tel: (01) 2014872; (01) 8655413 *Fax:* (01) 8226254
E-mail: hronis@otenet.gr
Key Personnel
Contact: Polychronis Papacristou
Founded: 1991
Specialize in educational books & editions.
Subjects: Education
Total Titles: 8 Print

Ianos+
Aristotelous 7, 546 24 Thessaloniki
Tel: (031) 277004 *Fax:* (031) 284832
Web Site: www.ianos.gr
Key Personnel
Contact: N Karatzas
Founded: 1984
Member of Thessaloniki's Booksellers Association.
Subjects: Biography, Ethnicity, History, Literature, Literary Criticism, Essays, Philosophy
Parent Company: Bookstore Ianos AE
Subsidiaries: Gallery Ianos
Branch Office(s)
Metamorphoseos 24 Kalamaria, 551 31 Thessaloniki *Tel:* (031) 426-780 *Fax:* (031) 426-780
Filippoupoleos 57 Ambelokipi, 561 23 Thessaloniki *Tel:* (031) 727-075 *Fax:* (031) 727-075

Idmon Publications+
Aristidoy 10-12, 105 57 Athens
Mailing Address: PO Box 48030, 132 31 Petroupoli, Athens
Fax: (01) 5015550
E-mail: idmon@in.gr
Key Personnel
Editor: Nikos Deligiannis
Subjects: History, Literature, Literary Criticism, Essays, Poetry
ISBN Prefix(es): 960-85270; 960-7547

Idryma Meleton Chersonisou tou Aimou
(Institute for Balkan Studies)
Meg Alexandrou 31A, 54641 Thessaloniki
Mailing Address: PO Box 50932, 54014 Thessaloniki
Tel: (0310) 832143 *Fax:* (0310) 831429
E-mail: imxa@imxa.gr
Founded: 1953
Subjects: Art, Economics, Education, Ethnicity, History, Social Sciences, Sociology, Bulkan Area from Ancient Times to Present Day
ISBN Prefix(es): 960-7387

Ikaros Ekdotiki
4 Voulis St, 10562 Athens
Tel: (01) 3225152 *Fax:* (01) 3235262
Founded: 1943
Subjects: Literature, Literary Criticism, Essays
ISBN Prefix(es): 960-7233

Institute of Neohellenic Studies, Manolis Triantaphyllidis Foundation+
Aristotelion University of Salonika, 54006 Thessaloniki
Tel: (031) 279695 *Fax:* (031) 997122
Telex: 418562
Key Personnel
Contact: K Prokovas
Founded: 1959
Subjects: Education, Language Arts, Linguistics
ISBN Prefix(es): 960-231
Orders to: S Patakis, Valtetsiou 14, 10680 Athens *Fax:* (01) 3628950

Irini Publishing House - Vassilis G Katsikeas SA+
130 Solonos St, 10681 Athens
Tel: (01) 3839259; (01) 3810465 *Fax:* (01) 3600651
Telex: 223639 Kats gr *Cable:* CATGROUP ATHENS
Key Personnel
President, Rights & Permissions: Vassilis G Katsikeas
Editorial, Production, Publicity: Vicky Pantazopulou
Sales: Georges V Katsikeas; Konstantin V Katsikeas
Subjects: Biography, Economics, Fiction, Government, Political Science, History, Poetry, Social Sciences, Sociology

Associate Companies: K and K Ltd, 130 Solonos St, 10681 Athens *Tel:* (01) 3609489 *Fax:* (01) 3606669
Subsidiaries: Ekdotiki Irini Ltd; Irini Foundation
Branch Office(s)
Aristotelous 7, 54624 Salonika *Tel:* (031) 261069

Editions Kalentis+
Mavromichali 5, 10679 Athens
Tel: (01) 36-01-551 *Fax:* (01) 36-23-553
Telex: 216831 hekogr
Key Personnel
Contact: Alexandros Kalentis; Marianna Kalentis; Nikos Kalentis; Emily Stamou
Founded: 1983
Subjects: Fiction, History
ISBN Prefix(es): 960-219
Distributor for Delithanasis Publications; Ereynites Publications; Kirki Publicatitons; Malliaris Publications
Showroom(s): CR Smirnis A Korai, 162 32 Biron
Bookshop(s): Parametros No 1, 62 Metonos Str, 15561 Holargos *Tel:* 6523145; Parametros No 11, 56 Perikleous Str, 15561 Holargos *Tel:* 6528176
Warehouse: A Kalendis-A Stamou, 62 Metonos Str, 15561 Holargos
Orders to: A Kalendis-A Stamou, 62 Metonos Str, 15561 Holargos

Ilias Kambanas Publishing Organization, SA+
66 Paparrigopoulou St, 121 33 Peristeri-Athens
Tel: (01) 5762791 *Fax:* (01) 5743988
E-mail: info@kambanas.gr
Key Personnel
President: Thalia Kambana
Vice President & Man Dir: Sophia Charokopou
Marketing Manager: Kirsten Janz
Founded: 1969
Member of Panhellenic Federation of Publishers & Booksellers. Specialize in textbooks for elementary schools, atlases, dictionaries, educational materials, novelty books, picture books, cut-out models.
Subjects: Crafts, Games, Hobbies
ISBN Prefix(es): 960-257
Imprints: Anemonylos; Superkids
Bookshop(s): 49 Char Trikoupi St, 106 81 Athens *Tel:* (01) 3647600 *Fax:* (01) 5743988
Warehouse: 65 Paparrigopoulou St, 121 33 Peristeri-Athens

Karatzas Charis+
23 Mavromichali St, 106 80 Athens
Tel: (010) 3678800 *Fax:* (01) 3678857
E-mail: info@nb.org
Key Personnel
Man Dir & International Rights Contract: Adonis Karatzas *Tel:* (01) 3678856 *E-mail:* adonik@nb.org
Founded: 1977
Internet & Legal Services, Professional Training Courses & Seminars.
Subjects: Economics, Labor, Industrial Relations, Law, Publishing & Book Trade Reference
ISBN Prefix(es): 960-272
Parent Company: Nomiki Bibliothiki Inc

Kardamitsa A+
Hippokratous 8, 10679 Athens
Tel: (01) 36 15 156 *Fax:* (01) 36 31 100
E-mail: info@kardamitsa.gr
Web Site: 194.219.182.214/kardamitsa/en/
Key Personnel
Contact: Mina Kardamitsa-Psychoyos; Basil Psychoyos
Founded: 1970
Subjects: Archaeology, History, Literature, Literary Criticism, Essays, Philosophy
ISBN Prefix(es): 960-7262; 960-354
Number of titles published annually: 10 Print

Total Titles: 270 Print
Parent Company: Institut du Livre, A Kardamitsa, 10679 Athens

Kastaniotis Editions SA+
3 Z Pigis, 106 78 Athens
Tel: (01) 3301208; (01) 3803234 *Fax:* (01) 3822530
E-mail: kastaniotis@ath.forthnet.gr
Key Personnel
Man Dir, Editorial: Athanasios Kastaniotis
Editorial: Anna Stamatopoulou
Sales: Stelios Kanakis
Production: Voula Vrachati
Publicity, Rights & Permissions: Sophie Catris
Founded: 1969
Member of Association of Publishers & Booksellers of Athens.
Subjects: Anthropology, Child Care & Development, Drama, Theater, Education, Fiction, Film, Video, Humor, Literature, Literary Criticism, Essays, Philosophy, Psychology, Psychiatry
ISBN Prefix(es): 960-03
Associate Companies: Ath Kastaniotis & Co General Partnership
Subsidiaries: Ath A Kastaniotis & Co Ltd Partnership

Katoptro Publications+
10, Korizi Str, 11743 Athens
Tel: (01) 9244827; (01) 9244852 *Fax:* (01) 9244756
E-mail: info@katoptro.gr
Web Site: www.katoptro.gr
Founded: 1986
Specialize in sciences.
ISBN Prefix(es): 960-7023; 960-7778

Kedros Publishers+
3-G Gennadiou Str, 10678 Athens
Tel: (01) 3802007; (01) 3089712 *Fax:* (01) 3831981
E-mail: kedros@ermis.accl.gr
Key Personnel
Man Dir: Evangelos Papathanassopoulos
Foreign Rights: Laura McDowell
Founded: 1954
Subjects: Drama, Theater, Literature, Literary Criticism, Essays, Philosophy, Poetry, Self-Help, Travel
ISBN Prefix(es): 960-04
Distributed by Cosmos Publishing Co (USA)

Kentro Byzantinon Erevnon
12 Kastritsiou Str, 546 23 Thessaloniki
Tel: (031) 270941 *Fax:* (031) 228922

Kleidarithmos+
27-b Stournari St, 10682 Athens
Tel: (01) 3832044 *Fax:* (01) 3617950
Key Personnel
Man Dir: Giannis Faldamis
Founded: 1985
Subjects: Architecture & Interior Design, Automotive, Civil Engineering, Computer Science, Electronics, Electrical Engineering, Management, Marketing, Mechanical Engineering, Microcomputers
ISBN Prefix(es): 960-209
Bookshop(s): Sturnara 37, 10682 Athens

Knossos Publications
50 Themistokleus, 10681 Athens
Tel: (01) 3610108; (01) 3804681 *Fax:* (01) 3804681
Founded: 1972
Subjects: Biography, History, Literature, Literary Criticism, Essays, Poetry, Travel
ISBN Prefix(es): 960-207

Parent Company: Stelios Chalkiadakis
Bookshop(s): 29, Evans Str, Iraklion Kreta 71201

Kritiki Publishing+
25 Koletti Str, 10677 Athens
Mailing Address: 10 Didotou Str, 10680 Athens
Tel: (01) 3622390; (01) 3836460 *Fax:* (01) 3621367
E-mail: kritiki@hol.gr
Key Personnel
Directing Manager: Themis Minoglou
Founded: 1987
Specialize in social sciences.
Subjects: Economics, Finance, Government, Political Science, History, Literature, Literary Criticism, Essays, Philosophy, Social Sciences, Sociology
ISBN Prefix(es): 960-218

Kyriakidis+
11 Kon Melenikou St, 54635 Thessaloniki
Tel: (031) 208540; (031) 210360; (031) 210067 *Fax:* (031) 245541
Key Personnel
President: Dimitrios Kyriakidis
Vice President: Anastasios Kyriakidis
Founded: 1970
Subjects: Accounting, Chemistry, Chemical Engineering, Economics, History, Mathematics, Theology
ISBN Prefix(es): 960-343

Kyriakidis Vasileios
96 Solonos, 106 80 Athens
Tel: (01) 3609126
E-mail: bkyriakid@otenet.gr
Key Personnel
Publisher: Sotiris Nikolopoulos
Founded: 1994
Publish books for Greek language as a foreign language.
Member of Book Publishers Association.
Subjects: History, Literature, Literary Criticism, Essays, Psychology, Psychiatry, Social Sciences, Sociology, Grammar, Vocabulary, Orthography, Ancient Greek History, Byzantine, European, Global, Ancient Greek Literature
ISBN Prefix(es): 960-7634
Total Titles: 100 Print

Leon, *imprint of* Costas Spanos

Libro Ltd
8 Patriarchou loakim St, 10674 Athens
Tel: (01) 7247116 *Fax:* (01) 7232066
ISBN Prefix(es): 960-7009

Livani Publishing Organization SA, see Nea Synora

Logos+
28 Em Benaki, 10678 Athens
Tel: (01) 3620989 *Fax:* (01) 4834000
E-mail: amglogos@otenet.gc
Founded: 1950
Evangelical Books & Magazines.
Subjects: Religion - Protestant
Parent Company: AMG International
Branch Office(s)
Emm. Benaki 28, 10678 Athens *Tel:* (01) 3823495; (01) 3820989
Egnatia 61, 54631 Thessalonoki *Tel:* (031) 232210
U.S. Office(s): 6815 Shallowford Rd, Chattanooga, TN 37421, United States *Tel:* 423-894-6060 *Fax:* 423-894-6863

Longman, *imprint of* Pearson Education Hellas SA

PUBLISHERS

GREECE

Macmillan Heinemann ELT
80 Kousidi St, 157 72 Zografou, Athens
Tel: (01) 748 2828 *Fax:* (01) 748 8735
E-mail: mhelt@ath.forthnet.gr
Web Site: www.mhelt.com
Key Personnel
Market Manager: Francis Baker *E-mail:* f.baker@
　athens.mhelt.com
Subjects: English as a Second Language
Parent Company: Macmillan Publishers Ltd

Mamuth Comix Ltd+
44 Ippokratous, 10680 Athens
Tel: (01) 3625055 *Fax:* (01) 3625054
E-mail: themask@athena.gr
Key Personnel
International Rights: Irene Tzourou
Founded: 1982
Subjects: Humor
ISBN Prefix(es): 960-321
Distributed by Ehapa Verlag Germany

Mavrogianni Publications+
37 Emm Benaki & Solonos St, 106 81 Athens
Tel: (01) 3304628 *Fax:* (01) 3838228
Key Personnel
Contact: G Mavrogiannis
Subjects: Education, Language Arts, Linguistics,
　Mathematics, Physics
ISBN Prefix(es): 960-514
Total Titles: 150 Print

Medusa/Selas+
48 Z Pigis St, 106 81 Athens
Tel: (01) 3608088; (01) 3608168 *Fax:* (01)
　3808970
E-mail: medusa@otenet.gr
Key Personnel
Conduct: Yannis Perdikogiannis
Founded: 1994
Subjects: Art, Fiction, Film, Video, Music, Dance,
　Nonfiction (General)
ISBN Prefix(es): 960-7246; 960-85004
Associate Companies: Topos, Lithi
Imprints: Topos, Lithi
Bookshop(s): Synergasia Andrea Metaxa 4,
　Athens
Warehouse: 63 Eressou Str, 10683 Athens

Melissa Publishing House+
10 Navarinou St, 10680 Athens 10680
Tel: (010) 3611692 *Fax:* (010) 3600865
Web Site: www.melissabooks.com
Key Personnel
Man Dir: George Ragias
Sales Dir: Chrys Ragias
Contact: Annie Ragia *E-mail:* annieragia@
　melissabooks.com
Founded: 1954
Book publishers.
Subjects: Architecture & Interior Design, Art,
　History, Maritime, Greek Civilization
ISBN Prefix(es): 960-204
Subsidiaries:
Divisions: Dictionary of Greek Artists
Distributed by Harry N Abrams Inc

Michalis Sideris
28 Andr Metaxa St, 10681 Athens
Tel: (01) 3301161; (01) 3301163 *Fax:* (01)
　3301164
Founded: 1978
Subjects: Earth Sciences, Education, Energy,
　English as a Second Language, Mathematics,
　Physics
ISBN Prefix(es): 960-7012

Minoas SA+
One Poseidonos St, N Jeaklio 14121
Tel: (010) 2711222 *Fax:* (010) 2711056
E-mail: info@minoas.ge
Web Site: www.minoas.ge
Key Personnel
Man Dir: Yannis Konstantaropoulos
Executive Manager: Andreas Konstantaropoulos
Sales Manager: Christos Hatzipantelides
Founded: 1958
Publications.
Subjects: Art, Biography, Fiction, History, Music,
　Dance, Nonfiction (General)
ISBN Prefix(es): 960-240; 960-542
Number of titles published annually: 80 Print
Total Titles: 800 Print
Bookshop(s): Patission 126, Athens 11257
　Tel: (010) 8215664 *Fax:* (010) 8215664

Mira, *imprint of* Harlenic Hellas Publishing SA

Editions Moressopoulos+
19 Yperidou St, 105 58 Athens
Mailing Address: PO Box 30564, 100 33 Athens
Tel: (01) 3234217 *Fax:* (01) 3232082
E-mail: mores.s@altavista.net
Telex: 216465 masgr
Key Personnel
Chief Executive: Stavros Moressopoulos
Rights & Permissions: Voula Moressopoulos
Founded: 1977
Member of Union of Book Publishers (Athens),
　Association of Photo Biennials (Paris, France),
　Union of Journalists, Owners of Periodical
　Press (Athens).
Subjects: Animals, Pets, Crafts, Games, Hobbies,
　How-to, Music, Dance, Photography, Sports,
　Athletics, Travel, Wine & Spirits
ISBN Prefix(es): 960-366
Parent Company: Moressopoulos SA
Associate Companies: Hellenic Centre of Photog-
　raphy (nonprofit making) European School of
　Photography, 19 Yperidou St, 105 58 Athens
Subsidiaries: Photografia Magazine

Morfotiki Estia AE+
61 Akadimias, 10679 Athens
Tel: (01) 3621180 *Fax:* (01) 3627706
Key Personnel
Contact: Makas
Founded: 1975
ISBN Prefix(es): 960-215
Bookshop(s): 49 Har Tricoupi St, Athens 10681
Warehouse: 13 Haralambous St, Athens

Morfotiko Idryma Ethnikis Trapezas (National
　Bank Cultural Foundation)+
13 Thucydidou St, 10558 Athens
Tel: (01) 3230841; (01) 3221335 *Fax:* (01)
　3245089; (01) 3227057
Founded: 1966
Subjects: Archaeology, History, Language Arts,
　Linguistics, Literature, Literary Criticism, Es-
　says, Nonfiction (General), Philosophy, Science
　(General)
ISBN Prefix(es): 960-250

Mousio Benaki
One Koumpari St, 106 74 Athens
Tel: (01) 3611617; (01) 3612694 *Fax:* (01)
　3622547
ISBN Prefix(es): 960-7671; 960-85160

Nakas Music House+
13 Navarinou St, 10680 Athens
Tel: (01) 364711; (01) 364716 *Fax:* (01) 3642521
Telex: 8018NAKAGR
Key Personnel
Contact: George Nakas
Founded: 1937
Subjects: Music, Dance
ISBN Prefix(es): 960-290
Distributor for Boosey & Hawkes; Henley Verlag;
　Ricordi

Ed Nea Acropolis+
Ag Melatiou 29, 11361 Athens
Tel: (01) 8231301 *Fax:* (01) 8810830
Key Personnel
President: Panagiotis Goumas
Vice President: Peter Kostinis
Editor: Costula Giannopulu
Founded: 1981
Subjects: Anthropology, Archaeology, Drama,
　Theater, History, Music, Dance, Mysteries,
　Parapsychology, Philosophy
ISBN Prefix(es): 960-8407
Branch Office(s)
Hania
Heraklion
Ioannina
Kallithea
Kavala
Patras
Rethymno
Salonica
Volos

Nea Synora+
98 Solonos St, 10680 Athens
Tel: (01) 3610589; (01) 3600398 *Fax:* (01)
　3617791
Telex: 21812269spa
Key Personnel
President: Giota Livani; Ilias Livani
Editor: Tonia Chourchouli
Founded: 1972
ISBN Prefix(es): 960-236; 960-237; 960-238;
　960-14
Parent Company: Livani Publishing Organization
　SA
Associate Companies: Mythos, Klydi
Subsidiaries: Multimedia Electronic Publishing
　SA
Warehouse: 135 Platonos St, 17673 Athens

Nea Thesis - Evrotas+
69a Ippokratous St, 106 80 Athens
Tel: (01) 3634932 *Fax:* (01) 3604665
Key Personnel
Contact: John Schinas
Subjects: Archaeology, Ethnicity, Government,
　Political Science, History, Philosophy
ISBN Prefix(es): 960-7076

Nikas
102 Solonos St, 10680 Athens
Tel: (01) 3634686; (01) 3633754
ISBN Prefix(es): 960-297

Notos
15 Omirou St, 10672 Athens
Tel: (01) 3636577; (01) 3629746 *Fax:* (01)
　3636737
Telex: 515418
ISBN Prefix(es): 960-8491

Odysseas Publications Ltd+
3 Moraitou St, 11471 Athens
Tel: (01) 3624326; (01) 3625575 *Fax:* (01)
　3648030
Key Personnel
Contact: Titos Mylonopoulos
Founded: 1973
Subjects: Biography, Child Care & Development,
　History, Human Relations, Philosophy, Psy-
　chology, Psychiatry, Romance, Women's Stud-
　ies
ISBN Prefix(es): 960-210

Okeanida+
27 Z Pigis St, Athens 10681
Tel: (01) 3827341 *Fax:* (01) 3805531
E-mail: oceanida@internet.gr
Key Personnel
Publisher: Mr Nikos Megapanos
Founded: 1986

GREECE

Subjects: Art, History, Literature, Literary Criticism, Essays
ISBN Prefix(es): 960-7213; 960-410
Total Titles: 250 Print
Online services available through World Wide Web.

Opera
32 Pentelis, 15343 Athens
Tel: (01) 6527516 *Fax:* (01) 3303634
E-mail: opera@acci.gr
Key Personnel
Contact & Opera Editions: George Miressiotis
Founded: 1989 (Private book publishing house)
Literary Books & Translations.
Subjects: *Specializes in:* European & Latin American authors
ISBN Prefix(es): 960-7073
Total Titles: 90 Print

Orfanidis Publications+
8 Lontou St, 10681 Athens
Tel: (01) 3836925 *Fax:* (01) 3845623
Founded: 1940
Subjects: Astrology, Occult, Automotive, Cookery, Gardening, Plants, Geography, Geology, Mysteries, Philosophy

Pagoulatos Bros+
56 Panepistimiou St, 10678 Athens
Tel: (01) 03818780; (01) 03801485 *Fax:* (01) 03838028
E-mail: pagoulatos_publ@ath.forthnet.gr
Telex: 222889 LATO GR
ISBN Prefix(es): 960-7208

Pagoulatos G-G P Publications
50 Sina St, 10672 Athens
Tel: (01) 3604895; (01) 3624624 *Fax:* (01) 3604897
Key Personnel
Editor: Gerasimos Pagoulatos
Subjects: English as a Second Language
ISBN Prefix(es): 960-294

Panepistimio Ioanninon
PO Box 1186, 45110 Ioannina
Tel: (06510) 97105-7 *Fax:* (06510) 97024
E-mail: intlrel@uoi.gr
Web Site: www.uoi.gr
Key Personnel
Publications Office: Mrs E Gouma
Subjects: Anthropology, Archaeology, Chemistry, Chemical Engineering, Education, History, Physics, Psychology, Psychiatry, Social Sciences, Sociology
ISBN Prefix(es): 960-233

D Papadimas+
Ippokratous St 8, 10679 Athens
Tel: (01) 3627318; (01) 3642692 *Fax:* (01) 3610271
Subjects: Antiques, Archaeology, Geography, Geology, History, Regional Interests, Theology
ISBN Prefix(es): 960-206

Haroula D Papadimitriou G P, see Harmi-Press Publications, Haroula D Papadimitriou G P

Kyr 1 Papadopoulos E E+
9 Kapodistriou St, 14452 Athens
Tel: (01) 2816234; (01) 2846074; (01) 2846075 *Fax:* (01) 2817127
Telex: 225176 Book Gr
Key Personnel
Man Dir: Kyr Papadopoulos
Sales: P Hatjibodojis
Production: George Papadopoulos
Rights & Permissions: Yiannis Papadopoulos

Founded: 1953
ISBN Prefix(es): 960-261

Papazissis Publishers SA
2 Nikitara Str, 10678 Athens
Tel: (01) 3609150; (01) 3838020; (01) 3808173 *Fax:* (01) 3809150
Telex: 219807 Itec
Key Personnel
Man Dir: Victor Papazissis
Sales, Advertising: Thalia Papazissis
Rights & Permissions: Stefanos Vlachos
Founded: 1929
Subjects: Economics, Education, Environmental Studies, Government, Political Science, History, Law, Regional Interests, Social Sciences, Sociology
ISBN Prefix(es): 960-02
Parent Company: Corais Ltd, 2 Nikitara Str, 10678 Athens

Patakis Publishers+
14, Valtetsiou Str, 106 80 Athens
Tel: (01) 36 500 00 *Fax:* (01) 36 500 69
E-mail: info@patakis.gr
Web Site: www.patakis.gr
Key Personnel
President: Stefanos Patakis
Production: Alexander Patakis
Sales: Peter Lazaridis
Publicity: Hara Mavrogonatou
Rights & Permissions: Yiannis Ntzoufras
Editorial: Nikitas Stellas
Foreign Rights Assistant: Vicky Stamatopoulou
 Tel: (01) 3615356 *E-mail:* vstamat@patakis.gr
Founded: 1974
Subjects: Anthropology, Art, Biography, Business, Child Care & Development, Cookery, Drama, Theater, Education, Fiction, Health, Nutrition, History, Language Arts, Linguistics, Literature, Literary Criticism, Essays, Management, Nonfiction (General), Philosophy, Poetry, Psychology, Psychiatry, Social Sciences, Sociology, Travel
ISBN Prefix(es): 960-293; 960-360; 960-600; 960-378; 960-16
Number of titles published annually: 500 Print
Total Titles: 3,000 Print
Branch Office(s)
N Monastiriou 122, Thessaloniki *Tel:* (031) 706354 *Fax:* (031) 706355
Distributor for Conceptum (CD-ROM); Goulandri-Horn Institute; Iolkos Publications; Triantafyllidis Institute
Bookshop(s): Akadimias 65, 10678 Athens
 Tel: (01) 3811740 *Fax:* (01) 3811850
Warehouse: These Tzaverdela, Aspropyrgos 19300

Pearson Education Hellas SA
229 Syngrou Ave, Nea Smyrni, 17121 Athens
Tel: (01) 937 3170 *Fax:* (01) 937 3194
Web Site: www.pearsoneduc.com
Key Personnel
Man Dir: Themis Zoulias
Sales Manager: Liz Hammon
Publisher: Loukas Ioannou
Founded: 1985
ELT supplementary titles.
ISBN Prefix(es): 0-582
Number of titles published annually: 10 Print
Total Titles: 20 Print
Parent Company: Pearson Plc
Imprints: Longman
Branch Office(s)
12 Mackenzie King St, 54622 Thessaloniki *Tel:* (031) 271163 *Fax:* (031) 241056
Foreign Rights: Loukas Ioannou

Pergamini, *imprint of* Costas Spanos

Galousis P Petros
48 Solomou, 10682 Athens
Tel: (01) 360 5004

Pontiki Publications SA+
10 Massalias, 10680 Athens
Tel: (01) 3609531; (01) 3609533 *Fax:* (01) 3645406
Key Personnel
Publisher: Kostas Papayoannou
Man Dir: Kostas Yabanis
Editorial Dir: Roussos Vranas
Founded: 1979
Subjects: Government, Political Science, History
ISBN Prefix(es): 960-8402

Proskinio
116 Solonos, 10681 Athens
Tel: (01) 3808348 *Fax:* (01) 3819724
Key Personnel
President: A Sideratos
Founded: 1990
Subjects: Government, Political Science, History
ISBN Prefix(es): 960-7107

M Psaropoulos & Co EE+
3 Kriezotou, 10671 Athens
Tel: (01) 3606808 *Fax:* (01) 3609645
Key Personnel
Man Dir: Tassos Psaropoulos
Editorial: Thalia Iacovidis
Sales: John Psaropoulos
Production: D Mavromatis
Publicity: P Pissanos
Rights & Permissions: M Psaropoulos
Founded: 1962
Subjects: Fiction, Medicine, Nursing, Dentistry
ISBN Prefix(es): 960-7147
Parent Company: Althayia SA
Subsidiaries: Finedawn Publishers

Psichogios Publications SA+
Mavromichali 1, 10679 Athens
Mailing Address: Zaimi 8, 10683 Athens
Tel: (01) 3602535; (01) 3302234 *Fax:* (01) 3640683; (01) 3302098
E-mail: psicho@otenet.gr
Telex: 225874 Mps Gr
Key Personnel
Man Dir: Athanassios Psichogios
 E-mail: thanospsicho@otenet.gr
Editorial, Rights & Permission: Elly Solomon
Founded: 1978
Subjects: Fiction, Philosophy, Human Science
ISBN Prefix(es): 960-7020; 960-274; 960-7021
Number of titles published annually: 100 Print
Total Titles: 800 Print
Branch Office(s)
Vassileos Irakliou 32, 54624 Thessaloniki
Bookshop(s): Pesmazoglou 5, 10564 Athens
Warehouse: Edessis 29, 11855 Votanikos

Red Dress Ink, *imprint of* Harlenic Hellas Publishing SA

Romiosyni (series), *imprint of* Denise Harvey

Nikolas 1 Rossi+
5 Sofokleous, 10559 Athens
Tel: (01) 3218572 *Fax:* (01) 3304440
Founded: 1895
Subjects: Education, Student's Aid
ISBN Prefix(es): 960-225

Sakkoulas Publications SA+
23, Ippokratous Str, GR-10679 Athens
Tel: (010) 3387500 *Fax:* (010) 3390075
E-mail: info@sakkoulas.gr
Web Site: www.sakkoulas.gr
Key Personnel
Man Dir: Panagiotis I Sakkoulas
Founded: 1958

Subjects: Business, Economics, Labor, Industrial Relations, Law, Management, Maritime, Public Administration, Social Sciences, Sociology
ISBN Prefix(es): 960-301
Associate Companies: Sakkoulas Publications EE, Ethn Amynis 42, 546 21 Thessaloniki *Tel:* (010) 244 228; (010) 244 229 *Fax:* (010) 224 230; Sakkoylas Publications SA, 1, Frangon Str, 546 26, Thessaloniki *Tel:* (010) 535381 *Fax:* (010) 546812
Subsidiaries: Sakkoulas Publications SA
Distributor for Nomos Verlagsgesellschaft; Verlag Recht und Wirtschaft mbH

Scripta+
25 Third Septemvriou, 10432 Athens
Tel: (01) 5230382 *Fax:* (01) 5233574
Key Personnel
Contact: Theophilos Palevratzis-Ashover
Founded: 1980
Subjects: English as a Second Language
ISBN Prefix(es): 960-7166

Siamantas Publications
61 Akadimias, 10679 Athens
Tel: (01) 3627164
Subjects: Fiction, History, Nonfiction (General)

J Sideris OE Ekdoseis
44 Stadiou St, 10564 Athens
Tel: (01) 3229638 *Fax:* (01) 3245052
Key Personnel
Contact: Andreas Sideris
Subjects: Language Arts, Linguistics, Literature, Literary Criticism, Essays, Science (General)
ISBN Prefix(es): 960-08

Sigma+
20 Mavromichali St, 10680 Athens
Tel: (01) 3638941; (01) 3607667 *Fax:* (01) 3638941
E-mail: sbooks@otenet.gr
Web Site: www.sigmabooks.gr
Key Personnel
Contact: D Stefanidis
Founded: 1973
Subjects: Fiction, Mythology, Folk Tales
ISBN Prefix(es): 960-425
Total Titles: 83 Print
Distributed by Cosmos Publishing Co Inc (US); Hellidon Press (UK)
Foreign Rep(s): Cosmos Publishing Co Inc (Canada, US)
Foreign Rights: Shin Won Agency Co (China, Japan, Korea)

Alex Siokis & Co+
54 Alex Svolou, 54013 Thessaloniki
Mailing Address: PO Box 50041, 54013 Thessaloniki
Tel: (031) 230257 *Fax:* (031) 281014
Key Personnel
Medical Publisher: Niki Sioki
Founded: 1960
Subjects: Medicine, Nursing, Dentistry
ISBN Prefix(es): 960-7461

Society for Macedonian Studies
4 Ethnikis Amynis Ave, 546 21 Thessaloniki
Tel: (031) 268710 *Fax:* (031) 971501
E-mail: ems@hyper.gr
Founded: 1939
Promotes the research in the topics of history, archaeology, linguistics & folklore concerning the region of Macedonia.
Subjects: Anthropology, Archaeology, History, Philosophy, Humanities
Total Titles: 4 Print
Foreign Rights: Dokomente-Verlag; Sweis; Ebsco; Faxon; Wasmuth; Dawson; Raabe; Readmore

Costas Spanos
7 Mavromichali, 10679 Athens
Tel: (01) 3623917; (01) 3614332 *Fax:* (01) 8953076 *Cable:* Bibliospan
Key Personnel
Man Dir, Editorial: C Spanos
Sales: John Papadakis
Publicity: Sophia Tjimoianni
Subjects: Regional Interests
ISBN Prefix(es): 960-262
Imprints: Leon; Pergamini

Spyropoulos A+
74, Ag Georgiou, 15451 North Psychiko
Tel: (01) 6712991 *Fax:* (01) 6719622
Founded: 1972
Specialize in ELT material.
ISBN Prefix(es): 960-7302

Stochastis+
39 Mavromichali, 10680 Athens
Tel: (01) 3601956 *Fax:* (01) 3610445
Key Personnel
President: Loukas Axelos
Founded: 1969
Subjects: Ethnicity, History, Literature, Literary Criticism, Essays, Philosophy, Social Sciences, Sociology, Travel
ISBN Prefix(es): 960-303
Associate Companies: Koinopraktiki (Union of Greek Publishers)
Imprints: Eurotyp
Book Club(s): Cosmos Book Club; Mos Book Club; The Friends of Book Book Club

Superkids, *imprint of* Ilias Kambanas Publishing Organization, SA

Technical Chamber of Greece
4 Karageorgi Servias St, 10248 Athens
Tel: (01) 3291601 *Fax:* (01) 3226185
E-mail: registry@central.tee.gr
Telex: 218374 Teegr
Key Personnel
General Dir: V Torolopoulos
Founded: 1923
The Technical Chamber of Greece (TEE) is a corporate body, under public law, supervised by the Ministry of Public Works.
Subjects: Science (General), Technology
ISBN Prefix(es): 960-7018

Tekmirio
17 Z Pigis, 10681 Athens
Tel: (01) 3637912; (01) 2287548

Thetili Publications
6 Emm Benaki, 10564 Athens
Tel: (01) 3215229
Founded: 1983
Subjects: History, Psychology, Psychiatry, Women's Studies, Drugs
ISBN Prefix(es): 960-85198

Thymari Publications+
14 Zalongou, 10678 Athens
Tel: (01) 3643015; (01) 3643901 *Fax:* (01) 3636591
E-mail: thymari@thymari.gr
Key Personnel
Dir & Editor in Chief: T H Grammenos
Psychologist, Marketing: I Grammenou
Key Author: G Pinteris PhD
Editorial Advisor: A Grammenou
Psychologist, Translator: M Koulentianou
Founded: 1978
Subjects: Human Relations, Psychology, Psychiatry, Social Sciences, Sociology

ISBN Prefix(es): 960-7161
Warehouse: Sarantaporou 98, 15561 Holargos *Tel:* (01) 6512216; (01) 6540811 *Fax:* (01) 6549207

To Rodakio+
35 Apollonos St, 10556 Athens
Tel: (01) 3221700 *Fax:* (01) 3246008
Key Personnel
International Rights: Julia Tsiakiri
Founded: 1992
Subjects: Drama, Theater, Literature, Literary Criticism, Essays, Poetry
ISBN Prefix(es): 960-7360

Topos, Lithi, *imprint of* Medusa/Selas

Toubis M
519 Vouliagmenis Ave, 163 41 Athens
Tel: (01) 9923876; (01) 9923806 *Fax:* (01) 9923867
E-mail: toubis@otenet.gr
Key Personnel
Secretary: Katerina Koumarianou
Founded: 1965
Development, production & distribution of high quality tourist publication.

Tropos Zois+
One Solomou St, 152 32 Chalandri
Tel: (01) 6840156 *Fax:* (01) 6858851
Web Site: www.book.culture.gr/tropos-zois
Subjects: Alternative medicine, natural eating & living, nutrition, yoga, reflexology
Number of titles published annually: 6 Print; 1 CD-ROM
Total Titles: 10 Print; 2 CD-ROM; 50 Audio

Typos
3-5 Gravias, 10678 Athens
Tel: (01) 3819083; (01) 3819085; (01) 3619083 *Fax:* (01) 3825012
ISBN Prefix(es): 960-246

D & J Vardikos
2 A Metaxa, 10681 Athens
Tel: (01) 3631146; (01) 3602150; (01) 3831146 *Fax:* (01) 9564354
Key Personnel
Man Dir: Dimitrios Vardikos
Founded: 1978
Subjects: Aeronautics, Aviation
ISBN Prefix(es): 960-7810
Branch Office(s)
Davaki 34, Kallithea, Athens
Bookshop(s): Inter-Attica, Davaki 34, Kallithea, Athens

J Vassiliou Bibliopolein+
15e Ippokratous St, 10679 Athens
Tel: (01) 3623382; (01) 3623480 *Fax:* (01) 3623580
Key Personnel
President: J Vassiliou
Founded: 1913
Member of Association of Publishers & Booksellers of Athens.
Subjects: Fiction, History, Philosophy

Vivliothiki Eftychia Galeou+
39 Halandriou, 15125 Maroussi
Tel: (01) 6841191 *Fax:* (01) 6825862
Key Personnel
Contact: N S Galeos
Subjects: Advertising, Business, Finance, Management, Marketing
ISBN Prefix(es): 960-7126
Bookshop(s): 19 Kolokotroni, Athens *Tel:* (01) 3227840

GREECE

Vlassis+
2 Lontou Str & 15 Z Pigis, 10681 Athens
Tel: (01) 3812900 *Fax:* (01) 3827557
Key Personnel
General Manager: Nickos Vlassis
Publisher, Marketing Manager & International Rights Contact: Anna-Maria Vlassis *Tel:* (01) 3833013 *E-mail:* amvlassi@otenet.gr
Founded: 1964
Hard cover & paper back.
Subjects: Biography, Fiction, Literature, Literary Criticism, Essays
ISBN Prefix(es): 960-302
Total Titles: 600 Print

S J Zacharopoulos SA Publishing Co+
5 Stadiou St, 10562 Athens
Tel: (01) 3231525 *Fax:* (01) 3243814
Key Personnel
President, Publicity, Rights & Permissions: Stavros Zacharopoulos
Production: Loucas Zacharopoulos
Editorial: Stefanos Zacharopoulos
Sales: George Zacharopoulos
Founded: 1959
Subjects: Drama, Theater, History, Poetry, Science (General)
ISBN Prefix(es): 960-208
Bookshop(s): Praxitelous 141, GR-18535 Piraeus

Zacharopoulos Z & G
22-24 Atlantos, 11254 Athens
Tel: (01) 2111895; (01) 2111897 *Fax:* (01) 2111897
ISBN Prefix(es): 960-281

ZOI
Subsidiary of "Zoe", Brotherhood of Theologians
14 Karytsi, 10561 Athens
Tel: (01) 3223560 *Fax:* (01) 3221283
Key Personnel
Man Dir: P Anastopoulos
Founded: 1907
Subjects: Religion - Other
Bookshop(s): St Sophia 41, Salonika *Tel:* (031) 54623 (also in three other Greek cities)

Har Zolindakis
65 Panepistimiou, 10564 Athens
Tel: (01) 3216504
Subjects: History

Zyrichidi Bros
30 Aristotelous, 54623 Thessaloniki
Tel: (031) 227915; (031) 266036 *Fax:* (031) 266036
Key Personnel
Contact: Zyrichidi Bros *Tel:* (031) 285 856
Founded: 1959
Publisher of books, selling all other book publishing companies.
General Partnership.
Subjects: Literature, Literary Criticism, Essays
Total Titles: 15 Print
Branch Office(s)
Zsimiski 115 *Tel:* (031) 285856 *Fax:* (031) 266036
Bookshop(s): Zsimiski 115 *Tel:* (031) 266036 *Fax:* (031) 266036

Guadeloupe

General Information

Capital: Basse-Terre
Language: French, Creole patois
Religion: Roman Catholic
Population: 400,000
Bank Hours: 0800-1200, 1400-1600 Monday-Friday
Shop Hours: 0900-1300, 1500-1800 Monday-Friday
Currency: 100 centimes = 1 French franc

Librairie Generale JASOR
44-46 rue Schoelcher, 97110 Pointe-a-Pitre
Tel: (590) 821770 *Fax:* (590) 917599
Telex: 919-2333
Subjects: Language Arts, Linguistics, Literature, Literary Criticism, Essays
ISBN Prefix(es): 2-912594

Guatemala

General Information

Capital: Guatemala City
Language: Spanish
Religion: Roman Catholic
Population: 10 million
Bank Hours: 0900-1500 Monday-Friday
Shop Hours: 0900-1300, 1500-1900 Monday-Friday; 0900-1300 Saturday
Currency: 100 centavos = 1 quetzal
Export/Import Information: Member of the Central American Common Market. Duty on catalogues is Q 0.03 per gross kilo. No import licenses, no exchange control.
Copyright: UCC, Buenos Aires, Florence (see Copyright Conventions, pg xi)

Cultura de La Universidad, *imprint of* Grupo Editorial RIN-78

Editorial Cultura
O Calle 16-40, Zona 15, Guatemala
Tel: (02) 692080 *Fax:* (02) 346135
Telex: 5805 *Cable:* CAN EXO

Fundacion para la Cultura y el Desarrollo
9 calle 2-75, zona 1, 01001 Guatemala
SAN: 003-1429
Tel: (02) 500216 *Fax:* (02) 325508
Key Personnel
General Manager: Carlos I Castaneda Acuna
E-mail: ccast@intelnet.net.gt
Founded: 1986
Subjects: History
ISBN Prefix(es): 84-88622
Parent Company: Asociacion de Amigos del Pais

Grupo Editorial RIN-78+
O Calle 16-40, Zona 15, Guatemala 692080
Tel: (02) 692080 *Fax:* (02) 601834
Key Personnel
Contact: Juan F Cifuentes
Founded: 1984
Subjects: Archaeology, Fiction, History, Literature, Literary Criticism, Essays, Military Science, Philosophy, Poetry, Science Fiction, Fantasy, Social Sciences, Sociology
Associate Companies: Servicios Editoriales "Palabra Tras Palabra"
Imprints: Cultura de La Universidad; Pedernal; Ymoescuento
Subsidiaries: Editorial "Palo de Hormigo"
Divisions: Centro de Documentacion de Estudios Literarios
Branch Office(s)
Roberto Quezada, 3442 N Delta Ave, Rosemead, CA 91770, United States *Fax:* 818-572-0964
Distributed by Oscar de Leon Castillo
Distributor for Artemis y Edimter

Editorial del Ministerio de Educacion
15 Ave 3-22, Zona 1, Guatemala

Pedernal, *imprint of* Grupo Editorial RIN-78

Editorial Piedra Santa
5 Calle, Zona 1, 7-55 Guatemala
SAN: 002-6204
Tel: (02) 29053; (02) 851524; (02) 851526; (02) 328603 *Fax:* (02) 329053
E-mail: piedrasanta.sal@salnet.net
Key Personnel
President: Irene Piedra Santa
E-mail: irene_piedra_santa@hotmail.com
Founded: 1947
ISBN Prefix(es): 84-8377
Subsidiaries: Editorial y Libreria Piedra Santa SA de CV
Bookshop(s): 11 Calle 6-50, Zona 1

Ymoescuento, *imprint of* Grupo Editorial RIN-78

Guinea-Bissau

General Information

Capital: Bissau
Language: Portuguese (official), Criolo, Tribal Languages
Religion: Indigenous Beliefs (65%), Muslim (30%), Christian (5%)
Population: 1 million
Currency: Peso (12,068 = $1 US)
Copyright: Berne (see Copyright Conventions, pg xi)

Instituto Nacional de Estudos e Pesquisa
PO Box 112, Bairro Cobornel, Bissau
Tel: (0245) 223032 *Fax:* (0245) 251125
E-mail: inep@sol.gtelecom.gw
Key Personnel
Dir: Mamadu Jao *E-mail:* mama_jao@hotmail.com
Subjects: Agriculture, Anthropology, Developing Countries, Environmental Studies, Health, Nutrition, History, Social Sciences, Sociology, Technology

Guyana

General Information

Capital: Georgetown
Language: English & Amerindian dialects
Religion: Christian, Hindu, Islamic
Population: 739,000
Shop Hours: 0800-1130, 1300-1600 Monday-Friday; 0800-1130 Saturday
Currency: 100 cents = 1 Guyana dollar
Export/Import Information: No tariff on books. Only advertising of commercial value, subject to duty. There are numerous businesses that import books. Import license required. Nominal exchange controls.
Copyright: Berne (see Copyright Conventions, pg xi)

Amerindian Research Unit
University of Guyana, PO Box 101110, Georgetown
Tel: (02) 4930 *Fax:* (02) 54885
Web Site: gold.sdnp.org.gy/uog/

Caribbean Community Secretariat
PO Box 10827, Ave of the Republic, Georgetown
Tel: (02) 692809 *Fax:* (02) 267816; (02) 257341; (02) 258031
E-mail: carisec1@caricom.org; carisec2@caricom.org; carisec3@caricom.org
Web Site: www.caricom.org *Cable:* CARIBSEC GUYANA
Key Personnel
Senior Project Officer (Documentation Center): Maureen Newton
Founded: 1973
Regional integration movement whose ultimate goal is the improvement of the standard of living of all peoples in the Community. At present the Community has fourteen member states. The Secretariat is the administrative arm of the Community.
ISBN Prefix(es): 976-600
Total Titles: 24 Print

Community Based Rehabilitation Progeamme
PO Box 10847, Georgetown
Tel: (02) 64004 *Fax:* (02) 62615
Founded: 1986
Subjects: Child Care & Development, Developing Countries, Disability, Special Needs, Education
ISBN Prefix(es): 976-8107

Hamburgh Press+
c/o Walter Roth Museum of Anthropology, 61 Main St, Georgetown
Tel: (02) 58486 *Fax:* (02) 58511
Key Personnel
Contact: Jennifer Wishart
Founded: 1996
Subjects: Anthropology, Archaeology
ISBN Prefix(es): 976-8152

New Guyana Co Ltd
Lot 8, Industrial Site, Ruimveldt, Georgetown
Mailing Address: PO Box 101088
Tel: (02) 262471; (02) 262473 *Fax:* (02) 262472
Cable: NEWCO GEORGETOWN GUYANA
Printers of Mirror Newspaper.
ISBN Prefix(es): 976-8000

Roraima Publishers Ltd
76 Robb St Lacytown, Georgetown
Mailing Address: PO Box 10322, Georgetown
Tel: (02) 273551; (02) 222363; (02) 225057
Fax: (02) 262319; (02) 258844
E-mail: roraima-distributors@solutions2000.net
Key Personnel
Man Dir: David Yhann
Founded: 1994
Subjects: Fiction, Nonfiction (General), Guyanese Works
Associate Companies: Roraima Distributors

Haiti

General Information

Capital: Port-au-Prince
Language: French and Creole
Religion: Predominantly Roman Catholic (about 75 percent)
Population: 6.4 million
Bank Hours: 0900-1300 Monday-Friday
Currency: 100 centimes = 1 gourde. US currency is widely used
Export/Import Information: Books charged ad valorem, children's picture books per kilo net. Advertising matter under 1 kilo gross weight duty-free. No import licenses or exchange controls, other than occasional exchange rationing, leading to delays.
Copyright: UCC (see Copyright Conventions, pg xi)

Editions Caraiibes SA
Lalue, BP 2013, Port-au-Prince
Tel: 23179
Telex: ITT 2030198
Key Personnel
Contact: Pierre J Elie
Founded: 1973
Subjects: Agriculture, Business, English as a Second Language, History, Marketing, Physics
Distributor for Hatier International; LaRousse; L'Ecole SA; LeRobert

Deschamps Imprimerie
PO Box 164, Port-au-Prince
Tel: 57-8999; 57-3596; 56-3853; 56-2253
E-mail: henrid@acn2.net
Key Personnel
Man Dir: Jacques Deschamps
Editorial Dir: Mael Fouchard; Henri R Deschamps
Production Dir: Wilhelm Frisch Jr; Claude Deschamps
Financial Dir: Jacques Deschamps Jr
Sales Dir: Peter J Frisch
Read extensively in English & French.
Subjects: Education, Fiction, Literature, Literary Criticism, Essays, Religion - Other
Divisions: Imprimerie Henri Deschamps

Editions du Soleil
Rue du Centre, BP 2471, Port-au-Prince
Tel: (01) 23147
Telex: Ppbooth 2030001 attn Lisocial *Cable:* LISOCIAL
Key Personnel
Contact: Edouard A Tardieu
Founded: 1952
Subjects: Education

Theodor (Imprimerie)
rue Dantes Destouches, Port-au-Prince
Subjects: Fiction, History, Literature, Literary Criticism, Essays

Holy See (Vatican City State)

General Information

Language: Italian and Latin
Religion: Roman Catholic
Population: 802
Currency: Vatican lira = Italian lira. Italian currency is used
Copyright: UCC, Berne (see Copyright Conventions, pg xi)

Biblioteca Apostolica Vaticana
Cortile del Belvedere, V-00120 Citta del Vaticano
Tel: (06) 69879402 *Fax:* (06) 69884795
E-mail: bav@librs6k.vatlib.it
Telex: 2024 Dirgental VA
Key Personnel
Dir & Chief Executive: Don Raffaele Farina
Subjects: Art, History, Language Arts, Linguistics, Law, Philosophy, Theology
ISBN Prefix(es): 88-210

Archivio Segreto Vaticano
Cortile del Belvedre, 00120 Citta del Vaticano
Tel: (06) 69883314 *Fax:* (06) 69885574
ISBN Prefix(es): 88-85042

LEV, *imprint of* Libreria Editrice Vaticana

Pontificia Academia Scientiarum (The Pontifical Academy of Sciences)
Casina Pio IV, V-00120 Vatican City S
Tel: 0669883195 *Fax:* 0669885218
E-mail: academy.sciences@acdscience.va
Web Site: www.vatican.va/roman_curia/pontifical_academies/index_it.htm
Telex: 2024
Key Personnel
President: Prof Nicola Cabibbo
Founded: 1936
"To promote the progress of the mathematical, physical & natural sciences & the study of epistemological problems relating thereto".
Subjects: Biological Sciences, Chemistry, Chemical Engineering, Earth Sciences, Environmental Studies, Mathematics, Medicine, Nursing, Dentistry, Physics, Science (General)
ISBN Prefix(es): 88-7761
Number of titles published annually: 3 Print
Total Titles: 100 Print

Scuola Vaticana Paleografia - Scuola Vaticana di Paleografia Diplomatica e Archivistica
Cortile del Belvedere, 00 120 Citta del Vaticano
Tel: (06) 69883595 *Fax:* (06) 69881377
Key Personnel
Dir: Rev Sergio B Pagano *E-mail:* pagano@librs6k.vatlib.it
Founded: 1884
Subjects: Human Relations, Language Arts, Linguistics, Library & Information Sciences
ISBN Prefix(es): 88-85054

Libreria Editrice Vaticana+
Via della Tipografia, 00 120 Vatican City
Tel: (06) 69885003 *Fax:* (06) 69884716
Telex: 5042024 Dirgentel Va
Key Personnel
Dir: Don Nicolo Suffi, SDB
Founded: 1926
Subjects: Art, History, Literature, Literary Criticism, Essays, Philosophy, Religion - Other, Theology
ISBN Prefix(es): 88-209
Parent Company: Via Della Tipografia, I-00120 Vatican City
Imprints: LEV

Honduras

General Information

Capital: Tegucigalpa
Language: Spanish (English on northern coast)
Religion: Predominantly Roman Catholic
Population: 5.0 million
Bank Hours: 0900-1200, 1400-1630 Monday-Friday
Shop Hours: Tegucigalpa: 0800-1800, 1330-1800 Monday-Friday; 0800-1200 Saturday; San Pedro Sula: 0700-1200, 1400-1900 Monday-Friday; 0800-1200 Saturday
Currency: 100 centavos = 1 lempira
Export/Import Information: Member of the Central American Common Market but has applied tariffs to imports from other CACM countries since December 1970. No tariff on books. Duty on catalogues is per kilo. No import licenses. No exchange controls.
Copyright: Berne, Buenos Aires (see Copyright Conventions, pg xi)

HONDURAS

Editorial Guaymuras+
PO Box 1843, Tegucigalpa
Mailing Address: Apartado Postal 1843, Tegucigalpa
Tel: 237 49 31 *Fax:* 238 42 45
E-mail: editorial@sigmanet.hn
Key Personnel
Dir: Isolda Arita Melzer
Manager: Rosendo Antunez *Tel:* 2375433
Founded: 1980
Member of the Library Group of America; also acts as printer, bookseller & distributor.
Subjects: Anthropology, Education, Environmental Studies, Ethnicity, Government, Political Science, History, Language Arts, Linguistics, Social Sciences, Sociology
Number of titles published annually: 54 Print
Total Titles: 320 Print
Distributed by Abya-Yala de Ecuador; Arco Iris de El Salvador; Libros sin Fronteras (USA); Piedra Santa de Guatemala
Distributor for Centro Editorial; ENLACE y Nuevos Libros de Nicaragua; Libreria de la UNAH; Roxsil; UCA de El Salvador
Bookshop(s): Libreria Guaymuras, Ave Cervantes No 1055, Tegucigalpa *Tel:* 2224140

Editorial Nuevo Continente
Ave Cervantes, Tegucigalpa
Tel: 22-5073
Key Personnel
Dir: Leticia Oyuela

Editorial Universitaria
c/o Universidad de Honduras, Tegucigalpa
Mailing Address: PO Box 3560, Tegucigalpa
Tel: 312110
Telex: 1289

Hong Kong

General Information

Language: English and Chinese (Cantonese Chinese community)
Religion: Predominately Buddhist, also some Confucianism, Islamic, Hinduism & Daoism
Population: 5.8 million
Bank Hours: 0900-1640 Monday-Friday; 0900-1200 Saturday
Shop Hours: 1000-2000 Monday-Saturday
Currency: 100 cents = 1 Hong Kong dollar
Export/Import Information: No tariffs on books and advertising. No import licenses required. No exchange controls.
Copyright: Berne, UCC (see Copyright Conventions, pg xi)

Adsale Publishing Co Ltd
4/F Stanhope House, 734 King's Rd, North Point, Hong Kong
Tel: (02) 8118897 *Fax:* (02) 5165119
E-mail: publishing@adsalepub.com.hk
Web Site: www.adsalepub.com.hk
Key Personnel
Contact: Mrs Annie Chu; Ms P Y Ho
Publish Chinese & English industrial trade magazines to foster trade links between foreign companies & China.
ISBN Prefix(es): 962-7036
Branch Office(s)
Adsale People Inc, 3080 Olcott St, Suite 225D, Santa Clara, CA 95054, United States, Monica Kan *Tel:* 408-986-8384 *Fax:* 408-986-1580

Asia Pacific Communications Ltd
Fook Lee Comm Centre, Suite 2803, 33 Lockhart Rd, Wanchai
Tel: (02) 8610102 *Fax:* (02) 5296816
E-mail: asiapac@attglobal.net
Key Personnel
Editor & Publisher: Kathleen Ng
Founded: 1991
Subjects: Finance, Asian Private Equity, Venture Capital
ISBN Prefix(es): 962-85096
Subsidiaries: Institute of Asian Private Equity Investment

B & I Publication Co Ltd, see Business & Industrial Publication Co Ltd

Benefit Publishing Co+
PO Box 92310, Tsim Sha Tsui Post Office, Kowloon
Founded: 1994
Subjects: Art, Film, Video, Music, Dance, Publishing & Book Trade Reference
ISBN Prefix(es): 962-598
Book Club(s): Hong Kong Book & Magazine Trade Association Ltd

Breakthrough Ltd - Breakthrough Publishers+
Breakthrough Centre, 11th Floor, 191 Woo Sung St, Kowloon
Tel: 2735 8848 *Fax:* 2690 2603
E-mail: admin@el2100.com
Web Site: www.teachlikethis.com
Key Personnel
Contact: Karen Chan
Founded: 1973
Member of Hong Kong Book & Magazine Trade Association Ltd, Hong Kong Article Numbering Association.
Subjects: Fiction, How-to, Human Relations, Humor, Literature, Literary Criticism, Essays, Poetry
ISBN Prefix(es): 962-264
Warehouse: Flats A, S-V, 14/F, Haribest Industrial Bldg, Shatin Town Lot 173, Fo Tan, Shatin

Business & Industrial Publication Co Ltd+
China Overseas Bldg, Rm B-C 5/F, 139 Hennessy Rd, Wan Chai, Hong Kong
Tel: (02) 25273377 *Fax:* (02) 28667732
Key Personnel
Dir: Alan Kwok
Founded: 1974
Subjects: Mechanical Engineering, Technology
ISBN Prefix(es): 962-7701
Associate Companies: Business & Industrial Trade Fairs Ltd

Business Traveller Asia Pacific
Member of Interasia Publications Ltd
13/F, Tung Sun Comm Bldg, 200 Lockhart Road, Wan Chai
Tel: (02) 25119317 *Fax:* (02) 25196846
E-mail: biztrvlr@netvigator.com
Key Personnel
Publisher: Georgina Wong
Editor: Jonathan Wall
Advertising Dir: Angela Hung
Founded: 1982
Member of HKABC & the Society of Publishers of Asia.
Subjects: Travel, Only regional consumer travel title in Asia Pacific. Written in English with 12 issues per year
Subsidiaries: Northeast Media Group
Branch Office(s)
Far East Shopping Center, 545 Orchard Rd, No 09-02 238 882, Singapore, Regional Advertising Manager: Jennet Kho *Tel:* 735 0471 *Fax:* 735 0472 *E-mail:* biztrvlr@mbox2.singnet.com.sg
U.S. Office(s): Thomas International Publishing Co, 5 Penn Plaza, New York, NY 10001, United States, Contact: Herb Weikes *Tel:* 212-629-1546 *Fax:* 212-629-1542 *E-mail:* hwikes@aernet.com

Butterworths Hong Kong
12/F, Hennessey Centre, 500 Hennessey Rd, Causeway Bay
Tel: 2965 1400 *Fax:* 2976 0840
E-mail: customer.care@butterworths-hk.com
Web Site: www.butterworths-hk.com
Key Personnel
Commissioning Editor: Anisha Sakhrani
Senior Editor (Hong Kong Cases): Victoria Lai
Advertising Sales Manager: Simon King
General Manager, Customer Service: Wong Wai Cheng
Subjects: Law
Parent Company: Reed Elsevier
Associate Companies: Butterworths India, 14th floor, Vijaya Bldg, 17, Barakhamba Rd, New Delhi 110001, India, Publishing Manager: Ambika Nair *Tel:* (011) 373 9614 *Fax:* (011) 332 6456 *Web Site:* www.butterworths-india.com; Malayan Law Journal Sdn Bhd, Unit A-5-1, 5th floor, Wisman HB, Megan Phileo Ave, 12 Jalan Yap Kwan Seng, 50450 Kuala Lumpur, Malaysia, Managing Editor, New Product Development: Julie Anne Thomas *Tel:* (03) 2162-2882 *Fax:* (03) 2162-3811 *Web Site:* www.mlj.com.my; Butterworths Singapore, No 1 Temasek Ave, 17-01 Millenia Tower, Singapore 039192, Singapore, Regional Publishing Dir: Conita Leung *Tel:* 336 9661 *Fax:* 336 9662 *Web Site:* www.butterworths.com.sg

Celeluck Co Ltd+
Rm 603, Opulent Bldg, 402 Hennessy Rd, Wan Chai
Tel: (02) 8939197; (02) 8939147 *Fax:* (02) 8915591
E-mail: open@open.com.hk
Web Site: www.open.com.hk
Key Personnel
Chief Editor: Jin Zhong
Subjects: Asian Studies, Government, Political Science, History, Journalism, Specializes in China affairs
ISBN Prefix(es): 962-7934

CFW Publications Ltd+
130 Connaught Rd Central, Hong Kong
Tel: (02) 5543004 *Fax:* (02) 5438007
Key Personnel
Man Dir: Allan Amsel
Founded: 1979
Subjects: Cookery, Travel
ISBN Prefix(es): 962-7031

China Express Media Ltd
18/F, Jing Long Comm Bldg, 52 Tang Lung St, Hong Kong
Mailing Address: 17/F, 83 Wanchai Rd, Hong Kong
Tel: (02) 5757288 *Fax:* (02) 5757088
E-mail: ossima@netvigator.com

Chinese Christian Literature Council Ltd+
Surson Commercial Bldg, 14/F, 140 Austin Rd, Kowloon
Tel: 23678031
Key Personnel
Contact: Mr Sau-Chung Fung
Administration Secretary: Ms Yvonne Mak
E-mail: yvonne@cclc.biz.com.hk
An interdenominational publishing house-mainly in the Chinese Language and also a nonprofit making organization.
Member of WACC, UK.
Subjects: Literature, Literary Criticism, Essays, Music, Dance, Religion - Protestant, Theology
ISBN Prefix(es): 962-294

Bookshop(s): 10 Tung Fong St G/F, Kowloon
Warehouse: 77 Wong Chuk Yeung St, Room 702, Yan Hing Centre, Fo Tan, Shatin

The Chinese University Press+
The Chinese University of Hong Kong, Sha Tin, New Territories
Tel: 26096508; 26096500 *Fax:* 26036692; 26037355
E-mail: cup@cuhk.edu.hk
Web Site: www.cuhk.edu.hk/cupress.w1.htm; www.chineseupress.com
Telex: 50301 cuhk hx *Cable:* SINOVERSITY
Key Personnel
Dir: Steven K Luk *Tel:* (02) 6096043
  E-mail: stevenkluk@cuhk.edu.hk
Sales, Rights & Permissions & Business Manager: Angelina Wong *Tel:* (02) 6096500
  E-mail: laifunwong@cuhk.edu.hk
Production: Kingsley Ma *Tel:* (02) 6096467
  E-mail: kwaihungma@cuhk.edu.hk
Editorial Manager: Y K Fung *Tel:* (02) 6096563
  E-mail: yatkongfung@cuhk.edu.hk
Accountant: Yvonne Tam *Tel:* (02) 6096507
  E-mail: yvonnetam@cuhk.edu.hk
Founded: 1977
Member of Association of American University Press, Association for Asian Studies, International Association of Scholarly Publishers, Society of Scholarly Publishing.
Subjects: Art, Asian Studies, Business, Child Care & Development, Education, Geography, Geology, Government, Political Science, History, Journalism, Language Arts, Linguistics, Law, Literature, Literary Criticism, Essays, Philosophy, Psychology, Psychiatry, Science (General), Social Sciences, Sociology
ISBN Prefix(es): 962-201
Total Titles: 500 Print; 4 CD-ROM; 2 Audio
Distributed by University of Michigan Press (USA only)
Foreign Rep(s): University of Michigan Press (US)

Chopsticks Publications Ltd (Chopsticks Cooking Centre)+
108 Boundary St, Ground Floor, Kowloon
Mailing Address: PO Box 73515, Kowloon, Hong Kong
Tel: (02) 3368433; (02) 3368037 *Fax:* (02) 3381462
Key Personnel
Manager: Caroline Au-Yeung
Founder & Dir, Rights & Permissions: Cecilia Jennie Au-Yang *E-mail:* cauyeung@netvigator.com
Sales, Production, Publicity: Chiu Mei Au-Yeung
Founded: 1971
Train caterers in the art of Chinese cooking. Offers classes that last one, four, eight & 13 weeks as well as a 17-week teacher training course.
Member of International Association of Culinary Professionals, USA; Specialize in Oriental cuisine.
Subjects: Cookery, Oriental Cuisine, Dim Sum, Health Cookery
ISBN Prefix(es): 962-7018
Associate Companies: Cherrytree Press Ltd
Distributed by Gazelle Book Services Ltd (UK)

Christian Communications Ltd
Wai Lee Commercial Bldg, 3/F, 128 Castle Peak Rd, Shamshuipo, Kowloon
Tel: (02) 7258558 *Fax:* (02) 3861804
Web Site: www.ccl.org.hk
Key Personnel
General Secretary: Thomas Tang
Founded: 1971
Also acts as Bookseller & Printing Service.
Subjects: Biblical Studies, Religion - Protestant
ISBN Prefix(es): 962-202

Branch Office(s)
1711 Branham Lane, Suite A-4A, San Jose, CA 95118, United States
Bookshop(s): 1/F 46 Morrison Hill Rd, Wan Chai; 2/F Hing Pong Commercial Bldg, 749A Nathan Rd, Kowloon; 1/F Kolok Bldg, 722 Nathan Rd, Kowloon; 1/F Hong Lok House, 475 Nathan Rd, Kowloon
Shipping Address: Block D 18/F Tsuen Tung Factory Bldg, 38-40 Chai Wai Kok St, Tsuen Wan NT
Warehouse: Block D 18/F Tsuen Tung Factory Bldg, 38-40 Chai Wai Kok St, Tsuen Wan
Orders to: Tsuen Tung Factory Bldg, Block D 18/F, 38-40 Chai Wai Kok St, Tsuen Wan NT

Chung Hwa Book Co (HK) Ltd+
Second Floor, 5B-5F Ma Hang Chung Rd, Tokwawan, Kowloon
Tel: (02) 7150176 *Fax:* (02) 7138202; (02) 7134675
E-mail: info@chunghwabook.com.hk
Web Site: www.chunghwabook.hk *Cable:* 5494
Key Personnel
Man Dir & Editor-in-Chief: Kwok-fai Chan
Publishing Manager: Shirley Cheung
Sales Manager: Belgrid Wong
Founded: 1927
Member of the Hong Kong Publishing Professionals Society Ltd, permanent member of Hong Kong Publishing Federation Ltd.
Subjects: Antiques, Art, Asian Studies, Business, Career Development, Computer Science, English as a Second Language, History, Language Arts, Linguistics, Literature, Literary Criticism, Essays, Management, Marketing, Philosophy, Religion - Buddhist, Self-Help, Social Sciences, Sociology
ISBN Prefix(es): 962-231
Parent Company: Sino United Publishing (Holdings) Ltd
Divisions: Publishing, Marketing & Sales, Retail
Distributor for Longman Asia Ltd; Open Learning Univeristy of Hong Kong (Macau & Hong Kong); Oxford University Press (Hong Kong); Publications (Holding) Ltd; University of H K Press
Bookshop(s): 5B Ma Hang Chung Rd, 2nd floor, Tokwawan, Kowloon; Reader's Service Centre, 450-452 Nathan Rd, Kowloon; Mongkok Branch, 740A Nathan Rd, Kowloon; 88 Fu Yan St, Kwun Tong, Kowloon; Tsuen Wan Branch, 245 Sha Tsui Rd, Tsuen Wan
Shipping Address: Unit 1-3, 2/F, Fu Hang Industrial Bldg, One Hok Yuen St
Warehouse: Unit 1-3, 2/F, Fu Hang Industrial Bldg, 1 Hok Yuen St East, Hunghom, Kowloon

Courseguides International Ltd
1505, Seaview Centre, 139-141 Hoi Bun Rd, Kwun Tong, Kowloon
Tel: (02) 7373322 *Fax:* (02) 7931188
Key Personnel
Publisher: T P C Street
Founded: 1982
Subjects: Sports, Athletics
Subsidiaries: Courseguides International (UK) Ltd

Design Human Resources Training & Development+
IOC, Mountain View Ct, Discovery Bay, Lantau Island, Hong Kong
Tel: (02) 29877018 *Fax:* (02) 29877018
Key Personnel
Author & International Rights: Robert Wright
  E-mail: wright@hkusua.hku.hk
Subjects: Management, Self-Help
ISBN Prefix(es): 962-85036
Distributor for Asia 2000
Orders to: Robert Wright School of Business, University of Hong Kong, 7/F Men Wah Complex, Pokfulam Rd, Hong Kong

The Dharmasthiti Buddist Institute Ltd+
Blk A, 2/F, Cambridge Court, 84 Waterloo Rd, Kowloon
Tel: (02) 7608878 *Fax:* (02) 7610825
E-mail: dharma@glink.nethk
Web Site: www.glink.net.hk/~dharma
Key Personnel
Contact: Ms Lai Jill; Cho Karen
Founded: 1982
A registered non-profit, religious & cultural organization; also participates in cultural education.
Subjects: Education, Ethnicity, Philosophy, Regional Interests, Religion - Buddhist, Academic, Chinese Culture, Life Growth
ISBN Prefix(es): 962-7541

Easy Finder Ltd
10 Tseung Kwan O Industial Estate West, 8 Chun Ying St, Tseung Kwan 0, Kowloon
Tel: (02) 29907100 *Fax:* (02) 9907212
ISBN Prefix(es): 962-85324

Economy and Press
A1, 5/F, Lo Yong Court Commercial Bldg, 212-220 Lockhart Road, Wanchai
Tel: (02) 28917556
ISBN Prefix(es): 962-7277

The Educational Publishing House Ltd
14 F Tsuen Wan Industrial Centre, 220-248 Texaco Rd, 14th floor, Tsuen Wan, Hong Kong
Tel: (02) 4088801 *Fax:* (02) 4080174
Telex: 35330 eph hx
ISBN Prefix(es): 962-12
Associate Companies: Fook Hing Offset Printing Co Ltd; The World Publishing Co; Kam Pui Enterprises Ltd; The Seashore Publishing Co; Harris Book Co Ltd; Hong Kong Housing Projects Corp Ltd; Pan-Lloyds (HK) Ltd

Electronic Technology Publishing Co Ltd+
9/F, Room 1, 15 Shing Yip St, Kwun Tong, Kowloon
Tel: 2342 8297 *Fax:* 2341 4247
E-mail: info@electronictechnology.com
Web Site: www.electronictechnology.com
Key Personnel
General Manager: Peter Luk *Tel:* 2342 8298
Founded: 1969
Branch offices located in China & Taiwan, Province of China.
Subjects: Communications, Computer Science, Electronics, Electrical Engineering, How-to, Marketing, Radio, TV, Technology
ISBN Prefix(es): 962-7007
Subsidiaries: Modern Electronic & Computing Publishing Co Ltd

Federal Publications Ltd+
Hunghom Commercial Centre, 37 Ma Tau Wai Rd, Units 903-905 Tower B, Kowloon
Tel: (02) 3342421 *Fax:* (02) 7645095
Key Personnel
Man Dir: Tom Y L Ng
Founded: 1959
Member of Hong Kong Educational P A, Educational Booksellers Association.
Subjects: Biblical Studies, Biological Sciences, Computer Science, Geography, Geology, Health, Nutrition, Mathematics, Religion - Protestant, Science (General)
ISBN Prefix(es): 962-302
Parent Company: Times Publishing Ltd, Singapore
Associate Companies: Federal Publications Sdn Bhd, Malaysia; Federal Publications (S) Pte Ltd; Times Books International
Bookshop(s): The Times Book Centre, Centre, Shops C & E, Mitlon Mansion, 96 Nathan Rd, Kowloon; The Times Book Centre, Shop G31,

HONG KONG

Hutchison House, Central District; Howard Book Store, G/F 74 Argyle St, Kowloon
Warehouse: Federal Publications Ltd, 2D Freder Centre, 68 Sung Wong Toi Rd, Kowloon

FormAsia Books Ltd+
Yu Yuet Lai Bldg, 45 Wyndham St, Suite 706, Central Hong Kong
Tel: (02) 5226422 *Fax:* (02) 5224234
E-mail: info@formasiabooks.com
Web Site: www.formasiabooks.com
Key Personnel
Dir: Frank Fischbeck
Founded: 1985
Essentially Hong Kong.
Subjects: Art, History, Specializes in Chinese colonial arts, culture & history
Distributed by Weatherhill

Friends of the Earth (Charity) Ltd
53-55 Lockhart Road, 2/F, Wan Chai
Tel: (02) 5285588 *Fax:* (02) 5292777
E-mail: foehk@hk.super.net
Subjects: Agriculture, Energy, Environmental Studies, Government, Political Science, Health, Nutrition
ISBN Prefix(es): 962-8119

Geocarto International Centre
Rm 17 2/F Wah Ming Centre, 421 Queens Rd West/Western District, Hong Kong
Fax: 25464262
E-mail: geocanto@hkstan.com
Key Personnel
Contact: K N Au
Subjects: Earth Sciences, Geography, Geology
ISBN Prefix(es): 962-8226

Good Earth Publishing Co Ltd
Rm A 10/F Chiap King Industrial Bldg, 714 Prince Edward Rd, San Po Kong, Kowloon
Tel: (02) 3386103 *Fax:* (02) 3383610
Key Personnel
General Manager: Yu Chen Fan
ISBN Prefix(es): 962-7878

Hong Kong China Tourism Press
24/F, Westlands Centre, 20 Westlands Rd, Quarry Bay
Tel: (02) 25618196 *Fax:* (02) 25618196
Key Personnel
Editor-in-Chief: Wang Miao
Vice General Manager & International Rights: Catherine Lee
Founded: 1980
Subjects: Travel
ISBN Prefix(es): 962-7799; 962-7166
Subsidiaries: HK China Tourism Company Ltd

Hong Kong Publishing Co Ltd
307 Yue Yuet Lai Bldg, 43-55 Wyndham St, Central Hong Kong
Tel: (02) 5259053
Telex: 78018 stkhx hx *Cable:* Hkpublish
Key Personnel
Man Dir: Dean Barrett
Editor: Julia Birch
Founded: 1975
Subjects: Asian Studies, Fiction, Travel
ISBN Prefix(es): 962-7035

Hong Kong University Press+
14/F Hing Wai Centre, 7 Tin Wan Praya Rd, Aberdeen
Tel: 25502703 *Fax:* 28750734
E-mail: hkupress@hkucc.hku.hk
Web Site: www.hkupress.org *Cable:* University, Hong Kong
Key Personnel
Publisher, Rights & Permissions: Colin Day
Editor: Dennis Cheung

Marketing: Winnie Chau *E-mail:* hkupress@hkucc.hku.hk
Founded: 1956
Academic publisher.
Specialize in Academic Publishing in Chinese & English.
Subjects: Anthropology, Archaeology, Architecture & Interior Design, Art, Asian Studies, Behavioral Sciences, Biography, Biological Sciences, Child Care & Development, Communications, Criminology, Disability, Special Needs, Education, English as a Second Language, Environmental Studies, Geography, Geology, Government, Political Science, History, Labor, Industrial Relations, Language Arts, Linguistics, Law, Library & Information Sciences, Medicine, Nursing, Dentistry, Natural History, Philosophy, Public Administration, Real Estate, Religion - Buddhist, Social Sciences, Sociology, Technology, Women's Studies
ISBN Prefix(es): 962-209
Total Titles: 250 Print
Distributed by Drake International Services (UK); Harry Howell (Australia & New Zealand); Universal Book Services; University of Washington Press (USA); Apac Publishers Services Pte Ltd (Singapore)
Distributor for Centre of Asian Studies at the University of Hong Kong (Hong Kong, Macau, UK); Kali for Women (India); Oriental Ceramic Society of Hong Kong (Worldwide); University Museum & Art Gallery at the University of Hong Kong (Worldwide); Zed Books Ltd (UK, Hong Kong & Macau); Comparative Education Research Centre (at the University of Hong Kong); Department of Comparative Literature at the University of Hong Kong (at the University of Hong Kong); Department of Social Work & Social Administration at the University of Hong Kong (at the University of Hong Kong); Faculty of Law (at the University of Hong Kong); INSTEP Faculty of Education (at the University of Hong Kong)

Island Press+
3/F, Flat A, 33 Hill Rd, Hong Kong
Tel: 8588176 *Fax:* 4829889
Key Personnel
Man Dir: Ho Leung-mau
Founded: 1983 (originally founded under the names Li Weijia, Lee Chik-Yuet, Ho Leung-mau)
Subjects: Education, Environmental Studies, Journalism, Literature, Literary Criticism, Essays, Publishing & Book Trade Reference, Travel
ISBN Prefix(es): 962-431

Joint Publishing (HK) Co Ltd
9/F Chung Sheung Bldg, 9 Queen Victoria St, 10F, Central Hong Kong
Mailing Address: 10/F, Tsuen Wan Industrial, Bldg, 220-248 Texaco Rd, Tsuen Wan, NT
Tel: (02) 5230105 *Fax:* (02) 8104201
E-mail: jpchk@hk.super.net *Cable:* JOINT PCO
Key Personnel
Man Dir: Mr Zhao Bin
Deputy General Manager: Mr Au Kang Lam
Assistant General Manager: Mr Li Chi Kin; Mr Ho Pui Tong
Dir & Deputy Chief Editor: Mr Li Xin
Rights & Permissions: Luk Judith
Bookshop Manager: Mr Wong Ming Pang
Founded: 1948
Overseas Office: Guangzhou, China.
Subjects: Architecture & Interior Design, Art, Asian Studies, Business, Environmental Studies, Film, Video, Finance, Health, Nutrition, History, Language Arts, Linguistics, Law, Literature, Literary Criticism, Essays, Management, Marketing, Medicine, Nursing, Dentistry
ISBN Prefix(es): 962-04
Parent Company: Sino United Publishing (Holdings) Ltd

Subsidiaries: JPC Collection Ltd (Flags & Gifts); JPC Data Chu Ltd
Bookshop(s): Readers Service Centre, 9/F Chung Sheung Bldg, 9 Queen Victoria St, Central; Lam Tin Branch, Kowloon; Whampoa Branch; Tsuen Wan Cultural Plaza, Tsuen Wan; Sino United (Canada) Ltd, Vancouver, BC, Canada; BC & Sino United Publishing (Toronto) Ltd, Toronto, ON, Canada; Foshan United Book Co Ltd, China; Foshan H, China; JPC Bookstore & SUP Bookstore, China; Guangzhou, China; Sino United Publishing (LA) Ltd, Monterey Park, CA, United States; Eastwind Books & Arts Inc, San Francisco, CA, United States; Oriental Culture Enterprise, New York, NY, United States; Joint Publishing Co, Bejing; Kwai-Fong Branch; Kwai Chung

Lands Department, Survey & Mapping Office
Survey & Mapping Office, 14/F, Murray Bldg, Garden Rd, Central Hong Kong
Tel: (02) 28482267; (02) 28482182 *Fax:* (02) 25218726
ISBN Prefix(es): 962-567

Lea Publications Ltd+
North Point, 499 King's Rd, 17/F, Flat A, Hong Kong
Tel: 25620121 *Fax:* 25650187
Key Personnel
Chairman: Bernard K S Chiu
Founded: 1976
Subjects: English as a Second Language, Fiction
ISBN Prefix(es): 962-213
Associate Companies: Book Marketing Ltd
Distributed by Book Marketing Ltd (Hong Kong)

Ling Kee Publishing Group+
Top floor, Zung Fu Industrial Bldg, 1067 King's Rd, Quarry Bay, Hong Kong
Tel: (02) 5616151 *Fax:* (02) 8111980 *Cable:* BOOKLAND
Key Personnel
Founder-owner, Chairman & Chief Executive: Bak Ling Au
Man Dir: Albert Au
Founded: 1945
Member of Hong Kong Educational Publishers Association.
Subjects: Antiques, Education, English as a Second Language, History, How-to, Nonfiction (General)
ISBN Prefix(es): 962-605; 962-608; 962-609; 962-610
Parent Company: Ling Kee Group Ltd
Subsidiaries: Ling Kee Publishing Co Ltd; Ling Kee Book Store Ltd; Unicorn Books Ltd; Unicorn Book (S) Ltd; Ling Lee Publishing Co (S) Ltd; Ling Kee (UK) Ltd; Ward Lock Educational Co Ltd; BLA Publishing Ltd; Thames Head Publishers; Unicorn Publications Inc; Ling Kee Publishing Co Inc
Distributor for Encyclopedia of China Publishing House (Beijing, China)
Showroom(s): 755 Nathan Rd, Kowloon
Bookshop(s): Ling Kee Book Store Ltd, 131 Des Voeux Rd

Logical Products (HK) Ltd
Dept Philosophy Univ, Pokfulam Rd, Hong Kong
Tel: 8592797 *Fax:* 5598452
E-mail: fctmoore@hkuxa.hku.hk
Key Personnel
Contact: Prof Laurence Goldstein
Subjects: Computer Science, Philosophy
ISBN Prefix(es): 962-375

Steve Lu Publishing Ltd
Rm 1203 Man Yee Bldg, 60-68 Des Voeux Rd Central, Hong Kong
Tel: (02) 5210681 *Fax:* (02) 8450492
E-mail: ltlahk@netvigator.com

Key Personnel
Dir: Steve Lu
Subjects: Art, Natural History, Photography, Travel
ISBN Prefix(es): 962-85043

Macmillan Publishers (China) Ltd
Unit 1812, 18/F Paul Y Centre, 51 Hung To Rd, Kwun Tong, Kowloon
Tel: 2811 8781 *Fax:* 2811 0743
Web Site: www.macmillan.com.hk
Key Personnel
Man Dir: Yiu Hei Kan *E-mail:* yhk@macmillan.com.hk
Founded: 1969
Subjects: Foreign Countries
ISBN Prefix(es): 962-03
Parent Company: Macmillan Publishers Ltd, United Kingdom

Med Info Publishing Co
401 Man Yee Bldg, 60 Des Voeux Rd C, Hong Kong
Tel: (02) 5222713
Key Personnel
Sales Manager: Stella Ng
ISBN Prefix(es): 962-363

Ming Pao Publications Ltd+
Subsidiary of Ming Pao Enterprise Corp Ltd
Ming Pao Industrial Centre, 15/F, Block A, 18 Ka Yip St, Chaiwan
Tel: 2595 3111; 2595 3318 *Fax:* 2898 2646
Web Site: security.mingpao.com/books
Key Personnel
General Man & Chief Ed: Mr Poon Yiu Ming
Tel: 25953318
Dir: Tiong Kiew Chiong
Founded: 1986
Ming Pao Publications Limited is a leading Chinese language publisher in Hong Kong. It was established in 1986 & has been publishing more than thousands titles of books including both fiction & nonfiction for the past years. A great variety of subjects, fiction, biography, investment, management, philosophy, psychology, health, comics, cookery are covered. The publications encompass a wide range of readerships, from professionals to general readers. Many book programmes turned into great success in sales & repute. Ming pao Publications Limited is a subsidiary company of Ming Pao Enterprise Corporation Limited, which owns & runs business worldwide.
Subjects: Biography, Business, Child Care & Development, Cookery, Economics, Fiction, Health, Nutrition, Management, Nonfiction (General), Philosophy, Psychology, Psychiatry, Regional Interests, Comics, Investment
ISBN Prefix(es): 962-357; 962-973
Associate Companies: Ming Pao Magazines Ltd, Mr Lung King Cheong *Tel:* 2515 5111 *Fax:* 2505 7841 *Web Site:* www.mpweekly.com; Ming Pao Newspapers Ltd, Mr Cheung Kin Bor *Fax:* 2898 3282 *Web Site:* www.mingpao.com; Yazhou Zhoukan Ltd, Mr Yau Lop Poon *Fax:* 2505 9662 *Web Site:* www.yzzk.com
Book Club(s): Ming Pao Book Club, Mr Poon Yiu Ming

Modern Electronic & Computing Publishing Co Ltd+
Blk 1, 9/F, 15 Shing Yip St, Kwun Tong, Kowloon
Tel: 23428297 *Fax:* 23414247
E-mail: info@computertoday.com.hk
Web Site: www.computertoday.com.hk
Key Personnel
General Manager: Mr Peter Luk *Tel:* 23429844
Founded: 1989
Branch Offices located in China & Taiwan.
Subjects: Communications, Computer Science, Education, How-to, Microcomputers, Technology
ISBN Prefix(es): 962-7007
Parent Company: Electronic Technology Publication Co, 15 Shing Yip St, 9/F, Room 1, Kwun Tong, Kowloon, Hong Kong, China

Nam Hing Holdings Limited
27/F, Yuen Long Trade Centre, 99/109 Castle Peak Rd, Yuen Long
Tel: (02) 4759105 *Fax:* (02) 4732001
E-mail: nhillhkg@nh-laminate.com.hk
Key Personnel
Overseas Marketing Manager: Martin Hol
Founded: 1977
Subjects: Electronics, Electrical Engineering, Mechanical Engineering
Branch Office(s)
Nam Hing Industrial Laminate Ltd

Next Magazine Publishing Ltd
8 Chun Ying St, TKO Industial Estate West, Tseung Kwan O
Tel: (02) 7442733 *Fax:* (02) 7907240
E-mail: editorial@nextmedia.com.hk
Web Site: www.nextmedia.com.hk

Peace Book Co Ltd+
Rm 901-3 & 916 Wing on House, 71 Des Vouex Rd, Central Hong Kong
Tel: (02) 8046687; (02) 25222130 *Fax:* (02) 8046409 *Cable:* PEACEBOOK
Key Personnel
Chief Executive Officer: Shen Wenyu
Dir: Qian Wangsi
Founded: 1979
Subjects: Asian Studies, Health, Nutrition
ISBN Prefix(es): 962-7176

Pearson Education China Ltd
18/F Cornwall House, Taikoo Place, 979 King's Road, Quarry Bay
Tel: 3181 0000 *Fax:* 2565 7440
E-mail: firstnamelastinitial@pearsoned.com.hk
Key Personnel
President, North Asia: T C Goh
Finance Dir, North Asia: Marion Cameron
Marketing & Sales Dir: KP Tse
Publishing Dir: Cynthia Lam; Kenneth Ma
Dir, Bilingual Dict & Home Ed: T C Wong
Dir, Asia ELT: Farrah Ching

Philopsychy Press+
CPO Box 1224, 2A Tower 1 22 Sui ho Rd, Shatin, New Territories
Tel: (02) 6044403 *Fax:* (02) 6044403
E-mail: ppp@hkbu.edu.hk
Key Personnel
International Rights: Dr Stephen Palmquist
Founded: 1993
Philopsychy means soul-loving.
Subjects: Biblical Studies, Philosophy, Psychology, Psychiatry, Religion - Protestant, Self-Help, Theology
ISBN Prefix(es): 962-7770

Photoart Ltd+
16-A, Shun Point Bldg Commercial Bldg, 5-11 Thomson Rd, Wanchaia
Mailing Address: G PO Box 12928, Hong Kong
Tel: (02) 23617782 *Fax:* (02) 8669230
Key Personnel
Man Dir: Mr Lee Geormning
Founded: 1960
Subjects: Photography, Publishing & Book Trade Reference
ISBN Prefix(es): 962-8165

Press Mark Media Ltd+
Flat D, 1/F, Prospect Mansion, 66-72 Paterson Street, Causeway Bay
Tel: (02) 8822230 *Fax:* (02) 28823949; (02) 28822471
E-mail: magazine@todayliving.com
Key Personnel
Man Dir: Kenneth Li
Founded: 1987
Publishing & advertising.
Subjects: Architecture & Interior Design, Art, House & Home, Publishing & Book Trade Reference, Regional Interests, Sports, Athletics, Travel, Wine & Spirits
ISBN Prefix(es): 962-7608

Publications (Holdings) Ltd+
Unit A1, 20/F, Chaiwan Industrial Centre, 20 Lee Chung St, Chaiwan
Tel: (02) 8366088 *Fax:* (02) 8384061; (02) 8730861
Key Personnel
Publishing Manager: Leung Ka Kei
Editor: Ms Tse Yin Fong
Marketing Manager: Mr Fung Ka Wai
Founded: 1980
Subjects: Accounting, Advertising, Animals, Pets, Antiques, Astrology, Occult, Business, Career Development, Child Care & Development, Cookery, Crafts, Games, Hobbies, Fiction, Finance, Gardening, Plants, Health, Nutrition, How-to, Management, Marketing, Mysteries, Nonfiction (General), Psychology, Psychiatry, Travel
ISBN Prefix(es): 962-17
Parent Company: TVE International Ltd
Associate Companies: CV Idayus; TV Week Ltd; Retail Corp Ltd; Audio-Visual Travel Ltd; Highlight Tours Ltd

Research Centre for Translation+
Institute of Chinese Studies, Chinese University of Hong Kong, Shatin, New Territories
Tel: 26097399
E-mail: renditions@cuhk.edu.hk
Telex: 50301 CUHK HX *Cable:* SINOVERSITY
Key Personnel
Dir: Eva Hung
Man Editor, Rights & Permissions: Pak-shan Tam
Tel: 26097407 *E-mail:* pstam@cuhk.edu.hk
Production Manager: Cecilia S S lp
Founded: 1971
Specialize in English translations of Chinese literature.
Subjects: Asian Studies, Fiction, Literature, Literary Criticism, Essays, Poetry
ISBN Prefix(es): 962-7255
Distributed by China Books (Australia); Chinese University Press (Worldwide)

Sesame Publication Co+
Rm 505, 4/F Winner House, 310 King's Rd, North Point, Hong Kong
Tel: (02) 5089920 *Fax:* (02) 5789337
E-mail: sesame01@hkstar.com
Key Personnel
Man Dir: Paul Wong
Founded: 1987
Specialize in children's books & printing services.
Subjects: Animals, Pets, Child Care & Development, English as a Second Language, Fiction
ISBN Prefix(es): 962-347
Warehouse: Blk B, 23/F, Jing Ho Ind Bldg, 78-84 Wang Lung St, Tsuen Wan, China *Tel:* (02) 408-7685 *Fax:* (02) 407-2565

Shanghai Book Co Ltd
5th flloor, Block A, 345 Des Voeux Rd, West, Hong Kong
Tel: 25486160
Key Personnel
Man Dir: Lap Shan Wong

HONG KONG

Founded: 1946
Subjects: Music, Dance
ISBN Prefix(es): 962-239
Associate Companies: Shanghai Book Co (Pte) Ltd, Singapore; Shanghai Book Co, (KL) Sdn Bhd, Malaysia; China Cultural Corporation
Imprints: The Won Yit Book Co
Distributor for People's Music Publishing House

Sin Min Chu Publishing Co
Rm 1015, Tower A, Hung Hom Comm Centre, 39 Ma Tau Wai Rd, Hung Hom, Kowloon
Tel: 33493270 *Fax:* 7658471
ISBN Prefix(es): 962-336

South China Morning Post Ltd+
Tong Chong St, Quarry Bay
Tel: 25652435; 25652450; 25622271
Fax: 5655380
Telex: hx 86008 *Cable:* Postscript Hong Kong
Key Personnel
Editorial: Howard Coats
Advertising, Sales Manager: Hilary Davies
Production: Edgar Chiu
Founded: 1976
Subjects: Asian Studies, Radio, TV
ISBN Prefix(es): 962-10
Bookshop(s): SCM Post Family Bookshops in Star Ferry, Furama Hotel, Ocean Centre

Springer-Verlag Hong Kong Ltd
Room 701 Mirror Tower, 61 Mody Rd, Tsimshatsui, Kowloon
Tel: (02) 27239698 *Fax:* (02) 27242366
Founded: 1986
ISBN Prefix(es): 962-430
Parent Company: Springer-Verlag GmbH & Co KG, Heidelberger Platz 3, 14197 Berlin, Germany

Summerson Eastern Publishers Ltd+
4/F, Block B, 434 Queen's Rd W, Hong Kong
Tel: 5408123 *Fax:* 5597869
Key Personnel
Man Dir: Mr M K Woo
Executive Dir: Ms M M Chong
Senior Manager: Bill M P Lo
Founded: 1976
Member of Hong Kong Educational Publishers Association Ltd.
ISBN Prefix(es): 962-221

Sun Mui Press
PO Box 366, Shatin, New Territories
Tel: 2694 8525 *Fax:* 2697 7976
E-mail: auly@chevalier.net
Key Personnel
Contact: Au Loong-Yu
Subjects: Economics, Government, Political Science, History
ISBN Prefix(es): 962-7529

Sun Ya Publications (HK) Ltd+
FRm 1306 Eastern Centre, 1065 King's Rd, North Point
Tel: (02) 5620161 *Fax:* (02) 5659951
Telex: 85849 Clwso Hx *Cable:* 6386
Key Personnel
Man Dir, Editorial, Rights & Permissions: Irene Yim
Man Dir: Yim Ng Seen Ha
Sales: Chan Chung-Chiu
Production: Miss Tsang Suet-Ying
Publicity: Wai Kim-Hung
Founded: 1961
Subjects: Fiction, Nonfiction (General)
ISBN Prefix(es): 962-08
Parent Company: Sino United Publishing (Holdings) Ltd

Subsidiaries: Sunbeam Publications (HK) Ltd
Bookshop(s): 111 N Atlantic Blvd, Suite 228, Monterey Park, CA 91754, United States

Ta Kung Pao (HK) Ltd
2nd floor, 342 Hennessy Rd, Wanchai
Tel: 28363166
Key Personnel
Marketing Manager, Circulation & Marketing Executive: Summy Ho
Subjects: China
ISBN Prefix(es): 962-582

Tai Yip Co+
30A Stanley St, 2/F, Central Hong Kong
Tel: (02) 5250496 *Fax:* (02) 8453296
Key Personnel
Dir: Ying-Lau Cheung
Subjects: Art
ISBN Prefix(es): 962-7239
Bookshop(s): Tai Yip Art Book Centre, Hong Kong Museum of Art, Museum Shop, Salisbury Rd, 1st floor, Tsim Sha Tsui, Kln *Tel:* 7322088

Technology Exchange Ltd+
Suite 1102, Fo Tan Industrial Centre, 26-28 Au Pui Wan St, Fotan, Shatin, Hong Kong
Tel: 2602 6300 *Fax:* 2609 1687
Key Personnel
General Manager: Francis K F Ng *E-mail:* fng@tech-ex.com
Founded: 1987
Specializing also in medical devices, instrumentation of automation & cable tv.
Subjects: Communications, Electronics, Electrical Engineering, Radio, TV
ISBN Prefix(es): 962-452
Total Titles: 5 Print

Thomson Corporation
17/F Lyndhurst Tower, One Lyndhurst Terrace Central, Hong Kong
Tel: (02) 5335416 *Fax:* (02) 5303588
Key Personnel
Editor-in-Chief: Tony Shale
General Manager & International Rights: Geoff Defreitas
Subjects: Finance

Times Ringier Ltd
11-13 Dai Kwai St, Tai Po, New Territories
Tel: 2660 2666 *Fax:* 2664 1993
E-mail: trhkmktg@timesringier.com.hk
Parent Company: TPL & Ringier AG

Unicorn Books Ltd+
14/F Zung Fu Ind Bld, 1067 King's Rd, Hong Kong
Tel: 2562-2641; 2561-6151 *Fax:* 2811-1980
Key Personnel
Chief Operating Officer: Albert K W Au
Member of the Ling Kee Group, Hong Kong.
Subjects: Antiques, Child Care & Development, Crafts, Games, Hobbies, Gardening, Plants, How-to, Self-Help, Chinese Language, Encyclopedia, Hong Kong History
ISBN Prefix(es): 962-232
Parent Company: Ling Kee Publishing Group
Distributed by Encyclopeida Publishing House of China (Beijing, China)

Union Press Ltd
3/F, Hong Lok Mansion, 74 Argyle St, Kowloon
Tel: 25673762 *Fax:* 23945084
ISBN Prefix(es): 962-207

Vision Pub Co Ltd+
Flat 33, 5/F, Tower B, Cambridge Plaza, Sheung Shui, New Territories
Tel: 26798119 *Fax:* 26798119

Key Personnel
Manager: Kai-man Pang
Founded: 1987
Member of HK Educational Publishers Association Ltd.
Subjects: Mathematics, Technology
ISBN Prefix(es): 962-407

Vista Productions Ltd
A7/F Melbourne Industrial Bldg, 16 Westlands Rd, Hong Kong
Tel: 25632492; 25623496 *Fax:* 25655803
Telex: 63321 Timbk Hx
Subjects: Education
ISBN Prefix(es): 962-05
Associate Companies: Times Educational Co Sdn Bhd, Malaysia

Wellday Ltd
Rm 1901, Kai Tak Commercial Bldg, 317-321 Des Voeux Rd Central, Hong Kong
Tel: 23628489 *Fax:* 23628564
Key Personnel
General Manager: Ms Shen Miao
Subjects: Advertising, Business
ISBN Prefix(es): 962-85051
Distributor for Miller Freeman Publishers Ltd

Witman Publishing Co (HK) Ltd+
9-11, Tsat Tse Mui Rd, Ground floor, North Point
Tel: (02) 5626279 *Fax:* (02) 5655482
E-mail: witmanp@hk.star.com
Key Personnel
Dir: Yau Suk Ching
Founded: 1978
Member of ACTPO. Specialize in English Language Books, Cassettes, Videos & Diskettes.
Subjects: Fiction, History, Language Arts, Linguistics, Mathematics
ISBN Prefix(es): 962-7044; 962-304

The Won Yit Book Co, *imprint of* Shanghai Book Co Ltd

Yazhou Zhoukan Ltd
15/F, Blk A, Ming Pao Industrial Centre, 18 Ka Yip St, Chai Wan
Tel: 2515 5111 *Fax:* 2515 2790
E-mail: yzzk@mingpao.com
Key Personnel
Chief Editor: Mr Lop Poon Yau
Dir Circulation Marketing: Mr Sammy Tsui
Founded: 1987
Subjects: Asian Studies, Business, Economics, Finance, Regional Interests
ISBN Prefix(es): 962-85434
Parent Company: Ming Pao Grou

Zie Yongder Co Ltd
14/F, Aik San Bldg, 14 Westlands Road, Quarry Bay, Hong Kong
Tel: 29630111
ISBN Prefix(es): 962-7359

ZYC Holding Ltd
14/F, Aik San Bldg, 14 Westlands Road, Quarry Bay, Hong Kong
Tel: 29630111

Hungary

General Information

Capital: Budapest
Language: Hungarian (German widely known)

Religion: Predominantly Roman Catholic, also Hungarian Reformed, Lutheran & Hungarian Orthodox
Population: 10.3 million
Bank Hours: 0800-1630 Monday-Friday
Shop Hours: 1000-1800 Monday-Friday; 1000-1500 Saturday
Currency: 100 filler = 1 forint
Export/Import Information: Any companies should be registered at the Registry Court. 12% VAT on books. Book importing & exporting is through Kultura - Hungarian Foreign Trading Co, H-1389 Budapest 62, Postfiók 149; atlases through Cartographica, H-1443 Budapest, Postafiok 132. Magyar Hirdeto, Budapest, is a full service advertising agency.
Copyright: UCC, Berne (see Copyright Conventions, pg xi)

Advent Kiado+
Borsfa-u 55, 1171 Budapest
Tel: (01) 2565205 *Fax:* (01) 2565205
Key Personnel
Publishing Dir: Laszlo Erdelyi
Founded: 1988
Subjects: Astrology, Occult, Biblical Studies, Cookery, Education, Health, Nutrition, Medicine, Nursing, Dentistry, Poetry, Religion - Protestant
ISBN Prefix(es): 963-7817; 963-9122

Agape Ferences Nyomda es Konyvkiado Kft
Matyas ter 26, 6725 Szeged
Tel: (062) 444-002 *Fax:* (062) 442-592
E-mail: agape@tiszanet.hu
Key Personnel
Dir: Karoly Harmath
Founded: 1991
Subjects: Religion - Catholic
ISBN Prefix(es): 963-458; 963-8112
Parent Company: Agape, Novi Sad, Cara Dusana 4-Yu

Agrargazdsagi Kutato es Informatikai Intezet
Zsil u 3-5, 1093 Budapest
Mailing Address: PF 5, 1355 Budapest
Tel: (01) 1171011 *Fax:* (01) 1377037
Telex: 22-6923
ISBN Prefix(es): 963-491

Akademiai Kiado+
Prielle K u 19-35, 1117 Budapest
Mailing Address: PO Box 245, 1519 Budapest
Tel: (01) 4668282 *Fax:* (01) 4668251
Key Personnel
President & Man Dir: Zsolt Bucsi Szabo
Sales, Promotion, Home & International: Rita Nemeth
Editorial Dir: Reka Atzel; Gyoengyi Pomazi
Founded: 1828
Publishing House of the Hungarian Academy of Sciences.
Subjects: Archaeology, Art, Biological Sciences, Earth Sciences, Economics, Engineering (General), History, Language Arts, Linguistics, Law, Literature, Literary Criticism, Essays, Medicine, Nursing, Dentistry, Music, Dance, Philosophy, Science (General), Social Sciences, Sociology, Veterinary Science
ISBN Prefix(es): 963-05
Branch Office(s)
ISBS (International Specialized Book Service Inc), 5804 NE Hassolo St, Portland, OR 97213-3644, United States

Aranyhal Konyvkiado Goldfish Publishing+
Dolmany u 5-7, H-1131 Budapest
Tel: (01) 2396721; (01) 2391851 *Fax:* (01) 2396721
E-mail: sprinter@com.kibernet.hu
Key Personnel
Owner & Manager: Gandor Radvan
Marketing Manager: Zulton Takacs
Artistic & Design Manager: Xenia Radvan
International Rights Contact: S Emege David
Founded: 1993
Specialize in children's books, mainly board books & activity books; Member of MKKE (Association of Hungarian Book Publishers & Distributors).
Subjects: Animals, Pets, Child Care & Development, Cookery, Crafts, Games, Hobbies, Education, Humor, Language Arts, Linguistics, Literature, Literary Criticism, Essays, Nonfiction (General), Outdoor Recreation, Physics
Number of titles published annually: 70 Print; 2 CD-ROM
Total Titles: 35 Print
Ultimate Parent Company: MKKE (Association of Hungarian Book Publishers & Distributors)
Subsidiaries: Sprinter Prest Romania SRL
Distributed by Sprinter Rft
Foreign Rep(s): Sprinter Prest Romania SRL (Romania)

Atlantisz Kiado+
Gerloczy u 4, 1052 Budapest
Tel: (01) 2663870 *Fax:* (01) 2663870
E-mail: atlantis@budapest.hu
Key Personnel
Publisher: Dr Tamas Miklos
Founded: 1990
Also International Bookshop.
Subjects: History, Philosophy, Religion - Other, Social Sciences, Sociology, Theology
ISBN Prefix(es): 963-7978; 963-9165

Balassi Kiado Kft+
Attila u 79, 1012 Budapest
Tel: (01) 1755064; (01) 1162885
E-mail: balassi@mail.datanet.hu
Key Personnel
Dir: Peter Koeszeghy
International Rights: Judit Borus
Founded: 1990
Member of The Association of Hungarian Bookpublishers & Booksellers.
Subjects: Art, History, Language Arts, Linguistics, Literature, Literary Criticism, Essays, Nonfiction (General), Philosophy, Social Sciences, Sociology
ISBN Prefix(es): 963-506; 963-7873
Total Titles: 533 Print; 1 CD-ROM
Distributed by Harrassowitz (Germany); Polis (Romania)
Distributor for Cambridge UP; Kaligram (Romania, Slovakia); Polis (Romania)
Bookshop(s): Margit u 1, 1023 Budapest, Contact: Hannus Zsuzaa *Tel:* (01) 212-0214 *Fax:* (01) 212-0214
Book Club(s): Balassi-Klub, Margit u 1, 1023 Budapest *Tel:* (01) 335-2885 *Fax:* (01) 335-2885

Cartographia Ltd+
Pf 80, 1590 Budapest
Tel: (01) 363 3639 *Fax:* (01) 363 4639
Web Site: www.cartographia.hu *Cable:* CARTOGRAPHIA
Key Personnel
Man Dir: Dr Arpad Papp-Vary
Sales, Publicity, Rights & Permissions: Ms Zsuzsa Nemenyi
Founded: 1954
ISBN Prefix(es): 963-352; 963-352; 963-353
Bookshop(s): Bajcsy-Zsilinszky u 37, H-1067 Budapest
Warehouse: Bosnyak ter 5, H-1149 Budapest

Central European University Press+
Formerly Open Society Institute
Szent Istvan ter 11b, H-1397 Budapest Pf 519/2
Tel: (01) 327 3136 *Fax:* (01) 327 3183
E-mail: ceupress@ceupress.com
Web Site: www.ceupress.com
Key Personnel
Dir: Peter Inkei
Founded: 1994
Dedicated to broadening the range of literature available in English or topics concerning the past & present history & culture of people living in the countries of central & eastern Europe.
Subjects: Economics, Government, Political Science, History, Literature, Literary Criticism, Essays, Social Sciences, Sociology, Cultural studies & medieval history
ISBN Prefix(es): 1-85866; 963-9241
Total Titles: 98 Print; 1 Online
Ultimate Parent Company: Central European University
U.S. Office(s): 400 W 59 St, New York, NY 10019, United States, Contact: Martin Greenwald *Tel:* 212-547-6932 *Fax:* 212-548-4607 (US & Canada)
Orders to: Plymbridge Distributors Ltd, Estover Rd, Plymbridge, United Kingdom *Tel:* (01752) 202301 *Fax:* (01752) 202333 (Orders for UK & Western Europe)
Books International, PO Box 605, Herndon, VA 20172, United States *Tel:* 703-661-1500 *Fax:* 703-661-1501 (Orders for US & Canada)

CEU-Press+
Oktober 6 u 12, 1051 Budapest
Mailing Address: PO Box 10/22, H-1515 Budapest 114
Tel: (01) 327-3014 *Fax:* (01) 327-3042
E-mail: sales@ceu.hu
Key Personnel
Dir: Klara Takacsi-Nagy
Marketing Dir: Martha Avery
Founded: 1997
Subjects: Developing Countries, Economics, Environmental Studies, Government, Political Science, History, Literature, Literary Criticism, Essays, Nonfiction (General), Social Sciences, Sociology

Corvina Books Ltd+
Voeroesmarty Ter 1, 1051 Budapest
Mailing Address: PO Box 108, Budapest 4 H-1364
Tel: (01) 3184148 *Fax:* (01) 3184410
E-mail: corvina@mail.matav.hu *Cable:* CORVINA BUDAPEST
Key Personnel
General Manager: Istvan Bart
Production Manager: Miklos Kozma
Founded: 1955
Subjects: Art, Cookery, Fiction, Travel, Specialize in Music
ISBN Prefix(es): 963-13

Europa Konyvkiado+
Kossuth ter 13-15, 1055 Budapest
Mailing Address: Postfach 65, 1363 Budapest
Tel: (01) 1312700; (01) 1312708 *Fax:* (01) 1314162
Telex: 225645 *Cable:* EUROLIBER
Key Personnel
Publisher: Levente Osztovits
Executive Dir: Dr P Roman
Production: T Nevery
Sales: M Kertesz
Publicity: G Joo
Founded: 1945
Subjects: Biography, Fiction, Philosophy, Poetry
ISBN Prefix(es): 963-07; 963-207

Foldmuvelesugyi Miniszterium Muszaki Intezet
Tessedik S u 4, PB 103, 2101 Goedoelloe
Tel: (028) 320644 *Fax:* (028) 320960
E-mail: dekani@eng.gau.hu
Telex: 022-5816 *Cable:* FMMI GODOLLO
Key Personnel
Dir: Dr Fozsef Hajdu
Founded: 1954

Subjects: Agriculture, Electronics, Electrical Engineering, Energy, Engineering (General), Environmental Studies, Mechanical Engineering, Science (General), Technology
ISBN Prefix(es): 963-611
Imprints: Mezogazdasagi; Technika
Orders to: FMMI, Postfach 103, H-2101 Godollo

Gondolat Kiado
Brody S u 16, 1088 Budapest
Mailing Address: PF 225, 1368 Budapest
Tel: (01) 138-3358 *Fax:* (01) 138-4540
Key Personnel
Editor-in-Chief: Miklos Hernadi, PhD
Dir: Gyorgy Feher
Subjects: Nonfiction (General)
ISBN Prefix(es): 963-280; 963-281; 963-282

Greger-Delacroix
Amfiteatrum u 3, 1031 Budapest
Tel: (01) 1608936
E-mail: gregerdelacroix@compuserve.com
Key Personnel
President & Dir: Andras J Kereszty
  E-mail: delacroix@greger.hu, biograph@greger.hu, greger@elender.h
Burea Chief: Erika Kormendy *Tel:* 361-302-5149
  E-mail: delacroix@greger.hu
Founded: 1990
Reliable books.
ISBN Prefix(es): 963-85811
Online services available through MATAU.HU.

Hatagu Sip Alapitvany
Vaci ut 19, 1134 Budapest
Tel: (01) 140-3728; (01) 140-1717; (01) 111-3033
ISBN Prefix(es): 963-7615

Hatter Lap- es Konyvkiado Kft+
PF 97, 1525 Budapest
Tel: (01) 1315101 *Fax:* (01) 1315101
Telex: 1311343
Key Personnel
Dir: Kalman Lantos
Founded: 1985
Subjects: Science (General), Transportation
ISBN Prefix(es): 963-7403

Helikon Kiado+
Papnoevelde u 8, Budapest 1053
Tel: (01) 1174756; (01) 1174678; (01) 1174865
  Fax: (01) 1174865
Key Personnel
Man Dir: Janos Szilagyi
Founded: 1982
Subjects: Art, History
ISBN Prefix(es): 963-207; 963-208
Bookshop(s): Helikon Bookshop, Suetoe u 2, H-1052 Budapest; Litea Bookshop & Teagarden, Hess A ter 4, H-1014 Budapest

Holnap Kiado Vallalat
Zenta utca 5, 1111 Budapest
Tel: (01) 1656624; (01) 1666928
Key Personnel
Dir: Eszter Milkovich
ISBN Prefix(es): 963-345; 963-346

Idegenforgalmi Propaganda es Kiado Vallalat+
Angol u 22, 1149 Budapest
Tel: (01) 1363652; (01) 363653 *Fax:* (01) 1837320
Telex: 225309 *Cable:* 1PV-BUDAPEST
Key Personnel
General Dir: Istvan Fazekas
Assistant Dir: Tamas Moldovan; Andras Vaczi
Founded: 1971
Member of WTO, Offices in Brussels & Milan, 32 different services in sport & Congressional events.
Subjects: Science (General), Travel
ISBN Prefix(es): 963-316
Imprints: IPV Herausgeben
Warehouse: IPV Buecherlager, H-1135 Budapest

Ifjusagi Lap-eskonyvkiado Vallalat (Youth Publishing House)+
Revay utca 16, 1374 Budapest
Tel: (01) 1116660 *Fax:* (01) 1530959
Telex: 226183
Key Personnel
Dir: Bela Koncz
Assistant Dir: Jozsef Gebler
Founded: 1957
Subjects: Crafts, Games, Hobbies, Fiction, House & Home, Mysteries, Romance, Science Fiction, Fantasy
ISBN Prefix(es): 963-422

Ikon Publishing Ltd
Toeroekvesz ut 46/D, 1025 Budapest
Tel: (01) 1761404 *Fax:* (01) 1158089
Key Personnel
Man Dir: Dr Andras Renyi
ISBN Prefix(es): 963-7948

IPV Herausgeben, *imprint of* Idegenforgalmi Propaganda es Kiado Vallalat

Janus Pannonius Tudomanyegyetem
Pf 9, 7601 Pecs
Tel: (072) 411433 *Fax:* (072) 15738
Key Personnel
President of Publishing Committee: Lovasz Gyoergy
Founded: 1991
Subjects: Earth Sciences, History, Law, Management, Marketing, Philosophy, Physical Sciences, Social Sciences, Sociology
ISBN Prefix(es): 963-641

Jelenkor Verlag+
Munkacsy u 30/a, H-7621 Pecs
Tel: (072) 314782 *Fax:* (072) 336803
E-mail: jelenkor@mail.datanet.hu
Key Personnel
Dir: Gabor Csordas
Founded: 1989
Subjects: Art, Drama, Theater, Fiction, Film, Video, History, Literature, Literary Criticism, Essays, Philosophy, Poetry
ISBN Prefix(es): 963-676; 963-7770

Joszoveg Muhely Kiado+
Kecskemeti ut 6, 1053 Budapest
Tel: (01) 3326467 *Fax:* (01) 3173536
E-mail: joszoveg@euroweb.hu
Key Personnel
Publications Manager: Dr Peter Foti
Distribution Manager: Eva Fay
Founded: 1997
Book Publisher.
Subjects: Government, Political Science, Philosophy, Psychology, Psychiatry, Social Sciences, Sociology, Bilingual books & ethnography
ISBN Prefix(es): 963-9134
Total Titles: 5 Print

Kepzoemueveszeti Kiado+
Roza u 4 -6, 1077 Budapest
Mailing Address: Postfach 110, 1366 Budapest
Tel: (01) 2522177; (01) 251-1677; (01) 1176222
  Fax: (01) 2522177
Telex: 22405
Key Personnel
Manager: Kemenczey Zolt an
Founded: 1954
Fine Arts Publishing House.
ISBN Prefix(es): 963-336
Bookshop(s): Poszterhaz, V, Bajcsy-Zsilinszky ut 62; Kepesbolt, Budapest V; 1, Deak Ferenc ter 6
Orders to: Kerepesi ut 62, 1148 Budapest

Kiiarat Konyvdiado
Verder u 20, 1035 Budapest
Tel: (01) 3886312
Key Personnel
Manager: Gyorgy Palinkas
Founded: 1995
Three book series: Hungarian architecture, Philosophical essays & Youngest generation of Hungarian literature.
Limited Partnership & membership(s): MKKE-Budapest.
Subjects: Architecture & Interior Design, Literature, Literary Criticism, Essays, Philosophy
ISBN Prefix(es): 963-85415; 963-85696; 963-9136
Total Titles: 69 Print
Foreign Rights: Agency Balla & Co (Hungary)
Showroom(s): Mucsarnok Kunsthalle, Dozsa gy-u-37, 1146 Budapest, Contact: Gabriella Nagy *Tel:* (01) 3437401 *Fax:* (01) 3435205
Bookshop(s): Irok Boltja, Andrassy ut 45, 1061 Budapest, Contact: Bernadette Nagy *Tel:* (01) 3221645
Warehouse: Helikon Bookhouse, Bajosy-zs. u 37, 1065 Budapest, Contact: lpdiko Hortobagyi *Tel:* (01) 3312329

Kijarat, see Kiiarat Konyvdiado

KJK-Keaszov+
pf 578, 1374 Budapest
Tel: (01) 1126430 *Fax:* (01) 464-5607
E-mail: vevoszolg@kjk.hn
Web Site: www.kerszov.hn (or kjk.hn)
Key Personnel
Man Dir: David G Young
Editorial: Judit Fogarasi
Founded: 1955
Rights & Permissions/Distribution: Artisjus, Budapest Bookstore for Specialists.
Subjects: Business, Economics, Education, Government, Political Science, Journalism, Law, Marketing, Psychology, Psychiatry, Social Sciences, Sociology
ISBN Prefix(es): 963-222; 963-220; 963-221; 963-224
Total Titles: 500 Print; 10 CD-ROM; 5 Online; 5 E-Book
Online services available through www.kerszov.hn.
Bookshop(s): Szechenyi Istvan Bookstore, Szent Istvan ter 4, H-1064 Budapest V; Economy & Law, Nador utca 8, 1051 Budapest
Warehouse: 1106 Jaszberenyi ut 29, Budapest

Officina Nova, Koenyv-es Lapkiado/Bertelsmann Media Kft+
PF 226, 1391 Budapest
Tel: (01) 1887989 *Fax:* (01) 1686674
Key Personnel
Dir: Katalin Balogh
Editor-in-Chief: Andras Szekely
Founded: 1987
Subjects: Antiques, Art, Cookery, Gardening, Plants, Health, Nutrition, History, Humor, Travel
ISBN Prefix(es): 963-7835; 963-7836; 963-8185
Parent Company: Bertelsmann Verlagsgruppe GmbH, Munich,, Germany
Associate Companies: Bertelsmann Professional Information
Divisions: Media Nova

Koenyveshaz Kft+
Vaci ut 19, H-1134 Budapest
Tel: (01) 1311566 *Fax:* (01) 1311566

Key Personnel
President: Mr Jozsef Ronga
Also a distribution house.

Magyar Tudomanyos Akademia Koezponti Fizikai Kutato Intezet Koenyvtara
Konkoly Thege M u 29-33, 1121 Budapest 1525
Mailing Address: PF 49, 1525 Budapest
Tel: (01) 1699499
E-mail: kolcs@sunserv.kfki.hu *Cable:* MTA KFKI KOENYVTAR
Key Personnel
Head of Library: Erika Eory
Founded: 1950
Subjects: Chemistry, Chemical Engineering, Computer Science, Electronics, Electrical Engineering, Mathematics, Microcomputers, Physical Sciences, Physics
ISBN Prefix(es): 84-7248; 963-371; 963-372
Orders to: KFKI Konyvtara, Spain

Kossuth Kiado RT+
Csanyi Laszlo utca 34, H-1043 Budapest
Mailing Address: PO Box 55, H-1327 Budapest
Tel: (01) 3700607 *Fax:* (01) 3700602
E-mail: rt@kossuted.hu
Web Site: www.kossuth.hu
Key Personnel
Man Dir: Mr Andras Sandor Kocsis *Tel:* (01) 3700600 *E-mail:* andrass@kossuted.hu
Book Publishing Dir: Mrs Jolanta Szabone Szuba *Tel:* (01) 3700603 *E-mail:* jolanta@kossuted.hu
Multimedia Manager: Mr Laszlo Foldes *Tel:* (01) 3700608 *E-mail:* hobo@kossuted.hu
International Relations Manager: Mr Balint Ordogh *E-mail:* balinto@kossuted.hu
Subjects: Business, Child Care & Development, Communications, Education, Finance, Geography, Geology, Health, Nutrition, Management, Natural History, Philosophy, Psychology, Psychiatry, Religion - Catholic, Travel, Wine & Spirits
Number of titles published annually: 80 Print; 12 CD-ROM
Total Titles: 80 Print; 45 CD-ROM
Showroom(s): Andrassy Ut 13, H-1061 Budapest *Tel:* (01) 266-3514 *Fax:* (01) 266-3515

Kulturtrade+
Margit krt 64/b, H-1027 Budapest
Tel: (01) 3757288 *Fax:* (01) 2027145
E-mail: hl2618vin@ella.hu
Key Personnel
Publisher & General Manager: Gabor Vince
Publishing Dir: Magda Molnar
Founded: 1991
Member of Museum Store Association.
Subjects: Art, Health, Nutrition, How-to, Physical Sciences
ISBN Prefix(es): 963-7826
Distributor for Bonechi; Konemann; Taschen International
Showroom(s): Muecsarnox, Konyvesbolt, Dozsa Cyoergy ut37, 1146 Budapest; Budacyongye Bevagarouozpont, 1026 Budapest Pazsit u 2
Bookshop(s): Kulturtrade Konyvesbolt, Krisztina Urt 34, 1013 Budapest
Warehouse: Bakfark Balint u 1-3, H-1027 Budapest

Lang Kiado+
Balassi Bu 7, 1055 Budapest
Tel: (01) 1534805; (01) 2695264 *Fax:* (01) 1112230 *Cable:* 1055 BUDAPEST, BALASSI BALINT U 7
Key Personnel
President: Dr Erdoes Akos
Vice President: Zsuzsanna Vadas
Founded: 1988
Subjects: Business, Literature, Literary Criticism, Essays, Public Administration
ISBN Prefix(es): 963-8054; 963-7840

Subsidiaries: Kner Printing House; Victoria Kft; Sorger-Kolon Kft: B & W Kft; Wien- Budapest Kft; Publicitas Kft; Cash Flow Kft; Europrospekt Kft; Indikator Kft; Magyar Installateur Kft; CompAlmanach CSFR; Televital Kft; Repro Express Kft
Bookshop(s): Pozsonyi ut 5 Ungarn, 1134 Budapest

Magveto Koenyvkiado+
Vorosmarty ter 1, 1851 Budapest
Mailing Address: 1806 BP, PF 123, 1055 Budapest
Tel: (01) 1176222 *Fax:* (01) 1185219
Telex: 22-3502-Magve H
Key Personnel
Man Dir: Geza Morcsanyi
Chief Dir: Zsuzsa Koermendy
Sales & Publicity: Rozalia Janos
Founded: 1955
Rights & Permissions: Artisjus (under Literary Agents).
Member of MKKE.
Subjects: Art, Fiction, History, Music, Dance, Philosophy, Poetry
ISBN Prefix(es): 963-14; 963-270; 963-271
Bookshop(s): Magvetoe Koenyvesbolt, Szent Istvan Koerut 26, H-1137 Budapest
Warehouse: Vaci ut 19, H-1134 Budapest

Magyar Kemikusok Egyesulete (Hungarian Chemical Society)
Fo u 68, H-1027 Budapest
Tel: (01) 2016883; (01) 2012535 *Fax:* (01) 2018056
E-mail: mail.mke@mtesz.hu
Web Site: www.mtesz.hu
Telex: 224343 MTESZ H
Key Personnel
President: Dr Alajos Kalman
Vice President: Dr Laszlo Pallos
Secretary General: Dr Gyula Koertvelyessy
Subjects: Travel
ISBN Prefix(es): 963-8191

Magyar Koenyvkiadok es Koenyvterjesztoek Egyesuelese Vereinigung der Ungarischen Buchverlage & Vertriebsunternehmen
Voeroesmarty ter 1, H 1051 Budapest
Mailing Address: PF 130, 1367 Budapest
Tel: (01) 1176222
ISBN Prefix(es): 963-7002; 963-7409

Marton Aron Kiado Publishing House
Division of The Hungarian Pastoral Institute
Korhaz u 37, Budapest H-1035
Tel: (01) 368 9584 *Fax:* (01) 367 8415
E-mail: olimak@freemail.hu
Key Personnel
General Dir: Laszlo Arato
Founded: 1992
Subjects: Education, Human Relations, Religion - Catholic, Theology
ISBN Prefix(es): 963-7947; 963-9011

Medicina Koenyvkiado+
Pf PB 9, 1361 Budapest
Mailing Address: Beloiannsz u 8, 1054 Budapest
Tel: (01) 1122650 *Fax:* (01) 1122450
Cable: MEDICINA H-1054 BUDAPEST, BELOISNNISZ 8
Key Personnel
Man Dir: Prof Istvan Arky, PhD
Editor: Bela Ortutay; Dr Bulcsu Buda
Production: Marton Orlai
Founded: 1957
Publishing House of Medical Literature.
Member of MKKE-HPBA(Hungarian Publishers & Booksalers Assoc).
Subjects: Medicine, Nursing, Dentistry, Sports, Athletics, Travel
ISBN Prefix(es): 963-240; 963-243; 963-253; 963-241

Mezoegazda Kiado (Farmer Publishing House)
Pf 116, Budapest 1631, 1165 Budapest
Mailing Address: H-1165 Budapest, Koronafurt u 44, Budapest
Tel: (01) 4076575 *Fax:* (01) 4071787
Fax on Demand: (01) 4071019/44
E-mail: mezogazda@matavnet.hu
Key Personnel
Dir: Dr Lajos Lelkes
Founded: 1992
Subjects: Agriculture, Animals, Pets, Environmental Studies, Gardening, Plants, Science (General), Veterinary Science, Wine & Spirits
ISBN Prefix(es): 963-7362; 963-8160; 963-8439; 963-9121; 963-9239; 963-9358
Number of titles published annually: 50 Print
Total Titles: 150 Print

Mezoegazdasagi Koenyvkiado Vallalat+
Bathori utca 10, 1054 Budapest
Mailing Address: PB 26, 1882 Budapest
Tel: (01) 1317330 *Fax:* (01) 1117270
Telex: 61 20 2536
Key Personnel
Manager: Dr Csaba Gallyas
Founded: 1950
Agricultural Publishing House.
Subjects: Agriculture, Science (General)
ISBN Prefix(es): 963-7518
Subsidiaries: Natura
Bookshop(s): Agricultural Bookshop, Vecsei u 5, Budapest

Mezogazdasagi, imprint of Foldmuvelesugyi Miniszterium Muszaki Intezet

Mora Ferenc Ifjusagi Koenyvkiado Rt+
Hermina ut 57-59, 1146 Budapest
Mailing Address: Mova Kiado, Postfach 277, 1392 Budapest
Tel: (01) 2523284 *Fax:* (01) 1115003
Telex: 227027
Key Personnel
Man Dir: Marton Bazso
Founded: 1950
Subjects: Science Fiction, Fantasy
ISBN Prefix(es): 963-11
Bookshop(s): Bobita Koenyvesbolt, Bajcsy-Zsilinszky ut 27, 1065 Budapest; Mora Ferenc Koenyvesbolt, Szabadsag ter 3/A, 6000 Kecskemet
Book Club(s): Mora Koenyvklub (Mora Bucklub)-Kinderbuecher

Mueszaki Koenyvkiado Ltd+
Szentendrei ut Ter 1, 1014 Budapest
Mailing Address: Pf 385, 1536 Budapest 3 Pf 48
Tel: (01) 563458; (01) 1557122 *Fax:* (01) 755713
E-mail: lakatosz@muszakikiado.hu
Telex: 226490
Key Personnel
Man Dir: Sandor Berczi
BCl, Textbooks: Maria Kekes
BC2, Vocational Textbooks: Norbert Baranyi
Rights & BC3, Professional: Zoltan Lakatos
Founded: 1955
Subjects: Architecture & Interior Design, Career Development, Chemistry, Chemical Engineering, Computer Science, Electronics, Electrical Engineering, Management, Mathematics, Physics, Science (General), Technology
ISBN Prefix(es): 963-10; 963-16

Mult es Jovo Kiado+
Keleti Karoly u 27, 1024 Budapest
Tel: (01) 316 70 19 *Fax:* (01) 316 70 19

HUNGARY

E-mail: mandj@multesjovo.hu
Web Site: www.multesjovo.hu
Key Personnel
Dir & Chief Editor: Janos Kobanyai
Founded: 1989
Subjects: History, Literature, Literary Criticism, Essays, Social Sciences, Sociology, Jewish Literature, History & Culture
ISBN Prefix(es): 963-85295; 963-85697; 963-85817; 963-9171
Foreign Rep(s): Liepman AG Literary Agency

Nemzeti Tankoenyvkiado+
Szalay u 10-14, 1055 Budapest
Mailing Address: Pf 20, 1363 Budapest
Tel: (01) 1291496; (01) 1530600 *Fax:* (01) 363 2423
E-mail: ntk@mail.datanet.hu
Key Personnel
Man Dir: Dr Abraham Istvan
Editorial: Mr Rethy Endre
Sales: Dr Danka Attila
Production: Mrs Etclka Babies Vasvan
International Rights Contact: Mrs Fudit Farago
Founded: 1949
Textbook Publishing House.
Subjects: Biological Sciences, Education, Geography, Geology, History, Language Arts, Linguistics, Law, Literature, Literary Criticism, Essays, Marketing, Mathematics, Mechanical Engineering, Music, Dance, Philosophy, Physics, Psychology, Psychiatry
ISBN Prefix(es): 963-17; 963-18
Shipping Address: Pontus Book Shop & Delivery Service, Gat u 25, 1095 Budapest

Nemzetkozi Szinhazi Intezet Magyar Kozpontja
Hevesi S ter 2, 1077 Budapest
Tel: (01) 1752372 *Fax:* (01) 1751184
Key Personnel
President: Gyoergy Lengyel
Dir: Erzsebet Bereczky
Subjects: Drama, Theater, Literature, Literary Criticism, Essays
ISBN Prefix(es): 963-691

Novorg Kiado+
pf 52, 1553 Budapest
Mailing Address: Postafiok 101, H-1518 Budapest
Tel: (01) 1603790; (01) 1603596; (01) 1602300 *Fax:* (01) 145581
E-mail: novorged@kjk.hu
Key Personnel
Manager: P Boris
Founded: 1986
Subjects: Business, Cookery, Economics, Finance, How-to, Law, Management, Marketing, Public Administration, Real Estate
ISBN Prefix(es): 963-485
Parent Company: Wolters Kluwer
Associate Companies: Koezgazdasagi Es Jogi Koenyvkiado
Showroom(s): W K Koenyvkereskedelmi Koezpont, Szentendrei ut 89-93, 1033 Budapest
Warehouse: W K Koenyvkereskedelmi Koezpont, Szentendrei ut 89-93, 1033 Budapest

OKKER Oktatasi, Kereskedelmi es Szervezesi Iroda
Csemgery u 68, 1064 Budapest
Tel: 01 332 4587
Key Personnel
Dir: Susanna Nouakne Gal
ISBN Prefix(es): 963-7315; 963-85136; 963-8351

Open Society Institute, see Central European University Press

Orszagos Mueszaki, Informacios Koezpont es Koenyvtar
Reviczky u 6, 1088 Budapest
Mailing Address: PF 12, 1428 Budapest
Tel: (01) 1336300; (01) 1137439 *Fax:* (01) 1382414
Telex: 22-4944 omikk-h
Key Personnel
Dir General: Dr Peter Horvath
Dir: Lajos Janszky
ISBN Prefix(es): 963-593; 963-592

Osiris Kiado (Osiris Publishing)+
Egyeten Ter 5, 2/10a, 1053 Budapest
Tel: (01) 266-6560 *Fax:* (01) 267-0935
E-mail: osiriskiado@mail.datanet.hu
Web Site: www.osiriskiado.hu
Key Personnel
Dir: Janos Gyurgyak *Tel:* (01) 266-6560, Ext 106
Founded: 1993
Subjects: Anthropology, Archaeology, Economics, Film, Video, History, Law, Library & Information Sciences, Literature, Literary Criticism, Essays, Philosophy, Psychology, Psychiatry, Religion - Catholic, Religion - Protestant, Social Sciences, Sociology, Theology
Number of titles published annually: 200 Print

Panem+
Zoldmali lejo 12/a, 1025 Budapest
Tel: (01) 120-8303 *Fax:* (01) 344-3923
E-mail: panem@mail.datanet.hu
Key Personnel
Dir: Zsuzsa Tarr
Founded: 1990
Subjects: Computer Science, Economics, Engineering (General), Science (General)
ISBN Prefix(es): 963-545; 963-7628

Park Konyvkiado Kft (Park Publisher)+
Sallei u 31, 1136 Budapest
Tel: (01) 1315767 *Fax:* (01) 2124363
E-mail: park@mail.matav.hu
Key Personnel
Manager: Andras Rochlitz
Marketing: Ms Aniko Zambo *Tel:* (01) 2125535
Founded: 1988
Subjects: Art, Child Care & Development, Gardening, Plants, History, House & Home, Management, Nonfiction (General), Self-Help
ISBN Prefix(es): 963-7737; 963-7737; 963-7970; 963-8227
Total Titles: 110 Print

Planetas Kiadoi es Kereskedelmi Kft
Koronafurt U 44, 1165 Budapest
Tel: (01) 1315767
Key Personnel
Dir: Klara Taxner
Founded: 1982
Subjects: Art, Music, Dance, Folklore
ISBN Prefix(es): 963-7931; 963-7737; 963-7970; 963-8227

Polgar Citizen Press+
Attila u 20, Budapest 1013
Tel: (01) 1752854; (01) 1568358
Key Personnel
Editor-in-Chief: Tamas Bekes
Subjects: Literature, Literary Criticism, Essays, Science (General)
Subsidiaries: Polgar Video Ltd

Saldo Penzugyi Tanacsado es Informatikai Rt+
Bartok B u 120, 1113 Budapest
Mailing Address: Postfach 64, 1364 Budapest
Tel: (01) 2038213; (01) 2038217
Telex: 226387
Key Personnel
General Dir: Dr Andras Mohos
Marketing Manager: Dr Jozsef Racz
Founded: 1959
Subjects: Accounting, Economics, Finance, Law, Public Administration
ISBN Prefix(es): 963-621

Springer Hungarica Kiado Kft
PF 142, 1410 Budapest
Tel: (01) 251-0099
Telex: 2515973
Founded: 1990
Subjects: Earth Sciences, Engineering (General), Medicine, Nursing, Dentistry
ISBN Prefix(es): 963-7775

Statiqum Kiado es Nyomda Kft+
Postfach 99, 1300 Budapest
Tel: (01) 1803311 *Fax:* (01) 1688635
Telex: 226699 Skv h
Key Personnel
Man Dir: Benedek Belecz
Sales Dir: Gyoergy Szehr
Rights & Permissions: Artisjus
Founded: 1991 (predecessor 1954)
Legal successor of Statistical Publishing House.
Subjects: Computer Science, Economics, Mathematics, Social Sciences, Sociology
ISBN Prefix(es): 963-340
Parent Company: State Property Agency, Vigado u 6, H-1051 Budapest
Bookshop(s): Statistical & Computing Bookshop, Keleti Karoly u 10, Budapest *Tel:* (01) 1158018
Orders to: KULTURA Aussenhandelsunternehmen fur Bucher und Zeintschriften, PO Box 149, H-1389 Budapest

Szabad Ter Kiado+
pf 95, 1525 Budapest
Tel: (01) 1550175; (01) 3755922 *Fax:* (01) 1560998; (01) 3560998
Telex: 223553
Key Personnel
Dir: Gabor Koltay
Deputy Dir, Productions Dir: Jozsef Lovasi
Founded: 1988
Cultural Service Guidance, Expense Sheet.
Subjects: Fashion, Government, Political Science, Literature, Literary Criticism, Essays, Mysteries
ISBN Prefix(es): 963-7810

Szabvanykiado+
9 Postfach 24, 1450 Budapest
Tel: (01) 1183011; (01) 1183442 *Fax:* (01) 1185125
Telex: 225723 norm h
Founded: 1972
Subjects: Nonfiction (General)
ISBN Prefix(es): 963-402

Szarvas Andras Cartographic Agency+
Repassy utca 2.IV.27, Budapest H-1149
Tel: (01) 363 0672; (01) 221 68 30 *Fax:* (01) 363 0672; (01) 221 68 30
E-mail: szarvas.andras@mail.datanet.hu
Key Personnel
Owner: Szarvas Andras *E-mail:* szarvas.andras@mail.datanet.hu
Founded: 1991
Map publishing & distribution.
Subjects: Earth Sciences, Geography, Geology, Regional Interests, Transportation, Travel
ISBN Prefix(es): 963-9251
Number of titles published annually: 20 Print
Total Titles: 40 Print

Szazadveg
Csalogany u 6-10, 1015 Budapest
Mailing Address: Menesi ut 12, 1118 Budapest
Tel: (01) 166-9902; (01) 166-5309; (01) 2010688 *Fax:* (01) 2100384
E-mail: stumpf@bsp.mtapti.hu

Key Personnel
Dir: GyurgyaK Janos
Marketing Manager: Pesti Zsuzsa
ISBN Prefix(es): 963-379; 963-7911; 963-8384

Szepirodalmi Koenyvkiado Kiado
pf 58, 1428 Budapest
Mailing Address: PB 58, Lenin Krt 9-11, 1073 Budapest
Tel: (01) 1221285
Key Personnel
Man Dir: Marton Tarnoc
Rights & Permissions: Ministry of Culture
Founded: 1950
Subjects: Education, Fiction, Poetry
ISBN Prefix(es): 963-15

Magyar Eszperanto Szoevetseg
Kenyermezo u 6, 1028 Budapest
Mailing Address: PB 193, 1368 Budapest
Tel: (01) 1564093; (01) 1563659 *Cable:* ESPERANTOCENTRO, BUDAPEST
Key Personnel
Dir: Mr Oszkar Princz
ISBN Prefix(es): 963-571

Tajak Korok Muzeumok Egyesuelet
PB 54, 1476 Budapest
Tel: (01) 2101330 *Fax:* (01) 2101329
Key Personnel
Publisher: Istvan Eri
Founded: 1977
Subjects: Archaeology, Architecture & Interior Design, Art, History, Natural History
ISBN Prefix(es): 963-555

Taltos Kiadasszervezesi Ltd
Bajza u 1, 1071 Budapest
Tel: (01) 1213515 *Fax:* (01) 1420676
ISBN Prefix(es): 963-7825

Technika, *imprint of* Foldmuvelesugyi Miniszterium Muszaki Intezet

Tevan Kiado Vallalat+
Iranyi u 4/6, 5600 Bekescsaba
Tel: (066) 23159; (066) 327766
Key Personnel
Dir: Dr Janos Cs Toth
Deputy Dir: Kantor Zsolt
Founded: 1989
Subjects: Fiction, Poetry
ISBN Prefix(es): 963-7900; 963-7278

Typotex Kft Elektronikus Kiado+
Ketek u 33, 1024 Budapest
Tel: (01) 2013317 *Fax:* (01) 3163759
E-mail: typotex@euroweb.hu
Web Site: www.vision.euroweb.hu/typotex
Key Personnel
Dir: Zsuzsa Votisky
Founded: 1989
Subjects: Mathematics, Philosophy, Physics
ISBN Prefix(es): 963-7546
Total Titles: 100 Print
Subsidiaries: Index Buchladen

Magyar Tudomanyos Akademia VilagGazdasagi Kutato Intezet
Kallo esp u 15, 1124 Budapest
Mailing Address: PB 36, 1531 Budapest
Tel: (01) 1668433 *Fax:* (01) 1620661
Telex: 227713 *Cable:* BUWORLDINST
Key Personnel
Dir: Prof Andras Inotai
ISBN Prefix(es): 963-301

Zenemukiado Vallalat+
Voeroesmarty ter 1, 1051 Budapest
Mailing Address: PB 322, 1370 Budapest
Tel: (01) 1176222
E-mail: musicpubl@emb.hu
Telex: 225500 *Cable:* EDITIOMUSICA
Key Personnel
Man Dir: Istvan Homolya
International Rights: Antal Boronkay
Founded: 1950
Subjects: Biography, Music, Dance
ISBN Prefix(es): 963-330
Bookshop(s): Andrassy ut h5, H-1061 Budapest
Tel: (01) 322-4091 *Fax:* (01) 322-4091

Zrinyi Kiado
pf 22, 1440 Budapest
Tel: (01) 2100020; (01) 1331170; (01) 3339165 *Fax:* (01) 3142432
Key Personnel
Manager: Mate Eszes
Publishing House of the Hungarian Army.
Subjects: Military Science, Science (General)
ISBN Prefix(es): 963-327; 963-326

Iceland

General Information

Capital: Reykjavik
Language: Icelandic (widespread knowledge of English
Religion: Lutheran
Population: 259,000
Bank Hours: 0915-1600 Monday-Friday (winter); 0800-1600 (summer); some open 1700-1800 Thursday
Shop Hours: 0900-1800 Monday-Thursday; 0900-1700/1900 Friday; most open 0900-1600 Saturday (winter)
Currency: 100 aurar = 1 krona
Export/Import Information: Member of the European Economic Area. 14% VAT on books. Sales Tax. No import licenses required. No exchange controls for books but they may not be imported on credit.
Copyright: UCC, Berne, Florence (see Copyright Conventions, pg xi)

AEskan
Eiriksgotu 5, 101 Reykjavik
Mailing Address: Postholf 523, 121 Reykjavik
Tel: 551-0248
Founded: 1930
ISBN Prefix(es): 9979-808; 9979-9395

Almenna Bokafelagid
Nybylavegur 16, 200 Kopavogur
Tel: 5643170 *Fax:* 5643190
Key Personnel
Man Dir: Fridriksson Fridrik
Editorial: Bjarni Thorstensson; Eirikur Hreinn Finnbogason
Sales Dir: Andri Thor Gudmundsson
Rights & Permissions: Stefania Petursdottir
Founded: 1955
Subjects: Biography, Fiction, History, Nonfiction (General), Poetry
ISBN Prefix(es): 9979-4
Book Club(s): The AB Book Club (BAB); The MAT Cookery Book Club; TAB (Music Club)

Arnamagnaean Institute in Iceland, see Stofnun Arna Magnussonar a Islandi

Hjalmar R Bardarson
Hrauntunga V/Alftanesveg, 210 Gardabaer, Reykjavik
Mailing Address: Postholf 998, 121 Reykjavik
Tel: 5550729
Key Personnel
Editor: Hjalmar R Bardarson
ISBN Prefix(es): 9979-818
Warehouse: Sidumuli 21, PO Box 8181, IS-128 Reykjavik
Orders to: Islensk Bokadrefin HF

Bokaforlag Birtingur+
Laugavegur 66, 101 Reykjavik
Tel: 5627700 *Fax:* 5627710
Founded: 1988
Subjects: Astrology, Occult, Health, Nutrition, Mysteries, Parapsychology, Philosophy, Psychology, Psychiatry, Religion - Other
ISBN Prefix(es): 9979-815; 9979-9002

Bokautgafan Orn og Orlygur ehf+
Dvergshoefda 27, IS-112 Reykjavik
Tel: 5671777 *Fax:* 5671240; 5684866
Telex: 2197 Ornice
Key Personnel
Man Dir: Pall Bragi Kristjonsson *E-mail:* pbk@centrum.is
Founded: 1966
Subjects: Biography, Cookery, Gardening, Plants, Health, Nutrition, How-to
ISBN Prefix(es): 9979-55

Bokaverslun Sigfusar Eymundssonar
Austurstraeti 18, 101 Reykjavik
Tel: 13135 *Fax:* 15078
Subjects: Education

Draupnisutgafan, **Loegberg**, *imprint of* Idunn

Filadelfia forlag
Hatun 2, 105 Raykjavik
Mailing Address: PO Box 5135, 125 Reykjavik
Tel: 5525155 *Fax:* 5620735
Telex: 3000 simtexisforlag
Key Personnel
Man Dir: Hronn Svansdottir
ISBN Prefix(es): 9979-803

Fjolvi
Njoervasundi 15A, 104 Reykjavik
Tel: 5688433 *Fax:* 5688142
Telex: 2159 Rethor
Key Personnel
Man Dir: Sturla Eiriksson
Editorial: Thorsteinn Thorarensen
Founded: 1966
Subjects: Fiction, History, Natural History, Poetry, Science (General)
ISBN Prefix(es): 9979-58
Book Club(s): Bokaklubbur Fjolva; Particip 'Verold'

Forlagid+
Laugavegi 18, 101 Reykjavik
Mailing Address: Postholf 786, 121 Reykjavik
Tel: 5525188 *Fax:* 5527937
E-mail: forlag@mm.is
Key Personnel
Man Dir: Johann Pall Valdimarsson
Founded: 1984
Subjects: Education, Fiction, Nonfiction (General), Travel
ISBN Prefix(es): 9979-53
Parent Company: Mal Og Menning

Frjals fjolmiolun hf-Urvalsbaekur
bverholti 11, 105 Reykjavik
Mailing Address: Postholf 5380, 125 Reykjavik
Tel: 5632700; 5227022 *Fax:* 9127079
Key Personnel
Editor: Sig Hreidar Hreidarsson
Founded: 1981 (an amalgamation of firms from 1910)

ICELAND

Subjects: Fiction, Mysteries, Romance
ISBN Prefix(es): 9979-9006; 9979-9023; 9979-840

Frodi Ltd+
Seljavegi 2, 101 Reykjavik
Tel: 5155500 *Fax:* 515-5599
E-mail: frodi@frodi.is
Web Site: www.frodi.is
Key Personnel
Contact: Magnus Hreggvidsson *E-mail:* magnus@frodi.is; Steinar J Ludviksson *E-mail:* steinar@frodi.is
International Contact: Halldora Viktorsdottir *E-mail:* halldora@frodi.is
Founded: 1989
Subjects: Architecture & Interior Design, Biography, Cookery, Education, Erotica, Fashion, Fiction, Gardening, Plants, Health, Nutrition, History, House & Home, How-to, Human Relations, Humor, Literature, Literary Criticism, Essays, Mysteries, Nonfiction (General), Outdoor Recreation, Poetry, Romance, Sports, Athletics
ISBN Prefix(es): 9979-71; 9979-802
Total Titles: 400 Print

Godord
Njardargata 39, 101 Reykjavik
Tel: 5516998
Key Personnel
Editor: Brynjar Viborg
Founded: 1989
Subjects: Poetry
ISBN Prefix(es): 9979-9017

Haskolautgafan - University of Iceland Press
Haskola Islands v/Sudvrgoetu, 101 Reykjavik
Tel: 5694361; 5694300 *Fax:* 5521331
E-mail: jorig@rhi.hi.is
Founded: 1988
ISBN Prefix(es): 9979-54

Heimskringla+
Laugavegi 18, 101 Reykjavik
Mailing Address: Postholf 392, 121 Reykjavik
Tel: 5515199; 5524040; 5689519 *Fax:* 5623523
E-mail: mm@centrum.is
Key Personnel
Publications Editor: Oloef Eldjarn
General Manager: Sigurdur Svavarsson
Founded: 1937
Academic publisher.
ISBN Prefix(es): 9979-3
Parent Company: Mal og menning

Hid Islenzka Bokmenntafelag+
Sidumula 21, 128 Reykjavik
Mailing Address: Postholf 8935, 128 Reykjavik
Tel: 5889060 *Fax:* 5889095
E-mail: hib@islandia.is
Web Site: www.arctic.is/hib
Key Personnel
President: Sigurdur Lindal
Chief Executive: Sverrir Kristinsson
Founded: 1816
Subjects: Art, Government, Political Science, History, Language Arts, Linguistics, Literature, Literary Criticism, Essays, Natural History, Psychology, Psychiatry, Social Sciences, Sociology
ISBN Prefix(es): 9979-804

Iceland Review+
Suourlandsbraut, 12, Reykjavik
Tel: 522 2000 *Fax:* 522 2022
E-mail: info@edda.is
Telex: 2121
Key Personnel
Chairman of Board: Haraldur J Hamar
Founded: 1963

Subjects: Art, Literature, Literary Criticism, Essays, Regional Interests
ISBN Prefix(es): 9979-51

Idunn+
Seljavegur 1, 101 Reykjavik
Mailing Address: PO Box 294, IS-121 Reykjavik
Tel: 5528555 *Fax:* 5528380
E-mail: idunn@vortex.is
Telex: 2308 *Cable:* REYKJAVIK PUBLISHERS
Key Personnel
Owner: Jon Karlsson
Founded: 1945
Subjects: Art, Child Care & Development, Fiction, Health, Nutrition, History, Nonfiction (General), Poetry, Self-Help
ISBN Prefix(es): 9979-1
Imprints: Draupnisutgafan, Loegberg
Subsidiaries: Islenski bokaklubburinn
Book Club(s): Draupnisutgafan

Independent Media Inc, see Frjals fjolmiolun hf-Urvalsbaekur

Isafoldarprentsmidja hf+
PO Box 455, 121 Reykjavik
Mailing Address: Bingholtsstraeti 5, 101 Reykjavik
Tel: 5517165 *Fax:* 5517226
Founded: 1877
Subjects: Education, Fiction
ISBN Prefix(es): 9979-809

Islendingasagnautgafan (Icelandic Saga's Publishers)+
Thorsberg 8, IS-220 Hafnarfjordur
Mailing Address: PO Box 488, 222 Hafnarfjord
Tel: 898 5868 *Fax:* 565 5868
E-mail: muninn@isl.is
Key Personnel
Owner & Dir: Benedikt Kristjansson
Founded: 1945 (*Founded to publish The Icelandic Sagas in old Icelandic*)
Subjects: Fiction, Nonfiction (General), Poetry, Self-Help, Icelandic sagas
ISBN Prefix(es): 9979-869
Imprints: Muninn Publishers; Skak Prent; Reykhdlt Publishers

Katholska kirkjan a Islandi - Landakot Publishers Thorlakssjodur
Landakoti, 101 Reykjavik
Tel: 550188
Key Personnel
Contact: Torfi Olafsson
Founded: 1987
Subjects: Religion - Catholic
ISBN Prefix(es): 9979-9261

Landakot Publishers Thorlakssjodur, see Katholska kirkjan a Islandi - Landakot Publishers Thorlakssjodur

Mal og menning+
Imprint of Edda-Media & Publishing
Sudurlandsbraut 12, 108 Reykjavik
Tel: 522 2000 *Fax:* 522 2022
E-mail: edda@edda.is
Web Site: www.edda.is
Key Personnel
Man Dir: Halldor Gudmundsson *E-mail:* halldor.gudmundsson@edda.is
Editorial Dir: Pall Valsson *E-mail:* pall.valsson@edda.is
Founded: 1937
Subjects: Education, Fiction, Literature, Literary Criticism, Essays, Nonfiction (General), Poetry, Travel
ISBN Prefix(es): 9979-3
Parent Company: Edda-Media & Publishing

Associate Companies: Forlagid, Laugavegi 18, 101 Reykjavik *Fax:* 515 2506 *E-mail:* forlag@mm.is
Imprints: Uglan Paperback Bookclub
Subsidiaries: Heimskringla
Bookshop(s): Bokabud Mals og menningar
Book Club(s): Mal og menning; Uglan

Muninn Publishers, *imprint of* Islendingasagnautgafan

Namsgagnastofnun
Laugavegi 166, 105 Reykjavik
Mailing Address: PO Box 5195, 125 Reykjavik
Tel: 5528088 *Fax:* 5624137
E-mail: simi@nams.is
Telex: 3000 Simtext Is-Edice *Cable:* EDICE
Key Personnel
Dir: Asgeir Gudmundsson
Editorial: Ingibjoerg Asgeirsdottir
Production: Bogi Indridason
Rights & Permissions: Eirikur Grimsson
Publicity, Sales: Hoerour Ragnarsson
Founded: 1937
National Centre for Educational Materials. Member of ICEM - International Council for Educational Media.
Subjects: Disability, Special Needs, Education
ISBN Prefix(es): 9979-0

Ormstunga+
Austurstrond 3, IS-170 Seltjarnarnes
Mailing Address: Postholf 88, 172 Seltjarnarnes
Tel: 561-0055 *Fax:* 561-0025
E-mail: ormstunga@mmedia.is
Key Personnel
International Rights: Gisli Mar Gislason
Founded: 1992
ISBN Prefix(es): 9979-63

Prentsmidjan Oddi
Hofdabakka 37, 110 Reykjavik
Mailing Address: Postholf 1572, 121 Reykjavik
Tel: 5683366 *Fax:* 5676694
Key Personnel
President: Torgeir Baldursson
Vice President: Hilmar Baldursson
Branch Office(s)
PO Box 415, Lincroft, NJ 07738, United States

Reykhdlt Publishers, *imprint of* Islendingasagnautgafan

Setberg
Freyjugoetu 14, IS-101 Reykjavik
Mailing Address: Postholf 619, 121 Reykjavik
Tel: 5517667; 5529150 *Fax:* 5526640
Telex: 3000 Simtex Is *Cable:* Setbergpublish
Key Personnel
General Manager: Arnbjoern Kristinsson
Subjects: Cookery, Fiction, Nonfiction (General)
ISBN Prefix(es): 9979-52

Skak Prent, *imprint of* Islendingasagnautgafan

Skjaldborg Ltd+
Grensasvegi 14, 108 Reykjavik
Mailing Address: Postholf 8427, 128 Reykjavik
Tel: 5882400; 5531599 *Fax:* 5888994
E-mail: skjaldborg@skjaldborg.is
Key Personnel
Dir: Bjorn Eiriksson
Editorial Manager: Helgi Magnusson
Subjects: Animals, Pets, Astrology, Occult, Biography, Crafts, Games, Hobbies, Fiction, Gardening, Plants, How-to, Humor, Nonfiction (General)
ISBN Prefix(es): 9979-57

Associate Companies: Heima er bezt *Tel:* 588-2400 *Fax:* 588-8998 (General magazine aimed at older generations)
Subsidiaries: Childrens Educational Bookclub
Book Club(s): Educational book club for childre

Skuggsja bokaforlag
Strandgata 31, 220 Hafnarfjorour
Mailing Address: Postholf 202, 222 Hafnarfiroi
Tel: 5550045
Subjects: Fiction
ISBN Prefix(es): 9979-829

Stofnun Arna Magnussonar a Islandi
Arnagarour v/Suougotu, 101 Reykjavik
Tel: 5525540 *Fax:* 525-4035
E-mail: rosat@rhi.hi.is
Key Personnel
Dir: Stefan Karlsson
Founded: 1972
Member of FIDEM; Specialize in research in & publication of Icelandic manuscripts & folklore.
Subjects: History, Language Arts, Linguistics, Literature, Literary Criticism, Essays, Music, Dance, Poetry, Regional Interests
ISBN Prefix(es): 9979-819

Thjodsagao ehf
Dvergshofda 27, IS-112 Reykjavik
Tel: 567-1777 *Fax:* 567-1240
E-mail: pbk@centrum.is

Uglan Paperback Bookclub, *imprint of* Mal og menning

Vaka-Helgafell
Sidumuli 6, 108 Reykjavik
Tel: 89733 *Fax:* 89733
E-mail: vaka@vaka.is
Telex: 3190 vakice
Key Personnel
International Rights: Petur Mar Olafsson
Marketing Dir: Edda Bjorgvinsdottir
ISBN Prefix(es): 9979-2

India

General Information

Capital: New Delhi
Language: Hindi & English are used for official purposes. Seventeen regional languages are accorded recognition by the constitution. Generally each administrative state includes speakers of a particular major language. In all, over 1500 languages & dialects are spoken
Religion: Predominantly Hindu, some Muslims (about 11%)
Population: 886.4 million
Bank Hours: 1000-1400 (1100-1500 Bombay) Monday-Friday; 1000-1200 (1100-1300 Bombay) Saturday
Shop Hours: Delhi: 0930-1930; Calcutta & Bombay: 1000-1830; Madras: 0900-1930. All effective Monday-Saturday, some open Sunday. Many close 2 hours for lunch
Currency: 100 paise = 1 Indian rupee
Export/Import Information: No tariff on books but advertising matter is dutied. Import Licenses required. Educational books may be imported by booksellers under open general license. Exchange transactions restricted.
Copyright: UCC, Berne, Buenos Aires (see Copyright Conventions, pg xi)

Aarti Books, *imprint of* Spectrum Publications

ABC, see Allied Book Centre

Abhinav Publications+
E-37 Hauz Khas, New Delhi 110016
Tel: (011) 666387; (011) 660932; (011) 6524658; (011) 6566387; (011) 6562784 *Fax:* (011) 6857009
Web Site: www.abhinavexports.com
Key Personnel
Dir: Shakti Malik *E-mail:* shakti@nde.vsnl.net.in
Founded: 1972
Subjects: Archaeology, Architecture & Interior Design, Art, Criminology, Drama, Theater, Ethnicity, Government, Political Science, History, Human Relations, Literature, Literary Criticism, Essays, Music, Dance, Philosophy, Religion - Other, Social Sciences, Sociology
ISBN Prefix(es): 81-7017
Number of titles published annually: 18 Print
Distributed by South Asia Books (USA)

Abhishek Publications
SCO 57-59 Sector 17-C, Chandigarh 160 017
Tel: (0172) 707562 *Fax:* (0172) 704668
Key Personnel
Chief Executive, Production, Publicity: SLM Prachand
Editorial: Mrs Geeta Mehndiratta
Sales, Rights & Permissions: Bharat Bhushan
Founded: 1977
Subjects: Government, Political Science, History, Philosophy
ISBN Prefix(es): 81-85733
Associate Companies: Nirjhar Prakashan, 3625 Sector 23-D, Chandigarh 160023

Academic Book Corporation+
C-1491, Rajaji Puram, Lucknow 22 6017
Tel: (0522) 418421; (0522) 416584 *Fax:* (0522) 22061; (0522) 210376 *Cable:* ACADEMIC
Founded: 1982
Subjects: Law, Management
ISBN Prefix(es): 81-238

The Academic Press+
887/5, Patel Nagar, PB No 13, Gurgaon, Haryana 122 001
Tel: (124) 6322779; (124) 6322005 *Fax:* (124) 6324782
E-mail: indoc@indiatimes.com
Key Personnel
Dir: Pankaj Jain *E-mail:* pancoj@indiatimes.com
Editorial: Satya Prakash
Sales: Kapil Jain
Production, Rights & Permissions: Sanjeev Jain Satyaprakash
Founded: 1968
Subjects: History, Human Relations, Philosophy, Religion - Other, Social Sciences, Sociology
ISBN Prefix(es): 81-85260

Academic Publishers
12/1A Bankim Chatterjee St, Calcutta 700073
Mailing Address: PO Box 12341, Calcutta 700073
Tel: (033) 241-4857 *Fax:* (033) 241-3702
E-mail: acabooks@cal.vsnl.net.in *Cable:* ACABOOKS
Key Personnel
Man Dir: Bimal Kumar Dhur
Sales Dir: B L Dutta
Founded: 1958
Subjects: Accounting, Business, Management, Medicine, Nursing, Dentistry
ISBN Prefix(es): 81-86358; 81-85086; 81-87504
Distributed by UBS Publishers Distributors Ltd (outside Calcutta)

Addison Wesley, *imprint of* Addison-Wesley (Singapore) Pte Ltd

Addison-Wesley (Singapore) Pte Ltd+
India Branch, 482 FIE Patparganj, Delhi 110 092
Tel: (011) 214 6067 *Fax:* (011) 214 6071
E-mail: info@pearsoned.co.in
Web Site: www.pearsonedindia.com
Key Personnel
General Manager: Subroto Mozumdar
 E-mail: subroto.mozumdar@pearsonedindia.com
Finance: Dipankar Rose
Founded: 1997
One of the world's largest educational publishers. It has played a very important role in publishing both higher education/academic titles as well as school products. The India Office is a liaison office, headquartered in Singapore. Since it inception in 1997, Addison Wesley Longman India has reprinted classic higher academic & professional titles & recently dictionaries & ELT products to make them available to students in India at affordable prices.
Subjects: Biological Sciences, Business, Chemistry, Chemical Engineering, Civil Engineering, Computer Science, Economics, Electronics, Electrical Engineering, English as a Second Language, Management, Mathematics, Physics, Science (General), Social Sciences, Sociology
Number of titles published annually: 200 Print
Total Titles: 303 Print
Parent Company: Pearson Plc
Imprints: Addison Wesley; Scott Foresman; Peachpit Press; Benjamin Cummings; Prentice Hall; Allyn & Bacon; Globe Fearon; Silver Burdett Ginn; Longman; Prentice Hall; Benjamin Cummings; SAMS; PTR; QUE; New Riders; Penguin Longman Publishing; Pitman; Financial Times PH; Merrill Education

Advaita Ashrama+
5 Dehi Entally Rd, Calcutta 700014
Tel: (033) 2440898; (033) 2452383; (033) 2164000 *Fax:* (033) 2450050
E-mail: advaita@vsnl.com
Web Site: education.vsnl.com/advaita/advtoc.html
Key Personnel
Manager: Swami Bodhasarananda
Founded: 1899
Publication Department of Ramakrishna Mission.
Subjects: Art, Religion - Hindu
ISBN Prefix(es): 81-85301; 81-7505
Number of titles published annually: 137 Print
Total Titles: 302 Print
Ultimate Parent Company: Ramakrishna Math
Distributed by Ramakristina Vedanta Centre (United Kingdom); Vedanta Society of Southern California (United States); Vivekananda Vedanta Society (United States)

Affiliated East West Press Pvt Ltd+
104 Nirmal Tower, 26 Barakhamba Rd, New Delhi 110001
Tel: (011) 3315398; (011) 3279113 *Fax:* (011) 3260538
E-mail: aewp.newdel@axcess.net.in *Cable:* BOOKMAIL
Key Personnel
Man Dir: Kamal Malik
Dir: Sunny Malik
Founded: 1962
Member of Delhi State Booksellers' & Publishers Association, Federation of Publishers & Booksellers Associations of India, Federation of Indian Publishers.
Subjects: Aeronautics, Aviation, Agriculture, Anthropology, Biological Sciences, Chemistry, Chemical Engineering, Civil Engineering, Computer Science, Economics, Electronics, Electrical Engineering, Management, Mathematics, Mechanical Engineering, Microcomputers, Physical Sciences, Physics, Science (General), Veterinary Science, Women's Studies

ISBN Prefix(es): 81-85095; 81-85336; 81-85938; 81-7671
Imprints: EWP
Branch Office(s)
New Delhi
Distributor for Academic Press; Adam Hilger; Addison Wesley Longman; American Ceramic Society; American Chemical Society; American Society for Photogrammetry & Remote Sensing; Blackwell Publications; Blackwell Science; Bowker-Saur; Converor Equipment Manufacturers Association; ELBS; Geological Society Publishing House; Harcourt Brace & Co; Hodder & Stoughton; Horwood Publishing; IEEE; Indiana University Press; International Thomson Pub; Iowa State University Press; John Wiley; Library Association Publications; Lippincott-Raven; MIT Press; Macmillan (UK); Marcel Dekker; Miller Freeman; Pergamon Press; Pira; Plenum Publishing; Portland; Prentice-Hall; Princeton University Press; Reed Educational Academic & Professional Publishers; Research Education Association (REA); Routledge; Royal Society of Chemistry; Society for Mining, Metallurgy & Exploration; TAPPI Press; Technomic Publications AG; University of California Press; University of Toronto Press; W B Saunders
Orders to: G-1/16 Ansari Rd, Darya Ganj, New Delhi 110 002

Agam Kala Prakashan
34, Central Market, Ashok Vihar, Delhi 110 005
Tel: (011) 7212195; (011) 7401485; (011) 7401486 *Fax:* (011) 7401485
Key Personnel
Editorial, Sales, Publicity, Rights & Permissions: Agam Prasad
Founded: 1977
Member of Capexal & Intach.
Subjects: Anthropology, Antiques, Archaeology, Art, Asian Studies, Earth Sciences, History, Language Arts, Linguistics
ISBN Prefix(es): 81-85415; 81-7186; 81-7320
Associate Companies: Agam Prakashan; Swati Publication; Rahul Publishing House
Distributed by M/S, Munshiram Manoharlal (P) Ltd; M/S, UBS Pub & Dist Ltd
Distributor for Rahul Publishing House; Swati Publications

Agricole Publishing Academy+
208 Defence Colony Flyover, New Delhi 110024
Tel: (011) 69 48 25
Key Personnel
Dir: Lalita Jain
Chief Executive: T C Jain
Founded: 1978
Subjects: Agriculture, Behavioral Sciences, Biological Sciences, Economics, Education, Energy, Engineering (General), Environmental Studies, Health, Nutrition, Labor, Industrial Relations, Real Estate, Social Sciences, Sociology, Technology
ISBN Prefix(es): 81-85005
Associate Companies: Yatan Publications; Agricole Reprints Corp

Ajanta Publications (India)+
One UB Jawahar Nagar, Bungalow Rd, Delhi 110 007
Mailing Address: 1743 Outram Lane, SGTB Nagar, Delhi 110 009
Tel: (011) 7415106; (011) 2926182; (011) 725 8630 *Fax:* (011) 7415016; (011) 7132908; (011) 7213076
Key Personnel
Chief Executive: Atwal Amit
Founded: 1975
Member of FIP; Also acts as Academic/General/Literary Agent & Printer.
Subjects: Anthropology, Archaeology, Art, Ethnicity, Government, Political Science, Language Arts, Linguistics, Literature, Literary Criticism, Essays, Management, Philosophy, Public Administration, Religion - Other, Social Sciences, Sociology
ISBN Prefix(es): 81-202
Parent Company: Ajanta Books International

Akshat Publications+
T4, Usha Chambers, Central Market, Ashok Vihar, Delhi 110052
Tel: (011) 7247234; (011) 7114425; (011) 7240483 *Fax:* (011) 7254734; (011) 7218836
Cable: SAYONARA
Key Personnel
Contact: Dr Roopa Vohra; Mr K L Jain
Founded: 1985
ISBN Prefix(es): 81-85069
Parent Company: Sayonara Group

AL Publishers+
44 Bhimangar, Opp Indira Park, Hyderabad 500380
Tel: (040) 7611600
Key Personnel
President: Mrs K Rama Dev
Author: Prof K M Lakshmana Rao
Founded: 1987
Subjects: Medicine, Nursing, Dentistry
ISBN Prefix(es): 81-900416

Allied Book Centre+
9/5 Rajpur Rd, 1st floor, Dehra Dun, Uttraranchal 248001
Tel: (0135) 656526; (0135) 650949; (0135) 9837066875 *Fax:* (0135) 656554
Key Personnel
Proprietor: Mohit Gahlot *E-mail:* gahlotmohit@rediffmail.com
Also acts as Printer & Distributor.
Subjects: Agriculture, Computer Science, Science (General), Technology, Botany, Forestry, Hydrology, Remote Sensing, Wildlife, Zoology
ISBN Prefix(es): 81-7089
Number of titles published annually: 10 Print
Total Titles: 20 Print

Allied Publishers Pvt Ltd+
1-13/14 Asaf Ali Rd, New Delhi 110 002
Mailing Address: PO Box 155, New Delhi 110 002
Tel: (011) 3239001; (011) 3233002
Web Site: www.alliedpublishers.com
Telex: 315153
Key Personnel
Man Dir: S M Sachdev
Editorial, Rights & Permissions: Sunil Sachdev
Manager: R N Purwar
Production: Ravi Sachdev
Publicity: S Banerjee
Founded: 1934
Subjects: Agriculture, Economics, Education, Energy, Government, Political Science, Management
ISBN Prefix(es): 81-7023
Associate Companies: Allied Publishers Subscription Agency
Branch Office(s)
15, J N Heredia Marg, Ballard Estate, Bombay 400038
81 Hill Rd, Ramnagar, Nagpur 440010
17 Chittaranjan Ave, Calcutta 700072
Jayadeva Hostel Bldg, 5 Main Rd, Gandhinagar 500009
Patiala House, 16-A, Ashok Marg, Lucknow 226 001 (UP)
13-14 Asaf Ali Rd, New Delhi 110002
3-5-1129 Kachiguda Cross Rd, Hyderabad 500027
751 Mount Rd, Madras 600002
Prarthana Flats, Opposite Thakor Baug, Navrangpura, Ahmedabad 380009

Allyn & Bacon, *imprint of* Addison-Wesley (Singapore) Pte Ltd

Amar Prakashan+
A-1/139-B Lawrence Rd, New Delhi 110035
Tel: (011) 713182 *Cable:* AMARPRA
Key Personnel
Chief Executive: M S Juneja
Editorial: Ganesh Rao
Sales: Maheep Singh
Publicity: Priya Chibbar
Production: Harbajan Singh
Founded: 1977
Member of FPBAI.
Subjects: Economics, Ethnicity, Government, Political Science, History, Management, Social Sciences, Sociology
ISBN Prefix(es): 81-85061; 81-85420
Divisions: Ideal Publications, Eternal Books
Branch Office(s)
UBS Publishers Dist, 5 Ansari Rd, Darya Ganj, Delhi 110002

Ambar Prakashan+
888, East Park Rd, Karol Bagh, New Delhi 110 005
Tel: (011) 7770067; (011) 522997; (011) 7525528 *Fax:* (011) 7776058
E-mail: bitambar@bol.net.in
Key Personnel
Contact: Ved Bhushan *Tel:* (011) 3535406 *Fax:* (011) 7776058
Founded: 1977
Subjects: Education, English as a Second Language, Mathematics, Science (General)
ISBN Prefix(es): 81-7289
Total Titles: 100 Print
Parent Company: Pitambar Publishing Co (P) Ltd, 888 E Park Rd, Karol Bagli, New Delhi 110 005
Distributed by Pitambar Publishing Co (P) Ltd

Anand Paperbacks, *imprint of* Orient Paperbacks

Ananda Publishers Pvt Ltd+
45 Beniatola Lane, Calcutta 700 009
Tel: (033) 2414352; (033) 2413417; (033) 344362 *Fax:* (033) 2253240; (033) 2253241
E-mail: ananda@cal3.vsnl.net.in
Web Site: www.anandapub.com
Key Personnel
Manager: Dwijendranath Basu
Subjects: Anthropology, Art, Biography, Cookery, Drama, Theater, Economics, Fiction, Finance, Gardening, Plants, History, Mysteries, Photography, Poetry, Psychology, Psychiatry, Science (General), Science Fiction, Fantasy, Social Sciences, Sociology, Sports, Athletics
ISBN Prefix(es): 81-7215; 81-7066

Ankur Publishing House
C/1, Anandvan CHS, Anandpark, Thane (West), Mumbai, Maharashtra 400 601
Tel: (022) 543 2817; (022) 536 9907 *Fax:* (022) 543 2817
E-mail: ankur@bom3.vsnl.net.in
Web Site: www.satyamplastics.com/ankurpublishing/
Key Personnel
Man Dir: Mrs Seema Mukherjee
Founded: 1976
Subjects: Government, Political Science, Literature, Literary Criticism, Essays, Science (General)
ISBN Prefix(es): 81-85043
Associate Companies: Sanjay Composers & Printers, Uphar Cinema Bldg, Green Park Extension, New Delhi 110016

PUBLISHERS

INDIA

Anmol Publications Pvt Ltd+
4374/4B Ansari Rd, Daryaganj, New Dehli 110 002
Tel: (011) 3255577; (011) 3261597; (011) 3278000 *Fax:* (011) 3280289
E-mail: anmol@nde.vsnl.net.in
Web Site: www.anmolbooks.com
Founded: 1985
Subjects: Education, Environmental Studies, Geography, Geology, Library & Information Sciences, Management, Science (General), Social Sciences, Sociology, Women's Studies
ISBN Prefix(es): 81-7041; 81-7488; 81-261

APH Publishing Corp+
5 Ansari Rd, Darya Ganj, New Delhi 110002
Tel: (011) 5100581; (011) 5410924; (011) 3285807 *Fax:* (011) 3274050
E-mail: aph@mantrasonline.com
Key Personnel
Editorial & International Rights: S B Nangia
Sales: Gopal Sharma
Founded: 1974
Publishers & Distributors.
Member of Federation of Indian Publishers.
Subjects: Accounting, Agriculture, Archaeology, Architecture & Interior Design, Biography, Chemistry, Chemical Engineering, Criminology, Economics, Education, Energy, Environmental Studies, Ethnicity, Fiction, Geography, Geology, Government, Political Science, Health, Nutrition, History, Labor, Industrial Relations, Law, Library & Information Sciences, Management, Marketing, Natural History, Philosophy, Public Administration, Religion - Hindu, Religion - Islamic, Religion - Other, Science (General), Social Sciences, Sociology, Travel, Women's Studies
ISBN Prefix(es): 81-7024; 81-7648
Number of titles published annually: 100 Print
Total Titles: 1,200 Print
Branch Office(s)
8/81, Punjabi Bagh, New Delhi 110026
Distributed by UBS Publishers Distributors Ltd

Arihant Publishers+
5, Opp Rajasthan University, Jawahar Lal Nehru Marg, Jaipur 302004
Tel: (0141) 515192
Key Personnel
Contact: Sumer Jain
Member of The Federation of Publishers & Booksellers Associations in India; Also acts as Distributor.
Subjects: Biological Sciences, Human Relations, Social Sciences, Sociology
ISBN Prefix(es): 81-7230
Parent Company: Bookmen Associates, 9 Opp Rajasthab University, JLN Marg, Jaipur 302004

Arya Medi Publishing House
4805/24 Bharat Ram Rd, Darya Ganj, New Delhi 110 002
Tel: (011) 5717012 *Fax:* (011) 5715850
Key Personnel
Man Dir: Naveen Gupta
Founded: 1980
Subjects: Science (General), Social Sciences, Sociology
ISBN Prefix(es): 81-7063; 81-7064; 81-86809

Asia Pacific Business Press Inc+
106-E, Kamla Nagar, New Delhi 110007
Mailing Address: PB No 2162, New Delhi 110007
Tel: (011) 3923955; (011) 3935654 *Fax:* (011) 3941561
E-mail: niir@vsnl.com
Web Site: www.niir.org
Key Personnel
Chief Executive Officer & President: Ajay Kr Gupta *E-mail:* akgupta@niir.org
Senior Vice President: P K Tripathi *E-mail:* pktripathi@niir.org
Senior Project Consultant: P K Chattopadhyay *E-mail:* chattopadhyay@niir.org
Founded: 2000
Subjects: Business, Chemistry, Chemical Engineering, Science (General), Technology
ISBN Prefix(es): 81-7833
Number of titles published annually: 50 Print
Distributed by National Institute of Industrial Research

Asian Educational Services+
31, Hauz Khas Village, New Delhi 110 016
Mailing Address: PO Box 4534, New Delhi 110 016
Tel: (011) 668594; (011) 660187; (011) 6851586 *Fax:* (011) 6852805; (011) 6855499
E-mail: asianeds@nda.vsnl.net.in *Cable:* ASIABOOKS NEW DELHI
Key Personnel
Publisher: Jagdish Jetley
Chief Executive: Gaurav Jetley
Publicity, Rights & Permissions: Mrs Saroj Jetley; Gautam Jetley
Founded: 1973
Subjects: Anthropology, Archaeology, Asian Studies, Astrology, Occult, Biography, Ethnicity, History, Language Arts, Linguistics, Military Science, Music, Dance, Natural History, Philosophy, Religion - Buddhist, Religion - Hindu, Religion - Islamic, Religion - Other, Social Sciences, Sociology, Theology, Travel
ISBN Prefix(es): 81-206
Subsidiaries: Antiquarian Publication and Reprographic Services Pvt Ltd
Branch Office(s)
31 Hauzkhas Village, New Delhi 110016
Tel: (011) 668594
PO Box 4534, 5 Scripuram First St, Madras
Tel: (044) 8265040 *Fax:* (044) 8211291
Distributed by Alexandra & Leigh Copeland; Bay Foreign Language Books; Editions Kailash; French & European Publications; Hippocrene Books, Inc; Jeremy Tenniswood; Kalaimahal Book Depot; Lake House Bookshop; La Librairie Du Trefle; Laurier Books Ltd; Libri Dall'Asia; Messages of Gods Love Multi; Sarasavi Book Shop (Pvt) Ltd; Schoenhof's Foreign Books; Selous Books Ltd; South Asia Books; Vijitha Yapa Book Shop; West Port Books; Wuest GmbH & Co Kg
Warehouse: 17 Shahpur Jat, New Delhi 110 017

Asian Trading Corporation+
St Thomas Bldg, 150 Brigade Rd, Bangalore 560 025
Mailing Address: PO Box 2587, Bangalore 560 025
Tel: (080) 51807; (080) 579410; (080) 5587807 *Fax:* (080) 5596363
E-mail: atc@mcdecom.net *Cable:* PASPIN
Key Personnel
Partner: C C Pais *Tel:* (080) 216846 *Fax:* (080) 216944; Nigel Fernandes *Tel:* (080) 5587807 *Fax:* (080) 5596363
Founded: 1946
Also exporters, importers & booksellers.
Subjects: Communications, Philosophy, Religion - Catholic, Religion - Other, Social Sciences, Sociology, Theology
ISBN Prefix(es): 81-7086
Total Titles: 125 Print
Imprints: Nil
Branch Office(s)
Mallikatte, Mangalore *Tel:* (824) 216846 *Fax:* (824) 216944

Associated Publishing House+
New Market, Karol Bagh, New Delhi 110005
Tel: (011) 2429392
Key Personnel
Man Dir, Sales: Ravinder K Paul
Editorial, Production Dir: Ashok K Paul
Publicity Dir, Rights & Permissions: Sharda Paul
Founded: 1966
Subjects: Art, Business, Economics, History, Philosophy, Poetry, Public Administration, Religion - Other, Social Sciences, Sociology, Travel
ISBN Prefix(es): 81-7045
Imprints: Associated Travel Series

Associated Travel Series, *imprint of* Associated Publishing House

Atma Ram & Sons
1376 Kashmere Gate, Delhi 110 006
Mailing Address: PO Box 1429, Delhi 110006
Tel: (011) 2523082; (011) 2946466
E-mail: yogesh2@ndf.vsnl.net.in *Cable:* BOOKS
Key Personnel
Man Dir, Publicity, Rights & Permissions: Ish Kumar Puri
Editorial, Production: Sushil Kumar Puri
Sales: Ashutosh Pury
Founded: 1909
Subjects: Art, Education, Engineering (General), History, How-to, Medicine, Nursing, Dentistry, Philosophy, Science (General), Social Sciences, Sociology, Technology
ISBN Prefix(es): 81-7043
Branch Office(s)
17 Ashok Marg, Lucknow

Authors Press
E-35/103, Shree Ganesh Complex, Jawahar Park, Laxmi Nagar, New Delhi 110092
Tel: (011) 2436299; (011) 2460145 *Fax:* (011) 2460145
E-mail: authorspress@yahoo.com
Key Personnel
Contact: Mr H S Negi
Publishers of Scholarly Books.
ISBN Prefix(es): 81-7273
Total Titles: 84 Print

Avinash Reference Publications+
W-70, MIDC, Shirali, Kolhapur 416122
Tel: (0231) 21024 *Fax:* (0231) 27262
Telex: 195272 IN
Key Personnel
Chief Editor: Dr J A Naik
Manager: Rajesh Naik
Founded: 1978
Subjects: Agriculture, Economics, Social Sciences, Sociology
ISBN Prefix(es): 81-85175
Associate Companies: Dr Naik & Co, W-70, MIDC, Shirali, Kolhapur 416122

B I Churchill Livingstone, *imprint of* B I Publications Pvt Ltd

B I Publications Pvt Ltd+
54 Janpath, New Delhi 110 001
Tel: (011) 3274443; (011) 3259352; (011) 3255118 *Fax:* (011) 3261290
E-mail: bigroup@del3.vsnl.net.in
Telex: 31-63352
Key Personnel
Chairman: R D Bhagat
Chief Executive: K S Mani
Publishing Dir: Y R Chadha *E-mail:* yrchadha@bipgroup.com
Founded: 1959
Subjects: Biological Sciences, Chemistry, Chemical Engineering, Electronics, Electrical Engineering, Engineering (General), Health, Nutrition, Mechanical Engineering, Medicine, Nursing, Dentistry, Physics
ISBN Prefix(es): 81-7225; 81-7042; 81-7431

Associate Companies: British Institute of Eng Technology (India) Pvt Ltd, 359, D N Rd, Bombay 400 023
Imprints: B I Churchill Livingstone; B I Waverly
Subsidiaries: B I Churchill Livingstone Pvt Ltd, (BICL); B I Waverly Pvt Ltd (BIW)
Branch Office(s)
One Aishwarya Apts 9/B, Kumkum Society Stadium Rd, Ahmedabad 380014 *Tel:* (079) 459847
147, Infantry Rd, Bangalore 560 001 *Tel:* (080) 2204652 *Fax:* (080) 2205696
18 Landsdowne Rd, Bombay 400 039 *Tel:* (020) 2021766 *Fax:* (020) 2046778
13-1A, Govt Pl Eas, Calcutta 700 069 *Tel:* (033) 2488742 *Fax:* (033) 2488743
150 Mount Rd, Madras 600 002 *Tel:* (044) 8521851 *Fax:* (044) 8525361
13 Daryaganj, New Delhi 110 002 *Tel:* (011) 3274443 *Fax:* (011) 3261290
Dharhara House, Nayatola (Police Chowki), Patna 800 004 *Tel:* (0612) 657814 *Fax:* (0612) 663794
Distributor for Edward Arnold; ASM International; Elsevier Science; Lippincott-Williams & Wilkins; Macmillan Group; Routledge Chapman & Hall; Roskill

B I Waverly, *imprint of* B I Publications Pvt Ltd

K P Bagchi & Co+
286, Ganguli St, Calcutta 700 012
Tel: (033) 267474; (033) 269496 *Fax:* (033) 2482973 *Cable:* KEPIBEE
Key Personnel
Chief Executive, Publicity, Rights & Permissions: P K Bagchi
Editorial, Sales, Production: K K Bagchi
Founded: 1972
Subjects: Anthropology, Economics, Government, Political Science, History, Language Arts, Linguistics, Literature, Literary Criticism, Essays, Social Sciences, Sociology
ISBN Prefix(es): 81-7074
Associate Companies: Kusum Book Agency, Kalyan Nagar, PO Pansila 743180, Dist North 24, Parganas, West Bengal

Baha'i Publishing Trust of India+
6, Canning Rd, New Delhi 110 001
Tel: (011) 6818990; (011) 6819391 *Fax:* (011) 6812703
E-mail: bptindia@del3.vsnl.net.in; publisher@bahaindia.org
Web Site: www.bahaindia.org
Telex: 0314881 Nsa In *Cable:* BAHAIFAITH
Key Personnel
General Manager: Mr Jiten Mishra
Founded: 1954
Subjects: Education, Religion - Other, Social Sciences, Sociology
ISBN Prefix(es): 81-85091
Parent Company: National Spiritual Assembly of the Baha'is of India, 6 Canning Rd, Baha i House, New Delhi 110 001
U.S. Office(s): Baha'i Publishing Trust, 415 Linden Ave, Wilmette, IL 60091, United States

The Bangalore Printing & Publishing Co Ltd+
88 Mysore Rd, Bangalore 560018
Mailing Address: PO Box 1807, Bangalore 560018
Tel: (0812) 601638; (0812) 6601027 *Fax:* (0812) 6679279
Web Site: www.bangalorepress.com *Cable:* MUDRASALA
Key Personnel
Man Dir: H R Ananth
General Marketing Manager: C A Krishnaswamy
Founded: 1917
Member of Federation of Indian Publishers.

Subjects: Agriculture, Biography, Fiction, Health, Nutrition, Philosophy, Psychology, Psychiatry, Religion - Other, Social Sciences, Sociology
ISBN Prefix(es): 81-87145
Branch Office(s)
The Bangalore Press, Statue Sq, Mysore *Tel:* 570-001
Distributed by U B S Publishers' Distributors Ltd (India)

Bani Mandir, Book-Sellers, Publishers & Educational Suppliers+
Ranibari Panbazar, Guwahati 781 001
Tel: (0361) 540465; (0361) 520241; (0361) 30485
Telex: 235-2455 NEWS IN *Cable:* LABANYA GUWAHATI
Key Personnel
Chief Executive: Chandra Kanta Hazarika
Editorial, Rights & Permissions: Surjya Kanta Hazarika
Sales: Ujjal Kumar Hazarika
Publicity: Utpal Kumar Hazarika
Founded: 1949
Member of Federation of Indian Publishers, Federations of Indian Booksellers & Publishers Association.
Subjects: Anthropology, Biological Sciences, Chemistry, Chemical Engineering, Cookery, Economics, Education, Environmental Studies, Ethnicity
ISBN Prefix(es): 81-7206
Parent Company: Bani Mandir
Subsidiaries: Chandra Kanta Press Pvt Ltd
Branch Office(s)
New Market, DIBRUGARH- 7860, Assam *Tel:* (0373) 22513/21255
Warehouse: Mr Utpal Jyoti Hazarti, Bani Mandir, Ranibari, Panbazar, Guwahati, 781001 Assam

Benjamin Cummings, *imprint of* Addison-Wesley (Singapore) Pte Ltd

Bharat Law House Pvt Ltd+
T-1/95 Mangolpuri Industrial Area, New Delhi 110 083
Tel: (011) 791 0001; (011) 791 0002; (011) 791 0003 *Fax:* (011) 791 0004
E-mail: blh@nda.vsnl.net.in
Web Site: www.bharatlawhouse.com
Key Personnel
Man Dir, Rights & Permissions: D C Puliani
Sales: Ashok Puliani
Editorial: Ravi Puliani
Publicity, Production: Mahesh Puliani
Founded: 1957
Subjects: Law
ISBN Prefix(es): 81-85224; 81-85397
Branch Office(s)
Shop 6, 1st floor, Amar Towers 1, First Cross, Gandhinagar, Bangalore 560009 *Tel:* (080) 2263434
Showroom(s): 4779/23 Ansari Rd, Daryaganj, New Delhi *Tel:* (011) 3275884; (011) 3278282

Bharat Publishing House+
123 Durga Chambers, Desh Bandhu Gupta Rd, Karol Bagh, New Delhi 110 005
Tel: (011) 575 7081 *Fax:* (011) 367 6058
E-mail: bitambar@bol.net.in
Key Personnel
Contact: Manish Aggarwal
Founded: 1990
Member of Federation of Indian Publishers, New Delhi (India).
Subjects: Geography, Geology, Language Arts, Linguistics, Mathematics, Physics, Science (General)
ISBN Prefix(es): 81-86378
Parent Company: Pitambar Publishing Co (P) Ltd, 888 E Oarj Rd, Karol Bagh, New Delhi 11005

Associate Companies: Ambar Parkashan
Distributed by Pitambar Publishing Co (P) Ltd

Bharatiya Samijik Vigyan Auusandhan Parishad (Indian Council of Social Science Research (ICSSR))
35 FerozShah Rd, New Delhi 110 001
Mailing Address: PO Box 10528, Aruna Asfa Ali Marg, New Delhi 110 067
Tel: (011) 6179834; (011) 6179838; (011) 6179679 *Fax:* (011) 6179836
E-mail: info@icssr.org
Web Site: www.ecssr.org *Cable:* ICSORES
Key Personnel
Chief Executive, Editorial, Production, Rights & Permissions & Chairman: Prof V R Panchmukhi
Director, NASSDOC: Dr K G Tyagi
Founded: 1969
Specialize to promote, sponsor & support social science research & social science information activities in India by providing financial assistance in the form of fellowship, sponsorship, study grants, & grants-in-ald etc to individuals as well as institutions.
Subjects: Anthropology, Business, Criminology, Economics, Education, Geography, Geology, History, Law, Management, Psychology, Psychiatry, Public Administration, Social Sciences, Sociology
ISBN Prefix(es): 81-85008
Total Titles: 500 Print
Branch Office(s)
Ambedkar National Institute of Social Sciences, Kongargaon AB Rd, Mhow Cantonment, Mhow 453441 *Tel:* (07324) 73186 *Fax:* (07324) 73645
AN Sinha Institute of Social Studies, Patna 800001 *Tel:* (0612) 221395 *Fax:* (0612) 226226
Centre for Development Studies, Prasanthnagar Rd, Ulloor, Trivandrum 695011 *Tel:* (0471) 448881 *Fax:* (0471) 447137 *E-mail:* sscds@ren.nic.in
Centre for Economic & Social Studies, Nizamia Obervatory Campus, Begumpet, Hyderabad 500016 *Tel:* (040) 3312789 *Fax:* (040) 3326808 *E-mail:* sscess@ren.nic.in
Centre for Policy Research, Dharma Marg, Chankayapuri, New Delhi *Tel:* (011) 6115273 *Fax:* (011) 6872746 *E-mail:* cpr@giasdlol.vsnl.net.in
Centre for Research in Rural & Industrial Development, 2-A, Sector 190A, Madhya Marg, Chandigarh 160019 *Tel:* (0172) 549450 *Fax:* (0172) 775215 *E-mail:* sscrrid@ren.nic.in
Centre for Social Studies South Gujarat, South Gujarat, University Campus, Udhna-Madgalla Rd, Surat 395007 *Tel:* (0261) 227173 *Fax:* (0261) 223851 *E-mail:* sscss@ren.nic.in
Centre for Studies in Social Sciences, R1, Baishnabghata, Patuli Township, Calcutta 700 094 *Tel:* (033) 4627252 *Fax:* (033) 4626183 *E-mail:* postmast@cssscal.unnet.in
Centre for the Study of Developing Societies, 29, Rajpur Rd, Delhi 110054 *Tel:* (011) 3951190 *Fax:* (011) 2943450 *E-mail:* sscsds@ren.nic.in
Council for Social Development, 53 Lodi Estate, New Delhi 110003 *Tel:* (011) 4615383 *Fax:* (011) 4616061 *E-mail:* sscsd@ren.nic.in
Gandhian Institute of Studies, Post Box 1116, Rajghat, Varanasi 221001 *Tel:* (0542) 331182 *Fax:* (0542) 330871 *E-mail:* ssgis@ren.nic.in
Giri Institute of Development Studies, Sector 'O', Aliganj, Housing Scheme, Lucknow 226020 *Tel:* (0522) 73640 *Fax:* (0522) 373640 *E-mail:* girilkw@iiml.unnet.in
Gujarat Institute of Development Research, Sarkhej, Gandhinagar Hwy, Ahmedabad *Tel:* (079) 7454192 *Fax:* (079) 7454191
ICSSR Eastern Regional Centre, R1 Baishnabghata Patuli, Township, Calcutta 700 094 *Tel:* (033) 466472 *Fax:* (033) 466695 *E-mail:* postmast@cssscal.uvnet.in

ICSSR North Eastern Regional Centre, Upper Nongthymmai, Shillong 793 041 *Tel:* (0364) 231631 *Fax:* (0364) 250076 *E-mail:* ssnerc@ren.nic.in

ICSSR Northern Regional Centre, Jawaharlal Nehru University, Library Bldg, New Mehrauli Rd, New Delhi 110 067 *Tel:* (011) 6107676 *E-mail:* sanrc@ren.nic.in

ICSSR North-Western Regional Centre, Punjab University, Library Bldg, Chandigarh 160 014 *Tel:* (0172) 541027 *E-mail:* ssnwrc@ren.nic.in

ICSSR Southern Regional Centre, Osmania University Library, Hyderabad 500 007 *Tel:* (40) 866766 *E-mail:* src@icssr.cmc.net.in

ICSSR Western Regional Centre, Vaidyanagri, Kalina 400 098 *Tel:* (022) 6113091 ext 375 *Fax:* (022) 6178712

Indian Institute of Education, 128/2, JP Naik rd, Kothrud, Pune 411029 *Tel:* (0212) 3369680 *Fax:* (0212) 4910872 *E-mail:* ssiie@ren.nic.in

Institute for Social & Economic Change, Nagarbhavi PO, Bangalore 560072 *Tel:* (080) 3215468 *E-mail:* ssisec@ren.nic.in

Institute for Studies in Industrial Development, PO Box 7151, Narendra Niketan, New Delhi 110002 *Tel:* (011) 3318073 *Fax:* (011) 3700092 *E-mail:* info@isidev.nic.in

Institute of Development Studies, 8-B, Jhalana Institutional Area, Jaipur 302004 *Tel:* (0141) 515726 *Fax:* (0141) 515348 *E-mail:* ssids@ren.nic.in

Institute of Economic Growth, University Enclave, Delhi 110007 *Tel:* (011) 7256288 *Fax:* (011) 7257410 *E-mail:* system@ieg.ernet.in

Institute of Public Enterprise, Osmania University Campus, Hyderabad 500007 *Tel:* (040) 7018145 *Fax:* (040) 7018938 *E-mail:* insprise@ipeou.uunet.in

Madhya Pradesh Institute of Social Science Research, 19-20, Mahashweta Nagar, Ujjain 456010 *Tel:* (0734) 510366 *Fax:* (0734) 512450 *E-mail:* ssmpi@ren.nic.in

Madras Institute of Development Studies, 79, Second Main Rd, PO Box 948, Channai 600020 *Tel:* (044) 412589 *Fax:* (044) 4910872 *E-mail:* ssmids@ren.nic.in

NKC Centre for Development Studies, Plot A, Changrasekharpur, Hyderabad 500016 *Tel:* (0674) 481471 *Fax:* (0674) 481617 *E-mail:* ssnkc@ren.nic.in

OKD Institute of Social Change & Development, KK Bhatta Rd, Chenikhuti, Guwahati 781003 *Tel:* (0361) 547493 *Fax:* (0361) 547393 *E-mail:* ssiscd@ren.nic.in

G B Pant Social Science Institute, 3, Yamuna Enclave, Juhsi, Sangram Nagar, Allahabad 221506 *Tel:* (0532) 667206 *Fax:* (0532) 667207 *E-mail:* jpandey@mri.ernet.in

Sardar Patel Institute of Economic & Social Research, Thaltej Rd, Ahmedabad 380054 *Tel:* (079) 6569598 *Fax:* (079) 6561714 *E-mail:* arpu@x400nicgw.nic.in

Bookshop(s): Centre for Multi-Disciplinary Development Research, D B Rodda Rd, Jubilee Circle, Dharwad 580001 *Tel:* (0836) 347639 *Fax:* (0836) 347627 *E-mail:* ssmdr@ren.nic.in; Centre for Women's Development Studies, 25, Bhai Vir Singh Marg, New Delhi 110001 *Tel:* (011) 3345530 *Fax:* (011) 3346044 *E-mail:* cwds@ndb.vsnl.net.in

Bharatiya Vidya Bhavan
Munshi Sadan Marg Kulapathikm, Mumbai, Bombay 400 007
Tel: (022) 3631261; (022) 8118261; (022) 8118262 *Fax:* (022) 3630058 *Cable:* BHAVIDYA BOMBAY GIRGAON
Key Personnel
Executive Secretary, Editorial, Rights & Permissions: S Ramakrishnan
Founded: 1938
Subjects: Art, Biography, Ethnicity, Fiction, History, Literature, Literary Criticism, Essays, Philosophy, Religion - Other, Social Sciences, Sociology
ISBN Prefix(es): 81-7276
Branch Office(s)
Belgaum
Rourkela
Ahmedabad
Bangalore
Serampore
Patna
Baroda
Bharuch
Pune
Ramachandrapuram
Bharwari
Bhatpara
Ratangarh
Bhimavaram
Bhopal
Bhubaneswar
Calcutta
Calicut
Cannanore
Chandigarh
Coimbatore
Dakor
Delhi
Ernakulam
Guntur
Hyderabad
Jaipur
Jammu
Jamnagar
Jodhpur
Kakinada
Kannyakumari
Kanpur
Kodaikanal
Kurkunta
Lucknow
Madras
Mangalore
Mukundgarth
Nagpur, New Delhi
Palghat
Renukoot
Tadapalligudam
Trichur
Trivandrum
Varanasi
Visakhapatnam
4-A Castle Town Rd, London W14 9HQ, United Kingdom *Tel:* (020) 83813086
U.S. Office(s): 79 Milk St, Boston, MA, United States *Tel:* (617) 426-4525
65-09 Queens Blvd, Woodside, NY 11377, United States

Bhawan Book Service, Publishers & Distributors+
30 Jadunath Dey Rd, Calcutta, West Bengal 700012
Tel: 2258836; 271559 *Fax:* 265315
Key Personnel
Contact: Sanjib Bose
Founded: 1942
Member of Federation of Indian Publishers, Federation of Educational Publishers.
Subjects: Agriculture, Chemistry, Chemical Engineering, Computer Science, Earth Sciences, Economics, Education, English as a Second Language, Geography, Geology
Branch Office(s)
Calcutta
Darbhanga
Muzaffarpur
New Delhi
Ranchi

Biblia Impex Pvt Ltd
2/18 Ansari Rd, Darya Ganj, New Delhi 110002
Tel: (011) 3278034; (011) 3262515 *Fax:* (011) 3282047
E-mail: bibimpex@giasd101.vsnl.net.in
Key Personnel
Man Dir: P K Goel
Exporters of Indian Publications.
ISBN Prefix(es): 81-85012

BIG Database Publishing Pvt Ltd
36-C Connaught Place, New Delhi 110001
Key Personnel
Man Dir, Publicity: Sudhir Malhorta
Editorial: Arun Coyal
Sales: S Khanna
Production: K D Sharma
Founded: 1984
Subjects: Economics
ISBN Prefix(es): 81-85166
Associate Companies: Orient Paperbacks; Vision Books Pvt Ltd

Bihar Hindi Granth Akademi
1 Premchand Marg, Rajender Nagar, Patna 800016
Tel: (0612) 671432
Key Personnel
Chairman: Lokesh Nath Jha
Dir, Rights & Permissions: Dr B N Thakur
Editorial: Yoganand Jha
Sales, Production, Publicity: Ramchandra Singh
Founded: 1970
Subjects: Human Relations, Science (General)
ISBN Prefix(es): 81-7351

Book Circle
Subsidiary of Disha Prakashan
109, Daryaganj, New Delhi 110002
Tel: (011) 3266258; (011) 3288283; (011) 3241513 *Fax:* (011) 3263050
E-mail: thebookcircle@yahoo.com
Web Site: www.meditechbooks.com
Key Personnel
Proprietor: Himanshu Chawla
Subjects: Medical & Technical Books
Ultimate Parent Company: Heritage Publishers

Book Faith India+
414-416 Express Tower, Azadpur Commercial Complex, Delhi 110033
Tel: (011) 7132459 *Fax:* (011) 7249674
E-mail: pilgrim@del2.vsml.net.in
Key Personnel
Publisher: Rawa Tiwari
Man Editor: Praveen Sareen *Tel:* (011) 7462427
Executive Editor: John Snyder Jr
Founded: 1990
Member of New Delhi Association of Publishers.
Subjects: Asian Studies, Religion - Buddhist, Religion - Hindu
ISBN Prefix(es): 81-7303
Associate Companies: Pilgrim Book House, B-27/98 A-8 Durgakund, Habasganj, Varanasi *E-mail:* Pilgrim@RW1.vsnl.net.in
Branch Office(s)
Pilgrims Book Distributors, P.O. Box 72, Lake City, MI 49651-0072, United States
Distributed by Moving Books; Pilgrims Book House (Nepal)
Orders to: PO Box 3872, Kathmandu, Nepal

Book Field Centre, *imprint of* Era Book Enterprises

Bookionics
Member of The Book Syndicate
3-5 1114/7, Opp Hotel Traveller Kachiguda X Rd, 500 027 Hyderabad
Tel: (040) 593654 *Fax:* (040) 595678
E-mail: bookionics@yahoo.com
Web Site: www.bookionics.com
Key Personnel
Owner: Chandrakant P Shah

INDIA

Founded: 1985
Subjects: Computer Science, Engineering (General), Management

Booklinks Corporation
3-5-1108 Maruthi Complex, Narayanguda, Hyderabad 500029
Tel: (0842) 558561 *Cable:* BOOKLINKS
Key Personnel
Chief Executive, Editorial: K B Satyanarayana
Sales, Production, Publicity: K Ramakrishna
Founded: 1965
Subjects: Social Sciences, Sociology, Humanities
ISBN Prefix(es): 81-85194

Books & Books+
C4A/20A, Janakpuri, New Delhi 110058
Tel: (011) 551252
Key Personnel
Contact: Indramohan Sharma; Aniruddha Bhaskar
Founded: 1980
Member of Federation of Indian Publishers; Specializes in Archaeology & Art.
Subjects: Anthropology, Archaeology, Architecture & Interior Design, Art, History, Philosophy, Religion - Buddhist, Religion - Hindu, Religion - Islamic
ISBN Prefix(es): 81-85016

BPB Publications+
20 Munish Plaza, Ansari Rd, Darya Ganj, New Delhi 110002
Tel: (011) 3281723; (011) 3272329 *Fax:* (011) 3266427
E-mail: bokks@bpbpub.com
Telex: 31 66971 GYANIN *Cable:* Radiocraft
Key Personnel
President: Manish Jain
Founded: 1958
Subjects: Computer Science, Electronics, Electrical Engineering
ISBN Prefix(es): 81-7029; 81-7656
Branch Office(s)
8/1 Ritchie St, Mount Rd, Madras 600002
4-3-269 Giriraj Lane, Bank St, Hyderabad 500001
Bookshop(s): Radio & Craft Publications, 4794 Bharat Ram Rd, 23 Daryaganj, New Delhi 110002

BR Publishing Corporation+
A-6, Nimri Commercial Centrem, Ashok Vihar Phase IV, Shastri Nagar, Delhi 110052
Tel: (011) 7430113; (011) 7143353
Telex: 31-66778 DK IN *Cable:* INDLIT
Key Personnel
Chief Executive, Editorial, Production & Publicity: Praveen Mittal
Founded: 1974
Subjects: Agriculture, Anthropology, Archaeology, Art, Economics, Government, Political Science, Health, Nutrition, History, Literature, Literary Criticism, Essays, Social Sciences, Sociology
ISBN Prefix(es): 81-7018
Parent Company: BRPC (India) Ltd
Associate Companies: Books for All; Low Price Publications
Branch Office(s)
South Asia Books, PO Box 502, Columbia, MO, United States
Showroom(s): One Ansari Rd, Daryaganj, New Delhi 110002
Orders to: D K Publisher's Distributors Pvt Ltd, One Ansari Rd, New Delhi 2

Brijbasi Printers Pvt Ltd+
E-46/11 Okhia Industrial Area, New Delhi 110 020
Tel: (011) 6914115; (011) 6841897 *Fax:* (011) 6837835
Key Personnel
Dir: Saurabh Garg; M L Garg
Founded: 1980
Subjects: Art, Cookery, Natural History, Religion - Hindu, Travel
ISBN Prefix(es): 81-7107
Associate Companies: S S Brijbasl & Sons

BS Publications+
Member of The Book Syndicate
Sultan Bazaar, Girraj Lane, 4-4-309, 2nd floor, 500 095 Hyderabad
Tel: (040) 4758216 *Fax:* (040) 4756271
E-mail: booksynd@hd2.dot.net.in
Key Personnel
Owner: Nikhil Nandan C Shah
Founded: 1999
Subjects: Agriculture, Engineering (General), Environmental Studies
ISBN Prefix(es): 81-7800
Total Titles: 25 Print

BSMPS - M/s Bishen Singh Mahendra Pal Singh+
23A Connaught Pl, Dehra Dun 248 001
Mailing Address: PO Box 137, Dehra Dun 248 001
Tel: (0135) 655748 *Fax:* (0135) 650107
E-mail: info@bishensinghbooks.com
Web Site: www.bishensinghbooks.com
Key Personnel
Man Dir, Sales: Gajendra Singh Gahlot
Editorial, Publicity, Rights & Permissions: R G S Gahlot
Production: Srimati Jaswanti Devi
Founded: 1957
Subjects: Agriculture, Biological Sciences, Earth Sciences, Environmental Studies, Geography, Geology, Natural History
ISBN Prefix(es): 81-211
Distributed by Koeltz Scientific Books (Germany)

Business Information Group, see BIG Database Publishing Pvt Ltd

Butterworths India, see LexisNexis Butterworths (India)

Central Tibetan Secretariat
c/o Library of Tibetan Works & Archives, Gangchen Kyishong, Dharamsala 176215, Himachal Pradesh
Tel: (01892) 22467 *Fax:* (01892) 23723
E-mail: ltwa@ndf.vsnl.net.in
Key Personnel
General Secretary: Sonam Topgyal
Sales Manager: Pasang Tsering
Production, Publicity, Rights & Permissions: Lodi G Gyari
Founded: 1961
Subjects: Ethnicity, Journalism, Religion - Other
Subsidiaries: Sheja Press, McLeod Ganj, Dharamsala Cantt, Himachal Pradesh; Tibetan Bulletin, c/o Library of Tibetan Works & Archives; Tibetan Freedom Press, Toon Soong, Tenzin Norgay Rd, Darjeeling, West Bengal

Chanakya Publications+
F10-14 Model Town, Delhi 110009
Tel: (011) 711976 *Cable:* CHANAKYA
Key Personnel
Proprietor: Akhileshwar Jha
Sales: R P Maurya
Production: Chakradhar
Editorial, Publicity, Rights & Permissions: S K Jha
Founded: 1980
Subjects: Ethnicity, Fiction, Human Relations, Poetry, Social Sciences, Sociology
ISBN Prefix(es): 81-7001
Subsidiaries: Prism India Paperbacks

S Chand & Co Ltd+
7361, Ram Nagar, Qutab Rd, Hotel Tourist Complex, New Delhi 110 055
Mailing Address: PO Box 5733, New Delhi 110 055
Tel: (011) 3672080-81-82 *Fax:* (011) 3677446
E-mail: schand@vsnl.com
Web Site: stepsindia.com/schand/group.html
Telex: 31-61310 *Cable:* ESCHAND, NEW DELHI
Key Personnel
Man Dir, Editorial & Publishing Dir, Rights & Permissions: Rajendra Kumar Gupta
General Administration & Export: B N Chatterjee
Sales & Marketing: R K Sahni
Founded: 1917
Subjects: Art, Business, Economics, Government, Political Science, Medicine, Nursing, Dentistry, Philosophy, Science (General), Social Sciences, Sociology, Technology
ISBN Prefix(es): 81-219
Associate Companies: Blackie & Son (Calcutta) Pvt Ltd; Rajendra Ravindra Printers Pvt Ltd, New Delhi; Shyamlal Charitable Trust, New Delhi (Publications)
Subsidiaries: Eurasia Publishing House Pvt Ltd
Divisions: S Chand Education Worldwide (Direct Sales for Encyclopedia Britannica Products)
Branch Office(s)
Bombay
Calcutta
Bangalore
Chandigarh
Cochin
Guwahati
Hyderabad
Lucknow
Madras
Nagpur
Patna
Distributor for Britannica (India)
Orders to: Nirja Construction & Development Co (P) Ltd, Publishers, Ram Nagar, New Delhi 110055

Charotar Publishing House
Opp Amul Dairy, Civil Court Rd, PO Box 65, Anand Gujarat 388001
Tel: (02692) 56237 *Fax:* (02692) 40089
E-mail: charotar@icenet.net
Web Site: www.charotarpublishinghouse.com
Key Personnel
Chief Executive, Publicity, Right & Permissions: Ramanbhai C Patel
Sales: Bhavin R Patel; Pradeep R Patel
Founded: 1944
Subjects: Civil Engineering
ISBN Prefix(es): 81-85594
Total Titles: 50 Print
Parent Company: Charotar Associate, Charotar Books Distributors
Subsidiaries: Charotar Book Distributors
Bookshop(s): Charotar Book Stall, nr Post Office, Vallabh Vidyanagar, Via Anand Gujarat 388120

Chetana Private Ltd
34 K Dubash Marg, Mumbai 400001
Tel: (022) 284 4968; (022) 282 4983 *Fax:* (022) 262 4316
E-mail: kavi@chetana.com
Web Site: www.chetana.com *Cable:* Indology
Key Personnel
Man Dir: Sudhakar S Dikshit
Publicity: K T Vaidya
Founded: 1946
Subjects: Philosophy, Religion - Other
ISBN Prefix(es): 81-85300

Children's Book Trust+
Nehru House, 4 Bahadur Shah Zafar Marg, New Delhi 110 002
Tel: (011) 3316974; (011) 3316970 *Fax:* (011) 3721090

PUBLISHERS

INDIA

E-mail: cbtnd@vsnl.com
Web Site: www.childrensbooktrust.com *Cable:* CHILDTRUST
Key Personnel
Chief Executive: Yamuna Shankar
General Manager, Rights & Permissions: Ravi Shankar
Editorial: G C Kurup
Sales Manager & Publicity: H R Khurana
Founded: 1957
ISBN Prefix(es): 81-7011
Branch Office(s)
G-14, Kamalalaya Centre, 156-A, Lenin Sarani, Calcutta 700013, Contact: Bimal Datta *Tel:* (033) 2365094
18-C, Rayala Towers, Anna Salai, Chennai 600002, Contact: V Badrinarynan *Tel:* (044) 8521850

Chowkhamba Sanskrit Series Office
K-37/99 Gopal Mandir Lane, Varanasi 221 001
Mailing Address: PO Box 1008, Varanasi 221 001
Tel: (0542) 333458 *Fax:* (0542) 333458
E-mail: cssoffice@satyam.net.in *Cable:* CHOWKHAMBA SERIES VARANASI
Key Personnel
Man Dir, Publicity: Brajmohan Das Gupta *Tel:* (0542) 335020
Sales, Production: Kamalesh Kumar Gupta *Tel:* (0542) 334032
Founded: 1892
Printing & selling Ayweredic books & book on Indology.
Subjects: Anthropology, Archaeology, Architecture & Interior Design, Art, Asian Studies, Astrology, Occult, Astronomy, Biography, Economics, Geography, Geology, Health, Nutrition, History, Music, Dance, Philosophy, Physical Sciences, Poetry, Religion - Other
ISBN Prefix(es): 81-7080
Number of titles published annually: 20 Print
Total Titles: 330 Print
Associate Companies: Krishnadas Academy, PO Box 1118, K-37/118 Gopal Mandir Lane, Varanasi 221001 *Tel:* (33) 5020
E-mail: cssoffice@satyam.net.in

The Christian Literature Society
PO Box No 501, Park Town, Tamil Nadu 600 003
Tel: (044) 5354296 *Fax:* (044) 5354297
Cable: Vedic
Founded: 1858
Subjects: Religion - Other
ISBN Prefix(es): 81-85884
Branch Office(s)
The Diocesan Press, PO Box 455, Madras 600007
Bookshop(s): CLS, Bangalore; CLS, Cochin; CLS, Coimbatore; CLS, Hyderabad; CLS, Madras; CLS, Madurai; CLS, Tiruvalla; CLS, Trivandrum

Chugh Publications
2, Strachey Rd, Civil Lines, Post E, Allahabad 211001
Tel: (0532) 623561
Key Personnel
Chief Executive, Production, Publicity, Rights & Permissions: Ramesh Chugh
Sales: Suman Chugh
Founded: 1973
Subjects: Human Relations, Social Sciences, Sociology
ISBN Prefix(es): 81-85076; 81-85613
Associate Companies: R S Publishing House, 20 Mahatma Gandhi Marg, Allahabad
Bookshop(s): Universal Book Shop

CICC Book House
Press Club Rd, Ernakulam, Cochin 682011
Tel: (0484) 353557; (0484) 355658

Key Personnel
Contact: T Jayachandran
Founded: 1962
Subjects: Drama, Theater, Fiction, Literature, Literary Criticism, Essays
ISBN Prefix(es): 81-7174
Book Club(s): Crime Book Club

Clarion, *imprint of* Hind Pocket Books Private Ltd

Clarion Books
G T Rd, Dilshad Garden, Delhi 110095
Tel: (011) 2282332 *Fax:* (011) 2282332
Cable: POCKETBOOK
Key Personnel
Chairman: D N Malhotra
Founded: 1970
Member of Federation of Indian Publishers.
Subjects: Archaeology
ISBN Prefix(es): 81-85120
Parent Company: Hind Pocket Books (P) Ltd

Classical Publishing Co
28 Shopping Complex, Karampura, New Delhi 110015
Tel: (011) 563689
Key Personnel
Man Dir, Editorial: Bal Krishan Taneja
Marketing: Miss Suman Sharma
Production: Nirmal Rani
Publicity: R P Singh
Founded: 1976
Subjects: Social Sciences, Sociology
ISBN Prefix(es): 81-7054

Comdex Computer Publishing, *imprint of* Pustak Mahal

Concept Publishing Co+
A 15-16, Commercial Block, Mohan Garden, New Delhi 59
Tel: (011) 5351460; (011) 5351794 *Fax:* (011) 5357103
E-mail: publishing@conceptpub.com *Cable:* CONPUBCO, New Delhi-59
Key Personnel
Proprietor & Chief Executive: Ashok Kumar Mittal
Editorial, Sales, Publicity: Nitin Mittal
Founded: 1975
Subjects: Alternative, Anthropology, Asian Studies, Behavioral Sciences, Communications, Earth Sciences, Economics, Education, Energy, Environmental Studies, Ethnicity, Geography, Geology, History, Journalism, Library & Information Sciences, Management, Philosophy, Psychology, Psychiatry, Public Administration, Self-Help, Social Sciences, Sociology, Women's Studies
ISBN Prefix(es): 81-7022
Number of titles published annually: 50 Print
Total Titles: 1,400 Print
Parent Company: D K Agencies (P) Ltd
Subsidiaries: Logos Press
Showroom(s): 23 Ansari Rd, New Delhi 110002 *Tel:* (011) 3272187
Bookshop(s): 23 Ansari Rd, New Delhi 110002 *Tel:* (011) 3272187

Cosmo Publications+
24-B Ansari Rd Daryaganj, New Delhi 110002
Mailing Address: PO Box No 7206, New Delhi 110002
Tel: (011) 3278779; (011) 3280455 *Fax:* (011) 3274597
E-mail: genesis.cosmo@axcess.net.in; genesis@ndb.vsnl.net.in
Key Personnel
Chairman & Man Dir: Rani Kapoor
Chief Editor & Sales Dir: Subodh Kapoor

Dir Foreign Sales, Rights & Permissions: Sunil Kapoor
Founded: 1972
Member of Federation of Indian Publishers, Federation of Publishers & Booksellers Association in India, Chemicals & Allied Export Promotions Council.
Subjects: Agriculture, Anthropology, Archaeology, Art, Asian Studies, Developing Countries, Drama, Theater, Economics, Education, Ethnicity, Government, Political Science, History, Language Arts, Linguistics, Library & Information Sciences, Literature, Literary Criticism, Essays, Music, Dance, Natural History, Nonfiction (General), Philosophy, Religion - Buddhist, Religion - Hindu, Religion - Islamic, Social Sciences, Sociology, Veterinary Science
ISBN Prefix(es): 81-7020; 81-7755
Total Titles: 1,225 Print
Parent Company: Genesis Publishing Pvt Ltd
Imprints: Siddhi Books
Subsidiaries: Cosmopolitan Book House
Divisions: Falcon Books; Cosmo Dictionaries
Warehouse: 4/16 West Patel Nagar, New Delhi 110 008

Current Books
Round West, Trichur 680001
Tel: (0487) 335642; (0487) 335292; (0487) 335660
Web Site: www.dcbooks.com/currentbooks.htm *Cable:* Current Books
Key Personnel
Chief Executive: D C Kizhakemuri
Editorial: M S Chandrasekhara Warrier
Sales: Kiliroor Radhakrishnan
Production, Publicity: Vadayar Vijayakumar
Rights & Permissions: Ponnamma Deecee
Founded: 1952
Subjects: Fiction, Nonfiction (General)
ISBN Prefix(es): 81-226
Associate Companies: DC Books; Kairali Children's Book Trust; Kairali Mudralayam
Branch Office(s)
Alleppey *Tel:* (0477) 4197
Alwaye *Tel:* (04854) 6006
Ernakulam *Tel:* (0484) 351590
Kottayam *Tel:* (0481) 5342
Kozhikode *Tel:* (0495) 76362
Quilon *Tel:* (0474) 76933
Tellicherry *Tel:* 20668
Trivandrum *Tel:* (0471) 77693
Book Club(s): VIP Book Club

D C Press, *imprint of* Kairali Children's Book Trust

Dastane Ramchandra & Co+
830, Sadashiv Peth, Chitrashala Chowk, Pune 411 030
Tel: (020) 4478193; (020) 4485950; (020) 5511964 *Fax:* (020) 4478193
Key Personnel
Man Dir, Editorial, Production: Vishwas Dastane
Sales, Publicity, Rights & Permissions: Mrs Bharati Dastane
Founded: 1960
Member of Marathi Publishers' Association; Specialize in Social Sciences, Career Development & Help-books.
Subjects: Career Development, Economics, History, Library & Information Sciences, Literature, Literary Criticism, Essays, Science (General), Science Fiction, Fantasy, Self-Help, Social Sciences, Sociology, Sports, Athletics, Women's Studies
ISBN Prefix(es): 81-85080
Associate Companies: Abhang Stores, Printers & Stationers, 830 Sadashiv Peth, Chitrashala Chowk, Pune 411030; Sports Publications, 830 Sadashiv Peth, Chitrashala Chowk, Pune

411030; Anuja Prakashan Publishers, 13A, Abhang Poona-Bombay Rd, Pune
Bookshop(s): 456 Raviwar Peth, Poona 411002

Daya Publishing House+
4762-63/23, Ansari Rd, Darya Ganj, New Delhi 110 002
Tel: (011) 3245578; (011) 3244987 *Fax:* (011) 7199029
E-mail: dayabooks@vsnl.com
Web Site: www.dayabooks.com
Key Personnel
Contact: Anil Mittal *Tel:* (011) 7103999
Founded: 1986
Subjects: Agriculture, Biological Sciences, Earth Sciences, Environmental Studies, Geography, Geology, Natural History, Veterinary Science
ISBN Prefix(es): 81-7035
Number of titles published annually: 25 Print

DC Books+
Good Shepard St, Kottayam, Kerala 686001
Mailing Address: PO Box 214, Kottayam Kerala 686001
Tel: 0481 3114; 0481 3226; 0481 8214
E-mail: dcbooks@sancharnet.com
Web Site: www.dcbooks.com *Cable:* Deecibooks
Key Personnel
Chief Executive, Rights & Permissions: D C Kizhakemuri
Editorial: M S Chandrasekhara Warrier
Sales: T K Murukesan
Production, Publicity: D Sreekumar
Founded: 1974
Subjects: Fiction, Literature, Literary Criticism, Essays, Poetry
ISBN Prefix(es): 81-7130
Associate Companies: Current Books; Kairali Children's Book Trust; Kairali Mudralayam
Book Club(s): Classics Club; D C Book Club

Diamond Comics (P) Ltd+
257, Dariba Kalan, Delhi 110006
Tel: 4580372; 4580834; 4583939 *Fax:* 4580372
Key Personnel
Man Dir: Narender Kumar
Editorial: Gulshan Rai
International Rights: Mr Marrish Verma
Founded: 1948
Subjects: Cookery, Crafts, Games, Hobbies, Criminology, Fiction, Health, Nutrition, How-to, Religion - Hindu
ISBN Prefix(es): 81-7184
Associate Companies: Diamond Books International, X-30, Okhala Industrial Estate Phase II, New Delhi 110020; Diamond Pocket (P) Ltd Books, X-30, Okhala Industrial Estate Phase II, New Delhi 110020; Punjabi Pustak Bhandar
Subsidiaries: Diamond Magazines
Book Club(s): Diamond Book Club

Disha Prakashan
138/16 Tri Nagar, Delhi 110035
Key Personnel
Man Dir, Publicity: B R Chawla
Founded: 1973
Subjects: Biography, Economics, History, Language Arts, Linguistics, Literature, Literary Criticism, Essays, Philosophy, Religion - Other, Social Sciences, Sociology
ISBN Prefix(es): 81-85045
Parent Company: Heritage Publishers
Associate Companies: Intellectuals' Rendezvous, Aggarwal Bhawa, 4C Ansari Rd, New Delhi 110002; Pankaj Publications International
Subsidiaries: Book Circle

DK Printworld (P) Ltd+
Srikunj, F-52 Bali Nagar, New Delhi 110015
Tel: (011) 5453975; (011) 5466019 *Fax:* (011) 5465926
E-mail: dkprintworld@vsnl.net
Key Personnel
Dir: Mr Susheel K Mittal
Founded: 1992
Specialize in books on Indology.
Subjects: Archaeology, Art, Asian Studies, Astrology, Occult, Drama, Theater, History, Music, Dance, Philosophy, Religion - Buddhist, Religion - Hindu, Religion - Islamic
ISBN Prefix(es): 81-246
Total Titles: 175 Print

Doaba House
1688, Nai Sarak, New Delhi 110 006
Tel: (011) 3274669 *Fax:* (011) 6968735
Key Personnel
Chief Executive, Editorial, Sales, Rights & Permissions: S N Malhotra
Production, Publicity: A C Seth; Rajiv Malhotra
Founded: 1924
Subjects: Education, English as a Second Language, Literature, Literary Criticism, Essays
ISBN Prefix(es): 81-85173

Dolphin Publications+
203-5 Shiv Darshan M G Rd, Opp Station Santacruz (West), Bombay 400054
Tel: (022) 6490184 *Fax:* (022) 6233674
Key Personnel
Editor: Mrs Renu Nauriyal
Founded: 1986
Member of Federation of Indian Publishers & Export Promotion Council; Specialize in children's books, general & nonfiction books.
Subjects: Animals, Pets, Biblical Studies, Crafts, Games, Hobbies, History, Mathematics, Natural History, Nonfiction (General)
ISBN Prefix(es): 81-85523
Associate Companies: India Book House, 203-5 Shiv Darshan M G Rd, Opp Station Santacruz (West), Bombay 400054
Subsidiaries: J Moolur & Co

Dreamland Publications+
J-128, Kirti Nagar, New Delhi 110 015
Tel: (011) 5121050; (011) 5435657; (011) 5455657 *Fax:* (011) 5428283
E-mail: dreamland@vsnl.com
Key Personnel
Contact: Ved Chawla
Founded: 1986
ISBN Prefix(es): 81-7301
Parent Company: Indian Book Depot

Dutta Baruah Publishing Co Pvt Ltd+
College Hostel Rd, Panbazar, Assam 781 001
Tel: (0361) 543995
Key Personnel
Man Dir: J N Dutta Baruah
Founded: 1938
Member of Federation of Indian Publishers. Also act as distributors.
Subjects: Art, Cookery, Language Arts, Linguistics, Literature, Literary Criticism, Essays, Poetry, Religion - Hindu, Religion - Other, Sports, Athletics
ISBN Prefix(es): 81-7373
Subsidiaries: M/S Parbati Prakashan

Eastern Book Centre+
20 Gole Market, New Delhi 110001
Tel: (011) 3314191
Key Personnel
Contact: Subir Ghosh
Founded: 1989
Member of Federation of Indian Publishers.
Subjects: Social Sciences, Sociology
ISBN Prefix(es): 81-85186

Eastern Book Co+
34 Lalbagh, Lucknow, Uttar Pradesh 226 001
Tel: (0522) 223171; (0522) 226517; (0522) 214218 *Fax:* (0522) 224328
E-mail: sales@ebc-india.com
Web Site: www.ebc-india.com *Cable:* LAWBOOK; LUCKNOW
Key Personnel
Chief Executive: P L Malik
Editorial: Surendra Malik
Production: Sumain Malik
Publicity, Exports: Vijay Malik
Founded: 1947
Specialize in Law Books & Law Reports in print media & electronic media (CD-Rom).
Member of Federation of Publishers & Booksellers Association of India, New Delhi, Avadh Chamber of Commerce & Industry, Lucknow Management Association, Indian Industries Association, Lalbagh Vyapar Mandal, Chemicals & Allied Products Export Promotion Council; Specialize in law books & legal journals.
Subjects: Law
ISBN Prefix(es): 81-7012
Total Titles: 1,200 Print; 1 CD-ROM
Associate Companies: Eastern Book Company Pvt Ltd; EBC Publishing Pvt Ltd; Manav Law House, 8-10, MG Marg, opp. Bishop Johnson School, Allahabad, Uttar Pradesh 211001
Distributed by Anupam Gyan Bhandar (Bangladesh); Blackwell's (Periodicals Division) (UK); Gurley & Associates (Trinidad & Tobago); Kokusai Shobo Ltd (Japan); Law Book Traders (Malaysia); Mabrochi International Co Ltd (Nigeria); Pakistan Law House (Pakistan); State Mutual Book & Periodical Services Ltd (US)

Eastern Law House Pvt Ltd+
54 Ganesh Chunder Ave, Calcutta 700 013
Tel: (033) 237 4989; (033) 237 2301 *Fax:* (033) 215 0491
E-mail: elh@cal.vsnl.net.in
Web Site: easternlawhouse.com *Cable:* LAURIPORTS CALCUTTA
Key Personnel
Director: Asok De
Founded: 1918
Subjects: Accounting, Government, Political Science, Law, Social Sciences, Sociology
ISBN Prefix(es): 81-7177
Number of titles published annually: 20 Print
Total Titles: 1,000 Print
Bookshop(s): 36 Netaji Subhash Marg, Daryaganj, New Delhi 11002
Orders to: 36 Netaji Subhash Marg, Daryaganj, New Delhi 110002 *Tel:* (011) 327 9982

Enkay Publishers Pvt Ltd
Enkay House, 3-4 Malcha Marg, Shopping Centre, Diplomatic Enclave, New Delhi 110 021
Tel: (011) 301-6994; (011) 301-2314 *Fax:* (011) 301-2314
Telex: 63124 *Cable:* ENTRAVEL
Key Personnel
Contact: S Narinder Singh Kohli
Member of Federation of Indian Publishers.
Subjects: Biography, History, Religion - Other, Social Sciences, Sociology
ISBN Prefix(es): 81-85148
Subsidiaries: Enkay International Pvt Ltd

Era Book Enterprises
52-47 Ramjas Rd, Karol Bagh, New Delhi 110-005
Tel: (011) 473993; (022) 5741764 *Cable:* Goldenhill
Key Personnel
Chief Executive, Rights & Permissions: Eranna R Jinde
Editorial: C V Bhimasankaram
Sales: V R Jinde
Production: B Ramakumar
Publicity: J E Rao

Founded: 1979
Subjects: Education, Mathematics
ISBN Prefix(es): 81-900270
Imprints: Book Field Centre
Subsidiaries: Book Field Centre
Branch Office(s)
2-30 Khariboudi St, Adoni 518301

Ess Ess Publications+
Darya Ganj Branch, Ansari Rd, New Delhi 110002
Tel: (011) 3260807 *Fax:* (011) 3274173
  Cable: ESS ESS PUBLICATIONS
Key Personnel
Man Dir, Publicity, Rights & Permissions: Mrs Sheel Sethi
Editorial, Sales, Production: Sumit Sethi
  E-mail: sumitsethi@vsnl.com
Founded: 1974
Specialize in all Indian books on Library & Information S.
Subjects: Economics, History, Human Relations, Library & Information Sciences, Management, Philosophy, Religion - Hindu, Social Sciences, Sociology
ISBN Prefix(es): 81-7000
Parent Company: Ess Ess Publishers' Distributors, KD-6A Ashok Vihar, Delhi 110052
Subsidiaries: Sumit Publications
Orders to: Ess Ess Publishers' Distributors, KD-6A Ashok Vihar, Delhi 110052 *Tel:* (011) 7437308

Eurasia Publishing House Pvt Ltd
Ravindra Mansion, Ram Nagar, New Delhi 110 055
Mailing Address: PO Box 5733, New Delhi 110 055
Tel: (011) 7772080; (011) 7779891 *Fax:* (011) 7777446
Telex: 3161310 Sccl In *Cable:* ESCHAND
Key Personnel
Man Dir, Sales Dir, Rights & Permissions: Rajendra Kumar Gupta
Founded: 1960
Subjects: Education, Engineering (General), Psychology, Psychiatry, Science (General), Social Sciences, Sociology
ISBN Prefix(es): 81-219
Parent Company: S Chand & Co Ltd, Ram Nagar, New Delhi 110055
Shipping Address: S Chand & Co Ltd, Ram Nagar, New Delhi 110055
Warehouse: S Chand & Co Ltd, Ram Nagar, New Delhi 110055
Orders to: S Chand & Co Ltd, Ram Nagar, New Delhi 110055

EWP, *imprint of* Affiliated East West Press Pvt Ltd

Financial Times PH, *imprint of* Addison-Wesley (Singapore) Pte Ltd

Firewall Media, *imprint of* Laxmi Publications Pvt Ltd

Firma KLM Privatee Ltd, Publishers & International Booksellers+
257-B BB Ganguly St, Calcutta 700012
Tel: (033) 274391; 4681209 *Fax:* (033) 274391; (033) 276544 *Cable:* INDOLOGY, CALCUTTA
Key Personnel
Man Dir, Rights & Permissions: R N Mukherti
Editorial, Production: K Roy
Founded: 1950
Subjects: Alternative, Human Relations, Social Sciences, Sociology, Humanities, Indology
ISBN Prefix(es): 81-7102

Associate Companies: Firma Mukhopadhyay, 2/1 Dr Aksay Pal Rd, Calcutta 700034
Distributed by Blue Dove Press (USA); Malshow Co Ltd (Japan); South Asia Books (USA)
Distributor for Asiatic Society Calcutta Publications; Burdwan University; Sanskrit College (Calcutta)

Focus, *imprint of* Popular Prakashan Pvt Ltd

Frank Brothers & Co (Publishers) Ltd+
4675-A Ansari Rd, 21 Darya Ganj, New Delhi 110 002
Tel: (011) 3263393; (011) 3279963; (011) 278150; (011) 260796; (011) 3279963 *Fax:* (011) 3269032
E-mail: fbros@ndb.vsnl.net.in
Telex: 0313265 Fran In
Key Personnel
Chairman: R C Govil
Dir: Neeraj Govil
Founded: 1930
Publishing.
Subjects: Accounting, Art, Biological Sciences, Business, Computer Science, Cookery, Economics, Education, English as a Second Language, Environmental Studies, Fiction, Geography, Geology, Government, Political Science, Health, Nutrition, History, Management, Mathematics, Nonfiction (General), Physics, Science (General)
ISBN Prefix(es): 81-7170
Number of titles published annually: 50 Print
Total Titles: 1,000 Print
Bookshop(s): IV/85 Chandni Chowk, Delhi 110006 *Tel:* (011) 3276791

Galgotia Publications Pvt Ltd+
5 Ansari Rd, Daryaganj, New Delhi 110 002
Mailing Address: PO Box 7221, Daryaganj 110 002
Tel: (011) 3263334; (011) 3288134 *Fax:* (011) 3281909; (011) 321909
E-mail: gppl.galgtia@axcess.net.in
Telex: 03171161 Star In
Key Personnel
Chief Executive, Editorial: Suneel Galgotia
Sales: Vinod Behl
Production: Padmini
Publicity: Jayanthi
Founded: 1972
Subjects: Computer Science, Engineering (General), Management, Medicine, Nursing, Dentistry
ISBN Prefix(es): 81-7515; 81-85623; 81-86011; 81-86340
Branch Office(s)
Galgotia Towers, G-64, Manserovar Business Complex Sector 18, Noida
Showroom(s): 17B Conn Place, New Delhi 110001
Bookshop(s): E D Galgotia & Sons

Ganesh & Co+
38 Thanikachalam Rd T Nagar, Madras 600017
Tel: (044) 4344519 *Fax:* (044) 4342009
E-mail: ksm@md2.vsnl.net.in; service@kkbooks.com
Key Personnel
Dir: K Srinivasamurthy
Founded: 1910
Subjects: Philosophy, Religion - Other
ISBN Prefix(es): 81-85988
Parent Company: Productivity & Quality Publishing Pvt Ltd

Geeta Prakasham
Hindi Book Centre, 4-5-769 1st floor, Badichowdi 500027
Tel: (0821) 33589

Key Personnel
General Manager: Gopala Krishna
Sales Manager: Gururaja Rao
Rights & Permissions: Sathyanarayana Rao
Founded: 1958
Subjects: Biography, History, Literature, Literary Criticism, Essays, Philosophy, Poetry, Religion - Other, Science (General), Social Sciences, Sociology

General Book Depot+
1691 Nai Sarak, Delhi 110007
Tel: (011) 3263695; (0110 3250635 *Fax:* (011) 2940861; (011) 3712710
Key Personnel
Contact: Ashwani Goyal *E-mail:* goyal@vsnl.com
Founded: 1936
Specialize in English & German Language Reprints & French Language Books.
Subjects: Business, Career Development, English as a Second Language, How-to, Language Arts, Linguistics, Nonfiction (General), Self-Help, Travel
ISBN Prefix(es): 81-85288
Imprints: GOYL Saab Publishers & Distributors
Subsidiaries: GOYL Saab Publishers & Distributors
Distributor for Oscar Brandstetter Verlag (Indian Sub-continent)

General Printers & Publishers+
263/F Raja Rammohan Roy Rd, Girgaon, Mumbai 400 004
Tel: (022) 3873113; (022) 3826854 *Fax:* (022) 3827197
Key Personnel
Executive Dir: Vijay P Thakker *E-mail:* thakker@bom3.vsnl.net.in
Founded: 1952
Member of Federation of Indian Publishers, Federation of Educational Publishers in India.
Subjects: Education, Workbooks, Testpapers
ISBN Prefix(es): 81-85619
Number of titles published annually: 20 Print
Total Titles: 100 Print

Gitanjali Publishing House
2/12 Vikram Vihar, Lajpat Nagar-IV, New Delhi 110024
Tel: (011) 621991; (011) 6237555
Founded: 1962
Subjects: Economics, Government, Political Science, History, Human Relations, Social Sciences, Sociology
ISBN Prefix(es): 81-85060
Bookshop(s): Indian Book Service, 2/12 Vikram Vihar, Lajpat Nagar-IV, New Delhi 110024

Globe Fearon, *imprint of* Addison-Wesley (Singapore) Pte Ltd

Goel Prakashen
359 Alam Gori Ganj, Bareilly, UP 250 002
Tel: (0121) 642946; (0121) 644766 *Fax:* (0121) 645855
Key Personnel
Man Dir, Editorial: B D Rastogi
Sales: Atul Krishna
Production: K Krishna
Publicity & Advertising Dir: Kamalni Rastogi
Founded: 1948
Subjects: Art, Chemistry, Chemical Engineering, Economics, Government, Political Science, History, Mathematics
ISBN Prefix(es): 81-85932
Subsidiaries: Krishna Prakashan Mandir
Bookshop(s): Goel Publishing, Krishna Prakashan Mandir, Subhash Bazar, Meerut 250002 UP

Golden Bells, *imprint of* Laxmi Publications Pvt Ltd

GOYL Saab, Publishers and Distributors, see General Book Depot

GOYL Saab Publishers & Distributors, *imprint of* General Book Depot

Gyan Bharati, *imprint of* National Publishing House

Gyan Books (P) Ltd, see Gyan Publishing House

Gyan Publishing House+
5 Ansari Rd, Daryaganj, New Delhi 110002
Tel: (011) 3261060; (011) 3282060 *Fax:* (011) 3285914
E-mail: gyanbook@del2.vsnl.net.in
Web Site: www.gyanbooks.com
Key Personnel
Chief Executive: B P Garg
Dir, Publications & International Rights: Amit Garg
Founded: 1984
Specialize in humanities & social science books.
Member of Federation of Indian Publishers, Federation of Indian Publishers & Booksellers Association, Delhi State Booksellers & Publishers Association.
Subjects: Agriculture, Anthropology, Archaeology, Art, Asian Studies, Astrology, Occult, Astronomy, Biography, Career Development, Child Care & Development, Communications, Cookery, Crafts, Games, Hobbies, Developing Countries, Drama, Theater, Earth Sciences, Economics, Education, Environmental Studies, Geography, Geology, Government, Political Science, History, Human Relations, Journalism, Language Arts, Linguistics, Law, Library & Information Sciences, Management, Music, Dance, Natural History, Philosophy, Psychology, Psychiatry, Public Administration, Religion - Buddhist, Religion - Hindu, Religion - Islamic, Self-Help, Social Sciences, Sociology, Sports, Athletics, Travel, Women's Studies
ISBN Prefix(es): 81-212
Number of titles published annually: 70 Print
Total Titles: 1,091 Print
Associate Companies: Gyan Books (P) Ltd; Gyan Exports
Warehouse: 30-C, Satyawati Colony, Ashok Vishar, Phase III, New Delhi 110052
E-mail: gyanbook@vsnl.com

Hans Prakashan
18 Nyaya Marg, Allahabad
Mailing Address: PO Box 103, Allahabad
Tel: (0532) 623077
E-mail: ar@nde.vsnl.net.in
Key Personnel
Chief Executive: Mahendra Pal Jha
Production: Amrit Rai
Founded: 1950
Subjects: Fiction
ISBN Prefix(es): 81-85954

HarperCollins Publishers India Pty Ltd+
7/61 Ansari Rd, Daryaganj, New Delhi 110002
Tel: (011) 3278586; (011) 3272161 *Fax:* (011) 3277294
Telex: 21-66641 Rupa In
Key Personnel
Man Dir: RK Mehra
Founded: 1991
Subjects: Biography, Education, Fiction, Poetry
ISBN Prefix(es): 81-7223
Associate Companies: East-West Press Pvt Ltd
Imprints: Indus Books; Peacock Books

Health Harmony, *imprint of* B Jain Publishers Overseas

Arnold Heinman Publishers (India) Pvt Ltd
AB-9, 1st floor Safdaoung Enclave, New Delhi 110 029
Tel: (011) 6883422; (011) 607806; (011) 664256 *Fax:* (011) 6877571
Telex: 31-72370 *Cable:* Heinemann
Key Personnel
Man Dir: G A Vazirani
Editorial, Rights & Permissions: Ms Rashmi Bhushan
Production: Mukesh Vazirani
Publicity: Ms Rani Roy
Sales: R K Rana
Founded: 1969
Subjects: Art, Engineering (General), Fiction, Government, Political Science, Literature, Literary Criticism, Essays, Medicine, Nursing, Dentistry, Philosophy, Poetry, Religion - Other, Social Sciences, Sociology
ISBN Prefix(es): 81-7031
Associate Companies: Edward Arnold (Publishers) Ltd, United Kingdom
Imprints: Mayfair Paperbacks; Sanskriti; Zebra Books for Children

Heritage Publishers+
32, Prakash Apartment, 5, Ansari Rd, Daryaganj, New Delhi 110002
Tel: (011) 3266258; (011) 3288283; (011) 3241513 *Fax:* (011) 3263050
E-mail: heritage@nda.vsnl.net.in *Cable:* HERIPUB
Key Personnel
Proprietor: B R Chawla
Founded: 1973
Subjects: Aeronautics, Aviation, Agriculture, Architecture & Interior Design, Art, Astronomy, Automotive, Biography, Chemistry, Chemical Engineering, Civil Engineering, Computer Science, Crafts, Games, Hobbies, Economics, Education, Electronics, Electrical Engineering, History, Language Arts, Linguistics, Literature, Literary Criticism, Essays, Philosophy, Religion - Other, Social Sciences, Sociology, Medical & Technical Books
ISBN Prefix(es): 81-7026
Associate Companies: Heritage Impex Worldwide
Subsidiaries: Book Circle; Intellectuals' Rendezvous, K-3/5
Distributor for Blackwell; CRC Press; Routledge; Taylor & Francis; Thames & Hudson

Himalaya Publishing House
Pooja Apartment, 4-B Murarilai St, Ansari Rd, Darya Ganj, New Delhi 110002
Tel: (011) 3860170; (011) 3863863; (011) 3270329 *Fax:* (022) 2080404; 3256286
Key Personnel
Chief Executive, Editorial, Publicity: D P Pandey
Production: Anuj Pandey
Rights & Permissions: Mrs Meena Pandey
Sales: K N Pandey; Sudhir Joshi
Founded: 1976
Subjects: Art, Business, Law, Management, Psychology, Psychiatry, Science (General), Social Sciences, Sociology
ISBN Prefix(es): 81-7040
Parent Company: Randoot, Kelewadi, Girgaon, Bombay 400004
Associate Companies: Geetanjali Press Pvt Ltd, Kundanlal Chandak Industrial Estate, Ghat Rd, Nagpur *Tel:* (0712) 24747
Branch Office(s)
Kudanlal Chandak Industrial Estate, Ghat Rd, Nagpur *Tel:* (0712) 24747
Bookshop(s): Randoot, Kelewadi, Girgaon, Bombay 400004
Shipping Address: Randoot, Kelewadi, Girgaon, Bombay 400004 *Tel:* (022) 360170/355798/ 363863

Warehouse: Randoot, Kelewadi, Girgaon, Bombay 400004 *Tel:* (022) 360170/355798/363863
Orders to: Randoot, Kelewadi, Girgaon, Bombay 400004

Himalayan Books+
17-L, Connaught Place, New Delhi 110 001
Tel: (011) 3329126; (011) 3722031 *Fax:* (011) 3321731 *Cable:* HIMALAYAN BOOKS
Key Personnel
Man Dir, Editorial: Ms Pawan Chowdhri
Sales, Production, Publicity, Rights & Permissions: Ms P Chowdhri
Founded: 1986
Subjects: Aeronautics, Aviation, Architecture & Interior Design, Military Science, Regional Interests, Religion - Other, Travel
ISBN Prefix(es): 81-7002
Associate Companies: English Book Store

Hind Pocket Books Private Ltd+
18-19 Dilshad Garden G T Rd, Delhi 110095
Tel: (011) 2282467 *Fax:* (011) 2282332
Cable: POCKETBOOK DELHI
Key Personnel
Man Dir: Dina N Malhotra
Marketing, Rights & Permissions: Shekhar Malhotra
Founded: 1957
Member of Federation of Indian Publishers.
Subjects: Biography, Fiction, How-to, Nonfiction (General), Self-Help
ISBN Prefix(es): 81-216
Associate Companies: Clarion Books, 18-19 Dilshad Garden Rd, Delhi 110095; Global Business Press, 18-19 Dilshad Garden Rd, Delhi 110095; Indian Book Company, 18-19 Dilshad Garden Rd, Delhi 110095; Sarswati, 18-19 Dilshad Garden Rd, Delhi 110095
Imprints: Clarion
Book Club(s): Gharelu Library Yojna; Clarion Book Club

Hindi Pracharak Sansthan+
C-21-30 Pisachmochan, Varanasi 221 010
Mailing Address: PO Box 1106, Varanasi
Tel: (0542) 54470; (0542) 52425; (0542) 52670; (0542) 355168; (0542) 56850; (0542) 361452
Key Personnel
Editorial: K C Beri; V P Beri; R P Beri; A K Beri
Sales: Vivek Beri
Subjects: Fiction
ISBN Prefix(es): 81-7337
Parent Company: Hindi Pracharak Sansthan
Associate Companies: Sahitya Bharati Publications Pvt Ltd; H P S Publications Pvt Ltd; Hindi Pracharak Publications Pvt Ltd
Subsidiaries: Kashi Offset Printers Pvt Ltd
Branch Office(s)
Pishach Mochan, Varanass (UP)
Cal Sahitya Bharati Publications Pvt Ltd, 211/1, Bidhan Sarin

IBD, see International Book Distributors

IBD Publisher & Distributors+
9-5, 3rd floor, Akarshanbhawan, 23, Ansari Rd, Daryaganj, New Delhi 110002
Tel: (011) 3251094 *Fax:* (011) 3259102
E-mail: piyush_gahlot@rediffmail.com
Founded: 2001
Member of Delhi Booksellers & Publisher Federations.
Subjects: Science (General), Technology
Number of titles published annually: 15 Print
Total Titles: 10 Print

IBH, see India Book House Pvt Ltd

PUBLISHERS								INDIA

Idara Ishaat-E-Diniyat Ltd
168/2 Jha House, Hazrat Nizamuddin, New Delhi 110 013
Tel: (011) 6926832; (011) 6926833 (office); (011) 461676; (011) 4631786 (showroom) *Fax:* (011) 6932787; (011) 4632786
E-mail: idara@del2.vsnl.net.in; sales@idara.com
Web Site: www.idara.com *Cable:* DINIYAT
Key Personnel
Man Dir: Mohammad Anas
Dir of Exports: Mohammad Yunus
Dir: Mohammad Yusuf
Founded: 1950
Specialize in Holy Qur'an & Islamic Religious Books. Cover Urdu, Arabic, English, French, Hindi & Gujrati Languages.
ISBN Prefix(es): 81-7101
Warehouse: D 80-81, Near Masjid Bilal, Abul Fazal Enclave Phase-1, Jamia Nagar, New Delhi 110 025

India Book House Pvt Ltd+
412 Tulsiani Chambers, Nariman Point, Bombay 400021
Tel: (022) 2840165 *Fax:* (022) 2835099
E-mail: padmini@ibhindia.com
Key Personnel
Man Dir: Deepak Mirchandani
Editorial & Publishing Director: Padmini Mirchandani
Founded: 1952
Distripress.
Subjects: Architecture & Interior Design, Art
ISBN Prefix(es): 81-7508
Parent Company: Mirchandani & Co Pvt Ltd
Associate Companies: Rishi Exports, Arch 29, Below Mahalaxmi Bridge, Mahalaxmi, Bombay 400 034, Mohan Shahani *Tel:* (022) 4927463 *Fax:* (022) 4950392; IBH Subscription Agency, Fleet Fasteners Bldg, MV Rd, Marol Naka, Andheri (East), Bombay 400 059, Moti Wadhwani *Tel:* (022) 8501999 *Fax:* (022) 8500645 *E-mail:* journals@ibhworld.com; IBH Magazine Services, Jesia House, 137 Modi St, Fort, Bombay 400 001, Lata Vasvani *Tel:* (022) 2840165 *Fax:* (022) 2633067 *E-mail:* subscriptions@ibhworld.com; India Book House Pvt Ltd, Mahalaxmi Chambers, 5th floor, 22 Bhulabhai Desai Rd, Bombay 400 026, Padmini Mirchandani *Tel:* (022) 4953827, 4923409 *Fax:* (022) 4938406 *E-mail:* ibhpub@vsnl.com
Distributed by Antique Collectors' Club (UK)
Distributor for Harper Collins (United States); Hodder & Stoughton Ltd (United Kingdom); Litle Hampton Publishers (United Kingdom); Random House Inc (United States); Simon Schuster (United States & United Kingdom); Transworld Publishers Ltd (United Kingdom)

The Indian Anthropolical Society, see Indian Museum

Indian Book Depot (Map House)+
J-128 Kirti Nagar, Delhi 110015
Tel: (011) 3673927; (011) 3523635 *Fax:* (011) 3552096
E-mail: ibdmaps@ndb.vsnl.net.in; ibd@indiabookfair.net
Web Site: www.indiabookfair.net
Key Personnel
Proprietor: Harish Chawla
Subjects: Mathematics, Travel
ISBN Prefix(es): 81-87172
Total Titles: 464 Print
Warehouse: 2937 Bahadur Garh Rd, New Delhi 110006
Orders to: 2937 Bahadur Garth Rd, New Delhi 110006

Indian Council for Cultural Relations
Azad Bhavan, Indraprastha Estate, New Delhi 110002
Tel: (011) 3319309 *Fax:* (011) 3712639
Web Site: education.vsnl.com/iccr/index.html
Telex: 3161860; 3166004 *Cable:* Culture
Founded: 1950
Subjects: Art, Drama, Theater, Ethnicity, Literature, Literary Criticism, Essays
ISBN Prefix(es): 81-85434
Branch Office(s)
Bangalore
Bombay
Calcutta
Madras
Varanasi
Chandigarh

Indian Council of Agricultural Research
Krishi Anusandhan Bhavan Dr, K S Krishnan Marg, Pusa, New Delhi 110012
Tel: (011) 388991 *Fax:* (011) 387293
Web Site: www.icar.org.in
Telex: 03162249 Icar In *Cable:* Agrisec
Key Personnel
Dir, Publication & Information: Dr V S Bhatt
Business, Advertising: S K Joshi
Publicity & Public Relations: S K Sharma
Subjects: Agriculture, Animals, Pets
ISBN Prefix(es): 81-7164

Indian Council of Social Science Research (ICSSR), see Bharatiya Samijik Vigyan Auusandhan Parishad

Indian Defence Review, *imprint of* Lancer Publisher's & Distributors

Indian Documentation Service+
887/5, Patel Nagar, Gurgaon 122001
Mailing Address: PO Box 13, Nai Subzi Mandi, Gurgaon 122 001
Tel: (0124) 6322005; (0124) 6322779 *Fax:* (0124) 6324782
E-mail: indoc@indiatimes.com
Web Site: www.indocservice.com
Key Personnel
Editorial, Production, Rights & Permissions: Satyaprakash
Dir: Pankaj Jain
Sales, Publicity: Pankaj Kumar
Founded: 1970
Member of Federation of Indian Publishers & Booksellers.
ISBN Prefix(es): 81-85258

Indian Institute of Advanced Study
Rashtrapati Nivas, Shimla, Himachal Pradesh 171005
Tel: (0177) 72303; (0177) 75139 *Fax:* (0177) 75139
E-mail: info@iias.org
Web Site: www.iias.org *Cable:* INSTITUTE
Key Personnel
Publication Officer: N K Maini
Sales: A K Sharma
Founded: 1965
Subjects: Social Sciences, Sociology
ISBN Prefix(es): 81-85952

Indian Institute of World Culture+
6 B P Wadia Rd, Basavangudi, Bangalore 560 004
Mailing Address: PO Box 402, Basavangudi, Bangalore 560 004
Tel: (080) 6678581
Web Site: www.ultindia.org
Key Personnel
Honorary Secretary: M S S Murthy
President: K R Ramachardran

Founded: 1945
Subjects: Ethnicity

Indian Museum
27 Jawaharlal Nehru Rd, Calcutta 700 016
Tel: (033) 2499902; (033) 2499904; (033) 249 9979; (033) 249 8948; (033) 249 8931 *Fax:* (033) 249 5699
E-mail: imbot@cal2.vsnl.net.in
Web Site: www.indianmuseum-calcutta.org
Telex: 0021-44721MIN *Cable:* Imbot
Key Personnel
Dir: Dr R C Sharma
Founded: 1814
Subjects: Anthropology, Archaeology, Art, Geography, Geology, Science (General)
ISBN Prefix(es): 81-85525

Indian Society for Promoting Christian Knowledge (ISPCK)+
PO Box 1585, Delhi 110006
Tel: (011) 2966323 *Fax:* (011) 2965490
E-mail: ispck@nde.vsnl.net.in
Web Site: www.acpl.com *Cable:* LITHOUSE DELHI
Key Personnel
Dir: Ashish Amos
Founded: 1711 (as autonomous body 1958)
Subjects: Biblical Studies, Biography, Government, Political Science, Religion - Other, Social Sciences, Sociology, Theology
ISBN Prefix(es): 81-7214
Subsidiaries: Navdin Prakashan Kendra
Bookshop(s): 51 Chowringhee Rd, Calcutta 700071; opp Liberty Cinema, Residency Rd, Sadar, Nagpur 440001

Indus Books, *imprint of* HarperCollins Publishers India Pty Ltd

Indus Publishing Co+
FS-5 Tagore Garden, New Delhi 110027
Tel: (011) 5935289; (011) 5151333 *Fax:* (011) 5449682
E-mail: mail@indusbooks.com; indusbooks@vsnl.com
Web Site: www.indusbooks.com
Key Personnel
Man Dir: M L Gidwani
Dir Sales & Product Development: Lokesh Gidwani *E-mail:* lgidwani@indusbooks.com
Founded: 1987
Publishers, booksellers & exporters.
Specialize in Himalayan Studies, Forestry, Environment, Mountaineering & Trekking.
Subjects: Agriculture, Archaeology, Environmental Studies, History, Natural History, Religion - Buddhist, Religion - Hindu, Social Sciences, Sociology, Travel, Botany, Himalayan Studies, Horticulture
ISBN Prefix(es): 81-85182; 81-7387
Number of titles published annually: 25 Print
Total Titles: 250 Print
Associate Companies: Indus International, 5-A (MIG), Rajouri Garden, New Delhi 110027, Lokesh Gidwani *Tel:* (011) 5151333 *Fax:* (011) 5449682 *E-mail:* mail@indus-intl.com *Web Site:* www.indus-intl.com (Exporters of Indian books & journals; worldwide delivery)
Book Club(s): Indus Club (Special discount for members)
Membership(s): Delhi State Booksellers' & Publishers' Association

Institute of Book Publishing, *imprint of* Sterling Publishers Pvt Ltd

Intellectual Publishing House+
23 Darya Ganj, Ansari Rd, New Delhi 110002
Tel: (011) 279911

INDIA

Key Personnel
International Rights: D R Chopra
Founded: 1974
Subjects: Archaeology, Art, Government, Political Science, History, Literature, Literary Criticism, Essays, Philosophy, Religion - Other, Social Sciences, Sociology
ISBN Prefix(es): 81-7076
Parent Company: Intellectual Book Corner Pvt Ltd

Inter-India Publications+
D-17 Raja Garden Extn, New Delhi 110 015
Tel: (011) 5441120; (011) 5467082
Key Personnel
Chief Executive, Editorial, Rights & Permissions: M C Mittal
Sales: Praveen Mittal
Founded: 1975
Member of Federation of Indian Publishers, New Delhi; specialize in tribes, women & forests.
Subjects: Agriculture, Anthropology, Archaeology, Art, Asian Studies, Crafts, Games, Hobbies, Economics, Ethnicity, Geography, Geology, Government, Political Science, History, Philosophy, Religion - Other, Social Sciences, Sociology, Transportation, Women's Studies
ISBN Prefix(es): 81-210
Parent Company: DK Publishers' Distributors Pvt Ltd

International Book Distributors+
Member of All India Federation of Booksellers & Publishers
9/3 Rajpur Rd, 1st floor, Dehra Dun, Uttaranchal 248001
Tel: (0135) 656526; (0135) 657497; (0135) 650949; (0135) 9897003322 *Fax:* (0135) 656554
E-mail: ibdbooks@sancharnet.in
Web Site: ibdbooks.com
Telex: 595280
Key Personnel
Proprietor: R P Singh
Founded: 1976
Specialize in printing, scanning & planning
Also acts as Distributor
Member of All India Federation of Booksellers & Publishers New Delhi.
Subjects: Agriculture, Animals, Pets, Biological Sciences, Environmental Studies, Gardening, Plants, Natural History, Science (General), Technology, Veterinary Science, Botany, Forestry, Wildlife
ISBN Prefix(es): 81-7089
Number of titles published annually: 50 Print
Total Titles: 400 Print
Associate Companies: Valley Offset Printers & Publishers, 15/2_B, Rajpur Rd, Dehra Dun Uttranchal 248001, Contact: Mr Prashant Gahlot *Tel:* (0135) 653998, 656172
Bookshop(s): Allied Book Centre, 9/5 Rajpur Rd, Dehra Dun, Uttranchal 248001

Interprint, *imprint of* Mehta Publishers

Intertrade Publications+
55 Gariahat Rd, Ballygunge, Calcutta 700019
Mailing Address: PO Box 10210, Calcutta 700 019
Tel: (033) 474872; (033) 475069 *Cable:* HELBELL
Key Personnel
Man Dir, Rights & Permissions: Dr K K Roy
Sales Dir: S Paul
Publicity Dir: Renu Kochhar
Advertising Dir: Pradip Raj
Founded: 1954
Subjects: Biography, History, Medicine, Nursing, Dentistry, Philosophy, Poetry, Religion - Other
Subsidiaries: Intertrade Publications (India) Pvt Ltd

Islamic Publishing House+
Islamic Service Trust Bldgs, 10-529 Maideen Pali Rd Calicut, Kerala 673 001
Tel: (0495) 720092; (0495) 724618 *Fax:* (0495) 724524
E-mail: iphcalicut@eth.net
Key Personnel
International Rights: Sheikh Mohamed
Manager: A P Moosa-Koya
Founded: 1945
Subjects: Biography, Government, Political Science, Health, Nutrition, History, Human Relations, Law, Philosophy, Religion - Islamic, Travel
ISBN Prefix(es): 81-7204
Number of titles published annually: 150 Print
Parent Company: Islamic Service Trust, Kerala, Kerala
Distributed by Current Books Kottayam
Distributor for Markazi Maktaba Islami (India)

ISPCK, see Indian Society for Promoting Christian Knowledge (ISPCK)

Jaico Publishing House
121-125 Mahatma Gandhi Rd, Bombay 400 023
Tel: (022) 270621; (022) 2676702; (022) 2676802; (022) 2674501 *Fax:* (022) 2041673; (022) 2656412
E-mail: jaicoborn@bom5.vsnl.net.in
Web Site: www.jaicobooks.com
Telex: 113369 Jai In *Cable:* JAICOBOOKS
Key Personnel
Man Dir: Ashwin J Shah
Executive Dir: S C Sethi
Editor: R H Sharma
Founded: 1945
Subjects: Astrology, Occult, Behavioral Sciences, Biography, Cookery, Criminology, Economics, Engineering (General), Ethnicity, Government, Political Science, Health, Nutrition, History, Humor, Language Arts, Linguistics, Law, Management, Philosophy, Psychology, Psychiatry, Religion - Other, Self-Help
ISBN Prefix(es): 81-7224
Subsidiaries: Jaico Press Pvt Ltd
Branch Office(s)
Jaico Book House, 14-1 1st Main Rd, 6th Cross, Gandhi Naga, Bangalore 560009
Jaico Book Enterprises, 3 Orient Row, Park Circus, Calcutta 700017
Jaico Book House, 1-8-27/4/1 opp Chikkadpally Bus Stand, Chikkadpally, Hyderabad 500020
Jaico Book Distributors, G-2, 16 Ansari Rd, Daryaganj, New Delhi 110002
Jaico Book Agency, Asha Mansion 1st Floor, 59A Montieth Rd, Egmore, Madras 600008
Bookshop(s): Jaicos

B Jain Publishers Overseas+
Member of B Jain Publishers Pvt Ltd
1921 Tenth St, Chuna Mandi Pahar Ganj, New Delhi 110055
Mailing Address: PO Box 5775, New Delhi 110055
Tel: (011) 3670430; (011) 3683200; (011) 3683300 *Fax:* (011) 3610471; (011) 3683400
E-mail: bjain@vsnl.com; info@bjainbooks.com
Web Site: www.bjainbooks.com; www.bjainindia.com *Cable:* BOOKCENTRE
Key Personnel
Owner: Dr P N Jain *Tel:* (011) 2169633 *Fax:* (011) 3683400
Dir & Editorial, Rights & Permissions: Ashok Jain *Fax:* (011) 3683100
Sales, Publicity: Kuldeep Jain *Tel:* (011) 3683100
E-mail: kjain@nda.vsnl.net.in
Founded: 1972
Subjects: Alternative, Health, Nutrition, Medicine, Nursing, Dentistry, Self-Help
ISBN Prefix(es): 81-7021
Number of titles published annually: 80 Print

BOOK

Total Titles: 1,250 Print
Imprints: Health Harmony

B Jain Publishers (P) Ltd+
1921 Tenth St, Chuna Mandi, Pahar Ganj, New Delhi 110055
Tel: (011) 3670430; (011) 3670572; (011) 3683100 *Fax:* (011) 3610471; (011) 3683400
E-mail: bjain@vsnl.com
Web Site: www.bjainbooks.com *Cable:* Bookcentre
Key Personnel
Man Dir: Dr Premnath Jain *Tel:* (011) 2169633
Dir & Editorial, Rights & Permissions: Ashok Jain *Fax:* (011) 3683100
Contact: Sh Kuldeep Jain *E-mail:* bjain@nda.vsnl.net.in
Founded: 1967
Subjects: Health, Nutrition, Medicine, Nursing, Dentistry, Religion - Buddhist, Religion - Hindu
ISBN Prefix(es): 81-7021
Total Titles: 1,175 Print
Associate Companies: B Jain Exports India
Subsidiaries: B Jain Publishers Overseas
U.S. Office(s): New Leaf Distributors, 401 Thoronton Rd, Lithia Springs, Atlanta, GA 30122-1557, United States
Bookshop(s): 1920 Tenth Chuna Mandi St, New Delhi 11055

Jaipur Publishing House
Chaura Rastha, Jaipur 302003
Tel: (0141) 62257
Key Personnel
Manager: Rajesh Agarwal
Production: R C Agarwal
Sales: Dhoop Chand Jain
Founded: 1960

Jaypee Brothers Medical Publishers Pvt Ltd+
G-16 EMCA House, 23-23B Ansari Rd, Daryaganj, New Delhi 110 002
Mailing Address: PO Box 7193, Daryaganj, New Delhi 110 002
Tel: (011) 3272143; (011) 3282021 *Fax:* (011) 3276490
Key Personnel
Editorial: Jitendar Vij
Sales: Pawaninder Vij
Subjects: Medicine, Nursing, Dentistry
ISBN Prefix(es): 81-7179
Associate Companies: BMJ; F A Davis Co; Mosby Year Book
Branch Office(s)
One-A Indian Mirror St, Wellington Square, PO Box 8880, Calcutta 700013 *Tel:* 2451926
202 Batavia Chambers, 8-Kumara Kruppa Rd, Kumara Park East, Bangalore 560001 *Tel:* 2281761

Kairali Children's Book Trust
PO Box 624- Railway Staion Rd, Current Books Bldg, Kottayam, Kerala 686 001
Tel: (0481) 563226 *Fax:* (0481) 564758
Key Personnel
Chief Executive, Rights & Permissions: D C Kizhakemuri
Editorial: Dr K Velayudhan Nair
Production: V P Sreedharan Nayanar
Publicity: G Sreekumar
Founded: 1980
Subjects: Biography, Fiction, Foreign Countries
ISBN Prefix(es): 81-7152
Associate Companies: Current Books; DC Books; Kairali Mudralayam
Imprints: D C Press
Book Club(s): Kairali Club
Orders to: Current Books, VIII/493 Railway Station Rd, Kottayam 686001

Kairalee Mudralayam
D C Books Complex, Good Shepherd St, Kottayam 686 001
Tel: (0481) 56314 *Fax:* (0481) 564758
Key Personnel
Man: D C Kizhakemuri
Editorial: M S Chandrasekhara Warrier
Sales: D C Ponnamma
Production, Publicity, Rights & Permissions: Mary John
Founded: 1978
Subjects: Biography, Fiction, Humor
ISBN Prefix(es): 81-85226
Associate Companies: Current Books; D C Books; Kairali Children's Book Trust

Kali For Women+
K-92, Hauz Khas Enclave, 1st floor, New Delhi 110016
Tel: (011) 6864497; (011) 6964947; (011) 6521008 *Fax:* (011) 6864497
E-mail: kaliw@del2.vsnl.net.in
Key Personnel
Contact: Ritu Menon; Urvashi Butalia
Editor: Preeti Gill
Founded: 1984
Subjects: Art, Biography, Drama, Theater, Environmental Studies, Fiction, Health, Nutrition, History, Law, Nonfiction (General), Social Sciences, Sociology, Women's Studies
ISBN Prefix(es): 81-85107; 81-86706

Kalyani Publishers+
4863-2B Bharat Ram Rd, 24 Daryaganj, New Delhi 110002
Tel: (011) 3278689; (011) 3274393; (011) 3271469
Key Personnel
Man Dir: Raj Kumar
Subjects: Education
ISBN Prefix(es): 81-7096; 81-7663
Bookshop(s): Lyall Book Depot, Chaura Bazar, Ludhiana *Tel:* (0161) 50221

Kerala University, Department of Publications
Trivandrum 695034, Kerala
Tel: (0471) 445631 *Fax:* (0471) 447158
Key Personnel
Chief Executive: Dr A Razaludeen
Production: Dr P Balachandran
Sales: Dr M A Karim
Founded: 1939
ISBN Prefix(es): 81-86397

Khanna Publishers+
2-B Nath Market, Nai Sarak, Delhi 110006
Tel: (011) 2912380; (011) 7224179
Key Personnel
Dir: R C Khanna; Vineet Khanna
Founded: 1959
Subjects: Civil Engineering, Communications, Computer Science, Electronics, Electrical Engineering, Energy, Engineering (General), Environmental Studies, Management, Mathematics, Mechanical Engineering, Technology
ISBN Prefix(es): 81-7409
Branch Office(s)
11 Community Centre, Ashok Vihar, Phase II, Delhi 110052 *Tel:* (011) 7224179

Kitab Ghar
Main Rd, Gandhi Nagar, New Delhi 110031
Tel: (011) 213206
Key Personnel
Chief Executive, Rights & Permissions: Satya Brat Sharma
Editorial, Production: Jagat Ram Sharma
Sales, Publicity: Dev Datt
Founded: 1970

Subjects: Biography, Drama, Theater, Fiction, Poetry, Science (General), Social Sciences, Sociology
ISBN Prefix(es): 81-7016

Konark Publishers, Pvt, Ltd+
Member of The Federation of Publishers & Booksellers Association in India
A149, Vikas Marg Shakarpur, Delhi 110092
Tel: (011) 2207103; (011) 2204101 *Fax:* (011) 2207103
E-mail: kprn07@hotmail.com; kprn@aol.net.in
Cable: THE KONARK DELHI
Key Personnel
Man: KPR Nair *Tel:* (011) 2455731
E-mail: kprn07@hotmail.com
Founded: 1986
Publisher.
Subjects: Government, Political Science, Human Relations, Labor, Industrial Relations, Social Sciences, Sociology
ISBN Prefix(es): 81-220
Number of titles published annually: 30 Print
Total Titles: 600 Print

Kosi Books, *imprint of* Vidyarthi Mithram Press

Krishna Prakashan Media (P) Ltd, *see* Goel Prakashen

Lalit Kala Akademi
35 Ferozshah Rd, New Delhi 110 001
Tel: (011) 387241; (011) 387243 *Fax:* (011) 383 450 *Cable:* Artakademi
Key Personnel
Chairman: Prof Sankho Chaudhuri
Acting Secretary: M Rajaram
Sales: Kewal Krishan
Founded: 1954
Subjects: Art, Ethnicity
ISBN Prefix(es): 81-87507

Lancer International, *imprint of* Lancer Publisher's & Distributors

Lancer Paperbacks, *imprint of* Lancer Publisher's & Distributors

Lancer Publishers, *imprint of* Lancer Publisher's & Distributors

Lancer Publisher's & Distributors+
PO Box 3802, New Delhi 110049
Tel: (011) 6867339; (011) 6854691 *Fax:* (011) 6862077
Key Personnel
Man Dir & International Rights: Capt Bharat Verma
Founded: 1983
Also acts as Printers & manufacturer for foreign publishers, importers, exporters & distributors.
Subjects: Asian Studies, Military Science, Self-Help
ISBN Prefix(es): 81-7062; 81-85096
Associate Companies: Spantech & Lancer, Spantech House Lagham Rd, South Godstone, Surrey RH9 8HB, United Kingdom *Tel:* (01342) 893239 *Fax:* (01342) 892584; Spantech & Lancer, 3986 Ernst Rd, Hartford, WI 53027, United States *Tel:* 414-673-9064 *Fax:* 414-673-9064
Imprints: Lancer Paperbacks; Lancer International; Lancer Publishers; Indian Defence Review
Divisions: Indian Defence Review
Distributor for Rawelette Books (UK); Greenhill Books (UK)
Orders to: Lancer Publishers, 56 Gautam Nagar, New Delhi 110049

Spantech & Lancer, Spantech House, Lagham Rd, South Godstone, Surrey RH9 8H8, United Kingdom
Spantech & Lancer, 3986 Ernst Rd, Hartford, WI 53027, United States

Law Publishers+
Sardar Patel Marg, Allahabad 211 001
Mailing Address: PO Box 1077, Allahabad 211 001
Tel: (0532) 4094; (0532) 2835; (0532) 3716; (0532) 2298 *Fax:* (0532) 622781; (0532) 609943
E-mail: lawpubxd@nde.vsnl.net.in
Telex: 229 laws *Cable:* PUBLISHERS
Key Personnel
Chief Executive: Subhash Sagar
Manager: K P Tewari
Founded: 1961
Export of Law & non-law journals & subscription service on back sets.
Subscription service for journals.
Subjects: Criminology, Engineering (General), Environmental Studies, History, Law, Library & Information Sciences, Mechanical Engineering, Philosophy, Physical Sciences, Religion - Buddhist, Religion - Hindu, Religion - Islamic, Technology, Women's Studies
ISBN Prefix(es): 81-7111

Laxmi Publications Pvt Ltd+
22, Golden House, Daryaganj, New Delhi 110002
Tel: (011) 3252574 *Fax:* (011) 3252572
E-mail: colaxmi@hotmail.com
Web Site: www.laxmipublications.com
Key Personnel
Chief Executive Officer: R K Gupta
  E-mail: rkg@laxmipublications.com
Dir, Business Development: Saurabh Gupta
  E-mail: guptas@global.t-bird.edu
Dir, Sales & Marketing: Saumya Gupta
  E-mail: saumyag@hotmail.com
Founded: 1974
Specialize in computer books, engineering, college & school textbooks.
Member of Federation of Indian Publishers.
Subjects: Civil Engineering, Computer Science, Electronics, Electrical Engineering, Mathematics, Mechanical Engineering
ISBN Prefix(es): 81-7008
Number of titles published annually: 25 Print; 5 CD-ROM
Total Titles: 600 Print; 5 CD-ROM
Imprints: Firewall Media; Golden Bells

Learners Press Private Ltd+
A-59 Okhla Industrial Area, Phase II, New Delhi 110020
Tel: (011) 6313023; (011) 6916209; (011) 6966165 *Fax:* (011) 6331241
E-mail: ghai@nde.vsnl.net.in *Cable:* PAPERBACKS
Key Personnel
Rights & Permissions: Vikas Ghai
Editorial: Marry Joseph
Production: Shammi Kapoor
Founded: 1990
Member of Federation of Indian Publishers.
ISBN Prefix(es): 81-7181

LexisNexis Butterworths (India)
Formerly Butterworths India
14th floor, Vijaya Bldg, 17, Barakhamba Rd, New Delhi 110001
Tel: (011) 373 9614; (011) 373 9615; (011) 373 9616; (011) 332 6454; (011) 332 6455 *Fax:* (011) 332 6456
E-mail: info@lexisnexis.co.on
Web Site: www.lexisnexis.co.in
Key Personnel
Publishing Manager: Ambika Nair
  E-mail: ambika.nair@lexisnexis.co.in

Editorial Manager: Sandeep Joshi
  E-mail: sandeep.joshi@lexisnexis.co.in
Commissioning Editor: Vidyaranya Chakravarthy
  E-mail: vidyaranya.chakravathy@lexisnexus.co.in
General Manager: Sudarshan Sharma
  E-mail: sudarshan.sharma@lexisnexis.co.in
Assistant Manager, Customer Service: Ruchika Malik *E-mail:* ruchika.malik@lexisnexis.co.in
Assistant Manager, Sales: Vikas Saddar
  E-mail: vikas.saddar@lexisnexis.co.in
Publishers: law, taxation, business.
Parent Company: Reed Elsevier
Associate Companies: Butterworths Hong Kong, 12/F, Hennessey Centre, 500 Hennessey Rd, Causeway Bay, Hong Kong, Commissioning Editor: Anisha Sakhrani *Tel:* 2965 1400 *Fax:* 2976 0840 *Web Site:* www.lexisnexis.com.uk; Malayan Law Journal Sdn Bhd, Unit A-5-1, 5th floor, Wisma HB, Megan Phileo Ave, 12 Jalan Yap Kwan Seng, 50450 Kuala Lumpur, Managing Editor, New Product Development: Julie Ann Thomas *Tel:* (03) 2162-2822 *Fax:* (03) 2162-3811 *Web Site:* www.mlj.com.my; LexisNexis Singapore, No 1 Temasek Ave, 17-01 Millenia Tower, Singapore 039192, Singapore, Regional Publishing Dir: Conita Leung *Tel:* 336 9661 *Fax:* 336 9662 *Web Site:* www.lexisnexis.com.sg

Longman, *imprint of* Addison-Wesley (Singapore) Pte Ltd

Lotus, *imprint of* Roli Books Pvt Ltd

Lustre Press, *imprint of* Roli Books Pvt Ltd

Lustre Press Pvt Ltd, see Roli Books Pvt Ltd

M/S Family Books Pvt Ltd, *imprint of* Pustak Mahal

Mahajan Publishers Private Limited+
Super Market Basement, Near Natraj Cinema, Ashram Rd, Ahmedabad 380009
Tel: (079) 6588537 *Fax:* (079) 6589101
E-mail: mahajan2000@hotmail.com *Cable:* PERIODICAL
Key Personnel
Man Dir: Mr Dinker Mahajan
  E-mail: mahajan2000@hotmail.com
Founded: 1953
Subjects: *Specializes In:* Textiles
ISBN Prefix(es): 81-85401
Associate Companies: Mahajan Book Distributors

Manohar Publishers & Distributors+
216 Ansari Rd, Daryaganj, New Delhi 110 002
Tel: (011) 275162 *Fax:* (011) 3265162
Key Personnel
Man Dir, Rights & Permissions, Publicity: Ajay Jain
Editorial: P P Jain
Publicity: Ramesh Jain
Founded: 1969
Subjects: Ethnicity, Government, Political Science, History, Social Sciences, Sociology
ISBN Prefix(es): 81-85054; 81-85425; 81-7304
Associate Companies: Manohar Book Service

Manosabdam Books, *imprint of* Vidyarthi Mithram Press

Mapin Publishing Pvt Ltd+
31 Somnath Rd, Usmanpura, Ahmedabad 380013
Tel: (079) 755-1793; (079) 755-1833 *Fax:* (079) 755-0955
E-mail: mapin@icenet.net
Web Site: www.mapinpub.com
Telex: 121618 rasa in

Key Personnel
Man Dir: Mallika Sarabhai
International Rights: Bipin Shah
Founded: 1985
Member of Federation of Indian Publishers; specialize in books on art, crafts, architecture, culture of India, heritage & archaeology.
Subjects: Archaeology, Architecture & Interior Design, Art, Crafts, Games, Hobbies, Photography
ISBN Prefix(es): 81-85322; 81-7380
Associate Companies: Grantha Corporation, 80 Cliffedgeway, Middletown, NJ 07701, United States *Tel:* (908) 747-9078 *Fax:* (908) 530-9374
Orders to: University of Washington Press, 4045 Brooklyn Ave NE, Seattle, WA 98105, United States *Tel:* 206-543-8870 *Fax:* 206-543-3932
Gazelle Book Service Ltd, LEL Industrial Estate, Unit 2, White Cross Mills, Lancs LA1 4XQ, United Kingdom *Tel:* (524) 68765 *Fax:* (524) 63232
Chidambaram, Usmanperra, Ahmedabad 380 013

Marg Publications
3rd Floor, Army & Navy Bldg, 148 Mahatma Gandhi Rd, Mumbai 400023
Tel: (022) 2821151 *Fax:* (022) 2047102
E-mail: margpub@bom5.vsnl.net.in
Web Site: www.tata.com/marg
Telex: 118-2618, 118-2731 TATA IN
Key Personnel
Publisher: J J Bhabha
Editorial: Ms Chandiramani Savita
Sales, Publicity: Baptist Sequeira
Design: Miss Naju Hirani
Contact: Radhika Sabavala
Business Development Manager: Baptist Sequeira
Tel: (022) 2045947
Founded: 1946
Marg meaning pathway leads the reader through the cultural heritage of India & its neighboring countries.
Books & Magazines on Indian art, paintings, sculpture, dance & architecture.
ISBN Prefix(es): 81-85026
Parent Company: National Centre for the Performing Arts, Nariman Point, Bombay 400021
Branch Office(s)
Tata Services Ltd, Jeevan Bharati Tower No 1, 10th floor, 124 Connaught Circus, New Delhi, Contact: Mr R K Gupta *Tel:* (011) 3327072-76 *Fax:* (011) 3226265
Distributed by Art Media Resources Ltd/Paragon Book Gallery

Sri Ramakrishna Math
16 Ramakrishna Math Rd, Madras 600-004
Mailing Address: PO Box 635, Mylapore, Chennai 600-004
Tel: (044) 4941231; (044) 4941959 *Fax:* (044) 4934589
E-mail: srkmath@giasmd01.vsnl.net.in
Key Personnel
President: Sri Ramakrishna Math
Founded: 1897
Subjects: Biography, Philosophy, Religion - Hindu
ISBN Prefix(es): 81-7120
Distributor for Advaita Ashrama (Calcutta, India)
Showroom(s): 99, Pondy Baza, T Nagar, Madras 600017; Chennai Central Railway Statioin, Chennai 600-004
Bookshop(s): 16 Ramakrishna Math Rd, Mylapore, Chennai 600 004; No 26, South Mada St, Mylapore, Chennai 600-004

Maya Publishers Pvt Ltd+
303/4 Kaushalya Park, Hauz Khas, New Delhi 110016
Tel: (011) 6490959; (011) 6494850 *Fax:* (011) 6491039

E-mail: surit@del2.vsnl.net.in
Key Personnel
Contact: Surit Mitra
ISBN Prefix(es): 81-86268
Associate Companies: Gulmohur Press Pvt Ltd

Mayfair Paperbacks, *imprint of* Arnold Heinman Publishers (India) Pvt Ltd

Mayoor Paperbacks, *imprint of* National Publishing House

Mehta Publishers+
Mehta House, A-16 (East) Naraina II, New Delhi 110028
Fax: (011) 5700644
E-mail: mopl@vsnl.com
Key Personnel
Man Dir, Production, Rights & Permissions: Gautam Mehta
Publicity & Marketing Manager: G P S Bawa
Founded: 1971
Subjects: Agriculture, Asian Studies, Computer Science, Education, Medicine, Nursing, Dentistry, Orientalia
ISBN Prefix(es): 81-7161; 81-7766; 81-88039
Number of titles published annually: 200 Print
Total Titles: 2,000 Print
Parent Company: Mehta Offset Pvt Ltd
Imprints: Interprint
Subsidiaries: Mehta Book Sellers
Book Club(s): T Book Club

Merrill Education, *imprint of* Addison-Wesley (Singapore) Pte Ltd

Minerva Associates (Publications) Pvt Ltd+
7-B Lake Pl, Calcutta 700 029
Tel: (033) 4763783
Key Personnel
Chairman, Publicity, Rights & Permissions: Sushil Mukherjea
Editorial Dir: O K Ghosh
Sales: T K Mukherjee
Founded: 1973
Publication of serious studies.
Subjects: Agriculture, Anthropology, Asian Studies, Economics, Education, Ethnicity, Government, Political Science, History, Journalism, Labor, Industrial Relations, Literature, Literary Criticism, Essays, Natural History, Philosophy, Psychology, Psychiatry, Public Administration, Religion - Buddhist, Religion - Hindu, Social Sciences, Sociology
ISBN Prefix(es): 81-7715
Number of titles published annually: 10 Print
Total Titles: 320 Print

Ministry of Information & Broadcasting
Publications Division, Patiala House, Tilak Marg, New Delhi 110 001
Tel: (011) 386879 *Cable:* EXINFOR
Key Personnel
Dir: Dr O P Kejariwal; Rao Maheshwar
Subjects: Art, Biography, Environmental Studies, Ethnicity, History, Science (General), Social Sciences, Sociology
ISBN Prefix(es): 81-230
Branch Office(s)
Commerce House, Currimbhoy Rd, Ballard Pier, Bombay
8 Esplanade East, Calcutta
Super Bazar 2nd floor, Connaught Circus, New Delhi
State Archaeological Museum Bldg, Public Garden, Hyderabad
Kanda, Chiyoda-Ku, Lucknow
LL Auditorium, Anna Salai, Madras
Bihar State Co-operative Bank Bldg, Ashoka Rajpath, Patna
Government Press, Press Rd, Trivandrum

PUBLISHERS

Mittal Publications
B-2-19-B Lawrence Rd, Delhi 110035
Tel: (011) 5552070; (011) 5592070
Key Personnel
Contact: K M Mittal
Founded: 1979
Member of India Federation of Publishers' & Booksellers' Association.
Subjects: Social Sciences, Sociology
ISBN Prefix(es): 81-7099
Orders to: A-110 Mohan Garden, New Delhi 110059

Motilal Banarsidass Publishers Pvt Ltd+
41 Bungalow Rd, Jawahar Nagar, Delhi 110007
Tel: (011) 391 1985; (011) 391 8335; (011) 397 4826 *Fax:* (011) 393 0689; (011) 5452771
Telex: 03166053 Enky In; 03165367 Kkrc In
Cable: GLORYINDIA
Key Personnel
Dir, Editorial, Rights & Permissions & Publishing: N P Jain
Home Sales: J P Jain
Finance: Ravi P Jain
Publishing: Anurag Jain
Founded: 1903
Subjects: History, Language Arts, Linguistics, Literature, Literary Criticism, Essays, Medicine, Nursing, Dentistry, Philosophy, Religion - Other
ISBN Prefix(es): 81-208
Branch Office(s)
16, St Mark's Rd, Bangalore, Karnataka 560001
PO Box 75, Chowk, Varanasi 221 001 *Tel:* (0542) 62898
Ashok Raipath, opposite Patna College, Patna, Bihar 800 004 *Tel:* (0612) 51442
120 Royapettah High Rd, Mylapore, Madras 600004
Warehouse: 45 A, Naraina Industrial Area phase-I, New Delhi 28

Mudgala Trust+
Kaveri 12, Fourth Cross St, Ramakrishna Nagar, Madras 600028
Tel: (044) 837257
Key Personnel
Founder: S R Balasubrahmanyam
Secretary, Treasurer: B Natarajan
President: Meenakshi Natarajan
Joint Secretary,Treasurer: Dr B Venkataraman
Member: Leela Venkataraman; Dr B Ramachandran; Asha Ramachandran
Founded: 1965
Subjects: Architecture & Interior Design, Art, Drama, Theater, Ethnicity, Music, Dance, Philosophy, Religion - Other
ISBN Prefix(es): 81-86392
U.S. Office(s): Mohan Venkataraman, 361 Bancroft Court, No 2, Rockford, IL 61107, United States *Tel:* 815-227-4553

Mudrak Publishers & Distributors+
MB-15 Antriksh Bhawan, 22 Kasturba Gandhi Marg, New Delhi 110 001
Mailing Address: W-152 Greater Kalish-1, New Delhi 110 048
Tel: (011) 3730818; (011) 3738319; (011) 6416317
Key Personnel
Prop: S P Kumria
Books of academic interest on subjects of humanities.
ISBN Prefix(es): 81-87161
Total Titles: 5 Print

A Mukherjee & Co Pvt Ltd
P-27 B C I T Rd, Scheme 52, Calcutta W B 700014
Tel: (033) 341606; (033) 341499
Key Personnel
Dir: Rajeev Neogi
Founded: 1940
Subjects: Education, Government, Political Science, Nonfiction (General), Religion - Other, Travel
ISBN Prefix(es): 81-86043

Multitech Publishing Co+
15 Yogesh Hingwala Lane, Ghatkopar East, Mumbai 400 077
Tel: (022) 5118820; (022) 513-0147 *Fax:* (022) 5115904
Key Personnel
Contact: Sevantilal Shah
Founded: 1977
Member of Federation of India Publishers.
Subjects: Chemistry, Chemical Engineering, Engineering (General), Management, Mechanical Engineering, Technology
Branch Office(s)
Ahmedabad Book Centre, D/122, Mahavir Chamber, Near Relief Cinema, Salapose Rd, Ahmedabad 380 001

Munshiram Manoharlal Publishers Pvt Ltd+
54 Rani Jhansi Rd, New Delhi 110055
Mailing Address: PO Box 5715, New Delhi 110055
Tel: (011) 3671668; (011) 3673650 *Fax:* (011) 3612745
E-mail: mrml@mantraonline.com
Web Site: mrmlbooks.com
Key Personnel
Chief Executive, Man Dir: Devendra Jain
Production, Publicity: Pankaj D Jain
  E-mail: pankaj.mrml@mantraonline.com
Sales Dir: Ashok Jain
Founded: 1952
Also acts as Major Book Dealer.
Subjects: Anthropology, Archaeology, Architecture & Interior Design, Art, Asian Studies, Astrology, Occult, Drama, Theater, History, Language Arts, Linguistics, Music, Dance, Philosophy, Religion - Buddhist, Religion - Hindu, Religion - Islamic, Religion - Other
ISBN Prefix(es): 81-215
Number of titles published annually: 80 Print
Total Titles: 1,200 Print
Bookshop(s): 4416 Nai Sarak, Delhi 110006 (Amir Chand Marg)

M/S Gulshan Nanda Publications+
7-Sheesh Mahal 5-A Pali Hill, Bandra, Bombay 50
Tel: (022) 6406994 *Fax:* (022) 4303696
Key Personnel
President: Himanshu Nanda
Vice President: Rahul Nanda
Founded: 1984
Member of Federation of Indian Publishers' Association.
Subjects: Fiction
ISBN Prefix(es): 81-7241
Associate Companies: Sonex Marketing & Publishing, United Kingdom *Tel:* (081) 4225172

Naresh Publishers+
111 Shankar Rd Market, New Rajendra Nagar, New Delhi 110060
Tel: (011) 5723235; (011) 5754442 *Fax:* (011) 574-6485
Key Personnel
Contact: Mohinder Kumar Chowdhry
Founded: 1972
Member of Federation of Educational Publishers in India, Federation of Indian Publishers, & Federation of Publishers & Booksellers in India.
ISBN Prefix(es): 81-7005
Associate Companies: Paramount Sales (India) Pvt Ltd, 484 Double Storey, PO Box 2860, New Rajinder Nagar, New Delhi 110060 *Tel:* (011) 5723235 *Fax:* (011) 5746485

Narosa Publishing House+
6 Community Centre, Panchsheel Park, New Delhi 110017
Tel: (011) 6433992; (011) 6433818 *Fax:* (011) 6468717
Telex: 3161661 *Cable:* Narosa New Delhi
Key Personnel
Man Dir: N K Mehra
Production Manager: M S Sejwal
Marketing Manager: S Mehra
Founded: 1977
Subjects: Biological Sciences, Chemistry, Chemical Engineering, Computer Science, Engineering (General), Environmental Studies, Mathematics, Medicine, Nursing, Dentistry, Philosophy, Physics, Psychology, Psychiatry, Religion - Other
ISBN Prefix(es): 81-85015; 81-85198; 81-7319
Associate Companies: Narosa Book Distributors Pvt Ltd (at above main address)
Branch Office(s)
2F-2G Shivam Chambers, 53 Syed Amir Ali Ave, Calcutta 700019 *Tel:* (033) 477209
35-36 Greams Rd, Thousand Lights, Madras 600006 *Tel:* (044) 475362
306 Shiv Centre, D B C Sector 17 PO KU Bazar, New Bombay 400705 *Tel:* (022) 7683646

National Academy of Letters, India, see Sahitya Akademi

National Academy of Art, see Lalit Kala Akademi

National Book Organization+
H-29 Green Park Extension, New Delhi 110-016
Tel: (011) 669962 *Fax:* (011) 6851795
Telex: 031 73034nbt-in
Founded: 1984
Acts as Distributor.
Subjects: Agriculture, Anthropology, Archaeology, Architecture & Interior Design, Behavioral Sciences, Child Care & Development, Developing Countries, Economics, Education, Environmental Studies, Geography, Geology, Government, Political Science, History, Human Relations, Labor, Industrial Relations, Law, Management, Military Science, Religion - Other, Social Sciences, Sociology, Women's Studies
ISBN Prefix(es): 81-85135; 81-237; 81-87521
Branch Office(s)
Delhi
Distributed by UBS Publishers Distributors Ltd
Bookshop(s): Municipal Flat No 18, Bungalos Rd, Delhi 110007

National Book Trust, see National Book Organization

National Book Trust India
H-29 Green Park Extension, New Delhi 110 016
Tel: (011) 669962; (011) 664540; (011) 664667 *Fax:* (011) 6851795
Telex: 031-73034 *Cable:* Nabotrust
Key Personnel
Chairman: Anand Sarub
Dir: Arvind Kumar
Joint Dir, Administration & Finance: S N Madan
Deputy Dir, Arts: Jyotish Datta Gupta
Deputy Dir, Exhibitions: Talewar Giri
Deputy Dir, Subsidies: R Gupta
Deputy Dir, Information & Publicity: D Das Gupta
Deputy Dir, Production: Dhruv Bhargava
Founded: 1957
Subjects: Foreign Countries, Human Relations
ISBN Prefix(es): 81-85135; 81-237
Bookshop(s): Jayanagar Shopping Complex, Bangalore; CIDCO Bldg, Sector 1, 2nd floor, Vashi, Bombay; S A Bhabari, Dutt Lane, Calcutta; A-4 Green Park, New Delhi

INDIA

National Council of Applied Economic Research, Publications Division
Parisila Bhawan, 11, Indraprastha Estate, New Delhi 110 002
Tel: (011) 3379861 *Fax:* (011) 3370164
E-mail: infor@ncaer.org
Web Site: www.ncaer.org
Key Personnel
Dir-General: Mr Suman Bery
Founded: 1956
Subjects: Agriculture, Business, Economics
ISBN Prefix(es): 81-85877

National Council of Educational Research & Training, Publication Department
Sri Aurobindo Marg, New Delhi 110016
Tel: (011) 6851070; (011) 662708 *Fax:* (011) 6868419
Telex: 31-73024 NCRT-IN *Cable:* EDUPRINT, NEW DELHI
Key Personnel
Dir: Dr K Gopalan
Founded: 1962
Member of Afro-Asian Book Council. Specializes in School Textbooks, Research Monographs, Supplementary Readers.
Subjects: Education
ISBN Prefix(es): 81-7450

National Institute of Industrial Research (NIIR)
Affiliate of NIIR Project Exports India (P) Ltd
106-E 1st floor, Kamla Nagar, Delhi 110007
Mailing Address: PB No 2162, Delhi 110007
Tel: (011) 3923955; (011) 3935654 *Fax:* (011) 3941561
E-mail: niir@niir.org
Web Site: www.nexusindia.com/niir.htm
Key Personnel
President & International Rights: Gupta Ajay Kumar *E-mail:* niir@vsnl.com
Founded: 1994
Publishers of process technology books, Business & Industrial Directory, Worldwide Importers Directory & Industrial Monthly Magazine.
Subjects: Business, Chemistry, Chemical Engineering, Science (General), Technology
ISBN Prefix(es): 81-86623
Number of titles published annually: 20 Print
Total Titles: 70 Print
Distributor for M/S Small Industry Research Institute

National Museum
Janpath, New Delhi 110011
Tel: (011) 3018159; (011) 3833436
Key Personnel
Editorial: C B Pandey
Sales: V P Dwivedi
Production: N R Banerjee
Subjects: Art, Ethnicity
ISBN Prefix(es): 81-85832

National Publishing House
23 Daryaganj, New Delhi 110 002
Tel: (011) 3274161; (011) 3275267
Key Personnel
Man Dir: K L Malik
Editorial, Production, Rights & Permissions: S K Malik
Sales: M K Malik
Founded: 1950
A-95 Sector 5, Noida 201301 (UP) Tel: 3683/4507.
Subjects: Ethnicity, Human Relations, Social Sciences, Sociology
ISBN Prefix(es): 81-214
Parent Company: K L Malik & Sons Pvt Ltd, 23 Daryaganj, New Delhi 110 002
Imprints: Mayoor Paperbacks; Gyan Bharati

Branch Office(s)
K L Malik & Sons Pvt Ltd, 34 Netaji Subhash Marg, Allahabad 3
Malik & Co, Chaura Rasta, Jaipur 302003
Bookshop(s): 23 Daryaganj, New Delhi 110002

Natraj Prakashan+
A-98, A Shok Vihar, Phase 1, Delhi 110052
Telex: 316 5503 FXRS 1N
Key Personnel
Owner: Mrs Kusum Goyanka
Founded: 1987
Subjects: Biography, Fiction, Literature, Literary Criticism, Essays, Poetry, Religion - Hindu
ISBN Prefix(es): 81-85979

Navajivan Trust+
Post Navajivan, Ahmedabad 380014
Tel: (079) 7541329
Key Personnel
Man Dir, Rights & Permissions: Jitendar T Desai
Sales, Publicity: Kapil Rawal
Founded: 1919
Subjects: Biography, History, Philosophy, Religion - Other
ISBN Prefix(es): 81-7229
Branch Office(s)
130 Princess St, Bombay 2

Navrang Booksellers & Publishers+
RB-7 Inderpuri, New Delhi 110 012
Tel: (011) 5835914; (011) 5836197 *Fax:* (011) 5836113; (011) 5836761
E-mail: navrang@del2.vsn.net.in
Key Personnel
Proprietor: Mrs Nirmal Singal
Founded: 1968
Subjects: Archaeology, Art, Developing Countries, Education, Ethnicity, History, Philosophy, Religion - Buddhist, Religion - Hindu
ISBN Prefix(es): 81-7013

Navyug Publishers
K-24 Hauz Khas, New Delhi 110016
Tel: (011) 278370
Key Personnel
Editorial: Pritam Singh
Sales: Gurbachan Singh
Founded: 1949
Subjects: Ethnicity
ISBN Prefix(es): 81-85267; 81-86216

Naya Prokash+
206 Bidhan Sarani, Calcutta 700 006
Mailing Address: PO Box 11468, Calcutta 700 006
Tel: (033) 349566 *Fax:* (033) 5523366; (033) 5524053 *Cable:* Napkas
Key Personnel
Production, Rights & Permissions, Editorial: Barin Mitra
Partner, Sales, Publicity: D Roy
Founded: 1962
Subjects: Agriculture, Environmental Studies, Gardening, Plants, Government, Political Science, History, Language Arts, Linguistics, Management, Military Science, Science (General), Social Sciences, Sociology
ISBN Prefix(es): 81-85109; 81-85421
Parent Company: Darbari Offset Pvt Ltd
Associate Companies: Mitrata Offset Print; Prokash Pvt Ltd
Subsidiaries: NP Sales Pvt Ltd

Neeta Prakashan+
A-4 Ring Rd, South Extension Part-1, New Delhi 110 049
Mailing Address: PO Box 3853, New Delhi 110 049
Tel: (011) 692013; (011) 692014; (011) 692015 *Fax:* (011) 4636011 *Cable:* Loveneeta

Key Personnel
Man Proprietor: Shanti Devi
Sales, Production, Publicity, Rights & Permissions Executive: Rakesh Gupta
Founded: 1960
Subjects: Education
ISBN Prefix(es): 81-7202

Neha Mini Katha, *imprint of* Spectrum Publications

Nem Chand & Brothers+
Civil Lines, Roorkee 247667 U P
Tel: (01332) 72258; (01332) 72752; (01332) 74343 *Fax:* (01332) 73258 *Cable:* ENGINJOUR
Key Personnel
Man Dir, Rights & Permissions: N C Jain
Editorial Dir: Dr Ashok K Jain
Sales Dir: Anil Jain
Production Dir: Shanil Jain
Publicity, Advertising Dir: Mrs Shashi Jain
Founded: 1951
Member of Chemical & Allied Products Export Promotion Council (Books Division); Also book packager.
Subjects: Agriculture, Architecture & Interior Design, Career Development, Earth Sciences, Fashion, Gardening, Plants, House & Home, Women's Studies
ISBN Prefix(es): 81-85240
Subsidiaries: Roorkee Press
Warehouse: Opposite Old Dy S P Office, Roorkee 247667

New Light Publishers+
B-8 Rattan Jyoti, 18 Rajendra Pl, New Delhi 110 008
Tel: (011) 5737448 *Fax:* (011) 5812385
E-mail: newlight@vsnl.net *Cable:* ENELPEE
Key Personnel
Man Partner: Vikas Chowdhary
Editorial: Prof R P Chopra
Publicity, Advertising: R K Chowdhry
Founded: 1964
Subjects: Language Arts, Linguistics, Self-Help
ISBN Prefix(es): 81-85018; 81-86332

New Riders, *imprint of* Addison-Wesley (Singapore) Pte Ltd

Newspread International+
E 2 Greater Kailish 11, New Delhi 110048
Tel: (011) 2331402 *Fax:* (011) 2607252
Telex: 22143 Bureau *Cable:* NEWSPREAD
Key Personnel
Executive Editor: Kul Bhushan
Production Manager: Benedict Mutisya Nzomo
Founded: 1971
ISBN Prefix(es): 81-86858
Showroom(s): Leader House, Moi Ave, Kenya

Nil, *imprint of* Asian Trading Corporation

Niyo Software
A3/3 Vrindavan Co Op Society, Range Hills Rd, Pune 411020
Tel: (020) 445 8742; (020) 400 1603 *Fax:* (020) 400 1603
E-mail: info@niyoindia.com
Web Site: www.niyoindia.com
Key Personnel
President: Milind Chudgar
Founded: 1995
Document conversion & e-enabling services, animation & graphic generation. Various formats including LIT, Adobe PDF, Palm Devices (PDB), XML, OEB & all possible ebook formats.

PUBLISHERS

INDIA

Omsons Publications+
T-7, Rajouri Garden, New Delhi 110027
Tel: (011) 5412452 *Fax:* (011) 3289353
E-mail: omsons@satyam.net.in
Key Personnel
Contact: Ramesh Kumar Virmani
Founded: 1983
Subjects: Agriculture, Anthropology, Behavioral Sciences, Biography, Business, Career Development, Drama, Theater, Economics, Education, Environmental Studies, Fiction, Foreign Countries, Geography, Geology, Government, Political Science, History, Humor, Library & Information Sciences, Literature, Literary Criticism, Essays, Management, Marketing, Philosophy, Psychology, Psychiatry, Social Sciences, Sociology, Travel, Veterinary Science, Women's Studies
ISBN Prefix(es): 81-7117
Parent Company: Western Book Depot, Panbazar, Guwahati 781001
Branch Office(s)
Jasomanta Rd, Panbazar, Guwahati 781001
Bookshop(s): Western Book Depot, Panbazar, Guwahati 781001
Orders to: Omsons, Prakash House, 4379/4B Ansari Rd, New Delhi 110002

Orient Paperbacks+
1590 Madarsa Rd, Kashmere Gate, Delhi 110006
Tel: (011) 3862267; (011) 3862201 *Fax:* (011) 3862935
E-mail: orientpbk@vsnl.com
Web Site: www.orientpaperbacks.com *Cable:* VISIONBOOK, DELHI 110006
Key Personnel
Man Dir: Vishwa Nath
Editorial, Production: Kapil Malhotra
Sales, Publicity, Rights & Permissions: Sudhir Malhotra *E-mail:* smalhotra@orientpaperbacks.com
Founded: 1977
Subjects: Astrology, Occult, Business, Career Development, Cookery, Crafts, Games, Hobbies, Drama, Theater, Fiction, Health, Nutrition, How-to, Humor, Nonfiction (General), Poetry, Self-Help, Sports, Athletics, Specialize in fitness
ISBN Prefix(es): 81-222
Number of titles published annually: 50 Print
Total Titles: 540 Print
Parent Company: Vision Books Pvt Ltd
Associate Companies: Rajpal & Sons; Ravindra Printing Press; Shiksha Bharati; Shiksha Bharati Press, G T Rd, Shadara, Delhi 110 032
Imprints: Anand Paperbacks
Branch Office(s)
Vasant, Ground floor, 3-B Pedder Rd, Bombay 400026 *Tel:* (022) 4929343 *Fax:* (022) 4960229
3-6-280/A/5 Himayatnagar, Hyderabad, K M Govindan *Tel:* (040) 322-3252
24 Feroze Gandhi Marg, Lajpat Nagar, New Delhi 110024 *Tel:* (011) 683-6470; (011) 683-6480 *Fax:* (011) 683-6490
Book Club(s): Orient Book Club

Oxford & IBH Publishing Co Pvt Ltd+
66 Janpath, 2nd floor, New Delhi 110001
Tel: (011) 332 45 78; (011) 332 05 18 *Fax:* (011) 371 32 75
E-mail: oxford@vsnl.com
Key Personnel
Dir: Mohan Primlani; Raju Primlani; Vijay Primlani
Founded: 1962
Subjects: Agriculture, Asian Studies, Biological Sciences, Civil Engineering, Earth Sciences, Engineering (General), Mechanical Engineering, Natural History, Psychology, Psychiatry, Science (General)
ISBN Prefix(es): 81-204; 81-205; 81-7087

Subsidiaries: Science Publishers Incorporated
Branch Office(s)
22 Park Mansion, Park St, Calcutta 700016

Oxford University Press+
2/11 Ansari Rd, Daryaganj, New Delhi 110002
Tel: (011) 2021029; (011) 2021198; (011) 2021396 *Fax:* (011) 3732312; (011) 3360897
E-mail: ibho@oup.wiprobt.ems.vsnl.net.in
Telex: OXORIENT
Key Personnel
Man Dir: Manzar Khan
Finance Dir: Ashok Rai Chaudhury
Dir Education Division: Aloke Roy Chowdhury
Dir Operations & IT: Neil Todd
Dir Academic Publishing: Rukun Advani
Regional Dir, East-Calcutta: J K Sen
Regional Dir, South-Madras: Sunil Paul
Branch Manager, North-Delhi: Sridhar Balan
Publicity Manager: Thomas Abraham
Founded: 1912
Subjects: Biography, Business, Developing Countries, Economics, History, Literature, Literary Criticism, Essays, Natural History, Philosophy, Religion - Hindu, Politics, Sociology, Culture Studies, Gender Studies. Ecology, Science, Medicine
ISBN Prefix(es): 81-7025
Parent Company: Oxford University Press, United Kingdom
Branch Office(s)
Oxford House, Apollo Bunder, Bombay 400001
5 Lala Lajpat Rai Sarani, Calcutta 700020
Oxford House, 219 Anna Salai, Madras 600006
U.S. Office(s): US University Press, 198 Madison Ave, New York, NY 11016, United States
Showroom(s): B/49 Mandir Marg, Mahanagar Ext, Lucknow 226006; 94 Koramangala Industrial Area, 4 "B" Cross, Fifth Block, Bqangalore 560095; Gayatri Sadan, 2060 Sadashiv Peth, V N Colony, Pune 411030; Hasan Manzil Complex, Frazer Rd, Patna 800001; 3-5-1107 Narayanagunda, Hyderabad 500029; Danish Rd, Panbazar, Guwahati 781001

Oxonian Press (P) Ltd+
N-56 Connaught Circus, New Delhi 110001
Tel: (011) 44957; (011) 3313584 *Fax:* (011) 3322639
E-mail: oxford.publ@axcess.net.in *Cable:* INDAMER
Key Personnel
Dir, Rights & Permissions: Gulab Primlani
Sales Dir: Dr A M Primlani
Publicity Manager: Ms Chandra Naharwar
Science Publishers, Inc, 10 Water St, No 10, Lebanon, NH 03766.
Subjects: Engineering (General), Music, Dance, Science (General)
ISBN Prefix(es): 81-7087
Parent Company: Oxford & IBH Publishing Co Pvt Ltd
Associate Companies: Amerind Publishing Co P Ltd
Branch Office(s)
29 Wodehouse Rd, Bombay
17 Park St, Calcutta 700016
165 Golf Links, New Delhi 110003
Showroom(s): Oxford Book & Stationery Co, Scindia House, New Delhi 110 001
Warehouse: Plot No 6, Sector 27A, Industrial Area, Faridabad

Paico Publishing House+
M G Rd, Ernakulam, Cochin 682 035
Mailing Address: PO Box 2560, Ernakulam, Cochin 682 035
Tel: (0484) 355835 *Cable:* PAICO
Key Personnel
Man Dir: Kanchana V Pai
Founded: 1955
Subjects: Fiction, History, Science (General)

Associate Companies: Broadway; Ernakulam; Pai & Co
Branch Office(s)
New Rd, Mattancherry, Cochin 682002
Paico Buildings, Press Rd, Trivandrum 1
Bookshop(s): Paico Books & Arts, Cochin; 181 Mount Rd, Madras 600002; Kallai Rd, Calicut 673002; K K Rd, Kottayam 686002

Panchasheel Prakashan
Film Colony, Chaura Rasta, Jaipur 302 003
Tel: (0141) 65072
Key Personnel
Editorial: M C Gupta
Sales: O P Agarwal
Founded: 1968
Subjects: Fiction
ISBN Prefix(es): 81-7056

Panjab University Publication Bureau
Chandigarh 160 014
Tel: (0172) 541782; (0172) 534373
Key Personnel
Manager: H R Grover
Founded: 1948
Member of Federation of Indian Publishers.
Subjects: Biography, History, Philosophy, Poetry, Religion - Other, Social Sciences, Sociology
ISBN Prefix(es): 81-85322

Pankaj Publications+
3 Regal Bldg, Sansad Marg, New Delhi 110001
Tel: (011) 3363395; (011) 3348805 *Fax:* (011) 5448265; (01) 3348805
E-mail: book@vsnl.in
Key Personnel
Manager: Vikas Bajaj *E-mail:* bajajvikas@hotmail.com
Subjects: Crafts, Games, Hobbies, Ethnicity, Music, Dance
ISBN Prefix(es): 81-87155
Number of titles published annually: 20 Print
Total Titles: 150 Print
Bookshop(s): Cambridge Book Depot, 3 Regal Bldg, Connaught Circus, New Delhi 110001, Mr Ranjana Bajaj *E-mail:* cambridgebooks@hotmail.com

Paramount Sales (India) Pvt Ltd+
484 Double Storey, New Rajinder Nagar, New Delhi 110060
Mailing Address: PO Box 2860, New Delhi 110060
Tel: (011) 5723235; (011) 5754442 *Fax:* (011) 5746485
Key Personnel
Dir: Naresh Kumar Chowdhry
Founded: 1986
Subjects: Art, Language Arts, Linguistics
ISBN Prefix(es): 81-7103
Associate Companies: Naresh Publishers, 111 Shankar Rd Market, New Rajinder Nagar, New Delhi 110060 *Tel:* (011) 5723235 *Fax:* (011) 5746485

Parimal Prakashan+
Parimal Bldg, Khadkeshwar, Aurangabad 431001
Tel: (0240) 323887
Key Personnel
Man Dir, Production: A B Dashrathe
Sales: S B Padalkar
Founded: 1974
Subjects: Archaeology, Astrology, Occult, Career Development, Education, Ethnicity, Human Relations, Literature, Literary Criticism, Essays, Medicine, Nursing, Dentistry, Social Sciences, Sociology
ISBN Prefix(es): 81-7088

Branch Office(s)
159/2 Shaniwar Peth Pune, Kennedy Bridge, Bombay
Bookshop(s): Marathwada Book Distributors, Parimal Bldg, Khadkeshwar, Amangabad 431001

Peachpit Press, *imprint of* Addison-Wesley (Singapore) Pte Ltd

Peacock Books, *imprint of* HarperCollins Publishers India Pty Ltd

Penguin Longman Publishing, *imprint of* Addison-Wesley (Singapore) Pte Ltd

People's Publishing House (P) Ltd
5-E Rani Jhansi Rd, New Delhi 110 055
Tel: (011) 529365 *Cable:* Quamikitab
Key Personnel
Chairman: T Madhavan
General Manager: P P C Joshi
Founded: 1942
Subjects: Biography, Engineering (General), History, Philosophy, Poetry, Social Sciences, Sociology
ISBN Prefix(es): 81-7007
Bookshop(s): 2 Marina Arcade, Connaught Place, New Delhi 110001 *Tel:* (011) 344064

Pitambar Publishing Co (P) Ltd+
888 E Park Rd, KarolBagh, New Delhi 110 005
Tel: (011) 367 0067; (011) 352 2997; (011) 367 3608 *Fax:* (011) 367 6058
E-mail: pitambar@bol.net.in
Web Site: www.pitambar.com *Cable:* PITAMBAR NEW DELHI
Key Personnel
Man Dir, Production, Rights & Permissions: Ved Bhushan
Man Dir, Publicity: Anand Bhushan
Sales: Manish Aggarwal; Prem Chand
Production: Jaideep Aggarwal
Founded: 1947
Member of Federation of Indian Publishers, New Delhi, Akhil Bhartia Hindi Prakashak Sangh, New Delhi.
Subjects: Accounting, Chemistry, Chemical Engineering, Computer Science, Economics, Electronics, Electrical Engineering, Fiction, History, Mathematics, Microcomputers, Religion - Buddhist, Religion - Hindu
ISBN Prefix(es): 81-209
Associate Companies: Ambar Prakashan, 888 E Park Rd, New Delhi 11005, Ved Bhushan; Computel Systems & Services, 10 Community Centre, Mayapuri, Phase I, New Delhi *Tel:* (011) 5136652 *Fax:* (011) 5133088; Piyush Printers Publishers Pvt Ltd, G-12 Udyog Nagar, Rohtak Road Industrial Area, New Delhi 110041, Jaideep Aggarwal; Bharat Publishing House, 123 Durga Chambers, Desh Bandhu Gupta Rd, New Delhi 110005, Karol Bagh; Reliant Microsystems Pvt Ltd, 10 Community Centre, Mayapuri, Phase-I, New Delhi 64, Prof V B Aggarwal
Branch Office(s)
H No 6/2, 111 Main Rd, SK Garden, Bensen Town Post, Bangalore 560046 *Tel:* 3534673
1-1-230/6 (407) Vivek Nagar, Chikkadapally, Hyderabad 500020 *Tel:* 7645614
Warehouse: 415-1-3, Mundika, New Delhi 110041

Pitman, *imprint of* Addison-Wesley (Singapore) Pte Ltd

Pointer Publishers+
1-Gha-22 Jawahar Nagar, Jaipur 302004
Tel: (0141) 568159 *Fax:* (0141) 562000

Key Personnel
Mgr: Vipin Jain
Founded: 1986
Publish reference & general books in arts, science & commerce.
Subjects: Accounting, Agriculture, Biological Sciences, Child Care & Development, Economics, Education, Environmental Studies, Geography, Geology, Government, Political Science, History, Library & Information Sciences, Literature, Literary Criticism, Essays, Management, Social Sciences, Sociology, Women's Studies
ISBN Prefix(es): 81-7132
Total Titles: 200 Print
Parent Company: Aavishkar Publishers' Distributors, Jaipur
Distributed by Aavishkar Publishers' Distributors

Popular Prakashan Pvt Ltd+
35-C Pandit Madan Mohan, Malviya Marg, Bombay 400034
Tel: (022) 4941656 *Fax:* (022) 4938049
Cable: NANDIBOOK
Key Personnel
Man Dir: Ramdas Ganesh Bhatkal
Joint Dir: Sadanand Ganesh Bhatkal
Dir: Harsha Ramdas Bhatkal
Founded: 1924
Subjects: Anthropology, Biography, Computer Science, Cookery, Economics, Government, Political Science, Health, Nutrition, History, Management, Medicine, Nursing, Dentistry, Music, Dance, Social Sciences, Sociology, Women's Studies
ISBN Prefix(es): 81-7154
Parent Company: Popular Book Depot
Associate Companies: Bhatkal & Sen
Imprints: Focus
Branch Office(s)
16 Southern Ave, Calcutta 700026 *Tel:* (033) 761413
4648-1 Ansari Rd, 21 Daryaganj, New Delhi 110002 *Tel:* (011) 3265245
67 Patil Estate, Pune 411005 *Tel:* (0212) 52088

Prabhat Prakashan+
205 Chawri Bazar, Delhi 110006
Tel: (011) 264676
Key Personnel
Chief Executive: Shyam Sunder
Executive: Pawan Agrawal
Editorial: Shyam Bahadur Verma
Sales: Raghuvir Verma
Production: Dharam Vir
Founded: 1952
Subjects: Art, Biography, Cookery, Fiction, Humor, Library & Information Sciences, Nonfiction (General), Poetry
ISBN Prefix(es): 81-7315
Branch Office(s)
Mathura
Showroom(s): 4-19 Asaf Ali Rd, New Delhi 2
Bookshop(s): 4-19 Asaf Ali Rd, New Delhi 2

Pratibha Pratishthan+
1685 Dakhni Rai St, Netaji Subhash Marg, New Delhi 110002
Tel: (011) 3265770
Key Personnel
President: Prabhat Kumar
Vice President: Piyush Agrawal
Sales Executive: Ajay Kumar; D S Negi
Founded: 1981
Subjects: Art, Biography, Cookery, Fiction, Humor, Library & Information Sciences, Nonfiction (General), Poetry
ISBN Prefix(es): 81-85827

Prentice Hall, *imprint of* Addison-Wesley (Singapore) Pte Ltd

Prima Communications Inc, *imprint of* Rajendra Publishing House Pvt Ltd

Promilla and Co
Sonali, C-127 Sarvodaya Enclave, New Delhi 110 017
Tel: (011) 668720 *Fax:* (011) 6448947
Key Personnel
President & Editor: Prof D H Butani
Production, Rights & Permissions Dir: Ashok Butani
General Manager: M M Khanna
Sales Manager: Sutikshan Naithani
Chief Executive: Nirmala Butani
Founded: 1970
Subjects: Art, Biography, Economics, Government, Political Science, History, Religion - Other, Social Sciences, Sociology, Women's Studies
ISBN Prefix(es): 81-85002

PTR, *imprint of* Addison-Wesley (Singapore) Pte Ltd

Publications & Information Directorate, CSIR+
Hillside Rd, New Delhi 110012
Tel: (011) 5786301 ext 287; (011) 5786301 ext 288
Telex: 031-77271 *Cable:* PUBLIFORM
Key Personnel
Editorial: G P Phondka
Sales: A K Srivastava
Founded: 1942
Subjects: Biological Sciences, Chemistry, Chemical Engineering, Physics, Science (General), Technology
ISBN Prefix(es): 81-7236; 81-85038
Parent Company: Council of Scientific & Industrial Research, New Delhi

Pustak Mahal+
10-B, Netaji Subhash Marg, Darya Ganj, New Delhi 110 002
Tel: (011) 3276539; (011) 3272783; (011) 3272784 *Fax:* (011) 3260518; (011) 2924673
E-mail: delaad37@giasdl01.vsnl.net.in
Telex: 031-78090 SBP IN
Key Personnel
Man Partner: Shri Ram Avtar Gupta
Marketing & Publishing Dir: Vikas Gupta
Dir: Ramesh Kumar Gupta; Dr Ashok Kumar Gupta
Production Dir: Venod Gupta
Founded: 1974
Publishes in twelve languages.
Member of Federation of Indian Publishers, Federation of Publishers & Booksellers Association, Federation of Educational Publishers of India, Akhil Bharatiye Hindi Prakashak Sangh, Delhi State Booksellers Association, Chemical & Allied Products Export Promotion Council, Association of Booksellers & Publishers of South India; Specialize in Supplementary educational literature for children & informative books of mass appeal.
Subjects: Architecture & Interior Design, Astrology, Occult, Biography, Computer Science, Cookery, Crafts, Games, Hobbies, Health, Nutrition, History, House & Home, Language Arts, Linguistics, Medicine, Nursing, Dentistry, Music, Dance, Parapsychology, Science (General)
ISBN Prefix(es): 81-223
Imprints: M/S Family Books Pvt Ltd; Comdex Computer Publishing
Subsidiaries: M/S Hind Pustak Bhandar
Divisions: Industrial Books Division
Branch Office(s)
23-25 Zaoba Wadi, Thakurdwar, Bombay 400 002 *Tel:* (022) 2010941 *Fax:* (022) 2053387
22/2, Mission Rd, Bangalore *Tel:* (080) 2234025 *Fax:* (080) 2240209 (Shama Rao's Compound)

Khemka House, Ashok Rajpath, Patna-4
Tel: (0612) 653644 *Fax:* (0612) 653644
Book Club(s): Comdex Book Club

QUE, *imprint of* Addison-Wesley (Singapore) Pte Ltd

Radiant Publishers+
E-155, State Bank of India Bldg, Kalkaji, New Delhi 110 019
Tel: (011) 6482861 *Fax:* (011) 6479870
E-mail: rpblcsind@yahoo.com
Key Personnel
Man Dir, Sales, Production, Publicity & Editorial, Rights & Permissions: Sunita Jain
Founded: 1973
Subjects: Economics, Education, Environmental Studies, Government, Political Science, Religion - Other, Social Sciences, Sociology, Women's Studies
ISBN Prefix(es): 81-7027
Number of titles published annually: 10 Print
Total Titles: 200 Print

Rahul Publishing House
WP-575 Wazirpur, Ashok Vihar, Delhi 110052
Tel: (011) 7212195
Key Personnel
Editorial & Production: Rahul Singhal
Founded: 1993
Subjects: Anthropology, Antiques, Archaeology, Art, Asian Studies, Earth Sciences, History, Language Arts, Linguistics, Regional Interests
ISBN Prefix(es): 81-7388
Associate Companies: Agam Prakashan; Agam Kala Prakashan; Swati Publication

Rajasthan Hindi Granth Academy+
A-26/2 Vidyalaya Marg, Tilak Nagar, Jaipur 302 004
Tel: (0141) 61410
Key Personnel
Chief Executive: Dr Ved Prakash
Sales, Publicity: K N Agrawal
Production: Mahesh Jain
Founded: 1969
Subjects: Agriculture, Art, Chemistry, Chemical Engineering, Economics, Education, Human Relations, Language Arts, Linguistics, Law, Library & Information Sciences, Medicine, Nursing, Dentistry, Philosophy, Physics, Science (General), Social Sciences, Sociology
ISBN Prefix(es): 81-7137

Rajendra Publishing House Pvt Ltd+
205 Neelam, Seaface Rd, Andheri (W), Mumbai Worli 400 018
Tel: (022) 6300741; (022) 6300742; (022) 6301930 *Fax:* (022) 6301940; 6322146
E-mail: rajendrabook@hotmail.com
Key Personnel
Chairman: Mr R K Tandon
Man Dir: Ms Swarn Tandon
Executive Dir: Ms Bindu Swaminathan Tandon; Mr Vivek Tandon *Tel:* (022) 8755935 *Fax:* (022) 8738551
Founded: 1988
Specialize in direct mail sale of high quality books.
Subjects: Astronomy, Geography, Geology, Health, Nutrition, History, How-to, Management, Science (General), Self-Help, Social Sciences, Sociology
ISBN Prefix(es): 81-900085; 81-86406; 81-900279
Total Titles: 10 Print
Imprints: Prima Communications Inc
Distributed by Gazelle Book Services Ltd
Distributor for Conari Press; Dorling Kindersley; Elements Books Ltd; Rodale Press Inc

Rajesh Publications+
One Ansari Rd, Daryaganj, New Delhi 110002
Tel: (011) 274550
Key Personnel
Man Dir: Mohan Lal *Tel:* 981111605 (mobile)
Contact: Sanjay Gupta
Founded: 1970
Subjects: Economics, Education, Geography, Geology, History, Management, Philosophy, Religion - Other
ISBN Prefix(es): 81-85891
Distributed by Janki Prakashan
Distributor for Seema Publications

Rajkamal Prakashan Pvt Ltd
One-B, Netaji Subbash Marg, New Delhi 110 002
Tel: (011) 3274463 *Fax:* (011) 3278144
Subjects: Education
ISBN Prefix(es): 81-7178
Branch Office(s)
M/D Ravkamal Prakashan Pvt Ltd

Rajpal & Sons+
Madarasa Rd, Kashmere Gate, Delhi 110006
Tel: (011) 223904; (011) 229174 *Fax:* (011) 2967791 *Cable:* RAJPALSONS DELHI
Key Personnel
Man Dir: Vishwa Nath
Sales: Satish Kumar
Editorial: Meera Johri
Publicity, Rights & Permissions: Kapil Malhotra
Founded: 1891
Specialize in dictionaries.
Subjects: Fiction, Human Relations, Literature, Literary Criticism, Essays, Science (General)
ISBN Prefix(es): 81-7028
Associate Companies: Orient Paperbacks; Shiksha Bharati; Vision Books Pvt Ltd
Branch Office(s)
3B Peddar Rd, Bombay 400026 *Tel:* (022) 4929343
3-6-280/A5, Himayat Nagar, Hyderabad 500 029
Bookshop(s): Lothian Rd, Kashmere Gate, Delhi 110006 *Tel:* (011) 2516602

Rastogi Publications+
Gangotri Shivaji Rd, Meerut 250002
Tel: (0121) 24142; (0121) 24688 *Fax:* (0121) 521545
Telex: 0549-209 *Cable:* RASTOGICO
Key Personnel
Editorial, Production, Rights & Permissions: R K Rastogi
Sales, Publicity: H K Rastogi
Sales, Publicitiy: Vivek Rastogi
Founded: 1966
Subjects: Agriculture, Animals, Pets, Biological Sciences, Earth Sciences, Education, Government, Political Science, Science (General)
ISBN Prefix(es): 81-7133; 81-85711
Subsidiaries: Pioneer Printers

Rebel Publishing House Pvt Ltd
50 Koregaon Park, Pune 411001
Tel: (0212) 628562 *Fax:* (0212) 624181
Key Personnel
Contact: Narain Das; Anando Ma Deva; Yoga Amit Swami
Founded: 1987
Subjects: Philosophy, Religion - Other, Theology
ISBN Prefix(es): 81-7261
Orders to: Sadhana Foundation, 17 Koreganon Park, Poona 411001

Regency Publications+
Member of Delphi State Publishers & Booksellers Association
20/36-G Old Market, West Patel Nagar, New Delhi 110 008
Tel: (011) 5712539; (011) 5740038 *Fax:* (011) 5783571
E-mail: regency@satyam.net.in
Key Personnel
Owner: Arun Verma
Founded: 1993
Subjects: Agriculture, Anthropology, Archaeology, Art, Biological Sciences, Education, Environmental Studies, Ethnicity, Fiction, Geography, Geology, Government, Political Science, History, Language Arts, Linguistics, Law, Philosophy, Regional Interests, Religion - Other, Social Sciences, Sociology, Sports, Athletics, Women's Studies
ISBN Prefix(es): 81-86030; 81-87498
Number of titles published annually: 20 Print
Total Titles: 150 Print
Distributed by DK Agencies; D K Publishers/Distributors; UBS Publishers' Distributors

Rekha Prakashan
16 Daryaganj, New Delhi 110 002
Tel: (011) 3279907; (011) 3279904 *Fax:* (011) 6321783
E-mail: rprakashan@satyam.net.in
Key Personnel
Chief Executive, Rights & Permissions: K C Aryan
Editorial: S Aryan
Sales: B N Aryan
Publicity Dir: G D Aryan
Founded: 1973
Subjects: Art, Regional Interests
ISBN Prefix(es): 81-900002; 81-900003
Number of titles published annually: 3 Print
Total Titles: 27 Print
Membership(s): Delhi State Booksellers' & Publishers' Association

Reliance Publishing House+
3026/7-H, Shiv Chowk, S Patel Nagar, New Delhi 110008
Tel: (011) 5852605; (011) 5772768; (011) 5737377 *Fax:* (011) 5786769
Fax on Demand: (011) 5852605
E-mail: reliance@indiatimes.com
Key Personnel
Man Dir, Rights & Permissions: Dr S K Bhatia
Sales: M K Bhatia
Publicity: Geeta Saxena *Tel:* (011) 5786769
Editorial: Bhatia Durgesh *Tel:* (011) 5737377
Founded: 1985
Publishers of reference books on the Indian book industry, humanities & social sciences.
Subjects: Accounting, Advertising, Agriculture, Anthropology, Archaeology, Architecture & Interior Design, Art, Asian Studies, Astrology, Occult, Astronomy, Behavioral Sciences, Biography, Biological Sciences, Business, Career Development, Child Care & Development, Communications, Criminology, Developing Countries, Disability, Special Needs, Drama, Theater, Earth Sciences, Economics, Education, Energy, Environmental Studies, Ethnicity, Fiction, Finance, Geography, Geology, Government, Political Science, History, Human Relations, Humor, Journalism, Labor, Industrial Relations, Library & Information Sciences, Literature, Literary Criticism, Essays, Management, Marketing, Medicine, Nursing, Dentistry, Military Science, Music, Dance, Mysteries, Mythology, Nonfiction (General), Philosophy, Poetry, Psychology, Psychiatry, Public Administration, Publishing & Book Trade Reference, Regional Interests, Religion - Buddhist, Religion - Hindu, Science Fiction, Fantasy, Social Sciences, Sociology, Sports, Athletics, Technology, Travel, Women's Studies
ISBN Prefix(es): 81-85047; 81-85972; 81-7510
Total Titles: 525 Print; 4 Online; 4 E-Book
Associate Companies: Geeta Graphics, J436, Baljit Nagar, New Delhi 110008, Manish K Bhatia *Tel:* (011) 5875330 *Fax:* (011) 5852605, 5786769; Geeta Enterprises, J436, Baljit Nagar, New Delhi 110008 *Tel:* (011)

5772748, 5875330 *Fax:* (011) 5786769
E-mail: reliance@indiatimes.com *Web
Site:* indianbookindustry.com
Distributed by DK Publishers' Distributors; UBS
Publishers Distributors Ltd
Warehouse: J-436, Baljit Nagar, New Delhi
110008 *Tel:* (011) 5875330 *Fax:* (011)
5786769; (011) 5772748 *E-mail:* reliance@
indiatimes.com

Research Signpost
37/661(2), Fort, PO, Trivandrum, Kerala 695023
Tel: (0471) 452918 *Fax:* (0471) 573051
E-mail: ggcom@vsnl.com
Web Site: www.researchsignpost.com
Key Personnel
Man Editor: Shankar Pandalai
Publications Manager: Anandavalli Hayathri
Publishers of scientific, technical, medical & agricultural books & journals. Also produces CD-ROMs.
Subjects: Agriculture, Medicine, Nursing, Dentistry, Science (General)
ISBN Prefix(es): 81-86481
Number of titles published annually: 150 Print

Researchco Reprints
25-B/2, New Rohtak Rd, Near Liberty Cinema,
New Dehli 110005
Tel: (011) 6781565; (011) 5781566; (011)
5781567 *Fax:* (011) 7276256
Telex: 31-79055 *Cable:* SEARCHBOOK
Key Personnel
Sales: Anil Jain *E-mail:* akjain@de12.vsnl.net.in
Founded: 1969
Specialize in stocking & supplying of back volume journals.
Subjects: Science (General), Technology
Warehouse: 1865 Trinagar, Delhi 110035

Response, *imprint of* Sage Publications India Pvt Ltd

Roli Books Pvt Ltd+
M-75 Greater Kailash-II (Mkt), New Delhi 110 048
Tel: (011) 6462782; (011) 6442271; (011) 6460886 *Fax:* (011) 6467185
E-mail: roli@vsnl.com
Web Site: rolibooks.com
Key Personnel
Contact: Pramod Kapoor *Tel:* (011) 6442271; Kiran Kapoor *Tel:* (011) 6225924
Publishing Manager: Ratna Sahai *Tel:* (011) 6420516
Founded: 1978
Publishing house & country distributor for foreign publishers.
Private limited company & sells titles to other houses under their logo.
Subjects: Art, Business, Cookery, Erotica, Fiction, History, Management, Music, Dance, Religion - Buddhist, Religion - Hindu, Religion - Islamic, Religion - Jewish, Travel, Plain text & coffee table books, destinations & monuments, Politics
ISBN Prefix(es): 81-7437
Total Titles: 122 Print; 122 Online; 4 Audio
Parent Company:
Ultimate Parent Company: Roli Books
Imprints: Lustre Press; Lotus

Roorkee Press, see Nem Chand & Brothers

Rupa & Co+
15 Bankim Chatterjee St, College Sq, Calcutta 700073
Tel: (033) 344821; (033) 346305 *Cable:* RUPANCO
Key Personnel
Man Dir: D Mehra

Sales: R N Barman
Productions & International Rights: R K Mehra
Accounts: S K Mehra
Publicity: C K Mehra
Founded: 1936
Subjects: Art, Crafts, Games, Hobbies, Education, Fiction, History, Literature, Literary Criticism, Essays, Philosophy, Religion - Other, Sports, Athletics
ISBN Prefix(es): 81-7167
Associate Companies: Harper Collins Publishers India
Imprints: Rupa Paperbacks
Branch Office(s)
G1 & 2 Ghaswalla Tower, P G Solanki Path, Bombay 400007
7/16 Makhanlal St, Ansari Rd, Daryaganj, New Delhi 2
94 South Malaka, Allahabad *Tel:* (0532) 53936
Distributor for Affiliated East-West (India); Elbs titles (UK); Faber & Faber (UK); Hamlyn (UK); Ladybird (UK); Macmillan (UK); McGraw-Hill Kogakusha (Singapore); Penguin (UK); Prentice-Hall (India); Tata McGraw-Hill (India); Unwin Hyman (UK); Wiley Eastern (India)

Rupa Paperbacks, *imprint of* Rupa & Co

SABDA+
Unit of Sri Aurobindo Ashram Trust
No 123, S V Patel Salai, Pondicherry 605 002
Tel: (0413) 334980; (0413) 223328 *Fax:* (0413) 223328
E-mail: sabda@sriaurobindoashram.org
Web Site: sabda.sriaurobindoashram.org
Telex: 0469221 Sas In *Cable:* SABDA
Key Personnel
Manager: Mira Gupta; Jay Raichura
International Rights & Permissions: Manoj Das Gupta
Founded: 1952
Specialize in works by or on the philosopher Sri Aurobindo & his spiritual collaborator known as "the Mother".
Member of the Federation of Indian Publishers, Akhil Bharatiya Hindi Prakashak Sangh & CAPEXIL (Export Promotion Council).
Subjects: Asian Studies, Education, Government, Political Science, Literature, Literary Criticism, Essays, Philosophy, Poetry, Psychology, Psychiatry, Religion - Hindu, Religion - Other, Social Sciences, Sociology, The spritual teachings & system of "Integral Yoga" of Sri Aurobindo
ISBN Prefix(es): 81-7058; 81-7060
Total Titles: 1,700 Print
Branch Office(s)
Sri Aurobindo Bhavan, 8 Shakespeare Sarani, Calcutta 700071, Contact: Indranil Sanyal *Tel:* (033) 2829261 *E-mail:* sabdacalcutta@vsnl.net
Distributed by Auromere (USA only); East-West Cultural Center (USA only); Lotus Press (USA only); Matagiri (USA only)
Distributor for Sri Aurobindo Ashram; Sri Aurobindo Society; Sri Mira Trust
Showroom(s): 13 Marine St, Pondicherry *Tel:* (0413) 334072 *Fax:* (0413) 223328 *E-mail:* sabda@sriaurobindoashram.org
Bookshop(s): Sri Aurobindo Society, 11 Sahakar, B Rd, Churchgate, Bombay 400 020 *Tel:* (022) 2043076; Sri Aurobindo Marg, New Delhi 110 016 *Tel:* (011) 6524810 *Fax:* (011) 6857449 *E-mail:* aurobindo@vsnl.com

Ratna Sagar Pvt Ltd+
A-8, Mukherjee Nagar, Commercial Complex, Delhi 110 009
Tel: (011) 7222505; (011) 7216094 *Fax:* (011) 7250787
Telex: 61604 AEROIN *Cable:* RATNABOOKS

Key Personnel
Contact: Dhanesh Jain
ISBN Prefix(es): 81-7070

Sage Publications India Pvt Ltd+
Affiliate of Sage Publications Inc
32 M-Block Market, Greater Kailash-I, New Delhi 110 048
Mailing Address: PO Box 4215, New Delhi 110 048
Tel: (011) 6485884; (011) 644 4958; (011) 6453915 *Fax:* (011) 6472426
E-mail: sageind@nda.vsnl.net.in *Cable:* SAGEPUB NEW DELHI 110048
Key Personnel
Man Dir: Tejeshwar Singh
Editorial: Omita Goyal
Sales: Sanjay Juneja
Marketing: Sunanda Ghosh
Founded: 1981
Subjects: Anthropology, Asian Studies, Behavioral Sciences, Business, Communications, Developing Countries, Economics, Environmental Studies, Government, Political Science, Management, Psychology, Psychiatry, Public Administration, Social Sciences, Sociology, Women's Studies
ISBN Prefix(es): 81-7036
Total Titles: 600 Print
Associate Companies: Sage Publications Ltd, United Kingdom; Sage Publications Inc, 2455 Teller Rd, Thousand Oaks, CA 91320, United States
Imprints: Vistaar; Response

Sahasrara Publications+
1143, Sector 37, Arun Vihar, Noida 201303
Tel: (011) 57-4902
Key Personnel
Contact: Opender Nath
Founded: 1996
Encyclopedia Bharatam Series:*The A's of India, The B's of India, The C's of India, The D's of India.*
Member of Federation of Publishers & Booksellers Association of India, Author is also the Publisher.
Subjects: Regional Interests, Encyclopedias on India, Treasury of Indian Quotations, Books of International Significance
ISBN Prefix(es): 81-86568
Total Titles: 4 Print; 2 E-Book
Parent Company: Sahasrara Publications
Branch Office(s)
Jamshedpur, De-Addiction Centre, Brahmani Rd, Bagun Nagar, Jamshedpur, Bihar 831017, Contact: Mrs Daya Mukherjee *Tel:* (0657) 845226
Distributed by Manohar Book Service (New Delhi, India); UBS Publishers' Distribution (New Delhi, India)

Sahitya Akademi
Rabindra Bhawan, 35, Feroz Shah Rd, New Delhi 110 001
Tel: (011) 3386626-629; (011) 3735297; (011) 3364207 (sales) *Fax:* (011) 3382428; (011) 3364207 *Cable:* SAHITYAKAR
Founded: 1955
National Academy of Letters.
Subjects: Literature, Literary Criticism, Essays
ISBN Prefix(es): 81-7201 (81-260)

Sahitya Pravarthaka Co-operative Society Ltd
PO Box 94, Kottayam, Kerala 686001
Tel: (0481) 4111; (0481) 4112 *Cable:* Sahithyam
Key Personnel
Secretary: P Gopinadh
Sales: N C Rayi
Production: Yalath Mopasang
Founded: 1945
Subjects: Literature, Literary Criticism, Essays
ISBN Prefix(es): 81-213

Bookshop(s): National Book Stall, PO Box 40, Kottayam 686001 (and branches throughout Kerala)
Orders to: c/o Sales Manager, National Book Stall, Kottayam

Sai Early Learners (P) Ltd, *imprint of* Sterling Publishers Pvt Ltd

Samkaleen Prakashan
2762, Rajguru Marg, Paharganj, New Delhi 110055
Tel: (011) 3523520; (011) 3518197
Key Personnel
Editor: Krishan Khullar
Founded: 1976
Subjects: Art, Language Arts, Linguistics, Law, Poetry, Religion - Other, Technology, Specialize in Indology
ISBN Prefix(es): 81-7083
Total Titles: 180 Print

SAMS, *imprint of* Addison-Wesley (Singapore) Pte Ltd

Samya, *imprint of* Stree

Sanskriti, *imprint of* Arnold Heinman Publishers (India) Pvt Ltd

Saraswati Publishers & Distributors+
434, Avadh Bihari Ki Gali, Govind Rao Ji Ka Rasta, Jaipur 302 001
Key Personnel
Contact: Onkar Nath Tripathi
Founded: 1986
ISBN Prefix(es): 81-85808

M C Sarkar & Sons (P) Ltd+
14 Bankim Chatterjee St, Calcutta 700 012
Tel: (033) 312490
Founded: 1910
Subjects: Fiction, Nonfiction (General)
ISBN Prefix(es): 81-7157

Sasta Sahitya Mandal+
N-77 Connaught Circus, New Delhi 110001
Tel: (011) 3310505 *Cable:* SATSAHITYA
Key Personnel
President: Dharam Vira
Secretary: Yashpal Jain
Founded: 1925
Subjects: Agriculture, Animals, Pets, Biography, Economics, Education, Ethnicity, History, Literature, Literary Criticism, Essays, Philosophy, Religion - Other
ISBN Prefix(es): 81-7309
Branch Office(s)
Zero Rd, Allahabad *Tel:* (0532) 50034

Sat Sahitya Prakashan+
205-B, Chawri Bazar, Delhi 110 006
Tel: (011) 3276316
Key Personnel
Chief Executive: S Sunder
Editorial: Nabab Singh Chauhan
Sales: P N Tiwari
Production: P Kumar; Rajan Chaudhary
Founded: 1970
Subjects: Art, Biography, Cookery, Fiction, Humor, Library & Information Sciences, Nonfiction (General), Poetry
ISBN Prefix(es): 81-85830

Sri Satguru Publications+
40/5 Shakti Nagar, 1st floor, Delhi 110007
Tel: (011) 7126497; (011) 7434930 *Fax:* (011) 7227336
E-mail: indianbookcentre@v.s.n.l.com

Key Personnel
Man Dir, Rights & Permissions: Anil Gupta
Export, Sales: Naresh Gupta
Publicity: Virender Gupta
Founded: 1980
Subjects: Art, History, Language Arts, Linguistics, Literature, Literary Criticism, Essays, Medicine, Nursing, Dentistry, Music, Dance, Philosophy, Religion - Buddhist, Religion - Other, Indology, Ayurveda
ISBN Prefix(es): 81-7030
Parent Company: Indian Books Centre
Associate Companies: Bibliotheca Indo-Buddhica Series, 40/5 Shakti Nagar, 1st floor, Delhi 110007; Sri Garib Dass Oriental Series, 40/5 Shakti Nagar, 1st floor, Delhi 110007

Satprakashan Sanchar Kendra+
Division of Divine Word Society
PO Box 507, Bhanwarkna Chowraha, Indore MP 452 001
Tel: 363733; 475744 *Fax:* 475731
E-mail: sskin@sancharnet.in
Web Site: www.educational.vsnl.com/satprakashan
Key Personnel
Dir: Sony Sebastian
Founded: 1980
Subjects: Biblical Studies, Communications, Religion - Catholic
ISBN Prefix(es): 81-85357; 81-85428
Number of titles published annually: 10 Print
Total Titles: 108 Print; 48 Audio

Sawan Kirpal Publications
Vijay Nagar, New Delhi 110 009
Tel: (011) 7110757; (011) 7210722 *Fax:* (011) 7210720
Key Personnel
Man Dir: Sant Rajinder Singh
Editorial: Dr Vinod Sena
Sales Dir: Rajesh Seth
Production: Jay Linksman
Publicity: Gary Moed
Founded: 1977
Subjects: Religion - Other
ISBN Prefix(es): 81-85380
Parent Company: Sawan Kirpal Publications Spiritual Society, H-11 Vijay Nagar, Delhi 110009
U.S. Office(s): SK Publications, 4S 175 Naperville Rd, Naperville, IL 60563, United States
Rt 1, PO Box 24, Bowling Green, VA 22427, United States

SBW Publishers+
7/9A Makhan Lal St, Ansari Rd, New Delhi 110002
Tel: (011) 3279603
Key Personnel
Contact: K L Sabharwal
Founded: 1980
Subjects: Philosophy, Regional Interests, Religion - Other, Social Sciences, Sociology
ISBN Prefix(es): 81-85708
Parent Company: Sabharwal Book Wholesalers

Scientific Book Agency+
56-D Mirza Ghalib St, Calcutta 700 016
Mailing Address: PO Box 239, Calcutta 700 001
Tel: (033) 292915; (033) 4642206
E-mail: debmalya@giase101.vsnl.net.in
Key Personnel
Man Dir: J Sinha
Editorial: P Sinha
Science Editor, Publicity & Advertising: Dr Snehamoy Sinha
Market Development Manager, Rights & Permissions: Swapan Mitra
Sales Dir: S P Sinha
Production: S Sinha
Publicity, Advertising & Chief Domestic Sales & Exports: Rajasi Sinha

Founded: 1954
Member of Federation of Publishers & Booksellers in India.
Subjects: Accounting, Agriculture, Anthropology, Archaeology, Architecture & Interior Design, Astronomy, Behavioral Sciences, Biological Sciences, Business, Chemistry, Chemical Engineering, Civil Engineering, Communications, Computer Science, Cookery, Developing Countries, Earth Sciences, Economics, Education, Electronics, Electrical Engineering, Energy, Engineering (General), Environmental Studies, Fiction, Finance, Foreign Countries, Geography, Geology, Government, Political Science, Health, Nutrition, History, Human Relations, Humor, Journalism, Labor, Industrial Relations, Law, Management, Marketing, Mathematics, Mechanical Engineering, Medicine, Nursing, Dentistry, Microcomputers, Military Science, Mysteries, Natural History, Parapsychology, Philosophy, Physical Sciences, Physics, Psychology, Psychiatry, Public Administration, Science (General), Social Sciences, Sociology, Technology, Veterinary Science
Total Titles: 8 Print
Parent Company: J Sinha & Co
Associate Companies: Industries Alliance, 49/13 Hindusthan Park, Calcutta 700029, Mrs Prakriti Sinha *Tel:* (033) 464-2206
Bookshop(s): 79/2 Mahatma Gandhi Rd, PO Box 239, Calcutta
Warehouse: 49/13 Hindusthan Park, Calcutta 700029 *Tel:* (033) 464-2206
Orders to: 49/13 Hindusthan Park, Calcutta 700029

Scientific Publishers India+
Maan Bhawan, Ratanda Rd, Jodhpur 342001
Mailing Address: PO Box 91, Jodhpur 342001
Tel: (0291) 512712; (0291) 433323 *Fax:* (0291) 512580
E-mail: scienti@sancharnet.in *Cable:* SCIENTIFIC-JODHPUR 342001
Key Personnel
Man Dir, Editorial: Pawan Kumar
Sales: Dawal Gawr
Founded: 1978
Booksellers, publishers & subscriptiion agents.
Subjects: Agriculture, Biological Sciences, Engineering (General), Natural History, Social Sciences, Sociology
ISBN Prefix(es): 81-85046; 81-7233
Total Titles: 350 Print
Parent Company: United Book Traders, 5A, New Pali Rd, Jodhpur 342001
Divisions: Publications & Export

Scott Foresman, *imprint of* Addison-Wesley (Singapore) Pte Ltd

Selina Publishers
4725/21A Dayanand Marg, Daryaganj, New Delhi 110 002
Tel: (011) 3280711
Key Personnel
Man Dir, Publicity, Rights & Permissions: H L Gupta
Editorial: Preeti Mehra
Production: Subhash Arora
Sales: D M D'Bras
Founded: 1975
Subjects: Education
ISBN Prefix(es): 81-85612
Associate Companies: Granth Bharati (Printing Press)
Subsidiaries: Mudra Prakashan
Branch Office(s)
48 Daryaganj, New Delhi 110002
Book Club(s): Sanket Library Yojna

Shaibya Prakashan Bibhag+
86/1, Mahatma Gandhi Rd, Calcutta 700009
Tel: (033) 388268; (033) 2411748

INDIA

Founded: 1984
Subjects: Biography, Computer Science, Electronics, Electrical Engineering, English as a Second Language, Publishing & Book Trade Reference, Religion - Hindu, Science (General), Science Fiction, Fantasy
ISBN Prefix(es): 81-87051

Sharda Prakashan
33/1, Bhul Bhullian Rd, Mehrauli, New Delhi 110030
Tel: (011) 653982
Key Personnel
Chief Executive, Production, Rights & Permissions: Vijay Dev Jhari
Editorial, Publicity: Ravinder Jhari
Sales: R D Jhari
Founded: 1971
Subjects: Biography, Drama, Theater, Fiction, Literature, Literary Criticism, Essays
ISBN Prefix(es): 81-85023
Associate Companies: Itihas Shodh Sansthan, 33/1 Mehrauli, New Delhi 110030; Jharison, Bhullehullian Rd, Mehrauli, New Delhi 110030
Subsidiaries: Nalanda Prakashan
Bookshop(s): 16-F3 Ansari Rd, Daryaganj, New Delhi 110002 *Tel:* (011) 279853

R R Sheth & Co+
110-112 Prince St, Bombay 400 002
Tel: (022) 2013441 *Fax:* (079) 5321732
Web Site: www.rrsheth.com
Key Personnel
Proprietor: Bhagatbhai Bhuralal Sheth *Tel:* (022) 6183182 *E-mail:* ppsheth_co@hotmail.com
Founded: 1926
Specialize in being publishers, booksellers & exporters in Gujarati language.
Subjects: Fiction, Literature, Literary Criticism, Essays
Total Titles: 100 Print
Associate Companies: Lokpriya Prakashan, 110, Princess St, Bombay 400 002 *Tel:* (022) 2058293
Branch Office(s)
Opp Phuvara, Gandhi Rd, Ahmedabad
Tel: (079) 5356573 *Fax:* (079) 5321732
E-mail: rrsheth_co@hotmail.com *Web Site:* www.rrsheth.com

Shiksha Bharati+
Kashmere Gate, Delhi 110006
Tel: (011) 386-7791 *Fax on Demand:* (011) 386-7791
Key Personnel
Man Dir, Rights & Permissions: Sudhir Malhotra
Editorial: Meera Johri
Founded: 1959
Subjects: Education
ISBN Prefix(es): 81-7483
Associate Companies: Orient Paperbacks; Rajpal & Sons; Vision Books Pvt Ltd
Subsidiaries: Shiksha Bharati Press
Bookshop(s): Lothian Rd, Kashmere Gate, Delhi 110006 *Tel:* (011) 2516602

Siddhi Books, *imprint of* Cosmo Publications

Silver Burdett Ginn, *imprint of* Addison-Wesley (Singapore) Pte Ltd

SIRI, see Small Industry Research Institute (SIRI)

Sita Publications+
308 Arjun Centre, Bombay 400 088
Mailing Address: POB TF B-8, Govind Station Rd, Govandi E, Mumbai 400 088
Tel: (022) 5555589 *Fax:* (022) 5561622
E-mail: ssrao@bom5.vsnl.net.in
Telex: SITAJAB

Key Personnel
Contact: S S Rao
Founded: 1993
Also acts as International Publishers Agent.
Subjects: Accounting, Advertising, Aeronautics, Aviation, Agriculture, Architecture & Interior Design, Automotive, Biological Sciences, Business, Chemistry, Chemical Engineering, Child Care & Development, Civil Engineering, Computer Science, Economics, Education, Electronics, Electrical Engineering, Energy, Engineering (General), Environmental Studies, Fashion, Finance, Labor, Industrial Relations, Library & Information Sciences, Literature, Literary Criticism, Essays, Management, Maritime, Marketing, Mathematics, Mechanical Engineering, Microcomputers, Physics, Psychology, Psychiatry, Publishing & Book Trade Reference, Technology
ISBN Prefix(es): 81-86052
Parent Company: Sita Books
Associate Companies: Sita Books & Periodicals Pvt Ltd, 308, Arjun Centre, Govandi(E), Mumbai 400 088 *Tel:* 5561622 *Fax:* 91-22-5561622
Branch Office(s)
Sita Books & Periodicals, 'Sita Villa', Chakrapani Road, Behind K.M.C Hospital, Mangalore 575 001 *Tel:* 426968
Bookshop(s): Herikripa,, 3 Krishna, Govandi(E), Mubai 400 088
Orders to: Sita Books & Periodicals Pvt Ltd, 308, Arjun Centre, Govandi(E), Mumbai 400 088

Small Industry Research Institute (SIRI)+
Institute Regd. Office, 4/43, Roop Nagar, Delhi 110 007
Mailing Address: PO Box 2106, Delhi 110 007
Tel: (011) 3910805; (011) 3916804; (011) 3971895 *Fax:* (011) 3910805; (011) 3971895
E-mail: siri@ndf.vsnl.net.in; siricon@vsnl.com
Web Site: www.indiaforum.com/siri
Key Personnel
Dir: D C Gupta
Founded: 1972
Industrial consultancy, publishing & exporting of industrial process technology books, directories, project reports, etc.
Member of Capexil, FIP, DSBPA, JBC (FICCI), ITA (London) Niesbud, BIS (Lib), Indo German Chamber of Commerce & Industry, Indo Italian Chamber of Commerce.
Subjects: Technology
ISBN Prefix(es): 81-85480
Number of titles published annually: 15 Print
Total Titles: 120 Print
Subsidiaries: SIRI Consultants & Engineers
Showroom(s): Small Industry Research Institute, 4/43, Roop Nagar, Delhi 110007

Somaiya Publications Pvt Ltd+
Bank Baroda Bldg, 6th floor, Parliament St, New Delhi 110 001
Tel: (011) 440030; (011) 3324939; (011) 3324973 *Fax:* (011) 3723351
Web Site: www.somaiya.com
Telex: 011-84588 (Bombay: SOC IN); 031-61996 (Delhi: SOIL IN) *Cable:* BOOKMARK, BOMBAY; Power Circle, Delhi
Key Personnel
Chairman: Dr S K Somaiya *Tel:* (022) 2048272 *Fax:* (022) 2047297 *E-mail:* mridughar@bol.net.in
Bombay Executive: K S Hattangadi
Delhi Executive: T V Kunni Krishnan
Ordering Contact: Mr N S Narayanan
Founded: 1967
Member of Federation of Indian Publishers.
Subjects: Agriculture, Anthropology, Archaeology, Asian Studies, Astrology, Occult, Behavioral Sciences, Business, Communications, Disability, Special Needs, Economics, Education, Engineering (General), English as a Second Language, Fiction, Government, Political Science, History, Journalism, Labor, Industrial Relations, Language Arts, Linguistics, Management, Marketing, Mechanical Engineering, Music, Dance, Nonfiction (General), Parapsychology, Philosophy, Psychology, Psychiatry, Religion - Buddhist, Religion - Hindu, Social Sciences, Sociology, Technology, Women's Studies
ISBN Prefix(es): 81-7039
Total Titles: 300 Print
Parent Company: The Godavari Sugar Mills Ltd, Fazalbhoy Bldg, Mahatma Gandhi Rd, Bombay 400023
Associate Companies: The Book Centre Ltd, Ranade Rd, Dadar, Bombay 400028 (Book Sales Division); The Book Centre Ltd, Plot No 103, Sixth Rd, Sion, Bombay, Contact: S S Sathe *Tel:* (022) 4076812; (022) 4077416 (printing press division)
Branch Office(s)
F-6 Bank of Baroda Bldg, Parliament St, New Delhi 110001

South Asia Publications+
29, Central Market, Ashok Vihar, Delhi 110052
Tel: (011) 7241869; (011) 7235539
Key Personnel
Contact: S P Garg
Founded: 1986
Subjects: Advertising, Agriculture, Anthropology, Art, Business, Economics, Finance, History, Management, Religion - Other
ISBN Prefix(es): 81-7433
Associate Companies: SanPark Press Pvt Ltd

South Asian Publishers Pvt Ltd+
36, Netaji Subhash Marg, Darya Ganj, New Delhi 110002
Tel: (011) 276292; (011) 276740
E-mail: vchigs@giasdla.vsnl.net.in
Key Personnel
Chief Executive, Editorial, Rights & Permissions: Vinod Kumar
Production, Publicity: K A Rastogi
Founded: 1980
Specialize in International Relations.
Subjects: Anthropology, Asian Studies, Biological Sciences, Chemistry, Chemical Engineering, Civil Engineering, Developing Countries, Electronics, Electrical Engineering, Engineering (General), Environmental Studies, Government, Political Science, Labor, Industrial Relations, Mathematics, Physics, Religion - Buddhist, Religion - Hindu, Science (General), Social Sciences, Sociology, Technology
ISBN Prefix(es): 81-7003
Warehouse: Sector IX, H 65, UP India

Spectrum Publications+
Hembarua Rd, Pan Bazar, Guwahati, Assam 781 001
Mailing Address: PO Box 45, Guwahati, Assam 781001
Tel: (0361) 26381; (0361) 24791 *Fax:* (0361) 544791 *Cable:* UNIPUB GUWAHATI
Key Personnel
Publisher: Krishan Kumar
Editorial: Ms Aarti Kumar
Sales: Ms Anita Kumar
Publicity: Ms Neha Kumar
Founded: 1976
Member of Federation of Indian Publishers.
Subjects: Anthropology, Asian Studies, Social Sciences, Sociology, Travel
ISBN Prefix(es): 81-85319; 81-87502; 81-900396; 81-900750
Imprints: Aarti Books; Neha Mini Katha; Sunny Classics
Branch Office(s)
298 Tagore Park, Model Town 1, Delhi 110009
Tel: (011) 7122641
GS Rd, Shilcong 793001 *Tel:* (0364) 223476

Distributor for Abilac; DIPR Arunachal Pradesh; Law Research Institute; Nehu Publications
Showroom(s): 4754-57 Daryaganj, 23 Ansari Rd, New Delhi 110002
Bookshop(s): The Modern Book Depot, Panbazar, Main Rd, Guwahati 781 001; United Publishers
Orders to: United Publishers, Panbazar, PO Box 82, Guwahati 781001

Sree Rama Publishers
1007 10th floor, Marketing Office, Babukhan Estate Bashiv Bagh, Hyderabad
Tel: 73128 *Cable:* BOOKS SECUNDERABAD
Key Personnel
Man Dir: Shiva Ramaiah Pabba
Editorial: Sreenivas Prabhu Pabba
Sales: Subash Chandra Sekhar Pabba
Production, Publicity, Rights & Permissions: Shivarajaiah Pabba
Founded: 1916
Subjects: Theology
ISBN Prefix(es): 81-7275
Parent Company: Sree Rama Book Depot, Market St, Secunderabad
Associate Companies: Popular Book House; Sree Sita Rama Book Depot; Secunderabad
Bookshop(s): Sree Rama Book Depot, Gunfoundry, Hyderabad 500001; Sree Rama Book Depot, Siddiamber Bazar, Hyderbad
Orders to: 113 Sarojinin Devi Rd, Secunderabad 500003

Sri Satguru Publications+
40/5 Shakti Nagar, Delhi 110 007
Tel: (011) 7126497; (011) 7434930 *Fax:* (011) 7227336
E-mail: ibcindia@giasdlo1.vsnl.net.in or ibcindia@ibcindia.com
Key Personnel
Man Dir, Rights & Permissions: Naresh Gupta
Export Dir: Sunil Gupta
Sales: Anil Gupta
Publicity: Virender Gupta
Founded: 1976
Subjects: Asian Studies, Music, Dance, Regional Interests, Religion - Buddhist
ISBN Prefix(es): 81-7030
Associate Companies: Bibliotheca Indo-Buddhica Series, 40/5 Shakti Nagar, Delhi 110 007; Sri Garib Dass Oriental Series, 40/5 Shakti Nagar, Delhi 110 007

Star Publications (P) Ltd+
4/5B Asaf Ali Rd, New Delhi 110002
Tel: (011) 3268651; (011) 3274874; (011) 3286757 *Fax:* (011) 3273335
E-mail: starpub@satyam.net.in
Web Site: www.starpublic.com
Key Personnel
Chairman & Man Dir: Amar N Varma *Tel:* (011) 3286757
Chief Executive: Anil K Varma *Tel:* (011) 3258993
Production, Publicity: Sanjay Varma *Tel:* (011) 3274874
Dir: Sunil Varma *Tel:* (011) 6468427
Founded: 1969
Publisher & distributor of English & Indian language books.
Subjects: English as a Second Language, History, Language Arts, Linguistics, Literature, Literary Criticism, Essays, Religion - Hindu, Politics, Religion-Islam, Religion-Jain, Religion-Sikh
ISBN Prefix(es): 81-85243; 81-85244
Total Titles: 600 Print; 50 Audio
Associate Companies: Star Book Centre, 4/5B Asaf Ali Rd, New Delhi 110002
Subsidiaries: Publications India; Hindi Book Centre; Star Publishers Distributors
Showroom(s): Hindi Book Centre, Star Publications (P) Ltd

Bookshop(s): Hindi Book Centre
Shipping Address: D-92/3 Okhla Industrial Area I, New Delhi 110020

Sterling Publishers Pvt Ltd+
Sterling House, A-59 Okhla Industrial Area Phase II, New Delhi 110020
Tel: (011) 6313023; (011) 6320118; (011) 6916165; (011) 6916209 *Fax:* (011) 6331241
Web Site: www.sterlingpublishers.com *Cable:* PAPERBACKS
Key Personnel
Chairman & Man Dir: S K Ghai *E-mail:* ghai@nde.vsnl.net.in
Rights & Permissions: Shuchita Ghai
Editorial: Marry Joseph
Sales: Vikas Ghai
Production: Shreeh Kumar
Publicity: Mr Mohammed Khan
Export: Kusum Malik
Founded: 1965
Member of Federation of Indian Publishers, Asian Association of Scholarly Publishers, Afro Asian Book Council; specialize in Humanities & Social Science.
Subjects: Agriculture, Art, Asian Studies, Astrology, Occult, Biography, Communications, Developing Countries, Economics, Education, English as a Second Language, Fiction, Gardening, Plants, Government, Political Science, History, Journalism, Library & Information Sciences, Literature, Literary Criticism, Essays, Management, Medicine, Nursing, Dentistry, Philosophy, Public Administration, Religion - Hindu, Religion - Islamic, Religion - Other, Science (General), Social Sciences, Sociology, Technology, Women's Studies
ISBN Prefix(es): 81-207
Associate Companies: Learners Press (P) Ltd, Sterling House, New Delhi
Imprints: Institute of Book Publishing; Sai Early Learners (P) Ltd; Sterling Press (P) Ltd

Sterling Information Technologies+
L-11, Green Park Extension, New Delhi 110 016
Tel: (011) 6313023; (011) 6320118 *Fax:* (011) 6331241 *Cable:* PAPERBACKS
Key Personnel
Rights & Permission: Vikas Ghai
Editorial: Malhotra Vandana
Founded: 1993
Subjects: Computer Science, Management, Marketing, Microcomputers, Technology
ISBN Prefix(es): 81-207
Distributed by Goodwill Book Store (Philippines); S S Mubaruks Bros Pte Ltd (Singapore); Vanguard Books Ltd (Pakistan)

Sterling Press (P) Ltd, *imprint of* Sterling Publishers Pvt Ltd

Stree+
Imprint of Bhatkal & Son
16 Southern Ave, Calcutta 700 001
Tel: (033) 4660812 *Fax:* (033) 4644614; (033) 4666677
E-mail: stree@cal2.vsnl.net.in
Key Personnel
Dir: Mandira Sen *E-mail:* bhatkal.sen@world.net
Founded: 1990 (Jointly founded by popular Prakashan, Mumbii & Mandira, Calcutta, who formed Bhatkal & Sen)
Publish women's studies in English & Bengali; also culture & dissent.
Subjects: Women's Studies
ISBN Prefix(es): 81-85604
Total Titles: 30 Print
Ultimate Parent Company: Bhatkal & Sen
Imprints: Samya
Branch Office(s)
Popular Prakashan, 46481 Ansari Rd, 21 Daryaganj, Delhi 110002, Contact: B Sengupta

Tel: (011) 3265245 *E-mail:* vansdel@nda.vsnl.net.in
Popular Pradashan, 35C Pandit MM Malariya Marq, Popular Press Building, Tardeo Mumbai 400034, Contact: Harsha Bhatkal *Tel:* (022) 4941556 *E-mail:* harshab@hotmail.com
Distributed by East-West Books (covers Southern India)

Sultan Chand & Sons Pvt Ltd
4859/24, Darya Ganj, New Delhi 110002
Tel: 3272532; 3251727 *Fax:* (11) 3254295
E-mail: scs@del2.vsnl.in
Key Personnel
Man Dir: Satish Agarwal *Tel:* 3278018
Founded: 1981
Member of Federation of Publishers & Booksellers Associations of India.
Subjects: Accounting, Behavioral Sciences, Biological Sciences, Business, Career Development, Chemistry, Chemical Engineering, Computer Science, Economics, Education, Electronics, Electrical Engineering, Engineering (General), English as a Second Language, Finance, Geography, Geology, Government, Political Science, Health, Nutrition, History, How-to, Human Relations, Labor, Industrial Relations, Law, Management, Marketing, Mathematics, Physics, Public Administration, Self-Help, Social Sciences, Sociology, Technology
Distributed by Prakash Sons

Suman Prakashan Pvt Ltd+
E-500 Hardevpuri Mandoli Rd, Shahadara, Delhi 110 093
Tel: (011) 5710759; (011) 5721750 *Fax:* (011) 5754739
Key Personnel
Dir: R N Malhotra
Founded: 1970
Specialize in Children's Textbooks
Member of PHDCCI & FICCI.
Subjects: Art, History, Mathematics, Science (General)
ISBN Prefix(es): 81-85869
Associate Companies: Pearl (India) Publishing House (P) Ltd

Sunny Classics, *imprint of* Spectrum Publications

Surjeet Publications+
7-K Kolhapur Rd, Kamla Nagar, Delhi 110 007
Mailing Address: PO Box 2157, Kamla Nagar, Delhi 110 007
Tel: (011) 2913081; (011) 2923105
Key Personnel
Man Partner: Harnam Singh
Founded: 1950
Also bookseller, distributor and remainder dealer.
Subjects: Literature, Literary Criticism, Essays, Social Sciences, Sociology
ISBN Prefix(es): 81-229

DB Taraporevala Sons & Co Pvt Ltd
210 Dr D Naoroji Rd, Mumbai 26 400 001
Tel: (022) 2041433; (022) 2041434 *Cable:* BOOKSHOP BOMBAY
Key Personnel
Chief Executive: Prof Russi J Taraporevala
Dir: Mrs Manekbai J Taraporevala; Miss Sooni J Taraporevala
Founded: 1864
Subjects: Art, Ethnicity, History, Social Sciences, Sociology

Theosophical Publishing House
Division of Theosophical Society (Worldwide)
Adyar c/o Theosophical Society, Madras 600020
Tel: (044) 4911338 *Fax:* (044) 4901399; (044) 4902706
E-mail: para.vidya@gems.vsnl.net.in *Cable:* THEOTHECA

Key Personnel
Manager: D K Govindaraj *E-mail:* theos.soc@gems.vsnl.net.in
Publications Officer: T Albert Echikwa *E-mail:* theos.soc@gems.vsnl.net.in
Founded: 1913 (*Provide books on Theosophy & Allied subjects at easily affordable prices.*)
Do not buy rights but permit the use of excerpts conditionally.
Subjects: Biography, History, Human Relations, Mysteries, Parapsychology, Philosophy, Religion - Other, Science (General), Theology
ISBN Prefix(es): 81-7059
Total Titles: 291 Print
Associate Companies: Theosophical Publishing House, 306 W Geneva Rd, PO Box 270, Wheaton, IL 60189, United States *Tel:* 630-665-0130 *Fax:* 630-665-8791 *E-mail:* olcott@theosophia.org; TPH Manila, Iba St, Quezon City, Metro, Manila, Philippines *Tel:* (02) 741-5740 *Fax:* (02) 740-3751 *E-mail:* tspeace@mnl.sequel.net
Bookshop(s): Adelaide, Australia; Brisbane, Australia; Perth, Australia; Sydney, Australia; Victoria, Australia; London, United Kingdom; Amsterdam, Netherlands; Quezon City, Philippines; Stockholm, Sweden; CA, United States; Accra, Ghana; Manila, Philippines

Central Tibetan Secretariat, see Central Tibetan Secretariat

Today & Tomorrow's Printers & Publishers+
24-B/5 Desh Bandhu, Gupta Marg, Karol Bagh, New Delhi 110 005
Tel: (011) 5721928; (011) 5727770 *Fax:* (011) 5721928
Key Personnel
Man Dir, Editorial, Rights & Permissions: R K Jain
Sales, Publicity, Production: S K Jain
Founded: 1967
Member of The Federation of Publishers & Booksellers Association of India, Chem & Allied Prod Exp Prom Council.
Subjects: Agriculture, Natural History, Science (General)
ISBN Prefix(es): 81-7019
U.S. Office(s): Scholarly Publications, 2825 Wilcrest, Suite 255, Houston, TX 77042, United States *Tel:* 713-781-0070 *Fax:* 713-781-2112
Distributed by Scholarly Pub (USA)

Transworld Research Network
37/661(2), Fort PO, Trivandrum, Kerala 695023
Tel: (0471) 452450 *Fax:* (0471) 573051
E-mail: ggcom@vsnl.com
Web Site: www.transworldresearch.com
Key Personnel
Man Editor: Shankar Pandalai
Publications Manager: Anandavalli Gayathri
Publisher review books in all areas of science, agriculture, medicine, pure science & technology. Also does CD-ROM production & software development.
Subjects: Agriculture, Medicine, Nursing, Dentistry, Science (General)
ISBN Prefix(es): 81-86848

N M Tripathi Pvt Ltd+
164 Shamaldas Gandhi Marg, Mumbai 400002
Tel: (022) 2013651; (022) 2050048
Key Personnel
Man Dir & Executive Manager: K R Tripathi
Founded: 1888
Gujrati language & literature.
Independent Company.
Subjects: Business, Ethnicity, Religion - Hindu, Gujrati poetry & novels
ISBN Prefix(es): 81-7118
Total Titles: 50 Print

Parent Company: Bombay Booksellers & Publishers' Association, Mumbai
Ultimate Parent Company: Federation of Publishers' & Booksellers' Associations, Delhi

UBS Publishers Distributors Ltd
5 Ansari Rd, Darya Ganj, New Delhi 110 002
Mailing Address: PO Box 7015, New Delhi
Tel: (011) 273601; (011) 3266646 *Fax:* (011) 3276593; (011) 3274261
E-mail: ubspddel@del3.vsnl.net.in
Web Site: www.ubspd.com *Cable:* ALLBOOKS
Key Personnel
Man Dir: C M Chawla
Exec Dir: Sukumar Das
Gen Mgr: Vivek Ahuja
Publish political, current affairs, cookery, religion, biography, fiction, self-improvement, management & general books. Distribute all types of books.
ISBN Prefix(es): 81-7476; 81-85273; 81-85674; 81-85944; 81-86112
Branch Office(s)
6 First Main Rd, PO Box 9713, Ghandi-Nagar Bangalore 560 009 *Tel:* (0172) 2263901, 2263902, 2253903 *Fax:* (0172) 2263904
8/1-B Chowringhee Lane, Calcutta 700-016 *Tel:* (033) 2441821, 2442910, 244973 *Fax:* (033) 2450027 *E-mail:* ubspdcal@cal.vsnl.net.in
6 Sivaganga Rd, Nugambakkam, Chennai 700 016 *Tel:* 8276355, 8270189 *Fax:* 8278920
80 Noronha Rd, Cantonment Kanpur 208 004 *Tel:* (0512) 369124, 362665, 352665, 357488 *Fax:* (0512) 315122
5 A Rajendra Nagar, Patna 800 016 *Tel:* 672856, 673973, 656170 *Fax:* 656169
Distributor for M/s Preface Books (Distribution in Western India)

UBSPD, see UBS Publishers Distributors Ltd

Vakils Feffer & Simons Ltd+
Hague Bldg, 9 Sprott Rd, Ballard Estate, Mumbai 400001
Tel: (022) 2611221; (022) 2619121 *Fax:* (022) 2614924; (022) 2610432 *Cable:* FLEETBOOKS
Key Personnel
Dir: Mr Arun K Mehta
Founded: 1960
Subjects: Art, Cookery, Gardening, Plants, Management, Religion - Hindu, Religion - Islamic, Religion - Other, Travel
ISBN Prefix(es): 81-87111
Showroom(s): Vakil & Sons Ltd, Vakils House, 18 Ballard Estate, Mumbai 400001
Bookshop(s): Vakil & Sons Ltd, Vakils House, 18 Ballard Estate, Mumbia 400001

Lok Vangamaya Griha Pvt Ltd
Bhupesh Gupta Bhawan, Mumbai 400 025
Mailing Address: 85 Sayani Rd, Prabhadevi Bombay 400045
Tel: (022) 4228222; (022) 4226468
Key Personnel
General Manager: Sukumar Damle
Founded: 1973
Subjects: Human Relations, Social Sciences, Sociology
ISBN Prefix(es): 81-86995
Bookshop(s): 5-22-32 Tilak Path, Aurangabad 431001; People's Book House, IS Cawasji Patel St, Fort Bombay 400001; Red Flag Bldg, Bindu Chowk, Kolhapur 416002; 562 Sadashiv Peth, Chirtashala Prakalp, Pune 411030

Vani Prakashan+
4697/5, 21-A Daryaganj, New Delhi 110 002
Tel: (011) 3273167; (011) 2110879; (011) 2286292; (011) 3275710; (011) 225151
Fax: (011) 3275710

Key Personnel
Chief Executive, Editorial, Production, Publicity & Sales: Arun Kumar Maheshwari
Founded: 1968
Subjects: Ethnicity, Fiction, History, Literature, Literary Criticism, Essays, Poetry, Hindi (with various subjects)
ISBN Prefix(es): 81-7055
Associate Companies: Navodaya Sales, 35, A, DDA Flat, Mansarovar Park, Shadhara, Delhi 32; Swarn Jyanti, 1/5971, Kabool Nagar, Shadhara, Delhi 32
Branch Office(s)
Book Corner, Sri Ram Center, Safdar Hashni Marg, New Delhi
Book Club(s): Jan Sulakh Pathak Manch

Vastu Gyan Publication
9/1, Institutional Area, New JNU, Aruna Asaf Ajli Marg, New Delhi
Mailing Address: 905 Suaya Kilan, 19 KG Maeg, New Delhi
Tel: (011) 3318730
Key Personnel
Author: Mr BB Puri
Subjects: Architecture & Interior Design
ISBN Prefix(es): 81-900614

Vidhi Sahitya Prakashan, see Vidhi

Vidhi
Vibhagiy Prakashan Bikri Kender, Vikas Bhawan, Secretariat, Patna 800015
Tel: (011) 389001 *Cable:* PATRIKA
Key Personnel
Sales Manager: C B Deogam
Assistant Manager: Ram Labhaya
Founded: 1968
Specialize in publications of the Acts in diglot form.
Subjects: Law
ISBN Prefix(es): 81-85956
Divisions: Vidhi Sahitya Prakashan

Vidya Puri+
Balu Bazar, Cuttack 753002
Tel: (0671) 620637; (0671) 617260 *Cable:* VIDYAPURI
Key Personnel
Man Partner, Editorial: Pitamber Mishra
Partner: Ramananda Mishra; Rupananda Mishra; Bhabananda Mishra; Jivananda Mishra
Sales: S K Sarangi
Founded: 1961
Subjects: Accounting, Animals, Pets, Biography, Biological Sciences, Business, Chemistry, Chemical Engineering, Computer Science, Literature, Literary Criticism, Essays
ISBN Prefix(es): 81-7411
Associate Companies: Goswami Press, Alamchand Bazar, Cuttack 753002; Graftek Pvt Ltd, Bhubaneswar 751002; Rainbow Offset (P) Ltd, Bhubaneswar 751002
Divisions: Vidyashre DTP Centre

Vidyarthi Mithram Press+
Baker Rd, Kottayam 686 001
Tel: (0481) 563281; (0481) 563282; (0481) 564713; (0481) 562616 (after office hours) *Fax:* (0481) 562616 *Cable:* VIDYARTHI
Key Personnel
Man Dir: Koshy P John
Founded: 1928
Subjects: Biography, Biological Sciences, Chemistry, Chemical Engineering, Child Care & Development, Computer Science, Cookery, Drama, Theater, Economics
Associate Companies: Auroville Publishers, Kottayam
Imprints: Kosi Books; Manosabdam Books
Branch Office(s)
Ernakulam

Kollam
Kozhikode
Palakkad
Thiruvalla
Thiruvananthapuram
Thrissur
Bookshop(s): Vidyarthi Mithram Book Depot, Baker Rd, Kottayam
Book Club(s): Vidyarthi Mithram Novel Club

Vikas Higher Education Books/Madhuban Educational Books, *imprint of* Vikas Publishing House Pvt Ltd

Vikas Publishing House Pvt Ltd+
576, Masjid Rd, Jangpura, New Delhi 110 014
Tel: (011) 4315313; (011) 4315570; (011) 4317857 *Fax:* (011) 4310879
Key Personnel
Dir: Piyush Chawla; Sajili Shirodkar
Man Dir: C M Chawla
Founded: 1969
Vikas focuses on textbooks & professional books on management, computers, engineering & technology. Madhuban it's Children's book imprint, offers a high quality range from preschool upwards.
Subjects: Agriculture, Animals, Pets, Anthropology, Architecture & Interior Design, Art, Biography, Chemistry, Chemical Engineering, Computer Science, Cookery, Crafts, Games, Hobbies, Economics, Education, Engineering (General), Ethnicity, Fiction, Geography, Geology, Government, Political Science, History, Journalism, Library & Information Sciences, Literature, Literary Criticism, Essays, Management, Mathematics, Medicine, Nursing, Dentistry, Military Science, Philosophy, Physics, Psychology, Psychiatry, Science (General), Technology
ISBN Prefix(es): 81-259
Number of titles published annually: 100 Print
Total Titles: 1,200 Print
Imprints: Vikas Higher Education Books/Madhuban Educational Books
Distributor for Thomson Learning (Routledge)

Vision Books Pvt Ltd+
24 Feroze Gandhi Rd, Lajpat Nagar-III, New Delhi 110024
Tel: (011) 386-2267; (011) 386-2201 *Fax:* (011) 386-2935
E-mail: mail@orientpaperbacks.com *Cable:* VISIONBOOK DELHI
Key Personnel
Chairman: Vishwa Nath
Man Dir, Rights & Permissions, Sales: Sudhir Malhotra
Publishing Dir: Kapil Malhotra
Publicity: Sidharth Malhotra
Editor: Dr O P Jaggi
Founded: 1975
Member of Federation of Indian Publishers, Delhi State Booksellers & Publishers Association.
Subjects: Anthropology, Cookery, Education, Fiction, Health, Nutrition, History, How-to, Management, Medicine, Nursing, Dentistry, Military Science, Religion - Other, Science (General), Travel, Career Guides, Fitness, Puzzle Books
ISBN Prefix(es): 81-7094
Total Titles: 700 Print
Associate Companies: Rajpal & Sons; Ravindra Printing Press; Shiksha Bharati; Vision Enterprises
Subsidiaries: Anand Paperbacks; Orient Paperbacks
Branch Office(s)
3-B Peddar Rd, Vasant Ground floor, Bombay *Tel:* (022) 492 9343 *Fax:* (022) 496 0229
24 Firoze Gandhi Rd, Lajpat Nagar, Lajpat Nagar *Tel:* (011) 683 6470-80 *Fax:* (011) 683 6490

3-6-280/A/5 Himayatnagar, Hyderabad *Tel:* (040) 322 3252
Distributed by Books from India (UK) Ltd (UK); Nalanda Bookshop (Mauritius)
Book Club(s): Anand Book Club; Orient Book Club

Vistaar, *imprint of* Sage Publications India Pvt Ltd

S Viswanathan (Printers & Publishers) Pvt Ltd+
38, McNichols Rd, Chetput, Chennai 600 031
Tel: (044) 8265623; (044) 8265633 *Fax:* (044) 8256002
E-mail: svprint@md2.vsnl.net.in
Key Personnel
Contact: V Subramanian
Subjects: Biological Sciences, Chemistry, Chemical Engineering, Computer Science, English as a Second Language, History, Mathematics, Medicine, Nursing, Dentistry, Physics, Religion - Hindu, Science (General)
ISBN Prefix(es): 81-87156
Associate Companies: Beta Photo-Comps Pvt Ltd
Bookshop(s): Ananda Book Depot, 38 McNichols Rd, Chetput Madras 600 031

Vivek Prakashan
7-UA Jawahar Nagar, Delhi 110 007
Mailing Address: Kamalanagar
Tel: (011) 2529649 *Fax:* (011) 6827347
Key Personnel
Contact: Asha Rani
Founded: 1979
Subjects: Economics, Fiction, Literature, Literary Criticism, Essays, Social Sciences, Sociology
ISBN Prefix(es): 81-7004

A H Wheeler & Co Ltd+
23 Lal Bahadur Shastri Marg, Allahabad 211 001
Mailing Address: 411 Surya Kiran Bldg, 19 K G Marg, New Delhi 110 001
Tel: (011) 3312629; (011) 3318357 *Fax:* (011) 3357798
E-mail: wheeler.jeet@axcess.net.in
Key Personnel
Contact: Arunjeet Banerjee
Founded: 1879
Member of Federation of Indian Publishers.
Subjects: Accounting, Advertising, Behavioral Sciences, Business, Career Development, Civil Engineering, Communications, Computer Science
ISBN Prefix(es): 81-7544; 81-85614; 81-85814
Associate Companies: Wheeler Leather Corporation Ltd
Subsidiaries: Symonds & Co
Divisions: Wheeler Exports; Wheeler Offset Press; Wheeler Publishing
Branch Office(s)
Bangalore
Calcutta
Chennai
Delhi
Mumbai

Zebra Books for Children, *imprint of* Arnold Heinman Publishers (India) Pvt Ltd

Indonesia

General Information

Capital: Jakarta
Language: Bahasa Indonesia (a form of Malay) is official language. English is common second language. About 25 local languages & over 250 dialects are spoken
Religion: About 87% Islamic, 10% Christian & some Hindu & Buddhist
Population: 195 million
Bank Hours: Generally 0800-1400 Monday-Thursday; 0800-1500 Friday; 0800-1300 Saturday
Currency: Rupiah
Export/Import Information: Books subject to import tax & VAT tax. No exchange control. Books & printed matter using Indonesian languages prohibited. Importers require no license but are categorized into four groups for credit arrangement controls.
Copyright: No copyright conventions signed but Indonesia has recently enacted tougher domestic copyright laws

Mandira Jaya Abadi+
Jl Letjen, Mt Haryono 501, Semarang, Jawa Janyah 50241
Tel: (024) 519547; (024) 316150 *Fax:* (024) 542189
Founded: 1961
ISBN Prefix(es): 979-490; 979-437

Advent Indonesia Publishing
Jl Raya Cimindi No 72, Bandung 40184 Java
Mailing Address: PO Box 1188, Bandung 40011 Java
Tel: (022) 630392; (022) 642006 *Fax:* (022) 630588 *Cable:* Indopub
Key Personnel
Manager: Djinan Sinaga
Chief Editor: Jahotner F Manullang
Treasurer: Agus Ricky
Founded: 1954
Subjects: Child Care & Development, Health, Nutrition, Human Relations, Religion - Protestant, Religion - Other
ISBN Prefix(es): 979-504

Akadoma CV
Jl Kalasan No 1, Jakarta Pussat
Tel: (021) 3904323
Key Personnel
Man Dir: Adam Saleh

Al-Bayan, *imprint of* Mizan

Alma'Arif PT
Jl Tamblong No 48-50, Bandung 40112
Tel: (022) 4207177 *Fax:* (022) 439194
Key Personnel
Man Dir: H M Baharthah
ISBN Prefix(es): 979-400

Alumni PT
Jl Bukit Pakar Timur II/109, Bandung 40197
Tel: (022) 2501251; (022) 2503039; (022) 2503038 *Fax:* (022) 2503044
Telex: 28640
Key Personnel
Man Dir, Rights & Permissions: Eddy Damian
Editorial: Yayat Ruchiyat
Sales: Punomo
Production Manager: Philips
Founded: 1966
Subjects: Economics, Law, Medicine, Nursing, Dentistry, Psychology, Psychiatry, Social Sciences, Sociology
ISBN Prefix(es): 979-414
Branch Office(s)
Jl Jend A Yani 206E, Banjarmasin
Wisma Sawah Besar, 8th floor, Jl Sukarjo Wiryopranoto 30, Jakarta *Tel:* (021) 372730 (Telex: 46810 Alumni Ia)
Putri Hijaubaru 37, Medan *Tel:* (061) 510615
Jl Kartini 22B, Tanjungkarang *Tel:* (0721) 53135
Bookshop(s): H Juanda St 54, Bandung *Tel:* (022) 58290

INDONESIA

Andi Offset+
Jln Beo No 38-40, Yogyakarta 55281
Tel: (0274) 561881 *Fax:* (0274) 588282
E-mail: andi_pub@indo.net.id
Key Personnel
Dir: J H Gondowijoyo
Founded: 1980
Member of Indonesian Publishers Association.
Subjects: Accounting, Chemistry, Chemical Engineering, Computer Science, Electronics, Electrical Engineering, Management, Marketing, Science (General), Technology
ISBN Prefix(es): 979-533
Distributor for Prenhallindo

CV Angkasa CV (Publishers)+
Jl Merdeka, No 6, Bandung 40111
Mailing Address: PO Box 354/Ed, Bandung
Tel: (022) 4208955; (022) 4204795 *Fax:* (022) 439183
Telex: 28276 Panghegar Bandung
Key Personnel
Chief Executive: Dr Fachri Said
Editorial Manager, Rights & Permissions: R Djajoesman
Sales Manager: Kofindar
Production Manager: Tom Gunadi
Founded: 1966
Subjects: Fiction, Nonfiction (General), Religion - Other
ISBN Prefix(es): 979-404; 979-547; 979-665
Associate Companies: PT Mutiara Sumber Widya
Bookshop(s): Balai Buku Angkasa, Jl Merdeka, No 6, Jawa Barat, Bandung

PT Pustaka Antara Publishing & Printing+
Taman Kebon Sirih III/13, 10250 Jakarta Pusat
Tel: (021) 3156994; (021) 3156995 *Fax:* (021) 322745
E-mail: nacelod@indo.net.id
Key Personnel
Dir: Aida Joesoef Ahmad
Founded: 1952
Member of Board of IKAPI (Indonesian Publishers Association)
Also acts as Director of Research, Training & International Relations.
Subjects: Religion - Islamic
ISBN Prefix(es): 979-8013
Associate Companies: CV Idayus *Tel:* (06221) 322745
Warehouse: P T Demina, Jl Rempoa Mulya, No 12, Bintaro, Jakarta Selatan *Tel:* (021) 7370966; (021) 7370967

Aries Lima, see New Aqua Press

Auroa+
Jln Bambu Betung VII No 8, Bojong Indah, Jakarta 11740
Tel: (021) 5810413
Key Personnel
International Rights: Ms Nanik Hardjono
Subjects: Asian Studies, Biblical Studies, Education, Religion - Catholic, Religion - Protestant
ISBN Prefix(es): 979-564

Badan Penerbit Kristen Gunung Mulia
(Gunung Mulia Christian Publishing House Ltd Co)+
Jalan Kwitang 22-23, Jakarta 10420
Tel: (021) 3901208 *Fax:* (021) 3901633
E-mail: trade@bpkgm.com
Web Site: www.bpkgm.com
Key Personnel
President: Ichsan Gunawan *E-mail:* ichsan@bpkgm.com
Dir: Viveka Nanda Leimena
Founded: 1951
Member of CBA.
Subjects: Christian, Theological General Literature
ISBN Prefix(es): 929-687
Number of titles published annually: 100 Print
Total Titles: 900 Print

Balai Pustaka+
Jl Gunung Sahari Raya No 4, Jakarta Pusat 10710
Tel: (021) 3447003; (021) 3447006; (021) 7650228; (021) 7650229 *Fax:* (021) 3446555; (021) 7650704
E-mail: mail@balaiperaga.com; pustakaperaga@lycos.com
Web Site: www.balaiperaga.com
Telex: 45905 Pnbp Jkt *Cable:* PERUM BALAI PUSTAKA
Key Personnel
President, Dir: Dr Zakaria Idris
Editorial, Production Dir: Kuntjono Sastrodarmodjo
Sales, Publicity Dir: Dr Chasan Mintara
Rights & Permissions Dir: Ismu Amran
Founded: 1917
Subjects: Education, Ethnicity
ISBN Prefix(es): 979-407; 979-651; 979-666
Branch Office(s)
Jl Pulogadung Kav Jl5, Pulogadung, Jakarta Timur
Jl Rawagate 17, Pulogadung, Jakarta Timur
Book Club(s): KPI (Klub Perpustakaan Indonesia)

Bhratara Karya Aksara+
Jl Rawabal, Kawawan Industri Pulogadung, Jakarta, Timur 13340
Tel: 021 81858
Telex: 48292 Bhranmia
Key Personnel
President: Ahmad Jayusman
Dir: Adit Jayusman; Robinson Rusdi
Founded: 1958
Member of IKAPI. Sales agent of UNU, UNESCO, ICPE, Journal IMMA, IDRC Pubs. Also printer & book importer/exporter.
Subjects: Agriculture, Economics, Education, Health, Nutrition, History, Language Arts, Linguistics, Science (General), Social Sciences, Sociology, Technology
ISBN Prefix(es): 979-410
Subsidiaries: P T Bhratara Tekno Komputer
Divisions: P T Karya Upaya Arta
Branch Office(s)
Jogja
Malang
Medan
Padang
Surabaya Ujung Pandang
Distributed by Indonesian Book Sellers
Distributor for ICPE; IDRC; Journal Muslim Minority Affairs; UNESCO
Showroom(s): Bhratara Bookshop, Jl Otista III/29, Jakarta, India *Tel:* (021) 8191858
Bookshop(s): Bhratara Bookshop, Jl Otista III/29, Jakarta, India *Tel:* (021) 8191858
Shipping Address: Bhratara Bookshop, Jl Otista III/29, Jakarta, Timur *Tel:* (021) 8191858
Warehouse: Bhratara Bookshop, Jl Otista III/29, Jakarta, Timur *Tel:* (021) 8191858
Orders to: Bhratara Bookshop, Jl Otista III/29, Jakarta, Timur *Tel:* (021) 8191858

Bina Aksara Parta+
Jln Raya Ubud, 80571 Bali
Tel: (361) 95240
Key Personnel
Contact: Silvio Santosa
Founded: 1983
Subjects: Fiction, Music, Dance, Religion - Hindu, Travel
ISBN Prefix(es): 979-8042

BOOK

Associate Companies: Orti Co, Jl Sandat 22, Ubud, Bali 80571
Orders to: Orti Co, PO Box 20, Ubud, Bali 80571

Bina Cipta PT
Jl Ganesha No 4, Bandung
Tel: (022) 2504319 *Fax:* (022) 2504319
Key Personnel
Dir: O Bardin
ISBN Prefix(es): 979-8000; 979-8928

Bina Ilmu
Jl Tunjungan No 53 E-F, Surabaya 60275
Tel: (031) 5323214; (031) 5340076 *Fax:* (031) 5315421
Key Personnel
Man Dir: H Mc Ariefin Noor
ISBN Prefix(es): 979-422

Bina Rena Pariwara
Jl Pejaten Raya No 5-E, Pasar Minggu, Jakarta Selatan 12510
Tel: (021) 7901938; (021) 7901939 *Fax:* (021) 7901939
Key Personnel
President & Dir: Yullia Himawati
Founded: 1988
Member of Indonesian Publishers Association (IKAPI).
Subjects: Communications, Economics, Education, Finance, Government, Political Science, Nonfiction (General), Religion - Islamic, Travel
ISBN Prefix(es): 979-8175; 979-9056
Parent Company: Yayasan Bina Pembangunan (Development Foundation)
Associate Companies: Center for Fiscal & Monetary Studies-CFMS
Divisions: BRP Consultant Division
Distributor for Pt Penakencana Nusadwipa
Bookshop(s): Most Big Book Stores in the Capital Cities of All Provinces in Indonesia
Book Club(s): Indonesian Publishers Association (IKAPI)
Warehouse: Depok Bogor

Biro Pusat Statistik
Jl Dr Sutomo No 8, Kotak Pos 1003, Jakarta 10010
Tel: (021) 3810291; (021) 3841195; (021) 3842508 *Fax:* (021) 3857046
Telex: 45159 *Cable:* KBPS
Key Personnel
Chief of Bureau: Yuwono Hadipramono
Bureau of Statistical Information System.
ISBN Prefix(es): 979-402

P T Bulan Bintang+
Jl Kramat Kitang 1/6, Jakarta Pusat 10420
Tel: (021) 3901651; (021) 3901652 *Fax:* (021) 3107027 *Cable:* BULANBINTANG
Key Personnel
President: Amran Zamzami
Vice President, Editor-in-Chief: Fauzi Amelz
Founded: 1954
Subjects: Art, Business, Economics, Education, Engineering (General), Fiction, Finance, Government, Political Science, History, Law, Literature, Literary Criticism, Essays, Nonfiction (General), Philosophy, Psychology, Psychiatry, Religion - Islamic, Science (General), Social Sciences, Sociology, Sports, Athletics, Technology
ISBN Prefix(es): 979-418

Bumi Aksara PT+
Jl Sawo Raya No 18, Rawamangun, Jakarta Timur 13220
Tel: (021) 4717049; (021) 4700988 *Fax:* (021) 4700989

Key Personnel
Dir: H Amir Hamzah
Founded: 1990
Member of Indonesian Book Association.
Subjects: Accounting, Agriculture, Business, Economics, Law, Management, Marketing, Religion - Islamic
ISBN Prefix(es): 979-526

Institut Dagang Muchtar
Jl Embong Wungu 8, Surabaya
Tel: (031) 42973
ISBN Prefix(es): 979-417

PT Dian Rakyat+
Jl Rawa Gelam I No 4, Kawasan Industri Pulogadung, Jakarta Timur
Tel: (021) 4604444
Telex: 62338 Fega la *Cable:* DIAN RAKYAT
Key Personnel
Dir: H Mohammad Ais
Publishing Division Man: Mlle Harmiel M Soekardjo
Founded: 1963
Subjects: Cookery, Economics, Literature, Literary Criticism, Essays, Medicine, Nursing, Dentistry
ISBN Prefix(es): 979-523

Dinastindo+
Jl Senopati No 54, Kebayoran Baru, Jakarta 12110
Tel: (021) 7250002; (021) 72799307 *Fax:* (021) 7262145
E-mail: dinastindo@yahoo.com
Web Site: www.dinastindo.net
Key Personnel
Contact: Rijanto Tosin
Founded: 1984
Member of ASP, IKAPI, Apkomindo.
Subjects: Business, Career Development, Computer Science, Management, Self-Help
ISBN Prefix(es): 979-552
Branch Office(s)
Surabaya & Bandung
Distributor for Abdi Tandu Publisher; Der Die Das; Pisi 2 Ribu Software; Solid Pro Publisher

Dioma, Kanisius, Obor, *imprint of* Penerbit Nusa Indah

Diponegoro CV+
Jl Mohammad Toha 44-46, Bandung 40252
Tel: (022) 5201215 *Fax:* (022) 5201215 *Cable:* C V DIPONEGORO BANDUNG
Key Personnel
Man Dir: H A Dahlan
Editorial, Sales, Production, Publicity: Dr Anwaruddin
Founded: 1963
Member of Indonesian Publishers Association.
Subjects: Religion - Other
ISBN Prefix(es): 979-8155

Djambatan PT
Jl Paseban No 29, Jakarta 10430
Tel: (021) 3908790; (021) 7203199; (021) 7208562 *Fax:* (021) 7227989
Key Personnel
Manager: Roswitha Pamoentjak
Founded: 1958
Subjects: Art, Literature, Literary Criticism, Essays, Philosophy, Religion - Other, Social Sciences, Sociology
ISBN Prefix(es): 979-428

Dunia Pustaka Jaya
Jl Kramat Raya 5-K (Gedung Maya Indah), Jakarta Pusat 10450
Tel: (021) 3909322; (021) 3909284 *Fax:* (021) 3909320 *Cable:* Depeje

Key Personnel
Dir: Ahad Rifai; Sumaryoto
Editor: Sugiarta Sriwibawa; S W Rukasah; Rohimah
Founded: 1971
Subjects: Art, Drama, Theater, Ethnicity, Fiction, Literature, Literary Criticism, Essays, Philosophy, Poetry
ISBN Prefix(es): 979-419

Duta Wacana University Press+
Jl Dr Wahidin 5-19, Yogyakarta 55224
Tel: (0274) 563929 *Fax:* (0274) 513235
E-mail: humas@ukdw.ac.id
Web Site: www.ukdw.ac.id
Telex: 25486 UKDW IA
Key Personnel
Dir: S H Hadi Purnomo
Founded: 1989
ISBN Prefix(es): 979-8139

Eresco PT
Jl Megger Girang No 98, Bandung 40254
Tel: (022) 5205985 *Fax:* (022) 5205984
   Cable: Erescopete Bandung
Key Personnel
Man Dir: Dr Arfan Razali
Editorial: Dr Prof H Rochmat Soemitro
Sales: Mr Amun; Mr Harsono
Founded: 1956
Subjects: Economics, Law, Philosophy, Psychology, Psychiatry
ISBN Prefix(es): 979-8020
Bookshop(s): Jl Perapatan 22 Pav, Jakarta
   Tel: (021) 368000
Book Club(s): Himpunan Masyarakat Pencinta Buku (HMPB)

Fortunajaya+
Jl Diponegoro 11, Klaten
Tel: (0272) 22030 *Fax:* (0272) 22543
Founded: 1985
ISBN Prefix(es): 979-557
Showroom(s): Jln Pemuda, Selatan 44 B, Klaten

Gaya Favorit Press+
Jl HR Rasuna Said, Kav B 32-33, Jakarta Selatan 12910
Mailing Address: Kuningan
Tel: (021) 4604444; (021) 5209370; (021) 5253816; (021) 5209366 *Fax:* (021) 5209366; (021) 5262131
E-mail: ptgfp1@rad.net.id
Telex: 62338 Fega IA
Key Personnel
Man Dir: Mirta Kartohadiprodjo
Editorial: Wied Harry Apriadji
Sales: Irwan SLT
Editorial, Publicity, Rights & Permissions: R H Yus Kayam
Founded: 1972
Subjects: Crafts, Games, Hobbies, Fiction, Non-fiction (General)
ISBN Prefix(es): 979-515
Parent Company: PT Gaya Favorit Press, Jln HR Rasuna Said blok B, Kav 32-33, Jakarta 12910

Gramedia+
Jl Palmerah Selatan 22-28, Jakarta Pusat 10270
Tel: (021) 5483008; (021) 5490666 *Fax:* (021) 5300545
E-mail: elex@elexmedia.com
Telex: Kompas Jkt 46327 *Cable:* KOMPAS JAKARTA
Key Personnel
President: Jakob Detama
Group Director: Teddy Surianto
Executive Manager: Al Adhi Mardhiyond
Production: Slamet M Jaeni
Rights & Permissions: Puspita Dewi
Publicity: Y Suliantoro

Founded: 1985
Publisher, Software House, Multimedia.
Specialize in Educational Software & Comics.
Subjects: Accounting, Animals, Pets, Antiques, Child Care & Development, Computer Science, Cookery, Crafts, Games, Hobbies, Electronics, Electrical Engineering, Fiction, Gardening, Plants, How-to, Management, Microcomputers, Mysteries, Technology
ISBN Prefix(es): 979-511; 979-403
Parent Company: Kompas-Gramedia Group

PT BPK Gunung Mulia (Gunung Mulia Christian Publishing House Limited Company)+
Jl Kwitang 22-23, Jakarta Pusat 10420
Tel: (021) 3901208 *Fax:* (021) 3901633
E-mail: bpkgm@centrin.net.id
Web Site: www.bpkgm.com
Key Personnel
Dir: Budi Arlianto
Founded: 1950
Subjects: Religion - Other
ISBN Prefix(es): 979-415
Bookshop(s): Toko Buku PT BPK Gunung Mulia

Harris+
Jln Veteran GOR 6, Medan
Tel: (061) 22272
Key Personnel
Man Dir: Ny Maswari
Founded: 1952
Member of Indonesian Publishers Association.

ILMU-ILMU Islam, *imprint of* Mizan

PT Indira+
Jl Borobudur No 20, Jakarta, Pusat 10320
Tel: (021) 3904290; (021) 3148868 *Fax:* (021) 3929373
E-mail: indirawb@mweb.co.id
Key Personnel
Man Dir: Dr Bambang P Wahyudi
Founded: 1950
Subjects: Automotive, Business, Career Development, Computer Science, Crafts, Games, Hobbies, Energy, English as a Second Language, Film, Video
ISBN Prefix(es): 979-8063
Parent Company: Grolier Inc, United States
Associate Companies: PT Widyadara
Subsidiaries: PT Radio Prambors-Commercial Radio Broadcasting

Indrajaya CV
Jl Jatibaru No 20, Jakarta Pusat
Tel: (021) 3457039; (021) 3457041 *Fax:* (021) 3457039

Institut Teknologi Bandung+
Jl Ganesa 10, Bandung 40132
Tel: (022) 2504048; (022) 2503147 *Fax:* (022) 431792
E-mail: itbpress@melsa.net.id; sofia@penerbit.itb.ac.id
Web Site: www.itb.ac.id
Key Personnel
Editor-in-Chief: Sofia Niksolihin
Founded: 1972
Subjects: Chemistry, Chemical Engineering, Education, Electronics, Electrical Engineering, Engineering (General), Health, Nutrition, Mathematics, Science (General), Technology
ISBN Prefix(es): 979-8001; 979-8591

Islamiyah
Jln Sutomo 329, Kotakpos 11, Medan
Tel: (061) 25421

Karunia CV
Jln Peneleh 18, Surabaya

Tel: (031) 5344120 *Fax:* (031) 5343409
ISBN Prefix(es): 979-9039

Karya Anda, CV+
Jl Praban No 55, Surabaya 60010
Tel: (031) 5344215; (031) 522580; (031) 5315402 *Fax:* (031) 5310594
Key Personnel
Man Dir: Moechlis
Subjects: Agriculture, Anthropology, Automotive, Behavioral Sciences, Education, Environmental Studies, Fiction, Humor
ISBN Prefix(es): 979-8002

Katalis PT Bina Mitra Plaosan
Jl Pratama 111/18 Pulo Mas, Jakarta, Timur 13220
Tel: (021) 7510477
Key Personnel
Publisher, Rights & Permissions: Elisabeth Soeprapto-Hastrich
Senior Editor: Ms Rasfiati Iskarno
Marketing Supervisor: Gertrud Moeljono
Business Manager, Production: Kisbandi Soeprapto
Editorial Assistant, Publicity: Gabriella Martiyah
Founded: 1986
Subjects: Career Development, How-to, Literature, Literary Criticism, Essays, Nonfiction (General), Science (General)
ISBN Prefix(es): 979-8060
Imprints: Siemens-Penuntun Berencana

Kesaint Blanc+
Jl Howitzer No 15A, Jakarta Pusat 10640
Tel: (021) 4204847; (021) 4204851; (021) 8207555 *Fax:* (021) 4216792; (021) 8207557
Key Personnel
Dir: Antonius Bangun
Founded: 1979
ISBN Prefix(es): 979-8295; 979-593
Associate Companies: Mitra Utama; Kesaint Krakatau; Kesaint Sibayak
Imprints: Megapoin; Oriental; Renaisans; Tamtan Gabara; Visipro
Branch Office(s)
Bandung
Medan
Surabaya
Yogyakarta
Bandar Lampung
Warehouse: Jl Mekar Sari
Cimanggis
Bogor

Kinta CV
Jl Kemanggisan Ilir V/110, Rt 005/13, Jakarta Barat 11480
Tel: (021) 5494751
Key Personnel
Man Dir: Dr Mohammad Saleh
ISBN Prefix(es): 979-8004

Kurnia Esanata
Jl Kramat II No 33, Jakarta Pusat 10420
Tel: (021) 361974; (021) 3104948
Telex: 44328
Key Personnel
Man Dir: Taufik H Das
ISBN Prefix(es): 979-446

Lembaga Demografi Fakultas Ekonomi Universitas Indonesia
Jl Salemba Raya 4, Jakarta Pusat, 10430
Tel: (021) 3900703; (021) 336434; (021) 336539 *Fax:* (021) 3102457
E-mail: demofeui@indo.net.id *Cable:* FEKODEM
Key Personnel
Dir: Dr Haidy A Pasay
Founded: 1964

Subjects: Child Care & Development, Developing Countries, Economics, Education, Environmental Studies, Ethnicity, Health, Nutrition, Labor, Industrial Relations, Library & Information Sciences, Social Sciences, Sociology, Women's Studies
ISBN Prefix(es): 979-525
Parent Company: Faculty of Economics University of Indonesia

Madju FA
Jl Amaliun No 37, Medan 20215
Tel: (061) 711990; (061) 710430 *Fax:* (061) 717753
ISBN Prefix(es): 979-8005

Marfiah, CV
Jln Kalibutuh No 131, Surabaya
Tel: (031) 46023
Key Personnel
Man Dir: Ellyati Wahyuni

Megapoin, *imprint of* Kesaint Blanc

Mizan+
Jl Yodkali 16, Bekamin Suci, Bandung 40124
Tel: (022) 7200931 *Fax:* (022) 72070238
E-mail: info@mizan.com
Web Site: www.mizan.com
Key Personnel
President & Dir: Haidar Bagir
Man Dir: Putut Widjanarko *E-mail:* pututw@mizan.com
Founded: 1983
Member of the Association of Indonesian Publishers (IKAPI).
Subjects: Asian Studies, Religion - Islamic
ISBN Prefix(es): 979-433
Imprints: Al-Bayan; Mizan: Khazanah; ILMU-ILMU Islam; Mizan Pustaka: Kronik Indonesia Baru; Mizan Sobat Bocah Muslim; Mizan Sahabat Remaja Muslim
Branch Office(s)
Jl Duren Tiga Selatan WII 8A, Jakarta
Bookshop(s): (Many throughout Indonesia, Singapore, Malaysia & Brunei)

Mizan: Khazanah, *imprint of* Mizan

Mizan Pustaka: Kronik Indonesia Baru, *imprint of* Mizan

Mizan Sahabat Remaja Muslim, *imprint of* Mizan

Mizan Sobat Bocah Muslim, *imprint of* Mizan

Mutiara Sumber Widya PT+
Jl Salemba Tengah 36-38, Jakarta Pusat 10440
Tel: (021) 3909864; (021) 3908651; (021) 3904247 *Fax:* (021) 3160313
Telex: 46709 Mutiara Ia
Key Personnel
Chief Executive: H Firdaus Oemar
Dir: Fahmi Umar
Subjects: Economics, Education, Mathematics, Music, Dance, Physics, Religion - Other
ISBN Prefix(es): 979-8011
Associate Companies: CV Angkasa (Publishers)
Subsidiaries: CV Mutiara Bhakti; Mutiara Permata Widya

New Aqua Press
Kawasan Indrustri Pulo Gadung, Jl Rawagela II/4, Jakarta Timur 13012
Tel: (021) 4897566
ISBN Prefix(es): 979-441

Oriental, *imprint of* Kesaint Blanc

PATCO
Jln Sawahan Sarimulyo 14, Surabaya
Tel: (031) 310021
Key Personnel
Man Dir: Adolf Pattyranie
Founded: 1972
Subjects: Regional Interests
Bookshop(s): TB Puncak Agung, Pasar Tambahrejo Blok A 21A, Jl Kapas Krampung, Surabaya

Pelita Masa PT
Jl Lodaya No 25, Bandung 40262
Tel: (022) 50823
Key Personnel
Man Dir: Rochdi Partamatmadja

Pembimbing Masa PT
Pusat Perdagangan Senen, Blok 1, Lantai IV No 2, Jakarta, Pusat
Mailing Address: PO Box 3281, Jakarta Pusat
Tel: (021) 367645; (021) 366042
Key Personnel
Man Dir: Setia Dharma Majiid
ISBN Prefix(es): 979-8023
Bookshop(s): Pembimbing Masa PT

Penerbit Erlangga
Jl H Baping Raya No 100, Ciracas, Jakarta 13740
Tel: (021) 8717006 *Fax:* (021) 8708660
E-mail: eriprom@rad.net.id
Web Site: www.erlangga.com
Key Personnel
Dir: Gunawan Hutauruk
ISBN Prefix(es): 979-411

Penerbit Nusa Indah+
Jl El Tari, Ende Flores-NTT 86318
Tel: (0381) 21502 *Fax:* (0381) 21645; (0381) 22373 *Cable:* NUSAINDAHENDE
Key Personnel
Dir: Henri Daros *Tel:* (0381) 21081
Vice Dir & Sales Manager: Frans Ndoi
Man Editor: Lucas Lege
Production, Design: Eman Diaz
Library & Documents: Rofinus Jamin
Founded: 1970
Member of Ikapi, Seksama, Kokosia, SVD Publishers, PLKI.
Subjects: Biblical Studies, Human Relations, Language Arts, Linguistics, Literature, Literary Criticism, Essays, Poetry, Religion - Catholic, Theology
ISBN Prefix(es): 979-429
Total Titles: 350 Print
Parent Company: PT ANI
Imprints: Dioma, Kanisius, Obor (East Indonesia)
Branch Office(s)
Gudang Buku Nusa Indah, Jln Polisi Istimewa 9, Surabaya 60265 *Tel:* (031) 5617746 *Fax:* (031) 5684307
Perwakilan Nusa Indah, Jln Matraman Raya 125, Jakarta *Tel:* (021) 8582447 *Fax:* (021) 8502403
Distributed by Dioma (East Java); Gramedia (all Gramedia bookshops in Jakarta, Surabaya, Kalimantan, Timor Timur, etc.); Kanisius (Central Java); Obor (Jakarta)
Showroom(s): Jln Matraman Raya 125, Jakarta 13012; Jln Polisi Istimewa 9, Surabaya 60265
Book Club(s): Kanisius Reading Community

PT Bhakti Baru
Jln Jend Akhmad Yani 15, Ujung Pandang
Tel: (0411) 5192 *Fax:* (0411) 7156
Telex: 7156 Hakalla UP *Cable:* Bhakti Baru
Key Personnel
Man Dir: Dr H M Jusuf Kalla
Publicity Manager: Alwi Hamu
Founded: 1972
Subjects: Religion - Other
Branch Office(s)
Jl Lembang 9, Jakarta, India *Tel:* (021) 336364

PUBLISHERS

PT Pradnya Paramita
Jl Bunga No 8-8A, Jakarta 13140
Tel: (021) 8583369; (021) 8504944 *Fax:* (021) 8583369 *Cable:* PRADNYA JKT
Key Personnel
President, Dir: Soenarto Sindoepranoto
Production Dir: Dr Mimien Saleh
Sales Dir: Soelistihardjo
Sales Executive: J Josojuwono
Editorial: A F Julianto
Founded: 1973
ISBN Prefix(es): 979-408
Bookshop(s): (See under Major Booksellers)

PT Pustaka LP3ES Indonesia
Jl Letjen S Parman 81, Slipi, Jakarta Barat 11420
Mailing Address: PO Box 493 Jkt, Jakarta 11420
Tel: (021) 5674211; (021) 5667139; (021) 5667141 *Fax:* (021) 5683785
Key Personnel
Dir: Dr Arselan Harahap
Managing Dir: Maruto M D
Founded: 1971
The Institute for Economics & Social Research, Education & Information.
Subjects: Science (General)
ISBN Prefix(es): 979-8015
Parent Company: LP3ES

Pusat Penelitian Perkebunan Sumbawa+
Palembang, 30001 Sumsel
Mailing Address: PO Box 1127, Palembang 30001
Tel: (0711) 312182; (0711) 361793 *Fax:* (0711) 361793
Key Personnel
Contact: Mr Anwar Chairil
ISBN Prefix(es): 979-529

Pustaka Utama Grafiti, PT+
Utan Kayu Utara, Jl Utan Kayu No 68, E, F, G, Jakarta timur 13120
Tel: (021) 8567502; (021) 8566998 *Fax:* (021) 8582430
Telex: 62797 TEMPO IA
Key Personnel
Man Dir: Zulkifly Lubis
Production Manager: A Rahman Tolleng
Commercial Manager: Yusril Djalinus
Founded: 1986
Member of IKAPI.
Subjects: Anthropology, Art, Biography, Business, Economics, Government, Political Science, History, Humor, Literature, Literary Criticism, Essays, Philosophy, Religion - Other, Social Sciences, Sociology
ISBN Prefix(es): 979-444
Parent Company: Grafiti Pers
Bookshop(s): Ancol, Pasar Seni, Jakarta Utara; Slipi Jaya Plaza, Basement, Jl S Parman Kav 17-18, Jakarta 11410; Pertokoan Italiano, Jl Margonda Raya No 166, Depok; Jl Sumatera 31 Block G-H, Surabaya
Warehouse: Jl Cipinang Kebembem I No 3 A, Jakarta Timur

Remaja Rosdakarya CV
Jl Ciateul 40, Bandung
Tel: (022) 5225810 *Fax:* (022) 58226
ISBN Prefix(es): 979-514

Renaisans, *imprint of* Kesaint Blanc

Rosda Jaya Putra
Jl Kembang No 4, Jakarta Pusat 10450
Tel: (021) 3904984; (021) 3901692; (021) 3904985 *Fax:* (021) 3901703
Key Personnel
Man Dir: H Rozali Usman
ISBN Prefix(es): 979-426

Sastra Hudaya PT
Jl Kalasan No 1, Jakarta Pusat
Tel: (021) 3904223
Key Personnel
Man Dir: Doddy Yudhista
ISBN Prefix(es): 979-8016

Universitas Sebelas Maret
Jln Ir Sutami 36A, Solo 57126
Tel: (0271) 46994 (ext 341) *Fax:* (0271) 46655
E-mail: due-uns@slo.mega.net.id; pptk-uns@slo.mega.net.id
ISBN Prefix(es): 979-498
Bookshop(s): Toko Buku, Jln Ir Sutami 36A, Solo 57126

Siemens-Penuntun Berencana, *imprint of* Katalis PT Bina Mitra Plaosan

Sumatera Utara University Press
Jl Universitas 21A Kampas USU, Medan, Sumatera Utara 20155
Mailing Address: Sumatera Utara
Tel: (061) 23210 (ext 261)
Telex: 51753
Key Personnel
Chairman: Mukmin Saraan
ISBN Prefix(es): 979-458

Tamtan Gabara, *imprint of* Kesaint Blanc

Tintamas Indonesia PT+
Jl Kramat Raya No 60, Jakarta Pusat 10420
Tel: (021) 3911459; (021) 7393701 *Fax:* (021) 3911459
Key Personnel
Dir: Marhamah Djambek
Founded: 1947
Member of IKAPI (Indonesian Publishers Association).
Subjects: Biography, History, Law, Philosophy, Religion - Other
ISBN Prefix(es): 979-590

Usaha Baru CV
Jln Apel Kedjoran 11/5, Surabaya
Tel: (031) 22128
Key Personnel
Man Dir: Imron Siregar

Visipro, *imprint of* Kesaint Blanc

Widjaya Penerbit
Jln Pecenongan 48-C, Jakarta
Tel: (021) 363446
Branch Office(s)
Jln Dalem Kaum 86, Bandung

CV Yasaguna
Jl Minangkabau, 44, Jakarta Selatan
Tel: (021) 8290422
Key Personnel
Manager: Hilman Madewa
Subjects: Agriculture
ISBN Prefix(es): 979-443

Yayasan Jaya Baya
Jln Penghela 2, Surabaya
Mailing Address: Kotakpos 250, Surabaya
Tel: (031) 41169

Yayasan Kawanku
Jln Setiabudi Raya, Gg Sumbangsih 11/3A, Jakarta
Tel: (021) 583100

Yayasan Lontar+
Jl Danau Maninjau 93, Pejombongan, Jakarta Pusat 10210
Tel: (021) 587-904; (021) 574-6880 *Fax:* (021) 573-0353
E-mail: lontar@ibm.net
Web Site: www.lontar.org
Key Personnel
Chairperson: Adila Suwarmo
Vice Chairperson: Indra Harbani
Secretary: Miriam Widodo
Treasurer: Fikri Jufri
Editor-in-Chief: John H McGlynn
Founded: 1987
Subjects: Art, Ethnicity, Literature, Literary Criticism, Essays
ISBN Prefix(es): 979-8083

Yayasan Obor Indonesia+
Jl Plaju, No 10, Jakarta Pusat 10230
Tel: (021) 326978; (021) 324488 *Fax:* (021) 324488
E-mail: obor@ub.net.id
Web Site: www.obor.or.id
Key Personnel
Chairman & International Rights: Mochtar Lubis
General Manager: Kartini Nurdin
Founded: 1978
Subjects: Advertising, Asian Studies, Business, Child Care & Development, Developing Countries, Earth Sciences, Economics, Education, Environmental Studies, Government, Political Science, History, Literature, Literary Criticism, Essays, Military Science, Natural History, Nonfiction (General), Philosophy, Publishing & Book Trade Reference, Science (General), Social Sciences, Sociology, Technology, Global Issues, Human Rights
ISBN Prefix(es): 979-461
U.S. Office(s): Obor Inc, 501 Cherry St, Philadelphia, PA 19102, United States

Islamic Republic of Iran

General Information

Capital: Tehran
Language: Persian (Farsi), Turkish and Armenian in Northwest, Arabic in Southwest, Kurdish in Kurdistan (English or French also)
Religion: Islamic (Shi'a sect and some Sunni sect)
Population: 61.2 million
Bank Hours: Generally Winter: 0800-1300 Saturday-Thursday; 1600-1800 Saturday-Wednesday; Summer: 0730-1300, 1700-1900 Saturday-Wednesday, 0730-1130 Thursday
Shop Hours: Generally Winter: 0800-2000 Saturday-Thursday; 0800-1200 Friday; Summer: 0800-1300, 1700-2100 Saturday-Thursday, 0800-1200 Friday
Currency: 100 dinars = 1 Iranian rial
Export/Import Information: No tariff on books and advertising but catalogs subject to VAT. Import licenses required. Publications offending public order, official religion or morality prohibited. Exchange controls, with new regulations issued each March.
Copyright: No copyright conventions signed

Amir Kabir Book Publishing & Distribution Co
PO Box 1136-54191, Tehran

ISLAMIC REPUBLIC OF IRAN

Tel: (021) 6463487; (021) 390752 *Fax:* (021) 6461931
Telex: 212421 NJR IR
Key Personnel
Dir: H Anwary
Production: Masdjed-Jamee
Publicity: A Poormomtaz
Sales: Emany
Founded: 1948
ISBN Prefix(es): 964-00
Parent Company: Sasman-e Tablighat-e Eslami
Subsidiaries: Shokufeh Books

Scientific and Cultural Publications
Ministry of Culture & Higher Education, 64 St, Sayyed Jamal-E-Din Asad Abadi Ave, Tehran
Tel: (021) 685475; (021) 686278
Founded: 1953
Subjects: History, Philosophy, Religion - Other, Science (General)
Bookshop(s): Enghelab St, Thehran

University of Tehran Publications & Printing Organization
Univ of Tehran, Control Administration, Enghelab Ave & 16 Azar St, Tehran
Tel: (021) 6462622 *Fax:* (021) 6462622
Web Site: www.ut.ac.lr
Key Personnel
Man Dir: Dr A Rastgou
Sales, Publicity: Mr R Farahani
Rights & Permissions: J Qajarieh
Founded: 1944
Bookshop(s): Enqelab Ave, Tehran

Iraq

General Information

Capital: Baghdad
Language: Arabic (official), and some Kurdish (English is the principal foreign language in Baghdad)
Religion: Islamic (predominantly the Shiite sect)
Population: 18.4 million
Bank Hours: Winter: 0900-1300 Saturday-Wednesday; 0900-1200 Thursday; Summer: 0800-1200 Saturday-Wednesday, 0800-1100 Thursday
Shop Hours: Winter: 0830-1430, 1700-1900 Saturday-Wednesday, 0830-1330 Thursday; Summer: 0800-1400, 1700-1900 Saturday-Wednesday, 0800-1300 Thursday
Currency: 1,000 fils = 20 dirhams = 1 Iraqi dinar
Export/Import Information: No tariffs on books & advertising. Import licenses required. Exchange control, influenced by annual foreign exchange budget. Importation by state trading company or established importer. The state trading company is the National House for Publishing, Distributing & Advertising, Aljamhuria St, 624, Baghdad.
Copyright: No copyright conventions signed

National House for Publishing, Distributing and Advertising
Al-Jumhuriyan St, Baghdad
Mailing Address: PO Box 624, Baghdad
Tel: (01) 4251846
Telex: 2392 *Cable:* Donta
Founded: 1972
Firm is attached to the Ministry of Information and is the sole importer & distributor of newspapers, magazines, periodicals & books.
Subjects: Agriculture, Business, Economics, Education, Government, Political Science, Science (General), Social Sciences, Sociology

Ireland

General Information

Capital: Dublin
Language: English & Irish (Gaelic)
Religion: Predominately Roman Catholic, some Church of Ireland
Population: 3.8 million
Bank Hours: 1000-1230, 1330-1500 Monday-Friday. Open until 1700 one night a week
Shop Hours: 0900 or 0930-1730 Monday-Saturday
Currency: 100 Eurocents = 1 Euro; 0.787564 Irish pounds = 1 Euro
Export/Import Information: Member of the European Community. BH & VMcK No tariff on books except on prayer & similar books from non-UK & children's picture books from non-EC. Pamphlets dutied from non-EEC. VAT is charged. No import licenses. Exchange controls.
Copyright: UCC, Berne (see Copyright Conventions, pg xi)

A & A Farmar+
Beech House, 78 Ranelagh Village, Dublin 6
Tel: (01) 4963625 *Fax:* (01) 4970107
E-mail: afarmar@iol.ie
Web Site: farmarbooks.com
Key Personnel
International Rights & Dir: Anna Farmar
Founded: 1992
Subjects: Business, Child Care & Development, Cookery, Literature, Literary Criticism, Essays, Wine & Spirits, Specializes in general literature, food & wine, business & social history
ISBN Prefix(es): 1-899047
Total Titles: 12 Print
Branch Office(s)
Irish Books & Media Inc, 1433 Franklin Ave East, Minneapolis, MN 55404-2135, United States
Orders to: Columba Mercier Distribution Ltd, 55A Spruce Ave, Stillorgan Industrial Park, Blackrock, Dublin

AIS
7 Merrion Square, Dublin 2
Tel: (01) 6616522 *Fax:* (01) 6612378
Also acts as distributor for all Irish language publications.
ISBN Prefix(es): 0-946339
Parent Company: Bord Na Gaeilge

An Gum+
44 Straid Ut Chonaill, Dublin 1
Tel: (01) 8734700 *Fax:* (01) 8731140
E-mail: gum@educ.irlgov.ie
Telex: 31136
Key Personnel
Editorial: Maire Nic Mhaolain
Production: John Dixon
Publicity: Seosamh O'Murchu
Founded: 1926
Subjects: Art, Cookery, Education, Geography, Geology, Mathematics, Science (General)
ISBN Prefix(es): 1-85791
Parent Company: The Department of Education, Dublin 1
Imprints: Oifig an tSolathair
Bookshop(s): Oifig Dhiolta Foilseachain Rialtais, Sr Theach Laighean, Dublin 2
Warehouse: Bishop S, Dublin 8
Orders to: An Ais, 31 Sr na bhFinini, Dublin 2

Anvil Books Ltd+
45 Palmerston Rd, Dublin 6
Tel: (01) 4973628 *Fax:* (01) 4968263 *Cable:* ANVIL

Key Personnel
Man Dir, Sales, Production, Publicity, Rights & Permissions: Rena Dardis
Editorial: Margaret Dardis
Founded: 1964
Subjects: Biography, History
ISBN Prefix(es): 0-900068; 0-947962; 1-901737
Associate Companies: The Children's Press

Atrium, *imprint of* Cork University Press

Attic Press, *imprint of* Cork University Press

Attic Press Ltd+
Imprint of Cork University Press (CUP)
c/o Cork University Press, Crawford Buiness Park, Crosses Green, Cork
Tel: (021) 4321 725 *Fax:* (021) 315 329
E-mail: atticirl@iol.ie
Web Site: www.iol.ie/~atticirl/
Key Personnel
Publisher: Sara Wilbourne *E-mail:* s.wilbourne@ucc.ie
International Rights: Dreie Axster
Founded: 1984
Subjects: Biography, Fiction, Government, Political Science, Health, Nutrition, History, Humor, Literature, Literary Criticism, Essays, Social Sciences, Sociology, Women's Studies
ISBN Prefix(es): 0-946211; 1-85594
Orders to: Gill & Macmillan, Goldenbridge, Inchicore, Dublin 8
Central Books Ltd, 99 Wallis Rd, London E9 5LN, United Kingdom
Koen Books, Twosome Dr, Moorestown, NJ 08057, United States

Avoca Publications+
Lonsdale Avoca Ave, Blackrock, Dublin
Tel: (01) 889218
Founded: 1983
Subjects: Aeronautics, Aviation
ISBN Prefix(es): 0-9509206

Ballinakella Paperbacks, *imprint of* Ballinakella Press

Ballinakella Press+
Whitegate, Clare
Tel: (061) 927030 *Fax:* (061) 927418
E-mail: info@ballinakella.com
Key Personnel
President: Dr Hugh W L Weir
Vice President: Mrs Hugh W L Weir
Founded: 1984
Specialize in Irish historical, topographical, genealogical & biographical books.
Subjects: Architecture & Interior Design, Biography, Genealogy, Geography, Geology, History, Regional Interests, Travel
ISBN Prefix(es): 0-946538
Number of titles published annually: 2 Print
Total Titles: 30 Print
Parent Company: Weir Publishing
Imprints: Ballinakella Paperbacks; Bell'acards; Weir's Guides
Subsidiaries: Bell'acards

Beehive Books, *imprint of* Veritas Co Ltd

Bell'acards, *imprint of* Ballinakella Press

Blackwater Press, *imprint of* Folens Publishers

Brandon, *imprint of* Mount Eagle Publications Ltd

Brandon Book Publishers Ltd+
Cooleen, Dingle, Co Kerry
Tel: (066) 51463 *Fax:* (066) 51234
Key Personnel
Man Dir, Editorial: Steve MacDonogh
Founded: 1982
Subjects: Biography, Fiction, Literature, Literary Criticism, Essays, Nonfiction (General)
ISBN Prefix(es): 0-86322
Parent Company: Mount Eagle Publications Ltd
Orders to: Gill & Macmillan Distribution, Goldenbridge, Inchicore, Dublin 8

Edmund Burke Publisher+
27 Priory Dr, Cloonagashel, Blackrock, County Dublin
Tel: (01) 2882159 *Fax:* (01) 2834080
E-mail: deburca@indigo.ie
Subjects: History, Regional Interests
ISBN Prefix(es): 0-946130
Subsidiaries: De Burca Rare Books

Campus, *imprint of* Campus Publishing Ltd

Campus Publishing Ltd+
26 Tirellan Heights, Galway
Tel: (091) 524662; (091) 767408 *Fax:* (091) 527505
Key Personnel
Publisher: Kevin T Brophy
Founded: 1990
Subjects: Drama, Theater, Education, Literature, Literary Criticism, Essays, Religion - Catholic, Religion - Protestant, Religion - Other, Self-Help, Social Sciences, Sociology, Playscripts
ISBN Prefix(es): 1-873223
Imprints: Campus; Playscripts

Careers & Educational Publishers Ltd+
Lower James St, Claremorris, County Mayo
Tel: (094) 71093
Key Personnel
Man Dir, Editorial, Publicity, Rights & Permissions: Eamonn Patrick O'Boyle
Sales: Christina O'Boyle
Production: William J O'Keeffe
Founded: 1976
Subjects: Career Development, Cookery, Crafts, Games, Hobbies, Education
ISBN Prefix(es): 0-906121
Imprints: Heritage Books
Bookshop(s): Eamonn P O'Boyle's Book Sales, Lower James St, Claremorris, County Mayo; Kilcolman Press Bookshop, Convent Rd, Claremorris, County Mayo

Cathedral Books Ltd
4 Sackville Place, Dublin 1
Tel: (01) 8787372 *Fax:* (01) 8787704
E-mail: cathedra@indigo.ie
Subjects: Biblical Studies, Philosophy, Psychology, Psychiatry, Religion - Catholic, Self-Help, Theology, Women's Studies
ISBN Prefix(es): 0-9517132; 1-871337

Children's Poolbeg, *imprint of* Poolbeg Press Ltd

The Children's Press+
45 Palmerston Rd, Dublin 6
Tel: (01) 4973628
Telex: (01) 4968263 *Cable:* CHILDREN'S PRESS DUBLIN
Key Personnel
Man Dir, Editorial, Sales, Production, Publicity, Rights & Permissions: Rena Dardis
Founded: 1981
Subjects: Biography, Fiction, History
ISBN Prefix(es): 0-900068; 0-947962; 1-901737
Parent Company: Anvil Books Lts

Clo Iar-Chonnachta Teo+
Indreabhan, Conamara, Galway, County Galway
Tel: (091) 593307 *Fax:* (091) 593362
E-mail: cic@iol.ie
Web Site: www.cic.ie
Key Personnel
Man Dir: Michaeal O Conghaile
General Manager: Deirdre O'Toole
Founded: 1985
Most publications are in the Irish language.
Subjects: Drama, Theater, Fiction, Gay & Lesbian, History, Music, Dance, Poetry, Regional Interests
ISBN Prefix(es): 1-874700; 1-900693; 1-902420
Distributed by Dufour Editions
Foreign Rep(s): Maggie Doyle (France); Dufour Editions (Canada, US); Harry Smith (US); Hansevik Tonnheiu (Sweden)

Clodhanna Teoranta
Chonradh na Gaeilge, 6 Sraid Fhearchair, Dublin 2
Key Personnel
Publicity Manager: Donnchadh O Laodha
ISBN Prefix(es): 0-905027; 0-9501264
Bookshop(s): Chonradh na Gaeilge, 6 Sraid Fhearchai, Dublin

The Collins Press+
West Link Park, Doughcloyne, Wilton, Cork
Tel: (021) 4347717 *Fax:* (021) 4347720
E-mail: enquiries@collinspress.le
Web Site: www.collinspress.com
Key Personnel
Contact: Con Collins
Founded: 1990
Independent Book Publisher.
Member of Irish Publishers Association (CLE).
Subjects: Archaeology, Biography, History, Human Relations, Natural History, Photography, Drama, Mind, Body & Spirit
ISBN Prefix(es): 0-9516036; 1-895256; 1-903464
Number of titles published annually: 17 Print
Total Titles: 91 Print
Distributed by Columbia Mercier Distribution (Ireland & Northern Ireland); Drake International Services (Britain, Common Wealth & Europe); Dufour Editions (US); Irish Books & Media (US)
Foreign Rep(s): Brookside Publishing Services (Ireland, Northern Ireland)
Foreign Rights: AMV Agencia Literaria SL; Gundhild Lenz-Mulligan

The Columba Book Service+
Stillorgan Industrial Park, 55A Spruce Ave, Blackrock, Dublin
Tel: (01) 2942556 *Fax:* (01) 2942564
E-mail: info@columba.ie
Web Site: www.columba.ie
Key Personnel
Sales Dir: Cecilia West *E-mail:* west@columba.ie
Man Dir: Sean O Boyle
Founded: 1985
Member of CLE (Irish PA) & Booksellers Association of Great Britain & Ireland.
Subjects: Religion - Catholic, Religion - Protestant, Religion - Other, Self-Help, Theology
Associate Companies: The Columba Press
Distributor for Continuum (In Ireland Only); Cowley Publications (USA); The Liturgical Press (USA); Michael Glazier (USA); Novalis (Canada); Paulist Press (USA); Pueblo Publishing (USA); Resource Publications (USA); St Mary's Press (USA); Sheed & Ward (USA); Twenty-Third Publications (USA)

The Columba Press+
55A Spruce Ave, Stillorgan Industrial Park, Blackrock, Dublin
Tel: (01) 2942556 *Fax:* (01) 2942564
E-mail: info@columba.ie

Web Site: www.columba.ie
Key Personnel
Chief Executive & Editorial: Sean O'Boyle
  E-mail: sean@columba.ie
Sales Dir & International Rights: Cecilia West
  E-mail: west@columba.ie
Marketing & Publicity: Brian Lynch
  E-mail: brian@columba.ie
Founded: 1985
Member of Cle, The Irish Book Publisher's Association.
Subjects: Art, History, Religion - Catholic, Religion - Protestant, Self-Help, Theology
ISBN Prefix(es): 0-948183; 1-85607
Total Titles: 200 Print
Imprints: Gartan, Preas Cholmcille
Subsidiaries: Columba Bookservice
Distributed by John Garratt Publishing (Australia)

Cork University Press+
Crawford Business Park, Crosses Green, Cork
Tel: (021) 4902980 *Fax:* (021) 4273553; (021) 4315329
E-mail: corkunip@ucc.ie
Web Site: www.corkuniversitypress.com
Key Personnel
Publisher: Sara Wilbourne *E-mail:* s.wilbourne@ucc.ie
Publicity: Nancy Hawkes *E-mail:* n.hawkes@ucc.ie
Editorial: Lucy Freeman *E-mail:* l.freeman@ucc.ie
Sales & Marketing: Mike Collins *E-mail:* mike.collins@ucc.ie
Founded: 1925
Member of CLE (Irish Publishers' Association).
Subjects: Archaeology, Geography, Geology, History, Social Sciences, Sociology, Women's Studies, Specializes in Irish studies, history, literature, cultural studies & politics
ISBN Prefix(es): 0-902561; 1-85918; 0-9502440
Number of titles published annually: 20 Print
Total Titles: 150 Print
Imprints: Atrium, Attic Press
Branch Office(s)
Stylus Publishing LLC, 22883 Quicksilver Drive, Sterling, VA 20166-2012, United States, Contact: John von Knorring *Fax:* 703-661-1501
  E-mail: stylusmail@presswarehouse.com *Web Site:* www.styluspub.com
Foreign Rep(s): Peter Prout (Spain & Portugal); Stylus (US)

Dee-Jay Publications+
3 Meadows Lane, Arklow, County Wicklow
Tel: (0402) 39125 *Fax:* (0402) 39064
Key Personnel
Contact: Jim Rees *E-mail:* jrees@eircom.net
Founded: 1992
Subjects: Biography, Genealogy, History, Maritime, Nonfiction (General), Travel
ISBN Prefix(es): 0-9519239
Branch Office(s)
Irish Books & Media Inc, 1433-E Franklin Ave, Minneapolis, MN 55404-2135, United States
Distributor for Arklow Enterprise Centre

Dominican Publications
42 Parnell Sq, Dublin 1
Tel: (01) 8721611 *Fax:* (01) 8731760
E-mail: dompubs@iol.ie
Key Personnel
Chief Executive, Editorial, Sales: Austin Flannery
Advertising, Production: Bernard Treacy
Founded: 1897
Subjects: Religion - Catholic, Books & periodicals on theology
ISBN Prefix(es): 0-9504797; 0-907271; 1-871552
Total Titles: 20 Print; 2 CD-ROM
Distributed by Columba
Book Club(s): Doctrine and Life Book Club; Religious Life Review Book Club; Scripture in Church Book Club

IRELAND

Dublin Institute for Advanced Studies
10 Burlington Rd, Dublin 4
Tel: (01) 6680748 *Fax:* (01) 6680561
Telex: 31687 Dias Ei
Key Personnel
Registrar: John Duggan
Founded: 1940
Specialize in research & advanced study in Celtic Studies & Physics.
Subjects: Ethnicity, Physics
ISBN Prefix(es): 0-901282; 1-85500

Eason & Son Ltd
80 Middle Abbey St, Dublin 1
Tel: (01) 8733811 *Fax:* (01) 8730620
Telex: 32566
Key Personnel
Man Dir: Gordon Bolton
Editorial, Sales, Production, Publicity, Rights & Permissions: Tom Owens
Founded: 1886
Subjects: Regional Interests
ISBN Prefix(es): 0-900346; 1-873430
Imprints: Irish Heritage Series
Subsidiaries: Eason & Son (NI) Ltd; Eason Advertising
Warehouse: Brickfield Dr, Crumlin, Dublin 12

The Economic & Social Research Institute
4 Burlington Rd, Dublin 4
Tel: (01) 6671525 *Fax:* (01) 6686231
E-mail: brendan.whelan@esri.ie
Web Site: www.esri.ie
Key Personnel
Assistant Dir, Secretary, Sales & Publicity: Gillian Davidson *E-mail:* admin@esri.ie
Dir: Prof Brendan J Whelan *E-mail:* brendan.whelan@esri.ie
Founded: 1960
Subjects: Economics, Education, Environmental Studies, Finance, Health, Nutrition, Social Sciences, Sociology
ISBN Prefix(es): 0-7070; 0-901809
Total Titles: 300 Print
Parent Company:

The Educational Company of Ireland
Ballymount Rd, Walkinstown, Dublin 12
Tel: (01) 4500611 *Fax:* (01) 4500993
E-mail: info@edco.ie
Key Personnel
Chief Executive: Frank Maguire
Executive Dir Sales & Marketing: Mr Oisin Mulcahy
Executive Dir: R McLoughlin
Founded: 1910
Firm is a trading unit of Smurfit Ireland Ltd.
Subjects: Business, Career Development, Computer Science, Ethnicity, Geography, Geology, History, Mathematics, Religion - Other, Science (General)
ISBN Prefix(es): 0-901802; 0-904916; 0-86167
Branch Office(s)
20-1 Talbot St, Dublin 1

Emerald Publications+
The Studio, 22 Summerstown Grove, Wilton Cork
Tel: (021) 962853 *Fax:* (021) 310983
E-mail: alongk@iol.ie
Key Personnel
Contact: Denis Linehan
Founded: 1980
Also acts as legal consultant.
Subjects: Criminology, Government, Political Science, Health, Nutrition, Law, Theology
ISBN Prefix(es): 0-9525813

Environmental Research Unit
St Martin's House, Waterloo Rd, Dublin 4
Tel: (01) 764211
Telex: 30846 *Cable:* Foras Dublin

Key Personnel
Chief Executive Officer: L M McCumiskey
Information & Training: S Smyth
Founded: 1964
National Institute for Physical Planning & Construction Research.
Subjects: Environmental Studies
ISBN Prefix(es): 0-906120; 0-9500200; 0-9501356; 1-85053; 0-900115

Estragon Press Ltd+
Durrus, Bantry, Co Cork 7
Tel: (027) 61186 *Fax:* (027) 61186
Key Personnel
Dir, Publisher, Author: John McKenna; Sally McKenna
Founded: 1991
Subjects: Cookery, Travel, Wine & Spirits
ISBN Prefix(es): 1-874076

European Foundation for the Improvement of Living & Working Conditions
Wyattville Rd, Loughlinstown, Dublin
Tel: (01) 2043100 *Fax:* (01) 2826456
E-mail: postmaster@eurofound.eu.int
Key Personnel
Contact: Mattanja De Boer
Founded: 1975
Subjects: EU Social Policy

European Healthcare Management Association
Vergemount Hall, Clonskeagh, Dublin 6
Tel: (01) 2839299 *Fax:* (01) 2838653
E-mail: ehma@iol.le
ISBN Prefix(es): 0-907727

Events of the Week+
18 Park Vale, Sandyford Rd, Dublin 16
Tel: (01) 2954962 *Fax:* (01) 2954963
Web Site: www.eventoftheweek.com
Key Personnel
Man Dir: Frank Cahill
Founded: 1958
Subjects: Communications, Marketing, Travel
Associate Companies: Mapmasters Ltd
Subsidiaries: Colour Craft Printers

Fact Pack Ireland Guides, *imprint of* Morrigan Book Co

C J Fallon
Lucan Rd, Palmerston, Dublin 20
Key Personnel
Man Dir: H McNicholas
Editorial: N White
Secretary: P Tolan
Founded: 1927
ISBN Prefix(es): 0-7144

Fingal Books, *imprint of* Raven Arts Press

FISH Publishing+
Durrus, Bantry, Co Cork
Tel: (027) 61246 *Fax:* (027) 61246
E-mail: info@fishpublishing.com
Web Site: www.fishpublishing.com
Founded: 1994
Annual Fish Short Story Prize (International).
Subjects: Fiction, Literature, Literary Criticism, Essays, Fiction
ISBN Prefix(es): 0-9523522
Number of titles published annually: 3 Print

Fitzwilliam Publishing Co Ltd+
1488 Assumpta Villas, Kildare
Tel: (01) 614575 *Fax:* (01) 614575
Key Personnel
Man Dir: Kevin McCaffrey
Marketing: Tom Madden

Subjects: Education, Ethnicity
ISBN Prefix(es): 1-871423

Flyleaf Press+
4 Spencer Villas, Glenageary, County Dublin
Tel: (01) 2806231
E-mail: flyleaf@indigo.ie
Web Site: www.flyleaf.ie
Key Personnel
Man Editor: James Ryan *E-mail:* ryanj@bwresira.ie
Founded: 1982
Subjects: Genealogy, Natural History, Family history
ISBN Prefix(es): 0-9508466; 0-9539974
Number of titles published annually: 2 Print
Total Titles: 10 Print
Distributed by Irish Books & Media (USA)

Folens Publishers+
8 Broomhill Business Park, Tallaght, Dublin 24
Tel: (01) 451-5311 *Fax:* (01) 451-5308
Key Personnel
Man Dir: John O'Connor *E-mail:* john.o'connor@folens.le
Financial Controller: Aoife Geraghty
Primary Publisher: Deirdre Whelan
Secondary Publisher: Anna O'Donovan
Founded: 1957
Subjects: Education
ISBN Prefix(es): 0-86121; 0-902592; 1-84131
Associate Companies: Folens Limited, United Kingdom; JUKA-91 Sp.z.o.o., Poland
Imprints: Blackwater Press

Four Courts Press Ltd+
Fumbally Court, Fumbally Lane, Dublin 8
Tel: (01) 453-4668 *Fax:* (01) 453-4672
E-mail: info@four-courts-press.ie
Web Site: www.four-courts-press.ie
Key Personnel
Man Dir: Michael Adams
Dir: Martin Healy *E-mail:* martin.healy@four-courts-press.ie
Founded: 1970
Subjects: Art, History, Law, Literature, Literary Criticism, Essays, Philosophy, Religion - Catholic, Theology, History including Medieval & Celtic studies
ISBN Prefix(es): 0-906127; 1-85182
Number of titles published annually: 50 Print
Total Titles: 400 Print
Imprints: Open Air
U.S. Office(s): ISBS, 5824 NE Hassalo St, Portland, OR 97213, United States
Warehouse: Gill & Macmillan Book Distributors, Hume Ave, Park West, Dublin 12
Orders to: Gill & Macmillan Book Distributors, Hume Ave, Park West, Dublin 12

Gallery Books, Ireland
Loughcrew, Oldcastle, Co Meath
Tel: (049) 8541779 *Fax:* (049) 8541779
E-mail: gallery@indigo.ie
Key Personnel
Chief Executive, Editorial: Peter Fallon
Administration: Jean Barry
Administrator: Suella Wynne
Sales: Anne Duggan
Founded: 1970
Specialize in contemporary Irish literature by Irish authors only.
Subjects: Drama, Theater, Poetry
ISBN Prefix(es): 0-902996; 0-904011; 1-85235
Associate Companies: Deerfield Publications Inc, Deerfield, MA 01342, United States
Distributed by Dufour Editions Inc (USA)

Gandon Editions+
The Cush Oysterhaven, Kinsale, Co Cork
Tel: (021) 770830 *Fax:* (021) 770755

PUBLISHERS

Key Personnel
Editor & International Rights: John O'Regan
Founded: 1983
Specialize in art & architecture books.
Subjects: Archaeology, Architecture & Interior Design, Art, Environmental Studies, History, Nonfiction (General)
ISBN Prefix(es): 0-946641; 0-946846; 0-948037

Gartan, Preas Cholmcille, *imprint of* The Columba Press

Gateway, *imprint of* Gill & Macmillan Ltd

Gill & Macmillan Ltd+
10 Hume Ave, Park West, Dublin 12
Tel: (01) 500 9500 *Fax:* (01) 500 9599
Web Site: www.gillmacmillan.ie
Key Personnel
Man Dir: Michael Gill *E-mail:* mhgill@gillmacmillan.ie
Publishing Dir, Educational Books: H J Mahony *E-mail:* hmahony@gillmacmillan.ie
Marketing & Sales Dir: P A Thew *E-mail:* pthew@gillmacmillan.ie
Finance Dir: M D O'Dwyer *E-mail:* dodwyer@gillmacmillan.ie
Production Dir: M O O'Keeffe *E-mail:* mokeefe@gillmacmillan.ie
Distribution Dir: J Manning *E-mail:* jmanning@gillmacmillan.ie
Publishing Dir, General Books: F M Tobin *E-mail:* ftobin@gillmacmillan.ie
Founded: 1968 (formerly Gill & Son)
Representation Overseas
Australia (Education titles): Macmillan Education Australia, Level 4 & 5, 627 Chapel St, Locked Bag 1400, South Yarra, Victoria 3141, Australia
Australia (General, Newleaf & Gateway titles): Banyan Tree Book Distributors, 13 College Rd, Kent Town, Adelaide, SA 5067, Australia
Canada (General, Newleaf & Gateway titles): Hushion House Publishing, 36 Northline Rd, Toronto, ON M4B 3E2, Canada
Europe (Switzerland, Germany, Austria, Belgium, Netherlands, France & Luxembourg): Michael Geoghegan, 14 Frognal Gardens, London NW3 6UX, UK
Scandinavia: Hanne Rotovnik, PO Box 5, Strandvejen 685B, DK-2930 Klampenbourg, Denmark
India, Pakistan, Sri Lanka (Newleaf & Gateway): Rajdeep Mukherjee, Pan Macmillan India, 5A/12 Ansari Rd, Daryaganj, New Delhi 110002, India
New Zealand: New Holland Publishers, Unit 1A, 218 Lake Rd, Northcote, Auckland, New Zealand
Singapore, Indonesia, Brunei & Malaysia: Pansing Distribution Sdn Bhd, 7 Tai Seng Dr, No 05-00, Nicosia Warehouse, Singapore 535217, Singapore
South Africa (Education Titles): Macmillan Boleswa, 2nd floor, Old Trafford No 4, Isle of Houghton, Corner of Boundary & Carsed Gowrie Rds, Houghton, Johannesburg 2017, South Africa
South Africa (General, Newleaf & Gateway titles): Pan Macmillan South Africa, 2nd floor, North Block, Hyde Park Corner, Corner Jan Smuts & First Rd, 2196 Hyde Park, Johannesburg, South Africa
UK (General, Newleaf & Gateway titles): Bounce Marketing, Islington Business Centre, 3-5 Islington High St, London N1 9LQ, UK
USA (General & Irish Interest titles): Irish Books & Media Inc, 1433 Franklin Ave East, Minneapolis, MN 55404-2102, USA
USA (Newleaf & Gateway titles): Hushion House Publishing, 36 Northline Rd, Toronto, ON M4B 3E2, Canada
West Indies: Macmillan Caribbean, Between Towns Rd, Oxford OX4 3PP, UK.
Subjects: Biography, Business, Child Care & Development, Cookery, Economics, Education, Fiction, Government, Political Science, Health, Nutrition, History, Law, Literature, Literary Criticism, Essays, Psychology, Psychiatry, Regional Interests, Self-Help, Travel
ISBN Prefix(es): 0-7171
Total Titles: 800 Print
Associate Companies: Macmillan Publishers Ltd, United Kingdom
Imprints: Gateway; Newleaf; Tivoli; Ri Ra
Foreign Rep(s): Hagenbach & Bender GmbH Literary and Media Agency

The Goldsmith Press Ltd+
Newbridge, Co, Kildare
Tel: (045) 433613 *Fax:* (045) 434648
E-mail: de@iol.ie
Key Personnel
Publicity Manager: Peter Mulreid
Business Manager: V M Abbott
Company Secretary: Patricia McGuane
Founded: 1972
Publisher of Irish poetry & books of Irish interest.
Subjects: Art, Cookery, Fiction, History, Literature, Literary Criticism, Essays, Poetry, Regional Interests
ISBN Prefix(es): 0-904984; 1-870491
Number of titles published annually: 6 Print
Total Titles: 100 Print

Government Publications Ireland
Division of Government Supplies Agency
51 St Stephens Green, Dublin 2
Tel: (01) 6476000 *Fax:* (01) 6476843
E-mail: opw@sol.ie
Web Site: www.opw.ie *Cable:* ENACTMENTS
Key Personnel
Contact: Fintan Butler *E-mail:* finton.butler@opw.ie
Founded: 1922
Heritage books, acts, Irish language books, government reports, dail & senate debates.
Subjects: Government, Political Science
ISBN Prefix(es): 0-7076
Ultimate Parent Company: Office of Public Works
Bookshop(s): Government Publications Sale Office, Sun Alliance House, Molesworth St, Dublin 2
Warehouse: Mount Shannon Rd, Rialto Dublin 8

The Hannon Press+
5 Carriff Bridge, Ballinor, Co Meath
Tel: (0405) 46089 *Fax:* (0405) 46089
Key Personnel
International Rights: Patricia Oliver *E-mail:* poliver@indigo.ie
Founded: 1995
Subjects: Biography, Business, How-to
ISBN Prefix(es): 0-9516472

Harbinger House, *imprint of* Roberts Rinehart Publishers

Heritage Books, *imprint of* Careers & Educational Publishers Ltd

Heritage Maps & Guides, *imprint of* Morrigan Book Co

Herodotus Press+
PO Box 4674, Dublin 8
Tel: (01) 4540120 *Fax:* (01) 4541134
Founded: 1995
Subjects: Archaeology, Genealogy, History, Maritime
ISBN Prefix(es): 0-9525414

History House Publishing+
5 Bindon St, Ennis, County Clare
Mailing Address: PO Box 50, Ennis, County Clare
Tel: (065) 24066 *Fax:* (065) 20388
Key Personnel
Man Dir: James Williams
Founded: 1983
Specialize in Genealogy.
Subjects: Genealogy, History
ISBN Prefix(es): 0-86366

IAP, *imprint of* Irish Academic Press

Institute of Public Administration
Vergemount Hall, Clonskeagh, Dublin 6
Tel: (01) 2697011 *Fax:* (01) 2698644
E-mail: information@ipi.ie
Web Site: www.ipa.ie
Telex: 90533 INPA EI *Cable:* ADMIN DUBLIN
Key Personnel
Publication Dir: Jim O'Donnell
Production: Kathleen Harte
Sales: Eileen Kelly
Founded: 1957
Subjects: Economics, Government, Political Science, History, Law, Public Administration, Social Sciences, Sociology
ISBN Prefix(es): 0-902173; 0-906980; 1-872002; 1-902448

Irish Academic Press+
44 Northumberland Rd, Ballsbridge, Dublin
Tel: (01) 668 8244 *Fax:* (01) 660 1610
E-mail: info@iap.ie
Web Site: www.iap.ie
Key Personnel
Managing Editor: Linda Longmore
Founded: 1974
Subjects: Art, History, Literature, Literary Criticism, Essays, Military Science
ISBN Prefix(es): 0-7165
Imprints: IAP; Irish University Press
Branch Office(s)
ISBS, 5804 NE Hassalo St, Portland, OR 97213, United States *Tel:* (503) 287-3093 *Fax:* 503) 280-8832
Orders to: Gill & Macmillan Book Distributors, Goldenbridge, Inchicore, Dublin 8

Irish Heritage Series, *imprint of* Eason & Son Ltd

Irish Management Institute+
Sandyford Rd, Dublin 16
Tel: (01) 2078400 *Fax:* (01) 2955147
E-mail: 3025reception@imi.ie
Web Site: www.imi.ie
Telex: 30325
Key Personnel
Chief Executive: Maurice O'Grady
Book Publishing & Distribution Manager: Alex Miller
Founded: 1952
The Institute is concerned with management, education, training & development. Publishing & bookselling are complementary activities. Member of Cle, The Irish Book Publishers Association.
Subjects: Accounting, Business, Communications, Economics, Finance, Labor, Industrial Relations, Management
ISBN Prefix(es): 0-903352; 0-9500327; 1-902664

Irish Times Ltd+
11-15 D'Olier St, Dublin 2
Tel: (01) 6758000 *Fax:* (01) 6773282
E-mail: b.mcniff@irish-times.ie
Web Site: www.ireland.com
Telex: 25167

IRELAND

Key Personnel
Prize Administrator: Gerard Cavanagh
Founded: 1859
Member of the Committee of Irish Book Publishers Association; Council Member Dublin City Center Business Association.
Subjects: Fiction, Genealogy, Literature, Literary Criticism, Essays
ISBN Prefix(es): 0-907011; 0-9503418
Branch Office(s)
Irish Trade Board, 880 Third Ave, 8th floor, New York, NY 10020, United States
Showroom(s): 16 D'Olier St, Dublin 2

Irish University Press, *imprint of* Irish Academic Press

Irish YouthWork Press
National Youth Federation, 20 Lower Dominick St, Dublin 1
Tel: (010) 8729933 *Fax:* (010) 8724183
E-mail: info@nyf.ie
Web Site: www.nyf.ie
Key Personnel
Services Executive: Mr Fran Bissett
Specialize in Youth Work Publications.
Subjects: Child Care & Development, Education, Social Sciences, Sociology
ISBN Prefix(es): 0-9522207; 1-900416
Total Titles: 17 Print
Online services available through World Wide Web.

Kells Publishing Company Ltd
John St, Kells, Co Meath
Tel: (046) 40117; (046) 40255 *Fax:* (046) 41522
ISBN Prefix(es): 1-872490

Albertine Kennedy Publishing
5 Henrietta St, Dublin 1
Tel: (01) 6607090 *Fax:* (01) 6607090
Key Personnel
Man Dir: Tom Kennedy
ISBN Prefix(es): 0-906002

Kennys Bookshop & Art Galleries
High St, Galway
Tel: (091) 562739 *Fax:* (091) 568544
E-mail: queries@kennys.ie
Web Site: www.kennys.ie
Key Personnel
Man Dir: Kenny Conor
ISBN Prefix(es): 0-906312

Kerryman Ltd
Clash, Tralee, Co Kerry
Tel: (071) 45500 *Fax:* (071) 45570
E-mail: ads@kerryman.ie
Web Site: www.kerryman.ie
Telex: 28100
Key Personnel
Man Dir: Bryan G Cunningham
Editorial: Gerard Colleran
Sales, Production: Brendan Doran
Founded: 1970
Subjects: History, Religion - Other
ISBN Prefix(es): 0-946277
Parent Company: Independent Newspapers Ltd, Middle Abbey St, Dublin 1

Libra House Ltd
4 St Kevin's Terrace, Dublin 2
Tel: (01) 542-717
Key Personnel
Contact: Cathal Tyrrell
Founded: 1972
Subjects: Labor, Industrial Relations, Transportation, Travel
ISBN Prefix(es): 0-904169

The Lilliput Press Ltd+
62-63 Sitric Rd, Arbour Hill, Dublin 7
Tel: (01) 6711647 *Fax:* (01) 671123
E-mail: info@lilliputpress.ie
Key Personnel
Publisher: Antony Farrell
Founded: 1984
Member of Irish Book Publishers' Association (Cle).
Subjects: Architecture & Interior Design, Biography, Fiction, History, Literature, Literary Criticism, Essays, Natural History, Poetry, Regional Interests
ISBN Prefix(es): 0-946640; 1-874675; 1-901866

Lindisfarne, *imprint of* Veritas Co Ltd

Little Rhino Books, *imprint of* Roberts Rinehart Publishers

Marino Books, *imprint of* Mercier Press Ltd

Mentor Publications+
Sandyford Industrial Estate, 43 Furze Rd, Dublin 18
Tel: (01) 2952112 *Fax:* (01) 2952114
E-mail: admin@mentorbooks.ie
Web Site: www.mentorbooks.ie
ISBN Prefix(es): 0-947548
Total Titles: 200 Print

Mercier, *imprint of* Mercier Press Ltd

Mercier Press Ltd+
5 French Church St, Cork
Tel: (021) 4275040 *Fax:* (021) 4274969
E-mail: books@mercier.ie
Web Site: www.mercier.ie
Key Personnel
Man Dir: John F Spillane
Founded: 1944
Subjects: Biography, Drama, Theater, Ethnicity, Fiction, History, Humor, Religion - Catholic
ISBN Prefix(es): 0-85342; 1-85635; 1-86023
Number of titles published annually: 40 Print
Total Titles: 300 Print
Imprints: Marino Books; Mercier
Branch Office(s)
Mercier/Marino, 16 Hume St, Dublin 2 *Tel:* (01) 6615299 *Fax:* (01) 6618583 *E-mail:* books@marino.ie
Distributed by Irish Books & Media (USA); Tower Books (Australia)
Foreign Rights: Amer-Asia (Asia); Lora Fountain (France); Natoli Stefan Oliva (Italy); Kristin Olson (Czech Republic); P&P Fritz (Germany); Rosenstone/Wender (US); Margit Schaleck (Denmark, Norway); Julio F Yanez (Latin America, Spain)
Bookshop(s): Mercier Bookshops Ltd, 5 French Church St, Cork *Tel:* (021) 427 5040 *Fax:* (021) 427 4673 *E-mail:* bookshop@mercier.ie
Warehouse: CMD (Columba Mercier Distribution), 55a Spruce Ave, Stillorgan Industrial Park, Blackrock, CO Dublin *Tel:* (01) 2942560 *Fax:* (01) 2942564 *E-mail:* cmd@columbia.ie

Messenger Publications
37 Lower Leeson St, Dublin 2
Tel: (01) 6767 491; (01) 6767 492 *Fax:* (01) 661 16 06
E-mail: sales@messenger.ie
Web Site: www.messenger.ie
Key Personnel
Editor: Brendan Murray SJ
Assistant Editor: Anne Duff
ISBN Prefix(es): 0-901335; 1-872245

Mizen Books, *imprint of* Roberts Rinehart Publishers

Morrigan Book Co+
Gore St, Killala, Ballina, County Mayo
Tel: (096) 32555
E-mail: morrigan@online.ie
Key Personnel
Publisher: Gerald Conan Kennedy *E-mail:* gerry.kennedy@online.ie
Founded: 1982
Subjects: Archaeology, Folklore, Mythology & General Irish Interest
ISBN Prefix(es): 0-907677
Online services available through World Wide Web.
Parent Company: Morigna Mediaco Teoranta
Imprints: Fact Pack Ireland Guides; Heritage Maps & Guides

Mount Eagle Publications Ltd+
Cooleen, Dingle, Co Kerry
Mailing Address: PO Box 32, Dingle, Co Kerry
Tel: (066) 9151463 *Fax:* (066) 9151234
Web Site: www.brandonbooks.com
Key Personnel
Publisher: Steve MacDonogh
Founded: 1997
Subjects: Biography, Fiction, History, Literature, Literary Criticism, Essays, Nonfiction (General)
ISBN Prefix(es): 0-86322; 1-902011
Imprints: Brandon
Subsidiaries: Brandon Book Publishers

National Library of Ireland
Kildare St, Dublin 2
Tel: (01) 6030200 *Fax:* (01) 6766690
E-mail: info@nli.ie
Web Site: www.nli.ie
Founded: 1877
Subjects: Regional Interests
ISBN Prefix(es): 0-907328

New Books/Connolly Books
43 E Essex St, Temple Bar, Dublin 2
Tel: (01) 6711943
Web Site: connollybookshop.1accesshost.com
Subjects: Economics, Government, Political Science, History, Philosophy
ISBN Prefix(es): 0-902912

New Writers' Press
61 Clarence Mangan Rd, Dublin 8
Key Personnel
Man Dir: Michael Smith
Founded: 1967
Subjects: Literature, Literary Criticism, Essays, Poetry
ISBN Prefix(es): 0-905582

Newleaf, *imprint of* Gill & Macmillan Ltd

Oak Tree Press+
19 Rutland St, Cork
Tel: (021) 431 3855 *Fax:* (021) 431 3496
E-mail: info@oaktreepress.com
Web Site: www.oaktreepress.com
Key Personnel
Man Dir: Brian O'Kane *E-mail:* brian.okane@oaktreepress.com
Founded: 1991
Business book publishers & developers of enterprise training & support materials.
Subjects: Accounting, Business, Career Development, Finance, Labor, Industrial Relations, Law, Management, Marketing
ISBN Prefix(es): 1-872853; 1-86076
Number of titles published annually: 15 Print
Total Titles: 170 Print
Parent Company: Cork Publishing

O'Brien Educational
20 Victoria Rd, Dublin 6
Tel: (01) 4923333 *Fax:* (01) 4922777
E-mail: books@obrien.ie
Web Site: www.obrien.ie
Key Personnel
Editorial, Rights & Permissions, Sales, Production: Michael O'Brien
Founded: 1976
Publishers to the Curriculum Development Unit, Trinity College, Dublin 2, & to other educational institutions in Ireland & the EEC.
Subjects: Art, Business, Career Development, Environmental Studies, History, Science (General)
ISBN Prefix(es): 0-905140; 0-86278; 0-9502046
Associate Companies: The O'Brien Press
Orders to: Gill & Macmillan Ltd, Goldenbridge Industrial Estate, Dublin 8 *Tel:* (01) 531005 *Fax:* (01) 541688
Central Books, 99 Wallis Rd, London E9 5LN, United Kingdom *Tel:* (020) 8986 4854 *Fax:* (020) 8533 5821
Michael Geoghegan, 15A Tower Terrace, Wood Green, London N22 6SX, United Kingdom *Tel:* (020) 8889 7094
Keith Ainworth (Pty), 66A Abel St, Suite 4, Penrith, NSW 2750, Australia *Tel:* (047) 323411 *Fax:* (047) 218259
Riverwood Publishers Ltd, 6 Donlands Ave, PO Box 70, Sharon, ON L0G 1V0, Canada *Tel:* 416-478-8396 *Fax:* 416-478-8380
Irsih Books & Media, 1433 Franklin Ave E, Minneapolis, MN 55404-2135, United States *Tel:* 612-871-3505 *Fax:* 612-871-3358

The O'Brien Press Ltd+
20 Victoria Rd, Rathgar, Dublin 6
Tel: (01) 4923333 *Fax:* (01) 4922777
E-mail: books@obrien.ie
Web Site: www.obrien.ie
Key Personnel
Man Dir, Rights & Permissions: Michael O'Brien
Editorial: Ide ni Laoghaire
Sales Manager: Chenile Keogh
Sales Dir: Ivan O'Brien
Founded: 1974
Subjects: Architecture & Interior Design, Biography, Business, Cookery, Criminology, Fiction, History, Humor, Music, Dance, Nonfiction (General), Self-Help, Sports, Athletics, Travel, Wine & Spirits, Women's Studies
ISBN Prefix(es): 0-905140; 0-86278; 0-9502046
Associate Companies: O'Brien Educational
Imprints: Pandas Flyers Red Flag
Foreign Rights: Akcali Ltd (Turkey); Big Apple Tuttle-Mori (Republic of China); Ilustrata SL (Portugal, Spain); Japan Foreign-Rights (Japan); Judith Ridge (Australia, New Zealand); Liepman AG; Literarni Agentura (Czech Republic); Lora Fountain (France, Italy, Russia); Valerie Hoskins & Associates (UK)
Orders to: Gill & Macmillan Ltd, Hume Ave, Park West, Dublin 12 *Tel:* (01) 500 9500 *Fax:* (01) 500 9599
Irish Books & Media, 1433 Franklin Ave E, Minneapolis, MN 55404-2135, United States *Tel:* 612-871-3505 *Fax:* 612-871-3358

Oifig an tSolathair, *imprint of* An Gum

The On Stream Local History Collection, *imprint of* On Stream Publications Ltd

On Stream Publications Ltd+
Currabaha, Cloghroe, Blarney, County Cork
Tel: (021) 4385798 *Fax:* (021) 4385798
E-mail: info@onstream.ie
Web Site: www.onstream.ie
Key Personnel
Man Dir: Roz Crowley
Founded: 1992
Specialize in quality publications.
Subjects: Agriculture, Behavioral Sciences, Biography, Cookery, Developing Countries, Health, Nutrition, History, How-to, Medicine, Nursing, Dentistry, Travel, Wine & Spirits
ISBN Prefix(es): 1-897685; 0-9510018
Imprints: The On Stream Local History Collection; Tackling Series of Practical Books
Subsidiaries: Forum Publications

Open Air, *imprint of* Four Courts Press Ltd

Ossian Publications+
40 MacCurtain St, Cork, County Cork
Mailing Address: PO Box 84, Cork, County Cork
Tel: (021) 4502040 *Fax:* (021) 4502025
E-mail: ossian@iol.ie
Web Site: www.ossian.ie
Key Personnel
Dir: John Loesberg
Founded: 1989
Irish music publisher & distributor.
Subjects: Ethnicity, How-to, Music, Dance, Irish Music
ISBN Prefix(es): 0-946005; 1-900428
Associate Companies: Bookmark
Branch Office(s)
Ossian USA, 118 Beck Rd, Loudon, NH 03301, United States *E-mail:* ossianusa@attbi.com
Distributed by Dufour Editions; Music Exhange; Music Sales Corp; Soar Valley Music
Distributor for Halshaw; Dave Malinson Publications; Music Sales Corp; Waltons

Pandas Flyers Red Flag, *imprint of* The O'Brien Press Ltd

Playscripts, *imprint of* Campus Publishing Ltd

Poolbeg Press Ltd+
Poolbeg Group Services, 123 Baldoyle Industrial Estate, Baldoyle, Dublin 13
Tel: (01) 8321477 *Fax:* (01) 8321430
E-mail: poolbeg@poolbeg.com
Web Site: www.poolbeg.com
Key Personnel
Man Dir: Philip MacDermott
Finance Dir: Kieran Devlin
Edit Dir: Kate Cruise O'Brien
Marketing Manager: Michael McLoughlin
Founded: 1976
Subjects: Fiction, History, Nonfiction (General)
ISBN Prefix(es): 1-85371; 0-905169
Imprints: Salmon; Torc; Children's Poolbeg
Subsidiaries: Torc Books Ltd; Salmon Publishing Ltd

PSAI Press
Political Studies Association of Ireland, c/o Dublin City University Business School, Glasnevin, Dublin 9
Tel: (01) 7005664
Web Site: www.politics.tcd.ie/psai/contact.html
Key Personnel
Contact: Prof Nicholas Rees *Tel:* (061) 202212 *E-mail:* nicholas.rees@ul.ie
Founded: 1982
Specializes in: Political Science.
Publications include: Journals & Irish Political Books.
ISBN Prefix(es): 0-9519748
Ultimate Parent Company: Political Studies Association of Ireland

Publishers Group South West (Ireland)+
Allihies, Bantry, Co Cork
Tel: (027) 73025 *Fax:* (027) 73131
E-mail: 73551.655@compuserve.com
Key Personnel
President: Tony Lowes
Vice President: Peter Haston
Secretary: Guy Cotten
Founded: 1984
Member of An Taise, The National Trust; Specialize in promotional T-shirts, buttons & balloons.
Subjects: Fiction, Philosophy, Poetry
ISBN Prefix(es): 1-870618; 0-9511629
Imprints: Christa-Jo Utley
Divisions: Cod's Head Preservation Society; Friends of Allihies Artists

Raven Arts Press+
2 Brookside, Dundrum Rd, Dundrum, Dublin 14
Key Personnel
Chief Executive: Dermot Bolger
Founded: 1978
Subjects: Ethnicity, Literature, Literary Criticism, Essays, Poetry
ISBN Prefix(es): 1-85186; 0-906897
Imprints: Fingal Books

Real Ireland Design
27 Beechwood Close, Boghall Rd, Bray
Tel: (01) 2860799 *Fax:* (01) 2829962
E-mail: realirel@indigo.ie
Web Site: www.realireland.ie/mainfrm.html
Key Personnel
Man Dir: Leonard Desmond
Founded: 1981
Subjects: Photography, Travel
ISBN Prefix(es): 2-87545; 0-946887

Relay Books+
Tyone, Nenagh Co Tipperary
Tel: (010) 6731734 *Fax:* (010) 6731734
E-mail: relaybooks@eiscom.net
Key Personnel
Dir & Editor: Donal A Murphy
Founded: 1982
Member of Cle, Book Publishers Association of Ireland.
Subjects: History, Literature, Literary Criticism, Essays, Regional Interests
ISBN Prefix(es): 0-946327
Distributed by Irish Books & Media (USA)

Rhino Books, *imprint of* Roberts Rinehart Publishers

Ri Ra, *imprint of* Gill & Macmillan Ltd

Roberts Rinehart Publishers+
Trinity House, Charlestown Rd, Ranelagh, Dublin 6
Tel: (01) 497-2399 *Fax:* (01) 497-0927
E-mail: books@townhouse.ie
Key Personnel
President: Rick Rinehart
Vice President: Jack van Zandt
Rights Dir: Mary Hegarty
Founded: 1983
Subjects: Anthropology, Art, Biography, Environmental Studies, Ethnicity, Fiction, History, Natural History, Photography, Regional Interests, Travel
ISBN Prefix(es): 0-911797; 1-879373; 1-57098
Parent Company: 6309 Monarch Park Place, Nivot, CO 80503, United States
Imprints: Rhino Books; Little Rhino Books; Mizen Books; Harbinger House
U.S. Office(s): 5309 Monarch Park Pl, Niwot, CO 80503, United States *Tel:* 303-652 2685 *Fax:* 303-652 2689 *E-mail:* books@robertrinehart.com

Round Hall Sweet & Maxwell+
4 Upper Ormond Quay, Dublin 7
Tel: (01) 873-0101 *Fax:* (01) 872-0078
Key Personnel
Dir: Elanor McGarry
Marketing Manager: Alison Gallagher
E-mail: alison.gallagher@itps.co.uk

IRELAND

Founded: 1982
Subjects: Criminology, Finance, Labor, Industrial Relations, Law
ISBN Prefix(es): 1-899738; 0-9508725
Total Titles: 200 Print
Parent Company: The Thomson Corporation
Orders to: Gill & Macmillan Distribution, Goldenbridge, Inchicore, Dublin 8, Contacts: Karen/ Karen Gallagher/ Donoghue *Tel:* (01) 4531005 *Fax:* (01) 4541688

Royal Dublin Society
Ballsbridge, Dublin 4
Tel: (01) 6680866 *Fax:* (01) 6604014
E-mail: marketing@rds.ie
Web Site: www.rds.ie *Cable:* SOCIETY DUBLIN
Key Personnel
Science Development Executive: Annette McDonnell *E-mail:* amcdonnell@rds.ie
Founded: 1731
Subjects: Biological Sciences, Science (General)
ISBN Prefix(es): 0-86027

Royal Irish Academy+
19 Dawson St, Dublin 2
Tel: (01) 6762570 *Fax:* (01) 6762346
E-mail: publications@ria.ie
Web Site: www.ria.ie
Key Personnel
Executive Secretary, Rights & Permissions: Patrick Buckley
Editor, Productions: Rachel McNicholl
Publications Officer: Hugh Shiels *Tel:* (01) 6380911 *E-mail:* h.shiels@ria.ie
Founded: 1785
Subjects: Archaeology, Biological Sciences, Earth Sciences, Environmental Studies, Ethnicity, Geography, Geology, Government, Political Science, History, Mathematics, Physical Sciences
ISBN Prefix(es): 0-901714; 1-874045
Number of titles published annually: 6 Print
Distributor for Environmental Institute; University College Dublin

Runa Press
2 Belgrave Terrace, Monkstown, Co Dublin
Tel: (01) 2801869
Subjects: Philosophy, Poetry
ISBN Prefix(es): 0-903543

Salmon, *imprint of* Poolbeg Press Ltd

Salmon Publishing+
Cliffs of Moher, Co Clare
Tel: (065) 7081941 *Fax:* (065) 7081621
E-mail: info@salmonpoetry.com
Web Site: www.salmonpoetry.com
Founded: 1980
Subjects: Poetry
ISBN Prefix(es): 1-897648; 0-948339

Sean Ros Press
Millquarter, Foulkesmill, Co Wexford
Tel: (051) 428666
Key Personnel
Contact: Bernard Browne
Founded: 1993
Subjects: Genealogy, History, Natural History
ISBN Prefix(es): 0-9525771
Total Titles: 9 Print

Tackling Series of Practical Books, *imprint of* On Stream Publications Ltd

Tir Eolas (Knowledge of the Land)
Newtownlynch, Doorus, Kinvara, Co Galway
Tel: (091) 637452 *Fax:* (091) 637452
E-mail: info@tireolas.com
Web Site: www.tireolas.com

Key Personnel
Dir: Anne Korff
Founded: 1987
Member of Cle.
Subjects: Anthropology, Archaeology, Biography, Environmental Studies, History, Natural History, Outdoor Recreation
ISBN Prefix(es): 1-873821
Total Titles: 9 Print
Distributed by Eason & Son (Ireland); Irish Books & Media (USA); Colin Smythe Publisher (England)
Orders to: Colin Smythe Publishers, PO Box 6, Gerrands Cross, Bucks SL9 8XA, United Kingdom
Eason & Sons, Furry Park Industrial Esate, Santry, Dublin 9
Irish Books & Media, 1433 Franklin Ave E, Minneapolis, MN 55404-2123, United States

Tivenan Publications+
Dually, New Castle West, Co Limerick
Tel: (069) 62596 *Fax:* (069) 62933
E-mail: birth@indigo.ie
Web Site: www.wellmotion.info
Key Personnel
Publisher: Nancy Murphy *Tel:* (069) 62933
Founded: 1993
Specializes in health, pregnancy & women's health.
Subjects: Child Care & Development, Health, Nutrition, Self-Help, Childbirth & Pregnancy
ISBN Prefix(es): 0-9522578
Total Titles: 1 Print; 1 E-Book
Distributed by Easons Dublin (Ireland)
Distributor for News Brothers Ltd
Bookshop(s): Easons Wholesalers, Furry Park Industrial Estate, Santry, Dublin 9 (Books)

Tivoli, *imprint of* Gill & Macmillan Ltd

Tomar Publishing Ltd+
Bloom House, 78 Eccles St, Dublin 7
Fax: (01) 744697
Key Personnel
Publisher: Mr Tom Breen
Founded: 1982
Subjects: History
ISBN Prefix(es): 1-871793

Topaz Publications+
10 Haddington Lawn, Glengeary, Co Dublin
Tel: (01) 2800460 *Fax:* (01) 2800460
Key Personnel
Managing Partner: Mrs Davida Murdoch
Founded: 1988
Subjects: Law
ISBN Prefix(es): 0-9514032
Distributed by Lexis Nexis Export Team

Torc, *imprint of* Poolbeg Press Ltd

Town House & Country House
Trinity House, Charleston Rd, Ranelagh, Dublin 6
Tel: (01) 4972399 *Fax:* (01) 4970927
E-mail: books@townhouse.ie
Key Personnel
Man Dir, Rights & Permissions: Treasa Coady
Editorial: Claire Haugh
Production: John McCurrie
Sales & Marketing: Brud Ni Chuilinn
Founded: 1984
Also acts as Publisher to Trinity College Dublin.
Subjects: Archaeology, Art, Biography, Fiction, Romance
ISBN Prefix(es): 0-948524; 1-86059; 0-946172
Associate Companies: Town House Publications Ltd
Imprints: Trinity College Dublin Press
Distributed by Roberts Rinehart Publishers (Canada & USA)

Distributor for Roberts Rinehart Publishers (USA)
Book Club(s): BCA
Warehouse: Gill & Macmillan, Goldenbridge Industrial Estate, Ichicore, Dublin
Orders to: Gill & Macmillan, Goldenbridge Industrial Estate, Inchicore, Dublin 8

Trinity College Dublin Press, *imprint of* Town House & Country House

Christa-Jo Utley, *imprint of* Publishers Group South West (Ireland)

Veritas Publications, *imprint of* Veritas Co Ltd

Veritas Co Ltd+
Veritas House, 7-8 Lower Abbey St, Dublin 1
Tel: (01) 8788177 *Fax:* (01) 8786507
Key Personnel
Dir: Father Sean Melody
Director: Maura Nyland
Editorial: Fiona Biggs
Retail: Brid Healy
Marketing, Publicity: Brian Lynch
Rights & Permissions: Rita Singleton
Founded: 1969
Veritas Publications is the publishing division of the Catholic Communications Institute of Ireland Inc.
Subjects: Religion - Other, Catechetical
ISBN Prefix(es): 0-905092; 0-86217; 0-901810; 1-85390
Parent Company: The Catholic Communications Institute of Ireland
Imprints: Veritas Publications; Beehive Books; Lindisfarne
Branch Office(s)
Leamington Spa, United Kingdom
Cork
Dublin
Ennis
Letterkenny
Sligo
Warehouse: 8 Hanover Quay, Dublin 2

Weir's Guides, *imprint of* Ballinakella Press

Wolfhound Press+
Imprint of Merlin Publishing
16 Upper Pembroke St, Dublin 2
Tel: (01) 6764373
E-mail: websales@wolfhound.ie
Web Site: www.wolfhound.ie; www.drumshee.com
Key Personnel
Publisher: Seamus Cashman
Sales, Marketing & Rights: Seamus O'Reilly
Founded: 1974
Subjects: Biography, Fiction, Photography
ISBN Prefix(es): 0-9503454; 0-905473; 0-86327
Total Titles: 300 Print
Orders to: Gill & Macmillan Ltd, Goldenbridge Industrial Estate, Inchicore, Dublin 8 *Tel:* (01) 4531005 *Fax:* (01) 4541688

Israel

General Information

Capital: Jerusalem
Language: Hebrew and Arabic (English and German widely known)
Religion: Predominantly Jewish (about 82%) and Muslim (about 14%)
Population: 4.7 million
Bank Hours: 0830-1230 Sunday-Thursday; also 1600-1700 Sunday-Tuesday & Thursday

Shop Hours: Usually Sunday 0900-1300, 1600-1800; weekdays 0900-1300, 1600-1900; many close Friday afternoon
Currency: 100 agorot = 1 new sheqel
Export/Import Information: Books (except for children's picture books) and advertising duty-free. 17% VAT on books. No import license required for books but must apply for importing number; exchange granted automatically. Import restrictions on Hebrew books.
Copyright: UCC, Berne, Florence (see Copyright Conventions, pg xi)

Academon Publishing House
Hebrew University, Jerusalem 91000
Mailing Address: PO Box 24130, Jerusalem 91000
Tel: (02) 5811326; (02) 5811327 *Fax:* (02) 5815558
Key Personnel
Man Dir: Itzik Lary
Founded: 1952
ISBN Prefix(es): 965-350
Bookshop(s): Academon, at the four Hebrew University campuses, Jerusalem & Rehovot

Academy of the Hebrew Language
Givat Ram, Jerusalem 91034
Mailing Address: PO Box 3449, Jerusalem 91034
Tel: (02) 6493555 *Fax:* (02) 5617065
E-mail: acad2u@vms.huji.ac.il
Web Site: hebrew-academy.huji.ac.il
Key Personnel
President: Prof Moshe Bar-Asher
Man Dir: Dr Nathan Efrati
Founded: 1953
Specialize in research & development of the Hebrew language.
Subjects: Hebrew Language & Linguistics
ISBN Prefix(es): 965-481
Number of titles published annually: 12 Print

Ach Publishing House+
PO Box 170, Kiriat Bialik 27000
Tel: (04) 727227; (04) 7222096 *Fax:* (04) 417839
Fax on Demand: (03) 9342850
Founded: 1967
Subjects: Behavioral Sciences, Education
ISBN Prefix(es): 965-267

Achiasaf Publishing House Ltd
6 Tsoran St. S Industrial Zone, Netanya
Mailing Address: PO Box 8414, Netanya 42504
Tel: (09) 8851390 *Fax:* (09) 8851391
E-mail: info@achiasaf.co.il
Web Site: www.achiasaf.co.il
Key Personnel
Man Dir: Matan Achiasaf; Shachna Achiasaf
Founded: 1933
Subjects: Fiction, Nonfiction (General), Science (General)

Achiever
22 Hahistadrut St, Jerusalem 94230
Tel: (02) 6253627 *Fax:* (02) 6255740
Key Personnel
Manager: D Kessler
Man Dir: Ayala Atzmon; Sara Atzmon

Agudat Sabah+
PO Box 2415, Natanya 42123
Tel: (09) 8620544 *Fax:* (09) 8620546
Key Personnel
Author & Editor: Sidney Pimienta
Founded: 1978
Subjects: Anthropology, Genealogy, History, Language Arts, Linguistics, Management, Regional Interests, Religion - Jewish
ISBN Prefix(es): 965-453

Subsidiaries: SIIAC (Societe Internationale d'Intervention et d'Action Commerciale)
Branch Office(s)
SIIAC-Pimienta

Am Oved Publishers Ltd
22 Mazeh St, Tel Aviv 65213
Tel: (03) 6291526 *Fax:* (03) 6298911
Telex: 1568 *Cable:* AMOVED TELAVIV
Key Personnel
Man Dir: Aharon Kraus
Founded: 1942
Subjects: Biography, Fiction, History, Philosophy, Poetry, Psychology, Psychiatry, Social Sciences, Sociology
ISBN Prefix(es): 965-13
Orders to: Distributor's Centre for Israeli Books Ltd, 22 Nachmani St, PO Box 2811, Tel Aviv

Amichai Publishing House Ltd
19 Yad Harotzim St, PO Box 8448, Netanyah 42505
Tel: (09) 8859099 *Fax:* (09) 8853464
Key Personnel
Man Dir: Dr Itzhak Oron *E-mail:* oron@idc.ac.ii
Founded: 1948
Subjects: Fiction, Language Arts, Linguistics, Science (General)

Ariel Publishing House
PO Box 3328, Jerusalem 91033
Tel: (02) 6434540 *Fax:* (02) 6436164
Key Personnel
Chief Executive: Ely Schiller *E-mail:* elysch@netvision.net.il
Founded: 1976
Subjects: Geography, Geology, History, Regional Interests, Religion - Other
ISBN Prefix(es): 965-439

Arsan Publishing House Ltd, see Kivunim-Arsan Publishing House

Astrolog Publishing House+
PO Box 1123, Hod Hasharon 45111
Tel: (09) 7412044 *Fax:* (09) 7442714
Key Personnel
Man Dir: Sara Ben-Mordechai *E-mail:* sarabm@netvision.net.il
Editor-In-Chief: Elisha Ben-Mordechai
Founded: 1994
A general publisher in the Hebrew language & New Age & alternative medicine in English & other languages. Also specializing in mysticism, prediction of the future, awareness & various religions.
Member of Israel Publishers' Association.
Subjects: Nonfiction (General)
ISBN Prefix(es): 965-494
Total Titles: 600 Print
Distributed by Independent Publishers Group (IPG) (United States)

Aurora Semanario Israeli de Actualidad+
PO Box 18066, Tel Aviv 61180
Tel: (03) 5462785; (03) 5463297 *Fax:* (03) 5625082
E-mail: aurorail@netvision.net.il
Founded: 1963
ISBN Prefix(es): 965-333
Parent Company: Aurora
Associate Companies: Aurora Em Poreuquce
Subsidiaries: Isnet
Divisions: Internet
Branch Office(s)
Buenos-Aires

Aviv Publishers Ltd, *imprint of* Bitan Publishers Ltd

Bar Ilan University Press
Bar Ilan University, Ramat Gan 52900
Tel: (03) 5318401; (03) 5318575 *Fax:* (03) 5353446
E-mail: press@mail.biu.ac.il
Web Site: www.biu.ac.il/Press
Key Personnel
General Manager: Margalit Avisar
Chairman, Book Committee: Prof Yehuda Friedlander
Founded: 1978
Member of Israel Association of Publishers.
Subjects: Archaeology, Behavioral Sciences, Biblical Studies, Economics, Education, Geography, Geology, History, Language Arts, Linguistics, Law, Literature, Literary Criticism, Essays, Philosophy, Psychology, Psychiatry, Religion - Jewish, Social Sciences, Sociology
ISBN Prefix(es): 965-226
Number of titles published annually: 25 Print

Ben-Zvi Institute+
12 Abarbanel St, Jerusalem 91076
Mailing Address: PO Box 7660, Jerusalem 91076
Tel: (02) 5398844 *Fax:* (02) 5612329
E-mail: mahonzvi@h2.hum.huji.ac.il
Web Site: www.ybz.org.il
Key Personnel
Dir: Haggai Ben-Shammai
Academic Secretary: Michael Glatzer
Founded: 1948
Specialize in Sephardi & Eastern Jewry.
Subjects: Ethnicity, Foreign Countries, History, Language Arts, Linguistics, Literature, Literary Criticism, Essays, Regional Interests, Religion - Jewish
ISBN Prefix(es): 965-235
Total Titles: 100 Print
Parent Company: Yad Izhak Ben-Zvi & the Hebrew University of Jerusalem

Bezalel Academy of Arts & Design
Mt Scopus, PO Box 24046, Jerusalem 91240
Tel: (02) 589 3313 *Fax:* (02) 582 3094
E-mail: ouriel@bezalel.ac.il
Web Site: www.bezalel.ac.il
Subjects: Architecture & Interior Design, Art, Photography
ISBN Prefix(es): 965-324

The Bialik Institute+
PO Box 53290, Jerusalem 91531
Tel: (02) 6783554 *Fax:* (02) 6783706
E-mail: bialik@actcom.co.il
Key Personnel
Man Dir: Yitzchak Taub
Founded: 1935
Subjects: Archaeology, Art, Biblical Studies, History, Literature, Literary Criticism, Essays, Philosophy, Poetry, Religion - Jewish
ISBN Prefix(es): 965-342
Number of titles published annually: 46 Print
Distributor for Moreshet; University of Ben Gurion Press; The Zionist Library

Bitan Publishers Ltd+
50 Yeshayahu St, Tel-Aviv 62494
Mailing Address: PO Box 3068, Ramat Hasharon 47130
Tel: (03) 6040089 *Fax:* (03) 5404792
Key Personnel
Manager: M Bitan
Founded: 1965
Also acts as director of the Israeli Publisher Association & Optimum Educational Software (1993) Ltd.
Subjects: Aeronautics, Aviation, Biography, Child Care & Development, Fiction, How-to, Human Relations, Literature, Literary Criticism, Essays, Mysteries, Nonfiction (General), Outdoor Recreation, Poetry, Self-Help, Travel, Women's Studies

Parent Company: ABM Publishers Ltd
Imprints: Orbach Editions Ltd; Aviv Publishers Ltd
Subsidiaries: Bitan United Multimedia Ltd
Divisions: Multimedia
Orders to: 14 Valenberg St, Tel-Aviv 69719

The Book Publishers Association of Israel
29 Carlebach St, 67132 Tel Aviv
Mailing Address: PO Box 20123, Tel Aviv 61201
Tel: (03) 5614121 *Fax:* (03) 5611996
E-mail: info@tbpai.co.il
Founded: 1939

Books in the Attic Publishers Ltd+
PO Box 23146, Tel-Aviv 61231
Tel: (03) 248324 *Fax:* (03) 623630
Key Personnel
President: Dr Yehuda Melzer
Founded: 1989
Subjects: Health, Nutrition, Medicine, Nursing, Dentistry
ISBN Prefix(es): 965-419

Boostan Publishing House
36 Meskek, Ben-Shemen Moshav 73115
Tel: (03) 9221821 *Fax:* (03) 9221299 *Cable:* Boostanmod Telaviv
Key Personnel
Man Dir: Mordechai Boostan
Sales Dir: Roni Birkenfield
Publicity Dir: Riva Almagor
Advertising Dir: Sara Wohlfeiler
Rights & Permissions: Dalia Sheingarten
Founded: 1969
Subjects: Biography, Education, Fiction, History, How-to, Medicine, Nursing, Dentistry, Poetry, Psychology, Psychiatry
ISBN Prefix(es): 965-275
Subsidiaries: Distributors' Centre for Israeli Books Ltd

Breslov Research Institute+
PO Box 5370, Jerusalem 91053
Tel: (02) 5824641 *Fax:* (02) 5825542
E-mail: info@breslov.org
Web Site: www.breslov.org/catalog.html
Key Personnel
Executive Dir: Rabbi Chaim Kramer
Founded: 1979
Subjects: Biblical Studies, Biography, Education, Health, Nutrition, History, Literature, Literary Criticism, Essays, Nonfiction (General), Philosophy, Psychology, Psychiatry, Religion - Jewish, Self-Help, Theology, Specialize in writings in English, French, Spanish, Russian & in Hebrew
ISBN Prefix(es): 0-930213; 965-290
Number of titles published annually: 5 Print
Total Titles: 70 Print; 70 Online; 70 E-Book
Imprints: Tsohar Publications
Branch Office(s)
PO Box 587, Monsey, NY 10952-0587, United States *Tel:* 914-425-4258 *Fax:* 914-425-3018
Distributed by Jewish Lights

Carta, The Israel Map & Publishing Co Ltd+
18 Ha'uman St, Jerusalem 91024
Mailing Address: PO Box 2500, Jerusalem 91024
Tel: (02) 6783355 *Fax:* (02) 6782373
E-mail: cartaben@netvision.net.il
Web Site: www.holyland-jerusalem.com
Key Personnel
Chairman: Emanuel Hausman
President, Chief Executive Officer: Shay Hausman
Editorial: Lorraine Kessel; Pirchia Cohen; Barbara Ball
Art Dir: Eli Kellerman
Founded: 1958
Cartographic & foreign language publisher - English, German & Russian, Hebrew.

Subjects: Archaeology, Education, Health, Nutrition, History
ISBN Prefix(es): 965-220
Number of titles published annually: 30 Print; 1 CD-ROM
Total Titles: 300 Print; 3 CD-ROM
Imprints: Nitzanim
Subsidiaries: Cana Publishing House; W Van Leer Publishing Ltd
Warehouse: Lonnie Kahn Ltd, 20, Eliahu Eitan, Rishon Le Zion 58851, Aaron Segal *Tel:* (03) 9520158/9518408 *Fax:* (03) 9520251/9518415/9518416

Center for Research & Study of Sephardi & Oriental Jewish History, see Misgav Yerushalayim

Centre for Educational Technology
Klausner St 16, Tel Aviv 61394
Tel: (03) 6460183 *Fax:* (03) 6460821
Key Personnel
Publishing Dir: Dani Dolev
ISBN Prefix(es): 965-354

Classikaletet+
14 Habanai St, Industrial Zone, Holon 58850
Tel: (03) 5582080 *Fax:* (03) 5582299
E-mail: kimbooks@netvision.net.it
Key Personnel
Man Dir: Yoram Ros
Founded: 1980
Subjects: Child Care & Development, Cookery, House & Home, How-to, Humor, Music, Dance, Nonfiction (General), Psychology, Psychiatry, Travel
ISBN Prefix(es): 965-286

Cordinata Ltd (Holy Land 2000)
27 Sutin St, 64684 Tel Aviv
Tel: (03) 5226885 *Fax:* (03) 5276661
E-mail: cordinata@isdn.net.il
Web Site: www.holy-land2000.com
Key Personnel
General Manager: Eliezer Sacks
Marketing Manager: Yaron Goldfisher
Founded: 1995
Specialize in books, mainly albums on the Holy Land. Also produce old & new maps, CD ROM, videos & calendars - all about the Holy Land.
Number of titles published annually: 10 Print; 5 CD-ROM; 5 Online; 15 E-Book; 5 Audio
Total Titles: 10 Print; 5 CD-ROM; 5 Online; 15 E-Book; 5 Audio
Online services available through Ingram.
U.S. Office(s): Argecy Co, 27280 Haggerty, Farmington Hills, MI 48331, United States, General Manager: Mr Coby Gutkovitch *Tel:* 248-324-1800 ext 124 *Fax:* 248-324-1900 *E-mail:* argecy@msn.com
Distributed by Riverside Distributors

Dalia Peled Publishers, Division of Modan+
36 Moshav, Ben-Shemen 73115
Tel: (08) 4221821 *Fax:* (08) 4221299
Key Personnel
Man Dir, Publicity, Rights & Permissions: Dahlia Peled
Editorial: Israel Peled
Sales: Raanan Rogel
Production: Ruti Bar-Lev
Founded: 1980
Subjects: Computer Science, Humor
ISBN Prefix(es): 965-269
Subsidiaries: People and Computers

DAT Publications+
PO Box 27019, Jaffa 61270
Tel: (03) 5071239 *Fax:* (03) 5070458
E-mail: DAT@y-dat.co.il

Web Site: www.y-dat.co.il
Key Personnel
General Dir & Rights Contact: Yigal Miller *Tel:* (03) 5072149
Dir: Benci Sharon *Tel:* (03) 5072680
Public Relations: Gila Bonen *Tel:* (03) 6035460 *Fax:* (03) 6035460
Founded: 1969
Publishers of original quality fiction, nonfiction & contemplative literature in Hebrew & English.
Publishers & international rights owners of Shlomo Kalo's works, Privately owned & Member of: Union of Israeli Publishing Houses.
Subjects: Biblical Studies, Fiction, History, Humor, Literature, Literary Criticism, Essays, Nonfiction (General), Philosophy, Religion - Other, Self-Help, Theology
ISBN Prefix(es): 965-7028
Total Titles: 42 Print; 3 Audio
Online services available through World Wide Web.
U.S. Office(s): Forevermore Bible Discovery Books, PO Box 1686, Grapevine, TX 76099, United States, Contact: Andrea Haber *Tel:* 972-869-8025 *Fax:* 972-869-6925 *E-mail:* ForEvrMor1@aol.com
Foreign Rep(s): Boris Hoffman (France); Forevermore (US)
Showroom(s): 22 Dov Mimezeritz, Jaffa, Contact: Nizah Miller *Tel:* (03) 6580221
Warehouse: 22 Dov Mimezeritz, Jaffa, Contact: Nizah Miller *Tel:* (03) 6580221

Dekel Academic Press, *imprint of* Dekel Publishing House

Dekel Publishing House+
17 Motzkin St, Tel Aviv 61450
Mailing Address: PO Box 45094, Tel Aviv 61450
Tel: (03) 5230063 *Fax:* (03) 5273011
E-mail: dekelpbl@netvision.net.il
Web Site: www.dekelpublishing.com
Key Personnel
Man Dir: Mr Zu Morik
Founded: 1975
Member of PMA.
Subjects: Cookery, Crafts, Games, Hobbies, How-to, Language Arts, Linguistics, Mathematics, Military Science, Securities, Self-Help, Sports, Athletics, Self-defense: Krav Maga
ISBN Prefix(es): 965-7178
Imprints: Dekel Academic Press; Tamai Books; Duvdevan
Distributed by Frog Co Ltd; North Atlantic Books

Devora Publishing Co, *imprint of* Pitspopany Press

Doko Video Ltd
33 Hayetzira St, Ramat Gan 52521
Tel: (03) 5753555; (03) 2721771 *Fax:* (03) 5753189
E-mail: dokoa@ibm.net
Key Personnel
Sales & Marketing Manager: Sharon Moss
Founded: 1981
Subjects: Music, Dance, Religion - Other
ISBN Prefix(es): 965-478

Domino, *imprint of* Keter Publishing House Ltd

Duvdevan, *imprint of* Dekel Publishing House

Dvir Publishing Ltd+
11 Lev Pesach St, North Industrial Area, Lod 71293
Mailing Address: PO Box 4020, Lod 71110
Tel: (08) 9246565 *Fax:* (08) 9251770
E-mail: info@zmora.co.il
Key Personnel
Man Dir & Editorial: Ohad Zmora

Sales: Eran Zmora
Founded: 1924
Subjects: Literature, Literary Criticism, Essays, Poetry, Religion - Jewish
ISBN Prefix(es): 965-01
Total Titles: 1,500 Print
Parent Company: Zmora-Bitan Publishers Ltd
Subsidiaries: Dvir Distribution; Karni Publishers Ltd; Megiddo Publishing Co Ltd

Dyonon/Papyrus Publishing House of the Tel-Aviv+
University Students Union, Tel Aviv 61392
Mailing Address: PO Box 39287, Tel Aviv 61392
Tel: (03) 6410351; (03) 6410352; (03) 6427545 (head office) *Fax:* (03) 6423149
Key Personnel
General Manager: Ittamar Herman
Import Manager: Brian Mellick
Editor-in-Chief: Chaviva Ashkenazi
Founded: 1977
Member of National Association of College Stores, USA.
Subjects: Behavioral Sciences, Business, Chemistry, Chemical Engineering, Child Care & Development, Criminology, Economics, Education, Finance, Genealogy, History, Medicine, Nursing, Dentistry, Nonfiction (General), Philosophy, Social Sciences, Sociology
ISBN Prefix(es): 965-306
Imprints: Papyrus
Branch Office(s)
Ben Gurion (Beer Sheva) University Campus
Bookshop(s): Tel Aviv University; Bar-Ilan University; Ben-Guryon University

Edanim Publishers Ltd+
5 Mikunis St, Tel Aviv 61376
Mailing Address: PO Box 37744, Tel Aviv 61376
Tel: (03) 688-8466 *Fax:* (03) 537-7820
Telex: 33847
Key Personnel
Publisher: Asher Weill
Founded: 1975
Subjects: Biography, History, Regional Interests
ISBN Prefix(es): 965-248
Parent Company: Weill Publishers

Encyclopedia Judaica, *imprint of* Keter Publishing House Ltd

Encyclopedia Judaica+
16 Beit Hadefus St, Jerusalem 91071
Mailing Address: PO Box 7145, Jerusalem 91071
Tel: (02) 6557822 *Fax:* (02) 6528962
E-mail: info@keter-books.co.il
Web Site: www.keter-books.co.il
Key Personnel
Man Dir: Yiftach Dekel
ISBN Prefix(es): 965-07
Parent Company: Keter Publishing House Ltd, Jerusalem

Eretz Hemdah Institute for Advanced Jewish Studies
5 HaMem Gimmel St, Jerusalem 94428
Tel: (02) 371-485; (02) 371-940 *Fax:* (02) 371-940
E-mail: eretzhemdah@ou.org
Key Personnel
Contact: Menachem Jacobowitz
Founded: 1987
Subjects: Law, Religion - Jewish
ISBN Prefix(es): 965-436
Distributor for Rubin Mass Ltd (Israel)

ESH (English for Speakers of Hebrew), *imprint of* University Publishing Projects Ltd

Eshkol Books Publishers & Printing Ltd
24 Avodat Israel St, Jerusalem 95155
Tel: (02) 5370451; (02) 5370179 *Fax:* (02) 5372732
Key Personnel
Manager: S Weinfeld
Subjects: Religion - Jewish

Feldheim Publishers Ltd
PO Box 35002, Jerusalem 91350
Tel: (02) 6513947 *Fax:* (02) 6536061
E-mail: feldheim@netvision.net.il
Web Site: www.feldheim.com
Key Personnel
Man Dir: Yaakov Feldheim
Sales Dir: Chaim Vomberg
Founded: 1939
Subjects: Biography, History, Philosophy, Religion - Other
ISBN Prefix(es): 0-87306; 1-58330
U.S. Office(s): 200 Airport Executive Park, Nanuet, NY 10954, United States *Tel:* 845-356-2282 *Fax:* 845-425-1908

The Arnold & Leona Finkler Institute of Holocaust Research
Bar-Ilan University, Ramat-Gan 52900
Tel: (03) 5340333 *Fax:* (03) 5351233
E-mail: michmad@mail.biu.ac.il
Key Personnel
Prof & Chair: Dan Michman
Founded: 1979
Subjects: History, Religion - Jewish, Holocaust, 20th Century Jewish History
Total Titles: 40 Print
Parent Company: Bar-Ilan University

Rodney Franklin Agency
53 Mazeh St, Tel Aviv 61376
Mailing Address: PO Box 37727, Tel Aviv 61376
Tel: (03) 5600724 *Fax:* (03) 5600479
E-mail: rodneyf@netvision.net.il
Founded: 1974
Publishers representatives, book & journal conference exhibitions.

Freund Publishing House Ltd+
PO Box 35010, Tel Aviv 61350
Tel: (03) 562-8540 *Fax:* (03) 562-8538
Key Personnel
Chief Executive Officer: Edmund Freund
Founded: 1968
Also Translation Agency.
Subjects: Aeronautics, Aviation, Behavioral Sciences, Biography, Chemistry, Chemical Engineering, Engineering (General), Environmental Studies, Mathematics, Mechanical Engineering, Medicine, Nursing, Dentistry, Science (General), Social Sciences, Sociology
ISBN Prefix(es): 965-294
Branch Office(s)
Suite 500, Chesham House, 150 Regent St, London W1R 5FA, United Kingdom

S Friedman Publishing House Ltd
27 Gruzenberg St, Tel Aviv 61292
Mailing Address: PO Box 29350, 65152 Tel Aviv
Tel: (03) 5176091 *Fax:* (03) 5179756
Key Personnel
General Manager: Shmuel Friedman
Man Dir: Dov Friedman; Malka Friedman Shapir

Gefen, *imprint of* Gefen Publishing House Ltd

Gefen Publishing House Ltd+
7 Ariel St, Jerusalem 91060
Mailing Address: PO Box 36004, Jerusalem 91060
Tel: (02) 5380247 *Fax:* (02) 5388423
E-mail: info@gefenpublishing.com
Web Site: www.gefenpublishing.com; www.israelbooks.com
Key Personnel
Chief Executive, Publicity: Murray S Greenfield
Publisher: Ilan Greenfield; Dror Greenfield
Founded: 1981
Subjects: Archaeology, Art, Biblical Studies, Biography, Cookery, English as a Second Language, Fiction, Government, Political Science, Health, Nutrition, History, How-to, Language Arts, Linguistics, Law, Medicine, Nursing, Dentistry, Military Science, Nonfiction (General), Photography, Poetry, Psychology, Psychiatry, Religion - Jewish, Theology, Travel, Wine & Spirits
ISBN Prefix(es): 965-229
Imprints: Gefen
Subsidiaries: Israbook Purchasing Service
U.S. Office(s): Gefen Books, 12 New St, Hewlett, NY 11557, United States, Contact: Maury J Storch *Tel:* 516-295-2805 *Fax:* 516-295-2739 *E-mail:* gefenbooks@compuserve.com
Distributor for Magnes Press Ltd; MOD Publishing Ltd; Yad Uashem
Shipping Address: Gefen Books, 12 New St, Hewlett, NY 11557, United States, Contact: Maury J Storch *Tel:* 516-295-2805 *Fax:* 516-295-2739 *E-mail:* gefenbooks@compuserve.com
Warehouse: Gefen Books, 12 New St, Hewlett, NY 11557, United States, Contact: Maury J Storch *Tel:* 516-295-2805 *Fax:* 516-295-2739 *E-mail:* gefenbooks@compuserve.com
Orders to: Gefen Books, 12 New St, Hewlett, NY 11557, United States, Contact: Maury J Storch *Tel:* 516-295-2805 *Fax:* 516-295-2739 *E-mail:* gefenbooks@compuserve.com

Gvanim Publishing House+
29 Bar Kochba St, 61111 Tel Aviv
Mailing Address: PO Box 11138, 61111 Tel Aviv
Tel: (03) 5281044; (03) 5283648 *Fax:* (03) 5283648
E-mail: traklinm@zahav.net.il
Key Personnel
Man Dir: Maritza Rosman
Founded: 1959
Subjects: Fiction, Poetry
Number of titles published annually: 100 Print
Total Titles: 6,000 Print
Parent Company: Traklin Ltd, Halonot
Associate Companies: Traklin Ltd, Gvanim
Foreign Rights: Pikarsky

Habermann Institute for Literary Research+
20 King David Blvd, Lod 71103
Mailing Address: PO Box 383, Lod 71103
Tel: (08) 9244569; (08) 9229384 *Fax:* (08) 9249466
E-mail: zmalachi@post.tau.ac.il
Key Personnel
Dir: Dr Michal Saraf
Founded: 1982
Subjects: Ethnicity, Literature, Literary Criticism, Essays, Poetry, Religion - Jewish
ISBN Prefix(es): 965-351
Number of titles published annually: 15 Print
Total Titles: 60 Print
Subsidiaries: MAHUT- Journal For Jewish Culture

Hadar Publishing House Ltd
11 Lev Pesach St, North Industrial Area, Lod 71293
Mailing Address: PO Box 4020, Lod 71110
Tel: (08) 9246565 *Fax:* (08) 9251770
E-mail: info@zmora.co.il
Key Personnel
Manager: Uzi Shavit
Man Dir: Zvi Zmora
Founded: 1950
Subjects: History, Literature, Literary Criticism, Essays
ISBN Prefix(es): 965-211

ISRAEL

Haifa University Press
Mount Carmel, Haifa 31905
Tel: (04) 8240111 *Fax:* (04) 8342245
Web Site: www.haifa.ac.il
Key Personnel
Chairman: Kenneth Stow
Coordinator: M Zeridan
Subjects: Archaeology, Biblical Studies, Education, History, Language Arts, Linguistics, Literature, Literary Criticism, Essays, Philosophy, Public Administration
ISBN Prefix(es): 965-311
Distributed by University Press of New England (Outside of Israel)

Hakibbutz Hameuchad Publishing House Ltd
Hayarkon 23, Bnei Brak 51114
Tel: (03) 5785810 *Fax:* (03) 5785811
Key Personnel
Man Dir: Uzi Shavit
Sales Manager: Nahman Gil
Founded: 1940
Subjects: Agriculture, Archaeology, Art, Biblical Studies, Biography, Biological Sciences, Drama, Theater, Economics, Education, Fiction, Foreign Countries, Geography, Geology, Government, Political Science, Health, Nutrition, History, Human Relations, Literature, Literary Criticism, Essays, Music, Dance, Natural History, Nonfiction (General), Philosophy, Poetry, Psychology, Psychiatry, Regional Interests, Religion - Jewish, Social Sciences, Sociology, Theology, Travel, Women's Studies
ISBN Prefix(es): 965-02

Otzar Hamore
c/o Israel Teachers' Union, 8 Ben Saruk St, Tel Aviv 62969
Tel: (03) 6922983 *Fax:* (03) 6922903
Key Personnel
Manager: Avigdor Biton
Man Dir: Joseph Salomon
Founded: 1951
Subjects: Education, Mathematics, Psychology, Psychiatry

Hanitzotz A-Sharara Publishing House
PO Box 41199, Jaffa 61411
Tel: (03) 6839145 *Fax:* (03) 6839148
E-mail: oda@netvision.net.il
Web Site: www.odaction.org; www.hanitzotz.com/challenge
Key Personnel
Publisher: Shimon Tzabar
Editor-in-Chief: Ms Roni Ben Efrat
Editor: Liz Leyh Levac
Language Editor: Stephen Langfur
Founded: 1990
Publishes a bimonthly magazine on the Israeli-Palestinian Conflict, Challenge.
Subjects: Developing Countries, Economics, Education, Film, Video, Foreign Countries, Labor, Industrial Relations, Social Sciences, Sociology, Politics; Israelai Palestinian Conflict

Beth Hatefutsoth
Tel Aviv University Campus, Klausner St, Ramat-Aviv, Tel-Aviv 61392
Mailing Address: PO Box 39359, Ramat Aviv, Tel Aviv 61392
Tel: (03) 646 2020 *Fax:* (03) 646 2134
E-mail: bhwebmas@post.tau.ac.il
Web Site: www.bh.org.il/General/index.asp
ISBN Prefix(es): 965-425

The Historial Society of Israel, *imprint of* The Zalman Shazar Center

Hod-Ami, Computer Books Ltd+
3 Bilu St, Herzliya 46426
Mailing Address: PO Box 6108, 46160 Herzliya
Tel: (09) 9564716 *Fax:* (09) 9571582
E-mail: info@hod-ami.co.il
Web Site: www.hod-ami.co.il
Key Personnel
CEO: Itzhak Amihud
Founded: 1968
Subjects: Computer Science
ISBN Prefix(es): 965-361
Total Titles: 180 Print

IMI, see Israel Music Institute (IMI)

Inbal Publishers+
24 Amal St, Park Afek-Rosh Haayin 48092
Mailing Address: PO Box 11415, Park Afek-Rosh Haayin 48092
Tel: (03) 9030111 *Fax:* (03) 9030888
E-mail: inbalpub@internet-zahav.net
Key Personnel
Man Dir: Shahrokh Sabzerov
Founded: 1980
Specialize in Children's Board Books.
ISBN Prefix(es): 965-332
Distributor for Pestalozzi Verlan (Germany)

Inbal Travel Information+
PO Box 1870, Ramat Gan 52117
Tel: (03) 5753032 *Fax:* (03) 5753130
Key Personnel
President: Michael Shichor
Founded: 1983
Subjects: Travel
ISBN Prefix(es): 965-288
Imprints: Michael's Guides

The Institute for Israeli Arabs Studies
PO Box 810, Ra'anana 43107
Tel: (09) 7486738 *Fax:* (09) 7486341
Founded: 1995
Subjects: Anthropology, Economics, Ethnicity, Government, Political Science, Labor, Industrial Relations, Regional Interests, Religion - Islamic, Social Sciences, Sociology, Women's Studies
ISBN Prefix(es): 965-454

The Institute for the Translation of Hebrew Literature+
23 Baruch Hirsch St, Bnei Brak
Mailing Address: PO Box 10051, Ramat Gan 52001
Tel: (03) 5796830 *Fax:* (03) 5796832
E-mail: hamachon@inter.net.il
Web Site: www.ithl.org.il
Key Personnel
Man Dir: Mrs Nilli Cohen
Office Manager: Mrs Debbie Dagan
Founded: 1962
Subjects: Literature, Literary Criticism, Essays, Poetry
ISBN Prefix(es): 965-255

Intermedia Audio, Video Book Publishing Ltd+
20 Ha-hashmal St, Tel Aviv 61367
Tel: (03) 5608501 *Fax:* (03) 5608513
E-mail: freed@inter.net.il
Key Personnel
Man Dir: Arie Fried
Founded: 1993
Subjects: Business, Education, English as a Second Language, Health, Nutrition, Journalism, Mathematics, Medicine, Nursing, Dentistry, Philosophy, Self-Help, Specialize in Alternative Medicine
ISBN Prefix(es): 965-7079
Total Titles: 25 Print; 6 Audio

The Israel Academy of Sciences & Humanities+
43 Jabotinsky Rd, Jerusalem 91040
Mailing Address: PO Box 4040, Jerusalem 91040
Tel: (02) 636 211 *Fax:* (02) 666 059
E-mail: isracad2@vms.huji.ac.il
Key Personnel
Man Dir: Dr Meir Zadok
Publications Dept: Tami Korman
Founded: 1959
Subjects: Biological Sciences, Environmental Studies, Geography, Geology, History, Philosophy, Religion - Jewish
ISBN Prefix(es): 965-208

Israel Antiquities Authority
Rockefeller Museum Bldg, PO Box 586, Jerusalem 91004
Tel: (02) 5638421 *Fax:* (02) 6289066
Web Site: www.israntique.org.il
Key Personnel
Editor-in-Chief: Tsvika Gal *Tel:* (02) 5638424 *Fax:* (02) 5630526 *E-mail:* tsvika@israntique.org.il
Dir: Shuka Dorfman *Tel:* (02) 6204600/1/8 *Fax:* (02) 6288391 *E-mail:* oshrat@israntique.org.il
Secretary: Harriet Menahem *Tel:* (02) 6204622 *Fax:* (02) 6289066 *E-mail:* harriet@israntique.org.il
Founded: 1990 (Formerly a Department of the Israel Ministry of Education)
Designated by the government of Israel to administer the Law of Antiquities responsible for all archeological matters, custodianship of all archeological sites, conducts excavations & surveys, issues excavation permits, curatorship, documentation & storage of all finds. Also, lends finds to museums, conservation & restoration of antiquities sites & antiquities, documentation, publication & education. Excavation reports.
Publications include excavation reports, surveys, bibliographies, monographs, guide books & two video cassettes.
Subjects: Archaeology, Archaeology of Israel (the Holy Land)
ISBN Prefix(es): 965-406
Total Titles: 74 Print
Online services available through World Wide Web.

Israel Book and Printing Centre
Industry House, 29 Hamered St, Tel Aviv 68125
Tel: (03) 5142895
Web Site: www.expot.gov.il
Key Personnel
Executive: Ronit Adler *Tel:* (03) 5142916 *Fax:* (03) 5142881 *E-mail:* adler@export.gov.il

Israel Exploration Society+
5 Avida St, Jerusalem 91070
Mailing Address: PO Box 7041, 91070 Jerusalem
Tel: (02) 6257991 *Fax:* (02) 6247772
E-mail: ies@vms.huji.ac.il
Web Site: www.hum.huji.ac.il/ies
Key Personnel
Man Dir: J Aviram
Founded: 1913
Subjects: Archaeology, Biblical Studies, Geography, Geology, History
ISBN Prefix(es): 965-221

The Israel Institute for Occupational Safety & Hygiene
22 Maze St, Tel-Aviv
Mailing Address: PO Box 1122, Tel Aviv 61010
Tel: (03) 6875037 *Fax:* (03) 6875038
Key Personnel
Dir: Menachem Schwartz *Tel:* (03) 5266444 *E-mail:* menachem@osh.org.il
Deputy Dir: Chaim Eliyahu *Tel:* (03) 5266432
Publications Manager: Andrei Matias *Tel:* (03) 5266476 *Fax:* (03) 6208232
Distribution Manager: Hizkiya Israel *Tel:* (03) 6575147 *Fax:* (03) 6575148

Subjects: Specialize in books about safety & hygiene in the work place
ISBN Prefix(es): 965-490

Israel Museum Products, Ltd
PO Box 71117, Jerusalem 91710
Tel: (02) 6708811 *Fax:* (02) 5631833
Web Site: www.imj.org.il
Key Personnel
Dir: Rita Gans
ISBN Prefix(es): 965-278

Israel Music Institute (IMI)
24 Kibutz Galuyot Rd, 68166 Tel Aviv
Mailing Address: PO Box 8269, Tel Aviv 61082
Tel: (03) 6811010 *Fax:* (03) 6816070
E-mail: musicinst@bezeqint.net
Web Site: aquanet.co.il/vip/imi
Key Personnel
Dir: Paul Landau
Founded: 1962
Member of IAMIC, International Federation Serious Music Publishers.
Subjects: Music, Dance
Associate Companies: Music in Israel (MII) (production of CDs)
Distributed by AB Nordiska Musikfoerlaget (Sweden); Albersen & Co BV (Holland); Cesky Hudebni Fond (Czech Republic, Hungary & Slovak Republik); Editions Musicales Europeennes (EME) (France, Belgium, Luxembourg, Spain & Portugal); Engstrom & Sodring Musikforlag AS (Denmark); Harald & Lyche & Co AS (Norway); Peer Musikverlag GmbH (Germany, Austria & Switzerland); Ricordi Americana SAEC (Argentina); Theodore Presser Co (USA, Canada & Mexico); Editions Musicales Europeennes (EME)
Distributor for Alkor-Baerenreiter

Israel Program for Scientific Translations, see Keter Publishing House Ltd

Israel Universities Press+
Givat Shaul B, Jerusalem 91071
Mailing Address: PO Box 7145, Jerusalem 91071
Tel: (02) 6557822 *Fax:* (02) 6528962
Key Personnel
Man Dir: Yiftach Dekel
Founded: 1969
Subjects: Government, Political Science, Regional Interests, Social Sciences, Sociology
ISBN Prefix(es): 965-07
Parent Company: Keter Publishing House Ltd

Israeli Music Publications Ltd
25 Keren Hayesod St, Jerusalem 94188
Mailing Address: PO Box 7681, Jerusalem 94188
Tel: (02) 625-1370 *Fax:* (02) 624-1378
E-mail: khanukaev@pop.isracom.net.il
Key Personnel
Dir: Sergei Khanukaev
Founded: 1949
Subjects: Music, Dance
ISBN Prefix(es): 965-259
Distributed by Theodore Presser Co (USA)

Jabotinsky Institute in Israel
38 King George St, Tel-Aviv
Mailing Address: PO Box 23110, Tel-Aviv 61230
Tel: (03) 6210611; (03) 5287320 *Fax:* (03) 5285587
E-mail: jabo@actcom.co.il
Web Site: www.jabotinsky.org
Founded: 1937
Subjects: Government, Political Science, History
ISBN Prefix(es): 965-416

(JDC) Brookdale Institute of Gerontology & Adult Human Development in Israel
JDC Hill, Jerusalem 91130
Mailing Address: PO Box 13087, Jerusalem 91130
Tel: (02) 6557400 *Fax:* (02) 5612391
E-mail: brook@jdc.org.il
Web Site: www.jdc.org.il/brookdale/
Key Personnel
Dir Human Resources & Administration: Rebecca Caspi
Subjects: Health, Nutrition, Social Sciences, Sociology
ISBN Prefix(es): 965-353

Jerusalem Center for Public Affairs
Beit Milken, 13 Tel Hai St, Jerusalem 92107
Tel: (02) 5619281 *Fax:* (02) 5619112
E-mail: jcpa@netvision.net.il
Web Site: www.jcpa.org
Key Personnel
Publications Coordinator: Mark Ami-El
Founded: 1976
Specializes in: Israel, Jewish communities, Jewish political tradition & federalism.
Publishes the Jewish Political Studies Review.
Total Titles: 60 Print

The Jerusalem Publishing House Ltd+
39 Tchernichovsky St, Jerusalem 91071
Mailing Address: PO Box 7147, Jerusalem 91071
Tel: (02) 5617744 *Fax:* (02) 5634266
E-mail: jphgagi@netvision.net.il
Key Personnel
Man Dir: Shlomo S Gafni *Fax:* (02) 54346016
Man Editor: Rachel Gilon
Founded: 1966
Israel Export Institute.
Subjects: Archaeology, History, Religion - Jewish

Biblioteca Judaica, see L B Publishing Co

Karni Publishers Ltd
11 Lev Pesach St, North Industrial Area, Lod 71293
Mailing Address: PO Box 4020, Lod 71110
Tel: (08) 9246565 *Fax:* (08) 9251770
E-mail: info@zmora.co.il
Key Personnel
Man Dir: Ohad Zmora
Founded: 1951
Subjects: Biography, Fiction, How-to, Poetry
ISBN Prefix(es): 965-254
Parent Company: Dvir Publishing House
Subsidiaries: Megiddo Publishing Co Ltd

The Harry Karren Institute for the Analysis of Propaganda, Yad Labanim
Yad Labanim, Wolfson Str, Herzliya 46489
Tel: (09) 500762 *Fax:* (09) 500043
Key Personnel
Contact: Elisa Mermelstein
Subjects: Film, Video, Journalism
ISBN Prefix(es): 965-414

Kernerman Semi-Bilingual Dictionaries, *imprint of* Kernerman Publishing Ltd

Kernerman/Password, see Password Publishers Ltd

Kernerman Publishing Ltd+
Affiliate of K Dictionaries Ltd
46 Hagolan St, Tel Aviv 69718
Tel: (03) 6492715 *Fax:* (03) 6493712
E-mail: kp@internet-zahav.net
Key Personnel
Chief Executive: Ari Kernerman
Production Manager: Nili Sadeh
Founded: 1969
Specialize in English learner's dictionaries for non-native speakers & general English-Hebrew dictionaries.
Subjects: Education, English as a Second Language
ISBN Prefix(es): 965-307
Associate Companies: Password Publishers Ltd
Imprints: Password; Kernerman Semi-Bilingual Dictionaries
Distributor for Chambers-Harrap; Oxford University Press (Israel); Simon & Schuster Education
Orders to: Lonnie Kahn Ltd, 20 Eliahu Eitan St, Rishon L'Tsion 75703 *Tel:* (03) 9518418 *Fax:* (03) 9518415 *E-mail:* kpu@internet-zahav.net

Kernerman Semi-Bilingual Dictionaries, *imprint of* Password Publishers Ltd

Keter, *imprint of* Keter Publishing House Ltd

Keter Publishing House Ltd+
16th Beit Hadfus, Givat Sahul B, Jerusalem 91071
Mailing Address: PO Box 7145, Jerusalem 91071
Tel: (02) 6557822 *Fax:* (02) 6528962
Key Personnel
Man Dir: Yiftach Dekel
Publisher & Editor: Zvika Meir
Founded: 1959
Subjects: Art, Fiction, How-to, Philosophy, Psychology, Psychiatry, Social Sciences, Sociology
ISBN Prefix(es): 965-07
Imprints: Domino; Encyclopedia Judaica; Keter
Subsidiaries: Domino Press; Encyclopaedia Judaica; Israel Program for Scientific Translations

Kiryat Sefer
66 Allenby St, Tel Aviv 65812
Tel: (03) 5178922 *Fax:* (03) 5100227
Key Personnel
Man Dir: Avi Sivan
Founded: 1933
Subjects: Fiction, Poetry, Religion - Other
ISBN Prefix(es): 965-17

Kivunim-Arsan Publishing House+
21 Hgalgal St, Industrial Area, Rehovot 76488
Tel: (08) 9470791 *Fax:* (08) 9469740
Key Personnel
Man Dir: Arieh Sandler
Founded: 1980
Subjects: Humor, Management
ISBN Prefix(es): 965-276
Showroom(s): Elhad Haam 20, Rehovot 76260
Bookshop(s): Elhad Haam 20, Rehovot 76260

Koren Publishers Jerusalem Ltd
33 Herzog St, Jerusalem 42622
Mailing Address: PO Box 4044, Jerusalem 91040
Tel: (02) 5660188 *Fax:* (02) 5666658
Key Personnel
Dir: Eli Koren
Man Dir: Eli Kahn
Founded: 1962
Subjects: Biblical Studies, Religion - Jewish
ISBN Prefix(es): 965-301
Parent Company: Maron Publishing Co Ltd
Distributed by Feldheim Publishers
Distributor for Maron Publishing Co Ltd

L B Publishing, *imprint of* L B Publishing Co

L B Publishing Co+
Imprint of Editorial D A Let C A
PO Box 32056, Jerusalem 91000
Tel: (02) 664 637 *Fax:* (02) 290 774
Key Personnel
President: Lili Brezinger
Editor: Salomon Lewinsky
Founded: 1993
Member of Publishers Association (Israel); Also acts as mediator & publisher for third parties; Specialize in Judaica.

Subjects: History, Regional Interests, Religion - Jewish
ISBN Prefix(es): 965-484
Number of titles published annually: 25 Print
Total Titles: 5 Print
Associate Companies: Reencuentro L B Editorial C A, Caracas, Venezuela
Imprints: L B Publishing
Subsidiaries: Biblioteca Judaica
Distributed by Galerna (Buenos Aires); Nuevas Estructuras (Madrid)
Distributor for Anaya; Planeta-Thesalia; Universidad de Salamanca
Foreign Rep(s): Galerna (Argentina); Gandhi (Mexico); Nuevas Estructuras (Spain)

Ledory Publishing House+
10 Trumpeldor St, PO Box 26507
Tel: (03) 5178555 *Fax:* (03) 9612182
Key Personnel
Manager: Gil Gepner
ISBN Prefix(es): 965-402

Maaliyot-Institute for Research Publications
Mitzpeh Nevo, Maaleh Adumim 90610
Mailing Address: PO Box 113, Maaleh Adumim 90610
Tel: (02) 5353655 *Fax:* (02) 5353947
E-mail: ybm@virtual.co.il
Subjects: Religion - Jewish

Ma'alot Publishing Company Ltd
29 Carlebach St, Tel Aviv 67132
Mailing Address: PO Box 20123, Tel Aviv 61201
Tel: (03) 5614121 *Fax:* (03) 5611996
E-mail: maalot@tbpai.co.il
Key Personnel
Man Dir: Amnon Ben-Shmuel
Founded: 1969
Established by the Book Publishers' Association of Israel as a jointly-owned publishing house in which most of the members of the Association are shareholders.
Parent Company: Book Publishers Association of Israel

Maarachot, *imprint of* Ministry of Defence Publishing House

Ma'ariv Book Guild (Sifriat Ma'ariv)
3A Yoni Netanyahu St, Or-Yehuda 60376
Tel: (03) 5333333 *Fax:* (03) 5333619
Telex: 033735 *Cable:* Ma'ariv Telaviv
Key Personnel
Publisher & Editor-in-Chief: Aryeh Nir
Man Dir: Yitzhak Kfir
Founded: 1954
Subjects: Biography, Education, Fiction, Geography, Geology, Government, Political Science, History, Religion - Other, Science (General), Travel
ISBN Prefix(es): 965-239
Book Club(s): Ma'ariv Book Club

Machbarot Lesifrut
11 Lev Pesach St, North Industrial Area, Lod 71293
Mailing Address: PO Box 4020, Lod 71110
Tel: (08) 9246565 *Fax:* (08) 9251770
E-mail: info@zmora.co.il
Key Personnel
Man Dir: Zvi Zmora
Subjects: Fiction, Government, Political Science, History, Language Arts, Linguistics, Literature, Literary Criticism, Essays
Number of titles published annually: 20 Print
Total Titles: 250 Print
Associate Companies: Zmora Bitan-Publishing House

The Magnes Press+
The Hebrew University, PO Box 39099, Jerusalem 91390
Tel: (02) 6586656 *Fax:* (02) 5633370
E-mail: magnes@vms.huji.ac.il
Key Personnel
Man Dir: Dan Benovici
Founded: 1929
Subjects: Archaeology, Art, Biography, History, Law, Music, Dance, Philosophy, Psychology, Psychiatry, Science (General)
ISBN Prefix(es): 965-223
Parent Company: The Hebrew University, Jerusalem
Imprints: Mount Scopus Press

MAP-Mapping & Publishing Ltd
17 Tchernichovsky St, Tel-Aviv 61560
Mailing Address: PO Box 56024, Tel-Aviv 61560
Tel: (03) 6210500 *Fax:* (03) 5257725
E-mail: info@mapa.co.il
Web Site: www.mapa.co.il
Key Personnel
Man Dir: Dani Tarcz
Editor-in-Chief: Mulli Meltzer
Founded: 1985
Subjects: History, Nonfiction (General), Travel
ISBN Prefix(es): 965-7009
Number of titles published annually: 35 Print
Total Titles: 120 Print
Imprints: Tel Aviv Books

Massada Press Ltd+
Jabotinsky 29, Jerusalem 92141
Mailing Address: PO Box 1232, Jerusalem 91000
Tel: (02) 6719441 *Cable:* ENCYCLOMAS
Key Personnel
Board Chairman, Chief Executive, Rights & Permissions: Alexander Peli
Man Dir: Nathan Regev
Founded: 1932
Subjects: Art, Biography, Cookery, Education, History, How-to, Music, Dance, Philosophy, Psychology, Psychiatry, Religion - Jewish, Religion - Other, Science (General), Social Sciences, Sociology
ISBN Prefix(es): 965-257
Associate Companies: Yeda Lakol Publishing Co Ltd

Massada Publishers Ltd
9 Bialik St, Givatayim 53447
Mailing Address: PO Box 187, Givatayin 53101
Tel: (03) 5716659 *Fax:* (03) 5716639
Telex: 361211 Mape Il *Cable:* PELIPRINT
Key Personnel
Man Dir: Yoav Barash
Founded: 1932
Subjects: Art, Cookery, Fiction, History, How-to
ISBN Prefix(es): 965-10
Associate Companies: Peli Printing Works Ltd; Reprocolor Ltd

Matar - Triwacks Enterprises
5 Hashela St, Tel Aviv 62283
Tel: (03) 5463433 *Fax:* (03) 5461679
Key Personnel
Man Dir: Moshe Triwacks
Subsidiaries: Triwacks Books Ltd

Medcom Ltd
PO Box 751, Petach-Tikva 49107
Tel: (03) 9342852; (03) 9342853 *Fax:* (03) 9343850
Founded: 1981
Subjects: Chemistry, Chemical Engineering, Medicine, Nursing, Dentistry
ISBN Prefix(es): 965-272

Megiddo Publishing Co Ltd, see Karni Publishers Ltd

Michael's Guides, *imprint of* Inbal Travel Information

Midrashiat Naom, Pardess Hanna
3 Achuzat Bayit St, Tel Aviv 65143
Tel: (09) 5172637 *Fax:* (09) 5100594
ISBN Prefix(es): 965-469

Ministry of Defence Publishing House+
27 David Elazar St, Hakiryah 67673
Mailing Address: PO Box 7103, Tel Aviv 67673
Tel: (03) 5655900; (03) 6917940 *Fax:* (03) 5655994; (03) 6375509
Key Personnel
Dir: Joseph Perlovitch
Deputy Dir & Chief Editor: Yishai Cordova
Tel: (03) 5655956
Founded: 1939
Subjects: Foreign Countries, History, Military Science, History of the Land of Israel & Geography; Holocaust; Albums, Picture Books
ISBN Prefix(es): 965-05
Total Titles: 1,500 Print
Imprints: MOD: Broadcast University; Maarachot; To Live (Holocaust)

Mirkam Publishers+
PO Box 10209, Nof-Kingreth, Post Office Rosh Pina 12000
Tel: (06) 6900967 *Fax:* (06) 6900967
Key Personnel
Owner, Chief Editor & General Manager: Yafa Shoham
Founded: 1993
Mostly translations of material to acquaint the Israeli reader with current metaphysical understanding & information.
Privately owned enterprise.
Subjects: Spiritual Growth & Channeling
Total Titles: 15 Print
Distributed by Lior Sharf Marketing & Distribution

Misgav Yerushalayim
Unit of Faculty of Humanities
Faculty of Humanities, The Hebrew University of Jerusalem, Mount Scopus, Jerusalem 91905
Tel: (02) 5883962 *Fax:* (02) 5815460
E-mail: misgav@h2.hum.huji.ac.il
Web Site: www.hum.huji.ac.il/misgav
Key Personnel
Dir: Prof Zeev W Harvey
Deputy Dir: Ms Nitza Genuth
Founded: 1972
University Research Center specializing in academic teaching & research on Shephardi & Oriental Jewry (multi-disciplinary).
Subjects: Art, Ethnicity, History, Language Arts, Linguistics, Literature, Literary Criticism, Essays, Philosophy, Religion - Jewish
ISBN Prefix(es): 965-296
Total Titles: 1 Print
Ultimate Parent Company: The Hebrew University, Jerusalem

Miskal Publishing Ltd+
20 Magshimim St, Petah-Tikwa 49348
Tel: (03) 9246980 *Fax:* (03) 9246985
Key Personnel
President: Dov Eichenwald
Man Dir: Haim Eichenwald
Founded: 1984
Parent Company: Yedioth Ahronot
Warehouse: 19 Merkava St, Holon

M Mizrahi Publishers
67 Levinsky St, Tel Aviv 66855
Tel: (03) 6870936 *Fax:* (03) 5475399 *Cable:* MIZEDITION TELAVIV
Key Personnel
Man Dir: Meir Mizrahi; Israel Mizrahi

Founded: 1960
Subjects: Fiction, History, Medicine, Nursing, Dentistry, Science (General)
Branch Office(s)
33 Hagivea St, Savyon *Tel:* 344661

MOD: Broadcast University, *imprint of* Ministry of Defence Publishing House

Modan Publishers Ltd
Meshek 33, Moshav Ben-Shemen 73115
Tel: (08) 9221821 *Fax:* (08) 9221299
E-mail: modan@modan.co.il
Key Personnel
Man Dir: Oded Modan
Dir: A Friedman
Subjects: Cookery, Religion - Jewish
ISBN Prefix(es): 965-341

The Moshe Dayan Center for Middle Eastern & African Studies
Tel Aviv University, Ramat Aviv, Tel Aviv 69978
Tel: (03) 640-9646 *Fax:* (03) 641-5802
E-mail: dayancen@ccsg.tau.ac.il
Web Site: www.dayan.org *Cable:* 342171 vesy il
Key Personnel
Head of Center: Dr Martin Kramer
Subjects: History, Modern Middle East
ISBN Prefix(es): 965-224
Distributed by Frank Cass; Oxford University Press; Syracuse University Press; Westview Press

Mossad Harav Kook, see Rav Kook Institute

Mount Scopus Press, *imprint of* The Magnes Press

Nehora Press
3 Kiryat Sara, Har Canaan, Safed 13410
Mailing Address: PO Box 2586, Safed 13410
Tel: (04) 6970255 *Fax:* (o4) 6970255
E-mail: nehora@canaan.co.il
Web Site: www.nehorapress.com
Key Personnel
Publisher: Amanda Goodman-Cohen
Founded: 2002
Publish authentic translations of Kabbalah from Hebrew into English.
Member of Publishers Marketing Association.
Subjects: Philosophy, Religion - Jewish
ISBN Prefix(es): 965-7222
Number of titles published annually: 3 Print
Shipping Address: 8153 Hansen Rd NE, Bainbridge Island, WA 98110, United States, D Steinecher *Tel:* 206-780-0124

Nitzanim, *imprint of* Carta, The Israel Map & Publishing Co Ltd

Open University of Israel+
16 Klausner St, Ramat Aviv, Tel Aviv 61392
Mailing Address: PO Box 39328, Tel Aviv 61392
Tel: (03) 6460460 *Fax:* (03) 6419279
Web Site: www.openu.ac.il
Key Personnel
President: Prof Eliahu Nissim
Founded: 1974
Occasionally engages in joint publications with Yale University Press & Boston University.
Specialize in Academic Publications & Textbooks in Hebrew.
Subjects: Accounting, Biblical Studies, Biological Sciences, Chemistry, Chemical Engineering, Computer Science, Economics, Education, Government, Political Science, History, Journalism, Literature, Literary Criticism, Essays, Management, Mathematics, Physics, Psychology, Psychiatry, Religion - Jewish, Social Sciences, Sociology

ISBN Prefix(es): 965-302; 965-06
U.S. Office(s): American Friends of the Open Univeristy of Israel, 180 W 80 St, New York, NY 10024, United States *Tel:* 212-712-1800 *Fax:* 212-496-3296

Or-Teva, *imprint of* Or'am Publishers

Or'am Publishers+
28 Itzhak Sade St, Tel Aviv 67212
Tel: (03) 5372277 *Fax:* (03) 5372281
E-mail: orampub@netvision.net.il
Web Site: www.oram.co.il
Key Personnel
Man Dir: Or'am Shatz; Shoshana Shatz
Founded: 1974
ISBN Prefix(es): 965-230
Total Titles: 1,700 Print; 10 Audio
Imprints: Or-Teva

Orbach Editions Ltd, *imprint of* Bitan Publishers Ltd

Papyrus, *imprint of* Dyonon/Papyrus Publishing House of the Tel-Aviv

Password, *imprint of* Kernerman Publishing Ltd

Password Publishers Ltd+
61 Shalma Rd, Tel Aviv 66089
Mailing Address: PO Box 5138, Tel Aviv 61051
Tel: (03) 6833566 *Fax:* (03) 6833702
E-mail: pass@password.co.il
Web Site: password.co.il
Key Personnel
Man Dir: Ilan Kernerman *E-mail:* ik@password.co.il
Founded: 1993
Localized language versions appear by local publishers worldwide.
Subjects: English as a Second Language, Language Arts, Linguistics, Specializing in the development & global marketing of English learner's dictionaries for different levels, in print & on CD
ISBN Prefix(es): 965-90207
Total Titles: 30 Print; 2 CD-ROM
Imprints: Kernerman Semi-Bilingual Dictionaries
Distributed by Alma Littera (Territory restricted to Lithuania); Aschehoug (Territory restricted to Norway); Atuakkiorfik (Territory restricted to Greenland); Bookman Books (Territory restricted to Taiwan); Boustany's Publishing House (Territory restricted to Egypt); Colibri (Territory restricted to Bulgaria); Corona (Territory restricted to Sweden); DZS (Territory restricted to Slovenia); Fragment (Territory restricted to Czech Republic); Hemus (Territory restricted to Bulgaria); Kernerman Publishing (Territory restricted to Israel); Kesaint Blanc (Territory restricted to Indonesia); Lund Humphries (Territory restricted to the UK); Mal og Menning (Territory restricted to Iceland); Martins Fontes Editora (Territory restricted to Brazil); McGraw-Hill Libri Italia (Territory restricted to Italy); Media Trade-SPN (Territory restricted to Slovak Republic); Mlada Fronta (Territory restricted to Czech Republic); Modulo Editeur (Territory restricted to Canada); Mrljes (Territory restricted to Yugoslavia); Penerbitan Pelangi (Territory restricted to Malaysia); PWN (Territory restricted to Poland); Skolska Knjiga (Territory restricted to Croatia); TEA (Territory restricted to Estonia & Russia)); Thai Watana Panich (Territory restricted to Thailand); Tramontana (Territory restricted to Italy); WSOY (Territory restricted to Findland); YBM Si-sa-yong-o-sa (Territory restricted to Korea); Zanichelli Editore (Territory restricted to Italy); Zvaigzne ABC Publishers (Territory restricted to Latvia)

Pitspopany Press+
c/o Simcha Publishing Co, PO Box 4636, Jerusalem 91044
Tel: (02) 6233507 *Fax:* (02) 6233510
E-mail: pitspop@netvision.net.il
Web Site: www.pitspopany.com
Key Personnel
President: Yaacov Peterseil
Administrator: Wendy Tohar
Founded: 1993
Subjects: Cookery, Fiction, Health, Nutrition, Humor, Mysteries, Religion - Jewish, Science Fiction, Fantasy, Self-Help, Adult Fiction & Non-Fiction
ISBN Prefix(es): 965-483; 1-930-143; 0-943-706
Number of titles published annually: 15 Print
Total Titles: 100 Print
Imprints: Devora Publishing Co; Simcha Pub
U.S. Office(s): 40 E 78 St, Suite 16D, New York, NY 10021, United States *Tel:* 212-472-4959 *Fax:* 212-472-6253
Shipping Address: 7253 Grayson Rd, Harrisburg, PA 17111, United States *Tel:* 712-564-2111

Prolog Publishing House
PO Box 300, Rosh Ha'ayin 48101
Tel: (03) 9022904 *Fax:* (03) 9022906
Web Site: www.prolog.co.il
Key Personnel
Man Dir: Ben Naim Raanan
Founded: 1988
Specialize in language teaching audio-video cassette courses, how-to books.
Subjects: How-to, Language Arts, Linguistics

Rav Kook Institute+
Maimon St, Jerusalem 91006
Mailing Address: PO Box 642, Jerusalem 91006
Tel: (02) 6526231 *Fax:* (02) 6526968
Key Personnel
Dir General: Rabbi Joseph Mowshovitz
Founded: 1937
A non-profit-making public corporation supported by the Jewish Agency, Ministry of Education & Culture & Ministry of Religious Affairs. Also provides financial support for works in above subjects.
Subjects: Biography, Philosophy, Religion - Jewish, Religion - Other, Theology
Number of titles published annually: 10 Print
Total Titles: 3,000 Print

Rolnik Publishers+
PO Box 17075, Tel Aviv 61170
Tel: (03) 6496663 *Fax:* (03) 6478661
E-mail: rolknik@attglobal.net
Web Site: www.rolnik.com; www.bible2000.net
Key Personnel
Publisher: Amos Rolnik
Founded: 1970
Subjects: Art, Biblical Studies, Film, Video, Israel, Hebrew Studies
ISBN Prefix(es): 965-326

Rubin Mass Ltd+
PO Box 990, Jerusalem 91009
Tel: (02) 627-7863 *Fax:* (02) 627-7864
E-mail: rmass@inter.net.il
Web Site: www.age.co.il/mas
Key Personnel
Man Dir: Mr Oren Mass
Founded: 1927
Also acts as exporters of Israeli publications & periodicals.
Subjects: Biblical Studies, Biography, Education, Government, Political Science, Medicine, Nursing, Dentistry, Philosophy, Psychology, Psychiatry, Publishing & Book Trade Reference, Religion - Jewish, Religion - Other
ISBN Prefix(es): 965-09
Distributor for Carta; Yad Vashm

ISRAEL

Saar Publishing House
39 Basel St, Tel-Aviv 62744
Mailing Address: PO Box 26243, Tel Aviv 62744
Tel: (03) 5445292 *Fax:* (03) 5445293
Key Personnel
Man Dir: Saar Hanoch
Founded: 1979
Specialize in the publication of original & translated poetry.
Subjects: Fiction, Humor, Travel

Sadan Publishing Ltd+
One David Hamelech St, Tel Aviv 64953
Mailing Address: PO Box 16096, Tel Aviv 64953
Tel: (03) 6954402 *Fax:* (03) 6953122
Key Personnel
President: David Sadan
Founded: 1962
Firm is also an international co-publisher & packager.
Subjects: Archaeology, Biblical Studies, Law
ISBN Prefix(es): 965-234
Subsidiaries: Sadan Publication International Inc

Schlesinger Institute
PO Box 3235, Jerusalem 91031
Tel: (02) 6555266 *Fax:* (02) 6523295
E-mail: medhal@szmc.org.il
Web Site: www.szmc.org.il
Key Personnel
Dir: Dr Mordechai Halperin
Subjects: Law, Medicine, Nursing, Dentistry, Religion - Jewish

Schocken Publishing House for Children, *imprint of* Schocken Publishing House Ltd

Schocken Publishing House Ltd+
24 Nathan Yelin Mor St, Tel Aviv 67015
Mailing Address: P O Box 2316, Tel Aviv 61022
Tel: (03) 5610130 *Fax:* (03) 5622668
Web Site: www.schockem.co.il *Cable:* SCHOCKENIS
Key Personnel
Man Dir: Racheli Edelman *E-mail:* racheli@iol.co.il
Production: Dita Eliaz
Rights & Permissions: Ms Gur Efrat
Founded: 1938
Member of Israeli Book Publishers Association.
Subjects: Anthropology, Behavioral Sciences, Child Care & Development, Criminology, Drama, Theater, Economics, Education, Fiction, Health, Nutrition, History, Law, Literature, Literary Criticism, Essays, Nonfiction (General), Philosophy, Poetry, Psychology, Psychiatry, Religion - Jewish, Travel, Western Fiction, Women's Studies
ISBN Prefix(es): 965-19
Imprints: Schocken Publishing House for Children; Shin, Shin, Shin
Divisions: Schocken Publishing House
Warehouse: Schocken Publishing House, 19 Lilienblum St, Tel Aviv

Shalem Press
22A Hatzfira Street, Jerusalem 93102
Tel: (02) 566-0601 *Fax:* (02) 566-0590
E-mail: shalemorder@shalem.org.il
Web Site: www.shalem.org.il
Key Personnel
Contact: Anat Altman *E-mail:* anata@shalem.org.il; Shmnel Reisman *E-mail:* shmuelr@shalem.org.il
Founded: 1994
Publish original books in Hebrew & English. Translate books into Hebrew.
Subjects: Economics, Government, Political Science, History, Philosophy, Cultural Issues
ISBN Prefix(es): 965-7052
Total Titles: 3 Print

Parent Company: The Shalem Center
U.S. Office(s): The Shalem Center, 1140 Connecticut Ave NW, Suite 801, Washington, DC 20036, United States *Tel:* 202-887-1270 *Fax:* 202-887-1277
Distributed by Armony Ltd

Shin, Shin, Shin, *imprint of* Schocken Publishing House Ltd

Sifri, *imprint of* Steimatzky Group Ltd

Sifri Ltd
PO Box 526, Tel Aviv 61004
Tel: (03) 5784679
Key Personnel
Dir: Yehoshua Matzliah; Eri M Steimatzky

Sifriat Poalim Ltd
24 Kibbutz Galuyot St, Merkazim Buil Gate 3, Tel Aviv 68166
Mailing Address: PO Box 37068, Tel Aviv 61369
Tel: (03) 5183143 *Fax:* (03) 5183191
E-mail: akantor@inter.net.il
Key Personnel
Man Dir: Avram Kantor
Management: Shlomo Zur
Encyclopedias: Amram Gordon
Production: Yaakov Shaia
Rights & Permissions: Yona Herzberg
Founded: 1939
Subjects: Art, Fiction, History, Labor, Industrial Relations, Philosophy, Social Sciences, Sociology
ISBN Prefix(es): 965-04

Simcha Pub, *imprint of* Pitspopany Press

Samuel Simson Ltd
5 Tel Giborim St, Teper House, Tel Aviv 68105
Tel: (03) 5181604 *Fax:* (03) 5181544
E-mail: sefer-lakol@mixam.co.il
Key Personnel
Man Dir: Rahamim Zalof
Founded: 1954

Sinai Publishing Co
72 Allenby Rd, Tel Aviv 65812
Tel: (03) 5163672 *Fax:* (03) 5176783
Key Personnel
Man Dir: Moshe Schlesinger
Founded: 1853
Subjects: Religion - Jewish
Subsidiaries: Sinai Export Co Ltd
Bookshop(s): Sinai Bookstore, 72 Allenby St, Tel Aviv

R Sirkis Publishers Ltd+
131 Bialik St, Ramat-Gan 52523
Tel: (03) 7510792 *Fax:* (03) 7513750
E-mail: sirkispb@inter.net.il
Key Personnel
Man Dir: Rafael Sirkis
President, Chief Editor: Ruth Sirkis
Founded: 1983
Subjects: Archaeology, Art, Child Care & Development, Cookery, Crafts, Games, Hobbies, Fashion, Gardening, Plants, Health, Nutrition, How-to, Psychology, Psychiatry, Self-Help, Travel
ISBN Prefix(es): 965-387

Y Sreberk+
16 Balfour St, Tel Aviv 65211
Tel: (03) 6293343 *Fax:* (03) 6299297
Key Personnel
Man Dir: Zeev Namir
Production Manager: Y Namir

Founded: 1951
Subjects: Literature, Literary Criticism, Essays, Music, Dance

Steimatzky, *imprint of* Steimatzky Group Ltd

Steimatzky Group Ltd+
11 Hakishon St, Bnei-Brak 51114
Mailing Address: PO Box 1444, Bnei-Brak 51114
Tel: (03) 5775777 *Fax:* (03) 5794567
E-mail: info@steimatzky.co.il
Web Site: www.ibooks.co.il
Key Personnel
CEO: Eri M Steimatzky
Man Dir: Yehoshua Matzliah
Founded: 1925
130 bookshops around the country. Also wholesaler, distributor, publisher, book club & mail order.
Subjects: Art, Biography, Fiction, Music, Dance, Religion - Other, Social Sciences, Sociology
ISBN Prefix(es): 965-236
Associate Companies: SIFFRI Ltd
Imprints: Sifri; Steimatzky

Steinhart-Katzir Publishers+
PO Box 8333, Netanya 42505
Tel: (09) 8854770 *Toll Free Tel:* 800-22-5854 *Fax:* (09) 8854771
E-mail: webmaster@haolam.co.il
Web Site: www.haolam.co.il
Key Personnel
Man Dir: Ohad Sharav
Founded: 1991
Subjects: Travel
ISBN Prefix(es): 965-420
Number of titles published annually: 20 Print
Total Titles: 100 Print
Distributor for National Geographic; Berndtson & Berndtson; Freytag & Berndt; ITM; Karto Alatier

Talmudic Encyclopedia Publications
1 Hapisga St, Jerusalem 91160
Mailing Address: PO Box 16066, Jerusalem 91160
Tel: (02) 6423242 *Fax:* (02) 6423919
Key Personnel
Man Dir: Yehoshua Hutner
Founded: 1949
Subjects: Religion - Jewish
ISBN Prefix(es): 965-445

Tamai Books, *imprint of* Dekel Publishing House

Tcherikover Publishers Ltd
12 Hasharon St, Tel Aviv 66185
Tel: (03) 6870621; (03) 6396099 *Fax:* (03) 6874729
Key Personnel
Man Dir: Moshe Barkay *E-mail:* barkay@inter.net.il
Manager, Editorial: S Tcherikover
Subjects: Art, Criminology, Economics, Education, Geography, Geology, History, Language Arts, Linguistics, Literature, Literary Criticism, Essays, Management, Nonfiction (General), Psychology, Psychiatry
ISBN Prefix(es): 965-16

c/o Teachers' Union, see Otzar Hamore

Tel Aviv Books, *imprint of* MAP-Mapping & Publishing Ltd

Tel Aviv Books Ltd
Imprint of MAP - Mapping and Publishing
18 Tchernikhovsky St, Tel Aviv 61560
Tel: (03) 6203252 *Fax:* (03) 5257725

PUBLISHERS
ISRAEL

Tel-Aviv University+
The Jaffee Center for Strategic Studies, Ramat Aviv, Tel-Aviv 69978
Mailing Address: PO Box 39040, Ramat Aviv, Tel-Aviv 69978
Tel: (03) 6424571; (03) 6409200; (03) 6426682 *Fax:* (03) 6422404; (03) 6408355
Key Personnel
Prof: Zeev Maoz
Founded: 1977
Subjects: Foreign Countries, Government, Political Science, History, Military Science, Regional Interests, Social Sciences, Sociology
ISBN Prefix(es): 965-459
U.S. Office(s): Westview Press, Boulder, CO, United States
Distributed by Jerusalem Post (Israel); Westview Press

Terra Sancta Arts+
PO Box 10009, Tel Aviv 61100
Tel: (03) 6499520; (03) 6499525 *Fax:* (03) 6490532
Key Personnel
Man Dir: Gil Ran; Nachman Ran
Founded: 1972
Subjects: Biblical Studies, Religion - Other
ISBN Prefix(es): 965-260
Shipping Address: 31 Ehud Str, Tel-Aviv 69936

Tirosh Communication Ltd
PO Box 6428, Tel-Aviv 61063
Tel: (03) 6044959 *Fax:* (03) 6053840
E-mail: hgeffen@netvision.net.il
Key Personnel
International Rights: Amos Geffen
Founded: 1969
ISBN Prefix(es): 965-330

To Live (Holocaust), *imprint of* Ministry of Defence Publishing House

Harry S Truman Research Institute for the Advancement for Jerusalem+
Hebrew University of Jerusalem, Mount Scopus, Jerusalem 91905
Tel: (02) 58823000; (02) 58823001; (02) 5882315 *Fax:* (02) 5828076
E-mail: mstruman@pluto.mscc.huji.ac.il
Web Site: atar.mscc.huji.ac.il/~truman
Telex: SCOPUS JERUSALEM
Key Personnel
Chairman: William A Brown
Dir: Prof Amnon Cohen *E-mail:* mstruman@mscc.huji.ac.il
Executive Dir: Dr Edy Kaufman *E-mail:* msek@mscc.huji.ac.il
Founded: 1966
ISBN Prefix(es): 965-222

Tsohar Publications, *imprint of* Breslov Research Institute

University of Haifa Library
Abba Khoushy Rd, Mt Carmel Central, 31999 Haifa
Tel: (04) 257753 *Fax:* (04) 342104
E-mail: webmaster@lib.haifa.ac.il
Web Site: www-lib.haifa.ac.il
Key Personnel
Dir: Baruch Kipnis *E-mail:* baruch@univ.haifa.ac.il
Head of Administration: Ms Humi Rekem
Subjects: Library & Information Sciences

University Publishing Projects Ltd+
28 HaNatziv St, Tel Aviv 67015
Tel: (03) 562-6622 *Fax:* (03) 562-6879
E-mail: uppbkshp@upp.co.il
Web Site: www.upp.co.il/home.htm

Key Personnel
Dir: Mordechai Mass; Natan Eden
Founded: 1970
Subjects: English as a Second Language, Religion - Jewish
ISBN Prefix(es): 965-372
Imprints: ESH (English for Speakers of Hebrew)

Urim Publications+
PO Box 52287, Jerusalem 91521
Tel: (02) 679-7633 *Fax:* (02) 679-7634
E-mail: publisher@urimpublications.com
Web Site: www.urimpublications.com
Key Personnel
Publisher: Tzvi Mauer
Children's Book Editor: Shari Dash Greenspan *E-mail:* children@urimpublications.com
Founded: 1997
Publisher & worldwide distributor of new & classic books with Jewish content.
Subjects: Biblical Studies, Biography, Ethnicity, Fiction, Human Relations, Literature, Literary Criticism, Essays, Religion - Jewish, Women's Studies
ISBN Prefix(es): 965-7108
Number of titles published annually: 8 Print
Total Titles: 22 Print; 1 CD-ROM
U.S. Office(s): Lambda Publishers, 3709 13 Ave, Brooklyn, NY 11218, United States *Tel:* 718-972-5449 *Fax:* 718-972-6307
Distributed by Ingram (North America)
Distributor for Lambda Publishers, Inc (Jewish bookstores in North America)

The Van Leer Jerusalem Institute
PO Box 4070, Jerusalem 91040
Tel: (02) 5605288; (02) 5605289 *Fax:* (02) 5619293
E-mail: values@vanleer.org.il
Web Site: www.vanleer.org.il/eng
Key Personnel
Executive Editor: Esther Shashar
Founded: 1959
Subjects: Foreign Countries, Government, Political Science, Psychology, Psychiatry, Science (General), Social Sciences, Sociology
ISBN Prefix(es): 965-271; 965-346

Yachdav, United Publishers Co Ltd
29 Carlebach St, Tel Aviv 67132
Mailing Address: PO Box 20123, Tel Aviv 61201
Tel: (03) 5614121 *Fax:* (03) 5611996
E-mail: maalot@tbpai.co.il
Key Personnel
Man Dir: Amnon Ben-Shmuel
Founded: 1960
Established by the Book Publishers' Association of Israel as a jointly-owned publishing house in which most of the members of the Association are shareholders.
Subjects: Philosophy, Psychology, Psychiatry, Public Administration, Social Sciences, Sociology
Parent Company: Book Publishers Association of Israel

Yad Eliahu Kitov
PO Box 894, Jerusalem 91008
Tel: (02) 6248868 *Fax:* (02) 6248838
Key Personnel
Man Dir: Chanoch Ben-Arza *E-mail:* benarza@netvision.net.il
Subjects: Religion - Other
ISBN Prefix(es): 965-252

Yad Izhak Ben-Zvi Press+
Ben-Zvi Institute, Abrabanel 12, Rehavia, Jerusalem 91076
Mailing Address: PO Box 7660, Jerusalem 91076
Tel: (02) 53988888 *Fax:* (02) 5638310
E-mail: yadbz@h2.hum.huji.ac.il

Web Site: ybz.org.il
Key Personnel
Dir: Dr Zvi Zameret
Chairman, Public Governing Council: Teddy Kollek
English Publications Coordinator: Yohai Goell
Tel: (02) 5398825
Founded: 1966
Specialize in the history of Palestine/Israel & the oriental Jewish Communities.
Subjects: Geography, Geology, History, Regional Interests, Religion - Jewish
ISBN Prefix(es): 965-235; 965-217
Total Titles: 300 Print

Yad Tabenkin
Ramat Efal 52960
Tel: (03) 5301217; (03) 5301227; (03) 5344458 *Fax:* (03) 5346376
E-mail: yadtab@inter.net.il
Web Site: www.ic.org/icsa.efal.html
Founded: 1976 (Research Institute)
Number of titles published annually: 4 Print

Yad Vashem - The Holocaust Martyrs' & Heroes' Remembrance Authority+
PO Box 3477, Jerusalem 91034
Tel: (02) 6443400 *Fax:* (02) 6443443
E-mail: general.information@yadvashem.org.il
Web Site: www.yad-vashem.org.il *Cable:* YADVASHEM JERUSALEM
Key Personnel
Chairman: Avner Shalev
Vice Chairman: Johanan Bein
Editorial: Prof Israel Gutman
Yad Vashem Studies: David Silberklang
Secretary-General: Ishai Amrami
Administrative Dir: Vashem Yad
Publications: Esther Aran
Founded: 1953
Subjects: Biography, Education, History, Nonfiction (General), Holocaust Research
ISBN Prefix(es): 965-308
Branch Office(s)
Heychal Wolyn, 10 Korazin St, PO Box 803, Givatayim
U.S. Office(s): American Society for Yad Vashem, 500 Fifth Ave, No 1600, New York, NY 10110, United States
Distributed by Rubin Mass Ltd, Publishers & Booksellers
Bookshop(s): Yad Vashem Distribution, PO Box 3477, Jerusalem 91034

Yaron Golan Publishers
3 Burla St, Tel Aviv 69364
Tel: (03) 6992867 *Fax:* (03) 6952664
Specializes in Hebrew books of prose & poetry.
ISBN Prefix(es): 965-395
Total Titles: 10 Print

Yavneh Publishing House Ltd+
4 Mazeh St, Tel Aviv 65213
Tel: (03) 6297856 *Fax:* (03) 6293638
E-mail: yavneh@attglobal.net
Web Site: www.dbook.co.il
Key Personnel
Man Dir: Eliav Cohen
Founded: 1932
Subjects: Fiction, Music, Dance, Religion - Jewish, Religion - Other, Science (General)

Yedioth Ahronoth Books+
3 Mikunis St, Tel Aviv 61376
Mailing Address: PO Box 37744, Tel Aviv 61376
Tel: (03) 6888 466 *Fax:* (03) 5377820
E-mail: books@yedioth.co.il
Web Site: www.yediothsfarim.co.il
Telex: 33847
Key Personnel
Man Dir: Mr Dov Eichenwald
Editor-in-Chief: Aliza Ziegler
Founded: 1952

ISRAEL

Subjects: Fiction, Health, Nutrition, How-to, Music, Dance, Nonfiction (General), Religion - Jewish
ISBN Prefix(es): 965-482
Total Titles: 150 Print
Parent Company: Yedioth Ahronoth (The Evening Newspaper of Israel)
Associate Companies: Books in the Attaic, Hakalir St 25, Tel aviv, Editor-in-Chief: Yehuda Melzer Tel: (03) 3524 8324 E-mail: ilai@actcom.co.il
Subsidiaries: Adi; Miskal
Warehouse: 19 Hamerkava St, Holon

Y L Peretz Publishing Co
14 Brenner St, Tel Aviv 63826
Tel: (03) 5281751 Fax: (03) 5257983
Key Personnel
Man Dir: Israel Stein
Founded: 1956
Subjects: Art, History, Literature, Literary Criticism, Essays, Philosophy, Poetry, Religion - Jewish, Social Sciences, Sociology
ISBN Prefix(es): 965-7012

Zakheim Publishing House+
8 Sokolov St, 52571 Ramat Gan
Mailing Address: PO Box 9933, 52111 Ramat Gan
Tel: (03) 6130434 Fax: (03) 6130443
Key Personnel
General Manager: Eli Zakheim
Founded: 1967
Publishing house, wholesaler & distributor of educational materials & electronic kits of educational subjects. Specializes in children's books, educational equipment, encyclopedias & dictionaries for youths & children.
Total Titles: 4 Print

The Zalman Shazar Center+
22 Rashba St, Jerusalem 91041
Mailing Address: PO Box 4179, Jerusalem 91041
Tel: (02) 5637171 Fax: (02) 5662135
E-mail: shazar@shazar.org.il
Web Site: www.shazar.org.il
Key Personnel
Chairman & Editorial, Hebrew: Prof Richard I Cohen
Executive Dir & Dir, Rights & Permissions: Zvi Yekutiel
Editorial Board Secretary: Maayan Avineri-Rebhun E-mail: maayan@shazar.org.il
Founded: 1973
Specialize in Jewish History.
Subjects: History, Religion - Jewish, Pictorial Albums, Historial Novels for Youth
ISBN Prefix(es): 965-227
Total Titles: 230 Print
Imprints: The Historial Society of Israel; Zion

Zion, imprint of The Zalman Shazar Center

Zmora-Bitan, Publishers Ltd
11 Lev Pesach St, North Industrial Area, Lod 71293
Tel: (08) 9246565 Fax: (08) 9251770
E-mail: info@zmora.co.il
Key Personnel
Man Dir: Ohad Zmora
Publisher & Publicity: Asher Bitan
Sales: Eran Zmora
Production: Maya Dvash
Founded: 1973
Subjects: Anthropology, Biography, Cookery, Economics, Fiction, Government, Political Science, History, Nonfiction (General), Self-Help
ISBN Prefix(es): 965-325; 965-03
Associate Companies: Bitan; Machbarot Lesifrut
Subsidiaries: Alpha Publishing House; Dvir Publishing House; Erez Books; Metziuth Books; Marganit Books

Italy

General Information

Capital: Rome
Language: Italian. Various others according to region
Religion: Predominantly Roman Catholic
Population: 57.6 million
Bank Hours: 0830-1330, 1500-1600 Monday-Friday
Shop Hours: 0830 or 0900-1300, 1500 or 1600-1930 or 2000 Monday-Saturday; many close Monday morning
Currency: 100 Eurocents = 1 Euro; 1936.27 Italian lira = 1 Euro
Export/Import Information: Member of the European Economic Community. 4% VAT on books; advertising matter other than single copies is dutied. No import license required.
Copyright: UCC, Berne, Florence (see Copyright Conventions, pg xi)

A & A+
Via Borgonvovo, 3, 20121 Milan
Tel: (02) 876999 Fax: (02) 877928
Founded: 1990
Acts as Photojournalist Agent.
Subjects: Photography
ISBN Prefix(es): 88-85279

Gruppo Abele+
Via Carlo Alberto 18, 10123 Turin
Tel: (011) 54,54,89; (011) 814,42,715 Fax: (011) 54.52.41
E-mail: egamedia@mbox.vol.it
Key Personnel
Man Dir & Editorial: Carla Martino
Sales: Doretta Graneris
Production: Pierangelo Bassignana
Publicity, Rights & Permissions: Silvia Mazza
Founded: 1983
Subjects: Child Care & Development, Communications, Education, Environmental Studies, Ethnicity, Health, Nutrition, Human Relations, Military Science
ISBN Prefix(es): 88-7670
Warehouse: Via Bologne 164, Turin

Edizioni Abete+
Via Prenestina 685, 00155 Rome
Tel: (06) 225821 Fax: (06) 2282960
Telex: 620370 ABETE I
Key Personnel
Chief Executive: Dr Luigi Abete
Editorial: Dr Giancarlo Abete
Sales: Dr Francesco Matassi; Franco Morbiducci
Founded: 1946
Subjects: Drama, Theater, Economics, Environmental Studies, Literature, Literary Criticism, Essays, Philosophy
ISBN Prefix(es): 88-7047
Parent Company: ABeTE SpA - Azienda Beneventana Tipografica Editoriale

Editrice Abitare Segesta
Corso Monforte 15, 20122 Milan
Tel: (02) 76.09.02.11 Fax: (02) 76.02.31.40
Web Site: www.abitare.it
Telex: 315302 ABIT I
Key Personnel
Publisher: Renato Minetto
Founded: 1976
ISBN Prefix(es): 88-86116

Accademia (Milano)
Via Columella 36, Milan 20128
Tel: (02) 2552593
Founded: 1967
Subjects: Literature, Literary Criticism, Essays

BOOK

Mario Adda Editore SNC
Via Tanzi 59, 70121 Bariums
Tel: (080) 5539502 Fax: (080) 5539502
Key Personnel
Man Dir & other offices: Mario Adda
Founded: 1963
Subjects: Archaeology, Architecture & Interior Design, Art, Crafts, Games, Hobbies, History, Literature, Literary Criticism, Essays, Music, Dance, Philosophy, Photography, Poetry, Regional Interests, Social Sciences, Sociology
ISBN Prefix(es): 88-8082

Adea Books, imprint of Adea Edizioni

Adea Edizioni+
Via Lepontina 17, 30159 Milan
Tel: (02) 69006933 Fax: (02) 69007135
Key Personnel
Editor: Mauro Maggio
Founded: 1992
Subjects: Astrology, Occult, Biography, Human Relations, Literature, Literary Criticism, Essays, Philosophy, Physical Sciences, Religion - Buddhist, Theology
ISBN Prefix(es): 88-86274
Imprints: Adea Books
Subsidiaries: Adea Education; Adea Incense; Adea Music; Adea SRL

Adelphi Edizioni SpA+
Via San Giovanni sul Muro 14, 20121 Milan
Tel: (02) 725731 Fax: (02) 89010337
E-mail: rightsdept@adelphi.it
Web Site: www.adelphi.it; www.adelphiaua.it
Key Personnel
Man Dir, Editorial Dir & Chairman: Roberto Calasso
Publicity: Matteo Codignola
Foreign Rights Manager: Francesca Sintini E-mail: rightsdept@adelphi.it
Founded: 1962
Subjects: Anthropology, Biography, Fiction, History, Literature, Literary Criticism, Essays, Mathematics, Mysteries, Philosophy, Physics, Poetry, Religion - Buddhist, Religion - Hindu, Science (General)
ISBN Prefix(es): 88-459
Bookshop(s): Via Brentano 2, 20121 Milano
Warehouse: Via Mecenate 87/4, I-20138 Milan
Orders to: Servizio Vendita Libri c/o RCS Libri & Grandi Opere SpA, Via Mecenate 91, I-20138 Milan Tel: (02) 50951

AdP, imprint of Segretariato Nazionale Apostolato della Preghiera

Adriana Gallina Editore, imprint of Adriano Gallina Editore sas

Adriatica Editrice
Via Andrea da Bariums 119/121, 70121 Bariums
Tel: (080) 5211341 Fax: (080) 5235640
E-mail: edit_adriatica@teseo.it
Web Site: www.teseo.it/edit_adriatica
Subjects: Ethnicity, Literature, Literary Criticism, Essays, Poetry

Aesthetica
Via Giusti 25, 90144 Palermo
Tel: (091) 308290 Fax: (091) 308290
E-mail: aesthetica@unipa.it
Key Personnel
President: Lucia Pizzo
Editorial Dir: Luigi Russo
Founded: 1985

Subjects: Art, Philosophy
ISBN Prefix(es): 88-7726

Edizioni della Fondazione Giovanni Agnelli
(Giovanni Agnelli Foundation Publishing)+
Via Giacosa 38, 10125 Turin
Tel: (011) 6500500 *Fax:* (011) 6502777
E-mail: staff@fga.it
Web Site: www.fondazione-agnelli.it
Key Personnel
President: Marco Demarie
Sales Mgr: Franco Picollo
Subjects: Economics, Geography, Geology, Government, Political Science, Social Sciences, Sociology
Number of titles published annually: 8 Print

De Agostini Scolastica
Via Federico from Montefeltro 6/A, 20156 Milan
Tel: (02) 380861 *Fax:* (02) 38086448
Web Site: www.scuola.com/inviarisposta.html
Subjects: Education, Geography, Geology, History, Science (General)
ISBN Prefix(es): 88-423; 88-402; 88-415

AIB Associazione Italiana Biblioteche+
Viale del Castro Pretorio 105, 00185 Rome
Tel: (06) 4463532 *Fax:* (06) 4441139
E-mail: aib@aib.it
Web Site: www.aib.it
Key Personnel
President: Igino Poggiali *E-mail:* poggiali@aib.it
Secretary: Andrea Paoli *E-mail:* paoli@aib.it
Subjects: Library & Information Sciences
ISBN Prefix(es): 88-7812
Number of titles published annually: 10 Print; 1 CD-ROM

Alba
Corso Porta Po 82/A, 44100 Ferrara
Tel: (0532) 249854 *Fax:* (0532) 249854
E-mail: alba_editrice@virgilio.it
Web Site: digilander.libero.it/albaeditrice
Key Personnel
Head of Company: Flavio Puviani
Founded: 1971
Subjects: Art, Literature, Literary Criticism, Essays, Poetry

Ermanno Albertelli Editore+
Via S Sonnino 34, 43100 Parma
Tel: (0521) 290387 *Fax:* (0521) 290387
Cable: ALBERTELLI PARMA
Key Personnel
Chief Executive, Production: Ermanno Albertelli
Sales: Viviana de Luca
Founded: 1968
Subjects: Military Science, Transportation
ISBN Prefix(es): 88-85909
Subsidiaries: Tuttostoria (Azienda di distribuzione)

Alberti Libraio Editore
Corso Garibaldi 74, 28921 Verbania
Tel: (0323) 402534 *Fax:* (0323) 401074
E-mail: alberti_libraio_editore@hotmail.com
Web Site: www.albertilibraioeditore.it
Founded: 1954
Subjects: History, Natural History, Regional Interests
ISBN Prefix(es): 88-7245; 88-85004

Aleph
Via S Agata 90, 94100 Enna
Tel: (0935) 500368 *Fax:* (0935) 500568
ISBN Prefix(es): 88-7154

Alessandro Tesauro Editore, *imprint of* Edizioni Ripostes

Libreria Alfani Editrice SRL
Via Alfani 84/86R, 50121 Florence
Tel: (055) 2398800 *Fax:* (055) 284397
E-mail: info@librerialfani.it
Key Personnel
Chief Executive: Umberto Panerai *E-mail:* info@librerialfani.it
Founded: 1968
Total Titles: 40 Print
Bookshop(s): Libreria Alfani, Via degli Alfani 84-86 R, I-50121 Florence

Alfieri & Ranieri, see mnemes - Alfieri & Ranieri Publishing

Edizioni Alice
Casella Postale 533, 6962 Viganello (Svizzera)
Tel: (091) 9729393 *Fax:* (091) 9718779

Alinari Fratelli SpA Istituto di Edizioni Artistiche
Largo Alinari 15, 50123 Florence
Tel: (055) 23951 *Fax:* (055) 262857
E-mail: info-more@alinari.it
Web Site: www.alinari.com
Telex: 572123 Alidea
Key Personnel
Man Dir: Claudio de Polo Saibanti
Founded: 1852
Subjects: Art, Education, Photography
ISBN Prefix(es): 88-7292
Bookshop(s): Fratelli Alinari, Via Vigna Nuova 48r, Florence; Fratelli Alinari, Via Alibert 16, Rome

Alinea+
Via P da Palestrina 17/19R, 50134 Florence
Tel: (055) 333428 *Fax:* (055) 331013
E-mail: info@alinea.it
Founded: 1980
Specialize in Architecture, Art & Engineering.
Subjects: Architecture & Interior Design, Art, Engineering (General)
ISBN Prefix(es): 88-8125
Distributed by Kappa-Clean
Book Club(s): Internazionale

Umberto Allemandi & C SRL+
Via Mancini 8, 10131 Turin
Tel: (011) 8199111 *Fax:* (011) 8193090
E-mail: allemandi@aztel.it
Key Personnel
Contact: Dr Christiano Casassa Mont
Founded: 1982
Subjects: Antiques, Archaeology, Architecture & Interior Design, Art, House & Home, Photography, Science (General)
ISBN Prefix(es): 88-422
Associate Companies: Umberto Allemandi & Co Publishing Srl

All'Insegna del Giglio
Via R Guiliani 152r, 50141 Florence
Tel: (055) 451.593 *Fax:* (055) 450,030
Founded: 1976
Subjects: Archaeology, History
ISBN Prefix(es): 88-7814

Amalthea srl+
Viale delle Camelie 13, 80040 Cercola
Tel: (081) 7334785 *Fax:* (081) 7334785
Web Site: www.amalthea.it
Key Personnel
President: Mario Casalini
Founded: 1991
Subjects: Art
ISBN Prefix(es): 88-86101

Edizioni Anabasi SpA
Via Durini 7, 20122 Milan
Tel: (02) 76.02.12.72 *Fax:* (02) 76.02.13.32
Key Personnel
Man & Editorial Dirs: Marjagiulia Castagnone; Sandro Mariotti d'Alessandro
Rights & Permissions: Simonetta Mazza
Editor: Riccardo Fedriga
Founded: 1991
Subjects: Fiction, Literature, Literary Criticism, Essays, Philosophy, Social Sciences, Sociology
ISBN Prefix(es): 88-417

Editrice Ancora+
Via Niccolini 8, 20154 Milan
Tel: (02) 3456081 *Fax:* (02) 34560866
E-mail: editrice@ancora-libri.it
Web Site: www.ancora-libri.it
Key Personnel
Man Dir: Gilberto Zini
Founded: 1934
Subjects: Religion - Other, Social Sciences, Sociology
ISBN Prefix(es): 88-7610; 88-514
Bookshop(s): Brescia *E-mail:* libreria.brescia@ancora-libri.it; Milan *E-mail:* libreria.hp@ancora-libri.it; Rome *E-mail:* libreria.zoma@ancora-libri.it; Trento *E-mail:* libreria.trento@ancora-libri.it

Franco Angeli SRL+
Viale Monza 106, 20127 Milan
Tel: (02) 28 37 141 *Fax:* (02) 26 14 47 93
E-mail: fran@francoangeli.it
Key Personnel
Man Dir: Dr Franco Angeli
Sales: Dr Stefano Angeli *Fax:* (02) 2613268
Founded: 1955
Subjects: Anthropology, Business, Economics, History, How-to, Management, Marketing, Psychology, Psychiatry, Social Sciences, Sociology
ISBN Prefix(es): 88-204; 88-464
Number of titles published annually: 600 Print
Total Titles: 9,000 Print

Editrice Antroposofica SRL
Via Sangallo 34, 20133 Milan
Tel: (02) 7491197
Key Personnel
Man Dir: Dr Iberto Bavastro
Founded: 1959
Subjects: Religion - Other
ISBN Prefix(es): 88-7787
Parent Company: Rudolf Steiner Verlag, Switzerland

APE, *imprint of* Organizzazione Didattica Editoriale Ape

Apimondia+
Corso Vittorio Emanuele, 101, 00186 Rome
Tel: (06) 6852286 *Fax:* (06) 6852286
E-mail: apimondia@mclink.it
Web Site: www.apimondia.org
Key Personnel
President: R Borneck *Tel:* (03) 84815007 *Fax:* (03) 84815007 *E-mail:* raymond.borneck@wanadoo.fr
Vice President: A S Jorgensen *Tel:* (045) 57561777 *Fax:* (045) 57561703 *E-mail:* asj@krl.dk
General Secretary: R Jannoni-Sebastianini
Founded: 1949
Member of International Federation of Bookkeepers Associations.
Subjects: Agriculture, Biological Sciences, Economics, Marketing, Technology, Veterinary Science
ISBN Prefix(es): 88-7643

Apogeo srl - Editrice di Informatica
Viale Papiniano 38, 20123 Milan
Tel: (02) 461920 *Fax:* (02) 4815382
E-mail: apogeo@apgeoline.com

ITALY

Key Personnel
Contact: Ivo Quartiroli
ISBN Prefix(es): 88-85146; 88-7303

Apostolato della Preghiera+
Segretariato Nazionale Apostolato della Preghiera, Via Degli Astalli, 16, 00186 Rome
Tel: (06) 697.607.1 *Fax:* (06) 67.81.063
E-mail: adp@adp.it
Web Site: www.adp.it
Key Personnel
Dir: Max Taggi *Tel:* (06) 7607202 *E-mail:* mt@adp.it
Contact: Roberto Izzi *Tel:* (06) 697607205
Founded: 1844 (founded in France in 1844, in Italy in 1861)
Bibles, books & leaflets.
Subjects: Psychology, Psychiatry, Religion - Other, Bibles, spirituality, pastoral activities, & prayer
Total Titles: 198 Print; 198 Online
Online services available through World Wide Web.
Parent Company: ADP International
Distributed by Messaggero Distribution SRL
Bookshop(s): Via Degli Astalli, 17, 00186 Rome *Tel:* (06) 697507201

Arcadia Edizioni Srl+
Via Caselline, 121, 41058 Vignola
Tel: (059) 76.60.34 *Fax:* (059) 77.92.79
E-mail: edizioni@arcadiabooks.com
Web Site: www.arcadiabooks.com
Key Personnel
Contact: Antony Shugaar
Subjects: Architecture & Interior Design, Art, Environmental Studies, Sports, Athletics, Travel
ISBN Prefix(es): 88-85684

Arcanta Aries Gruppo Editoriale
Via Makelle 97, 35138 Padova
Tel: (049) 8712477 *Fax:* (049) 8713851
Key Personnel
Chief Executive: Dr Franco Muzzio
Production: Sergio Fardin
Publicity: Stella Longato Muzzio
Founded: 1956
Subjects: Astrology, Occult, Health, Nutrition, Psychology, Psychiatry, Sports, Athletics
ISBN Prefix(es): 88-87564
Associate Companies: Franco Muzzio & C Editore SpA

Archimede Edizioni
Via Archimede 23, 20129 Milan
Tel: (02) 76 00 98 81 *Fax:* (02) 76 01 42 94
Key Personnel
Man Dir: Roberto Gulli
Editorial Dirs & International Rights: Paola Rosci
Sales Dir: Dario Ramilli
Editorial Dirs & International Rights: Emilio Zanette
Founded: 1990
Also acts as Educational Publisher.
Subjects: Biological Sciences, Earth Sciences, Education, English as a Second Language, Fiction, History, Mathematics
ISBN Prefix(es): 88-7952

Archimede Edizioni™, *imprint of* Paravia Bruno Mondadori Editori

Archinto snc+
Via Santa Valeria 3, 20123 Milan
Tel: (02) 86460237 *Fax:* (02) 86451955
E-mail: lettere@mcm.it; info@archinto.it
Web Site: www.archinto.it
Key Personnel
President: Rosellina Archinto
Founded: 1986
Subjects: Biography, Literature, Literary Criticism, Essays, Nonfiction (General), Poetry
ISBN Prefix(es): 88-7768
Number of titles published annually: 20 Print
Shipping Address: Vivalibri, Via Isonzo, 25, 00198 Rome, Pietro D'Amore
Tel: (06) 84242153 *Fax:* (06) 84085679
E-mail: vivalibri@tin.it
Orders to: Messaggerie Libri, Via Verdi, 8, Assago-Milano 20090 *Tel:* (02) 45774200, 45774210 *Fax:* (02) 45774230, 45774240

Archivio Guido Izzi Edizioni
Via Lazzarini 19, 00136 Rome
Tel: (06) 383193 *Fax:* (06) 39734433
Founded: 1984
Subjects: Art, History, Literature, Literary Criticism, Essays
ISBN Prefix(es): 88-85760

L'Archivolto+
Via Marsala 3, 20121 Milan
Tel: (02) 29010444; (02) 29010424 *Fax:* (02) 29001942
E-mail: info@archivolto.com
Web Site: www.archivolto.com
Founded: 1986
Specialize in architecture & interior design.
Subjects: Architecture & Interior Design, Gardening, Plants, Photography
ISBN Prefix(es): 88-7685
Subsidiaries: Edizioni L'Archivolto

Arcipelago Edizioni, *imprint of* Cooperativa Libraria IULM SCRL

Edizioni ARES+
Via Stradivari 7, 20131 Milan
Tel: (02) 29514202 *Fax:* (02) 29520163
E-mail: aresed@tin.it
Web Site: www.ares.mi.it
Key Personnel
Dir: Dr Cesare Cavalleri *E-mail:* cesare.cavalleri@ares.mi.it
Assistant Dir: Giuseppe Romano
E-mail: giuseppe.romano@ares.mi.it
Founded: 1957
Subjects: Architecture & Interior Design, Philosophy, Psychology, Psychiatry, Theology
ISBN Prefix(es): 88-8155

Argalia Editore delle Arti Grafiche Editoriali SRL
Via S Donato 148/c, 61029 Urbino Pesaro
Tel: (0722) 328733 *Fax:* (0722) 328756
Founded: 1942
Also book packager.
Subjects: Drama, Theater, Economics, Education, Fiction, History, Literature, Literary Criticism, Essays, Philosophy, Poetry, Science (General)

Aries, see Arcanta Aries Gruppo Editoriale

Edizioni Arka SRL+
Via Sanzio, 7, 20149 Milan
Tel: (02) 4818230 *Fax:* (02) 4816752
E-mail: arka.edizioni@tin.it
Key Personnel
Man Dir: Ginevra Viscardi
Founded: 1984
Subjects: Animals, Pets, Art
ISBN Prefix(es): 88-8072
Number of titles published annually: 20 Print

Arktos
Via Gardezzana 57, 10022 Carmagnola, Turin
Tel: (011) 9773941 *Fax:* (011) 9773941
Founded: 1976

Subjects: Astrology, Occult, Philosophy, Religion - Islamic
ISBN Prefix(es): 88-7049

Editore Armando Armando SRL+
Viale Trastevere, 236, 00153 Rome
Tel: (06) 5894525 *Fax:* (06) 5818564
E-mail: amministrazione@armando.it
Web Site: www.armando.it
Key Personnel
President: Enrico Iacometti
Founded: 1963
Subjects: Anthropology, Behavioral Sciences, Child Care & Development, Communications, Disability, Special Needs, Education, Health, Nutrition, Journalism, Language Arts, Linguistics, Medicine, Nursing, Dentistry, Philosophy, Psychology, Psychiatry, Radio, TV, Self-Help, Social Sciences, Sociology
ISBN Prefix(es): 88-7144
Number of titles published annually: 150 Print; 4 CD-ROM
Total Titles: 4 CD-ROM
Parent Company: Sovera Multimedia SRL, Via V Brunacci 55
Associate Companies: Sovera Multimedia, via Brunacci 55/55A, Claudia Iacometti *Tel:* (06) 5562429 *Fax:* (06) 5580723
Bookshop(s): Via Vincenzo Brunacci, 53, 00146 Rome *Tel:* (06) 5587850 *Fax:* (06) 5580723
Warehouse: Sovera Multimedia SRL, Via V Brunacci, 55, 00146 Rome

Gruppo Editoriale Armenia SpA+
Via Valtellina 63, 20159 Milan
Tel: (02) 683911 *Fax:* (02) 6684884
E-mail: armenia@armenia.it; armenia@mr-net.it
Web Site: www.armenia.it
Key Personnel
Chief Executive: Dr Giovanni Armenia
Rights & Permissions: Fabiola Marchet
E-mail: editoriale@armenia.it
International Rights: Simona Lari
Founded: 1972
Specialize in New Age, Positive Thinking & Fantasy.
Subjects: Animals, Pets, Astrology, Occult, Crafts, Games, Hobbies, Fiction, Health, Nutrition, How-to, Humor, Nonfiction (General), Parapsychology, Self-Help
ISBN Prefix(es): 88-344
Number of titles published annually: 80 Print
Total Titles: 500 Print; 2 CD-ROM
Online services available through World Wide Web.
Warehouse: Via Vialba 71, 20026 Novate Milanese, Milano *Tel:* (02) 38200208 *Fax:* (02) 38200208

Arnaud Editore SRL+
Via Nardi 27, 50132 Florence
Tel: (055) 216485 *Fax:* (055) 260466
Key Personnel
Chief Executive: Alfredo Meletti
Founded: 1944
Subjects: Art, Government, Political Science, History
ISBN Prefix(es): 88-8015
Associate Companies: Nuova Expolibro Toscana SRL, Via Ricasoli 7, I-50122 Florence
Branch Office(s)
Via J Nardi 27, I-50132 Florence
Warehouse: Via De' Pucci 2, 50122 Florence

Arsenale Editrice SRL+
San Polo 1789, 30125 Venice
Tel: (041) 5240610 *Fax:* (041) 5221579; (041) 5240865
Telex: 480481 Apiver I sub 128
Key Personnel
Man Dir, Rights & Permissions & Production: Andrea Grandese

Editorial: Cinzia Boscolo
Sales: Giorgio Tamaro
Production: Andrea Grandese
Founded: 1984
Subjects: Architecture & Interior Design, Art
ISBN Prefix(es): 88-7743
Parent Company: Editoriale Bortolazzi - Stei SRL, Via Monte Comun 30, I-37057 San Giovanni Lupatoto (VR)
U.S. Office(s): Moseley Assoc, 19 West 44 St, Suite 1200, New York, NY 10036, United States, Contact: Bert Paolucci
Bookshop(s): San Croce 29, I-30135 Venice

Artema
Centro Scientifico Arte, Via Borgone 57, 10139 Turin
Tel: (011) 386500 *Fax:* (011) 3853244
E-mail: cse@estorinese.inet.it
Key Personnel
President: Francesco Martiny
International Rights: Valentina Kalk
Founded: 1992
Subjects: Art
ISBN Prefix(es): 88-8052

Edizioni Artes+
Viale Forlanini 65, 20134 Milan
Tel: (02) 70209917 *Fax:* (02) 70209919
Key Personnel
Man Dir: Raffaele Grandi
Founded: 1985
Subjects: Art
ISBN Prefix(es): 88-7724
Associate Companies: Edi Ermes srl, Viale Forlanini 65, 20134 Milan

Artioli Editore in Modena
Via Emilia Ovest 669, 41100 Modena
Tel: (059) 827181 *Fax:* (059) 826819
E-mail: artiolip@pianeta.it
Founded: 1899
Subjects: Antiques, Architecture & Interior Design, Art, Drama, Theater, Photography, Regional Interests
ISBN Prefix(es): 88-7792

Casa Editrice Astrolabio-Ubaldini Editore+
Via Guido D'Arezzo 16, 00198 Rome
Tel: (06) 854 22 45; (06) 855 21 31 *Fax:* (06) 855 27 56
E-mail: astrolabio.gana@alphacomm.it
Key Personnel
Chief Executive: Francesco Gana
Editorial: Francesco Cardelli
Sales, Production: Fiorenzo Bertillo
Founded: 1946
Subjects: Philosophy, Psychology, Psychiatry, Social Sciences, Sociology, Oriental studies
ISBN Prefix(es): 88-340
Number of titles published annually: 35 Print
Total Titles: 820 Print

Editrice Atanor SRL+
Via Avezzano n 16, 00182 Rome
Tel: (06) 7024595 *Fax:* (06) 7014422
Key Personnel
Man Dir: Anna Maria Papini
Editorial: Francesco Albanese
Founded: 1912
Subjects: Asian Studies, Astrology, Occult, Science (General)
ISBN Prefix(es): 88-7169

Edizioni Dell'Ateneo Sr, see Instituti Editoriali E Poligrafici Internazionali SRL

Verlagsanstalt Athesia+
Portici, 41, 39100 Bolzano
Tel: (0471) 925203 *Fax:* (0471) 925207
Cable: ATHESIA VERLAG, BOZEN
Key Personnel
Man Dir, Production: Dr Peter Silbernagl
Sales Manager: Richard Fieg
Publicity Manager: Aron Mairhofer
Founded: 1907
Subjects: Art, Cookery, Geography, Geology, History, How-to, Humor, Law, Military Science, Outdoor Recreation, Poetry, Religion - Catholic, Travel
ISBN Prefix(es): 88-7014; 88-8266
Subsidiaries: Athesiabuch GmbH; Athesiadruck GmbH
Bookshop(s): Bozen; Brixen; Bruneck; Meran; Schlanders; Sterzing

Atlantica Editrice SARL
Casella Postale 34, 71100 Foggia
Founded: 1974
Subjects: Language Arts, Linguistics, Regional Interests, Science (General)
ISBN Prefix(es): 88-7085
Branch Office(s)
CP 38, I-71043 Manfredonia

Automobilia srl+
Via Alberto Mario 16, 20149 Milan
Tel: (02) 48021671 *Fax:* (02) 48194968
Key Personnel
President: Bruno Alfieri
Editorial: Ippolito Alfieri
Sales: Luisa Alfieri
Production: Verde Alfieri
Founded: 1979
Subjects: Architecture & Interior Design, Art, Automotive, Maritime, Transportation
ISBN Prefix(es): 88-85058; 88-85880; 88-7960

Aviani Editore+
Via Diaz 27, 33019 Tricesimo (Udine)
Tel: (0432) 46478 *Fax:* (0432) 43420
Founded: 1973
ISBN Prefix(es): 88-7772
Associate Companies: Grafiche Fulvio ove
Warehouse: Via Tavanacco, 63, 31000 Udine

Baha'i
Via Turati 9, 00040 Ariccia Rome
Tel: (06) 9334334 *Fax:* (06) 9334335
Founded: 1969
Subjects: Biography, Economics, Education, Religion - Other, Social Sciences, Sociology
ISBN Prefix(es): 88-7214

Bancaria Editrice SpA
Subsidiary of ABI Italian Banking Association
Piazza del Gesu 49, 00186 Rome
Tel: (06) 6767391; (06) 6767392; (06) 6767393 *Fax:* (06) 6767397
Key Personnel
Dir: Nicola Forti
Subjects: Business, Economics, Finance, Law, Management, Marketing
ISBN Prefix(es): 88-449

Bardi Editore srl
Via Piave 7, 00817 Rome
Tel: (06) 4817656 *Fax:* (06) 48912514
E-mail: bardied@tin.it
Web Site: www.bardieditore.com
Key Personnel
Man Dir: Garcia Y Garcia Laurent
Founded: 1921
Specialize in Oriental studies, scientific books, subscription & mail order books.
Subjects: Antiques, Archaeology, Architecture & Interior Design, History, Music, Dance
ISBN Prefix(es): 88-85699
Total Titles: 300 Print

Bastogi
Via Zara, 47, 71100 Foggia
Tel: (0881) 725070 *Fax:* (0881) 677513
Founded: 1979
Subjects: History, Literature, Literary Criticism, Essays, Religion - Other
ISBN Prefix(es): 88-86452; 88-8185

Casa Editrice Luigi Battei
Str Cavour 5/C, 43100 Parma
Tel: (0521) 233733 *Fax:* (0521) 231291
Key Personnel
Chief Executive: Antonio Battei
Founded: 1872
Subjects: Architecture & Interior Design, Literature, Literary Criticism, Essays, Regional Interests
Showroom(s): La Pillotta
Bookshop(s): La Pillotta
Warehouse: Borgo Serena 3, 43100 Parma
Tel: (0521) 234747

Battelloavapore, *imprint of* Edizioni Piemme SpA

BC News, *imprint of* Edizioni del Centro

BCSP, *imprint of* Edizioni del Centro

BEL srl, *imprint of* Belforte Editore Libraio srl

Belforte Editore Libraio srl+
Via Grande 91, 57123 Livorno
Tel: (0586) 887379 *Fax:* (0586) 889668
E-mail: belforte@librinformatica.it
Key Personnel
International Rights: Dr Riccardo Tagliati
Founded: 1834
Subjects: Antiques, Art, Behavioral Sciences, Biography, Child Care & Development, Education, Fiction, Human Relations, Library & Information Sciences, Literature, Literary Criticism, Essays, Nonfiction (General), Philosophy, Poetry, Psychology, Psychiatry, Regional Interests, Religion - Jewish, Wine & Spirits, Women's Studies
ISBN Prefix(es): 88-7997
Imprints: BEL srl
Subsidiaries: Librinformatica SRL

BeMa
Via Teocrito 50, 20128 Milan
Tel: (02) 2552451 *Fax:* (02) 27000692
Founded: 1975
Subjects: Antiques, Architecture & Interior Design, Earth Sciences, Engineering (General), English as a Second Language, Geography, Geology, Technology
ISBN Prefix(es): 88-7143
Imprints: Visual Itineraries

Bertello Edizioni
Via Bassigiano 46, 12011 Cuneo
Tel: (0171) 266861; (0171) 699002 *Fax:* (0171) 697729; (0171) 266861
ISBN Prefix(es): 88-8067

Bianco
Via Messina 31, 00198 Rome
Tel: (06) 8554962 *Fax:* (06) 8844703 *Cable:* DEL BIANCO UDINE
Founded: 1933
Subjects: Art, Engineering (General), History, Science (General)

Bibliopolis - Edizioni di Filosofia e Scienze Srl
Via Arangio Ruiz 83, 80122 Naples
Tel: (081) 664606 *Fax:* (081) 7616273
E-mail: info@bibliopolis.it
Web Site: www.bibliopolis.it

Key Personnel
Man Dir: Dr Francesco del Franco
Contact: Emilia del Franco
  E-mail: emiadelfranco@fiscolinet.it
Founded: 1976
Subjects: Archaeology, Literature, Literary Criticism, Essays, Mathematics, Philosophy, Physical Sciences, Physics, Science (General)
ISBN Prefix(es): 88-7088
Total Titles: 374 Print

Biblioteca Elle, *imprint of* Mondolibro Editore SNC

Biblioteca World, *imprint of* Mondolibro Editore SNC

Bibliotheca di Gabriele Chiusano+
Via Maresca, 66/B, 04024 Gaeta
Tel: (0771) 744350
Key Personnel
Man Dir: Gabriele Chiusano
Founded: 1992
Subjects: History, Literature, Literary Criticism, Essays, Philosophy, Poetry, Social Sciences, Sociology
ISBN Prefix(es): 88-87106

Biblos srl+
Via delle Pezze 33, 35013 Cittadella (Padova)
Tel: (049) 5975236 *Fax:* (049) 5972841
Subjects: Architecture & Interior Design, Art
ISBN Prefix(es): 88-86214
Showroom(s): Buchmesse Frankfurt

Editoriale Bios+
Via Sicilia, 5, 87100 Cosenza
Tel: (0984) 398300 *Fax:* (0984) 398300
Key Personnel
Contact: Irene Olivieri
Founded: 1981
Subjects: Engineering (General), Medicine, Nursing, Dentistry
ISBN Prefix(es): 88-7740

Edizioni Blues Brothers, *imprint of* Kaos Edizioni SRL

Bollati Boringhieri Editore Srl+
Corso Vittorio Emanuele 86, 10121 Turin
Tel: (011) 5591711 *Fax:* (011) 543024
E-mail: info@bollatiboringhieri.it; rightsdept@bollatiboringhieri.it *Cable:* EDIBOR
Key Personnel
Man Dir, Editorial: Romilda Bollati
Foreign Rights: Christa Pardatscher
Founded: 1957
Subjects: Economics, History, Literature, Literary Criticism, Essays, Philosophy, Science (General), Social Sciences, Sociology
ISBN Prefix(es): 88-339

Bompiani-RCS Libri+
Via Mecenate 91, 20138 Milan
Tel: (02) 50951 *Fax:* (02) 5065361
Web Site: www.reslibri.it
Telex: 311321 Fabbri I *Cable:* LIBRIFABBRI MILANO
Key Personnel
Dir: Mario Andreose
Editor-in-Chief: Elisabetta Sgarbi
  Tel: (02) 50952666 *Fax:* (02) 50952788
  E-mail: elisabetta.sgarb@res.it
Founded: 1929
Member of Gruppo Editoriale Fabbri, Bompiani, Sonzogno, Etas SpA.
Subjects: Art, Drama, Theater, Fiction, Nonfiction (General), Science (General)
ISBN Prefix(es): 88-450; 88-451; 88-452

Bonacci editore+
Via Mercuri 8, 00193 Rome
Tel: (06) 68300004 *Fax:* (06) 68806382
E-mail: info@bonacci.it
Web Site: www.bonacci.it
Key Personnel
Man Dir: Alessandra Bonacci
Founded: 1942
Specialize in the production of material for the teaching of Italian as a foreign language.
Subjects: History, Italian as a Foreign Language
ISBN Prefix(es): 88-7573
Total Titles: 4 Print; 1 Audio
Online services available through World Wide Web.
Foreign Rep(s): Attica (France); DEI (Spain); Grivas (Greece); Intext Book (Australia); Klett Verlag (Germany)
Warehouse: Via Pietro Cavallini 24/B *Tel:* (06) 321 57 08 *Fax:* (06) 321 57 08

Giuseppe Bonanno Editore+
Via Vittorio Emanuele 194, 95024 Acireale, Catania
Tel: (095) 601984 *Fax:* (095) 604380
Key Personnel
Editorial: Giuseppe Bonanno
Dir: Dr Mauro Bonanno *E-mail:* bonannomauro@tiscalinet.it
Founded: 1966
Subjects: Architecture & Interior Design, Art, Behavioral Sciences, Cookery, Economics, Fiction, Foreign Countries, Government, Political Science, History, Law, Literature, Literary Criticism, Essays
ISBN Prefix(es): 88-7796
Number of titles published annually: 10 Print
Total Titles: 198 Print
Divisions: AEB Editrice
Branch Office(s)
Bonanno Editore Roita, Via Torino 150, Rome *Tel:* (064) 740467
Bookshop(s): Libreria Bonanno, Via Vittorio Emanuele 194, 95024 Acireale, Catania *Tel:* (095) 601984 *Fax:* (095) 604380
Warehouse: Via Cozzale, 36 95024 Acireale, Catania

Casa Editrice Bonechi+
Via dei Cairoli 18b, 50131 Florence
Tel: (055) 576841 *Fax:* (055) 5000766
E-mail: bonechi@bonechi.it
Web Site: www.bonechi.it
Telex: 571323 CEB
Key Personnel
Man Dir: Giampaolo Bonechi
Editorial: Giovanna Magi; Marco Banti
Sales Dir: Claudio Magnani
Founded: 1973
Subjects: Art, Cookery, Travel
ISBN Prefix(es): 88-7009; 88-8029; 88-476
Imprints: CEB

Bonechi-Edizioni Il Turismo Srl
Via dei Rustici 5, 50122 Florence
Tel: (055) 2398224 *Fax:* (055) 216366
Key Personnel
Contact: Barbara Bonechi *E-mail:* barbara@bonechionline.com; Piero Bonechi *Tel:* (055) 216607 *E-mail:* bbonechi@dada.it
Founded: 1954
Subjects: Archaeology, Art, Travel
ISBN Prefix(es): 88-7204
Warehouse: Via Giuseppe di Vittorio, 31, Florence *Tel:* (055) 37-47-01 *Fax:* (055) 37-47-01

Ditta F Bongiovanni SAS
Via Rizzoli 28E, 40125 Bologna 40125
Tel: (051) 225722 *Fax:* (051) 226128
Key Personnel
Man Dir: Giancarlo Bongiovanni
Editorial: Barbara Bongiovanni
Production: Andrea Bongiovanni
Founded: 1905
Subjects: Music, Dance

Bonsignori Editore SRL+
Viale dei Quattro Venti 47, Rome 00152
Tel: (06) 5881496 *Fax:* (06) 5882839
E-mail: redazione@bonsignori.it
Key Personnel
Chief Executive: Mario Bonsignori; Simona Bonsignori
Founded: 1992
Subjects: Archaeology, Architecture & Interior Design, Art, History, Specializes in archeology, architecture & history of art
ISBN Prefix(es): 88-7597
Number of titles published annually: 20 Print

Book Editore
Via della Chiesa 49b, 40013 Castel Maggiore (Bologna)
Tel: (051) 714720 *Fax:* (051) 711216
Founded: 1987
Subjects: Language Arts, Linguistics, Literature, Literary Criticism, Essays, Philosophy, Poetry
ISBN Prefix(es): 88-7232

Edizioni Bora SNC di E Brandani & C
Via Jacopo di Paolo 42, 40128 Bologna
Tel: (051) 356133 *Fax:* (051) 374394
E-mail: daniele.brandani@mailbox.dsnet.it
Founded: 1971
Subjects: Art, Biography
ISBN Prefix(es): 88-85638; 88-85345
Total Titles: 4 Print

Edizioni Borla SRL+
Via delle Fornaci 50, 00165 Rome
Tel: (06) 39376728 *Fax:* (06) 39376620
Key Personnel
Man Dir: Dr Vincenzo D'Agostino
Founded: 1863
Subjects: Anthropology, Education, Government, Political Science, History, Philosophy, Psychology, Psychiatry, Religion - Other, Social Sciences, Sociology
ISBN Prefix(es): 88-263

Bovolenta
Via Belletti 14, 44100 Ferrara
Tel: (0532) 750737
Founded: 1975
Subjects: History, Literature, Literary Criticism, Essays, Philosophy
ISBN Prefix(es): 88-369

Edizioni Brenner+
Via Monte S Michele, 13A, 87100 Cosenza
Tel: (0984) 74537 *Fax:* (0984) 74537
Key Personnel
Man Dir, Editorial: Walter Brenner
Sales: Maria Gerbasi
Founded: 1956
Subjects: Ethnicity, History, Medicine, Nursing, Dentistry, Regional Interests

Edizioni Bresciane+
Via Pasubio 30, 25128 Brescia
Tel: (030) 393589 *Fax:* (030) 393589
Key Personnel
Man Dir, Editorial, Sales, Production: Bruno Enzo
Founded: 1980
Subjects: History, Journalism, Literature, Literary Criticism, Essays, Philosophy, Poetry, Religion - Catholic, Romance
Distributed by Casalini Libri

Editore Giorgio Bretschneider
Via Crescenzio 43, 00193 Rome

Mailing Address: Casella Postale 30011, Rm 47, 00193 Roma
Tel: (06) 6879361 *Fax:* (06) 6864543
E-mail: info@bretschneider.it
Web Site: www.bretschneider.it *Cable:* GIOBREROM
Key Personnel
Man Dir: Boris Bretschneider
Founded: 1974
Subjects: Archaeology, History, Greek & Roman Antiquities
ISBN Prefix(es): 88-85007; 88-7689
Number of titles published annually: 20 Print
Total Titles: 400 Print
Distributor for Universita di Messina; Universita di Macerata

Edizioni Bucalo SNC
Casella postale 51, 04100 Latina
Tel: (0773) 410036 *Fax:* (0773) 410036
Web Site: www.bucalo.it
Key Personnel
Chief Executive: Andrea Bucalo
Founded: 1965
Subjects: Law
ISBN Prefix(es): 88-7456
Parent Company: C Sopra

Buffetti
Via Fosso di S Maura, 00169 Rome
Tel: (06) 231951 *Fax:* (06) 23195490
Founded: 1973
Subjects: Economics, Law, Management
ISBN Prefix(es): 88-19

Bulzoni Editore SRL (Le Edizioni Universitarie d'Italia)+
Via Dei Liburni 14, 00185 Rome
Tel: (06) 4455207 *Fax:* (06) 4450355
Key Personnel
Man Dir, Editorial: Anna Bulzoni
Sales: Ivana Capitani
Production: Paola Bulzoni
Publicity: Anna Catarinozzi
Founded: 1969
Subjects: Art, Drama, Theater, Engineering (General), Fiction, Film, Video, Language Arts, Linguistics, Law, Literature, Literary Criticism, Essays, Philosophy, Science (General), Social Sciences, Sociology
ISBN Prefix(es): 88-7119; 88-8319
Bookshop(s): Libreria Ricerche, Via Liburni 10/12, I-00185 Rome *Tel:* (06) 491851

Cacucci Editore+
Via D Nicolai 17, 70122 Bari
Tel: (080) 5214220 *Fax:* (080) 5234777
Key Personnel
Man Dir: Dr Nicola Cacucci
Founded: 1929
Subjects: Economics, Law, Mathematics, Public Administration
Showroom(s): Salone del Libro Torino; Expolibro Bari
Bookshop(s): Via Cairoli 140, Bari; Via S Matarrese 2/D, Bari

Edizioni Cadmo SRL+
Via Benedetto da Maiano 3, 50014 Fiesole (Florence)
Tel: (055) 50181 *Fax:* (055) 50181201
Key Personnel
Man Dir: Mario Casalini
Founded: 1975
Subjects: Art, History, Language Arts, Linguistics, Music, Dance, Philosophy, Social Sciences, Sociology
ISBN Prefix(es): 88-7923

CADSR, *imprint of* Centro Ambrosiano di Documentazione e Studi Religiosi

Calosci+
Loc Vallone 35L, 52042 Camucia-Cortona
Tel: (0575) 678282 *Fax:* (0575) 678282
E-mail: info@calosci.com
Web Site: www.calosci.com
Founded: 1964
Subjects: Archaeology, Architecture & Interior Design, Art, History, Literature, Literary Criticism, Essays, Medicine, Nursing, Dentistry, Music, Dance, Regional Interests, Transportation
ISBN Prefix(es): 88-7785
Distributed by The Courier srl

Camera dei Deputati Ufficio Pubblicazioni Informazione Parlamentare+
Piazza Montecitorio, 00186 Rome
Tel: (06) 67609328 *Fax:* (06) 6781326
Web Site: www.camera.it
Telex: 612523
Key Personnel
Chief Executive: Dr Stefano Rizzo *Fax:* (06) 67602449 *E-mail:* rizzo_s@camera.it
Sales: Monica Fier *Tel:* (06) 67609909 *E-mail:* fier_m@camera.it
Founded: 1848
Specialize in bibliographies, books, pamphlets, proceedings, reference works.
Subjects: Economics, History, Law
Number of titles published annually: 20 Print
Total Titles: 250 Print
Bookshop(s): Libreria della Camera dei Deputati, Via Uffici del Vicario 17, Rome *Tel:* (06) 67603715 *E-mail:* sg-pi_libreria@camera.it

Campanotto+
Via Marano 46, 33037 Pasian di Prato, Udine
Tel: (0432) 699390; (0432) 690155 *Fax:* (0432) 644728
Key Personnel
Contact: Carlo Marcello Conti; Inga Conti
Founded: 1977
Subjects: Archaeology, Art, Fiction, History, Literature, Literary Criticism, Essays, Music, Dance, Philosophy, Photography, Poetry, Radio, TV, Religion - Catholic, Religion - Other
ISBN Prefix(es): 88-456
Subsidiaries: Grafiche Piratello

Camunia, Zanzibar, Edizioni Primavera, *imprint of* Giunti (Gruppo Editoriale)

Canova SRL
Via Calmaggiore 31, 31100 Treviso
Tel: (0422) 382383 *Fax:* (0422) 382383
Key Personnel
Man Dir, Editorial, Rights & Permissions: Ennio Zoppelli
Sales: Luigi Facchini
Founded: 1945
Subjects: Art, History
ISBN Prefix(es): 88-85066; 88-86177; 88-87061
Subsidiaries: Grafiche Zoppelli SRL
Bookshop(s): Via Cavour 6/b, 31015 Conegliano
Warehouse: Viale della Liberazione 40, 31030 Dosson

Edizioni Cantagalli+
Via Massetana Romana, 12, 53100 Siena
Tel: (0577) 42102 *Fax:* (0577) 45363
E-mail: cantagalli@edizionicantagalli.com
Web Site: www.edizionicantagalli.com
Key Personnel
Chief Executive: Pietro Cantagalli
E-mail: david@edizionicantagalli.com
Founded: 1927
Subjects: Biblical Studies, Disability, Special Needs, History, Music, Dance, Nonfiction (General), Philosophy, Regional Interests, Religion - Catholic, Science (General), Theology
ISBN Prefix(es): 88-8272

Franco Cantini Editore, see OCTAVO Franco Cantini Editore

Capone Editore SRL+
Via Caprarica 35, 73020 Cavallino di (Lecce)
Tel: (0832) 612618 *Fax:* (0832) 611877
Key Personnel
Editorial: Lorenzo Capone
Founded: 1980
Subjects: Art, Communications, Ethnicity, History, Literature, Literary Criticism, Essays, Philosophy, Regional Interests

Nuova Casa Editrice Licinio Cappelli GEM srl+
Via Farini 14, 40124 Bologna
Tel: (051) 239060 *Fax:* (051) 239286
E-mail: info@cappellieditore.com
Web Site: www.cappellieditore.com *Cable:* CAPPELLI EDITORE BOLOGNA
Key Personnel
Man Dir: Mario Musso
Editorial: Massimo Manzoni
Founded: 1851
Subjects: Art, Biography, Drama, Theater, Fiction, Film, Video, Government, Political Science, History, Medicine, Nursing, Dentistry, Music, Dance, Philosophy, Poetry, Psychology, Psychiatry, Religion - Other, Science (General), Social Sciences, Sociology
ISBN Prefix(es): 88-379
Associate Companies: Nicola Milano Editore

Edizioni Carmelitane
Via Anagnina, 662B, 00040 Marino, Rome
Tel: (06) 79847482 *Fax:* (06) 79845387
Founded: 1954
Subjects: History, Religion - Catholic
ISBN Prefix(es): 88-7229

Casa Musicale Edizioni Carrara SRL
Via Ambrogio da Calepio, 2/4, 24125 Bergamo
Tel: (035) 243618 *Fax:* (035) 270298 *Cable:* CARRARA MUSICA BERGAMO
Key Personnel
Editorial, Production: Vinicio Carrara
Sales, Publicity: Vittorio Carrara
Founded: 1912
Subjects: Music, Dance, Religion - Catholic

Edizioni Carroccio
Via Alfieri 1, 35010 Vigodarzere, Padova
Tel: (049) 700568 *Fax:* (049) 700568
Key Personnel
Man Dir: Luciano Lincetto
Founded: 1947
Subjects: Religion - Catholic, Religion - Other

Edizioni Cartedit SRL+
Via Industriale 7, 26010 Monte Cremasco (Cremona)
Tel: (0373) 277410 *Fax:* (0373) 277405
Key Personnel
Editor: Sig Pigon Lavinio
Founded: 1992
ISBN Prefix(es): 88-86170; 88-8070

Edizioni Cartografiche Milanesi+
Via Adda, 17, 20095 Cusano Milanino, Milan
Tel: (02) 6193747 *Fax:* (02) 66402281
E-mail: info@ortelio-ecm.it
Subjects: Geography, Geology
ISBN Prefix(es): 88-8151
Imprints: Ortelio

Cartoonseries, *imprint of* Stampa Alternativa - Nuovi Equilibri

ITALY

Casa Editrice Dr A Milani, see CEDAM (Casa Editrice Dr A Milani)

Casa Editrice Felice Le Monnier+
Via Meucci 2, 50015 Grassano
Tel: (055) 64910 *Fax:* (055) 643983
E-mail: monnier@tin.it
Key Personnel
President: Giuseppe De Rita
Vice President: Dr Enrico Paoletti
Man Dir: Dr Guglielmo Paoletti; Dr Vanni Paoletti
Man Dir & Promotions: Dr Simone Paoletti
Founded: 1836
Subjects: Biography, Education, History, Language Arts, Linguistics, Philosophy, Religion - Catholic
ISBN Prefix(es): 88-00
Imprints: Le Monnier

Casa Editrice Giuseppe Principato Spa+
Via Fauche 10, 20154 Milan
Tel: (02) 312025 *Fax:* (02) 33104295
E-mail: info@principato.it
Key Personnel
Publishing Dir: Franco Menin
Founded: 1887
Subjects: Biological Sciences, Chemistry, Chemical Engineering, Earth Sciences, English as a Second Language, Geography, Geology, History, Literature, Literary Criticism, Essays, Mathematics, Philosophy, Physics
ISBN Prefix(es): 88-416

Casa Editrice Libraria Ulrico Hoepli SpA+
Via Hoepli 5, 20121 Milan
Tel: (02) 864871 *Fax:* (02) 8052886
E-mail: hoepli@hoepli.it *Cable:* HOEPLI MILAN
Key Personnel
Man Dir: Dr Ulrico Hoepli; Gianni Hoepli; Dr Ulrico Carlo Hoepli
Rights & Permissions: Dr Susanna Schwarz Bellotti
Contact: Daniela Grazi
Founded: 1870
Subjects: Art, Engineering (General), How-to, Law, Social Sciences, Sociology, Technology
ISBN Prefix(es): 88-203
Bookshop(s): Hoepli Ulrico Libreria Internazionale
Shipping Address: Via Mameli 13, 1-20129 Milan

Casa Editrice Lint Srl
Via di Romagna 30, 34134 Trieste
Tel: (040) 360396 *Fax:* (040) 361354
Key Personnel
President: Prof Riccardo Maetzke
Advisor: Maria Rosa Casagrande Maetzke
Founded: 1962
Subjects: Art, Science (General)
ISBN Prefix(es): 88-86179; 88-85083; 88-8190

Casalini Libri
Via Benedetto da Maiano, Suite 3, 50014 Florence
Tel: (055) 50181 *Fax:* (055) 5018201 *Cable:* CASALINI FIESOLE
Key Personnel
Pres: Gerda von Grebmer
Man Dir: Barbara Casalini; Michele Casalini
Founded: 1968
Firm's main function is as a book exporter.
ISBN Prefix(es): 88-85297
Associate Companies: CADMO

Edistudio di Brunetto Casini+
Via Bruno 6/8, 56125 Pisa
Tel: (050) 48670 *Fax:* (050) 500585
E-mail: edistudio@sirius.pisa.it *Cable:* Edistudio CP 213 Pisa
Key Personnel
Chief Executive: Brunetto Casini
Founded: 1977
Specialize in local culture & local magazines.
Subjects: Drama, Theater, Education, Fiction, Geography, Geology, Language Arts, Linguistics, Literature, Literary Criticism, Essays, Music, Dance, Poetry, Science (General), Sports, Athletics
ISBN Prefix(es): 88-7036
Total Titles: 70 Print
Subsidiaries: Composit (Fotocomposizione elaborazione grafica)

Casa Editrice Castalia (Castalia Books Limited)+
Via Peyron 38, 10143 Turin
Tel: (011) 4374176 *Fax:* (011) 4374176
Key Personnel
Chairperson: Dr Mario Miglietti *Tel:* (011) 4342621
Dir: Silvia Camodeca
Founded: 1984
Publisher of children's books.
Subjects: Photography
ISBN Prefix(es): 88-7701
Number of titles published annually: 10 Print
Total Titles: 84 Print
Imprints: Mario Miglietti

Edizioni Castello di Antonio Careddu+
Via Campania 27, 09121 Cagliari
Tel: (070) 562296 *Fax:* (070) 562296
Key Personnel
Man Dir: Antonio Careddu
Editorial: Dr Caterina Marras
Sales: Dr Gianluca Careddu; Tiziana Careddu
Founded: 1982
Subjects: Art, Fiction, Philosophy, Poetry, Travel
ISBN Prefix(es): 88-86006

Il Castello srl+
Via Scarlatti 12, 20090 Trezzano sul Naviplio, Milan
Tel: (02) 48401629 *Fax:* (02) 4453617
E-mail: il_castello@tin.it
Key Personnel
Chief Executive: Luca Belloni
Editorial: Mose Menotti
Founded: 1955
Subjects: Art, Astronomy, Cookery, Crafts, Games, Hobbies, Outdoor Recreation, Photography, Fitness
ISBN Prefix(es): 88-8039
Number of titles published annually: 60 Print
Total Titles: 300 Print

Il Castoro+
Viale Abruzzi, 72, 20131 Milan
Tel: (02) 29513529 *Fax:* (02) 29529896
E-mail: castoro@riavarea.com
Key Personnel
Contact: Renata Gorgani
International Rights: Pico Floridi
Founded: 1993
Subjects: Biography, Fiction, Film, Video
ISBN Prefix(es): 88-8033

CCSP, *imprint of* Edizioni del Centro

CEB, *imprint of* Casa Editrice Bonechi

CED
Via Roma 210, 84121 Salerno
Tel: (089) 254252 *Fax:* (089) 254262
E-mail: ced@pamdoraezimet.it
ISBN Prefix(es): 88-8028

CEDAM (Casa Editrice Dr A Milani)
Via Jappelli 5/6, 35121 Padova
Tel: (049) 8239111 *Fax:* (049) 8752900
E-mail: info@cedam.com
Web Site: www.cedam.com
Key Personnel
President: Dott Antonio Milani
Administrator: Francesco Giordano; Carlo Porta
Founded: 1903
Subjects: Biological Sciences, Criminology, Economics, Finance, Government, Political Science, Law, Management, Marketing, Mathematics, Medicine, Nursing, Dentistry, Philosophy, Psychology, Psychiatry, Public Administration, Social Sciences, Sociology
ISBN Prefix(es): 88-13
Warehouse: Via Uruguay n 14, 35127 Camin PD

Edizioni CELI, *imprint of* Gruppo Editoriale Faenza Editrice SpA

CELID
Via Lodi 27, 10152 Turin
Tel: (011) 2489326 *Fax:* (011) 2489329
Key Personnel
Contact: Antonio Catalano; Vanda Cremona
Founded: 1974
Subjects: Architecture & Interior Design, Engineering (General), History
ISBN Prefix(es): 88-7661
Branch Office(s)
V Mattioli 39, 10125 Torino
Corso Duca Degli Abruzzi 24, 10129 Torino
Bookshop(s): Via S Ottavio 20, 10124 Turin

Celuc Libri
Via Santa Valeria 5, 20123 Milan
Tel: (02) 86450776 *Fax:* (02) 86451424
Key Personnel
Man Dir: Rita Barbatiello
Founded: 1969 (as CELUC), 1974 (as Celuc Libri SRL)
Subjects: Economics, Government, Political Science, History, Law, Literature, Literary Criticism, Essays, Mathematics, Philosophy, Religion - Other, Science (General), Social Sciences, Sociology
Bookshop(s): Libreria Celuc Libri, Via Santa Valeria 5, 20123 Milan

CEM, see Casa Editrice Maccari (CEM)

Istituto Centrale per il Catalogo Unico delle Biblioteche Italiane e per le Informazioni Bibliografiche
Viale del Castro Pretorio, 00185 Rome
Tel: (06) 4454701 *Fax:* (06) 4959302
E-mail: depinedo@itcaspur.caspur.it
Key Personnel
Dir: Dr Giovanna Mazzola Merola
Central Institute of the Union Catalog of Italian Libraries & Bibliographical Information.
Subjects: Library & Information Sciences
ISBN Prefix(es): 88-7107

Centro Ambrosiano di Documentazione e Studi Religiosi
Piazza Duca D'Aosta 8, 20124 Milan
Tel: (02) 6713161 *Fax:* (02) 66984388
Founded: 1972
Subjects: History, Religion - Other
ISBN Prefix(es): 88-7098
Imprints: CADSR

Centro Biblico
Via Masseria Vecchia 112, 80014 Naples
Tel: (081) 8048933 *Fax:* (081) 8048933
Key Personnel
Dir: David Freitag
Founded: 1952
Subjects: Biblical Studies, Religion - Protestant, Theology
ISBN Prefix(es): 88-7054

Centro Di
Lungarno Serristori 35, 50125 Florence
Tel: (055) 2342668 *Fax:* (055) 2342667
Cable: Centrodi Florence
Key Personnel
Man Dir: Alessandra Marchi
Founded: 1968
Subjects: Art
ISBN Prefix(es): 88-7038

Centro Documentazione Alpina
Corso Turati 49, 10134 Turin
Tel: (011) 3197823 *Fax:* (011) 3197827
Key Personnel
Editorial: Pietro Giglio; Mario Frasciome
Founded: 1970
Subjects: Geography, Geology
ISBN Prefix(es): 88-85504

Centro Editoriale Valtortiano SRL+
Viale Piscicelli 89-91, 03036 Isola del Liri, Frosinone
Tel: (0776) 807032 *Fax:* (0776) 809789
E-mail: cev@mariavaltorta.com
Web Site: www.mariavaltorta.com
Key Personnel
Editor: Emilio Pisani
Author: Maria Valtorta
Founded: 1985
Subjects: Religion - Catholic, Theology
ISBN Prefix(es): 88-7987
Number of titles published annually: 6 Print
Total Titles: 90 Print

Centro Italiano di Studi Sull'Alto Medioevo, see CISAM

Centro Italiano Studi Alto Medioevo
Piazza della Liberta 12, 06049 Spoleto (Perugia)
Tel: (0743) 23271 *Fax:* (0743) 232701
E-mail: cisam@cisam.org
Web Site: www.cisam.org
Key Personnel
President: Prof Enrico Menesto
Founded: 1952
To promote meetings & scientific publications on the high Middle Ages.
Subjects: Art, History, Literature, Literary Criticism, Essays, Philosophy
ISBN Prefix(es): 88-7988
Number of titles published annually: 24 Print
Total Titles: 500 Print
Imprints: CISAM

Centro Scientifico Editore, *imprint of* Centro Scientifico Torinese

Centro Scientifico Int
Via Borgone 57, 10139 Turin
Tel: (011) 3853656 *Fax:* (011) 3853244
E-mail: cse@estorinese.inet.it
Key Personnel
Administrator: Pierdvigo Massaza
Foreign Rights Manager: Valentina Kalk
Founded: 1993
Subjects: Medicine, Nursing, Dentistry, Psychology, Psychiatry
ISBN Prefix(es): 88-7640

Centro Scientifico Torinese+
Via Borgone 57, 10139 Turin
Tel: (011) 3853656 *Fax:* (011) 3853244
E-mail: cse@estorinese.inet.it
Key Personnel
President: Francesco Martiny
Editor: Dr Walter Martiny
Administrator: Pier Luigi Massaza
Founded: 1973
Subjects: Health, Nutrition, Human Relations, Medicine, Nursing, Dentistry, Psychology, Psychiatry

ISBN Prefix(es): 88-7640
Associate Companies: Artema Srl; Centro Scientifico Internazionale
Imprints: Centro Scientifico Editore; Soleverde; Edizioni Del Capricorno

Edizioni Centro Studi Erickson+
Loc Spini di Gardolo, 38014 Gardolo-Trento
Tel: (0461) 950690 *Fax:* (0461) 950698
E-mail: info@erickson.it
Web Site: www.erickson.it
Key Personnel
Dir: Dario lanes; Fabio Folgheraiter
Editor: Riccardo Mazzeo *E-mail:* ric@erickson.it; Francesca Cretti *E-mail:* cretti@erickson.it; Carmen Calovi *E-mail:* calovi@erickson.it
Founded: 1984
Subjects: Behavioral Sciences, Child Care & Development, Education, Nonfiction (General), Psychology, Psychiatry, Self-Help, Social Sciences, Sociology
ISBN Prefix(es): 88-7946
Number of titles published annually: 30 Print; 8 CD-ROM
Total Titles: 250 Print; 8 CD-ROM

Centro Studi Terzo Mondo (Study Center for the Third World)+
Via GB Morgagni 39, 20129 Milan
Tel: (02) 29409041; (330) 687866 *Fax:* (02) 29409041
E-mail: cstm@libero.it
Key Personnel
Chief Executive: Prof Umberto Melotti *E-mail:* melotti@uniroma1.it
Editorial, Rights & Permissions: Elena Sala
Founded: 1964
Books & journals on social sciences & on the problems of the Third World.
Subjects: Anthropology, Economics, Ethnicity, Geography, Geology, Government, Political Science, History, Literature, Literary Criticism, Essays, Poetry, Social Sciences, Sociology
Number of titles published annually: 12 Print
Total Titles: 120 Print
Imprints: CSTM; Ed La Cultura Sociologica

Le Cerchio Imigiative Editoriali+
Via Gambalunga, 91, 47900 Rimini
Tel: (0541) 21158; (0541) 708190 *Fax:* (0541) 21158
E-mail: ilcerchio@iper.net
Web Site: www.ilcerchio.it
Key Personnel
Man Dir, Production, Rights & Permissions: Dr Adolfo Morganti
Editorial: Dr Maurizio Mecozzi
Sales: Gloria Rubinato
Publicity: Dr Sergio de Vita
Desktop Publishing: Davide Peggi
Founded: 1979
Subjects: Anthropology, History, Philosophy, Religion - Other
ISBN Prefix(es): 88-86583
Parent Company: Cooperativa Culturale Il Cerchio, Via Gambalunga, 91, 47037 Rimini
Bookshop(s): Libreria Cooperativa Il Cerchio, Via Gambalunga, 91, 47900 Rimini

CG Ediz Medico-Scientifiche+
Via Viberti, 7, 10141 Turin
Tel: (011) 338507 *Fax:* (011) 3852750
Key Personnel
Contact: Pier Paola Pratis Palazzo
Founded: 1958
Specialize in medical books.
Subjects: Biological Sciences, Medicine, Nursing, Dentistry, Veterinary Science
ISBN Prefix(es): 88-7110

CIC Edizioni Internazionali+
Corso Trieste, 42, 00198 Rome

Tel: (06) 8412673 *Fax:* (06) 8412688
E-mail: info@gruppocic.it
Web Site: www.gruppocic.it
Telex: 622099 CICI
Key Personnel
President: Prof Andrea Salvati *E-mail:* a.salvati@gruppocic.it
Dir General: Dr Raffaele Salvati *E-mail:* r.salvati@gruppocic.it
Advertising Dept: Patrizia Arcangioli *E-mail:* arcangioli@gruppocic.it
Foreign Rights Dept: Marilena Cefa *E-mail:* cefa@gruppocic.it
Sales & Subscriptions Dept: Amelia Assi *E-mail:* assi@gruppocic.it
Founded: 1970
Member of ANES, USPI.
Subjects: Health, Nutrition, Medicine, Nursing, Dentistry, Psychology, Psychiatry
ISBN Prefix(es): 88-7141
Number of titles published annually: 150 Print; 10 CD-ROM; 15 Audio
Total Titles: 600 Print; 10 CD-ROM; 30 Audio
Subsidiaries: Centro Italiano Congressi; Kairos; Librerie CIC Edizioni Internazionali
Branch Office(s)
Viale E Caldara, 35/A, 20122 Milan, Contact: Antonietta Garzonio *Tel:* (02) 55187057 *Fax:* (02) 55187061
Centro Italiano Congress, CIC SUD, via le Escriva Nº 28, 70124 Bari, Contact: Olimpia Cassano *Tel:* (080) 5043737 *Fax:* (080) 5043736
Distributor for George Thieme Verlag (Italian territory)
Warehouse: Via Siracusa 2, 00161 Rome

Cideb Editrice SRL+
Piazza Garibaldi 11/2, 16035 Rapallo (Genova)
Tel: (0185) 55803 *Fax:* (0185) 67150
E-mail: info@blackcat-cideb.com
Key Personnel
Manager: Ornella Caffo
Founded: 1992
Subjects: Literature, Literary Criticism, Essays
ISBN Prefix(es): 88-7754
Orders to: Cideb SRL, Via Torre Civica 8, 16035 Rapallo, Genova

Il Cigno Galileo Galilei-Edizioni di Arte e Scienza
Piazza San Salvatore Lauro 15, 00186 Rome
Tel: (06) 6865493; (06) 68808432; (06) 6873842 *Fax:* (06) 6892109
E-mail: lzichic@tin.it
Key Personnel
Contact: Delfina Bergamaslhi
Founded: 1968
Specialize in printing graphic works & publish catalogues & art volumes.
Subjects: Art, Law, Mathematics, Science (General)
ISBN Prefix(es): 88-7831
Number of titles published annually: 40 Print; 4 CD-ROM
Total Titles: 385 Print; 4 CD-ROM
Showroom(s): Archivi Greco, Museo Mastroianni & Il Cigno Galileo Galilei La Stamperia

Ciranna e Ferrara
Via Solferino, 163, 20038 Seregno (Milan)
Tel: (0362) 230849 *Fax:* (0362) 326213
Founded: 1976
ISBN Prefix(es): 88-8144

Ciranna - Roma
Via Besio 127/143, 90145 Palermo
Tel: (091) 224499 *Fax:* (091) 311064
Key Personnel
Chief Executive, Rights & Permissions: Dr Lidia Fabiano
Founded: 1953

Subjects: Art, Business, Education, Geography, Geology, History, Language Arts, Linguistics, Law, Literature, Literary Criticism, Essays, Mathematics, Philosophy, Psychology, Psychiatry, Public Administration, Science (General), Technology
ISBN Prefix(es): 88-8322
Orders to: Via Capograssa 1115

Cisalpino, *imprint of* Monduzzi Editore SpA

Cisalpino - Monduzzi
Via Ferrarese 119/2, 40128 Bologna
Tel: (051) 4151111 *Fax:* (051) 370529
Founded: 1946
Subjects: Economics, History, Language Arts, Linguistics, Law, Literature, Literary Criticism, Essays, Management
ISBN Prefix(es): 88-205

CISAM, *imprint of* Centro Italiano Studi Alto Medioevo

CISAM
Piazza della Liberta, 12, 06049 Spoleto, Perugia
Tel: (0743) 23271 *Fax:* (0743) 232701
E-mail: cisam@etcisam.org
Web Site: www.cisam.org
Key Personnel
President: Enrico Menesio
Dir: Stefano Brufani
ISBN Prefix(es): 88-7988
Branch Office(s)
Palazzo Ancaiani, 06049 Spoleto, Perugia
Orders to: Indirizzo Sopra

Citta Nuova Editrice+
Via degli Scipioni 265, 00192 Rome
Tel: (06) 3216212 *Fax:* (06) 3207185
Key Personnel
Man Dir: Dr Vittorio Fasciotti; Dr Giovanni Battista Dadda
Founded: 1959
Subjects: Biblical Studies, Education, Philosophy, Psychology, Psychiatry, Religion - Other, Social Sciences, Sociology, Theology
ISBN Prefix(es): 88-311
Subsidiaries: Ciudad Nueva (Argentina); Unistad Verspreiding RV (Belgium); Cidade Nova Editora (Brazil); Ciudad Nueva (Colombia); Nouvelle Cite (France); Verlag Neue Stadt GmbH (Germany); Nieuwe Stad (Netherlands); New City (Philippines); Cidade Nova (Portugal); Editorial Ciutat Nova (Spain); Verlag Neue Stadt (Switzerland); New City (United Kingdom); New City Press (United States)
Shipping Address: Via V Ussani 88, 00151 Rome
Warehouse: Via V Ussani 88, 00151 Rome

Cittadella Editrice+
Imprint of Pro Civitate Christiana
Via Ancaiani 3, 06081 Assisi (Perugia)
Tel: (075) 813595 *Fax:* (075) 813719
E-mail: amministrazione@cittadellaeditrice.com
Web Site: cittadellaeditrice.com *Cable:*
CITTADELLA EDITRICE
Key Personnel
Trans Off: Gabriella Persico *E-mail:* redazione@cittadellaeditrice.com
Editorial Manager: Giuseppina Pompei
 E-mail: gpompei@cittadellaeditrice.com
Foreign Rights: Franco Ferrari *E-mail:* fferrari@cittadellaeditrice.com
Press Office Manager: Franco Ferrari *Tel:* (075) 813231
Founded: 1940
Subjects: Biblical Studies, Biography, Psychology, Psychiatry, Religion - Catholic, Religion - Other, Social Sciences, Sociology, Theology
ISBN Prefix(es): 88-308
Number of titles published annually: 32 Print

Total Titles: 466 Print
Bookshop(s): Libreria Cittadella, Via Ancaiani 3, 06081 Assisi (Perugia)

Claudiana Editrice+
Via Principe Tommaso 1, 10125 Turin
Tel: (011) 6689804 *Fax:* (011) 6504394
E-mail: claudiana.editirce@alpcom.it
Key Personnel
President: Pastore Eugenio Bernardini
Editorial, Sales, Rights & Permissions: Manuel Kromer
Founded: 1855
Member of AIE.
Subjects: Biblical Studies, History, Religion - Protestant, Theology
ISBN Prefix(es): 88-7016
Distributor for Edizioni GBU (Rome)
Bookshop(s): Libreria Claudiana, Via Francesco Sforza 12A, I-20122 Milan; Libreria Claudiana, Piazza Liberta, I-10066 Torre Pellice (Turin); Via Pr Tommaso 1, I-10125 Turin; Libreria di Cultura Religiosa, Piazza Cavour 32, I-00193 Rome

CLEUP - Cooperative Libraria Editrice dell 'Universita di Padova+
Via Prati 19, 35122 Padua
Tel: (049) 8753496 *Fax:* (049) 650261
Key Personnel
President: Fulvio Ursini
Vice President: Sergio Relai
Founded: 1962
Also book packager.
Subjects: Engineering (General), Government, Political Science, Language Arts, Linguistics, Mathematics, Medicine, Nursing, Dentistry, Psychology, Psychiatry, Science (General)
ISBN Prefix(es): 88-7178
Bookshop(s): Libreria CLEUP, Via San Francesco 64, I-35100 Padua *Tel:* 049-39557

CLUEB (Cooperativa Libraria Universitaria Editrice Bologna)+
Via Marsala 31, 40126 Bologna
Tel: (051) 220736 *Fax:* (051) 237758
E-mail: clueb@clueb.com
Web Site: www.clueb.com
Key Personnel
Man Dir: Luigi Guardigli *E-mail:* gua@clueb.com
Editorial Man: Giulio Forconi *E-mail:* g.forconi@clueb.com
Founded: 1959
Specialize also in theatre, detective stories & criticism of D.S.
Subjects: Accounting, Agriculture, Architecture & Interior Design, Art, Business, Economics, Education, History, Human Relations, Language Arts, Linguistics, Literature, Literary Criticism, Essays, Music, Dance, Philosophy, Psychology, Psychiatry, Science (General)
ISBN Prefix(es): 88-8091; 88-491
Number of titles published annually: 150 Print; 3 CD-ROM
Total Titles: 15 Print; 1 CD-ROM
Subsidiaries: Clueb DPE
U.S. Office(s): Paul & Company Publishers Consortium, PO Box 442, Concord, MA 01742, United States
Distributor for Universita' di Trento
Bookshop(s): Libreria Clueb, Bologna

CLUT Editrice+
Corso Duca degli Abruzzi 24, 10129 Turin
Tel: (011) 542192 *Fax:* (011) 542192
Key Personnel
Man Dir: Michele Ruffino
Editorial: Toscano Donatella
Founded: 1960
Subjects: Human Relations, Science (General), Technology

ISBN Prefix(es): 88-7992
Parent Company: Cooperativa Libraria Universitaria Torinese Scrl, Corso Duca degli Abruzzi 24, 10129 Turin

La Coccinella Editrice SRL
Via Crispi 77/79, 21100 Varese
Tel: (0332) 224690 *Fax:* (0332) 222025
Telex: 326169 per La Coccinella
Key Personnel
Editorial Dir: Domenico Caputo
Sales, Rights & Permissions: Giuliana Crespi
Production Dir: Valerio Morelli
Founded: 1977
Subjects: Crafts, Games, Hobbies, Education
ISBN Prefix(es): 88-7703
Subsidiaries: RCS Rizzoli Libri
Warehouse: RCS Rizzoli, Via Angelo Rizzoli 4, Milan

Nuova Coletti Editore Roma
Via Clitunno 24f, 00198 Rome
Tel: (06) 8557981 *Fax:* (06) 8557981
Founded: 1987
Subjects: Biblical Studies, Education, History, Literature, Literary Criticism, Essays, Philosophy, Religion - Catholic, Theology
ISBN Prefix(es): 88-7826
Warehouse: Borgo Pio 105, 00193 Rome

Collana, *imprint of* Mondolibro Editore SNC

Colonnese Editore+
Via San Pietro a Majella, 7, 80138 Naples
Mailing Address: PO Box 145, 80100 Napoli Centro
Tel: (081) 459858; (081) 293900 *Fax:* (081) 455420
E-mail: info@colonnese.it
Web Site: spacee.tin.it/lettura/gacolon
Key Personnel
Dir, Publishing & Sales: Gaetano Colonnese
Rights & Permissions: Edgar Colonnese
 E-mail: edgecolon@tin.it
Founded: 1965
Subjects: Archaeology, Drama, Theater, Fiction, History, Humor, Language Arts, Linguistics, Literature, Literary Criticism, Essays, Photography, Poetry, Women's Studies
ISBN Prefix(es): 88-87501
Number of titles published annually: 12 Print
Total Titles: 300 Print
Distributed by Zambon Verlag & Vertrieb (Germany)
Foreign Rights: Guido Lagomarsino (Italy)
Bookshop(s): Libreria Colonnese SAS, Via San Pietro a Majella 32/33, 80138 Naples *Tel:* (081) 459858 *Fax:* (081) 455420
Orders to: Colonnese, Via S Pa Majella 32-33, 80138 Naples *Tel:* (081) 459858 *Fax:* (081) 455420 *E-mail:* colophon@tin.it

Le Comete, *imprint of* Passigli Editori srl

Edizioni di Comunita SpA+
Division of Mondadori
Via Biancamano 2, 10121 Turin
Tel: (011) 56561 *Fax:* (011) 542903
E-mail: novarese@amemail.mondadori.it
Web Site: www.comunita.einaudi.it
Key Personnel
Res Administrator: R Veglia *Tel:* (011) 5656205
 E-mail: veglia@amemail.mondadori.it
Founded: 1946
Subjects: Architecture & Interior Design, Art, Computer Science, Economics, Government, Political Science, History, Law, Science (General), Social Sciences, Sociology
ISBN Prefix(es): 88-245
Total Titles: 70 Print
Ultimate Parent Company: Einaudi

Associate Companies: Arnoldo Mondadori Editore SpA
Distributed by A Mondadori

Consiglio Nazionale delle Ricerche Rep Pubblicazioni e Informazioni Scientifiche
Via Sommacampagna, 8, 00185 Rome

Continental SRL Editrice
Via Suardi 7, 24100 Bergamo
Tel: (035) 237088 *Fax:* (035) 237039
Key Personnel
Man Dir, Rights & Permissions: Luigi Maria Facheris
Editorial: Ornella Crispiatico
Sales, Publicity: Paola Sala
Production: Roberto Poli
Founded: 1974
Subjects: Education

Convivio (Nardini Editore), *imprint of* Nardini Editore srl

Cooperativa Libraria Editrice dell' Universita, see CLEUP - Cooperative Libraria Editrice dell 'Universita di Padova

Cooperativa Libraria IULM SCRL+
Via Filippo da Liscate, 1/2, 20143 Milan
Tel: (02) 89150013 *Fax:* (02) 89150013; (02) 8915002
E-mail: coopli-iulm@libezo.it
Key Personnel
President: Luciano Duo
Editor: Marisa Chiani
Founded: 1971
Subjects: English as a Second Language, Film, Video, Literature, Literary Criticism, Essays, Management, Marketing, Social Sciences, Sociology
ISBN Prefix(es): 88-7695
Number of titles published annually: 30 Print; 2 CD-ROM; 2 Audio
Total Titles: 2 CD-ROM; 2 Audio
Imprints: Arcipelago Edizioni

Cooperativa Libraria Universitaria Editrice Bologna, see CLUEB (Cooperativa Libraria Universitaria Editrice Bologna)

Cooperativa Libraria Universitaria Torinese, see CLUT Editrice

Edizioni Cooperative Scarl
Via Giuseppe Tomassetti, 12, 00161 Rome
Tel: (06) 442392227 *Fax:* (06) 44238504
E-mail: incm@legacoop.it
Web Site: www.legacoop.it
Key Personnel
President: Sandro Bonella
ISBN Prefix(es): 88-7361

Casa Editrice Corbaccio srl+
Corso Italia 13, 20122 Milan
Tel: (020) 8692413 *Fax:* (020) 804067
E-mail: info@corbaccio.it
Web Site: www.corbaccio.it
Key Personnel
President: Mario Spagnol
Man Dir: Stefano Mauri
Editorial: Cecilia Perucci
Sales: Giuseppe Somenzi
Production: Alfredo Bonfiglio
Publicity: Valentina Fortichiari
Rights & Permissions: Cristina Foschini
Founded: 1992
ISBN Prefix(es): 88-7972
Parent Company: Longanesi & C
Associate Companies: Finarte, GdP

Branch Office(s)
Nina Collins Association, 584 Broadway, Suite 607, New York, NY 10012, United States
Warehouse: Messaggerie Italiane Spa, Maggazzino Editoriale Via Bereguardina, Casarile 20080
Orders to: Pro Libro, Corso Italia 13, 20122 Milan

Libreria Cortina Editrice SRL+
Via A Mario 10, 37121 Verona
Tel: (045) 594177 *Fax:* (045) 597551
E-mail: libreriacortina@tin.it; cortinab@tin.it
Key Personnel
Chief Executive, Editorial: Cunego Pierpiorgio
Founded: 1971
Also book packager.
Subjects: Medicine, Nursing, Dentistry, Science (General)
ISBN Prefix(es): 88-85037; 88-7749
Bookshop(s): Palazzetto d'Ingresso, Policlinico Borgo Roma, Via delle Menegone, 1-37134 Verona *Tel:* (065) 505270 *Fax:* (065) 584594
E-mail: cortinab@tin.it

Costa e Nolan SpA+
Via Romani, 8, 16122 Genoa
Tel: (010) 873888 *Fax:* (010) 873889
Key Personnel
Man Dir, Rights & Permissions: Carla Costa
Editorial: Eugenio Buonaccorsi
Sales, Publicity: Stefano Tettamanti
Founded: 1982
Subjects: Art, Drama, Theater, Economics, Fiction, Literature, Literary Criticism, Essays
ISBN Prefix(es): 88-7648

CPE - Centro Programmazione Editoriale
Via Canaletto 20b, 41030 S Prospero (Modena)
Tel: (059) 908065 *Fax:* (059) 906029
Founded: 1973
Subjects: Education, Mathematics, Psychology, Psychiatry

Edizioni Cremonese SRL+
Borgo Santa Croce 17, 50122 Florence
Tel: (055) 2476371 *Fax:* (055) 2476372
Web Site: www.ed-cremonese.it *Cable:* EDIZIONI CREMONESE
Key Personnel
Man Dir: Alberto Stianti *E-mail:* cremonese@ed-cremonese.it
Founded: 1930
Subjects: Aeronautics, Aviation, Civil Engineering, Electronics, Electrical Engineering, Engineering (General), Mathematics, Mechanical Engineering, Science (General), Technology
ISBN Prefix(es): 88-7083

Crisalide+
Via Campodivivo 43, 04020 Spigno Saturnia (Latina)
Tel: (0771) 64463 *Fax:* (0771) 64693
E-mail: crisalide@crisalide.com; info@crisalide.com
Web Site: crisalide.com
Key Personnel
President & Owner: Raffaele Iandolo *Tel:* (0771) 639121
Founded: 1988
Subjects: Astrology, Occult, Parapsychology, Psychology, Psychiatry, Religion - Buddhist
ISBN Prefix(es): 88-7183
Number of titles published annually: 20 Print
Total Titles: 120 Print
Online services available through Crisalide.com.
Distributed by C D A

CSTM, *imprint of* Centro Studi Terzo Mondo

Edizioni Cultura della Pace+
Via del Salviatino 1, 50014 S Domenico, Florence
Tel: (055) 580550 *Fax:* (055) 597185
Key Personnel
President: Enrico Palmerini
Founded: 1986
Subjects: Anthropology, Biography, Communications, Developing Countries, Education, Environmental Studies, Ethnicity, Foreign Countries, Government, Political Science, History, Human Relations, Philosophy, Religion - Buddhist, Religion - Catholic, Religion - Hindu, Religion - Islamic, Religion - Jewish, Religion - Protestant, Religion - Other, Social Sciences, Sociology, Theology, Women's Studies
ISBN Prefix(es): 88-09; 88-87183
Imprints: ECP
Orders to: Edizioni Cultura della Pace, Via Brunetto Latini 49, 50131 Florence

Ed La Cultura Sociologica, *imprint of* Centro Studi Terzo Mondo

La Cultura Sociologica, *imprint of* La Culturale

La Culturale+
Via GB Morgagni 39, 20129 Milan
Tel: (02) 29409041 *Fax:* (02) 29409041
Key Personnel
Chief Executive: Prof Umberto Melotti *Tel:* (330) 687866 *E-mail:* melotti@uniroma1.it
Editorial, Rights & Permissions: Elena Sala
Founded: 1964
Books on social sciences.
Subjects: Biological Sciences, Economics, Ethnicity, Government, Political Science, History, Philosophy, Social Sciences, Sociology
Number of titles published annually: 8 Print
Total Titles: 100 Print
Associate Companies: Centro Studi Terzo Mondo
Imprints: La Cultura Sociologica

Edizioni Curci SRL+
Galleria del Corso 4, 20122 Milan
Tel: (02) 794746 *Fax:* (02) 76014504
E-mail: curci@iol.it
Web Site: www.edizionicurci.it
Key Personnel
President & General Manager: Giuseppe Gramitto Ricci
Classical Dept: Mrs Laura Moro
Founded: 1860
Subjects: Music, Dance
ISBN Prefix(es): 88-485
Associate Companies: Edizioni Accordo SRL
Warehouse: Via Ripamonti, 129, 20141 Milan, Lina Manfra *Tel:* (02) 57410561 *Fax:* (02) 5390043

Dami Editore SRL+
Via Gesu 10, 20121 Milan
Tel: (02) 76005497 *Fax:* (02) 784010
E-mail: damieditore@damieditore.it
Founded: 1972
Subjects: Animals, Pets, Fiction
ISBN Prefix(es): 88-09

D'Anna+
Via dei Della Robbia 26, 50132 Florence
Tel: (055) 242800 *Fax:* (055) 2480781
E-mail: gdanna@tin.it *Cable:* D'ANNA FLORENCE
Key Personnel
Man Dir, Sales, & Rights & Permissions: Albertina D'Anna
Editorial & Production: Gabriele D'Anna; Guido D'Anna
Founded: 1926

Subjects: Art, Chemistry, Chemical Engineering, Education, History, Literature, Literary Criticism, Essays
ISBN Prefix(es): 88-8104; 88-8321
Imprints: Editoriale Paradigma; G D'Anna-Sintesi
Warehouse: Loescher Editore, via Vajont 93, Cascine Vica Rivoli, Torino
Orders to: Loescher Editore, Via V Amedeo II, 18-1021 Torino

G D'Anna-Sintesi, *imprint of* D'Anna

Datanews+
Via S Erasmo, 22, 00184 Rome
Tel: (06) 70450318 *Fax:* (06) 70450320
E-mail: datanews.edit@mclink.it
Key Personnel
President: Corrado Perna
Man Dir: Pasquale Ragucci
Founded: 1985
Subjects: Economics, Environmental Studies, Ethnicity, Government, Political Science, History
ISBN Prefix(es): 88-7981

M d'Auria Editore SAS+
Calata Trinita Maggiore 52/53, 80134 Naples
Tel: (081) 5518963 *Fax:* (081) 5493827
E-mail: info@dauria.it
Web Site: www.dauria.it
Key Personnel
Dir: Gianni Macchiavelli
Publicity: Paola Raeli
Founded: 1837
Also acts as sales agent.
Subjects: Antiques, Archaeology, History, Literature, Literary Criticism, Essays, Religion - Other
ISBN Prefix(es): 88-7092
Number of titles published annually: 20 Print
Total Titles: 45 Print
Distributor for Edizioni Di Storia E Letteratura SRL; Instituto Universitario Orientale
Bookshop(s): Libreria Internazionale-International Book Center M d'Auria, Calata Trinita Maggiore 52/53, 80134 Naples

G De Bono Editore+
Via Masaccio 220, 50132 Florence
Tel: (055) 570670 *Fax:* (055) 5001665
Key Personnel
Chief Executive: Giuseppe De Bono
Editorial: Prof Aldo De Bono
Founded: 1958
Subjects: Education, Fiction, Philosophy

Giovanni De Vecchi Editore SpA+
Via Pisani 16, 20124 Milan
Tel: (02) 66984851 *Fax:* (02) 6701548
Founded: 1973
Subjects: Agriculture, Animals, Pets, Antiques, Astrology, Occult, Business, Career Development, Crafts, Games, Hobbies, Gardening, Plants, Health, Nutrition, How-to, Humor, Law, Medicine, Nursing, Dentistry, Outdoor Recreation, Sports, Athletics
ISBN Prefix(es): 88-412

DEA, see DEA Diffusione Edizioni Anglo-Americane

DEA Diffusione Edizioni Anglo-Americane
Via Lima 28, 00198 Rome
Tel: (06) 8551441 *Fax:* (06) 8543228
E-mail: deanet@deanet.it
Web Site: www.deanet.com
ISBN Prefix(es): 88-86188
Branch Office(s)
Massimo D'Azeglio 27, 40123 Bologna
Tel: (051) 236100 *Fax:* (051) 220882
Via Pascoli 56, 20133 Milan *Tel:* (02) 2364306 *Fax:* (02) 2362738

Via Domenico Cimarosa 91/c, 80127 Naples
Tel: (081) 5787576 *Fax:* (081) 5780739
Via G D Cassini 75/8, 10129 Torino *Tel:* (011) 503202 *Fax:* (011) 595559
Via Diaz 19/1, 34124 Trieste *Tel:* (040) 301257 *Fax:* (040) 310993

Edizioni Dedalo SRL+
Viale Luigi Jacobini 5, 70123 Bari
Mailing Address: Casella Postale BA/19, 70123 Bari
Tel: (080) 5311413 *Fax:* (080) 5311414
E-mail: info@edizionidedalo.it
Web Site: www.edizionidedalo.it
Key Personnel
Man Dir: Raimondo Coga
Editorial Manager: Claudia Coga
E-mail: claudiacoga@edizionidedalo.it
Founded: 1965
Also acts as printing house.
Subjects: Anthropology, Architecture & Interior Design, Art, Film, Video, Government, Political Science, History, Philosophy, Physical Sciences, Physics, Psychology, Psychiatry, Science (General), Social Sciences, Sociology
ISBN Prefix(es): 88-300; 88-220
Parent Company: Dedalo Litostampa Srl

Edizioni Dehoniane+
Via del Casale di S Pio V, 20, 00165 Rome
Tel: (06) 6624996 *Fax:* (06) 6628326 *Cable:* EDIZIONI DEHONIANE ROME
Key Personnel
Chief Executive: Vitantonio Giampietro
Editorial: Luigi Cortese
Sales, Publicity: Antonio Bozza
Production: Umberto Chiarello
Founded: 1964
Subjects: Education, Philosophy, Psychology, Psychiatry, Religion - Other, Social Sciences, Sociology, Theology
ISBN Prefix(es): 88-396
Parent Company: Provincia Meridonale Italiana della Congregazi one dei Sacerdoti del S Cuore di Gesu', via Marechiaro, 46 Naples
Bookshop(s): Libreria Dehoniana, Via Depretis 60, 1-80133 Naples

Edizioni Dehoniane Bologna (EDB)+
Via Nosadella, 6, 40123 Bologna
Tel: (051) 306811 *Fax:* (051) 341706
E-mail: ced-amm@dehoniane.it
Key Personnel
Man Dir: Alfio Filippi
Sales Dir, Rights & Permissions: Cesano Giacomo
Publicity Dir: Gabriella Zucchi
Contact: Vanda Persiani
Founded: 1965
Subjects: Biblical Studies, Education, Religion - Catholic, Religion - Other, Theology
ISBN Prefix(es): 88-10
Associate Companies: Data Service Center
Imprints: EDB
Distributed by Dehoniana Libri SpA
Bookshop(s): Dehoniana Libri, Via Nosadella, 6, 40123 Bologna
Shipping Address: Via Dal Ferro 4, 1-40138 Bologna

DEI Tipographia del Genio Civile
Via Nomentana 16, 00161 Rome
Tel: (06) 4402046 *Fax:* (06) 4403307
E-mail: dei@aec2000.it
Key Personnel
Man Dir, Production: Maria Cecilia Bartoli
Editorial, Publicity: Giuseppe Rufo
Sales: Grazia Jacomelli
Founded: 1879
Subjects: Architecture & Interior Design, Civil Engineering, Electronics, Electrical Engineering, Law, Technology

ISBN Prefix(es): 88-7722
Warehouse: Via Mesula 12, 00161 Roma

Edizioni Del Capricorno, *imprint of* Centro Scientifico Torinese

Edizioni del Capricorno
Via Borgone 57, 10139 Turin
Tel: (011) 386500 *Fax:* (011) 3853244
E-mail: cse@estorinese.inet.it
Key Personnel
Editor: Dr Walter Martiny
Foreign Rights Manager: Valentine Kalk
Subjects: Photography
ISBN Prefix(es): 88-7707
Parent Company: Centro Scientific Torinese SrL

Edizioni del Centro+
Via Marconi 7, 25044 Capo di Ponte (Brescia)
Tel: (0364) 42091 *Fax:* (0364) 42572
E-mail: ccspriest@tin.it
Web Site: www.rockart-ccsp.com *Cable:* CENTROSTUDI CAPODIPONTE
Key Personnel
Chief Executive: Prof Emmanuel Anati
Production: Ariela Fradkin
Founded: 1964
Research Institution with a Publishing Division.
Subjects: Anthropology, Antiques, Archaeology, Art, Biblical Studies, Ethnicity, History, Religion - Other
ISBN Prefix(es): 88-86621
Number of titles published annually: 3 Print
Total Titles: 90 Print
Parent Company: Centro Camuno di Studi Preistoric, Via Marconi 7, 25044 Capo di Ponte (Brescia)
Associate Companies: Arts & Crafts International; IDAPEE (Institut des Arts Prehistoriques et Ethnologique), Paris, France
Imprints: BCSP; BC News; CCSP
Subsidiaries: WARA: World Archives of Rock Art

Edizioni del Riccio SAS di G Bernardi+
Via di Soffiano 164a, 50143 Florence
Tel: (055) 702020 *Fax:* (055) 716362
Key Personnel
Chief Executive: Giuliano Bernardi
Founded: 1977
Subjects: Cookery, Medicine, Nursing, Dentistry, Psychology, Psychiatry, Travel
ISBN Prefix(es): 88-7099
Number of titles published annually: 8 Print

Istituto della Enciclopedia Italiana+
Piazza Enciclopedia Italiana 4, 00186 Rome
Tel: (06) 68981 *Fax:* (06) 68982175
E-mail: treccani5@pop.inet.it *Cable:* ENCICLOPEDIA
Key Personnel
Editorial Dir: Bray Massimo
Founded: 1925
Subjects: Art
ISBN Prefix(es): 88-12
Orders to: Piazza Enciclopedia Italiana 4, 00186 Rome

Casa Editrice Istituto della Santa
Via dei Caccia 5, Novara 28100
Tel: (0321) 22371 *Cable:* Dellasanta Novara
Founded: 1956
Subjects: Business

Edizioni Della Torre di Salvatore Fozzi & C SAS+
Via Contivecchi 8/2, 09122 Cagliari
Tel: (070) 270507 *Fax:* (070) 270507
Key Personnel
Chief Executive: Salvatore Fozzi *Tel:* (070) 271411 *Fax:* (070) 272542

PUBLISHERS — ITALY

Founded: 1974
Subjects: Archaeology, Art, Geography, Geology, History, Language Arts, Linguistics, Natural History, Poetry, Regional Interests
ISBN Prefix(es): 88-7343
Total Titles: 225 Print
Associate Companies: Scuola Domani, via Toscana 82, 09124 Cagliari
Subsidiaries: Agenzia Libraria Fozzi
Bookshop(s): Libreria Fozzi, Via Dante 72, 09100 Cagliari

Edizioni dell'Orso SAS+
Via Rattazzi 47, 15100 Alessandria
Tel: (0131) 252349 *Fax:* (0131) 257567
Key Personnel
Man Dir: Gian Paolo Calligaris
Editorial: Lorenzo Massobrio
Founded: 1979
Subjects: History, Language Arts, Linguistics, Poetry, Regional Interests
ISBN Prefix(es): 88-7694

Demetra SRL+
Via Stra 167, 37030 Colognola al Colli (Verona)
Tel: (045) 6174111 *Fax:* (045) 6174100
Key Personnel
Man Dir: Silvano Pizzighella
Founded: 1983
Subjects: Agriculture, Biological Sciences, Health, Nutrition, Literature, Literary Criticism, Essays
ISBN Prefix(es): 88-7122; 88-440

Di Baio Editore SpA+
Via Settembrini 11, 20124 Milan
Tel: (02) 6692254 *Fax:* (02) 6709257
Key Personnel
President: Giuseppe Maria Jonghi Lavarini
Man Dir: Fabio Alberti
Founded: 1973
Subjects: Architecture & Interior Design, Cookery, Crafts, Games, Hobbies, Gardening, Plants, House & Home, Technology
ISBN Prefix(es): 88-7080

Diakronia+
Via Albini 4b, 27029 Vigevano Pavia
Tel: (0381) 83034 *Fax:* (0381) 690576
Key Personnel
Administrator: Marisa Laveroni
Dir: Giorgio Bombi
Founded: 1984
Subjects: Architecture & Interior Design, Art, Cookery, History, Travel
ISBN Prefix(es): 88-8069
Subsidiaries: Dialogos sre

Organizzazione Didattica Editoriale Ape+
Viale Michelangelo 5, 50125 Florence
Tel: (055) 392670; (055) 689295 *Fax:* (055) 343485; (055) 683760 *Cable:* APE MURRI 565 BOLOGNA
Key Personnel
Chief Executive, Editorial, Production, Rights & Permissions: Gina Cesari
Sales: Giorgio Ognibene
Founded: 1964
Subjects: Fiction, Regional Interests
ISBN Prefix(es): 88-86515
Imprints: APE
Bookshop(s): Gottardi Concession, via Zanardi 60, IV Bologna

Dimensione Umana, *imprint of* Gruppo Editoriale Le Stelle SpA

Directorate of Archives, see Direzione Generale Archivi

Direzione Generale Archivi
Direzione generale pergli archivi, Divisione V, Via Gaeta, 8/A, 00185 Rome
Tel: (06) 4742177 *Fax:* (06) 4742177
E-mail: studi@archivi.beniculturali.it
Web Site: www.archivi.beniculturali.it
Telex: 623278
Key Personnel
Dir: Antonio Dentoni-Litta
Publishing branch of the Italian State Archives Administration.
Subjects: History, Law, Library & Information Sciences, Public Administration
ISBN Prefix(es): 88-7125
Number of titles published annually: 20 Print
Total Titles: 450 Print
Parent Company: Ministero Beni e Attivita Culturali
Orders to: Istituto poligrafico e Zecca dello stato, Via Marciana Marina, No A, 00199 Rome
Tel: (06) 85 081 *Fax:* (06) 85 084117
Direzione editoriale, Via Marciana Marina, No A, 00199 Rome *Tel:* (06) 85 081 *Fax:* (06) 85 084117
Libreria dello Stato, Via Marciana Marina, No A, 00199 Rome *Tel:* (06) 85 081 *Fax:* (06) 85 084117

Nuove Edizioni Dolomiti SRL+
Viale del Lavoro, 42, 32010 Pieve d'Alpago (Belluno)
Tel: (0437) 989216 *Fax:* (0437) 989099
Key Personnel
President: Ilario Sovicla
Vice President: Rosanna Sovilla
Founded: 1990
ISBN Prefix(es): 88-85080
Imprints: NED

Domus Academy
Via Savona 97, 20144 Milan
Tel: (02) 47719155 *Fax:* (02) 4222525
E-mail: info@domac.it
Web Site: www.domac.it
ISBN Prefix(es): 88-7184; 88-85187

Editoriale Domus Spa+
Via Grandi 5/7, 20089 Rozzano, Milan
Tel: (02) 824721 *Fax:* (02) 26863123; (02) 57500132
E-mail: editorialedomus@edidomus.it
Founded: 1929
Subjects: Aeronautics, Aviation, Architecture & Interior Design, Art, Automotive, Cookery, Transportation, Travel
ISBN Prefix(es): 88-7212

Dunod, *imprint of* Masson SpA

Edizioni E - Elle SRL
S Francesco d'Assisi 62, 34133 Trieste
Tel: (040) 637969 *Fax:* (0406) 378660
Telex: (040) 637969
Key Personnel
Man Dir: Giancarlo Stavro Santarosa
Editorial: Orietta Fatucci
Rights & Permissions: Sandra Goruppi
Founded: 1984
ISBN Prefix(es): 88-85326

Edizioni E/O+
Via Camozzi 1, 00195 Rome
Tel: (06) 3722829 *Fax:* (06) 7351096
Key Personnel
Man Dir, Rights & Permissions: Sandro Ferri
Editorial: Sandra Ozzola
Sales: Tom Joannucci
Production: Alfredo Lavarini
Publicity: Sergio Vezzali
Founded: 1979
Subjects: Fiction
ISBN Prefix(es): 88-7641

Edizioni EBE
Via dei Magazzini 22, 01016 Tarquinia (Viterbo)
Tel: (0766) 858878 *Fax:* (0766) 858877
Key Personnel
Chief Executive: Giovanni Di Capua
Sales: Norma Merli
Founded: 1973
Subjects: Government, Political Science, History
ISBN Prefix(es): 88-7977
Orders to: Via FS Nitti 12, I-00191 Rome
Tel: (06) 3272972

EBF, *imprint of* Biblioteca Francescana

ECIG+
Via Brignole De Ferrari, 9, 16125 Genoa
Tel: (010) 2512399 *Fax:* (010) 2512398
Key Personnel
Man Dir: Dr Gian Luigi Blengino
Founded: 1971
Specialize in: Sapiential Essays.
Subjects: Literature, Literary Criticism, Essays, Philosophy, Psychology, Psychiatry
ISBN Prefix(es): 88-7545
Showroom(s): Salone Del Libro Torino, Largo Regio Parco, 9-10152 Torino; Frankfurt Buchmesse, Frankfurt, Germany
Bookshop(s): Piazza Santa Sabina 2 sc A/2, Genoa *Tel:* (010) 203788; Salita Inf della Noce 8 rosso 16131, Genoa *Tel:* (010) 510355; Via S Gallo 21R, Florence *Tel:* (055) 261693; Viale Morgagni 31, Florence *Tel:* (055) 4361722; Via Ormea 90, Torino *Tel:* (011) 683527; Via Santa maria 7, Pisa *Tel:* (050) 501426; Via dei Mille 32, Pisa *Tel:* 050 35310; Via De Amicis 60, Naples *Tel:* (081) 5469304
Orders to: CLU - Salita Inferiore, Della NOCE 10 R, IDEM, 16143 Genoa

Ecole Francaise de Rome+
Piazza Navona 62, 00186 Rome
Tel: (06) 688851 *Fax:* (06) 68885405
E-mail: publ@ecole-francaise.it; secr@ekole-francaise.it
Web Site: www.ecole-francaise.it
Key Personnel
Dir: Andre Vauchez
Publisher: Francois-Charles Uginet *Tel:* (06) 68885305
Founded: 1881
Subjects: Archaeology, Art, History, Law
ISBN Prefix(es): 2-7283
Number of titles published annually: 30 Print
Total Titles: 400 Print

ECP, *imprint of* Edizioni Cultura della Pace

Edagricole - Edizioni Agricole+
Via Emilia Levante N 31/2, 40139 Bologna
Tel: (051) 62267 *Fax:* (051) 490200
E-mail: comm@calderini.agriline.it
Web Site: www.edagricole.it
Key Personnel
Man Dir & Editorial: Alberto Perdisa
Sales: Luigi Perdisa, Jr *Tel:* (051) 6226849 *Fax:* (051) 540000
Publicity: Franco Metri *Tel:* (051) 6226818
E-mail: stampa@calderini.agriline.it
Founded: 1935
Subjects: Agriculture, Animals, Pets, Biological Sciences, Gardening, Plants, Health, Nutrition, Science (General), Veterinary Science
ISBN Prefix(es): 88-206
Total Titles: 2,000 Print
Parent Company: Calderini SRL, Via Emilia Levante N 31/2, 40139 Bologna

ITALY

Associate Companies: Calderini Industrie Grafiche ed Editoriali SRL; Edizioni Calderini; Edagricole Periodici SpA
Bookshop(s): Via Zamboni 18, Bologna; Via Bronzino 14, Milan; Via Boncompagni 73, Rome

EDAS
Via San Giovanni Bosco 17, 98122 Messina
Tel: (090) 675653 Fax: (090) 675653
Founded: 1975
ISBN Prefix(es): 88-7820

EDB, imprint of Edizioni Dehoniane Bologna (EDB)

EDB, see Edizioni Dehoniane Bologna (EDB)

Edi Ermes SRL+
Viale Forlanini 65, 20134 Milan
Tel: (02) 70209911 Fax: (02) 70209919
Key Personnel
Chief Executive: Dr Italo Grandi
Founded: 1973
Also book packager.
Subjects: Art, Biological Sciences, Economics, Medicine, Nursing, Dentistry, Sports, Athletics, Veterinary Science
ISBN Prefix(es): 88-85019; 88-7051
Associate Companies: Edi Artes SRL, Viale Forlanini 65, 20134 Milan
Imprints: EE

Ediart Editrice
Imprint of Livro Grai
Loc Montelupino, 82/13, 06059 Todi (PG)
Tel: (075) 8943594 Fax: (075) 8942411
E-mail: ediart@ediart.it
Founded: 1983
Specialize in History of Art & Architecture.
ISBN Prefix(es): 88-85311
Number of titles published annually: 4 Print
Total Titles: 70 Print

Edicart
Nuova Edibimbi, Decora, Edivideo, Via Jucker, 28, 20025 Legnano, Milan
Tel: (0331) 465662 Fax: (0331) 465663
E-mail: edicart@galctica.it
ISBN Prefix(es): 88-474; 88-7774

Ediciclo Editore SRL+
Via Cesare Bellaria 13/15, 30026 Portogruaro (Venezia)
Tel: (0421) 74475 Fax: (0421) 282070
E-mail: posta@ediciclo.it
Key Personnel
Administrative Dir: Vittorio Anastasia
Founded: 1992
Subjects: Economics, Environmental Studies, History, Outdoor Recreation, Science (General), Social Sciences, Sociology, Sports, Athletics, Travel
ISBN Prefix(es): 88-85327; 88-85318
Imprints: Nuova Dimensione

EDIFIR SRL+
Edizioni Firenze, Via Fiume 8, Florence 50123
Tel: (055) 289506 Fax: (055) 289478
E-mail: edifir@cibernet.it
Key Personnel
President: Wanda Miletti Ferragamo
Administrator: Dr Pierfrancesco Pacini
International Rights: Dr Fabio Tongiorgi
Founded: 1985
Subjects: Architecture & Interior Design, History
ISBN Prefix(es): 88-7970

Edipuglia+
Via Dalmazia 22/B, 70050 (Bari) S Spirito
Tel: (080) 5333056 Fax: (080) 5333057
E-mail: edipugli@tin.it
Web Site: www.edipuglia.it
Key Personnel
Administrator: Ceglie Oronzo
Founded: 1979
Subjects: Antiques, Archaeology, History
ISBN Prefix(es): 88-7228
Number of titles published annually: 10 Print
Total Titles: 150 Print

Editrice Edisco+
Via Pastrengo 28, 10128 Turin
Tel: (011) 54 78 80 Fax: (011) 51 75 396
E-mail: info@edisco.it
Web Site: www.edisco.it
Key Personnel
General Manager: Corrado Jaria
Founded: 1952
Subjects: Chemistry, Chemical Engineering, Education, Electronics, Electrical Engineering, English as a Second Language, Literature, Literary Criticism, Essays, Mechanical Engineering, Physics, Science (General)
ISBN Prefix(es): 88-441
Number of titles published annually: 25 Print
Total Titles: 300 Print
Shipping Address: Via Barletta 124, 10136 Turin
Warehouse: Via Barletta 124, 10136 Turin

Edisport Editoriale SpA
Via Gradisca 11, 20151 Milan
Tel: (02) 380851 Fax: (02) 38010393
Telex: 353629 EDISP I
Key Personnel
Marketing: Donatella Tardini

Editalia (Edizioni d'Italia)
Via Tirso 26, 00198 Rome
Tel: (06) 8546146 Fax: (06) 8411225
Key Personnel
Man Dir: Lidio Bozzini
Rights & Permissions: Arrigo Pecchioli
Founded: 1952
Subjects: Art, Ethnicity, History
ISBN Prefix(es): 88-7060

Editori Laterza+
Via di Villa Sacchetti, 17, 00197 Rome
Tel: (06) 3223550; (06) 3218393 Fax: (06) 3223853
E-mail: laterza@laterza.it
Web Site: www.laterza.it
Key Personnel
President: Dr Giuseppe Laterza
Founded: 1901
Subjects: Anthropology, Archaeology, Communications, History, Law, Philosophy, Religion - Other
Number of titles published annually: 120 Print
Foreign Rep(s): Alice Chambers; Eulama Literary Agency

Editrice Bibliografica SpA
Viale Vittorio Veneto 24, 20124 Milan
Tel: (02) 28315996 Fax: (02) 28315906
E-mail: bibliografica@bibliografica.it
Web Site: www.bibliografica.it
Key Personnel
Administrator: Michele Costa
Editor: Giuliano Vigini
Founded: 1974
Member of Associazione Italiana Editori, Associazione Italiana per la difesa della reprografia delle opere, gestisce l'agenzia Italiana dell'ISBN.
Subjects: Library & Information Sciences
ISBN Prefix(es): 88-7075
Number of titles published annually: 40 Print
Total Titles: 300 Print; 1 CD-ROM

Associate Companies: Informazioni Editoriali-IE SRL, Via Bergonzoli 1/5, 20127 Milano, Contact: Mauro Zerbini Tel: (02) 283151 Fax: (02) 28315900

Editrice la Giuntina
Via Ricasoli 26/28, 50122 Florence
Tel: (055) 268684 Fax: (055) 219718
E-mail: giuntina@fol.it
Web Site: www.giuntina.it
Key Personnel
Contact: Daniel Vogelmann
Founded: 1980
Specialize in Jewish subjects.
Subjects: Religion - Jewish
ISBN Prefix(es): 88-85943; 88-8057
Total Titles: 240 Print

Editrice la Scuola SpA+
Via Luigi Cadorna 11, 25186 Brescia
Tel: (030) 29931 Fax: (030) 2993299 Cable: SCUOLA BRESCIA
Key Personnel
President: Dr Ing Luciano Silveri
Man Dir: Dr Ing Adolfo Lombardi
General Manager: Giuseppe Covone
Founded: 1904
Subjects: Education, Philosophy, Psychology, Psychiatry, Religion - Other
ISBN Prefix(es): 88-350
Associate Companies: Editrice Morcelliana SpA
Branch Office(s)
Bari
Bologna
Milan
Naples
Padua
Pescara
Rome

Edizioni Gruppo Abele, see Gruppo Abele

Edizioni Associate/Editrice Internazionale Srl+
Viale Gorizia 52, 00198 Rome
Tel: (06) 8841076 Fax: (06) 8841066
Key Personnel
President: Livio Fabjan
Administrative Delegate & Editorial Dir: Rean Mazzone
Founded: 1992
Subjects: Government, Political Science, Literature, Literary Criticism, Essays
ISBN Prefix(es): 88-267
Associate Companies: Editrice Ila Palma, Tea Nova Srl
Showroom(s): Torino e Francoforte
Bookshop(s): Distribuzione Libraria PDE
Warehouse: c/o Tea Nova Srl, Via Isidoro la Lumia 5/7, 90139 Palermo
Orders to: c/o Sede V Le, Via Casini 8, 00153 Rome

Edizioni d'Arte e Moderna, Edam+
Via di Monte Oliveto, 2, 50124 Florence
Tel: (055) 2298578 Fax: (055) 2208837
Founded: 1962
Subjects: Antiques, Architecture & Interior Design, Art
ISBN Prefix(es): 88-7244

Edizioni del Delfino, imprint of Adriano Gallina Editore sas

Edizioni di Torino, see EDT Edizioni di Torino

Edizioni Giuridiche Economiche Aziendali, see EGEA (Edizioni Giuridiche Economiche Aziendali)

Edizioni Il Punto d'Incontro SAS
Via Sansigoli 34, 36100 Venice
Tel: (0444) 928793 Fax: (0444) 928459

E-mail: edpunto@cdc.it
Subjects: Astrology, Occult, Ethnicity, Health, Nutrition, Philosophy, Religion - Buddhist, Religion - Catholic, Religion - Hindu, Religion - Islamic, Religion - Other
ISBN Prefix(es): 88-8093
Warehouse: Via Zamenhof 441, 36100 Venice

Edizioni L'Eta Dell'Acqua Rio, *imprint of* Lindau

Edizioni la Scala
Casella Postale 156, 70015 Noci (Bari)
Tel: (080) 4975838 *Fax:* (080) 4975839
Cable: BENEDETTINI NOCI
Key Personnel
Chief Executive, Editorial: Padre Giuseppe Quirino Poggi
Founded: 1947
Subjects: Biography, Music, Dance, Philosophy, Religion - Catholic

Edizioni l'Arciere SRL+
Via Bassignano 46, Cuneo 12100
Tel: (0171) 693174 *Fax:* (0171) 697729
Cable: ARCIERE EDIZIONI CUNEO
Key Personnel
Chief Executive, Sales, Rights & Permissions: Aldo Sacchetti
Editorial, Production, Publicity: Mario Donadei
Founded: 1973
Subjects: Art, Biography, Fiction, Geography, Geology, History, Literature, Literary Criticism, Essays, Military Science, Poetry, Regional Interests, Travel
ISBN Prefix(es): 88-86398

Edizioni l'eta Dell'Acquario Di I Bresci & C Sas+
Via Torchio 16, 28075 Grignasco (Novara)
Tel: (0163) 418978 *Fax:* (0163) 411095
Key Personnel
Dir: Count Bernardino del Boca Di Villaregia
Intl Rights: Isabella Bresci
Founded: 1971
Member of New York Academy of Science.
Subjects: Nonfiction (General), Parapsychology, Religion - Other
ISBN Prefix(es): 88-7136
Imprints: Edizioni L' Eta dell'Acquario
Showroom(s): c/o Lingotto, Salone del Libro Di Torino, Turin

Edizioni Mediterranee SRL+
Via Flaminia 109, 00196 Rome
Tel: (06) 3235433 *Fax:* (06) 3236277
E-mail: info@ediz-mediterranee.com
Web Site: www.ediz-mediterranee.com *Cable:* 0039-6
Key Personnel
General Manager: Giovanni Canonico *Tel:* (06) 3222797
Editorial: Paola Maria Canonico
Sales: Graziella Torre
Rights & Permissions: Assia Canonico; Eleasa Canonico
Founded: 1953
Subjects: Alternative, Archaeology, Art, Astrology, Occult, Biography, Gardening, Plants, Health, Nutrition, How-to, Medicine, Nursing, Dentistry, Military Science, Parapsychology, Philosophy, Psychology, Psychiatry, Religion - Other, Sports, Athletics, Martial arts, new age, UFO Meditation yoga, magic mediating, alchemy, esoterism
ISBN Prefix(es): 88-272
Total Titles: 1,500 Print
Subsidiaries: Hermes Edizioni SRL; Edizioni Studio Tesi

Edizioni Qiqajon+
Frozione Bose, 13887 Magnano (Biella)
Tel: (015) 679264 *Fax:* (015) 679290
E-mail: edizioni@qiqajon.it
Web Site: www.qiqajon.it
Key Personnel
President: Enzo Bianchi
International Rights: Guido Dotti *E-mail:* guido.dotti@qiqajon.it
Founded: 1983
Subjects: Religion - Catholic, Religion - Jewish, Religion - Protestant, Theology
ISBN Prefix(es): 88-85227; 88-8227
Number of titles published annually: 20 Print
Total Titles: 190 Print

Edizioni Realizzazioni Grafiche - Artigiana, see ERGA SNC di Carla Ottino Merli & C (Edizioni Realizzazioni Grafiche - Artigiana)

Edizioni Simone, *imprint of* Esselibri

Edizioni Studio Domenicano (ESD)+
Via Osservanza 72, 40136 Bologna
Tel: (051) 582034 *Fax:* (051) 331583
E-mail: esd@alinet.it
Web Site: www.esd-domenicani.it
Key Personnel
Dir: Benetollo Ottorino *E-mail:* esd.benetollo@tiscalinet.it
Founded: 1985
Subjects: Philosophy, Religion - Catholic, Social Sciences, Sociology, Theology, Works of St Thomas Aquinas (Latin & Italian)
ISBN Prefix(es): 88-7094
Number of titles published annually: 60 Print
Total Titles: 500 Print

Edizioni Universitarie di Lettere Economia Diritto, see LED - Edizioni Universitarie di Lettere Economia Diritto

EDT Edizioni di Torino+
Via Alfieri 19, 10121 Turin
Tel: (011) 5591811 *Fax:* (011) 5591824
Key Personnel
Chief Executive: Enzo Peruccio
Founded: 1976
Subjects: Medicine, Nursing, Dentistry, Music, Dance, Travel
ISBN Prefix(es): 88-7063

EE, *imprint of* Edi Ermes SRL

EE, *imprint of* Editrice Eraclea

Effata Editrice+
Via Tre Denti 1, 10060 Cantalupa, Turin
Tel: (0121) 353452 *Fax:* (0121) 353839
E-mail: info@effata.it
Web Site: www.effata.it
Key Personnel
Dir: Paolo Pellegrino
Founded: 1994
A publishing house that is engaged to spread significant words to answer the deepest questions of the human soul.
Subjects: Drama, Theater, Education, Fiction, Human Relations, Psychology, Psychiatry, Religion - Catholic, Self-Help, Words for helping & giving joy
ISBN Prefix(es): 88-86617
Number of titles published annually: 20 Print
Total Titles: 80 Print
Orders to: Mescat, Viale Bacchiglione 20/A, 20139 Milan, Contact: Francesco Crespi *Tel:* (02) 55210800 *Fax:* (02) 55211315

EFR, *imprint of* EFR-Editrici Francescane

EFR-Editrici Francescane
Via Orto Botanico, 11, 35123 Padova
Tel: (049) 8225702 *Fax:* (049) 8225713
E-mail: ebf@biblia.it
Key Personnel
President & International Rights: Aristide Cabassi *Tel:* (02) 29002736
Founded: 1995
Subjects: Religion - Catholic
ISBN Prefix(es): 88-8135
Associate Companies: Edizioni Bibliotea Francescana Milano, Piazza S Angelo, 2, 20121 Milano; Edizioni Messaggero Padova, Via Orto Botanico, 11, 35123 Padova; Edizioni Porziuncola Assisi, Piazza Porziuncola, 1, 06088 South Maria Degla Angeli; Libreria Internazionale Edizioni Francescane, Borgo S Lucia 38/40, 36100 Vicenza
Imprints: EFR
Distributor for Messaggero Distribuzione

EGEA (Edizioni Giuridiche Economiche Aziendali)+
Via Sarfatti 25, 20136 Milan
Mailing Address: Via Calatafimi, 10, 20122 Milan
Tel: (02) 58362034; (02) 89401158; (02) 89402431 *Fax:* (02) 58362033; (02) 89402431
E-mail: egea.edizioni@egea.uni-bocconi.it
Key Personnel
President: Prof Alberto Bertoni
Editor: Adriana Macchi
Founded: 1988
Subjects: Advertising, Career Development, Economics, Finance, History, Law, Management, Marketing, Philosophy, Public Administration
ISBN Prefix(es): 88-238
Associate Companies: Giuffre Editore SpA, Via Busto Arsizio 40, 20151 Milan
Bookshop(s): EGEA SpA, Via Sarfatti 25, 20136 Milan
Orders to: Messaggerie Libri SpA, Via G Carcano 32, 20141 Milan

EGGM, *imprint of* EuroGeoGrafiche Mencattini SRL

International EILES, see Edizioni Internazionali di Letteratura e Scienze

Giulio Einaudi Editore SpA+
Via Biancamano 2, 10121 Turin
Tel: (011) 56561 *Fax:* (011) 542903; (011) 5626220
Key Personnel
President: Giulio Einaudi
Vice President: Leonardo Mondadori
Editor: Vittorio Bo
Founded: 1933
Subjects: Art, Fiction, History, Music, Dance, Philosophy, Poetry, Psychology, Psychiatry, Social Sciences, Sociology
ISBN Prefix(es): 88-06
Parent Company: A Mondadori Editore SpA
Associate Companies: Elemond SpA/ Edizioni E Elle SpA
Bookshop(s): Libreria Einaudi, Via Manzoni 40, 20121 Milano
Warehouse: Arnoldo Mondadori, Via Montelun, 37131 Verona
Orders to: Ufficio Commerciale, Via Biancamano 2, 10121 Turin

EL, *imprint of* Editrice Liguria SNC di Norberto Sabatelli & C

El, *imprint of* Edizioni Lavoro SRL

Electa
Via Trentacoste 7, 20134 Milan
Tel: (02) 215631 *Fax:* (02) 26413121
Telex: 350523 Eleper I

ITALY

Key Personnel
Dir: Giorgio Fantoni; Massimo Vitta Zelman
Editorial: Carlo Pirovano
Rights & Permissions: Marisa Inzaghi; Mirella Tenderini
Founded: 1948
Subjects: Architecture & Interior Design, Art, Photography
ISBN Prefix(es): 88-435
Subsidiaries: Alfieri Edizioni d'Arte; Giulio Einaudi Editore SpA; Electa Firenze; Electa Editori Umbri Associati; Electa Napoli; Fantonigrafica; Electa Moniteu

Edizioni dell'Elefante+
Piazza dei Caprettari 70, 00186 Rome
Tel: (06) 68803710 *Fax:* (06) 6832526
Key Personnel
Chief Executive: Dr Enzo Crea
Editorial: Benedetta Origo Crea
Founded: 1964
Subjects: Art
ISBN Prefix(es): 88-7176

Eliseo, *imprint of* Loescher Editore SRL

Elle Di Ci - Libreria Dottrina Cristiana
10096 Leumann Turin
Tel: (011) 9552111 *Fax:* (011) 9572900; (011) 9574048
E-mail: mail@elledici.org
Web Site: www.elledici.org
Founded: 1941
Subjects: Biblical Studies, Child Care & Development, Education, Music, Dance, Religion - Catholic, Theology
ISBN Prefix(es): 88-01
Branch Office(s)
Corso C Alberto 77, 60127 Ancona *Tel:* (071) 2810306 *Fax:* (071) 2810306
Via Martiri d'Otranto, 69, 70123 Bari *Tel:* (080) 5740059 *Fax:* (080) 5797054
Via G Matteotti, 23/D, 40129 Bologna *Tel:* (051) 355242 *Fax:* (051) 355242
Viale M Rapisardi, 95124 Catania *Tel:* (095) 441379 *Fax:* (095) 441379
Via S Giovanni Bosco, 98122 Messina *Tel:* (090) 718874 *Fax:* (090) 718874
Via M Gioia, 62, 20124 Milano *Tel:* (02) 67072085 *Fax:* (02) 67071776
Via Donnaregina, 7, 80138 Napoli *Tel:* (081) 449167 *Fax:* (081) 291862
Via G Jappelli, 6, 35121 Padova *Tel:* (049) 875138 *Fax:* (049) 875138
Corso Francia, 214, 10090 Rivoli (*Tel:* (011) 9552333
Via Marsala, 40, 00185 Rome *Tel:* (06) 491400 *Fax:* (06) 4450370
Via Conciliazione, 26/28, 00193 Rome *Tel:* (06) 68806735 *Fax:* (06) 6874559
Via C Rolando, 63/r, 16151 GE Sampierdarena *Tel:* (010) 6459306 *Fax:* (010) 6459306
Via M Ausiliatrice, 10152 Torino *Tel:* (011) 5211925 *Fax:* (011) 5211925

Elmedi™, *imprint of* Paravia Bruno Mondadori Editori

ELS, *imprint of* Edizioni Librarie Siciliane

EMI, see Editrice Missionaria Italiana (EMI)

EMP, see Messaggero di San Antonio

Enne+
Via Mon Forte 7, 86100 Campobasso
Tel: (0874) 412357 *Fax:* (0874) 412357
Founded: 1965
ISBN Prefix(es): 88-7213; 88-85820

EQ, *imprint of* Edizioni Quasar di Severino Tognon SRL

ER, *imprint of* Editori Riuniti

Editrice Eraclea
Imprint of Compagnia Delle Cinque Vie SRL
Via del Bollo 8, 20123 Milan
Tel: (02) 8693635 *Fax:* (02) 86453613
E-mail: cinquevie@libero.it
Key Personnel
Man Dir: Mario Calori
Founded: 1974
Number of titles published annually: 10 Print
Total Titles: 85 Print
Imprints: EE

ERGA SNC di Carla Ottino Merli & C (Edizioni Realizzazioni Grafiche - Artigiana)+
Via Biga 52r, 16144 Genoa
Tel: (010) 8328441 *Fax:* (010) 8328799
Key Personnel
Chief Executive: Marcello Merli
Editorial: Marco Merli
Founded: 1964
Subjects: Art, Cookery, Ethnicity, History, Law, Literature, Literary Criticism, Essays, Music, Dance, Poetry, Regional Interests, Religion - Other, Romance, Science (General), Self-Help, Sports, Athletics
ISBN Prefix(es): 88-8163

ES, *imprint of* Editoriale Scienza

ESI SpA, see Edizioni Scientifiche Italiane

Essegi+
Via Faentina 362, 48010 S Michele (Ravenna)
Tel: (0544) 218849 *Fax:* (0544) 217358
Key Personnel
President: Dal Re Patrizia
Editorial Dir: Rieel Matteo
Founded: 1982
Specialize in Contemporary Art.
Subjects: Anthropology, Antiques, Archaeology, Architecture & Interior Design, Art, Astronomy, Drama, Theater, Fashion, History, Language Arts, Linguistics, Literature, Literary Criticism, Essays, Photography
ISBN Prefix(es): 88-7189
Divisions: Spazio Espositivo Essegi (Showroom also)

Esselibri
Via F Russo 33, 80123 Naples
Tel: (081) 5757255 *Fax:* (081) 5757944
Founded: 1989
Subjects: Philosophy
ISBN Prefix(es): 88-244
Imprints: Edizioni Simone

Etas Libri+
Division of RCS Libri Spa
Via Mecenate 91, 20138 Milan
Tel: (02) 50952309 *Fax:* (02) 50952898
Web Site: www.etas.it
Key Personnel
Contact: Lorena Ferrari *E-mail:* lorena.ferrari@rcs.it
Professor: Dr Direttore Divisione
Founded: 1963
Subjects: Business, Economics, Engineering (General), Management, Mathematics
ISBN Prefix(es): 88-453
Orders to: RCS Libri Spa, Via Mecenate 91, 20136 Milan *Tel:* (050) 952333 *Fax:* (050) 952300

ETR (Editrice Trasporti su Rotaie) (Rail Transport Publishing)+
Member of FerPress
Piazza Vittorio Emanuele 42, 25087 Salo (BS)
Tel: (03) 6541092 *Fax:* (03) 6541092
Web Site: www.itreni.com
Key Personnel
President: Erminio Mascherpa
Founded: 1980
Publish the monthly illustrative magazine TRENI.
Subjects: Crafts, Games, Hobbies, Transportation, Travel
ISBN Prefix(es): 88-85068

EUR, *imprint of* Edizioni Universitarie Romane

Eura Press, *imprint of* Todariana Editrice

EuroGeoGrafiche Mencattini SRL+
Via Po 47, 52100 Arezzo
Tel: (0575) 900010 *Fax:* (0575) 911161
Key Personnel
Contact: Silvano Mencattini
Founded: 1974
Member of USPI, AIE, AIPE; Specialize in Tourist Guide & Cartography.
Subjects: Geography, Geology
ISBN Prefix(es): 88-86263
Imprints: EGGM

Edizioni Europa
Via G.B. Martini 6, 00198 Rome
Tel: (06) 8419124
Founded: 1944
Subjects: Art, Economics, Government, Political Science, History, Music, Dance
Subsidiaries: Le Edigioni del Lavors

Editoriale Europress (Nardini Press), *imprint of* Nardini Editore srl

Fanucci
Via delle Fornaci 66, 00165 Rome
Tel: (06) 393366384 *Fax:* (06) 6382998
Key Personnel
Editor: Sergio Fanucci
Founded: 1972
Subjects: Science Fiction, Fantasy
ISBN Prefix(es): 88-347
Imprints: FE

Fatatrac+
Via Lanza 64A, 50136 Florence
Tel: (055) 669102 *Fax:* (055) 679289
Web Site: www.fatatrac.com
Key Personnel
Publisher: Nicoletta Codignola *E-mail:* n.codignola@fatatrac.com
Founded: 1978
Subjects: Animals, Pets, Art, Child Care & Development, Developing Countries, Education, Literature, Literary Criticism, Essays, Photography, Science Fiction, Fantasy
ISBN Prefix(es): 88-85089; 88-85657; 88-86228
Number of titles published annually: 18 Print
Foreign Rep(s): Nicoletta Codignola

FE, *imprint of* Fanucci

FEDA SA+
Via Frasca 8, 6900 Lugano
Tel: (091) 9235677 *Fax:* (091) 220171
Founded: 1990
Subjects: Archaeology, Architecture & Interior Design, Art, Photography
ISBN Prefix(es): 88-7269
Associate Companies: Edizioni Gottardo SA, Lugano; Giampiero Casagrande Editore, Lugano
Imprints: FIDIA

PUBLISHERS

ITALY

Federico Motta Editore SpA+
Via Branda Castiglioni 7, 20156 Milan
Tel: (02) 300761 *Fax:* (02) 38010046
E-mail: editor@mottaeditore.it
Web Site: www.mottaeditore.it
Telex: 350397 Motta 1
Key Personnel
Chief Executive Officer & Publisher: Federico Motta
Dir, Financial & Administration: Massimo Fumagalli
Sales, Encyclopaedia Dept: Patrizia Ruffo
Press & Advertising Relations: Natalina Costra
Dir, Sales, Book Dept: Lorena Vazzola
Founded: 1929
Subjects: Architecture & Interior Design, Art, Photography
ISBN Prefix(es): 88-7179

Feguagiskia' Studios+
Via Crosa di Vergagni 3R, 16124 Genoa
Tel: (010) 2757544 *Fax:* (010) 2510838
Key Personnel
Publisher: Gualtiero Schiaffino
Founded: 1982
Subjects: Child Care & Development, Literature, Literary Criticism, Essays

Giangiacomo Feltrinelli SpA
Via Andegari 6, 20121 Milan
Tel: (02) 86463485 *Fax:* (02) 72001064
Cable: Fedit Milan
Founded: 1954
Subjects: Art, Fiction, History, Philosophy, Poetry, Science (General)
ISBN Prefix(es): 88-07

La Fenice SRL
Via Prasso, 5, 00149 Rome
Tel: (06) 5565954 *Fax:* (06) 5565954
Telex: 680285 Fielde 1
Key Personnel
Editorial: Dr Marcello Veneziani
Sales: Dr Giuseppe Paolillo
Publicity: Rossella Giraldi
Founded: 1951
Subjects: History, Military Science, Philosophy
ISBN Prefix(es): 88-86171
Parent Company: Gruppo Italfin '80, Via Pinciana 25, I-00197 Rome
Associate Companies: Casa Editrice Acta Medica, Via Prasso, 5, 00149 Rome; Ciarrapico Editore; Casa Editrice Field Educational Italia, Piazza Montegrappa 4, I-00195 Rome
Subsidiaries: SPC (Stabilimenti Poligrafici Cassino

Fenice 2000+
Via della Maggiolina, 24, 20125 Milan
Tel: (02) 66984638; (02) 67075155 *Fax:* (02) 67074283
Key Personnel
President: Dr Enzo Angelucci
Man Dir: Dr Pierluigi Bozzia
Founded: 1986
Subjects: Aeronautics, Aviation, Animals, Pets, Art, Cookery, Crafts, Games, Hobbies, Gardening, Plants, Photography
ISBN Prefix(es): 88-8017

Festina Lente Edizioni+
Via della Croce 11, 50023 Impruneta (Florence)
Mailing Address: Via Condotta, 18/R, 50122 Florence
Tel: (055) 2313506; (055) 292612 *Fax:* (055) 292612
Key Personnel
Contact: Andrea del Sere; Paolo Gori Savellini
Founded: 1989
Subjects: Architecture & Interior Design, Art, History, Literature, Literary Criticism, Essays, Medicine, Nursing, Dentistry, Psychology, Psychiatry
ISBN Prefix(es): 88-85171
Showroom(s): Via Condotta 18/R, 50122 Florence
Bookshop(s): Via Condotta 18/R, 50122 Florence

Fiabesca, *imprint of* Stampa Alternativa - Nuovi Equilibri

FIDIA, *imprint of* FEDA SA

Fidia Edizioni d'Arte, see FEDA SA

Libreria Editrice Fiorentina di Vittorio Zani e C SAS+
Via Giambologna 5, 50132 Florence
Tel: (055) 579921 *Fax:* (055) 579921
Key Personnel
Editorial: Vittorio Zani
Founded: 1902
Subjects: Education, Regional Interests, Religion - Other, Social Sciences, Sociology
Imprints: LEF

Flaccovio Dario+
Via Abruzzi 17 26, 90144 Palermo
Tel: (091) 6700453 *Fax:* (091) 528100
Key Personnel
Contact: Marisa Flaccovio
Founded: 1980
ISBN Prefix(es): 88-7758
Bookshop(s): Via Ausonia, 70-90144 Palermo

Flaccovio Editore
Via Ruggiero Settimo 37, 90139 Palermo
Tel: (091) 589442 *Fax:* (091) 331992
Founded: 1939
Member of AIE.
Subjects: Archaeology, Architecture & Interior Design, Art, History, Regional Interests, Science (General)
ISBN Prefix(es): 88-7804
Parent Company: S F Flaccovio sas
Bookshop(s): Libreria SF Flaccovio, Via R Settimo, 34-90139 Palermo

Fogola Editore in Torino+
Piazza Carlo Felice 19, 10123 Turin
Tel: (011) 541512 *Fax:* (011) 530305
Founded: 1965
Subjects: Fiction, History, Literature, Literary Criticism, Essays
Total Titles: 115 Print
Showroom(s): Paztecipozione al Salone Del Libro Ditorino
Bookshop(s): Libreria Dante Alighieri, Piazza Carlo Felice 19, 10123 Turin

Folini+
Il Battaglino, 15052 Casalnoceto, Alessandria
Tel: (0131) 807001 *Fax:* (0131) 807001
E-mail: edifolini@edifolini.com
Web Site: www.edifolini.com
Key Personnel
President: Dr Fernando Folini *E-mail:* folinif@edifolini.com
Founded: 1986
Member of Associazione Italiana Editori.
Subjects: Biological Sciences, Environmental Studies, Health, Nutrition, Medicine, Nursing, Dentistry, Self-Help
ISBN Prefix(es): 88-7266
Imprints: Editoriale Fernando Folini; I Quanta

Editoriale Fernando Folini, *imprint of* Folini

Arnaldo Forni Editore SRL
Via Gramsci 164, 40010 Sala Bolognese (Bologna)
Tel: (051) 6814142 *Fax:* (051) 6814672
E-mail: info@fornieditore.com
Web Site: www.fornieditore.com
Key Personnel
Man Dir: Aurelia Forni
Founded: 1973
Subjects: Antiques, Archaeology, Architecture & Interior Design, Art, Astrology, Occult, Astronomy, Biography, Cookery, Drama, Theater, Earth Sciences, Economics, Gardening, Plants, Genealogy, Geography, Geology, History, Language Arts, Linguistics, Law, Literature, Literary Criticism, Essays, Mathematics, Medicine, Nursing, Dentistry, Music, Dance, Philosophy, Psychology, Psychiatry, Regional Interests, Religion - Catholic, Religion - Other
ISBN Prefix(es): 88-271
Number of titles published annually: 20 Print
Total Titles: 3,200 Print
Bookshop(s): Via Galliera 15, 40121 Bologna
Tel: (051) 221417 *Fax:* (051) 6814672
E-mail: rarebooks@fornieditore.com

Biblioteca Francescana+
Piazza S Angelo, 2, 20121 Milan
Tel: (02) 29002736 *Fax:* (02) 29002736
E-mail: ebf@biblia.it
Key Personnel
International Rights: P Aristide Cabassi
Founded: 1977
Specialize in Francescanesimo.
Subjects: History, Religion - Catholic, Theology
ISBN Prefix(es): 88-7962
Imprints: EBF
Distributor for Messaggero Distribuione (Italy)

Edizioni Frassinelli SRL+
Via Durazzo 4, 20134 Milan
Tel: (02) 217211 *Fax:* (02) 21721277
Key Personnel
President & Publisher: Valerio Anna Patrizia
Editorial Dir: Carla Tanzi
Marketing Dir: Giuseppe Baroffio
Rights & Permissions: Laura Casonato
Scout: Linda Clark
Contracts: Marica Fioroni
Founded: 1932
Subjects: Art, Biography, Fiction, Nonfiction (General)
ISBN Prefix(es): 88-7684
Parent Company: Sperling e Kupfer Editori SpA
Branch Office(s)
225 Lafayette St, Suite 602, New York, NY 10012, United States (Scout Office)

Fratelli Conte Editori SRL+
Via Andrea d'Isernia 59, 80122 Naples
Tel: (081) 7613667 *Fax:* (081) 669771
Key Personnel
Man Dir: Ferdinando Conte; Mario Conte
Founded: 1967
Subjects: Fiction

Edizioni Futuro SRL
Via Cesiolo, 10, 37126 Verona
Tel: (045) 915622 *Fax:* (045) 8300261
Telex: 480833
Key Personnel
Chief Executive: Vinicio de Lorentiis
Editorial: Francesca Pomini
Sales: Marta de Lorentiis
Rights & Permissions: Elena Zoccatelli
Founded: 1979
Subjects: Art, Biography, Environmental Studies, How-to
ISBN Prefix(es): 88-7650
Subsidiaries: Edizioni Vinicio de Lorentiis; Moderna International

Adriano Gallina Editore sas+
Salita Tarsia, 142, 80135 Naples
Tel: (081) 5496730 *Fax:* (081) 5448747

ITALY

Key Personnel
Man Dir: Rossana Gallina
Editorial: Maria Gallina
Sales: Giuseppe Gallina
Founded: 1968
Subjects: Archaeology, Art, Cookery, Ethnicity, Music, Dance, Poetry, Regional Interests, Travel
ISBN Prefix(es): 88-87350
Imprints: Adriana Gallina Editore; Edizioni del Delfino
Divisions: Edizioni del Delfino

Galzerano Editore+
84040 Casalvelino Scalo, Salerno
Tel: (0974) 62028 *Fax:* (0974) 62028 *Cable:* GALZERANO CASALVELINO SCALO (SA)
Key Personnel
Chief Executive: Giuseppe Galzerano
Founded: 1975
Subjects: Biography, Ethnicity, Fiction, Government, Political Science, History, Poetry
Number of titles published annually: 10 Print

Gamberetti Editrice SRL+
Via Faa di Bruno, 28, 00195 Rome
Tel: (06) 3728394 *Fax:* (06) 3728394; (06) 535469
E-mail: schiarim@ilmanifesto.it
Key Personnel
Contact: Chiarim Stefano
Founded: 1992
Specializes in the conflicts of the "New World Order", Middle East, Former Yugoslavia, Ireland, Italy, Latin America, Armenia, Polisario, & North-South relationship.
Subjects: Fiction, Literature, Literary Criticism, Essays
ISBN Prefix(es): 88-7990
Total Titles: 32 Print
Distributed by PDE Distribuzione (Firenze)

Gammalibri-Rock Books, *imprint of* Kaos Edizioni SRL

Gangemi Editore+
Piazza S Pantaleo 4, 00186 Rome
Tel: (06) 6872774; (06) 6872775 *Fax:* (06) 68806189
E-mail: gangemi@jnet.it
Key Personnel
Chief Executive: Giuseppe Gangemi
Marketing Executive Manager: Emilia Gangemi
Publishing Editor Manager: Fabio Gangemi
Founded: 1966
Subjects: Agriculture, Anthropology, Archaeology, Architecture & Interior Design, Art, Disability, Special Needs, History, Literature, Literary Criticism, Essays, Medicine, Nursing, Dentistry, Philosophy, Romance, Social Sciences, Sociology
ISBN Prefix(es): 88-7448
Branch Office(s)
Via Giulia 95, I-00186 Rome *Tel:* (06) 68308729
Bookshop(s): Via Cavour, 255, 00184 Rome *Tel:* (06) 4821661; Corso Garibaldi, 168, 89100 Reggio Calabria *Tel:* (0965) 894844 *Fax:* (0965) 894845

Editrice Garigliano SRL+
Via Aligerno 91/93, 03043 Cassino (Frosinone)
Tel: (0776) 21869 *Fax:* (0776) 21869 *Cable:* Editrice Garigliano Cassino
Key Personnel
Chief Executive: Marisa Canzano; Stefano Vitale
Editorial: Rodolfo Vitale
Sales: Brunella Martucci
Production: Antonio Violo
Publicity: Giovanni Violo
Rights & Permissions: Elena Vettese
Founded: 1968
Subjects: Education, Literature, Literary Criticism, Essays, Philosophy, Psychology, Psychiatry
ISBN Prefix(es): 88-7103
Bookshop(s): Libreria Universitaria, Vis Aligerno 91/93, 03043 Cassino (Frosinone)

Garolla
Via Pinamonte de Vimercate 6, 20145 Milan
Tel: (02) 48005574 *Fax:* (02) 48003915
Key Personnel
Contact: Federico Garolla
Subjects: Archaeology, Art
ISBN Prefix(es): 88-7682

Garzanti Editore+
Via Newton, 18A, 20148 Milan
Tel: (02) 487941 *Fax:* (02) 48794292
Telex: 325218 Gared *Cable:* Garzantieditore
Key Personnel
Publisher: Dr Livio Garzanti
Editorial: Dr Giananarea Piccioli
Sales Manager: Francesco Rampini
Rights & Permissions: Marie Louise Zarmanian
Founded: 1861
Subjects: Art, Biography, Fiction, Government, Political Science, History, Literature, Literary Criticism, Essays, Poetry
ISBN Prefix(es): 88-11
Associate Companies: A Vallardi, Via Newton, 18A, 20148 Milan
Bookshop(s): Libreria Garzanti, Galleria Vittorio Emanuele 66-68, 1020121 Milan; Libreria Garzanti, Palazzo Dell' Universita, Pavia; Libreria della Spiga, Via della Spiga 30, 1-20121 Milan

Edizioni GB+
Via Marzolo 15/B, 35131 Padova
Tel: (049) 772252 *Fax:* (049) 772252
Founded: 1985
Member of WWF.
Subjects: Alternative, Anthropology, Architecture & Interior Design, Biological Sciences, Environmental Studies, Government, Political Science, Library & Information Sciences, Medicine, Nursing, Dentistry, Philosophy, Physical Sciences, Science (General), Social Sciences, Sociology, Sports, Athletics, Travel
ISBN Prefix(es): 88-86272
Subsidiaries: Edizioni GB - Brasile

Istituto Geografico de Agostini SpA
Via Giovanni da Verrazzano 15, 28100 Novara
Tel: (0321) 4241 *Fax:* (0321) 471286
Telex: 200290 Edidea l *Cable:* GEOGRAFICO NOVARA
Key Personnel
Contact: Chiara Boroli
Founded: 1901
Subjects: Art, Gardening, Plants, Geography, Geology, History, Literature, Literary Criticism, Essays, Regional Interests, Religion - Other
ISBN Prefix(es): 88-402; 88-415; 88-410
Branch Office(s)
Uffici di Milano, Via Montefeltro 6/A, 20156 Milan *Tel:* (02) 380861 *Fax:* (02) 38086324

Gereria Cortina Editrice SRL, see Libreria Cortina Editrice SRL

Bruno Ghigi Editore+
Via Poletti 6, 47900 Rimini (Forli)
Tel: (0541) 781269
Key Personnel
All offices: Bruno Ghigi
Founded: 1955
Subjects: Geography, Geology, History
ISBN Prefix(es): 88-85640

Ghisetti e Corvi Editori SpA
Corso Concordia 7, 20129 Milan
Tel: (02) 76006232 *Fax:* (02) 76009468
Founded: 1937
ISBN Prefix(es): 88-8013

Giancarlo Politi Editore
Via Farini 68, 20159 Milan
Tel: (02) 6887341 *Fax:* (02) 66801290
Subjects: Art
ISBN Prefix(es): 88-7816
U.S. Office(s): 799 Broadway, Room 226, New York, NY 10003, United States

Editrice Giannotta di Sebastiano Pace Giannotta+
Viale Regina Margherita 2ef, 95125 Catania
Tel: (095) 447629 *Cable:* EDITRICE GIANNOTTA
Key Personnel
Man Dir, Editorial: Giannotta Sebastiano Pace
Founded: 1965
Subjects: Law, Literature, Literary Criticism, Essays, Philosophy, Science (General), Social Sciences, Sociology
Bookshop(s): Libreria Editrice Giannotta, Viale Regina Margherita 2 ef, 95125 Catania

G Giappichelli Editore SRL+
Via Po 21, 10124 Turin
Tel: (011) 8153511 *Fax:* (011) 8125100
Founded: 1921
Subjects: Economics, Government, Political Science, Law, Philosophy, Social Sciences, Sociology
ISBN Prefix(es): 88-348
Bookshop(s): Libreria Editrice Scientifica di G Giappichelli, Via Vasco 2, 1-10124 Turin

Giovanni Tranchida Editore, *imprint of* Tranchida

Edizioni del Girasole srl
Via Paolo Costa 10, 481000 Ravenna
Tel: (0544) 212830 *Fax:* (0544) 38432
E-mail: info@europart.it
Key Personnel
President: Lapucci Egle
Founded: 1965
Subjects: Archaeology, Art, History, Photography, Poetry, Romance
ISBN Prefix(es): 88-7567

A Giuffre Editore SpA+
Via Busto Arsizio 40, 20151 Milan
Tel: (02) 380891 *Fax:* (02) 38009582
Key Personnel
Man Dir: Giuseppe Giuffre
Chief Editor: Gaetano Giuffre
Founded: 1931
Subjects: Economics, Government, Political Science, History, Law, Social Sciences, Sociology
ISBN Prefix(es): 88-14
Branch Office(s)
Via V Colonna 40, I-00193 Rome *Tel:* (06) 659938; (06) 6569792
Bookshop(s): Giuffre Libreria, Pza S Stefano, 5, 20122 Milan

Giunti (Gruppo Editoriale)+
Via Bolognese, 165, 50139 Firenze
Tel: (055) 5062-1 *Fax:* (055) 5062274
E-mail: estero@giunti.it
Key Personnel
Publisher: Sergio Giunti *Fax:* (055) 5062298
Man Dir: Martino Montanarini *Fax:* (055) 5062298
Editorial Director: Bruno Mari *Fax:* (055) 5062298

International Rights: Roberto Borrani *Tel:* (055) 5062200; Debora Lascialfari *Tel:* (055) 5062347 *E-mail:* d.lascialfari@guinti.it
Founded: 1840
Subjects: Archaeology, Art, Education, Fiction, History, Science (General), Travel
ISBN Prefix(es): 88-09
Total Titles: 4,500 Print; 200 CD-ROM
Imprints: Camunia, Zanzibar, Edizioni Primavera
Distributor for Dami Editore

Giunti Publishing Group+
Via Bolognese 165, 50139 Florence
Tel: (055) 66791 *Fax:* (055) 6679298
Telex: 571438 Giunti *Cable:* MARZOLIB FLORENCE
Key Personnel
Dir: Dr Sergio Giunti
Rights & Permissions: Roberto Borrani
Founded: 1840
Group comprises: Giunti Marzocco, ME/DI Sviluppo, OS (Organizzazioni Speciali SRL), Lisciani e Giunti Editori, Edizioni Primavera.
Subjects: Art, Chemistry, Chemical Engineering, Education, Fiction, History, How-to, Language Arts, Linguistics, Literature, Literary Criticism, Essays, Mathematics, Psychology, Psychiatry, Science (General)
ISBN Prefix(es): 88-09
Imprints: Giunti Marzocco
Subsidiaries: Lisciani & Giunti; ME/DI Sviluppo; Edizioni Primavera; OS Org Speciali; Giunti Industrie Grafiche; Giunti Multimedia
Branch Office(s)
Ancona
Bari
Cagliari
Catania
Genoa
Lamezia Terme
Milan
Naples
Padua
Palermo
Rome

Edizioni Giuridico Scientifiche (SRL)+
Via Donizetti 37, 20122 Milan
Tel: (02) 55192219 *Fax:* (02) 76009444
Key Personnel
Editor: Ennio Alessio Mizzau
ISBN Prefix(es): 88-85874

Gius Laterza e Figli SpA+
Piazza Umberto I 54, 70121 Bari
Tel: (080) 5216713 *Fax:* (080) 5243461
E-mail: laterza@laterza.it
Telex: 623168
Key Personnel
Man Dir, Rome: Vito Laterza
Editorial Dir, Rome: Giuseppe Laterza; Alessandro Laterza
Production: Claudio Lodoli
Press, Publicity & Advertising (Rome): Karina Laterza
Rights & Permissions: Antonia Sollecito
Sales Dir, Bari: Caterina D'Ambrosio
Founded: 1885
Subjects: Archaeology, Architecture & Interior Design, Art, Biography, Economics, History, Philosophy, Psychology, Psychiatry, Religion - Other, Science (General), Social Sciences, Sociology
ISBN Prefix(es): 88-420
Bookshop(s): Libreria Internazionale Laterza, Via Sparano 134, 1-70121 Bari
Shipping Address: Via F Zippitelli 3, Zona Industriale, 1-70123 Bari

Giuseppe Laterza Editore Snc+
Via Crisanzio, 20/22, 70122 Bari
Tel: (080) 5237936 *Fax:* (080) 5237360
Key Personnel
Editor: Giuseppe Laterza
Founded: 1980
Subjects: Computer Science, Electronics, Electrical Engineering, Government, Political Science, Law, Literature, Literary Criticism, Essays, Poetry, Psychology, Psychiatry, Veterinary Science
ISBN Prefix(es): 88-86243; 88-8231
Imprints: Edizioni Fratelli Laterza
Subsidiaries: Laterza Litostampa; Libreria Fratelli Laterza; Cartoleria Fratelli Laterza

Glossa+
Piazza Paolo VI, 6, 20121 Milan
Tel: (02) 877609 *Fax:* (02) 72003162
E-mail: informazioni@glossaeditrice.it
Founded: 1987
Subjects: Theology
ISBN Prefix(es): 88-7105
Number of titles published annually: 12 Print
Total Titles: 130 Print

GM, *imprint of* Giorgio Mondadori & Associati

Gnocchi Editore
Via De Gasperi, 55, 80133 Naples
Tel: (081) 5524733 *Fax:* (081) 5518295
E-mail: idelgno@tin.it
Key Personnel
Contact: Guido Gnocchi
Founded: 1993
Subjects: Medicine, Nursing, Dentistry
ISBN Prefix(es): 88-7947

Gozzini, see Libreria Gozzini di Pietro e Francesco Chellini (SNC)

Grafica e Arte SRL+
Via Francesco Coghetti 108, 24128 Bergamo
Tel: (035) 255014 *Fax:* (035) 250164
E-mail: info@graficaearte.it
Web Site: www.graficaearte.it
Key Personnel
Man Dir: Emilio Agazzi
Founded: 1975
Subjects: Art, Ethnicity, History, Photography
Number of titles published annually: 10 Print
Total Titles: 220 Print
Distributed by Dehoniana Libri Sp
Showroom(s): Via Francesco Coghetti, 90, Bergamo 24128 *Tel:* (035) 255014 *Fax:* (035) 250164

Marchesi Grafiche Editoriali SpA
Via Bomarzo 32, 00191 Rome
Tel: (06) 331359 *Fax:* (06) 3336505
Founded: 1927
Specialize in publishing & printing for other firms.
ISBN Prefix(es): 88-86248

Grafis Edizioni+
Via 11 Giugno 4, 40033 Casalecchio di Reno (Bologna)
Tel: (051) 6165611 *Fax:* (051) 6167095
Key Personnel
Man Dir: Franco Trippa
Editorial: Enzo Massari
Press, Advertising: Cristina Agostina
Founded: 1965
Subjects: Architecture & Interior Design, Art, History, Photography, Regional Interests
ISBN Prefix(es): 88-8081
Book Club(s): Italia

Grafo Edizioni
Via Bassi 10, 25123 Brescia
Tel: (030) 393221 *Fax:* (030) 3701411
Key Personnel
Chief Executive: Matteo Montagnoli

Sales: Franco Agnelli
Founded: 1973
Subjects: Anthropology, Archaeology, Art, Ethnicity, History, Regional Interests
ISBN Prefix(es): 88-7385

Libreria Editrice Gregoriana
Via Roma 82, 35122 Padova
Tel: (049) 657493 *Fax:* (049) 662089
Key Personnel
Man Dir: Don Giancarlo Minozzi
Contact: Claudio Zanetto
Founded: 1922
Subjects: Philosophy, Psychology, Psychiatry, Religion - Other, Social Sciences, Sociology
ISBN Prefix(es): 88-7706
Parent Company: Euganea Editoriale Comunicazion SRL, Via Roma 82, 35122 Padova
Bookshop(s): Via Roma 37, Padova; Via Vescovado 33, Padova; Piazza Duomo 5, Padova

Ernesto Gremese Editore SRL+
Via Virginia Agnelli 88, V.Le Dei Colli Portuensi 537, 00151 Rome
Tel: (06) 65740507 *Fax:* (06) 65740509
E-mail: gremese@gremese.com
Web Site: www.gremese.com
Key Personnel
Chief Executive: Alberto Gremese
E-mail: alberto@gremese.com
Founded: 1954
Subjects: Art, Astrology, Occult, Cookery, Crafts, Games, Hobbies, Drama, Theater, Erotica, Fashion, Fiction, Film, Video, Health, Nutrition, House & Home, How-to, Literature, Literary Criticism, Essays, Music, Dance, Radio, TV, Sports, Athletics, Travel, Wine & Spirits
ISBN Prefix(es): 88-7605; 88-7742; 88-8440
Number of titles published annually: 80 Print
Total Titles: 700 Print
Imprints: L'Airone Editrice
Bookshop(s): Libreria Internazionale Ernesto Gremese SNC, Via Cola di Rienzo 136, 00192 Rome *Tel:* (06) 3235367 *Fax:* (06) 3235374 *E-mail:* info@liberia.gremese.it *Web Site:* www.liberiagremese.it

Gremese International Srl+
Via del Casaletto, 00151 Rome
Tel: (06) 65746320 *Fax:* (06) 65740509
Key Personnel
Executive Manager: Dr Cecilia Valci
Founded: 1991
Subjects: Art, Astrology, Occult, Cookery, Crafts, Games, Hobbies, Film, Video, Music, Dance, Nonfiction (General), Photography, Travel
ISBN Prefix(es): 88-7301
Parent Company: Gremese Editore Srl
Subsidiaries: Gremese Editore
U.S. Office(s): National Book Network, 4720 Boston Way, Lanham, MD 20706, United States

Piero Gribaudi Editore+
Via C Baroni, 190, 20142 Milan
Tel: (02) 89302244 *Fax:* (02) 89302376
E-mail: info@gribaudi.it
Web Site: www.gribaudi.it
Key Personnel
Publisher: Cesare Crespi; Maurizio Sola
Foreign Rights: Sandra Zerilli *E-mail:* szerilli@gribaudi.it
Founded: 1966
Subjects: Behavioral Sciences, Biblical Studies, Biography, Education, Human Relations, Humor, Religion - Catholic, Religion - Jewish, Self-Help, Theology
ISBN Prefix(es): 88-7152
Number of titles published annually: 50 Print
Total Titles: 650 Print
Imprints: PGE

ITALY

Gruppo Calderini Edagricole+
Via Emilia Levante 31/2, 40139 Bologna
Tel: (051) 62267 *Fax:* (051) 490200
E-mail: comunica@calderini.agriline.it
Web Site: www.calderini.it
Key Personnel
Man Dir: Giovanna Villani Perdisa *Tel:* (051) 6226800 *Fax:* (051) 540000
Rights & Permissions: Francesco Zueneli *Tel:* (051) 6226885 *E-mail:* rights@calderini.agriline.it
Founded: 1960
Subjects: Architecture & Interior Design, Art, Computer Science, Cookery, Crafts, Games, Hobbies, Education, Electronics, Electrical Engineering, Mechanical Engineering, Science (General), Self-Help, Sports, Athletics, Travel
ISBN Prefix(es): 88-7019
Total Titles: 988 Print
Parent Company: Calderini SRL, Via Emilia Levante 31/2, 40139 Bologna
Associate Companies: Edagricole - Edizioni Agricole; Edagricole Periodici SpA, Via Emilia Levante 31/2, 40139 Bologna; Officine Grafiche Calderini, 6 Emilia, 40064 Ozzano Emilia (Bo)
Branch Office(s)
Via Puglie 3, Rome
Bookshop(s): Via Zamboni 18, Bologna *Tel:* (051) 236817; Via Bronzino 14, Milan, Contact: Barbara Mazza *Tel:* (02) 29522981 *Fax:* (02) 29531856; Via Boncompagni 73, Rome, Maurizio Gentile *Tel:* (06) 42881098 *Fax:* (06) 42827240

Gruppo Editoriale Faenza Editrice SpA+
Via de Crescenzi 44, 48018 Faenza (Ravenna)
Tel: (0546) 670411 *Fax:* (0546) 660440
E-mail: info@faenza.com
Web Site: www.faenza.com
Key Personnel
Man Dir: Prof Goffredo Gaeta; Franco Rossi
Sales: Luisa Teston *E-mail:* lteston@faenza.com
Founded: 1965
Subjects: Advertising, Architecture & Interior Design, Art, Chemistry, Chemical Engineering, Electronics, Electrical Engineering, Medicine, Nursing, Dentistry
ISBN Prefix(es): 88-8138
Number of titles published annually: 98 Print
Imprints: Edizioni CELI

Gruppo Editoriale Internazionale SRL (GEI), see Instituti Editoriali E Poligrafici Internazionali SRL

Ugo Guanda Editore+
Corso Italia 13, 20122 Milan
Tel: (02) 8693072 *Fax:* (02) 76000306
E-mail: info@guanda.it
Telex: 353273 LONG I
Key Personnel
President: Mario Spagnol
Man Dir: Stefano Mauri
Editorial: Luigi Brioschi
Sales: Giuseppe Somenzi
Production: Alfredo Bonfiglio
Publicity: Valentina Fortichiari
Rights & Permissions: Cristina Foschini
Founded: 1932
Subjects: Art, Poetry
ISBN Prefix(es): 88-7746; 88-235; 88-8246
Parent Company: Longanesi & C
Subsidiaries: Gdp
U.S. Office(s): Nina Collins Association, 584 Broadway, Suite 607, New York, NY 10012, United States
Warehouse: Messaggerie Italiane Spa, Magazzino Editoriale, Via Bereguardina, 20080 Casarile (Mi)
Orders to: Pro Libro, Strada della Repubblica 56, 43100 Parma

Edizioni Guerini e Associati SpA+
Viale Filippetti 28, 20122 Milan
Tel: (02) 582980 *Fax:* (02) 58298030
E-mail: guerini@iol.it; info@guerini.it
Web Site: www.guerini.it
Key Personnel
President: Angelo Guerini
Printing Office: Federico Gagliardo *Tel:* (02) 58298017
Foreign Rights Manager: Claudia Premoli *Tel:* (02) 58298016
Founded: 1987
Essays, Books & Reviews.
Subjects: Anthropology, Management, Philosophy, Psychology, Psychiatry, Social Sciences, Sociology, Literary Criticism, Architecture & Gardens, Media Studies & Geopolitics
ISBN Prefix(es): 88-7802; 88-8107; 88-8335; 88-8195
Total Titles: 1,000 Print
Bookshop(s): Libreria Guerini, Piazza Soldini 5, 21053 Castellanza *Tel:* (0331) 508918 *Fax:* (0331) 508972 *E-mail:* libreria@liuc.it
Shipping Address: Pea Italia, Via Spallanzani 16, 20129 Milan

Guerra Edizioni Guru Azp
Via A Manna 25/27, 06132 S Andrea della Fratte (PG)
Tel: (075) 5289090 *Fax:* (075) 5288244
E-mail: guerra@tecnonet.it
Web Site: www.guru.it
Telex: Cuper 1 Rux
Key Personnel
Publicity Manager: Chellini Gastone
Founded: 1883
Subjects: Education, Language Arts, Linguistics
ISBN Prefix(es): 88-7715
Orders to: RUX edel, Via E Fermi 26, I-06100 Perugia *Tel:* (075) 751324

Guide del Cuore, *imprint of* Passigli Editori srl

Guide del Sole, *imprint of* Passigli Editori srl

GZ, *imprint of* Casa Musicale G Zanibon SRL

Herbita Editrice di Leonardo Palermo+
Via Errante 44, 90127 Palermo
Tel: (091) 6167732 *Fax:* (091) 6167716
Cable: HERBITA PALERMO
Key Personnel
Chief Executive: Leonardo Palermo
Founded: 1973
Subjects: Archaeology, Art, Computer Science, Economics, Geography, Geology, Government, Political Science, Law, Literature, Literary Criticism, Essays, Mathematics, Philosophy, Religion - Catholic
ISBN Prefix(es): 88-7994

Herder Editrice e Libreria
Piazza Montecitorio 120, 00186 Rome
Tel: (06) 6795304; (06) 6794628 *Fax:* (06) 6784751
E-mail: bookcenter@herder.it
Web Site: www.herder.it
Key Personnel
Man Dir: Oriol Schaedel
Founded: 1955
Subjects: Archaeology, Asian Studies, History, Language Arts, Linguistics, Philosophy, Religion - Other
ISBN Prefix(es): 88-85876
Associate Companies: Verlag Herder & Co, Austria; Verlag Herder GmbH & Co KG, Germany; Herder und Herder GmbH, Germany; Verlag A G Ploetz GmbH & Co KG, Germany; Editorial Herder SA, Spain; Herder AG, Switzerland

BOOK

Distributor for Academia Latinitati Fovendae (Rome); Academy Cardinalis Bessarionis (Rome); Center Studies "Girolamo Baruffaldi" (Hundreds); Center Studies Varroniani (Rieti); Church Abbaziale di Montecassino (Cassino); Department of Linguistica, University (Florence); Editions Universitaires Fribourg (Switzerland) (Italy); European Comunity (Rome); Faculty of Mastery University (Messina); Institute for East "C to Nallino" (Rome); Institute for the Ecclesiastical History Padovana (Padova); Institute of Indologia University (Turin); Instituto Espanol de Historia Eclesiastica (Rome); Institutum Historicum Polonicum (Rome); Italian Institute for the Mean & Far East (IsMEO) (Rome); Italian Institute of Germanic Studies (Rome); OECD, Paris (Rome); Properziana Academy of the Subasio (Assisi); Sargon Publishing limited liability company (Padova); University Institute Orients Them (Naples); University of the Studies of Rome "the Wisdom"; World Bank (Rome)

Hermes Edizioni SRL+
Via Flaminia 109, 00196 Rome
Tel: (06) 3222797 *Fax:* (06) 3236277
E-mail: edimedit@flashnet.it
Web Site: www.ediz-mediterranee.com
Key Personnel
General Manager: Giovanni Canonico
Editorial: Paola Maria Canonico
Sales: Graziella Torre
Rights & Permissions: Canonico Assia
Contact: Eleasa Canonico
Founded: 1979
Subjects: Anthropology, Health, Nutrition, How-to, Medicine, Nursing, Dentistry, Parapsychology, Psychology, Psychiatry, Religion - Buddhist, Religion - Hindu, Religion - Other, Sports, Athletics
ISBN Prefix(es): 88-7938
Total Titles: 300 Print
Parent Company: Edizioni Mediterranee SRL

Institutum Historicum S I
Via dei Penitenzieri, 20, 00193 Rome
Tel: (06) 6869357 *Fax:* (06) 6861342
E-mail: archivum@tin.it; ihsiroma@tin.it
Founded: 1932
Subjects: History
Total Titles: 50 Print

Hopeful Monster Editore
Via Santa Chiara 30, 10122 Turin
Tel: (011) 4367197; (011) 4358519 *Fax:* (011) 4369025
E-mail: hopmonst@tin.it
Web Site: www.hopefulmonster.net
Founded: 1986
Specializes in: Art books & catalogues concerning contemporary art.
Subjects: Art, History, Philosophy, Photography, Science (General), Travel
ISBN Prefix(es): 88-7757
Number of titles published annually: 15 Print
Distributed by Albolibro (Italy); Angelo Vecchi & C (Italy); Art Books International (UK & Eire); Campania Libri; Centro Di (Europe, Giappone & USA); Centro Distribuzione Editoriale (CDE) (Italy); Distribook (Italy); Distributed Art Publishers (DAP) (USA, Canada, South America & Asia); Erre Libri (Italy); Italia Libri SRL (Italy); Joker Art Diffusion (France & Belgium); L'Aquilone (Italy); Licosa (Europe (except UK, Eire)); Serena Libri (Italy)

Hora+
Milano 2, Res Tre Fili, 421, 20090 Segrate Milan
Tel: (02) 2155589 *Fax:* (02) 26412203
Key Personnel
Contact: Rosella Hoffer; Mariangela Ragazzi
Founded: 1989

PUBLISHERS

ITALY

Subjects: English as a Second Language
ISBN Prefix(es): 88-85144

Horus
Via Pramarino, 3, 10080 Baldissero Canavese Turin
Tel: (011) 511705 *Fax:* (011) 511705
Founded: 1978
Member of Casa Edittice Della Comunita Di Damanhur.
Subjects: Astrology, Occult, Earth Sciences, Mysteries, Social Sciences, Sociology
ISBN Prefix(es): 88-7012

I Quanta, *imprint of* Folini

Ibis+
Via Crispi 8, 22100 Como
Tel: (031) 3371367 *Fax:* (031) 306829
E-mail: ibisedizioni@galactica.it
Web Site: www.ibisedizioni.it
Key Personnel
President: Giulio Veronesi
Editorial Dir: Paolo M Veronesi
Founded: 1989
Subjects: Anthropology, Biological Sciences, Fiction, History, Literature, Literary Criticism, Essays, Philosophy, Social Sciences, Sociology, Travel
ISBN Prefix(es): 88-7164
Number of titles published annually: 15 Print
Total Titles: 130 Print

Idea Books+
Via Cappuccio, 18, 20123 Milan
Tel: (02) 89010670 *Fax:* (02) 86462515
Cable: IDEABOOKS MILANO
Key Personnel
Dir: Filippo Passigli
Founded: 1979
Also acts as a distributor.
Subjects: Architecture & Interior Design, Art, Crafts, Games, Hobbies, Fashion, Photography
ISBN Prefix(es): 88-7017
U.S. Office(s): 250 W 57 St, New York, NY 10107, United States

Casa Editrice Libraria Idelson di G Gnocchi+
Via A De Gasperi 55, 80133 Naples
Tel: (081) 5524733 *Fax:* (081) 5518295
E-mail: idelgno@tin.it
Web Site: www.idelson-gnocchi.com *Cable:* IDELSON NAPLES
Key Personnel
Chief Executive: Guido Gnocchi
Founded: 1908
Subjects: Biological Sciences, Medicine, Nursing, Dentistry
ISBN Prefix(es): 88-7069

Istituto Idrografico della Marina
Passo dell'Osservatorio 4, 16134 Genoa
Tel: (010) 24431 *Fax:* (010) 261400
E-mail: maridrografico.ge.sre@marina.difesa.it
Telex: 270435; 275521 Maridr I *Cable:* MARIDROGRAFICO
Key Personnel
Dir: Corrado Fiori
Vice Dir: Giuseppe Borsa
Production: Antonio Sfregola
Public Relations: Antonio Cairo
Map Division: Raffaele Gargiulo
Founded: 1872
Subjects: Maritime

IHT Gruppo Editoriale SRL
Via Monte Napoleone 9, 20121 Milan
Tel: (02) 794181 *Fax:* (02) 784021
E-mail: info@iht.it
Web Site: www.iht.it
Key Personnel
Dir: Lisa Massimiliano
Founded: 1985
Subjects: Art, Film, Video, Microcomputers, Military Science, Science (General), Technology
ISBN Prefix(es): 88-7803
Imprints: IHT Video
Distributed by Messaggerie Periodic
Orders to: IHT Publishing Group, Via Monte Napoleone 9, 20121 Milan

IHT Video, *imprint of* IHT Gruppo Editoriale SRL

Il Pensiero Scientifico Editore SRL+
Via Bradano 3/C, 00199 Rome
Tel: (06) 86282334 *Fax:* (06) 86282250
E-mail: pensiero@pensiero.it
Web Site: www.pensiero.it
Key Personnel
President: Annamaria De Feo
General Manager: Francesco De Fiore
Publicity Manager: Luciano De Fiore
Marketing & Sales Manager: Luca De Fiore
Foreign Rights: Andres De Fiore; Silvana Guida
Founded: 1946
The publishing missions of Il Pensiero Scientifico editore is the statement of the human values as the basis of Medical research and the development of all evidence based clinical practice.
Subjects: Education, Health, Nutrition, Psychology, Psychiatry, Medicine, Nursing and Oncology
ISBN Prefix(es): 88-7002
Number of titles published annually: 50 Print

Il Lavoro Editoriale, *imprint of* Il Lavoro Editoriale

Il Minotauro+
Via Quirino Majorana 221, 00152 Rome
Tel: (06) 5591864 *Fax:* (06) 5592337
E-mail: ilminotauro@tin.it
Web Site: www.ilminotauroeditore.it
Key Personnel
Contact: Dr Giorgio Ferrari
Founded: 1993
Subjects: Fiction, Government, Political Science, Literature, Literary Criticism, Essays, Philosophy, Travel
ISBN Prefix(es): 88-8073
Distributed by PDE Milano

Il Polifilo
Via Borgonuovo, 2, 20121 Milan
Tel: (02) 6551549 *Fax:* (02) 6598045
ISBN Prefix(es): 88-7050

Il Poligrafo
Via Turazza 19, 35128 Padova
Tel: (049) 776986 *Fax:* (049) 8070910
Key Personnel
Contact: Chiara Finesso
Founded: 1987
Subjects: History, Literature, Literary Criticism, Essays, Philosophy, Psychology, Psychiatry, Regional Interests, Science (General)
ISBN Prefix(es): 88-7115

Il Quadrante SRL
Via B Galliari 15 bis, 10125 Turin
Tel: (011) 6693910 *Fax:* (011) 6693929
Key Personnel
Man Dir, Editorial: Ezio Quarantelli
Sales: Grazia Angelini
Publicity: Marcella Longo
Rights & Permissions: Simonetta Violi
Founded: 1980
Subjects: Art, Biography, Fiction, Literature, Literary Criticism, Essays
ISBN Prefix(es): 88-381

Associate Companies: Edizioni Studio Tesi SRL
Subsidiaries: Mostre e Musei SRL

Il Saggiatore+
Via Helzo 9, 20129 Milan
Tel: (02) 29403460 *Fax:* (02) 29513061
E-mail: info@saggiatore.it
Web Site: www.saggiatore.it
Key Personnel
President: Luca Formenton
Editorial Dir: Marco Tropea
Founded: 1958
Subjects: Anthropology, Art, Asian Studies, Fiction, History, Literature, Literary Criticism, Essays, Music, Dance, Nonfiction (General), Philosophy, Poetry, Romance, Science (General), Social Sciences, Sociology
ISBN Prefix(es): 88-04; 88-428
Associate Companies: Marco Tropea Editore; Nuova Practiche Editrice

Ila - Palma, Tea Nova+
Via La Lumia 5/7, 90139 Palermo
Tel: (091) 332051 *Fax:* (091) 6259260
Key Personnel
Editor: Rean Mazzone
Founded: 1960
Subjects: Archaeology, Art, Economics, History, Literature, Literary Criticism, Essays, Management, Philosophy
ISBN Prefix(es): 88-7704
Subsidiaries: Nef; Tea; Tea Nova
Orders to: Via Benedetto Castiglia 6, I-90141 Palermo

In Dialogo+
Via S Antonio 5, 20122 Milan
Tel: (02) 8052529 *Fax:* (02) 58391345
E-mail: indial@tin.it
Founded: 1980
Subjects: Biblical Studies, Child Care & Development, Communications, Education, Government, Political Science, Human Relations, Religion - Catholic, Theology
ISBN Prefix(es): 88-8123; 88-85985
Shipping Address: Via Andolfato 3, 20126 Milan
Warehouse: Via Andolfato 3, 20126 Milan
Orders to: Dehoniana Libri SRL

Iniziative Culturali SRL, see Servitium

Editrice Innocenti SNC+
Via Zara 36, 38100 Trento
Tel: (0461) 36521 *Fax:* (0461) 30115 *Cable:* EDITRICE INNOCENTI TRENTO
Key Personnel
Chief Executive: Luciano Innocenti
Publicity: Silvia Nones
Founded: 1972
Subjects: Language Arts, Linguistics
Associate Companies: Casa Editrice Bulgarini, Via Petrolin, 8-50137 Firenze; Casa Editrice Principato, Via Fauche, Milan

Instituti Editoriali E Poligrafici Internazionali SRL+
Via Giosue Carducci, 60, 56010 Ghezzano (Pisa)
Tel: (050) 878066 *Fax:* (050) 878732
E-mail: iepi@iepi.it
Key Personnel
Man Dir: Lucia Carmignani
Founded: 1995
Specialize in: Philosophy, Archaeology, History, Sociology, Anthropology & Italian.
Subjects: Anthropology, Archaeology, Language Arts, Linguistics, Philosophy, Social Sciences, Sociology, Transportation
ISBN Prefix(es): 88-8147
Shipping Address: The Courier srl, viel A De-Basis 25, 50165 Firenze *Tel:* (055) 300443 *Fax:* (055) 300036

ITALY

Warehouse: The Courier srl, viel A DeBasis 25, 50165 Firenze *Tel:* (055) 300443 *Fax:* (055) 300036
Orders to: The Courier srl, Viel A DeBasis 25, 50165 Firenze *Tel:* (055) 300443 *Fax:* (055) 300036

International Ediemme
Via Innocenzo XI 41, 00165 Rome
Tel: (06) 39378788 *Fax:* (06) 6380839
E-mail: iscd@colosseum.it
Key Personnel
Editor-in-Chief: Pierfrancesco Morganti
ISBN Prefix(es): 88-7821

International University Press Srl+
Via Monte della Gioie 22, 00199 Rome
Tel: (06) 86211027; (06) 86211028 *Fax:* (06) 86211026
Key Personnel
President: Felice Alivernini
Founded: 1987
Member of USPI.
Subjects: Medicine, Nursing, Dentistry
ISBN Prefix(es): 88-85314
U.S. Office(s): Little, Brown & Company, 24 Beacon St, Boston, MA 02108, United States

Edizioni Internazionali di Letteratura e Scienze+
Via Cornelia 7, 00166 Rome
Tel: (06) 6241563 *Fax:* (06) 61520253
Founded: 1972
Specialize in historical experimentation of dynamic physiology comparison.
Subjects: History, Language Arts, Linguistics, Literature, Literary Criticism, Essays, Romance, Science Fiction, Fantasy, Social Sciences, Sociology
ISBN Prefix(es): 88-7130

Iperborea
Via Palestro 22, 20121 Milan
Tel: (02) 706684 *Fax:* (02) 798919
E-mail: iperborea@iol.it
Key Personnel
President & Editorial Dir: Emilia Lodigiani
Founded: 1987
Subjects: Literature, Literary Criticism, Essays
ISBN Prefix(es): 88-7091

ISAL (Ist Storia Arte Lombarda)
Palazzo Reale, Piazza Del Duomo, 14, 20122 Milan
Tel: (02) 878475 *Fax:* (02) 86463412
E-mail: isalbibl@tin.it
Key Personnel
Editor: Maria Luisa Gatti Perer
Founded: 1955
Subjects: Archaeology, Art
ISBN Prefix(es): 88-85153

ISMEO, see Istituto Italiano Per Il Medio Ed Estremo Oriente (ISMEO)

Isper SRL+
Corso Dante 122, 10126 Turin
Tel: (011) 633950 *Fax:* (011) 6670829
Key Personnel
Chief Executive: Dr Carlo Actis Grosso
Contact: Paola Riccardi
Founded: 1965
Subjects: Business, Management
Branch Office(s)
Via N Porpora 12, 1-00198 Rome
Corso del Popolo 46, 1-30172 Venice
Via Lambro 4, 1-20129 Milan
Book Club(s): Isper Club

Ist Patristico Augustinianum
Via Paolo VI 25, 1-00193 Rome
Tel: (06) 6800069 *Fax:* (06) 68006298
E-mail: pubblic.augnum@pcn.net
Key Personnel
Principal: Angelo Di Berardino
Founded: 1969
Subjects: Antiques, Literature, Literary Criticism, Essays, Religion - Catholic
ISBN Prefix(es): 88-7961
Imprints: SEA

Edizioni Italiane, *imprint of* Todariana Editrice

Istituto Italiano Edizioni Atlas+
Via Crescenzi 88, 24123 Bergamo
Tel: (035) 249711 *Fax:* (035) 216047
E-mail: edatlas@tin.it
Key Personnel
Contact: Dr Marco Carreri
ISBN Prefix(es): 88-268

Istituto Italiano Per Il Medio Ed Estremo Oriente (ISMEO)
Via Merulana 248, 00184 Rome
Tel: (06) 732742 *Fax:* (06) 4873138
Telex: 624163

Ithaca+
Piazza De Angeli, 1, 20146 Milan
Tel: (02) 48009484 *Fax:* (02) 48009493
Key Personnel
Communications: Barbara Crepaldi
Administrator: Girolamo Frisina
Founded: 1985
Specialize in total quality management.
Subjects: Business, Communications, Management, Marketing
ISBN Prefix(es): 88-7206

Editoriale Jaca Book SpA+
Via Gioberti, 7, 20123 Milan
Tel: (02) 48561520-29 *Fax:* (02) 48193361
E-mail: jacabook@jacabook.it
Web Site: www.jacabook.it
Key Personnel
President & Publisher: Sante Bagnoli
Editorial Dir: Maretta Campi
Administrative Dir: Guido Orsi *E-mail:* admin@jacabook.it
Academic Dep: Massimo Guidetti
Co-editions: Silvia Vassena *E-mail:* coeditions@jacabook.it
Rights: Ida Bonali *E-mail:* produzione@jacabook.it
Founded: 1978
Subjects: Anthropology, Archaeology, Architecture & Interior Design, Art, Asian Studies, Earth Sciences, Economics, Fiction, Geography, Geology, Government, Political Science, History, Human Relations, Literature, Literary Criticism, Essays, Music, Dance, Native American Studies, Natural History, Nonfiction (General), Philosophy, Photography, Physics, Poetry, Religion - Catholic, Religion - Other, Science (General), Social Sciences, Sociology, Theology
ISBN Prefix(es): 88-16
Total Titles: 130 Print
Subsidiaries: Jaca/Edizioni Universitarie

Gruppo Editoriale Jackson SpA
Via XXV Aprile, 39, 20091 Bresso
Tel: (02) 665261 *Fax:* (02) 66526222
E-mail: ordini@futura-ge.com
Telex: 316213
Key Personnel
Man Dir, President: Paolo Reina
Marketing Manager: Filippo Canavese
Dir Periodicals: Pierantonio Palerma
Dir Book Shops: Roberto Pancaldi
Administrative Dir: Luigi Gadola
Dir Production & Aquisitions: Luigi Beccaria
International: Stefania Scroglieri
Founded: 1975
ISBN Prefix(es): 88-7056; 88-256
Subsidiaries: Jackson Hispania SA; GEJ Publishing Group Inc
Warehouse: Piazza Amendola 45, Paderno Dugnano, Milano

Jandi-Sapi Editori
Via Crescenzio 62, 00193 Rome
Tel: (06) 68805509-15; (06) 6876054 *Fax:* (06) 6832612
E-mail: mail@jandisapi.com
Web Site: www.jandisapi.com
Founded: 1941
Subjects: Art, Law
ISBN Prefix(es): 88-7142
Imprints: JSE
Divisions: Archivi Arte Antica

Editrice Janus SpA+
Via dei Capodiferro 12, 24121 Bergamo
Tel: (035) 247180 *Fax:* (035) 247092
Key Personnel
Man Dir, Editorial: Marco Zingarelli
Sales, Production: Marcello Riva
Founded: 1956
Subjects: Literature, Literary Criticism, Essays

L Japadre Editore+
Corso Federico II, 49, 67100 l'Aquila
Tel: (0862) 26025 *Fax:* (0862) 25587
Key Personnel
Man Dir: Leandro Ugo Japadre
Founded: 1966
Subjects: Art, Economics, Ethnicity, Fiction, History, Language Arts, Linguistics, Literature, Literary Criticism, Essays, Philosophy, Poetry, Psychology, Psychiatry, Religion - Other, Science (General), Social Sciences, Sociology, Technology
ISBN Prefix(es): 88-7006
Branch Office(s)
Via G Boni 20, 1-00162 Rome *Tel:* (06) 44291182
Distributor for DASP (Deputazione Abruzzese Di Storia Patria)
Warehouse: Contrada Cappelli
Pal Prosperini

Jazz People, *imprint of* Stampa Alternativa - Nuovi Equilibri

Jouvence+
Via Monte Zebio 24, 00195 Rome
Tel: (06) 3202897 *Fax:* (06) 3202897
E-mail: ed.jouvence@flashnet.it
Key Personnel
Editorial Dir: Alessandro Gallo
Administrator: Claudia Pozzessere
Founded: 1979
Subjects: Archaeology, Asian Studies, History, Literature, Literary Criticism, Essays, Philosophy, Religion - Islamic
ISBN Prefix(es): 88-7801
Warehouse: Via Cassia, 1081-00189 Rome

Casa Editrice Dott Eugenio Jovene SpA
Via Mezzocannone 109, 80134 Naples
Tel: (081) 5521019 *Fax:* (081) 5520687
Cable: JOVENE
Key Personnel
Man Dir: Dr Alessandro Rossi
Founded: 1854
Subjects: Economics, Law
ISBN Prefix(es): 88-243

JSE, *imprint of* Jandi-Sapi Editori

Kaos Edizioni SRL+
Viale Abruzzi 58, 20131 Milan
Tel: (02) 29523063 *Fax:* (02) 29524822
Key Personnel
Man Dir: Lorenzo Ruggiero
Founded: 1985
Subjects: Biography, Drama, Theater, Film, Video, Government, Political Science, History, Music, Dance, Nonfiction (General), Social Sciences, Sociology
ISBN Prefix(es): 88-7953
Imprints: Gammalibri-Rock Books; Edizioni Blues Brothers

Kompass Fleischmann
Localita Ghiaie 166/d, 38014 Gardolo (Trento)
Tel: (0461) 961240 *Fax:* (0461) 961203
Key Personnel
Dir: Mario Cont
Administrator: Dr Petra Fleischmann
Founded: 1973
Subjects: Animals, Pets, Geography, Geology, Natural History, Travel
ISBN Prefix(es): 88-431

L'Airone Editrice, *imprint of* Ernesto Gremese Editore SRL

L'Airone Editrice+
Imprint of Gremese Editore
Via Virginia Agnelli, 88, 00151 Rome
Tel: (06) 6570758 *Fax:* (06) 65740509
E-mail: gremese@gremese.com
Web Site: www.gremese.com
Key Personnel
Publisher & Executive Manager: Alberto Gremese *Tel:* (06) 65740507 *E-mail:* alberto@gremese.com
Founded: 1992
Subjects: Astrology, Occult, Crafts, Games, Hobbies, Humor, Mysteries, Nonfiction (General), Parapsychology, Photography, Sports, Athletics, Travel
ISBN Prefix(es): 88-7944

Edizioni L' Eta dell'Acquario, *imprint of* Edizioni l'eta Dell'Acquario Di I Bresci & C Sas

LAC - Litografia Artistica Cartografica Srl
Via del Romito 11/13-R, 50134 Florence
Tel: (055) 483557 *Fax:* (055) 483690
Key Personnel
President: Maria G Garbarino
Contact: Mrs Cinzia Cassai
Founded: 1949
Subjects: Geography, Geology, Travel
ISBN Prefix(es): 88-7914

Lalli Editore SRL+
Via Fiume 60, 53036 Poggibonsi (Siena)
Tel: (0577) 933305 *Fax:* (0577) 983308
Cable: LALLIEDIT POGGIBONSI
Key Personnel
Chief Executive: Antonio Lalli
Editorial: Fioranna Casamenti
Founded: 1965
Subjects: Art, Biography, Drama, Theater, Education, Ethnicity, Fiction, Film, Video, Government, Political Science, Humor, Philosophy, Poetry, Regional Interests, Religion - Other, Science (General), Social Sciences, Sociology
Warehouse: Via Modena, 12-53036 Poggibonsi (SI)

Lanfranchi
Via Madonnina 10, 20121 Milan
Tel: (02) 8056083 *Fax:* (02) 8056083
ISBN Prefix(es): 88-363

Lang Edizioni™, *imprint of* Paravia Bruno Mondadori Editori

Laruffa Editore SRL+
Via dei Tre Mulini, 14, 89124 Reggio, Calabria
Tel: (0965) 814948 *Fax:* (0965) 814954
E-mail: laruffa@tin.it; laruffa@libero.it
Web Site: www.laruffaeditore.com
Founded: 1980
Subjects: Agriculture, Archaeology, Architecture & Interior Design, Education, History, Religion - Catholic, Social Sciences, Sociology, Travel
ISBN Prefix(es): 88-7221

Editrice LAS
Piazza Ateneo Salesiano 1, 00139 Rome
Tel: (06) 87290626 *Fax:* (06) 87290629
Founded: 1974
Subjects: Biblical Studies, Education, Philosophy, Psychology, Psychiatry, Religion - Catholic, Social Sciences, Sociology, Theology
ISBN Prefix(es): 88-213

Edizioni Fratelli Laterza, *imprint of* Giuseppe Laterza Editore Snc

Edizioni Lavoro SRL
Via Lancisi 25, 00161 Rome
Tel: (06) 44251174 *Fax:* (06) 44251177
Key Personnel
Man Dir, Rights & Permissions: Mario Bertin
Editorial: Alessandra Belardelli; Laura Lo Campo
Sales & Publicity: Stefania Vulterini
Founded: 1982
Subjects: Fiction, Government, Political Science, History, Philosophy, Social Sciences, Sociology
ISBN Prefix(es): 88-7910
Imprints: El

Il Lavoro Editoriale+
Via Piave 32, 60124 Ancona
Tel: (071) 2072210 *Fax:* (071) 2081342
E-mail: transeuropa@logica.it
Web Site: www.illavoreditoriale.com
Key Personnel
Editorial Board Chief: Giorgio Mangani
Founded: 1980
Subjects: Art, History, Human Relations, Literature, Literary Criticism, Essays, Essays; Specializes in art, history & literature about Mazche Regions, Italy
ISBN Prefix(es): 88-7663
Number of titles published annually: 15 Print
Imprints: Transeuropa; Il Lavoro Editoriale
Orders to: PO Box 297, Ancona

Lecce Spazio Vivo Srl
Via Palmieri 30, 73100 Lecce
Tel: (0832) 308885 *Fax:* (0832) 308885; (0832) 241562
Founded: 1945
Subjects: Disability, Special Needs, Education, English as a Second Language, History, Human Relations, Literature, Literary Criticism, Essays, Philosophy, Psychology, Psychiatry, Social Sciences, Sociology
ISBN Prefix(es): 88-7048
Bookshop(s): Libreria Milella, Via Palmieri 30, 73100 Lecce; Viale 1, 1-73100 Viale De Pietro
Warehouse: Universitaria Lecce, Via Palmieri 3, Obelisco Viale dell'Universitia, 1, 73100 Lecce

LED - Edizioni Universitarie di Lettere Economia Diritto+
Via Cervignano 4, 20137 Milan
Tel: (02) 59902055 *Fax:* (02) 55193636
Key Personnel
Man Dir: Maria Grazia Gelo
International Rights: Valeria Passerini
Founded: 1991
Subjects: Economics, History, Law, Literature, Literary Criticism, Essays, Philosophy, Psychology, Psychiatry
ISBN Prefix(es): 88-7916

L'Editrice Scientifica, see Nagard

LEF, *imprint of* Libreria Editrice Fiorentina di Vittorio Zani e C SAS

LER, see Libreria Editrice Rogate (LER)

L'Erma di Bretschneider SRL+
Via Cassiodoro 19, 00193 Rome
Tel: (06) 6874127 *Fax:* (06) 6874129
E-mail: edizioni@lerma.it
Web Site: www.lerma.it
Key Personnel
Chief Executive & Editorial: Dr Roberto Marcucci *E-mail:* erma@sysin.it
Founded: 1946
Subjects: Archaeology, Architecture & Interior Design, Art, History, Language Arts, Linguistics, Religion - Other
ISBN Prefix(es): 88-7062; 88-8265
Bookshop(s): Libreria L'Erma, Via Cassiodoro 19, 1-00193 Rome

L'eta D'oro Dell Illustrazione, *imprint of* Stampa Alternativa - Nuovi Equilibri

Casa Editrice Le Lettere SRL
Costa S Giorgio 28, 50125 Florence
Tel: (055) 2342710 *Fax:* (055) 2346010
Key Personnel
Chief Executive: Dr Giovanni Gentile
Sales, Administration: Carlo De Simone
Founded: 1956
Subjects: History, Language Arts, Linguistics, Literature, Literary Criticism, Essays, Philosophy
ISBN Prefix(es): 88-7166
Associate Companies: Progedi Srl, Viale Gramsci, 18, 50132 Florence
Shipping Address: Licosa Spa, Via Duca Di Calabria 1/1, 50125 Florence
Warehouse: Via Francesco Gioli 5-11, 50018 Scandicci

Letture Mensile di Informazione Culturale, Letteratura e Spettacolo
Via Giotto 36, 20145 Milan
Tel: (02) 48071 *Fax:* (02) 48072568
E-mail: letture@stpauls.it
Key Personnel
Contact: Antonio Rizzolo *Tel:* (02) 48072518 *Fax:* (02) 48072515
Founded: 1946
Subjects: Drama, Theater, Film, Video, Literature, Literary Criticism, Essays, Music, Dance, Poetry, Religion - Catholic, Science Fiction, Fantasy, Theology
Parent Company: Periodici, San Paolo

Levante+
Via Napoli 35, 70123 Bari
Tel: (080) 5213778 *Fax:* (080) 5213778
E-mail: levanted@tin.it
Web Site: www.levantebari.com
Key Personnel
Contact: Sara Cavalli
Founded: 1967
Subjects: Criminology, Drama, Theater, Mysteries, Philosophy, Psychology, Psychiatry, Travel
ISBN Prefix(es): 88-7949
Number of titles published annually: 20 Print

Levrotto e Bella Libreria Editrice Universitaria SAS+
Corso Vittorio Emanuele 26F, 10123 Turin
Tel: (011) 8121205 *Fax:* (011) 8124025
E-mail: levrotto@ipsnet.it

ITALY

Key Personnel
Man Dir, Editorial, Rights & Permissions: Elisabetta Gualini
Sales: Carmela Bueti; Giampiero Garnero
Founded: 1942
Also book packager.
Subjects: Science (General), Technology
ISBN Prefix(es): 88-8218
Bookshop(s): Libreria del Politecnico, Corso Einaudi 57, 1-10129 Turin

Edizioni Librex
Via Bellezza 15, 20136 Milan
Tel: (02) 58302006
Telex: 320208 *Cable:* Librex Milan
Key Personnel
General Manager: Antonio Mancia
Export: M Luisa Franceschini
Production: Luciano Baroni
Founded: 1966

Liguori Editore SRL+
Via Posillipo 394, 80123 Naples
Tel: (081) 7206111; (081) 7206202 (orders)
Fax: (081) 7206244
E-mail: liguori@liguori.it *Cable:* LIGUORI NAPOLI
Key Personnel
Man Dir: Amedleo Liguori
Editorial, Rights & Permissions: Guido Liguori
Sales: Franco Liguori
Publicity: Maria Liguori
Founded: 1949
Subjects: Anthropology, Economics, History, Language Arts, Linguistics, Law, Literature, Literary Criticism, Essays, Mathematics, Medicine, Nursing, Dentistry, Philosophy, Science (General), Social Sciences, Sociology, Theology
ISBN Prefix(es): 88-207
Bookshop(s): Librerie Commissionarie Liguori SRL, Via Mezzocannone 21-23, 1-80134 Naples *Tel:* (081) 5527702; Via Cinthiq 36/B, 80126 Naples *Tel:* (081) 7675228
Warehouse: Via Ciccarelli 16G, 80167 Naples

Editrice Liguria SNC di Norberto Sabatelli & C
Via De Mari 4r, 17100 Savona
Tel: (019) 829917 *Fax:* (019) 8387798
Key Personnel
Chief Executive: Norberto Sabatelli
Founded: 1934
Subjects: Art, Drama, Theater, Fiction, History, Literature, Literary Criticism, Essays, Poetry, Technology, Travel
ISBN Prefix(es): 88-8055
Imprints: EL

LIM, *imprint of* LIM Editrice SRL

LIM Editrice SRL+
Via di Arsina 296f, 55100 Lucca
Tel: (0583) 394464 *Fax:* (0583) 394469
E-mail: lim@lim.it
Key Personnel
Contact: Paola Borriero *E-mail:* paola.borriero@lim.it
Founded: 1988
Member of AIE.
Subjects: Music, Dance
ISBN Prefix(es): 88-7096
Associate Companies: Akademos, LIM Antiquaria, Una Cosa Rara
Imprints: LIM
Distributor for Adeva; Alamire; Broude Brothers; Garland; Fondazione Locatelli; Pendragon Press; Fondazione Rossini
Orders to: PO Box 198, 55100 Lucca

L'immaginazion, *imprint of* Piero Manni srl

Lindau, *imprint of* Lindau

Lindau+
Via Galliari, 15b, 10125 Turin
Tel: (011) 6693910 *Fax:* (011) 6693929
E-mail: lindau@lindau.it
Web Site: www.lindau.it
Key Personnel
Executive & Editorial Dir: Ezio Quarantelli
E-mail: quarantelli@lindau.it
Founded: 1989
Subjects: Fiction, Film, Video
ISBN Prefix(es): 88-7180
Number of titles published annually: 80 Print
Total Titles: 450 Print
Imprints: Lindau; Edizioni L'Eta Dell'Acqua Rio

Linea d'Ombra Libri (Linea D'Ombra Books)
Via della Madonna, 9, 31015 Conegliano
Tel: (0438) 412647 *Fax:* (0438) 412690
E-mail: info@lineadombra.it
Web Site: www.lineadombra.it
Founded: 1996
Publisher of art books & exhibition catalogues.
Subjects: Art, Photography, Poetry
ISBN Prefix(es): 88-09
Number of titles published annually: 20 Print
Parent Company: Linea D'Ombra

Linea Verde, *imprint of* Gruppo Editoriale Le Stelle SpA

Lisciani e Giunti Editori, see Giunti Publishing Group

Litografia Artistica Cartografia Srl - LAC, see LAC - Litografia Artistica Cartografica Srl

Vincenzo Lo Faro Editore
Via S Giovanni Laterano 276, 00184 Rome
Tel: (06) 70451187 *Fax:* (06) 70451641
Key Personnel
Chief Executive: Vincenzo Lo Faro
Editorial: Letizia Carile
Founded: 1967
Subjects: Art, Drama, Theater, Education, Environmental Studies, Fiction, Law, Medicine, Nursing, Dentistry, Philosophy, Poetry, Religion - Other, Social Sciences, Sociology
ISBN Prefix(es): 88-87428

Editrice la Locusta
Via del Castello 20, 36100 Vicenza
Tel: (0444) 324051
Key Personnel
Chief Executive: Rienzo Colla
Founded: 1954
Subjects: History, Literature, Literary Criticism, Essays, Poetry

Loescher Editore SRL+
Via Vittorio Amedeo II 18, 10121 Turin
Tel: (011) 5654111 *Fax:* (011) 5625822
E-mail: Loescher@inrete.it
Key Personnel
President: Lorenzo Enriques
Vice President: Federico Enriques
Dir General: Riccardo Botrini
Editorial Head: Aron Buttarelli
Commerical Dir: Giorgio Sacco
Founded: 1867
Subjects: Chemistry, Chemical Engineering, English as a Second Language, Geography, Geology, History, Language Arts, Linguistics, Literature, Literary Criticism, Essays, Philosophy
ISBN Prefix(es): 88-201; 88-7608; 88-8094; 88-7159
Parent Company: Zanichelli Editore SpA

Imprints: The Ma; Eliseo
Distributed by Cambridge (Italy); Klett Edition Deutsch (Italy)

Loffredo Editore Napoli SpA®
Via Consalvo 99 h, 80126 Naples
Tel: (081) 5937073 *Fax:* (081) 5936953
Key Personnel
Chief Executive: Mario Loffredo
Editorial, Sales, Rights & Permissions: Alfredo Loffredo
Production: Alfredo Loffredo, Jr
Publicity: Enzo Loffredo
Founded: 1880
Subjects: History, Language Arts, Linguistics, Literature, Literary Criticism, Essays, Philosophy, Religion - Other, Science (General)
ISBN Prefix(es): 88-8096
Bookshop(s): Libreria Luigi Loffredo, Via Kerbaker 19/21, 1-80129 Naples

Longanesi & C+
Corso Italia 13, 20122 Milan
Tel: (02) 8692640; (02) 8692144 *Fax:* (02) 72000306
E-mail: info@longanesi.it
Web Site: www.longanesi.it
Key Personnel
President: Stefano Passigli
Sales: Giuseppe Somenzi
Production: Alfredo Bonfiglio
Publicity: Valentina Fortichiari
Rights & Permissions: Cristina Foschini
E-mail: christina.foschini@longanesi.it
Editorial Dir: Luigi Brioschi
Founded: 1946
Subjects: Art, Biography, Fiction, History, How-to, Medicine, Nursing, Dentistry, Music, Dance, Philosophy, Psychology, Psychiatry, Religion - Other, Science (General), Social Sciences, Sociology
ISBN Prefix(es): 88-304
Number of titles published annually: 100 Print
Total Titles: 5 Print
Parent Company: Messaggerie Italiane
Associate Companies: Guanda, Cristina Foschini; Corbaccio, Cristina Foschini; Neri Pozza, Cristina Foschini; Ponte alle Grazie, Cristina Foschini
Subsidiaries: Finarte
Orders to: Pro Libro, Corso Italia 13, 20122 Milan

Longman Italia srl
Via G Fara, 28, 20124 Milan
Tel: (02) 67397 6390 *Fax:* (02) 67397 6500
E-mail: firstname.lastname@pearsoned-ema.com
Key Personnel
Man Dir, ELT: David Evans
Finance Manager, ELT: Lucia Donatellis
Publishing Manager, ELT: Barbara Cunsolo
Sales & Marketing Manager, ELT: Alan Osman

Angelo Longo Editore+
Via Paolo Costa 33, 48100 Ravenna
Tel: (0544) 217026 *Fax:* (0544) 217554
E-mail: longo-ra@linknet.it
Web Site: www.longo-editore.it
Key Personnel
General Manager: Alfio Longo
Founded: 1962
Subjects: Archaeology, Art, Drama, Theater, Fiction, Film, Video, History, Language Arts, Linguistics, Literature, Literary Criticism, Essays, Music, Dance, Philosophy, Photography, Poetry, Women's Studies
ISBN Prefix(es): 88-8063
Number of titles published annually: 60 Print
Total Titles: 980 Print
Bookshop(s): Libreria Dante di A M Longo, Via Diaz 39, 48100 Ravenna, Roberta Plazzi *Tel:* (0544) 33500

PUBLISHERS
ITALY

Carlo Lorenzini Editore+
Via Cividina 364, 33030 Torreano di Martignacco (Ud)
Tel: (0432) 678712 *Fax:* (0432) 678730
Founded: 1981
ISBN Prefix(es): 88-7093

Lorenzo Editore+
Via Monza 6, 10152 Turin
Tel: (011) 2485387 *Fax:* (011) 2485387
Cable: ITALSCAMBI CP 23 TURIN
Key Personnel
Chief Executive: Lorenzo Masetta
Founded: 1975
Specialize in Poetry.
Subjects: Fiction, Literature, Literary Criticism, Essays, Poetry
ISBN Prefix(es): 88-85199; 88-87362
Subsidiaries: 'Talento' (current events periodical)

LPE, *imprint of* Luigi Pellegrini Editore

Lubrina Editore Srl+
Via Cesare Correnti, 50, 24124 Bergamo
Tel: (035) 360782 *Fax:* (035) 241547
E-mail: obramas@spm.it
Key Personnel
Man Dir: Ornella Bramani
Founded: 1995
Member of EQ Consorzio di Editor di Qualita.
Subjects: Biblical Studies, Biography, Literature, Literary Criticism, Essays, Philosophy, Psychology, Psychiatry
ISBN Prefix(es): 88-7766

Edizioni de Luca SRL
E Q Visconti, 11, 00193 Rome
Tel: (06) 32650712 *Fax:* (06) 32650715
Founded: 1935
Subjects: Archaeology, Art, History
ISBN Prefix(es): 88-8016

La Luna+
Via DiGiovanni, 14, 90144 Palermo
Tel: (091) 301650 *Fax:* (091) 302075
Key Personnel
President: Valeria Ajovalasit
Vice President: Roberta Messina
Founded: 1986
Member of Arcidonna.
Subjects: Anthropology, Art, Fiction, Journalism, Literature, Literary Criticism, Essays, Nonfiction (General), Romance, Women's Studies
ISBN Prefix(es): 88-7823
Distributed by PDE

Luni
Corso MonForte, 20122 Milan
Tel: (02) 796040 *Fax:* (02) 780384
Key Personnel
Prof: Matteo Luteriani; Laura Niccolini
Founded: 1992
Subjects: Literature, Literary Criticism, Essays, Philosophy, Religion - Buddhist, Religion - Islamic, Religion - Other, Sports, Athletics
ISBN Prefix(es): 88-7984

Lusva Editrice
Via Roncaglia 27, 20146 Milan
Tel: (02) 4985386
Key Personnel
Chief Executive: Luca Maria Vizzotto
Founded: 1977
Subjects: Education, Fiction, Poetry

Lybra Immagine+
Via V Monti 6, 20123 Milan
Tel: (02) 48000818 *Fax:* (02) 48012748
E-mail: lybra@galactica.it
Web Site: www.lybra.it

Key Personnel
Editor: Mario Mastropietro
Founded: 1984
Subjects: Architecture & Interior Design, Fashion, Marketing, Photography
ISBN Prefix(es): 88-8223

Lyra Libri SAS
Via Volta 43, 22100 Como
Tel: (031) 279146 *Fax:* (031) 300135
Key Personnel
Chief Executive, Editorial: Maurizio Rosenberg Colorni
Founded: 1986
Subjects: Health, Nutrition, Psychology, Psychiatry, Self-Help, Women's Studies
ISBN Prefix(es): 88-7733

The Ma, *imprint of* Loescher Editore SRL

Casa Editrice Maccari (CEM)+
44 via Palermo, 43100 Parma
Tel: (0521) 771268 *Fax:* (0521) 771268
E-mail: maccarieditore@tin.it *Cable:* CEMPARMA
Key Personnel
Man Dir: Cesare Maccari, Jr
Production: Camilla Albera
Founded: 1946
Subjects: Biological Sciences, Literature, Literary Criticism, Essays, Medicine, Nursing, Dentistry
ISBN Prefix(es): 88-7532
Number of titles published annually: 12 Print
Total Titles: 4 Print
Subsidiaries: Editrice La Pilotta

Macmillan Heinemann ELT
Via di Campigliano (ang Via Meucci), 50015 Grassina (Fl)
Tel: (055) 649 1289 *Fax:* (055) 649 1501
E-mail: mheltinfo@dada.it
Web Site: www.mhelt.com
Key Personnel
Marketing Manager: Nick Broom *E-mail:* n.broom@dada.it
Subjects: English as a Second Language, Language Arts, Linguistics
Parent Company: Macmillan Publishers Ltd
Associate Companies: Casa Editrice Felice Le Monnier spa, Via Antonio Meucci, 2, 50015 Grassina (Fl)

Macro Edizioni+
Via Savona 66-Diegaro, 47023 Cesena (Forli)
Tel: (0547) 346290 *Fax:* (0547) 345091
E-mail: ordini@macroed12oni.it
Key Personnel
President & Editor: Giorgio Gustavo Rosso
E-mail: dizezione@macroedizione.it
Founded: 1987
Member of AIE (Association Itaugna Editori).
Subjects: Alternative, Archaeology, Biblical Studies, Cookery, Education, Environmental Studies, Health, Nutrition, House & Home, How-to, Philosophy, Psychology, Psychiatry, Religion - Other, Science (General)
ISBN Prefix(es): 88-7507
Total Titles: 300 Print
Associate Companies: Macro/Post
Distributor for Edizioni Essere Felici
Showroom(s): Salone Del Libro, Torino
Book Club(s): Il Giardino Dei Libri; Macro Librarsi, Via Savona 66-Diagaro, 47023 Cesena (Forli)
Orders to: Macro/Post, Via San Mauro 55, 47041 Bellaria *Tel:* (0541) 344820 *Fax:* (0541) 344824

Magnus Edizioni SpA+
Via Spilimbergo 180, 33034 Fagagna (Udine)
Tel: (0432) 800081 *Fax:* (0432) 810071

Key Personnel
Chief Executive & Editorial: Rene Leonarduzzi
Sales & Publicity: Antonio Stella
Founded: 1977
Subjects: Architecture & Interior Design, Art, Photography
ISBN Prefix(es): 88-7057
Subsidiaries: Grafiche Lema SpA

Giuseppe Maimone Editore+
Via A. di Sanqiuliano 278, 95124 Catania
Tel: (095) 310315 *Fax:* (095) 310315
Key Personnel
Administrator: Guiseppe Maimone
Founded: 1985
Subjects: Architecture & Interior Design, Art, Biography, Film, Video, History, Literature, Literary Criticism, Essays, Regional Interests
ISBN Prefix(es): 88-7751
Subsidiaries: Maimone & Associati; SAS di Maimone Giuseppe
Showroom(s): Salone Del Libro Torino, 19-24 Maggio, c/o Palazzo Lingotto, 10152 Torino; Mostra Parole Nel Tempo, 25-26 Settembre, c/o Castello Di Belgioiso, via Garibaldi 1, Belgioioso (Pavia); Il Libro, Salone Della Editoria Siciliana, 24 27 Marzo, c/o Ente Autonomo Fiera Di Messina Campionaria Internazionale, Viale Della Liberta, 98121 Messina

Manfrini Editori
SS del Brennero, 2, 38060 Calliano (Trento)
Tel: (0464) 839111 *Fax:* (0464) 85086
Telex: 400581 Manfri I *Cable:* Grafiche Manfrini
Key Personnel
Man Dir: Edoardo Manfrini
Founded: 1919
Subjects: Art, History, Literature, Literary Criticism, Essays, Nonfiction (General), Science (General), Travel
ISBN Prefix(es): 88-7024
Parent Company: R Manfrini SpA Vallagarina Arti Grafiche, SS del Brennero, 2, 38060 Calliano (Trento)
Branch Office(s)
Via Virgilio 6, I-39100 Bolzano

Manif, *see* Manifestolibri

Manifestolibri+
Via Tomacelli, 146, 00186 Rome
Tel: (06) 5881496 *Fax:* (06) 5882839
E-mail: redazione@manifestolibri.it
Web Site: www.manifestolibri.it
Key Personnel
Chief Editor: Marco Bascetta
General Manager: Simona Bonsignori
E-mail: bons@bonsignori.it
Founded: 1990
Publishing house in the group of "il Manifesto" daylly newspaper. Member of il Manifesto & carries books, online services, audio & CD-ROMs.
Subjects: Government, Political Science, Philosophy, Social Sciences, Sociology, Socio economic issues & affairs
ISBN Prefix(es): 88-7285
Total Titles: 250 Print; 2 CD-ROM; 10 Audio
Parent Company: Il Manifesto Dayly Newspaper
Branch Office(s)
Manifestolibri, Viale Dei 4, Venti 47, 00152 Rome, Contact: Simona Bonsignori

Manni/Lupetti, *imprint of* Piero Manni srl

Marchese Grafiche Editoriali SpA, *see* Marchesi Grafiche Editoriali SpA

Casa Editrice Marietti SpA+
Via Piandilucco 7, 16155 Genoa
Tel: (010) 6984226 *Fax:* (010) 667092
E-mail: marietti1820@split.it

Key Personnel
President: Flavio Repetto
Editor: Carla Villata
Foreign Rights: Carla Palazzesi
Founded: 1820
Subjects: Biblical Studies, History, Literature, Literary Criticism, Essays, Philosophy, Religion - Catholic, Religion - Islamic, Religion - Jewish, Theology
ISBN Prefix(es): 88-211
Number of titles published annually: 30 Print
Total Titles: 550 Print

Aldo Marino Editore
Via Caronda 136, 95128 Catania
Tel: (095) 438064 *Fax:* (095) 438064
Founded: 1977
Subjects: Literature, Literary Criticism, Essays, Science (General)
Bookshop(s): Libreria Scientifica di Aldo Marino, Via Firenze, 182/188, 95128 Catania

Tommaso Marotta Editore Srl+
Via dei Mille 78/82, 80121 Naples
Tel: (081) 418881 *Fax:* (081) 418411
Key Personnel
Man Dir: Thomas F Marianos
Editorial: Teresa Nuzzo
Founded: 1979
Subjects: Art, Biography, Fiction, History, Music, Dance, Poetry, Regional Interests

Marsilio Editori SpA+
Marittima Fabbricato 205, I-30135 Venice
Tel: (041) 2406511 *Fax:* (041) 5238352
Key Personnel
President & Sales Dir: Prof Cesare De Michelis
Editorial Dir: Emanuela Bassetti
Rights & Permissions & Acquisitions: Rita Vivian
Founded: 1961
Subjects: Art, Computer Science, Fiction, Film, Video, Literature, Literary Criticism, Essays, Nonfiction (General), Psychology, Psychiatry, Social Sciences, Sociology
ISBN Prefix(es): 88-317; 88-7693
U.S. Office(s): Marsilio Publishers, 853 Broadway, Suite 1509, New York, NY 10003, United States *Tel:* 212-473-5300 *Fax:* 212-473-7865
Distributor for Giovanni Tranchida Editore

Giunti Marzocco, *imprint of* Giunti Publishing Group

Marzorati Editore SRL+
Via Tirso, 26, 00198 Rome
Tel: (02) 8546146 *Fax:* (02) 8411225
Key Personnel
Man Dir & Editorial: Antonio Marzorati
Sales: Carlo Marzorati
Production: Franco Faglioni
Publicity: Patrizia Fatigati
Rights & Permissions: Francesca Marzorati
Founded: 1942
Subjects: Geography, Geology, History, Literature, Literary Criticism, Essays, Philosophy
ISBN Prefix(es): 88-280
Warehouse: Via Galilei 1/5, I-20010 Cornaredo

Editrice Massimo SAS di Crespi Cesare e C+
Viale Bacchiglione 20A, 20139 Milan
Tel: (02) 55210800; (02) 55211220 *Fax:* (02) 55211315
Key Personnel
Man Dir: Dr Cesare Crespi
Founded: 1951
Subjects: Astronomy, Biblical Studies, Biography, Drama, Theater, Fiction, History, Literature, Literary Criticism, Essays, Philosophy, Psychology, Psychiatry, Religion - Catholic, Religion - Other, Romance, Science (General), Social Sciences, Sociology, Theology

ISBN Prefix(es): 88-7030
Total Titles: 400 Print
Bookshop(s): Agenzia Mescat, Milan

Masson, *imprint of* Masson SpA

Masson SpA+
Via Fratelli Bressan, 2, 20126 Milan
Tel: (02) 270741 *Fax:* (02) 27074510
E-mail: info@masson.it
Key Personnel
Man Dir: Jean-Paul Baudouin
Publicity: Gianluigi Cervi
Rights & Permissions: Lidia Lupi
Founded: 1976
Subjects: Chemistry, Chemical Engineering, Medicine, Nursing, Dentistry, Physics, Science (General), Technology
ISBN Prefix(es): 88-214
Parent Company: Masson, France
Imprints: Dunod; Masson; Massonscoula

Massonscoula, *imprint of* Masson SpA

Edizioni Gabriele Mazzotta SRL+
Foro Buonaparte 52, 20121 Milan
Tel: (02) 8055803 *Fax:* (02) 8693046
Key Personnel
Rights & Permissions & Man Dir: Gabriele Mazzotta
Sales Dir: Antonio Vitagliano
Publicity Dir: Alessandra Pozzi
Founded: 1966
Subjects: Architecture & Interior Design, Art, Film, Video, Photography
ISBN Prefix(es): 88-202

McGraw-Hill Libri Italia Srl
Piazza Emilia 5, 20129 Milan
Tel: (02) 701601 *Fax:* (02) 733643
Key Personnel
International Rights Contact: Italo Raimondi
ISBN Prefix(es): 88-386; 88-7700
Parent Company: McGraw-Hill Inc, 1221 Avenue of the Americas, New York, NY 10020, United States
Associate Companies: McGraw-Hill Book Co Europe
Warehouse: McGraw-Hill Magazzine Editoriale, Via Milano 6/2, 20068 Peschiera Borroreo, Milan

McRae Books+
Via dei Rustici 5, Florence 50122
Tel: (055) 264384 *Fax:* (055) 212573
Key Personnel
Publisher: Anne McRae *E-mail:* mcrae@tin.it
Packagers of children's & adults illustrated non-fiction books for the international co-edition market.
Subjects: Art, Cookery, Geography, Geology, History, Nonfiction (General), Religion - Other, Science (General)

Edizioni Medicea SRL
Via Gordigiani 40e, 50127 Florence
Tel: (055) 363057 *Fax:* (055) 333862
Founded: 1975
Subjects: Architecture & Interior Design, Government, Political Science, Radio, TV, Science (General), Social Sciences, Sociology
ISBN Prefix(es): 88-900171

Mediserve SRL+
Via Quagliariello 35e, 80131 Naples
Tel: (081) 5452717 *Fax:* (081) 5462026
Key Personnel
Man Dir, Editorial: Luigi Martinucci
Sales: Giuseppe Cerasuolo
Rights & Permissions: Ivonne Carbonaro

Founded: 1978
Subjects: Medicine, Nursing, Dentistry, Science (General)
ISBN Prefix(es): 88-8204
Bookshop(s): Libreria Scienze Mediche Martinucci, Via T de Amicis 60, I-80145 Naples

Il Melangolo+
Via di Porta Soprana 3-1, 16123 Genoa
Tel: (010) 2514002 *Fax:* (010) 2514037
Founded: 1976
Subjects: Fiction, Literature, Literary Criticism, Essays, Philosophy, Poetry, Religion - Buddhist, Religion - Catholic, Religion - Jewish, Religion - Other, Theology
ISBN Prefix(es): 88-7018

Memorie Domenicane
Piazza San Domenico 1, I-51100 Pistoia
Tel: (0573) 28158 *Fax:* (0573) 975808
Key Personnel
Editorial: Eugenio Marino; Armando F Verde
Founded: 1884
Subjects: History, Theology
Parent Company: Centro Riviste della Provincia Romana dei Frati Predicatori, Piazza San Domenico 1, I-51100 Pistoia
Shipping Address: Centro Riviste della Provincia Romana dei Frati Predicatori, Piazza San Domenico 1, I-51100 Pistoia
Warehouse: Centro Riviste della Provincia Romana dei Frati Predicatori, Piazza San Domenico 1, I-51100 Pistoia
Orders to: Centro Riviste della Provincia Romana dei Frati Predicatori, Piazza San Domenico 1, I-51100 Pistoia

Casa Editrice Menna di Sinisgalli Menna Giuseppina+
Via Scandone 16, 83100 Avellino
Tel: (0825) 24080 *Fax:* (0825) 24080
Key Personnel
Chief Executive: Nunzio Menna
Founded: 1976
Subjects: Drama, Theater, History, Law, Literature, Literary Criticism, Essays, Poetry
Imprints: Verso il Futuro
Warehouse: CE MENNA, CP 80 Avellino

La Spiga Meravigli
Via Plezzo 36, 20132 Milan
Tel: (02) 2157240 *Fax:* (02) 2157833
ISBN Prefix(es): 88-7954; 88-7955

Messaggero di San Antonio+
Via Orto Botanico 11, 35123 Padua
Tel: (049) 8225000 *Fax:* (049) 8225688
Telex: 430855 Msa I *Cable:* Messaggero Padova
Key Personnel
Chief Executive: P Luciano Marini
Editorial: P Giacomo Panteghini
Sales, Production, Publicity, Rights & Permissions: P Agostino Varotto
Subjects: Biography, History, Journalism, Religion - Other
ISBN Prefix(es): 88-7026; 88-250
Bookshop(s): Libreria Messaggero, Piazza del Santo 17, I-35123 Padua

Mario Miglietti, *imprint of* Casa Editrice Castalia

Milano Libri
Via Mecenate 91, I-20138 Milan
Tel: (02) 50951 *Fax:* (02) 5065361
Subjects: Fiction, Literature, Literary Criticism, Essays
ISBN Prefix(es): 88-318; 88-7811; 88-17
Associate Companies: RCS Rizzoli Libri SpA

Nicola Milano Editore+
Via Farini 14, 40124 Bologna

Tel: (051) 239060 *Fax:* (051) 239286
E-mail: scuola@nicolamilano.com
Web Site: www.nicolamilano.com
Key Personnel
Chief Executive: Mario Musso
Founded: 1969
ISBN Prefix(es): 88-419

Milella di Lecce Spazio Vivo SRL+
Via Palmieri 30, 73100 Lecce
Tel: (0832) 308885 *Fax:* (0832) 308885
E-mail: leccespaziovivo@tiscalinet.it
Web Site: www.milellaeditore.com
Key Personnel
President: Antonio Pati
Professor: Gaetano Quarta
Founded: 1945
Subjects: Disability, Special Needs, Education, English as a Second Language, Human Relations, Literature, Literary Criticism, Essays, Philosophy, Psychology, Psychiatry, Social Sciences, Sociology
ISBN Prefix(es): 88-7048
Bookshop(s): Via M DePietro, Via Palmieri 30, 73100 Lecce; Via G Palmieri, Viale dell'UniVersite, 1, 30-73100 Lecce *Tel:* (0832) 308885 *Fax:* (0832) 308885
Warehouse: Via M DePietro, Via Palmieri, 30, 9-73100 Leece *Tel:* (0832) 308885
Orders to: Via M DePietro, Viale dell'UniVersite, 1, 9-73100 Lecce *Tel:* (0832) 308885

Minerva Italica SpA
Via Trentacoste 7, 20134 Milan
Tel: (02) 215631 *Fax:* (02) 21213699
Key Personnel
Man Dir: Arnoldi Gianni
Founded: 1951
Subjects: Art, Education, Fiction
ISBN Prefix(es): 88-298
Branch Office(s)
Via Lattanzio 90-94, I-70126 Bari
Via Alfani 68, I-50121 Florence
Via S Sebastiano is 247a, I-98100 Messina
Via Petrella 6, I-20124 Milan
Via A Emo 162-168, I-00136 Rome

Editrice Missionaria Italiana (EMI)+
Via di Corticella 181, 40128 Bologna
Tel: (051) 326027 *Fax:* (051) 327552
Key Personnel
Man Dir, Editorial, Production: Francesco Grasselli
Sales: Father Noe Cereda
Administrator: Father Giuseppe Mariani
Founded: 1977
Subjects: Anthropology, Religion - Other, Social Sciences, Sociology
ISBN Prefix(es): 88-307
Bookshop(s): Libreria Comboniana, Galleria Mazzini, 37121 Verona

mnemes - Alfieri & Ranieri Publishing+
Formerly Alfieri & Ranieri
Via F Bentivegna, 38, 90139 Palermo
Tel: (091) 588813 *Fax:* (091) 588813
E-mail: alfieri@mnemes.com
Web Site: www.mnemes.com
Founded: 1995
Subjects: Music, Dance
ISBN Prefix(es): 88-8161

Arnoldo Mondadori Editore SpA+
Via Mondadori, 1, 20090 Segrate (Milan)
Tel: (02) 75421 *Fax:* (02) 75422302
Web Site: www.mondadori.com
Telex: 320457 Mondmi I *Cable:* MONDADORI SEGRATE (MI)
Key Personnel
Chairman & President: Leonardo Mondadori
Vice President & Deputy Chairman: Luca Formenton
Chief Executive Officer: Maurizio Costa
Corporate Communications & Advertising Dir: Andrea Zagami
Press Relations Officer: Angelo Allegri *Tel:* (02) 75422729 *E-mail:* aallegri@mondadori.it
Founded: 1907
Legal Headquarters: Via Bianca di Savoia 12, 20122 Milan
Representative Office: Via Sicilia, 136, 00187 Rome
Foreign Offices: Artes Graficas Toledo SA (officine grafiche): Carretera Toledo Ocono km 8, Poligono Industriale SIN/N, Toledo, and Calle Principe De Vergara, 13, 28016 Madrid (both Spain); Mondadori UK Ltd, 43-45 Charlotte St, London W1P 1HA, UK; A Mondadori Deutschland GmbH, Tal 21, 80331 Munich, Germany; A Mondadori Editore, c/o Mondgraph, 9/11 Ave F Roosevelt, 75008 Paris, France; AME Publishing Ltd, 740 Broadway, New York, NY 10003, USA; Random House Mondori, Arago, 385, 08013 Barcelona.
Subjects: Art, Biography, Education, Fiction, History, How-to, Medicine, Nursing, Dentistry, Music, Dance, Mysteries, Philosophy, Poetry, Psychology, Psychiatry, Religion - Other, Romance, Science (General)
ISBN Prefix(es): 88-04
Parent Company: Fininvest
Associate Companies: Agenzia Lombarda Distribuzione, Via Stamira d'Ancona 30, 20127 Milan *Tel:* (02) 26113470 *Fax:* (02) 26113351; Gruner & Jahr Mondadori SpA, Corso Monforte 54, 20122 Milan *Tel:* (02) 762101 *Fax:* (02) 76013439; Harlequin Mondadori SpA, Corso Concordia, 7, 20129 Milan *Tel:* (02) 760381 *Fax:* (02) 780397; Mach 2 Libri SpA, Via B Quaranta, 40, 20139 Milan *Tel:* (02) 55210585 *Fax:* (02) 5396931; SIES Societa Italiana Editrice Stampatrice SpA *Fax:* (02) 66724360; Societa Europea di Edizioni SpA, Via Negri 4, 20123 Milan *Tel:* (02) 85661 *Fax:* (02) 73023880
Subsidiaries: Cemit Direct Media SpA; Club delgi Editori Sp; Edizioni di Comunita Srl; Edizioni Frassinelli Srl; Elemond SpA; Ellemme Srl; Giulio Einaudi Editore SpA; Random House Mondadori S A; Leonardo Arte Srl; Mondadori Franchising SpA; Mondadori Informatica SpA; Mondadori Pubblicita SpA; Riccardi Ricciardi Editore SpA; Sperling & Kupfer Editori SpA
Branch Office(s)
Corso Europa 5/7, 20122 Milan *Tel:* (02) 77941 *Fax:* (02) 7794359
Via Sicilia 136, 00187 Rome *Tel:* (06) 474971 *Fax:* (06) 47497336
Via Virgilio 8, 00195 Rome *Tel:* (06) 6838899 *Fax:* (06) 6874107
Via Mondadori 15, 37131 Verona *Tel:* (045) 934111 *Fax:* (045) 934697
Foreign Rights: AME Publishing Ltd (US); Continental Printing Ltd (UK); E-M Livres (France); Mondadori (Spain); Arnoldo Mondadori Deutschland GmbH (Germany); Mondgraph (France); Tuttle Mori Agency Inc (Japan)
Bookshop(s): Largo Corsia de Servi 11, 20122 Milan *Tel:* (02) 76005832 *Fax:* (02) 76014902; Piazza Cola Di Rienzo 81/83, 00192 Rome *Tel:* (06) 3220188 *Fax:* (06) 3210323; Via Appia Vuova 51, 00183 Rome *Tel:* (06) 7003690 *Fax:* (06) 7003450; Via XX Settembre 210/R, 16121 Genova *Tel:* (010) 585743 *Fax:* (010) 5704810; Via Vittorio Emanuele 36, 22100 Como *Tel:* (031) 273424 *Fax:* (031) 273314

Bruno Mondadori™, *imprint of* Paravia Bruno Mondadori Editori

Edizioni Scolastiche Bruno Mondadori™, *imprint of* Paravia Bruno Mondadori Editori

Giorgio Mondadori & Associati+
Via Ponti 10, 20143 Milan
Tel: (02) 891661 *Fax:* (02) 89125880
Telex: GlOMON 1 314369
Key Personnel
President: Giorgio Mondadori
Dir General Administration & Finance: Vito Leovino
Founded: 1978
Subjects: Antiques, Architecture & Interior Design, Art, Foreign Countries, Gardening, Plants, House & Home
ISBN Prefix(es): 88-374; 88-376
Imprints: GM
Subsidiaries: Gardenia srl; Giorgio Mondadori Periodici/Airone di Giorgio Mondadori & Associati; Editoriale Giorgio Mondadori; Giorgio Mondadori Editore; Giorgio Mondadori srl

Edizioni del Mondo Giudiziario
Viale Angelico 90, 00195 Rome
Tel: (06) 3721071 *Fax:* (06) 3250961
Key Personnel
Man Dir: Augusto Brusca
Editorial, Sales: Anna Tabili Brusca; Federico Carlo Brusca
Founded: 1946
Subjects: Law

Mondolibro Editore SNC+
Via Sillano 11a, 50022 Greve in Chianti (FI)
Tel: (055) 8546097 *Fax:* (055) 8546097
Web Site: www.mondolibraeditore.com
Key Personnel
Contact: Dr Ettore de Parentela
E-mail: eparentela@yahoo.it
Founded: 1987
Bookshops located in major cities throughout Italy, as well as New York, Los Angeles, London, Paris, Frankfurt & Tokyo.
Subjects: Art, Drama, Theater, Fiction, Film, Video, Literature, Literary Criticism, Essays, Nonfiction (General), Travel
ISBN Prefix(es): 88-85143
Imprints: Collana; Biblioteca Elle; Biblioteca World
Subsidiaries: Coloristi
Distributed by Albolibro SrL; Casalini Libri SpA; Cosma Libraria snc; DEM Libri SrL; L'Acquilone; Medialibri SrL; Midilibri SrL; Rossano Libri SrL

Monduzzi Editore SpA
Via Ferrarese 119/2, 40128 Bologna
Tel: (051) 4151123 *Fax:* (051) 370529
Telex: 512654 Mondbo I
Key Personnel
President: Dr Gianni Monduzzi
Man Dir: Dr Mauro Bettocchi
Founded: 1978
Subjects: Biological Sciences, Chemistry, Chemical Engineering, Economics, Engineering (General), Law, Literature, Literary Criticism, Essays, Medicine, Nursing, Dentistry, Physics, Psychology, Psychiatry, Social Sciences, Sociology
ISBN Prefix(es): 88-323
Imprints: Cisalpino
Divisions: International Proceedings Division

Le Monnier, *imprint of* Casa Editrice Felice Le Monnier

Editrice Morcelliana SpA+
Via Rosa 71, 25121 Brescia
Tel: (030) 46451 *Fax:* (030) 2400605
E-mail: edit.morcelliana@agora.stm.it
Key Personnel
Man Dir: Stefano Minelli
Founded: 1925
Subjects: History, Philosophy, Religion - Other, Social Sciences, Sociology

ISBN Prefix(es): 88-372
Associate Companies: Editrice La Scuola SpA

Moretti & Vitali editori srl+
Via Ambiveri, 15, 24126 Bergamo
Tel: (035) 321588 *Fax:* (035) 321647
Founded: 1989
Subjects: Architecture & Interior Design, Art, Biography, Human Relations, Literature, Literary Criticism, Essays, Psychology, Psychiatry
ISBN Prefix(es): 88-7186

Motta Junior Srl
Via Branda Castiglioni 7, 20156 Milan
Tel: (02) 300761 *Fax:* (02) 38010046
E-mail: editor@mottaeditore.it
Web Site: www.mottaeditore.it
Key Personnel
Dir, Sales Books Department: Lorena Vazzola
Pres: Massimo Fumagalli
Edit Dir: Madeleine Thoby

Motta Periodici Srl
Via Branda Castiglioni, 7, 20156 Milan
Tel: (02) 33400491 *Fax:* (02) 38010046
ISBN Prefix(es): 88-7179

Mucchi Editore SRL
Via Emilia Est 1527, 41100 Modena
Tel: (059) 374094 *Fax:* (059) 282628
E-mail: info@mucchieditore.it
Web Site: www.mucchieditore.it
Founded: 1646
Subjects: Crafts, Games, Hobbies, Education, History, Language Arts, Linguistics, Law, Literature, Literary Criticism, Essays, Philosophy, Science (General)
ISBN Prefix(es): 88-7000

Societa Editrice Il Mulino+
Str Maggiore 37, 40125 Bologna
Tel: (051) 256011 *Fax:* (051) 256034
E-mail: info@mulino.it
Web Site: www.mulino.it
Key Personnel
Man Dir: Giuliano Bassani
Sales Dir: Maria Selleri
Publicity Dir: Ida Meneghello
Rights & Permissions: Paola Pecchioli
  E-mail: paola.pecchioli@mulino.it
Editorial Dir: Giovanni Evangelisti
Founded: 1954
Subjects: Economics, Government, Political Science, History, Language Arts, Linguistics, Law, Philosophy, Psychology, Psychiatry, Social Sciences, Sociology
ISBN Prefix(es): 88-15

Ass Italiana Sclerosi Multipla
Vico Chiuso Paggi, 3, 16128 Genova
Tel: (010) 27131 *Fax:* (010) 2470226
ISBN Prefix(es): 88-7148

Mundici & Zanetti srl
Via dei Lapidari, 10, 40129 Bologna
Tel: (051) 325347 *Fax:* (051) 326109
Founded: 1977
Subjects: Astrology, Occult, Cookery, House & Home, Humor
ISBN Prefix(es): 88-7410

Gruppo Ugo Mursia Editore SpA+
Via Mellhiorre Gioia 45, 20124 Milan
Tel: (02) 67378500 *Fax:* (02) 67378605
Key Personnel
President & Publisher: Fiorenza Mursia
Publicity: Lorenza Sala
Rights & Permissions: Milena Molinari
Founded: 1922
Subjects: Art, Biography, Education, Fiction, History, Maritime, Philosophy, Poetry, Religion - Other, Science (General), Social Sciences, Sociology, Sports, Athletics
ISBN Prefix(es): 88-425
Warehouse: Via Cassanese antica, 20060 Vignate, Milano

Museo Storico in Trento
Via Clesio 3, 38100 Trento
Tel: (0461) 230482 *Fax:* (0461) 237418
E-mail: info@museostorico.tn.it
Web Site: www.museostorico.tn.it/editoria_ricerca
Founded: 1923
Subjects: History, Literature, Literary Criticism, Essays, Social Sciences, Sociology
ISBN Prefix(es): 88-7197
Number of titles published annually: 5 Print
Total Titles: 100 Print

Musumeci SpA+
Localita Amerique 99, 11020 Quart Acosta
Tel: (0165) 761216 *Fax:* (0165) 761112
ISBN Prefix(es): 88-7032

Franco Muzzio & C Editore SpA+
Via Makalle, 97, 35138 Padua
Tel: (049) 8712477 *Fax:* (049) 8713851
Telex: 432005 Muzzio
Key Personnel
Chief Executive & Publicity: Franco Muzzio
Editorial: Riccardo Degli Innocenti
Sales: Ennio Pengo
Production: Massi Miliano Muzzio
Rights & Permissions & Editorial: Stella Longato
Founded: 1973
Subjects: Computer Science, Electronics, Electrical Engineering, Energy, Music, Dance, Nonfiction (General), Science (General)
ISBN Prefix(es): 88-7021
Associate Companies: Arcana Editrice SRL, Viale Sondrio 7, I-20124 Milan; Casa Editice MEB SRL
Warehouse: Via Makalle 37, 35138 Padua

N, *imprint of* Pizzicato Edizioni Musicali

Giorgio Nada Editore SRL+
Via Treves 15/17, 20090 Vimodrone (Milan)
Mailing Address: Via Claudio Treves 15/17, 20090 Vimodrone (Milan)
Tel: (02) 27301126 *Fax:* (02) 27301454
E-mail: info@giorgionadaeditore.it
Web Site: www.giorgionadaeditore.it
Key Personnel
Chairman: Giorgio Nada *E-mail:* giorgio.nada@giorgioeditore.it
Founded: 1988
Specialize in books on history of Italian cars & motorcycle makes (Ferrari, Ducati, etc).
Subjects: Automotive, History, Transportation
ISBN Prefix(es): 88-7911
Number of titles published annually: 15 Print
Total Titles: 200 Print
Subsidiaries: Libreria dell'Automobile
Distributed by Haynes Publishing-Sparkford Yeovil (England); MBI Publishing Company (US)
Book Club(s): Corso Venezia, 43, 20121 Milan

Nagard
Via Larga 9, 20122 Milan
Tel: (02) 58371400 *Fax:* (02) 58304790
Founded: 1977
Subjects: Chemistry, Chemical Engineering, Education
ISBN Prefix(es): 88-85010

Casa Editrice Roberto Napoleone
Lungotevere della Vittoria 10, Rome 00195
Tel: (06) 37515191 *Fax:* (06) 37515143
Key Personnel
Chief Executive: Roberto Napoleone
Founded: 1974
ISBN Prefix(es): 88-7124

Nardini Editore srl+
Via del Salviatino 1, 50014 Fiesole (Florence)
Tel: (055) 598923 *Fax:* (055) 597185
Key Personnel
Manager: Ruth Mueller Nardini
Dir General: Fabio Nardini
Editorial Dir: Claudio Nardini
Founded: 1970
Subjects: Art, Biography, Economics, Education, Literature, Literary Criticism, Essays, Medicine, Nursing, Dentistry, Philosophy, Poetry, Religion - Other
ISBN Prefix(es): 88-404
Imprints: Convivio (Nardini Editore); Editoriale Europress (Nardini Press)

Accademia Naz dei Lincei
Via della Lungara 10, 00165 Rome
Tel: (06) 6838831 *Fax:* (06) 6893616
Founded: 1847
Subjects: Archaeology, Art, Biological Sciences, Economics, History, Management, Mathematics
ISBN Prefix(es): 88-218; 88-7052

Istituto Nazionale di Archeologia e Storia dell'Arte
Piazza S Marco 49, 00186 Rome
Tel: (06) 6798804 *Fax:* (06) 6798804
Key Personnel
President: Prof Alessandro Bettagno
Editor: Paolo Pellegrino
Founded: 1922
Member of International Association of Research Institutes in the History of Art (RIHA); the International Union of the Institutes of Archeology, History & History of Art in Rome; The International Association of Classical Archeology; The National Institute of Studies of the Renaissance; Associated with the National Committee of Research & The Jean Berard Centre in Naples.
Subjects: Archaeology, Art
ISBN Prefix(es): 88-7275

Istituto Nazionale di Studi Romani
Piazza dei Cavalieri di Malta 2, 00139 Rome
Tel: (06) 5743442; (06) 5743445 *Fax:* (06) 5743447
E-mail: studiromani@studiromani.it
Web Site: www.studiromani.it
Key Personnel
President: Prof Mario Petrucciani
Vice President: Prof Letizia Ezmiri Pani
Dir: Dr Fernanda Roscetti
Founded: 1925
Subjects: Architecture & Interior Design, Art, History, Literature, Literary Criticism, Essays
ISBN Prefix(es): 88-7311
Number of titles published annually: 7 Print
Total Titles: 829 Print

NED, *imprint of* Nuove Edizioni Dolomiti SRL

New Magazine+
Via dei Mille 69, 38100 Trento
Tel: (0461) 925007 *Fax:* (0461) 925007
E-mail: newmagaz@tin.it
Web Site: www.newmagazine.it; www.rivistamedica.it
Key Personnel
International Rights: Bruno Zanotti
Founded: 1982
Specialize in Medicine.
Subjects: Civil Engineering, Literature, Literary Criticism, Essays, Medicine, Nursing, Dentistry
ISBN Prefix(es): 88-8041
Distributed by Del Porto SpA (Worldwide)

PUBLISHERS

ITALY

Newton Compton Editori SRL
Via Conciliazione 15, 00193 Rome
Tel: (06) 6892045 *Fax:* (06) 6893076
Founded: 1969
Subjects: Anthropology, Archaeology, Fiction, Government, Political Science, History, How-to, Mathematics, Philosophy, Poetry, Psychology, Psychiatry, Science (General), Social Sciences, Sociology
ISBN Prefix(es): 88-7983; 88-8183; 88-8289

NIE, *imprint of* La Nuova Italia Editrice SpA

Nistri - Lischi Editori+
Via XXIV Maggio 28, 56123 Pisa
Tel: (050) 563371 *Fax:* (050) 562726 *Cable:* LISCHI PISA
Key Personnel
Man Dir: Luciano Lischi
Sales: Lucia Lischi
Founded: 1780
Subjects: Literature, Literary Criticism, Essays
Warehouse: Via Carducci, La Fontina, Pisa

NodoLibri+
Via Dottesio, 1, 22100 Como
Tel: (031) 306771 *Fax:* (031) 300554
Founded: 1989
Subjects: Art, History, Photography, Regional Interests
ISBN Prefix(es): 88-7185

Nord, *imprint of* Casa Editrice Nord SRL

Casa Editrice Nord SRL
Via Rubens 25, 20148 Milan
Tel: (02) 405708 *Fax:* (02) 4042207
E-mail: editrice.nord@agora.stm.it
Key Personnel
President: Gianfranco Viviani
Vice President: Marco Viviani
Editorial: Alex Voglino; Piergiorgio Nicolazzini
Founded: 1964
Subjects: Science Fiction, Fantasy
ISBN Prefix(es): 88-429
Imprints: Nord

Novartis Edizioni - Novartis Farma SpA+
Casella postale 88, 21047 Saronno (Varese)
Tel: (02) 96542736 *Fax:* (02) 96543320
Key Personnel
Man Dir, Production: Dr Giovanni Bravi
Editorial: Dr Leone Halfer
Sales: Maria Guzzetti
Founded: 1981
Subjects: Medicine, Nursing, Dentistry, Science (General)
ISBN Prefix(es): 88-7645

Novecento Editrice Srl+
Via Siracusa, 16, 90141 Palermo
Tel: (091) 587417 *Fax:* (091) 585702
E-mail: novedi@mbox.vol.it
Key Personnel
Administrator: Alessi Maria Caterina Domitilla
Founded: 1980
Subjects: Art, Literature, Literary Criticism, Essays, Photography
ISBN Prefix(es): 88-373
Bookshop(s): Libreria Novelento, via Siracusa 7/A, 90141 Palermo *Tel:* (091) 6256814
Warehouse: Via Agrigento 15, 90141 Palermo

Nugae, Interli Nee, Libri Di Bron, Cuccioli, *imprint of* Pagano Editore

Nuova Alfa Editoriale+
Via Trentacoste, 7, 20134 Bologna
Tel: (02) 215631 *Fax:* (02) 26413121
Key Personnel
Man Dir, Production: Maurizio Armaroli
Editorial, Publicity: Emanuela Spinsanti
Sales: Piera Raimondi
Founded: 1954
Subjects: Art, Literature, Literary Criticism, Essays
ISBN Prefix(es): 88-7779

Nuova Dimensione, *imprint of* Ediciclo Editore SRL

Nuova Ipsa Editore srl
Via G Crispi 50/52, 90145 Palermo
Tel: (091) 6819025 *Fax:* (091) 6816399
Key Personnel
Editorial Dir: Claudio Mazza
Founded: 1982
ISBN Prefix(es): 88-7676

La Nuova Italia Editrice SpA
Via Codignola, 50018 Scandicci, Florence
Tel: (055) 75901 *Fax:* (055) 7590208
Key Personnel
Man Dir: Carmelo Sambugar; Federico Codignola; Mario Ermini; Sergio Colleoni
Founded: 1926
Subjects: Art, Biography, History, Philosophy, Psychology, Psychiatry, Social Sciences, Sociology
ISBN Prefix(es): 88-221
Imprints: NIE
Branch Office(s)
Via E Bernardi 14, I-40133 Bologna
Via Del Fangario 25, I-09122 Cagliari
Via Degli Stan 26, I-87100 Cosenza
Via B Lupi 1, I-50129 Florence
Via di Serretto 41/2, I-16131 Genoa
Via Negroli 12, I-20133 Milan
Via S Alfonso Maria de'Liguori 3, I-80141 Naples
Via Olanda 15, I-90146 Palermo
Viale Carso 46, I-00195 Rome
Via Bassano 16, I-10136 Turin
Via Sacco Vantetti 8, I-60131 Ancona
Ste St Le 98 Km 79,400 (Complesso Big Center), I-70026 Modugno-Bari
Via Altichiero da Zevio 3, I-35100 Padua
Arbizzano- Negrar, Via L da Vinci, I-37020 Verona

Nuove Autonomie
Via Allegri da Correggio 13, 00196 Rome
Tel: (06) 36002539 *Fax:* (06) 3240145
Key Personnel
Chief Executive: Stelvio Minelli
Production: Bruno Puglielli
Founded: 1977
Subjects: Government, Political Science, Health, Nutrition
ISBN Prefix(es): 88-7976
Parent Company: Lega per le Autonomie e i Poteri Locali, Via Cesare Balbo 43, I-00184 Rome

Editrice Nuovi Autori
Via Gaudenzio Ferrari 14, 20123 Milan
Tel: (02) 89409338 *Fax:* (02) 58107048
E-mail: faglier@tin.it
Web Site: www.paginegialle.it/ednuoviaut
Key Personnel
Man Dir: Fulvio Aglieri
Editorial & Publicity: Alessandra Aglieri
Sales: Graziella Mosconi
Founded: 1980
Also acts as book packager.
Subjects: Biography, History, Literature, Literary Criticism, Essays, Poetry
ISBN Prefix(es): 88-7230

Nuovi Sentieri Editore
Via Ripa 2, 32100 Belluno
Tel: (0437) 590308
Key Personnel
Man Dir: Bepi Pellegrinon
Editorial: Loris Santomaso
Sales: Antonio Zullo
Founded: 1971
Subjects: Art, History, Literature, Literary Criticism, Essays, Photography, Poetry, Regional Interests
ISBN Prefix(es): 88-85510

Edizioni OCD
Carmelitani Scalzi, Via Anagnina, 662 b, 00040 Morena (Rome)
Tel: (06) 79847482 *Fax:* (06) 79845387
Key Personnel
Dir: Rodolfo Girardello *Tel:* (06) 79890821; Arnaldo Pigna *Tel:* (06) 79890834
Officer: Fiorenzo Bugin *Tel:* (06) 79890836; Massimo Angelelli *Tel:* (06) 79890830
Administration: Luigia Paolitti *Tel:* (06) 79890822; Teresa Alpini *Tel:* (06) 79890823; Onelia Paoletti *Tel:* (06) 79890824
ISBN Prefix(es): 88-7229
Branch Office(s)
Edizioni Cattoliche

OCTAVO Franco Cantini Editore+
Borgo Santa Croce 8, I-50122 Florence
Tel: (055) 2346022 *Fax:* (055) 2346109
Key Personnel
Man Dir: Franco Cantini
Founded: 1993
Specialize in art.
Subjects: Antiques, Archaeology, Architecture & Interior Design, Art, Education, Fiction, History, Photography
ISBN Prefix(es): 88-8030; 88-7737

OEMF, see OEMF srl International

OEMF srl International+
Via Palizzi 88, 20157 Milan
Tel: (02) 332101 *Fax:* (02) 33210200
Key Personnel
Dir: Carlo Marini
Founded: 1940
Subjects: Medicine, Nursing, Dentistry, Veterinary Science
ISBN Prefix(es): 88-7076

Officina Edizioni di Aldo Quinti+
Via Nicola Ricciotti 11, 00195 Rome
Tel: (06) 3215293 *Fax:* (06) 65740514
E-mail: officinaedizioni@yahoo.com
Key Personnel
Chief Executive: Aldo Quinti
Publicity: Jolanda Ridolfi
Founded: 1966
Subjects: Architecture & Interior Design, Art, Drama, Theater, Ethnicity, Film, Video, Language Arts, Linguistics, Social Sciences, Sociology
Warehouse: Via Virginia Agnelli, 52, 00151 Rome

Editoriale Olimpia SpA+
Viale Milton, 7, 50129 Florence
Tel: (055) 50161 *Fax:* (055) 5016280
E-mail: info@edolimpia.it
Web Site: www.edolimpia.it
Telex: 573084 Edol 1
Key Personnel
Man Dir, Editorial, Rights & Permissions: Renato Cacciaputi
Founded: 1939
Specialize in publications on hunting, fishing, dogs, scuba diving, weapons, handgliding-paragliding, etc.

ITALY

Subjects: Aeronautics, Aviation, Animals, Pets, Biological Sciences, Sports, Athletics
ISBN Prefix(es): 88-253
Number of titles published annually: 220 Print
Subsidiaries: Editoriale Olimpia

Edizioni Olivares
Via Mascagni, 7, 20122 Milan
Tel: (02) 76001753 *Fax:* (02) 76002579
Founded: 1986
Member of AIPE (Associatione Italiano Piccoli Editori) & AIE.
Subjects: Business, Management, Women's Studies
ISBN Prefix(es): 88-85982
Parent Company: Redifin SpA, Via Mascagni, 7, 20122 Milan
Showroom(s): Parole In Tasca-Salone del libro tascabile, c/o Castello di Belgioso, Via Garibaldi 1, 27011 Belgioso (Paira)
Warehouse: M ED Via dei Mille 20, Carugate (MI)

Leo S Olschki
Viuzzo del Pozzetto, 8, 50126 Florence
Tel: (055) 6530684 *Fax:* (055) 6530214
E-mail: celso@olschki.it
Web Site: www.olschki.it
Founded: 1886
Subjects: Anthropology, Archaeology, Architecture & Interior Design, Art, Astronomy, Biblical Studies, Geography, Geology, Government, Political Science, History, Language Arts, Linguistics, Library & Information Sciences, Literature, Literary Criticism, Essays, Music, Dance, Natural History, Philosophy, Physical Sciences, Religion - Catholic, Religion - Jewish, Science (General), Social Sciences, Sociology, Theology
ISBN Prefix(es): 88-222
Number of titles published annually: 150 Print
Total Titles: 3,000 Print

Organizzazioni Speciali SRL, see OS (Organizzazioni Speciali SRL)

Ortelio, *imprint of* Edizioni Cartografiche Milanesi

OS (Organizzazioni Speciali SRL)+
Via Sarpi, 7a, 50136 Florence
Tel: (055) 6236501 *Fax:* (055) 669446
Telex: 571438
Founded: 1950
Member of Giunti Publishing Group.
Subjects: Psychology, Psychiatry
ISBN Prefix(es): 88-09
Associate Companies: O S Consulting
Branch Office(s)
Ripa Porta Ticinese
Milano
Showroom(s): Via Campo nell'Elba, 27 Rome

Osanna Venosa+
Via Appia 3a, I-85029 Venosa, Potenza
Tel: (0972) 35952 *Fax:* (0972) 35723
Key Personnel
Editorial Dir: Antonio Vaccaro
Subjects: Archaeology, History, Literature, Literary Criticism, Essays
ISBN Prefix(es): 88-8167

Maria Pacini Fazzi Editore
Piazza S Romano 16, 55100 Lucca
Tel: (0583) 55530 *Fax:* (0583) 418245
E-mail: pacini.fazzi@lunet.it
Key Personnel
President: Maria Pacini Fazzi
Vice President: Giovan Pio Moretti
Editorial Dir: Francesca Fazzi
Founded: 1965

Subjects: Art, Cookery, Drama, Theater, History, Literature, Literary Criticism, Essays, Philosophy, Social Sciences, Sociology
ISBN Prefix(es): 88-7246

Pagano Editore+
Piazza S Domenico Maggiore 9, I-80134 Naples
Tel: (081) 5523840 *Fax:* (081) 54242949
Key Personnel
Man Dir: Flavio Pagano
Founded: 1985
Subjects: History, Literature, Literary Criticism, Essays, Music, Dance
ISBN Prefix(es): 88-85228
Parent Company: Edipica
Imprints: Nugae, Interli Nee, Libri Di Bron, Cuccioli
Subsidiaries: Vox Neapolis
Divisions: Scompaginate

Paideia Editrice+
Via Manzoni 20, 25020 Flero BS
Tel: (030) 3582434 *Fax:* (030) 3582691
E-mail: paideiaeditrice@tin.it
Key Personnel
Man Dir: Prof Giuseppe Scarpat, PhD
Editorial: Dr Marco Scarpat
Founded: 1945
Subjects: Art, Asian Studies, Biblical Studies, Music, Dance, Philosophy, Poetry, Religion - Catholic, Religion - Jewish, Religion - Protestant, Religion - Other
ISBN Prefix(es): 88-394

Palatina Editrice
Borgo Tommasini 9/A, 43100 Parma
Tel: (0521) 282388 *Fax:* (0521) 282388
Key Personnel
Chief Executive: Carlotta Capacchi
Editorial: Guglielmo Capacchi
Founded: 1965
Subjects: Art, Genealogy, History, Language Arts, Linguistics, Literature, Literary Criticism, Essays, Music, Dance, Regional Interests, Religion - Other, Travel
Number of titles published annually: 9 Print
Total Titles: 37 Print
Bookshop(s): Libreria Palatina Editrice, Borgo Tommasini 9/A, Parma 43100 *Tel:* (0521) 282388 *Fax:* (0521) 282388

Fratelli Palombi SRL
Via del Gracchi 181/185, 00192 Rome
Tel: (06) 3214150 *Fax:* (06) 3214752
Key Personnel
Man Dir: Dr Mario Palombi
Founded: 1914
Subjects: Art, History, Regional Interests
ISBN Prefix(es): 88-7621
Subsidiaries: Organizzazione Rab (sales)

G B Palumbo & C Editore SpA+
Via Ricasoli 59, 90139 Palermo
Tel: (091) 588850 *Fax:* (091) 6111848
Key Personnel
President: Concetta Formica
Chief Executive: Giorgio Palumbo
Founded: 1939
Subjects: Language Arts, Linguistics, Literature, Literary Criticism, Essays
ISBN Prefix(es): 88-8020
Warehouse: Via Maggiore G Galliano 17, Palermo

Franco Cosimo Panini Editore SpA+
Viale Corassori 24, 41100 Modena
Tel: (059) 343572 *Fax:* (059) 344274
E-mail: info@fcp.it
Web Site: www.fcp.it; www.francopanini.com
Founded: 1990

BOOK

Subjects: Archaeology, Architecture & Interior Design, Art, Literature, Literary Criticism, Essays, Poetry
ISBN Prefix(es): 88-7686; 88-248; 88-8290

Franco Panini SPA Editore in Bologna
Viale Corassori, 24, 41100 Modena
Tel: (059) 343572 *Fax:* (059)344274
Telex: 510260 Matex I *Cable:* MALIPIERO
Key Personnel
Chairman: Franco Panini
Man Dir: Dr Enrico Berardi
Editorial Dir: Dr Ermanno Mammarella
Founded: 1969
Subjects: Crafts, Games, Hobbies, Education
ISBN Prefix(es): 88-7686; 88-248; 88-8290
Parent Company: Gruppo Editoriale Franco Panini SPA, via Gozallozi 24, 41100 MO
Subsidiaries: Franco Panini Editore
Branch Office(s)
Malipiero France SA Editeur, S rue du Faubourg St, Honore, Paris, France

Edizioni Panini SpA+
Viale Corassori, 24, 41100 Modena
Tel: (059) 343572 *Fax:* (059) 344274
Telex: 510650 *Cable:* EDIPAN MODENA ITALIA
Key Personnel
Publisher: Franco Panini
Founded: 1963
Subjects: Education, Sports, Athletics
ISBN Prefix(es): 88-7686; 88-248; 88-8290

Editoriale Paradigma, *imprint of* D'Anna

Paramond™, *imprint of* Paravia Bruno Mondadori Editori

Paravia™, *imprint of* Paravia Bruno Mondadori Editori

Paravia Bruno Mondadori Editori+
Subsidiary of Edizioni Bruno Mondadori
Via Archimede 10/23/27/51, Corso Trapani 16 10139 Torino, 20129 Milan
Tel: (02) 748231 *Fax:* (02) 74823362
Web Site: paravia.it; paramond.it; langedizioni.it; edizioniscolastichebrunomondadori.it
Key Personnel
Chairman: Marco Galateri
Man Dir: Agostino Cattaneo; Roberto Gulli; T U Paravia
General Manager: Alberto Ansaldi
Editorial Dir: R Formento; A Fresco; M Garena; Paola Rosci; P Tartaglino; Emilio Zanette
Founded: 1998
Publishing.
AIE member Publisher Educational.
Subjects: Biological Sciences, Earth Sciences, Education, English as a Second Language, Geography, Geology, History, Literature, Literary Criticism, Essays, Mathematics, Philosophy
ISBN Prefix(es): 88-424
Total Titles: 200 Print
Associate Companies: Edizioni Electa-Bruno Mondadori
Imprints: Archimede Edizioni™; Elmedi™; Lang Edizioni™; Bruno Mondadori™; Edizioni Scolastiche Bruno Mondadori™; Paramond™; Paravia™
Distributor for Edizioni Electa-Bruno Mondadori

G B Paravia & C SpA
Corso Trapani 16, 10139 Turin
Tel: (011) 7710166 *Fax:* (011) 752812
Telex: 221652 Edito I
Key Personnel
Editorial: Dr Guido Gay
Founded: 1700
ISBN Prefix(es): 88-395; 88-8058

PUBLISHERS

Passigli Editori srl+
Via Chiantigiana 62, 50011 Antella (Florence)
Tel: (055) 640265 *Fax:* (055) 644627
Key Personnel
Man Dir: Prof Stefano Passigli
Editorial: Dr Luca Merlini; Dr Fabrizio Dall'Aglio
Sales: Dr Alvise Passigli
Rights: Domitilla Baldeschi
Founded: 1981
Subjects: Biography, History, Literature, Literary Criticism, Essays, Music, Dance, Poetry, Travel
ISBN Prefix(es): 88-368; 88-86161
Imprints: Guide del Sole; Guide del Cuore; Le Comete
Subsidiaries: Scala, Instituto Fotografico Editoriale

Patron Editore SrL+
Via Badini 12, 40050 Quarto Inferiore, Bologna
Tel: (051) 767003 *Fax:* (051) 768252
Key Personnel
General Dir: Riccardo Patron
Founded: 1925
Subjects: Agriculture, Art, Engineering (General), History, Language Arts, Linguistics, Law, Literature, Literary Criticism, Essays, Medicine, Nursing, Dentistry, Philosophy, Psychology, Psychiatry, Social Sciences, Sociology
ISBN Prefix(es): 88-555
Bookshop(s): Libreria Internazionale Patron, Via Zamboni 26, 40121 Bologna

PE, *imprint of* Pizzicato Edizioni Musicali

Editoriale PEG
Via Colonna 4, 20149 Milan
Tel: (02) 4859181 *Fax:* (02) 485918220
Telex: 323088
Key Personnel
President: Solly Cohen
Administrator: Giancarlo Meani
Founded: 1950
ISBN Prefix(es): 88-7067

Luigi Pellegrini Editore+
Via Roma 80/b, 87100 Cosenza
Tel: (0984) 454237 *Fax:* (0984) 454392
    Cable: PELLEGRINI EDITORE COSENZA
Key Personnel
Chief Executive, Rights & Permissions: Luigi Pellegrini
Editorial, Sales: Walter Pellegrini
Publicity: Erminia Petramala
Founded: 1952
Subjects: Drama, Theater, Fiction, History, Literature, Literary Criticism, Essays, Poetry
ISBN Prefix(es): 88-8101
Imprints: LPE

PGE, *imprint of* Piero Gribaudi Editore

Pheljna Edizioni d'Arte e Suggestione
Stradale Torino 11, 10018 Pavone Canavese (Turin)
Tel: (0125) 234114 *Fax:* (0125) 230085
Key Personnel
Editor: Ljdia Priuli
Founded: 1982
Subjects: Art, Cookery, Photography

PIAC, *imprint of* Pontificio Istituto di Archeologia Cristiana

Daniela Piazza Editore+
Via Sanfront, 11, 10138 Turin
Tel: (011) 4342706 *Fax:* (011) 4342471
Key Personnel
Publisher: Daniela Piazza
Founded: 1972
Subjects: Art, Biography, Cookery, History, Poetry, Regional Interests, Travel
ISBN Prefix(es): 88-7889

Piccin Nuova Libraria SpA+
Via Altinate 107, I-35121 Padua
Tel: (049) 655566 *Fax:* (049) 8750693
E-mail: info@piccinonline.com
Web Site: www.piccinonline.com
Key Personnel
Man Dir, Production: Dr Massimo Piccin
Editorial & Sales: Dr Antonella Noventa
    E-mail: a.noventa@piccinonline.com
Founded: 1980
Subjects: Biological Sciences, Law, Literature, Literary Criticism, Essays, Medicine, Nursing, Dentistry, Science (General)
ISBN Prefix(es): 88-299
Distributed by Gordon & Breach Publishing Group (English titles worldwide)
Foreign Rep(s): Scholium International Inc (Canada, Mexico, US)

Piemme Junior, *imprint of* Edizioni Piemme SpA

Edizioni Piemme SpA+
Via del Carmine 5, 15033 Casale Monferrato (AL)
Tel: (0141) 3361 *Fax:* (0142) 74223
E-mail: dirgen@edizpiemme.it
Web Site: www.edizpiemme.it
Key Personnel
Man Dir: Pietro Marietti
Piemme Editorial: Francesca Cristoffanini
Rights & Permissions: valeria Casonato
Press Officer: Valerie Caprioglio
Piemme Junior Editorial: Elisabetta Dami
Founded: 1982
Subjects: Biblical Studies, Cookery, Fiction, Gardening, Plants, Nonfiction (General), Religion - Catholic, Romance, Self-Help, Theology
ISBN Prefix(es): 88-384
Imprints: Battelloavapore; Piemme Junior

Piero Lacaita Editore+
Vieo Degli Albanesi 4, I-74024 Manduria (Taranto)
Tel: (099) 9711124 *Fax:* (099) 9711124
Key Personnel
Editorial Dir: Piero Lacaita
Founded: 1987
Subjects: History, Literature, Literary Criticism, Essays
ISBN Prefix(es): 88-87280

Piero Manni srl+
V Nino Bixio, 11B, 73100 Lecce
Tel: (0832) 387057 *Fax:* (0832) 387057
Key Personnel
Contact: Piero Manni; Grazia Manni; Anna Grazia D'Oria
Founded: 1983
Subjects: Human Relations, Literature, Literary Criticism, Essays, Poetry, Social Sciences, Sociology
ISBN Prefix(es): 88-8176
Imprints: Manni/Lupetti; L'immaginazion

Libreria Gozzini di Pietro e Francesco Chellini (SNC)
V Ricasoli 49, 50122 Florence
Tel: (055) 212433 *Fax:* (055) 211105
E-mail: gozzini@gozzini.it; info@gozzini.com
Web Site: www.gozzini.com
Founded: 1850
Member of Socio ALAI-LILA.
Total Titles: 2,000 E-Book

La Pilotta Editrice Coop RL+
Strada Universtia, 11, Via Palermo, 44, 43100 Parma
Tel: (0521) 771268 *Fax:* (0521) 771268
Key Personnel
President: Maria Pia Luchini
Editorial: Cesare Maccari
Founded: 1978
Subjects: Fiction, Literature, Literary Criticism, Essays, Poetry
Parent Company: Cemcasa Editrice Maccari

Francesco Pirella Editore
Via Casaregis 51/3, 16129 Genoa
Tel: (010) 363628 *Fax:* (010) 363644
E-mail: fpirella@split.it
Key Personnel
Man Dir: Francesco Pirella
Founded: 1972
Subjects: Art, Fiction, History, Literature, Literary Criticism, Essays, Poetry, Regional Interests
ISBN Prefix(es): 88-85514
Orders to: Serene Libri, Via Monte Zovetto 23 R, 77/4 I-16145 Genoa

Pirola
Via Castellanza, 11, 20151 Milan
Tel: (02) 30221 *Fax:* (02) 38011205
Founded: 1781
Subjects: Architecture & Interior Design, Business, Economics, Engineering (General), Law, Management, Social Sciences, Sociology
ISBN Prefix(es): 88-324

Pitagora Editrice SRL+
Via del Legatore 3, I-40138 Bologna
Tel: (051) 530003 *Fax:* (051) 535301
E-mail: pited@pitagoragroup.it
Web Site: www.pitagoragroup.it
Key Personnel
Chief Executive: Franco Stignani
Editorial: Mauro Bovini
Sales: Adolfo Francioni
Publicity: Antonella Valzania
Founded: 1958
Subjects: Engineering (General), Environmental Studies, Geography, Geology, Language Arts, Linguistics, Mathematics, Technology
ISBN Prefix(es): 88-371
Number of titles published annually: 60 Print
Total Titles: 900 Print
Associate Companies: Tecnoprint S N C, Via del Legatore 3, I-40138 Bologna *Tel:* (051) 531159 *Fax:* (051) 535301
Bookshop(s): Via Saragozza 112, I-40136 Bologna; Via Zamboni 57, I-40126 Bologna

Amilcare Pizzi SpA+
Via Pizzi 14, 20092 Cinisello Balsamo, Milan
Tel: (02) 618361 *Fax:* (02) 61836283
Telex: 330006 Ampiz I
Key Personnel
Chief Executive: Massimo Pizzi
Founded: 1914
Subjects: Art
Associate Companies: American Pizzi Offset Co, 370 Lexington Ave, Suite 505, New York, NY 10017, United States
Subsidiaries: Silvana Editoriale SpA

Pizzicato Edizioni Musicali
Via Monte Ortigara 10, 33100 Udine
Tel: (0432) 45288 *Fax:* (0432) 45288
E-mail: pizzikat@tin.it
Web Site: www.pizzicato.ch
Key Personnel
President: Anna Maria Fasano
Editor: Bruno Rossi
Founded: 1985
Subjects: Biography, Ethnicity, Music, Dance
ISBN Prefix(es): 88-7736
Imprints: N; PE; PVH

ITALY

Plurigraf SPA
Ss Flaminia, Km 90, 05035 Narni (Terni)
Tel: (0744) 715946 *Fax:* (0744) 722540
Key Personnel
President: Mr Mario Previsani
Founded: 1972
Subjects: Travel
ISBN Prefix(es): 88-7280

Istituto Poligrafico e Zecca dello Stato+
Piazza Verdi 10, 00198 Rome
Tel: (06) 85081 *Fax:* (06) 85082517
E-mail: infoipzs@ipzs.it
Telex: 611008 IPZSRO
Key Personnel
Dir: Salvatore Ficaio
Founded: 1928
State Publishing House & Italian State Stationery Office.
Subjects: Art, Government, Political Science, Language Arts, Linguistics, Law, Literature, Literary Criticism, Essays
ISBN Prefix(es): 88-240
Subsidiaries: Editalia SpA

Il Pomerio
Via Della Costa N, 4, 26900 Lodi
Tel: (0371) 420381 *Fax:* (0371) 422080
Key Personnel
Contact: Andrea Schiavi
Founded: 1994
Subjects: Architecture & Interior Design, Art, History
ISBN Prefix(es): 88-7121

Pontificio Istituto di Archeologia Cristiana
Via Napoleone III 1, 00185 Rome
Tel: (06) 4465574 *Fax:* (06) 4469197
E-mail: piac@piac.it; piac.biblio@piac.it
Web Site: www.piac.it
Key Personnel
Rector: Prof Philippe Pergola
Library Dir: Dr Giorgio Nestori
Founded: 1925
Subjects: Archaeology, History, Religion - Other, Christianity-last Roman painting, sculpture, mosaics; epigraphy
ISBN Prefix(es): 88-85991
Imprints: PIAC

Pontifico Istituto Orientale
Piazza Santa Maria Maggiore 7, 00185 Rome
Tel: (06) 447417104 *Fax:* (06) 4465576
Web Site: www.pio.urbe.it
Key Personnel
General Dir: Jaroslaw Dziewicki
  E-mail: jdziewi@tin.it
Founded: 1923
Subjects: Antiques, Archaeology, Asian Studies, Biblical Studies, Religion - Catholic, Religion - Other
ISBN Prefix(es): 88-7210

Neri Pozza Editore+
Contra Oratorio dei Servi, 21, 36100 Vicenza
Tel: (0444) 320787 *Fax:* (0444) 324613
Key Personnel
President: Giancarlo Ferretto
Man Dir: Mario Spagnol
Editorial: Angelo Colla
Sales: Giuseppe Somenzi
Production: Alfredo Bonfiglio
Publicity: Valentina Fortichiari
Rights & Permissions: Cristina Foschini
Founded: 1946
Subjects: Art, History, Literature, Literary Criticism, Essays
ISBN Prefix(es): 88-7305
Parent Company: Longanesi & C
Subsidiaries: Athesis, Longanesi, GdP

Edizioni Luigi Pozzi SRL+
Via Panama 68, 00198 Rome
Tel: (06) 8553548 *Fax:* (06) 8554105
Key Personnel
Chief Executive: Luigi Pozzi
Editorial: Maurizio Pozzi
Founded: 1893
Subjects: Medicine, Nursing, Dentistry
ISBN Prefix(es): 88-7025
Number of titles published annually: 15 Print

Pratiche Editrice+
Via Melzo, 9, 20129 Milan
Tel: (02) 29403460 *Fax:* (02) 29513061
Key Personnel
Chief Executive: Vittorio Bo
Editorial, Production, Publicity, Rights & Permissions: Susanna Boschi
Founded: 1976
Subjects: Drama, Theater, History, Philosophy
ISBN Prefix(es): 88-7380

Primavera, see Giunti Publishing Group

Edizioni Primavera SRL+
Via Bolognese, 165, 50139 Florence
Tel: (055) 66791 *Fax:* (055) 6679298
Key Personnel
President: Bruno Piazzesi
Editor: Roberto Cappello
Founded: 1981
Subjects: Travel
ISBN Prefix(es): 88-09
Imprints: Edizioni Quadrifoglio
Orders to: Giunti Marzocco, Via V Gioberti 34, I-50121 Florence

Principato+
Via Fauche 10, 20154 Milan
Tel: (02) 312025 *Fax:* (02) 33104295
E-mail: princi.red@comm2000.it
Key Personnel
Advisory Delegate: G Potesta
Publishing & Editorial Dir: Franco Menin
Founded: 1926
Subjects: Chemistry, Chemical Engineering, Earth Sciences, English as a Second Language, Geography, Geology, History, Literature, Literary Criticism, Essays, Mathematics, Physics
ISBN Prefix(es): 88-416

Prismi - Editrice Politecnica
Via Caracciolo 13, 80122 Naples
Tel: (081) 7612884 *Fax:* (081) 668339
ISBN Prefix(es): 88-7065

Priuli e Verlucca, Editori+
Stradale Torino 11, 10018 Pavone Canavese (Turin)
Tel: (0125) 239929 *Fax:* (0125) 230085
E-mail: priuli.e.verlucca@iol.it
Key Personnel
Chairman: Gherardo Priuli
Founded: 1971
Subjects: Anthropology, Antiques, Art, Cookery, Environmental Studies, Ethnicity, Photography, Regional Interests, Travel
ISBN Prefix(es): 88-8068

Psicologica Editrice+
Viale dele Medaglie, d'Oro, 428, 00136 Rome
Tel: (06) 35453558 *Fax:* (06) 35341466
E-mail: ontonet@tin.it
Web Site: www.ontopsicologia.org
Subjects: Art, Economics, Education, Philosophy, Psychology, Psychiatry, Science (General), Women's Studies, Ontopsychology
ISBN Prefix(es): 88-86766
Number of titles published annually: 5 Print
Total Titles: 60 Print

Il Punto D Incontro+
Via Sansigoli, 34, 36100 Vicenza
Tel: (0444) 928793 *Fax:* (0444) 928459
E-mail: edpunto@tin.it
Key Personnel
International Rights: Christina Levi; Patrizia Saterini
Contact: Sergio Peterlini
Specialize in books intended to sustain life's deepest foundations.
Subjects: Alternative, Astrology, Occult, Health, Nutrition, Philosophy, Religion - Buddhist, Religion - Hindu, Self-Help
ISBN Prefix(es): 88-8093

PVH, *imprint of* Pizzicato Edizioni Musicali

Edizioni Quadrifoglio, *imprint of* Edizioni Primavera SRL

Edizioni Quasar di Severino Tognon SRL+
Via Ajaccio 43, 00198 Rome
Tel: (06) 84241993 *Fax:* (06) 85833591
E-mail: qn@edizioniquasar.it
Web Site: www.edizioniquasar.it
Key Personnel
Contact: Stesso Indirizzo
Founded: 1972
Subjects: Archaeology, Art, History, Poetry, Travel
ISBN Prefix(es): 88-85020; 88-7097; 88-7140; 88-85086
Imprints: EQ
Bookshop(s): Libreria Archeologica Srl, Via Palermo 23, I-00184 Rome *Tel:* (06) 4828504

Edizioni Quattroventi SNC+
Via Dini 16, 61029 Urbino (Pesaro)
Tel: (0722) 2588 *Fax:* (0722) 320998
E-mail: quattroventi@info-net.it
Key Personnel
Man Dir, Editorial: Anna Veronesi
Sales, Production: Giorgio Balestrieri
Founded: 1981
Subjects: Archaeology, Art, History, Literature, Literary Criticism, Essays, Philosophy, Sports, Athletics
ISBN Prefix(es): 88-392
Bookshop(s): Libreria La Goliardica, Piazza Rinascimento 7, 61029 Urbino (PS)

Editrice Queriniana+
Via Ferri, 75, 25123 Brescia
Tel: (030) 2306925 *Fax:* (030) 2306932
E-mail: direzione@queriniana.it
Key Personnel
Man Dir: Rosino Gibellini
Sales & Advertising: Mario de Risio
Rights & Permissions: Giordana Maranesi
Founded: 1965
Subjects: Biblical Studies, Philosophy, Religion - Catholic, Religion - Other, Theology
ISBN Prefix(es): 88-399

Quesire
Queste Istituzioni Ricerche, Via Visconti, 20, 00193 Rome
Tel: (06) 3208732 *Fax:* (06) 3208628
ISBN Prefix(es): 88-391

Aldo Quinti, see Officina Edizioni di Aldo Quinti

Edition Raetia Srl-GmbH
23 Via Grappoli, 39100 Bolzano
Tel: (0471) 976904 *Fax:* (0471) 976908
E-mail: info@raetia.com
Subjects: Art, Government, Political Science, History, Humor, Photography, Regional Interests
ISBN Prefix(es): 88-7283

Edizioni RAI Radiotelevisione Italiano SpA,
see RAI.ERI

RAI.ERI+
Viale Mazzini 24, 00195 Rome
Mailing Address: Via Goiran, 3, 00195 Rome
Tel: (06) 3219414 *Fax:* (06) 321914; (06) 534732
Cable: EDRAD TURIN 06/37513749
Key Personnel
Dir General: Dr Guiseppe Marchetti Tricamo
Fax: (06) 36822072
Founded: 1949
Member of AIE-FEIG.
Subjects: Art, Communications, Fiction, Film, Video, Journalism, Nonfiction (General), Radio, TV, Social Sciences, Sociology
ISBN Prefix(es): 88-397
Parent Company: RAI Radiotelevisione Italiana, Viale Mazzini 14, 00195 Rome
Associate Companies: Raitrade, Via U Novaro 18, 00195 Rome; Sipra, Via Bertola 34, Turin; Telespazio, Via Alberto Bergamini 50, Rome

Rara-lst Editoriale di Bibliofilia e Reprints
Via Monti, 8, 20123 Milan
Tel: (02) 4983264 *Fax:* (02) 4814676
Founded: 1990
Subjects: Cookery, History, Literature, Literary Criticism, Essays, Medicine, Nursing, Dentistry, Technology
ISBN Prefix(es): 88-7270

RCS Libri SpA+
Via Mecenate 91, 20138 Milan
Tel: (02) 50951 *Fax:* (02) 5065361
Telex: 311321 Fabbri I *Cable:* LIBRIFABBRI MILAN
Key Personnel
Man Dir: Gianni Vallardi
International Dir of Coeditions: Massimo Rondinelli *Tel:* (02) 50952420 *Fax:* (02) 50952311 *E-mail:* massimo.rondinelli@rcs.it
Rights: Giovanna Canton *Tel:* (02) 50952288 *Fax:* (02) 50952288 *E-mail:* giovanna.canton@zcs.it
Founded: 1945
Other members of the group are Rizzoli, Bompiani, Fabbri, Sonzogno.
Subjects: Art, Business, Crafts, Games, Hobbies, History, Medicine, Nursing, Dentistry, Music, Dance, Outdoor Recreation, Science (General)
ISBN Prefix(es): 88-450; 88-451; 88-452
Parent Company: RCS Editori

RCS Rizzoli Libri SpA
Via Mecenate 91, 20138 Milan
Tel: (02) 50951 *Fax:* (02) 5065361
Telex: Rizzoli 333543 *Cable:* RCS EDITORI SPA, MILAN
Key Personnel
Chairman: Dr Giorgio Fattori
Dir General: Giovanni Ungarelli
Editorial: Rosaria Carpinelli; Evaldo Violo
Marketing: Bruno Appelius
Founded: 1909
Also literary agent.
Subjects: Art, Biography, Crafts, Games, Hobbies, Economics, Fiction, History, Medicine, Nursing, Dentistry, Music, Dance, Religion - Other, Social Sciences, Sociology
ISBN Prefix(es): 88-450; 88-451; 88-452
Associate Companies: Milano Libri; Sansoni Editore Nuova
Subsidiaries: Rizzoli International Publications
Bookshop(s): Libreria Rizzoli, Bologna, Milan, Rome, Torino

RE, *imprint of* Rugginenti Editore

Red Ezizioni, *imprint of* Red/Studio Redazionale SpA

Red/Studio Redazionale SpA+
Via Volta 43, 22100 Como
Tel: (031) 279146 *Fax:* (031) 300135
Key Personnel
Chief Executive, Editorial: Maurizio Rosenberg Colorni
Manager Foreign Rights: Mrs Meriem Peillet
Founded: 1977
Subjects: Agriculture, Child Care & Development, Earth Sciences, Environmental Studies, Health, Nutrition, Medicine, Nursing, Dentistry, Psychology, Psychiatry, Technology
ISBN Prefix(es): 88-7031
Imprints: Red Ezizioni

Regione Autonoma della Sardegna - Biblioteca Regionale
Via Roma 253, 09123 Cagliari
Tel: (070) 6065031 *Fax:* (070) 6065002
ISBN Prefix(es): 88-85994
Parent Company: Regione Autonoma della Sardegna

Reverdito Edizioni+
R.E.B. s.a.s. di Luigi Reverdito & C., Via Peratoner, 30, 38015 Lavis (TN)
Tel: (0461) 249995 *Fax:* (0461) 245281
Key Personnel
Contact: Luigi Reverdito
Founded: 1990
Specialize in Literature, Literary Criticism.
Subjects: Cookery, Health, Nutrition, History, Parapsychology, Poetry, Religion - Catholic
ISBN Prefix(es): 88-7978
Number of titles published annually: 8 Print

Franco Maria Ricci Editore (FMR)
Via Montecuccoli 32, 20147 Milan
Tel: (02) 414101 *Fax:* (02) 48301488
E-mail: ricci@fmrmagazine.it
Web Site: www.francomariaricci.it
Key Personnel
Publisher: Franco Maria Ricci
Contact: Pietro Ruffini *Tel:* (02) 41410354 *E-mail:* ruffini@frmmagazine.it
Founded: 1965
Subjects: Art
ISBN Prefix(es): 88-216
Number of titles published annually: 30 Print
Bookshop(s): Librerie Ricci
Book Club(s): Club dei Bibliofili; Collectors Club of Franco Maria Ricci

Riccardo Ricciardi Editore SpA
Via Mondadori, 1, 20090 Milan, Segrate
Tel: 02 0275421
Key Personnel
President: Prof Gian Arturo Ferrari
Founded: 1907
Subjects: History, Language Arts, Linguistics, Literature, Literary Criticism, Essays, Philosophy, Poetry
ISBN Prefix(es): 88-7817
Parent Company: Arnoldo Mondadori Editore SpA
Distributed by Arnoldo Mondadori Editore SpA

G e C Ricordi SpA+
Via Berchet 2, 20121 Milan
Tel: (02) 88812 *Fax:* (02) 88812270
Telex: 310177 Ricor I
Key Personnel
President: Guido Rignano
Vice President: Gianni Babini
Founded: 1808
Subjects: Art, Drama, Theater, Music, Dance
ISBN Prefix(es): 88-7592; 88-8192; 88-492; 88-87018
Associate Companies: Ricordi Americana SAEC, Argentina; Ricordi Brasileira S/A, Rua Conselheiro Nebias 1136, 012036 Sao Paulo SP, Brazil; Ricordi Canada, Canada; Ricordi Londra, United Kingdom; G Ricordi & Co, Paseo de la Reforma 481-A, 06500 Mexico, DF, Mexico; Ricordi Monaco, Monaco; Ricordi Parigi, France
Subsidiaries: Arti Grafiche Ricordi SpA; Dischi Ricordi SpA; Gruppo Editoriale Musica Leggera Ricordi
Warehouse: via Salomone 77, 20138 Milano

Edizioni Ripostes+
Via Lungomare Colombo, 225, 84219 Salerno
Tel: (089) 336049 *Fax:* (089) 756961
Key Personnel
Man Dir, Sales: Alessandro Tesauro
Editorial: Serafina Bartoli; Marco Amendolara; Elvira Spena
Founded: 1981
Subjects: Architecture & Interior Design, Art, History, Literature, Literary Criticism, Essays, Philosophy, Photography, Poetry, Psychology, Psychiatry
ISBN Prefix(es): 88-86819
Imprints: Alessandro Tesauro Editore
Branch Office(s)
Viale delle Tamerici 4, I-84100 Salerno
Warehouse: Viale delle Tamerici, 4-89100 Salerno

RIREA, *imprint of* Rirea Casa Editrice della Rivista Italiana di Ragioneria e di Economia Aziendale

Rirea Casa Editrice della Rivista Italiana di Ragioneria e di Economia Aziendale+
Via delle Isole 30, I 00198 Rome
Tel: (06) 8417690 *Fax:* (06) 8845732
E-mail: rirea_@infinito.it
Key Personnel
Dir: Dr Giovanna Nobile
Founded: 1901
Subjects: Accounting, Economics, Management
ISBN Prefix(es): 88-85333
Number of titles published annually: 20 Print
Imprints: RIREA

Editori Riuniti+
Via Tomacelli, 146, 00186 Rome
Tel: (06) 6875453 *Fax:* (06) 6868696
Key Personnel
Man Dir: Motarianni Michelangelo
Sales Dir, Publicity: Claudio Capotosti
Rights & Permissions: Ombretta Borgia
Founded: 1953
Subjects: Art, Economics, Education, Fiction, Government, Political Science, History, Language Arts, Linguistics, Law, Literature, Literary Criticism, Essays, Philosophy, Psychology, Psychiatry, Science (General), Social Sciences, Sociology
ISBN Prefix(es): 88-359
Imprints: ER

Laurus Robuffo Edizioni
Via della Macchiarella 146, 00119 Rome
Tel: (06) 5651492 *Fax:* (06) 5651233
Key Personnel
Chief Executive: Mario Robuffo
Founded: 1973
Subjects: Law
ISBN Prefix(es): 88-8087
Associate Companies: Edizioni FAG Srl, Via Garibaldi 5, 20090 Assago MI; NDM SRL, Via E Toti, 69/be, 70125 Bari; Epidromo SRL, Via Selva di Pescarola 6/6, 40131 Bologna; Giampaolo Fornasiero, Via Guido Rossa 2, 60020 Candia AN; Tecnolibri srl, Via Pratesi 217, 50145 Firenze; Libraria Ligure, Via Luigi Conepa, 11, 1, 16165 Geneva; Alfe snc, Via Stefano Breda 24/26, 35010 Limena PD; DLC snc, Via Nazionale Delle Puglie 200/a 105, 80026 Napoli Arpino Casoria; Libraria Dis-

tribuzioni snc, Via Olbia 33, 08100 Nuoro; M M Distribuzione Libraria Di C Marinaci & C snc, 90145 Palermo; Distributrice; Libraria Laziales srl, Via di Tor Fiorenza, 27 00199 Roma
Bookshop(s): Libreria Laurus Robuffo, Via S Martino delle Battaglia 35, 00185 Rome

Libreria Editrice Rogate (LER)+
Via dei Rogazionisti 8, 00182 Rome
Tel: (06) 7023430 *Fax:* (06) 7020767 *Cable:* ROGATE ROGAZIONISTI ROME
Key Personnel
Editorial: Vito Magno
Publicity: Nunzio Spinelli
Founded: 1976
Subjects: Religion - Other, Theology
ISBN Prefix(es): 88-8075

Edizioni Universitarie Romane
Via Poggioli, 3, 00161 Rome
Tel: (06) 491503 *Fax:* (06) 4453438
Key Personnel
Contact: Gian Vittorio Pallai
Founded: 1982
Subjects: Biological Sciences, Business, Chemistry, Chemical Engineering, Human Relations, Mathematics, Medicine, Nursing, Dentistry, Psychology, Psychiatry, Science (General), Social Sciences, Sociology
ISBN Prefix(es): 88-7730
Imprints: EUR

Archinto Rosellina+
Via S. Valeria 3, 20123 Milan
Tel: (02) 86460237 *Fax:* (02) 86451955
Founded: 1986
Subjects: Biography, Literature, Literary Criticism, Essays
ISBN Prefix(es): 88-7768

Rosenberg e Sellier Editori in Torino
Via Doria 14, 10123 Turin
Tel: (011) 8127820; (011) 532150 *Fax:* (011) 8127808 *Cable:* ROSENBERG SELLIER
Key Personnel
Man Dir: Katie Roggero
Sales, Marketing: Teresa Silletti
Production: Ada Lanteri
Founded: 1883
Subjects: Language Arts, Linguistics, Philosophy, Social Sciences, Sociology, Women's Studies
ISBN Prefix(es): 88-7011
Associate Companies: Rosenberg e Sellier Libreria Pera Documentazione Scientifica

Rossato+
Via Bella Venezia, 13/C, 36074 Novale di Valdagno (Vicenza)
Tel: (0455) 411000 *Fax:* (0455) 411550
E-mail: grossato@didanet.it
Key Personnel
Contact: Gino Rossato; Vania Rossato
Member of AIE.
Subjects: History, Military Science, Travel
ISBN Prefix(es): 88-8130

Rubbettino Editore+
Viale Rosario Rubbettino, 10, 88049 Soveria Mannelli (CZ)
Tel: (0968) 662034 *Fax:* (0968) 662055
E-mail: commerciale@rubbettino.it
Web Site: www.rubbettino.it *Cable:* RUBBETTINO SOVERIA MANNELLI
Key Personnel
President: Florindo Rubbettino
Editorial Dir: Giacinto Marra
Editorial: Gabriella Grandinetti; Angela Cimino
Sales: Antonio Colosino
Founded: 1972
Subjects: Anthropology, Art, Drama, Theater, Economics, Government, Political Science, History, Law, Literature, Literary Criticism, Essays, Philosophy, Poetry, Public Administration, Religion - Other, Romance, Social Sciences, Sociology, Theology, Women's Studies
ISBN Prefix(es): 88-7284; 88-498
Parent Company: Rubbettino SRL, Viale Rosario Rubbettino, 8, 88049 Soveria Mannelli (CZ)
Associate Companies: Calabria Letteraria Editrice
E-mail: cle@rubbettino.it

Rugginenti Editore+
Via Del Fontanili 3, 20141 Milan
Tel: (02) 89501283 *Fax:* (02) 89531273
E-mail: rugginenti@rugginenti.com
Web Site: www.rugginenti.com
Key Personnel
Editor: Gianni Rugginenti
Founded: 1968
Subjects: Music, Dance
ISBN Prefix(es): 88-7665
Total Titles: 40 Audio
Imprints: RE

Rusconi Libri Srl+
Viale Sarca 235, 20126 Milan
Tel: (02) 66191 *Fax:* (02) 66192758
E-mail: relazioniesterne@rusconi.it
Telex: 312233 *Cable:* RUSCONI EDITORE MILANO
Key Personnel
Editorial Dir: Alberto Conforti
Chief Editor: Pieranna Pagan
Sales: Marco Mattio
Foreign Rights: Olivia Olivieri
Founded: 1968
Subjects: Biography, History, Literature, Literary Criticism, Essays, Music, Dance, Nonfiction (General), Philosophy, Psychology, Psychiatry, Religion - Other
ISBN Prefix(es): 88-18
Parent Company: Rusconi Editore, Viale Sarca 235, 20126 Milan
Associate Companies: Eurolibri, Viale Sarca 235, 20126 Milan
U.S. Office(s): Rusconi Inc, 375 Park Ave, Suite 3307, New York, NY 10152, United States
Warehouse: Via Pacinotti, 16-20092 Cinisello Balsamo
Orders to: Eurolibri, Viale Sarca 235, 20126 Milan

Norberto Sabatelli & C, see Editrice Liguria SNC di Norberto Sabatelli & C

SAGEP
Piazza Merani 1, 16145 Genoa
Tel: (010) 313453 *Fax:* (010) 312621
Telex: 281343 SAGEP I
Key Personnel
Publisher: Eugenio de Andreis
Sales Manager: Carla Bisacchi
Founded: 1965
Subjects: Architecture & Interior Design, Art, Economics, Ethnicity, History, Science (General), Travel
ISBN Prefix(es): 88-7058

SAIE Editrice SRL
Subsidiary of Edizioni San Paolo SRL
Corso Regina Margherita 2, 10153 Turin
Tel: (011) 871022 *Fax:* (011) 830826
Key Personnel
Publicity: Fedele Molino
Founded: 1954
Subjects: Art, Earth Sciences, Economics, Education, Film, Video, Language Arts, Linguistics, Literature, Literary Criticism, Essays, Medicine, Nursing, Dentistry, Philosophy, Radio, TV, Religion - Other
Associate Companies: Edizioni Paoline SRL

Adriano Salani Editore srl+
Corso Italia, 13, 20122 Milan
Tel: (028) 693 238 *Fax:* (027) 201 8806
Telex: 353273 LONG I
Key Personnel
President: Mario Spagnol
Man Dir: Luigi Spagnol
Editorial: Maria Grazia Mazzitelli
Sales: Giuseppe Somenzi
Production: Alfredo Bonfiglio
Publicity: Allessandra Gnecchi
Rights & Permissions: Cristina Foschini
General Manager: Stefano Maure
Founded: 1862
Subjects: Fiction
ISBN Prefix(es): 88-7782
Parent Company: Longanesi & C
Subsidiaries: Messaggerie Italiane
U.S. Office(s): Nina Collins Association, 584 Broadway, Suite 607, New York 10012, United States
Warehouse: Messaggerie Italiane, Magazzino Editoriale, Via Bereguardina, 20080 Casarile (Mi)
Orders to: Pro Libro, Florence

Salerno Editrice SRL+
Via Valadier, 52, 00193 Rome
Tel: (06) 3608201 *Fax:* (06) 3223132
E-mail: salernoeditrice@mclink.it
Web Site: www.salernoeditrice.it
Key Personnel
Chief Executive: Prof Enrico Malato
Founded: 1972
Subjects: Biography, Fiction, History, Language Arts, Linguistics, Literature, Literary Criticism, Essays, Social Sciences, Sociology, Italian Literature & Historic Studies
ISBN Prefix(es): 88-85026; 88-8402
Number of titles published annually: 40 Print
Warehouse: Viale dei Colli Portuensi, 591, Rome 00151 *Tel:* (06) 55266684

Samaya SRL
Localita Lu Cupuneddu, 07028 Teresa di Gallura (Sassari)
Tel: (0789) 750039 *Fax:* (0789) 750081
Key Personnel
President: Milvia Pagan
Founded: 1980
Subjects: Child Care & Development, Health, Nutrition
ISBN Prefix(es): 88-85302

Collegio San Bonaventura di Grottaferrata
Via Vecchia di Marino 28/30, 00046 Grottaferrata (Rome)
Tel: (06) 94315318 *Fax:* (06) 9410781
Founded: 1877
Subjects: History, Religion - Other, Theology
ISBN Prefix(es): 88-7013

San Lorenzo
Via Gandhi 24/18 b, 42100 Reggio Emilia
Tel: (0522) 323140 *Fax:* (0522) 323140
E-mail: frtt15k1@re.nettuno.it (forte Luciano)
Founded: 1985
ISBN Prefix(es): 88-8071

Editrice San Marco SRL+
Via Abbadia 13, I-24069 Trescore Balneario (Bergamo)
Tel: (035) 940178 *Fax:* (035) 944385
E-mail: sanmarco@ibenet.it
Key Personnel
Man Dir: Giulio Belotti
Founded: 1955
Subjects: Agriculture, Biological Sciences, Education, Energy, Government, Political Science, Labor, Industrial Relations, Marketing, Technology
ISBN Prefix(es): 88-86285

PUBLISHERS

ITALY

Edizioni San Paolo SRL+
Piazza Soncino 5, I-20092 Cinisello Balsamo (Milan)
Tel: (02) 660751 *Fax:* (02) 66075211
E-mail: cb.spe.segreteria@stpauls.it
Key Personnel
Man Dir: Emilio Bettati
General Manager: Vincenzo Santarcangelo
Editorial: Elio Sala
Production: Angelo Zenzalari
Founded: 1914
Subjects: Art, Biography, Fiction, History, How-to, Medicine, Nursing, Dentistry, Music, Dance, Philosophy, Psychology, Psychiatry, Religion - Other
ISBN Prefix(es): 88-215
Parent Company: Societa San Paolo, Rome
Subsidiaries: DISP SRL; Multimedia San Paolo SRL; Periodici San Paolo SRL; SAIE Editrice SRL
Warehouse: DISP SRL, Piazza San Paolo 14, I-12051 Alba *Tel:* (0173) 361040 (Cuneo)

Sansoni Editore+
Division of RCS Libri Spa
Via Mecenate, 91, 20138 Milan
Tel: (02) 50952333 *Fax:* (02) 50952309
Web Site: www.sansonieditore.it
Founded: 1873
Subjects: Fiction
ISBN Prefix(es): 88-383
Associate Companies: RCS Rizzoli Libri SpA
Warehouse: RCS Libri Spa, Via Mecanate 91, 20138 Milan

Il Sapere Edizioni
Via Roma 210, 84121 Salerno
Tel: (089) 254252 *Fax:* (089) 254262
E-mail: sapere@elimet.sandera.it
ISBN Prefix(es): 88-8119

Sapere 2000 SRL
Via Turati 48, 00185 Rome
Tel: (06) 4465363 *Fax:* (06) 4465363
E-mail: sapere2000@flshnet.it
Key Personnel
Man Dir: Angelo Ruggieri
Founded: 1976
Subjects: Architecture & Interior Design, Ethnicity, Government, Political Science, Religion - Other, Social Sciences, Sociology
ISBN Prefix(es): 88-7673

Fausto Sardini Editrice+
Via Pace 73, 25046 Bornato (Brescia)
Tel: (030) 7750430 *Fax:* (030) 7254348
E-mail: sardini@sardini.it *Cable:* Fausto Sardini-Editore-Bornato
Key Personnel
Chief Executive: Fausto Sardini
Editorial: Davide Sardini
Founded: 1969
Subjects: Art, Fiction, History, Poetry, Regional Interests, Religion - Catholic, Science (General), Theology
ISBN Prefix(es): 88-7506
Subsidiaries: Intelligenza e Informatica SRL
Divisions: Informatica

Scala Group spa
Via Chiantigiana 62, 50011 Antella, Florence
Tel: (055) 623311 *Fax:* (055) 6233280
E-mail: scala@scalagroup.com
Web Site: www.scalagroup.com
Key Personnel
President: Dr Alberto Milla
VP & Chief Executive Officer: Alvise Passigli *E-mail:* a.passigli@scalagroup.com
Man Dir: Gianni Mancassola
Founded: 1953
Book packager & broadband files.

Subjects: Archaeology, Art, Education, Film, Video, Photography, Travel, Museums & Art Guides
ISBN Prefix(es): 88-8117
Number of titles published annually: 10 Print; 20 CD-ROM; 5 Online
Total Titles: 100 Print; 200 CD-ROM
Subsidiaries: E-ducation.it
Distributed by Hazan (Francophone countries); Riverside (US & Canada); Slovo (Russia)

Lo Scarabeo Srl+
Corso Svizzera 31, 10143 Turin
Tel: (011) 7716568 *Fax:* (011) 740843
Key Personnel
President: Pietro Alligo
Founded: 1987
Subjects: Art
ISBN Prefix(es): 88-86131

Schena Editore+
Viale Stazione 177, 72015 Fasano (Brindisi)
Tel: (080) 714681 *Fax:* (080) 714690
Key Personnel
Editor: Nunzio Schena
Founded: 1972
Subjects: Archaeology, Architecture & Interior Design, Art, Language Arts, Linguistics, Literature, Literary Criticism, Essays
ISBN Prefix(es): 88-7514; 88-8229

Salvatore Sciascia Editore
Corso Umberto I, 111, 93100 Caltanissetta
Tel: (0934) 21946 *Fax:* (0934) 551366 *Cable:* SCIASCIA EDITORE
Key Personnel
Man Dir: Quiseppe Sciascia
Editor: Salvatore Sciascia
Founded: 1946
Subjects: Art, History, Literature, Literary Criticism, Essays, Poetry
ISBN Prefix(es): 88-8241
Warehouse: Via Pietro Leone SN, 93100 Caltanissetta

Libreria Scientifica Cortina, see Libreria Cortina Editrice SRL

Edizioni Scientifiche Italiane+
Via Chiatamone 7, 80121 Naples
Tel: (081) 7645443 *Fax:* (081) 7646477
E-mail: info@esispa.com
Web Site: www.esispa.com
Key Personnel
President: Pietro Perlingieri
Administration: Francesco De Simone
Editorial Dir: Giovanna Delfino
Founded: 1945
Subjects: Architecture & Interior Design, Art, Cookery, Drama, Theater, Economics, Geography, Geology, History, Law, Literature, Literary Criticism, Essays, Medicine, Nursing, Dentistry, Music, Dance, Philosophy, Psychology, Psychiatry, Science (General), Social Sciences, Sociology, Technology
ISBN Prefix(es): 88-7104; 88-8114
Branch Office(s)
Via F lli Bronzetti, 11, 20129 Milan *Tel:* (02) 730846 *Fax:* (02) 730849
Via dei Taurini, 27, 00185 Rome *Tel:* (06) 4462664 *Fax:* (06) 4461308
Via Porta Rettori, 19, 82100 Benevento *Tel:* (0824) 43752 *Fax:* (0824) 43666

Editoriale Scienza (Science)+
Via Romagna 30, 34134 Trieste
Tel: (040) 364810 *Fax:* (040) 364909
E-mail: info@editscienza.it
Web Site: www.editscienza.it
Founded: 1990
Specialize in science books for children.

Member of Associazione Aie.
Subjects: Animals, Pets, Astronomy, Biological Sciences, Computer Science, Crafts, Games, Hobbies, Earth Sciences, Geography, Geology, Health, Nutrition, Mathematics, Nonfiction (General), Physical Sciences, Science (General), Science Fiction, Fantasy, Technology
ISBN Prefix(es): 88-7307
Number of titles published annually: 20 Print
Imprints: ES
Distributed by Messaggerie Libri

Casa Editrice Mariett Scuola SpA
Strada del Portone 177, 10095 Grugliasco, Turin
Tel: (02) 3158711 *Fax:* (02) 3158710
Key Personnel
Man Dir: Dr Federico Franchi
ISBN Prefix(es): 88-393

SEA, *imprint of* Ist Patristico Augustinianum

Edizioni Segno SRL+
Via E Fermi, 80, 33010 Tavagnacco Udine
Tel: (0432) 575179 *Fax:* (0432) 575589
E-mail: info@edizionisegno.it
Web Site: www.edizionisegno.it
Key Personnel
Dir: Pietro Mantero
Founded: 1988
Subjects: Biblical Studies, Mysteries, Nonfiction (General), Religion - Catholic, Theology
ISBN Prefix(es): 88-7282
Number of titles published annually: 50 Print; 1 Audio
Total Titles: 150 Print; 1 Audio

Segretariato Nazionale Apostolato della Preghiera+
Via degli Astalli 16, 00186 Rome
Tel: (06) 6976071 *Fax:* (06) 6781063
E-mail: adp@adp.it
Web Site: www.adp.it
Key Personnel
Administrative Dir: Massimo Taggi *Tel:* (06) 697607 Ext 202 *E-mail:* mt@adp.it
Founded: 1844
Subjects: Religion - Catholic
ISBN Prefix(es): 88-7357
Imprints: AdP

SEI - Societa Editrice Internazionale, see Societa Editrice Internazionale - SEI

Sellerio Editore
Via Siracusa, 50/2, 90141 Palermo
Tel: (091) 6259475 *Fax:* (091) 6258802
Founded: 1969
Subjects: Anthropology, Archaeology, Art, History, Literature, Literary Criticism, Essays, Photography, Social Sciences, Sociology
ISBN Prefix(es): 88-7681

SEMAR, *imprint of* SEMAR Publishers SRL

SEMAR Publishers SRL+
Via Arco Di Parma, 18, 00186 Rome
Tel: (06) 6876523 *Fax:* (06) 68308601
E-mail: info@semarweb.com
Web Site: semarweb.com *Cable:* SEMAR
Key Personnel
President: Luciano Sahlan Momo *Tel:* (06) 6879333 *E-mail:* momo@semarweb.com
Founded: 1986
Specialize in editions with conservation criteria.
Subjects: Art, Drama, Theater, Environmental Studies, Literature, Literary Criticism, Essays, Music, Dance, Philosophy, Poetry
ISBN Prefix(es): 88-7778
Number of titles published annually: 15 Print; 2 CD-ROM; 5 Audio
Total Titles: 180 Print; 6 CD-ROM; 176 Online; 10 Audio

Imprints: SEMAR
Distributed by Diest

Servitium
Via Ticino 2, 24020 Gorle (Bergamo)
Tel: (035) 4398011 *Fax:* (035) 792030
E-mail: servitium@spm.it
Subjects: Anthropology, Religion - Catholic, Romance, Theology, Spiritual
ISBN Prefix(es): 88-8166
Distributed by Dehoniana Libri SpA (Italy only)

Servizio Italiano Pubblicazioni Internazionali Srl, see SIPI (Servizio Italiano Pubblicazioni Internazionali) Srl

Sicania+
Via Catania 62, 98124 Messina
Tel: (090) 2936373 *Fax:* (090) 2932641
Key Personnel
Publisher: Ugo Magno
Editorial Dir: Gianvito Resta
Editor: Giovanni Molonia
Public Relations: Caterina Pastura
Founded: 1986
Subjects: Art, Drama, Theater, History, Language Arts, Linguistics, Literature, Literary Criticism, Essays, Philosophy, Photography, Regional Interests
ISBN Prefix(es): 88-7268
Subsidiaries: Edizioni GBM

Edizioni Librarie Siciliane+
Via Altofonte, 9, I-90030 Santa Cristina Gela (Palermo)
Tel: (091) 8570221 *Fax:* (091) 342670
Key Personnel
Dir General: Gaetano Mantovani
Founded: 1978
Subjects: Anthropology, Antiques, Archaeology, Architecture & Interior Design, Art, History, Human Relations, Natural History, Philosophy
Imprints: ELS

Silva Artegrafica SRL
Via Nazionale, 23, 43044 Collecchio (Parma)
Tel: (0521) 804106 *Fax:* (0521) 804406
ISBN Prefix(es): 88-7765

Silvana Editoriale SpA+
Via de Vizzi 86, 20092 Cinisello Balsamo Milan
Tel: (02) 6172464 *Fax:* (02) 61836283
Telex: 330006 Ampiz I
Key Personnel
Chief Executive: Massimo Pizzi
Founded: 1953
Subjects: Architecture & Interior Design, Art, Photography
ISBN Prefix(es): 88-366; 88-8215
Parent Company: Amilcare Pizzi SpA
Associate Companies: American Pizzi Offset Co, 141 E 44 St, New York, NY 10017, United States

SIPI, *imprint of* SIPI (Servizio Italiano Pubblicazioni Internazionali) Srl

SIPI (Servizio Italiano Pubblicazioni Internazionali) Srl
Viale Pasteur 6, 00144 Rome
Tel: (06) 5920509 *Fax:* (06) 5924819
Founded: 1951
Subjects: Economics, Government, Political Science, Labor, Industrial Relations, Regional Interests
ISBN Prefix(es): 88-7153
Imprints: SIPI

Societa Editrice Internazionale - SEI+
Corso Regina Margherita 176, 10152 Turin
Tel: (011) 52271 *Fax:* (011) 5211320
Telex: 216216 SEI TO I *Cable:* SEI TORINO
Key Personnel
President: Alessandro Braja
Man Dir & General Manger: Gian Nicola Pivano
Dir of Editorial Management, Marketing & Public Relations: Alessandro Rangaioli
Founded: 1908
Subjects: Education, Geography, Geology, History, Literature, Literary Criticism, Essays, Mathematics, Philosophy, Physics, Psychology, Psychiatry, Religion - Catholic
ISBN Prefix(es): 88-05

Societa Editrice la Goliardica Pavese SRL+
Viale Golgi, 6, 27100 Pavia
Tel: (0382) 529570 *Fax:* (0382) 423140
Key Personnel
Chief Executive: Dario De Bona
Founded: 1977
Subjects: Biological Sciences, Chemistry, Chemical Engineering, Medicine, Nursing, Dentistry, Physical Sciences, Physics, Science (General)
ISBN Prefix(es): 88-7830
Branch Office(s)
Via Lombroso 21, Pavia *Tel:* (0382) 525709
Viale Golgi 6 *Tel:* 529570
Bookshop(s): Via Lombroso u 21, 27100 Pavia
Shipping Address: Via Taramelli u 18, 27100 Pavia

Societa Napoletana Storia Patria Napoli
Maschio Angioino, 80133 Naples
Tel: (081) 5510353 *Fax:* (081) 5529238
E-mail: snsp@unina.it
Web Site: www.storia.unina.it/smsp/
Subjects: History, Monographies, diplomatics & history of art
ISBN Prefix(es): 88-8044

Societa Stampa Sportiva+
Via Guinizelli 56, 00152 Rome
Tel: (06) 5817311 *Fax:* (06) 5806526
E-mail: segreteria@stampasportiva.com
Web Site: www.stampasportiva.com
Key Personnel
President: Francesco Paolo Palumbo
Founded: 1967
Subjects: Physical Sciences, Sports, Athletics
ISBN Prefix(es): 88-8313
Number of titles published annually: 20 Print
Total Titles: 532 Print
Warehouse: Via Di Villa Pamphili 33/F, I-00152 Rome

Societa Storica Catanese
Via Etnea 248, 95131 Catania
Tel: (095) 311124
Key Personnel
Man Dir: Dr Michele D'Agata
Editorial: Giuseppe Trovato Pennisi
Sales: Francesco Romeo Giuzzetta
Production: Giovanni Assaro
Publicity: Dr Davide D'Agata
Rights & Permissions: Prof Rita Siciliano
Founded: 1955
Subjects: History, Law, Literature, Literary Criticism, Essays, Poetry, Regional Interests, Social Sciences, Sociology
Imprints: SSC

Edizioni Rosminiane Sodalitas
Corso Umberto I, 15, 28838 Stresa (Verbania)
Tel: (0323) 30091 *Fax:* (0323) 31623
E-mail: edizioni@rosmini.it
Key Personnel
Publicity: Muratore Umberto
Founded: 1906
Subjects: Philosophy, Theology

Edizioni del Sole 24 Ore
Via Lomazzo 52, 20154 Milan
Tel: (02) 30221 *Fax:* (02) 3022405
Telex: 331325 I 24 Ore
Key Personnel
Dir General: Gianni Rizzoni
Editorial: Francesco Bogliari
Founded: 1983
Subjects: Economics, Law, Management
ISBN Prefix(es): 88-7187

Soleverde, *imprint of* Centro Scientifico Torinese

Edizioni Sonda+
Via Ciamarella 23/3, 10149 Turin
Tel: (011) 211442 *Fax:* (011) 2217818
Key Personnel
Contact: Antonio Monaco
Founded: 1988
ISBN Prefix(es): 88-7106
Associate Companies: Il Tappeto Volante srl; Consorzio "Omniatech"; Consorzio "Leonardo"

Sonzogno
Via Mecenate 91, 20138 Milan
Tel: (02) 50951 *Fax:* (02) 5065361
Telex: 311321 Fabbri I *Cable:* Librifabbri Milan
Key Personnel
Dir: Mario Andreose
Rights & Permissions: Carla Tanzi
Founded: 1818
Member of Gruppo Editoriale Fabbri, Bompiani, Sonzogno, Etas SpA.
Subjects: Fiction, Mysteries, Nonfiction (General)
ISBN Prefix(es): 88-450; 88-451; 88-452

Edizioni Sorbona Milano+
Via dei Martinitt 3, 20146 Milan
Tel: (02) 48016464 *Fax:* (02) 48194485
Key Personnel
Contact: Dr F Bonadei
Founded: 1981
Subjects: Chemistry, Chemical Engineering, Medicine, Nursing, Dentistry, Physics, Science (General)
ISBN Prefix(es): 88-7150

Sperling e Kupfer Editori SpA+
Via Durazzo, 4, 20134 Milan
Tel: (02) 217211 *Fax:* (02) 21721277
Key Personnel
Chief Executive Officer: Roberto Avanzo
President: Valerio Anna Patrizia
Editorial Dir: Carla Tanzi
Rights & Permissions & Contract: Stefania Klein De Pasquale *E-mail:* sdepas@mondadori.it
Scout (US): Linda Clark
Scout (France): Zeline Guena
Scout (UK): Ros Ramsay
Founded: 1899
Subjects: Biography, Economics, Fiction, Health, Nutrition, How-to, Management, Nonfiction (General), Science (General), Sports, Athletics, Travel
ISBN Prefix(es): 88-200; 88-86845; 88-87592
Parent Company: Mondadori
Subsidiaries: Edizioni Frassinelli SRL
U.S. Office(s): 28 E 57 St, 7th floor, New York, NY 10022, United States (scout office)

Spirali Edizioni+
Via Gabba 3, 20121 Milan
Tel: (02) 8054417 *Fax:* (02) 8692631
E-mail: info@spirali.it
Web Site: www.spirali-vel.com
Key Personnel
Man Dir: Cristina Frua De Angeli
Editorial: Annalisa Scallo
Founded: 1978
Subjects: Art, Law, Literature, Literary Criticism, Essays, Music, Dance, Philosophy, Poetry, Psychology, Psychiatry

ISBN Prefix(es): 88-7770
Number of titles published annually: 10 Print

SSC, *imprint of* Societa Storica Catanese

Stampa Alternativa - Nuovi Equilibri+
Str Tuscanese, Km 4, 800, 01100 Viterbo
Tel: (0761) 352277 *Fax:* (0761) 352751
Key Personnel
Man Dir, Editorial: Marcello Baraghini
Sales: Angelo Leone
Founded: 1971
Subjects: Art, Health, Nutrition, Literature, Literary Criticism, Essays, Medicine, Nursing, Dentistry, Music, Dance
ISBN Prefix(es): 88-7226
Imprints: Fiabesca; Cartoonseries; Jazz People; L'eta D'oro Dell Illustrazione
Orders to: Nuovi Equilibri, PO Box 97, I-01100 Viterbo *Tel:* (0761) 352277 *Fax:* (0761) 352751

Edizoni Le Stelle, *imprint of* Gruppo Editoriale Le Stelle SpA

Gruppo Editoriale Le Stelle SpA
Via Vasari 15, 20135 Milan
Tel: (02) 55181460 *Fax:* (02) 5400017
Founded: 1954
Subjects: Education, Fiction, Geography, Geology, History, Music, Dance, Religion - Other, Science (General)
Imprints: Dimensione Umana; Linea Verde; Edizoni Le Stelle

Edizioni di Storia e Letteratura
Via Lancellotti 18, 00186 Rome
Tel: (06) 68806556 *Fax:* (06) 68806640
E-mail: edi.storialett@tiscalinet.it
Web Site: www.weeb.it/edistorialett
Key Personnel
Chief Executive: Maddalena De Luca
Founded: 1943
Subjects: Economics, Government, Political Science, History, Literature, Literary Criticism, Essays, Philosophy
ISBN Prefix(es): 88-900138; 88-87114

Istituto Storico Italiano per l'Eta Moderna e Contemporanea
Via Caetani 32, 00186 Rome
Tel: (06) 68806922 *Fax:* (06) 6875127
Key Personnel
Man Dir: Prof Luigi Lotti
Editorial: Dr Marina Maura
Founded: 1934
Subjects: History

Studio Bibliografico Adelmo Polla+
Via Prato 2, 67044 Cerchio
Tel: (0863) 78522 *Fax:* (0863) 78522
Key Personnel
Man Dir: Adelmo Polla
Editorial: Maria G Romanelli
Founded: 1974
Subjects: Archaeology, History, Language Arts, Linguistics, Literature, Literary Criticism, Essays, Travel

Studio Editoriale Programma
Via S. Eufemia, 5, 35121 Padova
Tel: (049) 8753110 *Fax:* (049) 8755870
Founded: 1981
Subjects: Art, History, Literature, Literary Criticism, Essays, Travel
ISBN Prefix(es): 88-7123

Edizioni Studio Tesi SRL
Via Flaminia, 109, 00196 Rome
Tel: (06) 3201656 *Fax:* (06) 3223540 *Cable:* EST
Key Personnel
Chief Executive & Editorial: Pier Paolo Benedetto
Founded: 1977
Subjects: Economics, Fiction, History, Literature, Literary Criticism, Essays, Music, Dance, Science (General)
ISBN Prefix(es): 88-7692
Subsidiaries: Edizioni dello Zibaldone

Edizioni Studium SpA+
Via Cassiodoro 14, I-00193 Rome
Tel: (06) 6865846 *Fax:* (06) 6875456
E-mail: edizionistudium@libero.it *Cable:* STUDIUM ROME
Founded: 1927
Periodicals.
Subjects: History, Literature, Literary Criticism, Essays, Philosophy, Religion - Other, Science (General), Social Sciences, Sociology
ISBN Prefix(es): 88-382
Number of titles published annually: 30 Print
Total Titles: 500 Print
Associate Companies: Editrice La Scuola SpA
Distributed by Editrice Le Seulo - Buscie

Sugarco Edizioni SRL
Via Fermi 9, 21040 Carnago (Varese)
Tel: (0331) 985511 *Fax:* (0331) 985385
Key Personnel
Man Dir: Dr Oliviero Cigada
Founded: 1956
Subjects: Biography, Fiction, History, How-to, Philosophy
ISBN Prefix(es): 88-7198

ME/D1 Sviluppo, see Giunti Publishing Group

Tappeiner
Zona Industriale, 6, 39011 Lana d Adige (Bolzano)
Tel: (0473) 563666 *Fax:* (0473) 563689
E-mail: tappeiner@pass.dnet.it
Subjects: Archaeology, Architecture & Interior Design, Art, Cookery, Geography, Geology, History, Outdoor Recreation
ISBN Prefix(es): 88-7073

La Tartaruga Edizioni SAS
Via Turati 38, 20121 Milan
Tel: (02) 6555036 *Fax:* (02) 653007
Founded: 1975
Subjects: Cookery, Drama, Theater, Literature, Literary Criticism, Essays, Women's Studies
ISBN Prefix(es): 88-7738; 88-85678

Tassotti Editore
Via San F Lazzaro 103, 36061 Bassano del Grappa (Vicenza)
Tel: (0424) 566105 *Fax:* (0424) 566205
Founded: 1984
Subjects: Art, History, Travel
ISBN Prefix(es): 88-7691
Divisions: Grafiche Tassotti SRL

TEA Tascabili degli Editori Associati SpA+
Corso Italia 13, 20122 Milan
Tel: (02) 80206625 *Fax:* (02) 8900844
Key Personnel
President: Stefano Mauri
Man Dir: Marco Taro
Editorial Dir: Stefano Res *E-mail:* stefano.res@tealibri.it
Sales: Giuseppe Somenzi
Production: Alfredo Bonfiglio
Publicity: Valentina Fortichiari
Rights & Permissions: Sabine Schultz
Publicity: Elena Dallorso
Founded: 1987
Subjects: Art, Cookery, Fiction, Health, Nutrition, History, How-to, Humor, Nonfiction (General), Philosophy, Photography, Poetry, Psychology, Psychiatry, Religion - Buddhist, Religion - Catholic, Religion - Hindu, Religion - Islamic, Religion - Jewish, Science Fiction, Fantasy, Self-Help
ISBN Prefix(es): 88-7818; 88-502
Number of titles published annually: 150 Print
Total Titles: 1,300 Print
Subsidiaries: Longanesi

Tecniche Nuove SpA+
Via Menotti 14, 20129 Milan
Tel: (02) 75701 *Fax:* (02) 7610351
E-mail: libri@tecnet.it; vendite-libri@tecnet.it
Web Site: www.tecnet.it
Key Personnel
Man Dir: Giuseppe Nardella
Editorial: E Guaglione
Publicity: S Savona
Founded: 1960
Subjects: Business, Computer Science, Electronics, Electrical Engineering, Energy, Health, Nutrition, Technology
ISBN Prefix(es): 88-7081; 88-85009; 88-481
Number of titles published annually: 150 Print; 15 CD-ROM; 20 E-Book
Total Titles: 700 Print; 30 CD-ROM; 30 E-Book
Subsidiaries: Grafica Quadrifoglio
U.S. Office(s): Tecniche Nuove USA, 844 Gage Drive, San Diego, CA 92106, United States
Warehouse: Via Castel Morrone 15

Tema Celeste
10 Piazza Borromeo, 20123 Milan
Tel: (02) 80651754; (02) 80651732 (subscriptions) *Fax:* (02) 80651787
E-mail: editorial@temaceleste.com; subscriptions@temaceleste.com
Web Site: www.temaceleste.com
Key Personnel
Publisher: Alberico Cetti Serbelloni
Editor: Simona Vendrame
Assistant Editor: Daniele Perra
Founded: 1983
Subjects: Art
ISBN Prefix(es): 88-85265; 88-7304

Edizioni del Teresianum
Piazza San Pancrazio 5/A, 00152 Rome
Tel: (06) 58540250 *Fax:* (06) 58540300
Key Personnel
Chief Executive: Cumer Dario
Sales, Publicity: Piergiorgio Mantovani
Founded: 1966
Subjects: Biblical Studies, Biography, History, Religion - Catholic, Theology
ISBN Prefix(es): 88-85317
Parent Company: Edizioni dei Padri Carmelitani Scalzi, Corso d'Italia 38, I-00198 Rome

Nicola Teti e C Editore SRL
Via Rezia, 4, 20135 Milan
Tel: (02) 55015575 *Fax:* (02) 55015595
Key Personnel
Man Dir: Nicola Teti
Editorial: Piero Lavatelli
Sales: Vincenzo Fracchiolla
Rights & Permissions & Production: Rita Vaccari
Production: Vanna Guzzi
Publicity: Nino Oppo
Founded: 1971
Subjects: Education, Government, Political Science, History, Natural History, Social Sciences, Sociology
ISBN Prefix(es): 88-7039

Edizioni Thyrus SRL+
Via della Rinascita 12, 05031 Arrone (Ternil)
Tel: (0744) 389496 *Fax:* (0744) 388700
Cable: UFFICIO POSTALE ARRONE
Key Personnel
Man Dir, Production, Rights & Permissions: Dr Osvaldo Panfili
Editorial: Prof Lido Pirro

Sales: Nobili Nevia
Founded: 1956
Subjects: Education, Fiction, History, Literature, Literary Criticism, Essays, Psychology, Psychiatry, Regional Interests, Social Sciences, Sociology, Theology
Book Club(s): Circolo Astrolabio

Tilgher-Genova sas
Via Assarotti 31/15, 16122 Genoa
Tel: (010) 839 11 40 *Fax:* (010) 87 06 53
E-mail: tilgher@tilgher.it
Web Site: www.tilgher.it
Key Personnel
Chief Executive: Lucio Bozzi
Founded: 1971
Subjects: Biological Sciences, Literature, Literary Criticism, Essays, Philosophy

Editrice Tirrenia Stampatori SAS
Via Ferrari 5, I-10124 Turin
Tel: (011) 8150826 *Fax:* (011) 8177010
Key Personnel
Editorial, Publicity: Anna Maria Bertolina
Founded: 1977
Specialize in University publishing.
Subjects: Geography, Geology, History, Language Arts, Linguistics, Literature, Literary Criticism, Essays, Mathematics, Philosophy, Psychology, Psychiatry, Social Sciences, Sociology
ISBN Prefix(es): 88-7763
Orders to: The Courier SRL, Distibozione Libr, VLA Debosis, 25-27, 80145 Firenze

Todariana Editrice+
Via Gardone, 29, 20139 Milan
Tel: (02) 56812953 *Fax:* (02) 55213405
E-mail: toeurs@tin.it
Key Personnel
Chief Executive: Teodoro Giuttari
Founded: 1967
Subjects: Fiction, Language Arts, Linguistics, Literature, Literary Criticism, Essays, Poetry, Psychology, Psychiatry, Science Fiction, Fantasy, Social Sciences, Sociology, Travel
ISBN Prefix(es): 88-7015
Number of titles published annually: 12 Print
Imprints: Eura Press; Edizioni Italiane
Subsidiaries: Eura Press; Edizioni Italiane

Tomo Edizioni srl+
Via Pienza, 255, 00138 Rome
Tel: (081) 00920 *Fax:* (081) 00920
Founded: 1989
Subjects: Art, Photography
ISBN Prefix(es): 88-7151

Trainer International SRL+
Corso Italia 29, 50123 Florence
Tel: (055) 288162 *Fax:* (055) 218951
Telex: 571136
Key Personnel
Editorial Dir: Enrico Bosi
Coordinator: Enrica Fuligni Nannelli
Founded: 1990
Subjects: Art, History, Travel, Wine & Spirits
ISBN Prefix(es): 88-85271
Warehouse: V Baldanzese, 118-50041 Calenzano Firenze

Tranchida+
Via Spalato, 11/2, I-20124 Milan
Tel: (02) 66802270 *Fax:* (02) 69003425
E-mail: rbuff@abanet.it
Key Personnel
Man Dir: Giovanni Tranchida
Founded: 1983
Member of AIE.
Subjects: Architecture & Interior Design, Fiction, Literature, Literary Criticism, Essays, Philosophy, Psychology, Psychiatry

ISBN Prefix(es): 88-8003; 88-85685
Imprints: Giovanni Tranchida Editore
Distributor for Nessaggerie Libri Spa

Transeuropa, *imprint of* Il Lavoro Editoriale

Transeuropa Libri+
Via Piave 32, 60124 Ancona
Tel: (071) 52735 *Fax:* (071) 52610
Key Personnel
Man Dir: Massimo Canalini
Founded: 1988
Subjects: Architecture & Interior Design, Biological Sciences, Fiction, Film, Video, History, Literature, Literary Criticism, Essays, Medicine, Nursing, Dentistry, Philosophy, Women's Studies
ISBN Prefix(es): 88-7828
Orders to: PO Box 118, Ancona

Editrice Trasporti su Rotaie, see ETR (Editrice Trasporti su Rotaie)

Casa Editrice Luigi Trevisini
Via Livio 10/12, 20137 Milan
Tel: (02) 5450704 *Fax:* (02) 55195782 *Cable:* TREVISINI-MILANO
Key Personnel
Chief Executive: Luigi Trevisini
Editorial: Dr Giusi Trevisini
Founded: 1849
ISBN Prefix(es): 88-292

Il Tripode Srl
Viale Gramsci 19, 80122 Naples
Tel: (081) 7613086 *Fax:* (081) 681267
Key Personnel
Contact: D H Gluieppe Martanoj
Subjects: Antiques, Economics, English as a Second Language, Philosophy, Poetry, Romance
Warehouse: Via San Domenico, 39-61 Naples

Marco Tropea Editore+
Via Melzo 9, J-20129 Milan
Tel: (02) 29403460 *Fax:* (02) 29513061
E-mail: info@saggiatore.it
Key Personnel
President: Luca Formenton
Editor: Marco Tropea
Founded: 1995
Subjects: Fiction, Nonfiction (General)
ISBN Prefix(es): 88-438
Associate Companies: Il Saggiatore SpA e Nuova Pratiche Editrice

Turris+
Corso Garibaldi 215, 26100 Cremona
Tel: (0372) 23845 *Fax:* (0372) 413084
Founded: 1981
Subjects: Art, Music, Dance
ISBN Prefix(es): 88-85635; 88-7929
Bookshop(s): Corso Garibaldi 215, 26100 Cremona

Edizioni Ubulibri SAS+
Via Ramazzini 8, 20129 Milan
Tel: (02) 9404372 *Fax:* (02) 9510265
E-mail: ubulibri@libero.it
Key Personnel
Man Dir, Editorial: Franco Quadri
General Manager & Publicity: Tania Rainini
Founded: 1979
Subjects: Drama, Theater, Film, Video, Music, Dance
ISBN Prefix(es): 88-7748
Number of titles published annually: 12 Print
Total Titles: 120 Print
Warehouse: Messaggerie Libri SPA, Via Beaeguardena, 20080 Casarile, Miss Catto *Tel:* (02) 90092243 262

Editoriale Umbra SAS di Carnevali e
Via Pignattara, 34, 06034 Foligno (Perugia)
Tel: (0742) 353174 *Fax:* (0742) 351156
E-mail: edit.umbra@cline.it
Web Site: www.italand.com/eu *Cable:* EDITORIALE UMBRA FOLIGNO
Key Personnel
Man Dir, Editorial, Rights & Permissions, Sales: Giovanni Carnevali
Publicity: M Lise Burget
Founded: 1982
Subjects: Art, History, Literature, Literary Criticism, Essays, Regional Interests
ISBN Prefix(es): 88-85659

Edizioni Unicopli SpA+
Via della Signora, 2a, 20122 Milan
Tel: (02) 76014680 *Fax:* (02) 76021612
Key Personnel
Chief Executive: Michele Salvatore
Chief Editor: Marzio Zanantoni
Editorial, Psychology, Psychiatry: Stefano Nutini
Publicity: Roselle Savari
Founded: 1985
Subjects: Literature, Literary Criticism, Essays
ISBN Prefix(es): 88-7061; 88-400; 88-7090

Unipress+
Via Battisti 231, I-35121 Padova
Tel: (049) 8752542 *Fax:* (049) 8752542
Key Personnel
Editorial Dir: Gian Luigi Borgato
Founded: 1987
Subjects: Agriculture, Biological Sciences, Chemistry, Chemical Engineering, Language Arts, Linguistics, Literature, Literary Criticism, Essays, Philosophy, Psychology, Psychiatry
ISBN Prefix(es): 88-8098

Editrice Uomini Nuovi
Via Mazzini 73, 21030 Marchirolo (Varese)
Tel: (0332) 723007 *Fax:* (0332) 723264
E-mail: info@eun.ch
Web Site: www.eun.ch
Key Personnel
Chief Executive, Editorial: Dr Giuseppe E Laiso
Sales: Ruth Laiso
Publicity: Anna Rossinelli
Founded: 1964
Subjects: Biblical Studies, Biography, Human Relations, Psychology, Psychiatry, Religion - Other, Self-Help
ISBN Prefix(es): 88-8077
Subsidiaries: Radio Uomini Nuovi (Radio Cristiana Internazionale)
Bookshop(s): EUN

Urbaniana University Press+
Division of Pontificia Universita Urbaniana
Via Urbano VIII, 16, 00120 Citta Del Vaticano
Tel: (06) 6988 2351; (06) 6988 1745; (06) 6988 2182 *Fax:* (06) 6988 2182
E-mail: uupdir@urbaniana.edu; uupamm@urbaniana.edu
Key Personnel
Chief Executive, Rights & Permissions & Publicity: Gaspare Mura, PhD
Production: Marisa Mignolli
Administration: Giuseppe de Summa
Founded: 1968
Specialize in periodicals & essays.
Subjects: Anthropology, Biblical Studies, Law, Philosophy, Psychology, Psychiatry, Religion - Catholic, Theology, Missiology
ISBN Prefix(es): 88-401
Number of titles published annually: 14 Print
Total Titles: 500 Print
Imprints: UUP
Distributed by Dehoniana Libri
Showroom(s): Franfurt Book Messe

Bookshop(s): Libreria Bookshop, Pontificia Universita Urbaniana, 00120 Citta Del Vaticano; Libreria Vaticana
Orders to: Dehoniana Libri, Via Delle Fornaci, 47-51, 00165 Rome *Tel:* (06) 6382607 *Fax:* (06) 6390402

UT Orpheus Edizioni+
Piazza di Porta Ravegnana, 1, 40126 Bologna
Tel: (051) 263720 *Fax:* (051) 263720
E-mail: mail@utorpheus.com
Web Site: www.utorpheus.com
Key Personnel
Contact: Dr Antonello Lombardi; Roberto De Caro
Sales Manager: Prof Valeria Tarsetti
E-mail: vtarsetti@utorpheus.com
Founded: 1994
Italian publisher specializing in the publication of books on different music subjects, classical music.
Subjects: Music, Dance, classical music editions
ISBN Prefix(es): 88-8109
Number of titles published annually: 100 Print
Total Titles: 820 Print
Distributor for Forni (Facsimiles); Spes (Facsimiles)
Foreign Rep(s): MKT (Italy)
Bookshop(s): Ut Orpheus Libreria Musicale, Via Marsala 31/E, 40126 Bologna *Fax:* (051) 239295; Hortus Musicus, Viole Licgi 7/A, 00198 Roma *Tel:* (06) 8840230 *Fax:* (06) 8543261
Warehouse: Via Aldina 26/A Calderara Di Reno, Elisabetta Pistolozzi *Tel:* (051) 726138
Orders to: Ut Orpheus Libreria Musicale, Via Marsala 31/E, 40126 Bologna *Fax:* (051) 239295

UTET Periodici Scientifici
Viale Tunisia, 37, 20124 Milan
Tel: (02) 6241171 *Fax:* (02) 62411720
E-mail: utetre@tin.it
Key Personnel
General Manager: Corrado Trevisan
International Rights: Grazia Raccolli
Founded: 1987
Subjects: Medicine, Nursing, Dentistry
ISBN Prefix(es): 88-7933; 88-85647
Parent Company: UTET SpA

UTET (Unione Tipografico-Editrice Torinese)
Corso Raffaello 28, 10125 Turin
Tel: (011) 65291 *Fax:* (011) 6529240 *Cable:* UTET Turin
Key Personnel
President: Dr Gianni Merlini
Founded: 1791
Subjects: Architecture & Interior Design, Art, History, Law, Music, Dance, Philosophy, Psychology, Psychiatry, Religion - Other, Science (General), Social Sciences, Sociology, Veterinary Science
ISBN Prefix(es): 88-02

UUP, *imprint of* Urbaniana University Press

Vaccari SRL
Via M Buonarroti 46, 41058 Vignola Modena
Tel: (059) 764106 *Fax:* (059) 760157
E-mail: info@vaccari.it
Web Site: www.vaccari.it
Key Personnel
Book Manager: Valeria Vaccari
Founded: 1989
Subjects: Crafts, Games, Hobbies, Philately
ISBN Prefix(es): 88-85335
Number of titles published annually: 10 Print
Total Titles: 2,000 Online

Valdonega SRL
Division of Stamperia Valdomega
Via Genova 17, 37020 Arbizzano, Verona
Tel: (045) 6020444 *Fax:* (045) 6020334
E-mail: valdoneg@valdonega.it
Specialize in books on books, limited art editions & quality productions.
ISBN Prefix(es): 88-85033
Number of titles published annually: 3 Print
Total Titles: 15 Print

Vallardi & Assoc
Via Galilei 6, 20124 Milan
Tel: (02) 6555545 *Fax:* (02) 6555640
Telex: 330326 GECVAL I
ISBN Prefix(es): 88-85202

Vallardi Industrie Grafiche+
Via Trieste 20, 20020 Lainate, Milan
Tel: (02) 9370284 *Fax:* (02) 93570442
Key Personnel
Publisher: Giuseppe Vallardi
Editorial: Emanuela Vallardi
Founded: 1969
ISBN Prefix(es): 88-7696

Valmartina Editore SRL+
Str del Portone 177, 10095 Grugliasco, Turin
Tel: (011) 3158711 *Fax:* (011) 3158710
Key Personnel
President: Luigi Vecchia
Editorial: Carlo Pasquinelli
Production: Giorgio Raccis
Rights & Permissions: Michela Melchiori
Founded: 1951
Subjects: Language Arts, Linguistics, Travel
ISBN Prefix(es): 88-494
Orders to: Via L Dottesio 1, I-35138 Padua *Tel:* (049) 8710099

Societa Editrice Vannini
Via Mandolossa, 117/A, 25064 Gussago
Tel: (030) 313374 *Fax:* (030) 314078 *Cable:* VANNINI BRESCIA
Founded: 1950
ISBN Prefix(es): 88-86430

Libreria Edtrice Vaticana
Via della Tipografia, 00120 Citta del Vaticano
Tel: (06) 69885003 *Fax:* (06) 69884716
E-mail: lev@publish.va
ISBN Prefix(es): 88-209

Giovanni De Vecchi Editore SpA, see Giovanni De Vecchi Editore SpA

Verso il Futuro, *imprint of* Casa Editrice Menna di Sinisgalli Menna Giuseppina

Veschi
Via Bressan, 2, 20126 Milan
Tel: (02) 270741 *Fax:* (02) 27074510
ISBN Prefix(es): 88-413

Vianello Libri+
Via Postioma 85, 31050 Ponzano (TV)
Tel: (0422) 440666 *Fax:* (0422) 440645
E-mail: vianello@mail.gpnet.it
Key Personnel
Contact: Giancarlo Buscaini; Livio Scibilia; Andrea Montagnani
Subjects: Architecture & Interior Design, Photography
ISBN Prefix(es): 88-7200
Orders to: Grafiche Vianello, Via Postioma 85, 31050 Ponzano

Vinciana Editrice sas+
Via Foppa, 14, 20144 Milan
Tel: (02) 4982306 *Fax:* (02) 48003275
E-mail: info@vinciana.com
Web Site: www.vinciana.com
Founded: 1976
Specialize in fine art.
Subjects: Art, Crafts, Games, Hobbies, How-to, Veterinary Science
ISBN Prefix(es): 88-86256
Total Titles: 42 Print

Vision Srl
Via Livorno, 20, 00161 Rome
Tel: (06) 44292688 *Fax:* (06) 44292688
E-mail: Vision.srl@stm.it
Web Site: www.visionpubl.com

Visual Itineraries, *imprint of* BeMa

Vita e Pensiero+
L go A Gemelli, 1, 20123 Milan
Tel: (02) 72342335; (02) 72342259 *Fax:* (02) 72342260
E-mail: editvep@mi.unicatt.it
Web Site: www.vitaepensiero.it
Telex: 321033 Ucatmi I
Key Personnel
President: Prof Sergio Zaninelli
Editorial Dir: Dr Aurelio Mottola *Fax:* (02) 72342660 *E-mail:* amottola@mi.unicatt.it
Founded: 1918
Member of Associazione Italiana Editori, Unione Editori Cattolici Italiani, Unione Stampa Periodica Italiana, Associazione Librai Italiani.
Subjects: History, Literature, Literary Criticism, Essays, Mathematics, Medicine, Nursing, Dentistry, Philosophy, Psychology, Psychiatry, Religion - Other
ISBN Prefix(es): 88-343
Number of titles published annually: 100 Print
Bookshop(s): Libreria Vita e Pensiero, L go A Gemelli, 1, 20123 Milan *E-mail:* eibreria.vp@mi.umicatt.it

La Vita Felice
Via Plinio Tadino 52, 20124 Milan
Tel: (02) 29524600 *Fax:* (02) 29401896
Subjects: Fiction, Literature, Literary Criticism, Essays, Poetry
ISBN Prefix(es): 88-86314; 88-7799

Vivalda Editori SRL+
Via Invorio 24 a, 10146 Turin
Tel: (011) 7720444 *Fax:* (011) 7720499
E-mail: vivalda@vivalda.com
Key Personnel
President: Dr Giorgio Vivalda
General Dir & Administrative Representative: Mario Dalmaviva
Founded: 1972
Subjects: Sports, Athletics
ISBN Prefix(es): 88-7808
Divisions: CDA

Vivere In SRL
Via di Acque Salvie, 1/A, 00142 Rome
Tel: (080) 065943323 *Fax:* (080) 065943323
E-mail: edizioniviverein@tin.it
Web Site: www.viverein.it
Subjects: Biblical Studies, Biography, Philosophy, Poetry, Regional Interests, Religion - Catholic, Social Sciences, Sociology, Theology, Essays
ISBN Prefix(es): 88-7263
Number of titles published annually: 15 Print
Total Titles: 350 Print
Distributed by Agenzia Libraria GALL SRL; Agenzia Libraria S Fozzi; Citta Nuova Centro; DEM Libri SRL; Distrimedia SRL; Ditta Restivo SRL; Ferrari Libri SRL; L'Editoriale SRL

Viviani Editore srl+
Piazza della Maddalena 6, 00186 Rome
Tel: (06) 6872855 *Fax:* (06) 6872856
Key Personnel
Contact: Lia Viviani
Founded: 1992
Member of AIE.
Subjects: Art, Biography, Drama, Theater, Literature, Literary Criticism, Essays
ISBN Prefix(es): 88-7993

Voce della Bibbia
Via Cavallotti 14, 41043 Formigine (Modena)
Tel: (059) 55 63 03 *Fax:* (059) 57 31 05
E-mail: bbitaly@tin.it
Web Site: www.vocedellabibbia.org
Key Personnel
General Dir: Ettore Calanchi
Founded: 1961
Subjects: Biblical Studies, Health, Nutrition, Music, Dance
Parent Company: Back to the Bible Broadcast, Box 82808, Lincoln, NE 68501, United States

Who's Who In Italy SRL
Via de Amicis 2, 20091 Bresso-Milan
Tel: (02) 66503753 *Fax:* (02) 6105587
E-mail: whoswhogc@ibm.net
Web Site: www.WHOSWHO-SUTTER.COM
Key Personnel
Man Dir: Giancarlo Colombo
Founded: 1977
Specialize in reference books, International publishers of Who's Who titles in 6 different nations in the English language & of particular interest to the world of business, politics, culture, art, science, education, etc, with cross-references between biographies & profiles of companies & institutions.
Member of Associazione Italiana Editori (Italian Publishers' Assn).
Subjects: Biography, Business, Management
ISBN Prefix(es): 88-85246
Number of titles published annually: 3 Print
Parent Company: Who's Who Sutters International Red Series Verlag AG, Seestr 357, 8038 Zurich, Switzerland
Subsidiaries: Who's Who Sutters International Red Series Verlag GmbH; Who's Who Strategic Area; Who's Who in Spain SA
Distributed by The Eurospan Group (England)
Distributor for UPS - United Publishers Services Ltd

Silvio Zamorani editore
Corso S Maurizio 25, 10124 Turin
Tel: (011) 8125700 *Fax:* (011) 8126144
Founded: 1984
ISBN Prefix(es): 88-7158

ZAN, *imprint of* Casa Musicale G Zanibon SRL

Zanfi Editori SRL+
Via Emilia Ovest 954, I-41100 Modena
Tel: (059) 891700 *Fax:* (059) 891701
Telex: 522272
Key Personnel
Contact: Celestino Zanfi
Founded: 1979
Member of Distripress.
Subjects: Cookery, Fashion, Gardening, Plants, Health, Nutrition, Outdoor Recreation, Religion - Buddhist, Travel
ISBN Prefix(es): 88-85168; 88-86169; 88-8169

Casa Musicale G Zanibon SRL+
Via Berchet, 2, 20121 Milan
Tel: (02) 88811 *Fax:* (02) 88814317
Telex: 88814317 *Cable:* IDROCIR MILANO
Key Personnel
Contact: Cristiano Giovannini
Founded: 1908
Subjects: Education, Music, Dance
ISBN Prefix(es): 88-86642
Imprints: GZ; ZAN
Subsidiaries: Edizioni Drago; Edizioni Orfeo

Zanichelli Editore SpA+
Via Irnerio 34, 40126 Bologna
Tel: (051) 293111 *Fax:* (051) 249782
E-mail: zanichelli@zanichelli.it
Key Personnel
Chairman: Lorenzo Enriques
Dir General & Vice President: Federico Enriques
Founded: 1859
Subjects: Anthropology, Architecture & Interior Design, Biological Sciences, Chemistry, Chemical Engineering, Computer Science, Earth Sciences, Economics, Education, Electronics, Electrical Engineering, Engineering (General), English as a Second Language, Geography, Geology, History, Language Arts, Linguistics, Law, Literature, Literary Criticism, Essays, Mechanical Engineering, Medicine, Nursing, Dentistry, Philosophy, Photography, Physics, Psychology, Psychiatry, Science (General), Social Sciences, Sociology
ISBN Prefix(es): 88-08
Subsidiaries: Loescher Editore srl; CEA Casa Editrice Ambrosiana srl; ESAC Edizioni Scientifiche A Cremonese srl
Distributor for Bovolenta; Decibel; Lucisano; Signorelli
Warehouse: Via Del Lavoro 15, 40050 Quarto Inferiore (BO)

Edizioni Zara
Via Toscana 80, 1-43100 Parma
Tel: (0521) 489956 *Fax:* (0521) 241750
Key Personnel
Chief Executive: Isabella Marchesi
Editorial: Giancarlo Zarattini
Founded: 1979
Also acts as distributor for Edizioni Artegrafica Silva, Parma.
Subjects: Drama, Theater, Environmental Studies, Geography, Geology, Language Arts, Linguistics, Literature, Literary Criticism, Essays, Natural History, Philosophy, Religion - Catholic
Distributor for Parita; Silva Editore

Jamaica

General Information

Capital: Kingston
Language: English
Religion: Predominantly Protestant
Population: 2.5 million
Bank Hours: 0900-1400 Monday-Thursday; 0900-1200, 1430-1700 Friday
Shop Hours: Downtown Kingston: 0900-1600 Monday and Tuesday, Thursday-Saturday; 0900-1200 Wednesday. Other areas: 0900-1700, with early closing Thursday
Currency: 100 cents = 1 Jamaican dollar
Export/Import Information: No tariff on books, but advertising matter dutied. No import license required for books; no obscene literature permitted. No exchange restrictions.
Copyright: Berne (see Copyright Conventions, pg xi)

American Chamber of Commerce of Jamaica+
77 Knutsford Blvd, Kingston 5
Tel: (876) 929-7866 *Fax:* (876) 929-8597
Key Personnel
Chief Executive Officer: Dr Ofe S Dudley
Member of Chamber of Commerce of The USA.
Subjects: Environmental Studies, Management, Marketing
ISBN Prefix(es): 976-8113
Parent Company: Chamber of Commerce of The USA (COCUSA)
Divisions: Association of American Chamber of Commerce of Latin America (AACCLA)

Association of Development Agencies
14 South Ave, Kingston 10
Tel: (876) 9602319; (876) 9683605 *Fax:* (876) 9298773
Founded: 1985
Forum for collective analysis, discussion, planning & collaboration.
Subjects: Communications, Developing Countries, House & Home, Regional Interests, Self-Help, Women's Studies
ISBN Prefix(es): 976-8112

Canoe Press+
Imprint of University of the West Indies
One A Aqueduct Flats, Mona, Kingston 7
Tel: (876) 977-2659 *Fax:* (876) 977-2660
E-mail: salex@uwimona.edu.jm
Key Personnel
Contact: Pansy Benn
Founded: 1992
Subjects: Scholarly Caribbean
ISBN Prefix(es): 976-640
Distributor for UWI Publications

Carib Publishing Ltd, *imprint of* West Indies Publishing Ltd

Caribbean Authors Publishing
12 Brentford Rd, Kingston 5
Tel: (876) 929-1226 *Fax:* (876) 929-3721
Key Personnel
Dir: Peter D Clarke
ISBN Prefix(es): 976-8037
Associate Companies: Multi Sector Consultants Ltd

Caribbean Food & Nutrition Institute
Jamaica Centre, Kingston 7
Mailing Address: PO Box 140, Kingston 7
Tel: (876) 927-3829
Telex: 3705 *Cable:* CAJANUS
ISBN Prefix(es): 976-626

The Caribbean Law Publishing Co Ltd
206 Old Hope Rd, Kingston 6
Tel: (876) 927-2085 *Fax:* (876) 977-0243
Key Personnel
International Rights: Ian Randle
Founded: 1996
Legal publishing on CD-ROM.
Subjects: Law
ISBN Prefix(es): 976-8167
Associate Companies: Ian Randle Publishers Ltd
Distributor for Juta Publishers

Carlong Publishers (Caribbean) Ltd+
33 Second St, Newport West, Kingston 13
Mailing Address: PO Box 489, Kingston 10
Tel: (876) 923-6505 *Fax:* (876) 923-7003
E-mail: sales@carlpub.com *Cable:* CARLONG KINGSTON
Key Personnel
Man Dir: Shirley Carby
Publishing Manager, Rights & Permissions: Dorothy Noel *E-mail:* commissioning@carlpub.com
Sales & Distribution: Lorna Allen
Editor: Lauren Kerr-Harvey *E-mail:* production@carlpub.com
Publisher: Jenni Anderson *E-mail:* publisher@carlbpub.com
Founded: 1990
Subjects: Business, Drama, Theater, Foreign Countries, Geography, Geology, History, Hu-

man Relations, Language Arts, Linguistics, Literature, Literary Criticism, Essays, Mathematics, Science (General), Social Sciences, Sociology
ISBN Prefix(es): 976-8010; 976-638
Total Titles: 92 Print
Distributor for Pearson Education (Restrictions: Publishing); Penguin Books Ltd (N B Now own the right to publish some titles formerly belonging to Carib Publishing Limited)
Foreign Rights: Albert Nathaniel (Saint Lucia & Saint Vincent); Andrea Permel (Trinadad & Tobago); Franklyn Laws (Saint Kitts-Nevis); Leroy Mulraine (Saint Lucia & Saint Vincent); Lloyd Austin (South America); Louis Forde (Barbados)
Showroom(s): 17 Ruthven Rd, Bldg 3, Kingston 10, Contact: Mrs Dorothy Noel
Tel: (876) 9609364-6 *Fax:* (876) 9681353
E-mail: commissioning@carlpub.com (Publishing)

CVM Publications+
c/o Dept of Management Studies, University of the West Indies, Mona, Kingston 7
Tel: (876) 977-3829 *Fax:* (876) 927-4117
Key Personnel
International Rights: Margaret Mendes
Founded: 1987
Specialize in Caribbean accounting texts.
Subjects: Accounting, Management
ISBN Prefix(es): 976-8053
Distributed by The Press; University of the West Indies

Eureka Press Ltd
5 1/2 Caledonia Rd, Mandeville
Mailing Address: PO Box 628, Mandeville
Tel: (876) 962-3947 *Fax:* (876) 961-5383
E-mail: eurekapr@cwjamaica.com
Subjects: Biography, Education, Religion - Other, Theology
ISBN Prefix(es): 976-8029

Gleaner Co Ltd
7 North St, Kingston
Mailing Address: PO Box 40, Kingston
Tel: (876) 922-2340 *Fax:* (876) 922-2319; (876) 922-6297; (876) 922-6223
Telex: 2319
ISBN Prefix(es): 976-612

Green Island Press, *imprint of* Ian Randle Publishers Ltd

Institute of Jamaica Publications+
2A Suthermere Rd, Kingston 10
Tel: (876) 926-5683; (876) 929-4786; (876) 929-4785 *Fax:* (876) 926-8817
Key Personnel
Man Dir: Patricia V Stevens
Founded: 1967
Subjects: Ethnicity, Fiction, History, Natural History, Nonfiction (General), Science (General), Social Sciences, Sociology
ISBN Prefix(es): 976-8017

The Jamaica Bauxite Institute
PO Box 355, Kingston 6
Tel: (876) 927-2073; (876) 927-2079 *Fax:* (876) 927-1159
E-mail: info@jbi.org.jm
Telex: 2309 *Cable:* JAMBAUX JA
Key Personnel
Chairman: Carlton E Davis
General Manager: Mr Parris A Lyew-Ayee
Public Relations Officer: Hilary Coulton
Founded: 1975
Subjects: Earth Sciences, Economics
ISBN Prefix(es): 976-8072

Jamaica Bureau of Standards
6 Winchester Rd, Kingston 10
Mailing Address: PO Box 113, Kingston 10
Tel: (876) 926-3140 *Fax:* (876) 929-4736
Telex: 2291 Stanbur Ja *Cable:* STANBUREAU
Key Personnel
Executive Dir: Dr Artnel Henry
Librarian: Andrea Robins
Founded: 1968
Member of the International Organization for Standardization.
ISBN Prefix(es): 976-604

Jamaica Information Service
58A Half Way Tree Rd, Kingston 10
Tel: (876) 926-3740; (876) 926-3749 *Fax:* (876) 926-6715
E-mail: jis@jis.gov.jm; jis@researchjis.gov.jm
Web Site: www.jis.gov.jm
ISBN Prefix(es): 976-633
U.S. Office(s): 1520 New Hampshire Ave, NW, Washington, DC 20036, United States *Tel:* 202-452-0660 *Fax:* 202-986-0184
Jamaica Consulate General, 842 Ingraham Bldg, 25 SE Second Ave, Miami, FL 33131, United States *Tel:* 305-374-8385 *Fax:* 305-374-9674
767 Third Ave, 3rd floor, New York, NY 10017, United States *Tel:* 212-935-9000 *Fax:* 212-935-7507

Jamaica Printing Services
77 1/2 Duke St, Kingston
Mailing Address: PO Box 487, Kingston
Tel: (876) 967-2250 *Fax:* (876) 967-2225
Subjects: Law

Jamaica Publishing House Ltd+
97 Church St, Kingston
Tel: (876) 922-1385; (876) 967-3866 *Fax:* (876) 922-5412
E-mail: jph@jol.com.jm *Cable:* JAPUB
Key Personnel
Chairman: Woodburn Miller
Manager: Elaine R Stennett
Founded: 1969
Subjects: Biography, Education, Geography, Geology, History, House & Home, Language Arts, Linguistics, Literature, Literary Criticism, Essays, Mathematics, Psychology, Psychiatry, Social Sciences, Sociology
ISBN Prefix(es): 976-606
Parent Company: Jamaica Teachers' Association

Jamrite Publications+
Suite 22, Spanish Court, One Lucia Ave, Kingston 5
Tel: (876) 926-1180; (876) 926-1181 *Fax:* (876) 968-4519
E-mail: blackolive@cwjamaica.com
Key Personnel
Contact: Christopher Issa *Tel:* (876) 968 9939
Founded: 1981
Subjects: Books on Jamaican Culture
Parent Company: Richard James & Associates Ltd

Kingston Publishers Ltd+
7 Norman Rd, LOJ Complex, Bldg 10, Kingston 5
Tel: (876) 927-8899 *Fax:* (876) 928-5719
Telex: Fitzgram 2293 *Cable:* KINGBOOKS
Key Personnel
Chairman: L M J Henry
Editor: Kim Robinson-Walcott; Julia Tan
Marketing Manager, Overseas: Dawn Chambers
Founded: 1972
Subjects: Cookery, Fiction, Music, Dance, Nonfiction (General), Romance, Travel
ISBN Prefix(es): 976-625
Shipping Address: International Freight Consolidators, 6885 NW 25 St, Miami, FL 33122, United States

Packer-Evans and Associates Ltd+
13 Stevenson Ave, Kingston 8
Tel: 924-1270 *Fax:* 926-3487
Key Personnel
Chairman, Rights and Permissions & Sales: Omri l Evans
Man Dir & Sales: Dr Claude Packer
Sales & Publicity: Norma Evans
Production: Gloria Foresythe; Carol Anglin
Publicity: Lisa Packer
Founded: 1984
Subjects: Mathematics
ISBN Prefix(es): 976-8022

The Press+
Imprint of University of the West Indies
One A Aqueduct Flats, Mona, Kingston 7
Tel: (876) 977-2659 *Fax:* (876) 977-2660
E-mail: salex@uwimona.edu.jm
Web Site: www.uwimona.edu.jm/press
Key Personnel
Dir: Pansy Benn
Founded: 1992
Member of the Book Industry Association of Jamaica. Also acts as marketer & distributor for departments of the University of the West Indies.
Subjects: Ethnicity, Government, Political Science, History
ISBN Prefix(es): 976-640

Ian Randle Publishers Ltd+
11 Cunningham Ave, Kingston 6
Mailing Address: PO Box 686, Kingston 6
Tel: (876) 978-0739; (876) 978-0745 *Fax:* (876) 978-1156
E-mail: irpl@colis.com
Web Site: www.colis.com/irp
Key Personnel
President & Publisher: Ian Randle
Business Manager: Carlene Randle
Founded: 1991
Specialize in Caribbean Studies; also acts as publishers agent.
Subjects: Biography, Cookery, History, Sports, Athletics, Women & Gender Studies
ISBN Prefix(es): 976-8100; 976-8123
Associate Companies: The Caribbean Law Publishing Co; Ian Randle Publishers (Barbados) Ltd
Imprints: Green Island Press
Distributor for Houghton Mifflin; Routledge

Alice J M Rhodd
c/o JBC Radio Waves, 37 St James St, Montego Bay
Key Personnel
Author: Alice J M Rhodd
Self publisher specializing in reading (Dyslexia).
Subjects: Disability, Special Needs, Radio, TV, Technology, Educational & Media Broadcasting
ISBN Prefix(es): 976-8042
Bookshop(s): Henderson's Bookstore, Montego Bay

Scientific Research Council
Hope Gardens, Kingston 6
Mailing Address: PO Box 350, Kingston 6
Tel: (876) 9271771; (876) 9271774 *Fax:* (876) 9271990
Telex: SCRSTIN JA
ISBN Prefix(es): 976-8126
Parent Company: Scientific Research Council
Subsidiaries: Marketech Ltd

Twin Guinep Ltd+
Red Hills PO, PO Box 34, St Andrew
Tel: (876) 944-4624 *Fax:* (876) 944-4324
Key Personnel
International Rights: Dennis Ranston

JAMAICA

E-mail: ranston@kasnet.com; Jacqueline Ranston
Founded: 1974
ISBN Prefix(es): 976-8007

University of the West Indies Press+
1A Aqueduct Flats, Mona, Kingston 7
Tel: 9772659; 7024082
Web Site: www.uwipress.com
Key Personnel
Dir: Linda E Speth *E-mail:* lspeth@cwjamaica.com
Finance Manager: Nadine Buckland
  E-mail: nbuckland@cwjamaica.com
Production Manager: Shivaun Hearne
  E-mail: hearnes@cwjamaica.com
Marketing & Sales Manager: Donna Muirhead
  E-mail: cuserv@cwjamaica.com
Founded: 1992
Academic book publisher.
Subjects: Anthropology, Environmental Studies, Ethnicity, History, Literature, Literary Criticism, Essays, Natural History, Social Sciences, Sociology, Women's Studies
ISBN Prefix(es): 976-8125; 976-640; 976-41
Number of titles published annually: 25 Print
Total Titles: 160 Print
Distributed by University of Oklahoma Press
Distributor for The Mill Press; Sir Arthur Lewis Institute
Foreign Rep(s): Eurospan (Middle East, UK & the continent); EWEB (Australia, Asia, New Zealand, Pacific); Lexicon (Trinidad West Indies); University of Oklahoma Press (Canada, North America)

UWI Publishers' Association
PO Box 42, Mona, Kingston 7
Tel: (876) 927-1020 *Fax:* (876) 977-2660
Key Personnel
Publication Officer: Annie Paul
Subjects: Literature, Literary Criticism, Essays
ISBN Prefix(es): 976-43

West Indies Publishing Ltd+
7-9 Norman Rd, Unit 33, Kingston CSO
Tel: (876) 928-9081 *Fax:* (876) 928-5269
Key Personnel
Chairman: Patrick H O Rousseau
Man Dir: D Andrew Rousseau
Publishing Manager: Diane Browne
Production & Communications Manager: Gina Harrison
Founded: 1976
Subjects: Cookery, Education, Fiction, Geography, Geology, History, Mathematics, Science (General)
ISBN Prefix(es): 976-605
Imprints: Carib Publishing Ltd
Subsidiaries: The Book Shop Ltd; Book Traders (Caribbean) Ltd; Carib Publishing Ltd
Distributor for Heinemann UK (Northern Caribbean)
Bookshop(s): The Springs, 15-17 Constant Spring Rd; Kingston 10; LOJ Shopping Centre, Shop No 17, 28-48 Barbados Ave, Kingston 5; Lane Plaza, 36 Manchester Rd, Mandeville, Manchester; 17 Burke Rd, Spanish Town; LOJ Shopping Centre, Shop No 12; Shops 12 & 13, Montego Bay Shopping Centre, Howard Cooke Blvd, Montego Bay, St James
Orders to: Book Traders (Caribbean) Ltd, Kingston

Japan

General Information

Capital: Tokyo
Language: Japanese
Religion: Shinto and Buddhism
Population: 125 million
Bank Hours: 0900-1500 Monday-Friday; 0900-1200 Saturday
Shop Hours: Same as bank hours
Currency: 100 yen = 1 dollar
Export/Import Information: 3% consumption; tax on books.
Copyright: UCC, Berne, Florence, Rome (see Copyright Conventions, pg xi)

ACCJ, *imprint of* The American Chamber of Commerce in Japan

ADA Edita Tokyo Co Ltd
12-14 Sendagaya 3 chome, Shibuya-ku, Tokyo 151-0051
Tel: (03) 34031581 *Fax:* (03) 34031582
Key Personnel
Dir: Yukio Futagawa
Sales Manager: Tatsuo Futagawa
Founded: 1972
Subjects: Architecture & Interior Design
ISBN Prefix(es): 4-87140
U.S. Office(s): G A International/Co Ltd, 180 Varick St, 4th floor, New York, NY 10014, United States *Tel:* 212-741-6329 *Fax:* 212-741-6283

Aiki News
3-201 Daikyo-Machi, Shinjuku-ku, Tokyo 160
Tel: (03) 33596265
Key Personnel
Editor-in-Chief: Stanley A Pranin
English Editor: Diane Skoss
Founded: 1988
Member of COSMEP.
Subjects: Sports, Athletics
ISBN Prefix(es): 4-900586

Akita Shoten Publishing Co Ltd
2-10-8 Iidabashi, 2 Chome, Chioyoda-ku, Tokyo 102-0072
Tel: (03) 32647249 *Fax:* (03) 32659076
Key Personnel
President: Sadami Akita
Editorial: Nobumichi Akutsu; Taizo Kabemura
Sales: Toshimichi Okubo
Foreign Rights: Noriyoshi Oda
Founded: 1948
Subjects: History, Literature, Literary Criticism, Essays, Social Sciences, Sociology
ISBN Prefix(es): 4-253

Alice-Kan+
2-14-13 Mejirodai, 2 Chome, Bunkyo Ku, Tokyo 112-0015
Tel: (03) 59767013 *Fax:* (03) 39438396
Key Personnel
President: Yu Kobayashi
Founded: 1981
Subjects: Child Care & Development
ISBN Prefix(es): 4-7520
Parent Company: Rodojunposh

The American Chamber of Commerce in Japan+
Tranomon Bldg, 3-25-2 Toranomon, Minato-ku, Tokyo 105-0001
Tel: (03) 34335381 *Fax:* (03) 34361446
Key Personnel
Dir, Publications: Jeanmarie Todd
Founded: 1948
Specialize in helping US business expand in Japan.
Subjects: Business, Foreign Countries, Marketing, Travel
ISBN Prefix(es): 4-915682
Imprints: ACCJ
U.S. Office(s): ACCJ, c/o US Chamber of Commerce, International Division, 1615 H St NW, Washington, DC 20062, United States *Tel:* 202-463-5460 *Fax:* 202-463-3114
Distributed by Charles E Tuttle Co (Japan & USA)

Aoki Shoten Co Ltd
1-60 Kanda-Jimbocho, 1 Chome, Chiyoda-ku, Tokyo 101-0051
Tel: (03) 32192341 *Fax:* (03) 32192585
Key Personnel
President: Masato Aoki
Foreign Trade: Kiyoshi Furukawa
Foreign Rights: Toyoichi Eguchi
Founded: 1947
Subjects: Social Sciences, Sociology
ISBN Prefix(es): 4-250

Asahiya Shuppan
3-4 Ichigaya-Sadohora-cho, 3 Chome, Shinjuku-ku, Tokyo 162-0842
Tel: (03) 32670865 *Fax:* (03) 32680928
Key Personnel
President: Takeshi Hayashima
ISBN Prefix(es): 4-7511

Asakura Publishing Co Ltd+
6-29 Shin-Ogawa machi, Shinjuku-ku, Tokyo 162-8707
Tel: (03) 32600141 *Fax:* (03) 32600180
Key Personnel
President: Kunizo Asakura
Foreign Trade: Hideo Shirahara
Foreign Rights: Haruo Obata
Founded: 1929
ISBN Prefix(es): 4-254

Atelier Publishing Co Ltd
c/o Shinichi Bldg, 8 Yotsuya, 2 Chome, Shinjuku-ku, Tokyo 160-0004
Tel: (03) 33572741 *Fax:* (03) 33572194
Key Personnel
President: Taisuke Hirabayashi
ISBN Prefix(es): 4-7518

AVACO - Christian Mass Communications Center
2-3-18 Nishi Waseda, Shinjuku-ku, Tokyo 169-0051
Tel: (03) 32034121 *Fax:* (03) 32034186
E-mail: avaco@ppp.fastnet.or.jp
Key Personnel
Executive Dir: Ohta Futoshi
Subjects: Education, Religion - Protestant

Baberu Inc+
Uetake Bldg, 3-6 Nishi-Kanda, 1 chome, Chiyoda-ku, Tokyo 101
Tel: (03) 32952306 *Fax:* (03) 32957128
Key Personnel
President: Ms Miyoko Yuasa
Dir, Planning & Editing Dept: Mr Maruhama Tetsuro
Founded: 1976
ISBN Prefix(es): 4-931049; 4-89449

Baifukan Co Ltd
4-3-12 Kudan-Hinami, Chiyoda, Tokyo 102-0074
Tel: (03) 32625270 *Fax:* (03) 32625276
Key Personnel
Chairman: Kenji Yamamoto
President, Sales: Itaru Yamamoto
Editorial: Masayuki Gotou; Takashi Murayama; Kazunori Matsumoto

Production: Fumio Shigematu
Editorial, Rights & Permissions: Tsuyoshi Nohara
Founded: 1924
Subjects: Biological Sciences, Chemistry, Chemical Engineering, Computer Science, Engineering (General), Mathematics, Physics, Psychology, Psychiatry, Social Sciences, Sociology
ISBN Prefix(es): 4-563

Baseball Magazine-Sha Co Ltd+
10-10 Misaki-cho, 3 Chome, Chiyoda-ku, Toyko 101-8381
Tel: (03) 32380285 *Fax:* (03) 32380084
Key Personnel
Chairman: Tsuneo Ikeda
President: Ikuo Ikeda
Founded: 1946
Subjects: History, Psychology, Psychiatry, Sports, Athletics
ISBN Prefix(es): 4-583
Subsidiaries: Kobunsha Co Ltd
Branch Office(s)
15 rue des Abessess, F-75018 Paris, France
Tokuma Bldg, 6-16 Nozaki-cho, Kita-ku, Osaka-shi, Osaka *Tel:* (06) 3156141

Bijutsu Shuppan-Sha, Ltd
Inaokakudan Bldg, 2-38 Kanda Jinbo-cho, Chiyoda-ku, Tokyo 101-8417
Tel: (03) 32342151 *Fax:* (03) 32349451
Web Site: www.bijutsu.co.jp *Cable:* FINEART BOOK TOKYO
Key Personnel
Chairman: Atsushi Oshita
President: Kentaro Oshita
Sales Manager: Hiroshi Mizukoshi
Founded: 1905
Subjects: Architecture & Interior Design, Art, Crafts, Games, Hobbies, How-to
ISBN Prefix(es): 4-568

Bun-ichi Sogo Shuppan
13-10, Nishi-Goken-cho, Shinjuku-ku, Tokyo 162-0812
Tel: (03) 32357341 *Fax:* (03) 32691402
E-mail: bunichi@vinet.or.jp
Key Personnel
President: Takeshi Okumura
Subjects: Biological Sciences, Electronics, Electrical Engineering, Environmental Studies, Natural History, Photography
ISBN Prefix(es): 4-8299

Bunkasha Publishing Co, Ltd+
29-6, Ichibancho Chiyoda-ku, Tokyo 102
Tel: (03) 32225111 *Fax:* (03) 32223666
E-mail: fukai@bunkasha.co.jp
Key Personnel
President: Kenichi Kai
Founded: 1948
Member of Japan Book Publishers Association, Japan Publishers Club, Japan Magazine Publishers Association, Japan Magazine Fair Trade Council for Promotion of Book Reading, Publishers Association for Cultural Exchange, National Council to Promote Ethic of Massmedia.
Subjects: Fashion, Fiction, Film, Video, Sports, Athletics
Parent Company: Bunkasha Publishing Co, Ltd

Bunkashobo-Hakubun-Sha
9-9 Mejirodai, 1 Chome, Bunkyo-ku, Tokyo 112-0015
Tel: (03) 39472034 *Fax:* (03) 39474976
Key Personnel
President: Sadayoshi Suzuki
Editor: Mr Y Amano
ISBN Prefix(es): 4-8301

Business Center for Academic Societies Japan
16-9 Honkomagome 5-chome, Bunkyo-ku, Tokyo 113
Tel: (03) 58145811 *Fax:* (03) 58145822
E-mail: gen@bcasj.or.jp
Key Personnel
Dir General: Mitsuoka Tomotari, PhD
Man Dir, Rights & Permissions: Konno Shozo
Production: B Todoroki
Founded: 1971
Subjects: Science (General)
ISBN Prefix(es): 4-930813
Associate Companies: Japan Scientific Societies Press, 2-10 Hongo 6-chome, Bunkyo-ku, Tokyo 113; Center for Academic Publications Japan, 4-16, Yayoi 2-chome, Bunkyo-ku, Tokyo 113

Chijin Shokan Co Ltd+
15, Naka-machi, Shinjuku-ku, Tokyo 162-0835
Tel: (03) 32354422 *Fax:* (03) 32358984
E-mail: KYY02177@nifty.ne.jp
Web Site: www.chijishokan.co.jp
Key Personnel
President: Osamu Kamijo
Editorial Manager: Akira Tsuda
Man Dir: Tomoaki Ogawa
Founded: 1930
Member of Japan Book Publishers Association.
Subjects: Engineering (General), Medicine, Nursing, Dentistry, Physical Sciences, Science (General), Technology
ISBN Prefix(es): 4-8052
Total Titles: 450 Print
Foreign Rep(s): Asano Agency (Worldwide); English Agency (Japan); Japan Uni Agency (Japan); Orion Press (Worldwide); Tuttle-Mori Agency (Japan)

Chikuma Shobo Publishing Co Ltd+
5-3 Kuramae, Komuro Bldg, 2 Chome, Taito-ku, Tokyo 111-0051
Tel: (03) 5687-2687 *Fax:* (03) 5687-2688
Web Site: www.chikumashobo.co.jp
Key Personnel
President: Akio Kikuchi *E-mail:* kikuchia@chikumashobo.co.jp
Editorial, Rights & Permissions: Tetsuo Matsuda
Sales, Publicity: Tatsuji Tanaka
Production: Isao Miyazono
Founded: 1940
Subjects: Biography, Communications, Economics, Education, Fiction, History, Human Relations, Nonfiction (General), Philosophy, Religion - Buddhist, Social Sciences, Sociology, Women's Studies
ISBN Prefix(es): 4-480

Chikyu-sha Co Ltd
3-5 Akasaka 4 chome, Minato-ku, Tokyo 107-0052
Tel: (03) 35850087 *Fax:* (03) 35892902
Key Personnel
President: Minoru Toda
Founded: 1946
ISBN Prefix(es): 4-8049

Child Honsha Co Ltd+
5-24-21 Koishikawa, 5 Chome, Bunkyo-ku, Tokyo 112-0002
Tel: (03) 38133781 *Fax:* (03) 38184970
Key Personnel
President: Yoshiaki Shimazaki
Editorial, Foreign Rights: Kazuhisa Vemura
Sales, Publicity & Foreign Trade: Katsuharu Mibu
Production: Shunzi Asaka
Rights & Permissions: Kotaro Ohashi
Founded: 1930
Subjects: Education
ISBN Prefix(es): 4-8054
Associate Companies: Kyodo Printing Co Ltd
Subsidiaries: Basic Inc; Hisakata Child Co Ltd

Chuo-Koron-Sha Inc
2-8-7 Kyobashi, Chuo-ku Tokyo 104-8320
Tel: (03) 35631431 *Fax:* (03) 35615922
Telex: J32505 Chuokor *Cable:* Chuokoron Tokyo
Key Personnel
President: Hoji Shimanaka
International Section Dir: Yukio Shimanaka
Founded: 1886
Subjects: Art, Economics, Government, Political Science, History, Philosophy, Religion - Other, Science (General), Social Sciences, Sociology
ISBN Prefix(es): 4-12

Chuo-Tosho Co Ltd+
Aburanokoji-Dori Motoseiganji-Sagaru Kamigyo-ku, Kyoto 602-0000
Tel: (075) 4412174 *Fax:* (075) 4413300
Key Personnel
President: Toshihiko Hirokou
Editorial, Publicity, Rights & Permissions: Takanori Ikeda
Sales: Tetsuo Hattori
Production: Tsuneo Takeuchi
Founded: 1950
ISBN Prefix(es): 4-482

CMC Co Ltd+
Hiyako Bldg, 5-4 Uchikanda 1 Chome, Chiyoda-ku, Tokyo 101
Tel: (03) 32932065 *Fax:* (03) 32932069
Key Personnel
President: Tsuruo Sakai
Founded: 1961
Subjects: Biological Sciences, Business, Electronics, Electrical Engineering
ISBN Prefix(es): 4-88231
Branch Office(s)
Osaka

Contex Corporation+
Suzuki Bldg 1-13-14, Akebono-cho, Tachikawa, Tokyo 190-0012
Tel: (03) 42-522-0051 *Fax:* (03) 42-526-2345; (03) 42-548-2400
E-mail: contex@qa2.so-net.ne.jp
Web Site: contex.co.jp/
Key Personnel
President: Shigeru Tsukakoshi
Contact: Yuko Tsukakoshi
Founded: 1982
Restaurant menu guide consisting of 10 language interpretations. English, Chinese, Korean, Japanese, French, Spanish, German, Italian and Portuguese cookery books & travel guides. Chinese, Korean & Japanese foods.
Subjects: Cookery, Travel
ISBN Prefix(es): 4-907653
Total Titles: 1 Print
Foreign Rep(s): Value Supply Inc

Corona Publishing Co Ltd
46-10 Sengoku, 4 Chome, Bunkyo-Ku, Tokyo 112-0011
Tel: (03) 39413131 *Fax:* (03) 39413137
Key Personnel
President: Tatsumi Gorai
Editorial Dir: Hiroshi Nakamata; Sumio Hatano
Founded: 1927
Subjects: Science (General), Technology
ISBN Prefix(es): 4-339

Daiichi Shuppan Co Ltd
One Chome, 39 Kanda Jimbo-cho, Chiyoda-ku, Tokyo 101-0051
Tel: (03) 32914577 *Fax:* (03) 32914579
E-mail: ishikawa@japan.email.ne.jp
Key Personnel
President, Foreign Trade & Foreign Rights Executive: Hideji Ishikawa
Founded: 1944
Subjects: Health, Nutrition, Medicine, Nursing, Dentistry
ISBN Prefix(es): 4-8041

Number of titles published annually: 10 Print; 1 CD-ROM
Total Titles: 150 Print; 5 CD-ROM

Dainippon Tosho Publishing Co, Ltd+
9-10 Ginza, One Chome, Chuo-ku, Tokyo 104-0061
Tel: (03) 35618672 *Fax:* (03) 35635596
Key Personnel
President: Kentaro Kaneko
Founded: 1890
Subjects: Chemistry, Chemical Engineering, Fiction, Psychology, Psychiatry
ISBN Prefix(es): 4-477

Diamond Inc+
4-2 Kasumigaseki, One Chome, Chiyoda-ku, Tokyo 100-0013
Tel: (03) 35046505 *Fax:* (03) 35046397
Key Personnel
President: Mr Yutaka Iwasa
Rights & Permissions: Mr Eiji Mitachi
Founded: 1913
Subjects: Business, Career Development, Economics, Environmental Studies, Management, Marketing, Nonfiction (General), Psychology, Psychiatry, Science (General), Self-Help
ISBN Prefix(es): 4-478
Subsidiaries: Diamond Agency; Diamond Big; Diamond Fund; Diamond Graphics; Diamond Service
Branch Office(s)
Osaka, India

Dobun Shoin
24-3 Koishikawa 5 Chome, Bunkyo-ku, Tokyo 112-0002
Tel: (03) 38127777 *Fax:* (03) 38127792
Key Personnel
President: Fumihiro Uno
Founded: 1924
Subjects: Business, Computer Science, How-to, Medicine, Nursing, Dentistry, Microcomputers, Nonfiction (General), Science (General), Sports, Athletics
ISBN Prefix(es): 4-8103

Dogakusha Inc
10-7 Suido, One Chome, Bunkyo-ku, Tokyo 112-0005
Tel: (03) 38167011 *Fax:* (03) 38167044
Key Personnel
President: Kusuji Kondo
ISBN Prefix(es): 4-8102

Dohosha Publishing Co Ltd+
206 Ubayanagi Nishihairu Muromachi Takoyakushidori, Nakagyo-ku Kyoto 604-0021
Tel: (075) 255-9801 *Fax:* (075) 255-9811
Key Personnel
President: Satoru Imada
Foreign Rights: Takuya Kosaka
Founded: 1918
Subjects: Architecture & Interior Design, Art, Asian Studies, Cookery, History, How-to, Medicine, Nursing, Dentistry, Religion - Buddhist
ISBN Prefix(es): 4-8104
Associate Companies: DDP Digital Publishing Inc; Ochanomizu Management Laboratory; OML Information Service Center
Subsidiaries:
Warehouse: 34-1, Shironokoshi-cho, Shimotoba, Fushimi-ku, Kyoto 612

Eichosha Company Ltd
Kusaka Bldg, 2-28 Kanda-Jimbo-cho, 2 Chome, Chiyoda-ku, Tokyo 101-0051
Tel: (03) 32636171 *Fax:* (03) 32636155
Key Personnel
President: Shozo Doki
Subjects: English as a Second Language, Language Arts, Linguistics, Literature, Literary Criticism, Essays
ISBN Prefix(es): 4-268

The Eihosha Ltd
1-1-8 Misaki-cho, One Chome ku, Chiyoda-ku, Tokyo 101-0061
Tel: (03) 32920167 *Fax:* (03) 32196095
Key Personnel
President: Sasaki Sumio
Contact: Masao Uji
Founded: 1949
Subjects: Literature, Literary Criticism, Essays
ISBN Prefix(es): 4-269

Elsevier Science
9-15 Higashi-Azabu 1-chome, Minato-ku, Tokyo 106-0044
Tel: (03) 5561 5033 *Fax:* (03) 5561 5047
E-mail: info@elsevier.co.jp
Web Site: www.elsevier.co.jp
Key Personnel
Man Dir: Ryoji Fukada
Sales & editorial services office of Elsevier Science BV, Netherlands.
Parent Company: Elsevier Science BV, Netherlands

Froebel-Kan Co Ltd+
6-14-9 Honkomagome, Bunkyo-ku, Tokyo 113-8611
Tel: (03) 53956614; (03) 53956600 *Fax:* (03) 53956627
Web Site: www.froebel-kan.co.jp
Telex: J24907
Key Personnel
President: Kennosuke Arai *E-mail:* arai-k@froebel.kan.co.jp
Dir: Mitsuhiro Tada *E-mail:* tada-m@froebel-kan.co.jp
Founded: 1907
Subjects: Animals, Pets, Education, Anpanman
ISBN Prefix(es): 4-577
Number of titles published annually: 120 Print
Total Titles: 1,000 Print; 1 CD-ROM
Parent Company: Toppan Printing Co, Ltd

Fuji Keizai Company Ltd
FK Bldg, 2-5 Nihombashi Kodemma-cho, Chou-ku, Tokyo 103-0001
Tel: (03) 36445811 *Fax:* (03) 36610165
Key Personnel
President: Hideo Abe
Founded: 1962
Subjects: Electronics, Electrical Engineering
ISBN Prefix(es): 4-89225; 4-8349
Subsidiaries: Fuji Khimera Institute
U.S. Office(s): Fuji Keizai, 141 E 55 St, Suite 3F, New York, NY, United States

Fukuinkan Shoten Publishers Inc+
6-6-3 Honkomagome, Bunkyo-ku, Tokyo 113-8686
Tel: (03) 39420032 *Fax:* (03) 39421401
Web Site: www.fukuinkan.co.jp *Cable:* FUKUINKANSHOTEN TOKYO
Key Personnel
Chairman: Katsumi Sato
President: Shiro Tokita
Sales Dir: Kazutoshi Tsukada; Munenori Yoshida
Dir (International Dept): Mariko Ogawa
Founded: 1952
Publisher specialized in children's & children related books. Very strong at high quality picture books for younger ages.
Subjects: Fiction, Literature, Literary Criticism, Essays, Nonfiction (General), Science (General), Science Fiction, Fantasy
ISBN Prefix(es): 4-8340

Number of titles published annually: 150 Print
Total Titles: 1,000 Print

Fukumura Shuppan Inc
5F Hongou TS Bldg, 2-30-7 Hongou, Tokyo 113-0033
Tel: (03) 38133981 *Fax:* (03) 38182786
Key Personnel
President: Jun-ichi Fukumura
ISBN Prefix(es): 4-571

Fumaido Publishing Company Ltd+
14-9 Otsuka, 2 Chome, Bunkyo-ku, Tokyo 112-0012
Tel: (03) 39462345 *Fax:* (03) 39470110
E-mail: fumaido@tkd.att.ne.jp
Key Personnel
President: Michio Miyawaki
Founded: 1960
Subjects: Education, Health, Nutrition, Sports, Athletics
ISBN Prefix(es): 4-8293

Fuzambo Publishing Co+
3 Kanda Jimbo-cho, One Chome, Chiyoda-ku, Toyko 101-0051
Tel: (03) 32912171 *Fax:* (03) 32912179
Key Personnel
President: Kiichi Sakamoto
Founded: 1886
Subjects: Art, Geography, Geology, History, Language Arts, Linguistics, Law, Literature, Literary Criticism, Essays, Philosophy, Religion - Other, Social Sciences, Sociology
ISBN Prefix(es): 4-572

Gakken Co Ltd+
40-5 Kamiikedai, 4 Chome, Ota-ku, Tokyo 145-8502
Tel: (03) 34933331 *Fax:* (03) 34933338
Key Personnel
President: Yoichiro Endo
Foreign Affairs Executive: Takeshi Kubodera
Foreign Rights: Shinobu Seki
Founded: 1946
Subjects: Astrology, Occult, Automotive, Business, Child Care & Development, Computer Science, Education, Electronics, Electrical Engineering, Environmental Studies, Gardening, Plants, House & Home, Nonfiction (General), Outdoor Recreation, Radio, TV
ISBN Prefix(es): 4-05

GakuseiSha Publishing Co Ltd
3-27-14 Shikahama, Adachi-ku, Tokyo 123
Tel: (03) 38573031 *Fax:* (03) 38573037
E-mail: info@gakusei.co.jp
Web Site: www.gakusei.co.jp
Key Personnel
President: Ichiro Tsuruoka
Foreign Rights Executive: Shigeru Ohas
Founded: 1952
Subjects: Archaeology, Geography, Geology, History, Language Arts, Linguistics, Law, Literature, Literary Criticism, Essays, Philosophy, Religion - Other, Social Sciences, Sociology
ISBN Prefix(es): 4-311

Genko-Sha
4-1-5 Iidabashi, Chiyoda-ku, Tokyo 102
Tel: (03) 32633515 *Fax:* (03) 32633045
E-mail: gks@genkosha.co.jp
Web Site: www.genkosha.co.jp
Key Personnel
President: Morio Kitahara *Tel:* (03) 3263 3511 *Fax:* (03) 3263 3830
Dir: Chuichi Kaneko *E-mail:* kaneko@genkosha.co.jp
Founded: 1931
Member of JBPA.
Subjects: Art, Film, Video, How-to, Photography
ISBN Prefix(es): 4-7683

Subsidiaries: Salon Agency Co Ltd (advertising agency)
Warehouse: Ono Poking Co Ltd, Inari Souka City
Tel: (0489) 32 2911 *Fax:* (0489) 36 5333
Orders to: Nippan IPS Co Ltd, 11-6, 3 Cho-Me, Iidabashi, Chiyoda-Ku, Toyko 102
Tel: (03) 3238 0700 *Fax:* (03) 3238 0707
E-mail: ips05@nippan-ips.co.jp

Gyosei Corporation
30-16, Ogikubo, 4 Chome, Suginami-ku, Tokyo 167-0051
Tel: (03) 53496666 *Fax:* (03) 53496677
E-mail: ldz06555@niftyserve.or.jp
ISBN Prefix(es): 4-324

Hakubunkan-Shinsha Publishers Ltd
14-6, Koishikawa, 2 Chome, Bunkyo-ku, Tokyo 112
Tel: (03) 38114721 *Fax:* (03) 38181431
Key Personnel
President: Kazuhiro Ohashi
ISBN Prefix(es): 4-89177
Parent Company: Hakuyusha Publishing Company Ltd

Hakusui-Sha Co Ltd
3-24 Ogawa-machi Kanda, Chiyoda-ku, Tokyo 101-0052
Tel: (03) 32917811 *Fax:* (03) 32918448
Cable: Hakusuisha Tokyo
Key Personnel
President: Kazuaki Fujiwara
Foreign Trade Executive: Souichi Kobayashi
Founded: 1915
Subjects: Art, Drama, Theater, Fiction, Literature, Literary Criticism, Essays, Music, Dance, Nonfiction (General), Philosophy
ISBN Prefix(es): 4-560

Hakutei-Sha+
65-1, Ikebukuro, 2 Chome, Toshima-ku, Tokyo 171-0014
Tel: (03) 39863271 *Fax:* (03) 39863272
Key Personnel
President: Yasuo Sato
Subjects: Health, Nutrition, Language Arts, Linguistics, Literature, Literary Criticism, Essays, Religion - Buddhist, Sports, Athletics
ISBN Prefix(es): 4-89174

Hakuyo-Sha
3F Hakuyo Dai 2 Bldg, 7-7 Kandasurugadai, One Chome, Chiyoda-ku, Tokyo 101-0062
Tel: (03) 5281-9772 *Fax:* (03) 5281-9886
E-mail: hakuyo@mars.dti.ne.jp
Web Site: www.hakuyo-sha.co.jp
Key Personnel
President: Hiroshi Nakamura
Founded: 1920
Subjects: Animals, Pets, Nonfiction (General), Psychology, Psychiatry, Science (General)
ISBN Prefix(es): 4-8269

Hakuyu-Sha
9 Ageba-cho, Shinjuku-ku, Tokyo 162-0824
Tel: (03) 32688271 *Fax:* (03) 32688273
Key Personnel
President: Kazuhiro Ohashi
Foreign Trade Executive: Montaro Ono
Publicity & Advertising: Kazuya Baba
Foreign Rights: Eiji Takamori
Founded: 1948
Subjects: Labor, Industrial Relations, Science (General)
ISBN Prefix(es): 4-8268

Hayakawa Publishing Inc
2 Kanda-Tacho, 2 Chome, Chiyoda-ku, Tokyo 101-0046
Tel: (03) 32541551 *Fax:* (03) 32541550
Telex: 02222331 Books J *Cable:* Hayakawa Tokyo
Key Personnel
President: Hiroshi Hayakawa
Founded: 1945
Subjects: Art, Biography, Drama, Theater, Fiction, Government, Political Science, History, Literature, Literary Criticism, Essays, Mysteries, Nonfiction (General), Philosophy, Religion - Other, Science (General), Science Fiction, Fantasy, Social Sciences, Sociology
ISBN Prefix(es): 4-15

Heibonsha Ltd, Publishers+
5-16-19 Himonya, Meguro-ku, Tokyo 152-8601
Tel: (03) 57211241 *Fax:* (03) 57211249
Web Site: www.heibonsha.co.jp/ *Cable:* BOOKSHEIBONSHA
Key Personnel
President: Naoto Shimonaka
Foreign Rights Manager: Yoshihiro Ninomiya
Founded: 1914
Subjects: Art, Education, History, Nonfiction (General), Philosophy, Social Sciences, Sociology
ISBN Prefix(es): 4-582

Hikarinokuni Ltd
3-2-14 Uehon-machi, Tennoji-ku, Osaka 543-0001
Tel: (06) 7681151 *Fax:* (06) 7686910
Key Personnel
President: Yoshio Okamoto
Man Dir: Yotaro Matsumoto
Editorial & Export Dir: Masaaki Tsuchiya
Founded: 1945
Subjects: Education
ISBN Prefix(es): 4-564

Hinoki Publishing Company Ltd
One Kanda-Ogawa-machi, 2 Chome, Chiyoda-ku, Tokyo 101-0052
Tel: (03) 32912488 *Fax:* (03) 32953554
Web Site: www.hinoki-shoten.co.jp
Key Personnel
Chairman: Hisako Suginomori
President: Tsunemasa Hinoki
Founded: 1626
Publisher of Noh & Kyogen Books.
ISBN Prefix(es): 4-8279

Hirokawa Publishing Co+
3-27-14 Hongo, Bunkyo-ku, Tokyo 113
Tel: (03) 38153652 *Fax:* (03) 38153650
Cable: HIGESEHI TOKYO
Key Personnel
President: Setsuo Hirokawa
Vice President: Hideo Hirokawa
Dir: Haruo Hirokawa
Founded: 1926
Subjects: Biological Sciences, Chemistry, Chemical Engineering, Medicine, Nursing, Dentistry, Science (General)
ISBN Prefix(es): 4-567
Total Titles: 50 Print

Hoikusha Publishing Co Ltd
1-6-12 Kawamata, Higashi-Osaka, Osaka 577-0063
Tel: (06) 788 4470 *Fax:* (06) 788 4970 *Cable:* Hoikusha
Key Personnel
President: Yuki Imai
Man Dir: Osamu Yoshino
Editorial: Hiroshi Murakami
Founded: 1947
Subjects: Art, Biography, Crafts, Games, Hobbies, History, How-to, Music, Dance, Natural History, Poetry, Science (General)
ISBN Prefix(es): 4-586
Branch Office(s)
1-1 Minami-Otsuka, Toshima-ku, Tokyo 170

Hokkaido University Press
Nishi 8-chome, Kita-Kujo, Kitakyu-shu Sapporo, Hokkaido 060-0808
Tel: (011) 7472308 *Fax:* (011) 7368605
Key Personnel
Vice President: Mutsuo Nakamura
ISBN Prefix(es): 4-8329

Hokuryukan Co Ltd+
8-14, Takanawa, 3 Chome, Minato-ku, Tokyo 108-0074
Tel: (03) 54494591 *Fax:* (03) 54494950
Key Personnel
President: Motojiro Fukuda
Foreign Department: Hisako Fukuda
Founded: 1891
Subjects: Science (General)
ISBN Prefix(es): 4-8326
Subsidiaries: New Science Publishing Co

The Hokuseido Press
32-4 Honkomagome, 3 Chome, Bunkyo-ku, Tokyo 113-0021
Tel: (03) 38270511 *Fax:* (03) 38270567
Cable: HOKSEDPRES TOKYO
Key Personnel
Dir: Masazo Yamamoto
Sales, Advertising: Eiichi Fujihira
Rights & Permissions: Keisuke Yamamoto
Founded: 1914
Subjects: Biography, Philosophy, Poetry, Religion - Other
ISBN Prefix(es): 4-590
Orders to: Book East, PO Box 13352, Portland, OR 97213, United States *Tel:* 503-287-0974 *Fax:* 503-281-3693 *E-mail:* kwakiyama@aol.com

Holp Book Co Ltd
Shinhana Bldg, 19-7 Shinjuku 1 chome Shinjuku-ku, Tokyo 160
Tel: (03) 5285-5011 *Fax:* (03) 3225-1663
E-mail: holp@holp.co.jp
Web Site: www.holp.co.jp
Key Personnel
President: Mr Seiji Ohyabu
Rights & Permissions, International Trade: Ms Junko Ishizaka
Founded: 1964
Subjects: Art, Education, Geography, Geology, Literature, Literary Criticism, Essays, Mathematics, Science (General)
ISBN Prefix(es): 4-89427
Subsidiaries: Holp Shuppan Publishers

Horitsu Bunka-Sha
71 Kamigamo-Iwagakakiuchi-cho, Kita-ku, Kyoto 603-8053
Tel: (075) 7025831
Key Personnel
President: Shigenobu Inoue
ISBN Prefix(es): 4-589

Hyoronsha Publishing Co Ltd
2-21 Tsukusdohachiman-cho, Shinjuku-ku, Tokyo 162-0815
Tel: (03) 32609406 *Fax:* (03) 32609408
Key Personnel
President: Harunobu Takeshita
Chief Editor: Kunio Hitomi
Sales Manager: Zenzo Uchida
Founded: 1948
Subjects: Education, History, Language Arts, Linguistics, Law, Philosophy, Religion - Buddhist, Religion - Other, Social Sciences, Sociology
ISBN Prefix(es): 4-566

Ichiryu-Sha
5-18 Yanaka, 2 Chome, Taito-ku, Tokyo 110-0001
Tel: (03) 38213916 *Fax:* (03) 38213964

Key Personnel
President: Tsuguo Hikosaka
Founded: 1951
Subjects: Law, Social Sciences, Sociology
ISBN Prefix(es): 4-7527

Ie-No-Hikari Association+
11 Funagawara-cho, Ichigaya, Shinjuku-ku, Tokyo 162-0826
Tel: (03) 32669028 *Fax:* (03) 52612307
Key Personnel
President: Shigenori Tokonabe
Man Dir: Masaya Kakunaka
Executive Dir: Katsuro Kawaguchi; Kazuyuki Morishita
Book Publication: Kenji Yokoyama
Founded: 1925
Subjects: Agriculture, Social Sciences, Sociology
ISBN Prefix(es): 4-259

Igaku-Shoin Ltd+
24-3 Hongo, 5 Chome, Bunkyo-ku, Tokyo 113-8719
Tel: (03) 38175664 *Fax:* (03) 38157804
Key Personnel
President: Yu Kanehara
Vice President, Medical Publications: Hideho Nakamura
Vice President, Sales: Kensaku Kobayashi
Senior Manager, Foreign Books & Journals: Kazuo Kuwabara *Tel:* (03) 3817 5676
    E-mail: k-kuwabara@igaku-shoin.co.jp
Founded: 1944
Subjects: Medicine, Nursing, Dentistry
ISBN Prefix(es): 4-260
Subsidiaries: Medical Sciences International Ltd; LWW Igaku-Shoin Ltd; Igaku-Shoin Medical Publishers Inc

Institute for Financial Affairs Inc-KINZAI
19 Minami-Motomachi, Shinjuku-ku Tokyo 160-0012
Tel: (03) 33580011 *Fax:* (03) 33580036
Key Personnel
President: Mr Hiromi Tokuda
General Manager: Mr Akifumi Kohno
Founded: 1950
Subjects: Accounting, Finance
ISBN Prefix(es): 4-322
Subsidiaries: KINZAI Corporation
Branch Office(s)
150 E 52 St, 27th floor, New York, NY 10022, United States
Osaka, Nagoya & Fukuoka

International Society for Educational Information (ISEI)
Affiliate of Ministry of Foreign Affairs, Japan
Shinko Ofisomu 502, 20-3 San'ei-cho, Shinjuku-ku, Tokyo 160-0008
Tel: (03) 33581138 *Fax:* (03) 33597188
E-mail: kaya@isei.or.jp
Web Site: www.isei.or.jp
Key Personnel
Chair, Board of Directors: Michiko Kaya
    E-mail: kaya@isei.or.jp
Founded: 1958
Specialize in publications about Japan.
Subjects: Art, Crafts, Games, Hobbies, Economics, Geography, Geology, History, Culture, Japan
Number of titles published annually: 10 Print
Total Titles: 48 Print

Ishihara Publishing Company Ltd
13-2 Nishisengoku, Kagoshima-shi, Kagoshima-ken 892
Tel: (0992) 391200 *Fax:* (0992) 391202
Key Personnel
President: Kan'ichiro Ishihara
Founded: 1990

ISBN Prefix(es): 4-900611
Imprints: Ishihara's Decade Diary
Distributed by Japan Publication & Selling Co Ltd; Mail Order House Catalog House Co Ltd; Tokyo Book Seller's Co Ltd

Ishihara's Decade Diary, *imprint of* Ishihara Publishing Company Ltd

Ishiyaku Publishers Inc
7-10 Honkomagome, One Chome, Bunkyo-ku, Tokyo 113-0021
Tel: (03) 39443131 *Fax:* (03) 53957611
Telex: 2723298 Mdp J *Cable:* MEPHARMA TOKYO
Key Personnel
President & Dir, International Office: Hiroshi Miura
Publisher, Dental Books: Yukuhide Yonekawa
Publisher, Medical: Akio Fukushima
Publisher, Dental Journals: Takao Suda
Marketing Dir: Akira Iwase; Tai Watanabe
International Rights: Ms S Ishimura
Founded: 1921
Subjects: Health, Nutrition, Medicine, Nursing, Dentistry, Veterinary Science
ISBN Prefix(es): 4-263; 4-281
Branch Office(s)
c/o Manden Bldg, 11-23 Nishi-Tenma 4-Chome, Kita-ku, Osaka-shi
Orders to: Tokyo Mail Service Co Ltd, 1-30-6 Sugamo, Toshimaku, Tokyo 170

Italia Shobo Ltd
2-23, Kanda-Jimbo-cho, 2 Chome, Chiyoda-ku, Tokyo 101
Tel: (03) 32621656 *Fax:* (03) 32346469
Cable: ITALIASHOBO
Key Personnel
President: Motomichi Ito
Founded: 1958
ISBN Prefix(es): 4-900143

Iwanami Shoten, Publishers+
2-5-5 Hitotsubashi, Chiyoda-ku, Tokyo 101-8002
Tel: (03) 52104000 *Fax:* (03) 52104039
E-mail: rights@iwanami.co.jp (foreign rights)
Web Site: www.iwanami.co.jp/
Key Personnel
President: Nobukazu Otsuka
Editorial Dir: Suzuki Minoru
Foreign Rights Manager: Sachiko Kagaya
Foreign Rights: Rika Ito *E-mail:* rika-ito@iwanami.co.jp; Noa Shimizu
Founded: 1913
Subjects: Art, Biography, Economics, Electronics, Electrical Engineering, History, Philosophy, Photography, Psychology, Psychiatry, Science (General), Social Sciences, Sociology
ISBN Prefix(es): 4-00
Number of titles published annually: 700 Print; 10 CD-ROM
Total Titles: 5,000 Print; 30 CD-ROM; 10 Audio
Orders to: Japan Publications Trading Co, Ltd, 1-2-1 Sarugakucho, Chiyoda-ku, Tokyo *Tel:* (03) 32923751 *Fax:* (03) 32920410

Iwasaki Shoten Publishing Co Ltd
9-2 Suido, One Chome, Bunkyo-ku, Tokyo 112-0005
Tel: (03) 38129131 *Fax:* (03) 38166033
E-mail: xlb02240@niftyserve.or.jp
Key Personnel
President: Hiro Iwasaki
Sales Manager: Tutomu Yasuda
Editorial: Toshio Iino
Founded: 1934
Member of Japan Children's Books Association.
Subjects: Art
ISBN Prefix(es): 4-265

Associate Companies: Iwasaki Gakujitsu Publishing Co
Subsidiaries: Iwasaki Art Publishing Co

Japan Bible Society
5-1 Ginza, 4 Chome, Chou-ku, Tokyo 104-0061
Tel: (03) 35670386
E-mail: info@bible.or.jp
Web Site: www.bible.or.jp
Key Personnel
General Secretary: Rev Makoto Watabe
Founded: 1875
Member of United Bible Societies.
ISBN Prefix(es): 4-8202

Japan Broadcast Publishing Co Ltd+
41-1 Udagawa-cho, Shibuya-ku, Tokyo 150-0042
Tel: (03) 3780-3356 *Fax:* (03) 34960123
Key Personnel
President: Tatsuo Ando
Contact: Chieako Ishizuka
Subjects: How-to, Language Arts, Linguistics, Literature, Literary Criticism, Essays, Science (General), Social Sciences, Sociology
ISBN Prefix(es): 4-14
Parent Company: NHK (Japan Broadcasting Corporation)

Japan Educational Publishing Co Ltd, *see* Nihon-Bunkyo Shuppan (Japan Educational Publishing Co Ltd)

Japan Industrial Publishing Co Ltd+
c/o Suzuki Bldg 10-1, Azabu-10-Ban 3 Chome, Minato-ku, Tokyo 106-0045
Tel: (03) 34561827
Key Personnel
President: Sakutarou Kobayashi
Founded: 1953
ISBN Prefix(es): 4-88045
Subsidiaries: Nikkoh Techno Research Co Ltd

Japan Publications Inc+
2-1 Sargaku-cho, One Chome, Chiyoda-ku, Tokyo 101-0064
Tel: (03) 32958411 *Fax:* (03) 32958416
Telex: J27161 *Cable:* NICHIBOSHUPPAN TOKYO
Key Personnel
President: Toshihiro Kuwahara
Vice President: Yoshiro Fujiwara
Editor-in-Chief: Yukishige Takahashi
Rights & Permissions: Masatoshi Sato
Founded: 1942
Subjects: Agriculture, Asian Studies, Child Care & Development, Cookery, Crafts, Games, Hobbies, Health, Nutrition
ISBN Prefix(es): 4-8170
Parent Company: Japan Publications Trading Co Ltd (Import & Export)
Orders to: Oxford University Press, 198 Madison Ave, New York, NY 10016, United States

Japan Scientific Societies Press, *see* Business Center for Academic Societies Japan

The Japan Times
5-4 Shibaura, 4 Chome, Minato-ku, Tokyo 108-0023
Tel: (03) 34532013 *Fax:* (03) 34538023
Key Personnel
President: Toshiaki Ogasawara
Subjects: Asian Studies, Nonfiction (General)
ISBN Prefix(es): 4-7890

Japan Travel Bureau Inc
Shibuya Bldg, 1-10-8 Dogenzaka, Shinjuku-ku Tokyo 150-0043
Tel: (03) 34779525 *Fax:* (03) 34779538
Telex: 2228020 Jtb Bok J *Cable:* Jtbbook Tokyo

Key Personnel
Vice President, Publishing: Mitsumasa Iwada
Editor-in-Chief, Books in English: Teruo Saito
Foreign Trade Manager: Kazuhiko Hamada
Founded: 1912
Subjects: Geography, Geology, History, Language Arts, Linguistics, Travel
ISBN Prefix(es): 4-533
Subsidiaries: Densan Process Co; Kotsu Print Co; Kotsu Seihon Co; Toyo Books Co
Branch Office(s)
The Royal Exchange Bldg, 56 Pitt St, Sydney, Australia
5 Rue Chantepoulet, Geneva, Switzerland
20 rue Quentin Bauchart, Paris 75008, France
50-51 Russell Square, London WC1B 4JQ, United Kingdom
c/o Guam Hilton Hotel, Ipao Beach, Guam
Hotel Miramar, Rm 2123, Nathan Rd, Kowloon, Hong Kong
Via Emilia 47, Rome, Italy
U.S. Office(s): 624 South Grand Ave, Suite 1410, Los Angeles, CA 90014, United States
402 Qantas Bldg, Union Sq, 360 Post St, San Francisco, CA 94018, United States
Waikiki Business Plaza, 2270 Kalakaua Ave, Honolulu, HI 96815, United States
The International Bldg, 45 Rockfeller Plaza, New York, NY 10020, United States

Journey Editions, *imprint of* Charles E Tuttle Publishing Co Inc

JUSE Press Ltd, see Nikkagiren Shuppan-Sha (JUSE Press Ltd)

Kadokawa Shoten Publishing Co
13-3 Fujimi, 2 Chome, Chiyoda-ku, Tokyo 102-0071
Tel: (03) 32388431 *Fax:* (03) 32627734
Key Personnel
Man Dir: Ohora Kunimitsu
Editorial: Kichinosuke Sato
President, Sales: Tsuguuhiko Kadokawa
Production: Yukio Hashimoto
Publicity: Masatoshi Tojo
Rights & Permissions: Hiroshi Tagami
Founded: 1945
Subjects: Art, Fiction, History, Literature, Literary Criticism, Essays, Religion - Other
ISBN Prefix(es): 4-04

Kaibundo Publishing Co Ltd
5-4 Suido, 2 Chome, Bunkyo-ku, Tokyo 112-0005
Tel: (03) 38153291 *Fax:* (03) 38153953
Key Personnel
President: Yoshihiro Okada
Editorial Dir: Yuji Tamura
Foreign Trade, Foreign Rights: Shinichi Arihara
Founded: 1914
Subjects: Business, Engineering (General), Maritime, Microcomputers, Technology
ISBN Prefix(es): 4-303

Kaisei-Sha Publishing Co Ltd+
3-5 Ichigaya Sadohara-cho, Shinjuku-ku, Tokyo 162-8450
Tel: (03) 32603229 *Fax:* (03) 32603540
E-mail: foreign@kaiseisha.co.jp
Web Site: www.kaiseisha.co.jp
Key Personnel
President: Masaki Imamura
Editorial Dir: Isamu Nakagawa
Editor, Foreign Rights: Hiroshi Konno
Founded: 1936
Subjects: Animals, Pets, Art, Biography, Crafts, Games, Hobbies, Disability, Special Needs, Environmental Studies, Foreign Countries, History
ISBN Prefix(es): 4-03

Kaitakusha+
5-2, Mukogaoka 1-chome, Bunkyo-ku, Tokyo 113-0023
Tel: (03) 58428900 *Fax:* (03) 58425560
E-mail: kaitakusha@kaitakusha.co.jp
Web Site: www.kaitakusha.co.jp
Key Personnel
President: Yoshiko Naganuma
Foreign Trade: Kenichi Naganuma
Foreign Rights: Yasuhiko Yamamoto
Founded: 1927
Subjects: Education, English as a Second Language, Language Arts, Linguistics, Literature, Literary Criticism, Essays
ISBN Prefix(es): 4-7589
Number of titles published annually: 30 Print; 3 CD-ROM; 3 Audio
Total Titles: 300 Print; 10 CD-ROM; 50 Audio

Kajima Institute Publishing Co Ltd
5-13 Akasaka, 6 Chome, Minato-ku, Tokyo 107-0052
Tel: (03) 55612554 *Fax:* (03) 55612561
Telex: 02422467 Kajima J attn Kajima Inst Pub Co
Key Personnel
President: Zenjiro Kawai
Foreign Trade: Waichi Kawamura
Foreign Rights: Sachie Furuta
Founded: 1963
Subjects: Architecture & Interior Design, Civil Engineering, Engineering (General)
ISBN Prefix(es): 4-306
Bookshop(s): Kasumigaseki Bookstore, 3-2-5 Kasumigaseki, Chiyoda-ku, Tokyo; Shinjuku Mitsui Building Bookstore, 2-1 Nishishinjuku, Shinjuku-ku, Tokyo; Shibuya Tohoseimei Building Bookstore, 2-15 Shibuya, Shibuya-ku, Tokyo

Kanehara & Co Ltd
31-14 Yushima, 2 Chome, Bunkyo-ku, Tokyo 113-0034
Tel: (03) 38117162 *Fax:* (03) 38130288
Cable: Kaneharaco Tokyo
Key Personnel
President & General Manager: Hideo Kanehara
Manager (Foreign Business): Hiroshi Kohno
Founded: 1875
Subjects: Labor, Industrial Relations, Medicine, Nursing, Dentistry, Technology
ISBN Prefix(es): 4-307

Kansai University Press
3-35, Yamate-machi, 3 Chome, Suita City, Osaka 564-0073
Tel: (06) 3681121 *Fax:* (06) 3377078
Key Personnel
Contact: Akio Onishi
ISBN Prefix(es): 4-87354

Kawade Shobo Shinsha
32-2 Sendagaya, 2 Chome, Shinjuku-ku, Tokyo 151-0051
Tel: (03) 34041201 *Fax:* (03) 34046386
Key Personnel
President: Masaru Shimizu
Founded: 1886
Subjects: Art, Fiction, History, Nonfiction (General), Philosophy, Science (General), Social Sciences, Sociology
ISBN Prefix(es): 4-309

Kazama Shobo+
34 Kanda-Jimbo-cho, One Chome, Chiyoda-ku, Tokyo 101-0051
Tel: (03) 32915729 *Fax:* (03) 32915757
Key Personnel
President: Tsutomu Kazama
Founded: 1933
Member of Japan Book Publishers Association.

Subjects: Education, History, Literature, Literary Criticism, Essays, Philosophy, Psychology, Psychiatry, Social Sciences, Sociology
ISBN Prefix(es): 4-7599

Keigaku Publishing Co Ltd+
46 Kanda Jimbo cho One chome, Chiyoda-ku, Tokyo 101-0051
Tel: (03) 32333731 *Fax:* (03) 32333730
Key Personnel
Publisher: Kazumi Mitsui
Editorial Dir, Foreign Rights Manager: Kiyoshi Yoshizaki
Sales Manager: Yoshiaki Tokunaga
Production Manager: Isoyoshi Yamamoto
Foreign Rights Associate: Naoko Sakaki
Founded: 1969
Subjects: Computer Science, Electronics, Electrical Engineering, Science (General)
ISBN Prefix(es): 4-7665
Associate Companies: Yugaku-sha Ltd

Keisuisha Publishing Company Ltd
1-4 Komachi, Naka-ku, Hiroshima 733-0041
Tel: (082) 2467909 *Fax:* (082) 2467876
E-mail: info@keisui.co.jp
Web Site: www.keisui.co.jp
Key Personnel
President: Itsushi Kimura *E-mail:* kimura@keisui.co.jp
Founded: 1975
Subjects: Asian Studies, Economics, Education, History, Language Arts, Linguistics, Literature, Literary Criticism, Essays, Philosophy, Social Sciences, Sociology
ISBN Prefix(es): 4-87440
Number of titles published annually: 40 Print
Total Titles: 710 Print

Kenkyusha Ltd
11-3, Fujimi, 2 Chome, Chiyoda-ku, Tokyo 102-0071
Tel: (03) 32887775 *Fax:* (03) 32694155
Key Personnel
President: Kunikatsu Araki
Foreign Trade Executive: Hiroji Yamazaki
Foreign Rights Executive: Josuke Okada
Founded: 1907
Subjects: Language Arts, Linguistics
ISBN Prefix(es): 4-327

Kin no Hoshi-Sha Co Ltd
4-3 Kojima, One Chome, Taito-ku, Tokyo 111-0056
Tel: (03) 38611861 *Fax:* (03) 38611507
Key Personnel
President: Masakazu Saito
Vice President: Matsuo Ishibashi
Editor: Masao Okohira
Founded: 1919
Subjects: Education
ISBN Prefix(es): 4-323
Warehouse: 1997-1 Hizaore 3-chome, Asaka-City, Saitama

Kindai Kagaku Sha Co, Ltd+
2-7-15 Ichigaya-Tamachi, Shinjuku City, Tokyo 162-0843
Tel: (03) 32606101 *Fax:* (03) 32606102
Key Personnel
Chief Executive Officer: Ryohji Sakurai
Founded: 1959
Member of Kohgakusho Kyokai (Association of Engineering Book Publishers) & Shokyoh (Japan Book Publishers Association.
Subjects: Computer Science, Electronics, Electrical Engineering, Mathematics, Physics
ISBN Prefix(es): 4-7649

JAPAN

Kinokuniya Co Ltd (Publishing Department)+
13 11 Higashi 3-Chome, Shibuya-ku, Tokyo 150-8513
Tel: (03) 54695919 *Fax:* (03) 54695959
E-mail: publish@kimokunya.co.jp
Web Site: www.kimokuniya.co.jp *Cable:* KINOKUNI
Key Personnel
General Manager: Shinjiro Kuroda
Sales: Yoshichika Ogasawara
Founded: 1926
Subjects: Art, Biography, History, Literature, Literary Criticism, Essays, Philosophy, Psychology, Psychiatry, Science (General), Social Sciences, Sociology
ISBN Prefix(es): 4-314
Associate Companies: Kinokuniya Book-Stores of America Co Ltd, 1581 Webster St, San Francisco, CA 94115, United States; Kinokuniya Publications Service of New York Co Ltd, 10 W 49 St, New York, NY 10020, United States; Kinokuniya Publications Service of London Co Ltd, Radnor House, 93-97 Regent St, London W1R 7TG, United Kingdom

Kinpodo
34 Shishigatani-Nishi-Teranomae-Machi, Sakyo-ku, kyoto 606
Tel: (075) 7511111 *Fax:* (075) 7516858
E-mail: kkimpodo@kb3.so-net.or.jp
Key Personnel
President: Katsusuke Shibata
Subjects: Medicine, Nursing, Dentistry
ISBN Prefix(es): 4-7653

KINZAI Corporation+
19, Minami-Motomachi, Shinjuku-ku, Tokyo 160-8520
Tel: (03) 33580011 *Fax:* (03) 33580036
E-mail: jdi04072@nifty.ne.jp
Key Personnel
President: Akira Kanai
General Manager: Shigeru Abe
Founded: 1971
Subjects: Finance, Banking, Security Business
ISBN Prefix(es): 4-322
Parent Company: Institute for Financial Affairs Inc
Branch Office(s)
Fukuoka Cities
Nagoya
Osaka
U.S. Office(s): KINZAI New York, 50 E 52 St, 27th floor, New York, NY 10022, United States

Kodansha+
12-21 Otowa 2-Chome, Bunkyo-Ku, Tokyo 112-0013
Tel: (03) 53953419 *Fax:* (03) 39444441
Web Site: www.kodansha.co.jp
Telex: J34509 Kodansha *Cable:* KODANSHAPUBLISH TOKYO
Key Personnel
President: Sawako Noma
Editorial: Akira Higashiura
Sales: Hironobu Hamada
Rights & Permissions: Takashi Kasahara
  E-mail: t-kasahara@kodansha.co.jp
Founded: 1909
Subjects: Art, Economics, Education, Fiction, Geography, Geology, History, House & Home, Humor, Language Arts, Linguistics, Literature, Literary Criticism, Essays, Medicine, Nursing, Dentistry, Nonfiction (General), Philosophy, Religion - Other, Social Sciences, Sociology
ISBN Prefix(es): 4-06
Subsidiaries: Kodansha America Ltd; Kodansha Europe Ltd; Kodansha International Ltd
Branch Office(s)
Osaka
U.S. Office(s): New York, NY, United States
Book Club(s): Kodansha Disney Children's Book Club

Kodansha International+
1-17-14 Otowa, Bunkyo-ku, Tokyo 112-8652
Tel: (03) 39446491 *Fax:* (03) 39446394
Web Site: www.thejapanpage.com
Key Personnel
President: Sawako Noma
Senior Executive Vice President: Fumio Hatano
Editorial Vice President: Kazuichi Ohmura
Sales Vice President: Kazuhide Sainowaki
Editorial Dir: Stephen Shaw *Tel:* (03) 3944-6493 (Tokyo, Japan) *E-mail:* shaw@kodansha-intl.co.jp
International Rights: Ayako Akaogi
Founded: 1963
Specialize in Japan & Asia.
Subjects: Art, Cookery, Crafts, Games, Hobbies, Fiction, History, How-to, Language Arts, Linguistics, Philosophy, Sports, Athletics, Martial arts
ISBN Prefix(es): 4-7700
Parent Company: Kodansha Ltd
Branch Office(s)
Kodansha Europe, 95 Aldwych, London WC2B 4JF, United Kingdom *Tel:* (020) 7304 4095 *Fax:* (020) 7304 4096
U.S. Office(s): Kodansha America, 575 Lexington Ave, New York, NY 10022, United States *Tel:* 917-322-6200 *Fax:* 212-935-6929

Kodansha Scientific Ltd
Otowa 2 Chome, Bunko-ku 112-01
Tel: (03) 39466201 *Fax:* (03) 39449915
Key Personnel
President: Sawako Noma
General Manager: Katsuhiro Ohbori
Founded: 1970
Subjects: Science (General)
ISBN Prefix(es): 4-06
Parent Company: Kodansha Ltd

Kogyo Chosakai Publishing Co, Ltd
14-7, Hongo, Bunkyo-ku, Tokyo 113-0033
Tel: (03) 38174701 *Fax:* (03) 38174709
E-mail: mya34844@pcvah.or.jp
Key Personnel
President: Yukio Shimura

Kokudo-Sha
2-5-8 Shimo-ochiai, Shinjuku-ku, Tokyo 161-0033
Tel: (03) 5996-3101 *Fax:* (03) 5983-7434
Key Personnel
President: Masaaki Suzuki
Founded: 1967
Subjects: Child Care & Development, Education, Literature, Literary Criticism, Essays, Psychology, Psychiatry, Social Sciences, Sociology
ISBN Prefix(es): 4-337

Kokusho Kankokai Co Ltd
10-5 Shimura 2 Chome Itabashi-ku, Tokyo 174-0056
Tel: (03) 59707421 *Fax:* (03) 59707427
Key Personnel
President: Kesao Sato
Chief Editor: Junichi Isozaki
Editor: Reiko Iwamoto
Founded: 1971
Subjects: Asian Studies, Education, Fiction, History, Language Arts, Linguistics, Literature, Literary Criticism, Essays, Military Science, Religion - Buddhist, Western Fiction
ISBN Prefix(es): 4-336
Warehouse: 3-11-26 Vchiya, Vrawa-sh, Saitama Prefecture 336

Komine Shoten Publishing Co Ltd
4-11, Ichigaya-Dai-Machi, Shinjuku-ku, Tokyo 162-0066
Tel: (03) 33573521 *Fax:* (03) 33571027
Key Personnel
President: Norio Komine
Founded: 1946
Subjects: Education
ISBN Prefix(es): 4-338

Kosei Publishing Co Ltd+
Affiliate of Rissho Kosei-kai
7-1 Wada, 2 Chome, Suginami-ku, Tokyo 166-0012
Tel: (03) 5385-2319 *Fax:* (03) 5385-2331
E-mail: dharmaworld@mail.kosei-shuppan.co.jp
Web Site: www.kosei-shuppan.co.jp/english/
Key Personnel
President: Teizo Kuriyama
Foreign Trade, Foreign Rights Executive: Toru Nakagawa
Dir, International Publishing Section: Koichiro Yoshida
Founded: 1966
Member of Japan Book Publishers Association.
Subjects: Art, Child Care & Development, Education, History, Human Relations, Literature, Literary Criticism, Essays, Medicine, Nursing, Dentistry, Music, Dance, Nonfiction (General), Philosophy, Psychology, Psychiatry, Religion - Buddhist, Self-Help, Travel
ISBN Prefix(es): 4-333
Total Titles: 481 Print; 2 Audio
Distributed by Charles E Tuttle Co Inc

Koseisha-Koseikaku Co Ltd
8 San'ei-cho, Shinjuku-ku, Tokyo 160-0008
Tel: (03) 33597371 *Fax:* (03) 33597375
Key Personnel
President: Hisao Satake
Editorial: Fukase Simao
Publishing: Hajime Torizuka
Founded: 1922
Subjects: Astrology, Occult, Labor, Industrial Relations, Philosophy, Science (General), Social Sciences, Sociology, Technology
ISBN Prefix(es): 4-7699

Koyo Shobo+
7 Kita-Yakake-cho, Saiin, Ukyo-ku, Kyoto 615-0026
Tel: (075) 3120788 *Fax:* (075) 3127447
Key Personnel
President: Yoshiki Ueda
Founded: 1960
Subjects: Archaeology, Art, Business, Developing Countries, Drama, Theater, Economics, Education, Environmental Studies, Ethnicity, Government, Political Science, History, Law, Management, Marketing, Philosophy, Psychology, Psychiatry, Social Sciences, Sociology
ISBN Prefix(es): 4-7710

Kyodo-Isho Shuppan Co Ltd+
21-10 Hongo 3 Chome, Bunkyo-ku, Tokyo 113-0033
Tel: (03) 38182361 *Fax:* (03) 38182368
E-mail: kyodo-ed@fd5.so-net.ne.jp
Web Site: www.kyodo-isho.co.jp
Key Personnel
President: Setsu Kinoshita *E-mail:* kyodo-ed@fd5.so-net.ne.jp
Founded: 1946
Subjects: Medicine, Nursing, Dentistry
ISBN Prefix(es): 4-7639

Kyoritsu Shuppan Co Ltd
6-19 Kohinata, 4 Chome, Bunkyo-ku, Tokyo 112-0006
Tel: (03) 39472511 *Fax:* (03) 39446043

PUBLISHERS

JAPAN

Key Personnel
President: Mitusaki Nanjo
Editorial Dir, Rights & Permissions: Mitsuaki Nanjo
Sales Dir: Hiroshi Todoroki
Founded: 1926
Subjects: Biological Sciences, Chemistry, Chemical Engineering, Computer Science, Engineering (General), Mathematics, Medicine, Nursing, Dentistry, Natural History, Physics, Technology
ISBN Prefix(es): 4-320

La Verve, *imprint of* Yohan Shuppan

Library & Information Science, *imprint of* Riso-Sha

Lotus, *imprint of* Yohan Shuppan

Maruzen Co Ltd
9-2 Nihombashi 3 Chome, Dai 2 Maruzen Bldg, Chuo-ku, Tokyo 103-0011
Tel: (03) 32720514 *Fax:* (03) 32740579
Web Site: www.maruzen.co.jp
Telex: J26516; J26517 *Cable:* MARUYA TOKYO
Key Personnel
Chairman: Kumao Ebihara
President: Nobuo Suzuki
Executive Dir: Ryozo Fujiwara
Man Dir: Isamu Tanahashi; Hiroshi Muko
Senior General Manager: Tsuneo Miyama
Founded: 1869
Subjects: Architecture & Interior Design, Biological Sciences, Chemistry, Chemical Engineering, Civil Engineering, Computer Science, Electronics, Electrical Engineering, Mechanical Engineering, Physics, Science (General)
ISBN Prefix(es): 4-621
Associate Companies: Maruzen Planet Co Lt, Tokyo
Subsidiaries: Maruzen Asia (Pte) Ltd; Maruzen International Co Ltd
Branch Office(s)
Fukuoka
Hiroshima
Kanazawa
Kobe
Kyoto
Nagoya
Okayama
Osaka
Sendai
Tsukuba
Yokohama
Warehouse: 5-7-1, Heiwajima, Ohta-ku, Tokyo 143

Medical Sciences International Ltd+
2F Houmei Bldg, 1-28-36 Hongo, Bunkyo-ku, Tokyo 113-0033
Tel: (03) 5804-6051 *Fax:* (03) 5804-6055 *Cable:* MEDSIJAPAN TOKYO
Key Personnel
President: Hiroshi Wakamatsu
Founded: 1979
Subjects: Medicine, Nursing, Dentistry
ISBN Prefix(es): 4-89592; 4-943921
Imprints: MEDSI

MEDSI, *imprint of* Medical Sciences International Ltd

Meiji Shoin Co Ltd
1-16 Kanda-Nishiki-cho, Chiyoda-ku, Tokyo 101-0054
Tel: (03) 32923741 *Fax:* (03) 32924429
Key Personnel
Man Dir: Yuzuru Miki
Editorial: Kunio Kawami
Sales: Harunori Saito
Founded: 1896
ISBN Prefix(es): 4-625
Branch Office(s)
Fukuoka
Osaka

Mejikaru Furendo-sha+
2-4 Kudan Kita 3 Chome, Chiyoda-ku, Tokyo 102-0073
Tel: (03) 32646611 *Fax:* (03) 32616602 (distribution); (03) 32640704 (editorial affairs)
E-mail: mfhensyu@mb.infoweb.ne.jp; mfeigyou@mb.infoweb.ne.jp; mfsoumu@mb.infoweb.ne.jp
Web Site: www.web.infoweb.ne.jplmedical-friend/
Key Personnel
President, Rights & Permissions: Yoshihiro Ogura
Foreign Rights: Hiromi Ikoma
Founded: 1947
Subjects: Art, Health, Nutrition, Medicine, Nursing, Dentistry
ISBN Prefix(es): 4-8392
Associate Companies: The International Nursing Foundation of Japan (INFJ)
Warehouse: 36-1 Hiraoka-cho, Hachioji, Tokyo 192

Minerva Shobo Co Ltd+
Member of Japan Book Publishers Association
One Tsutsumidani-cho, Hinooka, Yamashina-ku, Kyoto 607-8494
Tel: (075) 5815191 *Fax:* (075) 5810589
E-mail: info@minervashobo.co.jp
Web Site: www.minervashoboco.jp
Key Personnel
President: Nobuo Sugita *Tel:* (071) 581 5191 93
Foreign Trade: Keizo Sugita
Editorial Dir: Kiyoshi Igarashi
Foreign Rights: Miyako Shibata
Founded: 1948
Advisor of Japan Book Publishers Association.
Subjects: Child Care & Development, Disability, Special Needs, Economics, Education, Government, Political Science, History, Medicine, Nursing, Dentistry, Philosophy, Psychology, Psychiatry, Social Sciences, Sociology
ISBN Prefix(es): 4-623
Total Titles: 3,148 Print
Parent Company: Nobuo Sugita
Imprints: Tohan-Nippan
Branch Office(s)
3-6 Nishiki-cho, Kanda, Chiyoda-Ku, Tokyo 101-0034 *Tel:* (03) 8296-1615 *Fax:* (03) 3396-1620
Distributed by Nihon Shuppan Hanbai Co

Mirai-Sha
7-2 Koishikawa, 3 Chome, Bunkyo-ku, Tokyo 112-0002
Tel: (03) 38145521 *Fax:* (03) 38148600
Key Personnel
President: Yoshihide Nishitani
Founded: 1951
Subjects: History, Human Relations, Literature, Literary Criticism, Essays, Philosophy, Social Sciences, Sociology
ISBN Prefix(es): 4-624

Misuzu Shobo Ltd+
5-32-21 Hongo, Bunkyo-ku, Tokyo 113-0033
Tel: (03) 3815-9181 *Fax:* (03) 3818-8497
E-mail: nakagawa@msz.co.jp
Web Site: www.msz.co.jp
Key Personnel
President: Takashi Arai
Man Dir, Editor-in-Chief: Shogo Morita
Foreign Rights: Misako Nakagawa
Founded: 1946
Subjects: Art, Human Relations, Literature, Literary Criticism, Essays, Psychology, Psychiatry, Science (General), Social Sciences, Sociology
ISBN Prefix(es): 4-622

Mita Press, Mita Industrial Co, Ltd+
2-12, Hongo, 3 Chome, Bunkyo-ku, Tokyo 113
Tel: (03) 38177200 *Fax:* (03) 38177207
Key Personnel
President: Yoshihiro Mita
Man Dir: Akio Etori
International Relations Manager: Atsushi Mifune
Founded: 1988 (originally founded 1934 as Mita Industrial Co, Ltd)
Subjects: Astronomy, Biological Sciences, Medicine, Nursing, Dentistry, Nonfiction (General), Physical Sciences, Physics, Psychology, Psychiatry, Science (General), Technology
ISBN Prefix(es): 4-89583

Morikita Shuppan Co Ltd
1-4-11 Fujimi, Chiyoda-ku, Tokyo 102-0071
Tel: (03) 32658341 *Fax:* (03) 32648709
Key Personnel
President: Hajime Morikita
Foreign Trade Executive: Kazuo Mori
Foreign Rights Executive, Publicity: Sadao Hishino
Founded: 1940 (as Morikita Shoten)
Subjects: Science (General), Technology
ISBN Prefix(es): 4-627

Myrtos Inc+
10-5 Kudan-Kita, 1 Chome, Chiyoda-ku, Tokyo 102
Tel: (03) 32882200 *Fax:* (03) 32882225
E-mail: pub@myrtos.co.jp
Web Site: www.myrtos.co.jp
Key Personnel
President: Kazumitsu Kawai
Founded: 1985
Subjects: Archaeology, Education, History, Literature, Literary Criticism, Essays, Religion - Jewish, Religion - Protestant
ISBN Prefix(es): 4-89586
Branch Office(s)
Jerusalem, Israel

Nagai Shoten Co Ltd
21-15 Fukushima, 8 Chome, Fukushima-ku, Osaka 553-0003
Tel: (06) 4521881 *Fax:* (06) 4521882
Key Personnel
President: Tadao Nagai
Founded: 1946
Subjects: Medicine, Nursing, Dentistry
ISBN Prefix(es): 4-8159

Nagaoka Shoten Company Ltd+
7-14 Toyotama-kami, 1 Chome, Nerima-ku, Tokyo 176-8518
Tel: (03) 39925155 *Fax:* (03) 39483021
Key Personnel
President: Shuichi Nagaoka
Founded: 1963
Subjects: Animals, Pets, Cookery, Crafts, Games, Hobbies, Gardening, Plants, Health, Nutrition, House & Home, How-to, Travel
ISBN Prefix(es): 4-522
Subsidiaries: Cosumo Shuppan Company Ltd; Lesson Company Ltd; Okaichi Company Ltd

Nakayama Shoten Company Ltd
25-14 Hakusan, 1 Chome, Bunkyo-ku, Tokyo 113-0001
Tel: (03) 38131101 *Fax:* (03) 38133270
Key Personnel
President: Kurohiko Nakayama
Founded: 1948
Subjects: Biological Sciences, Medicine, Nursing, Dentistry, Science (General)
ISBN Prefix(es): 4-521

Nankodo Co Ltd+
42-6 Hongo, 3 Chome, Bunkyo-ku, Tokyo 113-8410
Tel: (03) 38117239 *Fax:* (03) 38117230
Telex: 2722203 Nankod J *Cable:* Booknankodo

Key Personnel
President: Atsushi Kodachi
Dir, Publications: Makoto Ueda
Dir, Foreign Division: Masao Takahashi
Sales Dir: Makoto Sagwara
Manager, Planning, Publicity: Shun Takahashi
Manager, Imports: Iwao Tojo
Founded: 1879
Subjects: Language Arts, Linguistics, Medicine, Nursing, Dentistry, Science (General), Technology
ISBN Prefix(es): 4-524
Branch Office(s)
Oike-minami Teramachi dori, Nakakyo-ku, Kyoto 604

Nan'un-Do Company Ltd+
361, Yamabuki-cho, Shinjuku-ku, Tokyo 162-0801
Tel: (03) 32682311 *Fax:* (03) 32605425
Key Personnel
President: Kazunori Nagumo
Founded: 1950
Member of J P A.
Subjects: Language Arts, Linguistics
ISBN Prefix(es): 4-523
Subsidiaries: Nan'un-Do Phoenix Company Ltd

Nanzando Co Ltd
1-11 Yushima 4 chome, Bunkyo-ku, Tokyo 113-0034
Tel: (03) 56897855 *Fax:* (03) 56897857
Key Personnel
Man Dir: Hajime Suzuki
Founded: 1901
Subjects: Medicine, Nursing, Dentistry
ISBN Prefix(es): 4-525

Nensho-Sha
3-5, Kitayama-cho, Tennoji-ku, Osaka 543
Tel: (06) 7719223 *Fax:* (06) 7719424
Key Personnel
President: Masaru Fujinami
Founded: 1934
ISBN Prefix(es): 4-88978

NHK Publishing, *imprint of* Nippon Hoso Shuppan Kyokai (NHK Publishing)

Nigensha Publishing Co Ltd+
2-31, Kanda Jimbo-cho, 2 Chome, Chiyoda-ku, Tokyo 101-0051
Tel: (03) 5395-2043 *Fax:* (03) 5210-4723
Key Personnel
President: Mr Takao Watanabe
Marketing Manager, Overseas: Yuji Nagai
Founded: 1953
Member of Japan Book Publishers Association & Azusakai Publishers Association.
Subjects: Art, Automotive, History
ISBN Prefix(es): 4-544

Nihon Bunka Kagakusha Co Ltd
15-17 Honkomagome, 6 Chome, Bunkyo-ku, Tokyo 113-0021
Tel: (03) 39463131 *Fax:* (03) 39463567
Cable: Nihonbunkamm Tokyo
Key Personnel
President: Hideyuki Motegi
Foreign Trade Executive: Yoshihiro Hoshi
E-mail: y_hoshi@nichibun.co.jp
Founded: 1948
Subjects: Education, Medicine, Nursing, Dentistry, Social Sciences, Sociology
ISBN Prefix(es): 4-8210

Nihon-Bunkyo Shuppan (Japan Educational Publishing Co Ltd)
7-5 Minami-Sumiyoshi, 4 Chome, Sumiyoshi-ku, Osaka 558-0041
Tel: (06) 6921261 *Fax:* (06) 6065172
E-mail: sskjep@po.iijnet.or.jp
Key Personnel
President: Ritsuro Shimono
Founded: 1948
Subjects: Art, Education, English as a Second Language, Social Sciences, Sociology
ISBN Prefix(es): 4-536
Subsidiaries: Kiroku Eigasha Production Co Ltd; Shugakusha Co Ltd

Nihon Hoso Shuppan Kyokai, see Japan Broadcast Publishing Co Ltd

Nihon Keizai Shimbun Inc Publications Bureau
3-6 Otemachi, 2 Chome, Chiyoda-ku, Tokyo 100-0004
Tel: (03) 5255-2827 *Fax:* (03) 3246-2861
Web Site: www.nikkei.co.jp
Key Personnel
General Manager: Takeshi Higuchi
ISBN Prefix(es): 4-532
Associate Companies: Nikkei Science Inc
Subsidiaries: Nikkei Publications Services Inc

Nihon Rodo Kenkyu Kiko
c/o Shinjuku Monolith Bldg, 3-1 Nishi-Shinjuku 2 chome, Shinjuku-ku, Tokyo 163-0023
Tel: (03) 53213074 *Fax:* (03) 53213015
E-mail: hom@po.iijner.or.jp
Key Personnel
Dir, Publishing Dept: Ms Atsuko Hojo
Subjects: Labor, Industrial Relations
ISBN Prefix(es): 4-538
Divisions: Research Institute

Nihon Tosho Center Co Ltd
8-2 Otsuka, 3 Chome, Bunkyo-ku, Tokyo 112-0012
Tel: (03) 39479387 *Fax:* (02) 39471774
E-mail: info@nihontosho.co.jp
Web Site: www.nihontosho.co.jp
Key Personnel
President: Yoshio Takano
Editorial Dir: Yochisada Kyuma
Sales Dir: Minami Nonaka
Founded: 1975
Subjects: Education, History, Literature, Literary Criticism, Essays, Social Sciences, Sociology, Autobiography, Social Welfare
ISBN Prefix(es): 4-8205
Branch Office(s)
Osaka

Nihon Vogue Co Ltd+
3-23 Ichigaya-Honmura-cho, Shinjuku-ku, Tokyo 162-8705
Tel: (03) 5261 5081 *Fax:* (03) 32698726
E-mail: wada-t@tezukuritown.com
Web Site: tezukuritown.com
Key Personnel
President: Nobuaki Seto *Tel:* (03) 5261 5089 *Fax:* (03) 3269 7874 *E-mail:* seto@tezukuritown.com
Manager, Overseas Department: Takuya Wada
Founded: 1954
Specialize in publication of handicrafts books.
Subjects: Cookery, Crafts, Games, Hobbies, Gardening, Plants, Sports, Athletics
ISBN Prefix(es): 4-529
Subsidiaries: NV Planing Co Ltd

Nikkagiren Shuppan-Sha (JUSE Press Ltd)
4-2 Sendagaya, Shibuya-ku, Tokyo 151-0051
Tel: (03) 33522231 *Fax:* (03) 33563419
Key Personnel
President: Teruhide Haga
Founded: 1955
Subjects: Business, Computer Science, Finance, Human Relations, Library & Information Sciences, Management, Mathematics, Self-Help, Technology
ISBN Prefix(es): 4-8171

The Nikkan Kogyo Shimbun Ltd
8-10 Kudan-kita, 1 Chome, Chiyoda-ku, Tokyo 102-0073
Tel: (03) 32227131 *Fax:* (03) 32348504
Web Site: www.nikkan.co.jp
Telex: NIKKANKO J29687 *Cable:* DAILYKOGYO TOKYO
Key Personnel
President, Chu-Shikoku: Toshio Fujiyoshi
President, Osaka: Kiyosi Muramoto
President, Tohoku: Tatsuo Uchida
Bureau Chief, New York: Joji Ito
Bureau Chief, Los Angeles: Etsuji Nakamura
Bureau Chief, London: Hidemasa Naka
Bureau Chief, SE Asia: Yasushi Abe
Editor, Chu-Shikoku: Keijyu Moriwaki
Editor, Osaka: Toshiyuki Takakura
Editor, Nagoya: Koichi Ota
Editor, Seibu: Tsutomu Sasaki
Editor, Tohoku: Susuma Suzuki
Founded: 1915
Subjects: Business, Technology
ISBN Prefix(es): 4-526
Branch Office(s)
No 44 Ludgate House, 107/111 Fleet St, London EC4, United Kingdom
1-17-18 Uesugi, Aoba-ku, Sendai
2-16 Kitahama-higashi, Chuo-ku, Osaka
2-21-28 Izumi, Higashi-ku, Nagoya, 1-1 Furumonndo-Cho, Hakata-ku, Fukuoka
10 Anson Rd, No 27-04, International Plaza, Singapore 0207, Singapore
U.S. Office(s): 611 W Sixth St, No 3201, Los Angeles, CA 90017, United States
60 E 42 St, No 1411, New York, NY 10165, United States

Nippon Hoso Shuppan Kyokai (NHK Publishing)+
41-1 Udagawa-cho, Shibuya-ku, Tokyo 150-0042
Tel: (03) 37803356 *Fax:* (03) 34960123
Cable: NHPUBLISHCO TOKYO
Key Personnel
President: Tatsuo Ando
Man Dir: Fumihiko Inatsugu
Editor of Project Development: Masahiro Kizaki
Founded: 1931
Subjects: Astronomy, Biological Sciences, Business, Chemistry, Chemical Engineering, Communications, Cookery, Crafts, Games, Hobbies, Drama, Theater, Earth Sciences, Economics, Education, Electronics, Electrical Engineering, English as a Second Language, Environmental Studies, Fashion, Fiction, Foreign Countries, Gardening, Plants, Government, Political Science, Health, Nutrition, Language Arts, Linguistics, Law, Literature, Literary Criticism, Essays, Management, Mathematics, Mechanical Engineering, Music, Dance, Mysteries, Regional Interests, Religion - Buddhist, Religion - Catholic, Religion - Hindu, Religion - Islamic, Religion - Jewish, Religion - Protestant, Religion - Other, Science (General), Social Sciences, Sociology, Sports, Athletics, Technology, Travel, Western Fiction
ISBN Prefix(es): 4-14
Parent Company: NHK (Japan Broadcasting Corporation)
Imprints: NHK Publishing
Subsidiaries: Hoso-Shuppan Circulation Center; Hoso-Shuppan Production; Niiza-Biso
Branch Office(s)
Fukuoka
Hiroshima
Matsuyama
Nagoya
Osaka
Sapporo
Sendai

Distributed by Weatherhill Inc
Warehouse: Hoso-Shuppan Circulation Center, 1-7-7 Hatanaka, Niiza-City, Saitama 352
Orders to: Japan Broadcast Publishing Co, Ltd, Shibuya-ku, Tokyo

Nippon Jitsugyo Publishing Co, Ltd+
2-12, Hongo, 3 Chome, Bunkyo-ku, Tokyo 113-0033
Tel: (03) 38145161 *Fax:* (03) 38181881
E-mail: nipojits@po.iijnet.or.jp
Key Personnel
Chairman: Yoichiro Nakamura
Founded: 1950
Subjects: Accounting, Business, Computer Science, Economics, Management, Marketing, Psychology, Psychiatry, Science (General)
ISBN Prefix(es): 4-534
Associate Companies: Four U (Publishing) Co Ltd

Nishimura Co Ltd+
754-39 Asahi-cho-dori, Nigata 951
Tel: (025) 2232388 *Fax:* (025) 2247165
Key Personnel
President: Masanori Nishimura
General Dir: Masanobu Nishiyama
Sales Manager: Masaru Gotoh; Kenji Sakai
Production & Publicity Manager: Tsutomu Maeda; Keiichi Ninomiya
Founded: 1979
Subjects: Art, Medicine, Nursing, Dentistry, Veterinary Science
ISBN Prefix(es): 4-89013
Associate Companies: West Village Co Ltd
  Fax: (025) 2235750
Branch Office(s)
Akita
Toyko
Bookshop(s): 68-2 Aza-Hasunuma, Hiroomote, Akita-shi 010; 754-39 Asahi-cho-dori, Nigata 951

Nobunkyo (Rural Village Culture Association)
6-1 Akasaka 7 Chome, Minato-ku, Tokyo 107-0052
Tel: (03) 35851141 *Fax:* (03) 35891387
E-mail: mbk@mail.ruralnet.or.jp
Key Personnel
Chief Dir: Takashi Sakamoto
Founded: 1940
Subjects: Agriculture, Education, Environmental Studies, Health, Nutrition, Medicine, Nursing, Dentistry
ISBN Prefix(es): 4-540
Bookshop(s): Nobunkyo Otemachi Branch, JA Bldg, Basement floor, 1-8-3 Otemachi, Chiyoda-ku, Tokyo 100

Obunsha Co Ltd
78 Yarai-cho, Shinjuku-ku, Tokyo 162
Tel: (03) 32666351 *Fax:* (03) 32666011
Cable: OBUNSHA TOKYO
Key Personnel
Chief Executive Officer: Fumio Akao
Advertising Manager: Masaru Wakabayashi
Contact: Kotaro Okada
Founded: 1931
Subjects: Computer Science, History, Science (General), Sports, Athletics
ISBN Prefix(es): 4-01
Associate Companies: The Asahi National Broadcasting Co Ltd, 1-1-1 Roppongi, Minato-ku, Toyko 106; English Educational Foundation of Japan, 55 Yokodera-cho, Shinjuku-ku, Toyko 162; Japan LL Education Center, Tokyo; Nippon Cultural Broadcasting Inc, 1-5 Wakabacho, Shinjuku-ku, Toyko 160; The Society for Testing English Proficiency, 1 Yarai-cho, Shinjuku-ku, Tokyo 162
Branch Office(s)
Fukuoka
Hiroshima
Nagoya
Osaka
Sapporo
Sendai

Ohmsha Ltd+
3-1 Kanda-Nishiki-cho, Chiyoda-ku, Tokyo 101-8460
Tel: (03) 3233-0641 *Fax:* (03) 3293-6224
E-mail: kaigaika@ohmsha.co.jp
Web Site: www.ohmsha.co.jp
Key Personnel
President: Seiji Sato
Dir, Foreign Rights & International Business: Osami Takeo *Tel:* (03) 3233-4036 *E-mail:* takeo@ohmsha.co.jp
Founded: 1914
Subjects: Engineering (General), Science (General)
ISBN Prefix(es): 4-274
Number of titles published annually: 300 Print
Total Titles: 3,000 Print
Distributed by IOS Press
Distributor for IOS Press

Ondorisha Publishers Ltd
11-11 Nishigoken-cho, Shinjuku-ku, Tokyo 162-0812
Tel: (03) 32683101 *Fax:* (03) 32353530
Key Personnel
President: Hideaki Takeuchi
Editor: Hideaki Sanada
Sales: Yoshihiro Ikuta
Founded: 1945
Subjects: Crafts, Games, Hobbies
ISBN Prefix(es): 4-277

Ongaku No Tomo Sha Corporation+
30 Kagurazaka, 6 Chome, Shinjuku-ku, Tokyo 162-0825
Tel: (03) 32352111 *Fax:* (03) 32352119
Key Personnel
President: Jun Meguro
Copyright Dept: Kazuyuki Nabeshima
Founded: 1941
Subjects: Education, Music, Dance
ISBN Prefix(es): 4-276
Subsidiaries: Musica Nova Co (at above main address); Suiseisha Music Publishers; T O A Music International Co; Tomo Music Enterprise Co (at above main address)
Branch Office(s)
Osaka
Distributed by Theodore Presser Co
Distributor for Theodore Presser Co

Otsuki Shoten Publishers+
11-9 Hongo 2 chome, Bunkyo-ku, Tokyo 113-0033
Tel: 03 38134651 (Sales) *Fax:* 03 38134656
E-mail: otsuki@meibun.or.jp
Key Personnel
President, Production: Sadamu Nakagawa
Editorial: Kunio Shuto
Sales: Atsuo Harada
Founded: 1946
Subjects: Economics, History, Literature, Literary Criticism, Essays, Philosophy, Social Sciences, Sociology
ISBN Prefix(es): 4-272

Oxford University Press KK
4-8 Kaname-cho 2 Chome, Toshima-ku, Tokyo 171-0043
Tel: (03) 59953801 *Fax:* (03) 59953919
Key Personnel
Man Dir: S Ziolkowski
ISBN Prefix(es): 4-7552
Parent Company: Oxford University Press, United Kingdom

Pacifica Ltd, see Seibu Time Co Ltd

Pearson Education Japan+
Nishi-Shinjuku, KF Bldg 101, Shinjuku-ku, Tokyo 160-0023
Tel: (03) 3365 9001 *Fax:* (03) 3365 9009
E-mail: firstname.lastname@pearsoned.co.jp
Web Site: pearsoned.co.jp
Key Personnel
Man Dir: Naoto Ono
Business Development Dir: Katsuhiro Kawahara
General Manager, Local Publishing: Yukio Miwa
General Manager, ELT: Mieko Otaka
Founded: 1978
Subjects: Business, Computer Science, Economics, English as a Second Language, Medicine, Nursing, Dentistry, Microcomputers
ISBN Prefix(es): 4-938712; 4-88735; 4-87471; 4-89471; 4-931356
Number of titles published annually: 100 Print
Total Titles: 400 Print
Parent Company: Pearson Education, One Lake St, Upper Saddle River, NJ 07458, United States
Branch Office(s)
1-13-19 Sekiguchi, Bunkyo-ku, Tokyo 112-0014
  Tel: (03) 3266 0404 *Fax:* (03) 3266 0326
Distributed by Hachette (France); SGEL (Spain)
Distributor for Chambers Harrap (UK); Hachette (France); SGEL (Spain)
Foreign Rights: Fumi Nishijima

Periplus Editions, *imprint of* Charles E Tuttle Publishing Co Inc

PHP Kenkyujo
3-10 Sanban-cho, Chiyoda-ku, Tokyo 102-0075
Tel: (03) 32396221 *Fax:* (03) 32396263
Telex: J5422 402 PHPJ
Key Personnel
President: Masaharu Matsushita
Man Dir: Katsuhiko Eguchi
Founded: 1946
Other branch offices located in Kizu, Kyushu & Nagoya.
Subjects: Business, Social Sciences, Sociology
ISBN Prefix(es): 4-569
Subsidiaries: PHP Editors Group Inc; PHP Institute of America Inc; PHP International (Singapore) Pte Ltd
Branch Office(s)
Tokyo

Poplar Publishing Co Ltd+
5 Suga-cho, Shinjuku-ku, Tokyo 160-0018
Tel: (03) 33572211 *Fax:* (03) 39245341
Cable: POPLARPUB
Key Personnel
President: Haruo Tanaka
Foreign Rights & Trade: Hiroyuki Sakai
Foreign Rights: Mari Sasaki
Founded: 1947
Subjects: Biography, Fiction, Geography, Geology, History, Science (General)
ISBN Prefix(es): 4-591

President Inc+
13-12 Hirakawa-cho, 2 Chome, Chiyoda-ku, Tokyo 102-0093
Tel: (03) 32373711 *Fax:* (03) 32373746
E-mail: matu-pre@po.iijnet.or.jp
Key Personnel
President: Yoshio Watabiki
International Rights: Keijiro Amano
Founded: 1963
Subjects: Business, Cookery, Economics, Finance, Government, Political Science, Management, Marketing, Philosophy
ISBN Prefix(es): 4-8334

Parent Company: Time Warner Publishing BV
Branch Office(s)
2-3-18 Nakanoshima, Kita-ku, Osaka

Reimei-Shobo Co Ltd+
EBS-Bldg, 3-6-27 Marunouchi, Naka-ku, Nagoya 460-0002
Tel: (052) 9623045 *Fax:* (052) 9519065
E-mail: reimei@mui.biglobe.ne.jp
Web Site: wwwl.biz.biglobe.ne.jp/~reimei/
Key Personnel
President: Kunihiro Buma
International Rights: Masako Yoshikawa
Founded: 1947
Member of Japan Book Publishers Association.
Subjects: Child Care & Development, Education, Psychology, Psychiatry
ISBN Prefix(es): 4-654
Number of titles published annually: 50 Print
Total Titles: 1,650 Print
Warehouse: 374 Sangen-cho, Kita-ku, Nagoya 462-0004

Rinsen Book Co Ltd+
Imadegawa-Dori, Kawabata-Higashi-Iru, Sakyo-Ku, Kyoto 606-0000
Tel: (075) 7816166 *Fax:* (075) 7816168
E-mail: rinsen@st.alpha-web.or.jp
Web Site: www.alpha-web.or.jp/rinsen *Cable:* RINSEN KYOTO
Key Personnel
President: Eizo Kataoka
International Rights: Ohashz Kyoko
Founded: 1932
Subjects: Asian Studies, History, Literature, Literary Criticism, Essays, Religion - Buddhist
ISBN Prefix(es): 4-653
Branch Office(s)
Saikachizaka Bldg, 2-11-16 Kanda-Surugadai, Chiyoda-Ku, Toyko *Tel:* (03) 3293-5021 *Fax:* (03) 3293-5023

Riso-Sha
614-17 Minoridai, Matsudo-shi, Tokyo 271-2231
Tel: (047) 3668003 *Fax:* (047) 3607301
Key Personnel
President: Sumio Miyamoto
Subjects: Education, Philosophy, Psychology, Psychiatry, Religion - Buddhist, Religion - Catholic, Social Sciences, Sociology
ISBN Prefix(es): 4-650
Parent Company: Iwao-Syobou
Imprints: Library & Information Science

Rural Village Culture Association, see Nobunkyo (Rural Village Culture Association)

Ryosho-Fukyu-Kai Co Ltd
8-2 Kasuga, 1 Chome, Bunkyo-ku, Tokyo 112-0003
Tel: (03) 38131251 *Fax:* (03) 38116490
Key Personnel
President: Ichigaku Kawanaka
Foreign Trade Executive: Isao Hiramatsu
Foreign Rights Executive: Fumio Kimura
Man Dir: Kiyoshi Funakoshi
Founded: 1914
Subjects: Government, Political Science, Law, Public Administration, Social Sciences, Sociology
ISBN Prefix(es): 4-656

Saera Shobo (Librairie Ca et La)+
3-1 Ichigaya-Sadohara-cho, Shinjuku-ku, Tokyo 162-0842
Tel: (03) 32684261 *Fax:* (03) 32684262
Web Site: www.saela.co.jp
Key Personnel
Chief Executive: Toshiichi Uraki *E-mail:* uraki@saela.co.jp
Founded: 1948
Subjects: Fiction, Mathematics, Science (General), Technology
ISBN Prefix(es): 4-378
Number of titles published annually: 24 Print
Total Titles: 450 Print
Imprints: Toshiichi Uraki

Sagano Shoin
39 Ushigase-Minami-No-Kuchi-Cho, Nishikyo-ku, Kyoto 615-8045
Tel: (075) 3917686 *Fax:* (075) 3917321
Key Personnel
President: Tadayoshi Nakamura
Contact: Takayo Shito
Founded: 1968
Subjects: Business, Computer Science, Economics, Education, Ethnicity, Law, Literature, Literary Criticism, Essays, Marketing, Sports, Athletics, Women's Studies
ISBN Prefix(es): 4-7823

Saiensu-Sha Co Ltd
1-3-25 Sendagaya, Shibuya-ku, Tokyo 151-0051
Tel: (03) 54748500 *Fax:* (03) 54748900
E-mail: rikei@saiensu.co.jp
Key Personnel
President: Yuzo Morihira
Contact: Nobuhiko Tajima
Founded: 1969
ISBN Prefix(es): 4-7819
Subsidiaries: Shinsei-sha Co Ltd

The Sailor Publishing Co, Ltd
OCM Bldg, 10-18 Mouri, 2 Chome, Koutou-ku, Tokyo 135
Tel: (03) 38462955 *Fax:* (03) 38460452
Key Personnel
President: Etsu Ogawa
ISBN Prefix(es): 4-88330; 4-915632
Parent Company: The Sailor Fountain Pen Co Ltd

Salesian Press/Don Bosco Sha+
9-7 Yotsuya, 1 Chome, Shinjuku-ku, Tokyo 160
Tel: (032) 33517041 *Fax:* (032) 33515430
Key Personnel
President: Aldo Cipriani
Founded: 1930
Subjects: Religion - Catholic
ISBN Prefix(es): 4-88626
Warehouse: 1-22-12 Wakaba Cho, Shinjuku-ku, Tokyo

Sangyo-Tosho Publishing Co Ltd
2 Chome 11-13, Iidabashi, Chiyoda-ku, Tokyo 102-0072
Tel: (03) 32617821 *Fax:* (03) 32392178
E-mail: info@san-to.co.jp
Web Site: www.san-to.co.jp
Key Personnel
President: Takehiko Ezura
Sales: Koji Nara
Founded: 1925
Subjects: Biological Sciences, Chemistry, Chemical Engineering, Computer Science, Electronics, Electrical Engineering, Engineering (General), Mathematics, Mechanical Engineering, Philosophy, Physical Sciences, Physics, Psychology, Psychiatry, Science (General), Technology
ISBN Prefix(es): 4-7828
Total Titles: 500 Print

Sankyo Publishing Company Ltd
3-2 Kanda-Jimbo-cho 3 chome, Chiyoda-ku, Tokyo 101-0051
Tel: (03) 32645711 *Fax:* (03) 32655149
Key Personnel
President: Machiko Hagiwara
Founded: 1947
Subjects: Chemistry, Chemical Engineering
ISBN Prefix(es): 4-7827

Sanseido Co Ltd
22-14 Misaki-cho 2 chome, Chiyoda-ku, Tokyo 101-0061
Tel: (03) 32309404 *Fax:* (03) 32309567
Key Personnel
Chairman: Hisanori Ueno
Man Dir: Masaaki Moriya
Editorial, Publicity: Eiichi Tsunoda
Sales: Toshio Gomi
Production: Akihiko Ejima
Founded: 1881
Subjects: Earth Sciences, Education, History, Language Arts, Linguistics, Law, Literature, Literary Criticism, Essays, Science (General), Social Sciences, Sociology
ISBN Prefix(es): 4-385

Sanshusha Publishing Co, Ltd+
5-34 Shitaya 1 chome, Taito-ku, Tokyo 110-0004
Tel: (03) 38421711 *Fax:* (03) 38453965
E-mail: toshi@sanshusha.co.jp
Telex: Oisco J33380
Key Personnel
President: Kanji Maeda
Advertising, Rights & Permissions Dir: Toshihide Maeda
Founded: 1938
Member of MEBIC (Multimedia & Electronic Book International Committee), JBPA (Japan Book Publishers Association), APPA (Asian Pacific Publishers Association)
Specialize in Electronic Publishing.
Subjects: Education, English as a Second Language, Language Arts, Linguistics, Literature, Literary Criticism, Essays, Philosophy, Religion - Buddhist, Science (General), Travel
ISBN Prefix(es): 4-384

Sanyo Shuppan Boeki Co Inc+
Taiko Bldg, 3F 3-11-16 Nishi-Shinjuku, Shiniuku-ku, Tokyo 160
Tel: (03) 36693761 *Fax:* (03) 53513028
Telex: 2524435 Sanyob *Cable:* Sanyobook Tokyo
Key Personnel
President: Hisatoshi Hattori
Foreign Trade: Koichi Ohnishi
Founded: 1956
Also importers and booksellers.
Subjects: Chemistry, Chemical Engineering, Cookery, Science (General)
ISBN Prefix(es): 4-87930
Associate Companies: ITO-Sanyo SA
Branch Office(s)
Niihama
Osaka

Seibido+
22, Kanda-Ogawa-cho 3 chome, Chiyoda-ku, Tokyo 101-0052
Tel: (03) 32912261 *Fax:* (03) 32935490
Key Personnel
President: Yoshimitsu Sano
Vice President: Eiichiro Sano
Editor: Toshiko Kobayashi; Mark Brown
Founded: 1955
Publisher of ESL textbooks for the university market.
Subjects: English as a Second Language, Language Arts, Linguistics
ISBN Prefix(es): 4-7919

Seibido Shuppan Company Ltd
8-2 Suido 1 chome, Bunkyo-ku, Tokyo 112-8533
Tel: (03) 38144351 *Fax:* (03) 38144355
Web Site: www.seibidoshuppan.co.jp
Key Personnel
President & Man Dir: Etsuji Fukami
Founded: 1966
Subjects: Agriculture, Animals, Pets, Astrology, Occult, Automotive, Business, Career Development, Child Care & Development, Computer

PUBLISHERS

JAPAN

Science, Cookery, Crafts, Games, Hobbies, Gardening, Plants, Health, Nutrition, House & Home, How-to, Medicine, Nursing, Dentistry, Music, Dance, Outdoor Recreation, Photography, Sports, Athletics, Travel
ISBN Prefix(es): 4-415
Number of titles published annually: 300 Print
Total Titles: 1,200 Print

Seibu Time Co Ltd
SSC, Bldg 11 Niban-cho, Chiyoda-ku, Tokyo 102-0084
Tel: (03) 52762120 *Fax:* (03) 52762209
Key Personnel
Publisher: Sueaki Takaoka
Editor-in-Chief: Masatoshi Takeuchi
Founded: 1983
Subjects: Fiction, Nonfiction (General)
ISBN Prefix(es): 4-8275
Parent Company: S S Communications

Seibundo
514, Waseda-Tsurumaki-cho, Shinjuku-ku, Tokyo 162-0041
Tel: (03) 32039201 *Fax:* (03) 32039206
Key Personnel
President: Koichi Abe
ISBN Prefix(es): 4-7923

Seibundo Shinkosha Publishing Co Ltd
13-7 Yayoicho 1 chome, Nakano-ku, Tokyo 164-0013
Tel: (03) 33737141 *Fax:* (03) 59995120
Key Personnel
President: Shigeo Ogawa
Editorial: Hajime Hishikawa
International Rights, Overseas Department: Kiyoshi Motoki
Founded: 1912
Subjects: Business, Crafts, Games, Hobbies, Electronics, Electrical Engineering, Gardening, Plants, Management, Science (General), Technology
ISBN Prefix(es): 4-416

Seibundo Shuppan+
2-8-5 Shimanouchi, Chuo-ku, Osaka-shi 542-0082
Tel: (06) 2116265 *Fax:* (06) 2116495
Key Personnel
President: Shigeo Maeda
Founded: 1876
Subjects: History, Language Arts, Linguistics, Literature, Literary Criticism, Essays, Regional Interests
ISBN Prefix(es): 4-7924
Distributed by Japan Publication Trading Co Ltd
Distributor for Tohan Co LTD

Seishin Shobo
20-6, Otsuka 3 chome, Bunkyo-ku, Tokyo 112-0012
Tel: (03) 39465666 *Fax:* (03) 39458880
Key Personnel
President: Shukuko Shibata
ISBN Prefix(es): 4-414

Seiwa Shoten Co Ltd
2-5 Kami-Takaido 1 chome, Suginami-ku, Tokyo 168-0074
Tel: (03) 33290031 *Fax:* (03) 33043822
Cable: Seiwapublishers
Key Personnel
President: Youji Ishizawa
Editor-in-Chief: Yoshinori Asanuma
Sales Manager: Masaharu Fujiwara
System Manager: Yukio Shimura
Foreign Books Manager: Yumi Matsuzawa
Founded: 1976
Subjects: Language Arts, Linguistics, Medicine, Nursing, Dentistry, Psychology, Psychiatry
ISBN Prefix(es): 4-7911
Bookshop(s): 1-11 Kamitakaido, 1-chome, Suginamiku, Tokyo 168; 2-5 Kami-Takaido 1 chome, Suginami-ku, Tokyo 168-0074
Book Club(s): Bookclub Psyche

Seizando-Shoten Publishing Co Ltd
Seizando Bldg, 4-51 Minami-Motomachi, Shinjuku-ku, Tokyo 160-0012
Tel: (03) 33575861 *Fax:* (03) 33575867
Key Personnel
President: Minoru Ogawa
Foreign Rights & Trade: Yoshihiro Munekata
Sales: Yoshio Kimura
Production: Yuhei Shibuya
Publicity: Masayuki Toyama
Rights & Permissions: Kokichi Shioji
Founded: 1953
Subjects: Maritime, Technology, Transportation
ISBN Prefix(es): 4-425

Sekai Bunka Publishing Inc
2-29 Kudan-Kita 4 chome, Chiyoda-ku, Tokyo 102-0073
Tel: (03) 32625111 *Fax:* (03) 32378446
Cable: Sebunpub
Key Personnel
President: Tsutomu Suzuki
Foreign Trade & Rights: Yumio Tanaka
Founded: 1946
Subjects: Art, Education, Geography, Geology, History
ISBN Prefix(es): 4-418
U.S. Office(s): 501 Fifth Ave, Suite 2102, New York, NY 10017, United States

Shakai Hoken Shuppan-Sha
Hikida Bldg, 9 Kanda-Surugada 2 chome, Chiyoda-ku, Tokyo 101-0062
Tel: (03) 32919841 *Fax:* (03) 32919847
Key Personnel
President: Hidefumi Sano
ISBN Prefix(es): 4-7846

Shakai Shiso-Sha
25-13 Hongo, 3 chome, Bunkyo-ku, Tokyo 113-0033
Tel: (03) 38138101 *Fax:* (03) 38139061
Key Personnel
President: Yasuo Miyakawa
Editorial: Hitoshi Tanaka
Sales: Tadashi Kamatsuka
Founded: 1947
Subjects: Architecture & Interior Design, Art, Drama, Theater, Fiction, History, Music, Dance, Poetry, Social Sciences, Sociology, Travel
ISBN Prefix(es): 4-390

Shibundo Co Ltd
4-2 Nishi-goken machi, Shinjuku-ku, Tokyo 162-0812
Tel: (03) 32682441 *Fax:* (03) 32683550
Key Personnel
President: Hitoshi Kurokouchi
Founded: 1915
Subjects: Art, Asian Studies, Literature, Literary Criticism, Essays, Regional Interests
ISBN Prefix(es): 4-7843

Shiko-Sha Co Ltd
10-12 Hiroo 2 chome, Shibuya-ku, Tokyo 150-0012
Tel: (03) 34007151 *Fax:* (03) 34007294
Telex: J24903 *Cable:* Lmdecw Tokyo
Key Personnel
Man Dir: Yasoo Takeichi
Founded: 1950
Subjects: Religion - Catholic, Religion - Protestant
ISBN Prefix(es): 4-7834

Shimizu-Shoin
1-11, Higashi-Goken-cho, Shinjuku-ku, Tokyo 162-0813
Tel: (03) 32605261 *Fax:* (03) 32605270
Key Personnel
President: Kyuya Nomura
Subjects: Biography, History, Nonfiction (General), Philosophy
ISBN Prefix(es): 4-389

Shincho-Sha Co Ltd+
71 Yarai-cho, Shinjuku-ku, Tokyo 162-8711
Tel: (03) 32665411 *Fax:* (03) 32665534
Telex: G27433 Shincho *Cable:* SHINCHOSHA
Key Personnel
President: Takanobu Sato
Sales: Tadahiko Arai
Publishing Dept: Masaya Kurihara
Foreign Rights: Hisashi Miyabe
Founded: 1896
Subjects: Biography, Business, Fiction, Film, Video, Literature, Literary Criticism, Essays, Mysteries, Nonfiction (General), Photography, Romance, Science (General), Science Fiction, Fantasy
ISBN Prefix(es): 4-10

Shingakusha Co Ltd+
11-39, Higashino, Naka-Inoue-cho, Yamashina-ku, Kyoto-shi 607-8142
Tel: (075) 5816111 *Fax:* (075) 5929910
Key Personnel
President: Miki Iwasaki
Executive Dir: Toshihiro Ueda; Takeshi Yoshikawa
Founded: 1957
Subjects: Education
ISBN Prefix(es): 4-7868
Branch Office(s)
Fukuoka
Sapporo
Tokushima
Tokyo

Shinkenchiku-Sha Co Ltd+
31-2 Yushima 2 chome, Bunkyo-ku, Tokyo 113-0034
Tel: (03) 38117101 *Fax:* (03) 38128229
Cable: JAPANARCH TOKYO
Key Personnel
President: Yoshio Yoshida
Man Dir: Nobuyuki Yoshida
General Manager, Foreign Rights Executive: Ryugo Maru
Founded: 1925
Subjects: Architecture & Interior Design
ISBN Prefix(es): 4-7869
Associate Companies: A&U Publishing Co, Ltd
Subsidiaries: The Japan Architect Co Ltd

Akane Shobo Co Ltd+
3-2-1 Nishi-Kanda, Chiyoda-ku, Tokyo 101
Tel: (03) 32630641 *Fax:* (03) 32635440
Key Personnel
President: Masaharu Okamoto
Editor-in-Chief: Tadao Sudo *Tel:* (03) 32630644 *Fax:* (03) 32632094
Founded: 1949
Subjects: Fiction, Literature, Literary Criticism, Essays, Nonfiction (General), Science (General)
ISBN Prefix(es): 4-251

Hara Shobo
25-13, Shinjuku 1 chome, Shinjuku-ku, Tokyo 160-0022
Tel: (03) 3354 0374 *Fax:* (03) 3226 7950
Key Personnel
President: Kyo Naruse
ISBN Prefix(es): 4-562

Shobunsha Publications Inc+
2nd Seiko Bldg, 211 Kudan-Kita 4-chome, Chiyoda-ku, Tokyo 102-0073
Tel: (03) 32622141 *Fax:* (03) 3262 2147
Key Personnel
President: Toshio Kuroda
Founded: 1960
Member of Japan Book Publishers Association, Mapping Enterprises Association of Japan & Japan Digital Road Map Association.
Subjects: Travel
ISBN Prefix(es): 4-398
Total Titles: 300 Print
Subsidiaries: Shobunsha Map Research Center

Shogakukan Inc+
3-1 Hitotsubashi 2 chome, Chiyoda-ku, Tokyo 101-0003
Tel: (03) 32305661 *Fax:* (03) 32305840
Key Personnel
President: Masahiro Ohga
Dir: Tetsuo Takaishi
Senior Manager, Foreign Rights: Toshiki Ishii
Founded: 1922
Subjects: Art, Earth Sciences, Education, Geography, Geology, History
ISBN Prefix(es): 4-09

Mitsumura Suiko Shoin+
Horikawa Higashi-iru, Kitayama-Dori, Kita-ku, Kyoto-shi 603-000
Tel: (075) 4938244 *Fax:* (075) 4936011
Key Personnel
President: Honda Kinzo
Editor: Ueda Keiichiro
Founded: 1958
Subjects: Architecture & Interior Design, Art, Philosophy, Religion - Buddhist
ISBN Prefix(es): 4-8381

Shokabo Publishing Co Ltd
8-1 Yonban-cho, Chiyoda-ku, Tokyo 102-0081
Tel: (03) 32629166 *Fax:* (03) 32629130
Key Personnel
President: Tatsuji Yoshino
Foreign Rights & Trade: Saneatsu Makiya
Founded: 1897
Subjects: Mathematics, Science (General), Technology
ISBN Prefix(es): 4-7853

Shokoku Publishing Co Ltd
25 Saka machi, Shinjuku-ku, Tokyo 160-0002
Tel: (03) 33593231 *Fax:* (03) 33573961
Key Personnel
President: Taishiro Yamamoto
Sales Dir: Mineharu Matsuba
Editorial Dir: Takeshi Goto
Founded: 1932
Subjects: Architecture & Interior Design, Art, Education, Engineering (General), Science (General)
ISBN Prefix(es): 4-395

Shorin-Sha Co ltd+
3-22, Koishikawa 2 chome, Bunkyo-ku, Tokyo 112-0002
Tel: (03) 38154921 *Fax:* (03) 38154923
Founded: 1985
Subjects: Medicine, Nursing, Dentistry
ISBN Prefix(es): 4-7965

Shueisha Inc
5-10 Hitotsubashi 2 chome, Chiyoda-ku, Tokyo 101-0003
Tel: (03) 32306393; (03) 32306320 *Fax:* (03) 32302547
Key Personnel
President: Tamio Kozima
Editorial: Toshio Kawaguchi
Sales & Foreign Trade: Katsunori Kawaziri
Foreign Rights: Norifumi Sunou; Takaaki Ike
Founded: 1926
Subjects: Art, Fiction, Language Arts, Linguistics, Literature, Literary Criticism, Essays, Nonfiction (General)
ISBN Prefix(es): 4-08
Associate Companies: Shogakukan Inc

Shufu-to-Seikatsu Sha Ltd
5-7 Kyobashi 3 chome, Chuo-ku, Tokyo 104-0031
Tel: (03) 35635124 *Fax:* (03) 35678793
Key Personnel
President: Akira Endo
Editor-in-Chief: Miss Miyako Kiyohara
Publishing Dept, Foreign Rights: Shujiro Murakawa
Founded: 1935
Subjects: Art, History, Literature, Literary Criticism, Essays, Medicine, Nursing, Dentistry, Philosophy, Religion - Other, Technology
ISBN Prefix(es): 4-391

Shufunotomo sha Co Ltd+
9 Kanda Surugadai 2 chome, Chiyoda-ku, Tokyo 101-0062
Tel: (03) 52807555 *Fax:* (03) 52807556
E-mail: international@shufunotom.co.jp
Web Site: www.shufunotom.co.jp
Key Personnel
President: Kunihiko Muramatsu
General Manager & International Dept: Shunichi Kamiya
Founded: 1916
Subjects: Architecture & Interior Design, Career Development, Child Care & Development, Cookery, Crafts, Games, Hobbies, Education, Fashion, Fiction, Gardening, Plants, Health, Nutrition, House & Home, How-to, Nonfiction (General), Photography, Religion - Buddhist, Travel
ISBN Prefix(es): 4-07
Total Titles: 1,200 Print; 10 CD-ROM; 3 E-Book

Shunjusha
18-6, Soto-Kanda 2 chome, Chiyoda-ku, Tokyo 101-0021
Tel: (03) 32559611 *Fax:* (03) 32531384
Key Personnel
President: Akira Kanda
ISBN Prefix(es): 4-393

Shuppan News Co Ltd
40-7 Kanda-Jimbo-cho 2 chome, Chiyoda-ku, Tokyo 101-0051
Tel: 03 32622076
Key Personnel
Editorial: Takeo Yoshizawa
Sales: Keiji Kinoshita
Rights & Permissions: Tetsuzo Suzuki
Founded: 1949
ISBN Prefix(es): 4-7852

Oru Shuppan+
2-4 Kudan-Kita 3 chome Chiyoda-ku, Tokyo 102-0073
Tel: (03) 32340971 *Fax:* (03) 32616602
Key Personnel
Contact: Mika Hirano
ISBN Prefix(es): 4-279

The Simul Press Inc
13-9 Araki-cho, Shinjuku-ku, Tokyo 160-0007
Tel: (03) 32262861 *Fax:* (03) 32262860
Key Personnel
President: Katsuo Tamura
Senior Man Dir: Eiko Ikuta
Dir, Overseas Affairs: Masumi Muramatsu
Senior Editor: Daitaro Suwabe
Marketing: Takayuki Kawazoe
Founded: 1967
Subjects: Business, Economics, Education, History, Language Arts, Linguistics, Literature, Literary Criticism, Essays, Philosophy, Regional Interests, Religion - Other, Social Sciences, Sociology
ISBN Prefix(es): 4-377
Associate Companies: Simul International, Inc

Sobun-Sha
6-7 Kojimachi 2 chome, Chiyoda-ku, Tokyo 102-0083
Tel: (03) 32637101 *Fax:* (03) 32636789
E-mail: sobunsha@juno.ocn.ne.jp
Web Site: www.sobunsha.co.jp
Key Personnel
President: Hirotoshi Kuboi
Vice President: Masaaki Kuboi
Founded: 1951
Academic Publishers.
Subjects: Asian Studies, Biblical Studies, Business, Developing Countries, Economics, Education, Ethnicity, Finance, Foreign Countries, Humanities
ISBN Prefix(es): 4-423

Sogensha Publishing Co Ltd+
3-6 Awaji-machi 4 chome, Chuo-ku Osaka-shi Osaka 541-0047
Tel: (06) 62319011 *Fax:* (06) 62333112
E-mail: sgse@email.msn.com
Web Site: www.sogensha.co.jp
Key Personnel
President: Keiichi Yabe
Founded: 1925
Subjects: Art, Education, History, Medicine, Nursing, Dentistry, Philosophy, Psychology, Psychiatry, Religion - Other
ISBN Prefix(es): 4-422
Associate Companies: Tokyo Sogensha Co Ltd

Sony Magazines Inc+
6-2 Goban-cho, Chiyoda-ku, Tokyo 102-0076
Tel: (03) 32345811 *Fax:* (03) 32346753
Key Personnel
President: Hiroshi Inagaki
ISBN Prefix(es): 4-7897
Parent Company: Sony Music Entertainment Inc

Soryusha
5 Koji-machi 3 chome, Chiyoda-ku, Tokyo 102
Tel: (03) 32631471 *Fax:* (03) 32632943
Key Personnel
President & Manager: Kotaro Tanaka
Subjects: How-to, Mathematics
ISBN Prefix(es): 4-88176
Parent Company: Tokyo Hyoujun
Associate Companies: Kougakusha; Tokyo Souken
Book Club(s): Japan Book Publishers Association

Soshisha Co Ltd+
26-26 Jingumae 4 chome, Shibuya-ku, Tokyo 150-0001
Tel: (03) 34706565 *Fax:* (03) 34702640
E-mail: soshisha@magical.egg.or.jp
Key Personnel
President: Masao Kase
Editor-in-Chief: Haruo Kitani
Sales Manager: Tomio Kobayashi
Founded: 1968
Subjects: Literature, Literary Criticism, Essays, Nonfiction (General), Science (General)
ISBN Prefix(es): 4-7942

Springer-Verlag Tokyo+
EBS Hongo Bldg, 3-3-13 Hongo 3-chome, Bunkyo-ku, Tokyo 113-0033
Tel: (03) 38120757 *Fax:* (03) 38120719
Founded: 1983
Subjects: Economics
ISBN Prefix(es): 4-431
Total Titles: 300 Print; 15 CD-ROM

PUBLISHERS

JAPAN

Online services available through Linkspringer.
Parent Company: Springer-Verlag GmbH & Co KG, Heidelberger Platz 3, 14197 Berlin, Germany

Surugadai-Shuppan Sha
7, Kanda-Surugadai 3 chome, Survgadai Bldg, Chiyoda-ku, Tokyo 101-0062
Tel: (03) 32911676 *Fax:* (03) 32911675
Key Personnel
President: Yoji Ida
ISBN Prefix(es): 4-411

Taimeido Publishing Co Ltd
3-22, Kanda-Ogawa-machi, Chiyoda-ku, Tokyo 101-0052
Tel: (03) 32912374 *Fax:* (03) 32912376
E-mail: taimell@ibm.net
Key Personnel
President: Yuzo Kanbe
Founded: 1918
Subjects: Agriculture, Economics, Geography, Geology, History, Philosophy, Religion - Other
ISBN Prefix(es): 4-470

Takahashi Shoten Co Ltd
22-13, Otowa 1 chome, Bunkyo-ku, Tokyo 112-0013
Tel: (03) 39434525 *Fax:* (03) 39434288
Key Personnel
President: Hideo Takahashi
Foreign Rights & Trade: Kazuo Kondo
Founded: 1939 (as Kowado Co Ltd)
Subjects: Education, Language Arts, Linguistics, Law, Medicine, Nursing, Dentistry, Technology
ISBN Prefix(es): 4-471

Tamagawa University Press+
1-1, Tamagawa-Gakuen 6 chome, Machida Shi 194-0041
Tel: (0427) 398935 *Fax:* (0427) 398940
E-mail: tup@adm.tamagawa.ac.jp
Key Personnel
President: Yoshiaki Obara
Dir & Editor: Kubo Kouichiro
Founded: 1923
Member of The Association of Japanese University Press (AJUP); International Association of Scholarly Publishers (IASP).
Subjects: Education, Social Sciences, Sociology
ISBN Prefix(es): 4-472

Tankosha Publishing Co Ltd
19-1, Murasakino miya-Nishi-machi, Kita-ku, Kyoto-shi 603-8158
Tel: (075) 432 5151 *Fax:* (075) 432 0275
E-mail: tankosha@magical.egg.or.jp
Web Site: tankosha.topica.ne.jp/
Key Personnel
President: Yoshito Naya
Founded: 1949
Subjects: Antiques, Architecture & Interior Design, Art, Cookery, Crafts, Games, Hobbies, Ethnicity, Gardening, Plants, History, Philosophy, Photography, Religion - Other
ISBN Prefix(es): 4-473
Total Titles: 4,000 Print
Subsidiaries: Weatherhill Inc
Branch Office(s)
Sugaya Bldg, 39-1 Ichigaya Yanagi-cho, Shinjuku-ku, Tokyo 162-0061

TBS-Britannica Co Ltd
Itochu Nenryo Bldg, 24-12 Meguro 1 chome, Meguro-ku Tokyo 153-0063
Tel: (03) 5436-5721 *Fax:* (03) 54365759
Key Personnel
President: Shinichi Hamanaka
ISBN Prefix(es): 4-484

Teikoku-Shoin Co Ltd
29 Kanda Jimbo-cho 3 chome, Chiyoda-ku Tokyo 101-0051
Tel: (03) 32620834 *Fax:* (03) 32627770
E-mail: kenkyu@teikokushoin.co.jp
Key Personnel
President: Mutsuo Shirahama
Dir & Manager, Research Section: Masami Komiya
Founded: 1926
Subjects: Geography, Geology, History
ISBN Prefix(es): 4-8071

The Oriental Economist, see Toyo Keizai Inc (The Oriental Economist)

Thomson Learning+
Dai 5, Nomura Bldg 3F, 1-3, Kanda Jinbo-cho, Chiyoda-ku, Tokyo 102
Tel: (03) 52825180 *Fax:* (03) 52825181
E-mail: yuko@tlj.co.jp
Web Site: www.tlj.co.jp
Key Personnel
General Manager: Yuko Matsuoka
  E-mail: yuko@tlj.co.jp
Founded: 1989
Publisher for ELT & academic texts.
Also acts as importing agent for Thompson affiliated companies.
Subjects: Communications, English as a Second Language, Language Arts, Linguistics
ISBN Prefix(es): 4-900718; 4-931321
Parent Company: The Thomson Corporation
Distributor for Boyd & Fraser; Brooks/Coe; Chapman & Hall/Blackie & Son Academic; Course Technology Inc; Delmar; Gale Research/St James; Heinle & Heinle/Newbury House; Little, Brown/Legal (Japan); MacMillan (ELT only-USA); Thomas Nelson & Sons Ltd (UK); Onword; PWS-Kent; South-Western; Van Nostrand Reinhold; Wadsworth

3A Corporation
6-3, Sarugaku-cho 2 chome, Chiyoda-ku, Tokyo 101
Tel: (03) 32925751 *Fax:* (03) 32925754
E-mail: 3ac@mail.at-m.or.jp
Web Site: www.at-m.or.jpl~3ac
Key Personnel
President: Michihiro Takai
Founded: 1973
Subjects: Language Arts, Linguistics, Management
Distributed by Chapman & Hall, London (except USA & Japan); Quality Resources, New York (USA)

Tohan-Nippan, *imprint of* Minerva Shobo Co Ltd

Toho Book Store+
1-3 Kanda-Jinbo-cho, Chiyoda-ku, Tokyo 101-0051
Tel: (03) 32331005 *Fax:* (03) 32950800
Key Personnel
President: Masakazu Fukushima
Founded: 1951
Member of Japan Book Publisher's Association; Specialize in China.
Subjects: Archaeology, Art, Asian Studies, Crafts, Games, Hobbies, Economics, Geography, Geology, History, Language Arts, Linguistics, Literature, Literary Criticism, Essays, Medicine, Nursing, Dentistry, Nonfiction (General), Philosophy, Regional Interests, Religion - Other
ISBN Prefix(es): 4-497
Branch Office(s)
Osaka
Bookshop(s): 1-10-2 Takashimadaira, Itabashi-Ku, Tokyo 175
Warehouse: 1-10-2 Takashimadaira, Itabashi-Ku, Tokyo 175
Orders to: 1-10-2 Takashimadaira, Itabashi-ku, Tokyo 175

Toho Shuppan+
Yasuda Seimei Tennouji Bldg, 1-8-15 Oomichi, Ten-nouji-ku, Osaka-Shi Osaka 543-0052
Tel: 06 3655421
Key Personnel
President: Shigeto Imahigashi
Founded: 1978
Subjects: Art, Asian Studies, Crafts, Games, Hobbies, History, Philosophy, Photography, Religion - Buddhist
ISBN Prefix(es): 4-88591

Tokai University Press
28-4 Tomigaya 2 chome, Shibuya-ku, Tokyo 151-0063
Tel: (03) 54780891 *Fax:* (03) 54780870
Key Personnel
President: Tatsuro Matsumae
Dir: Norimitsu Matsumae
Publicity & Foreign Rights & Trade: Yoshihiro Miura
Production: Fumio Kawakami
Founded: 1962
Subjects: Art, Biological Sciences, Earth Sciences, History, Language Arts, Linguistics, Literature, Literary Criticism, Essays, Philosophy, Religion - Other, Social Sciences, Sociology, Technology
ISBN Prefix(es): 4-486

Tokuma-Shoten+
1-16 Higashi Shimbashi 1 chome, Minato-ku, Tokyo 105-0021
Tel: (03) 35730111 *Fax:* (03) 35738771
Key Personnel
President: Yasuyoshi Tokuma
Editor & Foreign Trade: Kyoko Aoyama
Founded: 1954
Subjects: Art, Crafts, Games, Hobbies, Fiction, How-to, Literature, Literary Criticism, Essays, Nonfiction (General), Social Sciences, Sociology, Sports, Athletics
ISBN Prefix(es): 4-19
U.S. Office(s): 150 Skyline Tower, 10900 NE Fourth, Bellevue, WA 98004, United States

Tokyo Kagaku Dozin Co Ltd+
36-7 Sengoku, 3 chome Bunkyo-ku, Tokyo 112-0011
Tel: (03) 39465311 *Fax:* (03) 39465316
Key Personnel
President: Minako Ozawa
Manager, Editorial Dept & Foreign Rights & Trade: Mutsure Sumita
  E-mail: tokyokagakudozin@a.email.ne.jp
Founded: 1961
Subjects: Chemistry, Chemical Engineering, Medicine, Nursing, Dentistry, Science (General)
ISBN Prefix(es): 4-8079

Tokyo Shoseki Co Ltd+
2-17-1 Horifune, Kita-ku, Tokyo 114-8524
Tel: (03) 53907531 *Fax:* (03) 53907538
E-mail: home@tokyo-shoseki.co.jp
Web Site: www.tokyo-shoseki.co.jp
Key Personnel
President: Atsushi Choji
International Dept Manager: Shigeki Oyama
  E-mail: shoseki@tokyo-shoseki.co.jp
Founded: 1909
Associated with Toppan International Group.
Subjects: Art, Disability, Special Needs, Education, English as a Second Language, Fiction, History, Mathematics, Religion - Buddhist, Science (General), Travel

ISBN Prefix(es): 4-487
Total Titles: 1,000 Print; 100 CD-ROM
Subsidiaries: Astro Publishing Co Ltd (Domestic Only); Froebel-Kan Co Ltd
Branch Office(s)
Chubu (domestic only)
Chugoku (domestic only)
Hokkaido (domestic only)
Kansai (domestic only)
Kyushu (domestic only)
Tohoku (domestic only)

Tokyo Sogensha Co Ltd
1-5 Shin Ogawa-machi, Shinjuku-ku, Tokyo 162-0814
Tel: (03) 32688201 *Fax:* (03) 32688230
Key Personnel
Chairman: Takao Akiyama
President: Ichiro Hiramatsu
Editorial: Yasunobu Togawa
Sales: Haruo Hashimoto
Founded: 1925
Subjects: Literature, Literary Criticism, Essays, Mysteries, Science Fiction, Fantasy, Social Sciences, Sociology
ISBN Prefix(es): 4-488
Associate Companies: Sogensha Publishing Co Ltd

Tokyo Tosho Co Ltd
5-22 Suido, 2 chome, Bunkyo-ku, Tokyo 112-0005
Tel: (03) 38162561 *Fax:* (03) 38157330
Key Personnel
President & Foreign Trade Executive: Hiroyasu Katayama
Foreign Rights & Trade: Shizuo Sudo
Founded: 1955
Subjects: Biography, Science (General)
ISBN Prefix(es): 4-489

Toppan Co Ltd+
c/o Toppan Shibaura Bldg, 3-19-26 Shibaura, Minato-ku, Tokyo 108-0023
Tel: (03) 5418-2535 *Fax:* (03) 5418-2529
E-mail: yuri@top.co.jp
Web Site: www.toppan-pub.topica.ne.jp/
Key Personnel
Chief Executive: Hiroshi Yuri *Tel:* (03) 5418-253
Man Dir: Naomi Yoshikawa
Founded: 1963
Member of Japan Book Association of International Publications.
Subjects: Biological Sciences, Computer Science, Environmental Studies, Library & Information Sciences
ISBN Prefix(es): 4-8101
Total Titles: 350 Print
Parent Company: Toppan Printing Co Ltd
Associate Companies: Tokyo Shoseki Co Ltd
Distributor for Prentice Hall Japan Ltd (Japan)

Tosui Shobo Publishers
4-1, Nishi-Kanda 2 chome, Touho Gakki Honkan, Chiyoda-ku, Tokyo 101
Tel: (03) 32616190 *Fax:* (03) 32612234
Key Personnel
President: Michiya Kuwabara
Founded: 1978
Subjects: Anthropology, History
ISBN Prefix(es): 4-88708

Toyo Keizai Inc (The Oriental Economist)+
2-1 Nihonbashi-Hongoku-Cho 1 chome, Chuo-ku, Tokyo 103-0021
Tel: (03) 32465469; (03) 32465656 *Fax:* (03) 32704127
E-mail: xlk01673@niftyserve.or.jp
Key Personnel
President: Asano Junji
Rights Manager: Kurono Yukiharu
Founded: 1895
Subjects: Economics, Labor, Industrial Relations, Nonfiction (General), Social Sciences, Sociology
ISBN Prefix(es): 4-492
U.S. Office(s): Toyo Keizai America Inc, 380 Lexington Ave, Room 4505, New York, NY 10168, United States *Tel:* 212-949-6737

Tsukiji Shokan Publishing Co
7-4-4-201 Tsukiji, Chuo-ku, Tokyo 104-0045
Tel: (03) 35423731 *Fax:* (03) 35415799
Key Personnel
President: Jiro Doi
Founded: 1954
Subjects: Anthropology, Archaeology, Biological Sciences, Child Care & Development, Earth Sciences, Environmental Studies, Social Sciences, Sociology, Sports, Athletics
ISBN Prefix(es): 4-8067

Tutbooks, *imprint of* Charles E Tuttle Publishing Co Inc

Charles E Tuttle Publishing Co Inc+
Yaekari Bldg, 3F 5-4-12, Osaki, Shinagawa-ku, Tokyo 141-0032
Tel: (03) 5437 0171 *Fax:* (03) 5437 0755
E-mail: tuttle@gol.com
Key Personnel
President, Singapore: Eric Oey
Man Dir, Tokyo Office: John Moore
Rights & Permissions & International Right, Boston Office: Penny Probst
Founded: 1948
Subjects: Art, Asian Studies, Cookery, Crafts, Games, Hobbies, Fiction, Language Arts, Linguistics, Literature, Literary Criticism, Essays, Poetry, Public Administration, Social Sciences, Sociology, Sports, Athletics, Travel
Parent Company: Berkeley Books Pte Ltd
Imprints: Journey Editions; Periplus Editions; Tutbooks; Yenbooks
Subsidiaries: Periplus Editions (HK) Ltd
Divisions: Periplus (Singapore) Private Limited
U.S. Office(s): Charles E Tuttle Publishing Co Inc, 153 Milk St, Boston, MA 02109-4809, United States (editorial office)
Charles E Tuttle Publishing Co Ltd, Airport Industrial Park, 364 Innovation Dr, North Clarendon, VT 05759-9436, United States *Tel:* 802-773-8930 *Fax:* 802-773-6993 (executive office)

United Nations University Press+
29th floor, Toho Seimei Bldg, 15-1 Shibuya 2-chome, Shibuya-ku, Tokyo 150
Tel: (03) 4992811 *Fax:* (03) 34067345
Telex: 25442 unat unix *Cable:* UNATUNIV TOKYO
Key Personnel
Dir: Amadio A Arboleda
Founded: 1975
Specialize in books & journals in the social sciences, humanities & pure & applied natural sciences related to the University's research into the pressing global problems of human survival, development & welfare.
Subjects: Asian Studies, Developing Countries, Economics, Environmental Studies, Ethnicity, Geography, Geology, Health, Nutrition, Social Sciences, Sociology
ISBN Prefix(es): 92-808
Parent Company: United Nations University
Imprints: UNU/WIDER Publications; UNU-INTECH Publications
Branch Office(s)
UNU Office in North America, United Nations, Room DC2-1462-70, New York, NY 10017, United States
Distributor for Intermediate Technology Publications (ITC) (Japan)
Warehouse: c/o Hong Kong University Press, 139 Pokfulam Rd, Hong Kong

Universal Academy Press, Inc+
BR-Hongo-5 Bldg, 16-2 Hongo 6 chome, Bunkyo-Ku, Tokyo 113-0033
Tel: (03) 3813 7232 *Fax:* (03) 38135932
E-mail: general@uap.co.jp
Key Personnel
President: Masahito Sakui
Founded: 1986
Specialize in Publishing Japanese Research in English.
Subjects: Engineering (General), Medicine, Nursing, Dentistry, Science (General), Technology
ISBN Prefix(es): 4-946443
Orders to: CPO, Box 235, Tokyo 100-8691

The University of Nagoya Press
One Furo-cho, Chikusa-ku, Nagoya 464-8601
Tel: (052) 7815111 *Fax:* (052) 7802045
Key Personnel
President: Junpei Asai
Orders to: Japan Publications Trading Co Ltd, 1-2-1 Sarugaku-cho 1 chome, PO Box 5030, Chiyoda-ku, Tokyo 101-0064 *Tel:* (03) 32923751 *Fax:* (03) 32920410

University of Tokyo Press+
3-1 Hongo 7 chome, Bunkyo-ku 113-0033
Tel: (03) 38151902 *Fax:* (03) 38126958
Cable: UNIVERSITYPRESS
Key Personnel
Man Dir: Tadashi Yamashita
Associate Dir: Isao Watanabe
Manager, International Publications: Etsuko Hamao
Founded: 1951
Member of AAUP, STM, AJUP.
Subjects: Engineering (General), History, Medicine, Nursing, Dentistry, Philosophy, Psychology, Psychiatry, Religion - Other, Science (General), Social Sciences, Sociology
ISBN Prefix(es): 4-13
U.S. Office(s): Columbia University Press, 136 S Broadway, Irvington, NY 10533, United States

UNU-INTECH Publications, *imprint of* United Nations University Press

UNU/WIDER Publications, *imprint of* United Nations University Press

Toshiichi Uraki, *imprint of* Saera Shobo (Librairie Ca et La)

Waseda University Press
104-25 Totsuka-cho 1 chome, Shinjuku-ku, Tokyo 169-0071
Tel: (03) 32031551 *Fax:* (03) 32070406
E-mail: kyw03725@nifty.ne.jp
Web Site: www.waseda-up.co.jp
Key Personnel
President: Shigenor Watabe
Foreign Rights & Trade: Koji Terayama
Founded: 1886
Subjects: Anthropology, Archaeology, Economics, Education, Film, Video, Finance, Government, Political Science, History, Law, Literature, Literary Criticism, Essays, Philosophy, Psychology, Psychiatry, Social Sciences, Sociology, Sports, Athletics
ISBN Prefix(es): 4-657
Number of titles published annually: 35 Print
Total Titles: 550 Print

PUBLISHERS

Yakugyo Jiho Sha Company Ltd
Hokuskin Bldg, 36 Kanda-Jinbocho 2 chome, Chiyoda-ku, Tokyo 101-0051
Tel: (03) 32657755 *Fax:* (03) 32346573
Key Personnel
President: Shozo Takeda
Specialize in pharmaceutical industry & regulation, & pharmaceutical sciences.
ISBN Prefix(es): 4-8407

Yakuji Nippo Ltd
One Kanda-Izumi-cho, Chiyoda-ku, Tokyo 101-8648
Tel: (03) 38622141 *Fax:* (03) 38668408
Key Personnel
Contact: Daisuke Koyama *E-mail:* koyama_d@yakuji.co.jp
Subjects: Medicine, Nursing, Dentistry
ISBN Prefix(es): 4-8408

Yama-Kei Publishers Co Ltd+
Formerly Yama to Keikoku-Sha
1-1-33 Shiba-Daimon, Minato-ku, Tokyo 105-8503
Tel: (03) 3436-4021 *Fax:* (03) 34334057
E-mail: info@yamakei.co.jp
Key Personnel
General Manager, International Division: Tony S Endo
President: Yoshimitsu Kawasaki
Founded: 1930
Subjects: Earth Sciences, Geography, Geology, Sports, Athletics, Travel
ISBN Prefix(es): 4-635
Branch Office(s)
1-12-12 Esaka-cho, Fukita-Shi, Osaka

Yama to Keikoku-Sha, see Yama-Kei Publishers Co Ltd

Yamaguchi Shoten+
72 Ichijoji-Tsukuda-machi, Sakyo-ku, Kyoto-shi, Kyoto 606-8175
Tel: (075) 7816121 *Fax:* (075) 7052003
Key Personnel
President: Kanya Yamaguchi
Founded: 1949
Subjects: English as a Second Language, Language Arts, Linguistics, Literature, Literary Criticism, Essays
ISBN Prefix(es): 4-8411
Branch Office(s)
Fukuoka
Hiroshima
Nagoya
Tokyo

Yenbooks, *imprint of* Charles E Tuttle Publishing Co Inc

Yohan Shuppan+
14-9 Okubo 3-chome, Shinjuku-ku, Tokyo 169
Tel: (03) 32080181 *Fax:* (03) 32042582
E-mail: shinsuke@yohan-pub.co.jp
Telex: 2324818 Yohan J *Cable:* BOOKYOHAN
Key Personnel
President: Masanori Watanabe
Senior Man Dir: Shinsuke Suzuki
Editor-in-Chief: Yoshio Kida
Founded: 1963
Subjects: Art, Asian Studies, English as a Second Language, Language Arts, Linguistics
ISBN Prefix(es): 4-89684
Parent Company: Yohan (Western Publications Distribution Agency)
Imprints: Lotus; La Verve
Distributed by Weatherhill (North/South America)

Yokendo Ltd
30-15 Hongo 5 chome, Bunkyo-ku, Tokyo 113-0033
Tel: (03) 38140911 *Fax:* (03) 38122615
Key Personnel
President: Kiyoshi Oikawa
Foreign Rights: Akira Suzuki
Founded: 1914
Subjects: Agriculture, Engineering (General), Science (General)
ISBN Prefix(es): 4-8425

Yoshioka Shoten
87 Tanaka-Monzen-cho, Sakyo-ku, Kyoto 606-8225
Tel: (075) 7814747 *Fax:* (075) 7019075
Key Personnel
President: Makoto Yoshioka
ISBN Prefix(es): 4-8427

Yugaku-sha Ltd+
46 Kanda Jinbo-cho 1 chome, Chiyoda-ku, Tokyo 101-0051
Tel: (03) 32333731 *Fax:* (03) 32333730
Key Personnel
Publisher: Kazumi Mitsui
Editorial, Sales Manager: Yoshiaki Tokunaga
Production Manager: Isoyoshi Yamamoto
Foreign Rights Associate: Naoko Sakaki
Founded: 1969
ISBN Prefix(es): 4-8416
Associate Companies: Keigaku Publishing Co Ltd

Yuhikaku Publishing Co Ltd
17 Kanda Jimbo-cho 2 chome, Chiyoda-ku, Tokyo 101-0051
Tel: (03) 32641314 *Fax:* (03) 32628035
Cable: Yuhikakubook
Key Personnel
Chairman: Shiro Egusa
President: Tadataka Egusa
Foreign Trade & Rights: Osamu Nomura
Founded: 1877
Subjects: Economics, Education, History, Law, Psychology, Psychiatry, Social Sciences, Sociology
ISBN Prefix(es): 4-641

Yuki Shobo
39-12 Sekiguchi, Bunkyo-ku, Tokyo 112-0014
Tel: (03) 32030151 *Fax:* (03) 32030157
Key Personnel
President: Misue Takahashi
ISBN Prefix(es): 4-638

Yushodo Co Ltd+
29 San-ei-cho, Shinjuku-ku, Tokyo 160-0008
Tel: (03) 33571411 *Fax:* (03) 33515855; (03) 33571785
E-mail: intl@yushodo.co.jp
Web Site: www.yushodo.co.jp
Key Personnel
CEO: Mitsuo Nitta
President: Tamio Kawashima
Contact: R Carpenter
Founded: 1932
Specialize in Antiquarian Books, Periodicals, New Books, Microforms; Also acts as publisher, wholesaler, & dealer.
Subjects: Asian Studies, Economics, Regional Interests
ISBN Prefix(es): 4-8419
Associate Companies: JCC-Culture Japan; Newfield Building Co Ltd
Subsidiaries: Yushodo Fantas Corp; Yushodo Press Co Ltd
Branch Office(s)
Kansai
Ohtsuka
Kyoto
Warehouse: Yushodo Operation Center, 1542 Nakagawa, Isawa-cho, Higashiyatsushiro-gun, Yamanashi-Ken 406

JORDAN

Zeikei insatsu, *imprint of* Zeimukeiri-Kyokai

Zeimukeiri-Kyokai+
2-5-13 Simo-Ochiai, Shinjuku-ku, Toyko 161-0033
Tel: (03) 3953 3325 *Fax:* (03) 3565 3391
E-mail: postmaster@zeikei.co.jp
Web Site: www.zeikei.co.jp
Key Personnel
President: Yoshiharu Otsubo
Founded: 1945
Subjects: Accounting, Behavioral Sciences, Business, Economics, Human Relations, Law, Management, Marketing
ISBN Prefix(es): 4-419
Number of titles published annually: 100 Print
Total Titles: 1,700 Print
Imprints: Zeikei insatsu
Subsidiaries: Senbundo (Japan)

Zenkoku Kyodo Shuppan
10-32 Wakaba 1 chome, Shinjuku-ku, Tokyo 160-0011
Tel: (03) 33594811 *Fax:* (03) 33586174
Key Personnel
President: Takao Onaka
Founded: 1946
Subjects: Agriculture, Law, Management
ISBN Prefix(es): 4-7934

The Zion Press+
165-83 Arise Ikawadani-cho, Nishi-ku, Kobe 6512113
Tel: (078) 9757611 *Fax:* (078) 9757373
E-mail: greatobe@yo.rim.ur.jp
Key Personnel
President: Mirei Moritani
Vice President: Keiko Moritani
Editor: Mineo Moritani
Founded: 1982
Publicize Christian Truth.
Member of Japan Book Publishers Association.
Subjects: All fields of learning helpful to Christian purpose
ISBN Prefix(es): 4-7952
Total Titles: 1,000 Print
Parent Company: The Zion Press Corporation
Distributed by Seiun-Sha

Zoshindo JukenKenkyusha
19-15 Shinmachi 2 chome, Nishi-ku, Osaka Shi, Osaka 550-0013
Tel: (06) 65321581 *Fax:* (06) 65321588
E-mail: zoshindo@mbox.inet-osaka.or.jp
Web Site: www.zoshindo.co.jp/
Key Personnel
President: Akitaka Okamoto
Founded: 1890
Subjects: Education
ISBN Prefix(es): 4-424

Jordan

General Information

Capital: Amman
Language: Arabic. English widely used by business people
Religion: Predominantly Sunni Muslim
Population: 3.6 million
Bank Hours: 0830-1230 Saturday-Thursday
Shop Hours: 0900-1300, 1500-1900 Saturday-Thursday
Currency: 1000 fils = 1 dinar; 10 fils is known as a piastre
Export/Import Information: No tariffs on books and advertising matter, but tax applies. Import licenses required but granted freely. Air freight

JORDAN

must be by Jordanian national airline. Transportation insurance must be arranged in Jordan.
Copyright: No copyright conventions signed

Al-Tanwir Al Ilmi (Scientific Enlightenment Publishing House)+
PO Box 4237, al-Mahatta, Amman 11131
Tel: (026) 4899619 *Fax:* (026) 4899619
Key Personnel
Owner: Dr Taisir Subhi Mahmoud
E-mail: taisir@yahoo.com
Founded: 1990
Subjects: Education, Electronics, Electrical Engineering, Philosophy, Science (General), Social Sciences, Sociology
Total Titles: 55 Print

JBC, *imprint of* Jordan Book Centre Co Ltd

Jordan Book Centre Co Ltd+
Al-Jubeiha, Amman 11941
Mailing Address: PO Box 301, Amman 11941
Tel: (06) 5151882; (06) 5156882; (06) 5155882; (06) 606882; 06 676882 *Fax:* (06) 602016
E-mail: jbc@nets.com.jo; jbc@go.com.jo
Telex: 21153 *Cable:* JORDAN BOOK CENTRE/AMMAN
Key Personnel
Chief Executive: I Sharbain
Founded: 1982
Subjects: Business, Computer Science, Economics, Engineering (General), Fiction, Medicine, Nursing, Dentistry, Nonfiction (General)
Imprints: JBC
Showroom(s): University St, Amman

Jordan Distribution Agency Co Ltd
PO Box 375, Amman 11118
Tel: (06) 4630191; (06) 4630192 *Fax:* (06) 463152
E-mail: jda@go.com.jo
Telex: 22083 Distag Jo *Cable:* JODISTAG AMMAN
Key Personnel
Chairman & General Manager: Raja Elissa
Deputy Chairman, Dir: Nadia Elissa
Founded: 1951
Subjects: History

Jordan House for Publication
Basman St, Amman
Mailing Address: PO Box 1121, Amman
Tel: (06) 24224 *Fax:* (06) 51062
Telex: 22056 bestours jo
Key Personnel
Man Dir: Mursi El-Ashkar
Editorial: Dr Mohamad Takrouri
Founded: 1952
Subjects: Medicine, Nursing, Dentistry
Bookshop(s): 2 Basman St; Jabal Amman St, Amman

Kazakstan

General Information

Capital: Almaty
Language: Kazakh
Religion: Islamic (mostly Sunni Muslim)
Population: 17.1 million
Bank Hours: Generally open for short hours between 0930-1230 Monday-Friday
Shop Hours: Generally 0900-1800 Monday-Friday; often open weekends
Currency: 100 kopeks = 1 rubl
Export/Import Information: According to Ukrainian quotas and customs duties, companies engaged in trade should register with the Ukraine Ministry of Foreign Relations. Licenses for export and import are also required for trade with Russia.
Copyright: UCC (see Copyright Conventions, pg xi)

Gylym, Izd-Vo
Ul Puskina 111/113, 480100 Almaty
Tel: (03272) 618005; (03272) 618845
Fax: (03272) 618845; (03272) 618005
Telex: 251232 PTB Su
Key Personnel
Contact: Sagin-Girey Baimenov
Founded: 1946
Subjects: Biological Sciences, Chemistry, Chemical Engineering, Earth Sciences, Economics, Engineering (General), Mathematics, Physical Sciences, Science (General), Social Sciences, Sociology
ISBN Prefix(es): 5-628

Kazakh Al-Farabi State National University+
Al-Farabi Ave 71, 480078 Almaty
Tel: (03272) 472517
E-mail: evgenyaakazgu@ksisti.alma-ata.su
Subjects: Biological Sciences, Chemistry, Chemical Engineering, Economics, Environmental Studies, Government, Political Science, History, Human Relations, Journalism, Library & Information Sciences, Management, Marketing, Mathematics, Philosophy, Physical Sciences, Social Sciences, Sociology

Kazakhstan, Izd-Vo
Prospect Abaja 143, Dom Izdatel'stv, 480009 Almaty
Tel: (03272) 422929; (03272) 428562
Fax: (03272) 422929
Key Personnel
Dir: E H Syzdykov
Editors-in-Chief: M A Rashev; M D Sit'ko
Founded: 1920
Subjects: Economics, Government, Political Science, Medicine, Nursing, Dentistry, Science (General), Social Sciences, Sociology
ISBN Prefix(es): 5-615

Kramds-reklama Publishing & Advertising+
Ul Mira 115, 480091 Alma-Ata
Tel: (03272) 453968 *Fax:* (03272) 696753
Telex: 251233 RPAMS SU *Cable:* 251103 Y CNEX
Key Personnel
Dir: Lubov Shabykina
Chief Editor & Producer: Olga Tolanova
Chief Designer: Hasan Baimuratov
Manager: Tatyana Shah
Journalist: Rakip Nasyrow
Photographer: Oleg Belyalov; Vladimir Morozov
Founded: 1990
Subjects: Photography
ISBN Prefix(es): 5-86636
Parent Company: Kramds Corporation

Respublikanskij izdatei skij Kabinet
Ul Dzambula 25, 480100 Almaty
Tel: (03272) 610309 *Fax:* (03272) 631207
ISBN Prefix(es): 5-8380

Zazusy+
Prospect Abaya 143, Almaty 480009
Tel: (03272) 422849
Key Personnel
Dir: D I Isabekov
Editor-in-Chief: A T Saraev
Founded: 1934
Subjects: Literature, Literary Criticism, Essays, Poetry
ISBN Prefix(es): 5-605

Kenya

General Information

Capital: Nairobi
Language: Kiswahili (officially); English, Kikuyu & Luo also spoken
Religion: Most follow traditional beliefs; some Christian and Muslim also
Population: 26.2 million
Bank Hours: 0900-1400 Monday-Friday; 0900-1100 first and last Saturday of each month (except on coast, where banks open and close half an hour earlier)
Shop Hours: 0830-1230, 1400-1630 Monday-Friday; 0830-1200 or 1230 Saturday
Currency: 100 cents = 1 Kenya shilling
Export/Import Information: No tariff on books or advertising matter. Import licenses and exchange controls.
Copyright: UCC, Berne (see Copyright Conventions, pg xi)

AALAE, see African Association for Literacy & Adult Education (AALAE)

Academy Science Publishers+
PO Box 24916, Nairobi
Tel: (02) 884402-5 *Fax:* (02) 884406
E-mail: asp@arcc.or.ke
Key Personnel
Editor-in-Chief: Prof Keno E Mshigani
Publisher: Prof Thomas R Odhiambo
Publishing Manager: Mrs Serah W Mwanycky
Founded: 1989
Member of African Book Collectives Ltd London; APNET; KPA; African Academy of Sciences; Third World Academy of Sciences.
Subjects: Developing Countries, Environmental Studies, Science (General), Technology
ISBN Prefix(es): 9966-831
Number of titles published annually: 4 Print
Total Titles: 23 Print
Parent Company: The African Academy of Sciences
Associate Companies: African Books Collective Ltd (Agent), United Kingdom
Subsidiaries: Third World Academy of Sciences
Showroom(s): African Books Collective, The Jam Factory, 27 Park End St, Oxford OX1 1KU, United Kingdom
Bookshop(s): Prestige Bookshop, Nairobi; Textbook Centre Nairobi

Action Publishers+
PO Box 74419, Nairobi
Tel: (02) 506700
Key Personnel
Publisher: Dr J N K Mugambi
Founded: 1992
Subjects: Career Development, Developing Countries, Education, How-to, Music, Dance, Philosophy, Religion - Other, Self-Help, Theology
ISBN Prefix(es): 9966-888

ACTS, see African Centre for Technology Studies (ACTS)

AFER (African Ecclesial Review), *imprint of* Gaba Publications Amecea, Pastoral Institute

Africa Book Services (EA) Ltd+
Rattansi Educational Trust Bldg, Koinange St, Nairobi
Mailing Address: PO Box 45245, Nairobi
Tel: (02) 223641 *Fax:* (02) 330272
E-mail: abs@mref.co.ke

Key Personnel
Dir: Talat Lone
Founded: 1955
Member of Kenya Publishers Association & Kenya Book Sellers Association.
Subjects: Accounting, Library & Information Sciences, Nonfiction (General)
U.S. Office(s): Dars, 919 Blair Ave, Neenah, WI 54956-2000, United States
Distributor for IMF; UNESCO; World Bank

African Association for Literacy & Adult Education (AALAE)
PO Box 50768, Nairobi
Tel: (02) 222391; (02) 331512
Telex: 22096
ISBN Prefix(es): 9966-9901

African Centre for Technology Studies (ACTS)+
PO Box 45917, Nairobi 254 (2)
Tel: (02) 524700; (02) 524000 *Fax:* (02) 524701; (02) 524001
E-mail: acts@cgiar.org
Web Site: www.acts.or.ke
Key Personnel
Editor: Harrison Maganga
Founded: 1988
Specialize in academic books, also conduct research; offer training in editing, DTP & technical publishing.
Subjects: Agriculture, Biological Sciences, Developing Countries, Earth Sciences, Education, Environmental Studies, Health, Nutrition, Law, Science (General), Social Sciences, Sociology, Technology
ISBN Prefix(es): 9966-41
Divisions: Acts Press, Outreach, Training
Distributed by Zed Books (UK)

African Council for Communication Education
PO Box 47495, Nairobi
Tel: (02) 541440; (02) 540820 ext 289
Key Personnel
President: Francis Wete
Documentalist: Lydiah Gachung
Founded: 1976
ISBN Prefix(es): 9966-45

Book Sales (K) Ltd
PO Box 20377, Nairobi
Key Personnel
Chief Executive: Adrian Louis
Founded: 1976
Also bookseller.
ISBN Prefix(es): 9966-840
Subsidiaries: Kesho Book Centre

Bookman Consultants Ltd+
PO Box 31191, Nairobi
Tel: (02) 336771 *Fax:* (02) 217267
Key Personnel
Man Dir: Stanley Irura
Founded: 1988
Organizers of the Nairobi Book Fair.
Member of Kenya Publishers Association, Afro-Asian Book Council, also acts as Publishing Consultant & Publisher of the Kenya Bookseller.
Subjects: Publishing & Book Trade Reference
ISBN Prefix(es): 9966-867

British Institute in Eastern Africa
Laikipia Rd, Kileleshwa, Nairobi 43721
Mailing Address: PO Box 30710, Nairobi
Tel: (02) 43330; (02) 43721 *Fax:* (02) 43365
E-mail: britinst@insightkenya.com
Key Personnel
Dir: P J Lane
Secretary: Elizabeth Kiarie
Founded: 1962
Subjects: Archaeology, Ethnicity, History, Language Arts, Linguistics
Number of titles published annually: 1 Print
Distributed by Oxbow Books (UK); Oxbow Books (USA)

Camerapix Publishers International Ltd+
PO Box 45048, 3rd floor, ABC Place, Nairobi
Tel: (02) 448923; (02) 448924; (02) 448925 *Fax:* (02) 448926; (02) 448927
E-mail: info@camerapix.com
Web Site: www.camerapix.com
Telex: 22576 *Cable:* MOVIETONE NAIROBI
Key Personnel
Man Dir: Mohamed Amin
Editorial: Salim Amin
Sales: Rukhsana Haq
Production: Barbara Lawrence
Founded: 1960
Subjects: Art, Regional Interests, Travel
ISBN Prefix(es): 1-874041
Imprints: CPI
Subsidiaries: Camerapix Daares Salaam; Camerapix Karachi
Branch Office(s)
Camerapix London, 8 Ruston Mews, London W11 1RB, United Kingdom
Tel: (020) 7221 0077 *Fax:* (020) 7792 8105
E-mail: camerapixuk@btinternet.com
Distributor for Hunter & Struik

Cosmopolitan Publishers Ltd+
PO Box 18470, Nairobi
Tel: (02) 22143 *Fax:* (02) 333448
Telex: 22143
Key Personnel
Chairman: Dr Afrifa K Gitonga
Dir: Mr Murithi K Micheu
Marketing & Operations Dir: Boniface Wangaine
Founded: 1991
Subjects: Government, Political Science, Management, Mathematics, Psychology, Psychiatry
ISBN Prefix(es): 9966-881

CPI, *imprint of* Camerapix Publishers International Ltd

Danmar Publishers+
PO Box 75493, Nairobi
Tel: (02) 504818
Key Personnel
President: Daniel Irungu
Vice President & Author: Mary Irungu
Editor: Robert Irungu
Founded: 1990
Specialize in reading & spelling guides for beginners.
Subjects: English as a Second Language
ISBN Prefix(es): 9966-863
Parent Company: Danmar Publishers Printers & Stationer
Showroom(s): Chania Bookshop, PO Box 32413, Nairobi; Savanis Book Centre, PO Box 42157, Nairobi
Bookshop(s): Chania Bookshop, PO Box 32413, Nairobi; Savanis Book Centre, PO Box 42157, Nairobi

Dhillon Publishers Ltd, Paa Crescent+
PO Box 32197, Nairobi
Tel: (02) 505393
Founded: 1992
Subjects: English as a Second Language
ISBN Prefix(es): 9966-890

Egerton University
PO Box 536, Njoro
Tel: (037) 61620; (037) 61031; (037) 61032 *Fax:* (037) 61527; (037) 61442; (037) 61389
Telex: 33075
ISBN Prefix(es): 9966-838

Evangel Publishing House
Lumumba Drive, Roysambu, Nairobi
Mailing Address: Private Bag 28963, Nairobi
Tel: (02) 802033; (02) 802034 *Fax:* (02) 860840
E-mail: evanglit@maf.or.ke *Cable:* EVANGELIT NAIROBI
Key Personnel
Man Editor, Rights & Permissions: J Mugambi; R Nyamboki
Man Dir: Mr A Nandy
Founded: 1952
Subjects: Religion - Protestant, Religion - Other, Theology
ISBN Prefix(es): 9966-850; 9966-20

Focus Publications Ltd+
PO Box 48328, Nairobi
Tel: (02) 48233
Key Personnel
Man Dir: Serah T K Mwangi
Founded: 1991
Subjects: Accounting, Business, Education, English as a Second Language, Fiction, Finance, Law, Religion - Catholic
ISBN Prefix(es): 9966-882
Distributor for Scepter Ltd (UK); Sinag-Tala (Philippines)
Bookshop(s): Focus Books, PO Box 48328, Nairobi

Foundation Books
PO Box 73435, Nairobi
Tel: (02) 765485
Key Personnel
Man Dir: F O Okwanya
Editorial: C O Ojienda
Sales Promotion: Moses Gondi
Production: Sophia Wanjiku Ojienda
Founded: 1974
Sub-regional Co-ordinator, Regional Centre for Book Promotion in Africa; Co-publishing program Eastern Africa Region.
Subjects: Biography, Poetry
ISBN Prefix(es): 9966-849

Gaba Publications Amecea, Pastoral Institute+
PO Box 4002, Eldoret
Mailing Address: PO Box 4002, Eldoret
Tel: (0321) 61218; (0321) 62153 *Fax:* (0321) 62570
E-mail: gabapubs@africaonline.co.ke
Key Personnel
Assistant Dir & Editor: Sr Justin Nabushawo
Dir & Editor: Fr Eugene Ngoma
Founded: 1959
Subjects: Anthropology, Biblical Studies, Religion - Catholic, Religion - Other, Theology
ISBN Prefix(es): 9966-836
Imprints: AFER (African Ecclesial Review); Spearhead

Government Printer
PO Box 30128, Nairobi

Guru Publishers Ltd+
PO Box 32542, Nairobi
Tel: (02) 764146
Key Personnel
Man Dir, Proprietor & International Rights: Krishan Kumar Prabhakar
Founded: 1989
Member of Kenya Publishers Association; specialize in secondary math & mathematical tables.
Subjects: Mathematics
ISBN Prefix(es): 9966-9878
Distributed by Book Distributors Ltd-NBI (Kenya)

Heinemann Kenya Limited (EAEP)+
PO Box 45314, Nairobi

Mailing Address: PO Box 45314, Nairobi
Tel: (02) 222057; (02) 222144; (02) 228947
 Fax: (02) 448753; (02) 226286 *Cable:*
 EDPUBS NAIROBI
Key Personnel
Man Dir, Chief Executive & Rights & Permissions: Henry Chakava
Publishing Dir: Jimmi Makotsi
Sales & Marketing Dir: Winston Mutua Nzioki
Finance Dir: Fabian Murugu
Warehouse Dir: Charles Oduor Munjal
Publicity Manager: James Ogola
Publishing Manager, English Language Teaching: B O Muluka
Editor, Kiswahili: G Lilian Dhahabu
Editorial, Secondary: Anne Mithamo
Off Manager: Onyango Ogutu
Accountant: Mark Abonyo
Founded 1965
Member of Kenya Publishers Association; Co-publishers with James Currey Africa Books Collective Publishers (UK), Ohio University Press (USA), African Publishing Network (APNET) (Zimbabwe).
Subjects: Accounting, Agriculture, Art, Automotive, Biological Sciences, Business, Cookery, Drama, Theater, Economics, Education, Fashion, Fiction, Finance, Geography, Geology, Government, Political Science, History, Literature, Literary Criticism, Essays, Management, Music, Dance, Nonfiction (General), Philosophy, Physical Sciences, Physics, Poetry, Public Administration, Religion - Other, Social Sciences, Sociology, Theology
ISBN Prefix(es): 9966-46
Associate Companies: East African Educational Publishers (Uganda Branch) Ltd, Pioneer House, Suite 9, Plot 28, Jinja Rd, PO Box 11542, Kampala, Uganda
Imprints: Spear Books, EAEP Kenya Writers Series; Wandishi wa Kiafricka
Subsidiaries: Kenway Publications
Distributor for James Currey Publishers (UK); Heinemann International (UK)
Warehouse: East African Book Distributors Ltd, PO Box 10324, Nairobi *Tel:* (02) 220520 *Fax:* (02) 226286 (EABD)
Orders to: East African Book Distributors Ltd (EABD), PO Box 10324, Nairobi *Tel:* (02) 220520 *Fax:* (02) 226286

Horizon Books, *imprint of* Space Sellers Ltd

ICRAF, see International Centre for Research in Agroforestry (ICRAF)

International Centre for Research in Agroforestry (ICRAF)
United Nations Ave, Gigiri, Nairobi
Mailing Address: PO Box 30677, Nairobi
Tel: (02) 524000 *Fax:* (02) 524001
E-mail: icraf@cgiar.org
Web Site: cgiar.org/ICRAF
Key Personnel
Dir General: Dr Dennis P Garrity
Assistant Dir General: Bruce Scott
Founded: 1977
International not-for-profit organization.
Subjects: Agriculture, Environmental Studies
ISBN Prefix(es): 92-9059

Jacaranda Designs Ltd+
PO Box 76691, Nairobi
Tel: (02) 569736; (02) 568353 *Fax:* (02) 740524
Key Personnel
Man Dir & International Rights: Susan Scull Carvalho
Marketing Manager: Brown Onduso
Man Editor: Bridget King
Founded: 1991
Member of Multi-Cultural Publishers Exchange Association, Kenya Publishers Association & Association of International Schools in Africa (AISA).
Subjects: Fiction, Nonfiction (General)
ISBN Prefix(es): 9966-884
U.S. Office(s): Jacaranda Designs Ltd USA, PO Box 7936, Boulder, CO 80306, United States
Distributed by Southern Book Publishers (South Africa)

JKF, *imprint of* The Jomo Kenyatta Foundation

KEMRI, see Kenya Medical Research Institute (KEMRI)

Kenway Publications Ltd+
Woodvale Grove, Westlands, Brick Court, Nairobi
Mailing Address: PO Box 45314, Nairobi
Tel: (02) 444700 *Fax:* (02) 448753; (02) 532095
E-mail: eaep@africaonline.co.ke
Web Site: www.eastafricanpublishers.com
Telex: EDPUBS
Key Personnel
Chairman & Chief Executive Officer: Henry Chakava *Tel:* (02) 445260/1
Man Dir: Barrack O Muluka *Tel:* (02) 445260/1
Sales & Marketing Dir: Winston Mutua Nzioki *Tel:* (02) 544295
Publicity Manager: Rebecca Wabwoba *Tel:* (02) 445260/1
Founded: 1981
Specialize in tourism books, cit maps.
Member of African Publishing Network, Kenya Publishers Association.
Subjects: Animals, Pets, Anthropology, Biography, Cookery, Government, Political Science, History, Humor, Language Arts, Linguistics, Music, Dance, Natural History, Nonfiction (General), Regional Interests, Sports, Athletics, Travel
ISBN Prefix(es): 9966-46; 9966-848; 9966-25
Number of titles published annually: 4 Print
Total Titles: 56 Print
Parent Company: East African Educational Publishers Ltd, Nairobi, Man Dir: Barrack Muluka
Associate Companies: Transmedia Uganda, Plot 51/53, Nkrumah Rd, PO Box 28104, Kampala, Uganda, Ignatius Tumwesigye *Tel:* (041) 235860 *Fax:* (041) 347235 *E-mail:* transmed@swiftuganda.com *Web Site:* www.eastafricanpublishers.com
Distributed by African Books Collective (UK)
Foreign Rep(s): African Books Collective (UK/Europe)
Shipping Address: East African Book Distributors Ltd, PO Box 10324, Nairobi
Warehouse: East African Book Distributors Ltd, PO Box 10324, Nairobi, Warehouse Manager: Charles Munjal *Tel:* (02) 544321, (02) 545903, (02) 534020 *Fax:* (02) 532095 *E-mail:* eaep@nbnet.co.ke *Web Site:* www.eastafricanpublishers.com
Orders to: East African Book Distributors Ltd, PO Box 10324, Nairobi, Warehouse Manager: Charles O Munjal *Tel:* (02) 534020, (020) 544321, (020) 545903 *Fax:* (02) 532095 *E-mail:* eaep@nbnet.co.ke *Web Site:* www.eastafricanpublishers.com

Kenya Energy & Environment Organisation, Kengo
PO Box 48197, Nairobi 254-02
Tel: (02) 749747; (02) 748281 *Fax:* (02) 749382
Telex: 25222 *Cable:* KENGO KE
Key Personnel
Executive Dir: Mr Achoka Awori
Asstistant Marketing Officer: Julie Kariuki
Founded: 1981
Subjects: Agriculture, Energy, Environmental Studies
ISBN Prefix(es): 9966-841

Kenya Literature Bureau
Bellevue Area off Mombasa Rd, Nairobi
Mailing Address: PO Box 30022, Nairobi
Tel: (02) 506142; (02) 506143; (02) 506148; (02) 506156; (02) 506158; (02) 722657 *Fax:* (02) 505903; (02) 601474 *Cable:* Literature Nairobi
Key Personnel
Man Dir: S C Langat
Marketing Manager: Mr J K Muraya
Publishes, prints & distributes affordable books & other reading materials. Also encourages Kenyan authors through financial incentives, advice on how to write, etc.
Subjects: Agriculture, Animals, Pets, Education, Health, Nutrition, Law, Mathematics, Medicine, Nursing, Dentistry, Science (General), Science Fiction, Fantasy, Veterinary Science
ISBN Prefix(es): 9966-44
Total Titles: 700 Print

Kenya Medical Research Institute (KEMRI)
PO Box 54840, Nairobi (Subscriptions Office)
Tel: (02) 722541; (02) 722672; (02) 722532
 Fax: (02) 720030
E-mail: kemrilib@ken.healthnet.org
Key Personnel
Dir: Dr Davy Koech
Subjects: Biological Sciences, Environmental Studies, Health, Nutrition, Medicine, Nursing, Dentistry
ISBN Prefix(es): 9966-869
Orders to: PO Box 54840, Nairobi (Subscriptions Office)

Kenya Meteorological Department
PO Box 30259, Nairobi
Tel: (02) 567880 *Fax:* (02) 576955
E-mail: director@lion.meteo.go.ke; imtr@lion.meteo.go.ke
Web Site: www.meteo.go.ke
Telex: 22208 Weather *Cable:* WEATHER NAIROBI
Subjects: Electronics, Electrical Engineering, Environmental Studies
ISBN Prefix(es): 9966-830

Kenya Quality & Productivity Institute+
PO Box 57225, Nairobi
Key Personnel
Contact: Silas Gachanja Maina
Founded: 1992
Subjects: Developing Countries, Economics, Management, Mathematics, Self-Help
ISBN Prefix(es): 9966-894

The Jomo Kenyatta Foundation+
Industrial Area, Enterprise Rd, Nairobi
Mailing Address: PO Box 30533, Nairobi
Tel: (02) 557222; (02) 557223; (02) 557224
 Fax: (02) 531966 *Cable:* Foundation
Founded: 1966
Member of the Kenya Publishers Association.
ISBN Prefix(es): 9966-22
Parent Company: Ministry of Education, PO Box 30040, Nairobi
Imprints: JKF
Warehouse: Kijabe St, PO Box 30533, Nairobi
Orders to: c/o Sales & Marketing Manager, Industrial Area, Enterprise Rd, PO Box 30533, Nairobi

Lake Publishers & Enterprises Ltd+
Jomo Kenyatta Hwy, Kisumu
Mailing Address: PO Box 1743, Kisumu
Tel: (035) 22707; (035) 22291 *Fax:* (035) 22291
Key Personnel
President: James C Odaga
Dir: Mrs Asenath Bole Odaga
Editor: Aol Ohito
Founded: 1982
Member of Kenya Publishers Association, Kenya Booksellers Association, African Publishing Network (APNET), Harare, Zimbabwe.

Subjects: Biological Sciences, Drama, Theater, Education, Fiction, Government, Political Science, Labor, Industrial Relations, Literature, Literary Criticism, Essays, Mathematics, Music, Dance, Poetry, Religion - Protestant
ISBN Prefix(es): 9966-847
Associate Companies: Thu Tinda Bookshop; Thu Tinda Book Distribution Ltd
Subsidiaries: Innervision Communication
Distributor for ABC (outside Africa)
Showroom(s): Jomo Kenyatta Hwy, Kisumu; Kenya Industrial Estate, Airport Rd, Kisumu

Life Challenge AFRICA
PO Box 50770, Nairobi
Tel: (02) 561121; (02) 722314 *Fax:* (02) 721644
E-mail: lca@umsg.org
Key Personnel
Contact: Eric Walter
Subjects: Religion - Islamic, Religion - Other
ISBN Prefix(es): 9966-895
U.S. Office(s): SIM Int, Box 7900, Charlotte, NC 28241, United States

Macmillan Kenya Publishers Ltd+
Kijabe St, Nairobi
Mailing Address: PO Box 30797, Nairobi
Tel: (02) 220 012; (02) 224 485 *Fax:* (02) 212 179
Web Site: www.macmillan-africa.com
Key Personnel
Man Dir: David Muita *E-mail:* dmuita@macken.co.ke
Founded: 1970
ISBN Prefix(es): 9966-885
Parent Company: Macmillan Publishers Ltd, United Kingdom

Midi Teki Publishers+
PO Box 52906, Nairobi
Tel: (02) 506993
Founded: 1977
Subjects: Accounting, Business, Developing Countries, Government, Political Science, Public Administration, Social Sciences, Sociology
ISBN Prefix(es): 9966-861
Bookshop(s): Mihuti Bookshop, Box 31, Kangema, Muringo *Tel:* 0157-22164

Nairobi University Press+
PO Box 30197, Nairobi
Tel: (02) 334244 (ext 2258) *Fax:* (02) 336885
E-mail: nup@uonbi.ac.ke
Telex: 22095 Varsity KE
Key Personnel
Secretary: Omari E Gichogo *Tel:* (02) 334244 ext 222235
Founded: 1984
Subjects: Accounting, African American Studies, Behavioral Sciences, Developing Countries, Geography, Geology, Government, Political Science, History, Law, Mathematics, Philosophy, Physical Sciences, Physics, Real Estate, Religion - Protestant, Social Sciences, Sociology, Veterinary Science
ISBN Prefix(es): 9966-846
Parent Company: University of Nairobi (Company fully-owned by University of Nairobi)
Distributed by African Books Collective (Europe, USA)

Paulines Publications-Africa+
PO Box 49026, Nairobi
Tel: (02) 447202; (02) 447203 *Fax:* (02) 442319
E-mail: paulines@iconnect.co.uk
Key Personnel
President: Sr Maria Pezzini
Dir: Sr Teresa Marcazzan
Editor: Rev Leonard Byankya; C Moloney
Founded: 1985
Subjects: Biblical Studies, Biography, Child Care & Development, Communications, Education, History, Nonfiction (General), Psychology, Psychiatry, Religion - Catholic, Religion - Other, Theology, Women's Studies
ISBN Prefix(es): 9966-21
Parent Company: Paulines Publications
Ultimate Parent Company: Daughters of St. Paul, 6 Amore Str off Toyin Str, IKEJA, P M B 21243, Lagos, Nigeria
Branch Office(s)
Cathedral Bookshop, PO Box 2381, Dar Es Salaam, United Republic of Tanzania, Sister Carmel *Tel:* (051) 113204 *Fax:* (051) 113204 *E-mail:* paulines-dsm@cats-net.com
Catholic Book Centre, PO Box 2454, Addis Ahaha, Ethiopia
Catholic Book Centre, PO Box CY738, Causway, Harare, Zimbabwe
Catholic Bookshop, PO Box 30249, Nairobi, Thomasina, Sr *Tel:* (02) 225172 *Fax:* (02) 338514
Livraria Edicoes Paulistas, CP 3659, Maputo, Mozambique *Tel:* (01) 424671 *Fax:* (01) 423234 *E-mail:* paulines@virconn.com
Paulines Book & Media Centre, PMP 21243, Lagos State, Nigeria, Sister Clare *Tel:* (01) 7741636 *Fax:* (01) 7741636 *E-mail:* paulines@infoweb.abs.net
Paulines Cathedral Bookshop, PO Box 36291, Lusaka, Zambia, Sister Clara *Tel:* (01) 220264 *Fax:* (01) 250134 *E-mail:* paulines@zamnet.zm
Paulines Publications Africa, PO Box 49026, Nairobi, Sister Teresa Marcazzan *Tel:* 447202/3 *E-mail:* paulines@lconnect.co.ke
San Paolo Multimedia, Via Mascherino 94, 00193 Rome, Italy *Tel:* (06) 6872354 *Fax:* (06) 68308093 *E-mail:* pmultimedia@pen.net
Bookshop(s): Paulines Book & Media Centre, PO Box 4392, Kampala, Uganda, Sister Fidelis *Tel:* (041) 256346 *Fax:* (041) 349135 *E-mail:* paulines@swiftuganda.com; Paulines Multimedia Centre, PO Box 641, Bruma 2026, Johannesburg, Sister Paula *Tel:* (011) 6220488/9 *Fax:* (011) 6220490 *E-mail:* paulines@iafrica.com

Phoenix Publishers
Coffee Plaza 3rd floor, Heille Selassie Ave, Nairobi
Mailing Address: PO Box 18650 Nairobi
Tel: (02) 222309; (02) 223262 *Fax:* (02) 339875
Key Personnel
Secretary: Ann Wanjiru
Contact: G Woruingi
Founded: 1988
Member of Kenya Publishers' Association.
Subjects: Education, Environmental Studies, Geography, Geology, History, Mathematics, Physical Sciences, Poetry, Social Sciences, Sociology, Women's Studies
ISBN Prefix(es): 9966-47

Shirikon Publishers+
PO Box 46154, Nairobi
Key Personnel
Dir: Sylvester J Ouma
Subjects: Accounting, Anthropology, Biblical Studies, Business, Developing Countries, Economics, Education, History, Literature, Literary Criticism, Essays, Management, Philosophy, Religion - Catholic, Religion - Protestant, Social Sciences, Sociology, Theology, Women's Studies
ISBN Prefix(es): 9966-870; 9966-9842

Space Sellers Ltd+
PO Box 47186, Nairobi
Tel: (02) 555811; (02) 557517; (02) 557863 *Fax:* (02) 557815; (02) 558847
E-mail: sstms@africaonline.co.ke *Cable:* salespower
Key Personnel
Contact: Sylvia King *Tel:* (02) 530598
Founded: 1975
Member of NPA.
Subjects: Automotive, Business, Career Development, Gardening, Plants, How-to, Self-Help, Travel
ISBN Prefix(es): 9968-68
Number of titles published annually: 6 Print
Total Titles: 23 Print
Associate Companies: Target Mail Services, PO Box 30759, Nairobi, Ann Thieth *Tel:* (02) 556916 *Fax:* (02) 558847 *E-mail:* sstms@africaonline.co.ke
Imprints: Horizon Books

Spear Books, EAEP Kenya Writers Series, *imprint of* Heinemann Kenya Limited (EAEP)

Spearhead, *imprint of* Gaba Publications Amecea, Pastoral Institute

Sudan Literature Centre
PO Box 44838, GPO 00100 Nairobi
Tel: (02) 564141; (02) 569685; (02) 569688 *Fax:* (02) 564141
E-mail: across@maf.or.ke
Key Personnel
Coordinator: Rev Anthony Poggo
Founded: 1988
Producer of church & school books for Sudan.
Subjects: Education, Health, Nutrition, Literature, Literary Criticism, Essays, Religion - Protestant
ISBN Prefix(es): 9966-876

Transafrica Press
PO Box 48239, Nairobi Kenya
Key Personnel
Man Dir: John Nottingham
Founded: 1976
Subjects: Biography, Education, Fiction, History, How-to, Nonfiction (General), Poetry, Regional Interests, Religion - Other, Social Sciences, Sociology

Tree Shade Technical Services
PO Box 71222, Nairobi
Tel: (02) 225798; (02) 220712
Key Personnel
Dir: Timothy Gathirimu
Founded: 1992
Subjects: Environmental Studies
ISBN Prefix(es): 9966-892

Uzima, *imprint of* Uzima Press

Uzima Press+
PO Box 48127, Nairobi, Kenya
Tel: (02) 220239; (02) 216836
Key Personnel
Gen Mgr: Kiraka James
Founded: 1974
Member of KPA (Kenya Publishers Association) & CBA (Christian Booksellers Association).
Subjects: Fiction, Nonfiction (General), Religion - Protestant, Religion - Other, Social Sciences, Sociology, Theology
ISBN Prefix(es): 9966-855
Imprints: Uzima

Vipopremo Agencies
PO Box 47717, Nairobi
Tel: (02) 227189; (02) 333882
Subjects: Education, How-to
ISBN Prefix(es): 9966-845

Wandishi wa Kiafricka, *imprint of* Heinemann Kenya Limited (EAEP)

Gideon S Were Press+
PO Box 10622, Nairobi
Tel: (02) 740819; (072) 716730 (cellular)
E-mail: gswere@nbnet.co.ke
Founded: 1983
Home science; Christian religious education.
Subjects: Anthropology, Government, Political Science, History, Social Sciences, Sociology, Women's Studies
ISBN Prefix(es): 9966-852
Total Titles: 68 Print
Associate Companies: Star Academy

Democratic People's Republic of Korea

General Information

Capital: Pyongyang
Language: Korean
Religion: Buddhism, Christian & Chundo Kyo
Population: 22.2 million
Currency: 100 chon = 1 won
Export/Import Information: No tariff information; all importation and exportation must go through Korea Publications Export & Import Corporation, Pyongyang.

Academy of Sciences Publishing House
Nammundung, Dir Choe Kwan Sik, Pyongyang
Tel: (02) 51956
Founded: 1953
Subjects: Biological Sciences, Chemistry, Chemical Engineering, Economics, Education, Geography, Geology, History, Philosophy, Physics, Science (General)

Educational Books Publishing House
Pyongyang
Subjects: Education

The Foreign Language Press Group
Pyongyang Publishing Trade Association, Sochon-dong, Sosong District, Pyongyang
Tel: (02) 841342 *Fax:* (02) 812100
Telex: 37021 PP KP
Key Personnel
President: Sun Myong Hwang
Subjects: Archaeology, Art, Biography, Child Care & Development, Cookery, Education, History, Philosophy

Foreign Languages Publishing House
Pyongyang
Key Personnel
Dir: Hwang Sun Myong
Subjects: Asian Studies

Grand People's Study House
Jungsong Dong, Central District, Pyongyang
Tel: (08502) 321 5614 *Fax:* (08502) 381-4427; (08502) 381-2100
Subjects: Alternative, Asian Studies, Biblical Studies, Biography, Child Care & Development, Communications, Education, Electronics, Electrical Engineering

Industrial Publishing House
Pyongyang

Key Personnel
Dir: Kim Tong Su
Subjects: Business

Korea Science and Encyclopedia Publishing House (Guahak Baikkwa Sajon Chulpansa)+
Jangyongdong, Sosong District, Pyongyang
Mailing Address: PO Box 73, Pyongyang
Tel: (02) 381 8091 (Call between 18 & 21 hours Pyongyang local time, Mon, Wed & Fri only)
Fax: (02) 381 4550 (24 hours)
Key Personnel
President & Dir General: Kim Yong Il
Contact: Mr Jean Bahng
Founded: 1953
Editing & publishing; Dictionaries, Encyclopedias, various books & periodicals (magazines).
Subjects: Agriculture, Animals, Pets, Architecture & Interior Design, Art, Biological Sciences, Chemistry, Chemical Engineering, Civil Engineering, Communications, Economics, Education, Electronics, Electrical Engineering, Engineering (General), Geography, Geology, Government, Political Science, History, Law, Literature, Literary Criticism, Essays, Mathematics, Mechanical Engineering, Medicine, Nursing, Dentistry, Natural History, Philosophy, Physical Sciences, Physics, Science (General), Social Sciences, Sociology, Technology, Veterinary Science

Literature and Art Publishing House
Pyongyang
Key Personnel
President: Jong So Chon
Subjects: Art, Fiction

Transportation Publishing House
Namgyo-dong, Hyongjaesan District, Pyongyang
Key Personnel
Editor: Paek Jong Han
Subjects: Travel

Working People's Organization Publishing House
Pyongyang
Key Personnel
Dir: Pak Se Hyok
Subjects: Fiction, Government, Political Science

Republic of Korea

General Information

Capital: Seoul
Language: Korean (English also spoken in business)
Religion: Predominantly Mahayana Buddhist and Christian
Population: 44.1 million
Bank Hours: 0930-1600 Monday-Friday; 0930-1300 Saturday
Shop Hours: 1000-1900 Monday-Saturday
Currency: 100 chun = 10 hwan = 1 won
Export/Import Information: No tariffs on books and advertising matter. Authorizations for import of books and publications are reviewed annually by the Korean government. Import licenses are required. Exchange controls; prior deposits required at present.
Copyright: UCC (see Copyright Conventions, pg xi)

Ahn Graphics+
260-88 Sungbuk 2-Dong, Seongbug-gu, Seoul 136-022

Tel: (02) 7632320; (02) 7438066 *Fax:* (02) 7433352
E-mail: 100050.1023@compuserve.com; ahnO1dh@chollian.dacom.co.kr
Web Site: www.ag.co.kr
Key Personnel
President: Ok-Chul Kim
Founded: 1985
Member of Korean Publishers Association; Specialize in Art Books.
Subjects: Art, Computer Science
ISBN Prefix(es): 89-7059

Anam Publishing Co+
2F, 333-203, Sindang-dong, Jung-gu, Seoul 100-450
Tel: (02) 22380491 *Fax:* (02) 22524334
Key Personnel
President: Lee Chang-Sik
Founded: 1978
Subjects: Career Development
ISBN Prefix(es): 89-7235

Ario Company Ltd+
5-36 Hyochang-dong, Yongsan-gu, Seoul 140-120
Tel: (02) 7122001; (02) 712203 *Fax:* (02) 7023156
Key Personnel
Publisher: Yoong-Yeoup Lee
Founded: 1970
Subjects: Career Development
ISBN Prefix(es): 89-86063
Associate Companies: ARIO JSC Ltd, 5-36 Hyoch'ang-dong, Yongsan-gu, Seoul 140-120

B & B+
80-1, Cheongdam-dong, Gangnam-gu, Seoul 135-100
Tel: (02) 540-4425 *Fax:* (02) 517-8793
Key Personnel
Planning Dir: Jae-Woo Lee
Founded: 1996
Subjects: Computer Science
ISBN Prefix(es): 89-86929

Ba-reunsa Publishing Co
269-16 Nonhyeon-dong, Gangnam-gu, Seoul 135-010
Tel: (02) 5123217 *Fax:* (02) 5463217
Key Personnel
International Rights: Joung-Ouk Park
Founded: 1987
Subjects: History, Poetry, Science (General)
ISBN Prefix(es): 89-7109

Bakyoung Publishing Co
13-31 Pyeong-Dong, Jongroo-gu Seoul 110-102
Tel: (02) 7336771; (02) 7336773 *Fax:* (02) 7364818
Key Personnel
President: Jong-man Ahn
Founded: 1952
Subjects: Language Arts, Linguistics, Literature, Literary Criticism, Essays, Philosophy, Science (General), Social Sciences, Sociology
ISBN Prefix(es): 89-10

Bal-eon+
2F, 238-66 Yongdu-dong, Dongdaemun-gu, Seoul 130-070
Tel: (02) 9293546; (02) 9293547 *Fax:* (02) 9293548
Subjects: Architecture & Interior Design, Art
ISBN Prefix(es): 89-7763

BCM Media Inc+
1305-7 Seocho-dong, Seocho-gu, Seoul 137-080
Tel: (02) 567-0644; (02) 533-0089 *Fax:* (02) 552-9169
E-mail: bcmpub@nuri.net
Web Site: www.bcm.co.kr

Key Personnel
Chairman: Dr Byoung-Chul Min
Publishing & distributing of language educational materials.
Subjects: Education, Language Arts, Linguistics, English, Japanese & Chinese educational publications
ISBN Prefix(es): 89-7512
Distributor for Child's Play; Houghton Mifflin; Steck-Vaughn
Shipping Address: 752-27 Yuksam-Dong, B1 Jeil Bldg, Gangnam-gu, Seoul 135-080
Warehouse: 752-27 Yuksam-Dong, B1 Jeil Bldg, Gangnam-gu, Seoul 135-080

Bi-bong Publishing Co
Wijin Bldg, 2nd floor, 464-41, Seogyo-dong, Mapo-gu, Choong-ku, Seoul 121-210
Tel: (02) 3142-6555 *Fax:* (02) 3142-6556
Key Personnel
Publisher: Kie-Bong Park
Founded: 1980
Subjects: Business, Economics, Management
ISBN Prefix(es): 89-376

Big Tree Publishing+
215 Hongjae-Dong, Seodaemun-Ku, Seoul 120-090
Tel: (02) 7369653 *Fax:* (02) 7328694
E-mail: kennamu@unitel.co.kr
Key Personnel
Contact: Ik-Su Han
Founded: 1993
Subjects: Fiction, Nonfiction (General), Romance

BIR Publishing+
Formerly Biryongso Publishing
5 F Kangnam Publishing, Culture Center, 506 Sinsa-dong, Gangnam-gu, Seoul 135-8817
Tel: (02) 515 2000 *Fax:* (02) 515 2007
Web Site: www.bir.co.kr
Key Personnel
President: Park Sang Hee *Tel:* (02) 515 2003
Foreign Rights Senior Manager: Michelle Nam *Tel:* (02) 515 9108 *Fax:* (02) 3444 5185
E-mail: michellenam@minumsa.com
Founded: 1996
Picture & story books for young children.
ISBN Prefix(es): 89-491
Total Titles: 100 Print
Parent Company: Minumsa Publishing Co Ltd

BIR Publishing Co, *imprint of* Minumsa Publishing Co Ltd

Biryongso Publishing, see BIR Publishing

Bo-jinjae Printing Co Ltd
8, Dangsandong 5-ga, Yeongdeungpo-gu, Seoul 150-045
Tel: (02) 6792351; (02) 6792355 *Fax:* (02) 6762821
Key Personnel
President: Dai-Hoon Lee
Founded: 1912
ISBN Prefix(es): 89-7197

Bo Moon Dang+
448-6 Sinsoo-Dong, Mapo-Ku, Seoul 121-110
Tel: (02) 7047025 *Fax:* (02) 7042324
Key Personnel
President: Byung-Gye Kim
Subjects: Architecture & Interior Design, Chemistry, Chemical Engineering, Civil Engineering, Computer Science, Electronics, Electrical Engineering, Engineering (General), Mechanical Engineering, Science (General)

Bo Ri+
474-40 Seogyo-dong, Mapo-gu Seoul 121-842
Tel: (02) 3233676 *Fax:* (02) 3240285
Key Personnel
Contact: Kwang-Ju Cha
International Rights: Ri Bo
Founded: 1991
Specialize in books for children.
Subjects: Child Care & Development, Education, Labor, Industrial Relations, Literature, Literary Criticism, Essays
ISBN Prefix(es): 89-85494
Associate Companies: Dotori Publishing Co; Jakenchak Publishing Co

Borim Publishing Co+
Geumsan Bldg, 4th floor, 364-22 Seogyo-Dong, Mapo-gu, Seoul
Tel: (02) 31412221 *Fax:* (02) 31418474
Key Personnel
President: Kwon Jong-Taek
Executive Dir: Park Sang-Yong
Founded: 1976
Subjects: Animals, Pets, Fiction, History, Nonfiction (General), Science (General), Picture Book
ISBN Prefix(es): 89-433

Bum-Woo Publishing Co
21-1 Gusu-dong, Mapo-gu, Seoul 121-130
Tel: (02) 7172121; (02) 7172122 *Fax:* (02) 7170429
Key Personnel
Chief Executive: Hyung-Doo Yoon
Founded: 1966
Subjects: Communications, Drama, Theater, Fiction, History, Literature, Literary Criticism, Essays, Philosophy, Publishing & Book Trade Reference, Social Sciences, Sociology
ISBN Prefix(es): 89-08
Associate Companies: Yoon Communications

Cham Kae, *imprint of* O Neul Publishing Co

Chang-josa Publishing Co
20-1, Shinmunro 2-ga, Jongro-gu, Seoul 110-062
Tel: (02) 7380393
Key Personnel
President: Duk-kyo Choi
Founded: 1963
Subjects: History, Language Arts, Linguistics, Literature, Literary Criticism, Essays
ISBN Prefix(es): 89-85139

Cheong-mun-gag Publishing Co+
486-9 Gileum 3-Dong, Seongbug-gu, Seoul 136-113
Tel: (02) 9851451; (02) 9897423; (02) 9897421 *Fax:* (02) 9828679
E-mail: CMGbook@hitel.kol.co.kr
Key Personnel
Chief Executive: Hong-Seok Kim
International Rights: Han-Seung Kim
Founded: 1975
Subjects: Science (General), Technology
ISBN Prefix(es): 89-7088
Subsidiaries: Ham Seung Publishing Co
Divisions: Trade Books

Chong No Books Publishing Co Ltd
45-1 Gwancheol-Dong, Jongro-gu, Seoul 110-111
Tel: (02) 7325381 *Fax:* (02) 7326202
Key Personnel
Chief Executive: Ha-Gu Chang
Founded: 1954
Subjects: History, Language Arts, Linguistics, Literature, Literary Criticism, Essays, Philosophy, Religion - Other
ISBN Prefix(es): 89-305

The Chosun Ilbo Co, Ltd
61 Taepyongro 1-ga, Jung-gu, Seoul 100-756
Tel: (02) 7245114 *Fax:* (02) 7246199
Key Personnel
Contact: Sang-Hoon Bang

The Christian Literature Society of Korea
169-1 Samseong-Dong, Gangnam-Gu, Seoul 135-090
Tel: (02) 5530807 *Fax:* (02) 5643532
Key Personnel
President: So Young Kim
Founded: 1890
ISBN Prefix(es): 89-511
Bookshop(s): CLS Bookstore, 136-46, Yonjidong, Chongro-ku, Seoul

Chung Rim Publishing Co Ltd
Member of Chung Rim Interactive Co Ltd
Young Bldg 63, Nonhyn-Dong, Kangnam-ku, Seoul 135-010
Tel: (02) 544-3616 *Fax:* (02) 5468053
Key Personnel
Contact: Koh Young-Soo *Tel:* 02 5464341
Founded: 1971
Also acts as Director of Korea Publication Association.
Subjects: Accounting, Advertising, Art, Behavioral Sciences, Biography, Business, Career Development, Child Care & Development, Communications, Computer Science, Crafts, Games, Hobbies, Economics, Education, Electronics, Electrical Engineering, English as a Second Language, Fiction, Finance, History, How-to, Human Relations, Humor, Journalism, Labor, Industrial Relations, Law, Literature, Literary Criticism, Essays, Management, Marketing, Music, Dance, Nonfiction (General), Philosophy, Psychology, Psychiatry, Real Estate, Religion - Protestant, Romance, Science (General), Science Fiction, Fantasy, Social Sciences, Sociology, Technology, Travel, Women's Studies
ISBN Prefix(es): 89-352
Number of titles published annually: 80 Print; 3 CD-ROM; 6 Online; 6 E-Book
Total Titles: 1,300 Print; 3 CD-ROM; 6 Online; 6 E-Book
Associate Companies: Pan Rae Wolbo SA; Woo Jin Publishing Co; Kolis Co Ltd

Dae Won Sa Co Ltd+
358-17 Huam-Dong, Yongsan-gu, Seoul 140-190
Tel: (02) 7576717 *Fax:* (02) 7758043
Key Personnel
Vice President: S W Chang
Contact: Min-Do Cha
Founded: 1986
Subjects: Antiques, Architecture & Interior Design, Art, Crafts, Games, Hobbies, Environmental Studies, Philosophy, Science (General), Travel
ISBN Prefix(es): 89-369

Daehan Printing & Publishing Co Ltd
344-12, Sangdaewon-dong, Jungwon-gu, Sungnam-City, Kyungki-do
Tel: (031) 730-3830 (i-3) *Fax:* (031) 735-8104
Web Site: www.dhpop.com
Key Personnel
President: Lee Hae-Dong
ISBN Prefix(es): 89-378

Daeyoung Munhwasa+
200 Jeil Bldg, 178-2 Cheongpa-Dong 1-Ga, Yongsan-Gu, Seoul 140-131
Tel: (02) 716-3883 *Fax:* (02) 703-3839
E-mail: spotto29@hotmail.com
Key Personnel
Contact: Choon-Hwan Rim
Subjects: Public Administration, Philosophy of Administration
ISBN Prefix(es): 89-7644
Book Club(s): Korean Publish Association

REPUBLIC OF KOREA

Dai Hak Publishing Co
420-5 Ahyon 1- Dong, Mapo-ku, Seoul 121-011
Tel: (02) 364-9788 *Fax:* (02) 393-9045
Key Personnel
President: Jin Young Yoon
Subjects: Technology

Youl Hwa Dang Publisher+
506 Shinsa-Dong, Kangnam-Gu, Seoul
Tel: (02) 5153141; (02) 5153143; (02) 5153142
  Fax: (02) 5153144
E-mail: yhdp@hitel.net; horang2@unitel.co.kr
Key Personnel
President: Ki-Ung Yi
Editor & Foreign Rights: Ji-Hong Park
Founded: 1971
Specialize in Korean Traditional Art.
Subjects: Antiques, Architecture & Interior Design, Art, Crafts, Games, Hobbies, Film, Video, Music, Dance, Photography, Korean Art
ISBN Prefix(es): 89-301
Number of titles published annually: 20 Print
Total Titles: 500 Print

DanKook University Press
San 8 Hannam-dong, Yongsan-gu, Seoul 140-714
Tel: (02) 793-5034 *Fax:* (02) 792-5814
Key Personnel
President: Chang Choong-Sik
Subjects: History, Literature, Literary Criticism, Essays
ISBN Prefix(es): 89-7092

Dong-A Publishing & Printing Co Ltd
295-15, Dogsan 1-dong, Guro-gu, Seoul 152-011
Tel: (02) 8668800 *Fax:* (02) 8620410
Key Personnel
Chief Executive: Hyun-Shik Kim
Founded: 1980
ISBN Prefix(es): 89-00

Dong Hwa Publishing Co
130-4 Weonhyoro 1-ga, Yongsan-gu, Seoul 140-111
Tel: (02) 7135411; (02) 7135415 *Fax:* (02) 7017041
Key Personnel
President: In-Kyu Lim
Editorial Dir: Kyoung-Sik Roh
Sales Dir: Byong-Don Ann
Production Dir: Chong-Choon Seo
Publicity Dir: Kun-Han Park
Founded: 1968
Subjects: Art, History, Literature, Literary Criticism, Essays, Philosophy
ISBN Prefix(es): 89-431

Eulyu Publishing Co Ltd+
46-1 Susong-Dong, Jongro-Ju 110-603
Tel: (02) 7338150; (02) 7338151; (02) 7338152;
  (02) 7338153 *Fax:* (02) 7329154 *Cable:*
  EULYOO SEOUL
Key Personnel
President: Chin Sook Chung
Man Dir: Pil Young Choung
Editorial, Production: Ko Jung Gi
Sales: Sam Taek Huh
Founded: 1945
Subjects: History, Language Arts, Linguistics, Literature, Literary Criticism, Essays, Philosophy
ISBN Prefix(es): 89-324
Distributor for UN Publications

Ewha Womans University Press
11-1 Daehyun-Dong, Seodaemun-gu, Seoul 120-170
Tel: (02) 3626076 *Fax:* (02) 3124312
Key Personnel
President: Li Sook Cheung
Dir: Young-Il Kim
Founded: 1949

Subjects: Art, Education, Human Relations, Language Arts, Linguistics, Music, Dance, Philosophy, Religion - Other, Science (General), Social Sciences, Sociology
ISBN Prefix(es): 89-7300

Gim-Yeong Co+
170-4 Gahoe-dong, Jongro-gu, Seoul 110260
Tel: (02) 7454823; (02) 7454825 *Fax:* (02) 7454826
Key Personnel
President: Jung Sup Gimm
International Rights Contact: Mee Sung Kim
Founded: 1976
Subjects: Business, Environmental Studies, Fiction, How-to, Management, Marketing, Mysteries, Philosophy, Religion - Other, Science (General), Self-Help
ISBN Prefix(es): 89-349

Golden Bough Publishing Co, *imprint of* Minumsa Publishing Co Ltd

Gomdori, *imprint of* Woongjin Media Corporation

Gyeom-jisa
375-13 Seokyo-Dong, Mapo-gu Seoul 121-210
Tel: (02) 3351985 *Fax:* (02) 3351986
Key Personnel
Publisher: Chung Hae-Sang
Founded: 1964
Subjects: Science (General)
ISBN Prefix(es): 89-7169
Distributed by Min Jung Book Distribution Co

Haedong+
15-4 Namyeong-dong, Yongsan-gu, Seoul 140-160
Tel: (02) 953707 (Source lists phone w/o 1st digit) *Fax:* (02) 953707
Key Personnel
President & Author: B Ryong Chung
Founded: 1993
Subjects: Poetry
ISBN Prefix(es): 89-86861
Distributed by Bomoon-Dang; Han-yang Distributor

Hainaim Publishing Co Ltd
5-6 F Mijin Bldg, 464-41 Seogyo-dong, Mapo-gu, Seoul 121-210
Tel: (02) 326-1600; (02) 701-6819 *Fax:* (02) 326-1625
Key Personnel
President: Young-Seok Song
Rights Manager: Karen Lee *E-mail:* karenlee@hainaim.com
Founded: 1982
Subjects: Education, Fiction, History, Nonfiction (General), Science (General), Comics
ISBN Prefix(es): 89-7337

Hak Won Publishing Co
25-36, Chungsin-Dong, Jongro-gu, Seoul 110-490
Tel: (02) 7414621; (02) 7414623 *Fax:* (02) 7654584
Key Personnel
President: Young-Su Kim
Founded: 1945
Subjects: Art, Child Care & Development, Cookery, Literature, Literary Criticism, Essays, Social Sciences, Sociology
ISBN Prefix(es): 89-16

Hakgojae Publishing Inc+
70 Sogyeog-Dong, Jongro-gu, Seoul 110-200
Tel: (02) 7361713 *Fax:* (02) 7398592
E-mail: hkjass@hitel.kol.co.kr

Key Personnel
Contact: Chan-Kyu Woo
International Rights: Hyun-ki Park
Founded: 1991
Subjects: Archaeology, Architecture & Interior Design, Art, Asian Studies, Foreign Countries, History, Literature, Literary Criticism, Essays, Photography, Korean Studies
ISBN Prefix(es): 89-85846
Book Club(s): Kyobo Book Club

Hakmun Publishing, Co+
202 Sanggong Blvd, 251, Ceongjin-dong Jongro-gu, Seoul 110-130
Tel: (02) 733-1340 *Fax:* (02) 733-1350
E-mail: hakmun97@soback.kornet.nm.kr
Key Personnel
President: Young Chul Kim
Internal Dept: Ki-Hyoung Kim
Founded: 1963
Subjects: Business, Child Care & Development, Computer Science, Education, Engineering (General), English as a Second Language, Science (General), Social Sciences, Sociology
ISBN Prefix(es): 89-467; 89-87510
Branch Office(s)
Pusan *Tel:* (051) 502-8104
Taegu *Tel:* (053) 422-5000

Hanjin Publishing Co
3F, 51-18, 1-ga Weonhyoro, Yongsan-gu, Seoul 140-111
Tel: (02) 7137453 *Fax:* (02) 7135510
Key Personnel
President: Gab Han Jin
Subjects: Art, Literature, Literary Criticism, Essays, Religion - Other
ISBN Prefix(es): 89-86412

Hangil Art Vision
402 Gangnam Chulpan Munhwa Center, 506, Sinsa-dong, Gangnam-gu, Seoul 135-120
Tel: (02) 5154811 *Fax:* (02) 5154816
Key Personnel
Chief Executive: Euon-Ho Kim
Founded: 1976
Subjects: History, Literature, Literary Criticism, Essays, Philosophy, Social Sciences, Sociology
ISBN Prefix(es): 89-436; 89-437

Hanul Publishing Co+
201 Hyuam Bldg, 503-24 Changcheon-dong, Seodaemun-gu, Seoul 120-180
Tel: (02) 3260095; (02) 3366183 *Fax:* (02) 3337543
E-mail: newhanul@nuri.net
Key Personnel
Publisher: Kim Chong-Soo
Dir: Ms Lim Hee-Kun *Tel:* (02) 336-6183
Founded: 1980
Subjects: Asian Studies, Economics, Geography, Geology, Health, Nutrition, History, Journalism, Law, Literature, Literary Criticism, Essays, Medicine, Nursing, Dentistry, Philosophy, Social Sciences, Sociology, Theology, Women's Studies
ISBN Prefix(es): 89-460; 89-7058
Number of titles published annually: 150 Print
Total Titles: 1,200 Print
Associate Companies: Seoul Media Co; Siinsa Publishing Co

Haseo Publishing Co+
370-27, Shindang-Dong, Jung-gu, Seoul 100-454
Tel: (02) 2378161; (02) 2378165 *Fax:* (02) 2376575
Key Personnel
Chief Executive: Sang-Wook Kim
Founded: 1964
Subjects: Art, Literature, Literary Criticism, Essays, Social Sciences, Sociology
ISBN Prefix(es): 89-7330
Subsidiaries: Jigyung Publishing Co

PUBLISHERS

Hollym Corporation Publishers
13-13 Gwancheol-dong, Jongno-gu, Seoul 110-111
Tel: (02) 735-75514 *Fax:* (02) 7305149; (02) 7308192
E-mail: hollym@cholltan.net; info@hollym.co.kn
Key Personnel
President: Kiman Ham
Sales Dir: Ki Lee
Founded: 1963
Subjects: Art, Cookery, Economics, Fiction, History, Poetry, Travel
ISBN Prefix(es): 0-930878; 1-56591; 89-7094
U.S. Office(s): Hollym International Corp, 18 Donald Place, Elizabeth, NJ 07208, United States *Tel:* (908) 353-1655 *Fax:* (908) 353-0255

Hongik Media Plus Ltd+
1515 Hanseo River Park Bldg, 11-11, Yeoyido-dong, Youngdeungpo-gu, Seoul 120-010
Tel: (02) 786-1016 *Fax:* (02) 786-1709
E-mail: hongikcb@soback.kornet.nm.kr
Subjects: Biography, Career Development, Computer Science, Education, English as a Second Language
Subsidiaries: Hongik Media CNC Ltd

Hw Moon Publishing Co
30 Kyunji-dong, Chongno-ku, Seoul 110
Tel: (02) 724897
Key Personnel
Man Dir: Myong Hui Yi
Founded: 1961
Subjects: Biography, Fiction, History, Philosophy, Poetry, Religion - Other

Hyangmunsa Publishing Co
201 Jiseong Bldg, 645-20, Yeogsam-Dong, Gangnam-gu, Seoul 135-080
Tel: (02) 5385671; (02) 5385672 *Fax:* (02) 5385673
Key Personnel
President: Joong Ryol Nah
Founded: 1957
Subjects: Agriculture, Economics, Engineering (General), History, Science (General)
ISBN Prefix(es): 89-7187

Hyein Publishing House
Usin Bldg, Suite 202, 11-2 Gusan-Dong, Eunpyeoung-Gu, Seoul 122-060
Tel: (02) 3836928 *Fax:* (02) 3836929
E-mail: vvh103@chollian
Key Personnel
Contact: Choon-Won Cho
Founded: 1993
Subjects: Education, Health, Nutrition, Science (General), Travel
ISBN Prefix(es): 89-7853

Hyun Am Publishing Co
1660-15, 7-dong Bongceon, Gwanag, gu, Seoul 151-057
Tel: (02) 877-2565 *Fax:* (02) 877-2566
Key Personnel
Man Dir: Keun-Tae Cho
Publicity: Sang-Won Cho
Founded: 1951
Subjects: Literature, Literary Criticism, Essays, Philosophy, Religion - Other
ISBN Prefix(es): 89-87969

Iljisa Publishing House
46-1 Junghag-Dong, Jongro-gu, Seoul 110-150
Tel: (02) 7329320 *Fax:* (02) 7222807
Key Personnel
Man Dir: Sung-Jae Kim
Publicity Dirs: Byungki Yoo; Donhong Cho
Founded: 1956
Subjects: Archaeology, Fiction, History, Language Arts, Linguistics, Philosophy, Poetry, Social Sciences, Sociology
ISBN Prefix(es): 89-312

Iljo-gag Publishers+
9 Gongpyeuung-Dong, Jongro-gu, Seoul 110-160
Mailing Address: KPO Box 279, Seoul 110-160
Tel: (02) 733543011 *Fax:* (02) 7385857
E-mail: ilchokak@hitel.kol.co.kr; ilchokak@chollian.dacom.co.kr *Cable:* ICHOPUBLICO SEOUL
Key Personnel
President: Man-Nyun Han
Sales Dir: J Y Chot
Publicity Dir: J Y Choi
Founded: 1953
Subjects: Anthropology, Education, Engineering (General), History, Law, Medicine, Nursing, Dentistry, Psychology, Psychiatry, Science (General), Social Sciences, Sociology
ISBN Prefix(es): 89-337

Jeong-eum Munhwasa
810-12 Yeogsam-dong, Gangnam-gu, Seoul 135-080
Tel: (02) 5680070 *Fax:* (02) 5650352 *Cable:* Jeongeumsa
Key Personnel
President: Tong-Seek Chair
Sales Dir: Choong-tae Kim
Publicity & Advertising: Joo Park
Founded: 1928
Subjects: Fiction, Philosophy, Social Sciences, Sociology
ISBN Prefix(es): 89-7158

Jigyungsa Ltd+
790-14 Yeogsam-Dong, Gangnam-gu, Seoul 135-080
Tel: (02) 5576351 *Fax:* (02) 5576352
E-mail: jigyung@nextell.net
Key Personnel
President: Byung-Joon Kim
Dir, International & Planning Dept: Hyosik Kim
Dir, Marketing: Seong-Ho Lee
Dir, Production: Byung-Sik Kim
Founded: 1978
Subjects: Fiction, Nonfiction (General)
Subsidiaries: Miraejungbosa
Divisions: Walt Disney Books & Magazines

Jung-ang Munhwa Sa
172-11 Yeomri-dong, Mapo-gu, Seoul 121-090
Tel: (02) 7172114 *Fax:* (02) 7161369
Key Personnel
Chief Executive: Duck-Ke Kim
Founded: 1972
ISBN Prefix(es): 89-7511

Jung-ang Media, see Jung-ang Munhwa Sa

Kemongsa Publishing Co Ltd+
29-7 lga Euijuro, Jung-gu, Seoul 135-080
Tel: (02) 723-9367 *Fax:* (02) 561-0910
Key Personnel
President: Choon-sik Kim
Man Dir: Jong-uk Lee
Assistant Manager, Foreign Rights: Park Yeon
Founded: 1947
Specialize in children's books.
Subjects: Biography, English as a Second Language, Fiction, Geography, Geology, Nonfiction (General), Science (General)
ISBN Prefix(es): 89-06
Subsidiaries: Young Printing Co, Ltd; Kemong Enterprise Co Ltd; EMI - Kemongsa Co Ltd

Ki Moon Dang
286-20 Haengdang-Dong, Sungdong-ku, Seoul 133-070

Tel: (02) 2995496; (02) 2956175 *Fax:* (02) 2968188
Key Personnel
Chief Executive: Hae-Jak Kang
Founded: 1976
Subjects: Art, Engineering (General)

Korea Britannica Corp
701 Jeil-Sangho-Sinyong-Geumgo Bldg, 117, l-ga, Jangchung-dong, Jung-gu, Seoul 100-400
Tel: (02) 2789981; (02) 2789982 *Fax:* (02) 2789983
Key Personnel
President: Polly Sauer
Founded: 1968
Subjects: Education
ISBN Prefix(es): 89-7544
Parent Company: Encyclopaedia Britannica Inc, Britannica Centre, 310 South Michigan Ave, Chicago, IL 60604, United States

Korea Local Authorities Foundation for International Relations
720 Royal Bldg, 5 Dangju-dong, Jongro-gu, Seoul 110-720
Tel: 02 378973 *Fax:* 02 378970
E-mail: klfool@bova.dacom.co.kr
Subjects: Public Administration
ISBN Prefix(es): 89-86815

Korea Psychological Testing Institute+
797-25 Yeongsam-dung, Gangnam-gu, 135-082 Seoul
Tel: (02) 558-0286; (02) 558-0287 *Fax:* (02) 567-4877
E-mail: SHLK@hitel.kol.co.kr
Key Personnel
Contact: Myung-Joon Kim
Founded: 1972
Subjects: Psychology, Psychiatry
Associate Companies: Consulting Psychologists Press

Korea Testbook Co, see Kwangmyong Publishing Co

Korea Textbook Co Ltd
62-7 Manri-Dong 1-ga, Jung-gu, Seoul 100-371
Tel: (02) 3920996 *Fax:* (02) 3127415
Key Personnel
President: Keun-Woo Lee
Subjects: Art, Education, Government, Political Science
ISBN Prefix(es): 89-85182
Parent Company: Kwangmyong Printing & Publishing Co Ltd

Korea University Press
1-2 Anam-dong 5-ga, Seongbug-gu, Seoul 136-701
Tel: (02) 9201720 *Fax:* (02) 9236311
Key Personnel
President: Hie-Jip Kim
Founded: 1956
Subjects: Agriculture, Earth Sciences, Education, Engineering (General), History, Language Arts, Linguistics, Literature, Literary Criticism, Essays, Philosophy, Psychology, Psychiatry, Social Sciences, Sociology
ISBN Prefix(es): 89-7641

Korean Publishers Association+
105-2 Sagan-Dong, Jongno-Gu, Seoul 110-190
Tel: (02) 735 2702 *Fax:* (02) 738 5414
E-mail: kpa@kpa21.or.kr
Web Site: www.kpa21.or.kr
Key Personnel
President: Jung Il Lee
Secretary General: Jong Jin Jung
Founded: 1947
Subjects: Publishing & Book Trade Reference
ISBN Prefix(es): 89-85231

REPUBLIC OF KOREA

Koreaone Press Inc+
9F Gyeongun Bldg 70 Gyeongun-dong, Jongro-gu, Seoul 110-310
Tel: (02) 7391156 *Fax:* (02) 7343512
Key Personnel
Chief Executive: Nark-Cheon Kim
Founded: 1978
Subjects: Biography, Business, Career Development, Economics, Education, English as a Second Language, Environmental Studies, Fiction, Language Arts, Linguistics, Literature, Literary Criticism, Essays, Management, Mysteries, Nonfiction (General), Philosophy, Religion - Buddhist, Romance, Science (General), Science Fiction, Fantasy, Social Sciences, Sociology, Western Fiction
ISBN Prefix(es): 89-12
Associate Companies: Koreaone Media Inc; Koreaone Chest Inc
Divisions: Foreign Rights Department
U.S. Office(s): Koreaone International, 520 W Eighth St, Los Angeles, CA 90005, United States

Kukmin Doseo Publishing Co Inc+
822, Guro-dong, Guro-gu, Seoul 152-050
Tel: (02) 858-2461; (02) 858-2463 *Fax:* (02) 858-2464
E-mail: younhlee@chollian.net
Key Personnel
President: Young-Hoon Lee
Founded: 1978
Specializes in religious books.
Subjects: Religion - Protestant, Theology
ISBN Prefix(es): 89-401
Associate Companies: Kookmin Daily News Press
Subsidiaries: Yae-In Publishing Co
Distributor for Koonmin Daily News Press

Kukminseokwan Publishing Co Ltd
257-3 Gongdeog-dong Bldg, Mapo-Ku, Seoul 121-804
Tel: (02) 7107722; (02) 7107724 *Fax:* (02) 7155771
Key Personnel
Chief Executive: Yoo-Kwang Lee
Founded: 1961
Subjects: Social Sciences, Sociology
ISBN Prefix(es): 89-11

Kum Sung Publishing Co Ltd+
242-63 Gongdeog-Dong, Mapo-gu, Seoul 121-022
Tel: (02) 7139651 *Fax:* (02) 7041979
Key Personnel
Chairman: Moo-Sang Kim
Editorial Dir: Sung-Chul Kang
Man Dir: Bo-Hwan Lee
Manager: Dae-Shik Kim
Assistant Manager: Chae-Hyung Lee; Gwang-So Lee
Founded: 1965
Subjects: Fiction, Nonfiction (General)
ISBN Prefix(es): 89-07
Associate Companies: Shin Won Editorial Center, 250-4 Towha-dong, Mapo-ku, Seoul; Shinwon Agency Co, 372-6 Seogyo-dong, Mapo-gu, Seoul 121-022
Subsidiaries: Kumsung Textbook Co Ltd; Kumsung Artcom
Branch Office(s)
Kaiserstr 42, 60329 Frankfurt am Main, Germany

Kwangmyong Publishing Co
62-7 Manri-Dong 1-ga, Jung-gu, Seoul 100-371
Tel: (02) 3923081; (02) 3920996; (02) 3925855 *Fax:* (02) 3127415
Telex: K27229 Kortuna *Cable:* Kwangmyong, Seoul
Key Personnel
President: Keun-Woo Lee
Dir: Yun Bai Yoon
Founded: 1951
Subjects: Art, Regional Interests
Subsidiaries: Korea Textbook Co; Kwangmyong Toppan Moore Printing Co

Kyobo Book Centre
4F Gyobomungo, 179 Naesu-dong, Jangro-gu, Seoul 110-070
Tel: (02) 3973521; (02) 3973509 *Fax:* (02) 7362361
Subjects: Government, Political Science, Law, Literature, Literary Criticism, Essays
ISBN Prefix(es): 89-7085
Bookshop(s): Kyobo Book Centre Co Ltd

Kyohaksa Publishing Co Ltd+
150-67 Gongdeok-Dong, Mapo-Ku, Seoul 152-020
Tel: (02) 7174561; (02) 8592017 *Fax:* (02) 7183976
Key Personnel
President: Cheol-Woo Yang
Subjects: Business, Nonfiction (General)

Kyungnam University Press
449 Weolyeong-dong, Masan 631-701
Tel: (0551) 2432330 *Fax:* (0551) 2492073
Key Personnel
President: Tae-Rim Yun
Subjects: Philosophy, Social Sciences, Sociology

Literature Academy
133 Iwha-Dong, Jongro-Gu, Seoul 110-500
Tel: (02) 7645057 *Fax:* (02) 7458516
E-mail: munhac@ppp.kornet4.net
Web Site: www.munhakac.co.kr
Key Personnel
Contact: Je-Chun Park
Founded: 1988
Subjects: Art, Language Arts, Linguistics, Literature, Literary Criticism, Essays, Poetry
ISBN Prefix(es): 89-400
Total Titles: 280 Print

Maeil Gyeongje
51-9, Phil-Dong 1-ga, Jung-gu, Seoul 100-728
Tel: (02) 276-0210; (02) 2760211; (02) 2760212; (02) 2760213; (02) 2760214; (02) 2760215 *Fax:* (02) 271-0463
E-mail: mpd@unitel.co.kv
Key Personnel
President & Publisher: Dae-Whan Chang, PhD
Subjects: Business, Economics

Min Jung Seo Rim Publishing Co
161-7 Yeomni Dong, 4F Hancheong-Sireob Bldg, Mapo-gu, Seoul 121-874
Tel: (02) 7036541; (02) 7036547 *Fax:* (02) 7036549
E-mail: editmin@minjungdic.co.kr
Web Site: www.minjumgdic.co.kr
Key Personnel
President: Chul Hwan Kim
Editorial: Cha Hyun Yun
Founded: 1979
ISBN Prefix(es): 89-387
Parent Company: Beupmun Sa Publishing Co

Minjisa Publishing Co+
673-3 Mia-Dong, Kangbuk-Ky, Seoul 142-819
Tel: (02) 9806382 *Fax:* (02) 9861531
E-mail: minjisa@nownuri.net
Web Site: www.minjisa.co.kr
Key Personnel
President: Tai-Seung Ri *Tel:* (02) 9234385/ 9858035 *Fax:* (02) 9234386 *E-mail:* tsri201@yahoo.co.kr
Founded: 1982
Subjects: Child Care & Development, Education, Health, Nutrition, History, Literature, Literary Criticism, Essays, Psychology, Psychiatry
ISBN Prefix(es): 89-7362

BOOK

Number of titles published annually: 8 Print
Total Titles: 127 Print

Minumsa Publishing Co Ltd+
5F Kangnam Publishing Culture Center, 506 Sinsa-Dong, Gangnam-gu, Seoul 135-887
Tel: (02) 515-2000; (02) 515-2005; (02) 515-9108 *Fax:* (02) 515-2007; (02) 3444-5185
Web Site: www.minumsa.com
Key Personnel
President: Park Maeng-ho
Vice President: Park Geun-sup
Editorial: Park Sang Soon
Sales: Jung Dae Yong
Foreign Rights Manager: Michelle Nam *Tel:* (02) 515-2003, Ext 206 *E-mail:* michellenam@minumsa.com
Founded: 1966
Publishes a literary magazine, *World Literature*.
Subjects: Fiction, History, Literature, Literary Criticism, Essays, Nonfiction (General), Philosophy, Science (General), Social Sciences, Sociology
ISBN Prefix(es): 89-374
Total Titles: 200 Print
Imprints: BIR Publishing Co; Golden Bough Publishing Co; Science Books Ltd
Subsidiaries: BIR Publishing Co Ltd; Golden-Bough Publishing Co Ltd

Mirinae+
1011 Singeong Sangaa, 192-30, Inhyeondong 2 ga, Junggu, Seol 100-282
Tel: (02) 2279-2669 *Fax:* (02) 2234-1450
E-mail: mrn@lycos.co.kr
Key Personnel
Publisher: Kim Jin-Shik
Subjects: Literature, Literary Criticism, Essays, Poetry
ISBN Prefix(es): 89-7082

The Monthly Magazine for Ceramics Co, Ltd
1502-12 3-dong Seocho, Seocho-gu, Seoul 137-073
Tel: (02) 832747 *Fax:* (02) 978639
Founded: 1988
Parent Company: Daeho Yoeop Co Ltd

Moon Jin Media Co Ltd
3rd floor Shinwoo Bldg 5-7, Yongsan-Dong 3-Ka, Yongsan-Ku, Seoul 140-023
Tel: (02) 792-7611 *Fax:* (02) 7928885
E-mail: mjmedia@hitel.kol.co.kr
Key Personnel
President: Sang Chuu Lee
International Rights: Jong Yeon Park
Subjects: English as a Second Language
Bookshop(s): Kim & Johnson, 4F, Seojeong B1 1308-14, Seocho-4-dong, Seocho-ku, Seoul 137-074

Mun Un Dang
45-3 Myeongryundong 1-ga, Jongro-gu, Seoul 110-521
Tel: (02) 7433504; (02) 7433505 *Fax:* (02) 7450265
Key Personnel
President: Seoung-Beum Lee
Founded: 1962
Subjects: Engineering (General), Science (General)
ISBN Prefix(es): 89-7393

Munhag-gwan
34-22, Sinsu-dong, Mapo-gu, Seoul 121-110
Tel: (02) 7186810 *Fax:* (02) 7062225
Key Personnel
Chief Executive: Byong-Ik Kim
Founded: 1975

Subjects: Art, History, Literature, Literary Criticism, Essays, Philosophy, Social Sciences, Sociology
ISBN Prefix(es): 89-7077

Munye Publishing Co+
32-11 Chungjeongro 3-ga, Seodaemun-gu, Seoul 120-013
Tel: (02) 3935681; (02) 3935684 *Fax:* (02) 3935685
Key Personnel
Chief Executive: Byung-Suk Chun
Founded: 1966
Subjects: Art, Fiction, History, Literature, Literary Criticism, Essays, Nonfiction (General), Philosophy, Social Sciences, Sociology, Women's Studies
ISBN Prefix(es): 89-310

Nanam Publishing House+
501 Jihun Bldg, 1364-39 Seocho-dong, Seocho-gu, Seoul 137-070
Tel: (02) 3413-1711; (02) 552-8537 *Fax:* (02) 552-0711
E-mail: nanamcom@soback.kornet21.net; edit@nanamcom.co.kr; post@nanamcom.co.kr
Web Site: www.nanamcom.co.kr
Key Personnel
Chief Executive: Sang-Ho Cho
Founded: 1979
Subjects: Advertising, Art, Communications, Journalism, Literature, Literary Criticism, Essays, Poetry, Social Sciences, Sociology
ISBN Prefix(es): 89-300
Parent Company: Korea Society Review

O Neul Publishing Co+
458 Yonggang-dong, Mapo-gu, Seoul 121-070
Tel: (02) 716-2811 *Fax:* (02) 712-7392
Key Personnel
Editor: Yoon-Seon Park
Contact: Jong-Chun Lee
Founded: 1980
Subjects: Child Care & Development, Fiction, History, House & Home, Mysteries, Nonfiction (General), Poetry, Women's Studies
ISBN Prefix(es): 89-355
Imprints: Cham Kae

Ohmsa+
Sekee Bldg, 17 Kalweol-Dong, Yongsan-Ku, Seoul
Tel: (02) 7764868 *Fax:* (02) 7796757
Key Personnel
Contact: Jong-Hak Kwak
Founded: 1975
Subjects: Computer Science, Microcomputers, Telecommunication
Subsidiaries: Robot & Computer Company (R&C Sha)

Omun Gak
3rd floor, Madang Bldg, Yeoksam-Dong, Kangnam-Ku, Seoul 135-080
Tel: (02) 3453-8278 *Fax:* (02) 508-5210
Key Personnel
President: Sun-Ki Jeon
Editorial: Kyun Hee Kim
Publicity: Jai Yung You
Sales: Jai Yong Kim
Production: In Soo Kim
Rights & Permissions: Kae Choong Chang
Founded: 1959
Subjects: Literature, Literary Criticism, Essays, Social Sciences, Sociology
Associate Companies: Yueil Publishing and Marketing Cooperation, Room 509, Jungeun Bldg, 22-5 Chungmu-ro Fifth Avenue, Chung-ku, Seoul 100

The Organizing Committee of the 11th Int-l Zeolite Conference
Hwahaggonghaggwa KAIST, 373-1 Guseong-dong, Yuseong-gu, Daejeon 305-701
Tel: (042) 69-8161 *Fax:* (042) 69-8170
E-mail: skihm@sorak.kaist.ac.kr
Key Personnel
International Rights: Prof Son-Ki Ihm
ISBN Prefix(es): 89-950030

Oriental Books
375-45 Seogyo-Dong, Mapo-gu, Seoul 121-210
Tel: (02) 371737 *Fax:* (02) 346624
Key Personnel
Contact: Tae-Woong Kim
Founded: 1993
ISBN Prefix(es): 89-8300; 89-85705

Oruem Publishing House+
Hongjung Bldg, Suite 201, 1420-6, 1 dong Seoco, Seoco-gu, Seoul 137-070
Tel: (02) 5859122; (02) 5859123 *Fax:* (02) 5847952
Key Personnel
President: Seong-Ok Boo
Founded: 1993
Subjects: Asian Studies, Business, Communications, Economics, Education, Government, Political Science, Public Administration, Social Sciences, Sociology
ISBN Prefix(es): 89-7778

Pan Korea Book Corporation
1-222 Sinmunro 2-ga, Jongro-gu, Seoul 110-601
Tel: (02) 7332011; (02) 7332018 *Fax:* (02) 7368696
Telex: Pkbook K24149 *Cable:* Pankorbooks Seoul
Key Personnel
President: Yoon-Sun Kim
Subjects: Language Arts, Linguistics, Literature, Literary Criticism, Essays, Technology
ISBN Prefix(es): 89-7129

Panmun Book Co Ltd+
40 Chongno 1-ka, Chongno-ku, Seoul 110-121
Mailing Address: CPO Box 1016, Chongno-gu, Seoul 110-121
Tel: (02) 7338688; (02) 7338501; (02) 720-2859 *Fax:* (02) 7205756; (02) 953-2456
Telex: K27546 Panmuse *Cable:* PANMUSE SEOUL
Key Personnel
Man Dir: I H Liu
Sales Dir: S H Kim
Founded: 1955
Subjects: Medicine, Nursing, Dentistry, Science (General), Social Sciences, Sociology
Associate Companies: International Publications Service Inc
Subsidiaries: The STM Books & Journals Inc
Branch Office(s)
Kwangju
Pusan
Taegu
Taejon
Bookshop(s): 16 Kwangbok-dong 1-ka, Pusan; 40 Chongno 1-ga, Chongno-gu, Seoul
Warehouse: 15-7 Anam-dong 4-Ka, Sungbuk-ku, Seoul

Pearson Education Korea Ltd+
No 404 Sin La 2 Bldg, 137-5 Yeonhee-Dong, Seodaemun-Ku, Seoul 120-111
Tel: (02) 332 0841 *Fax:* (02) 332 0843
E-mail: firstname.lastname@pearsoned.co.kr
Key Personnel
General Manager: Yong-Jin Oh *E-mail:* yongjin.oh@pearsoned.co.kr
Senior Sales Manager, HE: Pock-Man Hur *Tel:* (02) 335 7987 *Fax:* (02) 335 7988 *E-mail:* pockman.hur@pearsoned.co.kr
Finance/Administration Manager: Eun-Ja Lee *Tel:* (02) 335 0267 *Fax:* (02) 335 7988 *E-mail:* eunja.lee@pearsoned.co.kr
Sales Manager: Bong- Jo Choi *Tel:* (02) 335 7987 *Fax:* (02) 335 7988 *E-mail:* bongjo.choi@pearsoned.co.kr; Chong-Dae Chung *E-mail:* chongdae.chung@pearsoned.co.kr
Rights/Publishing Manager: Yeon-Jung Lee *Tel:* (02) 3142 5776 *Fax:* (02) 335 7988 *E-mail:* yeonjung.lee@pearsoned.co.kr
Founded: 1997
Subjects: Computer Science, Engineering (General)
ISBN Prefix(es): 89-450
Number of titles published annually: 30 Print
Total Titles: 500 Print
Parent Company: Pearson Education, One Lake Street, Upper Saddle River, NJ 01867, United States
Ultimate Parent Company: Pearson Plc
Holding Company: Pearson Education Korea
Branch Office(s)
PEK Daegu Office, 3rd floor, 1160-12 Jisan-Dong, Susung-Ku, Daegu 706-090

Pochinchai Printing Co Ltd
8 Dangsan-Dong 5-Ka, Youngdeungpo-ku, Seoul 150-045
Mailing Address: CPO Box 2278, Yongsan-gu, Seoul 140-012
Tel: (02) 679-2351 *Fax:* (02) 676-2821
Telex: Pochcha K33448
Key Personnel
President: Won-Sun Kim
Chief Executive: Dal-Hoon Lee
Editorial: Kang Hurh
Founded: 1912
Subjects: Art, History, Social Sciences, Sociology, Technology

Prompter Publications+
PO Box 167, Chongnyangni, Tongdaemoon-gu, Seoul 130-650
SAN: 297-4584
Tel: (02) 82 2214 1794
Key Personnel
President & International Rights: Myungkark Park
Founded: 1989
US publisher.
Subjects: Chemistry, Chemical Engineering, Computer Science, Crafts, Games, Hobbies, Library & Information Sciences, Mathematics, Philosophy, Physics, Science (General)
ISBN Prefix(es): 1-877974
Number of titles published annually: 5 Print
Total Titles: 35 Print

Pyeong-hwa Chulpansa+
150 Palpan-Dong, Jongro-gu, Seoul 110-220
Mailing Address: CPO Box 5066, Seoul 121-110
Tel: (02) 7343341; (02) 7343343 *Fax:* (02) 7392129
Key Personnel
Publisher: Chang-Sung Huh
Founded: 1963
Subjects: Crafts, Games, Hobbies, English as a Second Language, Gardening, Plants, How-to, Literature, Literary Criticism, Essays, Outdoor Recreation, Sports, Athletics, Travel
ISBN Prefix(es): 89-367
Subsidiaries: Jinsun Publishers
Distributed by Seoul Publication Distribution Co Ltd

St Pauls+
103-36 Mia 9-Dong, Gangbug-gu, Seoul 142-109
Tel: (02) 9861361; (02) 9861364 *Fax:* (02) 984-4622
E-mail: miari@paolo.net; felix@paolo.net
Web Site: www.paolo.net
Key Personnel
General & Editiorial Dir: Chang-Ouk Lee

Tel: (02) 986-1361-4 *Fax:* (02) 986-1365
E-mail: felix@paolo.net
Founded: 1991
Publication of literary, children's books, theology & philosophy books, religious books. Publishes *My Friends,* monthly comic magazine.
Subjects: Biblical Studies, Fiction, Human Relations, Philosophy, Poetry, Religion - Catholic, Theology
Total Titles: 150 Print; 30 Audio
Book Club(s): St Pauls Book Club *Tel:* (02) 986-1361; 1365 *E-mail:* bookclub@paolo.net

Samho Music Publishing Co
718-8 Banpo 1-Dong, Seocho-gu, Seoul 137-080
Tel: (02) 5123515 *Fax:* (02) 512-3594
E-mail: webmaster@samhomusic.com
Web Site: www.samhomusic.com
Key Personnel
President: Jung-Tae Kim
International Rights: Sang-min Lee
Founded: 1977
Subjects: Art, Crafts, Games, Hobbies, Music, Dance, Outdoor Recreation, Publishing & Book Trade Reference, Sports, Athletics
ISBN Prefix(es): 89-326
Subsidiaries: Samho Media Co

Samhwa Publishing Co
15, 2-ga Eulijiro, Jung-gu, Seoul 110-192
Tel: (02) 7766686 *Fax:* (02) 7732993
Key Personnel
President: Kon Su Yu
Founded: 1962
Subjects: Art, Language Arts, Linguistics, Social Sciences, Sociology
ISBN Prefix(es): 89-87846

Samkwang Publishing Co
499-39 Seokyo-Dong, Mapo-Ku, Seoul
Tel: (02) 3237275 *Fax:* (02) 3251153
Key Personnel
Contact: Myung-Woo Lee
Founded: 1978
Subjects: Social Sciences, Sociology

Samseong Publishing Co Ltd+
1516-2, Seocho-dong, Seocho-gu, Seoul 137-070
Tel: (02) 3470-6852 *Fax:* (02) 7853565
Key Personnel
President: Bong-Kyu Kim
Planning & Coordination Dir: Seok Hyun Cho
Founded: 1952
Subjects: Art, Business, History, Literature, Literary Criticism, Essays, Women's Studies
ISBN Prefix(es): 89-15
Orders to: 60-32 Garibong-dong, Guro-gu, Seoul

Science Books Ltd, *imprint of* Minumsa Publishing Co Ltd

Se-Kwang Music Publishing Co+
232-32 Seokye-Dong, Yongsan-gu, Seoul 140-140
Tel: (02) 7140046 *Fax:* (02) 7192191
Key Personnel
President & Chairman: Shin-Joon Park
Sales Dir: Moon-Suk Kang
Publicity & Publication Manager: Nam-Jae Kang
Copyright Manager: Kichul Han
Founded: 1953
Subjects: Music, Dance
ISBN Prefix(es): 89-03
U.S. Office(s): Park Soon Tai, 3170 W Olympic Blvd, No E, Los Angeles, CA 90006, United States

Sejong Daewang Kinyom Saophoe
1-57 Chongryangli-dong, San, Iongno-ku, Seoul
Key Personnel
President: Gwan Ku Yi
Subjects: History, Religion - Other

Seogwangsa+
119-46 Yongdu 2-Dong, Dongdaemun-gu, Seoul 130-072
Tel: (02) 9246161; (02) 9246165 *Fax:* (02) 9224993
Key Personnel
President: Shin-Hyeok Kim
Editor: Min-Sook Bae
Founded: 1974
Subjects: Anthropology, Asian Studies, Education, Philosophy, Religion - Buddhist, Religion - Catholic, Religion - Hindu, Religion - Other
ISBN Prefix(es): 89-306

Seoul International Publishing House
94-60 Hwayang-dong, Seongdong-gu, Seoul 133-130
Tel: (02) 4698326; (02) 4698327
Key Personnel
President: Chung-Gil Shim
Founded: 1977
Formerly Seoul International Tourist Publishing Co.
Subjects: Art, Cookery, History, Language Arts, Linguistics, Photography, Regional Interests, Travel
ISBN Prefix(es): 89-85113
Orders to: European Book Service, Flevolaan 36-38, Postbus 124, 1380 AC Weesp, Netherlands
Charles E Tuttle Co Inc, PO Box 410, Rutland, VT 05701, United States

Seoul National University Press
San 56-1, Sinrim-dong, Gwanag-gu, Seoul 151-742
Tel: (02) 8774418 *Fax:* (02) 8884148
Key Personnel
President: Chong-Un Kim
Dir: Jong-Chul Lim
Founded: 1961
Subjects: Art, Earth Sciences, History, Language Arts, Linguistics, Literature, Literary Criticism, Essays, Medicine, Nursing, Dentistry, Philosophy, Science (General), Social Sciences, Sociology
ISBN Prefix(es): 89-7096

Shinkwang Publishing Co
278-1 Bomun-Dong 6-ka, Sungbuk-ku, Seoul 136-086
Tel: (02) 9255051; (02) 9255053 *Fax:* (02) 9255054
Key Personnel
Chief Executive: Yong-Ha Lee
Founded: 1972
Subjects: Cookery, Medicine, Nursing, Dentistry, Science (General)

Si-sa-yong-o-sa, Inc, see YBM/Si-sa

Sogang University Press
One Sinsoo-Dong, Mapo-gu, Seoul 121-742
Tel: (02) 715-0141; (02) 715-0147 *Fax:* (02) 701-8962
Key Personnel
President: Hong Park
Dir: Jae-Son Lee
Subjects: History, Language Arts, Linguistics, Literature, Literary Criticism, Essays, Science (General), Social Sciences, Sociology
ISBN Prefix(es): 89-7273

Sohaksa+
92-2 Namyoung-Dong, Yongsan-Ku, Seoul 140-160
Tel: (02) 7967661 *Fax:* (02) 7968700
Key Personnel
Contact: Young-Whan Suhl
Founded: 1988

Subjects: Anthropology, Archaeology, English as a Second Language, History, Management, Philosophy, Psychology, Psychiatry, Social Sciences, Sociology

Suhagsa
1586-4 Seocho 3-Dong, Seocho-Ku, Seoul 137-073
Tel: (02) 584-4642 *Fax:* (02) 521-1458
Key Personnel
President: Young-Ho Lee *Tel:* (02) 584-4642
Founded: 1953
Subjects: Fashion, Health, Nutrition, House & Home
ISBN Prefix(es): 89-7140
Total Titles: 143 Print
Book Club(s): KPA

Twenty-First Century Publishers, Inc+
5 Flil Bldg, 315-3, 1 dong, Ganseog, Namdong-gu, Inceon 405-231
Tel: (032) 429-9411 *Fax:* (032) 4299418
Key Personnel
President: Mr Y D Ahn
Editor: Ms Youngmi Kwon
Founded: 1988
Subjects: Business, Economics, Management
ISBN Prefix(es): 89-89457

Universal Publications Agency Press
UPA Bldg, 54 Gyeonji-dong, Jongro-gu, Seoul 110-170
Tel: (02) 328175 *Fax:* (02) 328176
Telex: K28504 Unipub *Cable:* CHANGHOSHIN SEOUL
Key Personnel
Manager: Il Chung Ha
ISBN Prefix(es): 89-7613

Woong Jin Publishing Co Ltd+
Dongweon Bldg, Ineui-Dong, 112-1, Jongru-Gu, Seoul 110-717
Mailing Address: CPO Box 1681, Chongno-Gu, Seoul 110-410
Tel: (02) 7427941 *Fax:* (02) 7441904
E-mail: wjmap@chollian.dacom.co.kr
Key Personnel
Foreign Rights Manager: Seang-Ju Hong
Founded: 1980
Subjects: Business, Education, English as a Second Language, How-to, Literature, Literary Criticism, Essays, Mysteries, Nonfiction (General), Romance, Travel
ISBN Prefix(es): 89-01; 89-345
Subsidiaries: Woong Nin Media Co Ltd

Woongjin Media Corporation+
28-9 Inevi-dong, Jongro-Gu, Seoul 110-410
Tel: (02) 745-6712 *Fax:* (02) 745-0777
E-mail: wjmhky@woongjin.co.kr
Key Personnel
Chairman: Suck-keum Yoon
President: Hwan-kee Ryu
Man Dir: Heungsung Lee
Founded: 1987
Specialize in multi-media packages, educational & home videos, CAI-software, compact discs.
Subjects: Business, Fiction, History, Nonfiction (General), Science (General)
ISBN Prefix(es): 89-02
Parent Company: Woongjin Publishing Co Ltd
Imprints: Gomdori
Subsidiaries: Woongjin (USA) Inc

Word of Life Press+
1-151 Sinmunro 2 ga Jongro-gu, Seoul 110-062
Tel: (02) 738-6555 *Fax:* (02) 7393824
Key Personnel
President & International Rights: Jay-Kwon Kim
E-mail: jaykkim@chollian.net
Founded: 1953
Specialize in Christian book publishing.

Subjects: Religion - Protestant, Missionary Work
ISBN Prefix(es): 89-04
Parent Company: TEAM Korea
Associate Companies: The Evangelical Alliance Mission (Team)
Divisions: World of Life Books in USA
U.S. Office(s): Los Angeles, CA, United States
Washington, DC, United States
Chicago, IL, United States

YBM/Si-sa+
Formerly Si-sa-yong-o-sa, Inc
55-1 Chongno 2-ga, Chongno-gu, Seoul 110-122
Tel: (02) 2000-0501 *Fax:* (02) 2265-7573
E-mail: suite@ybmsisa.com
Web Site: www.ybm.co.kr; www.ybmsisa.co.kr
Key Personnel
Chairman: Young-Bin Min
President: Sun-Shik Min
Editorial Dir: Hye-Ryoung Kim *E-mail:* hrkim@ybmsisa.com
Sales Dir: Jong-Chul Kim
Founded: 1961
Book & Magazine Publishing, Language Schools, Testing Activities, Music Company, IT Business, ELT Materials, Multi-media Publications, On-line Publishing, English Language Study Materials, TOET-L & TOEIC Prep Books.
Member of IPA, FIPP & ABC.
Subjects: Economics, Literature, Literary Criticism, Essays
ISBN Prefix(es): 89-17
Number of titles published annually: 1,000 Print
Total Titles: 12,000 Print
Subsidiaries: ICF/TOEIC Committee; Seoul Records; YBM/Education; YBM/ELS; IPS
Branch Office(s)
YBM/ELS (Canada (Vancouver, Toronto))
Distributed by Pearson
Distributor for Barron's; ETS/Chauncey; McGraw Hill; McMillan; National Geographic Society; Newsweek International; Pearson; Peterson's; Readers Digest; Simon & Schuster

Yearim-dang
233-5 Yongdab-dong, Seongdong-gu, Seoul 133-150
Tel: (02) 2493333 *Fax:* (02) 248-7400
Key Personnel
Chief Executive: Choon Na
Founded: 1973
Subjects: Cookery
ISBN Prefix(es): 89-507; 89-302; 89-87941

Yeha Publishing Co Ltd+
736-37, Yeogsam-dong, Gangnam-gu, Seoul 135-080
Tel: (02) 5535933; (02) 5535936 *Fax:* (02) 5525149
Key Personnel
Contact: Khil-Boo Park
Founded: 1987
Member of Korean Publishers Association.
Subjects: Business, Literature, Literary Criticism, Essays, Music, Dance
ISBN Prefix(es): 89-7359

Yonsei University Press
134 Sinchon-dong, Seodaemun-gu, Seoul 120-749
Tel: (02) 3926201 *Fax:* (02) 3931421
E-mail: ysup@bubble.yonsei.ac.kr
Key Personnel
President: Byung-Soo Kim
Dir: Suk-Hyun Kim
Business Manager: Ho-Sun Choi
Founded: 1955
Subjects: Art, History, Medicine, Nursing, Dentistry, Philosophy, Religion - Other, Science (General), Social Sciences, Sociology, Technology
ISBN Prefix(es): 89-7141

Kuwait

General Information

Capital: Kuwait
Language: Arabic. English also used commercially
Religion: Muslim
Population: 1.58 million
Bank Hours: 0800-1200 (0830-1230 during Ramadan) Saturday-Thursday
Shop Hours: 0800-1200 or 1230, 1530 or 16-2030 Saturday-Thursday; 0800-1200 Friday (markets and shopping centers also open 1530-2030); during Ramadan: 0830 or 0900-1230, 1930-1030 or 0200 Saturday-Thursday. Some shopping centers open 1600-2100 Friday
Currency: 1000 fils = approximately 3 US dollars
Export/Import Information: No tariffs on books or advertising in reasonable quantity; all immoral and seditious publications prohibited. Import license required. No exchange permit required.
Copyright: No copyright conventions signed

Kuwait Publishing House
PO Box 5209, 13053 Safat, Kuwait City
Tel: 2414697
Key Personnel
Dir: Amin Hamadeh

Ministry of Information
PO Box 193, 13002 Safat, Kuwait City
Tel: 2415300 *Fax:* 2421926
Telex: Mi 22030 Kt, Mi 46151 Kt *Cable:* ALIRSHAD
Subjects: Art, Education, Geography, Geology, History, Language Arts, Linguistics, Literature, Literary Criticism, Essays, Mathematics, Physics, Social Sciences, Sociology

Press Agency+
Fahd al-Salim St, PO Box 1019, Kuwait
Tel: 432269; 411495 *Fax:* 411495
Telex: Matboat 46046 Kt; Matboat 46246 Kt *Cable:* MATBOAT
Key Personnel
Man Dir: Abdullah M N Harami
Editorial: K A Harami; Ibrahim M Hadi
Founded: 1954
Bookshop(s): in Kuwait and Salmaiy

Laos People's Democratic Republic

General Information

Capital: Vientiane
Language: Lao (official), French, English and Tribal dialects
Religion: Theravada Buddhist
Population: 4.47 million
Bank Hours: 0800-1700 Monday-Friday
Shop Hours: 0800-2200 Monday-Friday, seven days a week for Vietnamese Morning Market
Export/Import Information: Import license required. Exchange controls.
Copyright: UCC (see Copyright Conventions, pg xi)

Lao-phanit
Vientiane Ministere de l'Education nationale, Bureau des manuels, scolaires, Vientiane
Subjects: Art, Cookery, Economics, Education, Fiction, Geography, Geology, History, Music, Dance, Physics, Social Sciences, Sociology

Pakpassak Kanphin
9-11 quai Fa-Hguun, Vientiane

Latvia

General Information

Capital: Riga
Language: Latvian (Lettish)
Religion: Predominantly Christian (mostly Lutheran)
Population: 2.7 million
Bank Hours: Generally open for short hours between 0930-1230 Monday-Friday
Shop Hours: Generally 0900-1800 Monday-Friday; often open weekends
Currency: 100 kopeks = 1 rubl
Copyright: Berne (see Copyright Conventions, pg xi)

Alberts XII+
Lacplesa iela 27-3, 1010 Riga
Tel: (02) 7285183 *Fax:* (02) 7332427
Key Personnel
Man Dir: Karlis Skruzis
Member of Latvian Book Publishers Association.
Subjects: Astrology, Occult, Cookery, Crafts, Games, Hobbies, Health, Nutrition, Nonfiction (General), Romance, Science Fiction, Fantasy
ISBN Prefix(es): 9984-557; 9984-645

Artava Ltd+
Bezdeligu 12, 1007 Riga
Tel: (02) 7830254 *Fax:* (02) 7830254
E-mail: arta@latnet.lv
Key Personnel
Dir: Vladis Spare
Foreign Rights: Elfrida Melbarzde
Founded: 1991
Member of Latvia Book Publishers Association.
Subjects: Biography, Fiction, How-to, Poetry, Romance, Science Fiction, Fantasy, Self-Help
ISBN Prefix(es): 9984-12; 9984-529

Avots+
Aspazijas bulv 24, LV 1050 Riga
Tel: (02) 7225824; (02) 7211394 *Fax:* (02) 7225824
Key Personnel
Man Dir: Janis Leja
Founded: 1980
Member of Book Publishers Association.
Subjects: Agriculture, Cookery, English as a Second Language, Gardening, Plants, House & Home, How-to, Language Arts, Linguistics, Nonfiction (General)
ISBN Prefix(es): 5-401

Bibliography Institute of the National Library of Latvia
Anglikanu iela 5, Riga 1816
Tel: (02) 7225135 *Fax:* (02) 7224587
E-mail: anitag@lnb.lv
Web Site: www.lnb.lv
Key Personnel
Deputy Dir, NLL: Anita Goldberga
  E-mail: anitag@lnb.lv
Founded: 1940
Statistical information & analysis of publishing activities & national bibliography.
Member of The Latvian Publishers Association.

LATVIA

Subjects: Publishing & Book Trade Reference, Publishing/reference library & information sciences
ISBN Prefix(es): 9984-607; 9984-9006; 9984-9007
Total Titles: 3 Print; 2 Online
Online services available through VIP.
Parent Company: The National Library of Latvia

Egmont Latvia Ltd+
3 Balasta Dambis, 1081 Riga
Mailing Address: PO Box 30, LV 1081 Riga
Tel: (02) 2468671 *Fax:* (02) 7860049
Key Personnel
General Manager: Janis Blums *E-mail:* janis@egmont.lv
Editor-in-Chief: Antra Chigure
Founded: 1991
Subjects: Advertising, Fiction, Film, Video, Sports, Athletics, Western Fiction, Children's Periodicals, Children's Literature
Parent Company: International Egmont Holding A/S

Finland-Lestvian, *imprint of* S/A Tiesiskas informacijas cerfus

Hermess Ltd+
Merkela iela 11-502, 1050 Riga
Mailing Address: Spoles iela 6, Riga LV 1058
Tel: (02) 7216801 *Fax:* (02) 7221290
Key Personnel
Executive Dir: Juris Zablovskis
Founded: 1993
Subjects: Science Fiction, Fantasy
ISBN Prefix(es): 9984-580; 9984-9036

Lielvards Ltd+
Skolas Iela 5, 5070 Lielvarde Ogresraj
Tel: (050) 53824 *Fax:* (050) 54310
E-mail: info@lielvards.lv
Web Site: www.lielvards.lv *Cable:* 030
Founded: 1992
Member of Lativia Book Publishers Association.
Subjects: Biological Sciences, Chemistry, Chemical Engineering, Computer Science, Geography, Geology, Health, Nutrition, History, Physics, Social Sciences, Sociology
ISBN Prefix(es): 9984-11; 9984-513
Showroom(s): Zaubes Iela 1-1, Riga

Liesma Publishers
Aspaziyas Blvd 24, Riga LV-1050
Tel: (02) 7223063 *Fax:* (02) 7223063
Key Personnel
Dir: Linde Skaidriite
Deputy Dir: Andrejs Brimerbergs
Founded: 1964
Member of Latvian Publishers' Association.
Subjects: Art, Fiction, Poetry, Travel

Madonas Poligrafistr Ltd, *imprint of* S/A Tiesiskas informacijas cerfus

Madris+
Tallinas 36a, Riga 1001
Tel: 7374000; 7374700 *Fax:* 7374000
E-mail: madris@latnet.lv
Key Personnel
General Manager: Skaidrite Naumova
Tel: 7374000
Founded: 1996
Subjects: Fiction, Poetry, Science (General), Travel
Number of titles published annually: 20 Print

Nordik/Tapals Publishers Ltd+
Daugavgrivas iela 36-9, Riga LV-1007
Tel: (02) 7602672; (02) 7602617 *Fax:* (02) 7602818

E-mail: nordik@nordik.lv
Web Site: www.nordik.lv
Key Personnel
Dir: Janis Juska *E-mail:* janis@tapals.lv
Ed-in-Chief: Ieva Janaite
Founded: 1991
Member of Latvian Publishers Association.
Subjects: Animals, Pets, Astrology, Occult, Biography, Communications, Crafts, Games, Hobbies, Criminology, Earth Sciences, Environmental Studies, Fiction, History, Human Relations, Law, Nonfiction (General), Poetry
ISBN Prefix(es): 9984-510
Number of titles published annually: 85 Print

Patmos
Baznicas iela 12a, Riga 1010
Tel: (02) 7289674 *Fax:* (02) 7820437
E-mail: bauc@mail.bkc.lv
Key Personnel
Publishing Dir: Zigurds Laudurgs
Editor: Dace Morica
Subjects: Biblical Studies, Health, Nutrition, Religion - Protestant, Theology

Preses Nams+
Division of Preses Nams Corp
Balasta dambis 3, Riga LV-1081
Tel: (02) 465732 *Fax:* (02) 465624
Key Personnel
Dir, Publishing House: Mara Caune
Founded: 1990 (Preses Nams Corp is a large printing house; the publishing house is one of its divisions)
Publisher of books, calendars, etc.
Member of Latvian Association of Book Publishers.
Subjects: Agriculture, Animals, Pets, Art, Astrology, Occult, Behavioral Sciences, Biography, Biological Sciences, Business, Child Care & Development, Civil Engineering, Crafts, Games, Hobbies, Disability, Special Needs, Drama, Theater, Education, Environmental Studies, Fiction, Film, Video, Gardening, Plants, Health, Nutrition, History, House & Home, Human Relations, Humor, Literature, Literary Criticism, Essays, Music, Dance, Philosophy, Photography, Poetry, Psychology, Psychiatry, Sports, Athletics, Travel, Women's Studies
ISBN Prefix(es): 9980-0
Total Titles: 600 Print
Parent Company: Preses Nams Corp
Ultimate Parent Company: AS Ventspils Nafta
Bookshop(s): Bookstore at Preses Nams Corp

S/A Tiesiskas informacijas cerfus
Baznicas icla 27/29, Riga 1010
Tel: (02) 7220422 *Fax:* (02) 7213854
E-mail: mariss@date.lv
Key Personnel
Dir: Signe Terihova
Founded: 1991
Subjects: Law
Parent Company: a/s SWHIS Kemerccentas
Imprints: Madonas Poligrafistr Ltd; Finland-Lestvian
Subsidiaries: LR Tieslictuministrijas A/S Dati
Book Club(s): Association of Latvian Book's publishers

Spriditis Publishers+
Kaleju iela 51, Riga 1050
Tel: (02) 7286516 *Fax:* (02) 7286818
Founded: 1990
Subjects: Biblical Studies, Fiction, History, Religion - Catholic, Religion - Protestant, Travel
ISBN Prefix(es): 5-7960
Bookshop(s): Kaleju St 51, Riga LV-1050

Vaidelote+
Kekava 17-9, 2123 Rigas Rajons

Tel: (02) 937943; (02) 2560475 *Fax:* (02) 570828
Founded: 1993
Subjects: Animals, Pets, Fiction
ISBN Prefix(es): 9984-507

Vieda+
Elijas Iela 17/2, 1018 Riga 1003
Tel: (02) 7210943 *Fax:* (02) 7210943
Key Personnel
Dir General: Aivars Gardo
Founded: 1989
Subjects: Astrology, Occult, History, Parapsychology, Philosophy
ISBN Prefix(es): 5-85745

Zvaigzne ABC Publishers, Ltd+
105 K Valdemara iela, Riga 1013
Tel: (02) 372396 *Fax:* (02) 7828431
E-mail: zvaigzne@com.latnet.lv
Key Personnel
President: Vija Kilbloka
Editorial Dir: Ilze Brige *Tel:* (02) 7372112
Foreign Rights & Sales Manager: Ruta Keisa *Tel:* (02) 7372358
Foreign Rights & Sales Executive: Vija Birnbauma *Tel:* (02) 7372358
Founded: 1965
Specialize in educational literature for the needs of Latvia.
Subjects: Education, English as a Second Language, Nonfiction (General)
ISBN Prefix(es): 5-405; 9984-04; 9984-17; 9984-560
Total Titles: 1,700 Print

Lebanon

General Information

Capital: Beirut
Language: Arabic (French widely used)
Religion: 43% Christian (mostly Roman Catholic, predominantly Maronite), 57% Muslim (mostly Sunni & Shiite)
Population: 3.4 million
Bank Hours: 0830-1230 Monday-Friday; 0830-1200 Saturday
Shop Hours: Vary. Generally 0900-1900 in winter, 0800-1500 in summer
Currency: 100 piastres = 1 Lebanese pound
Copyright: UCC, Berne (see Copyright Conventions, pg xi)

Arab Institute for Research and Publishing
Sakiyat Al Janzeer, Carlton Tower Bldg, Beirut
Mailing Address: PO Box 11-5460, Beirut
Tel: (01) 807900 *Fax:* (01) 96266; (01) 685501
Telex: 40067; (01) 807900 *Cable:* MOUKAYALI
Divisions: AlFaris Publishing & Distribution Co Ltd (Telex: 21497)
Warehouse: AlFaris Publishing & Distribution Co Ltd, PO Box 9157, Amman, Jordan *Fax:* (06) 685501

Arab Scientific Publishers BP+
Rue Sakiet Al Janzir, Ain Al-Tenah Reem Bldg CITY, 13-5574 Beirut
Tel: (01) 811385 *Fax:* (01) 860138; (01) 861311
Web Site: www.asp.com.lb
Key Personnel
President: Bassam Chebaro *Tel:* (01) 786607
E-mail: bchebaro@asp.com.lb
Founded: 1986
Subjects: Automotive, Biological Sciences, Computer Science, Cookery, Travel
ISBN Prefix(es): 2-84409; 9953-29
Number of titles published annually: 300 Print; 10 CD-ROM; 15 E-Book

Online services available through World Wide Web.
Associate Companies: Abjad Graphics; Mediterranean Press, Arabization & Software Center
Bookshop(s): Book Maze, Marriott Square

Dar Al-Kitab Alloubnani
BP 13-5352, Beirut
Tel: (01) 861563 *Fax:* (01) 351433
Telex: 22865 Ktl *Cable:* Kitaliban
Key Personnel
Man Dir: El-Zein Hassan
Founded: 1929
Associate Companies: Dar Al-Kitab Al-Masri, Egypt (Arab Republic of Egypt)
Branch Office(s)
Geneva, Switzerland
Paris, France
Casablanca, Morocco
Madrid, Spain

Dar Al-Maaref-Liban Sarl
PO Box 11-232, Beirut
Tel: (01) 931243 *Cable:* Damaref Beirut
Key Personnel
Man Dir: Dr Fouad Ibrahim
General Manager: Joseph Nachou
Sales: Joseph Ibrahim
Founded: 1959
Parent Company: Dar Al Maare, Egypt (Arab Republic of Egypt)

Dar Al Raed Al Lubnani
Kamel Al Assaad Bldgs, Hazmieh, Sammouri, Beirut
Mailing Address: BP 11-6585, Beirut
Tel: (01) 450757; (01) 451581
Telex: 43499 le Raed *Cable:* Kassammoury
Key Personnel
Chief Executive: Raed Sammouri
Editorial: Fadia Khoury
Sales: Ola Ramadan
Production: George Jabro
Publicity: Rima Khoury
Rights & Permissions: Hussein Ibrahim
Founded: 1971
Branch Office(s)
Dar Al Raed Al Rabi, Rawchi Blvd, Al Istiklal

Dar an-Nahar Sal
Rue de la Banque du Liban, BP 11-226, Beirut
Tel: (01) 340044; (01) 340960
Key Personnel
President: Mohamed Ali Hamade
Founded: 1967
ISBN Prefix(es): 2-84289

Editions de la Revue d'Etudes Palestiniennes, see Institute for Palestine Studies, Publishing & Research Organization (IPS)

Darl el-Machreq Sarl+
BP 166778, Achrafieh Beirut 1100 2150
Tel: (01) 202423; (01) 202424 *Fax:* (01) 329348
E-mail: machreq@cyberia.net.lb
Key Personnel
Man Dir, Rights & Permissions: Camille Hechaime
Founded: 1853
Subjects: Biblical Studies, History, Language Arts, Linguistics, Literature, Literary Criticism, Essays, Philosophy, Religion - Catholic, Religion - Islamic, Theology
ISBN Prefix(es): 2-7214
Orders to: Librairie Orientale, PO Box 1986, Beirut, Contact: M Maroun Nehme *Tel:* (01) 485793; (01) 492112 *Fax:* (01) 485793; (01) 485794; (01) 485795 *E-mail:* libor@cyberia.net.lb

Edition Francaise pour le Monde Arabe (EDIFRAMO)
Elissar Bldg, BP 113, 6140, Bliss St, Beirut
Tel: (01) 862437; (01) 341650; (01) 341614
Telex: 42530 le
Key Personnel
Manager: Tahseen S Khayat
Branch Office(s)
Julie Hse, 3 Themistocles Dervis St, PO Box 1612, Nicosia, Cyprus
22 blvd Poissonnieer, 75009 Paris, France

Geoprojects Sarl
PO Box 8375, Beirut
Mailing Address: Rue Jeane D'Arc Al-Wahad Bldg, Beirut
Tel: (01) 350721; (01) 344236 *Fax:* (01) 353000
Telex: 22661 Eltoup le
Key Personnel
Man Dir: Tahseen Khayat
Founded: 1978
Subjects: Regional Interests, Travel
Branch Office(s)
Geoprojects Ltd, Newtown Rd, Henley-on-Thomas, Oxon R69 1HG, United Kingdom *Tel:* (049) 122175

Institute for Palestine Studies, Publishing & Research Organization (IPS)
PO Box 11-07164, Beirut
Tel: (01) 868387 *Fax:* (01) 868387
Telex: Madaf 23317 le *Cable:* DIRASAT
Key Personnel
Honorary Chair: Constantine Dr Zurayk
Chair: Dr Hisham Nashabe
Executive Secretary: Prof Walid Khalidi
Founded: 1963
Subjects: Government, Political Science, Social Sciences, Sociology
ISBN Prefix(es): 2-905448
Branch Office(s)
13 Hera St, PO Box 5658, Nicosia, Cyprus, Greece *Tel:* (02) 456165 *Fax:* (02) 456324
U.S. Office(s): 3501 M Street NW, PO Box 25301, Georgetown Station, Washington, DC 20007, United States *Tel:* 202-342-3990 *Fax:* 202-342-3927

The International Documentary Centre of Arab Manuscripts
Immeuble Hanna, Beirut
Mailing Address: PO Box 2668
Key Personnel
Proprietor: Zouhair Baalbaki
Founded: 1965

Khayat Book and Publishing Co Sarl
90-94 rue Bliss, Beirut
Key Personnel
Man Dir: Paul Khayat
Subjects: Art, Crafts, Games, Hobbies, Education, Fiction, History, Medicine, Nursing, Dentistry, Religion - Other, Social Sciences, Sociology, Sports, Athletics

Librairie du Liban+
Riad Al-Solh Sq, Beyrouth
Mailing Address: PO Box 11945, Beyrouth
Tel: (0357) 862957 *Fax:* (0357) 9512906
Telex: 21037-45297 libsayle *Cable:* LIBRARIE DU LIBAN, BEIRUT
Key Personnel
Man Dir, Rights & Permissions: Khalil Sayegh
Man Dir, Publicity: George S Trad
Editorial: Ahmad Khatib; George Abdel Massih
Sales: Suheil Berjawi
Production: Wafic Mizhir
Founded: 1944
Sphinx Publishing Co, Egypt is also a member of the Group.

Subjects: Fiction, Language Arts, Linguistics, Literature, Literary Criticism, Essays, Travel
Showroom(s): Longman Arab World Centres, PO Box 11-945, Beirut; Amir Mohamed St, Al Houjairi Bldg, PO Box 6587, Amman *Tel:* (06) 637871; (06) 624216; 15 St, Central Khartoum, PO Box 1391, Sudan *Tel:* 80344
Bookshop(s): Lebanon Bookshop; Sayegh Bookshop, Diab Bldg, Al Salhieh, In Front of the Parliament, PO Box 784, Damascus, Syrian Arab Republic *Tel:* (011) 218456

Librairie Orientale sal+
Sin el-Fil, Jisr el-Wati, Librairie Orientale Bldg, Beirut
Mailing Address: PO Box 55206, Beirut
Tel: (01) 485793; (01) 485794; (01) 485795
Fax: (01) 485796
E-mail: libor@cyberia.net.lb
Key Personnel
Chief Executive Officer: Maroun Nehme
Founded: 1948
Specialize in dictionaries, research, philosophy, literature, children books & text books in Arabic, French & English.
Subjects: Archaeology, Education, English as a Second Language, History, How-to, Language Arts, Linguistics, Literature, Literary Criticism, Essays, Nonfiction (General), Philosophy, Regional Interests, Religion - Catholic
Number of titles published annually: 200 Print
Total Titles: 1,000 Print
Branch Office(s)
Ashrafieh-Park Bldg, Beirut, Contact: Mrs Achou *Tel:* (01) 200875, 216364 *Fax:* (01) 216021
Distributor for Dar el-Majani; Dar el-Mashreq
Foreign Rep(s): Aladdin Books UK (Middle East, North Africa); DTV Germany (Middle East, North Africa); Edicart-Italy (Middle East, North Africa)

Publitec Publications+
PO Box 166142, Beirut
Tel: (01) 495401; (01) 495403 *Fax:* (01) 493330
Telex: 44828
Key Personnel
President: Charles Gedeon
Manager: B Calfa
Assistant Manager: Ms M Sarkissian
Founded: 1953
ISBN Prefix(es): 2-903188
Subsidiaries: Publitec Publications
Distributed by Gale Research Inc (USA)

Rihani Printing and Publishing House
rue Jibb en Nakhl St, Beirut
Key Personnel
Proprietor: Albert Rihani
Manager: Daoud Stephan
Founded: 1963

World Book Publishing+
Rue Emile Edde, Beirut
Mailing Address: PO Box 11-3176, Beirut
Tel: (01) 349370; (01) 743357; (01) 743358
Fax: (01) 351226
E-mail: wbookpub@inco.com.lb
Web Site: www.arabook.com *Cable:* KITALIBAN
Key Personnel
Director-General: El Zein Said-Mohamed
 E-mail: editor@arabook.com
Vice President: Toufic El Zein *E-mail:* toufic@arabook.com
Vice President & Man Dir: Rafic El Zein
 E-mail: rafic@arabook.com
Founded: 1929
Subjects: Education, Literature, Literary Criticism, Essays, Philosophy, Poetry, Religion - Islamic
ISBN Prefix(es): 1-55206
Total Titles: 3,000 Print; 1,000 Online

Associate Companies: Editions Africaines/Dar Al Kitab Al-Alami
Subsidiaries: Librairie De L'ecole
Divisions: Livre Scolaire
Showroom(s): Hawd Al-Wilaga, Basta, Beirut
Bookshop(s): Librairie de l'Ecole, Rue Emile Edde, Beirut

Lesotho

General Information

Capital: Maseru
Language: English, Sesotho (a Bantu language)
Religion: Roman Catholic, Lesotho, Evangelical and Anglican
Population: 1.8 million
Bank Hours: 0830-1300 Monday-Friday; 0830-1100 Saturday
Shop Hours: Winter: 0830-1630 Monday-Friday; 0830-1300 Saturday; Summer: 0800-1630 Monday-Friday; 0800-1300 Saturday. Usually closed weekdays 1300-1400
Currency: 100 lisente = 1 loti South African currency is also legal tender
Export/Import Information: No tariffs on books or advertising matter. No import license required; no obscene literature permitted. Exchange controls being relaxed.
Copyright: Berne (see Copyright Conventions, pg xi)

Government Printer
PO Box 527, Maseru 100
Tel: 313023
ISBN Prefix(es): 99911-10

Mazenod Book Centre
PO Box 39, Mazenod 160
Tel: 350224
Telex: 427KO
Key Personnel
Manager: Fr B Mohlalisi
Founded: 1933
Subjects: History, Literature, Literary Criticism, Essays, Regional Interests, Religion - Other
ISBN Prefix(es): 99911-24

Saint Michael's Mission
Roma The Social Centre, Roma
Mailing Address: PO Box 25, Roma
Key Personnel
Man Dir: Rev Fr M Ferrange
Production: Peter Ntsaoana
Founded: 1968
Subjects: Anthropology, Biography, History, Regional Interests, Religion - Other, Social Sciences, Sociology

Libyan Arab Jamahiriya

General Information

Capital: Tripoli
Language: Arabic (official), also English and Italian
Religion: Muslim
Population: 4.5 million
Bank Hours: Generally Winter: 0830-1230; Summer: 0800-1200 Saturday-Thursday
Shop Hours: Vary greatly. Friday is weekly holiday but some Christian shops closed Sunday. Many are open 0830-1230, 1500-1730 Saturday-Thursday (slightly earlier hours in summer months)
Currency: 1,000 dirhams = 1 Libyan dinar
Export/Import Information: No tariff on books; advertising duited. Charity Tax and Municipal Tax levied on dutiable goods. Open General License for books. Exchange permit, liberally granted, is required. Import and export of books is handled by the General Company for Publishing, Advertising and Distribution, Tripoli.
Copyright: Berne (see Copyright Conventions, pg xi)

Al-Fatah University, General Administration of Libraries, Printing & Publications
PO Box 13543, Tripoli
Tel: (02133) 621988
Telex: 20629 TP Univ Ly
Founded: 1955
Bookshop(s): University Bookshop, PO Box 13113, Tripoli

Liechtenstein

General Information

Capital: Vaduz
Language: German
Religion: Predominantly Roman Catholic
Population: 28,642
Bank Hours: 0800-1200, 1330-1630 Monday-Friday
Shop Hours: 0800-1200, 1330-1830 Monday-Friday; 0800-1600 Saturday
Currency: 100 rapen = 1 francen (swiss franc)
Export/Import Information: 2% VAT on books. Most books exempt from Turnover Tax. Advertising matter usually dutiable, some exempt from Turnover Tax. No import licenses required. No exchange controls. Swiss regulations to a Customs Treaty.
Copyright: UCC, Berne, Florence (see Copyright Conventions, pg xi)

Bonafides Verlags-Anstalt
Auring 50, 9490 Vaduz
Tel: (075) 82510
Founded: 1991
Subjects: Accounting, Finance, Government, Political Science, Nonfiction (General)
ISBN Prefix(es): 3-905193

Botanisch-Zoologische Gesellschaft
Liechtenstein-Sargans-Werdenberg, Im Bretscha 22, 9494 Schaan
Tel: (00423) 2324819 *Fax:* (00423) 2332819
E-mail: renat@pingnet.li
Key Personnel
Contact: Georg Willi
Founded: 1970
Subjects: Animals, Pets, Earth Sciences, Gardening, Plants, Physical Sciences
ISBN Prefix(es): 3-905195

Buch und Verlagsdruckerei AG
Postfach 461, 9490 Vaduz
ISBN Prefix(es): 3-905238

Frank P van Eck Publishers+
Haldenweg, 9495 Triesen
Tel: (075) 29557 *Fax:* (075) 29557
Telex: 77030
Key Personnel
Manager: Elisabeth van Eck-Schaedler
Editor: Frank P van Eck
Founded: 1982
Subjects: Art, Sports, Athletics
ISBN Prefix(es): 3-905501
Associate Companies: Saentis Verlag
Subsidiaries: Edition Fuchs & Hase
Shipping Address: Schweizer Buchzertrum, Industrie Ost, 4614 Magendorf
Warehouse: Schweizer Buchzertrum, Industrie Ost, 4614 Magendorf
Orders to: Schweizer Buchzertrum, Industrie Ost, 4614 Magendorf

A R Gantner Verlag KG
Industriestrasse 105A, Postfach 131, 9491 Ruggell
Tel: (0423) 3771808 *Fax:* (0423) 3771802 *Cable:* GANTR FL
Key Personnel
Manager: Mrs Bruni Gantner-Caplan
ISBN Prefix(es): 3-7182
Associate Companies: Litag Anstalt

Verlag HP Gassner AG
Austr 7, 9494 Vaduz
Tel: (075) 2327253 *Fax:* (075) 2323720
Key Personnel
Publisher: Hans Peter Gassner; Traugott Schneidtinger
Founded: 1979
Subjects: Art, History, Literature, Literary Criticism, Essays
ISBN Prefix(es): 3-906250

Historischer Verein fur das Furstentum Liechtenstein (Historical Society for the Principality of Liechtenstein)
Messinastr 5, Postfach 626, FL-9495 Triesen
Tel: (0423) 8921747 *Fax:* (0423) 3921961
E-mail: hvfl@hvfl.li
Web Site: www.hvfl.li
Key Personnel
Secretary & Historian: Klaus Biedermann
Founded: 1901
Historical research. Publication of the yearbook. Non-profit organization, supported by our 800 members & the government of Liechtenstein.
Subjects: Archaeology, History
ISBN Prefix(es): 3-906393
Number of titles published annually: 1 Print

Kliemand Verlag
Sonnblickstr 6, 9490 Vaduz
Tel: (075) 21177 *Fax:* (075) 2321048
Subjects: Art, Poetry
ISBN Prefix(es): 3-906603

Kunstmuseum Liechtenstein Vaduz
Staedtle 32, 9490 Vaduz
Mailing Address: Postfach 370, 9490 Vaduz
Tel: (00423) 235 03 00 *Fax:* (00423) 235 03 29
E-mail: mail@kunstmuseum.li
Web Site: www.kunstmuseum.li
Specialize in 19th century to contemporary art.
Number of titles published annually: 5 Print
Total Titles: 40 Print

Liechtenstein Verlag AG+
Schwefelstr 33, 9490 Vaduz
Mailing Address: PO Box 133, 9490 Vaduz
Tel: 23 224 14 *Fax:* 23 243 40
E-mail: flbooks@verlag_ag.LOL.li
Key Personnel
Man Dir: Albart Piet Schiks
Founded: 1945
Also a literary agent.
Subjects: Finance, Government, Political Science, History, Law
ISBN Prefix(es): 3-85789

Verlag der Liechtensteinischen Akademischen Gesellschaft
Bahnhofstr 15a, FL-9494 Schaan

Mailing Address: Postfach 829, FL-9494 Schaan
Tel: (0423) 2323028 *Fax:* (0423) 2331449
Key Personnel
Dir: Norbert Jansen *E-mail:* jansen@mediateam.li
Founded: 1972
Subjects: Economics, Government, Political Science, Law
ISBN Prefix(es): 3-7211
Total Titles: 3 Print

Litag Anstalt- Literarische, Medien und Kuenstler Agentur
Industriestr 105A, 9491 Ruggell
Mailing Address: Postfach 131, 9491 Ruggell
Tel: (0423) 3771809 *Fax:* (0423) 3771802
Key Personnel
Dir: Mrs B Gantner-Caplan
Founded: 1956
ISBN Prefix(es): 3-7211
Parent Company: Verlag der Liechtensteinischen Akademischeen Gesellschaft, Am Schragenluegz, 9490 Vaduz

Megatrade AG+
Landstr 36, 9490 Vaduz
Tel: (075) 279976 *Fax:* (075) 20064
E-mail: wanger@wanger.net
Web Site: www.wanger.net *Cable:* JURT FL
Key Personnel
Contact: Dr Markus Wanger; Susanne Schedler
Subjects: Art, Business, Economics, Law
ISBN Prefix(es): 3-9520331
Parent Company: Wanger Group

Rheintal Handelsgesellschaft Anstalt
Industiestr Postfach 444, 9495 Triesen
Tel: (075) 3921882; (01) 8442786 *Fax:* (075) 3923646; (01) 8442806
E-mail: vetsch.p@bluewin.ch
Key Personnel
International Rights: Nick U Schweinfurth
Founded: 1889
Subjects: Career Development, Education, Interactive Audio Courses on CD-ROM
ISBN Prefix(es): 3-9520574
Orders to: Rheintal Hondelsgesellschaft Niederlassung ZH/Huttikon, Birkenweg 3, CH-8115 Huttikon, Switzerland

Saendig Reprint Verlag, Hans-Rainer Wohlwend
Am Schraegen Weg 12, 9490 Vaduz
Tel: (0423) 232 36 27 *Fax:* (0423) 232 36 49
E-mail: saendig@adon.li
Web Site: www.saendig.com
Key Personnel
Manager: Christian Wohlwend
Founded: 1981
Subjects: Art, History, Language Arts, Linguistics, Mathematics, Music, Dance, Physical Sciences, Religion - Other, Science (General)
ISBN Prefix(es): 3-253

Topos Verlag AG
Industriestr 105A, FL-9491 Ruggell
Mailing Address: Postfach 551, 9491 Ruggell
Tel: 3771111 *Fax:* 3771119
E-mail: topos@supra.net
Web Site: www.topos.li *Cable:* TOPOS
Key Personnel
Man Dir: Graham A P Smith
Founded: 1977
Subjects: Economics, Education, Law, Social Sciences, Sociology
ISBN Prefix(es): 3-289

Lithuania

General Information

Capital: Vilnius
Language: Lithuanian
Religion: Predominantly Roman Catholic
Population: 3.8 million
Bank Hours: 0900-1200/1300 Monday-Friday
Shop Hours: 0900-1300 and 1400-1800 Monday-Friday
Currency: 100 cents = 1 litas
Export/Import Information: There are no customs duties and very few export restrictions.
Copyright: Berne (see Copyright Conventions, pg xi)

Academia
A Gostauto 12, 2600 Vilnius
Tel: (02) 626851 *Fax:* (02) 226351
Key Personnel
Dir: A Garliauskas *Tel:* (02) 626861
Founded: 1990
Subjects: Agriculture, Art, Biological Sciences, Chemistry, Chemical Engineering, Energy, Geography, Geology, Language Arts, Linguistics, Medicine, Nursing, Dentistry, Philosophy, Social Sciences, Sociology

Algarve+
Rinktines 3/11, 2600 Vilnius
Tel: (02) 725910; (02) 721635 *Fax:* (02) 721462
Key Personnel
Publisher: Algimantas Matulevicius
Founded: 1995
Joint stock company.
Subjects: Advertising, Fiction, Health, Nutrition, Science (General), esoteric, applied health education literature
ISBN Prefix(es): 9986-856
Total Titles: 40 Print

Alma Littera+
Sermuksniu 3, 2600 Vilnius
Tel: (02) 617927; (02) 624695 *Fax:* (02) 617927
E-mail: post@almali.lt
Web Site: www.almali.lt
Key Personnel
Dir: Arvydas Andrijauskas *Tel:* (02) 627141
Founded: 1990
Member of EEPG.
Subjects: English as a Second Language, Fiction
Number of titles published annually: 2 CD-ROM
Total Titles: 600 Print; 8 Audio

Andrena Publishers+
Pasilaiciu 8-13, 2022 Vilnius
Tel: (02) 703834; (02) 627015
E-mail: andrena@takas.lt
Key Personnel
Contact: Nijole Petrosiene
Founded: 1995
Subjects: Poetry, Psychology, Psychiatry, Religion - Catholic, Romance
ISBN Prefix(es): 9986-37
Total Titles: 27 Print

AS Narbuto Leidykla (AS Narbutas' Publishers)+
Klevu 9, 5400 Siauliai
Tel: (075) 420868 *Fax:* (075) 429335
Key Personnel
Contact: Amalijus S Narbutas *E-mail:* amalijus@siauliai.aiva.lt
Founded: 1990
Subjects: Art, Astrology, Occult, Humor, Language Arts, Linguistics, Literature, Literary Criticism, Essays, Medicine, Nursing, Dentistry, Parapsychology

Baltos Lankos+
Mesiniu 4, 2001 Vilnius
Tel: (02) 220126 *Fax:* (02) 220152
E-mail: baltos.lankos@post.omnitel.net
Key Personnel
Dir: Saulius Zukas
Foreign Rights: Daiva Cibutaviciene
Founded: 1992
A humanities & social sciences publisher.
Subjects: Art, Biography, Fiction, History, Language Arts, Linguistics, Literature, Literary Criticism, Essays, Philosophy, Poetry
U.S. Office(s): 2016 W Huron, No 2F, Chicago, IL, United States, Contact: Jura Avizienis
Tel: 312-243-0799

Centre of Legal Information
Gedimino ave 30/1, 2695 Vilnius
Tel: (02) 617529; (02) 623650 *Fax:* (02) 625940
E-mail: webadm@utic.tm.lt
Subjects: Law
ISBN Prefix(es): 9986-452

Dargenis Publishers+
PO Box 2090, 3000 Kaunas
Tel: (037) 745271 *Fax:* (037) 745271
E-mail: dargenis@kaunas.omnitel.net
Key Personnel
Dir: Dalia Celiesiute
Founded: 1997
Subjects: English as a Second Language, Human Relations, Psychology, Psychiatry, Self-Help
ISBN Prefix(es): 9986-9196; 9955-403

Egmont Lietuva+
Algirdo 51A, 2600 Vilnius
Tel: (02) 231265; (02) 231266; (02) 231267 *Fax:* (02) 231269
Key Personnel
Dir: Irina Glagoleva
Founded: 1993
ISBN Prefix(es): 9986-22
Parent Company: Egmont International Holding A/S

Eugrimas+
Silutes 42a-1, 2042 Vilnius
Tel: (02) 300075 *Fax:* (02) 300075
E-mail: eugrimas@post.5ci.lt
Key Personnel
Dir: Eugenija Petruliene
Founded: 1995
Subjects: Criminology, Economics, Government, Political Science, History, Law, Philosophy
ISBN Prefix(es): 9986-752

Klaipedos Universiteto Leidykla+
H Manto 84, 5808 Klaipeda
Tel: (06) 398890 *Fax:* (06) 398999
E-mail: leidykla@rekt.ku.lt
Web Site: www.ku.lt
Key Personnel
Manager: Lolita Zemliene *Tel:* (06) 398891
E-mail: lolita@rekt.ku.lt
Founded: 1992
Subjects: Biological Sciences, Education, History, Maritime, Mathematics, Science (General), Social Sciences, Sociology
Number of titles published annually: 75 Print
Total Titles: 300 Print
Parent Company: Klaipeda University

Lietus Ltd+
Member of Lithuanian Publisher's Association
A Jakto 8/10, 2600 Vilnius
Tel: (02) 312298; (02) 8299 35423; (02) 745720 *Fax:* (02) 312298
Key Personnel
President: Liudas Pilius
International Rights: Agne Kudirkaite
Founded: 1991

LITHUANIA

Subjects: Education, Fiction, Nonfiction (General)
ISBN Prefix(es): 9986-431
Total Titles: 70 Print
Warehouse: Musu Knyga Ltd, Vilkpedes 20, Vilnius *Tel:* (02) 632921

Lietuvos Informacijos Institutas
Kalvariju 3, 2659 Vilnius
Tel: (02) 752284; (02) 753590; (02) 753382; (02) 752429 *Fax:* (02) 723017
E-mail: lii@lii.lt
Key Personnel
Contact: Dr Habic J Novickas
Subjects: Advertising, Business, Government, Political Science, Labor, Industrial Relations, Law, Library & Information Sciences, Management, Marketing

Lietuvos Rasytoju Sajungos Leidykla
(Lithuanian Writers' Union Publishers)+
K Sirvydo 6, 2600 Vilnius
Tel: (02) 628945; (02) 626154 *Fax:* (02) 628945
E-mail: zsleidykla@is.lt
Web Site: www.rsleidykla.lt
Key Personnel
Dir: Giedre Soriene
Editor-in-Chief: Valentinas Sventickas
Editor: Saulius Repecka *Tel:* (02) 628643
Founded: 1990
Member of Lithuanian Publishers Association.
Subjects: Fiction, Literature, Literary Criticism, Essays, Poetry
ISBN Prefix(es): 9-986
Number of titles published annually: 45 Print
Bookshop(s): Atzalynas, Antakalnio g 97, 2040 Vilnius; Fabijoniskiy, Staneviciouis g 24, 2029 Vilnius

Lithuanian National Museum Publishing House
Division of National Museum of Lithuania
Arsenalo 1, 2001 Vilnius
Tel: (02) 627774 *Fax:* (02) 611023
E-mail: muziejus@lnm.lt
Web Site: www.lnm.lt
Key Personnel
Dir & Contact: Birute Kulnyte
Subjects: Anthropology, Antiques, Archaeology, Art, History, Library & Information Sciences, Photography
Number of titles published annually: 10 Print
Total Titles: 2 Print

Lithuanian Publishers' Association
L Sierakauske 15, 2600 Vilnius
Tel: (02) 332943 *Fax:* (02) 263197
Key Personnel
Dir: Aleksandras Krasnovas
Founded: 1990
Member of International Publishers Association.

Martynas Mazvydas National Library of Lithuania (Lietuvos Nacionaline Martyno Mazvydo Biblioteka)+
Gedimino pr 51, 2600 Vilnius
Tel: 52496044 *Fax:* 52496055
E-mail: isbnetu@lnb.lt
Key Personnel
Dir: Vladas Bulavas *Tel:* 52497023
Fax: 52496129 *E-mail:* vlbula@lnb.lt
Founded: 1919
Subjects: Library & Information Sciences
ISBN Prefix(es): 9986-530

Mokslo ir enciklopediju leidybos institutas
(Science & Encyclopedia Publishing Institute)+
23 L Asanaviciutes St, 2050 Vilnius
Tel: (02) 458526; (02) 457980; (02) 458528
Fax: (02) 458537
E-mail: meli@meli.taide.lt

Key Personnel
Dir: Rimantas Kareckas *Tel:* 02 458525
Chief Editor: Jonas Varnauskas
Founded: 1992
Member of the Lithuanian Publishers' Association.
Subjects: Agriculture, Biological Sciences, History, Language Arts, Linguistics, Literature, Literary Criticism, Essays, Mathematics, Medicine, Nursing, Dentistry, Physics, Science (General)
Imprints: Vilnius

The Publishing House of the Lithuanian Writers' Union
c/o Lithuanian Publisher's Association, K Sirvydo 6, 2600 Vilnius
Tel: (02) 628945; (02) 626154 *Fax:* (02) 619696
Key Personnel
Dir: Vincas Akelis
Editor-in-Chief: Valentinas Sventickas
Founded: 1990
Member of Lithuanian Publishers' Association.
Subjects: Drama, Theater, Fiction, Literature, Literary Criticism, Essays, Poetry, Romance
Bookshop(s): Atzalynas, Antakalnio 97, 2600 Vilnius *Tel:* 76-88-57; Versme, Didzioji 27, 2600 Vilnius *Tel:* 62-64-10

Margi Rastai Publishers+
Laisves pr 60, 2056 Vilnius
Tel: (02) 429526; (02) 427909; (02) 429527; (02) 426705 *Fax:* (02) 426705
Subjects: Agriculture, Economics, Fiction, History, Sports, Athletics
ISBN Prefix(es): 9986-09

Scena+
Tuskulenu 13-14, 2051 Vilnius
Tel: (02) 751828; (02) 614145 *Fax:* (02) 610814
Key Personnel
Dir: Rasa Andrasiunaite
Founded: 1992
Specialize in books about theater.
Subjects: Art, Drama, Theater

Sviesa Publishers+
Vytauto Ave 25, 3000 Kaunas
Tel: (037) 341834 *Fax:* (037) 342032
E-mail: sviesa@balt.net
Web Site: www.sviesa.lt
Key Personnel
Dir: Vaidotas Gadliauskas
Founded: 1945
Subjects: Career Development, Child Care & Development, Crafts, Games, Hobbies, Education, English as a Second Language, House & Home, Sports, Athletics, Travel
ISBN Prefix(es): 5-430

Svietimo ir mokslo ministerijos Leidybos centras+
Gelezinio vilko 12, Vilnius 2600
Tel: (02) 617480; (02) 611060; (02) 616081
Fax: (02) 617480
E-mail: office@smmlc.elnet.lt
Key Personnel
Dir: Kareckas Rimantas
Founded: 1991
Member of Publishers Association of Lithuania.
Subjects: Education, English as a Second Language, History, Mathematics, Music, Dance, Religion - Protestant
Associate Companies: Enterprise of Printing Service, Strazdelio 1, Vilnius 2600
Subsidiaries: Book-Collecting Department
Distributor for Langenscheidt (Germany); Longman Group (UK)
Bookshop(s): Latako 6, Vilnius 2600; Pilies 22, Vilnius 2600
Warehouse: Vilkpedes 20, Vilnius 2637

Teisines Informacijos Centras, see Centre of Legal Information

TEV Leidykla+
Akademijos 4, 2600 Vilnius
Tel: (02) 729318; (02) 729803 *Fax:* (02) 729804
E-mail: tev@omnitel.net; tev@ktl.mii.lt
Key Personnel
Contact: Elmundas Zalys
Founded: 1991
Subjects: Computer Science, Education, Engineering (General), Mathematics, Physics
ISBN Prefix(es): 9986-546
Distributed by VSP International Publications; Zeist
Distributor for VSP International Publications; Zeist

Tyto Alba Publishers+
J Jasinskio 10, 2001 Vilnius
Tel: (02) 498602 *Fax:* (02) 498602
E-mail: tytoalba@taide.lt
Web Site: www.tytoalba.lt
Key Personnel
Dir: Lolita Varanaviciene
Rights Manager: Ausra Viliuniene *Tel:* (02) 497 597 *Fax:* (02) 498 602
Founded: 1993 (joint-stock company)
Subjects: Art, Biography, Business, Education, Fiction, How-to, Human Relations, Nonfiction (General), Philosophy, Self-Help
ISBN Prefix(es): 9986-16
Number of titles published annually: 50 Print
Total Titles: 300 Print

Vaga Ltd+
Gedimino pr 50, Vilnius 2600
Tel: (02) 626443; (02) 616002; (02) 613448; (02) 624101 *Fax:* (02) 616902
E-mail: vaga@post.omnitel.net
Key Personnel
Dir: Arturas Mickevicius
Dir General: Kornelijus Platelis
Founded: 1945
Subjects: Art, Biography, Fiction, Literature, Literary Criticism, Essays, Religion - Catholic
ISBN Prefix(es): 5-415
Associate Companies: Vaga Trading, Ltd; Vaga Publishers Ltd
Bookshop(s): Gedimino 35, Kaisiadorys; Donelaicio 3, Kaunas; Darbininku 16 & Vaga, Vilnius; Gedimino pr 50, 2600 Vilnius

Victoria Publishers+
Sviesos 4-6, Grigskes, 4058 Traku rajonas
Tel: (02) 221915; (02) 632632; (02) 221914
Fax: (02) 630797
Key Personnel
Contact: Natalija Stagiene
Founded: 1991
Subjects: Animals, Pets, Child Care & Development, Crafts, Games, Hobbies, Geography, Geology, Romance, Women's Studies

Vilnius, *imprint of* Mokslo ir enciklopediju leidybos institutas

Vilnius Art Academy Publishing House
Maironio 6, 2600 Vilnius
Tel: (02) 613004; (02) 613806 *Fax:* (02) 619966
E-mail: leidykla@vda.lt
Key Personnel
Contact: Timone Vaskeviciene

Vyturys Vyturio leidykla, UAB
J Tumo, Vaiganto 2, 2600 Vilnius
Tel: (02) 613615; (02) 627404; (02) 622542; (02) 629407 *Fax:* (02) 629407; (02) 613615
Founded: 1985
ISBN Prefix(es): 5-7900

Magazyn Wilenski
Laisves pr 60, 2056 Vilnius
Tel: (02) 427718; (02) 474007 *Fax:* (02) 474007
Key Personnel
Contact: Michal Mackiewicz
ISBN Prefix(es): 9986-542

Luxembourg

General Information

Capital: Luxembourg
Language: Luxembourgian, German, French, English
Religion: Predominantly Roman Catholic (about 97%)
Population: 437,389
Bank Hours: Vary. Generally 0830-1200, 1330-1630 Monday-Friday
Shop Hours: 0830-1200, 1330-1800 Monday-Saturday. Most close Monday morning. Some have late night shopping until 2000
Currency: 100 Eurocents = 1 Euro; 40.3399 Luxembourg francs = 1 Euro
Export/Import Information: Member of the European Union. In economic and monetary union with Belgium and Netherlands. No Tariff on books except children's picture books from non-EU; advertising other than single copied dutied. VAT on books and advertising. No import license required. No exchange controls.
Copyright: UCC, Berne, Florence (see Copyright Conventions, pg xi)

Editions APESS ASBL
17 rue Muller-Fromes, 9261 Diekirch
Tel: (045) 808358 *Fax:* (045) 802813
E-mail: apess@education.lu
Web Site: www.restena.lu/apess
Key Personnel
Contact: Carlo Felten
Founded: 1982
Subjects: Art, Education, History, Literature, Literary Criticism, Essays, Philosophy, Poetry, Science (General)
ISBN Prefix(es): 2-87979
Total Titles: 35 Print

ARA International
58, Domaine Mehlstrachen, L-6942 Niederanven
Tel: (352) 34 85 91 *Fax:* (352) 34 85 91
E-mail: amisrelart@pt.lu
Key Personnel
International President: Emile van der Vekene
E-mail: evekene@pt.lu
Founded: 1996
Associate Companies: ARA-Belgique, Ave de Messidor 188, bte 1, B-1180 Brussels, Belgium, Marianne Delvaulx *Tel:* (02) 346 10 02 *Fax:* (02) 346 10 02 *E-mail:* marianne.delvaulx@belgacom.net; ARA-Canada, rue Giroux 124 1/2, Loretteville, PQ G2B 2Y2, Canada, President: Johnathan Tremblay *Tel:* 416-843-2238 *E-mail:* laparure@hotmail.com *Web Site:* www.aracanda.org; ARA-Catalogne, Pasaje Marimon, 6, 2(degree)-2a, E-08021 Barcelona, Spain, President: Germana Cavalcanti *Tel:* (093) 200 18 68 *E-mail:* germanacavalcanti@yahoo.com; ARA-France, 122, blvd Murat, 75016 Paris, France, President: Jean-Pierre Rousseau *Tel:* (045) 20 92 31 *E-mail:* fc.terrasson@wanadou.fr; ARA-Grece, rue Anavriton, 17, GR-151 24 Maroussi, Greece, President: Sotiris Koutsiaftis *Tel:* (010) 802 03 16 *Fax:* (010) 362 01 88; ARA-Italia, c/o Fondazione Querini Stampalia, Castello 4778, I-30122 Venice, Italy, President: Gabriele Giannini *Tel:* (041) 522 52 35 *Fax:* (041) 522 49 54; ARA-Suisse, Chemin de la Perche, 28, CH-2900 Porrentruy, Switzerland, President: Maud Spira *Tel:* (032) 66 21 14 *Fax:* (032) 66 21 14 *E-mail:* araspira@hotmail.com *Web Site:* www.arasuisse.ch

Guy Binsfeld & Co Sarl+
14 pl du Parc, 2313 Luxembourg/Bonnevole
Mailing Address: BP 2773, 2313 Luxembourg
Tel: 496868 *Fax:* 488770
Key Personnel
Man Dir, Production, Publicity, Rights & Permissions: Guy Binsfeld
Founded: 1979
Subjects: How-to, Law, Nonfiction (General), Photography
ISBN Prefix(es): 3-88957; 2-87954
Divisions: Binsfeld-Conseils Communications Agency

Editions Emile Borschette
21 Fielserstrooss, 7640 Christnach
Tel: 87177 *Fax:* 879599
Founded: 1987
Subjects: Accounting, Career Development, Cookery, Drama, Theater, Education, Gardening, Plants, History, How-to, Humor, Language Arts, Linguistics, Literature, Literary Criticism, Essays, Mathematics, Music, Dance, Photography, Poetry, Regional Interests
ISBN Prefix(es): 2-87982
Subsidiaries: Atelier de Reliures

Cahiers Luxembourgeois
67, rue Roger Barthel, 7212 Bereldange
Tel: 338885 *Fax:* 336513
Key Personnel
Publisher: Nic Weber
Founded: 1993
Subjects: History, Literature, Literary Criticism, Essays
ISBN Prefix(es): 2-919976
Divisions: Edition Raymon Mehlen

Centre Culturel De Differdange
69, rue Prinzenberg, 4650 Niederkorn
Tel: (352) 587045 *Fax:* (352) 474692
Key Personnel
President & Editor: Cornel Meder
Founded: 1982
Subjects: Ethnicity, Literature, Literary Criticism, Essays
ISBN Prefix(es): 2-87991

Chambre des Employes Prives
13, rue de Bragance, 1255 Luxembourg
Tel: 444091-1 *Fax:* 459440
E-mail: info@cepp.pu
Key Personnel
President: Jos Kratochwil

Editpress
44, rue du Canal, 4050 Esch/Alzette
Tel: 547131 *Fax:* 547130
E-mail: tageblatt@tageblatt.lu

Eiffes Romain
293, Avenue de Luxembourg, L-4940 Bascharage
Tel: (023) 65 10 52
E-mail: rend@pt.lu
Key Personnel
Contact: Mr Romain Eiffes
Founded: 1995
Member of SACEM/Paris (Societe des Auteurs Compositeurs et Editeurs de Musique Paris).
Subjects: English as a Second Language, Music, Dance, Poetry
ISBN Prefix(es): 2-9599899

Essay und Zeitgeist Verlag
c/o Patrick Kontz BP 2116, 1021 Luxembourg
Fax: 425227
Founded: 1994
Subjects: Literature, Literary Criticism, Essays, Philosophy, Social Sciences, Sociology
ISBN Prefix(es): 2-9599981
Orders to: BP 2767, L-1207 Luxembourg

Galerie Editions Kutter
17 rue des Bains, 1212 Luxembourg
Tel: 23571 *Fax:* 471884
Subjects: Art, Photography, Regional Interests
ISBN Prefix(es): 2-87952

Grande Loge de Luxembourg
5, rue de la Loge, L-2018 Luxembourg
Mailing Address: PO Box 851, 2018 Luxembourg
Tel: 229451 *Fax:* 463566
ISBN Prefix(es): 2-9599875

Hubsch
24, rue des Genets, 3482 Dudelange
E-mail: 101755.3213@compuserve.com
Subjects: Humor, Romance, Science Fiction, Fantasy
ISBN Prefix(es): 2-9599996

Keyware sarl+
11, rue de la Montagne, 5460 Trintange
Tel: 358660
E-mail: texthaus@webcom.com
Founded: 1996
Subjects: Education
ISBN Prefix(es): 2-919891

Ministere des Affaires Culturelles
20 Montee de la Petrusse, 2327 Luxembourg
Tel: 4781 *Fax:* 402427
ISBN Prefix(es): 2-87984

Edition Objectif Lune+
One rue de Schoenfels, 8151 Bridel
Tel: 335230 *Fax:* 335230
E-mail: objectif.lune@cmdnet.lu
Key Personnel
President: Jean-Paul Kieffer
Specialize in photographic stills.
Subjects: Drama, Theater, Film, Video, Photography
ISBN Prefix(es): 2-9599934

Office des Publications Officielles des Communautes Europeenes+
2 rue Mercier, 2985 Luxembourg
Tel: 29291 42451 *Fax:* 488857
Key Personnel
Contact: Norbert Reiner
Founded: 1969
ISBN Prefix(es): 92-77; 92-78
U.S. Office(s): Burnan Associates, 4611-F Assembly Drive, Lanham, MD 20706, United States

Op der Lay+
19 rue d'Eschdorf, L-9650 Esch-Sure
Tel: 839742 *Fax:* 899350
E-mail: opderlay@pt.lu
Web Site: //webplaza.pt.lu/public/opderlay
Key Personnel
Contact: Robert Gollo Steffen; Renee Weber
Founded: 1987
Specialize in compact disc & music cassettes, literature & music from Luxembourg, also music publisher.
Subjects: Music, Dance, Poetry, Travel
ISBN Prefix(es): 2-87967
Total Titles: 7 Audio

Passerelle, *imprint of* Editions Promoculture

LUXEMBOURG

Editions Phi+
PO Box 321, 4004 Esch, Alzette
Tel: (00352) 541382-220 *Fax:* (00352) 541387
E-mail: editions.phi@editpress.lu
Key Personnel
Dir: Angelika Thome
Editorial: Jean Portante
Founded: 1980
Subjects: Art, Drama, Theater, Literature, Literary Criticism, Essays
ISBN Prefix(es): 3-88865; 2-87962

Editions Promoculture+
14 rue Duchscher, 1424 Luxembourg
Mailing Address: BP 1142, L-1011 Luxembourg
Tel: 480691 *Fax:* 400950
E-mail: promocul@pt.lu
Web Site: www.promoculture.net
Telex: 3112
Key Personnel
Dir: Albert Daming *E-mail:* daming@pt.lu
Founded: 1989
Law and fiscal publisher.
Also acts as Major Book Dealer.
Subjects: Accounting, Economics, Education, Finance, Law, Mathematics, Regional Interests
ISBN Prefix(es): 2-87974
Imprints: Passerelle
Warehouse: One rue Duchscher, L-1424 Luxembourg-Jare

Editions Saint-Paul+
14 rue Christophe Plantin, 2988 Luxembourg
Tel: 49931 *Fax:* 4993580
Telex: Wortlu 3471; 275256
Key Personnel
Man Dir: Paul Zimmer
Production: Jean Breser
Publicity: Patrick Ludovicy
Publishing Manager: Dirk Sumkoetter
 Tel: 4993256 *E-mail:* dirk.sumkoetter@editions.lu
Founded: 1886
Subjects: History, Literature, Literary Criticism, Essays
ISBN Prefix(es): 2-87963
Parent Company: Group Saint-Paul SA
Bookshop(s): Librarie Beaumont, 24 rue Beaumont, L-1249; Librairie Bourbon, rue du Fort Bourbon, L-1249; Librairie du Sud, 74 rue de l'Alzette, L-4010 Eschlalzette; Librairie Daman, 4 rue de Brabant, L-9213 Diekirch

Service Central de la Statistique et des Etudes Economiques (STATEC)
blvd Royal 6, 2449 Luxembourg 2013
Mailing Address: bp 304, 2449 Luxembourg 2013
Tel: 4781 *Fax:* 464289
E-mail: statec.post@statec.etat.lu
Web Site: www.statec.lu
Key Personnel
Dir: Robert Weides
Principal Inspector & Head of Information: Guy Zacharias *Tel:* 478-4281 *E-mail:* guy.zacharias@statec.etat.lu
Founded: 1964
National Statistical Institute of Luxembourg.
Under the authority of the Minister of the Economy.
Subjects: Agriculture, Business, Economics, Finance, Labor, Industrial Relations, Library & Information Sciences, Public Administration, Social Sciences, Sociology
ISBN Prefix(es): 2-87988
Number of titles published annually: 100 Print

Service Central des Imprimes et des Fournitures de Bureau de l'Etat
22, rue des Bruyeres, L-1274 Howald
Mailing Address: BP 1302, L-1013 Luxembourg
Tel: (00352) 498811916; (00352) 498811915
 Fax: (00352) 400881

Key Personnel
Contact: Claude Schaber *Tel:* (00352) 4988111
 E-mail: claude.schaber@scie.etat.lu
Founded: 1969
Specialize in textbooks.
Subjects: Archaeology, Art, Law, Natural History, Public Administration
ISBN Prefix(es): 2-495
Number of titles published annually: 70 Print
Total Titles: 1,023 Print

STATEC, see Service Central de la Statistique et des Etudes Economiques (STATEC)

Thesen Verlag Vowinckel
3 place de la Gare, L-6674 Mertert/Luxembourg
Mailing Address: Postfach 3570, D-54225 Trier, Germany
Tel: (00352) 748715 *Fax:* (00352) 26740429
Key Personnel
Man Dir: Dr Ilse Schirmer-Vowinckel
 E-mail: schirm.vow@pt.lu
Founded: 1969 (Founded in Germany since 1992 resident in the Grand-Duche of Luxembourg)
Specialize in scholarly books, book review "Kritikon Litterarum" literary criticism.
Member of Borsenverein des Deutschen Buchhandels.
ISBN Prefix(es): 3-7677

Editions Tousch+
8 rue Ernest Koch, 1864 Luxembourg
Tel: 452977 *Fax:* 458743
Subjects: Art, History, Humor, Photography, Poetry
ISBN Prefix(es): 2-919971

Varkki Verghese+
Maison 23A, 9769 Roder
Mailing Address: BP 13, L-9801 Hosingen
Tel: 923121 *Fax:* 929076
Founded: 1993
Member of GEMA (Music).
Subjects: Alternative, Asian Studies, Economics, Government, Political Science, Music, Dance, Poetry, Theology, Women's Studies
ISBN Prefix(es): 2-9599891
Associate Companies: Whitelion Ltd, United Kingdom
Divisions: Acanthus Records
Distributed by Oyster (India only)

Macau

General Information

Capital: Macau
Language: Portuguese and Chinese (Cantonese dialect) both official. English also widely spoken
Religion: Roman Catholic, Chinese Buddhist, Daoism, & Confucianism
Population: 373,904
Bank Hours: 0930-1700 Monday-Friday; 0930-1200 Saturday
Shop Hours: 0900-1730 Monday-Saturday
Currency: 100 avos= 1 pataca. Hong Kong currency is also widely used but there is no fixed exchange rate.
Export/Import Information: Macau is a free port.
Copyright: Berne (see Copyright Conventions, pg xi)

Livros Do Oriente+
Av Amizada 876-12 C, Macau
Tel: 518063 *Fax:* 518064
Key Personnel
Editor: Rogerio Coelho

BOOK

Founded: 1990
Subjects: Anthropology, Biography, Photography, Romance, Social Sciences, Sociology, Travel
ISBN Prefix(es): 972-9418
Branch Office(s)
R Fonte Santa, 91 Aveiras de Cima, 2050 Azambuja, Portugal

Museu Maritimo (Maritime Museum)
Largo do Pagode da Barra, n 1, Sul da China
Tel: (0853) 595481; (0853) 595483 *Fax:* (0853) 512160
E-mail: museumaritimo@marine.gov.mo
Web Site: www.museumaritime.gov.mo
Key Personnel
Dir: Wu Chu Pang
Subjects: Asian Studies, History, Maritime, Technology, Transportation
Number of titles published annually: 3 Print
Total Titles: 58 Print

Instituto Portugues Oriente
Av Cons Ferreira de Almeida, 95 G, Macau
Tel: 370642 *Fax:* 305426
Key Personnel
President: Dr Ana Paula Laborinho
 E-mail: ipor@macau.ctm.net
Founded: 1989
Subjects: Asian Studies, History, Language Arts, Linguistics
ISBN Prefix(es): 972-8013
Bookshop(s): Livraria Portuguesa, Rua de Sao Domingos, No 16-18, Contact: Mr Manuel Almeiya *Tel:* (0853) 566442; (0853) 515915 *Fax:* (0853) 378014 *E-mail:* iporlp@macau.net

Universidadede de Macau, Centro de Publicacoes
Au Padre Tomas Perreira, S.J., Taipa
Tel: 831622; 3974505 (Distribution); 3974430 (University Library) *Fax:* 831694
Founded: 1993
Subjects: Art, Economics, Education, Government, Political Science, History, Literature, Literary Criticism, Essays, Management, Public Administration, Social Sciences, Sociology
ISBN Prefix(es): 972-97631; 972-96791; 972-97050; 972-97834

The Former Yugoslav Republic of Macedonia

General Information

Capital: Skopje
Language: Macedonian
Religion: Predominantly Eastern Orthodox, some Muslim
Population: 2.1 million
Copyright: UCC, Berne (see Copyright Conventions, pg xi)

Detska radost+
ul Mito Hadzivasilev Jasmin bb, 91000 Skopje
Tel: (091) 112394; (091) 213059 *Fax:* (091) 225830; (091) 213059
Telex: YUNOVMAK 51154
Key Personnel
International Rights: Kiril Donev
Ed-in-Chief: Aleksandar Cvetkovski
Founded: 1945
Specializes in children's books.

Subjects: Fiction, Literature, Literary Criticism, Essays, Nonfiction (General), Poetry, Science Fiction, Fantasy
Associate Companies: NIP, Nova Makedonija, Skopje

Gjurgja Journalistic & Publishing Firm
11 Oktomvri 2/6-2, 91000 Skopje
Tel: (091) 228076
Key Personnel
Dir: Olga Kosteska
ISBN Prefix(es): 9989-676
Subsidiaries: Literary-Painting Salon

Ktitor+
Engelsova 8/18, 92000 Stip
Tel: (092) 21903; (092) 34746 *Fax:* (092) 34746
Telex: 53618 MAK.YU
Subjects: Drama, Theater, Literature, Literary Criticism, Essays, Music, Dance, Philosophy, Poetry, Religion - Other, Science (General)
ISBN Prefix(es): 9989-608

Macedonia Prima Publishing House+
ul Krst Misirkov 8, 96000 Ohrid
Tel: (096) 37109 *Fax:* (096) 31478
Key Personnel
President: Pasko Kuzman
Founded: 1993
Member of Association of Macedonian Publishers.
Subjects: Archaeology, Art, History, Literature, Literary Criticism, Essays, Photography, Poetry, Science Fiction, Fantasy, Social Sciences, Sociology
ISBN Prefix(es): 9989-619

Makedonska kniga (Knigoizdatelstvo)
ul 11 Oktomvri bb, 91000 Skopje (Macedonia)
Tel: (091) 224055; (091) 231610; (091) 235524 *Fax:* (091) 236951
Telex: 51637 *Cable:* MAKEDONSKA KNIGA
Key Personnel
Dir: Branislav Mihajlovic
Founded: 1947
Subjects: Art, Fiction
ISBN Prefix(es): 9989-46

Medis, Skopje+
M Hadzhivasilev 36/1-2, 91000 Skopje
Tel: (091) 118-104 *Fax:* (091) 272-253
E-mail: medis@informa.mk
Web Site: www.medis.com.mk
Key Personnel
President: Dr Mirko Spiroski
Founded: 1991
Specialize in medicine & computer science.
Subjects: Biological Sciences, Communications, Computer Science, Education, Electronics, Electrical Engineering, Mathematics, Medicine, Nursing, Dentistry, Microcomputers
Total Titles: 10 E-Book

Menora Publishing House
Bul Jane Sandanski 36-4/13, 91000 Skopje
Tel: (091) 418872 *Fax:* (091) 418872
E-mail: memoya@unet.com.mk
Web Site: members.xoom.com/menora
Key Personnel
Dir: Jordan Pop-Atanazov
Specialize in science.
Subjects: Science (General)
ISBN Prefix(es): 9989-632
Bookshop(s): Porta Bunjakovec, A-2, Dijadema, Lam I, BR 12-1, 91000 Skopje

Mi-An Knigoizdatelstvo
vl Ivan Agouski 1/1, 91000 Skopje
Tel: (091) 252565
E-mail: mtimes@soros.org.mk

Key Personnel
President: Vanja Tosevski
Vice President: Mishel Pavlovski
Editor-in-Chief: Jovan Pavlovski
Assistant Editor-in-Chief: Boshko Nacevski
Founded: 1991
Subjects: Journalism, Literature, Literary Criticism, Essays, Poetry, Publishing & Book Trade Reference
ISBN Prefix(es): 9989-613
Branch Office(s)
American Information Centre, str, Nikola Vaptsarov 8 *Tel:* 116-623

Murgorski Zoze+
ul Budimpestanska 37B, 91000 Skopje
Tel: (091) 241340
Founded: 1991
Subjects: Education, English as a Second Language, Language Arts, Linguistics
ISBN Prefix(es): 9989-651
Distributed by Kultura (Macedonia)

Narodna i univerzitetska biblioteka "Sv Kliment ohridski", see St Clement of Ohrid National & University Library

Nov svet (New World)+
Briselska 1, 1 000 Skopje Skopje
Tel: (02) 378-662
Key Personnel
Academic Poet: Hr Jon T Boskovski
Founded: 1966
Specialize in translations. The Company "Nov svet" (New World) was an illegal editorial of the Desidents Writers. Now is all regular Publish House - sponsored (on programes) by the Government of Republic of Macedonia.
Also acts as wholesaler & publishing house for books, newspapers & periodicals.
Subjects: Art, Journalism, Literature, Literary Criticism, Essays, Philosophy, Poetry, Science (General)
Total Titles: 2,000 Print
Associate Companies: Cross-Cultural Communications, 239 Wynsum Ave, Merrick, NY, United States

Prosvetno Delo
ul Veljko Vlahovic 15, 91000 Skopje
Tel: (091) 117255; (091) 118617 *Fax:* (091) 225434; (091) 129402
E-mail: prodelo@nic.mpt.com.mk
Key Personnel
Man Dir: Pavle Petrov
Subjects: Education
ISBN Prefix(es): 86-351
Bookshop(s): Dame Gruev BB, 91000 Skopje
Warehouse: Aco Sopov, 6 91000 Skopje

St Clement of Ohrid National & University Library+
Bul Goce Delcev 6, 91000 Skopje
Tel: (091) 115-177; (091) 115358 *Fax:* (091) 230874
E-mail: kliment@nubsk.edu.mk
Web Site: www.nubsk.edu.mk/; nubsk.nubskedu.mk/
Key Personnel
Dir & Chief Executive: Vera Kalajlievska
Contact: Veljan Ristevski
Database Contacts: Zaklina Gjalevska; Stana Jankoska
Founded: 1944
Scholarly & scientific works collections, including monograph titles, periodicals, newspapers & other printed materials (patents, standards, etc). Specialized collections include: old Slavonic manuscripts, printed & rare books & periodicals, oriental manuscripts, archive copies of Macedonia publications (1944 to present), prints & drawings, cartographic items, microfilms, doctoral dissertations, Master's theses, scientific & scholarly research projects. Online catalogue available.
Subjects: Library & Information Sciences
ISBN Prefix(es): 9989-652
Online services available through Telnet, World Wide Web.
Membership(s): IFLA

Seizmoloska Opservatorija+
PO Box 422, 91000 Skopje
Tel: (091) 231953 *Fax:* (091) 114042
E-mail: ljupco@iunona.pmf.ukim.edu.mk
Key Personnel
Editor & International Rights: Vera Cejkovska; Dragana Cernih
Member of International Association of Seismology & Physics of the Earth's Interior - IASPEI; International Union of Geodesy & Geophysics - IUGG.
Subjects: Computer Science, Earth Sciences, Electronics, Electrical Engineering, Geography, Geology
ISBN Prefix(es): 9989-631

Strk Publishing House+
ul Jurij Gagarin Br 17-2-17, 91000 Skopje
Tel: (091) 205393
Key Personnel
Dir: Nikola Strkovski
Editor: Snezana Strkovska
Founded: 1992
Also acts as importer/exporter of office supplies & paper; wholesale & retail.
Subjects: Astrology, Occult, Behavioral Sciences, Biography, Economics, History, Literature, Literary Criticism, Essays, Poetry, Romance
ISBN Prefix(es): 9989-662

Zumpres Publishing Firm+
ul Vanjamin Macukovski 6, P Fah 363, 91000 Skopje
Tel: (091) 163539; (091) 425175 *Fax:* (091) 425176; (091) 429196
E-mail: zumpres@yahoo.com
Founded: 1994
Subjects: Anthropology, Archaeology, Architecture & Interior Design, Art, Astrology, Occult, Astronomy, Behavioral Sciences, Biblical Studies, Biography, Computer Science, Fiction, History, Human Relations, Language Arts, Linguistics, Literature, Literary Criticism, Essays, Mysteries, Parapsychology, Philosophy, Poetry, Psychology, Psychiatry
ISBN Prefix(es): 9989-42

Madagascar

General Information

Capital: Antananavivo
Language: French and Malagasy
Religion: Most follow traditional beliefs, about 43% Christian and some Islamic
Population: 12.6 million
Bank Hours: 0800-1100, 1400-1600 Monday-Friday. Closed afternoon preceding a holiday
Shop Hours: 0800-1200, 1400-1800 Monday-Saturday
Currency: 100 centimes = 1 franc malgache (Malagasy franc)
Export/Import Information: For books and advertising matter, customs and import duties, also unique tax. Import license required.
Copyright: Berne, Florence (see Copyright Conventions, pg xi)

MADAGASCAR

Editions Ambozontany
c/o Librairie St Paul Ambatomena, BP 1170, Fianarantsoa 301
Tel: (07) 50027; (07) 51441
Key Personnel
Man Dir: Justin Bethaz
Editorial: Nicola Giambrone
Sales: Jose Minien
Founded: 1962
Subjects: Ethnicity, History, Religion - Other, Social Sciences, Sociology

Librairie Ambozontany
BP 1170, 301 Fianarantsoa
Tel: (07) 50027; (07) 51441

Maison d'Edition Protestante ANTSO+
19 Lalana Venance Manifatra, Antananarivo 101
Mailing Address: BP 660, Imarivolanitra Antananarivo 101
Tel: (022) 20886 *Fax:* (022) 26372
E-mail: fjkm@dts.mg *Cable:* FIJEKRIMA ANTSO
Key Personnel
Man Dir: Hans Andriamampianina
Founded: 1966
Subjects: Biblical Studies, Developing Countries, Education, Journalism, Literature, Literary Criticism, Essays, Religion - Protestant
Number of titles published annually: 6 Print
Total Titles: 13 Print
Bookshop(s): Bookshop Antso, Lot IIB 18, Totohabato Ranavalona 1, Tananarive 101 *Tel:* (022) 347 10; Librairie ANTSO, rue Bertho Anjoma, Toamasina 501 *Tel:* 33944

Centre National de Production de Materiel Didactique (CNAPMAD)
BP 665, Ankorondrano, Antananarivo 101
Tel: (02) 28954 *Fax:* (02) 20053
Key Personnel
Contact: Jersin Manjato Razafimahefa

CNAPMAD, see Centre National de Production de Materiel Didactique (CNAPMAD)

Foibe Filan-Kevitry NY Mpampianatra (FOFIPA)
BP 202, Antananarivo 101
Mailing Address: rue Jean Andriamady Faravohitra, BP760, Antananarivo
Tel: (02) 27500 *Fax:* (02) 35788
Subjects: Accounting, Agriculture, Cookery, English as a Second Language
Distributed by Les Libraries de Madagascar

Government Printer (Imprimerie Nationale)
BP 38, Ambatomena Antananarivo 101
Tel: (02) 23675

JEAG
120 rue Rainandriamampandry, 101 Antananarivo
Tel: (02) 24141 *Fax:* (02) 20397
Key Personnel
Director: Harilala Adrianarimanana
ISBN Prefix(es): 2-910885
Parent Company: Jureco SA
Distributor for Foi & Justice

Librarie Mixte
BP 3204, 37, rue 26 Jona 1960 Analakely, Antananarivo 101
Tel: (02) 25130 *Fax:* (02) 25130

Madagascar Print & Press Company+
rue Rabesahala - Antsakaviro, Antananarivo 101
Mailing Address: BP 953, Antananarivo 101
Tel: (02) 2222536 *Fax:* (02) 2234534
E-mail: roi@dts.mg

Key Personnel
Man Dir, Editorial: Georges Ranaivosoa
Founded: 1969
Sales, Publicity: Societe CEMOI.
Subjects: History, Literature, Literary Criticism, Essays
Imprints: Editions Revue de l'Ocean Indien
Subsidiaries: Communication et Media - Ocean Indien (Societe CEMOI)
Sales Office(s): Societe CEMOI

MADPRINT, see Madagascar Print & Press Company

Societe Malgache d'Edition+
BP 659, Ravoninahitriniarivo, Ankorondrano, Antananarivo 101
Tel: (020) 2222635 *Fax:* (020) 2222254
E-mail: tribune@bow.dts.mg
Telex: 22340 RAMEX MG TANANARIVE
Key Personnel
Man Dir: Rahaga Ramaholimihaso
Founded: 1943
Subjects: Communications, Economics, Education, Finance, Journalism, Law
Imprints: SME

Musee d'Art et d'Archaeologie
17 rue Dr Villette, Isoraka, BP 564, Antananarivo 101
Tel: (02) 21047 *Fax:* (02) 28218
E-mail: musedar@syfed.refer.mg
Key Personnel
Dir: Dr J A Rakotoarisoa
Subjects: Travel

Editions Revue de l'Ocean Indien, *imprint of* Madagascar Print & Press Company

SME, *imprint of* Societe Malgache d'Edition

Imprimerie Takariva
rue Radley Antanimena, Antananarivo 101
Mailing Address: BP 1029, Antananarivo
Tel: 02 23856
Key Personnel
Man Dir: Paul Rapatsalahy
Founded: 1933
Subjects: Fiction

Trano Printy Fiangonana Loterana Malagasy (TPFLM)-(Imprimerie Lutherienne)
Imprint of Fiangonana Loterana Malagasy
9 ave Grandidier Isoraka, Antananarivo 101
Mailing Address: BP 538, Antananarivo 101
Tel: (020) 223340 *Fax:* (020) 262643
E-mail: impluth@dts.mg
Key Personnel
Man Dir: Raymond Randrianatoandro
Tel: 2224569
Edit: Pastor Samoela Georges
Founded: 1877
Member of F L M, Union Professionnelle Des Imprimeurs De Madagascar.
Subjects: Fiction, Religion - Other
Number of titles published annually: 100 Print
Associate Companies: Fiangonana Loterana Malagasy, BP 1741, 101 Antananarivo, Contact: Raymond Randrianatoandro *Tel:* 022 24569
Bookshop(s): Analakely & Antsahamanitra

Tsileondriaka Edition
Lot II M 79 Andravoahangy, Antananarivo 101
Mailing Address: BP 1239, Antananarivo 101
Tel: (02) 31033; (02) 30659 *Fax:* (02) 31033

Tsipika Edition
48 rue Ny Havana-Antsahabe, Antananarivo 101
Tel: (02) 24595

BOOK

Key Personnel
Manager: Claude Rabenoro
Founded: 1990
Subjects: Environmental Studies, History
Distributed by Harmattan (France)

Malawi

General Information

Capital: Lilongwe
Language: English and Chichewa
Religion: About 50% Christian (Roman Catholic and Presbyterian), some Islamic and Hindu, remainder traditional beliefs
Population: 9.6 million
Bank Hours: 0800-1300 Monday-Friday; Saturday closed
Shop Hours: 0730 or 0800-1600 or 1700 Monday-Friday (with some closing for lunch); until midday Saturday
Currency: 100 tambala = 1 Malawi kwacha
Export/Import Information: No tariff on books; some advertising matter subject to duty. Import license required on certain category of goods. Exchange controls.
Copyright: UCC, Berne (see Copyright Conventions, pg xi)

Central Africana Ltd+
PO Box 631, Blantyre
Tel: 623227 *Fax:* 622236
E-mail: africana@sdwp.org.mw
Key Personnel
Chairman & Publisher: Frank M I Johnston
Tel: 821316
Founded: 1989
Subjects: History, Travel
ISBN Prefix(es): 99908-14
Number of titles published annually: 3 Print
Total Titles: 15 Print
Branch Office(s)
A231 St Martini Gardens, Queen Victoria St, Cape Town 8000, South Africa
Tel: (021) 4243595 *Fax:* (021) 4243595
E-mail: africana@iafrica.com
Foreign Rep(s): Struik & Southern Book Publishers (South Africa)

Christian Literature Association in Malawi
PO Box 503, Blantyre
Tel: 620839
Key Personnel
General Manager: J T Matenje
Sales Manager: E C Mtumbati
Founded: 1968
Subjects: Biography, Fiction, History, Poetry, Regional Interests, Religion - Other
ISBN Prefix(es): 99908-16

Dzuka Publishing Company Ltd
Private Bag 39, Blantyre
Tel: 01670855; 01670880 *Fax:* 67111433; 670021
Telex: 44112 AFNEWSMI
Key Personnel
General Manager: Egidio Mpanga
E-mail: dzuka@malawi.net
Founded: 1987
Subjects: Agriculture, Education, Fiction, Geography, Geology, History, Mathematics
ISBN Prefix(es): 99908-17
Parent Company: Blantyre Printing & Publishing Co Ltd

Government Printer (Imprimerie Nationale)
Government Printing Department, Ministry of Finance, Zomba
Mailing Address: PO Box 37, Zomba
Tel: (050) 523155 *Fax:* (050) 52230133

Telex: 45162 Geoprint Ml
ISBN Prefix(es): 99908-20

Mzuzu Publishing Co+
Box 225, Nkhata Bay
Tel: 352353 *Fax:* 352353
E-mail: kchiume@hotmail.com
Key Personnel
Executive Chairman: M W Kanyama Chiume
Founded: 1977 (transferred to Malawi under new name in 1995)
Member of Book Publisher's Association of Malawi.
Subjects: Biography, Fiction, History
ISBN Prefix(es): 9976-900

Popular Publications+
PO Box 5592, Limbe
Tel: 641126 *Fax:* 651171
E-mail: mpp@malawi.net
Telex: 44814 Montfort Ml
Key Personnel
General Manager, Publisher, Rights & Permissions: Vales Machila
Editorial: Prince C Shonga
Sales: M Kapelewera
Production: H Chinawa
Founded: 1976
Subjects: Biblical Studies, Fiction
ISBN Prefix(es): 99908-29
Parent Company: Montfort Press, PO Box 5592, Limbe
Bookshop(s): Moni Bookshop, PO Box 5592, Limbe

Malaysia

General Information

Capital: Kuala Lumpur
Language: Bahasa Malaysia (based on Malay) is official language; English widely used; Chinese, Tamil and Iban also spoken
Religion: Islam predomininates, there is a large Buddhist group among the Chinese, Hindu among the Indians
Population: 18.4 million
Bank Hours: West Malaysia (some states observe Muslim weekly holiday): 1000-1500 Monday-Friday; 0930-1130 Saturday. Sabah: 0800-1200, 1400-1500 Monday-Friday; 0900-1100 Saturday. Sarawak: 1000-1500 Monday-Friday; 0930-1130 Saturday
Shop Hours: West Malaysia varies; average 0830-1830 Monday-Saturday. Sabah: 0800-1830 Monday-Saturday. Sarawak: 0900-1800 Monday-Friday; 0900-1300 Saturday
Currency: 100 sen = 1 ringgit or Malaysian dollar
Export/Import Information: No tariff on books. Advertising matter dutied per lb, subject to CIF surtax. No obscene literature allowed. Import licenses required only in Sabah, for books not having the name, printer and publisher on first or last printed page. No exchange controls.
Copyright: Berne (see Copyright Conventions, pg xi)

S Abdul Majeed & Co+
7 Jln 3/82B, Bangsar Utama, Off Jalan Bangsar, 59200 Kaula Lumpur
Tel: (03) 2832230 *Fax:* (03) 2825670
Key Personnel
Man Partner: Peer Mohamed Majid
E-mail: peer@pc.jaring.my
Founded: 1952
Subjects: Asian Studies, Child Care & Development, Cookery, English as a Second Language, Health, Nutrition, Management, Marketing, Religion - Islamic, Travel
ISBN Prefix(es): 983-9629; 983-9550
Imprints: Malaysia Heritage Series
Branch Office(s)
35, Jalan Sekerat Off Tranofer Rd, 10050 Pinang
Showroom(s): 107c, Jalan Rajalaut, 50350 Kaula Lumpur

Academia Publications P Ltd
22, Jalan Bukit Bintang, 55100 Kuala Lumpur
Tel: (03) 572455
ISBN Prefix(es): 967-9925

Pustaka Aman Press Sdn Bhd
4200-A Simpang Tiga-Telipot, Jalan Sultan Yahya Petra, Peti Surat 67, 15700 Kota Bahru, Kelantan
Tel: (09) 781849 *Fax:* (09) 784058
ISBN Prefix(es): 983-63

Amiza Associate Malaysia Sdn Bhd+
71 Jalan SS 6/12, Kelana Jaya, 47301 Petaling Jaya, Selangor Darul Ehsan
Tel: (03) 7036100 *Fax:* (03) 7034268
Key Personnel
Marketing Manager: Jeremy Thor
Founded: 1982
Member of Malayasian Book Publishers Association.
Subjects: Business, Education
ISBN Prefix(es): 967-966
Parent Company: Johore State Economic Development Corp Johor Bahru, Malaysia

AMK Interaksi Sdn Bhd+
NO7, Jalan 3/82 B Bangsar Utama, Off Jalan Bangsar, 59200 Kuala Lumpur
Tel: (03) 215306 *Fax:* (03) 718067
Telex: MA 30226 MAHIR
Key Personnel
President: Miss Chin Choo Yuen
Founded: 1988
ISBN Prefix(es): 983-9617; 983-99555
Parent Company: Mahir Holdings Sdn Bhd
Shipping Address: Master Agencies Sdn Bhd, 110 Jl 27, Kawasan 16, Sungei Rasa, 41300 Kelang
Warehouse: 28, Jl SS26/13 Taman Mayang Jaya, 47301 Petaling Jaya

Pustaka Antara
399A Jalan Tuanku Abdul Rahman, 50100 Kuala Lumpar
Tel: (03) 2925823 *Fax:* (03) 2917997
Telex: MA 28140 *Cable:* Antara
ISBN Prefix(es): 967-937

Associated Educational Distributors (M) Sdn Bhd+
550 Taman Melaka Raya, 75000 Melaka
Tel: (06) 2844786 *Fax:* (06) 2844697
Subjects: Fiction
ISBN Prefix(es): 967-948

AWL Malaysia Sdn Bhd, see Pearson Education

Berita Publishing Sdn Bhd
31, Jalan Riong, 59100 Kuala Lumpur
Tel: (03) 2824322 *Fax:* (03) 2821605
Telex: MA 30259
Key Personnel
General Manager: Lo Cheng Choy
Sales: S Jeya Dev
Production: A Ravindranath
Publicity: Gerry Ho
Rights & Permissions: Gulrose Karim
Founded: 1973
Subjects: Business, Cookery, Education, Fiction
ISBN Prefix(es): 967-969
Parent Company: The New Straits Times Press (Malaysia) Berhad Balai Berita, 31 Jalan Riong, Kuala Lumpur 22-03
Subsidiaries: Berita Book Centre Sdn Bhd; Berita Distributors Sdn Bhd (both at above address)

Biro Penyediaan Teks ltm (Biroteks)+
Institut Teknologi Mara, 40450 Shah Alam, Selangor Darul Ehsan
Tel: (03) 59271 ext 495 *Fax:* (03) 500226; (03) 55692733
Key Personnel
Contact: Head of Biroteks
Founded: 1981
ISBN Prefix(es): 967-958

Butterworths, *imprint of* Malayan Law Journal Sdn Bhd

Castle, *imprint of* Glad Sounds Sdn Bhd

Darulfikir+
329-B Jl Abd Rahman Idris off Jl Raja Muda, 50300 Kuala Lumpur
Tel: (03) 2981636; (03) 26913892 *Fax:* (03) 26928757
E-mail: emel@darulfikir.com.my
Telex: MA 31533 Action
Key Personnel
Man Dir: Mohamad Ahmad
Founded: 1984
Subjects: Education, Language Arts, Linguistics, Religion - Islamic
ISBN Prefix(es): 983-99583; 983-9668
Number of titles published annually: 40 Print
Total Titles: 1,700 Print

Dewan Bahasa dan Pustaka+
Jl Dewan Bahasa, 50460 Kuala Lumpur
Mailing Address: PO Box 10803, 50926 Kuala Lumpur
Tel: (03) 21481011; (03) 2481820 *Fax:* (03) 21443875
Web Site: www.dbp.gov.my *Cable:* Bahasa
Key Personnel
Director General: Haji A Aziz *Tel:* (03) 2486785 *Fax:* (03) 2444460 *E-mail:* aziz@dbp.gov.my
Dir, Publishing: Rohani Zainal Abidin *Tel:* (03) 2488136 *Fax:* (03) 2449614 *E-mail:* rohani@dbp.gov.my
Business Manager: Ramly Ngah Idris *Tel:* (03) 2489512 *E-mail:* ramly@dbp.gov.my
Rights & Licensing: Abdul Nasir Mohd Razali *Tel:* (03) 2481497 *E-mail:* nasir1@dbp.gov.my
Founded: 1956
Specialize in Malay language & linguistics, Malay literature & Malay culture.
ISBN Prefix(es): 967-65; 983-62
Number of titles published annually: 500 Print
Branch Office(s)
Dewan Bahasa dan Pustaka Cawangan Sabah, PO Box 149, 88999 Kota Kinabalu, Sabah, Contact: Zaini Oje Ozea *Tel:* (088) 439217 *Fax:* (088) 439732
Dewan Bahasa dan Pustaka Wilayah Timur, PO Box 66, 15720 Kota Bharu, Kelantan, Contact: Sallehuddin Abang Shokeran *Tel:* (09) 7477373 *Fax:* (09) 7475252
Dewan Bahasa dan Pustaka Cawangan Sarawak, PO Box 1390, 93728 Kuching, Sarawak, Contact: Abdul Rahman Yusof *Tel:* (082) 444706 *Fax:* (082) 444707
Dewan Bahasa dan Pustaka Wilayah Utara, PO Box 144, 14007 Seberang Perai, Penang, Contact: Salmial Ismail *Tel:* (04) 6212000 *Fax:* (04) 6211013

Dewan Pustaka Islam+
10-2 Right Angle Jln 14/22, 46100 Petaling Jaya, Selangor Darul Ehsan
Tel: (03) 7557225 *Fax:* (03) 7586439

MALAYSIA

Key Personnel
Executive Chairman: Mohd Anuar Tahir
Man Dir: Ahmad Azam Abdul Rahman
Founded: 1971
Member of Book Contractor Association of Malaysia.
Subjects: Religion - Islamic
ISBN Prefix(es): 983-66
Associate Companies: Blue-T Sdn Bhd
Subsidiaries: Budaya Ilmu Sdn Bhd; Tradisi Ilmu Sdn Bhd
Distributed by Cekap Edar; Hizbi
Distributor for Institut Kajan Dasar; Institute of Strategic & International Studies (ISIS); Juta & Co (South Africa); Universiti Malaya Publication
Bookshop(s): Tradisi Ilmu Sdn Bhd, 10-2 Right Angle Jln 14/22, 46100 Petaling Jaya Selangor Darul Ehsan
Warehouse: Lot 1032, Jln Cempaka, Kg Sg Kayu Ara, 47400 Damansara Utama

Earlybird, *imprint of* Federal Publications Sdn Bhd

Eastview Malaysiana Library, *imprint of* Eastview Productions Sdn Bhd

Eastview Productions Sdn Bhd
11 Lorong 51A/227C, 46100 Petaling Jaya, Selangor Darul Ehsan
Tel: (03) 7762669; (03) 7762614; (03) 7556639 *Fax:* (03) 7550731
Key Personnel
Man Dir: Johnny Ong
Founded: 1980
ISBN Prefix(es): 967-60
Associate Companies: Anthonian Store Sdn Bhd; Pacific Book Centre, Singapore, Singapore; Pan Pacific Publications Pte Ltd, Singapore
Imprints: Eastview Malaysiana Library; Eastview Visual Library

Eastview Visual Library, *imprint of* Eastview Productions Sdn Bhd

Fairy Tales, *imprint of* Mecron Sdn Bhd

Federal, *imprint of* Federal Publications Sdn Bhd

Federal Publications Sdn Bhd+
Times Subang, Lot 46, Subang Hi-Tech Industrial Park, Batu Tiga, 40000 Shah Alam, Selangor
Tel: (03) 7351511 *Fax:* (03) 7364620
E-mail: kesoon@pc.jaring.my
Key Personnel
Vice President & General Manager: Stephen Lim
Tel: (03) 7364621
Founded: 1957
Subjects: Astronomy, Career Development, Child Care & Development, Computer Science, Education, English as a Second Language, Gardening, Plants, Mathematics, Science (General), Self-Help, Sports, Athletics
Total Titles: 500 Print
Online services available through World Wide Web.
Parent Company: Times Publishing Limited
Associate Companies: Federal Publications (S) (Pte) Ltd, Singapore; Federal Publications (HK) Ltd, Hong Kong
Imprints: Federal; Times; Earlybird
Divisions: Times Trade Direcories
Shipping Address: Federal Publications (HK) Ltd, Hong Kong
Warehouse: Federal Publications (HK) Ltd, Hong Kong
Orders to: Federal Publications (S) (Pte) Ltd, Singapore
Federal Publications (HK) Ltd, Hong Kong

FEP International Sdn Bhd
6 Jalan SS 4C/5, 47301 Petaling Jaya, Selangor Darul Ehsan
Mailing Address: PO Box 1091, Petaling Jaya, Selangor Darul Ehsan
Tel: (03) 7036150; (03) 7036152; (03) 7036154 *Fax:* (03) 7036989 *Cable:* BOOKMARK
Key Personnel
Man Dir: Mok Hai Lim
ISBN Prefix(es): 967-63
Associate Companies: FEP International Private Ltd, Singapore

Forum Publications+
11 Jalan 11-4E, 46200 Petaling Jaya, Selangor
Tel: (03) 7554007 *Fax:* (03) 7561879
E-mail: g2jomo@umcsd.um.edu.my
Key Personnel
President: Abdul Karim Hassan
Marketing Dir: Tong-Sin Chong
Founded: 1978
Subjects: Anthropology, Developing Countries, Economics, Government, Political Science, History, Labor, Industrial Relations, Regional Interests, Religion - Islamic
ISBN Prefix(es): 983-876
Parent Company: Institute of Social Analysis (INSAN)
Associate Companies: Malaysian Social Science Association
Subsidiaries: Ikraq

Geetha Publishers Sdn Bhd
13A Jalan Kovil Hilir, 51100 Kuala Lumpur
Tel: (03) 4417073
Key Personnel
Man Dir: Soma Narayanan
Subjects: Education, History, How-to, Publishing & Book Trade Reference
ISBN Prefix(es): 983-9594

Glad Sounds Sdn Bhd+
Jl Semangat, PO Box 1019, 46970 Petaling Jaya
Tel: (03) 7187070 *Fax:* (03) 7189948
Key Personnel
General Manager: Peter Khong
Founded: 1976
Subjects: Management, Religion - Other, Self-Help
ISBN Prefix(es): 983-897
Imprints: Castle
Branch Office(s)
Jaya Shopping Centre
Kota Raya Complex
Yik Foong Complex

Holograms (M) Sdn Bhd+
6, Jorong Bukit Pantai Satu, 59100 Kuala Lumpur
Tel: (03) 2824002 *Fax:* (03) 2822751
Key Personnel
International Rights: Chuah Guat Eng
Founded: 1994
Subjects: Developing Countries, Ethnicity, Fiction
ISBN Prefix(es): 983-9132

IBS Buku Sdn Bhd
B3-06, PJ Industrial Park, Jalan Kennajuan, 46200 Petaling Jaya, Selangor Darul Ehsan
Tel: (03) 7751763; (03) 7751566; (03) 7760514 *Fax:* (03) 7765551
E-mail: ibsbuku@po.jaring.my
Key Personnel
Man Dir, Production, Rights & Permissions: M N Meera
Editorial: Miss Chong
Dir, Sales & Publicity: Mohamed Mustafa
Founded: 1972
Subjects: Career Development
ISBN Prefix(es): 967-950
Subsidiaries: Pelanduk Publications (M) Sdn Bhd

International Book Service, see IBS Buku Sdn Bhd

International Law Book Services+
Lot 4.1, 4th floor, Wisma Shen 149, Jalan Masjid India, 50100 Kuala Lumpur
Mailing Address: PO Box 11664, 50752 Kuala Lumpur
Tel: (03) 2939864; (03) 2939862; (03) 2933661; (03) 2931661 *Fax:* (03) 2928035
E-mail: gbc@pc.jaring.my
Web Site: bookgold.com
Key Personnel
Sole Proprietor: Syed Ibrahim
Founded: 1981
Member of Malaysian Book Publishers Association.
Subjects: Law, Publishes the Malaysian Law Statutes & other general titles pertaining to law
ISBN Prefix(es): 967-89; 967-9960
Number of titles published annually: 75 Print
Total Titles: 600 Print; 1 CD-ROM

Jabatan Penerbitan Universiti Malaya, see University of Malaya, Department of Publications

K Publishing & Distributors Sdn Bhd+
Stadium Shan Alam, Aras 1, Quadron B, Seksyen 13, 40000 Shan Alam, Selangor
Tel: (03) 5501755; (03) 5501442 *Fax:* (03) 5501826
Telex: MA 30226 MAHIR
Key Personnel
President: En Ahmad Mahir Kamaruddin
Founded: 1985
Subjects: Fiction
ISBN Prefix(es): 967-9906; 983-852
Parent Company: Mahir Holdings Sdn Bhd
Shipping Address: Master Agencies Sdn Bhd, 110 Jl 27, Kawasan 16, Sungei Rasa, 41300 Kelang
Warehouse: 28, Jl SS26/13 Taman Mayang Jaya, 47301 Petaling Jaya

Kharisma Publications Sdn Bhd
22 Jl USJ 9/5P, Subang Business Centre, 47620 Subang Jaya
Tel: (03) 724660 *Fax:* (03) 724602
Parent Company: Kharisma Group of Companies

Lamina Series, *imprint of* Mecron Sdn Bhd

Little Board Books, *imprint of* Mecron Sdn Bhd

Mahir Publications Sdn Bhd+
Stadium Shah Alam 1 Quadran B Seksyen 13, 40000 Shah Alam, Selangor
Tel: (03) 5501826; (03) 5501442; (03) 5501755 *Fax:* (03) 5501826
Telex: MA30226MAHIR
Key Personnel
Man Dir: Ahmad Mahir Kamaruddin
Publishing Manager: Choo Yuen Chin
Founded: 1990
Specialize in School Titles.
Subjects: Education, English as a Second Language
ISBN Prefix(es): 983-70
Parent Company: Mahir Holdings Sdn Bhd
Subsidiaries: Quill Publishers
Shipping Address: Master Agencies Sdn Bhd, 110 Jalan 27, Kawasan 16, Sungai Rasa, 41300 Kelang
Warehouse: Taman Mayang Jaya, 28 Jalan SS 26/16, 47310 Petaling Jaya

Malaya Books Suppliers Co
272-E Jalan Air Itam, 11400 Pulau Pinang
Tel: (03) 7910420

Key Personnel
Manager: Tony Lau
ISBN Prefix(es): 983-835

Malaya Educational Supplies Sdn Bhd
306, Block C, Glomac Business Centre, 10, J1556/1 Kelana Jaya, 47301 Plaling Jaya, Selangor
Tel: (03) 7046628 *Fax:* (03) 7046629
Subjects: Education
ISBN Prefix(es): 967-9923

The Malaya Press Sdn Bhd
6 Jalan TPK 1/4, Taman Perindustrian Kinrara, 58200 Kuala Lumpur
Tel: (03) 5755890; (03) 5757817 *Fax:* (03) 5757194
Key Personnel
Man Dir: Lai Wing Chun
Editorial: Yiu Hong
Sales: Chong Tim Seng
Founded: 1958
Subjects: Education
ISBN Prefix(es): 967-934
Parent Company: Union Cultural Organization Sdn Bhd, 10 Jalan 217, Petaling Jaya
Associate Companies: Hong Kong Cultural Press Ltd, 9 College Rd, Kowloon, Hong Kong; Singapore Press (Pte) Ltd, 303 North Bridge Rd, Singapore 7, Singapore
Bookshop(s): Ipoh Book Co, 75 Market St, Ipoh, Perak; Malaya Book Co, 22-24 Jalan Bukit Bintang, Kuala Lumpur

Malayan Law Journal Sdn Bhd
Unit A-5-1, 5th floor, Wisma H, Megan Phileo Ave, 12 Jalan Yap Kwan Seng, 50450 Kuala Lumpur
Tel: (03) 2162 2822 *Fax:* (03) 2162 3811
Web Site: www.mlj.com.my
Key Personnel
Managing Editor, New Product Development: Julie Anne Thomas
Commissioning Editor: Prema Arumugam
Sale Dir: Ronald Tan
Area Sales Manager: Lawrence Tan
Commercial Dir: Pook Li Ping
Fulfillment Manager: Chow Wai Leng
Founded: 1932
Member of the LexisNexis Group.
Subjects: Law
ISBN Prefix(es): 967-962
Parent Company: Butterworth & Co (Publishers) Ltd, United Kingdom
Ultimate Parent Company: Reed Elsevier plc, 25 Victoria St, London SW1H 0EX, United Kingdom
Associate Companies: Butterworths Hong Kong, 12/F, Hennessy Centre, 500 Hennessy Rd, Causeway Bay, Hong Kong, Commissioning Editor: Anisha Sakhrani *Tel:* 2965 1400 *Fax:* 2976 0840 *Web Site:* www.butterworths-hk.com; Butterworths India, 14th floor, Vijaya Bldg, 17, Barakhamba Rd, New Delhi 110001, India, Publishing Manager: Ambika Nair *Tel:* (011) 373 9614 *Fax:* (011) 332 6456 *Web Site:* www.butterworths-india.com; Butterworths Singapore, No 1 Temasek Ave, 17-01 Millenia Tower, Singapore 039192, Singapore, Regional Publishing Dir: Conita Leung *Tel:* 336 9661 *Fax:* 336 9662 *Web Site:* www.butterworths.com.sg
Imprints: MLJ; Butterworths
Shipping Address: No 3, Jalan PJS 11/20, Bandar Sunway, 46150 Petaling Jaya, Selangor *Tel:* (03) 733 1893 *Fax:* (03) 733 1823
Warehouse: No 4, Lot 752, Jalan Subang 3, Taman Perindustrian Subang, 47610 Subang Jaya, Selangor Darul Ehsan, Warehouse Manager: Patrick Lee *Tel:* (03) 5636 1740
Orders to: No 3, Jalan PJS 11/20, Bandar Sunway, 46150 Petaling Jaya, Selangor *Tel:* (03) 733 1893 *Fax:* (03) 733 1823

Malaysia Heritage Series, *imprint of* S Abdul Majeed & Co

The Malaysian Current Law Journal Sdn Bhd+
221, Jalan Negara 2, Taman Melawati, 53100 Kuala Lumpur
Tel: (03) 4081400 *Fax:* (03) 4081451
Key Personnel
Chief Editor: V T Singam
Man Dir: Abdul Latiff Ibrahim
Subjects: Law
ISBN Prefix(es): 983-9680

MDC Publishers Printers+
MDC Bldg 2718, Jalan Permata 4, Taman Permata, Hulu Kelang, 53300 Kuala Lumpur
Tel: (03) 4086600 *Fax:* (03) 4081506
E-mail: mdcpp@2mws.com.my
Web Site: www.2mws.com.my/mdc
Key Personnel
Dir: Tajuddin Husain
Marketing Executive: Ameer Hussain; Ahmed Hussain
Founded: 1976
Member of Malaysian Book Publishers Association; Malaysian Booksellers Association; Malaysian Book Importers Association.
Subjects: Law, Management
Number of titles published annually: 300 Print
Branch Office(s)
L3-04, 3rd floor, Shaw Parade, Changkat Thambi Dollah, Kuala Lumpur *Tel:* (03) 2457745

Mecron Sdn Bhd+
15, Lengkongan Vethavanam, BT 3 1/2 mile, Jalan Ipoh, 51100 Kuala Lumpur
Tel: (03) 6269326 *Fax:* (03) 6219869 *Cable:* MECROMAN KUALA LUMPUR
Key Personnel
Chief Executive: Dr Y Mansoor Marican
Dir: Zaliha B Samsudeen
Founded: 1984
Specialize in children's books; also act as packager.
ISBN Prefix(es): 983-9072; 983-9556; 983-9387
Imprints: Fairy Tales; Lamina Series; Little Board Books; See & Read Series; Well Loved Tales
Warehouse: Binova No B5-3, No 1, Jalan 2/57B (Segambut), 51200 Kuala Lumpur

Pustaka Melayu Baru
One Bangunan Wisma Yakin, Jalan Melayu, 50100 Kuala Lumpur
Tel: (03) 2985281 *Fax:* (03) 2414457
ISBN Prefix(es): 967-9931

Minerva Publications
96 Jalan Dato' Bandar, Tunggal, 70000 Seremban, Negeri Sembilan
Tel: (06) 734439 *Fax:* (06) 734439
Key Personnel
Man Dir: Haji Tajuddin MS
Founded: 1964
Subjects: Business, Career Development, English as a Second Language, Religion - Islamic, Self-Help
ISBN Prefix(es): 983-68
Parent Company: News & Periodicals Store, 96 Jalan Dato Bandar Tunggal, Negeri Sembilan Darul Khusus
Divisions:

MLJ, *imprint of* Malayan Law Journal Sdn Bhd

Oscar Book International+
37A Jl 20-16, Paramount Garden, 46300 Petaling Jaya, Selangor Darul Ehsan
Tel: (03) 78753515; (03) 78762797 *Fax:* (03) 78762797

Key Personnel
Proprietor: Windfred Chee Moon Hock
Founded: 1980
Specialize in English & Malay.
Subjects: Language Arts, Linguistics
ISBN Prefix(es): 967-941
Total Titles: 120 Print

Pan Malayan Publishing Co Sdn Bhd
72C, Jalan Sungai Besi, 57100 Kuala Lumpur
Tel: (603) 92218377 *Fax:* (603) 92214333
ISBN Prefix(es): 967-922

Panther Publishing
130-1 Jalan Thamby Abdullah, 50470 Kuala Lumpur
Tel: (03) 2749854
Key Personnel
Chief Executive, Publicity: R Vijesurier
Editorial, Production: Bella Mary Peters
Sales: Mary Rajam
Founded: 1972
Subjects: Travel
ISBN Prefix(es): 983-99627
Branch Office(s)
Block 151, No 650-K, Lorong 4, Toa Payoh, Singapore 1231, Singapore

Parry's Press
60 Jalan Negara, Taman Melawati, 58100 Kuala Lumpur
Tel: (03) 4079179 *Fax:* (03) 4079180
E-mail: haja@pop.3.jaring.my
Telex: Parry's MA 33243 *Cable:* PABOKCENT
ISBN Prefix(es): 983-9342
Subsidiaries: Parry's Book Center Pte Ltd (Singapore)
Orders to: 528-A MacPherson Rd, Singapore 368217, Singapore

Pearson Education+
Lot 2, Jalan 215, Off Japan Templer, 46050 Petaling Jaya, Selangor Darul Ehsan
Tel: (03) 7782 0466 *Fax:* (03) 7781 8005
E-mail: name@pearsoned.com.my
Telex: 37600
Key Personnel
General Manager/Dir, School Pub: Wong Mei Mei
General Manager/HE: Edward Teoh Swee Ong
Publishing Manager: Poh Swee Hiang
Finance Dir: Mok Chek Khek
Founded: 1961
Subjects: Literature, Literary Criticism, Essays, Mathematics, Physics, Science (General)
ISBN Prefix(es): 967-976
Number of titles published annually: 300 Print
Total Titles: 2,000 Print
Parent Company: Pearson Education
Holding Company: Addison Wesley

Pelanduk Publications, *imprint of* Pelanduk Publications (M) Sdn Bhd

Pelanduk Publications (M) Sdn Bhd+
24 Jalan 2 20/16A, 46300 Petaling Jaya, Selangor Darul Ehsan
Tel: (03) 7761414; (03) 7761613
E-mail: pelpub@tm.net.my
Web Site: www.pelanduk.com
Key Personnel
Man Dir, Production: Ng Tieh Chuan
Editorial: Chong Meow Lian
Sales & Publicity: Jackson Tan
Editorial: Woo Kum Wah
Contact: Ms M H Chong
Founded: 1984
Subjects: Biography, Business, Economics, Language Arts, Linguistics, Management, Religion - Islamic, Social Sciences, Sociology

MALAYSIA

ISBN Prefix(es): 967-978
Imprints: Pelanduk Publications
Distributed by China Books; IBS Buku Sdn Bhd; Peace Book Co. Ltd.; Recreaids Pte Ltd; National Book Store; Weatherhill Inc

Pelangi Publishing Pte Ltd, see Penerbitan Pelangi Sdn Bhd (Pelangi Publishing Pte Ltd)

Penerbit Fajar Bakti Sdn Bhd+
4 Jalan U1/15, Seksyen U1, Hicom Glenmarie Industrial Park, 40000 Shah Alam, Selangor
Tel: (03) 7047011 *Fax:* (03) 7047010
Key Personnel
Man Dir: M Sockalingam
Founded: 1969
ISBN Prefix(es): 967-65; 967-933
Parent Company: Oxford University Press, United Kingdom
Subsidiaries: South-East Asian Publishing Unit

Penerbit Jayatinta Sdn Bhd+
No 18 Jalan 51A/223, 46100 Petaling Jaya, Selangor Darul Ehsan
Tel: (03) 7764036
Telex: MA20382 AB Delta
Key Personnel
Man Dir: Mr Lim Swee Sing; Mr Lim Kim Wah
Executive Dir: Ms Lee Yuet Yee
Group General Manager: Mr Phang Sang Choy; Mr Phang Sang Moi
Founded: 1988
Subjects: Economics, English as a Second Language, Environmental Studies, Geography, Geology, History, Philosophy, Religion - Islamic, Science (General)
ISBN Prefix(es): 983-883
Parent Company: Group of Delta Publishing
Subsidiaries: Pustaka Delta Pelajaran Sdn Bhd; Baron Production Sdn Bhd; Delta Distributors Sdn Bhd; Gunung Mutiara Sdn Bhd; Tempo Publishing (M) Sdn Bhd; Gedung Ilmu Sdn Bhd; Delta Publishing Sdn Bhd; Delta Editions Sdn Bh
Branch Office(s)
No 174 Jalan Pasar, 41400 Kelang, Selangor Darul Ehsan (Factory)

Penerbit Prisma Sdn Bhd+
129A Jalan SS 25/2 Taman Mewah, Petaling Jaya, 47301 Selangor Darul Ehsan, Petaling Jaya
Tel: (03) 7034393 *Fax:* (03) 7039367
Key Personnel
Man Dir: Wong Peng Khuen
Founded: 1986
ISBN Prefix(es): 983-9665; 983-99556; 983-823; 983-877

Penerbit Universiti Sains Malaysia+
d/a Perpustakaan Universiti Sains Malaysia, Minden, 11800 Pulau Pinang
Tel: (04) 6577888 *Fax:* (04) 6571526
E-mail: penerbitusm@notes.usm.my or rashidah@usm.my
Web Site: www.lib.usm.my:8080/katalog2000.nsf/tajukl
Telex: MA40254 *Cable:* UNISAINS
Key Personnel
Chairman: Prof Jamjan Rajikan
Secretary: Ms Rashidah Begum
Chief Editor: Mr Akhiar Salleh
Founded: 1974
Subjects: Biological Sciences, Chemistry, Chemical Engineering, Computer Science, Education, Electronics, Electrical Engineering, Management, Mathematics, Social Sciences, Sociology
Bookshop(s): Co-operative Bookshop Ltd, Universiti Sains Malaysia, d/a Perpustakaan Universiti Sains Malaysia, 11800 Pulau Pinang

Penerbitan Jaya Bakti+
No 28 & 30 Wisma Jaya Bakti, Jalan Cenderuh 2, Baut 4, Jalan Ipoh, 51200 Kuala Lumpur
Tel: (03) 6219399 *Fax:* (03) 6219585
Key Personnel
Man Dir: Silvaraju A L Kunjupillai
Founded: 1980
Member of Malaysian Book Publishers Association.
ISBN Prefix(es): 967-900
Showroom(s): 30, Wisma Jaya Bakti, Jalan Cenderuh 2, Batu 4, Jalan Ipoh, 51200 Kuala Lumpur

Penerbitan Pelangi Sdn Bhd (Pelangi Publishing Pte Ltd)+
64-66 Jalan Pingai, Taman Pelangi, 80400 Johor Bharu, Johor
Tel: (07) 3316288; (07) 3327938; (07) 3326805 *Fax:* (07) 3329201
Key Personnel
Man Dir: Lai Chin Heng
ISBN Prefix(es): 967-951; 983-50; 983-878

Penerbitan Tinta+
32-B, Jalan Cemur, Off Jalan Tun Razak, 50400 Kuala Lumpur
Tel: (03) 4424163 *Fax:* (03) 4424640
Key Personnel
Dir: Mohd Haneefa
Founded: 1974
Subjects: Business, Education, English as a Second Language, Management, Marketing
ISBN Prefix(es): 983-9588
Associate Companies: Fargoes Books Sdn Bhd
Subsidiaries: Penerbitan Fargoes Sdn Bhd

Institut Penyelidikan Minyak Kelapa Sawit Malaysia
PO Box 10620, 50720 Kuala Lumpur
Tel: (03) 8335155 *Fax:* (03) 8259446
E-mail: pub@porim.gov.my
ISBN Prefix(es): 967-961

Perfect Frontier Sdn Bhd
B201, Block B, No 11, Jalan Sepadu, Taman United, Off Jalan Klang Lama, 58200 Kuala Lumpur
Tel: (03) 7832926 *Fax:* (03) 7816448
ISBN Prefix(es): 983-865

Preston Corporation Sdn Bhd
18 Jalan 19/3, 46300 Petaling Jaya, Selangor Darul Ehsan
Tel: (03) 7563734 *Fax:* (03) 7573607
Telex: Prest MA 37433
Subjects: Education
ISBN Prefix(es): 967-917
Associate Companies: Times Educational Co Sdn Bhd; Vista Productions Ltd, A7/F Melbourne Industrial Bldg, 16 Westlands Rd, Quarry Bay, Hong Kong; Preston Corporation (Pte) Ltd, 9 Irving Place, Singapore 1336, Singapore

Professional Publications
97D, 4th floor, Jalan Tun H S Lee, 50000 Kuala Lumpur
Tel: (03) 2325376 *Fax:* (03) 2011928
Key Personnel
Editor: Vivien Khoo
Manager: Ah Tu Yeoh
Founded: 1985
Member of Malaysian Book Publishers Association.
Subjects: Accounting
ISBN Prefix(es): 967-9924
Associate Companies: Systematic Book Centre
Orders to: Systematic Book Center, 970, Jalan Tun H S Lee, 4th floor, 50000 Kuala Lumpur

BOOK

Pustaka Cipta Sdn Bhd+
58 C Jalan Kampung Attap, 50460 Kuala Lumpur
Tel: (03) 2744593 *Fax:* (03) 2749588
E-mail: rrapc@pc.jaring.my
Key Personnel
President: Baharuddin Zainal
Publication Dir: Rosihan Juara Baharuddin
Founded: 1985
Member of IKATAN, Malaysian Burriputra Publishers Association.
Subjects: Art, Biography, Communications, Computer Science, Education, English as a Second Language, Fiction, Journalism, Literature, Literary Criticism, Essays, Nonfiction (General), Poetry, Publishing & Book Trade Reference, Religion - Islamic, Science (General), Science Fiction, Fantasy, Technology, Travel, Women's Studies
ISBN Prefix(es): 967-9974; 967-99962; 983-101
Associate Companies: Essential Mark (M) Sdn Bhd; Puncak Indah Sdn Bhd
Subsidiaries: Dasar Buku Sdn Bhd; Dasar Cetak Sdn Bhd; Dasar Padu Sdn Bhd

Pustaka Delta Pelajaran Sdn Bhd+
Lot 18 Jalan 51A/223, Jalan Sultan, 46770 Petaling Jaya, Selangor Darul Ehsan
Mailing Address: PO Box 621
Tel: (03) 7570000 *Fax:* (03) 7576688
Telex: MA20382 AB Delta
Key Personnel
Man Dir: Mr Lim Swee Sing; Mr Lim Kim Wah
Executive Dir: Ms Lee Yuet Yee
Group General Manager: Mr Phang Sang Choy; Mr Phang Sang Moi
Founded: 1979
Subjects: Economics, English as a Second Language, Environmental Studies, Geography, Geology, History, Mathematics, Religion - Islamic, Science (General)
ISBN Prefix(es): 967-67
Parent Company: Group of Delta Publishing
Subsidiaries: Baron Production Sdn Bhd; Delta Distributors Sdn Bhd; Gunung Mutiara Sdn Bhd; Tempo Publishing (M) Sdn Bhd; Gedung Ilum Sdn Bhd; Delta Publishing Sdn Bhd; Delta Editions Sdn Bhd; Penerbit Jayatinta Sdn Bhd
Branch Office(s)
No 174 Jalan Pasar, 41400 Kelang, Selangor Darul Ehsan

Pustaka Sistem Pelajaran Sdn Bhd+
Lot 17.22-17.23 Jalan Satu, Bersatu Industrial Park, Cheras Jaya, 43200 Balakong, Selangor
Tel: (03) 9047558; (03) 9047017; (03) 9047018 *Fax:* (603) 9047573
Key Personnel
Man Dir: Michael Ong
Founded: 1973
ISBN Prefix(es): 967-902
Subsidiaries: Pustaka Yakin Pelajar Sdn Bhd; B H S Book Printing Sdn Bhd
Bookshop(s): The Bintang Store, 251 Jl Tun Sambanthan, 50470 Kuala Lumpur

See & Read Series, *imprint of* Mecron Sdn Bhd

Syarikat Cultural Supplies Sdn Bhd+
306 Block C Glomac Business Centre, 10 Jalan 217, Petalina, Jaya, 47301 Selangor Darul Ehsan
Tel: (03) 7046628; (03) 7554103; (03) 7915728 *Fax:* (03) 7046629
E-mail: malian@po.jaring.my
Key Personnel
Dir: Kow Ching Chuan
Founded: 1977
Subjects: Education
ISBN Prefix(es): 967-9917

454

Tempo Publishing (M) Sdn Bhd+
Bilik 118, Wisma Delta 18, Jalan 51A/223, Jalan 51A/223, 46100 Petaling Jaya, Selangor Darul Ehsan
Tel: (03) 7570000 *Fax:* (03) 7576688; (03) 7587001
Telex: MA20382 AB Delta
Key Personnel
Man Dir: Mr Lim Swee Sing; Mr Lim Kim Wah
Executive Dir: Ms Lee Yuet Yee
Group General Manager: Mr Phang Sang Choy; Mr Phang Sang Moi
Founded: 1990
Subjects: Fiction, Literature, Literary Criticism, Essays, Nonfiction (General)
ISBN Prefix(es): 983-888
Parent Company: Group of Delta Publishing
Subsidiaries: Pustaka Delta Pelajaran Sdn Bhd; Baron Production Sdn Bhd; Delta Distributors Sdn Bhd; Gunung Mutiara Sdn Bhd; Penerbit Jayatinta Sdn Bhd; Gedung Ilmu Sdn Bhd; Delta Publishing Sdn Bhd; Delta Editions Sdn Bhd
Branch Office(s)
No 174 Jalan Pasar, 41400 Kelang, Selangor Darul Ehsan

Text Books Malaysia Sdn Bhd
39 Jalan Buluh Kesap, 85007 Segamat, Johore Darul Ta'zim
Mailing Address: PO Box 30, 85007 Segamat, Johore
Tel: (074) 911181 *Fax:* (074) 911181
Founded: 1969
ISBN Prefix(es): 967-9929
Bookshop(s): Tai Kuang & Co, 41 Jalan Awang, 85000 Segamat, Johor D Ta'Zim

Time Track (M) Sdn Bhd
69, Medan Gopeng 5, Jalan Lapangan Terbang, 31350 Ipoh, Perak
Mailing Address: Lot 1.102, Ground floor, Wisma Central Jalan Ampang, 50450 Kuala Lumpur
Tel: (05) 3124329; (05) 3127541 *Fax:* (05) 2630305
ISBN Prefix(es): 983-069

Times, *imprint of* Federal Publications Sdn Bhd

Times Educational Co Sdn Bhd
22 Jalan 19/3, Petaling Jaya, Selangor Daral Ehsan, 46300 Selangor
Tel: (03) 7571766 *Fax:* (03) 7573607
Telex: MA 37433 *Cable:* Timesbooks
Subjects: Cookery
ISBN Prefix(es): 967-919
Parent Company: Times Educational Co Ltd, Hong Kong
Associate Companies: Preston Corporation Sdn Bhd; Preston-Times Printing & Publishing, Selangor; Preston Corporation (Private) Ltd, Singapore
Orders to: Preston Corporation Sdn Bhd, 18 Jalan 19/3, Petaling Jaya, Selangor

Trix Corporation Sdn Bhd+
Room 2, Level 6, Block G Central, Pusat Bandor, Damansara Heights, 50490 Kuala Lumpur 50490
Tel: (03) 2532019 *Fax:* (03) 2551068
Key Personnel
Man Dir: Mr B S Neoh
Subjects: Career Development, Education, Securities
ISBN Prefix(es): 983-9102

Tropical Press Sdn Bhd+
56-1 Jalan Maarof, Bangsar Baru, 59100 Kuala Lumpur
Tel: (03) 22825138; (03) 22825338 *Fax:* (03) 22823526
E-mail: feedback@tpress.po.my
Key Personnel
Man Dir: Winston Ee
Founded: 1975
Member of the Malaysian Book Publishers Association.
Subjects: Child Care & Development, Mathematics, Natural History, Physical Sciences, Science (General), Technology
ISBN Prefix(es): 967-73
Associate Companies: Art Printing Works Sdn Bhd

Uni-Text Book Co
42B Jl SS 20/10, Damansara Kim, 47400 Petaling Jaya, Selangor Darul Ehsan
Tel: (03) 7185426
Key Personnel
Man Dir: Bob E S Lim
Editorial: E S Lim
Production: E H Lim
Sales: Theresa Chung
Subjects: Education, History, Literature, Literary Criticism, Essays, Regional Interests, Religion - Other
ISBN Prefix(es): 967-935
Associate Companies: Uni-Text Distributors Private Ltd, 42B Jl SS 20/10, Damansara Kim, 47400 Petaling Jaya, Sellangor Darul Ehsan

Unit Penerbitan Akademik Cancelori~ Universiti Teknologi Malaysia+
Karung Berkunci 791, 80900 Johor Bahru
Tel: (07) 576160; (07) 576161; (07) 576162 *Fax:* (07) 5566157
Telex: MA60205
Key Personnel
Contact: Dr Yusof Yaacob
Subjects: Chemistry, Chemical Engineering, Civil Engineering, Computer Science, Education, Electronics, Electrical Engineering, Mathematics, Mechanical Engineering, Science (General)
ISBN Prefix(es): 983-9585; 983-52

University of Malaya, Department of Publications+
Lembah Pantai, 59100 Kuala Lumpur
Tel: (03) 79574361 *Fax:* (03) 79574473
Telex: MA 39845 *Cable:* VARSITIPRESS KUALA LUMPUR
Key Personnel
Head of Dept, Publicity, Rights & Permissions, Editorial: Dr Hamedi Mohd Adnan
E-mail: hamedi@um.edu.my
Founded: 1954
Subjects: Biography, Economics, Fiction, Foreign Countries, Government, Political Science, History, Medicine, Nursing, Dentistry, Poetry, Science (General), Social Sciences, Sociology
ISBN Prefix(es): 967-9940; 983-9705; 983-100

Utusan Publications and Distributors Sdn Bhd+
18 Jalan 6/91, Shamelin Perkasa, 56100 Kuala Lumpur
Tel: (03) 9856577; (03) 9852645
Key Personnel
General Manager: Othman Karim
ISBN Prefix(es): 967-61

Vinpress Sdn Bhd+
5 & 7 Lorong Datuk Sulaiman 7, Taman Tun Dr Ismail, 60000 Kuala Lumpur
Tel: (03) 7173333; (03) 7188877 *Fax:* (03) 7192942
Key Personnel
Man Dir: Thomas Soh
Founded: 1985
Member of Malaysian Book Publishers Association.
Subjects: Ethnicity, Health, Nutrition, Philosophy, Regional Interests, Religion - Other
ISBN Prefix(es): 967-81
Associate Companies: Vintrade SDN BHD

Well Loved Tales, *imprint of* Mecron Sdn Bhd

Maldive Islands

General Information

Capital: Male
Language: Dhivehi (Maldivian)
Religion: Islam is the state religion (most Sunni Muslim)
Population: 226,000
Currency: 100 laari (larees) = 1 rufiyaa (maldivian rupee)

Non-Formal Education Centre
Salahuddeen Bldg, Male 20-03
Tel: 328772; 324622
Key Personnel
Deputy Dir: Abdul Raheem Hasan
Founded: 1986
Subjects: Agriculture, Child Care & Development, Education, English as a Second Language, Environmental Studies, Health, Nutrition, Religion - Islamic, Science (General), Social Sciences, Sociology, Sports, Athletics
ISBN Prefix(es): 99915-50; 99915-58
Parent Company: Ministry of Education

Novelty Printers & Publishers+
Issuddeen Magu, Male, Dhilbahaaru Higun Male 2001
Tel: 322474; 318844 *Fax:* 322490
E-mail: novelty@dhivehinet.net.mv
Telex: 66045 NOVELTY MF
Key Personnel
Dir: Ali Hussain
General Manager: Asad Ali
Founded: 1965
Subjects: Animals, Pets, Foreign Countries, Regional Interests, Travel
ISBN Prefix(es): 99915-3
Subsidiaries: Novelty Bookshop

Mali

General Information

Capital: Bamako
Language: French
Religion: Predominantly Islamic
Population: 10 million
Currency: 100 centimes = 1 CFA franc
Export/Import Information: Member of the West African Economic Community. No tariff on books but subject to VAT at varying rates. Advertising matter (more than single copy) subject to tariff, import tax and VAT. All goods subject to local tax of percentage of customs value. Import license required. Importation is either by private importers or state enterprises. Exchange controls for non-franc zone.
Copyright: Berne (see Copyright Conventions, pg xi)

EDIM SA+
642 av Mardiagne, BP 2412, Bamako
Tel: 225522 *Fax:* 238503
Key Personnel
Man Dir: Aliou Tomota

MALI

Editor: Hr E Alain Kone
Founded: 1972
Subjects: Biography, Fiction, History, Nonfiction (General), Poetry, Religion - Other, Social Sciences, Sociology
ISBN Prefix(es): 2-913213
Subsidiaries: Editions populaires; Imprimerie Kasse Keita; Imprimerie nationale
Bookshop(s): Librairie Papeterie du Sondan, BP 21, Bamako

Malta

General Information

Capital: Valletta
Language: Maltese and English (official), Italian widely spoken
Religion: Predominantly Roman Catholic
Population: 365,000
Bank Hours: 0830-1230 Monday-Thursday; 0830-1230, 1700-1900 Friday; 0830-1200 Saturday
Shop Hours: 0900-1300, 1530-1900 Monday-Saturday
Currency: 1,000 mils = 100 cents = 1 Maltese lira
Export/Import Information: No tariff on books or advertising. No import license required. Exchange control by Central Bank. Trade Association agreement with the European Economic Community all Malta made goods that enter the European Economic Community are duty and quota free. Different rates of duty apply for imports with special preference for European Economic Community countries.
Copyright: Berne, UCC (see Copyright Conventions, pg xi)

Fondazzjoni Patrimonju Malti+
Formerly Patrimonju Publishing Ltd
115 Triq it-Teatru l-Qadim, Valletta VLT 09
Tel: 21 231515 *Fax:* 21 250118
E-mail: patrimonju@keyworld.net
Web Site: www.patrimonju.org.mt
Key Personnel
Administration Executive: Peter Calascione
Tel: 21 244777
Founded: 1996
Specialize in catalogues raisonne, collections of essays, art quality of Maltese history & cultural heritage subjects (known collectively as "Melitensia").
Subjects: Antiques, Archaeology, Art, Biography
Total Titles: 12 Print

Gaulitana
2, Triq Gedrin, Rabat, Gozo VCT 104
Tel: 554212 *Fax:* 554598
E-mail: joseph.bezzina@magnet.mt
Founded: 1985
Subjects: History, Religion - Catholic, Travel
ISBN Prefix(es): 99909-57
Number of titles published annually: 6 Print

Gozo Press
Mgarr Rd, Gh'sielem, Gh'sielem, Gozo GSM102
Mailing Address: Str 1 Main Gate St, 1st floor, Str 2 Victoria, Gozo VCT 103
Tel: 551534; 564395 *Fax:* 560857
E-mail: gozopress@orbit.net.mt
Key Personnel
Dir: Achilles F Cauchi
Manager: Carmel Mizzi
Member of The Periodical & Book Publishers Association.

Subjects: Crafts, Games, Hobbies, History, Literature, Literary Criticism, Essays, Religion - Other
Orders to: Gozo Press Office, Main Gate St, Victoria, Gozo

Media Centre+
Media Centre Complex, National Rd, Blata l-Bajda HMR 02
Tel: 249005; 223047; 247460; 224018; 220538; 244913 *Fax:* 243508
Key Personnel
President: Joseph Borg *E-mail:* joseborg@keyworld.net
Assistant Manager Administration: Ms Sylvana Magro
Founded: 1981
Subjects: Biblical Studies, Communications, Education, Religion - Catholic, Social Sciences, Sociology
ISBN Prefix(es): 99909-2
Book Club(s): Klaab Qari Nisrani (Maltese Language Publications)

Merlin Library Ltd
Publications Division, Mountbatten St, Blata l-Bajda HMR 08
Tel: 221205; 234438 *Fax:* 221135
Key Personnel
Dir: Arthur J Gruppetta
Founded: 1964
ISBN Prefix(es): 99909-1

Patrimonju Publishing Ltd, see Fondazzjoni Patrimonju Malti

PEG Ltd, see Publishers' Enterprises Group (PEG) Ltd

Progress Press Co Ltd+
Strickland House, 341 St Paul St, Valletta VLT 01
Tel: 241464; 241469; 241411; 241412 *Fax:* 241171
Telex: Mw 341 *Cable:* PROGRESS
Key Personnel
Man Dir: W B Asciak
Publication Manager: Joseph Tortell
 E-mail: jtortell@timesofmalta.com
Founded: 1957
Subjects: Literature, Literary Criticism, Essays
ISBN Prefix(es): 99909-3
Total Titles: 52 Print
Parent Company: The Allied Newspapers Ltd, 341 St Paul St, Valletta VLT07, Ronald Agius
Bookshop(s): 4 Castille Place, Valletta VLT 01

Publishers' Enterprises Group (PEG) Ltd
PEG Bldg, UB7 Industrial Estate, San Gwann SGN09
Tel: 440083; 448539 *Fax:* 488908
E-mail: pegltd@global.net.mt
Key Personnel
Man Dir, Editorial, Rights & Permissions: Emanuel Debattista
Sales: Victor Mifsud
Production, Publicity: Gaetan Cilia
Founded: 1983
Subjects: Cookery, Crafts, Games, Hobbies, Education, Outdoor Recreation, Travel
ISBN Prefix(es): 99909-0

The University of Malta Publications Section
The University of Malta, Administration Bldg, Msida MSD06
Tel: 343572 *Fax:* 344879
Telex: Mw 407 Hieduc *Cable:* University Malta
Founded: 1953
Subjects: Ethnicity, Language Arts, Linguistics, Law, Natural History, Regional Interests

Martinique

General Information

Capital: Fort-de-France
Language: French and Creole
Religion: Predominantly Roman Catholic
Population: 359,579
Currency: 100 centimes = 1 French franc
Export/Import Information: Tariff same as France. Overseas tax and reduced VAT on books. Small quantity of advertising free. No import licenses required. Exchange restrictions as in France.
Copyright: Berne (see Copyright Conventions, pg xi)

Editions Gondwana+
Morne Pavillon, 97220 Trinite
Tel: 583676 *Fax:* 580014
Key Personnel
Contact: Eric Leroy
Founded: 1987
Subjects: Agriculture, Archaeology, Gardening, Plants
ISBN Prefix(es): 2-908490
Distributed by Distique (France Metropolitan & Europe)

George Lise-Huyghes des Etages
108 rue de la Republique, 97200 Fort-de-France
Tel: 736819
Subjects: Behavioral Sciences, Education, Human Relations, Psychology, Psychiatry
ISBN Prefix(es): 2-909260

Virlogeux Francoise-COMEDIT
Rue de la Reine-Hortense, 97229 Les Trois Ilets
Tel: 683985 *Fax:* 683423
Founded: 1994
ISBN Prefix(es): 2-910746

Mauritania

General Information

Capital: Nouakchott
Language: Arabic (official and national), Poular, Wolof and Solinke (national)
Religion: Islamic
Population: 2.1 million
Bank Hours: 0800-1115, 1430-1630 Monday-Friday
Shop Hours: Vary. Generally 0800-1200, 0730-1500 Saturday-Thursday. Some closed Monday morning, some open Sunday morning
Currency: 5 khoums = 1 ouguiya
Export/Import Information: Member of the West African Economic Community. No tariff on books. Advertising matter (other than single copies) subject to fiscal, customs duty and added tax. Import licenses and exchange controls apply to imports outside of EEC and franc zone.
Copyright: Berne (see Copyright Conventions, pg xi)

Imprimerie Commerciale et Administrative de Mauritanie
BP 164, Nouakchott
Subjects: Education

Mauritius

General Information

Capital: Port Louis
Language: English (official) and Creole
Religion: Hindu, Christian and Muslim
Population: 1.1 million
Bank Hours: 1000-1400 Monday-Friday, 0930-1130 Saturday
Shop Hours: 0800-1600 or later Monday-Saturday
Currency: 100 cents = 1 Mauritian rupee
Export/Import Information: No tariff on books and advertising but there is a special levy. No import license required.
Copyright: UCC, Berne (see Copyright Conventions, pg xi)

African Cultural Centre
Bell Village, Port Louis
Tel: 2124131 *Fax:* 2088620
Founded: 1985
ISBN Prefix(es): 99903-904

Mauritus Bhojpuri Institute
15 Menagerie Rd, Cassis, Port Louis
Tel: 2082956 *Fax:* 4643445
Distributed by ELP; EOI; Mauritius; Mauritius Reading Association; Port Louis; Rose Hill; Vacoas

De l'edition Bukie Banane
8 Edwin Ythier St, Rose Hill
Tel: 4542327
Key Personnel
Man Dir: Dev Virahsawmy
Founded: 1979
Subjects: Drama, Theater, Poetry, Regional Interests
Orders to: Librairie le Cygne, Royal Rd, Rose Hill

Editions Capucines
20 Ave des Capucines, Quatre Bornes
Tel: 4641563 *Fax:* 4641563
E-mail: edcapsee@intnet.mu
Key Personnel
Manager: S Seewoochurn *Tel:* 464 1563
Founded: 1994
Subjects: Asian Studies, Education, History, Religion - Hindu, Religion - Other
Number of titles published annually: 5 Print
Total Titles: 8 Print
Distributed by Editions de l'Ocean Indien; Editions Le Printemps
Distributor for Editions de l'Ocean Indren (Mauritius)

EOI Ltd, see Editions de l'Ocean Indien Ltd

Golden Publications
4 Cite Pere Laval St, Port Louis
Tel: 2416640
ISBN Prefix(es): 99903-44

Government Printer (Imprimerie Nationale)
La Tour Koenig, Pointe aux Sables
Tel: 2345284

Hemco Publications
7 Virgil Naz St, Rose Hill
Tel: 4643141
Key Personnel
Editor: Dr H Gyaram
Founded: 1993
Subjects: Education, Medicine, Nursing, Dentistry, Religion - Buddhist, Religion - Catholic, Religion - Hindu, Religion - Islamic, Religion - Other

Imprimerie et Papeterie Commerciale, IPC
23 Menagerie Rd, Cassis
Tel: 2124190 *Fax:* 2083523
ISBN Prefix(es): 99903-38

Editions de l'Ocean Indien Ltd+
Stanley, Rose Hill
Tel: 4646761 *Fax:* 4643445
E-mail: eoibooks@intnet.me
Key Personnel
Gen Mgr: A Beeharry Panray
Founded: 1977
Subjects: Accounting, Agriculture, Art, Biography, Business, Career Development, Computer Science, Cookery, Economics, Education, Fiction, Geography, Geology, Health, Nutrition, Literature, Literary Criticism, Essays, Management, Marketing, Philosophy, Poetry, Science (General), Travel
ISBN Prefix(es): 2-7410
Number of titles published annually: 89 Print
Total Titles: 365 Print
Subsidiaries: Mauritius Printing Specialists Ltd
Branch Office(s)
Gound floor, Manhattan, Curepipe *Tel:* 6749065
Vel Plaza, Royal Rd, Goodlands *Tel:* 2838729
1st floor, NPF Bldg, Jules Koeing St, Port-Louis *Tel:* 2111310
30, Joseph Riviere St, Kung Hing Mall Bldg, Port-Louis *Tel:* 2423738
Student Complex, University of Mauritius, Reduit *Tel:* 4542258
Arcades Rond Point, Rose-Hill *Tel:* 4646391
Virginie Commercial Centre, Centre de Flacq *Tel:* 4132273
Distributed by Librarie L' Harmattan; African Books Collective Ltd
Distributor for Librarie L' Harmattan

EDITIONS Le Printemps+
4 Club Rd, Vacoas
Tel: 6961017 *Fax:* 6867302
E-mail: elp@bow.intnet.mu
Key Personnel
Man Dir: Ahmud Islam Sulliman
Subjects: Biography
ISBN Prefix(es): 99903-23
Subsidiaries: AIS Marketing
Divisions: Editions Le Printemps Ltd

Vizavi Editions+
29 Saint Georges St, Port Louis
Tel: 2080983 *Fax:* 2113047
E-mail: vizavi@intnet.mu
Key Personnel
Dir: Mrs P M Siew
Founded: 1993
Member of Association of Maurintian Publishers.
Subjects: Biography, Cookery, Government, Political Science, History, Literature, Literary Criticism, Essays, Nonfiction (General)
ISBN Prefix(es): 99908-37
Number of titles published annually: 3 Print

Mexico

General Information

Capital: Mexico City
Language: Spanish
Religion: Predominantly Roman Catholic
Population: 92.4 million
Bank Hours: 0900-1330 Monday-Friday
Shop Hours: 1000-1900 Monday, Tuesday, Thursday, Friday; 1100-2000 Wednesday and Saturday
Currency: 100 centavos = 1 Mexican peso
Export/Import Information: Member of the Latin American Free Trade Association. Foreign language books and textbooks generally dutied per kg legal weight, children's picture books ad valorem or per kg, whichever greater, and require import license. Three copies of non-Spanish advertising catalogs free but all others require license and dutied ad valorem. Customs request from Bank of Mexico all necessary information to decide cases of tariff.
Copyright: UCC, Berne, Buenos Aires (see Copyright Conventions, pg xi)

Aconcagua Ediciones y Publicaciones SA
Xochicalco 352, Col Narvarte, 03020 Mexico DF
Tel: (05) 5361292
Key Personnel
Dir: Julio Sanz Crespo
Subjects: Education, History, How-to, Literature, Literary Criticism, Essays, Religion - Other, Technology
ISBN Prefix(es): 968-6000
Associate Companies: Editorial Timun Mas SA, Spain
Branch Office(s)
Ediciones Ceac SA, Spain

Addison Wesley, *imprint of* Pearson Educacion de Mexico, SA de CV

Adivinar y Multiplicar, SA de CV
Av Cuauhtemoc 1129-406, Col Letran-Valle, 03650 Mexico, DF
Mailing Address: APDO Post 73-131, Mexico, DF 03311
Tel: (05) 604-4511 *Fax:* (05) 604-1583
E-mail: multipli@compuserve.com.mx
Key Personnel
Contact: Jesus E Rodriguez y Rodriguez
Founded: 1985
Subjects: Education, Mathematics
ISBN Prefix(es): 968-7458

Editorial AGATA SA de CV+
Pino Suares No 169, Colcentro Hidalgo, 44100 Guadalajara Jal
Tel: (03) 6584392 *Fax:* (03) 6138429
Key Personnel
Editor: Jaime Alvarez G Alvarez del Castillo
Founded: 1986
Member of National Commerce Association, National Art Graphics Association, Publishers Association.
Subjects: Drama, Theater, Journalism, Literature, Literary Criticism, Essays, Poetry, Regional Interests, Travel
ISBN Prefix(es): 968-7310; 970-657

AGT Editor SA
Apdo 189448. Av Progreso 202 1er Piso, Col Escandon Deleg Miguel Hidalgo, 11800 Mexico DF
Tel: (05) 5164261 *Fax:* (05) 2771696
Key Personnel
Contact: Roger Grasa Soler
Founded: 1978
Member of the Mexican National Publishing Industry.
Subjects: Agriculture, Biological Sciences, Veterinary Science
ISBN Prefix(es): 968-463
Imprints: Rustica

Aguilar Altea Taurus Alfaguara SA de CV
Av Universidad 767, 03100 Mexico DF
Tel: (05) 6888277 *Fax:* (05) 6011067
Key Personnel
Dir: Miguel Angel Cayuela
ISBN Prefix(es): 968-19
Parent Company: Grupo Santillana

MEXICO

ALFA OMEGA Grupo Editor+
Tabasco 106, Col Roma, 06700 Mexico DF
Tel: (05) 5119203 *Fax:* (052) 2077158
E-mail: 74054.1612@compuserve.com
Key Personnel
Dir: J Jorge Giannetto
Dir de Edicione: Ferreyrs C Gonzalo
 E-mail: gferreyrs@spin.com.mx
Founded: 1965
Subjects: Computer Science, Electronics, Electrical Engineering, Engineering (General), Management, Microcomputers, Technology
ISBN Prefix(es): 968-6062; 968-6223
Associate Companies: Publicaciones Marcombo SA

Alianza Editorial Mexicana
San Lorenzo No 160, Collztapalapa, 09860 Mexico, DF
Tel: (05) 6704887; (05) 6704712
Key Personnel
Man Dir: Alberto E Diaz
ISBN Prefix(es): 968-6001; 968-6354; 968-6423
Associate Companies: Alianza Editorial SA, Spain

Allyn & Bacon, *imprint of* Pearson Educacion de Mexico, SA de CV

Ediciones Alpe+
Avenue Morales No 58-702, 06200 Mexico DF
Tel: (05) 5365749; (05) 2033157 *Fax:* (05) 2033157
Founded: 1991
Subjects: Cookery, Fiction, Health, Nutrition, Humor, Poetry, Radio, TV, Religion - Hindu, Romance, Self-Help
ISBN Prefix(es): 968-6426

Arbol Editorial SA de CV+
Ave Cuauhtemoc, No 1434, Col Santa Cruz Atoyac, 03310 Mexico, DF
Tel: (05) 6884828; (05) 6886458
Key Personnel
Man Dir, Production: Gerardo Gally
Rights & Permissions: Gilda Moreno
Founded: 1979
Subjects: Drama, Theater, Environmental Studies, Health, Nutrition, Religion - Other
ISBN Prefix(es): 968-461

Ariel, see Grupo Editorial Planeta

Editorial Armonia SA+
Magdelena No 135, Col Del Valle, 03100 Mexico DF
Tel: (05) 687266
Key Personnel
Contact: Liliana Moreno Gomez
Founded: 1977
Member of the Mexican Association of Publishers.
Subjects: Cookery, Fashion, Health, Nutrition, House & Home
ISBN Prefix(es): 968-6598

Artes de Mexico y del Mundo, SA de CV+
Plaza Rio de Janeiro 52, 06700 Mexico, DF
Tel: (05) 208 3217 *Fax:* (05) 525 5925
E-mail: artesmex@internet.com.mx;
 artesdemexico@artesdemexico.com
Web Site: www.artesdemexico.com
Key Personnel
Contact: Alberto Ruy Sanchez Lacy
Founded: 1953
Subjects: Architecture & Interior Design, Art, Poetry

Editores Asociados Mexicanos SA de CV (EDAMEX)+
Heriberto Frias No 1104, Col Del Valle, 03100 Mexico, DF
Tel: (05) 5598588 *Fax:* (05) 5757035
Key Personnel
Man Dir: Manuel G Colmenares
Executive President: Octavio V Colmenares
Sales: Irene Fohri
Production: Antonio Escamilla
Founded: 1963
Also acts as Literary Agent for authors.
Subjects: Economics, Government, Political Science, Humor, Literature, Literary Criticism, Essays, Social Sciences, Sociology
ISBN Prefix(es): 968-409; 970-661
Associate Companies: Colmenares Editores SA; Editorial Meridiano SA
Divisions: Noroeste
Bookshop(s): Centro Cultural Edamex, Mexico DF

Editorial Avante SA de Cv
Luis Gonzalez Obregon No 9, Col Centro, 06020 Mexico DF
Tel: (05) 5855400 *Fax:* (05) 5855298
Key Personnel
Man Dir: Mario Alberto Saenz Hinojosa
Production: Ana Luisa Quiros Esteban
Sales, Publicity: Luis Quiros Esteban
Founded: 1950
Subjects: Biography, Drama, Theater, Education, Language Arts, Linguistics, Poetry, Social Sciences, Sociology
ISBN Prefix(es): 968-6006
Imprints: Impresora Galve SA; Impresora Multiple SA; Heidel Impresos SA de CV

Azteca, *imprint of* Fondo de Cultura Economica

Editorial Azteca SA+
Calle de la Luna No 225, Col Guerrero, 06300 Mexico, DF
Tel: (05) 5261157 *Cable:* Edasa
Key Personnel
Man Dir: Alfonso Alemon Jalomo
Sales Dir: Juan Alemon Jalomo
Founded: 1956
Subjects: Literature, Literary Criticism, Essays, Science (General)
ISBN Prefix(es): 968-6008

Editorial Banca y Comercio SA de CV
Napoles No 8, Col Juarez, 06600 Mexico DF
Tel: (05) 5353587
Key Personnel
Man Dir: Carlos Prieto Sierra
Assistant Manager: Amparo Quintanar
Founded: 1934
Subjects: Business, Law, Mathematics
ISBN Prefix(es): 968-6010

Biblioteca Interamericana Bilingual, *imprint of* Ediciones Euroamericanas

Libreria y Ediciones Botas SA
Justo sierra 5Z, Mexico 1 DF
Mailing Address: Apdo 941, Mexico 1 DF
Tel: (05) 5223896 *Fax:* (02) 702 54 03
E-mail: botas@mail.nextgeninter.net.mx
Key Personnel
Man Dir: Andres Botas Herandez
Sales Dir: Laura Botas Herandez
Founded: 1910
Subjects: Art, Economics, Fiction, History, Law, Medicine, Nursing, Dentistry, Philosophy, Science (General)

Ediciones el Caballito SA
Isabel la Catolica 922, Col Postal, 03410 Mexico, DF
Tel: (05) 5903653; (05) 5963400
Key Personnel
Rights & Permissions & Man Dir, Editorial: Manuel Lopez Gallo
Sales: Alfonso Garcia Espino
Production & Rights & Permissions: Teresa Dey
Founded: 1967
Subjects: Economics, History, Nonfiction (General), Regional Interests, Social Sciences, Sociology
ISBN Prefix(es): 968-6125
Associate Companies: Impoli SA, Isabel la Catolica 922, Col Postal, 03140 Mexico, DF
Subsidiaries: Presencia Latinoamerica
Bookshop(s): Libreria del Soltano SA; Ave Juarez 64, Satano Centro, Mexico, DF 1

Camion Escolar y Limusa, *imprint of* Editorial Limusa SA de CV

Casa & Gente, *imprint of* Cuernavaca Editorial S A

Editorial la Cebra SA de CV
Av Revolucion 528-700, Col San Pedro de los Pinos, 03800 Mexico, DF
Tel: (05) 2779529 *Fax:* (05) 2737866
E-mail: 74173.1014@compuserve.com
Key Personnel
Contact: Andrzej Rattinger
Founded: 1992
Publishers of ADCEBRA, Mexico's Marketing and Advertising magazine.

CEMLA, see Centro de Estudios Monetarios Latinoamericanos (CEMLA)

CEMO SA, see Centro Editorial Mexicano Osiris SA

Centro de Estudios Mexicanos y Centroamericanos+
Sierra Leona No 330 Col Lomas de Chapultepec, 11000 Mexico DF
Tel: (05) 5405921; (05) 5405922 *Fax:* (05) 5405923
E-mail: cemca@data.net.mx
Web Site: www.casadefiancia.org.mx/cemca
Key Personnel
Dir: Martine Dauzier
Editor: Joelle Gaillac
Head of Publications: Catherine Marielle
Founded: 1982
Edition De Boccard (Europe).
Subjects: Anthropology, Archaeology, Biological Sciences, Earth Sciences, Economics, Environmental Studies, Ethnicity, Foreign Countries, Government, Political Science, History, Music, Dance, Science (General), Social Sciences, Sociology
ISBN Prefix(es): 968-6029
Subsidiaries: Ministere des Affaires Etrangeres
Distributed by INAH

Centro Editorial Mexicano Osiris SA
Sierra Ventana No 545, Col Lomas de Chapultepec, 11000 Mexico DF
Tel: (05) 5406902; (05) 2027185 *Fax:* (05) 2027185
Key Personnel
Contact: Thania Nicolopulos Joannides
Founded: 1976
Subjects: Astrology, Occult, Cookery, Literature, Literary Criticism, Essays, Parapsychology, Poetry

Editora Cientifica Medica Latinoamerican SA de CV
Pensylvania No 109, Col Napoles, 03810 Mexico DF
Tel: (05) 5206135; (05) 5405600 *Fax:* (05) 5367579; (05) 5403764

Subjects: Computer Science, Medicine, Nursing, Dentistry
ISBN Prefix(es): 968-6166

El Coleccionista, Centro Historico, *imprint of* Cuernavaca Editorial S A

El Colegio de Mexico AC
Camino al Ajusco No 20, Col Pedregal de Santa Teresa, 10740 Mexico DF
Tel: (05) 5686033 ext 388; (05) 5686033 ext 297 *Fax:* (05) 6526233
E-mail: biblio@colmex.mx
Telex: 1777585 Colme *Cable:* COLMEX
Key Personnel
Publications Coordinator: Marta Lilia Prieto
Founded: 1940
Subjects: Asian Studies, Economics, Environmental Studies, Government, Political Science, History, Language Arts, Linguistics, Library & Information Sciences, Literature, Literary Criticism, Essays, Social Sciences, Sociology, Women's Studies
ISBN Prefix(es): 968-12

Colegio de Postgraduados en Ciencias Agricolas
Carr Mexico-Texcoco Km 35.5 Montecillo, 56230 Chapingo Edo de Mexico
Tel: (0595) 5854555 (ext 5509) *Fax:* (0595) 10275
E-mail: difusion@colpos.colpos.mx
Key Personnel
Secretary: Dr Alfonso Larque Saavedra
Founded: 1959
Member of Mexican National Association of Publishers.
Subjects: Agriculture, Biological Sciences, Economics, Education, Mathematics, Science (General), Social Sciences, Sociology, Technology, Veterinary Science
ISBN Prefix(es): 968-839
Branch Office(s)
Campus Puebla-Puebla, Pue
Campus San Luis Potosi-Salinas De Hgo
De Manlio Flavio Altamirano, Ver
SLP, Campus Tabasco-H
Campus Cordoba-Cordoba, Ver
Cardenas Tabasco, Campus Veracruz-Xalapa, Predito Tempetates, MPIO
Bookshop(s): LIC Enrique Moreno Sanchez, Carr, Mexico-Texcoco KM, 35.5 Montecillo, 56230 Chapingo Edo
Orders to: LIC Enrique Moreno

Comision Nacional Forestal
Av Mexico No 190, Col de Carmen, Coyoacan, 04100 Mexico DF
Tel: (05) 5349707; (05) 5247862
Subjects: Government, Political Science, History, Medicine, Nursing, Dentistry, Social Sciences, Sociology
ISBN Prefix(es): 968-6021

Compania Editorial Continental SA de CV+
Calzada de Tiapan 4620, Col Barrio del Nino Jesus, Mexico, DF 14000
Tel: (05) 5732300 ext 101 *Fax:* (05) 5618155
Key Personnel
President: Carlos Frigolet Lerma
Rights & Permissions: Demetrio Garmendia Guerrero
Production: Mario Munoz Rodriguez
Dir General de Editorial, Produccion y Ventas: Victorico Albores Santiago
Founded: 1954
Subjects: Engineering (General), Management, Mathematics, Science (General), Technology
ISBN Prefix(es): 968-26

Compania General de Ediciones SA de CV, see Selector SA de CV

Ediciones Contables y Administrativas SA
Heriberto Frias No 1451-1, Col Del Valle, 03100 Mexico, DF
Tel: (05) 6040140; (05) 6041998; (05) 6040260 *Fax:* (05) 6056730
Key Personnel
Man Dir: Pedro Gasca Rocha
Sales Dir: Gustavo Gasca Breton
Founded: 1967
Subjects: Accounting, Business
ISBN Prefix(es): 968-6014; 968-6317; 970-617
Branch Office(s)
Zaragoza 39-106, Guadalajara, Jalisco

Ediciones Corunda SA de CV+
Oaxaca No 1, Esq con Periferico Magdalena Contreras, 10700 Mexico, DF
Tel: (05) 5684741; (05) 5684751; (05) 5684640 *Fax:* (05) 6525211
Key Personnel
Contact: Silvia Molina
Founded: 1988
Subjects: Literature, Literary Criticism, Essays, Science Fiction, Fantasy
ISBN Prefix(es): 968-6044; 968-7444

Publicaciones Cruz O SA
Patriotismo No 875 - D, Colonia Mixcoac, 03910 Mexico DF
Tel: (05) 5637544; (05) 5930232 *Fax:* (05) 6806122
E-mail: pcosa@infosel.net.mx
Telex: 01776232
Key Personnel
General Dir: Oscar Rene Cruz
Founded: 1977
Cultural divulgation.
Member of National Association of Publishers.
Subjects: Biography, Economics, Law, Philosophy, Psychology, Psychiatry, Religion - Buddhist, Religion - Catholic, Religion - Jewish, Social Sciences, Sociology
ISBN Prefix(es): 968-20
Total Titles: 285 Print
Subsidiaries: Libreria Cruz O SA
Divisions: Publicaciones Cruz O SA de Guatemala CA

Cuernavaca Editorial S A+
Oxford No 23, Col Juarez, 06600 Mexico, DF
Tel: (05) 5113619; (05) 5142529; (05) 2867794 *Fax:* (05) 2117112
Telex: 1771422 PROME
Key Personnel
Editor: Nicolas H Sanchez-Osorio; Elia Cordova; Anne de Sanchez Osorio
Founded: 1985
Member of De Camara Nal Industria Editorial.
Subjects: Art
ISBN Prefix(es): 968-6188
Parent Company: Ediarte SA de CV
Imprints: Casa & Gente; El Coleccionista, Centro Historico

Ediciones Culturales Internacionales SA de CV Edicion Compra y Venta de Libros, Casetes, Videos+
Col Anzures Del Miguel Hidago, Leibnitz No 13-8 Piso, 11590 Mexico DF
Tel: (05) 2508099 *Fax:* (05) 5311597; (05) 5312454
Key Personnel
General Dir: Lic Mineya Cuentas M
Editorial Manager: Ma Aurora Aguilar Chavez
Founded: 1983
Subjects: Art, Child Care & Development, Ethnicity
ISBN Prefix(es): 968-418

Ediciones CUPSA, Centro de Comunicacion Cultural CUPSA, AC
Insurgentes Centro 86-5, Col San Rafael, 06030 Mexico DF
Tel: (05) 5925252; (05) 5662307 *Fax:* (05) 5462100
Key Personnel
Dir: Moises Valderrama
Founded: 1958
Subjects: Astrology, Occult, Biblical Studies, Poetry, Religion - Protestant, Religion - Other, Theology
ISBN Prefix(es): 968-7011
Warehouse: Heroes 83, Cal Guerrero 06300

Ediciones Dabar, SA de CV+
Calzada del Acueducto 165-D, Col San Lorenzo Huipulco, Del Tlalpan, 14370 Tlalpan
Tel: (05) 6550396 *Fax:* (05) 6550396
Key Personnel
Contact: Jose Vaderrey Falagan
Founded: 1991
Publishers & distributors of religious books in Spanish; theological, bibles, spiritual & catechisms.
Subjects: Religion - Other
ISBN Prefix(es): 968-6768

Maria Esther De Fleischmann
Atlaltunco No 57, Colonia San Miguel Techmacalco, 53970 Mexico
Mailing Address: San Francisco 109, Colonia Rancho San Francisco 01800
Tel: (05) 5852698; (05) 5852698 *Fax:* (05) 5854296
E-mail: fleischmann1@compuserve.com.mx
Key Personnel
Contact: Maria Esther Serafin Garcia
Subjects: Disability, Special Needs
ISBN Prefix(es): 968-499; 970-91523

Del Verbo Emprender SA de CV+
Fuente de Piramides No 20 Planta Baja Local B, Col Techamacalco, 53950 Mexico
Tel: (05) 2941160 *Fax:* (05) 2948633
Key Personnel
Contact: Salo Grabinsky Steider
Founded: 1989
Subjects: Child Care & Development, Human Relations, Management, Self-Help
ISBN Prefix(es): 968-6427

Editorial Diana SA de CV+
Arenal No 24, Edif Norte, Ex Hacienda Guadalupe Chimalistac, 01050 Mexico DF
Tel: (055) 5089-1220 *Fax:* (052) 5089-1230
E-mail: 4sales@diana.com.mx; editors@diana.com.mx *Cable:* EDISA
Key Personnel
President: Jose Luis Ramirez C
Vice President: Jose Luis Ramirez M
Literature Editor: Fausto Rosales
  E-mail: faustoro@diana.com.mx
General Interest Editor: Doris Bravo V
Technical Books Editor: V Manuel Fernandez
  E-mail: manfer@diana.com.mx
Sales: Vincente Perez *E-mail:* vincenteperez@diana.com.mx
Founded: 1946
Member of the National Association of the Mexican Publishing Industry.
Subjects: Advertising, Animals, Pets, Archaeology, Astrology, Occult, Biography, Career Development, Child Care & Development, Cookery, Economics, Education, Fiction, Health, Nutrition, History, Human Relations, Journalism, Literature, Literary Criticism, Essays, Management, Nonfiction (General), Parapsychology, Philosophy, Religion - Catholic, Self-Help, Sports, Athletics
ISBN Prefix(es): 968-13
Parent Company: Editorial Diana, SA de CV
Imprints: Edivision Cia, Editorial, SA de CV

MEXICO

Branch Office(s)
Buenos Aires, Argentina
Santafe de Bogota, Colombia
Barcelona, Spain
Caracas, Venezuela
Shipping Address: Roberto Cayol 1323, 03100 Col del Valle, Mexico DF

Direccion General de Publicaciones CNCA Coordinacion Juridica
Secretaria de Education Publica, Au Mexico Coyocan 371 col xoco, 033330 Mexico DF
Tel: (05) 6056565; (05) 6058589 *Fax:* (05) 6058731
ISBN Prefix(es): 968-29; 970-18
Parent Company: Educal, SA de CV, Av Ceylan 450, Col Euzkadi CP 02660

Directorio, *imprint of* Medios y Medios, Sa de CV

Ediciones Don Bosco SA de C
Moneda, No 24, Delegacion Cuauhtemoc, 06060 Mexico, DF
Tel: (05) 3963349
Key Personnel
Dir: Argeo Corona Thelian Cortes
Deputy Dir, Rights & Permissions: Milagros Magana del Campo
Sales: Jorge Rangel
Founded: 1958
Subjects: Religion - Other
ISBN Prefix(es): 968-6662; 968-6969
Associate Companies: Libreria Dectrina Cristiana, Corzo Francia 214, I-10096 Leuman (Turin), Italy; Edebe, Spain; Central Catequista Salesiana, Madrid Alcala 164, Madrid, Spain
Bookshop(s): Moneda, No 24, Delegacion Cuauhtemoc, 06060 Mexico, DF; 5 de Mayo 23, 06000 Mexico, DF; Ignacio Mariscal 8, Col revolucion, 06030 Mexico, DF

Ediciones Eca SA de CV+
Member of Cachoy Balcarcel, SA
Calle B No 20, Manzana II, Col Educacion, Cachoy Balcarcel SA, 04400 Mexico DF
Tel: (05) 5787325 *Fax:* (05) 5449561; (05) 6899935
Key Personnel
Contact: Gracia Ma Cacho
Founded: 1950
Subjects: Accounting, Business
ISBN Prefix(es): 968-14

Edamex SA de CV+
Heriberto Frias No 1104, Col Del Valle, Del Benito Juarez, 03100 Mexico, DF
Tel: (05) 55598588 *Toll Free Tel:* 800 024 8588 *Fax:* (05) 55750555; (05) 55757035
E-mail: info@edamex.com
Web Site: www.edamex.com
Key Personnel
President: Octavio Colmenares Vargas
Dir General: Monica Colmenares
Foreign Sales: Valeria Bastarrachea
Founded: 1963
Member of Camara Nacional de la Industria Editorial Socio No 40.
Subjects: Architecture & Interior Design, Art, Biography, Journalism, Management, Parapsychology, Public Administration, Self-Help, Social Sciences, Sociology, Sports, Athletics
ISBN Prefix(es): 968-409; 970-409
Number of titles published annually: 120 Print; 120 E-Book
Total Titles: 60 Print; 420 Online; 420 E-Book
Parent Company: Edamex
Foreign Rep(s): Books Information & Services (Puerto Rico); Distribuidora Lewis, SA (Panama); Giron Spanish Books; Internacional Libros; Libreria Alexandria (Costa Rica); Libreria Cientifica (Ecuador); Philobliblia, SA (Dominican Republic); Presa Peyran Editores, CA (Venezuela)

Editorial Edicol SA
esq Actipan No 45, Murcia No 2, 03920 Mexico, DF
Tel: (05) 5636990; (05) 5981512 *Fax:* (05) 5636966
Key Personnel
Man Dir: Jorge Silva Escamilla
Founded: 1970
Subjects: Architecture & Interior Design, Communications, Education, History, Language Arts, Linguistics, Social Sciences, Sociology
ISBN Prefix(es): 968-408

Edivision Cia, Editorial, SA de CV, *imprint of* Editorial Diana SA de CV

Education Pabla, see Direccion General de Publicaciones CNCA Coordinacion Juridica

El Colegio de Michoacan A C
Martinez de Navarrete 505 Esquina con Av del Arbol, 59699 Zamora, Michoacan
Tel: (0351) 515 71 00 *Fax:* (0351) 5157100, Ext 1712
E-mail: publica@colmich.cmich.udg.mx; publica@colmich.edu.mx
Web Site: www.colmich.edu.mx
Key Personnel
President: Carlos Herrejon Peredo
Secretary: Rafael Diego-Fernandez
Publications: Patricia Delgado Gonzalez
E-mail: pdelgado@colmich.edu.mx
Founded: 1979
Subjects: Americana, Regional, Anthropology, Archaeology, Behavioral Sciences, Developing Countries, Education, Environmental Studies, Government, Political Science, History, Language Arts, Linguistics, Native American Studies, Philosophy, Religion - Catholic, Social Sciences, Sociology, Theology
ISBN Prefix(es): 968-6959; 968-7230
Number of titles published annually: 30 Print

Editorial El Manual Moderno SA de CV+
Ave Sonora 206, Col Hipodromo Condesa, 06100 Mexico, DF
Tel: (05) 5648979; (05) 5642321 *Fax:* (05) 2641701; (05) 2651162
E-mail: mmoderuo@compuserve.com.ux
Key Personnel
Chairman: Dr Gustavo Setzer
President: Ing Hugo Setzer
Vice President: C P Hector Morales
Editorial: Iug Felipe Gerua
Marketing & Sales: Jose Pesez
Founded: 1958
Member of the International Association of Scientific, Technical & Medical Publishers, STM.
Subjects: Biological Sciences, Health, Nutrition, Medicine, Nursing, Dentistry, Psychology, Psychiatry, Self-Help, Veterinary Science
ISBN Prefix(es): 968-426
Subsidiaries: Editorial El Manual Moderno (Colombia), Ltda
Distributed by Ediciones Nueva Vision, CA (Venezuela); Ediciones Tecnicas Paraguayas (Paraguay); Ediciones Trecho, SA (Uruguay); Editorial Atlante Argentina, SRL (Argentina); H F Martinez de Murguia, SA (Espana)
Distributor for Appleton & Lange (Mexico); Atlante Argenti (Mexico); Celsus (Mexico); Ediciones Diaz de Santos, Medicina (America Latina); Harcourt Brace/Mosby-Doyma Libros (Mexico); Springer Verlag Iberica (America Latina)

Empresas Editoriales SA
Praga No 56, Planta Baja Col Juarez, 06600 Mexico DF
Tel: (05) 5288979; (05) 5288417 *Fax:* (05) 5288417
Founded: 1944
Subjects: Fiction
ISBN Prefix(es): 968-7035

Entretenlibro SA de CV
Wahsington No 1127-Altos, 64007 Monterrey, Nuevo Leon
Tel: (09183) 425570
Key Personnel
Contact: Jesus Rendon Contreras
Founded: 1983
Subjects: Education
ISBN Prefix(es): 968-462

Ediciones Era SA de CV+
Calle del Trabajo 31, Col La Fama Del Tlalpan, 14269 Mexico DF
Tel: (055) 55 28 1221 *Fax:* (055) 56 06 2904
E-mail: edicionesera@laneta.apc.org
Web Site: www.edicionesera.com.mx
Key Personnel
Man Dir: Mrs Nieves Espresate Xirau
Founded: 1960
Subjects: Art, Economics, Fiction, Government, Political Science, History, Literature, Literary Criticism, Essays, Social Sciences, Sociology
ISBN Prefix(es): 968-411
Number of titles published annually: 25 Print
Total Titles: 300 Print

Revista Mensual Escuela, *imprint of* Fernandez Editores SA de CV

Editorial Esfinge SA de CV
Esfuerzo 18-A, Colonia Ave 10 de Mayo, Colonia Industrial Atoto, Naucalpan, 53510 Naucalpan Edo de Mexico
Tel: (05) 3591313; (05) 3591111 *Fax:* (05) 5761343
Founded: 1957
Member of the National Chamber of the Industrial Editorial; Specialize in textbooks.
Subjects: Accounting, Chemistry, Chemical Engineering, Geography, Geology, History, Law, Literature, Literary Criticism, Essays, Mathematics, Physics
ISBN Prefix(es): 968-412
Parent Company: Grupo Cultural Esfinge SA de CV
Associate Companies: Altadir SA de CV; Inmobiliaria Acribia SA de CV; Distr Imagen Esfinge SA de CV
Distributor for Addison-Wesley Iberoamericana Mexico

Espasa-Calpe Mexicana SA
Pitagoras, No 1139, Col Del Valle, 03100 Mexico, DF
Tel: (05) 5752894; (05) 5755022
ISBN Prefix(es): 968-413
Branch Office(s)
Editorial Espasa-Calpe SA, Spain

Centro de Estudios Monetarios Latinoamericanos (CEMLA)+
Durango 54, Col Roma, 06700 Mexico, DF
Tel: (05) 5330300 *Fax:* (05) 5146554
E-mail: cemlasub@mail.internet.com.mx
Key Personnel
Man Dir: Lic Sergio Ghigliazza
Editorial, Rights & Permissions & Production: Juan Manuel Rodriguez *Tel:* 052 55114020 *Fax:* 052 52077024
Sales: Claudio Antonovich
Founded: 1952
Subjects: Computer Science, Economics, Finance
ISBN Prefix(es): 968-6154

PUBLISHERS MEXICO

Ediciones Euroamericanas+
Textitlan No 38, Col Santa Ursula Coapa, 04650 Mexico DF
Mailing Address: PO Box/Apartado 24-434, 06701
Tel: (05) 610-01-33 *Fax:* (05) 610-01-33
E-mail: thielemedina@prodigy.net.mx
Key Personnel
Man Dir: Klaus Thiele *E-mail:* thielemedina@prodigy.net.mx
Founded: 1971
Direct sales only to booksellers worldwide.
Subjects: Anthropology, Archaeology, History, Regional Interests
ISBN Prefix(es): 968-414
Imprints: Biblioteca Interamericana Bilingual; Paginas Mesoamericanas

Ediciones Exclusivas SA+
Monrovia 1105, Apdo Postal 21-148, Mexico 21
Tel: (05) 815878
Key Personnel
Contact: Jose Figueroa Marti
Founded: 1973
Member of La Camara Nacional de la Industria Editorial.
Subjects: Health, Nutrition, Human Relations, Medicine, Nursing, Dentistry, Psychology, Psychiatry
ISBN Prefix(es): 968-7039
U.S. Office(s): Latin Trading Corp, 539 H St, Suite B, Chula Vista, CA 91911, United States
Tel: 619-427-7867

Editorial Extemporaneos SA
Poniente 126-A-400, Col Nueva Vallejo, 07750 Mexico, DF
Tel: (05) 5875424; (05) 5878785 *Cable:* EDIEXTEMPO MEXICO
Key Personnel
Dir-General, Editorial: Lautaro Gondalez Porcel
Sales, Publicity, Production: Romeo Medina
Rights & Permissions: Eva Somlo
Founded: 1975
Subjects: Anthropology, Architecture & Interior Design, Art, Drama, Theater, Economics, Education, Government, Political Science, Humor, Literature, Literary Criticism, Essays, Philosophy, Social Sciences, Sociology
ISBN Prefix(es): 968-415
Bookshop(s): Librerias Extemporaneos SA, Hamburgo 260, Mexico 6, DF
Book Club(s): Club de Lectores Extemporaneos

Editorial Fata Morgana SA de CV+
Virgilio No 7-12, Col Polanco, 11560 Mexico DF
Mailing Address: Monte Elbruz 164-13, Lomas Chapultepec, 11000 Mexico DF
Tel: (055) 52 80 08 29 *Fax:* (055) 52 80 81 37
E-mail: editorial@fatamorgana.com.mx
Web Site: www.fatamorgana.com.mx
Key Personnel
Contact: Maria Abac Klemm
Founded: 1990
Subjects: Psychology, Psychiatry
ISBN Prefix(es): 968-6757
Number of titles published annually: 1 Print
Total Titles: 8 Print
Orders to: Virgilio No 7 Depto 12, Col Polanco, 11560 Mexico DF

Fernandez Editores SA de CV+
Calzada Mexico Coyoacan 321, 03310 Mexico DF
Tel: (05) 5244600; (05) 5342285 *Fax:* (05) 6889173
Key Personnel
President: Gonzalez Luis Fernandez
Man Dir: Luis Gerardo Fernandez
Production Manager: Luis Benjamin Fernandez
Commercial Manager: Luis Miguel Fernandez
Founded: 1943
Member of Camara Editorial of Mexico & manufacture of game tables & materials.
Subjects: Animals, Pets, Child Care & Development, Education, Environmental Studies, History, Literature, Literary Criticism, Essays, Mathematics, Nonfiction (General), Physics, Religion - Catholic, Science (General), Science Fiction, Fantasy, Social Sciences, Sociology
ISBN Prefix(es): 970-03; 968-416
Imprints: Revista Mensual Escuela

Fondo de Cultura Economica+
Carretera Picacho-Ajusco No 227,, Col Bosques del Pedregal, Mexico DF D1000
Tel: (05) 5242240; (05) 5243840; (05) 5246664
Fax: (05) 2274640; (05) 2274683; (05) 2274694
E-mail: fceedi@infoabc.com(fceedi)
Key Personnel
Man Dir: Miguel de la Madrid
Senior Editor: Adolfo Castanon
Production: Alejandro Ramirez
Sales: David Turner y Barragan
Publicity: Maria Luisa Armendariz
Foreign Rights: Socorro Cano
Founded: 1934
Specialize in editorial materials.
Subjects: Advertising, Agriculture, Anthropology, Archaeology, Architecture & Interior Design, Art, Behavioral Sciences, Biological Sciences, Communications, Developing Countries, Earth Sciences, Economics, Education, Energy, Ethnicity, Government, Political Science, History, Nonfiction (General), Philosophy, Poetry, Psychology, Psychiatry, Public Administration, Science (General), Science Fiction, Fantasy, Social Sciences, Sociology, Women's Studies
ISBN Prefix(es): 968-16
Imprints: Azteca; Galeras; La Gaceta; El Trimestre Economico
Branch Office(s)
Suipacha 617, Buenos Aires 1008, Argentina
Tel: (01) 3227262 *Fax:* (01) 3227262
Alameda Campinas 1077, Barrio Jardim Paulista, Sao Paulo SP CEP 01404, Brazil *Tel:* (011) 8859339 *Fax:* (011) 8843842
Ave Bulnes 152, Casilla Postal 10249, Santiago de Chile, Chile *Tel:* (02) 6962329 *Fax:* (02) 6962329
Carrera 16 No 80-18, Bogota, Colombia *Tel:* (01) 2570017 *Fax:* (01) 2572215
Edif Indubuilding Goico, 40 piso-15 via de los Poblados, s/n Hortaleza, Madrid 28033, Spain
Tel: (01) 7632800 *Fax:* (01) 7635133
Berlin No 238, Miraflores, Lima 18, Peru
Tel: (014) 472848 *Fax:* (014) 470760
Edif Torre Polar, PB, Local E, Pl Venezuela, Caracas, Venezuela *Tel:* (02) 5744753
Fax: (02) 5747442
Bookshop(s): Carret Picacho Ajusco, No 227, Mexico, DF CP 14200
Shipping Address: Jose Maria Joaristi 205, Paraje San Juan, San Lorenzo, Iztapalapa 09830

Fondo Editorial de la Plastica Mexicana+
Cda de Malitzin No 28, 04100 Mexico, DF
Tel: (05) 56-88-30-67 *Fax:* (05) 56-88-11-68
Founded: 1961
Subjects: Art, Regional Interests
ISBN Prefix(es): 968-6658
Number of titles published annually: 3 Print
Total Titles: 20 Print

La Gaceta, *imprint of* Fondo de Cultura Economica

Galeras, *imprint of* Fondo de Cultura Economica

Impresora Galve SA, *imprint of* Editorial Avante SA de Cv

Ediciones Gili SA de CV
Valle de Bravo No 21, Col Fracc El Mirador, 53050 Naucalpan Edo de Mexico
Tel: (05) 5606121; (05) 5606011 *Fax:* (05) 3601453
Telex: 1772918 Gilime *Cable:* GUSTO MEXICO
ISBN Prefix(es): 968-887
Associate Companies: Editorial Gustavo Gili SA, Spain

Gomez Gomez Hermanos Editores S de RL Edicion de Libros y Revistas+
Moneda 19-B, 06060 Mexico DF
Tel: (05) 6123946; (05) 6123906 *Fax:* (05) 633786
Key Personnel
Contact: Victor J Gomez
ISBN Prefix(es): 968-7030
Subsidiaries: El Mejor Regalo un Libro SRL

Editorial Grijalbo SA de CV+
Naucalpan No 282, Col Argentine Poniente, 11230 Mexico, DF
Tel: (05) 3584355 *Fax:* (05) 3584312
Telex: 1771415 Egsame *Cable:* GRIJALMEX
Key Personnel
Editorial: Rogelio Carvajal Davila; Ariel Rosales Ortiz
Sales: Rodolfo Munguia Calderon; Irma P Chavarria
Publicity: Alicia Velazquez; Oscar Davalos
Founded: 1954
Member of Camara Espanola de Comercio & Mexico y Camara Italiana de Comercio en Mexico.
Subjects: Fiction, Nonfiction (General)
ISBN Prefix(es): 968-419; 970-05
Parent Company: Ediciones Grijalbo SA, Spain
Associate Companies: Arnoldo Mondadori Editore
Branch Office(s)
Guadalajara, Jal
Mexicali, BC
Monterrey, NL

Grupo Editorial Iberoamerica, SA de CV+
Nebraska 199, Col Napoles, 03810 Mexico, DF
Tel: (05) 55230994
Key Personnel
President: Nicolas Grepe Philp
Founded: 1983
Book publisher & distributor to Latin America.
Subjects: Agriculture, Career Development, Chemistry, Chemical Engineering, Computer Science, Economics, Engineering (General), Environmental Studies, Finance, Management, Mathematics, Mechanical Engineering
ISBN Prefix(es): 968-7270
Branch Office(s)
Grupo Editorial Iberoamerica de Colombia, SA, Carrera 23 No 49-30, Barrio Palermo, Santa Fe de Bogota, Colombia *Tel:* (0571) 3202010 *Fax:* (0571) 3106553

Grupo Editorial Z Zeta SA de CV
Oculislas No 43, Col Sifon, 09400 Mexico DF
Tel: (05) 6705627; (05) 5817929 *Fax:* (05) 5758280
Key Personnel
Contact: Francisco Campos Fontanet
ISBN Prefix(es): 970-610
Warehouse: Ignacio Manuel Aaltamirano, 212 B Col Hank Gonzalez, 09750 Mexico DF

Heidel Impresos SA de CV, *imprint of* Editorial Avante SA de Cv

Editorial Hermes SA+
Calz Ermita Iztapalapa No 266, Col Sinatel, 09470 Mexico, DF

Tel: (05) 6741425; (05) 6741894; (05) 6744385 (ext 71) *Fax:* (05) 6743949 *Cable:* EDITERMES
Key Personnel
Man Dir: Sergio Sanchez Davila
Sales: Adolfo de la Becerril
Production, Rights & Permissions: Virginia Garcia Fiesco
Founded: 1944
Subjects: Art, Fiction, History
ISBN Prefix(es): 968-446
Associate Companies: Editorial Albastros SA ci, Buenos Aires, Argentina; Tercer Mundo Distribuidores, Santa Fe de Bogota, Colombia

Editorial Herrero SA
Rio Amazonas No 44, Col Cuauhtemoc, 06500 Mexico, DF
Tel: (05) 5664900 *Fax:* (05) 5664900
Key Personnel
General Dir: Donato Elias Herrero
Manager: Ricardo Arancon L
Founded: 1945
Subjects: Art
ISBN Prefix(es): 968-420

Hoja Casa Editorial SA de CV+
Av Cuauhtemoc No 1430, Col Santa Cruz Atoyac, 03310 Mexico, DF
Tel: (05) 6884828; (05) 6880318 *Fax:* (05) 6057600
Key Personnel
General Manager: Consuelo Saizar
Production: Gerardo Gally
Rights & Permissions: Gilda Moreno
Founded: 1990
Subjects: Astrology, Occult, Fiction, Literature, Literary Criticism, Essays, Self-Help
ISBN Prefix(es): 968-6565

Ibcon SA+
Paseo de La Reforma, No 104-4 Piso, 06600 Mexico DF
Tel: (05) 5665700 *Fax:* (05) 2554577
E-mail: ibcon@infosel.net.mx
Web Site: www.ibcom.com.mx
Key Personnel
Editor: Gabriel Zaid
Founded: 1954
Subjects: Business
ISBN Prefix(es): 968-6289
Total Titles: 17 Print

Instituto Indigenista Interamericano
Av Insurgentes Sur 1690, Col Florida, 01030 Mexico DF
Mailing Address: Apartado Postal 20315, CP 101 Mexico DF
Tel: (05) 6600007; (05) 6600132 *Fax:* (05) 6521274 *Cable:* INDIGENI
Key Personnel
Man Dir, Rights & Permissions: Dr Jose Matos Mar
Founded: 1940
Member of OEA; specialize in the development of the Pueblo Indian in America.
Subjects: Anthropology, History
ISBN Prefix(es): 968-6020

Informatica Cosmos SA de CV+
Calz del Hueso 122-A1, Col Ex-Hacienda Coapa, Mexico, DF 14300
Tel: (05) 6774868; (05) 6776043 *Fax:* (05) 6793575
E-mail: online@cosmos.com.mx
Web Site: www.cosmos.com.mx
Key Personnel
Man Dir: Raul Macazaga *E-mail:* macazaga@cosmos.com.mx
Dir of International Sales: Mary Christen *E-mail:* christen@cosmos.com.mx

Founded: 1956
Specialize in industry guides, products, producers, suppliers of industry, chemicals, food & feed, container & packaging, rubber, plastics & resins & equipment.
Online services available through World Wide Web.
U.S. Office(s): Schnell Publishing Co Inc, 2 Rector St, 26th floor, New York, NY 10006-1819, United States, Stacey Davis *Tel:* 212-791-4251 *Fax:* 212-791-4311 *E-mail:* sdavis@chemepo.com

Editorial Institucional y Desarrollo Humanistico SA de CV Edicion de Libros (IDH Ediciones)+
Av Juarez No 14-7 Piso, 11560 Mexico DF
Tel: (05) 5215060; (05) 5215009
Key Personnel
Contacts: Ms Alicia Sosa; Enrique Martinez Cruz
Founded: 1982
ISBN Prefix(es): 968-883
Parent Company: Grupo IDH

Intersistemas SA de CV+
Aguiar y Seijas No 75, Col Lomas Virreyes, 11000 Mexico, DF
Tel: (05) 2028243; (05) 5405600; (05) 5400798 *Fax:* (05) 5403764; (05) 5403464
Telex: 5403764
Key Personnel
Man Dir: Pedro Vera-Cervera
Editorial: Elvia Espino-Barros
Sales: Miguel Alberto Gonzalez
Founded: 1970
Subjects: Medicine, Nursing, Dentistry
ISBN Prefix(es): 970-655
Associate Companies: Vier Lista Anexa, EMC Columbia Federal Buenos Aires, Buenos Aires, Argentina; Graficas Enar SA, Pedro Muguruza 3-1, Madrid 16, Spain; Intermedica Inc, 322 West Port Avenue, Norwalk, CT 06851, United States

El Inversionista Mexicano SA de CV
Felix Cuevas 301-204, Col Del Valle, Del Benito Juarez, 03100 Mexico, DF
Tel: (05) 5243131; (05) 5245346; (05) 5349297 *Fax:* (05) 5243794
E-mail: elimmbi@iserve.net.mx
Key Personnel
Contact: Evangelina Astorga Dorantes
Founded: 1969

Editorial Iztaccihuatl SA+
Miguel E Schultz No 21, Col San Rafael, 06470 Mexico, DF
Tel: (05) 7050938; (05) 7051063 *Fax:* (05) 5352321 *Cable:* EIZTAMEXA
Key Personnel
President: Orlando Vieyra Legorreta
Founded: 1946
Subjects: Cookery, Literature, Literary Criticism, Essays, Wine & Spirits
ISBN Prefix(es): 968-421

Janibi Editores SA de CV
Matias Romero 1221-3, Col Del Valle, Del Benito Juarez, 03100 Mexico, DF
Tel: (05) 6046160 *Fax:* (05) 6882848
Key Personnel
Contact: Victor Munoz Polit
Founded: 1975
Subjects: Fashion, Music, Dance

Editorial Jilguero, SA de CV
Monte Pelvoux No 110-104, Col Lomas de Chapultepec, 11000 Mexico, DF
Tel: (05) 2026585 *Fax:* (05) 5401771
E-mail: mexdesco@compuserve.com.mx

Subjects: Animals, Pets, Anthropology, Antiques, Archaeology, Architecture & Interior Design, Cookery, Crafts, Games, Hobbies, History, Music, Dance, Outdoor Recreation, Travel

Editorial Joaquin Mortiz SA de CV+
Ave Insurgentes Sur No 1162, Col del Valle, 03100 Mexico, DF
Tel: (05) 5598781; (05) 5758585; (05) 5758019 *Fax:* (05) 5758980; (05) 5752426
Telex: 1764458 EDARME
Key Personnel
Man Dir, Production, Rights & Permissions: Joaquin Diez-Canedo
Founded: 1962
Member of the Grupo Editorial Planeta.
Subjects: Fiction, History, Nonfiction (General), Psychology, Psychiatry, Social Sciences, Sociology
ISBN Prefix(es): 968-27
Associate Companies: Editorial Planeta SA, Spain
Warehouse: Ave Gavilan 3, Bodega 1 & 2, Col Guadalupe del Mora, Delegacion Iztapalapa, 09360 Mexico, DF
Orders to: Editorial Planeta Mexicana, Ave Insurgentes Sur No 1162-3, Col Del Valle, 03100 Mexico DF

Editorial Jus SA de CV+
Plaza de Abasolo 14, Col Guerrero, 06300 Mexico DF
Tel: (05) 5260538; (05) 5260540 *Fax:* (05) 5291444
Key Personnel
President: Juan Landerreche
Man Dir: Tomas Reynoso
Sales Manager: Jorge Espinosa
Founded: 1941
Subjects: Biblical Studies, Economics, Education, Government, Political Science, History, Law, Literature, Literary Criticism, Essays, Philosophy, Religion - Catholic, Self-Help, Social Sciences, Sociology, Theology
ISBN Prefix(es): 968-423
Subsidiaries: Distribuidora Editorial Jus SA

Ediciones Larousse SA de CV+
Dinamarca No 81, Col Juarez, 06600 Mexico, DF
Mailing Address: PO Box 6-864, Mexico DF 06600
Tel: (05) 5330469 al 73; (05) 5330530 *Fax:* (05) 208-6225; (05) 208-0775
E-mail: larousse@compuserve.com
Key Personnel
President: Dominique Bertin
Founded: 1965
Subjects: English as a Second Language
ISBN Prefix(es): 970-607; 968-6042; 968-6147; 968-6347
Parent Company: Havas Publications Edition, France
Warehouse: Acalotenco 94-1, Mexico DF

Lasser Press Mexicana SA de CV
Praga 56-Piso 4, Col Juarez, 06600 Mexico, DF
Tel: (05) 5332097; (05) 5112312; (05) 5142705 *Fax:* (05)2076361; (05) 5148038
Telex: 1777529 Coseme *Cable:* LASPRESA
Key Personnel
President: Guillermo Menendez Castro
Editorial Dir: Elisa Tovar
Founded: 1972
Subjects: Biography, Literature, Literary Criticism, Essays, Nonfiction (General)
ISBN Prefix(es): 968-458; 968-7063

Phillip Richard Conover Lazo+
Member of Camara Nacional de la Industria Editorial Mexicana #2705
c/o The Huautla Press, Galeana No 25, Col San Angel, Del Alvaro Obregon, 01000 Mexico DF
Tel: (05) 5509705 *Fax:* (05) 5500641
E-mail: mel778@latinmail.com

Key Personnel
Owner, Editor & Writer: Phillip Richard Conover Lazo
Founded: 1990
Author, publisher, editor of Teo Nana Acatl. Searching for distributors & publishers desiring joint publishing ventures.
Subjects: Anthropology, History, Literature, Literary Criticism, Essays, Philosophy, Poetry, Religion - Buddhist, Religion - Hindu, Theology, Specialize in English language books
ISBN Prefix(es): 968-6744
Total Titles: 1 Print
Branch Office(s)
Aitken, Stone & Wylie Ltd, 29 Fernshaw Rd, London SW10 0TG, United Kingdom
Tel: (071) 351 7561 *Fax:* (071) 376 3594
E-mail: 100303.1765@compuserve.com
U.S. Office(s): Wylie, Aitken & Stone, 250 West 57 St, Suite 2114, New York, NY 10107, United States *Tel:* 212-246-0069
E-mail: 74454-3324@compuserve.com
Distributed by Libra Administraciones y Promociones'
Foreign Rep(s): Wylie, Aitken & Stone
Bookshop(s): Libreria el Juglar, Manuel M Ponce, 233 Col, Guadalupe Inn DF 01020, Facundo Caletti *Tel:* 660 7900
Orders to: Huantha Press, Galeana 25, San Angel DF 01000, Philip Conover *Tel:* (05) 509705

Ediciones Libra, SA de CV
Matias Romero 1221, Col Del Valle, Del Benito Juarez, 03100 Mexico, DF
Tel: (05) 6045952 *Fax:* (05) 68828486
Founded: 1986
Subjects: Crafts, Games, Hobbies, Fashion, Music, Dance

Libra Editorial SA de CV+
Melesio Morales No 16, Colonia Guadalupe Inn, 01020 Mexico DF
Tel: (05) 6641454; (05) 6514156 *Fax:* (05) 6641454
Key Personnel
President: Georgina Greco y Herrera
Editor: Gabriela Escalante de Figueroa
Founded: 1984
Subjects: Astrology, Occult, Child Care & Development, Cookery, Education, Gay & Lesbian, How-to, Humor, Language Arts, Linguistics, Nonfiction (General), Self-Help, Women's Studies
ISBN Prefix(es): 970-606; 968-6636
Warehouse: Av Centenario 514, Letra A

Libreria Parroquial de Claveria SA Edicion Compra y Venta de Libros+
Floresta No 79, Col Claveria, 02080 Mexico DF
Tel: (05) 3967027; (05) 3967718 *Fax:* (05) 3991243
Key Personnel
Contact: Padre Basilio Nunez Garcia
ISBN Prefix(es): 968-442

Libros y Revistas SA de CV
Mier y Pesado 130, Col del Valle, 03100 Mexico, DF
Tel: (05) 5437295
Telex: 01771403 dsayme
Key Personnel
General Dir, Editorial, Rights & Permissions: Marcial Frigolet Lerma
General Manager, Commercial Dir: Joaquin Roca Romero
Production: Miguel Montano
Founded: 1925
Subjects: Crafts, Games, Hobbies, Education, Fashion, Health, Nutrition
ISBN Prefix(es): 968-7066

Parent Company: Publicaciones Sayrols SA de CV
Associate Companies: Metropolitana de Publicaciones SA

Editorial Limusa SA de CV+
Balderas 95-Piso 1, Col Centro Dele Cuauhtemoc, Apdo N-29-182, 06040 Mexico DF
Tel: (05) 512 6858; (05) 585 3500 *Fax:* (05) 512 2903
E-mail: limusa@noriega.com.mx
Web Site: www.noriega.com.mx
Key Personnel
Chairman of the Board: Carlos Noriega Milera
Chairman & Chief Executive Officer: Carlos Noriega Arias
Vice President & Editorial Dir: Miguel Noriega Arias
Founded: 1962
Subjects: Accounting, Advertising, Aeronautics, Aviation, Agriculture, Architecture & Interior Design, Art, Astronomy, Automotive, Behavioral Sciences, Biological Sciences, Business, Career Development, Chemistry, Chemical Engineering, Child Care & Development, Civil Engineering, Communications, Computer Science, Cookery, Crafts, Games, Hobbies, Criminology, Drama, Theater, Earth Sciences, Economics, Education, Electronics, Electrical Engineering, Energy, Engineering (General), Finance, Geography, Geology, Government, Political Science, Health, Nutrition, House & Home, Human Relations, Journalism, Labor, Industrial Relations, Law, Management, Marketing, Mathematics, Mechanical Engineering, Medicine, Nursing, Dentistry, Microcomputers, Physical Sciences, Physics, Psychology, Psychiatry, Public Administration, Radio, TV, Real Estate, Religion - Catholic, Science (General), Social Sciences, Sociology, Sports, Athletics, Technology, Transportation, Veterinary Science
ISBN Prefix(es): 968-18
Total Titles: 2,500 Print
Parent Company: Grupo Noriega Editores
Imprints: Nori; Camion Escolar y Limusa; Uteha; Noriega Editores
Subsidiaries: Limex; Alamex; Grupo Noriega Editores de Colombia LTDA
Divisions: Uteha; Nori; Camion Escolar; Limusa; Noriega Editores
Branch Office(s)
E Robles Gil No 437, Col Americana SJ, Guadalajara, Contact: Francisco Haro *Tel:* (03) 269 032 *Fax:* (03) 268 899 *E-mail:* limusa@noriega.com.mx
M M Del Llano 417 Ote, NL Monterrey, Contact: Sra Agustin Medina *Tel:* (08) 345 7505 *Fax:* (08) 345 7505 *E-mail:* limusa@noriega.com.mx
Distributed by Anisa (Puerto Rico); Cuspide CIA (Argentina); Dimaxi (Ecuador); Ediciones Tecnicas Paraguayas (Paraguay); Hispania SRL; Fundacion Del Libro Universitario Libun (Peru)
Distributor for Meditor (America Latina); V Vives (Mexico)
Showroom(s): Ayuntamiento 112, Centro 06040
Bookshop(s): Libreria Bellas Artes, Av Juarez, No 18-D, 6770 Mexico DF *Tel:* (05) 518 2917; Integra Escolar, Felix Berenguer 106, Lomas Virreyes *Tel:* (05) 520 6592
Book Club(s): Librerias de Cristal, Tehuantepec 170, Roma Sur, 06770 Mexico D F *Tel:* (05) 564 4677
Warehouse: Oriente 171 No 108, Col Aragon Inguaran, Contact: Sra Carlos Sanchez *Tel:* (057) 81 61 57 *Fax:* (057) 81 08 74 *E-mail:* limusa@noriega.com.mx

Logos Consorcio Editorial SA+
General Molinos del Capo 64, Col San Miguel Chapultepec, 11850 Mexico DF
Tel: (05) 5151633

Key Personnel
Man Dir: Enrico Garcia Alonso S
ISBN Prefix(es): 968-425

Longman, *imprint of* Pearson Educacion de Mexico, SA de CV

Macmillan Editores SA de CV
Av Prolongacion San Antonio 170, Col Carola, 01180 Mexico DF
Tel: (05) 482 2200 *Fax:* (05) 482 2202
Key Personnel
Chief Executive: Christopher West
E-mail: cwest@macmillan.com.mx
Man Dir: Helen Melia *E-mail:* hmelia@macmillan.com.mx
Founded: 1982
Parent Company: Macmillan Publishers Ltd, United Kingdom
Associate Companies: Editorial Macmillan de Mexico SA de CV

Editorial Macmillan de Mexico SA de CV
Av Prolongacion San Antonio 170, Col Carola, 01180 Mexico DF
Tel: (05) 482 2200 *Fax:* (05) 482 2202
Web Site: www.macmillan.com.mx
Key Personnel
Chief Executive: Christopher West
E-mail: cwest@macmillan.com.mx
Man Dir: Helen Melia *E-mail:* hmelia@macmillan.com.mx
Founded: 1982
English language teaching publishers.
Parent Company: Macmillan Publishers Ltd, United Kingdom
Associate Companies: Macmillan Editores SA de CV

Mass + Medios, *imprint of* Medios y Medios, Sa de CV

Masson Editores
Dakota No 383, Col Napoles, 03810 Mexico, DF
Tel: (05) 6870933
Telex: 1777604
Key Personnel
President: Dr Jerome Talamon
Man Dir: Bruno Vanneuville
Founded: 1978
ISBN Prefix(es): 968-6099
Parent Company: Masson Editeur, France
Associate Companies: Editora Masson do Brasil Ltda, Brazil; Masson italia editori - ETM, via Pascoli 55, I-20133 Milan, Italy; Masson SA, Spain; Masson Publishing USA Inc, 211 E 43 St, Rm 1306, New York, NY 10017, United States

McGraw-Hill Interamericana de Mexico, SA de CV+
Calle Atlacomulco 499, Col San Andres Atoto, 53500 Naucalpan, Edo de Mexico
Mailing Address: Apdo 5-237, 06550 Mexico City
Tel: (05) 5767304; (05) 5769044 ext 156; 5413155 al 59 (Mexico City) *Fax:* (05) 6285367
E-mail: mcgraw-hill@infosel.net.mx
Web Site: www.mcgraw-hill.com.mx
Telex: 01774284 LMCHME
Key Personnel
Man Dir: Carlos Rios
Controller & Business Manager: Hugo Solis
Production Manager: Miguel Palafox
EDP Manager: Javier Carranza
Human Resources Manager: Rocio Gonzalez
Publisher, Professional Division: David Mejia
Publisher, College Division, BCV: Javier Neyra
Publisher, High School Division, BCV: Enrique Pereda

MEXICO

Publisher, Elementary-Junior High School Division, K-9: Joaquin Esponda
Distributor & Bookstore Sales Manager, Mexico: Rodolfo Munguia
Export Division Manager, Central America, Caribbean & South America: Lynette Kew
Founded: 1966
Sales Manager, Central America: Nathaniel Maxwell; Hotel Republica, Avenida Republica y Azuai, Quito, Ecuador. Tel: (02) 437667 Fax: (02) 436553. Sales Manager-College, Ecuador, Peru & Chile: Gilberto Capellan
Markets served: Mexico, Central America (Guatemala, Honduras, El Salvador, Costa Rica, Nicarauga, Panama), South America (Ecuador, Peru, Bolivia, Chile).
Subjects: Business, Engineering (General), Mathematics, Public Administration, Social Sciences, Sociology
ISBN Prefix(es): 968-25; 968-451; 968-422; 968-6046; 970-10
Parent Company: McGraw-Hill Inc, 1221 Avenue of the Americas, New York, NY 10020, United States
Sales Office(s): 13 Calle "A" 31-76, Zona 7, Apdo 1477, Colonia Tika III, Guatemala, Guatemala *Tel:* (02) 914793 *Fax:* (02) 519598

Medios Publicitarios Mexicanos SA de CV Editora de Directorios de Medios
Av Mexico No 99-303, Col Hipodromo Condesa, 06170 Mexico 11, DF
Tel: (05) 5742858 *Fax:* (05) 5742668
E-mail: mpmdirec@data.net.mx
Key Personnel
Contact: A Fernando Villamil
Founded: 1958
SRDS, LP 1700 Higgins Rd, Des Plaines, IL 60018.
Subjects: Advertising
Associate Companies: SRDS, United States

Medios y Medios, Sa de CV
Av Universidad 783-4, Col Del Valle, Del Benito Juarez, 03100 Mexico DF
Tel: (05) 56-01-85-11 *Fax:* (05) 56-88-59-85
E-mail: mass+medios@fc.camoapa.com.mx
Key Personnel
Dir: David Ramirez-Solis
Founded: 1993
Subjects: Advertising, Radio, TV
Imprints: Directorio; Mass + Medios

Mercametrica Ediciones SA Edicion de Libros
Av Universidad 1621-3, Col Hda. de Gpe. Chimalistac, 01050 Mexico, DF
Tel: (05) 6616293 *Fax:* (05) 6616293
Key Personnel
President: Ignacio Gomez
Founded: 1976
Subjects: Economics, Management, Marketing
ISBN Prefix(es): 968-7267

Editores Mexicanos Unidos SA
Luis Gonzalez Obregon No 5-B, 06020 Mexico DF
Tel: (05) 5217596; (05) 5218870 al 74; (05) 5211874 *Fax:* (05) 5128516
Key Personnel
Man Dir, Editorial: Fidel Miro Solanes
Dir: Sonia Miro de Laclau
Manager: Roque Laclau Gaona
Founded: 1954
Subjects: Fiction, Nonfiction (General)
ISBN Prefix(es): 968-15
Bookshop(s): Libro-Mex Editores SRL, Argentina 23, Mexico 1 DF

Editorial Minutiae Mexicana SA
Insurgentes Centro No 114-207, Col Revolucion, 06030 Mexico DF
Tel: (052) 55-5535-9488 *Fax:* (052) 722-232-0662
Key Personnel
Publisher: Virginia V De Barrios
  E-mail: barriosb@prodigy.net.mx
Founded: 1963
Specialize in Books in English only.
Subjects: Anthropology, Archaeology, Biological Sciences, Cookery, Crafts, Games, Hobbies, History, Natural History, Religion - Catholic, Travel
ISBN Prefix(es): 968-7074
Branch Office(s)
MEX/ICS, 124 Cota Ave, San Clemente, CA 92672, United States, Contact: Jean Stenzel *Tel:* 949-492-1257 *Fax:* 949-492-1257

Galeria de Arte Misrachi SA
Genova No 20-A, Col Juarez, 06600 Mexico DF
Tel: (05) 5334551 *Fax:* (05) 5257187
Key Personnel
Manager: Enrique Beraha Misrachi
Editorial, Sales, Production, Rights & Permissions, Publicity: Beraha Carlos Cohen
Founded: 1961
Subjects: Art
ISBN Prefix(es): 968-7047
Subsidiaries: Galeria Misrachi SA de CV

Impresora Multiple SA, *imprint of* Editorial Avante SA de Cv

Mundo Medico SA de CV Edicion y Distribucion de Revistas Medicas
Matias Romero 116, Col del Valle, 03100 Mexico DF
Tel: (05) 2038111; (05) 2038547; (05) 2036634; (05) 2554669; (05) 5592755 *Fax:* (05) 2036418
Key Personnel
Contact: Julieta Cano Garcia
Founded: 1973
Subjects: Medicine, Nursing, Dentistry
ISBN Prefix(es): 968-7204
Branch Office(s)
Mundo Medico, 600 B Lake St, Ramsey, NJ 07446, United States

Instituto Nacional de Antropologia e Historia
Cordoba 45, Col Roma, 06700 Mexico, DF
Mailing Address: Editor Coord Nat Difusion/Alvaro Obregon, No 151-3 Col Roma, CP 06700 Mexico DF
Tel: (05) 5335246; (05) 5332272; (05) 2074559; (05) 2074584 *Fax:* (05) 2074633
E-mail: difusion@inah.gob.mx
Key Personnel
International Rights: Sol Levin
Founded: 1822
Governmental Institution devoted to the preservation, research & promotion of Mexican historical heritage.
Subjects: Americana, Regional, Anthropology, Antiques, Archaeology, Art, History, Language Arts, Linguistics, Music, Dance, Native American Studies, Photography, Social Sciences, Sociology
ISBN Prefix(es): 968-6038; 968-6068; 968-6487
Total Titles: 120 Print
Distributed by Educal Libros y Arte
Orders to: Coord Control y Promocion, Calle Frontera, No 53, Col San Angel, Mexico DF CP 01000 *Tel:* (0525) 550-9714; (0525) 550-9676 *E-mail:* cncpbs@inah.gob.mx

Instituto Nacional de Estadistica, Geographia e Informatica
Patriotismo No 711 2 do Piso, Col San Jaun Mixcoac, 03910 Mexico DF
Tel: (05) 5631602; (05) 5638904 *Fax:* (05) 180739
E-mail: adconde@cis.inegi.gob.mx

BOOK

Key Personnel
Contact: Daniel de Lira Luna
Subjects: Developing Countries, Earth Sciences, Economics, Geography, Geology, Social Sciences, Sociology
ISBN Prefix(es): 970-13; 968-892

Naves Internacional de Ediciones SA+
Amores No 135, Col Del Valle, Del Benito Juarez, 03100 Mexico, DF
Tel: (05) 6690595; (05) 9180055595 *Fax:* (05) 6823728
E-mail: niesa@mpsnet.com.mx
Key Personnel
Contact: Pablo Llaca
Founded: 1981
Subjects: Advertising, Architecture & Interior Design, Art, Cookery, Photography
Associate Companies: Ramon Llaca y Cia SA
Distributor for Celeste; Folio; Idea Books; Juventud; Naturart; Tursen
Book Club(s): Club de Editores, AC

Nori, *imprint of* Editorial Limusa SA de CV

Noriega Editores, *imprint of* Editorial Limusa SA de CV

Nova Grupo Editorial SA de CV+
Panama 820-3, Portales, 03300 Mexico, DF
Tel: (05) 5320946 *Fax:* (05) 6050879
Key Personnel
Contact: Oscar Pruneda Portilla
Founded: 1987
Subjects: Communications, Education, Health, Nutrition, Language Arts, Linguistics, Mathematics, Nonfiction (General), Science (General), Self-Help
ISBN Prefix(es): 968-6197
Associate Companies: Oscar Edwin Pruneda Alvarez
Distributor for Oscar Edwin Pruneda Alvarez
Orders to: Zacahuitzco 165, Mexico 09440 DF
Tel: 5397678 *Fax:* 5497666

Editorial Nova, SA de CV
Goldsmith 37-401, Col Polanco, 11550 Mexico, DF
Tel: (05) 2806080 *Fax:* (05) 2803194
E-mail: bolind@viernes.iwm.com.mx
Key Personnel
Dir: Valades Humberto *E-mail:* hvaldes@iwm.com.mx
Subjects: Advertising

Editorial Nuestro Tiempo SA+
Av Copilco 300 Locales 6 y 7, 04360 Mexico, DF
Tel: (05) 5503165; (05) 5503170
Key Personnel
Man Dir: Esperanza Nacif Barquet
Founded: 1966
Subjects: Social Sciences, Sociology
ISBN Prefix(es): 968-427
Branch Office(s)
Agencia Guadalajara, Federalismo 958 Sur, Sol Moderna, 44100 Guadalajara, Jalisco *Tel:* (036) 126037

Editorial Nueva Imagen SA
Blvd Adolfo Lopez Mateos 202 50 Piso, Col San Pedro de los Pinos, 03800 Mexico DF
Tel: (05) 2714524; (05) 2711980
Telex: 1771427 Eni Me
Key Personnel
Administrative Dir: Enrique Sealtiel Alatriste L
Editorial Dir: Guillermo J Schavelzon
Founded: 1976
Subjects: Anthropology, Art, Economics, Fiction, Health, Nutrition, History, Humor, Language

Arts, Linguistics, Regional Interests, Science (General), Social Sciences, Sociology
ISBN Prefix(es): 968-429

Organizacion Cultural LP SA de CV+
Praga No 56-Piso 40, Col Juarez, 06600 Mexico DF
Tel: (05) 5112312; (05) 5147608 *Fax:* (05) 3584761
Key Personnel
Contact: Joaquin Martin Gamero Castillo
Subjects: Accounting, Astronomy, Biological Sciences, Child Care & Development, Computer Science, Cookery, Management, Sports, Athletics

Origen Editorial SA
Roberto Gayol 1219-A, Col del Valle, 03100 Mexico DF
Tel: (05) 5750711 ext 30; (05) 5750711 ext 31
ISBN Prefix(es): 968-847

Editorial Orion
Sierra Mojada No 325, Col Lomas de Chapultepec, CP 11000 Mexico 10, DF
Tel: (05) 5200224 *Fax:* (05) 5200224
Key Personnel
Man Dir: Silvia Hernandez Vda de Cardenas
Sales Dir, Rights & Permissions: Laura Hernandez Baltazar
Publicity Dir: Silvia Hernandez Baltazar
Founded: 1942
Subjects: Astrology, Occult, Literature, Literary Criticism, Essays, Parapsychology, Philosophy, Psychology, Psychiatry, Religion - Other
ISBN Prefix(es): 968-6053; 968-6957
Subsidiaries: Edit Cuzamil SA

Paginas Mesoamericanas, *imprint of* Ediciones Euroamericanas

Editorial Paidos Mexicana, SA
Guanajuato 202-302, Col Roma, 06700 Mexico, DF
Tel: (05) 5645607; (05) 5647908 *Fax:* (05) 5904361
E-mail: paimex@iserve.net.mx
Key Personnel
International Rights: Mauricio M Morlett
ISBN Prefix(es): 968-853

Palabra Ediciones Verlagsgesellschaft mbH
Triunfo de la Libertad No 5-2, Col Tlalpan, 14000 Tlalpan
Tel: (05) 5730985 *Fax:* (05) 5730985
Key Personnel
Contact: Henry C Bergonzi Braconi
Subjects: Religion - Catholic
ISBN Prefix(es): 968-6460; 968-7515
Associate Companies: Cosmos Libros SRL, Moreno, 1369 1 A Buenos Aires, Argentina

Instituto Panamericano de Geografia e Historia
Ex-Arzobispado 29, Col Observatorio, 11860 Mexico DF
Tel: (05) 2775888; (05) 5151910 *Fax:* (05) 2716172
E-mail: ipgh@laneta.apc.org *Cable:* IPAGHIS
Key Personnel
Secretary-General: Carlos Carvallo Yanez
Founded: 1928
Specialized Organization of the OEA.
Subjects: Anthropology, Archaeology, Ethnicity, Geography, Geology, History, Regional Interests
ISBN Prefix(es): 968-6384; 84-8420

Pangea Editores, Sa de CV+
Periferico Sur 3453-601, Col San Jeronimo, 10200 Mexico DF
Tel: (05) 6813035; (05) 6813160
E-mail: pangea@data.net.mx
Founded: 1986
Subjects: Anthropology, Archaeology, Astrology, Occult, Astronomy, Biography, Biological Sciences, Science Fiction, Fantasy, Self-Help
ISBN Prefix(es): 968-6177

Panorama Editorial, SA+
Manuel Maria Contreras, No 45 B, Col San Rafael, Del Cuauhtemoc, 06470 Mexico DF
Tel: (05) 5355135; (05) 5359074; (05) 5350377 *Fax:* (05) 5359202; (05) 5351217
Key Personnel
Dir General: Luis Castaneda
Commercial Dir: Pilar Marquez
Founded: 1979
Subjects: Business, Health, Nutrition, History, Human Relations, Humor, Management, Regional Interests, Self-Help, Travel
ISBN Prefix(es): 968-38

Editorial Libreria Parroquial de Claveria SA de CV+
Floresta 79, Col Claveria, 02080 Mexico DF
Tel: (05) 3967027; (05) 3967718 *Fax:* (05) 3967718
ISBN Prefix(es): 968-442

Editorial Patria SA de CV+
Av San Lorenzo No 160, Col Esther Zunorde Echeverria-1, 09860 Mexico, DF
Tel: (05) 6704712; (05) 6704887 *Fax:* (05) 5613218; (05) 5614063
Telex: 1764172
Key Personnel
Man Dir: Rene Solis
Deputy Manager & Administrator, Rights & Permissions: Isabel Lasa
Sales & Publicity Dir: Rogelio Villarreal
Founded: 1933
Subjects: Biography, History, How-to, Literature, Literary Criticism, Essays, Philosophy
ISBN Prefix(es): 968-6054; 968-39; 968-34
Divisions: Promexa; Nueva Imagen; Alianza

Libreria Patria SA
Av San Lorenzo No 160, Col Esther Zuno de Echeverria-I, 09860 Mexico, DF
Tel: (05) 6704712; (05) 6704887 *Fax:* (05) 5109417
Key Personnel
Man Dir: Francisco Majewski M
Founded: 1940
Also acts as distributor to Trillas, Limusa, Prmyreso, Avunte, Esfinge.
Subjects: Literature, Literary Criticism, Essays
ISBN Prefix(es): 968-6054; 968-39
Subsidiaries: Samara, Cia Papelera SA
Bookshop(s): Belisario Dominguez 53, Mexico, DF
Orders to: Belisario Dominguez 53, 06010 Mexico 1 DF

Editorial Pax Mexico+
Av Cuauhtemoc 1434, Col Santa Cruz Atoyac, 03310 Mexico DF
Tel: (05) 605 7677 *Fax:* (05) 605 7600
E-mail: editorialpax@editorialpax.com
Web Site: www.editorialpax.com
Key Personnel
Man Dir: Gerardo Gally *E-mail:* gerardogally@editorialpax.com
Founded: 1936
Subjects: Business, Career Development, Education, Health, Nutrition, How-to, Psychology, Psychiatry
ISBN Prefix(es): 968-860
Associate Companies: Hoja Casa Editorial SA
Subsidiaries: Arbol Editorial SA

Pearson Educacion de Mexico, SA de CV+
Calle 4, No 25, Fraccionamiento Industrial Alce Blanco, Naucalpan de Juarez, Estado de Mexico 53370
Tel: (05) 387-0700 *Fax:* (05) 358-6445
E-mail: firstname.lastname@pearsoned.com
Web Site: www.pearson.com.mx
Key Personnel
President, Mexico, Central America & Caribbean: Steve Marban
Dir, Finance & Operations: Sven Boes
Dir, ELT & School USP Division: Juan M Abarca
Dir, Edition & Manufacturing: Juan A Rodriguez
Founded: 1984
Subjects: Art, Biological Sciences, Business, Chemistry, Chemical Engineering, Computer Science, Economics, Education, History, Language Arts, Linguistics, Management, Mathematics, Microcomputers, Physics, Psychology, Psychiatry, Science (General), Securities, Sports, Athletics, Technology
ISBN Prefix(es): 968-444; 968-880; 970-17
Total Titles: 76 Print
Parent Company: Pearson Plc
Imprints: Prentice Hall Hispanoamericana; Addison Wesley; Allyn & Bacon; Longman; Scott Foresman; Silver Burdette Ginn; Penguin Readers
Branch Office(s)
El Monte Mall-Suite 21-B, Ave. Munoz Rivera, Hato Rey 00918-4621, Puerto Rico, Regional Man: Jose Javier Rivera *Tel:* (787) 751-4830 *Fax:* (787) 751-1677
Barrio La Guaria Moravia, 75 M. Norte del Porton Norte del Club la Guaria, Casa con Reja Blanca, San Jose, Costa Rica, Regional Man: Luis Diego Barrientos *Tel:* 382-3931 *Fax:* 280-6569
Warehouse: Calle Negra Modelo No 12 & 12B, Fracc Industrial Alce Blanco, Naucalpan de Juarez, Estado de Mexico 53770 *Tel:* (05) 363 0842 *Fax:* (05) 363 4579

Penguin Readers, *imprint of* Pearson Educacion de Mexico, SA de CV

Publicaciones Piramide, SA de CV+
3ra Cerrada del Lago Silverio, No 30 Col Anahuac, 11320 Mexico, DF
Tel: (05) 5313215 *Fax:* (05) 2725883
Key Personnel
Dir General: Clive Alexander Bayne
Founded: 1983
ISBN Prefix(es): 968-6070

Grupo Editorial Planeta
Clavijero No 70, Col Esperanza, Mexico, DF
Tel: (05) 5331250
Key Personnel
Man Dir, Editorial: Joaquin Diez-Canedo
Production, Rights & Permissions: Francisco Campos
Founded: 1977
Subjects: Fiction, History, Nonfiction (General), Psychology, Psychiatry, Social Sciences, Sociology
ISBN Prefix(es): 968-6640
Parent Company: Difusion Editorial SA
Branch Office(s)
Editoriales Ariel, Planeta, Seix Barral, Joaquin Planeta

Plaza y Valdes SA de CV+
cedro No 299, Col sta Maria Riviera, 06400 Mexico, DF
Tel: (05) 5359851; (05) 5664055 *Fax:* (05) 7050030
E-mail: pyvedito@servidor.unam.mx
Key Personnel
Dir General: Fernando Valdes
Founded: 1987
Member of Mexican Publishing Association.

Subjects: Agriculture, Anthropology, Archaeology, Communications, Public Administration, Religion - Buddhist, Science (General), Science Fiction, Fantasy, Social Sciences, Sociology
ISBN Prefix(es): 968-856
Associate Companies: Libermex SA-de-CV Libreria Bunuel
Branch Office(s)
Libros Sin Fronteras, PO Box 2085, Olympia, WA 98507-2085, United States *Tel:* 206-357-4332 *Fax:* 206-357-4332
Bookshop(s): Insurgentes sur 32 Col Juarez, 06600 Mexico DF

Editorial Porrua SA
Argentina No 15, 06020 Mexico, DF
Tel: (05) 7025467; (05) 7024574 *Fax:* (05) 7026529 *Cable:* PORRUAS MEXICO
Key Personnel
Dir General & President: Jose Antonio Perez Porrua
Founded: 1900
Subjects: Literature, Literary Criticism, Essays
ISBN Prefix(es): 968-432; 968-452; 970-07
Orders to: Libreria de Porrua Hnos y Cia SA, Apdo M-7990, Argentina 15

Ediciones Cientificas La Prensa Medica Mexicana SA de CV+
Paseo de las Facultades 26, Col Copilco Universidad Del Coyoacan, 04360 Mexico, DF
Tel: (05) 5504500 *Fax:* (05) 6589193 *Cable:* LAPREMEMEX
Key Personnel
Man Dir, Rights & Permissions: Carlos A Fournier Amor
Administration & Assistant Manager: Abel Zavaleta
Sales & Promotion: Angelica Ruiz
Founded: 1945
Member of National Chamber of the Mexican Editorial Industry.
Subjects: Biological Sciences, Education, Medicine, Nursing, Dentistry, Social Sciences, Sociology, Veterinary Science
ISBN Prefix(es): 968-435

Prentice Hall Hispanoamericana, *imprint of* Pearson Educacion de Mexico, SA de CV

Editorial Progreso SA de C V
Naranjo 248, Col Santa Ma La Rivera, 06400 Mexico, DF
Tel: (05) 5477304; (05) 5471780; (05) 5411187 *Fax:* (05) 5415342
E-mail: editprogresosav@infosel.net.mx
Key Personnel
Dir: Joaquin Flores Segura *Fax:* (055) 41 11 89 *E-mail:* progdir@webtelmex.net.mx
Founded: 1952
Subjects: Education, Religion - Catholic
ISBN Prefix(es): 968-436; 970-641
Number of titles published annually: 300 Print
Total Titles: 3,000,000 Print

Ediciones Promesa, SA de CV+
Justo Sierra, 53-A, Circuito Educadores, Ciudad Satelite, Edo de
Mailing Address: Apdo P.97 CP 53140 Boulevares, Edo de Mexico, Mexico
Tel: (05) 5623174 *Fax:* (05) 3938707
Key Personnel
Contact: Fernando B Rivera
Founded: 1979
Subjects: Biblical Studies, Biography, Education, Philosophy, Religion - Catholic, Securities, Self-Help, Theology
ISBN Prefix(es): 968-7224

Promociones de Mercados Turisticos SA de CV
Gral Juan Cano No 68, Col San Miguel Chapultepec, Del Miguel Hidalgo, 11850 Mexico, DF
Tel: (05) 5150925; (05) 5160162 *Fax:* (05) 2725942
E-mail: tm@mail.internet.com.mx
Web Site: www.travelguidemexico.com
Key Personnel
Dir: Chris A Luhnow
Specialize in publishing & editing.
Subjects: Travel, Most complete & sold guide book to Mexico
Total Titles: 3 Print

Publicaciones Cultural SA de CV
Lago Mayor 186 Planta Baja, Mexico, DF 17
Tel: (05) 5456860; (05) 5456861; (05) 5456862 *Fax:* (05) 5618155
Key Personnel
President: Carlos Frigolet Lerma
Rights & Permissions: Ofelia Garcia Martinez
Production: Mario Munoz Rodriguez
General Dir, Editorial, Production & Sales: Victorico Albores Santiago
Founded: 1965
ISBN Prefix(es): 968-439; 970-16

Publicaciones Importantes SA
Bolivar No 8-601, Apdo 1970, 06000 Mexico 1, DF
Tel: (05) 5101884; (05) 5109489 *Fax:* (05) 5129411
Key Personnel
Contact: Alfredo Farrugia Reed

Editorial Quehacer Politico SA
Manuel Gonzales No 545, Col Atlampa, 06450 Mexico, DF
Tel: (05) 5414245 *Fax:* (05) 5384855
Key Personnel
Contact: Miguel Canton Zetina
ISBN Prefix(es): 968-6553

Red Editorial Iberoamericana Mexico SA de CV+
Lago Mayor No 186, Col Anahuac, Mexico DF 11320
Tel: (05) 5456860; (05) 5456861 *Fax:* (05) 5619122
Key Personnel
President: Carlos Frigolet Lerma
Rights & Permissions: Victorico Albores Santiago
Production: Mario Munoz Rodriguez
Founded: 1986
ISBN Prefix(es): 968-456

Ediciones Roca, SA+
General Francisco Munguia No 7, Col Hipodromo Condesa, 06170 Mexico DF
Tel: (05) 2770744; (05) 2770946 *Fax:* (05) 2714070
Telex: 1772155
Key Personnel
General Manager: Victor Lemus Dominquez
Founded: 1972
Subjects: Education, Environmental Studies, Fiction, History, Literature, Literary Criticism, Essays, Religion - Other
ISBN Prefix(es): 968-21

Rustica, *imprint of* AGT Editor SA

Salvat Editores de Mexico+
Presidente Mazaryk No 101-5 Piso, Col Chapultepec Morales, 11590 Mexico DF
Tel: (05) 2039343; (05) 2034813 *Fax:* (05) 2506861
Key Personnel
President, Editorial, Rights & Permissions: Jean Claude Lhomme
Sales (Encyclopedias): Jacobo Jimenez Parker
Production: Teresa Ponce
Subjects: Cookery, Fiction, Geography, Geology, History, Medicine, Nursing, Dentistry
ISBN Prefix(es): 968-32
Parent Company: Salvat Editores SA, Spain
Subsidiaries: Promotora Editorial SA De C V
Bookshop(s): Libreria de Cd Universitatia, Odontologia 69, Local 9; Libreria Satelite, Plaza Satelite, Local D-155, Cd Satelite; Libreri de Morelia, Ave Francisco I Madero Pte 533, Centro, Mrelia, Mich

Editorial Santillana
Av Universidad No 767, Col Del Valle, 03100 Benito Juarez
Tel: (05) 6888966 *Fax:* (05) 6042304
Key Personnel
Dir of Publications: Fernando Garcia
ISBN Prefix(es): 968-430; 970-642
Parent Company: Grupo Santillana

Grupo Santillana
Av Universidad No 767, Col Del Valle, 03100 Benito Juarez
Tel: (05) 6888966 *Fax:* (05) 6042304
Key Personnel
Dir General: Miguel Angel Cayuela
Contact: Manuel Sabido Duran
ISBN Prefix(es): 968-430; 970-642
Divisions: Aguilar; Actea; Taurus; Alfaquara SA Dec v; Distribuidora Aguilar; Altea Taurus; Editorial Santillana SA Dec v; Aguilar Mexicana de Ediciones

Sayrols Editorial SA de CV+
Mier y Pesado No 128, Col Del Valle, 03100 Mexico, DF
Tel: (0525) 147 2300 *Fax:* (0525) 536 4622
E-mail: ventas@sayrols.com.mx
Web Site: www.sayrols.com.mx
Key Personnel
General Dir: Roberto Davo *E-mail:* rodavo@sayrols.com.mx
Corporate Sales Dir: Federico Falkner *E-mail:* ffalkner@sayrols.mx
Bus & Technology Sales Manager: Beatriz Coria *Tel:* (0525) 536 4115 *E-mail:* beatrizc@sayrols.com.mx
Administrative Dir: Lourdes Noriega *E-mail:* lnoriega@sayrols.com.mx
Finance Manager: Raul Saryols *E-mail:* rauls@sayrols.com.mx
Circulation Manager: Luis Sayrols *E-mail:* luiss@sayrols.com.mx
Founded: 1925
Established in 1925, today are the leaders in IT & Business titles, reaching different kind of niches as end users in small & medium business, corporate, IT channel of distribution, internet users & e-business, our portfolio includes women's magazines, sports, cars & entertainment & a news agency. Each one of our publications has its own site, & we can provide a complete service, including printing & distribution of any kind of media.
Editorial & distribution.
Subjects: Astrology, Occult, Automotive, Business, Computer Science, Cookery, Crafts, Games, Hobbies, Education, Fashion, Sports, Athletics, Women's Studies
ISBN Prefix(es): 968-6117
Total Titles: 30 Print
Associate Companies: Mystic Impresiones, SA (Printing); Publicaciones Sayrols, SA
Subsidiaries: Servicios Editoriales Sayrols Sa de W
Distributor for AIE (Italy); Ediciones Pleyades (Spain); Grupo Editorial Ideas, SA (Mexico); Hymsa Edipress (Spain); Servicios de Edicion Mexico, SA (Editorial); Servicios Editoriales Sayrols, SA (Editorial); Servicios Graficos Sayrols, SA (Design & pre press services)

PUBLISHERS MEXICO

Scott Foresman, *imprint of* Pearson Educacion de Mexico, SA de CV

SCRIPTA - Distribucion y Servicios Editoriales, SA de CV+
Copilco 178 Edif 21-501, Col Copilco Universidad, 04340 Mexico, DF
Mailing Address: Apdo Postal 70 649, 140000 Mexico, DF
Tel: (05) 5481716 *Fax:* (05) 6161496
E-mail: dyse@data.net.mx
Key Personnel
Contact: Bertha R Alavez Magana
Founded: 1986
Also acts as Exporter & Distributor.
Subjects: Art, Business, Film, Video, History
ISBN Prefix(es): 968-6269
Branch Office(s)
Scripta, 4011 Creek Rd, Youngstown, NY 14174, United States *Tel:* 716-754-8145 *Fax:* 716-754-2707

Selector SA de CV+
Dr Erazo 120 Colonia Doctores, Mexico City 06720
Tel: (05) 588-7272 *Fax:* (05) 761-5716
E-mail: info@selector.com.mx
Web Site: www.selector.com.mx
Key Personnel
President: Gonzalo Araico Montes de Oca
Marketing Dir: Francisco Merino Nieto
Publisher: Antonio Hernandez Estrella
Editorial Assistant: Rocio Flores
Financial Dir: Maricruz Vazquez
Production Dir: Victor Becerra
Founded: 1949
Subjects: Child Care & Development, Crafts, Games, Hobbies, English as a Second Language, Health, Nutrition, Human Relations, Humor, Nonfiction (General), Science Fiction, Fantasy, Self-Help
ISBN Prefix(es): 968-403; 970-643
Number of titles published annually: 77 Print
Branch Office(s)
Guadalajara, Prisciliano Sanchez 579, Col Centr, 44100 Guadalajara, Jalisco
Sucursal Monterrey, Washington 112 B, Altos, Col Centro, Monterrey, NL, Francisco Mendoza Salazar *Tel:* (08) 340 3260
Distributed by Ediciones Oceano Argentina SA; Editorial Diana Colombia Ltda; Carlos Federspiel y Co SA; Editorial Diana Chilena Ltd; Editorial Oceano Ecuatorian SA; Almacenes Siman SA; Distribuciones Alfaomega SA; Publicaciones Yuquivo; Central De Libros C POR A; Giron Spanish Book; Lectorum Publications Inc; Editorial Oceno Peruana SA; Vendiana Editorial AC; Editorial Oceano De Venezuela SA
Foreign Rep(s): Almacenes Siman (El Salvador); Central de Libros C. Por A. (Dominican Republic); Distribuciones Alfaomega, S.A. (Spain); Ediciones Oceano Argentina, SA (Argentina); Edit. Diana Colombiana Ltda (Colombia); Editorial Diana Chilena Ltda (Chile); Editorial Oceano Ecuatoriana, S.A. (Ecuador); Carlos Federspiel y Co., S.A. (Costa Rica); Giron Spanish Books Dist. Inc (US); Lectorum Publications Inc (US); Libreria Lehmann, S.A. (Costa Rica); Publicaciones Yuquivo (Puerto Rico); Santa Maria Representaciones Editoriales (Central America); Venediana Editorial, A.C. (Venezuela)
Bookshop(s): Lectorum, SA de CV, Calzada Del Hueso 809, Locales 8 y 9, Col Mirador Coapa, Mexico, DF *Tel:* (05) 6030790; Mexico, D.F., Un Paseo Por Libros, Pasaje Zocalo-Pino Suarez, Local 21 *Tel:* (05) 522 35781, 522 3486

Servicios Especiales Maciel SA de CV+
Dallas 85 201, Col Napoles, 03810 Mexico DF
Tel: 05 5435533

Key Personnel
General Dir: Maria Luisa Sabau Garcia
Foreign Rights Manager: Jorge Ruiz Esparza
Founded: 1987
Member of the National Association of the Publishing Industry.
Subjects: Architecture & Interior Design, Art, Cookery, Photography
ISBN Prefix(es): 968-6084

Siglo XXI Editores SA de CV+
Av Cerro del Agua, No 248, Col Romero de Terreros, 04310 Mexico DF
Tel: (05) 6587234 *Fax:* (05) 6587999
E-mail: sigloxxi@netcorp.net.mx *Cable:* SIGLOEDIT
Key Personnel
Man Dir, Editorial: Arnaldo Orfila; Jaime Labastida
General Manager, Rights & Permissions & Publicity: Guadalupe Ortiz
Sales & Contact: Marta De la Rosa
Production: Maria Oscos
Founded: 1966
Subjects: Anthropology, Architecture & Interior Design, Art, Criminology, Economics, Education, Government, Political Science, Health, Nutrition, History, Language Arts, Linguistics, Law, Literature, Literary Criticism, Essays, Philosophy, Psychology, Psychiatry, Regional Interests, Social Sciences, Sociology
ISBN Prefix(es): 968-23

Silver Burdette Ginn, *imprint of* Pearson Educacion de Mexico, SA de CV

Sistemas Tecnicos de Edicion SA de CV+
San Marcos No 102, Col Tlalpan, 14000 Mexico, DF
Tel: (05) 6559144 *Fax:* (05) 5739412
Telex: 1771410 *Cable:* SITEME
Key Personnel
President: J Ignacio Echeverria
Editor: Marsella Cruz
International Operations: Emma Moreno
Founded: 1985
Subjects: Animals, Pets, Behavioral Sciences, Biological Sciences, Cookery, Earth Sciences, History, Language Arts, Linguistics, Management, Mathematics, Self-Help
ISBN Prefix(es): 968-6579; 970-629

Sistemas Universales, SA+
Insurgentes Centro 123, Col San Rafael, 06470 Mexico, DF
Tel: (05) 705-4568; (05) 705-5937 *Fax:* (05) 705-3421
E-mail: 73661.405@coms
Key Personnel
Contact: Arturo Delgado
Founded: 1970
Specialize in Post Secondary technical books for distance education.
Subjects: Accounting, Automotive, Electronics, Electrical Engineering, English as a Second Language, Microcomputers
ISBN Prefix(es): 968-6064
Total Titles: 290 Print
Distributed by Hemphill California Corporation

Ediciones Suromex SA+
General Francisco Murguia No 7, Col Hipodromo C, 06170 Mexico, DF
Tel: 2770744; 2770946 *Fax:* 2710470
E-mail: suromex@mail.internet.com.mx
Web Site: www.intralector.com/suromex/
Key Personnel
General Manager: Victor Lemus Dominguez
Tel: 272 3630
Founded: 1982

Subjects: Animals, Pets, Art, Astrology, Occult, Astronomy, Biography, Cookery, Earth Sciences, Gardening, Plants, House & Home, Religion - Other, Self-Help, Sports, Athletics, House & home
ISBN Prefix(es): 968-855
Number of titles published annually: 70 Print
Total Titles: 350 Print
Parent Company: Susaeta Ediciones SA
Subsidiaries: Susaeta Ediciones SA

Time-Life Internacional de Mexico
Paseo de la Reforma, 195 Decimo Piso, Col Cuauhtemoc, 06500 Mexico DF
Tel: (05) 5469000
Key Personnel
General Manager: Koos H Siewers
Founded: 1962
Subjects: Nonfiction (General)
ISBN Prefix(es): 968-7123

Travelers Guide to Mexico, see Promociones de Mercados Turisticos SA de CV

Editorial Trillas SA de CV+
Calzada dela Viga 1132, Col Apatlaco, 09439 Mexico, DF
Tel: (05) 6884233 *Fax:* (05) 6579235
Telex: 1762109 Etrime *Cable:* ETRILLASA
Key Personnel
Man Dir: Francisco Trillas
Editorial: Carlos Trillas
Sales: Jesus Galera
Production: Alfonso Duran
Publicity: Sergio Shinji
Founded: 1953
Subjects: Architecture & Interior Design, Business, Child Care & Development, Crafts, Games, Hobbies, Education, English as a Second Language, House & Home, Law, Mathematics, Medicine, Nursing, Dentistry, Psychology, Psychiatry, Science (General), Social Sciences, Sociology, Veterinary Science
ISBN Prefix(es): 968-24
Associate Companies: Cia Editorial Carmex SA, Venezuela 1962, Buenos Aires, Argentina; Cia Editorial Atlante, Argentina S RL Junin 827; Apdo aereo 15-15, Bogota, Spain; Limex Venezolana CA, Ave Lima Quinta Lourdes, Los Caobos, Caracas, Venezuela; Trillas Colombia, Carreroi 15 No 33-71 Apdo, Aereo 15-151, Santa Fe de Boqota, Colombia, Joslyne Reyno; Biblouex SA, Raigizas 10.28026, Madrid, Spain
Branch Office(s)
Calzada de la Viga 1132, Col Apatlaco, Delegacon Iztapalapa, 09439 Mexico, DF *Tel:* (05) 6579188 *Fax:* (05) 6579235 (Commercial Division Telex: 1762109 ETRIME)
Showroom(s): Av Cuahutemoc, 12000
Orders to: Calz de la Viga 1132, Col Apatlaco, Deleg Iztapalapa, cp, 09439 Mexico DF *Tel:* 905 657 9188 *Fax:* 905 657 9235

El Trimestre Economico, *imprint of* Fondo de Cultura Economica

Universidad Nacional Autonoma de Mexico (National University of Mexico)+
Torre 11 de Humanidades P 14, Ciudad Universitaria, 04510 Mexico City, DF
Tel: (05) 6650584 *Fax:* (05) 5507428
Web Site: www.serpientedgsca.unm.mx
Key Personnel
Dir: Mario Mendoza Castaneda
Assistant Dir: Leonardo Duenas Garcia
Founded: 1935
Subjects: Anthropology, Archaeology, Architecture & Interior Design, Chemistry, Chemical Engineering, Drama, Theater, Economics, Education, Engineering (General), Ethnicity, Geog-

raphy, Geology, History, Journalism, Language Arts, Linguistics, Law, Literature, Literary Criticism, Essays, Mathematics, Medicine, Nursing, Dentistry, Music, Dance, Philosophy, Physics, Psychology, Psychiatry, Science (General), Social Sciences, Sociology, Technology, Veterinary Science
ISBN Prefix(es): 968-36
Branch Office(s)
Universidad Nacional Autonoma de Mexico, 600
U.S. Office(s): Hemisfair Plaza, PO Box 830426, San Antonio, TX 78283-0426, United States
Bookshop(s): Libreria Central, Corredor de Zona Comercial, Ciudad Universitaria, 04510 Mexico DF; Libreria del Palacio de Mineria, Tacuba 5, 06000 Mexico DF; Casa Universitaria del Libro, Orizaba y Puebla, Col Roma, 06710 Mexico DF; Libreria Julio Torri, Zona Cultura, Cuidad Universitaria, 04510 Mexico DF

Universidad Veracruzana Direccion General Editorial y de Publicaciones
Zamora 25, Apdo 97, Codigo Postal, 91001 Xalapa, Veracruz
Tel: (029) 28 71316 *Fax:* (029) 28 17 44 35
E-mail: direditaspeedy@coacade.uv.mx
Key Personnel
Encargado de Ventas y Suscripciones: Jaime Pasquel Brash
Founded: 1957
Subjects: Anthropology, Art, Drama, Theater, Education, Fiction, History, Music, Dance, Philosophy, Psychology, Psychiatry, Social Sciences, Sociology
ISBN Prefix(es): 968-834
Total Titles: 15 Print
Parent Company: Universidad Veracruzana
Distributed by Direccion Editorial Universidad Veracruzana ((Mexico))

Universo Editorial SA de CV Edicion de Libros Revistas y Periodicos+
c/o Arco Iris Editorial, Emelia Carranza No 105, 7829 San Luis Potosi
Tel: (048) 21593
Key Personnel
Contact: Edmundo Llamas
Founded: 1991
Subjects: Biological Sciences, Fiction, Journalism, Literature, Literary Criticism, Essays, Medicine, Nursing, Dentistry, Poetry
ISBN Prefix(es): 968-6504

Editorial Universo SA de CV
Roberto Gayol No 1219, Col Del Valle, 03100 Mexico, DF
Tel: (05) 5750711 ext 30; (05) 5750711 ext 31
Key Personnel
Man Dir, Rights & Permissions: Enrique Ivan H Garcia
Editorial: Fausto Rosales
Sales: Manuel Valdez Islas
Production: Enrique Escamilla
Publicity: Maria del Refugio Salinas
Founded: 1979
Subjects: Fiction, Nonfiction (General)
ISBN Prefix(es): 968-35
Parent Company: Editorial Diana SA
Associate Companies: Editorial Origen SA; Edivision Cia Editorial SA
Branch Office(s)
Buenos Aires, Argentina
Guadalajara, Monterrey
Caracas, Venezuela

Uteha, *imprint of* Editorial Limusa SA de CV

Editorial Varazen SA+
Herodoto No 42, Col Anzures, 11590 Mexico DF
Tel: (05) 5146573; (05) 5335274 *Fax:* (05) 2555172
Key Personnel
Man Dir: Luis Maria Molachino Agostena
Founded: 1968
Subjects: Education, Ethnicity
ISBN Prefix(es): 968-7128
Associate Companies: Editorial Juventud, SA, Barcelona, Spain

Ventura Ediciones, SA de CV
Rio Ganges No 64, Col Cuauhtemoc, Mexico, DF 06500
Tel: (05) 5112517; (05) 5530798 *Fax:* (05) 5431173
Key Personnel
General Dir: Nicolas Grepe
Founded: 1988
Subjects: Computer Science, Microcomputers
ISBN Prefix(es): 968-6346; 968-7393

Javier Vergara Editor SA de CV
Av Cuauhtemoc 1100, Col Vertiz Navarte, 03600 Mexico, DF
Tel: (05) 6053374; (05) 6048283
Key Personnel
General Manager: Elsa Marino
Founded: 1978
Subjects: Biography, Business, Fiction, History, Music, Dance, Nonfiction (General), Psychology, Psychiatry, Self-Help
ISBN Prefix(es): 968-497
Parent Company: Javier Vergara Editor Argentina

Editorial Vuelta, SA de CV+
Av Contreras 516, Col San Jeronimo Lidice, 10200 Mexico DF
Tel: (05) 6835633 *Fax:* (05) 6580074
Key Personnel
President: Octavio Paz
Manager: Patricia Rodriguez Ochoa
Secretary: Enrique Krauze
ISBN Prefix(es): 968-6229

Martha Zamora Edicion de Libros
Bosque del Castillo 35, La Herradura, 10 Mexico DF
Tel: (05) 2940231 *Fax:* (05) 2943856
Key Personnel
Contact: Martha Zamora

Zona Ediciones y Publications SA de CV
Beta No 97 Col Romero de Terreros-Coyoacan, 04310 Mexico DF
Tel: (05) 5547438
Key Personnel
Contact: Francisco Campos Fontanet
ISBN Prefix(es): 968-6174
Warehouse: Ignacio Manuel Altamirano, 212 B Col Hank Gonzalez, 09750 Mexico DF

Republic of Moldova

General Information

Capital: Kishinev
Language: Romanian
Religion: Predominantly Christian (mostly Eastern Orthodox)
Population: 4.5 million
Bank Hours: Generally open for short hours between 0930-1230 Monday-Friday
Shop Hours: Generally 0900-1800 Monday-Friday; often open weekends
Currency: 100 kopeks = 1 rubl
Export/Import Information: According to Ukrainian quotas & customs duties, companies engaged in trade should register with the Ukraine Ministry of Foreign Economic Relations. Licenses for export & import are also required for trade with Russia.
Copyright: UCC (see Copyright Conventions, pg xi)

Editura Hyperion
Bdl Stefan cel Mare 180, Kisinev 277004
Tel: (02) 244259
Key Personnel
Dir: Valeriu Matei
Founded: 1976
Subjects: Art, Fiction, Literature, Literary Criticism, Essays, Music, Dance
ISBN Prefix(es): 5-368

Izdatelstvo Kartia Moldoveniaske
Prosp Lenina 180, 277004 Kisinev
Tel: (02) 244022
Key Personnel
Dir: N N Mumzhi
Editor-in-Chief: I A Tsurkanu
Founded: 1924
Subjects: Agriculture, Economics, Government, Political Science, Human Relations, Literature, Literary Criticism, Essays, Social Sciences, Sociology
ISBN Prefix(es): 5-362

Lumina Publishing House
bd Stefan cel Mare, 180, 2004 Kisinev
Tel: (02) 246397
Key Personnel
Manager: Vladimir Chistruga
Editor-in-Chief: Chiril Vaculovschi
Founded: 1966
Specialize in Textbooks, University Presses, Scholarly Books.
Subjects: Biological Sciences, Chemistry, Chemical Engineering, Child Care & Development, Geography, Geology, History, Language Arts, Linguistics, Literature, Literary Criticism, Essays, Mathematics, Medicine, Nursing, Dentistry, Physics, Psychology, Psychiatry
ISBN Prefix(es): 5-372; 9975-65

Monaco

General Information

Capital: Monaco
Language: French. Monegasque, Italian and English also spoken
Religion: Roman Catholic
Population: 29,712
Bank Hours: 0830-1730 Monday-Friday
Shop Hours: 0830-1300, 1600-1930 Monday-Friday
Currency: 100 centimes = 1 franc
Copyright: Berne, UCC (see Copyright Conventions, pg xi)

Editions Alphee+
28 rue Comte-Felix-Gastaldi, 98015 Monaco Cedex
Mailing Address: BP 521, 98015 Monaco Cedex
Tel: (093) 30-40-06 *Fax:* (099) 99-67-18
ISBN Prefix(es): 2-907573
Associate Companies: Editions du Rocher
Tel: (099) 99-67-17 *E-mail:* info@editionsdurocher.net

Editions EGC+
9 Av du Prince Hereditair Albert, BP 438, 98011 Monaco Cedex
Tel: (093) 92057433 *Fax:* (093) 92052422
E-mail: multip@webstore.mc

Key Personnel
Administrator: Monsieur Gerard Comman
Subjects: Economics, History, Literature, Literary Criticism, Essays
ISBN Prefix(es): 2-911469

Victor Gadoury, see Editions Victor Gadoury

Editions Victor Gadoury
Formerly Victor Gadoury
57, rue Grimaldi, MC-98000 Monaco
Tel: (093) 251296 *Fax:* (093) 501339
E-mail: contact@gadoury.com
Web Site: www.gadoury.com
Founded: 1967
ISBN Prefix(es): 2-906602

Marsu Productions SAM
2 av du Prince-Hereditair-Albert, entree F Stade Louis II, 98000 Monaco
Tel: (093) 92056111 *Fax:* (093) 92057660
ISBN Prefix(es): 2-9502211

Editions de l'Oiseau-Lyre SAM
Les Remparts, 98015 Monaco Cedex
Mailing Address: BP 515, 98015 Monaco Cedex
Tel: (093) 300944 *Fax:* (093) 301915
E-mail: oiseau_lyre@compuserve.com
Key Personnel
Man Dir: Moroney Davitt
Subjects: Music, Dance
ISBN Prefix(es): 2-87855

Publications du Palais de Monaco
Archives du Palais Princier, BP 518, MC-98015 Monaco Cedex
Tel: 093 251831
ISBN Prefix(es): 2-903147

Les Editions du Rocher+
28 rue Comte Felix Gastaldi BP 521, 98015 Monaco Cedex
Mailing Address: BP 521, 98015 Monaco
Tel: (093) 303341 *Fax:* (093) 507371
Founded: 1943
Subjects: Antiques, Astrology, Occult, Biography, Crafts, Games, Hobbies, Drama, Theater, Fiction, Health, Nutrition, History, How-to, Literature, Literary Criticism, Essays, Military Science, Mysteries, Romance, Sports, Athletics, Western Fiction
ISBN Prefix(es): 2-268
Subsidiaries: Jean-Paul Bertrand Editeur
Shipping Address: 6 Place Saint, Sulpice, F-75279 Paris, France *Tel:* (01) 40465400 *Fax:* (01) 40469136

Rondeau Giannipiero a Monaco+
4 rue Langl e, 98000 Monaco
Tel: (093) 303075 *Fax:* (093) 257047
Key Personnel
President: S Roudeau
International Rights: G Roudeau
Founded: 1993
Subjects: Art, Fiction, History, Humor, Literature, Literary Criticism, Essays
ISBN Prefix(es): 2-910305

Editions Andre Sauret SA
One blvd Suisse, 98000 Monaco
Tel: (093) 506794 *Fax:* (093) 307104
Subjects: Art, Fiction, Library & Information Sciences
ISBN Prefix(es): 2-85051

Mongolia

General Information

Capital: Ulaanbaatar
Language: Mongolian
Religion: Buddhist Lamaism, Islamic, Christian
Population: 2.6 million
Bank Hours: 0900-1200, 1400-1700 Monday-Saturday
Shop Hours: 0900-1900 Monday-Saturday
Currency: 100 mongo = 1 togrog (tughrik)

Mongolgosknigotorg
41 Ul Lenina, Ulan-Bator
Also functions as distributor.

State Press
Ulan-Bator
Subjects: Geography, Geology, Government, Political Science, Law

Morocco

General Information

Capital: Rabat
Language: Arabic (official), Berber, French, Spanish (northern regions)
Religion: Islamic
Population: 27 million
Bank Hours: Summer: 0830-1130, 1500-1700 Monday-Friday; rest of year: 0815-1130, 1415-1630 Monday-Friday
Shop Hours: Tangiers: 0900-1200, 1600-2000; rest: 0900-1200, 1500-1800 or 1900
Currency: 100 centimes = 1 Moroccan dirham
Export/Import Information: No tariff on books; most advertising dutiable. Special Tax, and Stamp Duty of percentage of import duty. No import licenses required. Exchange controls but permission liberally granted.
Copyright: UCC, Berne (see Copyright Conventions, pg xi)

Access International Services+
80 Blvd La Resistance, Casablanca
Tel: (02) 316068 *Fax:* (02) 304685
Key Personnel
President: Rachid Bennis
Founded: 1985
Also acts as editor & exporter of Moroccan publications.
Subjects: Advertising, Art, Business, Communications, Economics, How-to, Human Relations, Law, Publishing & Book Trade Reference, Religion - Islamic
ISBN Prefix(es): 9981-9756
Imprints: Le Repere
Branch Office(s)
African Imprint Library Services, 236 Main St, Falmouth, MA 02540, United States

Editions Al-Fourkane+
8, rue Ibn Habbous, Av Yacoub El Mansour, App No 2, Casablanca
Mailing Address: BP 20362, Hay Salam, Casablanca
Tel: (02) 983351 *Fax:* (02) 983351
Key Personnel
Dir: Dr El Otmani Saad-Dine
Subjects: Biography, Government, Political Science, Religion - Islamic, Social Sciences, Sociology
ISBN Prefix(es): 9981-811
Parent Company: Al Fouruane

Annuaire Fax Telex, *imprint of* Office Marocain D'Annonces-OMA

Association de la Recherche Historique et Sociale+
BP 57, Ksar El Kebir 92-150
Tel: 918239
Key Personnel
Contact: Mohamed Akhrif
Subjects: Antiques, Archaeology, Art, Biography, History, Natural History, Poetry
ISBN Prefix(es): 9981-9778
Distributed by Editeurs Particuliers
Distributor for Imprimerie de Tanger SA

Cabinet Conseil CCMLA
44 rue Oued Ziz, Agdal, Rabat
Tel: (07) 770229; (07) 770264 *Fax:* (07) 770264
Key Personnel
Manager: Michele Malaval
Founded: 1992
Subjects: Accounting, Developing Countries, Economics
ISBN Prefix(es): 9981-9699

Dar El Kitab
pl de la Mosquee Habous, BP 4018, Casablanca
Tel: (02) 304581; (02) 305419 *Fax:* (02) 304581
Telex: 26630 Darki
Key Personnel
President: Boutaleb Abdou Abdelhay
Manager: Mrs Soad Kadiri
Publicity Manager: Mounjedine Abdel-Ghani
Production: Ferhat Mohamed
Founded: 1948
Subjects: History, Philosophy, Regional Interests, Science (General), Social Sciences, Sociology
ISBN Prefix(es): 9981-133

Dar Nachr Al Maarifa Pour L'Edition et La Distribution+
Rue Er-Rakha Quartier Industriel Cite Yacoub El Mansour, Rabat
Mailing Address: 10, Ave Fadela, QI CYM Rabat
Tel: (07) 795702; (07) 796914 *Fax:* (07) 790343
Key Personnel
Contact: Mr Zhiri M'Hamed
Founded: 1988
Member of Moroccan Association of Publishers; International Publishers Association. Also acts as distributor.
Subjects: Economics, Education, History, Law, Literature, Literary Criticism, Essays, Mathematics, Science (General), Social Sciences, Sociology
ISBN Prefix(es): 9981-808
Number of titles published annually: 10 Print
Total Titles: 3 Print
Distributor for APREJ
Bookshop(s): Librairie EL Maarif, SA, Rue Bab Chellah, BP 239, Rabat *Tel:* (07) 726524; 730701

Editions Eddif Maroc+
71 Av des Far, BP 7537, Casablanca 21000
Tel: (02) 442375; (02) 442376 *Fax:* (02) 313565
Telex: 23793M
Key Personnel
Pres: Retnani Abdelkader
Founded: 1979
Member of the Moroccan Association of Profession of Books (AMPL).
Subjects: Archaeology, Art, Drama, Theater, Education, Fiction, History, How-to, Humor, Law, Literature, Literary Criticism, Essays, Medicine, Nursing, Dentistry, Music, Dance, Philosophy, Psychology, Psychiatry, Religion - Other, Social Sciences, Sociology, Travel, Women's Studies
ISBN Prefix(es): 2-908801; 9981-09
Total Titles: 300 Print

MOROCCO

Associate Companies: Comptoir Marocain du Livre, Angles rues des Landes et Vignemale, Casablanca 20000 *Tel:* (022) 258781
Branch Office(s)
La Croisee Des Chemins
Distributor for Ceres Production (Tunisia)
Bookshop(s): Carrefour Des Arts, Rue Essanaani, Quartier Boorgogne Casablanca 20000 *Tel:* (022) 26 05 01 05 *Fax:* (022) 29 43 64 *E-mail:* mrctruni@caromail.com; Carrerour Des Livres, Angle rues des landes et Vignemale, Maarif Casablanca 20000 *Tel:* (022) 258781; Librairie 11 Janview, 53 av de madagascar, Rabat *Tel:* (07) 704580

Edition Diffusion de Livre au Maroc, see Editions Eddif Maroc

Europages, *imprint of* Office Marocain D'Annonces-OMA

Editions Le Fennec+
89, bd d'Anfa, 20000 Casablanca
Tel: (02) 209268; (02) 209314 *Fax:* (02) 277702
E-mail: fennec@techno.net.ma
Telex: 45468
Key Personnel
President, Editor: Laila Chaouni
Author: Fatima Mernissi
Founded: 1987
Subjects: Drama, Theater, Economics, Fiction, Health, Nutrition, Language Arts, Linguistics, Literature, Literary Criticism, Essays, Mysteries, Poetry, Psychology, Psychiatry, Religion - Islamic, Social Sciences, Sociology, Women's Studies
ISBN Prefix(es): 9981-838
Distributed by Vilo-Diffusion-Paris (Europe & Canada)

Formation Entreprises, *imprint of* Office Marocain D'Annonces-OMA

Le Gourmand, *imprint of* Office Marocain D'Annonces-OMA

Government Printer (Imprimerie Officielle)
Ave Jean Mermoz, Rabat-Chellah
Tel: (077) 65024

Les Editions du Journal L' Unite Maghrebine+
2, Lotissement El Menza H, Bettana, Sale
Tel: 780169 *Fax:* 780169
Telex: 780169
Key Personnel
Founder: Mohamed El Alami
Dir: Buthayma Ebrahim
Founded: 1988
Subjects: Economics, Ethnicity, Government, Political Science, Science (General), Sports, Athletics
Parent Company: Agence Afro-Asiatique de Press et d'Information (API)

Les Editions Maghrebines, EDIMA
Quartier Industriel, Blvd E, N 15, Sin Sebaa, Casablanca 05
Tel: (02) 351797; (02) 353230; (02) 353249 *Fax:* (02) 355541
Telex: 26954
ISBN Prefix(es): 9981-24
Bookshop(s): Librairie EDIMA-5, Place de la Mosquee Mohammadi, Habous, Casablanca

Office Marocain D'Annonces-OMA
332 Blvd Brahim Roudani, Casablanca
Tel: (02) 234891; (02) 232342 *Fax:* (02) 234892
Key Personnel
Contact: Assya Djellab
Member of Satellite de l'AEEA & de l'ATC Paris.
Subjects: Career Development
Imprints: Annuaire Fax Telex; Europages; Formation Entreprises; Le Gourmand; Les Pages Jannes Maroc
Distributor for Euredit pour le Maroc

Editions Okad+
4, Av Hassan Il, Route de Casablanca, Yacoubel el Mansouk, Quartier Industriel Cita, Rabat
Tel: (07) 796970; (07) 796971; (07) 796973; (07) 798589 *Fax:* (07) 798556
Telex: 32687
Key Personnel
Dir General: El Hadi Lasmer
Founded: 1981
Subjects: Economics, History, Language Arts, Linguistics, Poetry
ISBN Prefix(es): 9981-806

Editions Oum+
25 rue lbn Batouta, Casablanca 20000
Tel: (02) 274972 *Fax:* (02) 208882
Key Personnel
PDG: M Sijelmassi
Subjects: Art, How-to, Medicine, Nursing, Dentistry, Photography
Distributor for ACR; Flammarion; Gallimand

Les Pages Jannes Maroc, *imprint of* Office Marocain D'Annonces-OMA

Editions La Porte+
281 Ave Mohammed-V, BP 331, Rabat
Tel: (07) 709958; (07) 706476 *Fax:* (07) 709958; (07) 706478
Key Personnel
Man Dir: Mohamed Rafii Doukkali
Subjects: Economics, Government, Political Science, Language Arts, Linguistics, Law, Religion - Islamic, Religion - Other, Travel
ISBN Prefix(es): 9981-889
Subsidiaries: Librairie aux Belles Images (bookshop)

Le Repere, *imprint of* Access International Services

Editions Services et Informations pour Etudiants+
Cite Al Inara 1, No 155 Ave Dakhla, Casablanca 02
Mailing Address: BP 156691 CASA-PrP, Casablanca 20001
Tel: (02) 210163
Key Personnel
Dir: Mr Aitcaid Mustapma
Subjects: How-to

Societe Ennewrasse Service Librairie et Imprimerie
70 Ave Okba Bnou Nafie, Agdal, 10000 Rabat
Tel: (077) 6413 *Fax:* (077) 6413
Key Personnel
Contact: Mohamed Ali Omar
Subjects: Anthropology, Antiques, Business, Communications, Criminology, History, Human Relations, Law, Literature, Literary Criticism, Essays, Religion - Islamic, Women's Studies
Parent Company: Annawrasse (Sarl)

Mozambique

General Information

Capital: Maputo
Language: Portuguese
Religion: Catholic, Protestant & Islamic
Population: 16.6 million
Bank Hours: 0800-1200 Monday - Friday
Shop Hours: 0800-1230, 1400-1700 Monday-Saturday
Currency: One US dollar = 11,251 meticais
Export/Import Information: Children's picture books dutied per kg net weight, otherwise books and advertising matter duty-free. No additional taxes apply. Import licenses and strict exchange controls; authorities have classified books and advertising as List 3 in priorities.

Associacao dos Escritores Mocambicanos (AEMO)
CP 4187, 1420 Maputo
Tel: (01) 420727
Key Personnel
Man Dir: Pedro Chissano

Empresa Moderna Lda
Avda 25 de Setembro, Maputo CP 473
Tel: (01) 424594
Key Personnel
Man Dir: Louis Galloti
Founded: 1937
Subjects: Education, Fiction, History, Regional Interests

Centro De Estudos Africanos+
Universidade Eduardo Mondlane, CP 1993 Maputo
Tel: (01) 490828 *Fax:* (01) 491896
Telex: 6-740 CEA MO
Key Personnel
Dir: Coronel Sergio Vieira
Founded: 1976
Specializes in Social Science.
Subjects: Economics, Foreign Countries, Government, Political Science, History, Regional Interests

Editora Minerva Central
Rua Consiglieri Pedroso 84, CP 212 Maputo
Tel: (01) 22092; (01) 22093; (01) 26114; (01) 23637
Telex: 6-561 Miner Mo
Key Personnel
Man Dir: J F Carvalho
Founded: 1908
Subjects: Medicine, Nursing, Dentistry, Science (General)
Subsidiaries: J A Carvalho & Co Ltd

Myanmar

General Information

Capital: Yangon
Language: Burmese (English used for foreign correspondence)
Religion: Buddhism
Population: 42.6 million
Bank Hours: 1000-1400 Monday-Friday; 1000-1200 Saturday
Shop Hours: Generally 0800-1700 Monday-Saturday
Currency: 100 pyas = 1 kyat

Export/Import Information: Myanmar has own complex tariff system, but duties are paid by State Trading Corporation No 9, 550-552 Merchant St, Rangoon, and Printing and Publishing Corporation, 228 Theinbyu St, Rangoon, principally. No tariffs on advertising. Books exempt from sales tax. Import license required. Exchange controls; priorities apply.
Copyright: No copyright conventions signed

Hanthawaddy Book House
157 Bo Aung Gyaw St, Rangoon
Bookshop(s): Hanthawaddy Bookshop

Knowledge Printing & Publishing House
130 Bogyoke Aung San St, Yegyaw, Rangoon
Subjects: Art, Education, Government, Political Science, Religion - Other, Social Sciences, Sociology
Bookshop(s): Knowledge Book House

Kyi-Pwar-Ye Book House
84 St, Letse-gan Mandalay
Tel: (02) 21003 *Cable:* LUDU
Subjects: Art, Religion - Other, Travel

Sarpay Beikman Board
529 Merchand St, Rangoon
Tel: (01) 83611 *Cable:* Sarbeikman
Key Personnel
Chairman: Aung Htay
Secretary: Lt-Col Mg MgLay
Sales, Publicity & Advertising: U Tin Gyi
Editorial: Myo Thant
Founded: 1947
Subjects: Agriculture, Biography, Ethnicity, History, Law, Literature, Literary Criticism, Essays, Science (General)
Bookshop(s): Sarpay Beikman Bookshop
Book Club(s): Sarpay Beikman Book Club

Shumawa Publishing House
146 Bogyoke Aung San Market, Rangoon
Subjects: Mechanical Engineering
Bookshop(s): Shumawa Book House

Shwepyidan Printing & Publishing House
12 A Hninban, Yegwaw Quarter, Rangoon
Subjects: Government, Political Science, Law, Religion - Other

Smart & Mookerdum
221 Sule Pagoda Rd, Rangoon
Subjects: Art, Cookery, Science (General)

Thudhammawaddy Press
PO Box 419, 55-56, Rangoon
Subjects: Religion - Other

Universities Administration Office
Prome Rd, University Post Office, Rangoon
Key Personnel
Chief Editor, Translations and Publications Department: U Wun

Namibia

General Information

Capital: Windhoek
Language: English (official), Afrikaans and German widely used
Religion: Predominantly Christian
Population: 1.6 million
Bank Hours: 0900-1530 Monday-Friday
Shop Hours: 0830-1700 Monday-Friday, 0800-1300 Saturday
Currency: 100 cents = 1 Nambian dollar
Export/Import Information: Part of the Southern African Customs Union (SACU). Import licenses required. Payment of hard currency or any other currency for trade transactions strictly against documentation. Strict foreign exchange controls and regulations. No exchange control applicable to non-residents. Gradual easing exchange control of residents.
Copyright: Berne (see Copyright Conventions, pg xi)

Agrivet Publishers+
PO Box 178, Windhoek
Tel: (061) 228909 *Fax:* (061) 230619
E-mail: agriveti@iafrica.com.ma
Founded: 1992
Subjects: Foreign Countries, Travel, Veterinary Science

Bible Society of Namibia
PO Box 1926, Windhoek
Tel: (061) 235090 *Fax:* (061) 228663
ISBN Prefix(es): 99916-713

Bureau for Indigenous Languages
Department of Bantu Education, Windhoek
Mailing Address: PMB 13236, Windhoek
Tel: (061) 24601
Telex: 3178 *Cable:* Imfundo Windhoek
Key Personnel
Head: W Zimmermann
Founded: 1964
ISBN Prefix(es): 0-621
Branch Office(s)
Department of Education and Training, Pretoria, South Africa

Desert Research Foundation of Namibia (DRFN)
PO Box 20232, Windhoek
Tel: (061) 229855 *Fax:* (061) 230172
E-mail: drfn@drfn.org.na
Key Personnel
Contact: Dr Mary Seely *Fax:* (61) 230770
  E-mail: mseely@drfn.org.na
Founded: 1963
Subjects: Agriculture, Behavioral Sciences, Biological Sciences, Developing Countries, Earth Sciences, Education, Energy, Environmental Studies, Geography, Geology, Natural History, Physical Sciences, Regional Interests, Science (General), Botany, Zoology, Desertification Issues, Environmental Training, Water Management
ISBN Prefix(es): 99916-709
U.S. Office(s): Friends of Gobabeb, c/o Prof C S Crawford, Dept of Biology, University of New Mexico, Albuquerque, NM, United States

DRFN, see Desert Research Foundation of Namibia (DRFN)

Gamsberg Macmillan Publishers (Pty) Ltd
PO Box 22830, Windhoek
Tel: (061) 232165 *Fax:* (061) 233538
E-mail: gmp@iafrica.com.na
Key Personnel
Man Dir, Editorial, Rights & Permissions: Herman van Wyk
Production: Ingrid van Graan
Sales, Publicity: Kotie van der Merwe
Founded: 1977
Subjects: Literature, Literary Criticism, Essays
ISBN Prefix(es): 0-86848; 99916-0
Shipping Address: 19 Faraday S, Windhoek

Kuiseb-Verlag
PO Box 67, Windhoek
Tel: (061) 225372 *Fax:* (061) 226846
E-mail: nwg@iafrica.com.na
Key Personnel
Contact: Ingrid Demasius
Founded: 1925
ISBN Prefix(es): 99916-703

McGregor Publishers
PO Box 9338, Windhoek
Tel: (061) 62155 *Fax:* (061) 63059
E-mail: gmcgregor@unam.na
Key Personnel
Contact: Gordon McGregor
Founded: 1990
Specialize in German occupied South-West Africa.
Subjects: Military Science
ISBN Prefix(es): 99916-700

Media Institute of Southern Africa (MISA)
P/Bag 13386, Windhoek
Tel: (061) 32975 *Fax:* (061) 248016
E-mail: dush@ingrid.misa.org.na
Key Personnel
Dir: M Leepile

Multi-Disciplinary Research Centre Library
University of Namibia, Private Bag 13301, Windhoek
Tel: (061) 2063907 *Fax:* (061) 2063050
E-mail: root@ssdgate.ssd.mrc.unam.na
Key Personnel
Contact: Dr Ben Fuller
Founded: 1989
Subjects: Agriculture, Developing Countries, Economics, Environmental Studies, Geography, Geology, Government, Political Science, Science (General), Social Sciences, Sociology, Gender Issues, Life Sciences
Parent Company: University of Namibia
Divisions: Social Sciences Division; Science & Technology Division; Life Sciences Division
U.S. Office(s): J Diescho, University of Namibia Office, Africa/American Institute, 833 United Nations Plaza, New York, NY 10017, United States

Nepal

General Information

Capital: Kathmandu
Language: Nepali (official), also Maithir & Bhojpuri
Religion: Predominantly Hindu, also some Buddhist and Muslim
Population: 20.1 million
Bank Hours: 1000-1430 Sunday-Thursday; 1000-1230 Friday
Shop Hours: 1000-2000 Sunday-Friday
Currency: 100 paisa = 1 Nepalese rupee
Export/Import Information: No tariff on books and advertising. Import licenses required. Exchange controls.

International Standards Books & Periodicals (P) Ltd+
Kamabakshee Tole, Gha 3/333 Chowk Bhitra, Katmandu 44601
Mailing Address: PO Box 3000-ISB-NFSLA Kathmandu-3-30-15B, Katmandu 44601
Tel: (01) 212289; (01) 224005; (01) 223036
  Fax: (01) 223036
Telex: 3000 ISB-ASS-NP *Cable:* ANTERRASHTRIYASTARKOSAPHOOPASA, KATHMANDU

Key Personnel
Chairman: Sugat Dass Tuladhar
Chief Executive & Man Dir: Ganesh Lall Chhipa
Chief Man Dir: Suindra Lall Chhipa
Senior Man Dir: Yogendra Lall Chhipa
Junior Man Dir: Bijendra Lall Upasak
Man Dir: Ganesh Dass Chhipa
Company Secretary: Udhdab Lall Chhipa
Editorial Dir: Dharma Ratna Ranjit
Marketing Dir: Chandra Lexmee Ranjit
General Sales Dir: Pawan Ratna Tuladhar
General Order Dir: Bhawanyshowr Ranjit
Production Dir: Bhumaheshwor Ranjit
Promotion Dir: Suneeta Shobha Ranjit
Subscription Dir: Aneeta Shobha Ranjit
Distribution Dir: Miss Nanee Shobha Tuladhar
Customer Dir: Miss Bheem Shobha Tuladhar
Publishing Dir: Mrs Rameeta Shobha Tuladhar
Foreign Rights Dir: Rajendra K Ranjit
Supplies Dir: Shant Shobha Ranjit
Sales Manager: Basant Bahadur Basnet
Business Manager: Bijendra Man Tuladhar
General Trade Dir: Amrit Lall Ranjit
Circulation Dir: Surya Man Ranjit
Reference Dir: Ms Saraswati Shrestha
Acquisition Dir: Mrs Subarna Laxmi Chhipa
Export Dir: Jaya Ram Ranjit
Import Dir: Mrs Saroja Ranjit
Rights & Permission Dir: Shanta Dass Ranjit
Information Dir: Shanta Lall Ranjit
Publicity Manager: Mona Ranjit
Foreign Order Manager: Jambu Ranta Ranjitkar
Subsidiary Rights Manager: Ms Babee Shobha Ranjit
Marketing Manager: Jambu Ranta Ranjit
Founded: 1965
Centre for Central General Selling, Distribution & Wholesales, Order Supplies, Subscription & Publication.
Subjects: Agriculture, Anthropology, Archaeology, Architecture & Interior Design, Art, Business, Career Development, Chemistry, Chemical Engineering, Earth Sciences, Economics, Education, Engineering (General), Gardening, Plants, Geography, Geology, Government, Political Science, History, Human Relations, Language Arts, Linguistics, Law, Literature, Literary Criticism, Essays, Mathematics, Medicine, Nursing, Dentistry, Music, Dance, Natural History, Philosophy, Physics, Psychology, Psychiatry, Social Sciences, Sociology
Branch Office(s)
Arniko Main, Arniko Barhabise - 9, Ariko Rajmarg 87 KM
Ason Kamabakshee Tole, Katmandu City
Bhotahity Tole, Katmandu Valley
Showroom(s): Ason Kamalakshee Tole, Cha 1/112, Katmandu 3, Chowk Bhitra
Bookshop(s): S A A R C Books and Periodicals Shop, 09-53-01 Bhindyo Tole, Purano Bazar, Katmandu; A R N I K O, Barhabise-9, Arniko Rajmarg-87 KM, Bagmati Anchal, Barhabise, Katmandu 45303
Shipping Address: Naradevee Tole, Gha 3/460, Nyata Twa, Chowk Bhitra, PO Box 3000-ISB, City, Katmandu-3, 44601-3000 Katmandu
Warehouse: Bhurungkhel Tole, Cha 4/394, Ikhapokhary, Kshetrapaty, PO Box 5000-ISB, Katmandu-3, City, Katmandu 44601-5000
Orders to: Bhotahity Tole, Cha 1/333, Chowk Bhitra, 5th fl, PO Box 5000-ISB, Katmandu City 44601-5000
Maroohity Tole, Chha 3/333, Chowk Bhitra, 1st fl, PO Box 3000-ISB, Katmandu City 44601-3000

Royal Nepal Academy
Kamaladi, Katmandu 178 MEMS
Tel: (01) 221283; (01) 221241 *Fax:* (01) 221175
Key Personnel
Library Chief: T D Bhandari

Founded: 1957
Subjects: Art, History, Literature, Literary Criticism, Essays, Science (General), Social Sciences, Sociology

Sajha Prakashan, Co-operative Publishing Organization
Pulchowk, Kathmandu
Tel: (01) 521023; (01) 521118 *Cable:* SAJHA PRAKASHAN KATMANDU
Key Personnel
Chairman: Deepak Baskota
General Manager: Narayan S Gajurel
Manager, Marketing Department: Naseeb D Lama
Founded: 1966
Subjects: Literature, Literary Criticism, Essays

Worldwide Publishings Systems, see International Standards Books & Periodicals (P) Ltd

Netherlands

General Information

Capital: Amsterdam
Language: Dutch; Frisian in Friesland (though all speakers of Frisian also speak Dutch). English is common second language
Religion: Mainly Roman Catholic and Protestant
Population: 15.9 million
Bank Hours: 0900-1600 Monday-Friday; some open Saturday morning and on late night shopping evenings
Shop Hours: 0900-1730 or 1800 Monday-Saturday. Many close Monday morning
Currency: 100 Eurocents = 1 Euro; 2.20371 Dutch guilders = 1 Euro
Export/Import Information: Member of the European Economic Community. No tariff on books except children's picture books from non-EEC; advertising other than single copies is dutied; 6 % VAT on books. Import licenses required for certain countries (not USA or UK).
Copyright: UCC, Berne, Florence (see Copyright Conventions, pg xi)

Academic Publishers Associated, see APA (Academic Publishers Associated)

Aeolus Press BV+
Erichemsekade 14, 4117 GX Erichem
Mailing Address: Postbus 83, 2160 SZ Lisse
Tel: (0344) 572055 *Fax:* (0344) 572562
E-mail: aeolus@swets.hl
Key Personnel
President: Dr J K W van Leeuwen
Founded: 1979
Specialize in Ophthalmology, Consumer Safety & Occupational Medicine.
Subjects: Health, Nutrition, Labor, Industrial Relations, Medicine, Nursing, Dentistry
ISBN Prefix(es): 90-70430
Parent Company: Swets & Zeitlinger
U.S. Office(s): Swets & Zeitlinger Publishers, PO Box 613, Royersford, PA 19468, United States
Shipping Address: Swets & Zeitlinger, PO Box 825, SZ 2160 Lisse

Agathon, *imprint of* Unieboek BV

Agon, *imprint of* BV Uitgeverij de Arbeiderspers

Uitgeversmaatschappij Agon+
Herengracht 370-372, 1016 CH Amsterdam
Mailing Address: Postbus 2877, 1000 CW Amsterdam

Tel: (020) 5247500 *Fax:* (020) 6224937
Key Personnel
Publisher: R J W Dietz
Founded: 1987
Subjects: History
ISBN Prefix(es): 90-5157
Parent Company: Weekblad pers groep

Agora Gooi & Sticht, *imprint of* Uitgeefmaatschappij J H Kok BV

Allert de Lange BV
Damrak 62, 1012 LM Amsterdam
Tel: (02) 6246744 *Fax:* (020) 6384975
Key Personnel
Man Dir: W J van Loon
Founded: 1880
ISBN Prefix(es): 90-6133; 90-5336
Parent Company: Allert de Lange Beheer BV
Associate Companies: Nilsson & Lamm BV
Bookshop(s): Robert Premsela, Van Baerlestraat 78, 1071 BB Amsterdam; Ala Carte, Utrechtsestraat 110-112, 1017 VS Amsterdam

Altamira BV+
Blekersvaartweg 19A, 2101 CB Heemstede
Tel: (023) 5286882 *Fax:* (023) 5288097
Founded: 1985
Subjects: Literature, Literary Criticism, Essays
ISBN Prefix(es): 90-6963

Altamira-Becht, *imprint of* Gottmer Uitgevers Groop

Uitgeverij Ambo BV+
Herengracht 435-437, 1017 BR Amsterdam
Tel: (020) 5245411 *Fax:* (020) 4200422
Telex: 43272
Key Personnel
Publisher: Ms Eva Cossee
Founded: 1963
Member of Combo Group, Netherlands.
Subjects: History, Literature, Literary Criticism, Essays, Philosophy, Psychology, Psychiatry, Religion - Other, Social Sciences, Sociology
ISBN Prefix(es): 90-263; 90-6074; 90-414
Warehouse: Combo Nijkerk, Gezellestraat 16, 3861 RD Nijkerk
Orders to: Combo, Postbus 1, 3740 AA Baarn

Ankh-Hermes BV+
Postbus 125, 7400 AC Deventer
Tel: (0570) 678900 *Fax:* (0570) 624632
E-mail: ankh-hermes.nl@pi.net
Key Personnel
Dir: Nicole de Haas
Financial Dir: Mr A L Steenbergen
Founded: 1949
Subjects: Astrology, Occult, Gardening, Plants, Health, Nutrition, Parapsychology, Philosophy
ISBN Prefix(es): 90-202

Uitgeverij Anthos+
Keizersgracht 630, 1017 ER Amsterdam
Tel: (020) 5245411 *Fax:* (020) 4200422
E-mail: info@amboanthos.nl
Key Personnel
Man Dir: Robbert Ammerlaan
Member of the Combo Group.
Subjects: Biography, Fiction, Science (General)
ISBN Prefix(es): 90-6074

AO, *imprint of* Stichting IVIO

APA (Academic Publishers Associated)
Postbus 806, 1000 AV Amsterdam
Tel: (020) 6265544
E-mail: info@apa-publishers.com
Key Personnel
Man Dir: G van Heusden

Founded: 1967
Subjects: Art, Asian Studies, History, Human Relations, Language Arts, Linguistics, Law, Library & Information Sciences, Science (General), Social Sciences, Sociology, Theology
ISBN Prefix(es): 90-6037; 90-6023; 90-6042
Subsidiaries: Holland University Press BV; Oriental Press BV; Philo Press-van Heusden-Hissink & Co CV

Aramith, *imprint of* Gottmer Uitgevers Groop

BV Uitgeverij de Arbeiderspers+
Herengracht 372, 1016 CH Amsterdam
Mailing Address: Postbus 2877, 1000 CW Amsterdam
Tel: (020) 5247500 *Fax:* (020) 6224937
E-mail: info@arbeiderspers.nl
Key Personnel
Man Dir: R J W Dietz
Subjects: Biography, Fiction, History, Poetry
ISBN Prefix(es): 90-295
Parent Company: Weekbladpers Group
Imprints: Agon

Uitgeverij Arbor+
PO Box 1, 3740 AA Baarn
Tel: (035) 5422141 *Fax:* (035) 15433
Key Personnel
Man Dir: Robbert Ammerlaan
Member of the Combo Group.
Subjects: Religion - Other
ISBN Prefix(es): 90-5158

Architectura & Natura
Leliegracht 22, 1015 DG Amsterdam
Tel: (020) 6236186 *Fax:* (020) 6382303
E-mail: kemme@architectrua.nl
Key Personnel
Contact: G Kemme *E-mail:* kemme@architectrua.nl
Founded: 1939
Specialize in Architecture & Landscape Architecture.
ISBN Prefix(es): 90-71570
Number of titles published annually: 6 Print
Total Titles: 96 Print
Imprints: Goose Press
Subsidiaries: Goose Press

Arena, *imprint of* J M Meulenhoff BV

Uitgeverij Arena BV+
Herengracht 505, 1017 BV Amsterdam
Mailing Address: Postbus 100, 1000 AC Amsterdam
Tel: (020) 5540500 *Fax:* (020) 4216868
E-mail: arenaasd@wxs.nl
Key Personnel
President: Chantal d'Aulnis
Editor: Tanja Hendriks
Founded: 1989
Subjects: Biography, Literature, Literary Criticism, Essays, Nonfiction (General)
ISBN Prefix(es): 90-6974
Parent Company: J M Meulenhoff BV

Uitgevirj Aristos+
Provenierssingel 73-A, 3033 EJ Rotterdam
Tel: 073 6136416
E-mail: aristos@xs4all.nl
Web Site: www.xs4all.nl/~aristos
Key Personnel
Publisher: Gerrit Bussinh
Founded: 1997
Subjects: Fiction, Literature, Literary Criticism, Essays, Management, Nonfiction (General)
ISBN Prefix(es): 90-6935
Total Titles: 27 Print

Warehouse: Centraal Boehh, Erasmusweg 19, 4101 AK Culemberg *Tel:* (0345) 475911
Orders to: Uitgevserij Aristos

Ark Boeken Publishing House+
Donauweg 4, 1043 AJ Amsterdam
Tel: (020) 6114847 *Fax:* (020) 6114864
E-mail: arkboeken@wxs.nl
Key Personnel
General Dir: J Kor *Tel:* (020) 4802981
Publishing Dir: P Foget
Founded: 1913
Ark Boeken Publishing House combines the activities of Vereeniging tot Verspreiding der Heilige Schrift (Association for Distribution of the Holy Scripture) and Bijbel Kiosk Vereniging (Bible Kiosk Society).
Subjects: Religion - Protestant
ISBN Prefix(es): 90-338
Total Titles: 500 Print; 1 Audio
Bookshop(s): BKV-Lektuurcentrum, Hoofdstraat 55, 3971 KB Driebergen

Uitgeverij Jan van Arkel+
A Numankd 17, 3572 KP Utrecht
Tel: (030) 2731840 *Fax:* (030) 2733614
E-mail: i-books@antenna.nl
Web Site: www.antenna.bl/i-books
Key Personnel
Chief Executive: Jan van Arkel
Founded: 1974
Specialize in books on the environment & development, in books in the Dutch & English languages.
Subjects: Economics, Environmental Studies, Geography, Geology, Government, Political Science, Social Sciences, Sociology, Women's Studies
ISBN Prefix(es): 90-6224; 90-5727 (Internationals Books)
Total Titles: 150 Print
Imprints: International Books
Distributed by Bushbooks; Jon Carpenter Publishing (UK); International Books (Netherlands); Paul & Company, Publishers Consortium Inc (US)
Shipping Address: Central Books, 99 Wallis Rd, London E9 5LN, United Kingdom *Tel:* (020) 986 4854 *Fax:* (020) 533 5821
Orders to: c/o A Weitsel, 2 Home Farm Cottages, Sandy Lane, St Paul's Cray, Kent BR5 3HZ, United Kingdom *Tel:* (1689) 870437
Independent Publishers Group - IPG, 814 N Franklin St, Chicago, IL 60610, United States *Tel:* 312-337-0747 *Fax:* 312-337-5985
E-mail: frontdesk@ipgbook.com

Ars Scribendi bv Uitgeverij+
Productieweg 5, 3481 MH Harmelen
Mailing Address: PO Box 65, 3480 DB Harmelen
Tel: (0348) 443998 *Fax:* (0348) 444076
E-mail: info@arsscribendi.com
Web Site: www.arsscribendi.com
Key Personnel
President: R E C Richter
Founded: 1988
Member of KVB. Also acts as publishers' agents.
ISBN Prefix(es): 90-72718; 90-5495; 90-74777; 90-5566
Number of titles published annually: 20 Print
Total Titles: 300 Print
Parent Company: Richter's Alg Boek Centrale bv
Associate Companies: Intertext PvbA
Imprints: Corona; Fantom; Flash; Magnum
Subsidiaries: Handelsonderneming Dykhof bv; De Laude Scriptorum bv
Distributed by Agora bvba

Athenaeum-Polak & Van Gennep, *imprint of* Em Querido's Uitgeverij BV

B M Israel BV
NZ Voorburgwal 264, 1012 RS Amsterdam
Tel: (020) 6247040 *Fax:* (020) 6382355
E-mail: bmisrael@xs4all.nl
Web Site: www.nvva/israelbm
Key Personnel
General Manager: M Israel
Subjects: Art, Medicine, Nursing, Dentistry, Science (General)
ISBN Prefix(es): 90-6078
Bookshop(s): Boekhandel en Antiquariaat B M Israel BV, NZ Voorburgwal 264, 1012 RS Amsterdam

Backhuys Publishers BV+
Warmonderweg 80, 2341 KZ Oegstgeest
Mailing Address: PO Box 321, 2300 AH Leiden
Tel: (071) 5170208 *Fax:* (071) 5171856
E-mail: backhuys@backhuys.com
Web Site: www.backhuys.com
Key Personnel
President: Dr W Backhuys
Editor: Mike Ruijsenaars *E-mail:* mike@backhuys.com
Publisher: Wil R Peters *Tel:* (071) 5170927
E-mail: peters@backhuys.com
Founded: 1989
Publish & distribute scholarly books in the natural sciences (botany, zoology, geology).
Also acts as distributor of Museum Publications, University Presses & sells antiquarian books in same subjects.
Subjects: Biological Sciences, Earth Sciences, Geography, Geology, Natural History
ISBN Prefix(es): 90-73348; 90-73239; 90-220; 90-327; 90-5103; 2-85653; 90-5782; 2-86515
Number of titles published annually: 40 Print
Total Titles: 400 Print
Subsidiaries: Seashell Treasure Books
U.S. Office(s): Balogh Scientific Books, Champaign, IL 61822, United States, Contact: Pamela Burns *Tel:* 217-355-9331 *Fax:* 217-355-9413
Distributed by Balogh Scientific Books (North America)
Distributor for Editions Boubee (France); Hong Kong University Press (Zoology titles only); Israel Academy of Sciences & Humanities (Zoology & Botany titles only); Museum national d'Histoire naturelle (France); Naturalis (Netherlands); Service du Patrimoine Naturel (France)
Foreign Rep(s): Balogh Scientific Books

Bert Bakker, see Prometheus

Uitgeverij Balans+
Keizersgracht 117, 1015 CJ Amsterdam
Tel: (020) 6268982 *Fax:* (020) 6223481
E-mail: balans@uitgeverijbalans.nl
Web Site: www.uitgeverijbalans.nl
Key Personnel
Publisher: Jan G Gaarlandt
Rights & Permissions: Francoise Gaarlandt-Kist
Founded: 1986
Subjects: Biography, Fiction, History, Journalism, Literature, Literary Criticism, Essays, Nonfiction (General), Regional Interests, Religion - Other
ISBN Prefix(es): 90-5018
Total Titles: 40 Print
Orders to: Centraal Boekhuis, Postbus 100, 4100 BA Culemborg *Tel:* (0345) 475896

A A Balkema+
Imprint of Swets & Zeitlinger
Brugwachter 3-5, 3034 KD Rotterdam
Mailing Address: Postbus 1675, 3000 BR Rotterdam
Tel: (010) 4145822 *Fax:* (010) 4135947
E-mail: orders@swets.nl
Web Site: www.balkema.nl

Key Personnel
Man Dir: Martin Scrivener *Tel:* (0252) 435101
 E-mail: scrivy@swets.nl
Rights & Permissions: Rosemarie Daal
Sales Promotion: Ms Deet van Toledo
Founded: 1932
Specialize in Engineering.
Subjects: Archaeology, Biological Sciences, Civil Engineering, Earth Sciences, Engineering (General), Environmental Studies, Geography, Geology, Mechanical Engineering, Natural History, Physics
ISBN Prefix(es): 90-6191 (90-5809); 90-5410
Total Titles: 1,000 Print; 10 CD-ROM
Parent Company: Swets & Zeitlinger, Lisse
Branch Office(s)
A A Balkema Publishers, 2252 Ridge Rd, Brookfield, VT 05036-9704, United States *Tel:* 802-276-3162 *Fax:* 802-276-3837 *E-mail:* info@ashgate.com

Baltzer Science Publishers
Raphaelplein 3, 1077 PW Amsterdam
Tel: (020) 471051 *Fax:* (020) 4710152
E-mail: publish@baltzer.nl
Web Site: www.baltzer.nl
Key Personnel
President: B Stroomberg
Founded: 1980
Subjects: Chemistry, Chemical Engineering, Communications, Computer Science, Mathematics, Physics
ISBN Prefix(es): 90-5785

Benjamin & Partners Art Books, *imprint of* BoekWerk

John Benjamins BV+
Klaprozenweg 105, 1033 NN Amsterdam
Mailing Address: PO Box 36224, 1020 ME Amsterdam
Tel: (020) 6304747 *Fax:* (020) 6739773
E-mail: customer.services@benjamins.nl
Web Site: www.benjamins.com
Key Personnel
Man Dir, Amsterdam: John L Benjamins
Man Dir, USA: Paul Peranteau
Founded: 1964
Subjects: Art, Education, Language Arts, Linguistics, Literature, Literary Criticism, Essays, Philosophy, Psychology, Psychiatry, Social Sciences, Sociology, Applied Linguistics, Pragamatics, Translation Cognition, Historical Linguistics
ISBN Prefix(es): 90-272
Imprints: B R Gruener Publishing Co
Branch Office(s)
John Benjamins North America Inc, 821 Bethlehem Pike, Philadelphia, PA 19118, United States *Tel:* 215-836-1200 *Fax:* 215-836-1204

De Bezige Bij
Van Miereveldstraat 1, 1071 DW Amsterdam
Mailing Address: PO Box 75184, 1070 AD Amsterdam
Tel: (020) 3059810 *Fax:* (020) 3059824
E-mail: info@debezigebij.nl
Web Site: www.debezigebij.nl *Cable:* BEEBOOK
Key Personnel
President & Publisher: Robbert Ammerlaau
Founded: 1944
Subjects: Fiction, Literature, Literary Criticism, Essays, Nonfiction (General), Poetry
ISBN Prefix(es): 90-234

Big Balloon BV+
Fonteinlaan 5, 2012 JG Haarlem
Mailing Address: Postbus 701, 2003 RS Haarlem
Tel: (023) 5176620; (023) 5176642 *Fax:* (023) 5176630; (023) 5176640
Web Site: www.bigballoon.nl

Key Personnel
Man Dir: Cees De Groot
Founded: 1990
ISBN Prefix(es): 90-320; 90-5425

Erven J Bijleveld+
Janskerkhof 7, 3512 BK Utrecht
Mailing Address: Postbus 1238, 3500 BE Utrecht
Tel: (030) 2317688 *Fax:* (030) 2368675
Key Personnel
Man Dir: J B Bommelje, Sr
Founded: 1865
Subjects: Child Care & Development, Computer Science, History, Microcomputers, Philosophy, Psychology, Psychiatry, Religion - Jewish, Religion - Other, Social Sciences, Sociology, Theology
ISBN Prefix(es): 90-72019; 90-5548; 90-6131
Imprints: Bijleveld Press

Bijleveld Press, *imprint of* Erven J Bijleveld

BIS Publishers
Nieuwe Spiegelstr 36, 1017 DG Amsterdam
Tel: (020) 6205171 *Fax:* (020) 6279251
E-mail: bispub@XS4all-nl
Key Personnel
President & International Rights: Rudolf van Wezel
Founded: 1986
Subjects: Architecture & Interior Design, Communications
ISBN Prefix(es): 90-72007
Distributed by Hearst Books International

H W Blok Uitgeverij BV
Randstad 2025, 1314 BB Almere
Mailing Address: Postbus 12000, 1301 CA Almere
Tel: (036) 5485480 *Fax:* (036) 5485499
ISBN Prefix(es): 90-70008; 90-72763

Boek Promotions BV
Hilversumseweg 16, 1251 EX Laren Nh
Mailing Address: Postbus 88, 1250 AB Laren Nh
Tel: (035) 5310154
Key Personnel
Owner: Peter J Houbolt
Act mainly as packagers for sponsored books.
ISBN Prefix(es): 90-6459

Boekencentrum BV+
Goudstr 50, 2718 RC Zoetermeer
Mailing Address: Postbus 29, 2700 AA Zoetermeer
Tel: (079) 3615481 *Fax:* (079) 3615489
E-mail: info@boekcentrum.nl
Web Site: www.boeckencentrum.nl
Key Personnel
Dir: N A de Waal
Founded: 1948
Subjects: Education, Religion - Protestant, Theology
ISBN Prefix(es): 90-239; 90-211
Imprints: Meinema

De Boekerij BV+
Herengracht 540, 1017 CG Amsterdam
Tel: (020) 5353135 *Fax:* (020) 5353130
E-mail: info@boekery.nl
Key Personnel
Editorial Dir: Marijke Bartels
Man Dir & Sales: R C M Hogenes
Editorial, Children's: Dorine Louwerens
Publicity: Marc Van Biezen
Production: Hans Van den Broek
Contracts & Rights: Frederike Leffelaar
Founded: 1986
Subjects: Biography, Child Care & Development, Fiction, Health, Nutrition, History, Mysteries, Nonfiction (General), Romance

ISBN Prefix(es): 90-225
Ultimate Parent Company: PCM Algemene Boeken
Associate Companies: Bruna; T M Meulenhoff; Prometherus/Bert Bakker; Standaard; Unieboek/Van Reemst
Imprints: Forum; Piccolo; Parel Pockets; Van Goor

BoekWerk+
Emmastraat 31-2, 9722 EW Groningen
Tel: (050) 5265559 *Fax:* (050) 5268198
Key Personnel
Dir: G M Nuis
Founded: 1988
Subjects: Art, Business, Computer Science, Management, Marketing, Microcomputers
ISBN Prefix(es): 90-5402; 90-71677
Imprints: Benjamin & Partners Art Books

Bohn Scheltema en Holkema, see Bohn Stafleu Van Loghum BV

Bohn Stafleu Van Loghum BV
De Molen 77, 3995 AW Houten
Mailing Address: Postbus 246, 3990 GA Houten
Tel: (0172) 466321 *Fax:* (0172) 435527
Key Personnel
Man Dir: H J Demoet
Founded: 1752
Part of Wolters Kluwer Business Publishing.
Subjects: Biography, Human Relations, Medicine, Nursing, Dentistry, Social Sciences, Sociology
ISBN Prefix(es): 90-313; 90-368; 90-6016; 90-6065; 90-311; 90-6001; 90-6014; 90-6051; 90-6060; 90-6502

Boom Uitgeverij (Boom Publishers)+
Affiliate of Boom Law Publishers
Prinsengracht 747-751, 1017 JX Amsterdam
Mailing Address: Postbus 400, 7940 AK Meppel
Tel: (0522) 257012 *Fax:* (0522) 266198
Key Personnel
Man Dir: Dr J A Boom *Tel:* (0522) 266111
 E-mail: directic@boom.nl; Dr E A van Ingen
Man Dir, Law Department: Dr W J Soetenhorst
Founded: 1842
Subjects: Behavioral Sciences, Child Care & Development, Communications, Education, Environmental Studies, Government, Political Science, History, Language Arts, Linguistics, Law, Philosophy, Psychology, Psychiatry, Social Sciences, Sociology, Statistics
ISBN Prefix(es): 90-6009; 90-5352
Parent Company: Royal Boom Publishers
Distributor for Institute for Politics; Netherlands Institute for Banking; Royal Institute of the Tropes; TMC Asser Institute
Orders to: Boom Distributiecentrum, Postbus 400, 7940 AK Meppel

Bosch & Keuning+
Julianalaan 11, 3743 JG Baarn
Tel: (035) 12050 *Fax:* (030) 2202446
Key Personnel
Man Dir: Robbert Ammerlaan
Founded: 1925
(Sesam Pocketbooks).
Member of Combo Group.
Subjects: Art, Biography, Education, History, Medicine, Nursing, Dentistry, Music, Dance, Religion - Other, Science (General)
ISBN Prefix(es): 90-246
Imprints: Sesam

Bosch & Keuning Uitgevers, *imprint of* Uitgeverij Cantecleer BV

Bosch & Veuning Uitgeversgroep, see Veen Bosch & Keuning Uitgevers NV

Brill Academic Publishers+
Plantijnstr 2, 2300 PA Leiden
Mailing Address: Postbus 9000, 2300 PA Leiden
Tel: (071) 53 53 566 *Fax:* (071) 53 17 532
E-mail: cs@brill.nl
Web Site: www.brill.nl
Telex: 39296 *Cable:* BRILL LEIDEN
Key Personnel
Manager: R J Kasteleijn *E-mail:* kasteleijn@brill.nl
International Sales Manager: L Empringham
 E-mail: empringham@brill.nl
Marketing Manager: Alexander Dek
 E-mail: dek@brill.nl
Founded: 1683
Subjects: Archaeology, Asian Studies, Behavioral Sciences, Biological Sciences, History, Religion - Islamic, Religion - Jewish, Religion - Other, Science (General), Social Sciences, Sociology, Theology
ISBN Prefix(es): 90-04
Total Titles: 2,700 Print
Imprints: Leiden University Press
Subsidiaries: Brill Academic Publishers Inc
Branch Office(s)
VSP BV, International Science Publishers, Godfried van Seijstlaan 47, 3700 BR Zeist, Marketing Manager: Els van Egmond *Tel:* (060) 693 2081 *Fax:* (060) 692 5790 *E-mail:* vsppub@compuserve.com
U.S. Office(s): Brill USA Inc, 12 Water St, Suite 900, Boston, MA 02109, United States, Contact: Patrick Alexander *Tel:* 617-263-2323 *Fax:* 617-263-2324 *E-mail:* cs@brillusa.com

D van Brummen, *imprint of* Buijten en Schipperheijn BV Drukkerij en Uitg Mij v/h

Uitgeverij A W Bruna en Zoon NV
Kobaltweg 23-25, 3542 CE Utrecht
Mailing Address: PO Box 40203, 3504 AA Utrecht
Tel: (030) 2470411 *Fax:* (030) 2410018
E-mail: a.w.bruna@awbruna.nl; multimedia@awbruna.nl
Web Site: www.awbruna.nl
Telex: 73159
Key Personnel
Dir: J Raedschelders
Founded: 1966
Subjects: Literature, Literary Criticism, Essays
Branch Office(s)
A W Bruna en Zoon's Uitgeversmaatschappij BV

A W Bruna Informatica, *imprint of* A W Bruna Uitgevers BV

A W Bruna Uitgevers BV+
Postbus 40203, 3504 AA Utrecht
Tel: (030) 2470411 *Fax:* (030) 2410018
E-mail: a.w.bruna@awbruna.nl
Key Personnel
Dir: Joop Boezeman
Aquiring Editor, Fiction & Non-fiction: Steven Maat
Founded: 1868
Subjects: Computer Science, Fiction, History, Mysteries, Nonfiction (General), Philosophy, Psychology, Psychiatry, Science (General), Social Sciences, Sociology, Thrillers, Suspense
ISBN Prefix(es): 90-229; 90-449; 90-5672
Parent Company: PCM Algemene Boeken bv, Utrecht
Imprints: Zwarte Beertjes; A W Bruna Informatica; Signature
Branch Office(s)
Mary Anne Thompson Associates, 80 E 11 St, Suite 441, New York, NY, United States
Standaard Uitgeverij, Belgium

Buijten en Schipperheijn BV Drukkerij en Uitg Mij v/h+
Paasheuvelweg 44, 1105 Amsterdam
Mailing Address: PO Box 22708, 1011-DE Amsterdam
Tel: (20) 5241010 *Fax:* (20) 5241011
E-mail: info@bijten.nl
Key Personnel
Man Dir: G Sneep
Founded: 1902
Subjects: Biblical Studies, Human Relations, Philosophy, Poetry, Psychology, Psychiatry, Religion - Other, Theology, Travel
ISBN Prefix(es): 90-6064; 90-5881
Imprints: D van Brummen

Business Contact BV+
Herengracht 481, 1017 BT Amsterdam
Mailing Address: PO Box 13, 1000 AA Amsterdam
Tel: (020) 5249800 *Fax:* (020) 6276851
E-mail: businesscontact@contact-bv.nl
Web Site: www.boekenwereld.com
Key Personnel
Contact: Ms Annemie Michels
Subjects: Accounting, Business, Career Development, Economics, Finance, How-to, Management, Marketing
ISBN Prefix(es): 90-254
Number of titles published annually: 30 Print
Total Titles: 400 Print
Parent Company: Veen, Bosch & Keuning

BV Uitgevery NZV (Nederlandse Zondagsschool Vereniging)+
Postbus 3, 1200 AA Hilversum
Tel: (035) 6285285 *Fax:* (035) 6241319
Key Personnel
Manager: Sir E K van de Plassche
International Rights & Publisher: Sir J Graafland
Subjects: Crafts, Games, Hobbies, Religion - Other, Affectionate Development, Nature & Environment
ISBN Prefix(es): 90-6986
Parent Company: NZV
Imprints: Kwintessens
Distributor for Ark Boeken; Boekencentrum; Callenbach; Christofoor; Clavis; Groen/Jongbloed; Kok; NBG; Piramide

BZZTOH Publishers+
Laan van Meerdervoort 10, 2517 AJ The Hague
Tel: (070) 3632934 *Fax:* (070) 3631932
E-mail: info@bzztoh.nl
Web Site: www.bzztoh.nl
Key Personnel
Dir: Phil Muysson
Financial Dir: Arend Meijboom
Foreign Rights Manager: Karin Hasselo
 E-mail: karin@bzztoh.nl
Founded: 1970
Subjects: Animals, Pets, Astrology, Occult, Biography, Cookery, Fiction, Finance, Health, Nutrition, Humor, Literature, Literary Criticism, Essays, Music, Dance, Mysteries, Nonfiction (General), Philosophy, Real Estate, Religion - Buddhist, Religion - Hindu, Religion - Jewish, Romance, Self-Help, Sports, Athletics, Travel, Women's Studies
ISBN Prefix(es): 90-6291; 90-5501; 90-453
Number of titles published annually: 130 Print

Cadans, *imprint of* Sjaloom en Wildeboer Publishers

Cadans+
V Diemenstr 410, 1013CB Amsterdam
Mailing Address: Postbus 1895, 1000BW Amsterdam
Tel: (020) 6206263 *Fax:* (020) 6209253
Founded: 1992
Subjects: Fiction, Literature, Literary Criticism, Essays, Nonfiction (General), Poetry, Travel
ISBN Prefix(es): 90-5132
Parent Company: C V Sjaloom en Wildeboer

Uitgeverij G F Callenbach BV+
Gildestr 5, 8263 AH Kampen
Mailing Address: PO Box 5018, 8260 GA Kampen
Tel: (038) 3392555 *Fax:* (038) 3328912
Key Personnel
Man Dir: G F Callenbach
Foreign Rights, Rights & Permissions: Paula van Elven-Scholtes
Founded: 1854
Member of Combo Group, Netherlands.
Subjects: Biblical Studies, Fiction, Poetry, Religion - Protestant, Religion - Other, Theology
ISBN Prefix(es): 90-266

Uitgeverij Cantecleer BV+
Subsidiary of Veen Bosch & Keuning Uitgevers NV
Lt-Gen v Heutszln 8, 3743 JN Baarn
Tel: (035) 5486601 *Fax:* (035) 5486615
Key Personnel
Man Dir & Editor: J Van Beusekom
Editor: E Neele; J Junge; L Uyterlinde
Founded: 1948
Member of Bosch & Keuning NV.
Subjects: Art, Crafts, Games, Hobbies, Film, Video, House & Home, Nonfiction (General), Photography, Wine & Spirits
ISBN Prefix(es): 90-246; 90-213
Imprints: Bosch & Keuning Uitgevers
Shipping Address: Magazyn Centraal Boekhuis, Evasmusweg 10, Culemborg

Casterman NV+
Formerly Uiteverij Casterman Nederland BV
Subsidiary of Editions Casterman SA
Fazantendreef 13/1, 8251 JR Dronten
Tel: (0321) 313553 *Fax:* (0321) 318205
Key Personnel
General Manager: Pierre Rummens
ISBN Prefix(es): 90-303

Castrum Peregrini Presse+
Herengracht 401, 1017 BP Amsterdam
Mailing Address: PO Box 645, 1000 AP Amsterdam
Tel: (020) 235287 *Fax:* (020) 6247096
E-mail: mail@castrumperegrini.nl
Web Site: castrumperegrini.nl
Key Personnel
Man Dir & International Rights: M Defuster
Contact: Andrea Korte *E-mail:* a.korte@castrumperegrini.nl
Founded: 1951
Subjects: Antiques, Biography, Literature, Literary Criticism, Essays, Poetry
ISBN Prefix(es): 90-6034
Total Titles: 100 Print
Orders to: Hermannstr 61, 53225 Bonn, Germany

De Centaur, *imprint of* Omega Boek BV

Uitgeverij Christofoor
Steniaweg 32, 3702 AG Zeist
Mailing Address: PO Box 234, 3700 AE Zeist
Tel: (030) 6923974 *Fax:* (030) 6914834
ISBN Prefix(es): 90-6238

de Cocon, *imprint of* Unieboek BV

Uitgeverij Conserve+
Turelum 12, 1873 JW Groet Schoorl
Mailing Address: Postbus 74, 1870 AB Schoorl
Tel: (072) 5093693 *Fax:* (072) 5094370
Key Personnel
President: Kees De Bakker
Founded: 1983

Subjects: Biography, Fiction, History, Literature, Literary Criticism, Essays, Mysteries, Caribbean, Surinam, Second World War
ISBN Prefix(es): 90-71380; 90-5429
Total Titles: 250 Print

Contact Publishers
Herengracht 481, 1017 BT Amsterdam
Mailing Address: PO Box 13, 1000 AA Amsterdam
Tel: (020) 5249800
E-mail: info@contact-bv.nl
ISBN Prefix(es): 90-254
Ultimate Parent Company: Veen, Bosch & Keuning

Corona, *imprint of* Ars Scribendi bv Uitgeverij

Uitgeverij Coutinho BV (Coutinho Publishing)+
Slochterenln 7, Postbus 333, 1400 AH, 1405 AL Bussum
Tel: (035) 6949991 *Fax:* (035) 6947165
E-mail: info@coutinho.ul
Web Site: www.coutinho.ul
Key Personnel
Man Dir, Editorial: Dick Coutinho
  E-mail: coutinho!@coutinho.ul; Marleen Klein
Production: Tom Visser
Founded: 1976
Member of NUW.
Subjects: English as a Second Language, History, Human Relations, Language Arts, Linguistics, Literature, Literary Criticism, Essays, Philosophy, Specialize in Dutch as a second language
ISBN Prefix(es): 90-6283
Distributed by EPO (Belgium)

Otto Cramwinckel Uitgever
Herengracht 416, 1017 BZ Amsterdam
Tel: (020) 6276609 *Fax:* (020) 6383817
E-mail: otto.cram@cram.nl
Founded: 1985
Subjects: Communications, Radio, TV
ISBN Prefix(es): 90-71894; 90-75727

Davaco Publishers
Beukenlaan 3, 8085 RK Doornspijk
Tel: (0525) 661823 *Fax:* (0525) 662153
Founded: 1969
Specialize in 17th century Dutch Painting.
Subjects: Art
ISBN Prefix(es): 90-70288

De Brink (adult books), *imprint of* Uitgeverij Ploegsma BV

De Groot Goudriaan, *imprint of* Uitgeefmaatschappij J H Kok BV

De Ruiter, *imprint of* Educatieve Partners Nederland bv

De Toorts, *imprint of* Uitgeverij De Toorts

De Vier Windstreken, *imprint of* Meander Uitgeverij BV

De Walburg Pers
Zaadmarkt 86, 7201 DE Zutphen
Mailing Address: Postbus 4159, 7200 BD Zutphen
Tel: (0575) 510522 *Fax:* (0575) 541025
Key Personnel
Man Dir, Publicity, Rights & Permissions: Dr C F Schriks; J van't Leven; J Smal
Founded: 1961
Subjects: Architecture & Interior Design, Drama, Theater, Ethnicity, History
ISBN Prefix(es): 90-6011; 90-5730

Delft University Press+
Prometheu Splein 1, 2628 ZC Delft
Mailing Address: PO Box 98, 2600 MG Delft
Tel: (015) 2783254 *Fax:* (015) 2781661
E-mail: dup@dup.tudelft.nl
Key Personnel
Dir: Pam Maas
Editorial: Lydia M ter Horst
Founded: 1972
Subjects: Architecture & Interior Design, Chemistry, Chemical Engineering, Civil Engineering, Electronics, Electrical Engineering, Engineering (General), Mechanical Engineering, Physics, Science (General), Technology
ISBN Prefix(es): 90-6275; 90-407
Parent Company: Delft University of Technolog

van Dishoeck, *imprint of* Unieboek BV

Uitgeversmaatschappij Ad Donker BV+
Kon Emmaplein 1, 3016 AA Rotterdam
Mailing Address: Postbus 23096, 3001 KB Rotterdam
Tel: (010) 436 30 09 *Fax:* (010) 436 29 63
Web Site: www.uitgeverijdonker.nl
Key Personnel
Dir & Publisher: Willem A Donker
  E-mail: donker@bart.nl
Founded: 1938
Subjects: Biography, Education, Fiction, History, Psychology, Psychiatry, Social Sciences, Sociology
ISBN Prefix(es): 90-6100
Number of titles published annually: 25 Print
Total Titles: 150 Print
Imprints: Wilkerdon

Drempelreeks, *imprint of* Uitgeverij Vrij Geestesleven

De Driehoek BV+
Keizersgracht 756, 1017 EZ Amsterdam
Tel: (020) 6246426 *Fax:* (020) 6387155
Key Personnel
Dir: H J Heule; Dr W Heule
Founded: 1933
Subjects: Asian Studies, Health, Nutrition, Medicine, Nursing, Dentistry, Religion - Buddhist
ISBN Prefix(es): 90-6030

Uitgeverij Dwarsstap, *imprint of* Uitgeverij SUN

East-West Publications Fonds BV+
Postbus 85617, The Hague 2508 CH
Tel: (70) 3644590 *Fax:* (70) 3614864
Key Personnel
Chief Executive: L W Carp
Sales: A Neuvel
Founded: 1966
Subjects: Music, Dance, Regional Interests, Religion - Other, Esoteric/spiritual
ISBN Prefix(es): 90-70104; 90-5340
Number of titles published annually: 8 Print
Total Titles: 10 Print
Associate Companies: East-West Publications (UK) Ltd
Orders to: 8 Caledonia St, London N1 9DZ, United Kingdom *Tel:* (20) 7837 5061 *Fax:* (20) 7278 4429

ECI voor Boeken en Grammofoonplaten BV+
Laanakkerweg 14-18, 4131 PB Vianen Zh
Mailing Address: Postbus 400, 4130 EK Vianen Zh
Tel: (03473) 79214 *Fax:* (03471) 79380
Telex: 47449 ecihk nl
Key Personnel
Man Dir: Mr B M Tromp
Editorial, Nonfiction: Mrs B Eggels
Editorial, Fiction: Mr J Boezeman
Rights & Permissions: Mrs R Swaalf
Founded: 1967
Subjects: Fiction, Nonfiction (General)
ISBN Prefix(es): 90-70038; 90-5108
Parent Company: Bertelsmann AG, Munich, Germany
Book Club(s): ECI voor Boeken en Platen BV

EDECEA & WFE, *imprint of* West-Friesland/Boekproject-ontwikkeling

Educatieve Uitgeverij Edu'Actief BV+
Zomerdijk 9E, 7942 JR Meppel
Mailing Address: Postbus 1056, 7940 KB Meppel
Tel: (0522) 262222 *Fax:* (0522) 263052
Key Personnel
Man Dir: I Buwalda
Founded: 1848
Member of GEU.
Subjects: Communications, Economics, Education, Foreign Countries, Geography, Geology, Management, Marketing, Nonfiction (General)
ISBN Prefix(es): 90-5117; 90-372; 90-5766
Parent Company: Koninklyke Boom Pers BV

Educaboek, *imprint of* Educatieve Partners Nederland bv

Educatieve Partners Nederland bv+
De Molen 20, 3994 DB Houten
Mailing Address: Postbus 666, 3990 Dr Houten
Tel: (030) 6359777 *Fax:* (030) 6359700
Key Personnel
Man Dir: J H van Vloten
Founded: 1970
Part of Wolters Kluwer Educational Activities.
Subjects: Science (General)
ISBN Prefix(es): 90-11; 90-05; 90-207
Parent Company: Wolters Kluwer NV
Imprints: Stam Techniek; Stenfert Kroese; Schoolpers; De Ruiter; Robyns; Educaboek

Eekhoorn BV Uitgeverij+
Alexander Bellstraat 11, 3261 XX Oud Beijerland
Mailing Address: Postbus 1557, 3260 BB Oud Beijerland
Tel: (036) 5227545 *Fax:* (036) 5226986
Key Personnel
President: M G Stenvert
Editor: E H Kolk
Producer: F H A Kanters
Founded: 1920
Member of GAU.
ISBN Prefix(es): 90-6056
Showroom(s): Sutton 10, 7327 AB Apeldoorn, New Zealand
Warehouse: Sutton 10, 7327 AB Apeldoorn, New Zealand

Elektor, *imprint of* Segment BV

Elektuur, *imprint of* Segment BV

Element Uitgevers+
Oude Haven 32, 1411 WB Naarden-Vesting
Mailing Address: PO Box 5211, 1410 AE-Naarden
Tel: (035) 6941750 *Fax:* (035) 6945824
E-mail: element@wxs.nl
Key Personnel
Publisher: Jan van Willegen
Founded: 1995
Independent Publisher.
ISBN Prefix(es): 90-5689
Total Titles: 50 Print

Elmar BV+
Delftweg 147, 2289 Rijswijk ZH

Tel: (015) 2153232 *Fax:* (015) 2153230
E-mail: elmar@elmar.nl
Key Personnel
Man Dir: M Roodnat; H Masthoff
Founded: 1961
Subjects: Biography, Health, Nutrition, History, How-to, Humor, Nonfiction (General), Sports, Athletics, Travel
ISBN Prefix(es): 90-6120; 90-389

Elsevier, *imprint of* Elsevier Science BV

Elsevier Science BV
Sara Burgerhartstr 25, 1055 KV Amsterdam
Tel: (020) 5862911 *Fax:* (020) 4852457
E-mail: nlinfo-f@elsevier.nl
Telex: 10704
Key Personnel
Chairman & CEO: H P Spruijt
Dir: C J Blake; G P Joebsis; R C White; Frans H J Visscher; P Nientker; K J Leeflang; N Farmer; P Shepherd; R Dietz; H Gerbrandy; R Van Charldorp
Founded: 1946
Subjects: Biological Sciences, Chemistry, Chemical Engineering, Computer Science, Earth Sciences, Economics, Engineering (General), Mathematics, Medicine, Nursing, Dentistry, Physics, Science (General), Technology
ISBN Prefix(es): 0-444; 90-444
Parent Company: Reed Elsevier, Van de Sande Bakhuyzenstr 4, Postbus 470, 1000 AL Amsterdam
Associate Companies: Editora Campus, Brazil; Elsevier Science Ireland Ltd, Ireland; Elsevier Science SA, Switzerland; Elsevier Science Ltd, United Kingdom; Elsevier Science Inc
Imprints: Elsevier; Excerpta Medica; North Holland; Pergamon
Subsidiaries: Elsevier Geo Abstracts
Divisions: Secondary Publishing Division; Elsevier Science NL
U.S. Office(s): Elsevier Scientific Inc, 655 Ave of the Americas, New York, NY 10010, United States
Orders to: Elsevier Science BV, PO Box 211, Amsterdam *Tel:* (020) 4853753 *Fax:* (020) 4853705

Uitgeverij Hans Elzenga BV
Singel 262, 1016 AC Amsterdam
Tel: (020) 5511262 *Fax:* (020) 6203509
Key Personnel
Man Dir: Hans Elzenga
Founded: 1982
ISBN Prefix(es): 90-6692

Enschede en Zonen
Donauweg 6-8, 1043 AJ Amsterdam NL
Mailing Address: Postbus 8023, 1005 AA Amsterdam
Tel: (020) 5858600 *Fax:* (020) 5858605
Telex: 41049
ISBN Prefix(es): 90-70024

ENTERBOOKS, *imprint of* Uitgeverij De Toorts

Excerpta Medica, *imprint of* Elsevier Science BV

eXperience, *imprint of* J M Meulenhoff BV

Falkplan-Suurland BV
Baltesakker 17, 5625 TC Eindhoven
Mailing Address: Postbus 9510, 5602LM Eindhoven
Tel: (040) 264221 *Fax:* (040) 2417635
Telex: 51874 svehv
Key Personnel
Man Dir: D R A Suurland; J A Suurland

ISBN Prefix(es): 90-287
Associate Companies: Suurland Holding BV

Fantom, *imprint of* Ars Scribendi bv Uitgeverij

Frank Fehmers Productions+
Singel 512, 1017 AX Amsterdam
Tel: (020) 6238766 *Fax:* (020) 6246262
Telex: 16740 fepro nl *Cable:* Intpubcon
Key Personnel
Man Dir: Frank Fehmers
International Co-productions: Meghan Ferrill
Subjects: Business, Film, Video, Publishing & Book Trade Reference, Radio, TV
ISBN Prefix(es): 90-6151
Associate Companies: Frank Fehmers Productions Inc, 300 E 59 St, New York, NY 10022, United States; Frank Fehmers Productions Ltda, Estrada do Tombo 401, Bloco N Apt 102, 22450 Rio de Janeiro RJ, Brazil; Frank Fehmers Publishing BV, Groot Davelaarweg 20, Curacao, Netherlands Antilles

Fibula, *imprint of* Unieboek BV

Flash, *imprint of* Ars Scribendi bv Uitgeverij

Uitgeverij De Fontein BV
Prinses Marielaan 8, 3743 JA Baarn
Mailing Address: Postbus 1, 3740 AA Baarn
Tel: (035) 5422141 *Fax:* (035) 5423855
Key Personnel
Man Dir: W Hazeu
Founded: 1946
Member of the Combo Group.
Subjects: Fiction, Nonfiction (General)
ISBN Prefix(es): 90-261
Associate Companies: De Prom Uitgeverij

Fontes Pers, *imprint of* Holland University Press BV (APA)

Forum, *imprint of* De Boekerij BV

Fragment Cooperatieve Vereniging UA, Uitgeverij
Lindengracht 168, 1015 KL Amsterdam
Tel: (020) 6267133 *Fax:* (020) 6207989
Key Personnel
Contact: Mr S Hekking; Mrs P Vaandrager; Mrs S de Boer
Founded: 1981
Subjects: Art, Literature, Literary Criticism, Essays, Photography
ISBN Prefix(es): 90-6579

W Gaade, *imprint of* Unieboek BV

Gaberbocchus Press
Spuistr 272, 1001 AH Amsterdam
Mailing Address: Postbus 3547, 1001 AH Amsterdam
Tel: (020) 6245181 *Fax:* (020) 6230672
Subjects: Literature, Literary Criticism, Essays
ISBN Prefix(es): 90-6169
Parent Company: De Harmonie Publishers, Spuistraat 272, NL 1012 VW Amsterdam

GB Software Uitgever, *imprint of* BV Uitgeversbedryf Het Goede Boek

Uitgeverij Vrij Geestesleven+
V Tetslaan 15, 3707 VB Zeist
Mailing Address: Postbus 851, 3700 AW Zeist
Tel: (030) 6924953 *Fax:* (030) 6932304
Key Personnel
General Manager: Mr M Ockeloen
Founded: 1952

Subjects: Art, Biography, Education, Health, Nutrition, Literature, Literary Criticism, Essays, Psychology, Psychiatry
ISBN Prefix(es): 90-6038
Imprints: Drempelreeks
Bookshop(s): De Nieuwe Boekerij, Steynlaan 55, 3701 EC Zeist

Van Gennep Ltd+
Niuwezijds Voorburgwal 330, 1012 RW Amsterdam
Tel: (20) 6247033 *Fax:* (20) 6247035
E-mail: vangennep@wxs.nl
Key Personnel
Man Dir: BIM Kat
Founded: 1969
Subjects: Art, Government, Political Science, History
ISBN Prefix(es): 90-6012; 90-5515
Imprints: Sara

Uitgeverij De Geus BV+
Leistr 6, 4818 NB Breda
Mailing Address: Postbus 1878, 4801 BW Breda
Tel: (076) 5228151 *Fax:* (076) 5222599
Key Personnel
President: E Visser
Founded: 1983
Subjects: Fiction, Nonfiction (General)
ISBN Prefix(es): 90-5226; 90-6222; 90-70610

BV Uitgeversbedryf Het Goede Boek+
Koningin Wilhelminastraat 8, 1271 PH Huizen, NH
Mailing Address: Postbus 122, 1270 AC Huizen
Tel: (35) 5253508 *Fax:* (35) 5254013
Key Personnel
Dir: F Rikmans
Founded: 1932
Also acts as distributor.
Subjects: Aeronautics, Aviation, Maritime, Microcomputers, Sports, Athletics
ISBN Prefix(es): 90-240
Number of titles published annually: 3 Print
Total Titles: 48 Print
Imprints: GB Software Uitgever

Van Goor BV+
Herengracht 540, 1017 CG Amsterdam
Tel: (020) 5353135 *Fax:* (020) 5353130
E-mail: boekerij@boekery.nl
Key Personnel
Editorial Dir: Mrs Henny Bodenkamp; Mrs Dorine Louwerens
Publicity: Marc Van Biezen
Production: Hans van den Broek
International Rights Contact: Geri Brandjes
Parent Company: De Boekery BV
Ultimate Parent Company: Meulenhoff & Co BV
Associate Companies: Bruna; T M Meulenhoff; Prometheus/Bert Bakker; Standaard; Unieboek/Van Reemst
Imprints: Piccolo
Subsidiaries: De Boekeryij bv

Goose Press, *imprint of* Architectura & Natura

Uitgeverij CJ Goossens BV+
Delftweg 147, 2289 BD Rijswijkzh Zn
Tel: (015) 2123623 *Fax:* (015) 2124295
Founded: 1980
Subjects: Literature, Literary Criticism, Essays
ISBN Prefix(es): 90-6551

Gottmer Uitgevers Groop (Gottmer Publishing Group)+
Professor Van Vlotenweg 1A, 2061 EB Bloemendaal
Mailing Address: PO Box 160, 2060 AD Bloemendaal
Tel: (23) 5411190 *Fax:* (23) 5274404
E-mail: post@gottmer.nl

Web Site: www.gottmer.nl
Telex: 41856
Key Personnel
Man Dir: Mr C van Wijk
Founded: 1937
Subjects: Crafts, Games, Hobbies, Fiction, House & Home, Nonfiction (General), Religion - Other, Science (General), Travel, Body-Mind-Spirit, Lifestyle, Nautical
ISBN Prefix(es): 90-257; 90-230; 90-6834
Imprints: Altamira-Becht; Aramith; Hollandia

De Graaf Publishers
Zuideinde 40, 2420 AK Nieuwkoop
Mailing Address: Postbus 6, 2420 AA Nieuwkoop
Tel: (0172) 571461 *Fax:* (0172) 572231
E-mail: degraaf.books@xws.nl
Key Personnel
Man Dir: Maria Emilie de Graaf
Founded: 1959
Subjects: Religion - Other
ISBN Prefix(es): 90-6004
Total Titles: 350 Print
Subsidiaries: Miland Publishers

Griffioen Paperbacks, *imprint of* Em Querido's Uitgeverij BV

B R Gruener Publishing Co, *imprint of* John Benjamins BV

Den Gulden Engel, *imprint of* Uitgeverij Houtekiet

de Haan, *imprint of* Uitgeverij BV

Hadewijch, *imprint of* Uitgeverij Houtekiet

Hagen & Stam Uitgeverij Ten
Postbus 34, 2501 AG S Gravenhage
Tel: (070) 3045888; (070) 3045700 *Fax:* (070) 3045800; (070) 3045806
Member of the Wolters Kluwer Group.
Subjects: Architecture & Interior Design, Biological Sciences, Chemistry, Chemical Engineering, Civil Engineering, Computer Science, Electronics, Electrical Engineering, Energy, Engineering (General), Environmental Studies, Labor, Industrial Relations, Management, Mechanical Engineering, Microcomputers, Real Estate, Science (General), Technology, Transportation
ISBN Prefix(es): 90-70011; 90-71694; 90-76304; 90-76383
Parent Company: Wolter Kluwer

De Harmonie (De Harmonie Publishers)
Spuistr 272, 1012 VW Amsterdam
Mailing Address: Postbus 3547, 1001 AH Amsterdam
Tel: (020) 6245181 *Fax:* (020) 6230672
E-mail: info@deharmonie.nl
Web Site: www.deharmonie.nl
Key Personnel
Man Dir: Jaco Groot
Rights & Permissions: Elsbeth Lovis
Founded: 1972
Subjects: Humor, Literature, Literary Criticism, Essays, Poetry
ISBN Prefix(es): 90-6169; 90-803481
Subsidiaries: Gaberbocchus Press

Uitgeverij Ten Have+
Division of Bosch en Keuning NV
Julianalaan 11, 3743 JG Baarn
Mailing Address: Postbus 5019, 8260 GA Kampen
Tel: (038) 3392555 *Fax:* (038) 3327331
Key Personnel
Man Dir: C Sbiti
Man Editor: P de Boer
Founded: 1831
Member of: Bosch & Keuning Group.
Subjects: Religion - Other
ISBN Prefix(es): 90-259
Total Titles: 300 Print

Hayit Nederland BV
Damrak 62, 1012 LM Amsterdam
Mailing Address: Grosse Telegraphenstr 34-36, 50676 Kolm, Germany
Tel: (020) 6384980 *Fax:* (020) 6384975
Key Personnel
Product Manager: Dr J van der Wal
Founded: 1989
Subjects: Travel
ISBN Prefix(es): 90-5336
Parent Company: Hayit Verlag GmbH, Hansaring 82, D-50670 Cologne, Germany

Helmond B. V. Uitgeverij+
Lt-Gen v Heutszln 8, 3743 JN Baarn
Mailing Address: Postbus 309, 3740 AC Baarn
Tel: (035) 5417241 *Fax:* (035) 5418366
E-mail: pivo@knoware.nl
Key Personnel
Man Dir: Dr M H Hendriks; P I H Burgers
Founded: 1913
Subjects: How-to
ISBN Prefix(es): 90-252; 90-6075
Parent Company: Uitgcvcay Kok, Kampen
Shipping Address: Inteamedium, PO Box 130, 8260 AC Kampen

Hemma Holland
Postbus 70417, 1007 KK Amsterdam
Tel: (020) 6755326 *Fax:* (020) 6796254

HES & De Graaf Publishers BV+
Tuurdyk 16, 3997 MS 'tGoy-Houten, Utrecht
Tel: (030) 6011955 *Fax:* (030) 6011813
E-mail: HES@forum-hes.nl
Web Site: www.forum-hes.nl
Key Personnel
Chief Executive, Editorial & Publicity: S S Hesselink *E-mail:* hesselink@forum-hes.nl
Contact: E Kempers
Founded: 1971
Subjects: History, Language Arts, Linguistics, Literature, Literary Criticism, Essays, Philosophy, Theology
ISBN Prefix(es): 90-6194

Uitgeverij Heuff Nieuwkoop
Lauriehof 8, 1016 MA Amsterdam
Tel: (020) 6204625 *Fax:* (020) 6204625
Cable: Heuff/Nieuwkoop
Key Personnel
Man Dir: H Heuff
Founded: 1970
Subjects: Art, Fiction, History, Music, Dance
ISBN Prefix(es): 90-6141

Uitgeverij Heureka
Hooqstraat 20, 1381 VS Weesp
Mailing Address: Postbus 5347, 1380 GH Weesp
Tel: (0294) 450972 *Fax:* (0294) 415183
Key Personnel
Man Dir: F H B Cladder
Founded: 1976
Subjects: History
ISBN Prefix(es): 90-6262
Bookshop(s): Belboek - Int order Bookshop, Weesp *Tel:* (0294) 80000

Heureka Uitgeverij
Hoogstraat 20, 1381 VS Weesp
Mailing Address: Postbus 5347, 1380 GH Weesp
Tel: (0294) 450972 *Fax:* (0294) 415183
Key Personnel
Contact: F H B Cladder
Founded: 1976
Subjects: Government, Political Science, History
ISBN Prefix(es): 90-6262

Historische Uitgeverij+
Westersingel 37, 9718 CC Groningen
Tel: (050) 3181700 *Fax:* (050) 3146383
E-mail: info@histuitg.ne
Web Site: www.histuitg.ne
Key Personnel
Publisher: Patrick M Th Everard *E-mail:* p.everard@histuitg.ne
Founded: 1986
Subjects: History, Journalism, Literature, Literary Criticism, Essays, Nonfiction (General), Philosophy, Poetry, Psychology, Psychiatry
ISBN Prefix(es): 90-6554
Number of titles published annually: 20 Print
Total Titles: 150 Print

van Holkema en Waren Holkema en Warendorf, *imprint of* Unieboek BV

Holland B V Uitgeversmaatschappij
Spaarne 110, 2011 CM Haarlem
Tel: (023) 5323061 *Fax:* (023) 5342908
Key Personnel
Man Dir: Rolf van Ulzen
Sales Dir, Permissions: Ruurt van Ulzen
Founded: 1921
Subjects: Fiction, Poetry, Science (General)
ISBN Prefix(es): 90-251

Holland University Press BV (APA)
Postbus 806, 1000 AV Amsterdam
Tel: (020) 6265544
E-mail: info@apa-publishers.com
Subjects: History, Human Relations, Language Arts, Linguistics, Law, Theology
ISBN Prefix(es): 90-6037; 90-302; 90-6039; 90-6042
Parent Company: APA (Academic Publishers Associated)
Imprints: Fontes Pers

Hollandia, *imprint of* Gottmer Uitgevers Groop

Uitgeverij Hollandia BV+
Eemdijk 124, 3754 NL Eemdijk
Mailing Address: Postbus 91, 3750 GB Bunschoten Spakenburg
Tel: (033) 2996899 *Fax:* (033) 2996980
Key Personnel
Man Dir: Tonnis Muntinga
Founded: 1899
Subjects: Fiction, Maritime, Travel
ISBN Prefix(es): 90-6410; 90-6045

Uitgeverij Homeovisie BV+
Berenkoog 35, 1822 BH Alkamaar
Mailing Address: Postbus 9292, 1800 GG Alkamaar
Tel: (072) 5661133 *Fax:* (072) 5661295
Key Personnel
President: Mr F Bech
Editor: Marianne Meijer
Founded: 1976
Specialize in Homeopathy.
Subjects: Health, Nutrition, Medicine, Nursing, Dentistry
ISBN Prefix(es): 90-71669

Hotei Publishing+
Zoeterwoudsesingel 56, 2313 EK Leiden
Tel: (071) 5663190 *Fax:* (071) 5663191
E-mail: info@hotei-publishing.com
Web Site: www.hotei-publishing.com
Key Personnel
Dir: R Scholten; C Uhlenbeck
Publisher: Frank Vermeer *E-mail:* fvermeer@hotei-publishing.com

Founded: 1999
Member of Dutch Publishers Association.
Subjects: Art, Asian Studies, Gardening, Plants, History, Photography, Religion - Buddhist
ISBN Prefix(es): 90-74822
Number of titles published annually: 15 Print
Total Titles: 25 Print

Uitgeverij Houtekiet
Prinses Marielaan 8, 3740 AA Baarn
Mailing Address: PO Box 1, 3740 AA Baarn
Tel: (035) 5422141 *Fax:* (035) 5423855
Telex: 43272beka
Imprints: Hadewijch; Den Gulden Engel
Subsidiaries: Houtekiet Hadewijch

ICG Publications Holland+
Ln D Veren Naties 275, 3318 LA Dordrecht
Mailing Address: Postbus 509, 3300AM Dordrecht
Tel: (078) 6510454 *Fax:* (078) 6510972
Cable: INTERGRAPH DORDRECHT
Key Personnel
Man Dir: Henk J La Porte
Founded: 1978
Subjects: Language Arts, Linguistics, Medicine, Nursing, Dentistry
ISBN Prefix(es): 90-6765; 90-70176
Parent Company: Intercontinental Graphics Holland BV
Subsidiaries: I C G Printing BV

International Books, *imprint of* Uitgeverij Jan van Arkel

Uitgevery International Theatre & Film Books+
Nieuwpoortkade 2A, 1055 RX Amsterdam
Tel: (020) 60 60 911 *Fax:* (020) 60 60 914
E-mail: info@itfb.nl
Web Site: www.itfb.nl
Key Personnel
President: Mrs M Oele
Founded: 1975
Specialize in theatre & film books.
Subjects: Drama, Theater, Film, Video, Music, Dance
ISBN Prefix(es): 90-6403
Number of titles published annually: 25 Print
Total Titles: 500 Print

Uitgeverij Intertaal BV
Van Baerlestraat 76, 1071 BB Amsterdam
Mailing Address: Postbus 75410, 1070 AK Amsterdam
Tel: (020) 5756750 *Fax:* (020) 6752686
E-mail: int@intertaal.nl
Founded: 1963
Subjects: Language Arts, Linguistics
ISBN Prefix(es): 90-70885; 90-5451; 90-800002
Showroom(s): Inter L, Schuttershofstraat 43, 2000 Antwerpen
Warehouse: Lemelerbergweg 21-22, 1101 AJ Amsterdam Z O

IOS Press BV+
Nieuwe Hemweg 6B, 1013 BG Amsterdam
Tel: (020) 688 33 55 *Fax:* (020) 620 3419
E-mail: market@iospress.nl
Web Site: www.iospress.nl
Key Personnel
Dir: Dr E H Fredriksson
Assistant: Ms C Koolbergen *E-mail:* publisher@iospress.nl
Founded: 1987
Subjects: Biological Sciences, Chemistry, Chemical Engineering, Computer Science, Electronics, Electrical Engineering, Environmental Studies, Health, Nutrition, Language Arts, Linguistics, Management, Mathematics, Mechanical Engineering, Medicine, Nursing, Dentistry, Physics, Technology
ISBN Prefix(es): 90-5199; 1-58603
Number of titles published annually: 90 Print
Total Titles: 500 Print
Subsidiaries: IOS Press Inc
Branch Office(s)
IOS Press/Lavis Marketing, 73 Lime Walk, Oxford 0X3 7AD, United Kingdom *Tel:* (01865) 76 7575 *Fax:* (01865) 75 0079
IOS Press, Akademische Verlagsgesellschaft aka GmbH, Neue Promenade 6, 10178 Berlin, Germany *Tel:* (030) 2472 9840 *Fax:* (030) 2839 4100
Distributor for OHMSHA Ltd (Japan)

JeugdSalamander Paperbacks, *imprint of* Em Querido's Uitgeverij BV

SDU Juridische en Fiscale Uitgeverij
C Plantynstr 2, 2515 TZ The Hague
Mailing Address: Postbus 20024, 2500 EA The Hague
Tel: (070) 3789860 *Fax:* (070) 3458068
E-mail: sdu@sdu.nl
Web Site: www.sdu.nl
ISBN Prefix(es): 90-5409

Kadmos, *imprint of* M & P Publishing House

Kartoen
Salland 231, 9405 GL Assen
Tel: (050) 3110505 *Fax:* (050) 3112299
E-mail: mondria@worldonline.nl
Subjects: Humor, Self-Help

Katholieke Bijbelstichting (Catholic Bible Center Netherlands)+
Orthenstr 290, 5211 SX Hertogenbosch
Mailing Address: Postbus 1274, 5200 BH Hertogenbosch
Tel: (073) 6133220 *Fax:* (073) 6910140
Key Personnel
Manager: Ph L van Heusden *E-mail:* p.v.heusden@rkbyebel.nl
Founded: 1961
Subjects: Biblical Studies, Religion - Catholic
ISBN Prefix(es): 90-6173

Uitgeverij De Kern+
Pringes Marielaan 8, 3743 JA Baarn
Mailing Address: Postbus 133, 3740 AC Baarn
Tel: (035) 5486345 *Fax:* (035) 5420210
Key Personnel
Publisher: Heleen Buth
ISBN Prefix(es): 90-325
Parent Company: Bosch & Kenning

Kimio Uitgeverij bv+
Brediusweg 92, 1411 JN Naarden
Mailing Address: Postbach 1117, 1400 BC Bussum
Tel: (035) 6950760 *Fax:* (035) 6951548
Key Personnel
Publishing & Man Dir: J van den Boom
Founded: 1985
ISBN Prefix(es): 90-71368

KITLV Press Royal Institute of Linguistics & Anthropology+
Division of Royal Institute of Linguistics & Anthropology
Reuvensplaats 2, 2311 BE Leiden
Mailing Address: PO Box 9515, 2300 RA Leiden
Tel: (071) 5272295 *Fax:* (071) 5272638
E-mail: kitlvpress@kitlv.nl
Web Site: www.iias.leidenuniv.nl/institutes/kitlv
Key Personnel
Contact: Dr Harry A Poeze *Tel:* (071) 5272465 *E-mail:* poeze@rullet.leidenuniv.nl
Sales & Promotion Manager: Marc van Brunschot *Tel:* (071) 5272469 *E-mail:* brunschot@kitlv.nl
Founded: 1851
Subjects: Anthropology, Asian Studies, Economics, Environmental Studies, History, Language Arts, Linguistics, Social Sciences, Sociology, Women's Studies, Caribbean Studies
ISBN Prefix(es): 90-6718
Number of titles published annually: 15 Print
Total Titles: 250 Print
Distributed by The Asian Experts (Australia & the South Pacific); United Publishers Services Ltd (Japan); University of Washington Press
Distributor for Monash Asia Institute; Research School of Pacific & Asian Studies

Uitgeverij Kluitman Alkmaar BV
Kelvinstr 20, 1704 RS Heerhugowaard
Mailing Address: Postbus 231, 1700 AE Heerhugowaard
Tel: (072) 5710542 *Fax:* (072) 5743348
Key Personnel
Dir: Dr P F A Stanco; Mrs H Stanco-Gerla
Founded: 1864
ISBN Prefix(es): 90-206

Kluwer Academic/Plenum Publishers, *imprint of* Kluwer Academic Publishers

Kluwer Academic Publishers
Spulboulevard 50, 3311 GR Dordrecht
Mailing Address: Postbus 17, 3300 AA Dordrecht
Tel: (078) 6392 392 *Fax:* (078) 6392 254
Telex: 29245
Key Personnel
President: Jeffery K Smith
Vice President, Boston: M Stephen Dane
Vice President, New York: Robert W Holland
Vice President, Boston: Zachary Rolnik
Vice President, Dordrecht: Alexander W Schimmelpennick; Caroline F Vogelzang
Dir, Library Relations, Dordrecht: J F Hattink
Sales Dir, Dordrecht: S D Dissel
Sales Manager, Boston: Lawrence D Salas
Subjects: Behavioral Sciences, Law, Medicine, Nursing, Dentistry, Science (General), Social Sciences, Sociology, Technology
ISBN Prefix(es): 0-7923; 90-247; 90-286; 90-277
Parent Company: Wolters Kluwer NV
Imprints: Martinus Nijhoff; Kluwer Academic/Plenum Publishers
U.S. Office(s): Kluwer Academic Publishers, 101 Philip Dr, Norwell, MA 02061, United States *Tel:* 781-871-6600 *Fax:* 781-871-6528
Kluwer Academic Plenum Publisher, 233 Spring St, New York, NY 10013-1578, United States *Tel:* 212-620-8000
Orders to: Distributiecentrum KAP Group, Maxwellstraat 4-12, 3316 GP Dordrecht *Tel:* (078) 654 6427 *Fax:* (078) 6546 627
Kluwer Academic Publishers/Kluwer Academic Plenum Publishers, 101 Philip Dr, Norwell, MA 02061, United States *Tel:* 781-871-6600 *Fax:* 781-871-6528

Kluwer Bedrijfswetenschappen
Leeuwenbrug 99-103, 7411 TH Deventer
Mailing Address: PO Box 23, 7400 GA Deventer
Tel: (0172) 466321 *Fax:* (0172) 435527
Telex: 49774
Key Personnel
Publisher: P J A Snakkers
Chief Executive: A Langevoort
Subjects: Business, Economics, Technology
ISBN Prefix(es): 90-267
Parent Company: Wolters Kluwer NV
Warehouse: Intermedia bv, PO Box 4, 2400 MA Alphen 4d Ryn

Kluwer Law International+
Imprint of Kluwer Academic Publishers
PO Box 85889, The Hague 2508 CN
Tel: (070) 30 81 500 *Fax:* (070) 30 81 515

Key Personnel
Man Dir: Mr A Schimmelpenninck
Sales Manager: Mr N Nieuwenhuis
Marketing Manager: Ms A Timmers
Founded: 1995
Subjects: Specialize in International Law & International Relations
ISBN Prefix(es): 90-411
Parent Company: Wolters Kluwer NV
U.S. Office(s): Kluwer Law International, 233 Spring St, 7th floor, New York, NY 10013, United States
Warehouse: Maxwellstraat 4/10, PO Box 322, 3300 AH Dordrech
Orders to: Distributiecentrum KAP Group, PO Box 322, 3300 AH Dordrecht
Tel: (078) 6576000 *Fax:* (078) 6576476
E-mail: orderdept@wkap.nl *Web Site:* www.kluwerlaw.com
Distribution Center KAP Group, 101 Philip Dr, Assinippi Park, Norwell, MA 02061, United States *Tel:* 617-871-6600 *Fax:* 617-871-9045
E-mail: kluwer@wkap.com

Kluwer Technische Boeken BV+
Leeuwenbrug 99-103, 7411 TH Deventer
Mailing Address: PO Box 23, 7400 GA Deventer
Tel: (0172) 466321 *Fax:* (0172) 435527
Telex: 49560 KLUTB NL
Key Personnel
Man Dir & Chief Executive: N H L van Herk
Editorial: Benno van Lochem; Rob van Berkel; Jan Schukking
Sales: Hans Ulenberg
Production: Dick Laus
Part of Wolters Kluwer Trade Publishing.
Subjects: Management, Mechanical Engineering, Science (General), Technology
ISBN Prefix(es): 90-267; 90-201; 90-5576; 90-5577
Parent Company: Wolters Kluwer NV
Subsidiaries: Kluwer Technische Boeken Belgie
Warehouse: Intermedia bv, PO Box 4, 2400 MA Alphen 4d Ryn

Koenen, *imprint of* Van Dale Lexicografie BV

Uitgeefmaatschappij J H Kok BV+
Subsidiary of Veen Bosch & Keuning Uitgevers NV
Ysseldyk 31, 8266 AD Kampen
Mailing Address: PO Box 5019, 8260 GA Kampen
Tel: (038) 3392555 *Fax:* (038) 3327331
E-mail: algemeen@kok.nl
Key Personnel
Man Dir: B A Endedijk
Publisher: J Bijl; den Draak; F J Jonkers; C Verboom
Executive Secretary: Tineke Bouma *Tel:* (038) 3392528 *E-mail:* tbouma@kok.nl
Founded: 1894
Subjects: Fiction, History, Poetry, Religion - Other, Science (General), Social Sciences, Sociology
ISBN Prefix(es): 90-266; 90-242; 90-6140; 90-297; 90-435; 90-205; 90-391; 90-304
Imprints: De Groot Goudriaan; Agora Gooi & Sticht; Voorhoeve; VCL (series of novels)/Westfriesland
Subsidiaries: Callenbach; Kok Ten Have

Koninklijk Instituut Voor de Tropen
Unit of Royal Tropical Institute
Mauritskade 63, 1092 AD Amsterdam
Mailing Address: PO Box 95001, 1090 HA Amsterdam
Tel: (020) 5688272 *Fax:* (020) 5688286
E-mail: kitpress@kit.nl
Web Site: www.kit.nl
Telex: 15080 KIT NL

Key Personnel
Man Dir: R Smit
Business Manager: A Henselmans
Promotion & Sales Manager: E van 't Leven
E-mail: e.v.t.leven@kit.nl
Science Editor: R W Gunn
Educational Editor: P van den Boorn
Editor (Cultural Books): I Geerts
Founded: 1985
Publications department of Royal Tropical Institute (RIT) publishing books on international development cooperation & on non-Western cultures.
Subjects: Agriculture, Anthropology, Developing Countries, Environmental Studies, Health, Nutrition, Women's Studies, International Development Corporation
ISBN Prefix(es): 90-6832
Total Titles: 190 Print

Koninklijke Vermande bv+
Christoffel Plantijnstrz, 2515 TZ The Hague
Mailing Address: Postbus 20014, 2500 EA The Hague
Tel: (070) 3789860 *Fax:* (070) 3789783
Key Personnel
President: Dr J Emeis
Founded: 1750
Subjects: Accounting, Criminology, Environmental Studies, Law, Management, Science (General)
ISBN Prefix(es): 90-6040; 90-5458
Divisions: Kugler Publications BV

Kugler Publications+
Imprint of SPB Academic Publishing
PO Box 97747, 2509 GC The Hague
Tel: (070) 33-00253 *Fax:* (070) 33-00254
E-mail: kuglerspb@wxs.nl
Web Site: www.kuglerpublications.com
Key Personnel
President & International Rights: S P Bakker
Founded: 1974
Subjects: Criminology, Medicine, Nursing, Dentistry, Specializes in ophthalmology, otorhinolaryngolgy, neurology & neurosciences
ISBN Prefix(es): 90-6299
Number of titles published annually: 10 Print
Total Titles: 115 Print

Kwintessens, *imprint of* BV Uitgevery NZV (Nederlandse Zondagsschool Vereniging)

LCG Malmberg BV
Leeghwaterlaan 16, 5223 BA Hertogenbosch
Mailing Address: PO Box 233, 5201 AE Hertogenbosch
Tel: (073) 6288811 *Fax:* (073) 6210512
Cable: MALMBERG'S-HERTOGENBOSCH
Key Personnel
General Manager: Dr J V Nelthoven
Publisher: Dr J J Mathigssen
Founded: 1885
Firm is a part of Educational Publishing division of VNU BV.
Subjects: Biological Sciences, Chemistry, Chemical Engineering, Education, Physics
ISBN Prefix(es): 90-208; 90-345

Leiden University Press, *imprint of* Brill Academic Publishers

Uitgeverij Lemma BV+
Newtonlaan 57, 3584 BP Utrecht
Mailing Address: Postbus 3320, 3502 GH Utrecht
Tel: (30) 2545652 *Fax:* (30) 2586975
E-mail: infodesk@lemma.nl
Web Site: www.lemma.nl
Key Personnel
Publisher: Karin Vliig *E-mail:* karin.vliig@lemma.nl

Man Dir: R K Veen *E-mail:* rveen@lemma.nl
Founded: 1988
Subjects: Business, Communications, Economics, Education, Health, Nutrition, Labor, Industrial Relations, Law, Management, Marketing, Physical Sciences, Psychology, Psychiatry, Social Sciences, Sociology, Technology
ISBN Prefix(es): 90-5189
Total Titles: 400 Print

Lemniscaat+
Vyverlaan 48, 3062 HL Rotterdam
Mailing Address: Postbus 4066, 3006 AB Rotterdam
Tel: (010) 2062929 *Fax:* (010) 4141560
E-mail: info@lemniscaat.nl *Cable:* LEMNISCAAT ROTTERDAM
Key Personnel
Dir: J C Boele van Hensbroek *Tel:* (010) 2062920
E-mail: jcboele@lemniscaat.nl
Editor: Monique Postma *Tel:* (010) 2062925
E-mail: monique@lemniscaat.nl
Rights & Permissions: Susanne Padberg
Tel: (010) 2062924 *E-mail:* susanne@lemniscaat.nl
Contact: F M van den Hoek *Tel:* (010) 2062927
Founded: 1963
Subjects: Psychology, Psychiatry, Social Sciences, Sociology
ISBN Prefix(es): 90-6069; 90-5637
Total Titles: 380 Print

Uitgeverij Leopold BV
Singel 262, 1016 AC Amsterdam
Mailing Address: Postbus 3879, 1001 AR Amsterdam
Tel: (020) 5511250 *Fax:* (020) 4204699
Key Personnel
Man Dir: Liesbeth ten Houten
Permissions: Jacolien Kingmans
Founded: 1923
Subjects: Fiction
ISBN Prefix(es): 90-258
Parent Company: Nijgh en Van Ditmar NV
Associate Companies: BV Uitgeverij de Arbeiderspers

Littera Scripta Manet
Rijsseltweg 10, 7211 EP Eefde
Tel: (0575) 491950
Key Personnel
Man Dir: A Rutgers
Editorial: Mrs R L Rutgers-Schiff
Founded: 1947
Subjects: Animals, Pets, Science (General)
ISBN Prefix(es): 90-6036
Bookshop(s): International Hobby-Bookshop, Gorssel

Van Loghum Slaterus, see Bohn Stafleu Van Loghum BV

LSM, see Littera Scripta Manet

M & P Publishing House+
Onderdoor 9, 3995 DW Houten
Mailing Address: Postbus 170, 3990 DD Houten
Tel: (030) 6377736 *Fax:* (030) 6377764; (030) 6377736
Key Personnel
Chief Executive: G van Buuren
Production: D de Heus
Production, Rights & Permissions: T Ambaum
Editorial: D Rog
Publicity: Mrs G Brandjes
Sales: J Dubois
Founded: 1974
Subjects: Nonfiction (General)
ISBN Prefix(es): 90-6590; 90-359; 90-5112; 90-6790

Parent Company: Meulenhoff & Co, Van Der Does De Willeboissingel 13, 5211 CC Hertogenbosch
Imprints: Kadmos; Van Reemst; ZHU; Marco Polo
Subsidiaries: De Boekerij BV; Uniboek BV; A W Bruna BV; Prometheus BV; Standard BV; Bert Baliher BV; Meulenhoff Nederlad BV

Magnum, *imprint of* Ars Scribendi bv Uitgeverij

Otto Maier Benelux BV
Postfach 1860, D-881888 Ravensburg
Tel: (049) 0751860 *Fax:* (049) 075186 1289
E-mail: anja.fahs@ravensburger.de
Web Site: www.ravensburger.de
Telex: 47991
Subjects: Architecture & Interior Design, Crafts, Games, Hobbies, Nonfiction (General)
Parent Company: Ravensburger Buchverlag, Otto Maier GmbH, Germany

Marco Polo, *imprint of* M & P Publishing House

Meander Uitgeverij BV+
Industrieweg 7, 2254 AE Voorschoten
Tel: (071) 5601040 *Fax:* (071) 5619741
E-mail: info@vierwindstreken.com
Web Site: www.vierwindstreken.com
Key Personnel
Contact: Bob Markus
Founded: 1996
ISBN Prefix(es): 90-5579; 90-5116
Number of titles published annually: 50 Print
Imprints: De Vier Windstreken

Stichting Evangelische Uitgeverij H Medema
Postbus 113, 8170 AC Vaassen
Mailing Address: Emsterweg 96, 8171 PK Vaassen, NL
Tel: (0578) 574995 *Fax:* (0578) 573099
E-mail: medema@pi.net
Key Personnel
Contact: H P Medema
Founded: 1951
ISBN Prefix(es): 90-6353

Meinema, *imprint of* Boekencentrum BV

Meinema+
Postbus 29, 2700 AA Zoetermeer
Tel: (079) 3615481 *Fax:* (079) 3615489
E-mail: info@boekencentrum.nl
Key Personnel
Editor: C Korenhof *E-mail:* korenhof@boekencentrum.nl
Subjects: Religion - Catholic, Religion - Protestant, Theology
ISBN Prefix(es): 90-211
Number of titles published annually: 40 Print
Total Titles: 220 Print
Parent Company: Boekencentrum
Distributed by Denis & Co

Mets & Schilt Uitgevers en Distributeurs+
Formerly Jan Mets Uitgeverij
Westeinde 16, 1017 ZP Amsterdam
Tel: (020) 6256087 *Fax:* (020) 6270242
E-mail: info@metsenschilt.com
Web Site: www.metsenschilt.com
Key Personnel
Dir: J Mets; M J Schilt
Founded: 1981
Subjects: Art, Biography, Business, Cookery, Developing Countries, Foreign Countries, History, Journalism, Nonfiction (General), Social Sciences, Sociology, Travel
ISBN Prefix(es): 90-5330

Distributed by Van Halewyck (Belgium); Transaction Publishers (USA) (Africa, Asia, Australia, Ireland, New Zealand, North America, South America, Uk, US)

J M Meulenhoff, *imprint of* J M Meulenhoff BV

J M Meulenhoff BV+
Herengracht 505, 1017 BV Amsterdam
Mailing Address: PO Box 100, 1000 AC Amsterdam
Tel: (020) 5533500 *Fax:* (020) 6258511
E-mail: j.m.meulenhoff@meulenhoff.nl
Key Personnel
Man Dir, Editorial, Rights & Permissions & Publisher: Chantal d'Aulnis
Founded: 1895
Also specializing in commercial & Dutch language books.
Subjects: Fiction, Literature, Literary Criticism, Essays, Nonfiction (General)
ISBN Prefix(es): 90-290
Total Titles: 1,000 Print
Parent Company: Meulenhoff & Co BV
Imprints: Arena; eXperience; J M Meulenhoff; Meulenhoff M; Mpact
Subsidiaries: Arena; Meulenhoff International

Meulenhoff M, *imprint of* J M Meulenhoff BV

Miland Publishers
Zuideinde 40, 2421 AK Nieuwkoop
Mailing Address: Postbus 6, 2420 AA Nieuwkoop
Tel: (0172) 571461 *Fax:* (0172) 572231
E-mail: degraaf.books@wxs.nl
Founded: 1969
ISBN Prefix(es): 90-6003
Parent Company: De Graaf Publishers

Uitgeverij Mingus+
PO Box 242, 3440 AE Woerden
Mailing Address: Zaagmolenln 4, 3447 GS Woerden
Tel: (0348) 425507 *Fax:* (0348) 425507
Key Personnel
Contact: Teus Verweij
Founded: 1981
Subjects: Fiction, Nonfiction (General)
ISBN Prefix(es): 90-6564

Ministerie van Verkeer en Waterstaat
(Information & Documentation Div)
Plesmanweg 1, 2597 JG The Hague
Mailing Address: Postbus 20901, 2500 EX The Hague
Tel: (070) 3517086 *Fax:* (070) 3516430
Web Site: www.minverw.nl
Telex: 32562 minvwnl
Subjects: Transportation
ISBN Prefix(es): 90-369

Mirananda Publishers BV+
H Stijkelpln 29, 2597 NS 5 The Hague
Tel: (070) 3585943 *Fax:* (070) 3586843
E-mail: info@mirananda.nl
Web Site: www.mirananda.nl
Key Personnel
Man Dir: Jan-Carel Diecken
Contact: Reinoud Douwes
Founded: 1976
Subjects: Art, Astrology, Occult, Education, Language Arts, Linguistics, Philosophy, Psychology, Psychiatry, Religion - Other, Science (General)
ISBN Prefix(es): 90-6271
Number of titles published annually: 25 Print
Total Titles: 250 Print
Imprints: Moon Press (children's)
Orders to: Centraal Boekhuis, Erasmusweg 10, Culemborg

Mirran+
Oude Trambaan 23, 5085 NH Esbeek
Tel: (013) 5169534
E-mail: post@mirran.com
Web Site: www.mirran.com
Key Personnel
Director: Mieke de Jonge
Founded: 1996
Member of GAU.
Subjects: *Specializes in Danish children's books in Dutch translations.*
ISBN Prefix(es): 90-75837
Total Titles: 11 Print
Foreign Rep(s): Denis & Co (Belgium)
Shipping Address: Centraal Boekhuirs, PO Box 125, Culemborg

Mondria Publishers+
Westerkd 13A, 9718 AR Groningen
Tel: (050) 3110505 *Fax:* (050) 3112299
Key Personnel
Chief Executive, Sales, Publicity: E Vos
Founded: 1980
Subjects: Humor
ISBN Prefix(es): 90-6555; 90-432

Moon Press (children's), *imprint of* Mirananda Publishers BV

Mpact, *imprint of* J M Meulenhoff BV

De Muiderkring BV+
Hogeweyselaan 227, 1382 JL Weesp
Mailing Address: Postbus 313, 1380 AH Weesp
Tel: (0294) 450460 *Fax:* (0294) 412782
Key Personnel
Man Dir: Van Lidth de Jeude
Sales: B Hofman
Founded: 1929
Subjects: Computer Science, Crafts, Games, Hobbies, Electronics, Electrical Engineering
ISBN Prefix(es): 90-6082

Mulder Holland BV+
Transformatorweg 35, 1014 AJ Amsterdam
Mailing Address: Postbus 8064, 1005 AB Amsterdam
Tel: (020) 442022; (020) 441682; (020) 824805 *Fax:* (020) 465228
Telex: 14627 *Cable:* Emzet Amsterdam
Key Personnel
Publisher: John Winkel
Parent Company: Internatio Mueller

Uitgeverij Maarten Muntinga+
Postlous 2465, 1000 CL Amsterdam
Mailing Address: Nieuwezijds Voorburgwal 292, 1012 RT Amsterdam
Tel: (020) 5216767 *Fax:* (020) 6260596
E-mail: info@rainbow.nl
Key Personnel
President: Maarten Muntinga
Publisher: Hilbrand Gringhuis
Founded: 1983
Subjects: Literature, Literary Criticism, Essays, Nonfiction (General)
ISBN Prefix(es): 90-6766; 90-417
Imprints: Rainbow Crime; Rainbow Pocketboeken

Nai Publishers
Mauritsweg 23, 3012 JR Rotterdam
Tel: (010) 2010133 *Fax:* (010) 2010130
E-mail: info@naipublishers.nl
Web Site: www.naipublishers.nl
Key Personnel
Publisher & Director: Simon Franke
Editor, Production & Dept Director: Astrid Vorstermans
Editor & Production: Barbera van Kooij; Caroline Gautier

NETHERLANDS BOOK

Public Relations & Marketing: Mr Nieck de Bruijn *Tel:* (010) 2010132 *E-mail:* ndebruijn@publishersnai.nl
Office Manager: Marion Pot
Finance: Peter Pols
Bookshop: Thera Riemer-Magre; Marcel Witvoet
Founded: 1994
Publisher of books about architecture, art & urban design.
Subjects: Architecture & Interior Design, Art, Urban design
Foreign Rep(s): Art Data (UK, Ireland); Coen Sligting Bookimport (Austria, Belgium, Germany, Switzerland); DAP (Central America, North America, South America); Le Funambule (France); Modern Journal (Australia, New Zealand); Penny Padovani (Gibraltar, Greece, Italy, Portugal, Slovenia, Spain); Roger Ward International Book Marketing (Asia)

Narratio Theologische Uitgeverij+
Kwakernaat 10, 4205 PK Gorinchem
Mailing Address: Postbus 1006, 4200 CA Gorinchem
Tel: (0183) 628188 *Fax:* (0183) 628188
E-mail: narratio@worldonline.nl
Key Personnel
International Rights: L van den Herik
Founded: 1989
Subjects: Religion - Catholic, Religion - Protestant, Theology
ISBN Prefix(es): 90-5263
Total Titles: 220 Print; 7 Audio

Nederlands Literair Produktie-en Vertalingenfonds
Singel 464, 1017 AW Amsterdam
Tel: (020) 6206261 *Fax:* (020) 6207179
E-mail: nlpvf@xs4all.nl
Web Site: www.nlpvf.nl
Key Personnel
Man Dir: Rudi Wester
Deputy Dir: Reintje Gianotten
ISBN Prefix(es): 90-803223

Uitgeverij H Nelissen BV
Birkstraat 95-97, 3768 SD Soest
Mailing Address: Postbus 3167, 3760 DD Soest
Tel: (035) 5412386 *Fax:* (035) 5423877
E-mail: service@nelissen.nl
Key Personnel
Man Dir, Editorial, Permissions: Dick Boer
   E-mail: dickboer@nelissen.nl
Sales & Publicity: Pieter Zwart
Founded: 1922
Subjects: Education, Government, Political Science, Management, Philosophy, Religion - Other, Social Sciences, Sociology
ISBN Prefix(es): 90-244

Nico Israel
Keizersgracht 489, 1017 DM Amsterdam
Tel: (020) 6222255 *Fax:* (020) 6382666
Key Personnel
Man Dir: Nico Israel
Founded: 1950
Subjects: Geography, Geology, History, Travel
ISBN Prefix(es): 90-6072
Associate Companies: A Asher en Co BV

Nieuwe Stad
Utrechtseweg 171, 3818ED Amersfoort
Tel: (033) 4614615 *Fax:* (033) 4635885
Founded: 1960
ISBN Prefix(es): 90-71734
Parent Company: Citta Nuova Editrice, Italy

Nieuwe Wieken, *imprint of* Omega Boek BV

Nijgh & Van Ditmar Amsterdam+
Singel 262, 1016 AC Amsterdam
Mailing Address: Postbus 3879, 1001 AR Amsterdam
Tel: (020) 5511262 *Fax:* (020) 6203509
Key Personnel
President: Ary Langbroek
Vice President: Vic va de Reijt
Editor: Lidewijde Paris
Founded: 1837
Publisher of Zoetermeer: young/young debut writers' upmarket literary fiction & nonfiction.
Subjects: Literature, Literary Criticism, Essays, Social Sciences, Sociology
ISBN Prefix(es): 90-388
Parent Company: Em Querido bv
Imprints: Zoetermeer
Divisions: Dedalus (for Belgium)

Martinus Nijhoff, *imprint of* Kluwer Academic Publishers

North Holland, *imprint of* Elsevier Science BV

Omega Boek BV+
Fregat 35, 1113 EE Diemen
Tel: (020) 6905997 *Fax:* (020) 6957428
Founded: 1968
Subjects: Art, Fiction, Management, Military Science, Nonfiction (General)
ISBN Prefix(es): 90-6057; 90-6142
Imprints: De Centaur; Nieuwe Wieken; Omega Jeugdboekerij; Triton Pers
Book Club(s): EC1 voor boeken en platen BV
Orders to: Centraal Boekhuis, Erasmusweg 10, Culemborg

Omega Jeugdboekerij, *imprint of* Omega Boek BV

Ooievaar, *imprint of* Prometheus

Ooievaar+
Herengracht 406, 1017 BX Amsterdam
Mailing Address: Postbus 1662, 1000 BR Amsterdam
Tel: (020) 624 19 34 *Fax:* (020) 622 54 61
E-mail: pbo@pbo.nl
Web Site: www.pbo.nl
Associate Companies: Bert Bakker; Prometheus

Oriental Press BV (APA)
Postbus 806, 1000 AV Amsterdam
Tel: (020) 6265544
E-mail: info@apa-publishers.com
Subjects: Asian Studies, Religion - Islamic
ISBN Prefix(es): 90-6023
Parent Company: APA (Academic Publishers Associated)
Orders to: APA, Postbus 806, 1000 AV Amsterdam NL

Parel Pockets, *imprint of* De Boekerij BV

Partners Training & Innovatie
Dwerggras 30, 3068 PC Rotterdam
Mailing Address: Postbus 8639, 3009 AP Rotterdam
Tel: (010) 4071563
E-mail: partners@ced.nl
Key Personnel
Publisher: Mr C A van Dongen Uitgeven
Founded: 1992
Subjects: Education
ISBN Prefix(es): 90-5819; 90-75074
Total Titles: 104 Print; 11 Audio
Parent Company: LED

Passage, Uitgeverij+
Camphuysenstraat 58, 9721-KH Groningen

Mailing Address: Postbus 216, 9700 AE-Groningen
Tel: (050) 5271332
E-mail: passuit@xs4all.nl
Web Site: www.uitgeverijpassage.nl
Key Personnel
Publisher: Anton Scheepstra
Founded: 1991
Member of KVB & NUV (GAU).
Subjects: *Specialized in:*Dutch literature
ISBN Prefix(es): 90-5452
Total Titles: 60 Print
Distributed by Maklu
Foreign Rep(s): Maklu (Belgium)

Pearson Education Netherlands
Concertgebouwplein 25, 1070 LM Amsterdam
Tel: (020) 575-5800 *Fax:* (020) 664-5334
E-mail: firstname.lastname@mail.aw.nl
Key Personnel
Pres: Rita Snaddon
Finance & P&O: Hennie Haverkort
Marketing Manager, Professional Education: Sue Young
Publishing Manager: Arianne Strating
Founded: 1942
Subjects: Business, Computer Science, Economics, Education, Management, Technology
ISBN Prefix(es): 0-201
Parent Company: Pearson Plc

Penguin Books Netherlands BV
Herengracht 418-2H, 1017 BZ Amsterdam
Mailing Address: Postbus 3507, 1001 AH Amsterdam
Tel: (020) 6259566 *Fax:* (020) 6258676
ISBN Prefix(es): 90-75320

Penguin Books Netherlands BV
Herengracht 418-2H, 1017 BZ Amsterdam
ISBN Prefix(es): 90-75320

The Pepin Press+
PO Box 10349, 1001 EH Amsterdam
Tel: (020) 4202021 *Fax:* (020) 4201152
Key Personnel
Publisher & International Rights: Mr Pepin Van Roojen
Founded: 1986
Specialize in high quality art publications.
Subjects: Antiques, Archaeology, Architecture & Interior Design, Art, Asian Studies, Fashion, History
ISBN Prefix(es): 90-5496

Pergamon, *imprint of* Elsevier Science BV

Philo Press-Van Heusden-Hissink & Co CV (APA)
Postbus 806, 1000 AV Amsterdam
Tel: (020) 6265544
E-mail: info@apa-publishers.com
Founded: 1963
Firm incorporates Gerard Th Van Heusden (APA) & G W Hissink & Co (APA).
Subjects: Art, Asian Studies, Biblical Studies, History, Human Relations, Religion - Islamic, Religion - Jewish, Science (General), Theology
ISBN Prefix(es): 90-6022; 90-6024; 90-6025
Parent Company: APA (Academic Publishers Associated)

Picaron Editions+
Postbus 8024, 6710 AA Ede Gid
Tel: (020) 6201484
Founded: 1987
Subjects: Art, Philosophy
ISBN Prefix(es): 90-71466

Piccolo, *imprint of* De Boekerij BV

Piccolo, *imprint of* Van Goor BV

Plateau, *imprint of* Uitgeverij De Vuurbaak BV

Uitgeverij Ploegsma BV+
Keizersgracht 616, NL 1017 ER Amsterdam
Tel: (020) 6262907 *Fax:* (020) 6242994
Key Personnel
President: Peter Frohlich
Founded: 1901
Subjects: Child Care & Development, How-to, Science (General)
ISBN Prefix(es): 90-216
Imprints: Ploegsma (children's books); De Brink (adult books)

Ploegsma (children's books), *imprint of* Uitgeverij Ploegsma BV

Podium Uitgeverij+
Singel 450, 1017 AV Amsterdam
Tel: (020) 4213830
E-mail: post@uitgeverijpodium.nl
Key Personnel
Dir: Joost Nysen *Fax:* (020) 4213776
Founded: 1997
Specializes in Dutch Literature.
Subjects: Literature, Literary Criticism, Essays, Nonfiction (General)
ISBN Prefix(es): 90-5759
Number of titles published annually: 25 Print
Total Titles: 100 Print

De Prom
Subsidiary of Veen Bosch & Keuning Uitgevers NV
Prinses Marielaan 8, 3743 JA Baarn
Mailing Address: Postbus 1, 3740 AA Baarn
Tel: (035) 5482403 *Fax:* (035) 5418221
Key Personnel
Man Dir: U Hazeu
ISBN Prefix(es): 90-6801

Prometheus+
Formerly Bert Bakker
Herengracht 406, 1017 BX Amsterdam
Mailing Address: Postbus 1662, 1000 BR Amsterdam
Tel: (020) 624 19 34 *Fax:* (020) 622 54 61
E-mail: pbo@pbo.nl
Web Site: www.pbo.nl
Key Personnel
Man Dir: Ms Plien Van Albada
Sales Dir: Ms Carla De Jong
Publicity Dir: Ms Hella Jansen
Rights: Ms Hedda Sanders
Founded: 1893
Subjects: Gay & Lesbian, History, Language Arts, Linguistics, Literature, Literary Criticism, Essays, Nonfiction (General), Philosophy, Poetry, Psychology, Psychiatry, Science (General), Social Sciences, Sociology
ISBN Prefix(es): 90-6019; 90-351
Associate Companies: Ooievaar; Prometheus
Orders to: Ivec, Postbus 154, 1380 AD Weesp

Prometheus
Herengracht 406, 1017 BX Amsterdam
Mailing Address: Postbus 1662, 1000 BR Amsterdam
Tel: (020) 6241934 *Fax:* (020) 6225461
E-mail: pbo@pbo.nl
Web Site: www.pbo.nl
Key Personnel
Man Dir: Ms Plien van Albada
Publicity Dir: Maritge Wielaard
Editor in Chief: Onno Blom
Rights: Nelleke Geel
Founded: 1990
Subjects: Fiction, Nonfiction (General)
ISBN Prefix(es): 90-5333

Number of titles published annually: 300 Print
Associate Companies: Bert Bakker
Imprints: Ooievaar

Promotional Publications Int BV
Montalbaendreef 2, 3562 LC Utrecht
Tel: (030) 650650 *Fax:* (030) 620850
ISBN Prefix(es): 90-5344
Parent Company: Uitgeverij Het Spectrum BV, Postbus 2073, 3500 GB Utrecht

Publitronic, *imprint of* Segment BV

Em Querido's Uitgeverij BV
Singel 262, 1016 AC Amsterdam
Mailing Address: Postbus 3879, 1001 AR Amsterdam
Tel: (020) 5511262 *Fax:* (020) 6203509
Key Personnel
Man Dir: Ary T Langbroek
Founded: 1915
Subjects: Art, Biography, Fiction, Mathematics, Poetry
ISBN Prefix(es): 90-214; 90-253
Imprints: Athenaeum-Polak & Van Gennep; Griffioen Paperbacks; JeugdSalamander Paperbacks; Salamander Paperbacks; De Viergang

Rainbow Crime, *imprint of* Uitgeverij Maarten Muntinga

Rainbow Pocketboeken, *imprint of* Uitgeverij Maarten Muntinga

Rebo Productions BV+
le Poellaan 6, 2161 LB Lisse
Tel: (0252) 419105 *Fax:* (0252) 410231
Key Personnel
General Dir: H W J Wagner
Commerical Dir: E P A Veltman
International Rights: J A M Wagner
Founded: 1983
Subjects: Animals, Pets, Crafts, Games, Hobbies, Gardening, Plants
ISBN Prefix(es): 90-366
Associate Companies: Zuid Boekprodukties BV
Subsidiaries: Rebo Productions SRO; Celetna ii

Reed Elsevier Nederland BV+
Van de Sande Bakhuyzenstr 4, 1061 AG Amsterdam
Tel: (020) 515 9111 *Fax:* (020) 618 0325
Web Site: www.elsevier.com
Key Personnel
Chief Executive: Derk Haank
Legal Dir: Erik Ekker
Operating Companies: Argus; Bonaventura; Dagbladunie; Elsevier Opleidingen; Krips Repro; Misset; Pan European Publishing Company
Divisions, Subsidiaries & Branches: Elsevier Training NV, Brussels, International Equipment News Europe NV, Brussels (both Belgium); Editions Elsevier Thomas SA, Boulogne Billancourt, France; Elsevier Thomas Fachverlag GmbH, Mainz, Germany; Audet Tijdschriften, Arnheim, De Dordtenaar BV, Dordrecht, Toeristiek BV, Oostwoud, Dagblad van Rijn en Gouwe BV, Alphen aan den Rijn, Brabants Niewsblad BV, Roosendaal, Rotterdams Dagblad CV, Rotterdam, Nederlands Studiecentrum, Vlaardingen, CBBM BV, Zwijndrecht (all Netherlands); Elsevier Prensa SA, Barcelona, Arte y Cemento Bilbao (Both Spain).
Subjects: Science (General)

Van Reemst, *imprint of* M & P Publishing House

Uitgeverij La Riviere
PO Box 309, 3740 AH Baarn
Tel: (035) 5486676

Robyns, *imprint of* Educatieve Partners Nederland bv

Rodopi
Tijnmuiden 7, 1046 AK Amsterdam
Tel: (020) 6114821 *Fax:* (020) 4472979
E-mail: orders-queries@rodopi.nl
Web Site: www.rodopi.nl
Key Personnel
Dir: Fred van der Zee *E-mail:* f.van.der.zee@rodopi.nl
Founded: 1966
Subjects: Human Relations
ISBN Prefix(es): 90-6203; 90-5183; 90-420
Total Titles: 2,600 Print
U.S. Office(s): 6075 Roswell Rd, Suite 21-G, Atlanta, GA 30328, United States *Tel:* 404-843-4445 *Fax:* 404-843-4315 *E-mail:* orders-queries@rodopi.nl *Web Site:* www.rodopi.nl

Rostrum Publishing
Zuiddk 2A, 5705 CS Helmond
Tel: (0492) 545268 *Fax:* (0492) 528635
Telex: 71178
Key Personnel
Chief Executive & Rights & Permissions: Robert Hofman
Editorial, Film: Marja Geevers
Sales: Laura Smith
Production: Ellen Pardede
Publicity: Eleonore Hofman
Founded: 1975
Subjects: Film, Video, Nonfiction (General), Sports, Athletics
ISBN Prefix(es): 90-328

Rothschild & Bach+
Kleine Garmanplantsoen 21 VII, 1017 RP Amsterdam
Tel: (020) 6389329
ISBN Prefix(es): 90-5371
Associate Companies: International Theatre & Film Books

Salamander Paperbacks, *imprint of* Em Querido's Uitgeverij BV

Samsom BedrijfsInformatie BV
Prinses Margrietlaan 3, 2404 HA Alphen aan den Rijn
Mailing Address: PO Box 4, 2400 MA Alphen aan den Rijn
Tel: (0172) 466321 *Fax:* (0172) 435527
Key Personnel
Man Dir: C J Steur
Founded: 1882
Part of Wolters Kluwer Business Publishing.
Subjects: Advertising, Business, Finance, Labor, Industrial Relations, Management, Marketing, Public Administration, Social Sciences, Sociology, Technology
ISBN Prefix(es): 90-6500
Parent Company: Wolters Kluwer NV
Divisions: Hofstad Vakpers

Samsom Stafleu, see Bohn Stafleu Van Loghum BV

Sara, *imprint of* Van Gennep Ltd

Schoolpers, *imprint of* Educatieve Partners Nederland bv

Scriptum+
Dam 2, 3111 BD Schiedam
Mailing Address: PO Box 293, 3100 AG Schiedam
Tel: (010) 4271022 *Fax:* (010) 4736625

NETHERLANDS

E-mail: info@scriptum.nl
Web Site: www.scriptum.nl
Key Personnel
Publisher: Hans Ritman *E-mail:* ritman@scriptum.nl
Founded: 1985
Subjects: Antiques, Art, Business, Management, Marketing
ISBN Prefix(es): 90-71542; 90-5594
Number of titles published annually: 25 Print
Total Titles: 200 Print
Imprints: Scriptum Management; Scriptum Art; Scriptum Topography

Scriptum Art, *imprint of* Scriptum

Scriptum Management, *imprint of* Scriptum

Scriptum Topography, *imprint of* Scriptum

SDU Juridische & Fiscale Uitgeverij
c Plantynstr 2, 2515 TZ The Hague
Mailing Address: PB 20024, 2500 EA The Hague
Tel: (070) 3789860 *Fax:* (070) 3854321
Key Personnel
Marketing Manager: Mrs M J Geevers
Founded: 1991
Subjects: Finance, Law
ISBN Prefix(es): 90-5409

Segment BV+
Peter Treckpoelstr 2, 6191 VK Beek Lb
Mailing Address: PO Box 75, 6190 AB Beek Lb
Tel: (046) 43894444 *Fax:* (046) 4389401; (046) 4370161
E-mail: secretariant@segment.nl
Web Site: www.segment.nl
Key Personnel
Man Dir: Menno M J Landman
Founded: 1961
Part of Wolters Kluwer Trade Publishing.
Subjects: Electronics, Electrical Engineering, Philosophy, Science (General)
ISBN Prefix(es): 90-5381; 90-70160; 90-73035; 0-905705
Parent Company: Wolters Kluwer NV
Imprints: Elektuur; Elektor; Publitronic
Subsidiaries: Elektor (Germany, France & UK)

Semic Junior Press
Zwarteweg 6, 1412 GD Naarden
Tel: (035) 6944914 *Fax:* (035) 6944909
Telex: 4473114 cacjp nl
Key Personnel
Man Dir: Guillermo Hierro
Subjects: Astrology, Occult
ISBN Prefix(es): 90-305; 90-72073; 90-6236
Parent Company: Semic International AB, Sweden

Servire BV Uitgevers+
St Jacobstraat 125, 3511 Utrecht
Mailing Address: Postbus 14095, 3511 BP Utrecht
Tel: (030) 2349211 *Fax:* (030) 2349247
E-mail: servire@pi.net
Key Personnel
Chief Executive: Felix Erkelens
Founded: 1921
Subjects: Alternative, Astrology, Occult, Health, Nutrition, Human Relations, Psychology, Psychiatry, Religion - Buddhist, Religion - Hindu, Religion - Islamic, Religion - Jewish, Religion - Protestant, Religion - Other, Self-Help, Theology, Women's Studies
ISBN Prefix(es): 90-6077; 90-6325
Associate Companies: Hunter House Inc, Publishers, PO Box 2914, Alameda, CA 94501, United States

Sesam, *imprint of* Bosch & Keuning

Signature, *imprint of* A W Bruna Uitgevers BV

Sjaloom en Wildeboer Publishers+
V Diemenstr 410-412, 1013 CR Amsterdam
Mailing Address: Postbus 1895, 1000 BW Amsterdam
Tel: (020) 6206263 *Fax:* (020) 6209253
Founded: 1982
Subjects: Fiction, Health, Nutrition
ISBN Prefix(es): 90-6249
Imprints: Cadans

SMD Educational Publishers (Spruyt, Van Mantgem & De Does)
Rooseveltstraat 12, 2321 BM Leiden
Mailing Address: Postbus 63, 2300 AB Leiden
Tel: (071) 5797570 *Fax:* (071) 5797571
Founded: 1907
Subjects: Education, Medicine, Nursing, Dentistry
ISBN Prefix(es): 90-238

Smeets Illustrated Projects+
Molenveldstr 90, 6001 HL Weert
Tel: (04951) 570911 *Fax:* (04950) 46286
Telex: 37550
Key Personnel
Manager: V Pokorny
Subjects: Art
ISBN Prefix(es): 90-6220
Parent Company: Royal Smeets Offset
Associate Companies: VBI/Smeets

Sociaal en Cultureel Planbureau+
Postbus 16164, 2500 BD The Hague
Tel: (070) 3407000 *Fax:* (070) 3407044
E-mail: info@scp.ul
Founded: 1973
Subjects: Child Care & Development, Criminology, Education, Ethnicity, Government, Political Science, Health, Nutrition, Radio, TV, Real Estate, Social Sciences, Sociology, Women's Studies
ISBN Prefix(es): 90-377

Uitgeverij Het Spectrum BV
Montelbaendreef 2, 3562 LC Utrecht
Mailing Address: Postbus 2073, 3500 GB Utrecht
Tel: (030) 2650650 *Fax:* (030) 2620850
E-mail: het@spectrum.nl
Key Personnel
Dir: Joost C Bloemsma
Vice Dir, Sales Publicity: Yvonne Koolen
Editorial: George Pape; Renee Swaalf; Bart Drubbel; Mechteld Jansen; Marjon Aardema; Henk ter Borg
Production: Ludger van Zwetszelaar
Rights & Permissions: Jane Baird
Publisher, Multimedia: Ton von Bladel
Rights & Permissions: Anry van Esch
Founded: 1935
Subjects: Astrology, Occult, Computer Science, Criminology, Environmental Studies, History, Literature, Literary Criticism, Essays, Management, Mysteries, Nonfiction (General), Science Fiction, Fantasy, Travel
ISBN Prefix(es): 90-315; 90-274
Total Titles: 800 Print; 100 CD-ROM

Staatsdrukkerij en Uitgeverijbedrijf
Christoffel Plantijn Str 2, 2515 TZ The Hague
Mailing Address: Postbus 20025, 2500 EA The Hague
Tel: (070) 3789860 *Fax:* (070) 3789783
Telex: 32486
Subjects: Government, Political Science
ISBN Prefix(es): 90-12; 90-357; 90-399; 90-5332

Stam Techniek, *imprint of* Educatieve Partners Nederland bv

Stedelijk Van Abbemuseum
Bilderdijklaan 10, 5611 NH Eindhoven
Mailing Address: PO Box 235, 5600 AE Eindhoven
Tel: 040 2387310 *Fax:* 040 2460680
E-mail: vanabbe@worldaccess.nl
Key Personnel
Dir: J Debbaut
Founded: 1936
Subjects: Art, Library & Information Sciences
ISBN Prefix(es): 90-70149

Steltman Editions
Teniersstr 6, 1071 DX Amsterdam
Tel: (020) 6228683 *Fax:* (020) 6207588
E-mail: steltman@steltman.com
Key Personnel
President: Gerrit Steltman
Founded: 1982
Specialize in Art Design, Michael Parkes exclusive.
Subjects: Art
ISBN Prefix(es): 90-71867
U.S. Office(s): Steltman, 41 E 57 St, New York, NY 10022, United States

Stenfert Kroese, *imprint of* Educatieve Partners Nederland bv

Stenvert Systems & Service BV
Gildenveld 1, 3892 DC Zeewolde
Mailing Address: Postbus 1251, 3390 BB Zeewold
Tel: (036) 5225774 *Fax:* (036) 5226986
Key Personnel
President: M G Stenvert
Editor: E H Kolk
Producer: F H A Kanters
Founded: 1925
Member of GEU.
ISBN Prefix(es): 90-281
Showroom(s): Sutton 10, 7327 AB Apeldoorn
Warehouse: Sutton 10, 7327 AB Apeldoorn

Stichting IVIO+
De Meent 2, 8224 BR Lelystad
Mailing Address: Postbus 37, 8200 AA Lelystad
Tel: (0320) 229900 *Fax:* (0320) 229999
E-mail: dir@ivio.nl
Web Site: www.ivio.nl
Key Personnel
Manager: A L Greiner *Tel:* (0320) 229912
  E-mail: jmoes@ivio.nl
Founded: 1936
Subjects: Education
ISBN Prefix(es): 90-6121
Total Titles: 200 Print
Imprints: AO; Wereldschool

A J G Strengholt's Boeken, Anno 1928, BV+
Postbus 338, 1400 AH Bussum
Tel: (035) 6958411 *Fax:* (035) 6946173
Cable: EDITORAS
Key Personnel
Man Dir: Mrs C I C Bakker
Founded: 1928
Subjects: Biography, Health, Nutrition, History, How-to, Mathematics, Nonfiction (General)
ISBN Prefix(es): 90-6010
Parent Company: Strengholt BV, Postbus 338, 1400 AH Bussum

Uitgeverij SUN
Byleveldsingel 9, 6521 AM Nijmegen
Mailing Address: Postbus 1609, 6501 BP Nijmegen
Tel: (024) 3221700 *Fax:* (024) 3235439

PUBLISHERS — NETHERLANDS

Key Personnel
Publicity, Permissions: Wilfried Uitterhoeve
Founded: 1969
Subjects: Architecture & Interior Design, Ethnicity, History, Philosophy
ISBN Prefix(es): 90-6168
Imprints: Uitgeverij Dwarsstap

Swets & Zeitlinger Publishers+
Mailing Address: Postbus 825, 2160 SZ Lisse
Tel: (0252) 435111 *Fax:* (0252) 435447
E-mail: orders@swets.nl
Web Site: www.swets.nl
Telex: 41325 szlis nl *Cable:* SWEZEIT-LISSE
Key Personnel
Chairman of the Executive Board: Pieter Rustenburg *Fax:* (0252) 412775
Dir, Sales & Marketing: Steven A Hartman
Dir, Finance & Operations: Geert C D Visscher
Marketing & Sales Coordinator: Patrick Kleian
Tel: (0252) 435133 *E-mail:* pkleian@swets.nl
Founded: 1901
Subscription agent.
Subjects: Education, Engineering (General), Health, Nutrition, Labor, Industrial Relations, Language Arts, Linguistics, Medicine, Nursing, Dentistry, Music, Dance, Psychology, Psychiatry, Science (General), Technology
ISBN Prefix(es): 90-70430; 90-265
U.S. Office(s): PO Box 582, Downingtown, PA 19335-9998, United States

SWP, BV Uitgeverij+
Plantage Middenlaan 2-H, 1018 DD Amsterdam
Mailing Address: PO Box 257, 1000 AG Amsterdam
Tel: (020) 3307200 *Fax:* (020) 3308040
E-mail: swp@wxs.nl
Web Site: www.swpbook.com
Key Personnel
Publisher: Paul E Roosenstein
Founded: 1982
Specialize in early childhood education, health issues & social welfare.
Subjects: Child Care & Development, Criminology, Management, Psychology, Psychiatry
ISBN Prefix(es): 90-6665
Number of titles published annually: 40 Print; 1 CD-ROM
Total Titles: 300 Print; 2 CD-ROM

Sybex BV+
Birkstr 95, 3768 HD Soest
Tel: (035) 6027625 *Fax:* (035) 6026556
Key Personnel
General Manager & Publisher: G Beyering
Founded: 1988
Subjects: Computer Science
ISBN Prefix(es): 90-5160; 90-419
Branch Office(s)
Sybex Inc, Alameda, CA, United States
Warehouse: Centraal Boekhuis, Culemborg, Holland

Syntax Publishers, *imprint of* Tilburg University Press

Synthese-Miranda, see Mirananda Publishers BV

Telos Boeken+
c/o Buyten en Schipperheijn, PO Box 22708, 1000 Amsterdam
Tel: (020) 5241010 *Fax:* (020) 5241011
E-mail: info@buijten.nl
Key Personnel
International Rights: Guido Sneep
Founded: 1902
Subjects: Human Relations, Philosophy, Religion - Protestant, Theology, Travel
ISBN Prefix(es): 90-6064; 90-6353 (Medema); 90-324; 90-5560 (De Vuurbach); 90-5881

Terra Publishing Co+
Bonendaal 2A, 7231 GG Warnsveld
Mailing Address: PO Box 1080, NL 7230 AB Warnsveld
Tel: (0575) 58 13 10 *Fax:* (0575) 52 52 42
E-mail: terra@terraboek.nl
Web Site: www.terraboek.nl
Key Personnel
President: H Weesjes
Man Dir: T van Lexmond
Founded: 1971
Subjects: Architecture & Interior Design, Cookery, Crafts, Games, Hobbies, Gardening, Plants, Health, Nutrition
ISBN Prefix(es): 90-6255
Warehouse: Terra Magazijn, Distrimedia NV, Meulenbeeksesteenweg 20, 8700 Tielt

BV Uitgeverij en Boekhandel W J Thieme & Cie
Industrieweg 85, 7202 CA Zutphen
Mailing Address: Postbus 7, 7200 AA Zutphen
Tel: (0575) 594911 *Fax:* (0575) 519970
Cable: THIEME ZUTPHEN
Key Personnel
Dir: K Schillemans
Founded: 1792
Subjects: Science (General)
ISBN Prefix(es): 90-03

ThiemeMeulenhoff+
Herengracht 507, 1017 BV Amsterdam
Mailing Address: Postbus 7, 7200 AA Zutphen, Amsterdam
Tel: (030) 239 25 55 *Fax:* (030) 239 22 70
E-mail: w.de.jager@thiememeulenhoff.nl
Web Site: www.thiememeulenhoff.nl
Key Personnel
Man Dir: C J J van Steijn
Publishing Dir: P A Stadhouders
Subjects: Education
ISBN Prefix(es): 90-280
Parent Company: Meulenhoff & Co BV
Subsidiaries: NIB-Software

Thoth Publishers+
Lindelaan 18, 1405 AK Bussum
Tel: (035) 6944144 *Fax:* (035) 6943266
E-mail: thoth@euronet.nl
Key Personnel
Publisher: Kees van den Hoek
Founded: 1985
Subjects: Architecture & Interior Design, Art, Literature, Literary Criticism, Essays, Nonfiction (General)
ISBN Prefix(es): 90-6868

Uitgeverij de Tijdstroom BV+
Euclideslaan 201, 3584 BS Utrecht
Mailing Address: Postbus 1110, 3600 BC Maarssen
Tel: (030) 2586900 *Fax:* (030) 2586950
Founded: 1924
Subjects: Health, Nutrition, Management, Medicine, Nursing, Dentistry, Physics, Psychology, Psychiatry, Social Sciences, Sociology
ISBN Prefix(es): 90-6087; 90-352; 90-5256

Tilburg University Press
Warandelaan 2, 5037 AB Tilburg
Tel: (013) 4662909 *Fax:* (013) 4663288
E-mail: tup@kub.nl
Subjects: Behavioral Sciences, Biblical Studies, Economics, Language Arts, Linguistics, Library & Information Sciences, Philosophy, Psychology, Psychiatry, Theology
ISBN Prefix(es): 90-361
Imprints: Syntax Publishers

Tirion Uitgevers BV+
Subsidiary of Veen Bosch & Keuning Uitgevers NV
Lt Generaal van Heutszlaan 8, 3743 JN Baarn
Mailing Address: PO Box 309, 3740 AH Baarn
Tel: (035) 5486601 *Fax:* (035) 5486615
E-mail: tirion-uitgevers@wxs.ul
Key Personnel
Contact: Grietje de Kluijver
Founded: 1987
Subjects: Animals, Pets, Antiques, Biography, Child Care & Development, Cookery, Crafts, Games, Hobbies, Film, Video, Gardening, Plants, Health, Nutrition, Sports, Athletics
ISBN Prefix(es): 90-5121; 90-5210; 90-439
Distributed by Agora
Distributor for Davidsfonds (Belgium)

W E J Tjeenk Willink BV
Staverenstr 32015, 7418 CJ Deventer
Mailing Address: PO Box 23, 7400 GA Deventer
Tel: (0570) 647111 *Fax:* (0570) 63740
Part of Wolters Kluwer Rechtswebenschappen.
Subjects: Law
ISBN Prefix(es): 90-271
Parent Company: Wolters Kluwer Rechtswetenschappen BV
Ultimate Parent Company: Wolters Kluwer NV

Ton Bolland, *imprint of* Uitgeverij De Vuurbaak BV

Uitgeverij De Toorts+
Conradkade 6, 2031 CL Haarlem
Mailing Address: Postbus 9585, 2003 LN Haarlem
Tel: (023) 5532920 *Fax:* (023) 5320635
E-mail: uitgeverij@toorts.nl
Key Personnel
Man Dir & Production: J Hesseling
Sales, Editorial, Publicity, Rights & Permissions: Mrs M Klis
Founded: 1936
Subjects: Behavioral Sciences, Child Care & Development, Cookery, Health, Nutrition, Human Relations, Music, Dance, Psychology, Psychiatry, Self-Help, Wine & Spirits
ISBN Prefix(es): 90-6020
Imprints: De Toorts; ENTERBOOKS

Triton Pers, *imprint of* Omega Boek BV

Twente University Press
Unit of University of Twente
PO Box 217-CT 1134, 7500 AE Enschede
Tel: (053) 4893049 *Fax:* (053) 4892991
E-mail: tup@utwente.nl
Web Site: www.utwente.nl/tupress
Key Personnel
Publisher: HHJ Leferink
Founded: 1995
Subjects: Career Development, Computer Science, Education, Environmental Studies, Management, Mechanical Engineering, Medicine, Nursing, Dentistry, Public Administration, Regional Interests, Social Sciences, Sociology, Technology
ISBN Prefix(es): 90-365
Total Titles: 60 Print

Uiteverij Casterman Nederland BV, see Casterman NV

Jan Mets Uitgeverij, see Mets & Schilt Uitgevers en Distributeurs

Uitgeversmy Segment BV, see Segment BV

Uniboek BV+
Onderdoor 7, 3995 DB Houten
Mailing Address: Postbus 97, 3990 DB Houten

NETHERLANDS

Tel: (030) 6377660 *Fax:* (030) 6377600
E-mail: unieboek@worldaccess.nl
Telex: 40468 Uboek nl *Cable:* UNIEBOEK
Key Personnel
Dir: A C Akveld; Van Y R C Oort
Founded: 1891
Subjects: Archaeology, Architecture & Interior Design, Cookery, Fiction, Government, Political Science, History, Literature, Literary Criticism, Essays, Nonfiction (General)
ISBN Prefix(es): 90-226; 90-228; 90-269
Parent Company: Meulenhoff & Co BV
Associate Companies: De Boekerij BV; A W Bruna BV; Prometheus BV; Meulenhoff Nederland BV; M&P BV; Standard Uitgeverij
Imprints: Agathon; de Cocon; van Dishoeck; de Haan; van Holkema en Waren Holkema en Warendorf; het Wereldvenster; Fibula; W Gaade

Uniepers BV+
Postbus 69, 1390 AB Abcoude
Tel: (0294) 285111 *Fax:* (0294) 283013
Key Personnel
Chief Executive & Sales: Marinus H van Raalte
Editorial, Publicity, Rights & Permissions: Marieke Bemelman
Production: Albert v d Klashorst
Founded: 1961
Also book packagers.
Subjects: Anthropology, Antiques, Archaeology, Architecture & Interior Design, Art, History, Music, Dance, Natural History, Culture, Nature
ISBN Prefix(es): 90-6825

V S P International Science Publishers
47 Godfried van Seystlaan 47, 3703 BR Zeist
Mailing Address: PO Box 346, 3700 AH Zeist
Tel: (030) 6925790 *Fax:* (030) 6932081
E-mail: vsppub@compuserve.com
Web Site: www.vsppub.com
Key Personnel
Contact: Ms Els van Egmond
Founded: 1983
Member of STM; Specialize in STM Journal Publishing & STM Book Publising.
Subjects: Chemistry, Chemical Engineering, Earth Sciences, Mathematics, Medicine, Nursing, Dentistry, Physics, Science (General), Technology, Transportation
ISBN Prefix(es): 90-6764
Online services available through World Wide Web.
Orders to: Books International Inc, PO Box 605, Herndon, VA 22070, United States *Tel:* 703-661-1500 *Fax:* 703-661-1501

Van Buuren Uitgeverij BV+
Hallenhof 18, 6006 NC Weert
Mailing Address: PO Box 10356, 6000 GJ Weert
Tel: (03) 0495 548080 *Fax:* (03) 0495 547326
E-mail: vanbuuren.uitgeverij@wxs.nl
Founded: 1995
Member of Royal Dutch Booktrade Organization.
Subjects: Fiction, Nonfiction (General)
ISBN Prefix(es): 90-5695; 90-76077
Total Titles: 50 Print
Distributed by Standaard Uitgeverij NV (Dutch speaking part of Belgium)

De Grote Van Dale, *imprint of* Van Dale Lexicografie BV

Van Dale Grote Woordenboeken voor hedendaags taalgebruik, *imprint of* Van Dale Lexicografie BV

Van Dale Handbibliotheek, *imprint of* Van Dale Lexicografie BV

Van Dale Handwoordenboeken, *imprint of* Van Dale Lexicografie BV

Van Dale Kinderwoordenboeken, *imprint of* Van Dale Lexicografie BV

Van Dale Lexicografie BV
Subsidiary of Veen Bosch & Keuning Uitgevers NV
St Jacobsstraat 127, 3511 BP Utrecht
Mailing Address: PO Box 19232, 3501 DE Utrecht
Tel: (031) 2324711 *Fax:* (031) 2369642
E-mail: info@vandale.nl
Key Personnel
Man Dir, Export Sales, Rights & Permissions: A Wolthoorn
Editorial: M Jansen; M Moerland; R Schutz
Sales Dir: T Nijhuis
Production: J Butterfield
Founded: 1976
ISBN Prefix(es): 90-6648
Imprints: De Grote Van Dale; Van Dale Grote Woordenboeken voor hedendaags taalgebruik; Van Dale Handwoordenboeken; Koenen; Van Dale Kinderwoordenboeken; Van Dale Handbibliotheek
Branch Office(s)
Van Dale Lexicografie Belgie, Ternesselei 326, 2160 Wommelgem, Belgium *Tel:* 0032-3-3552830 *Fax:* 0032-3-3552841 (Distributor)
Orders to: PO Box 19232, 3501 DE Utrecht

Van Goor, *imprint of* De Boekerij BV

Van Gorcum & Comp BV+
Postbus 43, 9400 AA Assen
Tel: (0592) 379555 *Fax:* (0592) 372064
E-mail: assen@vgorcum.nl *Cable:* VANGORCUM
Key Personnel
Man Dir: L Dykema
Dir, Academic Books, Rights & Permission: G Winter
Sales: J van Veen
Founded: 1800
Subjects: Anthropology, Economics, Education, Geography, Geology, History, Language Arts, Linguistics, Law, Literature, Literary Criticism, Essays, Medicine, Nursing, Dentistry, Philosophy, Psychology, Psychiatry, Religion - Other, Social Sciences, Sociology
ISBN Prefix(es): 90-232; 90-255; 90-5693; 90-72371
Subsidiaries: Styx Publications

Uitgeverij G A van Oorschot bv+
Herengracht 613, 1017 CE Amsterdam
Tel: (020) 6231484 *Fax:* (020) 6254083
Key Personnel
President: W J van Oorschot
Vice President: Mrs G M Nefkens
Founded: 1945
Member of KNUB; Specialize in Literature.
Subjects: Literature, Literary Criticism, Essays, Nonfiction (General), Poetry
ISBN Prefix(es): 90-282

Uitgeverij Van Walraven BV
Ericastr 1, 3742 SG Baarn
Tel: (035) 5482411 *Fax:* (035) 5418221
Member of the Combo Group.
ISBN Prefix(es): 90-6049; 90-5564

Uitgeverij Van Wijnen+
Froonacker 12, 8801 KD Franeker
Mailing Address: Postbus 172, 8800 AD Franeker
Tel: (0517) 394588 *Fax:* (0517) 397179
Key Personnel
Dir: D Van Wijnen
Founded: 1988

BOOK

Subjects: Government, Political Science, History, Philosophy, Religion - Other, Theology
ISBN Prefix(es): 90-5194

Uitgeverij Vassallucci+
Herengracht 505, 1017 BV Amsterdam
Key Personnel
Dir: Lex Spaans *E-mail:* lex@vassallucci.nl; Oscar van Gelderen
Sales: Marrit de Weijer
Assistant Foreign Rights: Michiel Niesen
Founded: 1985
Subjects: Fiction, Literature, Literary Criticism, Essays, Nonfiction (General), Specializes in literary fiction
ISBN Prefix(es): 90-5000
Number of titles published annually: 70 Print
Total Titles: 300 Print
Parent Company: PCM General Books
Foreign Rep(s): Laura Susijn (London)
Shipping Address: Central Boekhuis, Culemborg

VCL (series of novels)/Westfriesland, *imprint of* Uitgeefmaatschappij J H Kok BV

Veen Bosch & Keuning Uitgevers NV
Formerly Bosch & Veuning Uitgeversgroep
Mariaplaats 21 C, 3511 LK Utrecht
Mailing Address: Postbus 8049, 3503 RA Utrecht
Tel: (030) 2349379 *Fax:* (030) 2300145
E-mail: algemeen@veenboschenkeuning.nl
ISBN Prefix(es): 90-246; 90-263; 90-266; 90-213; 90-261; 90-259
Associate Companies: Ambo-Anthos bv; Bekadidact bv; Uitgeverij Cantecleer BV; Contact bv; Uitgeverij Contact bv; Fontein bv; HBuitgevers bv; Houtekiet nv; J H Kok bv; Kosmos Z&K Uitgevers; Uitgeverij Luitingh-Sijthoff; NijghVersluys bv; Tirion Uitgevers bv; Uitgeverij Verlags; Van Dale Lexicografie; Veen Algemene Boeken; Veen Magazines; Veen Uitgevers Groep Belgie

Veen Bosch & Keuning Uitgevers NV+
Postbus 8049, 3503 RA Utrecht
Tel: (030) 2349311 *Fax:* (030) 2300145
Key Personnel
Man Dir: A de Groot *Fax:* (030) 2300145
An independent trade publisher of books, magazines, dictionaries & CD-ROM.
ISBN Prefix(es): 90-204; 90-245; 90-218; 90-215; 90-254
Number of titles published annually: 500 Print; 30 CD-ROM; 10 E-Book
Total Titles: 4,000 Print; 100 CD-ROM; 1 Online; 20 E-Book
Online services available through Van Dale Taalweb.
Subsidiaries: Ambo-Anthos bv; Atlas; Augustus; Bekadidact bv; Uitgeverij Cantecleer BV; Contact bv; Uitgeverij Contact bv; De Prom; Fontein bv; HBuitgevers bv; Houtekiet nv; J H Kok bv; Kosmos-Z&K Uitgevers; Uitgeverij Luitingh-Sijthoff; Nijgh Versluys bv; Poema Pandora; Tirion Uitgevers bv; Van Dale Lexicografie; Veen Algemene Boeken; Veen Magazines; Veen Uitgevers Groep Belgie

Uitgeverij Verloren+
Larenseweg 123, 1221 CL Hilversum
Mailing Address: Postbus 1741, 1200 BS Hilversum
Tel: (035) 6859856 *Fax:* (035) 6836557
E-mail: info@verloren.nl
Web Site: www.verloren.nl
Key Personnel
President: Mr L M VerLoren van Themaat
Founded: 1979
Subjects: Biography, Genealogy, History
ISBN Prefix(es): 90-6550
Number of titles published annually: 70 Print

Total Titles: 500 Print
Online services available through World Wide Web.

De Viergang, *imprint of* Em Querido's Uitgeverij BV

VNU Business Press Group BV+
Postbus 9194, 1006 CC Amsterdam
Mailing Address: Rynsburgstr 11, 1059 AT Amsterdam
Tel: (020) 4875487 *Fax:* (020) 4875700
Key Personnel
Man Dir: F X I Koot
Subjects: Business, Career Development, Computer Science, Library & Information Sciences, Marketing
ISBN Prefix(es): 90-72802

VNU Business Publications BV
Rynsburgstroat 11, 1059 AT Amsterdam
Mailing Address: Postbus 9194, 1006 CC Amsterdam
Tel: (020) 4875487 *Fax:* (020) 4875700
Telex: 41549
ISBN Prefix(es): 90-72802; 90-6434
Parent Company: VNU - Verenigde Nederlandse Uitgeversbedrijven BV
Subsidiaries: Educational Publishing (comprising LCG Malmberg BV qv); Uitgeverij Het Spectrum; Uitgeverij J van In; WNU Business Information Services; VNU Business Press Group BV; VNU Magazine Group; VNU Newspaper Group; VNU Printing Group; VNU Sales Group

Voorhoeve, *imprint of* Uitgeefmaatschappij J H Kok BV

VU Boekhandel/Uitgeverij BV+
De Boelelaan 1105, 1081 HV Amsterdam
Tel: (020) 6444355 *Fax:* (020) 6462719
E-mail: vu~uitgevererij@vuboekhandel.ne
Key Personnel
Man Dir & Editorials: P R Rienks; M Rienks
Production: Karen Sinnema
Sales: M Zitman
Founded: 1980
Subjects: Biological Sciences, Economics, History, Language Arts, Linguistics, Law, Medicine, Nursing, Dentistry, Philosophy, Psychology, Psychiatry, Public Administration, Science (General), Social Sciences, Sociology, Theology
ISBN Prefix(es): 90-6256; 90-5383
Imprints: VU Uitgeverij; VU University Press

VU Uitgeverij, *imprint of* VU Boekhandel/Uitgeverij BV

VU University Press, *imprint of* VU Boekhandel/Uitgeverij BV

Uitgeverij De Vuurbaak BV+
Hermesweg 20, 3770 AG Barneveld
Mailing Address: Postbus 257, 3770 AG Barneveld
Tel: (0342) 411731 *Fax:* (0342) 411631
E-mail: vuurbaak@nd.nl
Web Site: www.vuurbank.nl
Key Personnel
President & International Rights: B M van Hulst
Founded: 1965
Subjects: Religion - Protestant, Theology
ISBN Prefix(es): 90-6015; 90-5560; 90-5804
Number of titles published annually: 60 Print
Total Titles: 300 Print
Associate Companies: Plateau; Uitgeverij; Telos
Imprints: Ton Bolland; Plateau
Divisions: Nedag Beheer

Uitgeverij Waanders BV+
Faradaystr 17, 8013 PH Zwolle Zwolle
Mailing Address: Postbus 1129, 8001 BC Zwolle
Tel: (038) 4658628 *Fax:* (038) 4655989
E-mail: info@waanders.nl
Web Site: www.waanders.nl
Key Personnel
President: W J G M Waanders
Man Dir: H van de Wal
Deputy Director: M L M Waanders
Founded: 1836
Subjects: Antiques, Art, Ethnicity, History
ISBN Prefix(es): 90-6630; 90-400; 90-70072
Parent Company: Waanders Printers
Bookshop(s): Eiland 9, Zwolle

Wageningen Pers+
Mansholtlaan 12, 6708 PA Wageningen
Mailing Address: Postbus 42, 6700 AA Wageningen
Tel: (0317) 476515 *Fax:* (0317) 426044
E-mail: info@wageningenpers.nl
Web Site: www.wageningenpers.nl
Key Personnel
Man Dir: J Heeres
Marketing & Sales Dir: M Jacobs *E-mail:* mike.jacobs@wageningenpers.nl
Founded: 1994 (Book Department)
Publisher of scientific & technical books. Textbooks, Proceedings & Monographs.
Subjects: Agriculture, Animals, Pets, *Specialized in:* Animal Science & Agriculture
ISBN Prefix(es): 90-74134
Total Titles: 80 Print

Wereldbibliotheek+
Spuistraat 283, 1012 VR Amsterdam
Tel: (020) 6381899 *Fax:* (020) 6384491
E-mail: wereld@euronet.nl
Key Personnel
Man Dir: J B I M Kat
Founded: 1905
Subjects: Fiction, Nonfiction (General)
ISBN Prefix(es): 90-284
Total Titles: 200 Print

Wereldschool, *imprint of* Stichting IVIO

het Wereldvenster, *imprint of* Unieboek BV

West-Friesland/Boekproject-ontwikkeling+
Protonweg 32, 1627 LD Hoorn, Nh
Tel: (0229) 212625 *Fax:* (0229) 216949
Key Personnel
Man Dir, Editorial, Publicity: J W Hondelink
Sales: Maya Schaafsma-Rotte
Rights & Permissions: P Dubois
Founded: 1918
Specialize in packaging & local history.
Subjects: Literature, Literary Criticism, Essays, Nonfiction (General), Regional Interests
ISBN Prefix(es): 90-72420
Parent Company: Drukkery West-Friesland/EDECEA, Protonweg 32, 1627 LD Hoorn, Nh
Imprints: EDECEA & WFE

Uitgeverij Westers
Hammarskjoeldhof 35, 3527 HD Utrecht
Tel: (030) 2931043 *Fax:* (030) 2944586
E-mail: boekhandel@westers-utrecht.nl *Cable:* WESTERS UTRECHT
Key Personnel
Man Dir: R J N M Westers, Sr
Founded: 1967
Subjects: Fiction
ISBN Prefix(es): 90-6107

Wilkerdon, *imprint of* Uitgeversmaatschappij Ad Donker BV

Wolters Kluwer Academic Publishers BV, see Kluwer Academic Publishers

Wolters-Noordhoff B V+
Damsport 157, 9728 PS Groningen
Mailing Address: PO Box 58, 9700 MB Groningen
Tel: (050) 5226888 *Fax:* (050) 5226244
E-mail: webmaster@wolters.nl
Web Site: www.wolters.nl
Key Personnel
Acting Manager: Dr M J van Dalen
Founded: 1836 (1852)
Part of Wolters Kluwer Nederland.
ISBN Prefix(es): 90-01
Parent Company: Wolters-Kluwer
Subsidiaries: Martinus Nijhoff; Wolters-Noordhoff

Uitgeverij 010+
Watertorenweg 180, 3063HA Rotterdam
Tel: (010) 4333509 *Fax:* (010) 4529825
Key Personnel
Dir: P P De Winter
Founded: 1983
Subjects: Architecture & Interior Design, Art
ISBN Prefix(es): 90-6450

ZHU, *imprint of* M & P Publishing House

Zoetermeer, *imprint of* Nijgh & Van Ditmar Amsterdam

Zuid Boekproduktíes BV+
1E Poellaan 6, 2161 LB Lisse
Mailing Address: Postbus 314, 2160 AH Lisse
Tel: (0252) 431566 *Fax:* (0252) 431567
E-mail: info@rebo-publishers.com
Web Site: www.rebo-publishers.com
Key Personnel
Dir: F Voerman
Founded: 1983
Subjects: Animals, Pets, Cookery, Crafts, Games, Hobbies, Gardening, Plants
ISBN Prefix(es): 90-6248
Associate Companies: REBO Productions BV
Imprints: Zuidboek

Zuidboek, *imprint of* Zuid Boekproduktíes BV

Zwarte Beertjes, *imprint of* A W Bruna Uitgevers BV

Uitgeverij Zwijsen BV
Gasthuisring 58, 5041 DT Tilburg
Mailing Address: Postbus 805, 5000 AV Tilburg
Tel: (013) 5838800 *Fax:* (013) 5838800
Key Personnel
Man Dir: J N A Verwielen; G M Janssen
Publicity Manager: N J Filippo
Founded: 1846
ISBN Prefix(es): 90-276

Netherlands Antilles

General Information

Capital: Willemstad
Language: Dutch and Papiamento. English and Spanish widely spoken
Religion: Roman Catholic and Protestant
Population: 184,000
Bank Hours: 0830-1130, 1400-1600 Monday-Friday. St Maarten: 0800-1300 Monday-Friday (also 1600-1700 on Friday)

Shop Hours: 0800-1200, 1400-1800 Monday-Saturday
Currency: 100 cents = 1 Netherlands Antilles gulden or florin
Export/Import Information: No tariff on books or advertising. No import licenses. No exchange controls.
Copyright: UCC, Berne (see Copyright Conventions, pg xi)

Bredero+
Reigerweg 51, Willemstad, Curacao
Tel: (09) 7376751
Key Personnel
Author: L H Bredero
Subjects: Foreign Countries, History, Maritime, Nonfiction (General), Travel, Specializes in World War II memorabilia
ISBN Prefix(es): 99904-0
Orders to: Janus Publishing Co, 76 Titchfield Rd, London W1P 7AF, United Kingdom
Tel: (020) 7580 7664 Fax: (020) 7636 5756
E-mail: publisher@januspublishing.co.uk Web Site: www.januspublishing.co.uk

De Wit Stores NV
L G Smith Blvd 110, Oranjestad, Aruba
Tel: (0297) 823500 Fax: (0297) 821575
E-mail: dewitstores@sctarnet.aw Cable: Dewitstores
Key Personnel
Man Dir: R de Zwart
Founded: 1948
Subjects: Gardening, Plants, Health, Nutrition, Regional Interests, Self-Help, Travel, Women's Studies
ISBN Prefix(es): 90-6163
Bookshop(s): De Wit Book & Gift Store, Aruba; Aruba Post, Aruba; Boulevard Book and Drugstore, Aruba

Drukkerij Scherpenheuvel Haseth
Scherpenhuevel 1, Curacao
Tel: (09) 7671134
Key Personnel
Dir: Ronald Yrausquin
Subjects: Law
ISBN Prefix(es): 99904-915

New Caledonia

General Information

Capital: Noumea
Language: French
Religion: Predominantly Roman Catholic and Protestant
Population: 145,368
Currency: 100 centimes = CFP or Pacific franc
Export/Import Information: No tariff on books except luxury bindings and children's picture books. Advertising matter generally dutiable. Special Tax on all. No import licenses required.

Editions du Santal
BP 3072, Noumea
Tel: (0687) 262533 Fax: (0687) 262533
E-mail: santal@offratel.nc
Key Personnel
Director: Paul-Jean Stahl
Subjects: History, Travel
ISBN Prefix(es): 2-9508739

Savannah Editions SARL
49 rue de la Boudeuse magenta Que mo, 98684 Noumea
Tel: (0687) 252919 Fax: (0687) 282470
Founded: 1994

Subjects: How-to, Maritime, Outdoor Recreation, Sports, Athletics, Travel
ISBN Prefix(es): 2-9508530
Distributed by Editions Vilo Paris

New Zealand

General Information

Capital: Wellington
Language: English
Religion: Predominantly Christian (mostly Anglican & Roman Catholic)
Population: 3.3 million
Bank Hours: 0930-1600 Monday-Friday
Shop Hours: Vary. Most open 6-7 days a week
Currency: 100 cents = 1 New Zealand dollar
Export/Import Information: No tariffs on books and advertising. No import licenses, but literature which is indecent, advocates violence, lawlessness, disorder or seditiousness is prohibited. No special exchange controls.
Copyright: UCC, Berne, Florence (see Copyright Conventions, pg xi)

ABA Books
22/6 Brooklyn Rd, Hamilton
Mailing Address: PO Box 11-099, Hamilton
Tel: (07) 8549360 Fax: (07) 8549361
Web Site: www.ababooks.co.nz
Key Personnel
Dir: Elizabeth Maree Abbott
Man Dir: Graeme Hamilton Abbott
 E-mail: graeme@ababooks.co.nz
Founded: 1986
Educational book publishers.
Subjects: Chemistry, Chemical Engineering, Cookery, Language Arts, Linguistics, Mathematics, Physical Sciences, Physics, Science (General)
ISBN Prefix(es): 0-908866

Aoraki Press Ltd
PO Box 11-699, Wellington
Tel: (04) 3858528 Fax: (03) 3858528
E-mail: aorakipr@actrix.gen.nz
Key Personnel
Editor: Dr Maarire Goodall
Founded: 1990
Subjects: Drama, Theater, Foreign Countries, History, Law, Music, Dance, Regional Interests, Social Sciences, Sociology
ISBN Prefix(es): 0-908925
Distributor for Aoraki Productions; Otago Heritage Press
Orders to: PO Box 25-029, Christchurch Tel: (03) 3524001 Fax: (03) 3524001

Aspect Press
Subsidiary of Association of Handcraft Printers (AHP)
13 Kinross, St Levin
Tel: (06) 368-2887
Key Personnel
Editor & Author: P J Parr
Founded: 1971
Specialize in Private Press Booklets.
Subjects: History, Religion - Buddhist
ISBN Prefix(es): 0-908779
Total Titles: 48 Print
Book Club(s): TSP

Auckland University Press+
University of Auckland, 1-11 Short St, Auckland
Tel: (09) 373 7528 Fax: (09) 373 7465
E-mail: aup@auckland.ac.nz
Web Site: www.auckland.ac.nz/aup/

Key Personnel
Dir: Elizabeth P Caffin E-mail: e.caffin@auckland.ac.nz
Founded: 1966
Subjects: Archaeology, Art, Biography, Government, Political Science, History, Literature, Literary Criticism, Essays, Poetry, Social Sciences, Sociology, Women's Studies
ISBN Prefix(es): 1-86940
Distributed by HarperCollins (New Zealand)
Shipping Address: Anzac Ave entrance, 1-11 Short St, Auckland
Warehouse: HarperCollins, 31 View Rd, Glenfield, Auckland
Orders to: HarperCollins, PO Box 1, Auckland
Unireps, University of New South Wales, Sydney, NSW 2034, Australia Tel: (02) 9664 0999 Fax: (02) 9664 5420 E-mail: info.press@unsw.edu.au Web Site: www.unswpress.com.au
Eurospan, 3 Henrietta St, London WC2E 8LU, United Kingdom Tel: (020) 7240 0856 Fax: (020) 7379 0609 E-mail: info@eurospan.co.uk Web Site: www.eurospan.co.uk
Independent Publishers Group (IPG), 814 N Franklin St, Chicago, IL 60610, United States Tel: 312-337-0747 Fax: 312-337-5985 E-mail: frontdesk@ipgbook.com Web Site: www.ipgbook.com

Barkfire Press+
Newton, Auckland 1032
Mailing Address: PO Box 68582, Newton, Auckland 1032
Tel: (09) 3031039 Fax: (09) 3031059
E-mail: info@barkfire.com
Key Personnel
Man Dir: Ralph Talmont E-mail: ralph@barkfire.com
Founded: 1996
Packager, contract publisher, book producer.
Subjects: Americana, Regional, Architecture & Interior Design, Art, Asian Studies, Cookery, Ethnicity, Geography, Geology, Health, Nutrition, House & Home, How-to, Journalism, Music, Dance, Native American Studies, Natural History, Outdoor Recreation, Photography, Religion - Jewish, Travel, Wine & Spirits, Women's Studies, Yachting & Mythology
ISBN Prefix(es): 0-9583668
Parent Company: Mandragora Productions Ltd

David Bateman Ltd+
30 Tarndale Grove, Albany, North Shore, Auckland
Mailing Address: North Shore Mail Center, PO Box 100242, Auckland
Tel: (09) 4444680 Fax: (09) 4440389
Key Personnel
Chairman & Publisher: David L Bateman
Man Dir, Sales & Distribution: Paul C Parkinson Tel: (09) 415 5922
Man Dir, Publishing, Rights & Permissions: Paul Bateman
Secretary: Maureen Robinson
Founded: 1979
Member of Booksellers New Zealand & Book Publishers Association of New Zealand, also acts as agent for overseas publishers.
Subjects: Art, Business, Cookery, Gardening, Plants, Natural History, Travel
ISBN Prefix(es): 1-86953
Total Titles: 250 Print

Book Data Asia Pacific
Division of Book Data Ltd
300 Richmond Rd, upper fl, room 103, Grey Lynn Auckland
Tel: (09) 360 3294 Fax: (09) 360 8853
E-mail: info@bookdata.co.nz
Web Site: www.bookdata.com
Key Personnel
Man Dir: Ka Meechan
Founded: 1987

Specialize in a range of computer-based bibliographic information services for the international book trade; bibliographic CD-ROM database & online services.
Branch Office(s)
PO Box 746, Noosa Heads 4567, Australia, Glenda Roach *Tel:* (07) 5474 8544 *Fax:* (07) 5474 5202 *E-mail:* bookdata@bookfind.com.au

Bookmakers Design & Production Ltd
202 Jervois Rd, 1st floor, Herne Bay, Auckland 1
Tel: (09) 784572 *Fax:* (09) 784572
Telex: 63019
Key Personnel
Contact: Stephen Barnett

Brick Row Publishing Co Ltd+
PO Box 100057, Takapuna, Auckland 10
Tel: (09) 4106993 *Fax:* (09) 4106993
Key Personnel
Man Dir, Editorial: Oswald L Kraus
Sales, Publicity: Ruth Kraus
Founded: 1978
Subjects: Biography, Fiction, Literature, Literary Criticism, Essays, Nonfiction (General), Poetry, Science (General)
ISBN Prefix(es): 0-908595
Total Titles: 30 Print
Imprints: Southern Lights
U.S. Office(s): 1040 E Paseo El Mirador, Palm Springs, CA 92262, United States, Contact: O L Kraus *Tel:* 760-322-4342 *Fax:* 760-322-4342
Distributor for John Calder (UK); Excalibur (US); Free Spirit (US)

Brooker's Ltd
PO Box 43, Wellington
Tel: (04) 4998178 *Fax:* (04) 4998173
E-mail: service@brookers.co.nz
Key Personnel
Man Dir: Neil Story
Electronic Publishing Manager: Reiner Wolf
Publishing Manager: Geoff Adlam
Tax Manager: Nigal Royfee
Legislation Manager: Tony Mills
Founded: 1910
Specialize in looseleaf & electronic legal, tax & professional information.
Subjects: Business, Law
ISBN Prefix(es): 0-86472
Parent Company: The Thomson Corporation
Distributed by Carswell; LBC Information Services; Sweet & Maxwell; Westlaw
Distributor for Carswell; LBC Information Services; Sweet & Maxwell; Westlaw

Brookfield Press
PO Box 1201, Auckland 5
Tel: (09) 5765438 *Fax:* (09) 5736222
Key Personnel
Man Dir, Editorial: Richard Webster
Sales, Publicity: Don Kaye
Founded: 1971
Subjects: Astrology, Occult, Philosophy
ISBN Prefix(es): 0-86467
Parent Company: Brookings Bookshop 1971 Ltd
Distributed by Peaceful Living Publications (New Zealand)

Bush Press Communications Ltd
4 Bayview Rd, Hauraki Corner, Takapuna, Auckland 1309
Mailing Address: PO Box 33029, Takapuna, Auckland 1309
Tel: (09) 486 2667 *Fax:* (09) 486 2667
E-mail: bush.press@clear.net.nz
Key Personnel
Man Dir: Gordon Ell, onzm
Associate: Sarah Ell
Founded: 1979
Also represents Geological Society of NZ.

Also acts as Television Production & Publishing Services.
Subjects: Archaeology, Art, Cookery, Crafts, Games, Hobbies, Earth Sciences, Gardening, Plants, Genealogy, Geography, Geology, History, How-to, Natural History, Nonfiction (General), Outdoor Recreation, Photography, Regional Interests
ISBN Prefix(es): 0-908608
Number of titles published annually: 6 Print
Total Titles: 24 Print
Imprints: The Bush Press of New Zealand
Divisions: The Bush Press; Bush Films
Distributor for Geological Society of New Zealand
Warehouse: Forrester Books (NZ) Ltd, 10 Tarndale Dr, Albany, Auckland 1310 *Tel:* (09) 415 2080 *Fax:* (09) 415 2083 *E-mail:* forr@forrester.co.13

The Bush Press of New Zealand, *imprint of* Bush Press Communications Ltd

Business Bureau Christchurch+
PO Box 8226, Christchurch
Tel: (03) 3585287
Key Personnel
Contact: Geoff McDonnell
Founded: 1981
Subjects: Finance, Gardening, Plants
ISBN Prefix(es): 0-908852

Butterworths New Zealand Ltd
205-207 Victoria St, Wellington 1
Mailing Address: PO Box 472, Wellington 1
Tel: (04) 385 1479 *Fax:* (04) 385 1598
E-mail: Customer.Relations@butterworths.co.nz
Web Site: www.butterworths.co.nz
Key Personnel
Man Dir: Philip G Kirk
Legal Publishing Dir: Hellen Papadopoulos
National Sales Manager: Lara Stewart
E-mail: Lara.Stewart@butterworths.co.nz
Founded: 1914
Subjects: Law
ISBN Prefix(es): 0-409; 0-407; 0-408; 0-406
Parent Company: Reed Elsevier plc, 25 Victoria St, London SW1H 0EX, United Kingdom
Associate Companies: Butterworths Australia Ltd, Reed Elsevier Bldg, Tower 2, 475-495 Victoria Ave, Chatswood, NSW 2067, Australia *Tel:* (02) 9422 2222 *Fax:* (02) 9422 2444 *Web Site:* www.butterworths.com.au; Butterworths Canada Ltd, 75 Clegg Rd, Markham, ON L6G 1A1, Canada *Tel:* 905-479-2665 *Fax:* 905-479-2826 *Web Site:* www.butterworths.ca; Butterworths Asia, 3/F Baskerville House, 13 Duddell St, Central, Hong Kong, Hong Kong *Tel:* 537 6662 *Fax:* 537 6672; Butterworth India, C71-A Malviya Nagar, New Delhi 100 017, India *Tel:* (011) 623 6124 *Fax:* (011) 621 3861; Butterworth (Ireland) Ltd, 16 Upper Ormand Quay, Dublin 7, Ireland *Tel:* (031) 731 555 *Fax:* (031) 873 1876; Butterworths, C/- Shin Nichibo Bldg, 2-1 Sarugaku-cho, 1 Chome, Chiyoda-Ku, Tokyo 101, Japan *Tel:* (03) 3291 3970 *Fax:* (03) 3219 5260; Malayan Law Journal Sdn Bhd, No 18, Jalan Tuanku Abdul Rahman, 50100 Kuala Lumpur, Malaysia *Tel:* (03) 291 7273 *Fax:* (03) 291 6440; Butterworth & Co Publishers Ltd, 7 Jahangir St, Islamia Park, Poonch Rd, Lahore, Pakistan *Tel:* (042) 41 5226; Butterworths Asia/Malayan Law Journal, 10 Anson Rd, No 32-01 International Plaza, Singapore 0207, Singapore *Tel:* 220 3684 *Fax:* 225 5026; Butterworth Publishers Pty Ltd, 8 Walter Place, Waterval Park, Mayville, Durban 4001, South Africa *Tel:* (03) 1268 3111 *Fax:* (03) 1268 3108 *Web Site:* www.butterworths.co.za; Butterworth & Co (Publishers) Ltd, Halsbury House, 35 Chancery Lane, London, United Kingdom

Tel: (020) 7400 2500 *Fax:* (020) 7400 2842 *Web Site:* www.butterworth.co.uk; LEXIS Law Publishing, 701 E Water St, Charlottesville, VA 22906-7587, United States *Tel:* 804-972-7600 *Fax:* 804-972-7666 *Web Site:* www.michie.com

C&S Publications
121 Taupo Rd, Taumarunui
Tel: (0812) 56807 *Fax:* (0812) 8966583
Key Personnel
Contact: Ron Cooke
Founded: 1980
Subjects: History
ISBN Prefix(es): 0-908724

Canterbury University Press+
University of Canterbury, Private Bag 4800, Christchurch
Tel: (03) 364-2914 *Fax:* (03) 364-2044
E-mail: mail@cup.canterbury.ac.nz
Key Personnel
Dir: Jeff Field
Editor: Richard King
Office Manager: Kaye Godfrey
Founded: 1960
Specialize in botany, marine science, history, Maori & Pacific studies.
Subjects: Biography, Biological Sciences, History, Natural History, Nonfiction (General)
ISBN Prefix(es): 0-900392; 0-908812
Distributed by Book Representation & Distribution Ltd (UK & Europe); HarperCollins (NZ) Ltd (New Zealand); UNIREPS (Australia); University of New South Wales Press

Cape Catley+
83 Ngataringa Rd, Devonport, Auckland
Mailing Address: PO Box 32-622, Devonport, Auckland
Tel: (09) 445-9668 *Fax:* (09) 445-9668
E-mail: cape.catley@xtra.co.nz
Web Site: www.capecatleybooks.co.nz
Key Personnel
Man Dir: Christine Cole Catley
Founded: 1973
Subjects: Biography, Fiction, History, Literature, Literary Criticism, Essays, Mysteries, Nonfiction (General), Poetry
Number of titles published annually: 5 Print
Total Titles: 100 Print
Distributed by HarperCollins NZ Ltd (New Zealand)

Catholic Supplies (NZ) LTD+
PO Box 16-110, Wellington 6002
Tel: (04) 3843665 *Fax:* (04) 3843663
E-mail: sales@catholicsupplies.co.nz
Web Site: www.catholicsupplies.co.nz
Key Personnel
Contact: Peter Hoskins
Founded: 1918
Subjects: Education, Religion - Catholic
ISBN Prefix(es): 0-908696
Total Titles: 4 Print
Distributed by Twenty-Third Publications
Distributor for Alba House; Argus Communications; Art Studio Slabbinck; Ave Marie Press; Catholic Book Publishing; Catholic Truth Society; Claretian Publicaitons; James Clarke & Co Ltd; Columba Press; Conference Canadian Bishops; Credence Cassettes; Crossroad Publishing; Darton, Longman & Todd; Desbooks; Dimension Books Inc; Dominican Publications; E J Dwyer (Aust Pty Ltd); Fireside Bible Publishers Inc; Franciscan Press; Michael Glazer Books; Gracewing/Fowler Wright; Ignatius Press; Liguori Publications; Liturgical Press; Liturgy Training Publications; David Lovell Publishing; Lutterworth Press (Religious); Kevin Mayhew; McCrimmon Publishing Ltd; New City Press; Orbis Books; Oregon Catholic Press; Our Sunday Visitor; Paulist Press; Print-

ery; Pueblo Books; RCL (Tabor, Thomas More Books); Religious Education Press; Resource Publications; Resurrection Press; St Anthony Messenger Press; St Mary's Press; St Paul Publications; St Paul Publications; Sheed & Ward Inc; Source Publications; Spectrum Publications Pty Ltd; Tabor Publishing; University of Notre Dame Press; Veritas Publications
Warehouse: 85-89 Adelaide Rd, Wellington

The Caxton Press
PO Box 25088, Christchurch
Tel: (03) 3668516 *Fax:* (03) 3657840
Key Personnel
Man Dir: Bruce Bascand
Founded: 1935
Subjects: Biography, Gardening, Plants, Nonfiction (General)
ISBN Prefix(es): 0-908563

CCEAM, see Commonwealth Council for Educational Administration & Management

CCH New Zealand Ltd
24 The Warehouse Way, Northcote, Auckland
Mailing Address: PO Box 2378, Auckland 1
Tel: (09) 488 2760 *Fax:* (09) 489 3312
E-mail: nzsales@cch.co.nz
Web Site: www.cch.co.nz
Key Personnel
Man Dir: Sharon Bennett *E-mail:* sbennett@cch.co.nz
Founded: 1973
Subjects: Accounting, Law
ISBN Prefix(es): 0-86475; 0-86903
Parent Company: Walters Kluwer NV
U.S. Office(s): Walters Kluwer USA, 161 N Clark, 48th floor, Chicago, IL 60601, United States

Certes Press, *imprint of* Hazard Press Ltd

Church Mouse Press
38 Joseph St, Palmerston North
Tel: (06) 357-2445
Key Personnel
Proprietor: Anne De Roo
Founded: 1989
Direct sales & through bookshops & churches, books for adults & children.
Subjects: Biblical Studies, Fiction, Theology
ISBN Prefix(es): 0-908949
Total Titles: 16 Print

Cicada Press+
PO Box 34509, Auckland 10
Tel: (09) 4180890 *Fax:* (09) 4181142
Key Personnel
Man Dir: R K St Cartmail
Founded: 1978
Subjects: Art, Fiction, Poetry, Religion - Other
ISBN Prefix(es): 0-908599

Clerestory Press+
PO Box 21 120, Christchurch 8001
Tel: (03) 3553588 *Fax:* (03) 3553588
Key Personnel
International Rights: Dr Glyn Strange; Francine Bills
Founded: 1994
Member of BPANZ.
Subjects: Archaeology, Biography, Drama, Theater, Education, Genealogy, History, Law, Literature, Literary Criticism, Essays, Regional Interests, Women's Studies
ISBN Prefix(es): 0-9583706
Shipping Address: 31 Mersey St, Christchurch

Commonwealth Council for Educational Administration & Management
Auckland University of Technology, Education & Social Sciences, Private Bag 92006, 1020 Auckland N6 7TS
Tel: (09) 307 9999 ext 6879 *Fax:* (09) 307 9984
Key Personnel
President: Mrs Jo Howse *E-mail:* jo.howse@aut.ac.nz
Publisher of International Studies in Educational Administration.
Subjects: Education, Management
Distributed by The Education Publishing Co Ltd

Concept Publishing Ltd+
30 Tiri Rd, Milford, Auckland
Tel: (09) 4895330 *Fax:* (09) 4895335
E-mail: info@concept-publishing.co.nz
Key Personnel
Man Dir: Richard Beckett
Founded: 1997
Specialize in photoframe cards & personalized stationery.
Subjects: Cookery
Total Titles: 32 Print
Foreign Rights: Peter Elek & Associates

Craig Potton Publishing+
Box 555, Nelson
Tel: (03) 5489009 *Fax:* (03) 5489456
E-mail: info@cpp.co.nz
Web Site: www.craigpotton.co.nz
Key Personnel
Man Dir & Publisher: Robbie Burton
Founded: 1987
Specialize in wilderness photography & writing & high-quality, illustrated nonfiction; also acts as book packagers, produce calendars, posters, postcards.
Subjects: Architecture & Interior Design, Art, Biological Sciences, Crafts, Games, Hobbies, Natural History, Nonfiction (General), Outdoor Recreation, Photography
ISBN Prefix(es): 0-908802

Craig Printing Company Ltd
PO Box 99, Invercargill
Tel: (03) 2187029 *Fax:* (03) 2184811
Key Personnel
General Manager: Colin W Smith
Founded: 1876
Subjects: Aeronautics, Aviation, History, Nonfiction (General), Regional Interests, Travel
ISBN Prefix(es): 0-9597554

Wendy Crane Books
53 Wilford St, Lower Hutt
Tel: (04) 5664228
Key Personnel
Contact: Wendy Crane
Subjects: Biological Sciences, Earth Sciences, Geography, Geology, Physical Sciences
ISBN Prefix(es): 0-908895

Curly Tales, *imprint of* Magari Publishing

Current Pacific Limited+
PO Box 36-536 Northcote, Auckland 1330
Tel: (09) 480 1388 *Fax:* (09) 480 1387
Web Site: www.cplnz.com
Key Personnel
Editor: Amy M Yeung
Founded: 1992
Publisher of "New Zealand Trade Directory", a business/trade directory containing more than 6000 firms including manufacturers, importers, exporters, distributors, food processors, banks & financial firms, tourism services, trade promotion organizations, government departments, tertiary & secondary education institutions, professional institutions, libraries, etc.

Subjects: Business
Total Titles: 2 Print

David's Marine Books
121 Beaumont St, Westhaven, Auckland
Mailing Address: PO Box 1874, Auckland
Tel: (09) 3031459 *Fax:* (09) 3078170
E-mail: sales@transpacific.co.nz
Subjects: Crafts, Games, Hobbies, Electronics, Electrical Engineering, Fiction, How-to, Sports, Athletics, Travel, Marine Titles
Parent Company: Trans Pacific Marine
Distributor for Adlard Coles; Fernhurst; Sheridan House; Stationery Office

Doubleday New Zealand Ltd+
One Parkway Dr, Mairangi Bay Industrial Estate, Auckland 10
Mailing Address: Private Bag, North Shore Centre, Auckland 9
Tel: (09) 4782846
Telex: NZ60589
Key Personnel
Contact: Petrus van der Schaaf

Dunmore Press Ltd+
PO Box 5115, Palmerston North
Tel: (06) 3587169 *Fax:* (06) 3579242
E-mail: books@dunmore.co.nz
Web Site: www.dunmore.co.nz
Key Personnel
Dir & Editorial: Murray Gatenby
Dir & Marketing & Editorial, Rights & Permissions: Sharmian Firth
Founded: 1975
Subjects: Accounting, Business, Economics, Education, Ethnicity, History, Nonfiction (General)
ISBN Prefix(es): 0-908564; 0-86469
Number of titles published annually: 25 Print
Total Titles: 180 Print
Subsidiaries: Dunmore Printing Company Ltd
Foreign Rep(s): Federation Press (Australia)

Educational Distributors Ltd
1/1 Akatea Rd, Glendene, Auckland 7
Mailing Address: PO Box 45089, Auckland 8
Tel: (09) 8184473 *Fax:* (09) 8362399
E-mail: 100241.222@compuserve.com
Key Personnel
Contact: Ron Simpson
Founded: 1976
Member of BPANZ, specialize in distribution of educational & library lists within New Zealand.
Parent Company: School Supplies Ltd

ESA Publications (NZ) Ltd+
Box 9453, Newmarket, Auckland
Tel: (09) 579 3126 *Fax:* (09) 579 4713
Web Site: www.esa.co.nz
Key Personnel
Man Dir: Mark Sayes *E-mail:* mark@esa.co.nz
Founded: 1985
Publisher of educational books.
Subjects: Accounting, Biological Sciences, Chemistry, Chemical Engineering, Computer Science, Economics, English as a Second Language, Geography, Geology, Health, Nutrition, History, Mathematics, Physics, Science (General), Social Sciences, Sociology
ISBN Prefix(es): 0-908756; 0-9597692; 1-877234; 1-877291
Number of titles published annually: 30 Print
Total Titles: 95 Print
Parent Company: Sayes Corp Ltd
Warehouse: 665 Great South Rd, Unit G, Penrose, Auckland
Membership(s): Book Publishers Association of New Zealand

Eton Press (Auckland) Ltd
Birkenhead, Auckland 1330

Mailing Address: PO Box 36080, Northcote, Auckland 1330
Tel: (09) 4183635 *Fax:* (09) 4806488
E-mail: info@eton.co.nz
Key Personnel
Dir: Anthony Matthews
Founded: 1968
Member of BPANZ; Also acts for Tarquin & Dime Publications, Haese & Harris.
Subjects: Mathematics
Showroom(s): 18 Portsea Pl, Birkenhead, Auckland 1310

Evagean Publishing+
Bridge St, Ongaonga, Central Hawkes Bay
Mailing Address: PO Box 80, Ongaonga, Hawkes Bay
Tel: (09) 856-6639 *Fax:* (09) 856-6649
E-mail: evagean@iconz.co.nz
Web Site: www.evagean.co.nz
Founded: 1990
Specialize in compiling, publishing & marketing family histories & genealogies.
Subjects: Genealogy
Branch Office(s)
18 Waygrove Ave, Earlwood NSW 2206, Australia *Tel:* (02) 9789-4550 *Fax:* (02) 9789-4550
PO Box 1167, South Perth WA 6951, Australia *Tel:* (08) 3676578 *Fax:* (08) 3676578
PO Box 288, Warragul, Victory 3820, Victory 3820, Australia *Tel:* (03) 56236887 *Fax:* (03) 56236882
14 Kaweka St, Havelock Maith *Tel:* (06) 877 1210
PO Box 199, Te Aroha *Tel:* (07) 884-8783

Exisle Publishing Ltd+
PO Box 8077, Symonds St, Auckland
Tel: (09) 520 1162 *Fax:* (09) 520 1146
E-mail: mail@exisle.co.nz
Web Site: www.exisle.co.nz
Key Personnel
Publisher: Tim Chamberlain *E-mail:* tc@exisle.co.nz
International Rights: Benny Thomas
Founded: 1993
Member of Book Publishers of New Zealand.
Subjects: Biography, Business, Maritime, Natural History, Nonfiction (General), Outdoor Recreation, Pacific Studies
ISBN Prefix(es): 0-908988
Number of titles published annually: 4 Print
Total Titles: 12 Print
Parent Company: Exisle Holdings Ltd
Distributed by Berkeley Books (Singapore/SE Asia); Celebrity Books Ltd; Kirby Books Ltd

Flamingo, *imprint of* HarperCollins Publishers (New Zealand) Ltd

Fraser Books
Chamberlain Rd, RD 8, Masterton
Tel: (06) 3771359 *Fax:* (06) 3771359
Key Personnel
Managing Partner: Ian F Grant *E-mail:* ifgrant@xtra.co.nz
Founded: 1980
Specialize in book packaging.
Subjects: Agriculture, Biography, Economics, Government, Political Science, History, Regional Interests, Social Sciences, Sociology
ISBN Prefix(es): 0-9582052

Gauntlet Press, *imprint of* Hazard Press Ltd

GCL Publishing (1997) Ltd+
Level 1, 15 Bath St, Parnell, Auckland
Mailing Address: PO Box 37745, Parnell, Auckland
Tel: (09) 3092444 *Fax:* (09) 3092449
E-mail: info@gcl.co.nz

Web Site: www.gcl.co.nz; www.auto.co.nz
Key Personnel
Publisher: Mr Vern Whitehead *E-mail:* vern@gcl.co.nz
Founded: 1972
Publishers for the auto industry including newsletters, manuals, stock lists & pricing guides.
Subjects: Automotive
ISBN Prefix(es): 0-9598007
Number of titles published annually: 2 Print
Total Titles: 6 Print

Gnostic Press
100 Riverland Rd, Kumeu, Auckland
Mailing Address: 100 Riverland Rd, RD 2, Kumeu, Auckland
Tel: (09) 4127054 *Fax:* (09) 4126476
E-mail: gnostic.press.nz@xtra.co.nz
Key Personnel
Dir: John Searle
Founded: 1978
Created for the dispersment of the works of Abdullah Dougan (Sufi teacher).
Subjects: Philosophy, Religion - Buddhist, Religion - Hindu, Religion - Islamic, Religion - Other, Self-Help
ISBN Prefix(es): 0-473; 0-9597566; 0-477; 0-478; 0-475

Godwit Publishing Ltd+
39 Rawenen Rd, Birkenhead, Auckland 1310
Tel: (09) 4805410 *Fax:* (09) 4805930
E-mail: godwit@godwit.co.nz
Founded: 1990
Subjects: Art, Gardening, Plants, Genealogy, Natural History, Nonfiction (General)
ISBN Prefix(es): 0-908877; 1-86962
Orders to: Reed Publishing, Birkenhead, Auckland 1310

Gondwanaland Press, *imprint of* Gondwanaland Press

Gondwanaland Press
24 Glasgow St, Kelburn, Wellington 6005
Tel: (04) 4758092 *Fax:* (04) 4756194
Key Personnel
Manager: Hugh Price *E-mail:* randellprice@xtra.co.nz
Founded: 1992
Small private book publisher.
Subjects: Education, Government, Political Science, History, Public Administration, Chiefly education
ISBN Prefix(es): 0-9597766; 0-9582083
Number of titles published annually: 3 Print
Total Titles: 14 Print
Imprints: Gondwanaland Press

GP Publications, see Legislation Direct

Grantham House Publishing+
6/9 Wilkinson St, Oriental Bay
Mailing Address: PO Box 17256, Karosi, Wellington 6005
Tel: (04) 3813071 *Fax:* (04) 3813067
E-mail: gstewart@iconz.co.nz
Key Personnel
Chief Executive: Graham Stewart
Founded: 1985
Member of Booksellers New Zealand; Specialize in Railways, Tramways, Aviation, Shipping, Naval, Air Force, New Zealand history.
Subjects: History, Regional Interests, Transportation
ISBN Prefix(es): 1-86934
Total Titles: 40 Print
Parent Company: Bookprint Consultants Ltd

Shipping Address: PO Box 17256, Karosi, Wellington 6005
Warehouse: PO Box 17256, Karosi, Wellington 6005

Graphic Educational Publications
514 Dominion Rd, Auckland 3
Tel: (09) 6300488 *Fax:* (09) 6221559
Web Site: www.ak.planet.gen.nz/~com
Key Personnel
President, Editor & International Rights: Tom Newnham *E-mail:* tom@pl.net
Founded: 1963
Subjects: Asian Studies, Biography, Genealogy
ISBN Prefix(es): 0-9597819
Number of titles published annually: 3 Print
Total Titles: 10 Print

Halcyon Publishing Ltd+
PO Box 360, Auckland 1
Tel: (09) 4895337 *Fax:* (09) 4895218
E-mail: info@halcyonpublishing.co.nz
Key Personnel
Man Dir, Sales: Graham Gurr *E-mail:* gurr@halcyonpublishing.co.nz
Editorial Consultant: Antony Entwistle
Founded: 1984
Member of BPANZ & BSNZ.
Subjects: Cookery, Crafts, Games, Hobbies, Maritime, Outdoor Recreation, Sports, Athletics
ISBN Prefix(es): 0-908685; 0-908689; 1-877256
Imprints: Halcyon Sporting Heritage
Subsidiaries: The Halcyon Press; Halcyon Books; Hole in the Bank Books
Warehouse: Unit 11 Diana Court, 101-111 Diana Dr, Glenfield Auckland

Halcyon Sporting Heritage, *imprint of* Halcyon Publishing Ltd

Harlen Books, *imprint of* R P L Books

HarperCollins Publishers (New Zealand) Ltd+
31 View Rd, Glenfield, Auckland
Tel: (09) 4439400 *Fax:* (09) 4439403
E-mail: editors@harpercollins.co.nz
Web Site: www.harpercollins.co.nz *Cable:* Folio
Key Personnel
Chief Executive Officer: rian Murray
Man Dir: Tony Fisk
Commissioning & International Rights: Lorain Day *Tel:* (09) 443-9408
Founded: 1888
Subjects: Art, Biography, Cookery, Fiction, Gardening, Plants, History, Humor, Natural History, Regional Interests, Self-Help, Sports, Athletics, Travel
ISBN Prefix(es): 1-86950
Total Titles: 100 Print
Parent Company: HarperCollins Publishers, United States
Ultimate Parent Company: News Corporation
Imprints: HarperCollins New Zealand; Flamingo; Harper Sports
U.S. Office(s): HarperCollins Publishers, 10 E 53 St, New York, NY 10032, United States
Distributor for Auckland University Press; Canterbury University Press; Collinson Brown; Daphne Brasell Publishing; Lion Publishing; Otago University Press; Usborne; Western Publishers

Harper Sports, *imprint of* HarperCollins Publishers (New Zealand) Ltd

HarperCollins New Zealand, *imprint of* HarperCollins Publishers (New Zealand) Ltd

Hazard Press Ltd+
PO Box 2151, Christchurch
Tel: (03) 3770370 *Fax:* (03) 3770390
E-mail: quentinw@hazard.co.nz

Key Personnel
Publisher & Man Dir: Quentin Wilson
  E-mail: quentinw@hazard.co.nz
Founded: 1987
Member of Booksellers Association of New Zealand & Book Publishers Association of New Zealand.
Subjects: Art, Cookery, Drama, Theater, Government, Political Science, Literature, Literary Criticism, Essays, Nonfiction (General), Poetry
ISBN Prefix(es): 0-908790
Total Titles: 80 Print
Imprints: Showcase Publications; Gauntlet Press; Quoin Press; Certes Press; Orca Publishing
Distributed by Mosaic Press

Heinemann Education, *imprint of* Reed Publishing (NZ) Ltd

Heritage Press Ltd
9B Pounamu Ave, Greenhithe, Auckland 1311
Tel: (09) 4137503 *Fax:* (09) 4137503
E-mail: heritage.press@xtra.co.nz
Web Site: www.heritagepress.co.nz
Key Personnel
Contact: Prof John Dunmore
Founded: 1984
Subjects: Biography, Genealogy, History, Regional Interests
ISBN Prefix(es): 0-908708

Hodder Moa Beckett Publishers Ltd+
PO Box 3858, Auckland
Tel: (09) 4443640 *Fax:* (09) 4443646
Key Personnel
Man Dir: Neil Aston Aston
Publisher: Sarah Beresford
Founded: 1971
Subjects: Biography, Fiction, Nonfiction (General)
ISBN Prefix(es): 1-86958
Parent Company: Hodder Headline Ltd, United Kingdom

Huia Publishers+
39 Pipitea St, Thorndon, Wellington, Aotearoa
Mailing Address: PO Box 17335, Karori, Wellington
Tel: (04) 473-9262 *Fax:* (04) 473-9265
E-mail: huiapubs@huia.co.nz
Web Site: www.huia.co.nz
Key Personnel
International Rights: Robyn Bargh
Books Manager: Brian Bargh *E-mail:* brian.b@huia.co.nz
Founded: 1991
Specializes in books about & by Maori; educational resources in Maori language; children's books in English & Maori; histories of colonization in New Zealand.
Subjects: Biography, Drama, Theater, Education, Ethnicity, Fiction, History, Maori, Bi-cultural, Maori Language, indigenous
ISBN Prefix(es): 0-908975
Total Titles: 60 Print
Parent Company: Huia (NZ) Ltd
Divisions: Huia Communications

IPL Publishing Group+
28 Grey St, Wellington, The Terrace
Tel: (04) 499-3032 *Fax:* (04) 499-3032
Key Personnel
Contact: G Churchman
Founded: 1985
Member of BPANZ.
Subjects: History, Transportation, Technical & Practical
ISBN Prefix(es): 0-908876
Parent Company: G-B Churchman & Associates Ltd, c/o IPL Publishing Group Ltd, PO Box 10-215, Wellington, The Terrrace

Subsidiaries: IPL Books (Australia) Pty Ltd; IPL Wordprint
Divisions: IPL Books; IPL Video; IPL Publishing Services
Distributed by Gary Allen Pty Ltd (Australia)
Warehouse: 10 Tarndale Grove, Auckland

The Joint Board of Christian Education
75 Taranaki St, Wellington 3000
Mailing Address: PO Box 6133, Wellington 1
Tel: (04) 3850352 *Fax:* (04) 3856114
ISBN Prefix(es): 0-85819; 0-86407
Parent Company: Joint Board of Christian Education, 65 Oxford St, PO Box 1245, Collingwood, Vic 3006, Australia

Junior Publications Ltd
4/2 Frost Rd, Three Kings, Auckland 1004
Mailing Address: PO Box 56278, Dominion Rd, Auckland
Tel: (09) 6205459 *Fax:* (09) 6205459
Key Personnel
Dir: Jo Noble *E-mail:* jo@allsorts.co.nz
Specialize in magazines related to children's books.

Knowing Science, *imprint of* Magari Publishing

Kotuku Media Ltd+
Box 54/234, Plimmerton, Wellington
Tel: (04) 2331842
E-mail: kotuku.media@xtra.co.nz
Web Site: www.kotuku.media.co.nz
Key Personnel
Contact: Ross Miller
Founded: 1991
Subjects: Regional Interests
ISBN Prefix(es): 0-908967

Kowhai Publishing Ltd
10 Peacock St, Auckland 5
Tel: (09) 5759126 *Fax:* (09) 5753178
Key Personnel
Contact: Bruce Campbell
Specialize in photographic books of New Zealand scenery.
Subjects: Travel
ISBN Prefix(es): 0-908598

Landcare Research NZ
Canterbury Agricultural & Science Ctr Ellesmere Junction Rd, Lincoln 8152
Mailing Address: PO Box 40, Lincoln 8152
Tel: (03) 3256700 *Fax:* (03) 3252127
E-mail: mwpress@landcare.cri.nz
Web Site: www.landcare.cri.nz/mwpress/
Key Personnel
Manager: Greg Comfort
Sales: Catherine Montgomery
Founded: 1992
Specialize in scientific publications.
Subjects: Biological Sciences, Earth Sciences, Natural History, Science (General)
ISBN Prefix(es): 0-477; 0-478
Imprints: Manaaki Whenua Press
U.S. Office(s): Balogh Scientific Books, 1911 N Duncan Rd, Champaign, IL, United States
Distributor for Csiro Publishing (Australia)

Learning Guides (Writers & Publishers Ltd)+
141 Pope St, Camborne, Porirua City
Tel: (04) 23399400 *Fax:* (04) 2399400
E-mail: learning.guides@xtra.co.nz
Key Personnel
Manager: Lynda Litchfield
Founded: 1996
Subjects: Business, Computer Science, How-to, Management, Science (General)
ISBN Prefix(es): 0-9583643

Parent Company: Ecological Research Associates of New Zealand Inc, Upper Hutt
Orders to: PO Box 48-147, Upper Hutt

Learning Media Ltd+
PO Box 5013, Wellington
Tel: (04) 4962482
E-mail: info@learningmedia.co.nz
Web Site: www.learningmedia.co.nz; www.learningmedia.com
Key Personnel
Chief Executive: Neale Pitches
Founded: 1993
Member of NZ Book Publishers Association.
Subjects: Education
ISBN Prefix(es): 0-478
Total Titles: 2 CD-ROM
Branch Office(s)
Learning Media, 1235 Indiana Court, Suite 108, Redlands, CA 92374, United States
Distributed by Celebration Press (USA); Learning Media (New Zealand); Madeleine Lindley Ltd (UK); Thomas Nelson (UK)
Distributor for ITP Nelson (Canada); Lioncrest Pty Ltd (Australia); Pacific Stores Pty Ltd (Singapore)
Orders to: SSC Bldg, Level 3, Private Bag 3293, Wellington 6015

Legislation Direct+
Division of Blue Star Print Group
PO Box 12-418, Wellington
Tel: (04) 4965655 *Fax:* (04) 4965698
E-mail: lorders@legislationdirect.co.nz
Web Site: gplegislation.co.nz
Key Personnel
General Manager: Chris Eales
Administration Manager: Wendy Gaylor
  E-mail: wendy@legislationdirect.co.nz
Subjects: Career Development, Finance, Government, Political Science, Law, Nonfiction (General)
ISBN Prefix(es): 0-86956
Parent Company: Blue Star Print Group
Associate Companies: Whitcoulls (retail); Bennetts Government London Bookshops, London, United Kingdom
U.S. Office(s): Aubrey Books, 721 Ellsworth Dr, Suite 203A, Silver Spring, MD 20910-4436, United States
Distributor for Business Round Table; Ministry for the Environment; Ministry of Justice; NZ Statistics; Parliamentary Commission for the Environment
Bookshop(s): 47 Stephenson St, Birmingham B2 4DH, United Kingdom

Lincoln College Centre for Resource Management+
Lincoln University, Ellesmere Rd/Springs Rd, Lincoln, Canterbury
Mailing Address: Lincoln University, PO Box 84, Canterbury 8150
Tel: (03) 3252811 *Fax:* (03) 3252944
Web Site: www.lincoln.ac.nz
Telex: 4200 NZ
Key Personnel
Dir, Rights & Permissions: Dr John Hayward
Founded: 1960
Subjects: Environmental Studies
ISBN Prefix(es): 0-908584; 1-86931

Lincoln University Press+
PO Box 12214, Wellington
Tel: (04) 4710601 *Fax:* (04) 4710489
E-mail: braselld@lincoln.ac.nz
Web Site: www.learn.lincoln.ac.nz
Key Personnel
Man Dir & Publisher: Daphne Brasell
International Rights: Maureen Marshall
  E-mail: dba@clear.net.nz
Founded: 1987

Member of Book Publishers Association of New Zealand, & Booksellers New Zealand.
Subjects: Fiction, Gay & Lesbian, Literature, Literary Criticism, Essays, Women's Studies, Resource Management
ISBN Prefix(es): 0-9597837; 0-908896
Parent Company: Daphne Brasell Associates Ltd & Lincoln University
Ultimate Parent Company: Daphne Brasell Associates Ltd
Imprints: Whitireia Publishing
Subsidiaries: Lincoln University Press; Whitireia Publishing
Branch Office(s)
Orchard Hall, Lincoln University, PO Box 195, Lincoln, Canterbury, Contact: Daphne Brasell *Tel:* (03) 325 3873 *Fax:* (03) 325 3890
E-mail: braselld@lincoln.ac.nz
Distributed by Unireps (Australia)
Foreign Rep(s): Hemisphere (East Asia, Pacific); Unireps (Australia)

David Ling Publishing+
67 Hinemoa St, Auckland, Birkenhead
Mailing Address: PO Box 34-601, Birkenhead, Auckland
Tel: (09) 4182785 *Fax:* (09) 4182785
Key Personnel
Man Dir & International Rights: David Ling
 E-mail: davidling@xtra.co.nz
Founded: 1992
Publisher & packager.
Member of Booksellers NZ.
Subjects: Aeronautics, Aviation, Art, Biography, Fiction, History, Maritime
ISBN Prefix(es): 0-908990
Number of titles published annually: 10 Print
Total Titles: 80 Print
Distributed by David Bateman Ltd
Membership(s): Book Publishers Association of New Zealand

Longacre Press+
9 Dowling St, Dunedin
Mailing Address: PO Box 5340, Dunedin
Tel: (03) 4772911 *Fax:* (03) 4777222
E-mail: longacre.press@clear.net.nz
Key Personnel
Man Editor: Barbara Larson
Publicity Manager: Annette Riley
Founded: 1994
Subjects: Biography, Gardening, Plants, Gay & Lesbian, Natural History, Nonfiction (General), Sports, Athletics
ISBN Prefix(es): 0-9583405; 1-877135
Number of titles published annually: 10 Print
Total Titles: 75 Print
Distributed by Dennis Jones & Associates (Australia); Reed Publishing (NZ) Ltd (New Zealand)

Longman, *imprint of* Pearson Education

Macmillan Publishers New Zealand Ltd+
6 Ride Way, Albany, Auckland
Tel: (09) 414 0350; (09) 414 0356 (customer service); (09) 414 0352 (trade sales) *Fax:* (09) 414 0351
Web Site: www.macmillan.co.nz *Cable:* Macpublish
Key Personnel
Man Dir: David Joel *E-mail:* david@macmillan.co.nz
Trade Sales: Chris Baty *E-mail:* chris@macmillan.co.nz
School Sales: Robyn Garvan *E-mail:* robyn@macmillan.co.nz
Academic Sales: Victoria Johnson *E-mail:* vicki@macmillan.co.nz
Customer Service: Lyn O'Connor *E-mail:* lyn@macmillan.co.nz
Founded: 1977
ISBN Prefix(es): 0-908923
Parent Company: Macmillan Publishers Ltd, United Kingdom
Associate Companies: Macmillan Education Australia; Pan Macmillan Australia

Magari Publishing+
Imprint of Natural Expressions Ltd
PO Box 104, Taupo 2730
Tel: (07) 3770169 *Fax:* (07) 3773134
E-mail: frontdesk@magari.co.nz
Web Site: www.magari.co.nz
Key Personnel
Publisher: Margaret Woodhouse
 E-mail: margaret@magari.co.nz
Marketing Dir: Jack Gower
Founded: 1987
Subjects: Education, Humor, Self-Help
ISBN Prefix(es): 0-908801
Imprints: Curly Tales; Knowing Science
Warehouse: 3/29 Manuka St, Taupo

Mallinson Rendel Publishers Ltd+
15 Courtencey Pl, Level 5, Wellington
Mailing Address: PO Box 9409, Wellington
Tel: (04) 802 5012 *Fax:* (04) 802 5013
Key Personnel
Man Dir: E A Mallinson
Account: J D Harper
Publisher: Ann Mallinson *E-mail:* ann@mallinsonrendel.co.nz
Founded: 1980
Publisher of children's books.
ISBN Prefix(es): 0-908783; 0-908606
Number of titles published annually: 6 Print
Total Titles: 170 Print

Manaaki Whenua Press, *imprint of* Landcare Research NZ

Maori Publications Unit
PO Box 2061, Koyeopeo, Whakatane
Tel: (07) 3087254 *Fax:* (07) 3085098
Key Personnel
Contact: Dir
Subjects: English as a Second Language
ISBN Prefix(es): 1-877152; 0-908771
Showroom(s): Cor Domain Rd & McAlister St, Whakatane

John Martin Press
10 Beckenham Ave, Epsom, Auckland 1003
Tel: (09) 6255850 *Fax:* (09) 6255850
E-mail: nataliem@ihug.co.nz
Founded: 1988
Subjects: Poetry
ISBN Prefix(es): 0-9583616

McGraw-Hill Book NZ
Leyton House, 4th floor, Manukau City Shopping Center, Manukau City, Auckland
Mailing Address: PO Box 97-082, Manukau City
Tel: (09) 2622537 *Fax:* (09) 2622540

Mills Group+
PO Box 30818, Lower Hutt
Tel: (04) 5696744 *Fax:* (04) 5697464
Key Personnel
Chief Executive & Rights & Permissions: Harry Mills
Founded: 1982
Subjects: Nonfiction (General)
ISBN Prefix(es): 0-908722

Millwood Press Ltd
291B Tinakori Rd, Wellington
Tel: (04) 4735176 *Fax:* (04) 4735177
Telex: 31255 *Cable:* Siersprod
Key Personnel
Dir: Jim Siers; Judy Siers
Founded: 1972
Subjects: Foreign Countries

Moss Associates Ltd+
7 Dorset Way, Wadestown, Wellington 6001
Tel: (04) 4728226 *Fax:* (04) 4728226
E-mail: moss@xtra.co.nz
Key Personnel
Dir: Geoffrey R Moss
Founded: 1986
Subjects: Business, Career Development, Communications, Human Relations, Management
ISBN Prefix(es): 0-9583538
Distributed by Bagolyvar Publishing House (Hungary); Best Literary & Rights Agency (Korea); CCH (Australia); DPB Publications (India); Dragon's Eye Communications (Korea); Francolin Publishers (Pty) Ltd (South Africa); Joint Publishing (China); Kogan Page (UK); LDI Training (Indonesia); McGraw-Hill (USA); Moss Associates Ltd (New Zealand); Prommociones Jumerca (Spain); Singapore Institute of Management (Singapore & Malaysia); Tech Publications Pty Ltd (Singapore); Times Media Pvt Ltd (Singapore); UBS Publishers' Distributors Ltd (India); Vikas Publishing House Pvt Ltd (India); Yale International Publishing House (Taiwan)

Nagare Press+
PO Box 934, Palmerston North
Tel: (06) 3272531
Key Personnel
Editor & International Rights: Dr Wilhelmina Drummond
Subjects: Child Care & Development, Education, Fiction, Human Relations, Poetry, Wine & Spirits
ISBN Prefix(es): 0-908822

Nahanni Publishing Ltd+
PO Box 34-179, Birkenhead, Auckland 10
Tel: (09) 419 0681 *Fax:* (09) 419 0695
E-mail: info@nahanni-publishing.com; sales@nahanni.co.nz (for orders)
Key Personnel
Man Dir: Dr Ian Brooks *E-mail:* brooks@nahanni.co.nz
Founded: 1995
Subjects: Business
ISBN Prefix(es): 0-9583506; 0-9582036

Nestegg Books+
46 Owhiro Bay Pde, Wellington 6002
Tel: (04) 3836645
Key Personnel
Author, Editor & Publisher: Sheila Natusch
Founded: 1991
Subjects: Biography, History, Natural History, Regional Interests
ISBN Prefix(es): 0-473; 0-908629; 0-9597965; 0-9583757

New House Publishers Ltd+
PO Box 33376, Takapuna, Auckland 9
Tel: (09) 4106517 *Fax:* (09) 4106329
E-mail: service@newhouse.co.nz
Web Site: www.newhouse.co.nz
Key Personnel
Dir: David Heap *E-mail:* david@newhouse.co.nz
Founded: 1988
Specialist publishers of educational textbooks & materials.
Subjects: Accounting, Chemistry, Chemical Engineering, Earth Sciences, Economics, English as a Second Language, Geography, Geology, Language Arts, Linguistics, Management, Mathematics, Physics, Science (General), Technology
ISBN Prefix(es): 1-86946
Number of titles published annually: 25 Print
Total Titles: 300 Print

New Women's Press Ltd+
PO Box 47339, Auckland
Tel: (09) 767150 *Fax:* (09) 767150
Key Personnel
Man Dir: Wendy Harrex
Founded: 1982
Subjects: Women's Studies
ISBN Prefix(es): 0-908652
Warehouse: HarperCollins Publishers, PO Box 1, Auckland

New Zealand Council for Educational Research+
PO Box 3237, Wellington 6000
Tel: (04) 3847939 *Fax:* (04) 3847933
E-mail: peter.ridder@nzcer.org.ns
Key Personnel
Dir: Dr Anne Meade *E-mail:* anne.meade@vuw.ac.nz
Publicity Dir, Rights & Permissions: Bev Webber
Founded: 1934
Subjects: Education
ISBN Prefix(es): 0-908567; 0-908916; 1-877140
Imprints: NZCER
Distributor for ACER; NFER; SCRE
Showroom(s): Education House, 178 Willis St, Wellington
Bookshop(s): Education House, 178 Willis St, Wellington
Shipping Address: Education House, 178 Willis St, Wellington
Warehouse: Education House, 178 Willis St, Wellington
Orders to: Education House, 178-182 Willis St, Wellington 6000 (Distribution Services)

Northland Historical Publications Society
PO Box 204, Russell
Tel: (09) 4028244 *Fax:* (09) 4028296
Founded: 1989
Subjects: History
ISBN Prefix(es): 0-9583705; 0-9597926

NZCER, *imprint of* New Zealand Council for Educational Research

Orca Publishing, *imprint of* Hazard Press Ltd

Orca Publishing, Certes Press, *imprint of* Orca Publishing Services Ltd

Orca Publishing Services Ltd
PO Box 2151, Christchurch
Tel: (03) 3777770 *Fax:* (03) 3770390
Key Personnel
Man Dir & International Rights: Quentin Wilson
Editor: Antoinette Wilson *E-mail:* antoinette@orcapublishing.co.nz
Founded: 1994
Member of Book Publishers Association of NZ.
Subjects: Fiction, Nonfiction (General), Poetry
ISBN Prefix(es): 1-877162
Associate Companies: Hazard Press Ltd
Imprints: Orca Publishing, Certes Press
Distributed by Mosaic Press

Otago Heritage Books
500 Great King St, Dunedin
Mailing Address: PO Box 5361, Moray Place, Dunedin
Tel: (03) 4771500
Key Personnel
Editorial: G J Griffiths
Rights & Permissions: J A Cox
Founded: 1977
Specialize in regional books; also acts as retailer.
Subjects: History, Natural History, Regional Interests
ISBN Prefix(es): 0-908774; 0-9597723
Total Titles: 55 Print

Outrigger Publishers
PO Box 1198, Hamilton
Tel: (07) 856 6981
Key Personnel
Man Dir, Editorial: Norman Simms
 E-mail: nsimms@waikato.ac.nz
Founded: 1973
Publishes small magazines.
Subjects: Anthropology, Archaeology, Biblical Studies, History, Language Arts, Linguistics, Literature, Literary Criticism, Essays, Psychology, Psychiatry, Religion - Jewish
ISBN Prefix(es): 0-908571
Number of titles published annually: 2 Print

Oxford University Press
Ellerslie, Auckland 5
Mailing Address: PO Box 11149, Ellerslie, Auckland 5
Tel: (09) 5233134 *Fax:* (09) 5233134
Key Personnel
Publisher: Linda Cassells
Subjects: Agriculture, Art, Biography, Economics, History, Law, Literature, Literary Criticism, Essays, Natural History, Poetry
ISBN Prefix(es): 0-19
Parent Company: Oxford University Press, United Kingdom

Paerangi Books
PO Box 13-320, Johnsonville, Wellington 6004
Tel: (04) 4787789
Key Personnel
Contact: Trevor M Cobeldick
Founded: 1979
Subjects: Regional Interests
ISBN Prefix(es): 0-908965

Pearson Education+
48 Hillside Rd, Auckland 10
Mailing Address: Private Bag 102908, North Shore Mail Centre, Auckland 10
Tel: (09) 444 4968 *Fax:* (09) 444 4957
E-mail: firstname.lastname@pearsoned.co.nz
Key Personnel
Man Dir: Rosemary Stagg *E-mail:* rosemary.stagg@pearsoned.co.nz
Publisher, Schools: Ken Harrop
Marketing Manager Schools: Pat Fisk
Publisher, Tertiary: Bronwen Nicholson
Tertiary Sales Manager: Adrian Keane
Trade National Accounts Manager: John Cummerfield
Design/Production Manager: Polly Faulks
Administration Manager: Vera Bainbridge
Operations Manager: Ingeborg Van Elburg
Assistant to Man Dir: Sheila Jenkins
Founded: 1968
All New Zealand curriculum subjects in schools, higher education focus on business, economics & the social sciences.
ISBN Prefix(es): 0-582
Number of titles published annually: 60 Print
Total Titles: 600 Print
Parent Company: Pearson Education
Ultimate Parent Company: Pearson Plc
Imprints: Longman; Prentice Hall
Distributor for Sybex (New Zealand); WW Norton (New Zealand)

Penguin Books (NZ) Ltd
182-190 Wairau Rd (Glenfield), Private Bag, Takapuna, Auckland 9
Tel: (09) 4444965 *Fax:* (09) 4441470
Key Personnel
Man Dir: Tony Harkins
Sales Dir: Colin Cox
Publishing Dir: Geoff Walker
Marketing Dir: Karen Ferns
Founded: 1973

ISBN Prefix(es): 0-14
Parent Company: Penguin Publishing Co Ltd, United Kingdom

Polynesian Press+
PO Box 68 446, Auckland
Tel: (09) 3032349 *Fax:* (09) 3779528
Key Personnel
Contact: Robert Holding
Founded: 1976
ISBN Prefix(es): 0-908597
Distributed by University of Hawaii Press
Distributor for University of Hawaii Press

Prentice Hall, *imprint of* Pearson Education

Nelson Price Milburn Ltd+
One Te Puni St, Petone, Wellington
Mailing Address: PO Box 38-945, Wellington Mail Centre, Petone, Wellington
Tel: (04) 5687179 *Fax:* (04) 5682115
E-mail: npm@xtrq.co.nz
Key Personnel
General & Publishing Manager: Greg Browne
Secretary: John Heffernan
Founded: 1957
Distributor for Thomas Nelson UK & Thomas Nelson Australia.
Subjects: Accounting, Biological Sciences, Business, Chemistry, Chemical Engineering, Child Care & Development, Communications, Computer Science, Drama, Theater, Economics, Education, Electronics, Electrical Engineering, Finance, Geography, Geology, Health, Nutrition, History, Language Arts, Linguistics, Law, Management, Marketing, Mathematics, Outdoor Recreation, Physical Sciences, Physics, Poetry, Science (General), Social Sciences, Sociology, Sports, Athletics, Technology
ISBN Prefix(es): 0-7055; 1-86955; 1-86961
Parent Company: Thomas Nelson Australia, Australia
Ultimate Parent Company: The Thomson Corp, Suite 2706, Toronto Dominion Bank Tower, PO Box 24, Toronto Dominion Centre, Toronto, ON M5K 1A1, Canada
Associate Companies: 102 Dodds St, South Melbourne, Victoria 3205, Australia

Profile Publishing Ltd
Suite 2.1, 72 Dominion Rd, Mt Eden, Auckland
Mailing Address: PO Box 5544, Wellesley St, Auckland
Tel: (09) 6308940; (09) 3585455 *Fax:* (09) 3585462
E-mail: info@profile.co.nz
Web Site: www.profile.co.nz
Key Personnel
Man Dir: Reg Burchfield
Marketing & Promotions: Glenn Baker
ISBN Prefix(es): 0-9582045

Publishing Solutions Ltd
86-90 Lambton Quay, 9th Fl, Wellington
Tel: (04) 4710717 *Fax:* (04) 4710582
E-mail: gen@pubsol.co.nz
Web Site: www.pubsol.co.nz
Founded: 1992
Specialize in technical publishing.
Subjects: Maritime, Veterinary Science
ISBN Prefix(es): 0-9582063

Pursuit Publishing+
35 Norfolk St, Whangarei 0100
Mailing Address: PO Box 984, Whangarei 0100
Tel: (09) 4385725 *Fax:* (09) 4382543
Key Personnel
Author & President: Frank Newman
 E-mail: newman@mail.org
Founded: 1988
Subjects: Business

ISBN Prefix(es): 0-9597904
Distributed by Reed (NZ) Ltd (New Zealand)

Quoin Press, *imprint of* Hazard Press Ltd

R P L Books+
North Shore Mail Center, PO Box 100-243 NSMC, Auckland
Tel: (09) 4763510 *Fax:* (09) 4763590
E-mail: rplbooks@rplbooks.co.nz
Key Personnel
Man Dir: Duncan Sutherland *E-mail:* duncan@rplbooks.co.nz
Founded: 1970
Subjects: Biography, Sports, Athletics
ISBN Prefix(es): 0-908630; 0-908757; 0-9583371; 0-9597553; 0-9597884
Total Titles: 20 Print; 3 E-Book
Parent Company: Medialine Holdings Ltd
Imprints: Harlen Books; The Sporting Press
Subsidiaries: Harlen Publishing Company Ltd; The Sporting Press Ltd
Orders to: Forrester Books NZ Ltd, Private Bag 102907, NSMC, Auckland, David Forrester *Tel:* (09) 4152080 *Fax:* (09) 4152083

Reach Publications+
113 Wirihana Rd, Titirangi, Auckland
Mailing Address: PO Box 10-020, Dominion Rd, Auckland
Tel: 8176893
E-mail: giftednz@xtra.co.nz
Key Personnel
Managing Editor: Rory Cathcart
Founded: 1994
Subjects: Child Care & Development, Disability, Special Needs, Education
ISBN Prefix(es): 0-473
Parent Company: George Parkyn Centre for Gifted Education

Reed, *imprint of* Reed Publishing (NZ) Ltd

Reed Children's Books, *imprint of* Reed Publishing (NZ) Ltd

Reed Publishing (NZ) Ltd+
39 Rawene Rd, Birkenhead, Auckland 10
Mailing Address: PO Box 34901, Birkenhead, Auckland 10
Tel: (09) 480 4950; (09) 480 4988 (customer service) *Fax:* (09) 470 4999; (09) 480 4970 (customer service)
E-mail: lrobertson@reed.co.nz (customer service)
Web Site: www.reed.co.nz
Key Personnel
Man Dir: Alan Smith *E-mail:* asmith@reed.co.nz
Publishing Manager: Peter Janssen *E-mail:* pjanssen@reed.co.nz
Founded: 1988 (part of the company founded in 1907)
Subjects: Biography, Cookery, Fiction, History, Natural History, Nonfiction (General), Outdoor Recreation, Regional Interests, Travel
ISBN Prefix(es): 0-589; 0-7900; 0-86863; 1-86948; 0-474; 1-86944
Number of titles published annually: 100 Print
Total Titles: 280 Print; 2 Audio
Parent Company: Reed Education & Professional Publishing, United Kingdom
Ultimate Parent Company: Reed Elsevier plc, 25 Victoria St, London SW1H 0EX, United Kingdom
Associate Companies: Butterworths
Imprints: Reed; Heinemann Education; Reed Children's Books
Divisions: Reed Consumer Books; Heinemann Educational; Book Circle
U.S. Office(s): Heinemann USA, 361 Hanover St, Portsmouth, NH 03801-3912, United States
Distributor for BBC Books; John Murray

Resource Books Ltd+
37 Pembroke Crescent, Glendowie, Auckland 1005
Mailing Address: PO Box 25-598, St Heliers, Auckland 1130
Tel: (09) 5758030 *Fax:* (09) 5758055
E-mail: sales@resourcebooks.co.nz
Web Site: www.resourcebooks.co.nz
Key Personnel
Manager: Peter Biggs *E-mail:* pbiggs@resourcebooks.co.nz
Founded: 1984
Subjects: Art, Education, Medicine, Nursing, Dentistry
ISBN Prefix(es): 0-908618

RIMU Publishing Co Ltd
49 Casey Ave, Fairfield
Tel: (07) 8555536 *Fax:* (07) 8555536
Key Personnel
Man Dir: Theola Wyllie
Founded: 1984
Specialize in book publishing.
Subjects: Nonfiction (General)
ISBN Prefix(es): 0-908703

River Press
41 York St, Picton
Mailing Address: PO Box 10, Picton
Tel: (03) 5738383 *Fax:* (03) 5738383
Key Personnel
Contact: Carol Dawber *E-mail:* carol.dawber@xtra.co.nz
Founded: 1992
Also acts a book packager.
Subjects: History, Maritime, Mysteries, Nonfiction (General), Romance, Travel
ISBN Prefix(es): 0-9598041
Subsidiaries: Best Books

RSVP Publishing Company Ltd+
24 Tiri Rd, Oneroa, Waiheke Island, Auckland
Mailing Address: PO Box 47166, Ponsonby, Auckland
Tel: (09) 3723480 *Fax:* (09) 3723480
E-mail: rsvppub@iconz.co.nz
Web Site: www.rsvp-publishing.co.nz
Key Personnel
Publisher: Stephen Picard
Founded: 1990
Member of BPANZ.
Subjects: Alternative, Astrology, Occult, Environmental Studies, Fiction, Law, Nonfiction (General), Photography, Social Sciences, Sociology, Travel, Also specializes in eclectic & metaphysical books, illustrated books
ISBN Prefix(es): 0-9597948; 0-9582182
Number of titles published annually: 3 Print
Total Titles: 12 Print; 9 Online; 9 E-Book
Distributed by Banyan Tree Book Distributors
Foreign Rep(s): Banyan Tree (Australia)

Saint Publishing+
11 Akepiro St, Mt Eden, Auckland
Mailing Address: PO Box 8157, Symonds St, Auckland
Tel: (09) 623-2510 *Fax:* (09) 623-2890
E-mail: info@saintpublish.co.nz
Key Personnel
Sales & Marketing Manager: Karen Strawbridge
Contact: Selwyn Jacobson
Editor: Tom Hepburn
Founded: 1979
Specialize in calendars & lifestyle/coffee table books.
Subjects: Art, Humor, Sports, Athletics
ISBN Prefix(es): 1-877186; 1-877247
Total Titles: 6 Print
Distributor for Avalanche Publishing (New Zealand)

Seagull Press
Flat 2/27 Glade Ave, Richmond, Christchurch
Tel: (03) 3899338
Key Personnel
Author: R B Mehlhopt
Subjects: Poetry
ISBN Prefix(es): 0-908738; 0-9597686

Shearwater Associates Ltd+
108 Mana Esplanade, Paremata, Wellington
Mailing Address: PO Box 54-224, Plimmerton
Tel: (04) 2399024 *Fax:* (04) 2399024
Key Personnel
Contact: Michael Keith
Founded: 1990
Specialize in children's & educational publishing.
Subjects: Education, Fiction, History, Natural History, Nonfiction (General)
ISBN Prefix(es): 0-908864
Imprints: Shearwater Books; Titi Tuhiwai

Shearwater Books, *imprint of* Shearwater Associates Ltd

Shoal Bay Press Ltd+
62 Gloucester St, Christchurch 1
Mailing Address: PO Box 17661, Christchurch
Tel: (03) 3770370 *Fax:* (03) 3770390
E-mail: shoalbay@shoalbay.co.nz
Key Personnel
Contact: David Elworthy
Founded: 1984
Subjects: Business, Child Care & Development, Crafts, Games, Hobbies, Finance, Gardening, Plants, History, Management, Marketing, Natural History, Nonfiction (General), Outdoor Recreation, Photography, Sports, Athletics, Travel
ISBN Prefix(es): 0-908704; 1-877251
Warehouse: Macmillan Publishers, 6 Ridge Way, Albany, Auckland
Orders to: Macmillan Publishers, 6 Ridge Way, Albany, Auckland

Shortland Publications Ltd
360 Dominion Rd, Auckland 3
Mailing Address: PO Box 56133, Auckland
Tel: (09) 687128 *Fax:* (09) 6230143 *Cable:* NEWSPRESS
Key Personnel
Man Dir: Avelyn Davidson
Sales Manager: Jenny Boyd
Founded: 1977
Subjects: Sports, Athletics
ISBN Prefix(es): 0-86867
Parent Company: Wilson & Horton Ltd, 46 Albert St, PO Box 32, Auckland

Showcase Publications, *imprint of* Hazard Press Ltd

SIR Publishing+
Science House, 11 Turnbull St, Thorndon, Wellington
Mailing Address: PO Box 598, Thorndon, Wellington
Tel: (04) 4727421 *Fax:* (04) 4731841
E-mail: sirp@rsnz.govt.nz *Cable:* SIDSIR
Key Personnel
Manager: Robert Lynch
Founded: 1991
Publishers of Scientific Research journals, focusing on New Zealand, Australia, SW Pacific & Antarctica, Scientific Proceedings of Symposia & Workshops; Scientific Treatises; Science Education Resources. Incorporated within The Royal Society of New Zealand.
Subjects: Agriculture, Biological Sciences, Earth Sciences, Environmental Studies, Science (General)
ISBN Prefix(es): 0-477; 0-908654

Parent Company: The Royal Society of New Zealand, 4 Halswell St, Thorndon, PO Box 598, Wellington
Branch Office(s)
Eurospan Ltd, 3 Henrietta St, Covent Garden, London WC2E 8LU, United Kingdom *Tel:* (020) 7240 0856 *Fax:* (020) 7379 0609
Allen Press Inc, PO Box 1897, Lawrence, KS 66044-8897, United States *Tel:* 913-843-1234 *Fax:* 913-843-1274

Southern Lights, *imprint of* Brick Row Publishing Co Ltd

Southern Press Ltd
1037 Paekakariki Hill Rd, Pauatahanui, Porirua
Mailing Address: R D 1, Porirua 6221
Tel: (04) 239-9068 *Fax:* (04) 239-9835
Key Personnel
Man Dir, Editorial: R H Stott
Publicity: J Stott
Founded: 1971
Subjects: Aeronautics, Aviation, Archaeology, Civil Engineering, Maritime, Mechanical Engineering, Technology, Transportation
ISBN Prefix(es): 0-908616
Distributed by ARHS, NSW Division
Distributor for Australian Railway Historical Society, NSW Division
Shipping Address: High Ridge, Paekakariki Hill Rd, Pauatahanui, R D 1, Porirua Wellington

Spinal Publications+
8 Parata St, Waikanae
Mailing Address: PO Box 93, Waikanae
Tel: (04) 2937020 *Fax:* (04) 2932897
Key Personnel
General Manager: Jan McKenzie
Founded: 1980
Member of BPANZ.
Subjects: Health, Nutrition, Self-Help, Diagnosis & Treatment of Lumbar & Cervical Spine
ISBN Prefix(es): 0-9583647; 0-9598049; 0-9597446; 0-9597746
Distributed by Esaki Medical Instrument Co (Japan); Spine Care Products Benelux (Benelux, Switzerland, Austria); Spinal Publications Italia (Italy)

The Sporting Press, *imprint of* R P L Books

Statistics New Zealand
Aorangi Hse, 85, Molesworth St, Wellington
Mailing Address: PO Box 2922, Wellington
Tel: (04) 4954600 *Fax:* (04) 4729135
Key Personnel
Contact: Kay Whiteman
Subjects: Agriculture, Business, Economics, Education, Finance, Mathematics, Women's Studies
ISBN Prefix(es): 0-478

Sunshine Books International Ltd+
PO Box 74543, Auckland 1130
Tel: (09) 5203049 *Fax:* (09) 5224882
E-mail: orders@my-dictionary.com
Web Site: my-dictionary.com
Key Personnel
Co-Dir: Jenny Aston *E-mail:* jenny@my-dictionary.com
ISBN Prefix(es): 0-9597734

Sunshine Multi Media Ltd, Wendy Pye Ltd
413 Great South Rd, Penrose, Auckland
Mailing Address: Private Bag 17905, Greenlane, Auckland
Tel: (649) 525-3575 *Fax:* (649) 525-4205
E-mail: admin@sunshine.co.nz
ISBN Prefix(es): 1-877190
Branch Office(s)
433 Wellington St, Clifton Hill, Melbourne, Victoria 3068, Australia *Tel:* (0613) 9489-3968 *Fax:* (0613) 9482-2416
Maaholm Publishing House, Almevej 12, 2900 Hellerup, Denmark *Tel:* (0453) 9627 892 *Fax:* (0453) 9627 891
20 Heathbridge, Brooklands Rd, Weybridge, Surrey KT13 OUN, United Kingdom *Tel:* (044-1932) *Fax:* 850062

Tandem Press+
2 Rugby Rd, Birkenhead, Auckland 10
Tel: (09) 480-1452 *Fax:* (09) 480-1455
E-mail: customers@tandempress.co.nz
Web Site: www.tandempress.co.nz
Key Personnel
Man Dir, Editorial: Robert M Ross *E-mail:* bobross@tandempress.co.nz
Dir Marketing: Helen E Benton *E-mail:* helenb@tandempress.co.nz
Founded: 1990
Subjects: Business, Cookery, Ethnicity, Fiction, Health, Nutrition, Nonfiction (General), Outdoor Recreation, Photography, Psychology, Psychiatry, Self-Help, Travel, Women's Studies
ISBN Prefix(es): 1-877178; 0-908884; 9-781877
Total Titles: 135 Print
Distributor for New Women's Press (NZ)

Taylor Books+
51 Sixth Ave, Tauranga
Tel: (07) 5786024
Key Personnel
Head: Peter Rotherham
Founded: 1994
Subjects: English as a Second Language, Self-Help

Te Reo Publications+
c/o Postal Delivery Centre, South Hok Iurga Waimamaku
Tel: (0887) 54887
E-mail: jmcveagh@clear.net.nz
Key Personnel
Dir: Janine McVeagh
Subjects: Ethnicity, Fiction
ISBN Prefix(es): 0-908891

Te Ropu Kahurangi+
43 Landscape Rd, Papatoetoe
Tel: (09) 2782731
Key Personnel
Publisher & Editor: Bernard Gadd
Founded: 1983
We are a non-profit educational project.
Specialize in Learn-to-read books for ages 10 & over, novels & short stories for teenagers.
Subjects: Literature, Literary Criticism, Essays, Regional Interests
ISBN Prefix(es): 0-86477
Subsidiaries: Hallard Press
Showroom(s): Brick Row, 11 Cockayne Crescent, Sunnynook, Auckland 10

Te Waihora Press
PO Box 512, Christchurch
Tel: (03) 348-8675 *Fax:* (03) 348-8675
Key Personnel
Man Editor: Dr John Wilson *E-mail:* johnwilson56@xtra.co.nz
Founded: 1984
Subjects: Architecture & Interior Design, History
ISBN Prefix(es): 0-908714
Total Titles: 2 Print

Titi Tuhiwai, *imprint of* Shearwater Associates Ltd

Transworld Publishers (NZ) Ltd
Private Bag 102985, North Shore Mail Centre, Auckland
Tel: (09) 4156210 *Fax:* (09) 4156221
Key Personnel
Contact: Jacqui Dimes
ISBN Prefix(es): 0-908821
Parent Company: Bertelsmann AG, Germany
Associate Companies: Transworld Publishers, Australia; Bantam Doubleday Dell Inc, 1540 Broadway, New York, NY 10036, United States; Transworld Publishers, United Kingdom
Distributor for Avon; Dover (US); Langenscheidt; David Ling Publishing; Lonely Planet Publications; Workman; Trail Blazer; de Roos

University of Otago Press+
56 Union St W, Dunedin
Mailing Address: PO Box 56, Dunedin
Tel: (03) 479 8807 *Fax:* (03) 479 8385
E-mail: university.press@otago.ac.nz
Web Site: www.otago.ac.nz
Key Personnel
Man Editor & International Rights: Wendy Harrex *E-mail:* wendy.harrex@stonebow.otago.ac.nz
Publicist: Amanda Smith *Tel:* (03) 479 9094 *E-mail:* amanda.smith@stonebow.otago.ac.nz
Founded: 1958
Member of IASP (International Association of Scholarly Publishers).
Subjects: Anthropology, Art, Biography, Education, Environmental Studies, Fiction, Government, Political Science, History, Literature, Literary Criticism, Essays, Natural History, Photography, Poetry, Psychology, Psychiatry
ISBN Prefix(es): 0-908569; 1-877133; 1-877276
Total Titles: 117 Print
Branch Office(s)
UniReps, University of New South Wales Press, NSW 2034 South Wales, Australia *Tel:* (02) 96640999 *Fax:* (02) 96645420 *E-mail:* info.press@unsw.edu.au
U.S. Office(s): International Specialized Book Services, 5824 NE Hassalo St, Portland, OR 97213-3644, United States *Tel:* 503-287-3093 *Fax:* 503-280-8832 (North America)
Distributed by International Specialized Book Services (USA)
Orders to: HarperCollins, 31 View Rd, Glenfield, Auckland 10 *Tel:* (09) 4439400 *Fax:* (09) 4439402
Membership(s): Book Publishers Association of New Zealand

Victoria University Press+
Level 1, 154 Featherston St, Wellington
Mailing Address: PO Box 600, Wellington
Tel: (04) 4966580 *Fax:* (04) 4711701
E-mail: victoria-press@vuw.ac.nz
Web Site: www.vup.vuw.ac.nz
Key Personnel
Publisher: Fergus Barrowman
Editor: Rachel Lawson *E-mail:* rachel.lawson@vuw.ac.nz
Founded: 1979
Member of Booksellers New Zealand.
Subjects: Anthropology, Architecture & Interior Design, Drama, Theater, Government, Political Science, History, Language Arts, Linguistics, Law, Literature, Literary Criticism, Essays, Poetry, Social Sciences, Sociology
ISBN Prefix(es): 0-86473
Total Titles: 180 Print
Distributed by Random House (New Zealand)
Warehouse: Random House NZ Ltd, 18 Poland Rd, Glenfield, Auckland
Orders to: Archetype Book Agents, PO Box 105, 200 Auckland *Tel:* (09) 3773800 *Fax:* (09) 3773811

Viking Sevenseas Ltd, *imprint of* Viking Sevenseas NZ Ltd

Viking Sevenseas NZ Ltd
23B Ihakara St, Paraparaumu, Wellington

Mailing Address: PO Box 152, Paraparaumu 6150, Wellington
Tel: (04) 902-8240 *Fax:* (04) 902-8240
E-mail: vikings@paradise.net.nz *Cable:* VIKSEVEN
Key Personnel
Man Dir: Murdoch Riley
Founded: 1957
Subjects: Ethnicity, Natural History
ISBN Prefix(es): 0-85467
Imprints: Viking Sevenseas Ltd

Wellington Orchid Society Publications
PC Tomlinson, 14 Putnam St, Northland, Wellington 14
Tel: 04 4758765
Key Personnel
Manager: N D Neilson
Subjects: Culture Guides-Cymbidium, Lycaste/Anguloa, Oncidium, Paphiopedilum, Cattleya
ISBN Prefix(es): 0-908684

Whitireia Publishing, *imprint of* Lincoln University Press

Bridget Williams Books Ltd+
6 Glenbervie TCE, Thorndon, Wellington
Mailing Address: PO Box 5482, Wellington
Tel: (04) 4738317 *Fax:* (04) 4738417
E-mail: bwbooks@ihug.co.nz
Key Personnel
Dir: Bridget Williams
Business Manager: John Schiff
Publicist: Catriona Robertson
Administration: Anna Locker-Lampson
Founded: 1990
An independent publishing company focusing on New Zealand subjects, including Maori history & politics.
Subjects: Biography, Government, Political Science, History, Nonfiction (General), Women's Studies
ISBN Prefix(es): 0-908912; 0-908912
Number of titles published annually: 10 Print
Total Titles: 30 Print
Distributed by Independent Publishing Group (IPG)
Distributor for NIL

Wilson & Horton Publications Ltd
227 Dominon Rd, Auckland 3
Mailing Address: PO Box 56, Auckland 3
Tel: (09) 6388105 *Fax:* (09) 6302140
Telex: NZ 2325 *Cable:* HERALD
Key Personnel
Man Dir: H M Horton
Sales Manager: B Morgan
ISBN Prefix(es): 0-86864; 0-9583614
Branch Office(s)
NZ1 Bldg, Hamilton
22 Panama St, Wellington

Words Work
31 Robertson St, Rotorua
Mailing Address: PO Box 604, Rotorua 3201
Tel: (07) 3482953 *Fax:* (07) 3482953
E-mail: wordswrk@clear.net.nz
Key Personnel
Dir: Philippa Harrison *E-mail:* philippa@wordswo-k.co.nz; philippa@nzbike.co.nz
Founded: 1996
Prepress, graphic design, editing. Publish New Zealand's only cycling magazine.
50% partner in Phoenix Publishing.
Subjects: Child Care & Development, Fiction, How-to, Poetry, Religion - Protestant

Nicaragua

General Information

Capital: Managua
Language: Spanish
Religion: Predominantly Roman Catholic
Population: 3.8 million
Bank Hours: 0830-1500 Monday-Friday; 0830-1130 Saturday
Shop Hours: 0800-1200, 1430-1730 or longer Monday-Saturday
Currency: 100 centavos = 1 new cordoba
Export/Import Information: Catalogues dutied per gross kilo Compensatory tax on advertising. No import licenses or exchange controls.
Copyright: UCC, Buenos Aires, Florence (see Copyright Conventions, pg xi)

Academia Nicaraguense de la Lengua
(Nicaraguan Academy of Letters)
Apdo 2711, Managua
Subjects: Language Arts, Linguistics

ENN, see Editorial Nueva Nicaragua

Editorial Nueva Nicaragua
Paseo Salvador Allende, Km 3 1/2 Carretera Sur, Apdo RP-073, Managua
Tel: (02) 666520
Key Personnel
Dir Gen: Roberto Diaz Castillo
President: Sergio Ramirez Mercado
Production Dir: Irene Menocal Bravo
Financial: Mayra Rivera Juarez
Sales: Maria Jose Bermudez Moreno
Founded: 1981
Also acts as co-productions.
Subjects: Ethnicity, Fiction, Government, Political Science, Literature, Literary Criticism, Essays, Nonfiction (General), Poetry, Religion - Other, Social Sciences, Sociology

Niger

General Information

Capital: Niamey
Language: French (official) and 10 other national languages
Religion: 85% Islamic, most of remainder traditional beliefs
Population: 8.1 million
Bank Hours: 0800-1100, 1600-1700 (cool season 1530-1700) Monday-Friday
Currency: 100 centimes = 1 CFA franc
Export/Import Information: Member of West African Economic Community. No tariff on books; advertising matter subject to fiscal and customs duties (EEC members pay percentage of customs duty). Also statistical tax.
Copyright: UCC, Berne (see Copyright Conventions, pg xi)

Government Printer (Societe De L'Imprimerie Nationale Du Niger)
BP 61, Niamey
Tel: 734798
Telex: 5313

Nigeria

General Information

Capital: Abuja
Language: English (official), also Hausa, Yoruba, Ibo & Fulani
Religion: Islamic (mainly in north), Christian, and traditional beliefs
Population: 88.5 million
Bank Hours: 0800-1500 Monday; 0800-1300 Tuesday-Friday
Shop Hours: Vary locally. 0800-1230, 1400-1630 Monday-Friday; 0800-1230 Saturday
Currency: 100 kobo = 1 naira
Export/Import Information: No tariffs on books or advertising matter. Open general license. Obscene literature prohibited. Exchange controls.
Copyright: UCC, Berne, Florence (see Copyright Conventions, pg xi)

ABIC Books & Equipment Ltd+
18 Kenyatta St, Enugu
Mailing Address: PO Box 13740
Tel: (042) 331827 *Fax:* (042) 334811
Key Personnel
President: C N C Asomugha
Founded: 1987
Member of Nigerian Publishers Assoc. Specializes in Reference Books & Children's Books; also participates in Book Selling & as a Literary Agent.
Subjects: History, Poetry
ISBN Prefix(es): 978-2269
Branch Office(s)
PO Box 71391, Victoria Island, Lagos

Abisega Publishers (Nigeria) Ltd+
Isolak Bldg, 9 Queen Elizabeth Rd, Mokola, Rounabout
Mailing Address: PO Box 14398 UI, Ibadan
Tel: (022) 415802
Key Personnel
Man Dir: Adedeji Muyiwa
Member of Nigerian Publishers Association.
Subjects: Accounting
ISBN Prefix(es): 978-30339
Imprints: Opatoki Press

Adebara Publishers Ltd
PO Box 1970, Ibadan
Telex: 20311
Key Personnel
Man Dir, Editorial: Dele Adebara
Sales, Publicity: Bisi Oke
Production: Layi Bankole
Rights & Permissions: Kayode Ayeni
Founded: 1979
Subjects: Biography, Business, Education, Ethnicity, Fiction, Foreign Countries, Religion - Other
ISBN Prefix(es): 978-147
Imprints: Awoko; Gangan; Kakaki
Book Club(s): Amebo Book Club

African Books Collective Ltd, *imprint of* Nigerian Institute of International Affairs

African Education Publishers Ltd, see Africana-FEP Publishers Ltd

African Universities Press+
305 Herbert Macaulay St, Yaba, Lagos
Mailing Address: PO Box 3560, Lagos
Tel: (022) 317218
Telex: 20311 Box 078 *Cable:* PILGRIM IBADAN
Key Personnel
Executive Dir: Dr E A M Leigh

NIGERIA

Founded: 1963
ISBN Prefix(es): 978-148
Parent Company: Pilgrim Books Ltd, 305 Herbert Macaulay St, Yaba, Lagos
Subsidiaries: Aureol Publishers Ltd (West Africa)
Branch Office(s)
Klm 8 Zaria/Kaduna Rd, Nr Wasasa Junction, PMB 146 Kaduna State
187 Awka Rd, Onitsha, Anambra State

Africana-FEP Publishers Ltd+
Formerly African Education Publishers Ltd
1, Africana-FEP Drive, Onitsha Anambra State
Mailing Address: PMB 1639, Onitsha Anambra State
Tel: (046) 210669 *Cable:* AFRIBOOK, ONITSHA, NIGERIA
Key Personnel
Man Dir: Ralph O Ekpeh *Tel:* (080) 33125 705
Founded: 1971
Subjects: How-to, Science (General)
ISBN Prefix(es): 978-175
Branch Office(s)
3 Main St, Gidan Juma
9 Old Lagos Rd, PMB 5632 Ibadan *Tel:* (022) 311383
53 Barracks Rd Uyo, Presbook BP 13 Limbe, Cameroon

Ahmadu Bello University Press Ltd+
PMB 1094, Zaria, Kaduna State
Tel: (069) 550054
E-mail: abupl@abu.edu.ng
Telex: 57241 *Cable:* Unibello Press Zaria
Key Personnel
Man Dir, Editorial, Rights & Permissions: Saidu H Adamu
Editorial: George Ibrahim
Production: Oko Sandy
Marketing: Onwuaha I Sunday
Founded: 1974
Publishing & Printing.
Subjects: Education, Ethnicity, Foreign Countries, History, Social Sciences, Sociology, Veterinary Science
ISBN Prefix(es): 978-125

Albah Publishers+
136a Ibolo Rd, Bompal-Kano, Kano State
Mailing Address: PO Box 6177, Bompal-Kano, Kano State
Cable: Albah Kano
Key Personnel
Chairman, Editorial: Bashari F Roukbah
Sales & Publicity Manager: Idris A Muhammad
Production: Basiru Ahmad
Founded: 1978
Subjects: Education
ISBN Prefix(es): 978-2380
Parent Company: Elbash Limited
Associate Companies: Brunswick Publishing Co, PO Box 555, Lawrenceville, VA 23868, United States
Subsidiaries: Albah Research Centre
Bookshop(s): Baban Layi, Gyadi-Gyadi, Zariya Rd, Kano

Alliance West African Publishers & Co
Orindingbin Estate, New Aketan Layout, Oyo
Mailing Address: PMB 1039, Oyo
Tel: (085) 230798
Key Personnel
Chairman, Man Dir: Chief M O Ogunmola
Sales: L Oyeniji
Publicity & Permissions: Kehinde Ogunmola
Founded: 1971
Subjects: Biography, Ethnicity, Foreign Countries, History, How-to, Science (General)

Aromolaran Publishing Co Ltd+
Ibadan, Oyo State
Mailing Address: PO Box 1800, Ibadan, Oyo State
Tel: (02) 24392
Telex: 31158NG
Key Personnel
Man Dir: Dr Gabriel Adekunle Aromolaran
Sales: Mrs V M Aromolaran
Founded: 1970
Subjects: Art, Biography, How-to, Poetry, Religion - Other, Science (General)
ISBN Prefix(es): 978-127

Awoko, *imprint of* Adebara Publishers Ltd

Black Academy Press+
Owerri, Imo State
Mailing Address: PO Box 255, Owerri, Imo State, Niger
Tel: (083) 230606; (083) 232606 *Cable:* BAPRESS
Key Personnel
Man Dir: Dr S Okechukwu Mezu
Founded: 1970
Subjects: Biography, History, Nonfiction (General), Poetry
ISBN Prefix(es): 978-150
Parent Company: Mezu International Ltd, 6 Mezu Lane, Owerri, Imo State
Associate Companies: Black Academy Press Inc
Orders to: PO Box 66142, Baltimore, MD 21239, United States

Book Representation & Publishing Co Ltd
Agodi/Loyola College Rd, PMB 5349, Ibadan Oyo State
Tel: (022) 710242
Key Personnel
Executive Chairman, Dir: Chief B A Ajayi
Dirs: Chief M A Ajasin; Chief R F Fasoranti; Chief Funso Afelumo; Chief 'Bola Ige
General Manager: 'Bisi Taiwo
Administrative Manager: A L Salawu
Founded: 1973
Subjects: Education
ISBN Prefix(es): 978-172
Associate Companies: Circle Books Ltd, Ibadan

CEM Publishers Ltd
4 Yemi Ogunniyi St, Ajao Estate, Anthony Village, Lagos
Mailing Address: PO Box 4267, Lagos
ISBN Prefix(es): 978-176

Cross Continent Press Ltd+
PO Box 282, Yaba, Lagos State
Tel: (01) 862437 *Fax:* (01) 685679 *Cable:* Croconpres Lagos
Key Personnel
Man Dir: Dr T C Nwosu
Editorial: Prof Theo Vincent
Production: Kess Nwagwu
Publicity: Miss A C Ikeme
Marketing: Miss P N Ikekwem
Sales Coordinator: Dr J O Enwerem
General Consultant: Prof E J Nwosu
Founded: 1974
Subjects: Biography, Fiction, How-to, Nonfiction (General), Poetry
ISBN Prefix(es): 978-134
Parent Company: Tanhigh Holdings Ltd
Associate Companies: Vista Books Ltd
Subsidiaries: Editorial Consultancy & Agency Services
Branch Office(s)
Senator E P Echeruo, Executive Director, PO Box 2273, Owerri, Imo State
Showroom(s): 59 Awolowo Rd, SW Ikoyi, Lagos, Nigeria
Orders to: 59 Awolowo Rd, SW Ikoyi, Lago

BOOK

CSS Bookshops, Agency & Publishing Division+
19 Broad St, Lagos
Mailing Address: PO Box 174, Lagos
Tel: (01) 2633081; (01) 2637009; (01) 2637023; (01) 2633010 *Fax:* (01) 2637089 *Cable:* BOOKSHOPS
Key Personnel
Man Dir & Chief Executive: Alabi Dayo
Subjects: Biography, Ethnicity, Foreign Countries, History, Law, Medicine, Nursing, Dentistry, Nonfiction (General), Religion - Other, Science (General)
ISBN Prefix(es): 978-143
Subsidiaries: CSS Bookshops

Daily Times of Nigeria Ltd (Publication Division)
New Isheri Rd, PMB 21340, Agidingbi, Ikeja
Tel: (01) 900850-9
Telex: 21333 Times Ng *Cable:* Daily Times Lagos
Key Personnel
Chief Executive: Segun Osoba
Editorial: Faruk Mohammed
Sales: Funsho Akindele
Production: J M Teshola
Founded: 1925
Who's Who.
Subjects: Foreign Countries
ISBN Prefix(es): 978-144; 978-2171
Subsidiaries: Times Press Ltd; Newsstand Agencies Limited
Book Club(s): Times Book Club

Daystar Press (Publishers)+
Daystar House, Ibadan, Oyo State
Mailing Address: PO Box 1261, Ibadan, Oyo State
Tel: (022) 412670
Telex: 31176
Key Personnel
Man Dir, Editorial, Rights & Permissions & Publicity: Phillip Adelakun Ladokun
Trade: James Akinboye
Marketing: Tunde Felix
Founded: 1962
Subjects: Ethnicity, Health, Nutrition, House & Home, Religion - Other
ISBN Prefix(es): 978-122

Delta Publications (Nigeria) Ltd+
172 Ogui Rd, Enugu, Enugu State
Mailing Address: PO Box 3606, Lagos
Tel: (042) 3606
Key Personnel
Man Dir, Rights & Permissions: C D E Onyeama
Editorial Dir: Mrs E O Onyeama
Sales: Nicholas Ohaekweiro; Ebere Nwadigbo
Production, Publicity: Miss Nwanneka Okwu
Founded: 1982
Subjects: Biography, Fiction
ISBN Prefix(es): 978-2335
Bookshop(s): Enugu Airport Bookshop
Book Club(s): The Delta Book Club

ECWA Productions Ltd
10 Kano Rd, Jos Plateau State
Mailing Address: PMB 2010, Jos Plateau State
Tel: (073) 53897; (073) 52230
Telex: 81120 Ecwap Ng
Key Personnel
Man Dir: Dr Philip S Usman
General Manager, Publications: Jonathan A Babstunde
Challenge Publications is Publishing Division of ECWA Productions Ltd.
Subjects: Education, Religion - Other
ISBN Prefix(es): 978-137
Bookshop(s): Challenge Bookshops

PUBLISHERS

NIGERIA

Educational Research & Study Group
Institute of Ed, Univ of Ibadan, c/o Prof. Pai Obanya, Ibadan
Key Personnel
Man Dir: Areoye Oyebola
Founded: 1970
Subjects: Biography, Ethnicity, Foreign Countries, History, How-to, Nonfiction (General), Religion - Other, Science (General), Social Sciences, Sociology
ISBN Prefix(es): 978-30054

Egret Books, *imprint of* Paperback Publishers Ltd

Egret Stars Series, *imprint of* Paperback Publishers Ltd

Ethiope Publishing Corporation
34 Murtala Mohammed St, Benin City, Bendel State
Mailing Address: PMB 1192, Benin City, Bendel State
Tel: (052) 243036
Telex: 41110NG *Cable:* Ethiope
Key Personnel
General Manager: Sunday N Olaye
Founded: 1970
Subjects: Biography, Ethnicity, Fiction, Foreign Countries, History, How-to, Law, Nonfiction (General), Philosophy, Poetry, Science (General), Social Sciences, Sociology, Technology
ISBN Prefix(es): 978-123

Evans Brothers (Nigeria Publishers) Ltd
Jericho Rd, PMB 5164, Ibadan, Oyo State
Tel: (02) 2417570; (02) 2417601; (02) 2417626
Telex: 31104 Edbook *Cable:* EDBOOKS IBADAN
Key Personnel
Man Dir: B O Bolodeoku
Sales Dir: S A Oke
General Manager: V A Aladejana
Founded: 1966
Member of Nigerian Publishers Association (NPA).
Subjects: Accounting, Agriculture, Child Care & Development, Civil Engineering, Drama, Theater, Economics, Education, Electronics, Electrical Engineering, Environmental Studies, Fiction, Geography, Geology, Government, Political Science, History, Journalism, Law, Literature, Literary Criticism, Essays, Management, Mathematics, Medicine, Nursing, Dentistry, Philosophy, Romance, Science (General), Self-Help, Social Sciences, Sociology, Sports, Athletics, Technology
ISBN Prefix(es): 978-167
Associate Companies: Evans Brothers Ltd, UK, United Kingdom
Branch Office(s)
Kaduna, Lagos and Owerri

Olaiya Fagbamigbe Ltd (Publishers)
Agodi Gate, 11 Methodist Church Rd, Akure
Mailing Address: PO Box 14, Agodi Gate, Ibadan
Tel: (034) 2075 *Cable:* Fagbamigbe Akure
Key Personnel
Man Dir: Mrs M E Fagbamigbe
Editor: Yemi Fagbamigbe
Publicity: Gbenga Fagbamigbe
Rights & Permissions: Yetunde Fagbamigbe
Founded: 1976
Specialize in Childrens Books, Novels & Textbooks.
Subjects: Education
ISBN Prefix(es): 978-164
Warehouse: New Ife Rd, PO Box 1176, Agodi Gate, Ibadan

Fountain Series, *imprint of* Paperback Publishers Ltd

Fourth-Dimension Publishers, *imprint of* Fourth Dimension Publishing Co Ltd

Fourth Dimension Publishing Co Ltd+
Fourth Dimension Plaza, 16 Fifth Ave, City Layout, PMB 01164, Enugu 400001
Mailing Address: PMB 01164, Enugu
Tel: (042) 459969 *Fax:* (042) 456904
E-mail: info@fdpbooks.com; fdpbook@aol.com
Web Site: www.fdpbooks.com
Key Personnel
Chief Executive & Rights & Permissions: Victor U Nwankwo
Publishing & Editorial: Eva Igwilo
Production: Carolene Okorafor
Sales & Marketing: Jeremiah Udochu
Founded: 1976
Member of Nigerian Publishers' Association (NPA), African Publishers' Network (APNET) & Nigerian Book Foundation (NBF).
Subjects: Biography, Business, Cookery, Education, Fiction, Government, Political Science, Law, Social Sciences, Sociology
ISBN Prefix(es): 978-156
Number of titles published annually: 100 Print
Total Titles: 1,555 Print
Imprints: Fourth-Dimension Publishers
Foreign Rep(s): African Books Collective Ltd (Europe, US)
Foreign Rights: African Books Collective Ltd (Europe, US)
Showroom(s): ABC Ltd, 27 Park End St, Oxford OX1 1HU, United Kingdom, Justin Cox
Warehouse: ABC Ltd, Unite 3, Off Pytts Lane, Burford, Oxon OX18 4SJ, United Kingdom, Mary Jay
Orders to: ABC Ltd, 27 Park End St, Oxford OX1 1HU, United Kingdom

Gangan, *imprint of* Adebara Publishers Ltd

Gbabeks Publishers Ltd
L16 Ibadan St, Kaduna
Mailing Address: PO Box 3538, Kaduna, Kaduna State
Tel: (062) 217976
Key Personnel
Man Dir: Tayo Ogunbekun
Founded: 1982
Member of National Publishers Association.
Subjects: Education, Language Arts, Linguistics, Science (General), Social Sciences, Sociology
ISBN Prefix(es): 978-2416

Goldland Business Co Ltd+
85 Saint Finbarrs College Rd, Akoka, Lagos
Mailing Address: PO Box 2541, Yaba, Lagos
Tel: (01) 8023179087; (01) 821203
E-mail: goldland@consultant.com
Key Personnel
Author & International Rights Contact: Dr Jonathan A O Ifechukwu
Founded: 1982
Business consultants, researchers, trainers & publishers.
Specialize in publishing books in business & related fields.
Subjects: Business, Finance, Government, Political Science, How-to, Management, Marketing, Technology
ISBN Prefix(es): 978-30035
Number of titles published annually: 1 Print
Total Titles: 8 Print

Heritage Series, *imprint of* Heritage Books

Heritage Books+
2-8 Calcutta Crescent, Gate 1, 101251 Apapa, Lagos
Mailing Address: PO Box 610, 101251 Apapa, Lagos
Tel: (01) 5871333
E-mail: obw@infoweb.abs.net
Key Personnel
Editor: Naiwu Osahon
Senior Editor, Rights & Permissions: Bakin Kunama
Publicity: Edia Apolo
Founded: 1971
Subjects: Ethnicity, Fiction, Nonfiction (General), Poetry, Pan-Africanism
ISBN Prefix(es): 978-2358
Associate Companies: Third World First Publications, 2 Calcutta Crescent, Gate 1, 101251 Apaga, Lagos *Tel:* (01) 5871 333 *Fax:* (01) 5871 333 *E-mail:* obw@infoweb.abs.net
Imprints: Heritage Series; Oyoyo Series; Obobo Series
Subsidiaries: Obobo Books
Bookshop(s): Heritage (The Bookshop), PO Box 930, 101251 Apapa, Lagos *Tel:* (01) 5871 333 *E-mail:* obw@infoweb.abs.net

Hudanuda Publishing Co Ltd+
P.O. Box 984, Zaria, Kaduna State
Tel: (069) 5141
Key Personnel
Man Dir: Abdullahi Khalil
Founded: 1981
Member of Nigerian Publishers Association (NPA).
Subjects: Literature, Literary Criticism, Essays
ISBN Prefix(es): 978-2368
Associate Companies: Hodder & Stoughton Publishers, Mill Rd, Dunton Green, Sevenoaks, Kent TN13 2YA, United Kingdom
Branch Office(s)
Islamic Publsihing Co, Kukuru Byepass, Jos
Dal Arabia Publishing Co Ltd, Kano
Showroom(s): Zangon Shanu, Samaru, Zaria
Bookshop(s): No 28 Sobon Gari, Zaria
Warehouse: Zangon Shanu, PO Box 984, Zaria, Kaduna State

Ibadan University Press+
University of Ibadan, Ibadan, Oyo State
Tel: (022) 400550; (022) 400614 (ext 1244, 1042, 1032, 1093) *Cable:* Univpress Ibadan
Key Personnel
Head of Marketing: Bisi Ogunleye
Founded: 1952
Subjects: Agriculture, Ethnicity, Foreign Countries, History, Law, Medicine, Nursing, Dentistry, Philosophy, Psychology, Psychiatry, Science (General), Social Sciences, Sociology, Technology
ISBN Prefix(es): 978-121

Ilesanmi Press (Educational Publishers) Ltd
PO Box 204, Ilesha
Tel: (034) 232762; (034) 232044
Key Personnel
Man Dir, Rights & Permissions: G E Ilesanmi
Publishing, Production Dir: G O Ilesanmi
Marketing Dir: C A Ilesanmi
Editorial: C U Awioke
Founded: 1956
Subjects: Biography, Chemistry, Chemical Engineering, Engineering (General), Ethnicity, Foreign Countries, History, How-to, Language Arts, Linguistics, Music, Dance, Philosophy, Physics, Science (General), Social Sciences, Sociology
ISBN Prefix(es): 978-157
Branch Office(s)
Akure
Ibadan
Jos
Kano
Lagos
Minna
Onitsha

Uyo
Bookshop(s): Faji; Ilesha

Institute of African Studies, Onyeka, A
University of Nigeria, Nsukka
Tel: (022) 400550; (022) 400614 ext 12444
Key Personnel
Dir, Editorial, Rights & Permissions: Prof Bolanle Awe
Editorial, Sales, Production: Dele Layiwola
Founded: 1962
Subjects: Ethnicity
ISBN Prefix(es): 978-2450

JAD Publishers Ltd+
40 Adamson St, Keta, Victoria Island, Lagos
Mailing Address: PO Box 72320, Victoria Island, Lagos
Founded: 1989
Subjects: Behavioral Sciences, Biography, Biological Sciences, Developing Countries, Economics, Environmental Studies, Government, Political Science, History, Law, Mathematics, Social Sciences, Sociology
ISBN Prefix(es): 978-2863

Kakaki, *imprint of* Adebara Publishers Ltd

Kola Sanya Publishing Enterprise
2 Epe Rd, Oke-Owa, Ijebu-Ode
Mailing Address: PMB 2099, Ijebu-Ode
Tel: (037) 432638
Key Personnel
Man Dir: Chief K Osunsanya
Subjects: How-to, Nonfiction (General), Science (General)
ISBN Prefix(es): 978-171

Lantern Books, *imprint of* Literamed Publications Nigeria Ltd

Literamed Publications Nigeria Ltd+
Plot 45, Alausa Bus Stop, Oregun Rd, PMB 21068, Ikeja
Tel: (01) 4962512; (01) 4935258 *Fax:* (01) 4972217
E-mail: literamed@infoweb.abs.net
Web Site: www.lantern-books.com
Key Personnel
Production Mgr: M O Dawodu
Publishing Director: L A Aladesuyi
Finance Director: S O Ayorinde
Founded: 1969
Member of the Nigeria Publishers Association (NPA).
Subjects: Education, Government, Political Science, Social Sciences, Sociology
ISBN Prefix(es): 978-142
Number of titles published annually: 25 Print
Total Titles: 120 Print
Imprints: Lantern Books

Longman Nigeria Plc
52 Oba Akran Ave, Ikeja, Lagos State
Mailing Address: Private Mail Bag, Ikeja, Lagos State
Tel: (01) 497 89259 *Fax:* (01) 496 4370
E-mail: longman@infoweb.abs.net
Telex: 26639 longman ng *Cable:* Longman Ikeja
Key Personnel
Man Dir & Chief Executive: Abiodun Olowoniyi
Executive Dir (Northern Area Operations): Alhaji Musa Halliru
Deputy Chief Exec: Azed Echebiri
Marketing Dir: Dan Obidiegwu
Founded: 1961
Subjects: Biography, Ethnicity, Fiction, History, Nonfiction (General), Poetry, Psychology, Psychiatry, Religion - Other, Science (General), Social Sciences, Sociology, Technology
ISBN Prefix(es): 978-139

Merryland, *imprint of* Joe-Tolalu & Associates

Thomas Nelson (Nigeria) Ltd+
2, Kofo Abayomi Ave, Apapa, Lagos
Mailing Address: PO Box 336, Apapa, Lagos
Tel: (01) 961452
Telex: 26736 *Cable:* NELPITMAN IKEJA
Key Personnel
Executive Chairman Chief: C O Taiwo
General Manager: A Fasemore
Marketing Dir: L Solarin
Editor, Science: M O Omotoye
Editor, Humanities: F O Bada
Founded: 1965
Also acts as publishers for (NERDC) Nigerian Education Research & Development Council & the University of Lagos Press.
Subjects: Fiction, Nonfiction (General), Science (General), Social Sciences, Sociology
ISBN Prefix(es): 978-126
Parent Company: The Thomson Corp, Toronto Dominion Bank Tower, Suite 2706, PO Box 24, Toronto Dominion Centre, Toronto, ON M5K 1A1, Canada
Associate Companies: University Publishing Co
Branch Office(s)
120, Orlu Rd, Owerri 3
Edo Textile Mills Rd, Benin City, Edo State

New Africa Publishing Company Ltd
PO Box 1178, Owerri, Imo State
Tel: (083) 231891
Key Personnel
Chairman & Man Dir: H K Offonry
Dir: S O Igwe; B E Ogbuagu
Founded: 1981
Subjects: Art, Biography, Business, Education, Finance, Human Relations, Humor, Law, Management
ISBN Prefix(es): 978-2357

New Era Publishers+
PO Box 27720, Agodi, Ibadan
Tel: (022) 715706
Key Personnel
Executive Chairman: Prof O Imoagene
Founded: 1991
Also acts as Consultants.
Subjects: Fiction, Science (General)
ISBN Prefix(es): 978-2853
Parent Company: New-Era Holdings Ltd
Associate Companies: New-Era Equippers; Petro-Allied Services Ltd
Subsidiaries: New-Era Consultants Ltd
Distributed by Africa Book Centre (UK)

New Horn Press Ltd
Agodi Gate, Ibadan, Oyo State
Mailing Address: PO Box 4138, Ibadan, Oyo State
Key Personnel
Chairman: Dr Abiola Irele
Senior Editor, Rights & Permissions: Mrs Bassey Irele
Founded: 1974
Subjects: Fiction, How-to, Nonfiction (General), Poetry
ISBN Prefix(es): 978-2266

Nigerian Environmental Study Team
PMB 5297, Ibadan, Oyo State
Fax: (022) 410588; (022) 412644
ISBN Prefix(es): 978-31203

Nigerian Institute of Advanced Legal Studies
University of Lagos Campus, PMB 12820, Lagos
Tel: (01) 821752; (01) 821711; (01) 821753
Telex: 27506
Subjects: Law
ISBN Prefix(es): 978-31963

Nigerian Institute of International Affairs
13/15 Kofo Abayomi Rd, Victoria Island, Lagos
Mailing Address: GPO Box 1727, Lagos
Tel: (01) 611122; (01) 615606-10 *Fax:* (01) 611360
E-mail: niia@ric.nig.com
Telex: 22638 *Cable:* INTERNATIONS LAGOS
Key Personnel
Ag Dir-General Editorial: Prof R A Akindele
Editorial: Dr Bola Akinterinwa; Prof Bassey Ate; Dr Cyril Obi; Dr R O Olaniyan
Marketing & Sales: E A Ude
Founded: 1961 (Established as an independent, nonofficial, nonpolitical & nonprofit making organization. In Aug 1991, the Institute taken over by the Nigerian govt)
Encourage & facilitate the understanding of International Affairs; circumstances, conditions & attitudes of foreign countries & their people. Provide & disseminate information upon international questions, as we also promote the study & investigation of such international questions through such fora as conferences, lectures, discussions, to compliment our publications, journals & records.
Subjects: Economics, Law
ISBN Prefix(es): 978-2276
Imprints: African Books Collective Ltd

Nigerian Trade Review
10, Makinde St, Alausa, Ikeja, Lagos State
Mailing Address: PO Box 427, Ikeja, Lagos State
Tel: (01) 961147
Key Personnel
Man Dir: Chief P A Dawodu
Founded: 1958
ISBN Prefix(es): 978-2242

Northern Nigerian Publishing Co Ltd+
Gaskiya Bldg, Zaria, Kaduna State
Mailing Address: PO Box 412, Zaria, Kaduna State
Tel: (069) 32087
Telex: 75243
Key Personnel
Man Dir: Hussain Hayat
Man Editor: Muhammad Abubakar
Marketing Manager: Aliyu Haruna
Sales Manager: Johanna Madaki
Founded: 1966
Member of Nigerian Publishers Association.
Subjects: Nonfiction (General), Poetry, Regional Interests, Religion - Other
ISBN Prefix(es): 978-169
Parent Company: Gaskiya Corp Ltd
Branch Office(s)
Kano, Kaduna & Jos

NPS Educational Publishers Ltd (Nigeria Publishers Services)
South West Ring Rd, off Akinyemi Way, Ibadan
Mailing Address: PO Box 62, Ibadan
Tel: (032) 316006; (032) 316008
Telex: 31478 NG
Key Personnel
Chairman, Man Dir: Chief Duro Otesanya
Marketing Manager: Adebayo Falore
Also distributors.
ISBN Prefix(es): 978-2556
Branch Office(s)
37A Omeagana St, off Modebe Ave, PO Box 4073, Onitsha *Tel:* (046) 213774
BB2 Old Jos Rd, PO Box 722, Zaria *Tel:* (069) 34170

Nwamife Publishers Ltd+
10, Ibiam St, Uwani, Enugu, Anambra State
Tel: (042) 338454 *Cable:* Nwamife Enugu
Key Personnel
Chairman: Dr Felix C Adi
Sales, Production, Publicity: Samuel Umesike

Editorial, Rights & Permissions: Dr Nina Mba
Founded: 1970
Subjects: Biography, Education, Ethnicity, Fiction, History, How-to, Law, Nonfiction (General), Poetry, Science (General)
ISBN Prefix(es): 978-124

Obafemi Awolowo University Press Ltd+
Obafemi Awolowo University, Ile-Ife, Oyo State
Mailing Address: PMB 004, OAU Post Office, Ile-Ife
Tel: (036) 230290-9; (036) 230284
Telex: AVPL *Cable:* PRESS AWOVARSITY
Key Personnel
General Manager: Akin Fatokun
Editorial: Stephen Eyeh
Production: Isola Akinremi
Marketing: T A Kudoro
Founded: 1968
Specializes in Professional Texts
Member of International Publishers Association & National Publishers Association.
Also acts as International Publishing Agent, National Publishing Agent.
Subjects: Biography, Education, Ethnicity, History, Law, Medicine, Nursing, Dentistry, Philosophy, Religion - Other, Social Sciences, Sociology
ISBN Prefix(es): 987-136
Number of titles published annually: 6 Print
Total Titles: 100 Print
Foreign Rep(s): ABC London (Europe, US)

Obobo Series, *imprint of* Heritage Books

Obobo Books+
2/8 Calcutta Crescent, Gate 1, Apapa, 101251 Lagos
Mailing Address: PO Box 610, Apapa, 101251 Lagos
Tel: (01) 5871333
E-mail: obw@infoweb.abs.net
Key Personnel
Chief Executive: Ms Osahon Obobo
Editorial: Bakin Kunama
Sales, Publicity: Edia Apolo
Production: Edun Osahon
Founded: 1981
Also produce the television program *Obobo Playhouse*.
Subjects: Biography, Fiction, History, Coloring books
ISBN Prefix(es): 978-186
Number of titles published annually: 3 Print
Total Titles: 106 Print
Parent Company: Heritage Books, 2, Culcutta Crescent, Gate 1, PO Box 610 Apapa, 101251 Lagos
Associate Companies: Third World First Publications
Bookshop(s): Heritage, PO Box 930, 2-8 Calcutta Crescent, Gate 1, Apapa, 101251 Lagos

Ogunsanya Press, Publishers and Bookstores Ltd
64, Agbeni St, Ibadan
Mailing Address: PO Box 95, Ibadan
Tel: (022) 310924 *Cable:* Pombapress
Key Personnel
Man Dir, Editorial, Rights & Permissions: Chief Lucas Justus Popo-Ola Ogunsanya
Sales, Publicity: E A Faleke
Production: A S Banjo
Founded: 1970
Subjects: Geography, Geology, History, Language Arts, Linguistics, Mathematics, Science (General), Social Sciences, Sociology
ISBN Prefix(es): 978-170
Branch Office(s)
Popo-Ola Jubilee Lodge, Oke Imoru, PO Box 155, Ijebu Ode, Ogun State

Onibon-Oje Publishers
Felele Layout, Molete, Ibadan
Mailing Address: PO Box 3109, Ibadan
Tel: (022) 313956
Telex: 31657 Bonoje NG
Key Personnel
Chairman: Gabriel Onibonoje
Man Dir: J Olu Onibonoje
Founded: 1958
Subjects: Biography, Ethnicity, Fiction, Foreign Countries, History, How-to, Nonfiction (General), Poetry, Religion - Other, Science (General), Social Sciences, Sociology
ISBN Prefix(es): 978-145
Branch Office(s)
Benin City
Jos
Kano
Lagos
Onitsha
Sokoto
Zaria
Ikot Ekpene
Bookshop(s): SW8/77 Oke-Ado, Ibadan
Book Club(s): Onibonoje Book Club

Opatoki Press, *imprint of* Abisega Publishers (Nigeria) Ltd

Oyoyo Series, *imprint of* Heritage Books

Paperback Publishers Ltd+
Alafin Ave, Plot 7, Block 10, Oluyole Estate, SW, Ring Rd, Ibadan
Mailing Address: UI PO Box 14470, Ibadan
Tel: (022) 317363
Key Personnel
Man Dir: Agbo Areo
Sales Dir: S G Oyetunde
Founded: 1985
Members of the Nigerian Publishers Association.
Subjects: Education, Fiction
ISBN Prefix(es): 978-2432
Imprints: Egret Books; Fountain Series; Egret Stars Series
Branch Office(s)
Dayspring House, 15 Ogunsefunmi Str, Anifowose IKEJA

Riverside Communications+
100C Elelenwo, GRA Phase 1, Port Harcourt, Rivers State
Mailing Address: PO Box 7390, Port Harcourt, Rivers State
Tel: (084) 334042 *Fax:* (084) 334042
E-mail: isoun@aol.com; rvsdcom@aol.com
Key Personnel
President: Prof T T Isoun
Executive Director: Miriam Isoun
Founded: 1987
Subjects: Anthropology, Biological Sciences, Chemistry, Chemical Engineering, Cookery, Developing Countries, Environmental Studies, History, Language Arts, Linguistics, Mathematics, Medicine, Nursing, Dentistry, Nonfiction (General), Religion - Catholic, Religion - Protestant, Science (General), Veterinary Science
ISBN Prefix(es): 978-31226; 978-30333
Parent Company: Riverside Biotech Nigeria Limited 100
Branch Office(s)
Riverside Communications, 5575 Seminary Rd, No 104, Falls Church, VA 22041, United States, Miriam Isoun *E-mail:* isoun@aol.com

Saros International Publishers
24, Aggrey Rd, Port-Harcourt
Mailing Address: PO Box 193, Port-Harcourt
Tel: (084) 331763 *Fax:* (084) 331763
Key Personnel
Publisher: Ken Saro-Wiwa
Founded: 1985
Subjects: Drama, Theater, Fiction, Literature, Literary Criticism, Essays, Poetry
ISBN Prefix(es): 978-2460
Orders to: African Books Collective Ltd, The Jam Factory, 27 Park End St, Oxford OX1 1KU, United Kingdom

Spectrum Books Ltd+
Ring Rd, Spectrum House, Ibadan
Mailing Address: PO Box 1319, Ibadan
Tel: (02) 2310058; (02) 2311215; (02) 2312705
Fax: (02) 2312705; (02) 2318502
E-mail: admin1@spectrumbooksonline.com
Web Site: www.spectrumbooksonline.com
Key Personnel
Chief Executive: Joop Berkhout
Editorial: Tony Igboekwe
Sales, Publicity: Edgman Igbinosun
Founded: 1978
Subjects: Education, Fiction
ISBN Prefix(es): 978-029
Associate Companies: Safari Books (Export) Ltd, 17 Bond St, 1st floor, St Helier, Jersey, Channel Islands, United Kingdom
Distributed by ABC Oxford

Tabansi Press Ltd+
135 Awka Rd, Onitsha, Anambra State
Mailing Address: POB 243, Onitsha, Anambra State
Tel: (046) 211661
Key Personnel
Chief Executive: F N Tabansi
Deputy Chief Executive: P O Tabansi
Editor: Angus Abalum
Author: M O Odiaka
Founded: 1955
Specialize in educational book publishing.

Tana Press Ltd & Flora Nwapa Books Ltd+
2A, Menkiti Lane, Ogui, Enugu
Mailing Address: PO Box 62, Enugu
Tel: (042) 338857
Telex: 51164 Lake NG *Cable:* TANA
Key Personnel
Man Dir, nee Nwapa: Flora Nwakuche
Editorial: Dipl Ing Nina Mba
Production: E N Benyeogo; M A Ubah
Founded: 1979
Rights & Permissions: Tana Press, Ltd, Books Ltd.
Subjects: Fiction
ISBN Prefix(es): 978-2272
Branch Office(s)
PO Box 2, Oguta, Imo State
Warehouse: 22 Mbanugo, St Ogbete, Enugu
Orders to: Nigerian Publishers Services Ltd, Trusthouse, PO Box 62, Ibadan
Three Continents Press, 1346 Connecticut Ave NW, Washington, DC 20036, United States

Joe-Tolalu & Associates+
Plot 14, Block A, Surulere Industrial Rd, Ogba, Ikeja
Mailing Address: PO Box 3333, Mapo Post Office, Ibadan, Oyo State
Tel: (01) 4925078
Key Personnel
Man Dir: Tosin Awolalu
Founded: 1983
Also acts as literary agent & publishing consultant.
Subjects: Biography, Humor, Religion - Other, Travel
ISBN Prefix(es): 978-2415
Imprints: Merryland
Subsidiaries: Interprint Services
Divisions: Booktrust
Distributor for Delphi Publications; New Pen Publishing; Pelins Ltd

Unity Publishing & Research Company Ltd+
PO Box 1210, Festac City, Lagos
Tel: (01) 881504
Key Personnel
Executive Chairman: Dr M J A Iginla
Founded: 1990
Subjects: Developing Countries, Government, Political Science, Philosophy, Publishing & Book Trade Reference, Social Sciences, Sociology, Women's Studies
ISBN Prefix(es): 978-30855
Parent Company: Ipreco Group of Companies
Subsidiaries: International Publishing & Research Co
Branch Office(s)
c/o Foreign Partner, Mr J O Omodere, 7 Loradele Circle, Scarborough, ON, Canada
Bookshop(s): 7 Alhaja Risikatu Seriki Str, Ojo, Lagos
Shipping Address: 711 Road B Close, H 33 Festac City, Lagos
Warehouse: 7 Alhaja Risikatu Seriki Str, Ojo, Lagos

University of Lagos Press+
University of Lagos Press, University of Lagos, Akoka, Lagos
Mailing Address: PO Box 132, Unilag PO, Akoka, Lagos
Tel: (01) 825048 *Fax:* (01) 825048
Telex: 21210 *Cable:* UNILAG PRESS, LAGOS
Key Personnel
Dir: Mrs B A Awere
Editor: Bukola Olugasa E-mail: bukiolu@yahoo.com
Founded: 1980
Europe & UK.
Subjects: Biography, Education, Ethnicity, Foreign Countries, Human Relations, Law, Medicine, Nursing, Dentistry, Social Sciences, Sociology
ISBN Prefix(es): 978-2264
Distributed by African Books Collective
Showroom(s): Marketing Unit, University of Lagos Press, Commercial Rd, Unilag Akoka, Yaba, Lagos

University Publishing Co+
11, Central School Rd, Onitsha
Mailing Address: PO Box 386, Onitsha
Tel: (046) 230013 *Cable:* Varsity Box 386 Onitsha
Key Personnel
Dir: F C Ogbalu; W C Ifezue
Editorial: J Oranyeludike
Sales: D O Dandy
Production: I Nweke
Publicity: Christian Ogbalu
Permissions: Cecilia Ogbalu
Founded: 1959
Subjects: Biography, Ethnicity, Foreign Countries, History, Nonfiction (General), Philosophy, Poetry, Religion - Other
ISBN Prefix(es): 978-160
Associate Companies: Cynako International Press, Aba; Thomas Nelson (Nigeria) Ltd; African Literature Bureau, Aba
Branch Office(s)
Azikiwe Rd, Aba
Varsity Bookshop/Press, Oye Agu Junction, Abagana, Njikoka LGA
Afor Igwe, Ogidi
Oye Olisa Ogbunike, Onitsha-Enugu Rd, Awka
Eke-Amawbia, Awka
64 New Market Rd, Onitsha
Bookshop(s): Varsity Bookshop/Press at: Oye-Agu, Abagana, Njikoka LGA; Eke-Amawbia, Amawbia, Awka LGA; Aba; Abiriba, Ohafia LGA
Orders to: Varisty Bookshop, 64 New Market Rd, Onitsha

Vantage Publishers International Ltd+
98A Samonda, Old Airport Area, Ibadan, Oyo State
Mailing Address: PO Box 7669 Secretariat PO, Ibadan
Tel: (022) 415341
Key Personnel
Chairman & Publisher: Mr 'Poju Amori
Executive Dir: Mr Adewale Abiodun Amori
Founded: 1983
Member of International Scholary Publishers; Specialize in scholarly journals for Research Institutes & Faculty of Law & Publishing (editorial & production consulting).
Subjects: Biblical Studies, Biography, Biological Sciences, Business, Drama, Theater, Education, English as a Second Language, Fiction, Government, Political Science, Language Arts, Linguistics, Literature, Literary Criticism, Essays, Nonfiction (General), Poetry, Public Administration, Religion - Protestant, Social Sciences, Sociology
ISBN Prefix(es): 978-2458
Subsidiaries: Vantage Paper & Stationeries
Divisions: Vantage Productions
Bookshop(s): 98A Airport Area, Ibadan, Oyo State

West African Book Publishers Ltd+
One Babalola St, Mushin, Lagos
Tel: (01) 9007604; (01) 825020; (01) 526616
Telex: 26144 *Cable:* ACADPRESS
Key Personnel
Chairman: B A Idris Animashaun
Dir: Mrs A O Obadagbonyi
Editor: H O Mazi
Founded: 1967
Subjects: Advertising, Agriculture, Chemistry, Chemical Engineering, Child Care & Development, Economics, Geography, Geology, Government, Political Science, Human Relations, Mathematics, Science (General)
ISBN Prefix(es): 978-153; 978-31973
Associate Companies: Academy Press PLC; Lithotec LTD; Academy Computers LTD; Richware Pottery LTD

John West Publications Co Ltd+
208-212, Broad Street, Lagos
Mailing Address: PO Box 2416, Lagos
Tel: (01) 932011
Telex: 26446 wepal ng *Cable:* JAKPRESS
Founded: 1962
Subjects: Biography, How-to, Nonfiction (General)
ISBN Prefix(es): 978-163

Norway

General Information

Capital: Oslo
Language: Norwegian. There are two distinct forms, Bokmal (sometimes called Riksmal) and Nynorsk (formerly called Landsmal) whose relative importance has changed in recent years. About 90% of Norwegian books are now published in Bokmal and it is the medium of instruction in most schools. Danish and Swedish are usually intelligible to speakers of Norwegian
Religion: Predominantly Evangelical Lutheran
Population: 4.3 million
Bank Hours: 0830-1530 Monday-Friday; 0830-1500 (summer)
Shop Hours: 0830 or 0900-1700 or 1800 Monday-Friday; 0830 or 0900-1400 or 1600 Saturday
Currency: 100 ore = 1 Norwegian krone
Export/Import Information: Member of the European Free Trade Association. No tariff on books except children's picture books. Books exempt from VAT. No duty on advertising. No import license required. Nominal exchange controls.
Copyright: UCC, Berne, Florence (see Copyright Conventions, pg xi)

Ad-Notam Glydendal, see Glydendal Akademisk

Altera Forlag A/S
Postboks 2657, St Hanshaugen, 0131 Oslo
Tel: 22569590 *Fax:* 22565088
ISBN Prefix(es): 82-7608; 82-90494; 82-990826

Ansgarboker, *imprint of* Atheneum Forlag A/S

Ariel Lydbokforlag+
Postboks 1546 Vika, 0117 Oslo
Tel: 64943510 *Fax:* 64943510
Key Personnel
Chief Editor: Inger Schjoldager
Founded: 1988
Subjects: Education, Fiction, Poetry
ISBN Prefix(es): 82-7509

Aschehoug Forlag
Sehestedsgt 3, PB 363 Sentrum, N-0102 Oslo
Tel: 22400400 *Fax:* 22429467
Parent Company: H Aschehoug & Co (W Nygaard) A/S

H Aschehoug & Co (W Nygaard) A/S
Sehesteds gate 3, 0102 Oslo
Mailing Address: Postboks 363, Sentrum, 0102 Oslo
Tel: 22400400 *Fax:* 22206395
E-mail: epost@aschehoug.no
Web Site: www.aschehoug.no *Cable:* ACO OSLO
Key Personnel
Man Dir & Publisher: William Nygaard
Assistant Man Dir: Erik Holst
Dir, School Book Dept: Kari-Anne Haugen
Editorial: Freihow Halfdan; Marit Notaker; Irja Thorenfeldt; Egil Kristofferson; Ole Jacob Bull
Marketing: Terje Fredriksen
Rights & Permissions: Ivar Havnevik
Founded: 1872
Subjects: Fiction, Nonfiction (General), Science (General), Social Sciences, Sociology
ISBN Prefix(es): 82-03
Subsidiaries: Kunnskapsforlaget I/S (jointly owned with Gyldendal Norsk Forlag); Olaf Norlis Bokhandel A/S (jointly owned with Norake Skog A/S); Tano A/S Forlaget; Kirkelig Kulturverksted A/S; Universitetsforlaget A/S; Yrkesopplaring ANS; Oktober Forlag A/S; Lydbokforlaget A/S
Book Club(s): Den Norske Bokklubben A/S (with three other Norwegian publishers)

Atheneum Forlag A/S+
Nesset, 1433 Vinterbro
Tel: 64978000 *Fax:* 64978001
Key Personnel
Executive Dir, Publisher, Rights & Permissions: Svenn Otto Brechan
Founded: 1934
Subjects: Art, Biography, Fiction, Poetry, Psychology, Psychiatry, Religion - Other
ISBN Prefix(es): 82-503
Associate Companies: Ansgarboker
Imprints: Ansgarboker
Warehouse: Ansgar/Atheneum, Nesset, 1433 Vinterbro

Bedriftsokonomens Forlag A/S
Postboks 9047, Groenland, 0133 Oslo

Tel: 22985800 *Fax:* 22985841
Key Personnel
Man Dir: Kai Solheim
Subjects: Economics, Management, Nonfiction (General)
ISBN Prefix(es): 82-7037

Bladkompaniet A/S+
Staalfjaera 5, Kalbakken 0902 Oslo
Mailing Address: Postboks 148, Kalbakken, 0902 Oslo
Tel: 22902400 *Fax:* 22902401
Key Personnel
Man Dir: Ole Wagenes
Dir, Rights & Permissions: Finn Arnesen
Sales & Advertising: Bjoerg Vollan
Secretary: Britt Egge Kvalheim
Founded: 1915
Subjects: Fiction
ISBN Prefix(es): 82-509

F Bruns Bokhandel og Forlag A/S
Kongensgate 10, 7005 Trondheim
Mailing Address: Postboks 476, 7005 Trondheim
Tel: 73510022 *Fax:* 73509320
E-mail: brunslb@online.no
Key Personnel
Dir: Fridthjov Brun
Founded: 1873
Subjects: Science (General), Technology
ISBN Prefix(es): 82-7028

J W Cappelens Forlag A/S
Maribosgaten 13, 0101 Sentrum, Oslo
Mailing Address: Postboks 350, Sentrum, 0101 Oslo
Tel: 22365000 *Fax:* 22365040 *Cable:* CAPPELEN
Key Personnel
Chairman: Sigmund Stromme
Man Dir: Sindre Guldvog
Editorial: Per Glad; Aase Gjerdrum; Tove Storsveel; Anders Heger; Ola Haugen
Sales: Kirsti Soegstad
Production: Kjell Nordahl
Rights & Permissions: Kirsten Lier
Editorial: Jan O Bruvik
Founded: 1829
Subjects: Fiction, Nonfiction (General), Religion - Other
ISBN Prefix(es): 82-02
Parent Company: Albert Bonniers Foerlag AB, Sweden
Subsidiaries: Bedriftsoekonomens Forlag A/S; Boksenteret A/S; Aventura Forlag A/S; Chr Grondahls Forlag A/S; Sentraldistribusson ANS
Book Club(s): Den Norske Bokklubben A/S (with three other Norwegian publishers)

Credo, imprint of Genesis Forlag

N W Damm og Son A/S
Tordenskioldsgt 6B, 0055 Oslo
Tel: 22 47 11 00 *Fax:* 22 47 11 49; 22 47 11 42
E-mail: nwd@egmont.no
Web Site: www.damm.no
Key Personnel
Man Dir: Tom H Jenssen
Founded: 1845
Subjects: Fiction, Nonfiction (General)
ISBN Prefix(es): 82-517
Parent Company: Egmont Group, Copenhagen, Denmark

Det Norske Samlaget+
Trondheimsvn 15, N-0560 Oslo
Tel: 22687600 *Fax:* 22687502
E-mail: det.norske@samlaget.no
Web Site: www.samlaget.no
Key Personnel
Man Dir: Audun Heskestad

Editorial, Rights & Permissions: Svenn Fosseng
Sales: Sjur Mossige
Production: Olav Stokkmo
Founded: 1868
Member of Den norske Forleggerforening.
Subjects: Biography, Fiction, History, Philosophy, Poetry, Religion - Other
ISBN Prefix(es): 82-521
Number of titles published annually: 200 Print
Associate Companies: Noregs Boklag L/L

J W Eides Forlag A/S+
Postboks 4081, Dreggen 5023 Bergen
Tel: 55329040 *Fax:* 55319018
Key Personnel
Man Dir: Trine Kolderup Flaten
Subjects: Art, Education, Film, Video, History, Music, Dance, Radio, TV
ISBN Prefix(es): 82-514

Elanders Publishing AS
Brobekkvn 80, Sentrum, 0107 Oslo
Mailing Address: Postboks 1156, Sentrum, 0107 Oslo
Tel: 22636400 *Fax:* 22636594
Web Site: www.elanders.no
Key Personnel
Publisher: Aina Thorstensen *Tel:* 22636281
E-mail: aina.thorstensen@elanders.no
Founded: 1844 (AS Fabritius)
Subjects: Chemistry, Chemical Engineering, Law, Maritime, Medicine, Nursing, Dentistry, Transportation
ISBN Prefix(es): 82-90545; 82-07; 82-7180
Parent Company: Elanders Norge AS
Ultimate Parent Company: Elanders AB

Ex Libris Forlag A/S+
Nordregt 22, 0505 Oslo
Mailing Address: Postboks 2130, Gruenerloekka, 0505 Oslo
Tel: 22809500 *Fax:* 22385160
E-mail: office@exlibris.no
Key Personnel
Publisher: Hagen Oyvind
Editor: Toruun Andersen
Founded: 1982
Subjects: Alternative, Cookery, Health, Nutrition, Human Relations, Humor, Publishing & Book Trade Reference
ISBN Prefix(es): 82-7384; 82-474; 82-90473

Forlaget Fag og Kultur
Biskop Jens Nilssoensgt 5A, 0659 Oslo
Mailing Address: Postbox 6633 Etterstad, 0607 Oslo
Tel: 22683630 *Fax:* 22680625
E-mail: fffk@online.no
Key Personnel
Publisher: Mari Ettre Olsen
Founded: 1987
Subjects: Gardening, Plants, Language Arts, Linguistics, Science (General), Technology
ISBN Prefix(es): 82-11

Folhenuniversitetets Forlag+
Postboks 2959, Toyen, 0608 Oslo
Tel: 22575307 *Fax:* 22575310
Key Personnel
Man Dir, Rights & Permissions: Alt Westereng
Founded: 1948
Subjects: Education, Language Arts, Linguistics
ISBN Prefix(es): 82-7020

Fonna Forlag L/L
St Olavs Plass 3, 0130 Oslo
Mailing Address: Postboks 6912, St Olavs Plass, 0130 Oslo
Tel: 22201303 *Fax:* 22201201
Founded: 1940

Subjects: Biography, Fiction, Poetry
ISBN Prefix(es): 82-513

Fono Forlag+
Billingstadsletta 30, 1376 Billingstad
Mailing Address: Postboks 135, 1312 Slependen
Tel: 66846490 *Fax:* 66847507
E-mail: mail@fonoforlag.no
Key Personnel
General Manager: Halvor Haneborg *E-mail:* h.haneborg@fonoforlag.no
Member of Norsk Forleggerforening.
Subjects: Education, Fiction, Humor, Literature, Literary Criticism, Essays, Mysteries, Nonfiction (General)
ISBN Prefix(es): 82-7844; 82-91171

Genesis Forlag+
Sentrum, 0107 Oslo
Mailing Address: PO Box 1180, 0107 Oslo
Tel: 22310310 *Fax:* 22310305
Key Personnel
Publisher: Magne Lero
International Rights: Anne Mant Jordahl
Founded: 1996
Subjects: Biography, Health, Nutrition, Human Relations, Nonfiction (General), Psychology, Psychiatry, Religion - Protestant, Theology
ISBN Prefix(es): 82-476
Parent Company: Vaart Land
Imprints: Credo

Glydendal Akademisk+
Formerly Ad-Notam Glydendal
Subsidiary of Gyldendal Norsk Forlag
Kristian IVs g 13, 0164 Oslo
Mailing Address: PO Box 6730, St Olavs Pl, 0130 Oslo
Tel: (022) 034300 *Fax:* (022) 034305
Key Personnel
Man Dir: Fredrik Nissen *E-mail:* fredrik.nissen@gyldendal.no
Founded: 1988
Subjects: Accounting, Business, Economics, Education, Finance, Government, Political Science, Health, Nutrition, Law, Medicine, Nursing, Dentistry, Philosophy, Psychology, Psychiatry, Social Sciences, Sociology
ISBN Prefix(es): 82-05
Number of titles published annually: 100 Print

John Grieg Forlag AS
Valkendorfs gt 1a, 5012 Bergen
Mailing Address: Postboks 13, 5062 Bones
Tel: 55213181 *Fax:* 55218180 *Cable:* Bokgrieg
Key Personnel
Man Dir: Hermond J Berg Lindersen
Founded: 1721
Subjects: Fiction, Nonfiction (General), Sports, Athletics
ISBN Prefix(es): 82-533; 82-7129

Gyldendal Norsk Forlag A/S+
Sehestedsgt 4, 0130 Oslo
Mailing Address: Postboks 6860, St Olavs plass, 0130 Oslo
Tel: 22034100 *Fax:* 22034105
E-mail: gnf@gyldendal.no
Web Site: www.gyldendal.no
Telex: 72880 Gyldn n *Cable:* Gyldendal
Key Personnel
Man Dir: Bjorgun Hysing
Dir, Marketing: Jorgen Klafstad
Dir, Educational: Paul Hedlund
Dir, Fiction: Bjarne Buset
Dir, Nonfiction & Children: Unni Fjesme
Dir, Legal: Torger Andersen
Dir, University Press: Fredrik Nissen
Rights & Permissions: Eva Lie-Nielsen
Founded: 1925
Subjects: Art, Biography, Fiction, Government, Political Science, History, How-to, Music, Dance, Philosophy, Poetry, Psychology, Psychi-

atry, Religion - Other, Science Fiction, Fantasy, Social Sciences, Sociology
ISBN Prefix(es): 82-05
Subsidiaries: Kunnskapsforlaget I/S (jointly owned with H Aschehoug & Co A/S)
Book Club(s): Den Norske Bokklubben A/S (with three other Norwegian publishers)

Hilt & Hansteen A/S+
Postboks 2040, Gruenerlokka, 0505 Oslo
Tel: 22384010 Fax: 22374015
Telex: 72400 fotex n att: hiltoslo Cable: HILTOSLO
Key Personnel
Publisher: Bjorn Hansteen Fossum; Torstein Hilt E-mail: torstein.hilt@genrica.no
Founded: 1983
Subjects: Alternative, Health, Nutrition, Human Relations, Mysteries, Parapsychology, Self-Help
ISBN Prefix(es): 82-7413
Book Club(s): Bokklubben Energica A/S
Orders to: Forlagsentralen I/S, Postboks 1, 1010 Oslo

Hjemmenes Forlag
Postboks 25 Holmenkollen, 0324 Oslo
Tel: 22143151 Fax: 22920738
Key Personnel
Publisher: Yngve Woxholth
Subjects: Ethnicity, History
ISBN Prefix(es): 82-7006

Egmont Hjemmets Bokforlag AS
Tordenskioldsgate 6 B, 0055 Oslo
Tel: 22471000 Fax: 22471098
E-mail: egmont@egmont.com
Web Site: www.egmont.com
Key Personnel
Man Dir: Cato Praner
Founded: 1969
Subjects: Fiction, Nonfiction (General)
ISBN Prefix(es): 82-590; 82-7001
Parent Company: Egmont
Associate Companies: Egmont Serieforlaget AS, Oslo Tel: 22471300 Fax: 22471373; NY Lademann A/S, Denmark; Egmont Horizont Verlag GmbH, Germany Web Site: www.egmont-horizont.funonline.de; Richters AB, Sweden; N W Damm og Son A/S, Oslo; Fredhois A/S, Oslo; Edgemont Litor AS, Oslo Tel: 22471250 Fax: 22471289
Book Club(s): Hjemmets Bokklubb; Bokklubben Ny Krim; Bokklubben Virkelighetens Verden; Bokklubben Feminina; Bokklubben Bedre Ledelse; Damms Junior Bokklubb; Donald Duck Bokklubb; Bokklubben Damms Leselover; Jorden Rundt med Disney's Beste; Mikkes Trafikk Skole

Kolibri Forlag A/S
Huk Aveny 2B, Bygdoy, 0211 Oslo
Mailing Address: Postboks 33, Bygdoy, 0211 Oslo
Tel: 22438778 Fax: 22447740
ISBN Prefix(es): 82-7917; 82-90478

Kunnskapsforlaget ANS
Postboks 6736, 0130 St Olavs Plass, Oslo
Tel: 22036600 Fax: 22036605
E-mail: gunnar.sveen@Kunnskapsforlaget.no
Key Personnel
Man Dir: Harald S Stromme
Sales Dir: Tor Hallaraker
Chief Editor: Petter Henricksen
Multimedia Man: Finn Jorgen Solberg
Production: Svein F Heige
Founded: 1975
ISBN Prefix(es): 82-573
Parent Company: H Aschehoug & Co A/S, Gyldendal Norsk Forlag; Gyldendal Norah Forlag ASA

Libretto Forlag+
Eilert Sundts Gate 32, 0259 Oslo
Tel: (022) 443011 Fax: (022) 443012
Key Personnel
Publisher: Tom Thorsteinsen E-mail: tomthor@online.no
Founded: 1991
ISBN Prefix(es): 82-91091; 82-7886

Lunde Forlag og Bokhandel A/S+
Grensen 19, 0159 Oslo
Tel: 22007365 Fax: 22007373
E-mail: lunde@nlm.no
Telex: 74185 normi n Cable: NORSKLUTH
Key Personnel
President & Publisher: Asbjorn Kvalbein
Production & International Rights: Olaug Fonnes
Editor: Inger Holter
Founded: 1905
Subjects: Biography, Education, Fiction, Poetry, Religion - Other, Theology
ISBN Prefix(es): 82-520
Total Titles: 250 Print
Bookshop(s): Lunde Forlag og Bokhandel A/S, Sinsenveien 25, 0572 Oslo, Contact: Kjetil Gjaerde Tel: 22007350 Fax: 22007373 E-mail: lunde@nlm.no
Book Club(s): Perspektiv, P O Box 4007, 4602 Kristiansand, Contact: Mr Ingar Hjelset Tel: 38199055 Fax: 38199056

Luther Forlag A/S
Postboks 6640, St Olaus Pl, 0129 Oslo
Tel: 22330608 Fax: 22421000
E-mail: post@lutherforlag.no
Key Personnel
Man Dir: Kurt Hjemdal; Asle Dingstad
Founded: 1868
Subjects: Biography, Fiction, Religion - Protestant, Religion - Other
ISBN Prefix(es): 82-531
Number of titles published annually: 40 Print
Total Titles: 250 Print

Ernst G Mortensens Forlag A/S+
Soerkedalsveien 10 A, Majorstua, 3 Oslo
Tel: 22941000 Fax: 22113040
Telex: 77626 Cable: Pressmort
Key Personnel
Man Dir: Per Stokken
Editorial: Solveig Hoysaeter; Knut Enger
Sales: Egil Storaas
Information: Knut-Jorgen Erichsen
Advertising: R Marthinsen
Rights & Permissions: Per R Mortensen
Founded: 1933
ISBN Prefix(es): 82-527
Subsidiaries: NPS (Norsk Presseservice A/S; Forenede Trykkerier A/S

NKI Forlaget
Hans Burums Vei 30, N-1341 Bekkestua
Mailing Address: Postboks 111, N-1341 Bekkestua
Tel: 67588800 Fax: 67581902
Key Personnel
Publisher: Marit Anmarkrud
Sales & Marketing Manager: Randi Flugstad
Founded: 1967
Subjects: Chemistry, Chemical Engineering, Electronics, Electrical Engineering, English as a Second Language, Environmental Studies, Mathematics, Mechanical Engineering, Physics, Transportation
ISBN Prefix(es): 82-562

Norsk Bokreidingslag L/L
Postboks 684, 5807 Bergen
Tel: 55301899 Fax: 55320356
E-mail: post@bodonihus.no
Key Personnel
Manager: Jon Askeland Tel: (047) 55589303 E-mail: jon.askeland@sfu.vib.no
Founded: 1939
Subjects: Fiction, History, Language Arts, Linguistics, Poetry
ISBN Prefix(es): 82-90186; 82-7834
Number of titles published annually: 4 Print

Novus Forlag+
Herman Foss' Gate 19, 0171 Oslo
Tel: (022) 717450 Fax: (022) 718107
E-mail: novus@novus.no
Web Site: www.novus.no
Key Personnel
Publisher: Olav Rosset
Founded: 1972
Subjects: Education, Science (General)
ISBN Prefix(es): 82-7099
Total Titles: 300 Print

Forlaget Oktober A/S
kr Augustsgt 11, 0130 Oslo
Mailing Address: PO Box 6848, St Olaus Pl, 0130 Oslo
Tel: 22207760 Fax: 22207765
E-mail: oktober@aschehoug.no
Key Personnel
Publisher: Geir Berdahl
ISBN Prefix(es): 82-7094

Omnipax, *imprint of* Pax Forlag A/S

Origo Forlag
Postboks 28, 0905 Grorud, Oslo
Tel: 22160769 Fax: 22164837
Key Personnel
President: Leif-Runa R Forsth
Editor: Bodil Nordvik
ISBN Prefix(es): 82-597

Pax Forlag A/S+
Huitfeldtsgt 15, N-0201 Oslo
Mailing Address: Postboks 2336 Solli, N-0201 Oslo
Tel: (023) 136900 Fax: (023) 136919
Key Personnel
Man Dir: Bjorn Smith Simonsen
Editorial & Rights & Permissions: Birgit Bjerck
Founded: 1964
Subjects: Fiction, Nonfiction (General), Philosophy, Psychology, Psychiatry, Social Sciences, Sociology, Women's Studies
ISBN Prefix(es): 82-530
Imprints: Omnipax (Children's books)

Sambandet Forlag+
Vestlandskes bokhandel, Vetrisalm, 1, 5014 Bergen
Tel: 55317963 Fax: 55310944
E-mail: vestlandskes.bokhandel@c2i.net
Key Personnel
Publishing Dir: Ingar Hjelset
Founded: 1945
Subjects: Religion - Other
ISBN Prefix(es): 82-7752

Erik Sandberg+
Kongensgt 14, 0153 Oslo
Tel: 22335555 Fax: 22413562
Telex: 17580
Key Personnel
Chief Executive, Rights & Permissions: Trond Wikborg
Editorial: Arild Ronsen; Per Martinsen
Sales: Tor Nilsen
Production: Iril Kolle
Publicity: Solveig Thime
Founded: 1973
Subjects: Fiction, Nonfiction (General)
ISBN Prefix(es): 82-7316; 82-90160

PUBLISHERS

NORWAY

Sandviks Bokforlag+
Sverdrupsgt 23, 4007 Stavanger
Tel: 51510000 *Fax:* 51526009
Key Personnel
Publisher: Sigurd Sandvik
Editor: Eli Aleksandersen Cantillon
Project Manager: Nina Sandvik Bashforth
Publisher, International Log Book: Mark A Bashforth
President, Baby's First Book Club: Mikkel Sandvik
Founded: 1965
Subjects: Health, Nutrition, Maritime, Medicine, Nursing, Dentistry
ISBN Prefix(es): 82-7106
Subsidiaries: The International Log Book, Bath (UK & Stavanger); Go'boken Book Club, Helsingborg, Sweden & Stavanger; Baby's First Book Club
U.S. Office(s): Sandvik Publishing Ltd, Folcroft, PA, United States
Warehouse: DFU-huset, Figgjo

Scandinavian University Press, see Universitetsforlaget

Chr Schibsteds Forlag A/S+
Akersgaten 32, N-0107 Sentrum, Oslo 1
Mailing Address: Postboks 1178, N-0107 Sentrum, Oslo
Tel: 22863000 *Fax:* 22425492
Telex: 71230 aft n
Key Personnel
Man Dir, Rights & Permissions: Per G Damsgaard
Sales Dir: Lise Hammergren
Founded: 1839
Subjects: Biography, Earth Sciences, How-to
ISBN Prefix(es): 82-516
Parent Company: Schibsted ASA, Akersgaten 32, N-0107 Sentrum
Warehouse: Forlagsentralen, Postboks 1, Furuset, N-1001 Oslo 10
Orders to: Forlagsentralen, Postboks 1, Furuset, N-1001 Oslo 10

Skolebokforlaget A/S+
Postboks 1153, Sentrum, 0107 Oslo
Tel: 22335686 *Fax:* 22335805
Key Personnel
Man Dir: Hans B Butenschon
Textbooks Manager: Anne-Lise Gjerdrum
Founded: 1979
Subjects: Education
ISBN Prefix(es): 82-7317
Warehouse: Vestmarksvn 108, N-1300 Sandvika
Orders to: Sentraldistribusjon, Risalleen 5, N-0374 Oslo 3

Snofugl Forlag+
Postboks 95, 7084 Melhus 7221
Tel: 72872411 *Fax:* 72871013
Key Personnel
Manager: Asmund Snofugl
Founded: 1972
Member of Den Norske Forleggerforening.
Subjects: Biography, Fiction, Government, Political Science, History, Literature, Literary Criticism, Essays, Nonfiction (General), Poetry
ISBN Prefix(es): 82-7083
Total Titles: 150 Print
Associate Companies: A/S Bygdetrykk, N-7084 Melhus
Warehouse: Melhus skysstasjon, 7221 Melhus

Solum Forlag A/S+
Hoffsvn 18, 0212 Skoyen, Oslo
Mailing Address: Postboks 140, 0212 Skoyen, Oslo
Tel: 22500400 *Fax:* 22501453
E-mail: solumfor@online.no
Web Site: www.solumforlag.no
Key Personnel
Man Dir: Knut Endre Solum
Founded: 1974
Subjects: Disability, Special Needs, Fiction, Poetry, Science (General), Educational materials, Humanities
ISBN Prefix(es): 82-560
Distributed by International Specialized Book Service (USA)

Stabenfeldt A/S+
Haugesundsgate 43, 4004 Kjelvene, Stavanger
Mailing Address: Postboks 1544, 4004 Kjelvene, Stavanger
Tel: 51845400 *Fax:* 51526217 *Cable:* BOKORM
Key Personnel
Man Dir: Tor Tjeldflat
Marketing Dir: J O Skara Hansen
Founded: 1920
Subjects: Fiction, Nonfiction (General)
ISBN Prefix(es): 82-532
Parent Company: Bongs AB, Sweden
Divisions: Stabenfeldt AB, Malmoe, Sweden

Teknologisk Forlag
Tordenskioldsgt 6B, 0055 Oslo
Tel: 22471100 *Fax:* 22471149
Key Personnel
Man Dir, Rights & Permissions: Rudolf Jenssen
Assistant Dir: Tom Harald Jenssen
Editorial Dir: Tore Egeberg
Sales Dir: Karl H Ormen
Founded: 1958
Subjects: Engineering (General), How-to, Philosophy, Science (General)
ISBN Prefix(es): 82-512

Tell Forlag+
Nilsemarka 5c, 1390 Vollen
Mailing Address: Postboks 62, 1390 Vollen
Tel: 66780918 *Fax:* 66900572
E-mail: tell@online.no
Web Site: www.tell.no
Key Personnel
Publisher: Tell-Chr Wagle
Founded: 1987
Subjects: Art, Crafts, Games, Hobbies, Dance, Educational Books, Textbooks, Theatre
ISBN Prefix(es): 82-7522
Number of titles published annually: 25 Print

Tiden Norsk Forlag
Storgt 23d, Oslo
Mailing Address: PO Box 8813 Youngstorget, 0028 Oslo
Tel: 22007100 *Fax:* 22426458
E-mail: trine.lise.linnestad@tiden.no *Cable:* TIDEN
Key Personnel
Dir: Liv Lysaker
Editorial, Rights & Permissions: Per Bangsund; Bjorn Willadssen
Production: Torgeir Aass
Founded: 1933
Subjects: Fiction, Literature, Literary Criticism, Essays, Management, Nonfiction (General), Science Fiction, Fantasy
ISBN Prefix(es): 82-10; 82-990075
Book Club(s): Den Norske Bokklubben A/S (with three other Norwegian publishers)

Universitetsforlaget+
Kolstadgt 1, Toyen, 0600 Oslo
Mailing Address: Postboks 2959, Toyen, 0608 Oslo
Tel: 22575300 *Fax:* 22575353
E-mail: books@scup.no; journals@scup.no
Web Site: www.scup.no
Telex: 11896 Ufor N
  Cable: UNIVERSITYPRESS, OSLO
Key Personnel
Man Dir: Ms Siri Hatlen *Fax:* (022) 575354
E-mail: sha@scup.no
Publishing Dir, Books: Ms Inger M Tellefsen
Tel: 22575496 *Fax:* 22575352 *E-mail:* ite@scup.no
Publishing Dir, Journals: Mr Arne Henrik Frogh
Tel: 22575349 *Fax:* 22575454 *E-mail:* afr@scup.no
Personnel Dir: Ms Randi Bauer *Tel:* 22575386
Fax: 22575352 *E-mail:* rba@scup.no
Head of Marketing, Books: Ms Anne Borch-Nielson *Tel:* 22575490 *E-mail:* ani@scup.no
Head of Marketing, Journals: Ms Claire Sharp-Sundt *Tel:* 22575414 *Fax:* 22575454
E-mail: csu@scup.no
Rights Manager: Mr Lars Allden *Tel:* 22575401
Fax: 22575499 *E-mail:* lal@scup.no
Founded: 1950
Scandinavian University Press.
Publishers for Scandinavian Universities & other institutions of higher learning, Learned Societies of Scandinavia. Member of: STM, Norwegian Publishers' Association, European Union Publishers Forum & EEPG.
Subjects: Behavioral Sciences, Business, Education, Language Arts, Linguistics, Law, Mechanical Engineering, Medicine, Nursing, Dentistry, Philosophy, Science (General), Modern language & Healthcare
ISBN Prefix(es): 82-00
Total Titles: 2,000 Print; 10 CD-ROM; 35 Online; 20 Audio
Subsidiaries: Scandinavian University Press
Branch Office(s)
Scandinavian University Press United Kingdom, 60 St Aldates, Oxford OX1 1ST, United Kingdom, Mr George Drennan *Tel:* (01865) 791 891 *Fax:* (01865) 791 891
Stockholm, Sweden
Copenhagen, Denmark
U.S. Office(s): Scandinavian University Press North America, 875 Massachusetts Ave, Suite 84, Cambridge, MA 02139, United States, Contact: Mr Charles Germain *Tel:* 617-497-6515 *Fax:* 617-354-6875 *E-mail:* 75201.571@compuserve.com
Membership(s): American Association of University Presses

Verbum Forlag
Underhaugsv 15, Oslo
Mailing Address: PO Box 7062, Majorstuen, 0306 Oslo
Tel: 22932700 *Fax:* 22697313

Vett & Viten AS+
Vakaas vn 7, Hvalstad, Asker
Mailing Address: Postboks 203, 1379 Nesbru
Tel: 66849040 *Fax:* 66845590
E-mail: vv@vettviten.no
Web Site: www.vettviten.no
Key Personnel
Publisher: Jan Lien *Tel:* 66983984 *E-mail:* jan.lien@vettviten.no
Marketing & Sales: Tormod Tvinnereim
E-mail: tormod.tvinnereim@vettviten.no
Finance: Jan Kveine *Tel:* 66983982 *E-mail:* jan.kveine@vettviten.no
Founded: 1987
Subjects: Computer Science, Earth Sciences, Electronics, Electrical Engineering, Engineering (General), Environmental Studies, Film, Video, Geography, Geology, Medicine, Nursing, Dentistry, Radio, TV, Technology, Specialize in Dance
ISBN Prefix(es): 82-412
Number of titles published annually: 50 Print; 20 E-Book
Total Titles: 350 Print
Divisions: Norsk Bokdistribusjon (Computer Books)

Branch Office(s)
Vett & Viten Toensberg, Fjordgaten 13, N-3125 Toensberg, Ragnar Kihle *Tel:* 33381900 *Fax:* 33381901 *E-mail:* ragnar.kihl@vettviten.no
Sales Office(s): J A Sisson, 8713 Prudence Dr, Annadale, VA 22003, United States

Oman

General Information

Capital: Muscat
Language: Arabic, English in business
Religion: Predominantly Muslim (mostly Ibadi, some Sunni)
Population: 1.6 million
Currency: 1,000 baiza = 1 rial Omani

Apex Publishing
PO Box 2616 Ruwi, Way No 2706, 112 Muscat
Tel: 799388 *Fax:* 793316
E-mail: apexoman@gto.net.om
Key Personnel
President: Saleh M Talib
Editor: Anju Visen-Singh
Founded: 1980
Specialize in Oman.
Subjects: Art, Business, Gardening, Plants, History, Outdoor Recreation, Travel

Pakistan

General Information

Capital: Islamabad
Language: Urdu is national language but English is used extensively. Other principal languages are Punjabi, Pushto, Sindhi and Saraiki
Religion: Predominantly Islamic
Population: 121.7 million
Bank Hours: 0900-1300 Saturday-Wednesday; 0900-1100 Thursday
Shop Hours: 0930-1300, 1500-2000 Saturday-Thursday
Currency: 100 paisa = 1 Pakistan rupee
Export/Import Information: No tariff on books, magazines and advertising matter. Import license issued freely if required. Anti-Islamic and obscene literature prohibited. Exchange controls.
Copyright: UCC, Berne, Buenos Aires, Florence (see Copyright Conventions, pg xi)

Academy of Education Planning & Management (AEPAM)
Ministry of Education, Sariya Chowk G-8/1, Islamabad 44000
Mailing Address: PO Box 1566, Islamabad 44000
Tel: (051) 250731 *Fax:* (051) 856495 *Cable:* AEPAM
Key Personnel
Chief Documentation Officer: M H Shabab
Founded: 1982
Subjects: Economics, Education, English as a Second Language, Library & Information Sciences, Management, Microcomputers
ISBN Prefix(es): 969-444
Parent Company: Ministry of Education

Admission Times International, *imprint of* International Educational Services

AEPAM, see Academy of Education Planning & Management (AEPAM)

Aina-e-Adab
Chowk Minar Anarkali, Lahore 1
Tel: (042) 54069
Key Personnel
Proprietor: Sh Abdul Salam
ISBN Prefix(es): 969-430

Sheikh Shaukat Ali & Sons+
Urdu Bazar, MA Jinnah Rd, Karachi 74200
Tel: (021) 214585 *Fax:* (021) 212289
Subjects: Poetry, Religion - Islamic
ISBN Prefix(es): 969-440
Branch Office(s)
Mian Market, Ghazni St, Lahore

Sheikh Muhammad Ashraf Publishers
7 Aibak Rd, New Anarkali, Lahore 7
Tel: (042) 353171; (042) 353489 *Fax:* (042) 353489 *Cable:* ISLAMICLIT LAHORE
Key Personnel
Publisher: Sh Muhammad Ashraf
Man Dir: Sh Shahzad Riaz
Home Sales: Muhammad Hamayun
Export Sales: Muhammad Amin
Literary Adviser: A Hassan
Founded: 1923
Subjects: Biography, Geography, Geology, Government, Political Science, History, Law, Religion - Other
ISBN Prefix(es): 969-432
U.S. Office(s): Specialty Promotions Co Inc, 841 S Cregier Ave, Chicago, IL 60649, United States
Halalco Books, 108 E Fairfax St, Falls Churchs, VA 20046, United States
Bookshop(s): Ghazni St, Urdu Bazar; Kashmiri Bazar
Warehouse: 9 Aibak Rd, New Anarkali, Lahore 7

ASR Publications+
96-a, G block, Gulberg III, Lahore
Mailing Address: PO Box 3154, Gulberg-2, Lahore
Tel: (042) 5882617; (042) 5882618; (042) 877613; (42) 877496 *Fax:* (042) 5882617; (042) 5711575
E-mail: iwsl@asr.edunet.sdnpk.undp.org or iwsl@asr.brain.net.pk *Cable:* SOCFEM
Key Personnel
International Rights: Nighat Said Khan
Subjects: Women's Studies
ISBN Prefix(es): 969-8217
Distributed by Mr Books; Saeed Book Bank

The Book House+
8 Malik Jala Trust Bldg, Urdu Bazar, Lahore 2
Mailing Address: PO Box 734, Urdu Bazar, Lahore 54000
Tel: (042) 61212; (042) 232415 *Fax:* (042) 6360955 *Cable:* BOOKHOUSE
Key Personnel
Proprietor: Muhammad Saeed
General Manager: Muhammad Sheikh Saeed
Founded: 1951
Exporters of English & Urdu books & Textbooks.
Subjects: Antiques, Education
ISBN Prefix(es): 969-437

Centre for South Asian Studies
Quaid-e-Azam Campus, Univ Punjab, Lahore 54590
Tel: (042) 5864014 *Fax:* (042) 5867206 *Cable:* SASCUP
Key Personnel
Patron-in-Chief: Dr Rafique Ahmad
Dir & Editor: Dr Sarfaraz Hussain Mirza
Publication Officer: Ovais Nizaini
E-mail: ovaisn@hotmail.com

Subjects: Asian Studies, Ethnicity, Government, Political Science
ISBN Prefix(es): 969-471

Classic+
42 The Mall, Lahore 54000
Tel: (042) 323963; (042) 312977 *Fax:* (042) 7238236 *Cable:* CLASSIC LAHORE
Key Personnel
Man Dir, Editorial, Production, Permissions: Agha Amir Hussain
Sales, Publicity: S Rashid Hussain Agha
Founded: 1956
Subjects: Art, Fiction
ISBN Prefix(es): 969-28; 969-8136
Parent Company: Classic Publishers & Booksellers
Associate Companies: Menarva Publications, Lahore
Subsidiaries: Shish Mahal Kitab Ghar; Classic Bookshop

East & West Publishing Co+
22-Corner Chambers, L L Chundrigar Rd, Karachi 74200
Tel: (021) 212036 *Fax:* (021) 7784362 *Cable:* GOODBOOKS
Key Personnel
Publisher: Rafique Akhtar
Man Dir: Dr Nasir Rafique
Founded: 1971
Subjects: Biography, Regional Interests
ISBN Prefix(es): 969-8017

Fazlee Sons (Pvt) Ltd+
Temple Rd, Urdu Bazar, 74200 Karachi
Tel: (021) 214585; (021) 212289 *Fax:* (021) 6640522
E-mail: fazlee@tarique.khi.sdnpk.undp.org
Founded: 1948
Member of Association of Pakistan Printing & Graphic Arts Industry (PAPGAI); Pakistan Booksellers & Publishers Association (PBSPA).
Subjects: Literature, Literary Criticism, Essays, Religion - Other
ISBN Prefix(es): 969-441
Associate Companies: Printing Services (Pvt) Ltd
Subsidiaries: IS Asia
Bookshop(s): Fazlee Book Supermarket, 4 Mama Parsi Bldg, Temple Rd, Urdu Bazar, Karachi 74200
Orders to: 1-K-5/A, Commercial Area, Nazimabad No 1, Karachi *Tel:* 6622212-5

Ferozsons (Private) Ltd
60 Shahrah-e-Quaid-e-Azam, Lahore
Tel: (042) 6301196; (042) 6301197; (042) 6301198 *Fax:* (042) 6369204
E-mail: ferozsons@showroom.edunet.sdnpk.undp.org
Telex: 44382 Feroz PK *Cable:* FEROZSONS
Key Personnel
Man Dir, Publicity: A Salam
Editorial, Sales Dir: Mr Zaheer Salam
Founded: 1894
Subjects: Regional Interests, Religion - Islamic
ISBN Prefix(es): 969-0
Branch Office(s)
33/C-6, Karachi 29

H I Jaffari & Co Publishers+
Tahir Plaza 37/B, Blue Area, Islamabad 440000
Tel: (051) 811153 *Cable:* AMBOOKCO
Key Personnel
President: Hasan I Jaffri
Vice President: Raza I Jaffri
Contact: Muneer Hussain
Founded: 1959
Member of Pakistan Publishers & Booksellers Association (Federal Zone) Islamabad.

Subjects: History, Poetry, Religion - Islamic, Sports, Athletics
ISBN Prefix(es): 969-467
Subsidiaries: American Book Co

Hamdard Foundation+
Hamdard Centre, Nazimabad, Karachi 74600
Tel: (021) 6616001; (021) 6616002; (021) 6616003; (021) 6616004; (021) 641766
Fax: (021) 6611755
E-mail: hlpak@net3.ptc.pk
Telex: 29370 Hamd pk
Key Personnel
President: Hakim Mohammed Said
Founded: 1953
Subjects: Biography, Education, History, Library & Information Sciences, Literature, Literary Criticism, Essays, Medicine, Nursing, Dentistry, Philosophy, Religion - Islamic, Science (General), Social Sciences, Sociology
ISBN Prefix(es): 969-412
Parent Company: Hamdard Laboratories (Waqf)
Branch Office(s)
Karachi
Lahore
Peshawar
Rawalpindi
Bookshop(s): Hamdard Kitabistan, Seva Kunj Building, Shahrah-e-Liaqua, Karachi *Tel:* (021) 3371

HMR Publishing Co+
725, Shadman House, Main Bullavard Shadmad Colony, Lahore
Tel: (042) 7588972; (042) 7588967 *Fax:* (042) 7581212
Key Personnel
Man Dir: M Akhter *E-mail:* makhter@1hr.comsats.net.lk
Founded: 1986
Subjects: Biological Sciences, Health, Nutrition, Medicine, Nursing, Dentistry, Religion - Islamic, Science (General)
ISBN Prefix(es): 969-8019

Idara-e-Tehqiqat-e-Islami
Shah Faisal Masjid, Islamabad
Mailing Address: PO Box 1035, Islamabad
Tel: (051) 850751-5; (051) 850755
Telex: 54068 IIU Pak *Cable:* ISLAMSERCH
Key Personnel
Contact: Mr Zafar Ishaque Ansary
ISBN Prefix(es): 969-408

Idara Siqafat-e-Islamia
Club Rd, Lahore 3
Tel: (042) 53908
ISBN Prefix(es): 969-429

Institute of Islamic Culture
2 Club Rd, Lahore 3
Tel: (042) 305920; (042) 6363127 *Cable:* ICULT
Founded: 1950
Subjects: Religion - Islamic
ISBN Prefix(es): 969-469

International Educational Services+
617 Husain Centre, Shahrah-e-Iraq, Saddar, Karachi
Mailing Address: PO Box 10505, Karachi
Tel: (021) 521540
Key Personnel
Executive Dir: Mohammad S Mirza
Founded: 1980
Subjects: Advertising, Business, Education, English as a Second Language, Language Arts, Linguistics, Management, Marketing, Publishing & Book Trade Reference
ISBN Prefix(es): 969-33
Imprints: Admission Times International

International Institute of Islamic Thought+
28 Main Rd, F-10/2, Islamabad
Mailing Address: POB 1959, Islamabad
Tel: (051) 851621 *Fax:* (051) 280489
E-mail: iiipak@paknet1.ptc.pk
Key Personnel
Man Dir, Editorial, Publicity, Rights & Permissions: Muhammad Jamil
Production: Zeb Alam
Founded: 1981
Subjects: Ethnicity, Religion - Islamic
ISBN Prefix(es): 969-462

Islamabad, *imprint of* Pakistan Institute of Development Economics

Islamic Book Centre+
25B Masson Rd, Lahore 54000
Mailing Address: Post Box 1625, Lahore 54000
Tel: (042) 6316803 *Fax:* (042) 6360955
Cable: ISLAMIBOOK
Key Personnel
Man & Publicity Dir: Muhammad Sajid Saeed
Sales, Advertising Dir & Proprietor: Muhammad Hamid Saeed
Founded: 1961
Subjects: Religion - Other
ISBN Prefix(es): 969-436
Subsidiaries: Book House
Branch Office(s)
26 Paisa Akhbar (Anarkali), Lahore 2 *Tel:* (042) 61212
Malik, Jal-al Bldg, Urdu Bazar, Lahore 54000

Islamic Publications (Pvt) Ltd
13-E Shahalam Market, Lahore 54000
Tel: (042) 7325243; (042) 7664504; (042) 325243; (042) 3664504 *Fax:* (042) 7658674
E-mail: islamic@ms.net.pk *Cable:* ALILM
Key Personnel
Man Dir: Prof Muhammad Amin Javed
General Manager: Muhammad Munir Afzal *Tel:* (042) 7669546
Finance Manager: Abdul Ghaffar
Founded: 1960
Specialize in literature on Islam.
Member of Lahore Chamber of Commerce & Industry, Pakistan Publishers & Booksellers Association.
Subjects: Religion - Islamic
ISBN Prefix(es): 969-423
Number of titles published annually: 20 Print
Total Titles: 700 Print
Parent Company: Corporate Law Authority (Pakistan)
Showroom(s): Islamic Publications, 10-Chaterjee Rd, Urdu Bazar, Lahore
Bookshop(s): Islamic Publications, 10-Chaterjee Rd, Urdu Bazar, Lahore

Islamic Research Institute
International Islamic University, 28A, Main Road, F-10/2, 44000 Islamabad
Mailing Address: PO Box 1959, Faisal Mosque Complex, 44000 Islamabad
Tel: (051) 851621 *Fax:* (051) 853360
E-mail: dg-iri@iri-iiu.sdnpd.undp.org
Telex: 54068 IIU Pak *Cable:* Islamserch
Key Personnel
Dir-General: Dr Zafar Ishaque Ansari
Sales: Mumtaz Liaqat
Founded: 1960
The Institute is a Faculty of the International Islamic University, Islamabad.
Subjects: History, Law, Religion - Other
ISBN Prefix(es): 969-462

Jang Publishers+
13-Sir Aga Khan Rd, Lahore
Tel: (042) 6367480-83 *Fax:* (042) 6361026; (042) 6362316
E-mail: thenewslhr@jang.group.com
Web Site: www.jang-group.com
Telex: 44103 JANG PK *Cable:* Daily JANG
Key Personnel
Chief Editor: Shakeel ur Rehman *Tel:* (042) 6367480-3
Editor-in-Charge: Muzaffar Muhammad Ali *Tel:* (042) 630780-3,4; 7847219
Founded: 1985
Printing, marketing.
Specializes in Political Autobiography, Pakistani Politics & National Current History.
Subjects: Cookery, Government, Political Science, History, Humor, Literature, Literary Criticism, Essays, Mysteries, Nonfiction (General), Poetry, Regional Interests, Religion - Islamic, Sports, Athletics, Travel
ISBN Prefix(es): 969-36
Total Titles: 325 Print
Parent Company: Jang Group of Newspapers
Ultimate Parent Company: Jang Enterprises Ltd
Associate Companies: Daily AWAM; Daily AWAZ; Daily Jang (URDU); Daily The News International; Daily News; Weekly Akhbar-e-Jehan; Weekly Mag
Subsidiaries: Jang Publishers Press
Distributed by Welcome Book Port
Book Club(s): Jang Book Club, 13-Sir Aga Khan Rd, Lahore, Contact: Syed Mohammad Anis *Tel:* (042) 6367480-83

Library Promotion Bureau+
Karachi University Campus, Dastagir Society, Federal B Area, Karachi 75270
Mailing Address: PO Box 8421, Karachi 75270
Tel: (021) 6335605
Key Personnel
President: M Adil Usmani
Vice President: Dr G A Sabzwari
Secretary General: Nasim Fatima
Man Editor: R A Samdani
Founded: 1966
Subjects: Library & Information Sciences
ISBN Prefix(es): 969-459
Distributed by M S Royal Book Co

Maktaba-i-Danial, *imprint of* Pakistan Publishing House

Malik Sirajuddin & Sons+
Kashmiri Bazar, Lahore 8
Tel: (042) 7657527 *Fax:* (042) 7657490
E-mail: sirajco@brain.net.pk
Telex: 44942 CTOLH PK *Cable:* TAJIRKUTUB; LAHORE
Key Personnel
Man Dir: A R Malik *Tel:* (042) 7225809
Editorial, Publicity: S A Malik *Tel:* (042) 5867839 *Fax:* (042) 5861620
Sales: A A Malik *Tel:* (042) 7225812 *Fax:* (042) 7224586
Founded: 1934
Subjects: Biography, Fiction, How-to, Psychology, Psychiatry, Religion - Islamic
ISBN Prefix(es): 969-29
Associate Companies: Gul I Khandan, Urdu Monthly, Kashmiri Baza, Lahore 8; Islamic Juntri, Kashmiri Baza, Lahore 8
Subsidiaries: Siraj Mohammadi Press; Ayaz Book Binding Works
Branch Office(s)
Chowk Urdu Bazar, Lahore *Tel:* (042) 7666226, (042) 7669062 *Fax:* (042) 7224586
E-mail: sirajco@brain.net.pk
18-19 M J Hospital (WAQF), O/S Mori Gate, Circular Rd, Lahore
Shipping Address: 48C Lower Mall Rd, PO Box 2250, Lahore, Ayaz Ahmad Malik *Tel:* (042) 7225809, (042) 7225812 *Fax:* (042) 7224586
E-mail: sirajco@brain.net.pk

PAKISTAN

Maqbool Academy+
Member of Lahore Chamber of Commerce & Industries
199 Circular Rd, Chowk Anarkali, Lahore 2
Tel: (042) 7233165 *Fax:* (042) 7324164
Key Personnel
Proprietor: Maqbool Ahmed Malik *Tel:* (042) 7324164 *Fax:* (042) 7324164
Chief Executive: Dr Zafar Maqbool
 E-mail: zmaqbool@yahoo.com
Founded: 1954
Subjects: Asian Studies, Cookery, Drama, Theater, Education, Fashion, Fiction, Gardening, Plants, Government, Political Science, History, Humor, Literature, Literary Criticism, Essays, Poetry, Religion - Islamic, Religion - Other, Romance, Science (General)
ISBN Prefix(es): 969-442; 969-510
Total Titles: 100 Print
Associate Companies: Maqbool Books, Abuzar Lentre Modeltown Link Rd, Lahore *Tel:* (042) 5169923; (042) 5169924
Subsidiaries: Bustan-E-Adab
Branch Office(s)
Good Books, 3 Iqra Center, Ghazni St, Urdu Bazar, Lahore 2 *Tel:* (042) 7121966
Distributed by Book Centre
Showroom(s): Maqbool Academy, 10 Dayalsingh Mansion, The Mall, Lahore *Tel:* (042) 7357058/7238241 *Fax:* (042) 7238241
Bookshop(s): Igraa Centre, Ghazni St, Urdu Bazar, Lahore *Tel:* (042) 7121966

Nafees Academy
Tirath Das Rd, Karachi
Mailing Address: PO Box 91, Urdu Bazaar
Key Personnel
Proprietor: Tariq Iqbal Gahandri
Subjects: Education, History
ISBN Prefix(es): 969-421

Nashiran-e-Quran Pvt Ltd+
38-Urdu Bazar, Lahore
Tel: (042) 58581; (042) 58581
Key Personnel
Chairman: Abdul Hamid Khan
Man Dir: Adbul Rashid Khan
Dir: Khan Abdul Khaliq
Founded: 1967
Subjects: Literature, Literary Criticism, Essays, Religion - Islamic
ISBN Prefix(es): 969-431
Parent Company: Kitabistan Publishing Co 38-Urdu Bazar, Lahore
Warehouse: 4C Mela Ram Darbar Market, Lahore

National Book Foundation+
6-Mauve Area, G-8/4, PO Box 1169, Taleemi Chowk, Islamabad
Tel: (051) 9261533; (051) 9261534 *Fax:* (051) 2264283; (051) 2264283
E-mail: nbf@paknet2.ptc.pk
Web Site: nbf.org.pk *Cable:* BOOKFOUND ISLAMABAD PAKISTAN
Key Personnel
Man Dir: Dr Ahmad Faraz *Tel:* (051) 2255572
Secretary: Muhammad Aslam Rao
Deputy Dir Sales: Abdul Hafeez Tauqir *Tel:* (051) 9261535
Assistant Dir Production: Maqbool Ahmad *Tel:* (051) 9261036
Founded: 1972
Specialize in publishing & provision of books at low prices, book development & promotion, promotion of reading habit.
Member of Asia/Pacific Publishers Association.
Subjects: Accounting, Agriculture, Behavioral Sciences, Biological Sciences, Business, Career Development, Chemistry, Chemical Engineering, Civil Engineering, Religion - Islamic
ISBN Prefix(es): 969-37
Number of titles published annually: 135 Print

Total Titles: 320 Print
Branch Office(s)
First floor, Public Library, Jalal Baba Auditorium, Abbottabad *Tel:* (0992) 9310291
Quaid-i-Azam Medical College, Near Library, Bahawalpur
Shop No 10, Cantt Market, Railway Rd, Bannu, Mr Muhammad Barik Khan *Tel:* (0928) 621991
D I Khan
Agriculture University, Faisalabad
GOR Colony, Latifabad No 1, Hyderabad, Mr Lutuf Ali Narejo *Tel:* (0221) 783859 *Fax:* (0221) 783859
11-Aabpara, Islamabad, Mr Khizar Hayat *Tel:* (051) 9213458
Shop No 14, Liaquat University of Medical & Health Sciences, Jamshoro
Liaquat Memorial Library Premises, Ground Floor, Stadium Rd, Karachi, Mr Muhammad Yaqub *Tel:* (021) 9231806 *Fax:* (021) 9231806
56-57 Tufail Market, Shadman Colony, Lahore, Mr Muhammad Nasim *Tel:* (042) 7587735; (042) 7530329; (042) 755061 *Fax:* (042) 7587735
Chandka Medical College, Main Gate, Larkana, Mr Lutuf Ali Narejo *Tel:* (0741) 458215 *Fax:* (0741) 458215
Shop No 43, Cantonment Plaza, Mardan Cantt
1-A, Gulgasht Colony, Bosan Rd, Near UBL College Chowk, Multan, Mr Ghulam Murtaza *Tel:* (061) 9210119 *Fax:* (061) 9210119
Pupil's Medical Girls College, Nawabshah
48/D, F-6, Jamrud Rd, University Town, Peshawar, Mr Nazir Ahmad Yousufzai *Tel:* (091) 9216303 *Fax:* (091) 9216904
3-7/5, Faiz Muhammad Rd, Quetta, Mr Muhammad Idrees *Tel:* (081) 9201570 *Fax:* (081) 9201869
178-B Sarwar Rd, Rawalpindi, Kanwar Tariq Mahmood *Tel:* (051) 5568242 *Fax:* (051) 5568242
Public Library, Sukkur, Mr Jahan Khan Jamro *Tel:* (071) 25103

National Institute of Historical & Cultural Research
102, Rauf Centre, Fazlul Haq Road, Blue Area (West), Islamabad
Tel: (051) 218535
Key Personnel
Dir: Dr S M Zaman
Founded: 1973
Specialize in history & culture of South Asia with special emphasis on Pakistan.
Subjects: Biography, Ethnicity, History, Regional Interests
ISBN Prefix(es): 969-415

Pak American Commercial (Pvt) Ltd
53/2 Kashmir Rd, Rawalpindi, Cantt
Mailing Address: PO Box 294, Rawalpindi Cantt
Tel: (042) 563709 *Fax:* (021) 565190 *Cable:* PAKACINC KARACHI
Key Personnel
Dir: Agha M Jaffri
Editorial, Production: M Younus Shaikh
Sales, Publicity: Ahsan Jaffri
Rights & Permissions: Abbas Jaffri
Founded: 1949
Subjects: Government, Political Science, History
ISBN Prefix(es): 969-8152
Branch Office(s)
1st floor, Pak Chambers, 5 Temple Rd, Lahore

Pakistan Institute of Development Economics
Quaid-e-Azam University Campus, Islamabad
Mailing Address: PO Box 1091, Islamabad
Tel: (051) 9206610-27 *Fax:* (051) 9210886
E-mail: pide@apollo.net.pk
Web Site: www.pide.org.pk *Cable:* PIDE
Key Personnel
Editor: Dr A R Kemal

Literary Editor & Chief, Publications Division: Prof Aurangzeb A Hashmi
Founded: 1957
Member of Focal Point of DEVINSA (Sri Lanka), Focal Point of Human Resources Development Network (India).
Subjects: Agriculture, Anthropology, Developing Countries, Economics, Environmental Studies, Labor, Industrial Relations, Library & Information Sciences, Religion - Islamic, Social Sciences, Sociology, Women's Studies, Economics, Demography
ISBN Prefix(es): 969-461
Total Titles: 50 Print
Parent Company: Planning & Development Division
Ultimate Parent Company: Government of Pakistan
Imprints: PIDE; Islamabad

Pakistan Publishing House+
Victoria Chambers, Abdullah Haroon Rd, Saddar Karachi 74400
Tel: (021) 5681457
Telex: 23259 HONEY Pk Attn Noorani *Cable:* PRILECT
Key Personnel
Dir: Ms Hoori Noorani
Sales Manager: Aamir Hussain
Production Manager: Mohammad Yusuf
Rights & Permissions: Mohammad Iqbal
Founded: 1966
Subjects: History, Law, Literature, Literary Criticism, Essays
ISBN Prefix(es): 969-419
Associate Companies: Pakistan Law House, Pakistan Chowk, PO Box 90, Karachi 1
Imprints: PPH; Maktaba-i-Danial

PIDE, *imprint of* Pakistan Institute of Development Economics

PPH, *imprint of* Pakistan Publishing House

Publishers United Pvt Ltd+
176 Anarkali, Lahore 54000
Mailing Address: PO Box 1689, Lahore 54000
Tel: (042) 352238 *Cable:* PUBUN
Key Personnel
Man Dir: Javed Amin
Founded: 1942
Subjects: Biological Sciences, Chemistry, Chemical Engineering, Economics, Geography, Geology, History, Literature, Literary Criticism, Essays, Mathematics, Philosophy, Physics, Psychology, Psychiatry, Religion - Other, Technology
ISBN Prefix(es): 969-433
Book Club(s): National Book Foundation of Pakistan
Warehouse: 9 Rattigan Rd, Lahore *Tel:* (042) 353423

Quaid-i-Azam University Department of Biological Sciences
Islamabad
Tel: (051) 218911 *Cable:* Quaid-i-Azam University Islamabad
Key Personnel
Manager: Rashid Ahmed Khan
Founded: 1973
Subjects: Chemistry, Chemical Engineering, Social Sciences, Sociology
ISBN Prefix(es): 969-8329

Research Society of Pakistan
University of the Punjab, Old Campus, Lahore 3
Tel: (042) 322542
ISBN Prefix(es): 969-425

Royal Book Co+
232 Saddar Cooperative Market, Abdullah Haroon Rd, Karachi 74400
Tel: (021) 5684244; (021) 520628 *Fax:* (021) 5683706
Key Personnel
Proprietor: Jamshed Mirza
Founded: 1963
Subjects: Economics, Finance, Government, Political Science, History
ISBN Prefix(es): 969-407
Showroom(s): 402 Rehman Centre, Zaibunisa St, Karachi 74400
Warehouse: 402 Rehman Centre, Zaibunisa St, Karachi 74400

Sang-e-Meel Publications+
Chowk Urdu Bazar, Lahore 2
Mailing Address: PO Box 997, 54000 Lahore
Tel: (042) 7220100; (042) 7228143; (042) 7667970; (042) 7228147 *Fax:* (042) 7245101
E-mail: smp@sang-e-meel.com
Web Site: www.sang-e-meel.com
Key Personnel
Chief Executive: Niaz Ahmad
Sales Dir: Ijaz Ahmad
Production Dir: Afzaal Ahmad *E-mail:* aahmad@sang-e-meel.com
Founded: 1964
Member of Pakistan Publishers & Booksellers Association & Lahore Chamber of Commerce & Industry.
Subjects: Agriculture, Anthropology, Art, Asian Studies, Criminology, Drama, Theater, Fiction, Health, Nutrition, History, Journalism, Literature, Literary Criticism, Essays, Poetry, Travel
Branch Office(s)
25 Lower Mall, Lahore *Tel:* (042) 220100 *Fax:* (042) 245101

Sh Ghulam Ali & Sons (Pvt) Ltd+
Ashrafia Park, Ferozepur Rd, Lahore
Tel: (042) 7588979; (042) 7501664 *Fax:* (042) 7583611
Key Personnel
Dir: Sh Bashir Ahmad; Sh Niaz Ahmed; Mr Arshad Niaz
Subjects: Education, Religion - Islamic
ISBN Prefix(es): 969-31
Divisions: Printing & Packaging Division; Food Processing Division; Satellite Equipment
Branch Office(s)
Chotki Ghitti, Hyderabad *Tel:* (0221) 24431
M A Jinnah Rd, Karachi *Tel:* (0221) 722254
Yadkar Line, Chotki Ghitti, Hyderabad *Tel:* (0221) 24431

Shibil Publications (Pvt) Ltd
2nd floor, Uzma Arcade, Main Clifton Rd, Karachi 75600
Tel: (021) 533414; (021) 539570; (021) 571488 *Cable:* SHAMAILS KARACHI
Key Personnel
Author: Jawaid A Siddiqi
Founded: 1985
Member of Pakistan Publishers & Booksellers Association.
Subjects: Government, Political Science
ISBN Prefix(es): 969-451
Parent Company: Messrs Shamail Traders (Pvt) Ltd
Imprints: Urdu

Taj Co Ltd
B-4, Site Manghoo Pir Rd, Karachi 16
Tel: (021) 294221; (021) 295459; (021) 295619
Telex: 24839 Tajco Pk *Cable:* Kalampak
Key Personnel
Man Dir: Amjad Hussain Khokhar
Founded: 1929
Subjects: Religion - Other
ISBN Prefix(es): 969-452

Branch Office(s)
Rawalpindi
Lahore
Bookshop(s): Sale Depot, M A Jinnah Rd, Karachi

Urdu, *imprint of* Shibil Publications (Pvt) Ltd

Urdu Academy Sind+
16-Bahadur Shah Market, M A Jinah Rd, Karachi 2
Tel: (021) 2631485 *Cable:* LITERATURE
Key Personnel
Dir & International Rights: Aziz Khalid
Member of Pakistan Publishers & Booksellers Association; Also acts as printer.
Subjects: Education, Literature, Literary Criticism, Essays, Science (General)
ISBN Prefix(es): 969-30
Associate Companies: Falak Publishers, Karachi
Subsidiaries: Kitab Agency
Branch Office(s)
Urdu Markaz, Ganpat Rd, Lahore
Showroom(s): Rahmat Building, M A Jinnah Rd
Bookshop(s): Rahmat Building, M A Jinnah Rd
Shipping Address: Westwharf, Karachi

Vanguard Books Ltd+
45 The Mall, Lahore
Tel: (042) 7243779; (042) 7120776; (042) 7120781; (042) 7243783; (042) 7235767 *Fax:* (042) 7245097; (042) 7355197-8
Web Site: www.vanguardbooks.com
Key Personnel
Chief Executive Officer & International Rights: Najam Sethi *E-mail:* nasethi@lhr.comsats.net.pk
Chief Accountant: Aleem Ansari
Founded: 1978
Member of Pakistan Publishers & Booksellers Association.
Subjects: Asian Studies, Economics, Regional Interests, Religion - Islamic
ISBN Prefix(es): 969-402
Number of titles published annually: 30 Print
Total Titles: 325 Print
Online services available through World Wide Web.
Branch Office(s)
Vanguard Books, Mashriq Centre, Shah Suleman Rd, Gulshan Iqbal, Karachi
Vanguard Books, Jinnah Super Market, Islamabad
Vanguard Books, Mussee Road, Rawalpindi
Vanguard Books, 3 Commercial St, Karachi
Vanguard Books, 5-L Commercial, Lahore
Distributor for Blackwell; Macmillan Press; Penguin Books (UK); Pluto Press; Routledge; I B Tauris; Zed Press
Foreign Rep(s): Curzon Press (UK); Zed Press (UK)
Bookshop(s): Vanguard Books, Ejaz Center, Main Blvd, Gulberg, Lahore; Vanguard Books, Lok Virsa Bldg, Super Market, Islamabad; Vanguard Books, Mashriq Center, Gulshan Iqbal, Karachi

West-Pakistan Publishing Co (Pvt) Ltd
17 Urdu Bazar, Lahore
Mailing Address: GPO Box No 374, Lahore
Tel: (042) 52427 *Cable:* WESPUBLISH LAHORE
Key Personnel
Chief Executive: Syed Mahmud Shah
Founded: 1932
Government Printers.
Subjects: Religion - Islamic
ISBN Prefix(es): 969-434

Panama

General Information

Capital: Panama
Language: Spanish (English widely used)
Religion: Roman Catholic
Population: 2.7 million
Bank Hours: 0800-1600 Monday-Friday; 0900-1200 Saturday
Shop Hours: 9000-1800 Monday-Saturday
Currency: 100 centismos = 1 balboa. US currency also used
Export/Import Information: No tariffs on books and advertising matter. No import licenses or exhange controls.
Copyright: UCC, Buenos Aires (see Copyright Conventions, pg xi)

Focus Publications International SA
Ave Justo Arosemena y Calle 42, Apdo Aereo 6-3287, Bella Vista
Tel: 225 6638 *Fax:* 225 0466
E-mail: focusint@sinfo.net
Web Site: focuspublicationsint.com
Key Personnel
Publisher: Kenneth Jones *Tel:* 2256638 *Fax:* 2250466
Founded: 1970
Subjects: Marketing, Travel
ISBN Prefix(es): 958-95276

Fondo Educativo Interamericano
Edificio Eastern 6, Avda Federico Boyd y Calle 51, Apdo 6-3099, Panama
Tel: 2691511; 2230210
Telex: 2481
Key Personnel
Dir: Alicia Chavarria
President: Juan J Fernandez
Vice President: J Rose
Marketing Manager: C Merodio
Founded: 1985

Editorial Universitaria
Urb El Cangrejo Calle Jose, Apdo Aereo Estafeta Universitaria, Panama 4
Tel: 264-2087 *Fax:* 269-2684 *Cable:* Cuidad Universitaria
Key Personnel
Man Dir, Editorial: Dr Carlos M Gasteazoro
Sales: Eduvigis Vergara
Production: Prof Carlos N Ho
Publicity: Mary R de Natera
Founded: 1969
Subjects: Architecture & Interior Design, Art, Education, Geography, Geology, History, Law, Literature, Literary Criticism, Essays, Philosophy, Science (General), Social Sciences, Sociology
Bookshop(s): University Bookshop

Papua New Guinea

General Information

Capital: Port Moresby
Language: Pidgin, English and Motu (all official) as well as approximately 742 native languages
Religion: Predominantly Christian
Population: 4 million
Bank Hours: 0900-1400 Monday-Thursday; 0900-1700 Friday
Shop Hours: 0900-1800 Monday-Friday; 0900-1200 Saturday

PAPUA NEW GUINEA

Currency: 100 teoa = 1 kina
Export/Import Information: No tariff on books and advertising but import tax on non-educational books. No import license for books, but no obscene literature permitted.
Copyright: No copyright law

Assemblies of God Mission
PO Box 34, Maprik, East Sepik Province
Tel: 881256
Subjects: Religion - Other
ISBN Prefix(es): 9980-85
Parent Company: Assemblies Publications
Orders to: PO Box 254, Mitcham, Victoria 3132, Australia

The Christian Book Centre
PO Box 712, Madang, Madang Province
Tel: 822989 *Fax:* 823313
Key Personnel
Manager: Rex Bangs
Subjects: Literature, Literary Criticism, Essays, Religion - Other
ISBN Prefix(es): 9980-74; 0-85804
Parent Company: Kristen Press

Coffee Industry Board
c/o PNG Coffee Industry Board, PO Box 137, Goroka, Eastern Highlands Province
Tel: (675) 7321207 *Fax:* (675) 7321351
Telex: NE 72647 COFFEE
ISBN Prefix(es): 9980-85

IMPS Research Pty Ltd
POB 986, Port Moresby, National Capital District 121
Tel: 3213283 *Fax:* 3217360
E-mail: slandon@dotec.com.pg
Key Personnel
Contact: Thecla Kitas
Founded: 1989
ISBN Prefix(es): 9980-916
Divisions: Imprint Copy Centre; Impress Business Services
Distributor for Economic Insights; Insights PNL

Papua New Guinea Institute of Medical Research
PO Box 60, Eastern Highlands Province, Goroka
Tel: 7322800; 712200 *Fax:* 7321998
Subjects: Anthropology, Medicine, Nursing, Dentistry, Social Sciences, Sociology
ISBN Prefix(es): 0-909531; 9980-71
Number of titles published annually: 1 Print

KPI, *imprint of* Kristen Pres

Kristen Pres+
PO Box 712, Madang Province
Tel: (675) 822989 *Fax:* (675) 823313
Key Personnel
Executive Dir: Dennis T Brown
Publishing Manager & International Rights: Rev Kasek Kautil
Founded: 1969
Also act as printers and stationers.
Subjects: Agriculture, Biblical Studies, Biography, Business, Education, Fiction, Health, Nutrition, Religion - Protestant, Theology, Women's Studies
ISBN Prefix(es): 9980-74; 0-85804
Imprints: KPI; Yangpela Didiman
Bookshop(s): Christian Book Centre, PO Box 712, Madang Province; Christian Book Centre, PO Box 3098, Lae

Melanesian Institute
PO Box 571, 441 Goroka, Eastern Highlands Province
Tel: 7321777 *Fax:* 72-1214
Subjects: Anthropology, Religion - Catholic, Religion - Protestant, Religion - Other, Social Sciences, Sociology
ISBN Prefix(es): 9980-65

National Research Institute of Papua New Guinea
c/o National Research Institute, Economic Research Division, Boroko, National Capital District, 111
Mailing Address: PO Box 5854, Boroko, National Capital District 111
Tel: (675) 3263200
Key Personnel
Dir: Dr Wari Iamo
Publishing Manager: James Robins
Founded: 1975
Subjects: Anthropology, Criminology, Developing Countries, Economics, Education, Environmental Studies, Government, Political Science, Social Sciences, Sociology
ISBN Prefix(es): 9980-75

Nazarene Publications
PO Box 376, Mount Hagen, Western Highlands Province
Tel: (675) 546 2255 *Fax:* (675) 546 2255
E-mail: bcbes@datec.com.pg
Key Personnel
Nazarene Publications Dir: Brian Bett
Subjects: Religion - Protestant, Theology
ISBN Prefix(es): 9980-67
Number of titles published annually: 7 Print
Subsidiaries: Victory Books
Bookshop(s): Nazarene Book Store, PO Box 456, Mount Hagen, Western Highlands Province

Office of Libraries and Archives, Papua New Guinea
PO Box 734, Waigani, National Capital District
Tel: (675) 325-6200 *Fax:* (675) 325-1331
E-mail: ola@datec.com.pg
Key Personnel
Dir General: Daniel Paraide
Also acts as ISBN Agency.
ISBN Prefix(es): 9980-69

Summer Institute of Linguistics+
PO Box 413, Ukarumpa, Morobe Province
Tel: (675) 7373544 *Fax:* (675) 7374111
Founded: 1957
Subjects: Language Arts, Linguistics
ISBN Prefix(es): 9980-0; 0-909456; 0-7263
Orders to: Academic Publications, PO Box 413, Ukarumpa, Morobe Providence

University of Goroka
PO Box 1078, Goroka, Eastern Highlands Province
Tel: 7311700 *Fax:* 7322620
E-mail: amaras@uog.ac.pg
Web Site: www.uog.ac.pg
Key Personnel
Librarian: N Amarasinghe
ISBN Prefix(es): 0-9599993; 9980-915

University of Papua New Guinea Press
POB 320 University Post Office, Boroko
Tel: 6753260130 *Fax:* 6753260127
Key Personnel
Development Manager: John Evans
 Tel: 6753267260 *Fax:* 675367187 *E-mail:* john.evans@upng.ac.pg
Founded: 1995
Books on & about Papua New Guinea in any subject area.
ISBN Prefix(es): 9980-84
Total Titles: 30 Print
Parent Company: National Capital District

Yangpela Didiman, *imprint of* Kristen Pres

Paraguay

General Information

Capital: Asuncion
Language: Spanish & Guarani (both official)
Religion: Predominantly Roman Catholic
Population: 4.9 million
Bank Hours: 0930-1145 Monday-Friday
Shop Hours: 0900-2000 Monday-Saturday
Currency: $1.00 US = 2000 Guarani
Export/Import Information: Member of Latin American Free Trade Association; MERCOSUR; ALADI; GATT & WTO. Children's picture books and atlases are dutied, plus added tax and compensatory tax. Advertising catalogs subject to added tax compensatory tax. Additional taxes on all goods; also Consular fee. No import licenses required. Exchange controls; foreign exchange surcharge.
Copyright: UCC, Berne, Buenos Aires (see Copyright Conventions, pg xi)

Instituto de Ciencias de la Computacion (NCR)+
EE UU 961 c/ Tte Farina, 4 to piso, Asuncion
Tel: (021) 490076 *Fax:* (021) 497849
Key Personnel
Dir: Javier Cosp *E-mail:* jcosp@ecsalink.com.py
Founded: 1969
Entrenamiento en Computacioi.
Subjects: Computer Science, Microcomputers, Technology, Computation
Branch Office(s)
Mcal Estigarribia 134, Fernando de la Mora
Distributed by Rafael Peroni Editor

Intercontinental Editora+
Caballero 270, Asuncion
Tel: (021) 496991 *Fax:* (021) 449738
Key Personnel
Dir: Alejandro Gatti
Subjects: Government, Political Science, Law, Literature, Literary Criticism, Essays, Parapsychology, Poetry

NCR, see Instituto de Ciencias de la Computacion (NCR)

Peru

General Information

Capital: Lima
Language: Spanish, Quechua & Aymara (all official)
Religion: Predominantly Roman Catholic
Population: 22.8 million
Bank Hours: January-December 0900-1500 Monday-Friday
Shop Hours: 1000-1500 Monday- Friday
Currency: 100 centisimos = 1 new sol
Export/Import Information: Member of Andean Group within the Latin American Free Trade Association. Children's picture books and advertising matter dutied per kg plus VAT, sales tax applies on advertising matter. No freight tax on books, but there is a wholesaler's tax. No import licenses required. No exhange controls.
Copyright: UCC, Berne, Buenos Aires (see Copyright Conventions, pg xi)

PERU

Librerias ABC SA
Avda Paseo de la Republica 3440, Local B-32, Lima
Tel: (054) 422900; (054) 422902 *Fax:* (054) 422901
Key Personnel
Man Dir: Herbert H Moll
Founded: 1956
Subjects: Archaeology, Art, History

American Bookstore Center SA, see Librerias ABC SA

Biblioteca Nacional
Av Abancay Cdra 4, Lima 1
Tel: (01) 4287690 *Fax:* (01) 4277331
ISBN Prefix(es): 9972-601

Ediciones Brown SA+
Av Arequipa No 4455, Miraflores, 18 Lima
Tel: (01) 4462753 *Fax:* (01) 4462753
Key Personnel
Dir: Brown P Fortunato
Founded: 1985
Subjects: Communications, English as a Second Language, How-to, Language Arts, Linguistics, Nonfiction (General)
ISBN Prefix(es): 9972-9030

Asociacion Editorial Bruno+
Av Arica 751, Brena, Apdo 1759, Lima 5
Tel: (01) 4237890; (01) 4251248
Key Personnel
Dir: Maximo Segredo
Manager: Federico Diaz Pineo
Founded: 1950
Subjects: Education, Religion - Catholic
ISBN Prefix(es): 9972-1

Bulletin de l'Institut Francais d'Etudes Andines, *imprint of* Instituto Frances de Estudios Andinos, IFEA

Carvajal SA
Av Jorge Basadre 990 San Isidro, Lima 27
Tel: (01) 440-9685 *Fax:* (01) 440-4871
Telex: 055555; 055650 *Cable:* Carvajales Cali
ISBN Prefix(es): 9972-745
Subsidiaries: Editorial Norma SA

Catalogo, *imprint of* Ediciones Peisa (Promocion Editorial Inca SA)

Centro de la Mujer Peruana Flora Tristan
(Peruvian Women's Centre Flora Tristan)
Division of Comunicaciones
Parque Hernan Velarde 42, Lima 1
Tel: (01) 4332765; (01) 433 1457; (01) 433 9060 *Fax:* (01) 4339500
E-mail: postmast@flora.org.pe
Key Personnel
President: Cecilia Olea
Editor: Gaby Cevasco *E-mail:* gaby@flora.org.pe
Founded: 1979
NGO & Feminist.
Subjects: Government, Political Science, Health, Nutrition, Literature, Literary Criticism, Essays, Science (General), Social Sciences, Sociology, Specializes in issues on: health, research, women's rights, library, communication, development, gender, feminism, violence & tell-stories
ISBN Prefix(es): 9972-610

Editorial Desarrollo SA+
Ica 242, Pisol, Apdo Postal 3824, Lima 1
Tel: (01) 285380; (01) 286628 *Fax:* (01) 286628
Key Personnel
Man Dir: Luis Sosa Nunez
Assistant Manager: Bertha de Berrospi
Founded: 1965
Subjects: Accounting, Business
Bookshop(s): Libreria de Editorial Desarrollo, Ica 242, Pisol, Apodo Postal 3824, Lima

Instituto de Estudios Peruanos+
Horacio Urteaga 694, Jesus Maria, Lima 11
Tel: (014) 323070; (014) 244856 *Fax:* (014) 4324981
E-mail: libreria@iep.org.pe *Cable:* IEPERU
Key Personnel
Man Dir: Cecilia Blondet Montero *Tel:* (51-1) 424-4856 *Fax:* (51-1) 332-6173
E-mail: libreria@iep.org.pe
Founded: 1964
Subjects: Anthropology, Archaeology, Developing Countries, Economics, Education, Ethnicity, Government, Political Science, Health, Nutrition, History, Social Sciences, Sociology, Technology, Women's Studies
ISBN Prefix(es): 9972-51

Fondo Editorial de la Pontificia Universidad Catolica del Peru
Avda Universitaria, Cuadra 18s/n, San Miguel, Lima 32
Tel: (01) 4622540 (ext 220) *Fax:* (01) 4626390 (direct)
Key Personnel
Executive Dir: Agueero Gonzalex
Man Dir: Jose Enrique
Subjects: Anthropology, Archaeology, Computer Science, Economics, Education, Ethnicity, History, Language Arts, Linguistics, Law, Literature, Literary Criticism, Essays, Philosophy, Physical Sciences, Psychology, Psychiatry, Science (General), Social Sciences, Sociology, Theology
ISBN Prefix(es): 84-8390; 84-89309; 9972-42; 84-89292

Instituto Frances de Estudios Andinos, IFEA
Contralmirante Montero 141, Miraflores, Lima 18
Tel: (01) 4476070 *Fax:* (01) 4457650
E-mail: postmast@ifea.org.pe
Key Personnel
Dir: Jean Vacher
Founded: 1948
Subjects: Agriculture, Anthropology, Archaeology, Earth Sciences, Geography, Geology, History, Language Arts, Linguistics, Social Sciences, Sociology
ISBN Prefix(es): 84-89302; 9972-623
Number of titles published annually: 7 Print
Imprints: Bulletin de l'Institut Francais d'Etudes Andines; Travaux de l'Institut Francais d'Etudes Andines

Editorial Horizonte
Avda Nicolas de Pierola 995, Casilla 2118, Lima 1
Tel: (01) 279364; (01) 274341
Key Personnel
Manager: Humberto Damonte
Production Manager: Eduardo Collazos
Sales Manager: Fernando Damonte
Founded: 1968
Subjects: Anthropology, Art, Economics, Education, History, Language Arts, Linguistics, Literature, Literary Criticism, Essays, Philosophy, Social Sciences, Sociology
ISBN Prefix(es): 84-89307
Associate Companies: Codice Ediciones, Casilla 2118, Lima 100

Editorial Lima 2000 SA
Av Arequipa 2625, Lince, Lima 14
Tel: (01) 4403486 *Fax:* (01) 4403480
E-mail: oliver@amanta.rcp.net.pe
Key Personnel
Dir: Doris C Lopez
ISBN Prefix(es): 9972-654

Lluvia Editores Srl+
Av Inca Garcilaso de la Vega 1976, Of 501, Lima 1
Tel: (01) 4320732 *Fax:* (01) 4320732
Key Personnel
Contact: Esteban Quiroz Cisneros
Founded: 1978
Subjects: Literature, Literary Criticism, Essays
ISBN Prefix(es): 9972-627

Ediciones Peisa (Promocion Editorial Inca SA)
Av Dos de Mayo 1285, San Isidro, Lima 27
Tel: (01) 4404603; (01) 4410473 *Fax:* (01) 4425906
E-mail: peisa@terro.com.pe
Key Personnel
Man Dir: German Coronado Vallenas
Editor: Martha Munoz de Coronado
Founded: 1969
Subjects: Foreign Countries
ISBN Prefix(es): 9972-40
Imprints: Catalogo
Distributor for Aranco (Spain); Concorcio Natuzart (Spain); Folio (Spain); Tres Torres (Spain)

Libreria Studium SA+
Pl Francia 1164, Lima 1
Tel: (01) 326278; (01) 275960; (01) 325528 *Fax:* (01) 4325354
Key Personnel
Manager: Enrique Remy V
Purchasing & Exporting Manager: Sergio Costa B
Founded: 1936
Subjects: Ethnicity

Sur Casa de Estudios del Socialismo
Av Brasil 1329-201, Jesus Maria, Lima 11
Mailing Address: Apartado Postal 14-0098, Lima 14
Tel: (01) 423-5431 *Fax:* (01) 423-5431
E-mail: casasur@csur.org.pe
Key Personnel
Dir: Oscar Ugarteche
Executive Coordinator: Maria Martinez Castilla
Founded: 1986
Member of the Camara Peruana del Libro.
Subjects: Anthropology, Developing Countries, Economics, History, Literature, Literary Criticism, Essays, Philosophy, Social Sciences, Sociology
ISBN Prefix(es): 9972-619

Tarea Asociacion de Publicaciones Educativas+
Parque Oseres No 161, Pueblo Libre, Lima 21
Tel: (01) 4242827 *Fax:* (01) 4240997
E-mail: postmaster@tarea.org.pe
Key Personnel
President: Maria Amelia Palacios Vallejo
Dir: Estela Gonzalez Astete
Editor: Julio Del Valle
Founded: 1974
Subjects: Education
ISBN Prefix(es): 84-89296; 9972-618

Tassorello, SA
Av Flora Tristan 574, Maqdalena, Lima 17
Tel: (01) 4602040; (01) 4600255 *Fax:* (01) 4615714
Key Personnel
Contact: Andres Carbone
Founded: 1992
Subjects: Accounting, Education, Human Relations
ISBN Prefix(es): 9972-609

Travaux de l'Institut Francais d'Etudes Andines, *imprint of* Instituto Frances de Estudios Andinos, IFEA

PERU

Universidad de Lima-Fondo de Desarollo Editorial+
Av Javier Prado Este s/n, Surco, Lima 33
Tel: (01) 4376767 *Fax:* (01) 437-8066; (01) 435-6552
E-mail: fondo_ed@lima.edu.pe
Web Site: www.ulima.edu.pe
Key Personnel
Executive Dir: Jose Valdizan Ayala
Founded: 1962
Subjects: Communications, Computer Science, Economics, Engineering (General), Film, Video, Finance, Journalism, Law, Management, Marketing, Photography, Psychology, Psychiatry, Radio, TV, Science (General)
ISBN Prefix(es): 84-89358; 9972-45
Total Titles: 120 Print

Universidad Nacional Mayor de San Marcos
Jr Andahuaylas, 697 Lima 1
Tel: (01) 4314629
Key Personnel
Man Dir: Dr Wilson Reateggui Chavez; Rector de la Universidad
Founded: 1952
Subjects: Engineering (General), Law, Literature, Literary Criticism, Essays, Medicine, Nursing, Dentistry, Science (General)
Bookshop(s): Av Nicolas de Pierola 1222, Lima 1

Editorial Universo SA
Ave Nicolas Arriola 2285, Urb Apolo, La Victoria, Apdo 241, Lima 30
Tel: (014) 241639; (014) 233190
Key Personnel
Man Dir: Jose Antonio Aquino Benavides
Executive Manager: Salvador Lau Barraza
Founded: 1967
Subjects: Social Sciences, Sociology

Philippines

General Information

Capital: Quezon City
Language: Filipino (based on Tagalog) is the native national language. English widely used. Nine other major languages of the Malayo-Polynesian group, and about 60 other languages, are also spoken
Religion: Predominantly Roman Catholic and some Islamic
Population: 67.1 million
Bank Hours: 0900-1600 Monday-Friday
Shop Hours: Vary. Many open 0900-1200, 1400-1930 Monday-Saturday (some close 1730; some open Sunday)
Currency: 100 centavos = 1 Philippine peso
Export/Import Information: Duty on books except those which are philosophical, historical, economic, scientific, technical or vocational, approved by Department of Education for use of certain institutions (not exceeding 10 copies for an institution, or two for an individual) or for encouragement of sciences or fine arts; no tariffs on Bibles and similar religious books. No duty on advertising matter. No import licenses, but no obscene or immoral literature permitted. Release certificate issued on behalf of Central Bank required to clear goods. Imports subject to sales tax. No formal exchange controls but most imports need Letter of Credit (over $100 in any month, for example).
Copyright: UCC (see Copyright Conventions, pg xi)

Abiva Publishing House Inc+
851-881 Gregorio Araneta Ave, 1113 Quezon City
Tel: (02) 7120245 *Fax:* (02) 7320308
E-mail: abiva@asiagate.net
Key Personnel
President: Luis Q Abiva Jr
Executive Vice President: Nena A Garcia
Vice President, International Rights: Jorge Abiva Garcia
Founded: 1936
Subjects: Education, History, Religion - Other, Science (General)
ISBN Prefix(es): 971-553
Total Titles: 1 CD-ROM
Associate Companies: ACG Asian Tradelinks Inc
Subsidiaries: Hiyas Press; A C G Asian Tradelinks Inc
Branch Office(s)
2/F, Cebu Holdings Cente, Cebu Business Park, Cebu City
Matina Highway, Davao City

Anvil Publishing Inc+
2/F Team Pacific Bldg, 13 Jose Cruz St, Bo.Ugong, Pasig City, Metro Manila (Shipping & Warehouse same as Main)
Tel: (02) 9140155; (02) 6711899 *Fax:* (02) 6719235
E-mail: anvil@fc.emc.com.ph; pubdept@anvil.com.ph
Key Personnel
General Manager: Cecilia R Licauco
Publishing Manager: Karina A Bolasco
Marketing Consultant: Gwenn Jessica A Galvez
Founded: 1990
Also acts as wholesaler & distributor of paperbacks & tradebooks from the US & UK.
Subjects: Cookery, Crafts, Games, Hobbies, Fiction, Gardening, Plants, Health, Nutrition, How-to, Humor, Language Arts, Linguistics, Literature, Literary Criticism, Essays, Mysteries, Religion - Catholic, Romance, Science Fiction, Fantasy, Western Fiction, Women's Studies
ISBN Prefix(es): 971-27
Number of titles published annually: 150 Print
Total Titles: 600 Print
Parent Company: National Bookstore, 125 Pioneer St, Mandaluyong City, Metro Manila
Associate Companies: Megastrat Inc

Ateneo de Manila University Press+
Katipunan Rd, Loyola Heights, Quezon City
Tel: (02) 4265984; (02) 4261238 *Fax:* (02) 4265909
E-mail: unipress@pusit.admu.edu.ph (business/operations)
Key Personnel
Dir: Esther M Pacheco *E-mail:* empachec@pusit.admu.edu.ph
Founded: 1972
Member of the International Association of Scholarly Publishers & Book Development Association of the Philippines.
Subjects: Anthropology, Architecture & Interior Design, Asian Studies, Behavioral Sciences, Drama, Theater, Economics, Education, Environmental Studies, Fiction, Government, Political Science, History, Literature, Literary Criticism, Essays, Poetry, Psychology, Psychiatry, Religion - Catholic, Social Sciences, Sociology, Theology, Women's Studies, Social Sciences
ISBN Prefix(es): 971-550
Number of titles published annually: 25 Print
Total Titles: 150 Print
Parent Company: Ateneo de Manila University
Distributed by University of Hawaii Press

BFP Super Romance, *imprint of* Books for Pleasure Inc

Bookman Printing & Publishing House Inc+
373 Quezon Ave, 1114 Quezon City
Tel: (02) 7124813; (02) 7123587; (02) 7408108 *Fax:* (02) 7124843
E-mail: bookman@info.com.ph *Cable:* BOOKMAN
Key Personnel
President: Marietta P Martinez
Vice President: Lina P Enriquez
Editorial Dir: Ursula G Picache
Founded: 1945
Subjects: Education, English as a Second Language, Mathematics, Nonfiction (General), Science (General)
ISBN Prefix(es): 971-712

Bookmark Inc+
264-A Pablo Ocampo Sr Ave, Makati City
Tel: (0632) 8958061 *Fax:* (0632) 8970824
E-mail: bookmark@info.com.ph
Web Site: www.bookmark.com
Telex: Bookmark Manila
Key Personnel
President: Amb Bienvenido A Tan, Jr
General Manager: Jose Maria Lorenzo Tan
Vice President: Florencia D Reyes
Founded: 1945
Member of Association of Philippine Booksellers.
Subjects: Child Care & Development, Cookery, Gardening, Plants, History, Religion - Other, Travel
ISBN Prefix(es): 971-569
Branch Office(s)
Taft Ave, Makati, Metro Man
Delta Arcade Bldg, Makati, Metro Manila
Showroom(s): 357 T Pinpin Escolta, Manila; Delta Arcade Bldg, Makati, Metro Manila
Bookshop(s): 357 T Pinpin Escolta, Manila; Delta Arcade Bldg, Makati, Metro Manila

Books for Pleasure Inc+
Room 403, First Optima Realty Bldg, N Domingo Cor F Roman Sts, San Juan, Metro Manila
Tel: (02) 771807 *Fax:* (02) 7275240
Key Personnel
Vice President: Ramon A Fabella
Founded: 1976
Subjects: Cookery, Mysteries, Romance
ISBN Prefix(es): 971-502
Imprints: BFP Super Romance; Hiwaga Mystery Novels; Valentine Romance; Young Love

Bright Concepts Printing House+
Sto. Nino, San Fernando, 2000 Pampanga
Tel: (0917) 6473803
E-mail: dawnphilatelics@yahoo.com
Key Personnel
Author, Publisher: Jorge H Cuyugan *Tel:* (0918) 2318248
Founded: 1992
Subjects: Business, Crafts, Games, Hobbies
ISBN Prefix(es): 971-607
Subsidiaries: Dawn Philatelic
Orders to: Booklore Publishing Corp, Blk 2, Lot 13, Ridgemont Village, Cainta, Rizal *Tel:* 252-4280, 251-0771 *Fax:* 563-7629

Cacho Publishing House, Inc+
Pines Cor Union St, Mandaluyong City Metro Manila 1501
Tel: (02) 6318361 *Fax:* (02) 6315244
E-mail: cacho@s.com.ph
Key Personnel
President: Herbert T Veloso
General Manager: Ramon C Sunico
Founded: 1880
ISBN Prefix(es): 971-19
Parent Company: National Bookstore Inc
Associate Companies: Anvil Publishing Inc; Cacho Hermanos Inc *Tel:* (02) 6318361 *Fax:* (02) 6315244 *E-mail:* cacho@mozcom.com
Distributed by Impex (Japan)

PUBLISHERS

Capitol Publishing House Inc
54 Don Alejandro Roces Ave, 1103 Metro Manila
Tel: (02) 997061; (02) 997062; (02) 997063; (02) 997064; (02) 997065 *Fax:* (02) 990535

Claretian Communications Inc+
UPPO Box 4, 1101 Diliman, Quezon City
Tel: (02) 9213984 *Fax:* (02) 9217429
E-mail: cci@claret.org
Web Site: www.bible.claret.org
Key Personnel
Executive Dir, Rights & Permissions: Fr Alberto Rossa *Fax:* 02 921 9429
Founded: 1983
Subjects: Biblical Studies, Environmental Studies, Law, Theology, Women's Studies
ISBN Prefix(es): 971-501
Bookshop(s): Claretian Publications (CP) Bookstore, Fr Alberto Rossa

Communication Foundation for Asia Media Group (CFAMG)
4427 Second Old Sta Mesa, Manila
Mailing Address: PO Box SM 434
Tel: (02) 612342; (02) 607659
Telex: 27854 Cfa Ph *Cable:* SOCOTER MANILA
Key Personnel
Founder: Fr Cornelio Lagerwey
Founded: 1973
Member of The People in Communication Network (BOARD), The Association of Foundations, Philippine Partnership for the Development of Human Resources in Rural Areas (PHILDHRRA), OCICUNDA
Subjects: Agriculture, Biblical Studies, Biography, Communications, Environmental Studies, Film, Video, Philosophy, Religion - Other, Theology
ISBN Prefix(es): 971-577
Branch Office(s)
Dr John Tondowidjojo, Communication Training Center (Sanggar Bina Tama), Suddirman no 3, Surayaba 60136 Indonesia

De La Salle University+
2401 Taft Ave, De La Salle University, 4115 Dasmarinas
Tel: (02) 7419271; (02) 594832 *Fax:* (02) 5264237
E-mail: mcovatg@dlsu.edu.ph
Key Personnel
Contact: Mr Anthon Garcia
Founded: 1983
Member of International Association of Scholarly Publishers.
Subjects: Asian Studies, Business, Education, Fiction, Literature, Literary Criticism, Essays, Philosophy, Poetry, Religion - Catholic
ISBN Prefix(es): 971-92082

Encyclopaedia Britannica (Philippines) Inc
c/o New Business Center, 8th Floor Kings Court Bldg, 2129 Pasong Tamo, Makati, Metro Manila
Tel: (02) 895816 *Fax:* (02) 8102144
Key Personnel
President: Gabriel Ruvinetti

Estrella Publishing+
66 Niog St, Bacoor, 4102 Cavite
Key Personnel
Author & Publisher: Ervie Nangca-Antonio
Founded: 1993
Pocket book form.
Subjects: Fiction, Romance
ISBN Prefix(es): 971-645
Book Club(s): Kapisanan Ng Mga Manunulat Ng Nobelang Popular

Galleon Publications+
962 Josefa L Escoda St, NFWC Bldg, Suite 309, 1000 Ermita, Manila
Tel: (632) 523-1825 *Fax:* (632) 525-6129
Key Personnel
President & Publisher: Alfonso J Aluit
Founded: 1968
Publish guidebooks to Philippine destinations & works on topical Philippine history.
Subjects: Biography, History, Travel
ISBN Prefix(es): 971-8521
Total Titles: 30 Print
Distributed by Bookmark Inc
Membership(s): SATW

Garotech
903 Quezon Ave, Quezon 4332
Tel: (02) 993286 *Cable:* Romgar Manila
Key Personnel
Man Dir, Sales, Publicity: Rolando M Garcia
Editorial: Maridel Garcia
Founded: 1951
Subjects: Business, Education, Ethnicity, Foreign Countries, Government, Political Science, History
ISBN Prefix(es): 971-8711
Parent Company: Garcia Publishing House Inc
Orders to: PO Box 1860, Manila

Heritage Publishing House
6 St William, Cubao, Quezon City
Mailing Address: PO Box 3667, Manila
Tel: (02) 799484 *Fax:* (02) 7221484
Key Personnel
President: Mario R Alcantara
Man Dir: Ricardo S Sanchez
Previously MCS Enterprises Inc.
Subjects: Anthropology, Art, Government, Political Science, History

Hiwaga Mystery Novels, *imprint of* Books for Pleasure Inc

International Rice Research Institute (IRRI)
PO Box 933, 1099 Manila
Tel: (02) 884669; (02) 884511 *Fax:* (02) 7612404; (02) 8911292
E-mail: postmaster@irri.cgnet.com
Telex: (IIT) 45365 RICE INST PM
Key Personnel
Man Dir: Robert Huggans
Founded: 1960
Subjects: Agriculture
ISBN Prefix(es): 971-22
Parent Company: CGIAR: Consultative Group on International Research
Imprints: IRRI
Bookshop(s): Agribookstore IADS Inc, 1611 North Kent St, Arlington, VA 22209, United States; American Overseas Company, 550 Walnut St, Norwood, NJ 07648, United States; Harvest Farm Magazine, 14 Wenchow St, Taipei, Taiwan, Province of China; Haryana Scientific Corporation, Gandhi Chowk, Hisar, Haryana 125001, India; Oxford Book & Stationery Co, Scindia House, New Delhi 11001, India; S Toeche-Mittler Verlag, Hindenburgstr 33, 6100 Darmstadt, Germany

IRRI, *imprint of* International Rice Research Institute (IRRI)

J C Palabay Enterprises+
83 Molave St, Marikina Heights, Metro Manila
Mailing Address: 67 Gen Ordonez St, Marikina Heights, 1800 Marikina, Metro Manila
Tel: (02) 9478282 *Fax:* (02) 9424512
Telex: 29001 PXO PH; 23322 PXO PH
Key Personnel
President: Carmelita L Palabay
Vice President: Jescie L Palabay
Author: Romeo Cruz; Jose Villa Panganiban
Editor: Ponciano B P Pineda; Lourdes Arellano
Founded: 1974
Also import Science Laboratory Equipment & Globes.
Subjects: History
ISBN Prefix(es): 971-13
Parent Company: J C Palabay Enterprises Inc
Associate Companies: Four J Arts; Instructional Material Council; Mhelle L Publications
Showroom(s): 67 Gen Ordonez St, Marikina Heights, 1800 Marikina, Metro Manila
Warehouse: 67 Gen Ordonez St, Marikina Heights, 1800 Marikina, Metro Manila

Kadena Press+
2 Mayumi St, UP Village, 1101 Diliman, Quezon City
Mailing Address: PO Box 4, Diliman, Quezon City
Tel: (02) 9217429; (02) 9213984
Key Personnel
Executive Dir: Fr Alberto Rossa
Founded: 1991
Subjects: Fiction
ISBN Prefix(es): 971-32
Parent Company: Claretian Communications Inc

Logos (Divine Word) Publications Inc+
1916 Oroquieta St, Sta Cruz Manila
Tel: (02) 7111323 *Fax:* (02) 7322736
E-mail: dwpsvd@rp1.net
Key Personnel
Dir: Fr Gerry del Pinado SVD
Founded: 1987
Subjects: Business, Communications, Education, Religion - Other
ISBN Prefix(es): 971-510
Total Titles: 5 Audio
Parent Company: Society of the Divine Word

Marren Publishing House, Inc
851 Oroquieta St, Sta Cruz, 1003 Manila
Tel: (02) 3728937; (02) 3728938; (02) 3728939; (02) 3728940; (02) 3728441; (02) 4153116; (02) 4153117; (02) 4153118; (02) 4153119; (02) 7115829 *Fax:* (02) 9286611
Key Personnel
Sales & Marketing Manager: Joan Elena B Cellona
Subjects: Cookery, Fiction
ISBN Prefix(es): 971-649
Subsidiaries: MRE Trading Inc

Sonny A Mendoza+
Unit 31, Parian Commercial Center, Commonwealth Av, Diliman, Quezon City
Tel: (02) 8691111
Key Personnel
Publisher: Sonny Mendoza
Marketing Manager: Ramon N Orbeta
Production Manager: Armando S Peralta
Founded: 1991
Specialize in Filipino/Tagalog crosswords puzzles; also acts as distributor of Tagalog romance novels.
Subjects: Crafts, Games, Hobbies, Humor, Romance
ISBN Prefix(es): 971-599
Orders to: Apt 2, No 59 Paseo de Roxas, Urbaneta Village, Makati, Metro Manila

Mindanao State University - Mamitua Saber Research Center
Iligan City (MSU-ITT), 8801 Iligan City
ISBN Prefix(es): 971-8708

Mutual Books Inc+
425 Shaw Blvd, Mandaluyong, Metro Manila
Tel: (02) 796050 *Cable:* MUBINC
Key Personnel
President: Alfredo S Nicdao Jr
Founded: 1959
Subjects: Accounting, Business, Computer Science, Economics, Management, Mathematics

ISBN Prefix(es): 971-587
Associate Companies: Alfredo S Nicdao Jnr Inc
Shipping Address: PO Box 245, Greenhills, San Juan, 1502 Metro Manila

National Book Store Inc
Quad Alpha Centrum, 125 Pioneer St, Mandaluyong City 1550
Tel: (02) 6318061; (02) 6318062; (02) 6318063; (02) 6318064; (02) 6318065; (02) 6318066
E-mail: purchbooks@nationalbookstore.com.ph
Telex: 27890 NBS-PH; 41144 NBS-PM
Cable: Nabost Manila
Key Personnel
Man Dir: Mr Benjamin C Ramos
Sales Dir: Mitto Licauco
Publicity, Advertising: Mrs Socorro C Ramos
Rights & Permissions: Mr Alfredo C Ramos
Founded: 1945
Firm reprints over 300 titles annually for foreign publishers.
Subjects: Art, Fiction, How-to, Music, Dance, Nonfiction (General)
ISBN Prefix(es): 971-08

National Historical Institute
Affiliate of National Commission on Culture and the Arts
NHI Bldg TM Kalaw ST, Ermita, Manila
Mailing Address: PO Box 3398, Ermita, Manila
Tel: (0632) 590646; (0632) 572644
Key Personnel
Chairman & Executive Dir: Samuel K Tan
ISBN Prefix(es): 971-538
Ultimate Parent Company: Republic of the Philippines

National Museum of the Philippines
Padre Burgos St, 1000 Manila
Tel: (02) 494450 *Fax:* (02) 5270306
E-mail: nmuseum@i-next.net
Web Site: nmuseum.tripod.com
Key Personnel
Dir: Gabriel Casal *Tel:* (02) 5271215
Editor: Elenita D V Alba *Tel:* (02) 5270278
Acting Information Technology Officer: Carolina N Magdaleno *Tel:* (02) 5270241
The National Museum collects, identifies, preserves & exhibits the country's rich cultural heritage.
Subjects: Anthropology, Archaeology, Art, Biological Sciences, Geography, Geology, Natural History
ISBN Prefix(es): 971-567
Total Titles: 50 Print; 4 CD-ROM; 1 Online; 1 E-Book
Parent Company: Office of the President
Bookshop(s): National Museum Souvenir Shop, P Burgos St, Manila, Contact: Elenita D V Alba *Tel:* (02) 5270278 *Fax:* (02) 5270306 *E-mail:* nmuseum@i-next.net *Web Site:* nmuseumi-next.net

New Day Publishers+
11 Lands St, VASRA, 1100 Quezon City
Mailing Address: PO Box 1167, 1100 Quezon City
Tel: (02) 9988046; (02) 9275982 *Fax:* (02) 9246544
E-mail: newday@pworld.net.ph; newdayorders@edsamail.com.ph
Key Personnel
Executive Dir, Rights/Permissions & Manuscript Submissions: Ms Bezalie Bautista Uc-Kung *Tel:* (02) 9268049
Publicity, Marketing & Promotions: Mr Jesus Bacolores
Founded: 1969
Member of World Association for Christian Communication, Book Development Association of the Philippines & National Book Development Board.
Subjects: Anthropology, Asian Studies, Behavioral Sciences, Biblical Studies, Biography, Business, Career Development, Communications, Cookery, Economics, Education, Ethnicity, Fiction, History, How-to, Human Relations, Humor, Labor, Industrial Relations, Literature, Literary Criticism, Essays, Management, Marketing, Nonfiction (General), Philosophy, Poetry, Religion - Catholic, Religion - Protestant, Romance, Science Fiction, Fantasy, Self-Help, Theology
ISBN Prefix(es): 971-10
Number of titles published annually: 20 Print
Total Titles: 500 Print

Newark International Enterprises+
Room 507, FUBC Bldg, Escolta, Manila
Tel: (02) 2432077 *Fax:* (02) 2414893
Key Personnel
Gen Manager & Publisher: Mabini D Castillo
ISBN Prefix(es): 971-9071
Distributed by Goodwill Bookstore/Goodwill Trading Co Inc; Merriam & Webster Inc

Our Lady of Manaoag Publisher+
3078-B Reposo Ext, Sta Mesa, Manila
Tel: (02) 610214; (02) 610219 *Fax:* (06) 610219
Key Personnel
President: Dr Tomas Q D Andres
Marketing Dir: Pilar Corazon I Andres
Circulation Manager: Thomas Philamer Andres; Pilar Philamer I Andres
Founded: 1980
Also acts as a training centre that conducts Philippine based managment in Filipino language.
Subjects: Anthropology, Art, Asian Studies, Behavioral Sciences, Biblical Studies, Business, Career Development, Child Care & Development, Communications, Developing Countries, Education, Ethnicity, Film, Video, History, Humor, Management, Philosophy, Religion - Catholic
ISBN Prefix(es): 971-26; 971-91093
Parent Company: Values & Technologies Management Centre
Subsidiaries: Management Business Achievers Inc
Divisions: Philippine Institute of Management
Warehouse: 2004 C Arellano St, Sta Mesa, Manila

Pearson Education Asia
2/F J-L Bldg, 23 Matalino St, Bgy. Central, Dillman, 11011 Quezon City
Tel: (02) 434 5501 *Fax:* (02) 433 9757
E-mail: custserv@pearsoned.com.ph
Web Site: www.pearsoned.com
Key Personnel
Marketing Executive: Mary Antonette Tucit *E-mail:* dovie@pearsoned.com.ph; Ariel Pagdanganan *E-mail:* arielp@pearson.com.ph; Mary Ann Gonzalez *E-mail:* gonzalez@pearson.com.ph
Sales Manager: Dennis Elmer Lazo *E-mail:* denlazo@pearsoned.com.ph
Number of titles published annually: 30 Print
Total Titles: 60 Print
Parent Company: Pearson Education

Philippine Baptist Mission SBC FMB Church Growth International
2444 Taft Av, Metro Manila
Tel: (02) 599256; (02) 599257 *Fax:* (02) 512-1499
E-mail: csm@i-manila.com.ph
Key Personnel
Asst Dir: Abner G Lacson
Chief Accountant: Theresa Calleja
Subjects: Biblical Studies, History, Religion - Protestant, Theology
ISBN Prefix(es): 971-512
Shipping Address: Church Strengthening Ministry, 4796 Mercado St, Makati, Metro Manila
Orders to: Church Strengthening Ministry, 4796 Mercado St, Makati, Metro Manila

Philippine Education Co Inc
Esguerra Bldg 1, 140 Amorsolo St, 7th floor, Legaspi Village, 1229 Makati
Tel: (02) 487215; (02) 487317
Telex: 7222321 *Cable:* Pecoi Manila
Key Personnel
General Manager: Antero L Soriano
Subjects: Art, Education, Fiction, Social Sciences, Sociology
ISBN Prefix(es): 971-09

Rex Bookstores & Publishers+
84 P Florentino St, Sta Mesa Heights, Quezon City
Tel: (02) 712 4101 (ext 128) *Fax:* (02) 740 2702
E-mail: rex@usinc.net
Key Personnel
President: Dominador Buhain
International Sales & Foreign Rights Coordinator: Sonia A Santiago *E-mail:* sasantiago@rexpublishing.com.ph
Founded: 1950
Member of Asia/Pacific Publishers Association; International Publishers Association.
Subjects: Accounting, Agriculture, Anthropology, Archaeology, Behavioral Sciences, Biological Sciences, Business, Child Care & Development, Cookery, Criminology, Economics, Education, Environmental Studies, Finance, History, Human Relations, Labor, Industrial Relations, Law, Maritime, Marketing, Mathematics, Parapsychology, Physics, Psychology, Psychiatry, Science (General), Social Sciences, Sociology, Theology, Travel
ISBN Prefix(es): 971-23
Number of titles published annually: 100 Print
Ultimate Parent Company: Rex Group of Companies
Branch Office(s)
1906 Cecile Bldg, Mac-Arthur H-way, Balibago, Angeles City, Acting Officer In Charge: Almira Manaloto *Tel:* (045) 892-17-21
Ateneo Professional School, 1st floor, Rockwell Center, Bel-Air Makati, Helen Riosa *Tel:* 729-20-75
Duran Bldg, del Pilar Ext (crossing) Sangitan E, Cabanatuan, Officer In Charge: Gigi Yatco *Fax:* (044) 600-56-84
Cor J Serina St, Valmenta Blvd, Carmen, Cagayan de Oro, Officer In Charge: Lourdes Dicipulo *Tel:* (088) 858-67-75
11 Sanciangko St, Cebu City, Officer In Charge: Mabel Quijano *Tel:* (032) 254-67-73; (032) 254-67-74 *Fax:* (032) 254-64-66
Rustan's Superstore Bldg, Unit 4-A, Cubao, Officer In Charge: Luisa Lagat *Fax:* 911-10-70
156 CM Recto St, Davao City, Officer In Charge: Lourdes Dicipulo *Tel:* (082) 225-31-67, (082) 221-78-40 *Fax:* (088) 221-02-72
Aparente St, Dadiangas Heights, General Santos City, Officer In Charge: Hilda Malayao *Tel:* (083) 554-71-02
75 Brgy San Isidro Lopez-Jaena Jaro, Iloilo, Officer In Charge: Mabel Quijano *Tel:* (033) 329-03-32 *Fax:* (033) 329-03-36
Magallanes cor Alonzo St, Legaspi City, Officer In Charge: Ben Pring *Tel:* (052) 820-22-70
Star Centrum Bldg, Unit UG-2, Sen Gil Puyat Ave, Makati, Officer In Charge: Helen Riosa *Tel:* 893-37-44, 818-53-63
Facilities Center Bldg, 548 Shaw Blvd, Mandaluyong, Officer In Charge: Tina de la Cruz *Tel:* 531-13-06 *Fax:* 531-13-39
Zone 6 Pinmaludpod Urdaneta, Pangasinan, Officer In Charge: Che che Agcamaran *Fax:* (075) 568-39-75

856 Nicanor Reyes St, Samp, Manila, Officer
In Charge: Fatima Yumiaco *Tel:* 736-05-67
Fax: 736-41-91
1977 CM Recto Ave, Sampaloc, Manila, Officer
In Charge: Teodora Anastacio *Tel:* 735-55-27
Fax: 735-55-34
Lot 6, Blk 5 Cityview IV Brgy Tanauan, Tanza
Cavity, Officer In Charge: Easter Rapada
Book Club(s): Phil Educational Publishers Association, Contact: Dominador D Buhain
Warehouse: 84 P Florentino Av, QC,1008, 1008
Quezon City *Tel:* (02) 712 4101 (ext 128)
Fax: (02) 740 2702 *E-mail:* sasantiago@rexpublishing.com.ph

Saint Mary's Publishing Corp+
1308 P Guevarra St, Sta Cruz, Manila
Tel: (02) 7119730; (02) 7119743 *Fax:* (02) 7350955
Founded: 1995
Member of PEPA, BDAP, CLAPI.
Subjects: Economics, Education, English as a Second Language, Geography, Geology, History, Language Arts, Linguistics, Mathematics, Science (General), Social Sciences, Sociology
ISBN Prefix(es): 971-509

Salesiana Publishers Inc+
Pasay Rd cor Pasong Tamo con, Metro Manila
Makati
Tel: (02) 8161506; (02) 889234 *Fax:* (02) 8939876 *Cable:* SALESIANA PUBLISHERS MANILA
Key Personnel
Rector, Editor-in-Chief & all other offices: Demetrio M Carmona SDB
Founded: 1979
Subjects: Communications, Computer Science, Earth Sciences, Human Relations, Language Arts, Linguistics, Literature, Literary Criticism, Essays, Mathematics, Physics, Religion - Catholic, Science (General), Social Sciences, Sociology, Technology
ISBN Prefix(es): 971-8532; 971-522
Branch Office(s)
Salesiana-Bacolod, c/o RU Commercial Center, North Drive, Bacolod City (in front of Riverside Hospital)
Salesiana-Baguio, UB Commercial Complex, Gen Luuna St, Baguio City
Book Club(s): Philippine Bookfair Association

San Carlos Publications
University of San Carlos, 6000 Cebu City
Tel: (032) 70874
Key Personnel
Editor: B Resil Mojares PhD
Founded: 1973
Member of International Association of Scholarly Publishers & Council of Editors of Learned Journals.
Subjects: Anthropology, Archaeology, Biological Sciences, History, Social Sciences, Sociology
ISBN Prefix(es): 971-539

SIBS Publishing House Inc
N B Santos Bldg, 937 Quezon Ave, Quezon City 1104
Tel: (0632) 374-2902 *Fax:* (0632) 372-7301
E-mail: sibsbook@info.com.ph
Web Site: www.sibs.com.ph
Key Personnel
President: Carmen Mimette M Sibal
Vice President, Operations: Anita S Mangalindan
Head, Research & Development: Dr Juanita S Guerrero
Editor-in-Chief: Rogelio Mangahas
Managing Editor: Mamel Teh
Art Dir: Antonio M Concepcion
Head, Promotions Department: Cora A Sapo
Project Coordinator: Agnes S Apostol *Tel:* (062) 372-7313

Founded: 1996
Member of International Publishers Association & Philippine Educational Publishers Association.
Subjects: Art, Biological Sciences, Economics, Education, English as a Second Language, Environmental Studies, History, Journalism, Language Arts, Linguistics, Literature, Literary Criticism, Essays, Mathematics, Nonfiction (General), Religion - Other, Science (General), Social Sciences, Sociology, Christian Living Education, Civics & Culture, English, Filipino, Preschool books - reading, language, math & art, Values Education
Branch Office(s)
SIBS Publishing House Inc - Cebu, New Rd, Sangi, Barangay Pajo, Lapu-Lapu City 6015
Tel: (032) 3406809; (032) 8380; (032) 3408518
Fax: (032) 3408391; (032) 3406808

Silsilah Publication
Edificio Ciudad, San Jose Rd, 7000 Zamboanga City
Tel: (02) 5663; (02) 5942
ISBN Prefix(es): 971-31

Sinag-Tala Publishers Inc+
4th Floor, Regina Bldg, Cor Trasierra St, 3113 St Legaspi Village, Makati City Metro Manila
Tel: (02) 8192681 *Fax:* (02) 8192563
Key Personnel
Man Dir, Rights & Permissions: L A Uson
Marketing Dir: V A Tur
Founded: 1969
Subjects: Business, Economics, Religion - Catholic
ISBN Prefix(es): 971-554

Solidaridad Publishing House
531 Padre Faura, Ermita, 1000 Manila
Mailing Address: PO Box 3959, 1000 Manila
Tel: (02) 586581; (02) 591241 *Fax:* (02) 5255038
Cable: SOLDAD MANILA
Key Personnel
General Manager: F Sionil Jose
Founded: 1965
Subjects: Biography, Fiction, History
ISBN Prefix(es): 971-8845

University of the Philippines Press
Unit of University of the Philippines System
E De Los Santos St, UP Campus, Diliman, 1101 Quezon City
Tel: (02) 992558 *Fax:* (02) 9282558
E-mail: press@nicole.upd.edu.ph
Web Site: www.dilnet.upd.edu.ph. ~press
Key Personnel
Dir, Rights & Permissions: Laura L Samson
Sales, Publicity: Auramine F Soberano
Production: Conrado Calma
Founded: 1965
Subjects: Art, Business, Education, Fiction, Government, Political Science, How-to, Law, Medicine, Nursing, Dentistry, Music, Dance, Philosophy, Psychology, Psychiatry, Religion - Other, Science (General), Social Sciences, Sociology, Technology
ISBN Prefix(es): 971-542

UST Publishing House+
Beato Angelico Bldg, Espana St, Sampaloc, 1008 Manila
Tel: (02) 731-3522731 *Fax:* (02) 731-3522731
Key Personnel
Contact: Joselito B Zulueta
Founded: 1593
Subjects: Architecture & Interior Design, Asian Studies, Biblical Studies, Biological Sciences, Business, Chemistry, Chemical Engineering, Economics, Education, English as a Second Language, Health, Nutrition, History, Literature, Literary Criticism, Essays, Medicine, Nursing, Dentistry, Philosophy, Poetry, Religion - Catholic, Social Sciences, Sociology, Theology
ISBN Prefix(es): 971-506
Parent Company: University of Santo Tomas
Distributor for Bookmark; Heritage; Rarebook; Solidaridad
Book Club(s): Book Development Association of the Phillipines; Asian Catholic Publishers

Valentine Romance, *imprint of* Books for Pleasure Inc

Vera-Reyes Inc+
4/F Mariwasa Bldg, 717 Aurora Blvd, 1112 Quezon City
Tel: (02) 7218792 *Fax:* (02) 7218782
Telex: 63740 Vri pn *Cable:* Verareyes Manila
Key Personnel
Man Dir: L O Reyes
Publishing Dir: Gerardo P Legaspi
Dir, Medical Books: Gia Reyes
Founded: 1964
Subjects: Art, History, Medicine, Nursing, Dentistry, Philosophy, Religion - Other
ISBN Prefix(es): 971-575
Subsidiaries: International Typesetting Services; Vera-Reyes Medical Books
Bookshop(s): Vera-Reyes Medical Books

Vibal Publishing House Inc (VPHI)
865 Edsa, Diliman Quezon City
Tel: (02) 993764; (02) 7122722 *Fax:* (02) 7118852
Telex: ITT 40404 *Cable:* VIBAL INC, MANILA
Key Personnel
Chief Executive: Esther A Vibal
Editorial: Rhodora S Yatco
Sales: Dina C Tapang
Production: Rolando S Mata
Publicity, Rights & Permissions: Carian M Espino
Founded: 1955
Subjects: Ethnicity, Foreign Countries, Language Arts, Linguistics, Mathematics, Religion - Other, Science (General), Social Sciences, Sociology
ISBN Prefix(es): 971-07
Parent Company: Nasionale Boekhandel Ltd
Subsidiaries: ASN Graphics; SD Publications
Branch Office(s)
VPHI Cebu Branch, GV Bldg, P del Rosario St, Cebu City

VPHI, see Vibal Publishing House Inc (VPHI)

Young Love, *imprint of* Books for Pleasure Inc

Poland

General Information

Capital: Warsaw
Language: Polish and some German. English also used, especially among young people
Religion: Predominantly Roman Catholic
Population: 38.4 million
Bank Hours: 0800-1900 Monday-Friday, 0800-1600 Saturday
Shop Hours: 1100-1900 Monday-Friday; 0900-1300 Saturday
Currency: 100 groszy = 1 zloty
Export/Import Information: Import of books and newspapers, duty free, no tax. Individual private importers allowed to act. Advertising may be placed through AGPOL Foreign Trade Advertising agency, ul Kierbedzia 4, 7, 00-957 Warsaw. No import licenses as such required. All overseas trade is conducted in foreign cur-

POLAND   BOOK

rency. Small quantities of advertising materials duty free.
Copyright: UCC, Berne (see Copyright Conventions, pg xi)

Albatros
Kazury 2/12, 02-795 Warsaw
Tel: (022) 842-9867 *Fax:* (022) 842-9867
Key Personnel
Owner & Editor-in-Chief: Andrzej Kurylowicz
  E-mail: akurylowicz@wp.pl
Subjects: Fiction, Nonfiction (General)
Number of titles published annually: 80 Print
Total Titles: 110 Print

Alfa, *imprint of* Wydawnictwa Normalizacyjne Alfa-Wero

Wydawnictwa Normalizacyjne Alfa-Wero+
ul Nowogrodzka 22, 00-511 Warsaw
Tel: (02) 6218750; (02) 6216751 *Fax:* (02) 6218750
Telex: 812374 Wuen Pl
Key Personnel
Editor-in-Chief: Jerzy Wysokinski
Production Dir: Zdzislaw Adamski
Sales Manager: Malgorzata Lukaszczuk
Foreign Rights Manager: Wiktor Bukato
Founded: 1956
Subjects: Crafts, Games, Hobbies, Fiction, Science (General), Science Fiction, Fantasy
ISBN Prefix(es): 83-7001; 83-7179
Imprints: Alfa; Beta Books; Beta Comics
Bookshop(s): ul Sienna 63, Warsaw

Wydawnictwo Arkady+
ul Dobra 28, skr poczt, 137, 00-344 Warsaw
Tel: (022) 8268980; (022) 8267079; (022) 8269316; (022) 6358344 *Fax:* (022) 8274194
E-mail: arkady@arkady.com.pl
Web Site: arkady.com.pl
Key Personnel
President & Dir: Janina Krysiak
Editor-in-Chief: Elzbieta Leszczynska
Production Dir: Wieslaw Pyszka
International Rights: Jadwiga Marek
Founded: 1957
Subjects: Antiques, Architecture & Interior Design, Art, Crafts, Games, Hobbies, Environmental Studies, Photography
ISBN Prefix(es): 83-213

Arlekin-Wydawnictwo Harlequin Enterprises sp zoo
Ul Rakowiecka 4 (blB), 00-975 Warsaw
Tel: (022) 499498 *Fax:* (022) 499557
Key Personnel
Man Dir: Barbara Jozwiak
Founded: 1991
Subjects: Romance
ISBN Prefix(es): 83-7149; 83-7070

Wydawnictwa Artystyczne i Filmowe
ul Pulawska 61, 02-595 Warsaw
Tel: (022) 8455301; (022) 8455584; (022) 8455465; (022) 8453936 *Fax:* (022) 8455584; (022) 8455465; (022) 8453936
Key Personnel
Man Dir: Janusz Fogler
Editorial: Edward Rylukowski
Editorial, Publicity: Andrzej Dulewicz
Founded: 1959
Subjects: Art, Drama, Theater, Film, Video, Photography
ISBN Prefix(es): 83-221

Atena
Ul Warszawska 13, 85-959 Bydgoszcz
Tel: (061) 228685 *Fax:* (061) 524082
E-mail: atena@poz1.commet.pl
ISBN Prefix(es): 83-902443

Beta Books, *imprint of* Wydawnictwa Normalizacyjne Alfa-Wero

Beta Comics, *imprint of* Wydawnictwa Normalizacyjne Alfa-Wero

Biblioteka Narodowa
ul Niepodleglosci 213, 00-973 Warsaw
Tel: (022) 8255733; (022) 8259271 *Fax:* (022) 8255251
E-mail: biblnar@bn.org.pl; bndyrekt@bn.org.pl
Telex: 816761
Key Personnel
Dir: Michat Jagietto
Founded: 1928
Member of IFLA, FID, IAML, AIB & ASLIB.
Subjects: Library & Information Sciences
ISBN Prefix(es): 83-7009

BOSZ scp+
Olszania 311, 38622 Olszanica
Tel: (013) 469 90 00 *Fax:* (013) 469 61 88
E-mail: boszsc@ks.onet.pl
Web Site: www.bosz.com.pl
Subjects: Architecture & Interior Design, Art, Photography, Travel

Spoldzielnia Wydawnicza 'Czytelnik'+
ul Wiejska 12a, 00-490 Warsaw
Tel: (022) 6281441 *Fax:* (022) 6283178
E-mail: sekretariat@czytelnik.pl
Web Site: www.czytelnik.pl *Cable:* CZYTELNIK WARSAW
Key Personnel
Man Dir, Chairman: Zakowski Marek
Editor-in-Chief: Henryk Chlystowski
Foreign Rights: Anna Mencwel *Tel:* (022) 9289508 *E-mail:* am@czytelnik.pl
Founded: 1944
Subjects: Biography, Fiction, Journalism, Poetry, Social Sciences, Sociology
ISBN Prefix(es): 83-07
Number of titles published annually: 90 Print

Wydawnictwo Dolnoslaskie+
ul Straznicza 1/3, 50-206 Wroclaw
Tel: (071) 3288954; (071) 3288952 *Fax:* (071) 3288951
E-mail: sekretariat@wd.wroc.pl
Key Personnel
President: Andrzej Adamus
Vice President & Editorial Manager: Jan Stolarczyk
Executive Secretary: Barbara Kocowska
  Tel: (071) 3288951 *E-mail:* kocowska@wd.wvoc.pl
Founded: 1986
Member of the Polish Book Chamber.
Subjects: Art, History, Literature, Literary Criticism, Essays, Mysteries, Poetry
ISBN Prefix(es): 83-7023
Number of titles published annually: 70 Print
Orders to: Ars Polona SAV, Krakowskie Przedmiescie 7, 00-950 Warsaw

Dom Wydawniczy Bellona
ul Grzyowska 77, 00-844 Warsaw
Tel: (022) 620-20-44 *Fax:* (022) 652 26 95
E-mail: biuro@bellona.pl
Web Site: www.bellona.pl
Key Personnel
Dir: Jozef Skrzypiec

Drukarnia I Ksiegarnia Swietego Wojciecha, Dziat Wydawniczy
pl Wolnosci 1, 61-738 Poznan
Tel: (061) 8529186 *Fax:* (061) 8523746
E-mail: wydawnictwo.ksw@archpoznan.org.pl
Telex: 0414220 Kmp *Cable:* Albertinum Poznan
Key Personnel
Man Dir: Bogdan Reformat

Founded: 1895
Subjects: Biblical Studies, Religion - Catholic, Theology
ISBN Prefix(es): 83-7015
Branch Office(s)
ul Freta 48, 00-227 Warsaw
ul Krolewska 15, 20-109 Lubin
Bookshop(s): St Adalbert's Bookshop, pl Wolnosci 1, 61-738 Poznan

Polskie Wydawnictwo Ekonomiczne PWE SA+
ul Canaletta 4, Warsaw 00-099
Tel: (022) 8278001 *Fax:* (022) 8275567
E-mail: pwe@pwe.com.pl
Web Site: www.pwe.com.pl
Key Personnel
President & Editor-in-Chief: Alicja Rutkowska
Founded: 1949
Polish EconomicsPublishers.
Member of Polish Chamber of Books.
Subjects: Accounting, Advertising, Business, Economics, Environmental Studies, Finance, Management, Marketing
ISBN Prefix(es): 83-208
Number of titles published annually: 70 Print
Total Titles: 5,000 Print

Energeia sp zoo Wydawnictwo
ul Szturmowa 1, 02-678 Warsaw
Mailing Address: Skr Poczt 43, 00-976 Warsaw
Tel: (022) 847-00-53 *Fax:* (022) 847-00-53
Key Personnel
Man Dir: Jan E Okuniewski
Founded: 1991
Subjects: Drama, Theater, English as a Second Language, Language Arts, Linguistics, Literature, Literary Criticism, Essays
ISBN Prefix(es): 83-85118
Distributor for Julius Groos Verlag Heidelberg (Germany)

Gdanskie Wydawnictwo Psychologiczne SC
(Gdansk Psychology Publishing Company)+
ul Bema 4/1a, 81-753 Sopot
Tel: (058) 551-61-04; (058) 550-16-04; (058) 551-11-01 *Fax:* (058) 551-61-04; (058) 550-16-04
Web Site: www.gwp.pl
Key Personnel
General Manager: Magdalena Zylicz
  E-mail: magdaz@gwp.gda.pl
Founded: 1991
Publishes exclusively psychology books: academic textbooks, counselling books for psychotherapists & practical psychology for the general market.
Subjects: Psychology, Psychiatry, Self-Help
ISBN Prefix(es): 83-85416; 83-87957; 93-89120
Number of titles published annually: 20 Print
Total Titles: 100 Print

Wydawnictwa Geologiczne
ul Rakowiecka 4, 02-517 Warsaw
Tel: (022) 495351 ext 518
Key Personnel
Dir: Dr Marian Soldan
Founded: 1953
Subjects: Geography, Geology, Mathematics
ISBN Prefix(es): 83-220

Instytut Historii Nauki PAN+
Unit of Polish Academy of Sciences
ul Nowy Swiat 72, Pok 9 Palac Staszica, 00-330 Warsaw
Tel: (022) 8268754; (022) 6572746 *Fax:* (022) 8266137
E-mail: mah01@plearn.bitnet
Key Personnel
Editorial Manager: Anna Zawadzka
International Rights: Prof Andrzej Srodka

Subjects: Astronomy, Biography, Biological Sciences, Chemistry, Chemical Engineering, Earth Sciences, Education, Geography, Geology, History
ISBN Prefix(es): 83-900065; 83-900482; 83-900891; 83-86062
Total Titles: 10 Print

Wydawnictwo Harcerskie 'Horyzonty', see Spotdzielna Anagram

Impuls+
ul Krowoderska 21/3, 31-141 Krakow
Tel: (012) 4225947 *Fax:* (012) 4224180; (012) 4225947
Key Personnel
Dir: Wojciech Sliwerski
Editor-in-Chief: Piotr Niwinski
Founded: 1989
Member of Polish Book Chamber.
Subjects: Education, Environmental Studies, Literature, Literary Criticism, Essays, Philosophy, Religion - Catholic, Social Sciences, Sociology
ISBN Prefix(es): 83-86994; 83-85543; 83-88030

Instytut Wydawniczy Pax, Inco-Veritas+
Wybrzeze Kosciuszkowskie 21a, 00390 Warsaw
Tel: (022) 6257795; (022) 6253398; (022) 6251378 *Fax:* (022) 6253398; (022) 6251378; (022) 6257795
E-mail: iwpax@com.pl
Web Site: www.iwpax.com.pl
Key Personnel
Chief Editor: Amelia Szafranska
Founded: 1949
Subjects: Biblical Studies, Education, History, Literature, Literary Criticism, Essays, Philosophy, Poetry, Religion - Catholic, Theology
ISBN Prefix(es): 83-211
Bookshop(s): Piekna 16b, 00-449 Warsaw
Warehouse: Biuro Sprzedazy IW Pax, Wybrzeze Kosciuszkowskie 21a, 00390 Warsaw
Orders to: Biuro Handlu Zagranicznego Inco-Veritas, ul Wspolna 25, 00-159 Warsaw
Tel: (022) 293216 *Fax:* (022) 295202

Interpress+
al Bagatela 12, 00-585 Warsaw
Tel: (022) 6214876; (022) 6289331; (022) 6289202 *Fax:* (022) 6289331; (022) 6289202
Telex: 816336 pai pL *Cable:* INTERPRESS WARSZAWA
Key Personnel
Editor-in-Chief, Publicity: Bohdan Gawronski
Publicity, Rights & Permissions: Zofia Lewandowska
Production, Sales: Jawusz Malinowski
Founded: 1967
Subjects: History, Regional Interests, Science (General)
ISBN Prefix(es): 83-223
Branch Office(s)
Buero der Polnischen Informationen Agentur (PAI), Vinohradska 1616, Praha 2, Czech Republic *Tel:* 236117
Orders to: Dzial Handlowy, Wydawnictwo Interpress, ul Bagatela 12, 00-585 Warsaw

Iskry - Publishing House Ltd spotka zoo+
ul Smolna 11/13, 00-375 Warsaw
Tel: (022) 8279415 *Fax:* (022) 8279415
Key Personnel
President: Wieslaw Uchanski
Founded: 1952
Subjects: Aeronautics, Aviation, Biography, Cookery, History, Literature, Literary Criticism, Essays, Maritime, Mysteries, Parapsychology, Philosophy, Regional Interests, Science Fiction, Fantasy, Self-Help, Travel
ISBN Prefix(es): 83-207

ITB, *imprint of* Instytut Techniki Budowlanej, Dzial Wydawniczo- Poligraficzny

Panstwowe Przedsiebiorstwo Wydawnictw Kartograficznych
ul Solec 18, 00-410 Warsaw
Tel: (022) 6283251; (022) 6214850 *Fax:* (022) 6280236; (022) 6214850
E-mail: ppwk@pdsox.com *Cable:* PEPEWUKA WARSZAWA
Key Personnel
Dir: Alina Meljon
Founded: 1951
ISBN Prefix(es): 83-7000

Katolicki Uniwersytet Wydawniczo -Redakcja+
ul Konstatynow 1, PL-20-708 Lublin
Tel: (081) 5257151; (081) 5251809 *Fax:* (081) 541246
E-mail: sekret@kul.lublin.pl
Key Personnel
Dir: Edward Pudelko *E-mail:* pudelko@kul.lublin.pl
Founded: 1957
Subjects: Biblical Studies, History, Law, Philosophy, Psychology, Psychiatry, Religion - Catholic, Social Sciences, Sociology, Theology
ISBN Prefix(es): 83-228
Imprints: RW-KUL
Divisions: Redakcja Wydawnictw KUL; Zaklad Malej Poligrafii KUL
Orders to: Kolportaz Dzialu Wydawniczo-Poligraficznego KUL, ul Konstatynow 1, PL-20-708 Lublin *Tel:* (081) 5257166 *Fax:* (081) 5241246 *E-mail:* kolprw@kul.lublin.pl

KAW Krajowa Agencja Wydawnicza
ul Palacza 87a, 60-273 Poznan
Tel: (022) 32336
Telex: 813487 Kaw Pl
Key Personnel
Man Dir & Editor-in-Chief: Dobroslaw Kobielski
Editorial: Jedrzej Bednarowicz
Deputy Editor: Tadeusz Kaczmarek; Zbigniew Zlotnicki
Production: Wladyslaw Szeszko
Sales: Jozef Maka
Founded: 1974
Member of RSW.
Subjects: Education, Ethnicity, Government, Political Science, Science (General), Travel
ISBN Prefix(es): 83-03
Branch Office(s)
ul Podedwornego 12a, 15-269 Bialystok
ul sw Ducha 111/113, 80-801 Gdansk
ul 3 Maja 36, 40-097 Katowice
ul Florianska 33, 31-019 Krakow
ul Sienkiewicza 3/5, 90-113 Lodz
ul Buczka 28, 20-076 Lublin
ul Slowackiego 22, 60-823 Poznan
ul Komunistow 10, 35-030 Rzeszow
ul Orla Bialego 5, 70-562 Szczecin
pl Solny 14, 50-062 Wroclaw

Komputerowa Oficyna Wydawnicza Help+
Dworcowa 8, 05-816 Michalowice
Tel: (022) 723 89 21 *Fax:* (022) 723 87 64
Web Site: www.besthelp.pl
Key Personnel
Man Dir: Piotr Gomolinski *E-mail:* piotr@besthelp.pl
Founded: 1989
Specialize in computer books.
Subjects: Computer Science
ISBN Prefix(es): 83-87211
Number of titles published annually: 15 Print
Total Titles: 200 Print

Wydawnictwa Komunikacji i Lacznosci Co Ltd+
ul Kazimierzowska 52, 02-546 Warsaw

Tel: (022) 492751-56; (022) 492314; (022) 492324; (022) 492345 *Fax:* (022) 492322
E-mail: wkl@wkl.com.pl
Web Site: www.wkl.com.pl
Key Personnel
Dir: Jerzy Kozlowski
Editor-in-Chief: Bogumil Zielinski
Sales & Marketing Dir: Ewa Berus
Founded: 1949
Transport & Communications Publishers.
Subjects: Aeronautics, Aviation, Communications, Electronics, Electrical Engineering, Mechanical Engineering, Radio, TV, Transportation
ISBN Prefix(es): 83-206

Krajowa Agencja Wydawnicza, see KAW Krajowa Agencja Wydawnicza

'Ksiazka i Wiedza' Spotdzielnia Wydawniczo-Handlowa+
ul Smolna 13, 00-375 Warsaw
Tel: (022) 8275401; (022) 8279416 *Fax:* (022) 8279416
E-mail: publisher@kiw.com.pl
Web Site: www.kiw.com.pl
Telex: 817630 Kiw Pl *Cable:* KIW WARSZAWA
Key Personnel
Dir & Editor-in-Chief: Marta Stuhr; Stanistan Soltus
Editor: Jaroslaw Ladosz; Tadeusz Tarnogrodzki
Production: Andrzej Gierkowski
Founded: 1918
Member of RSW.
Subjects: Animals, Pets, Biography, Government, Political Science, History, Philosophy, Social Sciences, Sociology, Travel
ISBN Prefix(es): 83-05

Ksiaznica Publishing Ltd+
ul Powstancow 30/401, 40-039 Katowice
Tel: (032) 2572216 *Fax:* (032) 2572217
E-mail: ksiaznica@domnet.com.pl
Key Personnel
President: Mariusz Morga
Vice President: Bozena Sek
International Rights: Joanna Ociepka
Member of Polish Chamber of Books. Specialize in encyclopedic thematic dictionaries.
Subjects: Fiction, Health, Nutrition, Nonfiction (General), Romance
ISBN Prefix(es): 83-85348; 83-7132

Laumann-Polska+
ul Zymierskiego 53A/4, 58-573 Piechowice
Tel: (075) 7617182 *Fax:* (075) 7617192
Key Personnel
President: Maria Iburg
Subjects: Regional Interests, Travel
ISBN Prefix(es): 83-85716
Book Club(s): Polska Izba Ksiazki

Wydawnictwo Literackie+
ul Dluga 1, 31-147 Krakow
Tel: (012) 4225423 *Fax:* (012) 4225423
E-mail: redakcja@wl.interkom.pl
Key Personnel
Dir: Janusz Adamczyk
Finance Dir: Halina Ofiarska
Editorial Staff: Krzysztof Lisowski
Sales & Marketing: Barbara Leszczynska
Publicity: Boguslawa Stanowska-Cichon
Founded: 1953
Subjects: Art, Biography, Drama, Theater, Film, Video, History, Literature, Literary Criticism, Essays
ISBN Prefix(es): 83-08

Wydawnictwo Lodzkie+
ul Piotrkowska 171/173, Skr Poczi 372, 90-447 Lodz
Tel: (042) 6360331; (042) 6366189 *Fax:* (042) 6368524

Key Personnel
Editorial Dir: Jacek Zaorski
Sales & Publicity: Janina Sobczak
Production: Grazyna Bis-Stepniak
Rights & Permissions: Alfreda Gorzkiewicz
Founded: 1957
Subjects: Biography, Human Relations
ISBN Prefix(es): 83-218

Wydawnictwo Lubelskie
ul Okopowa 7, 20-022 Lublin
Tel: (081) 7436130
Key Personnel
Dir & Editor-in-Chief: Ireneusz Caban
Deputy Editor: Ludwik Zabielski
Founded: 1957
Subjects: Government, Political Science, Human Relations, Poetry, Science (General), Social Sciences, Sociology
ISBN Prefix(es): 83-87399

Ludowa Spoldzielnia Wydawnicza+
ul Grzybowska 4, 00-131 Warsaw
Tel: (022) 6205718; (022) 6205719 *Fax:* (022) 6207277 *Cable:* LSW, WARSZAWA
Key Personnel
Chairman & Editor-in-Chief: Rajewski Krzysztof
Editorial: Jerzy Dobrzanski
Founded: 1946
People's Publishing Cooperative.
Subjects: Agriculture, Biography, History, Literature, Literary Criticism, Essays, Poetry
ISBN Prefix(es): 83-205

Magnum Publishing House Ltd+
ul Narbutta 25A, 02-536 Warsaw
Tel: (022) 6460085; (022) 485505
E-mail: magnum@it.com.pl
Key Personnel
President: Jolanta Woloszanska
Vice President: Marcin Jarek
Founded: 1994
Member of Polish Chamber of Books.
Subjects: Biography, Government, Political Science, History
ISBN Prefix(es): 83-85852

Wydawnictwo Medyczne Urban & Partner+
ulm Sklodowskiej-Curie 55/61, 50-950 Wroclaw
Tel: (071) 3285487; (071) 223061; (071) 223068; (071) 223069; (071) 223065; (071) 3283068 *Fax:* (071) 3284391
Key Personnel
President: Wieslawa Hombek
President & International Rights: Miroslaw Gornicki
Founded: 1992
Subjects: Medicine, Nursing, Dentistry
ISBN Prefix(es): 83-85842
Parent Company: Urban & Schwarzenberg, Munich, Germany

Instytut Meteorologii i Gospodarki Wodnej
(Institute of Meteorology & Water Management)
ul Podlesna 61, 01-673 Warsaw
Tel: (022) 56-94-100 *Fax:* (022) 834-54-66
E-mail: sekretariat@imgw.pl
Web Site: www.imgw.pl
Telex: 814331
Key Personnel
Dir: Prof Jan Zielinski
Founded: 1945
Subjects: Earth Sciences, Environmental Studies, Foreign Countries, Geography, Geology, Library & Information Sciences, Physical Sciences, Meteorology, Hydrology, Oceanology, Water Management, Water Engineering, Water Quality
ISBN Prefix(es): 83-88887
Number of titles published annually: 20 Print

Parent Company: Ministry of Environment
Branch Office(s)
Gdynia
Katowice
Krakow
Poznan
Wroclaw

Muza SA+
ul Marszalkowska 8 IIp, 00-590 Warsaw
Tel: (022) 621-17-75; (022) 621-50-58; (022) 629-50-83 *Fax:* (022) 629-23-49
E-mail: muza@muza.com.pl
Key Personnel
President: Marcin Garlinski
International Rights: Agata Radkiewicz *E-mail:* a.radkiewicz@muza.com.pl
Founded: 1991
Subjects: Art, Cookery, Education, Fiction, House & Home, Nonfiction (General), Social Sciences, Sociology, Travel
ISBN Prefix(es): 83-7079; 83-7200; 83-85325
Imprints: Sport I Turystyka; Warszawskie Wydawnictwo Literackie
Book Club(s): Klub Czytelnikow Muza SA
Warehouse: ul Cybernetyki 9, 00-677 Warsaw

Polskie Wydawnictwo Muzyczne+
ul Krasinskiego 11a, 31-111 Krakow
Tel: (012) 4227171 *Fax:* (012) 4227044
E-mail: pwm@pwm.com.pl
Telex: 813370 *Cable:* PWM
Key Personnel
Man Dir: Dr Leszek Polony
Editorial: Ewa Nyozek
Financial: Andrzej Grobelski
Production: Grazyna Adamczyk
Publicity: Agata Stawska; Elzbieta Widlak
Sales: Andrzej Kosowski
Hire: Aleksandra Woznicka
Rights & Permissions & International Rights: Janina Warzecha
Founded: 1945
Polish Music Publishers.
Subjects: Music, Dance
ISBN Prefix(es): 83-224
Imprints: Poligrafia PWM
Subsidiaries: Centralnaa Biblioteka Muzyczna-Nutowa (PWM Hire Department)
U.S. Office(s): Theodore Presser, One Presser Place, Bryn Mawr, PA 19010-3490, United States *Fax:* 610-527-7841
Distributed by Kalmvs (Great Britain Commonwealth & Australia); Leduc (France); Schott (Germany & Switzerland); Universal (Austria)

Wydawnictwo Nasza Ksiegarnia Sp zoo+
ul Smulikowskiego 24c, 02-868 Warsaw
Tel: (022) 6439389 *Fax:* (022) 6437028
  Cable: NASZA KSIEGARNIA
Key Personnel
President: Miroslaw Tokarczyk
Editor-in-Chief: Malgorzata Samborska
Founded: 1921
Subjects: Education, Fiction, Science (General)
ISBN Prefix(es): 83-10

Norbertinum+
ul Ksiezycowa 15, 20-060 Lublin
Tel: (081) 5333895 *Fax:* (081) 5341243
E-mail: norbertinum@norbertinum.com.pl
Web Site: www.norbertinum.com.pl
Key Personnel
President & International Rights: Norbert Wojciechowski
Founded: 1989
Subjects: Biography, Fiction, History, Literature, Literary Criticism, Essays, Poetry, Religion - Catholic, Science (General), Social Sciences, Sociology, Theology
ISBN Prefix(es): 83-85131; 83-86837; 83-7222

Wydawnictwa Normalizacyjne, see
  Wydawnictwa Normalizacyjne Alfa-Wero

Ossolineum Zaklad Narodowy im Ossolinskich - Wydawnictwo+
Plac Solny 14a, 50-062 Wroclaw
Tel: (071) 3436961 *Fax:* (071) 448103
Toll Free Fax: 800 0712771
E-mail: osso-bn@pwr.wroc.pl
Telex: (071) 12771
Key Personnel
Man Dir: Wojciech Karwacki
Editor-in-Chief: Stanislaw Roscicki
Founded: 1817
Subjects: Archaeology, Architecture & Interior Design, Art, Biography, Biological Sciences, Environmental Studies, History, Language Arts, Linguistics, Literature, Literary Criticism, Essays, Medicine, Nursing, Dentistry, Philosophy, Poetry, Science (General), Social Sciences, Sociology
ISBN Prefix(es): 83-04
Bookshop(s): Sw Marka 12, 31-018 Krakow; ul Marcinkowskiego 30, 61-745 Poznan; Jaworzynska 4, 00-634 Warsaw; Rynek 6, 50-106 Wroclaw
Orders to: Export Dept c/o Ossolineum, Plac Solny 14a, 50-062 Wroclaw

P P H Penta
ul Kaniowska 40, 01-529 Warsaw
Mailing Address: skr poczt 81, 01-829 Warsaw
Tel: (022) 6390465 *Fax:* (022) 6390465
E-mail: penta@penta.pol.pl
Founded: 1988
Member of Polish Book Charitex.
ISBN Prefix(es): 83-85440; 83-900031

Pallottinum Wydawnictwo Stowarzyszenia Apostolstwa Katolickiego+
ul Przybyszewskiego 30 skr poczt /vel BP/23, 60-959 Poznan 2
Tel: (061) 8675233 *Fax:* (061) 8675238
E-mail: pallottinum@pallottinum.pl
Web Site: pallottinum.poznan.pl
Key Personnel
Dir: Stefan Dusza *Tel:* (061) 8672118
  E-mail: dusza@pallottinum.pl
Deputy Dir: Stanislaw Gawrylo
Editorial: Kazimierz Jacaszek
Founded: 1948
Publishers of the Catholic Apostolate Association.
Subjects: Biblical Studies, Philosophy, Religion - Catholic, Theology
ISBN Prefix(es): 83-7014

Panstwowy Instytut Wydawniczy (PIW)
(National Publishing Institute)+
ul Foksal 17, 00-372 Warsaw
Mailing Address: skr poczt 377, 00-372 Warsaw
Tel: (022) 8260201; (022) 8260202; (022) 8260203; (022) 8260204; (022) 8260205 *Fax:* (022) 8261536
E-mail: piw@piw.pl
Web Site: www.piw.pl
Telex: 8261536 *Cable:* PIW
Key Personnel
Dir: Radoslaw J Utnik *Tel:* (022) 8264879
  E-mail: dyrektor@piw.pl
Sales: Tomasz Kazmierczak
Production: Irena Rzepkowska
Rights: Stanislawa Lewicka
Founded: 1946
State Publishing Institute.
Subjects: Biography, Drama, Theater, Ethnicity, Fiction, History, Literature, Literary Criticism, Essays, Poetry, Science (General)
ISBN Prefix(es): 83-06
Number of titles published annually: 60 Print

Pearson Education Polska Sp z oo
ul Jana Olbrachta 94, 01-102 Warsaw

PUBLISHERS POLAND

Tel: (022) 533 1533 *Fax:* (022) 533 1534
E-mail: firstname.lastname@longman.com.pl
Key Personnel
Man Dir: Ms Danuta A Lapkiewicz *Tel:* (022)
 533 1555 *Fax:* (022) 533 1556
Finance & Operations Dir: Marcin Rudnik
 Tel: (022) 533 1551 *Fax:* (022) 533 1556
Commercial Dir: Rajmund Sawka *Tel:* (022) 553 1565
Marketing Manager: Anna Dadej *Tel:* (022) 533 1571
PA Marketing Dir: Katarzyna Glowinska
 Tel: (022) 533 1557 *Fax:* (022) 533 1556
Founded: 1991

PIW, see Panstwowy Instytut Wydawniczy (PIW)

Wydawnictwo Podsiedlik-Raniowski i Spolka+
Zmigrodzka 41/49, 60-171 Poznan
Mailing Address: skr poczt 6, 60-968 Poznan 47
Tel: (061) 8679546 *Fax:* (061) 8676850
E-mail: office@priska.com.pl
Key Personnel
Dir: Stecki Michal *E-mail:* michals@priska.com.pl
Founded: 1990
Specialize also in read-alongs & popular-scientific.
Subjects: Crafts, Games, Hobbies, Education, History, How-to, Poetry
ISBN Prefix(es): 83-85165; 83-7083

Poligrafia PWM, *imprint of* Polskie Wydawnictwo Muzyczne

Polish Scientific Publishers PWN+
PWN, ul Miodowa 10, 00-251 Warsaw
Tel: (022) 6954321; (022) 080020145 *Fax:* (022) 8267163 *Fax on Demand:* 080020145
Cable: PEWUEN WARSZAWA
Key Personnel
Man Dir: Grzegorz Boguta *E-mail:* gbpwn@pol.pl
Dir & Editor-in-Chief: Jan Kofman
Deputy Dir: Jan Malesinski; Elzbieta Goral
Editor: Barbara Petrozolin-Skowronska
International Dept, Rights & Contract Manager: Anna Raiter-Rosinska *E-mail:* arrpwn@pol.pl
Multimedia Publishing Coordinator: Zbigniew Zawadzki
Rights Acquisition Manager: Joanna Mielnik
Founded: 1951
Publish books in foreign languages & co-operate with foreign publishers.
Subjects: Business, Economics, Geography, Geology, Language Arts, Linguistics, Marketing, Mathematics, Medicine, Nursing, Dentistry
ISBN Prefix(es): 83-01
Subsidiaries: Springer PWN; daw Publishers PWN; School Publishers PWN
Branch Office(s)
Oddzial PWN ul Sw Tomasza 30, 31-027 Cracow
Oddzial PWN ul Wieckowskiego 13, 90-721 Lodz
Oddzial PWN ul Ratajczaka 35, 61-816 Poznan
Oddzial PWN ul Kotlarska 41, 50-151 Wroctaw
Showroom(s): ul Suwaks, 02-676 Warsaw
Bookshop(s): Ksiegarnia PWN, ul Miodowa 10, 00-251 Warsaw; ul Wieckowskiego 13, 90-721 Lodz; ul Kuznicza 56, 50-138 Wroclaw; ul SW Tomasza 30, 31-027 Krakow; ul Wodna 819, 61-782 Poznan
Warehouse: ul Suwaks, 02-676 Warsaw

Oficyna Wydawnicza Politechniki Wroclawskiej
wybrzeze wyspianskiego 27, 50-370 Wroclaw
Tel: (071) 3202304; (071) 3282940 *Fax:* (071) 3282940
Telex: 712254
Key Personnel
Dir: Halina Dudek *Tel:* (071) 3203823

Founded: 1968
Subjects: Architecture & Interior Design, Engineering (General), Environmental Studies, Microcomputers, Physical Sciences, Physics, Science (General), Technology
ISBN Prefix(es): 83-7085
Bookshop(s): Pl Grunwaldzki 13, PL 50-370 Wroclaw

Wydawnictwo Polskiego Towarzystwa Wydawcow Ksiazek
ul Mazowiecka 2/4, 00-048 Warsaw
Tel: (035) 260735 *Fax:* (035) 260735
Key Personnel
Contact: Jacek Gdaniec
ISBN Prefix(es): 83-7029; 83-85000

POMORZE-Pomorskie Wydawnictwo Prasowe
ul Paderewskiego 26, 85-075 Bydgoszcz
Tel: (052) 220237; (052) 211396; (052) 210452
Member of RSW.
ISBN Prefix(es): 83-7003

Pomorze Wydawnictwo Spoldzielnia Pracy
ul Paderewskiego 26, 85-075 Bydgoszcz
Tel: (052) 220237; (052) 211396; (052) 210452
Telex: 0562845
Key Personnel
Chief Executive: Zbigniew Cieslinski
Editorial: Dr Ryszard Zietek
Sales, Production, Publicity, Rights & Permissions: Ewa Grinberg
Founded: 1982
ISBN Prefix(es): 83-7003
Bookshop(s): Ksiegarnia Domu Ksiazki, ul Marii Konopnickiej 30, 85-124 Bydgoszcz

Wydawnictwo Prawnicze Co
ul Wisniowa 50, 02-520 Warsaw
Tel: (022) 496151; (022) 496152; (022) 496153; (022) 494094 *Fax:* (022) 499410
E-mail: wp@wp.com.pl
Key Personnel
President, Dir & Editor-in-Chief: Dr Jerzy Kowalski
Founded: 1952
Subjects: Criminology, Law, Marketing, Public Administration, Securities
ISBN Prefix(es): 83-219
Shipping Address: ul Sosnkowskiego 1, 02-495 Warsaw-Ursus
Warehouse: ul Sosnkowskiego 1, 02-495 Warsaw-Ursus

Przedsiebiorstwo Wydawniczo-Handlowe Wydawnictwo Siedmiorog+
ul Swiatnicka 7, 52-018 Wroclaw
Tel: (071) 341-68-71 *Fax:* (071) 341-68-87
Web Site: www.siedmiorog.com.pl
Key Personnel
Man Dir: Michalowski Tomasz
Subjects: Philosophy, Science Fiction, Fantasy
Showroom(s): ul Swiatniche 7, Wroclaw
Bookshop(s): ul Ch Toohue 39, Warsaw

PWE, see Polskie Wydawnictwo Ekonomiczne PWE SA

PZWL Wydawnictwo Lekarskie Ltd+
Unit of PWN Publishers Group
ul Dluga 38-40, 00-238 Warsaw
Mailing Address: Skr poczt 379, 00-950 Warsaw
Tel: (022) 8312161; (022) 8314281-85 *Fax:* (022) 8310054
E-mail: promocja@pzwl.pl
Web Site: www.pzwl.pl *Cable:* WYDLEK WARSZAWA
Key Personnel
President: Krystyna Regulska

Foreign Rights Manager: Anna Czyzewska
 Tel: (022) 8314345 *Fax:* (022) 8314345
 E-mail: anna.czyzewska@pzwl.pl
Founded: 1945
Medical Publishers Company Ltd.
Subjects: Biological Sciences, Chemistry, Chemical Engineering, Child Care & Development, Health, Nutrition, Medicine, Nursing, Dentistry, Psychology, Psychiatry, Veterinary Science
ISBN Prefix(es): 83-200
Total Titles: 400 Print; 2 CD-ROM
Parent Company: Scientific Publishers
Distributed by Scientific Publishers PWN
Distributor for Harcourt Brace & Co Ltd
Warehouse: ul Rolnicza 11, 05-092 Dziekanow Polski *Tel:* (022) 7511334 *Fax:* (022) 7511334

Wydawnictwa Radia i Telewizji
ul Chelmska 9, 00-724 Warsaw
Tel: (022) 412264
Key Personnel
Dir, Editor-in-Chief: Teresa Bartoszek
Production: Maciej Pcion
Founded: 1968
Subjects: Education, Fiction, Radio, TV, Science (General)
ISBN Prefix(es): 83-212

Oficyna Wydawnicza Read Me (Read Me Publishing House)+
ul Minska 25, 03-808 Warsaw
Mailing Address: Skr Poczt 144, 00-987 Warsaw
Tel: (022) 870624 *Fax:* (022) 6771425
E-mail: readme@rm.com.pl
Web Site: www.rm.com.pl
Key Personnel
Man Dir: Wlodzimierz Binczyk
Licensing Coordinator & International Rights: Joanna Kopanczyk *E-mail:* joanna@rm.com.pl
Contact: Janusz Fajfer; Tomasz Zajbt
Founded: 1991
Subjects: Computer Science, Economics, Education, Health, Nutrition, Microcomputers, Outdoor Recreation, Self-Help, Travel
ISBN Prefix(es): 83-85769; 83-7147; 83-87216; 83-900451
Number of titles published annually: 100 Print
Associate Companies: Wydawnicturo Eremis; Wydawnictwo RM

Res Polona+
ul Gdanska 80, 90-613 Lodz
Tel: (042) 6363634; (042) 6374587; (042) 6374607 *Fax:* (042) 6373010
Key Personnel
President: Jozef Fraszczynski
Founded: 1989
Subjects: Education
ISBN Prefix(es): 83-85063; 83-7071
Subsidiaries: Res Polona

Panstwowe Wydawnictwo Rolnicze i Lesne+
Al Jerozolimskie 28, 00-950 Warsaw
Mailing Address: Skr poczt 374, 00-950 Warsaw
Tel: (022) 8276338 *Fax:* (022) 8276338
Telex: 817509 Pl Pwril *Cable:* Pewril Warszawa
Key Personnel
Dir & Chief Editor: Mr Marian Bajorek
Deputy Editor: Halina Gutowski
Deputy Editor, Periodicals: Jan Czajka
Production: Danuta Kozlowska
Founded: 1947
State Agricultural and Forestry Publishers.
Subjects: Agriculture, Environmental Studies, Health, Nutrition, Veterinary Science
ISBN Prefix(es): 83-09
Branch Office(s)
ul Ratajczaka 33, 61-816 Poznan

Rosikon Press+
Aleja Debow 4, 05-080 Izabelin Warsaw
Tel: (022) 7226101; (022) 7226102; (022) 7226666 *Fax:* (022) 7226667

E-mail: rosikom@ikp.atm.com.pl; office@rosikompress.com
Web Site: rosikonpress.com
Key Personnel
Man Dir: Grazyna Kasprzycka-Rosikon *Tel:* (022) 7226666 *E-mail:* grosikon@ikp.atm.com.pl
Founded: 1990
Member of Polish Chamber of Books.
Subjects: Art, History, Photography, Religion - Catholic
ISBN Prefix(es): 83-900695
Number of titles published annually: 5 Print
Total Titles: 3 Print
Distributed by Azymut (Poland)

Wydawnictwo RTW+
ul Broniewskiego 9a, 01-780 Warsaw
Tel: (022) 633-70-10; (022) 39120123 *Fax:* (022) 6486277; (022) 39120123
E-mail: rtw@wydawrtw.media.pl
Web Site: www.wydawrtw.media.pl
Key Personnel
Rights Manager: Anna Wisniewska
Foreign Relations Assistant: Dorota Trusiak
Founded: 1992
Independent, Individual Company.
Subjects: Animals, Pets, Education, Geography, Geology, History, Science (General), Atlases
ISBN Prefix(es): 83-86822
Number of titles published annually: 50 Print; 20 Audio
Total Titles: 80 Print; 25 Audio
Online services available
through www.wydawrtw.media.pl.
Warehouse: ul Koleyowa 19/21, Warsaw, Contact: Dorota Trusiak

RW-KUL, *imprint of* Katolicki Uniwersytet Wydawniczo -Redakcja

Wydawnictwo SIC+
ul Chetmska 27/23, 00-724 Warsaw
Tel: (022) 8400753 *Fax:* (022) 8400753
E-mail: svc@zigzag.pl; scc@scc.ksiazka.pl; sic@zigzag.pl
Web Site: www.svc.ksiazka.pl
Key Personnel
Man Dir: Elzbieta Czerwirlska
Editor-in-Chief: Ranata Lis
Founded: 1993
Subjects: Human Relations, Self-Help
ISBN Prefix(es): 83-86056
Total Titles: 50 Print
Orders to: Hydawnictwo Siel, ul Tucka 2/4/6 m 21, 00-845 Warsaw, Contact: Katarzyna Jaskiewicz *Fax:* (022) 6546784 *E-mail:* sic@sic.ksiazka.pl

'Slask' Ltd+
Al W Korfantego 51, skr poczt 3667, 40-161 Katowice
Tel: (032) 580756; (032) 581913; (032) 585870 *Fax:* (032) 583229
E-mail: biuro@slaskwn.com.pl
Key Personnel
President: Tadeusz Sierny
Vice President: Ewa Bober
Editor: Wojciech Janota
Founded: 1954
Member of the Polish Chamber of the Book.
Subjects: Advertising, English as a Second Language, History, Literature, Literary Criticism, Essays, Nonfiction (General), Poetry, Regional Interests, Science (General)
ISBN Prefix(es): 83-900705; 83-900814; 83-85831; 83-7164

Spoleczny Instytut Wydawniczy Znak+
ul T Kosciuszki 37, 30-105 Krakow
Tel: (012) 4291469; (012) 4219776 *Fax:* (012) 4219814
E-mail: rucinska@znak.com.pl *Cable:* KOSCIUSZKI 37
Key Personnel
Contact: Jolanta Wlodarczyk
Founded: 1959
Subjects: History, Philosophy, Religion - Other
ISBN Prefix(es): 83-7006
Bookshop(s): ul Slawkowska 1, 31-007 Krakow

Sport 1 Turystyka, *imprint of* Muza SA

Spotdzielna Anagram
al 3 Maja 2 Pok, 4, 01-391 Warsaw
Tel: (022) 6250114
Key Personnel
Agency Editor-in-Chief: Zygmunt Konopka
Editorial: Andrzej Murawski
Sales: Halina Popiolek
Production: Wieslaw Felczak
Founded: 1974
Youth Publishing Agency & Publishing Co-operative.
This organization replaces the former Wydawnictwo Harcerskie 'Horyzonty'. It is also a Workers' Publishing Co-operative, allied to RSW. Mlodziezowa acts as both agency & publisher for Polish youth.
Subjects: Ethnicity, Government, Political Science, Science (General), Social Sciences, Sociology
ISBN Prefix(es): 83-203; 83-86086

Zaklad Wydawnictw Statystycznych
al Niepodleglosci 208, 00-925 Warsaw
Tel: (022) 6083223; (022) 6083210 *Fax:* (022) 6083867
Telex: 814581a *Cable:* GUS 12WS
Key Personnel
Man Dir: Andrzej Stasiun
Marketing: Christo Cwetkow
Founded: 1966
Statistical Publications Board of the Central Statistical Office.
Subjects: Economics, Mathematics, Social Sciences, Sociology
ISBN Prefix(es): 83-7027
Divisions: Zaklad Wydawnictwo

Oficyna Wydawnicza Szkoly Glownej Handlowej w Warszawie Oficyna Wydawnicza SGH+
Al Niepodleglosci 164, 02-554 Warsaw
Tel: (022) 494925; (022) 491251 (ext 486) *Fax:* (022) 495312
E-mail: wydawn@sgh.waw.pl
Web Site: www.akson.sgh.waw.pl
Telex: 816031sgh
Key Personnel
Contact: Andrzej Gawerski
Founded: 1917
Subjects: Economics, English as a Second Language, Finance, History, Law, Mathematics, Philosophy, Public Administration, Social Sciences, Sociology
ISBN Prefix(es): 83-86689; 83-7225

Instytut Techniki Budowlanej, Dzial Wydawniczo- Poligraficzny
ul Ksawerow 21, 02-656 Warsaw
Tel: (022) 8431471 *Fax:* (022) 8432931
Key Personnel
Man Dir: Stanislaw Wierzbicki
Founded: 1945
Subjects: Civil Engineering
ISBN Prefix(es): 83-7130; 83-7226
Imprints: ITB
Bookshop(s): ul Filtrowa 1, 00-611 Warsaw

Towarzystwo Naukowe w Toruniu
ul Wysoka 16, PL 87-100 Torun
Tel: (056) 6223941 (ext 8)
Key Personnel
Editorial Manager: Bozena Soltys
Founded: 1875
Specialize in humanities.
Subjects: Archaeology, Art, Biological Sciences, Geography, Geology, History, Language Arts, Linguistics, Law, Medicine, Nursing, Dentistry, Physical Sciences, Regional Interests
ISBN Prefix(es): 83-85196; 83-87639

Wydawnictwo TPPR Wspolpraca+
ul Marszalkowska 115, 00-932 Warsaw
Tel: (022) 200301 (ext 227)
Key Personnel
Chief Executive: Ryszard Pogonowski
Production: Kazimierz Andruk
Founded: 1984
Subjects: Government, Political Science, Literature, Literary Criticism, Essays
ISBN Prefix(es): 83-7018

Wydawnictwo Uniwersytetu Wroclawskiego SP ZOO
pl Uniwersytecki 9/13, 50-137 Wroclaw
Tel: (071) 3752991; (071) 2752809; (071) 3752773 *Fax:* (071) 3752735
E-mail: marketing@wuwr.com.pl
Web Site: www.wuwr.com.pl
Key Personnel
President: Marek Gorny
Founded: 1996
Scientific handbooks for students of Wroclawskiego University.
ISBN Prefix(es): 83-229

Verbinum Wydawnictwo Ksiezy Werbistow+
ul Ostrobramska 98, 04-118 Warsaw
Tel: (022) 6107878; (022) 8703286 *Fax:* (022) 6107775
Key Personnel
Editor: P Antoni Koszorz
Founded: 1983
Subjects: Developing Countries, Religion - Other
ISBN Prefix(es): 83-85009; 83-85762; 83-7192
Parent Company: Verbinum
Subsidiaries: Verbinum, Dzial Kolportazu

Videograf II Sp z o o Zaklad Poracy Chronionej
al W Korfantego 191, 40-153 Katowice
Tel: (03) 2036558; (03) 2036559; (03) 2036560 *Fax:* (03) 2036558; (03) 2036559; (03) 2036560
E-mail: videograf@videograf.dnd.com.pl
Key Personnel
Editor-in-Chief & International Rights: Jacek Illg
Man Dir: Franciszek Leki
Founded: 1996
Subjects: Biography, Education, Fiction, Film, Video, Gardening, Plants, Mysteries, Photography
ISBN Prefix(es): 83-7183; 83-86831

Vocatio Publishing House+
Skr Poczt 41, Polnej Rozy 1, PL-02792 Warsaw 78
Tel: (022) 648-5450 *Fax:* (022) 648-6382
E-mail: vocatio@vocatio.com.pl
Web Site: www.vocatio.com.pl
Key Personnel
President & Chief Executive Officer: Piotr Waclawik *E-mail:* wydawca@vocatio.com.pl
Founded: 1991
Member of ECPA, ICCC.
Subjects: Biblical Studies, Religion - Catholic, Religion - Protestant, Theology, Bible reference books; children's books, video books, music
ISBN Prefix(es): 83-85435; 83-7146

Wydawnictwo WAB (WAB Publishers)+
Lowicka 31 Str, 02-502 Warsaw

Tel: (022) 646 05 10; (022) 646 05 11; (022) 646 01 74; (022) 646 01 75 *Fax:* (022) 646 05 10; (022) 646 05 11; (022) 646 01 74; (022) 646 01 75
E-mail: wab@wab.com.pl
Web Site: www.wab.com.pl
Key Personnel
Editor: Beata Stasinska *Tel:* (022) 646 05 10
Founded: 1991
Specialize in promoting & publishing Polish contemporary literary fiction, as well as translations.
Subjects: Fiction, Health, Nutrition, Human Relations, Nonfiction (General)
ISBN Prefix(es): 83-88221
Number of titles published annually: 40 Print
Total Titles: 450 Print

Warszawskie Wydawnictwo Literackie, *imprint of* Muza SA

Wydawnictwa Przemyslowe WEMA+
ul Danilowiczowska 18, 00-950 Warsaw
Tel: (022) 8275456; (022) 8272117 *Fax:* (022) 6355779
Telex: 814548
Key Personnel
Chief Executive: Andrzej Januszewicz
Founded: 1967
Specialize in Printing.
Subjects: Electronics, Electrical Engineering, Mechanical Engineering
ISBN Prefix(es): 83-85250

'Wiedza Powszechna' Panstwowe Wydawnictwo+
ul Jasna 26, 00-054 Warsaw
Mailing Address: PO Box 162, 00-054 Warsaw
Tel: (022) 8269592 *Fax:* (022) 8269592; (022) 8268594
Key Personnel
Dir: Teresa Korsak
Deputy: Tadeusz Mazurek
Founded: 1952
Subjects: Language Arts, Linguistics, Science (General)
ISBN Prefix(es): 83-214

Wydawnictwo Wilga sp zoo+
ul J Smulikowskiego 1/3, 00-389 Warsaw
Tel: (022) 826-08-82; (022) 827-90-11 (ext 282) *Fax:* (022) 826-06-43
E-mail: wilga@ternet.pl
Key Personnel
President: Jan Wojnitko
Vice President: Anna Sikorska-Michalau
Editor-in-Chief: Olga Wojnitko
Foreign Rights: Anna Kedzior
Founded: 1993
Subjects: Education, Fiction
ISBN Prefix(es): 83-7156; 83-86664; 83-901029; 83-903028
Subsidiaries: Wilga Marketing
Warehouse: Panstwowe Magazyny Ustugowe, ul Przeyazdowa 25, 05-800 Pruszkow

WNT, *imprint of* Wydawnictwa Naukowo-Techniczne

WOSl "Wspolna Sprawa" Warsaw, *imprint of* Wydawn Na Sprawa' Wydawniczo-Oswiatowa Spotdzielnia Inwalidow

WUW, see Wydawnictwa Uniwersytetu Warszawskiego

Wydawn Na Sprawa' Wydawniczo-Oswiatowa Spotdzielnia Inwalidow+
ul Zelazna 40, 00-832 Warsaw
Tel: (022) 6209071 (ext 26) *Fax:* (022) 6209197

Key Personnel
President: Zdzislaw Kozanecki
Vice President, Publishing Manager: Marianna Malejko
Founded: 1956
Educational Publishing Co-operative of the Disabled.
Subjects: Crafts, Games, Hobbies
ISBN Prefix(es): 83-85048
Imprints: WOSl "Wspolna Sprawa" Warsaw
Showroom(s): Al Solidarnosci, 82

Wydawnictwa Naukowo-Techniczne+
ul Mazowiecka 2/4, 00-048 Warsaw
Tel: (022) 8267271 *Fax:* (022) 8268293
E-mail: wnt@pol.pl
Web Site: www.wnt.com.pl *Cable:* ENTE WARSZAWA
Key Personnel
General Manager: Dr Aniela Topulos
Rights & Permissions: Agnieszka Koztowska *Tel:* (022) 8272833
Founded: 1949
Subjects: Chemistry, Chemical Engineering, Computer Science, Electronics, Electrical Engineering, Mathematics, Mechanical Engineering, Microcomputers, Physics, Technology
ISBN Prefix(es): 83-204
Imprints: WNT

Wydawnictwa Szkolne i Pedagogiczne (Polish Educational Publishers-WSiP)+
pl Dabrowskiego 8, 00-959 Warsaw
Mailing Address: skr poczt 480, 00-959 Warsaw
Tel: (022) 8265451; (022) 8265452; (022) 8265453; (022) 8265454; (022) 8265455 *Fax:* (022) 8279280
E-mail: wsip@ikp.atm.com.pl; bossrwsip@ikp.atm.com.pl
Web Site: www.wsip.com.pl
Telex: 816132 *Cable:* WUESIPE WARSZAWA
Key Personnel
Man Dir: Andrzej Chrzanowski
Rights & Permissions: Maciej Lipko
Advertising: Wojciech Krasuski
Contact: Maria Bogobowicz
Founded: 1945
Member of EEPG, Polish Chamber of the Book.
Subjects: Education, Psychology, Psychiatry
ISBN Prefix(es): 83-02
Branch Office(s)
Delegatura WSiP, Basztowa 15, 31-143 Cracow
Orders to: Ars Polona, PO Box 1001, 00-068 Warsaw

Wydawnictwa Uniwersytetu Warszawskiego+
lmprint of Wydawnictwa Uniwersytetu Warszawskiego
ul Nowy Swiat 4, 00-497 Warsaw
Tel: (022) 5531318 *Fax:* (022) 5531318
E-mail: wuw@uw.edu.pl
Key Personnel
Dir: Elzbieta Nogowicz
Rights & Permissions Contact: Jolanta Okonska
Assistant Marketing Manager: Monika Glowacz
Founded: 1956
A predominant share in our offer is taken by the publications of the Polish Faculty (theory & history of literature, linguistics) & books on culture written from the point of view of various humanistic disciplines.
Subjects: African American Studies, Americana, Regional, Anthropology, Archaeology, Asian Studies, Biography, Biological Sciences, Economics, Education, English as a Second Language, Ethnicity, Genealogy, Geography, Geology, Government, Political Science, Religion - Other, Social Sciences, Sociology, Women's Studies
ISBN Prefix(es): 83-230; 83-235
Number of titles published annually: 45 Print
Total Titles: 455 Print

Orders to: Centrala Handlu Zagranicznego, Ars Polona SA, ul Krakowskie Przedmiescie 7, PL, PO Box 1001, 00-950 Warsaw *Tel:* (022) 8261201 *Fax:* (022) 8266240

Wydawnictwo Baturo (Baturo Publishers)+
uL Drobniewicza 26, 43-309 Bielsko-Biala
Tel: (33) 8125086 *Fax:* (33) 8140955
Fax on Demand: (33) 8140955
E-mail: baturo@baturo.com.pl
Web Site: www.baturo.com.pl
Key Personnel
Contact: Andrzej Baturo; Inez Baturo
Founded: 1991
Member of PTWK & PlK, Polish Book Chamber, Polish Association of Book Publishers.
Subjects: Animals, Pets, Architecture & Interior Design, Gardening, Plants, How-to, Photography
ISBN Prefix(es): 83-900564; 83-905021
Number of titles published annually: 5 Print

Wydawnictwo DiG (DiG Publishing; DiG Publishing)+
Nowy Swiat 39, 00-029 Warsaw
Tel: (022) 828-00-96 *Fax:* (022) 828-00-96
E-mail: biuro@dig.com.pl
Web Site: www.dig.com.pl
Key Personnel
Managing Dir: Slawomir Gorzynski
Dir: Krzysztof Dabrowski *E-mail:* kjd@dig.com.pl
Founded: 1991
Independent publishing company specializing in history & humanities.
Member of Polska Izba Ksiazki (Polish Book Chamber).
Subjects: Antiques, Archaeology, Art, Biography, Genealogy, History, Language Arts, Linguistics, Library & Information Sciences, Literature, Literary Criticism, Essays
ISBN Prefix(es): 83-7181; 83-85490
Number of titles published annually: 80 Print; 2 CD-ROM; 2 Online; 2 E-Book
Total Titles: 250 Print
Online services available through World Wide Web.
Distributed by Polnische Buchhandlung; Orbis Book Ltd
Bookshop(s): Al Niepodleglosci 213, 02-086 Warsaw

Wydawnictwo Naukowe PWN, see Polish Scientific Publishers PWN

Instytut Wydawniczy Zwiazkow Zawodowych
ul Noakowskiego 10 m 54, 00-378 Warsaw
Tel: (022) 279011
Key Personnel
Dir: Andrzej Wacowski
Founded: 1950
Publishing House of Trade Unions.
Subjects: Labor, Industrial Relations
ISBN Prefix(es): 83-202
Bookshop(s): Ksiegarnia Skladowa, Marienszat 8, 00-302 Warsaw

Portugal

General Information

Capital: Libson
Language: Portuguese
Religion: Predominately Roman Catholic, some Protestant
Population: 10 million
Bank Hours: 0830-1500 Monday-Friday

PORTUGAL

Shop Hours: 0900-1300, 1500-1900 Monday-Friday (some do not close midday); 0900-1300 Saturday. Generally closed Monday morning October-November
Currency: 100 Eurocents = 1 Euro; 200.482 Portuguese escudos = 1 Euro
Export/Import Information: Member of European Economic Community. Foreign language books from most countries dutied per kg (free from UK and reduced from EEC); atlases and children's picture books have higher tariff rate and children's picture books have an import surcharge. 5% VAT on books. Small quantity of advertising duty-free. No import license required for goods not exceeding a certain value, otherwise license including permission to transfer foreign exchange required.
Copyright: UCC, Berne (see Copyright Conventions, pg xi)

Academia das Ciencias de Lisboa
Rua Academia das Ciencias 19-1, 1200 Lisbon
Tel: (021) 3463866
ISBN Prefix(es): 972-623

Africa Literatura Arte Cultura - ALAC
Av Pedro V 11 2 D, 2795 Linda-A-Velha
Tel: (01) 4192274
ISBN Prefix(es): 972-9041

Edicoes Afrontamento+
Rua Costa Cabral 859, 4200 Porto
Tel: (02) 489271 *Fax:* (02) 491777
E-mail: afrontamento@mail.telepac.pt
Key Personnel
Man Dir, Editorial, Production: Jose Sousa Ribeiro
Sales, Publicity, Rights & Permissions: Marcela Figueiredo Torres
Founded: 1963
Subjects: Film, Video, Government, Political Science, Literature, Literary Criticism, Essays, Social Sciences, Sociology
ISBN Prefix(es): 972-36

ALAC, see Africa Literatura Arte Cultura - ALAC

Publicacoes Alfa SA+
Estrada Lisboa-Sintra, Km 14, Edificio CETOP, 2725-377 Mem Martins
Tel: (021) 917 2807 *Fax:* (021) 917 0130
Key Personnel
Administrator: Francisco Lyon de Castro
Founded: 1973
Subjects: History
ISBN Prefix(es): 972-626
Parent Company: Publicacoes Europa-America
Branch Office(s)
Commercial & Editorial Departments, Estrada Lisboa-Sintra, Km 14, Edificio CETOP, 2725-377 Mem Martins
Bookshop(s): Livraria Alfa, Avenida Antonio Augusto de Aguiar 150-A, 1050 Lisboa; Livraria Alfa, Rua Luis Pastor de Macedo, 1B, 1750 Lisboa

Livraria Almedina
Arco de Almedina 15, 3000 Coimbra
Tel: (039) 26199 *Fax:* (039) 851901
E-mail: livrarialmedina@mail.telepac.pt
Telex: 52207 acic p
Key Personnel
Man Dir: Joaquim Machado
Founded: 1955
Subjects: Education, Law
ISBN Prefix(es): 972-40

Associate Companies: Edicoes Globo Ltda, Rua S Filipe Nery 37A, 1250; Porto Ltda, Rua de Ceuta 79, 4050 Oporto
Bookshop(s): Arco de Almedina 15, Rua Ferreira Borges 121, 3049 Coimbra, Codex

Armenio Amado Editora de Simoes, Beirao & Ca Lda+
Rua Estrela 2-2, 3000 Coimbra
Tel: (039) 92150 *Fax:* (039) 851901
Key Personnel
Man Dir: Joaquim Machado
Founded: 1929
Subjects: Architecture & Interior Design, Government, Political Science, History, Language Arts, Linguistics, Law, Philosophy, Psychology, Psychiatry, Religion - Other, Social Sciences, Sociology
ISBN Prefix(es): 972-628

Edicoes Antigona
Rua Jorge Barradas, L 212-4d90 Dto, 1500 Lisbon
Tel: (021) 749483 *Fax:* (021) 749483
Key Personnel
Editorial, Sales: Manuel Luis de Oliveira
Founded: 1979
Subjects: Fiction, Government, Political Science, History, Literature, Literary Criticism, Essays, Social Sciences, Sociology
ISBN Prefix(es): 972-608

Apaginastantas - Cooperativa de Servicos Culturais
Apdo 4254, 1507 Lisbon Codex
Tel: (021) 668987
Key Personnel
Man Dir: Anabela Mendes
Editorial: Joao Barrento
Founded: 1982
Subjects: Literature, Literary Criticism, Essays, Social Sciences, Sociology
ISBN Prefix(es): 972-607

Apostolado da Oracao Secretariado Nacional
Largo das Teresinhas 5, 4719 Braga Codex
Tel: (053) 22485 *Fax:* (053) 615631
Key Personnel
Man Dir, Editorial: Manuel Morujao; Americo Nunes
Founded: 1874
Subjects: Biography, Poetry, Religion - Other, Theology
ISBN Prefix(es): 972-39

Livraria Arnado Lda
Rua Joao Machado 9-11, 3007 Coimbra Codex
Tel: (039) 27573 *Fax:* (039) 22598
Key Personnel
Man Dir: Vasco Antunes Domingos
Founded: 1966
Subjects: Law, Literature, Literary Criticism, Essays, Mathematics
ISBN Prefix(es): 972-701
Parent Company: Porto Editora Lda
Associate Companies: Empresa Literaria Fluminense, Lda

Arquivo Universidade de Coimbra
Rua S Pedro 11-2, 3000 Coimbra
Tel: (039) 25422 *Fax:* (039) 25841
Telex: 52273
Key Personnel
Contact: Manuel Augusto Rodrigues
ISBN Prefix(es): 972-594

Arvore Coop de Actividades Artisticas, CRL
Pr Azevedo Albuquerque 1, Porto 4000
Tel: (02) 383867 *Fax:* (02) 2002684
Key Personnel
President: Jose Rodrigues

Founded: 1963
Subjects: Architecture & Interior Design, Art
ISBN Prefix(es): 972-9089

Assirio & Alvim
Rua de Sao Nicolau 119-4, 1100-548 Lisbon
Tel: (021) 555580 *Fax:* (021) 3152935
Key Personnel
Editor: Herminio Monteiro
Subjects: Art, History, Literature, Literary Criticism, Essays, Photography
ISBN Prefix(es): 972-37

Atica, SA Editores e Livreiros
Rue Alvaro Coutinho, 2-3D, 1100 Lisbon
Tel: (021) 8153220 *Fax:* (021) 8153219
Key Personnel
Man Dir: Vasco Silva; Jose Rodrigues
Editorial, Rights & Permissions: Vasco Silva
Founded: 1935
Subjects: Drama, Theater, Literature, Literary Criticism, Essays, Poetry, Social Sciences, Sociology
ISBN Prefix(es): 972-617

Editorial 'Avante!'
Avenue Admiral, Continho stammerer, n 121, PT-1700-029 Lisbon
Tel: (021) 8429836 *Fax:* (021) 8429849
Telex: 65791
Key Personnel
Man Dir: Francisco Melo
Founded: 1974
Subjects: Economics, Fiction, Government, Political Science, Philosophy
ISBN Prefix(es): 972-550
Orders to: Alameda St Antonio dos Capuchos 6-B, 1100 Lisbon

Basica Editora
Rua de Entrecampos 36 - R/c E, 1700 Lisbon
Tel: (021) 779273
Key Personnel
Man Dir, Rights & Permissions: Francisco Prata Ginja
Editorial: Rui Ferreira Lopes da Costa
Production, Publicity: Maria Jorge Lopes da Costa
Founded: 1974
Subjects: Education
ISBN Prefix(es): 972-631
Imprints: BE
Sales Office(s): Platano Editora SARL
Bookshop(s): Livraria Basica, Ave Elias Garcia 49-B, 1000 Lisbon

BE, *imprint of* Basica Editora

Bertrand Editora Lda+
Rua Anchieta 29-1, 1200 Lisbon
Tel: (021) 3468286 *Fax:* (021) 3479728
Telex: 42748
Key Personnel
Man Dir: Joao Carlos Alvim
Sales, Rights & Permissions: Teresa Mendonca
Production: Mario Correia
Publicity: Laura Pinheiro
Founded: 1727
Subjects: Art, Literature, Literary Criticism, Essays, Social Sciences, Sociology
ISBN Prefix(es): 972-25
Bookshop(s): Sociedades Livreiras Bertrand

Bezerr-Editorae e Distribuidora de Abel Antonio Bezerra
Bairro Duarte Paeheco, Rua do Rosmaninho 110, Apdo 313, 4703 Braga
Tel: (053) 22604 *Fax:* (053) 617105
Key Personnel
Man Dir: Abel Antonio Bezerra
Founded: 1996

PUBLISHERS

PORTUGAL

Subjects: Drama, Theater, Education, Ethnicity, Fiction, History, Poetry, Travel
ISBN Prefix(es): 972-97378

Biblioteca Geral da Universidade de Coimbra
Division of Universidade de Coimbra
Largo Porta Ferrea, 3000-447 Coimbra Codex
Tel: (0239) 859800; (0239) 859800 *Fax:* (0239) 827135
E-mail: bguc@ci.uc.pt
Key Personnel
Dir: Prof Anibal Pinto De Castro
  E-mail: acastro@ci.uc.pt
Contact: Lucia Veloso
Subjects: Education, History, Library & Information Sciences, Literature, Literary Criticism, Essays, Music, Dance, Religion - Catholic
ISBN Prefix(es): 972-616

Biblioteca Publica Municipal do Porto
Rua D Joao IV, 4099 Porto Codex
Tel: (02) 565361; (02) 572147 *Fax:* (02) 5106139
Telex: 28108
Founded: 1833
ISBN Prefix(es): 972-634

Brasilia Editora (J Carvalho Branco)+
Rua Jose Falcao 173, 4050-317 Porto
Tel: (02) 2055854 *Fax:* (02) 2055854 *Cable:* BRASILIAEDITORA
Key Personnel
Man Dir: J Carvalho Branco *Tel:* 02 2001896 *Fax:* 02 2001904
Editorial, Rights & Permissions: Dr Zulmira C Branco
Sales, Publicity: Dr Isabel C Branco
Production: Joana Carvalho Branco
Founded: 1961
Subjects: Astrology, Occult, Biography, Fiction, Government, Political Science, Health, Nutrition, How-to, Philosophy, Poetry, Psychology, Psychiatry, Religion - Other, Social Sciences, Sociology
ISBN Prefix(es): 972-557
Parent Company: Livraria Leitura - Fernandes e Branco Lda, Rua de Ceuta 88, 4050
Associate Companies: Livraria Leitura - Fernandes e Branco Lda, Rua de Ceuta 88, 4050 Porto
Subsidiaries: Livraria Brasilia Editora
Bookshop(s): Livraria Brasilia Editora, Ave Almirante Reis 256B, 1000 Lisbon

Broteria Associacao Cultural e Cientifica
Rua Maestro Antonio Taborda, 14, 1293 Lisbon, Codex
Tel: (021) 3961660 *Fax:* (021) 3956629
ISBN Prefix(es): 972-9076

Camara Municipal de Castelo
Viana do Costelo Camara, 4900 Viana
Tel: (058) 828580 *Fax:* (058) 829811
Telex: 32582
Subjects: Antiques, Archaeology, Architecture & Interior Design, Art, History, Poetry
ISBN Prefix(es): 972-588
Associate Companies: Biblioteca Municipal, Museo Municipal
Subsidiaries: Livraria Municipal

Editorial Caminho SARL+
Al Santo Antonio dos Capuchos 6B, 1100 Lisbon
Tel: (021) 3152683 *Fax:* (021) 534346
E-mail: caminho@mail.telepac.pt
Key Personnel
Man Dir: Zeferino Antas de Coelho
Founded: 1977
Subjects: Fiction, Government, Political Science
ISBN Prefix(es): 972-21

Capu
Av Almirante Gago Coutinho 158, Lisbon 1700
Tel: (021) 8492869 *Fax:* (021) 8409361
Key Personnel
President: Torcato Lopes
ISBN Prefix(es): 972-580

Editora Caravela+
Rua Gen Mor Sarmento 9 C/v, 1500 Lisbon
Tel: (021) 155848 *Fax:* (021) 155848
Key Personnel
Man Dir & International Rights: Jose Chaves Ferreira
Founded: 1986
ISBN Prefix(es): 972-639

Celta Editora, Lda
Rua Vera Cruz 13-1j, 2780 Oeiras
Tel: (01) 4417433 *Fax:* (01) 4417733
Key Personnel
Contact: Rui Pena Pires
ISBN Prefix(es): 972-8027

Centro Estudos Geograficos
Faculdade de Letras Cidade Universitaria, 1600-214 Lisbon
Tel: (021) 7940218 *Fax:* (021) 7938690
E-mail: ceg@mail.telepac.pt
Key Personnel
President: Dr Diogo de Abreu
Founded: 1944
Subjects: Geography, Geology, Social Sciences, Sociology
ISBN Prefix(es): 972-636

Centro Psicologia Clinica+
Praceta dos Lirios, 2-r/c E, 2725 Mem Martins
Tel: (01) 9211182
ISBN Prefix(es): 972-725

Edicoes Cetop+
Apdo 7, 2726 Mem Martins Codex
Tel: (01) 9263222 *Fax:* (01) 9217940
Telex: 42255 pea p
Key Personnel
Man Dir: Tito Lyon de Castro
Editorial Dir, Rights & Production: Jose Antonio Rosa
Founded: 1965
Member of Euro-Business Publishing Network.
Subjects: Advertising, Business, Career Development, Computer Science, Finance, Management, Microcomputers, Technology, Travel
ISBN Prefix(es): 972-641
Subsidiaries: Lyon Multimedia Edicoes
Orders to: Publicacoes Europa America, Apdo 8, 2726 Mem Martins Codex

Chaves Ferreira Publicacoes SA
Rua D Carlos de Mascarehas, 16A porta-A, 1000 Lisbon
Tel: (021) 3871373 *Fax:* (021) 3871396
Key Personnel
Man Dir: Fernando Duval Chaves Ferreira
Founded: 1989
Subjects: Art, History, Technology
ISBN Prefix(es): 972-9402

Cidade Nova Editora
Rua Dr Camilo Dionizio Alvares 233, 2775 Parede
Tel: (01) 2478734 *Fax:* (01) 2476369
ISBN Prefix(es): 972-9159

Publicacoes Ciencia e Vida Lda+
Rua Victor Cordon 24-1d90 Dto, 1200 Lisbon
Tel: (021) 342-7989 *Fax:* (021) 3460224
Key Personnel
Man Dir, Editorial: Jeronimo Simoes
Founded: 1979

Subjects: Agriculture, Animals, Pets, Environmental Studies, Medicine, Nursing, Dentistry
ISBN Prefix(es): 972-590

Livraria Civilizacao (Americo Fraga Lamares & Ca Lda)+
Rua Alberto Aires de Gouveia 27, 4000 Porto
Tel: (02) 20002286 *Fax:* (02) 312382 *Cable:* Alamares
Key Personnel
Man Dir: Arquitecto Moura Bessa
Rights & Permissions: Maria Alice Moura Bessa
Founded: 1921
Subjects: Art, Economics, Fiction, Government, Political Science, History, Social Sciences, Sociology
ISBN Prefix(es): 972-26
Branch Office(s)
Ave Almirante Reis 102 r/c-Dto, Lisbon 1
Tel: (021) 823389 *Fax:* (021) 823389

Editora Classica+
Rua Gloria, 10 r/c, 1298 Lisbon, Codex
Tel: (021) 372386 *Fax:* (021) 3474729
Telex: 18570 escoli p.
Key Personnel
Editorial: Francisco Paulo
Subjects: Behavioral Sciences, Business, Communications, Drama, Theater, Fiction, History, Management, Science Fiction, Fantasy, Social Sciences, Sociology, Wine & Spirits
ISBN Prefix(es): 972-561
Bookshop(s): Cascais Shopping, Loja 12B, 2675 Cascais; Shopping dos Clerigos, 4000 Porto
Orders to: Distribuidora Internacional de Livros Lda, Rua Vale Formoso 37, 1900 Lisbon
Tel: (021) 8681183 *Fax:* (021) 8581257

Coimbra Editora Lda+
c/o Montenego Aura, Rua Amado, 3002 Coimbra Codex
Tel: (039) 25459 *Fax:* (039) 35371
Key Personnel
Man Dir: Antonio Frederico Araujo Serpa
Founded: 1920 (5)
Subjects: Education, Language Arts, Linguistics, Law, Literature, Literary Criticism, Essays, Psychology, Psychiatry
ISBN Prefix(es): 972-32; 972-96761
Bookshop(s): Rua Ferreira Borges 79, 3000 Coimbra

Edicoes Colibri+
Faculdade de Letras, Alameda da Universidade, 1600-214 Lisbon
Mailing Address: Apdo 42 001, Telheiras, 1601-801 Lisbon
Tel: (021) 796-4038 *Fax:* (021) 796-4038
E-mail: colibri@edi-colibri.pt
Web Site: www.edi-colibri.pt
Key Personnel
Man Dir: Fernando Mao de Ferro
Founded: 1991
Member of Associacao Portuguesa de Editores e Livreiros (APEL).
Subjects: Archaeology, Environmental Studies, Geography, Geology, History, Literature, Literary Criticism, Essays, Philosophy, Social Sciences, Sociology, Political science
ISBN Prefix(es): 972-772
Number of titles published annually: 50 Print
Total Titles: 400 Print; 400 Online
Online services available through World Wide Web.
Distributed by Dinapress; Sodilivros (Only in Portugal); Sodiexpor
Bookshop(s): Livraria Colibri-Faculdade de Ciencias Sociais e Humanas da Universidade Nova de Lisboa, Av de Berna, 26-C, 1069-061 Lisbon

PORTUGAL

Comissao para Igualdade e Direitos das Mulheres+
Av Republica 32-1 E, 1093 Lisbon Codex
Tel: (021) 7983000 *Fax:* (021) 7983099
E-mail: cidm@mail.telepac.pt
Key Personnel
President: Ana Maria Cruz
Editor: Madalena Barbosa
Founded: 1977
Subjects: Women's Studies
ISBN Prefix(es): 972-597

Editorial Confluencia Lda+
Calcada do Combro 99, 1116 Lisbon, Codex
Tel: (021) 663853 *Fax:* (021) 326921
Key Personnel
Man Dirs & Editorials: Rogerio Mendes de Moura; Eduardo Loureiro de Moura
Sales, Rights & Permissions: Manuela Duarte
Production: Paulo Caracas
Publicity: M Conceicao Silva
Founded: 1945
ISBN Prefix(es): 972-9014

Constancia Editores, SA
Estrada da Outurela, 118, 2795-605 Carnaxide
Tel: (021) 4246903 *Fax:* (021) 4246909
E-mail: info@constancia-editores.pt
Key Personnel
Contact: Jorge Manuel dos Santos
Founded: 1989
Subjects: Art, Astronomy, Biological Sciences, Chemistry, Chemical Engineering, Earth Sciences, Economics, Education, Energy, English as a Second Language, Geography, Geology, History, Language Arts, Linguistics, Mathematics, Music, Dance, Natural History, Philosophy, Physical Sciences, Social Sciences, Sociology, Technology
ISBN Prefix(es): 972-761; 972-8150; 972-9444
Branch Office(s)
Rua Goncalo Cristovao, 347, 2, Sala 215, 4000-270 Porto *Tel:* (022) 3325055 *Fax:* (022) 2325078

Contexto Editora+
Rua Rosa 105-2d90D, 1200 Lisbon
Tel: (021) 3479769 *Fax:* (021) 3479770
Key Personnel
Dir: Manuel de Brito
Founded: 1979
Subjects: Fiction, Poetry
ISBN Prefix(es): 972-575

Edicoes Cosmos+
Av Julio Dinis, 6C-4d90 Dto, 1050 Lisbon
Tel: (021) 7955140 *Fax:* (021) 7969713
Cable: COSMOS LISBOA
Key Personnel
Man Dir: Mario de Couceicas dos Reis
Founded: 1938
Subjects: Anthropology, Economics, Geography, Geology, History, Language Arts, Linguistics, Law, Literature, Literary Criticism, Essays, Music, Dance, Philosophy, Public Administration, Social Sciences, Sociology
ISBN Prefix(es): 972-762

Didactica Editora
Av da Ilha da Madeira, 26-A, 1400 Lisbon
Tel: (021) 3011731 *Fax:* (021) 3014887
Key Personnel
President: Francisco Prata Ginja
Founded: 1944
Member of APEL (Portguese Association of Publishers & Booksellers).
Subjects: Mathematics, Physical Sciences, Science (General)
ISBN Prefix(es): 972-650
Bookshop(s): Av da Ilha da Madeira, 22-A, 1400 Lisbon

DIFEL - Difusao Editorial SA+
Avenida das Tulipas, 40C, Miraflores, 1495 Alges
Tel: (021) 4120848 *Fax:* (021) 4120849
E-mail: difel.sa@netc.pt
Telex: 64030
Key Personnel
Man Dir & Editorial: Rita Fezas Vital
General Dir: Francisco Vicente
Founded: 1983
Subjects: Fiction, Nonfiction (General)
ISBN Prefix(es): 972-29

Difusao Cultural+
Rua Pinheiro Chagas 27-R/C, 1050 175 Lisbon
Tel: (021) 3173620 *Fax:* (021) 3528215
Key Personnel
General Manager: Dr Eduardo Martins Soares
Editorial Dir: Paulo Ramos
Founded: 1989
Subjects: Art, Behavioral Sciences, Child Care & Development, Cookery, Economics, Environmental Studies, Fiction, Management
ISBN Prefix(es): 972-709
Number of titles published annually: 40 Audio
Total Titles: 180 Print

Dinalivro+
Travessa Convento de Jesus 15 r/c, 1200 Lisbon
Tel: (021) 670348 *Fax:* (021) 3908489
E-mail: dinalivro@ip.pt
Key Personnel
President: Silverio Amaro
Founded: 1969
Subjects: Accounting, Aeronautics, Aviation, Architecture & Interior Design, Art, Astronomy, Biological Sciences, Computer Science, Education, Electronics, Electrical Engineering, Engineering (General), Gardening, Plants, Health, Nutrition, History, Literature, Literary Criticism, Essays, Medicine, Nursing, Dentistry, Photography, Physics, Psychology, Psychiatry, Science (General), Social Sciences, Sociology
ISBN Prefix(es): 972-576
Subsidiaries: Dinapress,
Bookshop(s): Centro Cultural Brasileiro-Largo Dr Antonio de Sousa de Macedo, 5-1200 Lisbon; Nova Fronteira-Shopping Center Brasilia, 5 Piso-Loja 505-A, 4000 Porto
Shipping Address: Travessa do Convento de Jesus, 14-1200 Lisbon
Warehouse: Travessa do Convento de Jesus, 14-1200 Lisbon
Orders to: Travessa do Convento de Jesus, 15, 1200 Lisbon

Direccao Geral Familia
Praca Londres 2-5, 1091 Lisbon Codex
Tel: (021) 8470430 *Fax:* (021) 8491516
Subjects: Child Care & Development, Social Sciences, Sociology
ISBN Prefix(es): 972-718

Distri Cultural Lda
Rua Vasco da Gama, 4-4A, 2685 Sacavem
Tel: (01) 9425394 *Fax:* (01) 9425214
Telex: 15094
Key Personnel
Man Dir: Karl-Heinz Petzler
Sales Dir: Carlos Alberto
Editorial: Jose Maria Rogagels
Founded: 1980
Subjects: Architecture & Interior Design, Art, Nonfiction (General), Travel
ISBN Prefix(es): 972-9472; 972-655
Parent Company: Grupo Distri
Bookshop(s): Internation Book Centre, Cenrto Comercial de Amoreiras, P-1000 Lisbon

Distri Editora Lda
Rua Vasco da Gama 4, 2685 Sacavem
Tel: (01) 9425394 *Fax:* (01) 9425214
Telex: 15094
Key Personnel
Man Dir: Pedro de Vasconcelos
Editorial, Rights & Permissions: Joao Pedro Bernardino
Founded: 1977
Sales & Publicity: Distri Cultural.
Subjects: Education, Nonfiction (General), Travel
ISBN Prefix(es): 972-9472; 972-655
Parent Company: Grupo Distri
Sales Office(s): Distri Cultural

Edicoes 70, Lda+
Rua Luciano, Cordeiro, 123-2 Esq, 1069-157 Lisbon
Tel: (0351) 21 319 02 40 *Fax:* (0351) 21 319 02 49
E-mail: edi.70@mail.telepac.pt
Web Site: www.edicoes70.pt
Founded: 1970
Subjects: Animals, Pets, Anthropology, Architecture & Interior Design, Art, Astrology, Occult, Education, History, Language Arts, Linguistics, Literature, Literary Criticism, Essays, Music, Dance, Nonfiction (General), Parapsychology, Philosophy, Photography, Social Sciences, Sociology
ISBN Prefix(es): 972-44
Number of titles published annually: 24 Print
Total Titles: 1,000 Print

Elo, *imprint of* Perspectivas e Realidades, Artes Graficas, Lda

Edicoes ELO+
Rua Almi'Rante Gago Coutinho, 2640 Mafra
Tel: (061) 812143 *Fax:* (061) 812820
E-mail: eloag@elografica.pt
Web Site: www.elografica.pt
Key Personnel
Man Dir: Joao Osorio de Castro
Founded: 1962
Subjects: Art, Education, History, House & Home, Travel
ISBN Prefix(es): 972-9181

Editorial Estampa, Lda+
Rua Escola do Exercito, 9 - r/c, Dt, 1100 Lisbon
Tel: (021) 3555663 *Fax:* (021) 521911
E-mail: estampa@mail.telepac.pt
Web Site: www.editorialestampa.pt
Telex: 66012 estampp
Key Personnel
Contact: Antonio Carlos Pinheiro
Founded: 1960
Subjects: Anthropology, Antiques, Architecture & Interior Design, Art, Astrology, Occult, Cookery, Drama, Theater, Economics, Education, Fiction, Geography, Geology, Health, Nutrition, History, Law, Literature, Literary Criticism, Essays, Medicine, Nursing, Dentistry, Nonfiction (General), Parapsychology, Philosophy, Psychology, Psychiatry, Religion - Other, Romance, Social Sciences, Sociology, Sports, Athletics
ISBN Prefix(es): 972-33
Warehouse: Travessa Escola Araujo, 34 C, 1150 Lisbon

Publicacoes Europa-America Lda
Apdo 8, Mem Martins, Codex
Tel: (01) 9211461; (01) 9211462 *Fax:* (01) 9217940
Telex: 42255 peap *Cable:* EUROPAMERICA
Key Personnel
Man Dir: Francisco Lyon de Castro
Sales Dir: Eduardo Lyon de Castro
Manager: Tito Lyon de Castro
Founded: 1945
Subjects: Art, Biography, Education, Engineering (General), Fiction, History, How-to, Medicine, Nursing, Dentistry, Music, Dance, Philosophy,

Poetry, Psychology, Psychiatry, Science (General), Social Sciences, Sociology, Technology
ISBN Prefix(es): 972-1
Subsidiaries: Editorial Inquerito Lda; Grafica Europam Lda; Publicacoes Forum Lda; Publicacoes Trevo Lda; Edicoes Cetop
Branch Office(s)
Delegacao de Lisboa, Rua das Flores, 45 - 2 Lisbon
Delegacao do Porto, Rua 31 de Janeiro, 221 Oporto
Bookshop(s): Lojas Europa-America, Ave Marques de Tomar 1-B; Ave 28 de Maio 61, Castelo Branco; Pr Ferreira de Almeida 21-22, Faro; Ave 25 de Abril 48, Almada; Rua Jose Relvas, 15 B-C Parede; Arcadas do Parque, Estoril; 225 Estrada Nacional 6-25, Cascais (Centro Comercial Pao de Acucar, Lojas 6, 7); Ave dos Bons Amigos 27-A, Cacem; Ave Antonio Enes 14-B; Ave Elias Garcia 104-B, Queluz

Europress Editores e Distribuidores de Publicacoes Lda+
Praceta da Republica, Loja A-1 Loja A, 2675 Pvoa de Santo Adriao
Tel: (01) 9387180; (01) 9387190; (01) 9387317; (01) 9877560 *Fax:* (01) 9381452; (01) 9877560
E-mail: europress@mail.telepac.pt
Key Personnel
Publisher, Man Dir, Editorial: Antonio Bento Vintem
Editor: Dulia Maia Rebocho
Sales: Carlos Vladimiro Ricardo Vintem
Production: Victor M Pinto Pedro
Publicity: Ana Christina Amaro
Founded: 1982
Member of APEL & APIGT; Also acts as National & International Distributor, Exporter & Printer.
Subjects: Chemistry, Chemical Engineering, Drama, Theater, Fiction, Health, Nutrition, History, Humor, Law, Literature, Literary Criticism, Essays, Medicine, Nursing, Dentistry, Nonfiction (General), Poetry, Religion - Other, Romance, Science (General), Sports, Athletics, Western Fiction
ISBN Prefix(es): 972-559
Associate Companies: Pentaedro-Publicidade e Artes Graficas Lda, Praceta da Republica, Lote A-1, Loja B, Povoa Sto Adriao, 2675 Odivelas; Revista de Biotecnologia e Bioquimica Aplicada, Rua D Luisa de Gusmao 6 - 1 Esq, 1600 Lisbon
Subsidiaries: Heuris; Lua Viajante, Ed Com de Livros e Material Audiovisual, Lda
Branch Office(s)
Maputo, Mozambique
Cidade Da Praia, Cabo Verde
Distributor for Ed-Maputo (Mozambique); Livraria LEIA; Sintra Editora
Bookshop(s): Bolsonoite l-Livraria Bar Lda, Avenida Rainha D Leonor 25-A, 1600 Lisbon; Bolsonoite ll, Rua Augusto Gil 6-A, 2675 Odivelas
Warehouse: Rua Augusto Gil 6-A, 2675 Odivelas
Tel: 9347366; 9347367 *Fax:* 9347368

Everest Editora
Rua Maria, 21-1 Dt Fte, 1100 Lisbon
Tel: (021) 8139554 *Fax:* (021) 8152345
E-mail: everesteditora@mail.telepac.pt
Key Personnel
Publisher: Carla Pires
Founded: 1994
Subjects: Cookery, Travel
ISBN Prefix(es): 972-750

FCA Editora de Informatica
Rua D Estefania 183-1 Esq, 1096 Lisbon, Codex
Tel: (021) 3151218 *Fax:* (021) 577827
Telex: 15432
Founded: 1991
Subjects: Computer Science
ISBN Prefix(es): 972-722

Fenda Edicoes+
Affiliate of APEL
Apdo 21334, 1131 Lisbon, Codex
Mailing Address: Rua S Nicolau 13-5 D, 1100-547 Lisboa
Tel: (021) 8823650 *Fax:* (021) 8823659
E-mail: info@fenda.pt
Web Site: www.fenda.pt
Key Personnel
Editor: Mr Vasco Santos *E-mail:* vasco.santos@fenda.pt
Public Relations: Elsa Sertorio *E-mail:* elsa.sertorio@fenda.pt
Founded: 1979
Specialize in edition of books.
Subjects: Literature, Literary Criticism, Essays, Poetry, Psychology, Psychiatry
ISBN Prefix(es): 972-9184
Total Titles: 93 Print
Distributed by Sodilivros
Foreign Rights: Capra Press (USA); Carmen Balcells (Europe); Gallimard (France); Rowohlt (Denmark)

Livraria Editora Figueirinhas Lda
Rua do Almada 47, 4050-036 Porto
Tel: (022) 3325300 *Fax:* (022) 3325907
E-mail: correio@liv-figueirinhas.pt
Key Personnel
Editorial, Rights & Permissions: Francisco Pimenta
Founded: 1944
Subjects: Literature, Literary Criticism, Essays
ISBN Prefix(es): 972-661

Empresa Literaria Fluminense, Lda
Rua S Joao Nepomuceno 8A, 1200 Lisbon
Tel: (021) 601138 *Fax:* (021) 3963371
Key Personnel
Man Dir: Antonio Nobre
Founded: 1905
ISBN Prefix(es): 972-555
Parent Company: Porto Editora Lda
Associate Companies: Livraria Arnado Lda

Editorial Franciscana+
Apdo 17, 4701 Braga Codex
Tel: (053) 22490 *Fax:* (052) 053519735
Key Personnel
Man Dir: Antonio Pedro da Anunciacao
Founded: 1922
Member of Filiada na APEL - Lisbon.
Subjects: Art, Biography, History, Music, Dance, Philosophy, Religion - Other, Theology
ISBN Prefix(es): 972-9190
Subsidiaries: Delegacao da Editorial Franciscana
Bookshop(s): Livraria Editorial Franciscana, Rua de Cedofeita 350, Oporto

Editorial Futura+
Rua Gen Morais Sarmento, 9-CV Esq, 1600 Lisbon
Tel: (021) 155848 *Fax:* (021) 155848
Key Personnel
Man Dir: Jose Chaves Ferreira
Founded: 1970
Subjects: Humor, Literature, Literary Criticism, Essays
ISBN Prefix(es): 972-587

Gabinete de Especializcao e Cooperacao Tecnica Internacional, see GECTI (Gabinete de Especializacao e Cooperacao Tecnica Internacional L)

GECTI (Gabinete de Especializacao e Cooperacao Tecnica Internacional L)+
Ave Republica 47-6d90Dto, 1000 Lisbon
Tel: (021) 768833 *Fax:* (021) 7963465
Key Personnel
Man Dir, Editorial: A Almeida Teixeira
Founded: 1963
Subjects: Business, Marketing, Public Administration
ISBN Prefix(es): 972-9012

Girassol Edicoes, LDA+
Affiliate of Susaeta Ediciones
Estrada Nacional, 249-4-Km 3 7, Sintra Parque - Arnazem 6, 2735-047 Rio de Mouro
Tel: (021) 9151540 *Fax:* (021) 9151548
E-mail: girassol@mail.telepac.pt
Key Personnel
General Manager: Fernando Sarmento
Founded: 1994
Number of titles published annually: 120 Print
Total Titles: 775,000 Print
Imprints: Susaeta Ediciones; Multinova
Branch Office(s)
Banco Santander *Tel:* (021) 4588390
Banco Espirito Santo *Tel:* (021) 4185367

Gradiva-Publicacnoes Lda+
Rua Almeida e Sousa 21 - r/c Esq, 1399 041 Lisbon
Tel: (021) 3974067 *Fax:* (021) 3953471
E-mail: gradiva@ip.pt
Web Site: www.gradiva.pt
Key Personnel
Man Dir: Deolinda Valente
Editor: Guilherme de Carvalho Negrnao Valente
Foreign Rights Department: Joana Gongalves
Vice Dir, Sales & Rights Permissions: Rodolfo Miguel D S B Begonha
Production: Fernando Guerreiro
Sales Manager: Carlos Rosa
Founded: 1981
Specialize in Science books.
Subjects: Anthropology, Asian Studies, Astronomy, Behavioral Sciences, Biological Sciences, Communications, Computer Science, Crafts, Games, Hobbies, Earth Sciences, Economics, Education, Engineering (General), Environmental Studies, Fiction, Geography, Geology, Government, Political Science, History, Human Relations, Humor, Journalism, Literature, Literary Criticism, Essays, Management, Mathematics, Natural History, Nonfiction (General), Philosophy, Physics, Psychology, Psychiatry, Romance, Science (General), Science Fiction, Fantasy, Self-Help, Social Sciences, Sociology
ISBN Prefix(es): 972-662
Number of titles published annually: 80 Print
Total Titles: 700 Print
Distributor for Sinais de Fogo

Guimaraes Editores, Lda+
Rua da Misericordia, 68-70, 1200 Lisbon
Tel: (021) 3432619; (021) 3462436 *Fax:* (021) 3432620
E-mail: guimaraes.ed@mail.telepac.pt
Web Site: www.guimaraes-ed.pt
Telex: 16337
Key Personnel
Man Dir: Isabel Leao
Man Dir, Editorial: Francisco da Cunha Leao
Founded: 1899
Subjects: Drama, Theater, Fiction, History, Philosophy, Poetry, Social Sciences, Sociology
ISBN Prefix(es): 972-665
Bookshop(s): Livraria Guimaraes, Rua da Misericordia 68, 1200 Lisbon
Shipping Address: Rua Conceiccao da Gloria 75, 1250 Lisbon
Warehouse: Rua Conceicao da Gloria 75, Lisbon
Orders to: Rua Conceiccao da Gloria 75, 1250 Lisbon

Impala
Rua Cristino da Silva, 1B, Monte Abraas, 2745 Queluz

PORTUGAL

Mailing Address: Praceta Antonio Feliciano de Castilho No 11/12, 2745 Queluz
Tel: (01) 4364401; (01) 4363860 *Fax:* (01) 4366572
Telex: 16088 cendi p
Founded: 1983
Member of APCT & AIND.
Subjects: Astronomy, Biography, Career Development, Child Care & Development, Economics, Education, Fashion, Gardening, Plants, Geography, Geology, How-to, Humor, Literature, Literary Criticism, Essays, Microcomputers, Music, Dance, Photography, Radio, TV, Sports, Athletics, Women's Studies
ISBN Prefix(es): 972-574
Imprints: Lisgrafica
Book Club(s): AIND

Imprensa Nacional-Casa da Moeda
Rua D Francisco Manuel de Melo 5, 1092 Lisbon Codex
Tel: (021) 658325 *Fax:* (021) 693166
Telex: 15328 incmp *Cable:* INCM
Key Personnel
President: Antonio Braz Teixeira
Dir: Vitalina Fernandes
Founded: 1768
Subjects: Anthropology, Archaeology, Art, Biography, Economics, Ethnicity, Government, Political Science, History, Language Arts, Linguistics, Law, Literature, Literary Criticism, Essays, Medicine, Nursing, Dentistry, Philosophy, Poetry, Public Administration, Social Sciences, Sociology
ISBN Prefix(es): 972-27
Branch Office(s)
Coimbra
Lisbon
Oporto
Bookshop(s): Rua D Francisco Manuel de Melo 5, 1092 Lisbon; Rua Marques Sa de Bandeira, 16-A e B Lisbon; Rua da Escola Politecnica, Lisbon; Centro Comercial das Amoreiras, loja 2112, Lisbon; Centro Comercial S Joaa de Deus, lojas 414, 416-417 Lisbon; Ave Fernao de Magalhaes, 486 Coimbra; Praca Guilherme Gomes Fernandes, 84 Porto; Livraria Camoes, Rua Bittencourt da Silva, 12-C Rio de Janeiro RJ, Brazil

Editorial Inquerito Lda+
Estrada Lisboa-Sintra, Km 14, Edificio CETOP, 2725-377 Mem Martins
Tel: (021) 917 0096 *Fax:* (021) 917 0130
E-mail: inquerito@iol.pt
Key Personnel
Man Dir: Francisco Lyon de Castro
Founded: 1938
Subjects: Economics, History, Law, Philosophy, Social Sciences, Sociology
ISBN Prefix(es): 972-670
Parent Company: Publicacoes Europa-America Lda
Associate Companies: Publicacoes Europa-America
Distributed by Publicacoes Europe-America
Orders to: Publicacoes Europa-America Lda, Estrada Lisboa-Sintra, Km 14, Apartado 8, 2726-901 Mem Martins

Instituto Tecnico de Alimentacao Humana, see Edicoes ITAU (Instituto Tecnico de Alimentacao Humana) Lda

Instituto de Investigacao Cientifica Tropical
(Tropical Sciences Research Institute)
Rua General Joao de Almeida, Palacio do Conde da Calheta, P-1300-266 Lisbon
Tel: (021) 362 2621; (021) 362 2622; (021) 362 2623; (021) 362 2624; (021) 362 2625; (021) 3645031 *Fax:* (021) 362 2626
E-mail: cdi@iict.pt; iictcdi@sapo.pt

Web Site: www.iict.pt
Telex: IICT 66932
Key Personnel
Contact: Maria Virginia Aires Magrio
Founded: 1883
Specialize in tropical areas.
Subjects: Agriculture, Anthropology, Archaeology, Biological Sciences, Earth Sciences, Environmental Studies, Ethnicity, Geography, Geology, History, Social Sciences, Sociology, Veterinary Science
ISBN Prefix(es): 972-672
Number of titles published annually: 23 Print
Bookshop(s): Imprensa Nacional-Casa da Moeda, Rua D Francisco Manuel de Melo, 5-D, P-1000 Lisbon; Livraria Portugal, Rua do Carmo, 70, P-1200 Lisbon; Livraria Bertrand, Rua Garrett, 73, P-1200 Lisbon
Warehouse: Travessa Paulo Martins, P-1300 Lisbon *Tel:* (021) 3635938
Orders to: Centro de Documentacao e Informacao, IICT, Rua General Joao de Almeida, Palacio do Conde da Calheta, P-1300-266 Lisbon

Edicoes ITAU (Instituto Tecnico de Alimentacao Humana) Lda
Rua Av Dr Oliverira Salazar Loja 2, 2665 Malveira
Tel: (01) 9661603 *Fax:* (01) 9661227
Key Personnel
Man Dir: Julio Roberto
Editorial, Sales, Production, Publicity: Jose Maria Paula
Founded: 1969
Subjects: Education, Health, Nutrition, Literature, Literary Criticism, Essays, Poetry, Social Sciences, Sociology
ISBN Prefix(es): 972-9055
Parent Company: Instituto Tecnico de Alimentacao Humana Lda
Orders to: Ave Elias Garcia 87-A, Lisbon 1

Americo Fraga Lamares & Ca Lda, see Livraria Civilizacao (Americo Fraga Lamares & Ca Lda)

Latina Livraria
Rua de Santa Catarina 2, 4000 Porto
Tel: (02) 2001294 *Fax:* (02) 2086053
Key Personnel
President: Henrique Fonseca Perdigao
Vice President: Maria Luisa Fonseca Perdigao
Founded: 1941
Subjects: Aeronautics, Aviation, Architecture & Interior Design, Art, History, House & Home, Literature, Literary Criticism, Essays, Music, Dance, Photography, Romance, Travel, Wine & Spirits
ISBN Prefix(es): 972-95647; 972-95657

Edicoes Manuel Lencastre+
Vale de Vigueria, 22, 2300, Tomar
Tel: 4688328
Founded: 1988
Subjects: Asian Studies, Astrology, Occult, Health, Nutrition, Philosophy, Religion - Buddhist, Religion - Catholic, Religion - Hindu, Religion - Islamic, Religion - Other
ISBN Prefix(es): 972-9054

Lidel Edicoes Tecnicas, Lda+
Rua D Estefania 183 r/c Dto, 1049-057 Lisbon, Codex
Tel: (021) 3151218 *Fax:* (021) 3577827
Key Personnel
Man Dir: Engo Frederico Annes
Editorial Dir: Jose Jomem de Mello
Founded: 1963
Member of Publishers & Booksellers Portuguese Association.

Subjects: Computer Science, Labor, Industrial Relations, Language Arts, Linguistics
ISBN Prefix(es): 972-9018

Lisgrafica, *imprint of* Impala

Livraria Apostolado da Imprensa+
Largo das Teresinhas 5, 4719 Braga Codex
Tel: (053) 22485 *Fax:* (053) 615631
Key Personnel
Man Dir, Editorial: Manuel Morujao; Americo Nunes
Founded: 1922
Subjects: Biography, Philosophy
ISBN Prefix(es): 972-571
Branch Office(s)
Rua da Lapa 111, 1200 Lisbon

Livraria Luzo-Espanhola Lda
Rua Nova do Almada 86, 1200 Lisbon
Tel: (021) 3424917 *Cable:* LIVRALUSO
Key Personnel
Man Dir: Inocencio Casimiro Araujo; Joao Pinto Soares
Founded: 1941
Subjects: Economics, Medicine, Nursing, Dentistry
ISBN Prefix(es): 972-9465
Bookshop(s): Livraria Luzo-Espanhola e Brasileira Lda, Ave 13 Maio 23 - 4, Rio de Janerio, Brazil; Livraria Luzo-Espanhola Lda, Rua da Sofia 121 - 1, Coimbra; Livraria Cientifico Medico do Porto, Rua do Carmo 14, Oporto

Livraria Minerva Editora+
Rua dos Gatos 10, 3000 Coimbra
Tel: (039) 26259 *Fax:* (039) 717267
E-mail: livrariaminerva@mail.telepac.pt
Key Personnel
Manager: Isabel Garcia; Jose Alberto Garcia
Founded: 1985
Subjects: Computer Science, Drama, Theater, Finance, Literature, Literary Criticism, Essays, Medicine, Nursing, Dentistry, Philosophy, Poetry, Romance
ISBN Prefix(es): 972-9316; 972-9318
Distributed by Faculdade de Letras da Universidade de Coimbra
Showroom(s): Rua Carlos Seixas, 74-P, 3000 Coimbra
Bookshop(s): Rua de Macau, 52, 3030 Coimbra

Editora Livros do Brasil Sarl
Rua Caetanos 22, 1200 Lisbon
Tel: (021) 3426113 *Fax:* (021) 3428487
Cable: Librasil
Key Personnel
Man Dir, Rights & Permissions: Antonio de Souza-Pinto
Editorial, Publicity: Joao Palma-Ferreira
Sales: Jose Manuel Lopes Filipe
Founded: 1944
Subjects: Biography, Government, Political Science, History, Philosophy, Science (General), Science Fiction, Fantasy
ISBN Prefix(es): 972-38
Associate Companies: Editores Associados Lda
Branch Office(s)
Rua de Ceuta 80, Oporto

Livros Horizonte Lda+
Rua Chagas 17-1 Dto, 1200 Lisbon
Tel: (021) 3466917 *Fax:* (021) 326921 *Cable:* LIVROSHORIZONTE
Key Personnel
Man Dir & Editorial: Rogerio Mendes de Moura; Eduardo Loureiro de Moura
Sales, Rights & Permissions: Manuela Duarte
Production: Paulo Caracas
Publicity: M Conceicao Silva
Founded: 1953

Subjects: Art, Education, History, Psychology, Psychiatry, Social Sciences, Sociology
ISBN Prefix(es): 972-24

Livraria Lopes Da Silva-Editora de M Moreira Soares Rocha Lda
Rua Cha 101-103, 4000 Porto
Tel: (02) 21678 *Fax:* (02) 2006017
Key Personnel
Man Dir: Adelino Silva
Founded: 1870
Subjects: Medicine, Nursing, Dentistry, Science (General), Technology
ISBN Prefix(es): 972-682

Lua Viajante-Edicao e Distribuicao de Livros e Material Audiovisual, Lda
Praceta Republca loja A, 2675 Povoa de Santo Adriao
Tel: (01) 9376180 *Fax:* (01) 9381452; (01) 9377560
E-mail: europress@mail.telepac.pt
Key Personnel
Publisher & Man Dir, Editorial: Antonio Bento Vintem
Editor: Dulia Maria Rebocho
Sales: Carlos Vladimiro Ricardo Vintem
Production: Victor M Pinto Pedro
Publicity: Ana Christina Amaro
Founded: 1992
Subjects: Computer Science
ISBN Prefix(es): 972-8038
Associate Companies: Europress-Editores & Distribuidores de Publicacoes Lda, Praceta Republca loja A, 2675 Povoa de Santo Adriao; Pentaedro-Publicidade e Artes Graficas Lda, Praceta Republica Loja A, 2675 Povoa de Santo Adriao
Distributed by Europress Editores & Distribuidores
Warehouse: Rua Augusto Gil 6-A, Odivelas *Tel:* (01) 9347366; (01) 9347367 *Fax:* (01) 9347368

Mafra, *imprint of* Perspectivas e Realidades, Artes Graficas, Lda

Livraria Tavares Martins+
Rua Clerigos 14, 4000 Porto
Tel: (022) 23459
Key Personnel
Man Dir: Jorge de Amorim
Founded: 1911
Subjects: Art, Biography, Drama, Theater, History, Law, Philosophy, Poetry, Religion - Other
ISBN Prefix(es): 972-694

McGraw-Hill Editora de Portugal
Estrada da Alfragide, Lote 107, Bloco A-1, 2720 Alfragide
Tel: (021) 4718964; (021) 14728500 *Fax:* (021) 14718981
Telex: 14724
Key Personnel
General Manager: Francisco Paes Mamede
Business Manager: Jose Temes
Sales Manager: Joao Esquivel
Editor: Hugo Xavier
Founded: 1977
Subjects: Agriculture, Architecture & Interior Design, Biological Sciences, Business, Chemistry, Chemical Engineering, Civil Engineering, Computer Science, Economics, Education, Electronics, Electrical Engineering, Engineering (General), Environmental Studies, Government, Political Science, Health, Nutrition, Human Relations, Law, Management, Marketing, Mathematics, Mechanical Engineering, Medicine, Nursing, Dentistry, Physics, Psychology, Psychiatry, Science (General), Social Sciences, Sociology
ISBN Prefix(es): 972-9241; 972-773
Parent Company: McGraw-Hill International Book Co, 1221 Avenue of the Americas, New York, NY 10020, United States
Associate Companies: Distribuidora Cuspide, Suipacha 764, 1008 Buenos Aires, Argentina, President: Joaquin Gil Paricio *Tel:* (01) 3228366 *Fax:* (01) 3223456; (01) 3223465; Makron Books do Brazil Editora Ltda, Rua Tabapua 1105, Itaim Bibi, CP 20689, 04533 Sao Paulo, Brazil, President: Milton Mira de Assumpcao, Filho *Tel:* (011) 8206622; (011)8208528; (011) 8296251 *Fax:* (011) 8294970

Melhoramentos de Portugal Editora, Lda+
Rua Embaixador Teixeira Sampaio 4, 1300 Lisbon
Tel: (021) 3963225 *Fax:* (021) 678254
Telex: 42802 SAGRIL-P
Key Personnel
Man Dir: Carolina Andrade
Founded: 1990
Subjects: Literature, Literary Criticism, Essays
ISBN Prefix(es): 972-713
Associate Companies: Companhia Melhoramentos de Sao Paulo, Brazil

Meriberica/Liber+
Av Duque d'Avila, 69-r/c E, 1000 Lisbon
Tel: (021) 8583849 *Fax:* (021) 8581536
Telex: 14598 merlib p
Key Personnel
President & Publisher: Telmo Protasio
Founded: 1977
Member of Apel Portuguesa de Editores e Livreiros Associagao.
Subjects: Architecture & Interior Design, Cookery, House & Home, Humor, Music, Dance
ISBN Prefix(es): 972-45

Editorial Minerva+
Rua Luz Soriano 31-33, 1200 Lisbon
Tel: (021) 3422535 *Fax:* (021) 3464720
Key Personnel
Dir: Joao Fernandes Domingues
Founded: 1927
Subjects: Fiction
ISBN Prefix(es): 972-591

Monitor
Rua Abade Faria, 6-2o Dto, 1900 Lisbon
Tel: (021) 894893 *Fax:* (021) 7934551
E-mail: monitor@esoterica.pt
Key Personnel
Contact: Carlos Verela Pinto
Subjects: Engineering (General), Human Relations, Management, Technology
ISBN Prefix(es): 972-9413; 972-95278

Monitor-Projectos e Edicoes, LDA+
Rua Abade Faria, 6-2 Dto, 1900 Lisbon
Tel: (021) 849-48-93 *Fax:* (021) 793-45-51
E-mail: monitor@esoterica.pt
Key Personnel
Prof: Victor Roldao *Tel:* (021) 7973656
Subjects: Career Development, Engineering (General), Human Relations, Management, Self-Help
ISBN Prefix(es): 972-9413; 972-95278
Total Titles: 50 Print
Branch Office(s)
Av da Igreja, 66-3 Esq, Lisbon *Tel:* (021) 7973656

Mosaico Editores, LDA
Rua de Campolide, 31, 5-E, 1070 Lisbon
Tel: (021) 388-19-02 *Fax:* (021) 387-10-81
E-mail: mosaico@mail.telepac.pt

Multinova, *imprint of* Girassol Edicoes, LDA

Multinova+
Av Santa Joana Princesa 12-E, Lisbon 1700
Tel: (021) 8483365 *Fax:* (021) 8483436
Cable: (021) 8483436
Key Personnel
Contact: Carlos Santos
Founded: 1970
Specialize in Director Commercials.
ISBN Prefix(es): 972-9035

Musicoteca Lda
Rua Joao Pereira da Rosa, 8, 1249-035 Lisbon
Tel: (021) 3220130 *Fax:* (021) 3476957
E-mail: musicoteca@mail.telepac.pt
Founded: 1990
Subjects: Music, Dance
ISBN Prefix(es): 972-9449

Editorial Noticias+
Rua Padre Luis Aparicio, n 10, 1º, 1150-248 Lisbon
Tel: (021) 3552130 *Fax:* (021) 3552168; (021) 3552169
E-mail: editnoticias@mail.telepac.pt
Web Site: www.editorialnoticias.pt
Telex: 64381
Key Personnel
Contact: Alexandro Leitz
Executive Editor: Marta Ramires *E-mail:* marta.ramires@editorialnoticias.pt
Founded: 1985
Also acts as Editor, Distributor, Bookseller.
Subjects: Cookery, Fiction, History, Journalism, Law, Religion - Other, Self-Help
ISBN Prefix(es): 972-46
Total Titles: 90 Print
Ultimate Parent Company: Lusomundo
Associate Companies: Oficina Do Livro
Subsidiaries: Oficina Do Livro
Bookshop(s): R da Olivenca 9, 2800 Almada; Avenida da Libserdade, 266-1250, 1250 Lisbon *Tel:* (021) 318 78 43; Rossio, 11, 1100 Lisbon *Tel:* (021) 342 17 77 *Fax:* (021) 322 57 33; Rossio, 13, 1100-199 Lisboa; Aveiro Forum, Rua Homem Cristo Filho, Centro Comercial Forum Loja 1, 01, 3810 Aveiro; Aveiro Glicinias, Centro Comercial Glicinias, Loja 41, 3810 Aveiro; Livraria Noticias, Centro Comercial Eborim, R do Eborim, 18, 7000-659 Evora; Livaria Noticias, Rua de Sao Francisco, nº 8 A, 9000-050 Funchal

Nova Acropole+
Rua Maria 48 3, Lisbon 1100
Tel: (021) 827097 *Fax:* (021) 8150401
Key Personnel
Contact: Paulo Loucao
Founded: 1979
Specialize in Human Sciences, Esoterism.
Subjects: Anthropology, Archaeology, Astrology, Occult, History, Philosophy
ISBN Prefix(es): 972-9026
Branch Office(s)
4710 Braga
R Prof Machado Nilela, 285-3d90

Nova Arrancada Sociedade Editora SA+
Largo do Carmo, 18-1 Esq, 1200 Lisbon
Tel: (021) 3470096; (021) 3472220 *Fax:* (021) 3472220
E-mail: novaarrancada@mail.telepac.pt
Key Personnel
Executive Dir: Jose Luis Henriques
Founded: 1995
Subjects: Drama, Theater, Economics, Government, Political Science, History, Literature, Literary Criticism, Essays, Religion - Catholic, Social Sciences, Sociology
ISBN Prefix(es): 972-8369
Number of titles published annually: 30 Print

PORTUGAL

Editorial O Livro Lda
Rua Claudio Nunes, 121, 1500 Lisbon
Tel: (021) 704749 *Fax:* (021) 7783536
Key Personnel
Man Dir: Carlos de Moura
Editorial: Carlos Perdigao
ISBN Prefix(es): 972-552

Observatorio Astronomico de Lisboa
Tapada da Ajuda, 1300 Lisbon
Tel: (021) 3637351 *Fax:* (021) 3621722
ISBN Prefix(es): 972-573

Edicoes Ora & Labora
Mosteiro de S Bento de Singeverga, 4795-309 Roriz Sts Santo Tirso
Tel: (252) 94 11 76 *Fax:* (252) 87 29 47
E-mail: msingeverga@net.sapo.pt
Founded: 1950
Member of Society of Portuguese Publishers & Booksellers.
Subjects: Anthropology, Biography, Religion - Catholic, Theology
ISBN Prefix(es): 972-9278

Palas Editores Lda+
Rua Quirino da Fonseca, 4 - c/v D, 1000 Lisbon
Tel: (021) 574903 *Fax:* (021) 795-4019
Key Personnel
Editor: Maria De Fatima De Sa Ressoa
Founded: 1973
Member of APEL.
Subjects: Education, History
ISBN Prefix(es): 972-9000

Paulinas+
Rua Alexandre Rey Colaco, 1700 Lisbon
Tel: (021) 8484355 *Fax:* (021) 8474151
Founded: 1950
Subjects: Biblical Studies, Biography, Human Relations, Literature, Literary Criticism, Essays, Religion - Catholic, Romance, Science Fiction, Fantasy, Securities
ISBN Prefix(es): 972-751
Bookshop(s): Paulinas Multimedia, Rua Morais Soares, 56 A-1900 Lisbon *Tel:* (021) 813 90 38 *Fax:* (021) 847 41 51; Paulinas Multimedia, Rua de Cedofeita, 355-4050 Porto *Tel:* (02) 31 49 56 *Fax:* (02) 32 08 31; Paulinas Multimedia, Rua Dr Fernao de Ornelas, 379050 Funchal-Maderia *Tel:* (091) 23 56 99 *Fax:* (091) 23 36 17; Paulinas Multimedia, Rua do Municipio, 12-8000 Faro *Tel:* (089) 82 30 27 *Fax:* (089) 80 56 79; Paulinas Multimedia, Praca Teofilo Braga, 12-13, 2900 Setubal *Tel:* (065) 53 42 14 (Centro Social S Francisco Xavier)

Paz-Editora de Multimedia, LDA+
Rua Bela Vista a Graca, 27-A Loja 23, 1170 Lisbon
Tel: (021) 8101282 *Fax:* (021) 8101287
E-mail: paz@esoterica.pt
Web Site: www.paseditora.pt
Key Personnel
Jr Partner: Peter C Wiesenthal
Partner: Helfried Bauer
Founded: 1996
Member of APEL.
Subjects: Health, Nutrition, Well being & reference
ISBN Prefix(es): 972-8416
Online services available through World Wide Web.
Associate Companies: Felecidade-Editora de Multimidia Ltda, Rio de Janeiro, Brazil

Editora Pergaminho Lda
Beco Torto, 3-1 Esq, 2750-505 Cascais
Tel: (021) 4847500 *Fax:* (021) 4836077
E-mail: pergaminho@mail.telepac.pt

Key Personnel
Contact: Mario Mendes Moura
Founded: 1990
Subjects: Art, Music, Dance, Radio, TV
ISBN Prefix(es): 972-711

Editorial Perpetuo Socorro+
Rua Dr Alves da Veiga 207, 4000 Porto
Tel: (02) 564251 *Fax:* (02) 564251
Key Personnel
Dir: Antonio Manual C Baptista
Founded: 1946
Subjects: Education, Religion - Other, Theology
ISBN Prefix(es): 972-563

Perspectivas e Realidades, Artes Graficas, Lda
Rua Ruben A Leitao 4-2 Esq, 1200 Lisbon
Tel: (021) 3471371 *Fax:* (021) 3471372
Telex: 42458 Perspe P
Key Personnel
Man Dir: Dr Joao Soares
Publicity: Rui Perdigao
Executive Dir: Dr Carlos Capelas
Founded: 1975
Subjects: Government, Political Science, Literature, Literary Criticism, Essays, Poetry
ISBN Prefix(es): 972-620
Associate Companies: Diglivro Lda
Imprints: Elo; Mafra

Petrony Livraria
Rua Assuncao 90, 1100 Lisbon
Tel: (021) 3422911 *Fax:* (021) 3431602
Founded: 1955
Subjects: Law
ISBN Prefix(es): 972-685

Planeta Editora, LDA+
Tv do Noronha, 21-1 Esq, 1200 Lisbon
Tel: (021) 397-87-56 *Fax:* (021) 395-10-26
Key Personnel
International Rights: Gloria Ribeiro
Subjects: Astrology, Occult, Astronomy, Biblical Studies, Earth Sciences, Fiction, Mysteries, Science Fiction, Fantasy
ISBN Prefix(es): 972-731

Platano Editora SA+
Ave de Berna 31 2 Esq, 1069 Lisbon
Tel: (021) 7979278 *Fax:* (021) 7954019
Key Personnel
President: Francisco Prata Ginja
Founded: 1972
Member of the Portuguese Association of Book Publishers.
Subjects: Drama, Theater, Poetry
ISBN Prefix(es): 972-621; 972-707; 972-770
Subsidiaries: Alicerce Editora Lda; Paralelo Editora Lda; Didactica Editora Lda; Platano Edicoes Tecnicas Lda; Editora de Ensino a Distancia Lda
Branch Office(s)
Platano Editora SA, Coimbra
Bookshop(s): Alicerce Editora Lda, Rua Guerra Junqueiro 456, 4100 Porto
Warehouse: Rua Joao Ortigao Ramos 29-B, 1500 Lisbon
Servicor Ceutrais de Preducco e Armazens Quinta dos Lagoas, Almada 2800

Porto Editora Lda+
Rua da Restauracao 365, 4099 Porto, Codex
Tel: (02) 2005813 *Fax:* (02) 313072
E-mail: pe@portoeditora.pt
Telex: 27205 ported p
Key Personnel
Man Dir: Graciete Teixeira; Jose A Teixeira; Rosalia G Teixeira; Vasco F Teixeira
Founded: 1944
Subjects: Education, Language Arts, Linguistics, Nonfiction (General)

ISBN Prefix(es): 972-0
Associate Companies: Empresa Literaria Fluminense Lda, Av Almirante Gago Coutinho 57 A, 1700 Lisbon *Tel:* (021) 8430900 *Fax:* (021) 8430901
Subsidiaries: Livraria Arnado Lda
Bookshop(s): Rua da Fabrica 90, Oporto *Tel:* (02) 2087669 *Fax:* (02) 2087669; Praca D Filipa de Lencastre 42, Oporto *Tel:* (02) 2087681 *Fax:* (02) 2087681

Portugalmundo+
Rua Heliodoro Salgado, 50-A, 1170-177 Lisbon
Tel: (021) 8155351 *Fax:* (021) 8144746
Key Personnel
Dir: Maria Jose Palmela Pinto
Founded: 1976
Member of APEL.
Subjects: Law
ISBN Prefix(es): 972-9288

Editorial Presenca+
Rua Augusto Gil 35-A, 1064-806 Lisbon
Tel: (021) 7992200 *Fax:* (021) 7977560
E-mail: info@editpresenca.pt
Web Site: www.editpresenca.pt
Telex: 62596 *Cable:* PRESENCA LISBOA
Key Personnel
President: Francisco Espadinha
Executive Dir: Manuel Aquino
Production: Maria Eugenia Queiroz
Rights & Permissions: Manuela Cardoso
Administration: Joao Espadinha
Finance Executive: Hugo Moura
Founded: 1960
Subjects: Animals, Pets, Architecture & Interior Design, Art, Astrology, Occult, Biography, Business, Child Care & Development, Computer Science, Cookery, Crafts, Games, Hobbies, Education, Fiction, Gardening, Plants, Government, Political Science, Health, Nutrition, History, How-to, Human Relations, Language Arts, Linguistics, Management, Marketing, Mysteries, Nonfiction (General), Philosophy, Poetry, Psychology, Psychiatry, Religion - Buddhist, Science (General), Self-Help, Social Sciences, Sociology, Sports, Athletics, Travel, Travel Guides, Art Techniques, Esoterics, Lesiure Books
ISBN Prefix(es): 972-23
Divisions: Marketing Department
Warehouse: Estrada das Palmeiras, 59, 2745-663 Barcarena *Tel:* (021) 4357544 *Fax:* (021) 4357540

Publicacoes Dom Quixote Lda+
Rua Luciano Cordeiro 116 - 2, 1098 Lisbon Codex
Tel: (021) 538079 *Fax:* (021) 574595
Telex: 14331 quixot p *Cable:* QUIXOTE
Key Personnel
Man Dir: Nelson de Matos; Isabel Dionisio
Production: Gina Martins
Publicity: Cecilia Andrade
Rights & Permissions: Cecilia Andrade
Founded: 1965
Subjects: Education, Fiction, History, Philosophy, Poetry, Science (General), Social Sciences, Sociology
ISBN Prefix(es): 972-20

Puma Editora Lda
Rua Vasco da Gama, 4-4a, 2685 Sacavem
Tel: (01) 9425394 *Fax:* (01) 9425214
Key Personnel
Man Dir: Karl-Heinz Petzler
Editorial, Rights & Permissions: Adriano Lopes
Founded: 1990
Subjects: Fiction, Nonfiction (General)
ISBN Prefix(es): 972-9469
Parent Company: Grupo Distri
Sales Office(s): Distri Cultural

PUBLISHERS
PORTUGAL

Quatro Elementos Editores+
Rua Arneiros 54 Lote F-2F, 1500 Lisbon
Tel: (021) 703695
Founded: 1978
Subjects: Art, Fiction, Literature, Literary Criticism, Essays, Photography, Poetry
ISBN Prefix(es): 972-9296

Quetzal Editores+
Affiliate of Livrania Bertrand, SGPS
Rua da Rosa 105, 2 Esq, 1200 Lisbon, Order Taker: Zita Seatra
Tel: (021) 3426172 *Fax:* (021) 3426173
E-mail: quetzal@ip.pt
Telex: 65732 pegest p
Key Personnel
Chairman: Maria Da Piedade Ferreira
Subjects: Art, Literature, Literary Criticism, Essays, Poetry, Romance, Travel
ISBN Prefix(es): 972-564
Shipping Address: Distribuidorz de Livnos Bertrand, Rua Terras do Vale, Amadora, Contact: Eduardo Morais *Tel:* (01) 4958787 *Fax:* (01) 4960255

Quid Juris - Sociedade editora+
Rua Marques da Fronteira 92-1 D, 1000 Lisbon
Mailing Address: Lote 51, Piso 1, Apartado 9803, 1911 Lisbon Codex
Tel: (021) 651946 *Fax:* (021) 3875538
E-mail: quidjuris@mail.telepac.pt
Key Personnel
Contact: Rua Sarmento Beires
Founded: 1988
Subjects: Criminology, Economics, Journalism, Law, Social Sciences, Sociology
ISBN Prefix(es): 972-724

Quimera Editores+
Rua Augusto Muchado, 5 r/c D, 1900 Lisbon
Tel: (021) 8472577 *Fax:* (021) 3431180
Key Personnel
Contact: Jose Alfaro
Founded: 1987
Subjects: Art, Biography, Drama, Theater, Fiction, History
ISBN Prefix(es): 972-589

Realizacoes Artis
Apdo 8, 2726 Mem Martins
Tel: (01) 363796 *Fax:* (01) 9170130
Key Personnel
Man Dir: Rogerio de Freitas; Ermelinda Penedo
Founded: 1950
Subjects: Art, Biography, Poetry
ISBN Prefix(es): 972-9298

Editora Replicacao Lda+
Av Infante Santo, 343 - r/c E, 1300 Lisbon
Tel: (021) 3977058 *Fax:* (021) 3969808
E-mail: replic@mail.telepac.pt
Key Personnel
Dirs: J C Anaia Cristo; Luisa Galhardo
Founded: 1982
La Spiga Language representative.
Subjects: Astrology, Occult, Biological Sciences, English as a Second Language, Health, Nutrition, Humor, Mathematics, Science (General), Sports, Athletics, Study of Foreign Languages
ISBN Prefix(es): 972-570
Associate Companies: Leianaia-Livreiros, Editores e Importadores Anaia, ldc

Revista Penteados
Rua dos Bacalhoeiros, 99-2 E, 1100 Lisbon
Tel: (021) 862963; (021) 8813511 *Fax:* (021) 870972
Telex: 64904
Key Personnel
International Rights: Leonor Veiga De Macedo
Parent Company: Rui Romano Lda

M Moreira Soares Rocha Lda, see Livraria Lopes Da Silva-Editora de M Moreira Soares Rocha Lda

Edicoes Rolim Lda
Rua Fialho de Almeida 38-2D, 1000 Lisbon
Tel: (021) 526375
Key Personnel
Man Dir: Maria Rolim Ramos
Founded: 1976
Subjects: Government, Political Science, History, Language Arts, Linguistics, Literature, Literary Criticism, Essays, Social Sciences, Sociology
ISBN Prefix(es): 972-687

Sa da Costa Editora
Prca Luis de Camoes 22 4, 1200 Lisbon
Tel: (021) 3460721
Telex: Sacost 15574 P *Cable:* Livrosacosta
Founded: 1913
Subjects: History, Literature, Literary Criticism, Essays, Philosophy
ISBN Prefix(es): 972-562
Bookshop(s): Livraria Sa da Costa

Edicioes Joao Sa da Costa Lda+
Av Brasil, 118-3 E, 1700 Lisbon
Mailing Address: Av 5 Outubro, 10-7/4, 1000 Lisbon
Tel: (021) 8400428; (021) 571118; (021) 563603 *Fax:* (021) 534194
Telex: 43534 fundis p
Key Personnel
Man Dir: Joao Sa da Costa
Executive Dir: Idalina Sa da Costa
Founded: 1984
ISBN Prefix(es): 972-9230

Edicoes Salesianas
Rua Dr Alves da Veiga 124, 4022 Porto Codex
Tel: (02) 565750 *Fax:* (02) 565800
Key Personnel
Man Dir: Jose Santos
Editorial, Production & Publicity: Jose Pedrosa Ferreira
Founded: 1947
Subjects: Biography, Education, Humor, Psychology, Psychiatry, Religion - Other
ISBN Prefix(es): 972-690
Branch Office(s)
Rua Saraiva de Carvalho 275, Lisbon *Tel:* (021) 3964142
Bookshop(s): Livraria Salesiana, Largo Luis de Camoes 7-9, 7000 Evora *Tel:* (066) 24570; Rua Saraiva de Carvalho 275, 1300 Lisbon *Tel:* (021) 609065

Edicoes 70+
Av Infante D Henrique 306-2, 1900 Lisbon
Tel: (021) 8590348 *Fax:* (021) 761736
Telex: 64489
Key Personnel
Contact: Jose Augusto Pereira
Founded: 1970
Subjects: Anthropology, Architecture & Interior Design, Art, Astrology, Occult, History, Literature, Literary Criticism, Essays, Philosophy, Social Sciences, Sociology
ISBN Prefix(es): 972-44

Silabo+
R Cidade de Manchester-2, 1170-100 Lisbon
Tel: (021) 8130345 *Fax:* (021) 8166719
E-mail: silabo@mail.telepac.pt
Key Personnel
Marketing Dir: Manuel Robalo
E-mail: manuelrobalo@mail.telepac.pt
Founded: 1983
Member of APEL.

Subjects: Computer Science, Economics, Management, Mathematics, Philosophy, Physics, Science (General)
ISBN Prefix(es): 972-618

Editora Soctip/Livraria Soctip, see Sociedade Tipografica, SA (Editora Soctip/Livraria Soctip)

Solivros+
Alto do Castelo, Villa de Trola, 4780 Santo Tirso
Tel: (052) 42385
Key Personnel
President & Editor: David Jorge Pereira
Founded: 1974
Specialize in publications of art works.
Subjects: Art, English as a Second Language, Literature, Literary Criticism, Essays, Poetry, Regional Interests, Religion - Catholic
ISBN Prefix(es): 972-693

Sousa & Almeida Livraria
Rua da Fabrica 40-42, 4050-245 Porto
Tel: 222050073 *Fax:* 222050073
Key Personnel
Contact: Sousa Almeida *E-mail:* sousaealmeida@net.sapo.pt

Susaeta Ediciones, *imprint of* Girassol Edicoes, LDA

Talento+
Av Gomes Pereira 41-1 E, 1500 Lisbon
Tel: (021) 7154281 *Fax:* (021) 7154257
Key Personnel
Dir: Francisco Santos
Financial Dir: Francisco Neves Ferro
Editorial Manager: Patricia Samos
Founded: 1988
Subjects: Biography, Music, Dance, Sports, Athletics
Branch Office(s)
Edipromo-Edicoes e Promocoes Ltda, 143 Vila Mariana, 0415 San Paulo SP, Brazil
Book Club(s): Club Mania Show

Almerinda Teixeira
Av 25 de Abril 5-16 E, 2800 Almada
Tel: (01) 2762352 *Cable:* Classica
Key Personnel
Editorial, Rights & Permissions: Francisco Paulo
Production, Publicity: Jose Ramos
Founded: 1903
Subjects: Agriculture, Economics, Electronics, Electrical Engineering, Fiction, History, Language Arts, Linguistics, Management, Poetry, Psychology, Psychiatry, Religion - Other, Science (General), Social Sciences, Sociology
ISBN Prefix(es): 972-95393

Teorema+
Pdr Luis Aparicio 9-1 F, 1100 Lisbon
Tel: (021) 3129131 *Fax:* (021) 3521480
E-mail: editorial.teorema@netc.pt
Key Personnel
President: Dr Carlos Da Veiga Ferreira
Founded: 1973
Subjects: Anthropology, Economics, Fiction, History, Literature, Literary Criticism, Essays, Nonfiction (General), Philosophy, Psychology, Psychiatry, Romance, Science (General), Social Sciences, Sociology
ISBN Prefix(es): 972-695

Texto Editora+
Estrada De Paco De Arvos, 66 E66A, 2735-336 Cacem
Tel: (021) 4272200 *Fax:* (021) 4272201
E-mail: info@te.pt
Web Site: www.te.pt
Key Personnel
Man Dir: Manuel Jose Ferrao; Luis Carlos Veloso; Carlos Santiago

PORTUGAL

Founded: 1977
Subjects: Cookery, Education, Fiction, Health, Nutrition, Management
ISBN Prefix(es): 972-47
Associate Companies: Publilivro - Editora e Distribuidora de Publicacoes Lda, Alto da Bela Vista, Casal Vale de Mourao, Apdo 237, 2735 Cacem
Branch Office(s)
Beco Veloso Salgado, 31, 4450-808 Ceca da Palmeira
Bookshop(s): Livraria Texto Editora, Rua Joaquim Paco D'Arcos, 13, 1500-365 Lisbon; Rua Damiao De Gois, 45, 4050-225 Porto

Sociedade Tipografica, SA (Editora Soctip/Livraria Soctip)
Rua de Dona Estefania 195-D, 1000 Lisbon
Tel: (021) 543280 *Fax:* (021) 577926
Telex: 65517 SOCTIP P
Key Personnel
Dir: Christina Ferreira
Founded: 1936
Subjects: Art
ISBN Prefix(es): 972-9435

Publicacoes Trevo Lda
Apdo 50, 2726 Mem Martins Codex
Tel: (01) 9211461 *Fax:* (01) 9217940
Telex: 42255 Peap
Key Personnel
Man Dir, Editorial: Tito Lyon de Castro
Sales: Eduardo Lyon de Castro
Founded: 1976
ISBN Prefix(es): 972-696
Parent Company: Publicacoes Europa-America Lda

Turinta-Turismo Internacional
Rua Goncalves Zarco Lote 5, Murches, 2750 Cascais
Tel: (01) 4870602 *Fax:* (01) 4872099
E-mail: turinta@mail.telepac.pt
Key Personnel
Contact: Hilario Sanches
International Rights: Eva Sanches
Founded: 1975
Member of IMTA.
ISBN Prefix(es): 972-8134
Distributed by Map Link (USA)

Editora Ulisseia Lda+
Ave Visconde de Valmor 47-1 Dto, 1000 Lisbon
Tel: (021) 734300; (021) 763467 *Fax:* (021) 56239
Telex: 15177 Verbo P
Key Personnel
Man Dir: Fernando Guedes
Editorial, Production: Martins de Oliveira
Sales: Jose Luis Fonseca
Publicity: Carlos Castro
Founded: 1950
Subjects: Literature, Literary Criticism, Essays
ISBN Prefix(es): 972-568
Parent Company: Editorial Verbo SA
Warehouse: Alto da Bela Vista, Calem 2735
Orders to: Rua Carlos Testa 1 - 2, 1000 Lisbon

Usus Editora+
Rua Viana do Castelo, 8 c/v E, 2775 Carcavelos
Tel: (01) 4535000 *Fax:* (01) 4426482
Key Personnel
Contact: Josi Caselas
Subjects: Law, Literature, Literary Criticism, Essays, Philosophy, Poetry, Theology
ISBN Prefix(es): 972-8070

Vega-Publicacao e Distribuicao de Livros e Revistas, Lda+
Alto dos Moinhos, 6A, 1500 Lisbon Codex
Tel: (021) 789414 *Fax:* (021) 786395

Key Personnel
Contact: Dr Assirio Bacelar
Founded: 1975
Subjects: Anthropology, Architecture & Interior Design, Art, Astrology, Occult, Behavioral Sciences, Biography, Child Care & Development, Communications, Computer Science, Cookery, Drama, Theater, Economics, Education, Fashion, Fiction, Gay & Lesbian, History, Humor, Law, Literature, Literary Criticism, Essays, Philosophy, Photography, Poetry, Religion - Buddhist, Religion - Other, Romance, Science Fiction, Fantasy, Social Sciences, Sociology
ISBN Prefix(es): 972-699

Editorial Verbo SA+
Rua Carlos Testa 1-2, 1000 Lisbon
Tel: (021) 562131 *Fax:* (021) 3865396; (021) 562139
Telex: 15177 Verbo P *Cable:* VERBO
Key Personnel
Man Dir: Fernando Guedes
Sales Dir: Jose Luis Fonseca
Founded: 1959
Door-to-door sales by EDC-Empresa de Divulgacao Cultural Sarl, Ave Duque de Avila 193, Lisbon; direct mail sales by Verbo Postal.
Subjects: Education, History, Science (General)
ISBN Prefix(es): 972-22
Subsidiaries: Editora Ulisseia Lda; Verbo Publicacoes Periodicas; Editora Verbo, S Paulo; Litecnica, Luanda

Livraria Verdade e Vida Editora
Rua Santa Isabel 16, 2495 Fatima
Tel: (049) 531417 *Fax:* (049) 531417
Founded: 1945
Subjects: Biography, Education, Fiction, History, Philosophy, Psychology, Psychiatry, Religion - Other, Theology
ISBN Prefix(es): 972-96166

Puerto Rico

General Information

Capital: San Juan
Language: Spanish and English
Religion: Predominantly Roman Catholic
Population: 3.6 million
Bank Hours: 0900-1430 Monday-Friday
Shop Hours: 0900-1730 or 1800 Monday-Saturday
Currency: US currency: 100 cents = 1 US dollar
Export/Import Information: No tariff on books and advertising matter. No import licenses required.
Copyright: UCC (see Copyright Conventions, pg xi)

Editorial Antillana, *imprint of* Editorial Cultural Inc

Editorial Cordillera Inc
Apdo 170, Hato Rey, PR 00919-0170
Tel: (787) 767-6188 *Fax:* (787) 767-8646
Key Personnel
President & Editorial: Hector E Serrano
Sales & Publicity: Isaac Serrano
Founded: 1962
Subjects: Literature, Literary Criticism, Essays, Social Sciences, Sociology
ISBN Prefix(es): 0-88495

Instituto de Cultura Puertorriquena
PO Box 4184, San Juan 00905
Tel: (787) 724-0910
Telex: 3859686

BOOK

Key Personnel
Dir: Carmelo Degardo Cintron
Editorial Dir: Marta Aponte Alsina
Sales: Ileana Colon de Barreto
Founded: 1955
Subjects: Anthropology, History, Literature, Literary Criticism, Essays, Music, Dance, Poetry
ISBN Prefix(es): 0-86581
Bookshop(s): Libreria del Instituto de Cultura Puertorriquena, San Francisco 305, San Juan 00901
Orders to: San Francisco 305, San Juan 00901

Editorial Cultural Inc
Calle Robles No 51, Rio Piedras 00925
Tel: (787) 765-9767 *Fax:* (787) 765-9767
E-mail: cultural@coqui.net
Key Personnel
Man Dir: Francisco Vazquez
Sales Dir: Maria Vazquez
Publicity Dir: Sonia M Delgado
Founded: 1949
Subjects: Biography, History, Literature, Literary Criticism, Essays
ISBN Prefix(es): 1-56758
Imprints: Editorial Antillana
Branch Office(s)
Editorial Antillana, Calle Robles No 51, Rio Piedras 00925
Bookshop(s): Libreria Cultural

EDUPR, see University of Puerto Rico Press (EDUPR)

Ediciones Huracan Inc+
Ave Gonzalez 1002, Rio Piedras 00925
Tel: (787) 763-7407 *Fax:* (787) 763-7407
Key Personnel
Dir: Carmen Rivera-Izcoa
Founded: 1975
Subjects: History, Literature, Literary Criticism, Essays, Social Sciences, Sociology
ISBN Prefix(es): 0-940238; 0-929157

Libros-Ediciones Homines+
PO Box 190374, Hato Rey 00919
Tel: (787) 250-1912 (ext 2347)
Web Site: coqui.ice.org/homines; coqui.metro.inter.edu.homines
Key Personnel
International Rights: Dr Aline Frambes-Buxeda
E-mail: a.frambes@inter.edu
Founded: 1977
Subjects: Behavioral Sciences, Government, Political Science, Regional Interests, Social Sciences, Sociology, Women's Studies
ISBN Prefix(es): 0-9623590
Number of titles published annually: 2 CD-ROM
Total Titles: 30 Print; 3 CD-ROM
Ultimate Parent Company: Universidad Interamericana de Puerto Rico

McGraw-Hill Intermericana del Caribe, Inc
Apdo 20712, Rio Piedras 00928
Tel: (787) 751-2451 *Fax:* (787) 764-1890
E-mail: c-davila@spiderlink.net
Key Personnel
Regional Manager: Carlos Davila
E-mail: carlos_davila@mcgrawhill.com
Subjects: Architecture & Interior Design, Business, Education, Engineering (General), English as a Second Language, Medicine, Nursing, Dentistry, Nonfiction (General), Technology

Modern Guides Company+
PO Box 9021340, San Juan 00902-1340
Tel: (787) 723-9105 *Fax:* (787) 723-4380
Key Personnel
Vice President: Cristina Banac
Founded: 1985
Marketing support, publishing, also acts as Distributor.

Subjects: Fiction, Travel
ISBN Prefix(es): 0-940788
Number of titles published annually: 2 Print; 2 Online
Total Titles: 3 Print; 2 Online
Online services available through Amazon.com.
Distributed by Spanish Periodicals

Piedras Press, Inc
UPR Sta, San Juan 00931-1735 Carr 173
Mailing Address: PO Box 21735, San Juan 00931-1735
Tel: (787) 731-9215
Key Personnel
President: Marc Schnitzer *Tel:* (787) 789-8928
Vice President & Treasurer: Emily Krasinski
Subjects: How-to, Language Arts, Linguistics, Self-Help
ISBN Prefix(es): 0-9630685
Number of titles published annually: 1 Print
Total Titles: 2 Print

Publishing Resources Inc
373 San Jorge St, 2nd Floor, Santurce 00912
Mailing Address: PO Box 41307, Minillas Sta, Santurce 00940
Tel: (787) 268-8080 *Fax:* (787) 774-5781
Key Personnel
Owner: Ronald J Chevako
Owner & Editor-in-Chief: Anne W Chevako
Retail Manager: Terry C Burns
Publishes magazines including *San Juan, Puerto Rico's City Magazine; Bienestar* (environmental) & *Dimension* (engineering).
Subjects: Ethnicity, Regional Interests, Science (General), Travel
ISBN Prefix(es): 0-89825

Ediciones Puerto+
PO Box 9066272, San Juan 00906-6272
Tel: (787) 7210844 *Fax:* (787) 7250861
E-mail: feriapr@caribe.net
Web Site: www.edicionespuerto.com
Key Personnel
President: Jose Carvajal
Founded: 1971
Subjects: Poetry, Social Sciences, Sociology
ISBN Prefix(es): 0-942347

University of Puerto Rico Press (EDUPR)+
University of Puerto Rico Sta, Rio Piedras 00931-3322
Mailing Address: PO Box 23322
Tel: (787) 758-6932; (787) 758-8345 (sales)
Fax: (787) 753-9116
Telex: 9573 *Cable:* EDUPR
Key Personnel
Dir: Marta Aponte-Alsina
Manager: Dalidia Colon-Pieretti
Production Manager: Juan Abascal
Editor-in-Chief: Gloria Madrazo-Vicens
Editor: Ana Garcia San Inocencio; Jesus Tome
Founded: 1932
Subjects: Art, Education, History, Nonfiction (General), Philosophy, Poetry, Psychology, Psychiatry, Social Sciences, Sociology
ISBN Prefix(es): 0-8477
Branch Office(s)
Edificio Vick Center-D Ave, Munoz Rivera No 867, Ofic 304, Rio Piedras, PR 00925, United States
Warehouse: Planta Piloto de Ron, Rd No 1 to Caguas, Rio Piedras

Publicaciones Voz de Gracia
PO Box 50581, Levittown 00950
Tel: (787) 784-4366 *Fax:* (787) 261-5401
E-mail: vozdegra@caribe.net
Founded: 1994
Subjects: Biblical Studies, Music, Dance
ISBN Prefix(es): 0-9633439
Divisions: Ministerios Alabanza y Adoracion

Reunion

General Information

Capital: Saint-Denis
Language: French
Religion: Predominantly Roman Catholic
Population: 626,000
Bank Hours: 0800-1500
Currency: 100 centimes = 1 French franc
Export/Import Information: No tariff on books and advertising. Books have reduced VAT. No import license. Nominal exchange control over certain value.
Copyright: Berne (see Copyright Conventions, pg xi)

Association des Ecrivains Reunionnais/ocean Indien (ADER)
36, rue de Gaulle, 97400 Saint Denis de La Reunion
Tel: 437607 *Fax:* 437607
Key Personnel
President: Alain Gili *E-mail:* agili@guetali.fr
Founded: 1975
Books, little review.
ISBN Prefix(es): 2-9507282
Number of titles published annually: 3 Print
Total Titles: 7 Audio

Editions Ocean
305, rue de la Communaute, 97440 Saint Andre
Tel: (0262) 588400 *Fax:* (0262) 588410
E-mail: ocean@guetali.fr
Key Personnel
Contact: Jean-Pierre Boyer
Founded: 1987
Subjects: Crafts, Games, Hobbies, History, Social Sciences, Sociology
ISBN Prefix(es): 2-907064
Distributor for ARS-Terres Creoles; CNH; CRI

Romania

General Information

Capital: Bucharest
Language: Romanian
Religion: Predominantly Romanian Orthodox
Population: 23.2 million
Bank Hours: 0900-1200, 1300-1500 Monday-Friday; 0900-1200 Saturday
Shop Hours: 0900-1900 Monday-Friday; early closing Saturday
Currency: 100 bani = 1 leu
Export/Import Information: Book import and export coordinated by Centrala Editoriala, Piata Sciinteii 1, R-79715 Bucharest. The commercial operations are carried out by Artexim-Foreign Trade Co, 33-16, R-70055 Bucharest. Import licenses required. Exchange controls: terms of payment established in the sales contract.
Copyright: Berne (see Copyright Conventions, pg xi)

Editura Academiei Romane
Calea 13 Septembrie nr 13, Sector 5, 791717 Bucharest
Mailing Address: CP 42, Sector 5, Bucharest
Tel: (01) 6317400; (01) 6314460 *Cable:* EDACAD
Key Personnel
Dir: Gral G Mihaila
Founded: 1948
Publishing House of the Academy of Romania.
Subjects: Anthropology, Archaeology, Art, Astronomy, Biological Sciences, Chemistry, Chemical Engineering, Computer Science, Earth Sciences, Electronics, Electrical Engineering, Energy, Foreign Countries, History, Language Arts, Linguistics, Law, Mathematics, Medicine, Nursing, Dentistry, Philosophy, Physical Sciences, Physics, Psychology, Psychiatry, Social Sciences, Sociology
ISBN Prefix(es): 973-27
Orders to: Orion Srl, Press International, Sos Oltenitei 35-37, Sect 4, PO Box 61-170, Bucharest *Tel:* (01) 534 63 45 *Fax:* (01) 312 51 09

Aion Verlag+
Str Cantacuzino no, 8F, bl PB nr 18, ap 7, Oradea, Bihor
Tel: (059) 14795
Key Personnel
President & Editor: Nicolae Olteanu
Founded: 1994
Subjects: Anthropology, Communications, How-to, Human Relations, Journalism, Philosophy, Psychology, Psychiatry, Religion - Other, Social Sciences, Sociology
ISBN Prefix(es): 973-97662
Parent Company: S C Varsatorul Impex SRL
Bookshop(s): Varsatorul Company

Editura Aius+
Str Nicolae, Bd N Titulescu 46/7, Et 1, Ap 7, 1100 Craiova
Tel: (051) 112786 *Fax:* (051) 113965
E-mail: aius@oltenia.ro
Key Personnel
Executive Manager: George Sorin Singer
Founded: 1991
Subjects: Economics, History, Literature, Literary Criticism, Essays, Medicine, Nursing, Dentistry
ISBN Prefix(es): 973-9251; 973-95229; 973-96340; 973-96913; 973-97385
Total Titles: 3 Print

Editura Albatros
One Piata Presei Libere 1, 79718 Bucharest
Tel: (01) 2228493 *Fax:* (01) 2228493
Key Personnel
Man Dir: Dan Petrescu
Chief Publisher: Georgetta Dimisianu
Founded: 1969
Subjects: History, Literature, Literary Criticism, Essays, Religion - Other
ISBN Prefix(es): 973-24

Alcor-Edimpex (Verlag) Ltd+
Bd 1 Mihalache 45, bl 16B+C, SC D, ap 116, sector 1, Bucuresti
Tel: (01) 665-34-40 *Fax:* (01) 665 34 40
E-mail: ed_alcor@yahoo.com
Web Site: www.rotravel.com/alcor
Key Personnel
General Manager: Corina Firuta
Founded: 1994
Subjects: Art, Crafts, Games, Hobbies, History, Religion - Other, Travel
ISBN Prefix(es): 973-96752; 973-97200; 973-97901; 973-98341; 973-95673; 973-96304; 973-98935; 973-8160
Number of titles published annually: 10 Print
Imprints: Arta Grafica Printing House, ao; Editura CNI Coresi

Editora All+
B-dul Timisoara 58, 76548 Bucharest
Tel: (01) 402 26 00 *Fax:* (01) 402 26 10
E-mail: info@all.ro

ROMANIA

Web Site: www.all.ro
Key Personnel
President: Mihail Penescu
Rights Manager: Carmen Penescu
Founded: 1992
Subjects: Computer Science, Education, Fiction, History, Medicine, Nursing, Dentistry, Nonfiction (General), Science (General)
ISBN Prefix(es): 973-96090; 973-9156; 973-571; 973-684; 973-8171
Number of titles published annually: 300 Print
Total Titles: 1,800 Print
Parent Company: Bic All

Alternative Editura+
Piata Presei Liberne nr 1, 71341 Bucharest
Tel: (01) 2234966; (01) 2229468 *Fax:* (01) 6756074; (01) 2234971
Key Personnel
Contact: Nicolae Lotreanu

Ararat Verlag und Druckerei+
Bdul Carlo 1 nr 45, Sector 2, Bucharest
Tel: (01) 3111425; (01) 6134050 *Fax:* (01) 3111420
Key Personnel
General Manager: Sirun Terzian
Dir: Stefan Agopian
Founded: 1994
Book Manufacturer.
Subjects: History, Literature, Literary Criticism, Essays, Philosophy, Social Sciences, Sociology
ISBN Prefix(es): 973-9310; 973-97869; 973-97127; 973-96682
Distributed by Humanitas (Romania)

Ars Longa Publishing House+
Str Elena Doamna 2, 6600 Iasi
Tel: (0232) 215078 *Fax:* (0232) 215078
E-mail: arslonga@mail.dntis.ro
Key Personnel
President: Christian Tamas
International Rights: Mrs Brandusa Tamas
Founded: 1994
Subjects: Fiction, History, Language Arts, Linguistics, Literature, Literary Criticism, Essays, Philosophy, Poetry, Religion - Catholic, Theology
ISBN Prefix(es): 973-96681; 973-97252; 973-9325
Number of titles published annually: 55 Print
Total Titles: 200 Print

Arta Grafica Printing House, ao, *imprint of* Alcor-Edimpex (Verlag) Ltd

Artemis Verlag
Piata Presei Libere 1, sector 1, Bucharest 71341
Tel: (01) 2226661
Key Personnel
Contact: Mirella Acsente
Founded: 1991
Subjects: Art, Biography, History, Nonfiction (General), Religion - Other
ISBN Prefix(es): 973-566

Editura Cartea Romaneasca
Calea Victoriei nr 115, Sector 1, 79721 Bucharest
Tel: (01) 3123733; (01) 6148802 *Fax:* (01) 3110025
Key Personnel
Dir: George Balaita
Founded: 1969
Subjects: Drama, Theater, Fiction, Literature, Literary Criticism, Essays, Poetry
ISBN Prefix(es): 973-23

Casa Editoriala Independenta Europa+
Str Brazda lui Novac, Bloc 6/lll/7, Craiova
Tel: (051) 153487; (051) 425801 *Fax:* (051) 425801
Key Personnel
Dir: Ion Deaconescu
Founded: 1990
Subjects: Art, History, Literature, Literary Criticism, Essays, Science (General)
ISBN Prefix(es): 973-9013; 973-95780
Associate Companies: Editura Libertatea, Yugoslavia; Editura Hyperion, Republica Moldova
Subsidiaries: Brasov
Branch Office(s)
Bucharest, Brasov
Showroom(s): rue A 1 Cuza nr 10, Craiova
Warehouse: Calea Bucuresti, bl M5, Craiova

The Center for Romanian Studies+
Member of Conference of Historical Journals
Oficiul Postal 1, Casuta Postala 108, Str Poligon nr 11A, 6600 Iasi
Tel: (032) 219000 *Fax:* (032) 219010
E-mail: csr@romanianstudies.ro
Web Site: www.romanianstudies.ro
Key Personnel
Dir: Dr Kurt W Treptow
Off Mgr: Petronela Postolache
Editor-in-Chief: Viorica Rusu
Founded: 1996
Member of Romanian Publishers Association.
Subjects: Biography, Foreign Countries, History, Language Arts, Linguistics, Literature, Literary Criticism, Essays, Poetry, Sports, Athletics
ISBN Prefix(es): 973-9432; 973-98391; 973-98091; 973-9155
Number of titles published annually: 12 Print
Total Titles: 60 Print; 2 CD-ROM
Imprints: Iasi; Oxford; Portland
Branch Office(s)
Center for Romanian Studies, c/o ISBS, 5804 NE Hassalo St, Portland, OR 97213-3644, United States, Contact: Tamma Greenfield *Tel:* 503-287-3093 *Fax:* 503-280-8832 *E-mail:* tamma@isbs.com
Center for Romanian Studies, 40 Drake International Services, Market Moose, Market Place, Deddington 0X15 OSE, United Kingdom, Contact: Norman Drake *Tel:* (01869) 338240 *Fax:* (01869) 338310 *E-mail:* romcen@drakeint.co.uk
Distributed by International Specialized Book Services (North America)

Editura Ceres
Piata Presei Libere nr 1, 79722 Bucharest
Tel: (01) 2224836
Key Personnel
Man Dir: Ecaterina Mosu
Founded: 1953
Subjects: Agriculture, Animals, Pets, Environmental Studies, Veterinary Science
ISBN Prefix(es): 973-40

Editura Clusium, Casa de Editura Atlas-Clusium SRL+
Piata Unirii nr 1, R-3400 Cluj
Tel: (095) 116940
E-mail: 1060 o.p.1@clug-Napoca
Key Personnel
Man Dir: Valentin Tascu; Nicolae Mocanu
Founded: 1990
Subjects: Art, History, Humor, Literature, Literary Criticism, Essays, Medicine, Nursing, Dentistry, Nonfiction (General), Philosophy, Poetry
ISBN Prefix(es): 973-555

Editura CN1 Coresi, *imprint of* Alcor-Edimpex (Verlag) Ltd

Coresi SRL+
Str Dem l. Dobrescu 4-6, Sector 1, CP 1-477, 70700 Bucharest CP 1-477
Tel: (01) 3127115 *Fax:* (01) 2230177
Key Personnel
General Manager: Vasile Poenaru
Executive Manager: Michiela Gaga
Founded: 1989
Specialize in children's literature & educational publications.
Subjects: Career Development, English as a Second Language, Language Arts, Linguistics
ISBN Prefix(es): 973-608
Number of titles published annually: 50 Print
Total Titles: 300 Print

Corint Verlag+
Str Prof Ion Bogdan 19, sector 1, Bucharest 71149
Tel: (01) 2119766 *Fax:* (01) 2119766
Key Personnel
President: Cristian Gresanu
Editor & International Rights: Daniel Penescu
International Rights: Andreea Riess
Founded: 1994
Specialize in scholarly books.
Subjects: Fiction, Geography, Geology, History, Mathematics, Outdoor Recreation, Physics
ISBN Prefix(es): 973-9281; 973-97054; 973-97588; 973-97379; 973-97792
Book Club(s): Corint

Editure Ion Creanga
Piata Presei Libere NR 1, 79725 Bucharest
Tel: (01) 2231112
Key Personnel
Deputy Dir: Daniela Crasnaru
Editor-in-Chief: Gheorghe Zarafu
Founded: 1969
Subjects: Art, Biography, Fiction, History, Literature, Literary Criticism, Essays, Music, Dance, Poetry
ISBN Prefix(es): 973-25

Editura Cronos SRL
CP 1-517, Sector 1, 70 700 Bucharest 1
Tel: (044) 262245; (094) 643310 (mobile phone); (044) 7690952 *Fax:* (01) 2231025
E-mail: crons@dial.kappa.rd
Web Site: www.cronos.roknet.rd
Key Personnel
Manager: Florin Chita
Founded: 1990
Cronos Publishing House by Cronos Foreign Service offers at request encyclopedic materials, informations & statistical data regarding Romania, also provides illustrations & maps of Romania, & proofs or actualizes different materials concerning Romania for foreign publishing houses, including encyclopedic articles.
Subjects: Advertising, Business, Travel
ISBN Prefix(es): 973-9000
Orders to: Str Progresului 39, Ap 6, 2064 BAlCOl Prahova

Editura Dacia
Str Paul Chinezu nr 2, 3400 Cluj-Napoca
Tel: (064) 194 912 *Fax:* (064) 11665
E-mail: dacia@multiarea.ro
Web Site: www.edituradacia.ro; www.cjnet.ro
Telex: 31347
Key Personnel
Dir: Vasile lgna
Publicity & Public Relations: Iliana Brasoveanu
Rights & Permissions: Petean Mircea
Founded: 1969
Subjects: Astrology, Occult, Biological Sciences, Chemistry, Chemical Engineering, Electronics, Electrical Engineering, Fiction, Finance, Geography, Geology
ISBN Prefix(es): 973-35

Editura Didactica si Pedagogica+
Str Spiru Haret nr 12, 70738 Bucharest
Tel: (01) 3122885 *Fax:* (01) 3122885
E-mail: edpdirector@mail.codecnet.ro

PUBLISHERS

ROMANIA

Key Personnel
General Manager: Adrian-Paul Iliescu
Founded: 1951
ISBN Prefix(es): 973-30
Number of titles published annually: 300 Print

Editura DOINA SRL
Plaiul Unirii rr 39, Bl miz, sc B35, Bucharest
Tel: (01) 3228107 *Fax:* (01) 3227541
Key Personnel
Dir: Jenica Panaitescu
Founded: 1992
Subjects: Biography, Literature, Literary Criticism, Essays
ISBN Prefix(es): 973-95318; 973-95859; 973-96301; 973-9193

Editure RAO, *imprint of* RAO Publishing Group

Editura Eminescu
Piata Presei Libere, nr1, 79731 Bucharest
Tel: (01) 2228540
Key Personnel
Man Dir: Valerin Rapeanu
Subjects: History, Poetry
ISBN Prefix(es): 973-22

Enciclopedia RAO, *imprint of* RAO Publishing Group

Enzyklopadie Verlag+
Piata Presei Libere 1, sector 1, Bucharest 79737
Tel: (01) 2223322 *Fax:* (01) 2243667
Key Personnel
Dir: Marcel Popa
International Rights: Irina Popa
Founded: 1968
Subjects: Antiques, Archaeology, Biography, Biological Sciences, Economics, History, Religion - Other
ISBN Prefix(es): 973-45
Total Titles: 24 Print

Euro Print Verlag
Str Sibiu 5, bl E3, ap 24, sector 6, Bucharest 77314
Tel: (01) 745-20-11 *Fax:* (01) 312-42-25
Key Personnel
Contact: Neculai Bratu
Founded: 1994
Editing & Distribution.
Limited Company.
Subjects: *Specializes In:*Stories, fairy tales, coloring & painting books for children

Editura Excelsior (Excelsior Verlag - Publishing House)+
Affiliate of The Association of the Romanian Publishers
Nr 5, Proclamatia de la Timisoara, 1900 Timisoara
Mailing Address: CP 262, OP 1, 1900 Timisoara
Tel: (056) 201078 *Fax:* (056) 201078
E-mail: excelsior@mail.dmltm.ro
Key Personnel
Dir: Corina Victoria Badulescu
Founded: 1990
Member of Writers Union of Romenien.
Subjects: Anthropology, Archaeology, Biblical Studies, Biography, Business, Communications, Cookery, Crafts, Games, Hobbies, Drama, Theater, Economics, Education, Ethnicity, Fiction, Health, Nutrition, History, Human Relations, Humor, Journalism, Language Arts, Linguistics, Library & Information Sciences, Literature, Literary Criticism, Essays, Mechanical Engineering, Medicine, Nursing, Dentistry, Mysteries, Nonfiction (General), Parapsychology, Philosophy, Poetry, Psychology, Psychiatry, Publishing & Book Trade Reference, Regional Interests, Religion - Other, Science (General), Science Fiction, Fantasy, Social Sciences, Sociology, Technology, Western Fiction, Science & fiction
ISBN Prefix(es): 973-99015; 973-592
Number of titles published annually: 50 Print
Total Titles: 490 Print
Distributor for Aletheia-Bistrita; Compact-Brasov; Dacia Traina-Sibiu; Libraria Eminescu; Librarii-TG Mures; Libris-Galati; Novus-Craiova; Prolibris-Ramnicu Valcea; Sedcomlibris-Iasi; Sedcomlibris-Suceava; Timlibris Timisoara

Fahrenheit, *imprint of* RAO Publishing Group

FF Press
Calea Mosilor 209, sc A et 7, ap 26, Sector 2, Bucharest
Tel: (01) 6191544 *Fax:* (01) 3129694
Key Personnel
President: Serban Florea
Editor: Ion Covaci
Contact: Dr Florea Doina
Founded: 1992
Subjects: Finance, History, Literature, Literary Criticism, Essays, Poetry, Science (General)
ISBN Prefix(es): 973-96089; 973-96745; 973-96837

Casa de editura Globus+
Pita Presei Libere, 1 et 8 cam 853, Sector 1, Bucharest 78202
Tel: (01) 2231510; (01) 2231530 *Fax:* (01) 6664265
Key Personnel
President: Tudor Stoica
Publisher: Petre Barbulescu
Author: Mihai Ungheanu
Founded: 1990
Subjects: Economics, Government, Political Science, History
ISBN Prefix(es): 973-49

Gryphon Publishing Ltd, see Editura Gryphon

Editura Gryphon+
Division of Gryphon Ltd
Str IL Caragiale, No 6-A-2, 2200 Brasov
Tel: (068) 68313642; (068) 68314049 *Fax:* (068) 68312888
E-mail: gryphon@gryphon.ro
Web Site: www.gryphon.ro
Key Personnel
President & General Manager: Eugen Ioan Popa
Tel: (092) 60 92 53
Founded: 1990
Specialize in importing books, provider for libraries & universities publishing house.
Subjects: Art, Civil Engineering, English as a Second Language, Health, Nutrition, Science (General), Technology
ISBN Prefix(es): 973-604
Number of titles published annually: 6 Print
Total Titles: 17 Print
Distributor for Grolier Inc USA

Hasefer
Bd I C Bratianu 35, et 2, ap 9, sector 3, 970478 Bucharest
Tel: (021) 312 22 84 *Fax:* (021) 312 22 84
E-mail: hasefer@fx.ro
Key Personnel
Dir: Sandu Singer
Subjects: Biblical Studies, Education, History, Literature, Literary Criticism, Essays, Religion - Other
ISBN Prefix(es): 973-8056
Number of titles published annually: 30 Print
Parent Company: Romanian Federation of Jewish Communities

Editura Humanitas+
One, Piata Presei Libere, R-79734 Bucharest
Tel: (01) 2228546 *Fax:* (01) 2229061; (01) 2228252
E-mail: editors@agora.humanitas.ro
Key Personnel
General Dir: Gabriel Liiceanu
Man Dir: Grigore Arsene
Editorial Dir: Adriana Irimia
Foreign Rights Executive: Daniela Popa Oancea
Founded: 1990
Specialize in Humanities & Fiction Books.
Subjects: Biography, History, Literature, Literary Criticism, Essays, Philosophy, Psychology, Psychiatry, Religion - Buddhist, Religion - Catholic, Religion - Hindu, Religion - Islamic, Religion - Jewish, Social Sciences, Sociology
ISBN Prefix(es): 973-28
Parent Company: Humanitas Publishing House
Associate Companies: Societatea Comerciala Librariile Humanitas
Subsidiaries: Rumaenisch-Franzisch duchvertriebs gesellschaft; Societatea Comerciala Librariile Humanitas; Societatea franco-romana de difuzare a cartii SA
Distributor for All; Nemira; Romanian, French & English Houses; Univers
Bookshop(s): Libraria Humanitas, Pasajul Kretzulescu Cl Victoriei nr 45; Libraria franceza, Institutul francez Bd Docia nr 77
Orders to: Librariile Humanitas, 1, Piata Presei Librere, R-79734 Bucharest

Humanitas Publishing House+
Piata Presei Libere nr 1, Bucharest 79734
Tel: (01) 2228546 *Fax:* (01) 2243632
E-mail: editors@agora.humanitas.ro
Web Site: www.humanitas.ro
Key Personnel
General Dir: Gabriel Liiceanu
Editorial Dir: Adriana Irimia
Foreign Rights Executive: Livia Stoia *Tel:* (01) 2243638 *E-mail:* lstoia@agora.humanitas.ro
Founded: 1990
Specialize in Humanities & Fiction.
Subjects: Biography, Government, Political Science, History, Literature, Literary Criticism, Essays, Philosophy, Psychology, Psychiatry, Religion - Buddhist, Religion - Catholic, Religion - Hindu, Religion - Islamic, Religion - Jewish, Science (General), Social Sciences, Sociology, Theology
ISBN Prefix(es): 973-28
Associate Companies: Societatea Comerciala Librariile Humanitas
Subsidiaries: Societatea Comerciala Librariile Humanitas; Societate franco romana de difuzare a cartii SA
Bookshop(s): Libraria Humanitas, Pasajul Kretzulescu Cl Victoriei nr 45; Libraria din fundul curtii, Cl Victoriei nr 120, Bucharest

Iasi, *imprint of* The Center for Romanian Studies

Editura Institutul European+
Str Cronicar Mustea nr 17, 6600 Iasi
Tel: (032) 127311 *Fax:* (032) 230197
E-mail: rtvnova@mail.cccis.ro
Key Personnel
President: Anca Untu-Dumitrescu
Editor-in-Chief: Sorin Parvu
Public Relations: Liliana Buruiana-Popovici
Founded: 1991
Member of The Association of Romaniau Editors.
Subjects: Education, English as a Second Language, Government, Political Science, History, Literature, Literary Criticism, Essays, Medicine, Nursing, Dentistry, Philosophy, Religion - Other, Theology
ISBN Prefix(es): 973-9148; 973-95528; 973-586; 973-95671
Distributed by Humanitas
Distributor for Ceu Press (Budapest)

ROMANIA

Editura Junimea+
Bdul copou 3-5, R-6600 Isai
Tel: (032) 117290
Key Personnel
Dir: Nicolae Cretu
Administrative Dir: Constantin Ursache
Foreign Rights: Christian Tamas
Founded: 1969
Subjects: Literature, Literary Criticism, Essays, Technology
ISBN Prefix(es): 973-37

Editura Kriterion SA+
One, Piata Presei Libere nr 1, 79726 Bucharest
Tel: (01) 2243638 *Fax:* (01) 2243628
E-mail: krit@dnt.ro
Key Personnel
Manager & Dir: H Szabo Gyula *Tel:* (095) 1634377 *E-mail:* szabogyula@yahoo.com
Founded: 1969
Subjects: Art, Ethnicity, Fiction, History, Literature, Literary Criticism, Essays, Poetry
ISBN Prefix(es): 973-26
Number of titles published annually: 40 Print
Total Titles: 200 Print
Branch Office(s)
Kriterion Cluj, Str S Mict, MNr 12A Cluj
Tel: (064) 197450 *Fax:* (064) 197450
E-mail: kriterion@mail.dntej.ro

Lider Verlag+
B-dul Libertati nr 4, bl 117, et 3, ap 7, sector 4 111, Bucharest 761061
Tel: (01) 4102214 *Fax:* (01) 3374822
Key Personnel
President & International Rights: Casandra Enescu
Founded: 1994
Subjects: Art, History, Language Arts, Linguistics, Literature, Literary Criticism, Essays, Medicine, Nursing, Dentistry, Philosophy, Romance
ISBN Prefix(es): 973-9343; 973-97836

Litera Publishing House
Vacaresti St, 310, Bucharest
Tel: (01) 3303502 *Fax:* (01) 3303502
E-mail: info@litera.ro
Key Personnel
Manager: Gheorghe Buzatu
Subjects: Literature, Literary Criticism, Essays
ISBN Prefix(es): 973-43

MAST Verlag+
Str Aleea Craesti 2, Bl A 47, ap 10, Bucharest 77418
Tel: (01) 7786950 *Fax:* (01) 4104588
Key Personnel
Contact: Florin Mateescu
Founded: 1994
Subjects: Agriculture, Animals, Pets, Antiques, Astrology, Occult, Gardening, Plants, Medicine, Nursing, Dentistry, Veterinary Science
ISBN Prefix(es): 973-97297; 973-97867; 973-97868

Editura Medicala (Medical Publishing House)+
Bdul Pache Protopopescu, Sector 2, 131 Bucharest
Tel: (01) 25 25 186 *Fax:* (01) 25 25 189
E-mail: edmedicala@fx.ro
Web Site: www.edmedicala.ro
Key Personnel
Man Dir: Alexandru Oproiu *E-mail:* oproiu@fx.ro
Founded: 1954
Medical Publishing House.
Subjects: Medicine, Nursing, Dentistry
ISBN Prefix(es): 973-39
Number of titles published annually: 30 Print

Mentor Kiado+
Member of Hungarian Book Guild From Romania
Str Vasile Stroiescu Nr 11, Sector 2, Bucharest
Tel: (01) 2232652 *Fax:* (01) 2232652
Key Personnel
Ed-in-Chief: Istvan Kiraly
Editor: Gyorgy Galfvi *Tel:* (065) 167091 *Fax:* (065) 167087; Andras Ferenc Kovacs *Tel:* (065) 167091 *Fax:* (065) 167087; Zsolt Lang *Tel:* (065) 167091 *Fax:* (065) 167087
Founded: 1993
Main mission is the publication of works of living Hungarian literature, particularly those of Transylvanian (province of Romania) writers. Special focus is the patronage of new writers & the Minomtates Mundi series, which presents the literary traditions of minority peoples.
Subjects: Art, Drama, Theater, Ethnicity, History, Literature, Literary Criticism, Essays, Philosophy, Poetry, Romance, Social Sciences, Sociology
ISBN Prefix(es): 973-95943; 973-96650; 973-97072; 973-9263
Total Titles: 5 Print
Ultimate Parent Company: Hungarian Book Guild From Romania

Editura Meridiane+
One, Piata Presei Libere nr 1, 71341 Bucharest
Tel: (01) 2243623 *Fax:* (01) 2223037
Key Personnel
Dir: Elena Victoria Jiquidi
Senior Editor, Acquisitions & Foreign Rights: Livia Szasz Campeanu; Andrei Niculescu
Founded: 1952
Subjects: Anthropology, Archaeology, Architecture & Interior Design, Art, Biography, Drama, Theater, Fashion, Film, Video, History, Language Arts, Linguistics, Literature, Literary Criticism, Essays, Medicine, Nursing, Dentistry, Music, Dance, Nonfiction (General), Religion - Other, Social Sciences, Sociology, Travel, Art History, Design, Cultural studies, Media
ISBN Prefix(es): 973-33
Number of titles published annually: 25 Print
Total Titles: 65 Print

Editura Militara+
Str Coblcescu 28A, 79735 Bucharest
Tel: (01) 6138924; (01) 3237822
Key Personnel
Dir: Cornel Barbulescu
Founded: 1950
Subjects: Education, Electronics, Electrical Engineering, Engineering (General), History, Military Science, Mysteries, Social Sciences, Sociology
ISBN Prefix(es): 973-32
Bookshop(s): Libraria Militara (Military Bookshop), Piate Natiunilor Unite nr 3, Bucharest

Editura Minerva+
Piata Presei Libere 1, 79732 Bucharest
Tel: (01) 2224823
Founded: 1969
Subjects: Astrology, Occult, Biography, Computer Science, Education, Film, Video, Finance, Library & Information Sciences
ISBN Prefix(es): 973-21
Parent Company: Editura Minerva
Subsidiaries: Series Biblioteca Pentru Toti

Monitorul Oficial, Editura+
Calea 13 Septembrie, Str Izvor 2-4 Casa Poporuli, Bucharest
Tel: (01) 6142429; (01) 6145759 *Fax:* (01) 3124703; (01) 3120901
Key Personnel
Manager: Eugenia Clubancan
Founded: 1832
Subjects: Law

ISBN Prefix(es): 973-567
Distributed by Kubon & Sagner (Germany)
Bookshop(s): Str Blanduziei nr 1, sector 1, Bucharest

Editura Muzicala
Str Calea Victoriei nr 141, 79733 Bucharest
Tel: (01) 3129867 *Fax:* (01) 3129867
E-mail: editura_muzicala@hotmail.com
Key Personnel
Man Dir: Vlad Ulpiu; Marius Vasileanu
Founded: 1958
Books, musical scores, compact discs & CD-ROM's.
Subjects: Biography, Music, Dance
ISBN Prefix(es): 973-42
Orders to: Bucharest

Nemira Verlag+
Piata Presei Libere Nr 1, Corp D Et 3, 76321 Bucharest
Tel: (01) 2116560 *Fax:* (01) 2228916
E-mail: nemira@dnt.ro
Key Personnel
Editorial Dir: Vlad T Popescu
International Rights: Iulia Stoica
Founded: 1991
Subjects: Accounting, Advertising, Economics, Education, Government, Political Science, Literature, Literary Criticism, Essays, Marketing, Science Fiction, Fantasy
ISBN Prefix(es): 973-569; 973-9301; 973-99576; 973-95169
Associate Companies: Nemira & Co; Nemira Multimedia
Bookshop(s): Edutura Nemira, PO Box 33-22, 71341 Bucharest
Book Club(s): Clubul cartii
Shipping Address: Edutura Nemira, PO Box 33-22, 71341 Bucharest
Warehouse: Edutura Nemira, PO Box 33-22, 71341 Bucharest
Orders to: Edutura Nemira, PO Box 33-22, 71341 Bucharest

Editura Niculescu+
Str Octav Cocarascu 79, Sector 1, 78182 Bucharest
Tel: (01) 224-47-53; (01) 666-72-13 *Fax:* (01) 224-28-98; (01) 222-03-72
E-mail: editura@niculescu.ro; Mayibuye@mweb.co.za
Web Site: www.niculescu.ro
Key Personnel
President: Dr Christian Niculescu *Tel:* (09) 2342900
Marketing & Distribution: Lavona George
Founded: 1993
Subjects: Accounting, Biography, Biological Sciences, Business, Career Development, Child Care & Development, Cookery, Economics, Education, Engineering (General), English as a Second Language, Fiction, Film, Video, Gardening, Plants, Geography, Geology, Government, Political Science, Health, Nutrition, History, House & Home, Humor, Language Arts, Linguistics, Law, Management, Marketing, Mathematics, Mysteries, Natural History, Nonfiction (General), Outdoor Recreation, Philosophy, Physics, Science (General), Self-Help, Social Sciences, Sociology, Wine & Spirits, Reference Work
ISBN Prefix(es): 973-568
Number of titles published annually: 180 Print; 18 CD-ROM
Total Titles: 70 Print; 12 CD-ROM
Associate Companies: Clubul de Carte Niculescu, Str Octav Cocarascu 79, 78182 Bucharest *Tel:* (01) 224-24-80

Editura Orion+
Str Ion Brezoianu 51 B, 70711 Bucharest 1
Tel: (01) 6146151; (01) 6594697

Key Personnel
President: Cristian Corneliu Bigica
Editor: Florin Lupescu
ISBN Prefix(es): 973-95052; 973-95532; 973-97273; 973-98353
Parent Company: Orion Enterprises Ltd

Oxford, *imprint of* The Center for Romanian Studies

Editura Paideia+
Str Teleajen nr 30, Sector 2, 73216 Bucharest
Tel: (01) 3308006; (01) 3301678 *Fax:* (01) 3301677
E-mail: paideia@fx.ro
Key Personnel
President: Ion Bansoiu *Tel:* (01) 2529850
Founded: 1990
Non-profit Organization.
Subjects: Literature, Literary Criticism, Essays, Philosophy, Religion - Other, Social Sciences, Sociology
ISBN Prefix(es): 973-9131; 973-95306; 973-9368; 973-9393
Number of titles published annually: 60 Print; 10 CD-ROM
Total Titles: 30 Print; 6 CD-ROM; 4 Audio
Foreign Rep(s): Anca Chelaru (US)
Foreign Rights: Radu Lungu (France)

Pallas-Akademia Koenyvkiadoes Koenyvkereskedes
Petoefi 4, Cp 140, 4100 Miercurea-Ciuc (Csikszereda)
Tel: (066) 171036; (066) 171955 *Fax:* (066) 171955
E-mail: pallas@nextra.ro
Founded: 1993
Subjects: Biography, Ethnicity, Fiction, Journalism, Literature, Literary Criticism, Essays, Regional Interests, Religion - Catholic
ISBN Prefix(es): 973-96702
Number of titles published annually: 30 Print
Distributed by Aligator kft Koenyvkereskedes (Cluj-Napoca, Romania); Babits Kiado (Szekszard, Hungary); Carthographia Kiado (Budapest, Hungary); Casa de Presa (Bucarest, Romania); Custos Koenyvkereskedes (Bucarest, Romania); Editura Humanitas (Bucarest, Romania); Editura Lyra (Targu-Mures, Romania); Sc Bon Ami (Stantu-Gheorghe, Romania); Sc Cartimpex Koenyvkeseskedes (Cluj-Napoca, Romania); Sc Libris srl (Satu-Mare, Romania); Sc Samlibris (Satu-Mare, Romania); Sc Zalanta Prest (Salonta, Romania)
Distributor for Akademiai Kiado (Budapest, Hungary); Babits Kiado (Szekszard, Hungary); Bagolyvar Kiado (Budapest, Hungary); Carthogrphia Kiado (Budapest, Hungary); Editura Dacia (Cluj-Napoca, Romania); Editura Humanita (Bucharest, Romania); Editura Ion Creanga (Bucharest, Romania); Editura Komp-Press (Cluj-Napoca, Romania); Editura Rao (Bucarest, Romania); Euro pa Kiado (Budapest, Hungary); Kossuth Kiado (Budapest, Hungary); Magveto Kiado (Budapest, Hungary); Magyar Koenyvklubb (Budapest, Hungary); Mentor Kiado (Targu-Mures, Romania); Mora Ferenc Kiado (Budapest, Hungary); Osiris Kiado (Budapest, Hungary); Park Kiado (Budapest, Hungary); Polis Kiado (Cluj-Napoca, Romania); Sprinter Koenyvkereskedes (Budapest, Hungary); Szent Istvan Tarsulat (Budapest, Hungary); Szukits Kiado (Szeged, Hungary)
Bookshop(s): str Petofi nr 4, Miercurea Ciuc 4100; P-ta Libertatii 5/A, Gheorgheni 4200; P-ta Marton Aron nr 2, Odorheiu-Secuiesc 4150; Str Koroesi Csoma Sandor nr 2, SPantu Gheorghe 4000; P-ta Trandafirilor nr 57, Targu-Mures 4300; Str M Sadoveanu nr 3, Brasov 2200; Str Universitatii nr 1, Cluj-Napoca 3400;
Str Horea nr 6, Satu-Mare; Sindicatelor nr 7, Salonta 3650; Libraria Eminescu, Bul Elisabeta nr 5, Sector 5, Bucharest

Pandora Publishing House+
B-dulLacul Tei nr 123, bloc 4, Apt 177, Bucharest 723241
Tel: (021) 243 3739 *Fax:* (021) 243 3739
Key Personnel
Dir: Ion Monafu *E-mail:* editurapandora@hotmail.com
Associate Dir: Valer Monafu
  E-mail: valmonafu@msn.com
Founded: 1991
Specialize in fiction, nonfiction, translation from contemporary foreign authors, science & children's books.
Also acts as translating & literary service/agency.
Subjects: Biography, Fiction, Humor, Literature, Literary Criticism, Essays, Nonfiction (General), Poetry, Science (General), Science Fiction, Fantasy
ISBN Prefix(es): 973-96336; 973-96932; 973-95148; 973-98403; 973-8147
Number of titles published annually: 15 Print
Total Titles: 120 Print
Associate Companies: Prolectura Foundation
Foreign Rep(s): Dan Monafu (Canada); Valer Monafu (US)

Petrion Verlag+
Calea Plevnei 124, sector 6, 70700 Bucharest
Tel: (01) 637-23-34 *Fax:* (01) 312-45-25
E-mail: petrion@stranets.ro
Key Personnel
President: Ion Petrica
Founded: 1990
Subjects: Education, Mathematics, Microcomputers, Physics
ISBN Prefix(es): 973-9116

Polirom Verlag+
Bd Copou 4, 6600 Iasi
Tel: (032) 217-440 *Fax:* (032) 214-100
E-mail: polirom@olntis.ro
Key Personnel
Manager: Silviu Lupescu
Founded: 1995
Subjects: Anthropology, Communications, History, Journalism, Literature, Literary Criticism, Essays, Management, Marketing, Medicine, Nursing, Dentistry, Philosophy, Psychology, Psychiatry, Social Sciences, Sociology
ISBN Prefix(es): 973-9248; 973-97108; 973-97410; 973-97522; 973-683

Portland, *imprint of* The Center for Romanian Studies

RAO International Publishing Co, *imprint of* RAO Publishing Group

RAO International Publishing Co+
Bdul 1 mai, nr 125, bl 7, sc A, ct 1, ap 1,2,3, Bucharest
Tel: (01) 2241704; (01) 2241002 *Fax:* (01) 2228059
Key Personnel
Contact: Ondine Dascalita
Subjects: Biography, Fiction, Literature, Literary Criticism, Essays, Mysteries, Nonfiction (General), Religion - Other, Romance, Science Fiction, Fantasy
ISBN Prefix(es): 973-576; 973-9164; 973-96203; 973-96204
Subsidiaries: Rao Educational
Book Club(s): Rao Buchklub

RAO Publishing Group+
B dul 1 Mai nr 125, et 1, Bl 7, sc A Ap 1, Sector 1, 78217 Bucharest
Mailing Address: PO Box 2-124, Bucharest
Tel: (01) 2241704; (01) 2241002 *Fax:* (01) 2228059
E-mail: rao@can.ro
Web Site: www.rao.inet.ro; www.rao.ro
Key Personnel
President: Anca Enculescu
Editorial Dir: Ondine Dascalita
Contact: Ovidiu Enculescu
Founded: 1993
Member of AER & IBBY.
Subjects: Biography, Education, Fiction, History, Nonfiction (General), Science Fiction, Fantasy, Self-Help, Classic & Contemporary Fiction, Textbooks
ISBN Prefix(es): 973-576; 973-9460; 973-98762; 973-98626
Total Titles: 280 Print
Online services available through World Wide Web.
Imprints: Editure RAO; Enciclopedia RAO; Fahrenheit; RAO International Publishing Co
Warehouse: Str Tiate Mics 4, Sibiu *Fax:* (069) 215605 *E-mail:* rao.sb@bx.logicnet.ro
Orders to: RAO International Publishing Co, PO Box 2-124, Bucharest, Contact: Catalina Manolache

Realitatea Casa de Edituri Productie Audio-Video Film+
Bd Dacia nr 126, 70267 Bucharest
Tel: (01) 6117105; (01) 6517105; (01) 6332468; (01) 6143793 *Fax:* (01) 2105411
E-mail: leu@dnt.ro
Key Personnel
President: Corneliu Leu
Editor: George Atanasiu; Leu Vlad
Founded: 1990
Specialize in Film Production & Video Cassettes; Member of Romanian Copyright Society.
Subjects: Education, Government, Political Science, Literature, Literary Criticism, Essays, Nonfiction (General), Philosophy, Romance
ISBN Prefix(es): 973-9025
Parent Company: Realitatea-Publishers & Producers Ltd
Branch Office(s)
Monolith Corporation, 37 4181 St, Suite A2, Jackson Heights, NY 11372, United States
Tel: 718-507-2870
Bookshop(s): Bucharest, Timisoara, Iassi, Busteni (Romania)

Rentrop & Straton Verlagsgruppe und Wirtschaftsconsulting+
B dul casol no 79 A, Str Batistei Nr 24A, Sector 2, Bucharest
Tel: (01) 6142515 *Fax:* (01) 3112635
Key Personnel
General Editor: George Straton
International Rights: Violeta Carutasu
Founded: 1995
Subjects: Business, Economics, How-to, Law, Literature, Literary Criticism, Essays, Management, Marketing
ISBN Prefix(es): 973-97748; 973-98033; 973-9495

Saeculum IO+
Str Ciucea 5, Bl L 19, ap 216, sect 3, 74696 Bucharest
Tel: (021) 3452827 *Fax:* (021) 3452827; (021) 2228597
E-mail: saeculum@tcnet.ro
Web Site: www.saeculum.ro
Key Personnel
Proprietor: Prof Ionel Oprisan, PhD
Founded: 1994
Member of SER (Publishers' Society of Romania).
Subjects: Anthropology, Art, Biography, Fiction, History, Literature, Literary Criticism, Essays,

Mysteries, Parapsychology, Philosophy, Poetry, Romance, Theology
ISBN Prefix(es): 973-9211; 973-9399; 973-642
Parent Company: Saeculum IO
Associate Companies: Saeculum Vizual; Vestala
Showroom(s): Str Teodosie Rudeanu 29, Bucharest
Warehouse: Str Teodosie Rudeanu 29, Bucharest

Editura 'Scrisul Romanesc'
Str Mihai Viteazui 4, 1100 Craiova
Tel: (051) 113763
Key Personnel
Dir: Ilarie Hinoveanu
Founded: 1972
'Romanian Writing' Publishing House.
Subjects: Government, Political Science, Literature, Literary Criticism, Essays, Social Sciences, Sociology
ISBN Prefix(es): 973-38

Editura Signata+
Str Chiriac nr 26, 1900 Timisoara
Tel: (056) 153081
Key Personnel
Dir: Ioan Iancu
Founded: 1990
Member of Romanian Writers' Association.
Subjects: Technology
ISBN Prefix(es): 973-551

Editura Stiintifica+
Piata Presei Libere nr 1, 79737 Bucharest
Tel: (01) 2223330
Key Personnel
Man Dir: Dinu Grama
Founded: 1990
Scientific publishing house.
Subjects: Biological Sciences, Geography, Geology, History, Mathematics, Nonfiction (General), Philosophy, Psychology, Psychiatry, Science (General)
ISBN Prefix(es): 973-44

Editura Stiintifica si Enciclopedica
Piata Scinteii 1, 79737 Bucharest
Tel: (01) 175168
Key Personnel
Manager: Dinu Grama
Production Manager, Sales Dir: Alexandru Banciu
Founded: 1975 (by amalgamation of Romanian Encyclopaedic Publishing House & Scientific Publishing House)
Scientific & Encyclopedia Publishing House.
The Foreign Encyclopedias Office supplies any encyclopedic materials, information, data, statistics, maps & illustrations concerning Romania required by foreign publishing houses.
Subjects: Language Arts, Linguistics, Literature, Literary Criticism, Essays, Science (General), Social Sciences, Sociology
ISBN Prefix(es): 973-29

Est-Samuel Tastet Verlag+
Bdul Uverturii nr 57-69, Bl 10, sc C, et 1, ap 87, sector 6, Bucharest
Mailing Address: ap 24, sector 1, Bucharest
Tel: (01) 6386250 *Fax:* (01) 3122012
Key Personnel
Contact: Samuel Tastet
Founded: 1995
Subjects: Art, Biography, Drama, Theater, Fiction, Literature, Literary Criticism, Essays, Poetry
ISBN Prefix(es): 973-96902; 973-98094

Editura Tehnica
1, Piata Presei Libere, 79738 Bucharest
Tel: (01) 2223321; (01) 2226630 *Fax:* (01) 2223776
Key Personnel
Man Dir: Dr Ioan Ganea
Founded: 1950
Also book packager.
Subjects: Engineering (General), Science (General), Technology
ISBN Prefix(es): 973-31

Editura Teora+
Calea Mosilor nr 211, Sector 2, Bucharest
Tel: (01) 6193004 *Fax:* (01) 2103828
E-mail: teora@teora.kappa.ro
Web Site: www.teora.ro
Key Personnel
Dir: Teodor Raducanu
Founded: 1990
Subjects: Computer Science, Electronics, Electrical Engineering, Science Fiction, Fantasy
ISBN Prefix(es): 973-601; 973-20

Editura Top Suspans
Aleea Terasei nr 6, Bloc R 2, ap 5, sector 4, Bucharest 75582
Tel: (01) 6830924; (01) 6103359
Key Personnel
Dir: Nicolae Carp
ISBN Prefix(es): 973-9060

Editura Univers+
One Piata Presei Libere nr 1, R-79739 Bucharest
Tel: (01) 2226629 *Fax:* (01) 2225652 *Cable:* 1 PIATA PRESEI LIBERE, 79739 BUCHAREST
Key Personnel
General Dir: Prof Martin Mircea
Editor: Denisa Comanescu
Foreign Rights Editor: Adrian Mihaltianu
Founded: 1961
Subjects: Biography, Education, Fiction, Literature, Literary Criticism, Essays, Philosophy, Poetry, Romance, Science Fiction, Fantasy
ISBN Prefix(es): 973-34
Subsidiaries: Univers Informatic

Universal Dalsi+
Str Bd Libertati 10, bl 114, sc 2, et 3, ap 28, sector 2, Bucharest
Tel: (01) 4103552; (01) 337 1682 *Fax:* (01) 4121658
Key Personnel
Dir: Maria Marian *Tel:* (01) 650 6091 *Fax:* (01) 312 9709
Founded: 1992
Private publishing house specialized in belles lettres in Romanian & other languages.
Subjects: Education, Fiction, Literature, Literary Criticism, Essays, Philosophy, Poetry, Science (General), Social Sciences, Sociology, Theology
ISBN Prefix(es): 973-9166; 973-9409; 973-95690; 973-96039
Total Titles: 10 Print
Distributor for Letos Mimai, Balasion

Editura Valahia SRL
Str Trivale bloc 61 sc B ap 9, Pitesti, Jud Arges, 0300 Pitesti
Tel: 097 680948
Key Personnel
Dir: George Nitu
Founded: 1990
ISBN Prefix(es): 973-95049

Editura de Vest+
Str Stantul Gheorge 1, 1900 Timisoara
Tel: (056) 191956; (056) 118218 *Fax:* (056) 14212
Key Personnel
Dir: Vasile Popovici
Founded: 1972
Subjects: Art, Fiction, Science (General), Technology
ISBN Prefix(es): 973-36

Vestala Verlag+
Str Ciucea 5, Bloc L19, AP 216, Sector 3, Bucharest
Mailing Address: PO Box 72-142, Bucharest
Tel: (01) 3452827 *Fax:* (01) 3452827; (01) 2228597
Key Personnel
Contact: Prof Dr Ionel Oprisan
Founded: 1993
Member of Publishers' Association of Romania (Asociatia Editorilor din Romania).
Subjects: Art, Biography, History, Literature, Literary Criticism, Essays, Mysteries, Parapsychology, Philosophy
ISBN Prefix(es): 973-9200; 973-96063; 973-96421; 973-96817; 973-9418
Number of titles published annually: 30 Print
Total Titles: 120 Print
Parent Company: Saeculum Verlag, 74696 Bucharest
Associate Companies: Saeculum i o Verlag

Vox Verlag und Vertrieb+
Str Garii de Nord nr: 6-8, blA, sc6, ap 2, sector 1, Bucharest 781232
Tel: (01) 6378584 *Fax:* (01) 6376829
Key Personnel
General Manager: Lucia Ovezea
Founded: 1994
Subjects: Gardening, Plants
ISBN Prefix(es): 973-96922; 973-97848

Vremea Publishers Ltd+
Str Constantin Daniel Nr 14, sec 1, 71121 Bucharest
Tel: (01) 3358131 *Fax:* (01) 3110219
E-mail: vremea@fx.ro
Key Personnel
President: Nicolae Henegariu
Vice President: Cristina Cantacuzino
Publishing Dir: Silvia Colfescu *Tel:* (092) 226088
Founded: 1990
member of AER Romanian Publishers Association.
Subjects: Astrology, Occult, Fiction, Health, Nutrition, History, Literature, Literary Criticism, Essays, Medicine, Nursing, Dentistry, Parapsychology, Philosophy, Poetry, Science Fiction, Fantasy
ISBN Prefix(es): 973-9162; 973-95063; 973-95581
Number of titles published annually: 45 Print
Total Titles: 250 Print

Russian Federation

General Information

Capital: Moscow
Language: Russian
Religion: Predominantly Christian (mostly Russian Orthodox), also Islam and Buddhist
Population: 149.5 million
Bank Hours: Generally open for short hours between 0930-1230 Monday-Friday
Shop Hours: Generally 0900-1800 Monday-Friday; often open weekends
Currency: 100 kopeks = 1 rubl
Export/Import Information: According to Ukrainian quotas and customs duties, companies engaged in trade should register with the Ukraine Ministry of Foreign Economic Relations. Licenses for export and import are also required for trade with Russia.
Copyright: UCC, Berne, Florence (see Copyright Conventions, pg xi)

PUBLISHERS

Agni Publishing House
23 Michurin St, 443110 Samara
Tel: (08462) 70-32-87; (08462) 70-23-87 (ext 445 - Orders) *Fax:* (08462) 70-23-85
E-mail: cdk@transit.samara.ru; support@agniart.ru (distribution & ordering)
Web Site: www.agni.samara.ru
Key Personnel
Manager: Sergey Tyoply
Also producers of fine art reproductions of paintings by Russian artists, photo-landscapes, framing & art albums.
Subjects: History, Philosophy

Airis Press+
106 Prospekt Mira, Office 555, 129626 Moscow
Tel: (095) 9561684; (095) 7852925 *Fax:* (095) 9561684; (095) 7852925
E-mail: rolf@airis.ru
Web Site: www.airis.ru
Key Personnel
Marketing Dir: Igor Chesnokov *E-mail:* iches@airis.ru
Founded: 1993
Specialize in educational literature, books helping school-leavers & students to prepare for the exams, handbooks & textbooks in foreign languages, popular educational books, reference books.
Subjects: Business, Career Development, Child Care & Development, Cookery, Crafts, Games, Hobbies, Education, English as a Second Language, Gardening, Plants, Health, Nutrition, How-to, Language Arts, Linguistics, Medicine, Nursing, Dentistry
ISBN Prefix(es): 5-7836; 5-8112
Number of titles published annually: 70 Print; 3 Audio
Total Titles: 180 Print; 3 Audio
Distributor for Foulsham; New Market Press; Parenting Press

ARGO-RISK Publisher
ul Stary Gaj 6-419, 111402 Moscow
Tel: (095) 4768538 *Fax:* (095) 2926511
E-mail: zayats@glas.apc.org
Key Personnel
Dir: Vladislav Artsatbanov
Editor-in-Chief: Dmitri Kuz'min
Founded: 1993
Subjects: Gay & Lesbian, Literature, Literary Criticism, Essays, Poetry
ISBN Prefix(es): 5-900506

Armada Publishing House+
37b Kronshtadtsky Blvd, Moscow 125499
Tel: (095) 4544301; (095) 45431526 *Fax:* (095) 4542481
E-mail: riv@armada.msk.su
Key Personnel
President: Dmitri Adamov
Editor: Anton Rybin
Foreign Rights: Olga Zasetskaya
Founded: 1992
Subjects: Animals, Pets, Fiction, Mysteries, Romance, Science Fiction, Fantasy
ISBN Prefix(es): 5-7632

Aspect Press Ltd+
ul Plehanova 23, corpus 3, Moscow 111398
Tel: (095) 3094062 *Fax:* (095) 3091166
E-mail: info@aspectpress.ru
Web Site: www.aspectpress.ru
Key Personnel
Dir & Owner: Leonid Shipov *E-mail:* shipov@aspectpress.ru
Founded: 1992
Specialize in university textbooks in humanities; Russian biographical dictionary in 33 vols.
Subjects: Economics, Government, Political Science, History, Philosophy, Social Sciences, Sociology

ISBN Prefix(es): 5-7567
Number of titles published annually: 50 Print
Total Titles: 110 Print
Distributed by Nauka Ltd (Japan)

Aurora Art Publishers+
Nevsky prospekt 7/9, 191065 Saint Petersburg
Tel: (0812) 3123753 *Fax:* (0812) 3125460
Telex: 121562 *Cable:* FOREIGN TRADE FIRM AURORA LENINGRAD
Key Personnel
President, Rights & Permissions: Boris Pidemsky
Commercial Dir: Zenobius Spetchinsky
Production: Faina Timofeeva
Founded: 1969
Publishes in foreign languages (English, French & German).
Subjects: Art
ISBN Prefix(es): 5-7300
Associate Companies: Aurora Design

N E Bauman Moscow State Technical University Publishers+
2-ja Baumanskaja ul 5, 107005 Moscow
Tel: (095) 2614597 *Fax:* (095) 2636707; (095) 2654298
Key Personnel
Dir: Tatyana I Popenchenko
Founded: 1989
Subjects: Biblical Studies, Business, Communications, Computer Science, Earth Sciences, Economics, Education, Electronics, Electrical Engineering, Energy, Engineering (General), Law, Management, Mathematics, Mechanical Engineering, Microcomputers, Science (General), Technology
ISBN Prefix(es): 5-7038
Parent Company: Moscow State Technical University

Beta-Service ZAO, see Mir Knigi Ltd

BLIC, russko-Baltijskij informaciionnyj centr, AO+
ul krasnogo flota 4, 190000 St Petersburg
Tel: (0812) 3112252 *Fax:* (0812) 3112252; (0812) 1135896
E-mail: blitz@blitz.spb.ru
Key Personnel
Press-Attache: Natalya Mikhailova *Tel:* (0812) 3121440
Founded: 1992
Specializes in various archival references, catalogs, historical books & monographies.
Subjects: Biography, Drama, Theater, Fiction, History, Maritime, Nonfiction (General), Poetry, Religion - Other, Romance, Science (General), Science Fiction, Fantasy, Sports, Athletics
ISBN Prefix(es): 5-86789
Total Titles: 70 Print
Branch Office(s)
Blumenstrape 126, 47798 Kreferd, Germany, Contact: Marina Potapova *Tel:* (0215) 1608453 *Fax:* (0215) 1608453
U.S. Office(s): 307 Mission Ave, San Rafael, CA 34901, United States, Contact: W Edward Nute *Tel:* 415-453-3579 *Fax:* 415-453-0343 *E-mail:* enute@igc.apc.org

CentrePolygraph Traders & Publishers Co+
18 Oktyabrskaya St, RU-127018 Moscow
Tel: (095) 2817411 *Fax:* (095) 2844074
Key Personnel
Editorial Dir: Igor Lazarev
Founded: 1991
Subjects: Astrology, Occult, Fiction, Mysteries, Science Fiction, Fantasy, Western Fiction
ISBN Prefix(es): 5-7001
Showroom(s): 20/1 Decabristov ul, Moscow
Bookshop(s): ul 32 Raspletina, Moscow
Warehouse: 70/1 Nizhegordoskaya ul, Moscow

RUSSIAN FEDERATION

Izdatelstvo Detskaya Literatura+
Malyi Cherkasskij pereulok 1, 103720 Moscow
Tel: (095) 9280803 *Fax:* (095) 9213007
Key Personnel
Dir: Tamara M Shatunova
Foreign Rights, Sales: Tatyana P Vladimirskaya *Tel:* (095) 9213007
Founded: 1933
Children's Literature Publishing.
Subjects: Art, Fiction, History, Literature, Literary Criticism, Essays, Poetry
ISBN Prefix(es): 5-08
Subsidiaries: Detskaya Literatura Publishers
Branch Office(s)
Dom Detskoy Knigi, 1 Tverskaya-Yamskaya 13, Moscow

Dom, Izdatel'stvo sovetskogo deskkogo fonda im & 1 Lenina+
Armjanskij per, 11/2a, 101963 Moscow
Tel: (095) 9236661 *Fax:* (095) 9285322
Key Personnel
Editor-in-Chief: A Likhanov
Founded: 1989
Subjects: Child Care & Development, Cookery, Crafts, Games, Hobbies, Education, Fiction, House & Home, How-to, Women's Studies
ISBN Prefix(es): 5-85201

Druzhba Narodov+
ul Petrovka 26, 101409 Moscow
Tel: (095) 9258671
Key Personnel
Dir: Gennady S Gots
Editor-in-Chief: Leonid A Teracopyan
Commercial Manager: Mikhail A Malygin
Founded: 1990
Member of the Association of Soviet Publishers.
Subjects: Crafts, Games, Hobbies, Theology
ISBN Prefix(es): 5-285
Parent Company: Ministry of Printing of Russian Federation
Associate Companies: Publishing houses of Russian Federation & other Soviet Republic All-Union Society "Book"; All-Union Culture Fund; Pushkin Fund

Izdatelstvo Ekologija
ul Kirova 40, 101000 Moscow
Tel: (095) 9287860
Key Personnel
Dir: L P Tizensgauzen
Editor-in-Chief: G P Dolgovykh
Founded: 1963
Forest Industry Publishing House.
Subjects: Environmental Studies
ISBN Prefix(es): 5-7120

Izdatelstvo 'Ekonomika'
Berezkovskaja naberezhnaya 6, 121864 Moscow
Tel: (095) 2404877 *Fax:* (095) 2404869
Key Personnel
Dir: I D Trotsenkd
Founded: 1963
Economics Publishing House.
Subjects: Agriculture, Business, Cookery, Economics, Management
ISBN Prefix(es): 5-282

Nalchik Book Publishing House Elbrus, *imprint of* Kabardino-Balkarskoye knizhnoye izdatelstvo

Energoatomizdat
ul Rozdestvenka 5/7, 103031 Moscow
Tel: (095) 9259993 *Fax:* (095) 2356585
Key Personnel
Dir: A P Aleshkin
Editor-in-Chief: G G Malkin
Founded: 1963
Publishing House for Atomic Literature.

RUSSIAN FEDERATION

Subjects: Computer Science, Electronics, Electrical Engineering, Environmental Studies, Literature, Literary Criticism, Essays, Physics, Science (General), Technology
ISBN Prefix(es): 5-283

FGUP Izdatelstvo Mashinostroenie
(Mashinostroenie Publishers)+
Stromynskij pereulok 4, 107076 Moscow
Tel: (095) 2683858 *Fax:* (095) 2694897
E-mail: mashpubl@mashin.ru
Web Site: www.mashin.ru
Key Personnel
Dir: Olga N Rumyantseva
Deputy Dir: Liubov I Kouzovkina *Tel:* (095) 268-4968 *E-mail:* kouzovkina@umail.ru
Founded: 1931
Publishing House for Mechanical Engineering.
Subjects: Aeronautics, Aviation, Automotive, Biography, Computer Science, Economics, Engineering (General), Environmental Studies, Mathematics, Mechanical Engineering, Technology
ISBN Prefix(es): 5-217
Associate Companies: Aspect

Finansy i Statistika Publishing House+
Porrovka 7, 101000 Moscow
Tel: (095) 925 4708 *Fax:* (095) 925 0957
E-mail: mail@finstat.ru
Web Site: www.finstat.ru
Key Personnel
Man Dir & Editor-in-Chief: Alevtina N Zvonova
Translator: Margarita Ter-Oganian *Tel:* (095) 923 0483
Founded: 1924
Finance and Statistics Publishing House.
Member of Russian Association of Book Publishers; Russian Association of Book Sellers; Guild of Russian Financiers.
Subjects: Accounting, Business, Career Development, Computer Science, Economics, Environmental Studies, Finance, Human Relations, Law, Library & Information Sciences, Management, Marketing, Mathematics, Microcomputers, Public Administration, Real Estate, Securities, Self-Help
ISBN Prefix(es): 5-279
Total Titles: 25 Print
Distributed by KnoRus
Distributor for KnoRus

Izdatelstvo Fizkultura i Sport+
ul Kaljaevskajastr 27, 101421 Moscow
Tel: (095) 2582690 *Fax:* (095) 2001217
Key Personnel
Dir: Valery L Shteinbakh
Editor-in-Chief: V I Vinokurov
Founded: 1923
Subjects: Outdoor Recreation, Sports, Athletics
ISBN Prefix(es): 5-278

Fizmatlit Publishing Co+
ul Profsojuznaja 90, 117485 Moscow
Tel: (095) 3347151 *Fax:* (095) 9550597
Key Personnel
Dir: L I Gladneva
Deputy Dir: A N Zotov
Founded: 1931
Subjects: Astronomy, Communications, Computer Science, Mathematics, Mechanical Engineering, Microcomputers, Physical Sciences, Physics
ISBN Prefix(es): 5-02
Parent Company: Nauka Publishers

Izdatelstvo Galart
ul Cernjahovskogo 4a, Moscow 125319
Tel: (095) 1512502; (095) 1514513 *Fax:* (095) 1513761
Key Personnel
Dir: V V Goryainov

Chief Editor: B Z Yashchina
Founded: 1969
Subjects: Art
ISBN Prefix(es): 5-269

Gidrometeoizdat+
ul Beringa 38, 199226 St Petersburg
Tel: (0812) 3520815 *Fax:* (0812) 3522688 *Cable:* LENINGRAD B-115 GIMIZ
Key Personnel
Dir: A I Ugriumov
Editor-in-Chief: Antonina S Andreeva
Publicity, Promotion: Sergey A Smoliakov
Founded: 1934
Subjects: Agriculture, Animals, Pets, Earth Sciences, Environmental Studies, Geography, Geology, Science (General)
ISBN Prefix(es): 5-286

Glas New Russian Writing+
PO Box 47, 119517 Moscow
Tel: (095) 4419157 *Fax:* (095) 4419157
Web Site: www.bham.ac.uk/glas; www.glas.msk.su
Key Personnel
Publisher & Editor: Natasha Perova
  E-mail: perova@glas.msk.su
Founded: 1992
Specialize in contemporary Russian literature in English translation, bringing publishers & interested readers up to date on the latest hits in Russian literary fiction. Features various literary trends with a view to show the entire literary map of Russia today. More than 100 authors in 23 issues have come out to date.
Subjects: Fiction, Literature, Literary Criticism, Essays
ISBN Prefix(es): 1-56663; 5-7172
Number of titles published annually: 4 Print
Total Titles: 28 Print
Branch Office(s)
University of Birmingham, Russian Dept, Birmigham B15 2TT, United Kingdom, Contact: Arch Tait *Tel:* (0121) 414 6047 *Fax:* (0121) 414 6047 *E-mail:* a.l.tait@bham.ac.uk
U.S. Office(s): 1332 N Halsted St, Chicago, IL 60622-2694, United States, Contact: Ivan Dee *Tel:* 312-787-6262 *Fax:* 312-787-6269 *E-mail:* elephant@ivanrdee.com
Distributed by Central Books Ltd (only UK & Europe)
Foreign Rep(s): Arch Tait (Worldwide); Ivan R Dee (USA) (Worldwide)
Shipping Address: National Book Network, 4720 Boston Way, Lanham, MD, United States *Tel:* 301-459-3366 *Fax:* 301-459-1705 *E-mail:* rfreese@nbnbooks.com
Warehouse: 15200 NBN Way, Blue Ridge Summit, PA 17214, United States

INFRA-M Izdatel'skij dom+
107 Dmitrovskoye Shosse, Moscow 127214
Tel: (095) 4855936 *Fax:* (095) 4855318
E-mail: books@orc.ru
Key Personnel
Foreign Rights Manager: Regina Bouglo
  Tel: (095) 4855918 *E-mail:* regina@orc.ru
Founded: 1992
Publisher of business books in accounting, management, law, public sector & produces audio & video courses of foreign languages.
Subjects: Accounting, Business, Economics, Education, Government, Political Science, Law, Management, Marketing
ISBN Prefix(es): 5-86225; 5-16
Distributed by Infra M Kniga

Interbook-Business AO
Spiridonovskij per 12/9, Kull 11, 103104 Moscow
Tel: (095) 2006469; (095) 2006462 *Fax:* (095) 9563752
Key Personnel
Dir: Gennadi Popov

Founded: 1992
Subjects: Art, Gardening, Plants, Sports, Athletics
ISBN Prefix(es): 5-89164

Izdatel'stvo Kazanskago Universiteta+
ul Lenina 18, 420008 Kazan Respublika Tatarstan
Tel: 325363
E-mail: kacimov@niimm.kazan.su
Key Personnel
Dir: Andrei Vatrushkin
Founded: 1957
Subjects: Chemistry, Chemical Engineering, Criminology, Economics, Environmental Studies, Mathematics
ISBN Prefix(es): 5-7464

Izdatel'stvo Mordovskogo gosudar stvennogo
ul Sovetskaja 24, Saransk Mordovia Republika 430000
Tel: 74771 *Fax:* 74771
Telex: teletype srn87aelita
Key Personnel
Dir: Aleksander N Zernov
Founded: 1990
Specialize in Scientific & Educational publications for high school.
Subjects: Agriculture, Civil Engineering, Economics, Education, Engineering (General), Geography, Geology, History, Language Arts, Linguistics, Literature, Literary Criticism, Essays, Mathematics, Medicine, Nursing, Dentistry, Philosophy, Social Sciences, Sociology
ISBN Prefix(es): 5-7103
Total Titles: 1,098 Print
Parent Company: Mordovian State University
Bookshop(s): ul Bolshevitskya 68, 430000 Saransk

Izdatel'stvo Ural'skogo+
Prosp Lenina 135, 620219 Ekaterinburg
Tel: (03432) 515448 *Fax:* (03432) 51-54-48
E-mail: info@idc.e-burg-ru
Key Personnel
Dir: Victor Kochkin
Chief Editor: Fiodor Eremeyev
Founded: 1986
Specialize in monographs & handbooks.
Subjects: Literature, Literary Criticism, Essays, Mathematics, Philosophy
ISBN Prefix(es): 5-7525

Izdatel'stovo Dal'nevostonogo Gosudarstvennogo Universite (Far-East State University Press)+
Oktjabrskaja ul 27, 690600 Vladivostok
Tel: 57779 (Director) *Fax:* 257200
Telex: 213218 FESU SU
Key Personnel
Dir: Tatyana V Prudkoglyad
Founded: 1982
Subjects: Human Relations, Mathematics
ISBN Prefix(es): 5-7444
Bookshop(s): Fesupress Bookshop, Oktjabrskaja ul 27, 690600 Vladivostok

Izdatelstvo Bolshaya Rossiyskaya Entsiklopedia
Pokrovskij bul'var' 8, 109817 Moscow
Tel: (095) 9177582; (095) 9179009 *Fax:* (095) 9177139
Key Personnel
Dir: Dr A Gorkin
Founded: 1925
The Great Encyclopedia of Russia Publishing House.
ISBN Prefix(es): 5-85270

Izdatelstvo Iskusstvo+
Sobinovskij per 3, 103009 Moscow
Tel: (095) 2035872 *Fax:* (095) 2918882
Key Personnel
Dir: O A Makarov

Deputy Dir: Bodnarouk Tatyana; Yamshchikov Anatoly
Founded: 1938 (as Izogiz & Iskusstvo)
Publishing House for Art Literature.
Specialize in Art.
Subjects: Architecture & Interior Design, Art, Drama, Theater, Film, Video, History, Philosophy
ISBN Prefix(es): 5-210
Distributed by Calmann & King (UK)
Distributor for Booth-Clibborn Editions; Giunti (Italy); Jaca Book (Italy)

Izdatelstvo Moskovskii Rabochii+
Cistoprudnyj bul'var' 8, 101854 Moscow
Tel: (095) 2210735 *Fax:* (095) 9254274
Key Personnel
President, All Moscow, Dir, Moskovskii Rabochiy: Dmitri V Evdokimov
General Dir, All Moscow: Ferdinand V Kaploun
Vice President: Oleg P Benukh; Alexei Vengerov
Editor-in-Chief: G I Broido
Founded: 1922
Moscow Worker Publishing House.
Subjects: Fiction, Nonfiction (General)
ISBN Prefix(es): 5-239; 5-7110
Branch Office(s)
Konstatin Evdokimov Bosmsco, 131 Beverly St, Boston, MA 02114, United States *Tel:* (617) 248-3988 *Fax:* (617) 248-3885

Izvestia Sovetov Narodnyh Deputatov Russian Federation (RF)
Pukinskaja pl 5, 103798 Moscow
Tel: (095) 2093738 *Fax:* (095) 2095394
Telex: 411121 Vesti SU
Key Personnel
Dir: Y F Yefremov
Subjects: Agriculture, Business, Economics, Government, Political Science, Law, Public Administration, Social Sciences, Sociology, Sports, Athletics
ISBN Prefix(es): 5-206

Kabardino-Balkarskoye knizhnoye izdatelstvo+
ul Malo-Kabardinskaja 1, 360000 Nalchik Kabardino Balkarskoye respublika
Tel: 54184
Key Personnel
Dir: Ibragim Matgerievich Gadiev
Chief Editor: Anatoly Muratovich Bitsuev
Founded: 1928
Subjects: Ethnicity
ISBN Prefix(es): 5-86778
Parent Company: Ministry of Press & Mass Informatio
Imprints: Nalchik Book Publishing House Elbrus

Kavkazskaya Biblioteka Publishing House+
prosp Karl Marks St 78, 355045 Stavropol'
Tel: (8652) 32314
Key Personnel
Dir: Eugen Panasko
Founded: 1990
Subjects: Fiction, Human Relations, Literature, Literary Criticism, Essays, Poetry, Science Fiction, Fantasy
ISBN Prefix(es): 5-8436
Distributor for Samarskiy Dom Pechaty & Sovremennic

Izdatelstvo Khudozhestvennaya Literatura+
ul Novo-Basmannaja 19, 107882 Moscow
Tel: (095) 268865; (095) 2613864 *Fax:* (095) 2618300
Key Personnel
Editor-in-Chief: V S Modestov
Dir: A N Petzov
Founded: 1930 (as The State Publishers of Fiction)
Publishing House for Fiction, Poetry & Literary Biography.
Subjects: Fiction, Literature, Literary Criticism, Essays, Music, Dance, Poetry
ISBN Prefix(es): 5-280

Izdatelstvo Kniga+
ul Tverskaja 50, 125047 Moscow
Tel: (095) 2516003 *Fax:* (095) 2500489
Telex: 411871
Key Personnel
Vice President: Vladimar Y Shvedov
Chairman of the Board, Dir: Viktor N Adamov
Editor-in-Chief: Ivan A Prokhorov
Founded: 1964
Subjects: Library & Information Sciences, Publishing & Book Trade Reference
ISBN Prefix(es): 5-212
Subsidiaries: Kniga Printshop (owned jointly-Kniga Publishers, Russia & Fargo Group, Toronto, Ontario, Canada); The Culture Center at Bol shaya Polianka (owned jointly-USSR & USA); Business Week- Russian Language Edition (jointly by McGraw-Hill Corp, USA Publishers & Kniga Publishers, Russia)

Izdatelstvo Knizhnaya Palata
ul. Oktjabr'skaja 4, Moscow 103009
Tel: (095) 2889247 *Fax:* (095) 1635827
Key Personnel
Dir: Alexey F Kurilko
Editor-in-Chief: V T Kabanov
Founded: 1987
Publishing House "Book Chamber".
Subjects: Fiction, Publishing & Book Trade Reference
ISBN Prefix(es): 5-7000

Izdatelskii Dom Kompozitor (Kompozitor Publishing House)
ul Sadovaja-Triumfalnaja, 12/14, 127006 Moscow
Tel: (095) 2092980; (095) 2094105 *Fax:* (095) 2095498
E-mail: music@sumail.ru
Key Personnel
Dir: G Voronov
Founded: 1957
Subjects: Biography, Education, Music, Dance
ISBN Prefix(es): 5-85285

KUbK Publishing House+
ul Gurjanova 5-134, 109548 Moscow
Tel: (095) 1640910; (095) 3679473 *Fax:* (095) 1528689
Key Personnel
President: Viktor Oubeiko
International Rights: Natalia Oubeiko
Founded: 1992
Subjects: Animals, Pets, Computer Science, Cookery, Romance
ISBN Prefix(es): 5-85554

Kul'tura redakcionno-izdatel skij kompleks
ul 35 Arbat, 121835 Moscow
Tel: (095) 2481151 *Fax:* (095) 2302180
ISBN Prefix(es): 5-8334
Branch Office(s)
Nevsky Pz, 15, St Petersburg

Ladomir Publishing House+
Zelenograd, Korpus 1435, K-617, Moscow 103617
Tel: (095) 5309833; (095) 5304742 *Fax:* (095) 5374742
Key Personnel
Editor-in-Chief: Yu Mirhailov
Founded: 1990
Subjects: Antiques, Asian Studies, Fiction, Government, Political Science, History, Philosophy, Religion - Buddhist, Religion - Hindu, Religion - Islamic, Science Fiction, Fantasy, Sports, Athletics
ISBN Prefix(es): 5-86218

Legprombytizdat
1-J Kadashevskii pereulok 12, 113035 Moscow
Tel: (095) 2330947
Key Personnel
Dir: T G Gromova
Editor-in-Chief: T P Drozdova
Founded: 1932
Light Industry and the Services Publishing House.
Subjects: Business, Labor, Industrial Relations, Social Sciences, Sociology
ISBN Prefix(es): 5-7088

Izdatelstvo Lenizdat+
ul Fontanka 59, 191023 St Petersburg
Tel: (0812) 3111451 *Fax:* (0812) 3151295
Telex: 122-693 IZDAT
Key Personnel
Gen Dir: V N Nabirukhin
Editor-in-Chief: V N Bunin
Founded: 1917
St Petersburg Publishing House.
Member of the Association of Bookpublishers of Russia. Founder of Russian International Book Exchange.
Subjects: Agriculture, Art, Fiction, Government, Political Science, Science (General), Science Fiction, Fantasy, Technology
ISBN Prefix(es): 5-289
Parent Company: Ministry of the Press & Mass Media of the Russian Federation

Publishing House Limbus Press+
Izmailovsky pr, 14, 198005 St Petersburg
Tel: (0812) 1126547 *Fax:* (0812) 1126706
E-mail: limbuspr@rol.ru; limbus@limbuspress.ru
Web Site: www.limbuspress.ru
Key Personnel
Publisher: Konstantin Tublin
Editor-in-chief: Victor Toporov
Foreign Rights: Julia Goumen
Subjects: Biography, Fiction, Nonfiction (General)
Number of titles published annually: 60 Print
Branch Office(s)
Moscow
Foreign Rep(s): Anna Benn (England); Catherine Fzagou (Greece); Anastasia Lester (France); Christian Marti-Menzel (Spain)

Izdatelstvo Malysh
ul Davydkovskaja 5, 121352 Moscow
Tel: (095) 4430654 *Fax:* (095) 4430655
Key Personnel
Dir: V M Maiiboroda
Editor-in-Chief: V A Rybin
Founded: 1957
Children's World Publishing House.
ISBN Prefix(es): 5-213

Izdatelstvo Medicina+
Petroverigskij pereulok 6/8, 103000 Moscow
Tel: (095) 9248785 *Fax:* (095) 9286003
Telex: 412282 MEDIZ SU
Key Personnel
Dir: A M Stochik *Tel:* (095) 9288648
Editor-in-Chief: N R Paleev *Tel:* (095) 9248785
Foreign Rights Manager: O H Sheshukova *Tel:* (095) 9239368
Founded: 1918
Publishing House for Medicine.
Subjects: Health, Nutrition, Medicine, Nursing, Dentistry, Psychology, Psychiatry, Science (General)
ISBN Prefix(es): 5-225
Associate Companies: Association for Medical Literature
Bookshop(s): Komsomolski pr 25, Moscow; Begovaya, 11, Moscow

RUSSIAN FEDERATION

Izdatelstvo Metallurgiya+
2j Obydenskij pereulok 14, 119857 Moscow
Tel: (095) 2025532 *Fax:* (095) 2025752
Key Personnel
Dir: A G Belikov
Editor-in-Chief: N N Marchenko
Founded: 1939
Publishing House for Metallurgy.
Subjects: Earth Sciences, Engineering (General), Technology
ISBN Prefix(es): 5-229

Mezdunarodnye Otno Denija+
ul Sadovaja-Spasskaja 20, Moscow 107078
Tel: (095) 2076793 *Fax:* (095) 2002204
Key Personnel
Dir: Boris Likhavchev
Founded: 1957
Subjects: Economics, Government, Political Science, Law
ISBN Prefix(es): 5-7133

Izdatelstvo Mezhdunarodnye Otnoshenia+
ul Sadovaja-Spasskaja 20, 107078 Moscow
Tel: (095) 2076793 *Fax:* (095) 2002204
Key Personnel
Chief Executive: B P Likhachev
Production: M Rodin
Founded: 1957
International Relations Publishing House.
Subjects: Biography, Government, Political Science
ISBN Prefix(es): 5-7133
Parent Company: Goscomizdat, Strastnoi bul 5, Moscow 101409

Middle Urals Publishing House, see Sredne-Uralskoye knizhnoye izatelstve (Middle Urals Publishing House)

Ministerstvo Kul 'tury RF+
Kitajskij Proezd 7, 103693 Moscow
Tel: (0812) 2204500
E-mail: rnb@q1as.apc.org
Member of IFLA.
Subjects: Genealogy, History, Library & Information Sciences, Social Sciences, Sociology
ISBN Prefix(es): 5-7196
Distributed by Kubon & Sagner

Izdatelstvo Mir (Mir Publishers)+
2 Pervy Rizhsky Pereulok, 107996 Moscow
Tel: (095) 286-17-83 *Fax:* (095) 288-95-22
Web Site: www.mir-pubs.dol.ru
Key Personnel
Dir: Dr Kh P Abdullaev *E-mail:* khpa@mir.msk.ru
Editor-in-Chief: Dr V I Propoi *Tel:* (095) 286 43 00 *E-mail:* vivp@mir.msk.ru
International Relations Supervisor: V V Gerasimovsky *Tel:* (095) 286 17 00 *E-mail:* vvg@mir.msk.ru
Founded: 1946 (under name Mir since 1964)
Translation & publication of scientific & technical books.
Member of ASKI (Book Publishers Association of Russia), Association "Task Force Against Piracy".
Subjects: Aeronautics, Aviation, Animals, Pets, Astronomy, Biological Sciences, Chemistry, Chemical Engineering, Communications, Computer Science, Earth Sciences, Electronics, Electrical Engineering, Engineering (General), Environmental Studies, Fiction, Geography, Geology, Health, Nutrition, Mathematics, Mechanical Engineering, Microcomputers, Physical Sciences, Physics, Psychology, Psychiatry, Science (General), Science Fiction, Fantasy, Self-Help, Technology
ISBN Prefix(es): 5-03

Number of titles published annually: 50 Print
Total Titles: 170 Print

Mir Knigi Ltd+
ul Sadovaja-Spasskaja 6, 107045 Moscow
Tel: (095) 2083879 *Fax:* (095) 7428579
Key Personnel
Media Project Dir: Slovovieva Rimma *E-mail:* rimma@beta.ru
Founded: 1999
Publishes the Mir Knigi magazine.
Subjects: Fiction, Nonfiction (General)
ISBN Prefix(es): 5-7043
Owned by: Beta-Service

Izdatelstvo Molodaya Gvardia+
ul Suscevskaja 21, 103030 Moscow
Tel: (095) 9722288 *Fax:* (095) 9720582
Key Personnel
General Dir: Valentin Yurkin
Founded: 1922
Young Guard Publishing House of the Young Communist League Central Committee.
Subjects: Art, Biography, Government, Political Science, History, Literature, Literary Criticism, Essays, Poetry, Social Sciences, Sociology, Sports, Athletics
ISBN Prefix(es): 5-235

Moscow University Press+
ul Gercena 5-7, 103009 Moscow
Tel: (095) 2295091
Telex: 411483 MGUSU
Key Personnel
Dir: N S Timofeyev
Founded: 1756
Member of University Press Council.
Subjects: Education
ISBN Prefix(es): 5-211
Branch Office(s)
Rights & Permissions: VAAP, Bolshaya Bronnaya 6a, Moscow 103670

Izdatelstvo Muzyka+
ul Neglinnaja 14, 103031 Moscow
Tel: (095) 9230497 *Fax:* (095) 9283304
E-mail: muzyka@insar.ru
Key Personnel
Dir: I Savintsen
Chief Distributor: Aleksey Grebennikov
Founded: 1861
State Music Publishing House.
Subjects: Education, Music, Dance
ISBN Prefix(es): 5-7140
Number of titles published annually: 150 Print
Subsidiaries:
Distributor for Schott
Showroom(s): ul Petrovka 26, 103031 Moscow
Bookshop(s): Music World, ul B.Nikitskaja, 13, 103871 Moscow
Warehouse: Ul Petrovka 26, 103031 Moscow
Orders to: ul Petrovka 26, 103031 Moscow

Izdatelstvo Mysl+
Leninskj Prospect 15, l19071 Moscow
Tel: (095) 2324248; (095) 952-5065; (095) 955-0458
Key Personnel
Dir: Timofeyev Yevgeny Alexeyevich
Founded: 1963
Subjects: Economics, Geography, Geology, History, Philosophy, Science (General)
ISBN Prefix(es): 5-244

Nauka Publishers+
ul Profsoyuznaya 90, 117485 Moscow
Tel: (095) 3347151 *Fax:* (095) 4202220
E-mail: nauka@nauka.msk.ru
Telex: 411612 IZAN *Cable:* Moscow-485
Key Personnel
Dir: V Vasiliev
Editor-in-Chief: T Filippova *Tel:* (095) 336 1022
Rights: V Anishchenko *Tel:* (095) 336 0266 *Fax:* (095) 334 7451
Sales: V Bogomolov *Tel:* (095) 334 7479 *Fax:* (095) 334 7479
Founded: 1727
Scientific books & journals in all fields of knowledge, university textbooks, popular science, academic monographs.
There are six self-supporting branches of Nauka in Moscow, two divisions in Novosibirsk & St Petersburg, Akademkniga Book selling firm & four printshops. The firm's other business activities include Direct Mail & Advertising.
Subjects: Aeronautics, Aviation, Archaeology, Art, Asian Studies, Astronomy, Biological Sciences, Chemistry, Chemical Engineering, Communications, Computer Science, Earth Sciences, Economics, Education, Electronics, Electrical Engineering, Energy, Engineering (General), Environmental Studies, Geography, Geology, Government, Political Science, Health, Nutrition, History, Language Arts, Linguistics, Law, Library & Information Sciences, Literature, Literary Criticism, Essays, Management, Marketing, Mathematics, Mechanical Engineering, Medicine, Nursing, Dentistry, Microcomputers, Natural History, Philosophy, Physics, Psychology, Psychiatry, Radio, TV, Science (General), Social Sciences, Sociology, Technology
ISBN Prefix(es): 5-02
Number of titles published annually: 1,000 Print
Total Titles: 80 Print
Subsidiaries: Akademkniga Booktrading Co; Oriental Literature Publishing Co Nauka; Physical & Mathematical Literature Publishing Co Nauka
Divisions: Printshops Nauka
Branch Office(s)
Siberian Publishing Co Nauka, Sovetskaya Ul 18, Novosibirsk 63009, Dir: Ye A Lazarchuk *Tel:* (03832) 225 181 *Fax:* (03832) 233 502
St Petersburg Publishing Co Nauka, Mendeleevskaya Liniya 1, St Petersburg 199034, Dir: S V Valchuk *Tel:* (0812) 328 3912 *Fax:* (0812) 328 0051
Ural Publishing Co Nauka, Ul Amundsena 100, Yekaterinburg 620016, Dir: Yu Ye Kezhun *Tel:* (03432) 288 149 *Fax:* (03432) 678 872
Bookshop(s): 2/10 B Cherkassky Per, Moscow, GSP 103624
Shipping Address: Nauka-Export Booktrading Co, Profsoyuznaya Ul 90, Moscow 117864, Dir: V V Bogomolov *Tel:* (095) 334 7479; (095) 334 7140 *Fax:* (095) 334 7479; (095) 334 7140 *E-mail:* nauka@naukae.msk.ru

Izdatelstvo Nedra+
Tverskaja Zastava 3, 125047 Moscow
Tel: (095) 2505255 *Fax:* (095) 2502772
Key Personnel
Dir: V D Menshicov
Founded: 1963
Natural Resources Publishing House.
Subjects: Earth Sciences, Energy, Geography, Geology
ISBN Prefix(es): 5-247

Izdatel'stvo Nizhegorodskogo Gosudarstvennogo Univ
Prosp Gagarina 23/2, komn. 230, 603600 Nizni Novgorod
Tel: (08312) 65 78 25 *Fax:* (08312) 65 85 92
Founded: 1990
Subjects: Archaeology, Biological Sciences, Chemistry, Chemical Engineering, Computer Science, Economics, Education, Electronics, Electrical Engineering, Engineering (General), English as a Second Language, Environmental Studies, Government, Political Science, History, Law, Marketing, Mathematics, Mechanical Engineering, Microcomputers, Philosophy, Phys-

ical Sciences, Physics, Psychology, Psychiatry, Social Sciences, Sociology
ISBN Prefix(es): 5-680

Novosti Izdatel 'stvo+
7 Bolshaja Pochtovaja, 107082 Moscow
Tel: (095) 2655008 *Fax:* (095) 2655208; (095) 2653880; (095) 9752065
Telex: 7581; 7582
Key Personnel
Dir: Alexander Eidinov
Man Dir: Alexander Proskurin
Rights Dept: Alexei Triumfov
Founded: 1964
Subjects: Art, Economics, Fiction, Government, Political Science, History, Nonfiction (General), Philosophy, Social Sciences, Sociology
ISBN Prefix(es): 5-7020

Obdeestro Znanie+
Lubjanskij poezed 4, 101835 Moscow
Tel: (095) 9281531
Key Personnel
Dir & Editor-in-Chief: V C Beliakov
Founded: 1951
The Knowledge.
Subjects: Business, Child Care & Development, Fiction, Science (General), Science Fiction, Fantasy, Self-Help
ISBN Prefix(es): 5-07

Okoshko Ltd Publishers (Izdatelstvo)+
Zubovskij Blvd 17, 119859 Moskva
Tel: (095) 2450998 *Fax:* (095) 2053424
Key Personnel
Dir: Ivan A Logashin
Founded: 1993
Russian - Belgian Joint Publishing Venture.
Also acts as an exclusive Zuidnederlandse Uitgeverij's representative in CIS & Baltic countries.
Subjects: Education, English as a Second Language, Language Arts, Linguistics
ISBN Prefix(es): 5-7400
Total Titles: 23 Print
Parent Company: Zuidnederlandse Uitgeverij NV, Belgium

Panorama Publishing House+
Bol Tishinskoj per 38, 123557 Moscow
Tel: (095) 2053707 *Fax:* (095) 2053708
Key Personnel
Dir: Valery S Buyanov
Founded: 1974
Subjects: Art, Child Care & Development, Fiction, Health, Nutrition, History, House & Home
ISBN Prefix(es): 5-85220

Izdatel'stvo Patriot
Olimpijskij prospekt 22, 129110 Moscow
Tel: (095) 2844904
Founded: 1951
Voluntary Society for the Promotion of the Army, Air Force & Navy.
Subjects: Military Science
ISBN Prefix(es): 5-7030

Pedagogika Press
Smolenskij Bulvar 4, 119034 Moscow
Tel: (095) 2465969 *Fax:* (095) 2465969
Key Personnel
Dir: V S Khelemendik
Founded: 1969
Subjects: Education, Science (General)
ISBN Prefix(es): 5-7155

Permskaja Kniga
ul K Marksa 30, 614000 Perm
Tel: (03422) 324245
Key Personnel
Editor-in-Chief: Almira G Zebzeeva

Subjects: Cookery, Crafts, Games, Hobbies, Fiction, Gardening, Plants, House & Home, Poetry, Romance
ISBN Prefix(es): 5-7625

Planeta Publishers+
ul Petrovka 8/11, Moscow 103031
Tel: (095) 9230470 *Fax:* (095) 2005246
Telex: 411733 *Cable:* PETROVKA 8/11 MOSCOW
Key Personnel
Dir: Vladimir Seredin
Editor-in-Chief: Gennadiy Alifanov
Founded: 1969
Subjects: Architecture & Interior Design
ISBN Prefix(es): 5-85250
Associate Companies: Interprint
Subsidiaries: Jupiter

Pressa Publishing House
ul Pravdy 24, 125867 Moscow
Tel: (095) 2573482 *Fax:* (095) 2505205
Key Personnel
Dir: VP Leontiev
Subjects: Earth Sciences, Fiction, Literature, Literary Criticism, Essays
ISBN Prefix(es): 5-253

Profizdat+
ul Kirova 13, 101000 Moscow
Tel: (095) 9245740 *Fax:* (095) 9752329
E-mail: iidprof@cityline.ru
Key Personnel
Dir: Vladimir N Soloviev
Founded: 1930
Information & Publishing House.
Subjects: Art, Cookery, Fiction, Gardening, Plants, Labor, Industrial Relations, Nonfiction (General), Poetry, Sports, Athletics
ISBN Prefix(es): 5-255

Progress Publishers
Zubovskij Bul'var 17, 119847 Moscow
Tel: (095) 2469032 *Fax:* (095) 2302403
Telex: 411800 Kegl
Key Personnel
Dir: A K Avelitchev
Editor-in-Chief: B V Oreshkin; V N Loskutov
Production: Mikhail Pavlovich Kryakovkin
Founded: 1931
Subjects: Biography, Economics, Fiction, Government, Political Science, History, Language Arts, Linguistics, Law, Literature, Literary Criticism, Essays, Philosophy, Social Sciences, Sociology
ISBN Prefix(es): 5-01

Prometej Izdatel 'stvo
ul Usacheva 64, 119048 Moscow
Tel: (095) 2454495
Key Personnel
Dir: V N Bukreev
Founded: 1987
ISBN Prefix(es): 5-7042; 5-8300

Izdatelstvo Prosveshchenie+
3-j proezd Marinoi Roshchi 41, 129846 Moscow
Tel: (095) 2891405 *Fax:* (095) 2004266
Telex: 111999 Park
Key Personnel
Dir: AP Sudakov
Dir, Marketing: L M Uzunova
Founded: 1963
Subjects: Education, English as a Second Language
ISBN Prefix(es): 5-09

Izdatelstvo Radio i Svyaz+
Poctant, a/ja 693, 101000 Moscow
Mailing Address: ul Myasnizkaya 40, 101000 Moscow

Tel: (095) 2585351
Key Personnel
Dir: E N Salnikov
Founded: 1981
Communications Publishing House.
Subjects: Communications, Computer Science, Electronics, Electrical Engineering, Radio, TV
ISBN Prefix(es): 5-256

Raduga Publishers+
Zubovskij bul'var 17, Moscow 119859
Tel: (095) 2450151 *Fax:* (095) 2416353
E-mail: vvm@aoraduga.msk.ru *Cable:* MOSCOW TITUL
Key Personnel
Dir: Nina S Litvinets
Marketing Dir: Nikolai P Iamskoi
Founded: 1982
Subjects: Biography, Cookery, Fiction, History, Literature, Literary Criticism, Essays, Philosophy, Poetry, Romance, Science Fiction, Fantasy
ISBN Prefix(es): 5-05

Respublika
Miusskaja Ploschad 7, Moscow 125811
Tel: (095) 2517956 *Fax:* (095) 2002254
Key Personnel
Dir: A P Poliakov
Editor-in-Chief: E P Loshkariev
Founded: 1918
Publishers of Political Literature.
Subjects: Government, Political Science, History
ISBN Prefix(es): 5-250

Russkaya Kniga Izdatelstvo (Publishers)+
Bolshoy Tishinsky pereulock, h 38, 123557 Moscow
Tel: (095) 2053377 *Fax:* (095) 2053424
Key Personnel
Dir: M F Nenashev
Founded: 1957
Russian Book State Publishing House.
Subjects: Art, Cookery, Fiction, Government, Political Science, Health, Nutrition, History
ISBN Prefix(es): 5-268

Russkij Jazyk+
Staropanskij pereulok 1/5, 103012 Moscow
Tel: (095) 9239705 *Fax:* (095) 9288906
Key Personnel
Dir: V I Nazarov
Chief Editor: A A Alexeeva
Founded: 1974
Russian Language Publishers.
Subjects: English as a Second Language
ISBN Prefix(es): 5-200

St Andrew's Biblical Theological College+
Jerusalem St 3, Moscow 109316
Tel: (095) 2702200 *Fax:* (095) 2707644
E-mail: standrews@standrews.ru
Web Site: www.standrews.ru
Key Personnel
Contact: Dr Alexei Bodrov *E-mail:* abodrov@standrews.ru
Sales & Marketing Manager: German Utenov
Founded: 1990
Independent Theological College/publishing house. Textbooks on biblical studies & themes & two journals.
Subjects: Archaeology, Art, Biblical Studies, Child Care & Development, Education, History, Philosophy, Publishing & Book Trade Reference, Religion - Other, Theology, High quality religious & theological literature
ISBN Prefix(es): 5-89647
Number of titles published annually: 25 Print
Total Titles: 100 Print

Scorpion Publishers+
Mozajskoe 9-41, 121471 Moscow
Tel: (095) 4436991

Key Personnel
President: Tatjana Piljajena
Founded: 1990
Member of the Association of Pubishers; specialize in publishing & trade; also acts as agent of buying or selling international rights & editions.
Subjects: Animals, Pets, Crafts, Games, Hobbies, Health, Nutrition, Philosophy, Theology, Veterinary Science
ISBN Prefix(es): 5-86408
Distributed by Solutions Ltd (West Europe)

Izdatelstvo Sovetskii Pisatel
ul Povarskaja 11, 121069 Moscow
Tel: (095) 2025051 *Fax:* (095) 2023200
Key Personnel
Director: A N Zhukov
Chief Editor: V I Mussalitin
Founded: 1935
USSR Writer's Union Publishing House.
Publishes monthly magazine *Soviet Motherland* in Yiddish.
Subjects: Art, Literature, Literary Criticism, Essays, Poetry
ISBN Prefix(es): 5-265

Sovremennik Publishers Too
Horosevskoe sosse 62, 123007 Moscow
Tel: (095) 9412992 *Fax:* (095) 9413544
Key Personnel
Dir: L A Frolov
Chief Editor: A P Karelin
Founded: 1970
Subjects: Drama, Theater, Fiction, Literature, Literary Criticism, Essays
ISBN Prefix(es): 5-270

SP Interbuk, Russian-Slovenien jv
ul Petrovka 26, 101409 Moscow
Tel: (095) 9245081 *Fax:* (095) 2002281; (095) 2302403
Key Personnel
Dir General: Alexander M Pershin
Editor-in-Chief: Sergei V Goncharenko
Commercial Dir: Mr Juri G Ivanov
15 in various cities of the former USSR.
Member of the Board of All-Russian Publishers' Association, All-Russian Books Distributors Association, All-Russia Publishers Club, Board of Izdatbank, All-Russia Union of Independent Publishers, Advisory Board of the Ministry of Information.
ISBN Prefix(es): 5-7664
Subsidiaries: Alma-Ata; Donetsk; Drozdy; Ekaterinograd; Forest; Kiev; Logos; Sibir; Slavia; Slavutich; St Petersburg; Tjumen
Divisions: Commercial Centre; Interbook Business; Printing Centre; Advertising Centre
Showroom(s): Starosadsky per 7/10, str 5, 101000 Moscow
Shipping Address: Interbuk Transport & Depots, Russian-Slovenien jv ul Petrovka 26, 101409 Moscow *Tel:* (095) 9245081 *Fax:* (095) 2002281

Sredne-Uralskoye knizhnoye izatelstve (Middle Urals Publishing House)+
ul Malyseva 24, 620219 Ekaterinburg
Tel: (03432) 514162 *Fax:* (03432) 512859
Key Personnel
Dir: Victor J Selivanov
Founded: 1920
Subjects: Fiction, Literature, Literary Criticism, Essays
ISBN Prefix(es): 5-7529
Subsidiaries:
Warehouse: Artinskaya St 23B, 620046 Ekaterinburg

Izdatelstvo Standartov+
Novopresnenskij pereulok 3, 123557 Moscow
Tel: (095) 2520348 *Fax:* (095) 2684724
Key Personnel
Dir: N V Zen'kovich
Editor-in-Chief: V P Videneyev
Founded: 1926
Official publications of the state service on standard data.
Subjects: Advertising, Law
ISBN Prefix(es): 5-7050

Stroyizdat Publishing House
ul Kaljaevskaja 23a, 101442 Moscow
Tel: (095) 2516967
Key Personnel
Dir: V A Kasatkin
Chief Editor: G A Zhigatcheva
Founded: 1932
Subjects: Architecture & Interior Design, Geography, Geology, Mechanical Engineering, Social Sciences, Sociology
ISBN Prefix(es): 5-274

Izdatelstvo Sudostroenie+
ul Gogolja 8, St Petersburg 191065
Tel: (0812) 3124479 *Fax:* (0812) 3120821
Key Personnel
Man Dir & Editor-in-Chief: Anatoly A Andreev
Founded: 1940
Publishing House for Shipbuilding.
Subjects: Advertising, Education, Engineering (General), History, Maritime, Mechanical Engineering, Military Science, Science (General), Technology, Transportation
ISBN Prefix(es): 5-7355
Bookshop(s): Varag, Malaja Morskaja 8, St Petersburg 191186

Teorija Verojatnostej i ee Primenenija+
ul Vavilova, 42, 117966 Moscow
Tel: (095) 1352380; (095) 3324410 *Fax:* (095) 1135125
E-mail: tvp@caravan.ru
Key Personnel
Dir & Partner: V I Khokhlov
Editor-in-Chief: Yu V Prokhorov
Founded: 1990
Worldwide except the territory of the former USSR.
Specialize in Mathematical Applied Sciences; also acts as Research Laboratories & as a Distribution Center for Western Scientific & Professional Editions & Software.
Subjects: Communications, Economics, Mathematics, Military Science, Physics, Securities
ISBN Prefix(es): 5-85484
Subsidiaries: TEV PLC; TBIMC; TVP-Interkniga
Distributed by SIAM USA; VSP (Netherlands)
Distributor for Academic Press; Blackwell; Cambridge University Press; Chapman & Hall; Harcourt Brace; O'Reilly; Pitman; Prentice Hall; John Wiley & Sons (all Russia)
Showroom(s): TVP, 1921 Nakhimovskii prosp 47, 117418 Moscow
Orders to: TVP, 1921, Nakhimovskii props 47, 117418 Moscow

Text Publishers Ltd Too+
A/ja Box 89, 125190 Moscow
Tel: (095) 9169168; (095) 6169411 *Fax:* (095) 9258814
E-mail: editor@textpub.msk.ru
Key Personnel
Editor-in-Chief: Mikhail Chernenko
President: Vitaly Babenko
Dir: Olgert Libkin
Commercial Dir: Valery Genkin
Art Dir: Vladimir Lubarov
Founded: 1988
Member of Association of Russian Publishers.
ISBN Prefix(es): 5-7516
Shipping Address: 56 Proezd Cherepanovykh, 125183 Moscow
Warehouse: 56 Proezd Cherepanovykh, 125183 Moscow
Orders to: 56 Proezd Cherepanovykh, 125183 Moscow

Top Secret Collection Publishers
ul B Nikitzkaya 22 of 12, 103009 Moscow
Tel: (095) 2022011; (095) 2024531 *Fax:* (095) 2913885
E-mail: topsec@glasnet.ru
Key Personnel
Rts Mgr: Elena Pavlova
Founded: 1993
Subjects: Biography, Fiction, Nonfiction (General), Travel
ISBN Prefix(es): 5-85275

Izdatelstvo Transport
Basmannyj Tupik 6a, 103064 Moscow
Tel: (095) 2625964 *Fax:* (095) 2611322
Key Personnel
Dir: V G Peshkov
Founded: 1923
Subjects: Aeronautics, Aviation, Automotive, Maritime, Transportation
ISBN Prefix(es): 5-277

Voronezh State University Publishers
ul Engelsa SA8, Voronez 394000
Tel: (0732) 560481
Key Personnel
Dir: Olga D Tekutyeva
Founded: 1958
Subjects: Biological Sciences, Chemistry, Chemical Engineering, Economics, Geography, Geology, Language Arts, Linguistics, Literature, Literary Criticism, Essays, Mathematics, Social Sciences, Sociology
ISBN Prefix(es): 5-7455

Voyenizdat+
ul Zorge 1, 103160 Moscow
Tel: (095) 1950154 *Fax:* (095) 1952454
Key Personnel
Dir: U J Stadnyuk
Chief Editor: S P Kulichkin; N P Sinitzin
Founded: 1919
Publishing House, Ministry of Defence.
ASCI publishing.
Subjects: Biography, Fiction, Government, Political Science, History, Military Science
ISBN Prefix(es): 5-203

Vsesoyuznii Molodejnii Knizhnii Centre
Petrovka 26, 101409 Moscow
Tel: (095) 924 7879
Key Personnel
Gen Dir: A D Tchavchanidze
Founded: 1989
All-Union Youth Book Centre.
Subjects: Fiction, Literature, Literary Criticism, Essays, Science (General)
ISBN Prefix(es): 5-7012

Vsesoyuznoe Obyedineniye Vneshtorgizdat
ul Fadeeva 1, 125047 Moscow
Tel: (095) 2505162 *Fax:* (095) 2539794
Telex: 411238 *Cable:* VNESHTORGIZDAT MOSCOW
Key Personnel
Dir-General: Vladimir I Prokopov
Chief Editor: Nickolai I Romanenko
Sales: Valentin A Sirotkin
Production: Vladimir A Melnichenko
Founded: 1925
Foreign Trade Publishing House.
Publish Catalogs, Prospectuses & Advertising Material in Russian & Foreign Languages on Soviet exports. Execute foreign firms' orders for printing services, translation & publishing in Russian of maintenance & other documents.

Subjects: Business
ISBN Prefix(es): 5-85025

Izdatelstvo Vysshaya Shkola+
ul Neglinnaja 29/14, 101439 Moscow
Tel: (095) 2000456 *Fax:* (095) 2090350
 Cable: 101430 GSP-4
Key Personnel
Dir: M I Kiselev
Chief Editor: A M Trubitsin
Founded: 1939
Higher School Publishing House.
Member of Publishers' Association of Russian Federation.
Subjects: Biological Sciences, Chemistry, Chemical Engineering, Economics, History, Language Arts, Linguistics, Literature, Literary Criticism, Essays, Philosophy, Physics, Technology
ISBN Prefix(es): 5-06

Rwanda

General Information

Capital: Kigali
Language: Kinyarwanda (a Bantu tongue) and French (both official) and Kiswahili
Religion: Traditional beliefs (about 50%), most of rest Roman Catholic
Bank Hours: 0800-1800 Monday-Friday; 0800-1300 Saturday
Shop Hours: 0800-1900 Monday-Saturday
Currency: 100 centimes = 1 Rwanda franc
Export/Import Information: No tariff on books and advertising, but Statistical tax. Import license, for statistical purposes, and Foreign Exchange License required. Application to National Bank, through authorized bank.
Copyright: UCC, Berne (see Copyright Conventions, pg xi)

Diocese de Kabjayi, see Imprimerie de Kabgayi

Government Printer (Imprimerie National du Rwanda)
BP 351, Kigali
Tel: 75350 *Fax:* 75820

Imprimerie de Kabgayi+
BP 66, Gitarama
Tel: 62252; 62877 *Fax:* 62345
Key Personnel
Man Dir: Thomas Habimana
Founded: 1932
Associate Companies: Diocese de Kabgayi ASBL, BP 66, Gitarama; Editions Bibliques et Liturgiques, BP 66, Gitarama

INADES (Institut Africain pour le Developpment Economique et Social)
BP 466, Kigali 08
Key Personnel
Sales: Michel Guery
Founded: 1975
Subjects: Literature, Literary Criticism, Essays, Regional Interests, Religion - Other, Social Sciences, Sociology

Samoa

General Information

Capital: Apia
Language: Samoan, English
Religion: Predominantly Christian (Congregational, Roman Catholic & Methodist)
Population: 165,000
Bank Hours: 0930-1500 Monday-Friday
Shop Hours: 0800-1200, 1330-1630 Monday-Friday; 0800-1230 Saturday
Currency: 100 sene = 1 tala (western Samoan dollar)
Export/Import Information: No tariff on most books, printed advertising generally free but some subject to duty. No import license or exchange controls.

Institute for Research Extension and Training in Agriculture (IRETA)
University of the South Pacific, Alafua Campus, Private Bag, Apia
Tel: (0685) 21882 *Fax:* (0685) 21671

IRETA, see Institute for Research Extension and Training in Agriculture (IRETA)

Saudi Arabia

General Information

Capital: Riyadh
Language: Arabic (English widely understood)
Religion: Islamic (officially) with about 85% of the Sunni sect
Population: 16.9 million
Bank Hours: 0830-1200, 1700-1900 Saturday-Wednesday; 0830-1130 Thursday. During Ramadan: 1000-1330 Saturday-Thursday
Shop Hours: 0900-1200, 1600-2100 Saturday-Thursday. During Ramadan closed until sunset, then open until 0200
Currency: 100 halalahs = 20 qurush = 1 Saudi riyal
Export/Import Information: No tariffs on books; advertising matter subject to ad valorem duty but if total duty on one consignment is less than 50 riyals, matter can enter free. Catalogues distributed gratis, usually admitted free. All printed matter except textbooks subject to censorship. No import licenses required.
Copyright: UCC (see Copyright Conventions, pg xi)

Asam Establishment for Publishing & Distribution
PO Box 87782, Riyadh 11652
Tel: (01) 4453732 *Fax:* (01) 4412583
Key Personnel
General Manager, Owner: Fahed M Abo Rdoun
Subjects: Religion - Islamic
ISBN Prefix(es): 9960-714

Dar Al-Mirrikh (Mars Publishing House)
PO Box 10720, Riyadh 11443
Tel: (01) 4647531; (01) 4658523 *Fax:* (01) 4657939
Telex: 403129
Key Personnel
President: Abdullah Majid
Vice President: Shams Zakaria
ISBN Prefix(es): 9960-24

Dar Al-Rayah for Publishing & Distribution
PO Box 40124, Riyadh 11499
Tel: (01) 4931869 *Fax:* (01) 4911985
ISBN Prefix(es): 9960-661

Dar Al-Shareff for Publishing & Distribution+
PO Box 58287, Riyadh 11594
Tel: (01) 4034931 *Fax:* (01) 4052234
Key Personnel
President: Ibrahim Al-Hazemi
Founded: 1992
Subjects: Animals, Pets, Astronomy, Behavioral Sciences, Biography, Drama, Theater, History, Humor, Literature, Literary Criticism, Essays, Medicine, Nursing, Dentistry, Nonfiction (General), Philosophy, Religion - Islamic, Romance, Sports, Athletics, Veterinary Science, Women's Studies
ISBN Prefix(es): 9960-640; 9960-741

International Publications Agency (IPA)
PO Box 70, Dhahran Airport
Tel: (03) 8954925
Telex: 871229
Key Personnel
Manager: Said Salah
Subjects: Regional Interests

Al Jazirah Organization for Press, Printing, Publishing
Al-Nassiriah St, Riyadh 11411
Mailing Address: PO Box 354, Riyadh
Tel: (01) 4419999 *Fax:* (01) 4412536
Key Personnel
Dir-Gen: Saleh Al-Ajroush
Editor-in-Chief: Khalid el Malek
Founded: 1964
Subjects: Government, Political Science, Law
ISBN Prefix(es): 9960-9190

King Saud University+
PO Box 2454, Riyadh 11451
Tel: (01) 4675634 *Fax:* (01) 4678633
Telex: 461019 KSU SJ
Key Personnel
President: Prof Abdullah Al-Faisal
Vice President: Prof Ibrahim Al-Mish'Al
Vice President, Research & Higher Studies: Prof Khalid Al Hamoudi
Dir, Translation Center: Prof Ahmed A Almohandis
Dean, Univ Libraries: Dr Sulaiman S Al Ugla
Founded: 1957
Subjects: Agriculture, Behavioral Sciences, Biological Sciences, Chemistry, Chemical Engineering, Geography, Geology, Language Arts, Linguistics, Mathematics, Medicine, Nursing, Dentistry, Technology
ISBN Prefix(es): 9960-05

Saudi Publishing and Distribution House+
3rd Floor, Jawhara Bldg No 1, Medina Rd, Baghdadiah, Jeddah 21451
Mailing Address: PO Box 2043, Jeddah 21451
Tel: (02) 6424043; (02) 6424255; (02) 6446308
 Fax: (02) 6432821 *Cable:* NASHRADAR
Key Personnel
Chairman & Man Dir: Mohammed Salahuddin
Founded: 1966
Also act as importers & distributors of English & Arabic books (academic, reference & general).
Subjects: Literature, Literary Criticism, Essays, Religion - Other, Science (General)
ISBN Prefix(es): 9960-26
Branch Office(s)
PO Box 899, Riyadh *Tel:* (01) 464 7894
Bookshop(s): Hyat Plaza Complex, King Saud St, Dammam Dhahran St Near Governorate, Dannan *Tel:* (03) 8323515; Zouman Shopping Centre, opposite S Fakhee Hospital, Jeddah *Tel:* (02) 6608964

Senegal

General Information

Capital: Dakar
Language: French
Religion: About 90% Islamic, 5% Christian (mostly Roman Catholic), the rest follow traditional beliefs
Population: 8.2 million
Bank Hours: Generally 0800-1115, 1430-1630 Monday-Friday
Shop Hours: Vary, and some open Sunday morning, some close Monday morning. Generally are 0800-1200, 1430-1800 Monday-Saturday
Currency: 100 centimes = 1 CFA franc
Export/Import Information: Member of West African Economic Community. No tariff on books except atlases. Added taxes apply to atlases. Advertising matter (more than one copy) subject to fiscal and customs duty plus added taxes. Import licenses and exchange controls apply for imports from outside EEC, Franc Zone, USA and Canada.
Copyright: Berne, UCC (see Copyright Conventions, pg xi)

Nouvelles Editions Africaines du Senegal (NEAS)+
10, Rue Amadou Assane Ndoye, BP 260, Dakar
Tel: (0221) 8211381; (0221) 8221580 *Fax:* (0221) 8223604
E-mail: neas@telecomplus.sn
Key Personnel
President: Souleymane Bachir Diagne
Dir General: Mr Doudou Ndiaye
Founded: 1989
Subjects: Literature, Literary Criticism, Essays, Social Sciences, Sociology
ISBN Prefix(es): 2-7236
Distributed by African Imprint Library Services

Agence de Distribution de Presse
4 rue Carnot, Dakar
Mailing Address: BP 374, Dakar
Tel: (08) 320278 *Fax:* (08) 324915
E-mail: adpresse@telecomplus.sn
Key Personnel
Man Dir: Philipe Schorp
Founded: 1943
Affiliated to NMPP, Paris.
Parent Company: NMPP (Paris, France)

Centre Africain d'Animation et d'Echanges Culturels Editions Khoudia+
CAEC-HLM Fass Paillote, immeuble 7, BP 5332 Poste de Fann, Dakar, Fann
Tel: 211023 *Fax:* 215109
Key Personnel
Production Dir: Ms Aissatou Dia
Founded: 1989
Subjects: Anthropology, Drama, Theater, Education, Ethnicity, Fiction, Literature, Literary Criticism, Essays, Poetry
ISBN Prefix(es): 2-87895
Distributed by Edilis (Ivory Coast); Presence Africaine (France)
Distributor for Edilis (Ivory Coast); Haho (Togo)

Centre de Linguistique Appliquee
Universite de Dakar, Faculte des Lettres et Sciences Humaines, Fann Parc, Dakar
Tel: 230126
Subjects: Language Arts, Linguistics, Literature, Literary Criticism, Essays

CODESRIA (Council for the Development of Social Science Research in Africa)+
PO Box 3304, Dakar, Avenue Cheikh Anta Diop X Canal IV, Dakar
Tel: 8259814; 8259822 *Fax:* 8241289; 8640143
E-mail: codesria@sonatel.senet.net
Web Site: www.cordesria.org
Telex: 61339 Codes SG
Key Personnel
Head of Publications & Communications: Felicia Oyekanmi *E-mail:* felicia.oyekanmi@codesria.sn
Founded: 1973
Publish in four languages: English, French, Portuguese & Arab. Specialize in social sciences.
Member of International Research Councils
Also acts as a coordinator of social science research in Africa.
Subjects: Behavioral Sciences, Developing Countries, Economics, Education, Environmental Studies, Ethnicity, Government, Political Science, History, Labor, Industrial Relations, Social Sciences, Sociology, Women's Studies
ISBN Prefix(es): 1-870784; 2-86978
Number of titles published annually: 10 Print
Total Titles: 186 Print
Warehouse: African Books Collective Ltd, The Jam Factory, 27 Park End St, Oxford OX1 1KU, United Kingdom *E-mail:* abc@africanbookscollective.com
Karthala, Edition Diffusion, 22-24 Blvd Arago, 75013 Paris, France

Council for the Development of Social Science Research in Africa, see CODESRIA (Council for the Development of Social Science Research in Africa)

Enda Tiers Monde
BP 3370, Dakar
Tel: (0221) 216027; (0221) 224229 *Fax:* (0221) 222695
Telex: 51456SG
Key Personnel
Chief Executive: Jacques Bugnicourt

Institut Fondamental d'Afrique Noire, Cheikh Anta Diop
Campus universitaire, Cheikh Anta Diop, BP 206, Dakar-Fann
Tel: (0221) 250090; (0221) 241652; (0221) 251990; (0221) 259890 *Fax:* (0221) 244918
Key Personnel
Dir: Prof Samb Djibril
Founded: 1936
Branch Office(s)
Musee de la Mer, Campus universitaire, BP 206 Dakar-Fann
Musee historique, Campus universitaire, BP 206 Dakar-Fann
Musees d'Art africain, Campus universitaire, BP 206 Dakar-Fann

NEAS, see Nouvelles Editions Africaines du Senegal (NEAS)

Les Nouvelles Editions Africaines du Senegal NEAS+
BP 260, 10 rue El Hadj Amadou Assane, Ndoye, Dakar
Tel: (08) 211381; (08) 221580 *Fax:* (08) 223604
E-mail: neas@sentoo.sn
Key Personnel
Dir General: Francois Boirot
Commercial Dir: Mamadou Kasse
Founded: 1972
Subjects: Biography, Education, Ethnicity, Fiction, History, Nonfiction (General), Philosophy, Poetry, Psychology, Psychiatry, Religion - Other, Science (General), Social Sciences, Sociology
ISBN Prefix(es): 2-7236
Number of titles published annually: 15 Print
Total Titles: 800 Print
Distributed by CEDA; Editions Donniya; Editions Jamana; Ganndal; NEI
Distributor for CEDA; Editions Donniya; Editions Jamana; Ganndal; NEI

Edition Sahel+
9 rue Thiong, BP 3683, Dakar
Tel: 212164
Telex: 469 teranga sg
Key Personnel
Contact: Niane Idrissa
Founded: 1982
ISBN Prefix(es): 2-906993

Societe Africaine d'Edition
14 Rue Jules Ferry, BP 1877, Dakar
Tel: 217977; 220284
Key Personnel
Man Dir: Pierre Biarnes
Founded: 1961
Subjects: Economics, Foreign Countries, Government, Political Science
Branch Office(s)
32 rue de l'Echiquier, F-75010 Paris, France
Tel: 5230233

Societe d'Edition d'Afrique Nouvelle
10 rue El Hadj Amadou Assane Ndoye, BP 260, Dakar
Tel: (08) 211381; (08) 221580 *Fax:* (08) 223604
Telex: 21 450 NEA SG
Key Personnel
Man Dir: Athanase Ndong
Senior Editor, Rights & Permissions: Rene Odou
Subjects: Foreign Countries, Religion - Other
ISBN Prefix(es): 2-7236

Sierra Leone

General Information

Capital: Freetown
Language: English
Religion: Predominantly traditional beliefs, also some Islamic and Christian
Population: 4.5 million
Bank Hours: 0800-1330 Monday-Thursday; 0800-1400 Friday
Shop Hours: 0800-1300, 1400-1830 Monday-Saturday
Currency: 100 cents = 1 leone
Export/Import Information: No tariff on books except children's picture books and advertising matter. Open general license. Exchange controls.

Macmillan Education
34-36 Rawdon St, Private Mail Bag 904, Freetown
Tel: (022) 225683 *Fax:* (022) 229186
E-mail: macmillan@sierratel.sl
Web Site: www.macmillan-africa.com
Key Personnel
General Manager: Kai Fomba
Parent Company: Macmillan Publishers Ltd, United Kingdom

Njala Educational Publishing Centre
Njala University PMB, Freetown

Sierra Leone University Press
Fourah Bay College, University of Sierra Leone, Mount Aureol, Freetown
Mailing Address: PO Box 87
Tel: (022) 27300; (022) 23494; (022) 27399; (022) 27323 *Cable:* Fourahbay

Key Personnel
Chairman & Honorary Editor: Prof Eldred Jones
Honorary Secretary, Rights & Permissions: Prof W S Marcus Jones
Founded: 1968
Subjects: Ethnicity, History, Nonfiction (General), Religion - Other, Social Sciences, Sociology

United Christian Council Literature Bureau
Bunumbu Press, Bo
Mailing Address: PO Box 28, Bo
Tel: 032462
Key Personnel
Man Dir: Joseph E Tucker

Singapore

General Information

Capital: Singapore
Language: Malay (national and official), also Chinese (Mandarin), Tamil and English (all official)
Religion: Daoism, Buddhist, Islamic, Christian, Hindu and Taoism
Population: 2.8 million
Bank Hours: 1000-1500 Monday-Friday; 930-1130 Saturday
Shop Hours: 0900-1800 Monday-Saturday
Currency: 100 cents = 1 Singapore dollar
Export/Import Information: No tariffs on books and advertising. Import licenses; no seditious publications permitted. Normal exchange control.
Copyright: Florence (see Copyright Conventions, pg xi)

APA Production Pte Ltd+
38 Joo Koon Rd, Singapore 628990
Tel: 8651600 *Fax:* 8616438
Telex: RS 36201APASIN
Key Personnel
Man Dir: Hans Hoefer; Yinglock Chan
Founded: 1971
Subjects: Travel
ISBN Prefix(es): 9971-925; 9971-982; 981-234
Parent Company: Langenscheidt KG
Associate Companies: APA Publications (HK), Hong Kong
Imprints: Insight Guides; Insight Pocket Guides; Insight Topics
U.S. Office(s): Langenscheidt Publishers, Inc, 46-35 54 Rd, Maspeth, NY 11378, United States
Distributor for Langenscheidt (Asia)

APAC Publishers Services+
Blk 12, Lorong Bakar Batu No 04-09, Kolam Ayer Industrial Estate, Singapore 348745
Tel: 7478662 *Fax:* 7478916
Key Personnel
Man Dir: Steven Goh E-mail: sgohapac@singnet.com.sg
Founded: 1990
Subjects: Architecture & Interior Design, Business, Chemistry, Chemical Engineering, Civil Engineering, Computer Science, Economics, Engineering (General), Environmental Studies, Management, Medicine, Nursing, Dentistry, Science (General), Social Sciences, Sociology, Technology
ISBN Prefix(es): 981-3045
Total Titles: 6 Print
Distributor for Aspen Publishers; BIOS Scientific Publishers; Blackwell Science; CAB International; Columbia University Press; Fairchild Books; Guilford Publications; Gulf Publishing; Haworth Press; Industrial Press; ISIS Medical Media Limited; John Hopkins University Press; Marcel Decker; Institute of Chemical Engineers; Ishiyaku EuroAmerica; S Karger; Lippincott Williams & Wilkins; MacLennan & Petty; Munksgaard; New York University Press; Noyes Data Corp/William Andrew; Pira International; Royal Society of Chemistry; M E Sharpe; Schattauer; Swets & Zeitlinger Publishers; Thomas Telford; W W Norton; Woodhead Publishing

Aquanut Agencies Pte Ltd
305 Clementi Avenue 4, No 08-427, Singapore S 120305
Tel: 7753614 *Fax:* 7753614
E-mail: aquanut@singnet.com.sg
Web Site: www.aquanut.com.sg
Key Personnel
Dir: Mr Leslie Lung
Founded: 1998
To carry on the business of publisher, book & print sellers. Also consultant for print, publishing & publicity.
Subjects: Asian Studies, Behavioral Sciences, How-to, Human Relations, Humor, Nonfiction (General), Self-Help, Social Sciences, Sociology
Number of titles published annually: 12 Print
Total Titles: 3 Print
Distributed by Horizon Books Pte Ltd

Archipelago Press, Les Editions du Pacifique, *imprint of* Archipelago Press

Archipelago Press+
26 Bukit Pasoh Rd, Singapore 089840
Tel: 2248044 *Fax:* 2247400
E-mail: edm@pacific.net.sg
Key Personnel
Chairman: Didier Millet
Man Dir: Charles Orwin
Editorial Dir: Timothy Auger
Founded: 1989
Subjects: Architecture & Interior Design, Art, Asian Studies, Cookery, Crafts, Games, Hobbies, History, Natural History, Photography, Travel
ISBN Prefix(es): 981-3018
Imprints: Archipelago Press, Les Editions du Pacifique

Asiapac Books Pte Ltd+
996 Bendemeer Rd, No 06-08/09, Kallang Basin Industrial Estate, Singapore 339944
Tel: 3928455 *Fax:* 3926455
E-mail: apacbks@singnet.com.sg
Web Site: www.asiapacbooks.com
Key Personnel
President: Chong Shin-Kian
Publisher: Lim Li-Kok
Publishing Dir: Lydia Lum
Founded: 1982
Member of Singapore Book Publishers Association; specialize in publishing & distribution.
Subjects: Asian Studies, Humor, Philosophy
ISBN Prefix(es): 9971-985; 981-3029; 981-3068; 981-229
Number of titles published annually: 50 Print
Total Titles: 280 Print; 4 Audio
Distributor for China Books & Periodicals, Inc (USA); Chinese Literature Press (SE Asia); CNPIEC (China); Foreign Languages Press (China); Millbank Books Ltd (UK); National Textbook Co (USA); Oriental Publications (Australia); Penton Overseas, Inc (USA); Sterling Publishing Co, Inc (USA)

Butterworths Singapore, see LexisNexis

Cannon International+
Legal Deposit Section, Singapore Resource Library, National Library Board, Stamford Rd, Singapore 178896
Tel: 3323639; 3447801 *Fax:* 3323273
E-mail: legaldep@nlb.gov.sq.hdtsdnl@technet.sq
Key Personnel
Chief Executive, Rights & Permissions: Wu Cheng Tan
Sales: Amirudin Bin Marzuki
Publicity: Pearlyn Peh
Founded: 1975
Subjects: Education, Language Arts, Linguistics, Literature, Literary Criticism, Essays
ISBN Prefix(es): 9971-84; 9971-83; 981-00; 9971-941; 9971-943
Imprints: Kingsway Publishers
Subsidiaries: Kingsway Publisher
Distributor for Robert Gibson (Singapore)

Marshall Cavendish Books, *imprint of* Times Media Pte Ltd

Marshall Cavendish Books
One New Industrial Rd, Singapore 536196
Tel: (065) 2848844 *Fax:* (065) 2854871
E-mail: te@corp.tpl.com.sg
Web Site: www.timesone.com.sg/te
Parent Company: Times Publishing Ltd

Marshall Cavendish Continuity Sets, *imprint of* Times Media Pte Ltd

Celebrity Educational Publishers
Block 474 Tampines St 41, No 01-108, Singapore 520470
Tel: 7857274 *Fax:* 7489108
Key Personnel
Man Dir, Editorial: Christopher S C Tan
Sales: Henry K H Ng
Production, Publicity: Lily Tay
Founded: 1983
Subjects: Language Arts, Linguistics, Science (General)
ISBN Prefix(es): 981-201
Subsidiaries: Willet Children's Books Australia

Chopsons Pte Ltd+
Siglap PO Box 264, Singapore 914503
Tel: 64483634 *Fax:* 64481071
E-mail: chopsons@singnet.com.sg
Key Personnel
Man Dir: Mr N T S Chopra
Founded: 1969
Supplies publications from Southeast Asia to the libraries all over the world - monographs & journals/serials.
Also acts as Literary Agent.
Subjects: Asian Studies, Education, Fiction, Government, Political Science, Poetry, Religion - Other, Science (General), Social Sciences, Sociology
ISBN Prefix(es): 9971-68
Distributor for Centre for Advanced Studies; Institute of Southeast Asian Studies; Singapore University Press; Sociology Department, National University of Singapore; World Scientific Publishing

Daiichi Media Pte Ltd
26-C Kim Keat Rd, Singapore 328807
Tel: 2563722 *Fax:* 2565922
E-mail: info@daiichimedia.com.sg; sales@daiichimedia.com.sg
Web Site: www.daiichimedia.com
Key Personnel
Business Development Manager: Edward Poon E-mail: edward@daiichimedia.com
Founded: 1993
Total Titles: 15 CD-ROM

Earlybird Books, *imprint of* Federal Publications (S) Pte Ltd

les editions du Pacifique, *imprint of* Times Media Pte Ltd

EPB Publishers Pte Ltd+
Block 162, Bukit Merah Central, 04-3545, Singapore 150162
Tel: (065) 2780881 *Fax:* (065) 2782456
Web Site: www.epb.com.sg
Telex: EPB RS 56289 *Cable:* EDUPUBS
Key Personnel
General Manager: Au Pui Chuan
Marketing: Kenny Koh
Production: Steven Tan
Founded: 1967
Member of Singapore Book Publishers' Association.
Subjects: Education
ISBN Prefix(es): 9971-0
Parent Company: Singapore National Printers Ltd, 303 Upper Serangoon Rd, Singapore 1334
Bookshop(s): EPB Bedok, North Street 1, 01-423 1646 *Tel:* 4437980; EPB Bukit Batok, 376 Bukit Batok St 31, 01-110 650376 *Tel:* 5624023; EPB Bukit Merah, 161 Bukit Merah Central, 01-3719 150161 *Tel:* 2730092; EPB Clementi Ave 3, 01-297 0512 *Tel:* 7770052; EPB Clementi West, 725 Clementi West St 2, 01-206 0521 *Tel:* 7788923; EPB Jurong West St 51, 01-213 2264 *Tel:* 5624106; 20 Outram Park, 02-187/213 0316 *Tel:* 2202377; EPB Tampine, 138 Tampines St 11, 01-132 1852 *Tel:* 7831939
Warehouse: PSA Multi Storey Complex, Blk 22 Pasir Pahjang Rd, No 06-29 Singapore

Europa Publications, *imprint of* Taylor & Francis Asia Pacific

Europhone Language Institute (Pte) Ltd+
3 Coleman St No 04-33, Peninsula Shopping Centre, Singapore 179803
Tel: 3373617; 3363992 *Fax:* 3374506 *Cable:* LANGUAGE SINGAPORE
Key Personnel
Chief Executive: K P Sivam
Founded: 1970
ISBN Prefix(es): 981-3019; 9971-9910; 9971-9912
Branch Office(s)
122 Campbell Complex, Kuala Lumpur, Malaysia

Federal Publications (S) Pte Ltd+
Times Centre, One New Industrial Rd, Singapore 536196
Tel: 62139288 *Fax:* 62889254
E-mail: fps@tpl.com.sg
Web Site: www.tpl.com.sg
Telex: 35846 *Cable:* FEDPUBS, SINGAPORE
Key Personnel
General Manager: June Oei *E-mail:* juneoei@tpl.com.sg
Publisher & Editorial Manager: Joy Tan
Sales Manager: Marina Ooi
Founded: 1957
Subjects: Education
ISBN Prefix(es): 981-01
Parent Company: Times Publishing Ltd, Times Centre, One New Industrial Rd 536196
Associate Companies: Federal Publications (HK) Ltd, Hong Kong; Federal Publications Sdn Bhd, Malaysia
Imprints: Earlybird Books; Times Academic Press
Distributor for Chambers Harrap Publishers Ltd

FEP International Private Ltd
108 Pasir Panjand Rd, No 05-01A, Singapore 118535
Tel: 4743135 *Fax:* 4752389
Telex: Fep rs 25601 *Cable:* Bookmark
Key Personnel
Publishing Manager, Rights & Permissions: Wong Sek Ohn
Publishing, Science & Math: Dr S Ramalingam
Publishing, Language & Arts: Ms Goh Bee Choo
Founded: 1960
Firm is also a large offset printer specializing in color work.
ISBN Prefix(es): 9971-1
Branch Office(s)
Australia
Egypt (Arab Republic of Egypt)
Ghana
Hong Kong
India
Jamaica
Kenya
Lesotho
Malaysia
Nigeria
Pakistan
Philippines
Swaziland
Trinidad & Tobago
United Kingdom
Zimbabwe

Garland Science, *imprint of* Taylor & Francis Asia Pacific

Global Educational Services Pte Ltd+
No 03-06, Irving Industrial Bldg, 3 Irving Rd, Singapore 369522
Mailing Address: Blk 844 Sims Ave, No 01-706, Singapore 400844
Tel: 2896351 *Fax:* 2896086
Key Personnel
Man Dir: Yoke Yin Ong
Founded: 1986
Joint projects with education institutions in design & publishing of educational materials; Exclusive Distributor for National University of Singapore on a series of operations research/management software for universities & management programs.
Specialize in Pre-school books design, Education Software, OEM Publishing projects, Operations Research Software.
Subjects: Language Arts, Linguistics, Mathematics, Science (General)
ISBN Prefix(es): 981-3006; 981-3032; 981-3059; 981-3098
Associate Companies: Global Educational Services Sdn Bhd, Malaysia
Subsidiaries: Global Educational Services Inc
Orders to: 222 Fourteenth St, Unit 5, Charlottesville, VA 22903, United States *Fax:* 434-979-0823

Gordon & Breach, *imprint of* International Publishers Distributor (S) Pte Ltd

Graham Brash Pte Ltd
32 Gul Dr, Singapore 629480
Tel: 8311336 *Fax:* 8614815
Telex: rs 23718 Feenix GB
Key Personnel
Man Dir: K C Campbell
Sales Dir, Publicity: Chuan Campbell
Subjects: Education
ISBN Prefix(es): 9971-947; 981-218; 9971-9901

Harwood Academic Publishers, *imprint of* International Publishers Distributor (S) Pte Ltd

Hillview Publications Pte Ltd+
Blk 20 Outram Park, No 02-115, Singapore 162020
Tel: 2241955 *Fax:* 3245103
Key Personnel
Man Dir: L M Ng
Founded: 1984
Member of Spore Book Publishers Association.
Subjects: Accounting, Economics, Education, English as a Second Language, Geography, Geology, Mathematics, Physics, Social Sciences, Sociology
ISBN Prefix(es): 981-202; 981-3013; 981-3052; 981-3079; 981-4013

Insight Guides, *imprint of* APA Production Pte Ltd

Insight Pocket Guides, *imprint of* APA Production Pte Ltd

Insight Topics, *imprint of* APA Production Pte Ltd

Institute of Southeast Asian Studies+
30 Heng Mui Keng Terrace, Pasir Panjang, Singapore 119614
Tel: 6778 0955 *Fax:* 6775 6259
E-mail: pubsunit@iseas.edu.sg
Web Site: www.iseas.edu.sg/pub.html
Key Personnel
Dir: Prof Chia Siow Yue *Tel:* 6870 2405
E-mail: chris@iseas.edu.sg
Man Editor: Triena Ong *Tel:* 6870 2448
E-mail: triena@iseas.edu.sg
Book Promotions & Secretary: Celina Kiong
E-mail: celina@iseas.edu.sg
Founded: 1968
Scholarly publishers.
Conduct post-doctoral research on politics, economics & social issues pertaining to the Asia-Pacific.
Subjects: Asian Studies, Economics, Energy, Environmental Studies, Finance, Foreign Countries, Government, Political Science, Social Sciences, Sociology
ISBN Prefix(es): 9971-902; 981-3035; 981-230
Number of titles published annually: 40 Print; 10 Online; 40 E-Book
Total Titles: 1,000 Print; 27 Online; 890 E-Book
Imprints: ISEAS
Distributed by James Bennett Library Services; Taylor & Francis Asia Pacific; United Publishers Services Ltd

Intellectual Publishing Co
113 Eunos Ave 3 04-08, Gordon Industrial Bldg, Singapore 409839
Tel: 7466025 *Fax:* 7489108
Telex: RS 55708 lpccp *Cable:* IPC INTELLE
Key Personnel
Manager: B C Poh
Editorial, Rights & Permissions: B L Poh
Sales, Publicity: B S Poh
Founded: 1971
Subjects: Language Arts, Linguistics
ISBN Prefix(es): 9971-907; 9971-960; 981-200
Associate Companies: Intellectual Publishing Sdn Bhd, 29A 1st floor, Jalan Selimang, Taman Tenaga, Cheras 3 1/2 ms, Kuala Lumpur, Malaysia
Subsidiaries: Intellectual Publishing Co Ltd

International Publishers Distributor (S) Pte Ltd+
08-01 Pines Industrial Bldg, 240 MacPherson Rd, Singapore 348574
Tel: 7416933 *Fax:* 7416922
Key Personnel
Man Dir: K C Ang *E-mail:* kcang@singnet.com
Founded: 1989
Subjects: Art, STM
Total Titles: 3,000 Print
Parent Company: Gordon & Breach Publishing Group

PUBLISHERS SINGAPORE

Imprints: Gordon & Breach; Harwood Academic Publishers
U.S. Office(s): PO Box 20029, River Front Plaza Station, Newark, NJ 07102-0301, United States

IPD, see International Publishers Distributor (S) Pte Ltd

ISEAS, *imprint of* Institute of Southeast Asian Studies

K C Ang Publishing Pte Ltd+
Imprint of Bunny Books
93 Hitam Manis, Chip Bee Garden, Singapore 278503
Tel: 4741680 *Fax:* 2542002
Key Personnel
Man Dir: K C Ang
Founded: 1985
Specialize in Children's Books.
ISBN Prefix(es): 9971-974

Kingsway Publishers, *imprint of* Cannon International

LexisNexis
Formerly Butterworths Singapore
No 1 Temasek Ave, 17-01 Millenia Tower, Singapore 039192
Tel: 6336 9661 *Fax:* 6336 9662
Web Site: www.lexisnexis.com.sg
Key Personnel
Man Dir: Michael Evans *Tel:* 6434 3800 *Fax:* 6339 0163
Regional Publishing Dir: Conita Leung *Tel:* 6434 3830
Publishing Manager: Balasakher Shunmugam *Tel:* 6434 3838
Managing Editor: Zabrina Hamid *Tel:* 6434 3841; Andrew Yeoh *Tel:* 6434 3842
Senior Editor: Sharon Kaur *Tel:* 6434 3847; Yee See Mun *Tel:* 6434 3809
Regional Sales Dir: Bryan Barrington *Tel:* 6434 3850
Founded: 1982
Subjects: Law
Parent Company: Reed Elsevier
Associate Companies: LexisNexis, 12/F, Hennessy Centre, 500 Hennessy Rd, Causeway Bay, Hong Kong, Business Development Manager: Anisha Sakhrani *Tel:* 2965 1400 *Fax:* 2976 0840 *Web Site:* www.lexisnexis.com.hk; LexisNexis, 14th floor, Vijaya Bldg, 17, Barakhamba Rd, New Delhi 110001, India, Publishing Manager: Ambika Nair *Tel:* (011) 373 9614 *Fax:* (011) 332 6456 *Web Site:* www.lexisnexis.co.in; Malayan Law Journal Sdn Bhd, Unit A-5-1, 5th floor, Wisma HB, Megan Phileo Ave, 12 Jalan Yap Kwan Seng, 50450 Kuala Lumpur, Malaysia, Managing Editor, New Business Development: Julie Anne Thomas *Tel:* (03) 2162 2833 *Fax:* (03) 2162 3811 *Web Site:* www.mjl.com.my

Marlin Dunitz, *imprint of* Taylor & Francis Asia Pacific

Maruzen Asia (Pte) Ltd
391 Orchard Rd No 04-08, Singapore 238872
Tel: 7751577
Telex: Mapore rs 26521 *Cable:* Maruzen Singapore
Key Personnel
Man Dir, Editorial: Yuki Hatori
Marketing: David Tan
Founded: 1978
Subjects: Asian Studies, Medicine, Nursing, Dentistry, Social Sciences, Sociology, Technology
ISBN Prefix(es): 9971-954

Parent Company: Maruzen Co Ltd, Japan
Associate Companies: Maruzen International Co Ltd, NY, United States

Masagung Books Pte Ltd
41 Sixth Ave, Off Bukit Timah Rd, Singapore 276483
Tel: 4683276 *Fax:* 345000
Telex: rs 34500 A; B Gasing *Cable:* Gasing Singapore
Key Personnel
Chairman: Haji Masagung
Manager: Tan Tho Quek
Founded: 1980
Subjects: Foreign Countries
ISBN Prefix(es): 9971-927
Parent Company: CV Haji Masagung, Indonesia

New York Institute of Finance Asia, *imprint of* Pearson Education Asia

Newscom Pte Ltd+
Blk 105, Boon Keng Rd, No 04-17, Singapore 339776
Tel: 6291 9861 *Fax:* 6293 1445
E-mail: circulation@newscom-mail.com
Web Site: www.newscomonline.com
Key Personnel
Chairman: Austin Morais
Circulation Manager: Dinesh Charles
E-mail: dineshcharles@newscom-mail.com
Founded: 1987
Acts as media representative; Member of the BPA & ABC (UK).
Subjects: Publishing & Book Trade Reference, Technology
Parent Company: NewSources Investments Ltd, Unit B, 19th floor, 133 Wanchai Rd, Wanchai, Hong Kong
Associate Companies: Newsteam SDN BHD, 87-89 Jalan Ipoh, 3rd floor, 51200 Kuala Lumpur, Malaysia *Tel:* (03) 4044-8599 *Fax:* (03) 4044-9599

Pan Pacific Publications (S) Pte Ltd+
16 Fan Yoong Rd, Singapore 629793
Tel: 2616288 *Fax:* 2616088
E-mail: ppps@pacific.net.sg
Telex: 36496
Key Personnel
Chairman: Steve Seow Kui Lim
General Manager: Catherine Ngien
Managing Editor: Margaret Tan
Operations Manager: Brenda Goh
Founded: 1971
Member of Publishers' Association (Singapore).
Subjects: Education
ISBN Prefix(es): 981-208; 9971-63
Parent Company: Pan Pacific Public Co Ltd
Associate Companies: Eastview Publications Sdn Bhd, Malaysia
Subsidiaries: Manhattan Press (S) Pte Ltd; Manhattan Press (HK) Ltd

Pearson Education Asia+
317 Alexandra Rd, No. 04-01 IKEA Bldg, Singapore 159965
Tel: 476 4688 *Fax:* 268 0370
E-mail: firstname.lastname@pearsoned.com.sg
Web Site: www.pearsoned.com
Telex: 24268
Key Personnel
Pres: Wong Wee Woon
Publishing & Business Development Dir: Stephen Troth
Finance Dir: James Kho
Regional Manager: Rasmiati Hartanto
Sales & Marketing Dir: Low Chwee Leong
Founded: 1975
Trade & academic publications.
Subjects: Business, Management

ISBN Prefix(es): 981-3026
Number of titles published annually: 30 Print
Total Titles: 160 Print
Parent Company: Pearson Education
Imprints: New York Institute of Finance Asia; Prentice Hall; Prentice Hall Asia ELT
Branch Office(s)
25 First Lok Yang Rd, Jurong 629734
Tel: 2682666
U.S. Office(s): Pearson Education, One Lake St, Upper Saddle River, NJ 07458, United States

Pearson Education Asia Pte Ltd
25 First Lok Yang Rd, Jurong 629734
Tel: 0268 2666 *Fax:* 0264 1740
E-mail: firstname.lastname@pearsoned.com.sg
Key Personnel
Publishing Manager, Higher Education: Yew Kee Chiang
Dir, Singapore Education: Andrew Yeo

PG Publishing Pte Ltd+
6A Napier Rd, Gleneagles Annexe, Block No 02-38 Gleneagles Hospital, Singapore 258500
Tel: 4726339 *Fax:* 4728279
Telex: rs 39967 *Cable:* PG PUB
Key Personnel
Chief Executive, Rights & Permissions: Ms Chiam Soo Lee
Editorial & Production: Mrs Sook-Cheng Lim
International Marketing: Lew Kok Liat
Production: Mary Cho
Founded: 1982
Subjects: Medicine, Nursing, Dentistry
ISBN Prefix(es): 9971-909; 9971-973; 981-3096; 981-206
Subsidiaries: PG Medical Books
Bookshop(s): PG Lucky Plaza Medical Books, 6A Napier Rd, Gleneagles Anexe, Block No 02-38 Gleneagles Hospital, Singapore 258500

Prentice Hall, *imprint of* Pearson Education Asia

Prentice Hall Asia ELT, *imprint of* Pearson Education Asia

Printworld Services Pte Ltd
Ruby Industrial Complex, 80 Genting Lane, No 04-02, Genting Block, Singapore 349565
Tel: 7442166 *Fax:* 7460845
E-mail: printw@mbox2.singnet.com.sg
Telex: 28990 (print)
Key Personnel
Man Dir: N T Nair
ISBN Prefix(es): 981-3093

Psychology Press, *imprint of* Taylor & Francis Asia Pacific

Pustaka Nasional Pte Ltd
Blk 2 Joo Chiat Rd 05-1131, Joo Chiat Complex, Singapore 420002
Tel: 7454321; 7454649; 7452417 *Fax:* 7452412
Telex: rs 26746 Smcc Pn *Cable:* HUDAYA
Key Personnel
Manager: Mr Syed Ali Bin Syed Zain
Subjects: Foreign Countries, Religion - Islamic
ISBN Prefix(es): 9971-77
Associate Companies: Pustaka Islamiyah SDN BHD
Distributor for Dewan Bahasa Dan Pustaka (Malaysia)
Showroom(s): Blk 1, Jalan Pasar Baru, No 01-41, Singapore 402001

Reed Elsevier, South East Asia+
51 Changi Business Park, Central 2, No 07-01, The Signature, Singapore 486066
Tel: 6789 9900 *Fax:* 6789 9966
Key Personnel
Executive Dir: Paul Beh
Founded: 1986

SINGAPORE

Members of Singapore Book Publishers Association & Afro Asian Book Council.
Subjects: Biological Sciences, Chemistry, Chemical Engineering, Electronics, Electrical Engineering, Law, Physical Sciences, Physics, Science (General), Social Sciences, Sociology, Technology, Travel
ISBN Prefix(es): 9971-64
Parent Company: Reed Elsevier plc, 25 Victoria St, London SW1H 0EX, United Kingdom

Ridge Books, *imprint of* Singapore University Press Pte Ltd

Routledge, *imprint of* Taylor & Francis Asia Pacific

Routledge-Falmer, *imprint of* Taylor & Francis Asia Pacific

Select Books Pte Ltd+
19 Tanglin Rd No 03-15, Tanglin Shopping Centre, Singapore 247909
Tel: 7321515 *Fax:* 7360855
E-mail: info@selectbooks.com.sg
Web Site: www.selectbooks.com.sg
Key Personnel
Man Dir: Lena U Wen Lim
Founded: 1976
Specialize in books on SE Asia.
Member of Publishers Association, Singapore.
Subjects: Antiques, Architecture & Interior Design, Art, Asian Studies, Developing Countries, Drama, Theater, Ethnicity, Government, Political Science
ISBN Prefix(es): 981-4022
Total Titles: 30 Print
Online services available through Asiaone.
Distributed by Asia Books (Thailand); Thames & Hudson (Europe)
Distributor for Asia Development Bank; Asian & Pacific Development Centre; Centre of Asian Studies; Food & Agriculture Organisation; Friedrich Naumann Stiftung; Gadjah Mada University Press; Hong Kong Institute of Asia Pacific Studies; Indra Publishing; Institute for Development Studies; Koninklijk Institute voor der Tropen; Koninklijk Institute voor Taal Land-en Volkenkunde; National Heritage Board; National University of Singapore Library; National University Museums; Pictures Publishers; Scalabrini Migration Center; SEAMEO Regional Centre; Singapore Association of Writers; Singapore Society of Asian Studies; The Art Gallery; United Nations Centre for Regional Development; United Nations Educational, Scientific & Cultural Organisation; United Nations Environment Programme; United Nations Publications; World Health Organisation; Worldwatch Institute; Yayasan Nusantara Jaya

The Shanghai Book Co (Pte) Ltd
Blk 231 Bain St, No 02-73, Bras Basah Complex, Singapore 180231
Tel: 3360144 *Fax:* 3360490
E-mail: shanghaibook@pacific.net.sg
Key Personnel
Man Dir: Mong Hock Chen
 E-mail: chenmonghock@pacific.net.sg
Founded: 1925
ISBN Prefix(es): 9971-906
Associate Companies: Shanghai Book Co (KL) SDN BHD, No 63C Jalan Sultan, 50000 Kuala Lumpur, Malaysia *Tel:* (03) 2384642 *Fax:* (03) 2320700

Shing Lee Group Publishers+
120 Hillview Ave 05-06/07, Kewalran Hillview, Singapore 669594
Tel: 7601388 *Fax:* 7825684
Telex: rs 39255 Bai *Cable:* SHINGBOOK
Key Personnel
Marketing Dir: Mr Peh Chin Thye
Executive Dir: Soh-Ngoh Peh
Founded: 1985
Subjects: Cookery
ISBN Prefix(es): 9971-61
Subsidiaries: Booktree; Concorde Publishers Pte Ltd; Dragon Investment PL; Dragon Link Granite PL; First Dragon Development PL; Second Dragon Development PL; Shing Lee Bookstore Pte Ltd; Shing Lee Investment Pte Ltd; Shing Lee Publishers Pte Ltd; Shing Lee Realty Pte Ltd; Super Food Investment International PL; Tech Media; Third Dragon Development PL; Third Dragon Holdings PL; Qingdao Huashan International Country Club

Singapore University Press, *imprint of* Singapore University Press Pte Ltd

Singapore University Press Pte Ltd+
Yusof Ishak House, NUS, 10 Lower Kent Ridge Rd, Singapore 119078
Tel: b7761148; b8742382; b8742472; 6874-2382 *Fax:* b7740652
E-mail: supbooks@nus.edu.sg
Web Site: www.nus.edu.sg/sup
Telex: rs 51112 NUSBUR *Cable:* SINGPRESS
Key Personnel
Chairman: Prof Lim Seh Chun
Man Dir: Peter Schoppert
 E-mail: peter_schoppert@nus.edu.sg
Founded: 1971
Publishing House of the National University of Singapore.
Member of IASP, SBPA; Specialize in Southeast Asian & Asia-Pacific titles (scholarly & academic).
Subjects: Asian Studies, Economics, Environmental Studies, Finance, Government, Political Science, History, Language Arts, Linguistics, Law, Literature, Literary Criticism, Essays, Management, Maritime, Psychology, Psychiatry, Science (General), Social Sciences, Sociology, Medicine & Architecture
ISBN Prefix(es): 9971-69
Total Titles: 150 Print; 1 Online; 100 E-Book
Online services available through Information Access Co.
Imprints: Ridge Books; Singapore University Press
Distributed by Hemisphere Publishing (Southeast & East Asia only); World Scientific Publishing Co (For co-published titles only)
Foreign Rep(s): James Bennett Library Services (Australia, New Zealand); Coronet Books Inc (US); Lavis Marketing (UK, Europe); United Publishers Services

SNP Pan Pacific Publishing Pte Ltd+
Jurong Bldg, No 04-00 CPF, 21 Jurong East St, Singapore 609646
Tel: 261-6288 *Fax:* 261-6088
Key Personnel
General Manager: Mr Rick Ang
Secretary: Quah Ai Hoon
Subjects: Education
ISBN Prefix(es): 981-3001; 981-208
Associate Companies: SNP Eastview Publications Sdn Bhd, Malaysia; SNP Manhattan Press (Hong Kong) Ltd, Hong Kong

Spen Press, *imprint of* Taylor & Francis Asia Pacific

Stamford College Publishers/Authors-Publishers+
Legal Deposit Section, Singapore Resource Library, National Library Board, Stamford Rd, Singapore 178896
Tel: 3323639 *Fax:* 3323273
E-mail: legaldep@nlb.gov.sq.hdtsdnl@technet.sq
Key Personnel
Man Dir, Publicity: L P Nicol
Editorial: L Thomas
Sales: J Dennis
Production: Mr Arangasamy
Founded: 1970
Subjects: Education
ISBN Prefix(es): 9971-83
Branch Office(s)
Stamford Executive Bookshop, Petaling Jaya, Malaysia

Success Publications Pte Ltd+
Blk 3013 Bedok Industrial Park E, No 04-2102, Bedok North Av 4, Singapore 489979
Tel: 4431003; 4430512 *Fax:* 4453156
Distributing, importing, exporting & publishing of educational books & materials; reading program; assessment books; Chinese.
Subjects: Education, English as a Second Language, Mathematics, Science (General)
ISBN Prefix(es): 981-216
Subsidiaries: Steven Tuition Centre
Orders to: Rest of the World, Bowker-Saur Ltd, Windsor Court, E Grinstead House, E Grinstead, West Sussex RH19 1XA, United Kingdom *Tel:* (01342) 326972 *Fax:* (01342) 336198

Taylor & Francis, *imprint of* Taylor & Francis Asia Pacific

Taylor & Francis Asia Pacific+
240 Macpherson Rd, No 08-01 Pines Industrial Bldg, Singapore 348574
Tel: 67415166 *Fax:* 67429356
E-mail: info@tandf.com.sg
Web Site: www.tandf.co.uk
Key Personnel
Man Dir: Barry D Clarke *E-mail:* barry.clarke@tandf.com.sg
Head, Sales: Jeffrey Lim *E-mail:* jeffrey.lim@tandf.com.sg
Founded: 1998
Subjects: Aeronautics, Aviation, Architecture & Interior Design, Art, Asian Studies, Biological Sciences, Business, Child Care & Development, Criminology, Economics, Education, Engineering (General), Environmental Studies, Ethnicity, Government, Political Science, History, Library & Information Sciences, Management, Medicine, Nursing, Dentistry, Philosophy, Physical Sciences, Psychology, Psychiatry, Religion - Other, Science (General), Social Sciences, Sociology, Specialize in book distribution, publisher services, confrences & author support
Parent Company: Taylor & Francis, United Kingdom
Imprints: Europa Publications; Garland Science; Marlin Dunitz; Psychology Press; Routledge; Routledge-Falmer; Spen Press; Taylor & Francis
Distributor for American Psychological Association (US); Ashgate (UK); Aslib (UK); Berghahn Books (UK); Brookings Institution (US); Edinburgh University Press (UK); Edward Elgar (UK); David Fulton (UK); Free Press (US); Gower (UK); Idea Group (UK); Information Age (US); Institute International Economics (US); Libraries Unlimited (US); Library Association (UK); Research Studies Press (UK); Transaction Publishers; Westview Press (US); World Bank (US)

Tech Publications Pte Ltd+
Sim Lim Tower, 10 Jalan Besar No B1-39, Singapore 208787
Tel: 7449113; 7428782 *Fax:* 2991550; 2763622
Telex: 7449835
Key Personnel
President: Gyan Jain

Vice President & Marketing Manager: Rajiv Jain
Founded: 1984
Subjects: Computer Science, Electronics, Electrical Engineering
ISBN Prefix(es): 981-214; 981-3005; 981-3091
Associate Companies: Micro Tech Publications, Dubai, United Arab Emirates
Bookshop(s): 04-35 Funan Centre 179097
Warehouse: 211 Henderson Rd, Henderson Bldg No 02-11 159552

Tecman, *imprint of* Tecman Bible House

Tecman Bible House+
Blk 231, 04-45/7/9, No 03-37, 02-71, Bain St, Singapore 180231
Mailing Address: BIK 231, Bain St, No 04-47, Bras Basah Complex, Singapore 180231
Tel: 3386764 *Fax:* 3388236
E-mail: tecman@tecman.com.sg
Web Site: www.tecman.com.sg
Key Personnel
President: Jane Tan
Founded: 1971
Import, export, retail & wholesale of Christian publications & products.
Subjects: Biblical Studies, Religion - Protestant, Theology
Imprints: Tecman

Times Academic Press, *imprint of* Federal Publications (S) Pte Ltd

Times Books International, *imprint of* Times Media Pte Ltd

Times Editions, *imprint of* Times Media Pte Ltd

Times Editions Pte Ltd, see Times Media Pte Ltd

Times Media Pte Ltd+
Formerly Times Editions Pte Ltd
Times Centre, One New Industrial Rd, Singapore 536196
Tel: 62848844 *Fax:* 62771186
E-mail: te@corp.tpl.com.sg
Web Site: www.timesone.com.sg/te
Telex: RS25713 *Cable:* TIMES
Key Personnel
Deputy Publisher: David Yip *E-mail:* davidyip@tpl.com.sg
International Sales & Rights: Angeline Lim *Tel:* 62139404 *E-mail:* angelinelim@tpl.com.sg
Founded: 1979
Subjects: Art, Cookery, Gardening, Plants, Government, Political Science, Health, Nutrition, Literature, Literary Criticism, Essays, Travel, Culture, Heritage, International Interests, Parenting
ISBN Prefix(es): 981-204; 2-85700; 981-232
Online services available through World Wide Web.
Parent Company: Times Publishing Group, One New Industrial Rd 536196
Associate Companies: Marshall Cavendish Books Ltd
Imprints: Marshall Cavendish Books; Marshall Cavendish Continuity Sets; les editions du Pacifique; Times Books International; Times Editions
Branch Office(s)
Bangunan Times Publishing, Lot 46, Subang Industrial Park, Bahu riga, 60000 Shah Alam, Malaysia, Contact: Christine Chong *Fax:* (03) 7354620
Times Books International, Malaysia

John Wiley & Sons (Asia) Pte Ltd+
2 Clementi Loop #02-01, Singapore 129809
Tel: 64632400 *Fax:* 64634605; 64634604
E-mail: enquiry@wiley.com.sg
Web Site: www.wiley.co.uk
Key Personnel
Vice President, Asia: Steven Miron
Publisher: Nick Wallwork
Foreign Rights Executive: Ira Tan
Number of titles published annually: 20 Print
Parent Company: John Wiley & Sons Inc, 605 Third Ave, New York, NY 10158, United States
Associate Companies: John Wiley & Sons, Ltd, United Kingdom; Jacaranda Wiley, Ltd, Australia

World Scientific Publishing Co Pte Ltd+
5 Toh Tuck Link, Singapore 596224
Tel: 6467-5775 *Fax:* 6467-7667
E-mail: wspc@wspc.com.sg
Key Personnel
Man Dir: Doreen Liu
Assistant Dir: Miss G K Tan
Dir & Publisher: Mrs Sook Cheng Lim
Manager, Sales: Ms Siew Lan Tan
Founded: 1980
Member of STM, Pub Assoc (Spore).
Subjects: Biological Sciences, Chemistry, Chemical Engineering, Computer Science, Electronics, Electrical Engineering, Engineering (General), Management, Mathematics, Medicine, Nursing, Dentistry, Physics
ISBN Prefix(es): 981-02; 9971-950; 9971-966; 9971-978
Subsidiaries: Imperial College Press
Branch Office(s)
World Scientific Publishing (HK) Co Ltd, PO Box 72482, Kowloon Central Post Office, Kowloon, Hong Kong *Tel:* 2771-8791 *Fax:* 2771-8155 *E-mail:* swped@pacific.net.hk
10, Royal Park, 34 Park Rd, Tasker Town, Bangalore 560 051, India *Tel:* (080) 286-3744 *Fax:* (080) 286-5189 *E-mail:* wspcind@blr.vsl.net.in
5F-6, No 88, Sec 3, Hsin-Sheng S Rd, Taipei, Taiwan, Province of China *Tel:* (02) 2369-1366 *Fax:* (02) 2369-0460 *E-mail:* wsptw@ms13.hinet.net
World Scientific Publishing Co Ltd, 57 Shelton St, London WC2H 9HE, United Kingdom *Tel:* (020) 7836-0888 *Fax:* (020) 7836-2020 *E-mail:* sales@wspc.co.uk
U.S. Office(s): World Scientific Publishing Co Inc, 1060 Main St, River Edge, NJ 07661, United States *Tel:* 201-487-9655 *Fax:* 201-487-9656 *E-mail:* wspc@wspc.com
Distributor for Imperial College Press (UK); The National Academy Press, USA (Asia-Pacific except Japan, Australia, New Zealand)

Slovakia

General Information

Capital: Bratislava
Language: Slovak
Religion: Predominantly Roman Catholic, some Lutheran
Population: 5.3 million
Currency: 100 Halerue = 1 koruna
Export/Import Information: There are plans to extablish custom-free zones to stimulate foreign investment. 6% VAT on books.
Copyright: UCC, Berne (see Copyright Conventions, pg xi)

ARCHA sro Vydavatel 'stro+
Staromestska 6, 813 36 Bratislava
Tel: (07) 5315586; (07) 54415609 *Fax:* (07) 5441586
E-mail: archa@internet.sk
Key Personnel
Editor-in-Chief: Marian Sapak
International Rights: Petra Bombikova
Subjects: Government, Political Science, History, Law, Philosophy, Science (General), Social Sciences, Sociology
ISBN Prefix(es): 80-7115

AV Studio Reklamno-vydavatel 'ska agentura
Lykovcova 7, 841 04 Bratislava
Tel: (07) 726297 *Fax:* (07) 726297
Founded: 1993
Subjects: Health, Nutrition, Religion - Other
ISBN Prefix(es): 80-88779

Danubiaprint
Fucikova 22, 81580 Bratislava
Tel: (07) 309167 *Fax:* (07) 362613
Key Personnel
Dir: Viliam Kacer
Firm is the publishing house of the Central Committee of the Communist Party of Slovakia.
Subjects: Biography, Economics, Fiction, Government, Political Science, History, Law, Philosophy, Social Sciences, Sociology
ISBN Prefix(es): 80-218
Book Club(s): CKP (Clenska kniznica Pravdy)

Dom Techniky Zvazu Slovenskych Vedeckotechnickych Spolocnosti Ltd
Kukucinova 8, 97400 Banska Bystrica
Tel: (088) 533512 *Fax:* (088) 42351
Key Personnel
Dir: Dipl Ing Lubomir Mravec
Manager: Dipl Ing Anna Kamasova
Founded: 1974
Subjects: Business, Finance, Management, Marketing, Mechanical Engineering
ISBN Prefix(es): 80-230

Egmont Neografia spol sro+
Nevadzova ul c 8, 827 99 Bratislava
Tel: (07) 238064; (07) 233933; (07) 295966 *Fax:* (07) 238755
E-mail: egmont@netlab.sk
Key Personnel
Man Dir: Stanislar Valko
Founded: 1990
Subjects: Humor
ISBN Prefix(es): 80-7134
Parent Company: Egmont Holding International, Denmark

Fortuna Print spol sra+
Viktorinova 1, 82108 Bratislava
Mailing Address: PO Box 223, 82108 Bratislava
Tel: (07) 5723140-3; (07) 5269295; (07) 5268727 *Fax:* (07) 5723145-6; (07) 5268561
ISBN Prefix(es): 80-7153; 80-85224

Kalligram Kiado spol sro+
Staromestska 6/d, POB 223, SK-810 00 Bratislava
Tel: (07) 54411-801 *Fax:* (07) 54411-801
Web Site: www.kalligram.sk
Key Personnel
Dir: Laszlo Szigeti *Tel:* (07) 54415028 *E-mail:* szig@kalligram.sk
Contact: Tomas Bona *E-mail:* bonatomas@usa.net
Founded: 1992
Private enterprise.
Subjects: Art, Philosophy, Social Sciences, Sociology, Politics
ISBN Prefix(es): 80-7149
Total Titles: 300 Print
Branch Office(s)
Pesti Kalligram, Tuzolto Utea, Budapest, Hungary *Tel:* (0361) 2153614 *Fax:* (0361)2166875 *E-mail:* szig@kalligram.sk
Orders to: Kalligram Publishers *Tel:* (07) 54415028

SLOVAKIA

LITA Ochranna Autorska Spolocnost' Agentura
Partizanska 21, 815 30 Bratislava
Tel: (07) 311719 *Fax:* (07) 3136458 *Cable:* LITA BRATISLAVA
ISBN Prefix(es): 80-219

Luc vydavatelske druzstvo+
Kozicova 2, 841 10 Bratislava
Mailing Address: PO Box 224, 811 06 Bratislava
Tel: (07) 65730331 *Fax:* (07) 65730331
Key Personnel
International Rights: Anna Kolkova
Founded: 1989
Member of Association of Slovak Catholic Publishers, Publishers of Catholic Libraries of Europe.
Subjects: Biography, Education, History, Philosophy, Poetry, Religion - Catholic, Theology
ISBN Prefix(es): 80-7114

Mlade leta Spd sro
Sasinkova 5, 81519 Bratislava
Tel: (07) 5664512; (07) 5664293 *Fax:* (07) 215714
Telex: 093421
Key Personnel
Man Dir: Ing Oldrich Polak
Editorial: Magda Baloghova
Sales Dir: Jana Misikova
Production: Ing Jozef Sipos
Publicity: Eva Hornisova
Founded: 1950
Young Years: Slovak Publishing House of Children's Literature.
ISBN Prefix(es): 80-06
Bookshop(s): Detska Kniha, Hurbanovo nam 7, Bratislava (The Child's Book)
Book Club(s): Club of Young Readers

Vydavatelstvo Obzor+
Spitalska 35, 81585 Bratislava
Tel: (07) 368395; (07) 55695; (07) 57015 *Fax:* (07) 368395 *Cable:* VYDAVATELSTVO OBZOR BRATISLAVA
Key Personnel
Acting Dir: Ing Richard Dame
Founded: 1953
Horizon: Slovak Book & Periodical Publishing House for People's Education.
Subjects: Archaeology, Art, Law, Literature, Literary Criticism, Essays, Mysteries, Parapsychology
ISBN Prefix(es): 80-215

Opus Records & Publishing House+
Mlynske Nivy 73, 82799 Bratislava
Tel: (07) 222680; (07) 61783 *Fax:* (07) 92219
Key Personnel
Man Dir: Prof Milos Jurkovic
Commercial Dir: Emilia Suta
Editorial: Slavka Dzadikova
Publicity: Dr Alena Jarosova
Founded: 1971
Member of IFPI & Sound Carriers.
Subjects: Music, Dance
ISBN Prefix(es): 80-7093
Parent Company: Bonton Slovagcia
Associate Companies: Music-Video-Express

Vydavatel'stvo SFVU Pallas
Trnavska 112, 82633 Bratislava
Mailing Address: PO Box 224, 82633 Bratislava
Tel: (07) 296627 *Fax:* (07) 294229; (07) 292820
Publishing House of the Slovak Fund of Fine Arts.
Subjects: Art, Biography, Literature, Literary Criticism, Essays
ISBN Prefix(es): 80-7095

Polygraf Print, s r o
Capajevova 44, SK-08001 Presov
Tel: (051) 44 13 280 *Fax:* (051) 77 13 241; (051) 77 13 270
E-mail: polygrafprint@polygrafprint.sk

Vydavatepstvo Praca spol sro+
Stefanikova 19, 812 71 Bratislava
Tel: (07) 292865; (07) 392890; (07) 392853 *Fax:* (07) 392840; (07) 392853
Key Personnel
Dir: Ing Miroslav Bernath
Founded: 1946
Praca Publishing House.
Subjects: Cookery, Crafts, Games, Hobbies, Finance, Law, Outdoor Recreation, Romance
ISBN Prefix(es): 80-7094
Divisions: Nakladatelstvo
Bookshop(s): Knizna predajna Praca, 81271 Bratislava, nam SNP 20

Priroda+
Dulovo nam 12, 82108 Bratislava
Tel: (02) 52496335; (02) 55566176 *Fax:* (02) 55566176
E-mail: priroda@nextra.sk
Web Site: www.priroda.sk
Key Personnel
Dir: Emilia Jankovitsova
Editorial: Jela Fellegiova
Founded: 1949
Publishing House.
Subjects: Business, Gardening, Plants, House & Home, How-to, Management, Outdoor Recreation, Self-Help, Travel, Veterinary Science, Nature
ISBN Prefix(es): 80-07
Number of titles published annually: 100 Print
Total Titles: 8,000 Print
Distributed by Aktis (Czech Republic); EUROMEDIA; Bertlesmann Group in Czech Republic
Warehouse: Plynarenska 6, 82109 Bratislava

Serafin+
Franticanska 2, 801 01 Bratislava
Tel: (02) 54432159 *Fax:* (02) 54434342
E-mail: vydserafin@gmx.net
Web Site: www.serafin.sk
Key Personnel
Contact: Adriana Alexyova; P Stefan Bankovic
Founded: 1990
Member of Zdruzenie katolickych vydavatelstiev Slovenska.
Subjects: Foreign Countries, Poetry, Religion - Catholic, Medicine
ISBN Prefix(es): 80-88944
Number of titles published annually: 15 Print
Total Titles: 125 Print
Parent Company: Zdruzenie katolickych vydavatelstiev Slovenska
Bookshop(s): Frantisek

Slo Viet
Palarikova 21, 811 04 Bratislava
Tel: (07) 52494886
Founded: 1990
Member of SSPOL & SSPUL.
Subjects: Asian Studies, Ethnicity, History, Language Arts, Linguistics, Poetry
ISBN Prefix(es): 80-900500
Number of titles published annually: 3 Print

Slovansky Tatran, Vydavatel 'stro spoi sro
Michalska 9, 81582 Bratislava
Tel: (07) 5335849; (07) 5330141 *Fax:* (07) 5335777
Key Personnel
Man Dir: Eva Mladekova
Founded: 1947
Slovak Publishing House of Belles Lettres.

Rights & Permissions, LITA, Slovak Literary Agency, Partizanska 21, 811 03 Bratislava.
Subjects: Art, Literature, Literary Criticism, Essays, Poetry
ISBN Prefix(es): 80-222
Bookshop(s): Tatran, Michalska 9, 81582 Bratislava

Slovenska kartografia as
Pekna cesta 17, 83407 Bratislava
Mailing Address: PO Box 224, 83407 Bratislava
Tel: (07) 282001; (07) 286783; (07) 285822; (07) 288215 *Fax:* (07) 286783; (07) 285822; (07) 288215
Telex: 93132 Karto c *Cable:* KARTOGRAFIA BRATISLAVA
Key Personnel
Proprietor: Peter Podolay
Dir: P Kmet'ko
Editorial: Zd Matula; Vertrieb S Nemec
Founded: 1957
Slovak Cartographic Publishing House.
ISBN Prefix(es): 80-85164; 80-7103
Bookshop(s): Slovenska kniha NP, Knihkupectvo, Obehodna 9, 81106 Bratislava
Orders to: Slovart AG, Gottwaldovo nam 6, 81764 Bratislava

Slovenske pedagogicke nakladateistvo (Slovak Pedagogical Publishing House)+
Sasinkova 5, 81560 Bratislava
Tel: (07) 55423892 *Fax:* (07) 55571894
E-mail: spn@spn.sk *Cable:* SPN BRATISLAVA
Key Personnel
General Dir: Maria Sedlakova
Sales Manager: Eva Sarandiova *Tel:* (07) 55563229
Founded: 1920
Slovak Publishing House for Educational Literature.
Subjects: Education, English as a Second Language, Ethnicity, History, Language Arts, Linguistics, Literature, Literary Criticism, Essays, Mathematics, Music, Dance, Physics, Psychology, Psychiatry, Social Sciences, Sociology, Sports, Athletics, Travel, Specializes in languages
ISBN Prefix(es): 80-08
Number of titles published annually: 160 Print; 1 CD-ROM
Total Titles: 1 CD-ROM
Parent Company: Media Trade sro, Krizna 28, Bratislava 1 81107
Bookshop(s): Krizna 47, Wagnerova, Contact: Andrej Martinka *Tel:* (02) 55425504
Orders to: Media Trade sro - SPN, Sasinkova 5, Bratislava *Tel:* (02) 55563229 *E-mail:* spn@spn.sk

Vydavatel'stvo Slovenskej akademie vied, see VEDA (Vydavatel'stvo Slovenskej akademie vied)

Slovensky Spisovatel Ltd as+
Andreja Plavku 12, 81367 Bratislava
Tel: (07) 399790 *Fax:* (07) 335411
Key Personnel
Editor-in-Chief: Stefan Strazay
Dir: Martin Chovanec
Founded: 1951
Subjects: Fiction, Literature, Literary Criticism, Essays, Poetry
ISBN Prefix(es): 80-220
Bookshop(s): Laurinska 2, 81367 Bratislava
Book Club(s): KMP (Kruh milovnikov poezie); SPKK (Spolocnost'priatel'ov krasnych knih)
Warehouse: Vajnorska 128, 83292 Bratislava

Smena Publishing House
Prazska 11, 81284 Bratislava
Tel: (07) 491455; (07) 497171

PUBLISHERS

Telex: 09341 *Cable:* BRATISLAVA SMENA
Key Personnel
Dir: Jaroslav Sisolak
Editor-in-Chief: Marie Caganova
Founded: 1949
Publishing House of Slovak.
Subjects: Biography, Crafts, Games, Hobbies, Fiction, History, Philosophy, Poetry, Psychology, Psychiatry, Social Sciences, Sociology
ISBN Prefix(es): 80-85686
Book Club(s): Maj

Sofa+
Vazska 11, 82107 Bratislava 211
Mailing Address: PO Box 4, 82011 Bratislava 211
Tel: (07) 242510 *Fax:* (07) 242510
E-mail: sofa@ba.sknet.sk
Founded: 1992
Subjects: Child Care & Development, Economics, Health, Nutrition, Human Relations, Library & Information Sciences, Philosophy, Physics, Psychology, Psychiatry, Publishing & Book Trade Reference, Social Sciences, Sociology
ISBN Prefix(es): 80-85752

Sport Publishing House Ltd+
Vajnorska ulica 100/A, 83258 Bratislava
Tel: (07) 49249618 *Fax:* (07) 49249586
Key Personnel
Man Dir: Ludovit Svenk
Founded: 1957 (Founded as publishing house of Slovak Central Committee of Czechoslovak Physical Culture Organization, 1992 transformed to Sport Publishing House Ltd)
Specializes in sports, travel & Western fiction.
Firm is the immediate successor of publishing house of the Slovak Central Committee of the Czechoslovak Physical Culture Organization.
Subjects: Fiction, Science Fiction, Fantasy, Sports, Athletics, Travel, Western Fiction
ISBN Prefix(es): 80-7096
Number of titles published annually: 6 Print
Total Titles: 2 Print

Technicka Univerzita
T G Masaryka 2117/24, 960 53 Zvolen
Tel: (0855) 635 *Fax:* (0855) 20027
Telex: 72267 VSLDC
Subjects: Agriculture, Animals, Pets, Architecture & Interior Design, Economics, Education, Environmental Studies, Science (General), Technology
ISBN Prefix(es): 80-228

Ustav informacii a prognoz skolstva mladeze a telovychovy+
Stare grunty 52, 842 44 Bratislava
Tel: (07) 65425166 *Fax:* (07) 65426180
Founded: 1975
Subjects: Career Development, Computer Science, Education, Labor, Industrial Relations, Library & Information Sciences, Management, Microcomputers, Outdoor Recreation, Psychology, Psychiatry, Social Sciences, Sociology
ISBN Prefix(es): 80-7098
Associate Companies: Slovenska pedagogicka kniznica

VEDA (Vydavatel'stvo Slovenskej akademie vied)
Bradacova 7, 85286 Bratislava
Tel: (07) 832254; (07) 831172 *Fax:* (07) 835391; (07) 832254
Telex: 93464 UKSAV *Cable:* VEDA BRATISLAVA
Key Personnel
Dir: Dr Eva Majeska
Publicity Manager: Dipl Ing Jaroslava Maderova
Founded: 1953

Publishing House of the Slovak Academy of Sciences.
Subjects: Archaeology, Earth Sciences, History, Language Arts, Linguistics, Philosophy, Psychology, Psychiatry, Technology
ISBN Prefix(es): 80-224
Bookshop(s): Knihkupectvo SAV, Dunajska 5, 814 30 Bratislava

Vydavatel' Sky odbor+
Mudronova 26, 03652 Martin
Tel: (0842) 31861 *Fax:* (0842) 32993
E-mail: vms@esix.matica.sk
Key Personnel
Publicity Manager: Tomas Winkler
Founded: 1863
Subjects: Biography, Ethnicity
ISBN Prefix(es): 80-7090

Vydavatelstvo Junior sro Slovart Print+
Pekna cesta c 6, 834 03 Bratislava
Tel: (07) 44872378; (07) 44872379; (07) 44872103 *Fax:* (07) 44872133
E-mail: junior@junior.sk
Key Personnel
Commercial Dir: Marta Horakova
Contact: M D Jaroslav Pijak *E-mail:* pijak@junior.sk
Founded: 1994
ISBN Prefix(es): 80-7146
Associate Companies: Nakladatelstvi Junior, Prague, Czech Republic
Distributor for Slowakei

Vydavatel'stvo Osveta (Verlag Osveta)+
Osloboditelov 21, 036 54 Martin
Mailing Address: PO Box 14, 036 54 Martin
Tel: (0842) 33503; (0842) 32921; (0842) 35037 *Fax:* (0842) 35036
Key Personnel
Proprietor: Martin Farkas
Founded: 1953
Specialize in distribution.
Subjects: Education, Fiction, Medicine, Nursing, Dentistry, Nonfiction (General), Science (General), Travel
ISBN Prefix(es): 80-217; 80-88824; 80-967377
Bookshop(s): Spitalska 18, 811 08 Bratislava; Knihkupectvi Klaty Klas, Osveta Exact Service, Lannova 6, 370 01 Ceske Budejovice, Czech Republic; M R Stefanika, 075 01 Trebisov
Warehouse: Expedicny Sklad Vydavatelstva Osveta, 038 41 Kost'any nad Turcom

Vysoka Vojenska Skola Letecka
Rampova 7, 041 21 Kosice
Mailing Address: PO Box 26, 041 21 Kosice
Tel: (095) 6512183; (095) 6333851 *Fax:* (095) 333851
Key Personnel
Contact: Frantisek Olejnik
ISBN Prefix(es): 80-7166

Wist+
Kozmonautov 35, 036 01 Martin
Tel: (0842) 4289652 *Fax:* (0842) 4289652
E-mail: wist@enelux.sk
Key Personnel
President: Robert Schwandner
Editor-in-Chief: Tomasz Trancygier *E-mail:* ttran@enelux.sk
International Rights Contact: Prava I Prevodi
Founded: 1993
Subjects: Fiction, Romance
ISBN Prefix(es): 80-8049
Number of titles published annually: 50 Print

Zilinska Univerzita
Moyzesova 20, 010 26 Zilina

Tel: (089) 625919; (089) 621247 *Fax:* (089) 620023
Key Personnel
Manager: Miroslav Kopecky
Dirs: Frantisek Schlosser; Milan Dado; Pavol Kostial
ISBN Prefix(es): 80-7100

Slovenia

General Information

Capital: Ljubljana
Language: Slovenian and Serbo-Croat
Religion: Predominantly Roman Catholic
Population: 2 million
Bank Hours: 0730-1800 Monday-Friday and 0730-1200 Saturday
Shop Hours: 0800-1900 Monday-Friday; 0800-1300 Saturday, some open Saturday afternoon
Currency: Tolar
Export/Import Information: 3% VAT on books.
Copyright: UCC, Berne (see Copyright Conventions, pg xi)

Cankarjeva Zalozba+
Kopitarjeva Ulica 2, 1000 Ljubljana
Tel: (061) 21-419 *Fax:* (061) 214250
Telex: 31821 Yu Cankar
Key Personnel
Man Dir: Dr Martin Znidersic
Editor: Janez Stanic
Rights & Permissions: Dagmar Dolinar
Subjects: Biography, Fiction, History, How-to, Philosophy, Poetry, Psychology, Psychiatry, Social Sciences, Sociology
ISBN Prefix(es): 86-361

Casopisni zavod Uradni list Republike Slovenije
Slovenska cesta 9, 1000 Ljubljana
Tel: (061) 1251419; (061) 1252357 *Fax:* (061) 224337
E-mail: url@uradni-list.si
Key Personnel
Chief Executive: Polutnik Marko
Editorial: Leskovic Alenka; Kurt Marija
Founded: 1946
Subjects: Law, Legislation
ISBN Prefix(es): 86-7085; 961-204

East West Operation (EWO) Ltd+
Copova 38, 1000 Ljubljana
Tel: (061) 217124; (061) 1264124; (061) 161181 *Fax:* (061) 217348
E-mail: ewo-arkadna@siol.net
Key Personnel
General Manager: Slavko Pregl
Foreign Rights: Irene Motaln-Sezun
Founded: 1991
Subjects: Art, Economics, Gardening, Plants, Health, Nutrition, History, Wine & Spirits
ISBN Prefix(es): 961-207
Subsidiaries: EWO Buechhandel GmbH

Franc-Franc podjetje za promocijo kulture Murska Sobota d o o+
Stefana Kovaca 30, 9000 Murska Sobota
Mailing Address: PP 27, 9000 Murska Sobota
Tel: (069) 22501 *Fax:* (069) 22501
E-mail: franc.franc@siol.net
Key Personnel
Owner, Dir & International Rights: Franci Just
Owner: Feri Lainscek
Founded: 1992
Member of Verbandes der Veleger und Buchhaendler Sloweniens. Specialize in Literature.

Subjects: Fiction, Journalism, Language Arts, Linguistics, Literature, Literary Criticism, Essays, Poetry, Regional Interests
ISBN Prefix(es): 961-219

Mladinska Knjiga International+
Slovenska 29, 1000 Ljubljana
Tel: (061) 1261300; (061) 1252796; (061) 1252798 *Fax:* (061) 215320
Key Personnel
Man Dir: Majda Sikosek
Editor: Vasja Krasevec
Subjects: Art, Astrology, Occult, How-to, Nonfiction (General), Science Fiction, Fantasy
ISBN Prefix(es): 86-11

Moderna galerija Ljubljana/Museum of Modern Art+
Tomsiceva 14, 1000 Ljubljana
Tel: (001) 2416800 *Fax:* (001) 2514120
Web Site: www.mg-lj.si
Key Personnel
Dir: Ms Zdenka Badovinac
Founded: 1948
Subjects: Art
Total Titles: 5 Print

Pomurska zalozba
Lendavska 1, 9000 Murska Sobota
Tel: (069) 32420 *Fax:* (069) 31086
Telex: 35-229 Yu Zgpmsb
Key Personnel
Dir: Ludvik Socic
Editor-in-Chief: Joze Hradil
Subjects: Fiction, Literature, Literary Criticism, Essays, Poetry
ISBN Prefix(es): 86-7195; 86-80755
Bookshop(s): Dobra knjiga, Titova c, 69000 Murska Sobota; Knjigarna Gornja Radgona 69250, Yugoslavia; Knjigarna Lendava 69220, Yugoslavia; Knjigarna Ljutomer 69240, Yugoslavia

Slovenska matica
Kongresni trg 8, 61001 Ljubljana
Tel: (061) 214200; (061) 214227; (061) 1263190 *Fax:* (061) 214200
Key Personnel
President: Dr Joza Mahnic
Vice President: Peter Vodopivec
Publisher: Drago Jancar
Founded: 1864
Subjects: Literature, Literary Criticism, Essays, Philosophy
ISBN Prefix(es): 86-80933; 961-213

Univerza v Ljubljani Ekonomska Fakulteta+
Kardeljeva pl 17, 1000 Ljubljana
Tel: (061) 1892400 *Fax:* (061) 1892698
E-mail: joze.cibej@uni-lj.s1
Key Personnel
International Rights: Dr Lea Bregar
Founded: 1946
Subjects: Accounting, Advertising, Business, Economics, Finance, Government, Political Science, Language Arts, Linguistics, Law, Management, Marketing, Mathematics, Securities
ISBN Prefix(es): 86-398; 961-6081; 961-6273

Zalozba Mihelac d o o+
Slomkova 15, 1000 Ljubljana
Tel: (061) 313654 *Fax:* (061) 1331197
Key Personnel
Contact: Mihelac Spela
Founded: 1990
Subjects: Art, Astrology, Occult, Astronomy, Biblical Studies, Child Care & Development, Communications, Drama, Theater, English as a Second Language, Fiction, Foreign Countries, Government, Political Science, History, Journalism, Language Arts, Linguistics, Literature, Literary Criticism, Essays, Medicine, Nursing, Dentistry, Parapsychology, Philosophy, Photography, Psychology, Psychiatry, Regional Interests, Religion - Buddhist, Religion - Catholic, Self-Help, Social Sciences, Sociology, Theology, Travel
ISBN Prefix(es): 961-6271
Showroom(s): Dunajska 23, 1000 Ljubljana
Bookshop(s): Dunajska 23, 1000 Ljubljana
Book Club(s): MOLJ
Orders to: Dunajska 23, 1000 Ljubljana

Zalozba Obzorja d d Maribor+
Partizanska 3-5, Gosposka 3, 2000 Maribor
Tel: (062) 28971; (062) 125681 *Fax:* (062) 223213
Key Personnel
Chief Executive: Pavla Pece
Editor: Bojan Osterc
Founded: 1950
Subjects: Biography, Cookery, English as a Second Language, History, Journalism, Language Arts, Linguistics, Literature, Literary Criticism, Essays, Management, Marketing, Music, Dance, Nonfiction (General), Poetry, Science (General)
ISBN Prefix(es): 86-377; 961-230
Divisions: Zalozba Obzorja p.o. Maribor
Bookshop(s): Zalozba Obzorja-Knjigarna, Gosposka 24 SLO, 2000 Maribor
Warehouse: Turnerjeva 17, SLO, 2000 Maribor

South Africa

General Information

Capital: Pretoria
Language: Afrikaans and English (both official) 11 other official languages exist
Religion: Predominatly Christian. Politically most important is the Dutch Reformed Church (about 30% of the white population). Also many Methodist, Anglican and African Independent Churches among African Christians
Population: 41.25 million
Bank Hours: 0900-1530 Monday-Friday
Shop Hours: Vary province to province. Often 0900-1700 Monday-Friday
Currency: 1 rand = 4.32 USDL (June 1996)
Export/Import Information: Printed books, brochures, leaflets and similar matter (tariff heading 49.01) are free of duty and surcharge with the exception of directories, guide books, year books, Christmas annuals and hand-books relating to South Africa which attract duty at a rate of 20% or 11c/Kg. No objectionable or undesirable literature permitted. No import permit required. Trade advertising matter, commercial catalogues and the like (tariff heading 4911.10.10 to 4911.10.30) are free of duty (otherwise 25% and 20% duty respectively). 5% surcharge is payable in all instances. 14% VAT on books. No import permit is required.

AA The Motorist Publications, *imprint of* Reader's Digest Southern Africa

Acacia Books, *imprint of* Nasou Via Afrika

Acorn Books+
PO Box 4845, Randburg 2125
Tel: (011) 8805768 *Fax:* (011) 8805768
E-mail: acorbook@iafrica.com
Key Personnel
Publisher: Eleanor-Mary Cadell
Founded: 1985
Specialize in: Natural History & African Wildlife.
Subjects: Natural History, Travel

ISBN Prefix(es): 1-874802
Total Titles: 6 Print

Addison Wesley, *imprint of* Maskew Miller Longman

Addison Wesley Longman, *imprint of* Pearson Education (Prentice Hall)

Africasouth Paperbacks, *imprint of* New Africa Books (Pty) Ltd

Afritech, *imprint of* Nasou Via Afrika

Afro, *imprint of* Nasou Via Afrika

Allyn & Bacon, *imprint of* Maskew Miller Longman

Anansi Uitgewers+
Forestweg 10, Oranjezicht, Capetown 8001
Tel: (021) 968511 *Fax:* (021) 969698
Key Personnel
Man Dir, Editorial: Dr Lydia Snyman
Man Dir, Financial: Andre Conradie
Founded: 1989
ISBN Prefix(es): 1-86843; 0-947454; 1-874885
Warehouse: c/o Newman and Swart Street, Durbanville
Orders to: PO Box 559, Durbanville 7550
Tel: (021) 968411 *Fax:* (021) 969698

Appleton Lange, *imprint of* Pearson Education (Prentice Hall)

Ashanti Publishing+
PO Box 5091, Rivonia 2128
Tel: (011) 8032506 *Fax:* (011) 8035094
Key Personnel
Man Dir: Nicholas Combrinck
Founded: 1987
Subjects: Environmental Studies, Foreign Countries, Government, Political Science, Military Science, Sports, Athletics
ISBN Prefix(es): 1-874800; 1-919686
Parent Company: Ashanti International Films Ltd, Gibraltar
Subsidiaries: Gibraltar
Branch Office(s)
Daring Publishing Group, 913 Tuscarawas St W, Canton, OH 44702, United States

Atlas, *imprint of* Nasou Via Afrika

Jonathan Ball Publishers
10-14 Watkins St, Denver Extension 4, Johannesburg 2094
Mailing Address: PO Box 33977, Jeppestown 2043
Tel: (011) 622-2900 *Fax:* (011) 622-7610
Key Personnel
Publishing & Rights: Francine Blum
Marketing: Eugene Ashton
Sales: Alastair Steyn
Founded: 1977
Subjects: Biography, Government, Political Science, History, Literature, Literary Criticism, Essays, Sports, Athletics
ISBN Prefix(es): 1-86842
Parent Company: Nasionale Boekhandel
Ultimate Parent Company: Nasionale Pers
Imprints: Delta Books; Ad Donker Publications

Jossey Bass, *imprint of* Pearson Education (Prentice Hall)

Bateleur, *imprint of* Nasou Via Afrika

Benjamin Cummings, *imprint of* Maskew Miller Longman

Bet-El Publishers+
PO Box 23227, Innesdale Pretoria 0031
Tel: (012) 3294508
Key Personnel
Chief Executive: Robbie Engelbrecht
Founded: 1973
Member of CBS (USA), CBSA (South Africa) & ICUMA (USA).
Subjects: Astrology, Occult, Behavioral Sciences, Biblical Studies, Child Care & Development, Drama, Theater, Earth Sciences, Ethnicity, Film, Video, Gay & Lesbian, History, Human Relations, Humor, Marketing, Medicine, Nursing, Dentistry, Parapsychology, Psychology, Psychiatry, Publishing & Book Trade Reference, Radio, TV, Religion - Buddhist, Religion - Catholic, Religion - Hindu, Religion - Islamic, Religion - Jewish, Religion - Protestant, Religion - Other
ISBN Prefix(es): 0-908421
Parent Company: Bet-el Media Group
Associate Companies: BAVCOM International; Bet-el Bookshop
Subsidiaries: Bet-el Film & Video Services
Distributed by Engeltal Press
Distributor for Bridge Publishing; Huntington House; B Kirkbride Bible; Omega Publishers; Whitaker House
Shipping Address: 385 Voortrekkers Rd, Pretoria 0084

Bible Society of South Africa
PO Box 6215, Roggebay, Cape Town 8012
Tel: (021) 212040 *Fax:* (021) 4194846
Telex: 527964 *Cable:* Testaments Cape Town
Key Personnel
Chief Executive, General Secretary, Rights & Permissions: Dr D Tolmie
Sales, Production: Rev A C Human
Publicity: N Turley
Founded: 1820 (as auxiliary of British & Foreign Bible Society, 1965 as autonomous body)
Subjects: Biblical Studies, Religion - Other
ISBN Prefix(es): 0-7982
Imprints: Bybelgenootskap
Branch Office(s)
Bloemfontein
Cape Town
Durban
Kempton Park
Kwazulu
Port Elizabeth
Soweto
Bookshop(s): 220 Kimberley Rd, Bloemfontein 9301; 15 Anton Anreith Arcade, Roggebay, Cape Town 8001; 97 Russell St, Durban 4001; Bible House, 18 Central Ave, Kempton Park 1620; Bible House, 31 Cotswold Ave, Cotswold, Port Elizabeth 6045; Bible House, Stand 5080, Zone 5, Pimville, Soweto 1808

The Brenthurst Press (Pty) Ltd
PO Box 87184, Houghton, Johannesburg 2041
Tel: (011) 6466024 *Fax:* (011) 4861651
E-mail: orders@brenthurst.co.az
Key Personnel
Sales Manager: Sally MacRoberts
 E-mail: sallymac@brenthurst.co.za
Founded: 1974
Subjects: History, Natural History, Regional Interests
ISBN Prefix(es): 0-909079

Butterworths South Africa
8 Walter Place, Mayville, 4001 Durban
Mailing Address: PO Box 4, Mayville, 4058 Durban
Tel: (031) 268 3111; (031) 268 3007 (customer service) *Fax:* (031) 268 3100; (021) 268 3109 (customer service)
Web Site: www.butterworths.co.za
Key Personnel
Man Dir: Billy Last *Tel:* (031) 268 3252
 Fax: (031) 29 8686
Sales & Marketing Dir: James Martens *Tel:* (031) 268 3246 *Fax:* (031) 268 3114
Electronic Publishing Dir: Chris Uniacke
 Tel: (031) 268 3256 *Fax:* (031) 268 3114
Publishing Dir: Theuns Viljoen *Tel:* (031) 268 3247 *Fax:* (031) 268 3114
Business Publishing Manager: Sarah Power-Wilson *Tel:* (031) 268 3112 *Fax:* (031) 268 3114
National Sales Manager: Wendy de Sornay
 Tel: (031) 268 3261 *Fax:* (031) 268 3118
Marketing Manager: Shannon MacLennan
 Tel: (031) 268 3251
Marketing Coordinator: Charmaine Chinappan
 Tel: (031) 268 3243
Subjects: Economics, Education, Law, Medicine, Nursing, Dentistry, Science (General)
ISBN Prefix(es): 0-409
Parent Company: Butterworth & Co (Publishers) Ltd, United Kingdom
Ultimate Parent Company: Reed Elsevier plc, 25 Victoria St, London SW1H 0EX, United Kingdom
Branch Office(s)
F10 Centurion Business, Bosmansdam Rd, Milnerton, 7441 Capetown *Tel:* (021) 551 5095 *Fax:* (021) 551 5121
Grayston 66, 2 Norwich Close, Sandton, 2196 Johannesburg *Tel:* (011) 784 6373 *Fax:* (011) 883 6540
Distributor for Butterworth-Heinemann

Bybelgenootskap, *imprint of* Bible Society of South Africa

Killie Campbell Africana Library, *imprint of* University of Natal Press

Cape Provincial Library Service
PO Box 659, Cape Town 8000
Tel: (021) 5910095 *Fax:* (021) 4102261
Key Personnel
Contact: Mrs Liesel de Villiers *E-mail:* lieseldu@cpls.wcapc.gov.za
Founded: 1950
Subjects: Library & Information Sciences
ISBN Prefix(es): 0-7984

Caversham Broshures
PO Box 1426, Pinetown 3600
Tel: (031) 7017021 *Fax:* (031) 7017036
Key Personnel
Product Manager: Mrs P Daehn
ISBN Prefix(es): 0-620; 1-86833; 1-874834
Parent Company: Kohler Packaging Ltd
Associate Companies: Braby's, PO Box 1426, Pinetown 3600; Swan Publishing, PO 1428, Pinetown 3600; Intratex, PO Box 1405, Pinetown 3600

Centaur, *imprint of* Heinemann Educational Publishers Southern Africa

Centre for Conflict Resolution
31-37 Orange St, Capetown 7700
Mailing Address: University of Cape Town, Private Bag 7701, Rondebosch 7701
Tel: (021) 6502503; (021) 6502750 *Fax:* (021) 6852142; (021) 6504053
E-mail: ccr@uctvax.uct.ac.za
Web Site: www.ccrweb.ccr.uct.ac.za
Telex: 5-21439
Key Personnel
Executive Dir: Mr Laurie Nathan *Tel:* (021) 4222512 *Fax:* (021) 4222622 *E-mail:* lnathan@ccr.uct.ac.za
Founded: 1968
Specialize in conflict management.
Subjects: Human Relations, Social Sciences, Sociology
ISBN Prefix(es): 0-7992
Number of titles published annually: 10 Print
Total Titles: 24 Print

Charles Merrill, *imprint of* Maskew Miller Longman

Clever Books+
999 Arcadia St, Arcadia, Pretoria 0083
Mailing Address: PO Box 20113, Alkantrant, Pretoria 0005
Tel: (012) 3424715 *Fax:* (012) 432376
E-mail: inlo631@mweb.co.2a
Key Personnel
Owner: J Steenhuisen
Founded: 1981
Specialize in educational books & worksheets.
Member of S A Publishers Association & S A Book Dealers Association; also specialize in Study Guides.
Subjects: Biological Sciences, Education, English as a Second Language, Language Arts, Linguistics, Mathematics, Physical Sciences, Science (General)
ISBN Prefix(es): 0-947056; 0-86817
Total Titles: 1,200 Print; 12 CD-ROM
Book Club(s): Clever Book Club

CMP Reprints, *imprint of* Sasavona Publishers & Booksellers

College of Careers (Pty) Ltd
PO Box 1144, Cape Town 8000
Tel: (021) 4624360 *Fax:* (021) 4619378
Key Personnel
Man Dir: Richard S Pooler
Founded: 1946
Subjects: Education
ISBN Prefix(es): 0-7985; 0-949945
Imprints: College of Careers Study Aids; College Tutorial Press; Faircape Books; Outlines

College of Careers Study Aids, *imprint of* College of Careers (Pty) Ltd

College Tutorial Press, *imprint of* College of Careers (Pty) Ltd

Conflict Management; Africa; Peacemaking; Peacebuilding, see Centre for Conflict Resolution

CUM Books (Pty) Ltd, see Digma Publications

Benjamin Cummings, *imprint of* Pearson Education (Prentice Hall)

Daan Retief, *imprint of* HAUM - Daan Retief Publishers (Pty) Ltd

Daan Retief, *imprint of* Jacklin Enterprises (Pty) Ltd

De Jager Publishers, see HAUM - De Jager Publishers

De Jager Haum, *imprint of* Maskew Miller Longman

Delta Books, *imprint of* Jonathan Ball Publishers

Delta Books (Pty) Ltd+
Imprint of Jonathan Ball Publishers (Pty) Ltd
PO Box 33977, Jeppestown 2043

SOUTH AFRICA

Tel: (011) 622-2900 *Fax:* (011) 622-7610
Key Personnel
Publishing & Permissions: Francine Blum
  E-mail: fplum@jonathanball.co.za
Marketing: Eugene Ashton
Sales: Alastair Steyn
Founded: 1980
Subjects: Nonfiction (General), General South African
ISBN Prefix(es): 0-908387
Parent Company: Nasionale Boekhandel
Ultimate Parent Company: Nasionale Pers
Associate Companies: Ad Donker (Pty) Ltd
Warehouse: Jonathan Ball Publishers, 10-14 Watkins St, Denver Ext 4, Johannesburg 2094

Digma Publications
Division of Butterworth Publishers
PO Box 65042, Benmore 2010
Tel: (011) 8834854 *Fax:* (011) 8836540
Telex: 425847 *Cable:* Chrispub
Key Personnel
Chairman: J J M Jacobs
Publisher: Freddie Crous; Koos van Niekerk
Founded: 1939
Subjects: Law, Religion - Other
ISBN Prefix(es): 0-86984; 1-86829

Ad Donker (Pty) Ltd+
Imprint of Jonathan Ball Publishers (Pty) Ltd
PO Box 33977, Jeppestown 2043
Tel: (011) 622-2900 *Fax:* (011) 622-7610
Key Personnel
Publishing & Permissions: Francine Blum
  E-mail: fplum@jonathanball.co.za
Marketing: Eugene Ashton
Sales: Alastair Steyn
Founded: 1973
Subjects: Nonfiction (General), General South African
ISBN Prefix(es): 0-86852
Parent Company: Nasionale Boekhandel
Ultimate Parent Company: Nasionale Pers
Associate Companies: Delta Books (Pty) Ltd
Warehouse: Jonathan Ball Publishers (Pty) Ltd, 10-14 Watkins St, Denver Ext 4, Johannesburg 2094

Ad Donker Publications, *imprint of* Jonathan Ball Publishers

Educum, *imprint of* Maskew Miller Longman

Educum Publishers Ltd
PO Box 3068, Halfway House 1685
Tel: (011) 3153647 *Fax:* (011) 3152757
Key Personnel
Group Man Dir: P Greyling
Sr General Manager: W Struik
General Manager: W C De Wet
Sales: C Mahlaba
Founded: 1947
Subjects: Accounting, Agriculture, Art, Biblical Studies, Biological Sciences, Business, Chemistry, Chemical Engineering, Computer Science, Cookery, Economics, Education, Engineering (General), Geography, Geology, Government, Political Science, History, Literature, Literary Criticism, Essays, Mathematics, Music, Dance, Natural History, Physical Sciences, Physics, Poetry, Religion - Protestant, Science (General), Social Sciences, Sociology, Technology
ISBN Prefix(es): 0-7980
Parent Company: Perskor Books (Pty) Ltd
Associate Companies: Varia Publishers, PO Box 3068, Halfway House, 1685; Lex Patria Publishers, PO Box 845, Johannesburg 2000

Casselt Elt, *imprint of* Pearson Education (Prentice Hall)

Ensiklopedie Afrikana
Prosbus 6050, Pretoria 0001
Tel: (011) 4021400; (011) 297093
Telex: 83031 *Cable:* Knowingly
Key Personnel
Man Dir: Hilton W Payne
ISBN Prefix(es): 0-908409; 0-86483
Parent Company: Sage Holdings (Pty) Ltd
Subsidiaries: Encyclopaedia Britannica (SA) (Pty) Ltd; Ensiklopedie Afrikana (Edms) Bpk; IQ Progressons (Pty) Ltd

Erudita Publications (Pty) Ltd+
Cor Beyers Naude Drive & 11 Ave, Melville 2092
Mailing Address: PO Box 29159, Melville, Johannesburg 2109
Tel: (011) 7264350 *Fax:* (011) 4821279
Key Personnel
Man Dir: Chris van Rensburg *E-mail:* cvrpub@mweb.co.za
Dir: Beverley J Lawrence
Founded: 1965
Subjects: Agriculture, Career Development, Communications, Health, Nutrition, Outdoor Recreation, Science (General), Technology, Travel, Aviation
ISBN Prefix(es): 0-908394
Total Titles: 4 Print

Faircape Books, *imprint of* College of Careers (Pty) Ltd

Woodhead Faulkner, *imprint of* Pearson Education (Prentice Hall)

Fernwood Press, *imprint of* Fernwood Press (Pty) Ltd

Fernwood Press (Pty) Ltd+
PO Box 15344, Vlaeberg, Capetown 8018
Tel: (021) 6833784 *Fax:* (021) 6718574
E-mail: ferpress@iafrica.com
Web Site: www.fernwoodpress.co.za
Key Personnel
Man Dir & International Rights: Pieter Struik
Founded: 1991
Subjects: Art, History, Natural History, Nonfiction (General), Regional Interests, Travel, Wine & Spirits
ISBN Prefix(es): 1-874950; 0-9583154
Number of titles published annually: 5 Print
Imprints: Fernwood Press
Distributed by Central Books Ltd/Global Book Marketing; Millbank Books (UK, Europe & Middle East)

Financial Times, *imprint of* Maskew Miller Longman

Financial Times-Pitman, *imprint of* Pearson Education (Prentice Hall)

Flesch Financial Publications (Pty) Ltd+
4 Gordon St, Cape Town 8001
Mailing Address: PO Box 3473, Cape Town 8000
Tel: (021) 4617472 *Fax:* (021) 4613758
E-mail: sflesch@aztec.co.za
Key Personnel
Man Dir: S Flesch *E-mail:* sflesch@iafrica.com
Editorial: M G K Maher
Sales Manager: Peter Duncan
Founded: 1966
Member of Publishers Association of South Africa.
Subjects: Aeronautics, Aviation, Animals, Pets, Business, Maritime
ISBN Prefix(es): 0-949989
Total Titles: 3 Print; 1 CD-ROM

Associate Companies: WJ Flesch & Partners (Pty) Ltd
Branch Office(s)
104 Greenway, Greenside 2193

Folio, *imprint of* Juventus/Femina Publishers

Russel Friedman Books
PO Box 73, Halfway House 1685
Tel: (011) 7022300 *Fax:* (011) 7021403
E-mail: rvulture@iafrica.com
Key Personnel
Contact: Russel Friedman
Founded: 1982
Subjects: Natural History
ISBN Prefix(es): 0-9583223; 1-875091
U.S. Office(s): 4651 Glenshire Place, Atlanta, GA 30338, United States

Galago, *imprint of* Galago Publishing Pty Ltd

Galago Publishing Pty Ltd+
8 First Ave, Alberton North
Mailing Address: PO Box 1645, 1450 Alberton
Tel: (011) 9072029 *Fax:* (011) 8690890
E-mail: lemur@mweb.co.za
Web Site: www.galago.co.za
Key Personnel
Man Dir: Francis Stiff
Founded: 1982
Specialize in general nonfiction, military, hunting & Africa.
Member of Publishers' Association South Africa.
Subjects: Aeronautics, Aviation, African American Studies, Biography, Foreign Countries, History, Military Science, Nonfiction (General), Hunting & Africa
Number of titles published annually: 6 Print
Total Titles: 20 Print
Parent Company: Lemur Books Pty Ltd
Imprints: Galago

Ginn, *imprint of* Heinemann Educational Publishers Southern Africa

GK Hall, *imprint of* Maskew Miller Longman

Government Printer
Private Bag X85, Pretoria 0001
Mailing Address: PO Box 571, Cape Town 8000
Tel: (012) 3239731 *Fax:* (012) 4614404
  Cable: QUAD
Subjects: Education, Geography, Geology
ISBN Prefix(es): 0-621

Hadeda Books, *imprint of* University of Natal Press

G K Hall, *imprint of* Pearson Education (Prentice Hall)

HarperCollins Religious
PO Box 33977, Jeppestown 2043
Tel: (011) 6222900 *Fax:* (011) 6223553
Key Personnel
Man Dir: Jonathan Ball
Sales, Marketing Dir: Alastair Steyn
Financial: Tony Van Tondor
Founded: 1962
Subjects: Biblical Studies, Fiction, Nonfiction (General)
ISBN Prefix(es): 0-00; 0-00
Parent Company: Nasionale Pens

Harvester Wheatsheaf, *imprint of* Maskew Miller Longman

Harvester Wheatsheaf, *imprint of* Pearson Education (Prentice Hall)

HAUM - Daan Retief Publishers (Pty) Ltd+
PO Box 629, Pretoria 0001
Tel: (012) 3228474 *Fax:* (012) 3222424
Key Personnel
Man Dir, Production: M A C Jacklin
Editorial, Sales, Publicity, Rights & Permissions: Dr H J M Retief
Founded: 1973
Subjects: Education, Regional Interests
Parent Company: HAUM (Hollandsch Afrikaansche Uitgevers Maatschapplij)
Associate Companies: HAUM-De Jager Publishers
Imprints: Daan Retief
Book Club(s): Kinderklub; Young People's Book Club

De Jager Haum, *imprint of* Pearson Education (Prentice Hall)

HAUM - De Jager Publishers
PO Box 629, Pretoria 0001
Tel: (012) 3284620 *Fax:* (012) 3284706; (012) 3283809
Key Personnel
Man Dir: Chris Richter
General Manager, Publishing: Lena Kohler
General Manager, Marketing: Johann Verreynne
Founded: 1894 (as HAUM)
Subjects: Literature, Literary Criticism, Essays, Religion - Other
ISBN Prefix(es): 0-7986
Parent Company: HAUM (Hollandsch Afrikaansche Uitgevers Maatschappij)
Associate Companies: HAUM-Daan Retief Publishers (Pty) Ltd
Branch Office(s)
Blomfontein
Cape Town
Durban
King William's Town
Pietersburg
Pretoria
Vereeniging
Witwatersrand
Orders to: PO Box 12635, Clubview 0014

HAUM (Hollandsch Afrikaansche Uitgevers Maatschappij)+
PO Box 629, Pretoria 0001
Tel: (012) 32284620 *Fax:* (012) 3284706; (012) 3283809
Key Personnel
Manager, Publisher: Chris Richter
Subjects: Biography, Education, Ethnicity, Fiction, History, Nonfiction (General), Poetry
ISBN Prefix(es): 0-7986
Subsidiaries: HAUM-Daan Retief Publishers (Pty) Ltd; HAUM-De Jager Publishers; HAUM Educational Publishers; IKUT; Juventus/Femina Publishers; Rostrum
Bookshop(s): HAUM Academic Bookshop; HAUM Booksellers

Heinemann-Centaur, *imprint of* Heinemann Educational Publishers Southern Africa

Heinemann Educational Publishers Southern Africa+
66 Park Lane, Sandton, Gauteng, 2196 Johannesburg
Mailing Address: PO Box 781940, Sandton, Gauteng, 2146 Johannesburg
Tel: (011) 322 8600 *Fax:* (011) 322 8717; (011) 322 8718
E-mail: customerliaison@heinemann.co.za
Web Site: ww.heinemann.co.za
Key Personnel
Publishing Dir: Saul Molobi
Founded: 1986
Member of South African Publishers Association.
Subjects: Economics, Education, English as a Second Language, Mathematics, Mechanical Engineering
ISBN Prefix(es): 0-435; 0-620
Parent Company: Reed Educational & Professional Publishing
Ultimate Parent Company: Reed Elsevier plc
Imprints: Ginn; Centaur; Heinemann-Centaur; Lexicon; Isando Books
Subsidiaries: Heinemann Higher and Further Education (Pty) Ltd

Heinemann Publishers (Pty) Ltd+
PO Box 371, Isando 1600
Tel: (011) 9741181 *Fax:* (011) 974311
Key Personnel
Man Dir, Rights & Permissions: Kevin Kroeger
Publishing: Robert Sulley
Production: Angela Tuck
Publicity: Andrew Meyer
Founded: 1966
Subjects: Computer Science, Medicine, Nursing, Dentistry, Nonfiction (General), Science (General), Technology
ISBN Prefix(es): 1-86813; 0-908379; 0-947034; 0-947472; 1-86834; 1-86853; 1-874820; 1-874914

The Hippogriff Press CC+
PO Box 191, Parklands, Johannesburg 2121
Tel: (011) 6464229 *Fax:* (011) 6464229
Key Personnel
Contact: E M MacPhail
Founded: 1989
Member of IPASA (Independent Publishers Association of South Africa).
Subjects: Fiction, Poetry
ISBN Prefix(es): 0-9583122

Homeros, *imprint of* Tafelberg Publishers Ltd

Ellis Horwood, *imprint of* Pearson Education (Prentice Hall)

Human & Rousseau (Pty) Ltd+
State House, 3-9 Rose St, Cape Town 8001
Mailing Address: PO Box 5050, Cape Town 8000
Tel: (021) 251280 *Fax:* (021) 4192619
E-mail: rhauman@nbh.naspers.co.za
Key Personnel
Gneral Manager: Kerneels Breytenbach
Operations Manager: Riel Hauman
Marketing Manager: Elsa Wolfaard
Founded: 1959
Subjects: Anthropology, Architecture & Interior Design, Art, Biography, Business, Child Care & Development, Communications, Cookery, Crafts, Games, Hobbies, Drama, Theater, Economics, Fiction, Gardening, Plants, History, House & Home, How-to, Language Arts, Linguistics, Literature, Literary Criticism, Essays, Management, Marketing, Music, Dance, Natural History, Nonfiction (General), Philosophy, Poetry, Religion - Protestant, Romance, Self-Help, Sports, Athletics
ISBN Prefix(es): 0-7981
Parent Company: Nasionale Boekhandel Ltd

Human Sciences Research Council+
Private Bag X41, Pretoria 0001
Tel: (012) 2022004; (012) 2022978 *Fax:* (012) 2022891
Web Site: www.hsrc.ac.za
Key Personnel
Publisher: Mrs R Keet *E-mail:* rkeet@beauty.hsrc.ac.za
Founded: 1965
Research Institution, Human Sciences only. Publish own research, selected external authors & co-publish with one UK publisher.
Subjects: Behavioral Sciences, Career Development, Criminology, Education, Government, Political Science, Human Relations, Philosophy, Psychology, Psychiatry, Regional Interests, Social Sciences, Sociology, Women's Studies
ISBN Prefix(es): 0-7969; 0-86965
Total Titles: 274 Print
Distributor for Zed Books (London)
Bookshop(s): HSRC Publishers, PO Box 5556, Petoria 0001, J Moagi *Tel:* (012) 3022004 *Fax:* (012) 3022933 *E-mail:* jels@beauty.hsrc.ac.za
Orders to: PO Box 5556, Pretoria 0001, J Moagi *Tel:* (012) 3022330 *Fax:* (012) 2022442 *E-mail:* jels@beauty.hsrc.ac.za

Institute for Reformational Studies CHE+
c/o Potchefstroom University for Christian Higher Education, Private Bag X6001, Potchefstroom 2522
Tel: (0148) 2992826 *Fax:* (0148) 2992824
E-mail: irsmcs@puknet.puk.ac.za
Telex: 346019 *Cable:* PUK
Key Personnel
Dir: Prof B J van der Walt
Publication Officer: Mrs M C Swanepoel
Founded: 1966
Subjects: Anthropology, Art, Biblical Studies, Developing Countries, Education, Government, Political Science, Religion - Protestant, Theology, Women's Studies
ISBN Prefix(es): 0-86990; 1-86822
Parent Company: Potchefstroom University for Christian Higher Education

Isando Books, *imprint of* Heinemann Educational Publishers Southern Africa

Ithemba! Publishing+
PO Box 1048, Auckland Park 2006
Tel: (011) 7266529 *Fax:* (011) 4824258
E-mail: firechildren@icon.co.za
Web Site: www.icon.co.za/~firechildren
Key Personnel
Contact: Bronwen Jones
Founded: 1994
Member of Publishers Association of South Africa & Children's Book Forum. Publisher of South African produced books only.
Subjects: Biography, Fiction, Regional Interests
Branch Office(s)
Lucretia Humphrey, 3026 Fifth Ave N, Great Falls, MT 59401, United States
Distributed by Africa Book Centre; Lucretia Humphrey (USA); National Book Trust of India (Asia)

Ivy Publications+
PO Box 397, Pretoria 0001
Tel: (012) 218931 *Fax:* (012) 3255984
E-mail: therese@statelib-pww.gov.za
Key Personnel
Contact: Ian Bruton-Simmonds
Founded: 1989
Subjects: Education, English as a Second Language, Journalism, Language Arts, Linguistics, Literature, Literary Criticism, Essays, Management, Nonfiction (General), Romance
ISBN Prefix(es): 0-620

Jacana Education+
Haughton Estate, 5 Saint Peter Rd, Johannesburg 2198
Mailing Address: PO Box 2004, Houghton 2198
Tel: (011) 4831294 *Fax:* (011) 4833441
E-mail: jacedu@iafrica.com
Subjects: Child Care & Development, Education, English as a Second Language, Environmental Studies, Gardening, Plants, Health, Nutrition, Medicine, Nursing, Dentistry, Travel
ISBN Prefix(es): 1-874955

Mike Jacklin, *imprint of* Jacklin Enterprises (Pty) Ltd

Jacklin Enterprises (Pty) Ltd+
19 Mifa Park, George Rd, Midrand 0046
Mailing Address: PO Box 521, Parklands 2121
Tel: (011) 6521800 *Fax:* (011) 3142984
E-mail: mjacklin@jacklin.co.za
Key Personnel
Man Dir: Mike Jacklin *Tel:* (011) 6521802
Editorial, Rights & Permissions: Daleen Zaaiman
Sales: Marie Erasmus
Production: Bashir Ismail
Founded: 1992
Specialize in children's book clubs (5); mail order fulfillment for books, magazines & partworks.
Subjects: Fiction, Romance, Technology, Transportation
ISBN Prefix(es): 1-86839; 1-874927
Total Titles: 2,000 Print; 2 Audio
Imprints: Mike Jacklin; Kennis Onbeperk; Daan Retief
Divisions: Disney Book Club; Daan Retief Book Clubs; Read & Learn Programme; Partworks Subscriptions
Distributor for BBC; Eaglemoss; Fabbri; Marshall Cavendish; Orbis (all South Africa only)

Janssen Publishers CC
PO Box 404, Simon's Town 7995
Tel: (021) 7861548 *Fax:* (021) 7862468
E-mail: janssenp@iafrica.com
Web Site: www.janssenbooks.co.za
Founded: 1981
Specialize in photo & art books of the male nude.
Subjects: Art, Erotica, Gay & Lesbian, Photography
ISBN Prefix(es): 1-919901
Number of titles published annually: 10 Print
Total Titles: 120 Print

Jasmyn, *imprint of* Tafelberg Publishers Ltd

Johannesburg Art Gallery
PO Box 23561, Joubert Park 2044
Tel: (011) 7253130; (011) 7253180 *Fax:* (011) 7206000
Key Personnel
Dir: Rochelle Keene
Curator of Publications: Sandy Shoolman *Tel:* (011) 7253130/80
Founded: 1910
Art Gallery.
Member of AAM, SAMA & ICOM.
Subjects: Art, Education, Photography
ISBN Prefix(es): 1-874836
Total Titles: 20 Print

Juta & Co+
Mercury Crescent, Hillstar Industrial Township, Kenwyn, Cape Province 7790
Mailing Address: PO Box 14373, Kenwyn 7790
Tel: (021) 7975101 *Fax:* (021) 7975569 (orders only); (021) 7970121
E-mail: books@juta.co.za
Web Site: www.juta.co.sa *Cable:* JUTA
Key Personnel
Man Dir, Rights & Permissions: Rory Wilson *Fax:* (021) 7677424 *E-mail:* rwilson@juta.co.za
Corporate Marketing Man: Navine Christian *E-mail:* nchristian@juta.co.za
Founded: 1853
Overseas Agents: Blackstone Press Ltd, 1st Floor, 104 Ebley St, Bondi Junction, Sydney, NSW 2022, Australia; BRAD, 244A London Rd, Hadleigh, Essex SS7 2DE, UK. Tel: (0702) 552912 Fax: (0702) 556095 (academic, medical & technical titles); Hammick's Law Bookshop, 191-192 Fleet St, London EC4A 2AH, UK (law titles).
Member of ABSA & SAPA.
Subjects: Accounting, Business, Education, Law, Medicine, Nursing, Dentistry
ISBN Prefix(es): 0-7021
Number of titles published annually: 500 Print; 10 CD-ROM
Total Titles: 44 CD-ROM
Parent Company: Juta Holdings (Pty) Ltd
Associate Companies: Juta (UK) Ltd, The Kidlington Centre, Suite E, Oxford 0X52DL, United Kingdom; Jutastat (Pty) Ltd
Branch Office(s)
Mercury Crescent Kenwyn, Cape Town 7790 *Tel:* (021) 7975101 *Fax:* (021) 7627424
PO Box 1010, Johannesburg 2000
Showroom(s): Madeira St, Umtata, Transkei *Tel:* (0471) 23634
Shipping Address: Hillstar Industrial Township, Wetton Cape, Jenny Newby *E-mail:* jnewby@juja.co.za
Warehouse: Hillstar Industrial Township, Wetton Cape, Winston Bell *Fax:* (021) 7616267 *E-mail:* wbell@juta.co.za

Juventus/Femina Publishers+
PO Box 629, Pretoria 0001
Tel: (012) 3284620 *Fax:* (012) 3283809
Telex: 30435
Key Personnel
Man Dir: Piet Scholtz
Manager, Editorial: Lena Kohler
Chief Publisher: Kobie Gouws
Sales: Robbie Goossen
Production: Manus Oberholzer
Publicity: Sas Klopper
Rights & Permissions: Hettie Scholtz
Founded: 1980
Subjects: Fiction, Nonfiction (General), Social Sciences, Sociology, Women's Studies
ISBN Prefix(es): 0-86816; 0-907996
Parent Company: HAUM (Hollandsch Afrikaansche Uitgevers Maatschappij)
Imprints: Folio

Kagiso, *imprint of* Maskew Miller Longman

Kagiso, *imprint of* Pearson Education (Prentice Hall)

Kennis Onbeperk, *imprint of* Jacklin Enterprises (Pty) Ltd

Kima Global Publishers+
Kima Global House, 11 Columbine Rd, Rondebosch 7700
Mailing Address: PO Box 374, Rondebosch 7701
Tel: (021) 686-7154 *Fax:* (021) 686-9066
E-mail: kima@global.co.za
Web Site: www.kimaglobal.co.za
Key Personnel
President & International Rights: Mr Robin Beck
Founded: 1993
Independent company specializing in personal growth books.
Member of NAPRA & PMA.
Subjects: Alternative, Astrology, Occult, Behavioral Sciences, How-to, Human Relations, Religion - Other, Self-Help
ISBN Prefix(es): 0-9584
Number of titles published annually: 10 Print
Total Titles: 23 Print
U.S. Office(s): c/o Holistic Marketing Cooperative, 1800 Central St, Suite 101, Kansas City, MO 64108, United States, Contact: Diana Trott *Tel:* 816-471-6776 *Fax:* 816-471-7091
Foreign Rep(s): Katia Schumer (Spain & Portugal)
Warehouse: Packaging Dynamics, 8800 NE Undergroud Dr, Kansas City, MO 64108, United States
Orders to: Holistic Marketing Cooperative, 1800 Central St, Suite 101, Kansas City, MO 64108, United States, Contact: Diana Trott *Tel:* 816-471-6776 *E-mail:* holistic_wisdom@yahoo.com

KZN Books, *imprint of* Nasou Via Afrika

Ladybird Books, *imprint of* Maskew Miller Longman

LAPA Publishers (Pty) Ltd+
Formerly J P van der Walt & Son (Pty) Ltd
Waltpark, 380 Bosman St, Pretoria 0002
Mailing Address: PO Box 123, Pretoria 0001
Tel: (012) 401 0700 *Fax:* (012) 3255498
E-mail: lapa@atkv.org.za
Key Personnel
Publication & Administrative Officer: Esme Smith *E-mail:* esmes@atkv.org.za
Founded: 1943
Subjects: Fiction, Law, Nonfiction (General), Philosophy, Religion - Other
ISBN Prefix(es): 0-7993
Ultimate Parent Company: ATKV
Imprints: Symbol Books
Book Club(s): Eike-Boekklub; Keurbiblioteek; President Boekklub; Romankeur; Symbol; Treffer-Boekklub

Lexicon, *imprint of* Heinemann Educational Publishers Southern Africa

Longman, *imprint of* Maskew Miller Longman

Longman, *imprint of* Pearson Education (Prentice Hall)

Maskew Miller Longman, *imprint of* Pearson Education (Prentice Hall)

Lux Verbi (Pty) Ltd+
33 Waterkant St, Cape Town 8000
Mailing Address: PO Box 1822, 8000 Cape Town
Tel: (021) 4215540 *Fax:* (021) 4191865
E-mail: luxverbi.publ@kinglsey.co.za
Telex: 526922
Key Personnel
Executive Chairman: Willem J van Zijl
Publishing: Hester Venter
Marketing: Maryna Volschenk
Founded: 1956
Subjects: Religion - Other, Theology
ISBN Prefix(es): 0-86997
Subsidiaries: Waterkant-Uitgewers (Edms) Bpk
Bookshop(s): 33 Waterkant St, Cape Town 8000; Suite 402, 30 Waterkant St, Cape Town; Central Square 37, Union St, London; OK Centre Shop, 404 Murchison St, Ladysmith; The Mall, c/o Malanand Sauer St, Vanderbijlpark
Book Club(s): New Day Readers Circle

MacMillan, *imprint of* Maskew Miller Longman

MacMillan Books, *imprint of* Maskew Miller Longman

MacMillan College, *imprint of* Maskew Miller Longman

MacMillan ELT, *imprint of* Maskew Miller Longman

MacMillan Reference, *imprint of* Maskew Miller Longman

Map Studio, see Struik Publishers (Pty) Ltd

PUBLISHERS

Maskew Miller Longman+
Howard Drive, Pinelands, Cape Town 7405
Mailing Address: PO Box 396, Cape Town 8000
Tel: (021) 531 7750 *Fax:* (021) 531 4877
E-mail: firstname@mml.co.za
Telex: 526053 SA
Key Personnel
Chief Executive: Fathima Dada *E-mail:* fathima@mml.co.za
Publishing Dir: Japie Pienaar *E-mail:* japie@mmi.co.za
Dir, Trade & Adult: Orenna Krut
  E-mail: orenna@mml.co.za
Dir MML International: Graham van der Vyver
  E-mail: graham@mmo.co.za
Financial Dir: Ms Cornelius Vamvadelis
Dir, Publishing Services, Editorial & Production: Jeremy Boraine
Founded: 1893
Subjects: Education, Language Arts, Linguistics, Literature, Literary Criticism, Essays
ISBN Prefix(es): 0-623; 0-636
Parent Company: Pearson Education
Ultimate Parent Company: Pearson Plc
Imprints: Unibook; De Jager Haum; Educum; Kagiso; Longman; Pearson Education South Africa; Perskor; Phumelela; Sached; Vlaeberg; Addison Wesley; Allyn & Bacon; Benjamin Cummings; Charles Merrill; Financial Times; GK Hall; Harvester Wheatsheaf; Ladybird Books; MacMillan; MacMillan Books; MacMillan College; MacMillan ELT; MacMillan Reference; Prentice Hall; Prentice Hall Australia; Prentice Hall Europe; Prentice Hall South Africa; QUE College; Regents Prentice Hall; Scribner; Woodhead Faulkner
Branch Office(s)
Private Bag X08, Amethyst St, Bertsham, 2013 Johannesburg *Tel:* (011) 4961730 *Fax:* (011) 4961117

Mayibuye Books+
Private Bag X 17, 7535 Bellville
Tel: (021) 9592529 *Fax:* (021) 9593411
E-mail: mayibuye@mweb.co.za
Key Personnel
Head, Marketing/Distribution: Lavona George
  E-mail: lavona@intekom.co.za
Dir: B Feinberg *E-mail:* bfeinberg@uwc.ac.za
Founded: 1992
A pioneering project helping to recover areas of South African history that have been neglected.
Subjects: Biography, History, Literature, Literary Criticism, Essays
ISBN Prefix(es): 1-86808
Total Titles: 94 Print; 1 CD-ROM

Media House Publications+
PO Box 782395, Sandton 2146
Tel: (011) 8826237 *Fax:* (011) 8829652
Key Personnel
Contact: K Everingham
Founded: 1983
Subjects: Humor, Nonfiction (General)

Charles Merrill, *imprint of* Pearson Education (Prentice Hall)

The Methodist Publishing House
Unit of The Methodist Church of Southern Africa
4 Shannon St, Salt River 7925
Mailing Address: PO Box 13128, Woodstock 7915
Tel: (021) 4483640 *Fax:* (021) 4483716
E-mail: methpub@iafrica.com
Key Personnel
General Manager: D R Leverton
Founded: 1894
Christian Booktrade.
Subjects: Religion - Protestant
ISBN Prefix(es): 0-949942; 0-947450; 1-947450
Total Titles: 10 Print

Distributor for Abingdon (South Africa); Eagle (South Africa); Highland (South Africa); Upper Room Books (South Africa); WCC (South Africa); Westminster/John Knox (South Africa)
Bookshop(s): PO Box 1452, Benoni 1500 *E-mail:* methbeno@iafrica.com; PO Box 130430, Bryanston 2074 *E-mail:* methran@iafrica.com; PO Box 708, Cape Town 8000 *E-mail:* methcape@iafrica.com; PO Box 108, Durban 4000; PO Box 8508, Johannesburg 2000; PO Box 1042, Kimberley 8300; 164 Chapel St, Pietermaritzburg 3200 *E-mail:* bookworms@futurenet.co.za

Nasionale Boekhandel Ltd
386 Voortekker Rd, Parow 7500
Mailing Address: PO Box 150, 7500 Parow
Tel: (021) 5911131
Telex: 526951 SA *Cable:* Nasboek
Key Personnel
Group Man Dir: P J Botha
Founded: 1950
Subjects: Education, Medicine, Nursing, Dentistry
Subsidiaries: Cape Booksellers Ltd: Human & Rousseau (Pty) Ltd; Nasboek (Natal) Ltd; Nasionale Boekwinkels Bpk; Nasou Ltd; Nasou Oudiovista; Natal Booksellers Ltd; J L van Schaik (Pty) Ltd; Van Schaik's Bookstore (Pty) Ltd; Tafelberg Publishers Ltd; Via Afrika Ltd; Via Afrika (Bophuthatswana) Ltd; Via Afrika (Ciskei) Ltd; Via Afrika (OFS) Ltd; Via Afrika (Transkei) Ltd, Umtata; Via Afrika (Lebowa) Ltd; Rygill's Educational Suppliers; Heer Printers (Pty) Ltd, Pretoria (all in Republic of South Africa); Nasionale Boekhandel (SWA) (Pty) Ltd
Book Club(s): Leserskring (Leisure Books)

Nasou - Oudiovista
Posbus 5197, Cape Town 8000
Tel: (012) 4063001; (012) 3429971 *Fax:* (012) 4062922
E-mail: nasouhk@nbh.naspers.co.za *Cable:* NASOU OUDIOVISTA
Key Personnel
Man Dir: W R van der Vyver
Head: P C Fouche
Founded: 1969
Subjects: Education
ISBN Prefix(es): 0-625; 0-7994
Parent Company: Nasionale Boekhandel Ltd

Nasou Via Afrika+
44 Hertzog Blvd, Cape Town 8001
Mailing Address: PO Box 5197, Cape Town 8000
Tel: (021) 406-3314 *Fax:* (021) 406-2922; (021) 406-3086
E-mail: MdeWitt@nasou.com
Web Site: www.nasou-viaafrika.com *Cable:* Via Afrika
Key Personnel
General Manager: D H Schroeder
  E-mail: dschroed@nasou.com
Senior Manager, Publishing: G Niebuhr
  Fax: (021) 406-3086 *E-mail:* gniebuhr@nasou.com
Marketing Manager: T Priem *Fax:* (021) 406-3086 *E-mail:* tpriem@nasou.com
Founded: 1970
Subjects: Fiction, Poetry, Science (General), Social Sciences, Sociology, Technology
ISBN Prefix(es): 0-86817; 0-625; 0-7994
Total Titles: 1,500 Print
Parent Company: National Education Group
Ultimate Parent Company: NASPERS
Imprints: Acacia Books; Afritech; Afro; Atlas; Bateleur; KZN Books
Bookshop(s): Western Cape, PO Box 487, Bellville 7535 *Tel:* (021) 918-8500 *Fax:* (021) 951-4731; Free State, PO Box 1058, Bloemfontein 9300 *Tel:* (051) 448-2345; Eastern Cape, 114 Adderley St, Cradock 5880 *Tel:* (048881) 3554; (0431) 43-3322 *Fax:* (048881) 3431; Eastern Cape, Loxford House, Hill St, 3rd fl, PO Box 1163, East London 5200 *Tel:* (0431) 43-9914; Western Cape, PO Box 82, George 6530 *Tel:* (044) 873-2812 *Fax:* (044) 873-2811; Eastern Cape, PO Box 147, Lusikisiki 4820 *Tel:* (039) 46-1364 *Fax:* (039) 46-1606
Warehouse: Berry Erasmus St, Berlin 5660 *Tel:* (043) 685 2461
PO Box 333, Butterworth 4960 *Tel:* (0474) 3334; 4193 *Fax:* (0474) 3611
PO Box 279, East London 5200 *Tel:* (0431) 43-3403 *Fax:* (0431) 43-1592
PO Box 135, Engcobo 5059 *Tel:* (0472) 48-1288 *Fax:* (0472) 48-1693
PO Box 17, Giyani 0826 *Tel:* (0158) 2-3322 *Fax:* (0158) 2-3322
16 Hope St, Kokstad 4700 *Tel:* (037) 727-2372; 2374 *Fax:* (037) 727-2313
16D Carrington St, Mafikeng 2745 *Tel:* (0140) 81-6122
North West, Private Bag X2136, Mafikeng 2745 *Tel:* (0140) 81-2801; 81-0674 *Fax:* (0140) 81-2970
PO Box 99, Mothibistad 8474 *Tel:* (01404) 3-1772 *Fax:* (01404) 3-1772
PO Box 420, Mount Frere 5090 *Tel:* (039) 255-0215
PO Box 2940, Newcastle 2940 *Tel:* (03431) 2-6191 *Fax:* (03431) 2-9523
Northern Province, PO Box 248, Pietersburg 0700 *Tel:* (015) 297-1082 *Fax:* (015) 297-1083
39 Yster St, PO Box 248, Pietersburg 0700 *Tel:* (015) 293-1178 *Fax:* (015) 293-0078
Rygill's, PO Box 556, Pinetown 3600 *Tel:* (031) 701-8201 *Fax:* (031) 701-8300
PO Box 95, Port Elizabeth 6000 *Tel:* (041) 54-2245 *Fax:* (041) 57-1798
PO Box 9296, Queenstown 5320 *Tel:* (0451) 8-3017/8-2728 *Fax:* (0451) 8-2691
Gauteng, PO Box 3626, Randburg 2125 *Tel:* (011) 792-2213 *Fax:* (011) 792-2239
PO Box 104, Sterkspruit 9762 *Tel:* (051) 611-0105
Vulindlela Heights, Errol Spring St, Umtata 5100 *Tel:* (0471) 2-2565; 31-0346; 31-3079 *Fax:* (0471) 2-4405
PO Box 259, Umtata 5100 *Tel:* (0471) 2-4406 *Fax:* (0471) 2-4405

National Botanical Institute
c/o Publications, PB X101, Pretoria 0001
Tel: (012) 804-3200 *Fax:* (012) 804-3211
E-mail: rpub@nbipre.nbi.ac.za
Web Site: www.nbi.ac.za
Key Personnel
Head Research, Support Services & Publications: M Joubert *E-mail:* mf@nbipre.nbi.ac.za
Directed toward research & conservation in the botanical field.
Subjects: Biological Sciences, Environmental Studies, Gardening, Plants, Natural History, Science (General)
ISBN Prefix(es): 0-9583205; 1-874907; 1-919684
Total Titles: 100 Print
Distributor for Briza Publications

New Africa Books (Pty) Ltd+
Formerly David Philip Publishers
99 Garfield Rd, Claremont, Cape Town 7700
Mailing Address: PO Box 23408, Claremont, Cape 7735
Tel: (021) 6744136 *Fax:* (021) 6743358
E-mail: newafrica@naep.co.za; orders@dpp.co.za (ordering)
Web Site: www.dpp.co.za
Key Personnel
Man Dir: Brian Wafawarowa
Marketing Manager: Dave Chislett
  E-mail: dave@dpp.co.za
Marketing Administrator: Erica Wicomb
  E-mail: erica@naep.co.za

Founded: 1971
Member of PASA.
Subjects: Agriculture, Anthropology, Archaeology, Architecture & Interior Design, Biography, Child Care & Development, Cookery, Developing Countries, Drama, Theater, Economics, Education, English as a Second Language, Environmental Studies, Fiction, Government, Political Science, History, Humor, Literature, Literary Criticism, Essays, Natural History, Nonfiction (General), Photography, Poetry, Publishing & Book Trade Reference, Regional Interests, Women's Studies
ISBN Prefix(es): 1-919876; 0-86486
Ultimate Parent Company: New Africa Investments Ltd
Imprints: Africasouth Paperbacks; David Philip; New Africa Education; Spearhead
Branch Office(s)
PO Box 32328, Braamfontein 2017 *Tel:* (011) 727 7062 *Fax:* (011) 727 7063
526 16 Rd, Constantia Sq, Halfway House, Midrand, Johannesburg, Gillian Temple *Tel:* (011) 805-6096 *Fax:* (011) 805-1622
E-mail: patience.tsotetsi@jhb.dpp.co.za
Distributed by Africa Book Centre
Distributor for James Currey (Johannesburg); Christopher Hurst; Oneworld Publications; Zed Books

New Africa Education, *imprint of* New Africa Books (Pty) Ltd

Oceanographic Research Institute
PO Box 10712, Marine Parade, Durban 4056
Tel: (031) 3373536 *Fax:* (031) 3372132
E-mail: seaworld@dbn.lia.net; ori@superbowl.und.ac.za; seaworld@neptune.lia.co.za
Key Personnel
Dir: Dr A J de Freitas
Librarian: Mrs A B D Kleu
Founded: 1951
Library services, exchange of scientific publications.
Subjects: Biological Sciences, Environmental Studies, Natural History, Science (General), Marine Biology, Conservation, Fisheries, Coastal Management, Pollution Studies
ISBN Prefix(es): 0-86989
Total Titles: 1 Print
Parent Company: South African Association of Marine Biological Research
Associate Companies: Sea World, Durban
  Tel: (031) 3373536 *Fax:* (031) 3372132
Distributed by Oceanographic Research Institute

Oudiovista Productions (Pty) Ltd, see Nasou - Oudiovista

Outlines, *imprint of* College of Careers (Pty) Ltd

Peachpit Press, *imprint of* Pearson Education (Prentice Hall)

Pearson Education (Prentice Hall)
Mill St, 8010 Cape Town
Mailing Address: PO Box 12122, Cape Town 7700
Tel: (021) 686 6356 *Fax:* (021) 686 4590
E-mail: firstname@mml.co.za
Key Personnel
Man Dir: Marian DeWet
Publisher, Higher Education: Hanli Venter
Founded: 1994
Distributes Prentice Hall titles in South Africa. Publish & distribute our subsidiaries. Specialize in higher education..
Subjects: Education
Parent Company: Pearson Plc
Associate Companies: Maskew Miller Longman (Pty) Ltd, Howard Dr, PO Box 96, Cape Town 8000, Man Dir: Fathima Dada *Tel:* (021) 5137750 *Fax:* (021) 5314049
Imprints: Addison Wesley Longman; Appleton Lange; Benjamin Cummings; Casselt Elt; Charles Merrill; De Jager Haum; Ellis Horwood; G K Hall; Harvester Wheatsheaf; Jossey Bass; Kagiso; Longman; Maskew Miller Longman; Peachpit Press; PH Macmillan ELT; PH Macmillan College; PH Macmillan Reference; Prentice Hall; Prentice Hall (Australia); Prentice Hall (Canada); Prentice Hall (Europe); Prentice Hall International; Prentice Hall (South Africa); Que College; Regents Prentice Hall; Schirmer; Scribner Reference; Woodhead Faulkner; Financial Times-Pitman
Showroom(s): Maskew Miller Longman (Midrand)

Pearson Education South Africa, *imprint of* Maskew Miller Longman

Perskor, *imprint of* Maskew Miller Longman

Perskor Books (Pty) Ltd
Postbus 3068, Halfway House 1685
Tel: (011) 3153647 *Fax:* (011) 3152757
Telex: 83561; 87483 *Cable:* Vaderland
Key Personnel
Man Dir: F Wessels
Editorial, Rights & Permissions: P V Heerden
Sales: S J Fourie
Production: A Bothma
Publicity: S Kloppers
Founded: 1940
Subjects: Education, Law
ISBN Prefix(es): 0-628
Subsidiaries: Educum Publishers Ltd; Perskor Publishers
Bookshop(s): Johannesburgse Boekwinkel; Perskor Bookshop
Book Club(s): Klub 707; Klub-Dagbreek; Klub Saffier
Orders to: Perskor-Boekwinkel, 4 Banfield Rd, Industrial North, Maraisburg 1700

PH Macmillan College, *imprint of* Pearson Education (Prentice Hall)

PH Macmillan ELT, *imprint of* Pearson Education (Prentice Hall)

PH Macmillan Reference, *imprint of* Pearson Education (Prentice Hall)

David Philip, *imprint of* New Africa Books (Pty) Ltd

David Philip Publishers, see New Africa Books (Pty) Ltd

Phumelela, *imprint of* Maskew Miller Longman

Prentice Hall, *imprint of* Maskew Miller Longman

Prentice Hall, *imprint of* Pearson Education (Prentice Hall)

Prentice Hall (Australia), *imprint of* Pearson Education (Prentice Hall)

Prentice Hall Australia, *imprint of* Maskew Miller Longman

Prentice Hall (Canada), *imprint of* Pearson Education (Prentice Hall)

Prentice Hall (Europe), *imprint of* Pearson Education (Prentice Hall)

Prentice Hall Europe, *imprint of* Maskew Miller Longman

Prentice Hall International, *imprint of* Pearson Education (Prentice Hall)

Prentice Hall (South Africa), *imprint of* Pearson Education (Prentice Hall)

Prentice Hall South Africa, *imprint of* Maskew Miller Longman

Publitoria Publishers+
PO Box 23334, Innesdale, Pretoria 0031
Tel: (012) 3290313 *Fax:* (012) 3290306
Key Personnel
Man Dir: L S van der Walt
Founded: 1982
Subjects: Education, Poetry
ISBN Prefix(es): 0-86880; 1-874991

Publitoria Editions
PO Box 23334, Innesdale, Pretoria 0031
Tel: (012) 3290313 *Fax:* (012) 3290306
Key Personnel
Man Dir: L S van der Walt
Founded: 1971
Also acts as Bookseller & Library Supplier.
Subjects: Education
ISBN Prefix(es): 0-86880; 1-874991

QUE College, *imprint of* Maskew Miller Longman

Que College, *imprint of* Pearson Education (Prentice Hall)

Queillerie Publishers+
PO Box 616, Gruenpunt, Cape Town 8051
Tel: (021) 4063326 *Fax:* (021) 4063111
E-mail: queiller@nbh.naspers.co.za
Key Personnel
Manager: Frederik de Jager
Founded: 1992
Member of Publishers Association of South Africa (PASA).
Subjects: Biography, Business, Cookery, Fiction, Gay & Lesbian, Human Relations, Labor, Industrial Relations, Nonfiction (General)
ISBN Prefix(es): 0-7958; 1-919710
Parent Company: Nasionale Boekhandel
Associate Companies: Tafelberg Publ; Human & Rousseau Publ; Kwela Books; J L Van Schaik; Nasou Via Afrika; Leo Books; Leisure Hour; Jonathan Ball Publishers; Van Schaik Bookstore
Branch Office(s)
Cape Town
Shipping Address: Nasionale Boekhandel, PO Box 487, Bellville 7535
Warehouse: Nasionale Boekhandel, PO Box 487, Bellville 7535
Orders to: Nasionale Boekhandel, PO Box 487, Bellville 7535

Ravan Press (Pty) Ltd+
104 Bordeaux Dr, PO Box 145, Randburg, Johannesburg 2125
Tel: (011) 7897636 *Fax:* (011) 7897653
Key Personnel
General Manager: Monica Seeber
Sales, Publicity & Rights: Ipuseng Kotsokoane
Book Design, Production: Matthew Seal
Founded: 1972
Member of the Publishers Association of South Africa.

Subjects: Anthropology, Biography, Business, Economics, Education, Environmental Studies, Ethnicity, Fiction, Government, Political Science, History, Labor, Industrial Relations, Management, Music, Dance, Nonfiction (General), Social Sciences, Sociology, Women's Studies
ISBN Prefix(es): 0-86975
Parent Company: Hodder & Stoughton Educational Southern Africa
Distributed by Hodder & Stoughton Educationa (Europe & UK); Ohio University Press (USA)
Warehouse: PSD, PO Box 15016, Hurlyvale 1611

Read Well Publishers
Business Centre Arcade, 66-C Landdros Marc St, Pietersburg 0700
Mailing Address: PO Box 4573, Pietersburg 0700
Tel: (0152) 2952193 *Fax:* (0152) 2952194
Key Personnel
Contact: Johannes Matemane
ISBN Prefix(es): 1-874921

Reader's Digest Southern Africa+
Private Bag X4, 8003 Capemail
Tel: (021) 4405145 *Fax:* (021) 4405401
Web Site: www.readersdigest.co.za
Key Personnel
Man Dir: Barry Lloyd *Fax:* (021) 6706204
  E-mail: barry@heritage.co.za
Editorial, Books & Rights & Permissions: D O Oakes *Tel:* (021) 6706252 *Fax:* (021) 6706203
  E-mail: dongie.oakes@readersdigest.com
Editorial, Magazines: A Spencer-Smith *Tel:* (021) 6706182 *E-mail:* tony.spencer-smith@readersdigest.com
Financial Dir: Jeff Mann *Tel:* (021) 6702789 *Fax:* (021) 6706209 *E-mail:* jeff.mann@readersdigest.com
Marketing, Publicity, Dir: Philip Bateman *Tel:* (021) 6702690 *Fax:* (021) 618763
  E-mail: philip@heritage.co.za
Sr Project Editor: Sandy Shepherd *Tel:* (021) 6706255 *E-mail:* sandy.shepherd@readersdigest.com
Direct mail books & catalogs.
Subjects: Computer Science, Cookery, Gardening, Plants, Health, Nutrition, Medicine, Nursing, Dentistry, Nonfiction (General), Travel
ISBN Prefix(es): 1-874912
Number of titles published annually: 5 Print
Total Titles: 53 Print
Parent Company: Reader's Digest Association, PO Box 235, Pleasantville, NY 10570, United States
Ultimate Parent Company: Heritage Collection Holdings Ltd
Imprints: AA The Motorist Publications
Branch Office(s)
Johannesburg Advertising Office, John Annandale *Tel:* (011) 799 2907 *Fax:* (011) 799 2999
Distributed by R D Vainons
Foreign Rights: Leigh Rautenbach (Southern Africa)
Warehouse: 8 Moorsom Ave, Epping 2 7475, Omar Kahaar *Fax:* (021) 548446 *E-mail:* omarwdmkahaar@heritage.co.za

Regents Prentice Hall, *imprint of* Maskew Miller Longman

Regents Prentice Hall, *imprint of* Pearson Education (Prentice Hall)

Renaissance, *imprint of* Tafelberg Publishers Ltd

Rostrum, see HAUM (Hollandsch Afrikaansche Uitgevers Maatschappij)

SA Kultuubeleggings, see Ensiklopedie Afrikana

Sable Media, see Struik Publishers (Pty) Ltd

Sached, *imprint of* Maskew Miller Longman

Sasavona Publishers & Booksellers
Private Bag X8, Braamfontein, Johannesburg 2017
Tel: (011) 4032502 *Fax:* (011) 3397274
Key Personnel
Manager: A E Kalteurider
Founded: 1974 (1875 as Swiss Mission Publishing)
Subjects: Education, Literature, Literary Criticism, Essays, Religion - Other
ISBN Prefix(es): 0-907985; 0-949985
Parent Company: Evangelical Presbyterian Church - Swiss Mission in SA, Private Bag X8, Braamfontein, Johannesburg 2017
Imprints: CMP Reprints; Sasavona Books; Swiss Mission Publications

Sasavona Books, *imprint of* Sasavona Publishers & Booksellers

Schirmer, *imprint of* Pearson Education (Prentice Hall)

Scribner, *imprint of* Maskew Miller Longman

Scribner Reference, *imprint of* Pearson Education (Prentice Hall)

Shuter & Shooter (Pty) Ltd
PO Box 618, Ferndale 2160
Tel: (011) 7928363 *Fax:* (011) 7927024
Cable: SHUSHOO
Key Personnel
Man Dir: M N Prozesky
Editorial, Rights & Permissions: J Inglis
Sales: D Ryder
Publicity: T Hepworth
Production: J Sharpe
Founded: 1925
Subjects: Biography, Ethnicity, History, Nonfiction (General), Science (General), Social Sciences, Sociology, Technology
ISBN Prefix(es): 0-947476; 0-7960; 0-86985
Parent Company: The Natal Witness (Pty) Ltd
Associate Companies: Ikhwezi Publishers, PO Box 648, Umtata 5100 *Tel:* (0471) 23988 *Fax:* (0471) 22786; Reach Out Publishers (at above address)
Subsidiaries: Shuter & Shooter (Gazankulu) (Pty) Ltd; Shuter & Shooter (Transkei) (Pty) Ltd
Branch Office(s)
219 Werdmuller Centre, Main Rd, Claremont, Cape Town 7700
2nd floor, Pharmacy House, 26 Juta St, Braamfontein 2017
O & S Building, Shop 18E, 18 Witklip St, Ladanna 0704
19 Fifth Avenue, Walmer 6070

South African Institute of International Affairs+
PO Box 31596, Braamfontein, Johannesburg 2017
Tel: (011) 3392021 *Fax:* (011) 3392154
E-mail: 160mig@cosmos.wds.ac.za
Web Site: www.wits.ac.za/saiia.htm
Key Personnel
National Dir: Dr Greg Mills *E-mail:* saiiagen@global.co.za
Founded: 1934
Subjects: Economics, Foreign Countries, Government, Political Science, Military Science
ISBN Prefix(es): 1-874890
Branch Office(s)
Cape Town, Mr Alan Harvey *Tel:* (021) 788-9295 *Fax:* (021) 788-9261

Durban, John Dickson *Tel:* (031) 201-4877 *Fax:* (031) 201-4914
Grahamstown
Pietermaritzburg
Port Elizabeth, Mr Peter Warmington *Tel:* (0331) 940381 *Fax:* (0331) 942332
Pretoria, Roland Henwood *Tel:* (012) 420-2687 *Fax:* (012) 420-3886
Witwatersrand, Philip Clayton *Tel:* (011) 636-2904 *Fax:* (011) 636-0512

South African Institute of Race Relations
PO Box 31044, Braamfontein 2017
Tel: (011) 4033600 *Fax:* (011) 4033671
E-mail: sairr@milkyway.co.za
Key Personnel
Dir: J S Kane-Berman
Founded: 1929
Specialize in Human Rights.
Subjects: Agriculture, Business, Ethnicity, Government, Political Science, Human Relations, Law, Public Administration, Social Sciences, Sociology
ISBN Prefix(es): 0-86982

Southern Book Publishers (Pty) Ltd+
Struik House, 7 Wessel Rd, Rivonia 2128
Mailing Address: P O Box 3103, Halfway House 1685
Tel: (011) 3153633 *Fax:* (011) 3153810
E-mail: Southern@struik.co.za
Key Personnel
Man Dir: C F B Van Rooyen
Editorial, Rights & Permissions: Louise Grantham
Local Sales, Publicity: Jane Winters
Production: Renee Ferreira
Office Manager: Bernice Janse Van Rensburg
  E-mail: bernicejvr@struik.co.za
Founded: 1987
Subjects: Animals, Pets, Gardening, Plants, Health, Nutrition, How-to, Natural History, Nonfiction (General), Travel
ISBN Prefix(es): 1-86812
Distributed by New Holland Publishers
Warehouse: SDC, PO Box 193, Maitland
Orders to: SDC, PO Box 193, Maitland

Spearhead, *imprint of* New Africa Books (Pty) Ltd

Struik Christian Books, see Struik Publishers (Pty) Ltd

Struik Publishers (Pty) Ltd+
PO Box 1144, Cape Town 8000
Tel: (021) 517128; (021) 462-4360 *Fax:* (021) 462-4379 *Cable:* DEKENA CAPETOWN
Key Personnel
Man Dir: Dick Wilkins
Sales Dir: Reinhard Marx
Founded: 1962
Subjects: Child Care & Development, Cookery, Environmental Studies, Foreign Countries, Gardening, Plants, Natural History
ISBN Prefix(es): 0-86977; 0-947458
Parent Company: The Struik Publishing Group (Pty) Ltd, PO Box 1144, Cape Town 8000
Associate Companies: Map Studio, PO Box 62, Bergvlei 2012; Struik Book Distributors; Struik Christian Books, PO Box 1144, Cape Town 8000; Sable Media, PO Box 1144, Cape Town 8000
Imprints: Timmins Publishers (Pty) Ltd
Subsidiaries: Timmins; Struik-Winchester
Distributed by National Book Distributors; New Holland Publishers
Warehouse: Struik Book Distributors, Graph Ave, Montague Gardens 7441

Struik-Winchester, see Struik Publishers (Pty) Ltd

SOUTH AFRICA

Swiss Mission Publications, *imprint of* Sasavona Publishers & Booksellers

Symbol Books, *imprint of* LAPA Publishers (Pty) Ltd

Tafelberg Publishers Ltd+
PO Box 879, Cape Town 8000
Tel: (021) 4241320 *Fax:* (021) 4241320
E-mail: tafelberg@tafelberg.com
Web Site: www.tafelberg.com *Cable:* BOEKNUUS CAPE TOWN
Key Personnel
General Manager: Harres Van Zyl
Founded: 1950
Tafelberg Publishes forms in African literature, author & political publications, books for young children & young readers in all the official languages & a wide variety of illustrated non-fiction.
Subjects: Cookery, Crafts, Games, Hobbies, Fiction, Gardening, Plants, Nonfiction (General), Romance
ISBN Prefix(es): 0-624
Number of titles published annually: 100 Print; 1 CD-ROM
Total Titles: 1,200 Print; 1 CD-ROM
Parent Company: Nasionale Boekhandel Ltd
Ultimate Parent Company: Nasionale Publisher
Imprints: Homeros; Jasmyn; Renaissance

Target Publishers (Edms) Bpk
PO Box 22688, Klerksdorp 2570
Tel: (018) 4627556 *Fax:* (018) 4627557
ISBN Prefix(es): 0-9583132

Taurus+
PO Box 39400, Bramley 2018
Tel: 7860018
Key Personnel
Chief Executive: Tienie du Plessis; Hans Pienaar; Gerrit Olivier; John Miles; Ampie Coetzee
Founded: 1975
ISBN Prefix(es): 0-947046
Parent Company: Licomil Co (Pty) Ltd

Thomson Publications
PO Box 56182, Pinegowrie 2123
Tel: (011) 7892144 *Fax:* (011) 7893196
ISBN Prefix(es): 0-9583086; 0-9583865
Parent Company: Times Media Ltd

Timmins Publishers (Pty) Ltd, *imprint of* Struik Publishers (Pty) Ltd

Unibook, *imprint of* Maskew Miller Longman

Unisa Press+
PO Box 392, Pretoria 0001
Tel: (012) 4293549 *Fax:* (012) 4293221
E-mail: moolmsj@alpha.unisa.ac.za; kempg@alpha.unisa.ac.za
Web Site: www.unisa.ac.za/dept/press/index.html
Cable: UNISA
Key Personnel
Head, Unisa Press: Mrs P Van Der Walt
Tel: (012) 429 3051 *E-mail:* vdwp@alpha.unisa.ac.za
Head of Publishing & Secretary International Rights: Ms S J Moolman *Tel:* (012) 429 3023
Founded: 1973
Specialize in academic publications.
Subjects: Economics, Education, History, Language Arts, Linguistics, Law, Nonfiction (General), Psychology, Psychiatry, Theology
ISBN Prefix(es): 0-86981; 1-86888
Total Titles: 128 Print
Parent Company: University of South Africa Pretonia
Orders to: The Business Section, Unisa Press, PO Box 392, Pretoria 0002

United Protestant Publishers (Pty) Ltd, see Lux Verbi (Pty) Ltd

University of Durban-Westville Library
PB X54001, Durban 4000
Tel: (031) 8202640; (031) 2045058 *Fax:* (031) 821873
Telex: 623228
Key Personnel
Chief Librarian: M Moodley *E-mail:* mmoodley@pixie.udw.ac.za
ISBN Prefix(es): 0-949947; 0-947445

University of Natal Press+
P B X01, Scottsville, Pietermaritzburg 3209
Tel: (0331) 2605226; (0331) 2605225 *Fax:* (0331) 2605599
E-mail: books@press.unp.ac/za; moberly@press.unp.ac.za
Key Personnel
Publisher: Glenn Cowley
Founded: 1947
Member of PASA (Publishers Association of South Africa).
Subjects: History, Literature, Literary Criticism, Essays, Natural History, Regional Interests, Women's Studies
ISBN Prefix(es): 0-86980
Imprints: Hadeda Books; Killie Campbell Africana Library
Distributed by Africa Book Centre (London); David Phillip Publishers (Republic of South Africa); International Specialist Book Services (USA)

University Publishers & Booksellers (Pty) Ltd
PO Box 29, Stellenbosch 7600
Tel: (021) 8870337 *Fax:* (021) 8832975
Cable: Biblia Stellenbosch
Key Personnel
Man Dir: B B Liebenberg
Founded: 1947
Subjects: Nonfiction (General)
ISBN Prefix(es): 0-86995

Van Schaik Publishers+
1064 Arcadia St, 1st floor, Hatfield 0083
Tel: (012) 342-2765 *Fax:* (012) 430-3563
E-mail: vanschaik@vanschaiknet.com
Web Site: www.vanschaiknet.com
Key Personnel
General Manager: Eloise Wessels
E-mail: ewessels@vanschaiknet.com
Founded: 1914
Specialize in publishing high-quality academic texts at affordable prices. Aim to provide academic content in any form, combination or format.
Subjects: Business, Economics, Education, Government, Political Science, History, Labor, Industrial Relations, Language Arts, Linguistics, Management, Medicine, Nursing, Dentistry, Public Administration, Social Sciences, Sociology, Natural Sciences
ISBN Prefix(es): 0-627
Number of titles published annually: 20 Print; 3 CD-ROM; 1 Online
Total Titles: 800 Print; 3 CD-ROM; 1 Online; 6 Audio
Ultimate Parent Company: Naspers
Imprints: Van Schaik Publishers Academica
Distributed by Van Schaik Publishers
Distributor for Jacana
Bookshop(s): Van Schaik Books
Warehouse: On the Dot Distribution, PO Box 487, Bellville, Marietha Van Wyk *Tel:* (021) 918 8500 *Fax:* (021) 951 4903
E-mail: mjvanwy@naspers.com
Orders to: PO Box 487, Bellville 7535, Madelyn Momsen *Tel:* (021) 918 8604 *Fax:* (021) 951 4903 *E-mail:* mmomsen@naspers.com

J P van der Walt & Son (Pty) Ltd, see LAPA Publishers (Pty) Ltd

Van Schaik Publishers Academica, *imprint of* Van Schaik Publishers

Vivlia Publishers & Booksellers+
One Amanda Avenue, Lea Glen Florida
Mailing Address: PO Box 4180, Randburg 2125
Tel: (011) 472-3912 *Fax:* (011) 472-4904
E-mail: vivlia@icon.co.ta
Key Personnel
Man Dir: Albert N Nemukula
National Sales & Mktg: S Mota
Editorial Service Mgr: G Nose
Founded: 1990 (To serve the disadvantaged group & publish mainly South African, 11 official languages)
Services schools & libraries.
Subjects: Education, Literature, Literary Criticism, Essays, Mathematics, Science (General)
ISBN Prefix(es): 0-9583125; 1-86867; 1-874868
Total Titles: 15 Print
Branch Office(s)
Surban, PO Box 72836, Mobeni, F Gumeoe *Tel:* (083) 267 3923
Umtata, 17 TT Mangala St, South Riose Park, Umtata, Z Maqabuka *Tel:* (083) 286 0917
Distributor for Africa World Press Inc
Showroom(s): Africa Book Centre, 38 King St, London, United Kingdom, A W Zurburg *Tel:* (020) 7497 0309

Vlaeberg, *imprint of* Maskew Miller Longman

Waterkant-Uitgewers (Edms) Bpk
33 Waterkant St, Posbus 4539, Cape Town 8000
Tel: (021) 215540 *Fax:* (021) 4191865
Key Personnel
Man Dir: W J van Zijl
Publicity: Mrs E M Volschenk
Founded: 1980
Subjects: Religion - Other
ISBN Prefix(es): 0-907992; 1-875081
Parent Company: Lux Verbi (Pty) Ltd
Associate Companies: Waterkant Publishers

Who's Who of Southern Africa
PO Box 411697, Craighall, Johannesburg 2024
Tel: (011) 8802406 *Fax:* (011) 8802366
Key Personnel
Editor: S V Hayes *E-mail:* shayes@jonathanball.co.za
Founded: 1907
Total Titles: 1 Print
Parent Company: Jonathan Ball Publishers SA

Witwatersrand University Press+
One Jan Smuts Ave, Johannesburg 2000
Mailing Address: PO Wits, Johannesburg 2050
Tel: (011) 4845907 *Fax:* (011) 4845971
E-mail: wup@iafrica.com
Web Site: www.wirs.oc.za/wup.html
Telex: 427125 SA
Key Personnel
Dir: Pat Tucker *Tel:* (011) 4845910
Commissioning Editor: Hyreath Anderson
Founded: 1922
Scholarly publisher specializing in the Humanities.
Member of Publisher's Association of South Africa.
Subjects: Anthropology, Archaeology, Business, Drama, Theater, History, Literature, Literary

Criticism, Essays, Medicine, Nursing, Dentistry, Natural History, Religion - Jewish
ISBN Prefix(es): 1-86814
Number of titles published annually: 20 Print
Total Titles: 160 Print
Distributed by Africa Book Centre (UK & Europe)
Showroom(s): 23 Junction Ave, Parktown, Johannesburg
Orders to: Book Promotions, PO Box 5, Plumstead 7800, Marlene Morgan *Tel:* (021) 706 0949 *Fax:* (021) 706 0941 *E-mail:* orders@bookpro.ca.za

Woodhead Faulkner, *imprint of* Maskew Miller Longman

Spain

General Information

Capital: Madrid
Language: Castilian Spanish (official) is the most widely used. Also Basque in the north, Catalan in the northeast, Galician in the northwest
Religion: Roman Catholic
Population: 40 million
Bank Hours: 0900-1400 Monday-Friday; 0900-1300 Saturday
Shop Hours: 0900-1300, 1700-2000 Monday-Saturday
Currency: 100 Eurocents = 1 Euro; 166.386 Spanish pesetas = 1 Euro
Export/Import Information: Member of European Economic Community. Tariffs on books same as other EEC members. 4% VAT on books. Import license not required; foreign books subject to censorship. No exchange controls.
Copyright: UCC, Berne, Florence (see Copyright Conventions, pg xi)

A-Z Ediciones y Publications
Espronceda, 20, 28003 Madrid
SAN: 001-5148
Tel: (091) 4427793 *Fax:* (091) 4425940
Key Personnel
International Rights: Rosa Perez
Founded: 1995
Subjects: Literature, Literary Criticism, Essays
ISBN Prefix(es): 84-86575

Aache Ediciones
Avenida Constitucion, 33 bajo B, 19003 Guadalajara
SAN: 000-006X
Tel: (0949) 220 438
E-mail: ediciones@aache.com
Web Site: www.aache.com
Key Personnel
Dir: Antonio Herrera Casado
Specialize in Guadalajara (Spain) books.
ISBN Prefix(es): 84-87743

Publicacions de l'Abadia de Montserrat
Ausias March, 92-98, interior C, 08013 Barcelona
SAN: 004-668X
Tel: (093) 2450303; (093) 2657923; (093) 2430302 *Fax:* (093) 2473594
E-mail: pamsa@pamsa.com
Web Site: www.pamsa.com
Key Personnel
Administrator: Jordi Ubeda i Baulo
Dir: Josep Massot i Muntaner
Founded: 1914
Subjects: Biography, History, Literature, Literary Criticism, Essays, Philosophy, Religion - Catholic, Theology
ISBN Prefix(es): 84-7202; 84-7826

Academia de la Llingua Asturiana
Apartau de Correos 574, E-33080 Uvieu
SAN: 000-0205
Mailing Address: C/ Marques de Santa Cruz 6-2, 33007 Uvieu/Oviedo Asturias
Tel: (098) 5211837 *Fax:* (098) 5226816
E-mail: alla@asturnet.es
Web Site: www.asturnet.es/alla
Key Personnel
President: Xose Lluis Garcia Arias
Founded: 1981
Subjects: Anthropology, Language Arts, Linguistics, Literature, Literary Criticism, Essays
ISBN Prefix(es): 84-8168
Orders to: Albora Llibros, Pz Romualdo Alvargonzalez 5, 33202 Xixon *Tel:* 85354213 *Fax:* 85354213

Acantilado+
Formerly Sirmio
Ferrar Valls i Taberner 8, 08006 Barcelona
Tel: (093) 2123808 *Fax:* (093) 4182317
E-mail: qcrema@mito.ibernet.com
Key Personnel
Man Dir: Jaume Vallcorba
Founded: 1989
Subjects: Art, Fiction, History, Literature, Literary Criticism, Essays, Philosophy, Poetry
ISBN Prefix(es): 84-7769
Parent Company: Quaderns Crema

Acantilado+
Subsidiary of Quaderns Crema
Muntaner, 462 3 1, 08006 Barcelona
Tel: (093) 4144906 *Fax:* (093) 4147107
E-mail: correo@elacantilado.com
Web Site: www.elacantilado.com
Key Personnel
Man Dir: Jaume Vallcorba
Founded: 1999
Subjects: History, Literature, Literary Criticism, Essays, Poetry, Narratives
ISBN Prefix(es): 84-95359; 84-930657
Number of titles published annually: 50 Print
Total Titles: 100 Print

Editorial Acanto SA
Bertran, 113, porta 2, 08023 Barcelona
SAN: 022-2322
Tel: (093) 4189093 *Fax:* (093) 4189088
E-mail: acanto@globalcom.es
Key Personnel
Editor: Silvia Blume
Founded: 1987
Subjects: Cookery, Crafts, Games, Hobbies, Gardening, Plants, Health, Nutrition, Sports, Athletics
ISBN Prefix(es): 84-86673

Acento Editorial+
Joaquin Turina 39, 28044 Madrid
SAN: 000-0361
Tel: (091) 5088996; (091) 5085145; (091) 4228800 *Fax:* (091) 5089927; (091) 5084974
E-mail: sm@hispanica.net
Key Personnel
Contact: MaPaz Serrano
Founded: 1993
Subjects: Fiction, How-to, Music, Dance, Nonfiction (General), Science (General), Self-Help, Travel
ISBN Prefix(es): 84-483

Editorial Acervo SL+
Juli Verne, 5-7, 08006 Barcelona
SAN: 022-2349
Tel: (093) 2122664 *Fax:* (093) 2122706
E-mail: editorial_acervo@hotmail.com
Key Personnel
Man Dir: Ana Perales
Founded: 1954
Subjects: History, Law, Literature, Literary Criticism, Essays, Science Fiction, Fantasy
ISBN Prefix(es): 84-7002
Total Titles: 1 Print

Editorial Acribia SA+
Royo Urieta 23, 50006 Zaragoza
SAN: 022-2357
Tel: (0976) 232089 *Fax:* (0976) 219212
E-mail: acribia@red3i.es
Key Personnel
Man Dir & other offices: Pascual Lopez Lorenzo
Founded: 1957
Subjects: Agriculture, Medicine, Nursing, Dentistry, Natural History, Science (General), Veterinary Science
ISBN Prefix(es): 84-200
Number of titles published annually: 30 Print
Total Titles: 980 Print

Centro de Estudios Adams-Ediciones Valbuena SA
Sagasta 23, 28004 Madrid
SAN: 002-046X
Tel: (091) 4459335 *Fax:* (091) 5933973
E-mail: adams@adams.es
Web Site: www.adams.es
Key Personnel
Director: Felix Perez Ruiz de Valbuena
Founded: 1957
Subjects: Accounting, Career Development, Computer Science, Labor, Industrial Relations, Psychology, Psychiatry, Public Administration, Transportation
ISBN Prefix(es): 84-7357; 84-8303

Editorial AEDOS SA+
Consell de Cent, 391, 08009 Barcelona
SAN: 022-2373
Tel: (093) 4883492 *Fax:* (093) 4877659
Key Personnel
Manager: Cristina Concellon
Founded: 1939
Subjects: Agriculture, Animals, Pets, Biological Sciences, Developing Countries, Earth Sciences, Economics, Energy, Environmental Studies, Foreign Countries, Human Relations, Labor, Industrial Relations, Management, Veterinary Science
ISBN Prefix(es): 84-7003
Parent Company: Mundiprensa Libros

AENOR (Asociacion Espanola de Normalizacion y Certificacion)+
Genova, 6, 28004 Madrid
Tel: (091) 914 32 60 00 *Fax:* (091) 913 10 40 32
E-mail: info@aenor.es
Web Site: www.aenor.es
Key Personnel
President: Manual Lopez Cachero
General Director: Ramon Naz Pajares
Dir of Operations: Avelino Brito Marquinas
Fax: (01) 913 10 31 72
Head of Publishing Dept: Silvia Sevilla
E-mail: ssevilla@aenor.es
Founded: 1986
Member of ISO, IEC, CEN, CENELEC, ETSI, COPANT, IQNET & GENE.
Subjects: Standardization & Certification
ISBN Prefix(es): 84-8143

Editorial Afers, SL+
La Llibertat, 12, Apartat de Correus 267, Catarroja, Valencia 46470
Tel: (096) 1268654 *Fax:* (096) 1272582
E-mail: afers@provicom.com
Web Site: www.provicom.com/afers
Key Personnel
Dir: Rafael Aracil i Marti i Josep Termes i Ardevol

Editorial Dir: Vicent S Olmos i Tamarit
 E-mail: vicent.olmos@provicom.com
Promotion & Rights: Tremedal Ortiz
Founded: 1985
Subjects: History, Regional Interests, Social Sciences, Sociology
ISBN Prefix(es): 84-86574
Foreign Rep(s): Agusti Colomines

Agata, *imprint of* Libsa Editorial SA

Agencia Espanola de Cooperacion
Av Reyes Catolicos, 4, 28040 Madrid
SAN: 001-6446
Tel: (091) 5838100; (091) 5838254; (091) 5838101; (091) 5838102 *Fax:* (091) 5838310; (091) 5838311; (091) 5838313
Key Personnel
Publishing Dir: Antonio Papell Cervera
Subjects: Art, Biography, Drama, Theater, Economics, Education, History, Law, Literature, Literary Criticism, Essays, Poetry, Social Sciences, Sociology
ISBN Prefix(es): 84-7232

Agora Editorial+
Carreteria 92, 29008 Malaga
SAN: 003-9683
Tel: (095) 2228699; (095) 2221847 *Fax:* (095) 2226411
Key Personnel
Publicity Dir: Antonio Gonzalez Alcalde
Commercial Dir: Jose Conzado Mora
Founded: 1979
Subjects: Literature, Literary Criticism, Essays, Mathematics
ISBN Prefix(es): 84-85698

Ediciones Agrotecnicas, SL
Seat of Spain 10 5 Izq, 28008 Madrid
SAN: 001-527X
Mailing Address: Plaza de Eskpana 10 5 Izq, 28008 Madrid
Tel: (091) 5175248; (091) 5473515 *Fax:* (091) 5474506
E-mail: agrotecnicas@agrotecnica.com
Web Site: www.agrotecnica.com
Subjects: Agriculture, Civil Engineering
ISBN Prefix(es): 84-87480
Subsidiaries: ISLA Agricola, SA

Editorial Aguaclara+
C/ Rosello, 55, 03010 Alacant
SAN: 002-242X
Tel: (096) 5240064 *Fax:* (096) 5259302
E-mail: edit.aguaclara@natural.es
Key Personnel
Dir: Luis T Bonmati Gutierrez
Founded: 1982
Subjects: Fiction, Literature, Literary Criticism, Essays, Poetry, Religion - Catholic
ISBN Prefix(es): 84-86234

Aguilar SA de Ediciones
Torrelaguna, 60, 28043 Madrid
SAN: 000-0779
Tel: (091) 7449060 *Fax:* (091) 7449093
E-mail: limarquezes@santillana.es
Web Site: www.gruposantillana.com
Telex: 47137 Agata *Cable:* GUILARDITOR
Key Personnel
President: Jesus de Polanco Gutierrez
Vice President: Francisco Perez Gonzalez
Dir General: Ambrosio Maria Ochoa Vazquez
Editorial Dir: Jaime Salinas Bonmati; Mauricio Santos Arrabal
Dir, Children's Books: Miguel Azaola
Sales Dir: Miguel Lendinez
Publisher of non-fiction books in Spanish.
Subjects: Art, Fiction, Geography, Geology, History, How-to, Humor, Journalism, Medicine, Nursing, Dentistry, Nonfiction (General), Philosophy, Religion - Other, Science (General), Self-Help, Travel
ISBN Prefix(es): 84-03
Branch Office(s)
Aguilar SA, Argentina
Isla Negra SA, Chile
Libreria Cientifica, Colombia
Edidac, Ecuador
Aguilar SA, Mexico
La Familia y Studium, Peru
Itaca SA
Editemas y Dilae SA, Venezuela

AITIM (Asociacion de Investigacion Tecnica de las industrias de la Madera y Corcho)+
Flora 3-2, 28013 Madrid
Tel: (091) 5425864 *Fax:* (091) 5590512
E-mail: informame@aitim.es
Web Site: www.aitim.es
Key Personnel
Dir: Fernando Peraza Sanchez; J Enrique Peraza Sanchez *E-mail:* e.peraza@aitim.es
Founded: 1964

Ediciones Akal SA+
Sector Foresta, 1, 28760 Tres Cantos, Madrid
SAN: 001-5326
Tel: (091) 6565611; (091) 6565157; (091) 8061996 *Fax:* (091) 6564911; (091) 8044028
E-mail: admon@akal.com
Key Personnel
Editor: Ramon Acal
International Rights: Juan Barja
Subjects: Anthropology, Archaeology, Architecture & Interior Design, Art, Asian Studies, Behavioral Sciences, Economics, Education, English as a Second Language, Film, Video, Law, Philosophy, Psychology, Psychiatry, Social Sciences, Sociology
ISBN Prefix(es): 84-460
Associate Companies: Ediciones Istmo

Editorial 'Alas'+
C/Villarroel No 124, Barcelona 08011
SAN: 002-2446
Mailing Address: Section 36,274, 08080 Barcelona
Tel: (093) 4537506; (093) 3233445 *Fax:* (093) 4537506
E-mail: sala@editorial-alas.com
Web Site: www.editorial-alas.com
Key Personnel
Contact: Jordi Sala
Founded: 1923
Specialize in sports subjects with emphasis on martial arts.
Subjects: Health, Nutrition, Parapsychology, Religion - Buddhist, Sports, Athletics, Martial arts
ISBN Prefix(es): 84-203

Alba, *imprint of* Libsa Editorial SA

Alberdania SL+
Istillaga plaza, 2 behea C, 20304 Irun, Gipuzkoa
SAN: 000-1201
Tel: (0943) 632814 *Fax:* (0943) 638055
E-mail: alberdania@ctv.es
Web Site: www.alberdania.com
Key Personnel
Contact: Jorge Gimenez Bech
Founded: 1993
Subjects: Anthropology, Art, Literature, Literary Criticism, Essays
ISBN Prefix(es): 84-95589

El Aleph Editores, *imprint of* Grup 62

El Aleph Editores
Imprint of Grup 62
Peu de la Creu, 4, 08001 Barcelona
Tel: (093) 443 71 00 *Fax:* (093) 443 71 30
E-mail: correu@grup62.com
Web Site: www.grup62.com
Key Personnel
Rights Manager: Laura Pujol

Alfaguara Ediciones SA - Grupo Santillana+
Torrelaguna, 60, 28043 Madrid
SAN: 001-5431
Tel: (091) 744 90 60 *Fax:* (091) 744 92 24
Web Site: www.alfaguara.santillana.es
Telex: 47137 Agata *Cable:* GUARA MADRID
Key Personnel
Man Dir: Guillermo Schavelzon
Editor: Amaya Elezcano
Editor Assistant: Asun Lasaosa
Rights & Permissions: Rosa Arrizabalaga
Founded: 1964
Subjects: Fiction, Literature, Literary Criticism, Essays, Travel
ISBN Prefix(es): 84-204
Subsidiaries: Alfaguara; Aguilar; Attea; El Pais-Aguilar; Taurus
Branch Office(s)
Santillana Publishing Co, 901 W Walnut St, Bldg A, Compton, CA 90220, United States

Ediciones Alfar SA
Centro Andaluz del Libro, Pol Ind La Chaparrilla, parcela 34-36, Carretera Sevilla-Malaga, KM 3, 41016 Sevilla
SAN: 001-544X
Tel: (05) 4406100; (05) 4406366; (05) 4406614 *Fax:* (05) 4402580
Key Personnel
President: Manuel Angel Vazquez Medel
Dir General: Manuel Diaz Vargas
Founded: 1982
Subjects: Anthropology, Archaeology, Behavioral Sciences, Fiction, History, Literature, Literary Criticism, Essays, Mathematics, Medicine, Nursing, Dentistry, Philosophy, Social Sciences, Sociology
ISBN Prefix(es): 84-7898; 84-8248; 84-86256

Edicions Alfons el Magnanim, Institucio Valenciana d'Estudis i Investigacio+
Corona, 36, 46003 Valencia
SAN: 002-0923
Tel: (06) 3883544; (06) 3883555 *Fax:* (06) 3883568
Web Site: www.alfonselmagnanim.com
Key Personnel
President: Fernando Giner
Vice President: Enrique Crespo
Dir: Agustin Andreu; Ricardo Belleveser
Subjects: Ethnicity, Government, Political Science, History, Social Sciences, Sociology
ISBN Prefix(es): 84-7822
Warehouse: Corona, 36, 46002 Valencia *Tel:* (06) 3912561; 3912562
Orders to: LLIG, Pl Manises, 3, 46003 Valencia *Tel:* (06) 3866170

Editorial Algazara+
Calle Albert Camus 1, 29002 Malaga
SAN: 002-2519
Tel: (095) 2358284 *Fax:* (095) 2333175
Founded: 1991
Member of Editors Association of Andalucia.
Subjects: History, Literature, Literary Criticism, Essays
ISBN Prefix(es): 84-87999

Alianza Editorial SA+
Division of General Edition
Juan Ignacio Luca de Tena, 15, 28027 Madrid
SAN: 000-1570
Tel: (091) 3938888 *Fax:* (091) 3207480
E-mail: alianza@anaya.es
Web Site: www.alianzaeditorial.es

PUBLISHERS

Key Personnel
Man Dir: Luis Sunen Garcia
Marketing: Ruth Zauner
Rights & Permissions: Laura Malejakis
Founded: 1965
Specialize in books for adults.
Subjects: Art, Fiction, Government, Political Science, History, Mathematics, Music, Dance, Philosophy, Poetry, Science (General), Social Sciences, Sociology
ISBN Prefix(es): 84-206
Parent Company: Grupo Anaya
Associate Companies: Alianza Editorial Argentina, Av Belgrano 355-Piso 10, Buenos Aires 1092, Argentina, Jorge Lafforgue *Tel:* (01) 4342 4426; Alianza Editorial Mexicana, 180 Remacimiento, Col San Juan Tlihuaca, Azcapotzalco 02400 DF, Mexico, Juan Carlos Arguelles *Tel:* (05) 561 8333 *Fax:* (05) 561 5231

Alinco SA - Aura Comunicacio
Placa Lesseps, 33, 08023 Barcelona
SAN: 000-5339
Tel: (093) 2172054 *Fax:* (093) 2373469
ISBN Prefix(es): 84-87711

Alta Fulla Editorial
Passatge Alio, 10, 08037 Barcelona
SAN: 000-1694
Mailing Address: Apdo 480 FD, 08080 Barcelona
Tel: (093) 4590708; (093) 4591363 *Fax:* (093) 2075203
E-mail: altafulla@altafulla.com
Web Site: www.altafulla.com
Key Personnel
Editor & Dir: Josep J Moli Cambray
Founded: 1977
Specialize in linguistics & paperback books.
Subjects: Anthropology, Architecture & Interior Design, Cookery, Crafts, Games, Hobbies, Economics, Mythology, Social Sciences, Sociology, Antropologia, Artes y Oficios, Cultura Popular, Etnografia, Facsimiles de Libros Antiguos, Folklore
ISBN Prefix(es): 84-85403; 84-86556; 84-7900

Altea, Taurus, Alfaguara SA
Torrelaguna, 60, 28043 Madrid
SAN: 005-0881
Tel: (091) 7449060 *Fax:* (091) 7449224
E-mail: clientes@santillana.es
Web Site: www.alfaguara.santillana.es
Key Personnel
Man Dir: Ambrosio Ochoa
Editorial: Jose Antonio Millan; Luis Sunen
Publicity & Promotion: Maria de Calonje
Rights & Permissions: Rosa Arrizabalaga
Founded: 1956
Subjects: Anthropology, Art, Biography, Education, Government, Political Science, History, Language Arts, Linguistics, Literature, Literary Criticism, Essays, Music, Dance, Philosophy
ISBN Prefix(es): 84-306; 84-372; 84-204

Ediciones Altera SL+
Comte d'Urgell, 64 1r 1a, 08011 Barcelona
SAN: 006-3428
Tel: (093) 4519537 *Fax:* (093) 4517441
E-mail: editorial@altera.net
Key Personnel
Commerical Manager: Mr Guillermo Losada
Founded: 1995
Subjects: Literature, Literary Criticism, Essays
ISBN Prefix(es): 84-920659; 84-89779
Number of titles published annually: 8 Print
Total Titles: 34 Print
Orders to: Prologo Distribuciones, Mascado 35, Bajas, 08032 Barcelona

Ambit Serveis Editorials, SA+
Consell de Cent, 282 Baixos, 08007 Barcelona
SAN: 000-183X
Tel: (093) 4881342 *Fax:* (093) 4874772
Key Personnel
Dir: Josep M A Benach Olivella
Founded: 1981
Subjects: Art, Cookery, Geography, Geology, Photography, Craftsmanship, Fine Arts, Nature
ISBN Prefix(es): 84-89681; 84-87342; 84-86147

Amnistia Internacional Editorial SL
Secretariado Estatal, Fernando VI, 8, 1º izda, 28004 Madrid
SAN: 002-2608
Tel: (091) 310 12 77 *Fax:* (091) 319 53 34
E-mail: amnistia.internacional@a-i.es
Web Site: www.a-i.es
Key Personnel
Dir: Cristina Martinez
Founded: 1987
Subjects: Developing Countries, Education, Foreign Countries, Government, Political Science, Law, Nonfiction (General), Regional Interests, Social Sciences, Sociology
ISBN Prefix(es): 84-86874
Branch Office(s)
AI-USA, 304 Pennsylvania Ave SE, Washington, DC, DC 20003, United States
Distributed by El Pais Aguilar; La Catarata

AMV Ediciones+
Calle Almansa 94, 28040 Madrid
Tel: (091) 5336926; (091) 5349368 *Fax:* (091) 5530286
Web Site: www.amvediciones.com
Key Personnel
Manager: Antonio Madrid Vicente
E-mail: amadrid@acta.es
Founded: 1986
Specialize also in cooling, heating & construction.
Subjects: Agriculture, Electronics, Electrical Engineering, Engineering (General), Gardening, Plants, Health, Nutrition, Medicine, Nursing, Dentistry, Science (General), Technology, Wine & Spirits
ISBN Prefix(es): 84-89922
Number of titles published annually: 15 Print; 1 CD-ROM
Total Titles: 90 Print; 3 CD-ROM

AMV Ediciones, see Ediciones A Madrid Vicente

Editorial Anagrama
Pedro de la Creu, 58, 08034 Barcelona
SAN: 022-2616
Tel: (093) 2037652 *Fax:* (093) 2037738
E-mail: anagrama@anagrama-ed.es
Web Site: www.anagrama-ed.es
Telex: 98753 Agram E
Key Personnel
Editor & Dir: Jorge de Herralde
Founded: 1968
Subjects: Anthropology, Literature, Literary Criticism, Essays, Philosophy, Psychology, Psychiatry, Social Sciences, Sociology
ISBN Prefix(es): 84-339

Ediciones Anaya SA+
Juan Ignacio Luca de Tena, 15, 28027 Madrid
Tel: (091) 393 86 00 *Fax:* (091) 320 91 29; (091) 742 66 31
E-mail: cga@anaya.es
Web Site: www.anaya.es
Telex: 22039 Anaya E *Cable:* Edinaya
Key Personnel
Chairman: Maria Isabel Andres Bravo
Vice President: Juan Jose Losada
Man Dir: Enrique Coque
Editorial, Rights & Permissions: Ramiro Sanchez
Sales: Antonio Gutierrez
Founded: 1959

SPAIN

Subjects: Education
ISBN Prefix(es): 84-207
Parent Company: Grupo Anaya, Juan Ignacio, Luca de Tena 15, 28027 Madrid
Associate Companies: Algaida Editores SA, Avda de San Francisco Javier s/n, Edificio Hermes, 41005 Seville, Juan Ignacio, Luca de Tena 15, 28027 Madrid; Ediciones Generales Anaya, Anaya Multimedia, Juan Ignacio, Luca de Tena 15, 28027 Madrid; Editorial Barcanova SA; Editorial Biblograf SA; Ediciones Catedra SA; Credsa, Calabria 108, 08015 Barcelona; Ediciones Piramide SA; Editorial Tecnos SA; Ediciones Versal SA; Edicions Xerais de Galicia, Doctor Maranon 10, 36211 Vigo

Anaya Educacion
Juan Ignacio Luca de Tena, 15, 28027 Madrid
Tel: (091) 393 86 00 *Fax:* (091) 742 66 31; (091) 320 91 29
E-mail: cga@anaya.es
Web Site: www.anaya.es
Key Personnel
Marketing Dir: Alejandro Sanchez
E-mail: asanchez@anaya.es
ISBN Prefix(es): 84-207

Anaya-Touring Club+
Unit of Grufo Anaya SA
Juan Ignacio Luca de Tena, 15, 28027 Madrid
Tel: (091) 393 86 00 *Fax:* (091) 742 66 31; (091) 320 91 29
E-mail: cga@anaya.es
Web Site: www.anaya.es
Key Personnel
Publisher: Pedro Pardo *Tel:* (01) 3938935
Fax: (01) 3207022 *E-mail:* ppardo@anaya.es
International Rights: Luis Bartolome
Founded: 1989
Specialize in travel books, guides, phrase books.
Subjects: Travel
ISBN Prefix(es): 84-8165
Number of titles published annually: 30 Print
Total Titles: 280 Print
Imprints: Guia Viva; Guiarama; Guiatotal

Anglo-Didactica, SL Editorial+
Santiago de Compostela, 16, BAJO-B, 28034 Madrid
Tel: (091) 3780188 *Fax:* (091) 3780188
E-mail: anglodidac@aregen.net
Key Personnel
Chief Executive Officer & Administration: Ana Merino Olmos *E-mail:* anamerino@worldonline.es
Founded: 1986
Specialize in bilingual books (Spanish-English) for learning or teaching both English & Spanish.
Subjects: Education, English as a Second Language, Language Arts, Linguistics
ISBN Prefix(es): 84-86623; 84-95959
Number of titles published annually: 4 Print
Total Titles: 60 Print
Distributed by Bilingual Publications Company

Editorial Anthropos del Hombre+
Poligono Industrial Can Roses, nave 22, 08191 Rubi Barcelona
SAN: 000-2313
Tel: (093) 6972296 *Fax:* (093) 6972296
Key Personnel
Editorial Dir: Esteban Mate
Founded: 1981
ISBN Prefix(es): 84-7658; 84-85887
Branch Office(s)
Jose Valencia, Literal Book Distributors, PO Box 713, Adelph, MD 20783, United States

Arambol, SL+
Garcia de Paredes, 86, 28010 Madrid
Tel: (091) 3194057 *Fax:* (091) 3194057

SPAIN

E-mail: arambolsl@hotmail.com
Key Personnel
Administrator: Monica Guijarro
Founded: 1988
Subjects: Music, Dance
ISBN Prefix(es): 84-88128
Distributed by Piles; Seemsa
Distributor for Schell Music

Editorial Aranzadi SA
Camino de Galar, n° 15, 31190 Cizur Menor (Navarra)
SAN: 002-273X
Tel: (0948) 297 297 *Fax:* (0948) 197 200
E-mail: clientes@aranzadi.es
Web Site: www.aranzadi.es
Key Personnel
President: Mariae de Aranzadi
General Dir: Jose Ruiz Cerrillo; Fernando Lopez Lorente
Sales & Marketing Dir: Rafael Rodriguez Galobart
Information Dir: Luis De La Guardia
Personnel Dir: Herminio De Vicente Medina
Publications Dir: Alberto Larrondo llondain
Sales Administrative Dir: Edurne Goni
Finance Dir: Pello Irujo Amezaga
Founded: 1929
Loose leaf publications, books & online products.
Subjects: Finance, Law, Management
ISBN Prefix(es): 84-7016; 84-8193
Total Titles: 25 CD-ROM; 15 Online
Online services available through World Wide Web.
Branch Office(s)
Elcano Navarra
Geova
Madrid
Editorial Aranzadi Madrid, C/Genova 25, Madrid, Contact: Inigo Mosloso *Tel:* (01) 3080835 *Fax:* (01) 3101071 *E-mail:* clientes@aranzadi.es

Editorial Franciscana Aranzazu
Santuario de Aranzazu, 20567 Onate Guipuzcoa
SAN: 000-2682
Tel: (043) 780797; (043) 780951 *Fax:* (043) 783370
Key Personnel
Dir: Juan lgnacio Larrea
ISBN Prefix(es): 84-7240

Arco Editorial SA+
Ganduser, 115-4, 08022 Barcelona
SAN: 000-2801
Tel: (093) 4184910 *Fax:* (093) 2118139
E-mail: arcoedit@idgrup.ibernet.com
Key Personnel
Contact: Francisco Asensio Cerver; Paco Asensio Acero; Juan Jose Orte Calvo
Founded: 1993
Subjects: Architecture & Interior Design
ISBN Prefix(es): 84-8185

Arco Libros SL+
Juan Bautista de Toledo, 28, 28002 Madrid
Tel: (091) 4153687; (091) 4161371; (091) 5196651 *Fax:* (091) 4135907
E-mail: arcolibros@arcomuralla.com
Web Site: www.arcomuralla.com
Key Personnel
Man Dir: Lidio Nieto Jimenez *Tel:* (091) 4161371
Founded: 1985
Subjects: History, Language Arts, Linguistics, Library & Information Sciences, Literature, Literary Criticism, Essays, Philology
ISBN Prefix(es): 84-7635

Editorial Argos Vergara SA+
Rambla Montserrat, 19 bajos, 08290 Cerdanyola, Barcelona
Tel: (093) 5808124 *Fax:* (093) 6921851

Key Personnel
President: Alfredo Plana Giner
Founded: 1941
ISBN Prefix(es): 84-7178; 84-7017; 84-7709

Arguval Editorial SA+
Heroes de Sostoa 122, 29002 Malaga
SAN: 002-2780
Tel: (095) 2318784; (095) 2360213 *Fax:* (095) 2323715
Key Personnel
Dir: Francisco Arguelles
Founded: 1983
ISBN Prefix(es): 84-86167; 84-89672

Editorial Ariel SA+
Member of Planeta Group
Provenza, 260, 3a planta, 08008 Barcelona
Tel: (093) 496 70 30 *Fax:* (093) 496 70 32
E-mail: editorial@ariel.es
Web Site: www.ariel.es
Key Personnel
General Manager: Jose Luis Castillejo
 E-mail: castillejo@ariel.es
Publisher, Foreign Rights: Asuncion Hernandez
 E-mail: ahernandez@ariel.es
Founded: 1941
Subjects: Economics, Geography, Geology, History, Literature, Literary Criticism, Essays, Philosophy, Psychology, Psychiatry, Science (General), Social Sciences, Sociology
ISBN Prefix(es): 84-344
Number of titles published annually: 80 Print; 80 Online; 80 E-Book
Total Titles: 700 Online; 700 E-Book
Online services available through World Wide Web.
Associate Companies: Editorial Seix Barral SA
Branch Office(s)
Planeta Publishing Corp, 939 Crandon Blvd, Unidades 18 & 19, Key Biscayne, FL 33149, United States, Eugeni Roca *Tel:* 305-361-0053 *Fax:* 305-361-0054 *E-mail:* eroca@netrox.net

Asociacion de Investigacion Tecnica de las industrias de la Madera y Corcho, see AITIM (Asociacion de Investigacion Tecnica de las industrias de la Madera y Corcho)

Asociacion para el Progreso de la Direccion (APD)
Jose Maria Olabarri, 2, 48001 Bilbao
SAN: 000-3662
Tel: (094) 423 22 50 *Fax:* (094) 423 62 49
E-mail: apd@bil.apd.es
Web Site: www.apd.es
Key Personnel
Dir, Publications: Vidal Perez Herrero
Subjects: Business
ISBN Prefix(es): 84-7019

Editorial Astri SA+
Riera Can Pahissa, 14-18 Nave 11, 08750 Molins de Rei Barcelona
SAN: 002-2829
Tel: (093) 6801207 *Fax:* (093) 6803194
E-mail: astri@astri.es; astri@mundivia.es
Web Site: www.astri.es *Cable:* ASTRl
Key Personnel
Manager: Joaquin Minano
Founded: 1983
Subjects: Art, Astrology, Occult, Cookery, Crafts, Games, Hobbies, Fashion, Film, Video, Gardening, Plants, Health, Nutrition, House & Home, How-to, Nonfiction (General), Science Fiction, Fantasy, Self-Help, Western Fiction
ISBN Prefix(es): 84-7590
Number of titles published annually: 80 Print
Bookshop(s): Passatje del Libre, Torret del Olla, 166, 08023 Barcelona

BOOK

Sociedad de Educacion Atenas SA+
Mayor 81, 28013 Madrid
SAN: 004-9646
Tel: (091) 5480127 *Fax:* (091) 5591771
Key Personnel
Man Dir, Editorial: Santiago L de Vega
Founded: 1935
Subjects: Biography, Education, Psychology, Psychiatry, Religion - Other
ISBN Prefix(es): 84-7020

Ediciones Atril+
Ctrade Fuenlabrada a Pinto, Km 21, 800, 28320 Pinto Madrid
SAN: 001-5741
Tel: (091) 6911000 *Fax:* (091) 6916380
Key Personnel
General Dir: Antonio Zorita Garcia
Founded: 1989
Specialize in publishing of color graphic impressions. Print color books for other publishers or publicity companies.
Subjects: Health, Nutrition, Medicine, Nursing, Dentistry
ISBN Prefix(es): 84-87589

Augustinus Editorial, see Avgvstinvs

Biblioteca de Autores Cristianos+
Don Ramon de la Cruz 57, 1a, 28001 Madrid
SAN: 003-9004
Tel: (091) 3090862; (091) 3090973 *Fax:* (091) 3091980
E-mail: bacventas@planalfa.es
Key Personnel
Dir: D Bernardo Herradez Rubio
Sales: Manuel Garcia Hernandez
Publicity: Bartolome Parera Galmes
Founded: 1945
Subjects: Astrology, Occult, History, Philosophy, Religion - Other, Theology
ISBN Prefix(es): 84-7914
Warehouse: Aragoneses, No 8, Poligono Industrial, 28100 Alcobendas

Avgvstinvs
General Davila 5, bajo D, 28003 Madrid
SAN: 000-443X
Tel: (091) 5342070 *Fax:* (091) 5544801
E-mail: revista@avgvstinvs.org
Web Site: www.avgvstinvs.org
Key Personnel
Dir: John J Oldfield *E-mail:* oar.seze.mad@teleline.es
Subjects: Theology
ISBN Prefix(es): 84-85096

Ayalga Ediciones SA+
Alcalde Luis Treillard, 14-16, 33400 Salinas Asturias
SAN: 000-4472
Tel: (085) 5500599; (085) 501299 *Fax:* (085) 5500869 *Cable:* AYALGA
Key Personnel
President: Francisco Javier Sitges
Vice President: Agustin Santarua
Man Dir: Ramon Baragano
Sales: Francisco Alzueta
Founded: 1976
Subjects: Regional Interests
ISBN Prefix(es): 84-7411
Divisions: Ayalga Ediciones SA
Orders to: Gran Via Escultor Salzillo, 19-11, 300004 Murcia

Editorial Ayuso
San Bernardo 48, 28015 Madrid
SAN: 000-5193
Tel: (091) 2228080
Subjects: Social Sciences, Sociology
ISBN Prefix(es): 84-336

PUBLISHERS — SPAIN

Ediciones B, SA+
Bailen, 84, 08009 Barcelona
SAN: 001-5911
Tel: (093) 484 66 00 *Fax:* (093) 232 46 60
Web Site: www.edicionesb.es; www.edicionesb.com
Telex: 53183
Key Personnel
Man Dir: Blanca Rosa Roca
Assistant Dir: Carlos Ramos
Production Dir: Jordi Omella
Head of Production: Jordi Aspa
Public Relations: Silvia Fernandez
Rights: Alejandra Segrelles
Founded: 1986
Subjects: Biography, Fiction, Humor, Nonfiction (General)
ISBN Prefix(es): 84-406; 84-7735

BAC, see Biblioteca de Autores Cristianos

Baile del Sol, Colectivo Cultural+
El Naciente, 8, 38280 Tegueste, Santa Cruz de Tenerife
SAN: 001-0103
Tel: (0922) 54-53-45
E-mail: bailesol@idecnet.com; bailesol@club.idecnet.com; bailesol@teleline.es
Key Personnel
General Coordinator: Tito Exposito
Founded: 1992
Subjects: Alternative, History, Poetry, Self-Help
ISBN Prefix(es): 84-88671
Distributed by Odon Molina, SL (Canary Islands); COBAl (Illes Balears); Youngest child Lopez Luengo Distributions (Galicia); Promarex (Catalonia); Carrer de Llibres (Valencian Community, Murcia & Albacete); Lidelsur, SL (Western Andalusia & Extremadura)

Editorial Barath SA+
Blasco de Garay 15, 28015 Madrid
SAN: 002-2977
Tel: (091) 4496049
Key Personnel
Man Dir: Victorino del Pozo
Sales: Cinta Barrobes
Production: Jorge Vines
Founded: 1980
Subjects: Astrology, Occult, Human Relations
ISBN Prefix(es): 84-85799
Associate Companies: Distribuciones Alfaomega SA, Calle Calvo Asensio 13, 28015 Madrid

Editorial Barcanova SA+
Placa Lesseps, 33 entl, 08023 Barcelona
SAN: 022-2985
Tel: (093) 2172054 *Fax:* (093) 2373469
E-mail: barcanova@barcanova.es
Web Site: www.barcanova.es
Key Personnel
Dir General: Ramon Besora Oliva
Editorial: Jordi Galofre
Production: Enric Canut
Founded: 1981
Subjects: Education
ISBN Prefix(es): 84-7533; 84-489; 84-85923
Parent Company: Grupo Anaya, Madrid
Associate Companies: Ediciones Anaya SA

Editorial Barcino SA+
Montseny, 9 baixos, 08012 Barcelona
SAN: 002-3000
Tel: (093) 2186888 *Fax:* (093) 2186888
E-mail: ebarcino@editorialbarcino.com
Web Site: www.editorialbarcino.com
Key Personnel
Literary Dir: Amadeu J Soberanas i Lleo
Founded: 1924
Subjects: Literature, Literary Criticism, Essays
ISBN Prefix(es): 84-7226

Beascoa SA Ediciones
Pujades, 81, 08005 Barcelona
SAN: 001-5997
Tel: (093) 3196517; (093) 3934380 *Fax:* (093) 3107694; (093) 3934389
E-mail: info@beascoa.com
Key Personnel
President: Francisco Beascoa-Anton
ISBN Prefix(es): 84-488; 84-7546
Associate Companies: Sol-Jouem, Lisbon, Portugal
Subsidiaries: Beascoa Internacional

Ediciones Bellaterra SA
Espronceda, 304, entlo 3, 08027 Barcelona
SAN: 001-6004
Tel: (093) 3390511; (093) 3499786 *Fax:* (093) 3520851
Key Personnel
Man Dir: Felio Riera Domenech
Editorial: Jeannine Rochefort
Sales: Angeles Galan Gallego
Founded: 1972
Subjects: Science (General), Social Sciences, Sociology, Technology
ISBN Prefix(es): 84-7290

Beta Editorial SA
Roux 67, 08017 Barcelona
SAN: 000-5746
Tel: (093) 2804640 *Fax:* (093) 2806320
Founded: 1943
ISBN Prefix(es): 84-7091

Biblioteca de Catalunya
Carrer of l'Hospital, 56, 08001 Barcelona
Tel: (093) 2702300 *Fax:* (093) 2702304
E-mail: bcpublic@bnc.es
Web Site: www.gencat.es/bc/
Key Personnel
Dir: Mrs Vinyet Panyella *E-mail:* vinyetp@bnc.es
Chief of Difussion Area: Montserrat Fonoll *E-mail:* mfonoll@bnc.es
Founded: 1914
Subjects: Art, History, Library & Information Sciences, Literature, Literary Criticism, Essays, Music, Dance
ISBN Prefix(es): 84-7845
Number of titles published annually: 6 Print
Parent Company: Department of Culture
Ultimate Parent Company: Generalitat De Catalunya

Biblioteca 'NT' (number of paperback series covering the arts and sciences, current affairs, religion and philosophy, etc), *imprint of* EUNSA (Ediciones Universidad de Navarra SA)

Editorial Biblioteca Nueva SL
Oquendo, 14B, 28006 Madrid
SAN: 002-3086
Tel: (091) 3100436; (091) 3081592; (091) 411-2020 *Fax:* (091) 3198235; (091) 745-2630
E-mail: editorial@bibliotecanueva.com; imago@teleline.es
Key Personnel
Man Dir: Antonio Roche
Sales Dir: Paz Casas Ruiz-Castillo
Founded: 1920
Subjects: Biography, Economics, History, Poetry, Psychology, Psychiatry
ISBN Prefix(es): 84-7030
Number of titles published annually: 140 Print
Total Titles: 3,895 Print

Biografia Joven, *imprint of* Editorial Casals SA

Boletin Oficial del Estado
Avda. de Manoteras, 54, 28050 Madrid
SAN: 000-6254
Tel: (091) 3841700; (091) 3841701; (091) 2365303 *Fax:* (091) 5382349
Web Site: www.boe.es
Key Personnel
Dir General: Beatriz Martin
Founded: 1661
Subjects: Law, Public Administration
ISBN Prefix(es): 84-340

Bookbank SL Agencia Literaria+
San Martin de Porres 14, 28035 Madrid
Tel: (091) 3733539 *Fax:* (091) 3165591
E-mail: bookbank@nexo.es
Key Personnel
Dir: Alicia Gonzalez Sterling
Founded: 1983
Specialize in representing foreign publishers & agents in Spain & Latin America & Spanish authors worldwide.

Antoni Bosch Editor SA+
Manuel Girona, 61, 08034 Barcelona
Tel: (093) 206 07 30 *Fax:* (093) 206 07 31
E-mail: info@antonibosch.com
Web Site: www.antonibosch.com
Key Personnel
President: Antoni Bosch-Domenech
Production, Rights & Permissions & Man Dir: Isabel Cruz Saez *E-mail:* icruz@antonibosch.com
Founded: 1978
Subjects: Economics, Music, Dance
ISBN Prefix(es): 84-85855; 84-95348
Associate Companies: Bon Ton
Distributor for Bon Ton

Bosch Casa Editorial SA+
Comte d'Urgell, 51 bis, 08011 Barcelona
SAN: 000-6297
Tel: (093) 4548437; (093) 4544629; (093) 4521050 *Fax:* (093) 3236736
E-mail: bosch@boschce.es
Web Site: www.boschce.es
Key Personnel
President: Agustin Bosch Domenech
Man Dir: J Manuel Ianez
Marketing Manager: Albert Ferre
Founded: 1934
Member of Publishers Association of Catalonia, focused in law books & legal matters.
Subjects: Criminology, Journalism, Language Arts, Linguistics, Law, Literature, Literary Criticism, Essays, Public Administration, Radio, TV
ISBN Prefix(es): 84-7162; 84-7676

J M Bosch Editor+
Ronda Universidad, 11, 08007 Barcelona
Tel: (093) 3175308 *Fax:* (093) 4122764
E-mail: jmb@libreriabosch.es
Web Site: www.libreriabosch.es/jmb
Key Personnel
Dir: Javier Bosch *E-mail:* direccion@libreriabosch.es
Founded: 1889
Subjects: Law
ISBN Prefix(es): 84-7698
Number of titles published annually: 35 Print
Total Titles: 530 Print
Parent Company: Libreria Bosch

Editorial M J Bosch, SL
Villarroel, 39-3r.3a, 08011 Barcelona
SAN: 006-6435
Tel: (093) 4512335
E-mail: mjbosch@colon.net
Key Personnel
Dir: Maria Jesus Bosch
Subjects: Criminology, Law
ISBN Prefix(es): 84-89591

SPAIN

Edicions Bromera SL+
Poligon Industrial l, Josep M Llopico, 21, 46600 Alzira, Valencia
SAN: 002-0974
Tel: (096) 2402254 *Fax:* (096) 2403191
E-mail: illa@bromera.com; bromera@bromera.com
Web Site: www.bromera.com
Founded: 1986
Member of the Valencia Publisher's Association.
Subjects: Literature, Literary Criticism, Essays
ISBN Prefix(es): 84-7660

Editorial Bruno+
Maestro Alonso, 21, 28028 Madrid
SAN: 022-3175
Tel: (091) 3610448 *Fax:* (091) 3613133
E-mail: info@editorial-bruno.es
Web Site: www.editorial-bruno.es
Key Personnel
Man Dir: Francisco Fernandez Cilleruelo
Founded: 1897
Subjects: Communications, Education, Religion - Catholic
ISBN Prefix(es): 84-216
Warehouse: Av Castilla, 15-17, Pol Ind S Fernando 1, 28850 Torrejon de Ardoz (Madrid)

Cabildo Insular de Gran Canaria Departamento de Ediciones
Cano, 24-1, 35002 Las Palmas
SAN: 000-6793
Tel: (0928) 381020 *Fax:* (0928) 381627
Web Site: www.grancanaria.com
Key Personnel
Dept Head: Jesus Bombin Quintana
Subjects: Geography, Geology, History, Natural History, Regional Interests
ISBN Prefix(es): 84-8103; 84-86127

Caja de Ahorros del Mediterraneo-Obras Sociales
San Fernando, 40, 03001 Alicante
SAN: 000-6290
Tel: (06) 5906363; (06) 5905785 *Fax:* (06) 5905828
Web Site: www.cam.es
ISBN Prefix(es): 84-7599; 84-88440

Calambur Editorial, SL+
Maria Teresa, 17-1C, 28028 Madrid
Tel: (091) 913553033 *Fax:* (091) 913553033
E-mail: calambur@calambureditorial.com
Web Site: www.calambureditorial.com
Key Personnel
Man Dir: Fernando Saenz *E-mail:* fsaenz@calambureditorial.com
Founded: 1998
Member of Emilio Torne, JF Escudero, Fernando Saenz.
Subjects: Fiction, Humor, Poetry
ISBN Prefix(es): 84-88015
Number of titles published annually: 12 Print
Total Titles: 86 Print

Calamo Editorial
C/Pintor Aparicio, 13, 03003 Alicante
SAN: 002-3213
Tel: (096) 5130581 *Fax:* (096) 5115345
E-mail: calamo@lobocom.es
Key Personnel
Dir: Ana Cristina Baidal Lopez *E-mail:* anacris@lobocom.es
Founded: 1990
Subjects: Fiction, Human Relations, Literature, Literary Criticism, Essays, Religion - Islamic, Travel, Arab & Mediterranean Culture
ISBN Prefix(es): 84-87839

Calesa SA Editorial La+
Camino Viejo de Zaratan, km 1 5, 47610 Zaratan Valladolid
SAN: 002-5119
Mailing Address: Parque Tecnologico de Boecillo, Parcela 134, 47151 Boecillo, Valladolid
Tel: (083) 351215; (083) 353575; (0983) 348102 *Fax:* (0983) 358550
E-mail: editorial@la-calesa.com
Key Personnel
Manager: Jacinto Altes-Bustelo
Founded: 1989
Subjects: Language Arts, Linguistics, Mathematics
ISBN Prefix(es): 84-8105; 84-87463
Subsidiaries: Boecillo Editora Multimedia, SA

Editorial Cantabrica SA+
Nervion 3-6, 48001 Bilbao Vizcaya
SAN: 002-3280
Tel: (04) 4245307 *Fax:* (04) 4231984
Key Personnel
Man Dir: Begona Grijelmo Mattern
Founded: 1960
Subjects: Cookery, Humor, Language Arts, Linguistics, Sports, Athletics
ISBN Prefix(es): 84-221
Warehouse: Andres Isasi, 11-3, 48012 Bilbao Vizcaya

Carroggio SA de Ediciones+
Numancia, 72-74, 08029 Barcelona
SAN: 000-7439
Tel: (093) 4949922 *Fax:* (093) 4949923
E-mail: editorial@carroggio.es
Web Site: www.carroggio.com
Key Personnel
General Administrator: Santiago Carroggio
Founded: 1911
Specialize in art & educational books.
Subjects: Art, History, Literature, Literary Criticism, Essays, Natural History
ISBN Prefix(es): 84-7254

Instituto Cartografico Latino, *imprint of* Editorial Vicens-Vives

Casa de Velazquez+
C/ de Paul Guinard, 3, Ciudad Universitaria, 28040 Madrid
Tel: (091) 4551580 *Fax:* (091) 5446870
E-mail: bcv@bibli.cvz.es
Web Site: www.casadevelazquez.org
Key Personnel
Dir: Gerard Chastagnaret
Head of Publishing: Vincent Lautie
Founded: 1928
Subjects: Archaeology, Geography, Geology, History, Language Arts, Linguistics, Literature, Literary Criticism, Essays, Social Sciences, Sociology
ISBN Prefix(es): 84-86839

Editorial Casals SA+
Casp 79, 08013 Barcelona
Tel: (093) 2449550 *Fax:* (093) 2656895
E-mail: casals@editorialcasals.com
Web Site: www.editorialcasals.com
Key Personnel
Man Dir: Ramon Casals *E-mail:* export@editorialcasals.com
Rights & Permissions: Angelica Regidor
Founded: 1870
Subjects: Art, Literature, Literary Criticism, Essays, Mathematics, Music, Dance, Philosophy, Religion - Catholic, Science (General), Social Sciences, Sociology
ISBN Prefix(es): 84-218; 84-7552
Number of titles published annually: 200 Print
Total Titles: 1,800 Print

BOOK

Associate Companies: Combel Editorial, SA; Editorial Magisterio Espanol, SA
Imprints: Biografia Joven; Punto Juvenil; Novelas y Cuentos
Warehouse: Juli Galve i Brusons 72-74, 08912 Badalona

Editorial Casariego+
c/Cristobal Bordiu, 3, 28003 Madrid
SAN: 002-3329
Tel: (091) 4424339; (091) 4425178; (091) 4411330; (091) 4416829 *Fax:* (091) 4426224
E-mail: casariego@btlink.net
Web Site: www.casariego.com
Key Personnel
Man Dir, Production, Rights & Permissions: Carmen Diaz-Casariego
Editorial, Sales: Isabel Rodriguez
Founded: 1959
Subjects: Art
ISBN Prefix(es): 84-86760
Bookshop(s): Libreria Facsimilia y Arte, Calle Cristobal Bordiu 36, 28003 Madrid

Casset Ediciones SL+
Pez Austral, 9, 28007 Madrid
SAN: 001-6225
Tel: (091) 5043584 *Fax:* (091) 2508841
Key Personnel
Editorial Dir: Javier Parra Alvarez
Founded: 1990
Subjects: Humor, Parapsychology
ISBN Prefix(es): 84-87859

Editorial Castalia
Zurbano, 39, 28010 Madrid
SAN: 022-3345
Tel: (091) 3198940; (091) 3195857 *Fax:* (091) 3102442
E-mail: castalia@infornet.es
Web Site: www.castalia.es
Key Personnel
Man Dir: Amparo Soler
Sales Dir: Federico Ibanez
Founded: 1941
Specialize in editions of the classics.
Subjects: Education, Literature, Literary Criticism, Essays
ISBN Prefix(es): 84-7039

Edicios do Castro
O Castro de Samoedo, 15168 Sada La Coruna
SAN: 001-4605
Tel: (0981) 621494; (0981) 620937; (0981) 620200 *Fax:* (0981) 623804
E-mail: edicios.ocastro@sargadelos.com
Web Site: www.sargadelos.com
Key Personnel
Dir: Isaac Diaz Pardo
Founded: 1963
Subjects: Art, Drama, Theater, Economics, Geography, Geology, History, Literature, Literary Criticism, Essays, Poetry, Science (General), Social Sciences, Sociology
ISBN Prefix(es): 84-7492
Imprints: Graficas do Castro/Moret

Graficas do Castro/Moret, *imprint of* Edicios do Castro

Catalogo, *imprint of* Ediciones Maeva

Ediciones Catedra SA+
Juan Ignacio Luca de Tena, 15, 28027 Madrid
SAN: 001-6144
Tel: (091) 3200119; (091) 3938800; (091) 3938787 *Fax:* (091) 7426631; (091) 7412118
E-mail: catedra@catedra.com
Web Site: www.catedra.com
Telex: 41071 MAEG

Key Personnel
Man Dir: Gustavo Dominguez Leon
Rights & Permissions: Marisa Barreno; Josune Garcia
Founded: 1973
Subjects: Art, Film, Video, History, Human Relations, Language Arts, Linguistics, Literature, Literary Criticism, Essays, Music, Dance, Philosophy, Poetry, Women's Studies
ISBN Prefix(es): 84-376
Parent Company: Grupo Anaya, Juan Ignacio, Luca de Tena 15, 28027 Madrid
Associate Companies: Ediciones Anaya SA; Tecnos; Piramide; Algaida
Bookshop(s): Iriarte 4, 28028 Madrid
Warehouse: Avda Ferrocarril s/n, 28346 Madrid
Orders to: Comercial Grupo Anaya, SA Calle Iriaste, 4, 28028 Madrid *Tel:* (01) 3597600 *Fax:* (01) 3559403

CCG, see Consello da Cultura Galega - CCG

Editorial CCS, see Central Catequistica Salesiana (CCS)

CEAC, Grupo Editorial SA+
Peru, 164, 08020 Barcelona
SAN: 003-3634
Tel: (093) 3073004 *Fax:* (093) 2660067
E-mail: atencioncliente@ceacedit.com; info@ceacedit.com
Web Site: www.ceacedit.com; www.editorialceac.com
Key Personnel
Man Dir: Santiago Pintanel
International Rights & Permissions Dir: Julia Esteve
Technical, Literary Dir: Norma Fenoglio
Founded: 1957
Member of Publishers Association of Spain.
Subjects: Architecture & Interior Design, Education, Electronics, Electrical Engineering, Engineering (General), Fiction, Health, Nutrition, Photography, Science Fiction, Fantasy
ISBN Prefix(es): 84-329
Parent Company: Grupo Editorial Ceac SA
Associate Companies: Grupo Ceac SA
Subsidiaries: Editorial Timun Mas SA; Ediciones Vidorama SA
Branch Office(s)
Aconcagua Ediciones y Publicaciones SA, Xochicalco, 352 Col Narvarte, 03020 Mexico, DF, Mexico
Warehouse: Poligono Can Magarola calle, 08100 Mollet del Valles

Cedel, Ediciones Jose O Avila Monteso ES+
Mallorca, 257, 08008 Barcelona
SAN: 001-625X
Tel: (093) 2156039 *Fax:* (093) 2156088
E-mail: cedel@wbsite.es
Key Personnel
President: Oriol Avila i Monteso, Sr
Man Dir, Rights & Permissions: Jose Avila
Founded: 1956
Subjects: Agriculture, Biological Sciences, Environmental Studies, Health, Nutrition
ISBN Prefix(es): 84-352

CEIC Alfons El Vell
Pza Rei en Jaume, 10, 46700 Gandia, Valencia
Tel: (06) 2876551 *Fax:* (06) 2875286
Key Personnel
Dir: Gabriel Garcia Frasquet

Celeste Ediciones+
Fernando VI, 8-1, 28004 Madrid
SAN: 000-7722
Tel: (01) 3100599; (002) 118298 *Fax:* (01) 3100459
E-mail: info@celesteediciones.com
Web Site: www.celesteediciones.com
Key Personnel
Manager: Miguel Angel San Jose
Dir of Export: Jesus Miranda
Rights: Cristina Fernandez Calderon
Founded: 1980
Subjects: Advertising, Architecture & Interior Design, Art, Economics, History, Mathematics, Music, Dance, Photography, Science (General), Travel
ISBN Prefix(es): 84-87553; 84-8211

Central Catequistica Salesiana (CCS)
Alcala, 166, 28028 Madrid
SAN: 002-3701
Tel: (091) 7252000 *Fax:* (091) 7262570
E-mail: sei@editorialccs.com
Web Site: www.editorialccs.com
Founded: 1944
Subjects: Biblical Studies, Biography, Crafts, Games, Hobbies, Drama, Theater, Education, Religion - Catholic
ISBN Prefix(es): 84-7043; 84-8316

Centro de Cultura Tradicional
Plaza de Colon, 4, 37001 Salamanca
SAN: 000-7951
Tel: (0923) 218707 *Fax:* (0923) 293256
Key Personnel
Director Editor: Angel Carril Ramos *Tel:* (0923) 293255 *E-mail:* acarril@dipsanet.es
ISBN Prefix(es): 84-87339

Centro de Estudios Avanzados en Ciencias Sociales (CEACS) del Instituto Juan March de Estudios e Investigaciones
Castello, 77, 28006 Madrid
Tel: (091) 4354240 *Fax:* (091) 5763420
E-mail: jackie@ceacs.march.es
Web Site: www.march.es
Key Personnel
President: Juan March
Vice-President: Carlos March
Man Dir: Jose Luis Yuste Grijalba

Centro de Estudios Politicos Y Constitucionales+
Centro de Estudioos Politicos Y Constitucionales, Plaza de la Marina Espanola, 9, 28071 Madrid
SAN: 000-8109
Tel: (091) 5401950 *Fax:* (091) 5478549
Key Personnel
Dir: Carmen Iglesias Cano
Assistant Dir: Feliciano Barrios Pintado
Founded: 1939
Subjects: Government, Political Science, History, Law, Philosophy, Social Sciences, Sociology
ISBN Prefix(es): 84-259

Centro UNESCO de San Sebastian
C/Urbieta, 11-1, 20006 San Sebastian
Mailing Address: PO Box 1.703 y 3.381, 20006 San Sebastian
Tel: (0943) 427003 *Fax:* (0943) 427003
E-mail: unescoeskola@retemail.es
Web Site: www.servicom.es/unesco
Key Personnel
Executive Dir: Juan Ignacio Martinez de Morentin de Goni
Founded: 1992
Specialize in Unesco training courses, manuals & student books.
Subjects: Education
Total Titles: 107 Print; 7 Online; 5 E-Book; 310 Audio
Parent Company: Unesco

Circe Ediciones, SA+
Milanesat, 25-27, 4, 08017 Barcelona
SAN: 000-9865
Tel: (093) 2040990; (093) 2040659 *Fax:* (093) 2041183
E-mail: circe@oceano.com
Telex: 51735 Exit-E
Key Personnel
Editor: Silvia Lluis
Founded: 1986
Subjects: Biography, Fiction, Literature, Literary Criticism, Essays, Nonfiction (General)
ISBN Prefix(es): 84-7765

Cisneros
Joaquin Costa, 36, 28002 Madrid
SAN: 003-9799
Tel: (091) 5619900 *Fax:* (091) 5613990
Key Personnel
Contact: A Enrique Chacon
Founded: 1914
ISBN Prefix(es): 84-7047

Editorial CISSPRAXIS SA+
Colon 1, 5 planta, 46004 Valencia
Tel: (06) 352 34 61 *Fax:* (06) 352 25 38
E-mail: dpto.directories@ciss.es
Web Site: www.ciss.es
Key Personnel
General Manager: Carlos Pintado Otero
Publishing Coordinator: Pablo Villanueva
E-mail: pvillanueva@ciss.es
Founded: 1973
Business & legal information services, training & professional fairs.
Subjects: Accounting, Business, Economics, Labor, Industrial Relations, Law, Management, Marketing
ISBN Prefix(es): 84-87410
Total Titles: 16 Print; 4 CD-ROM
Online services available through www.ciss.es.
Parent Company: Wolters Kluwer Espana SA
Ultimate Parent Company: Wolters Kluwer NV, Netherlands
Branch Office(s)
CISSPRAXIS (Madrid), Oreuse, 16 1, Madrid, Pablo Villanueva *Tel:* (091) 556 6411 *Fax:* (091) 555 4118 *E-mail:* pvillanueva@ciss.es
CISSPRAXIS (Barcelona), Via Layetana, 30 5, Barcelona *Tel:* (03) 93 295 5700 *Fax:* (03) 93 295 5701
Warehouse: Padre Larramendi, 5 bajo, Bilbao
Orders to: CISSPRAXIS, c/o Colon, 1, Valencia *Tel:* (096) 310 30 80 *Fax:* (096) 352 25 38 *E-mail:* editorial@ciss.es

Editorial Ciudad Nueva
Andres Tamayo, 4, 28028 Madrid
Tel: (091) 725 95 30; (091) 356 96 12 *Fax:* (091) 713 04 52
E-mail: editorial@ciudadnueva.com
Web Site: www.ciudadnueva.com
Key Personnel
Editorial Dir: Jose Luis Romero
Founded: 1964
Member of Espana.
Subjects: Religion - Other
ISBN Prefix(es): 84-86987; 84-85159
Parent Company: Citta Nuova Editrice, Italy
Subsidiaries: Ciutat Nova (Publicaciones en lengua Catalana)
U.S. Office(s): Living City Office, 99-28 64 Rd, Rego Park, NY 10465, United States

Civitas SA Editorial
Barbara de Braganza, 10, 28004 Madrid
SAN: 002-3205
Tel: (091) 902 011 787 *Fax:* (091) 725 26 73
E-mail: clientes@civitas.es
Web Site: www.civitas.es
Key Personnel
President & Counselor: Eduardo Garcia de Enterria
Founded: 1970
Subjects: Economics, Law, Public Administration

ISBN Prefix(es): 84-470; 84-7398
Bookshop(s): General Pardinas, 24, 28001 Madrid

Editorial Claret SA+
Roger de Lluria, 5, 08010 Barcelona
Tel: (093) 3010887 *Fax:* (093) 3174830
E-mail: editorial@claret.es; libreria@claret.es
Web Site: www.claret.es
Key Personnel
Man Dir & Production: Pere Codina Mas
Editorial Manager: Marcel-Li Lopez Rodriguez
Sales: Carlos Delgado Martinez
Publicity: Luis Vinoles del val
Founded: 1926
Subjects: Religion - Other
ISBN Prefix(es): 84-7263

Editorial Clie+
Galvani, 113, 08224 Terrassa, Barcelona
SAN: 004-0010
Tel: (093) 7884262; (093) 7885722 *Fax:* (093) 7800514
E-mail: libros@clie.es
Web Site: www.clie.es
Key Personnel
Sales Manager: Deborah Vila
Founded: 1924
Subjects: Religion - Protestant
ISBN Prefix(es): 84-7645; 84-7228; 84-8267
Book Club(s): Club de Lectores Clie

Climent, Eliseau Editor+
Perez Bayer 11, 46002 Valencia
SAN: 002-7936
Tel: (06) 3516492 *Fax:* (06) 3529872
Key Personnel
Editor: Elisen Climent Corbera
Founded: 1968
ISBN Prefix(es): 84-85211; 84-7502

Cofas SA, *imprint of* Vinaches Lopez, Luisa

Ediciones Colegio De Espana (ECE)+
Compania, 65, 37008 Salamanca
Tel: (023) 21 47 88 *Fax:* (023) 21 87 91
E-mail: info@colesp.eurart.es
Web Site: www.eurart.es/emp/colesp/
Key Personnel
Executive: Jose Luis de Celis
Founded: 1987
Subjects: Art, Language Arts, Linguistics, Literature, Literary Criticism, Essays
ISBN Prefix(es): 84-86408
Number of titles published annually: 20 Print
Total Titles: 50 Print

COLEX, see Editorial Constitucion y Leyes SA - COLEX

Columna Edicions, Libres i Comunicacio, SA+
Viladomat 0135, 08015 Barcelona
SAN: 001-0391
Tel: (093) 4264252; (093) 4261995; (093) 2076726 *Fax:* (093) 4238761
Founded: 1985
Subjects: Fiction, Poetry
ISBN Prefix(es): 84-7809; 84-8300; 84-86433
Subsidiaries: Aea

Combel, *imprint of* Editorial Esin, SA

Combel Editorial SA+
Affiliate of Editorial Casals SA
c/Casp 79, 08013 Barcelona
Tel: (093) 2449550 *Fax:* (093) 2656895
E-mail: combel@editorialcasals.com
Key Personnel
Man Dir: Ramon Casals
Rights: Angelica Regidar
Founded: 1989

ISBN Prefix(es): 84-7864
Number of titles published annually: 50 Print
Total Titles: 500 Print
Foreign Rep(s): Independent Publishers Group-Chicago (US)

Editora Comercial de Publicaciones+
Almirante Cadarso 11, 46005 Valencia
SAN: 001-0480
Tel: (06) 3957293; (06) 3952045 *Fax:* (06) 3952297
Key Personnel
Man Dir: Mora Pilar Taroncher
Founded: 1979
Subjects: Biblical Studies, History, Law, Philosophy, Religion - Catholic
ISBN Prefix(es): 84-7050

Los Libros del Comienzo+
Santa Engracia, 62, 28010 Madrid
SAN: 004-0487
Tel: (091) 5930251 *Fax:* (091) 5931603
E-mail: comienzo@teleline.es
Web Site: www.libroscomienzo.com
Key Personnel
Publisher: Eduardo Rosello
Founded: 1990
Subjects: Self-Help
ISBN Prefix(es): 84-87598

Compania Literaria+
Padilla, 56, 28006 Madrid
SAN: 001-0693
Tel: (091) 4015312 *Fax:* (091) 4015312
Key Personnel
Dir: Juan Bercelo
Founded: 1994
Subjects: Anthropology, Biography, History, Journalism, Literature, Literary Criticism, Essays, Nonfiction (General), Social Sciences, Sociology, Travel
ISBN Prefix(es): 84-8213

Complutense, SA Editorial+
Donoso Cortes, 63-3, 28015 Madrid
Tel: (091) 3946460; (091) 3946461 *Fax:* (091) 3946458
E-mail: ecsa@eucemos.sim.ucm.es
Web Site: www.ucm.es/info/ecsa
Key Personnel
Council Delegate: Antonio de Juan Abad
Dir General: Miguel Saugar
Dir Editorial: Isabel Merino Pella
E-mail: imerino@eucmos.sim.ucm.cs
Founded: 1995
Specialize in Biographics, Dictionaries, Medicine, Nursing.
Subjects: Anthropology, Art, Biography, History, Philosophy, Science (General), Social Sciences, Sociology, Women's Studies
ISBN Prefix(es): 84-89784; 84-89365; 84-7491
Number of titles published annually: 50 Print
Bookshop(s): Libreria Complutense, c/Donoso Lortes 65, 28015 Madrid *Tel:* (01) 5437558 *Fax:* (01) 5437476 *E-mail:* ecsa3@interbook.net

Ediciones de la Universidad Complutense de Madrid+
Donoso Cortes, 63-3 Planta, 28015 Madrid
Tel: (091) 394 64 60; (091) 394 64 61 *Fax:* (091) 394 64 58
E-mail: ecsa@rect.ucm.es
Web Site: www.ucm.es/info/ecsa
Key Personnel
Dir General: D Juan Diego Perez Gonzalez
Founded: 1986
Subjects: Anthropology, Biological Sciences, Economics, History, Psychology, Psychiatry, Social Sciences, Sociology
ISBN Prefix(es): 84-7754

Parent Company: Grupo Anaya
Orders to: Grupo Distribuidor ED, Ferrer del Rio 35, 28028 Madrid

Comunica Press SA+
Avda del Mediterraneo, 7, 28013 Madrid
SAN: 001-074X
Tel: (091) 5012171 *Fax:* (091) 5514209
E-mail: comunica@tsai.es
Web Site: www.comunica.es
Key Personnel
Dir General: Tito Drago
Founded: 1989
ISBN Prefix(es): 84-88817
Associate Companies: Inter Press Service
Subsidiaries: Comunica Press

Comunidad Autonoma de Madrid, Servicio de Documentacion y Publicaciones
Fortuny, 51, 28010 Madrid
SAN: 001-0820
Tel: (091) 319 51 54 *Fax:* (091) 319 85 68
Key Personnel
Contact: Gomez Garcia
Founded: 1983
Subjects: Agriculture, Animals, Pets, Archaeology, Architecture & Interior Design, Art, Biological Sciences, Business, Communications, Cookery, Crafts, Games, Hobbies, Economics, Education, Film, Video, Gardening, Plants, History, Law, Management, Medicine, Nursing, Dentistry, Music, Dance, Natural History, Poetry, Science (General), Sports, Athletics, Transportation, Travel, Wine & Spirits
ISBN Prefix(es): 84-451

Consejo Superior de Investigaciones Cientificas+
Vitruvio, 8, 28006 Madrid
SAN: 001-1347
Tel: (091) 5629633 *Fax:* (091) 5629634
E-mail: publ@orgc.csic.es
Web Site: www.csic.es/publica
Key Personnel
Contact: Teodoro Sacristan *E-mail:* t.sacristan@orgc.csic.es
Founded: 1911
D Teodoro Sacristan Santos, Servicio de Publicaciones CSIC, Vitruvio 8, 28006 Madrid.
Subjects: Science (General)
ISBN Prefix(es): 84-00

Consello da Cultura Galega - CCG
Pazo de Raxoi 2 Andar, Praza do Obradoiro, 15705 Santiago de Compostela
Tel: (0981) 56 90 20 *Fax:* (0981) 58 86 99
E-mail: consello.cultura.galega@xunta.es
Key Personnel
President: Carlos Otero Diaz
Subjects: Anthropology, Architecture & Interior Design, Art, Biological Sciences, Journalism, Law, Photography
ISBN Prefix(es): 84-87172

Editorial Constitucion y Leyes SA - COLEX
Sor Angela de la Cruz, 6-7a, 28020 Madrid
Tel: (091) 581.34.85 *Fax:* (091) 581.34.90
E-mail: colexeditor@interbook.net
Web Site: www.colex.es
Key Personnel
Dir: Rosario Fonseca-Herrero Raimundo
Founded: 1981
Subjects: Economics, Government, Political Science, Law, Management
ISBN Prefix(es): 84-7879; 84-86123

Costaisa, SA+
Euterpe 11, 08017 Barcelona
Tel: (093) 2536107 *Fax:* (093) 2057917
E-mail: costaisa@costaisa.com
Web Site: www.costaisa.com

PUBLISHERS

SPAIN

Key Personnel
Computer Science: Jordi Bisbe
Founded: 1968
Specialize in Multimedia, CD-ROM & the Internet.

Creaciones Monar Editorial
Escorial 26-28, 08024 Barcelona
SAN: 001-1894
Tel: (093) 2133928 *Fax:* (093) 2198460
Web Site: www.monar.com
Key Personnel
Contact: Vicente Monar Puerto
Founded: 1956
Subjects: Biblical Studies
ISBN Prefix(es): 84-85131; 84-89068

Ediciones Cristiandad+
Serrano 51-1 Izquierda, 28006 Madrid
Tel: (091) 781 99 70 *Fax:* (091) 781 99 77
E-mail: info@kgm.es
Web Site: www.edicionescristiandad.com
Subjects: Biblical Studies, History, Philosophy, Religion - Catholic, Social Sciences, Sociology
ISBN Prefix(es): 84-7057

Ediciones Cruilla SA+
Subsidiary of Ediciones SM
Balmes 245, 08006 Barcelona
Tel: (093) 2376344; (093) 2922172 *Fax:* (093) 2380116
E-mail: editorial@cruilla.com
Web Site: www.cruilla.com
Key Personnel
Man Dir: Josep Herrero Casanovas
Founded: 1984
Publishes only in the Catalan language.
ISBN Prefix(es): 84-7629; 84-8286
Total Titles: 1,152 Print

CSIC, see Consejo Superior de Investigaciones Cientificas

CTE-Centro de Tecnologia Educativa SA+
Via Augusta, 4 6a Planta, 08006 Barcelona
SAN: 000-9040
Tel: (093) 217 75 01 *Fax:* (093) 217 62 53
E-mail: cte@mx2.redestb.es.com
Web Site: www.centrocte.com
Key Personnel
Manager: Diego De Herrera Gimenez; Jose Luis Baron Sese
Founded: 1983
Specialize in technical books.
Member of ANCED.
Subjects: Business, Education
ISBN Prefix(es): 84-7608
Warehouse: Puig-gari, 21, 08014 Barcelona

Ediciones la Cupula SL+
Placa de las Beates, 3, 08003 Barcelona
SAN: 001-8066
Tel: (093) 268 28 05 *Fax:* (093) 268 07 65
E-mail: lacupula@eix.intercom.es
Web Site: www.lacupula.com
Key Personnel
Manager: Jose M Berenguer Sanchez
Subjects: Humor, Young & Adult Comics (Humor & Sex)

Curial Edicions Catalanes SA
Bruc 144, 08037 Barcelona
SAN: 001-2181
Tel: (093) 4588101 *Fax:* (093) 2077427
Key Personnel
Administrator: Carmina Garcia I Roca
Subjects: Art, Ethnicity, Geography, Geology, History, Literature, Literary Criticism, Essays
ISBN Prefix(es): 84-7256

Rafael Dalmau, Editor
Carrer del Pi, 13, 08002 Barcelona
SAN: 004-7295
Tel: (093) 3173338 *Fax:* (093) 3173338
Founded: 1959
Subjects: Anthropology, Biography, Ethnicity, Geography, Geology, History
ISBN Prefix(es): 84-232
Distributor for Garsineu

Ediciones Daly S L (Daly Technical Books Publishers)+
Cordoba 11 - 2 F, 29640 Fuengirola, Malaga
SAN: 001-6527
Tel: (095) 2582569 *Fax:* (095) 2583619
E-mail: daly@edicionesdaly.com
Web Site: edicionesdaly.com
Key Personnel
Dir: David Fernandez Garcia
Manager: Hugo Armando Quiroga Capovilla
Founded: 1986
Member of Association of Andalusia Publishers.
Subjects: Architecture & Interior Design, Art, Cookery, Crafts, Games, Hobbies, Education, Engineering (General), Gardening, Plants, Technology, Carpentry, Wrought iron
ISBN Prefix(es): 84-86584
Total Titles: 200 Print
Showroom(s): ABA, EEUU; Salones Internacionales del Libro; Bogota, Colombia; Frankfort, Germany; Guadalajara, Mexico; Liber; London, United Kingdom; Tokyo, Japan
Bookshop(s): Buenos Aires, Argentina
Warehouse: Poligono Industrial La Vega, Mijas, Malaga

Editorial De Vecchi, see Editorial De Vecchi SA

Editorial De Vecchi SA
Consell de Cent, 357-1A, 08007 Barcelona
Tel: (093) 272 46 70 *Fax:* (093) 487 74 94
Founded: 1967
Subjects: Agriculture, Animals, Pets, Cookery, Crafts, Games, Hobbies, Sports, Athletics
ISBN Prefix(es): 84-315

Editorial Deimos, SL
Glorieta del Puente de Segovia, 3, 28011 Madrid
Tel: (091) 479-23-42 *Fax:* (091) 5438214
E-mail: editorial@deimos-es.com
Web Site: www.deimos-es.com
Key Personnel
Administrator: Paulina Pardo Castaneda
Subjects: History, Mathematics, Religion - Catholic
Number of titles published annually: 6 Print
Total Titles: 46 Print

Editorial Revista de Derecho Privado Editorial de Derecho Financiero, *imprint of* EDERSA (Editoriales de Derecho Reunidas SA)

Espanola Desclee De Brouwer SA+
Henao 6-3 Apdo de Correos 277, 48009 Bilbao, Vizcaya
SAN: 002-4090
Tel: (094) 4233045; (094) 4246843 *Fax:* (094) 4237594
E-mail: desclee@tsai.es
Web Site: www.desclee.com
Key Personnel
Manager: Javier Gogeascoechea Arrien
E-mail: info@desclee.com
Founded: 1958
Subjects: Biblical Studies, Management, Psychology, Psychiatry, Religion - Other
ISBN Prefix(es): 84-330

Ediciones Desnivel, SL
Calle San Victorino, 8, 28025 Madrid
SAN: 001-2858
Tel: (091) 3602242 *Fax:* (091) 3602263
E-mail: direccion.desnivel@desnivel.com
Web Site: www.desnivel.com
Key Personnel
Coordinator: Ana Fernandez Soto
Editorial Dir: Dario Rodriguez
Editor: Hector del Campo; Jordi Pastor
Dir of Publicity: Ana Vinuesa
ISBN Prefix(es): 84-87746; 84-89969
Bookshop(s): Librerio Desnivel, c/Dmore de Dios, 11, 28011 Madrid

Ediciones Destino SA+
Provenza nº 260, 5a Planta, 08008 Barcelona
SAN: 001-6586
Tel: (093) 496 70 01 *Fax:* (093) 496 70 02
E-mail: edicionesdestino@stl.logiccontrol.es
Web Site: www.edestino.es
Key Personnel
President: Joaquin Palau Fau
Founded: 1942
Subjects: Architecture & Interior Design, Art, Fiction, History, Literature, Literary Criticism, Essays, Nonfiction (General)
ISBN Prefix(es): 84-233

Editorial Diagonal, *imprint of* Grup 62

Editorial Diagonal
Imprint of Grup 62
Peu de la Creu, 4, 08001 Barcelona
Tel: (093) 443 71 00 *Fax:* (093) 443 71 30
E-mail: correu@grup62.com
Web Site: www.grup62.com
Key Personnel
Rights Manager: Laura Pujol

Ediciones Diaz de Santos SA+
Juan Bravo, 3 A, 28006 Madrid
SAN: 001-6519
Tel: (091) 431-24-82 *Fax:* (091) 575-55-63
Telex: 45141 Dsan E ref Ediciones
Key Personnel
Man Dir: Joaquin Diaz Gomez
Sales: Julian Martin
Founded: 1983
Subjects: Business, Computer Science, Economics, Management, Medicine, Nursing, Dentistry, Science (General)
ISBN Prefix(es): 84-87189; 84-86251; 84-7978
Distributed by Grupo Editorial Iberoamerica (Mexico)
Bookshop(s): Diaz de Santos SA - Libreria Cientifico-Tecnica, Lagasca, 95, 28006 Madrid

Didaco Comunicacion y Didactica, SA+
Regas, 3 bajos, 08006 Barcelona
Tel: (093) 237 64 00 *Fax:* (093) 218 92 77
E-mail: didaco@cambrabcn.es
Web Site: www.didaco.es
Key Personnel
Manager: Lin Balague *E-mail:* lin@didaco.es
Administrator: Manuel Pastor *E-mail:* pastor@didaco.es
Publicity: Charo Latorre *E-mail:* charolatorre@didaco.es
International Sales: Victor Mesalles
E-mail: vmesalles@didaco.es
National Sales: Alfonso R Salmeron
E-mail: mail@didaco.es
Founded: 1986
Producers of multimedia English courses.
Subjects: Biological Sciences, English as a Second Language, Health, Nutrition, Language Arts, Linguistics, Nonfiction (General)
ISBN Prefix(es): 84-86983
Total Titles: 9 CD-ROM
Showroom(s): Bologna Children's Book Fair, Frankfurt Buchmesse, Liber, Barcelona

Dilagro SA
Comerc 48, 25007 Lleida

Tel: (0973) 24 51 00; (0973) 23 34 80
 Fax: (0973) 23 64 13
Web Site: www.dilagro.com
Key Personnel
Man Dir: Jorge Marimon
Subjects: Agriculture, Ethnicity, History, Regional Interests
ISBN Prefix(es): 84-7234
Bookshop(s): Libreria Tenica, Comercio 48, 25007 leida

Dinsic Publicacions Musicals
Sta Anna 10, E 3a, 08002 Barcelona
Tel: (093) 3180605 *Fax:* (093) 4120501
E-mail: dinsic@dinsic.com
Web Site: www.dinsic.com/
Key Personnel
International Rights: Francesca Galofre Mora
Founded: 1988
Subjects: Music, Dance
ISBN Prefix(es): 84-86949

Ediciones Diputacion de Salamanca
Division of Diputacion de Salamanca
Felipe Espino 1, 37002 Salamanca
SAN: 001-348X
Tel: (0923) 29 31 00 *Fax:* (0923) 29 31 29
E-mail: ediciones@dipsanet.es
Web Site: www.dipsanet.es
Key Personnel
Dir: Jesus Garcia Cesteros
Founded: 1982
Subjects: Geography, Geology, History, Regional Interests
ISBN Prefix(es): 84-7797
Distributed by Distribuciones Breogan

Diputacion Provincial de Cordoba
Plaza de Colon 5, 14001 Cordoba
SAN: 001-3307
Tel: (0957) 329646 *Fax:* (057) 211308
Key Personnel
Administration: Delores Martinez Coca
ISBN Prefix(es): 84-8154; 84-87034

Diputacion Provincial de Malaga
Unit of Provincial Government
Av de los Guindos, 48, 29004 Malaga
Tel: (0952) 069 207 *Fax:* (0952) 069 215
E-mail: cedma@cedma.com
Web Site: cedma.com
Key Personnel
Publication Dir: Victoria Rosado
 E-mail: vrosado@cedma.com
Founded: 1973
Subjects: Anthropology, Archaeology, Art, Drama, Theater, Geography, Geology, History, Literature, Literary Criticism, Essays, Poetry
ISBN Prefix(es): 84-7785
Total Titles: 50 Print
Distributed by Atenea; Bitacora; Breogan
Warehouse: Avda-Guindos, 48, 29004 Malaga

Diputacion Provincial de Sevilla, Servicio de Publicaciones
Av Menendez y Pelayo, 32, 41071 Sevilla
SAN: 001-3501
Tel: (095) 4550029 *Fax:* (095) 4550050
E-mail: caba174@dipusevilla.es
Web Site: www.dipusevilla.es
Key Personnel
Dir: Carmen Barriga Guillen
Founded: 1967
Subjects: History, Literature, Literary Criticism, Essays, Social Sciences, Sociology
ISBN Prefix(es): 84-7798

Diseno Editorial SA
Paseo del Alamo, 4, 28280 El Escorial, Madrid
Tel: (091) 918903936 *Fax:* (091) 918903936

Key Personnel
Dir: Ramon Nieto Alvarez-Uria
Founded: 1985
Books in Castellano & Catalan.
Subjects: Education, Literature, Literary Criticism, Essays
ISBN Prefix(es): 84-87666
Number of titles published annually: 4 Print
Total Titles: 2 Print
Warehouse: Colonia Guell, 08690 Sta Coloma De Cervello, Barcelona
Orders to: Exclusivas Escolares, Carretera Nacional 11, km 593-4, 08740 Sant Andreu de la Barca, Barcelona *Tel:* (093) 635 1300

DOC 6, SA
Mallorca. 272, Planta 3a, 08037 Barcelona
Tel: (093) 215 43 13 *Fax:* (093) 488 36 21
E-mail: mail@doc6.es
Web Site: www.doc6.es

Ediciones Doce Calles SL
c/o Palermo, 17, Entrada Napoles, 24, 28043 Madrid
SAN: 001-6659
Mailing Address: Apdo Correos 270, 28300 Aranjuez (Madrid)
Tel: (091) 300 33 83; (091) 892 4218 *Fax:* (091) 892 5149
E-mail: docecalles@infonegocio.com
Web Site: www.infonegocio.com/docecalles
Key Personnel
Dir General: Pedro Miguel Sanchez Moreno
Dir Marketing: Isabel Santos Esteras
 E-mail: isantos@infonegocio.com
Founded: 1987
Subjects: Aeronautics, Aviation, African American Studies, Anthropology, Architecture & Interior Design, Civil Engineering, Health, Nutrition, History, Medicine, Nursing, Dentistry, Natural History
ISBN Prefix(es): 84-87111; 84-89796
Number of titles published annually: 6 Print
Total Titles: 105 Print
Foreign Rep(s): Puvill Libros SA

Editorial Don Quijote+
Compas del Porvenir, 6, 41013 Sevilla
SAN: 002-3817
Tel: (05) 4235080
Key Personnel
Man Dir: Manuel Barrera Blasco
Founded: 1981
Subjects: Drama, Theater, Fiction, History, Literature, Literary Criticism, Essays, Poetry
ISBN Prefix(es): 84-85933; 84-88767

Editorial Donostiarra SA+
Pokopandegi, 4, Pabellon Igaralde, 20009 San Sebastian Guipuzcoa
SAN: 002-3825
Tel: (0943) 215 737; (0943) 213 011 *Fax:* (0943) 219 521
E-mail: info@donostiarra.com
Web Site: www.donostiarra.com
Key Personnel
President: Francisco Javier Rodriguez de Abajo
Marketing Dir: Jacobo Vidal Luzuriaga
Founded: 1965
Subjects: Accounting, Engineering (General), Film, Video, Finance, Health, Nutrition, Technology
ISBN Prefix(es): 84-7063
Distributor for EGA-Donostiarra-Profesores-Editores, SA; Larrauri Editorial SA
Book Club(s): Anele

Dorleta SA+
Nicolas Alcorta, 2, 48003 Bilbao Vizcaya
SAN: 001-4133
Tel: (04) 4448573 *Fax:* (04) 4223222

E-mail: dorletoi@sarenet.es
Key Personnel
Editor: Angel Tona
Dir: Jose Gondra
Dir Commercial: Yolanda Domingo
Founded: 1985
Subjects: Sports, Athletics
ISBN Prefix(es): 84-87812

Editorial Dossat SA
Plaza de Santa Ana 9, 28012 Madrid
SAN: 002-3833
Tel: (091) 3694011 *Fax:* (091) 3691398
Key Personnel
Man Dir: Barrera San Martin Eugeniano
Subjects: Architecture & Interior Design, Automotive, Civil Engineering, Disability, Special Needs, Electronics, Electrical Engineering, Engineering (General), Journalism, Medicine, Nursing, Dentistry, Science (General)
ISBN Prefix(es): 84-237

Ediciones Doyma SA+
Travesera de Gracia, 17-21, 08021 Barcelona
SAN: 001-6675
Tel: (093) 2000 711 *Fax:* (093) 2091 136
Web Site: www.doyma.es
Telex: 51964 lnk E
Key Personnel
Man Dir: Jose A Dotu
Journal Division Manager: Edgar Dotu
Book Division Manager: German Covas
Editorial Manager: Dr Oscar Vilarroya
Foreign Rights: Pilar Aparicio
Manager: Lorenzo Matas; Jose Latorre
Founded: 1971
Subjects: Medicine, Nursing, Dentistry
ISBN Prefix(es): 84-85285; 84-7592
Subsidiaries: AP (Americana de Publicaciones); Doyma Argentina SA; Doyma Andina SA; Doyma Mexicana SA CV; Ediciones Doyma de Venezuela CA

Edicions del Drac SA+
Via Augusta, 6, 08008 Barcelona
SAN: 002-0796
Tel: (093) 2171762 *Fax:* (093) 2171766
Key Personnel
President: Jesus Domingo
Dir General: Miguel Arango
Dir Barcelona: Francesc Salvado
Rights Manager: Eva Rubira
Founded: 1988
Publish in Catalan & Castellano.
Member of Editor Association of Spain & Commerce Association of Barcelona.
Subjects: Agriculture, Animals, Pets, Cookery, Economics, Film, Video, Gardening, Plants, Government, Political Science, Music, Dance, Mysteries, Photography, Psychology, Psychiatry, Sports, Athletics
ISBN Prefix(es): 84-86532
Parent Company: Ediciones Rialp SA
Branch Office(s)
Sebastian Elcano, 30, 28012 Madrid
Warehouse: Logistica de Ediciones SA, Bembibre, 28-30, Polg Cobo Calleja, 28940 Fuenlabrada, Madrid *Tel:* (01) 6420086 *Fax:* (01) 6421696
Orders to: Cauce, Distribuidora de Ediciones SA, Sebastian Elcano, 30, 28012 Madrid *Tel:* (01) 4672666 *Fax:* (01) 5302537

Durvan SA de Ediciones+
Subsidiary of Club Internacional Del Libro
Colon de Larreategui 13-3, 48001 Bilbao, Vizcaya
SAN: 001-4214
Tel: (094) 4230777; (094) 4236263 *Fax:* (094) 4243832
E-mail: editorial@durvan.com
Web Site: www.durvan.com

PUBLISHERS

SPAIN

Key Personnel
Man Dir: Lorenzo Portillo Sisniega *Tel:* (090) 2104020
Founded: 1960
ISBN Prefix(es): 84-85001; 84-7677
Total Titles: 2 CD-ROM
Associate Companies: Durclub, SA de Ediciones
Distributor for Carroggio, SA de Ediciones; Club Internacional del Libro; Ediciones Gredos DL, SA; Ediciones Rueda JM, SA; Lodisoft Internacional, SL; Urmo, SA
Warehouse: C/Nervion, 3-3, 48001 Bilbao

Dykinson SL+
Melendez Valdes 61, 28015 Madrid
Tel: (091) 544 28 46 *Fax:* (091) 544 60 40
E-mail: dykinson@telefonica.net
Web Site: www.dykinson.es; www.dykinson.com
Key Personnel
Contact: Rafael Tigeras Sanchez
Founded: 1973
Subjects: Economics, Education, Law, Psychology, Psychiatry
ISBN Prefix(es): 84-88030; 84-8155; 84-86133
Total Titles: 850 Print

Ediciones Ebenezer+
Apdo 20131, 08080 Barcelona
SAN: 001-6713
Tel: (093) 213669
E-mail: 101745.1635@compuserve.com
Key Personnel
Manager: Carlos A Piedad
Libreria & Distribution.
Subjects: Film, Video, Music, Dance
ISBN Prefix(es): 84-87498
Associate Companies: Libreria Biblica ALFA & OMEGA, Apdo 20159, 08080 Barcelona
Distributor for Broadman & Holman; Clie; Ed Carribe; Spanish House

ECE, see Ediciones Colegio De Espana (ECE)

Editorial EDAF SA+
Jorge Juan 30, 28001 Madrid
Tel: (091) 435 82 60 *Fax:* (091) 431 52 81
E-mail: edaf@edaf.net
Web Site: www.edaf.es
Key Personnel
President: Luciano Fossati
Dir: Jose Antonio Fossati
Publicity: Gerardo Fossati
Founded: 1959
Subjects: Astrology, Occult, Health, Nutrition, History, Literature, Literary Criticism, Essays, Self-Help
ISBN Prefix(es): 84-414; 84-7166; 84-7640
Total Titles: 1,000 Print
Branch Office(s)
Edaf del Plata, Lavalle, 1646-piso 7°, oficina, 21, 1048 Buenos Aires, Argentina, Contact: Alfonso Barredo *Tel:* (054) 11 43 75 55 00 *Fax:* (054) 11 43 75 55 00 *E-mail:* edafall@interar.com.ar
Edaf Y Morales, SA, Oriente 180 n 279, Col Moctezuma 2a Sec, Delg Venustiano Carranza 15530, Mexico, Contact: Gildardo Morales *Tel:* (052) 5 55 785 19 51 *Fax:* (056) 5 55 785 27 51 *E-mail:* edaf@edaf-y-morales.com.mx
Warehouse: Poligno Azque, Ctra de Daganzo KM, 3400 Naves 2Y3-Alcala de Henares, Madrid, Contact: Horacio Mallo *Tel:* (091) 8809514 *Fax:* (091) 8893851

Edebe
Passeig Sant Joan Bosco 62, 08017 Barcelona
SAN: 001-4435
Tel: (093) 2037408 *Fax:* (093) 2054670
E-mail: editorial@edebe.com
Web Site: www.edebe.com

Key Personnel
Dir: Antonio Garrido Gonzalez
Publication Dir: Jose Luis Gomez Cutillas
Specialize in education & literature.
Subjects: Education, Fiction, Literature, Literary Criticism, Essays, Technology
ISBN Prefix(es): 84-236
Associate Companies: Editorial Don Bosco SA, Mexico; Editorial Edebe, Argentina

EDERSA (Editoriales de Derecho Reunidas SA)
Conde de Serallo, 13, 28029 Madrid
SAN: 001-4451
Tel: (0902) 22 66 00 *Fax:* (091) 314 93 07
E-mail: dijusa@retemail.es
Web Site: www.edersa.com *Cable:* REVIPRIV
Key Personnel
Man Dir: Narciso Amoros Dorda
Marketing Dir: Narciso Amoros Koehler
Founded: 1913
Subjects: Biography, History, Law, Philosophy, Social Sciences, Sociology
ISBN Prefix(es): 84-7130
Imprints: Ediciones Pegaso; Editorial Revista de Derecho Privado Editorial de Derecho Financiero

Edex, Centro de Recursos Comunitarios+
Particular de Indautxu, 9 Lonja, 48011 Bilboa, Vizcaya
Tel: (094) 442 57 84 *Fax:* (094) 427 64 20
E-mail: edex@jet.es
Web Site: www.edex.es
Key Personnel
Editor: Claudia Alcepay
Subjects: Child Care & Development, Education
ISBN Prefix(es): 88-300

EDHASA (Editora y Distribuidora Hispano-Americana SA)+
Av Diagonal, 519-521, 2, 08029 Barcelona
Tel: (093) 4949720 *Fax:* (093) 4194584
E-mail: info@edhasa.es
Web Site: www.edhasa.es
Key Personnel
Editorial Dir: Daniel Fernandez *E-mail:* d.fdez@edhasa.es
General Manager: Anna Ardid *E-mail:* a.ardid@edhasa.es
Rights Department: Esther Lopez *E-mail:* e.lopez@edhasa.es
Publisher's Assistant: Cecilia Asker *E-mail:* c.asker@edhasa.es
Founded: 1946
Subjects: Fiction, History, Literature, Literary Criticism, Essays
ISBN Prefix(es): 84-350
Number of titles published annually: 60 Print
Total Titles: 600 Print

Edi-Liber Irlan SA+
Diagonal, 440 4 rt la, 08037 Barcelona
SAN: 001-4516
Tel: (093) 4161452 *Fax:* (093) 4160663
E-mail: ediliber@mx3.redestb.es
Key Personnel
Editor & International Rights: Monica Bertran
Founded: 1983
Member of Associacio D'Escriptors en Llengua Catalana.
Subjects: Cookery, Drama, Theater, Fiction, Literature, Literary Criticism, Essays, Poetry
ISBN Prefix(es): 84-7589
Distributor for L'arc de Bera'
Book Club(s): Club De Lectors Dels Paisos Catalans-Cercle De Lectors

Ediciones Ceac, *imprint of* Grupo Editorial CEAC SA

Ediciones Deusto SA
Alameda de Recalde, 27-7, 48009 Bilbao Vizcaya
SAN: 001-6594
Tel: (094) 4356177 *Fax:* (094) 4356173
E-mail: edicio01@sarenet.es
Web Site: www.ediciones-deusto.es
Key Personnel
General Dir: Xavier Arrufat
Founded: 1960
Subjects: Accounting, Finance, Management
ISBN Prefix(es): 84-234

Ediciones El Almendro de Cordoba+
El Almendro 6, Aptdo 5.066, 14006 Cordoba
SAN: 001-6810
Tel: (0957) 082 789; (0957) 274 692 *Fax:* (0957) 274 692
E-mail: ediciones@elalmendro.com
Web Site: www.elalmendro.com
Key Personnel
Man Dir, Editorial: Jesus Pelaez del Rosal
Founded: 1982
Also book packager.
Subjects: Biblical Studies, Religion - Catholic, Religion - Jewish, Religion & Judaism
ISBN Prefix(es): 84-8005; 84-86077
Subsidiaries: PI El Guijar
Distributed by Distal Libros (Argentina); Editorial Claretiana (Argentina)

Ediciones l'Isard, S L+
Affiliate of Gremi D'Editors de Catalunya
C/ Corsega, 663-665, E-08026 Barcelona
Tel: (093) 436 81 18 *Fax:* (093) 436 03 41
E-mail: isard@isard.net
Web Site: www.isard.net
Key Personnel
Dir: Jordi Marti i Canellas
Founded: 1995
Subjects: Architecture & Interior Design, Art, Cookery, Health, Nutrition, Wine & Spirits
ISBN Prefix(es): 84-921314; 84-89931
Number of titles published annually: 4 Print
Total Titles: 20 Print

Ediciones Turner, see Turner Publicaciones

Ediciones y Distribuciones Universitarias SA+
Viladomat, 247-249, 08029 Barcelona
SAN: 001-5091
Tel: (093) 4101727 *Fax:* (093) 4399429
Telex: 98772 CLLCE
Key Personnel
Administration Manager: Rufino Torres Castineira
Editorial Dir: Albert Ferre Cardona
Founded: 1985
Subjects: Art, Chemistry, Chemical Engineering, Language Arts, Linguistics, Marketing, Mathematics
ISBN Prefix(es): 84-7747; 84-85257

Edicions Camacuc+
Formerly JJ 2 SL Revista Camacuc
Arquebispe Olaetxea, 18-baux esq., 46017 Valencia
Tel: (096) 357 28 56 *Fax:* (096) 357 28 56
Key Personnel
Pastor: Amparo Sospedra
Founded: 1987
Subjects: History, Literature, Literary Criticism, Essays, Science Fiction, Fantasy
ISBN Prefix(es): 84-86970

Institut d'Edicions de la Diputacio de Barcelona
Londres, 55, 1r bis, 08036 Barcelona
SAN: 001-3188
Tel: (093) 4022 116 *Fax:* (093) 4022 290
E-mail: godovx@diba.es
Web Site: www.diba.es
Key Personnel
Dir: Josep Montanyes

Founded: 1991
ISBN Prefix(es): 84-7794

Edicola-62, *imprint of* Grup 62

Edicomunicacion SA+
Las Torres, 75-77, 08042 Barcelona
SAN: 002-1350
Tel: (093) 3590866 *Fax:* (093) 3590004
Key Personnel
Dir: Jose Luis Salgado
Subjects: Astrology, Occult, Humor, Nonfiction (General), Parapsychology, Poetry
ISBN Prefix(es): 84-7672

Edigol Ediciones SA+
Sant Gabriel, 50, 08950 Esplugues de Llobregat, Barcelona
SAN: 002-144X
Tel: (093) 372 63 04 *Fax:* (093) 371 76 32
E-mail: info@edigol.com
Web Site: www.edigol.com
Telex: Cllc E
Key Personnel
Man Dir: Jorge Onrubia
Sales: Joana Rius; Carmentxu Aparicio
Founded: 1976 (as Edigol Ediciones Cartograficas)
General service on Educational Cartography. Wall charts on drugs, anatomy, children's letters & numbers charts.
Subjects: Education, Geography, Geology, Educational Cartography, School Maps
ISBN Prefix(es): 84-85406
Parent Company: Industria Grafica Offset Lito SA, Sant Gabriel, 50, Esplugues de Llobregat, 08950 Barcelona

Edika-Med, SA+
Consell de Cent, 207, 08011 Barcelona
SAN: 002-1490
Tel: (093) 454 96 00 *Fax:* (093) 323 48 03
E-mail: edikamed@edikamed.com
Web Site: www.edikamed.com
Key Personnel
Manager: Dolores Gandia
Founded: 1988
Member of Grenio Publications; Specialize in Medical Literature.
Subjects: Medicine, Nursing, Dentistry, Psychology, Psychiatry
ISBN Prefix(es): 84-7877

Ediles-Ediciones Leonesas SA+
General Sanjurjo 7, 24001 Leon
SAN: 001-8198
Tel: (0987) 22 10 66 *Fax:* (0987) 22 54 60
Key Personnel
Dir: Pastor Jesus Vincente Benavides
Founded: 1981
Subjects: Art, Cookery, Literature, Literary Criticism, Essays, Travel
ISBN Prefix(es): 84-8012; 84-86013
Distributor for Hullera Vasco-Leonesa y Fundacion Hullera Vasco-Leonesa
Book Club(s): Club Bibliofilo Leones

Edilux+
Albahaca, 1, 18006 Granada
SAN: 003-8245
Tel: (0958) 08 20 00 *Fax:* (0958) 08 20 00
E-mail: ediluxsl@supercable.es
Founded: 1984
Subjects: Art, Photography, Travel
ISBN Prefix(es): 84-87282

EDIMSA - Editores Medicos SA+
Gabriela Mistral, 2, 28035 Madrid
SAN: 002-1601
Tel: (091) 376 81 40 *Fax:* (091) 373 99 07
E-mail: edimsa@edimsa.es
Web Site: www.edimsa.es
Key Personnel
General Dir: Carlos Gimenez Antolin
ISBN Prefix(es): 84-87054; 84-95076

Ediciones Edinford SA+
Marmolistas, 3 y 5, 29013 Malaga
SAN: 001-6748
Fax: (095) 254689
Key Personnel
Contact: Jose Luis Gonzalez Sodis
Founded: 1989
Subjects: College & Local Textbooks
ISBN Prefix(es): 84-87555

Editorial Ediseis SA
Pza Ciudad de Salta 3, 28043 Madrid
SAN: 001-4443
Tel: (091) 4165511; (091) 4165218 *Fax:* (091) 4165411
Telex: 47088 Edse E
Key Personnel
Man Dir: Luis Maria Saiz Martinez
Founded: 1981
Subjects: Language Arts, Linguistics
ISBN Prefix(es): 84-85786; 84-7711; 84-389
Branch Office(s)
Ediseis SA, Rosellon 55, 08029 Barcelona
Bookshop(s): The English Bookshop, Calaf 52, 08021 Barcelona

Editorial Editex SA+
PAE Neisa Sur Avda, Marconi, Nava 17, 28021 Madrid
SAN: 002-3914
Tel: (091) 505 10 35 *Fax:* (091) 798 19 80
E-mail: correo@editex.es
Web Site: www.editex.es
Key Personnel
Dir General: Severino Basarrate Elorrieta
Founded: 1946
Subjects: Child Care & Development, Health, Nutrition, Management
ISBN Prefix(es): 84-7131

Editora y Distribuidora Hispano Americana SA (EDHASA), see EDHASA (Editora y Distribuidora Hispano-Americana SA)

Editorial Everest SA+
Ctra Leon-La Coruna, Km 5, Apdo 339, 24080 Leon
Tel: (087) 844200 *Fax:* (087) 844202
E-mail: publicaciones@everest.es
Web Site: www.everest.es
Telex: 89916 *Cable:* EVEREST LEON
Key Personnel
Man Dir: Jose Antonio Lopez Martinez
Publication Dir: Raquel Lopez Varela
Export Dir: Severino Fernandez
Marketing Manager: Fernando Rodriguez Pereyra
Founded: 1981
Subjects: Animals, Pets, Astrology, Occult, Cookery, Crafts, Games, Hobbies, Gardening, Plants, History, Physics, Religion - Catholic
ISBN Prefix(es): 84-241
Associate Companies: Lectorum Publications Inc, 137 West 14 St, New York, NY 10011, United States (US Distributor)
Subsidiaries: Ediciones Gaviota SL
Orders to: Everest de Ediciones & Distribucion SL, Carretera Leon-Coruna, Km 5, POB 339, 24080 Leon, Manager: Javier Atienza

EDUNSA, see Ediciones y Distribuciones Universitarias SA

Ediciones Ega+
Juan de Garay, 15, 48003 Bilbao Vizcaya
SAN: 001-7124
Tel: (04) 4216787 *Fax:* (04) 4213010
Key Personnel
Dir & Editor: Jose Maria Gogeascoechea Arrien
Founded: 1988
Subjects: Religion - Other
ISBN Prefix(es): 84-7726

Egales (Editorial Gai y Lesbiana)+
Cervantes, 2, 08002 Barcelona
Tel: (093) 4127283 *Fax:* (093) 4127283
E-mail: complices@retemail.es
Key Personnel
Dir: Helle Bruun
International Rights: Connie Dagas
Founded: 1995
Subjects: Gay & Lesbian
Total Titles: 21 Print
Distributed by Alamo Square Distributors (Only USA)

Publicaciones de El Ciervo, S.A., see EL Ciervo 96

EL Ciervo 96
Calvet 56, 08021 Barcelona
SAN: 004-6345
Tel: (093) 200 51 45; (093) 201 00 96 *Fax:* (093) 201 10 15
E-mail: redaccion@elciervo.es
Web Site: www.elciervo.es
Key Personnel
Dir: Lorenzo Gomis
ISBN Prefix(es): 84-87178

El Hogar y la Moda SA
Muntaner, 40-42, 08011 Barcelona
SAN: 002-7715
Tel: (093) 508 70 00 *Fax:* (093) 454 87 72
E-mail: hymsa@hymsa.com
Web Site: www.hymsa.com
Telex: 50482
Key Personnel
Man Dir: Xavier Elies
Editorial: Josep Sarret
Sales, Rights & Permissions: Carlos Elies
Production: Jordi Balmana
Founded: 1909
Subjects: Women's Studies
ISBN Prefix(es): 84-7183
Parent Company: Editorial Everest, SA, Muntaner, 40-42, 08011 Barcelona
Associate Companies: Sociedad General de Publicaciones, Carretera Montcada s/n, Poligono Industrial, Barcelona; ASMI SA, Calle Aribau 20 pral, Barcelona
Subsidiaries: Servicios Editoriales SA; Publiventa SA
Bookshop(s): Libreria Hogar y Moda, Muntaner, 40-42, 08011 Barcelona

El Viso, SA Ediciones
Lopez de Hoyos, 350, 28043 Madrid
Tel: (091) 5196576; (091) 5196583 *Fax:* (091) 5196583
E-mail: lvisoh@anexo.es
Key Personnel
Contact: Custodia Caballero
Founded: 1981
Subjects: Art, Photography
ISBN Prefix(es): 84-86022
Distributed by Les Punxes, SL; Visor Distibuciones, SL

Ediciones Elfos SL+
Alberes, 34, 08017 Barcelona
Tel: (093) 4069479 *Fax:* (093) 4069006
E-mail: eltos-ed@teleline.es
Web Site: www.edicioneselfos.com
Key Personnel
Man Dir: Rita Schnitzer
Founded: 1980

Subjects: Cookery, Health, Nutrition, Humor, Decorative Art
ISBN Prefix(es): 84-85791; 84-87251; 84-88990; 84-8423
Number of titles published annually: 18 Print
Orders to: Naturart, SA, Avda Mare de Deu de Londa, 20, 08034 Barcelona *Tel:* (093) 2054000 *Fax:* (093) 2051441

Elkar, Euskal Liburu eta Kantuen Argitaldaria, SL+
lgara Bidea, 88 bis, 20009 Donostia-San Sebastian
Tel: (043) 310267 *Fax:* (043) 310216
Key Personnel
Administrator: Jose Maria Sors
Founded: 1972
Specialize in student languages.
Subjects: Education
ISBN Prefix(es): 84-7529; 89-7917; 84-85485
Warehouse: Zabaltzen, lgarabidea, 88 bis, Donostia *Tel:* (043) 2122144/212033 *Fax:* (043) 212192

Emece Editores+
Mallorca, 237-Entlo, 1, 08008 Barcelona
Tel: (093) 2151199 *Fax:* (093) 2154636
E-mail: emece@ran.es
Key Personnel
Contact: Sigrid Kraus de Carril
Founded: 1989
Subjects: Child Care & Development, Fiction, History, Romance
ISBN Prefix(es): 84-7888
Parent Company: Emece Editores, Argentina
Distributed by Emece Editores Argentina SA; Emece Editores Mexico SA

Editorial Empeno 14+
Pl Marques de Camarines, 7, 28023 Aravaca, Madrid
Tel: (091) 3079386 *Fax:* (091) 3079384
Key Personnel
Man Dir: Rafael Morales
Sales: Jose S Perez
Production: Carlos Saz
Publicity: Jacinto Cabetas
Founded: 1980
Subjects: Fiction, Language Arts, Linguistics, Poetry, Science (General), Social Sciences, Sociology, Technology
ISBN Prefix(es): 84-85823
Warehouse: Fermin Donaire, 3 Madrid

EmpresaActiva, *imprint of* Ediciones Urano, SA

Editorial Empuries, *imprint of* Grup 62

Editorial Empuries
Imprint of Grup 62
Peu de la Creu, 4, 08001 Barcelona
Tel: (093) 443 71 00 *Fax:* (093) 443 71 30
E-mail: correu@grup62.com
Web Site: www.grup62.com
Key Personnel
Rights Manager: Laura Pujol
Founded: 1983

Enciclopedia Catalana, SA+
Diputacio, 250, 08007 Barcelona
Tel: (093) 412 0030 *Fax:* (093) 301 4863
E-mail: secedit@grec.com
Web Site: www.enciclopedia-catalana.com
Key Personnel
Rights Department: Monica Rocamore
Founded: 1965
ISBN Prefix(es): 84-412

Ediciones Encuentro SA+
Cedaceros, 3, 28014 Madrid
Tel: (091) 532 26 07 *Fax:* (091) 532 23 46
E-mail: encuentro@ediciones-encuentro.es
Web Site: www.ediciones-encuentro.es
Key Personnel
President: Jose Miguel Oriol
Man Dir: Carmina Salgado
Sales: Joan R De la Serna
Production: Norberto Moreno
Editorial, Rights & Permissions: Gabriel Lanzas
Founded: 1978
Subjects: Anthropology, Art, Economics, History, Literature, Literary Criticism, Essays, Philosophy, Social Sciences, Sociology, Theology
ISBN Prefix(es): 84-7490
Number of titles published annually: 50 Print
Total Titles: 700 Print
Foreign Rep(s): Bookstore Banquet Jose Cubas (Argentina); Bookstore Miraflores Time Shred of Union (Peru); Bookstore Prow Mac lver (Chile); Bookstore Stadium (Ecuador); Bookstore the Apdo lnternationa (Costa Rica); Byblos Editorial Eduardo (Uruguay); Catholic Bookstore (Panama); Catholic University of Puerto Rico Bookstore (Puerto Rico); Cost Hispamer This of the UCA (South America); Disliber-Spec-Mexico SA of CU (Mexico); Distributing Paulinas (US); Distritexto Ltda (Colombia); Bookstore Juan Pablo ll (Dominican Republic); El Libro (Ecuador); Interservice Distribution SA of CU Col Copilco Univ (Mexico); Paulinas Jr (Peru); Warp Editions (Venezuela); World Book Centre (Chile)

Ediciones Endymion
Cruz Verde, 22, 28004 Madrid
Tel: (01) 5223668; (01) 5222210
Key Personnel
President: Jesus Moya Andrinal
Founded: 1986
Subjects: Poetry
ISBN Prefix(es): 84-7731

EOS Gabinete de Orientacion Psicologica
Avda Reina Victoria, 8, 28003 Madrid
Tel: (091) 554 12 04 *Fax:* (091) 554 12 03
E-mail: eos@eos.es
Web Site: www.eos.es
Founded: 1971
Subjects: Psychology, Psychiatry
ISBN Prefix(es): 84-85851

Erein+
Tolosa Etorbidea 107, 20018 San Sebastian Guipuzcoa
Tel: (0943) 218300; (0943) 218211 *Fax:* (0943) 218311
E-mail: erein@erein.com
Web Site: www.erein.com
Key Personnel
Man Dir, Production, Rights & Permissions: Aramaio Julen Lizundia
Editorial: Beitia lnaki Aldecoa
Sales, Publicity: Arzamendi Pello Elzaburu
Founded: 1976
Subjects: Education, Literature, Literary Criticism, Essays, Poetry
ISBN Prefix(es): 84-7568; 84-85324

Ediciones Eseuve SA
Batalla del Salado, 34, 28045 Madrid
Tel: (091) 539-01-03 *Fax:* (091) 528-87-59
Key Personnel
Contact: Angel Sabat Gomez
Founded: 1987
ISBN Prefix(es): 84-87301
Parent Company: Ediciones Rialp SA
Subsidiaries: Esmon Publicidad SA

Esic Editorial
Avda de Valdenigrales, s/n, 28223 Pozuelo de Alarcon, Madrid
Tel: (091) 4524100 *Fax:* (091) 3528534
E-mail: info.madrid@esic.es
Web Site: www.esic.es
Key Personnel
Contact: Maria Jesus Merino Sanz
 E-mail: mariajesusmerino@esic.es
Founded: 1970
Specializes in economy, marketing & enterprise.
Subjects: Accounting, Economics
ISBN Prefix(es): 84-7356

ESIN, *imprint of* Editorial Esin, SA

Editorial Esin, SA+
Casp, 79, 08013 Barcelona
Tel: (093) 244 95 50 *Fax:* (093) 265 68 95
E-mail: combel@editorialcasals.com
Web Site: www.editorialcasals.com
Key Personnel
Man Dir: Casals Ramon
Founded: 1987
Subjects: Education, Fiction, Religion - Catholic
ISBN Prefix(es): 84-7864
Number of titles published annually: 50 Print
Total Titles: 400 Print
Associate Companies: Editorial Casals, SA
Imprints: Combel; ESIN
Warehouse: Juli Galve i Brussons, 72, 08912 Badalona

Editorial Espasa-Calpe SA+
Carreterade lrun, Km 12, 200, Apdo de correos, 547, 28049 Madrid
Tel: (091) 3589689 *Fax:* (091) 3588679; (091) 3589505
E-mail: info@espasa.es
Web Site: www.espasa.com
Telex: 48850 Espac E *Cable:* ESPACALPE
Key Personnel
General Manager: Jorge Hernandez
Editorial Dir: Rafael Gonzalez Cortes
Rights & Permissions: Carlos Ezponda Ibanez
Founded: 1925
Member of Planeta Group (Spain).
Subjects: Art, Biography, Child Care & Development, Cookery, English as a Second Language, Fiction, History, Literature, Literary Criticism, Essays, Nonfiction (General), Science Fiction, Fantasy, Self-Help, Social Sciences, Sociology
ISBN Prefix(es): 84-239
Branch Office(s)
Roger de Lluria 33, 08009 Barcelona
Balbino Marron s/n, Edf Viapol portal A 5a, 41008 Sevilla
Simon Bolivar, 27 - dpto 34-35, 48013 Bilbao
Hebreista Perez Bayer, 9-10A, 46002 Valencia
Distributed by Planeta International S A (Restrictions Latin America)
Bookshop(s): Libreria Austral, Roger de Lluria 33, 08009 Barcelona; Casa del Libro Espasa-Calpe SA, Gran Via 29, 28013 Madrid; Casa del Libro, Maestro Victoria 3, 28013 Madrid; Casa del Libro, Colon de Larreategui 41, 48009 Bilbao; Casa del Libro, Paseo de Gracia 62, 08007 Barcelona

Editorial Espaxs SA
Rossello, 132, 08036 Barcelona
Tel: (093) 454 06 52 *Fax:* (093) 4510149
Telex: 50679 Espx E
Subjects: Medicine, Nursing, Dentistry
ISBN Prefix(es): 84-7179
Bookshop(s): Libreria Espaxs, Rosellon 132, 08036 Barcelona; Facultad de Medicina, 28804 Alcala de Henares, Madrid; Calle Zaragoza 5, 11003 Cadiz; Cami de Riudoms 6, local 2, 43201 Reus (Tarragona); Calle Fernando el Catolico 57, 50006 Zaragoza

Espiritualidad
Triana, 9, 28016 Madrid
Tel: (091) 350-49-22 *Fax:* (091) 350-49-22
E-mail: ede@edespiritualidad.org

SPAIN

Web Site: www.edespiritualidad.org
Founded: 1953
ISBN Prefix(es): 84-7068

Estudio de Bioinformacion, S L+
Transits, 3-5, 46002 Valencia
Tel: (096) 351 46 27 *Fax:* (096) 394 37 27
E-mail: bioinformacion@bioinformacion.com
Web Site: www.bioinformacion.com
Key Personnel
Dir: Ernesto Hanquet
Subjects: Psychology, Psychiatry
ISBN Prefix(es): 84-86772

Instituto de Estudios Fiscales+
Alcala N 5, 28014 Madrid
Tel: (091) 5273951 *Fax:* (091) 5273951
Web Site: www.minhac.es/ief
Key Personnel
Coordinator, Editorial Production: Alberto Romero Martin
Subjects: Accounting, Economics, Law, Public Administration
ISBN Prefix(es): 84-476
Parent Company: Ministerio de Economia y Hacienda
Warehouse: Centro de Publicaciones del Ministerio de Economia y Hacienda, Pza Campillo del Mundo Nuevo, 3-28005 Madrid
Orders to: Centro de Publicaciones del Ministerio de Economia y Hacienda Pza, Campillo del Mundo Nuevo, 3-28005 Madrid

Instituto de Estudios Riojanos
Muro De La Mata, 8 Principal, 26071 Logrono La Rioja
Tel: (0941) 262064; (0941) 262065 *Fax:* (0941) 246667
Key Personnel
Dir: Maria Jose Silvan Sada
Founded: 1946
Member of CECEL (Confederacioon Espanola de Centros de Estudios Locales).
Subjects: Archaeology, Art, Biological Sciences, Chemistry, Chemical Engineering, Earth Sciences, Geography, Geology, History, Language Arts, Linguistics, Literature, Literary Criticism, Essays, Mathematics, Physical Sciences, Regional Interests, Social Sciences, Sociology
ISBN Prefix(es): 84-87252; 84-89362

Institut d'Estudis Metropolitans de Barcelona
Bellaterra, 08193 Barcelona
Tel: (093) 691 83 61; (093) 691 97 97; (093) 691 91 82 *Fax:* (093) 580 65 72
E-mail: iermb@uab.es
Web Site: www.uab.es/iemb/
Key Personnel
Dir: Oriol Nel lo i Colom

Institut d'Estudis Vallencs (IEV)
Jaume Huguet, 1 (Antic Hospital Sant Roc), 43800 Valls, Tarragona
Tel: (0977) 600 660 *Fax:* (0977) 606 109
E-mail: iev@iev.es
Web Site: www.iev.es
Key Personnel
President: Jaume Saltoe Coscolin
Founded: 1960
Subjects: Archaeology, Environmental Studies, Geography, Geology, History
Number of titles published annually: 5 Print
Total Titles: 96 Print
Online services available through World Wide Web.

Publicaciones Etea
Escritor Castilla Aguayo, 4, Apdo 439, 14080 Cordoba
SAN: 002-8724
Tel: (0957) 222121 *Fax:* (0957) 222101

E-mail: webadmin@etea.com
Web Site: www.etea.com
Key Personnel
Dir: Jesus N Ramirez Sobrino *E-mail:* jramirez@etea.com
Subjects: Economics, Labor, Industrial Relations
ISBN Prefix(es): 84-86785

Etu Ediciones SL+
Grau de Sant Andreu 415, 08030 Barcelona
Tel: (093) 2741671 *Fax:* (093) 2741671
E-mail: etu@arrakis.es
Key Personnel
Dir General: Tristan Llop
Founded: 1996 (Founded by Kabaleb's son)
Courses of occult sciences.
Subjects: Astrology, Occult, Religion - Other, Angels
Total Titles: 7 Print
Distributed by Indigo (Spain & South America)
Distributor for Alfaomega S L (Spain)

Eumo Editorial+
P de Miquel de Clariana, 3, 08500 Vic, Barcelona
Tel: (093) 889 28 18; (093) 889 29 61 *Fax:* (093) 889 35 41
E-mail: eumo.editorial@uvrc.es
Web Site: www.eumoeditorial.com
Key Personnel
Dir General: Ricard Torrents
Man Dir (University Books): Carlota Torrents
Man Dir (School Text Books): Montse Ayats
Founded: 1979
Also book packager.
Subjects: Archaeology, Business, Economics, Education, Electronics, Electrical Engineering, Geography, Geology, Health, Nutrition, History, Library & Information Sciences, Literature, Literary Criticism, Essays, Nonfiction (General), Poetry, Women's Studies
ISBN Prefix(es): 84-7602
Number of titles published annually: 25 Print
Total Titles: 980 Print

Ediciones Eunate+
Pintor Crispin, 12-7 G, 31008 Pamplona, Navarra
Tel: (0948) 272352 *Fax:* (0948) 172636
E-mail: eunate@cin.es
Web Site: www.cin.es
Key Personnel
Dir General: Pedro Llorente Apat
Founded: 1987
ISBN Prefix(es): 84-7768

EUNSA (Ediciones Universidad de Navarra SA)+
Plaza de los Sauces, 1-2, 31010 Baranain Navarra
Tel: (0948) 256850 *Fax:* (0948) 256854
E-mail: eunsa@cin.es
Web Site: www.eunsa.es
Key Personnel
Editorial Dir: Jose Martinez Echalar
Production: Abel del Rio
Chairman: Damaso Rico
Founded: 1967
Subjects: Architecture & Interior Design, Biological Sciences, Business, Economics, Education, Engineering (General), History, Journalism, Language Arts, Linguistics, Law, Library & Information Sciences, Literature, Literary Criticism, Essays, Medicine, Nursing, Dentistry, Philosophy, Religion - Other, Theology
ISBN Prefix(es): 84-313
Imprints: Biblioteca 'NT' (number of paperback series covering the arts and sciences, current affairs, religion and philosophy, etc)

Fondo de Cultura Economica de Espana, SL+
Via de los Poblados, s/n, Edif Indubuilding-Goico, 4-15, 28033 Madrid

BOOK

Tel: (091) 7632800; (091) 7632766 *Fax:* (091) 7635133
Key Personnel
Man Dir: Arturo Azuela
Founded: 1934
Subjects: Anthropology, Economics, Government, Political Science, History, Language Arts, Linguistics, Law, Literature, Literary Criticism, Essays, Philosophy, Psychology, Psychiatry, Science (General), Social Sciences, Sociology, Technology
ISBN Prefix(es): 84-375
Parent Company: Fondo de Cultura Economica, Mexico
U.S. Office(s): Fondo de Cultura Economica, 2293 Verus St, San Diego, CA 92154, United States
Bookshop(s): Libreria Mexico, c/Fernando el Catolico, 86, 28015 Madrid

Miguel Font Editor
Pedro Ripoll Palov, 20, Apdo, PO Box 128, E-07008 Palma de Mallorca, Baleares
Tel: (071) 477300 *Fax:* (071) 476805
E-mail: miquel@globalnet.es
Key Personnel
Manager: Miguel Font i Cirer
Founded: 1984
ISBN Prefix(es): 84-86366; 84-7967

Forum Artis, SA+
Serrano, 7-1 izda, 28001 Madrid
Tel: (091) 4353180; (091) 4350548 *Fax:* (091) 4355124
E-mail: forum@adenet.es
Key Personnel
Dir: Mario Antolin Paz
Founded: 1991
Subjects: Art
ISBN Prefix(es): 84-88836

Naipes Heraclio Fournier SA
Poligono Industrial de Gojain, Avda San Blas 19, 01171 Legutiano
SAN: 004-3400
Mailing Address: PO Box 94, 01080 Vitoria
Tel: (0945) 465525 *Fax:* (0945) 465543
E-mail: fournier@nhfournier.es
Web Site: www.nhfournier.es
Telex: 35510 *Cable:* FOURNIER
ISBN Prefix(es): 84-85074; 84-88928

Fragua Editorial
Andres Mellado, 64, 28015 Madrid
Tel: (091) 544 22 97; (091) 549 18 06 *Fax:* (091) 549 18 06
E-mail: fragua@fragua.com
Web Site: www.fragua.com
Key Personnel
Man Dir: Mariano Munoz Alonso
Founded: 1971
Subjects: Advertising, Communications, Journalism, Language Arts, Linguistics, Library & Information Sciences, Philosophy, Photography, Radio, TV, Technology
ISBN Prefix(es): 84-7074

Fundacio La Caixa
Avda Diagonal, 621-629 Torre ll, pl 12, 08028 Barcelona
SAN: 003-1240
Tel: (093) 404 6079 *Fax:* (093) 3395703
E-mail: info@lacaixa.es
Web Site: portal1.lacaixa.es
Key Personnel
Vice President: Alejandro Plasencia
ISBN Prefix(es): 84-7664

Fundacion Biblioteca Alemana Gorres
Subsidiary of Fundacion Deutsche Stiftung
San Buenaventura, 9, 28005 Madrid
Tel: (091) 3668508; (091)3668509

PUBLISHERS

SPAIN

Key Personnel
Dir: Hans Juretschke
Librarian: Jutta Ploss
Founded: 1955

Fundacion Coleccion Thyssen-Bornemisza
Paseo del Prado, 8, 28041 Madrid
Tel: (091) 420 39 44 *Fax:* (091) 4202780
E-mail: umseo.thyssen-bornemisza@offcampus.es
Key Personnel
Contact: Laura Estevez Couras *E-mail:* lestevez@umseothyssen.org
Subjects: Art
ISBN Prefix(es): 84-88474
Distributed by Lunwerg SA

Fundacion de Estudios Libertarios Anselmo Lorenzo
Paseo de Alberto Palacios, 2, 28021 Madrid
Tel: (091) 7970424 *Fax:* (091) 5052183
E-mail: fal@cnt.es
Web Site: www.cnt.es/fal
Key Personnel
President: Ignacio Soriano
Librarian: Manuel Carlos Garcia
Founded: 1986
Subjects: Biography, Economics, History, Labor, Industrial Relations, Literature, Literary Criticism, Essays, Social Sciences, Sociology, Anarchism, Trade Unionism
ISBN Prefix(es): 84-86864
Number of titles published annually: 4 Print
Distributed by Taluzma (Barcelona)
Distributor for Lucina; Nossa y Jara Editores

Fundacion de los Ferrocarriles Espanoles
Santa Isabel, 44, 28012 Madrid
Tel: (091) 511 071 *Fax:* (091) 5284822; (091) 5391415
E-mail: fudou01@ffe.es
Web Site: www.ffe.es
Key Personnel
Dir: Carlos Zapatero
Specialize in Railways.
ISBN Prefix(es): 88-88675

Fundacion Gratis Date
Apdo 2154, 31080 Pamplona
Tel: (0948) 1233612 *Fax:* (0948) 123612
E-mail: fundacion@gratisdate.org
Web Site: www.gratisdate.org
Key Personnel
Dir: Jose Maria Iraburu
ISBN Prefix(es): 84-87903

Fundacion Juan March
Castello, 77, 28006 Madrid
Tel: (091) 435 42 40 *Fax:* (091) 576 34 20
E-mail: webmast@mail.march.es
Web Site: www.march.es
Key Personnel
Dir General: Jose Luis Yuste
ISBN Prefix(es): 84-7075

Fundacion Marcelino Botin
Pedrueca, 1, 39003 Santander, Cantabria
Tel: (0942) 226072 *Fax:* (0942) 226045
E-mail: fmabotin@fundacionmbotin.org
Web Site: www.fundacionmbotin.org
Key Personnel
Dir: Rafael Benjumea Cabeza De Saca
Contact: Isabel Cubria *E-mail:* prensa@fundacionmbotin.org
Founded: 1990
Subjects: Archaeology, Art, Environmental Studies, History, Human Relations, Science (General)
ISBN Prefix(es): 84-87678; 84-95516
Number of titles published annually: 12 Print
Distributed by Emiliano Garcia de la Torre (Spain)

Fundacion Rosacruz+
Apdo de Correos, 1219, 50080 Zaragoza
Tel: (076) 589100 *Fax:* (076) 589161
E-mail: correo@fundacionrosacruz.org
Web Site: www.fundacionrosacruz.org
Founded: 1993
Subjects: Literature, Literary Criticism, Essays, Mysteries, Philosophy, Religion - Other
ISBN Prefix(es): 84-87055
Parent Company: Stichting Rozkruis Pers, Netherlands
Associate Companies: Rozekruis Pers, France
Distributed by Totem (Balears Islands); Unicornio (Canary Islands)
Showroom(s): 49 bajos, Alicante *Tel:* (01) 5144805; del Oro, 23, Barcelona *Tel:* (03) 2184368; Porvenir, 12, entlo, Gerona; Tabares, 10 transversal izda. no2, La Cuesta (Tenerife); Santa Ana, 69, Leon *Tel:* (087) 213767; Francisco de Ricci, 7, Madrid *Tel:* (01) 5595992; Ladron de Guevara, 12, Malaga *Tel:* (05) 2253949; Goethe, 15 A, Palma De Mallorca *Tel:* (071) 285629; Po de la Pechina, 6 bajo, Valencia *Tel:* (06) 3910267; Santa Cruz, 8, Zaragoza *Tel:* (076) 574268

Editorial Fundamentos+
Caracas, 15-3 C D, 28010 Madrid
Tel: (091) 319 96 19 *Fax:* (091) 319 55 84
E-mail: fundamentos@editorialfundamentos.es
Web Site: www.editorialfundamentos.es
Key Personnel
Man Dir: Juan Serraller Ibanez
Editorial: Cristina Vizcaino
Founded: 1970
Subjects: Alternative, Crafts, Games, Hobbies, Drama, Theater, Fiction, Film, Video, Government, Political Science, Literature, Literary Criticism, Essays, Music, Dance, Philosophy, Psychology, Psychiatry, Social Sciences, Sociology
ISBN Prefix(es): 84-245

Galaxia SA Editorial+
Reconquista, 1, 36201 Vigo Pontevedra
Tel: (0986) 432100 *Fax:* (0986) 223205
E-mail: galaxia@editorialgalaxia.es
Web Site: www.editorialgalaxia.es
Key Personnel
Dir General: Carlos Casares
Founded: 1950
Subjects: Art, History, Literature, Literary Criticism, Essays, Philosophy, Poetry, Social Sciences, Sociology, Travel
ISBN Prefix(es): 84-7154; 84-8288
Warehouse: Trav Vigo, 71 (Sotano), 36206 Vigo Pontevedra

La Galera, SA Editorial+
Diputacio, 250, 08007 Barcelona
Tel: (093) 4120030 *Fax:* (093) 3173277
E-mail: lagalera@grec.com
Web Site: www.enciclopedia-catalana.com
Key Personnel
Man Dir: Roma Doria Forcada
Founded: 1963
Subjects: Education
ISBN Prefix(es): 84-246

Vicent Garcia Editores, SA
Guardia Civil, 22, 46020 Valencia
Tel: (096) 369 32 46 *Fax:* (096) 393 00 57
E-mail: vgesa@combios.es
Web Site: www.vgesa.com
Key Personnel
Dir General: Ricardo J Vicent
Founded: 1974
Specialize in facsimiles of manuscripts, incunabula & ancient books.
Subjects: Antiques, Art, Gardening, Plants, History, Language Arts, Linguistics, Law, Religion - Catholic, Travel

ISBN Prefix(es): 84-85094; 84-87988
Book Club(s): Club Konrad Haebler

Ediciones Garriga SA+
Rita Bonnat, 11, 08029 Barcelona
Tel: (093) 4392204 *Fax:* (093) 4107314
Telex: 54495 selee
Key Personnel
Man Dir: Jose Luis Ruiz de Ville
Founded: 1957
Subjects: Archaeology, Art, History, Maritime, Religion - Other
ISBN Prefix(es): 84-7079
Parent Company: Ediciones Nauta SA
Bookshop(s): Ediciones Nauta SA, Loveto No 16, 08029 Barcelona
Warehouse: Ediciones Nauta SA, Loveto No 16, 08029 Barcelona
Orders to: Ediciones Nauta SA, Loveto No 16, 08029 Barcelona

Ediciones Gaviota SA+
Manuel Tovar, 8, 28034 Madrid
Tel: (091) 358 01 08 *Fax:* (091) 729 38 58
E-mail: publicaciones@ediciones-gaviota.es
Web Site: www.everest.es
Key Personnel
Man Dir: Jose Antonio Lopez Martinez
Publication Dir: Matthew Todd Borgens
Export Dir: Severino Fernandez
Founded: 1980
Specialize in Children's & Juvenile Books.
ISBN Prefix(es): 84-392
Parent Company: Editorial Everest, SA
Associate Companies: Lectorum Publications Inc, 137 West 14 St, New York, NY 10011, United States (US Distributor)
Subsidiaries: Everestde Ediciones y Distribucion SL (exclusive distributor in Spain)
Orders to: Everset de Ediciones y Distribucion, Manuel Tovar 8, 28034 Madrid

Editorial Gedisa SA+
Bonanova Stroll, 9 1 1a, 08022 Barcelona
Tel: (093) 253 09 04 *Fax:* (093) 253 09 05
E-mail: gedisa@gedisa.com
Web Site: www.gedisa.com
Key Personnel
Publisher: Victor Landman
Founded: 1977
Subjects: Biography, Education, Human Relations, Nonfiction (General), Philosophy, Psychology, Psychiatry, Social Sciences, Sociology, Sports, Athletics
ISBN Prefix(es): 84-7432
Subsidiaries: Editorial Celtia SA; Editorial Gedisa Mexicana SA

Generalitat de Catalunya Diari Oficial de la Generalitat vern
Carrer Rocafort, 120, 08015 Barcelona
Tel: (093) 302 64 62 *Fax:* (093) 318 62 21
E-mail: llibrbcn@correu.cattel.com
Web Site: www.gencat.es/diari/
Key Personnel
General Dir: Ricard Lobo
Founded: 1977
Subjects: Art, Education, Health, Nutrition, History, Law, Public Administration, Regional Interests
ISBN Prefix(es): 84-393
Bookshop(s): Llibreria de la Generalitat de Catalunya, Rambla dels Estudis 118, 08002 Barcelona
Orders to: Llibreria de la Generalitat de Catalunya, Rambla dels Estudis 118, 08002 Barcelona

Ediciones Gestio 2000 SA+
Comte Borrell, 241, 08029 Barcelona
Tel: (093) 4106767 *Fax:* (093) 4109645

E-mail: info@gestion2000.com
Web Site: www.gestion2000.com
Key Personnel
Dir: Alexandre Amat *E-mail:* aamat@gestion2000.com
Founded: 1986
Specialize in Business Management.
Subjects: Accounting, Advertising, Career Development, Computer Science, Economics, Finance, Human Relations, Management, Marketing, Technology
ISBN Prefix(es): 84-86703; 84-8088; 84-86582
Total Titles: 400 Print; 10 CD-ROM
Online services available through World Wide Web.
Bookshop(s): Libreria de la Empresa c/Muntaner, 90 08011 Barcelona *E-mail:* libreria.empresa@gestion2000.com

Instituto de Cultura Juan Gil-Albert+
Avda Estacion, 6, 03005 Alicante
Tel: (096) 5121 216; (096) 5121 300 *Fax:* (096) 5121 216
E-mail: galbert@dip-alicante.es
Web Site: www.dip-alicante.es/galbert/
Key Personnel
President: Antonio Mira Perceval
Dir: Emilio La Parra Lopez
Founded: 1983
Also acts as Council for scientific research.
Subjects: Art, Poetry, Social Sciences, Sociology
ISBN Prefix(es): 84-7784

Editorial Gustavo Gili SA+
Rossello, 87-89, Apdo 35149, 08029 Barcelona
Tel: (093) 3228161 *Fax:* (093) 3229205
E-mail: info@ggili.com
Web Site: www.ggili.com
Key Personnel
President: Gustavo Gili
Editor-in-Chief & Man Dir: Monica Gili
Man Dir & Sales General Manager: Gabriel Gili
Sales Export: Saskia Adriaensen; Pepita Sanchez
Production: Andreas Schweiger
Foreign Rights: Elena Llobera
Founded: 1902
Publisher specializing in architectural books & magazines.
Also subscirption & periodical publications.
Subjects: Architecture & Interior Design, Art, Communications, Photography, Technology, Travel
ISBN Prefix(es): 84-252
Number of titles published annually: 50 Print
Total Titles: 1,200 Print
Associate Companies: Ediciones G Gili, SA de CV, Avda Valle de Bravo, 21-53050, Mexico (ISBN: 968-887)
Distributor for Colegio De Arquitectos de Almeria; Collegi D'Arquitectes de Catalunya

Gran Enciclopedia-Asturiana Silverio Canada
Menendez Valdes, 33-1, 33201 Gijon, Asturias
SAN: 004-9476
Tel: (085) 5349684 *Fax:* (098) 5356879
Telex: 89736 Edju E
Key Personnel
Man Dir, Editorial: Silverio Canada
Sales: Fernando Alvarez Conde
Production: Manuel Cardenas
Founded: 1970
Subjects: Regional Interests
ISBN Prefix(es): 84-7286
Orders to: Alto Atocha 7, Gijon

Grao Editorial+
Francesc Tarrega, 32-34, 08027 Barcelona
Tel: (093) 4080464; (093) 4050455 *Fax:* (093) 3524337
E-mail: grao@grao.com; editorial@grao.com
Web Site: www.grao.com

Key Personnel
Manager: Joaquim Mart
Editorial Dir: Cinta Vidal
Founded: 1977
Subjects: Education
ISBN Prefix(es): 84-7827
Number of titles published annually: 25 Print
Total Titles: 250 Print
Parent Company: Institut de Recursos I Investigacio per a la Foirmacio, SK (IRIF)

Editorial Gredos SA+
Sanchez Pacheco, 85, Apdo 2076, 28002 Madrid
Tel: (091) 7444920 *Fax:* (091) 5192033
E-mail: comercial@editorialgredos.com
Web Site: www.editorialgredos.com
Key Personnel
Man Dir: Mr Calonge; Mr Escolar; Mr Yebra; Mr Oliveira
Founded: 1944
Subjects: Economics, Education, History, Literature, Literary Criticism, Essays, Philosophy, Psychology, Psychiatry
ISBN Prefix(es): 84-249

Grijalbo Mondadori SA+
Arago 385, 08013 Barcelona
Tel: (093) 4767110 *Fax:* (093) 4767119
E-mail: marketing@grijalbo.com
Web Site: www.grijalbo.com
Key Personnel
General Manager: Riccardo Cavallero
 Tel: (093) 476 71 23 *Fax:* (093) 476 71 21
 E-mail: ricky@grijalbo.com
General Editor: Claudio Lopez de Lamadrid
 Tel: (093) 476 71 03 *E-mail:* claudio@grijalbo.com
Editor: Cristina Arminana *Tel:* (093) 476 71 00
 E-mail: cristina@grijalbo.com; Silvia Querini *Tel:* (093) 476 71 05 *E-mail:* silviaq@grijalbo.com
Rights: Isabelle Bordallo *Tel:* (093) 476 71 03
 E-mail: bordallo@grijalbo.com; Dora Hernando *E-mail:* dora@grijalbo.com
Contact: Carmen Garrido Montero
 E-mail: carmen@grijalbo.com
Founded: 1962
Subjects: Architecture & Interior Design, Fiction, Gardening, Plants, Human Relations, Humor, Literature, Literary Criticism, Essays, Nonfiction (General), Poetry
ISBN Prefix(es): 84-253; 84-397; 84-7515; 84-8441
Number of titles published annually: 400 Print
Branch Office(s)
Grijalbo SA, Av Belgrano, 1256/64, 1093 Buenos Aires, Argentina *Tel:* (0383) 74 03, 49 40 *Fax:* (0381) 27 26 *E-mail:* info@grijalbo.com.ar
Distribuidora Exclusiva Grijalbo SA, Centro Industiral Eldorado, Calle 64, 88 A-06, interior 1-2, Bogota D E, Colombia *Tel:* (0224) 74 28; (0252) 26 75 *Fax:* (0252) 95 97 *E-mail:* grijalbo@cdl.telecom.com.co
Editorial Grijalbo SA, Almirante Barroso, 27, Santiago De Chile, Chile *Tel:* (0672) 30 27 *Fax:* (0672) 18 50 *E-mail:* mondador@entelchile.net
Editorial Grijalbo SA DE C V, Av Homero, No 544, Col Chapultepec-Morales, 11570 Mexico D F, Mexico *Tel:* (05) 2030660; (05) 2030955 *Fax:* (05) 2547683
Ap Correos, 106-62260 Chacao, Av Principal Diego Cisnero, Edificio colegial Bolivariana, piso 2, local 2-2 Los Ruices, Caracas, Venezuela *Tel:* (0238) 13 22 *Fax:* (0239) 03 08 *E-mail:* griven@etheron.net
Distributor for Dedicersa De Cervantes Ediciones SA; Editorial Amazonas SA; Electa Espana SA; Forza Editores Inc
Foreign Rights: Ros Ramsay (UK); Mary Anne Thompson

Editorial Grupo Cero
Duque de Osuna N 4 Locales, 28015 Madrid
Tel: (091) 542 33 49 *Fax:* (091) 8700944
E-mail: pedidos@editorialgrupocero.com
Web Site: www.editorialgrupocero.com
Key Personnel
Dir: Miguel Oscar Menassa
Founded: 1976
Subjects: Literature, Literary Criticism, Essays, Medicine, Nursing, Dentistry, Poetry, Psychology, Psychiatry, Social Sciences, Sociology
ISBN Prefix(es): 84-85498

Grupo Comunicar
Apdo Correos 527, 21080 Huelva
Tel: (0959) 248380 *Fax:* (0959) 248380
E-mail: info@grupocomunicar.com
Web Site: www.grupo-comunicar.com
Key Personnel
President: Jose Ignacio Aguaded Gomez
Vice-President: Enrique Martinez-Salanova Sanchez
Founded: 1989
Subjects: Communications, Education
Total Titles: 20 Print
Distributor for Abis & Books; Amares; A-Z Dislibros; Carrer de Llibres; Centro Andaluz del Libro; Andres Garcia; Grial; Ikuska; Lemus

Grupo Editorial, see Ediciones SM

Grupo Editorial CEAC SA+
Paseig Manel Girona, 71 Baixos, 08034 Barcelona
SAN: 003-357X
Tel: (093) 2472424 *Fax:* (093) 2315115
E-mail: atencioncliente@ceacedit.com
Web Site: www.ceacedit.com; www.editorialceac.com
Key Personnel
President: Guillermo Menal, Sr
Executive Manager: Jaume Pintanel
Dir, International: Esteve Julia
Editorial Dir: Isabel Marti *E-mail:* imarti@ceacedit.com; Jose Lopez Jara *Tel:* (093) 307 52 59 *E-mail:* jljara@caecedit.com
Subjects: Education, Science Fiction, Fantasy, Technology
Imprints: Ediciones Ceac; Timun Mas; Libros Cupula

Grupo Santillana de Ediciones SA+
Torrelaguna, 60, 28043 Madrid
Tel: (091) 7449060 *Fax:* (091) 7449019
E-mail: grupo@santillana.es
Web Site: www.gruposantillana.com
Key Personnel
President: Jesus de Polanco Guterrez
Vice President: Francisco Perez Gonzalez; Ricardo Diez Hochleitner
Man Dir: Isabel de Polanco Moreno
Founded: 1960
Subjects: Education
ISBN Prefix(es): 84-294
Associate Companies: Editorial Santillana, Argentina; Editorial Santillana, Bolivia; Editorial Santillana, Colombia; Editorial Santillana, Costa Rica; Editorial Santillana, Chile; Editorial Santillana, Ecuador; Editorial Santillana, El Salvador; Editorial Santillana, Guatemala; Editorial Santillana, Mexico; Editorial Santillana, Paraguay; Editorial Santillana, Peru; Editorial Santillana, Puerto Rico; Editorial Santillana, Dominican Republic; Editorial Santillana, Uruguay; Editorial Santillana, Venezuela
Divisions: Aguilar; Alfaguara; Altea; Taurus; Richmond
U.S. Office(s): Santillana Publishing Co, 2105 NW 86 Ave, Miami, FL 33112, United States

Guadalquivir SL Ediciones
Asuncion, 61, 3, 41011 Sevilla

Tel: (095) 422 19 76; (095) 422 19 17 *Fax:* (095) 421 33 20
E-mail: guadalquivir.ed@svq.servicom.es
Founded: 1979
Subjects: Art, History, Literature, Literary Criticism, Essays
ISBN Prefix(es): 84-8093; 84-86080
Subsidiaries: Varflora
Orders to: Varflora, 17 Bajo, 41001 Seville

Guadarrama, *imprint of* Editorial Labor SA

Guia Viva, *imprint of* Anaya-Touring Club

Guiarama, *imprint of* Anaya-Touring Club

Guiatotal, *imprint of* Anaya-Touring Club

Editorial Gulaab
07192 Estellenchs, Baleares
Tel: (071) 61 86 55 *Fax:* (071) 61 86 55
E-mail: osho@arrakis.es
Key Personnel
Editor: J M Beltran Alorda
Subjects: Human Relations, Philosophy, Religion - Buddhist, Religion - Hindu, Religion - Other, Women's Studies
ISBN Prefix(es): 84-86797
Distributed by Alfa Omego (Spain); Ed Cerro Manupuehue (Chile); Ed luz de Luna (Argentina); Ed Moderna (Columbia); Unicornio (Spain)

Carl Hanser Verlag, *imprint of* Plastic Comunicacion SL

Harlequin Iberica SA
Hermosilla, 21, 28001 Madrid
Tel: (091) 4358712 *Fax:* (091) 4310484
Key Personnel
General Dir: Maria Teresa Villar
Founded: 1982
Subjects: Romance
ISBN Prefix(es): 84-396
Parent Company: Harlequin Enterprises Ltd, Toronto, ON, Canada

Heinemann Iberia SA, see Macmillan Heinemann ELT

Hercules de Ediciones, SA
Cl Orzan 117 1, 15003 A Coruna La Coruna
Tel: (0981) 220585; (0981) 226443 *Fax:* (0981) 220717
E-mail: empg05052@empresas-galicia.com
Key Personnel
President: Francisco Rodriguez Iglesias
Manager: Nicolas Salvador Egido
Subjects: Anthropology, Child Care & Development, Education
ISBN Prefix(es): 84-87244; 84-89468
Branch Office(s)
Hercules Astur
Warehouse: Rua Chinto Crespo, 2, A Gandara, San Pedro, L A Coruna

Editorial Herder SA+
Provenca, 388, 08025 Barcelona
Tel: (093) 476 26 26 *Fax:* (093) 207 34 48
E-mail: editorialherder@herder-sa.com
Web Site: www.herder-sa.com
Telex: 54120 Hegr E *Cable:* HERDER
Key Personnel
Man Dir: Friedl Antonio Valtl
Publicity: Carlos Rey
Founded: 1943
Subjects: Economics, Education, Language Arts, Linguistics, Medicine, Nursing, Dentistry, Philosophy, Psychology, Psychiatry, Religion - Other, Social Sciences, Sociology, Theology
ISBN Prefix(es): 84-254
Associate Companies: Verlag Herder & Co, Austria; Verlag Herder GmbH & Co KG, Germany; Herder und Herder GmbH, Germany; Herder Editrice e Libreria, Italy; Herder AG, Switzerland
Branch Office(s)
Hesperia SA Editorial y Libreria, Ave Callao 565, Buenos Aires, Argentina (Delegacione de Venta)
Herder Editorial y Livreria, Calle 12, No 6/89, Apdo Aereo, 6855 Bogota, Colombia (Delegacione de Venta)
Bookshop(s): Libreria Herder

Ediciones Hiperion SL+
Salustiano Olozaga, 14, 28001 Madrid
Tel: (091) 577 60 15; (091) 577 60 16 *Fax:* (091) 435 86 90
E-mail: info@hiperion.com
Web Site: www.hiperion.com
Key Personnel
Man Dir, Editorial: Jesus Munarriz
Sales: Maite Merodio
Founded: 1976
Subjects: Language Arts, Linguistics, Literature, Literary Criticism, Essays, Poetry, Religion - Islamic, Religion - Jewish
ISBN Prefix(es): 84-7517
Number of titles published annually: 30 Print
Total Titles: 600 Print
Bookshop(s): Libreria Hiperion, Calle Salustiano Olozaga 14, 28001 Madrid *Tel:* (091) 577 60 15

Editorial Hispano Europea SA+
Bori i Fontesta, 6-8, 08021 Barcelona
Tel: (093) 2013709; (093) 2018500 *Fax:* (093) 4142635
E-mail: hispaneuropea@mx3.redestb.es
Telex: 98772 cllcE
Key Personnel
Man Dir, Editorial & Publicity: Jorge J Prat
Sales: Xavier Campillo
Production: Jose Madueno
Founded: 1956
Subjects: Animals, Pets, Business, Gardening, Plants, Health, Nutrition, Sports, Athletics
ISBN Prefix(es): 84-255
Number of titles published annually: 50 Print
Total Titles: 536 Print

Hogar del Libro, SA+
Ramelleres, 17, 08001 Barcelona
Tel: (093) 3182700 *Fax:* (093) 3010399
Key Personnel
Dir: Sebastia Fabregues
Founded: 1945
Group of companies comprising one publisher, one major distributor & eight bookshops.
Subjects: Biography, Education, Fiction, Literature, Literary Criticism, Essays
ISBN Prefix(es): 84-7279
Associate Companies: Nova Terra
Bookshop(s): Hogar de Libro SA, Elisabets, 6, 08001 Barcelona

Editorial Horsori SL
Roger de Flor, 77-79, Esc Dcha 2-3, 08013 Barcelona
Mailing Address: Roger de Flor, 77-79, Esc Dcha, 2, 3, 08013 Barcelona
Tel: (093) 2322755 *Fax:* (093) 2651776
E-mail: horsori@retemail.es
Web Site: www.horsori.com
Key Personnel
Contact: Francisco Segu
Subjects: Education, Philosophy
ISBN Prefix(es): 84-85840
Warehouse: MADE Av Catalonya sln Pol Ind Can Coll, 08185, Lliga de Vall Barcelona

Ibaizabal Edelvives SA
Barrio San Miguel, s/n, 48290 Euba-Amorebieta, Vizcaya
Tel: (094) 6308036 *Fax:* (094) 6308028
E-mail: ibaizabal@euskalnet.net
Key Personnel
Dir: Jose Iraolagoitia Mendibe
Contact: Itziar Osa
Founded: 1990
Materials for school teaching literary editions.
Subjects: Education, History, Literature, Literary Criticism, Essays, Mathematics, Philosophy, Religion - Catholic, Technology
ISBN Prefix(es): 84-8325; 84-7992
Number of titles published annually: 123 Print
Total Titles: 1,261 Print
Warehouse: Edelvives, Avda Txori-Erri 46, Modulo 4, Letra E, 48150 Sondika *Tel:* (04) 4532009/4532174 *Fax:* (04) 4532091
Orders to: Edelvives, Avda Txori-Erri 46, Modulo 4, Letra E, 48150 Sondika *Tel:* (04) 4532009/4532174 *Fax:* (04) 4532091

Editorial Iberia, SA+
Plato, 26, 08006 Barcelona
Tel: (093) 2010599; (093) 2013807 *Fax:* (093) 2097362
E-mail: omega@ediciones-omega.es
Web Site: www.ediciones-omega.es
Telex: 98095
Key Personnel
Administrator: Antonio Paricio Larrea
Founded: 1945
Subjects: Health, Nutrition, Literature, Literary Criticism, Essays, Physics, Psychology, Psychiatry
ISBN Prefix(es): 84-7082
Parent Company: Ediciones Omega, SA
Associate Companies: Ediciones Medici, SL

Iberico Europea de Ediciones SA
Serrano, 44, 28001 Madrid
Tel: (091) 4357243
Founded: 1966
Subjects: Art, Biography, Business, How-to, Music, Dance, Social Sciences, Sociology
ISBN Prefix(es): 84-256

Icaria Editorial SA+
Ausias Marc, 16, 3r, 2q, 08010 Barcelona
Tel: (093) 3011723 *Fax:* (093) 3178242
Web Site: www.icariaeditorial.com
Key Personnel
Man Dir, Editorial, Rights & Permissions: Anna Monjo Omedes
Founded: 1977
Subjects: Anthropology, Cookery, Developing Countries, Economics, Energy, Environmental Studies, Literature, Literary Criticism, Essays, Poetry, Social Sciences, Sociology, Women's Studies, Analysis of International Politics, Critical Economy, Ecology, Relations of the North-South, Social Sciences, Voices & Proposals
ISBN Prefix(es): 84-7426
Warehouse: Lepanto, 135-7, 08013 Barcelona

Publicaciones ICCE (Calasanz Institute for Educational Sciences)+
Eraso 3, Madrid 28028
Tel: (091) 725 72 00 *Fax:* (091) 361 10 52
E-mail: info@ciberaula.net
Web Site: www.ciberaula.net
Key Personnel
Dir: Juan Yzuel *E-mail:* direccion@ciberaula.net
Publishing Dept Dir: Luis M Bandres
E-mail: editorial@ciberaula.net
Founded: 1967

Subjects: Education, History, Psychology, Psychiatry, Religion - Other, Social Sciences, Sociology
ISBN Prefix(es): 84-7278
Number of titles published annually: 10 Print
Total Titles: 85 Print
Parent Company: Calasanzian Fathers

Icono Perpetuo Socorro, *imprint of* Editorial El Perpetuo Socorro

Idea Books, SA+
Rosellon 186, 1-4, 08008 Barcelona
Tel: (093) 4533002 *Fax:* (093) 4541895
E-mail: ideabooks@ideabooks.es
Web Site: www.ideabooks.es
Key Personnel
Co-owner & International Rights & Permissions: Jorge Fernandez
Co-owner, Export & Editor: Juan B Lorente Herrera
Founded: 1990
Publisher of nonfiction books for professionals, students & children. Specialize in woodworking, furniture, iron & construction.
Member of Society of Editors.
Subjects: Agriculture, Biological Sciences, Child Care & Development, Crafts, Games, Hobbies, Earth Sciences, Education, Geography, Geology, Human Relations, Music, Dance, Philosophy, Physics, Religion - Other, Science (General)
ISBN Prefix(es): 84-8236
Number of titles published annually: 35 Print; 2 Audio
Imprints: Idea Musica; Idea Universitaria

Idea Musica, *imprint of* Idea Books, SA

Idea Universitaria, *imprint of* Idea Books, SA

Editorial Pablo Iglesias
Monte Esquinza, 30, 28010 Madrid
Tel: (091) 3 104 313 *Fax:* (091) 3 194 585
Web Site: www.fpabloiglesias.es
Key Personnel
Dir: Manuel Ortuno Armas
ISBN Prefix(es): 84-85691

Imagen y Deporte, SL+
Marte, 1 bajo, 50012 Zaragoza
Tel: (0976) 754000 *Fax:* (0976) 754000
E-mail: internocional@imagenydeporte.com
Web Site: www.imagenydeporte.com
Key Personnel
Man Dir: Carlos Torres
International Manager: Elena Rodrigo
 E-mail: produccion@imagenydeporte.com
Production Manager: Jose Torres
 E-mail: imagenydeporte@imagenydeporte.com
Founded: 1988
Production & distribution company of educational products, domentines & books.
Subjects: Education, Sports, Athletics
ISBN Prefix(es): 84-89117

Impredisur, SL+
Colegios, 3, 18001 Granada
Tel: (058) 290577
Key Personnel
President: Ignacio Llamas Labella
Founded: 1990
Subjects: Law, Regional Interests
ISBN Prefix(es): 84-7933
Bookshop(s): Libros Adaiz, Colegios 3, 18001 Granada
Orders to: Apdo de Correos 878, 18080 Granada

Editorial Incafo SA
Castello, 59, 28001 Madrid
Tel: (091) 4313460; (091) 5780961 *Fax:* (091) 4313589
Telex: 42459 lcf E
Key Personnel
Man Dir, Editorial: Luis Blas Aritio
Production: Javier Echevarri
Rights & Permissions: Margarita Mendez de Vigo
Founded: 1973
Subjects: Art, Environmental Studies, Natural History
ISBN Prefix(es): 84-85389; 84-8089
Book Club(s): Club del Libro de la Naturaleza

INEF Madrid, see Instituto Nacional del Educacion Fisica Madrid (INEF-Madrid)

Institucion Fernando el Catolico de la Excma Diputacion de Zaragoza
Palacio Provincial Plaza de Espana, 2, 50071 Zaragoza
Tel: (0976) 28 88 78; (0976) 28 88 79
 Fax: (0976) 28 88 69
E-mail: info@ifc.dpz.es
Web Site: www.dpz.es
Key Personnel
President: D Javier Lamban
Dir: Dr Gonzalo Borras
Secretary: D Jose Barranco
Founded: 1943
Subjects: Agriculture, Archaeology, Art, Geography, Geology, History, Law, Literature, Literary Criticism, Essays, Music, Dance
ISBN Prefix(es): 84-7820
Branch Office(s)
Centro de Estudios Borjanos, Casa de Aguilar, Borja
Centro de Estudios Bibilitanos, Puerta de Terrer, Calatayud
Grupo Cultural Caspolino, Palacio Barberan, 50700 Caspe
Centro de Estudios Darocenses, Puerta Baja, 50360 Daroca
Centro de Estudios Cinco Villas, Ramon y Caja, 17, 50600 Ejea Caballeros
Centro de Estudios Turiasonenses, Apdo 39, 50500 Tarazona

Institut de Recursos I investigacio per a la Formacio SL (IRIF)+
Francesc Tarrega, 32-34, 08027 Barcelona
Tel: (093) 4080464 *Fax:* (093) 3524337
E-mail: grao@grao.com
Web Site: www.grao.com
Key Personnel
Delegated Counselor: Antoni Zabala i Vidiella
Contact: Gloria Puig
Founded: 1977
Subjects: Education
ISBN Prefix(es): 84-7827
Divisions: Grao Editorial; Interactiva

Instituto de Estudios Economicos (Institute for Economic Studies)
Castello, 128, 28006 Madrid
Tel: (091) 782 05 80 *Fax:* (091) 562 36 13
E-mail: iee@ieemadrid.com
Key Personnel
Administrator: D Jose Maria Goizueta Besga
Founded: 1979
Subjects: Economics, Social Sciences, Sociology
ISBN Prefix(es): 84-85719

Instituto Nacional de Estadistica
Paseo de la Castellana, 183, 28071 Madrid
Tel: (091) 583 91 00
E-mail: info@ine.es
Web Site: www.ine.es
Key Personnel
President: Jose Ouevedo
Subjects: Mathematics

ISBN Prefix(es): 84-260
Distributed by Libreria Lines-Chiel; Mundi-Prensa Libros, SA

Instituto Nacional de Seguridad e Higiene en el Trabajo, see Ministerio de Trabajo y Asuntos Sociales

Instituto Vasco de Criminologia
Villa Soroa Avda Ategorrieta, 22, 20013 Donostia-San Sebastian
Tel: (0943) 321411; (0943) 321412 *Fax:* (0943) 321272
E-mail: szoivac@sc.ehu.es
Web Site: www.sc.edu.es
Key Personnel
Dir: Antonio Beristain
Founded: 1976
Subjects: Criminology, Human Rights
ISBN Prefix(es): 84-920328

Ediciones Internacionales Universitarias SA+
Pantoja 14, 28002 Madrid
Tel: (091) 5193907 *Fax:* (091) 4136808
Web Site: www.eunsa.es
Key Personnel
Contact: Damaso Rico
Subjects: Biography, Economics, Journalism, Nonfiction (General), Philosophy, Theology
ISBN Prefix(es): 84-87155
Holding Company: Plaza de los Sauces, 1-2, 31010 Baranain (Navarra) *Tel:* (0948) 256850 *Fax:* (0948) 256854 *E-mail:* eunsa@cin.es
Branch Office(s)
Pantoja 14, 28002 Madrid *Tel:* (091) 5193907 *Fax:* (091) 4136808 *E-mail:* eiunsa@inbernet.com

Intress, see Institut de Treball Social - Serveis Socials

IR Indo Edicions
Florida, 30, 36210 Vigo, Galicia
Tel: (0986) 21 48 34 *Fax:* (0986) 21 11 33
E-mail: correo@irindo.com
Web Site: www.irindo.com; irindo.net
Key Personnel
Contact: Bieito Ledo
Founded: 1985
ISBN Prefix(es): 84-7680

Iralka Editorial SL+
Ametzagana, 21-Local 10, 20012 San Sebastian
Tel: (0943) 32 30 14 *Fax:* (0943) 32 30 22
E-mail: iralka@euskalnet.net
Web Site: www.euskalnet.net/iralka
Key Personnel
Editor: Manuel Muner Sorazu
Founded: 1993
Subjects: Anthropology, Literature, Literary Criticism, Essays, Philosophy, Poetry, Social Sciences, Sociology
ISBN Prefix(es): 84-89806
Number of titles published annually: 5 Print
Total Titles: 31 Print

Ediciones Irusa+
Roger de Flor, 91, 08013 Barcelona
Tel: (093) 2318032 *Fax:* (093) 2653670
Key Personnel
Contact: Xabier Etxarri
Founded: 1982
Subjects: Cookery, Humor
ISBN Prefix(es): 84-8065; 84-86819

Editorial Isidoriana, Libreria
Plaza de San Isidoro, 4, 24003 Leon
Mailing Address: Apdo 126, 24080 Leon
Tel: (0987) 876161 *Fax:* (0987) 876162

PUBLISHERS

SPAIN

E-mail: sanisidoro@infonegocio.com
Key Personnel
Dir: Antonio Vinayo Gonzalez *Tel:* (987) 876070
  Fax: (987) 876061

Ediciones Istmo SA+
Colombia, 18, 28016 ESP Madrid
Tel: (091) 3454101; (091) 6568818 *Fax:* (091) 3592412; (091) 6564995
Key Personnel
Man Dir: Eduardo Casado Martindela Camara
Founded: 1969
Subjects: Anthropology, Art, History, Language Arts, Linguistics, Literature, Literary Criticism, Essays, Philosophy, Social Sciences, Sociology
ISBN Prefix(es): 84-7090

JJ 2 SL Revista Camacuc, see Edicions Camacuc

Ediciones JJB
Perez Galdos 12, 4, Apdo 1084, E-26002 Logrono, La Rioja
Tel: (041) 236429 *Fax:* (041) 226127
Key Personnel
Dir: Julian de Juan Berzosa
Founded: 1977
ISBN Prefix(es): 84-85305

Ediciones JLA+
Molina 18, E-28029 Madrid
Mailing Address: PO Box 54122, 2080 Madrid
Tel: (091) 3158577 *Fax:* (091) 7336239
Key Personnel
Dir: Jose Luis Alvarez *Tel:* (091) 3864292
  Fax: (091) 3161882 *E-mail:* vinilos@vinilos.com
Founded: 1975
Subjects: Radio, TV
ISBN Prefix(es): 84-7872; 84-86570
Warehouse: c/o Valdesahgil, 26-Local, 28039 Madrid

JOC Internacional, SA+
San Hipolit, 20, 08030 Barcelona
Tel: (093) 3458565; (093) 2741954 *Fax:* (093) 3465362
Web Site: www.jociycw.net
Key Personnel
Vice President: Montserrat Vila Planas
Manager: Francesc Matas Salla
Founded: 1989
Subjects: Crafts, Games, Hobbies
ISBN Prefix(es): 84-7831
Warehouse: Recared, 2, Local 35, 08030 Barcelona

Joyas Bibliograficas SA
Fomento, 5, 28013 Madrid
Tel: (091) 5470220
Key Personnel
Administrator: Carlos Romero de Lecea
Subjects: History, Literature, Literary Criticism, Essays, Poetry
ISBN Prefix(es): 84-7094

Ediciones Jucar+
Menendez Valdes, 33-1, 33201 Gijon Asturias
Tel: (08) 5170921; (08) 5349684 *Fax:* (08) 5349542
Telex: 89736 Edju E
Key Personnel
Man Dir: Silverio Canada Acebal
Editorial: Maria de Calonje
Production: Manuel Cardenas
Founded: 1974
Subjects: Fiction, Government, Political Science, Literature, Literary Criticism, Essays, Music, Dance, Poetry

ISBN Prefix(es): 84-334
Orders to: Honesto Batalon 7, Gijon *Tel:* (985) 355790

Ediciones Junior SA+
Arago 385, 08013 Barcelona
Tel: (093) 4767100 *Fax:* (093) 4767121
Key Personnel
President: Juan Grijalbo
Council Delegate: Jose Maria Vives
Assistant Council Delegate: Gonzalo Ponton
Manager: Josep Maria Pujol
Founded: 1974
Member of Grupo & Grijalbo-Mondadori Publications in Barcelona.
Subjects: Humor
ISBN Prefix(es): 84-7419
Warehouse: Grijalbo Comercial, SA, Progreso, 274, Badelona (Barcelona)

Junta de Castilla y Leon Consejeria de Educacion y Cultura
Avda de Soria, 15, 47193 La Disterniga (Valladolid)
Tel: (0983) 411586 *Fax:* (0983) 403070
Web Site: www.jcyl.es
Key Personnel
Dir: Agustin Garcia Simon *E-mail:* agustin.garcia@cec.jcyl.es
Founded: 1984
Subjects: Archaeology, Art, Biography, History, Literature, Literary Criticism, Essays, Poetry, Regional Interests, Science (General), Travel
ISBN Prefix(es): 84-7846; 84-9718
Distributor for Lidiza; Siglo

Editorial Juventud SA+
Provenca, 101, 08029 Barcelona
Tel: (093) 444 18 00 *Fax:* (093) 444 18 02
E-mail: juventud@bcn.servicom.es
Web Site: www.editorialjuventud.es *Cable:* JUVENTUD
Key Personnel
Dir General: Luis Zendrera Duniau
Founded: 1923
Subjects: Accounting, Aeronautics, Aviation, Animals, Pets, Architecture & Interior Design, Art, Biography, Fiction, History, Language Arts, Linguistics, Sports, Athletics, Travel
ISBN Prefix(es): 84-261
Associate Companies: Editorial Juventud SA, Mexico
Subsidiaries: Editorial Juventud de Espana Ltd
Distributed by Editorial Corimbo; Editorial Parsifal

Editorial Kairos SA+
Numancia 117-121, 08029 Barcelona
Tel: (093) 430 3746 *Fax:* (093) 410 5166
E-mail: kairos@sendanet.es *Cable:* KAIROS
Key Personnel
Man Dir: Salvador Paniker
Editorial, Rights & Permissions, Sales: Agustin Paniker
Production, Publicity: Pilar Tomas
Founded: 1966
Publishes a growing range of new consciousness titles.
Subjects: Philosophy, Psychology, Psychiatry, Religion - Other, Social Sciences, Sociology
ISBN Prefix(es): 84-7245

Editorial Labor SA+
Rambla Montserrat, 19 bajos, 08290 Cerdanyola, Barcelona
Tel: (093) 5808124 *Fax:* (093) 6921851
  Cable: EDILABOR
Key Personnel
Man Dir: Manuel Sanglas Muchart
Founded: 1915

Subjects: Art, Business, Engineering (General), History, Human Relations, Medicine, Nursing, Dentistry, Science (General), Technology
ISBN Prefix(es): 84-335; 84-250; 84-7593
Imprints: Guadarrama
Branch Office(s)
Editorial Labor SA Colombiana Ltda, Colombia
Editorial Labor SA, Uruguay
U.S. Office(s): DDL Books, Inc, 6521 NW 87 Ave, Miami, FL 33178, United States

Laertes SA de Ediciones+
Montseny, 43 baixos, 08012 Barcelona
Tel: (093) 2376869; (093) 2376944 *Fax:* (093) 2170384
E-mail: laertes@jet.es
Key Personnel
Man Dir & Editorial: Eduardo Suarez Alonso
Sales, Publicity: Carmen Miret
Founded: 1975
Subjects: Anthropology, Archaeology, Biography, Education, Fiction, Film, Video, Gay & Lesbian, Literature, Literary Criticism, Essays, Philosophy, Travel, Medicine & Nursing
ISBN Prefix(es): 84-85346; 84-7584
Total Titles: 525 Print
Foreign Rep(s): Ediciones Del Aguazul (Argentina); Ediciones Del Aguazul (Mexico)

Editorin Laiovento SL+
Rua do Horreo, 60, 15702 Santiago de Compostela Galiza
Tel: (0981) 564767; (0981) 589199 *Fax:* (0981) 572239
E-mail: laiovento@laiovento.com
Web Site: www.laiovento.com
Key Personnel
President: Afonso Ribas Fraga
Founded: 1989
Subjects: Economics, Education, History, Literature, Literary Criticism, Essays, Poetry, Science Fiction, Fantasy, Social Sciences, Sociology, Technology, Humanities & Social Sciences
ISBN Prefix(es): 84-87847; 84-89896
Imprints: Lengua Gallega Y Portuguesa
Distributor for Ninguna

Leandro Lara Editor+
Ave Antonio Gaudi, 76-126 NAVE 1 bis Pol. Ind. Rubi Sud, 08091 Rubi
Tel: (093) 6970036; (093) 6970364
E-mail: leandro@bbvnet.co
Key Personnel
Contact: Leandro Lara Merino
ISBN Prefix(es): 84-7699

Larousse Planeta SA+
Enric Granados, 84, 08008 Barcelona
Tel: (093) 908 99 10 54
E-mail: larousse@larousse.es
Key Personnel
Contact: Yolanda Portillo Jimenez
Founded: 1991
ISBN Prefix(es): 84-8016
Subsidiaries: Grandes De La Cite International

Las Ediciones de Arte (LEDA), see LEDA (Las Ediciones de Arte)

LEDA (Las Ediciones de Arte)+
Riera Sant Miguel 37, 08006 Barcelona
Tel: (093) 2379389; (093) 2155273
Key Personnel
Man Dir: Daniel Basilio Bonet
Founded: 1942
Subjects: Advertising, Architecture & Interior Design, Art, Child Care & Development, Crafts, Games, Hobbies
ISBN Prefix(es): 84-7095

SPAIN

Edicions de l'Eixample, SA+
Mallorca 297, pral, 08037 Barcelona
Tel: (093) 4589405 *Fax:* (093) 2076248
Key Personnel
Council Delegates: Salvador Saura; Ramon Torrente
Dir: Isabel Segura
Founded: 1983
Subjects: Fiction
ISBN Prefix(es): 84-86279

Lengua Gallega Y Portuguesa, *imprint of* Editorin Laiovento SL

Liber Ediciones, SA
Travesia Bayona, 1, 31011 Pamplona
Tel: (0948) 177 488 *Fax:* (0948) 176 667
E-mail: info@arsliber.com
Web Site: www.arsliber.com
Key Personnel
Contact: Juan Jose Izquierdo Broncano
Founded: 1989
Subjects: Art
ISBN Prefix(es): 84-89339

Ediciones Libertarias/Prodhufi SA+
C Bravo Murillo, 37-1 Dcha, 28015 Madrid
Tel: (091) 593 33 93 *Fax:* (091) 594 16 96
E-mail: libertarias@libertarias.com
Web Site: www.libertarias.com
Key Personnel
Publisher: Carmelo Martinez Garcia
Communication Dir: Annamaria Duran
Founded: 1979
Subjects: Cookery, Government, Political Science, Health, Nutrition, History, Literature, Literary Criticism, Essays, Poetry, Psychology, Psychiatry, Science Fiction, Fantasy, Social Sciences, Sociology
ISBN Prefix(es): 84-7954; 84-87095; 84-85641; 84-7683
Distributed by Conty SA de CV (Central America); Libertarias Prodhufi, SA

Libros Cupula, *imprint of* Grupo Editorial CEAC SA

Libsa, *imprint of* Libsa Editorial SA

Libsa Editorial SA+
San Rafael, 28108 Alcobendas Madrid
Tel: (091) 657 25 80 *Fax:* (091) 657 25 83
E-mail: libsa@libsa.es
Web Site: www.libsa.es
Key Personnel
President: Amado Sanchez *E-mail:* rocio@libsa.redestb.es
Foreign Rights: Alberto Boix
Foreign Rights Manager: Francisco Saavedra
Founded: 1980
Subjects: Art, Cookery, Crafts, Games, Hobbies, Gardening, Plants, Health, Nutrition, House & Home, Language Arts, Linguistics, Literature, Literary Criticism, Essays, Nonfiction (General), Self-Help, Children/Adult lists, Leisure & Practical Guides
ISBN Prefix(es): 84-7630
Imprints: Libsa; Agata; Alba

Lid Editorial Empresarial, SL+
Sopelana, 22, 28023 Madrid
Tel: (091) 372 90 03 *Fax:* (091) 372 85 14
E-mail: consejeros-lid@nexo.es
Key Personnel
President: Marcelino Elosua
Editor: Debbie Martinez
Founded: 1993
Member of Federacion de Gremios de Editores de Espana.
Subjects: Biography, Business, Career Development, Economics, Finance, Language Arts, Linguistics, Marketing, Self-Help, Economics & Business, Spanish Business History, Specialized Business Dictionaries
ISBN Prefix(es): 84-88717

Llibres del Segle+
La Rectoria, 17466 Gaueses Girona
Tel: (0972) 795079 *Fax:* (0972) 210354
E-mail: costapau@releline.es
Key Personnel
Production: Rosa M Tries
Subjects: Art, Education, History, Literature, Literary Criticism, Essays, Nonfiction (General), Poetry, Social Sciences, Sociology
ISBN Prefix(es): 84-89885
Total Titles: 12 Print
Distributor for L'Arc de Bera

Loguez Ediciones+
Carretera de Madrid 90, Apdo 1, 37900 Santa Marta de Tormes (Salamanca)
Tel: (0923) 138541 *Fax:* (0923) 138586
E-mail: loguezediciones@eresmas.com
Key Personnel
Man Dir, Sales: L Rodriguez Lopez
Editorial, Publicity: Maribel G Martinez
Founded: 1978
Specialize in children's literature, and musical books.
Subjects: Art, Earth Sciences, Education, Fiction, Gay & Lesbian, Literature, Literary Criticism, Essays, Music, Dance, Religion - Catholic, Religion - Other, Self-Help, Theology
ISBN Prefix(es): 84-85334; 84-89804
Number of titles published annually: 12 Print; 3 CD-ROM

Ediciones Luciernaga, *imprint of* Grup 62

Ediciones Luciernaga
Imprint of Grup 62
Peu de la Creu, 4, 08001 Barcelona
Tel: (093) 443 71 00 *Fax:* (093) 443 71 30
E-mail: correu@grup62.com
Web Site: www.grup62.com
Key Personnel
Rights Manager: Laura Pujol

Editorial Luis Vives (Edelvives)+
Xaudaro, 25, 28034 Madrid
Tel: (091) 334 48 83 *Fax:* (091) 334 48 92; (091) 334 48 94
E-mail: jmarketing@edelvives.es
Web Site: www.edelvives.es *Cable:* EDELVIVES
Key Personnel
Man Dir: Antonio Gimenez de Baguees
Editorial Dir: Jose Manuel Gomez Luque
Production Dir: Jesus Agudo
Commercial Dir: Jose Luis Illana
Founded: 1890
Subjects: Education
ISBN Prefix(es): 84-263
Number of titles published annually: 200 Print
Total Titles: 35,000 Print; 6 CD-ROM; 3 Audio
Associate Companies: Editorial Ibaizabal, Barrio de San Miguel s/n Euba-Amorebieta, 48290 Vizcaya *Tel:* (046) 308036 *Fax:* (046) 308028 *E-mail:* ibaizabal@euskalnet.net
Subsidiaries: Ediciones Baula
Branch Office(s)
Poligono de Cranda s/n, 33199 Asturias
Tel: (098) 579 46 16 *E-mail:* asturias@edelvives.es
Passeo Valldaura, 184, 08042 Barcelona
Tel: (093) 354 03 99 *E-mail:* barcelona@endelvives.es
Ayagaures 8 Nave D, Urb Ind Lomo Blanco-Las Torres, 35010 Las Palmas de Gran Canaria 9 *Tel:* (0928) 48 12 47 *E-mail:* canarias@edelvives.es
Manuel Tovar, esq. Estrada, 28034 Madrid
Tel: (091) 344 48 84 *E-mail:* madrid@edelvives.es
Veracruz, 32 (Pol. San Luis), 29006 Malaga
Tel: (095) 236 3409 *E-mail:* malaga@edelvives.es
Via Apia, 32, (Pol. Ind. Fuentequintillo), 41089 Montequintille (Sevilla) *Tel:* (095) 4 129 180 *E-mail:* sevilla@edelvives.es
Avda Txori-Erri, 46 No, Modulo 4, Letra E, 48150 Sondika (Vizcaya) *Tel:* (094) 453 20 09 *E-mail:* bilbao@edelvives.es
Poligono 1-2 (Tafaea) Parcela 28, 45600 Talavera de la Reina (Toledo) *Tel:* (0925) 81 74 34 *E-mail:* toledo@edelvives.es
Avda Ausias March 222, Pista de Silla, 46026 Valencia *Tel:* (096) 375 98 11 *E-mail:* valencia@edelvives.es
Acero 4, (Pol San Cristobal), 47012 Valladolid
Tel: (0983) 21 30 38 *E-mail:* valladolid@edelvives.es
Severino Cobas 142 (Lavadores), 36214 Vigo
Tel: (0986) 27 20 13 *E-mail:* vigo@edelvives.es
Ctra de Madrid, km 315 700, 50012 Zaragoza
Tel: (0976) 30 40 30 *E-mail:* zaragoza@edelvives.es

Editorial Lumen SA+
Ramon Miquel i Planas 10, 08034 Barcelona
Tel: (093) 2043496 *Fax:* (093) 2055619
E-mail: mbusquets.plaza@asertel.es
Key Personnel
Man Dir: Esther Tusquets
Founded: 1939
Subjects: Art, Fiction, Humor, Literature, Literary Criticism, Essays, Poetry, Social Sciences, Sociology
ISBN Prefix(es): 84-264

Lunwerg Editores, SA+
Sagasta 27, 2 izda, 28004 Madrid
Tel: (091) 5930058 *Fax:* (091) 5930070
E-mail: lunwerg.mad@retemail.es
Key Personnel
Man Dir: Juan Carlos Luna
Rights & Permissions: Carmen Garcia
Founded: 1980
Subjects: Archaeology, Architecture & Interior Design, Art, Cookery, Drama, Theater, History, Maritime, Photography, Travel
ISBN Prefix(es): 84-7782
Orders to: Mercedes Carregal, Beethoven 12, 08021 Barcelona *Tel:* (093) 2015933 *Fax:* (093) 2011587

Lynx Edicions
Montseny, 8, E-08193 Bellaterra, Barcelona
Tel: (093) 594 77 10 *Fax:* (093) 592 09 69
E-mail: pruizolalla@hbw.com
Web Site: www.hbw.com
Key Personnel
Contact: Pilar Ruiz-Olalla
Founded: 1989
Subjects: Animals, Pets, Natural History
ISBN Prefix(es): 84-87334
U.S. Office(s): Lynx Edicions, c/o Mail Management Group Inc, 81 N Forest Ave, Rockville Centre, NY 11570, United States

Antonio Machado, SA
Tomas Breton 55, 28045 Madrid
Tel: (091) 4681398 *Fax:* (091) 4681098
E-mail: editorial@visordis.es
Web Site: www.visordis.es
Key Personnel
Dir: Jose Miguel Garcia Sanchez
Books, Magazines, Journals, Newspapers.
Subjects: Architecture & Interior Design, Art, Drama, Theater, History, Language Arts, Linguistics, Literature, Literary Criticism, Essays, Music, Dance, Philosophy, Psychology, Psychiatry, Publishing & Book Trade Reference, Self-

PUBLISHERS

SPAIN

Help, Cultural History/Regionalia, Performing Arts, Political Science
ISBN Prefix(es): 84-7644

Macmillan Heinemann ELT
Martin de Vargas 5, Esc C 1, 28005 Madrid
Tel: (091) 517 85 40 *Fax:* (091) 517 85 54
E-mail: madrid@mad.heinemann.es
Web Site: www.heinemann.es
Parent Company: Macmillan Publishers Ltd
Distributor for Language Teaching Publications (LTP); Max Hueber Verlag/Verlag Fuer Deutsch

Mad SL Editorial+
Polig Merka C/B, naves 1-3, 41500 Alcala de Guadaira Sevilla
Tel: (095) 5630820 *Fax:* (095) 5630713
E-mail: info@mad.es
Web Site: www.mad.es
Key Personnel
Administrator: Dolores Lopez-Jurado
Dir: Luis Abril Mula *E-mail:* luis@mad.es
Gen Dir: Narciso Sanchez-Valdenaura *E-mail:* nsv@mad.es
Founded: 1983
Subjects: Law
ISBN Prefix(es): 84-86526

Ediciones Maeva+
Benito de Castro 6, 28028 Madrid
Tel: (091) 355 95 69 *Fax:* (091) 355 19 47
E-mail: maeva@infornet.es
Web Site: www.maeva.es
Key Personnel
Contact: Cuadros Lopez Maite
Founded: 1985
Subjects: Anthropology, Biography, Foreign Countries, History, Literature, Literary Criticism, Essays, Nonfiction (General), Regional Interests, Travel
ISBN Prefix(es): 84-86478; 84-95354
Imprints: Catalogo
Subsidiaries: Editoriales Exclusivas
Orders to: SGEL, c/o Avda Valdelaparda, 29, Poligono Industrial, 28108 Alcobendas-Madrid
Tel: (091) 6576955 *Fax:* (091) 6576958

Editorial Magisterio Espanol SA+
Casp 79, 08013 Barcelona
Tel: (093) 5776653 *Fax:* (093) 6420086
Web Site: www.editorialcasals.com
Key Personnel
General Manager: Ramon Casals
Founded: 1866
Subjects: Education, Fiction, Literature, Literary Criticism, Essays, Philosophy, Religion - Catholic
ISBN Prefix(es): 84-265
Parent Company: Editorial Casals, SA

Magoria, *imprint of* Obelisco Ediciones S

Edicions de la Magrana SA+
Padua, 83, 08006 Barcelona
Tel: (093) 4173000 *Fax:* (093) 4170106
E-mail: magrana@essi.es
Key Personnel
Man Dir: Carles-Jordi Guardiola
Production: Lluis Baselga
Assistant Dir: Eva Eduardo
Founded: 1975
Subjects: Biography, Cookery, Fiction, Literature, Literary Criticism, Essays, Philosophy, Science (General), Social Sciences, Sociology
ISBN Prefix(es): 84-7410

Mandala Ediciones+
Escalinata, 9, 28013 Madrid
Tel: (091) 5840954 *Fax:* (091) 5480326
E-mail: fcabal@lander.es
Web Site: www.lander.es:800/~fcabal
Key Personnel
Man Dir: Fernando Cabal *Tel:* (091) 5480954
Editorial: Gonzalo Rivero
Founded: 1980
Subjects: Architecture & Interior Design, Astrology, Occult, Behavioral Sciences, Cookery, Earth Sciences, Environmental Studies, Film, Video, Medicine, Nursing, Dentistry, Music, Dance, Psychology, Psychiatry, Religion - Buddhist, Religion - Hindu, Religion - Islamic, Biological Agriculture, Biological Medicine, Chinese Medicine, Dietetic Natural, Ecological Architecture, Ecology, Fitoterapia, Homeopatia, Manual Medicine, Massage, Relaxation
ISBN Prefix(es): 84-86961; 84-88769
Total Titles: 210 Print

Editorial Mapfre SA
Monte del Pilar s/n, 28023 El Plantio - Madrid
Tel: (091) 581 53 57 *Fax:* (091) 581 18 83
E-mail: edimap@mapfre.com
Web Site: www2.mapfre.com
Key Personnel
Man Dir: Miguel Angel Gimeno
Subjects: Financial Security & Services, Insurances
ISBN Prefix(es): 84-7100

Marcial Pons Ediciones Juridicas SA
San Sotero, 6, 28037 Madrid
Tel: (091) 304 33 03 *Fax:* (091) 754 12 18
Web Site: www.marcialpons.es
Key Personnel
Owner: Marcial Pons Abejer
Founded: 1990
Subjects: Law, Public Administration
ISBN Prefix(es): 84-7248; 963-371; 963-372

Marcombo SA de Boixareu Editores+
Gran Via, 594, 08007 Barcelona
Tel: (093) 3180079 *Fax:* (093) 3189339
E-mail: marcombo.boixareu@marcombo.es
Web Site: www.marcombo.es
Key Personnel
Man Dir: Josep Maria Boixareu Vilaplana
Marketing & Sales Manager: Jose Romero Gonzalez
Founded: 1945
Subjects: Anthropology, Automotive, Business, Civil Engineering, Communications, Computer Science, Economics, Electronics, Electrical Engineering, Energy, Finance, Management, Marketing, Mathematics, Microcomputers, Radio, TV
ISBN Prefix(es): 84-267
Branch Office(s)
Marcombo SA, Plaza de la Villa 1, 28005 Madrid
Distributed by Distribuciones Alba, S.A.; Alfaomego Grupo Editor (Colombia, Mexico, Guatemala, Costa Rica, Ecuador, Nicaragua, Honduras, El Salvador); Asturlibros, Poligono Silvota; Be Nvil, S.A. Llibres; Carrasco Libros, S.L.; Contemporanea de Ediciones (Venezuela); Distribuidora Cuspide, S.R.L. (Argentina); Galileo Libros, Ltd (Chile); Andres Libreros - Libro Tecnico; Lidiza, S.A.; Losa Libros Ltda (Uruguay); Marcombo, S.A.; Odon Molina, Distribuidor de Libros; Palma Distribucions, S.L.; Pato Libros; Distribuidora Del Sur; UNBE, S.A.; Unidisa, Demetrio Sillero; Viuber, S.L.Delegacion de Edit
Bookshop(s): Libreria Hispano Americana

Editorial Marfil SA+
Sant Eloi 17, 03804 Alcoi
Tel: (096) 5523311 *Fax:* (096) 5523496
E-mail: editorialmarfil@editorialmerfil.com
Web Site: www.editorialmarfil.com *Cable:* MARFIL
Key Personnel
Contact: Veronica Canto Domenych
Founded: 1947
Subjects: Education, Literature, Literary Criticism, Essays, Psychology, Psychiatry
ISBN Prefix(es): 84-268; 84-7816

Editorial Marin SA+
Avda San Julian, 234, Poligono Industrial El Congost, 08400 Granollers Barcelona
Tel: (093) 8468101 *Fax:* (093) 8468107
Cable: MARINEDI
Key Personnel
Administrator: Manuel Marin
Man Dir: Jorge Fernandez
Founded: 1900
Subjects: Art, Medicine, Nursing, Dentistry, Nonfiction (General)
ISBN Prefix(es): 84-7102
Branch Office(s)
Editorial Marin SA, Anaxagoras 1400, Colonia Santa Cruz Atoyac, 03310 Mexico, DF, Mexico
Warehouse: Calle Industria 5/n, Polzono Industrial, El Papiol

Ediciones Marova SL+
Cedaceros, 3-2, 28014 Madrid
Tel: (091) 5322606 *Fax:* (091) 5322346
E-mail: glanzas@infornet.es
Key Personnel
Man Dir: Jose Miguel Oriol
Founded: 1956
Subjects: Education, Psychology, Psychiatry, Religion - Other, Social Sciences, Sociology
ISBN Prefix(es): 84-269

Ediciones Martinez-Roca SA+
Provenca, 260 6a, 08008 Barcelona
Tel: (093) 496 70 12 *Fax:* (093) 496 70 14
E-mail: info@ediciones-martinez-roca.es
Web Site: www.edicionesmartinezroca.com
Key Personnel
Man Dir: Fernando Calvo Aparicio
Founded: 1988
Subjects: Animals, Pets, Astrology, Occult, Biography, Crafts, Games, Hobbies, Fiction, Health, Nutrition, How-to, Literature, Literary Criticism, Essays, Nonfiction (General), Psychology, Psychiatry, Romance, Science Fiction, Fantasy, Self-Help, Sports, Athletics
ISBN Prefix(es): 84-270; 84-8327

La Mascara, SL Editorial+
Pza. Diputado Luis Lucia, 21-B, 46015 Valencia
Tel: (096) 3486500 *Fax:* (096) 3487440
Key Personnel
Commercial Dir: Celso Andres
Founded: 1991
Subjects: Biography, Music, Dance, Poetry
ISBN Prefix(es): 84-7974
Subsidiaries: La Mascara France, Sarl

McGraw-Hill Iberic/Brazil Group+
Basauri, 17 Edif. Valrealty, plta1, 28023 Aravaca, Madrid
Tel: (01) 3728193; (01) 3728409 (customer service) *Fax:* (01) 3728513
Web Site: www.mcgraw-hill.es
Telex: 43817 DIE
Key Personnel
Group Man Dir: Antonio Garcia-Maroto
Publisher, Business & Professional Division: Eduardo Susanna
Publisher, High School Vocational Technical Division: Wenceslao Ortega
Distributor & Book Store Sales Manager: Fernando Serrano
Controller & Business Manager: Jose Castellano
Production Manager: Jose Martinez Alaminos
EDP Manager: Miguel Angel de Dios
Founded: 1974
Iberian/Mercosur Peninsula Group
Markets served: Spain, Portugal, Argentina, Uruguay, Paraguay.

Subjects: Biological Sciences, Education, Health, Nutrition, Medicine, Nursing, Dentistry, Science (General), Technology
ISBN Prefix(es): 84-7615; 84-85240; 84-7605; 84-486
Parent Company: McGraw-Hill Inc, 1221 Avenue of the Americas, New York, NY 10020, United States
Branch Office(s)
Mercosur, Argentina, Suipacha 764, 1008 Buenos Aires, Argentina *Tel:* (01) 3228868 *Fax:* (01) 3223456 (Distribudora Cuspide)
Mercosur, Paraguay, Suipacha 764, 1008 Buenos Aires, Argentina *Tel:* (01) 3228868 *Fax:* (01) 3223456 (Distribudora Cuspide)
Mercosur, Uruguay, Suipacha 764, 1008 Buenos Aires, Argentina *Tel:* (01) 3228868 *Fax:* (01) 3223456 (Distribudora Cuspide)

ME Editores, SL+
Marcelina, 23, 28029 Madrid
Tel: (091) 3151008 *Fax:* (091) 3230844
Founded: 1992
ISBN Prefix(es): 84-495

Editorial Medica JIMS, SL
Balmes, 266, 08006 Barcelona
Tel: (093) 2188800 *Fax:* (093) 2188928
   Cable: EDITOJIMS
Key Personnel
Man Dir, Editorial, Publicity: Antonio Jimenez Sanchez
Sales: Teresa Jimenez Sayo
Production: Luis Jimenez Sayo
Founded: 1956
Subjects: Medicine, Nursing, Dentistry
ISBN Prefix(es): 84-7092

Ediciones Medici SA+
Plato, 26, 08006 Barcelona
Tel: (093) 2 010 599; (093) 2 013 807; (093) 2 012 144 *Fax:* (093) 2 097 362
E-mail: omega@ediciones-omega.es
Web Site: www.ediciones-medici.es; www.ediciones-omega.es
Key Personnel
Man Dir: Ana Dexeus; Antonio Paricio; Gabriel Paricio
Founded: 1983
Subjects: Child Care & Development, Cookery, Education, Health, Nutrition, Human Relations, Medicine, Nursing, Dentistry, Nonfiction (General)
ISBN Prefix(es): 84-86193
Parent Company: Ediciones Omega SA
Orders to: Ediciones Omega/Medici, Plato, 26, 08006 Barcelona

Editorial Mediterrania SL+
Guillem Tell 15 - 17 entlo, 08006 Barcelona
Tel: (093) 218 34 58; (093) 237 86 65 *Fax:* (093) 237 22 10
Key Personnel
Man Dir & Sales: Eduard Fornes
Editorial, Rights & Permissions: Josep Abril
Production: Nuria Carpena
Publicity: Monica Estrich
Founded: 1980
Member of Association of Editors in the Catalan Language & Editors Guild of Catalunya.
Subjects: Art, Health, Nutrition, History, Literature, Literary Criticism, Essays, Outdoor Recreation, Photography, Religion - Catholic, Sports, Athletics, Travel
ISBN Prefix(es): 84-8334

Ediciones Mensajero+
Sancho de Azpeitia, 2, Apdo 73, 48014 Bilbao
Tel: (094) 4 470 358 *Fax:* (094) 4 472 630
E-mail: mensajero@mensajero.com
Web Site: www.mensajero.com *Cable:* MENSAJERO
Key Personnel
Man Dir: Angel Antonio Perez
Editorial, Production: Josu Leguina
   E-mail: josuleguina@mensajero.com
Publicity & Sales: Jose Manuel Diaz
Founded: 1915
Subjects: Education, How-to, Philosophy, Psychology, Psychiatry, Religion - Other, Social Sciences, Sociology
ISBN Prefix(es): 84-271

Editorial Milenio Arts Grafiques Bobala, SL+
Sant Salvador 8, 25005 Lleida
Tel: (0973) 236 611 *Fax:* (0973) 240 795
E-mail: editorial.milenio@cambrescat.es
Web Site: www.edmilenio.com
Key Personnel
Dir: Lluis Pages i Marigot *Fax:* (0973) 740 795
Founded: 1996
Specialize in Spanish & Latin American books.
ISBN Prefix(es): 84-89790
Total Titles: 20 Print
Associate Companies: Pages Editors, SL
Distributed by Espana y America
Book Club(s): Eventualmente

Ministerio de Economia y Hacienda Secretario General Tecnica Centro de Publicaciones
Paseo de la Castellana 162.1a, 28005 Planta, Madrid
Tel: (091) 3493592 *Fax:* (091) 3493502
Key Personnel
Technical General Secretario: Rosa Rodriguez-Moreno
ISBN Prefix(es): 84-476; 84-7196; 84-85482

Ministerio de Educacion y Culture Centro de Publicaciones
Ciudad Universitaria, 28071 Madrid
Tel: (091) 453 98 00 *Fax:* (091) 453 98 00
Key Personnel
Editorial Control Head: Antonio Arenas Carrera
ISBN Prefix(es): 84-369

Ministerio de Justicia e Interior, Centro de Publicaciones
San Bernardo, 62, Planta Baja, 28015 Madrid
Tel: (091) 390 44 29; (091) 390 20 83; (091) 390 20 97 *Fax:* (091) 390 20 92
Web Site: www.mju.es
Key Personnel
General Assistant Dir of Documentation & Publications: Gonzalo Puebla De Diego
Founded: 1947
Subjects: Law
ISBN Prefix(es): 84-7787
Distributed by BOE; DIJUSA; Diputacion de Barcelona; Edisofer, S.L.; Marcial Pons; Reydis Libros, Lazaro Pascual Yague S.L.; Tapia Libros, S.A.
Warehouse: C/Ocana, 151-28047 Madrid

Ministerio de Trabajo y Asuntos Sociales
Formerly Instituto Nacional de Seguridad e Higiene en el Trabajo
Agustin de Bethencourt, 4, 28071 Madrid
Tel: (091) 4037000 *Fax:* (091) 4030050
E-mail: gprensa@mtas.es
Web Site: www.mtas.es
Key Personnel
Dir: Javier Gomez-Hortiguela Amillo
ISBN Prefix(es): 84-7425

Ediciones Minotauro+
Rambla de Catalunya, 62, 08007 Barcelona
Tel: (093) 487 1089 *Fax:* (093) 487 1849
E-mail: edicionesminotauro@arrakis.es
Web Site: www.edicionesminotauro.com
Key Personnel
Man Dir: Francisco Porrua
Founded: 1983
Subjects: Biography, Fiction, Literature, Literary Criticism, Essays, Science Fiction, Fantasy
ISBN Prefix(es): 84-450
Total Titles: 150 Print

Editores Mira, SA
Concepcion Arenal, 22, 50012 Zaragoza
Tel: (0976) 460505 *Fax:* (0976) 460446
E-mail: miraeditores@ctv.es
Web Site: www.miraeditores.com
ISBN Prefix(es): 84-86778; 84-88688; 84-89859

MK Ediciones y Publicaciones
Castello 30-5, 28001 Madrid
Tel: (091) 4316305 *Fax:* (091) 5754978
Key Personnel
Editorial Dir: Marta Ferre Pich
Founded: 1975
Specialize in Theater.
Subjects: Drama, Theater
ISBN Prefix(es): 84-7389

M Moleiro Editor, SA+
Travesera de Gracia, 17-21, 08021 Barcelona
Tel: (093) 240 20 91 *Fax:* (093) 201 50 62
E-mail: mmoleiro@moleiro.com
Web Site: www.moleiro.com
Key Personnel
President: Manuel Moleiro
International Rights: Ms Monica Miro
Founded: 1992
Specialize in facsimile editions of medieval illuminated manuscripts & maps.
Subjects: Art
ISBN Prefix(es): 84-88526

Editorial Molino+
Calabria, 166, 08015 Barcelona
Tel: (093) 226 06 25 *Fax:* (093) 226 69 98
E-mail: molino@menta.net
Web Site: www.editorialmolino.com *Cable:* MOLINO BARCELONA
Key Personnel
Man Dir: Luis A del Molino Jover
Founded: 1933
Subjects: Education, Fiction, Sports, Athletics
ISBN Prefix(es): 84-272
Number of titles published annually: 100 Print
Total Titles: 1,345 Print

Editorial Moll SL+
Torre de l'Amor, 4, 07001 Palma de Mallorca
Tel: (0971) 724472 *Fax:* (0971) 726252
E-mail: info@editorialmoll.es; editorial.moll@ocesa.es
Web Site: www.editorialmoll.es
Key Personnel
Man Dir: Francesc de B Moll
Founded: 1934
Also acts as book distributor to the Balearic Islands.
Subjects: Art, Biography, Fiction, History, Language Arts, Linguistics, Literature, Literary Criticism, Essays, Natural History, Poetry, Regional Interests, Social Sciences, Sociology, Travel
ISBN Prefix(es): 84-273
Number of titles published annually: 60 Print
Total Titles: 950 Print
Bookshop(s): Llibres Mallorca, Esglesia de Sta Eulalia, 11, 07001 Palma de Mallorca, Contact: Victor Moll *Tel:* (0971) 728453 *Fax:* (0971) 728453
Warehouse: c/Asival, 22, Polignon can Valero, Palma *Fax:* (0971) 761422

PUBLISHERS   SPAIN

Monograma Ediciones
Padre Bartolome Pou, 24, 07003 Palma de Mallorca, Baleares
Tel: (071) 754124; (071) 712593 *Fax:* (071) 712593
E-mail: totem@atlas-iap.es
Key Personnel
Dir General: Leonardo Sainz Fernandez
ISBN Prefix(es): 84-88777
Orders to: Palau Reial, No 3, 07001 Palma de Mallorca, Baleares

Editorial Monte Carmelo
Padre Silverio, 2, 09001 Burgos
Tel: (0947) 25 60 61 *Fax:* (0947) 25 60 62
E-mail: editorial@montecarmelo.com
Web Site: www.montecarmelo.com
Key Personnel
Dir: Alberto Pacho Polvorinos
Subjects: Religion - Catholic
ISBN Prefix(es): 84-7239

Ediciones Morata SL+
Mejia Lequerica, 12, 28004 Madrid
Tel: (091) 448 09 26 *Fax:* (091) 448 09 25
E-mail: morata@infornet.es
Web Site: www.edmorata.es
Key Personnel
Man Dir: Flora Morata
Editorial Dir & Rights Manager: Florentina Gomez Morata
Founded: 1920
Subjects: Behavioral Sciences, Child Care & Development, Education, Government, Political Science, Mathematics, Medicine, Nursing, Dentistry, Parapsychology, Philosophy, Psychology, Psychiatry, Social Sciences, Sociology, Women's Studies
ISBN Prefix(es): 84-7112
Total Titles: 300 Print
Distributed by Berriak - Comercial de Edit. S.L.; Cerezo Libros; Distriforma, S.A.; Andres Garcia Libros, S.L.; Gea Llibres, S.L.; Lemus, Distribuciones, CB; Modesto Alonso Estraves, Distribuciones; Nogara Libros, SA; Norte, Promociones y Distrib. S.L.; Les Punxes Distribuidora, S.L.; Serrano Libros; La Tierra Libros, SL; UNIDISA

Anaya & Mario Muchnik+
Juan Ignacio Luca de Tena, 15, 28027 Madrid
Tel: (091) 393 89 00 *Fax:* (091) 742 66 31
E-mail: cga@anaya.es
Web Site: www.anaya.es
Key Personnel
General Dir: Victor Freixanes
Founded: 1990
Subjects: Literature, Literary Criticism, Essays
ISBN Prefix(es): 84-7979
Parent Company: Grupo Anaya SA
Distributor for America Latina

Instituto de la Mujer (Ministerio de Trabajo y Asuntos Sociales)
Condesa de Venadito, 34, 28027 Madrid
Tel: (091) 363 80 00
E-mail: inmujer@mtas.es
Web Site: www.mtas.es/mujer
Key Personnel
Dir General: Pilar Davila del Cerro
ISBN Prefix(es): 84-7799

Mundi-Prensa Libros SA+
Castello, 37, 28001 Madrid
Tel: (091) 4 36 37 00 *Fax:* (091) 5 75 39 98
E-mail: liberia@mundiprensa.es
Web Site: www.mundiprensa.com *Cable:* MUNDIPREN
Key Personnel
Man Dir: Jose Maria Hernandez
  E-mail: hernandez@mundiprensa.es
Manager: Ramon Reverte *E-mail:* resavbp@data.net.mx
Editorial & Publicity: Maria Isabel Hernandez
  E-mail: libreria@mundipresna.es
Associate to Commercial Dir: Jose Chai
  E-mail: jchai@mundiprensa.es
International Agency of Subscriptions: Pilar Garcia Gil *E-mail:* pilargarcia@mundiprensa.es
Administration: Ana Lopez *E-mail:* lopez@mundiprensa.es
Sales Mgr: Mariano Estaban *E-mail:* barcelona@mundiprensa.es
Information: Joaquin Alcaniz
  E-mail: informatica@mundiprensa.es
Accounting: Agustin de las Heras
  E-mail: delasheras@mundiprensa.es
Founded: 1948
Subjects: Agriculture, Animals, Pets, Biological Sciences, Economics, Gardening, Plants, Mechanical Engineering, Technology, Veterinary Science
ISBN Prefix(es): 84-7114
Subsidiaries: Mundi-Prensa Mexico, SA de CV; Libreria Agricola; Editorial Aedos, SA
Divisions: Mundi-Prensa Barcelona
Bookshop(s): Libreria Mundi-Prensa; Libreria Agricola, Fernando VI 2, 28004 Madrid; Libreria Inernacional, Aedos-Consejo de ciento 391, 08009 Barcelona

Mundo Negro Editorial+
Arturo Soria, 101, 28043 Madrid
Tel: (091) 4158115; (091) 4152412 *Fax:* (091) 5192550
E-mail: 100623.1651@compuserve.com
Key Personnel
Dir: Antonio Villarino
Founded: 1960
Subjects: Anthropology, Art, Biography, Developing Countries, Ethnicity, Foreign Countries, History, Religion - Catholic, Religion - Other, Theology
ISBN Prefix(es): 84-7295

Munoz Moya Editor+
28 de Febrero 8, 41310 Brenes
Tel: (05) 4797251 *Fax:* (05) 4796650
E-mail: editorial@mmoya.com
Web Site: www.mmoya.com
Key Personnel
Contact: Miguel Angel Munoz Moya
Founded: 1984
Specialize in Biblioteca Americana.
Subjects: Anthropology, Astrology, Occult, History, Literature, Literary Criticism, Essays, Mysteries, Poetry, Religion - Buddhist, Religion - Catholic, Religion - Jewish
ISBN Prefix(es): 84-8010; 84-86335; 84-931192
Number of titles published annually: 24 Online; 24 E-Book
Total Titles: 45 Online; 45 E-Book

Editorial la Muralla SA+
Constancia 33, 28002 Madrid
Tel: (091) 415 36 87; (091) 416 13 71 *Fax:* (091) 413 59 07
E-mail: muralla@arcomuralla.com
Web Site: www.arcomuralla.com
Key Personnel
Man Dir: Lidio Nieto
Publicity, Rights & Permissions: Nuria Nieto
Production: Julio Sanchez
Founded: 1968
Subjects: Art, Biological Sciences, Education, Geography, Geology, History, Language Arts, Linguistics, Literature, Literary Criticism, Essays, Mathematics, Music, Dance, Physical Sciences, Physics, Technology
ISBN Prefix(es): 84-7133
Distributed by Distribudora Malaguena Atenea; Distribuciones Cimadevilla SA; Egatorre; Andres Garcia Libros; Grial; Carmen Fernandez Lappi; Libregus SL; LOGI; Lyra; Marcelino Perich Rasclosa; Odon Molina; Palma Distribucion SL; Pedidos; PROLOGO; La Tierra Libros; UNIDISA

Editorial Musica Moderna
Garcia Luna, 1 y 3, 28080 Madrid
Tel: (091) 416 91 81; (091) 415 37 78
Key Personnel
Editor, Dir: Francisco Carmona
Founded: 1935
Subjects: Music, Dance
ISBN Prefix(es): 84-86292

Instituto Nacional de Administracion Publica
Atocha, 106, 28012 Madrid
Tel: (091) 349 32 41 *Fax:* (091) 349 32 70
Web Site: www.inap.map.es
ISBN Prefix(es): 84-7088
Branch Office(s)
Plaza de San Diego s/n, 28801 Alcala de Henares (Madrid) *Tel:* (091) 888 22 00 *Fax:* (091) 880 28 61
Calle de Jose Maranon, 12, 28010 Madrid
  Tel: (091) 594 97 00 *Fax:* (091) 445 08 39
Avenida del Doctor Marcelino Roca s/n, Peniscola (Casellon de la Plana *Tel:* (0964) 48 08 25 *Fax:* (0964) 48 06 49

Instituto Nacional del Educacion Fisica Madrid (INEF-Madrid)
Martin Fierro, s/n, 28040 Madrid
Tel: (091) 589 4057; (091) 589 4059
Web Site: www.inef.com
Key Personnel
Subdirector INEF: Teresa Gonzales Aja
Founded: 1961

Instituto Nacional de la Salud
Alcala, 56, 28014 Madrid
Tel: (091) 338 00 03
Web Site: www.msc.es
Key Personnel
Dir General: Josep Bonet Bertomeu
Head of Documentation & Publications: Carmen Limon Mendizabal
Subjects: Health, Nutrition
ISBN Prefix(es): 84-351

Naque Editora+
Pasaje Gutierrez Ortega, 1, 13001 Ciudad Real
Tel: (0926) 216714 *Fax:* (0926) 216714
E-mail: naque@cim.es
Web Site: www.naque.es
Key Personnel
Editor: Cristina Ruiz Perez
Founded: 1995
Also specializing in bimonthly magazines & translations.
Subjects: Art, Drama, Theater, Education, Literature, Literary Criticism, Essays
ISBN Prefix(es): 84-89987
Total Titles: 52 Print

Narcea SA de Ediciones+
Dr Federico Rubio y Gali 9, 28039 Madrid
Tel: (091) 554 64 84; (091) 554 61 02 *Fax:* (091) 554 64 87
E-mail: narcea@narceaediciones.es
Web Site: www.narceaediciones.es
Key Personnel
Editorial Dir: A de Miguel
Sales: N Nacher
Production: P Pazos
Rights & Permissions: C Vegas
Founded: 1968
Subjects: Education, Psychology, Psychiatry, Religion - Other, Social Sciences, Sociology
ISBN Prefix(es): 84-277

SPAIN

Ediciones Nauta Credito SA+
Joseph Tarradellas, 123-127 5 A, 08029 Barcelona
Tel: (093) 4392204 *Fax:* (093) 4107314
Telex: 54495 sele e *Cable:* EDINAUTA
Key Personnel
President: Jose Luis Ruiz de Villa Macho
Founded: 1962
Also book packager.
Subjects: Art, Nonfiction (General)
ISBN Prefix(es): 84-278
Warehouse: N Sra Montserrat 84-86, 08020 Barcelona

Navarra, Comunidad Autonoma, Servicio de Prensa, Publica Pamplona
Navas de Tolosa, 21, 31002 Pamplona, Navarra
Tel: (0948) 427121 *Fax:* (0948) 427123
E-mail: fpublio01@cfnavarra.es
Web Site: www.cfnavarra.es
Key Personnel
Press Dir: Felix Carmona Salinas
ISBN Prefix(es): 84-235
Orders to: Fondo de Publicaciones Gobierno de Navarra

NER, *imprint of* Editorial El Perpetuo Socorro

Editorial Nerea SA+
Juan de Laborda 2, 20280 Hondarribia Gipuzkoa
Tel: (0943) 64 57 43 *Fax:* (0943) 64 60 27
E-mail: nerea@nerea.net
Web Site: www.nerea.editores-euskadi.com
Key Personnel
Editor: Nerea Atxega
Contact: Marta Casares
Founded: 1987
Subjects: Architecture & Interior Design, Art, History, Women's Studies, Art History
ISBN Prefix(es): 84-86763; 84-89569

Editorial 92 SA+
Av Bogatell, 80 bis, 08005 Barcelona
Tel: (093) 3009092 *Fax:* (093) 3009109
Key Personnel
President: Josep Maria Fortia Vinolas
General Dir: Jaime Igea Noguera
Founded: 1989
Specialize in literary work consultations.
Subjects: Geography, Geology, History
ISBN Prefix(es): 84-87254
Divisions: Catalana d'Edicions, SA
Warehouse: Joan d'Austria 57-59, 08005 Barcelona

Noguer y Caralt Editores SA+
Santa Amelia, 22 Interior, 08034 Barcelona
SAN: 004-0568
Tel: (093) 280 13 99 *Fax:* (093) 280 19 93
E-mail: noguer-caralt@mx2.redestb.es
Key Personnel
President: Emilio Ardevol
Founded: 1942
Subjects: Art, Astrology, Occult, Biography, Cookery, Fiction, Geography, Geology, History, Literature, Literary Criticism, Essays, Nonfiction (General), Outdoor Recreation
ISBN Prefix(es): 84-217
Associate Companies: Editorial Noguer SA

Editorial Noray+
Cardenal Vives i Tuto, 59, 08034 Barcelona
Tel: (093) 280 59 66 *Fax:* (093) 280 61 90
E-mail: noray@europe.com
Web Site: www.noray.es
Key Personnel
Man Dir: Pablo Zendrera Zariquiey
Editorial: Panxo Pi-Suner Canellas
Founded: 1978
Subjects: Crafts, Games, Hobbies, Fiction, Maritime, Sports, Athletics

ISBN Prefix(es): 84-7486
Number of titles published annually: 20 Print
Bookshop(s): Libreria Maritima Noray

Ediciones Norma SA+
La Chopera 32, 28230 Las Rozas de Madrid
Tel: (091) 6370760 *Fax:* (091) 5470133; (091) 6370760
Key Personnel
Man Dir, Editorial, Rights & Permissions: Alonso Rafael Perez
Founded: 1978
Subjects: Alternative, Career Development, Child Care & Development, Cookery, How-to, Medicine, Nursing, Dentistry, Self-Help
ISBN Prefix(es): 84-7487
Associate Companies: Ediciones Eilea SA
Subsidiaries: Eilea SA; Libros Gamma
Showroom(s): Ronda de la Plazuela 8, 28230 Las Rozas, Madrid
Bookshop(s): Ronda de la Plazuela 8, 28230 Las Rozas, Madrid
Shipping Address: Ronda de la Plazuela 8, 28230 Las Rozas, Madrid
Warehouse: Ronda de la Plazuela 8, 28230 Las Rozas, Madrid
Orders to: Ronda de la Plazuela 8, 28230 Las Rozas, Madrid

Novelas y Cuentos, *imprint of* Editorial Casals SA

Nuer Ediciones
Fernando VI, 8-1, 28004 Madrid
Tel: (091) 310 05 99; 902 118 298 *Fax:* (091) 310 04 59
E-mail: nuer@pasadizo.com
Web Site: www.pasadizo.com
Key Personnel
Dir: Carlos Diaz Maroto *E-mail:* cdmaroto@pasadizo.com; Miguel San Jose Romano *E-mail:* miguel@pasadizo.com
International Rights: Cristina Fernandez Calderon
ISBN Prefix(es): 84-8068

Nueva Acropolis+
Pizarro 19, Bajo dcha, 28004 Madrid
Tel: (091) 5228730 *Fax:* (091) 5312952
E-mail: oinaes@jet.es
Web Site: www.acropolis.org
Founded: 1957
Member of the School of Philosophy.
Subjects: Anthropology, Archaeology, Astrology, Occult, Astronomy, History, Parapsychology, Philosophy, Religion - Other
ISBN Prefix(es): 84-85982

OASIS, Producciones Generales de Comunicacion+
Perez Galdos, 36, Barcelona 08012
Tel: (093) 2372020 *Fax:* (093) 2177378
Key Personnel
Contact: Tomas Mata; Ua Matthiasdottir
Founded: 1978
Subjects: Alternative, Cookery, Earth Sciences, Environmental Studies, Ethnicity, Health, Nutrition, Outdoor Recreation, Psychology, Psychiatry, Self-Help, Sports, Athletics
ISBN Prefix(es): 84-7901

Obelisco Ediciones S+
Pedro IV, 78, 4, 5, 08005 Barcelona
Tel: (093) 3098525 *Fax:* (093) 3098523
E-mail: obelisco@airtel.net; obelisco@edicionesobelisco.com
Web Site: www.edicionesobelisco.com
Key Personnel
Manager: Julio Peradejordi Salazar
Founded: 1981
Subjects: Self-Help, Astrology, New Age, Occult, Spiritualism, Alternative psychology, Judaica

ISBN Prefix(es): 84-7720; 84-86000
Number of titles published annually: 60 Print
Total Titles: 900 Print
Imprints: Magoria; Vital
Distributed by Aldisa (Guatemala); Aldisa Salvadorena (El Salvador); Corporacion Yupanqui SA (Peru); Ediciones Cruz Del Sur (Panama); Distribuciones del Futuro (Argentina); Forsa Editions Inc (Puerto Rico); Endiciones Gaviota (Columbia); Gaviota Librol (Colombia); Gussi Libros (Uruguay); LD Books (US); Lectorum (Mexico); Lectorum Publications Inc (US); Lectorum Sa De CV (Mexico); Libreria Alpha (US); Los Andes (Costa Rica); Pomaire (Venezuela); Ediciones Urano (Chile); Urano Venezuela (Venezuela)

Ediciones Oceano Grupo SA+
Milanesado, 21-23, 08017 Barcelona
Tel: (093) 280 20 20 *Fax:* (093) 204 10 73
E-mail: info@oceano.com
Web Site: www.oceano.com
Telex: 51735 Exit E
Key Personnel
Man Dir: Jose Lluis Monreal
Editorial: Carlos Gispert
Sales: Roberto Niubo
Production: Jose Gay
Rights & Permissions: Marta Bueno
Founded: 1950
Subjects: Art, Education, Fiction, Geography, Geology, History, Literature, Literary Criticism, Essays, Management, Science (General)
ISBN Prefix(es): 84-7069
Associate Companies: Ediciones Centrum Tecnicas y Cientificas SA, Milanesat, 21-23, 08017 Barcelona; Circe Ediciones SA, Milanesat, 21-23, 08017 Barcelona; Ediciones Manfer SA, Milanesat, 21-23, 08017 Barcelona
Subsidiaries: Instituto Gallach de Libreria y Ediciones SL
Orders to: Ediciones Oceano, SA, Paseo de Gracia, 26, 08007 Barcelona

Ediciones Offo, SA
Los Mesejo 23, 28007 Madrid
Tel: (091) 5514214 *Fax:* (091) 5010699
Key Personnel
Council Delegate: Joaquin Zuazo Martinez
Founded: 1957
ISBN Prefix(es): 84-7117

Oikos-Tau SA Ediciones+
Montserrat 12-14, 08340 Vilassar de Mar, Barcelona
Tel: (093) 7590791 *Fax:* (093) 7506825
Key Personnel
Man Dir, Editorial: Jordi Garcia-Bosch
Sales: Climent Garcia-Bosch
Production, Rights & Permissions: Jordi Garcia-Jacas
Founded: 1963
Member of Editors Guild of Cataluna & Federation of Editors of Spain.
Subjects: Agriculture, Anthropology, Architecture & Interior Design, Behavioral Sciences, Biography, Biological Sciences, Earth Sciences, Economics, Education, Geography, Geology, History, Language Arts, Linguistics, Literature, Literary Criticism, Essays, Marketing, Medicine, Nursing, Dentistry, Poetry, Psychology, Psychiatry, Social Sciences, Sociology
ISBN Prefix(es): 84-281

Ediciones Ojeda
Mater Salvatoris Cumbre del Tibidado, s/n, 08035 Barcelona
Mailing Address: PO Box 34055, E-08080 Barcelona
Tel: (093) 2120254; (093) 2370009 *Fax:* (093) 4159845
E-mail: lib.europa@mx3.redestb.es

PUBLISHERS

SPAIN

Key Personnel
International Rights: Angel Garcia Fuente de la Oyeda
ISBN Prefix(es): 84-920591

Ediciones Olimpic, SL+
Apdo Correos 9428, 08080 Barcelona
Tel: (093) 977650885 *Fax:* (093) 977650885
E-mail: edolimpic@worldonline.es
Key Personnel
Administrator: Rafael Barberan
Contact: Angels Gimeno *E-mail:* angelsjimeno@hotmail.com
Founded: 1987
Specialize in legal books for universities.
Subjects: Fiction, Science Fiction, Fantasy, Social Sciences, Sociology, Western Fiction
ISBN Prefix(es): 84-7750

Ediciones Omega SA+
Plato 26, 08006 Barcelona
Tel: (093) 2010599; (093) 2013807; (093) 2012144 *Fax:* (093) 2097362
E-mail: omega@ediciones-omega.es
Web Site: www.ediciones-omega.es
Key Personnel
Man Dir: Gabriel Paricio; Antonio Paricio
Founded: 1948
Also specialize in field guides.
Subjects: Agriculture, Biological Sciences, Chemistry, Chemical Engineering, Film, Video, Geography, Geology, Photography, Science (General), Technology
ISBN Prefix(es): 84-282

Omnicon, SA+
Hierro, 9-3-7, 28045 Madrid
Tel: (091) 5278249 *Fax:* (091) 5281348
E-mail: omnicon@skios.es
Web Site: www.omnicon.es
Key Personnel
Dir & International Rights: Juan M Varela
Founded: 1988
Subjects: Photography, Photography & Imaging Technical Books
ISBN Prefix(es): 84-88914

Opera Tres Ediciones Musicales+
Aptdo de Correos 18077, 28080 Madrid
Tel: (091) 542 4320 *Fax:* (091) 541 0580; (091) 680 76 26
Key Personnel
Contact: Blanca R Garcia
Subjects: Music, Dance
ISBN Prefix(es): 84-7893

Ediciones Orbis SA
Avda Diagonal, 652, edif A, 6, 08034 Barcelona
Tel: (093) 280 05 12 *Fax:* (093) 280 14 72
E-mail: orbis@edorbis.es
Web Site: www.edorbis.es
Key Personnel
Dir: Monica Casetti
ISBN Prefix(es): 84-402; 84-7530; 84-7634

Ediciones del Oriente y del Mediterraneo
cl Prado Luis, no 11, 28440 Guadarrama, Madrid
Tel: (091) 8543428 *Fax:* (091) 8548352
E-mail: sicamor@teleline.es
Web Site: www.webdoce.com/orienteymediterraneo
Key Personnel
Dir: Fernando Garcia Burillo
Subjects: Asian Studies, Biography, Developing Countries, Education, Ethnicity, Fiction, Foreign Countries, History, Literature, Literary Criticism, Essays, Nonfiction (General), Philosophy, Poetry, Religion - Islamic, Social Sciences, Sociology, Women's Studies
ISBN Prefix(es): 84-87198
Number of titles published annually: 12 Print
Total Titles: 74 Print
Distributed by Distribuciones Gracia Alvarez, SL; Arcadia Libros, SL; Distribuciones Cimadevilla, SA; Comercial Kalandraka, SL; Gaia Libros, SL; Gea Llibres, SL; Icaro Distribuidora, SL; Ikuska Libros, SL; Antonio Machado Libros, SA; Marketing i Distribucio Editorial, SL; Nadales Libros, SL; Odon Molina Distribuidor de Libros, SL; Palma Distribucions, SL; Puvill Libros, SA

Editorial Alfredo Ortells SL
Sagunto 5, 46009 Valencia
Tel: (06) 347 10 00 *Fax:* (06) 347 39 10
E-mail: editorial@ortells.com
Web Site: www.ortells.com
Key Personnel
Man Dir: Alfredo Ortells
Founded: 1952
ISBN Prefix(es): 84-7189

Oxford University Press Espana SA+
c/o Parque Empresarial San Fernando, Edificio Atenas 1, 28831 San Fernando de Henares, Madrid
Tel: (091) 6775053
Key Personnel
Man Dir: Jesus Lezcano
Founded: 1991
Subjects: Education, Language Arts, Linguistics
ISBN Prefix(es): 84-8104
Total Titles: 93 Print
Parent Company: Oxford University Press, United Kingdom
Subsidiaries: Parque Empresarial San Fernando; Girona; Mayor; Plaza de los Alfeceres; Pintor Rodriguez Acosta; Linares Rivas; Don Cristian; Uria; Doctor Manuel Candela; Paseo de Zorrilla; Reina Fabiola; Marques De Nervion

Pages Editors, SL+
Sant Salvador, 8, 25005 Lleida
Tel: (0973) 23 66 11 *Fax:* (0973) 24 07 95
E-mail: ed.pages.editors@cambrescat.es
Key Personnel
Dir: Lluis Pages i Marigot
Editor: Ramon Badia
Founded: 1991
Specialize in Catalan & Spanish books.
Subjects: Agriculture, Anthropology, Drama, Theater, Ethnicity, Fiction, History, Nonfiction (General), Philosophy, Psychology, Psychiatry, Religion - Catholic, Social Sciences, Sociology
ISBN Prefix(es): 84-7935
Associate Companies: Editorial Milenio Arts Grafiques Bobala, SL *E-mail:* editorial.milenio@cambrescat.es

Ediciones Paidos Iberica SA+
Mariano Cubi 92, 08021 Barcelona
Tel: (093) 2002804; (093) 241 9250 *Fax:* (093) 2022954
E-mail: paidos@paidos.com
Key Personnel
Man Dir: Javier Colomo
Production: Rosa Hurtado
Founded: 1979
Specialize in Social Sciences.
Subjects: Communications, Psychology, Psychiatry, Self-Help, Social Sciences, Sociology
ISBN Prefix(es): 84-7509
Parent Company: Editorial Paidos, Argentina
Associate Companies: Editorial Paidos Mexicana SA, Ruben Dario 118, Colonia Moderna, 03510 Mexico DF, Mexico

Editorial Paidotribo SL+
Consejo de Ciento, 245 bis 1º 1a, 08011 Barcelona
Tel: (093) 3233311 *Fax:* (093) 4535033
E-mail: paidotribo@paidotribo.com
Web Site: www.paidotribo.com
Key Personnel
Editor: Emilio Ortega Gomez
Founded: 1985
Subjects: Education, Health, Nutrition, Sports, Athletics, Anatomy
ISBN Prefix(es): 84-8019; 84-86475

Ediciones El Pais SA
Torrelaguna, 60, 28043 Madrid
Tel: (091) 7449060 *Fax:* (091) 7449093
E-mail: elpaisaguilar@santillana.es
Web Site: www.elpaisaguilar.es
Key Personnel
Dir: Guillermo Schauelzon
Founded: 1976
Subjects: How-to, Nonfiction (General), Travel
ISBN Prefix(es): 84-86459

Pais Vasco Servicio Central de Publicaciones
Division of Gobierno VASCO
Libreria Donostia 1, Vitoria-Gazteiz 01010
SAN: 003-2964
Tel: (0945) 018656 *Fax:* (0945) 018709
E-mail: hac-sabd@ej-gv.es
Web Site: www.ej-gv.net
Key Personnel
Contact: Pedro Castro Uribarren
Founded: 1980
Subjects: Agriculture, Art, Business, Education, Health, Nutrition, History, Law, Public Administration, Social Sciences, Sociology
ISBN Prefix(es): 84-457
Number of titles published annually: 200 Print; 10 CD-ROM
Total Titles: 3,450 Print; 30 CD-ROM
Distributed by Bidea 2000 SL
Bookshop(s): Gobierno Vasco Dto de Hacienda y Administracion Publica Libreria, Duque de Wellington 2, Vitoria 01010 *Tel:* (0945) 018557 *Fax:* (0945) 078709 *E-mail:* hac-sabd@ej-gv.es
Orders to: Bidea 2.000 SL, N Salcedo, 9, 48012 Bilbao *Tel:* (094) 4278177 *Fax:* (094) 4273745
Egartorre, Mirlo, 23, Madrid *Tel:* (01) 7116008 *Fax:* (01) 7116763
Zabaltzen, Portuetxe Kalea 88, 20009 San Sebastian *Tel:* (0943) 310301 *Fax:* (0943) 310452

El Paisaje Editorial+
Arrangoiti 8, Aranguren Vizcaya 48850
Tel: (04) 6390774
Key Personnel
Dir General: Agustin Garcia Alonso
Founded: 1981
Subjects: Biography, Drama, Theater, Fiction, Literature, Literary Criticism, Essays, Music, Dance, Poetry
ISBN Prefix(es): 84-7697
Parent Company: El Paisaje, Urazurrutia 37, 48003 Bilbao, Vizcaya
Branch Office(s)
Apdo 88, Cordoba
Bookshop(s): Centro Comercial del Libro, SA, Urbanizduion Torres de San Lamberto 3, 50011 Zaragoza

Ediciones Palabra SA+
Paseo de la Castellana, 210-2, E-28046 Madrid
Tel: (091) 350 7720 *Fax:* (091) 359 02 30
E-mail: epalsa@edicionespalabra.es
Web Site: www.edicionespalabra.es
Key Personnel
Chief Executive Officer: Belen Martin
E-mail: belenmartin@edicionespalabra.es
Manager: Ricardo Regidor
E-mail: ricardoregidor@edicionespalabra.es
Founded: 1963
Subjects: Biography, Education, History, Religion - Other, family & leisure time
ISBN Prefix(es): 84-7118; 84-8239
Number of titles published annually: 80 Print; 1 CD-ROM
Total Titles: 500 Print; 1 CD-ROM

Ediciones Paraiso, SL+
Munoz Degrain, 15, 33007 Oviedo
Tel: (985) 203 789
E-mail: paraiso@seteas.com
Key Personnel
Owner, Dir: Maria Emilia Fernandez Garcia
ISBN Prefix(es): 84-88472

Editorial Paraninfo SA+
Magallanes 25, 28015 Madrid
Tel: (091) 4463350 *Fax:* (091) 4456218; (091) 14478892
Web Site: www.paraninfo.es
Key Personnel
Man Dir: Alfonso Mangada Sanz
Sales Dir: Miguel Mangada Ferber; Manuel Montalban Velasco
Founded: 1948
Subjects: Biological Sciences, Business, Computer Science, How-to, Management, Physical Sciences, Science (General), Technology
ISBN Prefix(es): 84-283
Bookshop(s): Libreria Paraninfo, Magallanes 25, 28015 Madrid; Melendez Valdes 65, Madrid 28015

Parramon Ediciones SA+
Gran Via Corts Catalanes 322, 08004 Barcelona
Tel: (093) 289 27 20 *Fax:* (093) 426 37 30
E-mail: sales@parramon.es
Key Personnel
Man Dir: Fernando Penuela
Foreign Rights Dir: Remei Piqueras
  E-mail: remei@parramon.es
Foreign Rights: Gemma Isus; Ignacio Martin
  E-mail: ignacio@parramon.es
International Relations: Montse Soriano
Founded: 1958
Subjects: Art, Crafts, Games, Hobbies, Education, Health, Nutrition, How-to, Practical Art, Fiction & Non-Fiction Children & Juvenile Illustrated Books, Human Body, Partworks
ISBN Prefix(es): 84-342
Parent Company: Carvajal, SA
Warehouse: Parramon Ediciones, Marina 8-10 (Antigua Rambla Famadas), 08940 Cornella del Llobregat, Barcelona

Ediciones Partenon+
Paseo de la Habana 56, 28036 Madrid
Tel: (091) 5634450 *Fax:* (091) 5628405
Key Personnel
Man Dir: Rafael Torres Gorriz
Founded: 1969
Subjects: Language Arts, Linguistics, Literature, Literary Criticism, Essays, Social Sciences, Sociology
ISBN Prefix(es): 84-7119
Branch Office(s)
Ave Domenech 284, 00918 San Juan, Puerto Rico *Tel:* 787-753-8879 *Fax:* 787-754-8265
  E-mail: proex@icepr.com

Editorial Parthenon Communication, SL+
Cami del Pla de Can Sans No 24, Sant Andreu de Llavaneres, 08392 Barcelona
Tel: (093) 7952008 *Fax:* (093) 7952008
Founded: 1991
Specialize in graphics design.
Subjects: Architecture & Interior Design, Biography, Environmental Studies
ISBN Prefix(es): 84-88251

Centre de Pastoral Liturgica+
Rivadeneyra 6, 7, 08002 Barcelona
Tel: (093) 3022235 *Fax:* (093) 3184218
Web Site: www.cpl.es/
Key Personnel
President: Jose Aldazabal
Founded: 1966

Subjects: Literature, Literary Criticism, Essays, Religion - Other, Theology
ISBN Prefix(es): 84-7467
Warehouse: Pujades, 77-79, Barcelona

Pearson Educacion S A+
Nunez de Balboa, 120, 28006 Madrid
SAN: 002-2527
Tel: (091) 5903432 *Fax:* (091) 5903448
E-mail: firstname.lastname@pearsoned-ema.com
Telex: 47688 Wxyz E *Cable:* EDIMBRASA
Key Personnel
President: Bill Anderson
Man Dir, Higher Education Division: Luis Collado
Man Dir, School Division & VP: Luisa Crespo
Editorial Dir, School Division: Concho Ordonez
Man Dir, Professional & Trade Division: Ricardo Mendiola
VP, Finance/Operations: Robert Meek
Founded: 1942
Subjects: Art, Education, History, Language Arts, Linguistics, Medicine, Nursing, Dentistry, Philosophy, Psychology, Psychiatry, Science (General)
ISBN Prefix(es): 84-205
Parent Company: Pearson Plc
Branch Office(s)
Enrique Granados 46, 08008 Barcelona
Iruna 12, 48014 Bilbao
Saturnino Calleja 1, 28002 Madrid
Calle Amores 2027 Editorial Alhambra Mexicana SA de CV, Colonia del Valle, 03100 Mexico, DF, Mexico
Plaza de las Descalzas 2, 18009 Granada
Pasadizo de Pernas 13, 15005 La Coruna
Tomas Morales 48, 35003 Las Palmas
General Porlier 14, 38004 Santa Cruz de Tenerife
Reina Mercedes 35, 41012 Seville
Cabillers 5, 46003 Valencia
Julio Ruiz de Alda 12, 47013 Valladolid
Concepcion Arenal 25, 50005 Zaragoza
Bookshop(s): Nunez de Balboa, 120, 28006 Madrid SAN: 002-2527

Ediciones Pegaso, *imprint of* EDERSA
(Editoriales de Derecho Reunidas SA)

Ediciones Peninsula, *imprint of* Grup 62

Ediciones Peninsula
Imprint of Grup 62
Peu de la Creu, 4, 08001 Barcelona
Tel: (093) 443 71 00 *Fax:* (093) 443 71 30
E-mail: correu@grup62.com
Web Site: www.grup62.com
Key Personnel
Rights Manager: Laura Pujol

Pentalfa Ediciones+
Division of Grupo Helicon SA
Apdo de Correos 360, 33080 Oviedo
Tel: (0985) 985 386 *Fax:* (0985) 985 512
E-mail: pentalfa@helicon.es
Web Site: www.helicon.es/pentalfa.htm
Key Personnel
Dir: Gustavo Bueno Sanchez *Tel:* (0985) 245857
  Fax: (0985) 245649 *E-mail:* gbs@fgbueno.es
Founded: 1974
Subjects: Anthropology, Philosophy
ISBN Prefix(es): 84-85422; 84-7848
Total Titles: 3 Print; 2 CD-ROM

Perea Ediciones+
Apdo 8, 13620 Pedro Munoz, Ciudad Real
Tel: (026) 568261 *Fax:* (026) 586386
Key Personnel
Manager: Jose Perea Ramirez
Founded: 1987

Subjects: Astrology, Occult, Literature, Literary Criticism, Essays
ISBN Prefix(es): 84-7729

Editorial Peregrino SL (Pilgrim Publications)+
Ctra CM-412, km 65, 13350 Moral de Calatrava, Ciudad Real
Tel: (0926) 338 245 *Fax:* (0926) 338 002
E-mail: eplibros@teleline.es
Web Site: www.editorialperegrino.net
Key Personnel
Manager: Demetrio Canovas
Founded: 1979
Editing & distributing religious literature.
Subjects: Biblical Studies, Biography, Religion - Protestant
ISBN Prefix(es): 84-86589
Number of titles published annually: 10 Print
Total Titles: 60 Print
Parent Company: Evangelical Press
Distributed by Cristianismo Historico (USA); Distribuidora Bereana (USA)
Distributor for El Estandarte de la Verdad (Spain)
Book Club(s): Club Peregrino, Apdo 19, 13350 Moral de Calatrava, Ciudad Real

Editorial Perfils
El Bages, 7, 25005 Lerida
Mailing Address: PO Box 794, 25080 Lleida
Tel: (0973) 242160 *Fax:* (0973) 221670
E-mail: perfils@arrakis.es
Web Site: www.arrakis.es/~cvlmallorca/perfils-e.htm
Key Personnel
Dir: Mario Arque Domingo *Tel:* (973) 234453
ISBN Prefix(es): 84-87695

Permanyer Publications+
Mallorca 310, 08037 Barcelona
Tel: (093) 207 59 20 *Fax:* (093) 457 66 42
E-mail: permanyer@permanyer.com
Web Site: www.dolor.es; www.aidsreviews.com
Key Personnel
Dir General & Editor: Ricard Permanyer
Founded: 1973
Journals & Books.
Subjects: Medicine, Nursing, Dentistry, Veterinary Science
Associate Companies: Permanyer Portugal, Av Duque d'Avila 92, Lisboa, Portugal

Editorial El Perpetuo Socorro
Covarrubias 19, 28010 Madrid
Tel: (091) 445 51 26 *Fax:* (091) 445 51 27
E-mail: ed-ps@planalfa.es
Key Personnel
Dir: Vidal Ayala Sacristan
Founded: 1943
Member of AECE (Catholic Association of Publishers of Spain), Coedit Lit (Liturgical Coeditors of Spanish Episcopal Conference).
Subjects: Behavioral Sciences, Biblical Studies, Biography, Music, Dance, Religion - Catholic, Theology
ISBN Prefix(es): 84-284
Imprints: Icono Perpetuo Socorro; NER
Distributed by PPC
Distributor for Perpetuo Socorro (Mexico)

Ediciones Piramide SA+
Juan Ignacio Luca de Tena 15, 28007 Madrid
Tel: (091) 393 89 89 *Fax:* (091) 742 36 61
E-mail: infopiramide@piramide.es
Web Site: www.edicionespiramide.es
Telex: 41071 Maeg E
Key Personnel
Chairman: Maria Isabel Andres Bravo
Dir: Guillermo de Toca
Rights & Permissions: Paloma Rivero; Guillermo de Toca
Founded: 1973

PUBLISHERS

SPAIN

Subjects: Business, Economics, Law, Psychology, Psychiatry, Science (General), Technology
ISBN Prefix(es): 84-368
Parent Company: Grupo Anaya, Juan Ignacio, Luca de Tena 15, 28027 Madrid
Associate Companies: Ediciones Anaya

Pirene Editorial, sal+
Ausias March, 16, 3r. la., 08010 Barcelona
Tel: (093) 3178682 *Fax:* (093) 3178242
Key Personnel
Literary Dir: Francesc Boada
Founded: 1987
Editions in Spanish & Catalan.
Specialize in Infant & Children's Books.
Subjects: Biography, Education, Fiction, Humor
ISBN Prefix(es): 84-7766

Editorial Planeta SA+
Corcega, 273-277, 08008 Barcelona
Tel: (093) 228 58 00 *Fax:* (093) 2177140; (093) 2177748
Telex: 93458 Edtp *Cable:* EDIPLAN
Key Personnel
Chairman: Jose Manuel Lara Hernandez
General Manager: Jose Manuel Lara Bosch
Publishing General Manager: Ymelda Navajo
Founded: 1952
Members of the Planate Group: Editorial Ariel SA; Credito Internacional del Libro SA (CILSA), Balmes 155, 08008 Barcelona; Editorial Seix Barral SA; Editorial Planeta Argentina SAIC, Viamonte 1451, Buenos Aires, Argentina; Editorial Planeta Chilena SA, Olivares 1229 - 4, Santiago, Chile; Planeta Colombiana Editorial SA, Calle 22, 6-27 3 piso Edificio Distral, Bogota DE, Colombia; Editorial Planeta del Ecuador, Ave Francisco de Orellana, 1811 y 10 de Agosto, Edificio El Cid Planta baja, Quito, Ecuador; Difusion Editorial SA, Clavijero, 70 Col Transito, 06820 Mexico DF, Mexico; Ediciones Andinas SA, Camino Real, 159 Oficina 600, San Isidro-Lima, Peru; Editorial Planeta Venezolana SA Calle Madrid-Quinta Toscanella entre New York y Trinidad, Las Mercedes, Caracas 1050, Venezuela.
Subjects: Fiction, Nonfiction (General)
ISBN Prefix(es): 84-320
Associate Companies: Planeta/Agostini (Forum y Fasciculos Planeta), Aribau 185, 08021 Barcelona; Sudamericana/Planeta SA (Editores), Argentina; Lord Cochrane SA, Ave Providencia 727, Santiago, Chile; Editorial Artemisa SA, Ave Cuauhtemoc 1236 - 4, Colonia Vertiz Narvarte, Delegacion Benito Juarez, 03600 Mexico, DF, Mexico; Editorial Joaquin Mortiz SA, Mexico

Plastic Comunicacion SL+
La Llacuna, 162, Edif, 08018 Barcelona Activa
Tel: (093) 4019833 *Fax:* (093) 4019830
E-mail: plastunivers@app.es
Web Site: www.plastunivers.es
Key Personnel
Editor: Ferran Puig *E-mail:* ferran@app.es
Founded: 1990
Subjects: Plastics; magazines & books
ISBN Prefix(es): 84-87454
Number of titles published annually: 14 Print
Total Titles: 2 CD-ROM; 2 E-Book
Parent Company: Carl Hanser Verlag, Marburgerstr 13, D-6100 Darmstadt, Germany
Imprints: Carl Hanser Verlag

Plawerg SA
Beethoven, 10-1, 2a, 08021 Barcelona
Tel: (093) 414 72 26 *Fax:* (093) 209 50 01
E-mail: info@plawerg.es
Web Site: www.plawerg.com
Key Personnel
Man Dir: Juan Carlos Brinardeli
Founded: 1994

Specialize in Multimedia Editions.
ISBN Prefix(es): 84-89351

Editorial Playor SA+
Menendez Pelayo 83, Bajo-D, 28007 Madrid
Tel: (091) 4340201 *Fax:* (091) 5011342
E-mail: playor@attglobal.net
Key Personnel
Man Dir: Carlos A Montaner
Manager: Linda Periut
Founded: 1971
Subjects: Education, History, Language Arts, Linguistics, Literature, Literary Criticism, Essays, Mathematics, Science (General)
ISBN Prefix(es): 84-359

Plaza y Janes Editores SA+
Enric Granados, 86-88, 08008 Barcelona
Tel: (093) 45110 *Fax:* (093) 4156976
Key Personnel
Man Dir: Manfred Grebe
Dir Sales Division: Juan Pascual
Editorial Dir: Nuria Tey
Founded: 1959
Subjects: Biography, Fiction, History, Nonfiction (General)
ISBN Prefix(es): 84-01
Number of titles published annually: 100 Print
Total Titles: 500 Print
Parent Company: Verlagsgruppe Bertelsmann International GmbH, Munich, Germany

Pleniluni Edicions+
Roger de Lluria, 5, 08010 Barcelona
Tel: (093) 301 08 87 *Fax:* (093) 3174830
Founded: 1979
Member of the Association of Editors in Llengua Catalana and Gremi d Editors.
Subjects: Crafts, Games, Hobbies, Science Fiction, Fantasy, Sports, Athletics
ISBN Prefix(es): 84-85752

Editorial Pliegos+
Gobernador 29 4A, 28014 Madrid
Tel: (091) 4291545 *Fax:* (091) 4291545
Key Personnel
Dir: Cesar E Leante
Founded: 1983
Subjects: Drama, Theater, Fiction, Journalism, Literature, Literary Criticism, Essays, Poetry
ISBN Prefix(es): 84-88435

Polifemo, Ediciones
Avda de Bruselas, 47-5, 2, 28028 Madrid
Tel: (091) 7257101 *Fax:* (091) 3556811
E-mail: libros@polifemo.com
Web Site: www.polifemo.com
Founded: 1985
Subjects: Anthropology, Archaeology, Asian Studies, History, Travel
ISBN Prefix(es): 84-85647
Total Titles: 45 Print

Ediciones Pomares-Corredor+
Caspe, 162, 50 A, 08013 Barcelona
Tel: (093) 2652950 *Fax:* (093) 2653010
E-mail: edpomazes@mx3.zedestb.es
Key Personnel
Manager: Jose Manuel Pomares
Founded: 1990
Subjects: Education, Psychology, Psychiatry, Social Sciences, Sociology
ISBN Prefix(es): 84-87682

Editorial Popular SA
Dr Esquerdo, 173 6 Izda, 28007 Madrid
Tel: (091) 409 35 73 *Fax:* (091) 573 41 73
E-mail: epopular@infornet.es
Web Site: www.editorialpopular.com
Key Personnel
Man Dir: Ricardo Herrero-Velarde

Dir: Mercedes Calero
Founded: 1972
Subjects: Education, Literature, Literary Criticism, Essays, Social Sciences, Sociology
ISBN Prefix(es): 84-85016; 84-86524; 84-7884

Editorial Portic SA+
Imprint of Enciclopedia Catalana, SA
Diputacio, 250, 08007 Barcelona
Tel: (093) 412 00 30 *Fax:* (093) 301 48 63
E-mail: secedit@grec.com
Web Site: www.enciclopedia-catalana.com
Key Personnel
Rights Department: Monica Rocamora
Founded: 1963
Subjects: Biography, Journalism, Literature, Literary Criticism, Essays
ISBN Prefix(es): 84-7306

PPC Editorial y Distribuidora, SA+
Enrique Jardiel Poncela 4, 28016 Madrid
Tel: (091) 359-2300 *Fax:* (091) 350-5443
E-mail: ppcedit@ctv.es *Cable:* PEPECE
Key Personnel
President: Antonio Montero
Man Dir: Angel Alos
Sales Dir: Ignacio Martin
Rights & Permissions: Javier Cortes
Founded: 1955
Subjects: Education, Philosophy, Religion - Other
ISBN Prefix(es): 84-288
Bookshop(s): Librerias PPC

Editorial PRAXIS SA, see Editorial CISSPRAXIS SA

Pre-Textos+
Luis Santangel, 10, 46005 Valencia
Tel: (96) 333 32 26 *Fax:* (96) 395 54 77
E-mail: info@pre-textos.com
Web Site: www.pre-textos.com
Key Personnel
Man Dir: D Manuel Borras Arana
Production Manager: Manuel Ramirez
Founded: 1976
Subjects: Biography, Fiction, Language Arts, Linguistics, Literature, Literary Criticism, Essays, Music, Dance, Nonfiction (General), Philosophy, Poetry
ISBN Prefix(es): 84-85081; 84-87101; 84-8191
Number of titles published annually: 50 Print
Total Titles: 600 Print
Warehouse: CELESA, Moratines 22, 28005 Madrid

Editorial Prensa Espanola
Padilla 6, 28006 Madrid
Tel: (091) 4462616
Key Personnel
Dir: Rogelio Gonzalez-Ubeda
Founded: 1905
Subjects: Fiction, Nonfiction (General)
ISBN Prefix(es): 84-287

Prensas Universitarias de Zaragoza+
Edificio de Ciencias Geologicas Pedro Cerbuna, 12, 50009 Zaragoza
Tel: (034) 976761330 *Fax:* (034) 976761063
E-mail: puz@posta.unizar.es
Web Site: wzar.unizar.es/spub/
Key Personnel
Editorial Dir: Antonio Perez Lasheras
Founded: 1542
Subjects: History, Literature, Literary Criticism, Essays, Science (General), Social Sciences, Sociology, Academic
ISBN Prefix(es): 84-7733
Distributed by Bitacora

Editorial Presencia Gitana
Valderrodrigo 76 y 78, bajos A, 28039 Madrid

Tel: (091) 373 62 07 Fax: (091) 373 44 62
E-mail: anpregit@teleline.es
Web Site: www.presenciagitana.org/
Key Personnel
Responsable Legal: Manuel Martin Ramirez
Founded: 1987
Member of the European's Net Interface; specialize in gypsies.
Subjects: Anthropology, Biography, Education, Ethnicity, History, Humor, Social Sciences, Sociology, Antiracism, Gipsies (culture, language, story)
ISBN Prefix(es): 84-87347

Edicions Proa, SA+
Diputacio 250, 08007 Barcelona
Tel: (093) 4120030 Fax: (093) 3014863
E-mail: enciclo.catalan@bcn.servicom.es
Key Personnel
Literary Dir: Oriol Izquierdo Llopis
Founded: 1928
Subjects: Fiction, Literature, Literary Criticism, Essays, Poetry, Social Sciences, Sociology
ISBN Prefix(es): 84-8256
Parent Company: Enciclopedia Catalana, SA
Bookshop(s): Proa Espais, Diputacio 250, 08007 Barcelona

Progensa+
Parque Industrial PISA, c/Comercio 12, 41927 Mairena del Aljarafe, Sevilla
Tel: (0954) 186 200 Fax: (0954) 186 111
E-mail: progensa@progensa.com
Web Site: www.progensa.es
Key Personnel
Manager: Francisco Chica Gonzalez
Founded: 1980
Publishers of technical books.
Subjects: Electronics, Electrical Engineering, Energy, How-to, Technology
ISBN Prefix(es): 84-86505
Total Titles: 2 Print; 1 CD-ROM

Promocion Popular Cristiana, see PPC Editorial y Distribuidora, SA

Pronaos, SA Ediciones+
Alonso Cano, 30, 28003 Madrid
Tel: (091) 4427995 Fax: (091) 4203429
E-mail: pronaos@teleline.es; jaire@teleline.es
Key Personnel
International Rights: Rosario Alberdi Tel: (091) 5418199 Fax: (091) 5412766
Subjects: Architecture & Interior Design, Art, Gardening, Plants
ISBN Prefix(es): 84-85941
Total Titles: 2 CD-ROM
Bookshop(s): Naos-Libros, Quintana-12, 28013 Madrid Tel: (091) 5473916

Instituto Provincial de Investigaciones y Estudios Toledanos+
Plaza de la Merced, 4, 45002 Toledo
Tel: (0925) 25 93 00 (ext 367) Fax: (0925) 259348
E-mail: diputolepu@diputoledo.es
Key Personnel
President: Miguel A Ruiz Ayucar Alonso
Dir: Julio Porres de mateo
Founded: 1963
Subjects: Archaeology, Art, Biological Sciences, Cookery, Drama, Theater, Ethnicity, Geography, Geology, History, Poetry, Social Sciences, Sociology
ISBN Prefix(es): 84-87103
Distributed by Pedro Alcantarilla (Spain)

Publicaciones de la Universidad de Alicante
Apdo de correos 99, 03080 Alicante
Tel: 965 909 576 Fax: 965 909 445
E-mail: publicaciones.ventas@ua.es
Web Site: publicaciones.ua.es/
Key Personnel
Publication Dir: Jose Ramon Giner Mallol
 E-mail: JRamon.Giner@ua.es
Subjects: Agriculture, Chemistry, Chemical Engineering, Economics, Literature, Literary Criticism, Essays, Medicine, Nursing, Dentistry, Regional Interests, Science (General), Social Sciences, Sociology
ISBN Prefix(es): 84-7908
Distributed by Distribuciones de Enlace SA; Resto del mundo; Servei del Llibre l'Estaquirot; Sudamerica
Orders to: L'Estaquirot, Mare de Deu del Coll, 53, 08023 Barcelona

Publicaciones de la Universidad Pontificia Comillas-Madrid
Universidad Comillas 3, 28049 Madrid
Tel: (091) 734 39 50 Fax: (091) 734 45 70
E-mail: edit@pub.upco.es
Web Site: www.upco.es
Key Personnel
Dir: Eusebio Gil Coria
Founded: 1975
Subjects: Economics, History, Law, Medicine, Nursing, Dentistry, Philosophy, Social Sciences, Sociology, Theology, Women's Studies
ISBN Prefix(es): 84-87840; 84-89708
Distributed by Edisofer; Ikuska Libros; Melisa; Odon Molina; Sal Terrae; Sendra Marco

Pulso Ediciones, SL+
Rambla del Celler, 117-119, 08190 Sant Cugat del Valles, Barcelona
Tel: (093) 5896264 Fax: (093) 5895077
E-mail: pulso@pulso.com
Web Site: www.pulso.com
Key Personnel
Manager: Gloria Pasias Lomelino
Founded: 1978
Subjects: Animals, Pets, Architecture & Interior Design, Behavioral Sciences, Computer Science, Health, Nutrition, Medicine, Nursing, Dentistry, Psychology, Psychiatry, Science (General), Veterinary Science
ISBN Prefix(es): 84-86671

Punto Juvenil, *imprint of* Editorial Casals SA

Quaderns Crema SA+
Muntaner, 462 3 1, 08006 Barcelona
Tel: (093) 4144906 Fax: (093) 4147107
E-mail: qcrema@quadernscrema.com
Web Site: www.quadernscrema.com
Key Personnel
Man Dir: Jaume Vallcorba
Founded: 1979
Subjects: History, Literature, Literary Criticism, Essays, Poetry, Narratives
ISBN Prefix(es): 84-85704; 84-7727; 84-7769
Number of titles published annually: 32 Print
Total Titles: 325 Print
Subsidiaries: Acantilado

RA-MA, Libreria y Editorial Microinformatica+
Ctra Canillas 144, 28043 Madrid
Tel: (091) 381 03 00 Fax: (091) 381 03 72
E-mail: editorial@ra-ma.com; info@ra-ma.com
Web Site: www.ra-ma.com
Key Personnel
Contact: Jose L Ramirez
Founded: 1984
Subjects: Computer Science, Microcomputers
ISBN Prefix(es): 84-86381; 84-7897

RACC-62, *imprint of* Grup 62

RACC-62
Imprint of Grup 62

Peu de la Creu, 4, 08001 Barcelona
Tel: (093) 443 71 00 Fax: (093) 443 71 30
E-mail: correu@grup62.com
Web Site: www.grup62.com
Key Personnel
Rights Manager: Laura Pujol

Editora Regional de Murcia - ERM
Isaac Albeniz, 4, 30009 Murcia
Tel: (068) 280246 Fax: (068) 298293
E-mail: editora.regional@carm.es
Web Site: www.carm.es
Founded: 1980
Subjects: Anthropology, Archaeology, Architecture & Interior Design, Art, Cookery, Crafts, Games, Hobbies, Economics, Education, Environmental Studies, Gardening, Plants, Geography, Geology, History, Literature, Literary Criticism, Essays, Music, Dance, Outdoor Recreation, Philosophy, Poetry, Regional Interests, Religion - Islamic
ISBN Prefix(es): 84-7564
Distributed by Distribuidora M Atenea, SL; Carisma Libros; Distribuciones Cimadevilla; M Alonso Estravis Distribuidora; Herro Ediciones; Icaro Distribuidora, SL; Lidiza; Servei del Llibre; Distribuciones Lyra; Distribuidora Literaria de Editorial Siglo XXI; Miguel Sanchez Libros; La Tierra Libros; Troquel; Viuber
Orders to: Siglo XXI, c/Plaza 5, 28043 Madrid
Tel: (091) 7591809

Editorial Reus SA
Calle Preciados, 23, 28000 Madrid
Tel: (091) 2213619; (091) 2223054 Fax: (091) 5312408
Key Personnel
President: Jose Luis Allende y Garcia-Baxter
Founded: 1852
Subjects: Law
ISBN Prefix(es): 84-290
Distributed by Edisofer
Warehouse: Avda Democracia, Nave 305, 7-28031 Madrid

Ediciones Luis Revenga
Travesia de Andres Mellado, 9, 28015 Madrid
Tel: (091) 2434646 Fax: (091) 5434706
E-mail: cuadcerv@elr.es
Web Site: www.eunet.es/InterStand/CuadernoseCervantes
Key Personnel
Dir: Oscar Berdugo
ISBN Prefix(es): 84-87607

Editorial Reverte SA+
Loreto 13-15 Local B, 08029 Barcelona
Mailing Address: Apdo de Correos 1237, Barcelona
Tel: (093) 419 33 36; (093) 419 32 76 Fax: (093) 419 51 89
E-mail: istz0125@tsai.es; prom.reverte@teleline.es
Web Site: www.ludosoft.net/reverte/present.htm
Cable: EDIREVER
Key Personnel
Dir: Felipe Reverte
Editorial: Amado J Sala
Sales: Pablo Reverte
Rights & Permissions: Marta Sala
Founded: 1947
Subjects: Engineering (General), Science (General)
ISBN Prefix(es): 84-291
Associate Companies: Marsala, SA, Ave Angel Gallardo 613, 1405 Buenos Aires, Argentina; Salvatore Conforti, SL, Calle 37, No 22-72, (Barrio La Soledad), Bogota DE, Colombia; REPLA SA, de CV, Rio Panuco, 141-A, 06500 Mexico DF, Mexico; Editorial Miro CA, Venezuela

PUBLISHERS

SPAIN

Editorial Revista Agustiniana
Ramonet, 3, 28033 Madrid
Tel: (091) 550-5000 *Fax:* (091) 550-5225
E-mail: revista@agustiniana.com
Web Site: www.agustiniana.com
Key Personnel
Dir: Rafael Lazcano
Founded: 1960
Subjects: Biblical Studies, Philosophy, Religion - Catholic
ISBN Prefix(es): 84-86898
Distributed by Ediciones Y Distribuciones Isla

Ediciones Rialp SA+
Alcala 290, 28027 Madrid
Tel: (091) 3260504 *Fax:* (091) 3261321
E-mail: ediciones@rialp.com
Web Site: www.rialp.com/
Telex: 43229 Coim E (abonado 701) *Cable:* RIALPSA
Key Personnel
President: Jaime Vicens
Vice President: Jesus Domingo Garcia
Editorial: Miguel Arango
Children's Editorial: Carmen Gomez de Agueero
Public Relations: Teresa Arregui; Alfonso Rascon
Rights & Permissions: Eva Rubira
Member of Editors Association of Spain & Commerce Association of Spain.
Subjects: Cookery, Economics, Education, Gardening, Plants, Health, Nutrition, History, Literature, Literary Criticism, Essays, Military Science, Music, Dance, Philosophy, Poetry, Religion - Other, Science (General)
ISBN Prefix(es): 84-321
Branch Office(s)
Via Augusta, No 6, pral la 08006 Barcelona
Warehouse: Logistica de Ediciones, SA, Bembibre, 28-30, Polg Cobo Calleja, (28940 Fuenlabrada, Madrid *Tel:* (091) 6420086 *Fax:* (091) 6421696
Orders to: Cauce, Distribuidora de Ediciones SA, Sebastian Elcano, 30, 28012 Madrid *Tel:* (091) 4672666 *Fax:* (091) 5302537

Riquelme y Vargas Ediciones SL+
Avda de Andalucia 29, 23006 Jaen
Tel: (053) 270066 *Fax:* (053) 270066
Key Personnel
Contact: Elias Riquelme Ibanez
Founded: 1982
Subjects: Agriculture, Art, History, Law, Literature, Literary Criticism, Essays
ISBN Prefix(es): 84-86216

Editorial Roasa SL
Carretera de Huetor Vega, Edif Roma, 5-1A, 18008 Granada
Tel: (058) 0227846 *Fax:* (058) 132530 *Cable:* APDO 2069
Key Personnel
Man Dir, Sales: Felix J Rodriguez
Editorial: Jorge Alonso
Production: Manuel Alonso
Founded: 1982
Member of Association of Editions of Andalucia (AEA).
Subjects: Art, History
ISBN Prefix(es): 84-86043; 84-8042

Ediciones Joaquin Rodrigo
General Yague 11, 28020 Madrid
Tel: (091) 555 2728 *Fax:* (091) 556 4334
E-mail: ediciones@joaquin-rodrigo.com
Web Site: www.joaquin-rodrigo.com
Key Personnel
General Manager: Cecilia Rodrigo
Specialize in Classical Music.
ISBN Prefix(es): 84-88558

Ediciones ROL SA+
San Elias, 29 bajos, 08006 Barcelona
Tel: (093) 200 80 33 *Fax:* (093) 200 27 62
E-mail: rol@e-rol.es
Web Site: www.e-rol.es
Key Personnel
Man Dir: Julia Martinez Saavedra
Founded: 1977
Member of the Spanish Association of Technical Press.
Subjects: Health, Nutrition, Human Relations, Medicine, Nursing, Dentistry, Psychology, Psychiatry, Science (General), Social Sciences, Sociology
ISBN Prefix(es): 84-85535

Josep Ruaix Editor
Av de la Vila 18, 08180 Moia, Barcelona
Tel: (093) 820 81 36
Web Site: www.ruaix.com/
Key Personnel
Contact: J Ruaix
Founded: 1976
Subjects: Language Arts, Linguistics
ISBN Prefix(es): 84-920619
Number of titles published annually: 3 Print
Total Titles: 60 Print
Distributed by Gran Via Llibres; L'Arc de Bera, SA

Rueda, SL Editorial+
Porto Cristo, 13, 28924 Alcorcon, Madrid
Tel: (091) 619 27 79; (091) 619 25 64 *Fax:* (091) 610 28 55
E-mail: ed_rueda@infornet.es
Web Site: www.editorialrueda.es
Key Personnel
International Rights: Sanchez Rafael Rueda
Founded: 1970
Subjects: Agriculture, Architecture & Interior Design, Biological Sciences, Civil Engineering, Earth Sciences, Environmental Studies, Gardening, Plants, Geography, Geology
ISBN Prefix(es): 84-7207

Salvat Editores SA+
45, Calle Mallorca, 08029 Barcelona
Tel: (093) 4301441 *Fax:* (093) 4390579
Key Personnel
Financial Dir: Jean Paul Dupoizat
ISBN Prefix(es): 84-345
Parent Company: Hachette Livre SA, Paris, France
Divisions: Venta Directa; Fasciculos; Literatura

Editorial Miguel A Salvatella SA
Sant Domenec, 5, 08012 Barcelona
Tel: (093) 2189026 *Fax:* (093) 2177437
E-mail: editorial@salvatella.com
Web Site: www.salvatella.com
Founded: 1922
Subjects: Education
ISBN Prefix(es): 84-7210

Editorial San Martin+
Arenal 23, Apdo 97, 28013 Madrid
Tel: (091) 5483590
Key Personnel
Man Dir: Jorge Tarazona
Founded: 1854
Subjects: Aeronautics, Aviation, History, Military Science
ISBN Prefix(es): 84-7140
Bookshop(s): Libreria San Martin, Puerta del Sol 6, 28013 Madrid
Warehouse: Libreria San Martin, Puerta del Sol, 6 28013 Madrid

San Pablo Ediciones+
Protasio Gomez 15, 28027 Madrid
Tel: (091) 7987426; (091) 7987427; (091) 7987375 *Fax:* (091) 7425723
E-mail: editorial@sanpablo-ssp.es
Web Site: www.sanpablo-ssp.es
Key Personnel
President: Antonio Marono Pena *Fax:* (091) 305 2050 *E-mail:* ventao@sanpablo-ssp.es
Publication Dir: Ezequiel Varona
Administration: Antonio Diaz Martinez
Sales: Cecilio Ortiz
Production: Jose Maria Fernandez
Founded: 1936
Editorial.
Subjects: Biography, Education, Religion - Other, Theology
ISBN Prefix(es): 84-285
Number of titles published annually: 100 Print
Total Titles: 1,500 Print
Parent Company: Sociedad de San Pablo
Bookshop(s): Eight in Spain
Warehouse: Resina 1, 28021 Madrid
Orders to: Resina 1, 28021 Madrid

Ediciones San Pio X+
M de Mondejar, 32, 28028 Madrid
Tel: (091) 7262817; (091) 355 2727 *Fax:* (091) 7262817
E-mail: espx@planalfa.es
Key Personnel
Dir: Cesar Pallares Munoz
Founded: 1967
Subjects: Biblical Studies, Education, Philosophy, Religion - Catholic, Social Sciences, Sociology, Theology
ISBN Prefix(es): 84-7221
Number of titles published annually: 25 Print
Total Titles: 315 Print
Associate Companies: Bruno, Maestro Alonso, 21, 28028 Madrid *Tel:* (01) 3610448 *Fax:* (01) 3613133 *E-mail:* info@editorial.bruno.es
U.S. Office(s): 170-23 83 Ave, Jamaica, NY 11432, United States *Tel:* 212-291 9891 *Fax:* 212-291 9830

Universidad de Santiago de Compostela+
Servicio de Publicaciones e Intercambio Cientifico, Campus Universitario Sur, 15782 Santiago de Compostela
SAN: 005-2728
Tel: (0981) 593 500 *Fax:* (0981) 593 963
E-mail: spublic@usc.es
Web Site: www.usc.es/spubl
Key Personnel
Technical Dir: Marisa Melon-Rodriguez
Technical Coordinator: Juan L Blanco Valdes
Founded: 1945
Member of Association of Spanish Editorial University.
Subjects: Art, Education, Electronics, Electrical Engineering, Geography, Geology, History, Language Arts, Linguistics, Law, Philosophy, Physics, Science (General), Social Sciences, Sociology
ISBN Prefix(es): 84-7191; 84-8121; 84-9750
Number of titles published annually: 50 Print; 3 CD-ROM
Total Titles: 1,000 Print; 7 CD-ROM
Distributed by Klaus Dieter Vervuert (Europe)
Distributor for Breogan Distribuciones (Spain, Center); Editorial Galaxia (Galicia); L'Alebrije (South America); Libraria Couceiro (Portugal); Libreria Telematica Espanola; Midac, SL

SARPE, see Axel Springer Publicaciones

Ediciones Scriba SA+
Affiliate of Libreria Martinez Perez
Valencia, 246, 08007 Barcelona
Tel: (093) 215 19 33 *Fax:* (093) 487 37 66
Telex: 98772 Cllc E (Scriba)
Key Personnel
Man Dir: Manuel Martinez Bravo *Tel:* (093) 2152089 *E-mail:* mmb@scriba.jazztel.es
Founded: 1890

Subjects: Art, Medicine, Nursing, Dentistry, Science (General)
ISBN Prefix(es): 84-85835
Bookshop(s): Libreria Martinez Perez, Valencia, 246, 08007 Barcelona *E-mail:* lmp@scriba.jazztel.es

Secretariado Trinitario+
Av Filiberto Villalobos 80, 37007 Salamanca
Tel: (0923) 23 56 02 *Fax:* (0923) 23 56 02
E-mail: secretrinitario@planalfa.es
Key Personnel
Man Dir: Nereo Silanes
Rights & Permissions: Laurentino Silanes
Founded: 1967
Subjects: Religion - Catholic, Religion - Other, Theology
ISBN Prefix(es): 84-88643; 84-85376
Parent Company: Orden de la Santisima Trinidad

Editorial Seix Barral SA+
Member of Planeta Group
Provenza, 260, 4, 08008 Barcelona
Tel: (093) 496 7003 *Fax:* (093) 496 7004
E-mail: editorial@seix-barral.es
Web Site: www.seix-barral.es
Telex: 98255 Sxbl E
Key Personnel
Editorial Dir: Adolfo Garcia Ortega
E-mail: agarcia@seix-barral.es
Editorial: Pere Gimferrer
General Manager: Julian Leon *E-mail:* jleon@planeta.es
Founded: 1945
Specialize in foreign language, drama, essay. Member of the Planeta Group (see Editorial Planeta SA).
Subjects: Fiction, Poetry
ISBN Prefix(es): 84-322
Number of titles published annually: 60 Print
Orders to: Editorial Planeta SA, Corcega 273, 08008 Barcelona

Selecta-Catalonia Ed
Ronda de Sant Pere, 3 pral, 08010 Barcelona
Tel: (093) 3172331; (093) 3185183 *Fax:* (093) 3024793
Key Personnel
Delegate, Advisor: Sebastia Borras i Tey
Founded: 1943
Publications in Catalonian language.
Subjects: Ethnicity, Literature, Literary Criticism, Essays, Regional Interests
ISBN Prefix(es): 84-7667
Bookshop(s): Libreria Catalonia SA, Ronda de Sant Pere, 3 pral, 08010 Barcelona

Ediciones del Serbal SA+
Francesc Tarrega, 32, 08027 Barcelona
Mailing Address: Apdo de Correos 1386, 08080 Barcelona
Tel: (03) 408 08 34 *Fax:* (03) 408 07 92
E-mail: serbal@ed-serbal.es
Web Site: www.ed-serbal.es
Key Personnel
Man Dir, Editorial, Production: Jose Maria Riano de Castro
Publicity: Isabel Banos Regel
Sales: Xavier Espia Jemenez
Founded: 1980
ISBN Prefix(es): 84-85800; 84-7628

Servicio de Publicaciones Universidad de Cadiz+
Dr Maranon, 3, 11002 Cadiz
Tel: (056) 015268 *Fax:* (056) 220118
E-mail: pedro.cervera@uca.es
Web Site: www.uca.es/serv/publicaciones
Key Personnel
Dir: Mariano Frances Figueroa *E-mail:* mariano.frances@uca.es
Founded: 1980
Subjects: Chemistry, Chemical Engineering, Engineering (General), History, Law, Literature, Literary Criticism, Essays, Medicine, Nursing, Dentistry, Science (General)
ISBN Prefix(es): 84-7786
Distributed by Libreria Telmatica Espanola
Distributor for L'Alebrije (For America)

Servicio de Publicaciones Universidad de Cordoba+
Avda Menendez Pidal s/n, 14071 Cordoba
Tel: (0957) 21 81 25 *Fax:* (0957) 21 81 96; (057) 218666 (Director)
E-mail: publicaciones@uco.es; pa11gocag@lucano.uco.es (Director)
Web Site: www.uco.es/organiza/servicios/publica/presenta.htm
Key Personnel
Dir: Gustavo Gomez Castro
Founded: 1976
Subjects: Agriculture, Archaeology, Biological Sciences, Computer Science, Economics, Geography, Geology, Law, Veterinary Science
ISBN Prefix(es): 84-7801
Distributed by DOR SA; Francisco Baena SL

Servicio de Publicaciones y Produccion Documental de la Universidad de Las Palmas de Gran Canaria
Perez del Toro, 5, 35004 Las Palmas de Gran Canaria
Tel: (028) 458954; (028) 458952 *Fax:* (028) 458949
Key Personnel
Coordinator: German Santana Henriquez
ISBN Prefix(es): 84-89728; 84-88412

Ediciones Seyer+
Canizares 23, 29002 Malaga
Tel: (095) 2320887 *Fax:* (095) 2325511
Key Personnel
Dir: Antonio Abad
Founded: 1979
Subjects: Art, Literature, Literary Criticism, Essays, Maritime, Music, Dance, Poetry, Science Fiction, Fantasy, Sports, Athletics
ISBN Prefix(es): 84-86975
Warehouse: San Millan, 15 29013 Malaga

SGEL, see Sociedad General Espanola de Libreria SA - SGEL

Siglo XXI de Espana Editores SA+
Principe de Vergara 78, 28006 Madrid
Tel: (091) 562 37 23; (091) 561 77 48 *Fax:* (091) 561 58 19
E-mail: sigloxxi@sigloxxieditores.com
Web Site: www.sigloxxieditores.com *Cable:* SIGLOEDIT
Key Personnel
Man Dir, Production: Joaquin Garcia Ballestero
Sales: Eduardo Rivas
Man Dir: Javier Abasolo Fernandez
Founded: 1967
Subjects: Anthropology, Government, Political Science, History, Literature, Literary Criticism, Essays, Philosophy, Psychology, Psychiatry, Social Sciences, Sociology
ISBN Prefix(es): 84-323
Subsidiaries: Siglo XXI Editores SA de CV
Distributed by Distribuidora Literaria De Editorial Siglo XXI, SA

Signament 1 Comunicacio, SL Signament Edicions+
Enric Granados 11 entresol 1a, 08007 Barcelona
Tel: (093) 4516888 *Fax:* (093) 3234417
Key Personnel
Editor & Author: Xavier Escura-Dalmau
Founded: 1993
Subjects: History, Medicine, Nursing, Dentistry
ISBN Prefix(es): 84-921381

Ediciones Sigueme SA+
Francisco Garcia Tejado 23-27, 37007 Salamanca
Tel: (0923) 21 82 03 *Fax:* (0923) 27 05 63
E-mail: sigueme@ctv.es *Cable:* SIGUEME SALAMANCA
Key Personnel
Man Dir, Editorial: Santiago L de Vega
Sales: Jose Maria Hernandez
Production: Jesus Pulido
Publicity: Jorge Sans Vila
Founded: 1958
Subjects: Biblical Studies, Biography, History, Philosophy, Religion - Catholic, Religion - Protestant, Theology
ISBN Prefix(es): 84-301
Bookshop(s): Libreria Sigueme, Francisco Garcia Tejado 23-27, 37007 Salamanca

Silex Ediciones+
Alcala 202, 28028 Madrid
Tel: (091) 356.69.09 *Fax:* (091) 361.00.75
E-mail: silex@silexediciones.com
Web Site: www.silexediciones.com
Key Personnel
President: D Eleonor Dominguez Ramirez
Founded: 1972
Subjects: Aeronautics, Aviation, Archaeology, Art, Biography, History, Maritime, Photography, Travel
ISBN Prefix(es): 84-85041; 84-7737

Editorial Sintes SA
Ronda Universitat 4, 08007 Barcelona
Tel: (093) 3182838
Key Personnel
Man Dir, Editorial: Luis Sintes Pros; Jorge Sintes Pros
Founded: 1968
Subjects: Health, Nutrition, Sports, Athletics
ISBN Prefix(es): 84-302
Bookshop(s): Libreria Sintes, Ronda Universitat 4, 08007 Barcelona

Editorial Sintesis, SA+
Vallehermoso, 34, 28015 Madrid
Tel: (091) 593 20 98 *Fax:* (091) 445 86 96
E-mail: sintesis@sintesis.com
Web Site: www.sintesis.com
Key Personnel
President: Felisa Cedenilla Lorente
Contact: Francisco Belloso Cruzado
Founded: 1986 (Editorial Sintesis was founded in 1986 to provide high quality scientific & academic texts for University students in all areas of study.)
The publishing house stands out as one of the leading academic presses in the Spanish speaking world. Our mission is to offer research & learning materials of the highest standard that adapt to the specific needs of University students & their professors, as well as providing essential reading for professional & lay audiences. Our commitment is to provide the reading public with works of the highest quality, written by prestigious authors & educators & which can be distinguished by their innovative approach to a variety of subjects: art, philosophy, physical & social sciences, psychology, psychoanalysis & general studies.
Subjects: Biography, Biological Sciences, Chemistry, Chemical Engineering, Communications, Computer Science, Earth Sciences, Economics, Education, Engineering (General), Geography, Geology, History, Journalism, Language Arts, Linguistics, Library & Information Sciences, Literature, Literary Criticism, Essays, Management, Mathematics, Mechanical Engineering, Nonfiction (General), Philosophy, Physical Sciences, Psychology, Psychiatry, Science (General), Social Sciences, Sociology, Travel

ISBN Prefix(es): 84-7738
Number of titles published annually: 100 Print
Foreign Rep(s): Colofon (Mexico); Proeme (Latin America, US)

Equipo Sirius SA+
Avda Rafael Finat 34, 28044 Madrid
Tel: (091) 710 73 49 *Fax:* (091) 705 43 04
E-mail: sirius@equiposirius.com
Web Site: www.equiposirius.com
Key Personnel
Contact: Carmen de Pablo Urcelay
Founded: 1985
Subjects: Archaeology, Crafts, Games, Hobbies, Education, Photography, Physical Sciences, Science (General)
ISBN Prefix(es): 84-86639

Sirmio, see Acantilado

Ediciones Siruela SA+
Plaza de Manuel Becerra 15, 28028 Madrid
Tel: (091) 3555720; (091) 3554605; (091) 3552202 *Fax:* (091) 3552201
E-mail: siruela@siruela.com
Web Site: www.siruela.com
Key Personnel
Dir: Jacobo F J Stuart
Founded: 1982
Subjects: Art, Biography, Fiction, Nonfiction (General), Philosophy, Poetry, Religion - Buddhist, Religion - Catholic, Religion - Hindu, Religion - Islamic, Religion - Jewish, Religion - Other, Theology
ISBN Prefix(es): 84-7844

Edicions 62, *imprint of* Grup 62

Edicions 62+
Imprint of Grup 62
Peu de la Creu, 4, 08001 Barcelona
Tel: (093) 443 71 00 *Fax:* (093) 443 71 30
E-mail: correu@grup62.com
Web Site: www.grup62.com
Key Personnel
Man Dir: Juan Capdevila
Editorial Dir: Oriol Castanys
Sales & Publicity: Joaquim Sabria
Rights Manager: Laura Pujol
General Secretary: Josefina Revilla
Founded: 1962
Subjects: Art, Biography, Drama, Theater, Fiction, History, Literature, Literary Criticism, Essays, Music, Dance, Nonfiction (General), Philosophy, Poetry, Social Sciences, Sociology, Travel
ISBN Prefix(es): 84-297

Edicola-62
Imprint of Grup 62
Agusti Duran Sanpere, 1-5, 08001 Barcelona
Web Site: www.grup62.com
Key Personnel
Rights Manager: Laura Pujol

Grup 62+
Peu de la Creu, 4, 08011 Barcelona
Tel: (093) 443 71 00 *Fax:* (093) 443 71 30
E-mail: correu@grup62.com
Web Site: www.grup62.com
Key Personnel
Man Dir: Pere Sureda Vinolas
Editorial Dir: Martina Ros
Literary Dir: Xavier Folch
Sales & Publicity: Sergi Martinez
Rights Manager: Laura Pujol
Subjects: Biography, Drama, Theater, Fiction, History, Language Arts, Linguistics, Literature, Literary Criticism, Essays, Nonfiction (General), Parapsychology, Philosophy, Poetry, Psychology, Psychiatry, Science (General), Travel

Imprints: El Aleph Editores; Editorial Diagonal; Edicola-62; Editorial Empuries; Ediciones Luciernaga; Ediciones Peninsula; RACC-62; Edicions 62
Foreign Rep(s): Grupo Editorial Norma (South America, US)

Ediciones SM+
Joaquin Turina 39, 28044 Madrid
Tel: (091) 508 49 44 *Fax:* (091) 508 33 66
E-mail: comunicacion@grupo-sm.com
Web Site: www.ediciones-sm.com
Telex: 44710 Edsm E
Key Personnel
Dir General: Jorge Delkader Teig
Production Dir: Ignacio Fernandez
Publication Dir, Scholarly: Fernando Lopez-Aranguren
Publication Dir, General: Jose A Camacho
Rights: NcPaz Serrano
Communications & Public Relations: Juan A Cabrera
Founded: 1950
Specialize in publication of children's, juveniles, young adults & textbooks.
Subjects: Biography, Education, Humor, Literature, Literary Criticism, Essays, Philosophy, Religion - Other, Social Sciences, Sociology, Theology
ISBN Prefix(es): 84-348
Parent Company: Editions SM
Associate Companies: Cruilla, Calle Balmes 245 - 4, pta 3, 08006 Barcelona
Subsidiaries: Acento Editorial; Cesma; Ediciones SM; Editorial Crvilla; PPC
Orders to: CESMA SA, Aguacate 25, 28044 Madrid

Sociedad General Espanola de Libreria SA - SGEL
Avda Valdelaparra 29, 28108 Alcobendas, Madrid
Tel: (091) 657 69 00; (091) 657 69 12 *Fax:* (091) 657 69 28; (091) 657 69 19
Web Site: www.sgel.es
Key Personnel
Dir General: Enrique Valles
Founded: 1914
Subjects: English as a Second Language
ISBN Prefix(es): 84-7143
Parent Company: HDS

Anna Soler-Pont Literary Agecy
Travessera de Gracia 22, 08021 Barcelona
Tel: (093) 201 90 90 *Fax:* (093) 201 90 90
E-mail: pontas@intercom.es
Founded: 1992
Subjects: Fiction

Ramon Sopena SA+
Provenca 95, 08029 Barcelona
Tel: (093) 2303809 *Fax:* (093) 3223703
Key Personnel
Man Dir, Rights & Permissions: Ramon Sopena Rimblas
Production: Ramon Sopena, Jr
Founded: 1894
Subjects: Art, History, Language Arts, Linguistics, Science (General)
ISBN Prefix(es): 84-303
Total Titles: 200 Print

SPES Editorial SL+
Avda Diagonal, 407 bis, planta 10a, 08008 Barcelona
SAN: 000-5975
Tel: (093) 2922666 *Fax:* (093) 2922162
Telex: 54155 Cvox E *Cable:* Biblograf
Key Personnel
Man Dir: Alberto Cliarlau
Founded: 1952
Subjects: Language Arts, Linguistics

ISBN Prefix(es): 84-7153; 84-8332
Parent Company: Grupo Anaya, Juan Ignacio Luca de Terra 15, 28027 Madrid
Associate Companies: Ediciones Anaya SA

Axel Springer Publicaciones+
Pedro Teixeira 8, 28020 Madrid
SAN: 000-4448
Tel: (091) 514 06 30; (091) 556 00 48 *Fax:* (091) 514 06 30; (091) 556 0324
E-mail: info@axelspringer.es
Web Site: www.axelspringer.es
Telex: 46148 Srpe
Key Personnel
Man Dir: Alfredo Marron Gomez
Editorial: Marisa Perez Bodegas
Sales: Jose Aguilera Morena
Production: Andres Salcedo Pena
Publicity: Javier Jaen
Founded: 1952
Subjects: Art, Cookery, Crafts, Games, Hobbies, Gardening, Plants, History, Language Arts, Linguistics, Medicine, Nursing, Dentistry, Military Science, Music, Dance, Science (General), Sports, Athletics, Transportation
ISBN Prefix(es): 84-7291; 84-7700

Springer-Verlag Iberica, SA
Provenca, 388, 1 planta, 08025 Barcelona
Tel: (093) 4570227; (093) 4570759 *Fax:* (093) 4571502
E-mail: springer.bcn@springer.es
Key Personnel
Man Dir: Stephanie Van Duin
Founded: 1990
ISBN Prefix(es): 84-07
Parent Company: Springer-Verlag GmbH & Co KG, Heidelberger Platz 3, 14197 Berlin, Germany

Stanley Editorial+
Mendelu 15, 28280 Hondarribia
Tel: (0943) 64 04 12 *Fax:* (0943) 64 38 63
Key Personnel
Manager: Edward R Rosset *E-mail:* erossetc.stanley@nexo.es
Contact: Richard S Rosset *E-mail:* rrossetg.stanley@nexo.es
Founded: 1998
Specialize in Languages.
Subjects: History, Language Arts, Linguistics
ISBN Prefix(es): 84-7873; 84-86859
Total Titles: 100 Print
Subsidiaries: Cosmos (Mexico)
Distributor for ELI; Express Publishing
Warehouse: Popigono Olivares, c/o Sierra de Albarracin 3, Arganda del Rey, Madrid 28500
Tel: (091) 195928 *Fax:* (091) 195551

Editorial Rudolf Steiner+
Guipuzcoa 11-1 izda, 28020 Madrid
Tel: (091) 5531481 *Fax:* (091) 5531481
E-mail: rudolfsteiner@teleline.es
Key Personnel
President: Isabel Novillo Gavin
Founded: 1977
Subjects: Agriculture, Education, Philosophy, Psychology, Psychiatry, Religion - Other
ISBN Prefix(es): 84-89197
Number of titles published annually: 12 Print

Suaver, Javier Presa Suarez
Gran Via, 8, 9, Apartado postal: 427, 36203 Vigo, Pontevedra
Mailing Address: Apdo Postal n 427, 36280 Vigo
Tel: (086) 439507
Key Personnel
Dir: Javier Presa Suarez
Founded: 1990
Subjects: Poetry
ISBN Prefix(es): 84-88446
Distributed by Puvill Libros SA

SPAIN

Ediciones Susaeta SA
Campezo 13, 28022 Madrid
Tel: (091) 3009110 *Fax:* (091) 3009118
E-mail: susaeta@correo.net
Telex: 22148 Ssta e
Key Personnel
Sales Dir: Jose Ignacio Susaeta Erburu
Subjects: Cookery, Crafts, Games, Hobbies, Fiction, Travel
ISBN Prefix(es): 84-305

Ediciones Tabapress, SA+
Barquillo, 7, 28004 Madrid
Tel: (01) 5320876 *Fax:* (01) 5325890
E-mail: ediciones.tabapress@tsai.es
Key Personnel
Dir: Jesus Campos
Founded: 1988
Subjects: Art, History
ISBN Prefix(es): 84-7952; 84-86938

Ediciones Tarraco
San Francisco, 10, 43003 Tarragona
Tel: (077) 233813 *Fax:* (077) 233851
Key Personnel
Man Dir: Javier Elias
Founded: 1976
Subjects: Art, Education
ISBN Prefix(es): 84-7320
Parent Company: F Sugranes Editors SA, San Francisco, 10, 43003 Tarragona

TEA Ediciones SA+
Calle Fray Bernardino de Sahagun 24, 28036 Madrid
Tel: (091) 2705000 *Fax:* (091) 3458608
E-mail: madrid@teaediciones.com
Web Site: www.teaediciones.com
Telex: 22135 *Cable:* TEACEGOS
Key Personnel
Man Dir: Jaime Perena Brand
Sales: Milagros Anton
Production: Carlos Segura
Founded: 1957
Subjects: Psychology, Psychiatry
ISBN Prefix(es): 84-7174
Number of titles published annually: 15 Print
Total Titles: 300 Print
Parent Company: TEA-Cegos SA, Calle Fray Bernardino de Sahagun 24, 28036 Madrid
Branch Office(s)
Calle Paris, 211, 08008 Barcelona
Avda S Francisco Savier 21, 41005 Sevilla
Bidebarrieta 12, 48008 Bilbao
Bookshop(s): Paris 211, 08008 Barcelona

Ediciones Tecnicas Rede, SA
Ecuador, 91 1r-2, 08029 Barcelona
Tel: (093) 4103097 *Fax:* (093) 4392813
Key Personnel
Founding Editor: Pascual Gomez Aparicio
Subjects: Electronics, Electrical Engineering
ISBN Prefix(es): 84-247

Editores Tecnicos Asociados SA
Loreto, 13-15, Local B, 08029 Barcelona
Tel: (093) 4193336
Key Personnel
Man Dir: Carlos Palomar
Founded: 1963
Subjects: Architecture & Interior Design, Computer Science, Engineering (General), How-to
ISBN Prefix(es): 84-7146

Instituto Tecnologico de Galicia, ITG
Pocomaco, Sector 1, Portal 5, 15190 La Coruna
Tel: (0981) 17 32 06 *Fax:* (0981) 17 32 23
E-mail: itg1@itg.es
Web Site: www.itg.es
Key Personnel
Manager: Carlos Bald Orosa

Founded: 1991
ISBN Prefix(es): 84-89473

Editorial Tecnos SA+
Juan Ignacio Luca de Tena 15, 28027 Madrid
Tel: (091) 393 88 00; (091) 393 86 86 *Fax:* (091) 742 66 31
Web Site: www.tecnos.es
Telex: Maeg 41071
Key Personnel
Man Dir, Editorial: Alejandro Sierra Benayas
Production: Mariano Moreno
Publicity, Rights & Permissions: Pilar Lagarma
Founded: 1947
Subjects: Art, Business, Economics, Education, History, Law, Literature, Literary Criticism, Essays, Philosophy, Psychology, Psychiatry, Science (General), Social Sciences, Sociology, Technology
ISBN Prefix(es): 84-309
Parent Company: Grupo Anaya, Ferrer del Rio 35, 28028 Madrid
Associate Companies: Ediciones Anaya SA
Sales Office(s): Grupo Distribuidor Editorial SA, D Ramon de la Cruz 67, 28001 Madrid

Editorial Teide SA
Viladomat 291, 08029 Barcelona
Tel: (093) 4104507 *Fax:* (093) 3224192
E-mail: info@editorialteide.es
Web Site: www.editorialteide.es
Key Personnel
Man Dir, Publicity, Rights & Permissions, Editorial, Sales: Federico Rahola
Founded: 1942
Subjects: Education
ISBN Prefix(es): 84-307
Branch Office(s)
Calle Hierbabuena 50, 28039 Madrid *Tel:* (091) 5707920
Warehouse: Tambor del Bruch 8, 08970 San Juan Despi

Editorial Augusto E Pila Telena SL+
Pozo Nuevo 12, 28430 Alpedrete, Madrid
Tel: (091) 857 28 88; (607) 25 20 82 *Fax:* (091) 857 28 80
E-mail: pilatena@arrakis.es
Key Personnel
Man Dir: Augusto E Pila Telena
Editorial: Augusto Pila
Sales: Raquel Laviste
Founded: 1972
Specialize in Physical Education.
Subjects: Sports, Athletics
ISBN Prefix(es): 84-85514

Ediciones Temas de Hoy, SA+
Paseo de Recoletos, 4 planta, 28001 Madrid
Tel: (091) 4230318 *Fax:* (091) 4230309; (091) 5970654
E-mail: bnogueras@temasdehoy.es
Web Site: www.temasdehoy.es
Key Personnel
Council Delegate: Ymelda Navajo Lazaro
Founded: 1987
Subjects: Biography, History, Humor, Literature, Literary Criticism, Essays, Self-Help
ISBN Prefix(es): 84-7880; 84-86675

Editorial Sal Terrae+
Poligolo de Raos, Parcela 14-1, 39600 Maliano (Cantabria)
Mailing Address: Section 77, 39080 Santander (Cantabria)
Tel: (0942) 369 198 *Fax:* (0942) 369 201
E-mail: salterrae@salterrae.es
Web Site: www.salterrae.es
Key Personnel
Man Dir: Jesus Garcia-Abril
Founded: 1919

Subjects: Anthropology, Biography, History, Literature, Literary Criticism, Essays, Philosophy, Psychology, Psychiatry, Religion - Other, Theology
ISBN Prefix(es): 84-293

Tesitex, SL
Melchor Cano 15, 37007 Salamanca
Tel: (0923) 255115 *Fax:* (0923) 258703
E-mail: tesitex@tesitex.es
Web Site: www.tesitex.es
Key Personnel
Dir General: Jose Antonio Romero
Founded: 1988
Specialize in Electronic Book & Congress.
Subjects: Nonfiction (General), Publishing & Book Trade Reference
ISBN Prefix(es): 84-89609; 84-920313

Tf Editores+
Aragoneses 2, Acceso 11, Poligono Industrial de Alcobendas, 28108 Alcobendas, Madrid
Tel: (091) 484 1870; (091) 484 1878 *Fax:* (091) 661 3594
E-mail: editorial@tfeditores.com
Web Site: www.tfeditores.com
Key Personnel
Contact: Titto Ferreira; Chusa Hernandez
Founded: 1994
Publication Company, Edition, Printers.
Subjects: Architecture & Interior Design, Art, Literature, Literary Criticism, Essays, Photography
ISBN Prefix(es): 84-95183
Number of titles published annually: 40 Print
Total Titles: 215 Print
Parent Company: Tf Artes Graficas

Thales Sociedad Andaluza de Educacion Matematica
Facultad de Matematicas, Apdo postal de Correos 1160, 41080 Sevilla
Tel: (095) 4623658 *Fax:* (095) 4236378
E-mail: thales@cica.es
Web Site: thales.cica.es
Key Personnel
President: Rescuing Guerrero Hidalgo
Vice President: Mountain Vicenta Gil
Founded: 1981
Subjects: Education, Mathematics
ISBN Prefix(es): 84-920056

Editorial Thassalia, SA
Isradier 19-21, 08017 Barcelona
Tel: (093) 211.46.12 *Fax:* (093) 417.91.73
Key Personnel
Dir General: Joan Agut
Founded: 1994
Subjects: Fiction, History, Nonfiction (General), Religion - Buddhist, Religion - Hindu, Religion - Islamic, Spirituality
ISBN Prefix(es): 84-8237
Orders to: Distribuciones Prologo, Mascaro 35, 08032 Barcelona *Tel:* (093) 347 25 11 *Fax:* (093) 459 95 06

Timun Mas, *imprint of* Grupo Editorial CEAC SA

Tirant lo Blanch SL Libreriaa+
Artes Graficas 14, Bajo dcha, 46014 Valencia
Tel: (096) 3610048 *Fax:* (096) 3694151
E-mail: tlb@tirant.es
Web Site: www.tirant.es
Key Personnel
Manager: Candelaria Lopez-Quiles
Founded: 1976
Subjects: Criminology, Education, Labor, Industrial Relations, Law, Management, Social Sciences, Sociology
ISBN Prefix(es): 84-8002; 84-86558
Branch Office(s)
Campus Universitario Borrio, 12071 Castellon

PUBLISHERS

SPAIN

Gravador Esteve, 5, 46021 Valencia *Tel:* (0034) 963749840 *Fax:* (0034) 963341835
Warehouse: Calle Mendez Nunez, 34, 46024 Valencia

Titania, *imprint of* Ediciones Urano, SA

Ediciones Toray SA+
Rambla Montserrat, 19 bajos, 08290 - Cerdanyola Barcelona
Tel: (093) 5808124; (093) 6921851 *Fax:* (093) 6921851
Key Personnel
President: Alfredo Plana
Editorial Dir: M Antonia Estaun
Rights & Permissions: Heinz W Gehre
Founded: 1953
Subjects: Fiction, Medicine, Nursing, Dentistry
ISBN Prefix(es): 84-310
Parent Company: Grupo Telepublicaciones
Branch Office(s)
DDL Books Inc, 6521 NW 87 Ave, Miami, FL 33178, United States

Gregorio del Toro Editor
Hortaleza 81, 28004 Madrid
Tel: (091) 3080077; (091) 3190139 *Fax:* (091) 3080187
Subjects: Fiction, Nonfiction (General)
ISBN Prefix(es): 84-312

Ediciones de la Torre+
Espronceda 20, 28003 Madrid
Tel: (091) 692 20 34 *Fax:* (091) 692 20 34
E-mail: info@edicionesdelatorre.com
Web Site: www.edicionesdelatorre.com
Key Personnel
Manager: Jose Maria Gutierrez
Editorial: Rosa Perez
Founded: 1976
Subjects: Advertising, Child Care & Development, Communications, Drama, Theater, Education, Geography, Geology, History, Human Relations, Journalism, Literature, Literary Criticism, Essays, Nonfiction (General), Philosophy, Physics, Poetry, Radio, TV, Science (General), Social Sciences, Sociology
ISBN Prefix(es): 84-7960; 84-85866; 84-85277; 84-86587
Warehouse: C/Sorgo, 45, 28029 Madrid
Orders to: C/Sorgo, 454, 28029 Madrid

Torremozas SL Ediciones
Apdo de Correos 19032, 28080 Madrid
Tel: (091) 350 50 27; (091) 359 03 15 *Fax:* (091) 345 85 32
Founded: 1982
Specialize in Poetry.
Subjects: Literature, Literary Criticism, Essays, Poetry, Women's Studies
ISBN Prefix(es): 84-7839; 84-86072
Distributed by Maidhisa SL

Instituto Eduardo Torroja
Serrano Galvache, 28033 Madrid
Tel: (091) 302 04 40 *Fax:* (091) 302 07 00
E-mail: director.ietcc@csic.es
Web Site: www.ietcc.csic.es
Key Personnel
Dir: Marie Carmen Andrade Perdrix
E-mail: director.ietcc@csic.es
Vice Dir: Gustavo Verges Monk *E-mail:* vicedir.ietcc@csic.es
Manager: Jose Luis Gonzalez Lezcano
E-mail: gerente.ietcc@csic.es
Deputy Dir: Olga Rio Suarez *E-mail:* rio.ietcc@csic.es
Founded: 1934
Subjects: Architecture & Interior Design, Engineering (General)
ISBN Prefix(es): 84-7292

Trazo Editorial, SL+
Camino de los Molinos 155, 50015 Zaragoza
Tel: (076) 517586 *Fax:* (076) 517464
Key Personnel
Man Dir: D Francisco Javier Miguel
Founded: 1980
Subjects: Sports, Athletics, Travel
ISBN Prefix(es): 84-85821

Trea Ediciones, SL+
Donoso Cortes 7, 33204 Gijon, Asturias
Tel: (098) 5133453 *Fax:* (098) 5131182
E-mail: trea@trea.es
Key Personnel
Manager: Miguel A Blanco Vazquez
Editor: Alvaro Diaz Huici
International Rights: Ferwanda Poblet
Founded: 1990
Subjects: Art, Biological Sciences, Cookery, Education, Fiction, Geography, Geology, History, Library & Information Sciences, Literature, Literary Criticism, Essays, Nonfiction (General), Photography, Poetry, Public Administration, Travel
ISBN Prefix(es): 84-87733; 84-89427

Institut de Treball Social - Serveis Socials
Avda Diagonal, 482, 2º, tercera, 08006 Barcelona
Tel: (093) 217 26 64 *Fax:* (093) 237 36 34
E-mail: intressbar@intress.org
Web Site: www.intress.org
Key Personnel
President: Rosa Domenech Ferrer
Founded: 1984
ISBN Prefix(es): 84-87400

Trito Edicions, SL
Av de la Catedral 3, 08002 Barcelona
Mailing Address: Apartat de Correus, 2254, 08080 Barcelona
Tel: (093) 342 61 75 *Fax:* (093) 302 26 70
E-mail: trito@bcn.servicom.es
Web Site: www.trito.es
Founded: 1993
ISBN Prefix(es): 84-88955

Editorial Trivium, SA+
Campomanes 7, 28013 Madrid
Tel: (091) 5422388 *Fax:* (091) 5422862
Key Personnel
President: Carlos Tapia Navarro
Founded: 1982
Subjects: Economics, Law
ISBN Prefix(es): 84-7855
Bookshop(s): Libreria Trivium, SA
Warehouse: Pintores, 30 (Polig Urtinsa II), 28925 Alcorcon Madrid

Trotta SA Editorial+
Ferraz, 55, 28008 Madrid
Tel: (091) 5430361 *Fax:* (091) 5431488
E-mail: trotta@infornet.es
Web Site: www.trotta.es
Key Personnel
President: Alejandro Sierra Benayas
General Secretary: Christiane Schwamborn
Founded: 1990
Hardcover & Paperback.
Subjects: History, Law, Literature, Literary Criticism, Essays, Philosophy, Psychology, Psychiatry, Religion - Catholic, Religion - Islamic, Religion - Jewish, Religion - Other, Social Sciences, Sociology, Theology
ISBN Prefix(es): 84-87699; 81-8164
Total Titles: 500 Print

Ediciones Jose Porrua Turanzas SA
Marques de la Ensenada 16, Apdo 1307, 28004 Madrid
Tel: (091) 7021493 *Fax:* (091) 7021538
E-mail: info@porrualibros.com
Web Site: www.porrualibros.com
Key Personnel
Man Dir, Editorial: Jose Porrua
Sales, Production, Publicity, Rights & Permissions: Enrique Porrua Venero
Founded: 1954
Subjects: Foreign Countries, Literature, Literary Criticism, Essays
ISBN Prefix(es): 84-7317; 0-935568
Bookshop(s): Libreria Jose Porrua Turanzas SA

Turner Publicaciones+
Rafael Calvo 42, 2 Esc Izda, 28010 Madrid
Tel: (091) 308 33 36 *Fax:* (091) 319 39 30
Web Site: www.turnerlibros.com
Key Personnel
President: Andrea Nasi
Publisher: Manuel Arroyo
Chief Executive Officer: Santiago F de Cayela
E-mail: sfcaleya@turnerlibros.com
Editorial Dir: Juan G de Oteyza
E-mail: jgoteyza@turnerlibros.com
Founded: 1973
Specialize in production of catalogues & illustrated books; publishes general nonfiction.
Subjects: Architecture & Interior Design, Art, History, Literature, Literary Criticism, Essays, Nonfiction (General), Philosophy, Photography, Poetry, Regional Interests, Museum Catalogues
ISBN Prefix(es): 84-7506
Number of titles published annually: 60 Print
Total Titles: 200 Print

Tursen, SA
Mazarredo, 4-5 B, 28005 Madrid
Tel: (091) 3667148 *Fax:* (091) 3653148
Key Personnel
Contact: Alicia Parrilla
Founded: 1990
Member of la Camara, federacion y gremio de Editores; also acts as book illustrator.
Subjects: Advertising, Architecture & Interior Design, Art, Child Care & Development, Cookery, Crafts, Games, Hobbies, Disability, Special Needs, Environmental Studies, Gardening, Plants, Outdoor Recreation, Photography, Self-Help, Sports, Athletics, Travel
ISBN Prefix(es): 84-87756
Book Club(s): Circulo des Lectores
Warehouse: Poligono Industrial Las Monjas C/Invierno S/N Naves 14-15, Torrejon, Madrid

Tusquets Editores+
Cesare Cantu 8, 08017 Barcelona
Tel: (093) 2530400 *Fax:* (093) 4176703; (093) 4188698 (Rights & Editing)
E-mail: general@tusquets-editores.es
Web Site: www.tusquets-editores.com
Key Personnel
Man Dir: Beatriz de Moura; Antonio Lopez Lamadrid
Sales: Rosa Maria Segala
Publicity: Natalia Gil
Production: Orencio Sales
Foreign Rights & Permissions: Patricia Sanchez
E-mail: rightspat@tusquets-editores.es
Foreign Rights Acquisitions: Carmen Corral
Founded: 1969
Subjects: Biography, Fiction, History, Literature, Literary Criticism, Essays, Science (General)
ISBN Prefix(es): 84-7223
Branch Office(s)
Tusquets Editores SA, Venezuela 1664, 1096 Buenos Aires, Argentina *Tel:* (011) 43814520 *Fax:* (011) 43811760 *E-mail:* tusquets@interar.com.ar
Tusquets Editores Mexico, SA de CV, Edgar Allan Poe 91, Col Polanco 11560, Mexico *Tel:* (055) 281 50 40; (055) 281 53 44

Fax: (055) 281 55 92 *E-mail:* tusquets@mail.nextgeninter.net.mx
Warehouse: Carretera del Prat 39, Poligono Industrial Almeda nave n 5, 08940 Cornella, Barcelona

Ediciones Tutor SA+
Andres Mellado 9, 1D, 28015 Madrid
Tel: (091) 543 21 72 *Fax:* (091) 549 96 53
E-mail: tutor@autovia.com
Key Personnel
President: Jesus Domingo Garcia
Editorial Dir & Rights & Permissions: David Domingo Yanes
Marketing, Public Relations: Vivas Francisco Rubira
Founded: 1989
Subjects: Animals, Pets, Career Development, Cookery, Crafts, Games, Hobbies, Gardening, Plants, Health, Nutrition, Humor, Outdoor Recreation, Sports, Athletics
ISBN Prefix(es): 84-7902
Associate Companies: Editorial El Drac SL
Warehouse: ADT, c/o Pelaya ue4, Poligono Industrial Ri de Janeiro, 28110 algete, Madrid *Tel:* (091) 6280606
Orders to: I Taca SA Distribuciones Editoriales, Lopez de Hoyos, 141, 28002 Madrid *Tel:* (091) 3224400 *Fax:* (091) 3224370

Ediciones 29 - Libros Rio Nuevo+
Francesc Vila, Nave 14, Poligono Industrial Can Magi, 08190 Sant Cugat del Valles, Barcelona
Tel: (093) 675 41 35 *Fax:* (093) 590 04 40
E-mail: ediciones29@comunired.com
Web Site: www.ediciones29.com
Key Personnel
Man Dir: Alfredo Llorente Diez
Founded: 1968
Subjects: Astrology, Occult, Cookery, Erotica, Literature, Literary Criticism, Essays, Poetry, Religion - Catholic, Self-Help
ISBN Prefix(es): 84-7175
Total Titles: 200 Print

Editorial Txertoa+
Plz de Olaeta (Ferrerias) s/n-bajo, 20011 San Sebastian
Tel: (0943) 45 97 57; (0943) 46 09 41
Fax: (0943) 46 09 41
E-mail: txertoa@nexo.es
Key Personnel
Man Dir: Luis Aberasturi *Fax:* (043) 46094
Founded: 1968
Subjects: Anthropology, Art, Biography, Ethnicity, Geography, Geology, Language Arts, Linguistics, Literature, Literary Criticism, Essays, Regional Interests, Religion - Other, Social Sciences, Sociology
ISBN Prefix(es): 84-7148
Number of titles published annually: 12 Print
Total Titles: 250 Print

Ultramar Editores SA
Industria s/n, 08450 Llinars del Valles
Tel: (093) 8410351 *Fax:* (093) 8412334
E-mail: ultramar@javajan.com
Telex: 53132 Saedi E
Key Personnel
Man Dir: Emilio Teixidor
Founded: 1973
Subjects: Biography, Fiction, Film, Video, Literature, Literary Criticism, Essays, Science Fiction, Fantasy
ISBN Prefix(es): 84-7386

Umbriel, *imprint of* Ediciones Urano, SA

Universidad de Granada
Antiguo Colegio Maximo, Campus Universitario de Cartuja, 18071 Granada
Tel: (0958) 243932 *Fax:* (0958) 243931
Key Personnel
Dir: Rafael G Peinado Santaella
Deputy Dir: Antonio Martin
Subjects: Anthropology, Archaeology, Art, Biological Sciences, Education, Geography, Geology, History, Law, Literature, Literary Criticism, Essays, Medicine, Nursing, Dentistry, Music, Dance, Philosophy, Science (General), Social Sciences, Sociology
ISBN Prefix(es): 84-338

Universidad de Las Palmas de Gran Canaria, Escuela Universitaria de Informatica (ULPGC)
Campus Universitario de Tafira, 35017 Las Palmas de Gran Canaria
Tel: (0928) 45-87-19; (0928) 45-87-00
Fax: (0928) 45-87-11
E-mail: organizacion@sinf.ulpgc.es
Web Site: www5.ulpgc.es
Key Personnel
Dir: Eugenia Rua-Figueroa
ISBN Prefix(es): 84-8098

Universidad de Malaga+
Campus de Teatinos, Boulevard Louis Pasteur 30, 29071 Malaga
Tel: (095) 213 29 17 *Fax:* (095) 213 29 18
E-mail: spicum@uma.es
Web Site: www.uma.es
Key Personnel
Dir: Juan Antonio Lacomba Avellan
Founded: 1978
Subjects: Agriculture, Art, Earth Sciences, Economics, Education, History, Law, Medicine, Nursing, Dentistry, Philosophy, Social Sciences, Sociology
ISBN Prefix(es): 84-7496
Distributed by Distribuciones de Enlace SA

Ediciones Universidad de Navarra SA, see EUNSA (Ediciones Universidad de Navarra SA)

Universidad de Navarra, Ediciones SA+
Plaza de los Sauces 1-2, 31010 Baranain, Navarra
Tel: (0948) 256850 *Fax:* (0948) 256854
E-mail: eunsa@cin.es
Web Site: www.eunsa.es
Key Personnel
President: Manuel de Muga
Sales: Juan de Muga
Founded: 1967
Subjects: Art
ISBN Prefix(es): 84-313

Universidad de Oviedo Servicio de Publicaciones
Arguelles 19, 33003 Oviedo
Tel: (0985) 210160; (0985) 222428 *Fax:* (0985) 218352
Web Site: www.uniovi.es
Key Personnel
Dir: Ubaldo Gomez
Subjects: Behavioral Sciences, Language Arts, Linguistics, Physical Sciences, Science (General), Social Sciences, Sociology
ISBN Prefix(es): 84-7468

Ediciones Universidad de Salamanca+
Plaza de San Benito, 23, Salamanca 37008
Tel: (0923) 294598 *Fax:* (0923) 262579
E-mail: eus@usal.es
Web Site: www3.usal.es
Key Personnel
Man Dir: Jose Manuel Bustos Gisbert
E-mail: jbustos@gugu.usal.es
Founded: 1486
Subjects: Education, History, Literature, Literary Criticism, Essays, Philosophy, Science (General)
ISBN Prefix(es): 84-7481
Number of titles published annually: 100 Print
Bookshop(s): Salamanca

Universidad de Sevilla Secretariado de Publicaciones
Porvenir 27, 41013 Sevilla
Tel: (05) 487444; (05) 487442 *Fax:* (095) 487 7443
Web Site: publius.cica.es
Key Personnel
Dir: Enrique Valdivieso Gonzalez
ISBN Prefix(es): 84-472; 84-7405
Distributed by Distribuciones de Enlace SA; L'Alebrije; L'Estaquirot

Universidad de Valladolid Secretariado de Publicaciones e Intercambio Editorial+
c/Juan Mambrilla 14, 47003 Valladolid
Tel: (0983) 187810 *Fax:* (0983) 187812
E-mail: spie@uva.es
Web Site: www.uva.es
Key Personnel
Dir: Palacio Zuniga
Founded: 1949
Subjects: Accounting, Archaeology, Architecture & Interior Design, Art, Business, Chemistry, Chemical Engineering, Computer Science, Economics, Education, Electronics, Electrical Engineering, Engineering (General), Geography, Geology, Government, Political Science, History, Law, Literature, Literary Criticism, Essays, Medicine, Nursing, Dentistry, Philosophy, Physics, Psychology, Psychiatry, Science (General), Social Sciences, Sociology
ISBN Prefix(es): 84-7762; 84-8448

Publicacions de la Universitat de Barcelona+
Gran Via de les Corts Catalanes 585, 08071 Barcelona
Tel: (093) 403 54 41 *Fax:* (093) 403 54 46
Web Site: www.ub.es
Key Personnel
Dir: Joan Duran i Fontanals
Editorial: Carmen Garcia Gonzalez
Founded: 1935
Member de Gremi d'Editors de Catalunya & de Asociacion Editoriales Universitarias Espanoles.
Subjects: Art, Economics, Education, History, Law, Mathematics, Science (General), Social Sciences, Sociology
ISBN Prefix(es): 84-475
Bookshop(s): Balmes-21, 08071 Barcelona
Warehouse: Baldiri l Reixac, s/n 08028 Barcelona

Universitat de Valencia Servei de Publicacions
Artes Graficas 13, 46010 Valencia
Tel: (096) 3864115 *Fax:* (096) 3864067
E-mail: publicacions@uv.es
Web Site: www.uv.es
Key Personnel
Editor: Maite Simon Mendez
Technical Editorial: Immaculada Mesa Ballester
Subjects: Biological Sciences, Economics, Education, History, Literature, Literary Criticism, Essays, Medicine, Nursing, Dentistry, Philosophy
ISBN Prefix(es): 84-370

Edicions de la Universitat Politecnica de Catalunya SL
Jordi Girona Salgado nº 31, 08034 Barcelona
Tel: (093) 4016 883 *Fax:* (093) 4015 885
E-mail: edicions-upc@upc.es
Web Site: www.edicionsupc.es
Key Personnel
Dir: Josep Maria Serra-Munoz

Founded: 1994
Subjects: Architecture & Interior Design, Chemistry, Chemical Engineering, Civil Engineering, Computer Science, Electronics, Electrical Engineering, Engineering (General), Science (General)
ISBN Prefix(es): 84-7653

Urano, *imprint of* Ediciones Urano, SA

Ediciones Urano, SA+
Aribau 142, pral, 08036 Barcelona
Tel: (093) 2375 564 *Fax:* (093) 4153 796
E-mail: atencion@edicionesurano.com
Web Site: www.edicionesurano.com
Key Personnel
Manager: Joaquin Sabate
Literary Dir & International Rights: Gregorio Vlastelica *E-mail:* edit@edicionesurano.com
Fiction Editor: Aranzazu Sumalla
Founded: 1984
Subjects: Alternative, Astrology, Occult, Business, Fiction, Health, Nutrition, How-to, Management, Mysteries, Psychology, Psychiatry, Romance, Self-Help
ISBN Prefix(es): 84-7953; 84-86344; 84-95618; 84-95752
Number of titles published annually: 74 Print
Total Titles: 561 Print
Online services available through World Wide Web.
Imprints: EmpresaActiva; Titania; Umbriel; Urano
Branch Office(s)
Castillo 540, 1414 Buenos Aires, Argentina
  Tel: (011) 477 143 82 *Fax:* (011) 477 143 82
  E-mail: argentina@edicionesurano.com
Av Francisco Bilbao, 2809 Providencia, Santiago, Chile *Tel:* (562) 341 67 31 *Fax:* (562) 225 38 96 *E-mail:* chile@edicionesurano.com
Transversal 43, No 97-75, Santafe de Bogota DC, Colombia *Tel:* (571) 253 24 88 *Fax:* (571) 226 24 73 *E-mail:* colombia@edicionesurano.com
Vito Alessio Robles, No 140, Col Florida, 01030 Alvaro Obregon, Mexico *Tel:* (05) 661 0774 *Fax:* (05) 661 7590 *E-mail:* mexico@edicionesurano.com
Avda Luis Roche-Edif Santa Clara, PB Altamira Sur, 1062 Caracas, Venezuela *Tel:* (582) 264 03 73 *Fax:* (582) 261 69 62 *E-mail:* venezuela@edicionesurano.com

Urmo SA de Ediciones+
Nervion 3-6, 48001 Bilbao
Tel: (094) 424 53 07 *Fax:* (094) 423 19 84
E-mail: urmo@infonegocio.com
Web Site: www.urmo.com
Key Personnel
President: Begona Grijelmo Mattern
Chairman: Federico Guillermo Grijelmo Ribechnin
Founded: 1963
Subjects: Engineering (General), Microcomputers, Science (General)
ISBN Prefix(es): 84-314
Total Titles: 210 Print
Warehouse: Andres Isasi, 3-6, 48012 Bilbao

Parlamento Vasco
Becerro de Bengoa, s/n, 01005 Vitoria-Gasteiz, Alava
Tel: (0945) 004 000 *Fax:* (0945) 135 406
E-mail: legebiltzarra@parlam.euskadi.net
Web Site: parlamento.euskadi.net
Key Personnel
Dir: Juan Carols da Silva Ochoa
Subjects: History, Law, Social Sciences, Sociology
ISBN Prefix(es): 84-87122

Editorial Verbo Divino+
Ave de Pamplona 41, 31200 Estella Navarra
Tel: (0948) 556505; (0948) 55 65 11 *Fax:* (0948) 554506
E-mail: ventas@verbodivino.es
Web Site: www.verbodivino.es *Cable:* VERBODIVINO
Key Personnel
Man Dir: Father Tomas Langarica
Sales Dir: Martin Esparza
Advertising, Rights & Permissions: Maria Puy Larramendi
Founded: 1957
Subjects: Biblical Studies, Religion - Catholic, Social Sciences, Sociology, Theology
ISBN Prefix(es): 84-7151; 84-8169
Distributed by Alpa Libros (Spain); Bidea 2000 (Spain); Centro Biblico Verbo Divino (Ecuador); Centro Paulino (Venezuela); Claret Libreria (Spain); Comercial Gravi - Libros (Spain); Departamento Pastoral Biblica (Mexico); Distribucion Buho Azul (Spain); Distribucion Icaro (Spain); Distribucion Vilas Duran (Spain); Distribuciones Edit Lyra (Spain); Distriforma SA (Spain); Editorial Guadalupe (Argentina); Editorial Verbo Divino (Bolivia); Emaus Libros SL (Spain); Empresa Periodistica Mundo (Chile); Fundacion Editores Verbo Divino (Colombia); Libreria Catolica Gethsemani (United States); Libreria Centro Biblico Verbo Divino (Paraguay); Libreria Hispamer SA (Nicaragua); Libreria San Pablo (Venezuela); Libreria Verbum (Mexico); Libros D&D Unidisa (Spain); Manantial Cultura - Lib Loyola (Guatemala); Paulinas Distribuidora (United States); PPC Edit y Distribuidora SA (Spain); PPC Editorial y Distribuidora (Spain); Spanish Speaking Bookstore Distrib (United States)

Editorial Verbum SL+
Equilaz 6-2 Derecha, 28010 Madrid
Tel: (091) 446 88 41 *Fax:* (091) 594 45 59
E-mail: verbum@globalnet.es
Key Personnel
Dir: Pio E Serrano
Administrator: Aurora Calvino
Founded: 1991
Specialize in Spanish for foreigners.
Subjects: Drama, Theater, Fiction, Language Arts, Linguistics, Literature, Literary Criticism, Essays, Music, Dance, Philosophy, Poetry
ISBN Prefix(es): 84-7962
Total Titles: 136 Print; 1 Audio
Foreign Rep(s): Sara Grecco Editoriales (Puerto Rico); Interlogos (Italy)
Warehouse: Calle del Pez 21, 28004 Madrid

Javier Vergara Editor SA
Luis Santangel, 6, 46210 Valencia
Tel: (096) 159 05 11 *Fax:* (096) 159 06 97
Key Personnel
General Manager: Rodolfo Blanco
Publicity Manager: Maria Eugenia Delso
Founded: 1987
Subjects: Biography, Business, Fiction, History, Music, Dance, Nonfiction (General), Psychology, Psychiatry, Self-Help
ISBN Prefix(es): 84-7417
Parent Company: Javier Vergara Editor Argentina

Veron Editor+
Tarragona 97, 08820 El Prat de Llobregat
Tel: (093) 4781940 *Fax:* (093) 4781908
E-mail: veron@veroneditor.com
Key Personnel
Man Dir, Sales, Rights & Permissions: Lluis Veron Jane
Founded: 1965
Subjects: Literature, Literary Criticism, Essays, Nonfiction (General)
ISBN Prefix(es): 84-7255

Ediciones Versal SA
Rosello, 41-45, 08029 Barcelona
Tel: (093) 494 85 90 *Fax:* (093) 419 02 97
E-mail: cga.barcelona@cga.es
Web Site: www.anaya.es
Telex: 54155 CVOX E
Key Personnel
Dir General & Editorial: Antoni Munne
Production: Blanca Marques
Founded: 1984
Subjects: Biography, Literature, Literary Criticism, Essays, Nonfiction (General)
ISBN Prefix(es): 84-86311; 84-86717; 84-7876
Parent Company: Grupo Anaya, Juan Ignacio Luca de Tena, 15, 28027 Madrid
Associate Companies: Ediciones Anaya SA
Orders to: Grupo Distribuidor Editorial SA, Ferrer del Rio, 35, 28028 Madrid

Gobierno de Canarias - Viceconsejeria de Cultura y Deportes
Calle Villalba Hervas 4, 8 Planta, 38002 Santa Cruz de Tenerife
Tel: (092) 2474119 *Fax:* (092) 2474165
Key Personnel
Director General: Horacio Umpierrez Sanchez
ISBN Prefix(es): 84-7947; 84-87137
Distributed by Bitacora Servicios Editoriales (Spain); Dist Edit Breogan SL (Spain); Distribuciones Lemus (Spain); Rafael Roca Suarez E Hijos (Spain); Servei Del Llibre (Spain)

Vicens Basica, *imprint of* Editorial Vicens-Vives

Vicens Universidad, *imprint of* Editorial Vicens-Vives

Editorial Vicens-Vives+
Av de Sarria 130-132, 08017 Barcelona
Tel: (093) 2523700 *Fax:* (093) 2523711
E-mail: e@vicensvives.es
Web Site: www.vicensvives.es
Telex: 51425 Live E
Key Personnel
President: Roser Rahola; Pere Vicens
Dir: Albert Vicens; Anna Vicens
Founded: 1942
Subjects: Education, Ethnicity, Fiction, History, Mathematics, Science (General)
ISBN Prefix(es): 84-316
Imprints: Instituto Cartografico Latino; Vicens Basica; Vicens Universidad

Ediciones A Madrid Vicente+
Almansa, 94, 28040 Madrid
SAN: 000-2437
Tel: (091) 5336926 *Fax:* (091) 5330286
E-mail: amadrid@acta.es
Web Site: www.amvediciones.com
Key Personnel
Dir: Antonio Madrid Vicente
Founded: 1986
Subjects: Agriculture, Electronics, Electrical Engineering, Technology, Specialize in books about food technology, refrigeration, air conditioning, electricity, construction, coatings & pharmacy
ISBN Prefix(es): 84-89922; 84-87440
Total Titles: 100 Print
Online services available through Spain Telecom.
Foreign Rep(s): Mundi Prensa Calle Castello 37 (Latin America, Portugal, Spain, US)

Vinaches Lopez, Luisa+
Cervantes 34, 03570 Villajoyasa Alicante
Tel: (01) 3694488 *Fax:* (01) 3694488
Key Personnel
Dir: Lidia Falcon
International Rights: Elvira Siurana
Founded: 1976 (Vindicacion, 1997 Kira Edit)
Member of Spanish Feminist party.
Subjects: Anthropology, Biography, Drama, Theater, Fiction, Literature, Literary Criticism, Es-

says, Nonfiction (General), Poetry, Women's Studies, Feminism
ISBN Prefix(es): 84-922067
Parent Company: Vindicacion Feminista Publicaciones
Imprints: Cofas SA
Divisions: Aconcagua Publishing
Distributed by Aconcagia Publishing; Editorial Hacer; Kira Edit

Visor Distribuciones, SA+
Tomas Breton 55, 28045 Madrid
Tel: (091) 4681248; (091) 4681011; (091) 4681102 *Fax:* (091) 4681098
E-mail: editorial@visordis.es
Web Site: www.visordis.es
Key Personnel
Dir: Jose Miguel Garcia Sanchez
Founded: 1987
Subjects: Art, Education, Literature, Literary Criticism, Essays, Philosophy, Psychology, Psychiatry
ISBN Prefix(es): 84-7774

Visor Libros+
Isaac Peral, 18, 28015 Madrid
Tel: (091) 5492655 *Fax:* (091) 5448695
E-mail: visor-libros@visor-libros.com
Web Site: www.visor-libros.com
Key Personnel
Contact: Jesus Garcia Sanchez
Founded: 1970
Subjects: Language Arts, Linguistics, Literature, Literary Criticism, Essays, Poetry
ISBN Prefix(es): 84-7522

Vital, *imprint of* Obelisco Ediciones S

VOSA, SL Ediciones
Hermosilla 132-bajo, 28028 Madrid
Tel: (091) 7259430 *Fax:* (091) 7259430
Founded: 1993
ISBN Prefix(es): 84-8218

Ediciones Vulcano+
Matilde Hernandez 71, 28025 Madrid
Tel: (091) 461 44 58; (091) 500 16 49 *Fax:* (091) 461 44 58
E-mail: vulcano@vulcanoediciones.com
Web Site: www.vulcanoediciones.com
Key Personnel
Editor: Isidoro Correa
Founded: 1980
Subjects: Literature, Literary Criticism, Essays, Poetry, Technology, Travel
ISBN Prefix(es): 84-7828

Wolters Kluwer Espana SA
Collado Mediano 9, 28230 Lass Rozas Madrid
Tel: (091) 6020023 *Fax:* (091) 6020021
E-mail: pilarg@wke.es
Telex: 99020 EPWS
Key Personnel
Resident Dir: P C Minderhout
ISBN Prefix(es): 84-87670
Parent Company: Wolters Kluwer NV, Netherlands

Ediciones Xandro+
Apdo 40 020, Avda del Mediterraneo, 18, 28007 Madrid
Tel: (091) 5520261 *Fax:* (091) 5014145
Key Personnel
Contact: Belda German
Founded: 1987
Subjects: Psychology, Psychiatry
ISBN Prefix(es): 84-88665

Xarait Libros SA
Paseo de San Francisco de Sales 32, 28003 Madrid
Tel: (091) 534 15 67 *Fax:* (091) 535 08 31
Key Personnel
Man Dir: Miguel Ortiz Martinez
Founded: 1973
Subjects: Architecture & Interior Design, Art
ISBN Prefix(es): 84-85434

Edicions Xerais de Galicia
Doctor Maranon 12, 36211 Vigo
Tel: (086) 214888 *Fax:* (086) 201366
E-mail: xerais@xerais.es
Web Site: www.xerais.es
Key Personnel
Contact: Manuel Bragado Rodriguez
Founded: 1976
Subjects: Education, Fiction, History, Language Arts, Linguistics, Poetry, Social Sciences, Sociology
ISBN Prefix(es): 84-7507

Xunta de Galicia
Conselleria de Cultura Comunicacion Social e Turismo, San Caetano s-n, 15771 Santiago de Compostela
Tel: (081) 544816 *Fax:* (081) 544887
Key Personnel
Subdirector Xeral of Culture: Xabier Senin Fernandez
Conselleria de Cultura e Xuventude, Ed San Caetano, s/n.
Subjects: Agriculture, Art, Business, Economics, Education, Fiction, Finance, Geography, Geology, Health, Nutrition, History, Law, Literature, Literary Criticism, Essays, Management, Maritime, Marketing, Public Administration, Science (General)
ISBN Prefix(es): 84-453

Editorial Zendrera Zariquiey, SA+
Cardenal Vivesi Tuto 59 baixos, 08034 Barcelona
Tel: (093) 280.61.82 *Fax:* (093) 280.61.90
E-mail: anazz@wanadoo.es
Web Site: www.sirpus.com
Key Personnel
Man Dir: Mr F Zendrera
International Rights: Ms Fabregat
Founded: 1996
Subjects: Computer Science, Cookery, Travel
Total Titles: 120 Print
Associate Companies: Editorial Sirpus, SL

Sri Lanka

General Information

Capital: Colombo
Language: Sinhala & Tamila (official & national) & English (national)
Religion: Predominantly Buddhism
Population: 17.6 million
Bank Hours: 0900-1300 Monday-Friday
Shop Hours: 0800-1730 Monday-Friday
Currency: 100 cents = 1 Sri Lanka rupee
Export/Import Information: No tariff on books or advertising. Import license required for most book importation. Exchange controls.
Copyright: UCC, Berne, Florence (see Copyright Conventions, pg xi)

Buddhist Publication Society Inc
54 Sangharaja Mawatha, Kandy
Mailing Address: PO Box 61, Kandy
Tel: (08) 223679; (08) 237283 *Fax:* (08) 223679
E-mail: bps@ids.lk; bps@metta.lk

Key Personnel
President, Editor: Bhikkhu Bodhi
   E-mail: venbodhi@metta.lk
Administrative Secretary: L B W Seneviratne
Founded: 1958
Subjects: Religion - Buddhist
ISBN Prefix(es): 955-24
Foreign Rep(s): Vipassana Research Publications of America (US)
Foreign Rights: Dhamma Books (India); Wisdom Books (UK)

Business Directory of Lanka Limited+
Deanston House, 1st floor, Deanston Place, Colombo 3
Tel: (01) 577563; (01) 577793 *Fax:* (01) 586135
E-mail: info@lanka.com
Web Site: www.lanka.com
Key Personnel
Man Dir: Mangala Wickramarachchi
   E-mail: kompass@itmin.com
Founded: 1994
Member of Ceylon Chamber of Commerce.
ISBN Prefix(es): 955-9405
Subsidiaries: Raffles Lanka (Pvt) Ltd; Kompass Lanka (Pvt) Ltd

Calvary Press+
123 Highlevel Rd, Kirillapone, Colombo 6
Tel: (01) 553110
Subjects: Religion - Protestant
ISBN Prefix(es): 955-587

The Ceylon Chamber of Commerce
127, Lower Chatham St, Colombo 1
Mailing Address: PO Box 274, Colombo 2
Tel: (01) 412745; (01) 412747 *Fax:* (01) 449352
Key Personnel
Chairman: Mr A C Gunasinghe
Vice Chairman: Mr Mano Selvanathan
Deputy Chairman: Mr K Balendra
Secretary General: Mr C G Jayasuriya
ISBN Prefix(es): 955-604

Colombo Book Association+
PO Box 1946, Colombo 08
Tel: (01) 686878; (01) 072270652 *Fax:* (01) 696578
Key Personnel
President: Dhammadesha Ambalampitiya
Founded: 1983
Successful UNESCO project devoted to develop the literacy.
Subjects: Education, English as a Second Language
ISBN Prefix(es): 955-588
Imprints: Denuma

Danuma, *imprint of* Danuma Prakashakayo

Danuma Prakashakayo+
84 Serpentine Rd, Borella, Colombo 8
Mailing Address: PO Box 1946, Colombo
Tel: (01) 686878 *Fax:* (01) 696578
Founded: 1983
Subjects: Literature, Literary Criticism, Essays, Poetry, Science Fiction, Fantasy
ISBN Prefix(es): 955-556
Imprints: Danuma
Subsidiaries: Colombo Children's Book Society
Orders to: 84 Leslie, Ranagala Mawatha, Colombo 8

Denuma, *imprint of* Colombo Book Association

Department of Census & Statistics
No 6 Albert Crescent, Colombo 7
Mailing Address: PO Box 563, Colombo 7
Tel: (01) 692988; (01) 595291 *Fax:* (01) 687931
ISBN Prefix(es): 955-577

PUBLISHERS — SRI LANKA

Department of National Museums
PO Box 854, Colombo 7
Tel: (01) 595366
Key Personnel
Contact: W T T P Gunawardane
Subjects: Anthropology, Antiques, Natural History
ISBN Prefix(es): 955-578
Subsidiaries: National Museum (Galle); National Museum (Kandy); National Museum (Ratnapura); Folk Museum; Dutch Period Museum; National Museum of Natural History; School Science Museum; School Science Museum; School Science Museum; School Science Museum; Puppetry & Children's Museum; National Maritime Museum

Edirisooriya & Company
68, Elie house Rd, Colombo 15
Tel: (01) 522555; (01) 523216 *Fax:* (01) 446380; (01) 074618905
Telex: 21701 GLOBAL CE *Cable:* UNIMER
Key Personnel
Printing Manager: Lindwal Peiris *Tel:* (01) 074618905
Founded: 1985
Printing & binding of local circulation school books, web offset machines, etc.
Subjects: *Specialize in stickers, labels, diaries & calendars*
ISBN Prefix(es): 955-9228
Parent Company: S P Samy & Co (Pvt) Ltd
Subsidiaries: United Merchants Ltd
Branch Office(s)
Edirisooriya & Co, 30 Prince St, Colombo 11, Contact: Mr Ganesh *Tel:* (01) 441560; (01) 446380 *Fax:* (01) 446380

Gihan Book Shop
144C Hill St, Dehiwala
Key Personnel
Author: W O T Fernando
Founded: 1980
Subjects: Mathematics
ISBN Prefix(es): 955-593
Imprints: Sanjana Offset

M D Gunasena & Co Ltd
217 Olcott Mawatha, Colombo 11
Mailing Address: PO Box 246, Colombo 11
Tel: (01) 323981; (01) 323982; (01) 323983; (01) 323984; (01) 544840; (01) 544841; (01) 544824 *Fax:* (01) 323336
E-mail: mdgunasena@mail.ewisl.net
Web Site: mdgunasena.com
Founded: 1913
Associated imprints include Ananda Books Ltd, Sirisara Vidyalaya.
ISBN Prefix(es): 955-21

Inter-Cultural Book Promoters+
21 G4 Peramuna Mawatha, Eldeniya, Kadawatha
Tel: 925359 *Fax:* 925359
E-mail: inculture@eureka.lk
Founded: 1985
Subjects: Language Arts, Linguistics, Philosophy, Religion - Buddhist, Religion - Catholic, Religion - Hindu, Religion - Islamic, Religion - Jewish, Religion - Protestant, Religion - Other
ISBN Prefix(es): 955-9036
Parent Company: Inter-cultural Research Center

International Centre for Ethnic Studies+
554/1 Peradeniya Rd, Kandy
Tel: (08) 23095 *Fax:* (08) 234892
E-mail: ices@slt.lk
Key Personnel
Executive Dir: Prof K M De Silva
Librarian: Kanthi Gamage
Founded: 1982
A social science & policy research institute.
Subjects: Ethnicity, Women's Studies

ISBN Prefix(es): 955-580
Total Titles: 20 Print
Branch Office(s)
Kynsey Terrace, Colombo 8
Distributed by St Martin's Press
Distributor for Frances Pinter (UK)

J K Publications
J K 50, Katuwawala, Borelasgamuwa
Tel: (01) 518954
Key Personnel
Author: Jayasena Kottegoda
Subjects: Music, Dance
ISBN Prefix(es): 955-9438
Total Titles: 7 Print
Distributed by Godage; Gunasena; Lake House

Dayawansa Jayakody & Co+
101 & 112, Ven S Mahinda, Thero Mawatha, Maradana, Colombo 10
Tel: (01) 695773 *Fax:* (01) 696653
E-mail: dayawansa@eureka.lk
Key Personnel
Chairman: Dayawansa Jayakody
Man Dir: Veronica Damayanthi Jayakody
Founded: 1960
Member of IPA, APPA & Sri Lanka Association of Publishers.
Subjects: Drama, Theater, Fiction, Literature, Literary Criticism, Essays, Poetry
ISBN Prefix(es): 955-551
Number of titles published annually: 60 Print
Total Titles: 3,000 Print
Associate Companies: Helabima Publishers
U.S. Office(s): Dayawansa Jayakody & Company (USA), 131 Banwell Lane, Mount Laurel, NJ 08054, United States *Tel:* 856-234-8001 *Fax:* 856-234-8001 *E-mail:* dayawanska@eureka.lk (US Sales)
Distributor for Helabima Publishers
Foreign Rep(s): Uditha Daminda Sayakody (US)
Book Club(s): Dayawansa Jayakody Bookclub
Warehouse: 163/4, Siri Dhamma Mawatha, Colombo 10

Karunaratne & Sons Ltd+
647, kuluratne Mawatha, Colombo 10
Tel: 692295 *Fax:* 855520; 850256
E-mail: karusons@sri.lanka.net
Founded: 1971
Sri Lanka Association of Publishers.
Subjects: Archaeology, Economics, Education, Ethnicity, History, Philosophy, Religion - Buddhist, Social Sciences, Sociology, Women's Studies
ISBN Prefix(es): 955-9098

KVG de Silva & Sons+
415 Galle Rd, Colombo 4
Tel: (01) 84146 *Fax:* (01) 586598
Key Personnel
Man Partner: K V N Silva; Mrs Devini Dias; Mrs Veena Silva
Founded: 1898
Subjects: History, Regional Interests, Religion - Other
ISBN Prefix(es): 955-9112
Bookshop(s): Fort, Colombo & YMBA Shopping Complex, 44/9 YMBA Bldg, Borella, Colombo

Lake House Investments Ltd+
41 W A D Ramanayake Mawatha, Colombo 2
Tel: (01) 33271; (01) 35175 *Fax:* (01) 447848
E-mail: lhl@sri.lanka.net
Telex: 21266 Lakexpo CE *Cable:* COLOMBO 2 SRI LANKA
Key Personnel
Chairman: R S Wijewardene
Founded: 1965
Member of The Book Publisher's Association of Sri Lanka; Specialize in Text Books on Science & Law both in Sinhala & English.

Subjects: Education, Fiction, History, Law, Medicine, Nursing, Dentistry, Music, Dance, Science (General), Sports, Athletics
ISBN Prefix(es): 955-552
Associate Companies: Lake House Printers & Publishers Ltd
Divisions: Chitrafoto; Lakexpo; Lake House Bookshop
Bookshop(s): Lake House Bookshop, 100 Chittampalam Gardinar Mawatha, Colombo 2; Columbo University Bookshop, Columbo University, Cumarathuga Munidasa Mawatha, Columbo

Law Publishers Association+
21 Sownders Court, Colombo 2
Mailing Address: 21 Wekande Jumma Mosque Mawatha, Colombo 2
Tel: (01) 330363 *Fax:* (01) 436629
Founded: 1990
Subjects: Biography, Law
ISBN Prefix(es): 955-9210
Divisions: FAMYS
Orders to: FAMYS, 21 Sownders Court, Colombo 2

Ministry of Cultural Affairs
Transworks House, Colombo 1
Tel: (01) 437328 *Cable:* Sunlay
Key Personnel
Dir, Publications: R L Wimaladharma
Deputy Dir, Publications: K G Amaradasa
Editorial: Prof D E Hettiaratchi; Prof J D Dheerasekera; D P Ponnamperuma
Founded: 1971
Subjects: Art, Ethnicity, Literature, Literary Criticism, Essays, Religion - Other
ISBN Prefix(es): 955-9117
Bookshop(s): Jayanti Bookshop, 135 Dharmapala Mawatha, Colombo 7
Book Club(s): Book Club of the Ministry of Cultural Affairs of Sri Lanka

Ministry of Education+
Isurupaya, Sri Jayawardenapura Kotte, Battaramulla
Tel: 565141; 565150
Subjects: Accounting, Agriculture, Chemistry, Chemical Engineering, Computer Science, Geography, Geology, Mathematics, Physics, Science (General)
ISBN Prefix(es): 955-28
Subsidiaries: Educational Publications Dept

National Children's Educational Foundation+
International Headquarters, Mulleriyawa New Town
Tel: 578090 *Fax:* 578090
ISBN Prefix(es): 955-9104

National Library & Documentation Services Board
No 14, Independence Ave, Colombo 07
Mailing Address: PO Box 1764, Colombo 07
Tel: (01) 685198; (01) 685199; (01) 698847; (01) 685197 *Fax:* (01) 685201
E-mail: nldsb@mail.natlib.lk
Web Site: natlib.lk
Key Personnel
Chairman: Ms Tissa Kariyawasam
Dir, General: M S U Amarasiri *Tel:* (01) 687581
E-mail: dgnl@sltnet.lk
Librarian: Mrs M A Nalini
Founded: 1970
Member of IFLA, COMLA, CDNLAO, ACCU, AMIC.
Subjects: Communications, Computer Science, Ethnicity, Human Relations, Library & Information Sciences, Literature, Literary Criticism, Essays, Regional Interests, Social Sciences, Sociology
ISBN Prefix(es): 955-9011

SRI LANKA

Pradeepa Publishers+
34/34 Lawyers Off Complex, St Sebastian Hill, Colombo 12
Tel: (094) 435074; (094) 863261; (071) 735532
Fax: (094) 863261
Key Personnel
Author & Editor: K Jayatilake *E-mail:* pjayati@hotmail.com
Founded: 1968
Member of the Writers Association, Sri Lanka Book Publishers Association.
Subjects: Fiction, Literature, Literary Criticism, Essays, Religion - Buddhist
ISBN Prefix(es): 955-554

Saara Buddhi Publication
19/1, Haltotawatta Lane, Avissawella 10700
ISBN Prefix(es): 955-9415

Saman & Madara Publishers
997/26 Sri Jayawardenapura Mawatha, Welikada, Rajagiriya
Tel: (01) 862055 *Fax:* (01) 868071
E-mail: prince@eureka.lk
Telex: 21271 CE
Key Personnel
President: Mahinda Ralapanawe
Founded: 1970
Subjects: Fiction, Literature, Literary Criticism, Essays
ISBN Prefix(es): 955-563
Total Titles: 2 Print

Samayawardena Printers Publishers & Booksellers+
53 Maligakanda Rd, Maradana, Colombo 10
Tel: (01) 694682; (01) 687904; (01) 698977; (01) 683525 *Fax:* (01) 698977; (01) 683525
E-mail: samaya@applestr.lk
Founded: 1960
Member of Sri Lanka Book Publishers Association & Asia Pacific Book Publishers Association.
Subjects: Education, English as a Second Language, Nonfiction (General), Philosophy, Religion - Buddhist
ISBN Prefix(es): 955-570
Bookshop(s): Samayawardhana Book Shop, 61 Maligakanda Rd, Colombo 10 *Tel:* (01) 677539 *Fax:* (01) 683986

Sanjana Offset, *imprint of* Gihan Book Shop

Somawathi Hewavitharana Fund
Mahabodhi Mandiraya, 130 Maligakanda Rd, Colombo 10
Mailing Address: 36/6 Rosmead Pl, Colombo 7
Tel: (01) 691335; (01) 695161
Key Personnel
Trustee: Noel Wijenaike; Nanda Amerasinghe *Tel:* (01) 694026; Parinda Ranasinghe Tripitaka Publications.
Subjects: Religion - Buddhist
ISBN Prefix(es): 955-616
Number of titles published annually: 6 Print
Total Titles: 80 Print

Sri Lanka Jama'ath-e-Islami
77, Dematagoda Rd, Colombo 9
Tel: (01) 687091 *Fax:* (01) 686030
ISBN Prefix(es): 955-608
Bookshop(s): Sri Lanka Jama'ath-e-Islami Book Stall, 77, Dematagoda Rd, Colombo 9

State Printing Corp+
95 Sir Chittampalam Gardiner Mawatha, Colombo 2
Tel: (01) 503694 *Fax:* (01) 503694
Key Personnel
Marketing Manager: Jagath Gamanayake
ISBN Prefix(es): 955-610

Sunera Publishers+
64, Devala Rd, Nugegoda
Tel: 511527
Founded: 1989
Subjects: Career Development, Economics, Law, Management
ISBN Prefix(es): 955-9128

Swarna Hansa Foundation+
Vendervette Pl, Deniwala
Mailing Address: PO Box 16, Deniwala
Tel: (01) 712566 *Fax:* (01) 733649
Key Personnel
Program Executive: Gallege Punyawardana
Founded: 1978
Branch Offices: Hasalaka; Hiniduma; Kalawana; Nikaweratiya; Regional Centres at Kandy.
Subjects: Agriculture, Education, Environmental Studies, Health, Nutrition, History, Journalism, Literature, Literary Criticism, Essays, Poetry, Religion - Buddhist, Social Sciences, Sociology, Women's Studies
ISBN Prefix(es): 955-560
Branch Office(s)
Hiniduma

Trumpet Publishers (Pvt) Ltd+
A4, Perahera Mawatha, Off Sir James Peiris Mawatha, Colombo 3
Tel: (01) 563598; (01) 573208; (01) 547622 *Fax:* (01) 565778
Specialize in printing.
ISBN Prefix(es): 955-565
Parent Company: T F & 1 Printers
Associate Companies: Tanatha Finance & Investment Co Ltd

Unigraphics (Pte) Ltd
732, Maradana Rd, Colombo 10
Tel: (01) 694538 *Fax:* (01) 693731
E-mail: uni.graphics@lanka.ccom.lk
ISBN Prefix(es): 955-619

Vidura Science Publishers
55/A First Lane, Medawelikada Rd, Rajagiriya
Tel: (091) 564713
Subjects: Science (General)
ISBN Prefix(es): 955-567
Subsidiaries: Anura C Printers

Warna Publishers+
Aluth Rd, Wennappuwa
Subjects: Chemistry, Chemical Engineering, Government, Political Science, Mathematics, Science (General), Science Fiction, Fantasy
ISBN Prefix(es): 955-9375
Branch Office(s)
New Rd, Wennappuwa
Distributed by Godage Bookshop; Gunasena Book Shop; Lake House Book Shop

Waruni Publishers+
72/15 A Second Lane, Pushpanada Mawatha, Kandy
Tel: (08) 24370 *Fax:* (08) 32343
Telex: 22787 Matsui CE
Key Personnel
Man Dir: K P Vimala Jharma
Subjects: Agriculture, Biography, Genealogy
ISBN Prefix(es): 955-566

Sudan

General Information

Capital: Khartoum
Language: Arabic (official), English also used
Religion: Muslims (north), Animists or Christians (south)
Population: 28.3 million
Bank Hours: 0830-1200 Sunday-Thursday
Shop Hours: 0800-1300, 1700-2000 Saturday-Thursday
Currency: 1,000 milliemes = 100 piastres = 1 Sudanese pound
Export/Import Information: No tariff on books; some advertising matter may be dutied. Import licenses required. Exchange controls; annual foreign exchange budget.

ACAD1, see Arab Organization for Agricultural Development

AOAD, see Arab Organization for Agricultural Development

Arab Center for Agricultural Documentation, see Arab Organization for Agricultural Development

Arab Organization for Agricultural Development
4 El Gammaa Ave, Khartoum 11111
Mailing Address: PO Box 474, Khartoum 11111
Tel: (011) 78760; (011) 78761; (011) 78762; (011) 78763 *Fax:* (011) 471402
E-mail: aoad@sudanmail.net
Telex: 22554SD *Cable:* AOAD
Parent Company: Arab League

Al-Ayam Press Co Ltd
Aboul Ela Bldgs, United Nations Sq, Khartoum
Mailing Address: PO Box 363, Khartoum
Key Personnel
Man Dir: Beshir Muhammad Said
Founded: 1953
Subjects: Fiction, Nonfiction (General), Poetry

Khartoum University Press
PO Box 321, Khartoum
Tel: (011) 80558; (011) 81806
Key Personnel
Man Dir, General Editor: Ali El-Mak
Sales Manager: Abdel Raham Ibrahim
Editorial, Rights & Permissions: Jamal Abdel Malik; Judy El-Nagar
Founded: 1968
Subjects: Biography, Ethnicity, Fiction, History, Nonfiction (General), Philosophy, Poetry, Religion - Other, Science (General), Social Sciences, Sociology, Technology
Bookshop(s): University of Khartoum Bookshop

Suriname

General Information

Capital: Paramaribo
Language: Dutch. Hindustani and Javanese also spoken
Religion: Christian, Hindu & Islamic
Population: 410,000
Bank Hours: 0730-1400 Monday-Friday
Shop Hours: 0730-1630 Monday-Friday; 0730-1300 Saturday
Currency: 100 cents = 1 Suriname gulden or florin
Export/Import Information: No tariff on books except children's picture books; none on small quantities of advertising matter. Added taxes

charged. Import licenses liberally granted. Exchange controls.
Copyright: Berne (see Copyright Conventions, pg xi)

Apollo's Reklame en Uitgeversburo
Toreniastraat 3, Paramaribo
Mailing Address: PO Box 574, Paramaribo
ISBN Prefix(es): 99914-908

Drs F H R Oedayrajsingh Varma+
PO Box 9192, Paramaribo
Key Personnel
Dir: Dr Ferdinand H Varma
Subjects: Regional Interests
ISBN Prefix(es): 99914-903
Branch Office(s)
Postbus 70225, 1007 KE Amsterdam, Netherlands
Tel: (020) 628163

NV Drukkerij Eldorado
Eldoradolaan 1, Paramaribo
Tel: 472362
ISBN Prefix(es): 99914-51

Groto Publikasi
Moengostr 75, Paramaribo
Tel: 493569
Specialize in Dutch and Suriname language publications.
ISBN Prefix(es): 99914-914

R Ishaak
Oranje Nassaust 72, Nieuw Nickerie
Tel: 031917 *Fax:* 0231917
ISBN Prefix(es): 99914-924

C Kersten & Co
Steenbakkerijstr 83, Paramaribo
Tel: 471133
Telex: 142
ISBN Prefix(es): 99914-52

Lutchman, Drs LFS+
Elizelaan 10, Paramaribo
Tel: 465558; 44/453419
Key Personnel
Editor & Author: Sylvia Singh
Specialize in Poetry.
Subjects: Fiction, Poetry
ISBN Prefix(es): 99914-918
Associate Companies: Buitenweg; Handelsdrukkery; dr S Redmondstr 70
Bookshop(s): Vaco NV, Domineestr 26-32, Paramaribo; C Kersten & Co, NV-Steenbakkerij str 27

Mavis A Noordwijk
Regentessestr 3, Paramaribo
Mailing Address: PO Box 2653, Paramaribo
Tel: 479402
ISBN Prefix(es): 99914-907

Dr C D Ooft
Dr H D Benjaminstr 28, Paramaribo
Tel: 499139
ISBN Prefix(es): 99914-910

Orchid Press
PO Box 28, Paramaribo
ISBN Prefix(es): 99914-904

Pro Media Productions
Domineestr 12 boven, Paramaribo
Tel: 479355
ISBN Prefix(es): 99914-912

Publishing Services Suriname (Gowtu Stari Publishing)+
Van Idsingastraat 133, Paramaribo
Tel: 472746; 455792 *Fax:* 410366
E-mail: pssmoniz@sr.net
Web Site: www.parbo.com
Key Personnel
Author, Publisher: I Krishnadath
Illustration, Publisher: A Slyngard
Founded: 1992
Specialize in Children's Books, Educational Matters, Surinamese literature.
ISBN Prefix(es): 99914-915; 99914-920; 99914-928
Total Titles: 20 Print
Associate Companies: Uitgeverij Lees Mee

Educatieve Uitgeverij Sorava
Latourwegi 10, Paramaribo
Tel: 483879
ISBN Prefix(es): 99914-906; 99914-57

Stichting Kinderkrant Suriname
PO Box 3013, Paramaribo
ISBN Prefix(es): 99914-53

Stichting Wetenschappelijke Informatie+
Prins Hendrikst 38, Paramaribo
Tel: 475232 *Fax:* 422195
E-mail: swin@sr.net
Key Personnel
Man Dir, Editorial, Production, Publicity: J K Menke
Sales: W Boedhoe
Founded: 1977
Subjects: Anthropology, Developing Countries, Ethnicity, Government, Political Science, History, Labor, Industrial Relations, Literature, Literary Criticism, Essays, Science (General), Social Sciences, Sociology, Women's Studies
ISBN Prefix(es): 99914-900
Distributor for Local Surinamese Publications

Vaco, *imprint of* Vaco NV Uitgeversmij

Vaco NV Uitgeversmij+
Domineestr 26, Paramaribo
Mailing Address: PO Box 1841, Paramaribo
Tel: 472545 *Fax:* 10563
Telex: 123 INCO SN
Key Personnel
Man Dir: E Hogenboom
Publisher: J Trotman
Founded: 1952
Subjects: History, Regional Interests
ISBN Prefix(es): 99914-0
Parent Company: Interfund NV
Imprints: Vaco

Stichting Volksboekwinkel
Keizerstr 197, Paramaribo
Mailing Address: PO Box 3040, Paramaribo
Tel: 472469
ISBN Prefix(es): 99914-901

M Waagmeester-Verkuyl
Nickeriestr 22, Paramaribo
Mailing Address: PO Box 9166, Paramaribo
Tel: 498356
ISBN Prefix(es): 99914-905

Swaziland

General Information

Capital: Mbabane
Language: Siswati, English used in business
Religion: Christian (about 60%), most others follow traditional beliefs
Population: 913,000
Bank Hours: Until 1100 Saturday
Shop Hours: 0700-1800
Currency: 100 cents = 1 lilangeni = 1 South African rand
Export/Import Information: Same as South Africa.

Boleswa, *imprint of* Macmillan Boleswa Publishers (Pty) Ltd

Macmillan Boleswa Publishers (Pty) Ltd
Plot 230/231, First Ave, Matsapa Industrial Estate, Manzini
Mailing Address: PO Box 1235, Manzini
Tel: 84533 *Fax:* 85247
E-mail: macmillan@iafrica.sz
Web Site: www.macmillansa.co.za; www.macmillan-africa.com
Telex: 2221 MACSW WD
Key Personnel
Man Dir: Elias Nwandwe
Founded: 1978
Subjects: Education
ISBN Prefix(es): 0-333
Parent Company: Macmillan Publishers Ltd, United Kingdom
Imprints: Boleswa
Subsidiaries: Macmillan Swaziland National Publishing Co; Macmillan Botswana Publishing Co
Branch Office(s)
Matsapa

Sweden

General Information

Capital: Stockholm
Language: Swedish. Some Finnish and Lapp also spoken
Religion: Evangelical Lutheran Church of Sweden
Population: 8.8 million
Bank Hours: 0930-1500 Monday-Friday
Shop Hours: 0900-1800 Monday-Friday (later Friday); 0900-1400 or 1600 Saturday
Currency: 100 oere = 1 Swedish korona
Export/Import Information: Member of the European Free Trade Association. No tariff on books. Advertising tax. 25% VAT on books. No import licenses. No exchange controls.
Copyright: UCC, Berne, Florence (see Copyright Conventions, pg xi)

Acta Universitatis Gothoburgensis
Box 100, SE-40530 Goteborg
Tel: (031) 7731000 *Fax:* (031) 7734064
E-mail: library@ub.gu.se
Web Site: www.gu.se
Key Personnel
Man Dir: Jon Erik Norstrand
Publishes only works produced at or connected with Goteborg University.
Subjects: Art, Education, Language Arts, Linguistics, Literature, Literary Criticism, Essays, Social Sciences, Sociology, Women's Studies
ISBN Prefix(es): 91-7346
Parent Company: Goeteborgs Universitetsbibliotek

Akademiforlaget Corona AB
PO Box 5, 201 20 Malmo
Tel: (040) 189480 *Fax:* (040) 184570
E-mail: kundservice@cor.se
Web Site: www.cor.se

Key Personnel
Man Dir: Lars Welinder *E-mail:* lars.welinder@cor.se
Founded: 1961
Subjects: Education, Fiction, Nonfiction (General)
ISBN Prefix(es): 91-564; 91-7034

Akademiforlaget Goteborgslitteratur+
Esselte studium, 402 23 Goteborg
Mailing Address: Box 5103, 402 23 Goteborg
Tel: (031) 813410 *Fax:* (031) 811492
E-mail: sales@akg.se
Key Personnel
Dir: Sven Holmberg
Founded: 1990
Subjects: Behavioral Sciences, Cookery, Education, English as a Second Language, Human Relations, Language Arts, Linguistics, Mathematics, Medicine, Nursing, Dentistry, Music, Dance, Philosophy, Technology
ISBN Prefix(es): 91-24

Albert Bonniers Forlag+
Division of The Bonnier Group
Sveavagen 56, S-10363 Stockholm
Mailing Address: Box 3159, 10363 Stockholm
Tel: (08) 696 8620 *Fax:* (08) 696 8369; (08) 696 8347
E-mail: info@abforlag.bonnier.se
Web Site: www.albertbonniersforlag.com
Key Personnel
Publisher: Eva Bonnier
Man Dir: Kerstin Angelin
Rights & Permissions: Teresa Carlstrom
Founded: 1837
Publishing House.
Subjects: Fiction, Nonfiction (General)
ISBN Prefix(es): 91-7458
Parent Company: Bonnierforlagen AB

Alfabeta Bokforlag AB+
PO Box 4284, 102 66 Stockholm
Tel: (08) 7149353; (08) 7149336 *Fax:* (08) 6432431
E-mail: info@alfamedia.se
Web Site: www.alfamedia.se *Cable:* ALFABETA STOCKHOLM
Key Personnel
Man Dir, Rights & Permissions: Dag Hernried
Sales & Production: Lena Spaulding
 E-mail: lena@alfamedia.se
Founded: 1976
Subjects: Art, Ethnicity, Fiction, Film, Video, Music, Dance, Nonfiction (General), Psychology, Psychiatry, Travel
ISBN Prefix(es): 91-7712; 91-85328
Subsidiaries: Gammafon AB (audio cassettes)

Allt om Hobby AB+
Oerbyslottsvaeg 21, S-120 21 Stockholm
Mailing Address: PO Box 90133, 120 21 Stockholm
Tel: (08) 999333 *Fax:* (08) 998866
Key Personnel
Publisher: Freddy Stenbom *E-mail:* freddy.stenbom@hobby.se
Founded: 1966
Subjects: Aeronautics, Aviation, Communications, Crafts, Games, Hobbies, Electronics, Electrical Engineering, History, Maritime, Military Science, Photography, Transportation
ISBN Prefix(es): 91-85496
Book Club(s): Allt om Hobbys Bokklubb; Flygboklubben

Almquist & Wiksell, *imprint of* Liber AB

Almqvist och Wiksell International
PO Box 614, 15127 Sodertalje
Tel: (08) 7282500 *Fax:* (08) 338707
E-mail: scand.mongr@awi.se

Key Personnel
Dir: Mats Thomasson
Sales Manager: Hans Linder
Affiliated to the Akademibokhandeln Group & publishers to the universities of Stockholm, Uppsala & Lund.
Subjects: Science (General)
ISBN Prefix(es): 91-22

Apotekarsocietetens Forlag
PO Box 1136, 111 81 Stockholm
Tel: (08) 7235000 *Fax:* (08) 205511
Key Personnel
Man Dir: Yvonne Andersson *E-mail:* andersson.y@swepharm.se

AB Arcanum+
Tollestorpsvagen 2H, S-443 03 Stenkullen
Tel: (031) 871516 *Fax:* (031) 270925
Key Personnel
Man Dir: Bo Ramme
Founded: 1970
Subjects: Medicine, Nursing, Dentistry
ISBN Prefix(es): 91-85690

Arkitektur Forlag AB
Norrlandsgatan 18, 111 87 Stockholm
Mailing Address: PO Box 1742, 111 87 Stockholm
Tel: (08) 6796105 *Fax:* (08) 6115270
E-mail: redaktionen@arkitektur.se
Web Site: www.arkitektur.se
Key Personnel
Contact: Marianne Lundqvist *E-mail:* marianne.lundqvist@arkitektur.se
Founded: 1901
Subjects: Architecture & Interior Design
ISBN Prefix(es): 91-86050
Number of titles published annually: 4 Print

BBB Bokklubben Bra Bocker, *imprint of* Bokforlaget Bra Bocker AB

Berghs
Observatoriegatan 10, 104 30 Stockholm
Mailing Address: PO Box 45084, 104 30 Stockholm
Tel: (08) 316559 *Fax:* (08) 327745
Key Personnel
Chairman: Anders Oehman
Man Dir: Carl Hafstroem
Editorial Dir: Eva Vider
Founded: 1954
Subjects: Crafts, Games, Hobbies, Nonfiction (General)
ISBN Prefix(es): 91-502
Orders to: Foerlagssystem, PO Box 30195, 10425 Stockholm *Tel:* (08) 6574510

Bibliotekstjaenst AB
Traktorvaegen 13, 22182 Lund
Mailing Address: PO Box 200, 221 82 Lund
Tel: (046) 180000 *Fax:* (046) 180125
Telex: 32200 btjlund s
Founded: 1951
Subjects: Library & Information Sciences
ISBN Prefix(es): 91-7018
Associate Companies: BTJ Europe, Belgium; BTJ Norge, Norway; BTJ Inc, United States
Subsidiaries: BTJ Tryck AB
Divisions: BTJ Media; BTJ Database

Bokforlaget Atlantis AB+
Sturegatan 24, 114 36 Stockholm
Tel: (08) 7830440 *Fax:* (08) 6617285
E-mail: mail@atlantis-publishers.se *Cable:* ATLANTISBOOKS
Key Personnel
Man Dir: Kjell Peterson
Production: Lennart Rolf

Marketing Dir & Rights & Permissions: Hans Bjornell
Founded: 1977
Subjects: Art, Fiction, Nonfiction (General)
ISBN Prefix(es): 91-7486
Associate Companies: Clio History Book Club
Book Club(s): Clio History Book Club

Bokforlaget Bra Bocker AB
Sodra vagen, 26380 Hoganas
Mailing Address: Box 890, 201 80 Malmo
Tel: (040) 665 46 00 *Fax:* (040) 665 46 22
E-mail: kundservice@bbb.se
Web Site: www.bbb.se
Key Personnel
President & Marketing: Rolf Nilstam
Vice President, Production: Janson Anders
Editorial, Encyclopedia: Christer Engstoem
Editorial, Nonfiction: Lillemor Eagle
Editorial, Fiction: Goeran Green Claes
Founded: 1965
Subjects: Fiction, Geography, Geology, History
ISBN Prefix(es): 91-7024; 91-7119
Parent Company: International Masters Pubishers AB, PO Box 814, S-20180 Malmoe
Imprints: BBB Bokklubben Bra Bocker

Bokforlaget Cordia AB+
Vastrahamngatan21, 404 24 Goteborg
Mailing Address: PO Box 15169, 104 65 Stockholm
Tel: (08) 702 79 90 *Fax:* (08) 641 45 85
Key Personnel
President: Lars-G Stahl
Publisher: Goran Rask *E-mail:* g.rash@verbum.se
Founded: 1995
Subjects: History, Human Relations, Nonfiction (General), Specialize in Spirituality
ISBN Prefix(es): 91-7085
Parent Company: Verbum AB
Associate Companies: Verbum Foerlag; Foerlagshuset Gothia; Gleerups Foerlag

Bokforlaget Fabel AB
Bjursaetragatan 66, 124 64 Bandhagen
Tel: (08) 869080 *Fax:* (08) 7495021
Key Personnel
Man Dir: Sigvard Olsson
Founded: 1955
Subjects: Literature, Literary Criticism, Essays
ISBN Prefix(es): 91-46; 91-7842

Bokforlaget Opal AB
Tegelbergsvaegen 31, S-161 02 Bromma
Mailing Address: PO Box 20113, 161 02 Bromma
Tel: (08) 282179 *Fax:* (08) 296623
Key Personnel
Man Dir: Bengt Christell
Joint Publisher: Valborg Segerhjelm
Founded: 1973
ISBN Prefix(es): 91-7270
Book Club(s): Barnens Bokklub (jointly owned)

Bokforlaget Plus AB
Sankt Eriksgatan 48, 112 34 Stockholm
Tel: (08) 6547408
Key Personnel
Man Dir: Bengt Svensson
Founded: 1976
Subjects: Fiction, Nonfiction (General)
ISBN Prefix(es): 91-7406

Bokforlaget Rediviva, Facsimileforlaget
PO Box 15148, 161 15 Bromma
Tel: (08) 257007
Key Personnel
Man Dir: Karin Skrutkowska
Founded: 1968
Subjects: Geography, Geology
ISBN Prefix(es): 91-7120

PUBLISHERS SWEDEN

Bokforlaget Settern AB+
Member of Svenska Forlaggare foreningen, NOFF
Florshult, 286 92 Oerkelljunga
Tel: (0435) 80070; (0435) 80400 *Fax:* (0435) 80400
E-mail: info@settern.se
Web Site: www.settern.se
Key Personnel
Man Dir: Magdalena Roenneholm
 E-mail: magdalena@settern.se
Sales, Publicity, Advertising Dirs: Joergen Wahlen; Tomas Wahlen
Founded: 1974
Hunting & Fishing books.
Subjects: Nonfiction (General), Hunting & Fishing
ISBN Prefix(es): 91-7586
Number of titles published annually: 15 Print
Total Titles: 600 Print

Bokforlaget Spektra AB+
Olofsdalsvaegen 19, S-300 07 Halmstad
Mailing Address: PO Box 7024, 300 07 Halmstad
Tel: (035) 36030 *Fax:* (035) 36177
Key Personnel
Man Dir: Ake Hallberg; Solveig Hallberg
Founded: 1965
Subjects: Computer Science, Crafts, Games, Hobbies, Fiction, How-to, Publishing & Book Trade Reference, Science (General)
ISBN Prefix(es): 91-7136
Associate Companies: Grafisk Kompetens, Spektra Studio AB, Box 7039, 300 07 Halmstad

Bonnier Audio+
Sveavaegen 56, Box 3159, 10363 Stockholm
Tel: (08) 6968760 *Fax:* (08) 6968757
Key Personnel
President & Publisher: Christina Andersson
 E-mail: christine.anderson@audio.bonnier.se
Founded: 1986
Specialize in audio books.
Subjects: Fiction
ISBN Prefix(es): 91-7950
Number of titles published annually: 35 Print
Total Titles: 350 Print
Parent Company: Bonnierfoerlagen

Bonnier Audio
Sveavagen 56, S-10363 Stockholm
Mailing Address: PO Box 3159, S10363 Stockholm
Tel: 08 6968760; 08 6968757
Key Personnel
Man Dir: Christina Andersson
Founded: 1986
Subjects: Specialize in audio books
ISBN Prefix(es): 91-7950
Number of titles published annually: 45 Audio
Total Titles: 500 Audio
Book Club(s): Lyssnarklubben

Bonnier Carlsen Bokforlag AB
Drottninggatan 82, 111 83 Stockholm
Mailing Address: PO Box 1315, 111 83 Stockholm
Tel: (08) 59895500 *Fax:* (08) 4538945
Key Personnel
Man Dir: Pentti Molander
Sales: Johnny Gustafsson
Founded: 1968
Subjects: Humor
ISBN Prefix(es): 91-510; 91-48; 91-638
Parent Company: Bonnierforlagen AB

Bonnier Utbildning AB
Sveavagen 56, 10363 Stockholm
Mailing Address: PO Box 3159, 10363 Stockholm
Tel: (08) 6968590 *Fax:* (08) 6968610
Key Personnel
Publisher: Lars Malmius
Founded: 1987
Specialize in schoolbooks.
ISBN Prefix(es): 91-622
Parent Company: Bonnierforlagen AB

Albert Bonniers Forlag
Sveavaegen 56, 103 63 Stockholm
Mailing Address: PO Box 3159, 103 63 Stockholm
Tel: (08) 6968000 *Fax:* (08) 6968361 *Cable:* BONNIERS
Key Personnel
Man Dir: Kerstin Angelin
Publishing Dir: Eva Bonnier
Publisher: Karl Otto Bonnier
Rights & Permissions & Production: Arne Bjoerkman
Rights & Permissions: Teresa Carlstroem
Production: Robert Hedberg
Publicity: Ingela Palmquist; Carina Soederman
Subjects: Art, Cookery, Fiction, Nonfiction (General)
ISBN Prefix(es): 91-0
Parent Company: Bonnierfoerlagen AB
Warehouse: Samdistribution, PO Box 449, S-19104 Sollentuna

BOOX+
Kammakargatan 35, 11160 Stockholm
Tel: (08) 4113700 *Fax:* (08) 4115330
E-mail: info@boox.se
Key Personnel
Editor & Man Dir: Monica Norberg
Photographer & Picture Editor: Michel Hjorth
Designer: Bo Ljungstrom
Founded: 1998
Packagers of ideas for the international publishing world.
Subjects: Art, Cookery, Crafts, Games, Hobbies, Gardening, Plants, Nonfiction (General), Photography, Wine & Spirits
ISBN Prefix(es): 91-973496
Total Titles: 1 Print

Brombergs Bokforlag AB+
Industrigatan 4, 112 98 Stockholm
Mailing Address: PO Box 12886, 112 98 Stockholm
Tel: (08) 56262080 *Fax:* (08) 56262085
E-mail: info@brombergs.se
Web Site: www.brombergs.se
Telex: 12442 Fotex Bropublish S
Key Personnel
Man Dir, Publicity: Dorotea Bromberg
Production, Rights & Permissions: Ylva Aaberg
 E-mail: ylva.aberg@brombergs.se
Founded: 1973
Subjects: Fiction, Nonfiction (General)
ISBN Prefix(es): 91-7608
Number of titles published annually: 25 Print

Byggforlaget+
Narvavagen 19, 114 81 Stockholm
Mailing Address: PO Box 5456, 114 81 Stockholm
Tel: (08) 6653650 *Fax:* (08) 6616901
Web Site: www.byggforlaget.se
Key Personnel
Man Dir: Claes Dymling *Tel:* (08) 6653670
 E-mail: claes@byggforlaget.se
Founded: 1948
Subjects: Architecture & Interior Design
ISBN Prefix(es): 91-85194; 91-7988

Calago Foerlag, *imprint of* Ordfront Foerlag AB

Carlsson Bokfoerlag AB+
Stora Nygatan 31, 111 27 Stockholm
Mailing Address: Box 2112, 10313 Stockholm
Tel: (08) 4112349 *Fax:* (08) 7968457
Key Personnel
Man Dir: Trygve Carlsson
Founded: 1983
Subjects: Anthropology, Art, Government, Political Science, History, Journalism, Literature, Literary Criticism, Essays, Travel, Women's Studies, Ethnology
ISBN Prefix(es): 91-7798; 91-7203
Warehouse: Foerlagssystem, Loevasvagen 26, 791 45 Falun

Citadell, *imprint of* Raben och Sjoegren Bokfoerlag

Rene Coeckelberghs Bokfoerlag AB
Drottninggatan 81 B, 104 30 Stockholm
Mailing Address: PO Box 45059, 104 30 Stockholm
Tel: (08) 7230880 *Fax:* (08) 7230311
Telex: 14277 reco S
Key Personnel
Man Dir: Rene Coeckelberghs
Subjects: Fiction, Nonfiction (General), Poetry
ISBN Prefix(es): 91-7250; 91-7103; 91-7212; 91-7640

Combi International AB, see Forlagshuset Norden AB

Dahlia Books, International Publishers & Booksellers
Box 1025, SE-751 40 Uppsala
Tel: (018) 101098 *Fax:* (018) 100525
E-mail: dahlia@telia.com
Founded: 1973
Major function of this company is bookselling (antiquarian & new) at above address.
ISBN Prefix(es): 91-972293

Delta Forlags AB
Aladdinsvagen 14, 167 61 Bromma
Tel: (08) 25 11 18
Founded: 1973
Subjects: Fiction, Nonfiction (General), Science (General)
ISBN Prefix(es): 91-7228
Book Club(s): Delta Science Fiction Bok Klubb

Egmont Serieforlaget
Drottninggatan 4 B, 205 08 Malmo
Tel: (040) 6399400 *Fax:* (040) 939325
Telex: 32449 Hemmet S
Founded: 1920
Subjects: Fiction, Human Relations
ISBN Prefix(es): 91-7300; 91-7674; 91-7912
Parent Company: Gutenberghus Group, Denmark
Associate Companies: Ehapa-Verlag GmbH, Germany; Gutenberghus Publishing Service A/S, Denmark; NW Damm og Son A/S, Norway
Book Club(s): Part-owner of Kalle Ankas Pocket

Ekelunds Forlag AB+
Loetsjoev 1B, Sundbyberg, 16902 Solna
Mailing Address: PO Box 2050, 16902 Solna
Tel: (08) 821320 *Fax:* (08) 832956
E-mail: education@ekelunds.se
Key Personnel
Contact: Marit Ekelund
Founded: 1981
Subjects: Education, English as a Second Language
ISBN Prefix(es): 91-7724; 91-646

Liber Ekonomi, *imprint of* Liber AB

Ekonomibok Forlag AB
Grontevagen 5, 25484 Helsingborg
Tel: (042) 92950 *Fax:* (042) 92950
Key Personnel
Man Dir: Maj-Britt Hallgren *E-mail:* hallgren@ekonomibok.se

Founded: 1973
Subjects: Business, Fiction, Finance
ISBN Prefix(es): 91-86406

Ellerstroms+
Fredsgatan 6, S-222 20 Lund
Tel: 323295 *Fax:* 323295
E-mail: info@ellerstroms.se
Web Site: www.ellerstroms.se
Key Personnel
Editor: Erik Magnotrn *E-mail:* erik@ellerstroms.se
Founded: 1983
Publisher of fiction, prose & poetry. Swedish & translations.
Subjects: Fiction, Literature, Literary Criticism, Essays, Poetry
Number of titles published annually: 20 Print
Total Titles: 220 Print

Energica Foerlags AB/Halsabocker+
Stackmora 5588, 794 21 Orsa
Mailing Address: PO Box 8, 794 21 Orsa
Tel: (0250) 552000 *Fax:* (0250) 43191
Web Site: www.energica.com
Key Personnel
Man Dir: Monica Katarina Frisk
 E-mail: monica@energica.se
Founded: 1985
Subjects: Health, Nutrition, Psychology, Psychiatry
ISBN Prefix(es): 91-87056
Total Titles: 50 Print
Parent Company: Energica Foerlags AB

Eriksson & Lindgren Bokforlag+
Hantverkargatan 87, 102 23 Stockholm
Mailing Address: PO Box 12085, 102 23 Stockholm
Tel: (08) 6523226; (08) 6523227 *Fax:* (08) 6523223
E-mail: info@eriksson-lindgren.se
Key Personnel
Publisher & Man Dir: Claes Eriksson
Publisher: Marianne Eriksson
Founded: 1989
Subjects: Child Care & Development
ISBN Prefix(es): 91-87804; 91-87805; 91-87803

Bokforlaget Fingraf AB+
Forradsvagen 8, S-151 04 Soedertalje
Mailing Address: PO Box 4084, 151 04 Soedertalje
Tel: (08) 55030023 *Fax:* (08) 55069570
Key Personnel
Man Dir: Ossi Nikula
Editorial: Eivor Nikula
Founded: 1979
Subjects: Fiction, Humor, Medicine, Nursing, Dentistry
ISBN Prefix(es): 91-85964
Associate Companies: Fingraf Bookprinters AB, Forradsvagen 8, Box 4084, S-151 04 Soedertalje

Fischer & Co+
Norrlandsgatan 15, 111 43 Stockholm
Tel: (08) 242160 *Fax:* (08) 247825
E-mail: bokforlaget@fischer-co.se
Web Site: www.fischer.co.se
Key Personnel
Man Dir: Sara Nillson *E-mail:* sara@fischer-co.se
Founded: 1969
Subjects: Biography, Fiction, History, Nonfiction (General)
ISBN Prefix(es): 91-7054
Total Titles: 1 Audio
Book Club(s): Bockernas Klubb

Forlaget By och Bygd
PO Box 22087, 104 22 Stockholm
Tel: (08) 6520955
Key Personnel
Man Dir: Asa-Britt Karlsson
Subjects: Government, Political Science, Social Sciences, Sociology
ISBN Prefix(es): 91-85354

Forlaget Sanctus (Metodistkyrkans Forlag)
PO Box 45130, 10430 Stockholm
Tel: (08) 315570 *Fax:* (08) 315579
Telex: 909 Teleopr S
Founded: 1873
The Publishing House of the United Methodist Church in Sweden.
Subjects: Religion - Protestant, Theology
ISBN Prefix(es): 91-7214

Forlagshuset Norden AB+
Nobelvaegen 135, 201 23 Malmo
Mailing Address: PO Box 305, 201 23 Malmo
Tel: (040) 934250 *Fax:* (040) 930156
Key Personnel
General Manager: Sven-Erik Gunnervall
Founded: 1931
ISBN Prefix(es): 91-86442
Subsidiaries: Combi International AB

Folkuniversitetets foerlag+
Magle Lilla Kyrkogata 4, S-223 51 Lund
Tel: 148720 *Fax:* 132904
E-mail: info@fu-forlag.m.se
Web Site: www.fu-forlag.m.se
Key Personnel
Man Dir: Goran Fasth
Editorial, Production, Rights & Permissions: Kristin Nilsson
Sales, Publicity, Editor: Annalisa Mikaelsson
Founded: 1971
Subjects: Education, Language Arts, Linguistics
ISBN Prefix(es): 91-7434

Foreningen Svenska Laromedelsproducenter (The Swedish Association of Educational Publishers)
Drottninggatan 97 2 tr, 11360 Stockholm
Tel: (08) 7361940 *Fax:* (08) 7361944
E-mail: fsl@forlagskansli.se
Web Site: www.fsl.se
Key Personnel
Man Dir: Lena Westerberg *Tel:* (08) 7361943
 E-mail: lena.westerberg@forlagskansli.se
Founded: 1974
ISBN Prefix(es): 91-85386

Forlagshuset Gothia
PO Box 15169, 10465 Stockholm
Tel: (08) 4622660 *Fax:* (08) 4620322
ISBN Prefix(es): 91-526

Bengt Forsbergs Foerlag AB+
Soedra Tullgatan 4, 211 40 Malmoe
Tel: (040) 76320 *Fax:* (040) 303939
E-mail: info@forsbergsforlag.se
Web Site: www.forsbergsforlag.se *Cable:* GODBOK
Key Personnel
Man Dir: Joergen Forsberg
Rights: Claes Forsberg
Sales Dir: Matts Forsberg
Founded: 1944
Specialize in telephone sales.
Subjects: Animals, Pets, Art, History, Medicine, Nursing, Dentistry, Photography
ISBN Prefix(es): 91-7046
Subsidiaries: Editions Corniche

Bokforlaget Forum AB+
Gamla Brogatan 26, 107 23 Stockholm
Mailing Address: PO Box 70321, 107 23 Stockholm
Tel: (08) 6968440; (08) 6968410 (Orders)
Fax: (08) 6968367
Key Personnel
Publisher, Man Dir: Karin Leijon
Publisher, Editorial: Viveca Peterson
Information: Anneli Eldh
Marketing: Irene Westin Ahlgren
Rights & Permissions: Birgitta Lindgren
Production: Bengt Permatz
Sr Editor: Kerstin Bergfors; Karin Linge Nordh
Founded: 1944
Subjects: Fiction, Nonfiction (General)
ISBN Prefix(es): 91-37
Parent Company: Bonnierforlagen

C E Fritzes AB
10647 Stockholm
Tel: (08) 6909090 *Fax:* (08) 205021
Key Personnel
Man Dir: Christer Bunge-Meyer *E-mail:* christer.bunge-meyer@liber.se
Founded: 1837
Official publications from Swedish government & authorities.
ISBN Prefix(es): 91-38
Parent Company: Wolters Kluwer Scandinavia
Orders to: Kundtjaenst, S-10647 Stockholm

Gedins Forlag+
Tysta Gatan 10, 115 20 Stockholm
Tel: (08) 6621551 *Fax:* (08) 6637073
E-mail: gedins@perigab.se
Key Personnel
Publisher: Per I Gedin
Founded: 1987
Subjects: Fiction, Nonfiction (General)
ISBN Prefix(es): 91-7964
Book Club(s): Part-owner of Manadens Bok
Orders to: Sam Distribution, PO Box 449, 19124 Sollentuna *Tel:* (08) 6968400 *Fax:* (08) 6968358

SK-Gehrmans Musikforlag AB+
Haelsingegatan 1, 102 31 Stockholm
Mailing Address: Box 6005, 102 31 Stockholm
Tel: (08) 6100600 *Fax:* (08) 6100628
E-mail: order@sk-gehrmans.se
Web Site: www.sk-gehrmans.se
Key Personnel
Man Dir: Kettil Skarby *E-mail:* kettil.skarby@sk-gehrmans.se
Secretary: Cecilia Strom *E-mail:* cecilia.strom@sk-gehrmans.se
Founded: 1999
Music publisher.
Orchestral parts rental.
Subjects: Music, Dance, Folk music & ballads, music with Christian lyrics accordion music, orchestral music for brass & woodwinds, contemporary music, classical music, music for choirs, educational publications, sheet music publications & compilations, sheet whole sale distributions & printing plant
ISBN Prefix(es): 91-7748

Gidlunds Bokforlag
Djuphaellens gard, 776 23 Hedemora
Mailing Address: PO Box 123, 776 23 Hedemora
Tel: (0225) 771155 *Fax:* (0255) 771165
E-mail: hedemora@gidlunds.se
Web Site: www.gidlunds.sc
Key Personnel
Man Dir: Krister Gidlund
Founded: 1984
Subjects: Art, Biography, History, Philosophy, Social Sciences, Sociology
ISBN Prefix(es): 91-7844

Foerlagshuset Gothia, see Gothia Publishing House

PUBLISHERS

SWEDEN

Gothia AB, Forlagshuset
PO Box 15169, 104 65 Stockholm
Tel: (08) 4622660; (08) 7576270 *Fax:* (08) 4620322
Key Personnel
Chief Executive: Olle Sundling
Editorial, Production: Anna-Lena Pehrsson
Founded: 1977
Subjects: Education, Health, Nutrition
ISBN Prefix(es): 91-7584; 91-85174; 91-86028
Parent Company: Ax Trade Medical AB, Svetsarvaegen 20, 171 83 Solna

Gothia Publishing House+
Box 15169, S-104 65 Stockholm
Tel: (08) 4622660 *Fax:* (08) 4620322
E-mail: info.gothia@verbum.se
Web Site: www.gothia.nu
Key Personnel
President, Publisher & Man Dir: Olle Sundling
  E-mail: olle.sundling@verbum.se
Rights & Permissions: Agneta Lundin
Founded: 1985
Subjects: Child Care & Development, Education, Health, Nutrition, Medicine, Nursing, Dentistry, Regional Interests, Social Care
ISBN Prefix(es): 91-526; 91-7584; 91-7205

Hagaberg AB+
PO Box 6471, 113 82 Stockholm
Tel: (08) 6909000 *Fax:* (08) 7021940
Key Personnel
Man Dir: Ingrid Olausson
Editorial: Rune Olausson
Founded: 1983
Subjects: Gardening, Plants, Philosophy, Psychology, Psychiatry, Theology
ISBN Prefix(es): 91-86584

Hallgren och Fallgren Studieforlag AB
PO Box 209, 751 04 Uppsala
Tel: (018) 507100 *Fax:* (018) 127270
E-mail: info@hallgren-fallgren.se
Key Personnel
Man Dir, Editorial, Rights & Permissions: Karin Hallgren; Daniel Aberg
Founded: 1973
Subjects: Education, Science (General)
ISBN Prefix(es): 91-7382

Hanse Production AB
Tranhusgatan 29, 621 55 Visby
Tel: 0498 249318 *Fax:* 0498 249318
Key Personnel
Chief Executive: Thorbjoern Oedin
Founded: 1978
Subjects: Art, Regional Interests
ISBN Prefix(es): 91-85716

Bokforlaget Hegas AB
Box 201, 26321 Hoeganaes
Tel: (042) 330 340 *Fax:* (042) 330 141
E-mail: info@hegas.se
Key Personnel
Contact: Lena Hultberg
ISBN Prefix(es): 91-86650

Liber Hermods, *imprint of* Liber AB

Hillelforlaget+
Nybrogatan 19, 114 39 Stockholm
Mailing Address: PO Box 5053, 10242 Stockholm
Tel: (08) 6633866 *Fax:* (08) 6619366
Key Personnel
Man Dir: Marina Burstein *E-mail:* marina@chinuch.a.se
Founded: 1969
Subjects: Regional Interests, Religion - Jewish
ISBN Prefix(es): 91-85164
Total Titles: 20 Print

Lars Hoekerbergs Bokfoerlag
Fleminggatan 21, S-11226 Stockholm
Tel: (08) 244360 *Fax:* (08) 6503984
E-mail: hokerbook@ebox.tninet.se
Key Personnel
Man Dir: Jan Hoekerberg
Founded: 1882
Subjects: Fiction, Nonfiction (General)
ISBN Prefix(es): 91-7084; 91-7157
Number of titles published annually: 1 Print
Total Titles: 3 Print

Hundskolan i Solleftea AB
Overgard 7005, S-881 93 Solleftea
Tel: (0620) 83200 *Fax:* (0620) 83229
ISBN Prefix(es): 91-971825

ICA bokforlag+
Stora gatan 41, SE-721 85 Vasteras
Tel: (021) 194278 *Fax:* (021) 194283
E-mail: bok@forlaget.ica.se
Web Site: www.forlaget.ica.se/bok
Telex: 40486 ica s *Cable:* ICAFOeRLAGET
Key Personnel
Publisher: Goran Sunehag *Tel:* (021) 192470
  E-mail: goran.sunehag@forlaget.ica.se
Rights Manager: Ulla Joneby *E-mail:* ulla.joneby@forlaget.ica.se
Founded: 1945
Subjects: Animals, Pets, Cookery, Crafts, Games, Hobbies, Gardening, Plants, Health, Nutrition, House & Home, How-to, Self-Help
ISBN Prefix(es): 91-534
Number of titles published annually: 70 Print
Total Titles: 450 Print

Idrottsantikvariatet, *imprint of* Stroemberg B&T Forlag AB

Industrilitteratur Vindex, Forlags AB
Storgatan 19, S-114 85 Stockholm
Mailing Address: PO Box 5513, 114 85 Stockholm
Tel: (08) 7838100 *Fax:* (08) 6605911
Founded: 1887
Publications section of the Swedish Trade Council.
Subjects: Ethnicity, Marketing, Public Administration
ISBN Prefix(es): 91-7548
Parent Company: Swedish Trade Council; Federation of Swedish Industry

Informationsfoerlaget AB
Sveavaegen 61, S-113 86 Stockholm
Mailing Address: PO Box 6884, 113 86 Stockholm
Tel: (08) 340915 *Fax:* (08) 313903
E-mail: red@informationsforlaget.se
Key Personnel
Man Dir: Ulf Heimdahl
Senior Editor: Ylva Aberg
Founded: 1979
Specialize in sponsored books in cooperation with Swedish industry and authorities.
Subjects: Cookery, How-to, Wine & Spirits
ISBN Prefix(es): 91-7736

Ingenjoersforlaget AB+
106 12 Stockholm
Tel: (08) 7966500 *Fax:* (08) 7896224
Telex: 17191 Tecnews S *Cable:* Ingforlag
Key Personnel
Man Dir: Hakan Ryden
Founded: 1970
Subjects: Science (General)
ISBN Prefix(es): 91-7284

Interculture+
PO Box 4160, 10262-62 Stockholm
Tel: (08) 6427804 *Fax:* (08) 6423591

Telex: 909 Teleopr S attn Intconswed *Cable:* INTCONSWED
Key Personnel
Man Dir: Jan Valdelin
Founded: 1983
Subjects: Fiction, Film, Video
ISBN Prefix(es): 91-86608
Parent Company: ICS Interconsult Sweden A

International Bible Society
Fabriksgatan 17c, 524 23 Herrljunga
Mailing Address: PO Box 205, 524 23 Herrljunga
Tel: (0513) 21930 *Fax:* (0513) 21501
Key Personnel
Executive Dir: Hans-Lennart Raask
ISBN Prefix(es): 91-7165; 91-87412
Parent Company: Colorado Springs, CO, United States
Subsidiaries: IBS

Internationella bibelsaellskapet, see International Bible Society

Interskol Forlag AB
Schaktugnsgatan 2, 21616 Malmo
Tel: (040) 510195 *Fax:* (040) 150625
E-mail: info@interskol.se
Web Site: www.interskol.se
Key Personnel
Dir: Kenneth Arvidsson
Founded: 1975
Specialize in School Books.
ISBN Prefix(es): 91-7306

Invandrarfoerlaget+
Katrinedalsgatan 43, 50451 Boras
Tel: (033) 136070 *Fax:* (033) 136075
E-mail: migrant@immi.se
Web Site: www.immi.se
Key Personnel
Editor: Miguel Benito
Founded: 1973
Subjects: Education, Ethnicity
ISBN Prefix(es): 91-85242; 91-7906
Number of titles published annually: 4 Print
Total Titles: 140 Print
Online services available through World Wide Web.
Parent Company: Immigrant-institute, Katrinedalsgatan 43, 50451 Boras

ITK Laromedel AB+
Fleminggatan 21, S-104 20 Stockholm
Mailing Address: PO Box 8071, 104 20 Stockholm
Tel: (08) 244360 *Fax:* (08) 6503984
Key Personnel
Man Dir: Jan Hoekerberg
Contact: Annika Thiam
Founded: 1923
Subjects: Science (General), Technology
ISBN Prefix(es): 91-7084; 91-7157
Associate Companies: Lars Hoekerbergs Bokfoerlag

Iustus Forlag AB
Ostra Agatan 9, SE-75322 Uppsala
Tel: (018) 693091 *Fax:* (018) 693099
E-mail: iustus@iustus.se
Web Site: www.iustus.se
Key Personnel
Editor: Eva Thorell *Tel:* (018) 693068
  E-mail: eva.thorell@iustus.se
Marketing Dir: Ewa Waites *Tel:* (018) 693063
  E-mail: ewaw@iustus.se
Founded: 1973
Specialize in law books, aimed at both university level & practicing lawyers, judges, civil servants.

SWEDEN

Subjects: Business, Economics, Finance, Government, Political Science, Law, Management, Public Administration
ISBN Prefix(es): 91-7678
Number of titles published annually: 40 Print
Total Titles: 200 Print
Online services available through Norstedts Media.

IVA, *see* Kungl Ingenjoersvetenskapsakademien (IVA)

Jannersten Forlag AB+
Bjorkstigen 8, S-774 27 Avesta
Mailing Address: PO Box 45, 774 01 Avesta
Tel: (0226) 61900 *Fax:* (0226) 10927
E-mail: bridge@jannersten.se
Key Personnel
Dir: Per Jannersten
Founded: 1939
Subjects: Crafts, Games, Hobbies
ISBN Prefix(es): 91-85024

Johnston & Streiffert Editions+
Soedermalmsgatan 35, 431 69 Moelndal
Tel: (031) 826160 *Fax:* (031) 825150
Key Personnel
President: Turlough Johnston *E-mail:* turlough.johnston@swipnet.se
Contact: Eleonore Wagner
Founded: 1985
Also acts as Print Broker & Agent.
Subjects: Animals, Pets, Automotive, Crafts, Games, Hobbies, How-to, Maritime, Sports, Athletics
ISBN Prefix(es): 91-87036
Number of titles published annually: 3 Print
Total Titles: 10 Print
Associate Companies: Streiffert Foerlag, Stockholm
Subsidiaries: Johnston Print Consultants

Liber Kartor, *imprint of* Liber AB

Klassikerfoerlaget
Trycheingatan 4, S-10312 Stockholm
Mailing Address: PO Box 45022, 10430 Stockholm
Tel: (08) 4570300 *Fax:* (08) 4570334
E-mail: klassikerforlaget@raben.se
Key Personnel
Editor: Anders Stroem
Founded: 1953
Subjects: Literature, Literary Criticism, Essays
ISBN Prefix(es): 91-7102
Parent Company: P A Norstrdt & Soner AB

Konsultforlaget AB
Torsgatan 18, S-75002 Uppsala
Mailing Address: PO Box 2070, 750 02 Uppsala
Tel: (018) 555080 *Fax:* (018) 155081
E-mail: info@konsultforlaget.se
Key Personnel
Man Dir: Mats Josephson
ISBN Prefix(es): 91-7005

Kungl Ingenjoersvetenskapsakademien (IVA)
(Royal Swedish Academy of Engineering Sciences)
Grev Turegatan 14, 102 42 Stockholm SE
Mailing Address: PO Box 5073, 102 42 Stockholm
Tel: (08) 7912900 *Fax:* (08) 6115623
E-mail: info@iva.se
Web Site: www.iva.se *Cable:* Ivacademi
Key Personnel
President: Lena Torell
Editorial: Cissi Billgren Askwall
Editor: Eva Reinholdren *E-mail:* er@iva.se
Founded: 1919

Royal Swedish Academy of Engineering Sciences.
Subjects: Management, Science (General), Technology
ISBN Prefix(es): 91-7082

Hans Richter Laromedel+
Box 100, 64522 Straengnaes
SAN: 105-0893
Tel: (0152) 150 60; (0200) 11 55 30 (orders)
 Fax: (0152) 151 40; (0200) 11 55 31 (orders)
E-mail: info@richter.d.se
Web Site: www.richter.d.se
Key Personnel
Dir: Hans Richter Laromedel *E-mail:* post@richter.d.se
Founded: 1982
Member of Swedish Publishers Association & FSL; Also acts as Agent; Mail Order Distribution & Direct Marketing to Businesses & Schools.
Subjects: Education, English as a Second Language, Language Arts, Linguistics, Music, Dance
ISBN Prefix(es): 91-7884
Imprints: Nyforlaget

Bokforlaget Robert Larson AB+
Box 3063, 183 03 Taby
Tel: (08) 7328460 *Fax:* (08) 7327176
E-mail: info@larsonforlag.se
Web Site: www.larsonforlage.se *Cable:* LARSONBOOKS
Key Personnel
Dir: Birgitta Larson; Robert Larson; Joakim Larson
Founded: 1971
Subjects: Nonfiction (General)
ISBN Prefix(es): 91-514

Legenda, *imprint of* Bokfoerlaget Naturoch Kultur

Liber AB+
Haelsingegatan 49, 11398 Stockholm
Tel: (08) 6909200 *Fax:* (08) 6909470
E-mail: export@liber.se; infomaster@liber.se
Web Site: www.liber.se
Key Personnel
President: Jan Thurfell *E-mail:* hedwig.hermanson@liber.se
Subjects: Business, English as a Second Language, Geography, Geology, Health, Nutrition, History, Language Arts, Linguistics, Mathematics, Medicine, Nursing, Dentistry, Science (General), Social Sciences, Sociology, Technology
ISBN Prefix(es): 91-21; 91-40
Parent Company: Wolters Kluwer Scandinavia
Imprints: Almquist & Wiksell; Liber Ekonomi; Liber Hermods; Liber Kartor
Subsidiaries: Liber Distribution; Norstedts Tuvidik

Liber Hermods AB+
Besoksadress Norra Vallgatan 100, 205 10 Malmo
Tel: (040) 258600 *Fax:* (040) 304600
Key Personnel
President: Per Bergknut
Founded: 1898
Member of Euro Business Publishing Network; specialize in educational & business publishing & distance education.
ISBN Prefix(es): 91-23

Libris Bokforlaget+
Soederleden 14, S-701 12 Oerebro
Mailing Address: PO Box 1213, 701 12 Oerebro
Tel: (019) 208400 *Fax:* (019) 208430
E-mail: info@libris.se
Web Site: www.libris.se

BOOK

Key Personnel
Man Dir: Soren Liljedahl *E-mail:* soren.lijedahl@libris.se
Publicity Dir: Anna Stenlund
Rights & Permissions: Inger Lundin
Founded: 1916
Subjects: Fiction, Theology
ISBN Prefix(es): 91-7194
Parent Company: Libris Media AB
Book Club(s): Libris Bok & Musikklubb

Lidman Production AB+
PO Box 5098, 102 42 Stockholm
Tel: (08) 6633615 *Fax:* (08) 6633615
Key Personnel
Publisher: Sven Lidman
Founded: 1973
Subjects: Education

Metodistkyrkans Foerlag, *see* Forlaget Sanctus (Metodistkyrkans Forlag)

Mezopotamya Publishing & Distribution+
Saegstuvaegen 1A, S-141 04 Huddinge
Mailing Address: PO Box 4036, 141 04 Huddinge
Tel: (08) 7747354 *Fax:* (08) 7110836
Key Personnel
Editor: Nedim Dagdeviren
Specialize in publishing & distribution of Kurdish books, children's books & musical productions.
Subjects: Asian Studies, Ethnicity, History, Language Arts, Linguistics
ISBN Prefix(es): 91-971307

Natur och Kultur/LTs foerlag+
Ostermalmsgatan 45, 11426 Stockholm
Mailing Address: Box 27323, 10254 Stockholm
Tel: (08) 4538725 *Fax:* (08) 4538798
E-mail: lt@nok.se
Web Site: www.nok.se/lt
Key Personnel
Man Dir: Rolf Ellnebrand *Tel:* (08) 4538729 *E-mail:* rolf.ellnebrand@nok.se
Production Manager: Torbjorn Tesch *Tel:* (08) 4538728 *E-mail:* torbjorn.tesch@nok.se
Permissions: Viveka Pettersson *Tel:* (08) 4538733 *E-mail:* viveka.pettersson@nok.se
Founded: 1935
Subjects: Agriculture, Animals, Pets, Cookery, Crafts, Games, Hobbies, Gardening, Plants, Health, Nutrition, House & Home, Photography, Science (General)
ISBN Prefix(es): 91-27
Number of titles published annually: 30 Print
Total Titles: 300 Print; 300 Online
Parent Company: Bokfoerlaget Natur och Kultur

Bokfoerlaget Naturoch Kultur
Karlavaegen 31, S-102 54 Stockholm
Mailing Address: PO Box 27323, S-102 54 Stockholm
Tel: (08) 4538600 *Fax:* (08) 4538790
E-mail: info@nok.se
Web Site: www.nok.se
Key Personnel
Man Dir & Chief Executive Officer: Lars Grahn
Editorial Dir, Textbooks: Lars Kaellquist
Editorial Dir, Acadamic Books, fiction & nonfiction: Christian Reimers
Rights & Permissions, Children's Books: Maria Sjostrom *E-mail:* maria.sjostrom@nok.se
IT & New Media: Christina Forsberg
Rights & Permissions, Gen Nonfiction, Fiction, Academic Books: Katarina Grip *E-mail:* katarina.grip@nok.se
Founded: 1922
Subjects: Biography, Fiction, History, Nonfiction (General), Psychology, Psychiatry, Science (General)
ISBN Prefix(es): 91-27; 91-582
Number of titles published annually: 350 Print
Total Titles: 5,000 Print; 10 CD-ROM; 60 Audio

Online services available through World Wide Web.
Imprints: Legenda (commercial fiction & suspense novels)
Subsidiaries: LTs foerlag ab
Book Club(s): Boeckernas Klubb, Box 3317, S-10366 Stockholm; Natur och Kultur Direkt
Warehouse: Foerlagsdistribution, Skarpraettarvaegen 1, PO Box 706, Jaerfaella S-176 27

Nautiska Foerlaget AB+
Sluasplan 5, 104 65 Stockholm
Mailing Address: PO Box 15410, 104 65 Stockholm
Tel: (08) 6770000 *Fax:* (08) 6770010
E-mail: nautiska.ab@nautiskamf.se *Cable:* Namco
Key Personnel
Manager: H Hultkrantz
The Nautical Publishing Co Ltd.
Subjects: Maritime
ISBN Prefix(es): 91-970094

Nordiska Bokhandelns
Brotvagen 32, 161-39 Bromma
Tel: (08) 269809 *Fax:* (08) 254246 *Cable:* NORDBOK
Key Personnel
Man Dir: Hans Molander
Founded: 1851
ISBN Prefix(es): 91-516
Bookshop(s): AB Nordiska Bokhandeln

Norstedt
Tryckerigatan 4, 103 12 Stockholm
Mailing Address: PO Box 2052, 103 12 Stockholm
Tel: (08) 7893000 *Fax:* (08) 7983038
Key Personnel
Marketing Manager: Per Andersson
Founded: 1833
ISBN Prefix(es): 91-1; 91-20
Subsidiaries: Generalstabens Litografiska Anstalt; GLA Map Service

P A Norstedt & Soener AB
PO Box 2052, S-10312 Stockholm
Tel: (08) 7893000 *Fax:* (08) 214006
Key Personnel
Chief Executive: Kjell Bohlund
Contact: Lise-Lott Olofsson *Tel:* (08) 7698711
 E-mail: lise-lott.olofsson@norstedts.se
Founded: 1823
Subsidiaries: Bokfoerlaget Prisma; Bokfoerlaget Tivoli; Norstedts Foerlag; Norstedts Ordbok; Raben & Sjoegren; Tiden
Book Club(s): Barnens Bokklubb (Partially owned); Boeckernas Klubb (Partially owned); Clio (Partially owned); Manadens Bok (Partially owned); Samhaellsbok-Klubben Radix (Partially owned)

Norstedts Foerlag+
Tryckerigatan 4, S-103 12 Stockholm
Mailing Address: PO Box 2052, S-103 12 Stockholm
Tel: (08) 769 87 00 *Fax:* (08) 769 88 64
Web Site: www.norstedts.sc
Key Personnel
Man Dir: Svante Weyler *E-mail:* svante.weyler@norstedts.se
Rights & Permissions: Agneta Markas
 E-mail: agneta.markas@norstedts.se
Secretary: Gerd Ronnberg
Founded: 1823
Subjects: Fiction, Nonfiction (General)
ISBN Prefix(es): 91-1
Number of titles published annually: 100 Print
Parent Company: P A Norstedt & Soener AB
Imprints: Tivoli

Norstedts Juridik
PO Box 6472, 11382 Stockholm
Tel: (08) 6909100 *Fax:* (08) 6909070
Subjects: Law
ISBN Prefix(es): 91-7598

Norstedts Ordbok
PO Box 45022, 10430 Stockholm
Tel: (08) 7698950
E-mail: info.orabok@norstedtordbok.se
Web Site: www.norstedtsordbok.se
Parent Company: PA Norstedt & Soener
Ultimate Parent Company: KF Media

Bokforlaget Nya Doxa AB+
Praestgatan 26, 713 23 Nora
Mailing Address: PO Box 113, S-713 23 Nora
Tel: (0587) 10416; (0587) 12905 *Fax:* (0587) 14257
E-mail: info@nya-doxa.se
Web Site: www.aim.se/doxa
Key Personnel
Management Dir: David Stansvik
Editor: Tove Marling
International Rights: Karina Klok Madsen
Founded: 1991 (1974 as Bokfoerlaget Doxa AB)
Also distribution & sales for Bokfoerlaget Thales, Sweden.
Subjects: Art, Biblical Studies, Communications, Ethnicity, History, Literature, Literary Criticism, Essays, Nonfiction (General), Philosophy, Science (General), Social Sciences, Sociology, Theology, Women's Studies
ISBN Prefix(es): 91-88248; 91-578
Number of titles published annually: 30 Print
Total Titles: 200 Print

Nyforlaget, *imprint of* Hans Richter Laromedel

Ordfront Foerlag AB (Ordfront Publishing House)+
Bellmansgatan 30, S-118 91 Stockholm
Mailing Address: PO Box 17506, S-11891 Stockholm
Tel: (08) 4624420 *Fax:* (08) 4624490
E-mail: forlaget@ordfront.se
Web Site: www.ordfront.se *Cable:* ORDFRONT STOCKHOLM
Key Personnel
Man Dir: Leif Ericsson
Editorial, Rights & Permissions: Eva Stenberg
 E-mail: eva@ordfront.se
VP & Publishing Dir: Jan-Erik Pettersson
Founded: 1969
Member of Swedish Publishers Association; Specialize in history, politics, journalism & fiction.
Subjects: Fiction, History, Journalism, Publishing & Book Trade Reference, Social Sciences, Sociology
ISBN Prefix(es): 91-7324
Total Titles: 50 Print
Imprints: Calago Foerlag
Book Club(s): Ordfront Bookclub

Pagina Forlags AB+
Travgatan 92, S-194 27 Upplands Vasby
Mailing Address: PO Box 2103, 174 02 Sundbyberg
Tel: (08) 56421800 *Fax:* (08) 56421819
E-mail: pagina@pagina.se
Key Personnel
President: Lauri Pappinen
Founded: 1979
Subjects: Computer Science
ISBN Prefix(es): 91-86200; 91-86201; 91-636
Parent Company: Pagina AB
Subsidiaries: Pagina Oy

Pandang, *imprint of* Raben och Sjoegren Bokfoerlag

Bokforlaget Prisma+
Tryckerigatan 4, SE-103 12 Stockholm
Mailing Address: PO Box 2052, S-103 12 Stockholm
Tel: (08) 7698900 *Fax:* (08) 7698913
E-mail: prisma@prismabok.se
Web Site: www.prismabok.se
Key Personnel
Man Dir: Viveca Ekelund *E-mail:* viveca.ekelund@prismabok.se
Secretary: Gunnel Nordsater *E-mail:* gunnel.nordsater@prismabok.se
Founded: 1963
International Rights Contact: Pan Agency, PO Box 2052, SE-10312, Stockholm, Tel: (08) 769 8700, Fax: (08) 769 8804.
Subjects: Cookery, Fiction, Gardening, Plants, History, House & Home
ISBN Prefix(es): 91-518
Parent Company: P A Norstedt & Soener AB
Foreign Rights: Pan Agency

Psykologifoerlaget AB+
Mejerivaegen 7, S-100 74 Stockholm
Mailing Address: Box 47054, 100 74 Stockholm
Tel: (08) 6810000 *Fax:* (08) 6810002
E-mail: info@psykologiforlaget.se
Web Site: www.psykologiforlaget.se
Key Personnel
Man Dir: Catharina Mabon
Founded: 1957
Subjects: Education, Psychology, Psychiatry
ISBN Prefix(es): 91-7418

R & S Books, *imprint of* Raben och Sjoegren Bokfoerlag

Raben och Sjoegren Bokfoerlag+
Tryckerigatan 4, S-10312 Stockholm
Mailing Address: PO Box 2052, S-10312 Stockholm
Tel: (08) 7698800 *Fax:* (08) 7698813
E-mail: raben-sjogren@raben.se
Web Site: www.raben.se
Key Personnel
Publishing Dir: Suzanne Ohman-Sunden
 E-mail: suzanne.ohman-sunden@raben.se
Publisher: Ewa Malmborg *E-mail:* ewa.malmborg@raben.se; Annika Seward-Jensen *E-mail:* annika.seward-jensen@raben.se; Birgitta Westin *E-mail:* birgitta.westin@raben.se
Foreign Rights (Pan Agency): Lillevi Cederin *E-mail:* lillevi.cederin@raben.se; Kerstin Oberg *E-mail:* kerstin.oberg@raben.se
Secretary: Alva Settepassi *E-mail:* alva.settepassi@raben.se
Contact: Lisa-Lott Olofsson *Tel:* (08) 7698711
 E-mail: lise-lott.olofsson@norstedts.se
Founded: 1942
Subjects: Nonfiction (General)
ISBN Prefix(es): 91-29
Parent Company: P A Norstedt & Soener AB
Imprints: Citadell; R & S Books; Pandang; Tiden
Book Club(s): Barnens Bokklubb (jointly owned)

Richters Egmont
Ostra Foerstadsgatan 46, 205 75 Malmo
Tel: (040) 380600 *Fax:* (040) 933708
Telex: 33180 richt S
Key Personnel
Man Dir, Rights & Permissions: Lars G Gustafsson
Editorial: Annika Bladh; Ia Atterholm
Sales: Ulf Ottosson; Lena Oeman
Production: Anders Enquist
Founded: 1942
Subjects: Fiction
ISBN Prefix(es): 91-7705; 91-7706
Parent Company: Gutenberghus Group, Copenhagen, Denmark

Book Club(s): Richters Ungdomsbokklub; Kalle Ankas Bokklubb; Kokboksklubben God Mat; Richters Bokklubb; Laeslandet; Spaenningsbokklubben; Skoenhet och Haelsa

Samsprak Forlags AB
Skolgatan 44-A, S-701 44 Oerebro
Mailing Address: PO Box 247, S-701 44 Oerebro
Tel: (019) 132445 *Fax:* (019) 187255
E-mail: info@samsprak.se
Web Site: www.samsprak.se
Key Personnel
Contact: Sven Olov Stalfelt
Founded: 1980
Subjects: Communications, Education
ISBN Prefix(es): 91-86020
Total Titles: 10 Print; 1 CD-ROM; 14 Audio

Schultz Forlag AB
Ludvigsbergsgatan 43, S-11823 Stockholm
Mailing Address: 14, Quai d Orleans, 75004 Paris, France
Tel: (01) 43298392 *Fax:* (01) 40460821
Web Site: www.schultzforlag.com
Key Personnel
Dir: Barbro Schultz-Lundestam *Tel:* (01) 43298392 *E-mail:* Lundest@attglobal.net
Founded: 1982
Specializes in film/video production & novels, artbooks & poetry.
Subjects: Art, Film, Video, Literature, Literary Criticism, Essays, Photography, Poetry
ISBN Prefix(es): 91-87370
Number of titles published annually: 4 Print
Total Titles: 30 Print
Associate Companies: Schultz Forlag SARL
Distributed by Printed Matter (New York)

Bokforlaget Semic AB
Landsvaegen 57, S-172 25 Sundbyberg
Mailing Address: Box 1243, S-172 25 Sundbyberg
Tel: (08) 7993050 *Fax:* (08) 7993064
E-mail: bokforlaget@semic.se
Web Site: www.semic.se
Key Personnel
Publisher: Mans Gahrton
Founded: 1945
Subjects: Animals, Pets, Architecture & Interior Design, Cookery, Crafts, Games, Hobbies, Gardening, Plants, House & Home, Sports, Athletics
ISBN Prefix(es): 91-552
Parent Company: Semic International AB

Semic Bokforlaget International AB+
PO Box 1243, 17225 Sundbyberg
Tel: (08) 7793050 *Fax:* (08) 7993064 *Cable:* SEMICPRESS S
Key Personnel
Man Dir: Pentti Molander
Rights & Permissions, Magazines: Ulf Gransberg
Founded: 1950
Subjects: Cookery, Crafts, Games, Hobbies, Humor, Sports, Athletics
ISBN Prefix(es): 91-552
Parent Company: Bonnierforetagen, Torsgatan 21, S-113 90 Stockholm
Subsidiaries: Kustannus Oy Semic; Jultidningsfoerlaget AB; Bokforlaget Semic AB; Semic Press AB

Sjoestrands Foerlag
PO Box 1305 Duvgrand 1, 172 36 Sundbyberg
Tel: (08) 299932 *Fax:* (08) 984645
Key Personnel
Man Dir: Ulla-Britt Sjoestrand
Editor: Mr Stellan Forsman
Founded: 1978
Subjects: Astrology, Occult, Fiction, Nonfiction (General), Science Fiction, Fantasy
ISBN Prefix(es): 91-7574

SNS Foerlag+
Skoeldungagatan 1, 114 86 Stockholm
Mailing Address: PO Box 5629, 114 86 Stockholm
Tel: (08) 4539950 *Fax:* (08) 206206
E-mail: bok.info.order@sns.se
Key Personnel
Man Dir: Torgny Wadensjoe
Founded: 1948
Subjects: Economics, Social Sciences, Sociology
ISBN Prefix(es): 91-7150

Sober Foerlags AB
Birger Jarlsgatan 25, S-111 87 Stockholm
Mailing Address: PO Box 1747, 111 87 Stockholm
Tel: (08) 789 4958 *Fax:* (08) 204354
Key Personnel
Man Dir: Kjell E Johanson
Editorial: Ann-Marie Tjaernkvist
Founded: 1972
Subjects: Health, Nutrition, Social Sciences, Sociology
ISBN Prefix(es): 91-7296
Orders to: Sober Forlags AB, Metallvagen 4, S-435 83 Molnlycke

Stenstroems Bokfoerlag AB+
Linnegatan 98, 115 23 Stockholm
Mailing Address: PO Box 24086, S-104 50 Stockholm
Tel: (08) 6637601 *Fax:* (08) 6632201
Key Personnel
Publisher: Bengt Stenstroem
Founded: 1976
Specialize in reference books.
ISBN Prefix(es): 91-86448
Associate Companies: Interpublishing AB Stenstroem

Frank Stenvalls Forlag+
Foereningsgatan 12, S-211 44 Malmo
Mailing Address: PO Box 17111, S-20010 Malmo
Tel: (040) 127703 *Fax:* (040) 127700
E-mail: fstenval@algonet.se
Key Personnel
Man Dir: Frank Stenvall
Founded: 1966
Subjects: Aeronautics, Aviation, Maritime, Transportation
ISBN Prefix(es): 91-7266
Number of titles published annually: 5 Print
Total Titles: 60 Print
Bookshop(s): Stenvalls
Book Club(s): Swedish Military Bookclub

Stiftelsen Kursverksamhetens Foerlag, see Folkuniversitetets foerlag

Streiffert Forlag AB
Skeppargatan 27 37, S-102 47 Stockholm
Mailing Address: PO Box 5334, 102 47 Stockholm
Tel: (08) 6615880 *Fax:* (08) 7830433
Key Personnel
Man Dir: Bo Streiffert *E-mail:* bo@streiffert.se
Founded: 1985
Subjects: Travel
ISBN Prefix(es): 91-7886
Number of titles published annually: 8 Print
Total Titles: 41 Print

Stroemberg B&T Forlag AB+
PO Box 65, 162 11 Vallingby
Tel: (08) 6201900 *Fax:* (08) 7399836
E-mail: bokforlaget@stromberg.se
Web Site: www.stromberg.se
Key Personnel
Publisher: Hanserik Tonnheim
Founded: 1990
Subjects: Art, History, Religion - Other, Sports, Athletics
ISBN Prefix(es): 91-7151; 91-7148; 91-7198; 91-85110; 91-86184
Imprints: Idrottsantikvariatet; Stroembergs Bokforlag
Warehouse: Johnson & Johnsonhuset, Staffausvag 2, 19184 Sollentuna

Stroembergs Bokforlag, *imprint of* Stroemberg B&T Forlag AB

Stromberg+
PO Box 65, 16211 Vaellingby
Tel: (08) 6201900 *Fax:* (08) 7399836
Key Personnel
Publisher: Hanserik Tonnheim
Man Dir: Thomas Bjorklund
Founded: 1991
Subjects: Cookery, Economics, Education, Law, Nonfiction (General), Regional Interests
ISBN Prefix(es): 91-7151
Warehouse: Seelig & Co, Box 1308, Solna
Orders to: Seelig & Co, Box 1308, Solna

Studentlitteratur AB+
Akergraenden 1, S-221 00 Lund
Mailing Address: PO Box 141, 22100 Lund
Tel: 312000 *Fax:* 305338
E-mail: info@studentlitteratur.se
Web Site: www.studentlitteratur.se
Key Personnel
President: Stefan Persson
Publishing Dir: Sven-Ake Lennung
Rights Mgr: Kristina Karlssol *E-mail:* kristina.karlssol@studentlitteratur.se
Production: Thomas Lundgren
Rights Mgr: Susanne Worning *E-mail:* susanne.worning@studentlitteratur.se
Publishing Dir: Robert Kipowski
Founded: 1963
Subjects: Accounting, Behavioral Sciences, Biological Sciences, Business, Chemistry, Chemical Engineering, Computer Science, Education, Engineering (General), Language Arts, Linguistics, Law, Management, Mathematics, Medicine, Nursing, Dentistry, Philosophy, Physical Sciences, Psychology, Psychiatry, Social Sciences, Sociology, Technology
ISBN Prefix(es): 91-44
Number of titles published annually: 200 Print
Total Titles: 2,500 Print
Parent Company: Bratt International A/B, Lund

Studieforlaget i Goteborg Stiftelsen Kursverksamhetens Forlag
PO Box 2542, 403 17 Goteborg
Tel: (031) 106580 *Fax:* (031) 135359
Key Personnel
Contact: Bo Nordell
ISBN Prefix(es): 91-7602

Svenska alliansmissionens (SAM) foerlage
Vaestra Storgattan 14, 551 18 Joenkoeping
Mailing Address: PO Box 11054, 55011 Jonkoping
Tel: (036) 719870 *Fax:* (036) 719820 *Cable:* SAM
Key Personnel
Man Dir: Torbjoern Wetteroe
Subjects: Religion - Other
ISBN Prefix(es): 91-7484

Svenska Arbetsgivareforeningens forlag
Soedra Blasieholmshamnen, 10330 Stockholm
Tel: (08) 7626000 *Fax:* (08) 7626490 *Cable:* EMPLOYERS
Key Personnel
Manager: Kjell Frykhammar
ISBN Prefix(es): 91-7152

PUBLISHERS

Svenska Foerlaget liv & ledarskap ab+
Luntmakargatan 46, S-105 17 Stockholm
Mailing Address: PO Box 3313, 103 66 Stockholm
Tel: (08) 4122700 *Fax:* (08) 4114121
E-mail: kundservice@svenskaforlaget.com
Key Personnel
President: Lena Kjellgren
Publisher: Lena Kamhed
Founded: 1982
Subjects: Animals, Pets, Biography, Business, Career Development, History, Human Relations, Management, Nonfiction (General), Philosophy, Psychology, Psychiatry, Self-Help
ISBN Prefix(es): 91-7738
Parent Company: SMS Publishing AB/Schibsted ASA
Divisions: Executive Seminars
Book Club(s): Executive Book Club

Svenska Institutet+
Box 7434, 10391 Stockholm
Tel: (08) 789-20-00 *Fax:* (08) 20-72-48
E-mail: si@si.se
Founded: 1945
Specialize in information about Sweden-culture & society in many languages.
ISBN Prefix(es): 91-520

The Swedish Association of Educational Publishers (Foreningen Svenska Laromedelsproducenter), see Foreningen Svenska Laromedelsproducenter (The Swedish Association of Educational Publishers)

Teknografiska Institutet AB
Industrivaegen 5, 171 24 Solna
Mailing Address: PO Box 1243, 171 24 Solna
Tel: (08) 834285 *Fax:* (08) 7304131
Key Personnel
Man Dir: Jan Broden
Production: Ingrid Karpebaeck
Founded: 1946
ISBN Prefix(es): 91-7172

Tiden, *imprint of* Raben och Sjoegren Bokfoerlag

AB Timbro+
Grev Turegatan 19, S-102 45 Stockholm
Mailing Address: PO Box 5234, S-102 45 Stockholm
Tel: (08) 58789800 *Fax:* (08) 58789855
E-mail: info@timbro.se
Web Site: www.timbro.se
Key Personnel
Pres: Mattias Bengtsson
Production: Barbro Bengtson
Permissions & International Rights: Kristina von Unge *Tel:* (08) 58789834 *E-mail:* kristinau@timbro.se
Founded: 1978
Publishes a periodical for culture, politics & economics (Smedjan) www.smedjan.com).
Subjects: Economics, Government, Political Science, Nonfiction (General), Social Sciences, Sociology, Free Enterprise
ISBN Prefix(es): 91-7566

Tivoli, *imprint of* Norstedts Foerlag

Tryckeriforlaget AB+
Tumstockvaegen 19, S-183 07 Taby
Mailing Address: PO Box 7093, S-183 12 Taby
Tel: (08) 7567445 *Fax:* (08) 7560395
E-mail: tidkort@tidkort.se
Key Personnel
Dir: Leif Lindberg
Subjects: Antiques, Business, Wine & Spirits
ISBN Prefix(es): 91-970081; 91-971201

Var Skola Foerlag AB+
Riddargatan 17, 5tr, S-114 57 Stockholm
Tel: (08) 6623351 *Fax:* (08) 6621843
E-mail: var.skola@pi.se
Key Personnel
Man Dir: Gunnel Radahl; Stig Radahl
Subjects: Nonfiction (General)
ISBN Prefix(es): 91-7396; 91-7700

Verbum Foerlag AB+
Sankt Paulsgatan 2, S-104 65 Stockholm
Mailing Address: PO Box 15169, S-104 65 Stockholm
Tel: (08) 7436500 *Fax:* (08) 6414585
E-mail: info@verbum.se
Web Site: www.verbum.se
Key Personnel
Man Dir: Olof Ignerus
Editorial: Gillis Simonsson
Founded: 1911
Member of FSL, SBF, IPA, & Worlddidac.
Subjects: Music, Dance, Religion - Other, Theology
ISBN Prefix(es): 91-526
Parent Company: Verbum AB
Associate Companies: Gleerups Foerlag, Foerlagshuset Gothia
Subsidiaries: Libraria Konsthantverk AB
Divisions: Publishing, Stationery
Bookshop(s): V Hamngatan 21, Goeteborg

Wahlstrom & Widstrand
Sturegatan 32, 114 85 Stockholm
Mailing Address: PO Box 5587, 114 85 Stockholm
Tel: (08) 6968480 *Fax:* (08) 6968380 *Cable:* Bebolag
Key Personnel
Man Dir: Dag Bernce
Editorial: Margaret Bernce
Subjects: Art, Biography, Cookery, Fiction, History, Nonfiction (General)
ISBN Prefix(es): 91-500

AB Wahlstrom & Widstrand+
Sturegatan 32, 114 85 Stockholm
Mailing Address: PO Box 5587, 114 85 Stockholm
Tel: (08) 6968480 *Fax:* (08) 6968380
E-mail: info@wwd.se
Web Site: www.wwd.se *Cable:* WAHLWID S
Key Personnel
Publisher & Man Dir: Unn Palm
Sales Dir: Bengt Hennings
Rights & Permissions: Marina Kosjanov
  E-mail: marina.kosjanov@wwd.se
Founded: 1884
Specialize in novels, poetry, illustrated nature books, travel guides, health, psychology.
Subjects: Fiction, Health, Nutrition, Nonfiction (General), Poetry, Psychology, Psychiatry
ISBN Prefix(es): 91-46
Parent Company: Bonnierforlagen AB

B Wahlstroms
PO Box 30022, 104 25 Stockholm
Tel: (08) 6198600 *Fax:* (08) 6189761
E-mail: info@wahlstroms.se
Web Site: www.wahlstroms.se
Key Personnel
Chairman & Man Dir: Bertil Wahlstroem
Editor-in-Chief & Permissions: Brit-Marie Johansson
Founded: 1911
Subjects: Fiction, Nonfiction (General)
ISBN Prefix(es): 91-32
Parent Company: J A Lindblads Bokfoerlag AB
Bookshop(s): Kungsholmens Bokhandel AB, PO Box 49014, S-100 28 Stockholm
Warehouse: Loevsvaegen 26, S-791 29 Falun

SWITZERLAND

Zindermans AB
Forsta Langgatan 6, 41303 Goteborg
Tel: (031) 7750400 *Fax:* (031) 120660 *Cable:* ZINDERMANS
Key Personnel
Man Dir: Leif Stigsjoeoe
Founded: 1960
Subjects: Biography, Fiction, Government, Political Science, History, How-to, Nonfiction (General), Psychology, Psychiatry, Social Sciences, Sociology
ISBN Prefix(es): 91-528

Switzerland

General Information

Capital: Berne
Language: 3 official: German, French and Italian
Religion: Protestant and Roman Catholic
Population: 6.8 million
Bank Hours: 0800 or 0830-1200 or 1230, 1300 or 1330-1630 Monday-Friday
Shop Hours: 0800-1200, 1330-1830 Monday-Friday; in most cities, closed Monday morning; 0800-1200, 1330-1600 or 1700 Saturday
Currency: 100 rappen (centimes) = 1 Swiss franc
Export/Import Information: Member of the European Free Trade Association. No tariff on books. Most books exempt from Turnover Tax. Advertising matter usually dutiable, some exempt from Turnover Tax. 2% VAT on books. No import licenses required. No exchange controls.
Copyright: UCC, Berne, Florence (see Copyright Conventions, pg xi)

Aare-Verlag+
Werkhofstr 23, 4502 Solothurn
Mailing Address: Postfach 507, 5001 Aarau
Tel: (062) 8368626 *Fax:* (062) 8245780
Key Personnel
Publishing Manager: Hans Christof Saueriaender
Editor: Barbara Kueper
International Rights: Claudia Kukla
Founded: 1953
Subjects: Education
ISBN Prefix(es): 3-7260
Subsidiaries: Verlag Sauerlaende
Orders to: Koch, Neff & Oetringer, Schockenriedstr 39, D-70565 Stuttgart, Germany

AD, *imprint of* Editions Andre Delcourt & Cie

ADIRA+
29, rue du Rhone, Geneve 1204
Tel: (022) 312 25 43 *Fax:* (022) 312 26 13
E-mail: adira@adira.net
Web Site: www.adira.net
Key Personnel
President: Dominique Mottas
Author: Michel Potay
Founded: 1974
Also acts as distributor.
Subjects: Philosophy, Religion - Other, Spirituality
ISBN Prefix(es): 2-901821
Number of titles published annually: 2 Print
Total Titles: 12 Print
Parent Company: Editions Michel Potay
Ultimate Parent Company: Maison de la Revelation
U.S. Office(s): ADIRA New York, 590 Madison Ave, 21st floor, New York, NY 10022, United States
Distributed by Hervey's; Pathways

607

SWITZERLAND

Adonia-Verlag+
Gereenstrabe 9, CH-81238800 Ebmatingen
Tel: (01) 9801930 *Fax:* (01) 9800622
E-mail: advonia.verlag@bluewin.ch
Web Site: www.libroplus.ch/adonia
Founded: 1986
Member of SBVV, SSV, Pen.
Subjects: Poetry, Women's Studies
ISBN Prefix(es): 3-905009

Editions L'Age d'Homme - La Cite
10 rue de Geneve, 1000 Lausanne-9
Tel: (021) 3120095 *Fax:* (021) 3208440
Key Personnel
Man Dir: Vladimir Dimitrijevic
Founded: 1966
Subjects: Art, Biography, Drama, Theater, Fiction, Film, Video, Literature, Literary Criticism, Essays, Music, Dance, Philosophy, Poetry, Psychology, Psychiatry, Regional Interests, Religion - Other, Science Fiction, Fantasy, Social Sciences, Sociology
ISBN Prefix(es): 2-8251
Branch Office(s)
5 rue Ferou, 75006 Paris, France *Tel:* (01) 46 34 18 51 *Fax:* (01) 40 51 71 02
Bookshop(s): Librairie la Proue, Escaliers du Marche 17, CH-1000 Lausanne; Librairie Le Rameau d'Or, 19 blvd Georges Favon, CH-1200 Geneva

J H Goehre Albanus Verlag
Hulfteggstr 10, CH-8401 Winterthur 1
Tel: (052) 293503
Key Personnel
Contact: J H Goehre
Founded: 1946
Member of SBVV/VVDS.
ISBN Prefix(es): 3-85510

Amboss-Verlag E Widmer+
Industriestr 25, 9434 Au SG
Mailing Address: Postfach 404, 9434 Au SG
Tel: (071) 711236; (071) 714590 *Fax:* (071) 714590
Key Personnel
Contact: Charlotte Knoepfli-Widmer
Founded: 1968
ISBN Prefix(es): 3-85517

American Time, *imprint of* Europa Star, Bill Communication SA

Ammann Verlag & Co+
Neptunstr 20, 8032 Zurich
Mailing Address: Postfach 2074, 8032 Zurich
Tel: (01) 268 10 40 *Fax:* (01) 268 10 50
E-mail: info@ammann.ch
Web Site: www.ammann.ch
Key Personnel
Publisher: Egon Ammann; Marie-Luise Flammersfeld
Sales, Marketing: Susanne Schenzle
Production: Otto Doerries
Rights & Permissions: Monica Iseli
Editor: Stephanie von Harrach
Press: Joachim Leser
Founded: 1981
Subjects: Art, Fiction, Literature, Literary Criticism, Essays, Poetry, Science (General)
ISBN Prefix(es): 3-250
Number of titles published annually: 20 Print
Orders to: Ammann Verlag, Buchzentrum AG, B2, CH-4601 Olten
Ammann Verlag, c/o LKG mbH Verlagsauslieferung, Potzschauerweg Weg, 04579 Espenhain, Germany

Antonius-Verlag
Gaertnerstr 7, 4500 Solothurn
Tel: (032) 625 37 42

Key Personnel
Contact: Maria Gasser
Subjects: Education, Medicine, Nursing, Dentistry, Psychology, Psychiatry
ISBN Prefix(es): 3-85520
Branch Office(s)
Testzentrale der Deutschen Psychologen, Robert-Bosch-Breite 25, D-37079 Gottingen, Germany
Testzentrale der Schweizer Psychologen, Laenggassstr 76, Bern 9, Germany
Universitaetsverlag, Perolles 42, CH-1700 Fribourg Fribourg

Arche Verlag AG, Raabe und Vitali+
Hoelderlinstr 14, 8030 Zurich
Mailing Address: Postfach 112, 8030 Zurich
Tel: (01) 2522410 *Fax:* (01) 2611115
Telex: 815239
Key Personnel
Owner: Elisabeth Raabe; Regina Vitali
Founded: 1944
Subjects: Biography, Fiction, Literature, Literary Criticism, Essays, Music, Dance, Poetry, Travel
ISBN Prefix(es): 3-7160
Divisions: Arche Verlag GmbH

Archivio Storico Ticinese
Via del Bramantino 3, Bellinzona 6500
Tel: (092) 8256622 *Fax:* (092) 8251874
Telex: 846266
Key Personnel
Man Dir: Virgilio Gilardoni
Sales, Production: Libero Casagrande
Founded: 1960
Subjects: Art, Economics, History, Literature, Literary Criticism, Essays
ISBN Prefix(es): 88-7714
Parent Company: Edizioni Casagrande SA

Ariston Editions+
Villa Bellevue, Hauptstr 14, Kreuzlingen 8280
Mailing Address: Postfach 6030, 1211 Geneve 6
Tel: (071) 6727218 *Fax:* (071) 6727219
E-mail: 106420.3235@compuserve.com
Telex: 413428 arve ch *Cable:* ARISTON
Key Personnel
Man Dir, Editorial & Sales: Dr Monika Roell
Founded: 1964
Subjects: How-to, Medicine, Nursing, Dentistry, Nonfiction (General), Parapsychology, Psychology, Psychiatry, Self-Help
ISBN Prefix(es): 3-7205
Branch Office(s)
Ariston Verlag GmbH und Co Verlagsservice, Boschetsriederstr 12, 81379 Munich, Germany *Tel:* (089) 7241034 *Fax:* (089) 7241718
Ariston-P R Presse, Hauptrasse 14, 8280 Kreuzlingen

Armenia Editions+
PO Box 2621, 1260 Nyon 2
Tel: (079) 447 4593 *Fax:* (079) 447 4593
Key Personnel
Contact: Elisabeth Tavitian
Founded: 1991
Member of American Booksellers Association.
Subjects: Architecture & Interior Design, Art, Biography, Cookery, History, Language Arts, Linguistics, Literature, Literary Criticism, Essays, Music, Dance, Poetry, Regional Interests, Religion - Other, Romance, Theology, Travel
ISBN Prefix(es): 2-88421

Collection Artou, *imprint of* Editions Olizane

Ascona Presse
Passaggio San Pietro 7, 6612 Ascona
Tel: (091) 7911334 *Fax:* (091) 7911334
Founded: 1986

ASELF, see Association Suisse des Editeurs de Langue Francaise

Association pour la Diffusion Internationale de la Revelation d'Ares, see ADIRA

Association Suisse des Editeurs de Langue Francaise
Route Du Lac 2 1094 Paudex, Case Postale 1215, 1001 Lausanne
Tel: (021) 7963300 *Fax:* (021) 7963311
E-mail: aself@centrezational.cl
Key Personnel
President: Francine Bouchet
ISBN Prefix(es): 2-88303

Astrodata AG+
Chilenholzstr 8, 8907 Wettswil b Zurich
Tel: (01) 7001012 *Fax:* (01) 7001610
E-mail: wettswil@astrodata.ch
Web Site: www.astrodata.ch
Key Personnel
President: Claude Weiss
Founded: 1978
Subjects: Astrology, Occult, Psychology, Psychiatry
ISBN Prefix(es): 3-907029
Parent Company: Astrodata AG, Albisriederstr 232, CH-8047 Zurich
Distributor for Edition Astroterra
Bookshop(s): Chilenholzstr 8, 8907 Wettswil b Zurich

AT Verlag+
Division of AZ Fachverlage AG
Bahnhofstr 39-43, 5001 Aarau
Tel: (062) 836 6666 *Fax:* (062) 836 6667
E-mail: info.buchverlag@azag.ch
Web Site: www.at-verlag.ch
Key Personnel
Editorial Dir: Urs Hunziker *E-mail:* urs.hunziker@azag.ch
Editorial: Monika Schmidhofer *E-mail:* monika.schmidhofer@azag.ch
Production: Adrian Pabst *E-mail:* adrian.pabst@azag.ch; Edith Guenter *E-mail:* edith.guenter@azag.ch
Sales: Christine Gutknecht *E-mail:* christine.gutknecht@azag.ch; Karin Asti *E-mail:* karin.asti@azag.ch
Marketing: Eugen Jung *E-mail:* eugen.jung@azag.ch
Foreign Rights: Danielle Schwab *E-mail:* danielle.schwab@azag.ch
Founded: 1967
This is the book publishing section of the Aargauer Zeitung AG.
Subjects: Cookery, Health, Nutrition, How-to, Mysteries, Regional Interests
ISBN Prefix(es): 3-905214; 3-85502
Warehouse: Grafische Betriebe Aargauer Zeitung AG, Neumattstr 1/Betrieb Telli, CH-5004 Aarau

Athenaeum Verlag AG
Via Miravalle 23, 6900 Lugano-Massagno
Tel: (091) 571536 *Cable:* athenag
Key Personnel
Man Dir: J-E Nussbaumer
Administration: J Wuest-Wolfensberger
Editorial: J Steiner
Founded: 1972
Subjects: Art, Biography, Government, Political Science, History, Literature, Literary Criticism, Essays, Nonfiction (General), Science (General)
ISBN Prefix(es): 3-85532
Branch Office(s)
Buchauslieferung, Schweizer Buchzentrum, Olten

Atlantis-Verlag AG
Kreuzstr 39, 8008 Zurich

Tel: (010) 2622717 *Fax:* (01) 2512615
Telex: 815987
Founded: 1930
Subjects: Art, Geography, Geology
ISBN Prefix(es): 3-7611
Branch Office(s)
Atlantis-Verlag GmbH & Co KG, Germany

Atrium Verlag AG+
Feldeggstr 74, 8008 Zurich
Mailing Address: Postfach 262, 8030 Zurich
Tel: (01) 2613035; (01) 473035 *Fax:* (01) 2615436
Key Personnel
Contact: Uwe Weitendorf
Founded: 1936
ISBN Prefix(es): 3-85535

Augustin-Verlag
Schlatterweg 11, 8240 Thayngen
Mailing Address: PL 120, Thayngen
Tel: (052) 649 31 31 *Fax:* (052) 649 31 94
E-mail: augustin@augustin.ch
Key Personnel
President & Publisher: Karl Augustin
Founded: 1911
Publish journals (weekly newspapers for village people named Heimatblatt).
Subjects: Geography, Geology, History, Regional Interests
ISBN Prefix(es): 3-85540; 3-905116

Editions de la Baconniere SA+
Division of Medecine et Hygiene
46, chemin de la Mousse, 1225 Chene-Bourg
Tel: (022) 8690017 *Fax:* (022) 8690015
E-mail: DEB@medecinehygiene.ch
Key Personnel
Contact: Denis Bertholet
Founded: 1927
Subjects: Art, Biography, History, Music, Dance, Philosophy, Poetry, Social Sciences, Sociology
ISBN Prefix(es): 2-8252

U Baer Verlag+
Mainaustr 35, 8008 Zurich
Tel: (01) 3835500 *Fax:* (01) 3836883
Key Personnel
Man Dir: Dr Ulrich Baer
Editorial, Production: Marianne Widmer
Founded: 1971
Subjects: Art, Photography
ISBN Prefix(es): 3-905137

Barenreiter Verlag Basel AG+
Neuweilerstr 15, CH-4015 Basel
Mailing Address: Postfach 131, 4015 Basel
Tel: (061) 395898; (061) 395899 *Fax:* (061) 3079660
E-mail: baerenreiter_ch@compuserve.com
Web Site: www.baerenreiter.com
Key Personnel
President: Leonard Scheuch
Member Board: Peter G Isler
Founded: 1944
Member of Swiss Society of Music Publishers.
Subjects: Music, Dance
ISBN Prefix(es): 3-7618
Parent Company: Baerenreiter Praha
Associate Companies: Baerenreiter Verlag GmbH & KO KG, Heinrich-Schutz-Allee 35, 34131 Kassel-Wilhelmshohe, Germany, Barbara Scheuch *Tel:* (0561) 3105-0 *Fax:* (0561) 3105-240 *E-mail:* info@baerenreiter.com

Buchhandlung Baeschlin+
Bahnhofstrasse 19, 8750 Glarus
Tel: (058) 611126
Founded: 1853
ISBN Prefix(es): 3-85546

H R Balmer AG Verlag
Neugasse 12, 6301 Zug
Mailing Address: PO Box 1000, 6301 Zug
Tel: (042) 2144141; (042) 214735 *Fax:* (042) 210917
Telex: 868812 buch ch
Key Personnel
Man Dir: Christoph Balmer
Founded: 1974
Subjects: History, Literature, Literary Criticism, Essays, Psychology, Psychiatry
ISBN Prefix(es): 3-85548
Warehouse: Boesch 41, 6331 Huenenberg

Bargezzi-Verlag AG+
Postf 28, Wasserwerksgasse 19, 3000 Berne 13
Tel: (031) 221380; (031) 211434 *Fax:* (031) 3113071 *Cable:* Bargezzi Berne
Key Personnel
Man Dir, Editorial, Sales, Publicity, Rights & Permissions: Josef Gruebel
Production: Werner F Waegli
Founded: 1948
Subjects: Literature, Literary Criticism, Essays, Religion - Other
ISBN Prefix(es): 3-85550

Bartschi Publishing
Sternenstr 20b, 8903 Birmensdorf
Tel: 01 7373528
Key Personnel
Dir: Helen Bartschi
Founded: 1989
Subjects: Literature, Literary Criticism, Essays, Poetry, Psychology, Psychiatry
ISBN Prefix(es): 3-9520020

Basileia Verlag
Missionstr 21, 4003 Basel
Mailing Address: PO Box 128, 4003 Basel
Tel: (061) 251766 *Fax:* (061) 2688321; (061) 232523
Key Personnel
Man Dir: Rudolf Kellenberger
Subjects: Religion - Other, Social Sciences, Sociology
ISBN Prefix(es): 3-85555

Basilius Presse AG+
Gueterstr 86, 4002 Basel
Tel: (061) 228004; (061) 228005 *Fax:* (061) 232523 *Cable:* BASILIUS VERLAG
Key Personnel
Man Dir: P Weibel
Founded: 1957
Subjects: Art, Nonfiction (General), Science (General)
ISBN Prefix(es): 3-85560

Baumgartner Blicher, *imprint of* Terra Grischuna Verlag Buch-und Zeitschriftenverlag

Editions Belle Riviere
La Fontanelle, 1882 Gruyon
Tel: (024) 498 40 49 *Fax:* (024) 498 40 46
Key Personnel
Man Dir: Eugene Chave
Founded: 1974
ISBN Prefix(es): 2-88121

Benteli Verlag+
Seftigenstr, 310, 3084 Wabern-Bern
Tel: (031) 9608484 *Fax:* (031) 9617414
E-mail: info@benteliverlag.ch
Web Site: www.benteliverlag.ch
Key Personnel
Man Dir: Till Schapp
Public Relations Manager: Lisa Locher *Tel:* (031) 9608470 *E-mail:* lisa.locher@benteliverlag.ch
Founded: 1899
High quality books.
Subjects: Art, Photography
ISBN Prefix(es): 3-7165
Number of titles published annually: 35 Print
Total Titles: 350 Print

Benziger Verlag AG+
Bellerivstr 3, 8008 Zurich
Tel: (01) 2527050 *Fax:* (01) 2624792
Key Personnel
Contact: Christian Machalet
Founded: 1792
Subjects: Art, Music, Dance, Religion - Catholic, Religion - Protestant, Theology
ISBN Prefix(es): 3-545
Parent Company: Patmos Verlag

Beobachter Buchverlag
Forrlibuckstr 10, CH-8021 Zurich
Tel: (01) 8296111 *Fax:* (01) 8103791
Web Site: www.beobachter.ch
Key Personnel
Contact: H Hausherr *Tel:* (01) 4488984 *E-mail:* hhausherr@beobachter.ch
ISBN Prefix(es): 3-85569
Total Titles: 60 Print
Branch Office(s)
Industriestr 54, Postfach 8152, Glattbrugg-Zurich

Berchtold Haller Verlag+
Nageligasse 9, 3000 Bern 7
Mailing Address: Postfach 15, 3000 Bern 7
Tel: (031) 334 03 03 *Fax:* (031) 334 03 06
Key Personnel
Contact: Peter Schranz *E-mail:* schranz@theol-buch.ch
Founded: 1848
Subjects: Religion - Protestant, Romance
ISBN Prefix(es): 3-85570
Number of titles published annually: 3 Print
Total Titles: 40 Print; 13 Audio
Parent Company: Evangelisches Geweinschafhwerth EGW

Bergli Books AG+
Eptingerstr 5, 4052 Basel
Tel: (061) 373 27 77 *Fax:* (061) 373 27 28
E-mail: info@bergli.ch
Web Site: www.bergli.ch
Key Personnel
Man Dir: Dianne Dicks
Founded: 1990
Specialize in intercultural books on crossing cultures, emigration, intercultural marriages, bi-lingualism, short story anthologies.
Subjects: Behavioral Sciences, Ethnicity, Foreign Countries, Human Relations, Literature, Literary Criticism, Essays, Nonfiction (General), Travel, Women's Studies
ISBN Prefix(es): 3-9520002; 3-905252
Distributor for Survival Books; Travelers' Tales

Berichthaus Verlag, Dr Conrad Ulrich
Voltastr 43, 8044 Zurich
Tel: (01) 2526349 *Fax:* (01) 2526426
Subjects: History, History of Zurich & Switzerland
ISBN Prefix(es): 3-85572
Orders to: Schweiz Buchzentrum, CH 4601 Olten

Beroa-Verlag
Zellerstr 61, 8038 Zurich
Tel: (01) 4801313 *Fax:* (01) 4801312
Founded: 1957
Subjects: Biblical Studies
ISBN Prefix(es): 3-905335; 3-906336

Bettex, Editions Medicales Roland
78 rue de la Roseraie, CP 456, 1211 Geneva 4
Tel: (022) 7029311 *Fax:* (022) 7029355
ISBN Prefix(es): 2-88113

SWITZERLAND

Branch Office(s)
3, rue des Fontenalilles CP 193, 1000 Lausanne 13
Street 8, rue Copernic, 75116 Paris, France

Editions Beyeler
Baeumleingasse 9, 4001 Basel
Tel: (061) 206 97 00 *Fax:* (061) 206 97 19
Key Personnel
Owner: Ernst Beyeler
Founded: 1967
Subjects: Art
ISBN Prefix(es): 3-85575; 3-9520156

Bibellesbund Verlag+
Flugplatzstr 5, 8404 Winterthur, Schweiz
Mailing Address: Postfach, Flugplatzstr 6, 8404 Winterthur
Tel: (052) 2451445 *Fax:* (052) 2451446
E-mail: info@bibellesebund.ch
Web Site: www.bibellesebund.ch
Key Personnel
Secretary-General, Switzerland: Andreas Zimmermann
Secretary-General, Germany: Reinhold Frey
Man Dir, Sales, Production, Publicity, Switzerland: Martin Wassmer
Man Dir, Sales, Production, Publicity, Germany: Karl-Martin Gunther
Founded: 1930
Scripture Union of Switzerland & Germany.
Subjects: Religion - Protestant
ISBN Prefix(es): 3-87982
Associate Companies: Bibellesebund eV Industriestr 2, Postfach, D-51703 Marienheide-Roth, Germany *Tel:* (02264) 7045 *Fax:* (02264) 7155 *E-mail:* info@bibellesebund.de
Distributed by Haenssler Verlag; Brunnen Verlag

Bibliographisches Institut und F A Brockhaus AG
Rudolf Hans Furrer, Lowenstr 19, 8021 Zurich
Mailing Address: Postfach 4531, 6304 Zug
Tel: (01) 2120800 *Fax:* (01) 7108325
Key Personnel
Man Dir: Dr Ernst Grab
Founded: 1967
Subjects: Language Arts, Linguistics, Philosophy, Science (General)
ISBN Prefix(es): 3-411; 3-7653
Parent Company: Bibliographisches Institut und F A Brockhaus AG, Germany

Verlag Bibliophile Drucke von Josef Stocker AG
Hasenbergstr 7, 8953 Dietikon
Mailing Address: PO Box 66, 8953 Dietikon
Tel: (01) 7404444
Key Personnel
Man Dir: Mr Stocker
Subjects: Poetry
ISBN Prefix(es): 3-85577; 3-7276
Parent Company: Verlag Stocker-Schmid AG
Bookshop(s): Buchhandlung Stocker-Schmid, Hasenbergstr 7, PO Box 66, 8953 Dietikon

La Bibliotheque des Arts+
Ave de Rumine 48, 1005 Lausanne
Tel: (021) 3123667; (021) 239334 *Fax:* (021) 3213615
Key Personnel
Dir: Mr Francois Daulte
Founded: 1952
Subjects: Art
ISBN Prefix(es): 2-85047
Subsidiaries: La Bibliotheque des Arts
Branch Office(s)
Archer Fields Inc, 636 Broadway, New York, NY 10012, United States

Birkhauser Verlag AG+
Viaduktstr 42, 4051 Basel
Mailing Address: PO Box 133, 4010 Basel
Tel: (061) 2050707 *Fax:* (061) 2050799
E-mail: info@birkhauser.ch; sales@birkhauser.ch
Web Site: www.birkhauser.ch *Cable:* EDITA
Key Personnel
General & Editorial Manager: Hans-Peter Thuer
Marketing Manager: Alfred Schaefer
Rights & Licences: Irena Jankova *Tel:* (061) 2050718 *E-mail:* jankova@birkhauser.ch
Founded: 1879
Subjects: Architecture & Interior Design, Biological Sciences, Engineering (General), Environmental Studies, Mathematics, Nonfiction (General), Physics, Science (General)
ISBN Prefix(es): 3-7643
Parent Company: BertelsmannSpringer Science+Business Media, Germany
Imprints: Birkhauser Verlag fuer Architektur
Subsidiaries: Birkhauser Boston Inc
Branch Office(s)
Birkhauser Boston Inc, c/o Springer-Verlag New York Inc, 175 Fifth Ave, New York, NY 10010, United States
Distributor for Princeton Architectural Press (USA, UK)
Warehouse: Gewerbestrasse 18, Biel-Benken *Tel:* (061) 7215326 *Fax:* (061) 7217753

Birkhauser Verlag fuer Architektur, *imprint of* Birkhauser Verlag AG

Blaukreuz-Verlag Bern+
Lindenrain 5a, Postfach 1196, 3001 Bern
Mailing Address: PO Box 5524, 3001 Bern
Tel: (031) 3015866; (031) 3015243 *Fax:* (031) 3005869 *Cable:* BLAUKREUZVERLAG
Key Personnel
Man Dir: Ernst Zuercher
Founded: 1884
Publishes for the Blue Cross health & religious movement.
Subjects: Biography, Health, Nutrition, Religion - Protestant, Religion - Other
ISBN Prefix(es): 3-85580
Parent Company: Blaues Kreuz der deutschen Schweiz

Les Editions de la Fondation Martin Bodmer
19-21 Route Guignard, Postfach, 1223 Cologny-Geneva
Mailing Address: PO Box 7, 1223 Cologny-Geneva
Tel: (022) 7362370 *Fax:* (022) 7001540
Key Personnel
Contact: Dr Martin Bircher
Founded: 1971
Subjects: Language Arts, Linguistics
ISBN Prefix(es): 3-85682

Bohem Press Kinderbuchverlag+
Hardturmstr 122, 8005 Zurich
Tel: (01) 4407000 *Fax:* (01) 4407001
E-mail: bohem@dial.eunet.ch
Key Personnel
Dir: O Bozejovsky v Rawennoff *Tel:* (01) 4407004
Contact: Susanne Zeller
Founded: 1973
Subjects: Animals, Pets, Child Care & Development, Fiction
ISBN Prefix(es): 3-85581

Brunnen-Verlag Basel+
Wallstr 6, 4002 Basel
Tel: (061) 234406 *Fax:* (061) 2956069
Key Personnel
Man Dir: Hans-Peter Zueblin
Founded: 1921
Subjects: Religion - Other

ISBN Prefix(es): 3-7655
Bookshop(s): Buchhandlung Pilgermission, Spalenberg 20, 4002 Basel; Brunnen-Buchhandlung, Marktgasse 31, 8180 Buelach; Brunnen-Buchhandlung, St Gallerstr 6, 8500 Frauenfeld; Libreria La Fonte, Viale Stazione 1, 6512 Giubiasco; Buechegge AG, Loewengasse 37, 8810 Horgen; Christlicher Buecherladen zur Arche, Amtshausgasse 10, 4410 Liestal; Evangelische Buchhandlung, Hauptstr 25, 5734 Reinach AG; Christliche Buchhandlung, Ave Mercier de Molin 1, 3960 Sierre; Christliche Buchhandlung, Bahnhofstr 42, 6210 Sursee; Christliche Buchhandlung, Susann-Muellerstr 14, 9630 Wattwil; Christliche Buchhandlung "Brunne-Stube", Schmidstr 3, 8570 Weinfelden; Brunnen-Buchhandlung, untere Bahnofstr 20, 9500 Wil; Christliche Buchhandlung, HERTI-Zentrum, 6300 Zug; Sunnaewirbel, Buecher & Geschenke, Olympstr 4, 6440 Brunnen; Senfkorn-Laden, Hauptstr 33, 5262 Frick

Verlag Bucheli+
Zugerbergstr 7a, 6301 Zug
Tel: (042) 221736 *Fax:* (042) 417115
Key Personnel
Contact: Hans-Joerg Degen
Subjects: Automotive
ISBN Prefix(es): 3-7168

Buchhaus AG, see Office du Livre SA (Buchhaus AG)

Buchverlag Basler Zeitung
Hochbergerstr 15, Postfach, 4002 Basel
Tel: (061) 661111 *Fax:* (061) 6391343
E-mail: order@baz.ch
Key Personnel
Marketing: Jasmine Gasser
ISBN Prefix(es): 3-85815
Book Club(s): SBVV

Bugra Suisse Burchler Grafino AG+
Seftigenstr 310, 3084 Wabern
Tel: (031) 548111 *Fax:* (031) 544562
Telex: 911934
Key Personnel
Man Dir, Rights & Permissions: Dr Rudolf Gysi
Marketing: Erich Hirschi
Editorial: Peter Wyss
Founded: 1886
Subjects: Art, Education, Regional Interests
ISBN Prefix(es): 3-7170

Cahiers de la Renaissance Vaudoise
One Place Grand-Saint-Jean, 1002 Lausanne
Mailing Address: Postfach 3414, 1002 Lausanne
Tel: (021) 3121914 *Fax:* (021) 3126714
Key Personnel
President: Olivier Delacretaz
Subjects: Government, Political Science, History
ISBN Prefix(es): 2-88017

Les Editions Camphill
Fondation Perceval, 1211 St-Prex
Tel: (021) 8062269 *Fax:* (021) 8061897
Key Personnel
Contact: John Byrde
Founded: 1979
Subjects: Anthropology, Education, Social Sciences, Sociology
ISBN Prefix(es): 2-8299

Carre d'Art Edition Archigraphie+
c/o NLDA, One Pl de l'Ile, 1204 Geneva
Tel: (022) 3115750 *Fax:* (022) 3122121
Founded: 1989
Subjects: Architecture & Interior Design
ISBN Prefix(es): 2-88287
Branch Office(s)
3 ruede Fribourg, 1201 Geneva

PUBLISHERS SWITZERLAND

Edizioni Casagrande SA+
Via del Bramantino, 3, 6500 Bellinzona
Mailing Address: Postfach 1291, 6500 Bellinzona
Tel: (091) 8256622 *Fax:* (091) 8251874
E-mail: casagrande@casagrande-online.ch
Web Site: www.casagrande-online.ch
Telex: 846266
Key Personnel
Man Dir, Editorial: Libero Casagrande
Founded: 1972
Subjects: Art, History, Literature, Literary Criticism, Essays
ISBN Prefix(es): 88-7713
Subsidiaries: Archivio Storico Ticinese; Istituto Editoriale Ticinese (IET) SA; Istituto Grafico Casagrande SA
Bookshop(s): Libreria Casagrande, Viale Stazione, CH-6500 Bellinzona

Castle Publications SA
22 rue Centrale, 1248 Hermance
Tel: (022) 511036; (022) 7884222 *Fax:* (022) 7511111; (022) 7884240
Key Personnel
Man Dir: Nicolas Ferguson
Founded: 1972
Subjects: Communications, Language Arts, Linguistics
ISBN Prefix(es): 2-88344; 2-88047
Associate Companies: CEEL (Centre Experimental pour l'Enseignement des Langues)
Imprints: SAPL
Subsidiaries: Castle Mexico; Didasko (Castle Japan) 6-7-31-611 Itashibori; SAOL Publications, Canada; Castle France

Causa Verlag GmbH, see Tobler Verlag

Caux Books
Rue du Panorama, CH-1824 Caux
Tel: (041) 422213 *Fax:* (021) 9629465
E-mail: bookch@caux.ch
Subjects: Biography, Religion - Other, Social Sciences, Sociology
ISBN Prefix(es): 3-85601
Subsidiaries: Caux Edition SA

Caux Edition SA
Rue de Panorama, 1824 Caux
Mailing Address: Box 322, Mont-Royal, PQ H3P 3C5, Canada
Tel: (021) 9629469 *Fax:* (021) 9629465
Key Personnel
Man Dir, Editorial: Chas Piguet
Founded: 1965
Subjects: Biography, Drama, Theater, Religion - Other, Social Sciences, Sociology
ISBN Prefix(es): 2-88037
Parent Company: Caux Verlag AG
Branch Office(s)
22, av Robert-Schuman, 92100 Boulogne-Billancourt, France *Tel:* (01) 41104050 *Fax:* (01) 41108267
Bookshop(s): Librairie de Caux, Rue de Panorama, 1824 Caux

Verlag Bo Cavefors
c/o Mardatropa AG, 8001 Zurich
Tel: (01) 2017200
Key Personnel
Man Dir: Bo Cavefors
Subjects: Fiction, Poetry, Religion - Catholic
ISBN Prefix(es): 3-85593

Cedilivre SA, see Editions Foma SA

Centre Experimental pour l'Enseignement des Langues, see Castle Publications SA

Chamaeleon Verlag AG
Weinbergstr 11, 8001 Zurich
Tel: (01) 2525497 *Fax:* (01) 2725282
Key Personnel
Manager: Mrs Andree Mathis
Founded: 1985
ISBN Prefix(es): 3-905274

Christiana-Verlag+
Haus zur Ziegelhutte Rietstr 45, 8260 Stein am Rhein
Tel: (052) 7412092 *Fax:* (052) 7412092
E-mail: orders@christiana.ch; info@christiana.ch
Web Site: www.christiana.ch
Key Personnel
Man Dir & International Rights: Arnold Guillet
Tel: (052) 7414131
Founded: 1948
Subjects: Biological Sciences, Education, Philosophy, Religion - Catholic, Demonology, Angeology, Hagiographic
ISBN Prefix(es): 3-7171
Number of titles published annually: 12 Print
Online services available through World Wide Web.
Orders to: Christiana-Verlag, Postfach 110, D-78201 Singen, Germany

Christoph Merian Verlag+
St Alban-Vorstadt 5, 4052 Basel
Mailing Address: Postfach, 4002 Basel
Tel: (061) 221288; (061) 271288 *Fax:* (061) 2711273
E-mail: cmsbasel@swissonline.ch
Key Personnel
Chief Executive, Editorial: Dr Beat von Wartburg
Chief Executive: Claus Donau
Marketing: Franzijka Nyffenegger
E-mail: fnyffenegger@cmsbas.ch
Founded: 1976
Subjects: Art, History, Literature, Literary Criticism, Essays, Photography, Regional Interests
ISBN Prefix(es): 3-85616
Total Titles: 80 Print
Shipping Address: Schweizer Bridezentrum SBZ, Postbach, 4601 Olten, Contact: Yvonne Sardoz
Tel: (062) 209 2704 *Fax:* (062) 209 2788

Chronos Verlag+
Muenstergasse 9, 8001 Zurich
Tel: (01) 2654343 *Fax:* (01) 2654344
E-mail: loinfo@chronos-verlag.ch
Web Site: www.chronos-verlag.ch
Founded: 1985
Specialize in Gender studies, media & theatre studies.
Subjects: Fiction, Film, Video, History, Nonfiction (General), Social Sciences, Sociology
ISBN Prefix(es): 3-905312; 3-905314; 3-905315; 3-905313; 3-905311; 3-905310; 3-905278
Number of titles published annually: 50 Print
Total Titles: 350 Print
Orders to: AVA, Ch-8910 Affoltern aA *Tel:* (01) 762 60 60 *Fax:* (01) 762 60 65 (Orders for Switzerland Only)
GVA, Postfach 2021, Gottingen *Tel:* (0551) 48 71 77 *Fax:* (0551) 4 13 92 (Orders for foreign countries)

Clairefontaine, Editions
14, av de Florimont, 1006 Lausanne
Tel: (021) 230879
Key Personnel
Contact: Albert Mermoud

Werner Classen Verlag
Sp lu Genstr 10, 8027 Zurich
Tel: (01) 2015606 *Cable:* CLASSENVERLAG ZURICH
Key Personnel
Dir: Werner Classen
Founded: 1945
Subjects: Humor, Music, Dance, Poetry, Psychology, Psychiatry
ISBN Prefix(es): 3-7172

De Clivo Press
Usterstr 126, 8600 Duebendorf
Tel: (01) 8201124
Telex: CH 55256 Serco *Cable:* Declivopress Duebendorf
Key Personnel
Proprietor: Dr Walter Amstutz
ISBN Prefix(es): 3-85634

Cockatoo Press (Schweiz), Thailand-Publikationen (Thailand Publications (Switzerland))+
Im Leeacher 30, 8132 Zurich
Tel: (01) 9841725 *Fax:* (01) 9843420
E-mail: cockatoo@thailine.com
Web Site: www.thailine.com
Founded: 1991
Specialize in publishing & promotion, information service.
Subjects: Antiques, Archaeology, Asian Studies, Business, Cookery, Foreign Countries, Language Arts, Linguistics, Mysteries, Religion - Buddhist, Social Sciences, Sociology, Travel
ISBN Prefix(es): 3-905302
Parent Company: Thailine 2000, Im Leeacher 30, Hinteregg ZH, 8132 Zurich, Mrs Ratanaporn Muller-Kaewdam
Associate Companies: Chiang Saen Internet Ltd Part
Subsidiaries: Thailand Publications Switzerland
Distributor for Editions Duang Kamol; Pilot Publishing; Suriwong Books; White Lotus Press

Rene Coeckelberghs Editions
Museggstra 7, 6004 Lucerne
Tel: 515060 *Fax:* 516645
Packagers.
Subjects: Nonfiction (General)
ISBN Prefix(es): 2-8310; 3-905285

Conseil oecumenique de Eglises, see World Council of Churches (WCC Publications)

Consejo Mundial de Iglesias, see World Council of Churches (WCC Publications)

Cosa-Verlag, Giusep Condrau SA+
Casa Desertina, 7180 Disentis
Mailing Address: Postfach 10, 7180 Disentis
Tel: (081) 9476464; (081) 9476352 *Fax:* (081) 947-63-52
E-mail: info@casanova.ch
Web Site: www.casanova.ch *Cable:* DESERTINA DISENTIS
Key Personnel
Man Dir, Rights & Permissions, Editorial, Production, Publicity: Pius Condrau
Founded: 1953
Subjects: Art
ISBN Prefix(es): 3-9521636
Bookshop(s): Condrau, Disentis

Cosmos-Verlag AG
Krayigenweg 2, CP 425, CH-3074 Muri BE
Mailing Address: PO Box 5776, 3001 Bern
Tel: (31) 9506464 *Fax:* (31) 9506460
E-mail: info@cosmosverlag.ch
Key Personnel
Contact: Regina Haener *E-mail:* haener@cosmosverlag.ch
Founded: 1923
Subjects: Accounting, Business, Fiction, Finance, Management, Regional Interests
ISBN Prefix(es): 3-85621; 2-8296; 3-305
Number of titles published annually: 12 Print

SWITZERLAND

Comite international de la Croix-Rouge
17 Ave de la Paix, 1211 Geneva
Tel: (022) 7346001 *Fax:* (022) 7384416; (022) 7348280
Telex: CICR 414226
Key Personnel
Head of Publishing Unit: Charles Pierrat
Fax: (022) 73 8768
Founded: 1863
Subjects: Law
ISBN Prefix(es): 2-88145
Total Titles: 4 Print; 2,000 Online
U.S. Office(s): International Committee of the Red Cross, 780 Third Ave, 28th floor, New York, NY 10017, United States

Cultur Prospectiv, Edition
Gastometerstr 28, Zurich 8005
Tel: (01) 2718388 *Fax:* (01) 2719788
E-mail: cpinstitut@access.ch
Key Personnel
Contact: Dr Hans-Peter Meier
Founded: 1990
Subjects: Social Sciences, Sociology
ISBN Prefix(es): 3-905345

Edizioni Armando Dado, Tipografia Stazione
Via Orelli 29, 6600 Locarno
Tel: (091) 7514802 *Fax:* (091) 7521026
Key Personnel
Man Dir: Armando Dado
Subjects: Art, History, Literature, Literary Criticism, Essays, Photography
ISBN Prefix(es): 88-85115; 88-86315

Daimon Verlag AG+
Am Kosterplatz, Hauptstr 85, CH-8840 Einsiedeln
Tel: (055) 4122266 *Fax:* (055) 412-2231
E-mail: daimon@compuserve.com
Web Site: www.daimon.ch
Key Personnel
Publisher: Dr Robert Hinshaw *E-mail:* r@daimon.ch
Founded: 1979
Member of SBVV.
Subjects: Environmental Studies, History, Poetry, Psychology, Psychiatry, Specializes in Dream Interpretation
ISBN Prefix(es): 3-85630
Distributor for Chiron; Eranos; Parabola; Sounds True Rec; Spring Publication & Spring Audio/Journal
Orders to: Chiron Publications, 400 Linden Ave, Wilmette, IL 60091, United States *Fax:* 847-256-2202
Continuum, 22883 Quicksilver Dr, Dulles, VA 20166, United States *Fax:* 703-661-1501

Daphnis-Verlag
Kappelistra 15, 8002 Zurich
Tel: (01) 9153639 *Fax:* (01) 2014231
Key Personnel
Man Dir: J Fischlin
Founded: 1959
Subjects: Poetry
ISBN Prefix(es): 3-85631

De Vier Winstreken, *imprint of* Nord-Sued Verlag

Marcel Dekker AG+
Hutgasse 4, Postfach 812, 4001 Basel
Tel: (061) 258484 *Fax:* (061) 2618896
Key Personnel
President: Bruno Baumgartner
Founded: 1975
Subjects: Business, Chemistry, Chemical Engineering, Civil Engineering, Earth Sciences, Electronics, Electrical Engineering, Mathematics, Medicine, Nursing, Dentistry
ISBN Prefix(es): 0-8247
Parent Company: Marcel Dekker Inc, 270 Madison Ave, New York, NY 10016, United States

Editions Delachaux et Niestle SA+
79, rue de Oron, Case Postale 44, 1000 Lausanne 21
Tel: (021) 6533044 *Fax:* (021) 6534095
E-mail: contact@delachaux-niestle.com
Key Personnel
Man Dir: David Perret
Sales, Permissions: Yvette Perret
Founded: 1861
Subjects: Earth Sciences, Education, Medicine, Nursing, Dentistry, Psychology, Psychiatry, Science (General), Social Sciences, Sociology
ISBN Prefix(es): 2-603
Subsidiaries: Delachaux Niestle, France SA
Branch Office(s)
4 rue Laferriere, 75009 Paris, France
82 rue de Courcelles, 75008 Paris, France
Tel: (01) 48881239 *Fax:* (01) 48881277

Editions Andre Delcourt & Cie+
Rue de la Borde 27, Case Postale 113, 1018 Lausanne
Tel: (021) 6479772; (021) 721294 *Fax:* (021) 6478831
Key Personnel
Publisher: Andre Delcourt
Founded: 1986
Subjects: Architecture & Interior Design, Art, Literature, Literary Criticism, Essays, Medicine, Nursing, Dentistry, Photography
ISBN Prefix(es): 2-88161; 2-602
Imprints: AD; Delta; Delta et Spes; Spes

Delta, *imprint of* Editions Andre Delcourt & Cie

Delta et Spes, *imprint of* Editions Andre Delcourt & Cie

Verlag Harri Deutsch+
Riedstr 2, 3600 Thun
Tel: (033) 2223975 *Fax:* (033) 2223950
E-mail: verlag@harri-deutsch.de
Key Personnel
Man Dir: Harri Deutsch
Editor: Bernd Mueller
Founded: 1971
Subjects: Astronomy, Biological Sciences, Chemistry, Chemical Engineering, Computer Science, Economics, Electronics, Electrical Engineering, Mathematics, Physics, Science (General), Sports, Athletics, Technology
ISBN Prefix(es): 3-87144; 3-8171
Total Titles: 900 Print; 7 CD-ROM; 5 Online; 5 E-Book
Parent Company: Verlag Harri Deutsch, Germany
Bookshop(s): Naturwiss Fachbuchhandlung an der Universitaet, Graefstr 47, 60486 Frankfurt, Germany *Tel:* (069) 775021 *Fax:* (069) 7073739
Web Site: www.harri-deutsch.de
Orders to: Brockhaus Commission, Postfach 1220, 70806 Kornwestheim, Germany *Tel:* (07) 154-132720 *Fax:* (07) 154-132710

Didax, *imprint of* Editions Foma SA

Dimension World Ltd+
Wilhelm-His-Str 1, Postfach 339, 4003 Basel
Tel: (061) 3225214 *Fax:* (061) 3133862
Key Personnel
International Rights: David Haisch
Founded: 1982
Subjects: Art, Business, Communications, Ethnicity, Foreign Countries, How-to, Marketing, Photography, Real Estate, Travel
ISBN Prefix(es): 3-905450
Associate Companies: Pamelart
Subsidiaries: Icebear Group Branch
Branch Office(s)
Icebear Group, 103-2 Lewis Pl, CL-11500 Negoubo, Sri Lanka *Fax:* 0094-31-33862
Distributor for Pamelart

Diogenes Verlag AG+
Sprecherstr 8, 8032 Zurich
Tel: (01) 254 85 11 *Fax:* (01) 252 84 07
E-mail: info@diogenes.ch
Web Site: www.diogenes.ch *Cable:* DIOGENESVERLAG ZURICH
Key Personnel
Man Dir & Owner, Publisher: Daniel Keel
Man Dir & Owner, Administration & Finance: Rudolf C Bettschart
Man Dir, Organization & Marketing: Stefan Fritsch
Editorial Dir: Winfried Stephan
Publicity & Promotion: Ruth Geiger
Sales & Marketing: Ulrich Richter
Production: Res Schenk
Foreign Rights & Permissions: Susanne Bauknecht
Corporate Finance: Martha Pfyl
Founded: 1952
Subjects: Art, Drama, Theater, Fiction, Literature, Literary Criticism, Essays, Mysteries, Philosophy
ISBN Prefix(es): 3-257

Librairie Droz SA+
11 rue Massot, 1211 Geneva 12
Mailing Address: PO Box 389, 1211 Geneva 12
Tel: (022) 3466666 *Fax:* (022) 3472391
E-mail: droz@droz.org
Web Site: www.droz.org
Key Personnel
Man Dir, Rights & Permissions: Max Engammare
Sales Dir: Mrs Burquier
Founded: 1924
Subjects: Antiques, History, Literature, Literary Criticism, Essays, Social Sciences, Sociology
ISBN Prefix(es): 2-600
Number of titles published annually: 80 Print; 2 CD-ROM; 2 E-Book
Total Titles: 80 Print; 2 CD-ROM; 2 E-Book

Duboux Editions SA+
Frutigenstr 6, CH-3600 Thun
Tel: (033) 2256060 *Fax:* (033) 2256066
E-mail: duboux-editions@duboux.ch
Web Site: www.duboux.ch
Key Personnel
President & Publisher: Jean-Pierre Duboux
Founded: 1988
Subjects: Cookery, Travel
ISBN Prefix(es): 3-907950
Distributed by Verlag Handwerk & Technik

Gottlieb Duttweiler Institute for Trends & Futures
PO Box 531, 8803 Rueschlikon
Tel: (01) 7240020 *Fax:* (01) 7246262
E-mail: biblio@gdi.ch *Cable:* GREEN MEADOW
Key Personnel
President: Dr Christian Lutz
Marketing & Public Relations Manager: Rosemarie Krause
Library: Silvia Edelmann
Founded: 1963
Subjects: Economics, Management, Marketing, Social Sciences, Sociology
ISBN Prefix(es): 3-7184
Parent Company: Migros-Genossenschafts-Bund, Zurich
Imprints: GDI

E Lopfe-Benz AG Rorschach, Graphische Anstalt und Verlag
Pestalozzistr 5, 9401 Rorschach
Tel: (071) 8440444 *Fax:* (071) 8440445

PUBLISHERS

Key Personnel
Dir: Emil Enderle; Dieter Mildenberger
Editorial: Werner Meier
Sales: Peter Kruijsen
Advertising: Hans Schoebi; Peter Bick; Daniel Anderegg
Founded: 1875
Graphical Institute & Publisher.
Subjects: History, Humor, Poetry
ISBN Prefix(es): 3-85819
Subsidiaries: Nebelspalter Verlag

Editions l'Eau Vive
10 rue de Fribourg, 1201 Geneva
Tel: (022) 7329847 *Fax:* (022) 7410482
Key Personnel
Man Dir: Rolande Gloor
Founded: 1960
Subjects: Biography, Religion - Other
ISBN Prefix(es): 2-88035

Eboris-Coda-Bompiani+
17 rue du Gendrier, 1201 Geneva
Tel: (022) 9092840 *Fax:* (022) 7381425
Key Personnel
President: Isabella Coda-Bompiani
Founded: 1994
Subjects: Literature, Literary Criticism, Essays, Photography
ISBN Prefix(es): 2-940121

Eco Verlags AG+
Langstr 187, Zurich 8005
Tel: (01) 440400
Key Personnel
Man Dir: Verena Stettler
Founded: 1976
Subjects: Literature, Literary Criticism, Essays, Nonfiction (General)
ISBN Prefix(es): 3-85647
Imprints: Literatheke; Neue Szene

Verlag ED Emmentaler Druck AG
Dorfstr, 3550 Langnau im Emmental
Tel: (035) 21911 *Fax:* (035) 0524642
Key Personnel
Man Dir, Sales: Paul Hartmann
Editorial & Publicity: Markus F Rubli
Founded: 1845
Subjects: Fiction, Photography, Regional Interests
ISBN Prefix(es): 3-85654

Editions Edita+
Route de Geneve, Case Postale 85, 1000 Lausanne 9
Tel: (021) 6251392 *Fax:* (021) 6254291
Telex: 450296
Key Personnel
Contact: Michel Ferloni; Francois Mukundi
Founded: 1953
Subjects: Art, History
ISBN Prefix(es): 2-88001
Subsidiaries: Editions Office du Livre
Orders to: Office du Livre Distribution, 101 Route de Villars, 1701 Fribourg

Edition Epoca+
Werdstr 128, CH-8003 Zurich
Tel: (01) 4511717 *Fax:* (01) 4511717
E-mail: info@epoca.ch
Web Site: www.epoca.ch
Key Personnel
Contact: Urs Kummer; Adrian Stokar
Founded: 1995
Subjects: Fiction, Literature, Literary Criticism, Essays, Philosophy, Social Sciences, Sociology
ISBN Prefix(es): 3-905513
Number of titles published annually: 7 Print

Editions Ad Solem
2, rue des Voisins, 1211 Geneva 12
Mailing Address: Postfach 479, 1211 Geneva 12
Tel: (022) 321 19 30 *Fax:* (022) 321 19 31
E-mail: office@adsolem.ch
Subjects: Christian literature

eFeF-Verlag/Edition Ebersbach+
Schwarztorstr 75, Postfach 5966, 3001 Bern
Tel: (031) 3822004 *Fax:* (031) 3824555
Founded: 1984
Subjects: Biography, Fiction, Women's Studies
ISBN Prefix(es): 3-9521022
Orders to: Buch 2000, Obfeldstr 35, CH-8910 Affoltern

Drei Eidgenossen Verlag
Huegelweg 15, 4102 Binningen
Tel: (061) 475166 *Fax:* (061) 475166
Key Personnel
Man Dir: Mr Hosch
Founded: 1936
ISBN Prefix(es): 3-85643

Editions Eisele SA
Avenue Confrerie 42, Case Postale 128, 1008 Prilly
Tel: (021) 6256324 *Fax:* (021) 6256374
E-mail: editions.eisele@worldcom.ch
Key Personnel
International Rights: Jean-Luc Eisele
Subjects: Education, History, Science (General)
ISBN Prefix(es): 2-88002

Verlag Eisenbahn
Gut Vorhard 382, 5234 Villigen AG
Tel: (056) 2845584; 441595 *Fax:* (056) 2845884
Cable: VERLAGEISENBAHN VILLIGEN
Key Personnel
Man Dir: Rose Jeanmaire
Editorial: Jeannine dit-Quartier
Founded: 1866
Company acts as distribution centre for rail publications from all over the world.
Subjects: Crafts, Games, Hobbies, Maritime, Transportation
ISBN Prefix(es): 3-85649
Associate Companies: Bing-Werke
Bookshop(s): Railway Bookshop, Gut Vorhard, 5234 Villigen AG
Shipping Address: Postfach 1251, 79761 Waldshut, Germany
Warehouse: Postfach 1251, 79761 Waldshut, Germany

ELCE Editeurs et Libraires Catholiques d'Europe
Hans-Walter Luthi, Wattstr 6, 9012 Saint Gallen
Tel: (071) 279580 *Fax:* (071) 279580
E-mail: hawas@mhs.ch
Key Personnel
Contact: Hans-Walter Luthi

Elektrowirtschaft Verlag
Bahnhofplatz 9, Postfach, 8023 Zurich
Tel: (01) 2910102 *Fax:* (01) 2910903
Subjects: Electronics, Electrical Engineering
ISBN Prefix(es): 3-85651

Elsevier, *imprint of* Elsevier Science SA

Elsevier Science SA+
Ave de la Gare 50, 1001 Lausanne 1
Mailing Address: PO Box 564, 1001 Lausanne
Tel: (021) 3207381 *Fax:* (021) 3235444
Key Personnel
Man Dir: Herman Frank
Founded: 1964
Subjects: Chemistry, Chemical Engineering, Economics, Engineering (General), Physical Sciences

SWITZERLAND

ISBN Prefix(es): 0-444
Imprints: Elsevier; North-Holland

Elvetica Edizioni SA+
Case Postale 134, 6834 Morbio Inferiore
Tel: (091) 6839920; (091) 6835056 *Fax:* (091) 6837605
E-mail: info@swissfinance.com
Web Site: www.swissfinance.com
Key Personnel
General Manager: Dr M G Grosso
Founded: 1967
Member of Societa Editori Svizzera Italiana, Association Europeenne des Editeurs d'Annuaires & Schweizer Adressbuch Verleger Verband.
Subjects: Economics, Novels, Essays & Literature
ISBN Prefix(es): 88-86639
Total Titles: 1 CD-ROM; 1 E-Book
Online services available through World Wide Web.

Erker-Verlag
Division of Erker-Galerie AG
Bahnhofstr 8, 9000 Saint Gallen
Tel: (071) 2227979 *Fax:* (071) 2227919
Key Personnel
Contact: Franze Larese; Jurg Janett
Founded: 1946
Subjects: Art, Literature, Literary Criticism, Essays, Philosophy, Poetry
ISBN Prefix(es): 3-905542; 3-905543; 3-905544; 3-905545; 3-905546
Associate Companies: Erker-Galerie, Gallusstra 32, 9000 Saint Gallen
Orders to: Erker-Galerie AG, Gallusstr 32, CH-9000 Saint Gallen (Also returns)

Edition Hans Erpf Verlagsgenossenschaft+
Postfach 6018, 3001 Bern
Tel: (031) 3054410 *Fax:* (031) 3054410
Cable: BUCHERPF
Key Personnel
Man Dir: Hans Erpf
Founded: 1966
Subjects: Humor, Literature, Literary Criticism, Essays
ISBN Prefix(es): 3-905517; 3-905520
Number of titles published annually: 20 Print

Espaces Photographiques, *imprint of* Editions Olizane

Editions Esprit Ouvert+
3 chemin de Mornex, 1003 Lausanne
Tel: (021) 2308844 *Fax:* (021) 3235403
Founded: 1988
Subjects: Film, Video, Literature, Literary Criticism, Essays
ISBN Prefix(es): 2-88329

Ethosi-Verlag, see Schwengeler-Verlag

EULAR Publishers
Missionsstr 36, 4012 Basel
Mailing Address: PO Box, 4012 Basel
Tel: (061) 251317 *Fax:* (061) 251286
E-mail: eular@reinhardt.ch
Key Personnel
Publisher & International Rights: Ruedi Reinhardt
Founded: 1977
Official publishers of The European League Against Rheumatism (EULAR).
Subjects: Health, Nutrition, Medicine, Nursing, Dentistry
ISBN Prefix(es): 3-7177
Parent Company: F Reinhardt AG, Missionsstr 36, 4012 Basel
Orders to: Reinhardt Media-Service, Missionsstr 36, 4012 Basel

Europa Star, *imprint of* Europa Star, Bill Communication SA

SWITZERLAND

Europa Star, Bill Communication SA
Route des Acacias 25, 1211 Geneva 24
Mailing Address: PO Box 30, 1211 Geneva 24
Tel: (022) 307 78 37 *Fax:* (022) 300 37 48
Web Site: www.europastar.com
Key Personnel
Man & Sales Dir: P Maillard
  E-mail: phmaillard@mfi.com
Editor-in-Chief: Pierre Morgan Maillard
Marketing & Circulation Dir: Nathalie Glattfelder
  Tel: (022) 307 78 32 *E-mail:* nglattfelder@europastar.com
Founded: 1927
Trade magazine; specialize in watches & jewelry.
ISBN Prefix(es): 2-88205
Imprints: American Time; Europa Star; Eurotec; International Jeweler
Foreign Rep(s): International Jeweler

Europa Verlag AG
Raemistr 5, 8024 Zurich
Tel: (01) 4711629 *Fax:* (01) 2516081
Telex: 816534 fere ch *Cable:* Europaverlag Zurich
Key Personnel
Man Dir: Emmie Oprecht
Founded: 1933
Distributor for UNESCO, Paris.
Subjects: Art, Government, Political Science, History, Philosophy
ISBN Prefix(es): 3-85665
Associate Companies: Verlag Oprecht, Zurich (Theatrical)

Eurotec, *imprint of* Europa Star, Bill Communication SA

Edition Exodus
Imprint of Societe Cooperative Edition Exodus
Postfach 224, 3900 Brig 5
Tel: 4108767 *Fax:* 4108741
E-mail: editionexodus@compuserve.com
Key Personnel
Publisher: Markus Koferli
Founded: 1982
Subjects: Religion - Catholic, Religion - Protestant, Social Sciences, Sociology, Theology
ISBN Prefix(es): 3-905575

AZ Fachverlage AG, see AT Verlag

Faksimile Verlag AG
Alpenstr 5, 6004 Lucerne
Tel: (041) 511571 *Fax:* (041) 516902
E-mail: fvl@faksimile
ISBN Prefix(es): 3-85672

Editions Francois Feij
Pl del 'Eglise, 1166 Perroy
Tel: (021) 8254675
Subjects: Law
ISBN Prefix(es): 2-88030

Fischer Media AG fur Verlag und Publishing
Bahnhofplatz, Postfach 218, 3110 Muensingen
Mailing Address: Postfach 287, 3000 Bern 5
Tel: (031) 922211 *Fax:* (031) 7205112
E-mail: all@fischermedia.ch
Key Personnel
Manager: Heinrich Gasser
ISBN Prefix(es): 3-85681
Parent Company: Fischer Druck AG, Bahnhofplatz 1, 3110 Muensingen

Maurice et Pierre Foetisch SA
Rue de Bourg 6, Case Postale 2793, 1003 Lausanne
Tel: (021) 3239444; (021) 3239445 *Fax:* (021) 3115011
Telex: 524227
Key Personnel
Man Dir & other offices: Jean-Claude Foetisch
Founded: 1947
Subjects: Education, Music, Dance, Radio, TV
Associate Companies: Disco SA

Editions Foma SA
Ave de Longemalle 5, Postfach 226, 1020 Renens-Lausanne
Tel: (021) 6351361 *Fax:* (021) 6351704
Telex: CH-Cedil 25416
Key Personnel
Man Dir, Editorial: J-L Peverelli
Sales: M Sculati
Publicity: Ann-Mari Mingard
Rights & Permissions: F Buhler
Founded: 1948
Subjects: Film, Video, Literature, Literary Criticism, Essays, Photography, Psychology, Psychiatry, Sports, Athletics
ISBN Prefix(es): 2-88003
Imprints: Didax
Subsidiaries: 5 Continents, Cedilivre SA
Bookshop(s): Didax

Fondation de l'Encyclopedie de Geneve
Case Postale 3640, 1211 Geneva 3
Fax: (022) 3273391; (022) 3273365
Key Personnel
President: Catherine Santschi
Founded: 1979
Description of Geneva's past & present.
Subjects: History
ISBN Prefix(es): 2-940069
Total Titles: 11 Print

Fortuna Finanz-Verlag AG+
Haslerholz 7, Postfach 52, 8123 Ebmatingen
Tel: (01) 9803622 *Fax:* (01) 9103353
Key Personnel
Man Dir: Ueli Vonau
Founded: 1953
Subjects: Finance
ISBN Prefix(es): 3-85684

Fotorotar AG/EGG ZH, *imprint of* Schweizerisches Jugendschriftenwerk, SJW

Frobenius AG
Spalenring 31, 4012 Basel
Tel: (061) 7715677 *Fax:* (061) 7116218
Key Personnel
Publicity: Otto Rymann
Subjects: History, Law, Literature, Literary Criticism, Essays, Regional Interests
ISBN Prefix(es): 3-85695

G+B Arts International+
St Johanns Vorstadt 19, Postfach, Basel 4004
Tel: (061) 2610138 *Fax:* (061) 2610173
Key Personnel
Contact: Linda Lowery-Stuart
Subjects: Architecture & Interior Design, Art, Drama, Theater, History, Photography
Associate Companies: Harwood Academic; Harvey Miller Publishers; Craftsman House; Verlag der Kunst; neue bildende Kunst; Fine Arts Press
Orders to: Marston Book Services Ltd, PO Box 269, Abingdon, Oxon 0X14 4YN, United Kingdom *Tel:* (01) 2354 65500 *Fax:* (01) 2354 65555

Verlag Gachnang & Springer, Bern-Berlin
Junkerngasse 55, 3011 Bern
Tel: (031) 211780 *Fax:* (031) 3518385
Key Personnel
President: Johannes Gachnang
Editor: Christine Meyer-Thoss; Constance Lotz
Founded: 1983
Subjects: Art, Philosophy

ISBN Prefix(es): 3-906127
Distributed by Buchhandlung Walther Koenig (Europe, excluding Switzerland); buch 2000 (Switzerland); DAP Distributed Art Publishers (USA, Canada)

Garuda-Verlag+
10 Sonneggstr, Postfach 717, 8953 Dietikon 1
Tel: (01) 7411287 *Fax:* (056) 6401012
E-mail: garuda@bluewin.ch
Key Personnel
Dir: P Eisenegger; K Eisenegger
Founded: 1985
Also acts as book distributor & agent.
Subjects: Religion - Buddhist
ISBN Prefix(es): 3-906139
Distributor for Diamant Verlag; Fabri-Verlag; GARUDA-VERLAG

GC, *imprint of* Giampiero Casagrande Editore

GDI, *imprint of* Gottlieb Duttweiler Institute for Trends & Futures

Geneva Bible Society, *imprint of* La Maison de la Bible

Georg et Cie SA, see Georg Editeur SA

Georg Editeur SA+
chemin de la Mousse 46, 1225 Chene-Bourg
Tel: (022) 8690029 *Fax:* (022) 8690015
E-mail: livres@medecinehygiene.ch
Web Site: www.medecinehygiene.ch
Key Personnel
Man Dir: Henri Weissenbach *E-mail:* henri.weissenbach@medecinehygiene.ch; Jean-Francois Balavoine
Founded: 1857
Subjects: Economics, Environmental Studies, Ethnicity, Government, Political Science, History, Language Arts, Linguistics, Law, Music, Dance, Philosophy, Psychology, Psychiatry, Religion - Other, Science (General), Social Sciences, Sociology
ISBN Prefix(es): 2-8257
Number of titles published annually: 35 Print
Total Titles: 450 Print; 1 CD-ROM
Parent Company: Medecine & Hygiene
Associate Companies: Editions Eshel, Paris, France
Imprints: Editions Medecine et Hygiene

Giampiero Casagrande Editore+
Via Frasca 8, 6900 Lugano
Tel: (091) 9235677 *Fax:* (091) 9220171
Telex: 030
Founded: 1982
Subjects: Architecture & Interior Design, Art, History, Photography
ISBN Prefix(es): 88-7795
Imprints: GC
Subsidiaries: Fidia Edizioni d'Arte (FEDA SA)

Verlag Gleitschirm
Postfach 68, 7007 Chur
Tel: (081) 235241 *Fax:* (081) 221452
ISBN Prefix(es): 3-906334
Divisions: Gleitschirm-Reisen

Globi Verlag AG
Eidnstr 23, 8045 Zurich
Mailing Address: Postfach 8045, 8045 Zurich
Tel: (01) 4634135 *Fax:* (01) 4633502; (01) 4613971
Telex: 813282 *Cable:* GLOBIVERLAG ZURICH
Key Personnel
Man Dir: Emil Herzog
Founded: 1944
Subjects: Humor

ISBN Prefix(es): 3-85703
Warehouse: B D Buecherdienst Einsiedeln, 8840 Einsiedeln

Goethe-Verlag, Godhard von Heydebrand
Worbstr 20, Postfach 38, 3067 Boll
Tel: (031) 8333248
Key Personnel
Manager: Godhard von Heydebrand
Founded: 1955
ISBN Prefix(es): 3-85730

Victor Goldschmidt Verlagsbuchhandlung
Mostackerstr 17, 4003 Basel
Tel: (061) 236565 *Fax:* (061) 2616123
Key Personnel
Contact: Salomon Goldschmidt
Founded: 1902
Subjects: Religion - Jewish, "Judaica" & "Hebraica", Hebrew, German, English, French & Yiddish
ISBN Prefix(es): 3-85705

Pierre Gonin Editions d'Art
41 Rue de Valentin, 1004 Lausanne
Tel: (021) 3129996 *Fax:* (021) 3129996
Key Personnel
Contact: Francoise Gonin
Founded: 1990
ISBN Prefix(es): 2-88016

Gotthelf-Verlag
Badenerstr 69, 8026 Zurich
Tel: (061) 2428155 *Fax:* (061) 2646486
E-mail: rms@reinhardt.ch
Key Personnel
Man Dir: Alfred Ruedisuehli
Founded: 1928
Subjects: Religion - Other
ISBN Prefix(es): 3-85706
Associate Companies: CVB Buch und Druck, Missionsstr 36, 4012 Basel

Govinda-Verlag (Govinda Press)+
Postfach 257, 8212 Neuhausen 2
Tel: (052) 6726677 *Fax:* (052) 6726678
E-mail: info@govinda.ch
Web Site: www.govinda.ch
Key Personnel
Manager: Ronald Zuerrer *E-mail:* rz@govinda.ch
Founded: 1989
Subjects: Astrology, Occult, Mysteries, Parapsychology, Philosophy, Poetry, Religion - Hindu, Religion - Other
ISBN Prefix(es): 3-906347
Number of titles published annually: 5 Print
Total Titles: 50 Print

Graduate Institute of International Studies+
132 rue de Lausanne, 1202 Geneva 21
Mailing Address: Postfach 36, 1211 Geneva 21
Tel: (022) 7311730 *Fax:* (022) 7384306
E-mail: info@hei.unige.ch
Web Site: heiwww.unige.ch
Key Personnel
Dir Publications Dept: Vera Gowlland
Founded: 1927
Publishes only works originating from the Institute.
Subjects: Economics, History, Law
ISBN Prefix(es): 3-8288
U.S. Office(s): Columbia University Press, New York, NY, United States
Distributed by Kegan Paul International (UK); Kluwer (The Hague); Presses Universitaires de France (PUF) (France)

Editions du Grand-Pont
2 Place Bel Air, 1003 Lausanne
Tel: (021) 3123222 *Fax:* (021) 3113222
Founded: 1971
ISBN Prefix(es): 2-88148

Editions du Griffon (Neuchatel)
Faubourg du Lac 536, 2001 Neuchatel 2
Mailing Address: Postfach 536, 2001 Neuchatel
Tel: (032) 7252204
Founded: 1944
Subjects: Art
ISBN Prefix(es): 2-88006

Editions Francois Grounauer
One rue du Belvedere, 1203 Geneva
Tel: (022) 447948
Founded: 1972
Subjects: Government, Political Science, History, Social Sciences, Sociology
ISBN Prefix(es): 2-88076

GSMBA, Edition Bruno Gasser
Kasernenstr 23, 4058 Basel
Tel: (061) 6811103 *Fax:* (061) 6811103
E-mail: gasser@dial-switch.ck

Guides-Olizane, *imprint of* Editions Olizane

Th Gut Verlag
Seestr 86, Postfach 382, 8712 Staefa
Tel: (01) 9281101 *Fax:* (01) 9285200
Web Site: www.gutverlag.ch/
Telex: 875668
Key Personnel
Contact, All offices: Ulrich Gut
Founded: 1943
Subjects: Ethnicity, Government, Political Science, Regional Interests
ISBN Prefix(es): 3-85717

GVA Publishers Ltd+
PO Box 135, Champel, 1211 Geneva 12
Tel: (022) 3112424 *Fax:* (022) 3112556
Key Personnel
Executive Vice President: Alain Nicollier
Founded: 1979
Member of American Booksellers Association.
Subjects: Art, Travel
ISBN Prefix(es): 2-88115

Haffmans Verlag AG+
Seefeldstr 301, 8034 Zurich
Tel: (01 386 4000 *Fax:* (01) 386 4001
E-mail: verlag@haffmans.ch *Cable:* HAFFMANS VERLAG
Key Personnel
Man Dir, Publisher: Gerd Haffmans
Man Dir, Finance Production: Urs Jakob
Editor: Heiko Arntz
Editor & International Rights: Sophie von Heppe
Sales: Constantin Ragusa
Founded: 1982
Subjects: Art, Fiction, Humor, Literature, Literary Criticism, Essays, Mysteries, Poetry, Science Fiction, Fantasy
ISBN Prefix(es): 3-251
Number of titles published annually: 60 Print; 10 Audio
Total Titles: 350 Print; 17 Audio

Hagenbach & Bender GMBH
Gutenbergstr 20, CH 3011 Bern
Tel: (31) 3816666 *Fax:* (31) 3816677
E-mail: rights@hagenbach-bender.com
Web Site: www.hagenbach-bender.com
Key Personnel
Contact: Dieter A Hagenbach *E-mail:* dieter@hagenbach-bender.com
Founded: 2001
Literary & media agency.

Hallwag AG+
Nordring 4, 3001 Bern
Tel: (031) 423131 *Fax:* (031) 414133
E-mail: office@hallweb.ch
Web Site: www.hallweb.ch
Telex: 912661 Hawa CH *Cable:* HALLWAG BERNE
Key Personnel
President: Dr Juergen Schad
Editorial, Permissions: Beat Koelliker
Sales: Juerg Burri
Founded: 1912
Subjects: Animals, Pets, Art, Cookery, History, How-to, Nonfiction (General), Science (General), Travel
ISBN Prefix(es): 3-444
Branch Office(s)
Hallwag Verlagsgesellschaft mbH, Germany

Paul Haupt Berne+
Falkenplatz 14, 3001 Bern
Tel: (031) 3012345 *Fax:* (031) 3014669
E-mail: verlag@haupt.ch
Web Site: www.haupt.ch *Cable:* HAUPTBERN
Key Personnel
Man Dir, Permissions: Men Haupt
Production: Erich Hauri
Sales, Publicity: Cordula Frevel
Editor, Rights: Regina Balmer
Contact: Matthias Haupt
Founded: 1906
Subjects: Art, Crafts, Games, Hobbies, Economics, Education, How-to, Science (General), Social Sciences, Sociology
ISBN Prefix(es): 3-258
Total Titles: 2,500 Print; 5 CD-ROM
Foreign Rights: Gudruu Hebel (Scandinavia)
Bookshop(s): Falkenpl 14, Bern 3001; Hoeheweg 11, Interlaken 3800

Institut fuer Heilpaedagogik
Moosmattstr 20, 6005 Lucerne
Tel: (041) 415765
ISBN Prefix(es): 3-85745

Heilpaedagogisches Institut der Universitaet Freiburg
Petrus-Kanisius-Gasse 21, CH-1700 Fribourg
Tel: (026) 3007700 *Fax:* (026) 3009749
Key Personnel
Publisher: Prof Urs Haeberlin, PhD
Therapeutic Pedagogy Institute of Fribourg University.
Subjects: Disability, Special Needs, Education
ISBN Prefix(es): 3-906364

Helbing und Lichtenhahn Verlag AG+
Freiestr 82, 4051 Basel
Tel: (061) 231116; (061) 2721117 *Fax:* (061) 2721150
E-mail: helbing@access.ch
Web Site: www.helbing.ch
Key Personnel
Dir: Hans Christof Sauerlaender
Procuring Editor: Inge Hochreutener
Founded: 1822
Subjects: Anthropology, Economics, Environmental Studies, Government, Political Science, History, Language Arts, Linguistics, Law, Management
ISBN Prefix(es): 3-7190
Associate Companies: Sauerlaender AG

Verlag Helvetica Chimica Acta
c/o Ciba-Geigy AG, Malzgasse 21, Postfach 313, 4052 Basel
Tel: (061) 2724973 *Fax:* (061) 2724089
Key Personnel
Man Dir: Dr M V Kisakuerek
Subjects: Chemistry, Chemical Engineering
ISBN Prefix(es): 3-85727; 3-906390

SWITZERLAND BOOK

Herder AG
Muttenzerstr 109, 4133 Pratteln 2
Tel: (031) 8210900; (031) 2720818 *Fax:* (061) 8210907
Telex: 64358
ISBN Prefix(es): 3-906371; 3-906372
Associate Companies: Verlag Herder GmbH & Co KG, Germany; Verlag A G Ploetz GmbH & Co KG, Germany; Herder und Herder GmbH, Germany; Verlag Herder & Co, Austria; Herder Editrice e Libreria, Italy; Editorial Herder SA, Spain

Verlag Huber & Co AG+
Division of Huber & Co AG
Promenadenstr 16, Postfach 382, 8500 Frauenfeld
Tel: (052) 7235617 *Fax:* (052) 7235619
E-mail: buchverlag@huber.ch
Web Site: www.huber.ch
Key Personnel
Man Dir & Publisher: Hansrudolf Frey *Tel:* (052) 7235618
Production: Arthur Miserez *Tel:* (052) 7235656 *Fax:* (052) 7214977
Marketing: Charlotte Krahenbuhl
Founded: 1809
Subjects: Agriculture, Art, Environmental Studies, Ethnicity, Government, Political Science, History, Language Arts, Linguistics, Regional Interests
ISBN Prefix(es): 3-7193; 3-274
Total Titles: 200 Print
Bookshop(s): Buchhandlung Huber & Co AG, Freiestr 8, CH-8501 Frauenfeld *Tel:* (052) 7235858 *E-mail:* info@huberbooks.ch *Web Site:* www.huberbooks.ch

Hug & Co+
c/o Th Zaugg, Fuesslistr 4, 8022 Zurich
Tel: (01) 2212652 *Fax:* (01) 5121213
Telex: 829311 muvich
Key Personnel
Dir: Erika Hug
Founded: 1807
Subjects: Music, Dance
ISBN Prefix(es): 3-906415
Associate Companies: Edition Foetisch-Foetisch Freres, Case postale, CH-1002 Lausanne
Warehouse: Musica Vivam Flughofstr 61, CH-8152 Glattbrugg, Zurich
Orders to: Musica Vivam Flughofstr 61, CH-8152 Glattbrugg, Zurich

Editions Charles Hugenin Pro Arte
Rue du Sapin 2a, 2114 Fleurier
Tel: (032) 612727 *Fax:* (032) 8612727
Key Personnel
Man Dir: Jean-Charles Frochaux
Parent Company: Schola Cantorum-Triton
Associate Companies: Cantate Domino

Idegraf SA, Editions
route de Chancy, 28, 1213 Petit-Lancy Geneva
Tel: (022) 7920395 *Fax:* (022) 7936330
E-mail: 101512.3363@compuserve.com

Editions Ides et Calendes SA+
Evole 19, Case Postale 752, CH-2001 Neuchatel
Tel: (32) 7253861 *Fax:* (32) 7255880
E-mail: artides@artides.com; ides@livre.net
Web Site: www.artides.com; www.livre.net/ides
Key Personnel
Chief Executive: Alain Bouret
Founded: 1941
Subjects: Art, Law, Lives d'art & peiuture; photoarchive, photogalerie
ISBN Prefix(es): 2-8258

Verlag Industrielle Organisation+
Dietzingerstr 3, 8036 Zurich
Tel: (01) 4667711 *Fax:* (01) 4667412
E-mail: info@ofv.ch
Web Site: www.ofv.ch
Key Personnel
Contact: Gerhard Labitzke *Tel:* (01) 466 74 76 *E-mail:* glabitzke@ofv.ch
Founded: 1931
Subjects: Electronics, Electrical Engineering, Human Relations, Management, Marketing
ISBN Prefix(es): 3-85743
Parent Company: Orell Fussli Verlag

Interfrom AG Editions+
Scheideggstr 78, 8022 Zurich
Mailing Address: Postfach 5005, 8022 Zurich
Tel: (01) 2020900
Key Personnel
Publisher: Leo V Fromm
Executive Vice President & Editorial: A Harms-Hunold
Sales Manager: Annegret Busch
Public Relations: Ursula Malzahn
Founded: 1974
Popular Science by German-speaking Experts.
Subjects: Economics, Education, Environmental Studies, Ethnicity, Government, Political Science, History, Science (General), Social Sciences, Sociology
ISBN Prefix(es): 3-7201
Imprints: Zuerich
Branch Office(s)
Verlag A Fromm, Breiter Gang 10-16, 49076 Osnabrueck, Germany
Fromm International Publ Corp, 560 Lexington Ave, New York, NY 10022, United States
Warehouse: Schweizer Buchzentrum, CH-4601 Olten
Orders to: Schweizer Buchzentrum, CH-4601 Olten

International Jeweler, *imprint of* Europa Star, Bill Communication SA

Iris Verlag AG
CH-3177 Laupen
Tel: (031) 947744
ISBN Prefix(es): 3-85751

ISIOM Verlag fur Tondokumente, Weinreb Tonarchiv+
Case Postale 362, 6601 Locarno
Tel: (091) 7513524 *Fax:* (091) 7433913
E-mail: isiom@bluewin.ch
Key Personnel
President: Hans Haessig-Tellenbach
Author: Friedrich Weinreb; Graf Duerckneim
Founded: 1974
Specialize in audio books.
Subjects: Ethnicity, Religion - Jewish
ISBN Prefix(es): 88-85151

Jeanmaire & Co, see Verlag Eisenbahn

Jordanverlag AG+
Steffenstr 1, 8052 Zurich
Tel: (01) 3023676
Key Personnel
Contact: Peter Buff
Founded: 1984
Subjects: Biblical Studies, Religion - Catholic, Religion - Protestant
ISBN Prefix(es): 3-906561

Editions Jouvence+
Chemin du buillon 20, CH-1233 Bernex, Geneva
Tel: (022) 7576220 *Fax:* (0450) 432924
E-mail: jouvence@wanadoo.fr
Key Personnel
Dir: Jacques Maire
Editorial Dir: Olivier Clerc *Tel:* 0450 432862 *E-mail:* olivier.clerc@usa.net
Founded: 1989
Subjects: Child Care & Development, Environmental Studies, Health, Nutrition, Psychology, Psychiatry, Self-Help, Social Sciences, Sociology
ISBN Prefix(es): 2-88353
Associate Companies: Editions Jouvence, bat E, Business Parc International, 74166 Archamps, France *Tel:* (022) 432860 *Fax:* (0450) 432924
Branch Office(s)
Jouvence, BP 7, 79161 Saint Julien en genevirs, French Southern Territories

JPM Publications SA+
12 av William Fraisse, 1006 Lausanne
Tel: (021) 6177561 *Fax:* (021) 6161257
E-mail: information@jpmguides.com
Web Site: www.jpmguides.com
Key Personnel
Man Dir: Mr Jean-Paul Minder *Tel:* (021) 617 75 66 *E-mail:* jeanpaul.minder@jpmguides.com
Founded: 1992
Subjects: Travel
ISBN Prefix(es): 2-88452
U.S. Office(s): 245 E 19 St, 3D, New York, NY 10003, United States, Contact: Dorsey Smith
Distributed by Hunter Publishing

Jugend mit einer Mission Verlag+
Poststr 14, CH-2500 Biel 8
Mailing Address: Postfach 144, CH-2500 Biel 8
Tel: (032) 418988 *Fax:* (032) 418920
Key Personnel
Publisher: Eva Stopper
Founded: 1991
Subjects: Biblical Studies, Education, Religion - Protestant, Theology
ISBN Prefix(es): 3-906568

Junod Nicholas
12 rue Robert-de-Traz, 1206 Geneva
Tel: (022) 3470242 *Fax:* (022) 3470242
Telex: 23381 trib ch
Key Personnel
Man Dir, Rights & Permissions: Henri Heizmann
Founded: 1977
Subjects: Art, Cookery, Government, Political Science, Health, Nutrition, History, Humor, Radio, TV
ISBN Prefix(es): 2-8297
Parent Company: SA de la Tribune de Geneve

Juris Druck & Verlag AG
Baskerplatz 5, Postfach 816, 8039 Zurich
Tel: (01) 7409038; (01) 2117727; (01) 2117747 *Fax:* (01) 7409019
E-mail: juris@swissonline.ch
Key Personnel
Man Dir: Markus Christen
Founded: 1945
Member of SBVV.
Subjects: History, Law
ISBN Prefix(es): 3-260

Kalos-Verlag
Fritz Aerni-Schaffhauserstr 446, 8052 Zurich
Tel: (01) 3022751 *Fax:* (01) 3022751
ISBN Prefix(es): 3-906598

Kanisius Verlag+
ave de Beauregard 3-BP 1052, 1701 Fribourg
Tel: (037) 243128 *Fax:* (026) 4258738 *Cable:* KANISIUSWERK FRIBOURG
Key Personnel
Man Dir, Publicity: Dr Barbara Evers-Greder
Production Manager: Peter Ledergerber
Founded: 1898
Subjects: Biblical Studies, Biography, Cookery, Religion - Catholic, Self-Help, Theology
ISBN Prefix(es): 3-85764
Bookshop(s): Kanisiusbuchhandlung,, Bahnhofplatz 6, CH-1701 Fribourg *Tel:* (037) 221345; Kanisiusbuchhandlung, Haengebrueckstr 16,

CH-1702 Fribourg *Tel:* (037) 222954; Kanisiuswerk, Blarerstr 18, 78462 Konstanz, Germany

S Karger AG, Medical and Scientific Publishers+
Allschwilerstr 10, 4009 Basel
Tel: (061) 3061111 *Fax:* (061) 3061234
E-mail: karger@karger.ch
Web Site: www.karger.com
Key Personnel
Sales & Marketing Dir & President: Dr Thomas Karger
Man Dir: Steven Karger
Rights & Permissions: Berthold Moog
Founded: 1890
Anatomy Atlas.
Subjects: Biological Sciences, Medicine, Nursing, Dentistry, Psychology, Psychiatry, Veterinary Science, Medical & Scientific
ISBN Prefix(es): 3-8055
Associate Companies: Karger Japan, Inc, Yushima S Bldg 3F, 4-2-3, Yushima, Bunkyo-ku, Tokyo 113-0034, Japan *Tel:* (03) 3815-1800 *Fax:* (03) 3815-1802 *E-mail:* publisher@karger.jp; S Karger AG, 4 Rickett St, London SW6 1RU, United Kingdom *Tel:* (020) 7610 3331 *Fax:* (020) 7610 3337 *E-mail:* uk@karger.ch; S Karger Publishers Inc, 26 W Avon Rd, PO Box 529, Farmington, CT 06085, United States *Tel:* 860-675-7834 *Fax:* 860-675-7302 *E-mail:* karger@snet.net; Panther Publishers Private Ltd, 33 First Main, Koramangala First Block, Bangalore 560 034, India *Tel:* (080) 5505 836, 5505 837 *Fax:* (080) 5505 981 *E-mail:* panther_publishers@vsnl.com
Branch Office(s)
DA Information Services, 648 Whitehorse Rd, PO Box 163, Mitcham, Victoria 3132, Australia *Tel:* (03) 92107777 *Fax:* (03) 92107788 *E-mail:* service@dadirect.com.au *Web Site:* www.dadirect.com.au
Librairie Luginbuehl, 36 bd de Latour-Maubourg, F-75007 Paris, France *Tel:* (01) 45514258 *Fax:* (01) 45560780 *E-mail:* liblug@club-internet.fr
APAC Publishers Service, 31 Tannery Lane, 07-01 Dragon Land Building, 347788 Singapore, Singapore *Tel:* 6844 7333 *Fax:* 6747 8916 *E-mail:* service@apacmedia.com.sg
Bookshop(s): Karger Libri AG, Petersgraben 31, CH-4009 Basel *Tel:* (061) 306 1111 *Fax:* (061) 306 1516 *E-mail:* books@libri.karger.ch *Web Site:* www.libri.ch

KBV, see Kinderbuchverlag Luzern

Verlag Walter Keller, Dornach
Postfach, CH-4143 Dornach 2
Tel: (061) 7015713 *Fax:* (061) 7015716
E-mail: info@verlag-walterkeller.ch
Web Site: www.verlag-walterkeller.ch
Key Personnel
Contact: Ingrid Bergmann *E-mail:* i-bergmann@verlag-walterkeller.ch
Founded: 1969
Subjects: Art, Specialize in eurythmic
ISBN Prefix(es): 3-906633
Distributed by Anthroposophic Press Inc

Editions Ketty & Alexandre+
Case Postale, 1063 Chapelle-sur-Moudon
Tel: (021) 9051111 *Fax:* (021) 9056050
Key Personnel
Contact: Alexandre Gisiger
Founded: 1975
Subjects: History
ISBN Prefix(es): 2-88114

Kinderbuchfonds Baobab
Laufenstr 16, CH-4053 Basel
Tel: (061) 3332727 *Fax:* (061) 3332726
E-mail: baobab@access.ch
Founded: 1983
Editor of children's books from Africa, Asia & Latin America.
Total Titles: 3 Print

Kinderbuchverlag Luzern+
Griendelstr 15, 6000 Lucerne
Mailing Address: Postfach 5236, 6000 Lucerne
Tel: (041) 516861 *Fax:* (062) 8245780
Key Personnel
Publisher: Hans Uristof
Editorial & Foreign Rights Dir: Jasua Zagovc
Founded: 1979
Subjects: Animals, Pets, Art, Natural History, Nonfiction (General)
ISBN Prefix(es): 3-276

Kindler Verlag AG
Nelkenstr 20, 8006 Zurich
Tel: (01) 3633007
Telex: 045 57608 *Cable:* Kindlerverlag Zurich
Key Personnel
Publisher: Helmut Kindler; Nina Kindler
Subjects: Anthropology, Psychology, Psychiatry
ISBN Prefix(es): 3-463

Klett und Balmer & Co Verlag
Chamerstr 12A, Postfach 4464, 6304 Zug
Tel: (042) 214131 *Fax:* (042) 214131
E-mail: info@sklett.ch
Web Site: www.klett.ch
Key Personnel
Man Dir: Christoph Balmer; Michael Klett; Roland Klett; Dr Thomas Klett
Manager: Hans Egli
Founded: 1967
Subjects: Education, Government, Political Science, Philosophy, Science (General)
ISBN Prefix(es): 3-264
Parent Company: Ernst Klett KG, Stuttgart, Germany

Kober Verlag AG
Bumplizstr 101, 9018 Bern
Tel: (031) 554433 *Fax:* (055) 535181
Key Personnel
President: Harald Blum
Man Dir, Sales: Emil Zillig
Founded: 1816
Subjects: Philosophy, Religion - Other
ISBN Prefix(es): 3-85767
Associate Companies: The Kober Press, PO Box 2194, San Francisco, CA 94126, United States

Kolumbus-Verlag+
Muehlebuehlstr 10, 5737 Menziken
Tel: (062) 7711370 *Cable:* VDB MENZIKEN
Key Personnel
Man Dir: Dr G van den Bergh
Founded: 1945
Subjects: Language Arts, Linguistics, Philosophy
ISBN Prefix(es): 3-85769

Kommissionsverlag Leobuchhandling
Gallusstr 20, 9001 St Gallen
Mailing Address: Postfach 9001, 9001 St Gallen
Tel: (071) 22917 *Fax:* (071) 220587
Key Personnel
Man Dir: Eugen Hettinger
Founded: 1918
ISBN Prefix(es): 3-85788

Galerie Kornfeld & Co
Laupenstr 41, 3001 Bern
Mailing Address: Postfach 1471, 3001 Bern
Tel: (031) 254673 *Fax:* (031) 261891
Key Personnel
Proprietor: Eberhard W Kornfeld
Founded: 1864
Subjects: Art
ISBN Prefix(es): 3-85773

Kossodo Verlag AG
av Lignon 27-28, 1219 Le Lignon
Tel: (022) 962230
Key Personnel
Dir: Martha Duessel
Founded: 1956
Subjects: Art
ISBN Prefix(es): 3-7208

Verlag Karl Kraemer & Co+
Postfach 1209, CH-8034 Zurich
Tel: (0711) 78 49 60 (Germany) *Fax:* (0711) 78 49 620 (Germany)
E-mail: info@kraemerverlag.com
Web Site: www.kraemerverlag.com
Key Personnel
Publisher, President & Man Dir: Karl H Kramer *E-mail:* karl.kraemer@kraemerverlag.com
International Rights: Mrs Gudrun Kraemer
Founded: 1962
Specialize in publishing books & magazines on architecture, town planning & building construction.
Subjects: Architecture & Interior Design
ISBN Prefix(es): 3-85774
Associate Companies: Kark Kraemer Verlag GmbH und Co, Schulze-Delitzsch-Strasse 15, 70565 Stuttgart, Germany *Tel:* (0711) 78 49 60 *Fax:* (0711) 78 49 620
Bookshop(s): Karl Kraemer Fachbuchhandlung, Rotebuehlstr 40, 70178 Stuttgart, Germany *Tel:* (0711) 66993-0 *Fax:* (0711) 628955

Verlag Rene Kramer AG+
33, via del Tiglio, 6906 Lugano-Cassarate
Tel: (091) 518941 *Cable:* Edikramer Lugan 06
Key Personnel
Man Dir, Publicity: Rene Kramer
Founded: 1962
Subjects: Cookery
ISBN Prefix(es): 2-88290

Kranich-Verlag, Dres AG & H R Bosch-Gwalter+
Dufourstr 30, CH-8702 Zollikon
Tel: (01) 3918484 *Fax:* (01) 3920884
Founded: 1951
Specialize in Special Editions.
Subjects: Art, Biblical Studies, History, Literature, Literary Criticism, Essays, Poetry, Religion - Catholic, Religion - Protestant
ISBN Prefix(es): 3-906640

Kuemmerly & Frey (Geographischer Verlag)
Hallenstr 6-10, 3001 Bern
Tel: (031) 235111 *Fax:* (031) 9152220
Telex: 912765 *Cable:* KUMMERLYFREY
Key Personnel
Man Dir: Walter Frey
Founded: 1852
Subjects: Geography, Geology, Travel
ISBN Prefix(es): 3-259
Associate Companies: Kuemmerly & Frey Verlags-GmbH, Austria; BLay-Foldex, France; Kuemmerly & Frey Verlags-GmbH, Germany

Imprimerie A Kuendig
49 Chemin de l'Etang, Postfach 26, 1219 Chatelaine/Geneva
Tel: (022) 966013
Key Personnel
Manager: Georges Naef
Founded: 1923
ISBN Prefix(es): 2-88018

Edition Kunzelmann GmbH
Gruetstr 28, 8134 Adliswil
Tel: (01) 7103681 *Fax:* (01) 7103817
Founded: 1945

SWITZERLAND

Subjects: Music, Dance
ISBN Prefix(es): 3-85662; 3-9521049

Labor et Fides SA+
One rue Beauregard, CH-1204 Geneva
Tel: (022) 3113290; (022) 3113269 *Fax:* (022) 7813051
Key Personnel
Chairman: Gabriel de Montmollin
Founded: 1924
Subjects: Religion - Other, Social Sciences, Sociology, Theology
ISBN Prefix(es): 2-8309

Herbert Lang & Cie AG, Buchhandlung, Antiquariat
Munzgraben 2, Ecke Amthausgasse, 3000 Bern 9
Tel: (031) 3108484 *Fax:* (031) 3108494
E-mail: ius@buchlang.com
Web Site: www.buchlang.com
Telex: 912867 lang ch *Cable:* Librilang
Key Personnel
President: Christoph H Lang
Founded: 1813 (re-formed 1921)
Agents for libraries throughout the world.
Subjects: Science (General)
ISBN Prefix(es): 3-261

Peter Lang SA, see PlE-Peter Lang SA

Langenscheidt AG Zuerich-Zug
Loewenstr 19, 8021 Zurich
Mailing Address: Postfach 326, 8021 Zurich
Tel: (01) 2115000 *Fax:* (01) 2122149
Key Personnel
Administration: Doctor Ernst Grub
Member of the Langenscheidt Group, Germany.
Subjects: Language Arts, Linguistics
ISBN Prefix(es): 3-269; 3-906725
Parent Company: Langenscheidt KG, Germany

Franz Larese und Juerg Janett, see Erker-Verlag

Larousse (Suisse) SA
c/o Acces-Direct, 3 Route du Grand-Mont, 1052 Le Mont-sur-Lausanne
Tel: (021) 335336
Key Personnel
Man Dir: Jean-Claude Viatte
ISBN Prefix(es): 2-8276
Parent Company: Librairie Larousse, France

Lehrmittelverlag des Kantons Zurich+
Unit of State of Kanton Zurich
Raeffelstr 32, 8045 Zurich
Tel: (01) 4658585 *Fax:* (01) 4658583
E-mail: lehrmiHelverlag@lmv.zh.ch
Web Site: www.access.ch/lmvzh
Key Personnel
Assistant Dir: Robert Fuchs *Tel:* (01) 4658507
Sales Manager: Engemann Beat *Tel:* (01) 4658540 *E-mail:* beat.engemann@lmv.ch
Founded: 1851
Subjects: Film, Video, Radio, TV

Lenos Verlag+
Spalentorweg 12, 4051 Basel
Tel: (061) 253414 *Fax:* (061) 2613518
Key Personnel
Program Dir, Publicity: Heidi Sommerer
Sales: Tom Forrer
Founded: 1970
Subjects: Government, Political Science, Journalism, Nonfiction (General)
ISBN Prefix(es): 3-85787

Leonis Verlag+
Postfach 952, Kirchenweg, 8034 Zurich
Tel: (01) 475565 *Fax:* (01) 2624881 *Cable:* LEONISVERLAG ZURICH
Key Personnel
Proprietor, Man Dir: Dr Wolfgang M Metz
Founded: 1976
Subjects: How-to, Religion - Other, Self-Help
ISBN Prefix(es): 3-7210; 3-85627
Associate Companies: Doulos Verlag

Bernard Letu Editeur+
2 rue Calvin, 1204 Geneva
Tel: (022) 204757 *Fax:* (022) 208492
Founded: 1973
Subjects: Art, Photography
ISBN Prefix(es): 2-88051

Lia rumantscha
Obere Plessurstr 47, 7001 Chur
Tel: (081) 22442 *Fax:* (081) 2583223
E-mail: liarum@spin.ch
Key Personnel
Dir: Gion A Derungs
Founded: 1919
Company also gives financial support to other publications in Romansh in the Romansh-speaking area.
Subjects: History, Language Arts, Linguistics, Literature, Literary Criticism, Essays, Music, Dance, Poetry, Regional Interests, Religion - Other
ISBN Prefix(es): 3-906680

Die Libelle Verlag Ag Libellen Haus
Libellen Haus, lm Lochili 7, 8598 Bottighofen
Tel: (072) 753555 *Fax:* (072) 753565
E-mail: libelleverlag@bluewin.ch
ISBN Prefix(es): 3-909081

Limmat Verlag+
Quellenstr 25, 8031 Zurich
Tel: (01) 445 80 80 *Fax:* (01) 445 80 88
E-mail: mail@limmatverlag.ch
Web Site: www.limmatverlag.ch
Key Personnel
Sales: Jurg Zimmerli *Tel:* (01) 445 80 81 *E-mail:* zimmerli@limmatverlag.ch
Founded: 1975
Subjects: Art, Biography, Fiction, Government, Political Science, Literature, Literary Criticism, Essays, Social Sciences, Sociology, Women's Studies
ISBN Prefix(es): 3-85791
Total Titles: 400 Print

Literatheke, *imprint of* Eco Verlags AG

Maihof Verlag
Maihofstr 76, 6002 Lucerne
Tel: 395170 *Fax:* 4295367
E-mail: maihofdruck@logon.ch
Web Site: www.maihofdruck.ch
Key Personnel
Publisher: Margrit Boschung
Founded: 1959
Subjects: Biography, History, Maritime
ISBN Prefix(es): 3-9520027; 3-9520756

La Maison de la Bible, *imprint of* La Maison de la Bible

La Maison de la Bible+
Chemin de Praz-Roussy 4bis, 1032 Romanel-sur-Lausanne
Tel: (021) 867 10 10 *Fax:* (021) 867 10 15
E-mail: cmd@bible.ch
Web Site: www.bible.ch
Key Personnel
Chief Executive Dir & International Rights: Paul-Andre Eicher *Tel:* (021) 811 40 50 *E-mail:* adm@bible.ch

BOOK

Contact: Vivian Andre; Olivia Festal; Stefan Waldmann
Founded: 1917
Specialize in publishing & translating bibles, books, audio & CD-ROM.
Member of CBA & ECPA.
Subjects: Biblical Studies, Biography, Human Relations, Religion - Protestant, Theology, Family
ISBN Prefix(es): 2-8260; 2-608
Number of titles published annually: 25 Print
Total Titles: 340 Print; 4 CD-ROM; 47 Audio
Online services available through World Wide Web.
Imprints: Geneva Bible Society; La Maison de la Bible
Divisions:
Distributed by Haenssler/Bolanz (Germany); Service d'Orientation Biblique (Canada); La Centrale Biblique (Belgium); La Maison de la Bible (France & Italy); Servidis (Switzerland)
Distributor for Crossway; Focus on the Family; Harvest House; Lion, OM; Moody (US); STL; Thomas Nelson (US); Zondervan (US)

Manesse Verlag GmbH
Badergasse 9, CH-8001 Zurich
Tel: (01) 2525707; (01) 2525551 *Fax:* (01) 2625347
Key Personnel
Man Dir: Anne Marie Wells
International Rights: Angelika Rachor
Founded: 1944
Subjects: History, Literature, Literary Criticism, Essays, Poetry
ISBN Prefix(es): 3-7175
Total Titles: 350 Print
Parent Company: Deutsche Verlags-Anstalt GmbH (DVA), Germany

Manus Verlag
Bergstr 90, Postfach 630, 8708 Maennedorf
Tel: (01) 9202727 *Fax:* (01) 9202740
Key Personnel
Manager: Kurt Borer
Founded: 1970
ISBN Prefix(es): 3-907003; 3-906982

Librairie-Editions J Marguerat+
2 pl St Francois, 1002 Lausanne
Tel: (021) 3237717 *Fax:* (021) 3126732
Key Personnel
Dir: Jean Bakker
Founded: 1940
Subjects: Ethnicity, Geography, Geology, History, Music, Dance, Travel
ISBN Prefix(es): 2-88008

MARKT & TECHNIK AG, see Pearson Education

MARP, see Muslim Architecture Research Program (MARP)

Viktoria-Verlag Peter Marti, see Viktoria-Verlag Peter Marti

Les Editions la Matze
One rue du Mont, 1951 Sion
Tel: (027) 3231652 *Fax:* (027) 3231652
Key Personnel
Man Dir, Sales: Guy Gessler
Founded: 1975
Subjects: Archaeology, Art, Fiction, History, Military Science
ISBN Prefix(es): 2-88025

Meandre
14 Stalden, 1700 Fribourg
Tel: (026) 322174 *Fax:* (026) 323287
Key Personnel
Contact: Gerard Bourgarel
ISBN Prefix(es): 2-88359

Medecine et Hygiene
78 ave de la Roseraie, Casepostale 456, 1211 Geneva 4
Tel: (022) 7029311 *Fax:* (022) 7029355
E-mail: direction@medecinehygiene.dr
Key Personnel
Man Dir, Sales: P Y Balavoine
Publicity & Advertising Dir: G Antonietti
Editor-in-Chief: Dr B Kiefer
Founded: 1943
Subjects: Medicine, Nursing, Dentistry, Psychology, Psychiatry, Science (General)
ISBN Prefix(es): 3-88049

Editions Medecine et Hygiene, *imprint of* Georg Editeur SA

Peter Meili & Co, Buchhandluna
Fronwagpl 13, 8200 Schaffhausen
Tel: (053) 254144 *Fax:* (053) 254746
Telex: 76777 meibuch
Founded: 1838
Subjects: Government, Political Science, History, Language Arts, Linguistics, Regional Interests
ISBN Prefix(es): 3-85805
Bookshop(s): Buchhandlung Meili & Co

Memory/Cage Editions
Anwandstr 7, 8004 Zurich
Tel: (01) 2410445 *Fax:* (01) 2410445
E-mail: mail@memorycage.com
Web Site: www.memorycage.com
Key Personnel
Publisher: Daniel Kurjakoric *E-mail:* kurjakovic@memorycage.com.
Founded: 1994
Subjects: Art, Literature, Literary Criticism, Essays, Photography
ISBN Prefix(es): 3-907053
Orders to: DAP, 155 Sixth Ave, New York, NY 10013, United States, Contact: Amy Lozada *Tel:* 212-627-1999 *Fax:* 212-627-9484

Editions H Messeiller SA
11 St Nicolas, 2006 Neuchatel
Tel: (032) 7251296 *Fax:* (032) 7241937
Key Personnel
Dir: Cl-H Messeiller
Founded: 1887
Subjects: Art, Education, Law, Psychology, Psychiatry, Public Administration, Religion - Other
ISBN Prefix(es): 2-8261

Minervaverlag Bern+
Seftigenstr 25, 3007 Bern
Mailing Address: PO Box 6849, 3001 Bern
Tel: (031) 3726223 *Fax:* (031) 3726223
Key Personnel
Ambassador, American Biographic Institute: Louis R Jenzer
Founded: 1991
ISBN Prefix(es): 3-9520216
Total Titles: 2 Print; 8 Audio
Distributor for Prodest SA Lugano; WerdtVerlag Zuerich

Editions Minkoff
8 rue Eynard, 1211 Geneva 12
Mailing Address: Case postale 377, 1211 Geneva
Tel: (022) 3104660 *Fax:* (022) 3102857
E-mail: minkoff@minkoff-editions.com
Web Site: www.minkoff-editions.com
Key Personnel
Dir: Sylvie Minkoff *E-mail:* minkoff@ipzolink.ch
Founded: 1970 (in France, 1989)
Specialize in fac-similes.
Also acts as agents for: Editions des Abbesses; Centre de Music Baroque de Versailles; Patrimoine Musical Regional francais; Editions Universite-Conservatriœ de Musique de Geneve; Editions EBL-La Borie en Limousin; New Grove Dictionary of Music & Musicians, London; Editions de l'Oiseau-Lyre, Monaco; Bibliotheque Nationale music publications, Claude Debussy Documentation Centre, CNRS music publications & the French Musicological Society, Paris.
Subjects: Art, Drama, Theater, History, Music, Dance
ISBN Prefix(es): 2-8266
Number of titles published annually: 50 Print
Total Titles: 1,200 Print
Parent Company: Minkoff France Editeur
Bookshop(s): A La Regle d'Or, Librairie Musicale, Minkoff France Editeur, 23 rue de Fleurus, 75006 Paris, France *Tel:* (01) 45449433 *Fax:* (01) 45449430

Mondo SA (Editions-Verlag-Edizioni)
Passage Saint-Antoine, 1800 Vevey
Tel: (021) 9241450 *Fax:* (021) 9244662
Telex: 452100 Spn Ch
Key Personnel
Dir: Arslan Alamir
ISBN Prefix(es): 2-88168

Motovun Book GmbH+
Member of Motovun Group Association
Grendelstr 15, 6004 Lucerne
Tel: (041) 4109515 *Fax:* (041) 4109516
E-mail: motovun@bluewin.ch
Key Personnel
Man Dir & Publisher: Juergen Braunschweiger
Rights & Permissions: Brigitte Abeida
Founded: 1999
Also acts as publisher & packager. Member of Swiss Publishers Association.
Subjects: Archaeology, Art, Crafts, Games, Hobbies, Geography, Geology, History, Religion - Other, Travel
Subsidiaries: Motovun Productions & Trade

Verlag Rudolf Muehlemann
Haus zu Lagerstr 6, 8570 Weinfelden
Tel: (072) 225353 *Fax:* (072) 223004
Founded: 1949
ISBN Prefix(es): 3-85809

Lars Mueller Publishers+
Klosterstr 42, 5430 Wettingen
Mailing Address: PO Box 912, 5401 Baden
Tel: (056) 4301740 *Fax:* (056) 4301741
E-mail: books@lars-muller.ch
Web Site: www.lars-mueller-publishers.com
Key Personnel
Manager: Lars Mueller
Founded: 1983
Subjects: Architecture & Interior Design, Art, Photography, Graphic design & typography
ISBN Prefix(es): 3-906700; 3-907044; 3-907078; 3-03778
Number of titles published annually: 20 Print
U.S. Office(s): Distributed Art Publishers Inc, 155 Sixth Ave, 2nd floor, New York, NY 10013-1507, United States, Contact: Donna Wingate *Tel:* 212-627-1999 *E-mail:* dwingate@dapinc.com

Mueller Rueschlikon Verlags AG+
Gewerbestr 10, 6330 Cham
Mailing Address: Postfach 4161, 6304 Zug
Tel: (041) 740 30 40 *Fax:* (041) 741 71 15
Key Personnel
Rights & Licenses: Monika Hess
Publicity: Roland Dietschi
Founded: 1938
Subjects: Animals, Pets, Cookery, Crafts, Games, Hobbies, Fiction, How-to, Outdoor Recreation, Wine & Spirits
ISBN Prefix(es): 3-275

Editions Musicales De La Schola Cantorum
Av Agaune 9-A, 1890 Saint-Maurice
Mailing Address: Case Postale 112, 1890 Saint-Maurice
Tel: (024) 485 24 80 *Fax:* (024) 485 24 80
E-mail: labatiaz@bluewin.ch
Key Personnel
Contact: Roulin Blaise
Founded: 1970
Specializes In: Choral Music, Organ & Choral Methods.
Member of ASMEM.
Parent Company: Labatiaz
Associate Companies: Cantate Domino
Distributor for Gesseney; Labatiaz; Tales; Chorus (Pierre Kaelin); Musique Abbe Bovet; Henn

Muslim Architecture Research Program (MARP)+
Postfach 207, 8061 Zurich 4
Tel: (02) 4711228 *Fax:* (02) 4711228
Key Personnel
Contact: Alena Norod
Founded: 1973
Publisher of the first encyclopedia of architecture; also acts as Archaeological Institute & Architectural Office.
Subjects: Archaeology, Architecture & Interior Design, Art
ISBN Prefix(es): 3-906995
Warehouse: Muenchenbuchsea
Ostrov, Czech Republic

Edito Georges Naef SA+
quai Wilson, Case Postale 54, 1211 Geneva
Tel: (022) 7380502 *Fax:* (022) 7384224
E-mail: edito@kister.ch
Key Personnel
Contact: Georges Naef
Founded: 1986
Specialize in internet development.
ISBN Prefix(es): 2-8313
Total Titles: 24 CD-ROM
Parent Company: Kister SA
Subsidiaries: Naef Diffusion

Les Editions Nagel SA (Paris)
6 rue du Port, 1211 Geneva 7
Tel: (022) 734 17 30 *Fax:* (022) 7337424
E-mail: admi@nagel.ch; rights@nagel.ch
Web Site: www.nagel.ch
Key Personnel
Man Dir: Guillaume Briquet
Founded: 1928
Subjects: Archaeology, Art, Government, Political Science, Philosophy, Travel
ISBN Prefix(es): 2-8263

Verlag Nagel & Kimche AG, Zurich+
Imprint of Sanssouci
Nordstrasse 9, Postfach, 8035 Zurich
Tel: (01) 366 66 80 *Fax:* (01) 366 66 88
E-mail: info@nagel-kimche.ch
Web Site: www.nagel-kimche.ch
Telex: 897522 naki
Key Personnel
International Rights: Silvia Weber
Contact: Dr Dirk Vaihinges *E-mail:* vaihinges@nagel-kimche.ch
Founded: 1983
Subjects: Fiction
ISBN Prefix(es): 3-312
Ultimate Parent Company: Carl Hanser Verlag, Munich, Germany
Associate Companies: Zsolnay Verlag

Natura-Verlag Arlesheim
Pfeffingerweg 1, 4144 Arlesheim
Tel: (061) 717111 *Fax:* (061) 7064201
Subjects: Astrology, Occult, Education, Philosophy
ISBN Prefix(es): 3-85817

SWITZERLAND

Nebelspalter-Verlag
Pestalozzistr 5, 9401 Rorschach
Tel: (071) 8440444 *Fax:* (071) 8440445
Key Personnel
Dir: E Enderle; D Mildenberger
Founded: 1875
Subjects: Humor
ISBN Prefix(es): 3-85819
Parent Company: E Loepfe-Benz AG

Neptun-Verlag
Morellstr 6, Postfach 307, 8280 Kreuzlingen
Tel: (072) 727262 *Fax:* (072) 6642023
Telex: 882221 nept ch
Key Personnel
Manager: Herbert Berchtold
Founded: 1946
Subjects: History, Travel
ISBN Prefix(es): 3-85820

Neue Szene, *imprint of* Eco Verlags AG

Neue Zeitschrift Missionswissenschaft Verlag
Postfach 62, Missionshaus Bethlehem, 6405 Immensee
Tel: (041) 8541192 *Fax:* (041) 8504209
E-mail: nzmred@bluewin.ch
Web Site: www.mypage.bluewin.ch/nzm
Key Personnel
Contact: Fritz Foelmli
Founded: 1945
Subjects: Religion - Catholic, Theology
ISBN Prefix(es): 3-85824

Neue Zuercher Zeitung AG Buchverlag+
Zuercherstr 39, 8952 Schlieren
Tel: (01) 2581505 *Fax:* (01) 2581399
E-mail: buch.bestellung@nzz.ch
Web Site: www.nzz-buchverlag.ch
Key Personnel
Publicity Manager: Walter Koepfli *E-mail:* buch.verlag@nzz.ch
Book publishing division of Zurich daily newspaper.
ISBN Prefix(es): 3-85823; 3-03823
Total Titles: 200 Print; 10 CD-ROM

Verlag Arthur Niggli AG
Steinackerstr 8, CH-8583 Sulgen
Tel: (071) 6449111 *Fax:* (071) 6449190
E-mail: info@niggli.ch
Web Site: www.niggli.ch
Key Personnel
Man Dir: Bruno Waldburger
Founded: 1950
Subjects: Architecture & Interior Design, Art, Typography
ISBN Prefix(es): 3-7212

Les Editions Noir sur Blanc+
Le Motta, 1147 Montricher
Tel: (021) 8645931 *Fax:* (021) 8644026
Cable: EDINOBL
Key Personnel
Contact: Vera Michalski-Hoffmann
Founded: 1986
Subjects: Biography, Cookery, Drama, Theater, History, Humor, Literature, Literary Criticism, Essays
ISBN Prefix(es): 2-88250
Branch Office(s)
123 blvd Saint Germain, 75006 Paris, France
Tel: (01) 43269846 *Fax:* (01) 40518792
ul Frascati 18, 00483 Warsaw, Poland

Editions Nord-Sud, *imprint of* Nord-Sued Verlag

Nord-Sud Edizioni, *imprint of* Nord-Sued Verlag

Nord-Sued Verlag
Industriestr 8, 8625 Gossau, Zuerich
Tel: (01) 9366868 *Fax:* (01) 9366800 *Cable:* NORDSUED
Key Personnel
Dir: Davy Sidjanski
Editorial: Brigitte Hanhart Sidjanski; Jurgen Lassig
Public Relations: Sabine Reiner
Production: Ulrich Gaebler
Rights & Permissions: Monika Giuliani
Founded: 1961
ISBN Prefix(es): 3-85825; 3-314
Imprints: De Vier Winstreken; Editions Nord-Sud; North-South Books; Nord-Sud Edizioni
Divisions: Michael Neugebauer Verlag

North-Holland, *imprint of* Elsevier Science SA

North-South Books, *imprint of* Nord-Sued Verlag

Novalis Media AG
PO Box 1021, 8200 Schaffhausen
Tel: (052) 633212 *Fax:* (052) 6201491
E-mail: novalis@spectraweb.ch *Cable:* Novalis Schaffhausen
Key Personnel
Contact: Eva Frensch *Tel:* (052) 932780 *Fax:* (052) 932784; Mr M Frensch *Tel:* 052 6201490
Founded: 1946
Subjects: Anthropology, Art, Education, Philosophy, Social Sciences, Sociology
Number of titles published annually: 6 Print
Total Titles: 44 Print
Online services available through Novalis.
Branch Office(s)
PO Box 600, 78266 Buesingen, Contact: Mr Bracker *Tel:* (07734) 932780 *Fax:* (07734) 932781

NZN Buchverlag AG+
Hirschengraben 66, CH-8001 Zurich
Tel: (01) 266 12 92 *Fax:* (01) 266 12 93
E-mail: nzn@nzn.ch
Web Site: www.nzn.ch
Key Personnel
Editor-in-Chief: Magdalena Seibl
Founded: 1946
Subjects: Religion - Catholic
ISBN Prefix(es): 3-85827
Number of titles published annually: 4 Print

Objectif Terre, *imprint of* Editions Olizane

Octopus Verlag
Vazerolgasse 1, 7000 Chur
Tel: (081) 221029 *Fax:* (081) 2529466
ISBN Prefix(es): 3-279

Oekumenischer Rat der Kirchen, see World Council of Churches (WCC Publications)

Oesch Verlag AG+
Jungholzstr 28, 8050 Zurich
Tel: (01) 305 70 60 *Fax:* (01) 305 70 66
E-mail: info@oeschverlag.ch
Web Site: www.oeschverlag.ch *Cable:* OESCH
Key Personnel
Dir: Martin Brugger
Editorial: Natasha Fischer *E-mail:* lektorat@oeschverlag.ch
Rights & Permissions: Anne Brugger
Founded: 1935
Subjects: Career Development, Fiction, Health, Nutrition, Management, Marketing, Nonfiction (General), Self-Help
ISBN Prefix(es): 3-85833; 3-0350
Number of titles published annually: 40 Print
Total Titles: 2 Audio
Associate Companies: Conzett Verlag
E-mail: info@oeschverlag.ch *Web Site:* www.finanzbuch.ch; Jopp Verlag *E-mail:* info@oeschverlag.ch *Web Site:* www.joppverlag.ch

Office du Livre SA (Buchhaus AG)
Z13, Corminboeuf-Z1, 1701 Fribourg
Tel: (026) 4675111 *Fax:* (026) 4675466
Telex: 942291 Olf CH *Cable:* Livreoffice
Key Personnel
Dir: Jean-Marc Rod
Founded: 1947
Subjects: Architecture & Interior Design, Art, Asian Studies, Crafts, Games, Hobbies, Sports, Athletics
ISBN Prefix(es): 3-7215; 2-8264

Editions Olizane+
11 rue des Vieux-Grenadiers, 1205 Geneva
Tel: (022) 3285252 *Fax:* (022) 3285796
E-mail: guides@olizane.ch
Key Personnel
Man Dir: Matthias Huber
Founded: 1981
Subjects: Ethnicity, Photography, Travel
ISBN Prefix(es): 2-88086
Imprints: Objectif Terre; Collection Artou; Espaces Photographiques; Guides-Olizane; Etudes Orientales
Foreign Rights: Gaia Media Basel (Germany)

Edition Olms AG+
Fabenstr 28, 8008 Zurich
Tel: (01) 2610270 *Fax:* (01) 2617103
Key Personnel
Man Dir & other offices: Manfred Olms
Founded: 1977
Subjects: Art, Film, Video, Humor, Music, Dance, Photography
ISBN Prefix(es): 3-283
Warehouse: VVA/Bertelsmann, DFA/B, attn: Mrs Pia Brenne, PO Box 7600, D-33310 Guetersloh, Germany

Orell Fuessli Verlag+
Nuschelerstr 22, Postfach, 8022 Zurich
Tel: (01) 2113630 *Fax:* (01) 4667412
E-mail: info@orell-fuessli-verlag.ch
Web Site: www.orell-fuessli-verlag.ch
Telex: 813021 orla ch *Cable:* ORELLVERLAG ZURICH
Key Personnel
Man Dir & Sales, Marketing: Alex Aepli
Editorial: Katja Klingler; Werner Waldman
Rights & Permissions: Pia Hiefner-Hug
Founded: 1519
Subjects: Art, Biography, Economics, Education, Geography, Geology, History, How-to
ISBN Prefix(es): 3-280; 3-7249
Parent Company: Orell Fuessli Graphische Betriebe AG, Dietzingerstr 3, CH-8036 Zurich
Imprints: Eugen Rentsch Verlag AG
Bookshop(s): Orell Fuessli Buchhandlung, Pelikanstr 10, 8022 Zurich

Verlag Organisator AG
Loewenstr 16, Postfach, 8021 Zurich
Tel: (01) 2118155 *Fax:* (01) 4010815; (01) 4928758
Telex: 813834 *Cable:* orga/ch
Key Personnel
Man Dir, Editorial: F Borner
Sales, Publicity, Production: Bruno Waldburger
Founded: 1919
Subjects: Accounting, Government, Political Science, Labor, Industrial Relations
ISBN Prefix(es): 3-7220
Parent Company: Rudolf Haufe Verlag GmbH & Co KG, Germany
Bookshop(s): Basel; Lucerne; St Gallen; Schaffhausen; Winterthur; Zurich; others throughout Switzerland

Etudes Orientales, *imprint of* Editions Olizane

Origo Verlag+
Rathausgasse 30, 3011 Bern
Tel: (031) 224480 *Fax:* (031) 3114470
Key Personnel
Proprietor & Man Dir: Alexander Wild
Founded: 1947
Subjects: Mysteries, Parapsychology, Philosophy, Religion - Buddhist, Religion - Jewish, Religion - Other
ISBN Prefix(es): 3-282; 3-85835
Associate Companies: Verlag Alexander Wild

Orte-Verlag
Ekkehardstr 14, 8006 Zurich
Tel: (01) 3630234; (01) 559751
Key Personnel
Man Dir: Werner Bucher
Publicity: Ruth Good-Ramp
Subjects: Poetry
ISBN Prefix(es): 3-85830

Ostschweiz Druck und Verlag
Oberer Graben 8, Postfach 990, 9001 St Gallen
Tel: (071) 208585 *Fax:* (071) 236577
Telex: 77393
Key Personnel
Man Dir, Sales: Dr Emil Daehler
Founded: 1892
Subjects: Art, History, Music, Dance, Poetry, Social Sciences, Sociology
ISBN Prefix(es): 3-85837

Ott Verlag AG (Ott Publishers, Inc)+
Laenggasse 57, Postfach 802, CH-3607 Thun 7
Tel: (033) 221622 *Fax:* (033) 2253939
E-mail: info@ott-verlag.ch *Cable:* OTTPUBL THUN
Key Personnel
Man Dir, Publicity & Advertising: Hans M Ott
Founded: 1923
Specialize in printers & editors.
Subjects: Business, Earth Sciences, Economics, Gardening, Plants, Geography, Geology, Management, Military Science, Nonfiction (General), Sports, Athletics
ISBN Prefix(es): 3-7225
Associate Companies: Translegal Ltd (publishers of dictionaries)

Panorama Verlag, see Tobler Verlag

Editions du Panorama
Case Postale 3511, 2500 Biel 3
Tel: (032) 3581665 *Fax:* (032) 3581665
Key Personnel
Man Dir: Paul Thierrin
Founded: 1951
Subjects: Business, Fiction
ISBN Prefix(es): 2-88019

Parkett Publishers Inc+
Quellenstr 27, CH-8005 Zurich
Tel: (01) 2718140 *Fax:* (01) 2724301
E-mail: parkettmag@aol.com
Key Personnel
Man Dir: Dieter von Graffenried; Bice Curiger
Founded: 1984
Subjects: Art
ISBN Prefix(es): 3-907509
Branch Office(s)
Parkett Publishers, 155 Avenue of Americas, New York, NY 10013, United States *Tel:* 212-673-2660

Editions Parole et Silence+
Le Muveran, 1888 Les Plans
Tel: (024) 6982301 *Fax:* (024) 6982311
Key Personnel
Contact: Sabine Larive
ISBN Prefix(es): 2-84573

Editions du Parvis
1648 Hauteville
Tel: (026) 915 93 93 *Fax:* (026) 915 93 99
E-mail: book@parvis.ch
Web Site: www.parvis.ch
Key Personnel
Executive: Jean-Marie Castella
Founded: 1970
Subjects: Health, Nutrition, Religion - Catholic
ISBN Prefix(es): 2-88022; 3-907523
Number of titles published annually: 20 Print
Distributed by Gallus (Austria)
Distributor for Centro Editoriale Valtortiano (Europe)

Foundation Simon I Patino, see Editions Patino

Editions Patino+
8 rue Giovanni Gambini, Case Postale 182, 1211 Geneva 25
Tel: (022) 3470211 *Fax:* (022) 7891829
Key Personnel
Contact: John Dubouchet; Roger Guggisberg
Founded: 1986
Subjects: Fiction, Philosophy
ISBN Prefix(es): 2-88213
Orders to: Vilo L'Amateur, 25 rue Ginoux, F-75015 Paris, France *Fax:* (1) 45757553

Paulus Verlag, see Editions Saint-Paul

Editions Payot Lausanne+
18 ave de la Gare, CH-1001 Lausanne
Mailing Address: Case Postale 529, CH-1001 Lausanne
Tel: (021) 3290264 *Fax:* (021) 3290266
E-mail: ed.payot.nadir@bluewin.ch
Key Personnel
Publisher: Jacques Scherrer
Founded: 1875
Member of ASELF.
Subjects: Anthropology, Archaeology, Architecture & Interior Design, Education, History, Law, Literature, Literary Criticism, Essays, Medicine, Nursing, Dentistry, Music, Dance, Nonfiction (General), Philosophy, Regional Interests, Science (General), Social Sciences, Sociology
ISBN Prefix(es): 2-601
Total Titles: 490 Print
Parent Company: Nadir SA/Jacques Scherrer Editeur, Lausanne
Distributed by Doin Editeurs, Paris (for medical books in France, Belgium & Canada)
Distributor for Olympic Museum Publications (France & Belgium)
Orders to: Olf, ZI-3 Corminboeuf, CH-1701 Fribourg

Pearson Education+
Chollerstr 37, Ch 6301 Zug
Tel: 747 4747 *Fax:* 747 4777
E-mail: firstname.lastname@pearson.ch
Web Site: www.pearson.ch
Key Personnel
Business Manager: Tobias Eberhart
Chairman: Gunther Frank *Tel:* (089) 46003 121 *Fax:* (089) 46003 120
Vice Chairman: Josef Grand
Member of the Board: Martin Frey *Tel:* (01) 384 1414 *Fax:* (01) 384 1284
Founded: 1983
Other Business Activities: Distribution of M&T Books & Software; Sub-distribution of Microsoft, Lotus, Novell & Others.
Subjects: Computer Science

Parent Company: Pearson Plc
Distributor for Adobe Press; BradyGAMES; Hayden Books; New Riders; Que; Sams; Sams.net; Waite Group Press; Ziff-Davis Press

Pedrazzini Tipografia
Via Varenna, 7, 6600 Locarno
Tel: (093) 317735; (093) 317734 *Fax:* (093) 315118
Key Personnel
Man Dir & other offices: Benedetto Pedrazzini
Founded: 1880
Subjects: Education, History, Literature, Literary Criticism, Essays, Publishing & Book Trade Reference, Religion - Other
ISBN Prefix(es): 88-7408

Pendo Verlag GmbH+
Forchstr 40, 8032 Zurich
Mailing Address: Postfach, 8032 Zurich
Tel: (01) 3897030 *Fax:* (01) 3897035
E-mail: pendo-verlag@pendo.ch
Key Personnel
Publisher: Ernst Piper *Tel:* (089) 13999252 *Fax:* (089) 13999170 *E-mail:* ernst.piper@t-online.de
Editor: Katrin Eckert *Tel:* (01) 3897032 *Fax:* (01) 3897035
Founded: 1971
Specialize in Literature, Contemporary History, Essays.
Subjects: Government, Political Science, History, Poetry, Religion - Other
ISBN Prefix(es): 3-85842
Number of titles published annually: 35 Print
Total Titles: 200 Print
Imprints: Politics
Branch Office(s)
Volkarstr 13, 80634 Munich, Germany *Tel:* (089) 13999252 *Fax:* (089) 13999170 *E-mail:* ernst.piper@online.de *Web Site:* www.ernst-piper.de

Perret Edition
Promenadengasse 12, 8001 Zurich
Tel: (01) 2627357 *Fax:* (01) 2627357
Founded: 1995
Subjects: Art, Photography
ISBN Prefix(es): 3-9520910

Verlag Die Pforte im Rudolf Steiner Verlag
Postfach 135, CH-4143 Dornach 1
Tel: (061) 7012240 *Fax:* (061) 7012534
E-mail: steiner-verlag@magnet.ch
Key Personnel
International Rights: Benedikt Marzhn
Founded: 1960
Subjects: Anthropology, Philosophy
ISBN Prefix(es): 3-85636
Total Titles: 70 Print

Pharos-Verlag, Hansrudolf Schwabe AG
Therwilestr 5, CH-4011 Basel
Mailing Address: Postfach 68, CH-4011 Basel
Tel: (061) 541021 *Fax:* (061) 2797972
Key Personnel
Man Dir: Alexander Schwabe
Advertising Dir: Myrte Schwabe
Founded: 1958
Subjects: Transportation, Wine & Spirits
ISBN Prefix(es): 3-7230

Philosophisch-Anthroposophischer Verlag am Goetheanum+
Huegelweg 59, 4143 Dornach
Tel: (061) 7211116; (061) 7064200 *Fax:* (061) 7011436; (061) 7064201
Key Personnel
Editor: Joseph Morel
Founded: 1908

Subjects: Art, Literature, Literary Criticism, Essays, Medicine, Nursing, Dentistry, Philosophy, Science (General)
ISBN Prefix(es): 3-7235
Subsidiaries: Rudolf Geering Verlag

PIE-Peter Lang SA+
Formerly Peter Lang SA
EQRO Jupiterstr 15, CH-3015 Bern
Tel: (031) 9402121 *Fax:* (031) 9402131
E-mail: peterlang@datacomm.ch
Key Personnel
Editorial: Tony Albala de Rivas
Founded: 1977
Specialize in academic publications.
Subjects: Art, History, Language Arts, Linguistics, Law, Literature, Literary Criticism, Essays, Philosophy, Social Sciences, Sociology, Theology
ISBN Prefix(es): 0-8204; 3-261; 3-631; 3-906750; 3-906751; 3-906752; 3-906753; 3-906754; 3-906755; 3-906757; 3-906758; 3-906759
Subsidiaries: Peter Lang GmbH; Peter Lang Inc; PIE-Peter Lang SA

Politics, *imprint of* Pendo Verlag GmbH

Editions Pourquoi Pas+
Case Postale 60, 1247 Anieres-Geneve
Tel: (022) 7511031
Key Personnel
Contact: Astrid Mirabaud
Founded: 1981
Subjects: Literature, Literary Criticism, Essays
ISBN Prefix(es): 2-88173

Presses Polytechniques et Universitaires Romandes, PPUR+
EPFL-Ecublens, Centre Midi, CH-1015 Lausanne
Mailing Address: PO Box 119, CH-1015 Lausanne
Tel: (021) 693 21 30 *Fax:* (021) 693 40 27
E-mail: ppur@epfl.ch
Web Site: www.ppur.org
Telex: 450 456 attn. PPUR
Key Personnel
President: Pierre-Francois Pittet
Man Dir, Editorial: Olivier Babel
Production: Christophe Borlat
Promotion: Sylvain Collette
International Rights: Yasmine Babel-Sraih
  Tel: (021) 693 60 44 *E-mail:* yasmine.babel@epfl.ch
Founded: 1980
Also acts as book packager.
Subjects: Architecture & Interior Design, Biological Sciences, Chemistry, Chemical Engineering, Civil Engineering, Computer Science, Earth Sciences, Electronics, Electrical Engineering, Engineering (General), Management, Mathematics, Mechanical Engineering, Physics, Science (General), Technology
ISBN Prefix(es): 2-88074
Number of titles published annually: 30 Print
Distributed by Eyrolles-Geodif (France & Maroc); Patrimoine for Belgium (Benelux); PIP (Canada & USA)

Pro Juventute Verlag+
Seehofstr 15, Postfach, 8022 Zurich
Tel: (01) 2517244 *Fax:* (01) 2522824
ISBN Prefix(es): 3-7152

Editions Pro Schola
3 Place Chauderon, 1003 Lausanne 9
Mailing Address: PO Box 270, 1000 Lausanne 9 CH
Tel: (021) 323 66 55 *Fax:* (021) 323 67 77
E-mail: benedict@benedict-schools.com
Web Site: www.benedict-international.com

Key Personnel
Man Dir: Dr Jean J Benedict
Founded: 1928
Official distributor of the Benedict Method.
Member of SLESR.
Subjects: Education, English as a Second Language, Language Arts, Linguistics
ISBN Prefix(es): 2-88009
Total Titles: 85 Print
Distributed by Buchimport Peter Reimer
Warehouse: 24 Rue de Geneve, 1003 Lausanne

Promoedition SA+
35, rue des Bains, 1205 Geneva 11
Mailing Address: Case Postale 5615, 1211 Geneva
Tel: (022) 8099460 *Fax:* (022) 7811414
Key Personnel
International Rights Contact: Thierry B Opplkofer
Founded: 1972
Subjects: Business, Communications, Film, Video, Finance
ISBN Prefix(es): 2-88129

Psychosophische Gesellschaft
Schedlern, 9063 Stein
Tel: (071) 591301
Subjects: Astrology, Occult, Education, Philosophy, Psychology, Psychiatry, Theology
ISBN Prefix(es): 3-85846

Punktum AG, Buchredaktion und Bildarchiv+
Klusstr 50, CH-8032 Zurich
Tel: (01) 4224540 *Fax:* (01) 4224813
Key Personnel
Contact: Dr Niklaus Flueeler; Marianne Flueeler-Grauwiter
Specialize in Swiss Topics.
Subjects: Art, Ethnicity, History, Travel
ISBN Prefix(es): 3-907577
Divisions: Punktum Buchredoktion (Packaging), Punktum Bildarchiv (Picture Library)

Rabe Verlag AG Zuerich
Frankengasse 6, CH-8001 Zurich
Tel: (01) 2618540 *Fax:* (01) 2618541 *Cable:* RABEVERLAG ZURICH
Key Personnel
Man Dir, Sales: Dr J Kanitz
Editorial, Rights & Permissions: Dr Elsa Kanitz
Production: Dr P Portmann
Founded: 1962
Subjects: Art
ISBN Prefix(es): 3-85852
Branch Office(s)
PAPYRUS Franchise Corp, 954 16 St, Oakland, CA 94608, United States
Warehouse: CH-8608 Bubikon Zurich/Dorfstr. 15-15a *Tel:* (055) 243 23 83

Robert Raeber, Buchhandlung am Schweizerhof
Schweizerhofquai 2, 6002 Lucerne
Mailing Address: Postfach 4170, 6002 Lucerne
Tel: 512371
Key Personnel
Man Dir: Robert Raeber-Huber
Founded: 1973
Subjects: Fiction, Travel
ISBN Prefix(es): 3-7239
Bookshop(s): Raeber Buchhandlung, Schweizerhofquai 2, 6002 Lucerne

Raphael, Editions+
Case Postale 1, 1801 Le Mont-Pelerin
Tel: (021) 9215230 *Fax:* (021) 9215237
Key Personnel
Dir: Mr Denis Ducatel *E-mail:* denis.ducatel@dplanet.ch
Founded: 1990

Subjects: Literature, Literary Criticism, Essays, Psychology, Psychiatry, Religion - Protestant
ISBN Prefix(es): 2-88417
Total Titles: 24 Print
Distributed by Editions Empreinte; Editions La Clairiere; Interlivres (Canada); Jeunesse en Mission; Olbis

Rauhreif Verlag
Titlisstr 3, CH-4313 Moehlin
Tel: (061) 8515363
Subjects: Literature, Literary Criticism, Essays
ISBN Prefix(es): 3-907764

Verlag fuer Recht und Gesellschaft AG
Wallstr 14, 4010 Basel
Mailing Address: Postfach 646, 4010 Basel
Tel: (061) 231775 *Fax:* (061) 7262627
E-mail: info@vgr-verlag.com
Web Site: www.vgr-verlag.ch *Cable:* REGES VERLAG
Key Personnel
Man Dir: Dr Peter J Amuer
Founded: 1933
Subjects: Accounting, Law
ISBN Prefix(es): 3-7242
Associate Companies: Sciamed Verlag AG, Ringstr 75, Postfach, 4106 Therwil

Recom, *imprint of* RECOM Verlag

RECOM Verlag
Missionsstr 36, 4012 Basel
Tel: (061) 253390; (061) 251926; (061) 438760 *Fax:* (061) 2616213
Telex: 63755 rein ch
Key Personnel
Man Dir, Sales, Production, Publicity: Alfred Ruedisuehli
Founded: 1971 (1985)
Subjects: Medicine, Nursing, Dentistry
ISBN Prefix(es): 3-7245; 3-315
Parent Company: Friedrich Reinhardt AG
Imprints: Recom

Regenbogen Verlag+
Bodmerstr 9, Postfach 472, CH-8027 Zurich 2
Tel: (01) 2013676 *Fax:* (01) 2013703
Key Personnel
General Manager: Theo Ruff
Subjects: Art, Travel
ISBN Prefix(es): 3-85862
Orders to: Prolit Buchvertrieb GmbH, Siemensstr 18a, 35394 Giessen, Germany *Tel:* (0641) 77053

Reich Verlag AG+
Museggstr 12, 6004 Lucerne
Tel: (041) 4103721 *Fax:* (041) 4103227
Key Personnel
Man Dir: Alfons Wueest
Founded: 1974
Specialize in books of plates.
Subjects: Photography
ISBN Prefix(es): 3-7243
Total Titles: 60 Print
Imprints: Terra Magica

Verlag Friedrich Reinhardt AG
Missionsstr 36, 4012 Basel
Tel: (061) 253390; (061) 438760 *Fax:* (061) 2646488 *Cable:* Freinhardt Basle
Key Personnel
Man Dir, Rights & Permissions: Dr Ernst Reinhardt
Founded: 1900
Subjects: Biography, Environmental Studies, Fiction, History, How-to, Religion - Other
ISBN Prefix(es): 3-7245; 3-315
Subsidiaries: Eular Verlag (at above address); Reinhardt Communications

PUBLISHERS   SWITZERLAND

Eugen Rentsch Verlag AG, *imprint of* Orell Fuessli Verlag

Rex Verlag
St Karliquai 12, Postfach 5266, 6000 Lucerne 5
Tel: 514151 *Fax:* 4194711
Key Personnel
Man Dir: Markus Kappeler
Founded: 1931
Subjects: Education, Fiction, Religion - Catholic
ISBN Prefix(es): 3-7252
Bookshop(s): Rex Buchladen, St Karliquair 12, Postfach 5266, 6000 Lucerne

Rhein-Trio, Edition/Editions du Fou+
Postfach 34, 8197 Rafz, Spalenring 15a, 4055 Basel
Founded: 1993
Specialize in comics.
Subjects: Art, Astrology, Occult, Humor, Mysteries, Poetry
ISBN Prefix(es): 3-9520470
Distributed by Comics Virt (Austria)
Distributor for Comicwelt

Editiones Roche
c/o F Hoffmanes-La Roche Ltd, Grenzacherstr 124, Postfach, 4002 Basel
Tel: (061) 6883611 *Fax:* (061) 6919391; (061) 6919600
Telex: 962292 hir ch
Key Personnel
Publications Manager: Hans-Peter Fleury
E-mail: hans-peter.fleury@roche.com
Subjects: Business, Chemistry, Chemical Engineering, Disability, Special Needs, Health, Nutrition, History, Management, Science (General)
ISBN Prefix(es): 3-907046; 3-907770

Rodana Verlag AG, see Schweizer Spiegel Verlag Mit

Rodera-Verlag der Cardun AG+
Postfach 8411, Winterthur
Tel: (052) 292442 *Fax:* (052) 292592
Key Personnel
Contact: Franz H Duebi
Founded: 1991
Subjects: Biography, History, Literature, Literary Criticism, Essays, Theology
ISBN Prefix(es): 3-907803; 3-905270

Hans Rohr Verlag
Moehrlistr 130, CH-8006 Zurich 1
Tel: (01) 3614846 *Fax:* (01) 3639513
E-mail: buchhandlung.hans.rohr@dm.krinfo.ch
Key Personnel
Man Dir: Hans R Rohr
Founded: 1921
Subjects: Antiques, Film, Video, Language Arts, Linguistics, Regional Interests, Travel
ISBN Prefix(es): 3-85865

Rondo Verlag
Hittenbergstr 1, 8636 Wald
Tel: (055) 953937 *Fax:* (055) 2464293
Key Personnel
Contact: Elisabeth Wild
ISBN Prefix(es): 3-907935

Roth et Sauter SA
La Pale, CH-1026 Denges-Lausanne
Tel: (021) 8017561 *Fax:* (021) 8023279
Telex: 458179 rsd ch
Key Personnel
Man Dir: Michel Logoz; Pierre Sauter
Founded: 1890
Subjects: Art
ISBN Prefix(es): 2-88075
Imprints: Editions du Verseau

Rotpunktverlag+
Freyastr 20, CH-8004 Zurich
Mailing Address: Postfach 2134, CH-8026 Zurich
Tel: (01) 2418434 *Fax:* (01) 2418434
E-mail: info@rotpunktverlag.ch
Web Site: www.rotpunkfverlag.ch
Key Personnel
International Rights: Thomas Heilmann
Founded: 1977
Member of VVDS.
Subjects: Alternative, Developing Countries, Fiction, Government, Political Science, History, Nonfiction (General), Outdoor Recreation, Travel
ISBN Prefix(es): 3-85869
Orders to: AS Verlagsservice Holler, Schaldorferstr 16, A-8641 St Marien im Murzrtal, Austria
Tel: (03864) 67 77 *Fax:* (03864) 38 88
Buch 2000/AVA, Postfach 27, 8910 Affoltern
Tel: (01) 762 42 60 *Fax:* (01) 762 60 65
Prolit Verlagsauslieferung, Postfach 9, D-35461 Fernwald, Germany *Tel:* (0641) 9439325
Fax: (0641) 9439329

Rotten-Verlags AG
Terbinerstr 2, 3930 Visp
Tel: (028) 462252
ISBN Prefix(es): 3-907816

Ruegger Verlag+
Division of Sudostschweiz Presse AG
Albisriederstr 80A, 8040 Zurich
Mailing Address: Postfach 1470, 8040 Zurich
Tel: (01) 4912130 *Fax:* (01) 4931176
E-mail: info@rueggerverlag.ch
Web Site: www.rueggerverlag.ch
Key Personnel
Secretary: Marianne Pearson *E-mail:* mpearson@rueggerverlag.ch
Subjects: Specialize in economics, politics, sociology, ecology & educational research
ISBN Prefix(es): 3-7253
Number of titles published annually: 30 Print

SAB Schweiz Arbeitsgemeinschaft fuer die Berggebiete+
Laurstr 10, Postfach 174, 5200 Brugg
Tel: (056) 411079 *Fax:* (056) 413642
Subjects: Agriculture, Architecture & Interior Design, Economics, Energy, Environmental Studies, Labor, Industrial Relations, Regional Interests, Social Sciences, Sociology
ISBN Prefix(es): 3-85873

Sabe AG Verlagsinstitut+
Gotthardstr 52, 8002 Zurich
Tel: (01) 2024477 *Fax:* (01) 2021932
E-mail: sabeverlag@access.ch
Key Personnel
Dir: Heinrich M Zweifel
Founded: 1969
Member of Worlddidac & Swissdidac; Specialize in educational material of all kinds including software.
Subjects: Biological Sciences, Education, Geography, Geology, History, Language Arts, Linguistics, Mathematics, Natural History
ISBN Prefix(es): 3-252
Distributed by Heinevetter Verlag
Distributor for Verlag fuer Paedagogische Medien; Verlag an der Ruhr; Veritas Verlag

Editions Saint Augustin+
4, rue Simplon, 1890 Saint-Maurice
Tel: (024) 486 05 04 *Fax:* (024) 486 05 23
E-mail: editions@staugustin.ch
Key Personnel
General Dir: Marc Larive
Founded: 1934
Subjects: Religion - Catholic, Theology
ISBN Prefix(es): 2-88011

Bookshop(s): Librairie La Procure-Le Passage, Rue de Carouge 53, 1205 Geneve; Librairie Saint-Augustin, 88 rue de Lausanne, 1700 Fribourg; Librairie Saint-Augustin, ave du Simplon 4, 1890 Saint-Maurice

Oeuvre St-Augustin
4, rue Simplon, 1890 St-Maurice
Tel: (024) 4860504 *Fax:* (024) 4860523
Key Personnel
Contact: Renee Donnet-Descartes
ISBN Prefix(es): 2-88011

Editions Saint-Paul
Perolles 42, Case Postale 150, CH-1705 Fribourg
Tel: (026) 4264331 *Fax:* (026) 4264330
Key Personnel
Marketing Dir: Anton Scherer
Founded: 1873
Subjects: Education, Philosophy, Psychology, Psychiatry
ISBN Prefix(es): 3-7228; 2-88355
Parent Company: Imprimerie et Librairies Saint-Paul SA, 42, blvd Perolles, Case Postale 150, CH-1705 Fribourg
Associate Companies: Editions de la Sarine, 42, blvd Perolles, Case Postale 150, CH-1705 Fribourg; Editions Universitaires SA
Bookshop(s): Librairie Saint-Paul, Perolles 38, CH-1700 Fribourg; Librairie du Vieux Comte, rue de Vevey, CH-1630 Bulle

Salvioni arti grafiche SA
Via Ghiringhelli 9, 6500 Bellinzona
Tel: (091) 254141 *Fax:* (091) 261056
ISBN Prefix(es): 88-7967

SAPL, *imprint of* Castle Publications SA

Satyr-Verlag Dr Humbel+
Dufourstr 195, 8008 Zurich
Mailing Address: Postfach 6411, 8023 Zurich
Tel: 01 554620
Key Personnel
Manager: Dr Humbel
Founded: 1985
Subjects: Humor, Literature, Literary Criticism, Essays
ISBN Prefix(es): 3-906420
Parent Company: Satyr-Verlag Dr Humbel, 12 rue du Chateau, F-90200 Grosmagny, France
Orders to: Satyr-Verlag, Postfach 6411, CH-8023 Zurich

Sauerlaender AG+
Laurenzenvorstadt 89, CH-5001 Aarau
Tel: (064) 268626; (064) 268686 *Fax:* (064) 245780
E-mail: verlag@sauerlaendes.ch
Web Site: www.sauerlaender.ch
Telex: 981195 SAG CH
Key Personnel
Publisher & Man Dir: Hans Christof Sauerlaender
Editorial: Hansten Doornkaat; Peter Egger; Paula Peretti
Man Dir, Sales & Marketing: Klaus Wilberg
Sales: Monika Roesler
Advertising Manager: Heike Ossenkop
Rights & Permissions: Kerstin Michaelis
Founded: 1807
Subjects: Education, Nonfiction (General)
ISBN Prefix(es): 3-7941
Total Titles: 600 Print; 6 CD-ROM
Associate Companies: SABE Verlag AG, Todistrasse 23, 8002 Zurich *Tel:* (01) 202-1932
E-mail: verlag@sabe.ch
Subsidiaries: Verlag Sauerlaender GmbH

Scherz Verlag AG+
Member of Verlagsgruppe Droemer Weltbild
Theaterplatz 4-6, 3000 Bern 7

SWITZERLAND

Tel: (031) 3277150 *Fax:* (031) 3277171
E-mail: scherz@scherzverlag.ch
Web Site: www.scherzverlag.ch *Cable:*
SCHERZEDIT
Key Personnel
Editorial Dir: Peter Lohmann
Man Dir: Fuerg Zurlinden
Editorial Dept: Dorthe Binkert; Rachel Gratzfeld
Rights & Permissions: Barbara Frankhauser
Marketing Dir: Thomas Reisch
Contact: Isabella Milan E-mail: i.milan@scherzverlag.ch
Founded: 1938
Specialize in Hardcover fiction & nonfiction.
Subjects: Biography, History, Parapsychology, Philosophy, Psychology, Psychiatry
ISBN Prefix(es): 3-502
Total Titles: 1,200 Print
Subsidiaries: Otto Wilhelm Barth-Verlag KG

Schlaepfer & Co AG
Kasernenstr 64, CH-9100 Herisau
Tel: (071) 513131 *Fax:* (071) 525126
Key Personnel
Man Dir: P Schlaepfer
Founded: 1974
ISBN Prefix(es): 3-85882
Orders to: Schlapfer & Co AG Buchverlag, CH-9100 Herisau

Schnellmann-Verlag+
Rotackerstr 49, CH-8645 Jona-Kempraten
Tel: (055) 2111472; (079) 3175143 *Fax:* (055) 2111477
Web Site: www.dictionaries.ch
Key Personnel
Dir: Hans Schnellmann
Founded: 1973
ISBN Prefix(es): 3-85542

Verlag fuer Schoene Wissenschaften
Unterer Zielweg 36, Postfach, CH-4143 Dornach 2
Tel: (061) 723911 *Fax:* (061) 7011417
Key Personnel
Chief Executive: Dr Heinz Matile
Founded: 1928
Belles Lettres Publishing Co - Albert Steffen Foundation.
Subjects: Art, Education, Ethnicity, Health, Nutrition, Literature, Literary Criticism, Essays, Philosophy, Poetry, Religion - Other
ISBN Prefix(es): 3-85889

Editions Musicales de la Schola Cantorum
Epinassey, 1890 Saint-Maurice
Tel: (025) 652480; (025) 653060
Founded: 1896
Subjects: Music, Dance
Parent Company: Cantate Domino, Triton, Charles Huguenin

A Schudel & Co AG, Verlag
Schoepfgaesschen 8, 4125 Riehen
Tel: (061) 671011 *Fax:* (061) 671363
E-mail: a.schudel@bluewin.ch
Key Personnel
Manager: Ch Schudel
ISBN Prefix(es): 3-85895

Schulthess Polygraphischer Verlag AG
Zwingliplatz 2, 8022 Zurich
Tel: (01) 2519336 *Fax:* (01) 2616394
E-mail: schulthess@access.ch
Web Site: www.schulthess.com *Cable:* 2
Key Personnel
Dir, Advertising, Permissions: Werner Stocker
Founded: 1791
Firm has incorporated the former Leemann AG Druckerei/Verlag since 1978.

Subjects: Business, Law, Social Sciences, Sociology
ISBN Prefix(es): 3-7255

Hansrudolf Schwabe AG, see Pharos-Verlag, Hansrudolf Schwabe AG

Schwabe & Co AG
Steinentorstr 13, Postfach, 4010 Basel
Tel: (061) 278 95 65 *Fax:* (061) 272 55 73
E-mail: verlag@schwabe.ch
Web Site: www.schwabe.ch *Cable:*
SCHWABECO BASEL
Key Personnel
Man Dir: Hans-Rudolf Bienz; Dr Urs Breitenstein
Founded: 1488
Subjects: Archaeology, Art, History, Literature, Literary Criticism, Essays, Medicine, Nursing, Dentistry, Philosophy, Photography, Psychology, Psychiatry, Theology
ISBN Prefix(es): 3-7965
Orders to: Verlag, CH-4132 Muttenz

Verkehrshaus der Schweiz, see Verkehrshaus der Schweiz

Schweizer Spiegel Verlag Mit+
Rodana Verlag, Ramistr 18, 8024 Zurich
Tel: (01) 472195 *Fax:* (01) 7502943
Key Personnel
Contact: Allan Guggenbuhl
Subjects: Education, Psychology, Psychiatry
ISBN Prefix(es): 3-7270

Schweizerische Stiftung fuer Alpine Forschungen
Binzstr 23, 8045 Zurich
Tel: (01) 4610147
Key Personnel
President: Dr Juerg Marmet
Editorial: Dr Fritz Schwarzenbach
Founded: 1939
Swiss Foundation for Alpine Research.
Subjects: Earth Sciences, Geography, Geology
ISBN Prefix(es): 3-85515

Schweizerischen Gesellschaft fuer Volkskunde (Swiss Folklore Society), imprint of Verlagsbuchhandlung AG

Schweizerischer Verein fuer Schweisstechnik
St Alban-Vorstadt 95, 4006 Basel
Tel: (061) 233973 *Fax:* (061) 3178480
ISBN Prefix(es): 3-85896

Schweizerisches Ost-Institut, see Verlag SOI (Schweizerisches Ost-Institut)

Schweizerisches Jugendschriftenwerk, SJW+
Uetliberestr 20, 8045 Zurich
Tel: (01462) 49 40 (ISDN) *Fax:* (01462) 69 13 (ISDN)
E-mail: office@sjw.ch
Web Site: www.sjw.ch
Key Personnel
Dir: Tsultrin Shabga E-mail: t.shabga@sjw.ch
Art Dir: Hanna Burkard
Sales: Emilienne Eberia
Founded: 1956
ISBN Prefix(es): 3-7269
Number of titles published annually: 30 Print
Total Titles: 300 Print
Parent Company: Edition Fondation
Imprints: Fotorotar AG/EGG ZH
Orders to: BD Bucherdienst/Einsiel

Verlag Schweizerisches Katholisches Bibelwerk
Rue de l'hopital, 1700 Fribourg

Key Personnel
Dir: Othmar Keel
Member of AMB.
Subjects: Religion - Catholic
ISBN Prefix(es): 3-7203

Schwengeler-Verlag+
Rosenberg, 9442 Berneck
Tel: (071) 725666 *Fax:* (071) 725665
Key Personnel
Man Dir, Editorial, Rights & Permissions: Bruno Schwengeler
Sales, Production, Publicity: Walter Nitsche
Founded: 1968
Member of the Telos group.
Subjects: Literature, Literary Criticism, Essays, Religion - Other, Science (General)
ISBN Prefix(es): 3-85666
Subsidiaries: Ethos-Versandbuchhandlung; Ethos-Versand; D Ausione Letteratura Cristiana
Bookshop(s): TELOS-Buchhandlung, Oberer Graben 12, CH-8400 Winterthur

Sciamed Verlag AG
Wallstr 14, 4010 Basel
Mailing Address: Postfach 646, 4010 Basel
Tel: (061) 231775; (061) 235366 *Fax:* (061) 2722775 *Cable:* SCIAMED
Founded: 1983
Subjects: Medicine, Nursing, Dentistry
ISBN Prefix(es): 3-7242
Parent Company: Verlag Fuer Recht U Gesellschaft AG

Editions Scriptar SA+
Creux de Corsy 25, 1093 La Conversion-Lausanne
Tel: (021) 7911065 *Fax:* (021) 7914084
E-mail: info@jsh.ch
Web Site: www.jsh.ch
Key Personnel
Publicity Manager: F Mugnier Tel: (021) 7960097
Founded: 1946
Member of Swiss Watch & Jewelry Journal International Editio.
Subjects: Specializes in Watches & Jewelry
ISBN Prefix(es): 2-88012
Online services available through World Wide Web.

Editions Du Signal Rene Gaillard
2-4, rue de Geneve, 1003 Lausanne
Tel: (021) 3290194 *Fax:* (021) 3290194
Key Personnel
Proprietor: Rene Gaillard
Founded: 1972
Subjects: Human Relations
ISBN Prefix(es): 2-88023

Sinwel-Buchhandlung Verlag
Lorrainestr 10, Postfach 40, 3000 Bern 11
Tel: (031) 425205 *Fax:* (031) 3331376
Telex: 911469
Founded: 1978
Subjects: Crafts, Games, Hobbies, Outdoor Recreation
ISBN Prefix(es): 3-85911

SJW, see Schweizerisches Jugendschriftenwerk, SJW

SKAT (Swiss Centre for Development Cooperation in Technology & Management)
Vadianstr 42, CH-9000 St Gallen
Tel: (071) 2285454 *Fax:* (071) 2285455
E-mail: info@skat.ch
Web Site: www.skat.ch
Key Personnel
Head Information: Silvia Ndiaye E-mail: silvia.ndiaye@skat.ch
Founded: 1978

Consulting, documentation, & project implementation of water supply, sanitation & urban development.
Building materials, solid waste management, transport infrastructure, hand pumps.
Subjects: Manuals & reports
ISBN Prefix(es): 3-908001
Number of titles published annually: 10 Print
Total Titles: 66 Print
Online services available through World Wide Web.
Distributed by IT Publications Ltd

Editions D'Art Albert Skira SA
89 route de Chene, 1208 Geneva
Tel: (022) 3495533 *Fax:* (022) 3495535
 Cable: Edart Geneva
Key Personnel
Man Dir, Editorial: Mrs R Skira
Sales, Production & Publicity: Jean-Michel Skira
Founded: 1928
Subjects: Art, Education
ISBN Prefix(es): 2-605

Slatkine Reprints
5, rue des Chaudronniers, CP 3625, 1211 Geneva 3
Tel: (022) 7762551; (022) 3100476 *Fax:* (022) 7763527
Key Personnel
Man Dir: Michel E Slatkine
ISBN Prefix(es): 2-05

Verlag SOI (Schweizerisches Ost-Institut)
Jubilaeumsstr 41, Postfach, 3000 Bern
Tel: (031) 431212 *Fax:* (031) 3513801
Telex: 32728 *Cable:* Schweizost
Key Personnel
Man Dir: Peter Sager
Sales Manager: Peter Burgunder
Production Manager: Peter Dolder
Founded: 1958
Subjects: Government, Political Science, History, Social Sciences, Sociology
ISBN Prefix(es): 3-85913
Bookshop(s): Buchhandlung SOI, Jubilaeumsstr 41, 3000 Berne

Speer -Verlag
6954 Sala Capriasca
Tel: (091) 911026 *Fax:* (01) 3424531 *Cable:* SPERVERLAG
Key Personnel
Man Dir: R Roemer
Founded: 1944
Subjects: Fiction, Philosophy, Poetry
ISBN Prefix(es): 3-85916

Spes, *imprint of* Editions Andre Delcourt & Cie

Sphinx Verlag AG
Freiestr 82, 4051 Basel
Tel: (061) 259292 *Fax:* (061) 2721150
Key Personnel
Dir: H C Sauerlaender
Founded: 1975
Subjects: Astrology, Occult, Fiction, Health, Nutrition, Philosophy, Psychology, Psychiatry, Science (General)
ISBN Prefix(es): 3-85914
Associate Companies: Sauerlaender AG

Staatskunde Verlag E Krattiger AG, see Tobler Verlag

Staempfli Verlag AG+
Hallerstr 7, CH-3012 Bern
Mailing Address: PO Box 8326, CH-3001 Bern
Tel: (031) 3006311 *Fax:* (031) 3006688
E-mail: verlag@staempfli.com
Web Site: www.staempfli.com
Key Personnel
President, Editor, Rights & Permissions: Dr Rudolf Staempfli
Editor, Sales & Advertising Dir: Ursula Merz
Editor: Stephan Grieb
Marketing: Susanne Farner
Founded: 1799
Leading law publisher in Switzerland.
Member of Law Books in Europe.
Subjects: Government, Political Science, Law
ISBN Prefix(es): 3-7272
Parent Company: Staempfli Holding AG, Hallerstr 7, CH-3001 Bern
Bookshop(s): Buchstaempfli, Versandbuchhandlung, PO Box 560, 3000 Bern 9
Tel: (031) 3006677 *Fax:* (031) 3006688
E-mail: buchstaempfli@staempfll.com

Stahlbau Zentrum Schweiz (Swiss Institute of Steel Construction)
Seefeldstr 25, 8034 Zurich
Tel: (01) 261 89 80 *Fax:* (01) 262 09 62
E-mail: info@szs.ch
Web Site: www.szs.ch
Key Personnel
Man Dir: Urs Wyss
Swiss Institute of Steel Construction.
ISBN Prefix(es): 3-85920

Rudolf Steiner Verlag
Haus Duldeck, Postfach 135, CH-4143 Dornach 1
Tel: (061) 7012240 *Fax:* (061) 7012534
E-mail: steiner-verlag@magnet.ch
Key Personnel
Man Dir, Editorial: Benedikt Marzahn
Publicity, Sales: Winfried Altmann
Production: Carlo Frigeri; B Marzahn
Contact: Sabine Scherrer *Tel:* (061) 7069137
Founded: 1949
Administrators of the Rudolf Steiner Literary Estate.
Subjects: Philosophy
ISBN Prefix(es): 3-7274
Total Titles: 700 Print
Subsidiaries: Editrice Antroposofica SRL
Bookshop(s): Buchhandlung Duldeck, Haus Duldeck, Postfach 135, CH-4143 Dornach 1

Rudolf Steiner Verlag, see Verlag Die Pforte im Rudolf Steiner Verlag

Edition Stemmle AG+
Alte Landstr 55, 8802 Zurich
Mailing Address: Postfach 365, 8201 Schaffhausen
Tel: (01) 7154300 *Fax:* (01) 7154360
Key Personnel
Publisher: Dr Thomas N Stemmle
Marketing Dir: Robert Zueblin
Founded: 1993
Subjects: Architecture & Interior Design, Art, Photography
ISBN Prefix(es): 3-905514

Verlag Stocker-Schmid AG
Hasenbergstr 7, Postfach 66, CH-8953 Dietikon
Tel: (01) 7404444
Key Personnel
Man Dir: Mr Stocker
Subjects: Library & Information Sciences, Military Science, Regional Interests
ISBN Prefix(es): 3-85577; 3-7276
Subsidiaries: Verlag Bibliophile Drucke von Josef Stocker AG
Bookshop(s): Buchhandlung Stocker-Schmid, Hasenbergstr 7, Postfach 66, CH-8953 Dietikon

Strom-Verlag Luzern+
PO Box 1461, 6000 Lucerne 15
Tel: (041) 4408845 *Fax:* (041) 4408844
E-mail: pegasus.ebikon@edi.begasoft.ch
Key Personnel
Man Dir: Roland Grueter
Founded: 1956
Subjects: Ethnicity, Fiction, Natural History, Photography, Science (General), Travel
ISBN Prefix(es): 3-85921

Swedenborg - Verlag+
Apollostr 2, Postfach 247, 8032 Zurich
Tel: (01) 2515945
Key Personnel
President: Helen Guedemann
Editor: Dr Friedemann Horn
Manager: Heinz Grob
Founded: 1952
Subjects: Theology
ISBN Prefix(es): 3-85927
Orders to: Schweizer Buchzentrum, Olten

Swiss Centre for Development Cooperation in Technology & Management, see SKAT (Swiss Centre for Development Cooperation in Technology & Management)

Tages-Anzeiger
Werdstr 21, Postfach, CH-8021 Zurich
Tel: (01) 2484111
E-mail: tamedia@tdmedia.ch
ISBN Prefix(es): 3-85932

Terra Grischuna Verlag Buch-und Zeitschriftenverlag+
Felsenaustr 5, CH- 7004 Chur
Tel: (081) 2867050 *Fax:* (081) 2867057
E-mail: info@terra-grischuna.ch
Web Site: www.terra-grischuna.ch
Key Personnel
Owner: Reto Fetz
Founded: 1942
Subjects: Geography, Geology, Natural History, Regional Interests, Romance, Travel
ISBN Prefix(es): 3-7298
Imprints: Baumgartner Blicher
Distributed by Herold Verlags ausli efering

Terra Magica, *imprint of* Reich Verlag AG

Thailand Press, see Cockatoo Press (Schweiz), Thailand-Publikationen

Theologischer Verlag und Buchhandlungen AG+
Raeffelstr 20, 8045 Zurich
Tel: (01) 4617710
Key Personnel
Dir, Editorial: Werner Blum
Rights & Permissions: Mrs E Frick
Publicity: Reinhold Jost
Founded: 1934
Subjects: Religion - Other, Theology
ISBN Prefix(es): 3-290
Bookshop(s): Theologische Buchhandlung, Raeffelstr 20, 8045 Zurich (Antiquarian Bookshop)

Theseus - Verlag AG+
Im Eigeli 6A, 8700 Kystnacht
Tel: (01) 9109294 *Fax:* (01) 9108019
Founded: 1973
Subjects: Art, Fiction, Philosophy, Religion - Buddhist
ISBN Prefix(es): 3-85936
Subsidiaries: Theseus Verlag GmbH

3-D-World Und, see 3 Dimension World (3-D-World)

3 Dimension World (3-D-World)+
Wartenbergstr 39, 4020 Basel
Tel: (061) 424917

SWITZERLAND

Key Personnel
Publishing Dir: Gerd A Haisch
Founded: 1982
Member of SBVV/SGS.
Subjects: Art, Biography, Film, Video, Geography, Geology, Marketing, Travel
ISBN Prefix(es): 3-905450
Parent Company: Pamelart/Icebear-Group Inc

Istituto Editoriale Ticinese (IET) SA
Via del Bramantino, 3, 6500 Bellinzona
Tel: (092) 8256622 *Fax:* (092) 251874
Telex: 846266
Key Personnel
Man Dir: Libero Casagrande
Founded: 1900
Subjects: Fiction, Literature, Literary Criticism, Essays, Poetry
ISBN Prefix(es): 88-7713
Parent Company: Edizioni Casagrande SA

Tipografia Stazione, see Edizioni Armando Dado, Tipografia Stazione

Tobler Verlag+
Trogenerstrasse 80, Postfach 642, CH-9450 Altstaetten
Tel: (071) 755 6060 *Fax:* (071) 755 1254
E-mail: books@tobler-verlag.ch
Web Site: www.tobler-verlag.ch
Key Personnel
Publication Manager: Hans Joerg Tobler
Tobler Verlag has merged with Causa Verlag, Helion Verlag, Panorama Verlag & Staatskunde-Verlag E Krattiger AG.
Subjects: Health, Nutrition, Law, Management, Marketing, Nonfiction (General), Parapsychology, Philosophy, Photography, Psychology, Psychiatry
ISBN Prefix(es): 3-907506; 3-85612

Trachsel - Verlag AG+
Alpenblickweg 7, CH-3714 Frutigen
Mailing Address: Postfach 60, CH-3714 Frutigen
Tel: (33) 6711407 *Fax:* (33) 6712449
Key Personnel
Man Dir: Ernst Trachsel-Neukom
Founded: 1946
Subjects: Religion - Other
ISBN Prefix(es): 3-7271
Imprints: TVF

Trans Tech Publications SA
Brandrain 6, 8707 Zurich-uetikon
Tel: (01) 9221022 *Fax:* (01) 9221033
E-mail: ttp@ttp.ch
Web Site: www.ttp.net
Key Personnel
Dir: T Wohlbier *E-mail:* t.wohlbier@ttp.net
Founded: 1967
Subjects: Chemistry, Chemical Engineering, Mechanical Engineering, Physics
ISBN Prefix(es): 0-87849; 3-908158
Number of titles published annually: 30 Print
Total Titles: 412 Print
Branch Office(s)
c/o Enfield P & D Co, Inc, PO Box 699, Enfield
Tel: 603-632-7377 *Fax:* 603-632-5611

Translegal AG
Langgasse 57, CH-3600 Thun
Tel: (033) 221622 *Fax:* (033) 2253933
Key Personnel
Contact: Hans Ott
ISBN Prefix(es): 3-85942
Subsidiaries: Ott Verlag & Druck AG

Editions du Tricorne+
14, rue Lissignol, 1201 Geneva
Tel: (022) 7388366 *Fax:* (022) 7319749
E-mail: tricorne@freesurf.ch
Web Site: tricorne.org
Key Personnel
Man Dir: Serge Kaplun
Founded: 1976
Essays.
Subjects: Art, Crafts, Games, Hobbies, Economics, Management, Mathematics, Philosophy, Poetry, Psychology, Psychiatry, Regional Interests, Religion - Other, Social Sciences, Sociology
ISBN Prefix(es): 2-8293
Number of titles published annually: 12 Print
Total Titles: 234 Print
Parent Company: ASK
Distributed by Presses Universitaires de France (PUF)

Editions des Trois Collines Francois Lachenal
Sezegnin, 1285 Geneva
Tel: (022) 7561309 *Fax:* (022) 7561302
Key Personnel
Dir: Francois Lachenal
Founded: 1935
Subjects: Art, Government, Political Science, Philosophy, Psychology, Psychiatry
ISBN Prefix(es): 3-88013

TVF, *imprint of* Trachsel - Verlag AG

Editions 24 Heures
33, ave de la Gare, 1001 Lausanne
Tel: (021) 349500 *Fax:* (021) 3494224
Telex: 455745 Vgh Ch
Key Personnel
Man Dir: P Lamuniere
Founded: 1969
Subjects: Aeronautics, Aviation, Animals, Pets, Art, Automotive, Education, History, Military Science, Music, Dance, Transportation
ISBN Prefix(es): 2-8265; 2-88260

Werner Ulmer & Co
Mittlere Haltenstr 1, 3625 Heiligenschwendi
Tel: (033) 432220 *Fax:* (033) 434848
Key Personnel
Contact: Werner Ulmer
ISBN Prefix(es): 3-7222

Der Universitatsverlag Freiburg (University Editions of Freiburg)+
Perolles 42, 1705 Freiburg
Tel: (026) 426 43 11 *Fax:* (026) 426 43 00
E-mail: eduni@st-paul.ch
Web Site: www.st-paul.ch/uni-press-FR
Key Personnel
Director: Anton Scherer
Production Manager: Adolf Muller
Promotion Manager: Maurice Greder
Sales Manager & Subscriptions: Bernadette Meister
Founded: 1953
Subjects: Art, Economics, Ethnicity, Government, Political Science, History, Law, Literature, Literary Criticism, Essays, Medicine, Nursing, Dentistry, Music, Dance, Philosophy, Psychology, Psychiatry, Religion - Other, Theology
ISBN Prefix(es): 3-7278; 2-8271
Parent Company: Imprimerie et Librairies Saint-Paul SA, 42, boulevard de Perolles, CH-1705 Fribourg
Associate Companies: Editions Saint-Paul; Editions de la Sarine, 42, boulevard de Perolles, CH-1705 Fribourg
Bookshop(s): Librairie et Edition de la Suisse Romande

Uranium Verlag Zug
Postfach 42, 6317 Oberwil b Zug
Tel: (042) 217744
Telex: Topaz 58280
Key Personnel
Man Dir, Sales: L Young
Editorial: Mrs Young
Founded: 1976
Subjects: Nonfiction (General)
ISBN Prefix(es): 3-294
Branch Office(s)
Atzelbergstr 22, 60389 Frankfurt am Main, Germany

VCH Verlags-AG
Hardstr 10, Postfach 534, 4020 Basel
Tel: (061) 2710606 *Fax:* (061) 2710618
Telex: 911527 DMS CH
ISBN Prefix(es): 3-527
Parent Company: Wiley-VCH Verlag GmbH, Pappelallee 3, 69469 Weinheim, Germany

Vdf Hochschulverlag AG an der ETH Zurich
Voltastr 24, CH-8044 Zurich
Mailing Address: ETH Zentrum, CH-8092 Zurich
Tel: (01) 632 42 42 *Fax:* (01) 632 12 32
E-mail: verlag@vdf.ethz.ch
Web Site: www.vdf.ethz.ch
Key Personnel
Marketing: Claudia Signer *Tel:* (01) 632 77 72
  E-mail: signer@vdf.ethz.ch
International Rights: Ernst Schaerer
Founded: 1992
Subjects: Agriculture, Architecture & Interior Design, Computer Science, Economics, Engineering (General), Environmental Studies, Management, Mathematics, Physics, Science (General)
ISBN Prefix(es): 3-7281
Number of titles published annually: 70 Print

Verbandsdruckerei AG
Laupenstra 7a, 3000 Bern
Tel: (031) 252911
Telex: 32255
Key Personnel
Man Dir: Markus Rubli
Founded: 1919
Book publishing branch of Grafino Grafische Betriebe AG (Grafino Printing House).
Subjects: Agriculture, Nonfiction (General), Regional Interests
ISBN Prefix(es): 3-7280

Verkehrshaus der Schweiz
Lidostr 5, 6006 Lucerne
Tel: 314444 *Fax:* 316168
Key Personnel
Dir: Fredy Rey
Subjects: Communications, Transportation
ISBN Prefix(es): 3-85954
Branch Office(s)
Museum of Transportation & Communication

Verlagsbuchhandling AG
St Alban-Vorstadt 56, 4006 Basel
Tel: (061) 239723
Key Personnel
Dir: Franz Kaeser; Willy Kohler
Manager: Andre Horisberger
Founded: 1897
Subjects: Crafts, Games, Hobbies, Ethnicity, Music, Dance, Regional Interests
ISBN Prefix(es): 3-85715
Imprints: Schweizerischen Gesellschaft fuer Volkskunde (Swiss Folklore Society)
Orders to: Gesellschaft fuer Volkskunde, St Alban-Vorstadt 56, 4006 Basel

Editions Eliane Vernay+
79, rue des Eaux-Vives, 1207 Geneva
Tel: (022) 7350460 *Fax:* (022) 7350460
Key Personnel
Man Dir: Eliane Vernay
Founded: 1977
Subjects: Poetry
ISBN Prefix(es): 2-88291

Editions du Verseau, *imprint of* Roth et Sauter SA

Versus Verlag AG+
Merkurstr 45, 8032 Zurich
Tel: (01) 2510892 *Fax:* (01) 2626738
E-mail: info@versus.ch
Web Site: www.versus.ch
Key Personnel
Contact: Anne Buechi
Founded: 1993
Subjects: Accounting, Art, Business, Economics, Finance, Human Relations, Labor, Industrial Relations, Law, Management, Marketing, Public Administration
ISBN Prefix(es): 3-908143; 3-909066
Distributed by Linde Verlag Vienna (for Austria)

Verlag Alfred Vetter
Gartenstr 15, 8002 Zurich
Tel: (01) 2011184
ISBN Prefix(es): 3-85956

Vexer Verlag+
Brauerstr 27 B, 9000 Saint Gallen
Tel: (071) 2778151 *Fax:* (071) 2447987
E-mail: vexer@freesurf.ch
Key Personnel
Contact: Josef Felix Mueller
Founded: 1985
Subjects: Art, Film, Video, Literature, Literary Criticism, Essays
ISBN Prefix(es): 3-909090
Total Titles: 80 Print
Distributed by Buchandlung Walther Konig

Viktoria-Verlag Peter Marti
Loewenmattweg 5, 3110 Munsingen
Tel: (031) 7911932 *Fax:* (031) 7912564
Subjects: Humor, Regional Interests
ISBN Prefix(es): 3-85958

Editions Vivez Soleil SA+
15 rue Francois-Jacquier, Case Postale 313, 1225 Chene-Bourg, Geneva
Mailing Address: BP 18, 74103 Annemasse cedex, France
Tel: (022) 3492092 *Fax:* (022) 3492092
Key Personnel
President: Dr Christian Tal Schaller
Dir: Mr Marcel-Diedier, VRAC
Founded: 1987
Subjects: Health, Nutrition, Human Relations, Parapsychology, Psychology, Psychiatry
ISBN Prefix(es): 2-88058
Orders to: 21, rue des Tournelles, 74100 Ville-La-Grand

Verlag A Vogel
Postfach 63, Haetschen, 9053 Teufen
Tel: (071) 335 66 66 *Fax:* (071) 334684
E-mail: vavch@access.ch
Web Site: www.verlag-avogel.ch
Key Personnel
Contact: Silvia Loher *Tel:* (071) 335 66 70
ISBN Prefix(es): 3-906404
Number of titles published annually: 1 Print

Vogt-Schild Ag, Druck und Verlag+
Domacherstr 35-39, 4501 Solothurn 1
Tel: (065) 247247 *Fax:* (065) 247244
Telex: 934646 *Cable:* PRINTERS SOLEURE
Key Personnel
Dir: Dr Markus H Haefely
Public Relations: Hans A Roelli
Founded: 1906
Specialize in periodicals.
Subjects: Architecture & Interior Design, Chemistry, Chemical Engineering, Electronics, Electrical Engineering, Technology, Transportation
ISBN Prefix(es): 3-85962

Subsidiaries: Jeger Moll Druck und Verlag AG
Orders to: Vogt-Schild Ag

Verlag Die Waage+
Dorfstr 90, 8802 Kilchberg
Tel: (01) 7155569; (01) 7241969 *Fax:* (01) 7243127
Key Personnel
Publisher & International Rights: Felix M Wiesner
Founded: 1951
Subjects: Fiction, Literature, Literary Criticism, Essays, Philosophy
ISBN Prefix(es): 3-85966

Verlag im Waldgut AG+
Eisenwerk, Industriestr 21, 8500 Frauenfeld
Tel: (054) 222344 *Fax:* (054) 7288927
Key Personnel
President & Chief Editor: Beat Brechbuehl
Founded: 1980
Founded by Beat Brechbuehl, writer & publisher, in Wald near Zurich. In 1987 the publishing house moved to Frauenfeld & expanded its program.
Subjects: Developing Countries, Education, Ethnicity, Foreign Countries, Poetry
ISBN Prefix(es): 3-7294

Walter Verlag AG+
Dorfstr 81, CH-8706 Meilen
Mailing Address: PO Box 121, CH-8706 Meilen
Tel: (062) 341188 *Fax:* (062) 321184
Web Site: www.walter-verlag.ch
Key Personnel
Dir: Machalet Chnshan
Publicity: Charlotte Kraehenbuehl
Rights & Permissions: Erika Straumann
Founded: 1924
Subjects: Psychology, Psychiatry, Regional Interests, Religion - Other
ISBN Prefix(es): 3-530

WCC Publications, see World Council of Churches (WCC Publications)

Weber SA d'Editions
Case Postale 109, 1224 Chene-Dorugeries
Tel: (07) 93104541
Key Personnel
Man Dir: Marcel Weber
Founded: 1951
Subjects: Architecture & Interior Design, Art, Health, Nutrition, Library & Information Sciences, Photography
ISBN Prefix(es): 2-7190; 2-88301; 3-295

Weka Informations Schriften Verlag AG+
Hermetschloostr 77, 8010 Zurich
Tel: (01) 4328432 *Fax:* (01) 4328201
Key Personnel
Man Dir: Robert Boss
Founded: 1978
Specialize in Loose-Leaf Publication.
Subjects: Computer Science, Law, Management
ISBN Prefix(es): 3-297
Parent Company: WEKA Firmengruppe GmbH, Roemerstr 4, 86438 Kissing, Germany

Weltrundschau Verlag AG+
Postfach 659, 6341 Baar
Tel: 7615431 *Fax:* 7614404
E-mail: wrs@bluewin.ch *Cable:* WORLDREVIEW
Key Personnel
Man Dir: F Truniger
Editorial: E Gysling
Founded: 1959
Subjects: Government, Political Science, Sports, Athletics

ISBN Prefix(es): 3-7283
Associate Companies: Jeunesse Verlagsanstalt, Kirchstr 1, Vaduz, Liechtenstein (Rights & Permissions)

Weltwoche ABC-Verlag+
Edenstr 20, Postfach, CH-8021 Zurich
Tel: (01) 2078643; (01) 2078650; (01) 2078756
Fax: (01) 2078680
E-mail: order@baz.ch
Key Personnel
President: Rudolf Baechtold
Man Dir: Peter Zwicky
Founded: 1937
Subjects: Art, Nonfiction (General)
ISBN Prefix(es): 3-85504; 3-85975; 3-9520932
Book Club(s): SBVV

Wepf & Co AG
Eisengasse 5, Postfach 2064, 4001 Basel
Tel: (061) 3119576 *Fax:* (061) 3119585
E-mail: wepf@dial.eunet.ch *Cable:* WEPFCO BASEL
Key Personnel
Dir: H Herrmann; M Weber
Manager: Hans Jo Pfeiffer
Founded: 1902
Subjects: Architecture & Interior Design, Earth Sciences, Ethnicity, Geography, Geology
ISBN Prefix(es): 3-85977
Number of titles published annually: 5 Print

Werner Druck AG
Kanonengasse 32, 4051 Basel
Tel: (061) 2710690 *Fax:* (061) 2710601
Key Personnel
President & Co-Dir: Dr H G Hinderling
Co-Dir: N Werner
Founded: 1862
Subjects: Art
ISBN Prefix(es): 3-85979

Buchverlag der Druckerei Wetzikon AG
Rapperswilerstr 1, Postf, 8620 Wetzikon 1
Tel: (01) 9333111 *Fax:* (01) 9323232
Telex: 875547
Subjects: Environmental Studies
ISBN Prefix(es): 3-85981

Wiese Verlag AG+
Hochbergerstr 15, Postfach, 4002 Basel
Tel: (061) 661350 *Fax:* (061) 661343
E-mail: order@baz.ch
Key Personnel
Publisher: Peter Zwicky
Founded: 1988
Subjects: Architecture & Interior Design, Art, Crafts, Games, Hobbies
ISBN Prefix(es): 3-909158; 3-909164
Parent Company: Basler Zeitung
Book Club(s): SBVV

Verlag Alexander Wild+
Rathausgasse 30, CH-3011 Berne
Tel: (031) 224480 *Fax:* (031) 3114470
Key Personnel
Man Dir, Owner: Alexander Wild
Founded: 1977
Subjects: Literature, Literary Criticism, Essays
ISBN Prefix(es): 3-7284; 3-85982
Associate Companies: Origo-Verlag
Distributor for Origo-Verlag

WMO, see World Meteorological Organization

Die WochenZeitung
Postfach, CH-8031 Zurich
Tel: (01) 2721500 *Fax:* (01) 2721501
E-mail: woz@woz.links.ch

SWITZERLAND

J E Wolfensberger AG
Bederstr 109, 8027 Zurich
Tel: (01) 2857878 *Fax:* (01) 2012054
E-mail: wolfsberg@access.ch
Web Site: www.wolfensberger-ag.ch
Key Personnel
Dir: Ulla Wolfensberger
Founded: 1905
Subjects: Art, Lithographs, Limited editions, signed & numbered
ISBN Prefix(es): 3-85987

World Council of Churches (WCC Publications)+
Route de Ferney, 1211 Geneva 2
Mailing Address: PO Box 2100, 1211 Geneva 2
Tel: (022) 7916111 *Toll Free Tel:* 800-523-8211
Fax: (022) 7981346
Web Site: www.wcc-coe.org
Telex: 415730 OIK CH *Cable:* OIKOUMENE, GENEVA
Key Personnel
General Secretary: Konrad Raiser
Dir & Publisher: Jan H Kok
International Rights: Heather Stunt *Tel:* (022) 7916379 *E-mail:* hs@wcc-coe.org
Founded: 1948
Subjects: Religion - Other, Theology
ISBN Prefix(es): 2-8254
Total Titles: 15 Print
Branch Office(s)
World Council of Churches, Room 915, 475 Riverside Dr, New York, NY 10015-0050, United States
Distributed by Asian Trading Co (India); Christian Literature Society of Korea; Conference of Churches in Aotearoa-New Zealand; Ecumenical Council of Denmark; Intercultural Publications (India); ISPCK (India); Korea Christian Book Service; Methodist Publishing House (South Africa); National Council of Churches in Australia; United Church Distribution Center (Canada)
Bookshop(s): Epworth Bookshop, Wellington, New Zealand; Examiner Bookshop, Bombay, India
Shipping Address: Distribution Center, PO Box 348, Rte 222 & Sharadin Rd, Kuztown, PA 19530-0348, United States *Fax:* 610-683-5616

World Meteorological Organization
Case Postale No 5, 41 Avenue Giuseppe-Motta Tyotta, CH-1211 Geneva 20
Tel: (022) 246400 *Fax:* (022) 7308022
Telex: 414199 OMM CH; 23260 *Cable:* METEOMOND GENEVE
ISBN Prefix(es): 92-63

World Wild Life Films (Pty) Ltd
Eduard Zingg, Postfach 2942, CH-8023 Zurich
Tel: (01) 4331444 *Fax:* (01) 4331460
Key Personnel
Man Dir: Eduard Zingg
ISBN Prefix(es): 3-85986

Wyss Verlag AG Bern
Effingerstr 17, 3008 Bern
Tel: (031) 253715; (031) 254425 *Fax:* (031) 3814821; (031) 254821
Key Personnel
Dir: Christoph Wyss
Founded: 1849
Subjects: Art, History, Law
ISBN Prefix(es): 3-7285

Zbinden Druck und Verlag AG
St Alban-Vostadt 16, 4006 Basel
Tel: (061) 2722104; (061) 2722105 *Fax:* (061) 2726722
Key Personnel
Man Dir: Kurt Krause

Subjects: Anthropology, Biography, Education, Poetry
ISBN Prefix(es): 3-85989

Ziegler Druck- und Verlags-AG, Gemsberg-Verlag, Foto & Schmalfilm-Verlag
Postfach 778, Garnmarkt 10, 8401 Winterthur
Tel: (052) 857171 *Fax:* (052) 2133521
Key Personnel
Manager: Alfons Rueede
ISBN Prefix(es): 3-85701

Editions Zoe
11 rue des Moraines, 1227 Carouge, Geneva
Tel: (022) 3420578 *Fax:* (022) 3432964
Key Personnel
Man Dir: Marlyse Pietri-Bachmann
Founded: 1975
Subjects: History, Literature, Literary Criticism, Essays, Social Sciences, Sociology
ISBN Prefix(es): 2-88182

Zuerich, *imprint of* Interfrom AG Editions

Zumstein & Cie
Zeughausgasse 24, Postfach 187, 3000 Bern 7
Tel: (031) 222215; (031) 222217 *Fax:* (031) 212326
E-mail: post_zumstein@briefmarker.ch
Founded: 1905
Subjects: Crafts, Games, Hobbies
ISBN Prefix(es): 3-909278; 3-85994

Syrian Arab Republic

General Information

Capital: Damascus
Language: Arabic and some Kurdish.
Religion: Islamic (mostly of the Sunni sect) and Christian
Population: 13.7 million
Bank Hours: 0800-1400 Saturday-Thursday
Shop Hours: 1000-1900. Closed Friday. Generally long closing at lunchtime
Currency: 100 piastres = 1 Syrian pound
Export/Import Information: No tariffs on books except children's picture books, with additional taxes; most advertising matter is dutied. State organization for control and execution of publicity and advertising within Syria is Arab Advertising Organization, Damascus. The General Advertising Institute, 2842, must get samples of commercial advertising and promotional materials before distribution permitted. Import license must be submitted to Commercial Bank of Syria in order to obtain exchange license.
Copyright: No copyright conventions signed

Damascus University Press
Damascus
Tel: (011) 2215100 *Fax:* (011) 2236010
Telex: 411971
Key Personnel
Dir: Dr Hussain Omran
Subjects: Accounting, Agriculture, Anthropology, Archaeology, Architecture & Interior Design, Art, Behavioral Sciences, Business, Chemistry, Chemical Engineering, Civil Engineering, Communications, Computer Science, Earth Sciences, Economics, Education, Electronics, Electrical Engineering, Engineering (General), English as a Second Language, Environmental Studies, Finance, Geography, Geology, Government, Political Science, Health, Nutrition, History, Journalism, Language Arts, Linguistics, Law, Library & Information Sciences, Marketing, Mathematics, Mechanical Engineering, Medicine, Nursing, Dentistry, Natural History, Philosophy, Physics, Poetry, Psychology, Psychiatry, Public Administration, Religion - Islamic, Science (General), Social Sciences, Sociology, Transportation

Dar Al Maarifah (House of Knowledge)
PO Box 30268, Damascus
Tel: (011) 2210269 *Fax:* (011) 2241615
E-mail: staha@net.sy
Web Site: www.easyquram.com

Institut Francais d'Etudes Arabes de Damas
BP 344, Damascus
Tel: (011) 3330214; (011) 3331962; (011) 3334959 *Fax:* (011) 3327887
E-mail: ifead@net.sy
Web Site: www.univ-aioc.fr/iflead
Telex: 412.272 IFEAD SY
Key Personnel
Dir: Dominique Mallet
Founded: 1922
Specialize in academic publications.
Subjects: Anthropology, Archaeology, Geography, Geology, History, Language Arts, Linguistics, Literature, Literary Criticism, Essays, Philosophy, Religion - Islamic, Social Sciences, Sociology
ISBN Prefix(es): 2-901315; 2-84128
Number of titles published annually: 8 Print
Total Titles: 4 Print
Parent Company: Direction Generale des Relations Culturelles Scientifiques et Techniques, Ministere des affaires Etrangeres, Paris, France
Distributed by Al-Jaffan et al Jabi (Middle East)
Orders to: Librairie d'Amerique et d'Orient (Adrien Maisonneuve), 11, rue St-Sulpice, F-75006 Paris, France *Tel:* (01) 43268635 *Fax:* (01) 43545954

Taiwan, Province of China

General Information

Capital: Taipei
Language: Northern Chinese (Mandarin)
Religion: Predominantly Buddhist, also Muslim, Daoist, & Christian
Population: 20.9 million
Bank Hours: 0900-1530 Monday-Friday; 0900-1200 Saturday
Shop Hours: 1000-2130 Monday-Saturday
Currency: 100 cents = 1 new Taiwan dollar
Export/Import Information: No tariffs on books and advertising. Import licenses required; exchange available when license is presented at authorized bank. Publications approved for import will not violate the Republic of China's basic national policy, undermine public morality or contravene special regulations.
Copyright: No copyright conventions signed. Copyright is protected by the Copyright Law. Companies and individuals, including foreigners, can register their works with the Ministry of the Interior for portection. An amendment broading the scope of the Republic of China's Copyright Law was passed 28 June 1985 by the Legislative Yuan and put into effect on 12 July 1985. The amendment, aimed at curbing pirating activities, sharply increases the maximum sentence for violating copyrights from

three to five years and the maximum fine from US $75 to US $11,250, and brings computer software and video tapes under the scope of the law. Publications printed in Taiwan must acquire approval from the copyright holder before export.

Ai Chih Book Co Ltd
34, Alley 16, Lane 94, Techeng St, Kaohsiung
Tel: (07) 8121571 *Fax:* (07) 8121534
Key Personnel
Contact: Yang Baong Min
Subjects: Child Care & Development, Literature, Literary Criticism, Essays
ISBN Prefix(es): 957-608

Arsorigo Co Ltd+
5F, 14, Alley 2, Ho-ping E Rd, Sec 2, Taipei
Tel: (02) 7252387 *Fax:* (02) 7252387
Key Personnel
Chief Executive: Yuan ChiiShen

Art Book Co Ltd+
4F, 18, Lane 283, Roosevelt Rd, Section 3, Taipei
Tel: (02) 23620578 *Fax:* (02) 23623594
E-mail: artbook@ms43.hinet.net
Key Personnel
Publisher: Kung-shang Ho
Founded: 1972
Specialize in Fine Arts.
Subjects: Antiques, Art, History, How-to
ISBN Prefix(es): 957-672; 957-9045

The Artist Publishing Co
6F, 147, Chungching S Rd, Sec 1, Taipei
Tel: (02) 3932780; (02) 23932780 *Fax:* (02) 3932012; (02) 23932012
Key Personnel
Chief Executive: Ho Cheng-Kuang
Founded: 1975
Subjects: Art
ISBN Prefix(es): 957-9500; 957-8273; 957-9530

Asian Culture Co+
6F, 21, Nanching East Rd, Sec 3, Taipei
Tel: (02) 5072606 *Fax:* (02) 5074260
Key Personnel
President: Eric Tong-sheng Wu
International Rights: Mr Yuan-chun Ting
Subjects: Archaeology, Asian Studies, Business, Fiction, Health, Nutrition, History, Literature, Literary Criticism, Essays, Philosophy, Self-Help, Women's Studies
ISBN Prefix(es): 957-8983; 957-9027; 957-9449

Bookman Books, Ltd+
2F-5, 88, Hsinsheng S Rd, Sec 3, Taipei
Tel: (02) 3658617 *Fax:* (02) 3653548
Key Personnel
Man Dir: Jerome (Cheng-lung) Su
Founded: 1977
Also acts as exclusive agents in Taiwan for W W Norton, USA, & Faber & Faber, UK.
Subjects: Literature, Literary Criticism, Essays, Social Sciences, Sociology
ISBN Prefix(es): 957-586

Campus Evangelical Fellowship, Literature Department+
22, Roosevelt Rd, Sec 4, Taipei 10764
Tel: (02) 23653665-331 *Fax:* (02) 3680303
E-mail: publish@campus.org.tw
Key Personnel
Dir: Hui-Ping Peng
Vice Dir: Ruth Cha
Editor: Stephen Wu
Founded: 1965
Subjects: Biblical Studies, Biography, Child Care & Development, Human Relations, Religion - Protestant
ISBN Prefix(es): 957-587
Branch Office(s)
Overseas Campus Magazine, PO Box 638, Lomita, CA 90717-0638, United States

Cheng Chung Book Co, Ltd
20, Hengyang Rd, Taipei
Tel: (02) 3821147 *Fax:* (02) 3822805
Subjects: Education
ISBN Prefix(es): 957-09

Cheng Wen Publishing Company
3F, 277 Roosevelt Rd, Sec 3, Taipei
Mailing Address: 9, Lane 6, Hang Chow, South Rd, Sec 1, PO Box 22605, 22605 Taipei
Tel: (02) 3628032 *Fax:* (02) 3925428
Key Personnel
Chief Executive & Publisher: Larry C Huang
Founded: 1964
ISBN Prefix(es): 957-07

Cheng Yun Publishing Company Ltd+
Room 6, 12F, 601, Chungcheng Rd, Taipei
Tel: (02) 8117798 *Fax:* (02) 8123041
Key Personnel
Chief Executive: Lai Yen-Ping
Founded: 1991
ISBN Prefix(es): 957-9241
Associate Companies: Seven Brocades Products Inc

Chien Chen Bookstore Publishing Company Ltd+
80, Liming Rd, Kaohsiung
Tel: (07) 3820363 *Fax:* (07) 3892816
Key Personnel
Chief Exec: Mu-Shiung Chang
Founded: 1977
Subjects: Accounting, Agriculture, Animals, Pets, Behavioral Sciences, Biological Sciences, Business, Career Development
ISBN Prefix(es): 957-9574; 957-704

Chin Chin Publications Ltd
274-1, Hop'ing E Rd, Sec 1, Taipei
Tel: (02) 3633486 *Fax:* (02) 3636081
ISBN Prefix(es): 957-9427

China Law Magazine Ltd
130 Ch'ungch'ing S Rd Sec 1, Province of Taiwan, Taipei
Tel: (02) 23814211 *Fax:* (02) 23814211
E-mail: chinals@hk.china.com
ISBN Prefix(es): 957-99166
Parent Company: China Legal Service (UK) Ltd, United Kingdom

China Times Publishing Co+
4F, 240, Hop'ing W Rd, Sec3, Taipei
Tel: (02) 23087111 *Fax:* (02) 23027844
Web Site: www.chinatimes.com.tw
ISBN Prefix(es): 957-13

Chinese Christian Literature Council Taiwan Ltd
2F, 277, Hoping E Rd, Sec 2, Taipei
Tel: (02) 7080230 *Fax:* (02) 7551895
Key Personnel
Chief Executive: Lien-Hwa Chow
ISBN Prefix(es): 957-9186

Chu Liu Book Company+
Rm 312, 25, Poai Rd, Taipei 10035
Tel: (02) 3711031 *Fax:* (02) 3815823
E-mail: chuliu@ms13.hinet.net
Key Personnel
Off Manager: Paul Hsiung
Founded: 1973
Subjects: Child Care & Development, Education, History, Human Relations, Literature, Literary Criticism, Essays, Psychology, Psychiatry, Social Sciences, Sociology
ISBN Prefix(es): 957-732; 957-9464

Chung Hwa Book Co Ltd+
14F, 51, Chilung Rd, Sec 2, Taipei
Tel: (02) 3117365 *Fax:* (02) 7355887 *Cable:* 2821 TAIPEI
Key Personnel
Man Dir: James C Hsiung
Vice President: Erica Hsiung
Founded: 1912
Subjects: Art, Biography, Education, Engineering (General), Fiction, History, Literature, Literary Criticism, Essays, Medicine, Nursing, Dentistry, Music, Dance, Philosophy, Poetry, Psychology, Psychiatry, Religion - Other, Science (General), Social Sciences, Sociology
ISBN Prefix(es): 957-43

Commonwealth Publishing Company Ltd+
2F, 1, Lane 93, Sung Chiang Rd, Taipei 104
Tel: (02) 2517-3688 *Fax:* (02) 2517-3686
Web Site: www.bookzone.com.tw
Key Personnel
President: Charles Kao
Publisher: Cora Wang
Founded: 1982
General trade & translated titles.
Subjects: Biography, Business, Child Care & Development, Economics, Fiction, Health, Nutrition, Management, Nonfiction (General), Science (General), Self-Help
ISBN Prefix(es): 957-621
Number of titles published annually: 150 Print
Associate Companies: CommonWealth Magazine, 4F, No 87, Sung Chiang Rd, Taipei 104
Tel: (02) 2507 8627; Global Views Monthly Magazine

Cynosure Publishing Inc+
3F, 26, Lane 91, Neihu Rd, Sec 1, Taipei
Tel: (02) 26573275 *Fax:* (02) 26575300
E-mail: cynobook@tpts4.seed.net.tw
Key Personnel
Exec Dir: Jimmy C C Chen
Founded: 1989
Also acts as Packager.
ISBN Prefix(es): 957-9158; 957-9430
Parent Company: Long Ken Corp Ltd
Book Club(s): Hello! Book Club Inc, 5F, No 203, Chung Hsiao E Rd, Sec 3, Taipei, ROC
Tel: (02) 27401281 *Fax:* (02) 27401545
E-mail: heloclub@ms22.hinet.net *Web Site:* www.hellobookclub.com

Dayi Information Co
5F, 98, Kwangfu N Rd, Taipei
Tel: (02) 5796800 *Fax:* (02) 5796805
Key Personnel
Contact: Jeff Wang
Founded: 1992
Subjects: Business
ISBN Prefix(es): 957-99775

Designer Publisher Inc
7F, 159-2, Shita Rd, Taipei
Tel: (02) 23656268 *Fax:* (02) 23676500
Key Personnel
Chief Executive: Wang Su-Chao
Founded: 1992
ISBN Prefix(es): 957-9570
Imprints: Wang Su-Chao
Subsidiaries: Graphic Communications Monthly

Echo Publishing Company Ltd+
3F, 5-2, Alley 16, Lane 72, Pate Rd, Sec 4, Taipei
Tel: (02) 27361452 *Fax:* (02) 27568712
Key Personnel
Chief Executive: Ms Linda Wu
Founded: 1970

TAIWAN, PROVINCE OF CHINA

Subjects: Anthropology, Antiques, Archaeology, Architecture & Interior Design, Art, Asian Studies, Child Care & Development, Crafts, Games, Hobbies
ISBN Prefix(es): 957-588
Associate Companies: Echo Communications Co Ltd
Distributed by Charles E Tuttle Co (USA & UK)

Far East Book Co Ltd
10F, 66-1, Ch'ungch'ing S Rd, Sec 1, Taipei
Tel: (02) 3118740 *Fax:* (02) 3114184 *Cable:* 1418 TAIPEI
Key Personnel
Manager: Jonathan Riverbank
Subjects: Art, Education, History, Literature, Literary Criticism, Essays, Physics, Poetry
ISBN Prefix(es): 957-9666; 957-612

Farseeing Publishing Company Ltd+
4F, 50-1, Hsinsheng S Rd, Section 1, Taipei
Tel: (02) 3932166 *Fax:* (02) 3225455
E-mail: fars@msb.ninet.net
Key Personnel
Chief Executive: Hsiao Feng-Fu
Subjects: English as a Second Language, Health, Nutrition, Medicine, Nursing, Dentistry
ISBN Prefix(es): 957-640; 957-9506; 957-99215; 957-99266
Associate Companies: Weyfar Books Co Ltd
Subsidiaries: Farseeing Nursing Press
Divisions: Fayfar Publishing Co Ltd

Fuh-Wen Book Co+
63, Linsen Rd, Sec 2, Tainan, Taiwan
Tel: (06) 2386935 *Fax:* (06) 2347222
Key Personnel
President: Wu Chu-Ho
Vice President: James Chin
Editor: Shih Shu-Yen
Subjects: Accounting, Agriculture, Automotive, Chemistry, Chemical Engineering, Civil Engineering, Computer Science, Economics, Electronics, Electrical Engineering, Engineering (General), Environmental Studies, Finance, Marketing, Mathematics, Mechanical Engineering, Physical Sciences, Physics, Science (General)
ISBN Prefix(es): 957-536
Subsidiaries: Taiwan Fuh-Wen Sin-Yah Co Ltd
Branch Office(s)
985 Papen Rd, Bridgewater, NJ 08807, United States
Book Club(s): ABA
Shipping Address: The Kaohsiung Port
Warehouse: No 18 Alley 88 Lane 71, Fuh-Sin Rd, Yung-Kang Village, Tainan County

Great China Book Corporation
66, Ch'ungch'ing S Rd, Section 1, Taipei
Tel: (02) 23311433 *Fax:* (02) 23895866
ISBN Prefix(es): 957-521

Grimm Press Ltd+
7F, 134, Poai Rd, Taipei
Tel: (02) 23517251 *Fax:* (02) 23517244
E-mail: grimm@gmail.gcn.net.tw
Key Personnel
Publisher: K T Hao
International Rights: Catherine Van Hale
Subjects: Fiction
ISBN Prefix(es): 957-745

Chu Hai Publishing (Taiwan) Co Ltd
2F-1, 151, Anho Rd, Taipei
Tel: (02) 7039867 *Fax:* (02) 7084804
Key Personnel
International Rights: Gee H Luk
Subjects: Agriculture, Architecture & Interior Design, Art, Business, Civil Engineering, Computer Science, Engineering (General), Environmental Studies, Gardening, Plants, Health, Nutrition, Medicine, Nursing, Dentistry, Social Sciences, Sociology, Travel
ISBN Prefix(es): 957-657

Heavenly Lotus Publishing Co, Ltd
2F, 168, Chungch'eng Rd, Sec 2, Taipei
Tel: (02) 8736629 *Fax:* (02) 8736709
Key Personnel
President: Yun-Pen Lee
Founded: 1975
Subjects: Religion - Other
ISBN Prefix(es): 957-665; 957-9397

Highlight Publishing Company Ltd+
11F-7, 79, Hsintai Fifth Rd, Section 1, Hsichih 10650
Tel: (02) 6984565; (02) 26984633 *Fax:* (02) 6984980
E-mail: hilit@tpts5.seed.net.tw
Web Site: www.ptri.org.tw/hilit
Key Personnel
President: Dixson Sung
Founded: 1976
Subjects: Antiques, Art, Asian Studies, Cookery, Crafts, Games, Hobbies, Fiction, Gardening, Plants, How-to
ISBN Prefix(es): 957-629
Parent Company: Hilit Publishing Co Ltd
Associate Companies: Highlight International Co Ltd
Warehouse: 35, Lanc 142, Kun Yang St, Taipei

Hilit Publishing Co Ltd+
11F-7, No 79, Hsintai Fifth Rd, Sec 1, Hsichih
Tel: (02) 26984565; (02) 26984633 *Fax:* (02) 6984980
E-mail: hilit@tpts5.seed.net.tw
Key Personnel
Secretary: Jennifer Chien
Subjects: Cookery, Geography, Geology, Library & Information Sciences, Literature, Literary Criticism, Essays, Women's Studies

Ho-Chi Book Publishing Co+
2F, 207, Wuhsing St, Taipei 114
Tel: (02) 2974-0168 *Fax:* (02) 2792-4702
E-mail: hochi@ms12.hinet.net; hochi@email.gcn.net.tw
Key Personnel
Contact: Wu Kuei-tsung
Founded: 1956
Subjects: Behavioral Sciences, Biological Sciences, Child Care & Development, Health, Nutrition, Medicine, Nursing, Dentistry, Psychology, Psychiatry, Veterinary Science, Life Science
ISBN Prefix(es): 957-666; 957-9097
Distributor for Churchill Livingstone; Lippincott-Raven; McGraw-Hill; W B Saunders; Williams & Wilkins
Bookshop(s): Ho-Chi Book Store (Bei-yi Branch), Suite 249, Wu-Hsing St., Taipei 110 *Tel:* (02) 2723-9404 *Fax:* (02) 2723-0997; Tai-da Branch, Suite 7, Lane 12, Roosevelt Rd., Sec 4, Taipei 100 *Tel:* (02) 2365-1544 *Fax:* (02) 2367-1266; Rong-Zong Branch, Suite 120, Shih-Pai Rd, Sec 2, Taipei 112 *Tel:* (02) 2826-5375 *Fax:* (02) 2823-9604; Taichung Branch, Suite 24, Yu-Der Rd, Taichung *Tel:* (04) 203-0795 *Fax:* (04) 202-5093; Kaohsiung Branch, Suite 1, Pei-Peng 1st St, Kaohsiung 800 *Tel:* (07) 322-6177 *Fax:* (07) 323-5118

Hsiao Yuan Publication Co, Ltd+
5, Lane 7, Ch'ingt'ien St, Taipei
Tel: (02) 3949931 *Fax:* (02) 3417931
Key Personnel
Vice President: Feng Chu Huang-Yu
Subjects: Business, Chemistry, Chemical Engineering, Computer Science, Electronics, Electrical Engineering, English as a Second Language, Literature, Literary Criticism, Essays, Mathematics, Physical Sciences, Technology
ISBN Prefix(es): 957-12
Bookshop(s): No 96-3, Sec 3, Hsin Sheng S Rd, Taipei

Hsin Yi Publications+
75, Chung-ching S Rd, Sec 2, Taipei
Tel: (02) 23965303 *Fax:* (02) 23910799
Web Site: www.hsin-yi.org.tw//
Key Personnel
Publisher: Show Chung Ho
Chief Editor: Sin-Ju Ho
Director: Jung-Chen Cheng *E-mail:* jung@hsin-yi.org.tw
Founded: 1978
Distributed by Shen's Books & Supplies, 8625 Hubbard Rd, Auburn, CA 95602.
ISBN Prefix(es): 957-642; 957-9526
Total Titles: 1,000 Print
Online services available through www.hsin-yi.org.tw.
Parent Company: Hsin Yi Foundation
Associate Companies: Hsinex International Corporation, 75 Chung-Chin S Rd, Sec 2, Taipei, Santee Wen *Tel:* (02) 23913384 *Fax:* (02) 23913384 *E-mail:* santee@hsin-hi.org.tw

Hu Yu She Culture Co Ltd, see HYS Culture Co Ltd

HYS Culture Co Ltd+
2, Alley 3, Lane 130, Paoan Rd, Yungan, Kaohsiung
Tel: (07) 6914310 *Fax:* (02) 6914311
E-mail: hysccl@msl.hinet.net
Key Personnel
General Manager: Mr G L Hsu
Subjects: Animals, Pets
ISBN Prefix(es): 957-9561

Jillion Publishing Co+
2F, Lane 12, Nanching West Rd, Taipei
Tel: (02) 5432682 *Fax:* (02) 5231891
Key Personnel
Chief Exec: Ai Tien-Shi
Founded: 1985
Subjects: Career Development, English as a Second Language, How-to, Language Arts, Linguistics
ISBN Prefix(es): 957-9415; 957-786

Kuang Fu Book Co Ltd+
6F, 38, Fuhsing N Rd, Taipei
Tel: (02) 7716622 *Fax:* (02) 7315982
E-mail: lolatiao@kfgroup.com.tw
Web Site: www.kfgroup.com.tw
Key Personnel
President: Mr C H Lin
Foreign Affairs Executive: Mr Hong-Long Lin
Foreign Rights & Manager: Ming-Yen Tiao *Tel:* (02) 2741-0415
Founded: 1962
Also specializing in distance learning.
Subjects: Art, Education, Fiction, Health, Nutrition, History, Literature, Literary Criticism, Essays, Medicine, Nursing, Dentistry, Science (General)
ISBN Prefix(es): 957-42
Total Titles: 2,000 Print; 80 CD-ROM
Imprints: Kwang Fu Book Enterprises Co, Ltd
Subsidiaries: Kwang Toong Book Department Store Co Ltd
U.S. Office(s): Tron Link Enterprises Co, Ltd, 9401 De Vry Dr, Irvine, CA, United States, Contact: Mr Hong-tien Lin *Tel:* 949-856-9769; 949-854-1569 *Fax:* 949-856-9769 *E-mail:* hongtien@aol.com
Book Club(s): New Reader's Book Club, Contact: Lola Tiao *Tel:* (02) 2771-6622 *E-mail:* bookclub@kfgroup.com.tw

PUBLISHERS — TAIWAN, PROVINCE OF CHINA

Kuei Kuan Book Co Ltd, see Laureate Book Co Ltd

Kwang Fu Book Enterprises Co, Ltd, *imprint of* Kuang Fu Book Co Ltd

Laureate Book Co Ltd+
96-4 Hsinsheng S Rd, Sec 3, Taipei
Tel: (02) 2193338 *Fax:* (02) 2182859
E-mail: laureate@ms10.hinet.net
Key Personnel
Manager: Ping-Chung Chang
Founded: 1975
Subjects: Anthropology, Behavioral Sciences, Business, Child Care & Development, Education, Government, Political Science, History, Literature, Literary Criticism, Essays, Management, Philosophy, Psychology, Psychiatry, Social Sciences, Sociology, Women's Studies
ISBN Prefix(es): 957-551

Lead Wave Publishing Company Ltd+
3F 2 Roosevelt Rd, Sec 4, Taipei
Tel: (02) 23650177 *Fax:* (02) 23656407
Web Site: www.liwil.com.tw
Subjects: Computer Science, Microcomputers
ISBN Prefix(es): 957-9252
Parent Company: Liwei Publishing Co Ltd

Lee & Lee Communications+
51 Chung Ching S Rd, 7th fl, Sec 2, Taipei 100
Tel: (02) 7068833 *Fax:* (02) 7066205
E-mail: leelee@tpts1.seed.net.tw
Key Personnel
Distribution Manager: Shumin Huang
Founded: 1988
Member of Association of Multimedia, International.
Subjects: Antiques, Art
ISBN Prefix(es): 957-99049

Lien Ho Wen Hsueh Press Co Ltd, see UNITAS Publishing Co Ltd

Liming Cultural Enterprise Co Ltd
19, Lane 482, Chungshan Rd, Sec 2, Chungho
Tel: (02) 3821146 *Fax:* (02) 3821240
ISBN Prefix(es): 957-16
Subsidiaries: Tai-Chung Kaohsiung/Two Cities
Bookshop(s): 49 Chung-King S Rd, Section 1, Taipei 100
Warehouse: 19 Lane 482 Chung-Shan Rd, Section 2, Chung-Ho, Hsieh

Lin Pai Press Company Ltd+
1F, 15, Lane 71, Lungchiang Rd, Taipei
Tel: (02) 7765889 *Fax:* (02) 7712568
Member of Republic of China Publisher's Association.
Subjects: Fiction, Journalism, Literature, Literary Criticism, Essays, Mysteries, Romance
ISBN Prefix(es): 957-593; 957-812
Parent Company: Lin Pai Publishing Co Ltd
Shipping Address: 271 Chungyang Rd, Nan Gang, Taipei
Warehouse: 6F3 Lane 327, Sec 2, Jongshan Rd, Jongher, Taipei Shiang

Linking Publishing Company Ltd+
3F, 367, Tat'ung Rd, Sec 1, Hsichih
Tel: (02) 7634300-5052 *Fax:* (02) 27634590
Key Personnel
Editorial Dir: Linden T C Lin
Founded: 1974
Subjects: Art, Asian Studies, Biography, Business, Career Development, Child Care & Development, Cookery, Economics, English as a Second Language, Fiction, Health, Nutrition, History, Human Relations, Literature, Literary Criticism, Essays, Management, Nonfiction (General), Self-Help, Travel, Wine & Spirits, Women's Studies
ISBN Prefix(es): 957-08

Liwil Publishing Co Ltd, see Lead Wave Publishing Company Ltd

Morning Star Publisher Inc+
One, Industrial District, 30 Rd, Taichung
Tel: (04) 3595820 *Fax:* (04) 3597123
Key Personnel
President: Ming-Min Chen
Founded: 1980
Subjects: Environmental Studies, Fiction, Health, Nutrition, How-to, Human Relations, Management, Regional Interests, Romance, Self-Help
ISBN Prefix(es): 957-583
U.S. Office(s): 21311 Espada Place, Diamond Bar City, CA 91765, United States *Tel:* 909-396-7811 *Fax:* 909-396-9511
Book Club(s): A B A

National Museum of History
49, Nanhai Rd, Taipei 10728
Tel: (02) 3610270-514 *Fax:* (02) 3610171
Subjects: Antiques, Art, Asian Studies, History

National Palace Museum
Publications Division, 221, Chihshan Rd, Sec 2, Taipei
Tel: (02) 8821230 *Fax:* (02) 8821440
E-mail: service@npm.gov.tw
Web Site: www.npm.gov.tw
Key Personnel
Director: Mr Cheng-shang Tu
Head of Publications Division: Ms Sai-lan Hu
Founded: 1983
Subjects: Antiques, Archaeology, Art, History
ISBN Prefix(es): 957-562
Bookshop(s): World Journal Book Store, 379 Broadway, New York, NY 10013, United States; Paragon Books, 1507 S Michigan Ave, Chicago, IL 60605, United States

Newton Publishing Company Ltd+
11F, 190, Chungcheng Rd, Hsintien
Tel: (02) 9159500 *Fax:* (02) 9159486
Key Personnel
Chairman: Kao Yuan Chin
President: Chun-Tus Liu
Dir, International Rights Dept: Kao Yung Hsin
Subjects: Biography, Management, Marketing, Mathematics, Medicine, Nursing, Dentistry, Nonfiction (General), Physical Sciences, Science (General), Social Sciences, Sociology
ISBN Prefix(es): 957-627
Subsidiaries: Little Newton Co; Newton Culture Viedeo Co
Distributed by Leader Books Co (Hong Kong); Transforma (Malaysia)

Pearson Education
9F, No 91, Kee-Lung Rd, Section 2, Taipei
Tel: (02) 2736 5155 *Fax:* (02) 2738 1970
E-mail: firstname@pearsoned.com.tw
Key Personnel
General Manager: Angela Yang
Sales Manager/HED: Anderson Ho
Finance/Administration Manager: Chris Chen
Sales Manager/ELT: Jeff Huang
Publishing Manager/TRSL: Stella Chou
Parent Company: Pearson Plc
Branch Office(s)
Roosevelt Rd, 7th floor, No 245, Section 3, Taipei *Tel:* 2368 3904 *Fax:* 2367 3994

Petroleum Information Publishing Co
2F, 895-50, Chungcheng Rd, Hsinchuang
Tel: (02) 9042387 *Fax:* (02) 9021060
E-mail: pip@tptsl.seed.net.tw
Key Personnel
Chief Executive: Hong Tse-Wen
Subjects: Chemistry, Chemical Engineering, Environmental Studies, Science (General), Technology
ISBN Prefix(es): 957-9694
Subsidiaries: Petroleum Information Magazine

San Min Book Co Ltd+
386, Fuhsin North Rd, Taipei
Tel: (02) 25006600 *Fax:* (02) 25064000
E-mail: sanmin@ms2.hinet.net
Web Site: www.sanmin.com.tw
Key Personnel
Publicity Manager: Chen-Chiang Liu
International Rights: Wang Yun-Fen
Editor: Allie Hwang
Founded: 1953
Subjects: Agriculture, Anthropology, Art, Computer Science, Economics, Education, Government, Political Science, Law, Mathematics, Philosophy, Science (General), Technology
ISBN Prefix(es): 957-14
Number of titles published annually: 300 Print
Total Titles: 4,000 Print
Subsidiaries: Grand East Enterprise

Senate Books Co Ltd+
5F-20, 1, Lane 126, Fuhsin S Rd, Sec 1, Taipei
Tel: (02) 7417576 *Fax:* (02) 7112713
E-mail: senatebooks@usa.net
Key Personnel
International Rights: James Peiscy
Founded: 1985
Subjects: Law
ISBN Prefix(es): 957-789
Distributor for Matthew Bender

Shuttle Multimedia Inc
5F, 96, Kuangfu N Rd, Taipei
Tel: (02) 5796800 *Fax:* (02) 5796805
Key Personnel
Contact: Jeff Wang
Founded: 1993
Develop & sell software, CD-title mainly.
Subjects: Education, English as a Second Language
ISBN Prefix(es): 957-99430

Shy Chaur Publishing Co Ltd+
5F, 19, Minsheng Rd, Hsintien
Tel: (02) 22183377 *Fax:* (02) 22183239
E-mail: chien218@ms5.hinet.net
Key Personnel
President: Chien Tai-Hsiung
International Rights: Lin Cheng-Tsung; Chien Yu Shan
Founded: 1992
Subjects: Health, Nutrition, Law, Real Estate, Science (General), Self-Help, Travel
ISBN Prefix(es): 957-776
Parent Company: Shy Mau Publishing Co

Shy Mau Publishing Company+
5F, 19, Minshing Rd, 5F, Hsintien
Tel: (02) 22183277 *Fax:* (02) 22183239
E-mail: chien218@ms5.hinet.net
Key Personnel
President: Chien Tai-Hsiung
International Rights: Lin Cheng-Tsung; Chien Yu Shan
Founded: 1982
Subjects: Business, Career Development, Child Care & Development, Cookery, Management, Medicine, Nursing, Dentistry, Psychology, Psychiatry, Self-Help
ISBN Prefix(es): 957-776
Subsidiaries: Shy Chaur Publishing Co Ltd

Sinorama Magazine Co+
8F, 15-1, Hangchou S Rd, Taipei
Tel: (02) 3922256 *Fax:* (02) 3615734

TAIWAN, PROVINCE OF CHINA

Key Personnel
Publisher: Jason Hu
Editor-in-Chief: Wang Jia-fong
Deputy Editor-in-Chief: Anna Y Wang
Founded: 1976
ISBN Prefix(es): 957-9188
U.S. Office(s): Kwan Hwa Publishing (USA), Inc, 300 Wilshire Blvd, Suite 1510 A, Los Angeles, CA 90048, United States *Tel:* 213-782-8770 *Fax:* 213-782-8761

SMC Publishing Inc+
1F, Alley 14, Lane 283, Roosevelt Rd, Sec 3, Taipei
Tel: (02) 3620190 *Fax:* (02) 3623834
Key Personnel
Manager: Wei Te-wen
Founded: 1976
Publish in English & Chinese.
Subjects: Anthropology, Art, Asian Studies, Biological Sciences, History, Medicine, Nursing, Dentistry, Religion - Buddhist
ISBN Prefix(es): 957-638; 957-9482

The Third Wave Enterprise Co Ltd
19-1, Lane 231, Fushing N Rd, Taipei
Tel: (02) 87803636 *Fax:* (02) 87805656
Key Personnel
International Information Dept Manager: David Tsai
Founded: 1981
ISBN Prefix(es): 957-23
Parent Company: Acer Inc
Associate Companies: Acer Advanced Inc; Acer Peripheral; Sertek
Distributor for Data Communication; LAN Times

Torch of Wisdom+
10, Lane 270, Chienkuo S Rd, Sec 1, Taipei
Tel: (02) 7075802 *Fax:* (02) 7085054
E-mail: tow@ms2.hinet.net
Key Personnel
Contact: Pro Cheng Chen-Huang
Founded: 1951
Subjects: Asian Studies, Health, Nutrition, Religion - Buddhist
ISBN Prefix(es): 957-518

UNITAS Publishing Co Ltd+
6F 180 Chilung Rd Section 1, Taipei
Tel: (02) 27634300 *Fax:* (02) 27567914
Key Personnel
Chief Editor: Mr Ann-Ming Tsu
International Rights: Paula C Wang
Founded: 1984
Subjects: Fiction, Journalism, Literature, Literary Criticism, Essays, Nonfiction (General), Poetry, Romance, Women's Studies
ISBN Prefix(es): 957-522

Wang Su-Chao, *imprint of* Designer Publisher Inc

Wei-Chuan Publishing Company Ltd+
5F, 125, Sunchiang Rd, Taipei
Tel: (02) 5063564 *Fax:* (02) 5074902
Key Personnel
Chief Executive: Huang Su-Huei
Founded: 1971
Subjects: Child Care & Development, Cookery, Crafts, Games, Hobbies, How-to
ISBN Prefix(es): 957-9285
Subsidiaries: Wei-Chuan's Publishing

World Book Co Ltd+
Rm 701, 99, Ch'ungch'ing S Rd, Sec 1, Taipei
Tel: (02) 23113834 *Fax:* (02) 3317963
Key Personnel
President: Angela Chu Yen
Founded: 1921

Subjects: Art, Drama, Theater, History, Literature, Literary Criticism, Essays, Medicine, Nursing, Dentistry, Philosophy, Poetry, Chinese Classics
ISBN Prefix(es): 957-06

Wu Nan Book Co Ltd+
4F, 339, Hop'ingtung E Rd, Sec 2, Taipei
Tel: (02) 27055066 *Fax:* (02) 27094875
E-mail: wunan@wunan.com.tw
Web Site: www.wunan.com.tw
ISBN Prefix(es): 957-11

Yee Wen Publishing Co Ltd+
4F-3, 253, Roosevelt Rd, Sec 3, Taipei
Tel: (02) 3626012 *Fax:* (02) 3660977
E-mail: yeewen@msg.hinet.net
Key Personnel
Chief Executive: Feng-Chiao Yen
Sales Manager: Ming-Fang Tsai
Editorial Manager: Jammy Yen *Tel:* 650-367-5020 *Fax:* 650-364-0960 *E-mail:* yeewen@ricochet.net
Founded: 1953
Subjects: Archaeology, Asian Studies, Ethnicity, Philosophy, Regional Interests, Religion - Other
ISBN Prefix(es): 0-88691; 957-520
Number of titles published annually: 12 Print
Total Titles: 3,000 Print
U.S. Office(s): 518 Oak Park Way, Redwood City, CA 94062-4038, United States, Contact: Jammy Yen *Tel:* 650-367-5020 *Fax:* 650-364-0960 *E-mail:* yeewen_us@yahoo.com

Yi Hsien Publishing Co Ltd+
2F-2, 50, Roosevelt Rd, Sec 4, Taipei
Tel: (02) 22192577 *Fax:* (02) 22198511
E-mail: yihsient@ms17.hinet.net
Key Personnel
President & International Rights: Ed Tung
Founded: 1975
Subjects: Agriculture, Animals, Pets, Biological Sciences, Chemistry, Chemical Engineering, Earth Sciences, Health, Nutrition, Medicine, Nursing, Dentistry, Psychology, Psychiatry, Publishing & Book Trade Reference, Science (General), Veterinary Science
ISBN Prefix(es): 957-616
Bookshop(s): No 3, Lane 316, Roosevelt Rd, Sec 3, Taipei; No 178, Wu-ch'ang St, Taichung

Youth Cultural Publishing Co+
3F, 66-1, Ch'ungch'ing S Rd, Sec 1, Taipei
Tel: (02) 23146001 *Fax:* (02) 3612239
E-mail: youth@ms2.hinet.net
Web Site: www.youth.com.tw
Key Personnel
Chief Executive: Tchong-Koei Li
Founded: 1958
Subjects: Cookery, Education, Fashion, Literature, Literary Criticism, Essays, Psychology, Psychiatry, Science (General), Travel
ISBN Prefix(es): 957-530; 957-574
Parent Company: China Youth Corps
Showroom(s): No 219, Sung Chiang Rd, Taipei
Bookshop(s): No 6, Heng Yang Rd, Taipei; No 2-1, Feng Chia Rd, Taichung; No 157, Fu Hsing 2 Rd, Kaohsiung
Warehouse: No 21, Lane 111, Chung Ying St, Su Lin Town, Taipei

Yuan Liou Publishing Co, Ltd+
7F-5, No 184, Tingchou Rd, Sec 3, Taipei 100
Tel: (02) 3653707 *Fax:* (02) 3657979; (02) 3658989
E-mail: ylib@yuanliou.ylib.com.tw
Web Site: www.ylib.com.tw
Key Personnel
Publisher: Wang Jung-Wen
Founded: 1975
Subjects: Art, Business, Fiction, Health, Nutrition, History, How-to, Psychology, Psychiatry, Self-Help

ISBN Prefix(es): 957-32
Associate Companies: Meta Media International Co

Zen Now Press
3F, 6-2, Huaite St, Taipei 112
Tel: (02) 7182727 *Fax:* (02) 7174146
Key Personnel
President: Mr Su Chun-Jung
Subjects: Religion - Buddhist
ISBN Prefix(es): 957-9622
Distributed by Hsu Sheng Book Ltd

Tajikistan

General Information

Capital: Dushanbe
Language: Tajik
Population: 5.7 million
Bank Hours: Generally open for short hours between 0930-1230 Monday-Friday
Shop Hours: Generally 0900-1800 Monday-Friday; often open weekends
Currency: 100 kopeks = 1 rubl
Export/Import Information: According to Ukrainian quotas and customs duties, companies engaged in trade should register with the Ukraine Ministry of Foreign Economic Relations. Licenses for export and import are also required for trade with Russia.
Copyright: UCC (see Copyright Conventions, pg xi)

Irfon (Knowledge)
N Karabaev str 17, Dushanbe 734018
Tel: (03772) 33-39-06; (03772) 33-62-54
Key Personnel
Dir: J Sharifov
Editor-in-Chief: A Olimov
Founded: 1926
Subjects: Agriculture, Economics, Fiction, Government, Political Science, Medicine, Nursing, Dentistry, Philosophy, Social Sciences, Sociology, Technology
ISBN Prefix(es): 5-667

United Republic of Tanzania

General Information

Capital: Dar es Salem
Language: Swahili and English are both official languages
Religion: Islamic, Christian (mostly Roman Catholic), Hindu, the rest follow traditional beliefs
Population: 27.8 million
Bank Hours: Mainland Tanzania: 0900-1200 Monday-Friday; 0900-1100 Saturday. Zanzibar: 0830-1130 Monday-Friday; 0830-1000 Saturday
Shop Hours: 0800-1200, 1400-1715 or 1800 Monday-Saturday
Currency: 100 cents = 1 Tanzanian shilling
Export/Import Information: No tariff on books or advertising matter. Import license and exchange controls.
Copyright: Berne, Florence (see Copyright Conventions, pg xi)

PUBLISHERS

UNITED REPUBLIC OF TANZANIA

Africa Inland Church Literature Department, see Inland Publishers

Akajase Enterprises+
PO Box 7187, Dar Es Salaam
Tel: (051) 26121
Key Personnel
Dir: R A Akwilombe
Founded: 1988
Also bookseller.
Subjects: Fiction
ISBN Prefix(es): 9987-551

Ben and Company Ltd+
PO Box 3164, Dar Es Salaam
Tel: (051) 67407 *Fax:* (051) 112440
Telex: 41816
Key Personnel
Man Dir & Publicity: Ian Ben Moshi
Man Editor: James Odongo Ocholla
Senior Editor: Salim Kigenda
Sales & Marketing: Sadallah Sungura Alli
Founded: 1981
Specialize in Kiswahili, arts & crafts (life skills).
Member of Publishers Association of Tanzania (PATA).
Subjects: English as a Second Language, Mathematics, Science (General)
ISBN Prefix(es): 9976-920
Total Titles: 72 Print

Benedictine Publications Ndanda, *imprint of* Ndanda Mission Press

Bilal Muslim Mission of Tanzania+
PO Box 20033, Dar Es Salaam
Tel: (051) 30345; (051) 50924 *Fax:* (051) 116550
E-mail: bilal@raha.com
Telex: 41518 Geomic *Cable:* TABLIGH
Key Personnel
Chairman: Pyarali M Shivji *Tel:* (051) 114113
Editor: F H Abdullah
Chief Missionary: Sayid Saeed Akhtar Rizvi *Tel:* (051) 130345
Founded: 1968
An autonomous subsidiary of Shia Ithnaashery Supreme Council of Africa.
Subjects: Literature, Literary Criticism, Essays
ISBN Prefix(es): 9976-956

Bureau of Statistics+
PO Box 796, Dar Es Salaam
Tel: (051) 111634; (051) 111635 *Fax:* (051) 112352
E-mail: kento@raha.com
Telex: 41576 TASTAT TZ *Cable:* STATISTICS
Key Personnel
Publishing Officer: Eliab J C Chiduo
Founded: 1961
Subjects: Agriculture, Economics, Education

Central Tanganyika Press+
PO Box 15, Dodoma
Tel: (061) 22140 *Fax:* (061) 324565
Telex: 53328 TZ
Key Personnel
General Manager: James Lifa Chipaka
Marketing Sales Manager: David Tuppa
Founded: 1954
Subjects: Biblical Studies, Biography, Child Care & Development, Religion - Protestant
ISBN Prefix(es): 9976-66

Dodoma Tanzania, *imprint of* Kanisa la Biblia Publishers (KLB)

DUP (1996) Ltd+
PO Box 7028, Dar Es Salaam
Tel: (051) 49106; (051) 49107; (051) 49108 *Fax:* (051) 49106
E-mail: director@dup.udsm.ac.tz
Telex: 41327 Uniscie *Cable:* UNIVERSITY DAR ES SALAAM
Key Personnel
Dir: N G Mwitta
Marketing Manager: L D T Minzi
Founded: 1979
Member of Tanzania Publishers Association; also book packager.
Subjects: Accounting, Biological Sciences, Chemistry, Chemical Engineering, Civil Engineering, Developing Countries, Drama, Theater, Electronics, Electrical Engineering, History, Language Arts, Linguistics, Mathematics, Mechanical Engineering, Medicine, Nursing, Dentistry, Physical Sciences, Physics, Women's Studies
ISBN Prefix(es): 9976-60

East African Publishing House
SLP 3209, Dar Es Salaam
Tel: (02) 557417; (02) 557788 *Cable:* Afrobooks Nairobi
Key Personnel
Man Dir: E N Wainaina
Chief Editor, Rights & Permissions: Gacheche Waruingi
Marketing, Publicity, Sales, Distribution: James K Muraya
Production: John Mwazo
Founded: 1965
Subjects: Biography, Education, Fiction, How-to, Nonfiction (General), Poetry, Regional Interests, Religion - Other, Science (General), Social Sciences, Sociology
ISBN Prefix(es): 9976-5
Parent Company: E A Cultural Trust
Associate Companies: Afropress Ltd, PO Box 30502, Nairobi

Eastern Africa Publications Ltd
PO Box 1002, Arusha
Tel: (057) 3176; (057) 26708
Telex: 42121 Concentre *Cable:* EAPL ARUSHA
Key Personnel
General Manager: Abdullah Saiwaad
Sales, Marketing: J J Kimpinga
Production: S M S Payowela
Founded: 1979
Subjects: Biography, Geography, Geology, Government, Political Science, History, Nonfiction (General), Poetry, Science (General)
ISBN Prefix(es): 9976-2
Parent Company: Tanzania Karatasi Associated Industries, PO Box 2418, Dar es Salaam
Branch Office(s)
PO Box 1408, Dar Es Salaam

Emmaus Bible School
PO Box 1424, Dar Es Salaam
Tel: (026) 2354500 *Fax:* (026) 2350911
E-mail: cmml-dar@maf.or.tz
Key Personnel
Dir: Hansjoerg Schaerer
Contact: Anna Guttke
Member of TELM; Specialize in Correspondence Courses.
Subjects: Biblical Studies
ISBN Prefix(es): 9976-80
Associate Companies: Kanisa la Biblia (KLB) Publishers, PO Box 1424, Dodoma
Imprints: Emmaus Shule ya Biblia
Branch Office(s)
Emmaus Bible School, PO Box 9322, Dar es salaam *Tel:* (022) 2115920 *Fax:* (022) 2128767
Distributor for Everyday Publications Inc (Canada)

Emmaus Shule ya Biblia, *imprint of* Emmaus Bible School

General Publications Ltd+
PO Box 6804, Dar Es Salaam
Tel: (051) 68240; (051) 68249
Key Personnel
Man Dir: A A Macha
Founded: 1985
Specialize in publishing school books, Family Mirror Weekly newspaper & stationery sales.
Subjects: Agriculture, Business, Geography, Geology, Mathematics, Science (General)
ISBN Prefix(es): 9976-925

Government Printer
PO Box 9124, Dar Es Salaam

Idara ya vitabu, *imprint of* Kanisa la Biblia Publishers (KLB)

Inland Publishers
PO Box 125, Mwanza
Tel: (068) 40064
Key Personnel
Dir: Rev S M Magesa
A publishing division of Africa Inland Church Literature Department.
Subjects: Nonfiction (General), Religion - Other
ISBN Prefix(es): 9976-906; 9976-70

Institute of Kiswahili Research
PO Box 35110, Dar Es Salaam
Tel: (051) 49106 ext 2647
Key Personnel
Dir: Prof David P B Massamba
Founded: 1930
Subjects: Language Arts, Linguistics, Literature, Literary Criticism, Essays
ISBN Prefix(es): 9976-911

Kajura Publications
PO Box 8692, Dar Es Salaam
Tel: (051) 866181
Subjects: Astrology, Occult, Government, Political Science, Science Fiction, Fantasy
ISBN Prefix(es): 9987-8855

Kanisa la Biblia, *imprint of* Kanisa la Biblia Publishers (KLB)

Kanisa la Biblia Publishers (KLB)+
One Pagala, Dodoma
Mailing Address: PO Box 5214, Mtwara
Tel: (061) 354500 *Fax:* (061) 350911
E-mail: cmml-dodoma@maf.org
Key Personnel
Editor: Helmut Graef
Manager: Miss Inge Danzeisen
Founded: 1979
Specialize in Bible teaching books for lay people in Swahili.
Member of TELM (Tanzania Evangelical Literature Ministry) & Booksellers Association of Tanzania.
Subjects: Biblical Studies, Religion - Protestant, Theology
ISBN Prefix(es): 9976-74
Total Titles: 29 Print; 2 Audio
Associate Companies: Emmaus Bible School, PO Box 9322, Dar Es Salaam, Dir: Miss R Buchmuller *Tel:* (051) 128767 *Fax:* (051) 115920 *E-mail:* cmml-dar@maf.org
Imprints: KLB Publishers; Idara ya vitabu; Kanisa la Biblia; Dodoma Tanzania
Distributed by Emmaus Bible School
Distributor for Emmaus Bible School
Bookshop(s): PO Box 524, Mtwara, Sales Manager: Mr T E Nambanje *Tel:* (059) 333055 *E-mail:* cmml-mtwara@maf.org

Kisambo Publishers Ltd
PO Box 6542, Dar Es Salaam
Tel: (051) 114876; (051) 131382 *Fax:* (051) 112351
Founded: 1985

UNITED REPUBLIC OF TANZANIA

Subjects: Social Sciences, Sociology, Theology
ISBN Prefix(es): 9976-978
Imprints: Kiwavi; Tuitional Structures
Distributed by Diamond Publishers (Tepusa)
Distributor for Ben Co; CBP; Readit Books

Kiswahili, *imprint of* Press & Publicity Centre Ltd

Kiwavi, *imprint of* Kisambo Publishers Ltd

KLB Publishers, *imprint of* Kanisa la Biblia Publishers (KLB)

Ndanda Mission Press
Ndanda PO Box 4, Mtwara
Key Personnel
Manager: Fr S Hoibeck
Founded: 1934
Subjects: Fiction, History, Medicine, Nursing, Dentistry, Religion - Catholic, Religion - Other, Social Sciences, Sociology, Theology
ISBN Prefix(es): 9976-63
Imprints: Benedictine Publications Ndanda; Peramiho, Tanzania
Distributed by Peramiko Publications; Tabora Mission Press

Northwestern Publishers+
PO Box 277, Bukoba
Founded: 1990
Subjects: Language Arts, Linguistics, Religion - Protestant, Theology
ISBN Prefix(es): 9987-569
Parent Company: Evangelical Lutheran Church in Tanzania, Northwestern Diocese
Distributor for Ben & Co (Oxford); Central Tanganyika Press; Dar University; Tanzania Publishing House
Bookshop(s): ELCT Church Bookshop

Nyota Publishers Ltd+
CSTC Box 3574 (CSTC), Dar Es Salaam, D A Mcharo
Tel: (051) 25547; (051) 25549
Key Personnel
Dir & Author: P A Mcharo
Dir: E B Wilson; J E Kishada; Mrs P E McHaro
Subjects: Accounting, Business, Education, English as a Second Language, Fiction, Medicine, Nursing, Dentistry
ISBN Prefix(es): 9987-556
Associate Companies: Nyota Consultancy Co Ltd

Oxford University Press
PO Box 5299, Dar Es Salaam
Tel: (051) 29209 *Fax:* (051) 46822
Key Personnel
Manager: Salim Shaaban Salim
Founded: 1969
Subjects: Literature, Literary Criticism, Essays, Poetry
ISBN Prefix(es): 9976-4
Parent Company: Oxford University Press, United Kingdom

Peramiho Publications
PO Box 41, Peramiho
Tel: (054) 2730 *Fax:* (054) 2917
Key Personnel
Chief Executive: Fr Gerold Rupper
Contact: Bro Dominicus Weis; Bro Polycarr Stich
Founded: 1937
Local topics, printed mostly in Swahili.
Subjects: Agriculture, Religion - Other
ISBN Prefix(es): 9976-67
Associate Companies: Peramiho Printing Press
Subsidiaries: Benedictine Publication Ndanda/Peramiho
Divisions: Ndanda Mission Press

Branch Office(s)
Benedictine Priory, PO Box 528, Schuyler, NE 68661, United States *Tel:* 402-352-2127
Distributed by Ndanda Mission Press; TMP Tabora
Bookshop(s): Ndanda and Peramiho

Peramiho, Tanzania, *imprint of* Ndanda Mission Press

Press & Publicity Centre Ltd+
PO Box 20910, Dar Es Salaam
Tel: (051) 127765; (051) 122881; (051) 131078 *Fax:* (051) 113619; (051) 116749
Key Personnel
International Rights: Akberali Manji
Founded: 1981
Member of Publishers Association of Tanzania (PATA).
Subjects: Agriculture, Astrology, Occult, Computer Science, Education, Environmental Studies, Fiction, Geography, Geology, Health, Nutrition, Language Arts, Linguistics, Literature, Literary Criticism, Essays, Science (General)
ISBN Prefix(es): 9976-916
Total Titles: 30 Print
Imprints: Kiswahili
Distributed by Tepusa
Distributor for Africa Book Collective Ltd (UK)
Bookshop(s): Aggrey Street Shop, Nkrumah St, Dar Es Salaam

Readit Books
PO Box 20986, Dar es Salaam
Tel: (022) 2184077 *Fax:* (022) 2181077
E-mail: readitbooks@yahoo.com
Key Personnel
Man Dir: Abdallah Saiwaad
Marketing Dir: Khalfan Abdallah
Founded: 1993
Subjects: Astronomy, Fiction, Science (General)
ISBN Prefix(es): 9987-21

South African Extension Unit
SLP 70074, Dar Es Salaam
Tel: (051) 37325; (051) 37326 *Fax:* (051) 37325
ISBN Prefix(es): 9976-73
Subsidiaries: South African Extension Uni

Standard Book Numbering Agency, see Tanzania Library Services Board

Tanzania Library Services Board
Unit of Ministry of Education & Culture
Bibi Titi Mohamed St, PO Box 9283, Dar es Salaam
Tel: (051) 110572; (051) 110573
E-mail: tlsb@africaonline.co.tz *Cable:* TANLIS
Key Personnel
Dir General: E A Mwinyimvua
Founded: 1963
Subjects: Library & Information Sciences
ISBN Prefix(es): 9976-65
Branch Office(s)
PO Box 1273, Arusha, Contact: Mrs Sophia M Labokhe *Tel:* (057) 502642
PO Box 321, Bukuoba, Contact: Mr Vedastus Muijage *Tel:* (066) 20460
PO Box 1900, Do Doma, Contact: Mr John Mwelemi *Tel:* (061) 22063
PO Box 172, Iringa, Contact: Mr Metola Msusa Kanduru *Tel:* (061) 702421
PO Box 933, Kigoma, Contact: Ms Rhoda Z Zamuye *Tel:* (0695) 3168
PO Box 443, Lindi, Contact: Mr Geofrey Mushi *Tel:* (0525) 2156
PO Box 872, Mara/Musoma, Contact: Mr Hippolite Amin Latonge *Tel:* (068) 622183
PO Box 842, Mbeya, Contact: Mr Emmanuel Luvands *Tel:* (065) 502589
PO Box 858, Mo Rogord, Contact: Mr Leonard Ngowo *Tel:* (056) 602160
PO Box 863, Moshi, Contact: Mr Mariam Mundeme *Tel:* (055) 52432
PO Box 37, Mtwara, Contact: Mr Emmanuel Herbert *Tel:* (059) 333352
PO Box 1363, Mwanza, Contact: Mr Charles Katale *Tel:* (068) 41895
PO Box 804, Shinyanga, Contact: Mr William Melale *Tel:* (08) 762151
PO Box 179, Songea, Contact: Mr Hezekia Chawe *Tel:* (065) 602041
PO Box 332, Sumbawanga, Contact: Mr Peter Nkaki *Tel:* (065) 802259
PO Box 432, Tabora, Contact: Mr Carmilius C Nyigu *Tel:* (062) 3099
PO Box 5000, Tanga, Contact: Mr Joseph Maginge *Tel:* (053) 43127

Tanzania Publishing House+
SLP 2138, Dar Es Salaam
Tel: (051) 32164 *Cable:* PUBLISH DAR ES SALAAM
Key Personnel
General Manager & International Rights: Primus Isidor Karugendo
Founded: 1966
Member of Publishers Association of Tanzania-African Books Collective.
Subjects: Accounting, Agriculture, Animals, Pets, Art, Child Care & Development, Drama, Theater, English as a Second Language, Fiction, Gardening, Plants, Geography, Geology, Government, Political Science, Health, Nutrition, History, Journalism, Labor, Industrial Relations, Language Arts, Linguistics, Law, Management, Mathematics, Nonfiction (General), Photography, Physics, Poetry, Public Administration, Science (General), Sports, Athletics
ISBN Prefix(es): 9976-1
Parent Company: Tanzania Karatasi Associated Industries, Box 2418 DSM

Tema Publishers Ltd+
PO Box 63115, Dar Es Salaam
Tel: (051) 113608 *Fax:* (051) 75422
Key Personnel
Chief Executive: T Maliyamkono
Founded: 1994
Member of Publishers' Association of Tanzania (PATA).
Subjects: Education, Environmental Studies, Fiction, Nonfiction (General), Women's Studies
ISBN Prefix(es): 9987-25
Distributed by Tanzania Publishing House

Tuitional Structures, *imprint of* Kisambo Publishers Ltd

Thailand

General Information

Capital: Bangkok
Language: Thai is official language. English is widely used in government and commercial circles
Religion: Predominantly Buddhist of the Hinaya form
Population: 57.6 million
Bank Hours: 0830-1500 Monday-Friday
Shop Hours: Vary. Those catering to tourists generally open 0830-1800 or later
Currency: 100 satangs = 1 baht
Export/Import Information: No tariff on books but Standard Profit Tax and Business Tax apply (also a Municipal Tax of percentage of Business Tax). Advertising subject to same taxes

and ad valorem percentage of import duty. No import licenses for books, but special permit required by importer for orders over a certain sum. Certificate of payment (from Exchange Control Authority) required.
Copyright: Berne, Florence (see Copyright Conventions, pg xi)

Akson Charerntat (S/B Akson)
142 Phraeng Sapphasat Tanao Rd, Bangkok 10200
Tel: (02) 2214587 *Fax:* (02) 2255356
Key Personnel
Executive Dir: Surapon Dheva-Aksorn
ISBN Prefix(es): 974-405; 974-406

Bandansan
136-138 Nakhon Sawan Rd, Bangkok 10100
Tel: (02) 825511
ISBN Prefix(es): 974-225

Bannakhan
236 Woeng Nakhon Khasem, Bangkok 10100
Tel: (02) 227796
ISBN Prefix(es): 974-350

Bannakit Trading
34-42 Thanon Nakhonsawan Rd, Bangkok 10100
Tel: (02) 2825520; (02) 2827537; (02) 2814213 *Fax:* (02) 2820076
Subjects: Agriculture, Biography, Fiction
ISBN Prefix(es): 974-220

Chiang Mai University Library
130 Thanon Huay Kaew Rd, Amphoe Muang, Muang District, Chiangmai 50200
Tel: (053) 221154 *Fax:* (053) 222766; (053) 221013; (053) 221154
E-mail: prasit@lib.cmunet.edu
Key Personnel
Dir: Mr Prasit Malumpong
ISBN Prefix(es): 974-565; 974-656; 974-657; 974-658

Chokechai Thewet Co Ltd+
59 Ti Thong Rd, Pranakorn, Bangkok 10200
Tel: (02) 2226660
Key Personnel
Man Dir: Wichai Rojjanaprapayon
Marketing Executive: Dr Wiwat Rojjanaprapayon
Founded: 1963
Subjects: Fiction, Romance, Science Fiction, Fantasy
ISBN Prefix(es): 974-420

Office of Christian Education and Literature, *imprint of* Suriyaban Publishers

DK Book House
244-246 Siam Sq, Soi 2, Pathumwan, Bangkok 10500
Tel: (02) 2516335 *Fax:* (02) 2471033
Telex: 81198 Frtmast Th
ISBN Prefix(es): 974-210
Parent Company: Duang Kamon Co, Ltd
Associate Companies: D K Today Co, Ltd
Subsidiaries: D K Mah Boon Krong Co Ltd
Divisions: Technical Books
Bookshop(s): Mah Boon Krong Centre, 3rd floor, Prathumwan, Bangkok

Duang Kamon
244-246 Siam Sq, Soi 2, Pathumwan, Bangkok 10500
Tel: (02) 2516335
ISBN Prefix(es): 974-210

Graphic Art Publishing
105/19-2 Naret Rd, Bangkok 10500
Tel: (02) 2330302
Telex: 20657 Graphic Th
Key Personnel
Chief Executive: Mrs Angkana Sajjaraktrakul
Export Manager: H J Weber
Founded: 1972
Subjects: Biological Sciences, Chemistry, Chemical Engineering, Electronics, Electrical Engineering, Language Arts, Linguistics, Philosophy, Photography, Physics, Regional Interests, Science Fiction, Fantasy
ISBN Prefix(es): 974-295
Subsidiaries: Pandora Publishing
Book Club(s): Science Fiction Magazine Club

Khlang Withaya Pub
724-6 Mahachai Rd, Bangkok 10200
Tel: (02) 224546; (02) 2219331
Key Personnel
Manager: Prachark Chaovanabutvilai
ISBN Prefix(es): 974-205

New Generation Publishing Co Ltd+
486/70-73 Soi Perchburi 14, Petchburi Rd, Rachathevee Bangkok 10400
Tel: (02) 2150674; (02) 2150677 *Fax:* (02) 2150676
Key Personnel
Chief Executive: Kiatchai Prasertsrisak
Founded: 1990
Subjects: Animals, Pets, Art, English as a Second Language, Fiction, History, Natural History, Science (General)
ISBN Prefix(es): 974-7642
Parent Company: The Manager Media Group Public Co Ltd

Niyom Vidhya
192 Thanon Bamrungmuang Rd, Bangkok 10200
Tel: (02) 217661
ISBN Prefix(es): 974-7278

Non
901 Soi Songpinong, Samrong Nua, Samutprakarn, Bangkok
Tel: (02) 90130
ISBN Prefix(es): 974-395

Odeon Store LP
Wang Burapha, Bangkok 10500
Tel: (02) 2210742; (02) 2216567 *Cable:* Odeonstore
Key Personnel
Man Dir: Vichai Praepanich
Founded: 1947
Subjects: Nonfiction (General)
ISBN Prefix(es): 974-275
Branch Office(s)
Siam Sq soi 1, Bangkok

Pearson Education Indochina, Ltd
2390 Pattanakarn Rd, Suanluang, Bangkok 10250
Tel: (02) 722 7301 *Fax:* (02) 722 7307
E-mail: firstname@pearsoned.th.com
Key Personnel
Regional Manager: Narerat Ancharepirat *Tel:* (02) 722 7996
ELT Manager: Thansinee Thammapojsathid
ELT Marketing Executive: Udom Sathawara; Wanida Yingsiri
Publishing Manager: Sopis Rungruangvoratus
Parent Company: Pearson Plc

Pikkhanet Kanphim
97-9 Soi Phrangsapasat, Tanao Rd, Bangkok 10200
Tel: (02) 222850
ISBN Prefix(es): 974-476

Pra Cha Chang & Co Ltd
87 Phaholyothin Rd, Bangkok 10400
Subjects: Education
ISBN Prefix(es): 974-7655

Prasan Mit
3382 New Phet Buri Rd, Bangkok 10310
Tel: (02) 3915287; (02) 3925230
ISBN Prefix(es): 974-467

Ruamsarn (1977) Co Ltd+
864 Wang Burapha, Bangkok 10500
Tel: (02) 22216483 *Fax:* (02) 2222036
Key Personnel
Manager: Piya Taweevatanasarn
Founded: 1951
Subjects: Fiction, History
ISBN Prefix(es): 974-245

Sang Dad Publishing Company Ltd+
320 Lardprao Soi 94 (Town-in-Town), Lardprao Rd, Bangkok 10310
Tel: (02) 5381499; (02) 5387576 *Fax:* (02) 559 2643; (02) 5381499
E-mail: sangdad@asianet.co.th
Key Personnel
Chief Executive: Nidda Hongwiwat *Tel:* (02) 538 5553
President: Mr Thavitong Hongvivatana
Founded: 1984
Largest cookery book publisher in Thailand.
Subjects: Art, Child Care & Development, Cookery, History, Travel
Total Titles: 250 Print
Subsidiaries: NIS Media Group Co Ltd

Silkworm Books+
Chiang Mai 50100
Mailing Address: POB 217, Ratchadammoen Rd, Bangkok 10200
Tel: (053) 4765326 *Fax:* (053) 4765326
E-mail: silkworm@pobox.com
Key Personnel
Publisher & Dir: Trasvin Jittidecharaks
Founded: 1991
Registered as Trasvin Publications Ltd, 54/1-5 Sridonchai Rd, Chiang Mai, Thailand.
Subjects: Asian Studies
ISBN Prefix(es): 974-7047
Distributed by University of Washington Press (North America)

Soemwit Barwakhan
222 Woeng Nakhonkasemm, Bangkok 10100
Tel: (02) 214541
ISBN Prefix(es): 974-270

Suksapan Panit (Business Organization of Teachers Council of Thailand)
128/1 Thanon Ratchasima, Dusit, Bangkok 10300
Tel: (02) 811845
Telex: 72031 Suksapa Th
Key Personnel
Dir: Kamthon Sathirakul
Founded: 1950
ISBN Prefix(es): 974-8101

Suksit Siam Co Ltd
1715 Rama IV Rd, Bangkok 10500
Tel: (02) 511630
Key Personnel
Manager, Publicity: Mrs Nilchawee Sivaraksa
Subjects: Government, Political Science, Social Sciences, Sociology
ISBN Prefix(es): 974-260

Suriyaban Publishers
14 Pramuan Rd, Bangkok 10500
Tel: (02) 2347991; (02) 2347992 *Cable:* CCT Office

THAILAND

Key Personnel
Man Dir and all other offices: Pisnu Arkkapin
Founded: 1953
Subjects: Ethnicity, Literature, Literary Criticism, Essays, Religion - Other
ISBN Prefix(es): 974-500
Parent Company: Department of Christian Education and Literature, Church of Christ in Thailand
Imprints: Office of Christian Education and Literature
Bookshop(s): The Christian Bookstore

Sut Phaisan
683/8 Phra Chao Taksin Rd, Samre, Bangkok 10600
Tel: (02) 4682066; (02) 4675066
Subjects: Law
ISBN Prefix(es): 974-503

Thai Watana Panich Co, Ltd+
599 Maitrichit Rd, Bangkok 10100
Tel: (02) 6812288 *Fax:* (02) 6819973
Web Site: www.twp.co.th
Key Personnel
Man Dir: Thira T Suwan
Founded: 1935
Also acts as Distributor.
Subjects: Agriculture, Art, Biography, Education, Government, Political Science, Health, Nutrition, History, Language Arts, Linguistics, Management, Marketing, Mathematics, Music, Dance, Philosophy, Psychology, Psychiatry, Religion - Buddhist, Science (General), Social Sciences, Sociology
ISBN Prefix(es): 974-07
Distributor for Falcon; Kernerman; McGraw-Hills; Oxford; Pearson Education; Wendy Pye; Thomson Learning

Unesco Regional Office, Asia & the Pacific
24/1 Sukhumwit Soi 59, Bangkok 10110
Tel: (02) 3910577; (02) 3910703; (02) 3910880 *Fax:* (02) 3910866
Telex: 20591 *Cable:* UNESCO BANGKOK
ISBN Prefix(es): 974-680

Viratham
141 St Louis South Sathon Rd, Bangkok 10120
Tel: (02) 866848
ISBN Prefix(es): 974-380

Watthana Phanit
216-220 Bamrung Muang, Bangkok 10200
Tel: (02) 2217225
ISBN Prefix(es): 974-250; 974-02

White Lotus Co Ltd+
16 Soi 47 Sukhumwit Rd, Bangkok 10110
Mailing Address: PO Box 1141, Bangkok 10110
Tel: (02) 3324915
Key Personnel
Chief Executive: D Ande
Founded: 1972
Specialize in books on Asia (Southeast).
Subjects: Art, Ethnicity, Regional Interests
ISBN Prefix(es): 974-8495; 974-8496

Togo

General Information

Capital: Lome
Language: French, Kabiye and Ewe are official languages
Religion: About half follow traditional beliefs, Christian (about 35 percent) and Muslim (about 15 percent).
Population: 4 million
Bank Hours: 0730-1130, 1430-1600 Monday-Friday
Shop Hours: 0800-1200, 1430 or 1500-1730 or 1800 Monday-Friday; 0730-1230 Saturday
Currency: 100 centimes = 1 CFA franc
Export/Import Information: No tariff on books; advertising catalogs dutied. Additional taxes: Tax Forfaitaire, Statistical Tax, and Customs Stamp Tax of percentage of duties and added taxes; Small Wharfage Tax. Import license required for goods from non-franc zones above a certain value; from franc zone, need authorization of Togolese Government Office. Exchange controls on non-franc zone.
Copyright: Berne (see Copyright Conventions, pg xi)

Editions Akpagnon+
BP 3531, Lome
Tel: 220244 *Fax:* 220244
Key Personnel
Man Dir: Yves-Emmanuel Dogbe
E-mail: yedogbe.akpagnon@lapste.tg
Founded: 1979
Subjects: Biography, Developing Countries, Education, Literature, Literary Criticism, Essays, Parapsychology, Philosophy, Poetry, Self-Help, Social Sciences, Sociology
ISBN Prefix(es): 2-86427
Number of titles published annually: 10 Print
Total Titles: 5 Print
Orders to: CMD Claude M Diffusion Ltee, 1544 rue Villeray, Montreal, PQ H2E 1H1, Canada
L'Harmattan, 7 rue de l'Ecole Polytechnique, 75005 Paris, France
Nord-Sud Diffusion, 150 rue Berthelot, 1190 Brussels, Belgium
Presence Africaine, 25 bis, rue des Ecoles, 75005 Paris, France

Editogo
BP 891, Lome
Tel: 213718
Key Personnel
Man Dir: Kokou Amedegnato
Founded: 1962
Subjects: Education

Maison d'Edition de la Librairie-Imprimerie Evangelique du Togo
BP 378 Centre Togolais de communication evangelique CTCE, Haho, Editions Lome
Tel: 214582 *Fax:* 212967
Key Personnel
Dir General: F K Agbobli
Editorial: W Y Aladji; J C van de Werk
ISBN Prefix(es): 2-906718
Imprints: Editions Haho
Bookshop(s): Librairie Evangelique

Editions Haho, *imprint of* Maison d'Edition de la Librairie-Imprimerie Evangelique du Togo

Les Nouvelles Editions Africaines du TOGO (NEA-TOGO)+
239 Blvd du 13 Janvier, BP 4862, Lome
Tel: 216761; 221019 *Fax:* 221019
E-mail: ctce@cafe.tg
Telex: 5393 NEAOM
Key Personnel
Dir: Yawo Agbeko Tsolenyanou
Editor: Christiane Tchotcho Ekue
Founded: 1990
Subjects: Fiction, Poetry
ISBN Prefix(es): 2-7236; 2-7412

Parent Company: Les Nouvelles Editions Africaines, Senegal
Associate Companies: Les Nouvelles Editions Africaines, Ivory Coast

Presses de l'Universite du Benin
BP 1515, Lome
Tel: 254844 *Fax:* 258784
ISBN Prefix(es): 2-909886

Trinidad & Tobago

General Information

Capital: Port-of-Spain
Language: English (officially). French, Spanish, Hindi and Chinese also spoken
Religion: Roman Catholic and Anglican, also Hindu and Muslim
Population: 1.3 million
Bank Hours: 0800-1400 Monday-Thursday; 0800-1200, 1500-1700 Friday
Shop Hours: 0800-1630 Monday-Friday; 0800-1200 Saturday
Currency: 100 cents = 1 Trinidad and Tobago dollar
Export/Import Information: No tariff on books; duty and postal fee on advertising matter. No import license required for books; no obscene literature permitted. Exchange controls.
Copyright: UCC, Berne (see Copyright Conventions, pg xi)

Aquarela Galleries+
One A Dere St, Suite 4, Port of Spain
Tel: 6255982 *Fax:* 6245217
Key Personnel
Partner: Geoffrey MacLean
Founded: 1984
Also acts as Dealers in Fine Art.
ISBN Prefix(es): 976-8066
Associate Companies: MacLean Publishing Ltd

Joan Bacchus-Xavier+
37 Tragarete Rd, Port-of-Spain
Tel: 6225588 *Fax:* 6251330
Founded: 1988
Subjects: Anthropology, History, Outdoor Recreation, Travel
ISBN Prefix(es): 976-8074

Caribbean Epidemiology Centre
16-18 Jamaica Blvd, Port-of-Spain
Mailing Address: PO Box 164, Port-of-Spain
Tel: 6224261; 6224262 *Fax:* 622-2792
E-mail: cec_email@carec.paho.org
Telex: 22308
ISBN Prefix(es): 976-8114

Caribbean Telecommunications Union
17 Queen's Park West, Port-of-Spain
Tel: 6283185 *Fax:* 6286037
E-mail: ctunion@tstt.net.tt
Subjects: Electronics, Electrical Engineering, Public Administration, Technology
ISBN Prefix(es): 976-8121

Charran Educational Publishers+
58 Western Main Rd, St James
Tel: 6223832 *Fax:* 6235829
Telex: 3000 Postlx Wg
Key Personnel
Dir: Reginald Charran; Betty Charran
Sales: Terry R Ram

PUBLISHERS

TUNISIA

Founded: 1978
ISBN Prefix(es): 976-613
Bookshop(s): Charran's Bookshop (1978) Ltd, 58 Western Main Rd, St James; Muir Marshall Ltd, 64a Independence Sq, Port-of-Spain; Charran's Wholesale Center, 58 Western Main Rd, St James; Charran's Bookshop, 76 Henry St, Port-of-Spain
Warehouse: 58 S Quay, Port-of-Spain
Orders to: 58 S Quay, Port-of-Spain

Economic & Business Research
10 Flament St, Port-of-Spain
Mailing Address: PO Box 780, Port-of-Spain
Tel: 624-5064 *Fax:* 623-4137
E-mail: maxifill@opus.co.tt
Web Site: www.opus.co.tt./maxifill
ISBN Prefix(es): 976-8008

Inprint Caribbean Ltd
35-37 Independence Sq, Port-of-Spain
Tel: 6271569; 6231711 *Fax:* 6271451
Telex: 22661 *Cable:* EXPRESS
Key Personnel
Manager: Kim Morton
Founded: 1975
Subjects: Economics, Education, Government, Political Science, History, Social Sciences, Sociology
ISBN Prefix(es): 976-608
Parent Company: Caribbean Communications Network (CCN)
Associate Companies: Prime Radio 106.1 FM; CCN TV6
Subsidiaries: Trinidad Express Newspapers Ltd

Jett Samm Publishing Ltd+
37 Newbury Hill, Glencoe
Tel: 637-9548
Key Personnel
Editor-in-Chief: Nigel A Campbell
Founded: 1991
Subjects: Music, Dance, Travel
ISBN Prefix(es): 976-8106
Parent Company: Jett Samm Communications

Moksha Institute of Caribbean Arts & Letters
One Sapphire Dr, Diego Martin
Mailing Address: PO Box 3254, Diego Martin
Tel: 6374516
Key Personnel
Editor & President: Anson Gonzalez
Founded: 1991
ISBN Prefix(es): 976-609
Imprints: New Voices

Multi-Media Ltd
4 Christina Court, Diego Martin
Mailing Address: PO Box 3290, Diego Martin
Tel: 6288637; 6226774 *Fax:* 6281903
ISBN Prefix(es): 976-8098

New Voices, *imprint of* Moksha Institute of Caribbean Arts & Letters

Systematics Studies Ltd
Unit 9 Watts Trace, Curepe
Tel: 6453475 *Fax:* 6625654
E-mail: dooks@eclacps.undp.org
Key Personnel
Manager: Shirley Dookeran
ISBN Prefix(es): 976-8034
Distributor for The Brookings Institution; Inter-American Development Bank; International Center for Economic Growth/Institute for Contemporary Studies; International Monetary Fund; Organization for Economic Co-operation & Development; United Nations; The World Bank; World Trade Organization

University of the West Indies (Trinidad & Tobago)
St Augustine
Tel: 6622002 *Fax:* 6639684
Telex: (24520) (UWI-Wg) *Cable:* STOMATA
ISBN Prefix(es): 976-620

Tunisia

General Information

Capital: Tunis
Language: Arabic. French widely used
Religion: Islam
Population: 8.4 million
Bank Hours: 0800-1200/1400-1800 Monday-Friday
Shop Hours: 0800-1300/1500-1900 Monday-Saturday
Currency: 1,000 millimes = 1 Tunisian dinar
Export/Import Information: Tunisia had preferred tariffs and EEC agreement but most books are dutied. Advertising matter free. Custom formalities tax per 1,000 kg or less gross weight, with minimum rate. Consumption tax on and duty tax paid of percentage of duty and tax paid. Imports liberalized but in practice licenses granted dependent on foreigh exchange position.
Copyright: UCC, Berne (see Copyright Conventions, pg xi)

Ben Abdallah Editions
Rue 8601 ZI Charguia, 2035 Tunis
Tel: (01) 237011 *Fax:* (01) 786290
Telex: 18 074 *Cable:* KARIM TN
Key Personnel
General Dir: M Mohamed Sellami
ISBN Prefix(es): 9973-707

Alyssa Editions
Rue Habib Thameur, 2026 Sidi Bou Saiid
Tel: 740989 *Fax:* 733659
Key Personnel
Dir Marketing: Sabria Beu Youssef
Founded: 1993
Subjects: Archaeology, Fiction, History, Mysteries, Regional Interests
ISBN Prefix(es): 9973-758

Arcs Editions+
32 Rue Charles de Gaulle, 1000 RP Tunis
Tel: (01) 351617
Key Personnel
Dir: Sihem Bensedrine
Assistant Dir: Afaf Bensedrine
Founded: 1988
Subjects: History
ISBN Prefix(es): 9973-740

Academie Tunisienne des Sciences, des Lettres et des Arts Beit El Hekma+
25 av de la Republique, 2016 Carthage
Tel: (01) 277275; (01) 731696 *Fax:* (01) 731204
Key Personnel
President: Abdelwaheb Bouhdiba
Founded: 1983
Subjects: Art, Biography, Drama, Theater, Geography, Geology, History, Journalism, Language Arts, Linguistics, Law, Literature, Literary Criticism, Essays, Mathematics, Medicine, Nursing, Dentistry, Music, Dance, Philosophy, Physics, Poetry, Religion - Islamic, Social Sciences, Sociology, Veterinary Science
ISBN Prefix(es): 9973-929; 9973-911
Distributed by Dar Souhnoun; Demeter

Editions Bouslama+
15 Av de France, 1000 Tunis
Tel: (01) 245612 *Fax:* (01) 381100
Telex: 14230 *Cable:* Editions Bouslama
Key Personnel
Man Dir, Rights & Permissions: Ali Bouslama
Sales: Hichem Bouslama
Production: Riadh Bouslama
Publicity: Hatem Bouslama
Founded: 1960
Subjects: History
ISBN Prefix(es): 9973-714
Branch Office(s)
15 bis rue Lamine el Abassi, Tunis

CAEU, *imprint of* Maison d'Edition Mohamed Ali Hammi

Ceres Editions+
6 Rue Abderrahman Azzam, 1002 Tunis
Tel: (01) 782033 *Fax:* (01) 787516
E-mail: ceres@planet.tm
Key Personnel
Chief Executive Officer & Editorial: Karim Ben Smail *Tel:* (071) 960980
Man Dir: Mohamed Ben Smail
Editorial: Noureddine Ben Khader
Founded: 1964
Subjects: Agriculture, Antiques, Archaeology, Art, Biography, Biological Sciences, Business, Chemistry, Chemical Engineering, Developing Countries, Economics, Education, English as a Second Language, Environmental Studies, Ethnicity, Fiction, Geography, Geology, Government, Political Science, How-to, Law, Literature, Literary Criticism, Essays, Mathematics, Philosophy, Physical Sciences, Poetry, Religion - Islamic, Social Sciences, Sociology, Women's Studies
ISBN Prefix(es): 9973-19; 2-85703; 9973-700
Subsidiaries: Ceres Conseil; Demeter; Imprimeries Reunies
Distributed by France Edisud
Orders to: Demeter, 8 Av Abderrahman Azzam, 1002 Tunis *Tel:* (071) 760780 *E-mail:* ceres@planet.tm

Dar Arabia Lil Kitab
Maison Arabe du Livre, Rue 7101, El-Manar 2 El-Menzah, 1004 Tunis
Tel: (01) 888255
Telex: 14966 Kitab
Key Personnel
Man Dir: Mahdi Ben Youssef
Founded: 1975
Subjects: Biography, Economics, Education, History, Language Arts, Linguistics, Literature, Literary Criticism, Essays, Religion - Other
ISBN Prefix(es): 9973-10
Parent Company: Dar Arabia Lil Kitab, ave Ghouma Mahmoud, BP 3185, Tripoli, Libyan Arab Jamahiriya

Dar El Afaq+
4, rue Ahmed Bayram, 1006 Tunis
Tel: (01) 265904 *Fax:* (01) 569035
Key Personnel
President: Nabil Rebai
Founded: 1989
Subjects: Government, Political Science, Literature, Literary Criticism, Essays, Religion - Islamic
ISBN Prefix(es): 9973-743
Showroom(s): 8, Rue Francoi, Boucher, 1006 Tunis
Bookshop(s): 8, Rue Francoi, Boucher 1006
Shipping Address: 8, Rue Francoi, Boucher, 1006 Tunis
Warehouse: 8, Rue Francoi, Boucher, 1006 Tunis

Demeter
8 Av Keireddine Pacha, 1002 Tunis-Belvedere

TUNISIA

Tel: (01) 893083; (01) 283579 *Fax:* (01) 787516
ISBN Prefix(es): 9973-706

El-M'aaref Editions
7 rue de France, 4000 Sousse
Mailing Address: PO Box 215, Sousse 4000
Tel: (03) 256235 *Fax:* (03) 256530
ISBN Prefix(es): 9973-16; 9973-712
Parent Company: Dar El Maaref

Faculte des Sciences Humaines et Sociales de Tunis
Departement de Recheriche Publication et Bibliographie, 94 blvd du 9 Avril 1938, Tunis 1008
Tel: (01) 260858; (01) 262252; (01) 260950; (01) 260960; (01) 560840; (01) 560950
Fax: (01) 567551
Key Personnel
Dir: Melika Ouelbani
Founded: 1956
Subjects: Archaeology, Ethnicity, Geography, Geology, History, Language Arts, Linguistics, Literature, Literary Criticism, Essays, Philosophy, Psychology, Psychiatry, Social Sciences, Sociology
ISBN Prefix(es): 9973-922

FTERSI, see Publications de la Fondation Temimi pour la Recherche Scientifique et L'Information

Government Printer (Imprimerie Officielle de la Republique Tunisienne - IORT)
Route de Rades, KM 2 Ave Farhat Hached, 2040 Rades
Tel: (01) 299914
Telex: 14939 TN
ISBN Prefix(es): 9973-906; 9973-946

Maison d'Edition Mohamed Ali Hammi+
3 rue Dragut, 3001 Sfax
Mailing Address: 40 rue Chebbi, Sfax 3000
Tel: (04) 224534 *Fax:* (04) 211552
Key Personnel
President: Abid Nouri
Founded: 1983
Subjects: History, Language Arts, Linguistics, Literature, Literary Criticism, Essays, Mathematics, Philosophy
ISBN Prefix(es): 9973-727
Imprints: CAEU
Distributor for Centre Culturel Arabic (Liban); El Farabi (Liban)

IORT (Imprimerie Officielle de la Republique Tunisienne), see Government Printer (Imprimerie Officielle de la Republique Tunisienne - IORT)

Les Editions de l'Arbre
17 rue Mohamed Karkoub (ex 7112), El Manar 3, 2092 Tunis Tunisie
Tel: (01) 887 927 *Fax:* (01) 887 927
Key Personnel
Contact: A Beji
Founded: 1993
Subjects: Animals, Pets, Archaeology, Gardening, Plants, History, House & Home, Humor, Language Arts, Linguistics, Literature, Literary Criticism, Essays, Natural History, Outdoor Recreation, Poetry, Publishing & Book Trade Reference, Self-Help
ISBN Prefix(es): 9973-772

Maison Tunisienne de l'Edition+
36, rue Babel Khadra, 1006 Tunis
Tel: (01) 345333 *Fax:* (01) 353992
Telex: Mac 12032
Key Personnel
Man Dir: Larbi Azouz

Founded: 1966
Subjects: Agriculture, Anthropology, Archaeology, Biography, Drama, Theater, Education, History, Literature, Literary Criticism, Essays, Philosophy, Poetry, Public Administration, Religion - Islamic
ISBN Prefix(es): 9973-12

Publications de la Fondation Temimi pour la Recherche Scientifique et L'Information
BP 50, 1118 Zaghouan
Tel: (072) 676 446; (072) 680 110 *Fax:* (072) 676 710
E-mail: temimi.fond.@gnet.tn
Web Site: temimi.org (in Arabic); refer.org/6 (in French)
Key Personnel
Pres: Prof Abdeljelil Temimi
Founded: 1989
Subjects: Archaeology, History, Library & Information Sciences, Social Sciences, Sociology
ISBN Prefix(es): 9973-719
Number of titles published annually: 15 Print
Distributed by Geulhner & Rorin

Scientifique et l'Information-TRSI, see Publications de la Fondation Temimi pour la Recherche Scientifique et L'Information

Sud Editions
79 rue de Palestine, Tunis 1002
Tel: (01) 787626 *Fax:* (01) 792905
Telex: 12363 TN
Key Personnel
Man Dir: M Masmoudi
Editorial Dir: Nabil Asswad
Founded: 1976
Subjects: Art, Literature, Literary Criticism, Essays
ISBN Prefix(es): 9973-703
Warehouse: La Soukra, Km 15, 2036 Tunis

Editions Techniques Specialisees
2 bis, rue du Reservoir, 1008 Tunis Bab Menara
Tel: (01) 262155
Key Personnel
International Rights: Hajer Djilani
Founded: 1978
ISBN Prefix(es): 9973-711
Subsidiaries: Redaction

Societe Tunisienne de Diffusion
5, av de Carthage, 1000 RP Tunis
Tel: (01) 255000; (01) 261799 *Cable:* Studiffusion
ISBN Prefix(es): 9973-11

Turkey

General Information

Capital: Ankara
Language: Turkish
Religion: Predominantly Sunni Moslem
Population: 63.9 million
Bank Hours: 0900-1730 Monday-Friday
Shop Hours: 0800-1900 Monday-Saturday
Currency: Turkish lira
Export/Import Information: Books, magazines and similar publications are freely imported. International copyright laws enforced. 1% VAT on books.
Copyright: Berne, Florence (see Copyright Conventions, pg xi)

ABC Kitabevi AS
Tunel Meydan 1, 80030 Beyoglu, Istanbul

Tel: (0212) 2762404 *Fax:* (0212) 2851860
Telex: 24094 Abck Tr
Key Personnel
Man Dir: Artun Altiparmak
Editorial: Oender Renkliyildirim
Sales: K Karakush
Production: Hasan Guenaydin
Publicity: Ferit Guersu
Rights & Permissions: Necip Inselel
Founded: 1976
Subjects: Education
ISBN Prefix(es): 975-09

Ada Press Publishers+
Ilk Belediye Cad Vural Arikan, Apt No 5/7, 80050 Beyoglu, Istanbul
Tel: (0212) 243 1778; (0212) 243 1779
Fax: (0212) 249 3545
Key Personnel
Editor: Mr Ferit Edgue
Founded: 1976
Also acts as an art gallery.
ISBN Prefix(es): 975-438

Afa Yayincilik, see Afa Yayincilik Sanayi Tic AS

Afa Yayincilik Sanayi Tic AS+
Formerly Afa Yayincilik
Istiklal Cad. Bekar Sok. No: 17, Taksim/Istanbul
Tel: (0212) 2453967 *Fax:* (0212) 2444362
Key Personnel
President: Atil Ant
International Rights: Dilek Basak
Founded: 1985
Subjects: Biography, Child Care & Development, Drama, Theater, Film, Video, Government, Political Science, Nonfiction (General)
ISBN Prefix(es): 975-414
Distributed by DaDa Ltd
Bookshop(s): AFA Kitabevi, Istiklal Cad, Bekar Sok No 17, Beyoglu/Istanbul

Akdeniz Yayincilik+
Celal Ferdi Gokcay Sok Nebioglu Han K 1, Cagaloglu/Istanbul
Tel: (0212) 5268012; (0212) 5224045 *Fax:* (0212) 5268011; (0212) 6290027
Key Personnel
President: H Mursit Ul
Editor: Filiztekin Ferhan
Founded: 1995
Specialize in geographical atlases, school books & dictionaries.
ISBN Prefix(es): 975-469
Parent Company: Altin Kitaplar Yayinevi Ve Ticaret As

Alkim Kitapcilik-Yayimcilik+
Za Zafer Carsisi 14, Kizilay/Ankara
Member of Basar Arslan.
Subjects: Astrology, Occult, Business, Child Care & Development, Computer Science, Cookery, Crafts, Games, Hobbies, Drama, Theater, Economics, Finance, How-to, Law, Management, Marketing, Microcomputers, Nonfiction (General), Psychology, Psychiatry, Sports, Athletics
ISBN Prefix(es): 975-337

Altin Kitaplar Yayinevi
Sahaflar, Carsisi 9, Beyazit/Istanbul
Tel: (0212) 5224045; (0212) 3394359 *Fax:* (0212) 5268011
Key Personnel
Publisher: Fethi Ul; Muersit Ul; Turhan Bozkurt
Sales: K Husnu Terek
Production: Erden Heper; Batu Bozkurt
Editorial: Alpar Oya
Founded: 1959
Subjects: Criminology, Economics, Fiction, History, Nonfiction (General), Philosophy, Psychology, Psychiatry, Regional Interests, Science Fiction, Fantasy

ISBN Prefix(es): 975-7620
Showroom(s): Celal ferdi Goekcay SK, Nebio Is Hani, Istanbul

Arkadas Ltd+
Mithatpasa cad 28/C, Ankara 06441
Tel: (0312) 4344624 *Fax:* (0312) 4356057
Key Personnel
Chairman & Owner: Cumhur Ozdemir
 E-mail: cumhuro@arkadas.com.tr
Editor: Meltem Ozdemir *E-mail:* meltemo@arkadas.com.tr
Founded: 1979
Specialize in computer books, textbooks; also acts as Book Distributors, Bookshop. Authorized software replicator of Microsoft Co ln MENA (Middle East & North Africa).
Subjects: Animals, Pets, Computer Science, Cookery, English as a Second Language, Environmental Studies, Mathematics, Music, Dance, Physics
ISBN Prefix(es): 975-509
Number of titles published annually: 100 Print
Total Titles: 300 Print
Distributor for Microsoft Press
Foreign Rep(s): Microsoft Press (Turkey)
Bookshop(s): ODTUU Alisveris Merkezi, Ankara

Arkeoloji Ve Sanat Yayinlari (Archaeology & Art Publications)+
Hayriye Cad, Corlu Apt 4/5, 80060 Galatasaray Istanbul
Tel: (212) 293 0378 *Fax:* (212) 245 6877
E-mail: arkeolojisanat@superonline.com
Web Site: www.arkeolojisanat.com
Key Personnel
Publisher: Nezih Basgelen *Tel:* (212) 245 6838 *Fax:* (212) 245 6877 *E-mail:* nezihbasgelen@superonline.com
Senior Editor: Brian Johnson *Tel:* (212) 249 6960 *Fax:* (212) 245 6877 *E-mail:* brianjohnson@superonline.com
Founded: 1978
Since 1978 Arkeoloji ve Sanat Yayinlari (Archaeology & Art Publications) has been publishing books on archaeology, history, & art history of Turkey. With titles in Turkish, English, German & French, the company's list includes publications ranging from specialized scholarly monographs to popular guides to Turkey's famed tourist sites. Besides books, the press publishes a bimonthly journal, Arkeoloji ve Sanat, presenting the academic contributions of the world's leading scholars of Anatolian archaeology & art.
Subjects: Anthropology, Antiques, Archaeology, Architecture & lnterior Design, Art, History, Photography, Travel
ISBN Prefix(es): 975-7538
Number of titles published annually: 10 Print
Total Titles: 100 Print

Arkin Kitabevi
Ankara Cad. 60, Sirkeci, Istanbul 34410
Tel: (0212) 5229224; (0212) 5132384; (0212) 5413620 *Fax:* (0212) 5121901
Telex: 28362 Rga Tr *Cable:* BIRARKINLAR ISTANBUL
Key Personnel
Man Dir, Rights & Permissions: Ramazan Goikalp Arkin
Founded: 1957
Subjects: Education, Science (General)
ISBN Prefix(es): 975-402

Ataturk Kultur, Dil ve Tarih, Yusek Kurumu Baskanligi
Atatuerk Bulvari No: 217, Kavaklidere, Ankara
Tel: (0312) 4286100
Key Personnel
President: Prof Utkan Kocatuerk, PhD
Subjects: Archaeology, Ethnicity, History, Language Arts, Linguistics
ISBN Prefix(es): 975-16
Branch Office(s)
Atatuerk Research Ce
Turkish Culture Center
Turkish Historical Society
Turkish Language Society

Ataturk Universitesi+
K.K. Egitim Fakultesi Dekanligi, 25240 Erzurum
Tel: (0442) 2343677; (0442) 2184172 *Fax:* (0442) 17140
Key Personnel
Foreign Relations Coordinator: Dr Erol Cakmak
Founded: 1957
ISBN Prefix(es): 975-442

Aydin Yayincilik+
Balgat Nasuhi Akar Mahallesi, 1 Cad 5 SK No 12 A, Balgat/Ankara
Tel: (0427) 2506; (0427) 3850042 *Fax:* (0385) 3923; (0385) 2853925
Subjects: Mathematics, Science (General)
ISBN Prefix(es): 975-7948
Subsidiaries: Aydin Web Tesisleri (printing)
Book Club(s): Yayincilar Birligi
Warehouse: 100 yil Bolvari, Gl sok, No 29, Ostim

Bilden Bilgisayar (Bilden Computer, Programming, Digital Publishing Ltd)
Ziverbey Kasap Ismail Sok, Sadikoglu Ys Merkezi No 13 Buro No 41, 81040 Kadikoy/Istanbul
Tel: (0216) 449 52 50 *Fax:* (0216) 449 52 51
E-mail: bilden@bilden.com.tr
Web Site: www.bilden.com.tr
Key Personnel
General Manager: Sukru Korman
Specializes in the development of educational software on CD-ROM for ages 3-18.
Subjects: Education, Language Arts, Linguistics, Mathematics, Science (General), Social Sciences, Sociology
Distributor for Encyclopedia Britannica Co; LangMaster

Birsen Yayinevi+
Cagaloglu Yokusu 29, Evren Carsisi No 29/19, 34440 Cagaloglu, Istanbul
Tel: (0212) 5278578; (0212) 5137588 *Fax:* (0212) 5270895
Key Personnel
President: Mr Cengiz Algin
Vice President: Mr Bahadir Algin
Founded: 1973
ISBN Prefix(es): 975-511

Caglayan Kitabevi+
Istiklal Cad 166, 80070 Beyoglu, Istanbul
Tel: (0212) 2491794 *Fax:* (0212) 1491794
Key Personnel
President: Tuncay Caglayan
Founded: 1962 (Publishing since 1952)
Subjects: Chemistry, Chemical Engineering, Civil Engineering, Electronics, Electrical Engineering, Engineering (General), Management, Mathematics, Mechanical Engineering, Physics, Technology, Technical Books
ISBN Prefix(es): 975-436
Associate Companies: Caglayan Basimevi, Catalcesme Sokak 26, Cagaloglu, Istanbul; Caglayan Yayinev, PK 517, Beyoglu, Istanbul

Cep Kitaplari AS+
Piyerloti cad No 7-9, 34400 Cemberlitas, Istanbul
Tel: (0212) 5162004; (0212) 5163301; (0212) 4582409 *Fax:* (0212) 5162005; (0212) 5162004 Ext 17
Key Personnel
Editor-in-Chief: Osman Cetin Deniztekin *Tel:* (212) 5162004 Ext 13 *E-mail:* osmand@netscape.net
Founded: 1982
Member of Turkish Publishers Association.
Subjects: Fiction, Nonfiction (General), Religion - lslamic, Science (General), Science Fiction, Fantasy, Women's Studies
ISBN Prefix(es): 975-480
Number of titles published annually: 5 Print
Total Titles: 60 Print
Online services available through Varlik.
Parent Company: Varlik Yayinlari A S, Piyerloti Cd 7-9, 34400 lstanbul, Contact: Osman Deniztekin
Distributed by Varlik Yayinlari AS

Dergah Yayinlari AS, see Ezel Erverdi (Dergah Yayinlari AS) Muessese Muduru

Dokuz Eylul Universitesi
Dokuzcesmeler, 35160 Buca/lzmir
Tel: (0232) 4204180 *Fax:* (0232) 4201789
Founded: 1982
ISBN Prefix(es): 975-441

Dost Kitabevi Yayinlari+
Karanfil Sokak 29/4, 06650 Kizilay Ankara
Tel: (0312) 4188772 *Fax:* (0312) 4199397
E-mail: raulman@domi.net.tr; levent@easynet.fr
Key Personnel
CEO: Erdal Akalin *Tel:* (0312) 4252464 *Fax:* (0312) 4180355
Gen Mgr: Gunay Okumus *Tel:* (0312) 4188327 *Fax:* (0312) 4180355
Dir: Raul Mansur *Tel:* (0312) 4188772 *Fax:* (0312) 4199397 *E-mail:* raulman@domi.net.tr
Editor-in-Chief: Levent Yilmaz *Tel:* (0312) 4188772 *Fax:* (0312) 4199397 *E-mail:* levent@easynet.fr
Founded: 1979
Chain of bookshops. Started publishing books in 1997. Co-editions with Dorling Kindersley, Franco Maria Ricci.
Member of Turkish Publishers Association.
Subjects: History, Social Sciences, Sociology, Travel, Translated fiction
ISBN Prefix(es): 975-7501
Number of titles published annually: 60 Print
Total Titles: 80 Print
Branch Office(s)
105 Rue de l'Ouest, Paris, France, Mr Levent Yilmaz *Tel:* (01) 45410907 *E-mail:* levent@easynet.fr
Bookshop(s): Karanfil Sokak No: 11, 06650 Kizilay Ankara *Tel:* (0312) 4252464 *Fax:* (0312) 4180355
Orders to: Dost Dagitim, Bayindir sokak 40/B, Kizilay Ankara 06650, Murat Duman *Tel:* (0312) 4324868 *Fax:* (0312) 4357596

Dost Yayinlari San Ve Tic Ltd
Tuenel Gecidi is Hani, B/blok 9-210, Istanbul, Beyoglu 80050
Tel: (0212) 2453141 *Fax:* (0212) 2430278
Key Personnel
Dir: Salim Sengil
Marketing Manager: Asli Sengil Cansever
Founded: 1947
Subjects: Art, Humor, Literature, Literary Criticism, Essays
ISBN Prefix(es): 975-95481; 975-7499

Eren Yayincilik ve Kitapcilik Ltd Sti+
Tunel, Istiklal Cad, Sofyali Sok, No: 34, 80050 Beyoglu/Istanbul
Tel: (0212) 2520560; (0212) 2512858 *Fax:* (0212) 2433016
E-mail: eren@turk.net

Founded: 1983
Subjects: Engineering (General)
ISBN Prefix(es): 975-7622
Associate Companies: Ottomania
Branch Office(s)
Istanbul

Ezel Erverdi (Dergah Yayinlari AS) Muessese Muduru
Peykhane Cad Camii Sok No 57/1, 34490 Cemberlitas/Istanbul
Tel: (0212) 5161262; (0212) 5160047 *Fax:* (0212) 5161921
Key Personnel
Man Dir: Ezel Erverdi
Editorial: Mustafa Kutlu
Sales: Fatih Gokdag
Production: Kara Ismail
Publicity: Ashihan Erverdi
Founded: 1977
Subjects: Education, Ethnicity, Government, Political Science, History, Literature, Literary Criticism, Essays, Philosophy
ISBN Prefix(es): 975-7462; 975-7032
Subsidiaries: Ulke Yayin Haber Tic Ltd Sti; Emek matbaacilik ve ilancilik Ltd Sti
Bookshop(s): Ulke Yayin Haber Tic Ltd Sti, Ankara cad No 41/A Uygurhan Sirheci list

Iki Nokta Arastirma Basin Yayin Sanayi ve Ticaret Ltd Sti, *imprint of* IKI NOKTA Research Press & Publications Industry & Trade Ltd

IKI NOKTA Research Press & Publications Industry & Trade Ltd+
Moda, Cad 180/10, 81300 Kadikoy/Istanbul
Tel: (0216) 4180319; (0216) 4180320 *Fax:* (0216) 3376756
E-mail: ikinokta@superonline.com; ikinokta@turkinfo.com; ikinokta@gisoturkey.com; ikinokta @turkgis.com; ikinokta@infoturk.com
Web Site: www.ikinekta.com
Key Personnel
President: Yuecel Yaman
International Rights: Kerem Ahmet
Founded: 1986
Specialize in database updating.
Subjects: Archaeology, Communications, Geography, Geology, History
ISBN Prefix(es): 975-340
Number of titles published annually: 130 Print; 5 CD-ROM; 1 Online; 1 E-Book
Online services available through World Wide Web.
Imprints: Iki Nokta Arastirma Basin Yayin Sanayi ve Ticaret Ltd Sti

Iletisim Yayinlari+
Klodfarer Cd Iletisim Han No 7/2, Cagaloglu, Istanbul 34400
Tel: (0212) 5162263; (0212) 5162260; (0212) 5162264; (0212) 5162265 *Fax:* (0212) 5161258
E-mail: editors@iletisim.com.tr
Key Personnel
Contact: Nihat Tuna; Osman Yener
Founded: 1984
Subjects: Ethnicity, Fiction, Government, Political Science, History, Literature, Literary Criticism, Essays, Nonfiction (General), Philosophy, Science Fiction, Fantasy, Social Sciences, Sociology
ISBN Prefix(es): 975-470
Associate Companies: Birikim Yayinlari
Branch Office(s)
Ankara
Bodrum
Ismir

Imge Kitabevi
Konur Sok No 3, Kizilay, Kizilzy/Ankara 06650
Tel: (0312) 4181942 *Fax:* (0312) 4256532
E-mail: imge@www.imge.com.tr
Key Personnel
Contact: Refik Tabakci
ISBN Prefix(es): 975-533
Parent Company: Ilmge Kitabevi Ltd
Divisions: Ilmge Kitabevi Yayinlari

Inkilap Kitabevi Yayin Sanayii ve Ticaret AS, see Inkilap Publishers Ltd

Inkilap Publishers Ltd+
Formerly Inkilap Kitabevi Yayin Sanayii ve Ticaret AS
Ankara Cad No: 95, 34410 Sirkeci, Istanbul
Tel: (0212) 5140611; (0212) 5140610 *Fax:* (0212) 5140612
Web Site: www.inkilap.com
Key Personnel
Man Dir: Nazar Fikri; Julia Fikri; Errol Fikri
Foreign Rights: Sema Diker *E-mail:* sdiker@inkilap.com
Founded: 1935
Subjects: Animals, Pets, Archaeology, Art, Business, Child Care & Development, Cookery, Drama, Theater, Economics, Electronics, Electrical Engineering, Fiction, Gardening, Plants, Humor, Management, Mathematics, Music, Dance, Philosophy, Photography, Physics, Poetry, Psychology, Psychiatry, Religion - Islamic
ISBN Prefix(es): 975-10
Parent Company: Anka Offset AS, Teknografik Matbaacilik AS, Ankara Cad 95, Sirkeci, Istanbul
Associate Companies: Inkas, Ingilizce Nesriyat Kitapcilik AS, Ankara Cad 95, Sirkeci, Istanbul
Branch Office(s)
Yeni Zaman Kitabevi, Ankara Cad 155, Sirkeci, Istanbul (correspondence to Inkilap)

Isis Yayin Tic ve San Ltd+
Semsibey Sok 10, Beylerbeyi, 81210 Beylerbeyi/Istanbul
Tel: (0216) 3213851; (0216) 3213847; (0216) 3213847 *Fax:* (0216) 3218666
E-mail: isis@turk.net
Key Personnel
Dir: Sinan Kuneralp
Publishing: S Helvacioglu
Founded: 1983
Subjects: History, Social Sciences, Sociology
ISBN Prefix(es): 975-428

Kiyi Yayinlari+
Tellvikiye Cad 71/6, Beyoglu, Istanbul 80060
Tel: (0212) 2455845 *Fax:* (0212) 2454009
Key Personnel
Publisher: Sahin Beygu *E-mail:* sbeygu@ibm.net
Founded: 1987
Member of T Yay-Bir (Turkish Publishers Association).
Subjects: Literature, Literary Criticism, Essays, Nonfiction (General)
ISBN Prefix(es): 975-444

Kok Yayincilik+
Incesu Cad, No 10, Kolej/Ankara
Tel: (0312) 4302622 *Fax:* (0312) 4350497
E-mail: kokbilgi@kokyayincilik.com.tr
Web Site: www.kokyayincilik.com.tr
Key Personnel
International Rights: Celal Musaoglu
Founded: 1987
Subjects: Animals, Pets, Child Care & Development, Education, Health, Nutrition, House & Home, Human Relations, Mathematics, Music, Dance
ISBN Prefix(es): 975-499
Imprints: Offset

Kubbealti Akademisi Kultur ve Sasat Vakfi+
Peykhane Sok No 3, 34400 Cemberlitas, Istanbul
Tel: (0212) 5162356; (0212) 5189209 *Fax:* (0212) 5171460
Key Personnel
International Rights: Mrs Semahat Yuksel
Founded: 1978
Subjects: Architecture & Interior Design, Art, Biography, Environmental Studies, History, Literature, Literary Criticism, Essays, Music, Dance, Religion - Islamic, Culture
ISBN Prefix(es): 975-7663
Distributor for Istanbul Fetih Cemiyeti's Editions
Bookshop(s): Yeniceriler Cad No 43, 34490 Carsikapi, Istanbul

Metis Yayinlari (Metis Publishers)+
Ipek Sok No:9, Beyoglu/Istanbul 80060
Tel: (0212) 2454509; (0212) 2454696 *Fax:* (0212) 2454519
E-mail: metis@turk.net
Web Site: www.metisbooks.com
Key Personnel
International, Foreign Rights: Ms Muege Guersoy Soekmen
Founded: 1982
Member of Turkish Publishers' Association. Publisher of Psychiatry, Literature, Politics & Philosophy. Also acts as Verso agent in Turkey.
Subjects: Literature, Literary Criticism, Essays, Nonfiction (General), Philosophy, Poetry, Psychology, Psychiatry, Science Fiction, Fantasy, Social Sciences, Sociology, Western Fiction, Women's Studies, Political Studies
ISBN Prefix(es): 975-342; 975-7650
Number of titles published annually: 40 Print
Total Titles: 540 Print

Nurdan YayinlariSanayi ve Ticaret Ltd Sti+
Prof Kazim Gurkan Cad. Cagdas Han No: 13, Cagaloglu/Istanbul
Tel: (0212) 5225504; (0212) 5138653 *Fax:* (0212) 5126329; (0212) 5125186
Key Personnel
President & Owner: Cetin Tuezuener
International Rights: Nurdan Tuezuener
Founded: 1983
Member of Turkish Publishers' Association.
ISBN Prefix(es): 975-527
Subsidiaries: Meydan Larousse Co; Nu-Do Publishing Distribution Co

Offset, *imprint of* Kok Yayincilik

Oguz Yayinlari
Babiali Cad 30/7, 34410 Cagaloglu, Istanbul
Tel: (0212) 5264745; (0212) 5113418 *Fax:* (0212) 5114695
Key Personnel
Editor: Sevgili Turan
Subjects: Religion - Islamic, Theology
ISBN Prefix(es): 975-538

Pan Yayincilik+
Barbaros Bulvari No 74/4, Besiktas, 34400 Istanbul
Tel: (0212) 2618072 *Fax:* (212) 2275674
E-mail: pankitap@superonline.com
Key Personnel
Contact: Ferruh Gencer
Founded: 1986
Subjects: Fiction, Music, Dance, Science (General)
ISBN Prefix(es): 975-7652

Parantez Yayinlari Ltd+
Istiklal Cad 212 Aznavur Pasaji Alt Kat, Alt Kat, Beyoglu/Istanbul
Tel: (0212) 5168280 *Fax:* (0212) 5168280
E-mail: parantezyay@superonline.com.tr

Key Personnel
International Rights: Metin Zeynioglu
Founded: 1991
Member of Turkish Publishers Association & Turkish Pen Club.
Subjects: Biography, Fiction, Film, Video, Gay & Lesbian, Humor
ISBN Prefix(es): 975-7939

Payel Yayinevi+
Cagaloglu Yokusu Evren Han Kat 4 No 63, Cagaloglu, Istanbul
Tel: (0212) 5284409; (0212) 5118233 *Fax:* (0212) 5124353 *Cable:* PAYEL YAYINEVI-CAGALOGLU-ISTANBUL
Key Personnel
Editor, Owner: Ahmet Ozturk
Founded: 1966
Member of Publishers Association of Turkey & Cumhuriyet Book Club.
Subjects: Archaeology, Film, Video, History, Literature, Literary Criticism, Essays, Psychology, Psychiatry, Science (General), Social Sciences, Sociology, Women's Studies
ISBN Prefix(es): 975-388
Book Club(s): Cumhuriyet Book Club

Pearson Education Turkey+
Koza is Merkezi, B Blok Kat 4, Morbasan Sok Balmumcu, 80700 Istanbul
Tel: (0212) 288 6941 *Fax:* (0212) 267 1851
E-mail: firstname.lastname@pearsoned-ema.com
Key Personnel
Regional Dir, East Med/Arab World: Christine Ozden
Sales Dir, East Med/Arab World: Necip Inselel
Founded: 1995
Branch offices in Adana, Ankara, Antalya, Bursa, & Izmir.
Subjects: English as a Second Language
ISBN Prefix(es): 975-7015
Parent Company: Pearson Education
Ultimate Parent Company: Pearson Plc
Branch Office(s)
Ankara
Adana
Antalya
Bursa
Izmir
Distributor for Langenscheidt

Redhouse Press+
Rizapasa Yokusu 50, 34450 Eminonu/Istanbul
Tel: (0212) 5221498 *Fax:* (0212) 5190883
Telex: 23554 Peettr
Key Personnel
Co-Dir: Cerina Logico Blakney; Richard Blakney
Editor: Charles Brown; Serap Bezmez
Sales: Sait Sermet
Founded: 1822
Subjects: Education
ISBN Prefix(es): 975-413
Bookshop(s): Redhouse Boolesbave

Remzi Kitabevi+
Selvili Mescit Sok No 3, Cagaloglu, Istanbul 34440
Tel: (0212) 5220583; (0212) 5190981 *Fax:* (0212) 5229055
E-mail: post@remzi.com.tr
Web Site: www.remzi.com.tr *Cable:* REMZI KITABEVI ISTANBUL
Key Personnel
Man Dir: Erol Erduran
Dir: Ahmet Erduran
Production Manager: Oemer Erduran
Founded: 1927
Subjects: Art, Biography, Education, Fiction, History, Nonfiction (General), Philosophy, Psychology, Psychiatry, Science (General), Social Sciences, Sociology
ISBN Prefix(es): 975-14

Subsidiaries: Evrim Matbaacilik Ltd
Bookshop(s): Etiler Istanbul *Tel:* (0212) 282 2575 76 *Fax:* (0212) 282 2577; 44 Rumeli Caddesi, Nisantasi, Istanbul *Tel:* (0212) 234 5475-76 *Fax:* (0212) 232 5934; Erenkoy, Istanbul *Tel:* (0212) 448 0373-74 *Fax:* (0212) 448 0375; Akatlar, Istanbul *Tel:* (0212) 352 3355 *Fax:* (0212) 352 3356; Mecidiyekoy, Istanbul *Tel:* (0212) 217 1225 *Fax:* (0212) 216 8288; 452 Bagdat Cad, Suadiye, Istanbul *Tel:* (0212) 368 1491-92 *Fax:* (0212) 368 1467

Ruh ve Madde Yayinlari ve Saglik Hizmetleri AS (Spirit & Matter Publications)+
4/8 80060, Hasnun Galip Sok Pembe Cikmazi, Beyoglu, Istanbul
Tel: (0212) 2431814 *Fax:* (0212) 2520718
E-mail: bilyay@bilyay.org.tr
Web Site: www.ruhvemadde.com
Key Personnel
Foreign Rights: Yasemin Tokatli
Founded: 1994
Subjects: Alternative, Astrology, Occult, Earth Sciences, Nonfiction (General), Parapsychology, Philosophy, Religion - Islamic, Religion - Other, Self-Help
ISBN Prefix(es): 975-8007
Total Titles: 110 Print
Parent Company: Foundation for Spreading the Knowledge to Unify Humanity
Associate Companies: Society for Research on the Nature of the Human Individual, 4/8 80060, Gasnun Galip Sok Pembe Cikmazi, Beyoglu, Istanbul
Distributed by EGE META
Distributor for EGE META, META

Sabah Kitaplari+
Istiklal Cad. 21, Galatasaray/Istanbul
Tel: (0212) 5028572 *Fax:* (0212) 5028346
Key Personnel
Contact: Serpil Demirtas *E-mail:* sdemirtas@sabah.com.tr
Founded: 1974
Subjects: Biography, Business, Criminology, History, Management, Nonfiction (General)
ISBN Prefix(es): 975-579
Associate Companies: Suereli Yayinlar AS, Bueyuekdere Cad, Levent, Istanbul *Tel:* (01) 692420 (Periodical Press Inc)

Saray Medikal Yayin Tic Ltd Sti+
168 Sok No 5-7, Bornova/Izmir
Tel: (0232) 3394969; (0232) 3396949 *Fax:* (0232) 3733700
E-mail: eozkarahan@novell.cs.eng.dev.edu.tr
Key Personnel
Contact: Cetin Gultekin
Founded: 1993
Member of Turkish Publishers Association.
Subjects: Behavioral Sciences, Child Care & Development, Computer Science, Engineering (General), Medicine, Nursing, Dentistry, Philosophy, Self-Help, Social Sciences, Sociology
ISBN Prefix(es): 975-7816; 975-7074
Parent Company: Saray Medikal Yayin Sar ve Tic Ltd Sti
Subsidiaries: Bassaray Printing

Seckin Yayinevi+
Saglik Sok 19-B, 06410 Sihhiye, Ankara
Tel: (0312) 4353030 *Fax:* (0312) 4352472
E-mail: seckin@seckin.com.tr
Web Site: www.seckin.com.tr
Key Personnel
International Rights: Koray Seckin
Founded: 1959
Member of Turkish Publishers Association.
Subjects: Accounting, Computer Science, Economics, Law
ISBN Prefix(es): 975-347
Number of titles published annually: 70 Print

Total Titles: 233 Print
Online services available through World Wide Web.

Soez Yayin/Oyunajans+
PK 7, 80622 Levent/Istanbul
Tel: (0212) 1668931 *Fax:* (0212) 2454102
Web Site: www.oyunajans.com
Key Personnel
Contact: Mr Nevzat Erkmen *E-mail:* nerkmen@turk.net; Mr Ali Erkmen *E-mail:* aerkmen.@turk.net
Founded: 1983
Subjects: Advertising, Alternative, Art, Business, Career Development, Crafts, Games, Hobbies, Fiction, Film, Video, Finance, Health, Nutrition, How-to, Management, Psychology, Psychiatry, Self-Help, Specialize in translations of Turkish literature into English
ISBN Prefix(es): 975-7190; 975-95491
Total Titles: 50 Print

Toker Yayinlari+
Ankara cad 46/14, Sirkeci, Istanbul
Tel: (0212) 5223309
Key Personnel
President: Mr Yalcin Toker
Founded: 1962
Member of Turkish Publishers Association.
Subjects: Ethnicity, History, Literature, Literary Criticism, Essays
ISBN Prefix(es): 975-445
U.S. Office(s): C E M Toker, PO Box 39652, Phoenix, AZ 85069, United States

Toros Yayinlari Ltd Co
Yenicarsi Cad Luks Apt 33/1, 80050 Galatasaray, Istanbul
Tel: (0212) 2444155 *Fax:* (0212) 2452858; (0212) 2444155
Key Personnel
Author: Ali Neyzi
Editor: Rasit Goekceli *E-mail:* rgokceli@escortnet.com; Sahin Beygu
Founded: 1981
Subjects: Literature, Literary Criticism, Essays
ISBN Prefix(es): 975-433

Turkish Republic - Ministry of Culture+
Necatibey Cad. No 55 Kat 6-7, 06440 Kizilay/Ankara
Tel: (0312) 232 19 66; (0312) 231 54 50 *Fax:* (0312) 231 50 36
E-mail: yayimlar@kutuphanelergm.gov.tr
Web Site: www.kultur.gov.tr
Key Personnel
Dir, Publications Dept: Ali Osman Guzel
Founded: 1973
Subjects: Archaeology, Art, Drama, Theater, History, Literature, Literary Criticism, Essays
ISBN Prefix(es): 975-17
Distributed by Dosimm

Varlik Yayinlari AS+
Piyerloti Cad 7-9, Gemberlitas, Istanbul 34400
Tel: (0212) 5162004; (0212) 5163301; (0212) 5180048; (0212) 4582409 (Direct) *Fax:* (0212) 5162005; (0212) 5162004 (ext 117)
E-mail: varlik@varlik.com.tr; varlik@isbank.net.tr
Web Site: www.varlik.com.tr
Key Personnel
Publisher: Osman Deniztekin *Tel:* (0212) 5162004 ext 13 *E-mail:* osmand@netscape.net
Founded: 1946
Member of Turkish Publishers Association.
Subjects: Fiction, Nonfiction (General), Poetry, Science (General), Self-Help, Social Sciences, Sociology, Women's Studies
ISBN Prefix(es): 975-434
Number of titles published annually: 20 Print
Total Titles: 200 Print

TURKEY

Online services available through Varlik, World Wide Web.
Associate Companies: CEP Kitaplari AS
Distributor for CEP Kitaplari AS

Yapi-Endustri Merkezi Yayinlari-Yem Yayin+
Cumhuriyet Cad 329, 80230 Harbiye/Istanbul
Tel: (0212) 2193939 *Fax:* (0212) 2256623
E-mail: yem-od@yunus.mam.tubitak.gov.tr; kitap@yem.net
Web Site: www.yem.net
Key Personnel
President: Dogan Hasol
Deputy General Manager: Bulent Kumral
  E-mail: bulent_kumral@yem.net
Founded: 1968
Member of UICB. Also acts as bookshop & book importer.
Subjects: Architecture & Interior Design, Art, Civil Engineering
ISBN Prefix(es): 975-7438
Distributor for Melissa (Greece)

Kabalci Yayinevi
Himaye-i Etfal Sok 8-B, 34410 Istanbul
Tel: (0212) 5268586; (0212) 5226305 *Fax:* (0212) 5268495
Key Personnel
President: Sabri Kabalci
Coordinator: Elif Akin
Founded: 1987
Subjects: Anthropology, Art, Drama, Theater, History, Literature, Literary Criticism, Essays, Philosophy, Poetry, Social Sciences, Sociology
ISBN Prefix(es): 975-7942
Bookshop(s): Ortabahce Cad 22/4, Besiktas-Istanbul

Alev Yayinlari+
Yenicarsi Cad 26/5, Galatasaray/Istanbul
Tel: (0212) 2921016 *Fax:* (0212) 5168464
Key Personnel
Contact: Alev Yayinlari
Founded: 1989
Specialize in Alevite-Islamic Culture & Philosophy.
Subjects: Ethnicity, Government, Political Science, Literature, Literary Criticism, Essays
ISBN Prefix(es): 975-335
Parent Company: Genel Ajans Ltd
Distributed by Baris; Papiruea; Say; Yoen
Distributor for CAN; Pencere
Book Club(s): Cumhuriyet Book Club

Yetkin Printing & Publishing Co Inc+
Strazburg Cad No 31/A, Sihhiye/Ankara
Tel: (0312) 4181273; (0312) 2314234
  Fax on Demand: (0312) 4174388
Key Personnel
President, Editor: Y Ziya Gwlkok
Founded: 1984
Subjects: Accounting, Computer Science, Law, Management
ISBN Prefix(es): 975-464
Divisions: Kazimkarahekir Cd (Printing)
Bookshop(s): Gulkok Bookstore, Kocabeyoglu Pst 74, Kizilay, Ankara

Yuce Reklam Yay Dagt AS+
PK 76, 34492 Beyazit, Istanbul
Tel: (01) 5227506 *Fax:* (01) 5163959
Telex: 22418 NEKTR
Key Personnel
Dir: Fahri Savasci; Ali Seven; Munip Oniz
Founded: 1982
Subjects: Computer Science, Electronics, Electrical Engineering, Medicine, Nursing, Dentistry
ISBN Prefix(es): 975-411
Subsidiaries: A F M Yayincilik-Tanitim

Warehouse: Dizdariye Cesme Sok 6 Emre Han, Kat: 1, Sultanahmet, 34400 Istanbul
Orders to: Yuce Yayin AS, PK 40 Beyazit, 34492 Istanbul

Turkmenistan

General Information

Capital: Ashkhabad
Language: Turkmen
Religion: Predominantly Sunni Muslim
Population: 3.8 million
Bank Hours: Generally open for short hours between 0930-1230 Monday-Friday
Shop Hours: Generally 0900-1800 Monday-Friday; often open weekends
Currency: 23 marats = 1 US dollar
Export/Import Information: Companies engaged in trade should register with the Turkmenistan Ministry of Foreign Affairs.

Izdatelstvo Turkmenistan
ul Atabaeva 20, 744000 Aschabad
Tel: (03632) 294275
Key Personnel
Dir: A M Dzhanmuradov
Chief Editor: A Allanazarov
Founded: 1965
Turkmenistan Publishing House.
Subjects: Agriculture, Fiction, Government, Political Science, Science (General), Social Sciences, Sociology
ISBN Prefix(es): 5-87228

Uganda

General Information

Capital: Kampala
Language: English is official language
Religion: Predominantly Christian (about 60%) and some Muslim
Population: 19.4 million
Bank Hours: 0830-1400 Monday-Friday
Shop Hours: 0830-1230, 1400-1630 or longer; 0800-1230 Saturday
Currency: 100 cents = 1 new Uganda shilling
Export/Import Information: No tariff on books or advertising matter but subject to sales tax. Import license and exchange controls (granted automatically with import licenses).

Centenary Publishing House Ltd+
PO Box 6246, Kampala
Tel: (041) 241599 *Fax:* (041) 250427
Key Personnel
Man Dir, Editorial, Production, Rights & Permissions: Rev Sam Kakiza
Sales, Publicity: V Kagga-Senyonga
Founded: 1977
Subjects: Education, Religion - Other
ISBN Prefix(es): 9970-9004
Parent Company: Church of Uganda, PO Box 14123, Kampala

Centre for Basic Research
Kololo, Baskerville Ave Plot 15, Kampala
Mailing Address: PO Box 9863, Kampala
Tel: (041) 231228; (041) 235533; (041) 342987
  Fax: (041) 235413
E-mail: cbr@imul.com
Key Personnel
Dir: Dr John Jean Barya

BOOK

Sr Assistant Librarian: Judith Akello
Founded: 1988
Member of CODESRIA.
Subjects: Agriculture, Environmental Studies, Ethnicity, Geography, Geology, Government, Political Science, History, Labor, Industrial Relations, Law, Social Sciences, Sociology, Women's Studies, Social Sciences, Humanities

Fountain, *imprint of* Fountain Publishers Ltd

Fountain Publishers Ltd+
PO Box 488, Kampala
Tel: (041) 259163; (041) 251112 *Fax:* (041) 251160
E-mail: fountain@starcom.co.ug
Web Site: www.fountainpublishers.com
Key Personnel
Board Chairman & Man Dir: James Tumusiime
Business Manager: Fred Wangolo
Publishing Editor: Alex Bangirana
Marketing Manager: Paul Waddimba
Founded: 1988
Member of Uganda Publishers & Booksellers Association (UPABA) & African Publishers Network (APNET).
Subjects: Agriculture, Anthropology, Biography, Career Development, Cookery, Economics, Education, Fiction, Government, Political Science, Health, Nutrition, History, Humor, Language Arts, Linguistics, Mathematics, Nonfiction (General), Physical Sciences, Poetry, Psychology, Psychiatry, Science (General), Social Sciences, Sociology, Travel, Women's Studies
ISBN Prefix(es): 9970-02
Number of titles published annually: 20 Print
Total Titles: 170 Print
Online services available through World Wide Web.
Imprints: Fountain
Subsidiaries: Fountain Bookpoint; University Bookshop Makerere
Distributed by African Books Collective-ABC (Australia, Europe, UK & USA); James Currey
Distributor for James Currey Ltd (UK); Harper Collins; Christopher Hurst (UK); Lion Publishers Plc (UK); Penguin; Princeton University Press
Foreign Rights: The African Books Collective (ABC) (Australia, Commonwealth, Europe, North America)

Roce (Consultants) Ltd
PO Box 1481, Kampala
Tel: (041) 285630 *Fax:* (041) 259997
Telex: 61209 *Cable:* ROCE
Key Personnel
Man Dir: Robert K Rutaagi
Operations Dir: Celia K Rutaagi
Consulting Dir: Prof Ben Viregyera
Founded: 1984
Member of Uganda Publishers Book Sellers Association Specialize in Poetry & Swahili.
Subjects: Management, Marketing, Poetry
ISBN Prefix(es): 9970-402
Associate Companies: Roce Enterprises

T & E Publishers+
PO Box 5784, Kampala
Tel: (041) 542207 *Fax:* (041) 542207
Key Personnel
Chief Executive: Tobias Karindiriza
Subjects: Natural History
ISBN Prefix(es): 9970-9001

Ukraine

General Information

Capital: Kiev
Language: Ukrainian
Religion: Predominantly Christian (mostly Ukrainian Orthodox)
Population: 52 million
Bank Hours: Generally open for short hours between 0930-1230 Monday-Friday
Shop Hours: Generally 0900-1800 Monday-Friday; often open weekends
Currency: 100 kopeks = 1 rubl
Export/Import Information: According to Ukrainian quotas and customs duties, companies engaged in trade should register with the Ukraine Ministry of Foreign Economic Relations. 28% VAT on books. Licenses for export and import are also required for trade with Russia.
Copyright: UCC (see Copyright Conventions, pg xi)

ASK Ltd+
3 Nesterova St, 03057 Kyiv
Mailing Address: 2b Shamrylo-Str, PO Box 62, 04112 Kyiv
Tel: (044) 241-94-96; (044) 456-72-51 *Fax:* (044) 455-58-89
E-mail: ask.sale@i.com.ua
Key Personnel
Executive Dir: Lebedyev Oleg *E-mail:* ask.main@i.com.ua
Founded: 1991 (Founded by Lebedyev Oleg, Motzny Oleg, Sologub Igor, Sythevsky Oleg & Zyporucha Anatoliy)
Subjects: Accounting, Astrology, Occult, Biblical Studies, Business, Career Development, Child Care & Development, Computer Science, Cookery, Economics, English as a Second Language, Fiction, Gardening, Plants, Law, Marketing, Microcomputers, Nonfiction (General), Parapsychology, Science Fiction, Fantasy, Social Sciences, Sociology, Western Fiction
ISBN Prefix(es): 966-539
Number of titles published annually: 230 Print
Total Titles: 750 Print
Bookshop(s): 2 Sheljabov Str, 03057 Kyiv

Derzhavne Naukovo-Vyrobnyche Pidpryemstro Kartografia (State Scientific & Production Enterprise Kartographia)+
Formerly Kartografia Kartographischer Verlag
54 Popudrenka Str, Kyiv 02094
Tel: (044) 5524033 *Fax:* (044) 2388314
E-mail: admin@ukrmap.com.ua
Web Site: www.ukrmap.com.ua
Key Personnel
Dir: Rostyslav Sossa
Editor-in-Chief: Iryna Rudenko
Commercial Manager: Olexander Zacheshygryva
Founded: 1944
Development, production & realization of cartographic production.
Subjects: Geography, Geology
Parent Company: State Service of Geodesy, Cartography & Cadastre of Ukraine
Ultimate Parent Company: Ministry of Environment & Natural Resources of Ukraine
Distributed by Cartotravel (Germany); Kiwi Book Shop (Czech Republic); Omni Resources (US); Sklep Podroznika, InterMap (Poland)
Distributor for Freytag (Austria); GiziMap (Hungary); Hallwag (Switzerland); Ravenstein (Germany)

Dnipro
ul Vladimirskaja 42, 252034 Kyiv
Tel: (044) 2243182 *Fax:* (044) 2244157
Key Personnel
Dir: T I Sergiitchuk
Editor-in-Chief: S K Zholob
Founded: 1919
Subjects: Literature, Literary Criticism, Essays
ISBN Prefix(es): 5-308; 966-578

Kamenyar
ul Pidvalnaj 3, 290000 L'viv MSP
Tel: (0322) 721949 *Fax:* (0322) 727922
ISBN Prefix(es): 5-7745; 966-7255

Kartografia Kartographischer Verlag, see Derzhavne Naukovo-Vyrobnyche Pidpryemstro Kartografia

Lybid (University of Kyyiv Press)+
ul Krescatik 10, 252001 Kiev
Tel: (044) 2291171 *Fax:* (044) 2287272
Telex: 131498 PTB SU
Key Personnel
Dir: Olena A Boiko
ISBN Prefix(es): 5-325

Mystetstvo Publishers+
ul Zolotovoritska 11, 252034 Kiev
Tel: (044) 2255392; (044) 2290564 *Fax:* (044) 2290564
Key Personnel
Dir: Valentyn Kuzmenko
Deputy Dir: Nina D Prybega
Founded: 1932
Subjects: Art, Drama, Theater, Ethnicity, Film, Video, Travel
ISBN Prefix(es): 5-7715; 966-577

Naukova Dumka Publishers
Division of National Acedemy of Sciences of Ukraine
Ul Tereshchenkivska 3, 01601 Kiev
Tel: (044) 2244068; (044) 2251042; (044) 2254170 *Fax:* (044) 2247060
E-mail: ndumka@ukrpost.net
Key Personnel
Dir & Editor-in-Chief: Alexeenko Igor
Founded: 1922
Subjects: Agriculture, Biological Sciences, Chemistry, Chemical Engineering, Computer Science, Earth Sciences, Economics, Environmental Studies, Geography, Geology, Health, Nutrition, History, Language Arts, Linguistics, Law, Literature, Literary Criticism, Essays, Mathematics, Mechanical Engineering, Medicine, Nursing, Dentistry, Natural History, Philosophy, Photography, Physical Sciences, Psychology, Psychiatry
ISBN Prefix(es): 966-00
Number of titles published annually: 60 Print
Total Titles: 12 Print
Distributed by ASK; Oberegi Publishers; Osnova

Osnova, Kharkov State University Press+
Ul Universitetskaya 16, 310003 Harkiv
Tel: (057) 224647
Key Personnel
Man Dir: Nikolay N Sorokun *Tel:* (057) 219268
Dir: Valery K Gorbat'ko
Founded: 1949
Subjects: Aeronautics, Aviation, Agriculture, Archaeology, Architecture & Interior Design, Biological Sciences, Business, Chemistry, Chemical Engineering
ISBN Prefix(es): 5-7768

Osnovy Publishers+
bul'v Lihacova 5/18, Kiev 252133
Tel: (044) 2952582; (044) 2958636 *Fax:* (044) 2952582
Key Personnel
Executive Dir: Valentyna Kyrylova *Tel:* (044) 2958636
Rights Contact: Victor Ruzhitsky
Founded: 1993
Subjects: Business, Economics, Finance, Government, Political Science, History, Law, Management, Philosophy, Poetry, Public Administration, Social Sciences, Sociology, Women's Studies
ISBN Prefix(es): 966-500
Total Titles: 150 Print

Osvita (Education)
Yury Kotsyubynsky Str 5, 04053 Kyiv
Tel: (044) 216-58-02 *Fax:* (044) 216-98-15; (044) 216-54-44
E-mail: osvita@ukrpack.net
Founded: 1920
Member of Pan Educational Publishers Club (PEP-Club).
Subjects: Biological Sciences, Chemistry, Chemical Engineering, Child Care & Development, Education, English as a Second Language, History, Literature, Literary Criticism, Essays, Mathematics, Music, Dance, Physical Sciences, Physics, German, French
ISBN Prefix(es): 966-04
Number of titles published annually: 108 Print
Total Titles: 500,000 Print

Urozaj
vul Uryc Kogo 45, 252035 Kiev
Tel: (044) 2451196
Key Personnel
Dir: Vasily G Prikhodko
Subjects: Agriculture, Environmental Studies, Gardening, Plants, House & Home, Technology, Veterinary Science
ISBN Prefix(es): 5-337

Veselka Publishers+
ul Melnikova 63, 254655 Kiev
Tel: (044) 2139501 *Fax:* (044) 2133359
Founded: 1934
Subjects: Fiction
ISBN Prefix(es): 5-301
Bookshop(s): Munich; Frankfurt am Main; Toronto; Prague; Chicago

United Arab Emirates

General Information

Capital: Abu Dhabi
Language: Arabic and English
Religion: Islamic
Population: 2.23 million
Bank Hours: 0800-1200 Saturday-Thursday (1100 Thursday in Abu Dhabi)
Shop Hours: Abu Dhabi: Summer: 0800-1300, 1600-dusk Saturday-Thursday; Winter: 0800-1300, 1530-1900 Saturday-Thursday. Northern Emirates: Summer: 0900-1300, 1630-2000 or 2100 Saturday-Thursday; Winter: 0900-1300, 1600-2000 or 2100 Saturday-Thursday
Currency: 100 fils = 1 UAE dirham
Export/Import Information: No tariff on books or advertising matter, except duty on imports in Dubai and ad valorem rates in Ras al Khaimah anf Sharjah. No import licenses requires except for obscene publications in Dubai.

Arabian Heritage Books, *imprint of* Motivate Publishing

Department of Culture & Information Government of Sharjah
Sharjah
Mailing Address: PO Box 5119, Sharjah

UNITED ARAB EMIRATES

Tel: (06) 541116 *Fax:* (06) 362126
E-mail: shjbookfair@shariah-welcome.com
Telex: 68508 TOURSH *Cable:* THAQAFA
Key Personnel
Head: Mr Issam Bin Saqr Al Qassimi

Gulf Business Books, *imprint of* Motivate Publishing

Motivate Publishing+
PO Box 2331, Dubai
Tel: (04) 282 4060 *Fax:* (04) 282 4436
E-mail: books@motivate.co.ae
Web Site: www.booksarabia.com
Key Personnel
Man Partner: Ian Fairservice
Founded: 1981
Subjects: Biography, Business, Cookery, Foreign Countries, History, Natural History, Travel
ISBN Prefix(es): 1-873544; 1-86063
Imprints: Arabian Heritage Books; Gulf Business Books
Subsidiaries: Stewart's Court
Orders to: Book Representation & Distribution Ltd, 244A London Rd, Hadleigh, Essex S57 2DE, United Kingdom *Tel:* (020) 7552912 *Fax:* (020) 7556095

United Kingdom

General Information

Capital: London
Language: English; Welsh in most of Wales (where it is used alongside English for official purposes). About 80,000 speak Scots Gaelic (in Highlands and Islands of Scotland). Irish is used in parts of Northern Ireland
Religion: Protestant (The Church of England) officially, Roman Catholic, Methodist, United Reformed and Baptist have significant numbers of adherents
Population: 57.8 million
Bank Hours: 0900-1730 Monday-Friday
Shop Hours: 0900-1730 Monday-Saturday
Currency: 100 pence = 1 pound sterling
Export/Import Information: Member of the European Union. No tariffs on books; advertising matter dutiable over a certain weight. No import licenses required; nominal exchange controls. Advertising in the UK is regulated by statutes and voluntary codes; for information contact The Advertising Standards Authority Ltd, Torrington Place, London, WC1E 7HW.
Copyright: UCC, Berne, Florence (see Copyright Conventions, pg xi)

A A Publishing+
Fanum House, 4th Floor, Basingstoke, Hants RG21 2EA
Tel: (01256) 491522 *Fax:* (01256) 322575
E-mail: helen.taylor@theaa.com
Web Site: 195.89.185.89/aapub/home.asp
Telex: 858538 AA BASG
Key Personnel
Editorial Dir: Michael Buttler *Tel:* (01250) 491573 *E-mail:* michael.buttler@theaa.com
Man Dir: John Howard
Sales & Marketing Manager: Graham Sowerby
Founded: 1908
Subjects: Travel
ISBN Prefix(es): 0-86145; 0-7495; 0-901088
Total Titles: 530 Print

Parent Company: AA
Warehouse: T B S Limited, Colchester Rd, Frating Grean, Essex CO7 7DW, Mr Colchester
Tel: (01206) 255804 *Fax:* (01206) 255848

A & C, *imprint of* Helm Information Ltd

A-Mail Academic
City Bridge House, 57 Southwark St, London SE1 1RU
Tel: (020) 7871 9139 *Fax:* (020) 7871 9140
E-mail: a-mail@djlb.co.uk
Web Site: www.a-mail.co.uk
Key Personnel
Division Manager: Duncan Copplestone
 E-mail: dcopplestone@djlb.co.uk
Business Development Executive: Vivienne Medway *E-mail:* vmedway@djlb.co.uk
Sales Account Executive: Ian Wordsworth
 E-mail: iwordsworth@djlb.co.uk
Sales Administrator: James Murtagh
 E-mail: jmurtagh@djlb.co.uk
Supplier of targeted worldwide academic & library mailing lists & data.
Parent Company: Dudley Jenkins Group plc ("Your partners in academic marketing")

Abacus, *imprint of* Time Warner Books UK

Abbotsford Publishing
2A Brownsfield Rd, Lichfield WS13 6BT
Tel: (01543) 255749
Key Personnel
Partner: Kathy Simmons; Howard Clayton
Founded: 1992
Member of Independent Publishers Guild.
Subjects: Poetry, Local History
ISBN Prefix(es): 1-899596; 0-9503563
Total Titles: 12 Print

ABC-CLIO+
35A Great Clarendon St, Oxford OX2 6AT
Tel: (01865) 311350 *Fax:* (01865) 311358
E-mail: oxford@abc-clio.ltd.uk
Web Site: www.abc-clio.com
Key Personnel
Editorial: Simon Mason; Robert G Neville
 E-mail: bneville@abc-clio.ltd.uk
Marketing Manager: Suzanne Wheatley
 E-mail: swheatley@abc-clio.ltd.uk
Sales: Deborah Porter *E-mail:* dporter@abc-clio.ltd.uk
Founded: 1971
Specialize in abstracting services & bibliographies in print & electronic formats.
Subjects: Anthropology, Foreign Countries, History, Literature, Literary Criticism, Essays, Sports, Athletics
ISBN Prefix(es): 0-87436; 1-57607; 0-903450; 1-85109
Number of titles published annually: 18 Print; 10 CD-ROM; 1 E-Book
Total Titles: 350 Print; 30 CD-ROM; 3 E-Book
Parent Company: ABC-CLIO, 130 Cremona Dr, PO Box 1911, Santa Barbara, CA 93117, United States
Foreign Rep(s): DA Information Services Pty Ltd (India, South Africa); Disvan Enterprises (India); Andrew Durnell (Austria, Belgium, Croatia, Cyprus, Czech Republic, Denmark, Netherlands, Estonia, Finland, France, Germany, Greece, Hungary, Iceland, Italy, Latvia, Lithuania, Luxembourg, Malta, Monaco, Norway, Poland, Russia, Serbia, Slovak Republic, Slovenia, Sweden, Switzerland, Bosnia & Herzegovina); Iberian Book Services (Gibraltar, Portugal, Spain); Phambili Agencies CC (South Africa); Publishers Marketing Services Ltd (Brunei, Malaysia, Singapore); Publishers International Marketing (Asia, Middle East); 1 J Sagun Enterprises, Inc (Guam, Micronesia,

Philippines); United Publishers Services Ltd (Japan)
Warehouse: Plymbridge Distributors Ltd, Estover Rd, Plymouth PL6 7PZ
Orders to: Plymbridge Distributors Ltd, Estover Rd, Plymouth PL6 7PZ *Tel:* (01752) 202301 *Fax:* (01752) 202333 *E-mail:* orders@plymbridge.com

Abercastle Publications
Blaenrhos, Lady Rd, Blaenporth, Cardigan SA43 2BG
Tel: (01239) 811267
Key Personnel
Contact: Roni Roberts
Subjects: Specialize in books on Wales & Pembrokeshire
ISBN Prefix(es): 1-872887
Total Titles: 11 Print
Distributor for Happy Fish; Rosedale Publications

ABG Professional Information
PO Box 21375, London WC1N 1QP
Tel: (020) 7920 8991 *Fax:* (020) 7920 8992
E-mail: info@abgpublications.co.uk
Web Site: www.abgpublications.co.uk
Key Personnel
Publications Dir: Sally Johnson
Subjects: Accounting, Business, Finance, Management
ISBN Prefix(es): 1-85355; 0-85291
Parent Company: Institute of Chartered Accountants (England & Wales)/Accountancy Business Group
Bookshop(s): Blackwells' as the Institute, Moorgate Place, Copthall Ave, London EC2R 7DJ
Warehouse: 21 Erica Rd, Stacey Bushes, Milton Keynes
Orders to: Accountancy Books of ICAEW, PO Box 620, Central Milton Keynes MK9 2JX

Abington Publishing, *imprint of* Woodhead Publishing Ltd

Absolute Press+
Scarborough House, 29 James St W, Bath BA1 2BT
Tel: (01225) 316 013 *Fax:* (01225) 445 836
E-mail: info@absolutepress.demon.co.uk
Key Personnel
Man Dir, Publisher & International Rights: Jon Croft
Publicity: B Douglas
Founded: 1979
Also acts as agent in UK & Europe for Smith & Kraus & Streetwise Maps.
Subjects: Biography, Cookery, Gay & Lesbian, Travel, Wine & Spirits
ISBN Prefix(es): 0-948230; 0-9506785; 1-899791
Imprints: Gay Times Travel Guides
Distributed by Consortium Book Sales & Distribution (USA); Peribo Pty Ltd (Australia & New Zealand)
Distributor for Streetwise Maps (all UK & Europe)
Orders to: Central Books, 99 Wallis Rd, London E9 5LN

Academic Press, *imprint of* Academic Press Ltd

Academic Press Ltd+
24-28 Oval Rd, London NW1 7DX
Tel: (020) 7482-2893 *Fax:* (020) 7267-4752
E-mail: 25775ACPRESG,ap@acad.com
 Cable: HARBREX LONDON NW1
Key Personnel
Man & Editorial Dir: Jan Velterop
Sales Manager: Mary Ghing
Founded: 1959

PUBLISHERS UNITED KINGDOM

Academic Press is an imprint shared with Academic Press Inc in San Diego, CA, Orlando, FL, & Boston, MA (all in the USA).
Subjects: Animals, Pets, Biological Sciences, Business, Chemistry, Chemical Engineering, Computer Science, Earth Sciences, Economics, Environmental Studies, Finance, Physical Sciences, Science (General), Technology
ISBN Prefix(es): 0-12
Parent Company: Elsevier Science Ltd
Imprints: Academic Press
U.S. Office(s): 1250 Sixth Ave, San Diego, CA 92101, United States

Acair Ltd+
7 James St, Stornoway, Isle of Lewis HS1 2QN
Tel: (01851) 703 020 *Fax:* (01851) 703 294
E-mail: enquiries@acairbooks.com
Web Site: www.acairbooks.com
Key Personnel
Business Manager: Donalda Riddell
Founded: 1978
Publish a wide range of Gaelic, English & Bilingual books.
Subjects: Biography, Environmental Studies, Fiction, History, Poetry
ISBN Prefix(es): 0-86152

Access Press, *imprint of* HarperCollins Publishers

Ace Books, see Age Concern Books

Acorn Editions, *imprint of* James Clarke & Co Ltd

Acorn Editions, *imprint of* The Lutterworth Press

Act 3 Publishing+
One Wythborn Pl, London W1H 5WL
Tel: (020) 7402 2231
Key Personnel
Contact: R Keith Brian
Founded: 1985
Member of Independent Publishers Guild.
Subjects: Alternative, Child Care & Development, Fiction, Film, Video, Human Relations, Humor, Nonfiction (General), Poetry, Psychology, Psychiatry, Self-Help
ISBN Prefix(es): 0-948068
Number of titles published annually: 1 Print
Total Titles: 1 Print

Actinic Press, *imprint of* Cressrelles Publishing Company Ltd

Actinic Press Ltd+
10 Station Rd, Industrial Estate, Colwall, Malvern WR13 6RN
Tel: (01684) 540154 *Fax:* (01684) 540154
Key Personnel
Man Dir: Leslie Smith
Founded: 1926
Specialize in Chiropody.
ISBN Prefix(es): 0-900024
Total Titles: 4 Print
Parent Company: Cressrelles Publishing Co Ltd

ACU, see Association of Commonwealth Universities (ACU)

Adamantine Press Ltd+
Richmond Bridge House, 417-421 Richmond Rd, Twickenham TW1 2EX
Key Personnel
Dir: Jeremy Geelan
Founded: 1976
Subjects: Business, Communications
ISBN Prefix(es): 0-7449

Warehouse: Central Books Ltd, 99 Wallis Rd, London E9 5LN
Orders to: Central Books Ltd, 99 Wallis Rd, London E9 5LN

Addison-Wesley, *imprint of* Pearson Education Europe, Mideast & Africa

Adelphi Papers, *imprint of* International Institute for Strategic Studies

Adlard Coles Nautical+
Imprint of A&C Black (Publishers) Ltd
37 Soho Sq, London W1D 3QZ
Tel: (020) 7758 0200 *Fax:* (020) 7831 8478
E-mail: adlardcoles@acblack.co.uk
Web Site: www.adlardcoles.co.uk
Key Personnel
Dir: Janet Murphy
Rights Dir: Paul Langridge
Founded: 1947
Specialize in nautical books for the leisure market.
Subjects: Outdoor Recreation, Sports, Athletics
ISBN Prefix(es): 0-7136
Number of titles published annually: 25 Print
Total Titles: 220 Print
Distributor for Sheridan House
Warehouse: A&C Black, PO Box 19, Huntingdon, Cambs PE19 3SF

Adlib, *imprint of* Scholastic Ltd

Adobe Press, *imprint of* Pearson Education Europe, Mideast & Africa

Advisory Unit: Computers in Education+
126 Great North Rd, Hatfield, Herts AL9 5JZ
Tel: (01707) 266714 *Fax:* (01707) 273684
E-mail: sales@advisory-unit.org.uk
Web Site: www.advisory-unit.org.uk
Key Personnel
Export Sales Dir: M Aston *E-mail:* mike@kcited.demon.co.uk
Founded: 1991
Member of ESPA, BESA & NAACE; specialize in Educational Software.
Subjects: Computer Science, Disability, Special Needs, Economics, Geography, Geology, Mathematics, Microcomputers, Technology
ISBN Prefix(es): 1-874164
Number of titles published annually: 4 Print
Total Titles: 20 Print; 8 CD-ROM; 1 E-Book
Distributed by Orfeus (Denmark & Scandinavia)
Distributor for Harvard Associates (North America)

A4 Publications Ltd
Thornleigh, 35 Hagley Rd, Stourbridge DY8 1QR
Tel: (01384) 440591 *Fax:* (01384) 440582
Key Personnel
Publisher & Dir: Francesca Ash
 Tel: (01892) 783535 *Fax:* (01892) 783848
 E-mail: francesca.ash@a4publications.com
Advertising Sales: Julie Cruikshanks
 E-mail: nought2twelve@a4publications.com;
 Jerry Wooldridge *E-mail:* jerrywooldridge@a4publications.com
Founded: 1981
Member of LIMA.
ISBN Prefix(es): 0-510; 0-946197; 0-9502363

Age Concern Books+
Astral House, 1268 London Rd, London SW16 4ER
Tel: (020) 8765 7200
E-mail: infodep@ace.org.uk
Web Site: www.ageconcern.org.uk
Key Personnel
Marketing Manager: Michael Addison

Publisher: Richard Holloway
Founded: 1971
Specialize in practical handbooks for older people & their careers & professionals working with older people; training packs for professional careers.
Subjects: Finance, Health, Nutrition
ISBN Prefix(es): 0-86242
Total Titles: 70 Print
Parent Company: Age Concern England
Orders to: Biblios Publishers Distribution Service Ltd, Star Rd, Partridge Green, West Sussex RH13 8LD

Ai Interactive Ltd
Larkhill House, Cemetery Rd, Abingdon, Oxon OX14 1AS
Tel: (01235) 529595 *Fax:* (01235) 520205
E-mail: medical@andromeda-interactive.co.uk
Web Site: www.andromeda-interactive.co.uk
Key Personnel
Manager: Clive Helmington
Subjects: Medicine, Nursing, Dentistry, Graphic design
ISBN Prefix(es): 1-898137

Airlife Publishing Ltd+
101 Longden Rd, Shrewsbury, Salop SY3 9EB
Tel: (01743) 235651 *Fax:* (01743) 232944
E-mail: info@airlifebooks.com
Web Site: www.airlifebooks.com
Key Personnel
Rights & Permissions: Anne Walker
 E-mail: anne@airlifebooks.com
Founded: 1976
Subjects: Aeronautics, Aviation, Military Science, Transportation
ISBN Prefix(es): 0-9504543; 0-906393; 1-85310; 1-84037
Number of titles published annually: 100 Print
Total Titles: 600 Print

AJ Press, *imprint of* Books International

AK Press & Distribution+
PO Box 12766, Edinburgh EH8 9YE
Tel: (0131) 5555165 *Fax:* (0131) 5555215
E-mail: ak@akedin.demon.co.uk
Web Site: www.akuk.com
Founded: 1991
Mail order catalog available.
Subjects: Fiction, Philosophy, Poetry, Social Sciences, Sociology
ISBN Prefix(es): 1-873176; 1-902593
Branch Office(s)
London
U.S. Office(s): PO Box 40682, San Francisco, CA 94140-0682, United States *Tel:* 415-864-0892
Distributed by Bookspeed (UK); Turnaround (UK)

Al-Shir katul Islamiyyah, *imprint of* Islam International Publications Ltd

Aladdin Books Ltd+
28 Percy St, London W1P 0LD
Tel: (020) 7323 3319 *Fax:* (020) 7323 4829
E-mail: sales@aladdin1.dircon.co.uk
Key Personnel
Dir: C V Nicholas; E P Whittaker
Founded: 1980
Subjects: Nonfiction (General)

Aldwych Press Ltd+
3 Henrietta St, Covent Garden, London WC2E 8LU
Tel: (020) 7240 0856 *Fax:* (020) 7379 0609
E-mail: info@eurospan.co.uk
Web Site: www.eurospan.co.uk
Key Personnel
Man Dir: Michael Geelan

UNITED KINGDOM

Dir: Danny Maher
Marketing: Imogen Adams
Founded: 1979
Subjects: Economics, Government, Political Science, Law, Library & Information Sciences, Military Science, Philosophy, Social Sciences, Sociology
ISBN Prefix(es): 0-86172

Ian Allan Publishing Ltd+
Riverdene Business Park, Molesey Rd, Hersham, Surrey KT12 4RG
Tel: (01932) 266600 *Fax:* (01932) 266601
E-mail: info@ianallanpub.co.uk
Web Site: www.ianallan.com
Key Personnel
Chairman: David Allan
Man Dir: Tony Saunders
Dir Publishing: Bill Lucas
Production Director: Nicholas Lerwill
Retail Sales Manager: Wendy Myers
Publishing Manager: Peter Waller
Sales & Marketing Manager: Nigel Passmore
Founded: 1945
Subjects: Aeronautics, Aviation, Architecture & Interior Design, Automotive, Cookery, Gardening, Plants, Maritime, Photography, Transportation
ISBN Prefix(es): 0-7110
Parent Company: Ian Allan Group
Associate Companies: Ian Allan Motors; Ian Allan Travel; Chase Organics
Imprints: Dial House
Distributor for Mill Stream; Runpast; World of Transport; Yore Publications
Foreign Rep(s): Bill Bailey Publishers' Representatives (Austria, Belgium, Bulgaria, Croatia, Cyprus, Czech Republic, Netherlands, Estonia, France, Germany, Gibraltar, Greece, Hungary, Italy, Latvia, Liechtenstein, Lithuania, Luxembourg, Malta, Monaco, Poland, Portugal, Romania, Slovenia, Spain, Switzerland, Yugoslavia); D Richard Bowen (Scandinavia); Combined Books (US); DLS Australia Pty Ltd (Australia & New Zealand, Papua New Guinea); Electra Media Group Pty Ltd (Brunei, China, Hong Kong, Japan, Korea, Malaysia, Philippines, Singapore, Taiwan, Thailand, Eastern Asia); PIM (India, Middle East, Pakistan); Vanwell Publishing Ltd (Canada)
Bookshop(s): 47 Stephenson St, Birmingham *Tel:* (0121) 643 2496 *Fax:* (0121) 643 6855; Main Terminal Bldg, 3rd floor, Birmingham International Airport, Birmingham B26 3QJ *Tel:* (0121) 781 0921 *Fax:* (0121) 781 0928; 45-46 Lower Marsh, London SE1 7SG *Tel:* (207) 401 2100 *Fax:* (207) 401 2887; Unit 5, Piccadilly Station Approach, Manchester M1 2GH *Tel:* (0161) 237 9840 *Fax:* (0161) 237 9921
Warehouse: Littlehampton Book Services Ltd, Faraday Close, Durrington, Worthing, West Sussex BN13 3RB *Tel:* (01903) 828800 *Fax:* (01903) 721596

Umberto Allemandi & Co Publishing+
Subsidiary of Umberto Allemandi e C
70 S Lambeth Rd, London SW8 1RL
Tel: (020) 7735 3331 *Fax:* (020) 7735 3332
E-mail: feedback@theartnewspaper.com
Web Site: www.theartnewspaper.com
Key Personnel
Editor in Chief: Anna Somers Cocks *E-mail:* a.allemandi@theartnewspaper.co
Founded: 1982
Books on general cultural; two newspapers.
Subjects: Architecture & Interior Design, Art, Gardening, Plants
ISBN Prefix(es): 88-422
Total Titles: 150 Print
Branch Office(s)
Via Mancini 8, Torino 10131, Italy, Nicole Kerr-Munslow *Tel:* (011) 8199111 *Fax:* (011) 8193090 *E-mail:* gda.red@allemandi.com
Distributed by Antique Collectors Club (UK, USA & Australia only)

J A Allen, *imprint of* Robert Hale Ltd

Allen Lane, *imprint of* The Penguin Group UK

Allen Lane, *imprint of* Viking

Allied Mouse Ltd+
Mayfield, High St, Dingwall IV15 9SS
Tel: (01349) 865400 *Fax:* (01349) 866066
E-mail: info@heartstone.co.uk
Web Site: www.heartstone.co.uk
Key Personnel
Dir: Sita Sidle; Nick Sidle
Founded: 1988
Member of Publishers Association.
Subjects: Fiction
ISBN Prefix(es): 0-9513492

Allison & Busby+
Subsidiary of Editorial Prensa Iberica
Suite 111, Bon Marche Centre, 241 Ferndale Rd, London SW9 8BJ
Tel: (020) 7738 7888 *Fax:* (020) 7733 4244
E-mail: all@allisonbusby.co.uk
Web Site: www.allisonandbusby.com
Key Personnel
Publishing Dir: David Shelley *E-mail:* davids@allisonbusby.co.uk
Marketing: Fiona Hague
Editor: Debbie Hatfield
Founded: 1966
Subjects: Biography, Contemporary & Literary Fiction, Crime Fiction, Writers' Guides
ISBN Prefix(es): 0-7490 (Allison & Busby)
Number of titles published annually: 40 Print
Total Titles: 240 Print
Shipping Address: Turnaround Publisher Services, Olympia Trading Estate, Unit 3, Coburg Rd, London N22 6T2, Contact: Bill Godber *Tel:* (020) 8829 3000 *Fax:* (020) 8881 5088 *E-mail:* orders@turnaround-uk.com

Allyn & Bacon, *imprint of* Pearson Education Europe, Mideast & Africa

Almond Press, *imprint of* Sheffield Academic Press Ltd

Alpine Fine Arts Books Ltd+
43 Manchester St, London W1U 7LP
Tel: (020) 7935 0797 *Fax:* (020) 7935 0656
Key Personnel
Dir: Gordon M Saks
Founded: 1981
Subjects: Art
ISBN Prefix(es): 0-88168; 0-933516
Imprints: Cromwell Editions
Warehouse: Vine House Distribution, Waldenbury, North Common, Chailey, East Sussex BN8 4DR

Altamira Press, *imprint of* Sage Publications Ltd

Alun Books
Imprint of Goldleaf Publishing
3 Crown St, Port Talbot, W Glam SA13 1BG
Tel: (01639) 886186
E-mail: enquiries@alunbooks.co.uk
Web Site: www.alunbooks.co.uk
Key Personnel
Editor: Sally Jones
Founded: 1977
Publish books about Wales &/or by Welsh authors.
Subjects: Biography, Fiction, History, Poetry, Travel
ISBN Prefix(es): 0-907117; 0-9505643
Total Titles: 56 Print
Imprints: Barn Owl Press (Children's Books); Goldleaf Publishing (Local History)
Distributor for Port Talbot Historical Society

Amadeus Press, *imprint of* Timber Press Inc

Amber Books Ltd+
74-77 White Lion St, London N1 9PF
Tel: (020) 75207600 *Fax:* (020) 75207606
E-mail: amber-books@dial.pipex.com
Key Personnel
Rights & Operations Dir: Sara Ballard
Man Dir: Stasz Gynch
Founded: 1989
Subjects: Aeronautics, Aviation, Automotive, Crafts, Games, Hobbies, Criminology, How-to, Maritime, Military Science, Nonfiction (General), Parapsychology, Sports, Athletics, Transportation
ISBN Prefix(es): 1-897884
Total Titles: 120 Print
Parent Company: Brown Packaging Books Ltd

Amber Lane Press Ltd+
Cheorl House, Church St, Charlbury OX7 3PR
Tel: (01608) 810024 *Fax:* (01608) 810024
E-mail: jamberlane@aol.com
Key Personnel
Man Dir: Judith Scott
Founded: 1978
Subjects: Biography, Drama, Theater, Music, Dance
ISBN Prefix(es): 0-906399; 1-872868
Total Titles: 100 Print

Amber Waves, *imprint of* Heartland Publishing Ltd

Amberwood Publishing Ltd+
Unit 4, Alpha House, Laser Quay, Culpeper Close, Medway City Estate, Rochester, Kent ME2 4HH
Tel: (01634) 290115 *Fax:* (01634) 290761
E-mail: books@amberwoodpublishing.com
Web Site: www.amberwoodpublishing.com
Key Personnel
Man Dir: Henry Crisp *Fax:* (01483) 457101; June Crisp *Tel:* (01634) 290115 *Fax:* (01634) 290761
Sales: Anita Ashton *Tel:* (01634) 290115 *E-mail:* anita@amberwoodpublishing.com
Founded: 1991
Specialize in Natural/Health Publications, herbs, vitamins & minerals & self medication.
Subjects: Health, Nutrition, Aromatherapy, Herbal Medicine
ISBN Prefix(es): 1-899308; 0-9517723
Number of titles published annually: 3 Print
Total Titles: 29 Print

American Technical Publishers
27/29 Wilbury Piece, Wilbury Way, Hitchin, Herts SG4 0SX
Tel: (01462) 437933 *Fax:* (01462) 433678
E-mail: atp@ameritech.co.uk
Web Site: www.ameritech.co.uk
Distributor for American Ceramic Society; American Concrete Institute; American Society for Civil Engineers; American Society for Mechanical Engineers; American Society for Testing & Materials; American Water Works Association; William Andrew; Asian Productivity Organisation; ASM International; Casti Publishing Inc; ICBO; Instrument Society of America; National Association of Corrosion Engineers; Noble Publishing Corporation; Pegasus Communications; Productivity Press; Quality Resources;

Research Signpost/Transworld Research; Research Studies Press; Society for Mining, Metallurgy & Exploration; Society of Automotive Engineers; Society of Manufacturing Engineers; Synapse Information Resources Inc; Technical Association of the Pulp & Paper Industry; Water Environment Federation

Amistad, *imprint of* HarperCollins Publishers

Amnesty International Publications
99-119 Rosebery Ave, London EC1R 4RE
Tel: (020) 7814 6200 *Fax:* (020) 7833 1510
E-mail: information@amnesty.org.uk
Web Site: www.amnesty.org.uk *Cable:* AMNESTY LONDON WC1
Key Personnel
Marketing: Guy Montgomery
Founded: 1961
Subjects: Human Rights
ISBN Prefix(es): 0-86210; 0-900058
Branch Office(s)
80A Stranmillis Rd, Belfast BT9 5AD
 Tel: (02890) 666 216/666 001 *Fax:* (02890) 666 164 *E-mail:* enquiriesni@amnesty.org.uk
6 Castle St, Edinburgh EH2 3AT *Tel:* (0131) 466 6200 *Fax:* (0131) 466 6201 *E-mail:* rburnett@edinburgh.amnesty.org.uk
Orders to: PO Box 4, Rugby, Warwickshire CV21 1RU *Tel:* (01788) 545553 *Fax:* (01788) 579244

The Ampersand Press (CI) Ltd
39 Victoria St, Alderney, Guernsey GY9 3TA
Tel: (01481) 823462
Key Personnel
Editorial, Sales: Paul Davies
Production & Publicity: Colin Partridge
Founded: 1982
Subjects: History, Military Science, Regional Interests
ISBN Prefix(es): 0-946346
Bookshop(s): The Alderney Bookshop, 39 Victoria St, Alderney, Guernsey GY9 3TA

Amsco Publications, *imprint of* Omnibus Press

Anchor, *imprint of* Transworld Publishers Ltd

Andersen Artists Greeting Cards, *imprint of* Andersen Press Ltd

Andersen Giants, *imprint of* Andersen Press Ltd

Andersen Paperback Picture Books, *imprint of* Andersen Press Ltd

Andersen Press Ltd+
Affiliate of Random House
20 Vauxhall Bridge Rd, London SW1V 2SA
Tel: (020) 7840 8701 *Fax:* (020) 7233 6263
E-mail: andersenpress@randomhouse.co.uk
Web Site: www.andersenpress.co.uk
Key Personnel
Publisher & Man Dir: Klaus Flugge *Tel:* (020) 7840 8702 *E-mail:* kflugge@randomhouse.co.uk
International Rights: Sarah Pakenham *Tel:* (020) 7840 8704 *E-mail:* spakenham@randomhouse.co.uk
Publicity Manager: Rebecca Garrill *Tel:* (020) 7840 8704 *E-mail:* rgarrill@randomhouse.co.uk
Founded: 1976
Subjects: Fiction
ISBN Prefix(es): 0-86264; 0-905478
Total Titles: 396 Print
Online services available through Random House.
Associate Companies: Random House
Imprints: Andersen Artists Greeting Cards; Andersen Giants; Andersen Young Readers Library; Tigers; Andersen Paperback Picture Books; Andersen Press Board Books
Distributed by General Publishing (Canada); Random House (Australia); Random House (South Africa); Random House (New Zealand)
Foreign Rep(s): General Publishing (Canada); Akiko Iwamoto (Japan); Random House (Guam, Indonesia, Malaysia, Philippines, Singapore, Thailand); Random House Australia Pty Ltd (Australia); Random House (NZ) Ltd (New Zealand); Random House of Canada Ltd (Hong Kong, South Korea, Taiwan); Random House of South Africa Pty Ltd (South Africa); Wei Zhao (China)
Warehouse: The Book Service Ltd, Colchester Rd, Frating Green, Colchester, Essex CO7 7DW *Tel:* (01206) 255678 *Fax:* (01206) 255930
Orders to: The Book Service Ltd, Colchester Rd, Frating Green, Colchester, Essex CO7 7DW *Tel:* (01206) 255678 *Fax:* (01206) 255930

Andersen Press Board Books, *imprint of* Andersen Press Ltd

Andersen Young Readers Library, *imprint of* Andersen Press Ltd

Anderson Rand Ltd
The Scotts Bindery, Russell Court, Cambridge CB2 1HL
Tel: (01223) 467313 *Fax:* (01223) 316144
E-mail: ar.info@dial.pipex.com
Web Site: turboguide.com/data2/cdprod1/doc/cd-rom.publisher/A/Anderson.Rand.Ltd.html
Key Personnel
Man Dir: Dr R O Anderson *E-mail:* anderson.rand@usa.net
Founded: 1989
Comprehensive data on European book related organizations, mainly publishers, libraries & book sellers.
Subjects: Library & Information Sciences, Publishing & Book Trade Reference
ISBN Prefix(es): 1-873539
Total Titles: 4 Print; 4 CD-ROM

Andre Deutsch, *imprint of* Carlton Publishing Group

Chris Andrews Publications
15 Curtis Yard, North Hinksey Lane, Oxford OX2 0LX
Tel: (01865) 723404 *Fax:* (01865) 725294
E-mail: enquiries@cap-ox.com
Web Site: www.cap-ox.com
Key Personnel
Contact: C M Andrews
Founded: 1982
Member of BAPLA & IPG.
Subjects: Travel, Oxford, Cotswolds, Thames & Chilterns
ISBN Prefix(es): 0-9509643

Andromeda, *imprint of* Andromeda Oxford Ltd

Andromeda Oxford Ltd+
11-13 The Vineyard, Abingdon, Oxon OX14 3PX
Tel: (01235) 550 296 *Fax:* (01235) 550 330
E-mail: mail@andromeda.co.uk
Web Site: www.andromeda.co.uk
Key Personnel
Man Dir: David Holyoak *E-mail:* david.holyoak@andromeda.co.uk
Publishing Dir: Graham Bateman *E-mail:* graham.bateman@andromeda.co.uk
Production Dir: Clive Sparling *E-mail:* clive.sparling@andromeda.co.uk
Sales & Marketing Dir (USA, Canada, Australia, New Zealand): Christopher Collier *E-mail:* chris.collier@andromeda.co.uk
Sales Manager (Spain, Portugal, Latin America, Italy, Scandinavia, The Netherlands, Greece & Turkey, Israel, Far East): Anne-Marie Hansen *E-mail:* anne-marie.hansen@andromeda.co.uk
Sales Manager (UK): Rachel Lewis *E-mail:* rachel.lewis@andromeda.co.uk
Founded: 1986
Produce color illustrated, multi-volume reference works.
Subjects: Animals, Pets, Archaeology, Art, Behavioral Sciences, Earth Sciences, Gardening, Plants, Geography, Geology, History, Human Relations, Natural History, Religion - Islamic, Religion - Jewish, Science (General)
Total Titles: 500 Print
Parent Company: Mediainvest PLC
Imprints: Andromeda
Foreign Rights: D S Druck (Eastern Europe); Jacky Spigel (France & Germany)

Angels' Share, *imprint of* Neil Wilson Publishing Ltd

Anglo-German Foundation for the Study of Industrial Society (Deutsch Britische Stiftung)
34 Belgrave Sq, London SW1X 8DZ
Tel: (020) 7823 1123 *Fax:* (020) 7823 2324
E-mail: info@agf.org.uk
Web Site: www.agf.org.uk
Key Personnel
Dir: Keith Dobson *E-mail:* kd@agf.org.uk
Press & Publications Officer: Annette Birkholz *E-mail:* ab@agf.org.uk
Projects Manager: Ann Pfeiffer *E-mail:* ap@agf.org.uk
Founded: 1973
Subjects: Economics, Environmental Studies, Government, Political Science, Health, Nutrition, Labor, Industrial Relations, Management, Public Administration, Social Sciences, Sociology
ISBN Prefix(es): 0-905492; 1-900834
Number of titles published annually: 8 Print; 2 E-Book
Total Titles: 73 Print
Branch Office(s)
Humboldt Universitat Berlin/GBZ, Jagerstr 10/11, 10117 Berlin, Germany
Distributed by Palgrave (UK)
Orders to: YPS (York Publishing Services), 64 Hallfield Rd, Layerthorpe, York YO31 72Q *Tel:* (01904) 431213 *Fax:* (01904) 430868

Anthem Press, *imprint of* Wimbledon Publishing Company Ltd

Antique Collectors' Club Ltd+
5 Church St, Woodbridge, Suffolk IP12 1DS
Tel: (01394) 385501 *Fax:* (01394) 384434
E-mail: sales@antique-acc.com
Web Site: www.antique-acc.com
Key Personnel
Man Dir: Diana Steel
Dir: Brian Cotton
Sales Dir: Mark Eastnent
Founded: 1966 (privately owned)
Subjects: Antiques, Architecture & Interior Design, Art, Gardening, Plants
ISBN Prefix(es): 1-85149; 0-907462; 0-902028
Number of titles published annually: 30 Print
Total Titles: 200 Print
Imprints: Garden Art Press Ltd
U.S. Office(s): Antique Collectors' Club, Market Street Industrial Park, Wappingers Falls, NY 12590, United States, Contact: Dan Farrell *Tel:* 914-297-0003 *Fax:* 914-297-0068 *E-mail:* sales@antique-cc.com

Antiques & Collectors Guides Ltd+
Righolm, 40 High Barholm, Kilbarchan, Strathclyde PA10 2EQ
Tel: (0141) 8480880 *Fax:* (0141) 8892063

UNITED KINGDOM

Key Personnel
Editor & Author: Mr Loudon Temple
Founded: 1990
Subjects: Antiques
ISBN Prefix(es): 0-9514842

Anvil Press Poetry Ltd+
Neptune House, 70 Royal Hill, London SE10 8RF
Tel: (020) 8469 3033 *Fax:* (020) 8469 3363
E-mail: info@anvilpresspoetry.com
Web Site: www.anvilpresspoetry.com
Key Personnel
Founder & Editorial Dir: Peter Jay
Sales, Marketing & Promotion: Hamish Ironside
Administration & Rights: Kit Yee Wong
Founded: 1968
Subjects: Poetry
ISBN Prefix(es): 0-85646; 0-900977
Imprints: Poetica
Distributed by Littlehampton Book Services Ltd; Midpoint Trade Books
Warehouse: Littlehampton Book Services, Columbia Bldg, Faraday Close, Durrington, Worthing BN13 3HP
Orders to: Littlehampton Book Services, Columbia Bldg, Faraday Close, Durrington, Worthing BN13 3HP

AP Information Services+
Marlborough House, 1st floor, 298 Regents Park Rd, London N3 2UU
Tel: (020) 8349 9988 *Fax:* (020) 8349 9797
E-mail: info@ap-info.co.uk
Web Site: www.ap-info.co.uk
Key Personnel
Managing Partner: Alan Philipp *E-mail:* alan@ap-info.co.uk
Partner, Finance & Personnel: Gail Philipp *E-mail:* gail@ap-info.co.uk
Editorial Manager, Business Publications: Helen Irwin *E-mail:* helen@ap-info.co.uk
Editorial Manager, Finance Directories: Robyn Andrews *E-mail:* robyn@ap-info.co.uk
Head Sales & Marketing: Jacinta Tobin *E-mail:* jacinta@ap-info.co.uk
Marketing Manager: Philip Lowther *E-mail:* philip@ap-info.co.uk
Administrative Manager: Sally Rodohan *E-mail:* sally@ap-info.co.uk
Head of IT & Production: Kumar Divakaran *E-mail:* kumar@ap-info.co.uk
Founded: 1969
Member of Directory Publishers Association.
Subjects: Business, Education, Finance
ISBN Prefix(es): 0-906247
Distributed by Kennedy Publications (USA); Money Market Directories (USA)

Apex Publishing Ltd
PO Box 7086, Essex CO16 7WN
E-mail: enquiry@apexpublishing.co.uk
Web Site: www.apexpublishing.co.uk
Key Personnel
Man Dir: Chris Martin
Founded: 2002
Subsidy publishing for unknown & unpublished authors.
Subjects: Education, Fiction, Health, Nutrition, Nonfiction (General), Philosophy, Poetry, Religion - Other, Science Fiction, Fantasy, Self-Help

Apollos, *imprint of* Inter-Varsity Press

Apple Press+
112-116A Western Rd, 6 Blundell St, Hove, East Sussex BN3 1DU
Tel: (01273) 727268 *Fax:* (01273) 727269
E-mail: gailN@RotoVision.com
Web Site: www.quarto.com

Key Personnel
UK Sales Manager: Marian Silvester
Key Accounts Manager: Stuart Henderson
Editorial Office Manager: Gail Norman
Founded: 1984
Specialize in publishing illustrated non-fiction.
Subjects: Antiques, Art, Cookery, Crafts, Games, Hobbies, Fashion, Health, Nutrition, House & Home, Nonfiction (General), Transportation, Art Instruction, Beauty, Body/Mind/Spirit, Crafts, Design, Diet, Fitness, Food & Drink, Lifestyle, Pets, Photography
ISBN Prefix(es): 1-85076; 1-84092
Number of titles published annually: 25 Print
Total Titles: 500 Print
Parent Company: Quarto Publishing PLC
Distributor for Walter Foster Publishing (UK & Europe only)
Orders to: Grantham Book Services, Isaac Newton Way, Alma Park Industrial Estate, Grantham, Lincs NG31 9SD *Tel:* (020) 754 1080 *Fax:* (020) 754 1061 *E-mail:* orders@gbs.tbs-ltd.co.uk

Appletree Press Ltd+
The Old Potato Station, 14 Howard St S, Belfast BT7 1AP
Tel: (028) 9024 3074 *Fax:* (028) 9024 6756
E-mail: reception@appletree.ie
Web Site: www.appletree.ie
Key Personnel
Man Dir, Rights & Permissions: John D Murphy
Editorial: P Harron
Sales & Marketing: M Elliott
Founded: 1974
Publishers of gift & guidebooks in eight languages, including French, Russian, Japanese, Greek & Spanish.
Also acts as Book Packager.
Subjects: Art, Cookery, Crafts, Games, Hobbies, History, Literature, Literary Criticism, Essays, Music, Dance, Photography, Regional Interests, Social Sciences, Sociology
ISBN Prefix(es): 0-904651; 0-86281
Total Titles: 300 Print

Architectural Association Publications+
36 Bedford Sq, London WC1B 3ES
Tel: (020) 7887 4021; (020) 7887 4000 *Fax:* (020) 7414 0783
E-mail: publications@aaschool.ac.uk
Web Site: www.aaschool.ac.uk/publications
Key Personnel
Chairman: Mohsen Mostafavi
Publications Coordinator: Marilyn Sparrow
Founded: 1847
Also acts as a School of Architecture.
Subjects: Architecture & Interior Design
ISBN Prefix(es): 1-870890; 0-904503; 1-902902

Argentum, *imprint of* Aurum Press Ltd

Argo Spoken Word+
Polygram Spoken Word, One Sussex Pl, London W6 9XS
Mailing Address: PO Box 1420, W6 9XS London
Tel: (020) 8910 5000 *Fax:* (020) 8910 5400
Key Personnel
Product Manager: Alex Mitchison *E-mail:* Alexandra.mitchison@umusic.com
Founded: 1950
Subjects: Nonfiction (General), Poetry
ISBN Prefix(es): 1-85849
Parent Company: Decca/Polygram Group
Warehouse: EMI Music Services, Hermes Close, Tatchbrook Park, Leamington Spa CU34 6RP

Argyll Publishing
Glendaruel, Argyll PA22 3AE
Tel: (01369) 820229 *Fax:* (01369) 820372
E-mail: argyll.publishing@virgin.net

Web Site: freespace.virgin.net/bruntsfield.com/dt2001/argyll
Key Personnel
Publisher: Derek Rodger
Founded: 1992
Subjects: Biography, History, Poetry, Literature, Scottish Interest
ISBN Prefix(es): 1-874640; 1-902831

Aris & Phillips Ltd
Teddington House, Warminster, Wilts BA12 8PQ
Tel: (01985) 213409 *Fax:* (01985) 212910
E-mail: aris.phillips@btinternet.com
Web Site: www.arisandphillips.com
Key Personnel
Man Dir, Editorial: Adrian Phillips
Publicity Manager: Kathy Tuck
Rights & Permissions: Lucinda Phillips
Founded: 1972
Subjects: Anthropology, Archaeology, Asian Studies, Drama, Theater, History, Language Arts, Linguistics, Literature, Literary Criticism, Essays, Philosophy, Poetry, Ancient Near Eastern, Middle Eastern & Hispanic Studies, Classics, Egyptology
ISBN Prefix(es): 0-85668
Number of titles published annually: 24 Print
Total Titles: 600 Print
Distributor for Australian Centre for Egyptology (outside Australia); Gibb Memorial Trust; The Griffith Institute
Orders to: David Brown Book Co, 28 Main St, PO Box 511, Oakville, CT 06779, United States *Tel:* 860-945-9329 *Fax:* 860-965-9468 *E-mail:* david.brown.bk.co@snet.net *Web Site:* www.oxbowbooks.com (North America)
Iberian Book Services, Sector Islas Bloque 12-1°B, 28760 Tres Cantos, Madrid, Spain *Tel:* (091) 803 49 18 *Fax:* (091) 803 59 36 *E-mail:* pprout@jazzfree.com (Spain & Portugal)
Oxbow Books, Park End Pl, Oxford OX1 1HN *Tel:* (01865) 241249 *Fax:* (01865) 794449 *E-mail:* oxbow@oxbowbooks.com *Web Site:* www.oxbowbooks.com (Europe)

Arkana, *imprint of* Penguin Books Ltd

Arms and Armour Press, *imprint of* Cassell & Co

Arms & Armour Press+
Wellington House, 125 Strand, London WC2R 0BB
Tel: (020) 7420 5555 *Fax:* (020) 7420 5555
Telex: 9413701
Key Personnel
Chairman & Chief Executive: Philip Sturrock
Editorial Dir & Rights: Alison Goff
Sales Dir: Michelle Gustave
Founded: 1966
Subjects: Aeronautics, Aviation, Crafts, Games, Hobbies, Government, Political Science, History, Maritime, Military Science, Transportation, Naval Warfare
ISBN Prefix(es): 0-85368; 1-85409
Parent Company: Continuum International Publishing Group Ltd

Arnefold, *imprint of* George Mann Publications

Arnold+
338 Euston Rd, London NW1 3BH
Tel: (020) 7873 6000 *Fax:* (020) 7873 6325
E-mail: feedback.arnold@hodder.co.uk
Web Site: www.arnoldpublishers.com
Key Personnel
Chairman: Tim Hely-Hutchinson
Man Dir: Richard Stileman
Head of Marketing: Elizabeth Munn
STM Dir: Nick Dunton

Production Dir: Iain McWilliams
Foreign Rights & Permissions: Rebecca Duprey
Sales Dir: Andy White
Medical: Georgia Bentliff
Humanities: Christopher Wheeler
Marketing Assistant: Rachel Monk *Tel:* (020) 7873 6026 *E-mail:* rachel.monk@hodder.co.uk
Founded: 1890
Arnold is the academic, professional & medical division of Hodder Headline Plc.
Subjects: Environmental Studies, Geography, Geology, History, Human Relations, Language Arts, Linguistics, Literature, Literary Criticism, Essays, Medicine, Nursing, Dentistry, Psychology, Psychiatry, Social Sciences, Sociology, Cultural & Media Studies, Statistics
ISBN Prefix(es): 0-340; 0-7131; 0-85324
Parent Company: Hodder Headline Plc
Ultimate Parent Company: W H Smith
Branch Office(s)
Hodder & Stroughton (Australia) Pty Ltd, 12 Strathalbyn St, Kew East, Victoria 3102, Australia
Hodder Moa Becket, New Zealand
Hodder & Stoughton Educational, South Africa
Distributed by Bookpoint

Arrow Books, *imprint of* Random House UK Ltd

Art Books International Ltd+
One Stewarts Court, 220 Stewarts Rd, London SW8 4UD
Tel: (020) 7720 1503; (020) 7578 1222
Fax: (020) 7720 3158
E-mail: artbooks@a-b-i.demon.co.uk
Key Personnel
Man Dir: Stanley Kekwick
Founded: 1991
Specialize in distribution of art books.
Subjects: Antiques, Architecture & Interior Design, Art, Crafts, Games, Hobbies, Drama, Theater, Fashion, Music, Dance, Photography
ISBN Prefix(es): 1-874044
Total Titles: 12 Print
Branch Office(s)
Strauss Consultants, 48 West 25 St, New York, NY 10010, United States, Contact: Karen Struass *Tel:* 212-367-8270 *Fax:* 212-367-8273
Distributor for Apex Publishing; Art Books International; BE-MA Editrice; Beaux Arts; Biblioteque del l'Image; Black Dog Publishing; Zelda Cheatle Press; Bernard Jacobson Gallery; Cygnet Press; Design Line; Edwards; Form; Hand Held; Kala Press; Editions Menges; Khosla; Magnus Edizioni; Manchester City Art Galleries; McCabe; Memory Cage; Momentum; Museum of London; National Gallery of Ireland; Pallas Athene Arts; Raab Gallery; Royal Academy; Salts Mill Estates; SPES; Station Press; UIAH; Ziggurat

Art Sales Index Ltd+
194 Thorpe Lea Rd, Egham, Surrey TW20 8HA
Tel: (01784) 451145 *Fax:* (01784) 451144
E-mail: asi@art-sales-index.com
Key Personnel
Chairman: Richard Hislop *E-mail:* asi@art-sales-index.com
Man Editor & Technical Dir: Duncan Hislop
Founded: 1968
Also acts as International On-Line Service-Accessible World-Wide, 24 hours a day, 7 days a week.
Subjects: Art
ISBN Prefix(es): 0-903872

The Art Trade Press Ltd
9 Brockhampton Rd, Havant, Hants PO9 1NU
Tel: (023) 9248 4943
Key Personnel
Editorial, Sales: Mrs J M Curley
Founded: 1907
Subjects: Art
ISBN Prefix(es): 0-900083

Artech House+
46 Gillingham St, London SW1V 1AH
Tel: (020) 7596 8750 *Fax:* (020) 7630 0166
E-mail: artech-uk@artechhouse.com
Web Site: www.artechhouse.com
Key Personnel
Chief Executive: William M Bazzy
Dir, Sales & Marketing: Sharon J Horn
Senior Commissioning Editor: Dr Julie A Lancashire
Founded: 1969
Publisher of professional books for engineers & managers.
Subjects: Communications, Computer Science, Electronics, Electrical Engineering, Engineering (General), Management, Radio, TV, Science (General), Technology, Transportation
ISBN Prefix(es): 0-89006; 1-58053
Number of titles published annually: 70 Print; 5 CD-ROM
Parent Company: Artech House Inc, 685 Canton St, Norwood, MA 02062, United States
Associate Companies: Horizon House Publications, 46 Gillingham St, London SW1V 1HH
Warehouse: Mercury International, Yeomans, Dr, Brickhill St, Blakelands TN9 1TD *Tel:* (01908) 218844

Artetech Publishing Co
54 Frome Rd, Bradford on Avon, Wilts BA15 1LD
Tel: (01225) 862482 *Fax:* (01225) 865601
Key Personnel
President: Dr G Terence Meaden *E-mail:* terence.meaden@torro.org.uk
Founded: 1975
Also publishes the monthly international Journal of Meteorology.
Subjects: Archaeology, Earth Sciences, Environmental Studies
ISBN Prefix(es): 0-9510590
Total Titles: 3 Print
Associate Companies: Tornado & Storm Research Organization
Imprints: Meteorology

Arthur James Ltd+
Imprint of John Hunt Publishing Ltd
46a West St, New Alresford, Hants S024 9AU
Tel: (01962) 736880 *Fax:* (01962) 736881
E-mail: office@johnhunt-publishing.com
Web Site: www.johnhunt-publishing.com
Key Personnel
Contact: J Hunt *E-mail:* johnhuntpublishing@compuserve.com
Founded: 1935
Member of Independent Publishers Guild.
Subjects: Philosophy, Psychology, Psychiatry, Religion - Buddhist, Religion - Catholic, Religion - Hindu, Religion - Jewish, Religion - Protestant, Social Sciences, Sociology, Theology, Meditation
ISBN Prefix(es): 0-85305
Total Titles: 300 Print
Associate Companies: Cairns Publications
Shipping Address: Unit 9 Amor Way, Durhams Lane, Letchworth, Herts SG6 1VA
Warehouse: Unit 9 Amor Way, Dunhams Lane, Letchworth, Herts SG6 1VA

Arts Council of England
14 Great Peter St, London SW1P 3NQ
Tel: (020) 7333 0100 *Fax:* (020) 7973 6590
E-mail: enquiries@artscouncil.org.uk
Web Site: www.artscouncil.org.uk
Key Personnel
Chairman: Gerry Robinson
Chief Executive: Peter Hewitt
Executive Dir, Communications: Wendy Andrews
Dir, Information: Michael Clark
Assistant Officer, Infomation: J Lomas *Tel:* 9736517 *E-mail:* jackie.lomas@artscouncil.org.uk
Founded: 1946
Specialize in arts policy, arts management & research.
Subjects: Art, Photography, Dance, Drama, Visual Arts
ISBN Prefix(es): 0-7287
Distributed by Marston Book Services Ltd

AS Publishing+
73 Montpelier Rise, London NW11 9DU
Tel: (020) 8458 3552 *Fax:* (020) 8458 0618
E-mail: asp@dircon.co.uk
Key Personnel
Editor: Angela Sheehan
Packager of children's information books.
Imprints: Cherrytree Books

Ashgate Publishing Ltd+
Gower House, Croft Rd, Aldershot, Hants GU11 3HR
Tel: (01252) 331551 *Fax:* (01252) 317446
E-mail: info@ashgatepub.co.uk
Web Site: www.ashgate.com
Key Personnel
Chairman: Nigel Farrow *E-mail:* llong@ashgatepub.co.uk
President US Office: Barbara Church
Dir Editorial & Production: Sonia Hubbard
Editorial, Librarianship & Information Management: Suzie Duke
Editorial, Art & Architectural History: Pamela Edwardes
Editorial US, Literary Studies, Women & Gender Studies: Erika Gaffney
Editorial, History: Thomas Gray
Editorial US, Chemistry: G W A Milne
Editorial, Human Geography & Environmental Studies: Valerie Rose
Senior Editor, Economics & Business: Brendan George
Senior Editor, International Relations & Politics: Kirstin Howgate
Senior Editor, Sociology & Social Policy: Caroline Wintersgill
Senior Commissioning Editor, Philosophy & Theology: Sarah Lloyd
Publishing Dir, Business & Management: Josephine Burges
Publishing Dir, Art Books: Lucy Myers
Publisher, Music: Rachel Lynch
Publisher, Training & Professional: Jonathan Norman
Publisher, History & Variorum: John Smedley
Consultant Publisher, Aviation: John Hindley
Consultant Publisher, Law & Legal Studies: John Irwin
Founded: 1967
Subjects: Architecture & Interior Design, Art, Business, Criminology, Economics, Environmental Studies, Government, Political Science, History, Law, Library & Information Sciences, Literature, Literary Criticism, Essays, Management, Marketing, Music, Dance, Philosophy, Public Administration, Social Sciences, Sociology, Theology, Transportation
ISBN Prefix(es): 0-566; 1-85742; 1-85628; 0-86078; 1-85972; 0-291; 0-7546; 1-85521
Number of titles published annually: 750 Print
Associate Companies: Dartmouth Publishing Co Ltd; Gower Publishing Co Ltd
Imprints: Dartmouth (Law & Legal Studies); Gower (Business books & training resources); Lund Humphries (Art, architecture & design); Variorum (Collected studies in history)
U.S. Office(s): Ashgate Publishing Co, 131 Main St, Burlington, VT 05401-5600, United States *Tel:* 802-865-7641 *Fax:* 802-865-7847 *E-mail:* info@ashgate.com

Foreign Rep(s): ICK (Korea); IMA (Africa); Maya Publishers PVT Ltd (India); Taylor & Francis Asia Pacific (China, Malaysia, Singapore); United Publishers Services Ltd (Japan)
Orders to: Bookpoint Limited, Ashgate Gower Customer Service, 130 Milton Park, Abingdon, Oxon OX14 4SB *Tel:* (01235) 400400 *Fax:* (01235) 400454 *E-mail:* orders@bookpoint.co.uk
2252 Ridge Rd, Brookfield, VT 05036-9704, United States *Tel:* 802-276-3162 *Fax:* 802-276-3837 *E-mail:* orders@ashgate.com (North America)

Ashgrove Press+
3 Town Barton, Norton St Philip, Bath BA2 7LN
Tel: (020) 7713-7540 *Fax:* (020) 7713-7541
E-mail: gmo73@dial.pipex.com
Web Site: www.ashgrovepublishing.com
Key Personnel
Man Dir, Production Manager: Brad Thompson
Publisher: Robin Campbell
Man Editor: Tina Ryan
Founded: 1979
Book publishers specializing in metaphysical, spirituality & new age; also print-on-demand editions; Crucible Classics.
Subjects: Astrology, Occult, Cookery, Health, Nutrition, Medicine, Nursing, Dentistry, Religion - Other, Self-Help
ISBN Prefix(es): 0-906798; 1-85398
Number of titles published annually: 6 Print
Total Titles: 40 Print
Parent Company: Hollydata Publishers Ltd

Ashmolean Museum Publications+
Beaumont St, Oxford OX1 2PH
Tel: (01865) 278010 *Fax:* (01865) 278018
E-mail: publications@ashmus.ox.ac.uk
Web Site: www.ashmol.ox.ac.uk/ash/publications
Key Personnel
Sales & Marketing Officer: Declan McCarthy
Founded: 1683
Publishing & Retailing.
Subjects: Archaeology, Art, Asian Studies, Crafts, Games, Hobbies, History, Regional Interests, Travel
ISBN Prefix(es): 0-907849; 1-85444; 0-900090
Number of titles published annually: 15 Print
Parent Company: University of Oxford
Imprints: Griffith Institute
Branch Office(s)
Scholarly Book Services Inc, Canadian Distribution, 77 Mowat Ave, Suite 403, Toronto, ON M6K 3E3, Canada
U.S. Office(s): Arthur Schwarz & Co Inc, US Distribution, 15 Meades Mountain Rd, Woodstock, NY 12498, United States
Warehouse: Gazelle, Unit 2-3, Hightown, LEL Industrial Estate, Whitecross Mills, Lancaster
Orders to: Gazelle Book Services Ltd, Falcon House, Queen St, Lancaster LA1 1RN *Tel:* (01524) 68765 *Fax:* (01524) 63232
Woodstocker Books, Arthur Schwartz & Co Inc, 15 Meads Mountain Rd, Woodstock, NY 12498, United States *Tel:* 845-679-4024 *Fax:* 845-679-4093 *E-mail:* aschwartz@aschwartzbooks.com *Web Site:* www.aschwartzbooks.com (US)

Ashton & Denton Publishing Co (CI) Ltd
3 Burlington House, Saint Savior's Rd, Saint Helier, Jersey JE2 4LA
Tel: (01534) 735461; (01534) 727976
Fax: (01534) 875805
Key Personnel
Man Dir & Sales: A D W Mackenzie
Editorial & Publicity: Mrs Y E Ashden
E-mail: ashden@supanet.com
Production: M Mackenzie
Founded: 1948
Specialize in Channel Islands publications.
Subjects: Business, Finance, Regional Interests
ISBN Prefix(es): 0-85053
Number of titles published annually: 6 Print
Total Titles: 8 Print
U.S. Office(s): Ashton & Denton Publishing Co, PO Box 3, Cornish, UT, United States

Aslib, The Association for Information Management+
60/62 Toller Lane, Bradford BD8 9BY
Tel: (01274) 777 700 *Fax:* (020) 7903 0011
E-mail: aslib@aslib.com; pubs@aslib.com
Web Site: www.aslib.co.uk
Key Personnel
Managing Editor: Diane Heath
Head of Publications: Sarah Blair
Marketing Manager: Chris Grandy
Founded: 1924
Member of FID, EC1A, ALPSP, ICSTI.
Subjects: Business, Law, Library & Information Sciences, Management, Technology
ISBN Prefix(es): 0-85142
Distributed by DA Books & Journals Pty (Australia); Kinokuniyiya (Japan); Portland Press LD (Rest of World); Allied Publishers Pvt Ltd
Orders to: Portland Press Ltd, Commerce Way, Whitehall Industrial Estate, Colchester CO2 8HP

Aspect, *imprint of* Salamander Books Ltd

Aspect Guides, *imprint of* Peter Collin Publishing Ltd

Associated University Presses, *imprint of* Golden Cockerel Press Ltd

The Association for Information Management, see Aslib, The Association for Information Management

Association for Scottish Literary Studies+
Dept of Scottish History, University of Glasgow, 9 University Gardens, Glasgow G12 8QH
Tel: (0141) 330 5309 *Fax:* (0141) 330 5309
Web Site: www.asls.org.uk
Key Personnel
President: Dorothy McMillan
Treasurer: Tom Ralph
Secretary: Jim Alison
General Editorial: Dr Liam McIlvanney
General Manager: Duncan Jones *E-mail:* d.jones@scothist.arts.gla.ac.uk
Founded: 1970
ASLS is an educational charity supporting the study, teaching and writing of Scottish literature and language.
Subjects: Literature, Literary Criticism, Essays, Scottish literature and linguistics
ISBN Prefix(es): 0-948877; 0-9502629
Orders to: Scottish Book Source, Scottish Book Centre, 137 Dundee St, Edinburgh EH11 1BG *Tel:* (0131) 229 6800

Association of Commonwealth Universities (ACU)
John Foster House, 36 Gordon Sq, London WC1H 0PF
Tel: (020) 7380 6700 *Fax:* (020) 7387 2655
E-mail: info@acu.ac.uk
Web Site: www.acu.ac.uk *Cable:* ACUMEN LONDON WC1
Key Personnel
Secretary General: Prof Michael G Gibbons
Head Market Development: Sue Kirkland *Tel:* (020) 7380 6710 *E-mail:* s.kirkland@acu.ac.uk
Managing Editor: Paul Turner
Founded: 1913
Membership: 500 university institutions in 35 countries/regions in the Commonwealth. Associate Member of International Association of Universities; Member of Directory & Database Publishers Association. Specializes in promoting, in various practical ways, contact & cooperation between its member institutions.
Subjects: Developing Countries, Education, Higher Education
ISBN Prefix(es): 0-85143
Total Titles: 7 Print
Distributed by Palgrave Macmillan; UBS Publishers' Distributors

Association for Science Education+
College Lane, Hatfield, Herts AL10 9AA
Tel: (01707) 283001 *Fax:* (01707) 266532
E-mail: ase@asehq.telme.com
Web Site: www.ase.org.uk
Key Personnel
Chief Executive: Dr David S Moore
Deputy Chief Executive: John Lawrence
Publications Dir: Jane R Hanrott
Booksales Manager: Rob Oxley
Founded: 1901
Subjects: Biological Sciences, Chemistry, Chemical Engineering, Computer Science, Disability, Special Needs, Education, Energy, Physics, Science (General)
ISBN Prefix(es): 0-86357; 0-902786

Astic, *imprint of* Gwasg Gwenffrwd

ATAPepperpot Gift, *imprint of* Colour Library Direct

Atelier Books
6 Dundas St, Edinburgh EH3 6HZ
Tel: (0131) 5574050 *Fax:* (0131) 5578382
E-mail: mail@bournefineart.co.uk
Web Site: www.bournefineart.co.uk/books.html
Key Personnel
Man Dir: Patrick Bourne *E-mail:* bournefineart@enterprise.net
ISBN Prefix(es): 1-873830
Orders to: Scottish Book Source, 137 Dundee St, Edinburgh EH11 1BG *Tel:* (0131) 229 6800 *Fax:* (0131) 229 9070 *Web Site:* www.scottishbooks.org

The Athlone Press Ltd+
One Park Drive, London NW11 7SG
Tel: (020) 8458 0888 *Fax:* (020) 8201 8115
E-mail: athlonepress@btinternet.com
Web Site: www.transcomm.ox.ac.uk/wwwroot/athlone_press.htm
Key Personnel
Chairman: Brian Southam
Man Dir: Doris Southam
Editorial Dir: Tristan Palmer *E-mail:* tpalmer.athlonepress@btinternet.com
Production Manager: P J Albutt
Founded: 1949
Subjects: Anthropology, Archaeology, Art, Asian Studies, Economics, Film, Video, History, Law, Philosophy, Science (General), Social Sciences, Sociology, Academic
U.S. Office(s): The Athlone Press, 390 Campus Dr, Somerset, NJ 08873, United States *Tel:* 732-445-1245 *Fax:* 732-748-9801
Warehouse: Hoddle Doyle Meadows Ltd, Station Rd, Linton, Cambs CB1 69W
Orders to: c/o Book Systems Plus, BSP House, Station Rd, Linton, Cambs CB1 6NW *Tel:* (01223) 894870 *Fax:* (01223) 894871

Atlantic Transport Publishers
Trevithick House, West End, Penryn TR10 8HE
Tel: (01326) 373656 *Fax:* (01326) 378309; (01326) 373656
Key Personnel
Contact: David Joy *E-mail:* davjoy@aol.com
Founded: 1979

Subjects: History, Mechanical Engineering, Transportation
ISBN Prefix(es): 0-906899; 1-902827
Orders to: Atlantic Publishers, Trevithick House, West End, Penryn, Cornwall TR10 8HE

Atlas Press+
BCM Atlas Press, 27 Old Gloucester St, London WC1N 3XX
Tel: (020) 7490 8742 *Fax:* (021) 7490 8742
E-mail: atlaspress@compuserve.com
Web Site: www.atlaspress.co.uk
Key Personnel
Partner: Alastair Brotchie; Malcolm Green
Partner & Rights Contact: Antony Melville
Copy Editor & Proofreader: Chris Allen
Founded: 1983
Accessible translations of key works of the European avant-garde of the last 100 years. Mostly previously untranslated & often unobtainable in their original languages; where possible, editing done in collaboration with living authors/groups/artists; concise introductions & annotation as necessary.
Subjects: Alternative, Art, Biography, Drama, Theater, Erotica, Fiction, European Avant-Garde Literature & Art, Art History, Limited Editions
ISBN Prefix(es): 0-947757; 1-900565
Number of titles published annually: 8 Print
Total Titles: 75 Print
Imprints: The Printed Head
Distributed by Exact Change (trade titles only); Marginal Distribution (Canada); Peribo Pty Ltd (Australia)
Distributor for Cymbalum Pataphysicum
Foreign Rep(s): Exact Exchange (US)
Orders to: Consortium Inc, 1045 Westgate Dr, St Paul, MN 51140-0165, United States *Tel:* 612-221-9035 *Fax:* 612-221-0124
Turnaround Publisher Services, Olympia Trading Estate, Unit 3, Coburg Rd, London N22 6TZ, Contact: Bill Godber *Tel:* (020) 8829 3000 *Fax:* (020) 8881 5088

Atom, *imprint of* Time Warner Books UK

Attack!, *imprint of* Creation Books

Augener, *imprint of* Stainer & Bell Ltd

Aulis Publishers
Imprint of David Percy Associates
25 Belsize Park, London NW3 4DU
Tel: (01373) 451 777 *Fax:* (01373) 452 888
E-mail: info@aulis.com
Web Site: www.aulis.com
Key Personnel
Director: David Percy
Founded: 1992
Specialize in videotapes on space.
Subjects: History, Physical Sciences
ISBN Prefix(es): 1-898541
Total Titles: 3 Print

Aurora Northern Classics, *imprint of* The Orkney Press Ltd

Aurum Press Ltd+
25 Bedford Ave, London WC1B 3AT
Tel: (020) 7637 3225 *Fax:* (020) 7580 2469
Web Site: www.aurumpress.co.uk/top2.htm
Key Personnel
Man Dir & Sales Dir: Bill McCreadie *E-mail:* bill.mccreadie@aurumpress.co.uk
Editorial Dir: Piers Burnett *E-mail:* piers.burnett@aurumpress.co.uk
Sr Editor: Graham Coster
Sales Manager: Graham Eanes
Founded: 1976

Subjects: Art, Biography, Film, Video, Military Science, Nonfiction (General), Photography, Sports, Athletics, Travel, General adult nonfiction
ISBN Prefix(es): 1-85410; 1-903221 (Jacqui Small); 1-902538 (Argentum)
Number of titles published annually: 60 Print
Total Titles: 250 Print
Imprints: Argentum (Specialist photography); Jacqui Small (Books on interiors, lifestyle, gardens)
Warehouse: Littlehampton Book Services, Faraday Close, Durrington Worthing BN13 3HD *Tel:* (01903) 828500 *Fax:* (01903) 828625

Authentic Lifestyle, *imprint of* Paternoster Publishing

Autumn Publishing Ltd
North Barn, Appledram Barns, Birdham Rd, Appledram, Chichester PO20 7EQ
Tel: (01243) 531660 *Fax:* (01243) 774433
Web Site: www.autumnpublishing.co.uk
Key Personnel
Man Dir: Campbell Goldsmid *E-mail:* campbell@autumnpublishing.co.uk
Founded: 1976
ISBN Prefix(es): 0-946593; 1-85997
Imprints: Byeway Books

Avero Publications Ltd+
20 Great North Rd, Newcastle-upon-Tyne NE2 4PS
Tel: (0191) 2615790 *Fax:* (0191) 2611209
E-mail: nstc@newcastle.ac.uk
Key Personnel
Man Dir: F J G Robinson
Dir: Gwen Averley
Founded: 1981
Specialize in CD-ROM.
Subjects: Biography, History
ISBN Prefix(es): 0-907977
Subsidiaries: Romulus Press Ltd

Avon, *imprint of* HarperCollins Publishers

Award Publications Ltd+
27 Longford St, 1st floor, London NW1 3DZ
Tel: (020) 7388 7800 *Fax:* (020) 7388 7887
E-mail: info@award.abel.co.uk
Key Personnel
Man Dir: R Wilkinson
Production Manager: Deborah Wadsworth
Contact: Anna Wilkinson
Founded: 1955
ISBN Prefix(es): 0-86163; 1-84135
Imprints: Horus Editions
Warehouse: Award Publications Ltd, The Old Riding School, Welbeck Estate, NR Workshop, Notts S80 3LS *Tel:* (01909) 478 170 *Fax:* (01909) 484 632
Orders to: Award Publications Ltd, The Old Riding School, Welbeck Estate, NR Workshop, Notts S80 3LS *Tel:* (01909) 478 170 *Fax:* (01909) 484 632

Azure, *imprint of* The Society for Promoting Christian Knowledge (SPCK)

b small publishing+
Pinewood, 3A Coombe Ridings, Kingston-Upon-Thames KT2 7JT
Tel: (020) 8974 6851 *Fax:* (020) 8974 6845
E-mail: info@bsmall.co.uk
Web Site: homepage.ntlworld.com/codework/welcome.htm
Key Personnel
Partner/Publisher: Catherine Bruzzone *E-mail:* cath@bsmall.co.uk
Founded: 1990

Specialize in general activity books & foreign language learning.
ISBN Prefix(es): 1-874735; 1-902915
Distributed by Ragged Bears (UK trade)

BAAF, see BAAF: Adoption & Fostering

BAAF: Adoption & Fostering, *imprint of* BAAF: Adoption & Fostering

Bernard Babani (Publishing) Ltd+
The Grampians, Shepherds Bush Rd, London W6 7NF
Tel: (020) 7603 2581; (020) 7603 7296 *Fax:* (020) 7603 8203
E-mail: enquiries@babanibooks.com
Web Site: www.babanibooks.com *Cable:* RADIOBOOKS LONDON W6
Key Personnel
Man Dir, Edit: M H Babani
Sales, Rights & Permissions: S Babani
Production, Publicity: P Pragnell
Founded: 1977 (Babani Press 1971, Bernards Publishers 1942)
Subjects: Computer Science, Electronics, Electrical Engineering, Radio, TV
ISBN Prefix(es): 0-85934; 0-900162
Associate Companies: Babani Press

Babel Guides, *imprint of* Boulevard Books UK/The Babel Guides

Baha'i Publishing Trust+
4 Station Approach, Oakham, Rutland LE15 6QW
Tel: (01572) 722780 *Fax:* (01572) 724280
E-mail: sales@bahaibooks.co.uk
Web Site: www.bahai-publishing-trust.co.uk
Key Personnel
General Manager: Gordon James Kerr
Editorial Dir: George Ballentyne
Founded: 1937
Member of International Association of Baha'i Publishers.
Subjects: Government, Political Science, Human Relations, Philosophy, Religion - Other, Social Sciences, Sociology
ISBN Prefix(es): 0-900125; 1-870987
Parent Company: NSA Baha'is of UK
Imprints: Nightingale Books
Shipping Address: The Maltings, Station Rd, Ketton, Near Stamford, Kent, Lincs PE9 3RQ
Warehouse: The Maltings, Station Rd, Ketton, Near Stamford, Lincs PE9 3RQ

Bill Bailey Publishers' Representatives
16 Devon Sq, Newton Abbot, Devon TQ12 2HR
Tel: (01626) 331079 *Fax:* (01626) 331080
E-mail: billbailey.pubrep@eclipse.co.uk
Web Site: www.healthpress.co.uk
Key Personnel
Partner: W G Bailey; N Hammond; B J McGee; M J Parsons
Founded: 1981
Sales Representation in Europe.
A partnership with all types of books.
Distributed by International Publishers Representatives Ltd (Eastern Mediterranean & Middle East); JAMCO Distribution Inc (US); Maclennan & Petty Pty Ltd (Australia); The South African Medical Association (South Africa)

Bailey Brothers & Swinfen Ltd
Units 1A/1B Learoyd Rd, Mountfield Industrial Estate, New Romney TN28 8XU
Tel: (01797) 366905 *Fax:* (01797) 366638
Key Personnel
Dir: R P Mortimore; H J Mortimore
Founded: 1937
ISBN Prefix(es): 0-561
Parent Company: Bailey & Swinfen Holdings Ltd
Subsidiaries: Bailey Distribution Ltd

UNITED KINGDOM

Bailliere Tindall Limited+
Imprint of Elsevier Health Sciences
32 Jamestown Rd, London NW1 7BY
Tel: (020) 7424 4200 *Fax:* (020) 7482 4752
Key Personnel
Man Dir: Peter Lengemann
Man Dir Health & Medical Science: Andrew Stevenson
Vice President Sales & Mktg: Mary Ging
Head of Mktg: Tim Griswold
Founded: 1826
Subjects: Medicine, Nursing, Dentistry, Veterinary Science
ISBN Prefix(es): 0-7020
Parent Company: Harcourt Brace & Company, Orlando, FL 32887, United States
Shipping Address: Harcourt Brace & Co, Foots Cray, High St, Sidcup, Kent DA14 5HP
Warehouse: Harcourt Brace & Co, Foots Cray, High St, Sidcup, Kent DA14 5HP
Orders to: Harcourt Brace & Co, Foots Cray, High St, Sidcup, Kent DA14 5HP

The Banner of Truth Trust+
The Grey House, 3 Murrayfield Rd, Edinburgh EH12 6EL
Tel: (0131) 337 7310 *Fax:* (0131) 346 7484
E-mail: info@banneroftruth.co.uk
Web Site: www.banneroftruth.co.uk
Key Personnel
General Manager: John Rawlinson
Editorial: Philip Craig
Production Manager: Murdo MacLeod
Founded: 1957
Historic Christianity through literature.
Subjects: Religion - Protestant
ISBN Prefix(es): 0-85151
U.S. Office(s): PO Box 621, Carlisle, PA 17013, United States *Tel:* 717-249-5747 *Fax:* 717-249-0604 *E-mail:* info@banneroftruth.org
Warehouse: 17 Bankhead Dr, Sighthill Industrial Estate, Edinburgh EH11 4DW

Banson
3 Turville St, London E2 7HR
Tel: (020) 7729 7315; (020) 7613 1388
Fax: (020) 7729 7870
E-mail: banson@ourplanet.com
Key Personnel
Man Dir: Mr B Ullstein
Founded: 1987
Specialize in packaging for International Organizations.
Subjects: Environmental Studies

Bantam Paperbacks, *imprint of* Transworld Publishers Ltd

Bantam Press, *imprint of* Transworld Publishers Ltd

McCall Barbour+
28 George IV Bridge, Edinburgh EH1 1ES
Tel: (0131) 225-4816 *Fax:* (0131) 225-4816
E-mail: ashbethany43@hotmail.com
Key Personnel
Man Dir: Dr T C Danson-Smith
Founded: 1900
Christian Publishers.
Subjects: Religion - Protestant
ISBN Prefix(es): 0-7132
Total Titles: 2 Print

Barmarick Publications
Enholmes Hall, Patrington, Hull, East Yorkshire HU12 0PR
Tel: (01964) 630033 *Fax:* (01964) 631716
E-mail: hr24@dial.pipex.com
Key Personnel
Partner: Dr R Dobbins; A M Lunn; Dr B O Pettman

Founded: 1982
Subjects: Labor, Industrial Relations, Management, Social Sciences, Sociology
ISBN Prefix(es): 1-85385
Total Titles: 292 Print

Barn Dance Publications Ltd+
62 Beechwood Rd, Croydon CR2 OAA
Tel: (020) 8657 2813 *Fax:* (020) 8651 6080
E-mail: barndance@pubs.co.uk
Web Site: www.barndancepublications.co.uk
Key Personnel
Dir: Derek L Jones
Founded: 1984
Member of Book Data.
Subjects: Music, Dance, Fold Dance
ISBN Prefix(es): 0-9514275; 1-874565
Total Titles: 18 Print; 13 Audio

Barn Owl Press (Children's Books), *imprint of* Alun Books

Barnabas, *imprint of* Bible Reading Fellowship

Barrie & Jenkins, *imprint of* Random House UK Ltd

Bartsky Legal Texts Ltd, *imprint of* CyberClub

Basil Blackwell Ltd, see Blackwell Publishers

Batsford Ltd+
583 Fulham Rd, London SW6 5BY
Tel: (020) 7471 1100 *Fax:* (020) 7471 1101
E-mail: info@batsford.com
Key Personnel
Chief Executive: Jules Perel
Executive Editor: Richard Reynolds
Sales Manager: Alan Ritchie
Publicity Manager: Teresa Howes
Production & Distribution Dir: Roger Huggins
Editorial Dir: Naomi Roth
Founded: 1843
Subjects: Agriculture, Archaeology, Architecture & Interior Design, Art, Crafts, Games, Hobbies, Fashion, Film, Video, Gardening, Plants, History, House & Home, Nonfiction (General), Outdoor Recreation, Photography, Social Sciences, Sociology
ISBN Prefix(es): 0-7134
Parent Company: Batsford Holdings Plc
U.S. Office(s): 9 East 40 St, 10th floor, New York, NY, United States
Distributor for Chilton Book Co; Lennard/Queen Anne Press; Meredith Books (Europe); Taunton Press; Storey Books
Warehouse: PO Box 4, Braintree, Essex *Tel:* (01376) 321276 *Fax:* (01376) 552854
Orders to: PO Box 4, Braintree, Essex CM7 7QY *Tel:* (01376) 321276 *Fax:* (01376) 552854

Colin Baxter, *imprint of* Colin Baxter Photography Ltd

Colin Baxter Photography Ltd+
The Old Dairy, Woodlands Industrial Estate, Grantown-on-Spey, Morayshire PH26 3NA
Tel: (01479) 873999 *Fax:* (01479) 873888
E-mail: sales@colinbaxter.co.uk
Web Site: www.colinbaxter.co.uk; www.worldlifelibrary.co.uk
Key Personnel
Man Dir: Colin Baxter
Marketing Dir & Rights: Colin Kirkwood
E-mail: colin.kirkwood@colinbaxter.co.uk
Editorial & Production Dir: Mike Rensner
Founded: 1984
Independent Private Company.
Subjects: Natural History, Photography, Travel
ISBN Prefix(es): 0-948661; 1-900455; 1-84107

Number of titles published annually: 20 Print
Total Titles: 80 Print
Imprints: Colin Baxter; Worldlife Library
Distributed by Voyageur Press (US)
Foreign Rep(s): Ted Dougherty (Austria, Belgium, Netherlands, France, Germany, Greece, Italy, Luxembourg, Switzerland); Theo Philips (Branei, Hong Kong, Malaysia, Philippines, Singapore, Thailand); Peter Prout (Spain); Hanne Rotovnik (Denmark); Voyageur Press Inc (US)
Orders to: Freepost, PO Box 1, Nethybridge, Inverness-Shire PH25 3BR

Bay View Books Ltd+
The Red House, 25-26 Bridgeland St, Bideford EX39 2PZ
Tel: (01237) 479225; (01237) 421285
Fax: (01237) 421286
Key Personnel
International Rights: Charles Herridge
Founded: 1986
Subjects: Automotive
ISBN Prefix(es): 1-870979; 1-901432
Warehouse: Bailey Distribution Ltd, Units 1A/B Learoyd Rd, Mountfield Industrial Estate, New Romney, Kent TN28 8XU
Orders to: Chris Lloyd Sales & Marketing, 463 Ashley Rd, Parkstone, Poole, Dorset BH14 0AX

BBC Audiobooks+
Formerly Chivers Press Ltd
Windsor Bridge Rd, Bath BA2 3AX
Tel: (01225) 335 336 *Fax:* (01225) 310 771; (01225) 448 005; (01225) 422 585
E-mail: sales@chivers.co.uk; info@chivers.co.uk
Web Site: www.chivers.co.uk
Key Personnel
Man Dir: Paul Dempsey
Publishing Dir: Jan Paterson
Production & Publicity Manager: Lesley Barnes
Sales Manager: Mary Finch *E-mail:* mary@chivers.co.uk
Marketing Manager: Christine Graham
E-mail: christine@chivers.co.uk
Founded: 1979
Specialize in Large Print Books, Audio Books (complete & unabridged) & Facsimile Reprints.
Subjects: Biography, Fiction, Mysteries, Nonfiction (General), Romance, Western Fiction
ISBN Prefix(es): 0-563; 0-7451; 0-85995; 0-85997; 0-86220; 0-85119; 1-85549
Number of titles published annually: 1,215 Print; 216 Audio
Total Titles: 4,300 Print; 2,500 Audio
Parent Company: BBC Worldwide, 80 Wood Lane, London W12 0TT
Imprints: Black Dagger; Cavalcade Story Cassettes; Camden Large Print; Chivers Children's Audio Books; Chivers Large Print; Galaxy Large Print; Gunsmoke Western; Paragon; Read-Along; Sterling Audio Books; Windsor Large Print Bestsellers; Word for Word Audio Books
U.S. Office(s): Chivers North America, One Lafayette Rd, Box 1450, Hampton, NH 03842-0015, United States, Contact: Jim Brannigan *Tel:* 603-926-8744 *Fax:* 603-929-3890
Foreign Rep(s): Booktalk Pty Ltd (audio books) (Southern Africa); Chivers North America (US); Hargraves Library Service (Southern Africa); The Library Supply Co Ltd (New Zealand); Michael O'Brien (Ireland); Hargraves Library Service (large print) (Australia); Vanwell Publishing Ltd (Canada)

BBC Books, *imprint of* BBC Worldwide Publishers

BBC English+
80 Wood Lane, London W12 0TT
Tel: (020) 8576 2221 *Fax:* (020) 8576 3040

PUBLISHERS

UNITED KINGDOM

Key Personnel
Dir: Charles Hyde
Dir, International Publishing: Be Lenthall
Founded: 1943
Subjects: English as a Second Language
ISBN Prefix(es): 1-85497; 0-946675
Parent Company: BBC Worldwide Ltd

BBC Television Training
Imprint of BBC
17 Ribston Close, Shenley, Radlett, Herts WD7 9JW
Tel: (01923) 855632 *Fax:* (01923) 855632
Key Personnel
Dir, Rosedale Associates: Robin Gwyn
  E-mail: robin.gwyn@tesco.net
Media production training. Distribution of BBC TV training production books & videos. Also distribute wall charts on TV production.
Subjects: Radio, TV
ISBN Prefix(es): 0-948694
Total Titles: 20 Print

BBC Worldwide Publishers+
Woodlands, 80 Wood Lane, London W12 0TT
Tel: (020) 8576 2570 *Fax:* (020) 8749 8766
E-mail: bbcsales@bbc.co.uk
Web Site: www.bbcworldwide.com
Telex: 934678 BBCENTG *Cable:* BROADCASTS LONDON
Key Personnel
Head of Book Publishing: Chris Weller
Head of Sales & Marketing: Stuart Biles
Production Manager: Brian Dickson
Sales & Marketing Dir: Kevin Harrington
International Sales & Marketing Dir: Charles Hyde
International Rights & Export Manager: Richard Gay
Founded: 1925
Subjects: Cookery, Gardening, Plants, History, Language Arts, Linguistics, Natural History
ISBN Prefix(es): 0-563
Parent Company: BBC Worldwide
Imprints: Network Books; BBC Books
Bookshop(s): 4-5 Langham Place, Upper Regent St, London
Orders to: Exel-logistics Media Services, Invicta House, St Thomas Longley Rd, Medway City Industrial Estate, Rochester, Kent ME2 4DU *Tel:* (0634) 297123 *Fax:* (0634) 298000

BCA+
87 Newman St, London W1P 4EN
Tel: (020) 7637 0341 *Fax:* (020) 7291 3525
Key Personnel
Chief Executive: Alan Roe
Editorial Dir: Chris Holifield
Founded: 1966
Subjects: Aeronautics, Aviation, Animals, Pets, Antiques, Archaeology, Architecture & Interior Design, Art, Astrology, Occult, Automotive, Cookery, Crafts, Games, Hobbies, Fiction, Film, Video, Gardening, Plants, Geography, Geology, History, How-to, Humor, Literature, Literary Criticism, Essays, Microcomputers, Military Science, Music, Dance, Mysteries, Natural History, Nonfiction (General), Outdoor Recreation, Photography, Poetry, Romance, Science (General), Science Fiction, Fantasy, Self-Help, Sports, Athletics, Travel, Wine & Spirits
Ultimate Parent Company: Bertelsmann AG, Germany
Branch Office(s)
Guild House, Farnsby St Swindon SN1 5DD
  Tel: (01793) 512100 *Fax:* (01793) 616789
Book Club(s): Ancient & Medieval History; Christian Book Club; English Book Club; Executive World; Mind, Body & Spirit; Military & Aviation; Mystery & Thriller Guild; The Arts Guild; Discovery - The Book Club for Children; Fantasy & Science Fiction; The New Home & Garden Guild; Book Club of Ireland; Qpd; The History Guild; Literary Guild; World Books; Railway Book Club; Home Softwave World; Escape, The Travel Book Club

BCP, *imprint of* Gerald Duckworth & Co Ltd

Beaconsfield, *imprint of* Beaconsfield Publishers Ltd

Beaconsfield Publishers Ltd+
20 Chiltern Hills Rd, Beaconsfield, Bucks HP9 1PL
Tel: (01494) 672118 *Fax:* (01494) 672118
E-mail: books@beaconsfield-publishers.co.uk
Web Site: www.beaconsfield-publishers.co.uk
Key Personnel
President, Editor & Man Dir: John Churchill
Founded: 1979
Carefully developed titles in medicine, nursing, patient care & homeopathy.
Subjects: Alternative, Health, Nutrition, Medicine, Nursing, Dentistry
ISBN Prefix(es): 0-906584
Number of titles published annually: 2 Print
Total Titles: 34 Print
Imprints: Beaconsfield
Foreign Rep(s): Astam Books (Australia); Viking Seven Seas (New Zealand)
Orders to: Jackson Distribution, 3 Gibsons Rd, Heaton Moor, Stockport SK4 4JX, Contact: Brian Jackson *Tel:* (0161) 947-9669 *Fax:* (0161) 947-9669 *E-mail:* jacksonpub@aol.com
Membership(s): IPG

Ruth Bean Publishers+
Victoria Farmhouse, Carlton, Bedford MK43 7LP
Tel: (01234) 720356 *Fax:* (01234) 720590
E-mail: ruthbean@onetel.net.uk
Key Personnel
Dir: Nigel Bean; Ruth Bean
Founded: 1972
Specialize in needlecrafts & costume.
Subjects: Anthropology, Crafts, Games, Hobbies, Drama, Theater, Fashion
ISBN Prefix(es): 0-903585
Membership(s): IPG

Beano Books, *imprint of* Geddes & Grosset

Beaver Publishing Ltd+
Unit 350, Glenfield Park Site 2, Blakewater Rd, Blackburn BB1 5QH
Tel: (01625) 586670 *Fax:* (01625) 586782
Key Personnel
Dir: A M Palmer; A Palmer
Founded: 1993
Subjects: Fiction, Humor, Natural History, Nonfiction (General)
ISBN Prefix(es): 1-85962
Subsidiaries: Saga Bargain Books
Warehouse: Pegasus Distribution Ltd, Glenfield Park, Unit 350, Site 2, Blakewater Rd, Blackburn, Lancs BB1 5QH
Orders to: Pegasus Distribution Ltd, Glenfield Park, Unit 350, Site 2, Blakewater Rd, Blackburn, Lancs BB1 5QH

Mitchell Beazley+
2-4 Heron Quays, London E14 4JP
Tel: (020) 7531 8400; (020) 7531 8480 (UK sales); (020) 7531 8481 (special sales); (020) 7531 8479 (marketing); (020) 7531 8488 (publicity); (020) 7531 8482 (export sales); (020) 7531 8484 (foreign rights); (020) 7531 8476 (US sales) *Fax:* (020) 7531 8650
E-mail: enquiries@mitchell-beazley.co.uk
Web Site: www.mitchell-beazley.com

Key Personnel
Publisher & Man Dir: Jane Aspden
UK Sales & Marketing Dir: Mark Scott
International Sales Dir: Kate Newton
Editorial Dir: Louise Dixon
Art Dir: Vivien Brar
Production Dir: Julie Young
Financial Controller: Paula Warrender
UK Sales Manager: Helen Twewus
Publicity Manager: Fiona Smith
Marketing Manager: Nicola Wright
Special Sales Executive: Clare Webb
Founded: 1969
High quality book publishers.
Subjects: Antiques, Cookery, Gardening, Plants, House & Home, Wine & Spirits
ISBN Prefix(es): 0-85533; 1-85732; 1-84000
Parent Company: Octopus Publishing Group
Orders to: Littlehampton Book Services Ltd, Faraday Close, Durrington, Worthing, West Sussex BN13 3RB *Tel:* (01933) 828800 *Fax:* (0193) 828802

BECTA, *imprint of* British Educational Communication & Technology Agency (BECTA)

Belitha Press Ltd+
Subsidiary of C&B (Publishing) plc
London House, Great Eastern Wharf, Parkgate Rd, London SW11 4NQ
Tel: (020) 7978 6330 *Fax:* (020) 7223 4936
E-mail: info@belithapress.co.uk
Web Site: www.belithapress.co.uk
Telex: 8950511 ONEONE
Key Personnel
Chairman: Cameron Brown
Man Dir: Peter Osborn *E-mail:* peter.osborn@belithapress.co.uk
Editorial Dir: Mary-Jane Wilkins
Publishing Dir: Chester Fisher *E-mail:* chester.fisher@belithapress.co.uk
Foreign Rights Manager: Madeleine Ehm
  E-mail: madeleine.ehm@belithapress.co.uk
Sales & Marketing Dir: Penelope Buckland
  E-mail: penny.buckland@belithapress.co.uk
Marketing Manager: Ben Cameron *E-mail:* ben.cameron@belithapress.co.uk
Founded: 1980
Publishers of high-quality illustrated children's books for the international market.
Subjects: Art, Biography, Crafts, Games, Hobbies, Environmental Studies, Foreign Countries, Geography, Geology, Mathematics, Music, Dance, Natural History, Nonfiction (General)
ISBN Prefix(es): 1-85561; 1-84138; 0-947553
Warehouse: Biblios Distribution, Star Rd, Partridge Green, Horsham, West Sussex RH13 8LD *E-mail:* biblios@biblios.co.uk

Belknap, *imprint of* Harvard University Press

Bell & Howell Information & Learning, see ProQuest Information & Learning

Bellew Publishing Co Ltd+
8 Balham Hill, London SW12 9EA
Tel: (020) 8673 5611 *Fax:* (020) 8675 2142
Key Personnel
Chief Executive & Man Dir: I B Bellew
Chairman: Ian Mcquordale
Founded: 1983
Also book packager.
Subjects: Architecture & Interior Design, Art, Crafts, Games, Hobbies, Environmental Studies, Fiction, History, Travel
ISBN Prefix(es): 0-947792; 1-85725
Imprints: Deirdre McDonald Ltd
Orders to: Plymbridge Distributors Ltd, Estover Rd, Plymouth PL6 7PZ

Belton Books, *imprint of* Stainer & Bell Ltd

653

UNITED KINGDOM

BEN Gunn, *imprint of* SB Publications

Berg Publishers+
Imprint of Oxford International Publishers Ltd
150 Cowley Rd, Oxford OX4 1JJ
Tel: (01865) 245104 *Fax:* (01865) 791165
E-mail: enquiry@bergpublishers.com
Web Site: www.bergpublishers.com
Key Personnel
Man Dir: Kathryn Earle *E-mail:* kearle@berg1.demon.co.uk
Production Dir: Sara Everett *E-mail:* severett@bergpublishers.com
Founded: 1981
Subjects: Anthropology, Ethnicity, Fashion, Government, Political Science, History, Social Sciences, Sociology, Women's Studies
ISBN Prefix(es): 0-85496; 1-85973
Number of titles published annually: 50 Print
Total Titles: 400 Print
Ultimate Parent Company: Associated Technologies Ltd
Imprints: Oswald Wolff Books
Distributed by New York University Press (US, Canada & Australia)
Foreign Rep(s): Andrew Durnell (Europe); Maya Publishers (India); Troika (UK); United Publishers Services Ltd (Japan)
Shipping Address: PSL Freight Ltd, Bathe Wharf, Station Rd, Maldon, Essex CM9 4GQ *Tel:* (01621) 854451 *Fax:* (01621) 840771
Warehouse: Orca Book Services, Stanley House, 3 Fleet Lane, BH15 3AJ Poole RH13 8LD *Tel:* (01202) 665432 *Fax:* (01202) 666219 *E-mail:* orders@orcabookservices.co.uk
Orders to: New York University Press, 838 Broadway, 3rd floor, New York, NY 10003-4812, United States *Fax:* 212-995-3833

Berghahn Books Ltd+
3 Newtec Pl, Magdalen Rd, Oxford OX4 1RE
Tel: (01865) 250011 *Fax:* (01865) 250056
E-mail: info@berghahnbooks.com
Web Site: www.berghahnbooks.com
Key Personnel
Publisher: Dr Marion Berghahn
Editorial: Sean Kingston, PhD
Marketing Manager: Penny Costley-White
Publicity: David Towsey
Founded: 1994
Subjects: Anthropology, Economics, Government, Political Science, History, Literature, Literary Criticism, Essays, Military Science, Religion - Jewish, Social Sciences, Sociology, Women's Studies, Gender, Humanities, Migration
ISBN Prefix(es): 1-57181
Number of titles published annually: 100 Print
Total Titles: 400 Print; 1 CD-ROM
U.S. Office(s): Berghahn Books Inc, 604 W 115 St, New York, NY 10025, United States, Publisher: Dr Marion Berghahn *Tel:* 212-222-6502 *Fax:* 212-222-5209 *E-mail:* berghahnus@juno.com
Orders to: Berghahn Books Inc, PO Box 605, Herndon, VA 20172, United States *Tel:* 703-661-1500 *Fax:* 703-661-1501 *E-mail:* tod@booksintl.com
Plymbridge, Estover Rd, Plymouth PL6 7PZ, Contact: Juliet Lunn *Tel:* (01752) 202300 *Fax:* (01752) 202333 *E-mail:* orders@plymbridge.com

Berlitz (UK) Ltd+
Lincoln House, 296-302 High Holborn, London WC1 7JH
Tel: (020) 7611 9640 *Fax:* (020) 7611 9656
E-mail: publishing@berlitz.co.uk
Web Site: www.berlitz.com
Key Personnel
Man Dir: Roger Kirkpatrick *Tel:* (020) 7518 8304 *E-mail:* roger.kirkpatrick@berlitz.ie

Operations Dir: Anthony Finn *Tel:* (020) 7518 8306 *E-mail:* anthony.finn@berlitz.ie
Founded: 1970
Subjects: *Specialies in:* Phrase books, dictionaries, audio, video & childrens language products, travel guides & language reference
ISBN Prefix(es): 2-8315
Total Titles: 375 Print
Parent Company: Berlitz Publishing Company Ltd
Ultimate Parent Company: Berlitz International Inc
Distributed by Virgin Publishing Ltd (United Kingdom)

Bernards (Publishers) Ltd, see Bernard Babani (Publishing) Ltd

Betterway, *imprint of* David & Charles Ltd

BFBS, *imprint of* Bible Society

BFI Publishing+
21 Stephen St, London W1T 1LN
Tel: (020) 7957 4789 *Fax:* (020) 74367950; (020) 76362516
E-mail: publishing@bfi.org.uk
Web Site: www.bfi.org.uk
Key Personnel
Head of Publishing: Andrew Lockett
Marketing & Sales: Rebecca Watts *Tel:* (20) 79574817 *E-mail:* rebecca.watts@bfi.org.uk
Production, Rights & Permissions: Tom Cabot
Marketing & Promotions: Sarah Prosser
Founded: 1980
Subjects: Film, Video, Radio, TV, Social Sciences, Sociology, Women's Studies
ISBN Prefix(es): 0-85170
Number of titles published annually: 30 Print
Total Titles: 280 Print
Distributed by Indiana University Press (North America)
Warehouse: Plymbridge Distributors Ltd, Estover Rd, Plymouth PL6 7PZ *Tel:* (01752) 202301
Orders to: Plymbridge Distributors Ltd, Estover Rd, Plymouth PL6 7PZ *Tel:* (01752) 202301

Bible Distributors, *imprint of* Chapter Two

Bible Reading Fellowship+
Elsfield Hall, 1st floor, 15-17 Elsfield Way, Oxford OX2 8FG
Tel: (01865) 319700 *Fax:* (01865) 319701
E-mail: enquiries@brf.org.uk
Web Site: www.brf.org.uk
Key Personnel
Chief Executive Officer: Richard Fisher *E-mail:* richardfisher@brf.org.uk
Commissioning Editor: Sue Doggett *E-mail:* suedoggett@brf.org.uk; Naomi Starkey *E-mail:* naomi.starkey@brf.org.uk
Marketing & Operations Manager: Karen Laister *E-mail:* karen.laister@brf.org.uk
Founded: 1922
Subjects: Biblical Studies, Education, Religion - Protestant, Theology
ISBN Prefix(es): 0-7459; 1-84101
Total Titles: 120 Print
Imprints: Barnabas
Foreign Rights: Bob Clark (Europe)
Orders to: Marston Book Services, PO Box 269, Oxford OX14 4YN *Tel:* (01235) 46550 *Fax:* (01235) 465555 *Web Site:* www.marston.co.uk

Bible Society+
Stonehill Green, Westlea, Swindon SN5 7DG
Tel: (01793) 418100 *Fax:* (01793) 418118
E-mail: info@bfbs.org.uk
Web Site: www.biblesociety.org.uk
Telex: 44283

Key Personnel
Chief Executive: N Crosbie
Commercial Dir: Ashley Scott
Export: Janet Edwards
Production: D Hill
Rights & Permissions: Miss K Luckett
Founded: 1804
Subjects: Biblical Studies
ISBN Prefix(es): 0-564
Imprints: BFBS

Big Time, *imprint of* Peter Haddock Ltd

BILD Publications
Campion House, Green St, Kidderminster, Worcs DY10 1JL
Tel: (01562) 723010 *Fax:* (01562) 723029
E-mail: enquiries@bild.org.uk
Web Site: www.bild.org.uk
Key Personnel
Chief Executive: John Harris
Founded: 1972
Subjects: Behavioral Sciences, Child Care & Development, Disability, Special Needs, Health, Nutrition
ISBN Prefix(es): 1-873791; 0-906054; 1-902519; 1-904082
Orders to: Plymbridge Distributors, Plymbridge House, Estover Rd, Estover, Plymouth PL6 7PZ *Tel:* (01752) 202301 *Fax:* (01752) 202333 *Web Site:* www.plymbridge.com

Binky (Childrens), *imprint of* Grange Books PLC

Bio Scientifica, *imprint of* Society for Endocrinology

BIOS Scientific Publishers Ltd+
9 Newtec Pl, Magdalen Rd, Oxford OX4 1RE
Tel: (01865) 726286 *Fax:* (01865) 246823
Web Site: www.bios.co.uk
Key Personnel
Chairman: Derek Phillips
Man Dir & International Rights: Dr Jonathan Ray
Sales: Simon Watkins *E-mail:* simon.watkins@bios.co.uk
Founded: 1989
Publishers of Instant Notes, The Basics, Clinic Handbooks, Advanced Texts, Advanced Methods, Key Topics series, Genomes 2, Human Molecular Genetics 2, Clinic Intensive Care, Medical Mycology, Biotechnic & Histochemistry.
Member of International Group of STM Publishers.
Subjects: Agriculture, Biological Sciences, Medicine, Nursing, Dentistry
ISBN Prefix(es): 1-872748; 1-85996
Parent Company: Oxford Publishing Ventures Ltd
Distributed by Springer Verlag New York Inc (North America); University of New South Wales (Australia & New Zealand); Viva Books (India)
Distributor for Horizon Scientific Press; Experiemental Biology Reviews; Royal Microscopical Society (microscopy handbooks); Society of Experimental Biology
Foreign Rep(s): Academic Marketing Services (South Africa, Zimbabwe); APAC Publishers (SE Asia, Singapore); Durnell Marketing Ltd (Ireland, Europe, Northern Ireland); IPS (Middle East) Ltd (Middle East, North Africa); UNIREPS (Australia, New Zealand)
Orders to: Plymbridge Distributors Ltd, Estover Rd, Plymouth, Devon *Tel:* (01752) 202301 *Fax:* (01753) 202333 *E-mail:* orders@plymbridge.com
Springer-Verlag, PO Box 2485, Secaucus, NJ 07096-2485, United States *Fax:* 212-533-5587 *E-mail:* order@springer-ny.com

PUBLISHERS — UNITED KINGDOM

Birlinn Ltd+
West Newington House, 10 Newington Rd, Edinburgh EH9 1QS
Tel: (0131) 668 4371 *Fax:* (0131) 668 4466
E-mail: info@birlinn.co.uk
Web Site: www.birlinn.co.uk
Key Personnel
Man Dir & International Rights: Hugh Andrew
Office Manager: Sarah Tranter
Founded: 1992
Member of Scottish Publishers Association.
Subjects: Fiction, History, Regional Interests
ISBN Prefix(es): 1-874744
Number of titles published annually: 80 Print
Associate Companies: Maclean Press
Imprints: Canongate Books "A" Ltd; John Donald Publishers Ltd
Distributor for Maclean Press
Foreign Rep(s): Dufour Editions Distribution (North America)
Warehouse: Scottish Book Source, 32 Finlas St, Glasgow G22 5DU
Orders to: 137 Dundee St, Edinburgh, Scotland, Fiona Maxwell-Hoy *Tel:* (0131) 229 6800 *Fax:* (0131) 229 9070

Birmingham Books
Central Library, Chamberlain Sq, Birmingham B3 3HQ
Tel: (0121) 235 2868; (0121) 235 4511
Fax: (0121) 233 9702; (0121) 233 4458
ISBN Prefix(es): 0-7093

Birmingham Library Information Services
Central Library, Chamberlain Sq, Birmingham B3 3HQ
Tel: (0121) 303 4511; (0121) 233 9702; (0121) 235 2868 *Fax:* (0121) 233 4458
E-mail: central.library@birmingham.gov.uk
Web Site: www.birmingham.gov.uk
ISBN Prefix(es): 0-7093; 0-901011

Bishopsgate Press Ltd+
Bartholomew House, 15 Tonbridge Rd, Hiddenborough, Tonbridge, Kent TN11 9BH
Tel: (01732) 833778 *Fax:* (01732) 833090
Key Personnel
Chief Executive: Ian Straker
Publishing Manager: Bob Wilson
Founded: 1800
Subjects: Biography, Crafts, Games, Hobbies, Film, Video, Finance, Religion - Other
ISBN Prefix(es): 0-900873; 1-85219
Parent Company: Whitstable Litho Ltd, Milstrood Rd, Whitstable, Kent CT5 3PP

BLA Publishing Ltd+
Bic Ling Kee House, One Christopher Rd, East Grinstead, West Sussex RH19 3BT
Tel: (01342) 318980 *Fax:* (01342) 410980
Key Personnel
Chairman: Bak Ling Au
Contact: Penny Kitchenham
Founded: 1981
Specialist packagers (Illustrated Trade & Children's).
Subjects: Aeronautics, Aviation, Antiques, Biological Sciences, Crafts, Games, Hobbies, Maritime, Religion - Other
ISBN Prefix(es): 0-907733
Parent Company: Ling Kee (UK) Ltd
Associate Companies: Ward Lock Educational Co Ltd

A & C Black Publishers Ltd+
37 Soho Sq, London W1D 3QZ
Tel: (020) 7758 0200 *Fax:* (020) 7758 0222
E-mail: enquiries@acblack.co.uk
Web Site: www.acblack.co.uk
Key Personnel
Man Dir: Charles Black; Jill Coleman
Production: Oscar Heini
Rights Dir: Paul Langridge
Distribution Dir: Terry Rouelett
Publicity: Rosanna Bortoli
Founded: 1807
Independent.
Subjects: Art, Crafts, Games, Hobbies, Drama, Theater, Education, Maritime, Music, Dance, Natural History, Nonfiction (General), Sports, Athletics, Travel, Specializes in ornithology
ISBN Prefix(es): 0-7136; 0-212
Total Titles: 1,200 Print; 1 CD-ROM
Imprints: Adlard Coles Nautical; Christopher Helm (Publishers) Ltd; The Herbert Press
Subsidiaries: Christopher Helm (Publishers) Ltd
Distributed by Midpoint Trade Books
Distributor for Magi Children's Books; Sheridan House; Sunflower Books; V&A Publications
Shipping Address: Howard Rd, Eaton Socon, Huntingdon, Cambs PE19 3EZ, Contact: Terry Rouelett *Tel:* (01480) 212666 *Fax:* (01480) 405014
Warehouse: Howard Rd, Eaton Socon, Huntingdon, Cambs PE19 3EZ, Contact: Terry Rouelett *Tel:* (01480) 212666 *Fax:* (01480) 405014
Orders to: Howard Rd, Eaton Socon, Huntingdon, Cambs PE19 3EZ, Contact: Terry Rouelett *Tel:* (01480) 212666 *Fax:* (01480) 405014

Black Ace Books+
PO Box 6557, Forfar DD8 2YS
Tel: (01307) 465096 *Fax:* (01307) 465494
Web Site: www.blackacebooks.com
Key Personnel
Dir: Hunter Steele; Boo Wood
Founded: 1991
Specialize in high quality fiction.
Subjects: Fiction, History, Philosophy
ISBN Prefix(es): 1-872988
Number of titles published annually: 5 Print
Total Titles: 30 Print
Parent Company: Black Ace Enterprises
Associate Companies: Maran Steele Music

Black Dagger, *imprint of* BBC Audiobooks

Black Lace, *imprint of* Virgin Publishing Ltd

Black Spring Press Ltd+
152 Harringay Rd, London N15 3HL
Tel: (020) 7639 2492 *Fax:* (020) 7639 2508
E-mail: bsp@blackspring.demon.co.uk
Key Personnel
Dir: M Prausnitz *E-mail:* maja@blackspring.demon.co.uk; S R J Pettifar *E-mail:* bsp@blackspring.demon.co.uk
Founded: 1984
Subjects: Fiction, Music, Dance
ISBN Prefix(es): 0-948238; 0-931181
Orders to: Airlift Book Co, 8 The Arena, Mollison Ave, Enfield EN3 7NJ *Tel:* (020) 8804 0400 *Fax:* (020) 8804 0044

Black Swan, *imprint of* Transworld Publishers Ltd

Blackbirch Press, *imprint of* Gale Research

Blackie Children's Books+
27 Wrights Lane, London W8 5TZ
Tel: (020) 7416 3000 *Fax:* (020) 7416 3086
Telex: 917181
ISBN Prefix(es): 0-216
Parent Company: The Penguin Group
Shipping Address: Penguin Books, Bath Rd, Harmondsworth, Middx UB7 0DA
Warehouse: Penguin Books, Bath Rd, Harmondsworth, Middx UB7 0DA
Orders to: Penguin Books, Bath Rd, Harmondsworth, Middx UB7 0DA

Blackstaff Press+
Member of W & G Baird Group
Blackstaff House, Wildflower Way, Apollo Rd, Belfast BT12 6TA
Tel: (028) 9066 8074 *Fax:* (028) 9066 8207
E-mail: info@blackstaffpress.com
Web Site: www.blackstaffpress.com
Key Personnel
Man Dir: Anne Tannahill
Chairman: Roy Bailie
Marketing & Publicity Manager: Bairbre Ryan *E-mail:* marketing@blackstaffpress.com
Editorial: Patricia Horton
Production: Elizabeth McBlain
Rights: Susan Dalzell
Founded: 1971
Subjects: Art, Biography, Cookery, Drama, Theater, Fiction, History, Humor, Literature, Literary Criticism, Essays, Music, Dance, Natural History, Nonfiction (General), Photography, Poetry, Regional Interests, Religion - Buddhist, Religion - Catholic, Religion - Hindu, Religion - Islamic, Religion - Jewish, Religion - Protestant, Religion - Other, Travel
ISBN Prefix(es): 0-85640
Orders to: Dufour Editions Inc, Byers Rd, PO Box 7, Chester Springs, PA 19425-0007, United States *Tel:* 610-458-5005 *Fax:* 610-458-7103 *E-mail:* info@dufoureditions.com
Gill & Macmillan Distribution, Hume Ave, Park West, Dublin 12, Ireland *Tel:* (3531) 500 9500 *Fax:* (3531) 500 9599 *Web Site:* www.gillmacmillan.ie

Blackwell Business, *imprint of* Blackwell Publishers

Blackwell Finance, *imprint of* Blackwell Publishers

Blackwell Publishers+
108 Cowley Rd, Oxford OX4 1JF
Tel: (01865) 791100 *Fax:* (01865) 791347
Web Site: www.blackwellpublishers.co.uk
Telex: 837022 *Cable:* BOOKS OXFORD
Key Personnel
Chairman: Nigel Blackwell
Senior Sales Administrator - UK Office: Pamela Todd *E-mail:* ptodd@blackwellpublishers.co.uk
Divisional Marketing Manager - UK Office: Lorna Berrett *E-mail:* lberrett@blackwellpublishing.co.uk
Vice President, Marketing & Sales - US Office: Amy Yodanis *E-mail:* ayoda@blackwellpub.com
Publisher - UK Office: Andrew McNeillie *E-mail:* amcneill@blackwellpublishers.co.uk
Executive Editor - US Office: Al Bruckner *E-mail:* abruc@blackwellpub.com
Editorial Dir - US Office: Steve Smith *E-mail:* ssmit@blackwellpub.com
Senior Production Controller - UK Office: Brian Johnson *E-mail:* bjohnson@blackwellpublishers.co.uk
Editorial Dir, Journals - UK Office: Claire Andrews - UK Office *E-mail:* candrews@blackwellpublishers.co.uk
Journals Publisher - US Office: Otis Dean *E-mail:* odean@blackwellpub.com
Customer Service Manager - US Office: Barbara Sasso *E-mail:* bsass@blackwellpub.com
Journals Marketing Coordinator - US Office: Heather Day *E-mail:* hday@blackwellpub.com
Permissions Controller: Lindsay Doyle *E-mail:* Lindsay.Doyle@blacksci.co.uk
Rights Manager: Sr Karen Gibson *E-mail:* Karen.Gibson@blacksci.co.uk
Translation Rights Controller: Katherine Newman *E-mail:* Katherine.Newman@blacksci.co.uk
Founded: 1922
Allied Companies: Blackwell Scientific Publications Ltd; Polity Press; NCC Blackwell.
Member of the Blackwell Group.

Subjects: Business, Computer Science, Economics, Finance, Geography, Geology, Government, Political Science, History, Labor, Industrial Relations, Language Arts, Linguistics, Law, Literature, Literary Criticism, Essays, Philosophy, Psychology, Psychiatry, Religion - Other, Social Sciences, Sociology, Women's Studies
ISBN Prefix(es): 0-631; 0-85520; 0-7456
Imprints: Blackwell Finance; Blackwell Reference; Blackwell Business
U.S. Office(s): Blackwell Publishers Inc, 238 Main Street, Cambridge, MA 02142, United States Tel: 617-547-7110 Fax: 617-547-0789
Warehouse: Marston Book Services Ltd, Osney Mead, Oxford OX2 0DT Tel: (01865) 791155 Fax: (01865) 791927

Blackwell Reference, imprint of Blackwell Publishers

Blackwell Science Ltd+
Osney Mead, Oxford OX2 0EL
Tel: (01865) 206206 Fax: (01865) 721205
E-mail: shona.macdonald@blacksci.co.uk
Telex: 83355 MEDBOK G
Key Personnel
Chairman: Nigel Blackwell
Man Dir: Robert Campbell
Finance Dir: Martin Wilkinson
Editorial Dir: Peter Saugman
Production Dir: John Strange
Sales Dir: Edward Crutchley
Founded: 1939
Subjects: Architecture & Interior Design, Behavioral Sciences, Chemistry, Chemical Engineering, Child Care & Development, Earth Sciences, Fashion, Geography, Geology, Health, Nutrition, Law, Medicine, Nursing, Dentistry, Psychology, Psychiatry, Science (General), Sports, Athletics, Veterinary Science
ISBN Prefix(es): 0-86542; 0-632
Subsidiaries: Blackwell MZV; Blackwell Science (Australia) Pty Ltd; Munksgaard, International Booksellers & Publishers Ltd; Arnette Blackwell; Blackwell Science (Japan); Blackwell Science Ltd; Blackwell Wissenschafts-Verlag GmbH; Blackwell Science Inc
Bookshop(s): Broad St, Oxford; Art & Poster Shop, Broad St, Oxford; MOMA, Pembroke St, Oxford
Shipping Address: Marston Book Services Ltd, Osney Mead, Oxford OX2 0DT
Orders to: Marston Book Services Ltd, Osney Mead, Oxford OX2 0DT

Blake Publishing, imprint of John Blake Publishing Ltd

Blaketon Hall Ltd
Unit 1, 26 Marsh Green Rd, Marsh Barton, Exeter, Devon EX2 8PN
Tel: (01392) 210 602 Fax: (01392) 421 165
E-mail: sales@blaketonhall.co.uk
Web Site: www.blaketonhall.co.uk
Key Personnel
Man Dir: John Shillingford E-mail: martin@blaketonhall.co.uk
Dir: Pat Shillingford
Founded: 1976
Also acts as remainder dealer.
Subjects: Animals, Pets, Crafts, Games, Hobbies, How-to, Nonfiction (General)
ISBN Prefix(es): 0-907854

Blandford, imprint of Cassell & Co

Blandford Publishing Ltd+
Stanley House, 3 Fleets Lane, Poole, Dorset BH15 3A1
Tel: (01202) 665432 Fax: (01202) 666219

Telex: 9413701
Key Personnel
Chairman & Chief Executive: Philip Sturrock
Editorial Dir, Rights & Special Sales: Alison Goff
Sales Dir: Finbarr McCabe
Founded: 1919
Subjects: Animals, Pets, Astrology, Occult, Crafts, Games, Hobbies, Criminology, History, Music, Dance, Natural History, Outdoor Recreation, Sports, Athletics
ISBN Prefix(es): 0-7137
Parent Company: Continuum International Publishing Group Ltd

Bloodaxe Books Ltd+
Highgreen, Tarset, Northumberland NE48 1RP
Tel: (01434) 240 500 Fax: (01434) 240 505
E-mail: editor@bloodaxebooks.demon.co.uk
Web Site: www.bloodaxebooks.com
Key Personnel
Chairman: Simon Thirsk
Editor: Neil Astley
Marketing Manager: Alison Davis
Rights & Permissions Manager: Peg Osterman
Publicity: Christine MacGregor
Founded: 1978
Subjects: Poetry
ISBN Prefix(es): 0-906427; 1-85224
Number of titles published annually: 40 Print
U.S. Office(s): DuFour Editions Inc, PO Box 7, Chester Springs, PA 19425-0007, United States Tel: 610-458-5005 Fax: 610-458-7103
E-mail: dufour8023@aol.com
Orders to: Littlehampton Book Services, Centre Warehouse, Columbia Bldg, Faraday Durington Close, Worthing, West Sussex BN13 3RB
Tel: (01903) 828 800 Fax: (01903) 828 801
E-mail: orders@lbsltd.co.uk

Bloomsbury Publishing PLC+
38 Soho Sq, London W1D 3HB
Tel: (020) 7494 2111 Fax: (020) 7434 0151
E-mail: csm@bloomsbury.com
Web Site: www.bloomsburymagazine.com
Key Personnel
Chairman & Man Dir: Nigel Newton
Publishing Dir, Fiction: Liz Calder
Publishing Dir, Nonfiction: David Reynolds
Publishing Dir, Reference: Kathy Rooney
Publishing Dir, General: Alan Wherry
Production Dir: Penny Edwards
Publicity Dir: Becky Shaw
International Rights: Ruth Logan
Sales, UK: David Ward
Marketing: Sarah Beal
Founded: 1987
Subjects: Alternative, Architecture & Interior Design, Art, Astrology, Occult, Biography, Career Development, Child Care & Development, Communications, Cookery, Crafts, Games, Hobbies, Drama, Theater, Earth Sciences, Economics, Fashion, Fiction, Film, Video, Finance, Gardening, Plants, Gay & Lesbian, Health, Nutrition, History, House & Home, How-to, Human Relations, Humor, Literature, Literary Criticism, Essays, Management, Marketing, Medicine, Nursing, Dentistry, Music, Dance, Natural History, Nonfiction (General), Outdoor Recreation, Parapsychology, Photography, Psychology, Psychiatry, Religion - Other, Science (General), Self-Help, Social Sciences, Sociology, Theology, Travel, Wine & Spirits, Women's Studies
ISBN Prefix(es): 0-7475
Orders to: Exel-Logistics, Christchurch House, Beaufort Court, St Thomas Longley Rd, Medway City Estate, Rochester, Kent

Blorenge Books+
Blorenge Cottage, Church Lane, Llan-ffwyst, Y Fenni NP7 9NG
Tel: (01873) 856114

Key Personnel
Proprietor: Chris Barber
Founded: 1985
Subjects: Fiction, History, Mysteries, Outdoor Recreation, Travel
Number of titles published annually: 3 Print
Total Titles: 12 Print

Blueprint, imprint of Routledge

Blueprint+
Leatherhead, Randalls Rd, Surrey KT22 7RU
Tel: (01372) 802080 Fax: (01372) 802079
E-mail: publications@pira.co.uk
Key Personnel
Publisher: Annabel Taylor
Subjects: Photography, Publishing & Book Trade Reference
Parent Company: Pira International

BMJ Publishing Group+
BMA House, Tavistock Sq, London WC1H 9JR
Tel: (020) 7387 4499; (020) 7383 6245
Fax: (020) 7383 6661; (020) 7383 6662
E-mail: customerservices@bmjbooks.com
Web Site: www.bmjpg.com
Key Personnel
Chief Executive & Editor: Dr Richard Smith
Business Development Dir: Maurice Long
Publisher: John Hudson E-mail: jhudson@bmjbooks.com
Publishing Dir, Specialist Journals: Alexandra Williamson
Production Executive: Nathan Harris
  E-mail: nharris@bmjbooks.com
Sales & Marketing Executive: Clair Grant-Salmon
  E-mail: cgrantsalmon@bmjbooks.com
Sales & Marketing Manager: Helen Robertson
  E-mail: hrobertson@bmjbooks.com
Rights Executive: Kate Webster E-mail: rights@bmjbooks.com
Books Division Manager, Rights & Permisssions: John Hudson
Commissioning Editor: Mary Banks
  E-mail: mbanks@bmjbooks.com
Development Editor: Christina Karaviotis
  E-mail: ckaraviotis@bmjbooks.com
Founded: 1857
Subjects: Medicine, Nursing, Dentistry
ISBN Prefix(es): 0-7279; 0-900221
Parent Company: British Medical Association
Imprints: PSP
Subsidiaries: Professional & Scientific Publications
Distributed by AMA Services (WA) Pty Ltd (Australia); American College of Physicians (USA, Mexico); Apac Publishers Services (Far East, excluding Japan & Taiwan); BMJ Books (USA); Canadian Medical Association (Canada); HWA Eng Trading Co (Taiwan); Jaypee Brothers (India); Medical Association of South Africa (South Africa); Nankodo Co Ltd (Japan); Phi Shoten (Japan); F K Schattauer (Germany)
Distributor for American Academy of Ophthalmology; American Academy of Physicians; British Dental Journal; Schattauer
Foreign Rep(s): Anthony Rudkin Associates (Cyprus, Greece, Middle East, North Africa, Turkey, Iran); Associated Marketing Services (France & Spain, Italy & Portugal); Brookside Publishing Services (Ireland); David Towle International (Baltic States, Scandinavia); John Wilde Partnership (Austria, Germany & Switzerland); Kelvin Van Hasselt (Africa, Caribbean)
Bookshop(s): Burton St, London WC1
Tel: (020) 7383 6244 Fax: (020) 7383 6455
E-mail: orders@bmjbookshop.com Web Site: www.bmjbookshop.com

PUBLISHERS

Shipping Address: Unit 11c, North Orbital Trading Estate, Napsbury Lane, St Albans, Herts AL1 1XB
Warehouse: Unit 11c, North Orbital Trading Estate, Napsbury Lane, St Albans, Herts AL1 1XB

Boatswain Press, *imprint of* Kenneth Mason Publications Ltd

Bobcat Books, *imprint of* Omnibus Press

The Bodley Head, *imprint of* Random House UK Ltd

Bodley Head Childrens Books, *imprint of* Random House UK Ltd

Bonfini, *imprint of* Clematis Press Ltd

Book Club Associates, see BCA

Book Data
Globe House, One Chertsey Rd, Twickenham TW1 1LR
Tel: (020) 8843 8600 *Fax:* (020) 8843 8744
E-mail: info@bookdata.co.uk; sales@bookdata.co.uk
Web Site: www.bookdata.co.uk; www.ehaus.co.uk
Key Personnel
Man Dir: Francis Bennett
Sales Dir: Birgid MacLeod
International Key Accounts Dir: Pam Roud
Marketing Manager: Mo Siewcharran
 E-mail: marketing@bookdata.co.uk
International Sales Manager: Alison Kaye
Founded: 1987
Supplier of bibliographic information for English-language books & other published media. Services include: BookFind-Online; bibliographic CD-ROMS of international or UK published titles; customized record supply service; E-Haus web team providing web services & E-commerce solutions to the book industry.
Subjects: Library & Information Sciences, Publishing & Book Trade Reference
Total Titles: 8 CD-ROM; 2 Online
Associate Companies: Book Data Asia Pacific; Bibliographic Data Services (BDS); Book Data/SAP/net

The Book Guild Ltd+
Temple House, 25 High St, Lewes, East Sussex BN7 2LU
Tel: (01273) 472534 *Fax:* (01273) 476472
E-mail: info@bookguild.co.uk
Web Site: www.bookguild.co.uk
Key Personnel
Chairman: G M Nissen, CBE
Editorial Dir: Carol Biss
Founded: 1982
Member of Publishers' Association & Independent Publishers' Guild.
Subjects: Art, Biography, Fiction, History, Literature, Literary Criticism, Essays, Military Science, Travel
ISBN Prefix(es): 1-85776; 0-86332
Number of titles published annually: 100 Print
Orders to: Vine House Distribution, Waldenbury, North Common, Chailey, East Sussex BN8 4DR *Tel:* (01825) 723398 *Fax:* (01825) 724188 *E-mail:* sales@vinehouseuk.co.uk *Web Site:* www.vinehouseuk.co.uk

Book Marketing Ltd
2-4 Idol Lane, London EC3R 5DD
Tel: (020) 7398 0705 *Fax:* (020) 7626 3660
E-mail: bml@bookmarketing.co.uk
Key Personnel
Man Dir: Jo Henry

Founded: 1990
Subjects: Publishing & Book Trade Reference
ISBN Prefix(es): 1-873517
Total Titles: 15 Print

Book Packaging & Marketing+
3 Murswell Lane, Silverstone NN12 8UT
Tel: (01327) 858380 *Fax:* (01327) 858380
Key Personnel
Proprietor: Martin F Marix Evans
 E-mail: martin@marixevans.freeserve.co.uk
Founded: 1989
Book creator, authorship, photography, picture research, delivered as ready-for-press or film or printed books or as tiles for incorporation into website.
Subjects: History, Military Science, Photography, Travel, Specialize in Illustrated trade & reference books, editorial & authorship, picture research & production services
Number of titles published annually: 4 Print
Total Titles: 45 Print

Bookmarks Publications+
One Bloomsbury St, London WC1B 3QE
Tel: (020) 7637 1848 *Fax:* (020) 7637 3416
Web Site: www.bookmarks.uk.com
Key Personnel
Editorial: Emma Bircham *E-mail:* publications@bookmarks.uk.com
Founded: 1979
Publisher for the Socialist Workers' Party (GB).
Subjects: Economics, Government, Political Science, History, Labor, Industrial Relations
ISBN Prefix(es): 0-906224; 1-898876
Branch Office(s)
GPO Box 1473N, Melbourne 3001, Australia

Books for Europe Ltd+
3 Sutton Court, 92 Grange Rd, London W5 3PG
Tel: (020) 8840 6672 *Fax:* (020) 8840 6672
E-mail: bfekoma@dial.eunet.ch
Key Personnel
Man Dir: Juliusz Komarnicki *Fax:* (020) 8966 7865
Founded: 1984
Also acts as sales agent in UK, European Community & Middle East for publishers.
Subjects: Accounting, Advertising, Aeronautics, Aviation, Antiques, Archaeology, Architecture & Interior Design, Art, Asian Studies
Associate Companies: Book Representation & Distribution Ltd
Branch Office(s)
CP 196, CH-6900 Massagno, Switzerland

Books International+
101 Lynchford Rd, Farnborough, Hants GU14 6ET
Tel: (01252) 376564 *Fax:* (01252) 370181
E-mail: booksinter@aol.com
Web Site: www.books-international.co.uk/
Key Personnel
President: Mr Kris Machala
Founded: 1989
Subjects: Aeronautics, Aviation, Automotive, Crafts, Games, Hobbies, History, Maritime, Military Science, Publishing & Book Trade Reference, Transportation
ISBN Prefix(es): 0-9528867
Parent Company: Books International, Poland
Imprints: AJ Press
Branch Office(s)
Books International, ul Lubelska 30-32, 03-308 Warsaw, Poland
Distributor for AJ Press
Bookshop(s): 101 Lynchford Rd, Farnborough, Hants GU14 6ET

Books of Zimbabwe Publishing Co (Pvt) Ltd
22 Highfield Court, Church Rd, Haywards Heath, West Sussex RH16 3PA

UNITED KINGDOM

Tel: (079) 41959026
E-mail: info@booksofzimbabwe.co.za
Web Site: www.booksofzimbabwe.co.za
Key Personnel
Rights & Permissions: Joan Hopcraft
Founded: 1968
Subjects: Biography, Education, Fiction, Foreign Countries, History, Nonfiction (General)
ISBN Prefix(es): 0-86920
Subsidiaries: Africana Book Society (Pty) Ltd

Books on Screen, *imprint of* Butterworths Tolley

Boosey & Hawkes Music Publishers Ltd+
295 Regent St, London W1B 2JH
Tel: (020) 7580 2060 *Fax:* (020) 7291 7109
Web Site: www.boosey.com/publishing
Key Personnel
Sales & Marketing Dir: S A Richards
Founded: 1890
Also acts as a distributor for other music companies & book publishers of musical background books.
Subjects: Music, Dance
ISBN Prefix(es): 0-85162
Parent Company: Boosey & Hawkes PLC
Divisions: B & H Inc, Printed Music Division
U.S. Office(s): B & H Inc, 24 E 21 St, 2nd fl, New York, NY, United States *Tel:* 212-358-5302 *E-mail:* trade.uk@boosey.com
Orders to: The Hyde, Edgware Rd, London NW9 6JN *Tel:* (020) 8205 3861 *Fax:* (020) 8200 3737

Borland Press, *imprint of* Pearson Education Europe, Mideast & Africa

Boulevard Books UK, *imprint of* Boulevard Books UK/The Babel Guides

Boulevard Books UK/The Babel Guides+
71 Lytton Rd, Oxford OX4 3NY
Tel: (01865) 712931 *Fax:* (01865) 712931
E-mail: raybabel@dircon.co.uk
Web Site: www.raybabel.dircon.co.uk
Key Personnel
Dir, Boulevard Books UK: Ray Keenoy
Rights & Marketing Mgr, Babel Guides to Fiction in English Translation: Clara Corona
Founded: 1989
Publish contemporary world fiction in English translation, popular guides to fiction in translation.
Subjects: Fiction, Literature, Literary Criticism, Essays
ISBN Prefix(es): 1-899460
Number of titles published annually: 4 Print
Total Titles: 16 Print
Imprints: Babel Guides; Boulevard Books UK
Distributed by Drake International (UK & Europe); ISBS (US & Canada)
Orders to: Orca Book Services, 3 Fleets Lane, Poole Dorset BH15 3AJ *Tel:* (01202) 665432 *Fax:* (01202) 666219 *E-mail:* orders@orcabookservices.co.uk

Bounty Books, *imprint of* Octopus Publishing Group

Bounty Books+
Division of The Octopus Group Ltd
2-4 Heron Quays, London E14 4JP
Tel: (020) 7531 8600 *Fax:* (020) 7531 8607
Web Site: www.bountybooks.co.uk
Key Personnel
Man Dir: Laura Bamford *Tel:* (202) 7531 8406
Publishing Executive: Caroline Taylor *Tel:* (020) 7531 8603 *E-mail:* caroline.taylor@hamlyn.co.uk

657

UNITED KINGDOM

International Sales Dir: Des Higgins *Tel:* (020) 7531 8602 *E-mail:* des.higgins@bountybooks.co.uk
Export Sales Manager: Paula Whitehouse *Tel:* (020) 7531 8605 *E-mail:* paula.whitehouse@bountybooks.co.uk
Export Sales Coordinator: Catherine Saunders *Tel:* (020) 7531 8471 *E-mail:* catherine.saunders@bountybooks.co.uk
UK Sales Dir: Carolyne Meah *Tel:* (01257) 267 661 *Fax:* (01257) 263 770 *E-mail:* carolyne.emeah@bountybooks.co.uk
Key Accounts Manager: Tony Cartlidge *Tel:* (01772) 460 799 *E-mail:* tony.cartlidge@bountybooks.co.uk
Senior Sales Representative: David Atkinson *Tel:* (020) 7564 1365 *E-mail:* david.atkinson@bountybooks.co.uk
Publisher of promotional titles.
Distributed by Exel Logistics

Bowerdean Publishing Co Ltd
8 Abbotstone Rd, Putney, London SW15 1QR
Tel: (020) 8788 0938 *Fax:* (020) 8788 0938
Web Site: www.bowerdean.co.uk/
Key Personnel
Contact: Robert Dudley *E-mail:* rdudley@btinternet.com
Founded: 1993
Subjects: Management, Social Sciences, Sociology
ISBN Prefix(es): 0-906097
U.S. Office(s): c/o Kaimleen Hughes, IPM 22893 Quicksilver Dr, Dulles, VA 20166, United States *Tel:* 703-661-1500 *Fax:* 703-661-1501
Distributed by Central Books (UK); DA Information Services (Australia); International Publishers Marketing (US & Canada); Phambili Agencies (South Africa)
Warehouse: Central Books, 99 Wallis Rd, London E95LN, Bill Wallis *Tel:* (020) 8986 4854 *Fax:* (020) 8533 5821

Bowker, see CSA (Cambridge Scientific Abstracts)

Boxtree, *imprint of* Pan Macmillan

Boxtree Ltd+
25 Eccleston Pl, London SW1W 9NF
Tel: (020) 7881 8000 *Fax:* (020) 7881 8001
Key Personnel
Publishing Dir: Adrian Sington
Sales Dir: Michael Halden
Editor: Susanna Wadeson
Rights: Chantal Noel
Publicity: Sarah Bernie
Founded: 1986
Subjects: Film, Video, Humor, Radio, TV, Science Fiction, Fantasy
ISBN Prefix(es): 1-85283; 0-7522
Distributor for Museum Quilts (UK); Piccadilly (UK); Rosendale (UK); Smith Gryphon (UK)
Warehouse: Little Hampton Book Services

Marion Boyars Publishers Ltd+
24 Lacy Rd, London SW15 1NL
Tel: (020) 8788 9522 *Fax:* (020) 8789 8122
E-mail: marion.boyars@talk21.com
Web Site: www.marionboyars.co.uk
Key Personnel
Man Dir, Rights & Permissions, Publicity, Production: Catheryn Kilgarriff
Editorial Dir: Arthur Boyars
Editorial: Ken Hollings
Founded: 1975
Independent literary trade publisher.
Please include return postage for unsolicited submissions.
Subjects: Drama, Theater, Fiction, Literature, Literary Criticism, Essays, Music, Dance, Philosophy

ISBN Prefix(es): 0-7145
Number of titles published annually: 20 Print
Total Titles: 527 Print
U.S. Office(s): Marion Boyars Publishers Inc, 237 E 39 St, New York, NY 10016, United States, Dir, Publicity & Subsidiary Rights: Franklin Dennis *Tel:* 212-697-9676 *Fax:* 212-808-0664 *E-mail:* dennisfm@lanline.com
Distributor for Peribo Pty Ltd (Australia & New Zealand); Quartet Sales & Marketing (South Africa)
Foreign Rep(s): Peribo Pty (Australia)
Orders to: Central Books, 99 Wallis Rd, London E9 5LN *Tel:* (020) 8986 4854 *Fax:* (020) 8533 5821 *E-mail:* orders@centralbooks.com

Boydell & Brewer Ltd+
PO Box 9, Woodbridge IP12 3DF
Tel: (01394) 411320 *Fax:* (01394) 411477
E-mail: boydell@boydell.co.uk
Web Site: www.boydell.co.uk
Key Personnel
Man Dir: Dr R W Barber
Head of Sales & Marketing: Michael Richards
Founded: 1969
Subjects: History, Literature, Literary Criticism, Essays
ISBN Prefix(es): 0-85115; 0-85993
Number of titles published annually: 150 Print
U.S. Office(s): Boydell & Brewer Inc, 668 Mount Hope Ave, Rochester, NY 14620, United States
Foreign Rep(s): Nancy Bye (US); Duke Hill/Marsha Martin (US); Colin Flint (Baltic States, Denmark, Finland, Iceland, Norway, Sweden); Ben Greig (Baltic States, Scandinavia); Hushion House Publishing Inc (Canada); Iberian Book Services (Spain & Portugal); Inter Media Americana (Mexico, South Africa); Pat Malango (US); Flavio Marcello (France, Italy); Netwerk Academic Book Agency (Belgium, Netherlands, Luxembourg); Publishers International Marketing (Korea, Middle East, North Africa, Southeast Asia); Remley & Associates (US); I J Sagun Enterprises Ltd (Philippines); Roger Sauls (US); Ben Schrager (US); SHS (Austria, Germany & Switzerland); Siobhan Mullet (Ireland); TML (Pakistan)

BPP Publishing Ltd
Aldine Pl, London W12 8AA
Tel: (020) 8740 2222 *Fax:* (020) 8740 1111
E-mail: info@bpp.com
Web Site: www.bpp.com
Founded: 1976
Subjects: Accounting, Business, Economics, Marketing
ISBN Prefix(es): 0-7517; 0-86277; 1-871824

BPS Books (British Psychological Society)+
Division of British Psychological Society
St Andrews House, 48 Princess Rd E, Leicester LE1 7DR
Tel: (0116) 254 9568 *Fax:* (0116) 247 0787
E-mail: enquiry@bps.org.uk
Web Site: www.bps.org.uk
Key Personnel
Publisher: Joyce Collins
Senior Editor: Jon Reed
Founded: 1981
Member of IPG (Independent Publishers Guild).
Subjects: Behavioral Sciences, Education, Management
ISBN Prefix(es): 0-901715; 1-85433
Total Titles: 100 Print
Imprints: BPS Multimedia
Branch Office(s)
Stylus Publishing Inc, 22883 Quicksilver Dr, Dulles, VA 20166, United States
Distributed by Paul H Brookes (USA)
Warehouse: Plymbridge Distributors Ltd, Estover, Plymouth PL6 7PZ

BPS Multimedia, *imprint of* BPS Books (British Psychological Society)

Dr Barry Bracewell-Milnes
26 Lancaster Court, Banstead, Surrey SM7 1RR
Tel: (01737) 350736
Key Personnel
Dir: J B Bracewell-Milnes *E-mail:* jim_1001@hotmail.com
Subjects: Economics, Finance, Taxation

Bradford Books, *imprint of* MIT Press Ltd

Bradt Travel Guides Ltd+
19 High St, Chalfont St Peter, Gerrards Cross SL9 9QE
Tel: (01753) 893444 *Fax:* (01753) 892333
E-mail: info@bradt-travelguides.com
Web Site: www.bradt-travelguides.com
Key Personnel
President: Hilary Bradt
Editor: Patricia Hayne
Office Manager: Debbie Hunter
Sales & Marketing Manager: Peter Webb
Founded: 1972
Subjects: Outdoor Recreation, Travel
ISBN Prefix(es): 0-946983; 1-898323; 1-84162
Total Titles: 59 Print
Associate Companies: The Globe Pequot Press, PO Box 480, 246 Goose Lane, Guilford, CT 06437-0480, United States *Tel:* 203-458-4500 *Fax:* 203-458-4601 *E-mail:* info@globe-pequot.com
Distributed by Altair (Spain); Camerapix Publishers International (East Africa); Cartotheque E G G (France); Craenen, bvba Mechelsesteenweg (Belgium); Eco Trip 2001 (Israel); Globe Pequot Press (North America); Greene Phoenix Marketing (New Zealand); InterMediaAmericana Ltd (Baltic States, West & Southern Africa, Indian Ocean, Middle East (Except Israel), South & Central America, Caribbean); Inter Orbis (Italy); Dennis Jones & Associates Pty Ltd (Australia); Nilsson & Lamm bv (Netherlands); OLF SA (Switzerland); Platypus (Sweden, Norway); Scanvik Books aps Esplanaden (Denmark, Norway); TransQuest Asia Publishers Pte Ltd (Spain); Wild Dog Press (South Africa)
Foreign Rep(s): Altair (Spain); Camerapix Publishers International (East Africa); Cartotheque E G G (France); Craenen, bvba Mechelsesteenweg (Belgium); Eco Trip 2001 (Israel); The Globe Pequot Press (Canada, US); Greene Phoenix Marketing (New Zealand); Inter Orbis (Italy); InterMediaAmericana Ltd (Baltic States, Caribbean, Central/South America, Middle East exc Israel, South Africa); Dennis Jones & Associates Pty Ltd (Australia); Nilsson & Lamm bv (Netherlands); OLF SA (Switzerland); Platypus (Norway, Sweden); Scanvik Books aps Esplanaden (Denmark, Norway); TransQuest Asia Publishers Pte Ltd (Spain); Wild Dog Press (South Africa)
Orders to: Portfolio, Unit 5, Perivale Industrial Park, Horsenden Lane S, Greenford UB6 7RL *Tel:* (020) 8997 9000 *Fax:* (020) 8997 9097 *E-mail:* sales@portfoliobooks.com

BradyGames, *imprint of* Pearson Education Europe, Mideast & Africa

Brassey's UK Ltd+
583 Fulham Rd, London SW6 5BY
Tel: (020) 7471 1100 *Fax:* (020) 7471 1101
E-mail: info@batsford.com
Web Site: www.batsford.com
Key Personnel
Man Dir: Mr J Cook
Rights Manager: John Lee
Founded: 1886

Subjects: Aeronautics, Aviation, History, Maritime, Military Science
ISBN Prefix(es): 1-57488; 1-85753; 0-904609
Subsidiaries: Brassey's Inc
Divisions: Conway Maritime Press; Putnam Aeronautical
Branch Office(s)
Brassey's Inc, Suite 100, 22883 Quicksilver Dr, Dulles, VA 20166, United States
Warehouse: Marston Book Services, PO Box 269, Abingdon OX14 4SD
Orders to: Marston Book Services, PO Box 269, Abingdon OX14 4SD

Nicholas Brealey Publishing+
3-5 Spafield St, Clerkenwell, London EC1R 4QB
Tel: (020) 7239 0360 *Fax:* (020) 7239 0370
E-mail: sales@nbrealey-books.com
Web Site: www.nbrealey-books.com
Key Personnel
International Rights: Sue Coll *E-mail:* rights@nbrealey.books.com
Man Dir: Nicholas Brealey *E-mail:* nicholas.commissioningn@nbrealey-books.com
Marketing & Publicity Dir: Angie Tainsh *E-mail:* angiet@nbrealey-books.com
Founded: 1992
Member of IPG.
Subjects: Business, Career Development, Economics, Finance, Foreign Countries, Management, Self-Help, Foreign Countries
ISBN Prefix(es): 1-85788
Total Titles: 100 Print
U.S. Office(s): Intercultural Press Inc, 374 US Route One, PO Box 700, Yarmouth, ME 04096, United States, Publicity & Marketing: Terri Welch *Tel:* 207-846-5168 *Fax:* 207-846-5181 *E-mail:* books@interculturalpress.com (non-trade sales)
Distributor for Intercultural Press Inc (outside US)
Warehouse: The Book Service, Colchester Rd, Frating, Frating Green, Essex C07 7DW *Tel:* (01206) 256 000
Orders to: The Book Service, Colchester Rd, Frating, Frating Green, Essex C07 7DW *Tel:* (01206) 256 000
Nicholas Brealey Publishing, c/o National Book Network, 15200 NBN Way, Blue Ridge Summit, PA 17214, United States
Membership(s): IPG

Breedon Books Publishing Company Ltd+
Division of Breedon Publishing Group
Breedon House, 3 The Parker Centre, Mansfield Rd, Derby DE21 4SZ
Tel: (01332) 384235 *Fax:* (01332) 292755
E-mail: sales@breedonpublishing.co.uk
Web Site: www.breedonbooks.co.uk
Key Personnel
Chairman: Anton Rippon *E-mail:* anton@breedonpublishing.co.uk
Customer Services Manager: Beverley Rushworth *E-mail:* beverley@breedonpublishing.co.uk
Publicity Manager: Nicola J Rippon *E-mail:* nicola@breedonpublishing.co.uk
Founded: 1980
Subjects: Biography, Criminology, Genealogy, History, Sports, Athletics
ISBN Prefix(es): 0-907969; 1-873626; 1-85983
Number of titles published annually: 40 Print
Total Titles: 500 Print
Associate Companies: Soccer Publishing Inc, PO Box 1417, Princeton, NJ 08540, United States
Imprints: Breedon Sport; Breedon Heritage
Sales Office(s): Derek Searle Associates Ltd, Unit 13, Progress Business Centre, Whittle Parkway, Burnham, Berks SL1 6DQ *Tel:* (01628) 559500 *Fax:* (01628) 663876 *E-mail:* dsapublish@aol.com

Breedon Heritage, *imprint of* Breedon Books Publishing Company Ltd

Breedon Sport, *imprint of* Breedon Books Publishing Company Ltd

Breese Books Ltd+
164 Kensington Park Rd, London W11 2ER
Tel: (020) 7727 9426 *Fax:* (020) 7229 3395
Web Site: www.sherlockholmes.co.uk; www.abracadabra.co.uk
Key Personnel
Man Dir: Martin Breese *E-mail:* mbreese999@aol.com
Founded: 1985
Subjects: Fiction
ISBN Prefix(es): 0-947533
Number of titles published annually: 20 Print
Total Titles: 300 Print
Imprints: The Dreamer's Guides
Foreign Rights: Cathy Miller, Foreign Rights Agency (World)
Orders to: Clipper Distribution Services Ltd, Windmill Grove, Portchester, Hants PO16 9HT *Tel:* (01705) 200080 *Fax:* (01705) 200090
Midpoint Trade Books, NY, 27 W 20th St, Suite 1102, New York, NY 10011, United States *Tel:* 212-727-0190 *Fax:* 212-727-0195

Breslich & Foss+
20 Wells Mews, London W1T 3HQ
Tel: (020) 7580 8774 *Fax:* (020) 7580 8784
E-mail: sales@breslichfoss.com
Key Personnel
Man Dir: Paula G Breslich
Production Manager: Cathy Woodman *E-mail:* c.woodman@breslichfoss.com
Founded: 1978
Also acts as packager.
Subjects: Architecture & Interior Design, Art, Cookery, Crafts, Games, Hobbies, Gardening, Plants, Health, Nutrition, Wine & Spirits
ISBN Prefix(es): 1-85004

Brewin Books Ltd+
Doric House, 56 Alcester Rd, Studley, Warwicks B80 7LG
Tel: (01527) 854228 *Fax:* (01527) 852746
E-mail: enquiries@brewinbooks.com
Web Site: www.brewinbooks.com
Key Personnel
Dir: Alan Brewin
Founded: 1973
Subjects: Biography, Education, Fiction, Genealogy, Health, Nutrition, History, Military Science, Nonfiction (General), Regional Interests, Transportation, Travel, Publish a range of Midland Regional non-fiction titles on the regions history including hospital, health, housing, police, education, transport, local history, biographies, contemporary fiction & some military history. Distribute for several local authorities for walking guides & local history books
ISBN Prefix(es): 0-9505570; 0-947731; 1-85858
Number of titles published annually: 25 Print
Total Titles: 170 Print
Associate Companies: Supaprint (Redditch) Ltd, Enfield Estate, Unit 19, Redditch Worcs B97 6BZ, Man: Mike Abbott *Tel:* (1527) 8562212 *Fax:* (1527) 8560451 *E-mail:* mike@supaprint.com (Also warehouse)
Imprints: Alton Douglas Books
Distributor for City of Birmingham Libraries & Leisure; Hereford City Council; Rosmini House (Philosophy); Worcester County Council

Bridge Books+
61 Park Ave, Wrexham LL12 7AW
Tel: (01978) 262377 *Fax:* (01978) 358661
Key Personnel
Official Delegate, Partner: W A Williams *E-mail:* waw@bridgebooks.co.uk
Founded: 1983

Subjects: Aeronautics, Aviation, Ethnicity, Genealogy, History, Military Science, Regional Interests
ISBN Prefix(es): 1-872424; 0-9508285
Number of titles published annually: 12 Print
Associate Companies: Maelor Interactive Publishing Ltd, Wrexham
Subsidiaries: Maelor Interactive Publishing Ltd

Brilliant Publications+
One Church View, Sparrow Hall Farm, Edlesborough, Dunstable LU6 2ES
Tel: (01525) 229720 *Fax:* (01525) 229725
E-mail: sales@brilliantpublications.co.uk
Web Site: www.brilliantpublications.co.uk
Key Personnel
Publisher: Priscilla Hannaford *E-mail:* priscilla@brilliantpublications.co.uk
Founded: 1993
Subjects: Education, *Specialize in educational books for 3-13 year olds*
ISBN Prefix(es): 1-897675; 1-903893
Number of titles published annually: 20 Print
Total Titles: 100 Print
Membership(s): IPG; Publishers' Association

Brimax, *imprint of* Brimax Books

Brimax, *imprint of* Octopus Publishing Group

Brimax Books+
Division of The Octopus Publishing Group
2-4 Heron Quays, London E14 4JP
Tel: (020) 7531 8400 *Fax:* (020) 7531 8607
Web Site: www.brimax.co.uk
Pre-school publisher.
Subjects: Fiction, Nonfiction (General), Traditional board books, innovative interactive, classic stories & fairy tales, early learning, reference, new fiction
ISBN Prefix(es): 1-85854
Imprints: Brimax
Orders to: Littlehampton Book Services Ltd, Faraday Close, Durington, Worthing, West Sussex NN10 6RZ *Tel:* (01933) 828801

Britannia Press, *imprint of* East-West Publications (UK) Ltd

British Academic Press, *imprint of* I B Tauris & Co Ltd

The British Academy+
10 Carlton House Terrace, London SW1Y 5AH
Tel: (020) 7969 5200 *Fax:* (020) 7969 5300
E-mail: secretary@britac.ac.uk
Web Site: www.britac.ac.uk
Telex: 263194
Key Personnel
Publications Officer: James Rivington
Rights & Permissions: Janet English
Founded: 1902
The British Academy is a Registered Charity, No 233176.
Subjects: Archaeology, Art, History, Literature, Literary Criticism, Essays, Philosophy, Social Sciences, Sociology
ISBN Prefix(es): 0-85672; 0-902732
Orders to: OUP Distribution Services, Saxon Way West, Corby, Northamptonshire NN18 9ES
Oxbow Books, Park End Place, Oxford OX1 1HN

The British & Foreign Bible Society, see Bible Society

BAAF: Adoption & Fostering+
Skyline House, 200 Union St, London SE1 0LX
Tel: (020) 7593 2000 *Fax:* (020) 7593 2001
E-mail: mail@baaf.org.uk
Web Site: www.baaf.org.uk

UNITED KINGDOM

Key Personnel
Dir: Felicity Collier
Dir, Publications: Shaila Shah
Commissioning Editor of Adoption & Fostering (Journal): Prof Malcolm Hill
Publications Promotions Officer: Marianne Harper *Tel:* (020) 7593 2037 *E-mail:* marianne.harper@baaf.org.uk
Founded: 1980
Registered charity promoting best practice in both adoption & fostering services.
Umbrella body for all member agencies & all those working with children.
Subjects: Child Care & Development, Psychology, Psychiatry, Social Sciences, Sociology, Titles relating to adoption, fostering & childcare
ISBN Prefix(es): 0-903534; 1-873868; 0-9506807; 1-903699
Number of titles published annually: 12 Print
Total Titles: 120 Print
Imprints: BAAF: Adoption & Fostering

British Cement Association
Century House, Telford Ave, Crowthorne, Berks RG45 6YS
Tel: (01344) 762676 *Fax:* (01344) 761214
E-mail: library@bca.org.uk
Web Site: www.bca.org.uk
Key Personnel
Head of Information Service: Edwin Trout *E-mail:* etrout@bca.org.uk
Founded: 1935
Subjects: Civil Engineering, Engineering (General), Cement, Concrete
ISBN Prefix(es): 0-7210

The British Council, Design, Publishing & Print Department
10 Spring Gardens, London SW1A 2BN
Tel: (020) 7930 8466 *Fax:* (020) 7389 6347
Web Site: www.britishcouncil.org
Telex: 8952201BRICONG
Key Personnel
Head of Dept: Christine Borell
Head of Editorial: Nichola Liu
Founded: 1934
Headquarters: 10 Spring Gardens, London SW1A 2BN. Tel: (071) 9308466
Promotion abroad of a wider knowledge of Britain & the English language, development of closer cultural relations with other countries.
Among book & journal titles published or co-published are *British Book News, Media in Education Development, English Language Teaching Journal, ELT Documents, Language Teaching, British Writers, How to Live in Britain, The British Council Collection 1938-84, TV English, Video English.*
Subjects: English as a Second Language, Human Relations, Regional Interests
ISBN Prefix(es): 0-86355; 0-900229; 0-901618
U.S. Office(s): The British Council, The Cultural Attache, British Embassy, 3100 Massachusetts Ave, Washington, DC 20008, United States

British Educational Communication & Technology Agency (BECTA)
Millburn Hill Rd, Science Park, Coventry CV4 7JJ
Tel: (024) 7641 6994 *Fax:* (024) 7641 1418
E-mail: becta@becta.org.uk
Web Site: www.becta.org.uk
Key Personnel
Chief Executive: Owen Lynch
Press PR Officer: Nicola Newman
Founded: 1973
Subjects: Education, Government, Political Science, Technology
ISBN Prefix(es): 0-86184; 0-902204
Imprints: BECTA

British Film Institute, see BFI Publishing

British Horse Society
Stoneleigh Deer Park, Kenilworth, Warwicks CV8 2XZ
Tel: (08701) 202 244 *Fax:* (01926) 707 800
E-mail: enquiry@bhs.org.uk
Web Site: www.bhs.org.uk
Key Personnel
Chief Executive: Hywel Davies
ISBN Prefix(es): 0-900226
Subsidiaries: The British Horse Society Trading Company Ltd

The British Library National Bibliographic Service
Boston Spa, Wetherby, W Yorkshire LS23 7BQ
Tel: (01937) 546585 *Fax:* (01937) 546586
E-mail: nbs-info@bl.uk
Web Site: www.bl.uk
Key Personnel
Dir: Robert Smith
Founded: 1973
ISBN Prefix(es): 0-7123
Parent Company: The British Library
Orders to: Turpin Distribution Services Ltd, Blackhorse Rd, Letchworth, Herts SG6 1HN *Tel:* (01462) 672555 *Fax:* (01462) 480947

British Library Publications+
96 Euston Rd, London NW1 2DB
Tel: (020) 7412 7704 *Fax:* (020) 7412 7768
E-mail: blpublications@bl.uk
Web Site: www.bl.uk
Key Personnel
Publishing Manager: David Way *Tel:* (020) 7412 7532 *E-mail:* david.way@bl.uk
Founded: 1979
Publishing & book trade reference.
Subjects: Art, History
ISBN Prefix(es): 0-7123
Number of titles published annually: 50 Print; 3 CD-ROM
Total Titles: 600 Print; 10 CD-ROM
Parent Company: The British Library
Distributed by University of Toronto Press (Canada & USA)
Orders to: Turpin Distribution Services Ltd, Blackhorse Rd, Letchworth, Herts SG6 1HN

British Library Document Supply Centre, Publications Marketing
Boston Spa, Wetherby, W Yorks LS23 7BQ
Tel: (01937) 546060 *Fax:* (01937) 546333
Web Site: www.bl.uk
Key Personnel
Publications Officer: Dorothy Drydale *E-mail:* garth.frankland@bl.uk
Founded: 1962
ISBN Prefix(es): 0-7123; 0-9532; 0-904654
Parent Company: British Library, 96 Euston Rd, London NW1 2DB
Orders to: Turpin Distribution Services Ltd, Blackhorse Rd, Letchworth, Herts SG6 1HN *Tel:* (0146) 672555 *Fax:* (0146) 480947

British Museum Press+
46 Bloomsbury St, London WC1B 3QQ
Tel: (020) 7323 1234 *Fax:* (020) 7436 7315
Web Site: www.britishmuseum.co.uk
Telex: 28592 BMPUBS G
Key Personnel
Man Dir: Andrew Thatcher
Production: Susan Walby
Head of Sales, Marketing & Rights: Alasdair MacLeod *E-mail:* a.macleod@bmcompany.co.uk
Publicity: Penelope Vogler
Managing Editor: Teresa Francis
Founded: 1973
Subjects: Archaeology, Art, Asian Studies, Crafts, Games, Hobbies, Ethnicity
ISBN Prefix(es): 0-7141
Parent Company: The British Museum Company Limited
Bookshop(s): British Museum Shop, Great Russell St, London WC1
Orders to: Thames & Hudson Ltd, 44 Clockhouse Rd, Farnborough, Hants

British Psychological Society, see BPS Books (British Psychological Society)

British Tourist Authority
Thames Tower, Black's Rd, London W6 9EL
Tel: (020) 8846 9000 *Fax:* (020) 8846 0302
Web Site: www.visitbritain.com
Key Personnel
Chief Executive: David Quarmby
Founded: 1969
Subjects: Travel
ISBN Prefix(es): 0-7095; 0-85630
Branch Office(s)
Buenos Aires, Argentina
Sydney, Australia
Brussels, Belgium
Ontario, Canada
Zurich, Switzerland
Frankfurt, Germany
Copenhagen, Denmark
Madrid, Spain
Paris, France
Hong Kong, Hong Kong
Dublin, Ireland
Milano, Italy
Rome, Italy
Osaka, Japan
Tokyo, Japan
Seoul, Republic of Korea
Amsterdam, Netherlands
Oslo, Norway
Auckland, New Zealand
Lisbon, Poland
Singapore, Singapore
Stockholm, Sweden
Taipei, Taiwan, Province of China
Craighall, South Africa
U.S. Office(s): Chicago, IL, United States
New York, NY, United States

Bronant Books, *imprint of* Gwasg Gwenffrwd

Brooklands Books Ltd
PO Box 146, Cobham, Surrey KT11 1LG
Tel: (01932) 865051 *Fax:* (01932) 868803
E-mail: info@brooklands-books.com
Web Site: www.brooklands-books.com
Key Personnel
Man Dir: Ian Dowdeswell
Marketing Dir: Barbara Cleveland
Member of British Motor Heritage.
Subjects: Automotive, Motorcycles, Military, Racing
Number of titles published annually: 50 Print
Total Titles: 800 Print
Branch Office(s)
CarTech, 11605 Kost Dam Rd, North Branch, MN 55056, United States *Tel:* 651-583-3471 *Fax:* 651-583-2023
Distributor for Robert Bentley Inc

The Brown Reference Group PLC+
8 Chapel Pl, Rivington St, London EC2A 3DQ
Tel: (020) 7920 7500 *Fax:* (020) 7920 7501
E-mail: info@brownpartworks.co.uk
Web Site: www.brownpartworks.co.uk
Key Personnel
Marketing Dir: Sharon Hutton *Tel:* (020) 7920 7508 *E-mail:* shutton@brownpartworks.co.uk
Man Dir: Ashley Brown
Founded: 1995

Packager of books, partworks & continuity series.
Subjects: Cookery, Crafts, Games, Hobbies, History, Music, Dance, Natural History, Science (General), Social Sciences, Sociology, Military History, Popular Culture
ISBN Prefix(es): 1-84044

Brown, Son & Ferguson, Ltd
4/10 Darnley St, Glasgow G41 2SD
Tel: (0141) 4291234 *Fax:* (0141) 4201694
E-mail: enquiry@skipper.co.uk
Web Site: www.skipper.co.uk *Cable:* SKIPPER GLASGOW
Key Personnel
Chief Executive, Editorial, Production: T Nigel Brown
Sales & Publicity: David H Provan
Rights & Permissions: L Ingram-Brown
Founded: 1832
Subjects: Drama, Theater, Maritime
ISBN Prefix(es): 0-85174
Subsidiaries: James Munro & Co (at above address)

Brown Wells & Jacobs Ltd
Foresters Hall, 25-27 Westow St, London SE19 3RY
Tel: (020) 8771 5115 *Fax:* (020) 8771 9994
E-mail: postmaster@popking.demon.co.uk
Web Site: www.bwj.org
Key Personnel
Man Dir: Graham Brown *Fax:* (020) 8771 9994
Founded: 1978
Production of books.
Subjects: Nonfiction (General)
Number of titles published annually: 15 Print
Total Titles: 35 Print
Associate Companies: Book Street Ltd

Brunner-Routledge, *imprint of* Taylor & Francis Group

Bryntirion Press+
Bryntirion, Bridgend CF31 4DX
Tel: (01656) 656095 *Fax:* (01656) 656095
E-mail: press@draco.co.uk
Key Personnel
Man Editor: David Kingdon
Founded: 1955
Publish books in Welsh & English; also distribute for other publishers.
Subjects: Biblical Studies, Biography, History, Religion - Protestant, Theology
ISBN Prefix(es): 0-900898; 0-9502680; 1-85049
Total Titles: 80 Print
Parent Company: Evangelical Movement of Wales
Imprints: Evangelical Library of Wales

Buildings of England, *imprint of* Penguin Books Ltd

Buildings of England, *imprint of* The Penguin Group UK

Business Books, *imprint of* Random House UK Ltd

Business Monitor International+
179 Queen Victoria St, London EC4V 4DU
Tel: (020) 7248 0468 *Fax:* (020) 7248 0467
E-mail: subs@businessmonitor.com
Web Site: www.businessmonitor.com
Key Personnel
International Agents & Distribution Manager: Anne Wittman *Tel:* (020) 75577110
 E-mail: awittman@businessmonitor.com
Publisher: Jonathan Feroze *Tel:* (020) 75577111
 E-mail: jferoze@businessmonitor.com;
 Richard Londesborough *Tel:* (020) 75577105
 E-mail: rlondesborough@businessmonitor.com
Head of Marketing, Books: Sarah Bennett *Tel:* (020) 75577106 *E-mail:* sbennett@businessmonitor.com
Market Analysis: Terry Alexander
 E-mail: talexander@businessmonitor.com
Marketing: Peter Gaskell *E-mail:* pgaskell@businessmonitor.com
Syndication & Licensing: Andrew Leighton
 E-mail: aleighton@businessmonitor.com
Subscriptions: Joanna Miller *E-mail:* jmiller@businessmonitor.com
Consultant: Rob Anderson *E-mail:* randerson@businessmonitor.com
Technical Support: David Mulvaney
 E-mail: dmulvaney@businessmonitor.com
Macroeconomic Analysis: Matt Brooks
 E-mail: mbrooks@businessmonitor.com
Commercial Intelligence Service: Nick Jotischky
 E-mail: njotischky@businessmonitor.com
Founded: 1984
Specialize in essential news, data, analysis & forecasts on economic, business & political developments in global emerging markets countries.
Subjects: Business, Chemistry, Chemical Engineering, Developing Countries, Economics, Energy, Engineering (General), Finance, Foreign Countries, Government, Political Science, Journalism, Securities, Social Sciences, Sociology
Number of titles published annually: 35 Print; 28 CD-ROM; 68 Online
Total Titles: 35 Print; 28 CD-ROM; 68 Online
Online services available through Business Monitor International.
Associate Companies: Commercial Intelligence Service

Buster Books, *imprint of* Michael O'Mara Books Ltd

Butterworth Heinemann, *imprint of* Reed Educational & Professional Publishing

Butterworth-Heinemann Ltd+
Linacre House, Jordan Hill, Oxford OX2 8DP
Tel: (01865) 310366; 781-904-2500 (editorial & marketing) *Toll Free Tel:* 800-366-2665 (Customer Service & Sales) *Fax:* (01865) 310898; 781-904-2620 (sales); 781-904-2640 (editorial & marketing) *Toll Free Fax:* 800-446-6520 (customer service)
E-mail: collegerep@bhusa.com (academic sales); buseditors@bhusa.com (business); bhmarketing@repp.co.uk (business marketing); conventions@bhusa.com (conventions); dpeditors@bhusa.com (digital press); engeditors@bhusa.com (engineering); editors@focalpress.com (focal press); gen@bhusa.com (general sales); internetrep@bhusa.com (internet reseller sales); mededitors@bhusa.com (medical); newsneseditors@bhusa.com (newnes press); bhukorders@repp.co.uk (orders); securityeditors@bhusa.com (security); specialsales@bhusa.com (special & bulk sales); techsupport@bhusa.com; techeditors@bhusa.com (technoloby); tradesales@bhusa.com (trade (book store) sales)
Web Site: www.butterworth.heinemann.co.uk
Key Personnel
Man Dir: Philip Shaw
Sales Manager: David Burton *E-mail:* david.burton@repp.co.uk
Sales & Marketing Director: Clare Fletcher
 E-mail: clare.fletcher@repp.co.uk
International Sales Manager: Caroline Haw
 E-mail: caroline.haw@repp.co.uk
Sales Coordinator: Catherine Jackson
 E-mail: catherine.jackson@repp.co.uk
Foreign Rights Manager: Adele Parker *Fax:* 1865 314455 *E-mail:* adele.parker@repp.co.uk
Marketing Manager, Management & Professional: Jacquie Shanahan *E-mail:* jacquie.shanahan@repp.co.uk
Marketing Manager, Medical & Veterinary, Dentistry-Wright, Springhouse, Books for Midwives: Judy Chappell *E-mail:* judy.chappell@repp.co.uk
Marketing Manager, Technical, Focal Press, Newnes, Digital Press, Architectural Press, Laxton's, Brethericks: Duncan Enright
 E-mail: duncan.enright@repp.co.uk
Founded: 1991
Publisher of books, open learning material & electronic products for students & professionals in technology, medicine & business.
Subjects: Agriculture, Architecture & Interior Design, Computer Science, Electronics, Electrical Engineering, Engineering (General), Film, Video, Finance, Journalism, Management, Marketing, Medicine, Nursing, Dentistry, Photography, Physical Sciences, Technology, Travel, Veterinary Science
ISBN Prefix(es): 0-409; 0-250; 0-240; 0-7506; 1-56372; 0-433; 0-407; 0-408; 0-434; 1-55558; 0-480; 0-86729; 0-87591; 0-914236; 0-932376; 0-9626521
Parent Company: Reed Educational & Professional Publishing Ltd, Halley Court, Jordan Hill, Oxford OX2 8EJ
Ultimate Parent Company: Reed Elsevier plc, 25 Victoria Rd, London SW1H 0EX
Associate Companies: Butterworth-Heinemann Australia, 22 Salmon St, PO Box 251, Port Melbourne, Victoria 3207, Australia *Tel:* (03) 9245 7111 *Fax:* (03) 9345 7577 *E-mail:* sophie.kaliniecki@reededucation.com.au; Butterworth-Heinemann, G-2 Vardaan House, 7/28 Mahavir St, Ansari Rd, Daryaganj, New Delhi, India *Tel:* (011) 3282580 *Fax:* (011) 3282650 *E-mail:* bh_india@satym.net.in; Heinemann Reference, 39 Rawene Rd, Private Bag 34901, Birkenhead, Auckland 10, New Zealand *Tel:* (09) 480 4992 *Fax:* (09) 480 4970 *E-mail:* rjoel@reed.co.nz; Heinemann Publishers Pty Ltd, PO Box 781940, Sandton 2146, South Africa *Tel:* (011) 784 8619 *Fax:* (011) 784 8360; Butterworth-Heinemann Inc, 225 Wildwood Ave, Woburn, MA 01801, United States *Tel:* 781-904-2500 *Fax:* 781-904-2620
Orders to: Reed Book Services, Northampton Rd, Rushden, Northants NN10 6PU *Tel:* (0933) 58521 *Fax:* (0933) 50284

Butterworths Direct, *imprint of* Butterworths Tolley

Butterworths Tolley+
Halsbury House, 35 Chancery Lane, London WC2A 1EL
Tel: (020) 7400 2500; (020) 8662 2000 (customer service) *Fax:* (020) 7400 2842; (020) 8662 2012 (customer service)
E-mail: customer-services@butterworths.com
Web Site: www.butterworths.co.uk
Key Personnel
Man Dir: Paul Virik
Founded: 1818
Subjects: Accounting, Finance, Law
ISBN Prefix(es): 0-409; 0-510; 0-406; 0-85459; 0-85475; 0-7545
Number of titles published annually: 120 Print; 10 CD-ROM
Total Titles: 1,000 Print; 50 CD-ROM; 25 E-Book
Online services available through Butterworths Direct.
Parent Company: Reed Elsevier plc, 25 Victoria St, London SW1H 0EX
Associate Companies: Butterworths-Australia, Reed Elsevier Bldg, Tower 2, 475-495 Victoria Ave, Chatswood NSW 2067, Australia *Tel:* (02) 9422-2222 *Fax:* (02) 9422-2444; Butterworths-

UNITED KINGDOM

Canada, 75 Clegg Rd, Markham, ON L6G 1A1, Canada *Tel:* 905-479-2665 *Fax:* 905-479-2826; Butterworths-New Zealand, 205-207 Victoria St, Wellington, New Zealand *Tel:* (04) 385 1479 *Fax:* (04) 385 1598; Butterworths-Asia, N01 Temasek Ave, 17-01 Millenia Tower 039192, Singapore *Tel:* 336 9661 *Fax:* 336 9662; Butterworths-South Africa, 8 Walter Place, Mayville 4091 Natal, South Africa *Tel:* (031) 2683111 *Fax:* (031) 2683108
Imprints: Books on Screen; Butterworths Direct; Eclipse; Tolley
Branch Office(s)
Butterworths, 26 Upper Ormond Quay, Dublin 7, Ireland *Tel:* (03531) 873 1268 (editorial enquiries)
2, Addiscombe Rd, Croyden, Surrey CR9 5AF *Tel:* (020) 8686 9141 *Fax:* (020) 8686 3155
Butterworths LEXIS Direct, Globe House, Victoria Way, Woking, Surrey GU21 1DD *Tel:* (01483) 257725 (online publishing division)
Butterworths, 4 Hill St, Edinburgh EH2 3JZ, Dir: Philip Woods *Tel:* (0131) 225 7828 *Fax:* (0131) 220 1833 *E-mail:* sales.service@butterworths.co.uk
U.S. Office(s): Reed Elsevier Inc, 2 Park Ave, 2nd floor, New York, NY 10016, United States *Tel:* 212-448-2300 *Fax:* 212-448-2196
Bookshop(s): Butterworths Bookshop, 35 Chancery Lane, London WC2A 1EL *Tel:* (020) 7400 2868 *Fax:* (020) 7400 2870
Warehouse: Butterworths Warehouse, Unit 3, 2 Shipton Way, Express Park, Rusden, Northants NN10 6GL *Tel:* (01933) 411682 *Fax:* (01933) 411857
Orders to: Butterworths Warehouse, Unit 3, 2 Shipton Way, Express Park, Rusden, Northants NN10 6GL *Tel:* (01933) 411682 *Fax:* (01933) 411857

Bwrdd Croeso Cymru, see Wales Tourist Board

Byeway Books, *imprint of* Autumn Publishing Ltd

Bygone Kent, *imprint of* Meresborough Books

CABI Publishing
Division of CAB International
Wallingford, Oxon OX10 8DE
Tel: (01491) 832111 *Fax:* (01491) 833508
E-mail: publishing@cabi.org
Web Site: www.cabi-publishing.org
Key Personnel
Publishing Dir: Dr Philip Edge *E-mail:* p.edge@cabi.org
Book Publisher: Tim Hardwick *E-mail:* t.hardwick@cabi.org
Man Dir: Tony Llewellyn *E-mail:* t.llewellyn@cabi.org
Sales & Marketing Dir: Caroline McNamara *E-mail:* c.mcnamara@cabi.org
Commercial Dir: Mr Kelvin Tunley *E-mail:* allare@cabi.org
Contact: Sarah Harris *E-mail:* s.harris@cabi.org
Founded: 1928
A nonprofit international organization dedicated to improving human welfare worldwide through the dissemination, application & generation of scientific knowledge in support of sustainable development.
Subjects: Agricultural Economics, Engineering & Entomology, Animal Breeding, Genetics, Nutrition & Production, Biodiversity, Biological Control, Crop Production & Protection, Dairy Science, Ecology & Environment, Entomology, Forestry, Horticulture, Human Nutrition, Leisure/Tourism, Medicinal Plants, Nematology, Parasitology & Infectious Diseases, Plant Biotechnology, Breeding, Genetic & Pathology, Postharvest, Rural Development, Sugar Industry, Veterinary Medicine, Weed Science
ISBN Prefix(es): 0-85198; 0-85199
Total Titles: 300 Print; 20 CD-ROM; 1 Online; 6 E-Book
Branch Office(s)
10 E 40 St, Suite 3203, New York, NY 10016, United States, Contact: Joe Barrett *Tel:* 212-481-7018 *Fax:* 212-686-7993 *E-mail:* cabinao@cabi.org

Cadogan Guides+
Network House, One Ariel Way, London W12 7SL
Tel: (020) 8600 3550 *Fax:* (020) 8600 3599
E-mail: info@cadoganguides.com; editorial@cadoganguides.com; advertising@cadoganguides.com; publicity@cadoganguides.com; marketing@cadoganguides.com
Web Site: www.cadoganguides.com
Key Personnel
Editorial Dir: Vicki Ingle
Founded: 1985
Specialize in Travel Guides.
Subjects: Travel
ISBN Prefix(es): 0-947754; 0-946313; 1-86011
Parent Company: Morris Publications Ltd
Branch Office(s)
The Globe Pequot Press, 6 Business Park Rd, PO Box 833, Old Saybrook, CT 06475-0833, United States
Foreign Rep(s): Books for Europe (Austria, Czech Republic, France, Hungary, Poland, Switzerland); Capricorn Link (Aust) Pty Ltd (Australia); The Globe Pequot Press (Canada, US); Peter Hyde & Associates (Pty) Ltd (South Africa); Inter Media Americans (IMA) (Caribbean, South America); Nicky La Touche (Italy); Pernille Larsen (Scandinavia); Nilsson & Lamm (Holland); Sandro Salucci (Croatia, Greece, Portugal, Slovenia, Spain)
Orders to: Grantham Book Services, Isaac Newton Way, Alma Park Industrial Estate, Grantham, Lincs NG31 9SD

Calder Publications Ltd+
51 The Cut, London SE1 8LF
Tel: (020) 7633 0599
E-mail: info@calderpublications.com
Web Site: www.calderpublications.com
Key Personnel
Manager, Publishing Dir: John Calder *Tel:* (020) 76333
Production, Editorial, Design, Sales, Rights & Permissions: Toby Fenton
Founded: 1949
Publishers of international literature & books on cultural subjects.
No unsolicited manuscripts considered.
Subjects: Art, Biography, Drama, Theater, Fiction, Literature, Literary Criticism, Essays, Music, Dance, Nonfiction (General), Philosophy, Poetry
ISBN Prefix(es): 0-7145
Number of titles published annually: 30 Print
Total Titles: 400 Print; 200 Online; 200 E-Book
Online services available through Paris-anglo.com.
Parent Company: The Calder Educational Trust, 51 The Cut, London SE1 8LF, Contact: John Calder
Associate Companies: Riverrun Press, c/o Whitehurst & Clark, 100 Newfield Ave, Edison, NJ 00837, United States
Imprints: Riverrun Press
Distributed by Whitehurst & Clarke
Foreign Rep(s): Whitehurst & Clarke, Raritan Industrial (US)
Warehouse: Combined Book Services, Units 1-K Paddock, Wood Distribution Centre, Paddock Wood, Tonbridge, Kent TN12 6UU *Tel:* (01892) 837171 *Fax:* (01892) 837272 *E-mail:* orders@combook.co.uk

BOOK

Calmann & King Ltd, see Laurence King Publishing Ltd

Cambridge Scientific Abstracts, see CSA (Cambridge Scientific Abstracts)

Cambridge University Press+
The Edinburgh Bldg, Shaftesbury Rd, Cambridge CB2 2RU
Tel: (01223) 312393 *Fax:* (01223) 315052
E-mail: information@cup.cam.ac.uk; uksales@cambridge.org (sales); editorial@cambridge.org (editorial enquiries); rights@cambridge.org (rights & permission); www@cambridge.org (web services)
Web Site: www.uk.cambridge.org
Key Personnel
Chief Executive: R J Mynott
Editorial Dir: A M C Brown; C Hayes; M Y Holdsworth; S Mitton
International Dir: Nicholas Reckert
Production Dir: Christopher Hamilton-Emery
Rights Sales Manager: Christina Roberts
Permissions: Linda Nicol
Founded: 1534
Subjects: Agriculture, Anthropology, Archaeology, Architecture & Interior Design, Art, Biblical Studies, Biography, Biological Sciences, Chemistry, Chemical Engineering, Computer Science, Drama, Theater, Earth Sciences, Economics, Education, Engineering (General), English as a Second Language, Environmental Studies, Geography, Geology, Government, Political Science, History, Language Arts, Linguistics, Law, Literature, Literary Criticism, Essays, Mathematics, Medicine, Nursing, Dentistry, Music, Dance, Philosophy, Physical Sciences, Psychology, Psychiatry, Social Sciences, Sociology, Theology
Number of titles published annually: 1,600 Print; 10 CD-ROM; 50 Audio
Imprints: Canto
Branch Office(s)
Cambridge University Press, 10 Stamford Rd, Oakleigh, Victoria 3166, Australia *Tel:* (03) 9568 0322 *Fax:* (03) 9563 1517 *E-mail:* info@cambridge.edu.au *Web Site:* www.cambridge.edu.au
Cambridge University Press, Ruiz De Alarcon 13, 28014 Madrid, Spain
Cambridge University Press, 40 W 20 St, New York, NY 10011-4211, United States (US Branches)
Cambridge University Press, 1 The Moorings, Portswood Ridge, Victoria & Alfred Waterfront, Capetown 8001, South Africa
Distributor for CSLI Publications; Stanford University Press (outside North America)
Showroom(s): One & 2 Trinity St, Cambridge CB2 1SU

Camden Press Ltd+
43 Camden Passage, London N1 8EB
Tel: (020) 7226 2061 *Fax:* (020) 7226 2418
Key Personnel
Chairman: Robert Borzello
Founded: 1985
Subjects: Art, Biography, Health, Nutrition, Social Sciences, Sociology, Women's Studies
ISBN Prefix(es): 0-948491

Camden Large Print, *imprint of* BBC Audiobooks

Camerapix Publishers Intl Ltd+
6 Alston Rd, Barnet, Herts EN5 4ET
Tel: (020) 8449 5503 *Fax:* (020) 8449 8120
E-mail: camerapixuk@btinternet.com
Key Personnel
Man Dir: Mrs Rukhsana Haq
Dir: Salim Amin

Publisher of travel guides & photographic travel books.
Subjects: Travel
ISBN Prefix(es): 1-874041
Number of titles published annually: 3 Print
Total Titles: 65 Print

Cameron & Hollis+
Imprint of Cameron Books
PO Box 1, Moffat, Dumfries DG10 9SU
Tel: (01683) 220808 *Fax:* (01683) 220012
E-mail: editorial@cameronbooks.co.uk; sales@cameronbooks.co.uk (orders)
Web Site: www.cameronbooks.co.uk
Key Personnel
Dir: Ian Cameron; Jill Hollis
Founded: 1976
Primarily packagers.
Subjects: Architecture & Interior Design, Art, Environmental Studies, Film, Video, Natural History
ISBN Prefix(es): 0-906506
Associate Companies: Movie
Subsidiaries: Edition, Cameron & Hollis

Campbell Books, *imprint of* Macmillan Children's Books

Campbell Books, *imprint of* Pan Macmillan

Candle Books, *imprint of* Angus Hudson Ltd

Canongate Books Ltd+
14 High St, Edinburgh EH1 1TE
Tel: (0131) 557 5111 *Fax:* (0131) 557 5211
E-mail: salesandmark@canongate.co.uk; customerservices@canongate.co.uk
Web Site: www.canongate.net
Key Personnel
Publisher: Jamie Byng
Production Dir: Caroline Gorham
Rights Manager: Polly Hutchison *E-mail:* polly@canongate.co.uk
IT Manager: Francis Bickmore
Sales Manager: David Graham
Founded: 1973
Subjects: Art, Biography, Education, Fiction, History, Humor, Literature, Literary Criticism, Essays, Nonfiction (General), Photography, Poetry, Regional Interests, Travel
ISBN Prefix(es): 0-86241; 1-84195
Total Titles: 350 Print, 50 Audio
Imprints: Canongate Classics; Canongate Crime; Mojo Books; Payback Press (African-Black Interests); Rebel Inc
Distributed by Interlink (USA); Publishers Books West (USA)
Foreign Rights: Shirley Stewart (Western Europe); Robin Straus (Canada, US)
Orders to: Little Hampton Books Services, Faraday Close, Durrington, Worthing West Sussex BN13 3RB *Tel:* (01903) 828800 *Fax:* (01903) 828802

Canongate Academic, *imprint of* Tuckwell Press Ltd

Canongate Books "A" Ltd, *imprint of* Birlinn Ltd

Canongate Classics, *imprint of* Canongate Books Ltd

Canongate Crime, *imprint of* Canongate Books Ltd

Canterbury Press Norwich, *imprint of* Hymns Ancient & Modern Ltd

Canto, *imprint of* Cambridge University Press

Capall Bann Publishing+
Freshfields, Chieveley, Berks RG20 8TF
Tel: (01635) 247050 (sales); (1635) 248711 (editorial) *Fax:* (01635) 247050 (sales); (01635) 248711 (editorial)
E-mail: enquiries@capallbann.co.uk
Web Site: www.capallbann.co.uk
Key Personnel
Publisher: Jon Day; Julia Day
Founded: 1993
Family owned & run company.
Subjects: Alternative, Animals, Pets, Archaeology, Astrology, Occult, Education, Environmental Studies, Gardening, Plants, Maritime, Music, Dance, Mysteries, Parapsychology, Philosophy, Psychology, Psychiatry, Religion - Other, Self-Help, Women's Studies, Alternative Healing, Mind, Body & Spirit
ISBN Prefix(es): 1-898307; 1-86163
Number of titles published annually: 40 Print
Total Titles: 250 Print

Jonathan Cape, *imprint of* Random House UK Ltd

Jonathan Cape Childrens Books, *imprint of* Random House UK Ltd

Capstone Publishing Ltd+
Oxford Centre for Innovation, Mill St, Oxford OX2 0JX
Tel: (01865) 798623 *Fax:* (01865) 240941
E-mail: capstone_publishing@msn.com
Web Site: www.capstone.co.uk
Key Personnel
Dir: Mark Allin; Richard Burton
Sales & Marketing Dir: Simon Benham
  Tel: (0171) 6223082 *Fax:* (0171) 6223082
  E-mail: simonbenham@capstoneuk.fireserve.co.uk
Publishing Manager: Catherine Meyrick
Founded: 1996
Memberships: IPG.
Subjects: Business, Economics, Management
ISBN Prefix(es): 1-900961; 1-84112
Number of titles published annually: 20 Print
Total Titles: 90 Print
Distributor for Bard Press
Foreign Rights: Susie Adams (UK exclusive)
Warehouse: Marston Book Services, PO Box 269, Abingdon, Oxon OX14 4YN *Tel:* (01235) 465600 *Fax:* (01235) 465655
LPG Group, 40 Commerce Park, Milford, CT 06460, United States *Tel:* 203-878-6417 *Fax:* 203-874-2308
Orders to: Marston Book Services, PO Box 269, Abingdon, Oxon OX14 4YN *Tel:* (01235) 465600 *Fax:* (01235) 465655

Carcanet Press Ltd+
Conavon Court, 4th floor, 12-16 Blackfriars St, Manchester M3 5BQ
Tel: (0161) 834 8730 *Fax:* (0161) 832 0084
E-mail: pnr@carcanet.u-net.com
Web Site: www.carcanet.co.uk
Key Personnel
Editorial & Man Dir: Michael Schmidt
Sales: Siobhan Ginty *E-mail:* siobhan@carcanet.u-net.com
Marketing & Publicity Manager: Chris Gribble
  E-mail: chris@carcanet.u-net.com
Editorial & Production Manager: Sarah Rigby
  E-mail: sarah@carcanet.u-net.com
Financial Director: Joyce Nield *E-mail:* joyce@carcanet.u-net.com
Founded: 1969
Independent Poetry & fiction translation publisher.
Subjects: Fiction, Literature, Literary Criticism, Essays, Poetry
ISBN Prefix(es): 0-85635; 0-902145; 1-85754; 1-903039
Number of titles published annually: 45 Print
Total Titles: 700 Print
Online services available through World Wide Net.
Parent Company: Folio Holdings
Associate Companies: Folio Society
Imprints: From The Portuguese; Fyfield Books; Oxford Poets
Distributed by Littlehampton Book Services
Orders to: Paul & Co, PO Box 442, Concord, MA 01742, United States *Tel:* 508-369-3049 *Fax:* 508-369-2385

Cardiff Academic Press+
St Fagans Rd, Fairwater, Cardiff CF5 3AE
Tel: (029) 2056 03 *Fax:* (029) 2055 4909
E-mail: drakegroup@btinternet.com
Key Personnel
Man Dir: Mr R G Drake
Founded: 1979
Subjects: Biography, Education, Literature, Literary Criticism, Essays, Regional Interests, Religion - Other, Social Sciences, Sociology, Women's Studies, Welsh Studies
ISBN Prefix(es): 1-899025; 1-870495
Parent Company: Drake Group
Imprints: Plantin Publishers
Distributor for ECW Press (Canada); ILSI Press (USA); Plantin Publishers (UK); TUNS Press (Canada)

Cardinal Publishing Ltd+
59 Twyford Ave, London N2 9NR
Tel: (020) 8444 4666 *Fax:* (020) 8444 5637
Key Personnel
Man Dir: Tamar Karet *Tel:* (0171) 794-9510 *Fax:* (0171) 813-3530 *E-mail:* tamar@btinternet.com
Founded: 1998
Member of Book Packagers Association.
Subjects: Cookery, Gardening, Plants, Health, Nutrition, How-to, Natural History, Science (General)
Total Titles: 1 Print

Careers Research & Advisory Centre Ltd, see Hobsons

Careers & Occupational Information Centre (COIC)
Room W46, Moorfoot, Sheffield S1 4PQ
Tel: (0114) 259 4564 *Fax:* (0114) 259 3439
Key Personnel
Production Manager: David Baker
Founded: 1974
Subjects: Career Development
ISBN Prefix(es): 0-86110
Parent Company: Dept of Educational & Employment

Carfax Publishing, *imprint of* Taylor & Francis Group

Carfax Publishing Ltd
Imprint of Taylor & Francis Group
PO Box 25, Abingdon OX14 3UE
Tel: (01235) 401000 *Fax:* (01235) 401550
E-mail: sales@carfax.co.uk
Key Personnel
Man Editor: Ian White
Contact: Stephen Entwistle
Founded: 1973
Branch Office(s)
ITPS, Cheriton House, Northway, Andover SP10 5BE *Tel:* (01264) 342 926 *Fax:* (01264) 343 005 *E-mail:* book.orders@tandf.co.uk (European customer service operation for books)

UNITED KINGDOM

Carlton Books, *imprint of* Carlton Publishing Group

Carlton Publishing Group+
20 Mortimer St, London W1T 3JW
Tel: (020) 7612 0400 *Fax:* (020) 7612 0401
E-mail: enquires@carltonbooks.co.uk
Web Site: www.carltonbooks.co.uk
Key Personnel
Man Dir: Jonathan Goodman
Publishing Dir: Piers Murray Hill
International Sales Dir: Keith Allen-Jones
Founded: 1992
Subjects: Antiques, Architecture & Interior Design, Art, Biography, Criminology, Erotica, Fashion, Film, Video, Health, Nutrition, History, Humor, Music, Dance, Natural History, Radio, TV, Sports, Athletics, Wine & Spirits
ISBN Prefix(es): 1-85868; 1-84222
Parent Company: Carlton Communications PLC
Associate Companies: Carlton TV; Carlton International
Imprints: Andre Deutsch; Carlton Books; Granada Media; Manchester United Books

Jon Carpenter, *imprint of* Jon Carpenter Publishing

Jon Carpenter Publishing+
Alder House, Market St, Charlbury OX7 3PH
Tel: (01608) 811969 *Fax:* (016808) 811969
Key Personnel
Publisher: Jon Carpenter *E-mail:* jon@joncarpenter.co.uk
Founded: 1992
Subjects: Animals, Pets, Cookery, Developing Countries, Economics, Environmental Studies, Government, Political Science, Health, Nutrition, History, Social Sciences, Sociology, Specialize in the distribution & representative for overseas publishers
ISBN Prefix(es): 1-897766; 1-902279
Number of titles published annually: 10 Print
Total Titles: 60 Print
Imprints: Jon Carpenter; Wychwood Press
Distributed by Envirobook (Australia); I P G; New Horizons (South Africa)
Distributor for Apex Press (USA); Bootstrap Press (USA); Envirobook (Australia); International Books (Netherlands); New Society Publishers (Canada)
Shipping Address: Central Books, 99 Wallis Rd, London E9 5LN
Warehouse: Central Books, 99 Wallis Rd, London E9 5LN
Orders to: Central Books, 99 Wallis Rd, London E9 5LN

Carrick Media
1/4 Galt House, 31 Bank St, Irvine KA12 0LL
Tel: (01294) 311322 *Fax:* (01294) 311322
E-mail: enquiries@carrickmedia.demon.co.uk
Key Personnel
Proprietor: Kenneth Roy
Production Editor: Fiona McDonald *E-mail:* fm@carrickmedia.demon.co.uk
Founded: 1983
Specialize in Scotland & British media.
ISBN Prefix(es): 0-946724

Carroll & Brown, *imprint of* Metro Publishing Ltd

The Cartoon Cave+
PO Box 5257, Rutland LE15 8ZF
Tel: (01780) 460689; (01780) 460757
  Fax: (01780) 460689
Web Site: www.cartooncave.co.uk
Key Personnel
Contact: Larry Harris *E-mail:* larryh@cartooncave.co.uk

Founded: 1980 (*Larry Harris Productions Ltd*)
Publishes fiction for children between the ages of seven & fifteen.
ISBN Prefix(es): 0-9526834
Total Titles: 4 Print
Branch Office(s)
PO Box 9138, London W3 7WQ *Tel:* (020) 8740 8911
Distributed by Gardners Books

Frank Cass Publishers+
Formerly Frank Cass & Co Ltd
Crown House, 47 Chase Side, London N14 5BP
Tel: (020) 8920 2100 *Fax:* (020) 8447 8548
E-mail: info@frankcass.com
Web Site: www.frankcass.com
Key Personnel
Man Dir: Frank Cass
Editorial: Andrew Humphreys
Production: Mike Moran
Publicity Books: Eliza Dunlop
Publicity, Journals: Anne Kidson
Trade Manager: Joanna Legg
Rights & Permissions: Amna Whiston
Founded: 1957
Publisher of social science & humanities journals, monographs & edited collections.
Subjects: Developing Countries, Economics, History, Law, Literature, Literary Criticism, Essays, Military Science, British & International History, International Relations, Military Science & Development Studies, Politics, Sports Studies
ISBN Prefix(es): 0-7146
Associate Companies: Irish Academic Press
Subsidiaries: The Woburn Press; Vallentine, Mitchell & Co Ltd; The Littman Library of Jewish Civilization
U.S. Office(s): ISBS, 5824 NE Hassalo St, Portland, OR 97213-3644, United States *Fax:* 503-280-8832 *E-mail:* cass@isbs.com (North America)
Warehouse: Biblios Distribution, Star Rd, Partridge Green, West Sussex RH13 8LD *Tel:* (0403) 710971 *Fax:* (0403) 711143
Orders to: Plymbridge Distributors Ltd, Estover Rd, Plymouth PL6 7PY *Tel:* (01752) 202301 *Fax:* (01752) 202331 *E-mail:* orders@plymbridge.com
ISBS, 5824 NE Hassalo St, Portland, OR 97213-3644, United States *Fax:* 503-280-8832 *E-mail:* orders@isbs.com (North America)

Frank Cass & Co Ltd, see Frank Cass Publishers

Cassell & Co+
Wellington House, 125 Strand, London WC2R 0BB
Tel: (020) 7420 5555 *Fax:* (020) 7240 7261; (020) 7240 8531
Telex: 9413701
Key Personnel
Chairman & Chief Executive: Philip Sturrock
Imprint Dir, Arms & Armour Press, Blandford, Ward Lock & Cassell: Alison Goff
Imprint Dir, Cassell Academic & Contemporary Studies: Janet Joyce
Imprint Dir, Victor Gollancz: Jane Blackstock
Imprint Dir, Religious & Professional: Ruth McCurry
UK Trade Sales, Cassell: Finbarr McCabe
UK Trade Sales, Gollancz: Adrienne Maguire
UK Trade Sales, Academic: Georgian Brindley
Sales & Marketing Dir, Academic Division: Anne Godfrey
International Sales, General: Michael Goff
International Sales, Academic: Becca Seymour
Rights & Permissions, Gollancz: Jane Blackstock
Founded: 1848
Overseas Representation: Australia: New Holland Publishers Pty Ltd, NSW Australia; Canada: Books Inc, North Vancouver, Canada; Caribbean: HRA, London, UK; Central Europe: European Marketing Services, London, UK; Southern Europe: Penny Padovani, London, UK; Hong Kong, China, Korea, Taiwan: APS Ltd, Hong Kong; Hungary, Czech Republic, Slovakia, Croatia: CLB Marketing Services, Kecskemet, Hungary; India: Maya Publishers PVT Ltd, New Delhi, India; Japan: Ashton International Marketing Services, UK; Malaysia: APD Kuala Lumpur, Selangor Darul Ehsan, Malaysia; Middle East: Aston International Marketing Services, UK; Netherlands: Nilsson & Lamm, Netherlands; New Zealand: David Bateman, Auckland, New Zealand; Pakistan: Mackwin & Co, Karachi, Pakistan; Poland, Russia, Romania, Baltic States, Former USSR, Bulgaria: Bianca Katris, IMA, Greece; Singapore, Indonesia, Thailand: APD Singapore Ltd, Singapore; Scandinavia: PKB, Glostrup, Denmark; South America: HRA, London, UK; South Africa: Struik Book Distributors, Cape Town, South Africa; USA: Sterling Publishing Co Inc, New York, USA.
Subjects: Accounting, Advertising, Architecture & Interior Design, Art, Biblical Studies, Biography, Business, Career Development, Cookery, Crafts, Games, Hobbies, Developing Countries, Education, Environmental Studies, Fiction, Film, Video, Gardening, Plants, Gay & Lesbian, Geography, Geology, History, House & Home, How-to, Humor, Labor, Industrial Relations, Library & Information Sciences, Management, Marketing, Military Science, Music, Dance, Natural History, Nonfiction (General), Outdoor Recreation, Photography, Poetry, Publishing & Book Trade Reference, Religion - Catholic, Religion - Protestant, Science (General), Science Fiction, Fantasy, Social Sciences, Sociology, Sports, Athletics, Theology
ISBN Prefix(es): 0-7137; 0-7063; 0-289; 1-85409; 1-85079; 0-575; 0-85493; 0-86187
Parent Company: Hachette Livre
Associate Companies: Sterling Publishing, 387 Park Ave S, New York, NY 10016-8810, United States *Tel:* 212-532-7160 *Fax:* 212-213-2495
Imprints: Arms and Armour Press; Blandford; Geoffrey Chapman; Leicester University Press; Mansell; Mowbray; New Orchard Editions; Pinter, Studio Vista; Tycooly; Victor Gollancz; Ward Lock; Wisley Handbooks; Witherby
Subsidiaries: Arms & Armour Press; Blandford Press; Geoffrey Chapman; Ward Lock Ltd; Mowbray; New Orchard Editions; Studio Vista; Victor Gollancz; Mansell; Pinter; Leicester University Press
Distributed by Sterling Publishing (USA & Canada only)
Orders to: Cassell, Stanley House, 3 Fleets Lane, Poole, Dorset BH15 3AJ *Tel:* (0202) 670581 *Fax:* (0202) 666219
Sterling Publishing, 387 Park Ave S, New York, NY 10016-8810, United States *Tel:* 212-532-7160 *Fax:* 212-213-2495

Cassell Illustrated, *imprint of* Octopus Publishing Group

Castle House Publications Ltd
Quint House, Nevill Ridge, Nevill Park, Tunbridge Wells, Kent TN4 8NN
Tel: (01892) 539606 *Fax:* (01892) 517773; (01892) 517005
E-mail: enquiries@castlehouse.co.uk
Web Site: www.castlehouse.co.uk
Key Personnel
Man Dir: Donald Reinders
Production Editor: Jo Lethaby
Founded: 1973
Specializes In: Medicine.
Also run medical conferences.
Divisions: Castle House Medical Conferences

PUBLISHERS

Castlemead Publications+
Raynham House, Broadmeads, Ware, Herts SG12 9HY
Tel: (01920) 465525 *Fax:* (01920) 465545
E-mail: sales@castlemeadpublications.fsnet.co.uk
Web Site: www.castlemeadpublications.fsnet.co.uk
Key Personnel
Proprietor: Susan D M Lee
Founded: 1982
Publisher of pediatric growth charts.
Member of Publishers Association.
Subjects: Aeronautics, Aviation, Child Care & Development, Medicine, Nursing, Dentistry, Natural History, Regional Interests, Transportation
ISBN Prefix(es): 0-948555

Kyle Cathie Ltd+
122 Arlington Rd, London NW1 7HP
Tel: (020) 7692 7215 *Fax:* (020) 7692 7260
E-mail: general.enquiries@kyle-cathie.com
Web Site: www.kylecathie.co.uk
Key Personnel
Man Dir: Kyle Cathie *E-mail:* kcathie@aol.com
Editor: Caroline Taggart
Sales & Marketing Dir: Julia Barder
Founded: 1990
Subjects: Biography, Cookery, Gardening, Plants, Health, Nutrition, History, Natural History, Philosophy, Lifestyle, Health & Beauty, Mind, Body & Spirit
ISBN Prefix(es): 1-85626
Total Titles: 25 Print
Distributed by Simon & Schuster (Australia); Whitecap (Canada); Reed (New Zealand); Wild Dog (South America)
Orders to: Littlehampton Book Services Ltd, 14 Eldon Way, Lineside Estate, Littlehampton, West Sussex BN17 7HE

Catholic Institute for International Relations+
Cannonbury Yard, Unit 3, 190a New North Rd, London N1 7BJ
Tel: (020) 7354 0883 *Fax:* (020) 7359 0017
E-mail: ciir@ciir.org
Web Site: www.ciir.org
Key Personnel
Executive Dir: Christine Allen *E-mail:* christine@ciir.org
Production Editor: Adam Bradbury *E-mail:* adam@ciir.org
Press & Information Coordinator: Fiona Sinclair *E-mail:* fiona@ciir.org
Founded: 1940
Also acts as development agency.
Subjects: Developing Countries, Economics, Government, Political Science, Theology
ISBN Prefix(es): 0-904393; 0-946848; 1-85287
Orders to: Central Books, 99 Wallis Rd, London E9 5LN

Caucasus World, *imprint of* Routledge Curzon

Causeway Press Ltd+
129 New Court Way, Ormskirk, Lancs L39 5HP
Mailing Address: PO Box 13, Ormskirk, Lancs L39 5HP
Tel: (01695) 576048; (01695) 577360
Fax: (01695) 570714
E-mail: davidalcorn.causeypress@btinternet.com
Key Personnel
Editorial, Publicity, Rights & Permissions, Sales & Production: Michael Haralambos
Company Secretary: David Gray
Founded: 1982
Subjects: Business, Economics, Geography, Geology, Government, Political Science, Health, Nutrition, History, Mathematics, Psychology, Psychiatry, Social Sciences, Sociology, Technology

ISBN Prefix(es): 0-946183; 1-873929; 1-902796
Warehouse: The Trade Counter, Mendlesham, Suffolk IP14 5NA

Cavalcade Story Cassettes, *imprint of* BBC Audiobooks

Paul Cave Publications Ltd
74 Bedford Pl, Southampton SO15 2DF
Tel: (01703) 223591; (01703) 333457
Fax: (01703) 227190
E-mail: lanksmag@zone.co.uk
Key Personnel
Chairman & Editor: Paul Cave
Dir: Joan Cave
Founded: 1960
Member of Periodical Publishers Association.
Subjects: Regional Interests
ISBN Prefix(es): 0-86146; 0-9501735

Marshall Cavendish Partworks Ltd+
Member of Times Publishing Group
PO Box 1, Hastings, East Sussex TN35 4TJ
Tel: (01424) 756 565 *Fax:* (01424) 755 519
E-mail: enquiries@woodgt.co.uk
Web Site: www.marshallcavendish.co.uk
Telex: 23880 *Cable:* MARCAV LONDON W1
Key Personnel
Acting Chief Executive: John Armour
Circulation Manager: Christopher Jenner
Subjects: Antiques, Art, Astrology, Occult, Cookery, Crafts, Games, Hobbies, Gardening, Plants, Health, Nutrition
Associate Companies: ALP SNC, France; Marshall Cavendish Corporation, United States
Orders to: Circulation Department, 119 Wardour St, London W1V 3TD

Cavendish Publishing Ltd+
The Glass House, Wharton St, London WC1X 9PX
Tel: (020) 7278 8000 *Fax:* (020) 7278 8080
E-mail: info@cavendishpublishing.com
Web Site: www.cavendishpublishing.com
Key Personnel
Man Dir: Mr Sonny Leong *E-mail:* sonnyleong@cavendishpublishing.com
Man Editor: Ms Cara Annett *E-mail:* caraannett@cavendishpublishing.com
Editor: Jon Lloyd *E-mail:* johnlloyd@cavendishpublishing.com; Ruth Massey *E-mail:* ruthmassey@cavendishpublishing.com
Commissioning Editor: Beverley Brown *E-mail:* beverleybrown@cavendishpublishing.com
Brand & Product Manager: Cathy Thornhill *E-mail:* cathythornhill@cavendishpublishing.com
Founded: 1990
Member of Publishers Association of Great Britain.
Subjects: Criminology, Law, Medicine, Nursing, Dentistry, Securities, Social Sciences, Sociology
ISBN Prefix(es): 1-874241; 1-85941; 1-876213
Number of titles published annually: 100 Print
Total Titles: 500 Print
Subsidiaries: Cavendish Publishing (Australia) Pty Limited

Caxton Publishing Group Ltd, *imprint of* Verulam Publishing Ltd

CBD Research Ltd+
Chancery House, 15 Wickham Rd, Beckenham, Kent BR3 5JS
Tel: (020) 8650 7745 *Fax:* (020) 8650 0768
E-mail: cbd@cbdresearch.com
Web Site: www.cbdresearch.com
Key Personnel
Dir: Mrs S P Henderson

UNITED KINGDOM

Dir & Chmn: G P Henderson
Dir: A J Henderson
Founded: 1961
Subject Specialties: Associations, Directories & Official UN Organizations.
Member of Directory Publishers Association, European Association of Directory Publishers & Independent Publishers Group.
ISBN Prefix(es): 0-900246
Total Titles: 16 Print; 2 CD-ROM; 1 E-Book
Subsidiaries: Chancery House Press

CCH Editions Ltd+
Telford Rd, Bicester, Oxon OX6 0XD
Tel: (01869) 253300 *Fax:* (01869) 874700
E-mail: customer.services@cch.co.uk
Key Personnel
Man Dir: Hans Staal
Founded: 1982
Subjects: Business, Law
ISBN Prefix(es): 0-86325
Parent Company: Commerce Clearing House Inc, PO Box 5490, Chicago, IL 60680-5490, United States

Centaur Books, *imprint of* Old Vicarage Publications

Centaur Press (1954)
51 Achilles Rd, London NW6 1DZ
Tel: (020) 7431 4391 *Fax:* (020) 7431 5129
E-mail: books@opengatepress.co.uk
Web Site: www.opengatepress.co.uk
Key Personnel
Man Dir: T J L Wynne-Tyson
Founded: 1954
Linden Press at the above address has no connection with the Simon & Schuster imprint of the same name.
Subjects: Education, Environmental Studies
ISBN Prefix(es): 0-900000; 0-900001
Parent Company: Open Gate Press
Subsidiaries: The Linden Press
Bookshop(s): Keele's, Fontwell, Arundel, West Sussex BN18 0TA

Center for Advanced Welsh & Celtic Studies
National Library of Wales, Aberystwyth, Ceredigion SY23 3HH
Tel: (01970) 626717 *Fax:* (01970) 627066
E-mail: cawcs@wales.ac.uk
Web Site: www.aber.ac.uk/~awcwww/s/cyflwyniad.html
Key Personnel
Dir: Geraint H Jenkins *E-mail:* gcj@aber.ac.uk
Editorial Officer: Glenys Howells *E-mail:* glh@aber.ac.uk
Founded: 1985
Specialize in academic & celtic.
Parent Company: University of Wales

Centre for Alternative Technology+
Machynlleth, Powys SY20 9AZ
Tel: (01654) 705980; (01654) 705959 (mail order); (01654) 705993 (CAT shop) *Fax:* (01654) 702782; (01654) 705999 (mail order); (01654) 703605 (education & courses)
E-mail: pubs@cat.org.uk
Web Site: www.cat.org.uk
Key Personnel
Publisher: Caroline Oakley
Marketing Manager: Allan Shepherd
Production Manager: Graham Preston
Founded: 1974
Publisher of DIY Titles for environmentalists
Registered charity.
Subjects: Energy, Gardening, Plants, Nonfiction (General), Technology, Sustainable Lifestyles
Number of titles published annually: 4 Print
Online services available through World Wide Web.
Distributed by New Society Publishers (USA & Canada)

UNITED KINGDOM BOOK

Foreign Rep(s): New Society Publishers (Canada, US)
Shipping Address: CAT Mail Order *Tel:* (01654) 705959 *Fax:* (01654) 705999 *E-mail:* mail.order@cat.org.uk (24-hour mail order)

Centre for Information on Language Teaching & Research (CILT)+
20 Bedfordbury, London WC2N 4LB
Tel: (20) 7379 5101; (020) 7379 5110 (resources library & information services) *Fax:* (020) 7379 5082
E-mail: publications@cilt.org.uk; library@cilt.org.uk (library information)
Web Site: www.cilt.org.uk
Key Personnel
Dir: Dr Lid King
Head of Publishing: Emma Rees
Founded: 1966
Member of Publishers Association.
Subjects: Education, Language Arts, Linguistics
ISBN Prefix(es): 0-948003; 0-903466; 1-874016; 0-9500528; 1-902031
Number of titles published annually: 25 Print; 4 Audio
Total Titles: 100 Print; 8 Audio
Orders to: Central Books Ltd, 99 Wallis Rd, London E9 5LN *Tel:* (020) 8986 4854 *Fax:* (020) 8533 5821 *E-mail:* mo@centralbooks.com

Century, *imprint of* Random House UK Ltd

Chadwyck-Healey Ltd+
The Quorum, Barnwell Rd, Cambridge CB5 8SW
Tel: (01223) 215512 *Fax:* (01223) 215513
E-mail: mail@chadwyck.co.uk
Web Site: www.chadwyck.co.uk
Key Personnel
Vice President & General Manager: Steven Hall
Dir: Julie Carol Davis; Steve Sidaway
Group Promotions Manager: Nick Sinclair
Founded: 1973
Specialize in electronic publishing.
Subjects: Art, Drama, Theater, Economics, Film, Video, History, Literature, Literary Criticism, Essays, Music, Dance, Radio, TV, Science (General), Social Sciences, Sociology, Humanities
ISBN Prefix(es): 0-85964
Parent Company: Bell & Howell Information & Learning

Chambers Harrap Publishers Ltd
Subsidiary of Vivendi Universal Publishing
7 Hopetoun Crescent, Edinburgh EH7 4AY
Tel: (0131) 5565929 *Fax:* (0131) 5565313
E-mail: admin@chambersharrap.co.uk; webmanager@chambersharrap.co.uk
Web Site: www.chambersharrap.co.uk
Telex: 727967 Words G
Key Personnel
Man Dir: Maurice Shepherd
Publishing Manager: Patrick White
E-mail: pwhite@chambersharrap.co.uk
International Sales: Melissa Johnson
Marketing Manager: Jeanie Scott
Reference publisher.
ISBN Prefix(es): 0-550; 0-245
Number of titles published annually: 20 Print
Branch Office(s)
283-288 High Holborn, London, Marketing Dir: Robert Pearce *Tel:* (020) 7903 9999 *Fax:* (020) 7242 5009 *E-mail:* sales@kingfisherpub.com (UK sales head office)
Distributed by David Bateman Ltd (New Zealand); Bohemian Ventures (Czech Republic); Bordas Diffusion (France & French speaking countries); Ediciones Larousse SA (Mexico & Latin America); Gemcraft Books (Australia); Houghton Mifflin (US & English-speaking Canada); Inter Logos s.r.l. (Italy); Larousse-Bordas (France, Switzerland, Belgium & French-speaking Canada); Livraria Martins (Brazil); The Macmillan Press (United Kingdom); Paramount Books (PVT) Ltd (Pakistan); Readwide Bookshop Ltd (Ghana); Slovak Ventures (Slovakia); Spes SA (Spain); Times Media Private (Singapore, Malaysia & Brunai)
Orders to: The Macmillan Press, Brunel Rd, Houndmills, Basingstoke, Hants RG21 6XS *Tel:* (01256) 329242 *Fax:* (01256) 812521

Chameleon, *imprint of* Andre Deutsch Ltd

Chameleons Dramascripts, *imprint of* Ian Henry Publications Ltd

Chancellor Publications
32 Hatton Garden, 1st floor, London EC1N 8DL
Tel: (020) 7269 9150 *Fax:* (020) 7269 9151
E-mail: mail@chancellorpublication.com
Web Site: www.chancellorpublication.com
Key Personnel
Man Dir: Jonathan Bloch *E-mail:* jbloch@globalnet.co.uk
Founded: 1994
Supplier of legal & financial texts for practitioners & laymen.
Subjects: Law
ISBN Prefix(es): 1-899217
Total Titles: 5 Print
U.S. Office(s): ISBS Inc, 5804 NE Hassalo St, Portland, OR 97213-3644, United States *Fax:* 503-280-8832 *E-mail:* rod@isbs.com *Web Site:* www.isbs.com
Membership(s): IPG

Chancerel International Publishers Ltd+
120 Long Acre, London WC2E 9ST
Tel: (020) 7240 2811 *Fax:* (020) 7836 4186
E-mail: chancerel@chancerel.com
Web Site: www.chancerel.com
Key Personnel
Man Dir: W D B Prowse
Founded: 1976
Specialize in language teaching materials: English (British & American), German, French, Spanish, Italian & Japanese.
Subjects: Education, Language Arts, Linguistics
ISBN Prefix(es): 0-905703; 1-899888

Channel 4 Books, *imprint of* Pan Macmillan

Channel View Publications, *imprint of* Multilingual Matters Ltd

Chapman
4 Broughton Pl, Edinburgh EH1 3RX
Tel: (0131) 5572207 *Fax:* (0131) 5569565
E-mail: admin@chapman-pub.co.uk
Web Site: www.chapman-pub.co.uk
Key Personnel
Editor: Joy Hendry *E-mail:* editor@chapman.co.uk
Founded: 1970
Specialize in Scottish culture generally. Publish & develop Scottish literature in particular, also international writing. Quarterly magazine devoted to Scottish literature & arts. Features mainly poetry & plays.
Subjects: Drama, Theater, Literature, Literary Criticism, Essays, Poetry, Women's Studies
ISBN Prefix(es): 0-906772
Number of titles published annually: 4 Print
Total Titles: 60 Print; 1 Online; 1 E-Book

Geoffrey Chapman, *imprint of* Cassell & Co

Geoffrey Chapman, *imprint of* The Continuum International Publishing Group Ltd

Paul Chapman Publishing, *imprint of* Sage Publications Ltd

Chapter Two
Fountain House, Conduit Mews, London SE18 7AP
Tel: (020) 8316 5389 *Fax:* (020) 8854 5963
E-mail: chapter2UK@aol.com
Web Site: www.chaptertwo.org.uk
Key Personnel
Dir: Edwin N Cross
Founded: 1976
Publisher & bookseller.
Specialize in Plymouth Brethren Literature & their history.
Subjects: Language Arts, Linguistics, Religion - Protestant, Theology
ISBN Prefix(es): 1-85307; 0-947588
Number of titles published annually: 20 Print
Total Titles: 190 Print
Imprints: Bible Distributors
Branch Office(s)
Believers Bookshelf, PO Box 261, Sunbury, PA 17801, United States *Tel:* 717-672-2134 *E-mail:* deliver@mail.csrlink.net *Web Site:* www.usbusiness.com.bbs
Distributed by Believers Bookshelf of Canada
Distributor for Believers Bookshelf of Canada
Bookshop(s): 199 Plumstead Common Rd, London SE18 2UJ *Tel:* (020) 83164972

Deborah Charles Publications+
173 Mather Ave, Liverpool L18 6JZ
Tel: (0151) 724 2500 *Fax:* (0151) 729 0371
E-mail: dcp@legaltheory.demon.co.uk
Web Site: www.legaltheory.demon.co.uk
Key Personnel
Prof: B S Jackson
Founded: 1988
Subjects: Law, Philosophy, Social Sciences, Sociology, Legal Theory
ISBN Prefix(es): 0-9513793; 0-9528938

Charnwood Library Series, see Ulverscroft Large Print Books Ltd

Chartered Institute of Bankers (CIB) Publications, *imprint of* Financial World Publishing

The Chartered Institute of Building
Englemere, Kings Ride, Ascot, Berks SL5 7TB
Tel: (01344) 630700 *Fax:* (01344) 630777
E-mail: reception@ciob.org.uk
Web Site: www.ciob.org.uk
Key Personnel
Chief Executive: Keith Banbury
Editorial, Production, Rights & Permissions: David Petori
Bookshop: Sally Marsh *E-mail:* smarsh@englemer.co.uk
Librarian: Katherine Bowyer
Subjects: Architecture & Interior Design, Environmental Studies, Law, Management, Regional Interests
ISBN Prefix(es): 0-906600; 1-85380; 0-901822
Associate Companies: American Institute of Constructors

Chartered Institute of Library & Information Professionals in Scotland
Formerly Scottish Library Association
Scottish Centre for Information & Library Services, One John St, Hamilton ML3 7EU
Tel: (01698) 458888 *Fax:* (01698) 458899
E-mail: sla@slainte.org.uk
Web Site: www.slainte.org.uk
Key Personnel
Publications Officer: Alan Reid *Tel:* (0131) 271 3970 *Fax:* (0131) 440 4635 *E-mail:* alan.reid@midlothian.gov.uk
Founded: 1908

PUBLISHERS UNITED KINGDOM

Member of Scottish Publishers Association.
Subjects: History, Library & Information Sciences, Regional Interests
ISBN Prefix(es): 0-900649
Number of titles published annually: 3 Print
Total Titles: 12 Print
Orders to: Scottish Book Source, The Scottish Book Centre, 137 Dundee St, Edinburgh EH11 1BG *Tel:* (0131) 2296800 *Fax:* (0131) 2299070 *E-mail:* info@booksource.net *Web Site:* www.booksource.net

Chartered Institute of Personnel & Development+
CIPD House, Camp Rd, London SW19 4UX
Tel: (020) 8971 9000 *Fax:* (020) 8263 3333
E-mail: publish@cipd.co.uk
Web Site: www.cipd.co.uk
Key Personnel
Head of Publishing: Judith Dennett
Sales & Marketing Manager: Beryll Camplin
Founded: 1913
Specialize in books & reports covering the whole range of training, personnel & development issues, from practical guides & texts for students to books on best practice & strategic issues.
Subjects: Business, Human Relations, Management
ISBN Prefix(es): 0-85292
Number of titles published annually: 35 Print
Warehouse: CIPD Distribution, Plymbridge Distributors Ltd, Estove, Plymouth PL6 7PZ
Orders to: CIPD Distribution c/o Plymbridge Distributors Ltd, Estover, Plymouth PL6 7PZ

Chatham Publishing+
99 High St, Rochester, Kent ME1 1LX
Tel: (01634) 810760 *Fax:* (01634) 810761
Web Site: www.chathampublishing.com
Key Personnel
Editorial Dir: Julian Mannering *E-mail:* julian@chathampublishing.co.uk
Publisher: Robert Gardiner *E-mail:* robert@chathampublishing.co.uk
Founded: 1996
Small publishing house concerned principally with maritime history and narrative history.
Subjects: Maritime, Nonfiction (General), Nautical Archaeology, Naval or Mercantile History & Biography, Ship Modelling
ISBN Prefix(es): 1-86176
Number of titles published annually: 30 Print
Total Titles: 150 Print
Parent Company: Trident Publishing Ltd
Distributed by Grantham Book Services

Chatham House, see Royal Institute of International Affairs

Chatham House Papers, *imprint of* Royal Institute of International Affairs

Chatham Publishing, *imprint of* Gerald Duckworth & Co Ltd

Chatto & Windus/The Hogarth Press, *imprint of* Random House UK Ltd

The Chemical Society, see The Royal Society of Chemistry

Cherrytree, *imprint of* Evans Brothers Ltd

Cherrytree Books+
2A Portman Mansions, Chiltern St, London W1U 6NR
Tel: (020) 7487 0920 *Fax:* (020) 7487 0921
E-mail: sales@evansbrothers.co.uk
Web Site: www.evansbooks.co.uk
Key Personnel
Man Dir: Julian Batson
Rights Manager: Britta Martins
Publisher: Angela Sheehan
Production Dir: Lesley Barnes
Founded: 1988
Publish illustrated information books for children ages 5-15 years, mainly for the school library.
ISBN Prefix(es): 0-7451; 0-7540
Parent Company: The Gieves Group PLC, One Savile Row, London W1X 2JR
Associate Companies: Chivers Press Ltd; Evans Brothers Ltd; Zero to Ten Ltd
U.S. Office(s): Chivers North America Inc, One Lafayette Rd, Hampton, NH 03842, United States

Cherrytree Books, *imprint of* AS Publishing

Child's Play (International) Ltd+
Ashworth Rd, Bridgemead, Swindon, Wilts SN5 7YD
Tel: (01793) 616286 *Fax:* (01793) 512795
E-mail: allday@childs-play.com
Web Site: www.childs-play.com
Key Personnel
Chairman: Michael Twinn
UK Sales: Paul Gerrish
Publicity: Libby New
Editor: Sue Baker *Tel:* (01793) 616286
 E-mail: sue@childs-play.com
Education Officer: Imogen Cooper
Chief Executive Officer (Sales & Marketing): Richard Searle-Barnes *Tel:* (01793) 616286
 E-mail: richard@childs-play.com
Founded: 1972
Specialize in Early Years Education.
Member of BTHMA & IPG.
ISBN Prefix(es): 0-85953
Total Titles: 400 Print; 7 Audio
Subsidiaries: Childs Play Australia
U.S. Office(s): Childs Play USA, 67 Minot Ave, Auburn, ME 04210, United States, Contact: Ms Laurie Reynolds *Tel:* 207-784-7252 *Fax:* 207-784-7358 *E-mail:* cmpmaine@aol.com

Child's World Education Ltd
PO Box 1881, Gerrards Cross, Bucks SL9 9AN
Tel: (01753) 647060 *Fax:* (01753) 645522
Key Personnel
Contact: Susan Daughtrey
Subjects: Education
ISBN Prefix(es): 1-898696

Chivers Children's Audio Books, *imprint of* BBC Audiobooks

Chivers Large Print, *imprint of* BBC Audiobooks

Chivers Press Ltd, see BBC Audiobooks

Chorion IP+
Vernon House, 40 Shaftesbury Ave, London W1D 7ER
Tel: (020) 7434 1880 *Fax:* (020) 7434 1882
E-mail: info@enidblyton.co.uk
Web Site: www.chorion-ip.com
Founded: 1998
Crime novels.
Subjects: Fiction, Film, Video, Finance
Ultimate Parent Company: Chorion PLC

Chough Series (Educational Packs), *imprint of* Lodenek Press

Christian Education+
Formerly National Christian Education Council
1020 Bristol Rd, Selly Oak, Birmingham B29 6LB
Tel: (0121) 4724242 *Fax:* (0121) 4727575
E-mail: enquiries@christianeducation.org.uk
 (general enquiries & membership)
Web Site: www.christianeducation.org.uk/cep/cep_about.htm
Key Personnel
Dir: Peter Fishpool *E-mail:* director@christianeducation.org.uk
Senior Editor: Elizabeth Bruce *E-mail:* editorial@christianeducation.org.uk
Marketing: Lynette Adjei *E-mail:* marketing@christianeducation.org.uk
Orders: Robert Griffiths *E-mail:* sales@christianeducation.org.uk; Heidi Staaf *E-mail:* orders@christianeducation.org.uk
Founded: 1809
Subjects: Biblical Studies, Crafts, Games, Hobbies, Drama, Theater, Education, Religion - Protestant
ISBN Prefix(es): 0-7197; 0-85213
Imprints: Hillside
Subsidiaries: International Bible Reading Association
Bookshop(s): NCEL Bookroom, 1020 Bristol Rd, Selly Oak, Birmingham B29 6LB

Christian Education Movement, see Christian Education

Christian Focus, *imprint of* Christian Focus Publications Ltd

Christian Focus Publications Ltd+
Geanies House, Fearn, Tain, Ross-shire IV20 1TW
Tel: (01862) 871 011 *Fax:* (01862) 871 699
E-mail: info@christianfocus.com
Web Site: www.christianfocus.com
Key Personnel
Man Dir: William Mackenzie
 E-mail: whmmackenzie@christianfocus.com
General Manager: Ian Thompson *Tel:* (01862) 871 022 *E-mail:* ian.thompson@christianfocus.com
Production Manager: Jonathan Dunbar
 E-mail: jdunbar@christianfocus.com
Editorial Manager: Willie Mackenzie
 E-mail: Willie.Mackenzie@christianfocus.com
Children's Editor: Catherine Mackenzie
 E-mail: cmackenzie@christianfocus.com
Founded: 1979
Evangelical publisher.
Member of Christian Booksellers Association & Evangelical Christian Publishing Association.
Subjects: Fiction, Religion - Protestant, Theology
ISBN Prefix(es): 0-906731; 1-871676; 1-85792
Number of titles published annually: 90 Print
Total Titles: 800 Print; 1 CD-ROM; 1 Audio
Parent Company: Balintore Holdings PLC
Imprints: Mentor; Christian Focus; Christian Heritage
U.S. Office(s): Riverside, 636 South Oak, Iowa Falls, IA 50126, United States *Fax:* 515-648-5106 *E-mail:* maureenr@riversidedistributors.com
Foreign Rep(s): Cook Communications Ministries (Canada); Family Reading (Australia); Publishers International Marketing (Asia); Struik Christian Books (Southern Africa); SU (New Zealand)

Christian Heritage, *imprint of* Christian Focus Publications Ltd

The Chrysalis Press+
7 Lower Ladyes Hills, Kenilworth, Warwicks CV8 2GN
Tel: (01926) 855223 *Fax:* (01926) 748202
E-mail: chrysalis@which.net
Key Personnel
Man Dir: Brian Boyd
Founded: 1992

Subjects: Biography, Fiction, Literature, Literary Criticism, Essays
ISBN Prefix(es): 1-897765

Church House Publishing+
31 Great Smith St, London SW1P 3BN
Tel: (020) 7898 1306 *Fax:* (020) 7898 1305
E-mail: publishing@c-of-e.org.uk
Web Site: www.chpublishing.co.uk
Key Personnel
Publishing Manager: Alan Mitchell *Tel:* (020) 78981450 *E-mail:* alan.mitchell@c-of-e.org.uk
Production Manager: Katharine Allenby *Tel:* (020) 78981452 *E-mail:* katharine.allenby@c-of-e.org.uk
Sales & Marketing Manager: Matthew Tickle *Tel:* (020) 78981454 *E-mail:* matthew.tickle@c-of-e.org.uk
Editorial & Copyright Manager: Sarah Roberts *Tel:* (020) 78981578 *E-mail:* sarah.roberts@c-of-e.org.uk
National Society Publications Off: Hamish Bruce *Tel:* (020) 78981453 *E-mail:* hamish.bruce@c-of-e.org.uk
Contact: Aderyn Watson *E-mail:* aderyn.watson@c-of-e.org.uk
Subjects: Religion - Other
ISBN Prefix(es): 0-7151; 0-901819
Number of titles published annually: 40 Print; 1 CD-ROM
Total Titles: 300 Print; 1 CD-ROM; 1 Audio
Online services available through World Wide Web.
Parent Company: The Archbihops Council of the Church of England
Imprints: The National Society
Distributed by Novalis (Canada); Charles Paine Pty Ltd (Australia)
Orders to: The Canterbury Press, St Mary's Works, St Mary's Plain, Norwich NR3 3BH, Melanie Cole *Tel:* (01603) 612914 *Fax:* (01603) 624483

Church Literature Association, *imprint of* Church Union

Church Society
Dean Wace House, 16 Rosslyn Rd, Watford, Herts WD18 0NY
Tel: (01923) 235111 *Fax:* (01923) 800362
E-mail: enquiries@churchsociety.org
Web Site: www.churchsociety.org
Key Personnel
Publishing Secretary: David Phillips
Founded: 1835 (Present company started in 1950 as an amalgamation of two other similar organizations)
Specialize in books & booklets, Publishers 'Churchmen' quarterly since 1879. A society founded to keep the Church of England faithful to its formularies.
Subjects: Religion - Protestant, Theology
ISBN Prefix(es): 0-85190
Total Titles: 4 Print

Church Times, *imprint of* Hymns Ancient & Modern Ltd

Church Union
Faith House, 7 Tufton St, London SW1P 3QN
Tel: (020) 7222 6952 *Fax:* (020) 7976 7180
E-mail: churchunion@care4free.net
Web Site: www.churchunion.care4free.net
Key Personnel
Contact: Julien Chilcott-Monk
Founded: 1859
Member of Bookseller Association; specialize in religious books; also acts as Bookseller.
Subjects: Religion - Catholic, Religion - Protestant, Religion - Other
ISBN Prefix(es): 0-85191

Imprints: Church Literature Association; Tufton Books
Distributed by SCM - Canterbury Press
Bookshop(s): Faith House Bookshop, 7 Tufton St, London SW1P 3QN

Churchill Livingstone
Imprint of Elsevier Health Sciences
32 Jamestown Rd, London NW1 7BY
Tel: (020) 7424 4200 *Fax:* (020) 7485 4752
Founded: 1990
Subjects: Medicine, Nursing, Dentistry
ISBN Prefix(es): 88-7948
Parent Company: Elsevier Science Ltd

Cicerone Press
2 Police Sq, Milnthorpe, Cumbria LA7 7PY
Tel: (01539) 562 069 *Fax:* (01539) 563 417
E-mail: info@cicerone.co.uk
Web Site: www.cicerone.co.uk
Key Personnel
Dir, Sales & Marketing: Mrs Lesley Williams *E-mail:* lesley@cicerone.demon.co.uk
Dir, Editorial, Production & Finance: Jonathan E Williams *E-mail:* jonathan@cicerone.demon.co.uk
Founded: 1969
Publish specialized guides to walking, trekking, climbing, mountaineering & biking in the UK, Europe & other world regions.
Subjects: Outdoor Recreation, Travel
ISBN Prefix(es): 0-902363; 1-85284
Number of titles published annually: 20 Print
Total Titles: 280 Print
Distributed by Alpenbooks (USA); Midpoint Trade Books (USA)
Warehouse: 2B Summerlands Industrial Estat, North Kendal, Cumbria

CILIPS, see Chartered Institute of Library & Information Professionals in Scotland

CILT, see Centre for Information on Language Teaching & Research (CILT)

Cinderella, *imprint of* Novello & Co Ltd

CIWEM, *imprint of* Terence Dalton Ltd

Clarendon Press, *imprint of* Oxford University Press

Clarion, *imprint of* Elliot Right Way Books

James Clarke & Co Ltd+
PO Box 60, Cambridge CB1 2NT
Tel: (01223) 350865 *Fax:* (01223) 366951
E-mail: sales@jamesclarke.co.uk
Web Site: www.jamesclarke.co.uk
Key Personnel
Man Dir: Adrian C Brink
Founded: 1859
Subjects: Biblical Studies, Biography, History, Library & Information Sciences, Literature, Literary Criticism, Essays, Nonfiction (General), Philosophy, Publishing & Book Trade Reference, Religion - Catholic, Religion - Protestant, Theology
ISBN Prefix(es): 0-227
Number of titles published annually: 4 Print
Total Titles: 300 Print
Imprints: Acorn Editions; Patrick Hardy Books; Lutterworth Press
Distributed by Parkwest Publications Inc
Foreign Rep(s): Keith Ainsworth (Pty) Ltd (Australia); Applied Media (India, Sri Lanka); Catholic Supplies (NK) (New Zealand); CKK (Hong Kong, Indonesia, Malaysia, Philippines, Singapore, Thailand); Iberian Book Services (Portugal & Spain); Parkwest Publications Inc

(US); Kelvin van Hasselt Publishing Services (Africa, Caribbean)
Membership(s): IPG; Publishers' Association

Class Publishing+
Barb House, Barb Mews, London W6 7PA
Tel: (020) 7371 2119 *Fax:* (020) 7371 2878
E-mail: post@class.co.uk
Web Site: www.class.co.uk
Key Personnel
Manager: Richard Warner
Founded: 1989
Subjects: Health, Nutrition, Law, Medicine, Nursing, Dentistry
ISBN Prefix(es): 1-872362; 1-859590
Book Club(s): BCA
Warehouse: Plymbridge Distributors Ltd, Plymbridge House, Estover Rd, Plymouth, Devon PL6 7PZ *Tel:* (01752) 202 300 *Fax:* (01752) 202 330 *E-mail:* enquiries@plymbridge.com *Web Site:* www.plymbridge.com
Membership(s): IPG

Classey Books, *imprint of* E W Classey Ltd

E W Classey Ltd+
Oxford House, Marlborough St, Faringdon, Oxon SN7 7JP
Mailing Address: PO Box 93, Faringdon, Oxon SN7 7DR
Tel: (01367) 244700 *Fax:* (01367) 244800
E-mail: bugbooks@classey.demon.co.uk
Web Site: www.abebooks.com/home/bugbooks
Key Personnel
Publisher: E W Classey
Contact: Mr P Classey
Founded: 1949
Subjects: Biological Sciences, Earth Sciences, Environmental Studies, Natural History, Science (General), Arachnology, Botany, Entomology, Geology, Natural History, Ornithology, Zoology
ISBN Prefix(es): 0-900848; 0-86096
Imprints: Ferendune; Hedera Press; Classey Books

Classics, *imprint of* The Penguin Group UK

CLB Books, *imprint of* Colour Library Direct

CLB Publishing, *imprint of* Colour Library Direct

Clematis Press Ltd
18 Old Church St, London SW3 5DQ
Tel: (020) 7352 8755 *Cable:* CLEMATIS LONDON SW3
Key Personnel
Man Dir: Clara Waters
Founded: 1950
Trade Counter: Darton, Longman & Todd Ltd, One Amor Way, Dunhams Lane, Letchworth, Herts SG6 1UG.
Subjects: Art
ISBN Prefix(es): 0-568
Imprints: Bonfini
Warehouse: Amor Way, Dunhams Lane, Letchworth, Herts SG6 1UG

Clever Clogs, *imprint of* Funfax Ltd

Cloverleaf, *imprint of* Evans Brothers Ltd

Coachwise Ltd
Unit 2/3 Chelsea Close, Off Amberley Rd, Armley, Leeds LS12 4HW
Tel: (0113) 2311310 *Fax:* (0113) 2319606
Web Site: www.1st4sport.com
Key Personnel
Man Dir: Dr Tony Byrne
General Manager: Kath Leonard

PUBLISHERS

UNITED KINGDOM

Marketing Executive & International Rights Contact: Melanie Drake *E-mail:* mdrake@coachwise.ltd.uk
Founded: 1989
Specialize in leisure management & coaching targeting sports professionals.
Member of Direct Marketing Association (UK) Ltd.
Subjects: Health, Nutrition, Music, Dance, Outdoor Recreation, Sports, Athletics
Total Titles: 40 Print; 1 CD-ROM; 1 Audio
Parent Company: National Coaching Foundation

Cockbird Press+
PO Box 356, Heathfield TN21 9QF
Tel: (01435) 830430 *Fax:* (01435) 830027
Key Personnel
Man Dir: Lucy Faridany
General Editor: Diane White
Founded: 1990
Publish prints through catalogues by mail order.
Subjects: Biography, History, Travel
ISBN Prefix(es): 1-873054
Distributed by Seven Hills Book Distributors (US distributor)

Richard Cohen Books, *imprint of* Metro Publishing Ltd

COIC, see Careers & Occupational Information Centre (COIC)

Adlard Coles Nautical, *imprint of* A & C Black Publishers Ltd

Rosica Colin Ltd+
One Clareville Grove Mews, London SW7 5AH
Tel: (020) 7370 1080 *Fax:* (020) 7244 6441
Key Personnel
Dir: Joanna Marston
Founded: 1949
Literary agents.

Peter Collin Publishing Ltd+
32-34 Great Peter St, London SW1P 2DB
Tel: (020) 7222 1155 *Fax:* (020) 7222 1551
E-mail: info@petercollin.com
Web Site: www.petercollin.com
Key Personnel
Dir: S M H Collin; Peter Collin
Founded: 1985
Specialize in English & bilingual dictionaries.
ISBN Prefix(es): 0-948549; 1-901659
Imprints: Aspect Guides
U.S. Office(s): IPG, 814 N Franklin St, Chicago, IL 60610, United States *Fax:* 312-337-5985
Distributed by Foucher, Klett
Shipping Address: PO Box 1321, Oak Park, IL 60304, United States *Tel:* 708-366-9553 *Fax:* 708-366-9554 (US)
Orders to: Marston Books, PO Box 269, Abingdon, Oxon OX14 4YN *Tel:* (01235) 465600 *Fax:* (01235) 465655

Colonsay Books, *imprint of* House of Lochar

ColorCards, *imprint of* Speechmark Publishing Ltd

Colour Library Direct+
Godalming Business Center, Catteshall Lane, Woolsack Way, Godalming GU7 1XW
Tel: (01483) 426777 *Fax:* (01483) 426947
E-mail: prod@quad-pub.co.uk
Key Personnel
Man Dir: Brian Phipps
Publishing Dir: Will Steeds
Sales, Rights, Promotions: Des Higgins
Production: Grame Proctor
Production Manager: Karen Staff

Founded: 1959
Subjects: Animals, Pets, Art, Cookery, Environmental Studies, Photography, Travel
ISBN Prefix(es): 0-906558; 0-86283; 0-904681; 1-84100; 1-85833
Parent Company: Quadrillion
Imprints: ATAPepperpot Gift; CLB Books; CLB Publishing; QPI Books
Divisions: Bramley Books; CLB Editions; CLB Publishing; CLD Direct Marketing; IMC Video; Pepperpot Gift & Stationary; QPI Publishing; Quadrillion Multimedia Ltd

Colourpoint Books+
Unit D5, Ards Business Centre, Jubilee Rd, Newtownards BT23 4YH
Tel: (028) 9182 0505 *Fax:* (028) 9182 1900
E-mail: info@colourpoint.co.uk; sales@colourpoint.co.uk
Web Site: www.colourpoint.co.uk
Key Personnel
Partner: Malcolm Johnston *E-mail:* malcolm@colourpoint.co.uk; Sheila M Johnston *E-mail:* sheila@colourpoint.co.uk
Partner & International Rights: Norman Johnston *E-mail:* norman@colourpoint.co.uk
Administrator: Michelle Chambers
Sales Manager: Lawrence Greer
Editor: Ronnie Hanna
Founded: 1993
Specializes in educational textbooks/resources, transport titles, books of Irish interest.
Member of Publishers Association & Irish Educational Publishers' Association.
Subjects: Biography, Disability, Special Needs, Education, Government, Political Science, History, Maritime, Religion - Other, Transportation, Aviation
ISBN Prefix(es): 1-898392; 1-904242
Number of titles published annually: 30 Print
Total Titles: 100 Print
Distributed by Ian Allan Publishing (England, Scotland & Wales)
Distributor for Arthur Southern; Business Enthusiast Publishing; Nostalgia Road; Trans-Pennine Publishing

Combined Academic Publishers
15A Lewin's Yard, East St, Chesham, Bucks HP5 1HQ
Tel: (01494) 581601 *Fax:* (01494) 581602
E-mail: nickesson@combinedacademic.demon.co.uk
Web Site: www.combinedacademic.co.uk
Key Personnel
Dir: Nicholas Esson
Marketing Manager: Julia Mark
Founded: 1997
CAP is an innovative full service sales, marketing & distribution agency which serves the needs of university & academic presses seeking promotion/marketing, field sales representation & distribution in the UK & Europe.
Imprints: Duke University Press (UK & Europe); Indiana University Press (UK & Europe); McGill-Queens University Press (UK & Europe); Smithsonian Institution Press (UK & Europe); University of Nebraska Press (UK & Europe); University of Texas Press (UK & Europe); University of Washington Press (UK & Europe)
Shipping Address: Plymbridge Distributors Ltd, Estover House, Plymouth *Tel:* (01752) 202300 *Fax:* (01752) 202333 *E-mail:* orders@plymbridge.com

Comedia, *imprint of* Routledge

Commission for Racial Equality+
Elliot House, 10-12 Allington St, London SW1E 5EH
Tel: (020) 7828 7022 *Fax:* (020) 7630 7605

E-mail: info@cre.gov.uk
Web Site: www.cre.gov.uk
Key Personnel
Chairman: Sir Herman Ouseley
Marketing, Production, Rights & Permissions: Desrie Thomson
Founded: 1976
Subjects: Human Relations
ISBN Prefix(es): 0-907920; 1-85442; 0-902355
Imprints: CRE
Branch Office(s)
Birmingham
Edinburgh
Leeds
Leicester
Manchester
Orders to: PO Box 29, Norwich NR3 1GN *Tel:* (0870) 240 3697 *Fax:* (0870) 240 3698 *E-mail:* CRE@tso.co.uk

Commonwealth Secretariat+
Marlborough House, Pall Mall, London SW1Y 5HX
Tel: (020) 7747 6385 *Fax:* (020) 7839 9081
E-mail: info@commonwealth.int
Web Site: www.thecommonwealth.org
Key Personnel
Head of Publications: Mr R Jones-Parry *E-mail:* r.jones-parry@commonwealth.int
Founded: 1948
Intergovernmental organization with responsibility for the work & all activities of the Commonwealth.
Subjects: Agriculture, Developing Countries, Earth Sciences, Economics, Education, Energy, Environmental Studies, Finance, Government, Political Science, Law, Management, Public Administration, Social Sciences, Sociology, Technology, Women's Studies
ISBN Prefix(es): 0-85092
Number of titles published annually: 40 Print; 2 CD-ROM
Total Titles: 150 Print; 4 CD-ROM; 2 Audio
Foreign Rep(s): Addenda Ltd (New Zealand); Book Bird (Pakistan); Booker International (Brunei); Bookwell (India); Buma Kor & Co Ltd (Cameroon); DCS-Athens (Greece); E & D Limited (Tanzania); English House Services (Caribbean); Globe Enterprises (Malaysia); Grassroots Bookshop (Zimbabwe); Hargraves Library Services (South Africa); Iberian Book Services (Spain); Karim International (Bangladesh); Barbie Keene (Zimbabwe); Prestige Books (Zimbabwe); Reimmer Book Services (Ghana); Renouf Publishing Company Ltd (Canada); SARDC (Mozambique); Select Books Pte Ltd (Singapore); Stylus Inc USA (US); Tausco Book Distributors (India); Transglobal Publishers Service Ltd (Hong Kong); TRIOPS (Germany)
Warehouse: York Publishing Services, 64 Hallfield Rd, Layerthorpe, York YO31 72Q, Contact: Duncan Beal *Tel:* (01904) 431 213 *Fax:* (01904) 430 868 *Web Site:* www.yps-publishing.co.uk
Orders to: York Publishing Services, 64 Hallfield Rd, Layerthorpe, York YO31 7ZQ *Tel:* (01904) 431 213 *Fax:* (01904) 430 868 *E-mail:* obeal@yps-publishing.co.uk
Membership(s): Publishers' Association

Compass Equestrian Ltd+
Cadbrough Farm, Oldberrow, Henley-in-Arden B95 5NX
Tel: (0156) 479 5136 *Fax:* (0156) 479 5136
E-mail: compbook@globalnet.co.uk
Key Personnel
Dir: Valerie Wofford Watson
Contact: Clare Harris
Founded: 1996
Specializes in books on Equestrian topics.
Subjects: Nonfiction (General)
ISBN Prefix(es): 1-900667

UNITED KINGDOM

Total Titles: 13 Print
Distributed by Trafalgar Square Publishing

Compass Maps Ltd
The Coach House, Beech Court, Winford BS40 8DW
Tel: (01275) 474737
E-mail: info@papoutmaps.com
Web Site: www.mapgroup.net

Compendium Publishing+
43 Frith St, 1st floor, London WIV 5TE
Tel: (020) 72874570 *Fax:* (020) 74940583
E-mail: compendium@compuserve.com
Key Personnel
Man Dir: Alan Greene
Editorial: Simon Forty
Founded: 1998
Subjects: Aeronautics, Aviation, African American Studies, Anthropology, Antiques, Architecture & Interior Design, Art, Asian Studies, Automotive, Cookery, Crafts, Games, Hobbies, Erotica, History, How-to, Maritime, Military Science, Nonfiction (General), Sports, Athletics, Transportation, Travel
ISBN Prefix(es): 1-872004; 1-85915
Imprints: Wag Books; Windrow & Greene
Divisions: Compendium Publishing Ltd

Computer Science Press, *imprint of* W H Freeman & Co Ltd

Computer Step+
80 The Strand, London WC2R 0RL
Tel: (020) 7010 3000 *Fax:* (020) 7416 3193
E-mail: sevanti@computerstep.com
Key Personnel
Publisher: Harshad Kotecha
Partner & International Rights: Mrs Sevanti Kotecha
Founded: 1991
Subjects: Business, How-to, Technology, Computers, Educational Software
ISBN Prefix(es): 1-874029; 1-84078
Total Titles: 60 Print; 10 E-Book
Distributed by Computer Bookshops (UK non-booktrade); Federal Publications (Malaysia); IDG Books India (India, Pakistan, Bangladesh); Penguin Books (Australia, New Zealand, South Africa)

Condor Books, *imprint of* Souvenir Press Ltd

Connections, *imprint of* Eddison Sadd Editions Ltd

Conran Octopus, *imprint of* Octopus Publishing Group

Conran Octopus+
Imprint of Octopus Publishing Group
2-4 Heron Quays, London E14 4JP
Tel: (020) 7531 8400 *Fax:* (020) 7531 8627
E-mail: info@conran-octopus.co.uk
Web Site: www.conran-octopus.co.uk
Telex: 296249
Key Personnel
Sales & Mktg Dir: Catharine Snow
  E-mail: catharine.snow@conran-octopus.co.uk
Publishing Dir: Lorraine Dickey *E-mail:* lorraine.dickey@conran-octopus.co.uk
Creative Dir: Leslie Harrington *E-mail:* leslie.harrington@conran-octopus.co.uk
Publicity & Marketing Assistant: Virginia McIntosh *E-mail:* virginia.maintosh@conran-octopus.co.uk
UK Sales & Marketing Dir: Martin Hunka
  Tel: (020) 7531 8625 *E-mail:* martin.hunka@conran-octopus.co.uk
Founded: 1984
Subjects: Architecture & Interior Design, Crafts, Games, Hobbies, Gardening, Plants
ISBN Prefix(es): 1-85029; 1-84091; 1-84091
Distributed by APD Singapore Ptd Limited (Singapore, Malaysia, Indonesia, Vietnam, Burma, Laos & Thailand); Asia Publishers Services Ltd (Hong Kong, China & Taiwan); Books For Europe (Netherlands); Books for Europe (France & Benlux); CLB Marketing Services (Hungary, Czech Republic, Slovakia, Slovenia, Croatia & Poland); HardieGrant Books (Australia); Gill Hess Ltd (Ireland); HRA - Humphrys Roberts Associates (Central America); HRA - Humphrys Roberts Associates (South America); IKC Korea (Korea); Inter Media Americana (North Africa); Inter Media Americana; Victoria Kalish (USA); Marketing Services for Publishers (Philippines); Nilsson & Lamm: Stockholding (Netherlands); Octopus India (Indi & Sri Lanka); Octopus Publishing Group (Australia - special sales); Octopus Publishing Group (Japan); Publisher's Agent (Italy, Spain, Portugal & Gibraltar); Publisher's Services (Germany, Austria & Switzerland); Quartet Sales & Marketing (South Africa); Reed Publishing (NZ) Ltd; Derek Searle Associates Ltd; Vollmer Communications: Stockholding (Germany); Peter Ward Book Exports (Middle East, Greece, Israel, Cyprus & Malta)
Orders to: Littlehampton Bopok Services Ltd, Faraday Close, Durrington, Worthing, West Sussex BN13 3RB *Tel:* (01933) 828503

Conservative Policy Forum
32 Smith Sq Westminster, London SW1P 3HH
Tel: (020) 7984 8316 *Fax:* (020) 7984 8320
E-mail: cpf@conservatives.com
Web Site: www.conservativepolicyforum.com
Key Personnel
Dir: Greg Clark
Assistant Dir: Tracy-Jane Malthouse
  E-mail: tmalthouse@conservatives.com
Founded: 1945 (as Conservative Political Forum)
Subjects: Economics, Government, Political Science
ISBN Prefix(es): 0-85070

Constable, *imprint of* Constable Publishers

Constable & Robinson Ltd+
3 The Lanchester, 162 Fulham Palace Rd, London W6 9ER
Tel: (020) 8741 3663 *Fax:* (020) 8748 7562
E-mail: enquiries@constablerobinson.com
Web Site: www.constablerobinson.com
Key Personnel
Publisher: Nick Robinson *E-mail:* nick@constablerobinson.com
Sales Manager: Andrew Hayward
  E-mail: andrew@constablerobinson.com
Publishing Dir, Robinson: Jan Chamier
  E-mail: jan@constablerobinson.com
Publishing Dir, Magpie: Nova Jayne Heath
  E-mail: nova@constablerobinson.com
International Rights: Eryl Humphrey Jones
  E-mail: eryl@constablerobinson.com
Secretary fo Man Dir: Liz Le Breton
Founded: 1999
Subjects: Biography, Criminology, Fiction, Health, Nutrition, History, Military Science, Nonfiction (General), Outdoor Recreation, Psychology, Psychiatry, Science Fiction, Fantasy, Self-Help, Travel, Autobiography, Landscape Photography
ISBN Prefix(es): 1-85487; 0-948164; 1-84119; 1-85004
Imprints: Magpie
Divisions: Magpie Books Ltd
Distributed by Carroll & Graf (USA); General Publishing (Canada)
Foreign Rep(s): Keith Humphrey (UK); Genny kelliher (Ireland); Jill Parker (UK); Jim Peck (UK); Philip Robey (UK); Dennis & David Segrue (UK); Robert Wilkinson (UK)
Foreign Rights: Agence Litteraire Hoffman (France); Big Apple Tuttle-Mori Agency (Republic of China, Taiwan); ELST (Bulgaria); General Publishing Co Ltd (Canada); Michael Geoghegan (Italy, Portugal, Scandinavia, Spain); Humphrys Roberts Association (Caribbean); Japan English Service (Japan); Alexander Korzhenevski (CIS, Russia); Maya Publishers (India); KT Mc Neish (Italy, Scandinavia); Natoli Stefan & Oliva (Italy); OA Literary Agency (Greece); Penguin SA (South Africa); Theo Philips (SE Asia); Prava I Prevodi (Poland, Romania, Yugoslavia); Peter Prout (Portugal, Spain); Random House Pty Ltd (Australia); Thomas Schluck GmbH (Germany); Shelley Power Literary Agency (Netherlands); Tandem Press (New Zealand); Michael Timperley (Belarus, Ukraine); Transnet Contracts (Czech Republic, Slovak Republic); Tuttle-Mori Agency Ltd (Japan); Tuttle-Mori Big Apple Agency (Thailand); Eric Yang Agency (Korea)
Warehouse: TBS Direct, Colchester Rd, Frating Green, Colchester, Essex CO7 7DW *Tel:* (020) 8741 3663 *Fax:* (020) 8748 7562
Orders to: TBS Direct, Colchester Rd, Frating Green, Colchester, Essex CO7 7DW *Tel:* (020) 8741 3663 *Fax:* (020) 8748 7562

Constable Publishers+
3 The Lanchester, 162 Fulham Palace Rd, London W6 9ER
Tel: (020) 8741 3663 *Fax:* (020) 8748 7562
Telex: 27950 ref 830
Key Personnel
Chairman: B K Glazebrook
Editorial: Carol O'Brien *E-mail:* carol@constablerobinson.com
Sales Dir: Andrew Hayward
Man Dir: Nick Robinson
Rights Manager: Sandra der Herzhog
Founded: 1896
Subjects: Antiques, Archaeology, Art, Astrology, Occult, Behavioral Sciences, Child Care & Development, Erotica, Fiction, Gay & Lesbian, Health, Nutrition, History, Humor, Military Science, Nonfiction (General), Outdoor Recreation, Photography, Psychology, Psychiatry, Science Fiction, Fantasy, Travel
ISBN Prefix(es): 0-09
Total Titles: 130 Print
Parent Company: Constable & Robinson Ltd
Imprints: Constable; Robinson; Robinson's Children
Orders to: GBS, Isaac Newton Way, Alma Park Industrial Estate, Grantham NG31 9SD *Tel:* (01476) 541080 *Fax:* (01476) 541061

Consultants Bureau, *imprint of* Kluwer Academic/Plenum Publishers

The Continuum International Publishing Group Ltd
The Tower Bldg, 11 York Rd, London SE1 7NX
Tel: (020) 7922 0880 *Fax:* (020) 7922 0881
Web Site: www.continuum-books.com
Key Personnel
President (New York Office): Philip Sturrock
Executive Vice President & General Manager (New York): Ulla Schnell
Executive Vice President & Publishing Director (New York): Nicholas Weir Williams
Vice President & Senior Editor: Frank Oveis
  E-mail: frank@continuumbooks.com
Publisher-at-Large at New Yorrk Operation: Werner Mark Linz
Finance Dir: Frank Roney
Editorial Dir: Janet Joyce
Sale & Marketing Dir: John Parsons
Production Manager: Ian Sherratt

Subjects: Business, Drama, Theater, Education, Government, Political Science, History, Literature, Literary Criticism, Essays, Nonfiction (General), Psychology, Psychiatry, Women's Studies
Number of titles published annually: 300 Print
Imprints: Geoffrey Chapman; Leicester University Press; Mansell; Mowbray; Pinter; Tycooly
U.S. Office(s): The Continuum International Publishing Group Inc, 370 Lexington Ave, New York, NY 10017, United States *Tel:* 212-953-5858 *Fax:* 212-953-5944
Orders to: Orca Book Services, Stanley House, 3 Fleets Lane, Poole, Dorset BH15 3AJ *Tel:* (01202) 665432 *Fax:* (01202) 666219

Conway Maritime Press+
Division of Brassey's UK Ltd
583 Fulham Rd, London SW6 7BY
Tel: (020) 7471 1100 *Fax:* (020) 7471 1101
E-mail: info@batsford.com
Key Personnel
International Rights: Sarah Jane Coxon
Founded: 1968
Subjects: Maritime
ISBN Prefix(es): 0-85177
Associate Companies: Putnam Aeronautical Books
U.S. Office(s): Brassey's Inc, c/o Books International, 22833 Quicksilver Dr, Sterling, VA 20166, United States
Orders to: Marston Book Services, PO Box 269, Abingdon, Oxon OX14 4SD

Leo Cooper, *imprint of* Pen & Sword Books Ltd

Leo Cooper+
47 Church St, Barnsley, South Yorkshire S70 2AS
Tel: (01226) 734222 *Fax:* (01226) 734438
E-mail: enquiries@pen-sword.demon.co.uk
Web Site: www.pen-and-sword.co.uk
Key Personnel
Man Dir: Charles Hewitt *E-mail:* charles@pen-and-sword.co.uk
Publishing Manager: Henry Wilson *E-mail:* henry@pen-and-sword.co.uk
Book Production Manager: Barbara Bramall *E-mail:* production@pen-and-sword.co.uk
Sales Manager: Paula Brennan *E-mail:* sales@pen-and-sword.co.uk
Founded: 1990
Subjects: Biography, History, Maritime, Military Science, Nonfiction (General), Travel
ISBN Prefix(es): 0-85052
Number of titles published annually: 100 Print
Total Titles: 350 Print
Associate Companies: Wharncliffe Publishing
Imprints: Pen & Sword
Divisions: Pen & Sword Books Ltd
Distributed by Combined Books (USA); Vanwell Publishing Ltd (Canada)

Co-operative Union, *imprint of* Holyoake Books

Copper Beech Publishing Ltd+
PO Box 159, East Grinstead, Sussex RH19 4HF
Tel: (01342) 314734 *Fax:* (01342) 314794
E-mail: sales@copperbeechpublishing.co.uk
Web Site: www.btinternet.com/~copperbeechpublishing
Key Personnel
Contact: Jan Barnes
Subjects: Etiquette, Food & Drink, Victoriana
ISBN Prefix(es): 0-9516295; 1-898617
Membership(s): IPG

Cordee Ltd+
3a De Montfort St, Leicester LE1 7HD
Tel: (0116) 254 3579 *Fax:* (0116) 247 1176
E-mail: info@cordee.co.uk
Web Site: www.cordee.co.uk

Key Personnel
Contact: Ken Vickers *E-mail:* kenvickers@cordee.co.uk
Founded: 1973
Specialist publisher, distributor & wholesaler (worldwide).
Subjects: Outdoor Recreation, Travel
ISBN Prefix(es): 1-871890; 0-904405

Corgi, *imprint of* Transworld Publishers Ltd

Cornwall Books, *imprint of* Golden Cockerel Press Ltd

Coronet, *imprint of* Hodder & Stoughton General

Corwin Press, *imprint of* Sage Publications Ltd

Joanna Cotler Books, *imprint of* HarperCollins Publishers

Cottage Publications
Laurel Cottage, 15 Ballyhay Rd, Donaghadee, Co Down BT21 0NG
Tel: (01247) 888033; (0410) 057990 (mobile) *Fax:* (01247) 888063
E-mail: info@cottage-publications.com
Web Site: www.cottage-publications.com
Key Personnel
Contact: Timothy Johnston *E-mail:* tim@cottage-publications.com
Founded: 1990
Specialize in illustrated books on Ireland.
Subjects: Art, History, Regional Interests
ISBN Prefix(es): 0-9516402; 1-900935
Total Titles: 20 Print

Council for British Archaeology
Bowes Morrell House, 111 Walmgate, York YO1 9WA
Tel: (01904) 671417 *Fax:* (01904) 671384
E-mail: archaeology@compuserve.com; cbabooks@dial.pipex.com
Web Site: www.britarch.ac.uk
Key Personnel
Dir: George Lambrick *E-mail:* georgelambrick@britarch.ac.uk
Publications Officer: Kate Sleight
Founded: 1944
Subjects: Archaeology, Education
ISBN Prefix(es): 0-900312; 0-906780; 1-872414
Number of titles published annually: 12 Print
Total Titles: 65 Print

Countryside Books
2 Highfield Ave, Newbury, Berks RG14 5DS
Tel: (01635) 43816 *Fax:* (01635) 551004
Web Site: www.countrysidebooks.co.uk
Key Personnel
Man Dir, Editorial, Sales & Production: Nicholas Battle
Publicity, Rights & Permissions: Suzanne Battle
Founded: 1976
Publisher of regional interest books within UK
Specialize in walking guides.
Subjects: Genealogy, History, Regional Interests
ISBN Prefix(es): 0-905392; 0-86368; 1-85306
Number of titles published annually: 50 Print
Total Titles: 400 Print
Subsidiaries: Local Heritage Books

Countyvise Ltd+
14 Appin Rd, Birkenhead CH41 9HH
Tel: (0151) 6473333 *Fax:* (0151) 6478286
E-mail: cv@birkenheadpress.co.uk
Key Personnel
Man Dir: John Emmerson *E-mail:* je@birkenheadpress.co.uk
Founded: 1981

Subjects: Biography, History, Maritime, Regional Interests, Sports, Athletics, Transportation
ISBN Prefix(es): 0-907768; 1-871201; 0-9516129; 1-873245; 1-901231
Number of titles published annually: 7 Print
Total Titles: 110 Print
Imprints: Liver Press; Merseyside Port Folios; Picton Press

Covenant Publishing Co Ltd
8 Blades Court, Deodar Rd, London SW15 2NU
Tel: (020) 8877 9010 *Fax:* (020) 8871 4770
E-mail: admin@britishisrael.co.uk
Web Site: www.britishisrael.co.uk
Key Personnel
Chairman: M A Clark
Administrator: J B Dowse
Founded: 1922
Subjects: Religion - Other
ISBN Prefix(es): 0-85205

Richard & Erika Coward Writing & Publishing Partnership+
16 Sturgess Ave, London NW4 3TS
Tel: (020) 8202 9592
E-mail: info@writers.net
Key Personnel
Author: Richard Coward
Business Manager: Erika Coward
ISBN Prefix(es): 0-9515019

CRAC, *imprint of* Hobsons

CRE, *imprint of* Commission for Racial Equality

Creation Books+
72/80 Leather Lane, 4th floor, London EC1N 7TR
Tel: (020) 7430 9878 *Fax:* (020) 7242 5527
E-mail: info@creationbooks.com
Web Site: www.creationbooks.com
Key Personnel
President: James Williamson *E-mail:* james@creationbooks.com
Dir: Laurence Raine *E-mail:* laurence@creationbooks.com
Publishing Executive & Rights: Miranda Filbee *E-mail:* miranda@creationbooks.com
Founded: 1989
Subjects: Biography, Erotica, Fiction, Film, Video, Nonfiction (General), Photography
ISBN Prefix(es): 1-871592; 1-84068; 1-902588
Total Titles: 100 Print
Ultimate Parent Company: Creation Books
Associate Companies: Glitter Books, 85 Clerkenwell Rd, Suite 403, London EC1R 5AR, Contact: James Williamson *Tel:* (020) 7430 9878 *Fax:* (020) 7242 5527 *E-mail:* glitter@creationbooks.com
Imprints: Attack!; Velvet
U.S. Office(s): PO Box 1137, New York, NY 10156, United States
c/o Subterranean Co, Box 160, Monroe, OR 97456, United States
Distributed by Consortium Book Sales & Distribution (US & Canada); Creation Books Tokyo (Japan); Last Gasp (US & Canada); Marginal Distribution (US & Canada); Tower Books (Australia & New Zealand); Turnaround (UK & Europe); Tuttle-Shokai (Japan)
Foreign Rep(s): Julian Ashton (Far East, Middle East); Consortium Book Sales & Distribution (Canada, US); Creation Books Tokyo (Japan); Last Gasp (Canada, US); Marginal Distribution (Canada, US); Tower Books (Australia & New Zealand); Tuttle-Shokai (Japan)
Orders to: Book Clearing House, 45 Purdy St, Harrison, NY 10528, United States *Fax:* 914-835-0398 *E-mail:* bookch@aol.com *Web Site:* www.book-clearing-house.com

UNITED KINGDOM BOOK

Creative Monochrome, *imprint of* Creative Monochrome Ltd

Creative Monochrome Ltd
Courtney House, 62 Jarvis Rd, South Croydon, Surrey CR2 6HU
Tel: (020) 8686 3282 *Fax:* (020) 8681 0662
E-mail: sales@cremono.com
Web Site: www.cremono.com
Key Personnel
Man Dir: Roger Maile *E-mail:* roger@cremono.com
Founded: 1992
Subjects: Photography
ISBN Prefix(es): 1-873319
Total Titles: 24 Print
Imprints: Creative Monochrome; Digital Photoart; Photo Art International
Membership(s): IPG

Cressrelles Publishing Company Ltd+
10 Station Rd, Industrial Estate, Colwall, Nr Malvern WR13 6RN
Tel: (01684) 540154 *Fax:* (01684) 540154
Key Personnel
Man Dir: Leslie Smith
Business Manager: Simon Smith
  E-mail: simonsmith@cressrelles4drama.fsbusiness.co.uk
Founded: 1973
Subjects: Drama, Theater
ISBN Prefix(es): 0-85956
Number of titles published annually: 3 Print
Total Titles: 48 Print
Imprints: Actinic Press (chiropody); Kenyon-Deane (plays); J Garnet Miller Ltd (plays); New Playwrights Network (plays)
Divisions: Actinic Press; Kenyon-Deane; J Garnet Miller
Distributed by Empire Publishing Services
Distributor for Anchorage Press, Inc; I. E. Clark, Inc

Critical Studies in Latin American Culture, *imprint of* Verso

Paul H Crompton Ltd+
102 Felsham Rd, London SW15 1DQ
Tel: (020) 8780 1063 *Fax:* (020) 8780 1063
Key Personnel
Publicity & Rights: Paul Crompton
International Rights: Rose Brookhouse
Founded: 1968
Also producing martial arts videos.
Subjects: Cookery, Crafts, Games, Hobbies, Health, Nutrition
ISBN Prefix(es): 0-901764; 1-874250
Distributed by Talman Company (North America)
Orders to: c/o Airlift Book Co, 8 The Arena, Mollison Ave, Enfield, Middlesex EN3 7NJ
Tel: (081) 8040400 *Fax:* (081) 8040044

Cromwell Editions, *imprint of* Alpine Fine Arts Books Ltd

Croner CCH Group Ltd
Croner House, London Rd, Kingston-upon-Thames, Surrey KT2 6SR
Tel: (020) 85473333 *Fax:* (020) 85472638
E-mail: info@croner.co.uk
Web Site: www.croner.co.uk
Telex: 267778
Key Personnel
Man Dir: H F Staal
Production: George Rankin
Finance Dir: Peter Diggles
Founded: 1941
Subjects: Business, Finance, Health, Nutrition, Labor, Industrial Relations, Law, Transportation
ISBN Prefix(es): 0-900319
Parent Company: Wolters Kluwer (UK) PLC
Ultimate Parent Company: Wolters Kluwer NV, Netherlands
Subsidiaries: CCH Editions (Bicester)

Crossbridge Books+
345 Old Birmingham Rd, Bromsgrove B60 1NX
Tel: (0121) 447 7897 *Fax:* (0121) 445 1063
E-mail: em@crossbridgebooks.com
Web Site: www.crossbridgebooks.com
Key Personnel
Publisher & International Rights Contact: Eileen Mohr
Founded: 1995
Publisher of Christian books.
Member of Christian Booksellers Association.
Subjects: Biography, Religion - Protestant, Self-Help
ISBN Prefix(es): 0-9524604
Number of titles published annually: 2 Print
Total Titles: 8 Print
Imprints: Mohr Books
Membership(s): IPG

Crossway, *imprint of* Inter-Varsity Press

Crown House Publishing Ltd+
Crown Buildings, Bancyfelin, Carmarthen SA33 5ND
Tel: (01267) 211345 *Fax:* (01267) 211882
E-mail: books@crownhouse.co.uk
Web Site: www.crownhouse.co.uk
Key Personnel
Dir: David Bowman
Acquisitions Editor: Helen Kinsey
Founded: 1998
Subjects: Education, Psychology, Psychiatry
ISBN Prefix(es): 1-899836; 1-904424
Number of titles published annually: 20 Print
Total Titles: 90 Print
U.S. Office(s): 4 Berkeley St, First Floor, Norwalk, CT 06850, United States
Foreign Rep(s): Everybody's Books (South Africa); Footprint Books (Australia); Mark Tralten (Canada, US)
Orders to: PO Box 2223, Williston, VT 05495, United States *Tel:* 877-925-1213 *Fax:* 802-864-7626

The Crowood Press Ltd+
The Stable Block, Crowood Lane, Ramsbury, Marlborough, Wilts SN8 2HR
Tel: (01672) 520320 *Fax:* (01672) 520280
E-mail: enquiries@crowood.com
Web Site: www.crowood.com
Key Personnel
Publisher, Chief Executive: John F Dennis
Man Dir: Ken Hathaway
Sales Office Manager: Julie Sankey
Rights Manager: Madeleine Hacking
Founded: 1982
Subjects: Aeronautics, Aviation, Animals, Pets, Automotive, Crafts, Games, Hobbies, Gardening, Plants, Maritime, Natural History, Outdoor Recreation, Sports, Athletics
ISBN Prefix(es): 0-946284; 1-85223; 1-86126
Imprints: Helmsman Guides
Distributed by Grantham Book Services (United Kingdom); Peter Hyde Associates (South Africa); Motorbooks International (US transport & military titles); Nilsson & Lamm (Netherlands); Peribo Pty Ltd (Australia & New Zealand); Publishers Marketing Services (Singapore); Publishers Marketing Services Pte Ltd (Malaysia); Trafalgar Square Publishing (US); Vanwell Publishing Ltd (Canada)
Foreign Rep(s): Bookport Associates (Southern Europe); D Richard Bowen (Scandinavia); European Marketing Services (Austria, Belgium, France, Germany, Luxembourg, Switzerland)
Warehouse: Bookpoint Ltd, 39 Milton Park, Abingdon Oxon

CSA (Cambridge Scientific Abstracts)+
Windsor Court, East Grinstead House, East Grinstead, West Sussex RH19 1XA
Tel: (01342) 336159 *Fax:* (01342) 336197
E-mail: service@csa.com; tjones@csa.com (sales); marketing@bowker.uk.co
Web Site: www.csa.com
Key Personnel
Man Dir: Jacki Heppard *Tel:* (01342) 336043
  E-mail: jacki.heppard@bowker.co.uk
Marketing Manager: Jo Grange *Tel:* (01342) 336143 *E-mail:* jo.grange@bowker.com
Sales Dir: Doug Macmillan *Tel:* (01342) 336157
  E-mail: doug.macmillan@bowker.co.uk
Founded: 1988
Publisher of reference tools & professional development texts for the library & information world & publishing industry.
Subjects: Library & Information Sciences, Publishing & Book Trade Reference
ISBN Prefix(es): 1-85739; 0-905450; 0-8352; 0-85935
Total Titles: 150 Print; 8 CD-ROM; 4 Online; 5 E-Book
Online services available through CSA, Dialog, Optology.
Parent Company: Cambridge Information Group
Distributed by D W Thorpe (Australia)
Distributor for R R Bowker LLC (UK, Europe, Middle East, Africa, Southeast Asia)

CTBI Publications
Inter-Church House, 35-41 Lower Marsh, London SE1 7SA
Tel: (020) 7523 2121 *Fax:* (020) 7928 0010
E-mail: info@ctbi.org.uk
Web Site: www.ctbi.org.uk
Key Personnel
International Rights: Rev D J Rudiger *Tel:* (020) 7523 2041
Publications Secretary: Rev Collin Davey, PhD *Tel:* (020) 7523 2154
Founded: 1940 (as BCC Publications)
Subjects: Biblical Studies, Biography, Education, Environmental Studies, History, Microcomputers, Religion - Catholic, Religion - Protestant, Religion - Other, Theology, Women's Studies
ISBN Prefix(es): 0-85169
Parent Company: Churches Together In Britain & Ireland
Distributor for World Council of Churches (UK & Ireland)

CTS Publications, *imprint of* Incorporated Catholic Truth Society

Curiad
The Old Library, County Rd, Pen-y-Groes, Caernarfon, Gwynedd LL54 6EY
Tel: (01286) 882166 *Fax:* (01286) 882692
E-mail: curiad@curiad.co.uk
Web Site: www.curiad.co.uk
Key Personnel
Contact: Dyfed Wyn Edwards
Founded: 1992
Subjects: Music, Dance
ISBN Prefix(es): 1-897664

Current Science Group+
Middlesex House, 34-42 Cleveland St, London W1T 4LB
Tel: (020) 7323 0323 *Fax:* (020) 7580 1938
E-mail: info@current-science.com
Web Site: www.current-science-group.com
Key Personnel
Chairman: Vitek Tracz *E-mail:* vitek@sciencenow.com
Man Dir: Anne Greenwood *E-mail:* anne@cursci.co.uk
Operations Dir: Mike Lennie
Marketing Dir: Daryl Rainer

Subjects: Biological Sciences, Medicine, Nursing, Dentistry, Science (General)
ISBN Prefix(es): 1-870485; 1-85927
Subsidiaries: Current Drugs Ltd; Science Press
U.S. Office(s): 20 N Third St, Philadelphia, PA 19106-2113, United States *Tel:* 215-574-2266 *Fax:* 215-574-2270

James Currey Ltd+
73 Boxley Rd, Oxford OX2 0BS
Tel: (01865) 244 111 *Fax:* (01865) 246 454
E-mail: editorial@jamescurrey.co.uk
Web Site: www.jamescurrey.co.uk
Key Personnel
Chairman: James M Currey
Man & Editorial Dir: Dr Douglas H Johnson
  E-mail: douglas.johnson@jamescurrey.co.uk
Editorial Manager: Lynn Taylor *E-mail:* lynn.taylor@jamescurrey.co.uk
Founded: 1985
Subjects: Agriculture, Anthropology, Archaeology, Biography, Developing Countries, Drama, Theater, Economics, Education, Environmental Studies, Ethnicity, Foreign Countries, Government, Political Science, History, Law, Philosophy, Social Sciences, Sociology, Africa, Caribbean, Gender Studies, Literary Criticism, Theatre & Film, Third World Bibliographies
ISBN Prefix(es): 0-85255
Number of titles published annually: 50 Print
Total Titles: 360 Print
Imprints: Hans Zell Bibliographies
Foreign Rep(s): IMA (Africa); Intermedia Americana Ltd (Africa & Mideast exc South Africa & Israel, Africa exc South Africa); David Philip Publishers (Africa)
Orders to: Plymbridge Distributors Ltd, Estover, Plymouth PL6 7PZ *Tel:* (01752) 202301 *Fax:* (01752) 202333 *E-mail:* orders@plymbridge.com

CyberClub+
39A Welbeck St, London W1G 8DH
Tel: (020) 8731 6161 *Fax:* (020) 8905 5050
Key Personnel
Contact: Richard Astor
Member of Publishers Association (UK).
Subjects: Law
ISBN Prefix(es): 1-873994
Imprints: Bartsky Legal Texts Ltd

Cyfres y Gair, *imprint of* Cyhoeddiadau'r Gair

Cygnus Arts, *imprint of* Golden Cockerel Press Ltd

Cyhoeddiadau Barddas
Pen-Rhiw, 71 Ffordd Pentrepoeth, Treforys, Abertawe SA6 6AE
Tel: (01792) 792 829
Key Personnel
Contact: Alan Llwyd
Founded: 1976
Specializes in Welsh language & literature.
Subjects: Literature, Literary Criticism, Essays, Poetry
ISBN Prefix(es): 1-900437

Cyhoeddiadau FBA, *imprint of* Francis Balsom Associates

Cyhoeddiadau'r Gair (Work Publications)+
Cyngor Ysgolion Sul, Ysgol Addsg, Prifysgol Cymru Bangor, Safle'r Normal, Bangor, Gwynedd LL57 2PX
Tel: (01248) 382947 *Fax:* (01248) 383954
E-mail: eds00e@bangor.ac.uk
Key Personnel
Contact: Aled Davies *E-mail:* aled.davies@bonger.ac.uk
Founded: 1992
Specialize in Welsh language Christian books, cards & systems.
Subjects: Biblical Studies, Religion - Protestant
ISBN Prefix(es): 1-85994
Total Titles: 300 Print; 2 CD-ROM
Parent Company: Cyngor Ysgolion Sul
Imprints: Cyfres y Gair
Subsidiaries: Cardiau'r Gair gifts
Distributed by Welsh Books Council
Distributor for Curaid; Gwasg Efeng yl Aidd Cymru
Bookshop(s): Canolfan Addysg Grefyddol, Bangor
Warehouse: Libanus, Bontnewydd

Cymdeithas Lyfrau Ceredigion+
Ystafell B5, Y Coleg Diwinyddol, Stryd y Brenin, Aberystwyth, Ceredigion SY23 2LT
Tel: (01970) 617776 *Fax:* (01970) 624049
Key Personnel
Contact: Dylan Williams
Founded: 1954
Subjects: Ceredigion Interest
ISBN Prefix(es): 0-901410; 0-948930; 1-902416
Orders to: The Distribution Centre, Unit 16, Glan-yr-afon Industrial Estate, Hanbadarn Fawr, Aberystwyth, Ceredigion SY23 3AQ

Cynulliad Cenedlaethol Cymru, *imprint of* National Assembly for Wales

D&B Ltd
Holmers Farm Way, High Wycombe, Bucks HP12 4UL
Tel: (01494) 422000 *Fax:* (01494) 422260
E-mail: customerhelp@dnb.com
Web Site: www.dnb.com
Key Personnel
Man Dir: Claes Henckel
Sales: Nigel Dickinson
Publicity & Marketing: Barbara James
Founded: 1841
Member of Directory Publishers Association, European Association of Directory Publishers, Booksellers Association & Business Information Network.
ISBN Prefix(es): 0-901491; 0-900714; 1-86071
Parent Company: D&B Corporation, One Diamond Hill Rd, Murray Hill, NJ 07974-1218, United States
Branch Office(s)
Bangor
Birmingham
Glasgow
London
Manchester
Newport
Nottingham
Southampton

D C Thomson & Co Ltd
80 Kingsway East, Dundee DD4 8SL
Tel: ((01382) 223131 *Fax:* (01382) 462097
Web Site: www.dcthomson.co.uk
Key Personnel
Chairman: Brian H Thompson
Founded: 1905
Branch Office(s)
Courier Buildings, 2 Albert Sq, Dundee DD1 9QJ *Tel:* (01382) 223131 *Fax:* (01382) 322214
144 Port Dundas Rd, Glasgow G4 0HZ *Tel:* (0141) 332 9933 *Fax:* (0141) 331 1595
185 Fleet St, London *Tel:* (020) 7400 1030 *Fax:* (020) 7831 9440
137 Chapel St, Manchester M3 6AA *Tel:* (0161) 834 2831 *Fax:* (0161) 833 2884

Daily Telegraph (map service), *imprint of* Roger Lascelles

Dales Large Print Series, *imprint of* Magna Large Print Books

Dalesman Publishing Co Ltd+
Stable Courtyard, Broughton Hall, Skipton, North Yorks BD23 3AZ
Tel: (01756) 701381 *Fax:* (01756) 701326
E-mail: editorial@dalesman.co.uk
Web Site: www.dalesman.co.uk
Key Personnel
Chairman: T J Benn
Man Dir: Robert Flanagan
Editor: Terry Fletcher
Founded: 1939
Publish monthly magazines.
Subjects: Travel
ISBN Prefix(es): 0-85206; 1-85568

Terence Dalton Ltd+
Water St, Lavenham, Suffolk CO10 9RN
Tel: (01787) 249290 *Fax:* (01787) 248267
E-mail: tdl@lavenhamgroup.cp.uk
Web Site: www.terencedalton.co.uk
Key Personnel
Man Dir: Terence Dalton *E-mail:* terence@lavenhamgroup.co.uk
Director: Mrs Lis Whitehair *E-mail:* lis@lavenhamgroup.co.uk
Marketing Manager: Erica Hammond *E-mail:* erica@lavenhamgroup.co.uk
Business Development Officer: Barney Goodrich *E-mail:* barney@lavenhamgroup.co.uk
Conference & Book Sales: Claire Smith *E-mail:* claire@lavenhamgroup.co.uk
Book Sales: Gail Moss *E-mail:* gail@lavenhamgroup.co.uk
Webmaster: Steve Lodge *E-mail:* steve@lavenhamgroup.co.uk
Founded: 1967
Contract publishers for CIWEM (Chartered Institution of Water & Environmental Management). Some East Anglian, maritime & aviation titles still available.
Subjects: Aeronautics, Aviation, Environmental Studies, Maritime, Regional Interests, Magazines
ISBN Prefix(es): 0-900963; 0-86138; 0-903214; 0-904623
Parent Company: The Lavenham Group PLC
Associate Companies: The Lavenham Press Ltd, Water St, Lavenham, CO10 9RN Sudbury, Suffolk, Contact: Terence Dalton *Tel:* (01787) 247436 *Fax:* (01787) 248267 *E-mail:* postmaster@lavenhamgroup.co.uk
Imprints: CIWEM; Eastland Press; Mallard Reprints
Distributor for CIWEM

Dance Books Ltd, The Old Bakery+
4 Lenten St, Alton, Hants GU34 1HG
Tel: (01420) 86138 *Fax:* (01420) 86142
E-mail: dl@dancebooks.co.uk
Web Site: www.dancebooks.co.uk
Key Personnel
Man Dir, Production, Rights & Permissions: David Leonard *E-mail:* dl@dancebooks.co.uk
Sales: Richard Holland
Founded: 1960
Publishers & bookkeepers.
Subjects: Music, Dance
ISBN Prefix(es): 0-903102; 1-85273
Number of titles published annually: 10 Print
Total Titles: 130 Print
Distributed by Princeton Book Co; Astam Books
Distributor for Princeton Book Co

The C W Daniel Co Ltd+
One Church Path, Saffron Walden, Essex CB10 1JP
Tel: (01799) 521909; (01799) 526216 *Fax:* (01799) 513462
E-mail: cwdaniel@ukonline.co.uk
Web Site: www.cwdaniel.com

Key Personnel
Man Dir: Ian Miller
Editorial, Rights & Permissions: Jane Miller
Accounts: Jane Goodacre
Marketing, Publicity: Genevieve Miller
 Tel: (01799) 521909
Founded: 1903
Publisher of Mind, Body & Spirit Paperbacks.
Subjects: Animals, Pets, Astrology, Occult, Health, Nutrition, Self-Help
ISBN Prefix(es): 0-85207; 0-85032; 0-85435; 0-85978; 0-85243
Number of titles published annually: 10 Print
Total Titles: 250 Print
Imprints: L N Fowler & Co Ltd; Health Science Press; Neville Spearman Publishers
Distributed by Alternative Books (UK); APA Publications (Singapore); Beekman Publishers Inc (USA); Gemcraft Books (UK); Homeopathic Educational Services; National Book Network (USA); The New Leaf Distributing Co (USA); The Nutri Book Corp (USA); Peaceful Living Publications (UK)
Distributor for Brotherhood of Life, NM; Haug Verlag, Germany
Foreign Rep(s): Angell Eurosales (Northern Europe, Scandinavia); Bookport Associates (Greece & Cyprus, Spain, Italy & Portugal); Kerim Colakoglu (Turkey); Donald MacDonald (Scotland); Tony Moggach (Africa, Eastern Europe, Middle East); National Book Network (Canada, US); Theo Phillips (Hong Kong, Malaysia & Singapore, Philippines, Thailand); David Williams (South America)
Foreign Rights: Angell Euorsales (Northern Europe, Scandinavia); Angell Eurosales (Northern Europe, Scandinavia); Bookport Associates (Greece, Greece & Cyprus, Spain, Italy & Portugal); Kerim Colakoglu (Turkey); Donald MacDonald (Scotland); Genny Kelliher (Northern Ireland); Joe Portelli (Greece, Italy, Portugal, Spain); Tom Moggach (Africa); Tony Moggach (Eastern Europe, Middle East); National Book Network (Canada, US); Theo Philips (Hong Kong, Malaysia & Singapore, Philippines, Thailand); The Segrue Partnership (London); David Williams (South America)
Warehouse: Unit 7, Saffron Business Centre, Elizabeth Close, off Elizabeth Way, Saffron Walden, Essex CB10 2BL

Darf Publishers Ltd
277 West End Lane, London NW6 1QS
Tel: (020) 7431 7009 *Fax:* (020) 7431 7655
E-mail: darf@freeuk.com
Web Site: home.freeuk.net/darf
Key Personnel
Chief Executive: M B Fergiani
Editorial: Usama Al Fergiani
Sales, Publicity: Ghassan Fergiani
Production: A Bentaleb
Manager & Rights & Permissions: John Cowen
Founded: 1983
Specialize in reprints of out-of-print & rare books written in the 18th & 19th centuries.
Subjects: Archaeology, History, Religion - Islamic, Travel
ISBN Prefix(es): 1-85077
Number of titles published annually: 10 Print
Total Titles: 200 Print
Parent Company: Dar Al Fergian, PO Box 132, Tripoli, Libyan Arab Jamahiriya
Subsidiaries: Dar Al Fergiani

Dartmouth, *imprint of* Ashgate Publishing Ltd

Darton, Longman & Todd Ltd+
One Spencer Court, 140 Wandsworth High St, London SW18 4JJ
Tel: (020) 8875 0155 *Fax:* (020) 8875 0133
E-mail: tradesales@darton-longman-todd.co.uk

Key Personnel
Production: Leslie Kay
Sales & Marketing Dir: Alan Mordue
Editorial Dir: Brendan Walsh
Man Editor: Helen Porter
Rights & Permissions: Rachel Davis
Founded: 1959
Subjects: Biblical Studies, Religion - Catholic, Religion - Protestant, Religion - Other, Theology
ISBN Prefix(es): 0-232
Warehouse: 9 Amor Way, Dunhams Lane, Letchworth, Herts S96 1U9

Datapack Books, *imprint of* E J Morten (Publishers)

David & Charles Ltd+
Brunel House, Forde Close, Newton Abbot, Devon TQ12 4PU
Tel: (01626) 323200 *Fax:* (01626) 323319; (01626) 364463
E-mail: postermaster@davidandcharles.co.uk
Web Site: www.davidandcharles.co.uk
Telex: 42904 BOOKS G
Key Personnel
Sales & Marketing Dir: Susie Hallam
Non-Executive Dir: Neil McRae
Rights & Book Club Manager: Sue Narramore
Publishing Dir: Piers Spence
Operation Dir & Production Manager: Amanda Newton
Press & Promotions Officer: Susan Hallam
Founded: 1960
Subjects: Animals, Pets, Art, Cookery, Crafts, Games, Hobbies, Gardening, Plants, Health, Nutrition, How-to, Maritime, Outdoor Recreation, Photography, Transportation, Travel
ISBN Prefix(es): 0-7153; 0-907115; 1-85724; 0-276; 0-86438
Associate Companies: Levinson
Imprints: Betterway; How Design; North Light; Popular Woodworking; Writer's Digest
Divisions: The Readers' Union
Distributed by David Batemen Ltd (New Zealand); F & W Publications, Inc (USA & Canada); Kirby Book Distribution (Australia); Trinity Books (South Africa)
Foreign Rep(s): Angell Eurosales (Belgium, Denmark, Netherlands, Finland, France, Iceland, Norway, Sweden); Pat Bence (Botswana, Caribbean, Kenya, Mauritius, The Gambia); Candida Buckley (Denmark, Netherlands, Finland, Norway, Switzerland); Michelle Morrow Curreri (Asia, Latin America, Middle East); Lora Fountain (France); Gabriele Kern (Austria, Germany, Switzerland); Surit Mitra (Bangladesh, Indonesia, Nepal, Sri Lanka); Penny Padovani (France, Gibraltar, Greece, Italy, Spain); Marta Schooler (Asia, Latin America, Middle East)
Book Club(s): Readers Union Ltd
Orders to: Exel Logistics, DMS 3, Sheldon Way, Larkfield, Aylesford, Kent ME20 65E

David Bennett Books+
Subsidiary of C & B Publishing PLC
London House, Great Eastern Wharf, Parkgate Rd, London SW11 4NQ
Tel: (020) 7738 0314 *Fax:* (020) 7223 4936
Web Site: www.illustratedlibrary.com
Key Personnel
Man Dir: Peter Osborn *E-mail:* peter.osborn@belithapress.co.uk
Creative & Publishing Dir: David Bennett
 E-mail: david.bennett@db-books.co.uk
Foreign Rights Manager: Madeleine Ehm
 E-mail: madeleine.ehm@belithapress.co.uk
UK Sales & Marketing Dir: Tristan Hilderley
 E-mail: tristan.hilderley@db-books.co.uk
Founded: 1989
Specializes in picture books & novelties ages 0-7.

Warehouse: Biblios Distribution, Star Rd, Partridge Green, Horsham, West Sussex RH13 8LD, Contact: Julia Jackson *Tel:* (01403) 710851 *Fax:* (01403) 711143 *E-mail:* biblios@biblios.co.uk

Christopher Davies Publishers Ltd+
PO Box 403, Swansea SA1 4YF
Tel: (01792) 648825 *Fax:* (01792) 648825
E-mail: sales@cdaviesbookswales.com
Web Site: www.cdaviesbookswales.com
Key Personnel
Man Dir: Christopher Talfan Davies
 E-mail: chris@cdaviesbookswales.com
Founded: 1949
Subjects: Cookery, Health, Nutrition, History, Natural History
ISBN Prefix(es): 0-7154; 0-85339

Dawson Holdings PLC+
9th Floor South Wing, AMP House, Dingwall Rd, Croydon CR0 9XA
Tel: (0181) 6670770 *Fax:* (0181) 7743010
Web Site: dawson.investor-relations.co.uk
Key Personnel
Chief Executive: B C Ingleby
Chairman: Linden Hadden
Financial Dir: David Lowther
Internet Coordinator: Sally Wilson
Company Secretary: David Clark
Founded: 1809
Specialize in international library & information (subscriptions, book,. library software); news distribution.
Subsidiaries: Dawson Espana SF Faxon Company; Dawson France SA; Dawson IQ; Dawson UK Ltd; Eosi; Surridge Dawson; Turner Subscription Agency
Branch Office(s)
1001 W Pines Rd, Oregon, IL 61061-9570, United States

Debrett's Peerage Ltd+
King's Court, 2-16 Goodge St, London W1T 2QA
Tel: (020) 7915 9633 *Fax:* (020) 7753 4212
E-mail: people@debretts.co.uk
Web Site: www.debretts.co.uk
Key Personnel
Editorial, Peerage & Baronetage: Charles Kidd
Editorial: David Williamson
Operations Manager: Andrew Moulder
Business Development: Sharon Tidball
Founded: 1769
Subjects: Biography, Genealogy
ISBN Prefix(es): 1-870520; 0-905649
Orders to: Vinehouse Distribution Ltd, Waldenbury, North Common, Chailey, East Sussex BN27 3RP *Tel:* (01825) 723 398 *Fax:* (01825) 724 188

Decadence from Dedalus, *imprint of* Dedalus Ltd

Dedalus European Classics, *imprint of* Dedalus Ltd

Dedalus Ltd+
Langford Lane, St Judith's Lane, Sawtry, Cambs PEJ7 5XE
Tel: (01487) 832382 *Fax:* (01487) 832382
E-mail: sales@dedalusbooks.com
Web Site: www.dedalusbooks.com
Key Personnel
Chief Executive: Eric Lane
Chairman: Juri Gabriel
Editorial Dir: Robert Irwin
Founded: 1984
Subjects: Fiction, Literature, Literary Criticism, Essays
ISBN Prefix(es): 0-946626; 1-873982

Imprints: Dedalus European Classics; Decadence from Dedalus; Dedalus Nobel Prize Winner; Europe 1992-98; Empire of the Senses; Original English Language Fiction
U.S. Office(s): Subterranean Co, 265 S Fifth St, Monroe, OR 97651, United States
Distributed by Central Books
Foreign Rep(s): Richard D. Bowen (Scandinavia); Michael Geoghegan (Austria, Belgium, France, Germany, Switzerland, Holland); Marginal Distribution (Canada); Penny Padovani (Greece, Italy, Portugal, Spain); Peribo Pty Ltd (Australia, New Zealand); SCB Disributors (US)

Dedalus Nobel Prize Winner, *imprint of* Dedalus Ltd

Defiant Publications
190 Yoxall Rd, Shirley, Solihull, West Midlands B90 3RN
Tel: (0121) 745 8421
E-mail: info@defiantpublications.co.uk
Web Site: www.defiantpublications.co.uk
Key Personnel
Proprietor: Peter B Hands
Founded: 1980
Subjects: Humor, Transportation
ISBN Prefix(es): 0-946857

Delectation, *imprint of* Delectus Books

Delectus Books+
27 Old Gloucester St, London WC1N 3XX
Tel: (020) 8963 0979 *Fax:* (020) 8963 0502
Web Site: abebooks.com/home/DELECTUS/
Key Personnel
Publisher: Michael R Goss *E-mail:* mgdelectus@aol.com
Founded: 1988
Subjects: Anthropology, Criminology, Erotica, Gay & Lesbian, Psychology, Psychiatry, Dada, Decadence, Drugs & Alcohol, Ethnology, Fantasy, Folklore, Gothic & Horror, Occult & Witchcraft, Psychoanalysis, Scotland & Ireland, Sexology, Surrealism, Symbolists & the 1890's, True Crime, Vampires & Werewolves
ISBN Prefix(es): 1-897767
Number of titles published annually: 3 Print
Total Titles: 15 Print
Imprints: Delectation
Distributed by Marginal (Canada); Peribo (Australia & New Zealand); Turnaround (UK & Europe)
Orders to: Last Gasp of San Francisco, 777 Florida St, San Francisco, CA 94100, United States, Contact: Erick Gilbert *Tel:* 415-824-6636 *E-mail:* gasp@lastgasp.com

Denor Press+
PO Box 12913, London N12 ONP
Tel: (020) 8343 7368 *Fax:* (020) 8446 4504
E-mail: denor@dial.pipex.com
Web Site: www.xhf37.dial.pipex.com
Key Personnel
Rights Dir: Brendan Beder
Promotion & Marketing Executive: Elizabeth Plumstead
Founded: 1997
Subjects: Fiction, Health, Nutrition, Medicine, Nursing, Dentistry, Music, Dance, Nonfiction (General), Promotion & marketing services
ISBN Prefix(es): 0-9526056
Total Titles: 4 Print; 4 Online; 4 E-Book
Online services available through Denor Press.
Ultimate Parent Company: Denor Press
Membership(s): Publishers' Association

Andre Deutsch Children's Books, *imprint of* Scholastic Ltd

Andre Deutsch Ltd+
76 Dean St, London W1V 5HA
Tel: (020) 7316 4450 *Fax:* (020) 7316 4499
Key Personnel
Man Dir: Tim Forrester
Production Dir: Alastair Gourlay
Publicity Dir, Advertising: Nigel Stoneman
Founded: 1951
Subjects: Art, Biography, Cookery, Fiction, Government, Political Science, History, Humor, Music, Dance, Photography, Sports, Athletics, Travel
ISBN Prefix(es): 0-233
Parent Company: King Fisher Plc
Imprints: Chameleon
Warehouse: Littlehampton Book Services Ltd, 14 Eldon Way, Lineside Estate, Littlehampton, West Sussex BN17 7C11

Diagram Visual Information Ltd+
195 Kentish Town Rd, London NW5 2JU
Tel: (020) 74823633 *Fax:* (020) 74824932
E-mail: diagramuis@aol.com
Key Personnel
Dir & International Rights: Bruce Robertson
Founded: 1967
Book designer & creator.
Subjects: Art, Crafts, Games, Hobbies
ISBN Prefix(es): 1-900121
Number of titles published annually: 10 Print
Total Titles: 400 Print

Dial House, *imprint of* Ian Allan Publishing Ltd

Dickson Price Publishers Ltd
Hawthorn House, Bowdell Lane, Brookland, Rowney Marsh, Kent TN29 9RW
Tel: (01797) 344626 *Fax:* (01797) 344668
Key Personnel
Man Dir, Editorial, Rights & Permissions: Mr E E Dickson
Production: D S Wanstall
Founded: 1980
Subjects: Computer Science, Electronics, Electrical Engineering
ISBN Prefix(es): 0-85380

Digital Photoart, *imprint of* Creative Monochrome Ltd

DIME, *imprint of* Tarquin Publications

Dinas, *imprint of* Y Lolfa Cyf

Discovers, *imprint of* Moonlight Publishing Ltd

Discovery Walking Guides Ltd+
10 Tennyson Close, Dallington, Northampton NN5 7HJ
Tel: (01604) 752576
Web Site: www.walking.demon.co.uk
Key Personnel
Company Secretary: David Brawn
Contact: Ros Brawn
Founded: 1993
Specialize in walking guides, botanical guides, tour & trail maps.
Subjects: Gardening, Plants, Travel
ISBN Prefix(es): 1-899554
Number of titles published annually: 8 Print
Total Titles: 45 Print
Imprints: Tour & Trail Maps; Warm Island Walking Guides
Membership(s): IPG

Disney, *imprint of* Ladybird Books

DIY Publishing
Microworld House, 4 Foscote Mews, London W9 2HH
Tel: (020) 7266 2202 *Fax:* (020) 7266 2314
E-mail: info@diypublishing.com
Web Site: www.diypublishing.com
Service for authors to publish & sell their publications online.
Associate Companies: World Microfilms Publications Ltd

DMG Business Media Ltd
Queensway House, 2 Queensway, Redhill, Surrey RH1 1QS
Tel: (01737) 768611 *Fax:* (01737) 855477
Web Site: www.dmg.co.uk
Key Personnel
Managing Dir: Paul Camp
Subscriptions Mgr: Ben Martin *E-mail:* bmartin@dmg.co.uk
Subjects: Chemistry, Chemical Engineering, Civil Engineering, Communications, Engineering (General), Maritime, Publishing & Book Trade Reference, Radio, TV, Securities, Transportation
Parent Company: DMG World Media
Associate Companies: DMG Exhibition Group

Dobro Publishing
52 Howcroft Crescent, Finchley, London N3 1PB
Tel: (020) 8346 4010
E-mail: dobropublishing@aol.com
Web Site: www.drsandradelroy.com
Key Personnel
Contact: Dr Sandra Delroy
E-mail: psychologist@drsandradelroy.com
Subjects: Health, Nutrition, Medicine, Nursing, Dentistry, Psychology, Psychiatry

The Dolmen Press Ltd, see Colin Smythe Ltd

Dolphin Paperbacks, *imprint of* Orion Children's Books

John Donald Publishers Ltd, *imprint of* Birlinn Ltd

John Donald Publishers Ltd+
Imprint of Birlinn Ltd
West Newington House, 10 Newington Rd, Edinburgh EH9 1QS
Tel: (0131) 668 4371 *Fax:* (0131) 668 4466
E-mail: info@birlinn.co.uk
Web Site: www.birlinn.co.uk
Key Personnel
Commissioning Editor: Hugh Andrew
Office & Publicity Manager: Sarah Tranter
Founded: 1973
Subjects: History, Regional Interests, Sports, Athletics, Travel
ISBN Prefix(es): 0-85976
Number of titles published annually: 10 Print
Total Titles: 170 Print
Warehouse: Scottish Book Source, 32 Finlas St, Springlawn, Glasgow
Orders to: Scottish Book Source, 137 Dundee St, Edinburgh EH11 1BG, Fiola Slaxwell-Hoy *Tel:* (0131) 229 6800 *Fax:* (0131) 229 9070

Donhead Publishing Ltd
Lower Coombe, Donhead St Mary, Shaftesbury, Dorset SP7 9LY
Tel: (01747) 828422 *Fax:* (01747) 828522
E-mail: sales@donhead.com
Web Site: www.donhead.com
Key Personnel
Dir: Jill Pearce
Founded: 1992
Subjects: Architecture & Interior Design, Architectural & Building Conservation, Heritage & Landscapes

UNITED KINGDOM

ISBN Prefix(es): 1-873394
Number of titles published annually: 7 Print
Total Titles: 50 Print
Branch Office(s)
PRG Inc, PO Box 1768, Rockville, MD 20849, United States (North America only)
Membership(s): IPG

Dorling Kindersley Ltd+
80 Strand, London WC2R OLR
Tel: (020) 7010 3000 *Fax:* (020) 7010 6060
E-mail: onlineDKcustomer.service@dk.com
Web Site: www.dk.com
Key Personnel
Chairman: Peter Kindersley
Deputy Chairman: Christopher Davis
International Sales Dir: Ruth Sandys
Group Sales & Marketing Dir: David Holmes
Man Dir, Multi-Media: Alan Buckingham
Production Dir: Martyn Longly
International Sales (Adults): Michael Devenish
Chief Exec: James Middlehurst
Founded: 1974
Subjects: Art, Child Care & Development, Cookery, Crafts, Games, Hobbies, Gardening, Plants, Health, Nutrition, History, House & Home, Music, Dance, Nonfiction (General), Photography, Self-Help, Sports, Athletics, Wine & Spirits
ISBN Prefix(es): 0-7894; 0-86318; 0-7513
Associate Companies: DK Inc (USA), United States
Subsidiaries: DKP Inc; DK Family Library
Branch Office(s)
DK Austria & New Zealand
DK Canada
DK France
DK Germany
DK Russia
DK South Africa
Penguin Books Australia, 487 Maroondah Hwy, Ringwood VIC 3134, Australia *Tel:* (03) 9871 2400 *Fax:* (03) 9870 9618
U.S. Office(s): DK Family Library Inc, 7566 Southland Executive Park, Orlando, FL 32809, United States
Dorling Kindersley Inc, 375 Hudson St, New York, NY 10014, United States *Tel:* 212-213-4800 *Fax:* 212-213-5240
Distributed by Penguin Books
Bookshop(s): 10-13 Knox St WC2E 8HN
Warehouse: International Book Distributors Ltd, Magna Park, Coventry Rd, Butterworth, Leics LE17 4XH

Doubleday, *imprint of* Transworld Publishers Ltd

Alton Douglas Books, *imprint of* Brewin Books Ltd

Drake Educational Associates Ltd+
Saint Fagans Road, Fairwater, Cardiff CF5 3AE
Tel: (029) 2056 0333 *Fax:* (029) 2055 4909
E-mail: drakegroup@btinternet.com
Web Site: www.drakegroup.co.uk
Key Personnel
Man Dir: Mr R G Drake
Founded: 1970
Specialize in literacy & languages.
Subjects: Disability, Special Needs, Education
ISBN Prefix(es): 0-86174
Parent Company: Drake Group
Distributor for Highsmith Press (USA); Pembroke Publishers (Canada)

Dramatic Lines Publishers+
PO Box 201, Twickenham, Middlesex TW2 5RQ
Tel: (020) 8296 9502 *Fax:* (020) 8296 9503
E-mail: mail@dramaticlines.co.uk
Web Site: www.dramaticlines.co.uk

Key Personnel
Managing Editor: John Nicholas
Founded: 1994
Drama publisher.
Subjects: Drama, Theater
ISBN Prefix(es): 0-9522224; 0-9537770
Number of titles published annually: 6 Print
Membership(s): Publishers' Association

The Dreamer's Guides, *imprint of* Breese Books Ltd

Dref Wen, *imprint of* Gwasg y Dref Wen

Duck Editions, *imprint of* Gerald Duckworth & Co Ltd

Gerald Duckworth & Co Ltd+
61 Frith St, London W1D 3JL
Tel: (020) 7434 4242 *Fax:* (020) 7434 4420
E-mail: info@ducknet.co.uk
Web Site: www.duckw.com
Key Personnel
Chairman: Stephen Hill
Chief Executive Officer & Publisher: Tom Hedley
Chief Operating Officer: Gillian Hawkins
Founded: 1898
Specialize in Greek & Latin classics.
Subjects: Fiction, Language Arts, Linguistics, Literature, Literary Criticism, Essays, Maritime, Nonfiction (General), Philosophy, Psychology, Psychiatry, Religion - Other, Science (General), Classics, Linguistics
ISBN Prefix(es): 0-7156; 1-85399; 1-86176
Number of titles published annually: 300 Print
Total Titles: 1,500 Print
Associate Companies: Chatham Publishing
Imprints: BCP; Chatham Publishing; Duck Editions
Subsidiaries: Bristol Classical Press
Warehouse: Book Sellers International, PO Box 605, Herndon, VA 20172, United States *Tel:* 703-434-7064

Duke University Press, *imprint of* Combined Academic Publishers

Dun & Bradstreet Ltd, see D&B Ltd

Dunedin Academic Press+
Hudson House, 8 Albany St, Edinburgh EH1 3QB
Tel: (0131) 473 2397
Key Personnel
Contact: Anthony Kinahan *E-mail:* anthony@ajkinahan.demon.co.uk
Founded: 2000
Member of Scottish Publishers Association.
Subjects: Biography, Earth Sciences, Economics, Education, Geography, Geology, History, Law, Literature, Literary Criticism, Essays, Social Sciences, Sociology, Theology
ISBN Prefix(es): 1-903765
Number of titles published annually: 20 Print
Total Titles: 25 Print

Martin Dunitz Ltd+
Member of The Talor & Francis Group (USA & Canada)
The Livery House, 7-9 Pratt St, London NW1 0AE
Tel: (020) 7482 2202 *Fax:* (020) 7267 0159
E-mail: info@dunitz.co.uk
Web Site: www.dunitz.co.uk
Key Personnel
Man Dir: Martin Dunitz *E-mail:* martin.dunitz@tandf.co.uk
Editor Commissioning: Robert Peden *E-mail:* robert.peden@tandf.co.uk

Commissioning Editor: Alan Burgess *E-mail:* alan.burgess@tandf.co.uk
Managing Editor: Alison Campbell *E-mail:* alison.campbell@tandf.co.uk
Production: Rosemary Allen *E-mail:* rosemary.allen@tandf.co.uk
Marketing Manager: Daniel Tomkins *E-mail:* daniel.tomkins@tandf.co.uk
Journal Sales & Advertising: Ian Mellor *E-mail:* ian.mellor@tandf.co.uk
Rights Manager: Carla Oliveira *E-mail:* carla.oliveira@tandf.co.uk
Head of Special Sales: Beth Bacchus *E-mail:* beth.bacchus@tandf.co.uk
Journal Editorial Enquiries: Maire Collins *E-mail:* maire.collins@2tankd.co.uk
Customer Services: Teresa Davey *E-mail:* teresa.davey@tandf.co.uk
General Enquiries: Heather Cameron *E-mail:* heather.cameron@tandf.co.uk
Founded: 1978 (Founded by Ruth & Martin Dunitz)
Specialist Medical Publishers of postgraduate books & journals, Medicine, Dentistry.
Recipient of 1991 Queen's Award for Export Achievement. Incorporating Isis Medical Media.
Subjects: Medicine, Nursing, Dentistry, Psychology, Psychiatry
ISBN Prefix(es): 0-906348; 0-948269; 1-85317; 1-84184; 1-901865
Number of titles published annually: 130 Print
Total Titles: 420 Print; 1 CD-ROM
Associate Companies: Isis Medical Media
Distributed by The Talor & Francis Group (USA & Canada)
Distributor for Remedica
Warehouse: ITPS, Cheriton House, North Way, Andover Hants SP10 5BE *Tel:* (01264) 342937 *Fax:* (01264) 343005
Orders to: ITPS, Cheriton House, North Way, Andover Hants SP10 5BE *Tel:* (01264) 342937 *Fax:* (01264) 343005

Van Duren Publishers Ltd, see Colin Smythe Ltd

Gwasg Dwyfor
Industrial Estate, Pen-Y-Groes, Caernarfon LL54 6DB
Tel: (01236) 881 911 *Fax:* (01236) 880 120
E-mail: argraff@gwasgdwyfor.demon.co.uk
Key Personnel
Partner: Dafydd Owen; M P Roberts; J A Ellis
Founded: 1981
Subjects: Nonfiction (General)
ISBN Prefix(es): 1-870394

Eagle/Inter Publishing Service (IPS) Ltd+
St Nicholas House, 14 The Mount, Guildford, Surrey GU2 5HN
Tel: (01483) 306309 *Fax:* (01483) 579196
E-mail: eagle_ips@compuserve.com
Key Personnel
Man Dir: David Wavre
Editorial Manager: Lynne Barratt
Production Dir: James Ralton
Founded: 1990
Subjects: Religion - Catholic, Religion - Protestant, Religion - Other
ISBN Prefix(es): 0-86347
Orders to: STL, Kingstown Broadway, PO Box 300, Carlisle CA3 0QS

Eaglemoss Publications Ltd+
5 Cromwell Rd, London SW7 2HR
Tel: (020) 7590 8300 *Fax:* (020) 7590 8301
E-mail: enquiries@eaglemoss.co.uk
Web Site: www.eaglemoss.co.uk
Key Personnel
Chief Executive: Mark Stanley
Dir: E B Hilton

PUBLISHERS UNITED KINGDOM

Commercial Dir: J D Sibley
Financial Dir: S P Rose
Editorial Dir: Maggie Calmels
Marketing Dir: Suzie Deeming
Trade Enquiries: Gary Neale *E-mail:* garyneale@eaglemoss.co.uk
Founded: 1979
Specialize in publication of Partworks.
Subjects: Art, Computer Science, Cookery, Crafts, Games, Hobbies, Criminology, Outdoor Recreation, Photography, Sports, Athletics, Transportation
Branch Office(s)
Australia
Malaysia
Singapore
South Africa

EAL, *imprint of* Training Publications Ltd

Earthscan Publications Ltd+
120 Pentonville Rd, London N1 9JN
Tel: (020) 7278 0433 *Fax:* (020) 7278 1142
E-mail: earthinfo@earthscan.co.uk
Web Site: www.earthscan.co.uk
Key Personnel
Chief Executive: Jonathan Sinclair-Wilson
Sales Dir for Kogan Page: Julie McNair
Editorial: Frances McDermott
Production: Peter Chadwick
Publicity: Jeannette Hurdle
Marketing Issues/Bulk Orders: Helen Rose
  E-mail: hrose@earthscan.co.uk
Press/PR Inquiries: Martha Fumigali
  E-mail: mfumigali@kogan-page.co.uk
Press Review Copies: Helen Engstrand
  E-mail: engstrand@kogan-page.co.uk
Academic Inspection Copy Inquiries: Anna Murphy *E-mail:* amurphy@kogan-copy.co.uk
Founded: 1987
Subjects: Developing Countries, Environmental Studies
ISBN Prefix(es): 1-85383
Parent Company: Kogan Page Ltd, London
U.S. Office(s): Kogan Page, 163 Central Ave, Suite 2, Hopkins Professional Bldg, Dover, NH 03820, United States
Distributed by Island Press (USA)
Distributor for Island Press (outside North America)

East-West Publications (UK) Ltd+
8 Caledonia St, London N1 9DZ
Tel: (020) 7837 5061 *Fax:* (020) 7278 4429
Key Personnel
Chairman: L W Carp
Founded: 1976
Subjects: Music, Dance, Religion - Other
ISBN Prefix(es): 0-85692; 1-872571
Associate Companies: Cromwell Book Services Ltd
Imprints: Britannia Press; Gallery Children's Books
Warehouse: East-West & Britannia, TBS, Frating Distribution Centre, Frating Green, Colchester CO7 7DW
Gallery: The Trade Counter, The Airfield, Norwich Rd, Mendlesham IP14 5NA

Eastland Press, *imprint of* Terence Dalton Ltd

Ebury Press, *imprint of* Random House UK Ltd

Ebury Press Stationery, *imprint of* Random House UK Ltd

Ecco, *imprint of* HarperCollins Publishers

Eclipse, *imprint of* Butterworths Tolley

The Economist Intelligence Unit+
15 Regent St, London SW1Y 4LR
Tel: (020) 7830 1007 *Fax:* (020) 7830 1023
E-mail: london@eiu.com
Web Site: www.eiu.com
Telex: 266353 *Cable:* EIUG
Key Personnel
Chief Executive: Helen Alexander
Senior Editor - New York: Crispin Hawes
  E-mail: crispinhawes@eiu.com
Dir, Marketing: Nigel Ludlow
Editorial Dir: Daniel Franklin
Director, Marketing Development - New York: Jeremy Eagle *E-mail:* jeremyeagle@eiu.com
Sales Manager - New York: Julian Tate
  E-mail: juliantate@eiu.com
Founded: 1954
Economist Group Asia-Pacific, 10th Floor, Luk Kwok Centre, 72 Gloucester Rd, Wanchai, Hong Kong Tel: 529-0833 Fax: 865-1554; Economist Intelligence Unit, Schwarzenbergplatz 8/7, A-1030 Vienna, Austria Tel: (01) 71241610 Fax: (01) 7146769; 2/F Shokin Bldg, 8-11-12 Ginza, Chuo-ku, Tokyo 104, Japan Tel: (03) 32701008 Fax: (03) 32450358.
Subjects: Automotive, Business, Developing Countries, Economics, Finance, Management, Travel
ISBN Prefix(es): 0-85058; 0-86218; 0-900351
Parent Company: The Economist Group
Subsidiaries: Economist Publications Ltd
Branch Office(s)
Schwarzenbergplatz 8/7, 1030 Vienna, Austria *Tel:* (01) 712 41 610 *Fax:* (01) 714 6769
  E-mail: vienna@eiu.com
60/F Central Plaza, 18 Harbour Rd, Wanchai, Hong Kong *Tel:* 2802 7288; 2585; 3888 *Fax:* 2802 7638; 2802; 7720
  E-mail: hongkong@eiu.com
Postbus 1254, 1300 BG Almere, Netherlands
  E-mail: cmf@eiu.com
No 23-01 PWC Bldg, No 8 Cross St 04824, Singapore *Tel:* 534 5177 *Fax:* 534 5077
  E-mail: soniayao@eiu.com
U.S. Office(s): 481 Magnolia Ave, Larkspur, CA 94939, United States *Tel:* 415-924-3311 *Fax:* 415-331-2096 *E-mail:* owenweed@eiu.com
The Economist Bldg, 111 W 57 St, New York, NY 10019, United States *Tel:* 212-554-0600 *Fax:* 212-586-1181/2 *E-mail:* newyork@eiu.com
Bookshop(s): The Economist Bookshop, 25 St James St, London SW1A 1HG
Warehouse: Dartford, Unit 151, Dartford Trade Park, Hawley Rd, Dartford Kent DA2 2QB

Eddison Sadd Editions Ltd+
St Chads House, 148 King's Cross Rd, London WC1X 9DH
Tel: (020) 7837 1968 *Fax:* (020) 7837 6844
E-mail: langel@eddisonsadd.co.uk
Key Personnel
Man Dir: Nick Eddison
Editorial Dir: Ian Jackson
Founded: 1982
Packagers of international co-editions.
Subjects: Nonfiction (General), Illustrated Books, Kits
Associate Companies: Connections Book Publishing
Imprints: Connections

Edinburgh University Press Ltd+
22 George Sq, Edinburgh EH8 9LF
Tel: (0131) 650 4218; (0131) 650-6220 (Orders) *Fax:* (0131) 662 0053; (0131) 662-0053 (Orders)
E-mail: marketing@eup.ed.ac.uk; journals@eup.ed.ac.uk (Orders)
Web Site: www.eup.ed.ac.uk
Key Personnel
Editorial Dir: Jackie Jones *Tel:* (0131) 6504217
  E-mail: jackie.jones@eup.ed.ac.uk
Founded: 1948
Subjects: Anthropology, Archaeology, Architecture & Interior Design, Art, Computer Science, Economics, Education, Environmental Studies, Film, Video, Government, Political Science, History, Literature, Literary Criticism, Essays, Music, Dance, Natural History, Philosophy, Public Administration, Religion - Islamic, Science (General), Social Sciences, Sociology, Theology, Women's Studies
ISBN Prefix(es): 0-85224; 0-7486
Parent Company: The University of Edinburgh
Imprints: Polygon; Polygon at Edinburgh
Distributed by Columbia University Press (US & Canada)
Warehouse: Marston Book Services, PO Box 269, Abingdon, Oxon OX14 4YN *Tel:* (01235) 465500
Orders to: Marston Book Services, PO Box 269, Abingdon, Oxon OX14 4YN

Editon XII
23 Arundel Gardens, London W11 2LW
Tel: (020) 7833 0120 *Fax:* (020) 7923 5500; (020) 7923 5505
E-mail: info@editionxii.co.uk
Key Personnel
Man Dir: Edward More O'Ferrall
Marketing Manager: Simon Klemba
Specialize in academic publications.
Subjects: Business, Computer Science, Economics, Education, Engineering (General), Law, Social Sciences, Sociology
ISBN Prefix(es): 1-86149; 0-9520105; 1-899522
Orders to: Mike Sirott, 3691 S 3200 W, West Valley, UT 84119, United States
Baker & Taylor Books, 44 Kirby Ave, Somerville, NJ 08876, United States

Educational Explorers (Publishers) Ltd
11 Crown St, Reading, Berks RG1 2TQ
Tel: (0118) 987 3101 *Fax:* (0118) 987 3103
E-mail: explorers@cuisenaire.co.uk
Web Site: www.cuisenaire.co.uk
Key Personnel
Chairman: D M Gattegno
Man Dir: M J Hollyfield *E-mail:* hollyfield@cuisenaire.co.uk
Founded: 1960
Subjects: Language Arts, Linguistics, Mathematics, Psychology, Psychiatry
ISBN Prefix(es): 0-85225
Parent Company: Educational Solutions (UK) Ltd of Reading
Associate Companies: Cuisenaire Co, 11 Crown St, Reading, Berks RG1 2TQ; Educational Explorers Film Co, 11 Crown St, Reading, Berks RG1 2TQ; Educational Solutions Inc, 99 University Pl, New York, NY 10003-4555, United States

EITB, *imprint of* Training Publications Ltd

Eland
61 Exmouth Market, 3rd floor, London EC1R 4QL
Tel: (020) 7833 0762 *Fax:* (020) 7833 4434
E-mail: feedback@travelbooks.co.uk
Web Site: www.travelbooks.co.uk
Key Personnel
Contact: Rose Baring *E-mail:* info@travelbooks.co.uk
Subjects: Biography, Fiction, Travel
ISBN Prefix(es): 0-907871
Imprints: Sickle Moon Books

UNITED KINGDOM

ELC International
5 Five Mile Drive, Oxford OX2 8HT
Tel: (01865) 513186; (01865) 26520284
Fax: (01865) 513186; (01865) 26530180
E-mail: snyderpub@aol.com

Electronic Publishing Services Ltd
26 Rosebery Ave, London EC1R 4SX
Tel: (020) 7837 3345 *Fax:* (020) 7837 8901
E-mail: eps@epsltd.com
Web Site: www.epsltd.com
Key Personnel
Chairman: David R Worlock
Dir: David J Powell
Founded: 1985
Research & consultancy company which specializes in electronic publishing strategy development & high-level market research.
Member of The UK Publishers Association.
Subjects: Library & Information Sciences, Publishing & Book Trade Reference
ISBN Prefix(es): 0-9517344
Total Titles: 10 Print
Subsidiaries: Interactive Media Publications Ltd

Element Books Ltd+
Old School House, The Courtyard, Bell St, Shaftesbury, Dorset SP7 8BP
Tel: (01747) 851448 *Fax:* (01747) 855721
Key Personnel
Chairman: Michael Mann
Chief Executive: David Alexander
Man Dir: Julia McCutchen
Sales: Penny Stopa
Publicity: Jenny Carradice
Production Dir: Roger Lane *E-mail:* roger_lane@iconex.mactel.org
Founded: 1978
Subjects: Art, Astrology, Occult, Biography, Environmental Studies, Health, Nutrition, Literature, Literary Criticism, Essays, Management, Music, Dance, Philosophy, Psychology, Psychiatry, Religion - Other, Science (General), Self-Help, Travel, Women's Studies, Feminist Studies, Zen
ISBN Prefix(es): 1-85230; 1-86204; 0-906540
U.S. Office(s): Element Books Inc, 21 Broadway, Rockport, MA 01966, United States *Tel:* 508-546-1040
Distributed by India Book Distributors (Bombay) Ltd; India Book House Pvt Ltd; TBI Publishers' Distributors
Orders to: Penguin Books Ltd, Bath Rd, Harmondsworth, West Drayton, Middlesex UB7 0DA *Tel:* (0181) 8994000 *Fax:* (0181) 8994099

11:9, *imprint of* Neil Wilson Publishing Ltd

Elfande Ltd+
Surrey House, 31 Church St, Leatherhead, Surrey KT22 8EF
Tel: (01372) 220330 *Fax:* (01372) 220340
E-mail: sales@contact-uk.com
Web Site: www.contact-uk.com
Key Personnel
Man Dir: Nick Gould
Administration: Sarah Williams
Founded: 1985
Publish annual image source books in Europe.
Subjects: Architecture & Interior Design, Art, Photography
ISBN Prefix(es): 1-870458
Number of titles published annually: 6 Print; 3 CD-ROM
Total Titles: 6 Print; 3 CD-ROM; 3 E-Book

U.S. Office(s): Tonal Values, 133 N Montclair Ave, Dallas, TX, United States, Jill Peterson *Tel:* 214-943-2569 *Fax:* 214-942-6771
E-mail: info@tonalvalues.com

Edward Elgar Publishing Ltd
Glensanda House, Montpellier Parade, Cheltenham, Glos GL50 1UA
Tel: (01242) 226934 *Fax:* (01242) 262111
E-mail: info@e-elgar.co.uk
Web Site: www.e-elgar.co.uk
Key Personnel
Man Dir: Edward Elgar *E-mail:* edward@e-elgar.co.uk
Sales & Marketing Manager: Hilary Quinn
Contact: Sandy Elgar *E-mail:* sandy@e-elgar.co.uk
Founded: 1986
A privately owned scholarly publisher with a focus on economics.
Subjects: Business, Developing Countries, Economics, Environmental Studies, Finance, Government, Political Science, Labor, Industrial Relations
ISBN Prefix(es): 1-85898; 1-85278; 1-84064
Number of titles published annually: 250 Print
Total Titles: 1,360 Print
U.S. Office(s): Edward Elgar Publishing Inc, 136 West St, Suite 202, Northampton, MA 01060, United States, Rick Henning *Tel:* 413-584-5551 *Fax:* 413-584-9933 *E-mail:* rhenning@e-elgar.com
Orders to: DA Book Information Services, 648 Whitehorse Rd, Mitcham, Victoria 3132, Australia *Tel:* (03) 9210 7777 *Fax:* (03) 9210 7788 *E-mail:* Service@dadirect.com.au
Edward Elgar Publishing Inc, 2 Winter Sport Lane, PO Box 574, Williston, VT 05495-0575, United States *Fax:* 802-864-7626 *E-mail:* rhenning@e-elgar.com
Marston Book Services, PO Box 269, Abingdon, Oxon OX14 4YN *Tel:* (01235) 465500 *Fax:* (01235) 465555 *E-mail:* trade@marston.co.uk
Taylor and Francis Asia Pacific, Pines Industrial Bldg, 240 Macpherson Rd 348574, Singapore, Man Dir: Barry Clarke *Tel:* 741 5166 *Fax:* 742 9356 *E-mail:* info@tandf.com.sg
United Publishers Services Limited, Kenkyu-Sha Bldg, 9 Kanda Surugadai 2-Chome, Chiyoda-Ku, Tokyo, Japan *Tel:* (03) 3291 4541 *Fax:* (03) 3292 8610

Elkin, *imprint of* Novello & Co Ltd

Elliot Right Way Books+
Kingswood Bldgs, Brighton Rd, Lower Kingswood, Tadworth, Surrey KT20 6TD
Tel: (01737) 832202 *Fax:* (01737) 830311
E-mail: info@right-way.co.uk
Web Site: www.right-way.co.uk
Key Personnel
Dir: A Clive Elliot; Malcolm G Elliot
Editor: Judith Mitchell
Founded: 1945 (by Andrew George Elliot, father of the present owners)
Independent Book Publisher.
Subjects: Animals, Pets, Business, Career Development, Cookery, Crafts, Games, Hobbies, Finance, Genealogy, Health, Nutrition, House & Home, How-to, Humor, Self-Help, Sports, Athletics, Transportation, Drawing, Driving, Family Reference, Fishing, Hobbies, Horses, Pets, Public & Social Speaking, Quizzes
ISBN Prefix(es): 0-7160; 1-899606
Number of titles published annually: 20 Print
Total Titles: 120 Print
Ultimate Parent Company: Andrew Elliot & Sons Ltd
Imprints: Clarion (Bargain Books); Right Way Books

Foreign Rep(s): Hushion House Publishing Ltd (Canada); Peribo (Australia); Theo Phillips (CKK Ltd) (Asia); Kelvin Van Hasselt (Africa, Caribbean); Peter Ward (Middle East)

Aidan Ellis Publishing+
Whinfield, Herbert Rd, Salcombe, South Devon TQ8 8HN
Tel: (01548) 842755 *Fax:* (01548) 844356
E-mail: aidan@aepub.demon.co.uk
Web Site: www.demon.co.uk/aepub
Key Personnel
Partner: Aidan Ellis
Founded: 1971
Subjects: Art, Biography, Gardening, Plants, Health, Nutrition, Literature, Literary Criticism, Essays, Maritime, Nonfiction (General)
ISBN Prefix(es): 0-85628
Total Titles: 50 Print
Foreign Rep(s): Keith Aiusworth Pty Ltd; Peter Hyde Associates Pty Ltd (Australia, New Zealand, South Africa)
Orders to: Orca Book Services, 3 Fleets Lane, Poole, Dorset BH15 3AJ *Tel:* (01202) 665 432 *Fax:* (01202) 666 219 *E-mail:* orders@orca-book-services.co.uk

Elm Publications+
Seaton House, Kings Ripton, Huntingdon, Cambs PE28 2NJ
Tel: (01487) 773254; (01487) 773238
Fax: (01487) 773359
E-mail: elm@elm-training.co.uk
Web Site: www.elm-training.co.uk
Key Personnel
Man Dir & Rights & Permissions: Sheila Ritchie *E-mail:* sritchie@elm-training.co.uk
Production: Lesley Taylor
Founded: 1977
Subjects: Business, Career Development, Education, History, Language Arts, Linguistics, Law, Library & Information Sciences, Management, Travel
ISBN Prefix(es): 0-946139; 1-85450; 0-9505828
Number of titles published annually: 30 Print
Total Titles: 120 Print; 4 Online
Associate Companies: Elm Training

Elm Tree Books Ltd, see Hamish Hamilton Ltd

Elsevier Advanced Technology, *imprint of* Elsevier Science Ltd

Elsevier Advanced Technology+
The Boulevard, Langford Lane, Kidlington, Oxford OX5 1GB
Mailing Address: PO Box 150, Kidlington, Oxford OX5 1AS
Tel: (01865) 843848 *Fax:* (01865) 843010
E-mail: eatsales@elsevier.co.uk (sales)
Web Site: www.nepcon.co.uk/ex0210g.htm
Key Personnel
International Sales: Sophie Hayward
Contact: Philippa Sumner *Tel:* (01865) 843828 *Fax:* (01865) 843971 *E-mail:* p.sumner@elsevier.co.uk
Subjects: Business
Parent Company: Elsevier Science Ltd
Ultimate Parent Company: Reed Elsevier plc
Imprints: Trade and Technical Press
U.S. Office(s): Elsevier Science Inc, 655 Avenue of the Americas, New York, NY 10010-5107, United States *Tel:* 212-989-5800 *Fax:* 212-633-3990

Elsevier/Geo Abstracts, *imprint of* Elsevier Science Ltd

Elsevier Science Ltd+
The Boulevard, Langford Lane, Kidlington, Oxford OX5 1GB

Tel: (01865) 843000 *Fax:* (01865) 843010
E-mail: initial.lastname@elsevier.com
Web Site: www.elsevier.com
Key Personnel
Man Dir: Gavin Howe
Dir, Rights & Permissions: Anna Moon
Global Supplier Management: Lee Pierce
Production: Ian Hawley
Founded: 1971
Subjects: Agriculture, Architecture & Interior Design, Behavioral Sciences, Biological Sciences, Business, Chemistry, Chemical Engineering, Child Care & Development, Civil Engineering, Communications, Computer Science, Earth Sciences, Economics, Education, Electronics, Electrical Engineering, Energy, Environmental Studies, Health, Nutrition, Library & Information Sciences, Mechanical Engineering, Medicine, Nursing, Dentistry, Technology
ISBN Prefix(es): 0-08; 0-85334; 1-85166
Parent Company: Reed Elsevier, Netherlands
Imprints: Elsevier Advanced Technology; Elsevier/Geo Abstracts
Branch Office(s)
Elsevier/Geo Abstracts, The Old Bakery, 111 Queen's Rd, Norwich NR1 3PL
Elsevier Science London, 84 Theobald's Road, London WC1X 8RR

Empire of the Senses, *imprint of* Dedalus Ltd

Empirieus Books, *imprint of* Janus Publishing Company Ltd

Encyclopaedia Britannica (UK) International Ltd
Unity Wharf, 2nd floor, London SE1 2BH
Tel: (020) 7500 7800; (0845) 075 700 (orders CD or DVD inside UK); (0177) 901 3948 (orders CD or DVD outside UK); (0845) 075 8000 (order bks inside UK); (0845) 901 3948 (order bks outside UK) *Fax:* (020) 7500 7875
E-mail: enquiries@brittanica.co.uk
Web Site: corporate.britannica.co.uk
Telex: 422084
Key Personnel
Man Dir: James Strachan
Marketing Manager: Marcus Missen
ISBN Prefix(es): 0-85229
Parent Company: Encyclopaedia Britannica Inc, Britannica Centre, 310 S Michigan Ave, Chicago, IL 60604, United States
Associate Companies: Encyclopaedia Britannica (Australia) Inc, Level 1, 90 Mount St, North Sydney NSW 2060, Australia *Tel:* (02) 9923 5600 *Fax:* (02) 9929 3758 *E-mail:* feedbackaccount@brittanica.com.au; Encyclopaedia Britannica (France) Ltd; Encyclopaedia Britannica (India) Pvt. Ltd., Britannica Centre, 55-56 Ydyog Vihar Phase 4, Gurgaon 122016, India *Tel:* (0124) 639 9933 *Fax:* (0124) 639 9942 *E-mail:* corporate@brittanicain.com *Web Site:* www.britannicaindia.com; Encyclopaedia Britannica (Italy) Ltd; Encyclopaedia Britannica (Japan) Inc; Korea Britannica Corp; Encyclopaedia Britannica (Philippines) Inc; Encyclopaedia Britannica SA; Encyclopaedia Britannica de Espana, SA

The Energy Information Centre+
Rosemary House, Lanwades Business Park, Newmarket CB8 7PW
Tel: (01638) 751 400 *Fax:* (01638) 751 801
E-mail: info@eic.co.uk
Web Site: www.eic.co.uk
Key Personnel
Editorial Dir: Robert Buckley
Commercial Dir: Michael Southin
Founded: 1975
Subjects: Energy

ISBN Prefix(es): 0-905332
Parent Company: Cambridge Information & Research Services

English Teaching Professional
Tech West House, 10 Warple Way, London W3 0UE
E-mail: etp@etprofessional.com
Web Site: www.etprofessional.com
Key Personnel
Contact: Nicolas Ridley *Tel:* (020) 8762 9600
 E-mail: nicridley@etprofessional.com
Subjects: English as a Second Language
Parent Company: First Person Publishing Limited

Enigma Books, *imprint of* Severn House Publishers Ltd

Entra, *imprint of* Training Publications Ltd

Eos, *imprint of* HarperCollins Publishers

EPER
21 Hill Place, Edinburgh EH8 9DP
Tel: (0131) 650 8211; (0131) 650 6200
 Fax: (0131) 667 5927
E-mail: eper.enquiries@ed.ac.uk
Web Site: www.ials.ed.ac.uk
Key Personnel
Project Dir: David R Hill
Founded: 1984
Subjects: English as a Second Language, Language Arts, Linguistics
ISBN Prefix(es): 1-871914; 1-871019; 1-871035; 1-871027

Epworth Press
Affiliate of Methodist Publishing House
Methodist Publishing House, 4 John Wesley Rd, Werrington, Peterborough PE4 6ZP
Tel: (01733) 325002 *Fax:* (01733) 384180
E-mail: sales@mph.org.uk
Web Site: www.mph.org.uk
Key Personnel
Chairman: John Newton
Editorial: Rodd Cyril; Valerie Edden; Dorothy Graham; Emmanuel Jacob; Ivor Jones; Michael Townsend
Founded: 1750
Subjects: Biblical Studies, Religion - Other, Theology, Worship
ISBN Prefix(es): 0-7162
Total Titles: 100 Print
Sales Office(s): SCM Press Ltd

ERA Technology Ltd+
Cleeve Rd, Leatherhead, Surrey KT22 7SA
Tel: (01372) 36 74 38 *Fax:* (01372) 36 71 02
E-mail: 264045pub.sales@era.co.uk
Web Site: www.era.co.uk
Key Personnel
Divisional Manager: R W H Stafford
Founded: 1920
Specialize in Contract R & D.
Subjects: Aeronautics, Aviation, Automotive, Communications, Computer Science, Electronics, Electrical Engineering, Environmental Studies, Technology, Air Pollution Control, Energy Efficiency, Power Generation
ISBN Prefix(es): 0-7008
Subsidiaries: ERA Technology (Asia) Pte Ltd; ERA Technology Inc

Ernest Press
17 Carleton Drive, Glasgow G46 6AQ
Tel: (0141) 637 5492 *Fax:* (0141) 637 5492
E-mail: sales@ernest-press.co.uk
Web Site: www.ernest-press.co.uk
Key Personnel
Proprietor: Peter Hodghiss

Subjects: Mountaineering, Mounting Biking Guides
ISBN Prefix(es): 0-948153
Warehouse: Cordee, 3A De Montfort St, Leicester LE1 7HD

Ernst & Young+
Becket House, One Lambeth Palace Rd, London SE1 7EU
Tel: (020) 7951 2000 *Fax:* (020) 7951 1345
Also chartered accountants & business advisers.
Subjects: Accounting, Foreign Countries, Management
ISBN Prefix(es): 0-9505745; 1-873278

Eros Plus, *imprint of* Titan Books Ltd

The Erskine Press+
The Old Bakery, Banham, Norwich, Norfolk NR16 2HW
Tel: (01953) 88 72 77 *Fax:* (01953) 88 83 61
E-mail: erskpres@aol.com
Web Site: www.erskine-press.com
Key Personnel
Man Dir: Crispin de Boos
Consultant: Stephen Easton
Founded: 1986
Specialize in literature on Antarctic Exploration.
Member of Independent Publishers Guild.
Subjects: Architecture & Interior Design, Art, Astronomy, Cookery, History, Travel
ISBN Prefix(es): 1-85297; 0-948285
Total Titles: 54 Print
Parent Company: Archival Facsimiles Ltd

estamp+
204 St Albans Ave, London W4 5JU
Tel: (020) 8994 2379 *Fax:* (020) 8994 2379
E-mail: st@estamp.demon.co.uk
Key Personnel
Director: Sylvie Turner
Founded: 1990
Subjects: Specialize in art publishing, mail order, contemporary print making & paper
ISBN Prefix(es): 1-871831
Total Titles: 17 Print
Shipping Address: Central Book, 199 Wallis Rd, London E9 SLN, Kirsty *Tel:* (020) 8986 7859 *Fax:* (020) 8533 5821
Membership(s): IPG

Estates Gazette
147-151 Wardour St, London W1V 4BN
Tel: (020) 8652 3500; (020) 7411 2540 (Edit); (020) 7411 2626 (Adv); (01444) 445335 (Subns) *Fax:* (020) 7437 2432; (020) 7437 0294 (Edit); (020) 7437 2432 (Adv); (01444) 445567 (Subns)
Key Personnel
Publisher & Man Dir: Mark Kelsey
Publications Manager: Colin Greasby
Editorial Dir: Peter Bill *E-mail:* peter.bill@rbi.co.uk
Founded: 1858
ISBN Prefix(es): 0-7282; 0-900361
Parent Company: Reed Business Information Ltd
Orders to: Oakfield House, Perrymount Rd, Haywards Heath, West Sussex RH16 3DM

Eurobook Ltd+
PO Box 52, Wallingford, Oxon OX10 0XU
Tel: (01865) 749033 *Fax:* (01865) 749044
E-mail: eurobook@compuserve.com
Key Personnel
Man Dir, Rights & Permissions: Peter S Lowe
Editor: Ruth Spriggs
Sales, Publicity & Advertising: R McFarlane
International Rights: P S Lowe
Founded: 1968

UNITED KINGDOM

Subjects: Animals, Pets, Gardening, Plants, Natural History, Nonfiction (General), Science (General)
ISBN Prefix(es): 0-85654
Imprints: Peter Lowe

Euromonitor PLC+
60-61 Britton St, London EC1M 5UX
Tel: (020) 7251 8024 *Fax:* (020) 7608 3149
E-mail: info@euromonitor.com
Web Site: www.euromonitor.com
Telex: 262433 Monref G
Key Personnel
Man Dir: Trevor Fenwick
Marketing Dir: David Gudgin
Chairman: Robert Senior
Founded: 1972
Member of UK & European Directory Publishers Associations.
Subjects: Business, Marketing, Publishing & Book Trade Reference, Demographics,Macro-Economic Data, Market Research Reports
ISBN Prefix(es): 0-903706; 0-86338
Branch Office(s)
Singapore Technologies Bldg, 3 Lim Teck Rd, #08-02, Singapore 088934 *Tel:* 429 0590 *Fax:* 324 1867 *E-mail:* info@euromonitor.com.sg
U.S. Office(s): Euromonitor International, 122 S Michigan Ave, Suite 1200, Chicago, IL, United States, Contact: Kim Bergeman *Tel:* 312-922-1115 *Fax:* 312-922-1157 *E-mail:* insight@euromonitorintl.com *Web Site:* www.euromonitor.com
Distributed by Gale Research

Europa, *imprint of* Taylor & Francis Group

Europa Publications
11 New Fetter Lane, London EC4P 4EE
Tel: (020) 7822 4300; (020) 7842 2110 (marketing & sales) *Fax:* (020) 7822 4329; (020) 7842 2249 (marketing & sales)
E-mail: info.europa@tandf.co.uk
Web Site: www.europapublications.com
Key Personnel
Editorial Dir: Paul Kelly
Marketing Manager: Mary Sweny
Accounts Manager: Frances Bunting
Founded: 1926
Member of Directory Publishers Association.
Subjects: Developing Countries, Economics, Education, Foreign Countries, Government, Political Science, Publishing & Book Trade Reference, International affairs
ISBN Prefix(es): 0-946653; 1-85743; 0-900362; 0-905118
Number of titles published annually: 30 Print
Parent Company: Taylor & Francis Group

Europe 1992-98, *imprint of* Dedalus Ltd

European Schoolbooks Ltd
The Runnings, Cheltenham GL51 9PQ
Tel: (01242) 245252 *Fax:* (01242) 224137
E-mail: direct@esb.co.uk
Web Site: www.eurobooks.co.uk
Key Personnel
Man Dir: Frank A Preiss *E-mail:* fap@esb.co.uk
Founded: 1964
Also act as distributor for European publishers.
Subjects: Economics, Environmental Studies, Foreign Countries, Geography, Geology, Language Arts, Linguistics, Social Sciences, Sociology
ISBN Prefix(es): 0-85048
Subsidiaries: European Schoolbooks Publishing
Bookshop(s): The European Bookshop, 5 Warwick St, London W1R 5RA *Tel:* (020) 7734 5259 *Fax:* (020) 7287 1720; The Italian Bookshop, 7 Cecil Court, London WC2N 4EZ *Tel:* (020) 7240 1634 *Fax:* (020) 7240 1635 *E-mail:* italbookshop@freenet.co.uk

The Eurospan Group
3 Henrietta St, Covent Garden, London WC2E 8LU
Tel: (020) 7240 0856 *Fax:* (020) 7379 0609
E-mail: info@eurospan.co.uk
Key Personnel
Group Man Dir: Michael Geelan
Chairman: Danny Maher
Operations Manager: Kate Symonds
Business Manager: Patrick Tay
Marketing: Imogen Adams; Sally Greene; Tina Moran; Clare Sutton
Founded: 1963
Subjects: Agriculture, Anthropology, Archaeology, Art, Asian Studies, Behavioral Sciences, Biblical Studies, Biography, Biological Sciences, Business, Chemistry, Chemical Engineering, Child Care & Development, Communications, Computer Science, Developing Countries, Disability, Special Needs, Drama, Theater, Earth Sciences, Economics, Education, Energy, Engineering (General), Environmental Studies, Ethnicity, Film, Video, Finance, Foreign Countries, Gay & Lesbian, Genealogy, Geography, Geology, Government, Political Science, Health, Nutrition, History, Human Relations, Journalism, Labor, Industrial Relations, Language Arts, Linguistics, Law, Library & Information Sciences, Literature, Literary Criticism, Essays, Management, Maritime, Marketing, Mathematics, Medicine, Nursing, Dentistry, Microcomputers, Military Science, Music, Dance, Natural History, Nonfiction (General), Philosophy, Physics, Poetry, Psychology, Psychiatry, Public Administration, Radio, TV, Regional Interests, Religion - Buddhist, Religion - Catholic, Religion - Hindu, Religion - Islamic, Religion - Jewish, Religion - Protestant, Religion - Other, Science (General), Science Fiction, Fantasy, Social Sciences, Sociology, Technology, Theology, Veterinary Science, Women's Studies
Distributor for AMS Press; Aldwych Press; American Academy of Orthopaedic Surgeons; American Enterprise Institute; American Institute for Aeronautics & Astronautics; American Library Association; American Psychiatric Press; American Psychological Association; Amsterdam University Press (The Netherlands); Auburn House; Austin & Winfield; Bergin & Garvey; Boyton/Cook; CSIRO Publishing (Australia); Catholic University of America Press; Da Capo Press; Lawrence Erlbaum Associates Inc; Fordham University Press; Greenwood Press; Hampton Press; Heinemann USA; Human Sciences Press; Idea Group Publishing; International Scholars Publications; Iowa State University Press; Jason Aronson Publishers; Kent State University Press; Krieger Publishing Co; Libraries Unlimited; Louisiana State University Press; Lynne Rienner Publishers; ME Sharpe Publishing; Narosa Publishing House (India); Neal-Schuman Publishers; Rutgers University Press; The New York Academy of Sciences; The University of North Carolina Press; Ohio State University Press; Open Court Publishing Co; PMA Publishing; Penn State Press; Popular Culture Ink; Praeger Publishers; Quorum Books; Scholarly Resources; The Oryx Press; SIR Publishing (New Zealand); Slack Inc; Southern Illinois University Press; Syracuse University Press; Teacher Ideas Press; Teachers College Press; Temple University Press; Thomas International Publishing Company; University of Alabama Press; University of Georgia Press; University of Massachusetts Press; University of Missouri Press; University of Nevada Press; University of Notre Dame Press; University of Pittsburgh Press; University Press of Florida; University Press of Kansas; University Press of Virginia; University of South Carolina Press; University of Wisconsin Press; Wayne State University Press; Who's Who in Italy (Italy)
Orders to: EDS, 3 Henrietta St, London WC2E 8LU

Evangelical Library of Wales, *imprint of* Bryntirion Press

Evangelical Press & Services Ltd+
Grange Close, Faverdale North Industrial Estate, Darlington, County Durham DL3 0PH
Tel: (01325) 380232; 866-588-6778 *Fax:* (01325) 466153; 866-588-6778
E-mail: sales@evangelicalpress.org
Web Site: www.evangelicalpress.org
Key Personnel
General Manager & International Rights: Anthony L Gosling *E-mail:* anthony.gosling@evangelicalpress.org
Founded: 1967
Subjects: Biblical Studies, Religion - Protestant, Theology
ISBN Prefix(es): 0-85234; 0-946462; 0-85479
Number of titles published annually: 20 Print
Total Titles: 250 Print
Subsidiaries: Europresse SARL (French Publisher)
U.S. Office(s): PO Box 29, Phillipsburg, NJ, United States *Tel:* 908-454-0505 *Fax:* 908-859-2390
Distributor for Bryntirion Press; Carey Publications; Grace Publications Trust

Evans Brothers Ltd+
2A Portman Mansions, Chiltern St, London W1U 6NR
Tel: (020) 7487 0920 *Fax:* (020) 7487 0921
E-mail: sales@evansbrothers.co.uk
Web Site: www.evansbooks.co.uk
Telex: 8811713 Evbook G
Key Personnel
Dir: B D Jones; A Ojora
Man Dir: Stephen T Pawley *E-mail:* stephenp@evansbrothers.co.uk
Rights Manager: Britta Martins
Production Manager: Jenny Mulvanny
UK Publisher: Su Swallow
Founded: 1908
Subjects: Art, English as a Second Language, Geography, Geology, History, Library & Information Sciences, Mathematics, Music, Dance, Religion - Other, Science (General), Citizenship, Design & Technical, ICT, PSHE, R/E Multifaith, Social Issues
ISBN Prefix(es): 0-237
Number of titles published annually: 100 Print
Total Titles: 730 Print
Ultimate Parent Company: Imperial Securities
Associate Companies: Evans Brothers (Nigeria Publishers) Ltd, Nigeria
Imprints: Cherrytree; Cloverleaf
Subsidiaries: Evans Brothers (Kenya) Ltd; Zero to Ten Limited
Orders to: Thomson Publishing Services, Cheriton House, North Way, Andover, Hants SP10 5BE *Tel:* (01264) 33 24 24 *Fax:* (01264) 34 27 88 *E-mail:* evans@thomsonpublishingservices.co.uk *Web Site:* www.thomsonpublishingservices.co.uk

Ex Libris, *imprint of* Ex Libris Press

Ex Libris Press+
One The Shambles, Bradford on Avon, Wilts BA15 1JS
Tel: (01225) 863595 *Fax:* (01225) 863595
Web Site: www.ex-librisbooks.co.uk
Key Personnel
Proprietor: Roger Jones *E-mail:* roger.jones@ex-librisbooks.co.uk
Founded: 1981

Local & regional press covering west country & Channel Islands, also list of book on country life & lore.
Independent comany & member of Independent Publishers Guild.
Subjects: Biography, Geography, Geology, History, Literature, Literary Criticism, Essays, Walking guides & countryside paperback & occasional hardback
ISBN Prefix(es): 0-9506563; 0-948578; 1-903341
Number of titles published annually: 8 Print
Total Titles: 70 Print
Online services available through Gardners.
Imprints: Ex Libris; Seaflower Books
Distributed by Halsgrove (UK)
Membership(s): IPG

Exley Publications Ltd+
16 Chalk Hill, Watford, Herts WD1 4BN
Tel: (01923) 250505 *Fax:* (01923) 818733
 Toll Free Fax: 800-440
E-mail: enquiry@exleypublications.co.uk
Key Personnel
Chairman: Richard Exley
Man Dir & Editorial Dir: Helen Exley
Rights Dir: Frances Riley *E-mail:* frances.riley@exleypublications.co.uk
Export Sales Manager: Michael Illingworth
Contact: Julie Blake *E-mail:* julie.blake@exleypublications.co.uk
Founded: 1976
Specializes in gift books.
Subjects: Humor, Nonfiction (General)
ISBN Prefix(es): 1-85015; 1-86187
Total Titles: 350 Print
Associate Companies: Exley Handels GmbH, Schloss Merode, D52379 Langerwehe, Merode, Germany; Exley SA, 13 rue de Genval, B-1301 Bierges, Belgium
Subsidiaries: Exley Giftbooks
U.S. Office(s): Exley Giftbooks, 232 Madison Ave, New York, NY, United States
Distributed by Exley Handel GmbH (Germany); Exley SA (Belgium)

Expert Books, *imprint of* Transworld Publishers Ltd

Express Newspapers+
Ludgate House, 245 Blackfriars Rd, London SE1 9UX
Tel: (020) 7928 8000 *Fax:* (020) 7922 7966
Key Personnel
Licensing Manager: Sue McGeever *Tel:* (020) 7922 7887 *E-mail:* sue.mcgeever@express.co.uk
Subjects: Business, Cookery, Humor, Management, Sports, Athletics
ISBN Prefix(es): 0-85079
Parent Company: Northern & Shell, Ludgate House, 245 Blackfriars Rd, London SE1 9UX

Extraordinary People Press+
1B Portman Mansions, Chiltern St, London W1M 1PX
Tel: (020) 7935 4490 *Fax:* (020) 7486 5998
Key Personnel
Commissions Editor: Katrina Fox
 E-mail: katfox@easynet.co.uk
International Rights: K Butler
Founded: 1996
Subjects: Behavioral Sciences, Gay & Lesbian, Health, Nutrition, Human Relations, Nonfiction (General), Psychology, Psychiatry, Self-Help, Social Sciences, Sociology
ISBN Prefix(es): 0-9529482
Bookshop(s): Turnaround, Unit 3, Olympia Trading Estate, Cobury Rd, Wood Crear, London N22

Fabbri (GE) Ltd+
Elme House, 133 Long Acre, London WC2E 9AW
Tel: (020) 7836 0519; (020) 7468 5600
 Fax: (020) 7836 0280
E-mail: mailbox@gefabbri.co.uk
Web Site: www.gefabbri.co.uk
Key Personnel
Man Dir: Peter Edwards
International Dir: Philip Costick
Editorial Dir: Liz Glaze
Marketing Dir: Huw Thomas
Managing Editor: Hilary Newstead
Chief Accountant: Duncan Lewis
Production Manager: Judy Binning; Joy Kingsbury
Founded: 1987
Imprints: GE Fabbri; GE Magazines
Subsidiaries: GE Fabbri; GE Magazines

Faber & Faber Ltd+
3 Queen's Sq, London WC1N 3AU
Tel: (020) 7465 0045 *Fax:* (020) 7465 0034
Web Site: www.faber.co.uk *Cable:* FABBAF LONDON WC1
Key Personnel
Man Dir: Toby Faber
Publishing Dir: Joanna Mackle
Contract Manager: Alan Winwright
Publisher: Walter Donohue
Head of Sales: Chris McLaren
Founded: 1929
Also Distributor.
Subjects: Art, Biography, Drama, Theater, Fiction, Film, Video, History, How-to, Literature, Literary Criticism, Essays, Music, Dance, Philosophy, Poetry, Psychology, Psychiatry, Radio, TV, Religion - Other, Social Sciences, Sociology, Wine & Spirits
ISBN Prefix(es): 0-571
Parent Company: Geoffrey Faber Holdings
Subsidiaries: Faber Inc USA
U.S. Office(s): Faber & Faber Inc, 50 Cross St, Winchester, MA 01890, United States
Orders to: Macmillan Distribution Ltd, Brinel Rd Houndmills Ind Est, Baringstone Harts RG21 6XS *Tel:* (01256) 302692

Fabian Society
11 Dartmouth St, London SW1H 9BN
Tel: (020) 7227 4900 *Fax:* (020) 7976 7153
E-mail: info@fabian-society.org.uk
Web Site: www.fabian-society.org.uk
Key Personnel
Deputy General Secretary: Adrian Harvey
 Tel: (020) 7227 4908
Development Manager: Alison Sheppard
Finance Officer: Margaret McGillen *Tel:* (020) 7227 4903
General Secretary: Michael Jacobs *Tel:* (020) 7227 4905
Administrator: Claire Willgress
Editorial Manager: Ellie Levenson
Local Societies Officer: Deborah Stoate
Membership Officer: Giles Wright
Founded: 1884
Subjects: Economics, Government, Political Science
ISBN Prefix(es): 0-7163
Subsidiaries: NCLC Publishing Society Ltd

Facet Publishing+
Formerly Library Association Publishing
Imprint of Chartered Institute of Library & Information Professionals (CILIP)
7 Ridgmount St, London WC1E 7AE
Tel: (020) 7255 0594 *Fax:* (020) 7255 0591
E-mail: info@facetpublishing.co.uk
Web Site: www.facetpublishing.co.uk
Key Personnel
Man Dir & International Rights: Janet Liebster
Publisher: Helen Carley
Commissioning Editor: Rebecca Casey
Production Manager: Kathryn Beecroft
Sales Manager: Rohini Ramachandran
Founded: 1980
Specialize in library & information science.
Subjects: Computer Science, Library & Information Sciences, Management, Technology
ISBN Prefix(es): 0-85365; 0-85157; 1-85604
Warehouse: Bookpoint Ltd, 39 Milton Park, Abingdon OX14 4TD
Beman Associates, 4611-F Assembly Dr, Lanham, MD 20706, United States (North American orders)
Orders to: Bookpoint Ltd, 39 Milton Park, Abingdon, Oxon 0X14 4TD
Behman Associates, 4611-F Assembly Dr, Lanham, MD 20706, United States

The Factory Shop Guide
One Rosebery Mews, Rosebery Rd, London SW2 4DQ
Tel: (020) 8678 0593 *Fax:* (020) 8674 1594
E-mail: factshop@macline.co.uk
Key Personnel
Partners: Gillian Cutress; Rolf Stricker
Founded: 1985
Subjects: Gardening, Plants, Travel
ISBN Prefix(es): 0-948965

Facts On File
Michael O'Mara Books Ltd, 9 Lion Yard, Tremadoc Rd, London SW4 7NQ
Tel: (020) 7720 8643 *Fax:* (020) 76278953; (020) 76273041 (foreign sales); (020) 7622 6956 (UK sales & publicity)
Web Site: www.factsonfile.com
Key Personnel
Publicity & Sales: Suzanne Paterson
 E-mail: suzannepaterson@michaelomarabooks.com
Dir of Subsidary Rights & Export Sales: Ben Jacobs *Tel:* 212-967-8800, ext 4268
 E-mail: bjacobs@factsonfile.com
Founded: 1941
Acts as distributor for numerous US & Canadian publishers.
Subjects: Business, Career Development, Education, Government, Political Science, History, Language Arts, Linguistics, Literature, Literary Criticism, Essays, Maritime, Medicine, Nursing, Dentistry, Military Science, Music, Dance, Natural History, Self-Help
ISBN Prefix(es): 0-948894
Parent Company: Facts on File Inc, 11 Penn Plaza, 15th floor, New York, NY 10001-2006, United States
Distributed by Iberian Book Service; Overseas Book Service
Warehouse: Biblios, Star Rd, Partridge Green, West Sussex RH13 8LD
Orders to: Roundhouse Publishing Ltd, PO Box 140, Oxford 0X2 7FF

Fairacres Publication, *imprint of* SLG Press

Fairfield, *imprint of* Novello & Co Ltd

Falco, *imprint of* Hawk Books

Famedram Publishers Ltd+
PO Box 3, Ellon, Aberdeenshire AB41 9EA
Tel: (01651) 842429 *Fax:* (01651) 842180
E-mail: famedram@artwork.co.uk
Key Personnel
Man Dir: Bill Williams
Production: Eleanor Stewart
Editor (Artwork): Richard Carr
Advertising Sales: Sandra Moore *Tel:* (01436) 675743 *Fax:* (01436) 673327
Founded: 1971

Publisher of Artwork - bimonthly arts newspaper for Scotland & Northern England.
Subjects: Poetry, Travel, Wine & Spirits
ISBN Prefix(es): 0-905489; 0-9501944
Total Titles: 40 Print
Imprints: Northern Books

Family Law, *imprint of* Jordan Publishing Ltd

Family Walks, *imprint of* Scarthin Books

Fanny, *imprint of* Knockabout Comics

Farsight Press+
5 Lynette Ave, London SW4 9HE
Tel: (020) 8675 1693
Key Personnel
Dir & Sole Proprietor: Mr F Knox
Founded: 1996
Research & publication on criminology.
Subjects: Criminology
ISBN Prefix(es): 0-948669
Number of titles published annually: 4 Print
Total Titles: 4 Print

FBA Publications, *imprint of* Francis Balsom Associates

Ferendune, *imprint of* E W Classey Ltd

Fernhurst Books+
Duke's Path, High St, Arundel, West Sussex BN18 9AJ
Tel: (01903) 882277 *Fax:* (01903) 882715
E-mail: sales@fernhurstbooks.co.uk
Web Site: fernhurstbooks.co.uk
Key Personnel
Man Dir: Tim Davison
Business Development Manager: Phyl Ellis
Founded: 1979
Paperbacks on all aspects of water sports.
Subjects: Maritime
ISBN Prefix(es): 0-906754; 1-898660
Number of titles published annually: 14 Print; 1 CD-ROM
Total Titles: 100 Print; 1 CD-ROM
U.S. Office(s): Motorbooks International, 729 Prospect Ave, Osceola, WI 54020, United States *Tel:* 715-294-3345
Warehouse: Clipper Distribution, Windmill Grove, Porchester, Hants P016 9HT *Tel:* (02392) 200080 *Fax:* (02392) 200090

FHG Publications Ltd
Abbey Mill Business Centre, Seedhill, Paisley PA1 1TJ
Tel: (0141) 8870428 *Fax:* (0141) 8897204
E-mail: fhg@ipcmedia.com
Web Site: www.holidayguides.com
Key Personnel
General Manager: George Pratt
Founded: 1947
Subjects: Travel
ISBN Prefix(es): 1-85055; 0-900365
Parent Company: IPC Media Ltd, King's Reach Tower, Stampford St, London SE19LS
U.S. Office(s): Hunter Publishing, 239 S Beach Rd, Hobe Sound, FL, United States

Sadie Fields Productions Ltd+
4C/D West Point, 36/37 Warple Way, London W3 0RQ
Tel: (020) 8746 1171 *Fax:* (020) 8746 1170
E-mail: sales@tangobooks.co.uk
Key Personnel
Dir: Sheri Safran; David Fielder
Founded: 1981
Also book packager, childrens novelty (popups, holograms, touch & feel etc).
Associate Companies: Sadie Fields Management Inc
Divisions: Tango Books

Financial Times Prentice Hall, *imprint of* Pearson Education Europe, Mideast & Africa

Financial Training Co
New London House, 6 London St, London EC3R 7LQ
Tel: (020) 7481 6050 *Fax:* (020) 7265 0337
Key Personnel
Man Dir: William Macpherson
Founded: 1978
Subjects: Accounting
ISBN Prefix(es): 1-85179
Branch Office(s)
Swift House, Market Place, Berkshire RG40 1AP *Tel:* (0118) 977 4922 *Fax:* (0118) 989 4029
7 Hill St, Centre City Tower, Birmingham B5 4UA *Tel:* (0121) 644 4700 *Fax:* (0121) 644 4701
Saint David's House, Wood St, Suite 5, Cardiff *Tel:* (029) 2038 8067 *Fax:* (029) 2023 7408
91 Mitchell St, Glasgow G1 3LN *Tel:* (0141) 248 8080 *Fax:* (0141) 298 8040
32a Castle Way, Southampton, Hampshire SO14 2AW *Tel:* (023) 8022 0852 *Fax:* (023) 8063 4379
The Sherethorn Centre, Prospect St, Hull HU2 8PX
49 Saint Pauls St, Leeds LS1 2TE *Tel:* (0113) 388 9310 *Fax:* (0113) 242 8889
66 London Rd, 3rd floor, Beckville House, Leicester LE2 0QD
Coopers Bldg, Church St, 3rd floor, Liverpool L1 3AA *Tel:* (0151) 708 8839 *Fax:* (0151) 709 4264
18-20 Crucifix Lane, London SE1 3JW *Tel:* (020) 7407 5000 *Fax:* (020) 7407 0101
7-13 Mellor St, London SE1 eQP *Tel:* (020) 7407 5000 *Fax:* (020) 7407 0101
One Angel Square, Torrens St, London EC1 V1 NY *Tel:* (0207) 520 1146
10-14 White Lion St, London N1 9PD *Tel:* (020) 7520 1125 *Fax:* (020) 7520 1120
Saint James Bldg, Oxford St, 6th floor, Manchester M1 6FQ, United Republic of Tanzania *Tel:* (0161) 237 3366 *Fax:* (0161) 236 9047
Provincial House, Northumberland St, Newcastle Upon Tyne NE1 7DQ *Tel:* (0191) 232 9365 *Fax:* (0191) 232 2115
5 Clumber St, Alan House, 3rd floor, Nottingham NG1 3ED *Tel:* (0115) 941 0723 *Fax:* (0115) 941 5779
463a Glossop Rd, Pegasus House, Sheffield S10 2QD *Tel:* (0114) 266 9265 *Fax:* (0114) 268 4084

Financial World Publishing+
IFS House, 4-9 Burgate Lane, Canterbury, Kent CT1 2XJ
Tel: (01227) 762 600 *Fax:* (01227) 763 788
E-mail: institute@ifslearning.com
Key Personnel
Dir of Publishing: Eric Dobby
Publishing Manager: Philip Blake
  E-mail: pblake@ifslearning.co.uk
Mail Order Manager: Morton Griffiths
  E-mail: mgriffiths@ifslearning.co.uk
Founded: 1987 (as Bankers Books Ltd)
Subjects: Business, Finance, Law, Management
ISBN Prefix(es): 0-85297
Imprints: Chartered Institute of Bankers (CIB) Publications
Bookshop(s): 90 Bishopsgate, London EC2N 4DQ
Orders to: IFS Mail Order, c/o The Chartered Institute of Bankers, Emmanual House, Burgate Lane, Canterbury, Kent CT1 2XJ

Findhorn Press Inc+
305a The Park, Findhorn, Forres IV36 3TE
Tel: (01309) 690582 *Fax:* (01309) 690036
E-mail: books@findhorn.org
Web Site: www.findhornpress.com
Key Personnel
Publisher: Thierry Bogliolo *Tel:* (0467) 283488 (France) *Fax:* (0467) 490419 (France)
  E-mail: thierry@findhornpress.com
Founded: 1971
Publishes books that bring hope, healing & inspiration to the world.
Subjects: Self-Help, Alternative Health, Spirituality
ISBN Prefix(es): 0-905242; 1-899171; 1-84409
Number of titles published annually: 12 Print
Total Titles: 90 Print; 2 Audio
Distributed by Lantern Books (North America only)
Foreign Rep(s): Findhorn Publishing Services (Worldwide)

Firebird Books Ltd+
PO Box 327, Poole, Dorset BH15 2RG
Tel: (01202) 715349 (sales); (01258) 454675 (editorial) *Fax:* (01202) 736191
Key Personnel
Publisher: Stuart Booth
Production Dir: Kathryn Booth
Sales Dir: Chris Lloyd *E-mail:* chrlloyd@globalnet.co.uk
Founded: 1987
Subjects: History, Military Science
ISBN Prefix(es): 1-85314
Associate Companies: Wise Owl Quiz Promotions
Sales Office(s): Chris Lloyd Sales & Marketing, Poole *Tel:* (01202) 715349

Fireside, *imprint of* Simon & Schuster Ltd

First & Best in Education Ltd+
Earlstrees Court, Earlstrees Rd, Corby, Northants NN17 4HH
Tel: (01536) 399004 (editorial); (01536) 399005 (accounts) *Fax:* (01536) 399012
E-mail: firstandbest@themail.co.uk
Web Site: www.firstandbest.co.uk
Key Personnel
Man Dir & Marketing: Tony Attwood *Tel:* (01536) 399013 *E-mail:* tonyattwood@lineone.net
Editor: Anne Cockburn
Founded: 1979
Specialize in publishing books on marketing & direct mail & copiable books for schools & software for schools.
Subjects: Business, Education
ISBN Prefix(es): 0-906888; 1-898091; 1-86083
Ultimate Parent Company: Hamilton House Mailings Ltd
Imprints: School Improvement Reports
Distributor for National Council for Voluntary Organizations

First Discovery, *imprint of* Moonlight Publishing Ltd

First Discovery-Art, *imprint of* Moonlight Publishing Ltd

Fishing News Books Ltd+
Osney Mead, Oxford OX2 0EL
Tel: (01865) 206206 *Fax:* (01865) 721205
E-mail: fnb@blacksci.co.uk
Web Site: www.fishknowledge.com
Telex: 83355 MEDBOK G
Key Personnel
Editorial, Production: W E Redman
Marketing: Phillip Saugman
Founded: 1953
Subjects: Maritime
ISBN Prefix(es): 0-85238

Parent Company: Blackwell Scientific Publishing Ltd, Osney Mead, Oxford OX2 0EL
Bookshop(s): Blackwell Book Shops

The Fitzjames Press, *imprint of* Motor Racing Publications Ltd

Five Star, *imprint of* Gale Research

Flame, *imprint of* Hodder & Stoughton General

Flicks Books+
29 Bradford St, Trowbridge, Wilts BA14 9AN
Tel: (01225) 767 728 *Fax:* (01225) 760 418
E-mail: flicks.books@pipex.com
Key Personnel
Publisher: Matthew Stevens
Founded: 1986
Subjects: Film, Video, Cinema, TV
ISBN Prefix(es): 0-948911; 1-86236
Total Titles: 70 Print

Floris Books+
15 Harrison Gardens, Edinburgh EH11 1SH
Tel: (0131) 337 2372 *Fax:* (0131) 346 7516
E-mail: floris@floris.demon.co.uk
Key Personnel
Editorial: Christopher Moore
Production, Rights & Permissions: Christian Maclean
Schools/Libraries: Angelique Fowlie
Contact: Joanne Moore
Founded: 1976
Member of Scottish Publishers Association.
Subjects: Crafts, Games, Hobbies, Religion - Other, Science (General)
ISBN Prefix(es): 0-903540; 0-86315
Warehouse: Scottish Book Source, 32 Finlas St, Glasgow G22 5DU

Fodor's Travel Guides, *imprint of* Random House UK Ltd

Folens Ltd+
Apex Business Centre, Unit 20, Boscombe Rd, Dunstable, Beds LU5 4RL
Tel: (01582) 470471 *Fax:* (01582) 470818
E-mail: folens@folens.com
Web Site: www.folens.com
Key Personnel
Man Dir: Malcolm Watson
Publishing Dir: Steve Harrison
Founded: 1986
Publishers of educational books for both teachers & children up to the age of 16 years.
Subjects: Education
ISBN Prefix(es): 1-85276; 1-85008; 1-84163
Associate Companies: Educational Publishers
Distributed by Agius + Agius Limited (Malta); Al Kashkool Bookshop (Jordan); Al Manahil Educational Consultancy (Oman); All Prints Distributors & Publishers (United Arab Emirates); Bacon & Hughes Limited (Canada); Educational Supplies Pty Ltd (Australia); Incentive Publications Inc (USA); International Language Bookshop (Egypt); Stanford House (ELT Resource Centre) (Hong Kong); LKD Educational Resources (Jordan); Mars Publishing House (Saudi Arabia); Modern Teaching Aids (Australia); Proof Line (M) Sdn Bhd (Malaysia); Saeed & Samir Bookstore Co Ltd (Kuwait); September 21 Enterprise Pte Ltd (Singapore); Social Studies School Service (USA) (USA); South Pacific Books (Imports) Ltd (New Zealand); Southern Cross (Australia); TEK Books (Bookworld Espana) (Spain); University Book Store (M) Sdn Bhd (Malaysia)
Foreign Rep(s): IPR Beirut (Lebanon); IPR Cyprus (Cyprus)

Food Trade Press, *imprint of* Food Trade Press Ltd

Food Trade Press Ltd+
Station House, Hortons Way, Westerham, Kent TN16 1BZ
Tel: (01959) 563944 *Fax:* (01959) 561285
E-mail: foodtradereview@aol.com
Web Site: foodbooks.net
Key Personnel
Dir: Adrian M Binsted
Founded: 1944
Publisher, distributor & bookseller for the food trade.
Specialize in food production & technology.
ISBN Prefix(es): 0-900379; 0-903962
Number of titles published annually: 12 Print
Total Titles: 52 Print
Associate Companies: Attwood & Binsted Ltd
Imprints: Food Trade Press; Food Trade Review
Distributor for Campden & Chorleywood Food RA (UK); Chemical Publishing (USA); Chiriotti Editori (Italy); CTI Publications (USA); Food & Nutrition Press (USA); Leatherhead Food RA (UK)

Food Trade Review, *imprint of* Food Trade Press Ltd

Forbes Publications Ltd+
Abbott House, 1-2 Hanover Sq, London W1S 1YZ
Tel: (020) 7495 7945 *Fax:* (020) 7495 7916
E-mail: editorial@rapportgroup.com
Key Personnel
Dir: Judith Bloor; Mary Anne FitzGerald
Founded: 1947
Subjects: Business, Economics, Education, Health, Nutrition, Human Relations, Science (General), Technology
ISBN Prefix(es): 0-901762; 1-899527
Parent Company: The Rapport Group Ltd
Orders to: Plymbridge Distributors, Estover Rd, Plymouth, Devon PL6 7PZ *Tel:* (01752) 202300 *Fax:* (01752) 202330

Forth Naturalist & Historian
University of Stirling, Biological Sciences, Stirling FK9 4LA
Mailing Address: 30 Dunmar Drive, Alloa, Clackmannan, Scotland FK10 2EH
Tel: (01786) 467755 *Fax:* (01786) 464994
Web Site: www.stir.ac.uk/departments/naturalsciences/Forth_naturalist/index.htm
Telex: 777557 Stuniv G
Key Personnel
Honorary Editor & Secretary: Lindsay Corbett
 Tel: (01259) 215091 *E-mail:* lindsay.corbett@stir.ac.uk
Chairman: Prof David M Bryant *E-mail:* dmb1@stir.ac.uk
Founded: 1975
An informal charitable body of the University of Stirling to promote the environment, heritage & wildlife of Central Scotland. Specialize in maps, journals.
Member of Scottish Publishers Association.
Subjects: Archaeology, Biography, Biological Sciences, Earth Sciences, Environmental Studies, Geography, Geology, History, Natural History, Regional Interests
ISBN Prefix(es): 0-9506962; 0-9514147; 1-898008; 0-903650
Number of titles published annually: 1 Print
Total Titles: 35 Print; 80 E-Book
Online services available through Amazon.com, Barnes & Noble, BookPlace.
Ultimate Parent Company: University of Stirling
Distributed by Scottish Book Source; Scottish Publishers Association

Distributor for Clarkmannanshire Libraries; CFSS (Clarkmannanshire Field Studies Society); Creag Darach; Falkirk Local History Society; RIAS/Rutland Press; Stirling District Libraries

G T Foulis & Co, *imprint of* Haynes Publishing

Foulsham Publishers+
Bennetts Close, Slough Berks SL1 5AP
Tel: (01753) 526769 *Fax:* (01753) 535003
Telex: 41671 TCS G
Key Personnel
Man Dir & Commissioning Editor: B A R Belasco *E-mail:* belasco@foulsham.com
Dir Finance, Export Sales: Graham M Kitchen *E-mail:* kitchen@foulsham.com
Production Dir: Roy Mantel *E-mail:* mantel@foulsham.com
International Rights & Foreign Rights Manager (London): Cathy Miller
Editorial Dir: W Hobson *E-mail:* hobson@foulsham.com
Founded: 1819
Subjects: Alternative, Antiques, Astrology, Occult, Cookery, Crafts, Games, Hobbies, Education, Film, Video, Finance, Gardening, Plants, Health, Nutrition, House & Home, How-to, Humor, Self-Help, Technology, Travel, Wine & Spirits, Family Reference, Know How, Mind, Body, Spirit, Self Improvement
ISBN Prefix(es): 0-572
Number of titles published annually: 100 Print; 2 E-Book
Total Titles: 300 Print
Imprints: Quantum
Orders to: Associated Publishers Group, 1501 County Hospital Rd, Nashville, TN 37218, United States *Tel:* 615-254-2420 *Fax:* 615-254-2405

The Foundational Book Company for the John W Doorly Trust
16 Coach House Court, Hawthorn Way, Cambridge CB4 1BT
Founded: 1946
Subjects: Biblical Studies, Religion - Other
ISBN Prefix(es): 0-85241
Total Titles: 40 Print

Foundery Press & Chester House Publications, *imprint of* Methodist Publishing House

Fountain Press, *imprint of* Newpro UK Ltd

Four Seasons Publishing Ltd+
16 Orchard Rise, Kingston on Thames, Surrey KT2 7EY
Tel: (020) 8942 4445 *Fax:* (020) 8942 4446
E-mail: info@fourseasons.net
Key Personnel
Man Dir: Christopher Shepheard-Walwyn
 E-mail: csw@fourseasons.net
Founded: 1988
Expanding range of non-fiction gift books & social stationery for the international co-edition market.
ISBN Prefix(es): 1-85645

Fourth Estate Ltd+
6 Salem Rd, London W2 4BU
Tel: (020) 7727 8993 *Fax:* (020) 7792 3176
E-mail: general@4thestate.co.uk
Key Personnel
Man Dir: Victoria Barnsley
Dep Man Dir: Stephen Page
Rights Dir: Susie Dunlop
Publishing Dir: Christopher Potter
Production: Graham Cook
Publicity Dir: Nicky Eaton
Founded: 1984

UNITED KINGDOM

Subjects: Architecture & Interior Design, Biography, Cookery, Fiction, Gay & Lesbian, History, Humor, Literature, Literary Criticism, Essays, Radio, TV
ISBN Prefix(es): 0-947795; 1-872180; 1-84115; 1-85702
Imprints: Guardian Books
Distributor for John Brown Publishing; Duncar Baird Publisher (UK); Harvill Press (UK); Profile Books (UK)
Orders to: TBS, Frating Green, Colchester C07 7DW

L N Fowler & Co Ltd, imprint of The C W Daniel Co Ltd

Red Fox, imprint of Random House UK Ltd

W & G Foyle Ltd
113-119 Charing Cross Rd, London WC2H 0EB
Tel: (020) 7437 5660 Fax: (020) 7434 1574
E-mail: administration@foyles.co.uk
Web Site: www.foyles.co.uk Cable: FOYLIBRA LONDON WC2
Key Personnel
Chairman & Man Dir: WR Christopher Foyle
Marketing Dir: Bill Foyle Samuel Tel: (020) 7440 3226 E-mail: bill@foyles.co.uk
General Manager: Sharon Murray
Founded: 1903
General book store.
Divisions: Archaeology; Art; Astronomy; Autobiographies & Biographies; Children's Books - Fiction & Non-Fiction; Cinema; Computing; Cookery; Drama; Education; Engineering; English Language, EFL, Dictionaries & Reference; English Literature; Fiction - Hardback & Paperback; Foreign Languages; History; Humour; Maths & Physics; Medical, Nursing & Veterinary; Music; Natural History & Biology; Photography; Rare Books; Sociology; Sport; Technical; Theology; Transport; Travel

Francis Balsom Associates+
Unit 4, The Science Park, Aberstwyth SY23 3AH
Tel: (01970) 636400 Fax: (01970) 636414
E-mail: publishing@fbagroup.co.uk
Web Site: www.fbagroup.co.uk
Key Personnel
Man Dir: Sue Balsom
Chairman & Company Secretary: Denis Balsom
Business Manager: Priscilla Gibby
Founded: 1989
Subjects: Art, Government, Political Science, Health, Nutrition, Sports, Athletics
ISBN Prefix(es): 1-901862
Imprints: Cyhoeddiadau FBA; FBA Publications

The Fraser Press
182 Bath St, Glasgow G2 4HG
Tel: (0141) 3331992 Fax: (0141) 3331992
Key Personnel
Proprietor: M Hay
Founded: 1991
Subjects: Architecture & Interior Design, Art
ISBN Prefix(es): 1-873805

Free Association Books Ltd+
57 Warren St, London W1T 5NR
Tel: (020) 7388 3182 Fax: (020) 7388 3187
E-mail: fab@fa-b.com
Web Site: www.fa-b.com
Key Personnel
Chief Executive, Editorial & Man Dir: Tower Brown
Publisher: Trevor E Brown
Rights & Permissions: Cathy Miller
Sales & Marketing Manager: Elisabetta Minervini
Founded: 1983
Subjects: Behavioral Sciences, Child Care & Development, Ethnicity, Human Relations, Philosophy, Psychology, Psychiatry, Social Sciences, Sociology
ISBN Prefix(es): 0-946960; 1-85343
Branch Office(s)
NYUP, Elmer Holmes Bobst Library, 70 Washington Square S, New York, NY 10012-1091, United States
Foreign Rep(s): Astam Books Pty ltd (Australia, New Zealand, Papua New Guinea); Bookworm (Israel); Richard Bowen (Scandinavia); Roy de Boo (Germany); ISBS (North America); Jordan Book Centre (Middle East); Kay Kato (Japan); Dineke Kemper (Benelux, France, Switzerland, Holland); Flavio Marcello (Italy, Portugal, Spain); STM Publishers Services Pte (Far East); Viva Books (India)
Foreign Rights: Cathy Miller Agency
Warehouse: The Trade Counter, Unit D, Trading Estate Rd, London NW10 7LU
Orders to: ISBS, 5804 NE Hassalo St, Portland, OR 97213-3644, United States Fax: 503-280-8832 E-mail: fab@isbs.com
Plymbridge Distributors Ltd, Estover, Plymouth PL6 7PZ Tel: (01752) 202301 Fax: (01752) 202333 E-mail: cservs@plymbridge.com (UK & Europe)

Freedom Ministries, imprint of Moorley's Print & Publishing Ltd

Freedom Press
Angel Alley, 84b Whitechapel High St, London E1 7QX
Tel: (020) 7247 9249 Fax: (020) 7377 9526
Key Personnel
Manager: Charles Crute; Vernon Richards
Founded: 1886 (Independent non-profit making publisher)
Subjects: Economics, Government, Political Science, History, Philosophy, Social Sciences, Sociology
ISBN Prefix(es): 0-900384
Number of titles published annually: 7 Print
Total Titles: 80 Print
Distributed by Active Distribution; AK Distribution; Left Bank Distribution
Distributor for AK Press; Calabria Press; Michael E Coughlin; Five Leaves Publications; Left Bank Distribution; Libertarian Education; Phoenix Press; Red Lion Press; See Sharp Press

W H Freeman & Co Ltd
Houndmills, Basingstoke, Hants RG21 6XS
Tel: (01256) 332807 Fax: (01256) 330688
Key Personnel
Man Dir: Dominic Knight
Contact: Alex Hughes E-mail: a.hughes@macmillian.co.uk
Founded: 1959
Subjects: Behavioral Sciences, Biological Sciences, Chemistry, Chemical Engineering, Child Care & Development, Computer Science, Earth Sciences, Economics, Electronics, Electrical Engineering, Environmental Studies, Geography, Geology, Mathematics, Medicine, Nursing, Dentistry, Physical Sciences, Psychology, Psychiatry, Science (General)
ISBN Prefix(es): 0-7167; 0-87893; 0-935702; 1-57259; 0-87901; 0-89454
Parent Company: W H Freeman & Co, 41 Madison Ave, 35th Floor, New York, NY 10010, United States (Orders for North America & Far East)
Ultimate Parent Company: Verlagsgruppe Georg von Holtzbrinck GmbH, Germany
Holding Company: Scientific American, 41 Madison Ave, New York, NY 10014, United States
Imprints: Scientific American; Computer Science Press
Distributed by Palgrave (UK, Europe, Africa, Middle East, India & Pakistan)
Distributor for Sirauer Associates; Spectrum; University Science Books; Worth
Orders to: Marston Book Services, PO Box 87, Oxford OX4 1LB
W H Freeman & Co, 41 Madison Ave, New York, NY 10010, United States Tel: 212-576-9400 Fax: 212-481-1891 Web Site: www.whfreeman.com (North America & Far East)
Macmillan Education Publishers Australia Pty Ltd, Levels 4 & 5, 627 Chapel St, South Yarra, Victoria 3141, Australia Tel: (03) 9825 1025 Fax: (03) 9825 1010 E-mail: mea@macmillan.com.au Web Site: www.macmillan.com.au (Australia)

Samuel French Ltd
52 Fitzroy St, London W1T 5JR
Tel: (020) 7387 9373 Fax: (020) 7387 2161
E-mail: theatre@samuelfrench-london.co.uk
Web Site: www.samuelfrench-london.co.uk
Key Personnel
Chairman: Charles Van Nostrand
Man Dir: J W Bedding
Dir: Amanda Smith; Paul Taylor
Secretary to Man Dir: Vivien Goodwin
Founded: 1830
Subjects: Drama, Theater
ISBN Prefix(es): 0-573
Associate Companies: Samuel French (Canada) Ltd, 100 Lombard St, Lower Level, Toronto, ON, Canada; Samuel French Inc, 45 W 25 St, New York, NY 10010, United States; 7623 Sunset Blvd, Hollywood, CA 90046, United States
Bookshop(s): French's Theatre Bookshop, 52 Fitzroy St, London W1P 6JR

Sigmund Freud Copyrights
10 Brook St, Wivenhoe, Colchester CO7 9DS
Tel: (01206) 825433 Fax: (01206) 822990
E-mail: info@markpaterson.co.uk
Web Site: www.markpaterson.co.uk/sigmund.htm
Key Personnel
Dir: Mark Paterson E-mail: mark@markpaterson.co.uk
Archivist: Tom Roberts E-mail: tom@markpaterson.co.uk
Administrator: S Pearce
Associate Companies: Mark Paterson & Associates; Quentin Books Ltd

The Friendly Press
Member of Quakers Uniting in Publications Worldwide (QUIP)
26 Cleeve Hill, Bristol BS16 6UL
Tel: (0117) 908-2281 Fax: (0117) 908-2282
E-mail: phgassoc@aol.com
Key Personnel
Dir: Anne Hodkinson
Contact: E Anne Lang
Subjects: ELT Books & Materials, Religious Quaker
ISBN Prefix(es): 0-948728
Parent Company: PH Group

From The Portuguese, imprint of Carcanet Press Ltd

Frontier Publishing+
Windetts, Kirstead, Norfolk NR15 1EG
Tel: (01508) 558174
E-mail: frontier.pub@macunlimited.net
Web Site: www.frontierpublishing.co.uk
Key Personnel
Principal: Mr R Barnes
Founded: 1986
Subjects: Art, History, Nonfiction (General), Photography, Poetry, Travel
ISBN Prefix(es): 1-872914; 0-9508701
Total Titles: 20 Print
Imprints: Frontier 2000 Series
Membership(s): IPG

Frontier 2000 Series, *imprint of* Frontier Publishing

The FruitMarket Gallery
45 Market St, Edinburgh EH1 1DF
Tel: (0131) 225 2383 *Fax:* (0131) 220 3130
E-mail: fruitmarket@fruitmarket.co.uk
Web Site: www.fruitmarket.co.uk
Key Personnel
Dir & Rights: Graeme Murray
Founded: 1984
Mission: to bring the work of leading artists worldwide to Scotland & to exhibit the work of Scottish artists in an international context, engaging with contemporary issues.
Subjects: Art
ISBN Prefix(es): 0-947912

David Fulton Publishers Ltd+
Ormond House, 26-27 Boswell St, London WC1N 3JZ
Tel: (020) 7405 5606 *Fax:* (020) 7831 4840
E-mail: mail@fultonpublishers.co.uk
Web Site: www.fultonbooks.co.uk
Key Personnel
Chairman: David Fulton *E-mail:* david.fulton@fultonpublishers.co.uk
Man Dir: David Hill *E-mail:* david.hill@fultonpublishers.co.uk
Marketing Dir: Rachael Robertson *E-mail:* rachael.robertson@fultonpublishers.co.uk
Publisher: Helen Fairlie *E-mail:* helen.fairlie@fultonpublishers.co.uk
Senior Commissioning Editor: Nina Stibbe *E-mail:* nina.stibbe@fultonpublishers.co.uk
Commissioning Editor (Special Education Needs): Jude Bowen *E-mail:* jude.bowen@fultonpublishers.co.uk
Commissioning Editor: Margaret Haigh *E-mail:* margaret.haigh@fultonpublishers.co.uk
Marketing Executive: Fred O' Connor *E-mail:* fred.oconnor@fultonpublishers.co.uk; Georgina Allan *E-mail:* georgina.allan@fultonpublishers.co.uk
Production Manager: Alan Worth *E-mail:* alan.worth@fultonpublishers.co.uk
Founded: 1987
Specialize in SEN books for teachers.
Subjects: Disability, Special Needs, Education
ISBN Prefix(es): 1-85346
U.S. Office(s): Taylor & Francis Inc, 1900 Frost Rd, Suite 101, Bristol, PA 19007-1598, United States *Tel:* 215-785-5800 *Fax:* 215-785-5515
Foreign Rep(s): Andrew Durnell (Ireland, Europe, Scandinavia); Karim International (Bangladesh); Viva Group (India); Yale Representation Ltd (England)
Foreign Rights: Book Promotions (Pty) Ltd (South Africa); Hemisphere Publication Services (Asia & the Pacific); Macmillan Academic & Reference (Australia); Macmillan Publishers New Zealand Ltd (New Zealand); Taylor & Francis Inc (North America)
Warehouse: Marston Book Services Ltd, PO Box 269, Abingdon, Oxon OX14 4YN
Orders to: Marston Book Services Ltd, PO Box 269, Abington, Oxon OX14 4YN

Fun Files, *imprint of* Funfax Ltd

Funfax Ltd+
9 Henrietta St, London WC2E 8PS
Tel: (020) 7836 5411 *Fax:* (020) 7836 7570
E-mail: clairrey@dk-uk.com
Key Personnel
Man Dir & Foreign Rights: Roger Priddy
Commercial Dir: Jonathan Mitchell
Sales Dir: Steve Evans
Chief Editor: Lisa Telford
Production Manager: Mike Kudar
Art Dir: Roger Tainsh
Founded: 1990
ISBN Prefix(es): 1-85597; 0-7547; 1-86208
Parent Company: Dorling Kindersley Ltd, 80 Strand, London WC2R 0RL
Imprints: Clever Clogs; Fun Files; FX Pax; Junior Funfax; Know Alls; Lettermen; Mad Jack; Magic Joneuery; Microfax
U.S. Office(s): Dorling Kindersley Inc, 95 Madison Ave, New York, NY 10016, United States
Web Site: www.dk.com
Warehouse: International Book Distributors, Magna Park, Coventry Rd, Lutterworth, Lincs LE17

FX Pax, *imprint of* Funfax Ltd

Fyfield Books, *imprint of* Carcanet Press Ltd

Gaia Books Ltd+
66 Charlotte St, London W1T 4QE
Tel: (020) 7323 4010 *Fax:* (020) 7323 0435
E-mail: info@gaiabooks.com
Web Site: www.gaiabooks.co.uk
Key Personnel
Man Dir: Joss Pearson *E-mail:* jpearson@gaiabooks.com
Rights Dir: Suzy Boston *E-mail:* s.boston@gaiabooks.co.uk
Founded: 1982
Specialize in books that celebrate the vision of Gaia, the self-sustaining living Earth & seek to help their readers live in greater personal & planetary harmony; mainly four-color illustrated titles.
Subjects: Architecture & Interior Design, Environmental Studies, Gardening, Plants, Health, Nutrition, Mind, Body & Spirit, Natural Health & Living
ISBN Prefix(es): 1-85675
Number of titles published annually: 12 Print
Total Titles: 110 Print; 5 Audio
Branch Office(s)
20 High St, Stroud, Glos GL5 1AZ, UK Publisher: Lyn Hemming *Tel:* (01453) 752985 *Fax:* (01453) 752987 *E-mail:* addressee@gaiabooks.co.uk
Distributed by Simon & Schuster (USA, Canada, open market excluding Britain & Commonwealth)
Orders to: Grantham Book Services, Alma Park Industrial Estate, Isaac Newton Way, Lincolnshire NG31 9SD, Marilyn Baines *Tel:* (01476) 541080 *Fax:* (01476) 541061

Gairm Publications
29 Waterloo St, Glasgow G2 6BZ
Tel: (0141) 221 1971 *Fax:* (0141) 221 1971
Key Personnel
Editor: Derick S Thomson
Founded: 1952
Specialize in Scottish Gaelic publications.
Subjects: Biography, Fiction, Music, Dance, Poetry, Regional Interests
ISBN Prefix(es): 1-871901; 0-901771
Total Titles: 120 Print

Galaxy Large Print, *imprint of* BBC Audiobooks

Gale, *imprint of* Gale Research

Gale Research
50 Milford Rd, Reading, Berkshire RG1 8LJ
Mailing Address: PO Box 699, North Way, Andover SP10 5BE
Tel: (01264) 342962 *Fax:* (01264) 342763
E-mail: sales@psmedia.co.uk
Web Site: www.gale.com
Telex: 47214 ITPG
Key Personnel
Marketing Manager: Claire Gilman
Head of Sales: Lynne Guthrie
Customer Services Manager: Steven Kempson *Tel:* (0118) 957 7233 *Fax:* (0118) 959 1325 *E-mail:* steven.kempson@gale.com
Founded: 1989
Affiliate Company: Gale Research, 835 Penobscot Bldg, 645 Griswold St, Detroit, MI 48226-4094.
Subjects: Architecture & Interior Design, Art, Biography, Business, Child Care & Development, Drama, Theater, Fashion, Genealogy, History, Literature, Literary Criticism, Essays, Music, Dance, Women's Studies
ISBN Prefix(es): 1-55862; 0-912289; 1-873477
Parent Company: Gale Research
Imprints: Blackbirch Press; Five Star; Gale; Graham & Whiteside; Greenhaven Press; GK Hall & Co; Kidhaven Press; Lucent Books; Macmillan Reference USA; Oceano Grupo Editorial; Primary Source Microfilm; KG Saur; St James Press; Schirmer Reference; Charles Scribner's Sons; The TAFT Group; Thorndike Press; Twayne Publishers; UXL
Shipping Address: PO Box 699, Andover, Hants SP10 5YE
Warehouse: PO Box 699, Andover, Hants SP10 5YE
Orders to: PO Box 699, Andover, Hants SP10 5YE

Gallery Children's Books, *imprint of* East-West Publications (UK) Ltd

Galliard, *imprint of* Stainer & Bell Ltd

Garden Art Press Ltd, *imprint of* Antique Collectors' Club Ltd

Garden Art Press Ltd+
Imprint of Antique Collectors' Club Ltd
5A Church St, Woodbridge IP12 1DS
Tel: (01394) 385501 *Fax:* (01394) 384434
Key Personnel
Man Dir: Diana Steel
Subjects: Gardening, Plants
ISBN Prefix(es): 1-870673

Walter H Gardner & Co
16 Chalton Dr, London N2 0QW
Tel: (20) 8458 3202 *Fax:* (20) 8458 8499
Key Personnel
Man Partner: Walter H Gardner
Sales & Marketing: Mrs D Gardner
Founded: 2001
Also acts as Remainder Dealer & Periodical Back Issue Dealer.

Garland Science, *imprint of* Taylor & Francis Group

Garnet Publishing Ltd+
8 Southern Court, South St, Reading, Berks RG1 4QS
Tel: (0118) 959 7847 *Fax:* (0118) 959 7356
E-mail: enquiries@garnet-ithaca.demon.co.uk (general enquiries); orders@garnet-ithaca.demon.co.uk (ordering)
Web Site: www.garnet-ithaca.co.uk
Key Personnel
Editorial Manager: Emma Hawker *E-mail:* emmahawker@garnet-ithaca.demon.co.uk
Editor: Anna Hines *E-mail:* annahines@garnet-ithaca.demon.co.uk
Founded: 1991
Subjects: Anthropology, Archaeology, Architecture & Interior Design, Art, Biography, Cookery, English as a Second Language, Foreign Countries, History, Literature, Literary Criticism, Essays, Photography, Religion - Islamic, Travel

ISBN Prefix(es): 1-85964; 1-873938
Total Titles: 300 Print
Imprints: Ithaca Press; South Street Press
Distributed by ISBS (US & Canada)

Gateway Books+
The Hollies, Wellow, Bath BA2 8QJ
Tel: (01225) 835 127 *Fax:* (01225) 840 012
E-mail: sales@gatewaybooks.com
Key Personnel
Chief Executive, Publisher, Production: Alick Bartholomew
Sales & Marketing: Kevin Redpath
Editorial/PR: Tina Currie
Founded: 1982
Twenty-four years of an independent alternative publishing tradition.
Subjects: Anthropology, Earth Sciences, Environmental Studies, Health, Nutrition, Mysteries, Philosophy, Psychology, Psychiatry, Religion - Other, Self-Help
ISBN Prefix(es): 0-946551; 1-85860
Branch Office(s)
Gateway Books at WPR, 2819 Tenth St, Berkeley, CA 94710, United States *Tel:* 510-841-9347
Distributor for Amethyst Books (Banbury, UK)
Orders to: Airlift Book Co, 8 The Arena, Mollison Ave, Enfield, Middlesex EN3 7NJ
Tel: (0181) 8040 400 *Fax:* (0181) 8040 044

The Gay Men's Press, *imprint of* GMP Publishers Ltd

Gay Times Travel Guides, *imprint of* Absolute Press

Gazelle Books, *imprint of* Angus Hudson Ltd

GE Fabbri, *imprint of* Fabbri (GE) Ltd

GE Magazines, *imprint of* Fabbri (GE) Ltd

Geddes & Grosset+
Subsidiary of D C Thomson & Co Ltd
David Dale House, New Lanark, Lanark ML11 9DB
Tel: (01555) 665000 *Fax:* (01555) 665694
E-mail: info@gandg.sol.co.uk
Key Personnel
Publisher: Ron B Grosset *E-mail:* ron@gandg.sol.co.uk; Mike Miller *E-mail:* mike@gandg.sol.co.uk
Founded: 1987
Specializes in popular reference & children's books for the mass market.
Member of Scottish Publishers Association.
ISBN Prefix(es): 1-85534
Number of titles published annually: 80 Print
Imprints: Beano Books; Tarantula Books; Waverley Books
Distributed by Book Source; Peter Haddock Ltd

Geiser Productions+
7 The Corner, Grange Rd, London W5 3PQ
Tel: (020) 8579 4653 *Fax:* (020) 8567 6593
E-mail: geiser@globalnet.co.uk
Web Site: www.geiserproductions.com; www.sidsjournal.com
Key Personnel
Dir & International Rights: N H Geiser
Dir: Sidney DuBroff
Founded: 1967
In-house producers of sponsored and commissioned works, who accept assignments in all areas - whether large or small. Areas of endeavour include serious fiction, politics and, in something of a departure, country sports.
Subjects: Fiction, Government, Political Science, Journalism, Outdoor Recreation, Sports, Athletics

ISBN Prefix(es): 0-9503262
Membership(s): IPG

Gembooks
16 Green Park, Manor Rd, Bournemouth BH1 3HR
Tel: (01202) 399729 *Fax:* (01202) 399729
E-mail: readbooks@onmail.co.uk
Key Personnel
Editor & Author: Peter G Read
Founded: 1995
Specialize in diamond fiction.
Subjects: Criminology, Fiction, Mysteries, Novels based on diamond industry
ISBN Prefix(es): 0-9525315
Total Titles: 3 Print

Genesis Publications Ltd+
2 Jenner Rd, Guildford, Surrey GU1 3PL
Tel: (01483) 540970 *Fax:* (01483) 304709
E-mail: postmaster@genesiseditions.demon.co.uk
Web Site: www.genesis-publications.com
Key Personnel
Publisher: Brian Roylance
Founded: 1972
Subjects: Art, History, Literature, Literary Criticism, Essays, Natural History, Poetry, Science (General)
ISBN Prefix(es): 0-904351

Geographers' A-Z Map Company Ltd
Fairfield Rd, Borough Green, Sevenoaks, Kent TN15 8PP
Tel: (01732) 781000 *Fax:* (01732) 780677
E-mail: tradesales@a-zmaps.co.uk
Web Site: www.azmaps.co.uk
Key Personnel
Man Dir: D W Churchill; K Palmer
Founded: 1936
ISBN Prefix(es): 0-85039
Showroom(s): 44 Gray's Inn Rd, London WC1X 8HX *Tel:* (020) 7440 9500 *Fax:* (020) 7440 9501 *E-mail:* shop@a-zmaps.co.uk

The Geographical Association+
160 Solly St, Sheffield S1 4BF
Tel: (0114) 296 0088 *Fax:* (0114) 296 7176
E-mail: ga@geography.org.uk
Web Site: www.geography.org.uk
Key Personnel
Marketing Manager: Fran Royle
Senior Administrator: Frances Soar
Founded: 1893
National association for geography teachers with a membership of over 10,000.
Also book packager.
Subjects: Geography, Geology
ISBN Prefix(es): 0-900395; 0-948512; 1-899085; 1-905448
Number of titles published annually: 25 Print
Total Titles: 120 Print
Branch Office(s)
Bedfordshire Branch, Contact: Mr David Cooper *Tel:* (01536) 710226
Berkhamstead Branch
Blackpool & District Branch, Blackpool Sixth Form College, Blackpool Old Road, Highfurlong, Blackpool, Contact: Joan M Clarke *Tel:* (01253) 761330
Birmingham Branch, Contact: Julia Legg *Tel:* (0114) 2960088
Bradford Branch, Contact: Mr D E Cotton
Brighton & District Branch, Contact: Julia Legg *Tel:* (0114) 2960088
Cambridge & District Branch, Contact: Richard Dilley *Tel:* (01480) 461857
Cardiff Branch, Contact: Julia Legg *Tel:* (0114) 2960088
Chester, Halton & Warrington Branch, Contact: Elaine Jackson *Tel:* (01928) 425489
Durham Branch, Contact: Adam Nichols *Tel:* (0191) 374 7821

Geographical Association Branch Network, President: Alison Bailey *Web Site:* www.digitalbristol.org/members/ga/
Guildford Branch, Contact: Mr R E J Seymour
Hampshire Branch, Contact: Kim Adams *Tel:* (01962) 852764 *Web Site:* www.mcnaughtweb.freeserve.co.uk/hantsga/index.htm
Hereford Branch, Contact: Julia Legg *Tel:* (0114) 2960088 *E-mail:* jlegg@geography.org.uk
Hertfordshire GTA Branch
High Weald Branch, Chairman: Peter Goddard *Tel:* (01580) 764917 *Fax:* (01580) 764917 *E-mail:* c.g.@tobermory.demon.co.uk
Huddersfield & Halifax Branch, Contact: Janet Clarkson *Tel:* (01484) 608599
Hull & District Branch, Contact: Richard Hurrell *Tel:* (01482) 711688 *Fax:* (01482) 798991
Isle of Thanet Branch, Chairman: Jan Ingram *Tel:* (01843) 862845
Kingston-upon-Thames Branch, Contact: Dr Annie Hughes
Leicester Branch, Contact: Malcolm Pollard
Lincoln Branch *E-mail:* steephill@btinternet.com
Liverpool & District Branch, Contact: David Chambers *Tel:* (0151) 420 4941 *Fax:* (0151) 330 3366
Manchester Branch, Contact: Mrs M Blackburn
Norfolk Branch, Contact: Kirsten Remer *Web Site:* www.norfolkga.org.uk/
North Staffordshire Branch, Alleyne, Stone, Staffordshire ST15 8DT, Honorary Secretary: Robert G Jones *Tel:* (01785) 354200 *Fax:* (01785) 354222 *E-mail:* robertgjones@yahoo.com
Oxford Branch, St Edwards School, Woodstock Road, Oxford OX2 7NN, Contact: Dr G Nagle *Tel:* (01865) 319231
Plymouth & District Branch, Contact: Miss N S M Paterson *Tel:* (01752) 668482
Ribblesdale Branch, Contact: Mike Pearson
Tyneside Branch, Inspection & Advisory Service, Education Department, County Hall, Durham DH1 5UJ, Contact: Trevor Hemsley *Tel:* (0191) 383 4558
Worcester Branch, Contact: Richard Yarwood *Web Site:* www.worc.ac.uk/departs/envman/worcGA/
York & District Branch, 14 St James' Mount, York YO23 1EL, Secretary: Hilary Arnold *Tel:* (01904) 655114
Foreign Rep(s): Drake International (Europe, US)

Geological Society Publishing House
Unit 7, Brassmill Enterprise Centre, Brassmill Lane, Bath BA1 3JN
Tel: (01225) 445046 *Fax:* (01225) 442836
E-mail: rebecca.toop@geolsoc.org.uk
Web Site: www.geolsoc.org.uk
Key Personnel
Dir, Publishing: Neal Marriott *E-mail:* neal.marriott@geolsoc.org
Marketing Executive: Karen Wilson *E-mail:* karen.wilson@geolsoc.org.uk
Orders: Dawn Angel *E-mail:* angeld@geolsoc.org.uk
Founded: 1807
Member of European Federation of Geologists & Association of European Geological Societies.
Subjects: Civil Engineering, Earth Sciences, Geography, Geology, Science (General)
ISBN Prefix(es): 0-903317; 1-897799; 1-86239
Number of titles published annually: 30 Print
Total Titles: 250 Print; 2 CD-ROM
Parent Company: The Geological Society, Burlington House, Piccadilly, London W1J 0BG
Distributed by AAPG (North America)
Distributor for American Association of Petroleum Geologists (European distributor); Geological Society of America (European distributor); Society for Sedimentary Geology (European distributor)
Orders to: AAPG Bookstore, PO Box 979, Tulsa, OK 74101-0979, United States

Affiliated East-West Press PVT Ltd, G-1/16 Ansari Rd, New Delhi 110 002, India, Sunny Malik *Tel:* (011) 3279113 *Fax:* (011) 3260538
Kanda Book Trading Co, Cityhouse Tama 204, Tsurumaki 1-3-10, Tama-Shi, Tokyo 206-0034, Japan *Tel:* (04) 23577650 *Fax:* (04) 23577651

George Mann Publications+
6 Malthouse Close, Easton, Winchester, Hants SO21 1ES
Tel: (01622) 759591 *Fax:* (01622) 209193
Web Site: www.gmp.co.uk
Key Personnel
Chairman: George Mann
Man Dir: John Arne
Founded: 1972
Subjects: Astrology, Occult, Biography, Fiction, Human Relations, Nonfiction (General), Philosophy
ISBN Prefix(es): 0-7041
Parent Company: Arnefold Editions
Imprints: Arnefold; George Mann; Recollections

George Philip, see Philip's

Laura Geringer Books, *imprint of* HarperCollins Publishers

E J W Gibb Memorial Trust
Teddington House, Warminster, Wilts BA12 8PQ
Tel: (01985) 213409 *Fax:* (01985) 212910
Web Site: www.arisandphillips.com
Key Personnel
Secretary to the Trustees: P R Bligh
E-mail: prbligh@btinternet.com
Founded: 1902
A charity which supports & publishes books on the literature, religions, philosophy & history of the Persian, Turks & Arab peoples.
Subjects: History, Literature, Literary Criticism, Essays, Philosophy, Religion - Other
ISBN Prefix(es): 0-906094

Stanley Gibbons Publications
5 Parkside, Christchurch Rd, Ringwood, Hants BH24 3SH
Tel: (01425) 472363 *Fax:* (01425) 470247
E-mail: sales@stangib.demon.co.uk
Web Site: www.stanleygibbons.com
Key Personnel
Chief Executive: Paul Frasen
Editor: D Aggersberg
Sales Dir & Marketing: Gary Ashburn
Sales Manager: Rick Harris
Founded: 1856
Subjects: Crafts, Games, Hobbies, Philately
ISBN Prefix(es): 0-85259
Parent Company: Stanley Gibbons International Ltd, 399 Strand, London WC2R 0LX

Ginn & Company, *imprint of* Reed Educational & Professional Publishing

Ginn & Co Ltd+
Linacre House, Jordan Hill, Oxford OX2 8DP
Tel: (01865) 888000 *Fax:* (01865) 314222
E-mail: services@ginn.co.uk
Web Site: www.ginn.co.uk
Key Personnel
Publishing Dir: Kath Donovan; Rod Theodorou; Stephen Fahey
Man Dir: Paul Shuter *Tel:* (01865) 311366
E-mail: pshuter@ginn.co.uk
UK Sales Manager: Rachel Colyer *Tel:* (01865) 314096
Founded: 1862 (USA), 1920 (London)
Representation Outside the UK: Argentina: Kel Ediciones SA; Australia: Rigby Heinemann; Botswana, Lesotho & Swaziland: Heinemann Educational Botswana. Botswana; Brazil: Carlos Barbison; Canada: Irwin Publishing; Egypt: Cairo Trade Cuvae; India: Oxford University Press India; Jamaica: Schools Promotion Services; Kenya: Benjamin Kithyaka; New Zealand Reed Publishing (NZ) Ltd; Pakistan: Oxford University Press; Singapore & South East Asia: Susan Chua; South Africa: Heinemann Publishers Ltd; Uganda: Rotash Enterprises; Uruguay: Bookshop SA; Zimbabwe: Textbook Sales (PVT) Ltd; Reed Publishing Group (NZ) Ltd; Transglobal Publishers Service Ltd.
Subjects: Education
ISBN Prefix(es): 0-602
Parent Company: Reed Educational & Professional Publishing
Ultimate Parent Company: Reed Elsevier plc, 25 Victoria St, London SW1H 0EX
Foreign Rep(s): Agius & Agius Ltd (Europe); Basil Bonaparte (Grenada); Book Link Co Ltd (Thailand); Books & Bits (Chile); Brown Onduso (Kenya); Bushbooks (Australia); Cairo Trade Center - Alexandria (Egypt); Cairo Trade Center - Cairo (Egypt); Chris Chirwa (Southern Africa); Susan Chua (Brunei, Singapore, Sri Lanka); Crownbooks (Africa); George Davis (Jamaica); Drum Publishers (Tanzania); Editions de L' Ocean Indien Ltd (Africa); English Book Center (Colombia); Carole Ford (Europe, United Arab Emirates); R Yvonne Gaynes (Caribbean, Grenadines); Harcourt Canada (Canada); Heinemann Inc (US); Heinemann Botswana (Southern Africa); Carroll Heinemann (Ireland); Heinemann Ed Books (Nigeria) Ltd (Nigeria); Heinemann Lesotho (Southern Africa); Heinemann South Africa (South Africa); Heinemann Southern Africa (Southern Africa); Heinemann Swaziland (Southern Africa); Heinneman UK (UK); Irwin Publishing (Canada); Louise Jacobs (Africa, Far East, Middle East); Jango Heinemann (Southern Africa); Ishmael M Khan & Sons Ltd (Trinadad & Tobago); Rufus Khodra (Caribbean); Mark Kuo (Cambodia, Indonesia, Korea, Latin America, Malaysia, Myanmar, Vietnam); Gerry McCullough (Southern Africa); Nzomo Educational Supplies Ltd (Kenya); Onganda Y' Omambo Bookshop (Southern Africa); Oxford University Press (Pakistan); Publishers Marketing Associates (Pakistan); Adam Quilter (Caribbean, Central & South America, World); R E D I (Africa); Rearden Book Suppliers (Lebanon); Reed Publishing Group (NZ) Ltd (New Zealand); F Reimmer Book Services (Ghana); Rigby Heinemann (Australia); Rorash Educational Publishers (Uganda); S Seshadra (India); Clare Symonette (Caribbean); Transglobal Publishers Service Ltd (Hong Kong); Julie White (Barbados)
Warehouse: Unit 1, Block H, Industrial Estate, Long Eaton, Nottingham NG10 1GG

Glasgow City Libraries Publications+
The Mitchell Library, North St, Glasgow G3 7DN
Tel: (0141) 287 2999 *Fax:* (0141) 287 2815
Key Personnel
Commercial Manager: Verina Litster *Tel:* (0141) 287 2846 *E-mail:* verina.litster@cls.glasgow.gov.uk
Founded: 1980
Member of Scottish Publishers' Association.
Subjects: History, Regional Interests
ISBN Prefix(es): 0-906169

Mary Glasgow Publications, *imprint of* Nelson Thornes Ltd

Global Books Ltd+
Knoll House, 35 The Crescent, Sandgate, Folkestone, Kent CT20 3EE
Mailing Address: PO Box 219, Folkestone, Kent CT20 3LZ
Tel: (1303) 226799 *Fax:* (1303) 243087
E-mail: globook@aol.com
Web Site: simplyglobalbooks.com
Key Personnel
President & Publishing Dir: Paul Norbury
Sales Manager, International Sales-Marketing: Iris Warr
Founded: 1994
Subjects: Health, Nutrition, Language Arts, Linguistics, Religion - Other, Travel
ISBN Prefix(es): 1-86034; 1-901903; 1-898823
Number of titles published annually: 12 Print
Total Titles: 52 Print
Imprints: Global Oriental; Renaissance Books
Branch Office(s)
Midpoint Trade Books, 1263 Southwest Blvd, Kansas City, KS 66103, United States *Tel:* 913-831-2233 *Fax:* 913-362-7401
Distributed by International Press Distribution; Tutte Shokai; Ulysses Trowl Guides
Orders to: Grantham Book Services, Isaac Newton Way, Alma Park Industrial Estate, Grantham, Lincs NG31 9SD

Global Oriental, *imprint of* Global Books Ltd

Glowworm Books Ltd+
Unit 7 Greendykes Industrial Estate, Greendykes Rd, Broxburn, West Lothian EH52 6PG
Tel: (01506) 857570 *Fax:* (01506) 858100
E-mail: admin@GlowwormBooks.co.uk; sales@amaising.co.uk (packaging); sales@glowwormbooks.co.uk (publishing & schools division)
Web Site: www.GlowwormBooks.co.uk
Key Personnel
Man Dir: Mrs K Allan
Operations Dir: Mr G Allan
Sales Manager: Mrs Marion Farish
Buyer: Annie Crighton
Founded: 1984
Specialize in publishing children's picture books, also a school supplier for text books & libraries (in Scotland only).
Member of Booksellers Association & Scottish Publishers Association.
ISBN Prefix(es): 1-871512
Number of titles published annually: 3 Print
Total Titles: 43 Print

GMC Publications Ltd+
Castle Place, 166 High St, Lewes, East Sussex BN7 1XU
Tel: (01273) 477374; (01273) 488005 *Fax:* (01273) 486300
E-mail: pubs@thegmcgroup.com
Key Personnel
Senior Man Editor, Books: April McCroskie *Fax:* (01273) 487692 *E-mail:* aprilm@thegmcgroup.com
Publish magazines books & videos for general trade.
Subjects: Crafts, Games, Hobbies, Gardening, Plants, How-to, Photography
ISBN Prefix(es): 1-86108
Total Titles: 120 Print
Imprints: Guild of Master Publications Inc
Distributor for Sterling Publishing Co Inc; Taunton Press Publishers
Warehouse: Mail International Ltd, Braybon Business Park, Consort Way, Burgess Hill W Sussex

GMP Publishers Ltd+
PO Box 247, Swaffham PE37 8PA
Tel: (01366) 328101 *Fax:* (01366) 328102
E-mail: davidoraubrey@gmpub.demon.co.uk
Web Site: www.gmppubs.co.uk; www.gaymenspress.co.uk
Key Personnel
Dir, Editorial, Art & Photography: Aubrey Walter
Dir, Editorial, Fiction: David Fernbach
Founded: 1979
gay fiction & nonfiction.

Subjects: Art, Fiction, Gay & Lesbian, History, Nonfiction (General)
ISBN Prefix(es): 0-85449; 0-907040; 0-946097
Associate Companies: Heretic Books Ltd
Imprints: The Gay Men's Press; Editions Aubrey Walter
Distributed by LPC/Inbook (North America)
Orders to: Central Books Ltd, 99 Wallis Rd, London E9 5LN *Tel:* (020) 8986 4854 *Fax:* (020) 8533 5821

Godsfield Press Ltd+
Division of David & Charles Ltd
Godsfield House, Old Alresford, Hants SO24 9RQ
Tel: (01626) 323200 *Fax:* (01626) 323231
E-mail: mail@davidandcharles.co.uk
Web Site: www.davidandcharles.co.uk
Key Personnel
Proprietor: Debbie Thorpe *E-mail:* debbie@godsfield.com
Founded: 1995
Subjects: Health, Nutrition, Esoterics/New Age, Divination, Personal Growth, Sacred Living, Spiritual Wisdom
ISBN Prefix(es): 1-899434; 1-84181
Distributed by David & Charles (United Kingdom & Eire)
Orders to: HarperCollins Distribution Service, Glasgow GA ONB

Golden Books Publishing Company, Inc+
Division of Random House, Inc
20 Vauxhall Bridge Rd, London SW1V 2SA
Tel: (020) 7973 9000 *Fax:* (020) 7233 6125
Key Personnel
Accountant Financial: Alex Clark
Founded: 1907
ISBN Prefix(es): 0-307
U.S. Office(s): 850 Third Ave, New York, NY 10022, United States

Golden Cockerel Press Ltd+
16 Barter St, London WC1A 2AH
Tel: (020) 7405 7979 *Fax:* (020) 7404 3598
Telex: 23565
Key Personnel
Man Dir, UK: Andrew Lindesay; Tamar Lindesay *E-mail:* lindesay@btinternet.com
Founded: 1979
Subjects: Architecture & Interior Design, Art, Drama, Theater, Film, Video, Government, Political Science, History, Literature, Literary Criticism, Essays, Music, Dance, Philosophy, Social Sciences, Sociology, Theology
ISBN Prefix(es): 0-8453; 0-8387; 0-8386; 0-934223; 0-941664; 0-87413; 1-900541; 0-918016
Associate Companies: Associated University Presses Inc, 440 Forsgate Dr, Cranbury, NJ 08512, United States
Imprints: Associated University Presses (UK, Europe, India, Australia & New Zealand); Cornwall Books; Cygnus Arts
Distributor for Associated University Presses (UK, Europe, India, Australia & New Zealand)
Orders to: Gazelle Book Services, Falcon House, Queen Square, Lancaster LA1 1RN *Tel:* (01524) 68765 *Fax:* (01524) 63232
E-mail: gazelle4go@aol.com

Golden Dawn, *imprint of* Mandrake of Oxford

Golden Handshake, *imprint of* Jay Landesman

Goldleaf Publishing (Local History), *imprint of* Alun Books

Victor Gollancz, *imprint of* Cassell & Co

Victor Gollancz Ltd, see Gollancz/Witherby

Gollancz/Witherby+
Orion House, 5 Upper St Martin's Lane, London WC2H 9EA
Tel: (020) 7240 3444 *Fax:* (020) 7240 4822
Web Site: www.orionbooks.co.uk
Telex: 9413701 CASPUB
Key Personnel
Sales Dir: Andrew Macmillan
Rights & Permissions: Jane Blackstock
Publisher: Liz Knights
Production: Elizabeth Dobson
Science Fiction: Richard Evans
Children's: Chris Kloet
Subjects: Architecture & Interior Design, Biography, Fiction, History, Music, Dance, Mysteries, Natural History, Nonfiction (General), Outdoor Recreation, Science (General), Science Fiction, Fantasy, Sports, Athletics, Travel
ISBN Prefix(es): 0-575; 0-85493
Parent Company: Orion Publishing Group

Gomer Press (J D Lewis & Sons Ltd)+
Gwasg Gomer, Llandysul, Ceredigion SA44 4QL
Tel: (01559) 362371 *Fax:* (01559) 363758
E-mail: gwasg@gomer.co.uk
Web Site: www.gomer.co.uk *Cable:* GOMER LLANDYSUL
Key Personnel
Man Dir & Rights & Permissions: Jonathan Lewis
Editorial: Mairwen Prys Jones
Sales & Publicity: Sue Davies
Founded: 1892
Specialize in books from Wales, about Wales, in Welsh & in English.
Subjects: Education, Fiction, Language Arts, Linguistics, Nonfiction (General), Poetry, Regional Interests
ISBN Prefix(es): 0-86383; 0-85088; 1-85902
Number of titles published annually: 100 Print
Total Titles: 700 Print
Parent Company: J D Lewis & Sons Ltd
Imprints: Pont Books
Bookshop(s): Gomerian Press, Llandysul, Dyfed

Goodnight Sleeptight, *imprint of* Grandreams Ltd

A H Gordon
Kintradwell Farmhouse, Brora, Sutherland KW9 6LU
Tel: (01408) 622660
Key Personnel
President: Adam Gordon *E-mail:* adam@adamgordon.freeewire.co.uk
Founded: 1990
Specialize in Tramways, trolley buses and railways. Publisher of new books and dealer in second hand books & ephemera.
Subjects: Transportation, Buses, Railways, Christian
ISBN Prefix(es): 1-874422
Number of titles published annually: 6 Print
Total Titles: 41 Print

The Robert Gordon University+
Garthdee Rd, Aberdeen AB10 7QD
Tel: (01224) 262000 *Fax:* (01224) 263636
E-mail: sim@rgu.ac.uk
Web Site: www.rgu.ac.uk
Key Personnel
Head, School of Information & Media: Ian M Johnson
Course Leaders (Electronic Publishing): Sarah Pedersen
Course Leaders (Publishing Studies): Josephine M Royle
Founded: 1967
Subjects: Publishing & Book Trade Reference

Gower, *imprint of* Ashgate Publishing Ltd

Gower Publishing Ltd+
Gower House, Croft Rd, Aldershot, Hants GU11 3HR
Tel: (01252) 331551 *Fax:* (01252) 344405
E-mail: info@gowerpub.com
Web Site: www.gowerpub.com
Key Personnel
Man Dir: Christopher Simpson
Sales & Marketing Dir: Rachel Maund
Founded: 1967
Subjects: Business, Management
ISBN Prefix(es): 0-566
Associate Companies: Dartmouth Publishing Ltd
Orders to: Ashgate-Gower Asia Pacific, 3/303 Barrenjoey Rd, Newport, NSW 2107, Australia *Tel:* (02) 9999 2777 *Fax:* (02) 9999 3688 *E-mail:* info@ashgate.com.au (Australia, SE & NE Asia)
Ashgate Publishing Ltd, 2252 Ridge Rd, Brookfield, VT 05036-9704, United States *Tel:* 802-276-3162 *Fax:* 802-276-3837 *E-mail:* info@ashgate.com (North America & South America)
Bookpoint Ltd, Gower Publishing Customer Service, 130 Milton Park, Abingdon, Oxon OX14 4SB *Tel:* (01235) 827730 *Fax:* (01235) 400454 *E-mail:* orders@bookpoint.co.uk/enquiries@bookpoint.co.uk *Web Site:* pubeasy.books.bookpoint.co.uk (UK & Europe)

Gracewing Publishing
2 Southern Ave, Leominster HR6 0QF
Tel: (01568) 616835 *Fax on Demand:* (01568) 613289
E-mail: gracewingx@aol.com
Web Site: www.gracewing.co.uk
Subjects: Religion - Other, Theology, Church Biography, Ecclesiastical History
Distributed by Morehouse (US)
Distributor for Mercer University Press (in UK); Our Sunday Visitor; Smyth & Helwys; Source; Templegate

Graham & Whiteside, *imprint of* Gale Research

Graham-Cameron Publishing & Illustration+
The Studio, 23 Holt Rd, Sheringham, Norfolk NR26 8NB
Tel: (01263) 821 333 *Fax:* (01263) 821 334
E-mail: enquiry@graham-cameron-illustration.com
Web Site: www.graham-cameron-illustration.com
Key Personnel
Partner: Helen Graham-Cameron; Mike Graham-Cameron
Marketing Manager: Duncan Graham-Cameron
Founded: 1984 (Founded as a book publisher, became a packager & illustration agency)
Editorial & production assistance. Approximately 37 freelance professional illustrators under contract.
Member of Independent Publishers Guild (IPG), Cambridge Book Association (CBA) & Publishers in Cambridge Association (PICA).
Subjects: Education, English as a Second Language, Language Arts, Linguistics
ISBN Prefix(es): 0-947672

W F Graham (Northampton) Ltd
2 Pondwood Close, Moulton Park Industrial Estate, Northampton, Northamptonshire NN3 1RT
Tel: (01604) 645537 *Fax:* (01604) 648414
Key Personnel
Man Dir: R F Graham
Sales Dir: T A Graham
Founded: 1952
ISBN Prefix(es): 1-85128

Gramophone, *imprint of* Wilmington Business Information Ltd

Granada Media, *imprint of* Carlton Publishing Group

Grandreams Ltd+
4 North Parade, Bath, Avon BA1 1LF
Tel: (01225) 485923 *Fax:* (01225) 485928
E-mail: wrrake@robert-frederick.co.uk
Key Personnel
Rights Manager: Catherine Lyn-Jones
Production Manager: Josie Strong
Founded: 1977
Specialize in international coeditions & mass market children's books; dictionaries, reference books, foreign language books, novelty books, pop-ups, board books, storybooks, sticker books, coloring books.
Subjects: Fiction, Nonfiction (General)
Parent Company: Grandreams Ltd, 435-437 Edgware Rd, Little Venice, London W2 1TN
Imprints: Grandreams USA; Goodnight Sleeptight
Branch Office(s)
435-437 Edgware Rd, London W2 1TH
U.S. Office(s): 8 Arbour Dr, Wayne, NJ, United States

Grandreams USA, *imprint of* Grandreams Ltd

Grange Books PLC+
The Grange, Units 1-6, Kingsnorth Industrial Estate, Hoo, Nr Rochester, Kent ME3 9ND
Tel: (01634) 256 000 *Fax:* (01634) 255 500
E-mail: grangebooks@aol.com
Web Site: www.grangebooks.co.uk
Key Personnel
Marketing Manager: Bob Siwecki
General Sales Support & Coordination: Deborah Duthie *E-mail:* deborah.duthie@grangebooks.co.uk
Sales (North America): Stephen Ash *E-mail:* stephen.ash@grangebooks.co.uk
Sales (UK - Southwest & Ireland): Geoff Bailey
Sales (Australia, New Zealand, Far East, India & South Africa): John Norman *E-mail:* john.norman@grangebooks.co.uk
Sales (UK - Southeast, East Anglia & London): Don Peachey
Sales (Middle East, Central & Eastern Europe, Norway & Baltic States, Spain, Portugal, Central & South America): Bob Siwecki *E-mail:* bob.siwecki@grangebooks.co.uk
Sales (UK - Northern England, Scotland, Sweden, Finland, Denmark, Iceland, Holland & Belgium): Glenn Trueman
Founded: 1972
Discount & promotional book publisher & distributor.
Subjects: Aeronautics, Aviation, Animals, Pets, Architecture & Interior Design, Art, Astronomy, Automotive, Cookery, Crafts, Games, Hobbies, Gardening, Plants, Natural History, Nonfiction (General), Transportation, Travel, Wine & Spirits
ISBN Prefix(es): 1-85627
Imprints: Binky (Childrens); Park Lane (Art)
U.S. Office(s): Book Club of America, 230 Fifth Ave, Suite 1405, New York, NY, United States
Showroom(s): Bermondsey, Nr London Bridge Station *Tel:* (01634) 256 000

Grant & Cutler Ltd
55-57 Great Marlborough St, London W1F 7AY
Tel: (020) 7734 2012 *Fax:* (020) 7734 9272
E-mail: contactus@grantandcutler.com
Web Site: www.grant-c.demon.co.uk
Key Personnel
Dir: R C O Howard *Tel:* (020) 7494 3130
Founded: 1935
Specialize in bookselling & library supplies in Western European languages. Also specialize in Critical Guides to French, German, Tamesis texts, research bibliographies & checklists.
Member of Booksellers Association.

Subjects: Foreign Countries, Literature, Literary Criticism, Essays
ISBN Prefix(es): 0-7293; 0-900411
Number of titles published annually: 10 Print
Total Titles: 270 Print

Granta Books+
2/3 Hanover Yard, Noel Rd, London N1 8BE
Tel: (020) 7704 9776 *Fax:* (020) 7354 3469
E-mail: info@granta.com
Web Site: www.granta.com
Key Personnel
Publisher: Gail Lynch *E-mail:* glynch@granta.com
Senior Editor: Sara Holloway *E-mail:* sholloway@granta.com
Rights Dir: Angela Rose *E-mail:* arose@granta.com
Sales Dir: Frances Hollingdale *E-mail:* fhollingdale@granta.com
Publicity: Louise Campbell *E-mail:* lcampbell@granta.com
Subjects: Biography, Fiction, History, Literature, Literary Criticism, Essays, Nonfiction (General), Travel
ISBN Prefix(es): 1-86207
Parent Company: Granta Publications
Imprints: Granta Magazine
U.S. Office(s): Granta US, 1755 Broadway, 5th floor, New York, NY 10019, United States
Distributed by Allen & Unwin (Australia & New Zealand); Penguin Books (India); Raincoast (Canada)
Foreign Rep(s): Allen & Unwin Pty Ltd (Australia); Jonathan Ball/Harper Collins (South Africa); Michael Geoghegan (Austria, Belgium, France, Germany, Switzerland); I M A (Africa, Caribbean, Central & South America, Cyprus, Eastern Europe, Middle East, Turkey); Adam Murray (England, Scotland); Nilsson & Lamm (Netherlands); Penny Padovani (Gibraltar, Greece, Italy, Portugal, Slovenia, Spain); Penguin Books India (Bangladesh, India, Nepal, Pakistan, Sri Lanka); Raincoast Books (Canada); Repforce Ireland (Ireland); Hanne Rotovnik (Scandinavia); Roger Ward (Far East)
Warehouse: Macmillan Distribution Ltd, Houndmills Basingstroke, Hants RG21 6XS

Granta Magazine, *imprint of* Granta Books

The Greek Bookshop+
57a Nether St, North Finchley, London N12 7NP
Mailing Address: PO Box 29283, London N13 5BJ
Tel: (020) 8446 1985 *Fax:* (020) 8446 1986
E-mail: info@thegreekbookshop.com
Web Site: www.thegreekbookshop.com
Key Personnel
Partner: Loui D Loizou *E-mail:* zenobooksellers@aol.com; Maria Loizou
Founded: 1944
Publish books in Greek & English about Greece & Cyprus. Specialize in books about Byzantium, Modern History of Greece & Cyprus.
Subjects: Archaeology, Art, Cookery, History, Literature, Literary Criticism, Essays, Philosophy, Poetry, Romance, Travel
ISBN Prefix(es): 0-900834; 0-7228; 0-9521246
Total Titles: 25 Print
Subsidiaries: Loizou Publications

Green Books Ltd+
Foxhole, Dartington, Totnes, Devon TQ9 6EB
Tel: (01803) 863260 *Fax:* (01803) 863843
E-mail: greenbooks@gn.apc.org
Web Site: www.greenbooks.co.uk
Key Personnel
Chairman: Satish Kumar
Publisher (Editorial, Production, Rights): John Elford

Sales & Marketing Manager: Paul Rossiter
Founded: 1987
Subjects: Agriculture, Economics, Environmental Studies, How-to, Philosophy, Self-Help, Ecological, Spiritual & Cultural Issues
ISBN Prefix(es): 1-870098; 1-900322; 0-9527302; 1-903998
Associate Companies: Resurgence Magazine
Imprints: Green Earth Books; Resurgence Books; Themis Books
Distributed by Ceres Books; Gemcraft Books (Australia); Globe Enterprise (Malaysia)
Distributor for Chelsea Green Publishing Co (UK)

Green Earth Books, *imprint of* Green Books Ltd

Green Print, *imprint of* The Merlin Press Ltd

W Green, *imprint of* Sweet & Maxwell Ltd

W Green The Scottish Law Publisher+
21 Alva St, Edinburgh EH2 4PS
Tel: (0131) 225 4879 (orders); (0131) 225 4879 (marketing); (0207) 449 1104 (trade customers); (264) 342 828 (international book orders & information); (264) 342 766 (international subscription orders & information)
Fax: (0131) 225 2104 (orders); (0131) 225 2104 (marketing); (0207) 449 1144 (trade customers); (264) 342 761 (international book orders & information); (264) 342 761 (international subscription orders & information)
E-mail: enquiries@wgreen.co.uk; trade.sales@sweetandmaxwell.co.uk (trade customers)
Web Site: www.wgreen.co.uk
Key Personnel
Marketing Manager: Mdme Jane Scott
Publisher: Miss Jill Barrington
Dir: Gilly Michie
Man Editor: Stephen Chubb
Marketing Executive: Lyn Minay *E-mail:* lyn.minay@wgreen.co.uk
Subjects: Law
ISBN Prefix(es): 0-414
Total Titles: 140 Print; 1 CD-ROM
Ultimate Parent Company: The Thomson Corporation, Suite 2706, Toronto Dominion Bank Tower, PO Box 24, Toronto Dominion Centre, Toronto, ON M5K 1A1, Canada
Sales Office(s): Vicki McGee *Tel:* (01578) 730780 *Fax:* (01578) 730780 *E-mail:* vicki.mcgee@sweetandmaxwell.co.uk (customers in the Lothian, Tayside, Borders, Grampian and Fife areas; that is, postcoded areas: AB/DD/EH/KY/TD)
Stephen Wilson *Tel:* (01698) 320286 *Fax:* (01698) 320286 *E-mail:* stephen.wilson@sweetandmaxwell.co.uk (customers in the Central, Strathclyde, Dumfries & Galloway, Northern & Western Isles and Highlands & Islands areas; that is, postcoded areas: DG/G/HS/IV/KW/FK/KA/ML/PA/PH/ZE)
Foreign Rep(s): Barbara Gerken (Scotland)
Warehouse: W. Green - ITPS, Cheriton House, North Way, Andover Hants SP10 5BE
Orders to: W Green, 100 Ave Rd, Swiss Cottage, London NW3 3PF *Tel:* (020) 7449 1111 *Fax:* (020) 7449 1155 (customer service)

Greenhaven Press, *imprint of* Gale Research

Greenhill Books/Lionel Leventhal Ltd+
Park House, One Russell Gardens, London NW11 9NN
Tel: (020) 8458 6314 *Fax:* (020) 8905 5245
E-mail: info@greenhillbooks.com; sales@greenhillbooks.com
Web Site: www.greenhillbooks.com
Key Personnel
Chief Executive, Man Dir: Lionel Leventhal
Sales Dir: Mark Wray *E-mail:* mark.wray@greenhillbooks.com

Founded: 1984
Also acts as international distribution agent for Presidio Press, Novato, CA; Stackpole Books, Mechanicsburg, PA; Proctor Jones Publishing, San Francisco, CA; Emperor's Press, Chicago, IL; Concord, Hong Kong; Casemate Publishing, Havertown, PA; RZM Imports, Southbury, CT; Medals of America, Fountain Inn, SC; Countrysport Press, Camden, ME.
Subjects: Aeronautics, Aviation, Automotive, History, Maritime, Military Science, Transportation, Military history
ISBN Prefix(es): 0-947898; 1-85367
Number of titles published annually: 30 Print
Total Titles: 200 Print
Parent Company: Lionel Leventhal Ltd, Park House, One Russell Gardens, London NW11 9NN
Distributed by Peribo Pty Ltd (Australia); Publishers Marketing Services Pte Ltd (Malaysia & Singapore); South Pacific Books (New Zealand); Stackpole Books (US); Vanwell Publishing Ltd (Canada)

Greenwich Editions, *imprint of* Ramboro Books Plc

Greenwillow Books, *imprint of* HarperCollins Publishers

Greenwood Heinemann, *imprint of* Reed Educational & Professional Publishing

Gregg International, *imprint of* Gregg Publishing Co

Gregg Revivals, *imprint of* Gregg Publishing Co

Gregg Publishing Co
The Old Hospital Ardingly Rd, Chapelfields, Cuckfield, Haywards Heath RH17 5JR
Tel: (01444) 445070 *Fax:* (01444) 445050
E-mail: Rdowling@gowerpub.com
Key Personnel
Contact: Tracy Daborn
Founded: 1960
Subjects: Social Sciences, Sociology
ISBN Prefix(es): 0-576; 0-7512
Associate Companies: Ashgate Publishing Group
Imprints: Gregg International; Gregg Revivals
Orders to: Ashgate Distribution Services, Unit 3, Lower Farnham Rd, Aldershot, Hants GU12 4DL

Gresham Books, *imprint of* Gresham Books Ltd

Gresham Books, *imprint of* Woodhead Publishing Ltd

Gresham Books Ltd+
The Gresham Press, 46 Victoria Rd, Summertown, Oxford OX2 7QD
Tel: (01865) 513582 *Fax:* (01865) 512718
E-mail: info@gresham-books.co.uk
Web Site: www.gresham-books.co.uk
Key Personnel
Dir: M L Lewis; P A Lewis
E-mail: greshambks@btinternet.com
Founded: 1979
Specialize in hymnals, prayer books & school histories.
Subjects: History, Music, Dance, Religion - Catholic, Religion - Protestant, Local History
ISBN Prefix(es): 0-905418; 0-946095; 0-9502121
Number of titles published annually: 30 Print
Total Titles: 200 Print
Parent Company: Gresham Books
Imprints: Gresham Books

Griffith Institute, *imprint of* Ashmolean Museum Publications

Grub Street+
The Basement, 10 Chivalry Rd, London SW11 1HT
Tel: (020) 7924 3966; (020) 7738 1008
Fax: (020) 7738 1009
E-mail: post@grubstreet.co.uk
Web Site: www.grubstreet.co.uk
Key Personnel
Chief Executive & Rights & Permissions: John Davies *E-mail:* john@grubstreet.com.uk
Chief Executive: Anne Dolamore
Founded: 1986
Subjects: Cookery, Health, Nutrition, Nonfiction (General), Wine & Spirits, Military History/Aviation
ISBN Prefix(es): 0-948817; 1-898697; 1-902304
Number of titles published annually: 30 Print
Total Titles: 140 Print
Foreign Rep(s): Capricorn Link Pty Ltd (Australia); Forrester Books (New Zealand); Peter Hyde Associates (South Africa); Seven Hills Book Distributors (US); Vanwell Publishing (Canada)
Warehouse: Littlehampton Book Service (LBS), Faraday Close, Durrington, Worlting, West Sussex BN13 3RB

Guardian Books, *imprint of* Fourth Estate Ltd

Guild of Master Publications Inc, *imprint of* GMC Publications Ltd

Guinness Publishing Ltd
338 Euston Rd, London NW1 3BD
Tel: (020) 7891 4567 *Fax:* (020) 7891 4501
E-mail: guinness-publishing@guinness.com
Cable: MOSTEST ENFIELD
Key Personnel
Man Dir: Christopher Irwin
Sales Dir: Fred Buxton
Sales & Marketing Dir: Malcolm Roughead
National Sales Manager: Shaun Elder
Founded: 1954
Subjects: Military Science, Music, Dance, Sports, Athletics
ISBN Prefix(es): 0-900424; 0-85112
Parent Company: Guinness PLC, 39 Portman Square, London W1H 9HP
U.S. Office(s): 6 Landmark Square, Stamford, CT 06901, United States
Warehouse: Macmillan Distribution, Unit 8, Lye Industrial Estate, Pontardulais, Swansea SA4 1QD

Gunsmoke Western, *imprint of* BBC Audiobooks

Gwasg Carreg Gwalch+
6 Iard Yr Orsaf, Llanrwst, Gwynedd LL26 0EH
Tel: (01492) 642 031 *Fax:* (01492) 641 502
E-mail: books@carreg-gwalch.co.uk
Web Site: www.carreg-gwalch.co.uk
Key Personnel
Dir: Myrddin Ap Dafydd *E-mail:* myrddin@carreg-gwalch.co.uk
Founded: 1980
Privately owned publisher & printing company.
Subjects: Welsh & Celtic Interest, Welsh Language
ISBN Prefix(es): 0-86381
Number of titles published annually: 60 Print
Total Titles: 800 Print
Branch Office(s)
Ysgubor Plas, Llwyndyrys, Pwllheli, Gwynedd LL53 6NG *Tel:* (01758) 750440

Gwasg Prifysgol Cymru, *imprint of* University of Wales Press

Gwasg Prifysgol Cymru+
Imprint of University of Wales Press
10 Columbus Walk, Brigantine Place, Cardiff CF10 4UP
Tel: (029) 2049 6899 *Fax:* (029) 2049 6108
E-mail: press@press.wales.ac.uk
Web Site: www.uwp.co.uk; www.wales.ac.uk/press
Key Personnel
Dir: Susan Jenkins *E-mail:* s.jenkins@press.wales.ac.uk
Deputy Dir & International Rights Contact: Richard Houdmont *E-mail:* r.houdmont@press.wales.ac.uk
Commissioning Editor: Duncan Campbell *E-mail:* dcampbell@press.wales.ac.uk
Editorial Manager: Ceinwen Jones *E-mail:* c.jones@press.wales.ac.uk
Founded: 1922
The Welsh language imprint of the University of Wales Press.
Subjects: History, Language Arts, Linguistics, Literature, Literary Criticism, Essays
ISBN Prefix(es): 0-7083
Number of titles published annually: 10 Print; 1 CD-ROM
Total Titles: 300 Print
Ultimate Parent Company: University of Wales Registry
Orders to: Richard Houdmont *E-mail:* archebion@gwasa.cymru.ac.uk *Web Site:* www.wales.ac.uk/press
Paul & Company Publishers Consortium Inc, c/o IPG, 814 N. Franklin St, Chicago, IL 60610, United States *Tel:* 312-337-0747 *Fax:* 312-337-5985 *E-mail:* frontdesk@ipgbook.com *Web Site:* www.ipgbook.com (orders from bookstores)

Gwasg y Dref Wen+
28 Church Rd, Yr Eglwys Newydd, Cardiff CF4 2EA
Tel: (01222) 617860 *Fax:* (01222) 610507
E-mail: gwil-drefwen@btinternet.com
Key Personnel
Man Dir, Editorial: Roger Boore
Publicity, Sales: Gwilym Boore
Founded: 1970
Welsh-language publishers.
Member of Union of Welsh Publishers & Booksellers.
ISBN Prefix(es): 0-946962; 0-904910; 1-85596
Number of titles published annually: 50 Print; 4 Audio
Total Titles: 450 Print; 15 Audio
Imprints: Dref Wen

Gwasg Gwenffrwd+
Hendre Bach, Cerrigydrudion, Corwen, Clwyd LL21 9TB
Tel: (01490) 420 560
Key Personnel
Man Dir: Dr Goronwy Alun Hughes
Founded: 1947
Specialize in Pacific Islands, Oceanic Languages & Wales
Member of BLDSC (ASTIC Research Associates).
Subjects: Anthropology, Biography, Foreign Countries, Genealogy, History, Language Arts, Linguistics, Poetry, Regional Interests, *Specializes In:* Pacific Islands, Oceanic Languages & Wales
ISBN Prefix(es): 0-9501861; 1-85651
Number of titles published annually: 10 Print
Total Titles: 40 Print
Imprints: Astic; Bronant Books; A & Z Hughes; Translations Wales

Peter Haddock Ltd+
Pinfold Lane, Bridlington, East Yorkshire YO16 6BT
Tel: (01262) 678121 *Fax:* (01262) 400043
E-mail: enquiries@peterhaddock.com

Web Site: phaddock.sslserver.co.uk
Key Personnel
Man Dir: Peter Haddock
Sales Manager: David Haddock
Founded: 1952
ISBN Prefix(es): 0-7105
Imprints: Big Time

Hakluyt Society
c/o Map Library, British Library, 96 Euston Rd, London NW1 2DB
Tel: (01428) 641850 *Fax:* (01428) 641933
E-mail: office@hakluyt.com
Web Site: www.hakluyt.com
Key Personnel
Administrator: Richard Bateman
Founded: 1846
A registered charity inspired by and named after Richard Hakluyt (1552-1616), the famous collector and editor of narratives of voyages and travels and other documents relating to English interests overseas.
Subjects: Geography, Geology, History, Travel
ISBN Prefix(es): 0-904180
Number of titles published annually: 2 Print
Total Titles: 55 Print
Distributed by Ashgate Publishing Direct Sales

Peter Halban Publishers Ltd+
22 Golden Sq, London W1R 3PA
Tel: (020) 7437 9300 *Fax:* (020) 7431 9512
E-mail: books@halbanpublishers.com
Web Site: www.halbanpublishers.com
Key Personnel
Man Dir: Martine Halban; Peter Halban
 E-mail: peterhalbanpublishers@compuserve.com
Founded: 1986
Member of Independent Publishers Guild.
Subjects: Biography, History, Philosophy, Religion - Jewish
ISBN Prefix(es): 1-870015
Number of titles published annually: 10 Print
Total Titles: 52 Print
Online services available through Book Data.
Shipping Address: Littlehampton Book Services
 Tel: (01903) 828800 *Fax:* (01903) 828801
Warehouse: Littlehampton Book Services
 Tel: (01903) 828800 *Fax:* (01903) 828801
Orders to: Littlehampton Book Services
 Tel: (01903) 828800 *Fax:* (01903) 828801

Haldane Mason+
PO Box 34196, London NW10 3YB
Tel: (020) 8459 2131 *Fax:* (020) 8728 1216
E-mail: syd.hm@gtclick.com

Robert Hale Ltd+
Clerkenwell House, 45-47 Clerkenwell Green, London EC1R OHT
Tel: (020) 7251 2661 *Fax:* (020) 7490 4958
E-mail: enquire@halebooks.com
Web Site: www.halebooks.com
Key Personnel
Man Dir & Senior Editor: John Hale
Marketing Dir: Martin Kendall
Rights & Permissions Manager: Florence Pinard
Production Dir: Robert Hale
Founded: 1936
Subjects: Art, Biography, Cookery, Fiction, Geography, Geology, History, How-to, Music, Dance, Philosophy, Poetry, Sports, Athletics, Women's Studies
ISBN Prefix(es): 0-85131; 0-7198; 0-7090; 0-7091
Imprints: Horse Books; J A Allen; NAG Press
Distributor for Aperture; International Jewelry; Phoenix
Warehouse: Combined Book Services, Units 1/K, Paddock Wood Distribution Centre, Paddock Wood, Tonbridge, Kent TN12 6UU

GK Hall & Co, *imprint of* Gale Research

Halldale Publishing & Media Ltd
84 Alexandra Rd, Farnborough, Hants GU14 6DD
Tel: (01252) 532000 *Fax:* (01252) 512714
Key Personnel
Man Dir: Andrew Smith
Sales Dir: Stephen Marston *E-mail:* steve@halldale.com
Founded: 1993
Subjects: Aeronautics, Aviation, Maritime

Halsted Press, *imprint of* Wiley Europe Ltd

The Hambledon Press+
102 Gloucester Ave, London NW1 8HX
Tel: (020) 7586 0817 *Fax:* (020) 7586 9970
E-mail: office@hambledon.co.uk
Web Site: www.hambledon.co.uk
Key Personnel
Man Dir: Martin Sheppard *E-mail:* ms@hambledon.co.uk
Commissioning Editor: Tony Morris *Tel:* (020) 7482 2333 *E-mail:* ajm@hambledon.co.uk
Founded: 1981
Subjects: History
ISBN Prefix(es): 0-907628; 1-85285; 0-9506882
Total Titles: 200 Print
Parent Company: Hambledon & London Ltd
Sales Office(s): Yale University Press, 23 Pond St, London NW3 2PN *Tel:* (020) 7431 4422 *Fax:* (020) 7431 3755 (UK)

Hamish Hamilton, *imprint of* Penguin Books Ltd

Hamish Hamilton, *imprint of* The Penguin Group UK

Hamish Hamilton Ltd+
27 Wrights Lane, London W8 5TZ
Tel: (020) 7416 3000 *Fax:* (020) 7416 3099
Web Site: www.penguin.co.uk
Telex: 917181; 2
Key Personnel
Publisher: Simon Prosser
Export Sales: Max Adam *E-mail:* max.adam@penquin.co.uk
Founded: 1931
Subjects: Art, Biography, Fiction, History, Music, Dance
ISBN Prefix(es): 0-241
Parent Company: Penguin Books Ltd
Subsidiaries: Elm Tree Books Ltd; Hamish Hamilton Children's Books Ltd
Shipping Address: Bath Road, Harmondsworth, West Dayton, Middlesex UB7 0DA
Warehouse: Bath Road, Harmondsworth, West Dayton, Middlesex UB7 0DA

Hamlyn, *imprint of* Octopus Publishing Group

Hamlyn+
Imprint of Octopus Publishing Group
2-4 Heron Quays, London E14 4JP
Tel: (020) 7531 8400 *Fax:* (020) 7531 8650
Web Site: www.hamlyn.co.uk
Key Personnel
Publisher & Man Dir: Alison Goff *Tel:* (020) 7531 8410 *Fax:* (020) 7531 8562
 E-mail: alison.goff@hamlyn.co.uk
Sales & Marketing Dir: Wendy Rimmington
 Tel: (020) 7531 8573 *Fax:* (020) 7537 0514
 E-mail: wendy.rimmington@hamlyn.co.uk
Publicity & Marketing Manager: Sue Bobbermein
 Tel: (020) 7531 8584 *Fax:* (020) 7537 0514
 E-mail: sue.bobbermein@hamlyn.co.uk
Export Sales Manager: Caroline Babler
 Tel: (020) 7531 8574 *Fax:* (020) 7537 0514
 E-mail: caroline.babler@hamlyn.co.uk

Foreign Rights Manger - France, Spain, Portugal: Brigitte Perivier *Tel:* (020) 7531 8586
 E-mail: brigitte.perivier@hamlyn.co.uk
Area Rights Manager - Scandanavia & Italy: Sarah French *Tel:* (020) 7531 8587
 E-mail: sarah.french@hamlyn.co.uk
Area Rights Manager - Germany, Holland, Greece, South Africa: Isabelle Saulet *Tel:* (020) 7531 8576 *E-mail:* isabelle.saulet@hamlyn.co.uk
Foreign Rights Executive - Central & Eastern Europe: Daniel Bouquet *Tel:* (020) 7531 8575
 E-mail: daniel.bouquet@hamlyn.co.uk
North American Rights Manager: Nicole Stephens
 Tel: (020) 7531 8577 *Fax:* (020) 7537 0514
 E-mail: nicole.stephens@hamlyn.co.uk
UK Sales Dir: Kevin Hawkins *Tel:* (020) 7531 8582; (0780) 129 2031 *Fax:* 020 7537 0514
 E-mail: kevin.hawkins@hamlyn.co.uk
Special Sales Manager: Rebecca Collold
 Tel: (020) 7531 8585 *E-mail:* rebecca.cobbold@hamlyn.co.uk
Premium Sales Executive: Stuart Airley *Tel:* (020) 7531 8580 *E-mail:* stuart.airley@hamlyn.co.uk
Founded: 1947
International publisher of high quality illustrated, non-fiction for the general market.
Subjects: Architecture & Interior Design, Cookery, Crafts, Games, Hobbies, Fashion, Film, Video, Gardening, Plants, Health, Nutrition, History, Music, Dance, Natural History, Nonfiction (General), Sports, Athletics
ISBN Prefix(es): 0-600

Handbag Books, *imprint of* Kenneth Mason Publications Ltd

The Handsel Press+
62 Toll Rd, Kincardine, by Alloa FK10 4QZ
E-mail: handsel@dial.pipex.com
Web Site: www.handselpress.co.uk
Key Personnel
Chairman: David F Wright
Editor: Rev Jock Stein *Tel:* (1236) 723204
Founded: 1976
Subjects: Theology
ISBN Prefix(es): 0-905312; 1-871828
Distributed by Orca Book Services
Orders to: Scottish Book Source, 137 Dundee St, Edinburgh EH11 2QU *Tel:* (0131) 229 6800 *Fax:* (0131) 229 9070

Hans Zell Bibliographies, *imprint of* James Currey Ltd

Happy Cat Books Ltd+
Fieldfares Mill Lane, Bradfield, Nr Manningtree CO11 2UT
Tel: (01255) 870902 *Fax:* (01255) 870902
E-mail: mcwest@happycat.co.uk
Key Personnel
Man Dir: Martin C West *E-mail:* mcwest@happycat.co.uk
Founded: 1994
Publishing of board & picture books for ages under 6, fiction for 7-9 years.
ISBN Prefix(es): 1-899248; 1-903285
Number of titles published annually: 16 Print
Total Titles: 55 Print
Distributed by Star Bright Books (Distribution in USA only)
Orders to: Macmillan Distribution Ltd, Houndmills, Basingstoke, Hampshire RG21 6X6
 Tel: (01256) 302692 *Fax:* (01256) 812558

Harcourt Publishers Ltd+
32 Jamestown Rd, Camden Town, London NW1 7BY
Tel: (0171) 7424 4200 *Toll Free Tel:* 888-677-7357 *Fax:* (0171) 7482 2293
E-mail: ecare@harcourt.com
Web Site: www.harcourt.com

UNITED KINGDOM

Key Personnel
Main Dir: Peter Lengemann
Subjects: Education, Medicine, Nursing, Dentistry, Psychology, Psychiatry, Science (General), Social Sciences, Sociology, Veterinary Science, Academic Journals
ISBN Prefix(es): 0-443; 0-7216; 0-7020
Parent Company: Elsevier Science Ltd

Harden's Ltd
14 Buckingham St, London WC2N 6DF
Tel: (020) 7839 4763 *Fax:* (020) 7839 7561
E-mail: mail@hardens.com
Web Site: www.hardens.com
Key Personnel
Dir: Peter Harden; Richard Harden
Founded: 1991
Publish consumer guides, restaurant guides in particular. Specialize in corporate gift editions. Specialize in corporate gift editions.
Subjects: Foreign Countries, Travel
ISBN Prefix(es): 1-873721
Number of titles published annually: 5 Print; 2 E-Book
Total Titles: 6 Print; 2 E-Book
Membership(s): IPG

Patrick Hardy Books, *imprint of* James Clarke & Co Ltd

Patrick Hardy Books, *imprint of* The Lutterworth Press

Patrick Hardy Books+
Imprint of James Clarke & Co Ltd
PO Box 60, Cambridge CB1 2NT
Tel: (01223) 350865 *Fax:* (01223) 366951
E-mail: sales@lutterworth.com; publishing@lutterworth.com
Web Site: www.lutterworth.com
Key Personnel
Man Dir: Adrian Brink
Subjects: Fiction, Nonfiction (General), Religion - Other
ISBN Prefix(es): 0-7444
Distributed by Parkwest Publications Inc

Harley Books+
Martins, Great Horkesley, Colchester, Essex C06 4AH
Tel: (01206) 271216 *Fax:* (01206) 271182
E-mail: harley@keme.co.uk
Web Site: www.harleybooks.com
Key Personnel
Dir: Annette Harley
Founded: 1983
Member of Independent Publishers Guild (IPG); Specialize in Natural History especially entomology & botany.
Subjects: Biological Sciences, Environmental Studies, Natural History
ISBN Prefix(es): 0-946589
Number of titles published annually: 3 Print
Total Titles: 7 Print
Parent Company: BH & A Harley Ltd

HarperAudio, *imprint of* HarperCollins Publishers

HarperBusiness, *imprint of* HarperCollins Publishers

HarperCollins, *imprint of* HarperCollins Publishers

HarperCollins Children's Books, *imprint of* HarperCollins Publishers

HarperCollins Publishers+
Subsidiary of News Corporation
77-85 Fulham Palace Road, Hammersmith, London W6 8JB
Tel: (020) 8741 7070 *Toll Free Tel:* (0870) 900 2050 (cust serv) *Fax:* (020) 8307 4440 *Toll Free Fax:* (0141) 306 3767 (cust serv)
Web Site: www.harpercollins.com
Key Personnel
Executive Chairman & Publisher: Eddie Bell
Group Finance/Systems Director: Meyrick Veyers
Man Dir, Group Sales: Adrian Bourne
Man Dir, Educational & Children's: Natte Harris
Man Dir, Thorsons & Religious: James Catford
Dir, International Sales: David North
Founded: 1819
Member of Publishers Association.
Subjects: Animals, Pets, Anthropology, Art, Astrology, Occult, Behavioral Sciences, Biblical Studies, Biography, Business, Child Care & Development, Cookery, Crafts, Games, Hobbies, English as a Second Language, Fiction, Film, Video, Finance, Foreign Countries, Gardening, Plants, Gay & Lesbian, Government, Political Science, Health, Nutrition, History, House & Home, How-to, Human Relations, Literature, Literary Criticism, Essays, Management, Mysteries, Natural History, Nonfiction (General), Outdoor Recreation, Philosophy, Psychology, Psychiatry, Romance, Science Fiction, Fantasy, Self-Help, Sports, Athletics, Theology, Travel, Wine & Spirits, Women's Studies
ISBN Prefix(es): 0-00; 0-01; 0-246; 0-261; 0-586
Parent Company: HarperCollins
Imprints: Access Press; Amistad; Avon; Joanna Cotler Books; Ecco; Eos; Laura Geringer Books; Greenwillow Books; HarperAudio; HarperBusiness; HarperCollins; HarperCollins Children's Books; HarperEntertainment; HarperFestival; HarperLargePrint; HarperResource; HarperSanFrancisco; HarperTorch; HarperTrophy; William Morrow; Perennial; PerfectBound; Quill; Rayo; ReganBooks; Tempest
U.S. Office(s): 10 East 53 St, New York, NY 10022, United States *Tel:* (212) 207-7000
Warehouse: Westerhill Rd, Bishopbriggs, Glasgow G64 2QT *Tel:* (041) 7723200
Orders to: PO Box, Glasgow G4 0NB *Tel:* (0141) 7723200

HarperEntertainment, *imprint of* HarperCollins Publishers

HarperFestival, *imprint of* HarperCollins Publishers

HarperLargePrint, *imprint of* HarperCollins Publishers

HarperResource, *imprint of* HarperCollins Publishers

HarperSanFrancisco, *imprint of* HarperCollins Publishers

HarperTorch, *imprint of* HarperCollins Publishers

HarperTrophy, *imprint of* HarperCollins Publishers

Hart Publishing
Salter's Boatyard, Folly Bridge, Abingdon Rd, Oxford OX1 4LB
Tel: (01865) 245533 *Fax:* (01865) 794882
E-mail: mail@hartpub.co.uk
Web Site: www.hartpub.co.uk

Key Personnel
Man Dir: Richard Hart *E-mail:* richard@hartpub.co.uk
Sales & Marketing Dir: Jane Parker *E-mail:* jane@hartpub.co.uk
Customer Services Manager: Ann Poulter *E-mail:* ann@hartpub.co.uk
Editorial & Production Manager: Hannah Young *E-mail:* hannah@hartpub.co.uk
Finance Manager: Liam Barrett *E-mail:* liam@hartpub.co.uk
Journals Manager: Merav Pick *E-mail:* merav@hartpub.co.uk
Founded: 1996
Subjects: Law
Number of titles published annually: 60 Print
Distributed by Academic Marketing Services (Pty) Ltd (South Africa); Aditya Books Private Ltd (India); Roger Bayliss (Trade Representation (UK) - London, South East, South West, Scotland); CHIN Shan Informations Services Ltd (China, Hong Kong, Korea, Philippines, Singapore, Taiwan, Thailand, Vietnam); Charles Gibbes (Italy & France); International Specialized Book Services (North America); Intersentia Uitgevers NV (Benelux); IP Communications Pty Ltd (Australia & New Zealand); J & L Watt Publishing Consultants (Arab Middle East, Eastern Mediterranean & North Africa); Kay (Kaoru) Kato (Japan); Tony Lawrence (UK Trade Representation - Midlands, Wales, North West); Pakistan Law House (Pakistan); STM Publisher Services Pte Ltd (China, Hong Kong, Korea, Philippines, Singapore, Taiwan, Thailand, Vietnam); UBS Books (New Zealand)
Foreign Rep(s): Colin Flint (Scandinavia); Iberian Book Services (Spain & Portugal)

Hart Advertising Charity Agency, *imprint of* Hymns Ancient & Modern Ltd

Harvard University Press+
Fitzroy House, 11 Chenies St, London WC1E 7EY
Tel: (020) 7306 0603 *Fax:* (020) 7306 0604
E-mail: info@hup-mitpress.co.uk
Web Site: www.hup.harvard.edu
Key Personnel
General Manager: Ann Sexsmith
Publicity Manager: Lisa Jolliffe
Founded: 1913
Subjects: Anthropology, Asian Studies, Behavioral Sciences, Biological Sciences, Business, Earth Sciences, Economics, Education, Film, Video, Government, Political Science, History, Law, Literature, Literary Criticism, Essays, Medicine, Nursing, Dentistry, Natural History, Nonfiction (General), Philosophy, Psychology, Psychiatry, Religion - Jewish, Science (General), Social Sciences, Sociology, Women's Studies
ISBN Prefix(es): 0-674
Imprints: Belknap
Subsidiaries: The Loeb Classical Library
U.S. Office(s): 79 Garden St, Cambridge, MA 02138, United States *Tel:* 617-495-2480
E-mail: contact_hup@harvard.edu
Orders to: John Wiley & Sons Ltd, Southern Cross Trading Estate, 1 Oldlands Way, Bognor Regis, West Sussex PO22 9SA *Tel:* (01243) 779777 *Fax:* (01243) 820250

Harvey Map Services Ltd+
12-22 Main St, Doune, Perthshire FK16 6BJ
Tel: (01786) 841202 *Fax:* (01786) 841098
E-mail: sales@harveymaps.co.uk
Web Site: www.harveymaps.co.uk
Key Personnel
Sales Dir: Susan Harvey *Tel:* (01786) 841 202
Marketing: Catherine Nelson
Founded: 1977

Also acts as mapmakers.
Subjects: Education, Sports, Athletics
ISBN Prefix(es): 1-85137

The Harvill Press Ltd+
2 Aztec Row, Berners Rd, London N1 0PW
Tel: (020) 7704 8766 *Fax:* (020) 7704 8805
E-mail: info@harvill-press.com
Web Site: www.harvill-press.com
Key Personnel
Publisher: Christopher MacLehose
Sales Dir: Katharina Bielenberg *E-mail:* k.bielenberg@harvill-press.com
Editorial Dir: Margaret Stead; Guido Waldman
Marketing Dir: Paul Baggaley
Founded: 1946
Subjects: Anthropology, Biography, Fiction, Gardening, Plants, History, Literature, Literary Criticism, Essays, Mathematics, Mythology, Natural History, Nonfiction (General), Philosophy, Photography, Poetry, Self-Help, Travel, African Studies, Anthology, Art History, Crime Fiction, Current Affairs, Letters, Memoirs, Politics, Russian Studies
ISBN Prefix(es): 1-86046
Total Titles: 800 Print
Distributed by Farrar, Straus & Giroux (USA); Raincoast Books (Canada)
Orders to: Grantham Book Services, Isaac Newton Way, Alma Park Industrial Estate, Grantham, Lincs NG31 9SD

Hassle Free Press, *imprint of* Knockabout Comics

Hawk Books+
Kernick House, Kernick Rd, Penryn, Cornwall TR10 9DT
Mailing Address: PO Box 30, Penryn TR10 9YP
Tel: (01326) 376633 *Fax:* (01326) 376669
Key Personnel
Dir: P Hawkey
Founded: 1987
Specialize in character merchandise.
Subjects: Art, Humor
ISBN Prefix(es): 0-948248; 1-899441
Imprints: Falco; Sparrowhawk
Orders to: Bookpoint Ltd, 39 Milton Park, Abingdon, Oxon OX14 4TD

Hawker Publications Ltd+
Culvert House, Culvert Rd, Battersea SW11 5DH
Tel: (020) 7720 2108 *Fax:* (020) 7498 3023
E-mail: hawker@hawkerpubs.demon.co.uk
Web Site: www.careinfo.org
Key Personnel
Contact: Dr Richard Hawkins *E-mail:* richard@hawkerpubs.demon.co.uk
Founded: 1985
Specialize in providing a wide range of information to professionals working with elderly people & in the children's nursery sector.
Subjects: Child Care & Development, Medicine, Nursing, Dentistry
ISBN Prefix(es): 1-874790
Number of titles published annually: 12 Print
Total Titles: 18 Print
Warehouse: Plymbridge, Estover Rd, Plymouth PL6 7P2 *Fax:* (01752) 202330

Hawthorn Press+
Hawthorn House, One Lansdown Lane, Stroud, Glos GL5 1BJ
Tel: (01453) 757040 *Fax:* (01453) 751138
E-mail: hawthornpress@hawthornpress.com
Web Site: www.hawthornpress.com
Key Personnel
Dir: Judith Large; Martin Large
Sales & Accounts: Alan Lord
Project Management & Sales: Rachel Jenkins
Editor: Matthew Barton

Administration & Sales: Lynda McGill
Founded: 1980
Member of Independent Publishers Guild.
Subjects: Behavioral Sciences, Child Care & Development, Crafts, Games, Hobbies, Education, Psychology, Psychiatry, Self-Help, Women's Studies
ISBN Prefix(es): 1-869890; 1-903458; 0-950706
Number of titles published annually: 12 Print
Total Titles: 100 Print
Distributed by Anthroposophic Press (USA & North America); Astam Books Pty Ltd (Australia); Ceres Books (New Zealand); De Nieuwe Boekerij Import (Holland); Peter Hyde Associates (South Africa); New Leaf Distributing Co (USA & North America); Rudolf Steiner Publications (South Africa); Tri-fold Books (Canada)
Orders to: BookSource, 32 Finlas St, Glasgow G22 5DU *Tel:* (0141) 558 1366 *Fax:* (0141) 557 0189 *E-mail:* info@booksource.net

Hawthorns Publications Ltd+
Pond View House, 6A High St, Otford, Sevenoaks, Kent TN14 5PQ
Tel: (01959) 522368 *Fax:* (01959) 522368
Founded: 1973
Literacy & Numeracy textbooks & reading books for primary schools.
Member of the Publishers Association.
Subjects: Biography, Education, History
ISBN Prefix(es): 1-871044
Imprints: Pond View

Hayden Books, *imprint of* Pearson Education Europe, Mideast & Africa

Haymarket, *imprint of* Verso

Haynes, *imprint of* Haynes Publishing

Haynes Publishing+
Sparkford, Nr Yeovil, Somerset BA22 7JJ
Tel: (01963) 442030; (01963) 442080 (trade) *Fax:* (01963) 440001 (trade)
E-mail: sales@haynes-manuals.co.uk
Web Site: www.haynes.co.uk
Key Personnel
Chairman: John H Haynes
Group Chief Executive: Eric Oakley
Senior Publisher Bookbinder: Darryl Reach
Editorial Dir: Mark Hughes
Sales Dir, UK: Jeremy Yates-Round
Overseas Sales & Rights Dir: Graham Cook
Marketing Dir (Motortrade): David Hermelin
Production: Nigel Clements
Operations Dir: Ian Mauger
Finance Dir: James Bunkum
Book Trade Sales Manager: Tony Kemp
Head, UK Sales: Mike Webb
Customer Marketing Mgr: Maureen Wincott
Founded: 1960
Subjects: Aeronautics, Aviation, Automotive, Computer Science, History, House & Home, How-to, Maritime, Outdoor Recreation, Technology, Transportation, Motoring, Motorsports, Car & Motorcyle Service & Repair, Restoration
ISBN Prefix(es): 1-85010; 0-85696; 1-56392
Number of titles published annually: 100 Print
Total Titles: 2,280 Print
Parent Company: Haynes Publishing Group PLC
Associate Companies: MBI Publishing, 729 Prospect Ave, Saint Paul, MN 55101, United States, Bob Wilson *Tel:* 651-287-5000 *Fax:* 651-287-5001 *E-mail:* bwilson@motorbooks.com
Imprints: G T Foulis & Co; Haynes; Patrick Stephens Ltd
Subsidiaries: Editions Haynes SARL; Haynes Manuals Inc; Haynes Publishing Nordiska AB; Sutton Publishing Ltd

Distributor for Autosport; Bay View Books; David Bull Publishing; Car Chase; Dessert Winds; Duke 'Powersport' Videos; Hazleton Publishing; MBI Publishing; Motorbooks International (UK); Ordnance Survey; Porter & Porter; The Stationery Office
Foreign Rep(s): Graham Cook (world exc US & Canada)

Hazleton Publishing Ltd+
3 Richmond Hill, Richmond, Surrey TW10 6RE
Tel: (020) 8948 5151 *Fax:* (020) 8948 4111
E-mail: info@hazletonpublishing.com
Web Site: www.hazletonpublishing.com
Key Personnel
Chairman: Richard Poulter
Dir: Steven Palmer
Publisher: Nick Poulter
Managing Editor: Robert Yarham
Founded: 1975
Specialize in Year Books & Calendars.
Subjects: Motor Sports, Tennis & Golf
ISBN Prefix(es): 0-905138; 1-874557; 1-903135
Total Titles: 10 Print
Parent Company: Profile Media Group PLC

HB Publications
PO Box 21660, London SW16 1WJ
Tel: (020) 8769 1585 *Fax:* (020) 8769 2320
E-mail: sales@hbpublications.com
Web Site: www.hbpublications.com
Key Personnel
Contact: Lascelles Hussey
Specializes in the production of books for public sector managers.
Subjects: Accounting, Business, Finance, Management, Marketing
ISBN Prefix(es): 1-899448
Parent Company: HB Consulting

Headline, *imprint of* Headline Book Publishing Ltd

Headline Book Publishing Ltd+
338 Euston Rd, London NW1 3BH
Tel: (020) 7873 6000 *Fax:* (020) 7873 6124
E-mail: headline.books@headline.co.uk
Web Site: www.madaboutbooks.com
Key Personnel
Chief Executive: Tim Hely Hutchinson
Man Dir: Martin Neild
Dir, Non-fiction Publishing: Heather Holden-Brown
Dir, Production: Bryone Picton
Sales Dir: Kerr Macrae
Dir, Marketing: Louise Weir
Dir, Publicity: Georgina Moore
Dir, Fiction Publishing: Jane Morpeth
Dir, Rights: Sarah Thomson
Dir, Export Sales: Peter Newson
Founded: 1986
Book Publisher.
Subjects: Biography, Cookery, Fiction, Gardening, Plants, History, Nonfiction (General), Science (General), Sports, Athletics, Wine & Spirits
ISBN Prefix(es): 0-7472; 0-7553
Number of titles published annually: 500 Print
Parent Company: Hodder Headline Ltd
Ultimate Parent Company: WH Smith PLC, Greenbridge Rd, Swindon SN3 3LD
Imprints: Headline; Review
Orders to: Bookpoint Ltd, 130 Milton Trading Estate, Abingdon, Oxon OX14 4SB *Tel:* (01235) 400400 *Fax:* (01235) 400500

Headline Specials, *imprint of* Moorley's Print & Publishing Ltd

Headlions, *imprint of* Packard Publishing Ltd

Headway, *imprint of* Hodder & Stoughton Educational

UNITED KINGDOM

Health Development Agency+
Formerly Health Education Authority
Holborn Gate, 330 High Holborn, London WC1V 7BA
Tel: (020) 7430 0850 *Fax:* (020) 7061 3390
E-mail: hda.enquirydesk@hda-online.org.uk
Web Site: www.hda-online.org.uk
Key Personnel
General Manager & Publisher: Boyd Simon
Tel: (020) 7413 1846 *Fax:* (020) 7413 2028
E-mail: simon.boyd@hea.org.uk
Publishing Manager: Chris Owen *Tel:* (020) 7413 1909 *Fax:* (020) 7413 2028 *E-mail:* chris.owen@hea.org.uk
Man Editor: Delphine Verroest *Tel:* (020) 7413 2613 *Fax:* (020) 7413 2028 *E-mail:* delphine.verroest@hea.org
Sales & Customer Care Manager: Dolores Ashton *Tel:* (020) 7413 1986 *Fax:* (020) 7413 2028 *E-mail:* dolores.ashton@hea.org
Distribution Manager: John Billingham *Tel:* (020) 7413 1892 *Fax:* (020) 7413 2028 *E-mail:* john.billingham@hea.org.uk
New Media Editor & International Rights Contact: Andrea Horth *Tel:* (020) 7413 8986 *Fax:* (020) 7413 2028 *E-mail:* andrea.horth@hea.org.uk
Founded: 1987
Member of Publisher's Association & Educational Publisher's Council.
Subjects: Child Care & Development, Health, Nutrition, Medicine, Nursing, Dentistry, Sports, Athletics, Women's Studies
ISBN Prefix(es): 0-7521; 0-903652; 1-85448
Total Titles: 500 Print
Warehouse: Marston Book Services, PO Box 269, Abingdon, Oxon OX14 4YN

Health Education Authority, see Health Development Agency

Health Science Press, *imprint of* The C W Daniel Co Ltd

Heartland Publishing, *imprint of* Heartland Publishing Ltd

Heartland Publishing Ltd
PO Box 902, Sutton Valence, Kent ME17 3HY
Tel: (01622) 843040 *Fax:* (01622) 843040
E-mail: publish@heartland.co.uk
Web Site: www.heartland.co.uk
Key Personnel
Dir: Jeff Horne; Nick Evans
Founded: 1995
A small independent book publisher & visual media consultancy.
Member of Independent Publishers Guild (IPG).
Subjects: Music, Dance, Poetry, Travel
ISBN Prefix(es): 0-9525187
Imprints: Amber Waves; Heartland Publishing

Hedera Press, *imprint of* E W Classey Ltd

Heinemann Educational Publishing+
Halley Court, Jordan Hill, Oxford OX2 8EJ
Tel: (01865) 888130 (General Inquiries)
Fax: (01865) 314290 (General inquiries)
Web Site: www.heinemann.co.uk
Key Personnel
Regional Manager: Dawn Davidson *Tel:* (01865) 3144295 *E-mail:* dawn.davidson@repp.co.uk; Julian Ross *Tel:* (01865) 3144214 *E-mail:* julian.ross@repp.co.uk; Deborah Steele *Tel:* (01865) 3144509 *E-mail:* deborah.steele@repp.co.uk
Executive Administrator: Christine Fisher *Tel:* (01865) 314592 *E-mail:* christine.fisher@repp.co.uk
Man Dir: Bob Osborne *Tel:* (01865) 314120 *Fax:* (01865) 314078 *E-mail:* bob.osborne@repp.co.uk
Editorial Manager, International Division: Ruth Hamilton-Jones *Tel:* (01865) 314159 *Fax:* (01865) 314169 *E-mail:* ruth.hamilton-jones@repp.uk.co
Marketing Dir: Sally Green *Tel:* (01865) 314667 *Fax:* (01865) 314169 *E-mail:* sally.green@repp.co.uk
International Marketing Manager: Charlotte Svensson *Tel:* (01865) 3144153 *E-mail:* charlotte.svensson@repp.co.uk; Ejemhen O'Connell *Tel:* (01865) 314618 *Fax:* (01865) 314169 *E-mail:* ejemhen.o'connell@repp.co.uk
International Marketing Coordinator: Hayley Scott *Tel:* (01865) 314074 *Fax:* (01865) 314169 *E-mail:* hayley.scott@repp.co.uk
Business Development Dir: David Johns *Tel:* (01865) 3144588 *E-mail:* david.johns@repp.co.uk
Sales Dir: Neil Morley *E-mail:* neil.morley@repp.co.uk
Founded: 1961
Subjects: Education, Fiction, Nonfiction (General)
ISBN Prefix(es): 0-435; 0-431
Parent Company: Reed Educational & Professional Publishing
Ultimate Parent Company: Reed Elsevier plc, 25 Victoria Rd, London SW1H 0EX
Imprints: Heinemann Library
Sales Office(s): 5 March Rd, Edinburgh EH4 3TD *Tel:* (0131) 332 5098 *Fax:* (0131) 315 2618 (Scotland)
Distributed by Bushbooks; Golf View; Heinemann Educational Botswana; Crown Books; Irwin Publishing; Cairo Trade Centre; F Reimmer Book Services; Transglobal; Reed Edcational & Professional; The Book Merchant; Jacaranda Designs; Jhango Heinemann; Mark Kuo Arenabuki Sdn Bhd; Editions de l'Ocean Indien Ltd; New Namibia Books (Pty) Ltd; Reed Publishing Group (NZ) Ltd; Heinemann Educational Books (Nigeria) Plc; Redi Ltd; Susan Chua; Heinemann South Africa; Ishmael M Khan & Sons Ltd; Rorash Educational Publishers; Heinemann; Insaka Press; Eunice Pfende
Orders to: Heinemann Publishers, Halley Court, Jordan Hill, Oxford OX2 8EJ (UK orders, enquiries & manuscript submissions)
School Orders Dept, Freepost, PO Box 969, Oxford *Tel:* (01865) 888020 *Fax:* (01865) 314091 *E-mail:* he.service@heinemann.co.uk

Heinemann Educational, *imprint of* Reed Educational & Professional Publishing

Heinemann/Ginn, *imprint of* Reed Educational & Professional Publishing

Heinemann Library, *imprint of* Heinemann Educational Publishing

Heinemann Library, *imprint of* Reed Educational & Professional Publishing

William Heinemann Ltd+
20 Vauxhall Bridge Rd, London SW1V 2SA
Tel: (020) 7840 8628 *Fax:* (020) 7233 6127
Founded: 1890
Subjects: Biography, Fiction, Government, Political Science, History, Nonfiction (General), Travel
ISBN Prefix(es): 0-434; 0-437
Parent Company: Random House

Helicon Publishing Ltd+
Subsidiary of RM plc
Milton Park, Unit 140, Abingdon, Oxon OX14 4SE
Tel: (08709) 200200 *Fax:* (01235) 826999
E-mail: admin@helicon.co.uk
Web Site: www.helicon.co.uk
Key Personnel
Man Dir: David Attwooll
Rights Dir: Clare Painter
Sales & Marketing Dir: Sheila Lambie
E-mail: sheila@helicon.co.uk
Sales Admin Mgr: Hilary Isaac
Founded: 1992 (Management buyout of Hutchinson Reference Division of Random House)
Publishers of general & subject encyclopedias & dictionaries in book, CD-ROM & online form. Text & illustrations on the database are continuously updated offering flexible licensing, coedition & packaging opportunities.
Subjects: Art, Biography, Computer Science, Government, Political Science, History, Language Arts, Linguistics, Music, Dance, Science (General)
ISBN Prefix(es): 0-09; 1-85986
Total Titles: 70 Print; 5 CD-ROM
Imprints: Hutchinson Reference
Distributed by Penguin
Warehouse: Bookpoint, 130 Milton Park, Abingdon, Oxon OX14 45B
Orders to: Bookpoint, 130 Milton Park, Abingdon, Oxon OX14 45B

Helion & Co
26 Willow Rd, Solihull, West Midlands B91 1UE
Tel: (0121) 705 3393 *Fax:* (0121) 711 4075
E-mail: info@helion.co.uk
Web Site: www.helion.co.uk
Key Personnel
Owner & Rts Contact: Duncan Rogers
E-mail: duncan@helion.co.uk
Sales: Wilf Rogers *E-mail:* wilfrid@helion.co.uk
Founded: 1992
Specialize in military history; emphasis on German & Austrian history 1675-1945.
Subjects: Biography, History, Nonfiction (General)
ISBN Prefix(es): 1-874622
Total Titles: 15 Print

Christopher Helm (Publishers) Ltd, *imprint of* A & C Black Publishers Ltd

Christopher Helm (Publishers) Ltd+
37 Soho Sq, London W1D 3QZ
Tel: (020) 7758 0200 *Fax:* (020) 7758 0222
E-mail: enquiries@acblack.com
Key Personnel
Chairman: Nigel Newton
Man Dir: Jill Coleman
Commissioning Editor: Nigel Redman
E-mail: nredman@acblack.com
Rights & Permissions: Paul Langridge
Sales: David Wightman
Production Dir: Oscar Heini
Founded: 1986
Subjects: Natural History, Birds
ISBN Prefix(es): 0-7136; 0-7470; 1-873403; 1-903206
Parent Company: A & C Black Publishers Ltd
Ultimate Parent Company: Bloomsbury Publishing PLC
Imprints: Pica Press
Shipping Address: Howard Rd, Eaton Socon, Huntingdon, Cambs PE19 3EZ
Warehouse: Howard Rd, Eaton Socon, Huntingdon, Cambs PE19 3EZ
Orders to: Howard Rd, Eaton Socon, Huntingdon, Cambs PE19 3EZ

Helm Information Ltd+
The Banks, Mountfield, Nr Robertsbridge, East Sussex TN32 5JY
Tel: (01580) 880 561 *Fax:* (01580) 880 541
Web Site: www.helm-information.co.uk

Key Personnel
Dir: Amanda Helm *E-mail:* amandahelm@helm-information.co.uk; Christopher Helm *E-mail:* christopher.helm@helm-information.co.uk
Editorial, Ornithology: Roger Riddington
Permissions & Promotions Assistant: Elizabeth Imlay *E-mail:* permissions@helm-information.co.uk
Founded: 1990
Member of IPG (Independent Publisher's Guild).
Subjects: History, Literature, Literary Criticism, Essays, Natural History
ISBN Prefix(es): 1-873403; 1-903206
Total Titles: 20 Print
Associate Companies: Helm Wood Publishers Pty Ltd, PO Box 666, Wembley WA 601A, Australia
Imprints: A & C

Helmsman Guides, *imprint of* The Crowood Press Ltd

Help Yourself Books, *imprint of* Hodder & Stoughton Religious

Hemming Information Services
Formerly Newman Books Ltd
32 Vauxhall Bridge Rd, London SW1V 2SS
Tel: (020) 7973 6402 *Fax:* (020) 7233 5057
E-mail: h-info@hemming-group.co.uk
Web Site: www.h-info.co/uk/about_us.asp
Key Personnel
Publishing Dir: Graham Bond
Publisher: Yvonne Phillips
Head of Marketing: Susan Kirby
Managing Editor: Dean Wanless
Marketing: Phaedra Rees
Advertising: David Morris
Data Sales: Alethea Wiles *Tel:* (020) 7973 6624
Founded: 1939
Member of DMA, DPA & EADP.
Subjects: Cookery, Government, Political Science, Marketing
ISBN Prefix(es): 0-7079
Parent Company: Hemming Group Ltd

Hendon Publishing Co Ltd
Hendon Mill, Hallam Rd, Nelson, Lancs BB9 8AD
Tel: (01282) 613129; (01282) 697725 *Fax:* (01282) 870215
Key Personnel
Chief Executive, Sales: Henry Nelson
Editorial: Dorothy Nelson
Production: Jean Marsden
Publicity, Rights & Permissions: James Nelson
Founded: 1971
Subjects: Cookery, History
ISBN Prefix(es): 0-86067; 0-902907
Parent Company: Hendon Mill Co Ltd, Hendon Mill, Hallam Rd, Nelson, Lancs BB9 8AD
Showroom(s): Bookmarket, 24 Parker Lane, Burnley, Lancs
Bookshop(s): Colne Book Shop, One Newtown St, Colne, Lancs; Bookmarket, 4-6 Market St, Colne, Lancs

Ian Henry Publications Ltd+
20 Park Dr, Romford, Essex RM1 4LH
Tel: (01708) 749119 *Fax:* (01621) 850862
Key Personnel
Man Dir: Ian Wilkes
Founded: 1975
Subjects: Automotive, Drama, Theater, Genealogy, History, Regional Interests
ISBN Prefix(es): 0-86025
Number of titles published annually: 10 Print
Total Titles: 90 Print
Imprints: Chameleons Dramascripts

Branch Office(s)
PO Box 1132, Studio City 91614-10132, United States
Distributed by Players' Press (USA)
Distributor for Players' Press
Membership(s): IPG

Heraldry Today+
Parliament Piece, Ramsbury, Wilts SN8 2QH
Tel: (01672) 520617 *Fax:* (01672) 520183
E-mail: heraldry@heraldrytoday.co.uk
Web Site: www.heraldrytoday.co.uk
Key Personnel
Head of Firm: Rosemary Pinches
Founded: 1954
Member of Antiquarian Booksellers' Association.
Subjects: Art, Genealogy, History, Armour, Armed Forces, Heraldry, Orders of Knighthood, Peerages, Royalties
ISBN Prefix(es): 0-900455
Distributor for Society of Antiquaries

The Herbert Press, *imprint of* A & C Black Publishers Ltd

Herbert Press Ltd+
37 Soho Sq, London W1D 3QZ
Tel: (020) 7758 0200 *Fax:* (020) 7758 0222
Web Site: www.acblack.com
Key Personnel
Editor: Linda Lambert *Tel:* (020) 7758 0320 *E-mail:* llambert@acblack.com
Founded: 1975
Subjects: Archaeology, Architecture & Interior Design, Art, Specialize in Crafts
ISBN Prefix(es): 0-7136; 0-906969; 1-871569
Number of titles published annually: 3 Print
Total Titles: 100 Print
Parent Company: A & C Black Ltd
Orders to: A & C Black, Howard Rd, Eaton Socon, Huntingdon, Cambs PE19 3EZ

Heretic Books Ltd+
PO Box 247, Swaffham, Norfolk PE37 8PA
Tel: (01366) 328101 *Fax:* (01366) 328102
E-mail: davidoraubrey@gmpubs.demon.co.uk
Key Personnel
Editorial, Rights & Permissions: David Fernbach
Editorial: Peter Burton *E-mail:* peterburton@easicom.com; Aubrey Walter *E-mail:* aubrey@gmppubs.co.uk
Founded: 1979
Subjects: Environmental Studies, Gay & Lesbian
ISBN Prefix(es): 0-946097
Associate Companies: GMP Publishers Ltd *Web Site:* www.gmppubs.co.uk
Orders to: Bulldog Books, PO Box 300, Beaconsfield NSW 2014, Australia *Tel:* (02) 9699 3507 *Fax:* (02) 9699 3527
Central Books Ltd, 99 Wallis Rd, London E9 5LN *Tel:* (020) 8986 4854 *Fax:* (020) 8533 5821
InBook/LPC Group, 1436 Randolph Ave, Chicago, IL 60607, United States *Tel:* 312-432-7650 *Fax:* 312-432-4601

Heritage, *imprint of* Osborne Books Ltd

Heritage House Group Ltd
Heritage House, Lodge Lane, Derby DE1 3HE
Tel: (01332) 347087 *Fax:* (01332) 290688
E-mail: sales@hhgroup.co.uk
Web Site: www.hhgroup.co.uk
Key Personnel
Man Dir: B C Wood
Publications Manager: Nick McCann
Founded: 1950
Specialize in guidebooks to Stately Homes, Castles, Museums, Cathedrals etc, aimed at the tourist industry.
ISBN Prefix(es): 0-85101

Number of titles published annually: 6 Print
Total Titles: 88 Print

Heritage Press
4 Buckingham St, Brighton, Sussex BN1 3LT
Tel: (01273) 731296 *Fax:* (01273) 731296
Key Personnel
International Rights: Ann Dean
Founded: 1991
Canada & USA Representation: Strauss Consultants, 48 West 25th St, 11th Floor Front, New York NY 10010, USA. Tel: 212-367-8270 Fax: 212-367-8273.
Heritage Art Guides; specialize in books & postcard books on Burne-Jones, William Morris-Pre-Raphaelites Aubrey Beardsley listed on Book Data.
Subjects: Architecture & Interior Design, Art, Nonfiction (General), Art Travel, Art History, Decorative Arts, Stained Glass, especially William Morris & Burne-Jones
ISBN Prefix(es): 1-873089
Total Titles: 5 Print
Distributed by Strauss Consultants (Canada & USA)
Foreign Rep(s): Roger Ward; David Williams (Austria, Netherlands, Ireland, Far East, France, Germany, Italy, London, Northern Ireland, Southern Europe, Scandinavia, Spain); Bookport Associates; Books for Europe; Continent Books; Julian Cooper; Emma Ferguson; Hanne Rotovnik; IMA; Alan Levelle; Anthony Mcggach (Austria, UK, China, Far East, France, Germany, Greece, Italy, London, Northern Europe, Northern Ireland, Southern Europe, Scandinavia, Spain, Switzerland, Turkey, US); Tom Moggagh; Hibernian Book Services; MTM; Terry Rule; Strauss Consultants
Orders to: Art Books International Ltd, One Stewart's Court, 220 Stewart's Rd, London SW8 4UD *Tel:* (020) 7720 1503 *Fax:* (020) 7720 3158 *E-mail:* artbooks@a-b-i.demon.co.uk (all countries except USA & Canada)

Nick Hern Books Ltd+
The Glasshouse, 49a Goldhawk Rd, London W12 8QP
Tel: (020) 8749 4953 *Fax:* (020) 8735 0250
E-mail: info@nickhernbooks.demon.co.uk
Web Site: www.nickhernbooks.co.uk
Key Personnel
Publisher: Nick Hern *E-mail:* nick@nickhernbooks.demon.co.uk
Founded: 1988
Specialist performing arts publisher.
Subjects: Drama, Theater
ISBN Prefix(es): 1-85459
Number of titles published annually: 40 Print
Total Titles: 300 Print
Distributed by Currency Press (Australia); Playwrights Canada Press (Canada); Theatre Communications Group (USA)
Distributor for Drama Book Publishers (USA, Canada & Australia)
Shipping Address: Grantham Book Services, Isaac Newton Way, Alma Park Industria, Grantham Lincs NG31 9SD *Tel:* (01476) 54100 *Fax:* (01476) 541060
Warehouse: Grantham Book Services, Isaac Newton Way, Alma Park Industria, Grantham Lincs NG31 9SD *Tel:* (01476) 54100 *Fax:* (01476) 541060
Orders to: Grantham Book Services, Isaac Newton Way, Alma Park Industria, Grantham Lincs NG31 9SD *Tel:* (01476) 54100 *Fax:* (01476) 541060

High Risk, *imprint of* Serpent's Tail Ltd

Highland Books Ltd+
Williams Bldg, Woodbridge Meadows, Guildford, Surrey GU1 1BH

Tel: (0148) 342 4560 *Fax:* (0148) 342 4388
E-mail: highlandbooks@compuserve.com
Key Personnel
Dir: Philip Ralli
Founded: 1983
Publish books for Christian market, including "pick-me-ups" (books that encourage & restore).
Subjects: Biography, Religion - Protestant, Self-Help
ISBN Prefix(es): 0-946616; 1-897913
Total Titles: 60 Print
Foreign Rep(s): Alpha Logos (New Zealand, Nigeria, South Africa); Methodist Wholesale; Scripture Union (New Zealand)
Shipping Address: STL Limited, PO Box 300, Kingstown Broadway Carlisle *Tel:* (01228) 574949
Warehouse: STL Limited, PO Box 300, Kingstown Broadway Carlisle *Tel:* (01228) 574949
Orders to: STL Limited, PO Box 300, Kingstown Broadway Carlisle *Tel:* (01228) 574949

Hillside, *imprint of* Christian Education

Hilmarton Manor Press+
Calne, Wilts SN11 8SB
Tel: (01249) 760208 *Fax:* (01249) 760379
E-mail: mailorder@hilmartonpress.co.uk
Web Site: www.hilmartonpress.co.uk
Key Personnel
Man Dir: C Baile de Laperriere
Founded: 1969
Subjects: Antiques, Architecture & Interior Design, Art, Photography, Wine & Spirits
ISBN Prefix(es): 0-904722
Distributor for ADEC (France); Arte & Antiques Editions (Germany); Bibliotheque Des Arts (France & Switzerland); Edition Grund (France); Edition Mayer (France); Guide Emer (France); Servedit-Acatos (France); Tardy (France)

Hippo, *imprint of* Scholastic Ltd

HLT Publications
200 Greyhound Rd, London W14 9RY
Tel: (020) 7385 3377; (020) 7381 7404
Fax: (020) 7381 3377
E-mail: obp@hltpublications.co.uk
Web Site: www.holborncollege.ac.uk/OldbaileyPress.cfm
Key Personnel
Chairman: John Grenier
Chief Executive: Prof Cedric Bell
Founded: 1971
Member of Publishers Association of Great Britain.
Subjects: Business, Law
ISBN Prefix(es): 1-85352; 0-7510; 1-85248
Parent Company: HLT Group Ltd
Imprints: Old Bailey Press; Wise Owl Books
Subsidiaries: Old Bailey Press Ltd
Sales Office(s): Amalgamated Book Services Ltd, Royal Star Arcade, Suite 1, High Street, Maidstone, Kent ME14 1JL *Tel:* (01622) 764 555 *Fax:* (01622) 763 197
Warehouse: Anthony Rowe Ltd, Little Johns Lane, Unit L, Off Portman Rd, Reading, Berks RG30 1LG *Tel:* (0118) 950 3911 *Fax:* (0118) 950 5776

Hobsons+
159 173 Saint John St, London EC1V 4DR
Tel: (020) 7336 6633 *Fax:* (020) 7608 1034
Web Site: www.hobsons.com
Key Personnel
Chairman: Martin Morgan
Man Dir: Chris Letcher
Founded: 1974

Publishers under license for the Careers Research & Advisory Centre Ltd.
Subjects: Business, Career Development, Education, Science (General), Technology
ISBN Prefix(es): 1-86017; 0-86021; 1-85324; 0-903161
Parent Company: Daily Mail Trust
Imprints: CRAC
Warehouse: Biblios 2, Old London Rd, Washington NR Horsham, West Sussex RH20 3EN
Orders to: Biblios Publishers' Distribution Service Ltd, Star Rd, Partridge Green, West Sussex RH13 8LD

Hodder & Stoughton, *imprint of* Hodder & Stoughton Religious

Hodder & Stoughton Educational
338 Euston Rd, London NW1 3BH
Tel: (020) 7873 6272 *Fax:* (020) 7873 6299
E-mail: joanne.symmonds@hodder.co.uk
Web Site: www.hodderheadline.co.uk
Key Personnel
Man Dir: Philip Walters
Deputy Man Dir: Tim Gregson-Willams
Dir, Consumer Education: Katie Rodin
Dir, Schools Publishing: Lis Tribe
Dir, Health Sciences: Georgina Bentliff
Dir, Journal & Reference Books: Mary Attree
Production & Design Dir: Alyssum Ross
Sales & Marketing Dir: Catherine Newman
Founded: 1868
Subjects: Biblical Studies, Biological Sciences, Business, Career Development, Chemistry, Chemical Engineering, Computer Science, Crafts, Games, Hobbies, Engineering (General), Geography, Geology, Language Arts, Linguistics, Literature, Literary Criticism, Essays, Mathematics, Natural History, Photography, Physics, Science (General), Sports, Athletics, Theology
ISBN Prefix(es): 0-340; 0-7131; 0-450; 0-7122
Parent Company: Hodder Headline PLC
Imprints: Headway; Teach Yourself
Orders to: Bookpoint Ltd, 130 Milton Park, Abingdon, Oxon OX14 4TD

Hodder & Stoughton General
338 Euston Rd, London NW1 3BH
Tel: (020) 7873 6000 *Fax:* (020) 7873 6024
Key Personnel
Man Dir: Jamie Hodder-Williams *Tel:* (020) 7873 6125 *Fax:* (020) 7873 6198
Dir, Sales: Sheila Crowley *Tel:* (020) 7873 6159 *Fax:* (020) 7873 6194
Dir, Publicity: Karen Geary *Tel:* (020) 7873 6141 *Fax:* (020) 7873 6195
Publisher, Audio: Rupert Lancaster *Tel:* (020) 7873 6029
Publishing Dir: Roland Philipps *Tel:* (020) 7873 6139 *Fax:* (020) 7873 6198; Carolyn Mays *Tel:* (020) 7873 6132 *Fax:* (020) 7873 6198
Publisher, Sceptre: Carole Welch *Tel:* (020) 7873 6129 *Fax:* (020) 7873 6196
Head of Rights: Briar Silich
Founded: 1868
Subjects: Biography, Child Care & Development, Cookery, Fiction, History, Humor, Military Science, Mysteries, Self-Help
ISBN Prefix(es): 0-340; 0-450
Total Titles: 5,000 Print; 300 Audio
Parent Company: Hodder Headline LTD
Ultimate Parent Company: W H Smith PLC
Imprints: Coronet; Flame; New English Library; Sceptre; Mobius
Orders to: Bookpoint Ltd, 130 Milton Park, Abingdon, Oxon OX14 4SB

Hodder & Stoughton Religious+
338 Euston Rd, London NW1 3BH
Tel: (020) 7873 6000 *Fax:* (020) 7873 6059
E-mail: firstname.surname@hodder.co.uk

Key Personnel
Man Dir: Charles Nettleton
Publishing Dir: Judith Longman
Manager, Publicity: Suzanne Kennedy
Founded: 1868
Subjects: Biography, Child Care & Development, Human Relations, Humor, Religion - Catholic, Religion - Protestant, Religion - Other, Self-Help, Theology
ISBN Prefix(es): 0-340
Parent Company: Hodder Headline Ltd
Ultimate Parent Company: WH Smith PLC
Imprints: Help Yourself Books; Hodder Christian Books; Hodder & Stoughton; NIV Bibles
Orders to: Bookpoint Ltd, 39 Milton Park, Abingdon, Oxon OX14 4BR *Tel:* (01235) 400 400 *Fax:* (01235) 400 500 *E-mail:* orders@bookpoint.co.uk

Hodder Children's Books+
338 Euston Rd, London NW1 3BH
Tel: (020) 7873 6000 *Fax:* (020) 7873 6225
Web Site: www.hodderheadline.co.uk
Key Personnel
Man Dir: Mary Tapissier
Dir, Publishing: Margaret Conroy
Dir, Marketing: Andrea Reece
Dir, Rights: Nancy Miles
Dir Sales: Craig Atkinson
Dir, Fiction: Isabel Boissiur
Dir, Picture & Gift Publishing: Kate Burns
Dir, Hodder Wayland: Roberta Bailey
Dir, Editorial Development: Anne Clark
Founded: 1868
Subjects: Fiction, Nonfiction (General), Science Fiction, Fantasy
ISBN Prefix(es): 0-340
Parent Company: RM plc, Abingdon, Oxon
Imprints: Hodder Home Learning; Hodder Read Alone; Hodder Story Book; Hodder Toddler; Hodder Wayland; Signature; Silver
Orders to: Bookpoint Ltd, 39 Milton Park, Abingdon, Oxon OX14 4TD

Hodder Christian Books, *imprint of* Hodder & Stoughton Religious

Hodder Headline Ltd
338 Euston Rd, London NW1 3BH
Tel: (020) 7873 6000 *Fax:* (020) 7873 6024
Web Site: www.hodderheadline.co.uk
Key Personnel
Group Chief Executive: Tim Hely Hutchinson
Man Dir, Headline Book Publishing: Martin Neild
Man Dir, Hodder & Stoughton General: Jamie Hodder-Williams
Man Dir, Hodder Children's Books: Mary Tapissier
Man Dir, Hodder & Stoughton Religious: Charles Nettleton
Man Dir, Bookpoint Ltd: Tony Bryars
Man Dir, Hodder Arnold; Philip Walters
Acting Man Dir, John Murray: Martin Neild
Group Financial Dir: Colin Fairbairn
Founded: 1986
ISBN Prefix(es): 0-340
Associate Companies: Hodder Dargaud Ltd
Subsidiaries: Hodder Headline Australia Pty Ltd; Hodder Moa Becket Publishers Limited; Edward Arnold (Publishers) Limited; Bookpoint Limited; Headline Book Publishing Limited; Hodder & Stoughton Limited
Divisions: Arnold; Headline Book Publishing; Hodder Children's Books; Hodder & Stoughton Educational; Hodder & Stoughton General; Hodder & Stoughton Religious Books; Hodder Headline Audio
Orders to: Bookpoint Ltd, 130 Milton Park, Abingdon, Oxon OX14 4TD *Tel:* (01235) 835001 *Fax:* (01235) 832068

Hodder Home Learning, *imprint of* Hodder Children's Books

PUBLISHERS
UNITED KINGDOM

Hodder Read Alone, *imprint of* Hodder Children's Books

Hodder Story Book, *imprint of* Hodder Children's Books

Hodder Toddler, *imprint of* Hodder Children's Books

Hodder Wayland, *imprint of* Hodder Children's Books

Holland Enterprises Ltd
18 Bourne Court, Southend Rd, Woodford Green, Essex IG8 8HD
Tel: (020) 8551 7711 *Fax:* (020) 8551 1266
E-mail: enquires@holland-enterprises.co.uk
Web Site: www.holland-enterprises.co.uk
Key Personnel
Chairman: William C Holland
Man Dir: Jonathan Holland
ISBN Prefix(es): 1-85038

Hollis Publishing Ltd
Harlequin House, 7 High St, Teddington, Middlesex TW11 8EL
Tel: (020) 8977 7711 *Fax:* (020) 8977 1133
E-mail: hollis@hollis-pr.co.uk; orders@hollis-pr.co.uk
Web Site: www.hollis-pr.co.uk
Key Personnel
Man Dir: Gary Zabel
Publishing Dir: Rosie Sarginson
Sales Dir: Jane Ireland
Member of Directory Publishers Association.

Holyoake Books
Holyoake House, Hanover St, Manchester M60 0AS
Tel: (0161) 832 4300 *Fax:* (0161) 831 7684
E-mail: info@co-opu.demon.co.uk
Key Personnel
Publisher & Chief Information Officer: I V Williamson
Founded: 1869 (co-operative union)
Subjects: Human Relations, Social Sciences, Sociology
ISBN Prefix(es): 0-85195
Parent Company: Co-operative Union Ltd
Imprints: Co-operative Union

Home Health Education Service
Alma Park, Grantham, Lincs NG31 9SL
Tel: (01476) 591800; (01476) 591700; (01476) 590866 (orders) *Fax:* (01476) 577144
E-mail: 101654.543@compuserve.com
Key Personnel
Secretary: E Johnson
Founded: 1892
Subjects: Religion - Other
ISBN Prefix(es): 0-904748; 0-900703; 1-899505
Parent Company: Stanborough Press
U.S. Office(s): Review & Herald Publ Assn, Hagerstown, MD, United States

Honeyglen Publishing Ltd+
56 Durrels House, Warwick Gardens, London W14 8QB
Tel: (020) 7602 2876 *Fax:* (020) 7602 2876
Key Personnel
Publisher: Nadja Poderegin
Founded: 1982
Member of IPG.
Subjects: Biography, Fiction, History, Philosophy of History
ISBN Prefix(es): 0-907855
Total Titles: 13 Print
Orders to: Vine House Distribution Ltd, Waldenbury, North Common, Chailey, East Sussex BN8 4DR, Contact: Richard Squibb
Tel: (01825) 723398 *Fax:* (01825) 724188
E-mail: sales@vinehouseuk.co.uk

Honno Welsh Women's Press+
The Theological College, King St, Aberystwyth, Ceredigon SY23 2LT
Tel: (01970) 623 150 *Fax:* (01970) 623 150
E-mail: post@honno.co.uk
Web Site: www.honno.co.uk
Key Personnel
Editor: Janet Thomas
Information Officer: Ms Alyson Tyler
Founded: 1986
Specialize in writings by women living in Wales or having a Welsh connection.
Subjects: Biography, Fiction, Nonfiction (General), Poetry
ISBN Prefix(es): 1-870206
Number of titles published annually: 6 Print
Total Titles: 50 Print
Orders to: Turnaround Distribution, Unit 3, Olympia Trading Estate, Coburg Rd, London N22 6TZ *Tel:* (020) 8829 3000 *Fax:* (020) 8881 5088 *E-mail:* claire@turnaround-uk.com (England, Scotland, Ireland & overseas)
Welsh Books Council Distribution Centre, Glanyrafon Industrial Estate, Aberystwyth, Ceredigion SSY23 3AQ *Tel:* (01970) 624 455 *Fax:* (01970) 625 506 *E-mail:* canolfan.ddosbarthu@2cllc.org.uk (Wales)

Hoover's Business Press
5 Five Mile Dr, Oxford OX2 8HT
Tel: (01865) 513186 *Fax:* (01865) 513186
Web Site: www.hoovers-europe.com
Key Personnel
Man Dir: William Snyder *E-mail:* snyderpub@aol.com
ISBN Prefix(es): 1-57311

Horizon Scientific Press+
32 Hewitts Lane, Wymondham, Norfolk NR18 0JA
Mailing Address: PO Box 1, Wymondham, Norfolk NR18 0EH
Tel: (01953) 601106 *Fax:* (01953) 603068
E-mail: mail@horizonpress.com
Web Site: www.horizonpress.com
Key Personnel
Contact: Hugh Griffin
Founded: 1993
Specialize in academic journals & books.
Subjects: Biological Sciences, Medicine, Nursing, Dentistry, Science (General)
ISBN Prefix(es): 1-898486
Number of titles published annually: 8 Print
Total Titles: 30 Print; 2 Online

Horse Books, *imprint of* Robert Hale Ltd

Horus Editions, *imprint of* Award Publications Ltd

Hospitality Training Foundation+
International House, High St, 3rd floor, Ealing, London W5 5DB
Tel: (020) 8579 2400 *Fax:* (020) 8840 6217
E-mail: info@htf.org.uk
Web Site: www.htf.org.uk
Key Personnel
Promotions Assistant: Jenny Bech
Marketing Dir: Paul Hickey
Subjects: Career Development, Hotel & Catering
ISBN Prefix(es): 0-7033
Branch Office(s)
PO Box 67, Carmarthern SA31 1YU
E-mail: htfwales@htf.org.uk
28 Castle St, Edinburgh EH2 2HT
E-mail: htfscotland@htf.org.uk

House of Lochar
Isle of Colonsay, Argyll PA61 7YR
Tel: (01951) 200232 *Fax:* (01951) 200232
E-mail: lochar@colonsay.org.uk
Web Site: www.colosay.org.uk
ISBN Prefix(es): 1-899863
Imprints: Colonsay Books; West Highland Series
Distributed by Scottish Book Source; Natural Heritage (Canada)

Hove Foto Books, *imprint of* Newpro UK Ltd

How Design, *imprint of* David & Charles Ltd

How To Books Ltd+
3 Newtec Pl, Magdalen Rd, Oxford OX4 1RE
Tel: (01865) 793806 *Fax:* (01865) 248780
E-mail: info@howtobooks.co.uk
Web Site: www.howtobooks.co.uk
Key Personnel
Man Dir: Giles Lewis
International Rights: Derek Phillips
Founded: 1991
Series reference publisher of How-to books, Pathways, Essentials.
Subjects: Business, Career Development, Finance, How-to, Management, Self-Help, Travel, Living & Working Abroad, Successful Writing, Computer Basics
ISBN Prefix(es): 1-85703; 1-85876
Total Titles: 250 Print; 5 E-Book
Parent Company: Oxford Publishing Ventures
Associate Companies: Bios Scientific Publishers Ltd
Shipping Address: c/o Plymbridge Distributors, Plymbridge House, Estover Rd, Plymouth, Devon PL6 7PZ
Warehouse: How To Books Ltd, Customer Services, Plymbridge Distributors, Plymbridge House, Estover Rd, Plymouth, Devon PL6 7PZ
Orders to: c/o Plymbridge Distributors, Plymbridge House, Estover Rd, Plymouth, Devon PL6 7PZ

Angus Hudson Ltd+
Concorde House, Grenville Place, Mill Hill, London NW7 3SA
Tel: (020) 8959 3668 *Fax:* (020) 8959 3678
E-mail: sales@angushudson.com
Key Personnel
Production Dir: Stephen Price
Man Dir: Nicholas Jones
Controller: Christopher Atkinson
Founded: 1976
Subjects: Cookery, Religion - Protestant, Theology, Travel
Imprints: Candle Books; Gazelle Books
Subsidiaries: Monarch Books
Orders to: S T L Wholesale, Kingstown Industrial Estate, Kingstown Broadway, Carlisle

A & Z Hughes, *imprint of* Gwasg Gwenffrwd

Hugo's Language Books Ltd+
Redvers House, 13 Fairmile, Henley on Thames, Oxon RG9 2JR
Tel: (01491) 572656 *Fax:* (01491) 573590
E-mail: danadde@dk.com
Key Personnel
Dir Sales: Peter G Lock
Founded: 1875
Subjects: English as a Second Language, How-to, Language Arts, Linguistics
ISBN Prefix(es): 0-85285
Parent Company: Dorling Kindersley plc
Branch Office(s)
Hunter Publications, 239 S Beach Rd, Hobe Sound, FL 33455, United States

"Huh!" 1991, *imprint of* Pentathol Publishing

UNITED KINGDOM

Human Horizons Series, *imprint of* Souvenir Press Ltd

Hunt and Thorpe, *imprint of* John Hunt Publishing Ltd

John Hunt Publishing Ltd+
46a West St, New Alresford, Hants SO24 9AU
Tel: (01962) 736880; (01962) 736888 (orders)
Fax: (01962) 736881
E-mail: office@johnhunt-publishing.com
Web Site: www.johnhunt-publishing.com
Key Personnel
Publisher: John Hunt *Tel:* (01962) 736885
 E-mail: john@johnhuntpub.demon.co.uk
Sales Manager: Colin Nutt
Financial Controller: Sandra Geary
Edit Manager: Anne O'Rorke
Marketing Administrator: Maria Watson
Founded: 1989
Member of Independent Publishers Guild.
Subjects: Religion - Other, Inspirational, Educational, Children's Books including Novelty & Pop ups
ISBN Prefix(es): 0-85305; 1-85608; 1-903019
Number of titles published annually: 50 Print
Total Titles: 400 Print
Imprints: Hunt and Thorpe; Arthur James Ltd; "O" Books
Orders to: STL, Customer Service, PO Box 300, Carlisle, Cumbria CA3 0QS
 Tel: (0800) 282728 *Fax:* (0800) 282530 (UK)
 E-mail: salesline@stl.org

C Hurst & Co (Publishers) Ltd+
Covent Garden, 38 King St, London WC2E 8JZ
Tel: (020) 7240 2666 *Fax:* (020) 7240 2667
E-mail: hurst@atlas.co.uk
Web Site: www.hurstpub.co.uk
Key Personnel
Man Dir: Christopher Hurst
Sales & Rights: Michael Dwyer
Founded: 1968
Subjects: Economics, Government, Political Science, History, Regional Interests, Religion - Other
ISBN Prefix(es): 0-905838; 0-903983; 0-900966; 1-85065
Distributed by Alkem Co (S) Pte Ltd (Southeast Asia); Phambili Agencies (South Africa); Unifacmanu Trading Co Ltd (Taiwan); United Publishers Services Ltd (Japan); University & Reference Publishers' Services (UNIREPS) (Australia & New Zealand); Vanguard Books Pvt (Pakistan)
Foreign Rep(s): Applied Media (India); Sarah Bird (Italy); Peter & Bella Dietschi (Greece); Colin Flint (Denmark, Finland, Iceland, Norway & Sweden); Charles Gibbes (Portugal, Southern France); Dr Laszlo Horvath (Eastern Europe, Russia & Baltic States); Berj Jamkojian (Middle East); Cristina de Lara Ruiz (Spain); SHS Publishers Representatives (Austria, Germany, Switzerland); James Tovey (Paris, Northern France)
Shipping Address: Marston Book Services, PO Box 269, Abingdon, Oxon OX14 4YN
 Tel: (01235) 465500 *Fax:* (01235) 465555
 E-mail: trade.order@marston.co.uk

Hutchinson, *imprint of* Random House UK Ltd

Hutchinson Reference, *imprint of* Helicon Publishing Ltd

Hutchinson Childrens Books, *imprint of* Random House UK Ltd

Alan Hutchison Ltd
9 Pembridge Studios, 27A Pembridge Villas, London W11 3EP

Tel: (020) 7221 0129
Telex: 9419283AHPLTD
Key Personnel
Man Dir: Jemima Haddock
Founded: 1979
Subjects: Art
ISBN Prefix(es): 0-905885; 1-85272
Parent Company: Crown Products Group PLC
U.S. Office(s): Putnam Pub, 200 Madison Ave, New York, NY, United States

Hutton Press Ltd
130 Canada Dr, Cherry Burton, Beverly, East Yorks HU17 7SB
Tel: (01964) 550573 *Fax:* (01964) 550573
Key Personnel
Man Dir: Charles F Brook
Founded: 1979
Subjects: History, Maritime, Regional Interests
ISBN Prefix(es): 0-907033; 1-872167; 1-902709

Hyden House Ltd+
The Sustainability Centre, East Meon, Hants GU32 1HR
Tel: (01730) 823311 *Fax:* (01730) 823322
E-mail: info@permaculture.co.uk
Web Site: www.permaculture.co.uk
Key Personnel
Man Dir: Madeleine Harland
Creative Dir: Tim Harland
Founded: 1990
Specialize in permaculture & sustainable agriculture.
Subjects: Agriculture, Earth Sciences, Environmental Studies, Gardening, Plants, Permaculture
ISBN Prefix(es): 1-85623
Imprints: Permanent Publications
Distributed by Chelsea Green
Distributor for Candlelight Trust (Australia); Solar Survival Press (USA); Tagari Publications (Australia)

Hymns Ancient & Modern Ltd+
St Mary's Works, St Mary's Plain, Norwich NR3 3BH
Tel: (01603) 612914 *Fax:* (01603) 624483
E-mail: admin@scm-canterburypress.co.uk
Web Site: www.scm-canterburypress.co.uk
Key Personnel
Chief Executive Officer: Gordon Knights
Founded: 1861 (Public company 1975)
Member of Independent Publishers Guild (Main company is registered charity).
Subjects: Religion - Other
ISBN Prefix(es): 0-907547; 1-85311
Imprints: Canterbury Press Norwich; Church Times; Hart Advertising Charity Agency; Religious & Moral Education Press; SCM Press
Subsidiaries: G J Palmer & Sons Ltd; SCM-Canterbury Press Ltd
Distributed by Morehouse Publishing (United States)
Foreign Rep(s): Churches Stores (New Zealand); Hugh Dunphy (Jamaica, West Indies); International Publishers Marketing (US); Morehouse Publishing (US); Novalis (Canada); Openbook Publishers (Australia); Charles Paine Pty Ltd (Australia); Publishers International Marketing (London)

Iaith Cyf
Parc Busnes Aberarad, Uned 3, Castell Newydd Emlyn, Carmarthenshire SA38 9DB
Tel: (01239) 711668 *Fax:* (01239) 711698
E-mail: ymhol@cwmni-iaith.com
Web Site: www.cwmni-iaith.com
Key Personnel
Executive Dir: Gareth Ioan
Founded: 1993
Subjects: Education, Welsh Language
ISBN Prefix(es): 0-9522905; 1-900563

IC Publications Ltd, see International Communications

ICC United Kingdom
14-15 Belgrave Sq, London SW1X 8PS
Tel: (020) 7823 2811 *Fax:* (020) 7235 5447
E-mail: katharinehedger@iccorg.co.uk
Web Site: www.iccwbo.org; www.iccuk.net
Key Personnel
Chair: Phil Watts
Dir: Richard C l Bate
Policy Executive: Caroline T McGrath
Founded: 1919
Subjects: Advertising, Business, Communications, Economics, Environmental Studies, Finance, Government, Political Science, Law, Marketing
U.S. Office(s): US Council of the ICC, 1212 Avenue of the Americas, New York, NY 10036, United States

Icon Press+
One Huggetts Lane, Lower Willingdon, Eastbourne, East Sussex BN22 OLZ
Tel: (01323) 507270 *Fax:* (01323) 507270
E-mail: iconpress@philipbrown.screaming.net
Web Site: www.iconpress.co.uk
Key Personnel
Dir: Philip Brown
Founded: 1986
Publishers of art manuals, local history & poetry books.
Subjects: Art, Foreign Countries, History, Humor, Poetry, Regional Interests, Travel
ISBN Prefix(es): 1-873812
Number of titles published annually: 2 Print
Total Titles: 16 Print

ICP, *imprint of* Wilmington Business Information Ltd

Idol, *imprint of* Virgin Publishing Ltd

IEE, *imprint of* Institution of Electrical Engineers

IFLA International Programme for UAP
The British Library, Boston Spa, Wetherby, West Yorks LS23 7BQ
Tel: (01937) 546123 *Fax:* (01937) 546478
E-mail: ifla@bl.uk
Web Site: www.ifla.org/VI/2/uap.htm
Key Personnel
Acting Dir: Sara Gould
Founded: 1981
Subjects: Library & Information Sciences
ISBN Prefix(es): 0-7123; 0-9532; 0-9538

Illustrated History Paperbacks, *imprint of* Sutton Publishing Ltd

Imago Publishing Ltd
Member of Imago Group
Albury Court, Albury, Thame, Oxon OX9 2LP
Tel: (01844) 337000 *Fax:* (01844) 339935
E-mail: sales@imago.co.uk
Web Site: www.imago.co.uk
Key Personnel
Dir: Richard Hayes *E-mail:* richardh@imago.co.uk
Founded: 1980
Specialize in providing production services to publishers on a world-wide basis.
Parent Company: Imago Holdings Ltd
Ultimate Parent Company: Imago Investments Ltd
Branch Office(s)
Imago Services (HK) Ltd, Tung Chung Factory Bldg, 6th floor, Flat B, 653-659 King's Rd, North Point, Hong Kong, China, Contact: Kendrick Cheung *Tel:* 2811 3316 *Fax:* 2597 5256 *E-mail:* kcheung@imago.com.hk

Imago Productions (FE) Pte Ltd, 5 Lorong Bakar Batu, No 05-01, Macpherson Industrial Complex, 348742 Singapore, Singapore, Contact: KC Ng *Tel:* 748 4433 *Fax:* 748 6082 *E-mail:* kng@imago.com.sg
U.S. Office(s): Imago Sales (USA) Inc, 1431 Broadway-Penthouse, New York, NY 10018, United States, Contact: Joseph Braff *Tel:* 212-921-4411 *Fax:* 212-921-8226 *E-mail:* jbraff@imago-ny.com
Imago Sales (USA Mid West) Inc, 800 E Northwest Highway, Suite 700, Palatine, IL 60067, United States *Tel:* 847-705-3821 *Fax:* 847-963-2341
Imago Sales (USA West Coast) Inc, 31952 Camino Capistrano, Suite C22, San Juan Capistrano, CA 92675, United States *Tel:* 949-661-5998 *Fax:* 949-661-8013

Immediate Publishing
1-4 The Plain, Oxford, Oxon OX4 1AS
Tel: (01865) 200422 *Fax:* (01865) 200355
Key Personnel
Contact: Luci Allmark *E-mail:* luci@erlbaum.co.uk
Founded: 1993
Subjects: Computer Science
ISBN Prefix(es): 1-898931
Warehouse: Taylor & Francis, Rankin Rd, Basingstoke, Hamps RG24 8PR
Orders to: Direct Distribution, 27 Palmeira Mansions, Church Rd, Hove, East Sussex

Imperial College Press+
57 Shelton St, London WC2H 9HE
Tel: (020) 7836 3954 *Fax:* (020) 7836 2002
E-mail: edit@icpress.co.uk
Web Site: www.icpress.co.uk
Key Personnel
Contact: Dr John Navas *E-mail:* john@icpress.demon.co.uk
Founded: 1995
STM Publisher of Books & Journals.
Subjects: Biological Sciences, Chemistry, Chemical Engineering, Electronics, Electrical Engineering, Engineering (General), Mathematics, Physical Sciences, Science (General), STM. Specialize in Medicine
ISBN Prefix(es): 1-86094
Number of titles published annually: 85 Print; 2 CD-ROM
Total Titles: 175 Print; 2 CD-ROM
Distributed by World Scientific Publishing (Territory: United Kingdom); World Scientific Publishing Co Inc (Territory: United States); World Scientific Publishing Co Pte Ltd (Territories: India, Singapore, Taiwan); World Scientific Publishing (HK) Co Ltd (Territory: Hong Kong)
Orders to: World Scientific Publishing, 57 Shelton St, Covent Garden, London WC2H 9HE

In Old Photographs, *imprint of* Sutton Publishing Ltd

The In Pinn, *imprint of* Neil Wilson Publishing Ltd

Incorporated Catholic Truth Society+
40-46 Harleyford Rd, London SE11 5AY
Tel: (020) 7640 0042 *Fax:* (020) 7640 0046
E-mail: info@cts-online.org.uk
Web Site: www.cts-online.org.uk *Cable:* APOSTOLIC LONDON
Key Personnel
General Secretary: Fergal Martin
Founded: 1884
Subjects: Education, Religion - Catholic
ISBN Prefix(es): 0-85183; 1-86082
Imprints: CTS Publications
Distributor for Liberia Editrice Vaticana; L'Osservatore Romano Newspaper
Bookshop(s): 25 Ashley Place, London SW1P 1LT
Book Club(s): CTS Readers Club

Independence
PO Box 295, Cambridge CB1 3XP
Tel: (01223) 566 130 *Fax:* (01223) 566 131
E-mail: issues@independence.co.uk
Web Site: www.independence.co.uk
Key Personnel
Publisher: Craig Donnellan
Founded: 1989
Subjects: Social Issues
ISBN Prefix(es): 1-86168; 1-872995

Independent Voices, *imprint of* Souvenir Press Ltd

Independent Writers Publications Ltd+
97 Geary Rd, Dollis Hill, London NW10 1HS
Tel: (020) 8438 0179 *Fax:* (020) 8438 0179
Key Personnel
Contact: Alfred Shmueli
Founded: 1993
Subjects: Fiction

Indiana University Press, *imprint of* Combined Academic Publishers

Informa Publishing Group Ltd
19 Portland Place, London W1B 1PX
Tel: (020) 7453 2222 *Fax:* (020) 7436 2450
Web Site: www.informa.com
Key Personnel
Executive Chairman: Peter Rigby
Chief Executive: David Gilbertson
Corporate Development Director: Peter Miller

INSPEC, *imprint of* Institution of Electrical Engineers

Institute for Fiscal Studies
7 Ridgmount St, 3rd floor, London WC1E 7AE
Tel: (020) 7291 4800 *Fax:* (020) 7323 4780
E-mail: mailbox@ifs.org.uk
Web Site: www.ifs.org.uk
Key Personnel
Dir: Andrew Dilnot
Deputy Dir: James Banks
Research Dir: Richard Blundell
Deputy Research Dir: Costas Meghir
External Relations Manager: Emma Hyman *Tel:* (020) 7291 4850 *E-mail:* emma_h@ifs.org.uk
Executive Administrator: Robert Markless
Founded: 1969
Independent research institute.
Publish research findings on all aspects of taxation & economic public policy.
Subjects: Economics, Finance, Public Administration, working papers (on-line only)
ISBN Prefix(es): 1-873357
Number of titles published annually: 15 Print; 10 Online
Total Titles: 200 Print; 100 Online
Online services available through World Wide Web.

Institute of Development Studies
University of Sussex, Falmer, Brighton, Sussex BN1 9RE
Tel: (01273) 606261 *Fax:* (01273) 621202; (01273) 691647
E-mail: idsbtng.ids.books@sussex.au.uk
Web Site: www.ids.ac.uk/ids/publicat
Key Personnel
Head of Information Resource Unit: Michael Bloom
Communications Manager: Rosalind Goodrich
Founded: 1966
Subjects: Agriculture, Developing Countries, Economics, Education, Environmental Studies, Government, Political Science, Public Administration, Women's Studies
ISBN Prefix(es): 0-903354; 0-903715; 1-85864
Number of titles published annually: 50 Print
Total Titles: 500 Print

Institute of Economic Affairs+
2 Lord North St, London SW1P 3LB
Tel: (020) 7799 8900 *Fax:* (020) 7799 2137
E-mail: enquiries@iea.org.uk; iea@iea.org.uk
Web Site: www.iea.org.uk
Key Personnel
General Dir: John Blundell *Tel:* (020) 7799 8911 *E-mail:* jblundell@iea.org.uk
Editorial Dir: Prof Colin Robinson *Tel:* (020) 7799 8912 *E-mail:* crobinson@iea.org.uk
Development Dir: Tom Miers *Tel:* (020) 7799 8904 *E-mail:* tmeirs@iea.org.uk
Dir, Marketing & Subscriptions: Adam Myers *Tel:* (020) 7799 8920 *E-mail:* amyers@iea.org.uk
Sales Manager: Bob Layson *Tel:* (020) 7799 8909 *E-mail:* books@iea.org.uk
Founded: 1955
Subjects: Economics, Education
ISBN Prefix(es): 0-255

Institute of Education, University of London+
20 Bedford Way, London WC1H 0AL
Tel: (020) 7580 1122 *Fax:* (020) 7612 6560
Web Site: www.ioe.ac.uk/publications
Key Personnel
Dir: Prof Geoff Whitty
Publications Officer: Deborah Spring *E-mail:* d.spring@ioe.ac.uk
Founded: 1902
Subjects: Education
ISBN Prefix(es): 0-85473
Number of titles published annually: 15 Print
Total Titles: 80 Print
Orders to: Central Books, 99 Wallis Rd, London E9 5LN *Tel:* (020) 8986 4854 *Fax:* (020) 8533 5821

Institute of Irish Studies, The Queens University of Belfast+
Queen's University Belfast, 8 Fitzwilliam St, Belfast BT9 6AW
Tel: (028) 9027 3386 *Fax:* (028) 9043 9238
E-mail: iispubs@qub.ac.uk
Web Site: www.qub.ac.uk/iis
Key Personnel
Editor: Margaret McNulty *E-mail:* m.mcnulty@qub.ac.uk
Founded: 1987
A small press & publishing company which publishes academic & semi-academic books relative to all aspects of Irish studies.
Subjects: Anthropology, Archaeology, Art, Biography, Ethnicity, Film, Video, Geography, Geology, Government, Political Science, History, Language Arts, Linguistics, Regional Interests, Religion - Catholic, Religion - Protestant
ISBN Prefix(es): 0-85389
Number of titles published annually: 10 Print
Total Titles: 150 Print
U.S. Office(s): Dufour Editions, PO Box 7, Chester Springs, PA 19425-0007, United States *Tel:* 610-458-5005 *Fax:* 610-458-7103 *E-mail:* Dutour8023@aol.com *Web Site:* members.aol.com/dufour8023/index.html (Sales in USA)
Distributed by P D Meaney (One title only)
Distributor for Van Gorcum (North Ireland & Irish Republic for 1 book only)

Institute of Physics, see Institute of Physics Publishing

UNITED KINGDOM

Institute of Physics Publishing+
Dirac House, Temple Back, Bristol BS1 6BE
Tel: (0117) 929 7481 *Fax:* (0117) 929 4318
E-mail: custserv@iop.org
Web Site: www.iop.org
Key Personnel
Man Dir: Jerry Cowhig *E-mail:* jerry.cowhig@iop.org
Business Dir: Ken Lillywhite *E-mail:* ken.lillywhite@iop.org
Operations Dir: Dr Kurt Paulus *Tel:* (117) 930 1057 *E-mail:* kurt.paulus@iop.org
Head of Book Publishing: Nicki Dennis *E-mail:* nicki.dennis@iop.org
Rights: Brenda Trigg *E-mail:* brenda.trigg@iop.org
Sales: Nicola Newey *E-mail:* nicola.newey@iop.org
Founded: 1874
Member of ALPSP, PA & STM.
Subjects: Astronomy, Biography, Computer Science, Electronics, Electrical Engineering, Mathematics, Physical Sciences, Physics, Science (General), Technology
ISBN Prefix(es): 0-85274; 0-85498
Number of titles published annually: 45 Print
Total Titles: 700 Print
Parent Company: Institute of Physics
Subsidiaries: IOP Publishing Inc
U.S. Office(s): Institute of Phyiscs Publishing, Inc, Public Ledger Building, Suite 1035, 150 S Independence Mall W, Philadelphia, PA 19106, United States *Tel:* 215-627-0880 *Fax:* 215-627-0879 *E-mail:* info@ioppubusa.com
Warehouse: Marston Book Services Ltd, PO Box 269, Abingdon OX14 4YN *Tel:* (01235) 465 500 *Fax:* (01235) 465 555
Orders to: Institute of Physics Publishing c/o AIDC, 2 Winter Sport Lane, PO Box 20, Williston, VT 05495-0020, United States

Institution of Chemical Engineers
Davis Bldg, 165-189 Railway Terrace, Rugby CV21 3HQ
Tel: (01788) 578214 *Fax:* (01788) 560833
E-mail: jcressey@icheme.org.uk
Web Site: www.icheme.org
Telex: 311780
Key Personnel
Chief Executive & Secretary: Dr T J Evans
Senior Marketing Officer: Jacqueline Cressey
Founded: 1922
Subjects: Chemistry, Chemical Engineering
ISBN Prefix(es): 0-8169; 0-85295
U.S. Office(s): American Institute of Chemical Engineers, 345 E 47 St, New York, NY, United States
Distributed by Gulf Publishing Co (Canada & USA only)

Institution of Electrical Engineers+
Publishing Dept, Michael Faraday House, Six Hills Way, Stevenage, Herts SG1 2AY
Tel: (01438) 313311 *Fax:* (01438) 313465
E-mail: postmaster@iee.org.uk
Web Site: www.iee.org.uk/publish
Key Personnel
Man Dir: Steven Mair
Publishing Dir: Robin Mellors-Bourne
Marketing Enquiries: Janet Porter
Commissioning Editor: Roland Harwood
Founded: 1871
Subjects: Aeronautics, Aviation, Business, Communications, Computer Science, Electronics, Electrical Engineering, Energy, History, Management, Physical Sciences, Technology
ISBN Prefix(es): 0-85296; 0-906048; 0-86341
Number of titles published annually: 30 Print
Total Titles: 240 Print
Parent Company: Savoy Pl, London WC2R 0BL
Imprints: IEE; INSPEC; Peter Peregrinus Ltd
Bookshop(s): IEE, Savoy Pl, London WC2R 0BL

Warehouse: Unit 7, Fulton Close, Argyle Way, Stevenage SG1 2AF *Tel:* (01438) 355029 *Fax:* (01438) 355034
Orders to: PO Box 96, Stevenage, Herts SG1 2SD *Tel:* (01438) 767328 *Fax:* (01438) 742792 *E-mail:* sales@ieee.org *Web Site:* www.iee.org/shop/ (Publications Sales Dept)

Institution of Mechanical Engineers, see Professional Engineering Publishing Ltd

The Intef Institute, *imprint of* Karnak House

Intellect Ltd+
PO Box 862, Bristol BS99 1DE
Tel: (0117) 955 6811
E-mail: mail@intellectbooks.com
Web Site: www.intellectbooks.com
Key Personnel
Chairman: Masoud Yazdani
Man Dir: Robin Beecroft
Founded: 1984
A multidisciplinary publisher for individual & institutional readers.
Member of Independent Publishers Guild (IPG).
Subjects: Computer Science, Drama, Theater, Film, Video, Language Arts, Linguistics, Regional Interests, Women's Studies
ISBN Prefix(es): 1-871516
Total Titles: 300 Print
Online services available through World Wide Web.
Branch Office(s)
Bristol, The Tabacco Factory, Raleigh Rd, Bedminster, Bristol BS3 1TF, Robin Beecroft *Tel:* (0117) 9020326 *E-mail:* robin@intellect.fsbusiness.co.uk
Distributed by Astam Books (Australasia); International Specialised Book Services, Inc (North America); Judith Wengrove Agencies (South Africa); Plymbridge Distributors
Foreign Rep(s): Astam Books (Australia); ISBS (US); Dineke Kemp (Netherlands); Kemper Conseil (Netherlands); Marcello (Italy); SHS (Germany); Troika (UK); Judith Wengrowe Agencies (South Africa)

Inter-Varsity Press+
38 De Montfort St, Leicester LE1 7GP
Tel: (0116) 2551754 *Fax:* (0116) 2542044
E-mail: ivp@uccf.org.uk
Key Personnel
Chief Executive: B Wilson
Editorial: S Carter
Production: J Mansfield *Tel:* (0115) 978 1054 *Fax:* (0115) 942 2694 *E-mail:* jam@ivpbooks.com
Sales: T Banting *Tel:* (0115) 978 1054 *Fax:* (0115) 942 2694 *E-mail:* trb@ivpbooks.com
Personal Assistant to Chief Executive: Christine Ward *E-mail:* cw@uccf.org.uk
Marketing: V Smith-Dziuba *Tel:* (0115) 978 1054 *Fax:* (0115) 942 2694
Founded: 1928
Publisher of evangelical Christian books.
Subjects: Education, Religion - Other
ISBN Prefix(es): 0-85110; 0-85111
Number of titles published annually: 50 Print
Total Titles: 650 Print
Parent Company: UCCF
Imprints: Apollos (Academic books); Crossway (Popular books); IVP (General books)
Distributor for I V Press; DK Religious; Piquant; Third Way
Orders to: IVP Book Centre, Norton St, Nottingham NG7 3HR *Tel:* (0115) 9781054 *Fax:* (0115) 9422694 *Web Site:* www.ivpbooks.com

Intercept Ltd
PO Box 716, Andover, Hants SP10 1YG

Tel: (01264) 334748 *Fax:* (01264) 334058
E-mail: intercept@andover.co.uk
Web Site: www.intercept.co.uk
Key Personnel
Manager: Andrew Cook
Founded: 1983
Subjects: Agriculture, Biological Sciences, Environmental Studies, Gardening, Plants, Geography, Geology, Medicine, Nursing, Dentistry, Natural History, Science (General), Technology, Publish scientific, technical & medical
ISBN Prefix(es): 0-946707; 1-898298
Parent Company: Lavoisier, 14 rue de Provigny, 94236 Cachan, France
Distributor for Exegetics; Natural History Museum (London); Erich Nelson Foundation; NRC Research Press; Polytechnic International Press; Ray Society
Warehouse: Unit 2B, Duke Close, West Way, Walworth Industrial Estate, Andover, Hants SP10 5AR

Interfisc Publishing
4 Rickett St, London SW6 1RU
Tel: (020) 7610 2722 *Fax:* (020) 7610 3373
E-mail: editor@interfisc.com
Web Site: www.interfisc.com
Key Personnel
Contact: Adrian Ogley *E-mail:* aogley@interfisc.com
Founded: 1993
Professional & academic books on international tax.
Member of Association of Learned & Professional Society of Publishers.
Subjects: Business
ISBN Prefix(es): 0-9520442
Total Titles: 2 Print
Parent Company: Interfisc, 27 Old Gloucester St, London WC1N 3XX
Foreign Rep(s): American Distributor (Canada, US)
Orders to: International Information Services Inc, PO Box 3490, Silver Spring, MD 20918, United States *Tel:* 301-565-2975 *Fax:* 301-565-2973 *E-mail:* orders@interfisc.com (US & Canada)

Intermediate Technology Publications Ltd+
103-105 Southampton Row, London WC1B 4HL
Tel: (020) 7436 9761 *Fax:* (020) 7436 2013
E-mail: marketing@itpubs.org.uk
Web Site: www.itdgpublishing.org.uk
Key Personnel
Editorial, Rights & Permissions: Helen Marsden
Sales & Publicity: Toby Harris *E-mail:* tobyh@itpubs.org.uk
Founded: 1973
Malaysia, Singapore, Indonesia, Thailand, Brunei.
Subjects: Agriculture, Anthropology, Developing Countries, Engineering (General), Environmental Studies, Technology
ISBN Prefix(es): 0-903031; 0-946688; 1-85339
Number of titles published annually: 30 Print
Parent Company: Intermediate Technology Development Group, Schumacher Centre for Technology & Development, Bourton Hall, Bourton-on-Dunsmore, Warks CV23 9SD
Imprints: IT Publications
Distributed by Amin al-Abini (Middle East & North Africa); Astam Books Pty Ltd (Australia); Richard Bowen (Finland, Norway, Sweden, Iceland, Denmark); Grassroots Books Pvt Ltd (Zimbabwe); Horizon Books Ltd; InterMedia Americana (Central Africa); Lake House Bookshop (Sri Lanka); Maya Publishers Plc (India); Publishers Marketing Services Plc (Malaysia, Singapore, Indonesia. Thailand, Brunei); STM Publishers Services (Taiwan, Korea, Vietnam, Philippines, Hong Kong, Thailand, China); Stylus Publishing Inc (USA)
Distributor for IDRC (Canada); KIT Press (Amsterdam, The Netherlands); SKAT (Switzerland)

Foreign Rep(s): Stylus (US)
Orders to: Plymbridge Distributors Ltd, Estover Rd, Plymouth PL6 7PY

International Affairs, *imprint of* Royal Institute of International Affairs

International Bee Research Association
18 North Rd, Cardiff CF10 3DT
Tel: (02920) 372409 *Fax:* (02920) 665522
E-mail: mail@cardiff.ac.uk
Web Site: www.cf.ac.uk/ibra
Key Personnel
Dir: Richard Jones
Deputy Dir & Editor: Pamela A Munn, PhD
Founded: 1949
World information specialists on bees.
Member of IUBS.
Subjects: Agriculture, Biological Sciences, Education, Natural History, Bees, Bee Science, Pollination, Conservation
ISBN Prefix(es): 0-86098; 0-900149

International Biographical Centre, *imprint of* Melrose Press Ltd

International Communications
7 Coldbath Sq, London EC1R 4LQ
Tel: (020) 7713 7711 *Fax:* (020) 7713 7898; (020) 7713 7970
E-mail: icpubs@africasia.com
Web Site: www.africasia.com
Key Personnel
Dir: Emena Ben Yedder
Group Publisher: Ahmed Afif Ben Yedder
Sales: Shaunagh Cowell
Founded: 1974
Subjects: Art, Business, Sports, Athletics, Specializes in Current Affairs, Middle East & Africa
ISBN Prefix(es): 0-905268
Number of titles published annually: 4 Print
Subsidiaries: IC Publications

International Institute for Strategic Studies+
Arundel House, 13-15 Arundel St, Temple Place, London WC2R 3DX
Tel: (020) 7379 7676 *Fax:* (020) 7836 3108
E-mail: iiss@iiss.org
Web Site: www.iiss.org
Telex: 94081492 G *Cable:* MLINK
Key Personnel
Dir: Dr John Chipman *E-mail:* chipman@iiss.org
Assistant Dir: Steven Simon *E-mail:* simon@iiss.org; Terence Taylor *E-mail:* taylor@iiss.org
Manager, Editorial Service: James Green *Tel:* (020) 7379 7676 *E-mail:* green@iiss.org
Founded: 1958
Subjects: Government, Political Science, Military Science
ISBN Prefix(es): 0-86079; 0-900492
Number of titles published annually: 12 Print
Associate Companies: Oxford University Press, Great Clarendon St, Oxford OX2 6DP *Tel:* (01865) 267907 *Fax:* (01865) 267485
Imprints: The Military Balance; Strategic Survey; Survival; Adelphi Papers; Strategic Comments
Distributed by Oxford University Press
Orders to: Oxford University Press, Journals Marketing, 2001 Evans Rd, Cary, NC 27513, United States
OXFORD UNIVERSITY PRESS, Great Clarendon St, Oxford OX2 6DP *Tel:* (01865) 267907 *Fax:* (01865) 267485

International Labour Office
Millbank Tower, 5th floor, 21-24 Millbank, London SW1P 4QP
Tel: (020) 7828 6401 *Fax:* (020) 7233 5925
E-mail: ipu@ilo-london.org.uk
Web Site: www.ilo.org

Key Personnel
Dir: JUAN SOMAVIA
Publications Manager: Nick Evans *E-mail:* evansn@ilo-london.org.uk
Information Officer: Carl David
Founded: 1919
ISBN Prefix(es): 92-2
Parent Company: International Labour Organization, 4 Route des Morillons, CH-1211 Geneva 22, Switzerland

International Map Trade Association
5 Spinacre, Barton on Sea, Hants BH25 7DF
Tel: 01425) 620532 *Fax:* (01425) 620532
E-mail: imtaeurope@compuserve.com
Web Site: www.maptrade.org

Interpet Publishing+
Vincent Lane, Dorking, Surrey RH4 3YX
Tel: (01306) 881033 *Fax:* (01306) 885009
E-mail: publishing@interpet.co.uk
Key Personnel
Publisher: Kevin Kingham
Subjects: Animals, Pets, Gardening, Plants, Veterinary Science
ISBN Prefix(es): 0-948955; 1-86054; 1-84286; 1-902389; 1-903098

Investment Intelligence, *imprint of* Wilmington Business Information Ltd

IOM Communications Ltd
Subsidiary of The Institute of Materials
One Carlton House Terrace, London SW1Y 5DB
Tel: (020) 7451 7300 *Fax:* (020) 7839 1702
E-mail: admin@materials.org.uk
Web Site: www.materials.org.uk *Cable:* 451-7300
Key Personnel
Head of Publishing: Bill Jackson *Tel:* (020) 7451 7305 *E-mail:* bill_jackson@materials.org.uk
Managing Editor: Peter Danckwerts *Tel:* (020) 7451 7310 *E-mail:* peter_danckwerts@materials.org.uk
Marketing Manager: Peter Richardson *Tel:* (020) 7451 7372 *E-mail:* peter_richardson@materials.org.uk
Subjects: Chemistry, Chemical Engineering, Engineering (General)
ISBN Prefix(es): 0-904357; 0-900497; 0-901462; 0-901716; 1-86125

Iona Community, see Wild Goose Publications

IPS, see Eagle/Inter Publishing Service (IPS) Ltd

Irish Texts Society, *imprint of* Irish Texts Society (Cumann Na Scribeann nGaedhilge)

Irish Texts Society (Cumann Na Scribeann nGaedhilge)
c/o The Royal Bank of Scotland, 49 Charing Cross, London SW1A 2DX
E-mail: shuttonseanfile@aol.com
Key Personnel
President: Prof Padraig ORiain
Honorary Treasurer: Michael J Burns
Founded: 1898
Specialize in educational charity publishing Irish language texts with translations, & a subsidiary series of supporting commentaries, studies, indexes, etc; organization of annual seminar in conjunction with the combined departments of Irish, University College, Cork, Ireland; publication of catalogue & newsletter.
Subjects: Anthropology, History, Poetry
ISBN Prefix(es): 1-870166
Imprints: Irish Texts Society
Orders to: Michael J Burns, Tibradden Rd, Rockbrook, Dublin 16, Ireland *E-mail:* burnsfam@iol.ie

IRL Press, *imprint of* Oxford University Press

Isis Publishing Ltd+
7 Centremead, Osney Mead, Oxford OX2 0ES
Tel: (01865) 250 333 *Fax:* (01865) 790 358
E-mail: sales@isis-publishing.co.uk
Web Site: www.isis-publishing.co.uk
Key Personnel
International Rights: Veronica Babington Smith *E-mail:* vbs@isispublishing.fsnet.co.uk
Subjects: Biography, Fiction, Health, Nutrition, Mysteries, Nonfiction (General), Self-Help, Western Fiction
ISBN Prefix(es): 1-85089; 1-85695; 0-7531
U.S. Office(s): Ulverscroft Large Print (USA) Inc, 1881 Ridge Rd, PO Box 1230, West Seneca, NY 14224-1230, United States *Tel:* 716-674-4270 *Fax:* 716-674-4195

Islam International Publications Ltd
Islamabad, Sheephatch Lane, Tilford, Surrey GU10 2AQ
Tel: (01252) 783155 *Fax:* (01252) 783155
Key Personnel
Dir: Mr N A Qamar
Founded: 1889
Specialize in books on Islam, various translations & exegesis of Holy Quran in different languages.
Subjects: Religion - Islamic, Theology
ISBN Prefix(es): 1-85372
Parent Company: Al-Shirkatul Islamiyyah
Associate Companies: Islam International Publications Ltd
Imprints: Al-Shir katul Islamiyyah
Subsidiaries: London Mosque Publications
Branch Office(s)
Ahmadiyya Movement in Islam, Inc, Masjid Bait-Ur-Rehman, 15000 Good Hope Rd, Silver Spring, MD 20905, United States *Tel:* 301-879-0110 *Fax:* 301-879-0115

Islamic Foundation Publications
Markfield Conference Centre, Ratby Lane, Markfield, Lincs LE67 9SY
Tel: (01530) 244 944; (01530) 249 230
Fax: (01530) 244 946; (01530) 249 230
E-mail: info@islamic-foundation.org.uk; publication@islamic-foundation.com
Web Site: www.islamic-foundation.com *Cable:* ISLAMFOUND LEICESTER UK
Key Personnel
Dir General, Editorial: Dr M M Ahsan
Dir Publications: Farooq Murad
Contact: Chowdhury Mueen-Uddin *E-mail:* c.mueen@islamic-foundation.org.uk
Founded: 1973
Research, publication, post-graduation education, training.
Also brought PCIQ quiz game, video on "Islam in Europe".
Subjects: Economics, Education, Government, Political Science, History, Religion - Islamic
ISBN Prefix(es): 0-86037; 0-9503954
Number of titles published annually: 10 Print
Online services available through World Wide Web.
Imprints: Revival Publications
Distributed by International Institute of Islamic Thought (USA); IPS (Pakistan); Islamic Circle of North America (USA); Islamic Society of North America (USA); Sound Vision (USA)
Orders to: The Islamic Foundation Publications Unit, Markfield Dawah Center, Ratby Lane, Markfield, Leicester LE67 9SY

The Islamic Texts Society+
Elmhurst, 22A Brooklands Ave, Cambridge CB2 2DQ
Tel: (01223) 314387 *Fax:* (01223) 324342
E-mail: mail@its.org.uk
Web Site: www.its.org.uk

UNITED KINGDOM

Key Personnel
Man Dir: Fatima Azzam *E-mail:* fazzam@its.org.uk
Founded: 1981
Specialize in Islamic literature.
Subjects: Agriculture, Art, Biography, Fiction, History, Humor, Music, Dance, Natural History, Nonfiction (General), Photography, Poetry, Religion - Other, Sports, Athletics
ISBN Prefix(es): 0-946621
Number of titles published annually: 6 Print
Total Titles: 40 Print
Foreign Rep(s): Richard Carman (Sub-Saharan Africa); Iberian Book Services (Spain & Portugal); International Specialized Book Services (Canada, US); James Benson/Hugh Bulley (Malaysia, Singapore); Karim International (Bangladesh); Publishers International Marketing (Southeast Asia); Anthony Rudkin Associates (Greece & Cyprus, Malta, Mideast); Andrew Russell (Ireland, Northern Ireland); Murray Sutton (Denmark, Iceland, Scandinavia); Tahir Lodhi (Pakistan); The American University in Cairo Press (Egypt); Viva Marketing (India)
Warehouse: Haynes Publishing, Star Rd, Partridge Green, Horsham, Sparkford, Near Yeovil Somerset BA22 7JJ *Tel:* (01963) 442105 *Fax:* (01963) 440001 *E-mail:* sales@haynes-manuals.co.uk
Orders to: Haynes Publishing, Sparkford, Near Yeovil Somerset BA22 7JJ *Tel:* (01963) 442105 *Fax:* (01963) 440001 *E-mail:* sales@haynes-manuals.co.uk
Membership(s): Publishers' Association

IT Publications, *imprint of* Intermediate Technology Publications Ltd

Ithaca Press, *imprint of* Garnet Publishing Ltd

IUCN-The World Conservation Union
Publications Services Unit, 219c Huntingdon Rd, Cambridge CB3 0DL
Tel: (01223) 277894 *Fax:* (01223) 277175
E-mail: info@books.iucn.org
Web Site: www.iucn.org
Key Personnel
Publications Officer: Deborah Murith *Tel:* (022) 999 0119 *Fax:* (022) 999 0010 *E-mail:* dem@iucn.org
Founded: 1948
ISBN Prefix(es): 2-8317
Divisions:
Distributed by Island Press
Distributor for Cites; Ramsar; World Conservation Monitoring Centre

IVP, *imprint of* Inter-Varsity Press

J Whitaker & Sons Ltd
Endeavour House, 189 Shaftesbury Ave, London WC2H 8TJ
Tel: (01252) 742525; (01252) 742542
Fax: (01252) 742526; (01252) 742543
E-mail: custserv@whitaker.co.uk; help@whitaker.co.uk
Web Site: www.whitaker.co.uk *Cable:* WHITMANACK LONDON WC1
Key Personnel
Man Dir: Paul Pounsford
Sales Dir: Simon Skinner *Tel:* (01252) 742500 *Fax:* (01252) 742501
Editorial Dir: Michael Healy
Head of Sales: Terry Robinson
Head of Marketing: Simon Edwards
Founded: 1841
Subjects: Publishing & Book Trade Reference
ISBN Prefix(es): 0-85021; 0-949999

Associate Companies: Bookseller Publications
Subsidiaries: The Standard Book Numbering Agency Ltd; Teleordering Ltd, 3 The Windmills; BookTrack Ltd

Jade Publishers+
15 Stoatley Rise, Haslemere, Surrey GU27 1AF
Tel: (01428) 644846
Key Personnel
Partner: C P de Laszlo
Founded: 1988
Subjects: Crafts, Games, Hobbies, Fiction
ISBN Prefix(es): 0-903461
Subsidiaries: Bonnington Books
Orders to: Bookpoint Ltd, 39 Milton Park, Abingdon, Oxon OX14 4TD

JAI Press Ltd+
38 Tavistock St, Covent Garden, London WC2E 7PB
Tel: (020) 7379 8834 *Fax:* (020) 7379 8835
Web Site: www.jaipress.com
Key Personnel
Marketing in Sales: Della Sar
Founded: 1985
Specialize in research-level serials, monograph series, treatises & journals.
Subjects: Accounting, Behavioral Sciences, Biological Sciences, Business, Chemistry, Chemical Engineering, Child Care & Development, Economics, Education, Government, Political Science, Library & Information Sciences, Management, Psychology, Psychiatry, Social Sciences, Sociology
ISBN Prefix(es): 0-89232; 1-55938; 0-7623
Parent Company: Elsevier Science
Warehouse: Marston Book Services Ltd, PO Box 269, Abingdon OX14 4YN

James & James (Publishers) Ltd+
Gordon House Business Centre, 6 Lissenden Gardens, London NW5 1LX
Tel: (020) 7482 8888 *Fax:* (020) 7482 8889
E-mail: jxj@jamesxjames.co.uk
Web Site: www.jamesxjames.co.uk
Key Personnel
Man Dir: Hamish MacGibbon
Project Editor: Susie May
Marketing Manager: Ruth Weinberg
Founded: 1985
Publishers of illustrated books on history & the environment, specifically illustrated histories of companies, schools & other institutions.
Member of Independent Publishers Group.
Subjects: Business, Environmental Studies, History
ISBN Prefix(es): 0-907383
Total Titles: 10 Print
Associate Companies: James & James Science Publishers Ltd, Contact: Edward Milford *Tel:* (0171) 387 8558

James & James (Science Publishers) Ltd
35-37 William Rd, London NW1 3ER
Tel: (020) 7387 8558 *Fax:* (020) 7387 8998
E-mail: jxj@jxj.com
Web Site: www.jxj.com
Key Personnel
Publisher: Edward Milford *E-mail:* em@jxj.com
Founded: 1990
Subjects: Architecture & Interior Design, Electronics, Electrical Engineering, Energy, Environmental Studies, Physics
ISBN Prefix(es): 0-907383; 1-873936
Total Titles: 70 Print
Online services available through World Wide Web.
U.S. Office(s): American Book Center Inc, Brooklyn Navy Yard, Bldg 3, Brooklyn, NY 11205, United States *Tel:* 718-923-8332 *Fax:* 718-935-9647 *E-mail:* jxj@americanbookcenter.com
Distributed by A & I Ltd

Arthur James Ltd, *imprint of* John Hunt Publishing Ltd

Jane's Information Group
Sentinel House, 163 Brighton Rd, Coulsdon, Surrey CR5 2YH
Tel: (020) 8700 3700 *Fax:* (020) 8763 1005
E-mail: info@janes.co.uk
Web Site: www.janes.com
Key Personnel
Man Dir: Alfred Rolington *Tel:* 208-700-3701 *Fax:* 208-700-3704 *E-mail:* alfred.rolington@janes.co.uk
Publishing Dir, Reference: Alan Condron *Tel:* 208-700-3779 *Fax:* 208-700-3788 *E-mail:* alan.condron@janes.co.uk
Group Communications Manager: Claire Brunavs *Tel:* 208-700-3703 *Fax:* 208-763-1006 *E-mail:* claire.brunavs@janes.co.uk
Founded: 1897
Specialize in police, security, geopolitics, risk assessment, technical & infrastructure information. Full online subscription access & CD-ROMS.
Subjects: Aeronautics, Aviation, Foreign Countries, Maritime, Military Science, Transportation
ISBN Prefix(es): 0-7106; 0-309; 0-532; 0-265
Total Titles: 200 Print; 12 CD-ROM; 200 Online; 9 E-Book
Parent Company: The Woodbridge Co Ltd
Branch Office(s)
Jane's Information Group, Shenton Way, No 01-01 Vic Bldg, Singapore 068808, Singapore, Contact: David Fisher *Tel:* 6410 1240 *Fax:* 6226 1185 *E-mail:* info@janes.com.sg
Jane's Information Group, PO Box 3502, Rozelle NSW 2039, Australia, Contact: Pauline Roberts *Tel:* (02) 8587 7900 *Fax:* (02) 8587 7901 *E-mail:* info@janes.thomson.com.au
U.S. Office(s): Jane's Information Group (US), 1340 Braddock Pl, Suite 300, Alexandria, VA 22314, United States, Deborah Chiao *Tel:* 703-683-3700 *Fax:* 703-836-0029 *E-mail:* deborah.chiao@janes.com

Janus Books, *imprint of* Janus Publishing Company Ltd

Janus Publishing Company Ltd+
76 Great Titchfield St, London W1P 7AF
Tel: (020) 7580 7664 *Fax:* (020) 7636 5756
E-mail: sales@januspublishing.co.uk
Web Site: www.januspublishing.co.uk
Key Personnel
Man Dir: Sandy Leung
Production: Sue Braybrook
Publicity: Fleur Cage
Marketing: Sam Ketterer
Founded: 1991 (For authors overlooked by big publishing houses)
Janus-subsidized publishing *Empiricus*-non-subsidized.
Member of Independent Publishers Guild & publisher of radical ideas.
Subjects: Alternative, Astrology, Occult, Biography, Education, Fiction, Film, Video, Health, Nutrition, Nonfiction (General), Philosophy, Poetry, Religion - Buddhist, Religion - Jewish, Science Fiction, Fantasy, Theology, Social, Academic & Spiritual
ISBN Prefix(es): 1-85756
Ultimate Parent Company: Junction Books Ltd
Imprints: Janus Books; Empirieus Books
Branch Office(s)
Paul & Company Publishers Consortium Inc, PO Box 442, Concord, MA 01742, United States, Bob Paul *Tel:* 508-369-3049
Distributed by Vine House Distribution Ltd
Foreign Rep(s): Richard Bowden (Scandinavia, Sweden); Paul & Co (US); Vine House Distributors (Ireland, UK & the continent)

PUBLISHERS UNITED KINGDOM

Japan Library, *imprint of* Routledge Curzon

Jarrold Publishing+
Division of Jarrold & Sons Ltd
Whitefriars, Norwich NR3 1TR
Tel: (01603) 763300 *Fax:* (01603) 662748
E-mail: publishing@jarrold.com
Web Site: www.jarrold-publishing.co.uk
Key Personnel
Man Dir, Rights & Permissions: Caroline Jarrold
Founded: 1770
Specialize in the publishing of books & calendars.
Subjects: Regional Interests, Travel
ISBN Prefix(es): 0-85306; 0-7117
Number of titles published annually: 30 Print
Total Titles: 250 Print
Imprints: Pathfinder
Distributor for MacMillan Way Association; Northern Ireland Tourist Board; Wales Tourist Board
Bookshop(s): Jarrolds, London St, Norwich NR2 1JF

John Blake Publishing Ltd+
3 Bramber Court, 2 Bramber Rd, London W14 9PB
Tel: (020) 7381 0666 *Fax:* (020) 7381 6868
E-mail: words@blake.co.uk
Key Personnel
Man Dir: John Blake *E-mail:* john@blake.co.uk
Deputy Man Dir: Rosie Ries *E-mail:* rosie@blake.co.uk
Executive Editor: Adam Parfitt *E-mail:* adam@blake.co.uk
Production Editor: Michelle Signore
Founded: 1991
Subjects: Biography, Criminology, Fiction, Nonfiction (General), Radio, TV
ISBN Prefix(es): 1-85782
Number of titles published annually: 60 Print
Imprints: Blake Publishing; Metro Publishing
Branch Office(s)
c/o PMA, 220 W 19 St, New York, NY 10011, United States
Distributed by Trafalgar Square Publishing (US)
Orders to: Little Hamptons, Faraday Close Durrington Worthing, West Sussex BN13 3RB

John Wiley & Sons, *imprint of* Wiley Europe Ltd

Johnson Publications Ltd+
130 Wigmore St, London W1H 0AT
Tel: (020) 7486 6757 *Fax:* (020) 7487 5436
Key Personnel
Dir: M A Murray-Pearce; Z M Pauncefort
Subjects: Advertising, Biography, Marketing
ISBN Prefix(es): 0-85307
Orders to: Spring Court, Abbots Rd, Abbots Langley, Herts WD5 0BJ

Jones & Bartlett International+
Barb House, Barb Mews, London W6 7PA
Tel: (01892) 539356 *Fax:* (01892) 614944
E-mail: j&b@class.co.uk
Web Site: www.jbpub.com
Key Personnel
International Rights: Richard Warner
Founded: 1983
Subjects: Biological Sciences, Computer Science, Earth Sciences, Geography, Geology, Health, Nutrition, Mathematics, Medicine, Nursing, Dentistry
ISBN Prefix(es): 0-86720
Parent Company: Jones & Bartlett Publishers, Inc, 40 Tall Pine Dr, Sudbury, MA 01776, United States
Orders to: Plymbridge Distributors, Plymbridge House, Estover Rd, Plymouth, Devon PL6 7PZ
Tel: (0752) 695745 *Fax:* (0752) 695699

John Jones Publishing Ltd+
Unit 12, Clwydfro Business Centre, Ruthin, North Wales LL15 1NJ
Tel: (01824) 707255 *Fax:* (01824) 705272
E-mail: johnjonespublishing.ltd@virgin.net
Web Site: www.johnjonespublishing.ltd.uk
Key Personnel
Man Dir: John Idris Jones
Founded: 1979
Specialize in paperbacks for the tourist market & books in English with a Welsh background.
Member of IPG.
Subjects: Biography, History, Travel
ISBN Prefix(es): 1-871083
Total Titles: 49 Print
Distributed by John Reed (Australia)
Foreign Rep(s): John Reed Book Distribution

Jordan Publishing Ltd
21 St Thomas St, Bristol BS1 6JS
Tel: (0117) 923 0600 *Fax:* (0117) 925 0486
E-mail: customerservice@jordanpublishing.co.uk
Web Site: www.jordanpublishing.co.uk
Telex: 449119
Key Personnel
Man Dir: Richard Hudson
Publishing Dir: Martin West
Managing Editor: Mollie Dickenson
Marketing Manager: David Chaplin
 E-mail: dchaplin@jordanpublishing.co.uk
Founded: 1863
Subjects: Accounting, Business, Law
ISBN Prefix(es): 0-85308
Parent Company: Jordan & Sons Ltd, Bristol
Imprints: Jordans; Family Law
Branch Office(s)
20-22 Bedford Row, London WC1R 4JS
 Tel: (020) 7400 3333 *Fax:* (020) 7400 3366

Jordans, *imprint of* Jordan Publishing Ltd

Michael Joseph, *imprint of* Penguin Books Ltd

Michael Joseph Ltd+
27 Wrights Lane, London W8 5TZ
Tel: (020) 7416 3000 *Fax:* (0201) 7416 3099
Telex: 917181
Key Personnel
Publishing Dir: Tom Weldon
Marketing Dir: John Bond
Export Sales Dir: Max Adam *E-mail:* max.adam@penguin.co.uk
Rights Dir: Sophie Brewer
Founded: 1936
Subjects: Biography, Fiction, History
ISBN Prefix(es): 0-7207; 0-7181; 1-85145
Parent Company: Penguin Books Ltd
Imprints: Mermaid
Warehouse: Penguin Group Distribution Ltd, 27 Wrights Lane, London W8 5TZ
Orders to: Penguin Group Distribution Ltd, Bath Rd, Harmondsworth, Middlesex UB7 0DA

Richard Joseph Publishers Ltd
PO Box 6123, Basingstoke, Hants RG25 2WE
Tel: (01256) 811314 *Fax:* (01256) 336362
E-mail: rjoe01@aol.com
Web Site: www.sheppardsdirectories.co.uk
Key Personnel
Man Dir: Richard Joseph
Founded: 1990
Reference books for the secondhand & antiquarian trades.
Member of IPG.
ISBN Prefix(es): 1-872699
Total Titles: 26 Print; 1 CD-ROM
Imprints: Sheppard
Branch Office(s)
Richard Joseph Publishers, PO Box 1350, State College, PA 16804-1350, United States
Membership(s): IPG

Jossey-Bass, *imprint of* Wiley Europe Ltd

Junior Funfax, *imprint of* Funfax Ltd

Kahn & Averill
9 Harrington Rd, London SW7 3ES
Tel: (020) 8743 3278 *Fax:* (020) 8743 3278
Key Personnel
Man Dir: M Kahn
Founded: 1947
Subjects: Music, Dance
ISBN Prefix(es): 0-900707; 1-871082
Shipping Address: Bailey Distribution Ltd, Mountfield Industrial Estate, New Romney, Kent TN28 8XU
Warehouse: Bailey Distribution Ltd, Mountfield Industrial Estate, New Rowney, Kent TN28 8XU
Orders to: Bailey Distribution Ltd, Mountfield Industrial Estate, New Romney, Kent TN28 8XU

Karnac Books Ltd+
58 Gloucester Rd, London SW7 4QY
Tel: (020) 7584 3303 *Fax:* (020) 7823 7743
E-mail: books@karnac.demon.co.uk
Web Site: www.karnacbooks.com
Key Personnel
Man Dir: Cesare D S Sacerdoti
Founded: 1950
Subjects: Psychology, Psychiatry, Social Sciences, Sociology
ISBN Prefix(es): 0-946439; 1-85575; 0-9501647; 0-9507146
Imprints: Maresfield Lib
Distributed by Taylor & Francis (USA)
Distributor for Analytic Press; Clunie Press; Institute of Marital Studies
Bookshop(s): 118 Finchley Rd, London NW3 5HJ
 Tel: (020) 8969 4454 *Fax:* (020) 8969 5585
 E-mail: shop@karnacbooks.com

Karnak House+
300 Westbourne Park Rd, London W11 1EH
Tel: (020) 7243 3620 *Fax:* (020) 7243 3620
E-mail: karnakhouse@aol.com
Key Personnel
Dir: A S Saakana; Seheri Stroude
Founded: 1979
Specialize in African & Caribbean studies worldwide.
Subjects: Anthropology, Education, History, Language Arts, Linguistics, Nonfiction (General), Philosophy, Religion - Other, Science (General), Egyptology
ISBN Prefix(es): 0-907015; 1-872596
Number of titles published annually: 10 Print
Total Titles: 100 Print
Imprints: The Intef Institute
Distributed by Turnaround
Orders to: 631 E 75 St, Chicago, IL 60619, United States, Ras Seko Tafari *Tel:* 773-651-9888 *Fax:* 773-651-9850

Kegan Paul International Ltd+
121 Bedford Court Mansions, Bedford Ave, London WC1B 3SW
Mailing Address: PO Box 256, London WC1B 3SW
Tel: (020) 7580 55;1 *Fax:* (020) 7436 0899
E-mail: books@keganpaul.com
Web Site: www.keganpaul.com
Key Personnel
Chairman: Peter Hopkins
Editorial Dir: Kaori O'Connor
Founded: 1871
Subjects: Archaeology, Architecture & Interior Design, Art, Photography, Travel, Africa, Arabic Linguistics, Asian Studies, China, Egyptology, Environmental Studies & Natural Science, International Studies & Law, Islam, Japan, Ko-

rea, Literature & Poetry, Middle East, Oriental Philosophy & Religion, Pacific
ISBN Prefix(es): 0-7103
Number of titles published annually: 40 Print
Total Titles: 520 Print
U.S. Office(s): Columbia University Press, 562 W 113 St, New York, NY 10025, United States *Tel:* 212-666-1000 *Fax:* 212-316-3100
Distributed by Turpin Ltd
Shipping Address: John Wiley & Sons Ltd, Southern Cross Trading Estate, One Oldlands Way, Bognor Regis, West Sussex PO22 9SA, Contact: Diana Butterly *Tel:* (01243) 779777 *Fax:* (01243) 843303
Warehouse: John Wiley & Sons Ltd, Southern Cross Trading Estate, Oldlands Way Bagnor Regis, West Sussex PO22 9SA, Contact: Lori Powell *Tel:* (01243) 843223 *Fax:* (01243) 820250
Orders to: John Wiley & Sons Ltd, Southern Cross Trading Estate, One Oldlands Way, Bognor Regis, West Sussex PO22 9SA, Contact: Diane Butterly *Tel:* (01243) 843273 *Fax:* (01243) 843303
Columbia University Press, 61 W 62nd St, New York, NY 10023, United States *Tel:* 914-591-9111 *E-mail:* ms1004@columbia.edu *Web Site:* www.columbia.edu/cu/cup (North America)

Kelly's
Windsor Court, East Grinstead House, East Grinstead, West Sussex RH19 1XA
Tel: (01342) 335699 *Fax:* (01342) 335825
E-mail: kellys.mktg@reedinfo.co.uk
Web Site: www.kellysearch.com
Telex: 95127
Key Personnel
Publishing Dr: Brian Gallagher
Founded: 1799
Member of Directory Publishers Association & European Directory Publishers Association.
Subjects: Business
ISBN Prefix(es): 0-610
Warehouse: Vale Packaging, 420 Vale Rd, Tonbridge, Kent TN9 1TO

Kemps Publishing Ltd+
11 The Swan Courtyard, Charles Edward Rd, Yardley, Birmingham B26 1BU
Tel: (0121) 765 4144 *Fax:* (0121) 706 1408
E-mail: info@kempsgold.co.uk
Web Site: www.kempsgold.co.uk
Key Personnel
Contact: Marisha Gorcewicz
Founded: 1912
ISBN Prefix(es): 0-86259; 0-900273; 0-901268; 0-905255

The Kenilworth Press Ltd+
Addington, Buckingham MK18 2JR
Tel: (01296) 715101 *Fax:* (01296) 715148
E-mail: mail@kenilworthpress.co.uk
Web Site: www.kenilworthpress.co.uk
Key Personnel
Man Dir: David Blunt *E-mail:* david.blunt@kenilworthpress.co.uk
Dir: Deirdre Blunt
Founded: 1989
Publisher of instructional equestrian books.
Also acts as official publisher to The British Horse Society.
Subjects: Animals, Pets, Natural History, Sports, Athletics, Veterinary Science
ISBN Prefix(es): 1-872082; 0-901366; 1-872119
Number of titles published annually: 10 Print
Total Titles: 100 Print
Imprints: Threshold
Divisions: Threshold Books
Distributed by Half Halt Press Inc (USA)
Distributor for Half Halt Press Inc
Warehouse: Hoddle Doyle Meadows, Station Rd, Linton, Cambs CB1 6UX

Kenyon-Deane, *imprint of* Cressrelles Publishing Company Ltd

Kenyon-Deane+
10 Station Rd, Industrial Estate, Colwall, Nr Malvern, Worcs WR13 6RN
Tel: (01684) 540154 *Fax:* (01684) 540154
Key Personnel
Man Dir: Leslie Smith
Founded: 1930
Specialize in plays for women.
Subjects: Drama, Theater
ISBN Prefix(es): 0-7155
Total Titles: 400 Print
Parent Company: Cressrelles Publishing Co Ltd
Distributor for Anchorage Press (Europe)

Kershaw Publishing Co Ltd
3 Henrietta St, London WC2E 8LU
Tel: (020) 7240 0856 *Fax:* (020) 7764 8218
E-mail: chris@e-d-c.co.uk
Key Personnel
Man Dir: Peter K Taylor
Founded: 1969
Subjects: Mathematics, Philosophy, Social Sciences, Sociology
ISBN Prefix(es): 0-901665
Warehouse: H T Book Distribution, Bolholt, Warsaw Road, Bury, Lancs BL8 1RP
Orders to: H T Book Distribution, Bolholt, Warsaw Road, Bury, Lancs BL8 1RP

Kidhaven Press, *imprint of* Gale Research

Hilda King Educational+
Ashwells Manor Dr, Penn, Bucks HP10 8EU
Tel: (01494) 813947; (01494) 817947 *Fax:* (01494) 813947
E-mail: hildaking@clara.co.uk; orders@hildaking.co.uk
Web Site: www.hildaking.clara.net
Key Personnel
Director: Ron King *E-mail:* ron@hilda-king.co.uk
Contact: Hilda King *E-mail:* hilda@hilda-king.co.uk
Founded: 1990
Specializes in photocopiable educational resources.
Member of Publishers Association.
Subjects: Geography, Geology, History, Mathematics, Audio Tapes (phonics); English & French Language; English & French, nursery
ISBN Prefix(es): 1-873533
Total Titles: 100 Print; 8 Audio
Distributed by Morris Enterprises

Laurence King Publishing Ltd+
Formerly Calmann & King Ltd
71 Great Russell St, London WC1B 3BP
Tel: (020) 7430 8850 *Fax:* (020) 7430 8880
E-mail: enquiries@laurenceking.co.uk
Web Site: www.laurenceking.co.uk
Key Personnel
Chairman: Robin Hyman
Man Dir: Laurence King
Editorial Dir, Professional Trade Division: Philip Cooper
Editorial Dir, College & Fine Art: Lee Ripley Greenfield
Rights Manager: Janet Pilch *E-mail:* janet@laurenceking.co.uk
Foreign Rights: Sarah Davis *E-mail:* sarah@laurenceking.co.uk
Founded: 1976
Also acts as designer & producer of high-quality illustrated books; specialize in international co-editions.
Subjects: Architecture & Interior Design, Art, Fashion, Film, Video, House & Home, Religion - Other
ISBN Prefix(es): 1-85669
Total Titles: 200 Print
Warehouse: Thames & Hudson Ltd, 44 Clockhouse Rd, Farnborough, Hants GU14 7QZ

Kingfisher, *imprint of* Kingfisher Publications Plc

Kingfisher Publications Plc+
New Penderel House, 283-288 High Holborn, London WC1V 7HZ
Tel: (020) 7903 9999 *Fax:* (020) 7242 4979
E-mail: sales@kingfisherpub.com
Web Site: www.kingfisherpub.com
Key Personnel
Finance Dir: Geraud de Durand
Production Dir: John Richards
UK Trade, Export & Marketing Dir: Robert Pearce
Export Sales Manager: Melissa Johnson
International Sales & Marketing Dir: John Midgley
Foreign Rights Dir: Hilary Downie *E-mail:* hdownie@kingfisherpub.co.uk
Founded: 1974
Subjects: Regional Interests
ISBN Prefix(es): 0-7523; 0-86272; 1-85697; 1-85296
Number of titles published annually: 85 Print
Parent Company: Vivendi Universal Publishing, 31 rue du Colisee, 75383 Paris, France
Imprints: Kingfisher
Distributed by Larousse Kingfisher Cambers Inc (USA); Macmillan Distribution Ltd (England); Pansing Distribution SDN BHD (Brunei, Indonesia, Malaysia, Singapore); Paramount Books (PVT) Ltd (Pakistan); Publishers Associates Ltd (Hong Kong); Rupa & Co (India); Scholastic Australia Ltd (Australia); South Pacific Books (Imports) Ltd (New Zealand); Struik Book Distributors (South Africa)
Foreign Rep(s): Ashton International Marketing Services (China, Japan, Korea, Taiwan, Thailand); Humphrys Roberts Associates (Central America, South America, West Indies); Walton Marketing Services (Europe, Israel); Peter Ward Book Exports (Middle East)
Warehouse: Macmillan Distribution Ltd, Brunel Rd, Houndsmill, Basingstoke, Hants R921 2XS
Orders to: Macmillan Distribution Ltd, Brunel Rd, Houndsmill, Basingstoke, Hants R921 2XS

King's Fund Publishing+
11-13 Cavendish Sq, London W1G 0AN
Tel: (020) 7307 2400 *Fax:* (020) 7307 2801
E-mail: libweb@kingsfund.org.uk
Web Site: www.kingsfund.org.uk
Key Personnel
Head of Communications & Marketing: Stephen Lustig *Tel:* (020) 7307-2584 *E-mail:* slustig@kingsfund.org.uk
Founded: 1897
Health & social care titles mainly for professionals, managers, academics & libraries.
Not for profit charitable foundation.
Subjects: Health, Nutrition, Social Sciences, Sociology
ISBN Prefix(es): 1-85551; 1-85717; 1-870551; 1-870607; 1-873883
Number of titles published annually: 30 Print
Total Titles: 200 Print
Online services available through World Wide Web.
Parent Company: King's Fund
U.S. Office(s): Transaction Publishers, Contact: Mary Curtis *Tel:* 908-445-2280 *E-mail:* mcurtis@transactionpub.com

Jessica Kingsley Publishers+
116 Pentonville Rd, London N1 9JB

PUBLISHERS

UNITED KINGDOM

Tel: (020) 7833 2307 *Fax:* (020) 7837 2917
E-mail: post@jkp.com
Web Site: www.jkp.com
Key Personnel
Man Dir & International Rights: Jessica Kingsley
  E-mail: jessica@jkp.com
Sales & Marketing: Petra Green
Founded: 1987
Member of Independent Publishers Guild, Publishers Association.
Subjects: Behavioral Sciences, Child Care & Development, Criminology, Disability, Special Needs, Education, Medicine, Nursing, Dentistry, Psychology, Psychiatry, Social Sciences, Sociology
ISBN Prefix(es): 1-85302
Total Titles: 650 Print; 3 CD-ROM; 3 Audio
Imprints: Pentn Press
Distributed by Astam Books Pty Ltd (Australia & New Zealand); Book Promotions (Pty) Ltd (South Africa); Irwin Publishing (Canada); Publishers Marketing Services (Singapore, Malaysia, Brunei & Indonesia); Taylor & Francis Inc (USA); United Publishers Services (Japan); Viva Marketing (India)
Distributor for Paul H Brooke & MacLennan & Petty (UK); Love Publishing (UK)
Foreign Rep(s): Asia Publishers Service Ltd (China, Hong Kong, Korea, Philippines, Taiwan); Bill Baird (Scotland); Book Bird (Pakistan); Book Representation & Distribution (England, Northern Ireland); Brookside Publishing Services (Ireland); Andrew Durnell (Europe); STM Pte Ltd (Thailand)

Kingsway Publications+
26-28 Lottbridge Drove, Eastbourne, East Sussex BN23 6NT
Tel: (01323) 437700 *Fax:* (01323) 411970
E-mail: books@kingsway.co.uk
Web Site: www.kingsway.co.uk
Key Personnel
Chief Executive Officer: John Paculabo
Publishing Dir: Richard Herkes
List Administrator: Cathy Williams
Foreign Rights: Chris Jackson
Founded: 1977
Publisher & supplier of Christian books, music, crafts & children's ministry resources.
Member of Publishers Association.
Subjects: Religion - Protestant, Religion - Other, Theology
ISBN Prefix(es): 0-86065; 0-85476
Parent Company: Kingsway Communications Ltd
Associate Companies: David C Cook
Distributor for Barbour (USA/Canada); Bethany House (USA/Canada); Chariot Victor (USA/Canada)
Orders to: STL Wholesale, PO Box 300, Kingstown Industrial Estates, Kingstown Broadway, Carlisle CA3 0JH *Fax:* (01228) 514949
Membership(s): Publishers' Association

Kinship Library, see Centaur Press (1954)

KIT Press - Royal Tropical Institute
c/o Intermediate Technology Publications, 103-105 Southampton Row, London WC1B 4HH
Fax: (020) 7236 9761
Subjects: Agriculture, Anthropology, Art, Developing Countries, Health, Nutrition
ISBN Prefix(es): 90-6832
Warehouse: Plymbridge

Kluwer Academic/Human Sciences Press, *imprint of* Kluwer Academic/Plenum Publishers

Kluwer Academic/Plenum Publishers+
Imprint of Kluwer Academic Publishers
241 Borough High St, London SE1 1GB
Tel: (020) 7940 7494 *Fax:* (020) 7940 7495
E-mail: mail@plenum.co.uk
Web Site: www.wkap.nl
Key Personnel
Man Dir: Dr Ken Derham *E-mail:* k.derham@plenum.co.uk
Editor: Joanna Lawrence
Founded: 1960
European Editorial office of Kluwer academic/Plenum Publishers of New Turk.
Member of PA & STM.
Subjects: Biological Sciences, Chemistry, Chemical Engineering, Communications, Computer Science, Electronics, Electrical Engineering, Mathematics, Physical Sciences, Physics, Social Sciences, Sociology
ISBN Prefix(es): 0-306
Imprints: Consultants Bureau (journals); Kluwer Academic/Human Sciences Press (journals); Maik Nauka/Interperiodica (journals)
U.S. Office(s): 233 Spring St, 7th floor, New York, NY 10013-1522, United States *Tel:* 212-620-8000
Orders to: Distribution Center, PO Box 322, 3300AH Dordrecht, Netherlands
  Tel: (078) 6392392 *Fax:* (078) 6546474
  E-mail: orderdept@wkap.nl *Web Site:* www.wkap.nl (Except North, South & Central America)
Kluwer Academic Publishers, Assinippi Park, 101 Philip Dr, Norwell, MA 02061, United States *Tel:* 781-871-6600 *Fax:* 781-871-6528
  E-mail: kluwer@wkap.com *Web Site:* www.wkap.nl (North, South & Central America)

Knight Features+
20 Crescent Grove, London SW4 7AH
Tel: (020) 7622 1522 *Fax:* (020) 7622 1522
E-mail: peter@knightfeatures.co.uk
Web Site: www.knightfeatures.co.uk
Key Personnel
Dir, Proprietor: Peter Knight *E-mail:* peter@knightfeatures.co.uk
Associate: Ann King-Hall; Samantha Ferris; Gaby Martin; Andrew Knight
Founded: 1985
Specialize in full-length manuscripts, theater, films, television, radio, strip cartoons, puzzles & serializations; work in conjunction with agents worldwide Knight Features (no Short Stories, Poetry, Science Fiction or Cookery).
Subjects: Biography, Humor, Nonfiction (General), Sports, Athletics
Associate Companies: Peter Knight Agency

Knockabout Comics+
Unit 24, 10 Acklam Rd, London W10 5QZ
Tel: (020) 8969 2945 *Fax:* (020) 8968 7614
E-mail: knockcomic@aol.com
Key Personnel
Man Dir: Tony Bennett *E-mail:* tonyknock@aol.com
Distribution Manager: Joe Toussaint
International Rights: Lora Fountain *Tel:* (014) 3562196 *Fax:* (014) 3482272
Founded: 1975
Subjects: Gardening, Plants, Health, Nutrition, Humor, Social Sciences, Sociology, Specialize in comic books, graphic novels & drug information
ISBN Prefix(es): 0-86166
Number of titles published annually: 6 Print
Total Titles: 110 Print
Online services available
  through www.knockabout.com.
Parent Company: Toskanex Ltd
Imprints: Fanny; Hassle Free Press
Distributor for Last Gasp (North America); Quick American Archives (North America); Quick Trading Co (North America); Rip Off Press (excludes USA & Canada)
Foreign Rights: Lora Fountain (France & Spain, Germany, Holland)

Know Alls, *imprint of* Funfax Ltd

Kogan Page Ltd+
120 Pentonville Rd, London N1 9JN
Tel: (020) 7278 0433 *Fax:* (020) 7278 0433
E-mail: kpinfo@kogan-page.co.uk; kpsales@kogan-page.co.uk; orders@kogan-page.co.uk
Web Site: www.kogan-page.co.uk
Key Personnel
Man Dir: Philip Kogan
Publishing Dir, Professional & Reference: Pauline Goodwin
Publishing Dir, Training & Education: Philip Mudd
Production Dir: Peter Chadwick
Sales & Marketing Dir: Julie McNair
  E-mail: jmcnair@kogan-page.co.uk
Editor: Linda Batham; Philip Mudd
Finance: Gordon Watts
Rights Manager: Ben Heywood *Tel:* (020) 7843 1965 *E-mail:* bheywood@kogan-page.co.uk
Export Manager: Lynda Moynihan
Founded: 1967
Specialize in periodicals.
Subjects: Business, Career Development, Education, Finance, Management, Marketing, Self-Help, Transportation
ISBN Prefix(es): 0-85038; 1-85091; 0-7494
Subsidiaries: Earthscan Publications Ltd (environmental)
Branch Office(s)
Kogan Page India, c/o Viva Books, 432713 Ansari Rd, New Delhi 10002, India
U.S. Office(s): Kogan Page USA Office, 22 Broad St, Suite 34, Milford, CT 06460, United States
  Web Site: www.earthscan.co.uk
Distributed by Stylus Publishing Inc (USA)
Distributor for American Bankers Association (excluding North & South America)
Warehouse: Littlehampton Book Services Ltd, Faraday Close, Durrington, Worthing, West Sussex BN13 3RB *Tel:* (01903) 828 800 *Fax:* (01903) 828 801 *E-mail:* orders@lbsltd.co.uk

Kuperard+
Imprint of Bravo Ltd
311 Ballards Lane, London, England N12 8LY
Tel: (020) 8446 2440 *Fax:* (020) 8446 2441
Web Site: www.kuperard.co.uk
Key Personnel
Publishing: J Kuperard *E-mail:* kuperard@grove.clara.net
Sales & Marketing: Martin Kaye
  E-mail: martin@bravo.clara.net
Subjects: Education, Travel
ISBN Prefix(es): 1-85733
Number of titles published annually: 30 Print
Total Titles: 300 Print

Ladybird, *imprint of* Penguin Books Ltd

Ladybird Books+
80 Strand, London WC2R 0RL
Tel: (020) 7010 2900 *Fax:* (01509) 234672
Web Site: www.ladybird.co.uk
Telex: 341347
Key Personnel
Man Dir: Michael Herridge
Art Dir: Douglas Wilson
Sales Manager, Regional Export & Rights & Coeditions Manager: Yvonne Francis
Sales Manager, Regional Export: Nina Bueno del Carpio
Sales Manager: Ingrid Little
Marketing Dir: Diana Olivant
International Sales Dir: David King
UK Sales Dir: Deborah Wright
Product Manager: Michelle Thurston
Founded: (s)
Children's book publisher.

UNITED KINGDOM

Subjects: Education, English as a Second Language, Fiction, History, Natural History, Nonfiction (General)
ISBN Prefix(es): 0-7214
Parent Company: Penguin Group
Imprints: Disney
Divisions: Ladybird Disney Books
Foreign Rep(s): Penguin Books Deutchland (Austria, Germany); Penguin Books Netherlands (Holland); Penguin Books S A (Spain & Portugal); Penguin France (France); Penguin Italia (Italy); Sezai Selek Sokak 10/2 (Bulgaria, Romania, Turkey)

Jay Landesman+
8 Duncan Terrace, London N1 8BZ
Tel: (020) 7837 7290 *Fax:* (020) 7833 1925
Key Personnel
Man Dir: Jay Landesman
Founded: 1977
Subjects: Biography, Humor, Poetry
ISBN Prefix(es): 0-905150
Total Titles: 160 Print
Associate Companies: Polytantric Press
Imprints: Golden Handshake; Polytantric Press

Landy Publishing
3 Staining Rise, Staining, Blackpool, Lancs FY3 0BU
Tel: (01253) 895678 *Fax:* (01253) 895678
Key Personnel
Owner: Bob Dobson
Founded: 1981
Book publisher of regional titles.
Subjects: History, Regional Interests
ISBN Prefix(es): 1-872895
Number of titles published annually: 6 Print
Total Titles: 80 Print

Allen Lane, *imprint of* Penguin Books Ltd

Lang Syne Publishers Ltd+
120 Carstairs St, Dalmarnock, Glasgow G40 4JD
E-mail: enquiries@scottish-memories.co.uk
Web Site: www.scottish-memories.co.uk/langsyne/
Key Personnel
Dir: Kenneth W Laird
Founded: 1975
Subjects: Business, History, Humor, Music, Dance, Mysteries
ISBN Prefix(es): 0-946264; 1-85217
Branch Office(s)
Scott's Highland Enterprises, 1646 Beckworth Ave, London, ON N5V 2K7, Canada *Tel:* 519-453-0892 *Fax:* 519-453-6303
Scottish Flair, Quean Beyan, NSW *Tel:* (06) 2977-8780

Language Teaching Publications+
114A Church Rd, Hove BN3 2EB
Tel: (01273) 736344 *Fax:* (01273) 775361
E-mail: ltp@ltpwebsite.com
Web Site: www.ltpwebsite.com
Telex: 250 Elc
Key Personnel
Man Dir: Michael Lewis; Jimmie Hill
Founded: 1978
Alta Book Center, 14 Adrian Court, Burlingame, CA, United States 94010; Delta Systems Inc, 1400 Miller Parkway, McHenry, IL, United States 60050-7030.
Subjects: English as a Second Language, English as a foreign language
ISBN Prefix(es): 0-906717; 1-899396
Parent Company: Heinle Publishers, 25 Thomson Pl, Boston, MA 02210, United States
Imprints: LTP

Roger Lascelles+
47 York Rd, Brentford, Middlesex TW8 0QP
Tel: (0181) 8470935 *Fax:* (0181) 5683886
Key Personnel
Publisher: Roger Lascelles
Founded: 1970
Member of International Map Trade Association.
Subjects: Travel
ISBN Prefix(es): 0-903909; 1-872815; 1-85879
Imprints: Daily Telegraph (map service)
Distributor for LAC (Italy); Ravenstein (Germany)

The Latchmere Press
6 Dundalk Rd, London SE4 2JL
Tel: (020) 7639 7282
Key Personnel
Dir: Angela Cornforth
Founded: 1996
Subjects: Education
ISBN Prefix(es): 1-901090

Laurel, *imprint of* Novello & Co Ltd

Law Pack Publishing Ltd
76-89 Alscot Rd, London SE1 3AW
Tel: (020) 7394 4040 *Fax:* (020) 7394 4041
E-mail: mailbox@lawpack.co.uk
Web Site: www.lawpack.co.uk
Key Personnel
Man Dir: Thomas Coles *Tel:* (02) 7394 4050
Editor: Jamie Ross
Founded: 1993
Self-help legal publisher.
Subjects: Business, How-to, Law, Management, Self-Help, Taxes
ISBN Prefix(es): 1-898217; 1-902646

Lawrence & Wishart+
99a Wallis Rd, London E9 5LN
Tel: (020) 8533 2506 *Fax:* (020) 8533 7369
E-mail: office@l-w-bks.demon.co.uk
Web Site: www.l-w-bks.co.uk
Key Personnel
Man Editor: Sally J Davison *E-mail:* sally@l-w-bks.demon.co.uk
Sales & Publicity: Lindsay Thomas
Financial Dir: Avis Greenaway *E-mail:* avis@l-w-bks.demon.co.uk
Permissions: Vanna Derosas *E-mail:* vanna@l-w-bks.demon.co.uk
Founded: 1936
Subjects: Economics, Education, Environmental Studies, Ethnicity, Film, Video, Gay & Lesbian, Human Relations, Labor, Industrial Relations, Social Sciences, Sociology
ISBN Prefix(es): 0-85315
Distributed by New York University Press
Warehouse: Central Books Ltd *Tel:* (020) 8986 4854 *Fax:* (020) 8533 5821 *E-mail:* orders@centralbooks.com
Orders to: Troika Ltd, United House, North Rd, London N7 9DP *Tel:* (020) 7619 0800 *Fax:* (020) 7619 0810

LDA-Living & Learning (Cambridge) Ltd+
Abbeygate House, East Rd, Cambridge, Cambs CB1 1DB
Tel: (01223) 357788 *Fax:* (01223) 460557
E-mail: internationalsales@mcgraw-hill.com
Key Personnel
Man Dir: Carole Mills
Marketing Manager: Jayne Harris *E-mail:* jayne_harris@mcgraw-hill.com
Founded: 1973
Publisher of educational books, resources & games.
Subjects: Child Care & Development, Education
ISBN Prefix(es): 1-85503; 0-905114
Number of titles published annually: 60 Print
Total Titles: 2,000 Print
Parent Company: McGraw-Hill Children's Publishing
Imprints: LDA Multimedia
Branch Office(s)
Living & Learning, 5-7 Pembroke Ave, Waterbeach, Cambs, Anita Low *Tel:* (01223) 864886

LDA Multimedia, *imprint of* LDA-Living & Learning (Cambridge) Ltd

Learning Development Aids+
Abbeygate House, East Rd, Cambridge, Cambs CB1 1DB
Tel: (01223) 365445 *Fax:* (01223) 460557
E-mail: ldaorders@compuserve.com
Key Personnel
Man Dir: Carol Mills
Marketing Dir: Ms Catherine Jeffrey
Founded: 1980
Publish learning materials for numeracy, language, literacy & motivation for primary school children & those with special needs.
Subjects: Health, Nutrition
ISBN Prefix(es): 1-85503
Parent Company: Living & Learning (Cambridge) Ltd
Branch Office(s)
4383 Hecktown Rd, Unit GA1, Bethelem, PA 18017, United States
Bookshop(s): Chris Lloyd Sales & Marketing Services, 463 Ashley Rd, Poole, Dorset BH14 OAX
Shipping Address: Duke St, Cambs PE13 2AE
Warehouse: Duke St, Wisbech, Cambs PE13 2AE
Orders to: Duke St, Wisbech, Cambs PE13 2AE

Learning Matters, Crucial, *imprint of* Learning Matters Ltd

Learning Matters Ltd
58 Wonford Rd, Exeter EX2 4LQ
Tel: (01392) 215560 *Fax:* (01392) 215561
E-mail: info@learningmatters.co.uk
Web Site: www.learningmatters.co.uk
Key Personnel
Dir: Jonathan Harris *E-mail:* jonathan@learningmatters.co.uk
Founded: 1999
Publishers of training resources for teachers & course books for university students.
Subjects: Business, Computer Science, Education, Psychology, Psychiatry
ISBN Prefix(es): 1-903300; 1-903337
Number of titles published annually: 25 Print
Total Titles: 40 Print
Imprints: Learning Matters, Crucial
Distributor for Pippin Publishing Corporation, Canada
Membership(s): IPG

Learning Together+
FREEPOST, Belfast 3509, Holywood BT18 9BR
Tel: (020) 90402086 *Fax:* (2890) 402086
E-mail: info@learningtogether.co.uk
Web Site: www.learningtogether.co.uk
Key Personnel
Contact: Janet McConkey
Founded: 1989
Specialize in verbal & nonverbal reasoning.
Subjects: Education, Mathematics, Science (General)
ISBN Prefix(es): 1-873385
Orders to: Mallard Marketing, Woodside Church Hill, West End Southampton 5030 3AU *Tel:* (02380) 482528 *Fax:* (02380) 361855 *Web Site:* www.learningtogether.co.uk

Legal Action Group+
242 Pentonville Rd, London N1 9UN
Tel: (020) 7833 2931 *Fax:* (020) 7837 6094
E-mail: lag@lag.org.uk
Web Site: www.lag.org.uk
Key Personnel
Chief Executive: Andrew Heywood

International Rights: Jonathan Pearce
  E-mail: jpearce@lag.org.uk
Founded: 1972
Member of Independent Publishers' Guild.
Subjects: Law
ISBN Prefix(es): 0-905099
Total Titles: 30 Print

Legend, *imprint of* Random House UK Ltd

Leicester University Press, *imprint of* Cassell & Co

Leicester University Press, *imprint of* The Continuum International Publishing Group Ltd

Lemos & Crane+
20 Pond Sq, London N6 6BA
Tel: (020) 8348 8263 *Fax:* (020) 8347 5740
E-mail: paulc@lemos.demon.co.uk
Web Site: www.lemosandcrane.co.uk
Key Personnel
Marketing Manager: Carwyn Gravell
Founded: 1996
Subjects: Law, Management
ISBN Prefix(es): 1-898001
Warehouse: 20 Pond Sq, London N6 6BA
Orders to: Plymbridge Distributors Ltd, Estover Rd, Plymouth PL6 7PZ

Lennard Publishing, *imprint of* Queen Anne Press

Letterbox Library
71-73 Allen Rd, London N16 8RY
Tel: (020) 7503 4801 *Fax:* (020) 7503 4800
E-mail: info@letterboxlibrary.com
Web Site: www.letterboxlibrary.com
Key Personnel
Dir: Maikim Stern
Publicity & Marketing: Kerry Mason
Founded: 1983
Specialize in mulitcultural & non-sexist books.
Subjects: Art, Developing Countries, Disability, Special Needs, English as a Second Language, Environmental Studies, Ethnicity, Fiction, Foreign Countries, Gay & Lesbian, Geography, Geology, Health, Nutrition, History, Human Relations, Nonfiction (General), Religion - Hindu, Religion - Islamic, Religion - Jewish, Religion - Protestant, Religion - Other

Letterland International Ltd
33 New Rd, Barton, Cambs CB3 7AY
Tel: (01223) 262675 *Fax:* (01223) 264126
E-mail: info@letterland.com
Web Site: www.letterland.com
Key Personnel
Man Dir: Mark Wendon
Founded: 1985
Subjects: Education, Language Arts, Linguistics
ISBN Prefix(es): 0-907345; 1-86209
Distributed by Harper Collins Publishers (UK & Eire)

Lettermen, *imprint of* Funfax Ltd

Letts Educational
Member of Granada Media Group
The Chiswick Centre, 414 Chiswick High Rd, London W4 5TF
Tel: (020) 8996 3333 *Fax:* (020) 8742 8390
E-mail: mail@lettsed.co.uk
Web Site: www.lettsed.co.uk
Key Personnel
Man Dir: Richard Carr
Production Dir: Julia Millette
Administrative Dir: Andrew Riddle
Founded: 1972
Subjects: Accounting, Computer Science, Economics, Finance, Labor, Industrial Relations, Law, Library & Information Sciences, Management, Marketing, Mathematics
ISBN Prefix(es): 1-85805
Parent Company: BPP Holdings PLC, Aldine House, Aldine Pl, London W12 8 AW
Subsidiaries: LETTS Educational; BPP Publishing; Blackstone Press
Warehouse: c/o The Trade Counter Ltd, The Airfield, Mendlesham IP14 5NA

J D Lewis & Sons Ltd, see Gomer Press (J D Lewis & Sons Ltd)

John Libbey & Co Ltd+
13 Smiths Yard, Summerly St, London SW18 4HR
Tel: (020) 8947 2777 *Fax:* (020) 8947 2664
E-mail: johnlibbey@aol.com
Web Site: www.johnlibbey.com
Key Personnel
Man Dir & Publisher: John Libbey
Marketing Manager: Angie Needs
Founded: 1979
Subjects: Film, Video, Medicine, Nursing, Dentistry, Medical (specializes in Epilepsy, Neurology, nuclear medicine) & Cinema/Animation
ISBN Prefix(es): 0-86196; 1-86462
Total Titles: 100 Print
Subsidiaries: John Libbey Eurotext Ltd
Branch Office(s)
John Libbey & Co PTY Ltd, Level 10, 15-17 Young St, Sydney, NSW 2000, Australia *Tel:* (02) 9251 4099 *Fax:* (02) 9251 4428 *E-mail:* jlsydney@mpx.com.au
U.S. Office(s): John Libbey at Demos Medical Publishing, 386 Park Ave S, Suite 201, New York, NY 10016, United States *Tel:* 212-683-0072 *Fax:* 212-683-0118
Distributed by Butterworth-Heinemann (Medical titles only); Indiana University Press (North America - film/cinema/animation titles only); Tower Books Wholesalers Pty Ltd (Asia & Southern Hemisphere)
Orders to: Plymbridge Distributors Ltd, Plymbridge House, Estover Rd, Plymouth PL6 7PY *Tel:* (01752) 202301 *Fax:* (01752) 202333 *E-mail:* orders@plymbridge.com (Europe)

Liberty+
21 Tabard St, London SE1 4LA
Tel: (020) 7403 3888 *Fax:* (020) 7407 5354
E-mail: info@liberty-human-rights.org.uk
Web Site: www.liberty-human-rights.org.uk
Key Personnel
Dir: John Wadham
Founded: 1934
Subjects: Law
ISBN Prefix(es): 0-901108; 0-946088
Associate Companies: Civil Liberties Trust

Library & Information Statistics Unit
Loughborough University, Loughborough, Leics LE11 3TU
Tel: (01509) 223071 *Fax:* (01509) 223072
E-mail: lisu@lboro.ac.uk
Web Site: www.lboro.ac.uk/departments/dis/lisu/lisuhp.html
Key Personnel
Dir: Dr J Eric Davies *E-mail:* j.e.davies@lboro.ac.uk
Deputy Dir & Senior Statistician: Claire Creaser
Research Associate & Copyright Adviser: Dr Sally Maynard
Founded: 1987
Previously Library Management Research Unit (1969-79) & Centre for Library & Information Management (1979-87).
Subjects: Library & Information Sciences, Management, Public Administration
ISBN Prefix(es): 0-948848; 0-904924; 1-901786
Total Titles: 33 Print
Parent Company: Department of Information Science
Ultimate Parent Company: Loughborough University

Library Association Publishing, see Facet Publishing

Libris Ltd+
10 Burghley Rd, London NW5 1UE
Tel: (020) 7482 2390 *Fax:* (020) 7485 4220
Key Personnel
Dir: Nicholas Jacobs
Founded: 1986
Specialize in German-language literature in translation (pre-1945, from Goethe) & in German author studies (biography, criticism); German dictionaries.
Subjects: Biography, Fiction, History, Literature, Literary Criticism, Essays, Poetry
ISBN Prefix(es): 1-870352
Number of titles published annually: 4 Print
Total Titles: 47 Print
Distributed by Paul & Co Publishers Consortium Inc (USA)
Shipping Address: Bookshippers Association Inc, 38 Wilks Ave, Unit 3b, Dartford Trade Park, Hawley Rd, Dartford, Kent DA1 1JS *Tel:* (01322) 274414 *Fax:* (01322) 274415
Orders to: Central Books Ltd, 99 Wallis Rd, London E9 5LN, Mr Bill Norris *Tel:* (020) 8986 4854 *Fax:* (020) 8533 5821

Frances Lincoln Ltd+
4 Torriano Mews, Torriano Ave, London NW5 2RZ
Tel: (020) 7284 4009 *Fax:* (020) 7485 0490
E-mail: rowans@frances-lincoln.com
Telex: 21376
Key Personnel
Man Dir: John Nicoll
Editorial Dir, Adult Nonfiction: Anne Fraser
Editorial Dir, Children's: Janetta Otter-Barry
Production: Siobhan Egan; Kim Oliver
Sales Dir: Martin Destricher
Rights: Andrew Dunn; Carey Smith
Founded: 1978
Subjects: Architecture & Interior Design, Child Care & Development, Crafts, Games, Hobbies, Gardening, Plants, Health, Nutrition, House & Home
ISBN Prefix(es): 0-7112; 0-906459
Orders to: Bookpoint Ltd, 39 Milton Park, Abingdon, Oxon OX14 4TD

Linden Press, see Centaur Press (1954)

Linen Hall Library+
17 Donegall Sq N, Belfast BT1 5GB
Tel: (028) 9032 1707 *Fax:* (028) 9043 8586
E-mail: info@linenhall.com
Web Site: www.linenhall.com
Key Personnel
President: Dr Maurna Crozier
Librarian: Mr John Gray; Ms Yvonne Murphy
Deputy Librarian: Mr John Killen
Reference Librarian: Mr Gerry Healey
Systems Librarian: Mrs Linda Dale
General Services Manager: Mrs Patricia Saunders
Finance Officer: Ms Susan Finlay
Founded: 1788
Subjects: Biography, History, Library & Information Sciences, Literature, Literary Criticism, Essays
ISBN Prefix(es): 0-9508985; 1-900921
Imprints: Linen Hall Review

Linen Hall Review, *imprint of* Linen Hall Library

UNITED KINGDOM

Linford Mystery Library Series, see Ulverscroft Large Print Books Ltd

Linford Romance Library Series, see Ulverscroft Large Print Books Ltd

Linford Western Library Series, see Ulverscroft Large Print Books Ltd

Linguaphone Institute Ltd+
Liongate Enterprise Park, 80 Morden Rd, Mitcham CR4 4PH
Tel: (020) 8687 6000 *Fax:* (020) 8687 6310
E-mail: ads@linguaphone.co.uk (Advertising); cst@linguaphone.co.uk (Customer Support)
Web Site: www.linguaphone.co.uk
Key Personnel
Chief Executive Officer: Peter Jamieson
Dir, Sales & Marketing: Richard Avery
  E-mail: ra@linguaphone.co.uk
Founded: 1924
Subjects: Language Arts, Linguistics
ISBN Prefix(es): 0-7473
Imprints: Linguatape
Subsidiaries: Linguaphone Institute Ltd; Linguapac Distributors Sdn Bhd; Linguapac Distributors Plc

Linguatape, *imprint of* Linguaphone Institute Ltd

Lion Giftlines, *imprint of* Lion Publishing PLC

Lion Publishing PLC+
Mayfield House, 256 Banbury Rd, Oxford OX2 7DH
Tel: (01865) 302750 *Fax:* (01865) 302757
E-mail: international@lion-publishing.co.uk
Web Site: www.lion-publishing.co.uk
Key Personnel
Man Dir: Paul Clifford *E-mail:* p.clifford@lion-publishing.co.uk
International Dir: Tony Wales *E-mail:* t.wales@lion-publishing.co.uk
Editorial Dir: Rebecca Winter *E-mail:* r.winter@lion-publishing.co.uk
Sales Dir: John O'Nions *E-mail:* j.o'nions@lion-publishing.co.uk
International Rights: Vanessa Norman *E-mail:* v.norman@lion-publishing.co.uk; Paul Whitton *E-mail:* p.whitton@lion-publishing.co.uk
Founded: 1971
Specialize in Adult Religion & Spirituality, Illustrated Reference, Biography, Health, Gift Books under Lion Giftlines Imprint, Children's Books - Bible Stories & Prayers, Information & Reference, Activity, Novelty & Picture Books.
Subjects: Biblical Studies, Nonfiction (General), Religion - Catholic, Religion - Protestant, Self-Help, Theology
ISBN Prefix(es): 0-7459; 0-85648
Number of titles published annually: 110 Print
Total Titles: 500 Print
Imprints: Lion Giftlines
Distributed by Hodder Headline Australia (Australia); HarperCollins New Zealand (New Zealand); Struik Christian Books (South Africa); OMF Literature (Philippines)

Lippincott Williams & Wilkins
3rd floor, 241 Borough High St, London SE1 1GB
Tel: (020) 7940 7500 *Fax:* (020) 7940 7575
Web Site: www.llw.co.uk
Key Personnel
Dir, Journals Publishing: Caroline Black
Sales & Marketing Dir: Ian Banbery
  E-mail: ibanbery@lww.co.uk
Founded: 1893
Subjects: Medicine, Nursing, Dentistry, Veterinary Science

ISBN Prefix(es): 0-316; 1-901831
Parent Company: Wolters Kluwer
Branch Office(s)
Lippincott Williams & Wilkins Pty Ltd, Suite 4, Level 2, 22-36 Mountain St, Broadway, NSW 2007, Australia *Tel:* (02) 9212-5955 *Fax:* (02) 9212-6966
Lippincott Williams & Wilkins Asia Ltd, Suite 907-910, New T&T Centre, Harbour City, 7 Canton Rd, Tsimshatsui, Kowloon, Hong Kong *Tel:* 2610-2339 *Fax:* 2421-1123
U.S. Office(s): 351 W Camden St, Baltimore, MD 21201, United States *Tel:* 410-528-4000
16522 Hunters Green Parkway, Hagerstown, MD 21740, United States *Tel:* 301-223-2300 *Fax:* 301-223-2398 *E-mail:* orders@LWW.com
345 Hudson St, 16th floor, New York, NY 10014, United States *Tel:* 212-886-1200 (healthcare group also)
530 Walnut St, Philadelphia, PA 19106-3621, United States *Tel:* 215-521-8300 *Fax:* 215-521-8902 (head office)
Springhouse, 1111 Bethlehem Pike, PO Box 808, Springhouse, PA 19477, United States *Tel:* 215-646-8700 *Fax:* 215-654-1328

Little Brown & Co (UK), see Virago Press

The Littman Library of Jewish Civilization+
Subsidiary of Frank Cass Publishers
PO Box 645, Oxford OX2 0UJ
Tel: (01865) 514688 *Fax:* (01865) 514688
E-mail: enquiries@littman.co.uk; editorial@littman.co.uk; marketing@littman.co.uk
Web Site: www.littman.co.uk
Key Personnel
Chief Executive Officer: Ludo Craddock *Tel:* (01865) 722964 *E-mail:* ludo.craddock@littman.co.uk
Dir: Colette Littman; Roby Littman
Editorial: Connie Webber
Subjects: Biography, Drama, Theater, Ethnicity, History, Literature, Literary Criticism, Essays, Philosophy, Poetry, Religion - Jewish, Theology
ISBN Prefix(es): 1-874774
U.S. Office(s): ISBS, 5824 NE Hassalo St, Portland, OR 97213-3644, United States
Distributor for ISBS (Exclusive distributor for the US & Canada)
Warehouse: Plymbridge Distributors, Estover Rd, Plymouth PL6 7PY *Tel:* (01752) 202000 *Fax:* (01752) 202333 *E-mail:* orders@plymbridge.com *Web Site:* www.plymbridge.com

Liver Press, *imprint of* Countyvise Ltd

Liverpool University Press+
4 Cambridge St, Liverpool L69 7ZU
Tel: (0151) 794 2233; (0151) 794 2237 *Fax:* (0151) 794 2235
E-mail: j.m.smith@liverpool.ac.uk
Web Site: www.liverpool-unipress.co.uk
Key Personnel
Publisher: Robin J C Bloxsidge *Tel:* (0151) 794 2231 *E-mail:* R.J.C.Bloxsidge@liverpool.ac.uk
Marketing: Sandra Robinson *E-mail:* sandrob@liverpool.ac.uk
Production: Andrew Kirk *E-mail:* andrewk@liv.ac.uk
Founded: 1899
Subjects: Archaeology, Architecture & Interior Design, Art, Education, Environmental Studies, Geography, Geology, History, Literature, Literary Criticism, Essays, Medicine, Nursing, Dentistry, Regional Interests, Science (General), Science Fiction, Fantasy, Social Sciences, Sociology, Veterinary Science, Art history, cultural affairs, current events, population studies, urban & regional planning
ISBN Prefix(es): 0-85323

Number of titles published annually: 40 Print
Total Titles: 200 Print
Distributed by International Specialized Book Distributors; University of Pennsylvania Press (USA & Canada)
Distributor for Fremantle Arts Centre Press (Australia)
Orders to: Marston Book Services, PO Box 269, Abingdon, Oxon 0X14 4YN

Livewire, *imprint of* The Women's Press Ltd

LLP Ltd
69-77 Paul St, London EC2A 4LQ
Tel: (020) 7553 1000 *Fax:* (020) 7553 1109
E-mail: info@lloydslist.com
Web Site: www.lloydslist.com *Cable:* LLOYDSLIST LONDON EC3
Key Personnel
Editor in Chief, Publisher: Leigh Smith
Publishing Dir: Steven Warshaw
Chief Executive: David Gilbertson
Executive Editor: Christopher Mayer *Tel:* (020) 7553 1402
Editor: Julian Bray *Tel:* (020) 7553 1374
Production Editor: Linda Roulston *Tel:* (020) 7553 1480
Advertising Director: Jon Hughes *Tel:* (020) 7553 1334
Founded: 1973
Business to business international publishers.
Subjects: Finance, Law, Maritime, Insurance
ISBN Prefix(es): 1-85044
Parent Company: LLP Limited, Sheepen Place, Colchester UK CO3 3LP
Branch Office(s)
LLP Limited c/o Distributech Fulfilment Services, 41-21 28 St, Unit D, Long Island City, NY 11101, United States *Tel:* 718-786-0076 *Fax:* 718-786-4252

Local Heritage Books, see Countryside Books

Ward Lock, *imprint of* Cassell & Co

Locomotion Papers, *imprint of* Oakwood Press

Lodenek Press
Trevinette, Chapel Amble, Wadebridge, Cornwall PL27 6ES
Tel: (01208) 880850
Key Personnel
Man Dir, Sales, Production, Rights & Permissions: D R Rawe
Editorial: H J Ingrey
Founded: 1970
Subjects: Regional Interests
ISBN Prefix(es): 0-902899; 0-946143
Total Titles: 18 Print
Imprints: Chough Series (Educational Packs)
Distributed by Tabb House (in Cornwall only)
Distributor for Tabb House

Y Lolfa Cyf+
Talybont, Ceredigion SY24 5AP
Tel: (01970) 832 304 *Fax:* (01970) 832 782
E-mail: ylolfa@ylolfa.com
Web Site: www.ylolfa.com
Key Personnel
Man Dir, Production: Garmon Gruffudd *E-mail:* garmon@ylolfa.com
Editorial: Lefi Gruffudd
Administration, Rights & Permissions: Nia Williams
Marketing & Publicity: Dilwyn Phillips
Founded: 1965
Publishers of Welsh books & English books of Welsh & Celtic interest.
Subjects: Cookery, Crafts, Games, Hobbies, Fiction, Language Arts, Linguistics, Music, Dance,

Poetry, Regional Interests, Science Fiction, Fantasy
ISBN Prefix(es): 0-86243; 0-904864; 0-9500178
Number of titles published annually: 35 Print
Total Titles: 500 Print; 4 Audio
Imprints: Dinas

London Chamber of Commerce & Industry Examinations Board
6 Graphite Sq, London SE11 5EE
Tel: (020) 7793 3850 *Fax:* (020) 7582 1806
Web Site: www.lccieb.org.uk
Key Personnel
Publishing Manager: Christine Winters
 E-mail: christinew@lccieb.org.uk
Publishing arm of the LCCI Examinations Board, publish support materials for students, candidates of LCCI exams (& their teachers), student financial textbooks & teachers handbooks. Specialize in English language for business & secretarial.
Subjects: Business, Finance
Number of titles published annually: 10 Print
Total Titles: 60 Print

Stacey London, *imprint of* Stacey International

Lonely Planet, UK+
10a Spring Pl, London NW5 3BH
Tel: (020) 7428 4800 *Fax:* (020) 7428 4828
E-mail: go@lonelyplanet.co.uk
Web Site: www.lonelyplanet.com
Key Personnel
Publisher: Tony Wheeler; Maureen Wheeler
Dir: Jim Hart
Manager, UK: Charlotte Hindle
Founded: 1973
Subjects: Travel
ISBN Prefix(es): 0-86442; 2-84070
Parent Company: Lonely Planet Publications Pty Ltd, Melbourne, Australia
Divisions: Lonely Planet (France); Lonely Planet (United States)
Warehouse: Grantham Book Services, Issac Newton Way, Alma Park Industrial Estate, Grantham NU31 9SD
Orders to: World Leisure Marketing, West Meadows Industrial Estate, Derby DE2 6HA

Longman, *imprint of* Pearson Education Europe, Mideast & Africa

Lorenz Books+
Hermes House, 88-89 Blackfriars Rd, London SE1 8HA
Tel: (020) 7401 2077 *Fax:* (020) 7633 9499
E-mail: info@anness.com
Key Personnel
Contact: Paul Anness
International Contact: Denise Lie
Subjects: Animals, Pets, Cookery, Crafts, Games, Hobbies, Gardening, Plants, Health, Nutrition, How-to, New Age
ISBN Prefix(es): 1-85967; 0-7548
Imprints: Ultimate
Subsidiaries: Anness Publications Pty; Anness Publications
Branch Office(s)
Anness Publishing, 27 W 20 St, Suite 504, New York, NY 10011, United States
Distributed by Bateman (New Zealand); Five Mile Press (Australia); Raincoast (Canada)
Orders to: Aurum Press, 25 Bedford Ave, London WC1B 3AT

Lorna, *imprint of* Novello & Co Ltd

Loughborough University
Department of Information Science, Ashby Rd, Loughborough, Lincs LE11 3TU
Tel: (01509) 263171; (01509) 223052
 Fax: (01509) 223053
E-mail: dis@lboro.ac.uk
Web Site: www.lboro.ac.uk
Key Personnel
Dept Head: Prof Ron Summers
Prof: Christine L Borgman *Tel:* (01509) 223050
 E-mail: r.summers@lboro.ac.uk; John Feather *Tel:* (01509) 223058 *E-mail:* j.p.feather@lboro.ac.uk; Cliff McKnight *Tel:* (01509) 223061 *E-mail:* c.mcknight@lboro.ac.uk; Jack Meadows *Tel:* (01509) 223082 *E-mail:* a.j.meadows@lboro.ac.uk; Charles Oppenheim *Tel:* (01509) 223065 *E-mail:* c.oppenheim@lboro.ac.uk
ISBN Prefix(es): 0-902761

Peter Lowe, *imprint of* Eurobook Ltd

LTP, *imprint of* Language Teaching Publications

Luath Press Ltd+
543/2 Castlehill, The Royal Mile, Edinburgh EH1 2ND
Tel: (0131) 225 4326 *Fax:* (0131) 225 4324
Web Site: www.luath.co.uk
Key Personnel
Dir: Gavin MacDougall *E-mail:* gavin.macdougall@luath.co.uk
Founded: 1981
Publisher of *On the Trail of* series.
Member of Scottish Publishers Association.
Subjects: Biography, Fiction, Genealogy, History, Literature, Literary Criticism, Essays, Natural History, Nonfiction (General), Outdoor Recreation, Poetry, Regional Interests, Science Fiction, Fantasy, Sports, Athletics, Travel, Wine & Spirits
ISBN Prefix(es): 0-946487; 1-84282
Number of titles published annually: 30 Print
Total Titles: 80 Print
Distributed by Addenda (New Zealand); Hushion House (Canada); Midpoint Trade Books (USA only); Peribo (Australia); Petersen (Germany, Austria, Switzerland)
Shipping Address: Scottish Book Source, 32 Finlas St, Glasgow G22 5DU
Warehouse: Scottish Book Source, 32 Finlas St, Glasgow G22 5DU
Orders to: Scottish Book Source, 32 Finlas St, Glasgow G22 5DU, Contact: Gerry McLean *Tel:* (0141) 558 1366 *Fax:* (0141) 557 0189 *E-mail:* info@booksource.net *Web Site:* www.booksource.net

Lucent Books, *imprint of* Gale Research

Lucis Press Ltd
3 Whitehall Court, Suite 54, London SW1A 2EF
Tel: (020) 7839 4512; (020) 7839 4513
 Fax: (020) 7839 5575
E-mail: lucis@lucistrust.org
Web Site: www.lucistrust.org
Key Personnel
General Secretary: Chris Morgan
Dir: Helen Durant *E-mail:* lucispress@lucistrust.org
Founded: 1938
Publisher of 24 books of Esoteric Philosophy by Alice A Bailey.
Subjects: Astrology, Occult, Education, Philosophy, Religion - Other, Social Sciences, Sociology
ISBN Prefix(es): 0-85330
Total Titles: 38 Print; 1 CD-ROM
Parent Company: Lucis Publishing Co, 120 Wall St, 24th floor, New York, NY 10005, United States, Sarah McKechnie
Associate Companies: Lucis Trust, One rue de Varembe 3e, Case Postale 31, 1211 Geneva 20, Switzerland (for European translations)
Distributed by Lucis Press SA (South Africa); Sydney Goodwill Unit of Service (Australia); The Triangle Centre (New Zealand)
Distributor for Agni Yoga Society

Lund Humphries, *imprint of* Ashgate Publishing Ltd

Lund Humphries+
Imprint of Ashgate Publishing
Gower House, Croft Rd, Aldershot, Hants GU11 3HR
Tel: (01252) 331551 *Fax:* (01252) 368595
E-mail: info@lundhumphries.com
Web Site: www.lundhumphries.com
Key Personnel
Publishing Dir, Art Books: Lucy Myers *Tel:* (020) 7841-9802 *E-mail:* lmyers@lundhumphries.com
Founded: 1943
Subjects: Architecture & Interior Design, Art, Photography
ISBN Prefix(es): 0-85331
Number of titles published annually: 20 Print
Total Titles: 70 Print
Parent Company: Ashgate Publishing Ltd
U.S. Office(s): 131 Main St, Burlington, VT 05401-5600, United States *Tel:* (802) 865 7641 *Fax:* (802) 865 7847 *E-mail:* info@lundhumphries.com
Distributor for Hartley & Marks (Europe only); Powerhouse Publishing World (Outside Australia & New Zealand)
Warehouse: Bookpoint Ltd, 130 Milton Park, Abingdon, Oxon OX14 4SB

Lutterworth Press, *imprint of* James Clarke & Co Ltd

The Lutterworth Press+
PO Box 60, Cambridge CB1 2NT
Tel: (01223) 350865 *Fax:* (01223) 366951
E-mail: publishing@lutterworth.com
Web Site: www.lutterworth.com
Key Personnel
Man Dir, Rights: Adrian C Brink
Sales Manager: Colin Lester
Founded: 1799
Member of PA, IPG.
Subjects: Archaeology, Art, Biblical Studies, Biography, Crafts, Games, Hobbies, Education, History, Natural History, Nonfiction (General), Religion - Protestant, Theology
ISBN Prefix(es): 0-7444; 0-7188
Number of titles published annually: 15 Print
Total Titles: 600 Print
Parent Company: James Clarke & Co Ltd
Imprints: Acorn Editions; Patrick Hardy Books
Distributed by Parkwest Publications Inc (USA exclusive; Canada non-exclusive)

Luxor Press L, see Charles Skilton Ltd

Lyle Publications Ltd
4 Shepherds Mill, Selkirk, Selkirkshire TD7 5EA
Tel: (01750) 23355 *Fax:* (01750) 23388
E-mail: lyle.publications@talk21.com
Key Personnel
Dir: Tony Curtis; Annette Curtis
Subjects: Antiques, Art
ISBN Prefix(es): 0-86248

Thomas Lyster Ltd
Units 3/4a, Old Boundary Way Industrial Park, Ormskirk, Lancs L39 2YW
Tel: (01695) 575112 *Fax:* (01695) 570120
E-mail: books@tlyster.co.uk
Web Site: www.tlyster.co.uk
Key Personnel
General Manager: Ian Lyster
Founded: 1988

UNITED KINGDOM

Specialize in offering distribution services to other smaller publishers.
ISBN Prefix(es): 1-871482
Total Titles: 15 Print
Parent Company: Plymbridge Distributors Ltd, Estover Rd, Plymouth DL6 7DY
Distributor for Aquila Books; Broadview Publishing; Colour Affects Ltd; Cornish Books; Enanef Ltd; Fort Publishing Ltd; Lancashire Books; Landscape Press; Pigeon Publications; Royal & Ancient Golf Club; Sheldrake Press; South Bank University (Distance Learning Centre); Taghan Publishing
Membership(s): IPG

Macdonald Young Books, *imprint of* Wayland Publishers Ltd (Incorporating Macdonald Young Books)

Macdonald Young Books, see Wayland Publishers Ltd (Incorporating Macdonald Young Books)

Macgregor Science, *imprint of* Thistle Press

Macmillan, *imprint of* Pan Macmillan

Macmillan Audio Books+
18-21 Cavaye Place, London SW10 9PG
Tel: (020) 7373 6070 *Fax:* (020) 7244 6379
Subjects: Art, Biography, Cookery, Fiction, History, Military Science, Mysteries, Natural History, Poetry
ISBN Prefix(es): 0-333
Parent Company: Macmillan Publishers Ltd

Macmillan Children's Books, *imprint of* Pan Macmillan

Macmillan Children's Books+
Imprint of Pan Macmillan
20 New Wharf Rd, London N1 9RR
Tel: (020) 7014 6000 *Fax:* (020) 7014 6001
Web Site: www.panmacmillan.com
Key Personnel
Man Dir: Kate Wilson
Sales & Marketing Dir: Emma Hopkin
Associate Publisher: Marion Llyod
Publishing Dir: Sarah Davies; Alison Green
Publishing Dir, Campbell Books: Mandy Suhr
Subjects: Fiction, Nonfiction (General)
ISBN Prefix(es): 0-330; 0-333
Number of titles published annually: 300 Print
Total Titles: 2,700 Print
Imprints: Campbell Books
Divisions: Black & White Colour

Macmillan Heinemann ELT
Macmillan Oxford, Between Towns Rd, Oxford OX4 3PP
Tel: (01865) 405700 *Fax:* (01865) 405701
E-mail: elt@mhelt.com
Web Site: www.mhelt.com
Key Personnel
Man Dir (ELT): Mike Esplen *E-mail:* mike.esplen@mhelt.com
Man Dir (Education): Chris Harrison *E-mail:* chris.harrison@mhelt.com
Publishing Dir: Sue Bale *E-mail:* sue.bale@mhelt.com
Finance Dir: Paul Emmett *E-mail:* paul.emmett@mhelt.com
Curriculum Publishing Dir: Alison Hurbert
Specialize in the publication of core curriculum texts for primary, JSS, SSS.
ISBN Prefix(es): 0-333
Parent Company: Macmillan Education Ltd

Macmillan Ltd
4 Crinan St, London N1 9XW
Tel: (020) 7843 3600 *Fax:* (020) 7843 4640
E-mail: books@macmillan.com
Web Site: www.macmillan.com
Key Personnel
Chairman: Dieter von Holtzbrinck
Chief Executive: Richard Charkin *E-mail:* richard@macmillan.com
Executive Dir (Australia): Ross Gibb
Executive Dir: Mike Barnard; Christopher Paterson *E-mail:* c.paterson@macmillan.co.uk; David North *E-mail:* d.north@macmillan.co.uk; Geoff Todd *E-mail:* g.todd@macmillan.co.uk; Annette Thomas *E-mail:* a.thomas@nature.com
Executive Dir & Man Dir, Reference: Dominic Knight *E-mail:* d.knight@macmillan.co.uk
Man Dir, ELT: Mike Esplen *E-mail:* mike.esplen@mhelt.com
Man Dir, Education: Christopher Harrison *E-mail:* chris.harrison@mhelt.com
Man Dir, Children's: Kate Wilson *E-mail:* k.wilson@macmillan.co.uk
Subjects: Fiction, Nonfiction (General)
ISBN Prefix(es): 0-330; 0-333
Associate Companies: Macmillan Heinemann ELT; Macmillan Reference; Palgrave; Pan Macmillan
Orders to: Macmillan Distribution Ltd, Brunel Rd, Houndmills, Basingstoke, Hants RG21 6XS

Macmillan Press Ltd, see Palgrave Publishers Ltd

Macmillan Publishers (UK) Ltd+
Division of Grove
25 Eccleston Pl, London SW1W 9NF
Tel: (020) 7881 8000 *Fax:* (020) 7881 8001
E-mail: books@macmillan.com
Web Site: www.macmillan.com
Key Personnel
Chief Executive: R D P Charkin
Rights Dir, Trade: Chantal Noel *E-mail:* c.noel@macmillan.co.uk
Founded: 1843
ISBN Prefix(es): 0-333; 0-900178
Parent Company: Macmillan Ltd
Ultimate Parent Company: Georg van Holtzbrink & Co
Associate Companies: Macmillan India Ltd, India; Gill & Macmillan Ltd, Ireland; Macmillan Publishers Nigeria Ltd, Nigeria; The Northern Nigerian Publishing Co Ltd, Nigeria; The College Press plc, Zimbabwe; Pan Macmillan Ltd
Subsidiaries: Grove's Dictionaries of Music Ltd; Macmillan Education Ltd; Macmillan Magazines Ltd; Macmillan Press Ltd; Macmillan Distribution Ltd; Macmillan General Books Ltd; Macmillan Children's Books Ltd; Stockton Press Ltd; Stockton Press Netherlands BV; Macmillan Publishers Australia Pty Ltd; Macmillan Publishers Hong Kong Ltd; Macmillan Publishers China Ltd; Peninsula Production & Distribution Ltd; Macmillan Language House Co Ltd; Macmillan Shuppan KK; Nature Japan KK; Macmillan Kenya Publishers Ltd; Editorial Macmillan de Mexico SA de CV; Macmillan Publishers New Zealand Ltd; Pansing Distribution Sdn Bhd; Macmillan Boleswa Publishers Pty Ltd; Macmillan Swaziland National Publishing Co Ltd; Nature America Inc; St Martin's Press Inc; College Press Pvt Ltd; Stockton Press Netherlands Holdings BV
Orders to: Macmillan Distribution Ltd, Brunel Rd, Houndmills, Basingstoke, Hants RG21 2XS *Tel:* (0125) 6329242

Macmillan Reference Ltd
Porters South, Crinan St, London N1 9XW
Tel: (020) 7881 8000 *Fax:* (020) 7881 8001
E-mail: books@macmillan.co.uk
Web Site: www.macmillan-reference.co.uk
Key Personnel
Man Dir: Ian Jacobs *E-mail:* i.jacobs@macmillan.co.uk
Science Publisher: Gina Fullerlove *E-mail:* g.fullerlove@macmillan.co.uk
Art Publisher: Jane Turner *E-mail:* j.turner@macmillan.co.uk
Humanities & Social Sciences Publisher: Sara Lloyd *E-mail:* s.lloyd@macmillan.co.uk
Marketing: Alex Lankester *E-mail:* a.lankester@macmillan.co.uk
Production: Jeremy Macdonald *E-mail:* j.macdonald@macmillan.co.uk
Subjects: Art, Economics, Finance, Government, Political Science, History, Human Relations, Music, Dance, Science (General), Social Sciences, Sociology
ISBN Prefix(es): 0-333

Macmillan Reference USA, *imprint of* Gale Research

Macmillan Technical Publishing USA, *imprint of* Pearson Education Europe, Mideast & Africa

Julia MacRae, *imprint of* Random House UK Ltd

Mad Jack, *imprint of* Funfax Ltd

Magi Publications+
1 The Coda Centre, 189 Munster Rd, London SW6 6AW
Tel: (020) 7385 6333 *Fax:* (020) 7385 7333
E-mail: info@littletiger.co.uk
Web Site: www.littletigerpress.com
Key Personnel
Rights Manager: M S Bhatia
Founded: 1987
Specialize in co-production of children's picture books.
Subjects: English as a Second Language, Fiction
ISBN Prefix(es): 1-870271; 1-85430
Subsidiaries: Little Tiger Press
Orders to: A & C Black, Howard Rd, Eaton Socon, Huntingdon, Cambs PE19 3EZ

Magic Joneuery, *imprint of* Funfax Ltd

Magna Large Print Books+
Magna House, Long Preston, Skipton, North Yorks BD23 4ND
Tel: (01729) 840 225; (01729) 840 526; (01729) 840 251 *Fax:* (01729) 840 683
Web Site: www.ulverscroft.co.uk
Key Personnel
Man Dir: John Cressey
Rights: Diane Allen
Founded: 1973
ISBN Prefix(es): 0-86009; 1-85057; 1-85389; 0-7505
Number of titles published annually: 240 Print; 72 Audio
Total Titles: 1,000 Print
Parent Company: The Ulverscroft Group Ltd
Imprints: Dales Large Print Series; Story Sound Audio Tapes
Branch Office(s)
Ulverscroft (Large Print USA Inc), Seneca Pl, 1881 Ridge Rd, West Seneca, NY 14224, United States
Distributed by Ulverscroft (USA)
Showroom(s): Cawdor Books, 96 Dykehead St, Queenslie, Glasgow G33 4AQ *Tel:* (01729) 840225 *Fax:* (01729) 840683

Magpie, *imprint of* Constable & Robinson Ltd

Maik Nauka/Interperiodica, *imprint of* Kluwer Academic/Plenum Publishers

PUBLISHERS UNITED KINGDOM

Mainstream Publishing Co (Edinburgh) Ltd+
7 Albany St, Edinburgh EH1 3UG
Tel: (0131) 557 2959 *Fax:* (0131) 556 8720
E-mail: mainstream.pub@btinternet.com
Key Personnel
Dir: Bill Campbell; Peter MacKenzie
Sales Manager: Raymond Cowie
Off Manager: Elaine Scott
Founded: 1978
Subjects: Art, Biography, Government, Political Science, History, Literature, Literary Criticism, Essays, Photography, Sports, Athletics
ISBN Prefix(es): 1-85158
Distributed by Hurlion House (Canada); Trafalgar Square (USA)
Orders to: Tiptree, St Luke's Chase, Tiptree, Colchester, Essex C05 0SR

Making Sense of Science, *imprint of* Portland Press Ltd

Mallard Reprints, *imprint of* Terence Dalton Ltd

Management Books 2000 Ltd+
Forge House, Limes Rd, Kemble, Cirencester, Glos GL7 6AD
Tel: (01285) 771441 *Fax:* (01285) 771055
E-mail: m.b.2000@virgin.net
Web Site: www.mb2000.com
Key Personnel
Man Dir: Nicholas Dale-Harris
Founded: 1986
Publisher & distributor of management guides, textbooks & references.
Subjects: Business, Career Development, Management, Marketing, Real Estate
ISBN Prefix(es): 1-85251; 1-85252
Number of titles published annually: 40 Print
Total Titles: 200 Print
Online services available through World Wide Web.
Imprints: Mercury Books
Orders to: Combined Book Services, Paddock Wood Distribution Centre, Paddock Wood Kent TN12 6UU *Tel:* (01892) 837171

Management Pocketbooks Ltd+
Laurel House, Station Approach, Alresford, Hants SO24 9JH
Tel: (01962) 735 573 *Fax:* (01962) 733 637
E-mail: sales@pocketbook.co.uk
Web Site: www.pocketbook.co.uk
Key Personnel
International Rights: Rosalind Baynes
  E-mail: ros@pocketbook.co.uk
Founded: 1987
Small, highly accessible management guides written by trainers, full of graphics, mnemonics, bullet points for clarity & ease of recall.
Member of Independent company.
Subjects: Business, Management
ISBN Prefix(es): 1-870471
Number of titles published annually: 10 Print
Total Titles: 70 Print; 2 Audio
U.S. Office(s): Stylus Publishing, 22883 Quicksilver Dr, Sterling, VA 20166-2012, United States, Contact: John von Knorring *Tel:* 703-660-1500 *Fax:* 703-661-1501
  E-mail: styluspub@aol.com
Membership(s): IPG

Manchester United Books, *imprint of* Carlton Publishing Group

Manchester University Press+
Oxford Rd, Manchester M13 9NR
Tel: (0161) 273 5539 *Fax:* (161) 274 3346
E-mail: mup@man.ac.uk
Web Site: www.manchesteruniversitypress.co.uk
Key Personnel
Chief Executive & Production Director: David Rodgers *E-mail:* D.Rodgers@man.ac.uk
Editorial Dir: Matthew Frost *E-mail:* M.Frost@man.ac.uk
Editor: Tony Mason *E-mail:* T.Mason@man.ac.uk; Alison Whittle *E-mail:* A.Whittle@man.ac.uk
Trade: Norma Ashton *E-mail:* N.Ashton@man.ac.uk
Sales & Marketing Dir: Clare Blick *E-mail:* c.blick@man.ac.uk
Rights & Publicity: Alison Sparkes *E-mail:* A.Sparkes@man.ac.uk
Founded: 1903
Subjects: Art, Economics, Film, Video, Government, Political Science, History, Literature, Literary Criticism, Essays, Radio, TV, Social Sciences, Sociology, Academic publishers
ISBN Prefix(es): 0-7190
Associate Companies: Palgrave, 257 Park Ave S, New York, NY 10010, United States
Imprints: Mandolin
Distributed by University of British Columbia Press (Canada)

Mandolin, *imprint of* Manchester University Press

Mandrake of Oxford+
PO Box 250, Oxford OX1 1AP
Tel: (01865) 243671
E-mail: mandrake@mandrake.uk.net
Web Site: www.mandrake.uk.net
Key Personnel
Contact: M Morgan
Founded: 1986
Also acts as Bookseller & Mail-Order Subscription Agent.
Subjects: Art, Astrology, Occult, Fiction, Health, Nutrition, Parapsychology, Religion - Hindu, Religion - Other, Science (General), Science Fiction, Fantasy
ISBN Prefix(es): 1-869928
Number of titles published annually: 10 Print
Imprints: Golden Dawn; Nuit-Isis
Orders to: Gazelle, Falcon House, Queen Square, Lancaster *Tel:* (01524) 68765 *Fax:* (01424) 63232 *E-mail:* Gazelle4go@AOL.com
New Leaf, 401 Thornton Rd, Lithia Springs, GA 30057, United States *Tel:* 770-948-7845 *Fax:* 770-944-2313 (Trade only)

Maney, *imprint of* Maney Publishing

Maney Publishing+
Hudson Rd, Leeds LS9 7DL
Tel: (0113) 249 7481 *Fax:* (0113) 248 6983
E-mail: maney@maney.co.uk
Web Site: www.maney.co.uk
Key Personnel
Man Dir: Michael Gallico *E-mail:* m.gallico@maney.co.uk
Marketing Controller: Mary Starkey *E-mail:* m.starkey@maney.co.uk
Founded: 1900
Academic book & journal publisher.
Subjects: Antiques, Archaeology, Architecture & Interior Design, Art, Drama, Theater, Ethnicity, History, Language Arts, Linguistics, Library & Information Sciences, Literature, Literary Criticism, Essays, Natural History, Theology
Total Titles: 65 Print
Imprints: Maney; Northern Universities Press; Modern Humanities Research Association; Pasold Research Fund

Mango Publishing
425 New Kings Rd, London SW6 4RN
Tel: (020) 7751 2070 *Fax:* (020) 7751 2071
Web Site: www.mangopublishing.net
Key Personnel
Contact: Gavin Caldwell *E-mail:* gavin@mangopublishing.net
Subjects: Biography, Literature, Literary Criticism, Essays, Poetry, Poetry, literature & biography by Caribbean heritage writers especially women; literary criticism of Caribbean literature
ISBN Prefix(es): 1-902294
Total Titles: 10 Print

George Mann, *imprint of* George Mann Publications

Mansell, *imprint of* Cassell & Co

Mansell, *imprint of* The Continuum International Publishing Group Ltd

The Mansk Svenska Publishing Co Ltd+
17 North View, Peel, Isle of Man M5 1DQ
Tel: (0162) 4842855 *Fax:* (0162) 844241
E-mail: hanneke@advsys.co.uk
Key Personnel
Man Dir: G V C Young, OBE
Founded: 1980
Subjects: Biography, Fiction, History
ISBN Prefix(es): 0-907715
Branch Office(s)
Spellinge Gard, S-590 20 Mantord, Sweden
Bookshop(s): 50 Michael St, Peel 1M5 1HD

Manson Publishing Ltd+
73 Corringham Rd, London NW11 7DL
Tel: (020) 8905 5150 *Fax:* (020) 8201 9233
E-mail: manson@man-pub.demon.co.uk
Web Site: www.manson-publishing.co.uk
Key Personnel
Man Dir: Michael Manson
Publishing Coordinator: Clair Chaventre
Founded: 1992
Membership(s): Publishers Association & Independent Publishers Guild.
Subjects: Agriculture, Biological Sciences, Chemistry, Chemical Engineering, Earth Sciences, Medicine, Nursing, Dentistry, Veterinary Science, Microbiology, Plant Science
ISBN Prefix(es): 1-874545; 1-84076
Total Titles: 90 Print
Subsidiaries: Veterinary Press Ltd
Distributed by Blackwell Science (Asia) Pty (Australia & New Zealand); Nankodo Co Ltd (Japan - medicine & veterinary medicine books); United Publishers Services Ltd (Japan - Science books only)
Orders to: Marston Book Services Ltd, Unit 160, Milton Park Industrial Centre, Abingdon *Tel:* (01235) 465500 *Fax:* (01235) 465555
Membership(s): IPG; Publishers' Association

Peter Marcan Publications
PO Box 3158, London SE1 4RA
Tel: (020) 7357 0368
Key Personnel
Proprietor: Peter Marcan
Founded: 1978
Member of Author-Publisher Enterprise (UK).
Subjects: Art, History, Music, Dance
ISBN Prefix(es): 0-9510289; 1-871811; 0-9504211

Marcham Books+
Appleford, Abingdon, Oxon OX14 4PB
Tel: (01235) 848319
Key Personnel
Chief Executive, Editorial: G E Duffield
Sales, Publicity: G Elwes
Production: E Collie
Founded: 1963

711

UNITED KINGDOM

Subjects: Asian Studies, Biblical Studies, Biography, History, Music, Dance, Philosophy, Religion - Catholic, Religion - Protestant, Theology
ISBN Prefix(es): 0-900531
Parent Company: Appleford Publishing Group
Associate Companies: Appleford Printers, Courtenay Bookroom
Divisions: Sutton Courtenay Press

Maresfield Lib, *imprint of* Karnac Books Ltd

Maritime Books
Lodge Hill, Liskeard, Cornwell PL14 4EL
Tel: (01579) 343663 *Fax:* (01579) 346747
E-mail: warshipworld.marbooks@virgin.net
Web Site: www.navybooks.com
Key Personnel
Chief Executive: M Critchley
Manager: P Garnett
Founded: 1980
Subjects: Maritime
ISBN Prefix(es): 0-907771
Total Titles: 26 Print
Subsidiaries: Warship World Magazine

Market House Books Ltd+
Market House, Market Sq, Aylesbury, Bucks HP20 1TN
Tel: (01296) 484911 *Fax:* (01296) 437073
E-mail: information@mhbref.com
Web Site: www.mhbref.com
Key Personnel
Dir: Dr Alan Isaacs *E-mail:* isaacs@mhbref.com; Peter Sapsed
Dir & Production: Dr John Daintith
 E-mail: daintith@mhbref.com
Founded: 1969
Book producer & Packager.

Mars Business Associates Ltd
62 Kingsmead, Lechlade, Glos GL7 3BW
Tel: (01367) 252 506 *Fax:* (01367) 252 506
E-mail: sales@marspub.co.uk
Web Site: www.marspub.co.uk
Key Personnel
Contact: Dr John Robertson *E-mail:* johnr@cccp.net
Founded: 1988
Subjects: Accounting, Finance

Marshall Editions Ltd+
The Orangery, 161 New Bond St, London W1S 2UF
Tel: (020) 72948222 *Fax:* (020) 72918233
Web Site: www.marshalleditions.com
Key Personnel
Chairman: Richard Harman *E-mail:* rharman@smediakey.u-net.com
Publisher: Barbara Marshall
Chief Executive: Nick Croydon
Sales Dir: Belinda Rasmussen
Founded: 1977
Also acts as book packager.
Subjects: Business, Crafts, Games, Hobbies, Gardening, Plants, Geography, Geology, Health, Nutrition, History, Management, Military Science, Natural History, Religion - Other, Science (General), Travel, Wine & Spirits
ISBN Prefix(es): 0-9507901
Parent Company: Just Group plc
Associate Companies: Melrose Ltd; Video Arts Ltd
Subsidiaries: Marshall Media Ltd; Marshall Publishing Ltd

Marston House, *imprint of* Marston House

Marston House+
Marston Magna, Yeovil, Somerset BA22 8DH
Tel: (01935) 851331 *Fax:* (01935) 851372
Key Personnel
Man Dir, Production: A E Birks-Hay
Editorial Dir: M L Birks-Hay
Founded: 1991
Subjects: Architecture & Interior Design, Art, Gardening, Plants, Nonfiction (General), crafts
ISBN Prefix(es): 0-9517700; 1-899296
Number of titles published annually: 3 Print
Total Titles: 20 Print
Parent Company: Alphabet & Image Ltd
Imprints: Marston House
Distributor for Taylor Curwen Ltd
Orders to: Chris Lloyd Sales & Marketing Services, Stanley House, 1st floor, 3 Fleets Lane, Poole, Dorset BH15 3AJ, Chris Lloyd
Tel: (01202) 649930 *Fax:* (01202) 649950
E-mail: chrlloyd@globalnet.co.uk

Martin Books, *imprint of* Simon & Schuster Ltd

Martin Dunitz, *imprint of* Taylor & Francis Group

Kenneth Mason Publications Ltd+
The Book Barn, White Chimney Row, Wetbourne, Hants PO10 8RS
Tel: (01243) 377977; (01243) 377978
Fax: (01243) 379136
E-mail: boatswain@dial.pipex.com
Key Personnel
Chairman: Kenneth Mason
Man Dir: Piers Mason
Founded: 1958
Subjects: Astrology, Occult, Child Care & Development, Cookery, Health, Nutrition, House & Home, Law, Maritime, Self-Help
ISBN Prefix(es): 0-85937; 1-873432
Imprints: Handbag Books; Boatswain Press
Warehouse: Book Barn

Adam Matthew Publications
Pelham House, London Rd, Marlborough, Wilts SN8 2AA
Tel: (01672) 511921 *Fax:* (01672) 511663
Web Site: www.adam-matthew-publications.co.uk
Key Personnel
Director: William Pidduck
 E-mail: adam_matthew@msn.com; David Tyler
 E-mail: amp_david@msn.com
Founded: 1990
Original manuscript collections, rare printed books & other primary source material in microform & electronic format.
Subjects: African American Studies, Asian Studies, Economics, Ethnicity, History, Music, Dance, Religion - Other, Science (General), Social Sciences, Sociology, Technology, Women's Studies
ISBN Prefix(es): 1-85711
Number of titles published annually: 1 CD-ROM; 1 Online
Distributed by Maruzen Co Ltd (Japan only)
Foreign Rep(s): Maruzen Co Ltd (Japan); Transmission Books Co Ltd (Taiwan)

Mayhew-McCrimmon Ltd, see McCrimmon Publishing Co Ltd

MCB University Press Ltd
60-62 Toller Lane, Bradford, West Yorks BD8 9BY
Tel: (01274) 777700 *Fax:* (01274) 785201
E-mail: info@emeraldinsight.com; help@emeraldinsight.com (academic sales); editorial@emeraldinsight.com (editorial)
Web Site: www.mcb.co.uk
Key Personnel
Chairman: Barrie Pettman
Productions, Rights & Permissions: Tracy Cogan
Publicity: Michelle Kelly
Customer Operations Manager: Suzanne Halliday
 E-mail: shalliday@emeraldinsight.com
Founded: 1969
Subjects: Business, Human Relations, Library & Information Sciences, Management, Marketing
ISBN Prefix(es): 0-86176; 0-905440; 0-903763

McCrimmon Publishing Co Ltd+
10-12 High St, Great Wakering, Southend-on-Sea SS3 0EQ
Tel: (01702) 218956 *Fax:* (01702) 216082
E-mail: sales@mccrimmons.com (Sales); orders@mccrimmons.com (Orders); perms@mccrimmons.com (Permission-related inquiries); clipart@mccrimmons.com (Clip Art)
Web Site: www.mccrimmons.com
Key Personnel
Dir: Donald McCrimmon; Joan McCrimmon
 E-mail: mccrimmon@dial.pipex.com
Founded: 1968
Member of PRS, MCPS.
Subjects: Biblical Studies, Education, Music, Dance, Religion - Catholic, Religion - Other, Textbooks-Liturgy
ISBN Prefix(es): 0-85597
Number of titles published annually: 20 Print
Total Titles: 100 Print
Distributed by Liturgical Press (USA)
Distributor for Harcourt Brace; LTP Chicago (USA); Printery House (USA); St Michael's Altar Breads
Bookshop(s): All Saints Pastoral Centre Bookshop, London Colney, Herts
Warehouse: 10 Terminal Close, Shoeburyness

Deirdre McDonald Ltd, *imprint of* Bellew Publishing Co Ltd

McGill-Queens University Press, *imprint of* Combined Academic Publishers

McGraw-Hill Publishing Company+
McGraw Hill House, Shoppenhangers Rd, Maidenhead SL6 2QL
Tel: (01628) 502500 *Fax:* (01628) 635895
Telex: 848484 *Cable:* McGrawHill
Key Personnel
Group VP, Northern Europe/MEA: I Raimondi
Publishing Dir: A Waller
Founded: 1899
Subjects: Career Development, Computer Science, Engineering (General), Management, Mathematics, Medicine, Nursing, Dentistry, Psychology, Psychiatry, Science (General), Social Sciences, Sociology
ISBN Prefix(es): 0-07
Parent Company: McGraw-Hill Inc, 1221 Avenue of the Americas, New York, NY 10020, United States
Associate Companies: McGraw-Hill Book Co Australia Pty Ltd, Australia; McGraw-Hill Ryerson Ltd, Canada; Editorial McGraw-Hill Latinoamericana SA, Colombia; Tata McGraw-Hill Publishing Co Ltd, India; McGraw-Hill Book Co Japan Ltd, Japan; Libros McGraw-Hill de Mexico SA de CV, Mexico; McGraw-Hill Book Co, New Zealand Ltd, New Zealand; Editora McGraw-Hill de Portugal Lda, Portugal; Editorial McGraw-Hill Latinoamericana SA, Puerto Rico; McGraw-Hill Interamericana de Espana SA, Spain
Distributed by Amacom (UK, Europe); Berrett-Koehler (UK, Europe); Harvard Business School Press (UK, Europe)

Meadowfield Press, *imprint of* Merrow Publishing Co Ltd

Media Research Publishing Ltd+
Lister House, 117 Milton Rd, Weston-super-Mare, North Somerset BS23 2UX
Tel: (01934) 644 309 *Fax:* (01934) 644 402

Key Personnel
Contact: Cliff Dane *E-mail:* cliffd@globalnet.co.uk
Founded: 1993
Specialize in financial aspects of the music industry.
Subjects: Accounting, Business, Music, Dance
ISBN Prefix(es): 0-9521414; 0-9534171
Total Titles: 2 Print

The Medici Society Ltd
Grafton House, Hyde Estate Rd, London NW9 6JZ
Tel: (020) 8205 2500 *Fax:* (020) 8205 2552
E-mail: export@medici.co.uk
Web Site: www.medici.co.uk
Founded: 1908
Subjects: Art, Poetry, Fine Art
ISBN Prefix(es): 0-85503
Bookshop(s): The Medici Galleries, 7 Grafton St, London W1X 3LA; 26 Thurloe St, London SW7 2LT

Willem A Meeuws Publisher
11-12 Broad St, Oxford OX1 3AR
Tel: (01865) 242939 *Fax:* (01865) 204021
E-mail: thorntons@booknews.demon.co.uk
Web Site: www.thorntonsbooks.co.uk
Key Personnel
Publisher: Willem A Meeuws
Founded: 1968
Subjects: History
ISBN Prefix(es): 0-902672
Total Titles: 70 Print
Subsidiaries: Thorntons of Oxford Ltd
Distributor for Folio Society; Slavica (USA)
Orders to: Thorntons of Oxford Ltd, Oxford

Melrose Press Ltd+
St Thomas Pl, Ely, Cambs CB7 4GG
Tel: (01353) 646600 *Fax:* (01353) 646601
E-mail: tradesales@melrosepress.co.uk
Key Personnel
Chairman: Richard Kay
Managing Director: Nicholas Law
Chief Executive: Jean Pearson
Editorial & Head of Research: Jon Gifford
Founded: 1969
Subjects: Biography
ISBN Prefix(es): 0-948875
Imprints: International Biographical Centre
Shipping Address: Bath Road, Harmondsworth, West Drayton, Middlesex UB7 0DA

Mentor, *imprint of* Christian Focus Publications Ltd

MEP, *imprint of* Professional Engineering Publishing Ltd

Mercat Press+
10 Coates Crescent, Edinburgh EH3 7AL
Tel: (0131) 225 5324 *Fax:* (0131) 226 6632
E-mail: enquiries@mercatpress.com
Web Site: www.mercatpress.com
Key Personnel
Man Dir: Sean Costello; Tom Johnstone
Founded: 1970
Member of Scottish Publishers' Association.
Subjects: Cookery, Gardening, Plants, Literature, Literary Criticism, Essays, Music, Dance, Natural History, Nonfiction (General), Outdoor Recreation, Regional Interests
ISBN Prefix(es): 0-901824; 0-906664; 1-873644; 0-902347; 1-85752
Number of titles published annually: 30 Print
Total Titles: 250 Print
Parent Company: Mercat Press Ltd

Merchiston Publishing
School of Communication Arts, Napier University, Craighouse Rd, Edinburgh EH10 5LG
Tel: (0131) 455 6150 *Fax:* (0131) 455 6193
Key Personnel
Contact: Mairi Sutherland *E-mail:* m.sutherland@napier.ac.uk
Founded: 1987
Member of Scottish Publishers' Association.
Subjects: Publishing & Book Trade Reference, Regional Interests
ISBN Prefix(es): 0-9511266; 1-872800

Mercury Books, *imprint of* Management Books 2000 Ltd

Merehurst, *imprint of* Merehurst Publishers

Merehurst Publishers+
Ferry House, 51-57 Lacy Rd, London SW15 1PR
Tel: (020) 8355 1480 *Fax:* (020) 8355 1499
E-mail: intsales@merehurst.co.uk
Key Personnel
International Sales Dir: Mark Newman
  Tel: (0612) 96922353 *Fax:* (0612) 96922558
  E-mail: markn@mm.com.au
COO: Sharon Miller *E-mail:* smiller@merehurst.co.uk
Publisher & CEO: Anne Wilson *Tel:* (0612) 96922336 *Fax:* (0612) 96922558
  E-mail: annew@mm.com.au
Founded: 1979
Subjects: Cookery, Crafts, Games, Hobbies, Gardening, Plants, House & Home, Nonfiction (General), Catering, Wines
ISBN Prefix(es): 0-948075; 1-85391; 1-898018
Total Titles: 600 Print
Parent Company: Murdoch Books Pty, Australia
Ultimate Parent Company: Murdoch Magazines Pty Ltd
Imprints: Merehurst
Foreign Rep(s): Booktraders Ltd (Middle East); Cavendish Books (Canada); HRA (Caribbean & South America); Murdoch Books (Australia & New Zealand); Onslow Books (Europe); Tuttle Publishing (USA); Wild Dol Press (Southern Africa)
Orders to: D Services, 6 Euston St, Freeman's Common, Leicester LE2 7SS, John Timmis *Tel:* (0116) 2547671 *Fax:* (0116) 2544670

Meresborough Books
17-25 Station Rd, Rainham, Kent ME8 7RS
Tel: (01634) 371591 *Fax:* (01634) 262114
E-mail: shop@rainhambookshop.co.uk
Key Personnel
Dir: Hamish Mackay-Miller; Barbara Mackay-Miller
Founded: 1977
Subjects: Regional Interests
ISBN Prefix(es): 0-905270; 0-948193
Associate Companies: Rainham Bookshop
Imprints: Bygone Kent

Meridian Books
40 Hadzor Rd, Oldbury B68 9LA
Tel: (0121) 429 4397
Key Personnel
Contact: Peter Groves
Founded: 1983
Subjects: Travel, Walking
ISBN Prefix(es): 1-869922
Distributed by Local Heritage Books

The Merlin Press Ltd+
PO Box 30705, London WC2E 8QD
Tel: (020) 7836 3020 *Fax:* (020) 7497 0309
E-mail: info@merlinpress.co.uk
Web Site: www.merlinpress.co.uk

Key Personnel
Dir & Rights: Anthony W Zurbrugg *E-mail:* tz@merlinpress.co.uk
Founded: 1956
Subjects: Economics, Government, Political Science, History, Labor, Industrial Relations, Philosophy, Social Sciences, Sociology, Labor Studies
ISBN Prefix(es): 0-85036; 1-85425
Number of titles published annually: 10 Print
Imprints: Green Print
Distributed by Central Books Ltd (United Kingdom); Independent Publishers Group (USA)

Mermaid, *imprint of* Michael Joseph Ltd

Merrell Publishers Ltd+
42 Southwark St, London SE1 1UN
Tel: (020) 7403 2047 *Fax:* (020) 7407 1333
E-mail: mail@merrellpublishers.com; sales@merrellpublishers.com
Key Personnel
Publisher: Hugh Merrell *E-mail:* hm@merrellpublishers.com
Editorial Dir: Julian Honer *E-mail:* jh@merrellpublishers.com
Managing Editor: Anthea Snow
Art Dir: Matt Hervey *E-mail:* mh@merrellpublishers.com
Production Manager: Kate Ward
Sales & Marketing Executive: Eddy Obermueller *E-mail:* eo@merrellpublishers.com
Sales & Marketing Manager: Emilie Nangle *E-mail:* en@merrellpublishers.com
Founded: 1993
Have also published several exhibition catalogues in association with galleries in Europe & North America.
Subjects: Architecture & Interior Design, Art, Photography
ISBN Prefix(es): 1-85894
Number of titles published annually: 20 Print
Total Titles: 80 Print
U.S. Office(s): Rizzoli International Publications, 300 Park Ave S, New York, NY 10010, United States, Jerry Hoffnagle *Tel:* 212-387-3622 *Fax:* 212-387-3535 *E-mail:* jhoffnagle@rizzoliusa.com
Foreign Rep(s): Asia Publishers Services Ltd (China, Hong Kong, Korea, Taiwan); Books for Europe (Baltic States, Scandinavia); Bookwise International (Australia, New Zealand); Critiques Livres Distribution (France); DesignEXchange (Japan); Gustavo Guillen Coutino (Caribbean, Central America); Humphrys Roberts Associates (South America); Gabriele Kern (Austria, Germany, Switzerland); Csaba & Jackie Lengyel de Bagota (Eastern Europe); Nilsson & Lamm (Belgium, Netherlands, Luxembourg); Penny Padovani (Greece, Italy, Portugal, Spain); Quartet Books (Southern Africa); Rizzoli International Publications (US); Peter Ward Book Exports (Cyprus, Israel, Malta, Middle East, Turkey)
Orders to: Marston Book Services, PO Box 269, Abingdon, Oxon OX14 4YN *Tel:* (01235) 465500 *Fax:* (01235) 465555 *E-mail:* trade.order@marston.co.uk; trade.enq@marston.co.uk
St Martin's Press, c/o VHPS, 16365 James Madison Highway, Gordonsville, VA 22942-8501, United States (US & Canada)

Merrion Press
100 Hackford Rd, London SW9 0QU
Tel: (020) 7735 7791 *Fax:* (020) 77357 059
Key Personnel
Dir: Susan Shaw
Subjects: Art, Literature, Literary Criticism, Essays
ISBN Prefix(es): 0-903560

UNITED KINGDOM BOOK

Merrow Publishing Co Ltd
2 Abbey Rd, Darlington, Co Durham DL3 8LR
Tel: (01325) 351661 *Fax:* (01325) 351661
Key Personnel
Man Dir & Rights: J Gordon Cook
Founded: 1951
Subjects: Mechanical Engineering, Science (General), Technology
ISBN Prefix(es): 0-900541; 0-904095
Associate Companies: Meadowfield Press Ltd
Imprints: Meadowfield Press

Merseyside Port Folios, *imprint of* Countyvise Ltd

Meteorology, *imprint of* Artetech Publishing Co

Methodist Publishing House
4 John Wesley Rd, Werrington, Peterborough PE4 6ZP
Tel: (01733) 335002 *Fax:* (01733) 384180
E-mail: sales@mph.org.uk; chief.exec@mph.org.uk
Web Site: www.mph.org.uk
Key Personnel
Chief Executive & Rights: Brian Thornton
Founded: 1733
Subjects: Biblical Studies, Religion - Protestant, Theology
ISBN Prefix(es): 0-7162; 0-901027; 0-946550; 1-85852
Number of titles published annually: 40 Print; 1 CD-ROM; 2 Audio
Total Titles: 200 Print; 1 CD-ROM; 10 Audio
Online services available through World Wide Web.
Parent Company: The Methodist Church of Great Britain
Imprints: Foundery Press & Chester House Publications
Distributor for Upper Room

Methuen Publishing Ltd+
215 Vauxhall Bridge Rd, London SW1V 1EJ
Tel: (020) 7798 1600 *Fax:* (020) 7828 2098
Web Site: www.methuen.co.uk
Key Personnel
Man Dir: Peter Tummons *E-mail:* ptummons@methuen.co.uk
Publishing Dir: Max Eilenberg *E-mail:* maxe@methuen.co.uk
Founded: 1889
Subjects: Archaeology, Biography, Drama, Theater, Fiction, History, Humor, Music, Dance, Travel, Discovery, autobiography
ISBN Prefix(es): 0-413
Total Titles: 500 Print
Subsidiaries: Methuen Drama Ltd
Distributed by Peribo Proprietary Ltd (Australia, New Zealand)
Shipping Address: *Tel:* (01206) 255678 *Fax:* (01206) 255930
Warehouse: TBS Distribution Centre, Colchester Rd, Frating Green, Colchester, Essex CO7 7DW *Tel:* (01206) 255678 *Fax:* (01206) 255930
Orders to: Cash Sales, TBS, Colchester Rd, Frating Green, Essex CO7 7DW
Tel: (01206) 255678 *Fax:* (01206) 255930

Metro Publishing, *imprint of* John Blake Publishing Ltd

Metro Publishing Ltd+
19 Gerrard St, London W1V 7LA
Tel: (020) 7734 1411 *Fax:* (020) 7734 1811
E-mail: metro@metro.books.demon.co.uk
Key Personnel
Publishing Dir: Alan Brooke
Man Dir: Susanne McDadd
Chairman: Ian Savage

Founded: 1995
Independent publisher of commercial non-fiction.
Subjects: Biography, Child Care & Development, Cookery, Gardening, Plants, Health, Nutrition, Nonfiction (General), Psychology, Psychiatry, Travel
ISBN Prefix(es): 1-900512
Imprints: Carroll & Brown; Richard Cohen Books
Distributed by Trafalgar (U S); Trinity (South Africa)
Warehouse: Biblios Publishers' Services Ltd, Star Rd, Partridge Green, West Sussex RH13 8LD, Contact: Jane Frost *Tel:* (01403) 710971 *Fax:* (01403) 711143 *E-mail:* biblios@biblios.co.uk
Orders to: Biblios Publishers' Services Ltd, Star Rd, Partridge Green, West Sussex RH13 8LD, Contact: Jane Frost *Tel:* (01403) 710971 *Fax:* (01403) 711143 *E-mail:* biblios@biblios.co.uk

MGM+
10 Cumberland Ct, Great Cumberland Place, London W1H 7DP
Tel: (020) 7262 8386
Key Personnel
Contact: Marcus Gregory
Founded: 1996
Subjects: Poetry, Psychology, Psychiatry
ISBN Prefix(es): 0-9528799-0-5
Imprints: Our Wonderful Psychoneural Systems
U.S. Office(s): 4500 Seminary Rd, Alexandria, VA 22304-1533, United States, M Y Yassa

Micelle, *imprint of* Micelle Press

Micelle Press+
10-12 Ullswater Crescent, Weymouth, Dorset DT3 5HE
Tel: (01305) 781574 *Fax:* (01305) 781574
E-mail: tony@wdi.co.uk
Web Site: www.wdi.co.uk/micelle
Key Personnel
Proprietor: Anthony L L Hunting *E-mail:* tony@wdi.co.uk
Founded: 1984
A specialist publisher and bookseller of books on cosmetics, toiletries, perfumes, surfactants and other specialty materials. In addition to our own books, we publish on behalf of the International Federation of Societies of Cosmetic Chemists (IFSCC), and represent the Cosmetic, Toiletry & Fragrance Association (CTFA) in the EC, Quensen & Ourdas for Haarmann & Reimer books in the UK, and some other publishers.
Member of Independent Publishers Guild.
Subjects: Biological Sciences, Chemistry, Chemical Engineering, Health, Nutrition, Natural History, Physical Sciences, Science (General), Technology
ISBN Prefix(es): 1-870228; 0-9608752
Total Titles: 20 Print
Imprints: Micelle; Michelle
Divisions: Janet Barber Translations
U.S. Office(s): Micelle Press, PO Box 1519, Port Washington, NY 11050-0306, United States, Contact: Art Candido *Tel:* 516-767-7171 *Fax:* 516-944-9824 *E-mail:* info@scholium.com
Distributed by Scholium International Inc (USA & Canada); Springfields Aromatherapy Pty Ltd (Australia); Talulah Books (South Africa); United Books & Periodicals (India)
Distributor for CTFA Inc (USA, restriction UK only); Quensen & Ourdas (Germany, restriction UK only); H Ziolkowsy GmbH (Germany, restriction not Germany)

Michael Joseph, *imprint of* The Penguin Group UK

Michelin Tyre PLC, Tourism Dept, Maps & Guides Division
Edward Hyde Bldg, 38 Clarendon Rd, Watford, Herts WD1 1SX
Tel: (01923) 415000 *Fax:* (01923) 415250
Web Site: www.michelin.co.uk
Key Personnel
Head of Tourism & Sales Manager: John Lewis
Founded: 1910
Subjects: Travel
ISBN Prefix(es): 0-206
Parent Company: Michelin et Cie, France
Branch Office(s)
Michelin Travel Publications - Michelin Tire Corp, One Parkway South, Greenville, SC 29615, United States

Michelle, *imprint of* Micelle Press

Microfax, *imprint of* Funfax Ltd

Middleton Press
Easebourne Lane, Midhurst, West Sussex GU29 9AZ
Tel: (01730) 813169 *Fax:* (01730) 812601
Key Personnel
President & Editor: Vic Mitchell
Founded: 1981
Produce books for the Tramway enthusiast & modeller.
Subjects: Military Science, Regional Interests, Transportation, Railways, Tramways, Trolleybuses
ISBN Prefix(es): 0-906520; 1-873793; 1-901706

Midland Publishing+
Imprint of Ian Allan Publishing Ltd
4 Watling Dr, Hinckley LE10 3EY
Tel: (01455) 254490 *Fax:* (01455) 254495
E-mail: midlandbooks@compuserve.com
Web Site: www.ianallan.com/publishing
Key Personnel
Publisher: N P Lewis
Founded: 1992
Subjects: Aeronautics, Aviation, Military Science, Transportation
ISBN Prefix(es): 1-85780

Miles Kelly Publishing Ltd+
Bardfield Centre, Great Bardfield CM7 4SL
Tel: (01371) 811309 *Fax:* (01371) 811393
E-mail: info@mileskelly.net
Web Site: www.mileskelly.net

The Military Balance, *imprint of* International Institute for Strategic Studies

J Garnet Miller+
10 Station Rd, Industrial Estate, Colwall, Malvern, Worcs WR13 6RN
Tel: (01684) 540154 *Fax:* (01684) 540154
Key Personnel
Man Dir: Leslie Smith
Business Manager: Simon Smith
Founded: 1955
Subjects: Drama, Theater
ISBN Prefix(es): 0-85343
Number of titles published annually: 10 Print
Total Titles: 250 Print
Parent Company: Cressrelles Publishing Co Ltd
Distributed by Empire Publishing Services (Restrictions, Africa & Asia)
Distributor for I E Clark Inc (UK & Europe)
Foreign Rights: Bates Plays (US); DALRO (Southern Africa); Play Bureau (New Zealand); Warners Chappel (Australia)

Harvey Miller Publishers+
Imprint of Brepols Publishers NV

Editorial Department Harvey Miller, Brepols Publishers NV, 2, Byron Mews, Fleet Rd, Hampstead, London NW3 2NQ
Tel: (020) 7284 4359 *Fax:* (020) 7267 8764
E-mail: harvey.miller@brepols.com
Key Personnel
Dir: Harvey Miller
Editorial Dir: Elly Miller
Founded: 1969
Subjects: Art, History
ISBN Prefix(es): 0-905203; 1-872501; 0-85602
Associate Companies: G+B Arts International
Distributed by International Publishers Distributor
Orders to: Marston Book Services, PO Box 269, Abingdon, Oxon OX14 4YN *Tel:* (01235) 465500 *Fax:* (01235) 465555

J Garnet Miller Ltd, *imprint of* Cressrelles Publishing Company Ltd

Miller, *imprint of* Octopus Publishing Group

Miller's Publications
2-4 Heron Quays, London E14 4JP
Tel: (020) 7531 8400 *Fax:* (020) 7531 8650
Key Personnel
General Manager: Valerie Lewis
Executive Editor: Alison Starling
Subjects: Antiques, Architecture & Interior Design
ISBN Prefix(es): 0-85533; 1-85732; 0-86134; 0-905879
Parent Company: Octopus Publishing Group
Distributed by Antique Collectors Club (USA)

MIND Publications+
15-19 Broadway, London E15 4BQ
Tel: (020) 8519 2122 *Fax:* (020) 8522 1725; (020) 8534 6399 (orders)
E-mail: contact@mind.org.uk; publications@mind.org.uk (mail order)
Web Site: www.mind.org.uk
Key Personnel
Chief Exec: Richard Brook
Information Dir: Anny Brackx *Tel:* (020) 8221 9660 *Fax:* (020) 7221 9681 *E-mail:* a.brackx@mind.org.uk
Founded: 1946
Specialize in mental health, psychiatry, psychology.
Subjects: Psychology, Psychiatry, Self-Help, Women's Studies
ISBN Prefix(es): 1-874690
Number of titles published annually: 15 Print
Total Titles: 200 Print; 200 Online; 200 E-Book

Mirabel Books Ltd+
103 Mirabel Rd, London SW6 7EQ
Tel: (0171) 385 2515 *Fax:* (0171) 386 5027
Key Personnel
Dir: John Turner
Vice President: Cynthia Parzych
Sales Dir, Italy: Pino Vittoriette
Founded: 1989
Packager/publisher of quality illustrated, nonfiction books for the adult & children's markets.
Subjects: Animals, Pets, Anthropology, Antiques, Archaeology, Art, Asian Studies, Astrology, Occult, Earth Sciences, Gardening, Plants, Geography, Geology, History, Maritime, Military Science, Music, Dance, Natural History, Nonfiction (General), Science (General), Wine & Spirits
ISBN Prefix(es): 1-873901

MIT Press Ltd
Fitzroy House, 11 Chenies St, London WC1E 7EY
Tel: (020) 7306 0603 *Fax:* (020) 7306 0604
E-mail: info@hup-mitpress.co.uk
Web Site: www-mitpress.mit.edu
Key Personnel
General Manager: Ann Sexsmith *E-mail:* asexsmith@Hup-MITpress.co.uk
Publicity Manager: Ann Twiselton
Exhibits & Text Manager: Judith Bullent
Founded: 1932
Subjects: Architecture & Interior Design, Art, Behavioral Sciences, Computer Science, Earth Sciences, Economics, Environmental Studies, Finance, Language Arts, Linguistics, Philosophy, Psychology, Psychiatry, Science (General), Social Sciences, Sociology, Technology
ISBN Prefix(es): 0-262
Number of titles published annually: 250 Print
Parent Company: MIT Press
Imprints: Bradford Books; Semiotext(e); Zone Books
Orders to: John Wiley & Sons Ltd, Southern Cross Trading Estate, One Oldlands Way, Bognor Regis, West Sussex PO22 9SA *Tel:* (1243) 779777 *Fax:* (1243) 820250 *E-mail:* cs-books@wiley.co.uk

Mitchell Beazley, *imprint of* Octopus Publishing Group

Mobius, *imprint of* Hodder & Stoughton General

Modern Humanities Research Association, *imprint of* Maney Publishing

Mohr Books, *imprint of* Crossbridge Books

Mojo Books, *imprint of* Canongate Books Ltd

Monarch Books+
Subsidiary of Angus Hudson Ltd
Concorde House, Grenville Pl, Mill Hill, London NW7 3SA
Tel: (020) 8959 3668 *Fax:* (020) 8959 3678
E-mail: monarch@angushudson.com
Key Personnel
Editorial Dir: Tony Collins *E-mail:* tonyc@angushudson.com
Founded: 1988
Christian publisher producing up-market paperbacks for the international market.
Subjects: Biblical Studies, Biography, Education, Gay & Lesbian, Humor, Management, Psychology, Psychiatry, Religion - Protestant, Theology
ISBN Prefix(es): 1-85424; 0-9508396; 0-947697
Number of titles published annually: 35 Print
Total Titles: 100 Print
Warehouse: Kregel Publications, PO Box 2607, Grand Rapids, MI 49501, United States *Tel:* 616-451-4775 *Fax:* 616-451-9330
Send the Light, PO Box 300, Kingstown Broadway, Carlisle, Cumbria CA13 0QS *Tel:* (01228) 512512 *Fax:* (01228) 514949 *E-mail:* salesline@stl.org
Orders to: Kregel Publications, PO Box 2607, Grand Rapids, MI 49501, United States *Tel:* 616-451-4775 *Fax:* 616-451-9330
Send the Light, PO Box 300, Kingstown Broadway, Carlisle, Cumbria CA13 0QS *Tel:* (01228) 512512 *Fax:* (01228) 514949 *E-mail:* salesline@stl.org

Monument, *imprint of* Witherby & Co Ltd

Moonlight First Encyclopedia, *imprint of* Moonlight Publishing Ltd

Moonlight Publishing Ltd
The King's Manor, East Hendred, Oxon OX12 8JY
Tel: (01235) 821 821 *Fax:* (01235) 821 155
E-mail: moonlight.publishing@virgin.net
Key Personnel
Dir: Christine Baker; Robin Baker; P Stanley Baker
Founded: 1980
Subjects: Nonfiction (General)
ISBN Prefix(es): 1-85103; 0-907144
Imprints: Discovers; First Discovery; First Discovery-Art; Moonlight First Encyclopedia; Pocket Bears; Pocket Worlds; Tales of Heaven & Earth
Orders to: Ragged Bears Ltd, Ragged Appleshaw, Andover, Hants SP11 3HX *Tel:* (01264) 772269

Moorley's Print & Publishing Ltd+
23 Park Rd, Ilkeston, Derbyshire DE7 5DA
Tel: (0115) 9320643 *Fax:* (0115) 9320643
E-mail: info@moorleys.co.uk
Key Personnel
Chairman & Man Dir: John R Moorley *E-mail:* john@moorleys.co.uk
Founded: 1966
Member of European Christian Bookseller Association.
Subjects: Biblical Studies, Drama, Theater, Music, Dance, Poetry, Religion - Protestant, Theology
ISBN Prefix(es): 0-901495; 0-86071
Number of titles published annually: 12 Print
Total Titles: 300 Print
Associate Companies: Truedata Computer Services
Imprints: Freedom Ministries; Headline Specials
Distributor for Cliff College Publishing; Nimbus Press; Social Workers Christian Fellowship; T Young

Morgan Publishing, *imprint of* Welsh Academic Press

William Morrow, *imprint of* HarperCollins Publishers

E J Morten (Publishers)+
6 Warburton St, Didsbury, Manchester M20 6WA
Tel: (0161) 445 7629 *Fax:* (0161) 448 1323
E-mail: timlovat@aol.com
Key Personnel
Man Dir, Rights & Permissions: John Anthony Morten
Founded: 1969
Facsimile reprints undertaken.
Subjects: History, Regional Interests
ISBN Prefix(es): 1-85972; 0-901598
Parent Company: E J Morten (Booksellers), Didsbury, Manchester
Imprints: Datapack Books; Pride Publications
Divisions: Morten Hire

Motilal (UK) Books of India
PO Box 324, Borehamwood, Herts WD6 1NB
Tel: (0208) 9051244 *Fax:* (0208) 9051108
E-mail: info@mlbduk.com
Web Site: www.mlbduk.com
Key Personnel
Man Dir: Ray McLennan
Founded: 1980
Comprehensive coverage of Indology subjects. Imports from all Indian publishers against special orders. Also acts as UK agent for Motilal Banarsidass, Sundeep Prakashan, Concept Publications, Kant Publications & South Asia Books (India).
Subjects: Archaeology, Architecture & Interior Design, Art, Asian Studies, Education, History, Language Arts, Linguistics, Literature, Literary Criticism, Essays, Philosophy, Religion - Buddhist, Religion - Hindu, Religion - Islamic, Romance, Social Sciences, Sociology, Women's Studies, Specializes in Indology, Hinduism, Buddhism, Jainism, Translations of Sanskrit & Pali texts
ISBN Prefix(es): 81-208; 0-946482

UNITED KINGDOM

Total Titles: 8,000 Print
Ultimate Parent Company: Money Savers (London) Ltd

Motor Racing Publications Ltd+
Unit 6, The Pilton Estate, 46 Pitlake, Croydon CR0 3RY
Tel: (0208) 681 3363 *Fax:* (0208) 760 5117
E-mail: mrp.books@virgin.net
Web Site: www.oberon.co.uk/mrp
Key Personnel
Man Dir, Publicity, Rights & Permissions: John Blunsden
Editorial & Customer Services: John Plummer
Sales, Production: Jim Starr
Founded: 1948
Specialize in sports.
Subjects: Automotive, Technology, Transportation
ISBN Prefix(es): 0-900549; 0-947981; 0-948358; 1-899870
Number of titles published annually: 11 Print
Total Titles: 80 Print
Imprints: The Fitzjames Press
Distributed by Motorbooks International USA (overseas distribution); Vine House Distribution Ltd
Foreign Rep(s): Bookport Associates (Gibraltar, Italy, Malta, Portugal & Spain); Bookworld Wholesale; D Richard Bowen (Scandinavia); Dennis Buckingham; Patrick Bygate (Croatia & Slovenia, Greece); Juliusz Komarnicki (Austria, Czech Republic, France, Hungary, Poland, Slovak Republic, Switzerland); Mike Lapworth; Clive Malins; Robert J Pleysier (Benelux, Germany); Mike Ryba

Mowbray, *imprint of* Cassell & Co

Mowbray, *imprint of* The Continuum International Publishing Group Ltd

MQ Publications Ltd
12 The Ivories, 6-8 Northampton St, London N1 2HY
Tel: (020) 7359 2244 *Fax:* (020) 7253 7358
E-mail: mqp@btinternet.com
Key Personnel
Man Dir: Susan Jenkins; Gerson Kesner
Subjects: Cookery, Crafts, Games, Hobbies, History
Warehouse: Biblios, Star Rd, Patridge Green, West Sussex

MRP, see Motor Racing Publications Ltd

Multilingual Matters Ltd+
Frankfurt Lodge, Clevedon Hall, Clevedon BS21 7HH
Tel: (01275) 876519 *Fax:* (01275) 871673
E-mail: info@multilingual-matters.com
Web Site: www.multilingual-matters.com
Key Personnel
Man Dir: Mike Grover *E-mail:* mike@multilingual-matters.com
Editorial Manager: Marjukka Grover
 E-mail: marjukka@multilingual-matters.com
Production Manager: Ken Hall *E-mail:* ken@multilingual-matters.com
Marketing & Distribution Manager: Kathryn King *E-mail:* kathryn@multilingual-matters.com
Founded: 1982
Member of Independent Publishing Guild.
Subjects: Education, Environmental Studies, Geography, Geology, Language Arts, Linguistics, Social Sciences, Sociology, Travel, Specializing in bilingualism & bilingual education, second & foreign language learning & translation studies, also tourism research
ISBN Prefix(es): 0-905028; 1-85359; 1-873150
Number of titles published annually: 30 Print
Total Titles: 300 Print; 10 Online

Imprints: Channel View Publications
Branch Office(s)
Channel View Publications, 5201 Dufferin St, North York, ON M3H 5T8, Canada
 Tel: (416) 667-7791 *Fax:* (416) 667-7832
 E-mail: utpbooks@utpress.utoronto.ca (American Distributors)
UTP, 5201 Dufferin St, North York, ON M3H 5T8, Canada *Tel:* 416-667-7791 *Fax:* 416-667-7832 *E-mail:* utpbooks@utpress.utoronto.ca
Orders to: Plymbridge Distributors, Plymbridge House, Estover Rd, Estover, Plymouth PL6 7PZ *Tel:* (01752) 202301 *Fax:* (01752) 202331 *E-mail:* cservs@plymbridge.com

Multimedia, see Prion Books Ltd

James Munro & Co
4-10 Darnley St, Glasgow G41 2SD
Tel: (0141) 429 1234 *Fax:* (0141) 420 1694
E-mail: enquiry@skipper.co.uk (general enquiries); sales@skipper.co.uk (orders)
Web Site: www.skipper.co.uk
Key Personnel
Sales Dir: L Ingram-Brown
Founded: 1832
Subjects: Maritime
ISBN Prefix(es): 0-85174
Parent Company: Brown, Son & Ferguson, Ltd

Murchison's Pantheon Ltd+
45 Beech St, London EC2Y 8AD
Tel: (020) 7628 1492 *Fax:* (020) 7628 6270
E-mail: 100450.1105@compuserve.com
Key Personnel
Contact: Charles Blount *E-mail:* charlesblount@compuserve.com
Specialize in audio travel guides.
Subjects: History, Travel
ISBN Prefix(es): 1-900652

John Murray (Publishers) Ltd+
30 Albemarle St, London W1S 4BD
Tel: (020) 7493 4361 *Fax:* (020) 7499 1792
E-mail: johnmurray@dial.plpex.com
Web Site: www.johnmurray.co.uk
Key Personnel
Chairman & Marketing Dir, General Books: John R Murray
Man Dir: Nick Perren *E-mail:* nick.perren@dial.pipex.com
Head of Finance: Philip Carter
Head of Rights: Jane Blackstock
Editorial Dir: Grant McIntyre
Marketing Dir, Educational Books: Judith Reinhold
Humanities Publisher: Jim Belben
Mathematics Publisher: Rose Wands
Modern Languages Publisher: Carolyn Burch
Publisher: Katie Mackenzie Stuart
Publicity Manager: Stephanie Allen
Founded: 1768
Independent publisher.
Subjects: Accounting, Biography, Biological Sciences, Chemistry, Chemical Engineering, Child Care & Development, Communications, Economics, Electronics, Electrical Engineering, Geography, Geology, History, Marketing, Mathematics, Nonfiction (General), Physics, Science (General), modern languages
ISBN Prefix(es): 0-7195
Distributor for Abbeville Press Inc
Orders to: Grantham Book Services Ltd, Isaac Newton Way, Alma Park Industrial Estate, Grantham, Lincs NG31 9SD *Tel:* (01476) 541000 *Fax:* (01476) 541060

Music Sales Ltd, see Omnibus Press

Muze UK Ltd+
Cygnet House, 9th Floor, 12-14 Sydenham Rd, Croydon, Surrey CR0 2EE
Tel: (0870) 7277 256 *Fax:* (0870) 7277 257
E-mail: colin@muze.co.uk
Web Site: www.muze.com
Key Personnel
President: Colin Larkin
Research Editor: Nic Oliver
Administration: Susan Pipe
Founded: 1990
Subjects: Biography, Music, Dance
ISBN Prefix(es): 1-872747
Parent Company: Muze Inc, 304 Hudson St, 8th Floor, New York, NY 10013, United States

MWH London Publishers+
233 Seven Sisters Rd, London N4 2DA
Tel: (020) 7272 5170 *Fax:* (020) 7272 3214
Telex: 8812176
Key Personnel
Man Dir: Mohamed Tamin
Founded: 1970
Subjects: Regional Interests
ISBN Prefix(es): 0-906194
Associate Companies: Muslim Information Centre
Orders to: MIC, London

NAG Press, *imprint of* Robert Hale Ltd

NAG Press+
Imprint of Robert Hale Ltd
Clerkenwell House, 45-47 Clerkenwell Green, London EC1R 0HT
Tel: (20) 7251 2661 *Fax:* (20) 7490 4958
E-mail: enquire@halebooks.com
Web Site: www.halebooks.com/n_a_g_press_files.html
Key Personnel
Dir: Martin Kendall
Founded: 1937
Subjects: Horological & gemmological
ISBN Prefix(es): 0-7198
Total Titles: 100 Print
Warehouse: CBS, Units 1/K, Paddockwood Distribution Centre, Townbridge, KY, United States, Contact: Alan Smith *Tel:* (01892) 837171 *Fax:* (01892) 837212 *E-mail:* orders@combook.co.uk

NATE, see National Association for the Teaching of English (NATE)

National Archives of Scotland
H M General Register House, Edinburgh, Scotland EH1 3YY
Tel: (0131) 5351314 *Fax:* (0131) 5351360
E-mail: publications@nas.gov.uk
Web Site: www.nas.gov.uk
Key Personnel
Head of Publications & Education Branch: Rosemary Gibson
Publications Officer: Alison Lindsay *Tel:* (0131) 535-1353
Founded: 1787
General historical & educational publications designed to make the holdings of the NAS more accessible.
Member of Scottish Publishers Association.
Subjects: History
ISBN Prefix(es): 1-870874
Number of titles published annually: 3 Print
Total Titles: 42 Print
Branch Office(s)
West Search Room, West Register House, Charlotte Square, Edinburgh, Scotland EH2 4DJ *Tel:* (0131) 535 1413 *Fax:* (0131) 535 1411 *E-mail:* wsr@nas.gov.uk

National Assembly for Wales, *imprint of* National Assembly for Wales

PUBLISHERS

UNITED KINGDOM

National Assembly for Wales
Cardiff Bay, Cardiff CF99 1NA
Tel: (029) 20 825111 *Fax:* (029) 20 825350
E-mail: stats.pubs@wales.gsi.gov.uk
Web Site: www.wales.gov.uk
Key Personnel
Man Dir & General Editor: E Swires-Hennessy
Tel: (029) 2082 5087 *Fax:* (029) 2082 5087
E-mail: ed.swires-hennessy@wales.gsi.gov.uk
Founded: 1981
Specialize in statistics on Wales.
Subjects: Business, Economics, Education, Government, Political Science, Health, Nutrition, Public Administration, Social Sciences, Sociology
ISBN Prefix(es): 0-7504
Total Titles: 35 Print
Imprints: Cynulliad Cenedlaethol Cymru; National Assembly for Wales

National Association for Mental Health, see MIND Publications

National Association for the Teaching of English (NATE)+
Broadfield Business Centre, 50 Broadfield Rd, Sheffield S8 OXJ
Tel: (0114) 255 5419 *Fax:* (0114) 255 5296
E-mail: natehq@btconnect.com
Web Site: www.nate.org.uk
Key Personnel
Development & Communications Dir: Trevor Millum
Founded: 1963
Member of Publishers Association; specialize in English teaching.
Subjects: Drama, Theater, Education, English as a Second Language, Film, Video, Literature, Literary Criticism, Essays, Poetry, Literacy, Information & communication technology
ISBN Prefix(es): 0-901291
Number of titles published annually: 10 Print
Total Titles: 50 Print
Distributed by Australian Reading Association
Distributor for BELTA; Paul Chapman Publishing; Devon County Council; Drake Publishing; English & Media Centre; Falmer Press; Framework Press/Fultons; David Fulton; Garth Publishing; Nelsons; Open University Press; PCET Wallcharts; Thimble Press; Ward Lock

National Christian Education Council, see Christian Education

National Computing Centre, see Blackwell Publishers

National Extension College+
Michael Young Centre, Purbeck Rd, Cambridge CB2 2HN
Tel: (01223) 400 200 *Fax:* (01223) 400 399
E-mail: info@nec.ac.uk
Web Site: www.nec.ac.uk
Key Personnel
Executive Dir: Ros Morpeth
Assistant Dir: Roger Merritt
Founded: 1963
Member of ICDE, NIACE & BAOL.
Subjects: Accounting, Business, Career Development, Education, English as a Second Language, Environmental Studies, Self-Help
ISBN Prefix(es): 0-86082; 1-85356; 0-902404
Imprints: NEC

National Foster Care Association+
87 Blackfriars Rd, London SE1 8HA
Tel: (020) 7620 6400 *Fax:* (020) 7620 6401
E-mail: nfca@fostercare.org.uk
Key Personnel
Communications Manager: Katrina Phillips
Founded: 1976
Subjects: Child Care & Development
ISBN Prefix(es): 1-897869; 0-946015

National Foundation for Educational Research
The Mere Upton Park, Slough SL1 2DQ
Tel: (01753) 574123 *Fax:* (01753) 691632
E-mail: enquiries@nfer.ac.uk
Web Site: www.nfer.ac.uk
Key Personnel
Head of Publication: Dr Enver Carim
Subjects: Education
ISBN Prefix(es): 0-7005; 0-7087; 0-85633; 0-901225
Branch Office(s)
Slough Rd, Datchet, Berks SL3 9AU *Tel:* (01753) 574123 *Fax:* (01753) 691632 (Please do not send post to this address)
Genesis 4, York Science Park, University Rd, Heslington, York YO10 5DG *Tel:* (01904) 433435 *Fax:* (01904) 433436 *E-mail:* j.harland@nfer.ac.uk
Chestnut House, Tawe Business Village, Phoenix Way, Enterprise Park, Swansea SA7 9LA *Tel:* (01792) 459800 *Fax:* (01792) 797815 *E-mail:* scya@nfer.ac.uk

National Galleries of Scotland+
Publications Dept, The Dean Gallery, Belford Rd, Edinburgh EH4 3OS
Tel: (0131) 624 6257; (0131) 624 6261 *Fax:* (0131) 315 2963
E-mail: enquiries@nationalgalleries.org
Web Site: www.nationalgalleries.org
Key Personnel
Head of Publications & Picture Library: Janis Adams *E-mail:* jadams@nationalgalleries.or
Subjects: Art, Photography
ISBN Prefix(es): 0-903598; 1-903278
Total Titles: 90 Print; 1 CD-ROM

National Institute of Adult Continuing Education+
21 De Montfort St, Lincs LE1 7GE
Tel: (0116) 204 4200; (0116) 204 4201 *Fax:* (0116) 285 4514
E-mail: enquiries@niace.org.uk; niace@niace.org.uk
Web Site: www.niace.org.uk
Key Personnel
Dir: Alan Tuckett *E-mail:* alan.tuckett@niace.org.uk
Dir Research, Development & Information: Peter Lavender *E-mail:* peter.lavender@niace.org.uk
Dir Programmes & Policy: Sue Cara
Dir Finance: Margaret Conner *E-mail:* margaret.conner@niace.org.uk
Founded: 1921
NIACE, the national organization for adult learning, has a broad remit to promote life long learning opportunities for adults. NIACE works to develop increased participation in education & training. It aims to do this for more who do not have easy access due to class, gender, age, race, language & culture, learning difficulties, disabilities or insufficient financial resources.
Subjects: Education
ISBN Prefix(es): 1-872941; 1-86201; 0-900559
Number of titles published annually: 40 Print
Total Titles: 100 Print
Branch Office(s)
NIACE Dysgu Cymru, 35 Cathedral Rd, Ground Floor, Cardiff, Wales CF11 9HB *Tel:* (0292) 0370900 *Fax:* (0292) 0370909 *E-mail:* enquiries@niacecy.demon.co.uk *Web Site:* www.niacedc.org.uk

National Library of Scotland
George IV Bridge, Edinburgh, Scotland EH1 1EW
Tel: (0131) 226 4531 *Fax:* (0131) 622 4803
E-mail: enquiries@nls.uk
Web Site: www.nls.uk
Key Personnel
Librarian: Martyn Wade
Dir Public Services: Dr Alan Marchbank
Head of Public Programs: Dr Kenneth Gibson
Subjects: History, Regional Interests

National Library of Wales
Aberystwyth, Ceredigion SY23 3BU
Tel: (01970) 632 800 *Fax:* (01970) 615 709
E-mail: holi@llgc.org.uk
Web Site: www.llgc.org.uk
Key Personnel
President: R Brinley Jones
Vice President: John Phillips
Treasurer: Conrad L Bryant
Editor: Gwyn Jenkins
Librarian: Mr Andrew M W Green
Founded: 1907
Copyright/Legal Deposit Library.
Subjects: Art, Genealogy, Government, Political Science, Library & Information Sciences, Literature, Literary Criticism, Essays, Photography, Publishing & Book Trade Reference
ISBN Prefix(es): 0-907158

National Museum & Gallery
Cathays Park, Cardiff CF10 3NP
Tel: (029) 2039 7951 *Fax:* (029) 2037 3219
E-mail: post@nmgw.ac.uk
Web Site: www.nmgw.ac.uk
Key Personnel
Contact: John Williams-Davies

National Museum of Scotland Publishing, see NMS Publishing Ltd

National Portrait Gallery Publications+
St Martin's Place, London WC2H 0HE
Tel: (020) 7306 0055 (ext 253) *Fax:* (020) 7306 0092
E-mail: publications@npg.org.uk
Web Site: www.npg.org.uk
Key Personnel
Head of Publications: Robert Carr-Archer
Rights & Permissions: Tom Morgan
Sales & Marketing Officer: Pallavi Vadhia
E-mail: pvadhia@npg.org.uk
Publications Assistant: Shirley Ellis
E-mail: sellis@nqg.org.uk
Founded: 1976 (book publishing division)
Also acts as Picture Library.
Subjects: Art, Biography, History, Photography
ISBN Prefix(es): 0-904017; 1-85514
Number of titles published annually: 14 Print
Total Titles: 31 Print
Branch Office(s)
Antique Collector's Club, Market St Industrial Park, Wappingers Falls, New York, NY 12590, United States *Fax:* 845-297-0068
Warehouse: Grantham Book Services, Isaac Newton Way, Alva Park Industrial Estate, Grantham Lines N931 9SD *Tel:* (01476) 541 080 *Fax:* (01476) 541 061

The National Society, *imprint of* Church House Publishing

National Trust+
36 Queen Anne's Gate, London SW1H 9AS
Tel: (020) 7222 9251 *Fax:* (020) 7222 5097
Key Personnel
Publisher: Margaret Willes
Founded: 1987
Subjects: Art, Cookery, Gardening, Plants, History, Photography, Social Sciences, Sociology, Travel
ISBN Prefix(es): 0-7078
Number of titles published annually: 12 Print
Total Titles: 75 Print
Parent Company: National Trust Enterprises, The Stable Block, Heywood House, Westbury, Wilts BA13 4NA

UNITED KINGDOM

Branch Office(s)
Rowallane House, Ballynahinch, Co Down, Northern Ireland *Tel:* (028) 9751 0721 *Fax:* (028) 9751 1242
Wemyss House, 28 Charlotte Square, Edinburgh, Scotland *Tel:* (0131) 243 9300 *Web Site:* www.nts.org.uk/
Lanhydrock, Bodmin *Tel:* (01208) 74281 *Fax:* (01208) 77887 (regional office for Cornwall)
Hughenden Manor, High Wycombe, Bucks *Tel:* (01494) 528051 *Fax:* (01494) 463310 *Web Site:* www.nationaltrust.org.uk/regions/thameschilterns/ (regional office for Thames & Solent)
The Hollens, Grasmere, Ambleside, Cumbria *Tel:* (0870) 609 5391 *Fax:* (015394) 35353 (regional office for the North West)
Killerton House, Broadclyst, Exeter EX5 3LE *Tel:* (01392) 881691 *Fax:* (01392) 881954 (regional office for Devon)
Scots' Gap, Morpeth, Northumberland *Tel:* (01670) 774691 *Fax:* (01670) 774317 (regional offices for North East)
Blickling, Norwich *Tel:* (0870) 609 5388 *Fax:* (01263) 734924 *Web Site:* www.nationaltrust.org.uk/regions/eastanglia/ (regional office for East Anglia)
Clumber Park Stableyard, Worksop, Notts *Tel:* (01909) 486411 *Fax:* (01909) 486377 (regional office for the East Midlands)
Attingham Park, Shrewsbury, Salop *Tel:* (01743) 708100 *Fax:* (01743) 708150 *E-mail:* sevinfo@stmp.ntrust.org.uk *Web Site:* www.nationaltrust.org.uk/regions/westmidlands/ (regional office for the West Midlands)
Polesden Lacey, Dorking, Surrey *Tel:* (01372) 453401 *Fax:* (01372) 452023 (regional office for the South East)
Eastleigh Court, Bishopstrow, Warminster, Wilts *Tel:* (01985) 843600 *Fax:* (01985) 843624 *Web Site:* www.nationaltrust.org.uk/regions/wessex/ (regional office for Wessex)
Goddards, 27 Tadcaster Rd, Dringhouses, York *Tel:* (01904) 702021 *Fax:* (01904) 771970 (regional office for Yorkshire)
Trinity Square, Llandudno, Wales LL30 2DE *Tel:* (01492) 860123 *Fax:* (01492) 860233
Trafalgar Square Publishing, Howe Hill Rd, North Pomfret, VT 05053, United States
Warehouse: MacMillian Distribution Ltd, Houndmills, Basingstoke R921 GXS, Mrs Beverly Morris *Tel:* (01256) 329242 *Fax:* (01256) 812558
Orders to: MacMillian Distribution Ltd, Houndmills, Basingstoke R921 GXS, Hazel Maynard

NCLC Publishing Society Ltd
11 Dartmouth St, London SW1H 9BN
Tel: (020) 7222 8877 *Fax:* (020) 7976 7153
E-mail: fabian-society@geo2.poptel.org.uk
Key Personnel
General Secretary: Michael Jacobs
Subjects: Government, Political Science, Regional Interests
ISBN Prefix(es): 0-7163

NCVO+
Regent's Wharf, 8 All Saints St, London N1 9RL
Tel: (020) 7713 6161 *Fax:* (020) 7713 6300
E-mail: ncvo@ncvo-vol.org.uk
Web Site: www.ncvo-vol.org.uk
Key Personnel
Head of Marketing & Publications: Jim Minton
Marketing Officer: Lou Large
Chief Executive: Stuart Etherington
Online Development Manager: Simon Cope *Tel:* (0207) 520 2544 *E-mail:* simon.cope@ncvo-vol.org.uk
Founded: 1919 (NCVO), 1969 (BSP), 1991 (NCVO Publications)
Also publish in association with other organizations.

Member of Publishers Association, Independent Publishers Association (IPG).
Subjects: Disability, Special Needs, Finance, Management, Public Administration
ISBN Prefix(es): 0-7199
Orders to: Hamilton House Mailings, 17 Staveley Way, Northampton NN6 7TX

NEC, *imprint of* National Extension College

Negotiate Ltd+
99 Caiyside, Edinburgh EH10 7HR
Tel: (0131) 445 7571; (0131) 477 7858 *Fax:* (0131) 445 7572
E-mail: florence@negweb.com
Web Site: www.negotiate.co.uk
Key Personnel
Man Dir: Gavin Kennedy
Founded: 1986
Subsidiaries: Negotiate P S C

Nelson Thornes Ltd+
Delta Pl, 27 Bath Rd, Cheltenham GL53 7TH
Tel: (01242) 267100; (01242) 267311 *Fax:* (01242) 221914
E-mail: cservices@nelsonthornes.com
Web Site: www.nelsonthornes.com
Key Personnel
Man Dir General Management: Oliver Gadsby
Founded: 1972
Subjects: Business, Child Care & Development, Education, Environmental Studies, Geography, Geology, History, Language Arts, Linguistics, Mathematics, Medicine, Nursing, Dentistry, Music, Dance, Physics, Religion - Other, Science (General), Social Sciences, Sociology, Technology
ISBN Prefix(es): 0-7487; 0-85950; 1-871402
Parent Company: Wolters Kluwer PLC
Ultimate Parent Company: Wolters Kluwer NV, Netherlands
Imprints: Mary Glasgow Publications
Warehouse: Alexandra Industrial Estate, Alexandra Way, Ashchurch, Tewkesbuy GL20 8PE

Net.Works, *imprint of* Take That Ltd

Network Books, *imprint of* BBC Worldwide Publishers

Neville Spearman Publishers, *imprint of* The C W Daniel Co Ltd

New Cavendish Books+
3 Denbigh Rd, London W11 2SJ
Tel: (020) 7229 6765 *Fax:* (020) 7792 0027
Web Site: www.newcavendishbooks.co.uk
Key Personnel
Dir: Narisa Chakra *Tel:* (020) 7229 6765 *E-mail:* narisa@new-cav.demon.co.uk
Founded: 1973
Subjects: Nonfiction (General), Technology, Toys, collecting & popular culture
ISBN Prefix(es): 0-904568; 1-872727
Number of titles published annually: 4 Print
Total Titles: 70 Print
Imprints: White Mouse Editions
Distributed by Antique Collectors Club

New English Library, *imprint of* Hodder & Stoughton General

New Era Publications UK Ltd+
Saint Hill Manor, East Grinstead, Sussex RH19 4JY
Tel: (01342) 314 846 *Fax:* (01342) 314 857
E-mail: books@newerapublications.com
Web Site: www.newerapublications.com
Key Personnel
Man Dir: Margaret Blunden

BOOK

Dir, Public Affairs: Robert Springall
Sales Dir: Nic Webb *E-mail:* nic@nrgw.demon.co.uk
Marketing Director: Robert Black
Founded: 1985
Subjects: Business, Education, Fiction, Health, Nutrition, Management, Nonfiction (General), Philosophy, Religion - Other, Science Fiction, Fantasy, Self-Help, Western Fiction
ISBN Prefix(es): 1-870451; 1-900944
Total Titles: 90 Print; 1 CD-ROM; 18 Audio
Parent Company: New Era Publications International ApS, Denmark
Associate Companies: Author Services Inc, 7051 Hollywood Blvd, Suite 400, Los Angeles, CA 90028, United States *Tel:* 213-466-3310 *E-mail:* asi@earthlink.net
Branch Office(s)
Continental Publications Pty Ltd, Budget House, 6th floor, 130 Main St, Johannesburg 2001, South Africa *Tel:* (0113) 316 621 *Fax:* (0113) 316 621
New Era Central Europe, Leonardo Da Vinci u 8-12, 1084 Budapest, Hungary *Tel:* (01) 210-3446 *Fax:* (01) 210-3501
Nueva Era Dinamica SA, C/montera 20, 1 Dcha, 28013 Madrid, Spain *Tel:* (07) 77 0941
New Era Publications Australia Pty Ltd, Ballarat House, Level 3, 68-72 Wentworth Ave, Surry Hills, NSW 2010, Australia *Tel:* (02) 211 0692 *Fax:* (02) 211 0686
New Era Publications Deutschland GmbH, Hittfelder Kirchweg 5a, 21220 Seevetal-Maschen, Germany *Tel:* (04105) 68330 *Fax:* (04105) 683322 *E-mail:* buch@newerapublications.de
New Era Publications France EURL, 14, Rue des Moulins, 75001 Paris, France *Tel:* (01) 42 974250 *Fax:* (01) 42 974260 *E-mail:* librairie@newerapublications.com
New Era Publications Group, Str Kasatkina, 16, Bldg 1, 129301 Moscow, Russian Federation *Tel:* (095) 286 88 31 *Fax:* (095) 286 88 31
New Era Publications Italia, Via Cadorna, 61, 20090 Vimodrone (MI), Italy *Tel:* (02) 274 09272 *Toll Free Tel:* 800-828-195 *Fax:* (02) 274 09198 *E-mail:* sales@newera.it
New Era Publications Japan Inc, 4-38-15-2F Higashi Ikebukuro, Toshima-Ku, Tokyo 170, Japan *Tel:* (03) 5960 5660 *Fax:* (03) 5960 5561 *E-mail:* nepjp@newerapublications.com
Source Publications Co, 2nd Floor 65, Section 4, Min-Shen East Rd, Taipei ROC, Taiwan, Province of China *Tel:* (02) 25465851
U.S. Office(s): Bridge Publications, A751 Fountain Ave, Los Angeles, CA, United States
Warehouse: Bailey Distribution, Learoyd Rd, New Romney, Kent TN28 8XU

New European Publications Ltd+
14-16 Carroun Rd, London SW8 1JT
Tel: (020) 7582 3996 *Fax:* (020) 7582 7021
Key Personnel
Dir: Sir Richard Body; John Coleman
Founded: 1987
Specialize in European affairs & subjects with a special interest in 'communitarian' politics.
Subjects: Aeronautics, Aviation, Government, Political Science, Travel
Number of titles published annually: 5 Print
Total Titles: 23 Print
Orders to: Central Books Ltd, 99 Wallis Rd, London E9 5LN

New Holland, *imprint of* New Holland Publishers (UK) Ltd

New Holland Publishers (UK) Ltd+
Garfield House, 86-88 Edgware Rd, London W2 2EA
Tel: (020) 7724 7773 *Fax:* (020) 7724 6184
E-mail: postmaster@nhpub.co.uk

PUBLISHERS — UNITED KINGDOM

Key Personnel
Man Dir: John Beaufoy *E-mail:* john@nhpub.co.uk
Editorial: Jo Jennings; Yvonne McFarlane; Rosemary Wilkinson
Rights & Co-Editions Dir: Elena Mannion
  E-mail: elena@nhpub.co.uk
Sales & Marketing Dir: Martin Oestreicher
  E-mail: martin@nhpub.co.uk
Publicity & Promotions Manager: Harriet Boston
  E-mail: harriet@nhpub.co.uk
Founded: 1956
Specialize in illustrated books.
Subjects: Cookery, Crafts, Games, Hobbies, House & Home, How-to, Natural History, Travel
ISBN Prefix(es): 1-85368; 1-85974
Parent Company: The New Holland Struik Publishing Group (Pty) Ltd, South Africa
Imprints: New Holland
Subsidiaries: New Holland Australia
Distributor for Southern Book Publishers (Europe, UK, North America & Asia); Stonebridge Press (Europe, UK & South Africa); Struik Publishers (Europe, UK & North America); Weatherhill (Europe, UK & South Africa)
Shipping Address: F J Tytherleigh & Co Ltd, Hubert Rd, Brentwood, Essex CM14 4RF
Orders to: Littlehampton Book Services Ltd, Faraday Close, Durrington, West Sussex BN13 3RB

New Leaf Books Ltd+
11 Chesterford Gardens, London NW3 7DD
Mailing Address: Box BCM-New Leaf, London WC1N 3XX
Tel: (020) 7435 3056 *Fax:* (020) 7431 3625
E-mail: newleafbooks@btinternet.com
Key Personnel
Man Dir: Michael Wright *Tel:* (7970) 855246
Founded: 1973
Also acts as book packager.
Subjects: Antiques, Cookery, Gardening, Plants, Health, Nutrition, House & Home, How-to, Natural History, Photography, Science (General), Technology, Travel, Veterinary Science, Wine & Spirits
ISBN Prefix(es): 0-907916
Foreign Rep(s): Andrew Nurnberg Associates (London, World)
Foreign Rights: Andrew Nurnberg Associates (London, World)

New Orchard Editions, *imprint of* Cassell & Co

New Playwrights Network, *imprint of* Cressrelles Publishing Company Ltd

New Playwrights' Network+
10 Station Rd, Industrial Estate, Colwall, Malvern WR13 6RN
Tel: (01684) 540154 *Fax:* (01684) 540154
Key Personnel
Man Proprietor: L G Smith
Founded: 1972
Subjects: Drama, Theater
ISBN Prefix(es): 0-86319; 0-903653; 0-906660
Total Titles: 400 Print

New Roders, *imprint of* Pearson Education Europe, Mideast & Africa

Newman Books Ltd, see Hemming Information Services

Newpro UK Ltd+
Old Sawmills Rd, Faringdon, Oxon SN7 7DS
Tel: (01367) 242411 *Fax:* (01367) 241124
E-mail: sales@newprouk.co.uk
Key Personnel
Man Dir: Chris Coleman *E-mail:* chriscoleman@newprouk.co.uk
Founded: 1984
Also distributes for other photography publishers.
Subjects: Crafts, Games, Hobbies, History, Photography
ISBN Prefix(es): 0-86343; 1-87403; 0-90644
Imprints: Fountain Press; Hove Foto Books

Nexus, *imprint of* Virgin Publishing Ltd

Nexus Special Interests+
Nexus House, Azalea Drive, Swanley, Kent BR8 8HU
Tel: (01322) 660070 *Fax:* (01322) 617633
Web Site: www.nexusonline.com
Key Personnel
Books Manager & International Rights Contact: Bill Burkinshaw *Fax:* (01296) 738704
Customer Services Manager: Jayne Hewish
Subjects: Crafts, Games, Hobbies, Engineering (General), Gardening, Plants, Wine & Spirits, Specialize in Hobby & Craft books, magazines, plans, exhibitions & awards evenings
ISBN Prefix(es): 1-87403; 0-85344; 1-85486; 0-85076
Total Titles: 130 Print
Parent Company: Nexus Media Ltd
Distributed by Chris Lloyd
Foreign Rep(s): Chris Lloyd
Warehouse: Cassell Warehouse, Fleets Industrial Estate, One, Willis Way, Poole, Dorset BH15 3SS

The NFER-NELSON Publishing Co Ltd+
Darville House, 2 Oxford Rd East, Windsor, Berks SL4 1DF
Tel: (01753) 858961; (01753) 827249 (customer service) *Fax:* (01753) 856830; (01753) 620160 (customer service)
E-mail: information@nfer-nelson.co.uk; edu&hsc@nfer-Nelson.co.uk (customer service)
Web Site: www.nfer-nelson.co.uk
Telex: 937400 ONECOM G ref 24966001
Key Personnel
Man Dir: Michael Jackson
Commercial Dir: Penn Fiona
Business Development Dir: Ian Florance
Founded: 1981
A joint venture of the National Foundation for Educational Research in England and Wales and the Thomson Corporation.
Subjects: Business, Child Care & Development, Education, Health, Nutrition, Psychology, Psychiatry
ISBN Prefix(es): 0-7005; 0-7087; 0-85633; 0-901225
Parent Company: Thomson Corporation
Associate Companies: Thomas Nelson & Sons Ltd, Routledge
Divisions: ASE
Warehouse: Units 1 & 2, Wyndham Rd, Hawkswoan Estate, Swindon, Wiltshire SN2 1BR

NIACE, see National Institute of Adult Continuing Education

Nicholas Enterprises Ltd+
28 Percy St, London W1P 0LD
Tel: (020) 7323 3319 *Fax:* (020) 7323 4829
E-mail: aladdin@duron.co.uk
Key Personnel
Contact: Charles Nicholas
Founded: 1980
Subjects: Crafts, Games, Hobbies, Nonfiction (General)

Nico Editions, *imprint of* Thoemmes Press

Nightingale Books, *imprint of* Baha'i Publishing Trust

Nightingale Press, *imprint of* Wimbledon Publishing Company Ltd

Nile & Mackenzie Ltd+
13 John Prince's St, London W1M 9HB
Tel: (020) 7493 0351 *Fax:* (020) 7495 0128
Key Personnel
Man Dir: Daljit Sehbai
Rights & Permissions: Donna Stewart
Founded: 1974
Subjects: Education
ISBN Prefix(es): 0-86031

James Nisbet & Co Ltd+
78 Tilehouse St, Hitchin, Herts SG5 2DY
Tel: (01462) 438331 *Fax:* (01462) 431528
Key Personnel
Chairman: E M Mackenzie-Wood
Founded: 1810
Subjects: Education
ISBN Prefix(es): 0-7202

NIV Bibles, *imprint of* Hodder & Stoughton Religious

NMS Publishing Ltd+
Royal Museum, Chambers St, Edinburgh EH1 1JF
Tel: (0131) 247 4026 *Fax:* (0131) 247 4012
E-mail: publishing@nms.ac.uk
Web Site: www.nms.ac.uk
Key Personnel
Publishing Dir: Lesley A Taylor *Tel:* (0131) 247 4186 *E-mail:* ltaylor@nms.ac.uk
Production: Liz Robertson
Marketing & Publicity: Cara Helm *E-mail:* cara@nms.ac.uk; Claire Saunderson
Administrator: Elizabeth Dewar
Founded: 1998
Subjects: Archaeology, Art, Biography, Cookery, Geography, Geology, History, Natural History, Nonfiction (General), Poetry, Science (General), Technology, Scottish history & culture, photographic archive
ISBN Prefix(es): 0-948636; 1-901663
Number of titles published annually: 15 Print
Total Titles: 110 Print; 1 CD-ROM; 1 Audio
Parent Company: NMS Enterprises Ltd
Distributed by Gazelle Book Service; Arthur Schwartz & Co Inc; Scottish Book Source; Reg Tigwell Art Agencies; University of British Columbia

No Exit Press, *imprint of* Oldcastle Books Ltd

No Exit Press, see Oldcastle Books Ltd

North Light, *imprint of* David & Charles Ltd

Northcote House Publishers Ltd+
Horndon House, Horndon, Tavistock, Devon PL19 9NQ
Tel: (01822) 810066 *Fax:* (01822) 810034
E-mail: northcote.house@virgin.net
Web Site: www.northcotehouse.com
Key Personnel
Publisher: Brian Hulme
Founded: 1985
Subjects: Drama, Theater, Education, Literature, Literary Criticism, Essays, Music, Dance
ISBN Prefix(es): 0-7463
Number of titles published annually: 20 Print
Total Titles: 150 Print
Imprints: Writers & Their Work
Distributed by University Press of Mississippi (USA)

UNITED KINGDOM

Orders to: Plymbridge Distributors Ltd, Estover, Plymouth PL6 7PY *Tel:* (01752) 202301 *Fax:* (01752) 202331
Membership(s): IPG

Northern Books, *imprint of* Famedram Publishers Ltd

Northern Universities Press, *imprint of* Maney Publishing

Norton & Liveright, Countryman Press, *imprint of* W W Norton & Company Ltd

W W Norton & Company Ltd+
Castle House, 75/76 Wells St, London W1T 3QT
Tel: (020) 7323 1579 *Toll Free Tel:* 800-233-4830 (orders) *Fax:* (020) 7436 4553 *Toll Free Fax:* 800-458-6515 (orders)
E-mail: office@wwnorton.co.uk
Web Site: www.wwnorton.co.uk
Key Personnel
President: W Drake McFeely
Man Dir: R A Cameron
Sales Manager: Judith Pamplin
Publicity: Ariadne Van de Ven
Marketing Manager: Victoria Keown-Boyd
Founded: 1980
Subjects: Architecture & Interior Design, Art, Biography, Economics, Government, Political Science, History, Literature, Literary Criticism, Essays, Maritime, Music, Dance, Photography, Psychology, Psychiatry
ISBN Prefix(es): 0-393
Number of titles published annually: 120 Print; 20 CD-ROM
Total Titles: 4,000 Print
Parent Company: W W Norton & Company Inc, 500 Fifth Ave, New York, NY 10110, United States
Imprints: Norton & Liveright, Countryman Press
Distributor for New Directions
Foreign Rep(s): APAC Publishers Services Pte Ltd (Indonesia, Malaysia & Singapore, Thailand); B K Norton Ltd (Korea & Taiwan); Delaney Global Publishers Service (Guam, Philippines); M K International Ltd (Japan); Pearson Education New Zealand (New Zealand); Transglobal Publishers Service Ltd (Hong Kong); US PubRep Inc (Caribbean, Mexico, South & Central America); Transglobal Publishers Service Ltd (Australia)
Orders to: John Wiley & Sons Ltd, One Oldlands Way, Bognor Regis, West Sussex PO22 9SA

Norwood Publishers
3 Chapel St, Norwood Green, Halifax, West Yorks HX3 8QU
Tel: (01274) 602454
Key Personnel
Partner: Mr M H Wolfenden; A M Wolfenden
Founded: 1991
Subjects: Education, Health, Nutrition, Social Sciences, Sociology
ISBN Prefix(es): 1-873784

Novello & Co Ltd+
8/9 Frith St, London W1V 5TZ
Tel: (020) 7434 0066 *Fax:* (020) 7287-6329
E-mail: music@musicsales.co.uk
Web Site: www.musicsales.co.uk
Key Personnel
Man Dir & Executive Dir: James Rushton
Contact: Nichole Wade
Founded: 1811
Subjects: Music, Dance
ISBN Prefix(es): 0-85360
Parent Company: Music Sales Ltd
Imprints: Cinderella; Elkin; Fairfield; Laurel; Lorna; Paxton

Branch Office(s)
c/o Shawnee Press Inc, 49 Waring Drive, Delaware Gap, PA 18327-1099, United States
Orders to: Music Sales Ltd, Newmarket Rd, Bury St-Edmunds, Suffolk IP33 3YB *Tel:* (01284) 702600 *Fax:* (01284) 768301

NTC Publications Ltd+
Farm Rd, Henley-on-Thames, Oxon RG9 1EJ
Tel: (01491) 411000 *Fax:* (01491) 571188
E-mail: info@ntc.co.uk
Key Personnel
Man Dir: David Roberts *E-mail:* david_roberts@ntc.co.uk
Production Dir: Andrew Denham
Librarian: Alison Haan *Tel:* (01491) 411000 *E-mail:* alison_haan@ntc.co.uk
Founded: 1984
Member of the Periodical Publishers Association (PPA).
Subjects: Advertising, Economics, Government, Political Science, Marketing, Radio, TV
ISBN Prefix(es): 1-870562
Parent Company: Information Sciences Ltd
Divisions: NTC Conferences Ltd; NTC Research Ltd
U.S. Office(s): 1615 "L" St NW, Suite 1220, Washington, DC 20036, United States *Tel:* 202-778-0680 *Fax:* 202-778-4546

Nuit-Isis, *imprint of* Mandrake of Oxford

"O" Books, *imprint of* John Hunt Publishing Ltd

Oakwood Library of Railway History, *imprint of* Oakwood Press

Oakwood Press
PO Box 13, Usk, Monmouthshire NP15 1YS
Tel: (01291) 650444 *Fax:* (01291) 650484
E-mail: oakwood-press@dial.pipex.com
Web Site: www.oakwood-press.dial.pipex.com
Key Personnel
Proprietor, Man Dir & Rights: Jane Kennedy
Founded: 1934
Specialist transport publisher.
Subjects: History, Transportation
ISBN Prefix(es): 0-85361
Number of titles published annually: 20 Print
Total Titles: 150 Print
Imprints: Locomotion Papers; Oakwood Library of Railway History
Divisions: Oakwood Video Library

Oceano Grupo Editorial, *imprint of* Gale Research

The Octagon Press Ltd+
PO Box 227, London N6 4EW
Tel: (020) 8341 5971 *Fax:* (020) 8348 9392
E-mail: octagon@schredds.demon.co.uk
Web Site: www.octagonpress.com
Key Personnel
Man Dir: George Schrager
Publicity: Patti Schneider
Founded: 1972
Subjects: Anthropology, Asian Studies, Behavioral Sciences, Education, Philosophy, Poetry, Psychology, Psychiatry, Religion - Islamic, Religion - Other, Travel, Sufis
ISBN Prefix(es): 0-900860
Number of titles published annually: 2 Print
Total Titles: 150 Print
Distributed by ISHK Book Service (USA, North America, South America)

Octopus Publishing Group+
2-4 Heron Quays, London E14 4JP
Tel: (020) 7531 8400 *Fax:* (020) 7531 8650
Web Site: www.octopus-publishing.co.uk

BOOK

Subjects: Aeronautics, Aviation, Antiques, Architecture & Interior Design, Automotive, Cookery, Crafts, Games, Hobbies, Drama, Theater, Fiction, Film, Video, Gardening, Plants, Geography, Geology, Health, Nutrition, Literature, Literary Criticism, Essays, Music, Dance, Mysteries, Natural History, Nonfiction (General), Photography, Poetry, Science Fiction, Fantasy, Sports, Athletics, Travel, Wine & Spirits
Parent Company: Hachette Livre
Imprints: Bounty Books; Brimax; Cassell Illustrated; Conran Octopus; Hamlyn; Miller; Mitchell Beazley; Philip
Orders to: Littlehamptom Book Services Ltd, Durrington Worthing, West Sussex BN13 3RB *Tel:* (01903) 828800

Oilfield Publications Ltd
PO Box 11, Ledbury, Herefordshire HR8 1BN
Tel: (01531) 634563 *Fax:* (01531) 634239; (01531) 633744
E-mail: opl@dial.pipex.com
Web Site: www.oilpubs.com
Key Personnel
Man Dir: Julia Lourd
Subjects: Energy, Maritime, book & vessel registers for the international offshore oil & gas industry
ISBN Prefix(es): 1-870945
Branch Office(s)
Oilfield Publications Inc, 888 W Sam Houston Parkway S, Suite 280, Houston, TX 77042, United States *Tel:* 713-334-8970 *Fax:* 713-334-8968 *E-mail:* oplusa@oilpubs.com

Old Bailey Press, *imprint of* HLT Publications

Old Vicarage Publications
The Old Vicarage, Reades Lane, Dane in Shaw, Congleton, Cheshire CW12 3LL
Tel: (01260) 279276 *Fax:* (01260) 298913
Key Personnel
Proprietor: William Ball *E-mail:* william.ball@btinternet.com
Founded: 1983
Subjects: Ethnicity, Film, Video, Regional Interests, Travel
ISBN Prefix(es): 0-900269; 0-947818; 0-9508635
Imprints: Centaur Books
Branch Office(s)
State Book & Periodical Service, New York, NY, United States

Oldcastle Books Ltd+
18 Coleswood Rd, Harpenden, Herts AL5 1EQ
Tel: (01582) 761264 *Fax:* (01582) 712244
E-mail: info@noexit.co.uk
Web Site: www.noexit.co.uk
Key Personnel
Dir & Foreign Rights: Ion Mills
  E-mail: ionmills@noexit.co.uk
Founded: 1985
No unsolicited manuscripts.
Subjects: Crafts, Games, Hobbies, Fiction, Mysteries, Non Fiction, Gambling, Crime Fiction
ISBN Prefix(es): 0-948353; 1-874061; 1-901982
Imprints: No Exit Press
Sales Office(s): 21 Great Ormond St, London WC1N 3JB *Tel:* (020) 7430 1021 *Fax:* (020) 7430 0021 *Web Site:* www.thebigbookshop.co.uk
Foreign Rep(s): Capricorn Link (Australia); Codasat (Canada); Four Walls Eight Windows/No Exit Press (North America); Michael Geoghegan (Belgium, France); Gill & Macmillan (Ireland); Gabriele Kern (Austria, Germany & Switzerland); Pernille Larson (Scandinavia); PIMS (Far East, Middle East); Peter Prout (Gibraltar, Spain); PSD Promotions (Pty) Ltd (South Africa); Southern Publishers Group (New Zealand); Trafalgar Square Publishing (US); Turnaround (UK)
Foreign Rights: Shirley Stewart

PUBLISHERS UNITED KINGDOM

The Oleander Press+
16 Orchard St, Cambridge CB1 1JT
Tel: (01223) 357768
E-mail: editor@oleanderpress.com
Web Site: oleanderpress.com
Key Personnel
Man Dir: Jerry Toner
Founded: 1960
Subjects: Biography, Drama, Theater, Language Arts, Linguistics, Literature, Literary Criticism, Essays, Poetry, Regional Interests, Travel, Specialize in travel, especially Arabia Peninsula, Games, Monographs
ISBN Prefix(es): 0-900891; 0-902675; 0-906672
Number of titles published annually: 4 Print
Total Titles: 120 Print

Oliver Books Ltd
Unit 16-18 Wimbledon Stadium Business Centre, Riverside Rd, London SW17 0BA
Tel: (020) 8879 3949 *Fax:* (020) 8879 0792
E-mail: info@oliverbooks.co.uk; sales@oliverbooks.co.uk
Web Site: www.oliverbooks.co.uk
Key Personnel
Man. Director: Peter Fenton
Founded: 1978
Subjects: Biography, Film, Video, Music, Dance
ISBN Prefix(es): 1-870049

Michael O'Mara Books Ltd+
9 Lion Yard, Tremadoc Rd, London SW4 7NQ
Tel: (020) 7720 8643 *Fax:* (020) 7627 8953 (Editorial); (020) 7627 4900 (Foreign Sales)
E-mail: foreignsales@michaelomarabooks.com
Web Site: www.michaelomarabooks.com
Key Personnel
Chairman: Michael O'Mara
Man Dir: Lesley O'Mara
Foreign Sales Man: Louise Green
UK Sales Dir: David Crombie
Editorial Dir: Gabrielle Mander
Childrens Man Editor: Philippa Wingate
Production Consultant: David Bann
Founded: 1985
Subjects: Biography, Crafts, Games, Hobbies, History, Humor, Nonfiction (General), Self-Help
ISBN Prefix(es): 1-85479; 0-948397
Number of titles published annually: 80 Print
Imprints: Buster Books
Subsidiaries: Mary Ford Publications
Orders to: Grantham Book Services, Isaac Newton Way, Alma Park Industrial Estate, Grantham, Lincs NG31 9SD *Tel:* (01476) 541080 *Fax:* (01476) 541061/63
Membership(s): IPG

Omnibus Press+
8-9 Frith St, London W1D 3JB
Tel: (020) 7434 0066 *Fax:* (020) 7439 2848
E-mail: music@musicsales.co.uk
Web Site: www.musicsales.com
Telex: 21892
Key Personnel
Man Dir: Robert Wise
Dir: Malcolm Grabham
Editorial: Chris Charlesworth
Sales & Marketing Manager: Hilary Power
Rights & Permissions Manager: Andrew King
Production Manager: Mark Pickard
Founded: 1979
Subjects: Biography, Music, Dance
ISBN Prefix(es): 0-7119; 0-86001; 0-9657122
Parent Company: Music Sales Ltd, London
Imprints: Amsco Publications; Bobcat Books; Proteus; WISE Publications; Zomba Books
Subsidiaries: Music Sales Corp; Music Sales Pty
Branch Office(s)
Music Sales Pty Ltd, c/o Bookwise, 54 Coultenden Rd, Fundon, Austria

U.S. Office(s): Music Sales Corporation, 275 Park Ave S, New York, NY 10010, United States
Distributor for BBC Music Guides; Firefly; Gramophone; OZONE; Parker Mead; RED Independent Music Press; Rogan House; Showcase Publications
Warehouse: Book Sales Ltd, Newmarket Rd, Bury St, Edmunds, Suffolk IP33 3YB

Oneworld Publications
185 Banbury Rd, Oxford OX2 7AR
Tel: (01865) 310597 *Fax:* (01865) 310598
E-mail: info@oneworld-publications.com
Web Site: www.oneworld.publications.com
Key Personnel
Partner: Novin Doostdar *E-mail:* ndoostdar@yahoo.com; Juliet Mabey
Man Dir: Helen Coward
Founded: 1986
Subjects: Anthropology, Education, History, Philosophy, Psychology, Psychiatry, Religion - Buddhist, Religion - Catholic, Religion - Hindu, Religion - Islamic, Religion - Jewish, Religion - Protestant, Religion - Other, Self-Help
ISBN Prefix(es): 1-85168
Number of titles published annually: 40 Print
Total Titles: 200 Print
Online services available through World Wide Web.
Branch Office(s)
PO Box 2510, Novato, CA 94948, United States

Open Books Publishing Ltd
Willow Cottage, Cudworth, Nr Ilminster, Somerset TA19 0PS
Tel: (01460) 52565 *Fax:* (01460) 52565
Key Personnel
Man Dir: Patrick Taylor *E-mail:* patrickta@aol.com
Founded: 1974
Subjects: Gardening, Plants, Nonfiction (General)
ISBN Prefix(es): 0-7291

Open Gate Press+
51 Achilles Rd, London NW6 1DZ
Tel: (020) 7431 4391 *Fax:* (020) 7431 5129
E-mail: books@opengatepress.co.uk
Web Site: www.opengatepress.co.uk
Key Personnel
Contact: Jeannie Cohen
Founded: 1988
Subjects: Anthropology, Archaeology, Economics, Government, Political Science, Philosophy, Psychology, Psychiatry, Social Sciences, Sociology
ISBN Prefix(es): 1-871871
U.S. Office(s): Paul & Company Publishers Consoritum Inc, PO Box 442, Concord, MA 10742, United States
Distributor for Cambridge International Publishers
Orders to: Book Representation & Distribution Ltd, 244-A London Rd, Hadleigh, Essex SS7 2DE

Open University Press+
Celtic Court, 22 Ballmoor, Buckingham MK18 1XW
Tel: (01280) 823388 *Fax:* (01280) 823233
E-mail: enquiries@openup.co.uk
Web Site: www.openup.co.uk
Key Personnel
Man Dir & Publisher: John Skelton *E-mail:* jskelton@openup.co.uk
Financial Dir: Barry Clarke *E-mail:* bclarke@openup.co.uk
Publishing Dir & Publisher: Jacinta Evans *E-mail:* jevans@openup.co.uk
Publisher: Shona Mullen *E-mail:* smullen@openup.co.uk; Justin Vaughan *E-mail:* jvaughan@openup.co.uk
Production Dir: Sue Hadden

Marketing Manager: Sarah Wilman *E-mail:* swilman@openup.co.uk
Sales Dir: Barbara Martin *E-mail:* bmartin@openup.co.uk
Founded: 1977
Subjects: Behavioral Sciences, Criminology, Developing Countries, Education, Government, Political Science, Health, Nutrition, Management, Psychology, Psychiatry, Public Administration, Social Sciences, Sociology, Women's Studies
ISBN Prefix(es): 0-335
Parent Company: Clarke, Skelton & Wright Ltd, 246 Bishopgate, London EC2
Foreign Rep(s): Dave Smith (Finland, Norway, Republic of Ireland, Sweden)
Orders to: Marston Book Services, PO Box 269, Abingdon, Oxon OX14 4YN
Raincoast Books Distribution Ltd, 9050 Shaughnessy St, Vancouver, BC V6P 6E5, Canada *E-mail:* custserv@raincoast.com *Web Site:* www.ubcpress.ubc.ca/ (Canada)
Taylor & Francis Inc, 7625 Empire Dr, Florence, KY, United States *Web Site:* www.taylorandfrancis.com (USA Orders and Customer Service)

Open University Worldwide+
The Berrill Bldg, Walton Hall, Milton Keynes MK7 6AA
Tel: (01908) 858785 *Fax:* (01908) 858787
E-mail: ouwenq@open.ac.uk
Web Site: www.open.ac.uk
Key Personnel
Dir: Bob Masterton
Marketing Manager: Katherine Bull
Rights & Permissions, Print: Sue Hitchen
Rights & Permissions, Audio Visual: Diana Rualt
Founded: 1977
Subjects: Architecture & Interior Design, Astronomy, Biological Sciences, Chemistry, Chemical Engineering, Computer Science, Developing Countries, Disability, Special Needs, Earth Sciences, Economics, Education, Electronics, Electrical Engineering
ISBN Prefix(es): 0-7492
Parent Company: The Open University, Walton Hall, Milton Keynes, Bucks MK7 6AA
Branch Office(s)
40 University Rd, Belfast BT7 1SU, Ireland *Tel:* (028) 9024 5025 *Fax:* (028) 9023 0565 *E-mail:* ireland@open.ac.uk
66 High St Harborne, Birmingham *Tel:* (0121) 428 1550 *Fax:* (0121) 427 9484 *E-mail:* west-midlands@open.ac.uk
10 Drumsheugh Gardens, Edinburgh, Scotland *Tel:* (0131) 225 2889 *Fax:* (0131) 220 6730 *E-mail:* scotland@open.ac.uk
Cintra House, 12 Hills Rd, Cambridge CB2 1PF *Tel:* (01223) 361650 *Fax:* (01223) 355207 *E-mail:* east-of-england@open.ac.uk
St James's House, 150 London Rd, East Grinstead RH19 1HG *Tel:* (01342) 410545 *Fax:* (01342) 317411 *E-mail:* south-east@open.ac.uk
2 Trevelyan Sq, Boar Lane, Leeds LS1 6ED *Tel:* (0113) 245 1466 *Fax:* (0113) 234 1862
Parsifal College, 527 Finchley Rd, London NW3 7BG *Tel:* (020) 7431 3215 *Fax:* (020) 7556 6196 *E-mail:* london@open.ac.uk
351 Altrincham Rd, Sharston, Manchester M22 4UN *Tel:* (0161) 998 7007; 998 7478 *Fax:* (0161) 945 3356 *E-mail:* north-west@open.ac.uk
Eldon House, Regent Centre, Gosforth, New Castle Upon Tyne NE3 3PW *Tel:* (0191) 213 1380 *Fax:* (0191) 284 6592 *E-mail:* north@open.ac.uk
Clarendon Park, Clumber Ave, Sherwood Rise, Nottingham NG5 1AH *Tel:* (0115) 962 5451 *Fax:* (0115) 971 5575 *E-mail:* east-midlands@open.ac.uk

Foxcombe Hall, Boars Hill, Oxford OX1 5HR
Tel: (01865) 735140 *Fax:* (01865) 736288
E-mail: south@open.ac.uk
24 Cathedral Rd, Cardiff, Wales CF11 9SA
Tel: (029) 2066 5636 *Fax:* (029) 2022 7930
E-mail: wales@open.ac.uk

Opus Book Publishing Ltd
20 East Rd, West Mersea, Colchester CO5 8EB
Tel: (01206) 383629 *Fax:* (01206) 383629
E-mail: opus@mac.co.uk
Key Personnel
Contact: Diana van der Klugt
Subjects: Maritime
ISBN Prefix(es): 1-898574

Opus Publishing Ltd
36 Camden Sq, London NW1 9XA
Tel: (020) 7267 1034 *Fax:* (020) 7267 6026
E-mail: opuspub@dircon.co.uk
Key Personnel
President: Martin Heller

Orbit, *imprint of* Time Warner Books UK

Orchard Books, see The Watts Publishing Group Ltd

Ordnance Survey
Customer Contact Centre, Ordnance Survey, Romsey Rd, Southampton SO16 4GU
Tel: (08456) 05 05 05 (customer information); (023) 8079 5519 (trade orders) *Fax:* (023) 8079 2615 (trade customer information); (023) 8079 2388 (trade orders)
E-mail: enquiries@ordsvy.gov.uk
Web Site: www.ordnancesurvey.co.uk
Key Personnel
Dir General: Vanessa Lawrence
Head of Marketing: Eric Bates
Head of Sales: Phil Watts
Press Officer: Philip Round
Sales Off Manager: Nicky Long *Tel:* (23) 8030 5278 *E-mail:* nlong@ordsvy.gov.uk
ISBN Prefix(es): 0-319

Original English Language Fiction, *imprint of* Dedalus Ltd

Orion, *imprint of* Orion Publishing Group Ltd

Orion Children's Books+
c/o The Orion Publishing Group, Orion House, 5 Upper St Martins Lane, London WC2H 9EA
Tel: (020) 7240 3444 *Fax:* (020) 7240 4822
Web Site: www.orionbooks.co.uk
Key Personnel
Man Dir & Publisher: Judith Elliott
Founded: 1993
ISBN Prefix(es): 1-85881
Number of titles published annually: 50 Print
Imprints: Dolphin Paperbacks

Orion Publishing Group Ltd+
Orion House, 5 Upper St Martins Lane, London WC2H 9EA
Tel: (020) 7240 3444 *Fax:* (020) 7240 4822
E-mail: info@orionbooks.co.uk
Web Site: orionbooks.co.uk
Key Personnel
Chairman: Nicholas Barber
Chief Executive: Anthony Cheetham
Man Dir & Group Finance Dir: Peter Roche
Founded: 1991
Subjects: Archaeology, Art, Biography, Biological Sciences, Business, Crafts, Games, Hobbies, Fiction, Film, Video, History, Management, Mysteries, Nonfiction (General), Poetry, Religion - Other, Romance, Science (General), Science Fiction, Fantasy, Self-Help, Sports, Athletics, Western Fiction
ISBN Prefix(es): 0-7528
Parent Company: Hachette Livre
Associate Companies: Dent Children; Everyman; Millenium; Phoenix; Phoenix House
Imprints: Orion
Subsidiaries: JM Dent & Sons; Orion Books; Weidenfeld & Nicolson
Warehouse: Littlehampton Book Service, 14 Eldon Way, Lineside Estate, Littlehampton, West Sussex BN17 7HE
Orders to: Littlehampton Book Service, 14 Eldon Way, Lineside Estate, Littlehampton, West Sussex BN17 7HE

The Orkney Press Ltd+
8 Broad St, Kirkwall, Orkney KW15 1NX
Tel: (1856) 875747 *Fax:* (1856) 876284
Key Personnel
Sales Dir: Mrs Sidsel Firth
Founded: 1981
Subjects: Anthropology, Archaeology, History, Maritime, Natural History, Philosophy, Science (General)
ISBN Prefix(es): 0-907618
Imprints: Scottish Falcon; Aurora Northern Classics

Orpheus Books Ltd+
2 Church Green, Witney, Oxon OX28 4AW
Tel: (01993) 774949 *Fax:* (01993) 700330
E-mail: info@orpheusbooks.com
Web Site: www.orpheusbooks.com
Key Personnel
Chairman: Nicholas Harris *E-mail:* nicholas@orpheusbooks.com
Founded: 1992
Principally book packagers.
Subjects: Animals, Pets, Astronomy, Earth Sciences, Geography, Geology, History, Natural History, Science (General), Transportation
ISBN Prefix(es): 1-901323
Number of titles published annually: 7 Print

Osborne Books Ltd
Unit 1B, Everoak Estate, Bromyard Rd, St Johns, Worcs WR2 5HP
Tel: (01905) 748071 *Fax:* (0190) 748952
E-mail: books@osborne.u-net.com
Web Site: www.osbornebooks.co.uk
Key Personnel
Contact: Michael Fardon
Founded: 1987
Subjects: Accounting, Business, History, Literature, Literary Criticism, Essays, Photography
ISBN Prefix(es): 1-872962; 0-9510650
Imprints: Heritage

Osprey Publishing Ltd+
Elms Court, Chapel Way, Botley, Oxford OX2 9LP
Tel: (01865) 727022 *Fax:* (01865) 727017
E-mail: info@ospreydirect.co.uk
Web Site: www.ospreypublishing.com
Key Personnel
Man Dir: William Shepherd
Financial Dir: Sarah Lough
Sales & Marketing Dir: Joanna Sharland
Illustrated military history from around the world with all-time greatest battles of land & air, from antiquity to the present day.
Subjects: Aeronautics, Aviation, Crafts, Games, Hobbies, History, Military Science
ISBN Prefix(es): 1-85532; 0-85045; 0-540; 1-84176
Total Titles: 600 Print
U.S. Office(s): Specialty Book Marketing, 443 Park Ave S, New York, NY 10016, United States, Contact: Bill Corsa *Tel:* 212-685-5560 *Fax:* 212-685-5836 *E-mail:* ospreyusa@aol.com
Distributor for Compendium Publishing
Orders to: Grantham Book Services, Isaac Newton Way, Alma Park Industrial Estate, Grantham, Lincs NG31 9SD *Tel:* (01476) 541 080 *Fax:* (01476) 541 061
Motorbooks International, 729 Prospect Ave, Osceola, WI 54020-0001, United States *Tel:* 715-294-3345 *Fax:* 715-294-4448

Our Wonderful Psychoneural Systems, *imprint of* MGM

Overstone Press, *imprint of* Thoemmes Press

Peter Owen Ltd+
73 Kenway Rd, London SW5 0RE
Tel: (020) 7373 5628; (020) 7370 6093 *Fax:* (020) 7373 6760
E-mail: admin@peterowen.u-net.com
Web Site: www.peterowen.com
Key Personnel
Sales & Publicity: Daniel McCabe
Editorial: Antonia Owen
Editorial & Rights: Simon Smith
Rights: Peter Owen
Production: Keith Savage
Founded: 1950
Subjects: Art, Biography, Drama, Theater, Fiction, Gay & Lesbian, Language Arts, Linguistics, Literature, Literary Criticism, Essays, Music, Dance, Publishing & Book Trade Reference, Social Sciences, Sociology, Women's Studies
ISBN Prefix(es): 0-7206
Number of titles published annually: 25 Print; 30 Audio
Foreign Rep(s): World Wide

Owl Books
c/o Coveropen Ltd, 6 Sefton View Orrell, Wigan WN5 8UG
Tel: (01695) 622022 *Fax:* (01542) 821819
Key Personnel
Proprietor: J A Roby
Founded: 1989
Member of IPG.
Subjects: Biography, History, Sports, Athletics
ISBN Prefix(es): 0-9514333; 1-873888
Associate Companies: Coveropen Ltd, PO Box 60, Wigan WN1 2QB

Oxfam+
Member of Oxfam International
Oxfam Supporter Services Department, Oxfam House, 274 Banbury Rd, Oxford OX2 7DZ
Tel: (01865) 312610 *Fax:* (01865) 313925
E-mail: oxfam@oxfam.org.uk
Web Site: www.oxfam.org.uk
Telex: 83610 *Cable:* OXFAMG OXFORD
Key Personnel
Publishing Executive: Robert Cornford *E-mail:* r.cornford@oxfam.org.uk
Marketing: Deborah Logan
Contact: Caroline Knowles
Founded: 1942
Subjects: Developing Countries, Economics, Government, Political Science, Social Sciences, Sociology, Women's Studies
ISBN Prefix(es): 0-85598
Total Titles: 130 Print
Distributed by David Philip Publishers (Southern Africa); Stylus Publishing LLC (USA & Canada)
Orders to: BEBC, PO Box 1496, Parkstone, Dorset BH12 3YD

Oxford International Centre for Publishing Studies
School of Art, Publishing & Music, Oxford Brookes University, The Richard Hamilton Bldg, Headington Hill Campus, Oxford OX3 0BP
Tel: (01865) 484951 *Fax:* (01865) 484952
E-mail: apm@brookes.ac.uk

Web Site: www.brookes.ac.uk/schools/apm/ publishing
Key Personnel
Dir: Prof Paul Richardson *E-mail:* ptrichardson@ brookes.ac.uk
Founded: 1994
A centre for publishing education, training, consulting & research.

Oxford Poets, *imprint of* Carcanet Press Ltd

Oxford University Press+
Great Clarendon St, Oxford OX2 6DP
Tel: (01865) 556767 *Fax:* (01865) 556646
Web Site: www.oup.co.uk
Telex: 837330 Oxpres G
Key Personnel
Man Dir, ELT: Peter R Mothersole
Man Dir, UK Academic Division: Ivan S Asquith
Group Finance Dir: R C Boning
Group Personal Dir: M J Havelock
Public Affairs Manager: Caroline Scotter Mainprize
Chief Executive: Henry Reece
Man Dir, UK Educational Division: Fiona Clarke
Man Dir, International Division: Susan Froud
President, OUP USA: Edward Barry
Man Dir, OUP Spain: Jesus Lazcano
Founded: 1478
Subjects: Art, Biography, Economics, Education, Engineering (General), Government, Political Science, History, Language Arts, Linguistics, Law, Literature, Literary Criticism, Essays, Mathematics, Medicine, Nursing, Dentistry, Military Science, Music, Dance, Philosophy, Poetry, Psychology, Psychiatry, Publishing & Book Trade Reference, Religion - Other, Science (General), Social Sciences, Sociology
ISBN Prefix(es): 0-19
Associate Companies: Cornelsen und Oxford University Press GmbH, Germany
Imprints: Clarendon Press; IRL Press
Subsidiaries: Oxford University Press Inc
Branch Office(s)
70 Wynford Dr, Don Mills, ON M3C 1J9, Canada
Warwick House, 18th Floor, Taikoo Place, 979 King's Rd, Hong Kong, China
Oxford University Press Espana SA, Pargue Empresarial San Fernando de Henares: Edificio Atenas la Plantz, San Fernando de Henares, 28830 Madrid, Spain
PO Box 43, New Delhi 110001, India
Oxford University Press KK (Japan), 2-4-8 Kanamecho, Toshima-ku, Toyko 171, Japan
PO Box 72532, Nairobi, Kenya
Penerbit Fajar Bakti Sdn Bhd, Malaysia
PO Box 13033, Karachi 75350, Pakistan
37 Jal an Pemimpin, No 03-03 Union Industrial Bldg B Block A, Singapore 577177, Singapore
PO Box 5299, Dar es Salaam, Thailand
PO Box 1141, Cape Town 8000, South Africa
GPO Box 2784Y, Melbourne, Victoria (Australia & New Zealand)
Bookshop(s): 116-117 High St, Oxford OX1 4BZ
Tel: (01865) 242913
Orders to: OUP Distribution Services, Saxon Way West, Corby, Northamptonshire NN18 9ES
Tel: (01536) 741519 *Fax:* (01536) 746337

Oxford University Press Children's Books
Great Clarendon St, Oxford OX2 6DP
Tel: (01865) 556767 *Fax:* (01865) 267732
E-mail: enquiry@oup.co.uk
Web Site: www.oup.co.uk

Oyster Books+
Sparrow Hillway, Weare, Axbridge BS26 2LA
Tel: (01934) 732251 *Fax:* (01934) 732123
E-mail: pearls@oysterbooks.co.uk
Web Site: www.oysterbooks.co.uk
Key Personnel
Man Dir: Tim Wood
Production Dir: Ali Brooks
Sales Dir: Donna Webber
Sales & Marketing: Rachel Holmes
  E-mail: rachel@oysterbooks.co.uk
Founded: 1985
Also acts as book packagers.
Subjects: Fiction, Nonfiction (General)
ISBN Prefix(es): 0-948240

P N Review, see Carcanet Press Ltd

Packard Publishing Ltd+
Forum House, Stirling Rd, Chichester, West Sussex PO19 7DN
Tel: (01243) 537977 *Fax:* (01243) 537977
E-mail: info@packardpublishing.co.uk
Web Site: www.packardpublishing.com
Key Personnel
Man Dir: Michael Packard
Founded: 1977
Academic book publisher & distributor.
Subjects: Agriculture, Architecture & Interior Design, Biological Sciences, Environmental Studies, Gardening, Plants, Geography, Geology, Natural History
ISBN Prefix(es): 0-906527; 0-948690; 1-85341
Number of titles published annually: 6 Print
Imprints: Headlions; PPL
Distributed by Stipes Publishing LLC (USA)
Distributor for Librairie DuLiban (UK); Oxygraphics Ltd (UK)
Shipping Address: c/o Clipper Distribution Services, Windmill Grove, Portchester, Hants PO16 9HT
Warehouse: c/o Clipper Distribution Services, Windmill Grove, Portchester, Hampshire PO16 9HT

Palgrave Publishers Ltd+
Brunel Rd, Houndmills, Basingstoke, Hants RG21 6XS
Tel: (01256) 329242 *Fax:* (01256) 479476
E-mail: orders@palgrave.com (ordering online); catalogue@palgrave.com (catalogue requests); conferences@palgrave.com (conference & exhibition information); rights@palgrave.com (copyright & permissions); lectureservices@palgrave.com (inspection copy service); reviews@palgrave.com (review copy requests); booksellers@palgrave.com (bookseller queries)
Web Site: www.palgrave.com
Key Personnel
Man Dir: Dominic Knight *E-mail:* d.knight@palgrave.com
Publishing Dir, College Publishing Division (Business, Computer Science & Engineering): Christopher Glennie *E-mail:* c.glennie@palgrave.com
Publishing Dir, College Publishing Division (Humanities & Social Science): Frances Arnold *E-mail:* f.arnld@palgrave.com
Publishing Dir, College Publishing Division (Professional & Business Management): Stephen Rutt *E-mail:* s.rutt@palgrave.com
Publishing Dir, Academic Division: Josie Dixon *E-mail:* j.dixon@palgrave.com
Sales & Marketing Dir: Margaret Hewinson *E-mail:* m.hewinson@palgrave.com
Marketing Dir: Carol Monoyios *E-mail:* c.monoyios@palgrave.com
International Sales Dir: Alastair Gordon *E-mail:* a.gordon@palgrave.com
UK Sales Dir: Sam Burridge *E-mail:* s.burridge@palgrave.com
Publishing Services Dir: Tim Fox *E-mail:* t.fox@palgrave.com
Subjects: Business, Computer Science, Economics, Engineering (General), History, Human Relations, Management, Science (General), Social Sciences, Sociology, Technology
ISBN Prefix(es): 0-333
Parent Company: Macmillan Ltd
Imprints: W H Freeman
U.S. Office(s): 175 Fifth Ave, New York, NY, NY 10010, United States *Tel:* 212-982-3900 *Fax:* 212-777-6359

Pallas Athene+
59 Linden Gardens, London W2 4HJ
Tel: (020) 7229 2798 *Fax:* (020) 7792 1067
Key Personnel
President & Publisher: Alexander Fyjis-Walker
Founded: 1991
Subjects: Art, Travel
ISBN Prefix(es): 1-873429; 0-9529986
Total Titles: 20 Print
Imprints: Pallas Guides; WOL Books
Orders to: Trafalgar Square Publishing, PO Box 257, Howe Hill Rd, North Pomfret, VT 05053, United States
Vine House Distribution Ltd, Waldenbury, North Common, Chailey, E Sussex BN8 4DR

Pallas Guides, *imprint of* Pallas Athene

Pan, *imprint of* Pan Macmillan

Pan Books Ltd, see Pan Macmillan

Pan Macmillan+
25 Eccleston Place, London SW1W 9NF
Tel: (020) 7881 8000 *Fax:* (020) 7881 8001
Web Site: www.panmacmillan.com
Key Personnel
Man Dir & Chief Executive: Adrian Soar *E-mail:* a.soar@macmillan.co.uk
Marketing: Iain Chapple *E-mail:* i.chapple@macmillan.co.uk
Production: Daria Neklesa *E-mail:* d.neklesa@macmillan.co.uk
Publicity: Kate Wright-Morris *E-mail:* k.wright-morris@macmillan.co.uk
Founded: 1947
No unsolicited manuscripts. Query first for appropriate contact details & submission process. New authors & agents for children's books should go through an agent.
Subjects: Education, Nonfiction (General), Romance, Self-Help
ISBN Prefix(es): 0-330
Parent Company: Macmillan Ltd
Holding Company: Macmillan Ltd
Associate Companies: Macmillan General Books Ltd
Imprints: Boxtree; Campbell Books; Channel 4 Books; Macmillan; Macmillan Children's Books; Pan; Papermac; Picador; Sidgwick & Jackson
Subsidiaries: Pan Macmillan (Australia) Pty Ltd; Pan Books New Zealand Ltd; Pan Books Pty Ltd
Warehouse: Houndmills, Basingstoke, Hampshire *Tel:* (01256) 464481 *Fax:* (01256) 460675
Orders to: Houndmills, Basingstoke, Hants *Tel:* (01256) 464481 *Fax:* (01256) 460675

Panos Institute
9 White Lion St, London N1 9PD
Tel: (020) 7278 1111 *Fax:* (020) 7278 0345
E-mail: panos@panoslondon.org.uk
Web Site: www.panos.org.uk
Key Personnel
Head of Information: Heather Budge-Reid
Subjects: Developing Countries, Environmental Studies
ISBN Prefix(es): 1-870670
Distributed by Fernwood Books Ltd (Canada); Ideas Centre (Australia); Paula & Co (USA); Russel Friedman Boks (South Africa)

Papermac, *imprint of* Pan Macmillan

UNITED KINGDOM

Paperstyle Gift Line, *imprint of* Ryland Peters & Small Ltd

Paragon, *imprint of* BBC Audiobooks

Parapress, *imprint of* Parapress Ltd

Parapress Ltd+
5 Bentham Hill House, Stockland Green Rd, Tunbridge Wells, Kent TN3 OTJ
Tel: (01892) 512118 *Fax:* (01892) 512118
E-mail: office@parapress.co.uk
Web Site: www.parapress.co.uk
Key Personnel
Man Dir: Elizabeth Imlay *E-mail:* e.imlay.parapress@virgin.net
General Assistant: James Ewing
Publicity Assistant: David Walsh
Founded: 1999
Specialize in animals, biography, history & militaria.
Subjects: Animals, Pets, Biography, Crafts, Games, Hobbies, Education, Health, Nutrition, History, How-to, Humor, Literature, Literary Criticism, Essays, Maritime, Military Science, Music, Dance, Nonfiction (General), Outdoor Recreation, Self-Help, Sports, Athletics, Women's Studies
ISBN Prefix(es): 1-898594
Number of titles published annually: 4 Print
Total Titles: 20 Print
Imprints: Parapress
Membership(s): IPG

PARAS
BM Box 6596, London WC1N 3XX
Tel: (020) 8342 9600 *Fax:* (020) 8342 9600
Key Personnel
Contact: Deborah O'Brien Bell
Founded: 1990
Subjects: Poetry, Poetry/Spirituality
ISBN Prefix(es): 1-874292

Park Lane (Art), *imprint of* Grange Books PLC

The Parthenon Publishing Group Ltd+
Richmond House, South Rd, White Cross, Lancs LA1 4XQ
Tel: (01524) 585700 *Fax:* (01524) 66882
E-mail: mail@parthpub.com
Web Site: www.parthpub.com
Key Personnel
Man Dir: David GT Bloomer *E-mail:* dbloomer@crcpress.com
Managing Editor: J Wright *E-mail:* jwright@crcpress.com
Production Manager: M Clarke *E-mail:* mclarke@crcpress.com
Foreign Rights: A Garnett *E-mail:* agarnett@crcpress.com
Marketing Manager: J Tissington
 E-mail: jtissington@crcpress.com
Founded: 1983
Subjects: Environmental Studies, Medicine, Nursing, Dentistry
ISBN Prefix(es): 1-85070; 1-84214
Number of titles published annually: 80 Print
Parent Company: CRC Press LLC
Ultimate Parent Company: Information Holdings
Subsidiaries: The Parthenon Publishing Group Inc
Foreign Rep(s): Academic Marketing Services (Pty) Ltd (South Africa); Steven Anderson (Ireland); APAC Publishers Services PTE LTD (Indonesia, Malaysia & Singapore, Thailand); Asia Publishers Services Ltd (China, Hong Kong, Philippines, Taiwan); Michael Boone (Canada, US); CRC Press LLC (Japan); DA Information Services (Australia & New Zealand); Bernd Feldmann (Austria, Germany, Switzerland); Bianca Gallo (Finland, Iceland, Scandinavia); Dr A Ghandi (Iran); Laszlo Horvath (Belarus, Bulgaria, Croatia, Czech Republic, Estonia, Hungary, Latvia, Lithuania, Macedonia, Poland, Russia & CIS, Slovak Republic, Slovenia, Ukraine, Yugoslavia, Bosnia & Herzegovina, Albania, Moldova); Information & Culture Korea (Korea); Patrick Jandebeur (Canada, US); Frans Janssen (Benelux); Tony Maggach (Kenya, Nigeria, Ethiopia, Ghana, Uganda, Tanzania, Zambia); Flavio Marcello (France, Italy, Portugal, Spain); Ryan Prior (Canada, US); Ms Zitsa Seraphimidis (Greece); R Seshadri (India); James & Lorin Watt (Middle East, Mediterranean); Dennis Weiss (Canada, US); Angela Williams (Canada, US)
Orders to: CRC Press, ltps, Cheriton House, North Way, Andover, Hants SP10 5BE
 Tel: (01264) 342932 *Fax:* (01264) 342788
 E-mail: crcpress@itps.co.uk (Europe, Middle East & Africa)
CRC Press LLC, 2000 NW Corporate Blvd, Boca Raton, FL 33431, United States *Tel:* 561-994-0555 *Fax:* 561-989-8732 *E-mail:* orders@crcpress.com (North America, South America & Asia)
DA Information Services, 648 Whitehorse Rd, Mitcham, Victoria 3132, Australia
 Tel: (03) 9210 7777 *Fax:* (03) 9210 7788
 E-mail: service@dadirect.com.au *Web Site:* www.dadirect.com.au (Australia & New Zealand)

Parthian Books+
53 Colum Rd, Cardiff CF10 3EF
Tel: (2920) 341314 *Fax:* (2920) 341314
E-mail: parthianbooks@yahoo.co.uk
Web Site: www.parthianbooks.co.uk
Key Personnel
Dir & International Rights: Richard Davies
Founded: 1993
Translations In: English from Welsh & Membership In: Literary Publishers-Wales.
Subjects: Drama, Theater, Fiction
ISBN Prefix(es): 0-9521558; 1-902638
Number of titles published annually: 6 Print
Total Titles: 26 Print
Owned by: St Clair Press, PO Box 287, Rozella, NSW 2039, Australia
Distributed by Dufour Editions
Foreign Rep(s): Dufour Editions Inc (US)
Orders to: Dufour Editions, St Clair Press, PO Box 287, Rozella NSW 2039, Australia

Partridge Press, *imprint of* Transworld Publishers Ltd

Pasold Research Fund, *imprint of* Maney Publishing

PasTest
Egerton Court, Parkgate Estate, Knutsford, Cheshire WA16 8DX
Tel: (01565) 752000 *Fax:* (01565) 650264
E-mail: enquiries@pastest.co.uk
Web Site: www.pastest.co.uk
Key Personnel
Dir, Rights: Freydis Campbell
Founded: 1972
Subjects: Business, Medicine, Nursing, Dentistry
ISBN Prefix(es): 0-906896; 1-901198

Paternoster Periodicals, *imprint of* Paternoster Publishing

Paternoster Press, *imprint of* Paternoster Publishing

Paternoster Publishing+
Subsidiary of Send the Light Ltd
PO Box 300, Carlisle, Cumbria CA3 0QS
Tel: (01228) 512118 *Fax:* (01228) 514949
E-mail: orderline@stl.org
Web Site: www.paternoster-publishing.com
Key Personnel
Publisher: Mark Finnie *Tel:* (01228) 512512 ext 2249 *E-mail:* mark.finnie@paternoster-markpublishing.com
General Manager: Rob Cook *Tel:* (01228) 512512 ext 2253 *E-mail:* rob.cook@paternoster-publishing.com
US Sales Manager: John Lewis *Tel:* 706-554-5827 *E-mail:* john@omlit.om.org
Founded: 1935
Specialize in religious (Christian) books & periodicals.
Subjects: History, Philosophy, Religion - Other
ISBN Prefix(es): 0-85364
Total Titles: 200 Print
Imprints: Authentic Lifestyle; Paternoster Periodicals; Paternoster Press; Regnum; Rutherford House

Pathfinder, *imprint of* Jarrold Publishing

Pathfinder London+
47 The Cut, London SE1 8LL
Tel: (020) 7261 1354 *Fax:* (020) 7261 1354
E-mail: pathfinderlondon@compuserve.com
Web Site: www.pathfinderpress.com
Key Personnel
Contact: T Hunt
Subjects: Developing Countries, Economics, Government, Political Science, History, Labor, Industrial Relations, Social Sciences, Sociology, Women's Studies
ISBN Prefix(es): 0-87348
Book Club(s): Pathfinder Readers Club
Warehouse: Plymbridge, Estover, Plymouth PL6 7PZ
Orders to: Pathfinder, c/-Baker & Taylor International, Suite 143/102 Longueville Rd, Lane Cove, NSW 2066, Australia *Tel:* (02) 9924 0505 *Fax:* (02) 9924 0515 (Australia, New Zealand, the Pacific, Southeast Asia)
Plymbridge Distributors Ltd, Estover Rd, Plymouth PL6 7PZ *Tel:* (01752) 202301 *Fax:* (01752) 202331 *E-mail:* orders@plymbridge.com (Europe, the Middle East, Africa, South Asia)

Stanley Paul, *imprint of* Random House UK Ltd

Pavilion Books Ltd+
London House, Great Eastern Wharf, Parkgate Rd, London SW11 4NQ
Tel: (020) 7350 1230 *Fax:* (020) 7350 1260; (020) 7801 0315
E-mail: info@pavilionbooks.co.uk
Web Site: www.pavilionbooks.co.uk
Key Personnel
Man Dir: Colin Webb *E-mail:* colin.webb@pavilionbooks.co.uk
Children's Publishing Dir: Pamela Webb
 E-mail: pamela.webb@pavilionbooks.co.uk
Adult Publishing Dir: Vivien James
 E-mail: vivien.james@pavilionbooks.co.uk
International Co-editions: Melanie Beveridge
 E-mail: melanie.beveridge@pavilionbooks.co.uk
Founded: 1981
Subjects: Art, Biography, Cookery, Film, Video, Gardening, Plants, House & Home, Photography, Travel
ISBN Prefix(es): 1-85145; 1-85793; 0-907516; 1-86205
Total Titles: 200 Print
Parent Company: C & B Publishing Plc
Warehouse: Biblios, Star Rd, Partridge Green, West Sussex RH13 8LD *Tel:* (01403) 710971 *Fax:* (01403) 711143 *E-mail:* biblios@biblios.co.uk

PUBLISHERS   UNITED KINGDOM

Pavilion Publishing (Brighton) Ltd
The Ironworks, Cheapside, Brighton, East Sussex
  BN1 4GD
Tel: (01273) 623222 *Fax:* (01273) 625526
E-mail: info@pavpub.com
Web Site: www.pavpub.com
Subjects: Social Sciences, Sociology, Disability,
  Health, Nursing, Special Needs
ISBN Prefix(es): 1-84196; 1-900600
Distributed by Gizmo
Distributor for Gizmo; NEC

Paxton, *imprint of* Novello & Co Ltd

Payback Press, *imprint of* Canongate Books Ltd

PC Publishing+
Division of Music Technology Books Limited
Export House, 130 Vale Rd, Tonbridge, Kent TN9
  1SP
Tel: (01732) 770893 *Fax:* (01732) 770268
E-mail: info@pc-publishing.com
Web Site: www.pc-publishing.co.uk
Key Personnel
Publisher: Philip Chapman
Founded: 1988
Subjects: Computer Science, Electronics, Electri-
  cal Engineering, Music, Dance
ISBN Prefix(es): 1-870775
Number of titles published annually: 10 Print
Total Titles: 40 Print
Distributed by Cimino Publishing Group (USA);
  Keyfax (US & Canada); Music Books Plus (US
  & Canada); Music Software (Australia & New
  Zealand)
Orders to: Littlehampton Book Services, Faraday
  Close, Durrington, Worthing, W Sussex BN13
  3RB *Tel:* (01903) 828800 *Fax:* (01903) 828801
  E-mail: enquiries@lbsltd.co.uk *Web Site:* www.
  lbsltd.co.uk (UK)

PCR, *imprint of* Wilmington Business
  Information Ltd

Pearson Education
128 Long Acre, London WC2 9AN
Tel: (020) 7447 2000 *Fax:* (020) 7240 5771
E-mail: firstname.lastname@pearsoned-ema.com
Telex: 81259
Key Personnel
President Professional Education: Peter Marshall
Administration Manager, Prod Ed: Juliane
  Heineke
Finance Dir, Higher/Prof Ed: John Knight
VP, UK Sales & Marketing: Adrian Meillor
Editor-in-Chief, Business & Ref: Richard Stagg
Editor-in-Chief, Computing: Steve Temblett
Founded: 1724
Subjects: Accounting, Aeronautics, Aviation,
  Agriculture, Anthropology, Art, Biological Sci-
  ences, Business, Career Development, Chem-
  istry, Chemical Engineering, Computer Science,
  Criminology, Economics, Education, Engineer-
  ing (General), Environmental Studies, Geogra-
  phy, Geology, Government, Health Sciences,
  Health, Nutrition, History, Language Arts, Lin-
  guistics, Law, Literature, Literary Criticism,
  Essays, Management, Mathematics, Music,
  Dance, Natural History, Philosophy, Physics,
  Poetry, Psychology, Psychiatry, Religion -
  Other, Science (General), Social Sciences, So-
  ciology, Veterinary Science, Women's Studies
ISBN Prefix(es): 0-582; 0-05
Parent Company: Pearson Plc
Branch Office(s)
Fourth Ave, Pinnacles, Harlow, Essex CM19 5AA
  Tel: (01279) 623623 *Fax:* (01279) 431067
Showroom(s): 5 Bentinck St, London W1M 5RN
  Tel: (020) 7935 0121 *Fax:* (020) 7486 4204

Pearson Education Europe, Mideast & Africa+
Edinburgh Gate, Harlow, Essex CM20 2JE
Tel: (01279) 62 3623 *Fax:* (01279) 43 1059
E-mail: firstname.lastname@pearsoned-ema.com
Web Site: www.pearsoned-ema.com
Key Personnel
President & Chief Executive Officer, Group Exec-
  utive: Nigel Portwood
Chief Operating Officer, Group Executive: Brian
  Landers
Vice President, Finance, Group Executive: Lianne
  Gammon
President, Pearson Education Ltd: Rod Bristow
Rights & Contracts Dir, Pearson Education Ltd:
  Lynette Owen
VP, Finance, Pearson Education Ltd: John Knight
Senior Vice President, People & Change: Graham
  Abbey
President, ELT & Schools: Dugie Cameron
Man Dir, ELT Publishing: Gill Negas
Marketing Dir, ELT Marketing: Martha Ware
Man Dir, UK Schools: Jeff Andrew
Dir, International: Kern Roberts
Publishing Dir, International: Jenny Pares
Publishing Dir, UK Schools: Lorna Cocking
President, Higher Education: Jim Green
VP, Production: Colin Lander
Head of Facilities Management, Operations: John
  Fessey
Divisional Coordinator, FM Operations: Miranda
  Fishburn
Dir, Customer Service, Corporate Services: Jennie
  Heals
President, Schools EMA: John Penrose
Man Dir, Direct English, Consumer Language
  Learning: Clive Sawkins
Founded: 1998 (result of merger of Addison Wes-
  ley Longman, Financial Times Management &
  Prentice Hall Europe)
Subjects: Art, Business, Communications, Drama,
  Theater, Economics, Education, Government,
  Political Science, History, Language Arts, Lin-
  guistics, Medicine, Nursing, Dentistry, Music,
  Dance, Philosophy, Psychology, Psychiatry,
  Religion - Other, Science (General), Social Sci-
  ences, Sociology, Technology
ISBN Prefix(es): 0-13
Parent Company: Pearson Education
Ultimate Parent Company: Pearson PLC
Imprints: Allyn & Bacon; Prentice Hall; Pren-
  tice Hall Europe; Prentice Hall Regents; Long-
  man; Addison-Wesley; Financial Times Pren-
  tice Hall; Scott Foresman; Que; Que Lycos
  Books; Ziff-Davis Press; New Roders; Macmil-
  lan Technical Publishing USA; Que Educa-
  tion & Training; BradyGames; Sams Publish-
  ing; Sams.net; Borland Press; Hayden Books;
  Adobe Press; Waite Group Press
Branch Office(s)
Pearson Education Software Publishing Divi-
  sion, 124 Cambridge Science Park, Milton
  Rd, Cambridge CB4 4ZS *Tel:* (01223) 425558
  Fax: (01223) 425349 *E-mail:* info@logo.com
128 Longacre, London WC2 9AN *Tel:* (020)
  7477 2000 *Fax:* (020) 7240 5771
Campus 400, Maylands Ave, Hemel Hemp-
  stead, Herts HP2 7EZ *Tel:* (01442) 881900
  Fax: (01442) 882099
U.S. Office(s): Pearson Education, One Lake St,
  Upper Saddle River, NJ 07458, United States

Peartree Publications
61 Peartree Lane, Bexhill, East Sussex TN39
  4RQ
Tel: 01424 844274
Key Personnel
Partner: Roger Stepney
Founded: 1986
Subjects: Music, Dance
ISBN Prefix(es): 1-85254
Total Titles: 6 Print; 2 Audio

Peepal Tree Press+
17 Kings Ave, Leeds LS6 1QS
Tel: (0113) 2451703 *Fax:* (0113) 2468368
Key Personnel
Man Editor: Jeremy Poynting *E-mail:* jeremy@
  peepal.demon.co.uk
Marketing Manager: Hannah Bannister
  E-mail: hannah@peepal.demon.co.uk
Founded: 1985
Specialize in Caribbean, African, South Asian &
  Black British fiction, poetry & criticism.
Subjects: Education, Fiction, History, Literature,
  Literary Criticism, Essays, Poetry, Social Sci-
  ences, Sociology
ISBN Prefix(es): 0-948833; 0-900715
Imprints: South Asians Overseas Series
Orders to: Central Books, 99 Wallis Rd, London
  E9 5LN
Paul & Co PCS Data Processing Inc, 360 W 31
  St, New York, NY 10001, United States

Pelican History of Art, *imprint of* Yale
  University Press London

Pen & Sword, *imprint of* Leo Cooper

Pen & Sword Books Ltd+
47 Church St, Barnsley, South Yorks S70 2AS
Tel: (01226) 734222 *Fax:* (01226) 734438
E-mail: ps-it@pen-and-sword.co.uk
Web Site: www.pen-and-sword.co.uk
Key Personnel
Chairman: Sir Nicholas Hewitt Bt
Man Dir: Charles Hewitt *Tel:* (01226) 734555
  E-mail: charles@pen-and-sword.co.uk
Founded: 1990
Subjects: History, Maritime, Military Science,
  Military History, Local History
ISBN Prefix(es): 0-85052; 1-871647
Imprints: Leo Cooper; Pen & Sword Paperbacks;
  Wharncliffe Books
Divisions: Leo Cooper Imprint; Pen & Sword Pa-
  perbacks; Wharncliffe

Pen & Sword Paperbacks, *imprint of* Pen &
  Sword Books Ltd

Pencil Press, *imprint of* Roundhouse Publishing
  Ltd

Penguin, *imprint of* Penguin Books Ltd

Penguin Books Ltd+
27 Wright's Lane, London W8 5TZ
Tel: (020) 7416 3000 *Fax:* (020) 7416 3099;
  (020) 7416 3293
Web Site: www.penguin.com
Telex: 917181
Key Personnel
Chief Executive Officer: Anthony Forbes Watson
President: David Wan
Man Dir, Penguin General Division: Helen Fraser
Man Dir, Penguin Press: Andrew Rosenheim
Man Dir, Puffin: Philippa Milnes Smith
Man Dir, Frederick Warne: Sally Floyer
Rights Division (Warne): Susan Winton
Rights Dir (Adult): Sophie Brewer
Publicity Dir: Joanna Prior
Founded: 1935
General trade publisher; baby & toddler titles
  through to adult.
ISBN Prefix(es): 0-14; 0-7207; 0-241; 0-670; 0-
  7181
Parent Company: Penguin Publishing Co Ltd
Ultimate Parent Company: Pearson
Imprints: Viking; Puffin Books; Arkana; Lady-
  bird; Hamish Hamilton; Michael Joseph; Allen
  Lane; Frederick Warne; Buildings of England;
  Penguin; Ventura

UNITED KINGDOM

Branch Office(s)
Penguin USA, 375 Hudson St, New York, NY 10014, United States
Orders to: Penguin Group Distribution Ltd, Bath Rd, Harmondsworth, Middlesex UB7 0DA

The Penguin Group UK+
Formerly Penguin UK
80 Strand, London WC2R 0RN
Tel: (020) 7010 3000
Web Site: www.penguin.co.uk
Key Personnel
Chief Executive Officer, The Penguin Group: John Makinson
Chief Executive Officer, The Penguin Group (UK): Anthony Forbes Watson
Man Dir, Penguin: Helen Fraser
Man Dir, Ventura/Warne: Sally Floyer
Man Dir, Puffin: Francesca Dow
Group Sales & Operations: Peter Brown
Man Dir, Dorling Kindersley: Andrew Welhan
Founded: 1935
ISBN Prefix(es): 0-241; 0-670; 0-7181
Parent Company: Pearson PLC
Imprints: Michael Joseph; Hamish Hamilton; Viking; Allen Lane; Rough Guides; Buildings of England; Classics; Puffin
Subsidiaries: LadyBird Books Ltd
Divisions: Penguin General Books; Penguin Press; Frederick Warne; Dorling Kindersley; Puffin
U.S. Office(s): Penguin Putnam Inc, 375 Hudson St, New York, NY 10014, United States
Distributor for Rough Guides; Wisden
Warehouse: Penguin Books Ltd, Bath Rd, Harmondsworth MDDX UB7 (Customer Services)
Orders to: Penguin Books Ltd, Bath Rd, Harmondsworth, Middlesex UB7 0DA

The Penguin Press, *imprint of* Viking

Penguin Publishing Co Ltd
80 Strand, London WC2R 0RL
Tel: (020) 7010 3000 *Fax:* (020) 7010 6060
Telex: 917181
Key Personnel
Chief Executive: Anthony Forbes-Watson
UK Group Man Dir: Helen Fraser
Founded: 1935
Holding company for Penguin Books Ltd, UK; Penguin Books Australia Ltd; Penguin Books Canada Ltd; Penguin Books New Zealand Ltd; Penguin Putnam Inc, USA.
ISBN Prefix(es): 0-14; 0-670
Parent Company: Pearson Group
Ultimate Parent Company: Pearson PLC, Millbank Tower, London SW1P 4QZ
U.S. Office(s): Penguin Books USA, 375 Hudson St, New York, NY 10014, United States *Tel:* 212-366-2000
Shipping Address: Bath Road, Harmondsworth, West Drayton, Middlesex UB7 0DA
Warehouse: Bath Road, Harmondsworth, West Drayton, Middlesex UB7 0DA
Orders to: Bath Road, Harmondsworth, West Drayton, Middlesex UB7 0DA

Penguin UK, see The Penguin Group UK

The Pensions Management Institute
PMI House, 4/10 Artillery Lane, London E1 7LS
Tel: (020) 7247 1452 *Fax:* (020) 7375 0603
E-mail: enquiries@pensions-pmi.org.uk
Web Site: www.pensions-pmi.org.uk
Key Personnel
Deputy Secretary: P Whiteing
ISBN Prefix(es): 0-946242; 1-898785

Pentathol Publishing+
40 Gibson St, Wrexham, Wrexham County LL13 7NS
Mailing Address: PO Box 92, Wrexham County LL13 7NS
Key Personnel
Contact: A E Cowen
Founded: 1991
Member of Publishers Association.
Subjects: Poetry
ISBN Prefix(es): 1-873021
Number of titles published annually: 1 Print
Total Titles: 1 Print
Imprints: "Huh!" 1991

Pentn Press, *imprint of* Jessica Kingsley Publishers

Perennial, *imprint of* HarperCollins Publishers

PerfectBound, *imprint of* HarperCollins Publishers

Pergamon Flexible Learning+
Imprint of Butterworth-Heinemann
Linacre House, Jordan Hill, Oxford OX2 8DP
Tel: (01865) 310366; (01865) 388190
 Fax: (01865) 314290
E-mail: bhmarketing@repp.co.uk
Web Site: www.bh.com/pergamonfl
Key Personnel
Dir: Kathryn Grant *E-mail:* kathryn.grant@repp.co.uk
Marketing Manager: Duncan Enright
 E-mail: duncanenright@repp.co.uk
International Marketing Manager: Jacquie Shanahan *E-mail:* jacquie.shanahan@repp.co.uk
Founded: 1987
Subjects: Business, Education, Management, Marketing, Customer Service, Sales, Health & Safety, Training & Development, Open Learning Materials
ISBN Prefix(es): 0-08; 0-7506
Parent Company: Butterworth-Heinemann, Linacre House, Jordan Hill, Oxford OX2 8DP
Ultimate Parent Company: Reed
Associate Companies: Butterworth-Heinemann Inc, 313 Washington St, Newton, MA 02158, United States *Tel:* 617-928-2500 *Fax:* 617-928-2620

Permanent Publications, *imprint of* Hyden House Ltd

Perpetuity Press+
Member of IPS
PO Box 376, Leicester LE2 1UP
Tel: (0116) 217778 *Fax:* (0116) 217171
E-mail: info@perpetuitypress.com
Web Site: www.perpetuitypress.com
Key Personnel
Publisher: K A Gill
Founded: 1994
Subjects: Business, Criminology, Law, Management, Maritime, Security Management, Risk Management & Policing, crime prevention
ISBN Prefix(es): 1-899287
Membership(s): IPG

Peter Peregrinus Ltd, *imprint of* Institution of Electrical Engineers

Petroc Press+
Imprint of LibraPharm Ltd
Gemini House, 162 Craven Rd, Newbury, Berks RG14 5NR
Tel: (01635) 522651 *Fax:* (01635) 36294
E-mail: petroc@librapharm.com
Web Site: www.librapharm.com
Key Personnel
Man Dir: Dr P L Clarke
Founded: 1995
Subjects: Medicine, Nursing, Dentistry

ISBN Prefix(es): 1-900603
Number of titles published annually: 10 Print
Total Titles: 50 Print
Shipping Address: Plymbridge Distributors, Estover Rd, Plymouth PL6 7PZ
 Tel: (01752) 202300 *Fax:* (01752) 202330
 E-mail: enquiries@plymbridge.com
Warehouse: Plymbridge Distributors, Estover Rd, Plymouth PL6 7PZ *Tel:* (01752) 202300 *Fax:* (01752) 202330 *E-mail:* enquiries@plymbridge.com
Orders to: Plymbridge Distributors, Estover Rd, Plymouth PL6 7PZ *Tel:* (01752) 202301 *Fax:* (01752) 202333

Pevsner Architectural Guides, *imprint of* Yale University Press London

Phaidon Press Ltd+
Regent's Wharf, All Saints St, London N1 9PA
Tel: (020) 7843 1231 *Fax:* (020) 7843 1111
E-mail: esales@phaidon.com
Web Site: www.phaidon.com
Key Personnel
Man Dir: Andrew Price
Export Sales Dir: Sheila McKenna
Operations Dir: Fran Johnson
Publisher: Richard Schlagman
Vice President Sales & Marketing, Phaidon Pres Inc: Mary Albi
Deputy Publisher: Amanda Renshaw
Marketing Manager: Truda Spruyt
UK Sales Manager: Simon Kingsley
Sales & Marketing Dir: John Roberts
International Editions Manager: Helen Garrett
Founded: 1923
Subjects: Architecture & Interior Design, Art, Biography, Drama, Theater, History, Photography
ISBN Prefix(es): 0-7148
Subsidiaries: Phaidon Press Inc
U.S. Office(s): 7195 Grayson Rd, Harrisburg, PA 17111, United States *E-mail:* ussales@phaidon.com
Warehouse: Unit 4, Lodge Causeway Trading Estate Fishponds, Bristol, Avon BS16 3JB

Pharmaceutical Press+
Division of The Royal Pharmaceutical Society
PO Box 151, Wallingford, Oxon OX10 8QU
Tel: (01491) 829 272 *Fax:* (01491) 829 292
E-mail: rpsgb@cabi.org
Web Site: www.pharmpress.com
Key Personnel
Dir of Publications: Charles Fry *E-mail:* cfry@rpsgb.org.uk
Editorial Production Manager: John Wilson
 E-mail: jwilson@rpsgb.org.uk
Head of Sales & Marketing: Jane Weir
 E-mail: jweir@rpsgb.org.uk
Sales Executive: Jane Mulholland
 E-mail: jmulholland@rpsgb.org.uk
Marketing Executive: Sarah Owen *Tel:* (0171) 735 9141 *E-mail:* sowen@rpsgb.org.uk
Founded: 1841
Subjects: Chemistry, Chemical Engineering, Health, Nutrition, Law, Medicine, Nursing, Dentistry, Veterinary Science, Pharmaceutical
ISBN Prefix(es): 0-85369
Number of titles published annually: 15 Print
Total Titles: 60 Print; 10 CD-ROM; 1 Online

Philip & Tacey Ltd
North Way, Andover, Hants SP10 5BA
Tel: (01264) 332171 *Fax:* (01264) 332226
E-mail: info@philipandtacey.co.uk
Web Site: www.philipandtacey.co.uk
Key Personnel
Man Dir: Gerry Vaughan
Founded: 1829
Member of BESA.
Subjects: Education
ISBN Prefix(es): 0-902073

Associate Companies: Philograph Publications Ltd, Pottington Industrial Estate, Riverside Rd, Barnstable EX31 1LR
Branch Office(s)
Didax Inc, 395 Main St, Rowley, MA 01969, United States

Philip, *imprint of* Octopus Publishing Group

Philip's+
Division of Hachette Livre (France)
2-4 Heron Quays, London E14 4JP
Tel: (020) 7531 8459; (020) 7531 8439 (rights & data sales) *Fax:* (020) 7531 8460; (020) 7531 8464 (rights & data sales)
E-mail: george.philip@philips-maps.co.uk
Web Site: www.philips-maps.co.uk
Key Personnel
Man Dir & Publisher: John Gaisford *Tel:* (020) 7531 8436 *E-mail:* john.gaisford@philips-maps.co.uk
Mapping Director: David Gaylard *Tel:* (01923) 819423 *Fax:* (01923) 819541 *E-mail:* david.gaylard@philips-maps.co.uk
Trade Sales Dir: Roger Fox *E-mail:* roger.fox@philips-maps.co.uk
Trade Sales Administrator: Wendy Graham *E-mail:* wendy.graham@philips-maps.co.uk; Dimity Castellano *E-mail:* dimity.castellano@philips-maps.co.uk
Rights, Foreign Rights, Premiums & Data Sales Dir: Victoria Dawbarn *E-mail:* victoria.dawbarn@philips-maps.co.uk
Digital Data Sales: Ruth King *E-mail:* ruth.king@philips-maps.co.uk
Founded: 1834
Specialize in World Atlases, Road Atlases, Astronomy, Encyclopedias & illustrated reference. Member of Royal Geographical Society & International Map Traders Association.
Subjects: Astronomy, Geography, Geology, Travel
ISBN Prefix(es): 0-540
Total Titles: 200 Print
Parent Company: Octopus Publishing Group
Ultimate Parent Company: Largardere Group
Orders to: Littlehampton Book Services, Durrington, Worthing, West Sussex BN13 3RB *Tel:* (01903) 828500 *Fax:* (01903) 828625 *E-mail:* orders@lbsltd.co.uk *Web Site:* www.lbsltd.co.uk

Phillimore & Co Ltd+
Shopwyke Manor Barn, Chichester, West Sussex PO20 2BG
Tel: (01243) 787636 *Fax:* (01243) 787639
E-mail: bookshop@phillimore.co.uk
Web Site: www.phillimore.co.uk
Key Personnel
Chairman: Philip Harris
Manager & Editorial: Noel H Osborne
Founded: 1897
Subjects: Archaeology, Architecture & Interior Design, Regional Interests
ISBN Prefix(es): 0-85033; 0-900592; 1-86077; 0-900809
Associate Companies: British Association for Local History; Historical Publications Ltd

Philograph Publications Ltd
Pottington Industrial Estate, Riverside Rd, Barnstaple EX31 1LR
Tel: (01271) 45061 *Fax:* (01271) 23076
Key Personnel
Man Dir: Chris Tacey
Founded: 1829
Specialize in teaching aids & resources for primary schools.
ISBN Prefix(es): 0-85370
Parent Company: Philip & Tacey Ltd, North Way, Andover, Hants

U.S. Office(s): Didax Inc, 395 Main St, Rowley, MA 01969, United States
Orders to: Philip & Tracey Ltd, Riverside Rd, Pottington Industrial Estate, Devon EX31 1LR

Photo Art International, *imprint of* Creative Monochrome Ltd

Phronesis, *imprint of* Verso

Piatkus Books+
5 Windmill St, London W1T 2JA
Tel: (020) 7631 0710 *Fax:* (020) 7436 7137
E-mail: info@piatkus.co.uk
Web Site: www.piatkus.co.uk
Key Personnel
Man Dir: Judy Piatkus
Editorial Dir: Gill Bailey
Sales Dir: Philip Cotterell
Publicity Manager: Jana Sommerlad
Production Manager: Simon Colverson
Rights Manager: Jon Mitchell
Founded: 1979
An independent publishing company. Specialize in general trade nonfiction & popular fiction including mass market.
Subjects: Astrology, Occult, Biography, Business, Career Development, Cookery, Criminology, Fashion, Fiction, Health, Nutrition, Humor, Management, Nonfiction (General), Psychology, Psychiatry, Self-Help
ISBN Prefix(es): 0-7499; 0-86188
Number of titles published annually: 175 Print
Total Titles: 3,000 Print
Online services available through World Wide Web.
Parent Company: Judy Piatkus (Publishers) Ltd
Distributed by Angell Eurosales (Austria, Benelux, France, Germany, Iceland, Scandinavia, Switzerland); Ashton International Marketing Services (Middle East); David Bateman Ltd (New Zealand); Bookport Associates (Gibraltar, Greece, Italy, Malta, Portugal, Spain); General Publishing (Canada); Kelvin van Hasselt (Mauritius, Seychelles & West Africa); Hodder Headline (Australia) Pty Ltd (Australia); India Book Distribution (Bombay) Ltd (India); MTM; Pansing Distribution Sdn Bhd (Malaysia & Singapore); Penguin South Africa (Pty) Ltd (South Africa & Zimbabwe); Ralph & Sheila Summers (Far East)
Shipping Address: Grantham Book Services Ltd, Isaac Newton Way, Alma Park Industrial Estate, Grantham, Lincs NG31 9SD *Tel:* (01476) 541000 *Fax:* (01476) 590223
Warehouse: Grantham Book Services Ltd, Isaac Newton Way, Alma Park Industrial Estate, Grantham, Lincs N931 9SD *Tel:* (1476) 541000 *Fax:* (1476) 590223
Orders to: Grantham Book Services Ltd, Isaac Newton Way, Alma Park Industrial Estate, Grantham, Lincs NG31 9SD *Tel:* (01476) 541000 *Fax:* (01476) 590223

Pica Press, *imprint of* Christopher Helm (Publishers) Ltd

Picador, *imprint of* Pan Macmillan

Piccadilly Press+
5 Castle Rd, London NW1 8PR
Tel: (020) 7267 4492 *Fax:* (020) 7267 4493
E-mail: books@piccadillypress.co.uk
Web Site: www.piccadillypress.co.uk
Key Personnel
Man Dir & Publisher: Brenda Gardner
Editorial: Yasemin Ucar
Production: Geoff Barlow
Rights: Margot Edwards
Book Clubs & Special Sales: Caroline Bidwell
Founded: 1983

Subjects: Humor, Nonfiction (General), Parental Books
ISBN Prefix(es): 1-85340
Number of titles published annually: 30 Print
Total Titles: 250 Print
Foreign Rights: Akcali Copyright (Turkey); Carmen Balcells Agencia Lit (Spain); Luigi Bernabo Associates (Italy); The English Agency (Japan) Ltd (Japan); JLM Literary Agency (Greece); KCC (Korea); Jacqueline Miller Agency (France); Andrew Nurnberg Associates (Czech Republic, Hungary, Poland, Romania, Russia); I Pikarski (Israel)
Orders to: TBS Ltd, Frating Green, Colchester Rd, Colchester, Essex C07 7DW *Tel:* (01206) 256 000 *Fax:* (01206) 255 715

Pickering & Chatto (Publishers) Ltd+
21 Bloomsbury Way, London WC1A 2TH
Tel: (020) 7405 1005 *Fax:* (020) 7405 6216
E-mail: info@pickeringchatto.co.uk
Web Site: www.pickeringchatto.com
Key Personnel
Chairman: Lord Rees-Mogg
Man Dir: James Powell *E-mail:* james@pickeringchatto.co.uk
Editorial Dir: Mark Pollard *E-mail:* mark@pickeringchatto.co.uk
Commissioning Editor: Anna Crago *E-mail:* anna@pickeringchatto.co.uk
Marketing Manager: Deborah Fajerman *E-mail:* deborah@pickeringchatto.co.uk
Founded: 1985
Specialize in history of politics, history of science & history of economics.
Subjects: History, Literature, Literary Criticism, Essays, Philosophy, Women's Studies
ISBN Prefix(es): 1-85196
Number of titles published annually: 20 Print
Imprints: William Pickering
Distributed by Ashgate Publishing Co (North & South America); DA Information Services (Australia & New Zealand); Taylor & Francis Asia Pacific (Singapore, Hong Kong, Indonesia, Philippines & Malaysia); Turpin Distribution; Unifacmanu Trading Co Ltd (Taiwan)
Foreign Rep(s): Applied Media (India); Iberian Book Services (Spain & Portugal); Publishers International Marketing (China, Middle East, South Korea)
Warehouse: Turpin Distribution, Blackhorse Rd, Letchworth, Herts SG6 1HN *Tel:* (01462) 672 555 *Fax:* (01462) 480 947 *E-mail:* info@turpinltd.com
Membership(s): IPG

William Pickering, *imprint of* Pickering & Chatto (Publishers) Ltd

Picton Press, *imprint of* Countyvise Ltd

Picton Publishing (Chippenham) Ltd+
Queens Bridge Cottages, Patterdown, Chippenham, Wilts SN15 2NS
Tel: (01249) 443430 *Fax:* (01249) 443430
Key Personnel
Dir & Rights: Anne Picton-Phillips
Founded: 1972
Subjects: Crafts, Games, Hobbies, Drama, Theater, Gardening, Plants, Military Science
ISBN Prefix(es): 0-902633; 0-948251; 1-85464
Subsidiaries: Bareboner Books; Nutshell Press

Picture Corgi, *imprint of* Transworld Publishers Ltd

Pimlico, *imprint of* Random House UK Ltd

Pine Forge Press, *imprint of* Sage Publications Ltd

UNITED KINGDOM

Pinter, *imprint of* The Continuum International Publishing Group Ltd

Pinter, Studio Vista, *imprint of* Cassell & Co

Pinwheel Ltd+
Subsidiary of Andromeda Holdings Ltd
Station House, 8-13 Swiss Terrace, London NW6 4RR
Tel: (020) 7586 5100 *Fax:* (020) 7483 1999
E-mail: sales@pinwheel.co.uk
Web Site: www.pinwheel.co.uk
Key Personnel
Sales Manager: Kristina Dahlqvist
　E-mail: kristina.dahlqvist@pinwheel.co.uk; Giovanna Franchina *E-mail:* giovanna.franchina@pinwheel.co.uk
European Sales Manager: Rachel Pidcock
　E-mail: rachel.pidcock@pinwheel.co.uk
Sales Administrator: Janina Sochanik
　E-mail: janina.sochanik@pinwheel.co.uk
Commissioning Editor: Shaheen Bilgrami
　E-mail: shaheen.bilgrami@pinwheel.co.uk
Art Dir: Angela Brooksbank *E-mail:* angela.brooksbank@pinwheel.co.uk
Production Manager: Toby Reynolds
　E-mail: toby.reynolds@pinwheel.co.uk
Founded: 1995
Children's novelty books for preschool age.
Number of titles published annually: 15 Print
Total Titles: 60 Print

Pion Ltd+
207 Brondesbury Park, London NW2 5JN
Tel: (020) 8459 0066 *Fax:* (020) 8451 6454
E-mail: admin@pion.co.uk
Web Site: www.pion.co.uk
Key Personnel
Dir: Dr Jonathan Briggs; Dr Jan Schubert
Man Dir: Adam Gelbtuch
International Sales & Rights: Diana Harrop
　E-mail: sales@pion.co.uk
Founded: 1960
Journal publisher.
Member of ALPSP, IPG.
Subjects: Geography, Geology, Mathematics, Physical Sciences
ISBN Prefix(es): 0-85086
Total Titles: 100 Print
Associate Companies: Turpion Ltd (Joint venture with Royal Society of Chemistry)
Foreign Rights: Japan Uni Agency (Japan)
Warehouse: Turpin Distribution Services, Blackhorse Rd, Letchworth, Herts SG6 1H *Tel:* (01462) 672555 *Fax:* (01462) 480947 *E-mail:* custservturpin@turpinltd.com
Orders to: Turpin Ltd, Blackhorse Rd, Letchworth, Herts SG6 1HN *Tel:* (01462) 672555 *Fax:* (01462) 480947 *E-mail:* custservturpin@turpinltd.com (Also warehouse address)

PIRA Intl
Randalls Rd, Leatherhead, Surrey KT22 7RU
Tel: (01372) 802080 *Fax:* (01372) 802079
E-mail: publications@pira.co.uk
Web Site: www.piranet.com
Key Personnel
Contact: Philip Swinden
A consultancy business with major publishing & conference activities, serving the printing, publishing, packaging & paper industries.
Subjects: Publishing & Book Trade Reference, Technology
ISBN Prefix(es): 1-85802; 0-902799
U.S. Office(s): Books International, PO Box 605, Herndon, VA 20172, United States *Tel:* 703-689-4204

Pitkin Unichrome Ltd+
Healey House, Dene Rd, Andover, Hants SP10 2AA
Tel: (01264) 409200 *Fax:* (01264) 334110
E-mail: enquiries@pitkin-unichrome.com
Web Site: www.britguides.com
Key Personnel
Dir: Heather Hook
Founded: 1947
Subjects: Biography, History, Travel
ISBN Prefix(es): 0-85372; 0-85373; 1-871004
Number of titles published annually: 10 Print; 1 CD-ROM
Total Titles: 280 Print; 1 CD-ROM; 270 Online; 1 E-Book
Parent Company: Jarrold Publishing
Ultimate Parent Company: Jarrold & Sons Ltd

Planet+
PO Box 44, Aberystwyth, Ceredigion SY23 3ZZ
Tel: (01970) 611255 *Fax:* (01970) 611197
E-mail: planet.enquiries@planetmagazine.org.uk
Web Site: www.planetmagazine.org.uk
Key Personnel
Chairman & Dir: John Barnie
Founded: 1985
Publishing House.
Subjects: Art, Literature, Literary Criticism, Essays, Poetry
ISBN Prefix(es): 0-9505188
Total Titles: 7 Print
Parent Company: Berw Cyf

Plantin Publishers, *imprint of* Cardiff Academic Press

Plantin Publishers+
St Fagans Rd, Fairwater, Cardiff CF5 3AE
Tel: (029) 2056 0333 *Fax:* (029) 2055 4909
E-mail: drakegroup@btinternet.com
Web Site: www.drakegroup.co.uk
Key Personnel
Man Dir: R G Drake
Founded: 1987
Specialize in publishing re-prints of out-of-print titles, usually out-of-copyright.
Subjects: Biography, Literature, Literary Criticism, Essays
Parent Company: Cardiff Academic Press

Platform 5 Publishing Ltd
3 Wyvern House, Sark Rd, Sheffield S2 4HG
Tel: (0114) 255 2625 *Fax:* (0114) 255 2471
E-mail: platform5@platfive.freeserve.co.uk
Key Personnel
Publisher & Editor-in-Chief: Peter Fox
Editor: David Haydock
Founded: 1984
Subjects: Transportation
ISBN Prefix(es): 0-906579; 1-872524; 1-902336
Distributor for Quail Map Co (UK, except South of England); South Coast Transport Publishing

Plexus Publishing Ltd+
55a Clapham Common Southside, London SW4 9BX
Tel: (020) 7662 2440 *Fax:* (020) 7622 2441
E-mail: info@plexusuk.demon.co.uk
Web Site: www.plexusbooks.com
Key Personnel
Sales, Production: Terence Porter
Editorial, Rights & Permissions: Sandra Wake
Coordinator Editor: Rebecca Martin
Founded: 1973
Publish illustrated nonfiction books specializing in international co-editions with an emphasis on biography, popular music, rock 'n' roll, popular culture, art, photography & cinema.
Subjects: Biography, Drama, Theater, Fashion, Film, Video, Music, Dance, Photography, Radio, TV
ISBN Prefix(es): 0-85965
Number of titles published annually: 15 Print
Total Titles: 100 Print
Distributed by Publishers Group West (USA & Canada)
Warehouse: Bookpoint Ltd, 39 Milton Park, Abingdon, Oxon OX14 4TD *Tel:* (01235) 400 400 *Fax:* (01235) 832 068
Orders to: Bookpoint Ltd, 39 Milton Park, Abingdon, Oxon OX14 4TD *Tel:* (01235) 400 400 *Fax:* (01235) 832 068
Publishers Group West, 1700 Fourth St, Berkeley, CA 94710, United States *Tel:* 510-528-1444 *Fax:* 510-528-9555

Plough Publishing House of Bruderhof Communities in the UK+
Darvell Bruderhof, Robertsbridge, East Sussex TN32 5DR
Tel: (01580) 883 344 *Fax:* (01580) 883 317
Toll Free *Fax:* 800-018-3347
E-mail: ploughuk@plough.com
Web Site: www.plough.com
Key Personnel
Man Dir, Rights & Permissions: Josef Ben Elieser
Sales, Publicity & Advertising Dir: Detlef Manke
Founded: 1937
Firm is the Publishing House of the Bruderhof Communities in the UK.
Subjects: Fiction, Poetry, Religion - Other, Self-Help, Theology

Pluto Press+
345 Archway Rd, London N6 5AA
Tel: (020) 8348 2724 *Fax:* (020) 8348 9133
E-mail: pluto@plutobooks.com
Web Site: www.plutobooks.com
Key Personnel
Man Dir: Roger van Zwanenberg
Editorial Dir: Anne Beech
Managing Editor: Robert Webb
Head, Sales & Marketing: Kathleen May
　Tel: (020) 8374 2188 *E-mail:* kathleen@plutobooks.com
Marketing Manager: Kathleen May
Founded: 1971
Independent progressive publishing.
Subjects: Anthropology, Biography, Developing Countries, Economics, Environmental Studies, Government, Political Science, History, Labor, Industrial Relations, Law, Social Sciences, Sociology, Women's Studies
ISBN Prefix(es): 0-85305; 0-86104; 0-7453; 0-902818; 0-904383
Number of titles published annually: 60 Print
Total Titles: 400 Print
Associate Companies: Journeyman Press
U.S. Office(s): c/o Stylus Publishing, 22833 Quicksilver Dr, Sterling, VA 20166-2012, United States *Tel:* 703-661-1581 *Fax:* 703-661-1501
Distributed by Footprint Books (Australia); Phambili Agencies Co (South Africa); Stylus Publishing (USA); UBC Press, University of British Columbia (Canada)
Orders to: ITPS, Cheriton House, North Way, Andover, Hampshire SP10 5BE *Tel:* (01264) 342832 *Fax:* (01264) 342788 *E-mail:* Pluto@itps.co.uk

Pocket Bears, *imprint of* Moonlight Publishing Ltd

Pocket Biographies, *imprint of* Sutton Publishing Ltd

Pocket Books, *imprint of* Simon & Schuster Ltd

Pocket Classics, *imprint of* Sutton Publishing Ltd

Pocket ColorCards, *imprint of* Speechmark Publishing Ltd

Pocket Histories, *imprint of* Sutton Publishing Ltd

PUBLISHERS

UNITED KINGDOM

Pocket Worlds, *imprint of* Moonlight Publishing Ltd

Poetica, *imprint of* Anvil Press Poetry Ltd

Poetry Wales Press Ltd+
38-40 Nolton St, 1st floor, Bridgend CF31 3BN
Tel: (01656) 663018 *Fax:* (01656) 649226
E-mail: enquiries@seren.force9.co.uk
Web Site: www.seren-books.com
Key Personnel
Chief Executive, Editorial: Cary Archard
Man Dir: Mick Felton
Poetry Editor: Amy Wack
Publicity Officer: Simon Hicks
Founded: 1981
Book Publisher.
Subjects: Art, Biography, Drama, Theater, Fiction, History, Literature, Literary Criticism, Essays, Poetry
ISBN Prefix(es): 0-907476; 1-85411
Number of titles published annually: 25 Print
Total Titles: 250 Print
Imprints: Seren
U.S. Office(s): Dufour Editions, PO Box 449, Chester Springs, PA 19425, United States *Tel:* 610-458-5005 *Fax:* 610-458-7103
E-mail: dufour8023@aol.com *Web Site:* go.to/dufour

Point, *imprint of* Scholastic Ltd

Police Review Publishing Company Ltd
5th Foor, Celcon House, 289-293 High Holborn, London WC1V 7HZ
Tel: (020) 7440 4700 *Fax:* (020) 7405 7167; (020) 7405 7163
Key Personnel
Publisher: Fabiana Angelini *E-mail:* fabiana.angelini@policereview.co.uk
Man Dir: Alfred Rolington
Founded: 1893
Subjects: Criminology, Law
ISBN Prefix(es): 0-7106; 0-309; 0-85164
Parent Company: The Thomson Corporation
Associate Companies: Jane's Information Group, 1340 Braddock Pl, Suite 300, Alexandria, VA 22314-1651, United States *Tel:* 703-683-3700 *Fax:* 703-836-1593

The Policy Press+
University of Bristol, 34 Tyndall, Bristol BS8 1PY
Tel: (0117) 954 6800 *Fax:* (0117) 973 7308
E-mail: tpp-info@bristol.ac.uk
Web Site: www.policypress.org.uk
Key Personnel
Publishing Dir: Alison Shaw
Marketing & Sales Manager: Julia Mortimer
Editorial Manager & International Rights: Dawn Rusher
Founded: 1996
A specialist policy studies publisher, publishing books, journals, reports & guides from leading academics & researchers. Publications provide the latest research in accessible formats, reaching those who formulate or implement policy at executive & grass-roots levels, as well as academics & students.
Subjects: Civil Engineering, Disability, Special Needs, Economics, Education, Ethnicity, Geography, Geology, Government, Political Science, Health, Nutrition, Labor, Industrial Relations, Management, Public Administration, Social Sciences, Sociology, Women's Studies
ISBN Prefix(es): 0-86922; 1-86134; 1-873575
Associate Companies: The Joseph Rowntree Foundation
Orders to: DA Information Services, 648 Whitehorse Rd, Mitcham, Victoria 3132, Australia *Tel:* (03) 9210 7777 *Fax:* (03) 9210 7788

E-mail: service@dadirect.com.au (Australia, New Zealand & Papua New Guinea)
ISBS (International Specialised Book Services), 5824 NE Hassals St, Portland, OR 97213-3644, United States *Fax:* 503-280-8832 *E-mail:* orders@isbs.com *Web Site:* www.isbs.com
Marston Book Services, PO Box 269, Abingdon, Oxon OX14 4YN *Tel:* (01235) 465500 *Fax:* (01235) 465556 *E-mail:* direct.orders@marston.co.uk
Unifacmanu Trading Co Ltd, 4F, 91, Ho-Ping East Rd Section 1, Taipei, Taiwan, Province of China

Policy Studies Institute
100 Park Village E, London NW1 3SR
Tel: (020) 7468 0468 *Fax:* (020) 7388 0914
E-mail: postmaster@psi.org.uk
Web Site: www.psi.org.uk
Key Personnel
Dir: Prof Jim Skea *E-mail:* j.skea@psi.org.uk
Secretary: Penny Swann
Founded: 1978
Subjects: Art, Business, Economics, Education, Government, Political Science, Labor, Industrial Relations, Public Administration, Social Sciences, Sociology
ISBN Prefix(es): 0-85374; 0-9503317
Orders to: BEBC Ltd, PO Box 1496, Poole, Dorset BH12 3YD

Polity Press, see Blackwell Publishers

Polo Publishing+
30 Chichester Close, Hampton, Middlesex TW12 3QJ
Tel: (0181) 783-1903 *Fax:* (0181) 979-9425
Key Personnel
Contact: Alan Symons
Subjects: History, Religion - Jewish
ISBN Prefix(es): 0-9523751
Distributed by Seven Hills

Polybooks Ltd+
2 Caversham St, London SW3 4AH
Tel: (020) 7351 4995 *Fax:* (020) 7351 4995
Key Personnel
Managing Editor: James Hughes
Founded: 1964
Book publishers.
Subjects: Art, Biography, Communications, Erotica, Fiction, History, Literature, Literary Criticism, Essays, Nonfiction (General), Wine & Spirits
ISBN Prefix(es): 0-284
Total Titles: 20 Print
Parent Company: Charles Skilton Publishers
Associate Companies: Christchurch Publishers Ltd; Luxor Press

Polygon, *imprint of* Edinburgh University Press Ltd

Polygon+
22 George Sq, Edinburgh EH8 9LF
Tel: (0131) 650 8436 *Fax:* (0131) 662 0038
E-mail: polygon.press@eup.ed.ac.uk
Web Site: www.eup.ed.ac.uk
Key Personnel
General Editor: Jackie Jones *E-mail:* jackie.jones@eup.ed.ac.uk
Sales & Marketing Manager: Jane Camillin *E-mail:* jane.camillin@eup.ed.ac.uk
International Rights: Alison Bowden *E-mail:* alison.bowden@eup.ed.ac.uk
Founded: 1969
Publisher.
Subjects: Drama, Theater, Fiction, Film, Video, History, Humor, Literature, Literary Criticism,
Essays, Music, Dance, Nonfiction (General), Philosophy, Poetry, Women's Studies
ISBN Prefix(es): 0-7486
Total Titles: 100 Print
Online services available through World Wide Web.
Parent Company: Edinburgh University Press Ltd
Distributed by Columbia University Press (USA)
Foreign Rep(s): Columbia University Press (Canada, North America); Hemisphere Publication Services (Australia & New Zealand, Far East); John Wilde Partnership (Germany, Northern Europe)
Warehouse: Scottish Book Source, 137 Dundee St, Edinburgh EH11 1BG, A Mc Dougall *Tel:* (0131) 558 1366 *Fax:* (0131) 557 0189
Orders to: Edinburgh University Press, 22 George Sq, Edinburgh EH8 9LF

Polygon at Edinburgh, *imprint of* Edinburgh University Press Ltd

Polytantric Press, *imprint of* Jay Landesman

Pomegranate Europe Ltd
8, Galliford Rd, Maldon, Essex CM9 7XD
Tel: (01621) 851646 *Fax:* (01621) 852426
E-mail: sales@pomeurope.co.uk
Key Personnel
Sales Dir: Ms Ley Bricknell
Founded: 1985
Also acts as distributor of books, calendars, cards, postcards, posters & social stationery throughout Europe.
Subjects: Architecture & Interior Design, Art, Astrology, Occult, Environmental Studies, Ethnicity, Photography, Women's Studies
ISBN Prefix(es): 1-56640; 1-85257

Pond View, *imprint of* Hawthorns Publications Ltd

Pont Books, *imprint of* Gomer Press (J D Lewis & Sons Ltd)

Pookie Productions Ltd+
PO Box 27018, Edinburgh EH10 5YU
Tel: (0131) 221868 *Fax:* (0131) 221868
Key Personnel
Author & Dir: Ivy Wallace
Man Dir & International Rights: Heather Bonning; Cherry Hope
Founded: 1994
Licensing agent & copyright holders specializing in the work of Ivy Wallace, author & illustrator of the Pookie series & the Animal Shelf series.
Subjects: Fiction
ISBN Prefix(es): 1-872885
Distributed by Scholastic (Australia, New Zealand, Papua New Guinea); Verbatim Distributors (South Africa)
Orders to: Biblios Publishers Distribution Services, Star Rd, Partridge Green, West Sussex RH13 8LD

Popular Dogs, *imprint of* Random House UK Ltd

Popular Woodworking, *imprint of* David & Charles Ltd

David Porteous Editions+
PO Box 5, Chudleigh, Newton Abbot TQ13 0YZ
Tel: (01626) 853310 *Fax:* (01626) 853663
E-mail: dp@davidporteous.com
Web Site: www.davidporteous.com
Key Personnel
Publisher: David Porteous
Founded: 1992
Subjects: Art, Crafts, Games, Hobbies, How-to
ISBN Prefix(es): 1-870586
Total Titles: 18 Print

Distributed by Keith Ainsworth Pty Ltd (Australia); Everybody's Books CC (Republic of South Africa); Forrester Books NZ Ltd (New Zealand); Vanwell Publishing Ltd (Canada)
Warehouse: Parkwest Publications Inc, 451 Communipaw Ave, Jersey City, NJ 07304, United States *Tel:* 201-432-3257 *Fax:* 201-432-3708 *E-mail:* parkwest@parkwestpubs.com *Web Site:* www.parkwestpubs.com
Orders to: Parkwest Publications Inc, 451 Communipaw Ave, Jersey City, NJ 07304, United States *Tel:* 201-432-3257 *Fax:* 201-432-3708 *E-mail:* parkwest@parkwestpubs.com *Web Site:* www.parkwestpubs.com
Membership(s): IPG

Porthill Publishers
36 West Way, Edgware, Middlesex HA8 9LB
Mailing Address: PO Box 311, Edgware, Middlesex HA9 9EA
Tel: (020) 89586783 *Fax:* (020) 89054516
Key Personnel
Publisher: Mr Radomir Putnikovich
Member of British Publishers Association.
Subjects: Art, History, The History of Serbian Culture
ISBN Prefix(es): 1-870732
Foreign Rep(s): Aleksandar Gacic (US)

Portland Press Ltd+
59 Portland Pl, London W1B 1QW
Tel: (020) 7580 5530 *Fax:* (020) 7323 1136
E-mail: editorial@portlandpress.com
Web Site: www.portlandpress.com
Key Personnel
Man Dir: Rhonda Oliver
Dir, Marketing & Customer Service: Adam Marshall *E-mail:* adam.marshall@portlandpress.com
Founded: 1990
Member of ALPSP, UKSG, IPG.
Subjects: Biological Sciences, Chemistry, Chemical Engineering, Health, Nutrition, Medicine, Nursing, Dentistry, Physical Sciences, Science (General), *Biochemistry & molecular biology; school to research level*
ISBN Prefix(es): 1-85578; 0-904498
Number of titles published annually: 7 Print
Total Titles: 112 Print; 3 Online; 3 Audio
Parent Company: The Biochemical Society
Imprints: Making Sense of Science
Branch Office(s)
Portland Customer Services, Commerce Way, Colchester CO2 8HP, Dir, Marketing & Customer Services: Adam Marshall *Tel:* (01206) 796351 *Fax:* (01206) 799331 *E-mail:* sales@portland-services.com *Web Site:* www.portland-services.com
Distributed by DA Information Services (Australia)
Distributor for Bioscientifica Ltd; Information Today, Inc (Europe); Institute of Petroleum; International Water Association Publishing; Journal of Reproduction & Fertility Ltd; Society for Endocrinology
Orders to: Portland Customer Services, Commerce Way, Colchester CO2 8HP *Tel:* 01206 796351 *Fax:* 01206 799331 *E-mail:* sales@portland-services.com *Web Site:* www.portland-services.com
Membership(s): IPG

T & AD Poyser Ltd+
Foots Cray High St, Sidcup, Kent DA14 5HP
Tel: (020) 8308 5700 *Fax:* (020) 8308 5702
E-mail: cservice@harcourt.com
Telex: 25775 Acpres G
Key Personnel
Man Dir: Christopher Gibson
Editor & Foreign Rights: Andrew Richford
Founded: 1972

Subjects: Aeronautics, Aviation, Environmental Studies, Natural History
ISBN Prefix(es): 0-85661
Number of titles published annually: 6 Print
Total Titles: 50 Print
Parent Company: Harcourt Inc, 6277 Sea Harbor Drive, Orlando, FL 32887, United States

PPL, *imprint of* Packard Publishing Ltd

PRC Publishing Ltd+
64 Brewery Rd, London N7 9NT
Tel: (020) 7697 3000
E-mail: info@prcpub.com
Key Personnel
Man Dir: Joanne Messham *E-mail:* jo.messham@prcpub.com
Senior Sales Executive: Cairen Behrens
Founded: 1990
Subjects: Architecture & Interior Design, Art, Cookery, Crafts, Games, Hobbies, Gardening, Plants, How-to, Military Science, Music, Dance, Natural History, Nonfiction (General), Transportation, Wine & Spirits
ISBN Prefix(es): 1-85648
Parent Company: Chrysalis Books

Prentice Hall, *imprint of* Pearson Education Europe, Mideast & Africa

Prentice Hall Europe, *imprint of* Pearson Education Europe, Mideast & Africa

Prentice Hall Regents, *imprint of* Pearson Education Europe, Mideast & Africa

Mathew Price Ltd+
The Old Glove Factory, Bristol Rd, Sherborne, Dorset DT9 4HP
Tel: (01935) 816010 *Fax:* (01935) 816310
E-mail: mathewp@mathewprice.com
Key Personnel
President: Mathew Price
Rights Manager: Tabbie Hunt
Production Manager: Karen Pearce
Administration Manager: Sue Davies

Pride Publications, *imprint of* E J Morten (Publishers)

Prim-Ed Publishing UK Ltd
Tower Court, 4th flr, Foleshill, Enterprise Park, Courtaulds Way, Coventry CV6 5NX
Mailing Address: PO Box 051, Nuneaton CV11 6ZU
Tel: (01203) 322860; (0870) 0131208 *Fax:* (01203) 322861; (0870) 0131209
E-mail: sales@prim-ed.com
Web Site: www.prim-ed.com
Key Personnel
Administration Manager: Joanne Turnbull
Contact: Seamus McGuinness
Subjects: Education, History, Language Arts, Linguistics, Mathematics, Religion - Other, Science (General), Specialize in Geography
Total Titles: 350 Print

Primary Source Microfilm, *imprint of* Gale Research

Primrose Hill Press Ltd+
58 Carey St, London WC2A 2JB
Tel: (020) 7405 7484 *Fax:* (020) 7405 7459
E-mail: info@primrosehillpress.co.uk
Web Site: www.primrosehillpress.co.uk
Key Personnel
Dir: William Butler
Man Dir: Brian Hill *E-mail:* bhill@primrosehillpress.co.uk

Founded: 1997
Specialize in books dedicated to the art & artists of fine wood engraving.
Subjects: Animals, Pets, Art, Gardening, Plants, Poetry
ISBN Prefix(es): 1-901648
Number of titles published annually: 10 Print
Total Titles: 28 Print

The Printed Head, *imprint of* Atlas Press

Prion, *imprint of* Prion Books Ltd

Prion Books Ltd+
Imperial Works, Perren St, London NW5 3ED
Tel: (020) 7482 4248 *Fax:* (020) 7482 4203
E-mail: books@prion.co.uk
Web Site: www.prionbooks.com
Key Personnel
Man Dir: Barry Winkleman
Founded: 1980
Specialize in humor, food & drink, literary & historical reprints, cultural travel, health & nutrition.
ISBN Prefix(es): 1-85375
Number of titles published annually: 50 Print
Total Titles: 200 Print
Imprints: Prion
Distributed by Peter Hyde-Verbatim (South Africa); Peribo (Australia); South Pacific (New Zealand); Trafalgar Square (USA)
Shipping Address: Macmillan, Basingstoke, Hants RG21 6XS
Warehouse: Macmillan, Houndmills, Basingstoke, Hampshire RG21 6XS

Prism Press Book Publishers Ltd+
The Thatched Cottage, Partway Lane, Hazelbury Bryan, Sturminster Newton, Dorset DT10 2DP
Tel: (01258) 817164 *Fax:* (01258) 817635
Key Personnel
Dir: Diana King; Julian King
Founded: 1974
Subjects: Astrology, Occult, Cookery, Environmental Studies, Government, Political Science, Philosophy, Self-Help, Technology, Wine & Spirits
ISBN Prefix(es): 0-904727; 0-907061; 1-85327
U.S. Office(s): Associated Publishers Group, 1501 County Hospital Rd, Nashville, TN 37218, United States
Orders to: Bailey Distribution Ltd, Units 1A/1B, Learoyd Rd, Mountfield Industrial Estate, New Romney, Kent TN28 8XU

Professional Book Supplies Ltd
8 Station Yard, Steventon, Abingdon, Oxford OX13 6RX
Tel: (01235) 861234 *Fax:* (01235) 861601
E-mail: probooks@aol.com
Key Personnel
Man Dir & Dir of Sales & Marketing: Christopher Smith
Production Dir: Lyn Simister
Founded: 1965
Also acts as Second Hand Law Dealers & Book Manufacturers.
Subjects: Accounting, Law
ISBN Prefix(es): 0-86205; 0-903486

Professional Engineering Publishing Ltd+
Northgate Ave, Bury St Edmunds, Suffolk IP32 6BW
Tel: (01284) 763277 *Fax:* (01284) 718692 (sales & marketing)
E-mail: orders@pepublishing.com
Web Site: www.pepublishing.com
Key Personnel
Publications Dir, Publishing & Information Systems: Allan Singleton
Books Publisher: Judith Entwisle-Baker

PUBLISHERS								UNITED KINGDOM

Sales, Publicity: Peter Williams
 E-mail: pa_william@imeche.org.uk
Production: Mike Heath
Journals Publisher: Rosie Grimes
Founded: 1974
Book, journal & magazine publisher.
Member of ALPSP, PA, UKSG, NAG, STM Group.
Subjects: Energy, Engineering (General), Management, Mechanical Engineering, Technology, Transportation
ISBN Prefix(es): 0-85298; 1-86058
Number of titles published annually: 60 Print; 2 CD-ROM; 14 Online
Total Titles: 300 Print; 2 CD-ROM; 14 Online
Parent Company: Institution of Mechanical Engineers
Imprints: MEP
Branch Office(s)
American Society of Mechanical Engineers, New York, NY, United States
Distributed by ASME (USA & Canada)
Distributor for ASME (Europe)

Professional, Managerial & Healthcare Publications
PO Box 100, Chichester, West Sussex PO18 8HD
Tel: (01243) 576444 *Fax:* (01243) 576456
E-mail: admin@pmh.uk.com
Web Site: www.pmh.uk.com
Key Personnel
Editor & Publisher: Peter Harkness
Founded: 1994
Number of titles published annually: 4 Print
Total Titles: 2 CD-ROM

Profile Books Ltd+
58A Hatton Garden, London EC1N 8LX
Tel: (020) 7404 3001 *Fax:* (020) 7404 3003
E-mail: info@profilebooks.co.uk
Web Site: www.profilebooks.co.uk
Key Personnel
Publisher & Man Dir: Andrew Franklin
 E-mail: andrew.franklin@profilebooks.co.uk
International Rights: Nicky White *E-mail:* nicky.white@profilebooks.co.uk
Editorial Dir: Stephen Brough *E-mail:* stephen.brough@profilebooks.co.uk
Editorial: Penny Daniel *E-mail:* penny.daniel@profilebooks.co.uk
Production: Edwin Laing *E-mail:* edwin.laing@profilebooks.co.uk
Publicity & Marketing: Kate Griffin *E-mail:* kate.griffin@profilebooks.co.uk
Sales: Claire Beaumont *E-mail:* claire.beaumont@profilebooks.co.uk
Founded: 1996
Subjects: Biography, Business, Criminology, Developing Countries, Economics, Environmental Studies, Ethnicity, Finance, History, Management, Marketing, Nonfiction (General), Psychology, Psychiatry, Social Sciences, Sociology, Travel, Current Affairs
ISBN Prefix(es): 1-86197
Online services available through amazon.co.uk.
Divisions: The Economist Books
Distributor for The Economist Books
Foreign Rep(s): Allen & Unwin (Australia); APD Singapore Pte Ltd (Malaysia, Singapore, Thailand, Vietnam); Asia Publishers Services Ltd (China, Hong Kong, Korea, Philippines, Taiwan, Macao); Jonathan Bell Publishers Pty Ltd (South Africa); Andrew B Durnell (Europe); Ivan Kerr (Northern Ireland, Republic of Ireland); PIM (Japan, Middle East); Renouf Publishing (Canada, US); Signature Book Representation (UK); Viva Books Ltd (Bangladesh, India, Nepal, Pakistan, Sri Lanka)
Orders to: Kate Griffin, 62 Queen Anne St, London W1M 9LA

TBS Ltd, Frating Distribution Centre, Colchester Rd, Frating Green, Colchester CO7 7DW *Tel:* (01206) 256 000; (01206) 255 678 *Fax:* (01206) 255 930

ProQuest Information & Learning
Formerly Bell & Howell Information & Learning
Division of ProQuest Co
The Quorum, Barnwell Rd, Cambridge CB5 8SW
Tel: (01223) 215512 *Fax:* (01223) 215514
E-mail: marketing@proquest.co.uk
Web Site: www.proquest.co.uk
Key Personnel
Sales Dir: Sue Orchard
Man Dir: Tim Smartt
Subjects: Business, Economics, Electronics, Electrical Engineering, Management, Marketing, Music, Dance, Physics, Science (General), Social Sciences, Sociology
ISBN Prefix(es): 0-576

Proteus, *imprint of* Omnibus Press

PSP, *imprint of* BMJ Publishing Group

Psychological Corporation Ltd
Foots Cray High St, Sidcup, Kent DA14 5HP
Tel: (020) 8308 5750 *Fax:* (020) 8308 5702
E-mail: tpc@harcourt.com
Web Site: www.tpc-international.com
Key Personnel
Contact: Jessica Spencer
Subjects: Disability, Special Needs, Language Arts, Linguistics, Psychology, Psychiatry
ISBN Prefix(es): 0-7491
Branch Office(s)
555 Academic Court, San Antonio, TX, United States
Orders to: Chinese Behavioural Science Corp, 9F-1, 206, Nan-Chuan Rd, Sec 2, Taipei 100 *Tel:* (08862) 2365 6349 *Fax:* (08862) 2365 0525 *E-mail:* cbsc@cm1.hinet.net
Dansk Psykologisk Forlag, Stockholmsgade 29, Copenhagen, Denmark *Tel:* 3538 1655 *Fax:* 3538 1665 *E-mail:* dk-psych@dpf.dk *Web Site:* www.dpf.dk

Psychology Press, *imprint of* Taylor & Francis Group

Publishing Training Centre at BookHouse+
45 E Hill, Wandsworth, London SW18 2QZ
Tel: (020) 8874 2718 *Fax:* (020) 8870 8985
E-mail: publishing.training@bookhouse.co.uk
Web Site: www.train4publishing.co.uk
Key Personnel
Chief Executive: Dag Smith; John Whitley
Courses Development Manager: Graham Smith
Founded: 1980
Act as co-publisher with UNESCO & is a member of ABPTOE.
Subjects: Career Development, Publishing & Book Trade Reference
ISBN Prefix(es): 0-907706

Puffin, *imprint of* The Penguin Group UK

Puffin Books, *imprint of* Penguin Books Ltd

QHS-London, *imprint of* Quaker Home Service

QPI Books, *imprint of* Colour Library Direct

Quaker Home Service
Quaker Book Shop, Friends House, 173 Euston Rd, London NW1 2BJ
Tel: (020) 7663 1030 *Fax:* (020) 7663 1001
E-mail: bookshop@quaker.org.uk
Web Site: www.quaker.org.uk

Founded: 1882
Subjects: Religion - Other
ISBN Prefix(es): 0-85245
Parent Company: Religious Society of Friends
Imprints: QHS-London

Qualum Publishing+
665 Finchley Rd, London NW2 2HN
Tel: (020) 7431 7171 *Fax:* (020) 7681 1316
E-mail: info@qualum.com
Web Site: www.qualum.com
Key Personnel
Contact: Jonathan Stoppi
Founded: 1993
Subjects: Education, Technology
ISBN Prefix(es): 1-899168
Number of titles published annually: 1 Print
Total Titles: 5 Print
Book Club(s): Independent Publishers Group

Quantum, *imprint of* Foulsham Publishers

Quartet Books Ltd+
27 Goodge St, London W1P 2LD
Tel: (020) 7636 3992 *Fax:* (020) 7637 1866
E-mail: quartetbooks@easynet.co.uk
Key Personnel
Chairman: Naim Attallah
Man Dir: Jeremy Beale
Publishing Dir: Stella Kane
Editor: Zelfa Hourani; Chris Parker
Publicity: Arielle Gottlieb
Founded: 1972
Member of the Namara Group, 45 Poland St, London W1V 4AU.
Subjects: Biography, Fiction, History, Music, Dance, Philosophy
ISBN Prefix(es): 0-7043
Parent Company: Namara Ltd
Associate Companies: Robin Clark Ltd
Subsidiaries: Namara Publications
Distributed by Southern Publishers Group (New Zealand); Tower Books (Australia); Trinity Books (South Africa)
Warehouse: Plymbridge Distributors Ltd, Estover Rd, Plymouth, Devon PL6 7PZ *Tel:* (01752) 202300
Orders to: Plymbridge Distributors Ltd, Estover Rd, Plymouth, Devon PL6 7PZ *Tel:* (01752) 202300 *Fax:* (01752) 202333 *E-mail:* orders@plymbridge.com

Quarto Publishing plc+
6 Blundell St, London N7 9BH
Tel: (020) 7700 6700 *Fax:* (020) 7700 4191; (020) 7700 0077
E-mail: quarto@quarto.com
Web Site: www.quarto.com
Key Personnel
Chairman & Chief Executive: Laurence F Orbach
Deputy Chief Executive: Robert J Morley
Publisher, Quintet: Oliver Salzmann
Publisher, Quarto: Piers Spence *E-mail:* pierss@quarto.com
Publisher, Childrens: Jeffrey Nobbs
Founded: 1976
International co-editions publisher.
Subjects: Alternative, Animals, Pets, Antiques, Art, Astrology, Occult, Cookery, Crafts, Games, Hobbies, Drama, Theater, Fashion, Gardening, Plants, Gay & Lesbian, Health, Nutrition, House & Home, How-to, Natural History, Nonfiction (General), Outdoor Recreation, Science (General), Self-Help, Wine & Spirits, Gardening; Illustrated, how-to; Interior Design & Reference
Number of titles published annually: 150 Print
Total Titles: 5,000 Print

731

UNITED KINGDOM

Parent Company: Quarto Group Inc, 276 Fifth Ave, Suite 206, New York, NY 10001, United States
Subsidiaries: Apple Press Ltd; The Artists & Illustrators Magazine Ltd; Quarto Children's Books; Quintet Publishing Ltd

Quartz Editions+
Premier House, 112 Station Rd, Edgware HA8 7BJ
Tel: (020) 8951 5656 *Fax:* (020) 8381 2588
E-mail: quartzeditions@btconnect.com
Key Personnel
Dir: Susan Pinkus
Founded: 1992
Packager & publisher of high-quality, illustrated titles for the international market.
Subjects: Astrology, Occult, Geography, Geology, Health, Nutrition, History, Natural History, Nonfiction (General), Parapsychology, Dinosaurs
ISBN Prefix(es): 0-9534241

Que, *imprint of* Pearson Education Europe, Mideast & Africa

Que Education & Training, *imprint of* Pearson Education Europe, Mideast & Africa

Que Lycos Books, *imprint of* Pearson Education Europe, Mideast & Africa

Queen Anne Press+
Windmill Cottage, Mackerye End, Harpenden, Herts AL5 5DR
Tel: (01582) 715866 *Fax:* (01582) 715866
E-mail: queenanne@lenqap.demon.co.uk
Key Personnel
Chairman, Man Dir & Editorial Rights: Adrian Stephenson *E-mail:* stephenson@lennardqap.co.uk
Editor: Celia Kent
Founded: 1976
Specialize in sports.
Subjects: Sports, Athletics
ISBN Prefix(es): 1-85291
Total Titles: 40 Print
Parent Company: Lennard Associates
Imprints: Lennard Publishing
Divisions: Lennard Books
Warehouse: TBS Book Distribution, Colchester Rd, Frating Green, Colchester Essex CO7 7DW *Tel:* (01206) 255606 *Fax:* (01206) 255930
Orders to: Virgin Books, Thames Wharf Studios, Rainville Rd, London W6 9HT *Tel:* (020) 7386 3300 *Fax:* (020) 7386 3360

Quentin Books Ltd
11 Brook St, Wivenhoe, Colchester CO7 9DS
Tel: (01206) 825433 *Fax:* (01206) 822990
Key Personnel
Man Dir & International Rights: Mark Paterson *E-mail:* markpaterson@compuserve.com
Founded: 1978
Also acts as book packager.
Subjects: Geography, Geology, History, Regional Interests
ISBN Prefix(es): 0-947614
Associate Companies: Sigmund Freud Copyrights; Mark Paterson & Associates
Showroom(s): Alma St, Wivenhoe CO7 9BE
Bookshop(s): Alma St, Wivenhoe CO7 9BE

Quill, *imprint of* HarperCollins Publishers

Quiller Publishing Ltd+
Wykey House, Wykey, Shrewsbury SY4 1JA
Tel: (01939) 261616 *Fax:* (01939) 261606
E-mail: info@quillerbooks.com
Key Personnel
Man Dir, Editor & Rights & Permissions: Andrew Johnston
Founded: 2001
Specialize in sponsored books.
Subjects: Biography, Business, History, House & Home, Outdoor Recreation, Travel, Country sports, Shooting, Fishing, Equestrian, Fallonry
ISBN Prefix(es): 0-907621; 1-899163; 1-85310; 1-870948; 1-904057
Total Titles: 80 Print
Distributed by Peribo Pty Ltd (Australia); Stackpole Books (USA)
Warehouse: Airlife Publishing Ltd, 101, Longden Rd, Shrewsbury SY4 1JA *Tel:* (01743) 235 651 *Fax:* (01743) 232 944
Orders to: Airlife Publishing Ltd, 101, Longden Rd, Shrewsbury SY4 1JA *Tel:* (01743) 235 651 *Fax:* (01743) 232 944

Quintessence Publishing Co Ltd+
Quintessence House, Grafton Rd, New Malden Surrey KT3 3AB
Tel: (0181) 9496087 *Fax:* (0181) 3361484
E-mail: quintessence@btinternet.com
Key Personnel
Dir: Joyce Ronald
Founded: 1948
Subjects: Medicine, Nursing, Dentistry
ISBN Prefix(es): 0-86715; 1-85097; 4-87417
Parent Company: Quintessenz Verlag Berlin, Germany
Associate Companies: Quintessence Publishing Inc, IL, United States; Quintessence Publishing Co, Ltd, Tokyo, Japan

Quintet Publishing Ltd+
Division of Quarto Publishing PLC
The Fitzpatrick Bldg, 188-194 York Way, London N7 9QR
Tel: (020) 7700 9000 *Fax:* (020) 7700 5785
E-mail: quintet@quarto.com
Key Personnel
Chairman & Chief Executive: Laurence F Orbach
Publishing Dir: Oliver Salzmann *E-mail:* olivers@quarto.com
Founded: 1984
Publishes co-edition books.
Subjects: Crafts, Games, Hobbies, Fashion, Gardening, Plants, Geography, Geology, Health, Nutrition, History, House & Home, How-to, Maritime, Military Science, Music, Dance, Mysteries, Natural History, Outdoor Recreation, Photography, Sports, Athletics, Technology, Transportation, Travel, Wine & Spirits
Number of titles published annually: 60 Print
Total Titles: 750 Print

RAC Publishing+
RAC House, Bartlett St, South Croydon, Surrey CR2 6XW
Mailing Address: PO Box 100, South Croydon, Surrey CR2 6XW
Tel: (020) 8686 0088 *Fax:* (020) 8688 2882
Key Personnel
Publisher: Lynne Elder *E-mail:* lynne@west-one.com
Founded: 1904
Publishers of guides, handbooks & maps for motorists & travelers.
Subjects: Automotive
ISBN Prefix(es): 0-86211; 0-902628
Parent Company: RAC Enterprises
Orders to: Bookpoint Ltd, 39 Milton Park, Abingdon, Oxon OX14 4TD

Radcliffe Medical Press Ltd+
18 Marcham Rd, Abingdon, Oxon OX14 1AA
Tel: (01235) 528820 *Fax:* (01235) 528830
E-mail: contact.us@radcliffemed.com
Web Site: www.radcliffe-oxford.com

Key Personnel
Man Dir: Andrew Bax
Editorial Dir: Gill Nineham
Financial Dir: Margaret McKeown
Editorial Manager: Jamie Etherington *E-mail:* jetherington@radcliffemed.com
Head of Marketing: Gregory Moxon
Founded: 1987
Subjects: Medicine, Nursing, Dentistry
ISBN Prefix(es): 1-870905; 1-85775
Total Titles: 300 Print; 2 CD-ROM

Ragged Bears Ltd+
Ragged Appleshaw, Andover, Hants SP11 9HX
Tel: (01264) 772269 *Fax:* (01264) 772391
E-mail: books@ragged-bears.co.uk
Web Site: www.ragged-bears.co.uk
Key Personnel
Man Dir: Pamela Shirley
Dir Editorial & Rights: Henrietta Stickland
Founded: 1985
ISBN Prefix(es): 1-85714; 1-870817
Imprints: Spindlewood
Distributor for ACC - Children's Classics; Allen & Unwin Children's Books; b small Publishing; David Bennett Books; Children's Corner; Chronicle Books; Clunie Press; Era Publications; Gallery Children's Books; Key Porter Books; Lemniscaat; Lothian Books; Matthew Price Children's Books; Moonlight Publishing; North-South Books; Owl Man; R&S Books; Siphano Picture Books; Star Bright Books; Templar Publishing; Tundra Books; Upland Books; The Wordhouse
Warehouse: c/o The Trade Counter, The Airfield, Norwich Rd, Mendlesham, Suffolk IP14 5NA

Rainham Bookshop, see Meresborough Books

Ramakrishna Vedanta Centre
Unity House, Blind Lane, Bourne End, Bucks SL8 5LG
Tel: (0162) 852-6464
Web Site: www.ramakrishna.org
Key Personnel
Book Sales Manager: Tony Leong
Founded: 1948
Subjects: Philosophy, Religion - Hindu
ISBN Prefix(es): 0-902479; 0-7025

Ramboro Books Plc
10 Blenheim Court, Brewery Rd, London N7 9NT
Tel: (020) 7700 7444 *Fax:* (020) 7700 4552
E-mail: enquiries@ramboro.co.uk
Web Site: www.ramborobooks.com
Key Personnel
Chairman: John Needleman
International Sales Dir: Tim Finch *E-mail:* tfinch@chrysalisbooks.co.uk
US Sales Dir: Robin Cortie
Founded: 1964
Also remainder dealer, promotion publisher.
Subjects: Art, Cookery, History, Transportation
ISBN Prefix(es): 0-86288; 0-905694
Associate Companies: Greenwich Editions
Imprints: Greenwich Editions

Ramsay Head Press+
9 Glenisla Gardens, Edinburgh EH9 2HR
Tel: (0131) 662 1915 *Fax:* (0131) 662 1915
E-mail: ramsayhead@btinternet.com
Key Personnel
Editorial Dir & International Rights: Conrad K Wilson
Founded: 1968
Member of Scottish Publishers Association.
Subjects: Architecture & Interior Design, Art, Biography, Fiction, History, Literature, Literary Criticism, Essays, Poetry
ISBN Prefix(es): 0-902859; 1-873921
Total Titles: 24 Print

Random House Audiobooks, *imprint of* Random House UK Ltd

Random House Business Books, *imprint of* Random House UK Ltd

Random House UK Ltd+
Random House, 20 Vauxhall Bridge Rd, London SW1V 2SA
Tel: (020) 7973 9000 *Fax:* (020) 7233 6125
E-mail: enquiries@randomhouse.co.uk
Web Site: www.randomhouse.co.uk
Telex: 299080 RANDOM G
Key Personnel
Chief Executive: Gail Rebuck
Group Deputy Chairman, General Books Division: Simon Master
President, International Sales Division: Brian Davies
Man Dir, Ebury Special Books Division: Amelia Thorpe
Financial Dir: Anthony McConnell
Group Operations Dir: David Pemberton
Group Sales Dir: Mike Broderick
Man Dir, Century, Hutchinson & Arrow Books: Simon King
Group Marketing Dir: Caroline Michel
Group Production Dir: Stephen Esson
International Dir: Simon Littlewood
Founded: 1987
US Affiliate: Random House Inc, 201 E 50 St, New York, NY 10022.
Subjects: Art, Astrology, Occult, Biography, Cookery, Fashion, Fiction, Government, Political Science, Health, Nutrition, Humor, Nonfiction (General), Philosophy, Poetry, Travel
ISBN Prefix(es): 1-85686; 0-7126
Parent Company: Random House Inc
Imprints: Arrow Books; Business Books; Jonathan Cape; Century; Chatto & Windus/The Hogarth Press; Hutchinson; Legend; Pimlico; Vintage; Barrie & Jenkins; Ebury Press; Ebury Press Stationery; Popular Dogs; Rider; Stanley Paul; Vermilion; Bodley Head Childrens Books; Hutchinson Childrens Books; Jonathan Cape Childrens Books; Julia MacRae; Riverswift; Red Fox; Random House Audiobooks; Tell-A-Story; Fodor's Travel Guides; Random House Business Books; The Bodley Head; William Heinemann
Divisions: General Books Division: Arrow Books, Business Books, Jonathan Cape; Legend, Pimlico, Vintage; Ebury Press Special Books Division: Barrie & Jenkins; Ebury Press; Childrens Books Division: Bodley Head Childrens Books; Red Fox; Tell-A-Story, Fodor's Travel Guides; Electronic Publishing & Multimedia Division: Random House Audiobooks
Orders to: The Book Service Ltd, TBS Distribution Centre, Colchester Rd, Frating Green, Colchester, Essex C07 7DW *Tel:* (01206) 255678

Ransom Publishing Ltd+
Ransom House, Unit 1, Brook St, Watlington, Oxon OX49 5PP
Tel: (01491) 613 711 *Fax:* (01491) 613 733
E-mail: ransom@ransompublishing.co.uk
Web Site: www.ransom.co.uk
Key Personnel
Man Dir: Jenny Ertle *E-mail:* jenny@ransompublishing.co.uk
Marketing, Sales & Export Dir: Robert Ertle
Marketing Manager: Katy Chan *E-mail:* katy@ransompublishing.co.uk
Founded: 1995
Multimedia CD-ROM publisher for use in education & at home.
ISBN Prefix(es): 1-86398; 1-900127
Number of titles published annually: 8 CD-ROM
Total Titles: 30 CD-ROM
Distributed by Gauntlet Entertainment

Foreign Rep(s): Afro-Asian Book Co (Pakistan); Apex-Vision (Korea); Hed Arzi Multimedia Ltd (Israel); Bertelsman (Germany); Demac Educational Software (Ireland); EDCO Interactive (Ireland); Halifax srl (Italy); Kastinatos Editions SA (Greece); The Leaning Foundation (South Africa); LKD Educational Resources (Jordan); DBC Medier (Denmark); NIIT (India); The Original Traffic Company (Netherlands); Planeta Quarks Com Imp Exp Ltda (Brazil); Ransom Publishing (Ireland & UK); Anthony Rudkin Associates (Middle East); Studi (France); Topics Entertainment (US); Typotex Electronic Publishing (Hungary); Webster Publishing Pty Ltd (Australia)

Rapra Technology Ltd
Shawbury, Shrewsbury, Shropshire SY4 4NR
Tel: (01939) 250383 *Fax:* (01939) 251118
E-mail: publications@rapra.net
Web Site: www.rapra.net
Key Personnel
Chief Executive: Andrew Ward
Publications Sales & Marketing Business Manager: Dr Sarah Ward
Produces books, reports, databases relating to all aspects of rubber & plastics processes, products & properties.

Rationalist Press Association
Bradlaugh House, 47 Theobald's Rd, London WC1X 8SP
Tel: (020) 7430 1371 *Fax:* (020) 7430 1271
E-mail: info@rationalist.org.uk
Web Site: www.rationalist.org.uk
Key Personnel
Editor: Jim Herrick *E-mail:* jim.herrick@rationalist.org.uk
Founded: 1899
Subjects: Literature, Literary Criticism, Essays, Philosophy, Psychology, Psychiatry, Religion - Other, Science (General), Social Sciences, Sociology, From a Humanist Perspective
ISBN Prefix(es): 0-301

Ravette Publishing Ltd+
Unit 3, Tristar Centre, Star Rd, Partridge Green, Horsham RH13 8RA
Tel: (01403) 711443 *Fax:* (01403) 711554
E-mail: ravettepub@aol.com
Key Personnel
Man Dir: Margaret Lamb
Founded: 1980
Subjects: Animals, Pets, Criminology, Education, Environmental Studies, Fiction, Foreign Countries, Humor, Nonfiction (General), Self-Help, Adventure, Autobiography/Memoirs/Letters, Beauty, Body, Mind & Spirit, Food & Drink
ISBN Prefix(es): 0-906710; 0-948456; 1-85304; 1-84161
Number of titles published annually: 40 Print
Total Titles: 126 Print

Rayo, *imprint of* HarperCollins Publishers

Read-Along, *imprint of* BBC Audiobooks

The Reader's Digest Association Ltd
11 Westferry Circus, Canary Wharf, London E14 4HE
Tel: (020) 7715 8000 *Fax:* (020) 7715 8181
Web Site: www.readersdigest.co.uk
Telex: 264631
Key Personnel
Marketing Dir: Martin Pasteiner
General Books Editor: Noel Buchanan
Ad Editor: Cortina Butler
Subjects: Animals, Pets, Antiques, Archaeology, Architecture & Interior Design, Cookery, Crafts, Games, Hobbies, Earth Sciences, Fiction, Film, Video, Gardening, Plants, Health, Nutrition, House & Home, How-to, Mysteries, Nonfiction (General), Science (General), Travel
ISBN Prefix(es): 0-276
Parent Company: The Reader's Digest Association Inc, Pleasantville, NY 10570, United States

Reader's Digest Children's Books+
King's Court, Parsonage Lane, Bath BA1 1ER
Tel: (01225) 312200 *Fax:* (01225) 460942
Key Personnel
Contact: Jill Eade *E-mail:* eade@readersdigest.co.uk
Founded: 1981
Subjects: Education
ISBN Prefix(es): 1-85724; 1-84088; 0-907874
Parent Company: Readers Digest Inc
Imprints: Readers Digest Young Families
U.S. Office(s): Readers Digest Young Families, 355 Riverside Ave, Westport, CT 06880, United States
Shipping Address: Littlehampton Book Services, 10-14 Eldon Way, Lineside Estate, Littlehampton, West Sussex BN17 7HE

Readers Digest Young Families, *imprint of* Reader's Digest Children's Books

Reading & Language Information Centre+
University of Reading, Bulmershe Court, Earley, Reading RG6 1HY
Tel: (0118) 931 8820 *Fax:* (0118) 931 6801
E-mail: reading-centre@reading.ac.uk
Web Site: www.ralic.rdg.ac.uk
Key Personnel
Dir: Prof Viv Edwards *E-mail:* v.k.edwards@reading.ac.uk
Membership & Publications: Barbara Shaw *E-mail:* ehsshaba@reading.ac.uk
Publications: Judy Tallet
Founded: 1969
Specialize in language & literacy learning.
Subjects: Education, English as a Second Language, Language Arts, Linguistics
ISBN Prefix(es): 0-7049

Reaktion Books Ltd+
79 Farringdon Rd, London EC1M 3JU
Tel: (020) 7404 9930 *Fax:* (020) 7404 9931
E-mail: info@reaktionbooks.co.uk
Web Site: www.reaktionbooks.co.uk
Key Personnel
Editorial Dir: Michael R Leaman
Publicity & Rights Manager: Maria Kilcoyne *E-mail:* maria@reaktionbooks.co.uk
Production Manager: Ken MacPherson
Marketing Manager: Gaelle Beauclair
Sales Manager: David Hoek
Designer: Fin Lewis
Picture Researcher: Harry Gilonis
Founded: 1985
Subjects: Architecture & Interior Design, Art, Asian Studies, Film, Video, Geography, Geology, Government, Political Science, History, Language Arts, Linguistics, Literature, Literary Criticism, Essays, Nonfiction (General), Photography, Travel, Specialize in non-fiction
ISBN Prefix(es): 0-948462; 1-86189
Number of titles published annually: 40 Print
Total Titles: 170 Print
Online services available through Amazon.
Distributed by Consortium Book Sales & Distribution (USA & Canada)
Foreign Rep(s): APD Singapore Pte Ltd (Brunei, Cambodia, Indonesia, Philippines, Singapore, Thailand, Vietnam); APD Singapore (Malaysia) Ltd (Malaysia); Consul Books (Netherlands); Ewa Ledochowicz (Croatia, Czech Republic, Estonia, Hungary, Poland, Romania, Slovak Republic, Slovenia); Maruzen Company Ltd (Japan); Onslow Books (Austria, Belgium, Germany, Switzerland); Penny Padovani (Greece, Italy, Portugal, Spain); Hanne Rotovnik (Den-

mark, Ireland, Finland, Norway, Sweden); Southern Publishers Group (New Zealand); James Tovey (France); Unireps (Australia); United Publishers Services (Japan)
Warehouse: Grantham Book Services Ltd, Isaac Newton Way, Alma Park Industrial Estate, Grantham, Lincs NG31 9SD *Tel:* (01476) 541080 *Fax:* (01476) 541061 *E-mail:* orders@gbs.tbs-ltd.co.uk

Rebel Inc, *imprint of* Canongate Books Ltd

Recollections, *imprint of* George Mann Publications

RED, *imprint of* Wilmington Business Information Ltd

Redcliffe Press Ltd+
81G Pembroke Road, Clifton, Bristol BS8 3EA
Tel: (0117) 9737207 *Fax:* (0117) 9238991
Key Personnel
Man Dir: John Sansom
Rights & Permissions & Sales: Angela Sansom
Editorial: Clara Sansom
Founded: 1976
Subjects: Art, Literature, Literary Criticism, Essays, Regional Interests
ISBN Prefix(es): 0-905459; 0-948265; 1-872971; 1-900178
Imprints: White Tree Books

Redstone Press+
7a St Lawrence Terrace, London W10 5SU
Tel: (020) 7352 1594 *Fax:* (020) 7352 8749
E-mail: redstone.press@virgin.net
Web Site: www.redstonepress.co.uk
Key Personnel
Proprietor: Julian Rothenstein *E-mail:* jr@redstonepress.co.uk
Founded: 1987
Subjects: Art
ISBN Prefix(es): 1-870003
Online services available through TM Web Services.
Associate Companies: Shambhala Publications (USA)
Subsidiaries: Shambhala Redstone Editions
Distributed by Central Books Ltd; Distribuciones Loring (Spain); Bo Rudin (Scandinavia)
Orders to: Central Books Ltd, 99 Wallis Rd, London E9 5LN

Reed Business Information
Windsor Court, East Grinstead House, East Grinstead, West Sussex RH19 1XA
Tel: (01342) 326972 *Fax:* (01342) 335960
E-mail: rbi.subscriptions@qss-uk.com (subscription queries)
Web Site: www.reedbusiness.com
Key Personnel
Chief Executive: Keith Jones
Chief Operating Officer: Mark Kelsey
Man Dir: James Blazeby; Neil Stiles; Sandy Whetton
Marketing Dir: Jane Burgess
Finance Dir: Carolyn Pickering
ISBN Prefix(es): 0-610; 0-611; 0-948056
Parent Company: Reed Elsevier plc, 25 Victoria St, London SW1H 0EX
Branch Office(s)
Quadrant House, The Quadrant, Sutton, Surrey SM2 5AS *Tel:* (020) 8652 3500 *Fax:* (020) 8652 8932
Statham House, Talbot Rd, Stretford, Manchester M32 0FP *Tel:* (0161) 877 6399 *Fax:* (0161) 877 6288

24, rue de Milan, Paris 75009, France *Tel:* (01) 55 95 95 13 *Fax:* (01) 55 95 95 15
U.S. Office(s): 3730 Kirby Drive, Suite 1030, Houston, TX 77098, United States *Tel:* 713-525-2600 *Fax:* 713-525-2659

Reed Educational & Professional Publishing+
Halley Court, Jordan Hill, Oxford OX2 8EJ
Tel: (01865) 311366 *Fax:* (01865) 314641
E-mail: reededucational@repp.co.uk
Web Site: www.repp.com
Key Personnel
Chief Executive: John Philbin
Finance Dir: Graham Shaw
Group Financial Controller: Michael Sheehy
Tel: (01865) 314-230 *E-mail:* michael.sheehy@repp.co.uk
Subjects: Education, English as a Second Language
Parent Company: Reed Elsevier plc, 25 Victoria St, London SW1H 0EX
Associate Companies: Rigby Heinemann, Australia; Heinemann Educational, Botswana; Rigby Education, United States; Heinemann Publishers Ltd, South Africa; Greenwood Heinemann; Reed Publishing, New Zealand
Imprints: Butterworth Heinemann; Ginn & Company; Greenwood Heinemann; Heinemann Educational; Heinemann Library; Rigby; Rigby Heinemann; Heinemann/Ginn

Reed Elsevier Group plc
Formerly Reed Elsevier plc
Affiliate of Reed Elsevier NV
25 Victoria St, London SW1H 0EX
Tel: (020) 7222 8420 *Fax:* (020) 7227 5799
Web Site: www.reed-elsevier.com
Key Personnel
Chief Executive Officer: Crispin Davis
Chief Financial Officer: Mark Armour
Corporate Headquarters, jointly owned by Reed Elsevier plc, London, UK and Reed Elsevier NV, Amsterdam, Netherlands.

Reed Elsevier plc, see Reed Elsevier Group plc

William Reed Directories+
Broadfield Park, Crawley, West Sussex RH11 9RT
Tel: (01293) 610 400 *Fax:* (01293) 610 322
E-mail: directories@william-reed.co.uk
Web Site: www.william-reed.co.uk
Key Personnel
Man Dir: Mark de Lange
Editorial Manager: Sulann Staniford
Group Sales Manager: Simon Hughes
Marketing Executive: Tracy Larner *E-mail:* tracy.larner@william.reed.co.uk
Founded: 1991
Member of DPA.
Subjects: Business, Catering, Food & Drink
ISBN Prefix(es): 0-901595
Parent Company: William Reed Publishing Ltd
Associate Companies: Knowledge Store; William Reed International

ReganBooks, *imprint of* HarperCollins Publishers

Regency House Publishing Ltd+
3 Mill Lane, Broxbourne, Herts EN10 7AZ
Tel: (01992) 479988 *Fax:* (01992) 479966
E-mail: regencyhouse@btinternet.com
Key Personnel
Man Dir: Nicolette Trodd
Publisher: Brian Trodd
Founded: 1992
Publisher & packager of mass-market non-fiction.
Subjects: Animals, Pets, Architecture & Interior Design, Art, Automotive, Cookery, Crafts, Games, Hobbies, Photography, Poetry, Regional Interests, Transportation

ISBN Prefix(es): 1-85361
Parent Company: Grange Books PLC

Regency Press CP Ltd
Gordon House, Lissenden Gardens, London NW5 1LX
Tel: (020) 7404 4882 *Fax:* (020) 7404 4885
E-mail: info@regency.org
Web Site: www.regency.org
Key Personnel
Contact: Cristina Paiva *Tel:* (020) 7468 0220 *E-mail:* cp@regency.org
Founded: 1990
Publications intended for developing controls & emerging markets.
Specialize in human rights, world health, poverty reduction & racial equality; books for refugees & helping children.
Subjects: Environmental Studies
ISBN Prefix(es): 0-9532905
Number of titles published annually: 10 Print; 1 CD-ROM; 5 Online; 5 E-Book; 1 Audio
Total Titles: 40 Print; 1 CD-ROM; 30 Online; 6 E-Book; 1 Audio
Subsidiaries: The Regency Corporation Ltd

Regnum, *imprint of* Paternoster Publishing

RELATE
Herbert Gray College, Little Church St, Rugby, Warwicks CV21 3AP
Tel: (01788) 573241 *Fax:* (01788) 535007
Web Site: www.relate.org.uk
Key Personnel
Chief Executive: Sarah Bowler
Head of Publications: Suzy Powling
Founded: 1938
Subjects: Human Relations, Psychology, Psychiatry, Social Sciences, Sociology
ISBN Prefix(es): 0-85351

Religious & Moral Education Press, *imprint of* Hymns Ancient & Modern Ltd

Renaissance Books, *imprint of* Global Books Ltd

Research Studies Press Ltd (RSP)+
16 Coach House Cloisters, 10 Hitchin St, Baldock, Herts S67 6AE
Tel: (01462) 895060 *Fax:* (01462) 892546
E-mail: rsp@rspltd.demon.co.uk
Web Site: www.research-studies-press.co.uk
Key Personnel
Publisher: William G Askew
Man Dir: Stephen Holmes *E-mail:* stephen@rspltd.demon.co.uk
Founded: 1983
Subjects: Biological Sciences, Chemistry, Chemical Engineering, Civil Engineering, Computer Science, Electronics, Electrical Engineering, Energy, Engineering (General), Mathematics, Mechanical Engineering, Technology, Botany, Forestry
ISBN Prefix(es): 0-86380
Number of titles published annually: 15 Print
Total Titles: 100 Print
Foreign Rep(s): American Technical Publishers Ltd (UK & Europe); Hemisphere Publication Services (Asia & the Pacific); Taylor & Francis Inc (North America); United Publishing Services Ltd (Japan); Viva Books Pvt Ltd (India)
Orders to: American Technical Publishers Ltd, 27/29 Knowl Piece, Wilbury Way, Hitchin, Herts 5G4 0SX *Tel:* (01462) 437933 *Fax:* (01462) 433678 (UK & Europe)
Hemisphere Publication Services, Golden Wheel Building, 41 Kallang Pudding Rd #04-03, Singapore *Tel:* 741 5166 *Fax:* 742 9356 (Asia & Pacific)

Taylor & Francis Inc, 7625 Empire Dr, Florence, KY 52053, United States *E-mail:* bkorders@taylorandfrancis.com
Membership(s): IPG

Resurgence Books, *imprint of* Green Books Ltd

Retail Entertainment Data Publishing Ltd
Subsidiary of Wilmington Business Information Ltd
Paulton House, 8 Shepherdess Walk, London N1 7LB
Tel: (020) 7566 8216 *Fax:* (020) 7566 8259 (Inquiry); (020) 7566 8316 (Editorial)
E-mail: info@redpublishing.co.uk
Web Site: www.redpublishing.co.uk
Key Personnel
Publisher & Dir: Rory A Cornwell
Publisher: Doug Marshall *E-mail:* dmarshall@redpublishing.co.uk
Editor: Matthew Garbutt
Sales Manager: Becca Bailey
Founded: 1971
Subjects: Music, Dance
ISBN Prefix(es): 0-904520; 1-900105
Bookshop(s): Music Sales, Newmarket Rd, Bury St Edmunds, Suffolk IP33 3YB

Review, *imprint of* Headline Book Publishing Ltd

Revival Publications, *imprint of* Islamic Foundation Publications

RIBA Publications+
Construction House, 56-64 Leonard St, London EC2A 4LT
Tel: (020) 7251 0791 *Fax:* (020) 7608 2375
Web Site: www.ribabookshop.com
Key Personnel
Man Dir: Geoffrey Denner
Production Dir: M Stribbling
Editor: Mark Lane
Marketing Executive: Diane Williams *E-mail:* diane@ribabooks.com
Founded: 1967
Subjects: Architecture & Interior Design
ISBN Prefix(es): 0-900630; 0-947877; 1-85946
Parent Company: RIBA Companies Ltd, 66 Portland Place, London W1N 4AD
Associate Companies: RIBA Information Services National Building Specification
Bookshop(s): RIBA Bookshop, 66 Portland Place, London W1N 4AD

The Richmond Publishing Co Ltd+
PO Box 96, Slough SL2 3RS
Tel: (01753) 643104 *Fax:* (01753) 646553
E-mail: rpc@richmond.co.uk
Key Personnel
Man Dir: Mrs S J Davie
Founded: 1970
Subjects: Environmental Studies, Natural History
ISBN Prefix(es): 0-85546
Total Titles: 100 Print

RICS Books
Surveyor Court, Westwood Business Park, Coventry CV4 8JE
Tel: (020) 7222 7000 *Fax:* (020) 7334 3851
E-mail: mailorder@rics.org.uk
Web Site: www.ricsbooks.com
Key Personnel
Man Dir: Angela Martland
Founded: 1981
Specialize in surveying, property & construction.
Member of The Royal Institution of Chartered Surveyors.
Subjects: Architecture & Interior Design, Civil Engineering, Earth Sciences, Real Estate
ISBN Prefix(es): 0-85406
Parent Company: RICS Business Services, 12 Great George St, London SW1P 3AD
Bookshop(s): Lower Ground Floor, 12 Great George St, Parliament Square, London SW1P 3AD, Manager: Lee Coxon *Fax:* (020) 7222 9430 *E-mail:* bookshop@rics.org.uk

Rider, *imprint of* Random House UK Ltd

Rigby, *imprint of* Reed Educational & Professional Publishing

Rigby Heinemann, *imprint of* Reed Educational & Professional Publishing

Right Way Books, *imprint of* Elliot Right Way Books

Riverrun Press, *imprint of* Calder Publications Ltd

Riverswift, *imprint of* Random House UK Ltd

Roadmaster Publishing
PO Box 176, Chatham, Kent ME5 9AQ
Tel: (01634) 862843 *Fax:* (01634) 201555
E-mail: roadmasterpublishing@blueyonder.co.uk
Key Personnel
Contact: Malcolm Wright
Subjects: Automotive, Environmental Studies, Geography, Geology, History, Natural History, Regional Interests, Transportation

Robinson, *imprint of* Constable Publishers

Robinson's Children, *imprint of* Constable Publishers

Robson Books+
Division of Chrysalis Group
64 Brewery Rd, London N7 9NT
Tel: (020) 7697 3000 *Fax:* (020) 7697 3001
E-mail: robson@chrysalisbooks.co.uk
Web Site: www.batsford.com/robson.htm
Key Personnel
Publisher: Jeremy Robson *E-mail:* jrobson@chrysalisbooks.co.uk
Editor: Lorna Russell
Head of Publicity: Harriet Boston
Founded: 1973
Subjects: Biography, Cookery, Government, Political Science, Humor, Military Science, Sports, Athletics, Travel
ISBN Prefix(es): 0-903895; 0-86051
Number of titles published annually: 75 Print
Total Titles: 800 Print
Warehouse: MacMillan Distribution Ltd, Houndmill, Basingstoke, Hampshire *Tel:* (01256) 329242 *Fax:* (01256) 327961

George Ronald Publisher Ltd+
46 High St, Kidlington, Oxford OX5 2DN
Tel: (01865) 841515
E-mail: sales@grbooks.com
Web Site: www.grbooks.com
Key Personnel
General Manager: Erica Leith *Tel:* (01235) 529137 *E-mail:* erica@grooks.com
Founded: 1947
Subjects: Religion - Other
ISBN Prefix(es): 0-85398
Branch Office(s)
8325 17 St North, St Petersburg, FL 33702, United States

Rooster Books Ltd
The Old Police Station, Priory Lane, Royston, Herts SG8 9DU
Tel: (01763) 242939 *Fax:* (01763) 243332
E-mail: rooster@solutions-for-business.co.uk
Web Site: www.solutions-for-books.co.uk/rooster
Key Personnel
Dir: Guy Garfit
Founded: 1978
Subjects: Business, Computer Science, Economics, Travel
ISBN Prefix(es): 1-871510
Number of titles published annually: 12 Print
Subsidiaries: Digital Colour Press; Solutions for Business

Rosendale Press Ltd+
8 Ponsonby Place, London SW1P 4PT
Tel: (020) 7834 1123 *Fax:* (020) 7834 1240
E-mail: info@rosendale.demon.co.uk
Key Personnel
Chairman: Timothy Green
Editorial Dir: Maureen Green *E-mail:* maureeen@rosendal.demon.co.uk
Founded: 1987
Member of Independent Publishers Guild; Specialize in International co-editions.
Subjects: Cookery, Health, Nutrition, Human Relations, Self-Help
ISBN Prefix(es): 0-9509182; 1-872803
Warehouse: Littlehampton Book Services Ltd, 10-14 Eldon Way, Lineside Estate, Littlehampton, West Sussex BN17 7HE

RotoVision SA
Sheridan House, 112-116A Western Rd, Hove, East Sussex BN3 1DD
Tel: (01273) 716 010 *Fax:* (01273) 727 269
E-mail: sales@rotovision.com
Web Site: www.rotovision.com
Key Personnel
Chief Executive: Ken Fund *E-mail:* kenf@rotovision.com
Publisher: Aidan Walker *E-mail:* aidanw@rotovision.com
Founded: 1974
Subjects: Advertising, Architecture & Interior Design, Photography
ISBN Prefix(es): 2-88046

Rough Guides, *imprint of* The Penguin Group UK

Rough Guides Ltd+
62-70 Shorts Gardens, London WC2H 9AB
Tel: (020) 7556 5000 *Fax:* (020) 7556 5050
E-mail: mail@roughguides.co.uk
Web Site: www.roughguides.com
Key Personnel
Publisher: Mark Ellingham
Editorial Dir: Martin Dunford
Rights Dir: Richard Trillo
Founded: 1982
Specialize in worldwide travel guides for independently minded travelers, music & cultural reference books & maps.
Subjects: Developing Countries, Foreign Countries, Geography, Geology, History, Music, Dance, Outdoor Recreation, Travel
ISBN Prefix(es): 1-85828
Branch Office(s)
345 Hudson St, 4th Floor, New York, NY 10014, United States
Distributed by Penguin Companies
Orders to: Penguin Books Australia Ltd, 487 Maroondah Hwy, Ringwood, Victoria 3134, Australia
Penguin Books Canada Ltd, 10 Alcorn Ave, Siuite 300, Toronto, ON M4V 3B2, Canada
Viking Penguin USA, 375 Hudson St, New York, NY 10014-3657, United States

Roundhall Sweet & Maxwell, *imprint of* Sweet & Maxwell Ltd

UNITED KINGDOM

Roundhouse, *imprint of* Roundhouse Publishing Ltd

Roundhouse Publishing Ltd
Millstone, Limers Lane, Northam, North Devon EX39 2RG
Tel: (01237) 474 474 *Fax:* (01237) 474 774
E-mail: roundhouse.group@ukgateway.net
Web Site: www.roundhouse.net
Key Personnel
President & Chief Executive: Alan T Goodworth
Founded: 1991
Distributor of small & medium publisher lists from the USA, Canada & Australia.
Also acts as agent & representative for English-language publishers. Full service representation & warehousing for publishers to UK, Europe, Middle East & Africa.
Subjects: Biography, Business, Film, Video, Health, Nutrition, History, Language Arts, Linguistics, Literature, Literary Criticism, Essays, Radio, TV, Self-Help, Travel, Also parenting, medical & psychology, music, religion & spirituality
ISBN Prefix(es): 1-85710
Imprints: Pencil Press; Roundhouse
Subsidiaries: Pencil Press; Roundhouse Reference Books
Distributor for Adams Media Corporation (UK & Europe); Applause Cinema & Theatre Books (UK & Europe); Bayeux Arts (UK & Europe); Chelsea House (UK & Europe); Creative Homeowner (UK & Europe); Douglas & McIntyre (UK & Europe); Fairview Press (UK & Europe); Formac Publishing (Selected titles); Free Spirit Publishing (UK & Europe); Global Exchange (UK & Europe); Gryphon House (UK & Europe); Hale & Iremonger (UK & Europe); Harcourt Brace (selected titles); Hardie Grant Books (UK & Europe); Haworth Press (Selected titles); Home Planners (UK & Europe); Interlink Publishing (UK & Europe); Listen & Live Audio (UK & Europe); Little Hills Press (UK & Europe); Lothian Books (UK & Europe); Marshall Cavendish Corp (Selected titles); Mosaic Press (UK & Europe); North Star (UK & Europe); Paragon House (UK & Europe); Rebus (UK & Europe); Self-Counsel Press (UK & Europe); Seven Locks Press (UK & Europe); Sourcebooks (UK & Europe); SPI Books (UK & Europe); Stephan Philips (UK & Europe); Ulysses Travel Guides (UK & Europe); University Press of Mississippi (UK & Europe); Walker & Co (UK & Europe); Warwick Publishing (UK & Europe); Wynn Publishing (UK & Europe)
Shipping Address: Orca Book Services, Stanley House, Fleets Lane, Poole Dorset BH15 3AJ
Warehouse: Orca Book Services, Stanley House, Fleets Lane, Poole Dorset BH15 3AJ

Routledge, *imprint of* Taylor & Francis Group

Routledge+
Member of Taylor & Francis Group
11 New Fetter Lane, London EC4P 4EE
Tel: (020) 7583 9855 *Fax:* (020) 7842 2298
E-mail: info@routledge.co.uk
Web Site: www.routledge.com
Key Personnel
Chief Executive: A Selby
Publishing Dir: S Neil
IT: Tony Short
Founded: 1988
Represents the publishing interests and activities previously undertaken under the names of Routledge & Kegan Paul Ltd, Methuen Academic, Tavistock Publications Ltd, Croom Helm Ltd & Unwin Hyman Academic.
Subjects: Archaeology, Biography, Business, Communications, Developing Countries, Economics, Education, Film, Video, Geography, Geology, Government, Political Science, History, Language Arts, Linguistics, Law, Literature, Literary Criticism, Essays, Philosophy, Psychology, Psychiatry, Religion - Other, Social Sciences, Sociology, Women's Studies
ISBN Prefix(es): 0-415; 0-7448; 1-85178; 0-906890; 0-7099; 0-85664; 0-416; 0-85362; 0-422
Associate Companies: Thomson Finance Company, Metro Center, One Station Place, Stamford, CT 06902, United States
Imprints: Blueprint; Comedia
U.S. Office(s): Routledge, 29 West 35 St, New York, NY 10001, United States *Tel:* 212-216-7800 *Fax:* 212-564-7854 *Web Site:* www.routledge-ny.com
Orders to: Copp Clark, 2775 Matheson Blvd East, Mississauga, ON L4W 4P7, Canada
Taylor & Francis, 7625 Empire Dr, Florence, KY, United States *Tel:* 800-634-7064 *Fax:* 800-248-4724 *E-mail:* cserve@routledge-ny.com (US)
Taylor & Francis Customer Services, ITPS, Cheriton House, North Way, Andover, Hants SP10 5BE *Tel:* (01264) 343071 *Fax:* (01264) 343005 *E-mail:* book.orders@tandf.co.uk (UK, Europe & Asia)

Routledge Curzon, *imprint of* Taylor & Francis Group

Routledge Curzon
11 New Fetter Lane, London EC4P 4EE
Tel: (020) 7583 9855 *Fax:* (020) 7842 2298
E-mail: info@routledge.co.uk
Web Site: www.routledge.com
Key Personnel
Chairman: Malcolm Campbell
Dir: Martina Campbell
Chief Editor: Jonathan Price
Marketing Manager: Marie Lenstrup
 E-mail: marie.lenstrup@planet.nl
Founded: 1970
Subjects: Anthropology, Asian Studies, Business, Developing Countries, Economics, Ethnicity, Foreign Countries, History, Language Arts, Linguistics, Philosophy, Regional Interests, Religion - Buddhist, Religion - Hindu, Religion - Islamic, Religion - Jewish, Religion - Other, Social Sciences, Sociology, Travel, Women's Studies
ISBN Prefix(es): 0-7007; 1-873410
Number of titles published annually: 120 Print
Total Titles: 1,000 Print
Imprints: Caucasus World; Japan Library
U.S. Office(s): 29 W 35th St, New York, NY 10001, United States *Tel:* 212-216-7800 *Fax:* 212-564-7854 *Web Site:* www.routledge-ny.com
Distributed by Paul & Co (Canada & USA, Middle East titles only); University of Hawaii Press (Canada & USA except for Middle East titles)
Distributor for University of Hawaii Press (UK, Europe, Africa, Middle East, South Asia)
Orders to: ITPS - International Thompson Publishing Service, Cheriton House, North Way, Andover, Hampshire SP10 5BE *Tel:* (01264) 342 991 *Fax:* (01264) 364 418 *E-mail:* curzon@itps.co.uk

Routledge Falmer, *imprint of* Taylor & Francis Group

Royal College of General Practitioners+
14 Princes Gate, Hyde Park, London SW7 1PU
Tel: (020) 7581 3232 *Fax:* (020) 7225 3047
E-mail: info@rcgp.org.uk
Web Site: www.rcgp.org.uk
Key Personnel
Head of Communications: Jane Austin
 E-mail: jaustin@rcgp.org.uk
Founded: 1952
Subjects: Education, Health, Nutrition, Medicine, Nursing, Dentistry, Psychology, Psychiatry
ISBN Prefix(es): 0-85084
Branch Office(s)
Elmwood House, 46 Elmwood Ave, Belfast BT9 6AZ, Ireland, Northern Ireland Regional Manager: Ms Valerie Fiddis *Tel:* (02890) 667389 *E-mail:* nireland@rcgp.org.uk (Northern Ireland)
The David Anderson Bldg, Foresterhill Rd, Aberdeen, Scotland, Honorary Secretary: Dr Graeme Miller *Tel:* (01224) 558042 *Fax:* (01224) 558047 *E-mail:* rcgp@pcrc.grampian.scot.nhs.uk (NE Scotland regional office)
Fintry Mill Medical Centre, Finavon St, Dundee, Scotland, Honorary Secretary: Dr Gordon Crosby *Tel:* (01382) 501002 *Fax:* (01382) 501002 *E-mail:* escotland@rcgp.org.uk (E Scotland regional office)
25 Queen St, Edinburgh, Scotland, Chairman: Dr Bill Reith *Tel:* (0131) 260 6800 *Fax:* (0131) 260 6836 *E-mail:* scottishc@rcgp.org.uk (Scotland's main headquarters, also the SE Scotland regional office)
Lancaster House, 4 Lancaster Crescent, Glasgow, Scotland, Honorary Secretary: Dr John Langan *Tel:* (0141) 211 3374 *Fax:* (0141) 211 3375 *E-mail:* gmacpherson@rcgp.org.uk (W Scotland regional office)
North of Scotland Institute of Postgraduate Medical Education Postgraduate Centre, Raigmore Hospital, Inverness, Scotland, Honorary Secretary: Dr Calum MacAulay *Tel:* (01463) 704347 *Fax:* (01463) 705539 *E-mail:* nscotland@rcgp.org.uk (N Scotland regional office)
Cardiff Postgraduate Centre, Cardigan House, University Hospital of Wales, Heath Park, Cardiff, Wales CF14 4XW, Mrs Angela Evelyn *Tel:* (029) 20 746452 *E-mail:* sewales@rcgp.org.uk (SE Wales regional office)
Tyldesley House, Clarence Rd, Craig y Don, Llandudno, Wales LL30 1TW, Angela Thompson *Tel:* (01492) 877854 *Fax:* (01492) 877854 *E-mail:* nwales@rcgp.org.uk (N Wales regional office)
Princess House, Princess Way, Swansea, Wales *Tel:* (01792) 482456 *Fax:* (01792) 482456 *E-mail:* jr62@dial.pipex.com (SW Wales regional office)
Distributed by San Medrea (Spain)

Royal Genealogies, *imprint of* Stacey International

Royal Institute of International Affairs+
Chatham House, 10 St James's Sq, London SW1Y 4LE
Tel: (020) 7957 5700 *Fax:* (020) 7957 5710
E-mail: contact@riia.org
Web Site: www.riia.org
Key Personnel
Head Publications: Margaret May
Media Enquiries: Keith Burnet *Tel:* (020) 7314 2798 *E-mail:* kburnet@riia.org
Founded: 1920
Subjects: Asian Studies, Business, Developing Countries, Economics, Energy, Environmental Studies, Foreign Countries, Government, Political Science
ISBN Prefix(es): 0-905031; 1-86203
Imprints: Chatham House Papers; International Affairs; The World Today
Branch Office(s)
Cassell, PO Box 605, Herndon, VA 20172, United States
Brookings Institution Press, 1775 Massachusetts Ave, NW, Washington, DC 20036, United States
U.S. Office(s): Chatham House Foundation, 16 Sutton Place 9/A, New York, NY, United States, Contact: Richard W Murphy

Distributed by Brookings; Cambridge University Press; Cassell Academic; Oxford University Press; Routledge
Warehouse: Plymbridge Distributors Ltd, Plymbridge House, Estover Rd, Plymouth, Devon PL6 7PZ *Fax:* (01752) 202 3333
Orders to: Plymbridge Distributors Ltd, Plymbridge House, Estover Rd, Plymouth, Devon PL6 7PZ *Fax:* (01752) 202 3333

Royal Institution of Chartered Surveyors, see RICS Books

The Royal Society
6-9 Carlton House Terrace, London SW1Y 5AG
Tel: (020) 7839 5561 *Fax:* (020) 7930 2170
E-mail: info@royalsoc.ac.uk
Web Site: www.royalsoc.ac.uk
Key Personnel
President: Robert May
Executive Secretary: Stephen Cox
Dir of Communications: Dr D S Boak
 E-mail: david.boak@royalsoc.ac.uk
Founded: 1660
Subjects: Education, Energy, Engineering (General), Geography, Geology, Mathematics, Mechanical Engineering, Physical Sciences, Physics, Psychology, Psychiatry, Science (General)
ISBN Prefix(es): 0-85403

The Royal Society of Chemistry+
Burlington House, Piccadilly, London
Tel: (020) 74378656 *Fax:* (020) 74378883
E-mail: sales@rsc.org
Web Site: www.rsc.org
Key Personnel
Head of Information Services: Robert Welham
Editorial, Books: Dr Robert Andrews
Editorial, Journals: Robert Parker
Editorial, Secondary Services: Sharon Bellard
Sales & Promotion: Barry Anderson; Jenny McCluskey
Production: John Futter
Founded: 1841
Subjects: Chemistry, Chemical Engineering, Engineering (General), Health, Nutrition, Mechanical Engineering
ISBN Prefix(es): 0-85186; 0-85404; 0-85990
Branch Office(s)
Thomas Graham House, Science Park, Milton Rd, Cambridge CB4 0WF *Tel:* (01223) 420066 *Fax:* (01223) 423623
Distributed by Springer-Verlag New York Inc (North America)
Orders to: Turpin Distribution Services Ltd, Blackhorse Rd, Letchworth, Herts SG6 1HN *Tel:* (01462) 672555 *Fax:* (01462) 480947

RSP, see Research Studies Press Ltd (RSP)

The Rubicon Press+
R/O 105, Squires Gate Lane, Blackpool, Lancs FY4 1QW
Mailing Address: PO Box 147, Lytham St Annes, Lancashire FY8 3WZ
Tel: (01253) 780247 *Fax:* (01253) 780247
E-mail: robinrub@aol.com
Key Personnel
Partner: Juanita Homan; Robin A Page
 E-mail: robin.page@whsmithnet.co.uk
Founded: 1985
Member of Specializing in Egyptology & English History.
Subjects: Antiques, Archaeology, Biography, Fiction, History, Literature, Literary Criticism, Essays, Travel, Women's Studies
ISBN Prefix(es): 0-948695
Book Club(s): Ancient & Medieval History Book Cl; Book Club Associates, Greater London House, Hampstead Rd, London NW1 7TZ,
Contact: Michael Greenwood *Tel:* (020) 7760 6500 *Fax:* (020) 7760 6777; The History Guild
Membership(s): IPG

Michael Russell Publishing Ltd+
Wilby Hall, Wilby, Norwich NR16 2JP
Tel: (01953) 887776 *Fax:* (01953) 887762
Key Personnel
Man Dir: Michael Russell
 E-mail: michaelrussell@ukgateway.net
Founded: 1976
Subjects: Nonfiction (General)
ISBN Prefix(es): 0-85955
Number of titles published annually: 15 Print
Total Titles: 135 Print

Rutherford House, *imprint of* Paternoster Publishing

The Rutland Press+
15 Rutland Sq, Edinburgh EH1 2BE
Tel: (0131) 229 7545 *Fax:* (0131) 228 2188
Web Site: www.rias.org.uk/about_the_rutland_press.htm
Key Personnel
Sales & Marketing Manager: Eilidh Donaldson
Publishing Manager: Helen Leng *E-mail:* hleng@rias.org.uk
Publishing Coordinator: Susan Skinner
Founded: 1982
Subjects: Architecture & Interior Design, Travel
ISBN Prefix(es): 1-873190
Parent Company: Royal Incorporation of Architects in Scotland

Ryland Peters & Small Ltd+
Kirkman House, 12-14 Whitfield St, London W1T 2RP
Tel: (020) 7436 9090 *Fax:* (020) 7436 9790
E-mail: info@rps.co.uk
Web Site: www.rylandpeters.com
Key Personnel
Man Dir: David Peters
Rights Dir: Joanna Everard *E-mail:* joanna.everard@rps.co.uk
Art Dir: Gabriella Le Grazie
Publishing Dir: Alison Starling
Sales Manager: Jacqueline Maceacharn
Founded: 1995
Publish high quality illustrated books for the international market.
Subjects: Architecture & Interior Design, Cookery, Gardening, Plants, House & Home, Wine & Spirits, Lifestyle
ISBN Prefix(es): 1-84172
Number of titles published annually: 50 Print
Total Titles: 150 Print
Imprints: Paperstyle Gift Line
U.S. Office(s): Ryland Peters & Small Inc, 519 Broadway, 5th floor, New York, NY, United States *Tel:* 646-613-8682; 646-613-8684; 646-613-8685 *Fax:* 646-613-8683 *E-mail:* info@rylandpeters.com
Warehouse: Macmillan Distribution Ltd, Brunel Rd, Houndmills, Basingstoke, Hants RG21 6XS *Tel:* (01256) 329 242 *Fax:* (01256) 327 961 *E-mail:* mdl@macmillam.co.uk

Sage Publications Ltd+
6 Bonhill St, London EC2A 4PU
Tel: (020) 7374 0645; (020) 7330 1234 (book orders hotline) *Fax:* (020) 7374 8741
E-mail: info@sagepub.co.uk
Web Site: www.sagepub.co.uk
Telex: 296207 Sage G
Key Personnel
Man Dir: Stephen Barr
Editorial Dir: Ziyad Marar
Marketing Dir: Ian Eastment
Founded: 1971
Member of IPG.
Subjects: Anthropology, Behavioral Sciences, Biological Sciences, Business, Communications, Computer Science, Criminology, Economics, Education, Engineering (General), Environmental Studies, Ethnicity, Finance, Government, Political Science, Health, Nutrition, History, Human Relations, Language Arts, Linguistics, Management, Marketing, Medicine, Nursing, Dentistry, Philosophy, Psychology, Psychiatry, Religion - Protestant, Social Sciences, Sociology, Women's Studies
ISBN Prefix(es): 0-8039; 0-7619
Imprints: Altamira Press; Paul Chapman Publishing; Corwin Press; Pine Forge Press; Sage Science Press
Divisions: Scolari
Branch Office(s)
M-32 Market, Greater Kailash-1, New Delhi 110024, India *Tel:* (011) 6419884 *Fax:* (011) 6472426 *E-mail:* sageind@giasdl01.vsnl.net.in
U.S. Office(s): 2455 Teller Rd, Thousand Oaks, CA 91320, United States *Tel:* 805-499-0721 *Fax:* 805-499-0871 *E-mail:* info@sagepub.com *Web Site:* www.sagepub.com

Sage Science Press, *imprint of* Sage Publications Ltd

Sainsbury Publishing Ltd+
Auldearn Main St, Bleasby, Nottingham NG14 7GH
Tel: (01636) 830499 *Fax:* (01636) 830175
Key Personnel
Dir: George Sainsbury *E-mail:* george@gsbooks.demon.co.uk
Founded: 1987
Subjects: Humor, Natural History
ISBN Prefix(es): 1-870655

Saint Andrew Press+
121 George St, Edinburgh EH2 4YN
Tel: (0131) 225 5722 *Fax:* (0131) 220 3113
E-mail: cofs.standrew@dial.pipex.com
Web Site: www.churchofscotland.org.uk
Key Personnel
Head of Publishing: Ann Crawford
Sales & Production Manager: Derek Auld
Distribution: Ian Dunnet
Marketing & Publicity Officer: Alison Fleming
Founded: 1954
Member of Scottish Publishers Association.
Subjects: History, Regional Interests, Religion - Protestant, Religion - Other, Theology
ISBN Prefix(es): 0-7152; 0-86153
Number of titles published annually: 12 Print
Total Titles: 100 Print
Parent Company: The Board of Communication of the Church of Scotland
Ultimate Parent Company: The Church of Scotland
Distributor for Church of Scotland Stationery; Pathway Productions; Wild Goose Publications

St David's Press, *imprint of* Welsh Academic Press

St George's Press
Rotten Row House, Rotten Row, Lewes, East Sussex BN7 1TN
Tel: (01273) 473159 *Fax:* (01273) 471918
E-mail: sgp17@aol.com
Web Site: www.eppingforest.co.uk/stgeorgespress
Founded: 1969
The works of Julian Fane, Novelist, Short Story writer; Memorialist & Literary figure of distinction.
Subjects: Fiction, Literature, Literary Criticism, Essays
ISBN Prefix(es): 0-241; 0-902619

UNITED KINGDOM

St Jerome Publishing
2 Maple Rd W, Brooklands, Manchester M23 9HH
Tel: (0161) 973 9856 *Fax:* (0161) 905 3498
E-mail: stjerome@compuserve.com
Web Site: www.stjerome.co.uk
Key Personnel
Man Dir & International Rights: Ken Baker
Founded: 1994
Specialize in books on interpreting & related fields; intercultural communication.
Subjects: Language Arts, Linguistics, Cultural Studies, Literary Studies
ISBN Prefix(es): 1-900650
Number of titles published annually: 15 Print
Total Titles: 52 Print
Distributed by Binghamton University Press; European Institute for the Media; Exeter University Press; Kent State University Press; Multilingual Matters; Northern Illinois University Press; Rodopi; Routledge; Rutgers University Press
Membership(s): IPG; Publishers' Association

St Paul's Bibliographies Ltd+
17 Greenbanks, Lyminge, Kent CT18 8HG
Tel: (0130) 386 2258 *Fax:* (0130) 386 2660
E-mail: stpauls@stpaulsbib.com
Web Site: www.oakknoll.com/spbib.html
Key Personnel
Dir: J von Hoelle; R Fleck; C Reynard
Founded: 1979
ISBN Prefix(es): 0-906795; 0-946053; 1-873040
Parent Company: Oak Knoll Press, 414 Delaware St, New Castle, DE 19720, United States
Distributed by Oak Knoll Press
Distributor for Oak Knoll Press (USA)
Orders to: Scott Brinded, 106 Dover Rd, Folkestone, Kent CT20 1NN *Tel:* (01303) 220567 *Fax:* (01303) 220600

Salamander Books Ltd+
Division of Chrysalis Books
64 Brewery Rd, London N7 9NT
Tel: (020) 7697 3000 *Fax:* (020) 7700 3572
Key Personnel
Chairman: John Needleman
Man Dir: David Spence *E-mail:* dspence@chrysalisbooks.co.uk
Sales Dir: Colin Gower
Production Manager: Peter Thompson
International Rights: Candida Buckley
Founded: 1974
Subjects: Aeronautics, Aviation, Animals, Pets, Cookery, Crafts, Games, Hobbies, Gardening, Plants, Health, Nutrition, House & Home, Natural History, Sports, Athletics, Transportation
ISBN Prefix(es): 0-86101; 1-84065
Imprints: Aspect; Vega
Bookshop(s): Macmillan Distribution Ltd, Houndmills, Basingsoke

The Salariya Book Co Ltd+
25 Marlborough Pl, Brighton, East Sussex BN1 1UB
Tel: (01273) 603 306 *Fax:* (01273) 693 857
E-mail: salariya@salariya.com
Web Site: www.salariya.com
Key Personnel
President: David Salariya
Editor: Karen Barker
Foreign Rights: Nina De La Mer *Tel:* (01273) 621619
Book Rights: Jo Furse *E-mail:* jo.furse@salariya.com
Founded: 1989
Illustrated children's books for international co-edition market.
Subjects: Architecture & Interior Design, Fiction, Foreign Countries, Geography, Geology, History, Natural History, Science (General), Technology
Total Titles: 150 Print

The Saltire Society
9 Fountain Close, 22 High St, Edinburgh EH1 1TF
Tel: (0131) 556 1836 *Fax:* (0131) 557 1675
E-mail: saltire@saltire.org.uk
Web Site: www.saltire-society.demon.co.uk
Key Personnel
Administrator: Kathleen Munro
Founded: 1936
Subjects: History, Poetry
ISBN Prefix(es): 0-85411
Branch Office(s)
Blvd Brand Whitlock 152, BTE 3, 1200 Brussels, Belgium, Convener: Alasdair Geater *Tel:* (2) 735 82 72 *Web Site:* at www.amg1.net/scotland.htm (Brussels)
'Eredene', Huntly Rd, Aboyne, Convener: Ian Kinniburgh *Tel:* (0133) 988 6484 *E-mail:* iankinniburgh@beeb.net (Aberdeen)
Feddans, Cardross, Chair: Alison Cowey *Tel:* (01436) 841 440 (Helensburgh)
Magdalene House, Lochmaben, Dumfries, Converner: Mdme May McKerrell of Hillhouse *Tel:* (01387) 810439 (Dumfries & Galloway)
28 India St, Edinburgh EH3 6HB, Chairman: Dr Neil MacGillivray *Tel:* (0131) 225 3837 (Edinburgh)
Birchdale, 69 Culduthel Rd, Inverness, Chairman: Dr Alastair Scott-Brown *Tel:* (01463) 223 294 *E-mail:* ardynsb@onetel.net.uk (Highland)
Whitelums, Maryton, Kirriemuir, Chairman: Mrs Marion Wallace *Tel:* (01575) 572 302 (Kirriemuir)
25 St Mary's St St, St Andrews, Chairman: Rev Dr James Marshall *Tel:* (01334) 476 136 (St Andrews)
Solwayside, Harbour Rd, Wigtown, Acting Convener: Mrs Mary Norris *Tel:* (01988) 402253 (Galloway)
Warehouse: SBS, 32 Finlas St, Galsgow UK G225DU
Orders to: Scottish Book Source, 137 Dundee St, Edinburgh EH11 1BG *Tel:* (0131) 229 6800 *Fax:* (0131) 229 9070

Salvationist Publishing & Supplies Ltd
117-121 Judd St, King's Cross, London WC1H 9NN
Tel: (020) 7387 1656 *Fax:* (020) 7383 3420
E-mail: addmin@sp-s.co.uk
Key Personnel
Man Dir: Lieutenant General Michael Williams
Company Secretary: Gordon Camsey
Subjects: Music, Dance, Religion - Other
ISBN Prefix(es): 0-85412
Subsidiaries: S P & S Mail Order (also ordering)

Sams Publishing, *imprint of* Pearson Education Europe, Mideast & Africa

Sams.net, *imprint of* Pearson Education Europe, Mideast & Africa

Sangam Books Ltd+
57 London Fruit Exchange Brushfield St, London E1 6EP
Tel: (020) 7377-6399 *Fax:* (020) 7375-1230
E-mail: sangambks@aol.com
Key Personnel
Chief Executive, Sales, Publicity: A A de Souza
Founded: 1981
Member of Publishers Association UK.
Subjects: Fiction, Medicine, Nursing, Dentistry, Nonfiction (General), Science (General), Social Sciences, Sociology, Technology
ISBN Prefix(es): 0-86131; 0-86311; 0-86125; 0-86132
Number of titles published annually: 30 Print
Parent Company: Orient Longman Ltd, India

Sapphire, *imprint of* Virgin Publishing Ltd

W B Saunders & Co Ltd+
Imprint of Elsevier Health Sciences
32 Jamestown Rd, London NW1 7BY
Tel: (020) 7267 4200 *Fax:* (020) 7485 4752
Telex: 25775 Acpres G
Key Personnel
Man Dir: Peter Lengemann
Man Dir Health & Medical Science: Andrew Stevenson
Vice President, Sales & Marketing: Mary Ging
Head of Marketing: Tim Griswold
Founded: 1888
Subjects: Medicine, Nursing, Dentistry, Veterinary Science
ISBN Prefix(es): 0-7216; 0-7020; 0-218
Parent Company: Elsevier Science Ltd

KG Saur, *imprint of* Gale Research

Savannah Publications
90 Dartmouth Rd, Forest Hill, London SE23 3HZ
Tel: (020) 8244 4350 *Fax:* (020) 8244 2448
E-mail: savpub@dircon.co.uk
Subjects: Publishers of military works of reference & military genealogy
ISBN Prefix(es): 1-902366
Total Titles: 100 Print

Savitri Books+
115J Cleveland St, London W1P 5PN
Tel: (020) 7436 9932 *Fax:* (020) 7580 6330
Key Personnel
Man Dir: M S Srivastava
Founded: 1983
Also acts as packagers.
Subjects: Crafts, Games, Hobbies, How-to, Natural History
ISBN Prefix(es): 0-9534103

SAWD Publications+
Suite 1, 62 Bell Rd, Sittingbourne, Kent ME10 4HE
Tel: (01795) 472 262 *Fax:* (01795) 422 633
E-mail: wainman@sawd.demon.co.uk
Web Site: www.sawd.demon.co.uk
Key Personnel
Partners: Allison Wainman; Susannah Wainman
Founded: 1989
Subjects: Cookery, Gardening, Plants, Humor, Nonfiction (General)
ISBN Prefix(es): 1-872489

SB Publications+
19 Grove Rd, Seaford, East Sussex BN25 1TP
Tel: (01323) 893498 *Fax:* (01323) 893860
E-mail: sales@sbpublications.swinternet.co.uk
Web Site: www.sbpublications.swinternet.co.uk
Key Personnel
Owner: Lindsay Woods
Founded: 1987
Subjects: History, Maritime, Regional Interests, Transportation, Travel, UK local history & guides
ISBN Prefix(es): 1-85770; 1-870708
Number of titles published annually: 25 Print
Total Titles: 140 Print
Imprints: BEN Gunn
Membership(s): IPG

Scarthin Books+
The Promenade Scarthin, Cromford, Derbyshire DE4 3QF
Tel: (01629) 823272 *Fax:* (01629) 825094
E-mail: clare@scarthinbooks.com

Web Site: www.scarthinbooks.com; www.books.co.uk
Key Personnel
Proprietor: D J Mitchell
Marketing: G N Cooper
Founded: 1981
Member of Booksellers Association of Great Britain & Ireland (BAGBI).
Subjects: History, Outdoor Recreation
ISBN Prefix(es): 0-907758
Number of titles published annually: 5 Print
Total Titles: 110 Print
Imprints: Family Walks

Sceptre, *imprint of* Hodder & Stoughton General

Schirmer Reference, *imprint of* Gale Research

Schofield & Sims Ltd+
Dogley Mill, Fenay Bridge, Huddersfield HD8 0NQ
Tel: (01484) 607080 *Fax:* (01484) 606815
E-mail: post@schofieldandsims.co.uk
Web Site: www.schofieldandsims.co.uk
Key Personnel
Chairman: John S Nesbitt
Man Dir: J Stephen Platts
Sales Dir: Jack Brierley
Founded: 1901
ISBN Prefix(es): 0-7217
Membership(s): IPG

Scholastic Ltd+
Villiers House, Clarendon Ave, Leamington Spa, Warwickshire CV32 5PR
Tel: (01926) 887799; (01926) 813910 (warehouse) *Fax:* (01926) 883331
E-mail: scholastic@tens.co.uk
Web Site: www.scholastic.co.uk
Key Personnel
Man Dir: David Kewley
Educational Publishing Dir: Annie Peel
Sales & Marketing Dir: Gavin Lang
Buying Dir, Direct Marketing: Victoria Birkett
Editorial Dir, Children's Books: David Fickling
Senior Commissioning Editor, Educational Books: Gina Nuttall
Editor, Book Clubs: Helen Ward
Editor, Hippo Books: Anne Finnis
Production: Doug Brown
Advertising: Chris Pratt
Finance, IT: Ian Bloodworth
Senior Trade Vice President: Michael Jacobs
Marketing Vice President: Jennifer Pasanen
Founded: 1964
Subjects: Fiction, Nonfiction (General)
ISBN Prefix(es): 0-590
Parent Company: Scholastic Inc, 557 Broadway, New York, NY 10012-3999, United States
Imprints: Adlib; Andre Deutsch Children's Books; Hippo; Point
Branch Office(s)
Scholastic Childrens Books, Commonwealth House, 1-19 New Oxford St, London WC1A 1NU *Tel:* (020) 7421 9000 *Fax:* (020) 7421 9001

School Improvement Reports, *imprint of* First & Best in Education Ltd

School Improvement Reports, see First & Best in Education Ltd

School of Oriental & African Studies+
Thornhaugh St, Russell Sq, London WC1H 0XG
Tel: (020) 7637 2388 *Fax:* (020) 7436 3844
E-mail: md2@soas.ac.uk; aol@soas.ac.uk
Web Site: www.soas.ac.uk *Cable:* SOASUL LONDON WC1
Key Personnel
Publications Manager: M J Daly

Publications: Andrew Osmond
Founded: 1916
Subjects: Art, History, Language Arts, Linguistics, Literature, Literary Criticism, Essays, Religion - Other, Asia & Africa
ISBN Prefix(es): 0-901877; 0-7286

SchoolPlay Productions Ltd+
15 Inglis Rd, Colchester, Essex CO3 3HU
Tel: (01206) 540111 *Fax:* (01206) 766944
E-mail: schoolplay@inglis-house.demon.co.uk
Web Site: www.schoolplayproductions.co.uk
Key Personnel
Man Dir: Jeremy Lucas *E-mail:* jrl@inglis-house.demon.co.uk
Founded: 1989
Specialize in publishing plays & musicals for performance by youth groups & schools; play scripts & musical scores.
Subjects: Drama, Theater, Music, Dance
ISBN Prefix(es): 1-872475; 1-902472
Number of titles published annually: 12 Print
Total Titles: 130 Print

Science & Technology Letters, *imprint of* Science Reviews Ltd

Science Reviews, *imprint of* Science Reviews Ltd

Science Reviews Ltd
PO Box 314, St Albans, Herts AL1 4TS
Tel: (01727) 847322 *Fax:* (01727) 847323
E-mail: scilet@scilet.com
Key Personnel
Publisher: Dr Peter J Farago
Founded: 1978
Subjects: Chemistry, Chemical Engineering, Environmental Studies, Medicine, Nursing, Dentistry, Science (General)
Associate Companies: Science & Technology Letters; Science Reviews Inc, 1115 S Plymouth Court, Suite 412, Chicago, IL 60605, United States *Tel:* 312-913-1404 (also orders)
Imprints: Science Reviews; Science & Technology Letters; Symposium Press

Scientific American, *imprint of* W H Freeman & Co Ltd

SCM Press, *imprint of* Hymns Ancient & Modern Ltd

SCM Press+
Imprint of Hymns Ancient & Modern Ltd
9-17 St Albans Pl, London N1 0NX
Tel: (020) 7359 8033 *Fax:* (020) 7359 0049
E-mail: scmpress@btinternet.com
Web Site: www.scm-canterburypress.co.uk
Key Personnel
Publisher: Alex Wright
Publicity & Marketing Manager: Susan Molyneux Warner
Production: Stephen Rogers
Rights & Permissions: Jenny Willis
 E-mail: rights@scm-canterburypress.co.uk
Sales Manager: Sheena Daley *E-mail:* sales@scm-canterburypress.co.uk
Founded: 1929 (Publishers International Marketing)
Member of Publishers Association.
Subjects: Biblical Studies, Religion - Catholic, Religion - Jewish, Religion - Protestant, Religion - Other, Theology
ISBN Prefix(es): 0-334; 1-85931
Total Titles: 400 Print
Parent Company: SCM-Canterbury Press Ltd, St Mary's Works, St Mary's Plain, Norwich NR3 3BH (also sales, orders & customer enquiries)
Imprints: Xpress Reprints

Sales Office(s): SCM-Canterbury Press Ltd, St Mary's Works, St Mary's Plain, Norwich NR3 3BH *Tel:* (01603) 612914 *Fax:* (01603) 624483
Distributed by Trinity Press (USA); SPCK
Distributor for Australian Theological Forum; Concilium; Deo Publishing; Epworth Press; Trinity Press Intl (UK & Europe)
Foreign Rep(s): Church Stores (New Zealand); Hugh Dunphy (West Indies); International Publishers Marketing (US); Moorehouse Publishing (US); Novalis (Canada); Openbook Publishers (Australia); Charles Paine Pty Ltd (Australia); Publishers International Marketing (Africa, Far East, Middle East)
Warehouse: The Trade Counter, Mendlesham, Suffolk IP14 5NA
Orders to: SCM-Canterbury Press Ltd, St Mary's Works, St Mary's Plain, Norwich NR3 3BH *Tel:* (01603) 612914 *Fax:* (01603) 624483

Scott Foresman, *imprint of* Pearson Education Europe, Mideast & Africa

Scottish Affairs
Formerly Unit for the Study of Government in Scotland
Chisholm House, One Surgeons Sq, Edinburgh EH1 1LZ
Tel: (0131) 650 2456 *Fax:* (0131) 650 6345
Web Site: www.institute-of-governance.org
Key Personnel
Business Manager: Lindsay Adams
 E-mail: ladams@ed.ac.uk
Founded: 1976
Subjects: Government, Political Science
ISBN Prefix(es): 0-9518053; 0-9509626

Scottish Braille Press
Division of Royal Blind Asylum & School
Craigmillar Park, Edinburgh EH16 5NB
Tel: (0131) 6624445 *Fax:* (0131) 6621968
E-mail: scot.braille@dial.pipex.com
Web Site: www.scottish-braille-press.org
Key Personnel
Manager: Mr J H Adams
Founded: 1891
Also Printer.

Scottish Council for Research in Education
61 Dublin St, Edinburgh, Scotland EH3 6NL
Tel: (0131) 5572944 *Fax:* (0131) 5569454
E-mail: scre@scre.ac.uk
Web Site: www.scre.ac.uk
Key Personnel
Dir: Valerie Wilson *Tel:* (0131) 623 2964
 E-mail: valerie.wilson@scre.ac.uk
Head of Administrative Services: David Gilhooly
Head of Information Services: Rosemary Wake
Founded: 1932
Subjects: *Research in the service of education, using Research Series, Research Reviews & Research Reports*
ISBN Prefix(es): 0-901116; 0-947833; 1-86003
Total Titles: 153 Print

Scottish Cultural Press+
Imprint of SCP Publishers Ltd
Unit 13d, Newbattle Abbey Business Annexe, Newbattle Rd, Dalkeith EH22 3LJ
Tel: (0131) 660-6366 (editorial); (0131) 660-6414 (editorial); (0131) 660-4666 (orders)
 Fax: (0131) 5555018
E-mail: info@scottishbooks.com
Web Site: www.scottishbooks.com
Key Personnel
Dir: Avril Gray
Dir & Company Secretary: Brian Pugh
Founded: 1992
Publisher of Scottish non-fiction & fiction.
Subjects: Archaeology, Biography, Environmental Studies, History, Literature, Literary Criticism,

UNITED KINGDOM

Essays, Nonfiction (General), Poetry, Regional Interests, Social Sciences, Sociology
ISBN Prefix(es): 1-898218; 1-840170; 1-898827
Total Titles: 100 Print
Associate Companies: Scottish Children, Unit 13d, New Battle Abbey Business Annexe, New Battle Rd, Dalkeith EH22 3LT *Tel:* (0131) 660-4757, 660-6414 (Editorial); (0131) 660-4666 (orders) *Fax:* (0131) 660-6414 (editorial); (0131) 660-4666 (orders) *E-mail:* info@scottishbooks.com *Web Site:* www.scottishbooks.com
U.S. Office(s): Wilson & Associates, PO Box 2569, Alvin, TX 77512, United States *Tel:* 281-388-0196 *Fax:* 413-683-8503 *E-mail:* info@thebookdistribution.com *Web Site:* www.thebookdistribution.com (Canada & US)
Distributor for Scottish Children's Press; Scottish Cultural Press

Scottish Falcon, *imprint of* The Orkney Press Ltd

Scottish Library Association, see Chartered Institute of Library & Information Professionals in Scotland

Scottish Office Library & Information Services
Room X1/10, Saughton House, Broomhouse Dr, Edinburgh EH11 3XD
Tel: (0131) 2448159 *Fax:* (0131) 2448240
Key Personnel
Senior Librarian: Jean Smith *E-mail:* jsmith@gtnet.gov.uk
Information Services Librarian: Brian Bourner
Library Management Group Librarian: Morag Macdonald
Systems Librarian: Hazel Martin
Founded: 1984
Subjects: Agriculture, Criminology, Disability, Special Needs, Economics, Education, Energy, Environmental Studies, Finance, Government, Political Science, Health, Nutrition, Social Sciences, Sociology, Transportation
Distributed by HMSO Books

Scottish Text Society+
27 George Sq, Edinburgh EH8 9LD
Mailing Address: School of English Studies, University of Nottingham, Nottingham NG7 2RD
Tel: (0115) 951 5922
Tel: (0115) 951 5922
E-mail: sts@arts.gla.ac.uk
Key Personnel
Editorial Secretary: Nicola Royan *E-mail:* nicola.royan@nottingham.ac.uk
Founded: 1882
Subjects: Genealogy, History, Literature, Literary Criticism, Essays, Poetry, Religion - Protestant, Theology, Medieval Literature
ISBN Prefix(es): 0-9500245; 1-897976
Total Titles: 23 Print
Orders to: Book Source, 32 Finlas St, Cowlairs Estate, Glasgow 922 5DU *Tel:* (08702) 402 182 *Fax:* (0141) 577 0189 *E-mail:* orders@booksource.net

Scribner, *imprint of* Simon & Schuster Ltd

Charles Scribner's Sons, *imprint of* Gale Research

Scripta Technica, *imprint of* Wiley Europe Ltd

Scripture Union+
207-209 Queensway, Bletchley, Milton Keynes, Bucks MK2 2EB
Tel: (01908) 856000 *Fax:* (01908) 856111
E-mail: info@scriptureunion.org.uk
Web Site: www.scriptureunion.org.uk
Key Personnel
Publishing Dir: Malcolm Hall
E-mail: malcolmh@scriptureunion.org.uk
Copyright Permissions, Overseas Rights Administration: Rosemary North *E-mail:* rosemaryn@scriptureunion.org.uk
Founded: 1867
Specialize in holiday club resources.
Subjects: Biblical Studies, Education, Religion - Protestant, Theology
ISBN Prefix(es): 0-85421; 0-86201
Number of titles published annually: 100 Print
Total Titles: 450 Print; 450 Online
Branch Office(s)
157 Albertbridge Rd, Belfast BT5 4PS, Ireland *Tel:* (028) 9045 4806 *Fax:* (028) 9073 9758 *E-mail:* admin@suni.co.uk *Web Site:* www.suni.co.uk (Northern Ireland)
87 Lower George's St, Dun Laoghaire, Co Dublin, Ireland *Tel:* (01) 280 2300 *Fax:* (01) 280 2409 *E-mail:* suirl@aol.ie *Web Site:* www.scriptureunion.ie (Republic of Ireland)
9 Canal St, Glasgow, Scotland G4 0ABD *Tel:* (0141) 332 1162 *Fax:* (0141) 332 1162 *E-mail:* info@scriptureunionscotland.org.uk *Web Site:* www.scriptureunionscotland.org.uk (Scotland)
Orders to: Scripture Union Mail Order, PO Box 5148, Milton Keynes, MLO MK2 2YZ *Tel:* (01908) 856006 *Fax:* (01908) 856020 *E-mail:* subs@scriptureunion.org.uk (UK & Wales)
Send the Light (STL) Ltd, PO Box 300, Kingstown Broadway, Carlisle, Cumbria CA3 0GS *Tel:* (01228) 611758

Seaflower Books, *imprint of* Ex Libris Press

Search Press Ltd+
Wellwood, North Farm Rd, Tunbridge Wells, Kent TN2 3DR
Tel: (01892) 510850 *Fax:* (01892) 515903
E-mail: searchpress@searchpress.com
Web Site: www.searchpress.com
Key Personnel
Man Dir: Martin de la Bedoyere
E-mail: martind@searchpress.com
Commissioning Editor: Rosalind Dace
Production: Inger Arthur
Founded: 1970
Subjects: Art, Crafts, Games, Hobbies, Gardening, Plants, How-to
ISBN Prefix(es): 0-85532

Martin Secker & Warburg+
Imprint of Random House
20 Vauxhall Bridge Rd, London SW1V 2SA
Tel: (020) 7840 8400 *Fax:* (020) 7233 8791
E-mail: enquiries@randomhouse.co.uk
Web Site: www.randomhouse.co.uk
Key Personnel
Editorial Dir: Geoff Mulligan *Fax:* (020) 7233 6117
Editor: David Milner
Founded: 1910
Subjects: Fiction, Nonfiction (General)
ISBN Prefix(es): 0-436
Ultimate Parent Company: Bertelsmann

Semiotext(e), *imprint of* MIT Press Ltd

Senate, *imprint of* Tiger Books International PLC

Seren, *imprint of* Poetry Wales Press Ltd

Seren+
Imprint of Poetry Wales Press Ltd
38-40 Nolton St, 1st & 2nd Floors, Bridgend CF31 3BN
Tel: (01656) 663018 *Fax:* (01656) 649226
E-mail: seren@seren.force9.co.uk
Web Site: www.seren-books.com
Key Personnel
International Rights: Mick Felton
E-mail: mickfelton@seren.force9.co.uk
Founded: 1982
Subjects: Art, Biography, Drama, Theater, Fiction, Government, Political Science, History, Literature, Literary Criticism, Essays, Music, Dance, Photography, Poetry, Sports, Athletics, Women's Studies, Anthologies
ISBN Prefix(es): 0-907476; 1-85411
Number of titles published annually: 30 Print
Total Titles: 200 Print; 1 CD-ROM; 1 Audio
Distributed by Dufour Editions Inc (US); St Clair Press (Australia)

Serif+
47 Strahan Rd, London E3 5DA
Tel: (020) 8981-3990 *Fax:* (020) 8981-3990
Key Personnel
Publisher & International Rights: Stephen Hayward *E-mail:* stephen@serif.demon.co.uk
Founded: 1993
Subjects: Cookery, Developing Countries, Foreign Countries, Government, Political Science, History
ISBN Prefix(es): 1-897959
Orders to: Central Books, 99 Wallis Rd, London E9 5LN
Interlink Publishing Group, 46 Crosby St, Northampton, MA 01060-1804, United States *Tel:* 413-582-7054 *Fax:* 413-582-7057 *E-mail:* sales@interlinkbooks.com *Web Site:* www.interlinkbooks.com

Serindia Publications+
Unit 1, Ashburton Centre, 276 Cortis Rd, London SW15 3AY
Tel: (020) 8785-6313 *Fax:* (020) 8785-0999
E-mail: info@serindia.com
Web Site: www.serindia.com
Key Personnel
Man Dir: Anthony Aris
Founded: 1976
Subjects: Art, Asian Studies
ISBN Prefix(es): 0-906026
Associate Companies: Aris & Philips Ltd

Serpent's Tail Ltd+
4 Blackstock Mews, London N4 2BT
Tel: (020) 7354-1949 *Fax:* (020) 7704-6467
E-mail: info@serpentstail.com
Web Site: www.serpentstail.com
Key Personnel
Editorial Dir: Peter Ayrton *E-mail:* pete@serpentstail.com
Production: Ruth Petrie
Publicity: Anna Vallois
Sales & Marketing: Jenny Boyce
Founded: 1986
Subjects: African American Studies, Asian Studies, Biography, Criminology, Ethnicity, Fiction, Gay & Lesbian, Literature, Literary Criticism, Essays, Music, Dance, Mysteries, Nonfiction (General), Women's Studies, High Risk/Cult
ISBN Prefix(es): 1-85242
Number of titles published annually: 40 Print
Total Titles: 350 Print
Imprints: High Risk
Branch Office(s)
Lisa Garbutt Book Promotion, PO Box 976, North Kingstown, RI 02852, United States *Tel:* 401-885-3482 *Fax:* 401-885-7996
Distributed by Quartet Sales & Marketing (South Africa); Tower Books Pty Ltd (Australia)
Orders to: LBS, Faraday Close, Durrington, Worthing, West Sussex BN13 3RB *Tel:* (01903) 828800 *Fax:* (01903) 828801

Severn House Publishers Ltd+
9-15 High St, Sutton, Surrey SM1 1DF
Tel: (0208) 7703930 *Fax:* (0208) 7703850

E-mail: sales@severnhouse.com
Web Site: www.severnhouse.com
Key Personnel
Chairman: Edwin Buckhalter
Publisher: Amanda Stewart
Acquisitions Editor: Hugo Cox
Rights Manager: Michelle Duff
Founded: 1974
Member of RNA CWA, RWA, ALA.
Subjects: Fiction
ISBN Prefix(es): 0-7278
Number of titles published annually: 120 Print
Total Titles: 400 Print
Parent Company: Severn House Books (Holdings) Ltd
Imprints: Enigma Books
U.S. Office(s): Chivers North America, PO Box 1450, Hampton, NH 03843-1450, United States *Fax:* 603-929-3890 (Regular print)
Severn House Publishers Inc, 595 Madison Ave, 15th floor, New York, NY 10022, United States *Tel:* 212-888-4042 *Fax:* 212-759-5422 *E-mail:* sales@severnhouse.com *Web Site:* www.severnhouse.com (large print)
Orders to: Grantham Book Services Ltd, Isaac Newton Way, Alma Park Industrial Estate, Grantham, Lincs NG31 9SD *Tel:* (01476) 541080 *Fax:* (01476) 541061 (Also warehouse)

Shakti Communications
28a Popin Business Centre, South Way, Wembley HA9 0HF
Tel: (020) 8903 5442 *Fax:* (020) 8903 4684
E-mail: shakticom@btinternet.com
Key Personnel
Man Dir: Mr Ravi Jain
ISBN Prefix(es): 0-7128; 0-906666; 0-9505709

Shaw & Sons Ltd
Shaway House, 21 Bourne Park, Bourne Rd, Crayford, Kent DA1 4BZ
Tel: (01322) 621100 *Fax:* (01322) 550553
E-mail: sales@shaws.co.uk
Web Site: www.shaws.co.uk
Key Personnel
Publishing Dir: D Hubber
Publications Dir: Crispin Williams
    E-mail: crispin@shaws.co.uk
Sales, Publicity: P Brown
Founded: 1750
Member of the Publishing Association.
Subjects: Government, Political Science, Law, Nonfiction (General)
ISBN Prefix(es): 0-7219
Number of titles published annually: 10 Print
Total Titles: 60 Print

Shearwater Press Ltd
4 Auckland Terrace, Ramsey, Isle of Man IM8 1AF
Tel: (01624) 812114 *Fax:* (01624) 815525
Telex: 629824 Bell
Key Personnel
Man Dir, Editorial: Peter Crellin
Founded: 1973
Subjects: Art, Fiction, Geography, Geology, History, Regional Interests
ISBN Prefix(es): 0-904980

Sheed & Ward Ltd+
14 Coopers Row, London EC3N 2BH
Tel: (020) 7702 9799 *Fax:* (020) 7702 3583
Key Personnel
Dir & Rights: M T Redfern
Dir: K G Darke; A M Redfern
Founded: 1926
Also acts as distributor for other publishers.
Subjects: History, Philosophy, Religion - Other
ISBN Prefix(es): 0-7220

Sheffield Academic Press Ltd+
Mansion House, 19 Kingfield Rd, Sheffield S11 9AS
Tel: (0114) 255 4433 *Fax:* (0114) 255 4626
E-mail: admin@sheffac.demon.co.uk
Web Site: www.sheffieldacademicpress.com
Key Personnel
Man Dir: Jean Allen
Dir: David J A Clines; Dr Philip R Davies; Michael M Mallett
Marketing Manager: Maureen Allum
    E-mail: mallum@sheffac.demon.co.uk
Founded: 1976
Subjects: Archaeology, Biblical Studies, Biological Sciences, Chemistry, Chemical Engineering, Drama, Theater, Foreign Countries, Language Arts, Linguistics, Literature, Literary Criticism, Essays, Medicine, Nursing, Dentistry, Religion - Jewish, Science (General), Technology, Theology
ISBN Prefix(es): 0-905774; 1-85075; 1-84127
Number of titles published annually: 110 Print
Total Titles: 850 Print
Imprints: Almond Press
U.S. Office(s): Cornell University Press Services, 750 Cascadilla St, PO Box 6525, Ithaca, NY 14851, United States (Distribution)
Distributor for Worldwide-Semitic Study Aids Series of University of Birmingham
Foreign Rep(s): Trevor Brown Associates (Europe); Erickson Marketing; Korean Christian Book Service (Korea); Justin Moulder (UK); Brian Pugh (Ireland, Northern Ireland, Scotland); Russell Book Representation (UK); Sheffield Academic Press (Australia, Canada, New Zealand); Derek Walker (Northeast England)

Sheffield Hallam University Press, see SHU Press

Sheldon Press, *imprint of* The Society for Promoting Christian Knowledge (SPCK)

Sheldon Press+
Imprint of The Society for Promoting Christian Knowledge (SPCK)
Holy Trinity Church, Marylebone Rd, London NW1 4DU
Tel: (020) 643 0382 *Fax:* (020) 643 0391
E-mail: sheldon@spck.org.uk
Web Site: www.sheldonpress.co.uk *Cable:* FUTURITY LONDON NW1
Key Personnel
Publisher: Joanna Moriarty *E-mail:* jmoriarty@spck.org.uk
Sales Manager: George Taylor *E-mail:* gtaylor@spck.org.uk
Publicity Manager: Sarah Dennis
    E-mail: sdennis@spck.org.uk
Commissioning Editor: Elizabeth Marsh
    E-mail: emarsh@spck.org.uk
Founded: 1973
Subjects: Health, Nutrition, Psychology, Psychiatry, Self-Help
ISBN Prefix(es): 0-85969
Number of titles published annually: 15 Print
Total Titles: 200 Print
Warehouse: Marston Book Services Ltd
Orders to: 160 Milton Park Estate, Oxford OX14 4YN *Tel:* (01235) 465500 *Fax:* (01235) 465555

Shelfmark Books
60 St Paul's Rd, London N1 2QW
Tel: (020) 7226 7767 *Fax:* (020) 7226 7767
Key Personnel
Contact: John Wardroper
Founded: 1994
Subjects: History, Literature, Literary Criticism, Essays

ISBN Prefix(es): 0-9526093
Orders to: Central Books, 99 Wallis Rd, London E9 5LN

Shepheard-Walwyn (Publishers) Ltd+
The Chandlery, 50 Westminster Bridge Rd, Suite 604, London SE1 7QY
Tel: (020) 7721 7666 *Fax:* (020) 7721 7667
E-mail: books@shepheard-walwyn.co.uk
Web Site: www.shepheard-walwyn.co.uk
Key Personnel
Man Dir & International Rights: Anthony Werner
Founded: 1971
Non-fiction book publishers.
Subjects: Economics, Government, Political Science, History, Nonfiction (General), Philosophy, Religion - Other
ISBN Prefix(es): 0-85683
Number of titles published annually: 5 Print
Total Titles: 95 Print
Shipping Address: Swift Book Distribution, The Grange, Units 1-6, Kingsnorth Industrial Estate, Hoo, Rochester ME3 9ND *Tel:* (01634) 256477 *Fax:* (01634) 256488 *E-mail:* swiftbookdist@aol.com
Membership(s): IPG

Sheppard, *imprint of* Richard Joseph Publishers Ltd

Sherbourne Publications+
Sherbourne, Trefonen Rd, Morda, Oswestery, Salop SY10 9AG
Tel: (01691) 657 853 *Fax:* (01691) 657 853
Key Personnel
Contact: Dorothy McNeil
Founded: 1989
Member of Society of Authors & ALCS Independent Publishers Guild.
Subjects: Animals, Pets, Poetry
ISBN Prefix(es): 1-872547
Distributor for B Small Publishing (UK); Tarquin Publications (UK)

Sheridan Book Company, *imprint of* Tiger Books International PLC

Sherwood Publishing+
Subsidiary of A D International
Sherwood House, 7 Oxhey Rd, Watford, Herts WD19 4QF
Tel: (07000) 234683 *Fax:* (07000) 234689
E-mail: enquiries@adinternational.com
Web Site: www.sherwoodpublishing.com
Key Personnel
Chief Executive: Julie Hay
Founded: 1993
Subjects: Behavioral Sciences, Career Development, Education, Human Relations, Management, Psychology, Psychiatry, Self-Help, Personal development for trainers
ISBN Prefix(es): 0-9521964
U.S. Office(s): Sherwood Publishing, 4036 Kerry Court, Minnetonka, MN 55343, United States

Shire Publications Ltd+
Cromwell House, Church St, Princes Risborough, Bucks HP27 9AA
Tel: (01844) 344301 *Fax:* (01844) 347080
E-mail: shire@shirebooks.co.uk
Web Site: www.shirebooks.com
Key Personnel
Publisher: John Rotheroe
Sales & General Manager: Sue Ross
Publicity Manager: Patience Dizon
Founded: 1962
Subjects: Antiques, Archaeology, Architecture & Interior Design, Biography, Crafts, Games, Hobbies, Electronics, Electrical Engineering, Ethnicity, Gardening, Plants, Genealogy, History, House & Home, Labor, Industrial Re-

lations, Maritime, Military Science, Music, Dance, Natural History, Photography, Social Sciences, Sociology, Sports, Athletics, Transportation, Canals, Coins & Medals, Costume & Fashion Accessories, Egyptology, London, Scottish Heritage, Furniture & Furnishings, Glass, Ceramics, Guide & Walking, Motoring, Railway & Steam, Toys, Collectables, Textile History
ISBN Prefix(es): 0-85263; 0-7478
Number of titles published annually: 30 Print
Total Titles: 500 Print

SHU Press
Learning Centre, Sheffield Hallam University, City Campus, Pond St, Sheffield S1 1WB
Tel: (0114) 225 4702 *Fax:* (0114) 225 4478
E-mail: shupress@shu.ac.uk
Web Site: www.shu.ac.uk
Key Personnel
Administrator: Monica Moseley *E-mail:* m.moseley@shu.ac.uk
Founded: 1980
Also produces videos & computer software games.
Subjects: Accounting, Business, Criminology, Education, Engineering (General), Government, Political Science, Health, Nutrition, History, Labor, Industrial Relations, Library & Information Sciences, Management, Mathematics, Public Administration, Regional Interests, Social Sciences, Sociology, Sports, Athletics, Technology, Women's Studies, Special Needs, Computer Software, Culture, European Studies, Urban Studies, English
ISBN Prefix(es): 0-86339; 0-903761
Parent Company: Sheffield Hallam University

Sickle Moon Books, *imprint of* Eland

Sidgwick & Jackson, *imprint of* Pan Macmillan

Sidgwick & Jackson Ltd+
Imprint of Pan Macmillan
25 Eccleston Place, London SW1W 9NF
Tel: (020) 7881 8000 *Fax:* (020) 7881 8001
Key Personnel
Man Dir: William Armstrong
Publicity: Phillipa McEwan
Promotions Officer: James Strachan
Founded: 1908
Subjects: Archaeology, Biography, Cookery, Economics, Fiction, Government, Political Science, History, Military Science, Music, Dance, Sports, Athletics, Travel
ISBN Prefix(es): 0-283
Orders to: Macmillan Distribution Ltd, Brunel Rd, Houndmills, Basingstoke, Hants RG21 6XS

Sigma Leisure, *imprint of* Sigma Press

Sigma Press+
One South Oak Lane, Wilmslow, Cheshire SK9 6AR
Tel: (01625) 531035 *Fax:* (01625) 536800
E-mail: info@sigmapress.co.uk
Web Site: www.sigmapress.co.uk
Key Personnel
Man Dir, Production: Graham Beech
Editorial: Diana Beech
Founded: 1980
Specialize in books on all aspects of leisure activities, particularly of the outdoors.
Subjects: Crafts, Games, Hobbies, Music, Dance, Outdoor Recreation, Regional Interests, Sports, Athletics, Transportation
ISBN Prefix(es): 1-85058; 0-905104
Total Titles: 250 Print
Imprints: Sigma Leisure

Warehouse: Thomas Lyster & Co, Unit 9, Ormskirk Industrial Estate, Old Boundary Way, Burscough Rd, Ormskirk L39 2TW
Tel: (01695) 575112 *Fax:* (01695) 570120
Membership(s): IPG

Signature, *imprint of* Hodder Children's Books

Silver, *imprint of* Hodder Children's Books

Silver Link Publishing Ltd+
The Trundle, Ringstead Rd, Great Addington, Kettering, Northamptonshire NN14 4BW
Tel: (01536) 330588 *Fax:* (01536) 330588
E-mail: sales@slinkp-p.demon.co.uk
Web Site: www.nostalgiacollection.com
Key Personnel
Man Dir: Peter Townsend
Company Secretary: Frances Townsend
Production Manager: Mick Sanders
Founded: 1985
Also acts as book packager.
Subjects: Animals, Pets, Biography, Business, Crafts, Games, Hobbies, Health, Nutrition, History, Humor, Maritime, Nonfiction (General), Transportation, Towns/Cities in the UK & Farming
ISBN Prefix(es): 0-947971; 1-85895; 1-85794
Associate Companies: Past & Present Publishing Ltd

Simon & Schuster, *imprint of* Simon & Schuster Ltd

Simon & Schuster Audio, *imprint of* Simon & Schuster Ltd

Simon & Schuster Ltd+
Division of Simon & Schuster Inc
4th Floor, Africa House, 64-78 Kingsway, London WC2B 6AH
Tel: (020) 7316 1900 *Fax:* (020) 7316 0332
E-mail: firstname.surname@simonandschuster.co.uk
Telex: 21702
Key Personnel
Man Dir & CEO: Ian Chapman *Fax:* (020) 7316 0331
Publishing Dir, Trade: Susanne Baboneau
Senior Editor, Scribner: Tim Binding
Publisher Non Fiction: Helen Gummer
Children's Publisher: Martina Challis
Editorial Dir, Martin Books: Janet Copleston
International Publisher: Jonathan Atkins
Sales & Marketing Dir: James Kellow
Rights: Diane Spivey
Production: Karen Ellison
Publicity: Rachael Healey
Dir, Finance: Bob Ness
Founded: 1943
Subjects: Biography, Business, Fiction, Nonfiction (General), Science (General)
ISBN Prefix(es): 0-671; 0-517; 0-684
Total Titles: 200 Audio
Parent Company: Simon & Schuster, 1230 Avenue of the Americas, New York, NY 10020, United States
Ultimate Parent Company: Viacom Inc, 1515 Broadway, New York, NY 10036, United States
Associate Companies: Simon & Schuster Australia, 20 Barcoo St, East Roseville NSW 2069, Australia
Imprints: Fireside; Martin Books; Pocket Books; Scribner; Simon & Schuster; Touchstone; Simon & Schuster Audio
Divisions: Martin Books
Distributed by S&S Australia; Distieau
Distributor for Pocket Books (US & Europe)
Shipping Address: HarperCollins Publishing Ltd, Westerhill Rd, Bishopbriggs, Glasgow G64 2QT

Warehouse: IBD Ltd, Magna Park, Coventry Rd, Lutterworth, Leics LE17 4XH *Tel:* (01442) 887900
Orders to: HarperCollins Publishing Ltd, Westerhill Rd, Bishopbriggs, Glasgow G64 2Q1

Charles Skilton Ltd+
2 Caversham St, London SW3 4AH
Tel: (020) 7351 4995 *Fax:* (020) 7351 4995
Key Personnel
Managing Editor: James Hughes
Publicity Manager: Leonard Holdsworth
Founded: 1943
Subjects: Antiques, Art, Biography, Cookery, Erotica, History, Poetry
ISBN Prefix(es): 0-284
Total Titles: 40 Print
Subsidiaries: Albyn Press Ltd; Fortune Press; Luxor Press Ltd; Polybooks Ltd

Skoob Esoterica, *imprint of* Skoob Russell Square

Skoob Pacifica, *imprint of* Skoob Russell Square

Skoob Russell Square+
10 Brunswick Centre, off Bernard St, London WC1N 1AE
Tel: (020) 7278 8760
E-mail: books@skoob.com
Web Site: www.skoob.com
Key Personnel
President & Editorial Dir: I K Ong *E-mail:* ike@skoob.com
Artistic Manager: Mark Lovell *E-mail:* mark@skoob.com
Founded: 1987
Independent & multi-media.
Subjects: Anthropology, Antiques, Art, Asian Studies, Astrology, Occult, Computer Science, Economics, Fiction, Government, Political Science, History, Literature, Literary Criticism, Essays, Mathematics, Philosophy, Poetry, Publishing & Book Trade Reference, Science (General), Technology, Secondhand academic books
ISBN Prefix(es): 1-871438
Total Titles: 48 Print
Imprints: Skoob Esoterica; Skoob Seriph; Skoob Pacifica
Distributed by APG (USA); Gazelle Book Services Ltd (UK)

Skoob Seriph, *imprint of* Skoob Russell Square

SLG Press+
Convent of the Incarnation, Fairacres, Oxford OX4 1TB
Tel: (01865) 721301 *Fax:* (01865) 790860
E-mail: editor@slgpress.co.uk; orders@slgpress.co.uk
Key Personnel
Editor: Sr Isabel Mary
Founded: 1967
Subjects: Religion - Other, Theology
ISBN Prefix(es): 0-7283
Number of titles published annually: 6 Print
Total Titles: 66 Print
Imprints: Fairacres Publication
Distributed by Canterbury Press (UK); Cistercian Publications (USA & Canada)

SLS Legal Publications (NI)
School of Law, The Queen's University Belfast, 28 University Sq, Belfast BT7 1NN
Tel: (01232) 335224 *Fax:* (01232) 326308
Web Site: www.law.qub.ac.uk
Key Personnel
Program Dir: Ms D M Dudley *E-mail:* m.dudley@qub.ac.uk
Publications Editor: Sara Gamble *E-mail:* s.gamble@qub.ac.uk

Legal Editor: Deborah McBride *E-mail:* d.
 mcbride@qub.ac.uk
Founded: 1980
Subjects: Law
ISBN Prefix(es): 0-85389

Jacqui Small, *imprint of* Aurum Press Ltd

Smith-Gordon+
13 Shalcomb St, London SW10 0HZ
Tel: (020) 7351-7042 *Fax:* (020) 7351-1250
E-mail: publisher@smithgordon.com
Key Personnel
Dir & Publisher: Eldred Smith-Gordon
Founded: 1988
Subjects: Health, Nutrition, Medicine, Nursing,
 Dentistry, Science (General), Technology
ISBN Prefix(es): 1-85463
Total Titles: 80 Print
U.S. Office(s): Books International Inc, PO Box
 605, Herndon, VA 22106, United States
Orders to: Smith-Gordon, 47 Worthing Rd, East
 Preston, Nr Worthing, West Sussex BN16
 1DE, Rosemary Harris *Tel:* (01903) 856646
 Fax: (01903) 856646

Smith Settle Ltd+
Ilkley Rd, Otley, West Yorks LS21 3JP
Tel: (01943) 467958 *Fax:* (01943) 850057
E-mail: sales@smith-settle.co.uk
Key Personnel
Man Dir: Kenneth Smith
Editorial Dir: Mark Whitley
Founded: 1986
Subjects: Art, Biography, History, Humor, Nonfiction (General), Regional Interests
ISBN Prefix(es): 1-870071; 1-85825
Number of titles published annually: 12 Print
Total Titles: 120 Print
Distributor for Spredden Press (UK); Woodstock
 Books (UK)
Membership(s): IPG

Smithsonian Institution Press, *imprint of*
Combined Academic Publishers

Colin Smythe Ltd+
38 Mill Lane, Gerrards Cross, Bucks SL9 8BA
Mailing Address: PO Box 6, Bucks SL9 8XA
Tel: (01753) 886000 *Fax:* (01753) 886469
E-mail: sales@colinsmythe.co.uk
Web Site: www.colinsmythe.co.uk
Key Personnel
Man Dir & International Rights: Colin Smythe
 E-mail: cs@colinsmythe.co.uk
Production Dir: Leslie Hayward
Founded: 1966
Book publishers & author's agent.
Subjects: Biography, Drama, Theater, Literature,
 Literary Criticism, Essays, Religion - Catholic,
 Folklore & Mysticism
ISBN Prefix(es): 0-900675; 0-901072; 0-905715;
 0-86140; 0-85105
Number of titles published annually: 12 Print
Total Titles: 480 Print
Distributed by Dufour Editions (USA & Canada);
 Oxford University Press (USA & Canada)
Distributor for ELT Press (Europe); Tir Eolas
 (Britain & Europe)
Warehouse: c/o Clipper Distribution Services Ltd,
 Windmill Grove, Portchester, Hants PO16 9HT
 Tel: (02392) 200080 *Fax:* (02392) 200090
Membership(s): IPG; Publishers' Association

William Snyder Publishing Associates
5 Five Mile Drive, Oxford OX2 8HT
Tel: (01865) 513186 *Fax:* (01865) 513186
Key Personnel
Man Dir: William Snyder *E-mail:* snyderpub@
 aol.com

ISBN Prefix(es): 0-948058
Associate Companies: ELC International

Society for Research into Higher Education,
see SRHE

Society for Endocrinology, *imprint of* Society
for Endocrinology

Society for Endocrinology
17/18 The Courtyard, Woodlands, Bradley Stoke,
 Bristol BS32 4NQ
Tel: (01454) 642200 *Fax:* (01454) 642222
E-mail: info@endocrinology.org; sales@
 endocrinology.org
Web Site: www.endocrinology.org
Key Personnel
Executive Dir: Sue Thorn
Publications Dir: Steve Byford
Sales & Marketing Officer: Lesley Drake
Founded: 1946
Established to promote the study of the endocrine
 system, publishes journals, books, conference
 proceedings & newsletters & offers a publication service to pharmaceutical companies.
Learned society.
ISBN Prefix(es): 1-898099
Total Titles: 12 Print
Online services available through World Wide
 Web.
Imprints: Bio Scientifica; Society for Endocrinology
Distributed by Portland Press Ltd

**The Society for Promoting Christian
Knowledge (SPCK)+**
Holy Trinity Church, Marylebone Rd, London
 NW1 4DU
Tel: (020) 7643 0382 *Fax:* (020) 7643 0391
E-mail: spck@spck.co.uk; sales@spck.co.uk
Web Site: www.spck.org.uk
Key Personnel
Publishing Dir: Simon Kingston
 E-mail: skingston@spck.org.uk
Publicity Manager: Sarah Dennis
 E-mail: sdennis@spck.org.uk
Sales Manager: George Taylor *E-mail:* gtaylor@
 spck.org.uk
Founded: 1698
Throughout the UK 28 Outlets.
Subjects: Biblical Studies, Biography, Religion -
 Catholic, Religion - Protestant, Self-Help, Theology
ISBN Prefix(es): 0-85969; 0-281; 1-902694
Number of titles published annually: 80 Print
Total Titles: 500 Print
Imprints: Azure; Sheldon Press
Distributed by The Pilgrim Press (US)
Warehouse: Marston Christian Warehouse
Orders to: Marston Book Services, PO Box 269,
 Abingdon, Oxford OX14 47N *Tel:* (01235)
 465511 *Fax:* (01235) 465518

The Society of Metaphysicians Ltd+
Archers' Court, Stonestile Lane, The Ridge, Hastings, East Sussex TN35 4PG
Tel: (01424) 751577 *Fax:* (01424) 722387
E-mail: newmeta@btinternet.com; info@
 metaphysicians.org.uk
Web Site: www.newmeta.btinternet.co.
 uk; www.metaphysicians.org.uk; www.
 metaphysicalresearchgroup.org.uk
Key Personnel
President: J J Williamson
Dir of Research: I D Cumberland
General Secretary: Eleanor Swift
Correspondence Education: Terrance Kiernan
Business Secretary: Trevor Sully
Founded: 1944
Publisher of Neometaphysical Digest (quarterly).

Subjects: Astrology, Occult, Earth Sciences, Electronics, Electrical Engineering, Environmental
 Studies, Government, Political Science, Human
 Relations, Parapsychology, Philosophy, Physical Sciences, Physics, Psychology, Psychiatry,
 Science (General), Social Sciences, Sociology,
 New titles, Neometaphysics
ISBN Prefix(es): 1-85228; 1-85810; 0-900684
Number of titles published annually: 150 Print
Total Titles: 2,325 Print
Associate Companies: Istituto Italiano di Ricerche
 Metafisiche, Trieste, Italy *Tel:* (040) 630315
 Fax: (040) 630315 *E-mail:* metaresearch@tin.
 it; Society of Metaphysicians; Society of Metaphysicians (Nigeria) Ltd
Divisions: Metaphysical Research Group
Distributor for Health Research (USA); Sun
 Books (USA)

Sophia Books, *imprint of* Rudolf Steiner Press

South Asians Overseas Series, *imprint of* Peepal
Tree Press

South Street Press, *imprint of* Garnet Publishing
Ltd

Southgate Publishers+
The Square, Sandford, Crediton, Devon EX17
 4LW
Tel: (01363) 776888 *Fax:* (01363) 776889
E-mail: info@southgatepublishers.co.uk
Web Site: www.southgatepublishers.co.uk
Key Personnel
Dir: Drummond Johnstone *E-mail:* dj@
 southgatepublisher.co.uk
Founded: 1991
Specialize in resources for teachers, home learning & life-long learning.
Subjects: Education, Environmental Studies,
 Mathematics, Music, Dance, Science (General)
ISBN Prefix(es): 1-85741
Total Titles: 120 Print
Subsidiaries: Mosaic Educational Publications
Distributed by Bacon & Hughes (Canada)

Souvenir Press Ltd+
43 Great Russell St, London WC1B 3PA
Tel: (020) 7580 9307; (020) 7637 5711; (020)
 7637 5712; (020) 7637 5713 *Fax:* (020) 7580
 5064
E-mail: souvenirpress@ukonline.co.uk *Cable:*
 PUBLISHER LONDON WC1
Key Personnel
Man Dir, Rights & Permissions: Ernest Hecht
Production: Ken Ruskin
Publicity Executive: James Doyle
Founded: 1951
Subjects: Art, Biography, Fiction, History, Howto, Medicine, Nursing, Dentistry, Music, Dance,
 Philosophy, Poetry, Psychology, Psychiatry,
 Religion - Other, Social Sciences, Sociology,
 Sports, Athletics
ISBN Prefix(es): 0-285
Number of titles published annually: 55 Print
Total Titles: 700 Print
Imprints: Condor Books; Human Horizons Series;
 Independent Voices; The Story-Tellers
Subsidiaries: Souvenir Press (Educational & Academic) Ltd; Souvenir Press (Films) Ltd; Euro-Features Ltd; Pictorial Presentations Ltd; Pop-Universal Ltd; Condor Books
Warehouse: BookPoint Ltd, 130 Milton Trading Park, Abingdon, Oxon OX14 4SB, Nicola
 Comber *Fax:* (01235) 400512 *E-mail:* orders@
 bookpoint.co.uk
Membership(s): Publishers' Association

Sovereign International Books, *imprint of*
Sovereign World Ltd

UNITED KINGDOM

Sovereign World Ltd+
Unit 5, Goblands Farm, Cemetry Lane, Hadlow, Kent TN11 0DP
Mailing Address: PO Box 777, Tonbridge, Kent TN11 OZS
Tel: (01732) 850598 *Fax:* (01732) 851077
E-mail: sovereignworldbooks@compuserve.com
Web Site: www.sovereign-world.org
Key Personnel
President: Chris Mungeam
Man Dir: Tim Pettingale *E-mail:* tim@sovereign-world.com
Founded: 1986
Subjects: Religion - Protestant
ISBN Prefix(es): 1-85240
Imprints: Sovereign International Books

SPA Books Ltd+
PO Box 47, Stevenage, Herts SG2 8UH
Tel: (01438) 225727 *Fax:* (01438) 310104
E-mail: strongoakpress@hotmail.com
Key Personnel
Man Dir: Stephen Apps
Founded: 1980
Also distributor & retailer.
Subjects: Art, Biography, History, Military Science, Nonfiction (General), Regional Interests, Travel
ISBN Prefix(es): 0-907590; 1-871048
Associate Companies: The Strong Oak Press
Imprints: Strong Oak Press

Sparrowhawk, *imprint of* Hawk Books

SPCK, see The Society for Promoting Christian Knowledge (SPCK)

Speechmark Publishing Ltd+
Telford Rd, Bicester, Oxon OX26 4LQ
Tel: (01869) 244644 *Fax:* (01869) 320040
E-mail: info@speechmark.net
Web Site: www.speechmark.net
Key Personnel
Publisher: Ian Franklin *E-mail:* ianf@speechmark.net
Sales Manager: Sally Dickinson *E-mail:* sallyd@speechmark.net
Marketing Manager: Su Underhill *E-mail:* suu@speechmark.net
Publishing Manager: Sarah Miles *E-mail:* sarahm@speechmark.net
Customer Services Manager: Jan Jervis *E-mail:* janj@speechmark.net
Founded: 1984
BESA.
Subjects: Behavioral Sciences, Child Care & Development, Disability, Special Needs, Education, Language Arts, Linguistics, Medicine, Nursing, Dentistry, Psychology, Psychiatry, Social Sciences, Sociology, Practical handbooks for teachers, speech & language therapists, psychologists occupational therapists & nursing staff covering speech & language, gerontology, special needs & mental health
ISBN Prefix(es): 0-86388
Number of titles published annually: 35 Print; 1 CD-ROM
Total Titles: 200 Print; 1 CD-ROM; 5 Audio
Imprints: ColorCards; Pocket ColorCards; Winslow Editions
Membership(s): IPG

Spellmount Ltd Publishers+
The Old Rectory, Staplehurst, Kent TN12 0AZ
Tel: (01580) 893730 *Fax:* (01580) 893731
E-mail: enquiries@spellmount.com
Web Site: www.spellmount.com
Key Personnel
Publisher: Jamie Wilson
Editorial Dir: Jag Wilson
Founded: 1983

Also acts as book packager.
Subjects: Biography, History, Military Science, Nonfiction (General)
ISBN Prefix(es): 0-946771; 1-873376; 1-86227
Associate Companies: Tom Donovan Publishing; Howell Press; National Army Museum PUBLICATIONS; Ken Trotman Ltd
Warehouse: CBS Ltd, 406 Vale Rd, Tonbridge, Kent TN9 1XR
Orders to: Amalgamated Book Services, Royal Star Arcade, High St, Suite 1, Maidstone, Kent ME14 1JL ME14 1JL, Sales Manager: Frank McNamara *Tel:* (01622) 764 555 *Fax:* (01622) 763 197 (North & East Midlands, Scotland, UK & Ireland)
Ashton International Marketing Services, PO Box 298, Sevenoaks, Kent TN13 1WV *Tel:* (01732) 746 093 *Fax:* (01732) 746 096 (Middle East & Far East)
Barry Brittlebank, 17 Whitehall Crescent, Bradford Rd, Wakefield, West Yorkshire WF1 2AF *Tel:* (01622) 764 555 *Fax:* (01622) 763 197 (Northern UK)
Jonathon Brooks, 57 Greenway, Berkhamsted, Herts (London)
D Richard Brown, Post Box 30037, 5-20061 Malmo 30, Sweden *Tel:* (040) 161 200 *Fax:* (040) 161 208 (Denmark, Finland, Iceland, Norway, Sweden)
European Marketing Services, 55 Overhill Rd, Dulwich, London SE22 0PQ *Tel:* (020) 8516-5433 *Fax:* (020) 8516-5434 (Austria, Belgium, France, Germany & Switzerland)
Owen Hazell, 180 Vale Rd, Tonbridge, Kent TN9 1SP (Southeast, East Anglia)
Robin House, 37 From Park, Bartestree, Hereford HR1 4BF (Southwest, Midland & South Wales)
Iberian Book Services, Sector Islas, Bloque 12, 1, B, 28760 Tres Cantos, Madrid, Spain *Tel:* (09) 1803 49 18 *Fax:* (09) 1803 59 36 (Spain & Portugal)
Carr O'Connell, 342 North Circular Rd, Philsboro, Dublin 7, Ireland (Northern Ireland & Ireland)
Penny Padovani, 56 Rosebank, Holyport Rd, Fulham, London SW6 6LH *Tel:* (020) 7381-3936 (Italy & Greece)
Peribo Pty Ltd, 58 Beaumont Rd, Mount Kuring-gai, NSW 2080, Australia, Andrew Coffey *Tel:* (02) 9457 0011 *Fax:* (02) 9457 0022 (Australia & New Zealand)

Spindlewood, *imprint of* Ragged Bears Ltd

Spokesman+
Imprint of Bertrand Russell Peace Foundation Ltd
Russell House, Bulwell Lane, Nottingham NG6 0BT
Tel: (0115) 9708318; (0115) 9784504 *Fax:* (0115) 9420433
E-mail: elfeuro@compuserve.com
Web Site: www.spokesmanbooks.com; www.russfound.org
Key Personnel
Editorial: Ken Coates
Publications Manager, Rights & Permissions: Anthony Simpson
Production: Ken Fleet
Founded: 1970
Subjects: Business, Economics, Environmental Studies, Government, Political Science, Labor, Industrial Relations, Social Sciences, Sociology, Peace & Human Rights
ISBN Prefix(es): 0-85124
Associate Companies: Russell Press Ltd, Radford Mill, Norton St, Nottingham NG7 3HN

Spon Press, *imprint of* Taylor & Francis Group

Spon Press
Member of The Taylor & Francis Group
11 New Fetter Lane, London EC4P 4EE
Tel: (020) 7583 9855 *Fax:* (020) 7842 2298
E-mail: info@routledge.co.uk
Web Site: www.sponpress.com
Key Personnel
Man Dir: Marianne Russell
Editorial Dir: Phillip Read
Marketing Dir: Robert Creffield
Production: Gavin Macdonald
Sales Man: Chris Hall
Area Sales Export: Graham Boaler; Mima Birks
Rights & Permissions: Anna Bisztyga
Founded: 1834
Subjects: Architecture & Interior Design, Civil Engineering, Crafts, Games, Hobbies, Environmental Studies, Real Estate, Sports, Athletics, Transportation
ISBN Prefix(es): 0-413; 0-419

The Sportsman's Press+
25 King Charles Walk, London SW19 6JA
Tel: (020) 8789 0229 *Fax:* (020) 8789 0229
Key Personnel
Publisher & Rights: Kenneth Kemp
Founded: 1984
Subjects: Humor, Sports, Athletics, Equestrian, Country Sports
ISBN Prefix(es): 0-948253
Orders to: Vine House, Waldenbury, North Common, Chailey, BN8 4DR East Sussex *Tel:* (01825) 723398 *Fax:* (01825) 724188

Springer-Verlag London Ltd+
Sweetapple House, Catteshall Rd, Goldaming, Surrey GU7 3DJ
Tel: (0483) 418800; (01483) 418822 (sales) *Fax:* (01483) 415151; (01483) 415144
E-mail: postmaster@svl.co.uk
Key Personnel
Man Dir: John Watson
Founded: 1987
Subjects: Astronomy, Computer Science, Engineering (General), Mathematics, Medicine, Nursing, Dentistry
ISBN Prefix(es): 1-85233
Parent Company: Springer-Verlag GmbH & Co KG, Heidelberger Platz 3, 14197 Berlin, Germany

Square One Publications+
The Tudor House, 16 Church St, Upton Office Services, Upton-upon Severn, Worcester WR8 0H7
Tel: (01684) 593704 *Fax:* (01684) 594060
Key Personnel
Contact: Mary Wilkinson *E-mail:* marywilk@rinyonline.co.uk
Founded: 1988
Subjects: Militaria, autobiographies
ISBN Prefix(es): 1-899955
Warehouse: Upton Office Services, 18 Riverside Close Upton-On Severn, Worcester WR8 0JN, Contact: Deidre Thompson *Tel:* (01684) 592035 *E-mail:* deidre@uptonjazz.farmcom.net

SRHE
3 Devonshire St, London W1N 2BA
Tel: (020) 7637 2766 *Fax:* (020) 7637 2781
E-mail: srheoffice@srhe.ac.uk
Web Site: www.srhe.ac.uk
Key Personnel
Dir: Prof Heather Eggins
Founded: 1965
The Society is a registered charity & publishes mainly in cooperation with Open University Press.
Subjects: Education
ISBN Prefix(es): 0-9510798

St James Press, *imprint of* Gale Research

St Pauls Publishing+
187 Battersea Bridge Rd, London SW11 3AS

Tel: (020) 7978 4300 Fax: (020) 7978 4370
E-mail: editions@stpauls.org.uk
Web Site: www.stpauls.ie
Key Personnel
Man Dir & Rights & Permissions: Fr Andrew Pudussery
Founded: 1967
Subjects: Human Relations, Humor, Philosophy, Religion - Catholic, Religion - Other, Social Sciences, Sociology, Theology
ISBN Prefix(es): 0-85439
Number of titles published annually: 35 Print
Total Titles: 265 Print
Parent Company: Society of St Paul, Via della Fanella 39, I-00148 Rome, Italy
Branch Office(s)
Moyglare Rd, Maynooth, Co Kildare, Ireland, Francisco Chacko E-mail: sales@stpauls.ie Web Site: www.stpauls.ie (Same address as Distribution Center)
Bookshop(s): St Pauls, Morpeth Terrace, Victoria, London SW1P 1EP, Sebastian Karamvelil Tel: (020) 7828 5582 Fax: (020) 7828 3329 E-mail: bookshop@stpauls.org.uk

Stacey International+
128 Kensington Church St, W8 4BH London
Tel: (020) 7221 7166 Fax: (020) 7792 9288
E-mail: stacey-inter@btconnect.com
Web Site: www.thebookplace.com/stacey
Key Personnel
Chairman: Tom Stacey
Chief Executive: Max Scott
Marketing Manager: Kitty Carruthers
Customer Service: Meave Beckett
    E-mail: meave@stacey-international.co.uk
Founded: 1973
Subjects: Archaeology, Architecture & Interior Design, Art, Business, Cookery, Education, Foreign Countries, Gardening, Plants, Genealogy, Geography, Geology, History, Natural History, Religion - Islamic, Travel
ISBN Prefix(es): 0-905743; 0-9503304; 0-900988
Total Titles: 40 Print
Parent Company: Stacey Arts Ltd
Imprints: Royal Genealogies; Stacey London
Branch Office(s)
Interlink Publishing Group, 46 Crosby St, Northampton, MA 01060-1804, United States Tel: 413-582-7054 Fax: 413-582-7057 E-mail: info@interlinkbooks.com
Orders to: Central Books, 99 Wallis Rd, London E9 5LN, Katie Sneyd Tel: (020) 8986 4854 Fax: (020) 8533 5821 E-mail: orders@centralbooks.com

Stainer & Bell Ltd
Victoria House, 23 Gruneisen Rd, London N3 1DZ
Mailing Address: PO Box 110, London N3 1DZ
Tel: (020) 8343 3303 Fax: (020) 8343 3024
E-mail: post@stainer.co.uk
Web Site: www.stainer.co.uk
Key Personnel
Joint Man Dir, Production: Carol Wakefield
    E-mail: carol@stainer.co.uk
Joint Man Dir, Publicity, Rights & Permissions: Keith Wakefield E-mail: keith@stainer.co.uk
Publishing Dir: Nicholas Williams
    E-mail: nicholas@stainer.co.uk
Founded: 1907
Subjects: Education, Music, Dance, Religion - Other
ISBN Prefix(es): 0-85249
Imprints: Augener; Belton Books; Galliard; A Weekes; Joseph Williams
Distributor for Hope Publishing Co, USA (UK & Europe only)

Harold Starke Publishers Ltd
203 Bunyan Court, Barbican, London EC2Y 8DH
Tel: (01379) 388334; (020) 7588 5195
Fax: (01379) 388335
E-mail: red@eclat.force9.co.uk
Key Personnel
Editorial, Rights & Permissions: Miss N Galinski
Export Sales: Harold Starke
Founded: 1960
Member of the British Publishers Association.
Subjects: Medicine, Nursing, Dentistry
ISBN Prefix(es): 0-287; 1-872457

The Stationery Office+
51-9 Elms Lane, London SW8 5DT
Mailing Address: PO Box 276, London SW8 4DT
Tel: (020) 7600 5522; (020) 7873 8787
Fax: (020) 7873 8200 (orders)
Web Site: www.tso.co.uk; www.officialdocuments.co.uk
Key Personnel
Chief Executive: Fred J Perkins
Dir, Business Development: Kevan Lawton
Editorial: Philip Brooks Tel: (1603) 605532
    E-mail: phil.brooks@theso.co.uk
Founded: 1786
UK sales agent for most major international organizations.
Subjects: Agriculture, Archaeology, Architecture & Interior Design, Business, Computer Science, Earth Sciences, Economics, Education, Energy, Environmental Studies, Finance, Government, Political Science, Health, Nutrition, History, Law, Library & Information Sciences, Medicine, Nursing, Dentistry, Social Sciences, Sociology, Technology, Transportation
ISBN Prefix(es): 0-10; 0-11; 0-337
Associate Companies: The Parliamentary Press - London, Mandela Way, London SE1 5SS Tel: (020) 7394 4200; TSO, G50, Phase Two, Government Bldgs, Ty-Glas, Llanishen, Cardiff CF14 5ST Tel: (02920) 765892; TSO Content Solutions, 84-90 East St, Epsom, Surrey KT17 1HF Tel: (01372) 845700; TSO Ireland, 16 Arthur St, Belfast BT1 4GD, Ireland Tel: (02890) 238451 Fax: (02890) 235401 E-mail: belfast.bookshop@tso.co.uk (also book shop); TSO - Norwich, St Crispins, Duke St, Norwich NR3 1PD Tel: (01603) 622211; TSO Scotland, 71-73 Lothian Rd, Edinburgh, Scotland EH3 9AZ Tel: (0870) 6065566 Fax: (0870) 606 5588 E-mail: edinburgh.bookshop@tso.co.uk
Bookshop(s): 68-69 Bull St, Birmingham B4 6AD, Manager: James Furnival Tel: (0121) 236 9696 Fax: (0121) 236 9699 E-mail: birmingham.bookshop@tso.co.uk; 18-19 High St, Cardiff CF10 1PT Tel: (02920) 39 5548 Fax: (02920) 38 4347 E-mail: cardiff.bookshop@tso.co.uk; 123 Kingsway, London WC2B 6PQ, Manager: Tiffany Holt Tel: (020) 7242 6393; (020) 7242 6410 Fax: (020) 7242 6394 E-mail: london.bookshop@tso.co.uk; 9-21 Princess St, Albert Sq, Manchester M60 8AS, Manager: Ian Penney Tel: (0161) 834 7201 Fax: (0161) 833 0634 E-mail: manchester.bookshop@tso.co.uk; TSO Scotland, 71-73 Lothian Rd, Edinburgh, Scotland EH3 9AZ Tel: (0870) 6065566 Fax: (0870) 606 5588 E-mail: edinburgh.bookshop@tso.co.uk

Rudolf Steiner Press+
35 Park Rd, London NW1 6XT
Mailing Address: Hillside House, The Square, Forest Row, East Sussex RH18 5ES
Tel: (01342) 824433 Fax: (01342) 826437
E-mail: office@rudolfsteinerpress.com
Web Site: www.rudolfsteinerpress.com
Key Personnel
Chief Editor: Sevak Gulbekian
Marketing Assistant/Administrator: K Bernard
Founded: 1920
Subjects: Agriculture, Art, Biography, Education, Health, Nutrition, Music, Dance, Philosophy, Self-Help
ISBN Prefix(es): 0-85440; 1-85584
Number of titles published annually: 15 Print
Total Titles: 400 Print
Imprints: Sophia Books
Distributor for Anthroposophic Press (US); Mercury Arts Publications (UK); New Knowledge Books (UK)
Orders to: Scottish Book Source, 137 Dundee St, Edinburgh EH11 1BG Tel: (0131) 229 6800 Fax: (0131) 229 9070 E-mail: orders@scottishbooksource.com

Stenlake Publishing+
54-58 Mill Sq, Catrine, Ayrshire KA5 6RD
Tel: (01290) 551122 Fax: (01290) 551122
E-mail: info@stenlake.co.uk
Web Site: www.stenlake.co.uk
Founded: 1984
Also acts as international dealer in antique postcards (1900-1940).
Subjects: Antiques, History, Maritime, Regional Interests
ISBN Prefix(es): 1-872074; 1-84033
Associate Companies: Grotte Hall (Postcards)

Patrick Stephens Ltd, imprint of Haynes Publishing

Sterling Audio Books, imprint of BBC Audiobooks

Stobart & Son Ltd, imprint of Stobart Davies Ltd

Stobart Davies Ltd+
Priory House, 2 Priory St, Hertford SG14 1RN
Tel: (01992) 501518 Fax: (01992) 501519
E-mail: sales@stobartdavies.com
Web Site: www.stobart-davies.com
Key Personnel
Publicity: Claire Davies
Rights & Permissions: Brian J Davies
    E-mail: brian@stobart-davies.com
Founded: 1989
Subjects: Crafts, Games, Hobbies, How-to, Natural History, Woodwork, Craft & Forestry
ISBN Prefix(es): 0-85442
Number of titles published annually: 5 Print
Total Titles: 65 Print
Imprints: Stobart & Son Ltd

Stokesby House Publications
Stokesby, Norfolk NR29 3ET
Tel: (01493) 750645 Fax: (01493) 750146
E-mail: stokesbyhouse@btinternet.com
Key Personnel
Contact: Pamela Minett
Subjects: Biological Sciences, Environmental Studies
ISBN Prefix(es): 0-9514490; 1-873600

Story Sound Audio Tapes, imprint of Magna Large Print Books

The Story-Tellers, imprint of Souvenir Press Ltd

Strategic Comments, imprint of International Institute for Strategic Studies

Strategic Survey, imprint of International Institute for Strategic Studies

Strong Oak Press, imprint of SPA Books Ltd

Studio Editions Ltd+
Random House, 20 Vauxhall Bridge Rd, London SWIV 2SA
Tel: (020) 7973 9690 *Fax:* (020) 7233 6057
Telex: 261212
Key Personnel
Chairman: Sonia Land
Dir: J Roderick Webb
Rights Dir: K T Forster
Founded: 1982
Subjects: Antiques, Architecture & Interior Design, Art
ISBN Prefix(es): 0-946495; 1-85170; 1-85891
Subsidiaries: BPL Remainders; Studio Designs
Warehouse: Grantham Book Services Ltd, Isaac Newton Way, Alma Park Industrial East, Grantham Lincs NG31 9SD

Sunflower Books
12 Kendrick Mews, London SW7 3HG
Tel: (020) 7589 1862 *Fax:* (020) 7589 1862
E-mail: mail@sunflowerbooks.co.uk
Web Site: www.sunflowerbooks.co.uk; www.wwwalking.com
Key Personnel
Joint Man Dir: John Seccombe *Tel:* (01392) 274686; Patricia Underwood
Founded: 1982
Subjects: Travel, Landscapes; walking & touring guides to (mainly) European destinations
ISBN Prefix(es): 0-948513; 1-85691
Number of titles published annually: 6 Print
Total Titles: 45 Print
Parent Company: P A Underwood Ltd
Orders to: PO Box 115, Exeter EX2 6YU
Tel: (01392) 423002 *Fax:* (01392) 423002
A & C Black, Howard Rd, Eaton Socon, Huntingdon, Cambs PE19 3EZ *Tel:* (01480) 212666 *Fax:* (01480) 405014

Supportive Learning Publications+
23 West View, Chirk, Wrexham LL14 5HL
Tel: (01691) 774778 *Fax:* (01691) 774849
E-mail: sales@slpuk.demon.co.uk
Web Site: www.slpuk.demon.co.uk
Key Personnel
Contact: Phil Roberts
Founded: 1988
Subjects: Disability, Special Needs, Drama, Theater, Education, English as a Second Language, Geography, Geology, History, Humor, Mathematics, Poetry, Science (General)
ISBN Prefix(es): 1-86109; 1-871585
Distributed by Galt Educational; Hope Education; The Yorklshire Purchasing Group

Survival, *imprint of* International Institute for Strategic Studies

Sutton Publishing Ltd+
Subsidiary of Haynes Publishing
Phoenix Mill, Thrupp, Stroud, Glos GL5 2BU
Tel: (01453) 731114 *Fax:* (01453) 731117
E-mail: sales@sutton-publishing.co.uk; editorial@sutton-publishing.co.uk; publishing@sutton-publishing.co.uk
Web Site: www.suttonpublishing.co.uk
Key Personnel
Man Dir: Keith Fullman
Publishing Dir, Permissions: Peter Clifford
Sales & Marketing Dir: Jeremy Yates-Round
Foreign Rights Manager: Viktoria Tischer
Contact: Rachel Graham *Tel:* (01453) 732409
E-mail: rachelgraham@sutton-publishing.co.uk
Founded: 1978
Subjects: Agriculture, Archaeology, Architecture & Interior Design, Art, Biography, Business, Engineering (General), Fiction, Genealogy, History, House & Home, Human Relations, Labor, Industrial Relations, Literature, Literary Criticism, Essays, Maritime, Military Science, Nonfiction (General), Photography, Regional Interests, Religion - Protestant, Social Sciences, Sociology, Sports, Athletics, Technology, Transportation, Travel
ISBN Prefix(es): 0-86299; 0-904387; 0-7509
Number of titles published annually: 200 Print
Total Titles: 800 Print
Imprints: Pocket Classics; In Old Photographs; Illustrated History Paperbacks; Pocket Biographies; Pocket Histories
Distributor for Army Records Society; History of Parliament Trust

Sweet & Maxwell, *imprint of* Sweet & Maxwell Ltd

Sweet & Maxwell Ltd+
11 New Feather Lane, London EC4P 4EE
Tel: (020) 7393 7000; (020) 7449 1104
Fax: (020) 7449 1144
E-mail: info@routledge.co.uk
Founded: 1799
Subjects: Law, Law
ISBN Prefix(es): 0-421; 0-420; 0-414
Parent Company: Thomson Corporation Publishing Ltd
Ultimate Parent Company: The Thomson Corporation, Toronto Dominion Bank Tower, Suite 2706, PO Box 24, Toronto Dominion Centre, Toronto, ON M5K 1A1, Canada
Imprints: Sweet & Maxwell; W Green; Roundhall Sweet & Maxwell
Subsidiaries: W Green; Roundhall Sweet & Maxwell
Distributor for Carswell (Europe); LBC (Europe); WGL (Europe)
Orders to: Cheriton House, North Way, Andover, Hants SP10 5BE

Sydney Jary Ltd+
9 Upper Belgrave Rd, Clifton, Bristol BS8 2XH
Tel: (0117) 974-1640 *Fax:* (0117) 973-7116
E-mail: admin@s-jary.co.uk
Key Personnel
Contact: Michael C Ross
Founded: 1960
Subjects: Biography, Business, History, Management, Military Science
Associate Companies: Avon World Limited

Symposium Press, *imprint of* Science Reviews Ltd

Tabb House+
7 Church St, Padstow, Cornwall PL28 8BG
Tel: (01841) 532316 *Fax:* (01841) 532316
E-mail: tabbhouse@connexions.co.uk
Key Personnel
Chief Executive, Dir: Caroline White
Founded: 1980
Book Publisher.
Subjects: Biography, Fiction, Literature, Literary Criticism, Essays, Nonfiction (General), Poetry, Children's Fiction
ISBN Prefix(es): 0-907018; 1-873951; 0-9534079
Number of titles published annually: 4 Print
Total Titles: 103 Print
Orders to: Gardeners Books Ltd, 1 Whittle Dr, Willington Dr, Eastbourne, Sussex BN23 6QH *Tel:* (01323) 521 555 *Fax:* (01323) 521 666 *E-mail:* sales@gardners.com *Web Site:* gardners.com

The TAFT Group, *imprint of* Gale Research

Take That Ltd, *imprint of* Verulam Publishing Ltd

Take That Ltd+
Imprint of Verulam Publishing Ltd
PO Box 200, Harrogate HG1 2YR
Tel: (01423) 507545 *Fax:* (01423) 526035
E-mail: sales@takethat.co.uk
Web Site: www.takethat.co.uk
Key Personnel
Man Dir: Chris Brown
Founded: 1987
Subjects: Business, Computer Science, Finance, Media/Sport, Gambling
ISBN Prefix(es): 1-873668; 0-9516461; 0-9519489; 1-903994
Number of titles published annually: 15 Print; 6 E-Book
Total Titles: 55 Print; 12 E-Book
Imprints: Net.Works
Distributed by Trafalgar Square
Distributor for Cardoza (Europe); Maximedia (UK)
Foreign Rep(s): Trafalgar Square Publishing (US)
Orders to: Verulam, 152a Park Street Lane, Park St, St Albans, Herts AL2 2AU

Tales of Heaven & Earth, *imprint of* Moonlight Publishing Ltd

Tango Books+
Division of Sadie Fields Productions Ltd
4 C/D West Point, 36-37 Warple Way, London W3 ORG
Tel: (020) 87461171 *Fax:* (020) 87461170
E-mail: sales@tangobooks.co.uk
Key Personnel
Dir: David Fielder *Tel:* (020) 8735 4935
E-mail: david@tangobooks.co.uk; Sheri Safran *Tel:* (020) 8735 4931 *E-mail:* sheri@tangobooks.co.uk
Founded: 1991
ISBN Prefix(es): 1-85707
Imprints: Tango Cards
Distributor for Innovative Kids; Soundprints; Van der Meer
Warehouse: The Trade Center Ltd, Mendlesham Industrial Estate, Norwich Rd, Mendlesham, Suffolk IP14 5NA

Tango Cards, *imprint of* Tango Books

Taprobane Ltd
PO Box 717, London W5 3E4
Tel: (020) 8998-3024

Tarantula Books, *imprint of* Geddes & Grosset

Tarquin, *imprint of* Tarquin Publications

Tarquin Publications+
Stradbroke, Diss, Norfolk IP21 5JP
Tel: (01379) 384 218 *Fax:* (01379) 384 289
E-mail: enquiries@tarquin-books.demon.co.uk
Web Site: www.tarquin-books.demon.co.uk
Key Personnel
Chief Executive, Editorial, Rights & Permissions: Gerald Jenkins *E-mail:* gerald@tarquin-books.demon.co.uk
Sales: Margaret Jenkins
Founded: 1970
Subjects: Education, Mathematics, Science (General)
ISBN Prefix(es): 0-906212; 1-899618
Number of titles published annually: 7 Print
Total Titles: 99 Print
Imprints: Tarquin; DIME
Membership(s): IPG

Tarragon Press+
Moss Park, Ravenstone, Whithorn DG8 8DR
Tel: (01988) 850368 *Fax:* (01988) 850304
Key Personnel
Dir & Editor: David Sumner *E-mail:* dsummer@gn.apc.org
Founded: 1987
Member of Scottish Publishers Association.

PUBLISHERS

UNITED KINGDOM

Subjects: Biological Sciences, Environmental Studies, Health, Nutrition, Medicine, Nursing, Dentistry, Physical Sciences, Science (General)
ISBN Prefix(es): 1-870781
Orders to: Lavis Marketing, 73 Lime Walk, Headington, Oxford OX3 7AD

Taschen Evergreen, *imprint of* Taschen UK Ltd

Taschen UK Ltd+
13 Old Burlington St, London W1S 3AJ
Tel: (020) 7437 4350 *Fax:* (020) 7437 4360
E-mail: contact@tashen.com
Web Site: www.taschen.com
Key Personnel
Contact: Paul Torjussen *E-mail:* paul.torjussen@taschen-uk.com
Founded: 1994
Subjects: Art, Fashion, Photography, Architecture, Design
ISBN Prefix(es): 3-8228
Parent Company: Taschen Verlag, Cologne, Germany
Associate Companies: TASHEN Deutschland, Hohenzollernring 53, D-50672 Koln, Germany, Public Relations: Dr Christine Waiblinger *Tel:* (0221) 201 80 170 *Fax:* (0221) 201 80 42 *E-mail:* c.waiblinger@taschen-deutschland.com; TASCHEN Espana, c/ Victor Hugo, 1, 2º Dcha, Madrid, Spain, Customer Services: Mr Fernando Gonzalez *Tel:* (091) 360 50 63 *Fax:* (091) 360 50 64 *E-mail:* f.gonzalez@taschen-espana.com; TASCHEN France, 82, Rue Mazarine, F-75006 Paris, France, Customer Services: Ms Regina Masanes *Tel:* (01) 40 51 70 93 *Fax:* (01) 43 26 73 80 *E-mail:* r.masanes@taschen-france.com; TASCHEN Japan, Atelier Ark Bldg, 5-11-23, Minami Aoyama Minato-Ku, J-Tokyo 107-0062, Japan, Public Relations: Ms Asuka Shibata *Tel:* (03) 57 78 30 00 *Fax:* (03) 57 78 30 30 *E-mail:* order@taschen-japan.com
Imprints: Taschen Evergreen
U.S. Office(s): Taschen USA, 230 Fifth Ave, Suite 1411, New York, NY 10001, United States, Paul Norton
Warehouse: Grantham Book Services, Isaac Newton Way, Alma Park Industrial Estate, Grantham, Lincs N931 9SD *Tel:* (01476) 541000 (UK only)

Tate Gallery Publishing Ltd, see Tate Publishing Ltd

Tate Publishing Ltd+
Formerly Tate Gallery Publishing Ltd
Millbank, London SW1P 4RG
Tel: (020) 7887 8869; (020) 7887 8870; (020) 7887 8871 *Fax:* (020) 7887 8878
E-mail: tgpl@tate.org.uk
Web Site: www.tate.org.uk *Cable:* TATEGAL LONDON
Key Personnel
Chief Executive: Celia Clear *E-mail:* celia.clear@tate.org.uk
Editor: Judith Severne *Tel:* (020) 7887 8868 *E-mail:* judith.severne@tate.org.uk
Picture Rights: Chris Webster *Tel:* (020) 7887 8867 *Fax:* (020) 7887 8900 *E-mail:* chris.webster@tate.org.uk
Sales & Rights Dir: James Attlee *E-mail:* james.attlee@tate.org.uk
Publishing Dir: Roger Thorp *Tel:* (020) 7887 8617 *E-mail:* roger.thorp@tate.org.uk
Founded: 1931
Publishers of art books, exhibition catalogues & gallery guides of modern art & British art since 1550.
Subjects: Architecture & Interior Design, Art, Education, Art History
ISBN Prefix(es): 1-85437
Number of titles published annually: 30 Print

Total Titles: 150 Print
Parent Company: Tate Enterprises
Ultimate Parent Company: Tate Gallery
Subsidiaries: Tate Gallery Liverpool; Tate Gallery Modern; Tate Gallery St Ives
Distributed by Thames & Hudson Pty Ltd (Australia); Harry N Abrams Inc (USA & Canada)

Tauris Academic Studies, *imprint of* I B Tauris & Co Ltd

I B Tauris & Co Ltd+
6 Salem Rd, London W2 4BU
Tel: (020) 7243 1225 *Fax:* (020) 7243 1226
E-mail: mail@ibtauris.com
Web Site: www.ibtauris.com
Key Personnel
Chairman & Publisher: I Bagherzade *E-mail:* ibagherzade@ibtauris.com
Man Dir: Jonathan McDonnell *E-mail:* jmcdonnell@ibtauris.com
Production: N Denny *E-mail:* ndenny@ibtauris.com
Marketing: A Deter *E-mail:* adeter@ibtauris.com
Editor: P Brewster; L Crook; D Stonestreet
International Rights: Isabella Steer *E-mail:* isteer@ibtauris.com
International Sales Manager: Martin Ashworth *E-mail:* mashworth@ibtauris.com
Publicist: L Gallagher
Founded: 1983
Independent publisher of both scholarly & general interest books
Specialize in Middle East studies, history, politics, international relations, film & visual culture.
Subjects: Architecture & Interior Design, Asian Studies, Developing Countries, Film, Video, Government, Political Science, History, Nonfiction (General), Religion - Islamic, Cultural Studies & Middle East Studies
ISBN Prefix(es): 1-85043; 1-86064
Number of titles published annually: 175 Print
Imprints: British Academic Press; Tauris Academic Studies; Tauris Parke; Tauris Parke Paperbacks
Branch Office(s)
Palgrave Macmillan, 175 Fifth Ave, New York, NY 10010, United States
U.S. Office(s): I B Tauris & Co Ltd, St Martin's Press, 175 Fifth Ave, New York, NY 10010, United States *Tel:* 212-982-3900 *Fax:* 212-777-6359
Distributor for The New Press (excl USA); Saqi Book (US only); Philip Wilson Publishers (World)
Orders to: Thomson Publishing Services, Cheriton House, North Way, Andover SP10 5BE

Tauris Parke, *imprint of* I B Tauris & Co Ltd

Tauris Parke Paperbacks, *imprint of* I B Tauris & Co Ltd

Taylor & Francis, *imprint of* Taylor & Francis Group

Taylor & Francis Asia Pacific, *imprint of* Taylor & Francis Group

Taylor & Francis Group+
11 New Fetter Lane, London EC4P 4EE
Tel: (020) 7583 9855 *Fax:* (020) 7842 2298
E-mail: info@tandf.co.uk
Web Site: www.tandf.co.uk; www.taylorandfrancis.com
Key Personnel
Chief Executive: A R Selvey
Man Dir Journals: S B Neal
Journal Sales: K R Courtney
Man Dir Books: R Horton

Journal Marketing Manager Dir: Bev Acreman
Books Sales Dir: C Kheshe
Man Dir Psychology Press: Mike Forster
Founded: 1798
Subjects: Education, Engineering (General), Medicine, Nursing, Dentistry, Physics, Psychology, Psychiatry, Science (General), Social Sciences, Sociology, Humanities
ISBN Prefix(es): 0-85066; 1-85000; 0-7484
Number of titles published annually: 1,800 Print
Parent Company: Taylor & Francis Group Ltd
Imprints: Brunner-Routledge; Carfax Publishing; Europa; Garland Science; Martin Dunitz; Psychology Press; Routledge; Routledge Curzon; Routledge Falmer; Spon Press; Taylor & Francis; Taylor & Francis Asia Pacific; UCL Press
Subsidiaries: Routledge Inc
Foreign Rep(s): Routledge Inc (North America); Routledge India Liaison (India); Taylor & Francis Group (East Asia, North America); United Publishers Services (Japan)
Foreign Rights: Lillian Koe (Malaysia); Ed Summerson (Hong Kong); Takahiko Kaneko (Japan); Rachel Zillig (Caribbean, Middle East, North Africa, West Indies); David Barrett-Jolley (Botswana); Marco Castellan (Central & South America); Marco Castellan (France, Italy, Portugal, Spain); Christoph Chesher (UK); Sandra Collins (Austria, Germany & Switzerland); Graham Crossley (UK); Peter Havinga (Belgium, Netherlands, Greece, Luxembourg); Sophie Hopkin (Israel); M Anwer Iqbal (Pakistan); Se-Yung Jun (Korea); Barbie Keene (Zimbabwe); Jeffrey Lim (China, Taiwan); Roy Mansell (Lesotho, Namibia, South Africa); Vera Medeiros (Brazil); Michelle Swinge (Australia, Asia); Chinke Ojiji (Nigeria); Nick Pepper (Denmark, Finland, Iceland, Norway, Sweden); Ian Pringle (Brunei, Indonesia, Singapore, Thailand); Sophie Rogers (London); I J Sagun (Philippines); Hema Shah (Eastern Europe)
Orders to: ITPS, Cheriton House Northway, Andover SP10 5BE *Tel:* (01264) 342926

Taylor Graham Publishing
48 Regent St, Cambridge CB2 1FD
Web Site: www.taylorgraham.com
Key Personnel
Dir: Peter J Taylor
Founded: 1984
Subjects: Computer Science, Library & Information Sciences, Management, Technology
ISBN Prefix(es): 0-947568
Branch Office(s)
PMB 187, 12021 Wilshire Blvd, Los Angeles, CA 90025, United States

John Taylor Book Ventures+
63 Berners Way, Faringdon, Oxon SN7 7NR
Tel: (01367) 244387 *Fax:* (01367) 244387
Key Personnel
Man Dir: John Taylor
Founded: 1987
Also acts as editorial & production consultant.
Subjects: Art, Communications, Publishing & Book Trade Reference
ISBN Prefix(es): 1-871224

Teach Yourself, *imprint of* Hodder & Stoughton Educational

Teeney Books Ltd+
Arlington House, 72 Fore St, Trowbridge BA14 8HD
Tel: (01225) 775657 *Fax:* (01225) 775676
E-mail: teeneybo@primex.co.uk
Key Personnel
Man Dir: Tiny de Vries
Production Dir: Martyn Lewis
Founded: 1990
ISBN Prefix(es): 1-873338; 1-85952

UNITED KINGDOM

Telegraph Books+
1 Canada Sq, Canary Wharf, London E14 5DT
Tel: (020) 7538 6826 *Fax:* (020) 7538 6064
Web Site: www.telegraph.co.uk
Telex: 22874 Telldn G
Key Personnel
Publisher: Susannah Charlton
Product Manager: Clare Sims *E-mail:* clare.sims@telegraph.co.uk
Founded: 1930
Subjects: Automotive, Career Development, Cookery, Economics, Education, Fiction, Gardening, Plants, How-to, Humor, Journalism, Law, Medicine, Nursing, Dentistry, Natural History, Poetry, Self-Help, Sports, Athletics, Technology
ISBN Prefix(es): 0-86367; 0-901684
Number of titles published annually: 50 Print
Parent Company: Telegraph Group Ltd, One Canada Sq, Canary Wharf, London E14 5DT
Ultimate Parent Company: Hollinger
Book Club(s): Telegraph Books Direct (United Kingdom)
Warehouse: Units 5 & 6 Industrial Estate, Brecon, Powys LD3 8LA
Orders to: Telegraph Books Direct

Tell-A-Story, *imprint of* Random House UK Ltd

Tempest, *imprint of* HarperCollins Publishers

Tern Press
St Mary's Cottage, Great Hales St, Market Drayton, Shropshire TF9 1JN
Tel: (01630) 652153
Key Personnel
Rights: Nicholas Parry; Mary Parry
Founded: 1972
Subjects: Biblical Studies, Literature, Literary Criticism, Essays, Natural History, Poetry
Total Titles: 90 Print
Branch Office(s)
Joshua Heller Rare Books Inc, PO Box 39114, Washington, DC 20016-9114, United States (US Affiliate)

Texere Publishing Ltd
71-77 Leadenhall St, London EC3A 3DE
Tel: (020) 7204 3644 *Fax:* (020) 7208 6701
Key Personnel
Man Dir: Martin Liu
Dir, Production & Operations: Pom Somkabcharti
Executive Editor: David Wilson
Sales Manager & Administrative Coord: James Coulson
Founded: 2000
Total Titles: 80 Print
U.S. Office(s): Texere LLC, 55 E 52 St, New York, NY 10055, United States *Tel:* 212-317-5106 *Fax:* 212-317-5178
Distributed by W W Norton

Textile & Art Publications Ltd+
12 Queen St, Mayfair, London W1J 5PG
Tel: (020) 7499 7979 *Fax:* (020) 7409 2596
E-mail: post@textile.art.com
Web Site: www.textile-art.com
Key Personnel
Publisher: Michael Franses
Founded: 1993
Subjects: Art, Asian Studies, Religion - Buddhist, Textile art
ISBN Prefix(es): 1-898406
Number of titles published annually: 2 Print
Total Titles: 4 Print

TFPL
17-18 Britton St, London EC1M 5NQ
Tel: (020) 7251 5522 *Fax:* (020) 7251 8318
E-mail: central@tfpl.com
Web Site: www.tfpl.com

Key Personnel
Marketing Manager: Bindy Pease *E-mail:* bindy.pease@tfpl.com
Marketing Executive: Kim Mullings *E-mail:* kim.mullings@tfpl.com
Founded: 1987
Member of Directory Publishers Association.
Subjects: Computer Science, Library & Information Sciences
ISBN Prefix(es): 1-870889
Branch Office(s)
55 Broad St, Suite 20C, New York, NY 10004-2501, United States *Tel:* 212-269-4666 *Fax:* 212-269-2777 *E-mail:* tfplinc@tfpl.com
Distributor for TFPL Inc

Thames & Hudson Ltd+
181A High Holborn, London WC1V 7QX
Tel: (020) 7845 5000 *Fax:* (020) 7845 5050
E-mail: sales@thameshudson.co.uk
Web Site: www.thamesandhudson.com
Key Personnel
Man Dir: Thomas Neurath
Editorial: Jamie Camplin
Sales Dir: Trevor Naylor
Production: Neil Palfreyman
Marketing: Johanna Neurath
Rights & Permissions: Christian Frederking *E-mail:* c.frederking@thameshudson.co.uk
Publicity: Kate Burvill
Founded: 1949
Subjects: Archaeology, Architecture & Interior Design, Art, Crafts, Games, Hobbies, Ethnicity, Fashion, History, Music, Dance, Philosophy, Photography, Psychology, Psychiatry, Religion - Other, Science (General), Technology, Travel, Graphics
ISBN Prefix(es): 0-500
Associate Companies: Editions Thames & Hudson, 12 Rue du Seine, Paris 75006, France
Subsidiaries: Thames & Hudson Ltd (Eastern Mediterranean, Middle East and Pakistan); Thames & Hudson Ltd (Italy, Spain, Portugal, Mexico and Central America); Thames & Hudson (S) Private Ltd (Malaysia); Thames & Hudson (S) Private Ltd (Singapore & South-East Asia); Thames & Hudson (Australia) Pty Ltd (Australia)
U.S. Office(s): Thames & Hudson Inc, 500 Fifth Ave, New York, NY 10110, United States
Distributor for Harry N Abrams Inc; British Museum Press; Co & Bear; Flammarion; Laurence King; MOMA; National Gallery of Australia; Royal Academy of Arts; Royal Collection Enterprises; Scalo Publishing; Scriptum Editions; Skira Editore; Steidl Verlag; Violette Editions
Orders to: 44 Clockhouse Rd, Farnborough, Hants GU14 7QZ *Tel:* (01252) 541602 *Fax:* (01252) 377380

Tharpa Publications
Conishead Priory, Ulverston, Cumbria LA12 9QQ
Tel: (01229) 588599 *Fax:* (01229) 483919
E-mail: tharpa@tharpa.com
Web Site: www.tharpa.com
Key Personnel
Dir: Hugh Clift
Founded: 1984
Subjects: Religion - Buddhist
ISBN Prefix(es): 0-948006
Associate Companies: Editions Tharpa, BP 278, 75525 Paris Cedex 11, France *Tel:* (01) 43 67 87 87 *Fax:* (01) 43 67 87 87 *E-mail:* info@tharpa.org *Web Site:* www.tharpa.org; Editorial Tharpa Brasil, Rua Mourato Coelho 910, Cep 10.41 7.001, Sao Paulo, SP, Brazil *Tel:* (011) 814 6326 *Fax:* (011) 814 6326 *E-mail:* jangchub@iconet.com.br; Editorial Tharpa Espana, C/Empecinado n2, atico derecha, 41004 Sevilla, Spain *Tel:* (05) 421 1415 *Fax:* (05) 421 1415 *E-mail:* tharpa@teleline.es; Editorial Tharpa Mexico, Madero No 687 Colonia Centro, CP44100 Guadalajara, Jalisco, Mexico *Tel:* (03) 825 1301 *Fax:* (03) 827 1026 *E-mail:* tharpa@closeup.com.mx; Tharpa Canada Inc, 2255-B Queen St E, Suite 147, Toronto, ON, Canada *Tel:* (416) 504 0966 *Fax:* (416) 504 0966 *E-mail:* 76467.262@compuserve.com; Tharpa Verlag, Dennlerstr 38, 8047 Zurich, Switzerland *Tel:* (01) 401 0220 *Fax:* (01) 401 0220 *E-mail:* tharpa@tharpa.org *Web Site:* www.tharpa.org
U.S. Office(s): Tharpa Books, PO Box 430, 47 Sweeney Rd, Glen Spey, NY 12737, United States *Tel:* 845-856-5102 *Fax:* 845-856-2110 *E-mail:* tharpabooks@aol.com

Themis Books, *imprint of* Green Books Ltd

Thistle Press+
4 Old Mill Cottages, Culsalmond, Insch, Aberdeenshire AB52 6TS
Tel: (01464) 821053 *Fax:* (01464) 821053
E-mail: info@oldmilldesign.co.uk
Key Personnel
Partner & International Rights Contact: Dr Keith Nicholson
Partner: Angela Nicholson
Founded: 1992
Member of Scottish Publishers Association.
Subjects: Archaeology, Biography, Earth Sciences, Environmental Studies, History, Outdoor Recreation, Regional Interests, Travel, Scottish Travel Guides
Total Titles: 10 Print
Associate Companies: Scottish Travel Books, West Bank, Western Rd, Insch AB52 6JR
Imprints: Macgregor Science

Thoemmes Press+
11 Great George St, Bristol BS1 5RR
Tel: (0117) 929 1377 *Fax:* (0117) 922 1918
E-mail: info@thoemmes.com
Web Site: www.thoemmes.com
Key Personnel
Man Dir: Rudi Thoemmes *E-mail:* rthoemmes@thoemmes.com
Production: Alan Rutherford *E-mail:* arutherford@thoemmes.com
Financial Dir: Linda Keeble
Marketing Manager: Alison Lewis *E-mail:* alisonlewis@thoemmes.com
Editorial: Philip de Bary *E-mail:* philip@thoemmes.com; Merilyn Holme *E-mail:* mholme@thoemmes.com; Kirsten Robertson *E-mail:* krobertson@thoemmes.com
Founded: 1989
Specialize in reprints.
Subjects: Business, Education, Geography, Geology, History, Language Arts, Linguistics, Management, Philosophy, Science (General), Social Sciences, Sociology, Theology
ISBN Prefix(es): 1-85506; 1-84371
Number of titles published annually: 60 Print
Total Titles: 1,000 Print
Parent Company: Thoemmes Ltd
Imprints: Nico Editions; Overstone Press
Orders to: Alton Logistics Ltd, Battle Rd, Unit 4, Heathfeld, Newton Abbot TQ12 6RY
The University of Chicago Press, 1427 60 St, Chicago, IL 60637-2954, United States

Thorndike Press, *imprint of* Gale Research

Threshold, *imprint of* The Kenilworth Press Ltd

Tiger Books International PLC+
26A York St, Twickenham, Middlesex TW1 3LJ
Tel: (0181) 8925577 *Fax:* (0181) 8916550
E-mail: enquires@tigerbooks.co.uk
Key Personnel
Dir: Grahame Parish; Sue Parish
Founded: 1985
Specialize in Remainders & Promotional Reprints.

Subjects: Fiction, Nonfiction (General)
ISBN Prefix(es): 1-85501; 1-870461; 1-84056
Associate Companies: Sheridan Book Company Ltd
Imprints: Sheridan Book Company; Senate
Warehouse: Bartholomews Storage & Distribution Ltd, Woodside Rd, Boyatt Wood Industrial Estate, Eastleigh, Hants SO5 5XZ

Tigers, *imprint of* Andersen Press Ltd

Timber Press Inc+
2 Station Rd, Swavesey, Cambridge CB4 5QJ
Tel: (01954) 232959 *Fax:* (01954) 206040
E-mail: timberpressuk@BTInternet.com
Web Site: www.timberpress.com
Key Personnel
Marketing Manager (UK): Pam Segers
Founded: 1978
Subjects: Agriculture, Gardening, Plants, Music, Dance
ISBN Prefix(es): 0-88192; 0-931340
Imprints: Amadeus Press
Branch Office(s)
Timber Press, 133 SW Second Ave, Suite 450, Portland, OR 97204, United States *Tel:* 503-227-2878 *Fax:* 503-227-3070 *E-mail:* info@timberpress.com

Time-Life (UK)+
Brettenham House, 4th floor, Lancaster Place, London WC2E 7TL
Tel: (020) 7911 8000 *Fax:* (020) 7911 8100
E-mail: email@timelife.demon.co.uk
Web Site: www.twbookmark.com
Key Personnel
Man Dir: Joseph Peckl
Rights & Permissions: Curtis Kopf
European Head Off: Time-Life Books BV, Netherlands.
ISBN Prefix(es): 0-8094; 0-7835; 0-7054; 0-900658
Parent Company: Time Warner, United States
Branch Office(s)
Time Life Books, 777 Duke St, Alexandria, VA 22314, United States
Time Life Building, Rockefeller Center, New York, NY 10020, United States
Orders to: Bookpoint Ltd, 39 Milton Park, Abingdon, Oxon OX14 4TD *Tel:* (0235) 835001 *Fax:* (0235) 832068

Time Out Group Ltd+
Universal House, 251 Tottenham Court Rd, London W1T 7AB
Tel: (020) 7813 3000 *Fax:* (020) 7813 6001
E-mail: net@timeout.co.uk
Web Site: www.timeout.com
Key Personnel
Publisher: Lesley Gill
Man Dir: Mike Hardwick
Financial Dir: Kevin Ellis
Guides Editorial Dir: Pete Fignnes *E-mail:* pete@timeout.com
Online Commercial Dir: David Pepper *E-mail:* davidpepper@timeout.com
Group Commercial Dir: Lesley Gill
Marketing Dir: Christine Cort
Production Dir: Steve Proctor
Group General Manager: Nichola Coulthard *Tel:* (020) 7813 6103 *E-mail:* nicholacoulthard@timeout.com
Editor, Time Out Magazine London: Laura Lee Davies
Editor, Time Out New York: Cyndi Stivers
International Agenda Editor: Sharon Lougher *E-mail:* sharonlougher@timeout.com
Founded: 1968
Subjects: Art, Drama, Theater, Fashion, Film, Video, Gay & Lesbian, Poetry, Radio, TV, Travel
Number of titles published annually: 10 Print
Total Titles: 40 Print
Divisions: Time Out Guides; Time Out Magazine
Branch Office(s)
Time Out, 627 Broadway, 7th floor, New York, NY 10012, United States

Time Warner Books UK+
Brettenham House, Lancaster Pl, London WC2E 7EN
Tel: (020) 7911 8000 *Fax:* (020) 7911 8100
E-mail: email.uk@timewarnerbooks.co.uk
Web Site: www.timewarnerbooks.co.uk
Key Personnel
Chief Executive & Publisher: David Young
Publisher: Ursula Mackenzie
Sales Dir: David Kent
Editorial Dir: Richard Beswick; Barbara Boote *Tel:* (020) 7911 8030 *E-mail:* barbara.boote@timewarnerbooks.co.uk; Lennie Goodings; Hilary Hale; Tim Holman; Alan Samson
Finance: Nigel Batt
Marketing Dir: Terry Jackson
Rights Dir: Nann du Sautoy
Founded: 1988
Also acts as book distributor.
Subjects: Business, Crafts, Games, Hobbies, Fiction, Mysteries, Nonfiction (General), Romance, Science Fiction, Fantasy, Travel
ISBN Prefix(es): 0-8212; 0-316; 0-7515; 1-85723; 1-86049
Number of titles published annually: 400 Print
Parent Company: AOL/Time Warner Inc
Associate Companies: Little Brown & Co, Boston, MA, United States
Imprints: Abacus; Atom; Orbit; Virago
U.S. Office(s): Little, Brown & Company, Time-Life Bldg, 1271 Avenue of the Americas, New York 10020, United States
Orders to: TBS Distribution Centre, Colchester Rd, Frating Green, Colchester, Essex C07 7LW

Titan Books Ltd+
Titan House, 144 Southwark St, London SE1 0UP
Tel: (020) 7620 0200 *Fax:* (020) 7620 0032
E-mail: 101447.2455@compuserve.com
Key Personnel
Publisher: Nick Landau
Editorial, Rights & Permissions: Katy Wild
Sales: Siobhan Flynn
Production: Robert Kelly
Publicity: Mark Chapman
Founded: 1981
Subjects: Art, Biography, Film, Video, Radio, TV, Science Fiction, Fantasy
ISBN Prefix(es): 1-85286; 0-907610
Parent Company: Titan Entertainment Group, London
Imprints: Eros Plus
Divisions: Titan Magazines; Titan Merchandise; Titan Studio
Bookshop(s): Birmingham; Cambridge; Coventry; Croydon; Edinburgh; Glasgow; Liverpool; London; Newcastle; Southampton
Orders to: Forbidden Planet Mail Order, 71-75 New Oxford St, London WC1A 1DG *Tel:* (020) 7497-2150 *Fax:* (020) 7497-2632

Tobin Music
The Old Malthouse, Knight St, Sawbridgeworth, Herts CM21 9AX
Tel: (01279) 726625
E-mail: candidatobin@candidatobin.co.uk
Web Site: www.candidatobin.co.uk
Key Personnel
Man Dir, Editorial: Candida Tobin *E-mail:* candidatobin@compuserve.com
Sales, Production, Publicity, Rights & Permissions: Christopher Dell
Founded: 1973
Music education books covering all musical theory & simple composition for home & school use for all ages & abilities.
A unique system of teaching using patterns & colors, tutors on various instruments.
Subjects: Tutors, workbooks & information books *Specializes In:* Classroom music teaching recorder, classical guitar & piano
ISBN Prefix(es): 0-905684
Total Titles: 30 Print; 1 CD-ROM
Imprints: Tobin Music Books

Tobin Music Books, *imprint of* Tobin Music

Tolley, *imprint of* Butterworths Tolley

Toucan Press
White Cottage, Rue de Carteret, Guernsey GY5 7YG
Tel: (01481) 57017
Key Personnel
Man Dir: G Stevens Cox
Founded: 1850
Subjects: History, Literature, Literary Criticism, Essays
ISBN Prefix(es): 0-85694; 0-900749
Total Titles: 90 Print

Touchstone, *imprint of* Simon & Schuster Ltd

Tour & Trail Maps, *imprint of* Discovery Walking Guides Ltd

Towy Publishing
PO Box 24, Carmarthen SA31 1YS
Tel: (01267) 236569 *Fax:* (01267) 220444
Subjects: Antiques

TPL, *imprint of* Training Publications Ltd

Trade and Technical Press, *imprint of* Elsevier Advanced Technology

Training Publications, *imprint of* Training Publications Ltd

Training Publications Ltd
3 Finway Court, Whippendell Rd, Watford; Herts WD18 7EN
Tel: (01923) 209800 *Fax:* (01923) 213 144
Key Personnel
General Manager: Mr B Peck
Editorial, Rights & Permissions: Mrs Lesley Page *E-mail:* lpage@emta.org.uk
Warehouse, Distribution: Mr J A Atkinson
Founded: 1965
Subjects: Engineering (General)
ISBN Prefix(es): 0-85083; 1-84019
Parent Company: Engineering & Marine Training Authority
Imprints: EAL; EITB; Entra; TPL; Training Publications
Warehouse: PO Box 75, Stockport, Chesire SK4 1PH *Tel:* (0161) 480 5285 *Fax:* (0161) 474 7502 (Also orders)

Transedition, *imprint of* Transedition Ltd

Transedition Ltd+
43 Henley Ave, Oxford OX4 4DJ
Tel: (01865) 770549 *Fax:* (01865) 712500
E-mail: enquiries@transed.co.uk
Web Site: www.translateabook.com
Key Personnel
Sales & Acquisitions: Ed Glover *E-mail:* ed@transed.co.uk
Production: Richard Johnson *Tel:* (020) 8969 4817 *Fax:* (020) 8969 0487 *E-mail:* graphics@dircon.co.uk
Translations: Kathy Pearmain *Tel:* (01865) 396700 *E-mail:* kathy@translateabook.com

Accounts: Yasmin Qureski *E-mail:* yas@transed.co.uk
Founded: 1992
Packaged books & translations, illustrated books. Member of Motouun.
Subjects: Cookery, Gardening, Plants, History, Religion - Other, Theology
ISBN Prefix(es): 1-898250
Number of titles published annually: 6 Print
Total Titles: 100 Print
Imprints: Transedition
Divisions: Translate-A-Book
Foreign Rights: Illustrata (Portugal, Spain)

Translations Wales, *imprint of* Gwasg Gwenffrwd

Transport Bookman Publications Ltd+
8A South St, Isleworth, Middlesex TW7 7BG
Tel: (020) 8560 2666 *Fax:* (020) 8569 8273
Key Personnel
Man Dir: C F Stroud
Founded: 1971
Member of Book Data & Booksellers Association.
Subjects: Transportation
ISBN Prefix(es): 0-85184
Parent Company: Chater & Scott Ltd

Transworld Publishers Ltd
61-63 Uxbridge Rd, Ealing, London W5 5SA
Tel: (020) 8579 2652 *Fax:* (020) 8579 5479
Telex: 267974
Key Personnel
Deputy Man Dir, Publishing & Bantam Press Publisher: Mark Barty-King
Deputy Man Dir: Patrick Janson-Smith
Editorial Dir, Bantam Press: Ursula Mackenzie
Editorial Dir, Doubleday: Marianne Velmans
Juvenile Editorial Dir: Philippa Dickinson
UK Sales Dir: Garry Prior
Marketing Dir: Larry Finlay
International Sales Dir: John Blake
Publicity Dir: Judy Turner
Rights Dir: Rebecca Winfield
Art Dir: Liz Laczynska
Founded: 1950
Subjects: Biography, Computer Science, Criminology, Fiction, Film, Video, Government, Political Science, Health, Nutrition, Humor, Nonfiction (General), Science Fiction, Fantasy, Sports, Athletics
ISBN Prefix(es): 0-553; 0-385; 0-440; 0-552; 0-593; 1-85225
Parent Company: Bantam Doubleday Dell Publishing Group Inc, 1540 Broadway, New York, NY 10036, United States
Ultimate Parent Company: Bertelsmann AG, Germany
Associate Companies: Transworld Publishers (Australia) Pty Ltd; Bantam Books (Canada) Inc/Doubleday Canada Ltd, Toronto, ON, Canada; Transworld Publishers (New Zealand) Pty
Imprints: Anchor; Bantam Paperbacks; Bantam Press; Black Swan; Corgi; Doubleday; Expert Books; Picture Corgi; Partridge Press; Young Corgi
Warehouse: PO Box 17, Wellingborough, Northants NN8 4BU

Treehouse Children's Books Ltd+
Page Farm, Newton, West Pennard, Glastonbury, Somerset BA6 8NN
Tel: (01458) 835 757 *Fax:* (01458) 835 758
Key Personnel
Dir: Andrew Bailey; David Bailey; Deborah Bailey; Dawn Powell; Richard Powell
E-mail: richard.powell4@virgin.net
Founded: 1989
ISBN Prefix(es): 1-85576; 1-872300

Associate Companies: Emma Books Ltd
Warehouse: Macmillan Distribution Ltd, Brunel Rd, Houndmills, gbrBasingstone, Hants RG21 GX5

Trentham Books Ltd+
Westview House, 734 London Rd, Oakhill, Stoke-on-Trent, Staffs ST4 5NP
Tel: (01782) 745567; (01782) 844699
Fax: (01782) 745553
E-mail: tb@trentham-books.co.uk
Web Site: www.trentham-books.co.uk
Key Personnel
Editorial Director: Dr Gillian Klein
E-mail: gillian@trentham-books.co.uk
Dir & Sales Manager: Barbara Wiggins
Production Manager: John Stipling
Founded: 1981
Member of Publishers Association of UK.
Subjects: Child Care & Development, Drama, Theater, Education, Ethnicity, Humor, Law, Psychology, Psychiatry, Social Sciences, Sociology, Technology, Women's Studies, Inclusive Education
ISBN Prefix(es): 0-948080; 1-85856; 0-7287
Number of titles published annually: 35 Print
Total Titles: 300 Print
Subsidiaries: Trentham Print Design Ltd
Distributor for Arts Council of England

Trigon Press+
117 Kent House Rd, Beckenham, Kent BR3 1JJ
Tel: (0181) 7780534 *Fax:* (0181) 7767525
E-mail: trigon@easynet.co.uk
Key Personnel
Man Dir, Sales & Partner: Roger Sheppard
Editorial, Production: Judith Sheppard
Publicity: Angela Roberts
Rights & Permissions: Pat Palmer
Designer: Jacqui Burton
Founded: 1974
Member of Independent Publishers Guild, Bibliographical Society; also acts as distributors for US museums & galleries.
Subjects: Art, Library & Information Sciences, Literature, Literary Criticism, Essays, Science Fiction, Fantasy
ISBN Prefix(es): 0-904929
Total Titles: 4 Print
Subsidiaries: The London Office
Distributed by Oak Knoll Books

Trotman Publishing+
2 The Green, Richmond, Surrey TW9 1PL
Tel: (020) 8486 1150 *Fax:* (020) 8486 1161
E-mail: sales@trotman.demon.co.uk
Web Site: www.careers-portal.co.uk/trotmanpublishing
Key Personnel
Chairman: Andrew Fiennes Trotman *Tel:* (020) 8486 1170
Dir: Tom Lee *Tel:* (020) 8486 1157
Editorial Dir: Amanda Williams *Tel:* (020) 8486 1168
Man Editor: Rachel Lockhart *Tel:* (020) 8486 1213
Advertising Manager: Alistair Rogers *Tel:* (020) 8486 1164
Marketing Manager: Deborah Jones *Tel:* (020) 8486 1158
Sales & Distribution Manager: Sean McKone *Tel:* (020) 8486 1166
Sales & Distribution Coordinator: Tracy Deadman *Tel:* (020) 8486 1160
Press Officer: Lorna Damiani *Tel:* (020) 8486 1165
Trade Sales Manager: Mike Baggallay *Tel:* (020) 8486 1165
Production Manager: Francisca Perez *Tel:* (020) 8486 1203
Man Dir: Toby Trotman *Tel:* (020) 8486 1171
Founded: 1971

Subjects: Career Development, Education
ISBN Prefix(es): 0-85660
Parent Company: Trotman & Co Ltd
Associate Companies: Trotman (Australia) Ltd, Sydney, Australia
Subsidiaries: Careers Consultants Ltd; Syston Publishing Co Ltd

True Crime, *imprint of* Virgin Publishing Ltd

Tuba Press+
Tunley Cottage, Tunley, Cirencester, Glos GL7 6LW
Tel: (01285) 760424 *Fax:* (01285) 760766
Key Personnel
Partner, Books: Peter Ellson
Partner, Magazines: Charles Graham
Founded: 1976
Specialize in poetry, chiefly unpublished authors. Member of Association of Little Presses & Small Press Group of Britain.
Subjects: Fiction, Poetry
ISBN Prefix(es): 0-907155; 0-9505956
Total Titles: 33 Print

Tuckwell Press Ltd+
The Mill House, Phantassie, East Linton, East Lothian EH40 3DG
Tel: (01620) 860 164 *Fax:* (01620) 860 164
E-mail: customerservices@tuckwellpress.co.uk
Web Site: www.tuckwellpress.co.uk
Key Personnel
Publishing Dir: John Tuckwell
International Rights: Val Tuckwell
Founded: 1995
Specialize in Scottish history; mainly academic with emphasis on Scotland & the North of England.
Subjects: Archaeology, Architecture & Interior Design, Biography, Environmental Studies, History, Literature, Literary Criticism, Essays, Religion - Protestant
ISBN Prefix(es): 1-898410; 1-86232
Number of titles published annually: 40 Print
Total Titles: 150 Print
Imprints: Canongate Academic
Distributed by Footprint (Australia & New Zealand); Hushion House (USA & Canada)
Warehouse: Scottish Book Source, 32 Finlas St, Glasgow G22 5DU
Orders to: Scottish Book Source, 137 Dundee St, Edinburgh EH11 1BG

Tufton Books, *imprint of* Church Union

Twayne Publishers, *imprint of* Gale Research

Two-Can Publishing Ltd+
Division of Zenith Entertainment Ltd
43-45 Dorset St, London W1H 4AB
Tel: (020) 7224 2440 *Fax:* (020) 7224 7005
E-mail: helpline@two-canpublishing.com
Web Site: www.two-canpublishing.com
Key Personnel
Chairman: Andrew Jarvis
Marketing Dir: Ian Grant
International Rights: Helen Cross
Founded: 1987
Specialize in children's magazines, books & multimedia.
Subjects: Animals, Pets, Geography, Geology, History, Natural History, Physics, Science (General), Technology
ISBN Prefix(es): 1-85434
Orders to: Title Book Services, Church Rd, Tiptree, Colchester, Essex CO5 0SR

Tycooly, *imprint of* Cassell & Co

Tycooly, *imprint of* The Continuum International Publishing Group Ltd

PUBLISHERS

UNITED KINGDOM

UXL, *imprint of* Gale Research

UCL Press, *imprint of* Taylor & Francis Group

UCL Press Ltd+
Imprint of Taylor & Francis Group Ltd
11 New Fetter Lane, London EC4P 4EE
Tel: (020) 7583 9855 *Fax:* (020) 7842 2298
E-mail: info@tandf.co.uk
Web Site: www.tandf.co.uk
Key Personnel
Publishing Dir: Stephen B Neal *E-mail:* stephen.neal@tandf.co.uk
Senior Editor, Social & Political Sciences: Mari Shullaw
Founded: 1991
Subjects: Archaeology, Art, Environmental Studies, Geography, Geology, Government, Political Science, History, Human Relations, Philosophy, Social Sciences, Sociology, Technology
ISBN Prefix(es): 1-85728; 1-84142
Orders to: Taylor & Francis Ltd, Rankine Rd, Basingstoke, Hants RG24 8PR *Tel:* (01256) 813000 *Fax:* (01256) 479438

UK Academy of Science, see The Royal Society

Ulster Historical Foundation+
Balmoral Bldgs, 12 College Square E, Belfast BT1 6DD
Tel: (02890) 332288 *Fax:* (02890) 239885
E-mail: enquiry@uhf.org.uk
Web Site: www.ancestryireland.com
Key Personnel
Executive Dir: Fintan Mullan
Research Dir: Dr Brian Trainor
Project Manager: Andrew Vaughan
Founded: 1956
Subjects: Education, Genealogy, History, Regional Interests, Conferences, Genealogy, Historical Publishing
ISBN Prefix(es): 0-901905

Ultimate, *imprint of* Lorenz Books

Ulverscroft Large Print Books Ltd+
The Green Bradgate Rd, Anstey, Leicester LE7 7FU
Tel: (0116) 236 4325 *Fax:* (0116) 234 0205
E-mail: sales@ulverscroft.co.uk
Web Site: www.ulverscroft.co.uk
Key Personnel
Chairman: D F Thorpe
Man Dir: Patricia Henderson
Founded: 1964
Publishers of Ulverscroft Large Print Books, Charnwood Library Series, Linford Mystery Library Series, Linford Romance Library Series, Linford Western Library Series.
Subjects: Biography, Fiction, Literature, Literary Criticism, Essays, Mysteries, Nonfiction (General), Romance, Travel, Western Fiction
ISBN Prefix(es): 0-85456; 0-7089
U.S. Office(s): Ulverscroft Large Print (USA) Inc, 1881 Ridge Rd, PO Box 1230, West Seneca, NY 14224-1230, United States
Distributor for Magna Large Print (Australia, Canada, New Zealand, South Africa, USA)
Showroom(s): Cawdor Books, 96 Dykehead St, Queenslie, Glasgow G33 4QA *Tel:* (01729) 840225 *Fax:* (01729) 840683

Umberto Allemandi, see Umberto Allemandi & Co Publishing

Unicorn Books
56 Rowlands Ave, Hatch End, Pinner HA5 4BP
Tel: (020) 8420 1091 *Fax:* (020) 8428 0125
Web Site: www.unicornbooks.co.uk/

Key Personnel
Man Dir: Raymond Green
Founded: 1985
Member of Antiquarian Bookseller's Association & Provincial Bookseller's Fairs Association.
Subjects: Military Science, Music, Dance, Transportation
ISBN Prefix(es): 1-85241
Parent Company: Factwell Ltd
Subsidiaries: MSR Books
Distributor for Archway Publishing; John Hallewell Publications

Unit for the Study of Government in Scotland, see Scottish Affairs

United Writers Publications Ltd+
Ailsa, Castle Gate, Penzance, Cornwall TR20 8BG
Tel: (01736) 365 954 *Fax:* (01736) 365954
E-mail: info@unitedwriters.co.uk
Key Personnel
Man Dir, Editorial, Sales: Malcolm Sheppard *E-mail:* malcolm@unitedwriters.co.uk
Production: Tina Sully
Publicity: Peter Keane
Rights & Permissions: Julian Tremayne
Founded: 1962
Subjects: Biography, Fiction, Sports, Athletics, Travel
ISBN Prefix(es): 0-901976; 1-85200
Number of titles published annually: 6 Print
Total Titles: 150 Print

Universitas, *imprint of* Voltaire Foundation Ltd

The University of Birmingham
(External Relations & Development Office) Information Office, Edgbaston, Birmingham B15 2TT
Tel: (0121) 414 3344 *Fax:* (0121) 414 3971
Web Site: www.general.bham.ac.uk
Key Personnel
Dir: Frank Albrighton *E-mail:* f.c.albrighton@bham.ac.uk
ISBN Prefix(es): 0-7044; 0-85057; 0-903054

University of Exeter Press+
Reed Hall, Streatham Dr, Exeter EX4 4QR
Tel: (01392) 263066 *Fax:* (01392) 263064
E-mail: uep@ex.ac.uk
Web Site: www.ex.ac.uk/uep
Key Personnel
Publisher: Simon C Baker *E-mail:* s.c.baker@ex.ae.uk
Marketing & Sales Manager: Genevieve Davey *Tel:* (1392) 264364 *E-mail:* uepsales@exeter.ac.uk
Founded: 1956
Subjects: Archaeology, Drama, Theater, Education, Film, Video, History, Language Arts, Linguistics, Literature, Literary Criticism, Essays, Maritime, Philosophy, Poetry, Regional Interests, Publish academic or scholarly
ISBN Prefix(es): 0-85989; 0-900771
Total Titles: 250 Print
Distributed by David Brown Book Co (North America)
Foreign Rep(s): Warren Bertram (Benelux); D Richard Bowen (Scandinavia); Eleanor Brasch Enterprises (Australia & New Zealand); Bernd Feldmann (Austria, Germany, Switzerland); Peter Prout (Gibraltar, Spain & Portugal); Roger Ward (China & Hong Kong, Indonesia, Japan, Korea & Taiwan, Malaysia & Singapore, Philippines, Thailand)
Orders to: Plymbridge Distributors Ltd, Estover Rd, Plymouth PL6 7PY *Tel:* (01752) 202301 *Fax:* (01752) 202333 *E-mail:* orders@plymbridge.com

University of London Careers Service
49 Gordon Sq, London WC1H 0PN
Tel: (020) 7554 4500 *Fax:* (020) 7383 5678
E-mail: careers@lon.ac.uk
Web Site: www.careers.lon.ac.uk
Key Personnel
Dir: Anne-Marie Martin *E-mail:* directors.office@careers.lon.ac.uk
Communications Services Manager: Ingrid Ross *Tel:* (020) 7554 4521 *E-mail:* i.ross@careers.lon.ac.uk
Head of Systems & Resources: Yanina Hinrichsen
Subjects: Career Development, How to Change Your Career, How to Analyse & Promote Your Skills for Work, How to Complete an Application Form, How to Write a Curriculum Vitae, How to Succeed at Interviews & Other Selection Methods
ISBN Prefix(es): 0-7187
Number of titles published annually: 1 Print
Total Titles: 5 Print

University of Nebraska Press, *imprint of* Combined Academic Publishers

University of Newcastle Upon Tyne
Registrar's Office, 6 Kensington Terrace, Newcastle Upon Tyne NE1 7RU
Tel: (0191) 222 6000 *Fax:* (0191) 222 6229
Web Site: www.ncl.ac.uk
Key Personnel
Publications Officer: Dinah A Michie *E-mail:* dinah.michie@ncl.ac.uk
Founded: 1963
ISBN Prefix(es): 0-7017; 0-900565

University of Texas Press, *imprint of* Combined Academic Publishers

University of Wales Press+
Member of Literary Publishers (Wales) Ltd
10 Columbus Walk, Brigantine Pl, Cardiff CF10 4UP
Tel: (029) 2049-6899 *Fax:* (029) 2049-6108
E-mail: press@press.wales.ac.uk
Web Site: www.wales.ac.uk/press
Key Personnel
Dir: Susan Jenkins *E-mail:* s.jenkins@press.wales.ac.uk
Deputy Dir: Richard Houdmont *E-mail:* r.houdmont@press.wales.ac.uk
Editorial Manager: Ceinwen Jones *E-mail:* c.jones@press.wales.ac.uk
Production/Design Manager: Liz Powell *E-mail:* liz.powell@press.wales.ac.uk
Commissioning Editor: Duncan Campbell *E-mail:* d.campbell@press.wales.ac.uk
Sales Support Executive: Bethan James *E-mail:* b.james@press.wales.ac.uk
Founded: 1922
Subjects: Archaeology, Architecture & Interior Design, Art, Biblical Studies, Economics, Education, Geography, Geology, History, Language Arts, Linguistics, Literature, Literary Criticism, Essays, Philosophy, Science (General), Social Sciences, Sociology, Theology, Women's Studies
ISBN Prefix(es): 0-7083; 0-900768
Number of titles published annually: 60 Print; 1 CD-ROM
Total Titles: 500 Print; 1 CD-ROM
Parent Company: University of Wales Registry, King Edward VII Ave, Cathays Park, Cardiff CF10 3NS
Imprints: Gwasg Prifysgol Cymru (Welsh-language imprint of UWP)
Distributed by Paul & Company Publishers Consortium (USA & Canada)

University of Washington Press, *imprint of* Combined Academic Publishers

UNITED KINGDOM

University Presses of California, Columbia & Princeton Ltd
c/o John Wiley & Sons Ltd, Distribution Centre, One Oldlands Way, Bognor Regis, West Sussex PO22 9SA
Tel: (01243) 842165 *Fax:* (01243) 842167
E-mail: webmaster@pupress.princeton.edu
Web Site: pup.princeton.edu
Key Personnel
Office Manager: Lois Edwards *E-mail:* lois@upccp.demon.co.uk
Founded: 1976
Subjects: Social Sciences, Sociology
ISBN Prefix(es): 0-231; 0-691; 0-520
Parent Company: Columbia University Press, New York, NY, United States

Uplands Books+
One The Uplands, Maze Hill, Saint Leonards TN38 0HL
Tel: (01424) 422306 *Fax:* (01424) 719879
E-mail: sales@uplands-books.com
Key Personnel
International Rights: Christopher Maxwell-Stewart
Founded: 1990
Specialize in children's books.
ISBN Prefix(es): 1-897951; 0-9512246
Warehouse: Trade Counters, Mendelsham Industrial Estate, Norwich Rd, Mendelsham Suffolk 1P14 5NA
Orders to: Ragged Bears
Membership(s): IPG

Usborne Publishing Ltd+
Usborne House, 83-85 Saffron Hill, London EC1N 8RT
Tel: (020) 7430 2800 *Fax:* (020) 7430 1562; (020) 7242 0974
E-mail: mail@usborne.co.uk
Web Site: www.usborne.com
Key Personnel
Man Dir: Peter Usborne
General Manager: Robert Jones
Production Manager: Garry Lewis
Publishing Dir: Jenny Tyler
International Rights: Elizabeth Wright
Founded: 1973
ISBN Prefix(es): 0-7460; 0-86020

Vacation Work Publications+
9 Park End St, Oxford OX1 1HJ
Tel: (01865) 241978 *Fax:* (01865) 790885
E-mail: info@vacationwork.co.uk
Web Site: www.vacationwork.co.uk
Key Personnel
Dir & Rights: Charles James
Publicity Dir: David Woodworth
Contact: Andrew James *E-mail:* andrew@vacationwork.co.uk
Founded: 1967
Publisher of books for students abroad, the working traveler.
Independent Company.
Subjects: Advertising, Career Development, Crafts, Games, Hobbies, Developing Countries, Foreign Countries, Outdoor Recreation, Travel
ISBN Prefix(es): 0-907638; 1-85458; 0-901205
Total Titles: 55 Print
Associate Companies: Peterson's *Web Site:* www.petersons.com (Also distribution)
Distributed by Seven Hills (US)

Vacher Dod Publishing Ltd
One Douglas St, London SW1P 4PA
Tel: (020) 7828 7256 *Fax:* (020) 7828 7269
E-mail: politics@vacherdod.co.uk
Web Site: www.vacherdod.co.uk
Key Personnel
Publisher: Andrew Cox *E-mail:* andrewcox@vacherdod.co.uk; Edward Peck
Founded: 1832
Publisher of UK Parliamentary Reference.

Subjects: Foreign Countries, Government, Political Science
ISBN Prefix(es): 0-905702

Vallentine, Mitchell & Co Ltd+
Subsidiary of Frank Cass Publishers
Crown House, 47 Chase Side, Southgate N14 5BP
Tel: (020) 8920 2100 *Fax:* (020) 8447 8548
E-mail: info@vmbooks.com; vminfo@frankcass.com
Web Site: www.vmbooks.com; www.frankcass.com/vm
Key Personnel
Man Dir: Frank Cass
Editorial: Hilary Hewitts
Trade: Joanna Legg
Production: Ray Green
Publicity: Hayley Osen
Founded: 1950
Subjects: Cookery, History, Literature, Literary Criticism, Essays, Religion - Jewish, Theology, Military History, Political Science
ISBN Prefix(es): 0-85303
Associate Companies: Irish Academic Press; The Woburn Press
Warehouse: Biblios Distribution, Partridge Green, West Sussex RH13 8LD *Tel:* (0403) 710971 *Fax:* (0403) 711143
Orders to: ISBS, 5824 NE Hassalo St, Portland, OR 97213-3644, United States *Tel:* 503-287-3093 *Fax:* 503-280-8832 *E-mail:* orders@isbs.com
Plymbridge Distributors Ltd, Estover Rd, Plymouth PL6 7PZ *Tel:* (07152) 202301 *Fax:* (07152) 202331 *E-mail:* orders@plymbridge.com

ValuSource, *imprint of* Wiley Europe Ltd

Kelvin Van Hasselt Publishing Services
Mayflower Close, Lymington, Hants SO41 3SN
Tel: (0590) 6 71695; (0590) 6 70004 *Fax:* (0590) 6 71533
E-mail: kvhbooks@aol.com
Telex: 47674 MATCOM G
Key Personnel
Contact: Kelvin Van Hasselt
ISBN Prefix(es): 1-870357

Van Molle Publishing+
PO Box 29, Aberteifi, Cardigan, Ceredigion SA43 1YN
Tel: (01239) 851482 *Fax:* (01239) 851482
Key Personnel
Contact: Cheryl Foster
Founded: 1995
Subjects: Fiction, Children's Picture Books, Adult Fiction (General)
ISBN Prefix(es): 0-9526925
Total Titles: 4 Print

Variorum, *imprint of* Ashgate Publishing Ltd

Vega, *imprint of* Salamander Books Ltd

The Vegetarian Society
Parkdale, Dunham Rd, Altrincham, Cheshire WA14 4QG
Tel: (0161) 925 2000 *Fax:* (0161) 926 9182
E-mail: info@vegsoc.org
Web Site: www.vegsoc.org
Key Personnel
Chief Executive Officer: Tina Fox *Tel:* (016) 9252002 *E-mail:* tina@vegsoc.org
Head Public Affairs: Samantha Calvert *E-mail:* sam@vegsoc.org
Editor: Dave Bowler *E-mail:* editor@vegsoc.org
Founded: 1847
Registered educational charity

Also publish in association with Harper Collins, Sigma Press & other publishers.
Subjects: Cookery, Education
ISBN Prefix(es): 0-900774

Veloce Publishing Ltd+
33 Trinity St, Dorchester, Dorset DT1 1TT
Tel: (01305) 260068 *Fax:* (01305) 268864
E-mail: info@veloce.co.uk
Web Site: www.veloce.co.uk; www.velocebooks.com
Key Personnel
Publisher: Rod Grainger
Dir: Judith Brooks
Founded: 1991
Also specialize in motorsports & workshop manuals.
Subjects: Automotive, Biography, Mechanical Engineering, Outdoor Recreation, Transportation
ISBN Prefix(es): 1-874105; 1-901295; 1-903706
Number of titles published annually: 20 Print
Total Titles: 175 Print
Distributed by Motorbooks International Inc (USA)
Distributor for Howell Press (USA); Porter Publishing (UK)

Velvet, *imprint of* Creation Books

Ventura, *imprint of* Penguin Books Ltd

Venture Press Ltd
16 Kent St, Birmingham B5 6RD
Tel: (0121) 622 3911 *Fax:* (0121) 622 4860
E-mail: info@basw.co.uk
Web Site: www.basw.co.uk
Key Personnel
Assistant Dir: Sally Arkley
ISBN Prefix(es): 0-900102; 0-9501603; 1-86178; 1-873878

Verbatim+
PO Box 156, Chearsley, Aylesbury, Bucks HP18 0DQ
Tel: (01844) 208474
Web Site: www.verbatimbooks.com
Key Personnel
Man Dir, Editorial: Laurence Urdang
Sales, Rights & Permissions: Hazel Hall
Founded: 1974
Subjects: Language Arts, Linguistics
ISBN Prefix(es): 0-930454
Total Titles: 17 Print
Parent Company: Laurence Urdang Inc
U.S. Office(s): Verbatim Books, 4 Laurel Heights, Old Lyme, CT 06371-1462, United States, Contact: Laurence Urdang *Tel:* 860-434-2104 *E-mail:* luverbatim@aol.com

Veritas Foundation Publication Centre+
63 Jeddo Rd, London W1Z 9EE
Tel: (020) 8749 4957; (020) 8749 4965 *Fax:* (020) 8749 4965
Key Personnel
Man Dir & Rights: Thomas Wachowiak *E-mail:* thomas@veritas.knsc.co.uk
Sales: A Zabihe
Founded: 1947
Also publishes weekly newspaper.
Subjects: Education, Religion - Other
ISBN Prefix(es): 0-948202; 0-901215

Vermilion, *imprint of* Random House UK Ltd

Verso+
6 Meard St, London W1F 0EG
Tel: (020) 7437 3546; (020) 7434 1704; (020) 7439 8194 *Fax:* (020) 7734 0059
E-mail: enquiries@verso.co.uk
Web Site: www.versobooks.com
Key Personnel
Executive Chairman: George Galfavi

International Rights: Gil McNeil
Founded: 1971
Subjects: Economics, Ethnicity, Film, Video, Government, Political Science, History, Literature, Literary Criticism, Essays, Nonfiction (General), Philosophy, Psychology, Psychiatry, Social Sciences, Sociology, Women's Studies
ISBN Prefix(es): 0-86091; 0-85984; 0-902308
Number of titles published annually: 70 Print
Parent Company: New Left Review
Imprints: Critical Studies in Latin American Culture; Haymarket; Phronesis
U.S. Office(s): 180 Varick St, 10th floor, New York, NY 10014-4606, United States *Tel:* 212-807-9680 *Fax:* 212-807-9152
E-mail: versoinc@aol.com
Distributed by Penguin Books (Canada); W W Norton/National Book Company (United States)
Foreign Rep(s): APD Singapore Ptd Ltd (Brunei, Malaysia, Singapore, Thailand); IMA (South America); Macmillan Publishers Australia (Australia & New Zealand); Maya Publishers Pvt Ltd (India); Missing Link (Germany); B K Norton Ltd (China & Taiwan, Hong Kong, Korea); Stephans Philip Publishers Ltd (South Africa, Zimbabwe); Publishers European Sales Agency (Europe); Segment Book Distributors (India); United Publishers Services (Japan); James & Lorin Watt (Cyprus, Malta, Middle East, Turkey); John Wilde Partnership (Austria, Germany & Switzerland)
Orders to: Marston Book Services, Unit 160 Milton Park, Abingdon, Oxford OX14 4SD *Tel:* 01235 465500

Verulam Publishing Ltd+
152A Park Street Lane, Park St, Saint Albans, Herts AL2 2AU
Tel: (01727) 872770 *Fax:* (01727) 873866
E-mail: 100124.2375@compuserve.com; sales@verulampub.demon.co.uk
Key Personnel
Man Dir: David Collins *E-mail:* david.collins@verulampub.demon.co.uk
Dir: Penny Collins *E-mail:* penny.collins@verulampub.demon.co.uk
Founded: 1991
Subjects: Advertising, Animals, Pets, Business, Cookery, Humor, Marketing, Photography, Sports, Athletics
ISBN Prefix(es): 1-873668; 1-85882; 1-86019; 1-84067; 1-84186
Imprints: Caxton Publishing Group Ltd; Take That Ltd (US)
Distributor for Caxton Publishing Group World (US); Cumberland Houe Publishers Europe (US); Rutledge Hill Press (Europe); Stoddart (Europe); Take That Ltd (US); Top Floor Publishing Europe (US)

Vif, *imprint of* Voltaire Foundation Ltd

Viking, *imprint of* Penguin Books Ltd

Viking, *imprint of* The Penguin Group UK

Viking+
27 Wrights Lane, London W8 5TZ
Tel: (020) 7416 3000 *Fax:* (020) 7416 3274
Telex: 917181
Key Personnel
Chief Executive: Peter Mayer
Editorial Dir: Claire Alexander
Production: Joy Harrison
Marketing Dir: Clare Harrington
Rights & Permissions: Ruth Salazar
Founded: 1969
Formerly Allen Lane.
Subjects: Art, Biography, Cookery, Fiction, History, Nonfiction (General), Social Sciences, Sociology, Travel

ISBN Prefix(es): 0-670
Parent Company: Penguin Books Ltd
Imprints: Allen Lane; The Penguin Press
U.S. Office(s): 375 Hudson St, New York, NY 10014, United States *Tel:* 212-366-2000
Orders to: Penguin Books, Bath Rd, Harmondsworth, Middlesex UB7 0DA *Tel:* (01) 7591984

Viking Children's Books+
27 Wright's Lane, London W8 5TZ
Tel: (020) 7416 3000 *Fax:* (020) 7416 3086
Telex: 917181
Key Personnel
Chief Executive: Peter Mayer
Editorial Dir: Phillipa Milnes-Smith
Publishing Dir: Elizabeth Attenborough
Rights & Permissions: Nikki Griffiths
Founded: 1969
ISBN Prefix(es): 0-670
Parent Company: Penguin Books Ltd
U.S. Office(s): Viking Children's Books, 375 Hudson St, New York, NY 10014, United States *Tel:* 212-366-2000
Orders to: Penguin Books, Bath Rd, Harmondsworth, Middlesex UB7 0DA *Tel:* (01) 7591984

Vintage, *imprint of* Random House UK Ltd

Virago, *imprint of* Time Warner Books UK

Virago Press+
Brettenham House, Lancaster Pl, London WC2E 7EN
Tel: (020) 7911 8000 *Fax:* (020) 7911 8100
E-mail: virago.press@timewarnerbooks.co.uk
Web Site: www.virago.co.uk
Telex: 885233
Key Personnel
Publisher: Ms Lennie Goodings
Senior Editor: Jill Foulston
Founded: 1973
Subjects: Biography, Education, Fiction, Government, Political Science, Health, Nutrition, History, Philosophy, Public Administration, Social Sciences, Sociology, Travel, Women's Studies
ISBN Prefix(es): 0-86068; 1-86049; 1-85381
Parent Company: Little Brown & Co

Virgin Publishing Ltd+
Thames Wharf Studios, Rainville Rd, London W6 9HA
Tel: (020) 7386 3300 *Fax:* (020) 7386 3360
E-mail: info@virgin-books.co.uk; info@virgin-pub.co.uk
Web Site: www.virginbooks.com
Key Personnel
Chairman: Robert Devereux
Man Dir: Rob Shreeve
Publicity Manager: Susan Atkinson
Marketing Manager: Amy Nelson-Bennett
Sales Dir: Ray Mudie
Export Sales: Natalie Rogers
International Sales & Rights Dir: K T Forster
Editorial Dir: Humphrey Price
Publishing Dir, Travel: Louise Cavanagh
Rights Manager: Helen Monroe
  E-mail: hmonroe@virgin-pub.co.uk
Founded: 1990
Specialize in music.
Subjects: Astrology, Occult, Biography, Child Care & Development, Criminology, Erotica, Film, Video, History, Humor, Music, Dance, Nonfiction (General), Radio, TV, Science Fiction, Fantasy, Sports, Athletics, Travel
ISBN Prefix(es): 0-352; 0-426; 1-85227; 0-7535; 0-85031; 0-86369
Parent Company: Virgin Media Group, 20 Soho Square, London W1A 1BS

Imprints: Black Lace; Idol; Nexus; Sapphire; True Crime
Distributor for Berlitz Publishing (UK & export)
Foreign Rep(s): Ashton International Marketing Services (Far East, India, Middle East); IMA (Africa, Eastern Europe); MRA (Brazil, Central & South America, West Indies); Onslow Books (Europe)
Foreign Rights: ACER (Spain); Agence Literaire Lora Fountain (France); Akcali Copyright (Turkey); Bengt Nordin Agency (Scandinavia); Big Apple Tuttle Mori Agency (China & Taiwan, Thailand); BPA of Israel (Israel); Dilia Literary Agency (Czech Republic); Helfa A W Literary Agency (Poland); Interrights Literary & Translation (Bulgaria); KCC (Korea); Lex Copyright (Hungary); Lijnkamp Literary Agency (Netherlands); Living Agency (Italy); Motovun Co Ltd (Japan); Read 'n' Right Agency (Greece); Thomas Schluck GmbH (Germany); Synopsis Literary Agency (Russia); Eric Yang Agency (Korea)

The Vital Spark, *imprint of* Neil Wilson Publishing Ltd

VNU Business Publications
32-34 Broadwick St, London W1A 2HG
Tel: (020) 7316 9170 *Fax:* (020) 7316 9440
Web Site: www.vnu.co.uk
Key Personnel
Man Dir: Brin Bucknor
Financial Dir: Tosh Bruce-Morgan
Founded: 1980
Subjects: Accounting, Business, Communications, Computer Science, Economics, Finance, Management, Technology
ISBN Prefix(es): 0-86271
Parent Company: VNU Business Publications, Netherlands
Subsidiaries: Learned Information (Europe)
Orders to: Booksales Dept, VNU House, 32-34 Broadwick St, London W1A 2HG

Voltaire Foundation, *imprint of* Voltaire Foundation Ltd

Voltaire Foundation Ltd+
University of Oxford, 99 Banbury Rd, Oxford OX2 6JX
Tel: (01865) 284600 *Fax:* (01865) 284610
E-mail: email@voltaire.ox.ac.uk
Web Site: www.voltaire.ox.ac.uk
Key Personnel
Dir: Dr Nicholas Cronk *Tel:* (1865) 284602
  E-mail: nicholas.cronk@voltaire.ox.ac.uk
Publisher: Mr Alan Steel *Tel:* (1865) 284601
  E-mail: alan.steel@voltaire.ox.ac.uk
Deputy Publisher: Mrs Janet Godden *Tel:* (1865) 284606 *E-mail:* janet.godden@voltaire-foundation.oxford.ac.uk
Electronic Publishing Manager: Dr Robert McNamee *Tel:* (1865) 284603 *E-mail:* robert.mcnamee@voltaire.ox.ac.uk
Founded: 1971
Publishing & seminars on the European Enlightenment.
Subjects: History, Language Arts, Linguistics, Literature, Literary Criticism, Essays, Philosophy
ISBN Prefix(es): 0-7294; 0-903588; 0-9502162
Total Titles: 400 Print; 1 CD-ROM
Parent Company: University of Oxford
Imprints: Universitas; Vif; Voltaire Foundation
Foreign Rep(s): Aux Amateurs de Livres International (France)
Warehouse: Plymbridge Distributors Ltd, Plymbridge House, Estover Rd, Plymouth PL6 7PY
  Tel: (01752) 202301 *Fax:* (01752) 202331
Orders to: Plymbridge Distributors Ltd, Plymbridge House, Estover Rd, Plymouth PL6 7PZ
  Tel: (01752) 202301 *Fax:* (01752) 202331
  E-mail: cservs@plymbridge.com

UNITED KINGDOM

W H Freeman, *imprint of* Palgrave Publishers Ltd

Wag Books, *imprint of* Compendium Publishing

Waite Group Press, *imprint of* Pearson Education Europe, Mideast & Africa

John Waite Ltd+
Tower House, Ivychurch, Romney Marsh TN29 0AX
Tel: (1797) 344 177 *Fax:* (1797)) 344 177
Key Personnel
Man Dir: John A Waite
Founded: 1983
Publisher of spoken work CDs & nonfiction.
Subjects: Nonfiction (General)
ISBN Prefix(es): 0-946714
Number of titles published annually: 2 Print

Wales Tourist Board
Brunel House, 2, Fitzalan Rd, Cardiff CF24 0UY
Tel: (029) 2049 9909 *Fax:* (029) 2048 5031
Key Personnel
Chief Executive: John French
Dir Communications & Corporate Affairs: Jonathan Jones
Head of Production Services & Sales: Rhys Jones
Founded: 1969
Subjects: Travel
ISBN Prefix(es): 1-85013; 0-900784
Orders to: Jarrold Publishing, Whitefriars, Norwich NR3 1TR

Walker Books Ltd+
87 Vauxhall Walk, London SE11 5HJ
Tel: (020) 7793 0909 *Fax:* (020) 7587 1123
Key Personnel
Chairman & Editorial: David Lloyd
Man Dir: David Heatherwick
Merchandising: Judy Burdsall
Publicity Manager: Charlie Price
Foreign Rights: Caroline Muir
Art Dir: Amelia Edwards
Sales, UK: Ian Spanton
Sales & Marketing Dir: Henryk Wesolowski
Founded: 1978
Subjects: Fiction, Nonfiction (General)
ISBN Prefix(es): 1-56402; 0-7636; 0-7445
U.S. Office(s): Candlewick Press, 2067 Massachusetts Ave, Cambridge, MA 02140, United States *Tel:* 617- 661-3330 *Fax:* 617-661-0565
Orders to: Faber Book Services, Burnt Mill, Elizabeth Way, Harlow, Essex CM20 2HX

Editions Aubrey Walter, *imprint of* GMP Publishers Ltd

The Warburg Institute+
University of London, Woburn Sq, London WC1H 0AB
Tel: (020) 7862 8949 *Fax:* (020) 7862 8955
E-mail: warburg@sas.ac.uk
Web Site: www.sas.ac.uk/warburg/
Key Personnel
Secretary: Anita Pollard
Founded: 1921
The Institute is a non-commercial organization.
Subjects: Art, History, Philosophy, Science (General)
ISBN Prefix(es): 0-85481
Number of titles published annually: 2 Print
Total Titles: 36 Print
Parent Company: University of London
Distributed by Nino Aragno Editore

Ward Lock Educational Co Ltd+
Bic Ling Kee House, One Christopher Rd, East Grinstead, West Sussex RH19 3BT
Tel: (01342) 318980 *Fax:* (01342) 410980

E-mail: wle@lingkee.com
Key Personnel
Chairman: Bak Ling Au
General Manager: Penny Kitchenham
E-mail: psk@lingkee.com
Founded: 1952
Subjects: Computer Science, Geography, Geology, History, Mathematics, Music, Dance, Poetry, Religion - Other, Science (General)
ISBN Prefix(es): 0-7062
Parent Company: Ling Kee Ltd
Associate Companies: B L A Publishing Ltd

Ward Lock Ltd+
Wellington House, 125 Strand, London WC2 OBB
Tel: (020) 7420 5555 *Fax:* (020) 7240 7261
Telex: 9413701
Key Personnel
Chairman & Chief Executive: Philip Sturrock
Publishing Dir: Alison Goff
Founded: 1854
Overseas Representation: Australia: New Holland Publishers Pty Ltd, NSW Australia 2086; Canada: Cavendish Books Inc, North Vancouver, Canada; Caribbean: HRA, London, UK; Central Europe: European Marketing Services, London, UK; Southern Europe: Penny Padovani, London, UK; Hong Kong, China, Korea, Taiwan: APS Ltd, Hong Kong; Hungary, Czech Republic, Slovakia, Croatia: CLB Marketing Services, Kecskemet, Hungary; India: Maya Publishers PVT Ltd, New Dehli, India; Japan: Ashton International Marketing Services, UK; Malaysia: APD Kuala Lumpur, Selangor Darul Ehsan, Malaysia; Middle East: Ashton International Marketing Services, UK; Netherlands: Netherlands: Nilsson & Lamm, Netherlands; New Zealand: David Bateman, Auckland, New Zealand; Pakistan: Mackwin & Co, Karachi, Pakistan; Poland, Russia, Romania, Baltic States, Former USSR, Bulgaria: Bianca Katris, IMA, Greece; Singapore, Indonesia, Thailand: APD Singapore Ltd, Singapore; Scandinavia: PKB, Glostrup, Denmark; South America: HRA, London, UK; South Africa: Struik Book Distributors, Cape Town, South Africa; USA: Sterling Publishing Co Inc, New York, USA.
Subjects: Cookery, Gardening, Plants, Health, Nutrition, House & Home, How-to, Nonfiction (General), Outdoor Recreation, Self-Help, Sports, Athletics
ISBN Prefix(es): 0-7063
Parent Company: Continuum International Publishing Group Ltd

Warm Island Walking Guides, *imprint of* Discovery Walking Guides Ltd

Frederick Warne, *imprint of* Penguin Books Ltd

Frederick Warne Publishers Ltd+
80 Strand, London WC2R 0RL
Tel: (020) 7010 3000 *Fax:* (020) 7010 6706
Key Personnel
Chief Executive: Anthony Forbes-Watson
Marketing: Gill Thomas
Production: Alan Lee
Man Dir: Sally Floyer
Founded: 1865
Specializes in classic characters and licensed merchandise programs.
ISBN Prefix(es): 0-7232
Parent Company: Penguin Books Ltd
U.S. Office(s): Penguin USA, 375 Hudson St, New York, NY 10014, United States *Tel:* 212-366-2000
Orders to: Penguin Books Ltd, Bath Rd, Harmondsworth, West Drayton, Middlesex UB7 0DA *Tel:* (02) 208 757 4000

BOOK

Waterlow, *imprint of* Wilmington Business Information Ltd

A P Watt Ltd
20 John St, London WC1N 2DR
Tel: (020) 7405 6774 *Fax:* (020) 7831 2154
E-mail: apw@apwatt.co.uk
Key Personnel
Man Dir: Derek Johns; Caradoc King
Foreign Rights Dir: Linda Shaughnessy
Dir: Jo Frank; Georgia Garrett; Sam North
Media: Nick Harris
Founded: 1875

Franklin Watts, see The Watts Publishing Group Ltd

The Watts Publishing Group Ltd+
96 Leonard St, London EC2A 4RH
Tel: (020) 7739 2929 *Fax:* (020) 7739 2318
E-mail: gm@wattspub.co.uk
Web Site: www.wattspub.co.uk
Key Personnel
Group Man Dir: Marlene Johnson
Deputy Publishing Dir, Orchard Books: Rosemary Davies
Publishing Dir, Franklin Watts: Philippa Stewart
Publishing Dir, Orchard Books: Francesca Dow
Trade Sales Dir, Watts Publishing Group: George Spicer
Promotions & Marketing Associate Director: Linda Banner
Royalties & Contracts Manager: Marian Head
Rights Director: Claire Hurst
Founded: 1969
The Watts Group is comprised of Franklin Watts & Orchard Books.
Subjects: Fiction, Nonfiction (General)
ISBN Prefix(es): 0-7496; 1-85213; 1-86039; 0-85166; 1-84121; 0-86313
Parent Company: Hachette Livre
Subsidiaries: Grolier Australia Pty
U.S. Office(s): 387 Park Ave S, New York, NY 10016, United States
Orders to: Littlehampton Book Services, Worthing, West Sussex, Colchester, Essex C05 0SR

Waverley Books, *imprint of* Geddes & Grosset

Wayland Publishers Ltd (Incorporating Macdonald Young Books)+
61 Western Rd, Hove BN3 1JD
Tel: (01273) 722561 *Fax:* (01273) 329314; (01273) 723526
Key Personnel
Man Dir: D J Smith
Dir & General Manager: Roberta Bailey
Publishing Dir: Steve White-Thomson
Production Dir: Philip Hughes
UK Sales Dir: Terry Frost
Founded: 1969
Subjects: Fiction, Nonfiction (General), Poetry
ISBN Prefix(es): 0-85340; 0-7502; 1-85210; 0-85078
Parent Company: Wolters Kluwer NV, Netherlands
Imprints: Macdonald Young Books
Warehouse: Littlehampton Book Services, 10-14 Eldon Way, Lineside Estate, Littlehampton, West Sussex BN17 7HE

Weatherbys Allen Ltd+
Sanders Rd, Wellingborough, Northamptonshire NN8 4BX
Tel: (01933) 440077 (cxt 351) *Fax:* (01933) 270300
E-mail: turfnews@weatherbys-group.com
Key Personnel
Chief Executive: Caroline Burt
Founded: 1926
Subjects: Animals, Pets, Sports, Athletics
ISBN Prefix(es): 0-85131

PUBLISHERS

UNITED KINGDOM

Associate Companies: Mannin Industries Ltd, Isle of Man
Subsidiaries: The Caduceus Press
Distributor for The Pony Club (UK)
Bookshop(s): 4 Lower Grosvenor Place, London
Warehouse: The Trade Counter Ltd, 16 Airfield Norwich Rd, Mendlesham, Suffolk P14 5NA

Webb & Bower (Publishers) Ltd+
9 Duke St, Dartmouth, Devon TQ6 9PY
Tel: (01803) 835525 *Fax:* (01803) 835552
Key Personnel
Man Dir: Richard Webb
Founded: 1975
Subjects: Nonfiction (General)
ISBN Prefix(es): 0-86350
Parent Company: R W Ltd
Associate Companies: Country Diary of an Edwardian Lady Ltd

Adrian Webster Ltd, see Websters International Publishers Ltd

Websters International Publishers Ltd+
Axe & Bottle Court, 70 Newcomen St, London SE1 1YT
Tel: (020) 7940 4700 *Fax:* (020) 7940 4701
E-mail: info@websters.co.uk
Web Site: www.websters.co.uk; www.ozclarke.com
Key Personnel
Chairman & Publisher: Adrian Webster
 E-mail: adrianqwe@msmail.websters.eurkom.ie
Editorial Dir, Group: Clare Harcup
Man Dir: Jean-Luc Barbanneau
Financial Dir: Alan Fennell
Co-Editions Coordinator: Karen Connell
 E-mail: karenco@websters.co.uk
Editor-in-Chief: Susannah Webster
Founded: 1983
Specialize in wine information in all formats.
Subjects: Cookery, Health, Nutrition, Travel, Wine & Spirits
ISBN Prefix(es): 1-870604; 1-85320
Number of titles published annually: 6 Print; 1 CD-ROM
Total Titles: 20 Print
Associate Companies: Adrian Webster Ltd; Websters Multimedia Ltd
Distributed by Little Brown & Co (UK) Ltd
Foreign Rights: Elizabeth Brayne Foreign Rights Agency (all territories)

Websters Multimedia Ltd, see Websters International Publishers Ltd

A Weekes, *imprint of* Stainer & Bell Ltd

Welsh Academic Press+
PO Box 733, Cardiff CF14 2YX
Tel: (029) 2056 0343 *Fax:* (029) 2056 1631
E-mail: post@ashley.drake.com
Web Site: www.welsh-academic-press.co.uk
Key Personnel
Man Dir: Ashley Drake
Dir: Norman Drake; Siwan Drake
Founded: 1994
Specialize in the publishing of scholarly & academic books. that are also accessible to the general reader, "International in Outlook...Welsh in Identity'.
Subjects: Biography, Government, Political Science, History, Literature, Literary Criticism, Essays, Celtic Studies
ISBN Prefix(es): 1-86057
Number of titles published annually: 15 Print
Total Titles: 40 Print
Parent Company: Ashley Drake Publishing Ltd
Imprints: Morgan Publishing; St David's Press
Foreign Rep(s): Marika Janouskova (Eastern Europe); Cranbury International (Caribbean, South & Central America); Cristina de Lara Ruiz (Spain); Ted Dougherty (Austria, Benelux, Germany & Switzerland); Fathima News Enterprise (Singapore); Charles Gibbes (Greece); Globe Enterprises (Malaysia); Golden Book Services (Philippines); International Specialized Book Services (US); Maya Publishers Pvt Ltd (India); Tony Moggach Associates (Sub-Saharan Africa); Mullet & Fitzpatrick (Ireland); Onslow Books (Scandinavia); Victor Osorio (Portugal); David Pickering (Italy); Anthony Rudkin Associates (Middle East); St. Clair Press (Australia); James Tovey (France); University of Toronto Press (Canada)
Warehouse: International Specialized Book Services, Hassalo St, Portland, OR, United States
Orders to: International Specialized Book Services, Hassalo St, Portland, OR, United States
Orca Book Services Ltd, 3 Fleets Lane, Poole, Dorset BH15 3AJ *Tel:* (01202) 665432 *Fax:* (01202) 666219 *E-mail:* orders@orcabookservices.co.uk (Order processing dept)
Membership(s): Publishers' Association

Welsh Womens Press, see Honno Welsh Women's Press

Werner Shaw Ltd
Park Hall Estate, Suite F22, 40 Martell Rd, West Dulwich, London SE21 8EN
Tel: (020) 8761 5570 *Fax:* (020) 8761 5570
Key Personnel
Contact: Barry Shaw
Founded: 1980
Total Titles: 6 Print

West Highland Series, *imprint of* House of Lochar

Westview Press
12 Hid's Copse Rd, Cumnor Hill, Oxford OX2 9JJ
Tel: (01865) 865466 *Fax:* (01865) 862763
E-mail: westview@opp.i-way.co.uk
Web Site: www.westviewpress.com
Telex: 2 39479 WVP UR
Key Personnel
VP, Sales & Marketing - Perseus Books Group: Matthew Goldberg *Tel:* 212-207-7604
 E-mail: matty.goldberg@perseusbooks.com
Manager: Gary Hall; Sue Miller
Founded: 1990
Subjects: Agriculture, Art, Economics, Environmental Studies, Government, Political Science, History, Social Sciences, Sociology
ISBN Prefix(es): 0-89158; 0-86531; 0-8133
Parent Company: Westview Press, 5500 Central Ave, Boulder, CO 80301, United States, Contact: Cathleen Tetro
Distributed by HarperCollins Publishers Order Department (New York)
Orders to: Perseus Books Group, PO Box 317, Oxford OX2 9RU *Tel:* (01865) 865466 *Fax:* (01865) 862763 *E-mail:* perseus@oppuk.co.uk
Perseus Books Group Customer Service, 5500 Central Ave, Boulder, CO 80301, United States *Fax:* 303-449-3356 *E-mail:* westview.orders@perseusbooks.com

Wharncliffe Books, *imprint of* Pen & Sword Books Ltd

Wharncliffe Publishing Ltd+
47 Church St, Barnsley, South Yorks S70 2AS
Tel: (01226) 734222 *Fax:* (01226) 734438
E-mail: sales@pen-and-sword.co.uk
Key Personnel
Man Dir: Mr C Hewitt *Tel:* (01226) 734555
Founded: 1988
Subjects: History, Outdoor Recreation, Regional Interests, Local History, Countryside Books, Military History
Parent Company: Barnsley Chronicle Holdings Ltd
Associate Companies: Pen & Sword Books Ltd
Distributed by Combined Publishing
Distributor for Public Record Office Action
Membership(s): IPG

Which? Books, *imprint of* Which? Ltd

Which? Ltd+
2 Marylebone Rd, London NW1 4DF
Tel: (08453) 010 010 *Fax:* (020) 7770 7485
E-mail: books@which.net
Web Site: www.which.net
Telex: 918197
Key Personnel
Head of Publishing: Gill Rowley *Tel:* (020) 7830-7585 *E-mail:* rowleyg@which.co.uk
Founded: 1957
Member of Publishers' Association.
Subjects: Business, Computer Science, Finance, Gardening, Plants, Health, Nutrition, Law, Self-Help, Travel, Consumer Advice (Law, Finance, Practical), Accommodation & Restaurant Guides, Do-It-Yourself
ISBN Prefix(es): 0-85202
Total Titles: 80 Print
Parent Company: Consumers' Association
Imprints: Which? Books
Showroom(s): Castlemead, Gascoyne Way, Hertford SG14 1YB
Warehouse: Castlemead, Gascoyne Way, Hertford SG14 1YB *Fax:* (0171) 830 8585
Orders to: Castlemead, Gascoyne Way, Hertford SG14 1YB
Penguin Books Ltd, 27 Wrights Lane, London W8 5TZ

White Cockade Publishing+
71 Lonsdale Rd, Oxford OX2 7ES
Tel: (01865) 510411 *Fax:* (01865) 463644
E-mail: mail@whitecockade.co.uk
Web Site: www.whitecockade.co.uk
Key Personnel
Dir: Ms Perilla Kinchin
Founded: 1988
Member of Independent Publishers Guild.
Subjects: Antiques, Architecture & Interior Design, Crafts, Games, Hobbies, History, Regional Interests, Social Sciences, Sociology, Women's Studies, Design History
ISBN Prefix(es): 0-9513124; 1-873487
Number of titles published annually: 1 Print
Total Titles: 10 Print
Distributed by Paul & Co Publishers Consortium Inc (USA & Canada)

White Eagle Publishing Trust+
New Lands, Brewells Lane, Liss, Hants GU33 7HY
Tel: (01730) 893300 *Fax:* (01730) 892235
E-mail: enquiries@whiteagle.org
Web Site: www.whiteaglelodge.org/books
Key Personnel
Man Dir: Ylana Hayward
Foreign Rights: Geoffrey Dent *E-mail:* geoffrey@whiteagle.org
Founded: 1953
Subjects: Astrology, Occult, Religion - Other
ISBN Prefix(es): 0-85487
Total Titles: 46 Print; 10 Audio
Parent Company: White Eagle Lodge
Distributed by De Vorss & Co Inc (North America)

White Mouse Editions, *imprint of* New Cavendish Books

White Tree Books, *imprint of* Redcliffe Press Ltd

UNITED KINGDOM

Whiting & Birch Ltd+
Forest Hill, 90 Dartmouth Rd, London SE23 3HZ
Mailing Address: PO Box 872, London SE23 3HL
Tel: (020) 8244 2421 *Fax:* (020) 8244 2448
E-mail: savpub@dircon.co.uk
Key Personnel
Man Dir: David Whiting
Founded: 1987
Subjects: Child Care & Development, Criminology, Education, Ethnicity, Language Arts, Linguistics, Literature, Literary Criticism, Essays, Social Sciences, Sociology
ISBN Prefix(es): 1-871177; 1-86177
U.S. Office(s): Independent Publishers Group, 814 N Franklin St, Chicago, IL 60610, United States *Tel:* 312-337-0747 *Fax:* 312-337-5785 *E-mail:* frontdesk@ipgbook.com *Web Site:* www.ipgbook.com
Distributed by IPG (North America)

Whittet Books Ltd+
Hill Farm, Stonham Rd, Cotton, Stowmarket, Suffolk 1P14 4RQ
Tel: (01449) 781877 *Fax:* (01449) 781898
Key Personnel
Chairman: A Whittet
Man Dir: Annabel Whittet
Founded: 1976
Subjects: Animals, Pets, Natural History, Horses
ISBN Prefix(es): 0-905483; 1-873580
Parent Company: A Whittet & Co Ltd
Distributed by Diamond Farm Book Publishers (Canada & USA)
Warehouse: Biblios, Star Rd, Partridge Green, Horsham, W Sussex RH13 8LD

Whittles Publishing+
Roseleigh House, Harbour Rd, Latheronwheel, Caithness KW5 6DW
Tel: (01593) 741240 *Fax:* (01593) 741360
E-mail: info@whittlespublishing.com
Web Site: www.whittlespublishing.com
Key Personnel
Publisher & Dir: Dr Keith Whittles
Founded: 1986
Specialize in engineering, geomatics, surveying, applied science & nautical. Also a nontechnical (nonfiction) & technical author.
Member of Scottish Publishers Association.
Subjects: Civil Engineering, Maritime, Natural History, Regional Interests, Geomatics
ISBN Prefix(es): 1-870325
Number of titles published annually: 10 Print
Total Titles: 50 Print
Orders to: BookSource, 32 Finlas St, Cowlairs Industrial Estate, Glasgow G22 5DU *Tel:* (141) 558 1355 *Fax:* (0141) 557 0189 *E-mail:* customerservices@booksource.net

Whurr Publishers Ltd+
19B Compton Terrace, London N1 2UN
Tel: (020) 7359 5979 *Fax:* (020) 7226 5290
E-mail: info@whurr.co.uk
Web Site: www.whurr.co.uk
Key Personnel
Man Dir & Publisher: Colin Whurr
Company Secretary: Lynn Brett
Founded: 1987
Independent.
Subjects: Business, Education, Medicine, Nursing, Dentistry, Psychology, Psychiatry
Total Titles: 400 Print
Subsidiaries: Cole & Whurr Ltd
Distributed by MacLennan & Petty (Australia & New Zealand); Taylor & Francis (Exclusive for North America)
Orders to: Turpin Distribution Services Ltd, Blackhorse Rd, Letchworth, Herts SG6 1HN *Tel:* (01462) 672555 *Fax:* (01462) 480947 *E-mail:* turpin@rsc.org

WI Enterprises Ltd
104 New Kings Rd, London SW6 4LY
Tel: (020) 7371 9300 *Fax:* (020) 7471 9300
E-mail: d.page@nfwi.org.uk
Web Site: www.womens-institute.co.uk/shop/policies/about.shtml
Key Personnel
Chairman: Anne Salmon
Group Manager: Mark Linacre
Sales & Marketing Man: Dahla Page *E-mail:* d.page@nfwi.org.ok
Company Secretary: David Wood
Founded: 1977
Subjects: Cookery, Crafts, Games, Hobbies, Economics, Gardening, Plants, Women's Studies
ISBN Prefix(es): 0-947990; 0-900556
Parent Company: National Federation of Women's Institutes
Warehouse: WI Enterprises Ltd, Penzance TR93 0WW *Tel:* (01736) 333 333

Wild Goose Publications+
Savoy House, 4th floor, 140 Sauchiehall St, Glasgow G2 3DH
Tel: (0141) 332 6292 *Fax:* (0141) 332 1090
E-mail: admin@ionabooks.com
Web Site: www.ionabooks.com
Key Personnel
Publishing Manager: Sandra Kramer *E-mail:* sandra@ionabooks.com
Assistant Publishing Manager: Jane Riley *E-mail:* jane@ionabooks.com
Marketing Officer: Alex O'Neill *E-mail:* alex@ionabooks.com
Founded: 1985
Produces books on social justice, political & peace issues, holistic spirituality, healing & innovative approaches to worship. Part of the IONA community established in the Celtic Christian tradition of Saint Columba.
Member of Independent Publishers Guild.
Subjects: Biblical Studies, Government, Political Science, Music, Dance, Religion - Catholic, Religion - Protestant, Theology
ISBN Prefix(es): 0-947988; 1-901557
Number of titles published annually: 10 Print; 2 Audio
Total Titles: 125 Print; 25 Audio
Parent Company: The Iona Community
Distributed by GIA Publications (North America); Novalis Publishing (Canada); Pleroma Christian Supplies (New Zealand); Willow Connection Pty Ltd (Australia)
Orders to: Saint Andrew Press, 121 George St, Edinburgh EH2 4YN *Tel:* (0131) 225 5722 *Fax:* (0131) 220 3113
Membership(s): IPG

Wiley Europe Ltd+
Baffins Lane, Chichester, West Sussex PO19 1UD
Tel: (01243) 779777 *Fax:* (01243) 775878
E-mail: customer@wiley.co.uk
Web Site: www.wiley.co.uk
Key Personnel
Man Dir: Dr John Jarvis
Publishing Dir: Dr Steven Mair
STM Book Publishing Dir & Dir of Planning: Dr Ernest Kirkwood
Publisher, Technology: Dr Ann-Marie Halligan
Dir, New Media Development: Dr Rosemary Altoft
STM Journal Publishing Dir: Dr Michael Davis
Publisher, Medicine: Dr Deborah Reece
Publisher, College Division: Dr Simon Plumtree
Publisher, Chemistry: Dr Helen McPherson
Publisher, Medicine: Dr Richard Edelstein
Publisher, Life/Science: Dr Charlotte Brabants
Commercial Dir: Dr Sarah Stevens
Publisher, Psychology: Dr Michael Coombs
Dir Sales, Marketing & Publicity: Dr Robert Long
Publicity & Exhibition Man: Dr Julia Lampam
Production Dir: Helen Balley
Finance Dir: Jim Dicks
IT & Customer Service Dir: Peter Ferris
Marketing Development Dir: Paul Holmes
Sales Dir: Philip Kisray
Publishing Technologies Dir: Cliff Morgan
Human Resource Dir: Angela Poulter
Customer Service Dir: Margaret Radbourne
Distribution Dir: Mike Ridge
Publisher, Earth/Environmental Science: Sally Wilkinson
Senior Publishing Editor, Architecture: Maggie Toy
Founded: 1960
Other Main Office: WILEY-VCH, Pappelallee 3, 69469 Weinheim, Germany. *Tel:* (06201) 6060; *Fax:* (06201) 606328.
2000 titles in print.
Subjects: Accounting, Architecture & Interior Design, Biological Sciences, Business, Chemistry, Chemical Engineering, Computer Science, Cookery, Earth Sciences, Economics, Finance, Management, Marketing, Mathematics, Mechanical Engineering, Medicine, Nursing, Dentistry, Physics, Psychology, Psychiatry, Religion - Other, Technology
ISBN Prefix(es): 1-870604; 1-85320
Total Titles: 11,000 Print; 300 E-Book
Online services available through Wiley-InterScience.
Parent Company: John Wiley & Sons Inc, 605 Third Ave, New York, NY 10158, United States
Associate Companies: John Wiley & Sons Australia Ltd, Australia *Tel:* (07) 3859 9755 *Fax:* (07) 3859 9715; John Wiley & Sons Canada Ltd, ON, Canada *Tel:* (416) 236-4433 *Fax:* (416) 236-4447; WILEY-VCH, Germany *Tel:* (06201) 606 0 *Fax:* (06201) 606 328 *E-mail:* info@wiley-vch.de; John Wiley & Sons (Asia) Pte Ltd, Singapore *Tel:* 463-2400 *Fax:* 463-4603; Tokyo Liaison Office, Kudonshita Tokyu Shin-Sakura, Bldg 6F, 1-3-3 Kudan-Kita, Chiyoda-ku Tokyo 102-0073, Japan *Tel:* (03) 3556 9762 *Fax:* (03) 3556 9763 *E-mail:* fwga5479@mb.infoweb.or.jp
Imprints: Wiley-Interscience; Wiley Liss; John Wiley & Sons; Halsted Press; Scripta Technica; Wiley-Heyden; ValuSource; Jossey-Bass
Distributor for California, Columbia & Princeton University Press (Europe, Middle East, Africa); Indiana University Press (Continental Europe); Kegan Paul International Ltd (Europe); W W Norton & Co Ltd (Europe, Middle East, Africa, Asia, West Indies); O'Reilly UK Ltd (Europe, Middle East, Africa, Asia, West Indies); Research Studies Press Ltd (Europe, Middle East, Africa); Sybex International Corp (Continental Europe); The University of Chicago Press (Europe); Yale University Press (Europe, Middle East, Africa); Harvard University Press/MIT Press Ltd & LOEB Classical Library (Europe, Middle East, Africa)
Orders to: John Wiley & Sons Ltd Distribution Center, Southern Cross Trading Estate, One Oldlands Way, Bognor Regis, West Sussex PO22 9SA *Tel:* (01243) 779777 *Fax:* (01243) 820250

Wiley-Heyden, *imprint of* Wiley Europe Ltd

Wiley-Interscience, *imprint of* Wiley Europe Ltd

Wiley Liss, *imprint of* Wiley Europe Ltd

William Heinemann, *imprint of* Random House UK Ltd

Joseph Williams, *imprint of* Stainer & Bell Ltd

Wilmington Business Information Ltd+
Paulton House, 8 Shepherdess Walk, London N1 7LB

Tel: (020) 7549 8704 *Fax:* (020) 7490 2979
Web Site: www.waterlow.com/signature/
Key Personnel
Dir: Rory A Conwell; Brian Gilbert; Michael Harrington; Paul Holden; Peter Lunn; Ahmed Zahedieh
Business Services Manager: E M Dutta *Tel:* (020) 7566 8277 *E-mail:* sdutta@waterlow.com
Founded: 1843
Member of Directory & Database Publishers Association.
Subjects: Business, Disability, Special Needs, Drama, Theater, Fiction, Finance, Law, Music, Dance
Online services available through World Wide Web.
Parent Company: Wilmington Group PLC
Associate Companies: Wilmington Publishing Ltd
Imprints: Gramophone; ICP; Investment Intelligence; PCR; RED; Waterlow
Subsidiaries: Retail Entertainment Data Publishing Ltd; Waterlow Specialist Information Publishing Ltd
Divisions: International Company Profile; Investment Intelligence; RED; Waterlow Co Services; Waterlow Professional Publishing; Waterlow Signature: Waterlow Direct Mail

Neil Wilson Publishing Ltd+
Pentagon Centre, Suite 303a, 36 Washington St, Glasgow G3 8AZ
Tel: (0141) 221 1117 *Fax:* (0141) 221 5363
E-mail: info@nwp.sol.co.uk
Web Site: www.nwp.co.uk
Key Personnel
Contact: Neil Wilson *E-mail:* neil@nwp.sol.co.uk
Founded: 1992
Member of Scottish Publishers Association.
Subjects: Biography, Cookery, Fiction, History, Humor, Outdoor Recreation, Regional Interests, Sports, Athletics, Wine & Spirits
ISBN Prefix(es): 1-897784; 1-903238
Number of titles published annually: 15 Print
Total Titles: 100 Print
Online services available through World Wide Web.
Imprints: Angels' Share; 11:9; The In Pinn; The Vital Spark
Distributed by Interlink Books (USA)
Foreign Rep(s): Capricorn (Australia); Interlink Publishing (US)
Warehouse: Book Source, 32 Finlas St, Cowlairs Estate, Glasgow G22 5DU *Tel:* (0870) 240 2182 *Fax:* (0141) 557 0189
Orders to: Book Source, 32 Finlas St, Cowlairs Estate, Glascow G22 5DU *Tel:* (0870) 240 2182 *Fax:* (0141) 557 0189 *E-mail:* orders@booksource.net

Philip Wilson Publishers+
7 Deane House, 27 Greenwood Pl, London NW5 1LB
Tel: (020) 7284 3088 *Fax:* (020) 7284 3099
E-mail: pwp@monoclick.co.uk
Key Personnel
Man Dir: Philip Wilson *E-mail:* pwilson@monoclick.co.uk
Sales & Publicity Manager: Juliana Powney *E-mail:* jpowney@monoclick.co.uk
Commissioning Editor: Anne Jackson *E-mail:* ajackson@monoclick.co.uk
Production Man: Norman Turpin *E-mail:* nturpin@monoclick.co.uk
Founded: 1975
Subjects: Antiques, Archaeology, Architecture & Interior Design, Art, Fashion
ISBN Prefix(es): 0-85667
Number of titles published annually: 16 Print
Total Titles: 150 Print
Distributed by Antique Collectors Club
Foreign Rep(s): APD Singapore Pte Ltd (Brunei, Indonesia, Malaysia, Singapore, Thailand); Asia Publishers Services Ltd (China & Hong Kong, Japan, Korea, Taiwan, Macao); Consul Books (Netherlands); Csaba Lengyel de bagota (Croatia, Czech Republic, Hungary, Romania, Slovak Republic, Slovenia, Yugoslavia, Bosnia & Herzegovina); Exhibitions International (Belgium); Interart SRL (France); Livraria Gaudi Ltda (Brazil); Peter Hyde Associates (South Africa); Thames & Hudson (Australia); The Art Book Studio (India)
Foreign Rights: David Wine (Israel); Hanne Rotovnik (Finland, Iceland, Scandinavia); Michael Geoghegan (Austria, Germany, Switzerland); Michael Morris Associates (Middle East); Penny Padovani (Greece, Italy, Portugal, Spain)

Wimbledon Publishing Company Ltd+
Isis House, 67-69 Southwark St, London SE1 0HX
Tel: (020) 7401 8855 *Fax:* (020) 7928 9226
E-mail: enquiries@wpcpress.com
Web Site: www.wpcpress.com
Key Personnel
Man Dir: Mr K Sood
Sales & Marketing: Mr N McPherson
Edit, Nightingale Press: Mr L Chaput
Founded: 1993
Specialize in Political Science & Humanities plus gift & humor books for the discerning wit.
Subjects: Biography, Biological Sciences, Business, Economics, Government, Political Science, Health, Nutrition, History, Humor, Language Arts, Linguistics, Literature, Literary Criticism, Essays, Self-Help, Women's Studies
ISBN Prefix(es): 1-898855; 1-903222
Number of titles published annually: 50 Print
Total Titles: 150 Print
Imprints: Anthem Press (Academic humanities); Nightingale Press (Gift books & humor); WPC Classics (School & college classics); WPC School Books (Secondary education textbooks)
U.S. Office(s): 4117 Hillsboro Pike, Suite 103-106, Nashville, TN 37215, United States *Tel:* 801-749-2983 *Fax:* 801-749-2983 *E-mail:* enquiries@wpcpress.com
Orders to: Pathway Book Service, 4 White Brook Lane, Gilsum, NH 03348, United States *Tel:* 603-357-0236 *Fax:* 603-357-2073 *E-mail:* pbs@pathwaybooks.com

Windhorse Publications+
11 Park Rd, Moseley, Birmingham B13 8AB
Tel: (0121) 449 9191 *Fax:* (0121) 449 9191
E-mail: windhorse@compuserve.com
Web Site: www.windhorsepublications.com
Key Personnel
Dir, Rights Manager & Commissioning Editor: Dr Jnanasiddhi
Business Manager: Robert Mason
Founded: 1976
Subjects: Religion - Buddhist
ISBN Prefix(es): 0-904766; 1-899579
Number of titles published annually: 9 Print
Total Titles: 100 Print
Associate Companies: Windhorse Books, PO Box 574, Newtown, NSW 2042, Australia, Contact: Ratnajyoti *Tel:* (02) 9519 8826 *Fax:* (02) 9519 8826 *E-mail:* books@windhorse.com.au *Web Site:* www.windhorse.com.au (Australia)
Distributed by Book Representation & Distribution Ltd (United Kingdom); Mayajala Books; Weatherhill Inc (North America)
Distributor for Dharma Publishing (Europe); Dharmachakra; Weatherlight Press; Western Buddhist Review
Orders to: Weatherhill Inc, 41 Monroe Turnpike, Trumbull, CT 06611, United States *Tel:* 800-437-7840 *Fax:* 800-557-5601 *E-mail:* weatherhill@weatherhill.com *Web Site:* www.weatherhill.com (US)

Windrow & Greene, *imprint of* Compendium Publishing

The Windrush Press Ltd+
Windrush House, 12 Main St, Adlestrop GL56 0YN
Tel: (01608) 658758; (01608) 652012 *Fax:* (01608) 659345
E-mail: windrush@windrushpress.com
Web Site: www.windrushpress.com
Key Personnel
Man Dir: Geoffrey Smith
Publishing Dir: Victoria Huxley *E-mail:* victoriama.huxley@btinternet.com
Founded: 1987
Specialize in military history & ancient mysteries.
Subjects: Biography, History, Humor, Mysteries, Nonfiction (General), Travel
ISBN Prefix(es): 0-900075; 1-900624
Total Titles: 50 Print
Online services available through World Wide Web.
Parent Company: Orion Group, 5 Upper St Martin's Lane, London WC2H 9EA
Distributor for Windrush Publishing Services
Orders to: Littlehampton Book Services, Faraday Close, Durrington, West Sussex BN13 3RB *Tel:* (01903) 828890 *Fax:* (01903) 828802

Windsor Books International
The Boundary, Wheatley Rd, Garsington, Oxford, Oxon OX44 9EJ
Tel: (01865) 361122 *Fax:* (01865) 361133
E-mail: windsorbooks@compuserve.com
Key Personnel
Man Dir: A Geoff Cowen *E-mail:* geoffcowen@windsorbooks.co.uk
Founded: 1991
Also acts as distributor in the UK & Europe for publishers in the US & other countries.
Subjects: Architecture & Interior Design, Art, Music, Dance, Radio, TV, Travel
ISBN Prefix(es): 1-874111
Subsidiaries: Springfield Books
Distributor for Allworth Press, New York (UK & Europe); Billboard Music Books, New York (UK & Europe); Creative Publishing International, Minnesota (UK & Europe); C & T Publishing, California (UK & Europe); Getty Publications, California (UK & Europe); The Globe Pequot Press, Connecticut (UK); Hudson Hills Press, New York (UK & Europe); Hunter Publishing, Florida (UK & Europe); The Lyons Press, Connecticut (UK); Meyer & Meyer, Aachen (UK); Sally Milner Publishing, Australia (UK & Europe); Open Road Publishing, New York (UK & Europe); Watson-Guptill Publications, New York (UK & Europe)

Windsor Large Print Bestsellers, *imprint of* BBC Audiobooks

Winslow Editions, *imprint of* Speechmark Publishing Ltd

Wise Owl Books, *imprint of* HLT Publications

WISE Publications, *imprint of* Omnibus Press

Wisley Handbooks, *imprint of* Cassell & Co

WIT Press+
Ashurst Lodge, Ashurst, Southampton S040 7AA
Tel: (023) 8029 3223 *Fax:* (023) 8029 2853
E-mail: witpress@witpress.com
Web Site: www.witpress.com
Key Personnel
Chief Executive: Prof C Brebbia
Man Dir, Publicity, Rights & Permissions: Lance Sucharov
Sales, UK Office: Myra Mouland *E-mail:* myra@wessex.ac.uk

Sales, US Office: Linda Ovellette *E-mail:* info@compmech.com
Marketing Manager, US Office: Dee Halzack *Tel:* (978) 667-5841 *E-mail:* info@compmech.com
Marketing Manager, UK Office: Helen Arnold *E-mail:* marketing@witpress.com
Founded: 1976
Publisher in advanced engineering subjects, including engineering analysis & computational methods. Also publishes the serial *Boundary Element Communications*, as well as the proceedings of conferences organized by the Wessex Institute of Technology & edited/authored volumes.
Subjects: Architecture & Interior Design, Automotive, Biological Sciences, Civil Engineering, Computer Science, Earth Sciences, Electronics, Electrical Engineering, Engineering (General), Environmental Studies, Maritime, Mathematics, Mechanical Engineering, Technology, Transportation, Acoustics, Biomedicine, Earthquake Engineering, Environmental & Ecological Engineering, Fluid Mechanics, Fracture Mechanics, Heat Transfer, Marine Engineering, Transport Engineering
ISBN Prefix(es): 0-931215; 0-945824; 1-56252; 1-85312; 0-905451
Number of titles published annually: 50 Print
Total Titles: 500 Print; 6 CD-ROM
Parent Company: Computational Mechanics International
U.S. Office(s): Computational Mechanics, 25 Bridge St, Billerica, MA 01821, United States *Tel:* 978-667-5841 *Fax:* 978-667-7582 *E-mail:* info@compmech.com

Witherby, *imprint of* Cassell & Co

Witherby & Co Ltd+
Book Dept, 2nd floor, 32-36 Aylesbury St, London EC1R 0ET
Tel: (020) 7251 5341 *Fax:* (020) 7251 1296
E-mail: books@witherbys.co.uk
Web Site: www.witherbys.com
Key Personnel
Man Dir: Alan Witherby
Founded: 1740
Member of Bookseller Association; Institute of Experts.
Subjects: Business, Economics, Management, Maritime, Technology, Transportation
ISBN Prefix(es): 0-900886; 1-85609
Number of titles published annually: 20 Print; 2 Audio
Total Titles: 250 Print; 1 CD-ROM; 2 Audio
Imprints: Monument
Bookshop(s): 20 Aldermanbury, London EC2V 7HY, Christine Burge *Tel:* (020) 7417 4431 *Fax:* (020) 7417 4431 *E-mail:* books@witherbys.co.uk

H F & G Witherby Ltd, see Gollancz/Witherby

The Woburn Press+
Subsidiary of Frank Cass Publishers
Crown House, 47 Chase Side, London N14 5BP
Tel: (020) 8920 2100 *Fax:* (020) 8447 8548
E-mail: info@woburnpress.com
Web Site: www.frankcass.com/wp
Key Personnel
Man Dir: Stewart Cass
Editorial: Andrew Humphreys
Trade: Joanna Legg
Production: Daphna Weiss
Publicity: Hayley Osen
Founded: 1969
Subjects: Education
ISBN Prefix(es): 0-7130
Associate Companies: Vallentine, Mitchell & Co Ltd; Irish Academic Press

U.S. Office(s): 5824 NE Hassalo St, Portland, OR 97213-3644, United States *Tel:* 503-287-3093 *Fax:* 503-280-8832 *E-mail:* orders@isbs.com
Warehouse: Biblios Distributions, Star Rd, Partridge Green, West Sussex RH13 8LD *Tel:* (0403) 710971 *Fax:* (0403) 711143

WOL Books, *imprint of* Pallas Athene

Oswald Wolff Books, *imprint of* Berg Publishers

The Women's Press Ltd+
Member of Namara Group
34 Great Sutton St, London EC1V 0LQ
Tel: (020) 7251 3007 *Fax:* (020) 7608 1938
E-mail: sales@the-womens-press.com
Web Site: www.the-womens-press.com
Key Personnel
Man Dir: Emma Drew *E-mail:* emma@the-womens-press.com
Founded: 1977
Subjects: Alternative, Art, Biography, Disability, Special Needs, Environmental Studies, Ethnicity, Fiction, Gay & Lesbian, Government, Political Science, Health, Nutrition, Literature, Literary Criticism, Essays, Music, Dance, Nonfiction (General), Psychology, Psychiatry, Self-Help, Women's Studies
ISBN Prefix(es): 0-7043
Number of titles published annually: 36 Print
Imprints: Livewire (books for teenagers & young women)
Distributed by Codasat (Canada); Ted Dougherty (Europe-excluding Spain & Portugal); Iberian Book Services (Spain & Portugal); IMA (Africa, Eastern Europe, Caribbean & Latin America); Quartet (South Africa); Hanne Rotovnik (Scandinavia); Southern Publishers Group (New Zealand); Tower Books (Australia); Trafalgar Square (US)
Foreign Rights: Writer's House (US)
Orders to: Plymbridge Distributors Ltd, Estover Rd, Estover, Plymouth PL6 7PZ *Tel:* (01752) 202301 *Fax:* (01752) 202331 *E-mail:* control@plymbridge.com

Woodhead Publishing Ltd+
Abington Hall, Abington, Cambridge CB1 6AH
Tel: (01223) 891358 *Fax:* (01223) 893694
E-mail: wp@woodhead-publishing.com
Web Site: www.woodhead-publishing.com
Key Personnel
Man Dir: Martin J Woodhead *Tel:* (01223) 891358 ext 16 *E-mail:* martinw@woodhead-publishing.com
Editorial Dir: Francis Dodds *E-mail:* francisd@woodhead-publishing.com
Editorial & Production: Mary Campbell; Alex Harrington
Marketing Manager: Nick Birch *E-mail:* nickb@woodhead-publishing.com
Financial Manager: Rob Burleigh *E-mail:* robb@woodhead-publishing.com
Founded: 1989
Specialize in engineering materials, welding, food science, food technology, textiles, environment, finance & investment.
Subjects: Energy, Engineering (General), Finance, Health, Nutrition, Technology, Food Science
ISBN Prefix(es): 1-85573
Number of titles published annually: 45 Print; 2 CD-ROM; 8 Online; 3 E-Book
Total Titles: 350 Print; 4 CD-ROM; 8 Online; 3 E-Book
Imprints: Abington Publishing; Gresham Books
Distributed by CRC Press LLC
Distributor for American Welding Society
Warehouse: Combined Book Services Ltd, Units I/K, Paddock Wood Distribution Centre, Paddock Wood, Tonbridge TN12 6UU *Tel:* (01892) 837171 *Fax:* (01892) 837272
Membership(s): IPG

Word for Word Audio Books, *imprint of* BBC Audiobooks

Wordsworth Editions, *imprint of* Wordsworth Editions Ltd

Wordsworth Editions Ltd+
Cumberland House, Crib Street, Ware, Herts SG12 9ET
Tel: (020) 7706 8822 *Fax:* (020) 7706 8833
E-mail: enquiries@wordsworth-editions.com
Web Site: www.wordsworth-editions.co.uk/distributors.htm
Founded: 1987
Specialize in Wordsworth Editions & Classics with CD-ROM, folklore, myths & legends.
Subjects: History, Literature, Literary Criticism, Essays, Poetry
ISBN Prefix(es): 1-85326; 1-84022
Number of titles published annually: 50 Print; 20 CD-ROM
Total Titles: 700 Print; 10 CD-ROM
Imprints: Wordsworth Editions; Wordsworth Education
Distributed by Agius & Agius Ltd (Malta & Gozo); Allphy Book Distributors Ltd (New Zealand & Fiji); Bohemian Ventures sro (Czech Republic); Copernicus Diffusion (France); Inter Orbis Media Dist srl Ed (Italy); NTC/Contemporary (USA); OM Books International (India); Peribo Pty Ltd (Australia & Papua New Guinea); Readwide Bookshop Ltd (Ghana, The Gambia, Liberia, Cameroon & Sierra Leone); Ribera Libros SL (Spain); Slovak Ventures sro (Slovak Republic); Taschenbuch-Vertrieb Ingeborg Blank GmbH Lager und Buro (Germany & Austria)
Foreign Rep(s): Don O'Mahoney (Ireland); Advanced Global Distribution (US); IMA (Caribbean, South America); Publishers International Marketing (Far East, Middle East)
Showroom(s): Cumberland House, Crib Street, Ware, Herts SG12 9ET
Warehouse: Wordsworth Editions, The Airfield, Mendlesham, Suffolk IP14 5NA

Wordsworth Education, *imprint of* Wordsworth Editions Ltd

Wordwright Books, *imprint of* Wordwright Publishing

Wordwright Publishing+
25 Oakford Rd, London NW5 1AJ
Tel: (020) 7284 0056 *Fax:* (020) 7284 0041
E-mail: wordwright@clara.co.uk
Key Personnel
Dir, International Rights: Charles Perkins *E-mail:* cfp@wordwright.clara.co.uk
Dir: Veronica Davis
Founded: 1987
Member of the Book Packagers Association; also acts as book packager.
Subjects: Art, Cookery, Gardening, Plants, Geography, Geology, History, Humor, Natural History, Nonfiction (General), Social Sciences, Sociology, Sports, Athletics, Women's Studies
ISBN Prefix(es): 0-9527128
Total Titles: 40 Print
Imprints: Wordwright Books

World Microfilms Publications Ltd+
Microworld House, 4 Foscote Mews, London W9 2HH
Tel: (020) 7266 2202; (0845) 606 0612
Fax: (020) 7266 2314
E-mail: microworld@ndirect.co.uk
Web Site: www.microworld.ndirect.co.uk
Key Personnel
Man Dir: Stephen C Albert
Founded: 1969

200 Microfilms, 200 slide sets, 200 tapes, 100 video & slide packs.
Subjects: Architecture & Interior Design, Art, Drama, Theater, Economics, Film, Video, History, Music, Dance, Religion - Other, Science (General), Self-Help, Microfilm Collections
ISBN Prefix(es): 1-85035; 1-86013; 0-905272
Number of titles published annually: 10 Print
Total Titles: 700 Print; 3 CD-ROM; 400 Audio
Associate Companies: Audio-Forum; Pidgeon Audio Visual; Sussex Tapes; Sussex Video; Stotts Correspondence College
Foreign Rep(s): Norman Ross Publishing Inc (Canada, US)

World of Information+
2 Market St, Saffron Walden, Essex CB10 1HZ
Tel: (01799) 521150 Fax: (01799) 524805
E-mail: queries@worldinformation.com
Web Site: www.worldinformation.com
Key Personnel
Man Dir & Rights: Anthony Axon
Founded: 1972
Subjects: Business, Economics, Government, Political Science
ISBN Prefix(es): 1-86217
Number of titles published annually: 140 Print; 1 CD-ROM
Total Titles: 160 Print; 3 CD-ROM
Subsidiaries: Central European Business Ltd

World of Islam Altajir Trust+
33 Thurloe Pl, London SW7 2HQ
Tel: (020) 7581 3522 Fax: (020) 7584 1977
Key Personnel
Dir: Alistair Duncan
Founded: 1974
Subjects: Archaeology, Art, Religion - Islamic, Theology
ISBN Prefix(es): 0-905035
Orders to: Scorpion Publishing Ltd, Victoria House, Victoria Rd, Buckhurst Hill, Essex IG9 5ES Fax: (0181) 5060553

The World Today, *imprint of* Royal Institute of International Affairs

Worldlife Library, *imprint of* Colin Baxter Photography Ltd

WPC Classics, *imprint of* Wimbledon Publishing Company Ltd

WPC School Books, *imprint of* Wimbledon Publishing Company Ltd

Gordon Wright Publishing Ltd+
55 Marchmont Rd, Edinburgh EH9 1HT
Tel: (0131) 6671300 Fax: (0131) 6671459
E-mail: gordonwrightpublisher@compuserve.com; 101370.330@compuserve.com
Key Personnel
Man Dir: Gordon Wright
Founded: 1969
Member of Scottish Publishers Association.
Subjects: Fiction, Humor, Literature, Literary Criticism, Essays, Nonfiction (General)
ISBN Prefix(es): 0-903065
Warehouse: Scottish Book Source, 32 Finlas St, Cowlairs Industrial Estate, Springburn, Glasgow
Orders to: Scottish Book Source, Scottish Book Centre, 137 Dundee St, Edinburgh EH11 1BG

Writers & Their Work, *imprint of* Northcote House Publishers Ltd

Writer's Digest, *imprint of* David & Charles Ltd

Wychwood Press, *imprint of* Jon Carpenter Publishing

Xpress Reprints, *imprint of* SCM Press

Y Cyfarwyddwr Urdd Gobaith Cymru
Swyddfa'r Urdd, Ffordd Llanbadarn, Aberystwyth, Ceredigion SY23 1EN
Tel: (01970) 613100 Fax: (01970) 626120
E-mail: urdd@urdd.org
Web Site: www.urdd.org
Key Personnel
Chief Executive: Jim O'Rourke E-mail: jim@urdd.org
Founded: 1923

Yale English Monarchs, *imprint of* Yale University Press London

Yale University Press London+
23 Pond St, London NW3 2PN
Tel: (020) 7431 4422 Fax: (020) 7431 3755
E-mail: sales@yaleup.co.uk
Key Personnel
Man Dir: John Nicoll
Deputy Man Dir: Robert Baldock
Editorial Dir: Gillian Malpass
Sales & Marketing Dir: Kate Pocock
E-mail: kate.pocock@yaleup.co.uk
Publicity: Hazel Hutchison
Sales: Andrew Jarmain
Rights: Anne Bihan
Founded: 1961
Subjects: Anthropology, Architecture & Interior Design, Art, Asian Studies, Biography, Environmental Studies, Government, Political Science, History, Language Arts, Linguistics, Law, Literature, Literary Criticism, Essays, Music, Dance, Natural History, Nonfiction (General), Philosophy, Photography, Physical Sciences, Psychology, Psychiatry, Religion - Jewish, Social Sciences, Sociology, Theology, Women's Studies
ISBN Prefix(es): 0-300
Parent Company: Yale University Press, 92 A Yale Station, New Haven, CT 06520, United States
Imprints: Pelican History of Art; Pevsner Architectural Guides; Yale English Monarchs
Subsidiaries: Yale Representation Ltd
U.S. Office(s): Yale University Press, PO Box 209040, 302 Temple St, New Haven, CT 06520-9040, United States Tel: 203-432-0960 Fax: 203-432-0948
Distributor for Metropolitan Museum of Art; National Gallery Publications
Orders to: John Wiley & Sons Ltd Distribution Centre, Southern Cross Trading Estate, Bognor Regis, West Sussex PO22 9SA

Anglia Young Books+
Imprint of Motivation in Learning Ltd (Bangor)
Durham's Farmhouse, Ickleton, Saffron Walden, Essex CB10 1SR
Tel: (01799) 531192 Fax: (01799) 531192
E-mail: r.hayes@btinternet.com
Web Site: www.btinternet.com/~r.hayes
Key Personnel
Contact: Rosemary Hayes E-mail: R.Hayes@BInternet.com
Founded: 1989
Subjects: Disability, Special Needs, Fiction, History, Religion - Other
ISBN Prefix(es): 1-871173
Distributor for Kallisto Ltd
Orders to: Broadgali House, 72 Church St, Deeping St James, Peterborough PE6 8HD

Young Corgi, *imprint of* Transworld Publishers Ltd

Zed Books Ltd+
7 Cynthia St, London N1 9JF
Tel: (020) 7837 4014; (020) 7837 0384
Fax: (020) 7833 3960
E-mail: zed@zedbooks.demon.co.uk
Web Site: zedweb.hypermart.net/zed/contact.htm
Key Personnel
Sales: Farouk Sohawon
Editor: Robert Molteno; Michael Pallis
Editor, Rights & Permissions: Mohammed Umar
E-mail: mohammed@zedbooks.demon.co.uk
Marketing: Julian Hosie
Production: Anne Rodford
Founded: 1976
Subjects: Environmental Studies, Social Sciences, Sociology, Women's Studies, Development Studies
ISBN Prefix(es): 0-905762; 0-86232; 1-85649; 1-84277
Total Titles: 350 Print
Distributed by St Martin's Press/Palgrave (USA)
Shipping Address: Plymbridge, Estover, Plymouth PL6 7PZ
Warehouse: Plymbridge, Estover, Plymouth PL6 7PZ

Zeno Booksellers, see The Greek Bookshop

Ziff-Davis Press, *imprint of* Pearson Education Europe, Mideast & Africa

Zomba Books, *imprint of* Omnibus Press

Zone Books, *imprint of* MIT Press Ltd

Zwemmer Holdings Co Ltd
24 Litchfield St, London WC2H 9NJ
Tel: (020) 7240 4158 Fax: (020) 7836 7049
E-mail: sales@zwemmer.com
Web Site: www.zwemmer.com
Key Personnel
Man Dir: Rupert Gather
Founded: 1921
Subjects: Architecture & Interior Design, Art, Film, Video, Photography, Performing Arts
ISBN Prefix(es): 0-302
Bookshop(s): Zwemmers, 80 Charing Cross Rd, London WC2; OUP Bookshop, 72 Charing Cross Rd, London WC2H OBE; Whitechapel Art Gallery, Whitechapel High St, London E1 7QX

Uruguay

General Information

Capital: Montevideo
Language: Spanish
Religion: Predominantly Roman Catholic
Population: 3.1 million
Bank Hours: 1300-1700 Monday-Friday
Shop Hours: 0900-1200, 1400-1900 Monday-Friday; 0900-1230 Saturday
Currency: 100 centesimos = 1 new Uruguayan peso
Export/Import Information: Member Southern Cone Common Market (MERCOSUR) No tariffs on books or single copies catalogues but surcharge on advertising matter. Additional surcharge on all imports, plus VAT Cif, plus Stamp Tax of percentage of total invoice value. No import licenses. No exchange controls.
Copyright: UCC, Berne, Buenos Aires (see Copyright Conventions, pg xi)

Albe Libros Technicos
Cerrito 566, 11000 Montevideo

Tel: (02) 957485 *Fax:* (02) 957528
Key Personnel
Contact: Daniel Aljanatl
Branch Office(s)
Albe Libros Technicos-Salto, Joaquin Suarez 28, Salto

Editorial Arca SRL+
Andes 1118, Montevideo 11100
Tel: (02) 900318 *Fax:* (02) 901887; (02) 930188
Key Personnel
Man Dir: Claudio Rama
Founded: 1964
Subjects: Anthropology, Drama, Theater, Economics, Geography, Geology, Health, Nutrition, History, Humor, Music, Dance, Poetry, Regional Interests, Religion - Other, Technology
ISBN Prefix(es): 9974-40

Arpoador+
Roque Graseras 693, Montevideo 11300
Tel: (02) 707826 *Fax:* (02) 717278
Key Personnel
Contact: Martha Paulick
Founded: 1995
Subjects: Economics, History, Literature, Literary Criticism, Essays
ISBN Prefix(es): 9974-7533

Barreiro y Ramos SA
Juan Carlos Gomez 1430, 11100 Montevideo
Tel: (02) 986621 *Fax:* (02) 962358, (02 958283)
Cable: BAREIRAMOS
Key Personnel
Man Dir: Dr Gaston Barreiro Zorrilla
Sales Dir: Raul Catelli
Founded: 1871
Subjects: Literature, Literary Criticism, Essays, Religion - Other
ISBN Prefix(es): 84-8292; 9974-33

Cotidiano Mujer
Salto 1265, 11200 Montevideo
Tel: (02) 4130374; (02) 4024180 *Fax:* (02) 4095651
E-mail: cotidian@chasque.apc.org.uy
Key Personnel
Contact: Elena Fonseca
Founded: 1985
Subjects also include ecology, feminism & human rights.
Subjects: Journalism, Women's Studies

Ediciones de Juan Darien+
Hocquart 1771, 11800 Montevideo
Tel: (02) 2090223
E-mail: dayraq@chasque.apc.org
Key Personnel
Contact: Dayman Cabrera
Founded: 1990
Subjects: Art, Cookery, Economics, Education, History, Literature, Literary Criticism, Essays, Nonfiction (General), Poetry, Social Sciences, Sociology
ISBN Prefix(es): 9974-580

Instituto del Tercer Mundo+
Juan D Jackson 1136, 11200 Montevideo
Tel: (02) 496192 *Fax:* (02) 419222
Key Personnel
Dir: Roberto Bissio
Editor: Victor Bacchetta *E-mail:* victorb@chasque.apc.org
Founded: 1986
New Zealand/Aotearoa.
Member of Association for Progressive Communications (APC).
Subjects: Human Relations, Civil Society
ISBN Prefix(es): 9974-574
U.S. Office(s): Humanities Press International Inc, 165 First Ave, Atlantic Highlands, NJ 07716, United States *Tel:* 908-872-1441 *Fax:* 908-872-0717
DHL, 8424 NW 56 St, Suite MVD 023040, Miami, FL 33166, United States
Distributed by Andenbuch-Romanische Bucchandlung (Alemania); Arning Publications (Norway); CEDIB (Bolivia); Fondo de Cultura Economica (Peru); Hillco Media Group (Sweden); Humanities Press International Inc (US); Ibercultura GmbH (Switzerland); IEPALA (Spain); Instituto del Tercer Mundo (Uruguay); Lamuv Verlag (Germany); Leer Ltda (Colombia); Libreria De La Paz (Argentina); Libreria Lectura SA (Venezuela); Libreria Milnovecientos (Chile); Libri Mundi (Ecuador); MARCIAL PONS Libreros (Spain); Mellemfolkeligt Samvirke (Denmark); NCOS (Belgium); New Internationalist Aotearoa; New Internationalist Australia (Australia); New Internationalist Canada (Canada); New Internationalist Publications (UK); Novib Publications (Netherlands); Oxfam Publications (UK); Sipro (Servicios Informativos Procesados AC) (Mexico); Tyron SA (Argentina)
Distributor for Revista delsur; Social Watch
Orders to: Hersilia Fonseca/Marketing

Departemento de Publicaciones de la Universidad de la Republica
JE Rodo 1827-29, 11200 Montevideo
Tel: (02) 485714 *Fax:* (02) 480303
Key Personnel
Dir: Daniel Cabalero
ISBN Prefix(es): 9974-0

Editorial Dismar+
18 de Julio 2172/308, 11200 Montevideo
Tel: (02) 407946
Key Personnel
Editor: Martha Campos
Founded: 1989
Member of Camara Uruguaya del Libro.
Subjects: Journalism, Medicine, Nursing, Dentistry, Psychology, Psychiatry
ISBN Prefix(es): 9974-560

EQ Opciones en Educacion
Luis A de Herrera 2368, 11600 Montevideo
Mailing Address: PO Box 16035, 11600 Montevideo
Tel: (02) 4808720; (02) 9009934 *Fax:* (02) 4873965
E-mail: opciones@adinet.com.uy
Key Personnel
Contact: Esperanza Querol
Founded: 1995
Member of Camara Uruguaya del Libro; Specialize in educational material; Also acts as importer, seller & distributor.
Subjects: Astronomy, Education, Language teaching methods
Distributor for Editora Nova Fronteira; Editora Pedagogica Universitario; Hachette Livre

Libreria Amalio M Fernandez, Editorial
25 de Mayo 477, Plta baja Ofc 11, 11000 Montevideo
Tel: (02) 9151782; (02) 852684 *Fax:* (02) 9151782
Key Personnel
Man Dir & Editorial: Carlos W Deamestoy Perez
Sales: Jorge M Garcia
Founded: 1951
Subjects: Law, Social Sciences, Sociology
ISBN Prefix(es): 84-8293

La Flor del Itapebi+
Patria 746, 11300 Montevideo
Tel: (02) 7115847 *Fax:* (02) 4090191
Key Personnel
Contact: Isabel Larghero
Founded: 1992
Subjects: Computer Science, Fiction, Mathematics
ISBN Prefix(es): 9974-592
Parent Company: Olmer SA

Fundacion de Cultura Universitaria+
25 de Mayo 568, Casilla de Correo 1155, 11000 Montevideo
Tel: (02) 9161152; (02) 959038 *Fax:* (02) 952549
E-mail: fcuedit@adinet.com.uy
Key Personnel
Man Dir: Carlos (Fallecido) Fuques
Administrator: Jorge Mahy
Founded: 1968
Subjects: Accounting, Criminology, Economics, Finance, Government, Political Science, History, Law, Regional Interests, Romance, Social Sciences, Sociology
Branch Office(s)
Artigas N 1251, regional Norte-Salto

Hemisferio Sur Edicion Agropecuaria
Buenos Aires 335, 11000 Montevideo
Tel: (02) 964515 *Fax:* (02) 964520
ISBN Prefix(es): 9974-556

Linardi y Risso Libreria
Juan Carlos Gomez 1435, 11000 Montevideo
Tel: (02) 957129 *Fax:* (02) 957328; (02) 957431; (02) 957598
E-mail: lyrbooks@chasque.apc.org
Founded: 1944
Specialize in Latin American books.
Subjects: Government, Political Science, History, Literature, Literary Criticism, Essays
ISBN Prefix(es): 9974-559
Orders to: Linardi Y Risso, 4405 73 Ave, Suite 12-333, Miami, FL 33166-6400, United States

A Monteverde y Cia SA+
25 de Mayo 577, 11000 Montevideo
Tel: (02) 952012 *Fax:* (02) 952012
Key Personnel
Man Dir: Daniel Mussini
Sales Dir: Liliana Mussini
Founded: 1879
Subjects: Astronomy, Biological Sciences, Chemistry, Chemical Engineering, Earth Sciences, Geography, Geology, History, Literature, Literary Criticism, Essays, Mathematics, Music, Dance, Natural History, Philosophy, Physical Sciences, Physics
ISBN Prefix(es): 9974-34
Subsidiaries: Talleres Graficos; Impresos; Encuaderna; Cion
Bookshop(s): Palacio del Libro
Orders to: Trienta y Tres 1475, 11000 Montevideo *Tel:* (02) 952939

Mosca Hermanos
Av 18 de Julio 1578, 11200 Montevideo
SAN: 004-2757
Tel: (02) 489671 *Fax:* (02) 489671 *Cable:* Moscaher
Key Personnel
Man Dir: Gustavo Mosca
Sales Dir: Gonzalo Mosca
Founded: 1888
Subjects: Literature, Literary Criticism, Essays, Religion - Other
ISBN Prefix(es): 9974-555; 84-89275

Nordan-Comunidad+
Millan 4115, 12900 Montevideo
Tel: (02) 305 6265 *Fax:* (02) 308 1640
E-mail: nordan@chasque.net
Web Site: www.nordan.com.uy
Key Personnel
Editor: Prieto Ruben
Coordinator: Zaya Arremyr *E-mail:* admin@nordan.com.uy

Subjects: Agriculture, Alternative, Anthropology, Architecture & Interior Design, Communications, Developing Countries, Economics, Education, Environmental Studies, Foreign Countries, Government, Political Science, Health, Nutrition, Language Arts, Linguistics, Literature, Literary Criticism, Essays, Philosophy, Poetry, Psychology, Psychiatry, Radio, TV, Social Sciences, Sociology, Women's Studies
ISBN Prefix(es): 9974-42

Prensa Medica Latinoamericana+
Guayabo 1790 Apto 504, 11200 Montevideo
Mailing Address: Casilla de Correo 6022, Montevideo
Tel: (02) 4092933 *Fax:* (02) 4000916
E-mail: prensmed@adinet.com.uy
Founded: 1988
Subjects: Child Care & Development, Health, Nutrition, Medicine, Nursing, Dentistry, Psychology, Psychiatry
ISBN Prefix(es): 9974-568

Punto de Encuentro Ediciones
Andresito Guacarary 1836, 11200 Montevideo
Tel: (02) 405167
Key Personnel
Editorial: Marylin Dias Capo
Founded: 1989
Subjects: Art, Literature, Literary Criticism, Essays
ISBN Prefix(es): 9974-603

Luis A Retta Libros
Paysandu 1827, 11200 Montevideo
Mailing Address: PO Box 591042, Miami, FL 33159-1042, United States
Tel: (02) 400-0766 *Fax:* (02) 409-0174
E-mail: rettalib@chasque.apc.org
Founded: 1975
Subjects: Anthropology, History, Literature, Literary Criticism, Essays, Poetry, Women's Studies
ISBN Prefix(es): 9974-557

Rosebud Ediciones+
Luis B Cavia 2805, Apto 801, 11300 Montevideo
Tel: (02) 771773 *Fax:* (02) 771773
Key Personnel
Contact: Jacqueline Listur
Founded: 1993
Subjects: Biography, Ethnicity, Fiction, History, Humor, Nonfiction (General), Poetry, Self-Help
ISBN Prefix(es): 9974-638

Ediciones Sol del Sur+
Gral Prim 3145, 11600 Montevideo
Tel: (02) 621627
Key Personnel
Marketing Dir: Daniel Gonzalez Moras
Founded: 1968
Specializes in Poetry & Essay Writing.
Subjects: History, Literature, Literary Criticism, Essays, Regional Interests
Showroom(s): Barreiro y Ramos, SA, Juan Carlos Gomez, 1430 Montevideo
Bookshop(s): Linardi y Risso, Juan Carlos Gomez 1435
Orders to: Retta Libros, Paysandu 1827, Montevideo *Fax:* (02) 4090174

Ediciones Trilce+
Durazno 1888, 11200 Montevideo
SAN: 002-0230
Tel: (02) 427722; (02) 427662 *Fax:* (02) 427662
E-mail: trilce@adinet.com.uy
Key Personnel
Dir: Pablo Harari
Founded: 1985
Subjects: Developing Countries, Fiction, Government, Political Science, History, Literature, Literary Criticism, Essays, Psychology, Psychiatry, Social Sciences, Sociology, Women's Studies
ISBN Prefix(es): 9974-32; 84-89269

La Urpila Editores
Rbla Rep. Argentina 1225, 11100 Montevideo
Tel: (02) 9085347
Key Personnel
Editor & Writer: Prof Norma Suiffet
Founded: 1979
Subjects: Literature, Literary Criticism, Essays, Poetry
ISBN Prefix(es): 9974-566
Parent Company: Casa del Poeta Latinoamericano

Editia Uruguay+
Bartolome Mitre 1377, 11000 Montevideo
Tel: (02) 9159633; (02) 9159759 *Fax:* (02) 9164419
E-mail: libros@editia.com
Key Personnel
Contact: Ernesto Sanjines
Founded: 1970
Specialize in computer science & technical books; Also acts as Distributor & Wholesaler.
Subjects: Computer Science
ISBN Prefix(es): 9974-621
Distributed by Diana (Mexico, USA, Central America & Colombia)
Distributor for Diana; Editores Mexicanos Unidos (Uruguay, Paraguay & Bolivia); GYR (Uruguay); Marcombo; Prentice Hall

Vinten Editor+
Hocquart 1771, 11800 Montevideo
Tel: (02) 2090223 *Fax:* (02) 290223
E-mail: dayraq@chasque.apc.org
Key Personnel
Contact: Dayman Cabrera
Founded: 1976
Subjects: Art, Economics, Education, Literature, Literary Criticism, Essays, Nonfiction (General), Poetry, Social Sciences, Sociology
ISBN Prefix(es): 9974-570

Uzbekistan

General Information

Capital: Tashkent
Language: Uzbek
Religion: Predominantly Islamic (mostly Sunni Muslim)
Population: 21.6 million
Bank Hours: Generally open for short hours between 0930-1230 Monday-Friday
Shop Hours: Generally 0900-1800 Monday-Friday; often open weekends
Currency: 100 kopeks = 1 rubl

Izdatelstvo Literatury i isskustva
ul Navoi 30, 700129 Taskent
Tel: (0371) 445172
Key Personnel
Dir: Sh Z Usmanhodjayev
Editor-in-Chief: H T Turabekov
Founded: 1926
Subjects: Literature, Literary Criticism, Essays
ISBN Prefix(es): 5-638

Izdatelstvo Uzbekistan+
ul Navoi 30, 700129 Taskent
Key Personnel
Dir: Shomukhitdin Sh Mansurov
Chief Editor: Zufar A Juraev
Founded: 1924
Uzbek Publishing House.
Subjects: Art, Economics, Government, Political Science, History, Law
ISBN Prefix(es): 5-640
Associate Companies: Matbaa Uzbek-Turkey JV Rastr Uzbek-Britain JV

Venezuela

General Information

Capital: Caracas
Language: Spanish
Religion: Predominantly Roman Catholic
Population: 20.7 million
Bank Hours: 0830-1130, 1400-1630 Monday-Friday
Shop Hours: 0900-1300, 1500-1900 Monday-Saturday
Currency: 100 centimos = 1 bolivar
Export/Import Information: Member of the Latin American Free Trade Association.
Copyright: UCC, Berne (see Copyright Conventions, pg xi)

Academia Nacional de la Historia
Av Universidad, Bolsa a San Francisco, Palacio de las Academias, Caracas 1010-A
Tel: (02) 4817547; (02) 4839435; (02) 486720 *Fax:* (02) 4817547
Telex: 27252
ISBN Prefix(es): 980-222

Alfadil Ediciones+
Calle Los Mangos, Edif Grupo Alfa, Piso 1, Las Delicias Sabana Grande, Apdo 50304, Caracas 1050-A
Mailing Address: Las Delicias Sabana Grande, Apdo 50304, Caracas
Tel: (02) 762-3036; (02) 761-3576; (02) 715-676 *Fax:* (02) 7620210
E-mail: alfagrupo@compuserve.com
Key Personnel
Contact: Yolanda Segnini; Leonardo Milla
Founded: 1978
Subjects: Astrology, Occult, Economics, Fiction, Geography, Geology, History, Journalism, Literature, Literary Criticism, Essays, Music, Dance, Nonfiction (General), Philosophy, Poetry, Self-Help, Social Sciences, Sociology
ISBN Prefix(es): 980-6005; 980-354
Parent Company: Alfa, Grupo Editorial
Associate Companies: Distribuidora de Ediciones Noray, CA
Subsidiaries: Libreria Ludens
Bookshop(s): Ludens, SRL, Torre Polar, Local F, Plaza Venezuela, Caracas

Armitano Editores CA+
Cuarta Transversal de Boleita Sur, Edificio Centro Industrial Piso 1, Apdo 50853, Caracas 1070
Tel: (02) 2342565; (02) 2342568; (02) 2340865 *Fax:* (02) 2341647
E-mail: armiedit@telcel.net.ve
Web Site: www.armitano.com *Cable:* ARMITPRESS CARACAS VENEZUELA
Key Personnel
Man Dir: E Armitano
Sales Dir: P Salazar
Founded: 1957
Member of Graphic Arts Association of Venezuela.
Subjects: Anthropology, Architecture & Interior Design, Art, Environmental Studies, History
ISBN Prefix(es): 980-216
Number of titles published annually: 12 Print
Total Titles: 350 Print

VENEZUELA

Editorial Ateneo de Caracas
Edificio Ateneo de Caracas, Piso 5, Apdo 662, Carmelitas, Caracas 1010-A
SAN: 000-4197
Tel: (02) 5734622 (ext 33); (02) 5754475 (orders); (02) 5734400; (02) 5734600 *Fax:* (02) 5754475
Key Personnel
President: Maria Teresa Castillo
Editorial Dir, Sales, Production: Antonio Polo
Founded: 1978
Subjects: Art, Government, Political Science, History, Literature, Literary Criticism, Essays, Poetry, Psychology, Psychiatry, Science (General)
ISBN Prefix(es): 980-255; 84-8350
Bookshop(s): Libreria Ateneo de Caracas, Edificio Ateneo de Caracas 5 piso, Plaza Morelos Apdo 662, Caracas 1010

Monte Avila Editores Latinoamericana CA+
Av Eugenio Mendoza con lera tansversal, Qta Cristina, La Castellana Apdo 70712, Caracas 1070
Tel: (02) 2659871 *Fax:* (02) 2667226; (02) 2659871
E-mail: alemar@telcel.net.ve
Telex: 24220 Conac
Key Personnel
Man Dir & President: Alexis Marquez Rodrigez
Editorial, Rights & Permissions: Wilfredo Machado
Sales: Glenda Sanchez
Production: Mirna Ferrer
Founded: 1968
Tenemos Una Distribuidora En New York Lectorum Publications Inc, 111 Eighth Ave, Suite 804, New York, NY: Gerente Teresa Mlawer; Libros Sin Fronteras, PO Box 2085, Olympia, WA 98507-2085: Contact Michael Shapiro.
Subjects: Anthropology, Art, Economics, Education, Fiction, Geography, Geology, Government, Political Science, History, Literature, Literary Criticism, Essays, Music, Dance, Philosophy, Poetry, Psychology, Psychiatry, Regional Interests, Science (General), Social Sciences, Sociology
ISBN Prefix(es): 980-01
Distributed by Anahuac (Madrid)
Distributor for Editorial Anthropos Y Visor Libros De Espana; Editorial Montesinos; En Venezuela; Monte Avila Distribuye

Biblioteca Ayacucho
Av Urdaneta, Animas a Pl Espana, Centro Financiero Latino Piso 12, Ofc 1, 2, 3, Apdo 14413/2122 Caracas 1010-A
Tel: (02) 5644402; (02) 5643583 *Fax:* (02) 5634223
Telex: 26217 B1A4A *Cable:* BIAYACUCHO
Key Personnel
President of Editorial Commission, Editorial, Rights & Permissions: Dr Jose Ramon Medina
Editorial Dir: Oswaldo Teejo
Sales, Publicity: Miriam Valdez
Founded: 1975
Subjects: Anthropology, Architecture & Interior Design, Art, Developing Countries, Drama, Theater, Fiction, History, Literature, Literary Criticism, Essays, Philosophy, Photography, Poetry
ISBN Prefix(es): 980-276

Editorial Biosfera CA+
Ave Chama, Qta Coral, PB de Colinas de Bello Monte, Apdo 50634, Caracas 1050
Tel: (02) 7528892; (02) 7519119 *Fax:* (02) 7519320
Key Personnel
Man Dir, Editorial: Dr Serafin Mazparrote
Founded: 1979

Subjects: Art, Biological Sciences, Language Arts, Linguistics, Mathematics, Nonfiction (General), Science (General)
ISBN Prefix(es): 980-210
Subsidiaries: Litho-Mundo SA
Bookshop(s): Ediciones Amanecer (Libreria) Centro Polo, Av Principal, Colinas de Bello Monte

Sociedad Fondo Editorial Cenamec
Av Arichuna, Cruce con Calle Cumaco, Edif Sociedad Venezolana de Ciencias Naturales, Caracas 1080-A
Tel: (02) 229133; (02) 229511 *Fax:* (02) 225077
Key Personnel
President: Dr Enrique Planchart
Vice President: Prof Tania Calderin
Founded: 1974
Subjects: Biological Sciences, Chemistry, Chemical Engineering, Mathematics, Physics
ISBN Prefix(es): 980-218

Colegial Bolivariana CA
Ave Diego Cisneros, principal, Los Ruices, Edif Co-Bo, Piso 1, Apdo 70324, Caracas 1071-A
Tel: (02) 2391055; (02) 2391244 *Fax:* (02) 2396502 *Cable:* COLEGIAL
Key Personnel
Man Dir: Hans L Schnell
Founded: 1961
ISBN Prefix(es): 980-262
Branch Office(s)
Puente Yanes A Tracabordo, Edificio BEL-VEL, Planta Baja, Caracas 1011
Ave Constitucion, Local No 28, Pto La Cruz 6023 Edo Anzoategui
Calle 97 (Bolivar) No 6-48, Apdo de Correos 834, Maracaibo 4001-A Edo Zulia

Ediciones Ekare+
Final Av Luis Roche, Edif Banco del Libro, Altamira Sur, Apdo 68284, Caracas 1062
SAN: 001-6780
Tel: (02) 2630080; (02) 2636170; (02) 2630091 *Fax:* (02) 2633291
Key Personnel
President: Carmen Diana Dearden
Edit Dir & Foreign Rights: Maria Francisca Majobre
Marketing & Sales Manager: Maria Cristina Serrano
Founded: 1978
Specialize in children's picture books. Publish in Spanish only.
Subjects: Fiction
ISBN Prefix(es): 980-257; 84-8351
Subsidiaries: Ekare Sur; Ekare Espana

Fundacion Centro Gumilla
Edif Centro Valores Local 2 Esq de Luneta, Apto 4838, Caracas 1010A
Tel: (02) 5649803; (02) 5644757 *Fax:* (02) 5647557
Subjects: Economics, Education, Government, Political Science, Labor, Industrial Relations, Religion - Catholic, Social Sciences, Sociology, Theology
ISBN Prefix(es): 980-250

Fundacion Servicio para el Agricultor
Av Francisco de Miranda, Edif Cavendes, Piso 8 Ofc 806, Los Palos Grandes, Apdo 2224, Caracas 1062
Tel: (02) 2843089; (02) 2841134; (02) 2852016 *Fax:* (02) 2853946
E-mail: izamora@etheron.net
Key Personnel
President: Luis Marcano Marcano Gonzalez
Founded: 1952
Subjects: Agriculture
ISBN Prefix(es): 980-260

Shipping Address: Fusagri Cerretera Via La Segundera, Km 3, Apdo 162, Cagua, Edo Aragua
Orders to: Fusagri Estacion Experimental de Cagua, Apdo 162, Cagua Estado Aragua

Grijalbo SA
2da Av de Campo Claro, Qta Herminia, Caracas 1071
Tel: (02) 2381542; (02) 2381732 *Fax:* (02) 2390308
Key Personnel
Man Dir: Manuel Morales
Founded: 1964
ISBN Prefix(es): 980-293
Parent Company: Ediciones Grijalbo SA, Spain

Editorial Kapelusz Venezolana SA
Ave Cajigal No 29, QTa K, San Bernadino, Apdo 14234, Caracas 1011-A
Tel: (02) 517601; (02) 526281
Telex: 24039 Ekave VC *Cable:* KAPELUSZ
Key Personnel
Man Dir: Horacio Perotti Beraldo
Founded: 1963
ISBN Prefix(es): 980-285
Parent Company: Editorial Kapelusz SA, Argentina

Editorial Labor de Venezuela SA
Ave Andres Bello, Edificio Garten, Caracas
Tel: (02) 7811398; (02) 7815819
Key Personnel
Man Dir: Jaime Salgado Palacio

McGraw-Hill/Interamericana de Venezuela CA
2da Calle de Bello Monte, entre, Ave Casanova y blvd de Sabana Grande, Local G-2, Apdo 50785, Caracas 1050
Tel: (02) 2383494; (02) 7618181; (02) 7616992 *Fax:* (02) 2382374; (02) 7616993
E-mail: mikan@attmail.com
Telex: 29976
Key Personnel
Man Dir, Bogata: Carlos Marquez
General Manager: Mauricio Mikan
Controller-Business Manager: Rafael Ramos
College Division Manager: Javier Lindarte
Market Served: Venezuela.
ISBN Prefix(es): 980-6168
Parent Company: McGraw-Hill Inc, 1221 Avenue of the Americas, New York, NY 10020, United States
Associate Companies: Libros McGraw-Hill de Mexico SA de CV, Bogota, Colombia

Ministerio de Educacion Biblioteca Central
Esq de Salas, Edif Ministerio, Torre de Servicio, Edif sede, Carmelitas, Caracas 1010
Tel: (02) 5628970 (ext 8149); (02) 5621767; (02) 5640025 *Fax:* (02) 5641224
Telex: 21943
Key Personnel
Dir: Lozada Bernarda
ISBN Prefix(es): 980-02

Editorial Nueva Sociedad+
Pi la Castellana, Edificio IASA, Piso 6, Ofc 606, 602. La Castellana, Apdo 61712, Caracas 1060-A
Tel: (02) 2659975; (02) 2650593; (02) 2651265 *Fax:* (02) 313397
E-mail: nuso@nuevasoc.org.ve
Web Site: nuevasoc.org.ve
Telex: 24163
Key Personnel
Dir: Dietmar Dirmoser *E-mail:* dirmoser@nuevasor.org.ve
Man Editor: Sergio Chejfec *E-mail:* chejfec@nuevasoc.org.ve
Books Coordinator: Helena Gonzalez *E-mail:* helena@nuevasoc.org.ve

PUBLISHERS

VIET NAM

Sales, Promotion: Ester de Rodriguez
 E-mail: ester@nuevasoc.org.ve
Founded: 1972
Subjects: Developing Countries, Economics, Environmental Studies, Ethnicity, Government, Political Science, Social Sciences, Sociology, Technology, Women's Studies
ISBN Prefix(es): 980-6110; 980-317

OCEI (Oficina Central de Estadistica e Informatica)
Av Boyaca, Edif Fundacion La Salle, Mariperez, Apdo 4593, San Martin, Caracas 101
Tel: (02) 7821133; (02) 7821167; (02) 7825756; (02) 7821156 *Fax:* (02) 7930428
Telex: 21241
Key Personnel
Chief: Pedro Guillermo Paul Bello
General Dir: Miguel Bolivar Chollett
Dir, Social Communication: Ana Maria Rodriguez
Founded: 1978
Specialize in the production of national statistics & policy information.
ISBN Prefix(es): 980-280
Warehouse: O C E 1, Sotano 2

Oficina Central de Estadistics e Informatica, see OCEI (Oficina Central de Estadistica e Informatica)

Editorial Planeta Venezolana
Calle Madrid, entre Trinidad y New York, Qta Toscanella, Las Mercedes Apdo 51285, Las Mercedes, Caracas 1050
Tel: (02) 913982; (02) 924872 *Fax:* (02) 913792
Telex: 29944
ISBN Prefix(es): 980-271

Editorial Pomaire Venezuela SA
Ave Luis Roche, Edif Santa Clara, PB Altamira Sur, Apdo 51.960, Caracas 1062
Tel: (02) 2622122; (02) 2621253 *Fax:* (02) 2616962
Key Personnel
Man Dir: Jose Luis Garcia Froiz
ISBN Prefix(es): 980-290
Parent Company: Editorial Pomaire SA, Spain

Editorial Reverte Venezolana SA
Peligro a Pele el Ojo, Edif Torre Carabobo, PB Local 2, La Candelaria, Apdo 14520, Caracas 1010
Tel: (02) 5726670; (02) 5724468 *Fax:* (02) 5722598; (02) 5724468; (02) 5726670
ISBN Prefix(es): 980-294
Associate Companies: Editorial Reverte SA, Spain

Teduca, Tecnicas Educativas, CA
Av Romulo Gallegos, Edif Zulia, Sector Monte Cristo Piso 1, Boleita Norte, Apdo 1071, Caracas 1062
Tel: (02) 2355878; (02) 2354395; (02) 2356265 *Fax:* (02) 2397952
Telex: 27876 Cpbth Vc
Key Personnel
Chairman: Eduardo Robles Piquer
General Manager: Enrique de Polanco Soutullo
Founded: 1977
Subjects: Education
ISBN Prefix(es): 980-275
Associate Companies: Santillana SA de Ediciones, Spain
Orders to: Urbanizacion Industrial Cloris, Ave 2, Local 84-03 Ave Norte, Guarenas, Edo, Miranda

Ediciones Tripode
Calle Terepaima, Edif Tripode, Piso 3, El Marquez, Apdo 75003, Caracas 1070-A

Tel: (02) 2378860; (02) 2378972 *Fax:* (02) 2377697
Key Personnel
Dir: Ing Mario Gonzalez Casado
Consultant: Padre Cesareo Gil
Manager: Coralia Salcedo R
Founded: 1972
Subjects: Religion - Catholic, Religion - Other
ISBN Prefix(es): 980-208

Universidad de los Andes, Consejo de Publicaciones
Ave Andres Bello, Antiguo Central Azucarero (Cala), Via la Parroquia, Merida, Estado Merida
Tel: (074) 402409; (074) 402408 *Fax:* (074) 711955
Key Personnel
Man Dir: Dr Eduardo Zuleto
Sales, Production: Macario Molina
Publicity: Ana Allegue de Pietri
Rights & Permissions: Asunta Briceno
Founded: 1977
Subjects: Medicine, Nursing, Dentistry, Regional Interests, Science (General), Social Sciences, Sociology, Technology
ISBN Prefix(es): 980-221

Vadell Hermanos Editores CA+
Esquinas de Peligro a Pele el Ojo, Edif Golden, sotano 1, La Candelaria, Caracas
Tel: (02) 5723108; (02) 5725243 *Fax:* (02) 5725243
Key Personnel
General Manager: Dr Manuel M Vadell Graterol
Founded: 1973
Member of Association Venezuelan Editors.
Subjects: Education, Science (General)
ISBN Prefix(es): 980-212

Ediciones Vega SRL
Av Universitaria Edif Odeon, PB Los Chaguaramos, Apdo 51662, Caracas 1010-A
Tel: (02) 6622092; (02) 6621397 *Cable:* EDIVEGA
Key Personnel
Man Dir: Fernando Vega Alonso
Founded: 1965
ISBN Prefix(es): 980-6044
Bookshop(s): Libreria Tecnica Vega

Viet Nam

General Information

Capital: Hanoi
Language: Vietnamese
Religion: Predominantly Buddhist
Population: 69 million
Currency: 100 xu = 1 new dong
Export/Import Information: None available at present.
Copyright: Florence (see Copyright Conventions, pg xi)

Giao Duc Publishing House
81, Tran Hung Dao St, Hanoi
Tel: (04) 262011
Key Personnel
Dir: Nguyen Si Ty
Founded: 1957
Subjects: Education

Lao Dong (Labor) Publishing House
31, Hai Ba Trung St, Hanoi
Tel: (04) 253972

Pho Thong (Popularization) Publishing House
Hanoi

Popular Army Publishing House
Hanoi
Subjects: Military Science

Science & Technics Publishing House (Nha Xuat Ban Khoa Hoc Va Ky Thuat)+
70 Tran Hung Dao St, Hanoi 84-4
Tel: (04) 9 424 786; (04) 9 423 172 *Fax:* (04) 8 220 658
E-mail: nxbkhkt@hn.vnn.vn
Web Site: www.nxbkhkt.com.vn
Key Personnel
Dir: Prof To Dang Hai, PhD *E-mail:* todanghai@hn.vnn.vn
Founded: 1960
Member of Vietnam Publishers Association.
Subjects: Accounting, Advertising, Aeronautics, Aviation, Agriculture, Animals, Pets, Archaeology, Architecture & Interior Design, Astronomy, Automotive, Behavioral Sciences, Biological Sciences, Business, Career Development, Chemistry, Chemical Engineering, Civil Engineering, Communications, Computer Science, Crafts, Games, Hobbies, Earth Sciences, Economics, Education, Electronics, Electrical Engineering, Energy, Engineering (General), English as a Second Language, Environmental Studies, Finance, Gardening, Plants, Geography, Geology, Health, Nutrition, How-to, Management, Maritime, Marketing, Mathematics, Mechanical Engineering, Medicine, Nursing, Dentistry, Microcomputers, Natural History, Physical Sciences, Physics, Radio, TV, Science (General), Securities, Technology, Transportation, Veterinary Science
Number of titles published annually: 280 Print
Total Titles: 10,000 Print
Branch Office(s)
28 Dong Khoi St, Q 1 Ho Chi Minh City 84-8
 Tel: (08) 8 225 062 *E-mail:* chinhanhkhkt@hcm.fpt.vn
Bookshop(s): 31-33 Yen Bai St, Danang City
 Tel: (04) 8 220 686; 40 Ngo Quyen St, Hanoi
 Tel: (04) 9 349 147; 28 Dong Khoi St, Q1, Ho Chi Minh City *Tel:* (08) 8 225 062

Su Hoc (Historical) Publishing House
Hanoi
Subjects: Government, Political Science, Philosophy

Su That (Truth) Publishing House
24 Quang Trung St, Hanoi
Tel: (04) 252008
Founded: 1945
(Under the Central Committee of the Communist Party of Viet Nam).
Subjects: Government, Political Science, Philosophy, Social Sciences, Sociology

Trung-Tam San Xuat Hoc-Lieu
Tran-binh-Trong 240, Ho Chi Minh City 5

Y Hoc Publishing House
4 Le Thanh Ton, Hanoi
Tel: (04) 253274
Subjects: Medicine, Nursing, Dentistry

Yugoslavia

General Information

Capital: Belgrade
Language: Serbo-Croatian in most of the country; Slovene in Slovenia, Macedonian in Macedonia.
Religion: Eastern Orthodox, Roman Catholic, Islamic
Population: 10.4 million
Bank Hours: 0800-1500 Monday-Friday
Shop Hours: 0800-2000 Monday-Friday; 0800-1500 Saturday. Some open weekdays continuously and early Sunday morning
Currency: 100 para = 1 new Yugoslav dinar
Export/Import Information: No tariffs on books except on publications of Yugoslav publishers printed abroad. Advertising catalogs for such books dutied, otherwise free; non-Yugoslavian language advertising materials dutied. Special equalization tax, customs clearance charge and import surcharge when goods are subject to duty. No import licenses required. Exchange controls. The basic commercial unit is known as an enterprise but there are no state monopolies.
Copyright: UCC, Berne (see Copyright Conventions, pg xi)

AGAPE+
Cara Dusana 4, 21000 Novi Sad
Tel: (021) 469-474 *Fax:* (021) 469-382
E-mail: agape@eunet.yu
Web Site: www.agape.hu
Key Personnel
President & International Rights: Karoly Harmath
 E-mail: harmath@eunet.yu
Founded: 1977
Member of ELCE; Association of Hungarian Catholic Publishers; International Association of Franciscan Publishers, UCIP.
Subjects: Religion - Catholic, Theology
ISBN Prefix(es): 86-463
Number of titles published annually: 50 Print
Parent Company: AGAPE Kft, Hu-Szeged, 6725 Szeged, Matyas Ter

Alfa-Narodna Knjiga
Safarikova 11, PO Box 247, 11000 Belgrade
Tel: (011) 3221-484; (011) 3227-426; (011) 3223-910 *Fax:* (011) 3227-946
E-mail: alfankkl@eunet.yu
Web Site: www.narodnaknjiga.co.yu
Key Personnel
Editor-in-Chief: Milicko Mijovic
Subjects: Art, Astrology, Occult, Child Care & Development, Cookery, Criminology, Fiction, Government, Political Science, Health, Nutrition, History, How-to, Journalism, Language Arts, Linguistics, Literature, Literary Criticism, Essays, Medicine, Nursing, Dentistry, Mysteries, Nonfiction (General), Philosophy, Poetry, Psychology, Psychiatry, Religion - Other, Science (General), Self-Help
ISBN Prefix(es): 86-331
Number of titles published annually: 300 Print
Total Titles: 1,000 Print
Foreign Rep(s): Tea Jovanovic (Worldwide)
Foreign Rights: Tea Jovanovic (World)

Association of Yugoslav Publishers & Booksellers
Kneza Milosa 25/1, 11000 Belgrade
Mailing Address: PO Box 570, 11000 Belgrade
Tel: (011) 642533; (011) 646841 *Fax:* (011) 646339
Key Personnel
General Dir: Mr Ognjen Lakecevic
 E-mail: ognjenl@eunet.yu
Publisher: Mrs Mirjana Popovic

Founded: 1954
Organizer of the International Book Fair in Belgrade.
Member of IPA, Geneve.
ISBN Prefix(es): 86-7115

Beogradski Izdavacko-Graficki Zavod
Bulevar Vojvode Misica 17, 11000 Belgrade
Tel: (011) 650-399; (011) 651-666 *Fax:* (011) 651-841
Telex: 11855 Yu Bigz *Cable:* BEOGRAF
Key Personnel
Man Dir: Gojko Zecar
Editorial Dir, Permissions: Vidosav Stevanovic
Founded: 1831
Subjects: Philosophy, Poetry, Social Sciences, Sociology
ISBN Prefix(es): 86-13
Imprints: BIGZ
Book Club(s): Book Lovers' Club

BIGZ, *imprint of* Beogradski Izdavacko-Graficki Zavod

Borba
Trg Nikole Pasica 7, 11000 Belgrade
Tel: (011) 3243-437; (011) 3234-531; (011) 3239-038 *Fax:* (011) 3244-913
Key Personnel
Dir: Novica Dukic
ISBN Prefix(es): 86-80105

Decje Novine, see Niro Decje Novine

Forum
Vojvode Misica 1, 21000 Novi Sad
Tel: (021) 57216 *Fax:* (021) 57216
Telex: yu-14199
Key Personnel
Dir: Kalman Petkovics
Subjects: Fiction, Government, Political Science
ISBN Prefix(es): 86-323

Gradevinska Knjiga
Trg Nikole Pasica 8/11, 11000 Belgrade
Tel: (011) 3233-565; (011) 3244-345; (011) 3244-359 *Fax:* (011) 3233-565
Key Personnel
Man Dir: Milan Visnic
Editor & Chief: Milica Dodic
Commercial Manager: Jovo Karadzic
Founded: 1948
Subjects: Engineering (General)
ISBN Prefix(es): 86-395
Bookshop(s): Narodnog fronta 14, Belgrade; Student, 27 marta 78, Belgrade

Izdavacka preduzece Gradina+
Ulica pobede 38/3, 18000 Nis
Tel: (018) 25-864 *Fax:* (018) 25-456
Key Personnel
Dir: Gordana Jovanovic
Subjects: Art, Science (General)
ISBN Prefix(es): 86-7129
Bookshop(s): Ulica pobede 38/3, 18000 Nis; ul pobede 113Y, Nis; Veljka Vlahovica 2, Nis; Dimitrija Tucovica bb, Nis

Jugoslavijapublik+
Knez Mihailova 10, 11000 Belgrade
Tel: (011) 633266 *Fax:* (011) 622858; (011) 622669
Telex: 11125
Key Personnel
General Manager: Slobodan Zaric
Founded: 1962
Subjects: History, Philosophy, Religion - Other
ISBN Prefix(es): 86-7121

Jugoslovenska Revija
Karatordeva 41, 11000 Belgrade
Tel: (011) 625-829
Telex: 12954 Yurew
Key Personnel
Dir: Rajko Bobot
Permissions: Milovan Ignjatovic
Subjects: Art, Travel
ISBN Prefix(es): 86-7413

Tehnicka Knjiga (Technical Book)+
pf 307 Vojvode Stepe 89, 11000 Belgrade Serbia
Tel: (011) 468596 *Fax:* (011) 473442
E-mail: tkmjiga@eumet.yu
Key Personnel
Editor-in-Chief: Mrdjenovic Dragi
Man Dir: Grbovic Radivoje
Sales Manager: Cosovic Llida
Subjects: Computer Science, Electronics, Electrical Engineering, Engineering (General), How-to, Science (General)
ISBN Prefix(es): 86-325

Kultura
XIV Vojvojanaske udarne brigade 4-6, 21470, 21000 Backi Petrovac
Tel: (021) 780-156 *Fax:* (021) 780-291 *Cable:* Obzor Novi Sad
Key Personnel
Dir: Anna Makanova
ISBN Prefix(es): 86-7103
Bookshop(s): Backi Petrovac Bodvis Jan

Libertatea
Zarka Zrenjanina 7, 26000 Pancevo
Tel: (013) 33-51; (013) 46-447 *Fax:* (013) 46-447 *Cable:* Libertatea Pancevo
Key Personnel
Dir: Todor Gilezan
ISBN Prefix(es): 86-7001

Minerva
Trg 29 novembra 3, 24000 Subotica
Tel: (024) 28834; (024) 25712 *Fax:* (024) 23-208 *Cable:* Minerva Subotica
Key Personnel
Dir: Josip Prcic
Subjects: Science (General)
ISBN Prefix(es): 86-7099
Bookshop(s): YU-24000 Subotica: ul oktobra 4; Maksima Gorkog 20; Put M Pijade 25

Narodna Biblioteka Srbije (National Library of Serbia)
ul Skerliceva 1, 11000 Belgrade
Tel: (011) 431-083; (011) 451-242
Telex: NBS 12208
Key Personnel
Dir: Svetislav Duric
Subjects: History
ISBN Prefix(es): 86-7035

Naucna Knjiga+
Uzun Mirkova 5/1, Postanski fah 690, 11000 Belgrade
Tel: (011) 637230; (011) 186585; (011) 623922; (011) 621342 *Fax:* (011) 638070 *Cable:* NAUCNA KNJIGA
Key Personnel
Man Dir: Dr Blazo Perovic
Founded: 1947
Subjects: Education, Engineering (General), Medicine, Nursing, Dentistry, Science (General)
ISBN Prefix(es): 86-23; 86-321
Bookshop(s): Znanje, Gracanicka br 16, Belgrade; Naucna Knjiga, Knez Mihailova gr 19 & 40, Belgrade; Naucna knjiga, Jug Bogdanova 68, Prokuplje

PUBLISHERS

YUGOSLAVIA

Nio Pobjeda - Oour Izdavacko-Publicisticka Djelatnost
Bulevar revolucije 11, 81000 Podgorica
Tel: (081) 45955; (081) 44433; (081) 44474
Fax: (081) 52803
Telex: 61243 YU pob
Key Personnel
Dir: Ljubo Buric
Publishing Dir: Mileta Radovanovic
Editor: Branko Banjevic; Djerdj Djokaj; Ratko Vujosevic; Vojislav Minic
Sales, Trade Dir: Miodrag Raonic
Founded: 1962
Subjects: Science (General)
ISBN Prefix(es): 86-309
Branch Office(s)
Safarikova 15, YU-21000 Novi Sad *Tel:* (021) 51086
Miladin Popovica bb, YU-38000 Pristina *Tel:* (038) 24062
Karadordev trg 7, YU-11080 Zemun *Tel:* (011) 600652

Niro Decje Novine
pf 24, Tihomira Matijevica 4, 32300 Gornji Milanovac
Tel: (032) 712246; (032) 712247; (032) 714970; (032) 711256; (032) 711248; (011) 3221476; (011) 342010 *Fax:* (032) 711248
Telex: 13731 GM, 12206 BGB
Subjects: Education
ISBN Prefix(es): 86-367

Nolit Publishing House+
Terazije 27/ll, Postanski fah 369, 11000 Belgrade
Tel: (011) 3245017; (011) 3228872 *Fax:* (011) 3221365; (011) 627285 *Cable:* NOLIT BGD
Key Personnel
Man Dir: Radivoje Nesie
Editorial: Radivoje Mikic
Dir: Branko Nikezic
Founded: 1928
Subjects: Agriculture, Art, Fiction, History, Philosophy, Psychology, Psychiatry, Social Sciences, Sociology
ISBN Prefix(es): 86-19

Obod
Njegoseva 3, 81250 Cetinje
Tel: (086) 21953; (086) 21331 *Fax:* (086) 21953; (086) 21649; (086) 33951 *Cable:* OBOD CETINJE
Key Personnel
Dir: Slobodan Koljevic
Subjects: Fiction
ISBN Prefix(es): 86-305
Branch Office(s)
Dobracina 32, Belgrade
Bookshop(s): Njegoseva 11, Belgrade

Izdavacka Organizacija Rad
Mose Pijade 12, 11000 Belgrade
Tel: (011) 3239-758; (011) 3239-998 *Fax:* (011) 3230-923
Key Personnel
Man Dir: Bravislav Milosevic
Sales Dir: Milovan Vlahovic
21 Bookshops throughout Yugoslavia.
Subjects: Biography, Economics, Engineering (General), Government, Political Science, Philosophy, Poetry, Social Sciences, Sociology
ISBN Prefix(es): 86-09
Bookshop(s): Papirus, Terazije 26, Belgrade; Frankopanska 5, Zagreb

Panorama NIJP/ID Grigorije Bozovic
Dom Stampe bb, 38000 Pristina
Tel: (038) 24-619; (038) 24-618 *Fax:* (038) 29637 *Cable:* Jedinstvo Pristina
Key Personnel
Dir: Milan Seslija

Subjects: Government, Political Science, History, Medicine, Nursing, Dentistry, Philosophy, Social Sciences, Sociology
ISBN Prefix(es): 86-7019

Parenon-Preduzece za proizvodnju trgovinu iusluge, see Partenon MAM Sistem

Partenon MAM Sistem+
Formerly Parenon-Preduzece za proizvodnju trgovinu iusluge
Simina 9a/1, 11000 Belgrade
Tel: (011) 632535; (011) 625942; (011) 633465 *Fax:* (011) 632535; (011) 623980
E-mail: partenon@infosky.net
Key Personnel
Dir: Momcilo Mitrovic
Subjects: Agriculture, Fiction, Science (General), Linguistics
ISBN Prefix(es): 86-7157
Number of titles published annually: 30 Print

Izdavacko Preduzece Matice Srpske+
Trg Toze Markovica 2, pf 149, 21000 Novi Sad
Tel: (021) 420 199; (021) 420 837 *Fax:* (021) 27281
Key Personnel
Dir: Milorad Grujic *E-mail:* m.grujic@sezampro.yu
Editor: Ivan Negrisorac; Milica Micic Dimovski; Dragan Mojovic
Founded: 1826
Subjects: History, Human Relations, Literature, Literary Criticism, Essays
ISBN Prefix(es): 86-363
Bookshop(s): Zmaj Jovina 4, Novi Sad, Milenko Ranin *Tel:* 29-436; Matice srpske 1, Novi Sad, Davor Pekoric *Tel:* 26-182; Trg Toz Markovica 24, Novi Sad, Zdravko Gaseric *Tel:* 29-307

Privredni Pregled
Marsala Birjuzova 3-5, 11000 Belgrade
Tel: (011) 628477; (011) 620364 *Fax:* (011) 623375; (011) 3281912
Telex: 11509 Yu Pp *Cable:* Privredni Pregled Bgd
Key Personnel
Dir: Toma Markovic
ISBN Prefix(es): 86-315
Branch Office(s)
Orce Nikolova 79, Skopje
Mose Pijade, 21 Zagreb
Hala 'Tivoli', Ljubljana
Marsala Tita 86, Sarajevo

Prosveta
Dobracina 30, 11000 Belgrade
Tel: (011) 642722; (011) 625766; (011) 625760 *Fax:* (011) 627-465
Telex: 11609 Yu
Key Personnel
General Dir: Vidosav Stevanovic
Editor-in-Chief: Milisav Savic
Export Manager: Milutin Trifunovic
Rights & Permissions: Branka Simic
Founded: 1945
Subjects: Human Relations
ISBN Prefix(es): 86-07
Book Club(s): Prosveta

Radnicka Stampa
Trg Nikole Pasica 5, 11000 Belgrade
Tel: (011) 3230-927; (011) 3233-038
Telex: RSNIRO YU 72638 *Cable:* Radnicka stampa Belgrade
Key Personnel
Dir: Radoslav Roso
Sales Manager: Cedo Males
Subjects: Economics, Government, Political Science, Social Sciences, Sociology
ISBN Prefix(es): 86-7073

Republicki Zavod za Unapredivanje Vaspitanja i Obrazovanja
Kneza Milosa 101, 11000 Belgrade
Tel: (011) 659322
Key Personnel
Chief Executive: Milivoje Brajove
Editor-in-Chief: Krsto Lekovie
Sales Manager: Radmila Miranovie
Founded: 1973
Republic Institution for the Improvement of Education.
Subjects: Education
ISBN Prefix(es): 86-80871
Bookshop(s): Knjizara Zavoda, Kneza Milosa 101, 11000 Belgrade

Savez Inzenjera i Tehnicara Jugoslavije+
Kneza Milosa 9/ll, 11000 Belgrade
Tel: (011) 3243653; (011) 3243652 *Fax:* (011) 3243652
E-mail: internet@eunet.yu *Cable:* SITJ BEOGRAD
Key Personnel
President: Mihailo Milojevic, PhD
Vice President: Budimir Cetkovic, MSc; Radomir Simic, PhD
General Secretary: Milorad Terzic, PhD
Founded: 1919
Union of Engineers & Technicians of Yugoslavia.
Member of World Federation of Engineering Organizations; World Federation of Scientific Workers; Regional Council of Coordination of Central & East-European Engineering Organizations.
Subjects: Civil Engineering, Communications, Economics, Electronics, Electrical Engineering, Engineering (General), Mechanical Engineering, Science (General), Technology
ISBN Prefix(es): 86-80067

Savremena Administracija
Knez Mihailova 6/V-4 pf 479, 11000 Belgrade
Tel: (011) 623-287 *Fax:* (011) 667-277; (011) 623-776
Telex: 12233 Yu Sa
Key Personnel
Dir: Vojin Moraca
Founded: 1954
Subjects: Economics, Law
ISBN Prefix(es): 86-387

Sluzbeni List
pf 226 Jovana Ristica 1, 11000 Belgrade
Tel: (011) 651885 *Fax:* (011) 651482
Telex: 11756 Yu Slist
Key Personnel
Dir: Dusan Masovic
Subjects: Law
ISBN Prefix(es): 86-355
Bookshop(s): Prodavnica 1, Brankova 16, Belgrade, Croatia; Prodavnica 2, 9 Novembra 1a

Sportska Knjiga
Radnicka 24, Postfach 20148, 11030 Belgrade
Tel: (011) 3220226; (011) 3225361 *Cable:* Sportska Knjiga
Key Personnel
Dir: Dragoslav Bajic
Editor: Sava Bjelajac
Founded: 1949
Subjects: Sports, Athletics
ISBN Prefix(es): 86-7107

Srpska Knjizevna Zadruga
Srpskih vladara 19/I, Postfach 653, 11000 Belgrade
Tel: (011) 3233-545; (011) 3234-977 *Fax:* (011) 626-224
Founded: 1892
Subjects: History
ISBN Prefix(es): 86-379

YUGOSLAVIA

Svetovi (The Worlds)+
Arse Teodorovica 11 pf 33, Novi Sad 21000
Tel: (021) 28032; (021) 28036 *Fax:* (021) 28036; (021) 28032
E-mail: aum.mar@eunet.yu
Key Personnel
Dir: Jovan Zivlak
Founded: 1951
Subjects: Anthropology, Art, Fiction, Philosophy, Poetry
ISBN Prefix(es): 86-7047
Number of titles published annually: 40 Print
Total Titles: 2,000 Print
Bookshop(s): Pasiceva 32, Novi Sad *Tel:* (021) 23-071

Tehnika, see Savez Inzenjera i Tehnicara Jugoslavije

Turisticka Stampa+
Dure Dakovica 100, 11000 Belgrade
Tel: (011) 750740; (011) 767466 *Fax:* (011) 762236
Key Personnel
Man Dir & Editorial: Dragan Kankaras
Founded: 1953
Subjects: Art
ISBN Prefix(es): 86-7041

Vesti
Trg partizana 12, Postanski fah 105, 31000 Uzice
Tel: (031) 21263; (031) 42488; (031) 42203
Key Personnel
Dir: Mihajlo Rebic
ISBN Prefix(es): 86-7319

VINC, *imprint of* Vojnoizdavacki i novinski centar

Vojnoizdavacki i novinski centar+
Bircaninova 5, 11000 Belgrade
Tel: (011) 644188 *Fax:* (011) 644042
Key Personnel
President: Dr Nikola Popovic
Editor-in-Chief: Milisav Djordjevic
Editor, Foreign Writers' Edition: Novica Stevanovic
Founded: 1945
Subjects: Military Science
ISBN Prefix(es): 86-335; 86-80641
Imprints: VINC
Bookshop(s): Poslovni biro "Vojna Knjiga", Vase Carapica 22, 11000 Belgrade

Vuk Karadzic+
Kraljevica Marka 9, Postfach 762, 11000 Belgrade
Tel: (011) 628066; (011) 628043 *Fax:* (011) 623150; (011) 634232 *Cable:* VUK KARADZIC BELGRADE
Key Personnel
Man Dir: Ancic Vojin
Founded: 1956
Subjects: Art, History, Philosophy, Psychology, Psychiatry, Science (General), Social Sciences, Sociology
ISBN Prefix(es): 86-307
Branch Office(s)
Dure Dakovica 5, Banja Luka *Tel:* (078) 60080
Bul 23, oktobra 35, Novi Sad *Tel:* (021) 611763
Francuska 10, Smederevska Palanka
Novosadska bb, Svetozarevo *Tel:* (035) 223313

Zavod za Izdavanje Udzbenika
pf 175, Sremska 7, 21000 Novi Sad
Tel: (021) 23-844; (021) 22-068 *Fax:* (021) 22-062; (021) 623-454
Key Personnel
Man Dir: Vasilije Lalatovic
Contact: Slobodan Babic
Founded: 1965

Subjects: Education
ISBN Prefix(es): 86-413

Zavod za udzbenike i nastavna sredstva
Obilicev venac 5, 11000 Belgrade
Tel: (011) 636-971; (011) 630-317; (011) 639-577 *Fax:* (011) 630-014; (011) 637-429; (011) 637-426
Key Personnel
Dir: Dr Dobrosav Bjeletic
Founded: 1957
Subjects: Education
ISBN Prefix(es): 86-17
Bookshop(s): Kosovska 45, 11000 Belgrade; Vukasoviceva 50, 11090 Belgrade

Zambia

General Information

Capital: Lusaka
Language: English is official language
Religion: Most follow traditional animist beliefs (70%), about 20% Christian (Protestant and Roman Catholic)
Population: 8.7 million
Bank Hours: 0815-1245 Monday, Tuesday, Wednesday, Friday; 0815-1200 Thursday; 0815-1100 Saturday
Shop Hours: Generally 0800-1700 Monday-Friday; 0800-1300 Saturday
Currency: 100 ngwee = 1 Zambian kwacha
Export/Import Information: No tariffs on books but all imports subject to sales tax. Single copies of advertising free. Import license required. Exchange controls.
Copyright: UCC, Berne (see Copyright Conventions, pg xi)

Aafzam Ltd+
PO Box 31012, Lusaka
Tel: (01) 223261
Key Personnel
Chairman: H Earl Johnson
Founded: 1971
Subjects: Biography, Business, Developing Countries, Government, Political Science, Music, Dance, Wine & Spirits
ISBN Prefix(es): 9982-9903
Associate Companies: A Afzamwines Ltd; Satis Suppliers Ltd

Apple Books+
Art & Design Centre, 405 4th Floor, Cairo Rd/Chainda Place, Lusaka 10101
Mailing Address: PO Box 35687, Lusaka 10101
Tel: (01) 211216 *Fax:* (01) 224855
Key Personnel
Man Dir: G B Mwangilwa
General Manager: Rodrick Chris Chibesa
Founded: 1987
Member of Booksellers & Publishers Association of Zambia; specialize in book exports; also acts as Literary Agent.
Subjects: Biography, Fiction, History, Humor
ISBN Prefix(es): 9982-06
Parent Company: Virgo Ltd

Bookworld+
Box 31838, Lusaka
Tel: (01) 225195 *Fax:* (01) 225282
Founded: 1991
Member of Booksellers & Publishers Association of Zambia.
Subjects: Educational
ISBN Prefix(es): 9982-16

Wilfred Bwalya Chilangwa Publications+
Private Bag CH 50, Chelston, Lusaka
Tel: (01) 282998
E-mail: hope@samnet.zm
Key Personnel
Contact: Wilfred B Chilangwa
Founded: 1995
Subjects: Education, Human Relations

Government Printer
PO Box 30136, Lusaka
Tel: (01) 215401; (01) 215805; (01) 215685; (01) 216972
ISBN Prefix(es): 9982-10

Historical Association of Zambia
PO Box 30680, Lusaka
Key Personnel
Chairman: Dr Y A Chondoka
Founded: 1969
Subjects: Agriculture, Anthropology, History
ISBN Prefix(es): 9982-802

Lundula Publishing House+
Mzenga Banda, PO Box 30100, Lusaka
Fax: (01) 26012; (01) 26200
Key Personnel
Man Dir: Ngand 'Osamba Lundula
Founded: 1991
Member of US & British Library & Zambian Book Sellers & Printers Association.
Subjects: Education, English as a Second Language, Language Arts, Linguistics, Social Sciences, Sociology
ISBN Prefix(es): 9982-9904
Parent Company: Editions Passou, BP 236, LuBumbash, The Democratic Republic of the Congo
Distributed by Zambia Educational Publishing House; Book World in Zambia; University of Zambia Bookshop
Distributor for Editions Passou (Democratic Republic of the Congo)
Book Club(s): US & British Libraries in Zambia; Writer's Association of Zambia

M & M Management & Labour Consultants Ltd+
PO Box 35128, Lusaka
Tel: (01) 217218 *Fax:* (01) 224495
Telex: ZA 40618
Key Personnel
Managing Consultant: Tresford K Mwaba
Founded: 1987
Also act as Management Consulting.
Subjects: Human Relations, Labor, Industrial Relations, Management
ISBN Prefix(es): 9982-805

Macmillan Publishers (Zambia) Ltd
Plot 8357, Sentor Investments Complex, Great North Rd, Lusaka
Mailing Address: Provate Bag RW 348X Ridgeway, Lusaka
Tel: (01) 223 669 *Fax:* (01) 223 657; (01) 641 018
E-mail: macpub@zamnet.zm
Web Site: www.macmillan-africa.com
Key Personnel
Man Dir: Miles Banda *E-mail:* mkbanda@zamnet.zm
Sales Manager: Richard Chanda
Educational publishers.
Parent Company: Macmillan Publishers Ltd, United Kingdom
Branch Office(s)
Plot No 22, Nawaitwika Rd, Northrise, Ndola

MFK Management Consultants Services+
Luangwa House, Cairo Rd, PO Box 31411, Lusaka
Tel: (01) 223530; (01) 252934

Key Personnel
Author: Frederick K Mwanza
Subjects: Business, Developing Countries, Economics, Finance, Government, Political Science, Management, Philosophy, Social Sciences, Sociology
ISBN Prefix(es): 9982-823

Movement for Multi-Party Democracy+
c/o Goodwin Bwalya Mwangilwa, MMD Secretariat, Private Bag E365, Lusaka
Tel: (01) 224850; (01) 224851; (01) 224852; (01) 224853 *Fax:* (01) 224855
Founded: 1991
Subjects: Government, Political Science, Public Administration
ISBN Prefix(es): 9982-17

Multimedia Zambia+
PO Box 320199, Lusaka
Tel: (01) 253666 *Fax:* (01) 363050
Telex: 40630 ZA
Key Personnel
Executive Dir: Jumbe Ngoma
Founded: 1971
Subjects: Biography, Communications, Cookery, Fiction, Religion - Other, Social Sciences, Sociology
ISBN Prefix(es): 9982-30
Parent Company: Christian Council of Zambia/Zambia Episcopal Conference
Shipping Address: African Books Collective Ltd, The Jam Factory, 27 Park End St, Oxford OX1 1KU, United Kingdom
Warehouse: African Books Collective Ltd, The Jamm Factory, 27 Park End St, Oxford OX1 1HM, United Kingdom
Orders to: African Books Collective Ltd, The Jam Factory, 27 Park End St, Oxford OX1 1KU, United Kingdom

Printpak (Z) Ltd
PO Box 70069, Ndola
Tel: (01) 611001; (01) 611002; (01) 600113; (01) 612027 *Fax:* (01) 617096
Telex: 41860
Key Personnel
Contact: J Muyuni
ISBN Prefix(es): 9982-13

University of Zambia Press (UNZA Press)
PO Box 32379, Lusaka 10101
Tel: (01) 290740; (01) 219624; (01) 252514
Fax: (01) 253952
Telex: ZA 44370 *Cable:* UNZAS
Key Personnel
Publisher: Miss M A Sifuniso
Editorial: Samuel Kasankha; Christopher Bwalya
Production: John C Mukuka
Founded: 1938
Subjects: Education, Social Sciences, Sociology
ISBN Prefix(es): 9982-03
Parent Company: University of Zambia Company, PO Box 32379, Lusaka 10101
Bookshop(s): University Bookshop

Yorvik Publishing Ltd+
Plot 531, David Kaunda Rd, Chingola
Mailing Address: PO Box 10583, Chingola
Tel: (02) 311628; (02) 312852; (02) 313707
Fax: (02) 311628
Key Personnel
Man Dir: A M Morton
Founded: 1993
Subjects: Special Education, Secondary School Sciences
ISBN Prefix(es): 9982-20
Associate Companies: Anthony Morton Ltd
Bookshop(s): AML Graphics, Armshal Rd, Noola

Zambia Association for Research & Development
First Floor Design House, Dar es Salaam Pl, Cairo Rd, Lusaka
Mailing Address: PO Box 37836, Lusaka
Tel: (01) 222883
E-mail: zard@zamnet.zm
Key Personnel
Contact: Mercy Khozi
Founded: 1984
Subjects: Government, Political Science, Health, Nutrition, Social Sciences, Sociology, Women's Studies
ISBN Prefix(es): 9982-818
Book Club(s): Booksellers & Publishers Association of Zambia

Zambia Educational Publishing House+
Chishango Rd, Lusaka 10101
Mailing Address: PO Box 32708, Lusaka 10101
Tel: (01) 229490; (01) 229211 *Fax:* (01) 225073
Telex: ZA 40056 *Cable:* HOUSE LUSAKA
Key Personnel
Man Dir: H M Chipewo
Publishing Manager: A Sikabanga
Marketing Manager: R Munamwimbu
Founded: 1967
Member of Booksellers & Publishers Association of Zambia.
Subjects: Agriculture, Biography, Drama, Theater, Education, Ethnicity, Fiction, Government, Political Science, History, Language Arts, Linguistics, Literature, Literary Criticism, Essays, Poetry, Social Sciences, Sociology
ISBN Prefix(es): 9982-00; 9982-01
Distributed by Gamsberg Publishers (Namibia)
Distributor for Multimedia Zambia; Printpak Ltd; Longman Zambia; Macmillan Zambia
Book Club(s): Read-a-Book Club

Zambian Ornithological Society
PO Box 33944, Lusaka
Subjects: Natural History
ISBN Prefix(es): 9982-811

ZPC Publications+
PO Box 34798, Kabelenga Rd, Lusaka
Tel: (01) 227673; (01) 227674; (01) 227675
Fax: (01) 225026
Telex: ZA 40068
Founded: 1988
Commercial Printing also.
Subjects: Agriculture, Child Care & Development, Drama, Theater, Education, Environmental Studies, Gardening, Plants, History, Women's Studies
ISBN Prefix(es): 9982-02
Parent Company: Zambia Printing Co Ltd

Zimbabwe

General Information

Capital: Harare
Language: English is the official language. Chishona and Sindebele are major African languages.
Religion: Majority (55%) Christian, most of the rest follow traditional beliefs
Population: 10 million
Bank Hours: 0830-1400 Monday, Tuesday, Thursday, Friday; 0830-1200 Wednesday; 0830-1100 Saturday
Shop Hours: 0800 or 0830-1700 Monday-Friday; 0800-1300 Saturday
Currency: 100 cents = 1 Zimbabwe dollar
Export/Import Information: Surcharge duty of 20% CIF to order, and 12 1/2% tax on retail sales on books. Advertising matter in bulk has duty and VAT charged. Import license is normally required for books and printed matter. Exchange controls.
Copyright: Berne (see Copyright Conventions, pg xi)

Academic Books Pvt Ltd+
PO Box 567, Harare
Tel: (04) 706729; (04) 704910 *Fax:* (04) 702071
Key Personnel
Editorial Dir: Irene Staunton
Member of Zimbabwe Publisher's Association.
Subjects: Art, Education, Fiction, Geography, Geology, History, Literature, Literary Criticism, Essays, Nonfiction (General), Science (General)
ISBN Prefix(es): 0-949229; 0-908311
Parent Company: F E I C Ltd
Divisions: Baobab Books
Distributed by ABC (England); David Philip (South Africa)
Warehouse: 4 Conald Rd, Graniteside, Harare

Action Magazine+
Mukuvisi Environment Centre, Harare
Mailing Address: PO Box 4696, Harare
Tel: (04) 747213-7-274 *Fax:* (04) 747409
E-mail: actionmg@cst.co.zw
Web Site: www.cst.co.zw/action
Key Personnel
Coordinator: Steve Murray
Documentation & Resource Officer: K Chigwitana *E-mail:* resource.action@cst.co.zw
Founded: 1987
Developing & producing environment & health education materials, training in environmental education.
Information about environmental education in Zimbabwe & region.
Subjects: Environmental Studies, Health, Nutrition
Parent Company: NGO, Zimbabwe Trust, 4 Lanark Rd, Harare

Africa Film & TV t/a Z Promotions
PO Box 6109, Harare
Tel: (04) 726972; (04) 726795 *Fax:* (04) 726796
E-mail: info@africfilmtv.com
Web Site: www.africafilmtv.com
Key Personnel
Contact: Russell Honeyman
Founded: 1986
Quarterly Magazine, Annual Directory.
Subjects: Film, Video, Radio, TV

Books for Africa Publishing House+
21 Inez Terrace, Harare
Tel: (04) 794329 *Fax:* (04) 61881
Telex: 22386
Key Personnel
Publishing Manager: Chris Nyabezi
Member of the Book Publishers Association.
ISBN Prefix(es): 0-949933

Anvil Press+
PO Box 4209, Harare
Tel: (04) 792551; (04) 739681
Key Personnel
Man Dir: Paul Brickhill
Manager: Felix Nyabadza
Founded: 1987
Subjects: Drama, Theater, Environmental Studies, Literature, Literary Criticism, Essays, Social Sciences, Sociology
ISBN Prefix(es): 0-7974
Associate Companies: Grassroots Books
Bookshop(s): Grassroots Books, Africa House, 100 J Moyo Ave, Box A267, Avondale
Warehouse: 78 Kaguvi St, Harare

ZIMBABWE

Argosy Press
PO Box 2677, Harare 704715
Tel: (04) 704766; (04) 704715 *Fax:* (04) 752162
Telex: 26334
ISBN Prefix(es): 0-7974
Associate Companies: Modus Publications Pvt Ltd

Bold ADS
PO Box 1027, Harare
Tel: (04) 621321; (04) 621327 *Fax:* (04) 621328
Telex: 26013
Key Personnel
General Manager: L M Manduku
Production Manager: N Magadzine
Sales & Marketing: L Ndlovu
Founded: 1950
Subjects: Foreign Countries
Parent Company: Zimbabwe Newspapers (Pvt) Ltd
Subsidiaries: B & T Directories (Pvt) Ltd; Publications (C A) (pvt) Ltd
Branch Office(s)
PO Box 1027, Bulawayo

The Bulletin Newspaper+
PO Box 1595, Bulawayo
Tel: (9) 78831; (9) 880591 *Fax:* (9) 78835
E-mail: dirpub@mweb.co.zw
Key Personnel
Chief Executive: Bruce Gordon Beale
Editorial Manager: Anne Venables
Rights & Permissions: Wendy Grimsell
Subjects: Education
Parent Company: Directory Publishers (Pvt) Ltd
Subsidiaries: BCF Ltd

Christian Audio-Visual Action (CAVA)
Box 649, Harare
Tel: (04) 752233 *Fax:* (04) 727030
Key Personnel
Contact: Rev H W Murray
Founded: 1977
Subjects: Biblical Studies, Theology

College Press Publishers (Pvt) Ltd+
15 Douglas Rd, Workington, Harare
Mailing Address: PO Box 3041
Tel: (04) 754145; (04) 773231; (04) 773236; (04) 757153; (04) 754255 *Fax:* (04) 754256
E-mail: nellym@collegepress.co.zw
Telex: 22558 colprs zw *Cable:* LIBRIS
Key Personnel
Man Dir: Benias Benison Mugabe
Sales Dir: Cletus Jack Ngwaru
Publishing Manager: Cynthia Sithole *Tel:* (04) 754255 *Fax:* (04) 757150
Production Dir & International Division: Engelbert Lemon Luphahla
Financial Dir: Edwin Busangabanye
Founded: 1968
Primarily an Educational Publisher.
Member of Zimbabwe Book Publishers Association & APNET.
Subjects: Accounting, Agriculture, Biblical Studies, Biography, Biological Sciences, Business, Chemistry, Chemical Engineering, Child Care & Development, Cookery, Drama, Theater, Economics, English as a Second Language, Environmental Studies, Fiction, Geography, Geology, History, Mathematics, Physics, Poetry, Science (General), Teachers Education
ISBN Prefix(es): 0-86925; 1-77900
Number of titles published annually: 30 Print
Total Titles: 700 Print
Associate Companies: Macmillan Publishers Ltd, United Kingdom
Imprints: Scholastic Books; Ventures
Branch Office(s)
PO Box 298, Bulawayo, Contact: H P Dube
Tel: (09) 74174
PO Box 1239, Gweru, Contact: G K Madzime
Tel: (054) 23457
PO Box 355, Masvingo, Contact: G Muzenda
Tel: (035) 62264
PO Box 963, Mutare, Contact: S J Chikuse
Tel: (020) 64211
Distributed by Macmillan Publishers (Worldwide)
Distributor for Macmillan Publishers
Foreign Rep(s): Macmillan Publishers (Worldwide)
Orders to: College Press Publishers, Contact: Cletus Ngwaru

Dorothy Duncan Braille & Transcription Library
119 Fife Ave, Harare
Mailing Address: Box CY 1551 Causeway, Harare
Tel: (04) 251116 *Fax:* (04) 251117
E-mail: chiedza@samara.co.zw
Key Personnel
Coordinator: Sister Catherine Jackson
Contact: Ster C Jackson
Parent Company: Dorothy Duncan Centre for the Blind & Physically Handicapped

Farmesa Regional Prog on Farm Research Methods
PO Box 3730, Harare
Tel: (04) 791407; (04) 791485; (04) 791495 *Fax:* (04) 703497
E-mail: makradho@havare.iafrica.com
Web Site: www.farmesa.co.zw
Key Personnel
Project Coordinator: Dr John Dixon
Information Specialist: Ms M Zunguzel
Subjects: Agriculture

Flame Lily, *imprint of* The Literature Bureau

Geological Survey Department
PO Box 8039, Causeway, Harare
Telex: 22416 MINESZW *Cable:* MINES
Key Personnel
Dir: Dr J L Orpen
Founded: 1910
Subjects: Geography, Geology
Parent Company: Ministry of Mines, Zimbabwe, P Bag 7709, Causeway, Harrare

The Graham Publishing Company (Pvt) Ltd
PO Box 2931, Harare
Tel: (04) 706207 *Fax:* (04) 752439
Key Personnel
Man Dir: Gordon M Graham
Founded: 1968
Subjects: Fiction, History, Nonfiction (General), Travel
ISBN Prefix(es): 0-86921

Happy Books+
PO Box BW59, Harare Borrowdale
Tel: (04) 8871414
Key Personnel
Editorial Manager: Florence Ford
Founded: 1987
Member of ZBPA.
ISBN Prefix(es): 1-77902
Divisions: Frameset Educational Aids
Orders to: Nationwide, Box 1819, Harare

HarperCollins Publishers Zimbabwe Pvt Ltd+
161 A Josiah Chinamano Ave, Harare
Mailing Address: PO Box UA 201, Union Ave, Harare
Tel: (04) 721413; (04) 727516 *Fax:* (04) 721413
Key Personnel
General Manager: Susan D McMillan
Founded: 1964 (formerly William Collins International)
Subjects: Accounting, Business, Education, English as a Second Language, Law
ISBN Prefix(es): 1-77904

Journal on Social Change
Mass Media House, 19 Selous Ave, Harare
Mailing Address: PO Box 4405, Harare
Tel: (04) 720417; (04) 700047 *Fax:* (04) 730808
E-mail: schange@africaonline.co.zw
Key Personnel
Chairperson of Editorial Board: Joyce Kazembe
Coordinating Editor: John Vekris
Founded: 1981 (Founded one year after independence to complement govt efforts to transform & reconstruct Zimbabwean society)
Non-profit, independent organization.
Quarterly Journals.
Subjects: Art, Developing Countries, Economics, Government, Political Science, Labor, Industrial Relations, Social Sciences, Sociology, Analysis of National & Regional Current Affairs
Number of titles published annually: 4 Print

Legal Resources Foundation Publications Unit
PO Box 918, Harare
Tel: (04) 790947; (04) 728211; (04) 728212 *Fax:* (04) 728213
Subjects: Law
ISBN Prefix(es): 0-908312

The Literature Bureau
Ministry of Education, Sport & Culture, Causeway, Harare
Mailing Address: PO Box CY121, Causeway, Harare
Tel: (04) 726929; (04) 729120 *Cable:* LITBURO
Key Personnel
Chief Publications Officer: B C Chitsike
Principal Editorial Officers: E Tafa; E Bhala
Founded: 1954
Subjects: Animals, Pets, Drama, Theater, Literature, Literary Criticism, Essays, Poetry
ISBN Prefix(es): 0-86926
Imprints: Flame Lily
Branch Office(s)
PO Box 828, Bulawayo
Book Club(s): Shona Readers' Book Club

Longman Zimbabwe (Pvt) Ltd+
Tourle Rd, Southerton, Harare
Mailing Address: PO Box ST125, Harare Southerton
Tel: (04) 621 661; (04) 621 670 *Fax:* (04) 62716
Telex: 22560 *Cable:* Longman Harare Zimbabwe
Key Personnel
General Manager: Emily Chandauka
E-mail: emilyc@longman.co.zw
Founded: 1964
Subjects: Accounting, Agriculture, Business, Cookery, Economics, Education, English as a Second Language, Environmental Studies, History, Mathematics, Natural History, Poetry, Religion - Other, Science (General)
ISBN Prefix(es): 0-582; 0-908308; 0-908310
Total Titles: 700 Print
Parent Company: Pearson Education, United Kingdom
Ultimate Parent Company: Pearson Plc

Mambo Press+
Senga Rd, Gweru
Mailing Address: Box 779, Gweru
Tel: (054) 24016; (054) 25807 *Fax:* (054) 21991
E-mail: mambo@icon.co.zw
Key Personnel
General Manager: Fr R Gentile
Editor: Emmanuel Makadho
Marketing Manager: Charles Zhou
Founded: 1958

Subjects: Fiction, History, Natural History, Nonfiction (General), Poetry, Religion - Other
ISBN Prefix(es): 0-86922
Number of titles published annually: 12 Print
Total Titles: 320 Print
Foreign Rep(s): Africa B/Centre (UK); Botswana B/Ceentre (Botswana); Botswana B/Centre (US); Pauline Multimedia (Zambia)
Bookshop(s): Mambo Bookshop, Speke Ave/First St, PO Box UA 320, Harare, Contact: Mrs R Mabuza Tel: (04) 705899; Mambo Bookshop, PO Box 1010, Masvingo, Contact: Mr H Muromo Tel: (039) 64566; Mambo Bookshop, Bulawayo, PO Box FM 87, Bulawayo, Contact: Mrs S Kamutingondo Tel: (09) 61162

Manhattan Publications
170 Chinoyi St Harare, PO Box 5, Harare
Tel: (04) 781805 Fax: (04) 496292
E-mail: nchudy@mweb.co.zw
Key Personnel
Proprietor: Alexander Katz
Founded: 1983
Zimbabwe economics.
Subjects: Business, Economics
Number of titles published annually: 5 Print
Total Titles: 12 Print
Parent Company: Manhattan Realty (Pvt) Ltd

Mercury Press Pvt Ltd+
Gickon House 22, Kaguvi St, Harare
Mailing Address: PO Box 2373, Harare
Tel: (04) 751515; (04) 751516 Fax: (04) 737670
Cable: TUTORIAL
Key Personnel
Man Dir & International Rights: D F Sutherland
Founded: 1972
Subjects: Education, English as a Second Language, Language Arts, Linguistics, Poetry
ISBN Prefix(es): 0-7974
Parent Company: Central African Correspondence College P/L, Gickon House 22, Kaguvi St, Harare
Associate Companies: Phoenix Printers P/L, Gickon House 22, Kaguvi St, Harare

National Archives of Zimbabwe+
Private Bag 7729, Causeway, Harare
Tel: (04) 792741 Fax: (04) 792398
Founded: 1949
Subjects: History
ISBN Prefix(es): 0-908302

Nehanda Publishers+
Union Ave, Harare
Mailing Address: PO Box UA517, Harare
Tel: (04) 708165 Fax: (04) 707698
Key Personnel
President: Dr L M Lenneiye
Vice President: Dr Kimani Gecau
Founded: 1984
Subjects: Economics, Environmental Studies, Foreign Countries, Government, Political Science, Literature, Literary Criticism, Essays, Regional Interests
ISBN Prefix(es): 0-908305

Phantom Publishers+
PO Box BW59, Borrowdale, Harare
Tel: (04) 737241
Key Personnel
Author, Publisher: Jeremy Ford
Founded: 1988
Subjects: Poetry
ISBN Prefix(es): 0-7974
Orders to: Nationwide, PO Box 1819, Harare

Quest Publishing Pvt Ltd, see ZRD Trust

Sapes Trust Ltd
PO Box MP111, Harare
Tel: (04) 726060; (04) 790815 Fax: (04) 726060; (04) 732735
Telex: 26464 AAPS 2W
Key Personnel
Administrative Manager: J Kadye
Executive Dir: Dr I Mandaza
Subjects: Developing Countries, Economics, Environmental Studies, Government, Political Science, Public Administration, Social Sciences, Sociology
ISBN Prefix(es): 1-77905
Subsidiaries: Southern Africa Publishing & Printing Houses (SAPPHO)

SAZ, see Standards Association of Zimbabwe (SAZ)

Scholastic Books, imprint of College Press Publishers (Pvt) Ltd

Social Change & Development, see Journal on Social Change

Standards Association of Zimbabwe (SAZ)
Northridge Park, Northerd Close, Borrowdale, Harare
Mailing Address: PO Box 2259, Harare
Tel: (04) 885511; (04) 885512 Fax: (04) 882020
E-mail: sazinfo@mweb.co.zw
Key Personnel
Dir General: M P Mutasa Tel: (04) 885517 Fax: (04) 882581 E-mail: standards@mail.pci.co.zw
Manager of Standards Information: Miss R Marunda Tel: (04) 885511 Fax: (04) 882020 E-mail: sazinfo@mweb.co.zw
Founded: 1957
Subjects: Agriculture, Automotive, Chemistry, Chemical Engineering, Civil Engineering, Electronics, Electrical Engineering, Engineering (General), Mechanical Engineering
ISBN Prefix(es): 0-86928
Number of titles published annually: 110 Print
Total Titles: 1,082 Print
Branch Office(s)
Standards Association of Zimbabwe, PO Box 591, Mutare, Contact: Mr P Chiadzwa Tel: (020) 60516 Fax: (020) 66252 E-mail: saznytave@technopcork.co.zw
Standards Association of Zimbabwe, PO Box RY 129, Raylton, Bulawayo, Contact: Mr A G Ncube Tel: 09 70447 Fax: 09 71876 E-mail: sazbti@accacia.mweb.co.zw

Thomson Publications Zimbabwe (Pvt) Ltd
130 Harare St, Harare 217373WE
Mailing Address: PO Box 1683, Harare
Tel: (04) 736835 Fax: (04) 749803
E-mail: tpubl@mweb.co.zw
Key Personnel
General Manager: Brian Gamble Tel: (04) 749741
Founded: 1954
Subjects: Accounting, Agriculture, Automotive, Business, Communications, Economics
ISBN Prefix(es): 0-7974
Total Titles: 7 Print
Subsidiaries: Amalgamated Publications

University of Zimbabwe Library
PO Box 167, Mount Pleasant, Harare
Tel: (04) 303211 Fax: (04) 335383
E-mail: mainlib@uzlib.uz.zw
Web Site: www.uz.ac.zw/library
Key Personnel
Librarian: Dr B Mbambo
Founded: 1957
Number of titles published annually: 14,300 Print
Total Titles: 597,356 Print
Parent Company: National University of Science & Technology
Associate Companies: Africa University; Solusi University College
Divisions: National University of Science & Technology Library

University of Zimbabwe Publications+
Mount Pleasant, Harare
Mailing Address: PO Box MP 203, Harare
Tel: (04) 303211 Ext 1236 Fax: (04) 333407; (04) 335249
E-mail: uzpub@admin.uz.ac.zn
Telex: 4152 ZW Cable: UNIVERSITY
Key Personnel
Dir, Publications: M S Mtetwa
Founded: 1969
Subjects: History, Language Arts, Linguistics, Literature, Literary Criticism, Essays, Medicine, Nursing, Dentistry, Philosophy, Religion - Other, Science (General), Social Sciences, Sociology, Technology
ISBN Prefix(es): 0-908307
Distributed by African Books Collective (UK)

Ventures, imprint of College Press Publishers (Pvt) Ltd

Vision Publications+
753 Senga 2, Gweru
Founded: 1996
Subjects: Education, Fiction, Language Arts, Linguistics, Literature, Literary Criticism, Essays, Nonfiction (General), Poetry, Religion - Protestant, Theology
Parent Company: Vision Enterprises

Z Promotions, see Africa Film & TV t/a Z Promotions

ZEB, imprint of Zimbabwe Publishing House (Pvt) Ltd

Zimbabwe Foundation for Education with Production (ZIMFEP)+
52 Alamorgan Ave, Belvedere
Mailing Address: PO Box 298, Harare
Tel: (04) 753991; (04) 771833/4 Fax: (04) 749147
E-mail: zimfep@africaonline.co.zw
Key Personnel
Dir: Dr Vimbisai Nhundu
Founded: 1981
Member of Zimbabwe Book Publishers Association.
Subjects: Drama, Theater, Education
ISBN Prefix(es): 0-908303

Zimbabwe International Book Fair+
PO Box CY 1179, Harare
Tel: (04) 702104; (04) 702108 Fax: (04) 702129
E-mail: zibf@samara.co.zw
Key Personnel
Contact: T Mbanga
Subjects: Developing Countries

Zimbabwe Publishing House (Pvt) Ltd+
183 Arcturus Rd, Kamfinsa Centre, Greendale
Mailing Address: PO Box GD 510, Harre
Tel: (04) 497555-8; (04) 497548 Fax: (04) 497554
E-mail: apg@ld.co.zw
Telex: 6035 Zph Zw
Key Personnel
General Manager: Mwazvita Madondo
Editorial Manager & Rights & Permissions: Promise Mayo
Founded: 1981
Subjects: Cookery, Education, Geography, Geology, History, Literature, Literary Criticism, Essays, Mathematics, Natural History, Science (General)
ISBN Prefix(es): 0-949225; 0-949932; 0-908300; 1-77901

ZIMBABWE

Total Titles: 187 Print
Associate Companies: African Publishing Group, PO Box 90150, Contact: Helena Perry *Tel:* (04) 497 55518 *Fax:* (04) 497 5554 *E-mail:* apg@ld.co.zw
Imprints: ZEB; ZPH
Subsidiaries: Zimbabwe Educational Books
Branch Office(s)
PO Box 1442, Bulawayo, Contact: Zwelithini Mpofu *Tel:* (04) 74666
PO Box 384, Masvingo, Contact: Stephan Rubaba *Tel:* (034) 68137
PO Box 1029, Mutare, Contact: Absalom Kunzwu *Tel:* (020) 08716
PO Box 1191, Gweru *Tel:* (054) 24978
Bookshop(s): Frontline Bookshop, PO Box 350, Harare
Warehouse: 97 Coventry Rd, Workington Harare *Tel:* (04) 667170

Zimbabwe Women Writers+
78 Kaguvi St, Harare
Mailing Address: PO Box 4209, Harare
Tel: (04) 774261 *Fax:* (04) 750282
E-mail: zww@telco.co.zw
Key Personnel
Contact: Keresia Chateuka
Founded: 1996
Subjects: Nonfiction (General)
Orders to: PO Box 4209, Harare

Zimbabwe Women's Bureau+
43 Hillside Rd, Cranborne, Harare
Tel: (04) 747905; (04) 747809 *Fax:* (04) 747809
Key Personnel
Dir: Mrs Lydia Chikwavaire
Subjects: Agriculture

ZIMFEP, see Zimbabwe Foundation for Education with Production (ZIMFEP)

ZPH, *imprint of* Zimbabwe Publishing House (Pvt) Ltd

ZRD Trust+
Formerly Quest Publishing Pvt Ltd
107, Leopold Takawira St, Harare
Mailing Address: PO Box 2054, Harare
Tel: (04) 774775; (04) 744519 *Fax:* (04) 774764
Telex: 2033 ZW
Key Personnel
Editor & Publisher: R S Roberts *E-mail:* rsrob@mweb.co.zw
Founded: 1970
Specialize in Reference Works
Member of Central Africa Historical Association, Historical Association of Zimbabwe & Zimbabwe Independent Publishers.
Subjects: History, Zimbabwe
ISBN Prefix(es): 0-908306
Number of titles published annually: 2 Print
Total Titles: 15 Print

Type of Publication Index

ASSOCIATION PRESSES

Australia
Centenary of Technical Education in Bairnsdale Group, pg 17

Austria
Verband der Wissenschaftlichen Gesellschaften Oesterreichs (VWGOe), pg 60

Belgium
Documenta CV, pg 68

Chile
Alfabeta Impresores Ltda, pg 99

China
Sichuan Science & Technology Publishing House, pg 109

Czech Republic
Kalich SRO, pg 125
Narodni Knihovna CR, pg 126

France
Gippe-Marche Du Livre Ancien, pg 166
La Voix du Regard, pg 189

Germany
Blaukreuz-Verlag Wuppertal, pg 204
Chmielorz GmbH Verlag, pg 210
Verlag Deutsche Unitarier, pg 214
Deutscher Psychologen Verlag GmbH (DPV), pg 215
Dr Ernst Hauswedell & Co Verlag, pg 238
Erika Heydick Sax-Verlag Beucha, pg 240
Lebenshilfe-Verlag Marburg, Verlag der Bundesvereinigung Lebenshilfe fuer Menschen mit geistiger Behinderung eV, pg 256
Neuland-Verlagsgesellschaft mbH, pg 268
Philipp Reclam Jun Verlag GmbH, pg 273
Verlag Stahleisen GmbH, pg 289
Wiley-VCH Verlag GmbH, pg 302

Greece
Karatzas Charis, pg 312

Hong Kong
Ta Kung Pao (HK) Ltd, pg 322

India
Addison-Wesley (Singapore) Pte Ltd, pg 329

Italy
Belforte Editore Libraio srl, pg 377

Republic of Korea
Anam Publishing Co, pg 434
Korean Publishers Association, pg 437

The Former Yugoslav Republic of Macedonia
Mi-An Knigoizdatelstvo, pg 449

Morocco
Association de la Recherche Historique et Sociale, pg 469

Nigeria
Riverside Communications, pg 501

Russian Federation
N E Bauman Moscow State Technical University Publishers, pg 537
BLIC, russko-Baltijskij informaciionnyj centr, AO, pg 537

Spain
Aguilar SA de Ediciones, pg 562
Oikos-Tau SA Ediciones, pg 584

Turkey
Iletisim Yayinlari, pg 640

United Kingdom
Portland Press Ltd, pg 730

AUDIO BOOKS

Australia
Australian Large Print Pty Ltd, pg 14
Bible Society in Australia National Headquarters, pg 15
Boinkie Publishers, pg 15
Louis Braille Audio, pg 16
Greater Glider Productions Australia Pty Ltd, pg 24
F H Halpern, pg 25
Hodder Headline Australia, pg 26
Barry Long Books, pg 30
Narkaling Inc, pg 34
Network Promotions P/L, pg 34
New Creation Publications Ministries & Resource Centre, pg 34
Tarka Publishing, pg 44

Austria
Edition S der OSD, pg 51
Niederosterreichisches Pressehaus Druck- und Verlagsgesellschaft mbH, pg 55
oebv & hpt Verlagsgesellschaft mbH & Co KG, pg 56

Barbados
Business Tutors, pg 63

Belgium
Editions De Boeck-Larcier SA, pg 67

Benin
Les Editions du Flamboyant, pg 76

Brazil
Editora Elevacao, pg 82

Chile
Instituto Geografico Militar, pg 100

China
Beijing Publishing House, pg 102
China Braille Press, pg 103
Chinese Pedagogics Publishing House, pg 104
Fudan University Press, pg 105
Qingdao Publishing House, pg 108
Shanghai Educational Publishing House, pg 109
Tsinghua University Press, pg 110

Costa Rica
Promesa, Ediciones, pg 116

Czech Republic
Karmelitanske Nakladatelstvi, pg 125
Karolinum, nakladatelstvi, pg 125
Knihovna A Tiskarna Pro Nevidome, pg 125

Denmark
Forlaget alokke AS, pg 129
Dansk Historisk Handbogsforlag ApS, pg 131
Kaleidoscope Publishers Ltd, pg 133
New Era Publications International ApS, pg 134

France
Editions Amrita SA, pg 147
Emgleo Breiz, pg 151
Brud Nevez, pg 152
Des Femmes, pg 164
Sofradif Editions Philippe Auzou, pg 185

French Polynesia
Simone Sanchez, pg 190

Germany
Assimil GmbH, pg 196
Deutsche Blinden-Bibliothek, pg 213
Droemersche Verlagsanstalt Th Knaur Nachfolger GmbH & Co, pg 218
Egmont vgs verlagsgesellschaft mbH, pg 221
Esogetics GmbH, pg 224
Guenther Butkus, pg 235
Heinz-Theo Gremme Verlag, pg 239
Verlag Herder GmbH & Co KG, pg 239
Klaus Isele, pg 245
KBV-Verlags-und Mediengesellschaft mbH, pg 248
Kidemus Verlag GmbH, pg 248
Kleiner Bachmann Verlag fur Kinder und Umwelt, pg 250
Koptisch-Orthodoxes Zentrum, pg 252
Verlag Antje Kunstmann GmbH, pg 254
Lahn-Verlag GmbH, pg 255
Ingrid Langner, pg 256
Gustav Luebbe Verlag, pg 259
Verlagsgruppe Luebbe GmbH & Co KG, pg 259
Naumann & Goebel Verlagsgesellschaft mbH, pg 267
Osho Verlag GmbH, pg 271
Verlag Parzeller GmbH & Co KG, pg 271
Patmos Verlag GmbH & Co KG, pg 272
Pendragon Verlag, pg 272
Philipp Reclam Jun Verlag GmbH, pg 273
Schirner Verlag, pg 283
TR - Verlagsunion GmbH, pg 294
Verlag Klaus Wagenbach GmbH, pg 300

Ghana
World Literature Project, pg 308

Greece
Hestia-I D Hestia-Kollaros & Co Corporation, pg 311
Pagoulatos G-G P Publications, pg 314
Patakis Publishers, pg 314
Scripta, pg 315
Toubis M, pg 315

Hong Kong
Benefit Publishing Co, pg 318
The Dharmasthiti Buddist Institute Ltd, pg 319
Joint Publishing (HK) Co Ltd, pg 320

India
Addison-Wesley (Singapore) Pte Ltd, pg 329
Star Publications (P) Ltd, pg 351

Indonesia
PT Indira, pg 355

Ireland
Clo Iar-Chonnachta Teo, pg 359
Roberts Rinehart Publishers, pg 363

Israel
Breslov Research Institute, pg 366

Italy
Editrice Eraclea, pg 388
In Dialogo, pg 393
Editoriale Olimpia SpA, pg 401
RAI.ERI, pg 405
Rossato, pg 406
Rugginenti Editore, pg 406

Jamaica
Alice J M Rhodd, pg 413

Japan
Hyoronsha Publishing Co Ltd, pg 417
Seibido Shuppan Company Ltd, pg 424
Shincho-Sha Co Ltd, pg 425

BOOK

Kenya
Jacaranda Designs Ltd, pg 432

Republic of Korea
Gim-Yeong Co, pg 436
Kemongsa Publishing Co Ltd, pg 437
Koreaone Press Inc, pg 438
Moon Jin Media Co Ltd, pg 438

The Former Yugoslav Republic of Macedonia
Medis, Skopje, pg 449

Martinique
George Lise-Huyghes des Etages, pg 456

Mexico
Libra Editorial SA de CV, pg 463

Netherlands
Uitgeverij De Toorts, pg 485

New Zealand
Taylor Books, pg 496

Norway
Ariel Lydbokforlag, pg 502
Fono Forlag, pg 503

Peru
Instituto de Estudios Peruanos, pg 511

Philippines
Anvil Publishing Inc, pg 512

Poland
Wydawnictwo Podsiedlik-Raniowski i Spolka, pg 519
Wydawnictwo RTW, pg 520

Singapore
Asiapac Books Pte Ltd, pg 545
Europhone Language Institute (Pte) Ltd, pg 546

Slovenia
Zalozba Mihelac d o o, pg 552
Zalozba Obzorja d d Maribor, pg 552

South Africa
Bet-El Publishers, pg 553

Spain
Aguilar SA de Ediciones, pg 562
Consello da Cultura Galega - CCG, pg 568
Didaco Comunicacion y Didactica, SA, pg 569
Edilux, pg 572
Editorial la Muralla SA, pg 583
Editorial Verbum SL, pg 595

Switzerland
Bergli Books AG, pg 609
ISIOM Verlag fur Tondokumente, Weinreb Tonarchiv, pg 616

Taiwan, Province of China
Campus Evangelical Fellowship, Literature Department, pg 629
Echo Publishing Company Ltd, pg 629
Zen Now Press, pg 632

Turkey
IKI NOKTA Research Press & Publications Industry & Trade Ltd, pg 640

United Kingdom
Berlitz (UK) Ltd, pg 654
Bible Reading Fellowship, pg 654
Cherrytree Books, pg 667
Chorion IP, pg 667
Folens Ltd, pg 683
George Mann Publications, pg 687
Grandreams Ltd, pg 689
Gwasg y Dref Wen, pg 690
HarperCollins Publishers, pg 692
Hawk Books, pg 693
Headline Book Publishing Ltd, pg 693
Hodder & Stoughton General, pg 696
Hodder Children's Books, pg 696
Hodder Headline Ltd, pg 696
Hugo's Language Books Ltd, pg 697
Isis Publishing Ltd, pg 701
Kuperard, pg 705
Ladybird Books, pg 705
Letterbox Library, pg 707
Magna Large Print Books, pg 710
Murchison's Pantheon Ltd, pg 716
New Era Publications UK Ltd, pg 718
Orion Publishing Group Ltd, pg 722
Penguin Books Ltd, pg 725
The Penguin Group UK, pg 726
The Reader's Digest Association Ltd, pg 733
Telegraph Books, pg 748
World Microfilms Publications Ltd, pg 758

Zimbabwe
Christian Audio-Visual Action (CAVA), pg 768

AV MATERIALS

Australia
Art Gallery of South Australia Bookshop, pg 12
Artmoves, pg 12
Board of Studies, pg 15
R J Cleary Publishing, pg 18
Encyclopaedia Britannica (Australia) Inc, pg 22
Greater Glider Productions Australia Pty Ltd, pg 24
Hampden Press, pg 25
Ready-Ed Publications, pg 40
RMIT Publishing, pg 41
Wizard Books Pty Ltd, pg 48

Austria
Osterreichischer Bundesveilag Ges.mbh, pg 57

Belgium
Carto BVBA, pg 65

Brazil
A & A & A Edicoes e Promocoes Internacionais Ltda, pg 77
Empresa Brasileira de Pesquisa Agropecaria, pg 83

Burundi
Editions Intore, pg 98

Chile
Instituto Geografico Militar, pg 100

China
China Machine Press (CMP), pg 103
People's Education Press, pg 107
Wuhan University Press, pg 110

Colombia
Consejo Episcopal Latinoamericano Celam, pg 111
Unidad Universitaria del Sur (UNISUR), pg 114

Costa Rica
Centro Agronomico Tropical de Investigacion y Ensenanza (CATIE), pg 115

Denmark
Gyldendalske Boghandel - Nordisk Forlag A/S, pg 132
IBIS, pg 133
Kaleidoscope Publishers Ltd, pg 133
Square Dance Partners Forlag, pg 135
Systime, pg 136

Estonia
National Library of Estonia, pg 140

Fiji
University of the South Pacific, pg 141

Finland
Otava Publishing Co Ltd, pg 143
Werner Soederstroem Osakeyhtioe (WSOY), pg 145

France
Editions Belin, pg 150
Codes Rousseau, pg 155
Editions J Dupuis, pg 160
INRA Editions (Institut National de la Recherche Agronomique), pg 169
IRD Editions, pg 170
Editions MDI (La Maison des Instituteurs), pg 175
Sofradif Editions Philippe Auzou, pg 185

Germany
Belser Wissenschaftlicher Dienst, pg 200
Calwer Verlag Stuttgart eV, pg 209
Carl-Auer-Systeme Verlag, pg 209
Cornelsen Verlag GmbH & Co OHG, pg 211
Egmont vgs verlagsgesellschaft mbH, pg 221
Filmfaust Verlag - Internationale Filmzeitschrift, pg 227
Lehrmittelverlag Wilhelm Hagemann GmbH, pg 236
kopaed verlagsgmbh, pg 252
Kulturbuch-Verlag GmbH, pg 254
Lahn-Verlag GmbH, pg 255
Langenscheidt KG, pg 256
Ingrid Langner, pg 256
Libertas- Europaeisches Institut GmbH, pg 257
Medien-Verlag Bernhard Gregor GmbH, pg 262
Missio eV Aachen, pg 264
Nusser Verlag, pg 269
TR - Verlagsunion GmbH, pg 294
Ziethen-Panorama Verlag GmbH, pg 305

Greece
Ekdoseis Domi AE, pg 310

Hong Kong
The Chinese University Press, pg 319

Israel
Rolnik Publishers, pg 371

Italy
Istituto della Enciclopedia Italiana, pg 384
IHT Gruppo Editoriale SRL, pg 393
Casa Editrice Maccari (CEM), pg 397
Scala Group spa, pg 407

Jamaica
Alice J M Rhodd, pg 413

Japan
AVACO - Christian Mass Communications Center, pg 414
International Society for Educational Information (ISEI), pg 418
Ongaku No Tomo Sha Corporation, pg 423
President Inc, pg 423
Seibido, pg 424
Seibundo Shinkosha Publishing Co Ltd, pg 425
Sekai Bunka Publishing Inc, pg 425

Republic of Korea
Korea Britannica Corp, pg 437
Twenty-First Century Publishers, Inc, pg 440

Malta
Media Centre, pg 456

Mexico
Ediciones Culturales Internacionales SA de CV Edicion Compra y Venta de Libros, Casetes, Videos, pg 459
Organizacion Cultural LP SA de CV, pg 465
Ediciones Promesa, SA de CV, pg 466

Netherlands
Ministerie van Verkeer en Waterstaat, pg 481

New Zealand
Learning Media Ltd, pg 492

Philippines
Encyclopaedia Britannica (Philippines) Inc, pg 513
Our Lady of Manaoag Publisher, pg 514

PUBLISHERS

Poland
PZWL Wydawnictwo Lekarskie Ltd, pg 519

Portugal
Paulinas, pg 528

Reunion
Association des Ecrivains Reunionnais/ocean Indien (ADER), pg 531

Romania
Editura Cronos SRL, pg 532

Russian Federation
Airis Press, pg 537
BLIC, russko-Baltijskij informaciionnyj centr, AO, pg 537
Okoshko Ltd Publishers (Izdatelstvo), pg 541

Slovenia
Franc-Franc podjetje za promocijo kulture Murska Sobota d o o, pg 551

South Africa
Nasou - Oudiovista, pg 557

Spain
Anaya Educacion, pg 563
Editorial Astri SA, pg 564
Central Catequistica Salesiana (CCS), pg 567
Editorial Claret SA, pg 568
Comunidad Autonoma de Madrid, Servicio de Documentacion y Publicaciones, pg 568
Editorial De Vecchi SA, pg 569
Didaco Comunicacion y Didactica, SA, pg 569
Edebe, pg 571
Erein, pg 573
Imagen y Deporte, SL, pg 578
Editorial la Muralla SA, pg 583
Pearson Educacion S A, pg 586

Sweden
Mezopotamya Publishing & Distribution, pg 604
Bokfoerlaget Naturoch Kultur, pg 604
Verbum Foerlag AB, pg 607

Switzerland
Bibellesbund Verlag, pg 610

United Kingdom
Barn Dance Publications Ltd, pg 652
BBC English, pg 652
Books of Zimbabwe Publishing Co (Pvt) Ltd, pg 657
Coachwise Ltd, pg 668
Drake Educational Associates Ltd, pg 676
Encyclopaedia Britannica (UK) International Ltd, pg 679
Hodder & Stoughton Educational, pg 696
Islamic Foundation Publications, pg 701
Moorley's Print & Publishing Ltd, pg 715
Pavilion Publishing (Brighton) Ltd, pg 725

Pergamon Flexible Learning, pg 726
Ramakrishna Vedanta Centre, pg 732
World Microfilms Publications Ltd, pg 758

Viet Nam
Trung-Tam San Xuat Hoc-Lieu, pg 763

Zimbabwe
Christian Audio-Visual Action (CAVA), pg 768

BELLES LETTRES

Albania
Botimpex Publications Import-Export Agency, pg 1

Algeria
Enterprise Nationale du Livre (ENAL), pg 2

Argentina
Editorial Acme SA, pg 3
Ada Korn Editora SA, pg 3
Editorial Atlantida SA, pg 3
Ediciones de la Flor SRL, pg 6
Ediciones de Arte Gaglianone, pg 6
Editorial Losada SA, pg 7
Marymar Ediciones SA, pg 7
Editorial Sopena Argentina SACI e I, pg 9

Australia
Access Press, pg 10
AHB Publications, pg 11
Dragon Press, pg 20
EK Press, pg 21
Hat Box Press, pg 25
New Endeavour Press, pg 34
Spinifex Press, pg 43

Austria
Aarachne Verlag, pg 49
Aeneas Verlagsgesellschaft GmbH, pg 49
Amalthea-Verlag, pg 49
Astor-Verlag, Willibald Schlager, pg 49
Dachs-Verlag GmbH, pg 50
Denkmayr GmbH Druck & Verlag, pg 51
Docker Verlag GmbH & Co KG, pg 51
Literature Verlag Droschl, pg 51
Edition S der OSD, pg 51
Ennsthaler GesmbH & Co KG, pg 51
Guthmann & Peterson Liber Libri, Edition, pg 52
Haymon-Verlag GesmbH, pg 52
Johannes Heyn, Gert und Volkmar Zechner, pg 52
Leopold Stocker Verlag, pg 54
Literas-Verlag GmbH, pg 54
Merbod Verlag, pg 55
Thomas Mlakar Verlag, pg 55
Otto Mueller Verlag GesmbH & Co KG, pg 55
oebv & hpt Verlagsgesellschaft mbH & Co KG, pg 56
Oesterreichischer Bundesverlag GmbH, pg 56
Anna Pichler Verlag GmbH, pg 57
Richard Pils Publication P, pg 57
Georg Prachner KG, pg 57
Residenz Verlag GmbH, pg 58
Ritter Verlag, pg 58

Verlag Roeschnar, pg 58
Verlag Styria, pg 59
Verlag Anton Schroll & Co, pg 60
Wieser Verlag, pg 61
Paul Zsolnay Verlag GmbH, pg 61

Azerbaijan
Sada, Literaturno-Izdatel'skij Centr, pg 61

Belarus
Junactva, Vydavectva, pg 63
Kavaler Publishers, pg 63

Belgium
Libraire Ancienne Noel Anselot, pg 64
Le Cri Editions, pg 67
Maison d'Editions Cl Dejaie, pg 67
Editions les eperonniers, pg 68
Imprimerie Hayez SPRL, pg 69
Editions Labor, pg 70
Lansman Editeur, pg 70
La Longue Vue, pg 71
Paradox Pers vzw, pg 72
La Part de L'Oeil, pg 72
Imprimeur - Editeur Vaillant-Carmanne SA, pg 75
Vita, pg 75
Editions Luce Wilquin, pg 75

Bolivia
Gisbert y Cia SA, pg 76

Bosnia and Herzegovina
Svjetlost, pg 77

Brazil
Ars Poetica Editora Ltda, pg 79
Ediouro Publicacoes, SA, pg 81
Livraria Martins Fontes Editora Ltda, pg 83
Imago Editora Importacao e Exportacao Ltda, pg 85
Editora Nova Alexandria Ltda, pg 88
Editora Nova Fronteira SA, pg 88
Pool Editorial Ltda, pg 90
Editora Revan Ltda, pg 90
Livraria Sulina Editora, pg 92
34 Literatura S/C Ltda, pg 92
Editora da Universidade de Sao Paulo, pg 93
Vozes Editora Ltda, pg 93

Bulgaria
Andina Publishing House, pg 94
Bulgarski Pissatel, pg 94
Darzavno Izdatelstvo Narodna Kultura, pg 95
EA Publishing House, pg 95
Fama, pg 95
Interpres, pg 96
Kibea Publishing Co, pg 96
Kralica MAB, pg 96
Narodna Kultura, pg 97
Ivan Vazov Publishing House, pg 98
Peyo K Yavorov Publishing House, pg 98

Burundi
Editions Intore, pg 98

Chile
Ediciones Bat, pg 99

TYPE OF PUBLICATION INDEX

China
China Theatre Publishing House, pg 104
Fudan University Press, pg 105
Jinan Publishing House, pg 107

Colombia
Instituto Caro y Cuervo, pg 112
Editorial Santillana SA, pg 113

The Democratic Republic of the Congo
Centre Protestant d'Editions et de Diffusion (CEDI), pg 115
Presses Universitaires du Zaiire (PUZ), pg 115
Editions Saint Paul-Afrique, pg 115

Costa Rica
Promesa, Ediciones, pg 116
Editorial de la Universidad de Costa Rica, pg 117
Editorial Universitaria Centroamericana (EDUCA), pg 117

Croatia
AGM doo, pg 118
ALFA dd za izdavacke, graficke i trgovacke poslove, pg 118
ArTresor naklada, pg 118
Durieux d o o, pg 118
Faust Vrani, pg 118
Graficki zavod Hrvatske, pg 118
Knjizevni Krug Split, pg 119
Matica hrvatska, pg 119
Mladost d d Izdavacku graficku i informaticku djelatnost, pg 119
Skolska Knjiga, pg 120
Znanje d d, pg 120

Cuba
Holguin, Ediciones, pg 121
Editorial Oriente, pg 121
Ediciones Union, pg 121

Czech Republic
Atlantis sro, pg 123
Aurora, pg 123
Bakalar spol sro, pg 123
Cesky spisovatel, pg 123
Columbus, pg 123
Nakladatelstvi Josef Hribal, pg 124
Jota, pg 125
Kalich SRO, pg 125
Karmelitanske Nakladatelstvi, pg 125
Konsultace, pg 125
Labyrint, pg 125
Lidove noviny Nakladatelstvi, pg 125
Josef Lukasik A Spol, pg 125
Mariadan, pg 126
Melantrich, pg 126
Mlada fronta, pg 126
Nakladatelstvi Svoboda, pg 126
Nase vojsko, nakladatelstvi a knizni obchod, pg 126
Odeon, nakladatelstvi krasne literatury a umeni, pg 127
Nakladatelstvi a vydavatelstvi Panorama, pg 127
Paseka, pg 127
Prace, pg 127
Prostor, Ltd, pg 128
Svoboda Servis GmbH, pg 128
Vitalis SRO, pg 129
Votobia sro, pg 129
Zvon, pg 129

773

TYPE OF PUBLICATION INDEX
BOOK

Denmark
Grevas Forlag, pg 132
Gyldendalske Boghandel - Nordisk Forlag A/S, pg 132
Politisk Revy, pg 134
Det Schonbergske Forlag, pg 135
Forlaget Vindrose A/S, pg 136
Wisby & Wilkens, pg 136

Egypt (Arab Republic of Egypt)
Al Arab Publishing House, pg 138
General Egyptian Book Organization, pg 138
Middle East Book Centre, pg 139
Senouhy Publishers, pg 139

Estonia
Oue Eesti Raamat, pg 139
Ilmamaa, pg 140
Olion Publishers, pg 140
Perioodika, pg 140
Tuum, pg 141

Finland
Fenix-Kustannus Oy, pg 142
Schildts Foerlagsaktiebolag, pg 144
Soederstroem et Co Foerlagsaktiebolag, pg 144

France
Editions Al Liamm, pg 146
Alsatia SA, pg 146
L'Amitie par le Livre, pg 147
Editions Arcam, pg 147
Editions Aubier-Montaigne SA, pg 149
Autrement Editions, pg 149
Editions Belfond, pg 150
Berg International Editeurs, pg 150
William Blake & Co, pg 150
De Boccard Edition-Diffusion, pg 151
Emgleo Breiz, pg 151
Editions Buchet/Chastel, pg 152
Le Cadratin, pg 152
Cicero Editeurs, pg 155
Editions de Compostelle, pg 156
Librairie Jose Corti, pg 156
Nouvelles Editions Debresse, pg 158
La Delirante, pg 158
Georges-Charles Demay, pg 158
Les Editeurs Reunis, pg 161
Editions Fanlac, pg 163
Fata Morgana, pg 163
FBT de R Editions/Editions des Limbes d'Or, pg 163
Librairie Fischbacher, International Art Book Distribution (import-export), pg 164
Edition Galilee, pg 165
Editions Gallimard, pg 165
Librairie Guenegaud Sarl, pg 167
Editions Hatier SA, pg 168
Editions de l'Herne, pg 168
Pierre Horay Editeur, pg 168
Editions Infrarouge, pg 169
Editions Interferences, pg 169
Editions J'ai Lu, pg 170
Editions Klincksieck, pg 171
Langues & Mondes/L'Asiatheque, pg 171
Editions Fernand Lanore Sarl, pg 172
Editions des Limbes d'Or/FBT de R Editions, pg 173
Mercure de France SA, pg 176
Librairie Minard, pg 176
Nil Editions, pg 177
Librairie A-G Nizet Sarl, pg 177
Noir Sur Blanc, pg 177
Nouvelles Editions Latines, pg 178
Editions Odile Jacob, pg 178
Editions de l'Orante, pg 178
Editions Paradigme, pg 179
Editions Jean Picollec, pg 179
Editions Christian Pirot, pg 180
Presence Africaine Editions, pg 180
Editions Sand et Tchou SA, pg 183
Editions Scala, pg 184
Seghers, pg 184
Nouvelles Editions Seguier, pg 184
Editions de Septembre, pg 184
Le Serpent a Plumes, pg 184
Service Technique pour l'Education, pg 185
Editions Andre Silvaire Sarl, pg 185
Societe des Editions Grasset et Fasquelle, pg 185
Association d'Editions Sorg, pg 186
Editions Stock, pg 186
Les Editions de la Table Ronde, pg 187
Editions Tallandier, pg 187
Publications de l'Universite de Pau, pg 188
La Vague a l'ame, pg 188
Editions Verdier, pg 189

Germany
A Francke Verlag (Tubingen und Basel), pg 191
Verlag und Antiquariat Frank Albrecht, pg 192
Alpha Literatur Verlag/Alpha Presse, pg 193
Anabas-Verlag Guenter Kaempf GmbH & Co KG, pg 193
Verlag APHAlA Svea Haske, Sonja Schumann GbR, pg 194
arani-Verlag GmbH, pg 194
Ars Vivendi Verlag, pg 195
Asso Verlag, pg 196
Atelier Verlag Andernach (AVA), pg 196
Aufbau-Verlag GmbH, pg 196
J J Augustin GmbH Verlag, pg 196
Verlag der Autoren GmbH & Co KG, pg 197
AvivA Britta Jurgs GmbH, pg 197
Dr Bachmaier Verlag GmbH, pg 197
Dr Wolfgang Baur Verlag Kunst & Alltag, pg 199
be.bra verlag GmbH, pg 199
Bechtle Graphische Betriebe und Verlagsgesellschaft mbH und Co KG, pg 200
Beck & Gluckler Verlag GmbH & Co KG, pg 200
Verlag C H Beck (OHG), pg 200
Beerenverlag, pg 200
Belser Wissenschaftlicher Dienst, pg 200
Bergstadtverlag Wilhelm Gottlieb Korn GmbH Wuerzburg, pg 200
C Bertelsmann Verlag GmbH, pg 201
Blanvalet VerlagGmbH, pg 204
Bleicher Verlag GmbH, pg 204
Brandes & Apsel Verlag GmbH, pg 206
Brigg Verlag Franz-Josef Buchler KG, pg 206
Brunnen-Verlag GmbH, pg 207
Fachverlag Hans Carl GmbH, pg 209
Christusbruderschaft Selbitz ev, Abt Verlag, pg 210
Claassen Verlag GmbH, pg 210
ComMedia & Arte Verlag Bernd Mayer, pg 211
J G Cotta'sche Buchhandlung Nachfolger GmbH, pg 212
Dagmar Dreves Verlag, pg 212
Dana Verlag, pg 212
Das Arsenal, Verlag fuer Kultur und Politik GmbH, pg 212
Deutsche Verlags-Anstalt GmbH (DVA), pg 214
Deutscher Literatur-Verlag, pg 215
Deutscher Taschenbuch Verlag GmbH & Co KG (dtv), pg 215
Edition Dia, pg 216
Eugen Diederichs Verlag GmbH & Co KG, pg 216
Dieterichsche Verlagsbuchhandlung Mainz, pg 216
Maximilian Dietrich Verlag, pg 216
Dolling und Galitz Verlag GmbH, pg 217
Droste Verlag GmbH, pg 218
Karl Elser Druck GmbH, pg 218
Echter Wurzburg Frankische Gesellschaftsdruckerei und Verlag GmbH, pg 220
Econ Taschenbuchverlag, pg 220
Econ Verlag GmbH, pg 220
Edition Klaus Blahak Dr Fredric Kroll, pg 220
Edition Solitude - Akademie Schloss Solitude, pg 221
Egmont vgs verlagsgesellschaft mbH, pg 221
Ehrenwirth Verlag GmbH, pg 221
Eichborn AG, pg 222
EinfallsReich Verlagsgesellschaft MbH, pg 222
Engelhorn Verlag, pg 222
Verlag Peter Engstler, pg 223
Eremiten-Presse und Verlag GmbH, pg 223
Europa Verlag GmbH, pg 224
Extent Verlag und Service Wolfgang M Flamm, pg 225
Fabel-Verlag Gudrun Liebchen, pg 226
Fannei & Walz Verlag, pg 227
Wolfgang Fietkau Verlag, pg 227
Karin Fischer Verlag GmbH, pg 228
Fleischhauer & Spohn GmbH & Co, pg 228
FVA-Frankfurter Verlagsanstalt GmbH, pg 229
Frieling & Partner GmbH, pg 230
GLB Parkland Verlags-und Vertriebs GmbH, pg 232
Verlagsgesellschaft R Gloess & Co, pg 233
Wilhelm Goldmann Verlag GmbH, pg 233
Grabert-Verlag, pg 233
Brigitte Grabitz - ikoo Buchverlag, pg 233
Haag und Herchen Verlag GmbH, pg 235
Haering, Siegfried, Literaten-Verlag Ulm, pg 236
Hansa Verlag Ingwert Paulsen Jr, pg 237
Carl Hanser Verlag, pg 237
Heinz-Theo Gremme Verlag, pg 239
Heliopolis-Verlag, pg 239
Hellerau-Verlag Dresden GmbH, pg 239
F A Herbig Verlagsbuchhandlung GmbH, pg 239
Hans-Alfred Herchen & Co Verlag KG, pg 239
Verlag Peter Hoell, pg 241
Hoffmann und Campe Verlag GmbH, pg 242
Horlemann Verlag, pg 243
Husum Druck- und Verlagsgesellschaft mbH Co KG, pg 244
Jan Thorbecke Verlag GmbH & Co, pg 246
KBV-Verlags-und Mediengesellschaft mbH, pg 248
Martin Kelter Verlag GmbH u Co, pg 248
Kidemus Verlag GmbH, pg 248
Gustav Kiepenheuer Verlag GmbH, pg 249
Verlag Kiepenheuer und Witsch GmbH & Co KG, pg 249
Verlag Kleine Schritte Ursula Dahm & Co, pg 249
Klosterhaus-Verlagsbuchhandlung Dr Grimm KG, pg 250
Albrecht Knaus Verlag GmbH, pg 250
Druckerei & Verlag Ernst Knoth GmbH, pg 251
Kolibri-Verlags GmbH, pg 252
KONTEXTverlag, pg 252
Karin Kramer Verlag, pg 253
Krug & Schadenberg, pg 254
Verlag Antje Kunstmann GmbH, pg 254
Landbuch-Verlagsgesellschaft mbH, pg 255
Verlag Langewiesche-Brandt KG, pg 256
Ingrid Langner, pg 256
Leibniz-Buecherwarte, pg 257
Dr Gisela Lermann, pg 257
Libertas- Europaeisches Institut GmbH, pg 257
Linden-Verlag, pg 258
Logos-Verlag Literatur & Layout GmbH, pg 258
Luchterhand Literaturverlag GmbH/ Verlag Volk & Welt GmbH, pg 259
Lutherische Verlagsgesellschaft mbH, pg 259
Annemarie Maeger, pg 260
Mannerschwarm Skript Verlag Bartholomae & Co OHG, pg 260
Edition Maritim GmbH, pg 261
Matthes und Seitz Verlag GmbH, pg 261
Merlin Verlag Andreas Meyer Verlags GmbH und Co KG, pg 263
Miranda-Verlag Stefan Ehlert, pg 264
Missio eV Aachen, pg 264
Mitteldeutscher Verlag GmbH, pg 264
Monia Verlag, pg 265
Gunter Narr Verlag, pg 266
Nebel Verlag GmbH, pg 267
Neue Erde Verlags GmbH, pg 267
Verlag Neues Leben GmbH, pg 268
New Era Publications Deutschland GmbH, pg 268
Nie/Nie/Sagen-Verlag, pg 268
C W Niemeyer Buchverlage GmbH, pg 268
Rainar Nitzsche Verlag, pg 269
nymphenburger, pg 269
Orlanda Frauenverlag GmbH, pg 270
Osho Verlag GmbH, pg 271
Ostfalia-Verlag Jurgen Schierer, pg 271
Pandion-Verlag, Ulrike Schmoll, pg 271
Paranus Verlag - Bruecke Neumuenster GmbH, pg 271
Passavia Druckerei GmbH, Verlag, pg 271
Pfaffenweiler Presse, pg 272
Pfalzische Verlagsanstalt GmbH, pg 272
Philipp Reclam Jun Verlag GmbH, pg 273

PUBLISHERS

Pollner Verlag, pg 274
Projektion J Buch- und Musikverlag GmbH, pg 275
Propylaeen Verlag, Zweigniederlassung Berlin der Ullstein Buchverlage GmbH, pg 275
Quintessenz Verlags-GmbH, pg 276
Reclam Verlag Leipzig, pg 277
Rogner und Bernhard GmbH & Co Verlags KG, pg 279
ROSPO Verlag, pg 280
Verlag Roter Morgen, pg 280
Rowohlt Verlag GmbH, pg 280
Ruetten & Loening Berlin GmbH, pg 281
Eugen Salzer-Verlag GmbH & Co KG, pg 281
Richard Scherpe Verlag GmbH, pg 283
Buchverlag Andrea Schmitz, pg 284
Schneekluth Verlag, pg 284
Schoeffling & Co, pg 284
Carl Ed Schuenemann KG, pg 285
Theodor Schuster, pg 285
Gerd Simon & Claudia Magiera, Verlagsbuero, pg 287
Adolf Sponholtz Verlag, pg 288
Steidl Verlag, pg 289
Verlag Stendel, pg 290
Steyler Verlag, pg 290
Suedverlag GmbH, pg 291
Suedwest Verlag GmbH & Co KG, pg 291
Otto Teich, pg 292
Druck-und Verlagshans Thiele & Schwarz GmbH, pg 293
K Thienemanns Verlag, pg 293
Verlag Theodor Thoben, pg 293
Hans Thoma Verlag GmbH Kunst und Buchverlag, pg 294
Tomus Verlag GmbH, pg 294
Treves Editions Verein Zur Foerderung der Kuenstlerischen Taetigkeiten, pg 295
Ullstein Heyne List GmbH & Co KG, pg 295
Ulrike Helmer Verlag, pg 296
Unrast Verlag e V, pg 296
Verlag und Studio fuer Hoerbuchproduktionen, pg 298
VS Verlagshaus Stuttgart GmbH, pg 299
W Ludwig Verlag GmbH, pg 300
Verlag Klaus Wagenbach GmbH, pg 300
Friedenauer Presse Katharina Wagenbach-Wolff, pg 300
Weidler Buchverlag Berlin, pg 301
Rosa Winkel Verlag GmbH, pg 303
Wolf's-Verlag Berlin, pg 304
Wolgang Fietkau, pg 304
The World of Books Literaturverlag, pg 304
Das Wunderhorn Verlag GmbH, pg 304
Wunderlich Verlag, pg 304
Zambon Verlag, pg 305
Zebulon Verlag GmbH & Co KG, pg 305

Ghana
Anowuo Educational Publications, pg 306
Ghana Publishing Corporation, pg 307
Moxon Paperbacks, pg 307
Waterville Publishing House, pg 308

Greece
Bergadis, pg 309
Boukoumanis' Editions, pg 309
Denise Harvey, pg 311
Hestia-1 D Hestia-Kollaros & Co Corporation, pg 311
Minoas SA, pg 313
Stochastis, pg 315
To Rodakio, pg 315

Guadeloupe
Librairie Generale JASOR, pg 316

Guatemala
Grupo Editorial RIN-78, pg 316

Haiti
Editions Caraiibes SA, pg 317

Holy See (Vatican City State)
Biblioteca Apostolica Vaticana, pg 317

Hong Kong
Research Centre for Translation, pg 321

Hungary
Europa Konyvkiado, pg 323
Helikon Kiado, pg 324
Jelenkor Verlag, pg 324
Magveto Koenyvkiado, pg 325
Park Konyvkiado Kft (Park Publisher), pg 326
Szepirodalmi Koenyvkiado Kiado, pg 327

Iceland
Almenna Bokafelagid, pg 327
Forlagid, pg 327

India
Ananda Publishers Pvt Ltd, pg 330
Atma Ram & Sons, pg 331
Geeta Prakasham, pg 337
Arnold Heinman Publishers (India) Pvt Ltd, pg 338
Intertrade Publications, pg 340
Jaico Publishing House, pg 340
People's Publishing House (P) Ltd, pg 346

Indonesia
Pustaka Utama Grafiti, PT, pg 357

Israel
Am Oved Publishers Ltd, pg 365
The Bialik Institute, pg 365
Boostan Publishing House, pg 366
Classikaletet, pg 366
DAT Publications, pg 366
Gvanim Publishing House, pg 367
Hakibbutz Hameuchad Publishing House Ltd, pg 368
The Institute for the Translation of Hebrew Literature, pg 368
Karni Publishers Ltd, pg 369
Massada Press Ltd, pg 370
Schocken Publishing House Ltd, pg 372
Sifriat Poalim Ltd, pg 372
University Publishing Projects Ltd, pg 373
Y L Peretz Publishing Co, pg 374
Zmora-Bitan, Publishers Ltd, pg 374

Italy
Adelphi Edizioni SpA, pg 374
Bollati Boringhieri Editore Srl, pg 378
Bonacci editore, pg 378
Bonsignori Editore SRL, pg 378
Book Editore, pg 378
Campanotto, pg 379
Nuova Casa Editrice Licinio Cappelli GEM srl, pg 379
Casa Editrice Felice Le Monnier, pg 380
Nuova Coletti Editore Roma, pg 382
M d'Auria Editore SAS, pg 384
Giulio Einaudi Editore SpA, pg 387
Giangiacomo Feltrinelli SpA, pg 389
Festina Lente Edizioni, pg 389
Arnaldo Forni Editore SRL, pg 389
Istituto Geografico de Agostini SpA, pg 390
Gius Laterza e Figli SpA, pg 391
Ugo Guanda Editore, pg 392
Il Minotauro, pg 393
Edizioni Internazionali di Letteratura e Scienze, pg 394
Linea d'Ombra Libri, pg 396
Longanesi & C, pg 396
La Luna, pg 397
Tommaso Marotta Editore Srl, pg 398
Arnoldo Mondadori Editore SpA, pg 399
Gruppo Ugo Mursia Editore SpA, pg 400
Newton Compton Editori SRL, pg 401
Leo S Olschki, pg 402
Paideia Editrice, pg 402
Palatina Editrice, pg 402
Neri Pozza Editore, pg 404
RAI.ERI, pg 405
Rara-lst Editoriale di Bibliofilia e Reprints, pg 405
RCS Rizzoli Libri SpA, pg 405
Riccardo Ricciardi Editore SpA, pg 405
Salerno Editrice SRL, pg 406
Edizioni San Paolo SRL, pg 407
SEMAR Publishers SRL, pg 407
Studio Bibliografico Adelmo Polla, pg 409
Edizioni Studio Tesi SRL, pg 409
Sugarco Edizioni SRL, pg 409
UTET (Unione Tipografico-Editrice Torinese), pg 411
Viviani Editore srl, pg 412

Japan
Chuo-Koron-Sha Inc, pg 415
The Hokuseido Press, pg 417
Iwanami Shoten, Publishers, pg 418
Kodansha International, pg 420
Charles E Tuttle Publishing Co Inc, pg 428
Yushodo Co Ltd, pg 429

Kenya
Foundation Books, pg 431
Transafrica Press, pg 433

Republic of Korea
Hollym Corporation Publishers, pg 437
Hw Moon Publishing Co, pg 437
Iljisa Publishing House, pg 437
Jeong-eum Munhwasa, pg 437
Mirinae, pg 438
Sejong Daewang Kinyom Saophoe, pg 440

Latvia
Artava Ltd, pg 441
Nordik/Tapals Publishers Ltd, pg 442

TYPE OF PUBLICATION INDEX

Preses Nams, pg 442
Vaidelote, pg 442

Liechtenstein
Liechtenstein Verlag AG, pg 444

Lithuania
AS Narbuto Leidykla (AS Narbutas' Publishers), pg 445
Baltos Lankos, pg 445
Lietuvos Rasytoju Sajungos Leidykla, pg 446
The Publishing House of the Lithuanian Writers' Union, pg 446
Tyto Alba Publishers, pg 446
Vaga Ltd, pg 446

Luxembourg
Editions APESS ASBL, pg 447
Cahiers Luxembourgeois, pg 447
Eiffes Romain, pg 447
Op der Lay, pg 447
Editions Phi, pg 448

The Former Yugoslav Republic of Macedonia
Detska radost, pg 448
Makedonska kniga (Knigoizdatelstvo), pg 449
Mi-An Knigoizdatelstvo, pg 449
Strk Publishing House, pg 449
Zumpres Publishing Firm, pg 449

Malaysia
Holograms (M) Sdn Bhd, pg 452

Mali
EDIM SA, pg 455

Mexico
Ediciones Era SA de CV, pg 460
Fondo de Cultura Economica, pg 461
Editorial Hermes SA, pg 461
Phillip Richard Conover Lazo, pg 462
Universidad Veracruzana Direccion General Editorial y de Publicaciones, pg 468
Universo Editorial SA de CV Edicion de Libros Revistas y Periodicos, pg 468

Monaco
Les Editions du Rocher, pg 469
Rondeau Giannipiero a Monaco, pg 469

Netherlands
Uitgeverij Arena BV, pg 473
De Bezige Bij, pg 474
Uitgeverij G F Callenbach BV, pg 475
Castrum Peregrini Presse, pg 475
Van Gennep Ltd, pg 477
HES & De Graaf Publishers BV, pg 478
Historische Uitgeverij, pg 478
Holland B V Uitgeversmaatschappij, pg 478
Uitgeefmaatschappij J H Kok BV, pg 480
Nijgh & Van Ditmar Amsterdam, pg 482
Em Querido's Uitgeverij BV, pg 483
A J G Strengholt's Boeken, Anno 1928, BV, pg 484

Uitgeverij G A van Oorschot bv, pg 486
Wereldbibliotheek, pg 487

New Zealand
The Caxton Press, pg 490
Outrigger Publishers, pg 494

Nigeria
Aromolaran Publishing Co Ltd, pg 498
Black Academy Press, pg 498
Cross Continent Press Ltd, pg 498
Ethiope Publishing Corporation, pg 499
Heritage Books, pg 499
Longman Nigeria Plc, pg 500
New Horn Press Ltd, pg 500
Northern Nigerian Publishing Co Ltd, pg 500
Nwamife Publishers Ltd, pg 500
Onibon-Oje Publishers, pg 501
University Publishing Co, pg 502

Norway
Det Norske Samlaget, pg 503
Gyldendal Norsk Forlag A/S, pg 503

Philippines
Anvil Publishing Inc, pg 512
Cacho Publishing House, Inc, pg 512
Marren Publishing House, Inc, pg 513
Philippine Education Co Inc, pg 514
University of the Philippines Press, pg 515

Poland
Spoldzielnia Wydawnicza 'Czytelnik', pg 516
Wydawnictwo Dolnoslaskie, pg 516
Instytut Wydawniczy Pax, Inco-Veritas, pg 517
Iskry - Publishing House Ltd spotka zoo, pg 517
KAW Krajowa Agencja Wydawnicza, pg 517
'Ksiazka i Wiedza' Spotdzielnia Wydawniczo-Handlowa, pg 517
Wydawnictwo Literackie, pg 517
Wydawnictwo Lodzkie, pg 517
Wydawnictwo Lubelskie, pg 518
Muza SA, pg 518
Panstwowy Instytut Wydawniczy (PIW), pg 518
Wydawnictwo SIC, pg 520
'Slask' Ltd, pg 520
Spoleczny Instytut Wydawniczy Znak, pg 520
Spotdzielna Anagram, pg 520
Videograf II Sp z o o Zaklad Poracy Chronionej, pg 520
Wydawnictwo WAB, pg 520

Portugal
Bezerr-Editorae e Distribuidora de Abel Antonio Bezerra, pg 522
Brasilia Editora (J Carvalho Branco), pg 523
Chaves Ferreira Publicacoes SA, pg 523
Editora Classica, pg 523
Edicoes Colibri, pg 523
DIFEL - Difusao Editorial SA, pg 524
Editorial Estampa, Lda, pg 524
Publicacoes Europa-America Lda, pg 524
Fenda Edicoes, pg 525
Editorial Inquerito Lda, pg 526
Latina Livraria, pg 526
Publicacoes Dom Quixote Lda, pg 528
Realizacoes Artis, pg 529
Sa da Costa Editora, pg 529
Solivros, pg 529
Almerinda Teixeira, pg 529

Puerto Rico
University of Puerto Rico Press (EDUPR), pg 531

Romania
Ars Longa Publishing House, pg 532
Editura Clusium, Casa de Editura Atlas-Clusium SRL, pg 532
Editure Ion Creanga, pg 532
Editura Dacia, pg 532
Editura Excelsior, pg 533
Hasefer, pg 533
Editura Kriterion SA, pg 534
Mentor Kiado, pg 534
Editura Militara, pg 534
Editura Minerva, pg 534
Nemira Verlag, pg 534
Editura Niculescu, pg 534
Pallas-Akademia Koenyvkiadoes Koenyvkereskedes, pg 535
Pandora Publishing House, pg 535
Polirom Verlag, pg 535
RAO International Publishing Co, pg 535
Saeculum IO, pg 535
Editura Signata, pg 536
Est-Samuel Tastet Verlag, pg 536
Editura Univers, pg 536

Russian Federation
ARGO-RISK Publisher, pg 537
Armada Publishing House, pg 537
BLIC, russko-Baltijskij informaciionnyj centr, AO, pg 537
Druzhba Narodov, pg 537
Kabardino-Balkarskoye knizhnoye izdatelstvo, pg 539
Kavkazskaya Biblioteka Publishing House, pg 539
KUbK Publishing House, pg 539
Ladomir Publishing House, pg 539
Publishing House Limbus Press, pg 539
Mir Knigi Ltd, pg 540
Panorama Publishing House, pg 541
Profizdat, pg 541
Raduga Publishers, pg 541
Russkaya Kniga Izdatelstvo (Publishers), pg 541
Izdatelstvo Sovetskii Pisatel, pg 542
Voyenizdat, pg 542

Senegal
Centre Africain d'Animation et d'Echanges Culturels Editions Khoudia, pg 544
Les Nouvelles Editions Africaines du Senegal NEAS, pg 544

Slovakia
Kalligram Kiado spol sro, pg 549
Luc vydavatelske druzstvo, pg 550
Vydavatelstvo Obzor, pg 550
Vydavatepstvo Praca spol sro, pg 550
Slovansky Tatran, Vydavatel 'stro spoi sro, pg 550
Slovensky Spisovatel Ltd as, pg 550
Smena Publishing House, pg 550

Slovenia
Cankarjeva Zalozba, pg 551
Franc-Franc podjetje za promocijo kulture Murska Sobota d o o, pg 551
Zalozba Mihelac d o o, pg 552
Zalozba Obzorja d d Maribor, pg 552

South Africa
HAUM (Hollandsch Afrikaansche Uitgevers Maatschappij), pg 555
Human & Rousseau (Pty) Ltd, pg 555
Nasou Via Afrika, pg 557
Queillerie Publishers, pg 558

Spain
Acantilado, pg 561
Aguilar SA de Ediciones, pg 562
Ediciones Akal SA, pg 562
Ediciones Alfar SA, pg 562
Alianza Editorial SA, pg 562
Ambit Serveis Editorials, SA, pg 563
Editorial Biblioteca Nueva SL, pg 565
Calamo Editorial, pg 566
Editorial Castalia, pg 566
Complutense, SA Editorial, pg 568
Ediciones Encuentro SA, pg 573
Editorial Grupo Cero, pg 576
Ediciones Hiperion SL, pg 577
Institucion Fernando el Catolico de la Excma Diputacion de Zaragoza, pg 578
Editorial Lumen SA, pg 580
Editorial Milenio Arts Grafiques Bobala, SL, pg 582
Editorial la Muralla SA, pg 583
Nueva Acropolis, pg 584
Editora Regional de Murcia - ERM, pg 588
Editorial Seix Barral SA, pg 590
Torremozas SL Ediciones, pg 593
Trea Ediciones, SL, pg 593
Turner Publicaciones, pg 593
Tursen, SA, pg 593
Publicacions de la Universitat de Barcelona, pg 594
Editorial Verbum SL, pg 595
Visor Libros, pg 596

Sudan
Al-Ayam Press Co Ltd, pg 598
Khartoum University Press, pg 598

Sweden
Ellerstroms, pg 602
Samsprak Forlags AB, pg 606

Switzerland
Editions L'Age d'Homme - La Cite, pg 608
Ammann Verlag & Co, pg 608
Arche Verlag AG, Raabe und Vitali, pg 608
Armenia Editions, pg 608
Atrium Verlag AG, pg 609
Editions de la Baconniere SA, pg 609
Verlag Bibliophile Drucke von Josef Stocker AG, pg 610
Blaukreuz-Verlag Bern, pg 610
Werner Classen Verlag, pg 611
Cosa-Verlag, Giusep Condrau SA, pg 611
Cosmos-Verlag AG, pg 611
Daphnis-Verlag, pg 612
eFeF-Verlag/Edition Ebersbach, pg 613
Erker-Verlag, pg 613
Edition Hans Erpf Verlagsgenossenschaft, pg 613
Europa Verlag AG, pg 614
Giampiero Casagrande Editore, pg 614
Haffmans Verlag AG, pg 615
Editions Ides et Calendes SA, pg 616
Jordanverlag AG, pg 616
Kranich-Verlag, Dres AG & H R Bosch-Gwalter, pg 617
Lia rumantscha, pg 618
Limmat Verlag, pg 618
Manesse Verlag GmbH, pg 618
Librairie-Editions J Marguerat, pg 618
Editions H Messeiller SA, pg 619
Verlag Nagel & Kimche AG, Zurich, pg 619
Les Editions Noir sur Blanc, pg 620
Orte-Verlag, pg 621
Ostschweiz Druck und Verlag, pg 621
Editions du Panorama, pg 621
Verlag Friedrich Reinhardt AG, pg 622
Rex Verlag, pg 623
Roth et Sauter SA, pg 623
Rotpunktverlag, pg 623
Sinwel-Buchhandlung Verlag, pg 624
Speer -Verlag, pg 625
Strom-Verlag Luzern, pg 625
Editions des Trois Collines Francois Lachenal, pg 626
Editions 24 Heures, pg 626
Viktoria-Verlag Peter Marti, pg 627
Verlag Die Waage, pg 627
Verlag im Waldgut AG, pg 627
Buchverlag der Druckerei Wetzikon AG, pg 627
Zbinden Druck und Verlag AG, pg 628

Taiwan, Province of China
Chien Chen Bookstore Publishing Company Ltd, pg 629
Chung Hwa Book Co Ltd, pg 629

United Republic of Tanzania
East African Publishing House, pg 633

Togo
Editions Akpagnon, pg 636
Les Nouvelles Editions Africaines du TOGO (NEA-TOGO), pg 636

Tunisia
Academie Tunisienne des Sciences, des Lettres et des Arts Beit El Hekma, pg 637
Ceres Editions, pg 637
Les Editions de l'Arbre, pg 638
Maison Tunisienne de l'Edition, pg 638
Editions Techniques Specialisees, pg 638

Turkey
Altın Kitaplar Yayinevi, pg 638
Kabalci Yayinevi, pg 642

Ukraine
Osnova, Kharkov State University Press, pg 643
Osnovy Publishers, pg 643

PUBLISHERS

United Kingdom
Books for Europe Ltd, pg 657
Canongate Books Ltd, pg 663
Carcanet Press Ltd, pg 663
The Chrysalis Press, pg 667
Andre Deutsch Ltd, pg 675
Aidan Ellis Publishing, pg 678
Faber & Faber Ltd, pg 681
GMP Publishers Ltd, pg 687
The Greek Bookshop, pg 689
Robert Hale Ltd, pg 691
The Harvill Press Ltd, pg 693
Northcote House Publishers Ltd, pg 719
Octopus Publishing Group, pg 720
Peter Owen Ltd, pg 722
Parapress Ltd, pg 724
Planet, pg 728
St George's Press, pg 737
Seren, pg 740
Souvenir Press Ltd, pg 743
Telegraph Books, pg 748
Tuba Press, pg 750
Frederick Warne Publishers Ltd, pg 754
The Windrush Press Ltd, pg 757

Uruguay
La Flor del Itapebi, pg 760
Ediciones Trilce, pg 761

Venezuela
Biblioteca Ayacucho, pg 762

Yugoslavia
Alfa-Narodna Knjiga, pg 764
Association of Yugoslav Publishers & Booksellers, pg 764
Beogradski Izdavacko-Graficki Zavod, pg 764
Izdavacka preduzece Gradina, pg 764
Jugoslavijapublik, pg 764
Nio Pobjeda - Oour Izdavacko-Publicisticka Djelatnost, pg 765
Obod, pg 765
Izdavacka Organizacija Rad, pg 765
Panorama NIJP/ID Grigorije Bozovic, pg 765
Partenon MAM Sistem, pg 765
Izdavacko Preduzece Matice Srpske, pg 765
Srpska Knjizevna Zadruga, pg 765
Svetovi, pg 766

Zimbabwe
Anvil Press, pg 767

BIBLES

Albania
NL SH, pg 1

Argentina
Argentine Bible Society, pg 3
Editorial Ruy Diaz SAEIC, pg 5
Editorial Guadalupe, pg 6
Ediciones Preescolar SA, pg 8
San Pablo, pg 8

Australia
Bible Society in Australia National Headquarters, pg 15
Hodder Headline Australia, pg 26
St Pauls, pg 41

Austria
Oesterreichisches Katholisches Bibelwerk, pg 56

Belgium
NV Uitgeverij Altiora Averbode, pg 64
Brepols Publishers NV, pg 65

Brazil
Action Editora Ltda, pg 77
Associacao Arvore da Vida, pg 79
Ediouro Publicacoes, SA, pg 81
Edicoes Loyola SA, pg 87
Editora Mundo Cristao, pg 88
Paulinas Editorial, pg 89
Paulus Editora, pg 89
Editora Scipione Ltda, pg 91

Bulgaria
Sluntse Publishing House, pg 98

Colombia
Eurolibros Ltda, pg 111
Instituto Misionerao Hijas De San Pablo, pg 113

Czech Republic
Ceska Biblicka Spolecnost, pg 123
Zvon, pg 129

Denmark
Bibelselskabets Forlag og Vajsenhusets Forlag, pg 130
Scandinavia Publishing House, pg 135

Estonia
Estonian Bible Society, pg 140

Finland
Foersamlingsfoerbundets Foerlags AB, pg 142
Lasten Keskus Oy, pg 143

France
Editions Al Liamm, pg 146
Societe Biblique Francaise, pg 150
Editions du Cerf, pg 153
Le Laurier, pg 172
Editions Mediaspaul, pg 175
Muller Edition, pg 176
Editions Le Sarment, pg 184
Sofradif Editions Philippe Auzou, pg 185

Germany
Agentur des Rauhen Hauses Hamburg GmbH, pg 192
Bertelsmann Lexikon Verlag GmbH, pg 201
R Brockhaus Verlag, pg 206
Deutsche Bibelgesellschaft, pg 213
Evangelische Haupt-Bibelgesellschaft und von Cansteinsche Bibelanstalt, pg 225
Friedrich Frommann Verlag, pg 230
Grass-Verlag, pg 234
Verlag Katholisches Bibelwerk GmbH, pg 248
Verlag Parzeller GmbH & Co KG, pg 271
Pattloch Verlag GmbH & Co KG, pg 272
Silberburg-Verlag Titus Haeussermann GmbH, pg 287
Steyler Verlag, pg 290
Verein der Benediktiner zu Beuron-Beuroner Kunstverlag, pg 297
Verlag und Studio fuer Hoerbuchproduktionen, pg 298

Ghana
Ghana Institute of Linguistics Literacy & Bible Translation (GILLBT), pg 307
World Literature Project, pg 308

Greece
Alamo Hellas, pg 308
Apostoliki Diakonia tis Ekklisias tis Hellados, pg 309
Chrysi Penna - Golden Pen Books, pg 309
Logos, pg 312

Hungary
Advent Kiado, pg 323
Agape Ferences Nyomda es Konyvkiado Kft, pg 323

India
Dolphin Publications, pg 336
Satprakashan Sanchar Kendra, pg 349

Indonesia
Penerbit Nusa Indah, pg 356

Ireland
Dominican Publications, pg 359
Four Courts Press Ltd, pg 360

Israel
Carta, The Israel Map & Publishing Co Ltd, pg 366
Koren Publishers Jerusalem Ltd, pg 369
Rolnik Publishers, pg 371

Italy
Centro Biblico, pg 380
Citta Nuova Editrice, pg 382
Cittadella Editrice, pg 382
Elle Di Ci - Libreria Dottrina Cristiana, pg 388
Piero Gribaudi Editore, pg 391
In Dialogo, pg 393
Lubrina Editore Srl, pg 397
Giuseppe Maimone Editore, pg 397
Editrice Massimo SAS di Crespi Cesare e C, pg 398
Paideia Editrice, pg 402
Edizioni Piemme SpA, pg 403
Fausto Sardini Editrice, pg 407
Societa Editrice Internazionale - SEI, pg 408
Editrice Uomini Nuovi, pg 410

Japan
Japan Bible Society, pg 418
Myrtos Inc, pg 421

Kenya
Paulines Publications-Africa, pg 433

Republic of Korea
Kukmin Doseo Publishing Co Inc, pg 438
St Pauls, pg 439
Word of Life Press, pg 440

Lebanon
Darl el-Machreq Sarl, pg 443

Malta
Gozo Press, pg 456
Media Centre, pg 456

TYPE OF PUBLICATION INDEX

Mexico
Ediciones Dabar, SA de CV, pg 459
Fernandez Editores SA de CV, pg 461
Editorial Limusa SA de CV, pg 463
Naves Internacional de Ediciones SA, pg 464
Organizacion Cultural LP SA de CV, pg 465
Palabra Ediciones Verlagsgesellschaft mbH, pg 465
Ediciones Promesa, SA de CV, pg 466

Netherlands
Boekencentrum BV, pg 474
Katholieke Bijbelstichting, pg 479
Telos Boeken, pg 485

Pakistan
Sheikh Muhammad Ashraf Publishers, pg 506

Philippines
Communication Foundation for Asia Media Group (CFAMG), pg 513
Logos (Divine Word) Publications Inc, pg 513
Our Lady of Manaoag Publisher, pg 514

Poland
Instytut Wydawniczy Pax, Inco-Veritas, pg 517
Vocatio Publishing House, pg 520

Singapore
Tecman Bible House, pg 549

South Africa
Bet-El Publishers, pg 553
Institute for Reformational Studies CHE, pg 555

Spain
Publicacions de l'Abadia de Montserrat, pg 561
Editorial Claret SA, pg 568
Editora Comercial de Publicaciones, pg 568
Complutense, SA Editorial, pg 568
Ediciones Cristiandad, pg 569
Idea Books, SA, pg 578
Ediciones Mensajero, pg 582
San Pablo Ediciones, pg 589
Ediciones San Pio X, pg 589
Ediciones Sigueme SA, pg 590
Editorial Verbo Divino, pg 595

Sweden
International Bible Society, pg 603

Switzerland
Berchtold Haller Verlag, pg 609
Beroa-Verlag, pg 609
La Maison de la Bible, pg 618

Taiwan, Province of China
Campus Evangelical Fellowship, Literature Department, pg 629

United Republic of Tanzania
Northwestern Publishers, pg 634
Peramiho Publications, pg 634

TYPE OF PUBLICATION INDEX BOOK

United Kingdom
McCall Barbour, pg 652
Bible Society, pg 654
Cambridge University Press, pg 662
Chapter Two, pg 666
Christian Education, pg 667
Cyhoeddiadau'r Gair, pg 673
Darton, Longman & Todd Ltd, pg 674
HarperCollins Publishers, pg 692
Hodder & Stoughton Religious, pg 696
Hodder Headline Ltd, pg 696
Angus Hudson Ltd, pg 697
The Islamic Texts Society, pg 701
Marcham Books, pg 711
Oxford University Press, pg 723
St Pauls Publishing, pg 744
Tern Press, pg 748

Yugoslavia
AGAPE, pg 764

Zimbabwe
Christian Audio-Visual Action (CAVA), pg 768

BIBLIOGRAPHIES

Albania
Botimpex Publications Import-Export Agency, pg 1
NL SH, pg 1

Argentina
Alfagrama SRL ediciones, pg 3
Instituto Nacional de Ciencia y Tecnica Hidrica (INCYTH), pg 7
Theoria SRL Distribuidora y Editora, pg 9

Australia
Australian Institute of Family Studies (AIFS), pg 13
Australian Scholarly Publishing, pg 14
Chingchic Publishers, pg 18
Magpie Books, pg 31
Mulini Press, pg 34
National Library of Australia, pg 34
New Albion Press, pg 34
D W Thorpe, pg 44

Austria
Akademische Druck-u Verlagsanstalt Dr Paul Struzl GmbH, pg 49
Universitaetsverlag Wagner GmbH, pg 60
Zirkular - Verlag der Dokumentationsstelle fuer neuere oesterreichische Literatur, pg 61

Bangladesh
The University Press Ltd, pg 62

Belgium
Maison d'Editions Baha'ies ASBL, pg 64
Bourdeaux-Capelle SA, pg 65
Brepols Publishers NV, pg 65
La Charte Editions juridiques, pg 66
Maison d'Editions Cl Dejaie, pg 67
Dexia Bank, pg 68
Claude Lefrancq Editeur, pg 71
Zuid En Noord VZW, pg 76

Botswana
National Library Service, pg 77

Brazil
Edicon Editora e Consultorial Ltda, pg 81
Fundacao Joaquim Nabuco Editora, pg 84
Edicoes Loyola SA, pg 87
Livraria Sulina Editora, pg 92

Bulgaria
Bojko Kacarmazov, pg 94
Hristo G Danov State Publishing House, pg 95

China
Qingdao Publishing House, pg 108
Shandong Friendship Press, pg 108

Colombia
Editorial Santillana SA, pg 113

The Democratic Republic of the Congo
Facultes Catoliques de Kinshasa, pg 115

Costa Rica
Centro Agronomico Tropical de Investigacion y Ensenanza (CATIE), pg 115
Litografia Artex, SA, pg 116

Cote d'Ivoire
Les Nouvelles Editions Africaines, pg 118

Croatia
AGM doo, pg 118
Leksikografski Zavod Miroslav Krleza, pg 119
Matica hrvatska, pg 119

Cyprus
Chrysopolitissa Publishers, pg 122

Czech Republic
Divadelni Ustav, pg 124
Jota, pg 125
Karmelitanske Nakladatelstvi, pg 125
Narodni Knihovna CR, pg 126
Statni Vedecka Knihovna Usti Nad Labem, pg 128

Denmark
Borgens Forlag A/S, pg 130
Danish National Library Authority, pg 131
Forum Publishers, pg 132

Egypt (Arab Republic of Egypt)
Dar El Shorouk Publishing & Distributing House, pg 138

Estonia
Estonian Academic Library, pg 139
Estonian Academy Publishers, pg 139
National Library of Estonia, pg 140

Finland
Forlagsaktiebolaget Scriptum, pg 142
Suomalaisen Kirjallisuuden Seura, pg 144

France
Academie Nationale de Reims, pg 145
Actes Graphiques, pg 145
ADPF Publications, pg 146
Agence Bibliographique de L'Enseignement Superieur, pg 146
Editions Belfond, pg 150
Editions Bertout, pg 150
Bibliotheque Nationale de France, pg 150
Editions Andre Bonne, pg 151
Michele Broutta Oeuvres Graphiques Contemporaines, pg 152
Le Cadratin, pg 152
Editions des Cahiers Bourbonnais, pg 152
CERDIC-Publications, pg 153
Chadwyck-Healey France, pg 154
CTNERHI - Centre Technique National d'Etudes et de Recherches sur les Handicaps et les Inadaptations, pg 157
Electre Editions du Cercle de la Librairie, pg 161
Institut d'Etudes Slaves, pg 163
Sarl Editions Jean Grassin, pg 167
Hachette Livre, pg 167
Institut International de la Marionnette, pg 170
Lettres Modernes, pg 172
Editions G P Maisonneuve et Larose, pg 174
Librairie Minard, pg 176
F De Nobele, pg 177
Editions A et J Picard SA, pg 179
Jean-Michel Place, pg 180
PRODIG UMR 8586 CNRS-Paris 1,4,7 ephe, pg 182
References cf, pg 182
Service des Publications Scientifiques du Museum National d'Histoire Naturelle, pg 184
Universitas, pg 188

French Polynesia
Scoop/Au Vent des Iles, pg 190

Germany
Verlag und Antiquariat Frank Albrecht, pg 192
Antiquariat und Verlag Auvermann Keip GmbH, pg 194
ARCult Media, pg 194
Barenreiter-Verlag Karl-Votterle GmbH & Co KG, pg 198
Bertelsmann Lexikon Verlag GmbH, pg 201
Biblio-Zeller Verlag, pg 202
Buchhaendler-Vereinigung GmbH, pg 207
Buchverlage Langen-Mueller/Herbig, pg 207
Centaurus-Verlagsgesellschaft GmbH, pg 210
Cicero Presse Verlag & Antiquariat, pg 210
Copress Verlag, pg 211
Degener & Co, Manfred Dreiss Verlag, pg 213
Karl Elser Druck GmbH, pg 218
Dumjahn Verlag, pg 219
Duncker und Humblot GmbH, pg 219
Edition Klaus Blahak Dr Fredric Kroll, pg 220
Fraunhofer IRB Verlag Fraunhofer Informationszentrum Raum und Bau, pg 229
Friedrich Frommann Verlag, pg 230
Guetersloher Verlagshaus Gerd Mohn, pg 235
Harrassowitz Verlag, pg 237
Dr Ernst Hauswedell & Co Verlag, pg 238
Erika Heydick Sax-Verlag Beucha, pg 240
Anton Hiersemann, Verlag, pg 240
Friedrich Hofmeister Musikverlag GmbH, pg 242
Edition ID-Archiv/ID-Verlag, pg 244
Iudicium Verlag GmbH, pg 245
JKL Publikationen GmbH, pg 246
Vittorio Klostermann GmbH, pg 250
K F Koehler Verlag, pg 251
Verlag Valentin Koerner GmbH, pg 252
Koptisch-Orthodoxes Zentrum, pg 252
Institut fuer Landes- und Stadtentwicklungsforschung, ILS Nordrhein-Westfalen, pg 255
Dr Gisela Lermann, pg 257
Merlin Verlag Andreas Meyer Verlags GmbH und Co KG, pg 263
Musikantiquariat und Dr Hans Schneider Verlag GmbH, pg 266
Verlag Neue Musik GmbH, pg 267
C W Niemeyer Buchverlage GmbH, pg 268
Max Niemeyer Verlag GmbH, pg 269
Georg Olms Verlag AG, pg 270
Pawel Panpresse, pg 272
Guido Pressler Verlag, pg 275
Rossipaul Kommunikation GmbH, pg 280
Eugen Salzer-Verlag GmbH & Co KG, pg 281
K G Saur Verlag GmbH, A Gale/Thomson Learning Company, pg 282
Schott Musik International GmbH & Co KG, pg 284
Stadt Duisburg - Amt Fuer Statistik, Stadtforschung und Europaangelegenheiten, pg 288
C A Starke Verlag, pg 289
Suedverlag GmbH, pg 291
Treves Editions Verein Zur Foerderung der Kuenstlerischen Taetigkeiten, pg 295
Trotzdem-Verlags Genossenschaft eG, pg 295
Ulrike Helmer Verlag, pg 296
Edition Curt Visel, pg 298
VWB-Verlag fur Wissenschaft & Bildung, Amand Aglaster, pg 300
Das Wunderhorn Verlag GmbH, pg 304
Zeller Verlag GmbH & Co, pg 305

Ghana
Bureau of Ghana Languages, pg 306

Greece
Hestia-1 D Hestia-Kollaros & Co Corporation, pg 311

Guatemala
Grupo Editorial RIN-78, pg 316

Haiti
Editions Caraiibes SA, pg 317

PUBLISHERS

Hong Kong
The Chinese University Press, pg 319
Sun Mui Press, pg 322

Hungary
CEU-Press, pg 323
Europa Konyvkiado, pg 323
Jelenkor Verlag, pg 324

Iceland
Frodi Ltd, pg 328

India
Agricole Publishing Academy, pg 330
Book Circle, pg 333
Disha Prakashan, pg 336
Gyan Publishing House, pg 338
Heritage Publishers, pg 338
Indian Documentation Service, pg 339
Natraj Prakashan, pg 344
Reliance Publishing House, pg 347
Vidya Puri, pg 352
Vidyarthi Mithram Press, pg 352

Ireland
Sean Ros Press, pg 364

Israel
Ben-Zvi Institute, pg 365
The Institute for the Translation of Hebrew Literature, pg 368
The Magnes Press, pg 370
Misgav Yerushalayim, pg 370
Yad Izhak Ben-Zvi Press, pg 373
The Zalman Shazar Center, pg 374

Italy
AIB Associazione Italiana Bibliotheche, pg 375
Umberto Allemandi & C SRL, pg 375
Archinto snc, pg 376
Belforte Editore Libraio srl, pg 377
Bonsignori Editore SRL, pg 378
Edizioni Bora SNC di E Brandani & C, pg 378
Edizioni Carmelitane, pg 379
Casalini Libri, pg 380
Istituto Centrale per il Catalogo Unico delle Biblioteche Italiane e per le Informazioni Bibliografiche, pg 380
Colonnese Editore, pg 382
Editrice Bibliografica SpA, pg 386
Arnaldo Forni Editore SRL, pg 389
Lalli Editore SRL, pg 395
Angelo Longo Editore, pg 396
Lubrina Editore Srl, pg 397
OCTAVO Franco Cantini Editore, pg 401
Leo S Olschki, pg 402
Maria Pacini Fazzi Editore, pg 402
Rubbettino Editore, pg 406
Salerno Editrice SRL, pg 406
Collegio San Bonaventura di Grottaferrata, pg 406
Edizioni Rosminiane Sodalitas, pg 408
Editrice Uomini Nuovi, pg 410

Japan
Toho Book Store, pg 427

Republic of Korea
Gim-Yeong Co, pg 436
Kemongsa Publishing Co Ltd, pg 437
Korean Publishers Association, pg 437
Kukmin Doseo Publishing Co Inc, pg 438

Latvia
Bibliography Institute of the National Library of Latvia, pg 441

Lebanon
Publitec Publications, pg 443

Liechtenstein
Topos Verlag AG, pg 445

Lithuania
Lietuvos Informacijos Institutas, pg 446
Lithuanian National Museum Publishing House, pg 446
Martynas Mazvydas National Library of Lithuania, pg 446

Luxembourg
Service Central des Imprimes et des Fournitures de Bureau de l'Etat, pg 448

The Former Yugoslav Republic of Macedonia
St Clement of Ohrid National & University Library, pg 449

Malaysia
Geetha Publishers Sdn Bhd, pg 452

Malta
Fondazzjoni Patrimonju Malti, pg 456

Mexico
Centro de Estudios Mexicanos y Centroamericanos, pg 458
Instituto Nacional de Antropologia e Historia, pg 464

Morocco
Association de la Recherche Historique et Sociale, pg 469

Netherlands
APA (Academic Publishers Associated), pg 472
De Graaf Publishers, pg 478
HES & De Graaf Publishers BV, pg 478
Nico Israel, pg 482
Philo Press-Van Heusden-Hissink & Co CV (APA), pg 482

New Zealand
Cape Catley, pg 489

Nigeria
Evans Brothers (Nigeria Publishers) Ltd, pg 499

Pakistan
Academy of Education Planning & Management (AEPAM), pg 506
National Institute of Historical & Cultural Research, pg 508
Sang-e-Meel Publications, pg 509

Papua New Guinea
National Research Institute of Papua New Guinea, pg 510
Office of Libraries and Archives, Papua New Guinea, pg 510

Peru
Instituto de Estudios Peruanos, pg 511

Poland
Biblioteka Narodowa, pg 516
Katolicki Uniwersytet Wydawniczo-Redakcja, pg 517
Ossolineum Zaklad Narodowy im Ossolinskich - Wydawnictwo, pg 518
Oficyna Wydawnicza Szkoly Glownej Handlowej w Warszawie Oficyna Wydawnicza SGH, pg 520
Towarzystwo Naukowe w Toruniu, pg 520
Wydawnictwa Uniwersytetu Warszawskiego, pg 521
Wydawnictwo DiG, pg 521

Portugal
Biblioteca Geral da Universidade de Coimbra, pg 523
Edicoes Colibri, pg 523
Edicoes Cosmos, pg 524
Imprensa Nacional-Casa da Moeda, pg 526
Instituto de Investigacao Cientifica Tropical, pg 526
Edicoes Ora & Labora, pg 528
Paulinas, pg 528
Talento, pg 529

Romania
Editura Academiei Romane, pg 531
Editura Excelsior, pg 533
Editura Humanitas, pg 533
Humanitas Publishing House, pg 533
Editura Niculescu, pg 534
Saeculum IO, pg 535
Vestala Verlag, pg 536

Russian Federation
BLIC, russko-Baltijskij informaciionnyj centr, AO, pg 537
Izdatel'stvo Mordovskogo gosudar stvennogo, pg 538
Izdatel'stvo Ural'skogo, pg 538
Izdatelstvo Kniga, pg 539
Izdatelstvo Knizhnaya Palata, pg 539
Izdatelskii Dom Kompositor, pg 539
Ministerstvo Kul'tury RF, pg 540

Senegal
CODESRIA (Council for the Development of Social Science Research in Africa), pg 544

Slovakia
Vydavatel' Sky odbor, pg 551

TYPE OF PUBLICATION INDEX

South Africa
New Africa Books (Pty) Ltd, pg 557
South African Institute of International Affairs, pg 559

Spain
Arco Libros SL, pg 564
Biblioteca de Catalunya, pg 565
Editorial Casariego, pg 566
Editora Comercial de Publicaciones, pg 568
Instituto de Estudios Riojanos, pg 574
EUNSA (Ediciones Universidad de Navarra SA), pg 574
Joyas Bibliograficas SA, pg 579
Junta de Castilla y Leon Consejeria de Educacion y Cultura, pg 579
Editorial Monte Carmelo, pg 583
Mundo Negro Editorial, pg 583
Oikos-Tau SA Ediciones, pg 584
Pre-Textos, pg 587
Editorial Revista Agustiniana, pg 589
Trea Ediciones, SL, pg 593
Ediciones Xandro, pg 596

Sri Lanka
National Library & Documentation Services Board, pg 597

Sweden
Bokforlaget Rediviva, Facsimileforlaget, pg 600
Dahlia Books, International Publishers & Booksellers, pg 601
Invandrarfoerlaget, pg 603
Mezopotamya Publishing & Distribution, pg 604

Switzerland
Armenia Editions, pg 608
Librairie Droz SA, pg 612
Garuda-Verlag, pg 614
Presses Polytechniques et Universitaires Romandes, PPUR, pg 622

Taiwan, Province of China
Campus Evangelical Fellowship, Literature Department, pg 629

Tunisia
Academie Tunisienne des Sciences, des Lettres et des Arts Beit El Hekma, pg 637
Dar Arabia Lil Kitab, pg 637

Turkey
Ataturk Kultur, Dil ve Tarih, Yusek Kurumu Baskanligi, pg 639
IKI NOKTA Research Press & Publications Industry & Trade Ltd, pg 640

United Kingdom
ABC-CLIO, pg 644
Arts Council of England, pg 649
Ashgate Publishing Ltd, pg 649
Aslib, The Association for Information Management, pg 650
Avero Publications Ltd, pg 651
The British Library National Bibliographic Service, pg 660
British Library Publications, pg 660
British Library Document Supply Centre, Publications Marketing, pg 660

779

TYPE OF PUBLICATION INDEX   BOOK

Cambridge University Press, pg 662
Chadwyck-Healey Ltd, pg 666
CTBI Publications, pg 672
Facet Publishing, pg 681
Flicks Books, pg 683
Gale Research, pg 685
The Geographical Association, pg 686
GMP Publishers Ltd, pg 687
Grant & Cutler Ltd, pg 689
Gwasg Gwenffrwd, pg 690
Hilmarton Manor Press, pg 696
Angus Hudson Ltd, pg 697
Institute of Development Studies, pg 699
International Bee Research Association, pg 701
Manchester University Press, pg 711
Maney Publishing, pg 711
Peter Marcan Publications, pg 711
Melrose Press Ltd, pg 713
National Library of Scotland, pg 717
Pen & Sword Books Ltd, pg 725
Plough Publishing House of Bruderhof Communities in the UK, pg 728
The Reader's Digest Association Ltd, pg 733
St Paul's Bibliographies Ltd, pg 738
School of Oriental & African Studies, pg 739
Thistle Press, pg 748
Transport Bookman Publications Ltd, pg 750
Trigon Press, pg 750
Voltaire Foundation Ltd, pg 753
Werner Shaw Ltd, pg 755
Philip Wilson Publishers, pg 757

Venezuela
Biblioteca Ayacucho, pg 762

Yugoslavia
Narodna Biblioteka Srbije, pg 764

Zimbabwe
National Archives of Zimbabwe, pg 769

BRAILLE BOOKS

China
China Braille Press, pg 103
Qingdao Publishing House, pg 108

Czech Republic
Knihovna A Tiskarna Pro Nevidome, pg 125

Germany
Deutsche Blinden-Bibliothek, pg 213
Verlag Esoterische Philosophie GmbH, pg 224
Sturtz Verlag GmbH, pg 291

India
Nem Chand & Brothers, pg 344

Lithuania
Svietimo ir mokslo ministerijos Leidybos centras, pg 446

United Kingdom
Scottish Braille Press, pg 739

Zimbabwe
Dorothy Duncan Braille & Transcription Library, pg 768

CD-ROM, ELECTRONIC BOOKS

Albania
State Textbook Publishing House, pg 1

Argentina
Abeledo-Perrot SAE e I, pg 2
Laffont Ediciones Electronicas SA, pg 7
San Pablo, pg 8

Australia
Artmoves, pg 12
Australian Institute of Family Studies (AIFS), pg 13
Blackwell Science Pty Ltd, pg 15
Board of Studies, pg 15
Butterworths Australia Ltd, pg 16
China Books, pg 18
Chiron Media, pg 18
CSIRO Publishing (Commonwealth Scientific & Industrial Research Organisation), pg 19
D&B Marketing Pty Ltd, pg 20
Emerald City Books, pg 22
Encyclopaedia Britannica (Australia) Inc, pg 22
Era Publications, pg 22
Flora Publications International Pty Ltd, pg 23
Gangan Publishing, pg 23
Hampden Press, pg 25
Law Book Co Information Services, pg 29
New Creation Publications Ministries & Resource Centre, pg 34
Pascal Press, pg 37
Price Publishing, pg 39
Rankin Publishers, pg 40
Reed Educational Publishing Australia, pg 40
Spinifex Press, pg 43
Standards Association of Australia, pg 43
State Library of NSW Press, pg 43
Thames & Hudson (Australia) Pty Ltd, pg 44
D W Thorpe, pg 44

Austria
Abakus Verlag GmbH, pg 49
Braintrust Marketing Services Ges mbH Verlag, pg 50
Compass-Verlag GmbH, pg 50
Herold Business Data AG, pg 52
Linde Verlag Wien GmbH, pg 54
Verlag der Oesterreichischen Akademie der Wissenschaften (OEAW), pg 56
Verlag des Oesterreichischen Gewerkschaftsbundes GmbH, pg 56
Signum Verlag GmbH & Co KG, pg 58

Bangladesh
Gatidhara, pg 62

Belgium
Brepols Publishers NV, pg 65
Campinia Media VZW, pg 65
CED-Samsom, pg 66
Editions De Boeck-Larcier SA, pg 67
Easy Computing NV, pg 68
Koepel van de Vlaamse Noord - Zuidbeweging 11.11.11, pg 70
Uitgeverij Lannoo NV, pg 70
Larcier-Department of De Boeck & Larcier SA, pg 71

Brazil
Comissao Nacional de Energia Nuclear, pg 81
Editora Companhia das Letras/Editora Schwarcz Ltda, pg 82
Empresa Brasileira de Pesquisa Agropecaria, pg 83
Editora Forense, pg 83
Hemus Editora Ltda, pg 85
Horus Editora Ltda, pg 85
Libreria Editora Ltda, pg 86
Editora Nova Fronteira SA, pg 88
Saraiva SA, Livreiros Editores, pg 91

Bulgaria
Ciela Publishing House, pg 94
DATAMAP - Europe, pg 95
Interpres, pg 96

Chile
Norma de Chile, pg 101

China
Aviation Industry Press, pg 102
Beijing Publishing House, pg 102
Chemical Industry Press, pg 102
China Ocean Press, pg 103
Cultural Relics Publishing House, pg 105
Electronics Industry Publishing House, pg 105
Fudan University Press, pg 105
Higher Education Press, pg 106
Jilin Science & Technology Publishing House, pg 106
Patent Documentation Publishing House, pg 107
People's Education Press, pg 107
Qingdao Publishing House, pg 108
Shandong University Press, pg 109
Shanghai Foreign Language Education Press, pg 109
Tsinghua University Press, pg 110
Wuhan University Press, pg 110

Colombia
Centro Regional para el Fomento del Libro en America Latina y el Caribe, pg 111

Costa Rica
Centro Agronomico Tropical de Investigacion y Ensenanza (CATIE), pg 115
Union Mundial para la Naturaleza (UICN), Oficina Regional para Mesoamerica, pg 117

Croatia
Masmedia, pg 119

Cuba
Casa Editora Abril, pg 120
Instituto de Informacion Cientifica y Tecnologica (IDICT), pg 121

Czech Republic
Diderot sro, pg 124
Narodni Knihovna CR, pg 126
Cesky normalizacni institut, pg 127

Denmark
Atuakkiorfik A/S Det Greenland Publishers, pg 130
Djof Publishing Jurist-og Okonomforbundets Forlag, pg 131
Christian Ejlers' Forlag aps, pg 131
Forlaget FSR A/S (ITID A/S), pg 132
GEC Gads Forlag Aktieselskab af 1994, pg 132
Kraks Forlag AS, pg 133
Scandinavia Publishing House, pg 135
J H Schultz Information A/S, pg 135
A/S Skattekartoteket, pg 135
Systime, pg 136

Estonia
Estonian Bible Society, pg 140
National Library of Estonia, pg 140

Finland
Kirja-Leitzinger, pg 143
Otava Publishing Co Ltd, pg 143

France
ACR Edition Internationale (Art Creation Realisation), pg 145
Agence Bibliographique de L'Enseignement Superieur, pg 146
Les Editions de l'Atelier SA, pg 148
Atelier National de Reproduction des Theses, pg 148
Bibliotheque Nationale de France, pg 150
Cirad, pg 155
Codes Rousseau, pg 155
Editions Dalloz Sirey, pg 157
La Decouverte et Syros, pg 158
Delagrave Edition SA, pg 158
Encyclopedia Universalis France SA, pg 162
Flammarion SA, pg 164
Association Frank, pg 165
Joly Editions, pg 170
Le Livre de Paris, pg 173
Editions de la Reunion des Musees Nationaux, pg 176
References cf, pg 182
Editions Scientifiques et Medicales Elsevier, pg 184
Sofradif Editions Philippe Auzou, pg 185
Association d'Editions Sorg, pg 186
Editions Springer France, pg 186
Sybex, pg 186

Germany
A Francke Verlag (Tubingen und Basel), pg 191
ABC der Deutschen Wirtschaft, Verlagsgesellschaft mbH, pg 191
Andernach Atelier Verlag (AVA), pg 193
ARCult Media, pg 194
Bank-Verlag GmbH, pg 198
Verlag C H Beck (OHG), pg 200
Beleke KG Verlag, pg 200
Belser Wissenschaftlicher Dienst, pg 200
Bergverlag Rudolf Rother GmbH, pg 200
Bertelsmann Lexikon Verlag GmbH, pg 201
W Bertelsmann Verlag GmbH & Co KG, pg 201
BertelsmannSpringer Science & Business Media GmbH, pg 202

Bibliographisches Institut & F A Brockhaus AG, pg 203
BW Bildung und Wissen Verlag und Software GmbH, pg 203
Blackwell Wissenschafts-Verlag GmbH, pg 203
Bock und Herchen Verlag, pg 204
Born-Verlag, pg 205
Oscar Brandstetter Verlag GmbH & Co KG, pg 206
R Brockhaus Verlag, pg 206
Buchhaendler-Vereinigung GmbH, pg 207
Bundesanzeiger Verlagsgesellschaft, pg 208
Campus Verlag GmbH, pg 209
Chmielorz GmbH Verlag, pg 210
Compact Verlag GmbH, pg 211
Cornelsen Verlag GmbH & Co OHG, pg 211
Cornelsen Verlag Scriptor GmbH & Co KG, pg 212
Corona Verlag, pg 212
Data Becker GmbH & Co KG, pg 212
Datacom Buchverlag GmbH, pg 212
Degener & Co, Manfred Dreiss Verlag, pg 213
Verlag Horst Deike KG, pg 213
Verlag fuer Deutsch GmbH, pg 213
Verlag Harri Deutsch, pg 213
Deutsche Blinden-Bibliothek, pg 213
Deutscher Adressbuch-Verlag fuer Wirtschaft und Verkehr GmbH, pg 214
Deutscher Instituts-Verlag GmbH, pg 215
Die Verlag H Schafer GmbH, pg 216
DSI Data Service & Information, pg 219
Ecomed Verlagsgesellschaft AG & Co KG, pg 220
Econ Taschenbuchverlag, pg 220
Econ Verlag GmbH, pg 220
Egmont vgs verlagsgesellschaft mbH, pg 221
Europ Export Edition GmbH, pg 224
Extent Verlag und Service Wolfgang M Flamm, pg 225
FAB-Verlag, pg 226
Fachbuchverlag Leipzig im Carl Hanser Verlag, pg 226
Festo Didactic GmbH & Co, pg 227
Verkehrs-Verlag J Fischer GmbH & Co KG, pg 228
Verlag Franz Vahlen GmbH, pg 229
Fraunhofer IRB Verlag Fraunhofer Informationszentrum Raum und Bau, pg 229
Betriebswirtschaftlicher Verlag Dr Th Gabler GmbH, pg 231
Verlag Ernst und Werner Gieseking GmbH, pg 232
Govi-Verlag Pharmazeutischer Verlag GmbH, pg 233
Walter de Gruyter GmbH & Co KG, pg 234
Carl Hanser Verlag, pg 237
Rudolf Haufe Verlag GmbH & Co KG, pg 238
Dr Ernst Hauswedell & Co Verlag, pg 238
F A Herbig Verlagsbuchhandlung GmbH, pg 239
Hestra-Verlag Hernichel & Dr Strauss GmbH & Co KG, pg 240
Carl Heymanns Verlag KG, pg 240
Ing W Hofacker GmbH Verlag, pg 241
Verlag Hoppenstedt GmbH, pg 242
Huss-Medien GmbH, pg 243
Huss-Verlag GmbH, pg 244
Huthig GmbH & Co KG, pg 244
Impuls-Theater-Verlag, pg 244
Industrieschau Verlagsgesellschaft mbH, pg 244
International Thomson Publishing (ITP), pg 245
SachBuchVerlag Kellner, pg 248
Verlag im Kilian GmbH, pg 249
Klages-Verlag, pg 249
Vittorio Klostermann GmbH, pg 250
Knowledge Media International, pg 251
W Kohlhammer GmbH, abt Haussortiment, pg 252
kopaed verlagsgmbh, pg 252
Lahn-Verlag GmbH, pg 255
Verlag Laterna magica GmbH & Co KG, pg 256
Logophon Lehrmittelverlag GmbH, pg 258
Hermann Luchterhand Verlag GmbH, pg 259
Matthias-Gruenewald-Verlag GmbH, pg 261
C F Mueller Verlag, Huethig GmbH & Co, pg 265
Verlagsgesellschaft Rudolf Mueller GmbH & Co KG, pg 265
Munzinger-Archiv GmbH Archiv fuer publizistische Arbeit, pg 266
Verlag Stephanie Naglschmid, pg 266
Gunter Narr Verlag, pg 266
Naumann & Goebel Verlagsgesellschaft mbH, pg 267
Nebel Verlag GmbH, pg 267
Verlag Neue Wirtschafts-Briefe GmbH & Co, pg 267
Georg Olms Verlag AG, pg 270
Patmos Verlag GmbH & Co KG, pg 272
Pearson Education Deutschland GmbH, pg 272
Philipp Reclam Jun Verlag GmbH, pg 273
pmi Verlag, pg 274
Polygraph Verlag GmbH, pg 274
Reed Elsevier Deutschland GmbH, pg 277
Rossipaul Kommunikation GmbH, pg 280
Verlag Werner Sachon GmbH & Co, pg 281
K G Saur Verlag GmbH, A Gale/Thomson Learning Company, pg 282
Schaeffer-Poeschel Verlag fuer Wirtschaft Steuern Recht, pg 282
Verlag der Schillerbuchhandlung Hans Banger OHG, pg 283
Schirner Verlag, pg 283
Verlag Dr Otto Schmidt KG, pg 283
Erich Schmidt Verlag GmbH & Co, pg 284
Siegler & Co Verlag fuer Zeitarchive GmbH, pg 286
Johannes Sonntag Verlagsbuchhandlung GmbH, pg 287
Springer-Verlag GmbH & Co KG, pg 288
Staatliche Museen Kassel, pg 288
Straelener Manuskripte Verlag, pg 290
Sybex Verlag GmbH, pg 291
Systhema Verlag GmbH, pg 291
Konrad Theiss Verlag GmbH, pg 293
Georg Thieme Verlag KG, pg 293
TR - Verlagsunion GmbH, pg 294
Trotzdem-Verlags Genossenschaft eG, pg 295
Urban und Fischer Verlag fur Medizin, pg 296
Friedr Vieweg & Sohn Verlagsgesellschaft mbH, pg 298
Vista Point Verlag GmbH, pg 299
Vogel Medien GmbH & Co KG, pg 299
Voggenreiter-Verlag, pg 299
Walhalla Fachverlag GmbH & Co KG Praetoria, pg 300
Waxmann Verlag GmbH, pg 300
WEKA Firmengruppe GmbH & Co KG, pg 301
Wer liefert was? GmbH, pg 301
Wiley-VCH Verlag GmbH, pg 302
Zeller Verlag GmbH & Co, pg 305

Greece

Apostoliki Diakonia tis Ekklisias tis Hellados, pg 309
Ekdotike Athenon SA, pg 310
Hestia-I D Hestia-Kollaros & Co Corporation, pg 311
Karatzas Charis, pg 312
Editions Moressopoulos, pg 313
Patakis Publishers, pg 314
Sakkoulas Publications SA, pg 314
Toubis M, pg 315

Hong Kong

The Chinese University Press, pg 319
Chung Hwa Book Co (HK) Ltd, pg 319
Joint Publishing (HK) Co Ltd, pg 320
Research Centre for Translation, pg 321

Hungary

Aranyhal Konyvkiado Goldfish Publishing, pg 323
Balassi Kiado Kft, pg 323
KJK-Keaszov, pg 324
Kossuth Kiado RT, pg 325
Nemzeti Tankoenyvkiado, pg 326
Novorg Kiado, pg 326
Panem, pg 326
Polgar Citizen Press, pg 326

Iceland

Mal og menning, pg 328
Namsgagnastofnun, pg 328

India

Affiliated East West Press Pvt Ltd, pg 329
Nem Chand & Brothers, pg 344
Research Signpost, pg 348
Sita Publications, pg 350
Spectrum Publications, pg 350
Transworld Research Network, pg 352
Vidyarthi Mithram Press, pg 352
A H Wheeler & Co Ltd, pg 353

Indonesia

Gramedia, pg 355
PT Indira, pg 355
Lembaga Demografi Fakultas Ekonomi Universitas Indonesia, pg 356

Ireland

Cathedral Books Ltd, pg 359

Israel

Academy of the Hebrew Language, pg 365
Agudat Sabah, pg 365
Bitan Publishers Ltd, pg 365
Carta, The Israel Map & Publishing Co Ltd, pg 366
Doko Video Ltd, pg 366
Israel Music Institute (IMI), pg 369
Kernernan Publishing Ltd, pg 369
Open University of Israel, pg 371
Password Publishers Ltd, pg 371
Rolnik Publishers, pg 371
R Sirkis Publishers Ltd, pg 372

Italy

Umberto Allemandi & C SRL, pg 375
Editore Armando Armando SRL, pg 376
Arsenale Editrice SRL, pg 376
Casa Editrice Bonechi, pg 378
Bonsignori Editore SRL, pg 378
Istituto Centrale per il Catalogo Unico delle Biblioteche Italiane e per le Informazioni Bibliografiche, pg 380
Centro Biblico, pg 380
Centro Scientifico Int, pg 381
Centro Scientifico Torinese, pg 381
CIC Edizioni Internazionali, pg 381
Il Cigno Galileo Galilei-Edizioni di Arte e Scienza, pg 381
D'Anna, pg 383
Edizioni Studio Domenicano (ESD), pg 387
Gangemi Editore, pg 390
Istituto Geografico de Agostini SpA, pg 390
Giunti (Gruppo Editoriale), pg 390
Il Saggiatore, pg 393
Liguori Editore SRL, pg 396
Manifestolibri, pg 397
Editoriale Olimpia SpA, pg 401
RAI.ERI, pg 405
Rusconi Libri Srl, pg 406
Fausto Sardini Editrice, pg 407
Scala Group spa, pg 407
Edizioni Librarie Siciliane, pg 408
Vivere In SRL, pg 411
Zanichelli Editore SpA, pg 412

Jamaica

The Caribbean Law Publishing Co Ltd, pg 412

Japan

Dobun Shoin, pg 416
Gakken Co Ltd, pg 416
Igaku-Shoin Ltd, pg 418
International Society for Educational Information (ISEI), pg 418
Iwanami Shoten, Publishers, pg 418
Kinokuniya Co Ltd (Publishing Department), pg 420
Nobunkyo (Rural Village Culture Association), pg 423
Ongaku No Tomo Sha Corporation, pg 423
Sanshusha Publishing Co, Ltd, pg 424
Seibido Shuppan Company Ltd, pg 424
Shincho-Sha Co Ltd, pg 425
Toho Book Store, pg 427
Tokyo Shoseki Co Ltd, pg 427
Yakuji Nippo Ltd, pg 429
Zeimukeiri-Kyokai, pg 429

TYPE OF PUBLICATION INDEX — BOOK

Republic of Korea
Cheong-mun-gag Publishing Co, pg 435
Chung Rim Publishing Co Ltd, pg 435
Gim-Yeong Co, pg 436
Korea Britannica Corp, pg 437
Maeil Gyeongje, pg 438
Moon Jin Media Co Ltd, pg 438
Woong Jin Publishing Co Ltd, pg 440

Liechtenstein
Rheintal Handelsgesellschaft Anstalt, pg 445

Lithuania
Lithuanian National Museum Publishing House, pg 446
TEV Leidykla, pg 446

Luxembourg
Edition Objectif Lune, pg 447
Editions Promoculture, pg 448

The Former Yugoslav Republic of Macedonia
Medis, Skopje, pg 449

Malaysia
Malayan Law Journal Sdn Bhd, pg 453
Pustaka Cipta Sdn Bhd, pg 454

Mexico
Instituto Nacional de Antropologia e Historia, pg 464
Instituto Nacional de Estadistica, Geographia e Informatica, pg 464
Organizacion Cultural LP SA de CV, pg 465
Pearson Educacion de Mexico, SA de CV, pg 465
SCRIPTA - Distribucion y Servicios Editoriales, SA de CV, pg 467

Netherlands
Brill Academic Publishers, pg 475
A W Bruna Uitgevers BV, pg 475
Elmar BV, pg 476
Hagen & Stam Uitgeverij Ten, pg 478
Katholieke Bijbelstichting, pg 479
Kluwer Academic Publishers, pg 479
Kluwer Law International, pg 479
Koninklijke Vermande bv, pg 480
Uitgeverij Lemma BV, pg 480
Van Dale Lexicografie BV, pg 486

New Zealand
Brooker's Ltd, pg 489
CCH New Zealand Ltd, pg 490
Learning Media Ltd, pg 492
Nelson Price Milburn Ltd, pg 494

Norway
Elanders Publishing AS, pg 503
Fono Forlag, pg 503

Paraguay
Instituto de Ciencias de la Computacion (NCR), pg 510

Philippines
Encyclopaedia Britannica (Philippines) Inc, pg 513

Poland
Polish Scientific Publishers PWN, pg 519
PZWL Wydawnictwo Lekarskie Ltd, pg 519
Wydawnictwa Szkolne i Pedagogiczne (Polish Educational Publishers-WSiP), pg 521
Wydawnictwo DiG, pg 521

Portugal
Constancia Editores, SA, pg 524

Romania
Alcor-Edimpex (Verlag) Ltd, pg 531
The Center for Romanian Studies, pg 532
Editura Militara, pg 534
Editura Muzicala, pg 534

Russian Federation
FGUP Izdatelstvo Mashinostroenie, pg 538

Singapore
Archipelago Press, pg 545
Daiichi Media Pte Ltd, pg 545
LexisNexis, pg 547
Shing Lee Group Publishers, pg 548
Tecman Bible House, pg 549

Slovakia
Ustav informacii a prognoz skolstva mladeze a telovychovy, pg 551

South Africa
Bet-El Publishers, pg 553
Juta & Co, pg 556
South African Institute of International Affairs, pg 559
Van Schaik Publishers, pg 560

Spain
Editorial AEDOS SA, pg 561
Ediciones Agrotecnicas, SL, pg 562
Anaya Educacion, pg 563
Editorial Aranzadi SA, pg 564
Editorial Astri SA, pg 564
Bosch Casa Editorial SA, pg 565
Calesa SA Editorial La, pg 566
CEAC, Grupo Editorial SA, pg 567
Editorial CISSPRAXIS SA, pg 567
Complutense, SA Editorial, pg 568
Didaco Comunicacion y Didactica, SA, pg 569
Durvan SA de Ediciones, pg 570
Esic Editorial, pg 573
Editorial Espasa-Calpe SA, pg 573
Fundacion Coleccion Thyssen-Bornemisza, pg 575
Idea Books, SA, pg 578
Larousse Planeta SA, pg 579
Lid Editorial Empresarial, SL, pg 580
Editorial Luis Vives (Edelvives), pg 580
Marcombo SA de Boixareu Editores, pg 581
Mundi-Prensa Libros SA, pg 583
Editorial Parthenon Communication, SL, pg 586
Pentalfa Ediciones, pg 586
Pronaos, SA Ediciones, pg 588
Pulso Ediciones, SL, pg 588
San Pablo Ediciones, pg 589
Servicio de Publicaciones Universidad de Cordoba, pg 590
Tesitex, SL, pg 592

Sweden
Ekelunds Forlag AB, pg 601
Hallgren och Fallgren Studieforlag AB, pg 603
Hans Richter Laromedel, pg 604
Norstedts Juridik, pg 605
Norstedts Ordbok, pg 605
Studentlitteratur AB, pg 606

Switzerland
Bibellesbund Verlag, pg 610
Verlag Harri Deutsch, pg 612
Helbing und Lichtenhahn Verlag AG, pg 615
Verlag Industrielle Organisation, pg 616
La Maison de la Bible, pg 618
Presses Polytechniques et Universitaires Romandes, PPUR, pg 622
Verlag fuer Recht und Gesellschaft AG, pg 622
Schwabe & Co AG, pg 624
Schweizerisches Jugendschriftenwerk, SJW, pg 624
Vdf Hochschulverlag AG an der ETH Zurich, pg 626

Taiwan, Province of China
Kuang Fu Book Co Ltd, pg 630
Lead Wave Publishing Company Ltd, pg 631
Lee & Lee Communications, pg 631
Shuttle Multimedia Inc, pg 631
The Third Wave Enterprise Co Ltd, pg 632

United Republic of Tanzania
Bureau of Statistics, pg 633

Thailand
Thai Watana Panich Co, Ltd, pg 636

Tunisia
Editions Techniques Specialisees, pg 638

Turkey
Alkim Kitapcilik-Yayimcilik, pg 638
Bilden Bilgisayar, pg 639
IKI NOKTA Research Press & Publications Industry & Trade Ltd, pg 640
Soez Yayin/Oyunajans, pg 641

United Kingdom
ABC-CLIO, pg 644
Advisory Unit: Computers in Education, pg 645
Ai Interactive Ltd, pg 645
Umberto Allemandi & Co Publishing, pg 646
Anderson Rand Ltd, pg 647
Arnold, pg 648
Art Sales Index Ltd, pg 649
Aslib, The Association for Information Management, pg 650
Avero Publications Ltd, pg 651
BBC English, pg 652
Belitha Press Ltd, pg 653
Berlitz (UK) Ltd, pg 654
Blackwell Science Ltd, pg 656
Book Data, pg 657
Books for Europe Ltd, pg 657
Business Monitor International, pg 661
Butterworth-Heinemann Ltd, pg 661
Chadwyck-Healey Ltd, pg 666
Chambers Harrap Publishers Ltd, pg 666
Chapter Two, pg 666
Child's World Education Ltd, pg 667
Chorion IP, pg 667
Coachwise Ltd, pg 668
Peter Collin Publishing Ltd, pg 669
Computer Step, pg 670
Croner CCH Group Ltd, pg 672
CSA (Cambridge Scientific Abstracts), pg 672
D&B Ltd, pg 673
The Economist Intelligence Unit, pg 677
Electronic Publishing Services Ltd, pg 678
Encyclopaedia Britannica (UK) International Ltd, pg 679
Estates Gazette, pg 679
Euromonitor PLC, pg 680
Facet Publishing, pg 681
First & Best in Education Ltd, pg 682
Gale Research, pg 685
Geological Society Publishing House, pg 686
Golden Books Publishing Company, Inc, pg 688
W Green The Scottish Law Publisher, pg 689
Harcourt Publishers Ltd, pg 691
HarperCollins Publishers, pg 692
Helicon Publishing Ltd, pg 694
Hobsons, pg 696
Law Pack Publishing Ltd, pg 706
Letterbox Library, pg 707
Mandrake of Oxford, pg 711
McCrimmon Publishing Co Ltd, pg 712
NCVO, pg 718
NMS Publishing Ltd, pg 719
Oilfield Publications Ltd, pg 720
Orion Publishing Group Ltd, pg 722
The Parthenon Publishing Group Ltd, pg 724
Pavilion Publishing (Brighton) Ltd, pg 725
Pharmaceutical Press, pg 726
Plough Publishing House of Bruderhof Communities in the UK, pg 728
ProQuest Information & Learning, pg 731
Retail Entertainment Data Publishing Ltd, pg 735
The Rutland Press, pg 737
Sage Publications Ltd, pg 737
Silver Link Publishing Ltd, pg 742
Stainer & Bell Ltd, pg 745
The Stationery Office, pg 745
Sweet & Maxwell Ltd, pg 746
Telegraph Books, pg 748
Two-Can Publishing Ltd, pg 750
VNU Business Publications, pg 753
Wayland Publishers Ltd (Incorporating Macdonald Young Books), pg 754
Websters International Publishers Ltd, pg 755
Wilmington Business Information Ltd, pg 756
WIT Press, pg 757
World Microfilms Publications Ltd, pg 758
Yale University Press London, pg 759

Uruguay
EQ Opciones en Educacion, pg 760
La Flor del Itapebi, pg 760

Viet Nam
Science & Technics Publishing House, pg 763

Yugoslavia
Izdavacko Preduzece Matice Srpske, pg 765

CHILDREN'S BOOKS

Albania
Fan Noli Verlag Rexhep Hida, pg 1
NL SH, pg 1

Algeria
Les Editions Algeriennes En-Nahdha, pg 2

Argentina
Editorial Abril SA, pg 2
Editorial Albatros SACl, pg 3
Argentine Bible Society, pg 3
Editorial Atlantida SA, pg 3
Beas Ediciones SRL, pg 4
Bonum Editorial SACl, pg 4
Editorial Caymi SACl, pg 4
Cesarini Hermanos, pg 4
Editorial Ruy Diaz SAEIC, pg 5
Ediciones Don Bosco Argentina, pg 5
Ediciones del Eclipse, pg 5
Editorial Ciudad Nueva de la Sefoma, pg 5
Emece Editores SA, pg 5
Errepar SA, pg 5
Angel Estrada y Cia SA, pg 6
Ediciones de la Flor SRL, pg 6
Editorial Guadalupe, pg 6
Libreria Huemul SA, pg 6
Librograf, pg 7
Editorial Losada SA, pg 7
Ediciones LR SA, pg 7
Editorial Norte SA, pg 8
Editorial Plus Ultra SA, pg 8
Ediciones Preescolar SA, pg 8
San Pablo, pg 8
Editorial Sigmar SACl, pg 9
Editorial Sopena Argentina SACl e l, pg 9
Editorial Sudamericana SA, pg 9

Armenia
Arevik, pg 10

Australia
ABC Books (Australian Broadcasting Corporation), pg 10
Aboriginal Studies Press, pg 10
Access Press, pg 10
Allen & Unwin Pty Ltd, The Australian Newspaper, Vogel Breads, pg 11
Bandicoot Books, pg 14
Bible Society in Australia National Headquarters, pg 15
Boinkie Publishers, pg 15
Budget Books Pty Ltd, pg 16
Childerset Publishers, pg 18
China Books, pg 18
R J Cleary Publishing, pg 18
Coolabah Publishing, pg 18
Crawford House Publishing, pg 19
Crossroad Distributors Pty Ltd, pg 19
D'Artagnan Publishing, pg 20
Dragon Press, pg 20
Edwina Publishing, pg 21
Egan Publishing Pty Ltd, pg 21
David Ell Press Pty Ltd, pg 21
Encyclopaedia Britannica (Australia) Inc, pg 22
Era Publications, pg 22
The Five Mile Press Pty Ltd, pg 23
Fremantle Arts Centre Press, pg 23
Great Western Press Pty Ltd, pg 24
Greater Glider Productions Australia Pty Ltd, pg 24
Geoffrey Hamlyn-Harris, pg 25
Hartys Creek Press, pg 25
Roland Harvey Studios, pg 25
Hodder Headline Australia, pg 26
Institute of Aboriginal Development (IAD Press), pg 28
Kangaroo Press, pg 29
Little Red Apple Publishing, pg 30
Thomas C Lothian Pty Ltd, pg 30
Macmillan Education Australia, pg 31
Magabala Books Aboriginal Corporation, pg 31
Margaret Hamilton Books, pg 31
J M McGregor Pty Ltd, pg 32
Mimosa Publications Pty Ltd, pg 33
Mountain House Press, pg 33
New Era Publications Australia Pty Ltd, pg 34
Newman Centre Publications, pg 35
Off the Shelf Publishing, pg 35
Omnibus Books, pg 35
Pan Macmillan Australia Pty Ltd, pg 36
Papyrus Publishing, pg 37
Pearson Education Australia, pg 37
Penguin Books Australia Ltd, pg 37
Plantagenet Press, pg 38
Rainforest Publishing, pg 39
Random House Australia, pg 40
Reed Educational Publishing Australia, pg 40
St Joseph Publications, pg 41
St Pauls, pg 41
Shakespeare Head Press Pty Ltd, pg 42
Simon & Schuster Australia Pty Ltd, pg 42
Social Club Books, pg 42
Stafford Books, pg 43
Tarka Publishing, pg 44
Troll Books of Australia, pg 45
University of Queensland Press, pg 46
University of Western Australia Press, pg 46
The Useful Publishing Co, pg 46
Vista Publications, pg 47
Vital Publications, pg 47
Walker Books Australia Pty Ltd, pg 47
Franklin Watts Australia, pg 47
Windhorse Books, pg 48
Wizard Books Pty Ltd, pg 48

Austria
Astor-Verlag, Willibald Schlager, pg 49
Annette Betz Verlag im Verlag Carl Ueberreuter, pg 49
Dachs-Verlag GmbH, pg 50
Denkmayr GmbH Druck & Verlag, pg 51
Development News Ltd, pg 51
Edition Graphischer Zirkel, pg 52
Verlag Jungbrunnen - Wiener Spielzeugschachtel GesellschaftmbH, pg 53
Verlag Kerle im Verlag Herder & Co, pg 53
Edition Koenigstein, pg 54
Mangold Verlag GmbH, pg 54
Edition Neues Marchen, pg 55
Niederosterreichisches Pressehaus Druck- und Verlagsgesellschaft mbH, pg 55
Obelisk-Verlag, pg 56
oebv & hpt Verlagsgesellschaft mbH & Co KG, pg 56
Oesterreichischer Kunst und Kulturverlag, pg 56
Anna Pichler Verlag GmbH, pg 57
Richard Pils Publication P, pg 57
J Steinbrener OHG, pg 59
Edition Thurnhof KEG, pg 59
Verlag Carl Ueberreuter GmbH, pg 59

Azerbaijan
Sada, Literaturno-Izdatel'skij Centr, pg 61

Bangladesh
Ankur Prakashani, pg 62
Bangladesh Publishers, pg 62
Gatidhara, pg 62
Agamee Prakashani, pg 62
The University Press Ltd, pg 62

Belarus
Belaruskaya Encyklapedyya, pg 63
Interdigets Publishing House, pg 63
Junactva, Vydavectva, pg 63
Kavaler Publishers, pg 63
Narodnaya Asveta, pg 63
Yunatstva, pg 63

Belgium
Abimo, pg 63
Altina, pg 64
Averbode Publishers, pg 64
Maison d'Editions Baha'ies ASBL, pg 64
Bakermat NV, pg 65
Editions Gerard Blanchart & Cie SA, pg 65
Caramel SA, pg 65
Cartoon Creation, pg 66
Editions Casterman SA, pg 66
Editions Chantecler, pg 66
Uitgeverij Clavis, pg 66
Coda, pg 66
Conservart SA, pg 67
Davidsfonds - Infodok NV, pg 67
Editions Delta SA, pg 67
Eenhoorn BVBA, pg 68
Facet NV, pg 68
Graton Editeur SA, pg 69
Koepel van de Vlaamse Noord - Zuidbeweging 11.11.11, pg 70
Uitgeverij Lannoo NV, pg 70
Claude Lefrancq Editeur, pg 71
Parasol NV, pg 72
Rainbow Grafics Intl - Baronian Books SC, pg 72
Editions Scaillet, SA, pg 74
Uitgeverij De Sikkel NV, pg 74
Standaard Uitgeverij, pg 74
Zuid En Noord VZW, pg 76
Zuid-Nederlandse Uitgeverij NV/ Central Uitgeverij, pg 76

Benin
Les Editions du Flamboyant, pg 76

Bermuda
Bermudian Publishing Co, pg 76

Bosnia and Herzegovina
Bemust doo Novinsko-Izdavacko stamparsko i trgovacko preduzece, pg 77

Brazil
A & A & A Edicoes e Promocoes Internacionais Ltda, pg 77
Agalma Psicanalise Editora Ltda, pg 78
AGIR S/A Editora, pg 78
Livraria Alema, pg 78
Editora Alfa Omega Ltda, pg 78
Editora Antroposofica Ltda, pg 78
Ao Livro Tecnico Industria e Comercio Ltda, pg 78
Associacao Arvore da Vida, pg 79
Editora Atica SA, pg 79
Brinque Book Editora de Livros Ltda, pg 80
Callis Editora Ltda, pg 80
Centro de Estudos Juridicosdo Para (CEJUP), pg 80
Concordia Editora Ltda, pg 81
Conquista, Empresa de Publicacoes Ltda, pg 81
Edicon Editora e Consultorial Ltda, pg 81
Ediouro Publicacoes, SA, pg 81
Editora Brasil-America (EBAL) SA, pg 82
Editora Companhia das Letras/ Editora Schwarcz Ltda, pg 82
Editora Elevacao, pg 82
Livraria Martins Fontes Editora Ltda, pg 83
Formato Editorial ltda, pg 83
Global Editora e Distribuidora Ltda, pg 84
Editora Globo SA, pg 84
Editora e Grafica Carisio Ltda, pg 84
Grafica Editora Primor Ltda, pg 84
Editora Harbra Ltda, pg 84
Imago Editora Importacao e Exportacao Ltda, pg 85
Editora Kuarup Ltda, pg 86
Editora Leitura Ltda, pg 86
Livraria Nobel S/A, pg 86
Edicoes Loyola SA, pg 87
Editora Manole Ltda, pg 87
Editora Meca Ltda, pg 87
Editora Melhoramentos Ltda, pg 87
Memorias Futuras Edicoes Ltda, pg 88
Editora Mercado Aberto Ltda, pg 88
Editora Moderna Ltda, pg 88
Editora Mundo Cristao, pg 88
Editora Nova Fronteira SA, pg 88
Edit Palavra Magica, pg 89
Pallas Editora e Distribuidora Ltda, pg 89
Paulinas Editorial, pg 89
Livraria Pioneira Editora/Enio Matheus Guazzelli e Cia Ltd, pg 89
Editora Primor Ltda, pg 90
Qualitymark Editora Ltda, pg 90
Editora Revan Ltda, pg 90
RHJ Livros Ltda, pg 90
Editora Rocco Ltda, pg 91
Salamandra Consultoria Editorial SA, pg 91
Editora Santuario, pg 91
Editora Scipione Ltda, pg 91
Editora Sinodal, pg 91
Sobrindes Linha Grafica E Editora Ltda, pg 92
Thex Editora e Distribuidora Ltda, pg 92
34 Literatura S/C Ltda, pg 92
Totalidade Editora Ltda, pg 92
Editora Vigilia Ltda, pg 93
Zip Editora Ltda, pg 93

TYPE OF PUBLICATION INDEX

BOOK

Bulgaria
Abagar Pablioing, pg 94
Aleks Print Publishing House, pg 94
Antroposofsko Izdatelstvo Dimo R Daskalov OOD, pg 94
Bulgarski Houdozhnik Publishers, pg 94
Hristo G Danov State Publishing House, pg 95
Fama, pg 95
Fondacija Zlatno Kljuce, pg 95
Hermes Publishing House, pg 95
Heron Press Publishing House, pg 96
Kibea Publishing Co, pg 96
Kralica MAB, pg 96
Lettera, pg 96
MATEX, pg 96
Mladezh, pg 96
Musica Publishing House Ltd, pg 96
Pet Plus, pg 97
Prosveta Publishers as, pg 97
Prozoretz Ltd Publishing House, pg 97
Sanra Book Trust, pg 97
Seven Hills Publishers, pg 97
Slavena, pg 98
Sluntse Publishing House, pg 98
Svetra Publishing House, pg 98
TEMTO, pg 98
Trud - Izd kasta, pg 98
Ivan Vazov Publishing House, pg 98
Peyo K Yavorov Publishing House, pg 98
Zunica, pg 98

Burundi
Editions Intore, pg 98

Cameroon
Editions Buma Kor, pg 99

Chile
Arrayan Editores, pg 99
Dolmen Ediciones SA, pg 100
Norma de Chile, pg 101
Editorial Patris SA, pg 101
Pehuen Editores Ltda, pg 101
Ediciones Universitarias de Valparaiso, pg 101
Zig-Zag SA, pg 102

China
Beijing Juvenile & Children's Books Publishing House, pg 102
Beijing Publishing House, pg 102
China Film Press, pg 103
China Ocean Press, pg 103
Dolphin Books, pg 105
Education Science Publishing House, pg 105
Foreign Languages Press, pg 105
Fujian Children's Publishing House, pg 106
Guizhou Education Publishing House, pg 106
Heilongjiang Science & Technology Press, pg 106
Jilin Science & Technology Publishing House, pg 106
Jinan Publishing House, pg 107
Language Publishing House, pg 107
Morning Glory Publishers, pg 107
People's Education Press, pg 107
People's Fine Arts Publishing House, pg 108
Qingdao Publishing House, pg 108
Science Press, pg 108
Shandong Friendship Press, pg 108

Shanghai Educational Publishing House, pg 109
Tomorrow Publishing House, pg 110
Writers' Publishing House, pg 110
Zhejiang Education Publishing House, pg 110

Colombia
Amazonas Editores Ltda, pg 111
Eurolibros Ltda, pg 111
Kapelusz Ltda Editorial, pg 112
Lito Technion Ltda, pg 112
Migema Ediciones Ltda, pg 113
Editorial Norma SA, pg 113
Editorial Oveja Negra, pg 113
Editorial Santillana SA, pg 113
Carlos Valencia Editores, pg 114

The Democratic Republic of the Congo
Saint-Paul, pg 115

Costa Rica
Promesa, Ediciones, pg 116
Scout Interamericana, pg 117
Editorial de la Universidad de Costa Rica, pg 117
Editorial Universitaria Centroamericana (EDUCA), pg 117

Cote d'Ivoire
Akohi Editions, pg 117
Centre de Publications Evangeliques, pg 117

Croatia
ALFA dd za izdavacke, graficke i trgovacke poslove, pg 118
Graficki zavod Hrvatske, pg 118
Matica hrvatska, pg 119
Nasa Djeca Publishing, pg 119
Znaci Vremena, Institut Za Istrazivanje Biblije, pg 120
Znanje d d, pg 120

Cuba
Casa Editora Abril, pg 120
Editorial Gente Nueva, pg 121
Editorial Oriente, pg 121

Czech Republic
Albatros Publishing House, Co Ltd, pg 122
Aurora, pg 123
Aventinum Nakladatelstvi, pg 123
Bakalar spol sro, pg 123
Nakladatelstvi Blok, pg 123
Doplnek, pg 124
Erika, pg 124
Granit SRO, pg 124
Iuventus, pg 124
Jan Vasut Publishing, pg 124
Jota, pg 125
Kalich SRO, pg 125
Karmelitanske Nakladatelstvi, pg 125
Konsultace, pg 125
Mariadan, pg 126
Mlada fronta, pg 126
Nakladatelstvi Svoboda, pg 126
Nakladatelstvi a vydavatelstvi Panorama, pg 127
Pressfoto Vydavatelstvi Ceske Tiskove Kancelare, pg 128
Svojtka & Co, pg 128
Touzimsky & Moravec, pg 128
Ladislav Vasicek, pg 129

Denmark
Agertofts Forlag A/S, pg 129
Alinea A/S, pg 129
Alma, pg 129
Forlaget alokke AS, pg 129
Forlaget Apostrof ApS, pg 130
Aschehoug Dansk Forlag A/S, pg 130
Atuakkiorfik A/S Det Greenland Publishers, pg 130
Bierman og Bierman I/S, pg 130
Bogfabrikken Fakta ApS, pg 130
Bonnier Publications AS, pg 130
Borgens Forlag A/S, pg 130
Bornegudstjeneste-Forlaget, pg 130
Forlaget Carlsen A/S, pg 131
The Danish Literature Centre, pg 131
Egmont Serieforlaget A/S, pg 131
Forum Publishers, pg 132
P Haase & Sons Forlag A/S, pg 132
Forlaget Hjulet, pg 132
Host & Son Publishers Ltd, pg 133
Forlaget Klematis A/S, pg 133
Lohses Forlag, pg 133
Mellemfolkeligt Samvirke, pg 133
Scandinavia Publishing House, pg 135
Sommer og Soerensen Forlag ApS, pg 135
Unitas Forlag, pg 136
Wisby & Wilkens, pg 136

Egypt (Arab Republic of Egypt)
Al Arab Publishing House, pg 138
Dar Al-Kitab Al-Masri, pg 138
Dar Al-Matbo at Al-Gadidah, pg 138
Dar El Shorouk, pg 138
Dar El Shorouk Publishing & Distributing House, pg 138
The Egyptian Society for the Dissemination of Universal Culture and Knowledge (ESDUCK), pg 138
Elias Modern Publishing House, pg 138
Dar Al Maaref, pg 139

El Salvador
Clasicos Roxsil Editorial SA de CV, pg 139

Estonia
Oue Eesti Raamat, pg 139
Estonian Bible Society, pg 140
Kunst Publishers Ltd, pg 140
Kupar Publishers, pg 140
Sinisukk, pg 140
Tuum, pg 141
Valgus Publishers, pg 141

Finland
Aika Oy Kristilliset Kirjat, pg 141
Foersamlingsfoerbundets Foerlags AB, pg 142
Kustannus Oy Kolibri, pg 143
Kustannus Oy Semic, pg 143
Kustannus Oy Uusi Tie, pg 143
Lasten Keskus Oy, pg 143
Otava Publishing Co Ltd, pg 143
Schildts Foerlagsaktiebolag, pg 144
SV-Kauppiaskanava Oy, pg 144
Tammi Publishers, pg 144

France
Actes Graphiques, pg 145
Editions Albin Michel, pg 146
Editions d'Annabelle, pg 147
Les Editions de l'Atelier SA, pg 148

Autrement Editions, pg 149
Editions A Barthelemy, pg 149
Societe Biblique Francaise, pg 150
Editions Andre Bonne, pg 151
Emgleo Breiz, pg 151
Editions BRGM, pg 152
Brud Nevez, pg 152
BS1 - ELOR Editions Jeunesse, pg 152
Editions Casterman, pg 153
Editions du Cerf, pg 153
Dargaud, pg 157
Delagrave Edition SA, pg 158
Editions Delville, pg 158
Dessain et Tolra SA, pg 159
Les Editions des Deux Coqs d'Or, pg 159
Devenirs Visuels SA, pg 159
Disney Hachette Edition, pg 159
Editions Farel, pg 163
FBT de R Editions/Editions des Limbes d'Or, pg 163
Librairie Fischbacher, International Art Book Distribution (import-export), pg 164
Flammarion SA, pg 164
Groupe Fleurus-Mame, pg 164
Editions Gammaprim, pg 166
Editions Jean Paul Gisserot, pg 166
Editions Grandir, pg 166
Hachette Jeunesse Image, pg 167
Hachette JeunesseRoman, pg 167
L'Harmattan, pg 168
Editions Hatier SA, pg 168
Hemma Jeune, SA, pg 168
Kaleidoscope, pg 171
Librairie Larousse, pg 172
Editions des Limbes d'Or/FBT de R Editions, pg 173
Editions Lito, pg 173
Les Livres du Dragon d'Or, pg 173
LLB France (Ligue pour la Lecture de la Bible), pg 173
Editions Josette Lyon, pg 174
Editions Mango, pg 174
Editions Mediaspaul, pg 175
Editions Memo, pg 175
Editions de la Reunion des Musees Nationaux, pg 176
Naufal Group Sarl, pg 177
Editions Nord-Sud, pg 177
Editions du Centre Pompidou, pg 180
Les Presses d'Ile-de-France Sarl, pg 181
Editions du Rouergue, pg 183
Editions du Seneve, pg 184
Sofradif Editions Philippe Auzou, pg 185
Association d'Editions Sorg, pg 186
Ulisse Edition, pg 188
La Vague a l'ame, pg 188
Librairie Vuibert, pg 189
Pierre Zech Editeur, pg 189

French Polynesia
Scoop/Au Vent des Iles, pg 190
Haere Po No Tahiti, pg 190
Simone Sanchez, pg 190

Germany
Abakus Musik Barbara Fietz, pg 191
Agentur des Rauhen Hauses Hamburg GmbH, pg 192
Albarello Verlag GmbH, pg 192
Altberliner Verlag GmbH, pg 193
Anrich Verlag GmbH, pg 193
Antex Verlag-Hans Joachin Schuhmacher, pg 193
Antiquariats-Union Vertriebs GmbH & Co KG, pg 194

PUBLISHERS

Arena Verlag GmbH, pg 194
Ars Edition GmbH, pg 195
Asso Verlag, pg 196
B & B Verlag Anita und Klaus Buscher, pg 197
Beerenverlag, pg 200
Berliner Handpresse Wolfgang Joerg und Erich Schonig, pg 201
Bertelsmann Lexikon Verlag GmbH, pg 201
Bibliographisches Institut & F A Brockhaus AG, pg 203
Verlag Wolfgang Bleiweis, pg 204
Bolanz Verlag fur Alle, pg 205
Born-Verlag, pg 205
Brigg Verlag Franz-Joset Buchler KG, pg 206
R Brockhaus Verlag, pg 206
Brunnen-Verlag GmbH, pg 207
Buchergilde Gutenberg Verlagsgesellschaft mbH, pg 207
Butzon & Bercker GmbH, pg 208
Carlsen Verlag GmbH, pg 209
Christophorus-Verlag GmbH, pg 210
CMA Edition, pg 211
Compact Verlag GmbH, pg 211
Coppenrath Verlag, pg 211
Corona Verlag, pg 212
Delphin Verlag GmbH, pg 213
Deutsche Bibelgesellschaft, pg 213
Deutscher Taschenbuch Verlag GmbH & Co KG (dtv), pg 215
Dipa-Verlag GmbH, pg 217
Domino Verlag, Guenther Brinek GmbH, pg 217
Echter Wurzburg Frankische Gesellschaftsdruckerei und Verlag GmbH, pg 220
Egmont EHAPA Verlag GmbH, pg 221
Egmont Franz Schneider Verlag GmbH, pg 221
Egmont Pestalozzi-Verlag, pg 221
Egmont vgs verlagsgesellschaft mbH, pg 221
Elefanten Press Verlag GmbH, pg 222
Verlag Heinrich Ellermann GmbH & Co KG, pg 222
Engel & Bengel Verlag, pg 222
Ensslin und Laiblin Verlag GmbH & Co KG, pg 223
ERF-Verlag GmbH, pg 223
Esslinger Verlag J F Schreiber GmbH, pg 224
Christa Falk-Verlag, pg 226
Favorit-Verlag Huntemann und Markus & Co GmbH, pg 227
Finken Verlag GmbH, pg 228
Verlag der Francke Buchhandlung GmbH, pg 229
Verlag Freies Geistesleben, pg 230
Margarethe Freudenberger - selbstverlag fur jedermann, pg 230
Garbe Verlag Ellen Vogt, pg 231
Genius Verlag, pg 231
Gerstenberg Verlag, pg 232
GLB Parkland Verlags-und Vertriebs GmbH, pg 232
Grass-Verlag, pg 234
Lehrmittelverlag Wilhelm Hagemann GmbH, pg 236
Carl Hanser Verlag, pg 237
F A Herbig Verlagsbuchhandlung GmbH, pg 239
Verlag Herder GmbH & Co KG, pg 239
Max Hieber KG, pg 240
Dieter Hoffmann Verlag, pg 242
Horlemann Verlag, pg 243
Johannis, pg 246

Jowi-Verlag, pg 246
Karl-May-Verlag Lothar Schmid GmbH, pg 248
Verlag Katholisches Bibelwerk GmbH, pg 248
Verlag Ernst Kaufmann GmbH, pg 248
Verlag Kerle im Verlag Herder, pg 248
Kidemus Verlag GmbH, pg 248
Der Kinderbuch Verlag GmbH, pg 249
Kleiner Bachmann Verlag fur Kinder und Umwelt, pg 250
Knowledge Media International, pg 251
Koptisch-Orthodoxes Zentrum, pg 252
Franckh-Kosmos Verlags-GmbH & Co, pg 252
Roman Kovar Verlag, pg 253
Lahn-Verlag GmbH, pg 255
Landbuch-Verlagsgesellschaft mbH, pg 255
Lappan Verlag GmbH, pg 256
Leibniz-Buecherwarte, pg 257
Lentz Verlag, pg 257
Siegbert Linnemann Verlag, pg 258
Logos-Verlag Literatur & Layout GmbH, pg 258
Johannes Loriz Verlag der Kooperative Duernau, pg 259
Verlag Waldemar Lutz, pg 260
Wolfgang Mann-Verlag GmbH, pg 260
Menschenkinder Verlag und Vertrieb GmbH, pg 262
Gertraud Middelhauve Verlag GmbH & Co KG, pg 263
Missio eV Aachen, pg 264
Moritz Verlag, pg 265
Karl Muller Verlag, pg 266
Naumann & Goebel Verlagsgesellschaft mbH, pg 267
Nebel Verlag GmbH, pg 267
Verlag Neue Stadt GmbH, pg 267
Neuer Honos Verlag GmbH, pg 267
Verlag Neues Leben GmbH, pg 268
Oekotopia Verlag, Wolfgang Hoffman, pg 270
Oncken Verlag KG, pg 270
One Way Medien OHG, pg 270
Patmos Verlag GmbH & Co KG, pg 272
Pattloch Verlag GmbH & Co KG, pg 272
Pelikan Vertriebsgesellschaft mbH & Co KG, pg 272
Postreiter-Verlag GmbH, pg 274
Ravensburger Buchverlag Otto Maier GmbH, pg 277
Konrad Reich Verlag GmbH, pg 278
Verlag an der Ruhr GmbH, pg 281
Saatkorn-Verlag GmbH, pg 281
Verlag der Sankt-Johannis-Druckerei C Schweickhardt, pg 281
Scheffler-Verlag, pg 282
Agora Verlag Manfred Schlosser, pg 283
Buchverlag Andrea Schmitz, pg 284
Verlag Schulte und Gerth GmbH & Co KG, pg 285
Sellier Verlag GmbH, pg 286
Siebert und Engelbert Dessart Verlag GmbH, pg 286
Tangens Systemverlag GmbH, pg 291
K Thienemanns Verlag, pg 293
Tipress Dienstleistungen fur das Verlagswesen GmbH, pg 294
Titania-Verlag Ferdinand Schroll, pg 294

Treves Editions Verein Zur Foerderung der Kuenstlerischen Taetigkeiten, pg 295
Verlag Beltz & Gelberg, pg 297
Verlag und Studio fuer Hoerbuchproduktionen, pg 298
Voggenreiter-Verlag, pg 299
A Weichert Verlag GmbH & Co KG, pg 301
Friedrich Wittig Verlag GmbH, pg 303
Verlag DAS WORT GmbH, pg 304
Xenos Verlagsgesellschaft mbH, pg 304

Ghana

Adwinsa Publications (Ghana) Ltd, pg 306
Afram Publications (Ghana) Ltd, pg 306
Asempa Publishers, pg 306
Beginners Publishers, pg 306
Black Mask Ltd, pg 306
Educational Press & Manufacturers Ltd, pg 307
Ekab Business Ltd, pg 307
EPP Books Services, pg 307
Frank Publishing Ltd, pg 307
Goodbooks Publishing Co, pg 307
Kwamfori Publishing Enterprise, pg 307
Paul Ntem Maanoh, pg 307
Quick Service Books Ltd, pg 308
Sam Woode Ltd, pg 308
Sedco Publishing Ltd, pg 308
Sub-Saharan Publishers, pg 308
Woeli Publishing Services, pg 308
World Literature Project, pg 308

Greece

Akritas, pg 308
Anixis Publications, pg 309
Apostoliki Diakonia tis Ekklisias tis Hellados, pg 309
Athina, Mary Mavrogiannis, pg 309
Atlantis M Pechlivanides & Co SA, pg 309
Axiotelis G, pg 309
Boukoumanis' Editions, pg 309
Chrysi Penna - Golden Pen Books, pg 309
Chryssos Typos AE Ekodeis, pg 309
Dorikos Publishing House, pg 310
Elafaki, pg 310
Elliniki Leschi Tou Vivliou, pg 310
Giovanis Publications, Pangosmios Ekdotikos Organismos, pg 310
Govostis Publishing SA, pg 311
Harmi-Press Publications, Haroula D Papadimitriou G P, pg 311
Hestia-I D Hestia-Kollaros & Co Corporation, pg 311
I Prooptiki, pg 311
Institute of Neohellenic Studies, Manolis Triantaphyllidis Foundation, pg 311
Editions Kalentis, pg 312
Ilias Kambanas Publishing Organization, SA, pg 312
Kastaniotis Editions SA, pg 312
Kedros Publishers, pg 312
Kritiki Publishing, pg 312
Logos, pg 312
Editions Moressopoulos, pg 313
Nakas Music House, pg 313
Odysseas Publications Ltd, pg 313
Orfanidis Publications, pg 314
Pagoulatos G-G P Publications, pg 314
Kyr l Papadopoulos E E, pg 314
Patakis Publishers, pg 314
M Psaropoulos & Co EE, pg 314

TYPE OF PUBLICATION INDEX

Psichogios Publications SA, pg 314
Nikolas I Rossi, pg 314
Sigma, pg 315
D & J Vardikos, pg 315
Vlassis, pg 316
S J Zacharopoulos SA Publishing Co, pg 316

Guyana

Roraima Publishers Ltd, pg 317

Haiti

Editions Caraiibes SA, pg 317

Hong Kong

Benefit Publishing Co, pg 318
CFW Publications Ltd, pg 318
Chinese Christian Literature Council Ltd, pg 318
Christian Communications Ltd, pg 319
Federal Publications Ltd, pg 319
Island Press, pg 320
Joint Publishing (HK) Co Ltd, pg 320
Peace Book Co Ltd, pg 321
Publications (Holdings) Ltd, pg 321
Sesame Publication Co, pg 321
Sun Ya Publications (HK) Ltd, pg 322

Hungary

Advent Kiado, pg 323
Aranyhal Konyvkiado Goldfish Publishing, pg 323
Idegenforgalmi Propaganda es Kiado Vallalat, pg 324
Ifjusagi Lap-eskonyvkiado Vallalat, pg 324
Officina Nova, Koenyv-es Lapkiado/Bertelsmann Media Kft, pg 324
Lang Kiado, pg 325
Mora Ferenc Ifjusagi Koenyvkiado Rt, pg 325
Park Konyvkiado Kft (Park Publisher), pg 326
Tevan Kiado Vallalat, pg 327

Iceland

AEskan, pg 327
Almenna Bokafelagid, pg 327
Forlagid, pg 327
Frjals fjolmiolun hf-Urvalsbaekur, pg 327
Frodi Ltd, pg 328
Idunn, pg 328
Islendingasagnautgafan, pg 328
Mal og menning, pg 328
Setberg, pg 328
Skjaldborg Ltd, pg 328

India

Addison-Wesley (Singapore) Pte Ltd, pg 329
Advaita Ashrama, pg 329
Allied Publishers Pvt Ltd, pg 330
Ambar Prakashan, pg 330
Ananda Publishers Pvt Ltd, pg 330
Baha'i Publishing Trust of India, pg 332
Bani Mandir, Book-Sellers, Publishers & Educational Suppliers, pg 332
Bharat Publishing House, pg 332
Bhawan Book Service, Publishers & Distributors, pg 333
Children's Book Trust, pg 334
The Christian Literature Society, pg 335
Dastane Ramchandra & Co, pg 335

TYPE OF PUBLICATION INDEX

BOOK

DC Books, pg 336
Diamond Comics (P) Ltd, pg 336
Dolphin Publications, pg 336
Dreamland Publications, pg 336
Dutta Baruah Publishing Co Pvt Ltd, pg 336
Frank Brothers & Co (Publishers) Ltd, pg 337
HarperCollins Publishers India Pty Ltd, pg 338
Hindi Pracharak Sansthan, pg 338
Indian Book Depot (Map House), pg 339
Islamic Publishing House, pg 340
Lancer Publisher's & Distributors, pg 341
Laxmi Publications Pvt Ltd, pg 341
Learners Press Private Ltd, pg 341
Sri Ramakrishna Math, pg 342
A Mukherjee & Co Pvt Ltd, pg 343
M/S Gulshan Nanda Publications, pg 343
Naresh Publishers, pg 343
Nem Chand & Brothers, pg 344
Omsons Publications, pg 345
Paico Publishing House, pg 345
Paramount Sales (India) Pvt Ltd, pg 345
Parimal Prakashan, pg 345
Pitambar Publishing Co (P) Ltd, pg 346
Prabhat Prakashan, pg 346
Pratibha Pratishthan, pg 346
Rajpal & Sons, pg 347
M C Sarkar & Sons (P) Ltd, pg 349
Sasta Sahitya Mandal, pg 349
Sat Sahitya Prakashan, pg 349
Satprakashan Sanchar Kendra, pg 349
Scientific Book Agency, pg 349
Shaibya Prakashan Bibhag, pg 349
Sharda Prakashan, pg 350
Shiksha Bharati, pg 350
Somaiya Publications Pvt Ltd, pg 350
Spectrum Publications, pg 350
Star Publications (P) Ltd, pg 351
Vidya Puri, pg 352
Vidyarthi Mithram Press, pg 352
Vikas Publishing House Pvt Ltd, pg 353
Vivek Prakashan, pg 353

Indonesia

Mandira Jaya Abadi, pg 353
CV Angkasa CV (Publishers), pg 354
PT Pustaka Antara Publishing & Printing, pg 354
Auroa, pg 354
Balai Pustaka, pg 354
Bina Rena Pariwara, pg 354
PT Dian Rakyat, pg 355
Dunia Pustaka Jaya, pg 355
Fortunajaya, pg 355
Gramedia, pg 355
PT Indira, pg 355
Karya Anda, CV, pg 356
Mizan, pg 356
Pustaka Utama Grafiti, PT, pg 357
Yayasan Obor Indonesia, pg 357

Ireland

An Gum, pg 358
Clo Iar-Chonnachta Teo, pg 359
Gill & Macmillan Ltd, pg 361
Kerryman Ltd, pg 362
Mercier Press Ltd, pg 362
The O'Brien Press Ltd, pg 363
Poolbeg Press Ltd, pg 363
Publishers Group South West (Ireland), pg 363
Roberts Rinehart Publishers, pg 363
Wolfhound Press, pg 364

Israel

Achiever, pg 365
Amichai Publishing House Ltd, pg 365
Bitan Publishers Ltd, pg 365
Breslov Research Institute, pg 366
Classikaletet, pg 366
Dekel Publishing House, pg 366
Dvir Publishing Ltd, pg 366
Feldheim Publishers Ltd, pg 367
Gefen Publishing House Ltd, pg 367
Hadar Publishing House Ltd, pg 367
Hakibbutz Hameuchad Publishing House Ltd, pg 368
Inbal Publishers, pg 368
The Institute for the Translation of Hebrew Literature, pg 368
Ma'ariv Book Guild (Sifriat Ma'ariv), pg 370
Modan Publishers Ltd, pg 371
Pitspopany Press, pg 371
Rolnik Publishers, pg 371
Saar Publishing House, pg 372
Schocken Publishing House Ltd, pg 372
R Sirkis Publishers Ltd, pg 372
Y Sreberk, pg 372
Steimatzky Group Ltd, pg 372
Urim Publications, pg 373
Yad Vashem - The Holocaust Martyrs' & Heroes' Remembrance Authority, pg 373
Yavneh Publishing House Ltd, pg 373
Yedioth Ahronoth Books, pg 373
Zakheim Publishing House, pg 374
Zmora-Bitan, Publishers Ltd, pg 374

Italy

Alba, pg 375
Archino snc, pg 376
Edizioni Arka SRL, pg 376
Editore Armando Armando SRL, pg 376
Bovolenta, pg 378
Edizioni Bresciane, pg 378
Campanotto, pg 379
Casa Musicale Edizioni Carrara SRL, pg 379
Edizioni Cartedit SRL, pg 379
Casa Editrice Castalia, pg 380
Edizioni Castello di Antonio Careddu, pg 380
Centro Biblico, pg 380
Edizioni Centro Studi Erickson, pg 381
Citta Nuova Editrice, pg 382
La Coccinella Editrice SRL, pg 382
Colonnese Editore, pg 382
Continental SRL Editrice, pg 383
Dami Editore SRL, pg 383
G De Bono Editore, pg 384
Edizioni E - Elle SRL, pg 385
Edizioni EBE, pg 385
Edizioni Il Punto d'Incontro SAS, pg 386
Editrice Eraclea, pg 388
Fatatrac, pg 388
Feguagiskia' Studios, pg 389
Istituto Geografico de Agostini SpA, pg 390
Giunti (Gruppo Editoriale), pg 390
In Dialogo, pg 393
Edizioni Internazionali di Letteratura e Scienze, pg 394
Editoriale Jaca Book SpA, pg 394
Editrice Janus SpA, pg 394
Linea d'Ombra Libri, pg 396
Vincenzo Lo Faro Editore, pg 396
Macro Edizioni, pg 397
Giuseppe Maimone Editore, pg 397
Casa Editrice Menna di Sinisgalli Menna Giuseppina, pg 398
Messaggero di San Antonio, pg 398
Motta Junior Srl, pg 400
Edizioni Piemme SpA, pg 403
Edizioni Primavera SRL, pg 404
Il Punto D Incontro, pg 404
RAI.ERI, pg 405
Rara-Ist Editoriale di Bibliofilia e Reprints, pg 405
Editori Riuniti, pg 405
Rubbettino Editore, pg 406
Rugginenti Editore, pg 406
Adriano Salani Editore srl, pg 406
Lo Scarabeo Srl, pg 407
Editoriale Scienza, pg 407
Societa Editrice Internazionale - SEI, pg 408
Edizioni Sonda, pg 408
Editrice Uomini Nuovi, pg 410
Zanfi Editori SRL, pg 412

Jamaica

Eureka Press Ltd, pg 413
Institute of Jamaica Publications, pg 413
Kingston Publishers Ltd, pg 413
Twin Guinep Ltd, pg 413
West Indies Publishing Ltd, pg 414

Japan

Alice-Kan, pg 414
Child Honsha Co Ltd, pg 415
Dainippon Tosho Publishing Co, Ltd, pg 416
Dohosha Publishing Co Ltd, pg 416
Froebel-Kan Co Ltd, pg 416
Fukuinkan Shoten Publishers Inc, pg 416
Fuzambo Publishing Co, pg 416
Gakken Co Ltd, pg 416
Hyoronsha Publishing Co Ltd, pg 417
International Society for Educational Information (ISEI), pg 418
Iwanami Shoten, Publishers, pg 418
Kaisei-Sha Publishing Co Ltd, pg 419
Kin no Hoshi-Sha Co Ltd, pg 419
Kokudo-Sha, pg 420
Kosei Publishing Co Ltd, pg 420
Nagaoka Shoten Company Ltd, pg 421
Nishimura Co Ltd, pg 423
Obunsha Co Ltd, pg 423
Ongaku No Tomo Sha Corporation, pg 423
Poplar Publishing Co Ltd, pg 423
Saera Shobo (Librairie Ca et La), pg 424
Seibido Shuppan Company Ltd, pg 424
Shiko-Sha Co Ltd, pg 425
Shingakusha Co Ltd, pg 425
Akane Shobo Co Ltd, pg 425
Soryusha, pg 426
Tokyo Shoseki Co Ltd, pg 427
Yugaku-sha Ltd, pg 429
Zoshindo JukenKenkyusha, pg 429

Jordan

Al-Tanwir Al Ilmi (Scientific Enlightenment Publishing House), pg 430

Kenya

Africa Book Services (EA) Ltd, pg 430
Danmar Publishers, pg 431
Evangel Publishing House, pg 431
Focus Publications Ltd, pg 431
Heinemann Kenya Limited (EAEP), pg 431
Jacaranda Designs Ltd, pg 432
Kenway Publications Ltd, pg 432
Kenya Literature Bureau, pg 432
Kenya Quality & Productivity Institute, pg 432
Lake Publishers & Enterprises Ltd, pg 432
Phoenix Publishers, pg 433
Space Sellers Ltd, pg 433
Sudan Literature Centre, pg 433
Uzima Press, pg 433

Democratic People's Republic of Korea

Grand People's Study House, pg 434

Republic of Korea

Ba-reunsa Publishing Co, pg 434
BIR Publishing, pg 435
Bo Ri, pg 435
Borim Publishing Co, pg 435
Dae Won Sa Co Ltd, pg 435
Dong-A Publishing & Printing Co Ltd, pg 436
Dong Hwa Publishing Co, pg 436
Haseo Publishing Co, pg 436
Hollym Corporation Publishers, pg 437
Iljisa Publishing House, pg 437
Jigyungsa Ltd, pg 437
Jung-ang Munhwa Sa, pg 437
Kemongsa Publishing Co Ltd, pg 437
Korea Britannica Corp, pg 437
Koreaone Press Inc, pg 438
Kukmin Doseo Publishing Co Inc, pg 438
Kukminseokwan Publishing Co Ltd, pg 438
Kum Sung Publishing Co Ltd, pg 438
Kyohaksa Publishing Co Ltd, pg 438
Literature Academy, pg 438
Minjisa Publishing Co, pg 438
Moon Jin Media Co Ltd, pg 438
Omun Gak, pg 439
St Pauls, pg 439
Samhwa Publishing Co, pg 440
Samseong Publishing Co Ltd, pg 440
Twenty-First Century Publishers, Inc, pg 440
Woong Jin Publishing Co Ltd, pg 440
Woongjin Media Corporation, pg 440
Word of Life Press, pg 440
Yearim-dang, pg 441

Latvia

Alberts XII, pg 441
Artava Ltd, pg 441
Egmont Latvia Ltd, pg 442
Hermess Ltd, pg 442
Madris, pg 442
Preses Nams, pg 442
Spriditis Publishers, pg 442
Vaidelote, pg 442
Zvaigzne ABC Publishers, Ltd, pg 442

PUBLISHERS

Lebanon
Librairie du Liban, pg 443
Librairie Orientale sal, pg 443
World Book Publishing, pg 443

Liechtenstein
Frank P van Eck Publishers, pg 444

Lithuania
Alma Littera, pg 445
Dargenis Publishers, pg 445
Egmont Lietuva, pg 445
Lietus Ltd, pg 445
Lietuvos Rasytoju Sajungos Leidykla, pg 446
The Publishing House of the Lithuanian Writers' Union, pg 446
Margi Rastai Publishers, pg 446
Sviesa Publishers, pg 446
Victoria Publishers, pg 446

Luxembourg
Editions Emile Borschette, pg 447
Op der Lay, pg 447
Editions Saint-Paul, pg 448
Varkki Verghese, pg 448

The Former Yugoslav Republic of Macedonia
Detska radost, pg 448
Nov svet (New World), pg 449

Madagascar
Maison d'Edition Protestante ANTSO, pg 450
Foibe Filan-Kevitry NY Mpampianatra (FOFIPA), pg 450
Librarie Mixte, pg 450

Malawi
Dzuka Publishing Company Ltd, pg 450
Popular Publications, pg 451

Malaysia
S Abdul Majeed & Co, pg 451
Amiza Associate Malaysia Sdn Bhd, pg 451
Associated Educational Distributors (M) Sdn Bhd, pg 451
Darulfikir, pg 451
Dewan Bahasa dan Pustaka, pg 451
Dewan Pustaka Islam, pg 451
Eastview Productions Sdn Bhd, pg 452
Federal Publications Sdn Bhd, pg 452
FEP International Sdn Bhd, pg 452
Forum Publications, pg 452
IBS Buku Sdn Bhd, pg 452
Mahir Publications Sdn Bhd, pg 452
Mecron Sdn Bhd, pg 453
Oscar Book International, pg 453
Pearson Education, pg 453
Penerbit Jayatinta Sdn Bhd, pg 454
Penerbit Prisma Sdn Bhd, pg 454
Penerbitan Tinta, pg 454
Perfect Frontier Sdn Bhd, pg 454
Pustaka Cipta Sdn Bhd, pg 454
Pustaka Delta Pelajaran Sdn Bhd, pg 454
Pustaka Sistem Pelajaran Sdn Bhd, pg 454
Tempo Publishing (M) Sdn Bhd, pg 455
Tropical Press Sdn Bhd, pg 455
Vinpress Sdn Bhd, pg 455

Maldive Islands
Non-Formal Education Centre, pg 455

Malta
Merlin Library Ltd, pg 456
Publishers' Enterprises Group (PEG) Ltd, pg 456

Mauritius
Editions Capucines, pg 457
Golden Publications, pg 457
Editions de l'Ocean Indien Ltd, pg 457
Vizavi Editions, pg 457

Mexico
Adivinar y Multiplicar, SA de CV, pg 457
Editorial Avante SA de Cv, pg 458
Comision Nacional Forestal, pg 459
Ediciones Corunda SA de CV, pg 459
Ediciones Culturales Internacionales SA de CV Edicion Compra y Venta de Libros, Casetes, Videos, pg 459
Editorial Diana SA de CV, pg 459
Entretenlibro SA de CV, pg 460
Fernandez Editores SA de CV, pg 461
Fondo de Cultura Economica, pg 461
Editorial Hermes SA, pg 461
Editorial Iztaccihuatl SA, pg 462
Ediciones Larousse SA de CV, pg 462
Libros y Revistas SA de CV, pg 463
Editorial Limusa SA de CV, pg 463
Naves Internacional de Ediciones SA, pg 464
Organizacion Cultural LP SA de CV, pg 465
Panorama Editorial, SA, pg 465
Editorial Patria SA de CV, pg 465
Ediciones Cientificas La Prensa Medica Mexicana SA de CV, pg 466
Editorial Progreso SA de C V, pg 466
Ediciones Promesa, SA de CV, pg 466
Sayrols Editorial SA de CV, pg 466
Sistemas Tecnicos de Edicion SA de CV, pg 467
Ediciones Suromex SA, pg 467
Editorial Trillas SA de CV, pg 467

Republic of Moldova
Editura Hyperion, pg 468
Lumina Publishing House, pg 468

Morocco
Editions Eddif Maroc, pg 469
Editions Okad, pg 470

Nepal
International Standards Books & Periodicals (P) Ltd, pg 471

Netherlands
Altamira BV, pg 472
Ars Scribendi bv Uitgeverij, pg 473
Big Balloon BV, pg 474
Uitgeverij G F Callenbach BV, pg 475
East-West Publications Fonds BV, pg 476

Educatieve Uitgeverij Edu'Actief BV, pg 476
Eekhoorn BV Uitgeverij, pg 476
Van Goor BV, pg 477
Gottmer Uitgevers Groop, pg 477
Katholieke Bijbelstichting, pg 479
Kimio Uitgeverij bv, pg 479
LCG Malmberg BV, pg 480
Meander Uitgeverij BV, pg 481
Mirran, pg 481
Omega Boek BV, pg 482
Uitgeverij Ploegsma BV, pg 483
Prometheus, pg 483
Rebo Productions BV, pg 483
Sjaloom en Wildeboer Publishers, pg 484
Telos Boeken, pg 485
Uitgeverij De Toorts, pg 485
Van Buuren Uitgeverij BV, pg 486
Uitgeverij De Vuurbaak BV, pg 487
Uitgeverij Westers, pg 487

New Zealand
Brick Row Publishing Co Ltd, pg 489
Bush Press Communications Ltd, pg 489
Cape Catley, pg 489
Craig Printing Company Ltd, pg 490
HarperCollins Publishers (New Zealand) Ltd, pg 491
Hazard Press Ltd, pg 491
Huia Publishers, pg 492
Learning Media Ltd, pg 492
Magari Publishing, pg 493
Mallinson Rendel Publishers Ltd, pg 493
Maori Publications Unit, pg 493
Nelson Price Milburn Ltd, pg 494
Reed Publishing (NZ) Ltd, pg 495
RSVP Publishing Company Ltd, pg 495
Shearwater Associates Ltd, pg 495
Shortland Publications Ltd, pg 495
Sunshine Books International Ltd, pg 496
Te Reo Publications, pg 496

Nigeria
ABIC Books & Equipment Ltd, pg 497
Adebara Publishers Ltd, pg 497
Evans Brothers (Nigeria Publishers) Ltd, pg 499
Fourth Dimension Publishing Co Ltd, pg 499
Literamed Publications Nigeria Ltd, pg 500
New Era Publishers, pg 500
Northern Nigerian Publishing Co Ltd, pg 500
Obobo Books, pg 501
Saros International Publishers, pg 501
Tana Press Ltd & Flora Nwapa Books Ltd, pg 501
Joe-Tolalu & Associates, pg 501
Unity Publishing & Research Company Ltd, pg 502
Vantage Publishers International Ltd, pg 502
West African Book Publishers Ltd, pg 502

Norway
Ariel Lydbokforlag, pg 502
Atheneum Forlag A/S, pg 502
John Grieg Forlag AS, pg 503
Gyldendal Norsk Forlag A/S, pg 503

Lunde Forlag og Bokhandel A/S, pg 504
Luther Forlag A/S, pg 504
Sandviks Bokforlag, pg 505
Snofugl Forlag, pg 505
Solum Forlag A/S, pg 505

Pakistan
Hamdard Foundation, pg 507
Islamic Publications (Pvt) Ltd, pg 507
Malik Sirajuddin & Sons, pg 507
Maqbool Academy, pg 508
National Book Foundation, pg 508
Sang-e-Meel Publications, pg 509
Sh Ghulam Ali & Sons (Pvt) Ltd, pg 509

Papua New Guinea
Kristen Pres, pg 510

Peru
Asociacion Editorial Bruno, pg 511
Carvajal SA, pg 511
Ediciones Peisa (Promocion Editorial Inca SA), pg 511
Tarea Asociacion de Publicaciones Educativas, pg 511

Philippines
Abiva Publishing House Inc, pg 512
Anvil Publishing Inc, pg 512
Bookman Printing & Publishing House Inc, pg 512
Bookmark Inc, pg 512
Cacho Publishing House, Inc, pg 512
Communication Foundation for Asia Media Group (CFAMG), pg 513
Encyclopaedia Britannica (Philippines) Inc, pg 513
Marren Publishing House, Inc, pg 513
New Day Publishers, pg 514
Our Lady of Manaoag Publisher, pg 514
Philippine Baptist Mission SBC FMB Church Growth International, pg 514
Rex Bookstores & Publishers, pg 514

Poland
Wydawnictwa Normalizacyjne Alfa-Wero, pg 516
Instytut Wydawniczy Pax, Inco-Veritas, pg 517
Iskry - Publishing House Ltd spotka zoo, pg 517
Ludowa Spoldzielnia Wydawnicza, pg 518
Muza SA, pg 518
Wydawnictwo Nasza Ksiegarnia Sp zoo, pg 518
Wydawnictwo Podsiedlik-Raniowski i Spolka, pg 519
Przedsiebiorstwo Wydawniczo-Handlowe Wydawnictwo Siedmiorog, pg 519
Res Polona, pg 519
Wydawnictwo RTW, pg 520
'Slask' Ltd, pg 520
Spotdzielna Anagram, pg 520
Vocatio Publishing House, pg 520
Wydawnictwo Wilga sp zoo, pg 521
Wydawn Na Sprawa' Wydawniczo-Oswiatowa Spotdzielnia Inwalidow, pg 521

TYPE OF PUBLICATION INDEX	BOOK

Portugal

Edicoes Afrontamento, pg 522
Livraria Arnado Lda, pg 522
Contexto Editora, pg 524
Dinalivro, pg 524
Distri Cultural Lda, pg 524
Editorial Estampa, Lda, pg 524
Publicacoes Europa-America Lda, pg 524
Europress Editores e Distribuidores de Publicacoes Lda, pg 525
Everest Editora, pg 525
Girassol Edicoes, LDA, pg 525
Gradiva-Publicacnoes Lda, pg 525
Livros Horizonte Lda, pg 526
Meriberica/Liber, pg 527
Editorial Noticias, pg 527
Editorial O Livro Lda, pg 528
Paulinas, pg 528
Perspectivas e Realidades, Artes Graficas, Lda, pg 528
Porto Editora Lda, pg 528
Portugalmundo, pg 528
Editorial Presenca, pg 528
Publicacoes Dom Quixote Lda, pg 528
Puma Editora Lda, pg 528
Editora Replicacao Lda, pg 529
Teorema, pg 529
Texto Editora, pg 529
Publicacoes Trevo Lda, pg 530
Vega-Publicacao e Distribuicao de Livros e Revistas, Lda, pg 530

Romania

Editura Aius, pg 531
Alcor-Edimpex (Verlag) Ltd, pg 531
Editora All, pg 531
Editura Clusium, Casa de Editura Atlas-Clusium SRL, pg 532
Coresi SRL, pg 532
Corint Verlag, pg 532
Editure Ion Creanga, pg 532
Editura Dacia, pg 532
Editura DOINA SRL, pg 533
Enzyklopadie Verlag, pg 533
Editura Excelsior, pg 533
FF Press, pg 533
Editura Kriterion SA, pg 534
Lider Verlag, pg 534
MAST Verlag, pg 534
Mentor Kiado, pg 534
Editura Minerva, pg 534
Nemira Verlag, pg 534
Editura Niculescu, pg 534
Pandora Publishing House, pg 535
RAO International Publishing Co, pg 535
RAO Publishing Group, pg 535
Saeculum IO, pg 535
Vox Verlag und Vertrieb, pg 536

Russian Federation

Airis Press, pg 537
CentrePolygraph Traders & Publishers Co, pg 537
Dom, Izdatel'stvo sovetskogo deskkogo fonda im & 1 Lenina, pg 537
Druzhba Narodov, pg 537
Finansy i Statistika Publishing House, pg 538
Kabardino-Balkarskoye knizhnoye izdatelstvo, pg 539
Izdatelstvo Khudozhestvennaya Literatura, pg 539
KUbK Publishing House, pg 539
Ladomir Publishing House, pg 539
Publishing House Limbus Press, pg 539
Izdatelstvo Malysh, pg 539
Obdeestro Znanie, pg 541

Okoshko Ltd Publishers (Izdatelstvo), pg 541
Panorama Publishing House, pg 541
Permskaja Kniga, pg 541
Raduga Publishers, pg 541
Russkaya Kniga Izdatelstvo (Publishers), pg 541
Scorpion Publishers, pg 541
Sredne-Uralskoye knizhnoye izatelstve (Middle Urals Publishing House), pg 542
Izdatelstvo Sudostroenie, pg 542
Text Publishers Ltd Too, pg 542

Saudi Arabia

Dar Al-Shareff for Publishing & Distribution, pg 543
Saudi Publishing and Distribution House, pg 543

Senegal

Centre Africain d'Animation et d'Echanges Culturels Editions Khoudia, pg 544

Singapore

Asiapac Books Pte Ltd, pg 545
Cannon International, pg 545
Celebrity Educational Publishers, pg 545
Europhone Language Institute (Pte) Ltd, pg 546
Federal Publications (S) Pte Ltd, pg 546
FEP International Private Ltd, pg 546
Global Educational Services Pte Ltd, pg 546
K C Ang Publishing Pte Ltd, pg 547
Pan Pacific Publications (S) Pte Ltd, pg 547
Shing Lee Group Publishers, pg 548
SNP Pan Pacific Publishing Pte Ltd, pg 548
Success Publications Pte Ltd, pg 548
Tecman Bible House, pg 549

Slovakia

ARCHA sro Vydavatel'stro, pg 549
AV Studio Reklamno-vydavatel'ska agentura, pg 549
Egmont Neografia spol sro, pg 549
Luc vydavatelske druzstvo, pg 550
Mlade leta Spd sro, pg 550
Vydavatelstvo Obzor, pg 550
Priroda, pg 550
Slo Viet, pg 550
Slovansky Tatran, Vydavatel'stro spoi sro, pg 550
Sofa, pg 551
Vydavatelstvo Junior sro Slovart Print, pg 551
Vydavatel'stvo Osveta (Verlag Osveta), pg 551

Slovenia

East West Operation (EWO) Ltd, pg 551
Franc-Franc podjetje za promocijo kulture Murska Sobota d o o, pg 551
Mladinska Knjiga International, pg 552
Zalozba Mihelac d o o, pg 552
Zalozba Obzorja d d Maribor, pg 552

South Africa

Anansi Uitgewers, pg 552
Bet-El Publishers, pg 553
Educum Publishers Ltd, pg 554
Erudita Publications (Pty) Ltd, pg 554
HarperCollins Religious, pg 554
HAUM - Daan Retief Publishers (Pty) Ltd, pg 555
HAUM - De Jager Publishers, pg 555
Human & Rousseau (Pty) Ltd, pg 555
Ithemba! Publishing, pg 555
Jacklin Enterprises (Pty) Ltd, pg 556
Maskew Miller Longman, pg 557
New Africa Books (Pty) Ltd, pg 557
Publitoria Publishers, pg 558
Publitoria Editions, pg 558
Ravan Press (Pty) Ltd, pg 558
Struik Publishers (Pty) Ltd, pg 559
Tafelberg Publishers Ltd, pg 560
Vivlia Publishers & Booksellers, pg 560

Spain

Publicacions de l'Abadia de Montserrat, pg 561
Editorial Acanto SA, pg 561
Editorial Aguaclara, pg 562
Aguilar SA de Ediciones, pg 562
Alberdania SL, pg 562
Alinco SA - Aura Comunicacio, pg 563
Anaya Educacion, pg 563
Editorial Astri SA, pg 564
Ediciones Atril, pg 564
Ediciones B, SA, pg 565
Editorial Barcanova SA, pg 565
Beascoa SA Ediciones, pg 565
Edicions Bromera SL, pg 566
Editorial Bruno, pg 566
Calamo Editorial, pg 566
Editorial Casals SA, pg 566
CEAC, Grupo Editorial SA, pg 567
Editorial Claret SA, pg 568
Combel Editorial SA, pg 568
Compania Literaria, pg 568
Creaciones Monar Editorial, pg 569
Ediciones Cruilla SA, pg 569
Ediciones Daly S L, pg 569
Ediciones Destino SA, pg 569
Didaco Comunicacion y Didactica, SA, pg 569
Diputacion Provincial de Malaga, pg 570
Edicions del Drac SA, pg 570
Ediciones Ebenezer, pg 571
Editorial EDAF SA, pg 571
Edebe, pg 571
Edicions Camacuc, pg 571
Editorial Everest SA, pg 572
El Hogar y la Moda SA, pg 572
Ediciones Elfos SL, pg 572
Elkar, Euskal Liburu eta Kantuen Argitaldaria, SL, pg 573
Editorial Empeno 14, pg 573
Erein, pg 573
Editorial Esin, SA, pg 573
Editorial Espasa-Calpe SA, pg 573
Fundacion Coleccion Thyssen-Bornemisza, pg 575
Fundacion Rosacruz, pg 575
Galaxia SA Editorial, pg 575
La Galera, SA Editorial, pg 575
Ediciones Gaviota SA, pg 575
Grijalbo Mondadori SA, pg 576
Grupo Editorial CEAC SA, pg 576
Grupo Santillana de Ediciones SA, pg 576

Editorial Gulaab, pg 577
Hercules de Ediciones, SA, pg 577
Ediciones Hiperion SL, pg 577
Ibaizabal Edelvives SA, pg 577
Idea Books, SA, pg 578
Ediciones JJB, pg 579
Ediciones JLA, pg 579
Editorial Juventud SA, pg 579
LEDA (Las Ediciones de Arte), pg 579
Libsa Editorial SA, pg 580
Llibres del Segle, pg 580
Loguez Ediciones, pg 580
Editorial Luis Vives (Edelvives), pg 580
Editorial Magisterio Espanol SA, pg 581
Edicions de la Magrana SA, pg 581
Editorial Marfil SA, pg 581
Editorial Marin SA, pg 581
Editorial Mediterrania SL, pg 582
Editorial Molino, pg 582
Editorial Moll SL, pg 582
Editorial Alfredo Ortells SL, pg 585
Parramon Ediciones SA, pg 586
Pearson Educacion S A, pg 586
Editorial Peregrino SL, pg 586
Pirene Editorial, sal, pg 587
Plastic Comunicacion SL, pg 587
Editorial Playor SA, pg 587
Plaza y Janes Editores SA, pg 587
Ediciones Rialp SA, pg 589
Editorial Miguel A Salvatella SA, pg 589
San Pablo Ediciones, pg 589
Ediciones San Pio X, pg 589
Ediciones Seyer, pg 590
Silex Ediciones, pg 590
Equipo Sirius SA, pg 591
Ediciones Siruela SA, pg 591
Grup 62, pg 591
Ediciones SM, pg 591
Ramon Sopena SA, pg 591
Ediciones Susaeta SA, pg 592
Ediciones Toray SA, pg 593
Ediciones de la Torre, pg 593
Editorial Verbo Divino, pg 595
Veron Editor, pg 595
Xunta de Galicia, pg 596
Editorial Zendrera Zariquiey, SA, pg 596

Sri Lanka

Colombo Book Association, pg 596
Danuma Prakashakayo, pg 596
Dayawansa Jayakody & Co, pg 597
Lake House Investments Ltd, pg 597
Pradeepa Publishers, pg 598
Saman & Madara Publishers, pg 598
Sunera Publishers, pg 598
Swarna Hansa Foundation, pg 598
Warna Publishers, pg 598

Sweden

Alfabeta Bokforlag AB, pg 600
Bonnier Audio, pg 601
Bonnier Carlsen Bokforlag AB, pg 601
Eriksson & Lindgren Bokforlag, pg 602
Hagaberg AB, pg 603
Hallgren och Fallgren Studieforlag AB, pg 603
Bokforlaget Hegas AB, pg 603
Mezopotamya Publishing & Distribution, pg 604
Bokfoerlaget Naturoch Kultur, pg 604
Raben och Sjoegren Bokfoerlag, pg 605

PUBLISHERS

Richters Egmont, pg 605
Bokforlaget Semic AB, pg 606
Semic Bokforlaget International AB, pg 606
Sjoestrands Foerlag, pg 606

Switzerland

Armenia Editions, pg 608
Bibellesbund Verlag, pg 610
Blaukreuz-Verlag Bern, pg 610
Bohem Press Kinderbuchverlag, pg 610
Caux Edition SA, pg 611
Christoph Merian Verlag, pg 611
Cosa-Verlag, Giusep Condrau SA, pg 611
Diogenes Verlag AG, pg 612
Editions Esprit Ouvert, pg 613
Jugend mit einer Mission Verlag, pg 616
Verlag Walter Keller, Dornach, pg 617
Kinderbuchverlag Luzern, pg 617
Lia rumantscha, pg 618
La Maison de la Bible, pg 618
Motovun Book GmbH, pg 619
Verlag Nagel & Kimche AG, Zurich, pg 619
Neptun-Verlag, pg 620
Nord-Sued Verlag, pg 620
Orell Fuessli Verlag, pg 620
Pro Juventute Verlag, pg 622
Rex Verlag, pg 623
Rodera-Verlag der Cardun AG, pg 623
Sauerlaender AG, pg 623
Schlaepfer & Co AG, pg 624
Strom-Verlag Luzern, pg 625
Uranium Verlag Zug, pg 626

Taiwan, Province of China

Ai Chih Book Co Ltd, pg 629
Campus Evangelical Fellowship, Literature Department, pg 629
Cheng Yun Publishing Company Ltd, pg 629
Chien Chen Bookstore Publishing Company Ltd, pg 629
Commonwealth Publishing Company Ltd, pg 629
Cynosure Publishing Inc, pg 629
Echo Publishing Company Ltd, pg 629
Grimm Press Ltd, pg 630
Highlight Publishing Company Ltd, pg 630
Hsin Yi Publications, pg 630
HYS Culture Co Ltd, pg 630
Kuang Fu Book Co Ltd, pg 630
Linking Publishing Company Ltd, pg 631
Newton Publishing Company Ltd, pg 631
Yuan Liou Publishing Co, Ltd, pg 632

United Republic of Tanzania

Ben and Company Ltd, pg 633
Central Tanganyika Press, pg 633
DUP (1996) Ltd, pg 633
General Publications Ltd, pg 633
Kisambo Publishers Ltd, pg 633
Ndanda Mission Press, pg 634
Nyota Publishers Ltd, pg 634
Press & Publicity Centre Ltd, pg 634
Readit Books, pg 634
Tanzania Publishing House, pg 634
Tema Publishers Ltd, pg 634

Thailand

Bannakit Trading, pg 635
New Generation Publishing Co Ltd, pg 635
Suriyaban Publishers, pg 635
Thai Watana Panich Co, Ltd, pg 636

Togo

Editions Akpagnon, pg 636

Trinidad & Tobago

Charran Educational Publishers, pg 636
Inprint Caribbean Ltd, pg 637

Tunisia

Arcs Editions, pg 637
Editions Bouslama, pg 637
Dar Arabia Lil Kitab, pg 637
Maison d'Edition Mohamed Ali Hammi, pg 638
Les Editions de l'Arbre, pg 638
Maison Tunisienne de l'Edition, pg 638

Turkey

Afa Yayincilik Sanayi Tic AS, pg 638
Altin Kitaplar Yayinevi, pg 638
Arkadas Ltd, pg 639
Aydin Yayincilik, pg 639
Ezel Erverdi (Dergah Yayinlari AS) Muessese Muduru, pg 640
Inkilap Publishers Ltd, pg 640
Kok Yayincilik, pg 640
Nurdan YayinlariSanayi ve Ticaret Ltd Sti, pg 640
Pan Yayincilik, pg 640
Redhouse Press, pg 641
Remzi Kitabevi, pg 641
Sabah Kitaplari, pg 641
Saray Medikal Yayin Tic Ltd Sti, pg 641
Soez Yayin/Oyunajans, pg 641
Turkish Republic - Ministry of Culture, pg 641
Varlik Yayinlari AS, pg 641
Kabalci Yayinevi, pg 642

Uganda

Centenary Publishing House Ltd, pg 642
Fountain Publishers Ltd, pg 642

Ukraine

ASK Ltd, pg 643
Veselka Publishers, pg 643

United Arab Emirates

Motivate Publishing, pg 644

United Kingdom

Abbotsford Publishing, pg 644
Acair Ltd, pg 645
Act 3 Publishing, pg 645
Aladdin Books Ltd, pg 645
Allied Mouse Ltd, pg 646
Alun Books, pg 646
Andersen Press Ltd, pg 647
Andromeda Oxford Ltd, pg 647
Apple Press, pg 648
Argo Spoken Word, pg 648
AS Publishing, pg 649
Autumn Publishing Ltd, pg 651
Award Publications Ltd, pg 651
b small publishing, pg 651
Baha'i Publishing Trust, pg 651

TYPE OF PUBLICATION INDEX

Barn Dance Publications Ltd, pg 652
BCA, pg 653
Beaver Publishing Ltd, pg 653
Belitha Press Ltd, pg 653
Bible Reading Fellowship, pg 654
BLA Publishing Ltd, pg 655
A & C Black Publishers Ltd, pg 655
Blackie Children's Books, pg 655
Bloomsbury Publishing PLC, pg 656
Books for Europe Ltd, pg 657
Breslich & Foss, pg 659
Brimax Books, pg 659
BAAF: Adoption & Fostering, pg 659
British Museum Press, pg 660
Brown Wells & Jacobs Ltd, pg 661
Bryntirion Press, pg 661
Cassell & Co, pg 664
Cherrytree Books, pg 667
Child's Play (International) Ltd, pg 667
Chorion IP, pg 667
Christian Education, pg 667
Christian Focus Publications Ltd, pg 667
Church Union, pg 668
Colour Library Direct, pg 669
Constable & Robinson Ltd, pg 670
Constable Publishers, pg 670
Crossbridge Books, pg 672
Cyhoeddiadau'r Gair, pg 673
Cymdeithas Lyfrau Ceredigion, pg 673
David Bennett Books, pg 674
Dorling Kindersley Ltd, pg 676
Gwasg Dwyfor, pg 676
East-West Publications (UK) Ltd, pg 677
Encyclopaedia Britannica (UK) International Ltd, pg 679
Eurobook Ltd, pg 679
Evans Brothers Ltd, pg 680
Express Newspapers, pg 681
Faber & Faber Ltd, pg 681
Sadie Fields Productions Ltd, pg 682
Floris Books, pg 683
W H Freeman & Co Ltd, pg 684
Funfax Ltd, pg 685
Gairm Publications, pg 685
Geddes & Grosset, pg 686
The Geographical Association, pg 686
Stanley Gibbons Publications, pg 687
Glowworm Books Ltd, pg 687
Golden Books Publishing Company, Inc, pg 688
Gollancz/Witherby, pg 688
Gomer Press (J D Lewis & Sons Ltd), pg 688
Graham-Cameron Publishing & Illustration, pg 688
W F Graham (Northampton) Ltd, pg 688
Grandreams Ltd, pg 689
Grange Books PLC, pg 689
Gwasg y Dref Wen, pg 690
Peter Haddock Ltd, pg 690
Happy Cat Books Ltd, pg 691
Patrick Hardy Books, pg 692
HarperCollins Publishers, pg 692
Hawk Books, pg 693
Hodder Children's Books, pg 696
Hodder Headline Ltd, pg 696
Holland Enterprises Ltd, pg 697
Honno Welsh Women's Press, pg 697
Angus Hudson Ltd, pg 697

Islamic Foundation Publications, pg 701
Jade Publishers, pg 702
The Kenilworth Press Ltd, pg 704
Kingfisher Publications Plc, pg 704
Kuperard, pg 705
Ladybird Books, pg 705
LDA-Living & Learning (Cambridge) Ltd, pg 706
Learning Together, pg 706
Letterbox Library, pg 707
Letterland International Ltd, pg 707
Frances Lincoln Ltd, pg 707
Lion Publishing PLC, pg 708
Y Lolfa Cyf, pg 708
Lorenz Books, pg 709
The Lutterworth Press, pg 709
Macmillan Children's Books, pg 710
Macmillan Heinemann ELT, pg 710
Macmillan Ltd, pg 710
Magi Publications, pg 710
The Mansk Svenska Publishing Co Ltd, pg 711
McCrimmon Publishing Co Ltd, pg 712
The Medici Society Ltd, pg 713
Methodist Publishing House, pg 714
Mirabel Books Ltd, pg 715
National Foster Care Association, pg 717
New Era Publications UK Ltd, pg 718
NMS Publishing Ltd, pg 719
Octopus Publishing Group, pg 720
Michael O'Mara Books Ltd, pg 721
Opus Book Publishing Ltd, pg 722
Orion Children's Books, pg 722
Orion Publishing Group Ltd, pg 722
Orpheus Books Ltd, pg 722
Oyster Books, pg 723
Pan Macmillan, pg 723
Pavilion Books Ltd, pg 724
Penguin Books Ltd, pg 725
The Penguin Group UK, pg 726
Philip & Tacey Ltd, pg 726
Philograph Publications Ltd, pg 727
Piccadilly Press, pg 727
Pinwheel Ltd, pg 728
Pookie Productions Ltd, pg 729
Porthill Publishers, pg 730
Portland Press Ltd, pg 730
Mathew Price Ltd, pg 730
Quarto Publishing plc, pg 731
Quartz Editions, pg 732
Ramboro Books Plc, pg 732
Random House UK Ltd, pg 733
Ravette Publishing Ltd, pg 733
The Reader's Digest Association Ltd, pg 733
Reader's Digest Children's Books, pg 733
Regency House Publishing Ltd, pg 734
Saint Andrew Press, pg 737
Salamander Books Ltd, pg 738
The Salariya Book Co Ltd, pg 738
Sangam Books Ltd, pg 738
Scholastic Ltd, pg 739
Scottish Cultural Press, pg 739
Scripture Union, pg 740
Seren, pg 740
Sherbourne Publications, pg 741
Speechmark Publishing Ltd, pg 744
St Pauls Publishing, pg 744
Stacey International, pg 745
Studio Editions Ltd, pg 746
Supportive Learning Publications, pg 746
Tabb House, pg 746
Tango Books, pg 746
Tarquin Publications, pg 746
Teeney Books Ltd, pg 747

TYPE OF PUBLICATION INDEX · BOOK

Tiger Books International PLC, pg 748
Transworld Publishers Ltd, pg 750
Treehouse Children's Books Ltd, pg 750
Two-Can Publishing Ltd, pg 750
Uplands Books, pg 752
Usborne Publishing Ltd, pg 752
Van Molle Publishing, pg 752
Viking Children's Books, pg 753
Walker Books Ltd, pg 754
Frederick Warne Publishers Ltd, pg 754
The Watts Publishing Group Ltd, pg 754
Wayland Publishers Ltd (Incorporating Macdonald Young Books), pg 754
WI Enterprises Ltd, pg 756
Wordsworth Editions Ltd, pg 758
Y Cyfarwyddwr Urdd Gobaith Cymru, pg 759
Anglia Young Books, pg 759

Uruguay
A Monteverde y Cia SA, pg 760
Nordan-Comunidad, pg 760
Rosebud Ediciones, pg 761

Venezuela
Alfadil Ediciones, pg 761
Editorial Ateneo de Caracas, pg 762
Ediciones Ekare, pg 762

Viet Nam
Science & Technics Publishing House, pg 763

Yugoslavia
Alfa-Narodna Knjiga, pg 764
Minerva, pg 764
Izdavacko Preduzece Matice Srpske, pg 765
Svetovi, pg 766
Vuk Karadzic, pg 766

Zambia
Apple Books, pg 766
Yorvik Publishing Ltd, pg 767
Zambia Educational Publishing House, pg 767
ZPC Publications, pg 767

Zimbabwe
Academic Books Pvt Ltd, pg 767
Anvil Press, pg 767
College Press Publishers (Pvt) Ltd, pg 768
Happy Books, pg 768
The Literature Bureau, pg 768
Longman Zimbabwe (Pvt) Ltd, pg 768
Mambo Press, pg 768
Mercury Press Pvt Ltd, pg 769
Vision Publications, pg 769
Zimbabwe Publishing House (Pvt) Ltd, pg 769
ZRD Trust, pg 770

DATABASES

Argentina
Alfagrama SRL ediciones, pg 3
Instituto Nacional de Ciencia y Tecnica Hidrica (INCYTH), pg 7

Australia
Australasian Medical Publishing Company Ltd (AMPCO), pg 13
Curriculum Corporation, pg 19
Encyclopaedia Britannica (Australia) Inc, pg 22
Universal Business Directories, Australia Pty Ltd, pg 46

Austria
Compass-Verlag GmbH, pg 50

Azerbaijan
Sada, Literaturno-Izdatel'skij Centr, pg 61

Belgium
Brepols Publishers NV, pg 65
CED-Samsom, pg 66

Brazil
Comissao Nacional de Energia Nuclear, pg 81
Editora Nova Fronteira SA, pg 88

Bulgaria
DATAMAP - Europe, pg 95

China
Chemical Industry Press, pg 102
China Machine Press (CMP), pg 103
Electronics Industry Publishing House, pg 105
Fudan University Press, pg 105
Higher Education Press, pg 106
Patent Documentation Publishing House, pg 107

The Democratic Republic of the Congo
Facultes Catoliques de Kinshasa, pg 115

Costa Rica
Centro Agronomico Tropical de Investigacion y Ensenanza (CATIE), pg 115
Union Mundial para la Naturaleza (UICN), Oficina Regional para Mesoamerica, pg 117

Croatia
Masmedia, pg 119

Cuba
Instituto de Informacion Cientifica y Tecnologica (IDICT), pg 121

Czech Republic
Divadelni Ustav, pg 124
Cesky normalizacni institut, pg 127

Denmark
Danish National Library Authority, pg 131
J H Schultz Information A/S, pg 135
Systime, pg 136

Estonia
Ilmamaa, pg 140
National Library of Estonia, pg 140

France
Agence Bibliographique de L'Enseignement Superieur, pg 146
CERDIC-Publications, pg 153
Les Editions ESF, pg 161
Editions Legislatives, pg 172
References cf, pg 182
Editions Springer France, pg 186

Germany
AOL-Verlag Frohmut Menze, pg 194
ARCult Media, pg 194
AZ Bertelsmann Direct GmbH, pg 197
Beleke KG Verlag, pg 200
BertelsmannSpringer Science & Business Media GmbH, pg 202
BW Bildung und Wissen Verlag und Software GmbH, pg 203
Buchhaendler-Vereinigung GmbH, pg 207
Fachverlag Hans Carl GmbH, pg 209
Carl Link Verlag-Gesellschaft mbH Fachverlag fur Verwaltungsrecht, pg 209
Deutscher Adressbuch-Verlag fuer Wirtschaft und Verkehr GmbH, pg 214
Die Verlag H Schafer GmbH, pg 216
Dingfelder-Verlag Inh Gerd Gmelin, pg 217
DSI Data Service & Information, pg 219
Ecomed Verlagsgesellschaft AG & Co KG, pg 220
Feltron-Elektronik Zeissler & Co GmbH, pg 227
Fraunhofer IRB Verlag Fraunhofer Informationszentrum Raum und Bau, pg 229
Gesundheits-Dialog Verlag GmbH, pg 232
Verlag Ernst und Werner Gieseking GmbH, pg 232
Carl Hanser Verlag, pg 237
Verlag Hoppenstedt GmbH, pg 242
Klages-Verlag, pg 249
K F Koehler Verlag, pg 251
Munzinger-Archiv GmbH Archiv fuer publizistische Arbeit, pg 266
pmi Verlag, pg 274
Reed Elsevier Deutschland GmbH, pg 277
Verlag Werner Sachon GmbH & Co, pg 281
K G Saur Verlag GmbH, A Gale/Thomson Learning Company, pg 282
Springer-Verlag GmbH & Co KG, pg 288
Georg Thieme Verlag KG, pg 293
Wer liefert was? GmbH, pg 301
Verlag fuer Wirtschaft & Verwaltung Hubert Wingen GmbH & Co KG, pg 303
Wison Verlag GmbH, pg 303
Zeller Verlag GmbH & Co, pg 305

Greece
Hestia-I D Hestia-Kollaros & Co Corporation, pg 311

Hungary
Polgar Citizen Press, pg 326
Typotex Kft Elektronikus Kiado, pg 327

India
Asia Pacific Business Press Inc, pg 331
National Institute of Industrial Research (NIIR), pg 344

Ireland
European Foundation for the Improvement of Living & Working Conditions, pg 360
Royal Irish Academy, pg 364

Israel
The Institute for the Translation of Hebrew Literature, pg 368
MAP-Mapping & Publishing Ltd, pg 370

Kenya
Academy Science Publishers, pg 430
Kenya Meteorological Department, pg 432

Republic of Korea
Chung Rim Publishing Co Ltd, pg 435
Korea Britannica Corp, pg 437
Maeil Gyeongje, pg 438

Latvia
Bibliography Institute of the National Library of Latvia, pg 441
S/A Tiesiskas informacijas cerfus, pg 442

Lithuania
Centre of Legal Information, pg 445
Lietuvos Informacijos Institutas, pg 446
Lithuanian National Museum Publishing House, pg 446

The Former Yugoslav Republic of Macedonia
Medis, Skopje, pg 449

Malaysia
Malayan Law Journal Sdn Bhd, pg 453

Mexico
Mercametrica Ediciones SA Edicion de Libros, pg 464

Morocco
Access International Services, pg 469
Office Marocain D'Annonces-OMA, pg 470

Netherlands
A W Bruna Uitgevers BV, pg 475
IOS Press BV, pg 479

Oman
Apex Publishing, pg 506

Philippines
Encyclopaedia Britannica (Philippines) Inc, pg 513

Poland
Instytut Meteorologii i Gospodarki Wodnej, pg 518
Wydawnictwo DiG, pg 521

PUBLISHERS

Romania
Editura Excelsior, pg 533

Russian Federation
BLIC, russko-Baltijskij informaciionnyj centr, AO, pg 537

Senegal
CODESRIA (Council for the Development of Social Science Research in Africa), pg 544

Singapore
LexisNexis, pg 547
Tecman Bible House, pg 549

Slovakia
Ustav informacii a prognoz skolstva mladeze a telovychovy, pg 551

South Africa
Centre for Conflict Resolution, pg 553
Jacklin Enterprises (Pty) Ltd, pg 556

Spain
Editorial Aranzadi SA, pg 564

Sweden
Bibliotekstjaenst AB, pg 600

Switzerland
Cockatoo Press (Schweiz), Thailand-Publikationen, pg 611

Taiwan, Province of China
Chien Chen Bookstore Publishing Company Ltd, pg 629

United Republic of Tanzania
Bureau of Statistics, pg 633

Turkey
IKI NOKTA Research Press & Publications Industry & Trade Ltd, pg 640
Saray Medikal Yayin Tic Ltd Sti, pg 641

United Kingdom
ABC-CLIO, pg 644
Advisory Unit: Computers in Education, pg 645
Anderson Rand Ltd, pg 647
Art Sales Index Ltd, pg 649
Book Data, pg 657
Butterworth-Heinemann Ltd, pg 661
Chadwyck-Healey Ltd, pg 666
Electronic Publishing Services Ltd, pg 678
Encyclopaedia Britannica (UK) International Ltd, pg 679
EPER, pg 679
Euromonitor PLC, pg 680
First & Best in Education Ltd, pg 682
Foulsham Publishers, pg 683
Gale Research, pg 685
Hobsons, pg 696
Institute of Physics Publishing, pg 700
Institution of Electrical Engineers, pg 700
J Whitaker & Sons Ltd, pg 702

James & James (Science Publishers) Ltd, pg 702
Jane's Information Group, pg 702
NCVO, pg 718
Oilfield Publications Ltd, pg 720
ProQuest Information & Learning, pg 731
William Reed Directories, pg 734
Trigon Press, pg 750
VNU Business Publications, pg 753
Wilmington Business Information Ltd, pg 756

DICTIONARIES, ENCYCLOPEDIAS

Albania
Fan Noli Verlag Rexhep Hida, pg 1
NL SH, pg 1
State Textbook Publishing House, pg 1

Algeria
Enterprise Nationale du Livre (ENAL), pg 2

Argentina
Abeledo-Perrot SAE e I, pg 2
Editorial Caymi SACI, pg 4
Editorial Claridad SA, pg 4
Editorial Ruy Diaz SAEIC, pg 5
Editorial Kier SACIFI, pg 7
Laffont Ediciones Electronicas SA, pg 7
Ediciones Larousse Argentina SA, pg 7
Librograf, pg 7
Instituto Nacional de Ciencia y Tecnica Hidrica (INCYTH), pg 7
Ediciones Preescolar SA, pg 8
Editorial Sopena Argentina SACI e I, pg 9
Tipografica Editora Argentina, pg 9

Australia
Robert Berthold Photography, pg 14
Bridgeway Publications, pg 16
Butterworths Australia Ltd, pg 16
China Books, pg 18
Encyclopaedia Britannica (Australia) Inc, pg 22
Era Publications, pg 22
Flora Publications International Pty Ltd, pg 23
Great Western Press Pty Ltd, pg 24
Hodder Headline Australia, pg 26
Hospitality Press Pty Ltd, pg 26
Illert Publications, pg 27
Institute of Aboriginal Development (IAD Press), pg 28
John Wiley & Sons Australia Ltd, pg 28
Reed Educational Publishing Australia, pg 40
Stafford Books, pg 43
Wileman Publications, pg 47

Austria
Akademische Druck-u Verlagsanstalt Dr Paul Struzl GmbH, pg 49
Fassbaender Verlag, pg 51
Edition Dr Heinrich Fuchs, pg 52
Osterreichischer Bundesveilag Ges.mbh, pg 57

Belarus
Belaruskaya Encyklapedyya, pg 63
Interdigets Publishing House, pg 63
Kavaler Publishers, pg 63
Narodnaya Asveta, pg 63

TYPE OF PUBLICATION INDEX

Belgium
Editions De Boeck-Larcier SA, pg 67
Dexia Bank, pg 68
Intersentia Uitgevers NV, pg 69
Maklu, pg 71
La Renaissance du Livre, pg 73
Standaard Uitgeverij, pg 74
Vlaamse Esperantobond VZW, pg 75

Bosnia and Herzegovina
Bemust doo Novinsko-Izdavacko stamparsko i trgovacko preduzece, pg 77
Svjetlost, pg 77

Brazil
Abril SA, pg 77
Agalma Psicanalise Editora Ltda, pg 78
Ao Livro Tecnico Industria e Comercio Ltda, pg 78
Editora Campus Ltda, pg 80
Edicon Editora e Consultorial Ltda, pg 81
Ediouro Publicacoes, SA, pg 81
EDUSC - Editora da Universidade do Sagrado Coracao, pg 82
Livraria Martins Fontes Editora Ltda, pg 83
Editora Globo SA, pg 84
Hemus Editora Ltda, pg 85
IBRASA (Instituicao Brasileira de Difusao Cultural Ltda), pg 85
Libreria Editora Ltda, pg 86
Edicoes Loyola SA, pg 87
Editora Meca Ltda, pg 87
Editora Melhoramentos Ltda, pg 87
Editora Moderna Ltda, pg 88
Editora Nova Fronteira SA, pg 88
Pallas Editora e Distribuidora Ltda, pg 89
Paulus Editora, pg 89
Saraiva SA, Livreiros Editores, pg 91
Editora Scipione Ltda, pg 91
Tempus Editores, pg 92
Thex Editora e Distribuidora Ltda, pg 92
Editora Vigilia Ltda, pg 93

Bulgaria
Abagar Pablioing, pg 94
Abagar, Veliko Tarnovo, pg 94
Dolphin Press Group Ltd, pg 95
EA Publishing House, pg 95
Kibea Publishing Co, pg 96
Lettera, pg 96
LIK IZDANIJA, pg 96
Litera Prima, pg 96
Naouka i Izkoustvo, Ltd, pg 97
Nov Covek Publishing House, pg 97
Pensoft Publishers, pg 97
Prozoretz Ltd Publishing House, pg 97
Reporter, pg 97
Seven Hills Publishers, pg 97
Sluntse Publishing House, pg 98
Technica, pg 98

Chile
Arrayan Editores, pg 99
Norma de Chile, pg 101
Publicaciones Lo Castillo SA, pg 101

China
Anhui People's Publishing House, pg 102
Beijing Education Publishing House, pg 102
Beijing Juvenile & Children's Books Publishing House, pg 102
Beijing Publishing House, pg 102
Beijing University Press, pg 102
Chemical Industry Press, pg 102
China Foreign Economic Relations & Trade Publishing House, pg 103
China Light Industry Press, pg 103
China Machine Press (CMP), pg 103
China Materials Management Publishing House, pg 103
China Ocean Press, pg 103
China Theatre Publishing House, pg 104
China Translation & Publishing Corp, pg 104
CITIC Publishing House, pg 104
Commercial Press (Hong Kong) Ltd, pg 104
Electronics Industry Publishing House, pg 105
Encyclopedia of China Publishing House, pg 105
Fudan University Press, pg 105
Guizhou Education Publishing House, pg 106
Heilongjiang Science & Technology Press, pg 106
Higher Education Press, pg 106
Inner Mongolia Science & Technology Publishing House, pg 106
Jilin Science & Technology Publishing House, pg 106
Jinan Publishing House, pg 107
Language Publishing House, pg 107
The People's Communications Publishing House, pg 107
Qingdao Publishing House, pg 108
Science Press, pg 108
Shandong Friendship Press, pg 108
Shandong Literature & Art Publishing House, pg 109
Shanghai Foreign Language Education Press, pg 109
Sichuan University Press, pg 109
Tianjin Science & Technology Publishing House, pg 109
Wuhan University Press, pg 110
Zhejiang Education Publishing House, pg 110

Colombia
Asociacion Instituto Linguistico de Verano, pg 111
Eurolibros Ltda, pg 111
Editorial Libros y Libres SA, pg 112
Ediciones Monserrate, pg 113
Pearson Educacion de Colombia LTDA, pg 113
Editorial Santillana SA, pg 113

Croatia
Globus-Nakladni zavod, pg 118
Graficki zavod Hrvatske, pg 118
Informator dd, pg 119
Leksikografski Zavod Miroslav Krleza, pg 119
Masmedia, pg 119
Matica hrvatska, pg 119
Mladost d d Izdavacku graficku i informaticku djelatnost, pg 119
Nakladni zavod Matice hrvatske, pg 119
Vitagraf, pg 120

TYPE OF PUBLICATION INDEX BOOK

Cuba
Instituto de Informacion Cientifica y Tecnologica (IDICT), pg 121

Czech Republic
Academia, pg 122
Aleko, Nakladatelska Divize, pg 122
Barrister & Principal, pg 123
Columbus, pg 123
Diderot sro, pg 124
Divadelni Ustav, pg 124
Granit SRO, pg 124
Jan Vasut Publishing, pg 124
Karmelitanske Nakladatelstvi, pg 125
Karolinum, nakladatelstvi, pg 125
Libri s r o, pg 125
Maxdorf Ltd, pg 126
Nase vojsko, nakladatelstvi a knizni obchod, pg 126
NLN, Ltd The Lidove noviny Publishing House, pg 127
Omnipress Praha, pg 127
Nakladatelstvi a vydavatelstvi Panorama, pg 127
Paseka, pg 127
Prostor, Ltd, pg 128
Svojtka & Co, pg 128
SystemConsult, pg 128
Votobia sro, pg 129

Denmark
GEC Gads Forlag Aktieselskab af 1994, pg 132

Dominican Republic
Sociedad Editorial Dominicana SA, pg 137

Ecuador
Biblioteca Ecuatoriana 'Aurelio Espinosa Polit', pg 137
CIESPAL (Centro Internacional de Estudios Superiores de Comunicacion para America Latina), pg 137
Corporacion Editora Nacional, pg 137

Egypt (Arab Republic of Egypt)
Al Arab Publishing House, pg 138
Dar El Shorouk, pg 138
Dar El Shorouk Publishing & Distributing House, pg 138
Elias Modern Publishing House, pg 138

Estonia
Estonian Bible Society, pg 140
Estonian Encyclopaedia Publishers Ltd, pg 140
Ilmamaa, pg 140
National Library of Estonia, pg 140
Perioodika, pg 140
TEA Publishers, pg 140
Valgus Publishers, pg 141

Finland
Aika Oy Kristilliset Kirjat, pg 141
Otava Publishing Co Ltd, pg 143
Suomalaisen Kirjallisuuden Seura, pg 144
Tietoteos Publishing Co, pg 144
Werner Soederstroem Osakeyhtioe (WSOY), pg 145
Yliopistopaino/Helsinki University Press, pg 145

France
Editions Al Liamm, pg 146
Les Editions de l'Atelier SA, pg 148
Editions Belin, pg 150
Editions Bordas, pg 151
Emgleo Breiz, pg 151
Bureau des Longitudes de France, pg 152
Chasse Maree-Armen, pg 154
Counseil International de la Langue Francaise, pg 157
Editions Dalloz Sirey, pg 157
Editions du Dauphin, pg 158
Devenirs Visuels SA, pg 159
Dictionnaires Le Robert, pg 159
Les Dossiers d'Aquitaine, pg 160
Encyclopedia Universalis France SA, pg 162
Institut d'Etudes Slaves, pg 163
Paul Geuthner Librairie Orientaliste, pg 166
Hachette Education, pg 167
Fernand Hazan Editeur SA, pg 168
INRA Editions (Institut National de la Recherche Agronomique), pg 169
Joly Editions, pg 170
Karthala Editions-Diffusion, pg 171
Lacour-Olle, pg 171
Langues & Mondes/L'Asiatheque, pg 171
Librairie Larousse, pg 172
Editions Legislatives, pg 172
Letouzey et Ane Sarl, pg 172
Le Livre de Paris, pg 173
LLB France (Ligue pour la Lecture de la Bible), pg 173
La Maison du Dictionnaire, pg 174
Editions Mango, pg 174
Masson-Williams et Wilkins, pg 175
Editions de la Reunion des Musees Nationaux, pg 176
Fernand Nathan, pg 177
Naufal Group Sarl, pg 177
Editions du Centre Pompidou, pg 180
Presses Universitaires de France (PUF), pg 181
Editions Robert Laffont, Nil, Fixot, Seghers, Julliard, pg 183
Sofradif Editions Philippe Auzou, pg 185
Editions Technip SA, pg 187
Universitas, pg 188
Editions de Vergeures, pg 189
Editions Philateliques Yvert et Tellier, pg 189

Germany
AOL-Verlag Frohmut Menze, pg 194
J J Augustin GmbH Verlag, pg 196
Axel Juncker Verlag Jacobi KG, pg 197
Barenreiter-Verlag Karl-Votterle GmbH & Co KG, pg 198
Bauverlag GmbH, pg 199
Verlag C H Beck (OHG), pg 200
Bertelsmann Lexikon Verlag GmbH, pg 201
Verlag Beruf + Schule Belz KG, pg 202
Bibliographisches Institut & F A Brockhaus AG, pg 203
Bibliographisches Institut GmbH, pg 203
Verlag Hermann Boehlaus Nachfolger Weimar GmbH & Co, pg 205
Oscar Brandstetter Verlag GmbH & Co KG, pg 206
Helmut Buske Verlag GmbH, pg 208
Calwer Verlag Stuttgart eV, pg 209
Marianne Cieslik, pg 210
Compact Verlag GmbH, pg 211
Cornelsen Verlag GmbH & Co OHG, pg 211
Verlag Darmstaedter Blaetter Schwarz und Co, pg 212
Deutscher Taschenbuch Verlag GmbH & Co KG (dtv), pg 215
Droemersche Verlagsanstalt Th Knaur Nachfolger GmbH & Co, pg 218
E Schweizerbart'sche Verlagsbuchhandlung (Nagele und Obermiller), pg 220
Ecomed Verlagsgesellschaft AG & Co KG, pg 220
Elpis Verlag GmbH, pg 222
Encyclopedia Britannica, pg 222
Verlag Esoterische Philosophie GmbH, pg 224
F A Brockhaus, GmbH, pg 225
FAB-Verlag, pg 226
Fachbuchverlag Pfanneberg & Co, pg 226
Festo Didactic GmbH & Co, pg 227
Harald Fischer Verlag GmbH, pg 228
Verlag Franz Vahlen GmbH, pg 229
Friedrich Frommann Verlag, pg 230
Betriebswirtschaftlicher Verlag Dr Th Gabler GmbH, pg 231
Gebrueder Borntraeger Science Publishers, pg 231
Walter de Gruyter GmbH & Co KG, pg 234
Hallwag Verlag GmbH, pg 236
Harenberg Kommunikation Verlags- und Medien GmbH & Co KG, pg 237
Verlag Herder GmbH & Co KG, pg 239
Kindler Verlag GmbH, pg 249
Ernst Klett Verlag GmbH, pg 250
Verlag Fritz Knapp GmbH, pg 250
Knowledge Media International, pg 251
W Kohlhammer GmbH, abt Haussortiment, pg 252
Laaber-Verlag, pg 255
Langenscheidt Fachverlag GmbH, pg 255
Langenscheidt KG, pg 256
Magnus Verlag, pg 260
Margraf Verlag, pg 261
Neuer Honos Verlag GmbH, pg 267
Max Niemeyer Verlag GmbH, pg 269
Georg Olms Verlag AG, pg 270
Polyglott-Verlag, pg 274
Polygraph Verlag GmbH, pg 274
Propylaeen Verlag, Zweigniederlassung Berlin der Ullstein Buchverlage GmbH, pg 275
Quintessenz Verlags-GmbH, pg 276
Dr Ludwig Reichert Verlag, pg 278
Reise Know-How Verlag Peter Rump GmbH, pg 278
Verlagsgruppe Reise-Know-How, pg 278
Romiosini Verlag, pg 280
K G Saur Verlag GmbH, A Gale/Thomson Learning Company, pg 282
Schott Musik International GmbH & Co KG, pg 284
Theodor Schuster, pg 285
Silberburg-Verlag Titus Haeussermann GmbH, pg 287
Springer-Verlag GmbH & Co KG, pg 288
Verlag Stahleisen GmbH, pg 289
Straelener Manuskripte Verlag, pg 290
VS Verlagshaus Stuttgart GmbH, pg 299
Wachholtz Verlag GmbH, pg 300
Wiley-VCH Verlag GmbH, pg 302
Xenos Verlagsgesellschaft mbH, pg 304

Ghana
Bureau of Ghana Languages, pg 306
EPP Books Services, pg 307

Greece
Alamo Hellas, pg 308
Athina, Mary Mavrogiannis, pg 309
Diavlos, pg 309
Dodoni Publications, pg 310
Ekdoseis Domi AE, pg 310
Ekdotike Athenon SA, pg 310
Eleftheroudakis, GCSA International Bookstore, pg 310
Hestia-I D Hestia-Kollaros & Co Corporation, pg 311
Hiotellis P, pg 311
I Prooptiki, pg 311
Institute of Neohellenic Studies, Manolis Triantaphyllidis Foundation, pg 311
Ilias Kambanas Publishing Organization, SA, pg 312
Kastaniotis Editions SA, pg 312
Kyriakidis Vasileios, pg 312
Michalis Sideris, pg 313
Nakas Music House, pg 313
Pagoulatos G-G P Publications, pg 314
Patakis Publishers, pg 314
Nikolas I Rossi, pg 314
Sakkoulas Publications SA, pg 314
J Vassiliou Bibliopolein, pg 315
S J Zacharopoulos SA Publishing Co, pg 316

Haiti
Editions Caraiibes SA, pg 317

Hong Kong
The Chinese University Press, pg 319
Chung Hwa Book Co (HK) Ltd, pg 319
Joint Publishing (HK) Co Ltd, pg 320
Peace Book Co Ltd, pg 321

Hungary
Akademiai Kiado, pg 323
Aranyhal Konyvkiado Goldfish Publishing, pg 323
Balassi Kiado Kft, pg 323
Greger-Delacroix, pg 324
Joszoveg Muhely Kiado, pg 324
Officina Nova, Koenyv-es Lapkiado/Bertelsmann Media Kft, pg 324
Kossuth Kiado RT, pg 325
Novorg Kiado, pg 326
Panem, pg 326

Iceland
Bokautgafan Orn og Orlygur ehf, pg 327
Frodi Ltd, pg 328
Isafoldarprentsmidja hf, pg 328
Mal og menning, pg 328

PUBLISHERS

India
Addison-Wesley (Singapore) Pte Ltd, pg 329
Agam Kala Prakashan, pg 330
Agricole Publishing Academy, pg 330
Allied Publishers Pvt Ltd, pg 330
Ananda Publishers Pvt Ltd, pg 330
Anmol Publications Pvt Ltd, pg 331
Asian Educational Services, pg 331
Avinash Reference Publications, pg 331
Bani Mandir, Book-Sellers, Publishers & Educational Suppliers, pg 332
Bharat Publishing House, pg 332
BR Publishing Corporation, pg 334
Cosmo Publications, pg 335
Diamond Comics (P) Ltd, pg 336
DK Printworld (P) Ltd, pg 336
Dutta Baruah Publishing Co Pvt Ltd, pg 336
General Book Depot, pg 337
Gyan Publishing House, pg 338
Islamic Publishing House, pg 340
Law Publishers, pg 341
Munshiram Manoharlal Publishers Pvt Ltd, pg 343
National Book Organization, pg 343
Natraj Prakashan, pg 344
Omsons Publications, pg 345
Oxford University Press, pg 345
Parimal Prakashan, pg 345
Pitambar Publishing Co (P) Ltd, pg 346
Prabhat Prakashan, pg 346
Pratibha Pratishthan, pg 346
Publications & Information Directorate, CSIR, pg 346
Pustak Mahal, pg 346
Rahul Publishing House, pg 347
Rajendra Publishing House Pvt Ltd, pg 347
Rajpal & Sons, pg 347
Reliance Publishing House, pg 347
M C Sarkar & Sons (P) Ltd, pg 349
Sat Sahitya Prakashan, pg 349
Scientific Book Agency, pg 349
Shaibya Prakashan Bibhag, pg 349
Shiksha Bharati, pg 350
Sita Publications, pg 350
Star Publications (P) Ltd, pg 351
Vidya Puri, pg 352
Vidyarthi Mithram Press, pg 352

Indonesia
PT Indira, pg 355
Karya Anda, CV, pg 356
Mizan, pg 356
Penerbit Nusa Indah, pg 356

Ireland
An Gum, pg 358
Topaz Publications, pg 364

Israel
Academy of the Hebrew Language, pg 365
Achiasaf Publishing House Ltd, pg 365
Achiever, pg 365
Amichai Publishing House Ltd, pg 365
The Bialik Institute, pg 365
Carta, The Israel Map & Publishing Co Ltd, pg 366
Classikaletet, pg 366
Dvir Publishing Ltd, pg 366
Gefen Publishing House Ltd, pg 367
Hakibbutz Hameuchad Publishing House Ltd, pg 368
Intermedia Audio, Video Book Publishing Ltd, pg 368
The Jerusalem Publishing House Ltd, pg 369
Kernerman Publishing Ltd, pg 369
Keter Publishing House Ltd, pg 369
Kiryat Sefer, pg 369
Ma'ariv Book Guild (Sifriat Ma'ariv), pg 370
MAP-Mapping & Publishing Ltd, pg 370
Massada Press Ltd, pg 370
Misgav Yerushalayim, pg 370
M Mizrahi Publishers, pg 370
Password Publishers Ltd, pg 371
Prolog Publishing House, pg 371
Rolnik Publishers, pg 371
Rubin Mass Ltd, pg 371
Schlesinger Institute, pg 372
Schocken Publishing House Ltd, pg 372
Talmudic Encyclopedia Publications, pg 372
Yad Vashem - The Holocaust Martyrs' & Heroes' Remembrance Authority, pg 373
Yavneh Publishing House Ltd, pg 373
Zakheim Publishing House, pg 374

Italy
De Agostini Scolastica, pg 375
Alba, pg 375
Bompiani-RCS Libri, pg 378
Edizioni Bora SNC di E Brandani & C, pg 378
Casa Editrice Felice Le Monnier, pg 380
Casa Editrice Libraria Ulrico Hoepli SpA, pg 380
Citta Nuova Editrice, pg 382
Cittadella Editrice, pg 382
Istituto della Enciclopedia Italiana, pg 384
Edi Ermes SRL, pg 386
Editrice Eraclea, pg 388
Federico Motta Editore SpA, pg 389
Festina Lente Edizioni, pg 389
Arnaldo Forni Editore SRL, pg 389
Garzanti Editore, pg 390
Istituto Geografico de Agostini SpA, pg 390
Edizioni del Girasole srl, pg 390
Giunti Publishing Group, pg 391
Ernesto Gremese Editore SRL, pg 391
Gruppo Editoriale Faenza Editrice SpA, pg 392
Editoriale Jaca Book SpA, pg 394
Casa Editrice Le Lettere SRL, pg 395
Edizioni Librex, pg 396
Vincenzo Lo Faro Editore, pg 396
Loescher Editore SRL, pg 396
Angelo Longo Editore, pg 396
Macmillan Heinemann ELT, pg 397
Tommaso Marotta Editore Srl, pg 398
OCTAVO Franco Cantini Editore, pg 401
Editoriale Olimpia SpA, pg 401
Leo S Olschki, pg 402
Paravia Bruno Mondadori Editori, pg 402
Edizioni Piemme SpA, pg 403
Amilcare Pizzi SpA, pg 403
RCS Libri SpA, pg 405
Editori Riuniti, pg 405
SAIE Editrice SRL, pg 406
Edizioni San Paolo SRL, pg 407
Sansoni Editore, pg 407
Edizioni Librarie Siciliane, pg 408

Societa Editrice Internazionale - SEI, pg 408
Nicola Teti e C Editore SRL, pg 409
Who's Who In Italy SRL, pg 412
Zanichelli Editore SpA, pg 412

Japan
Dohosha Publishing Co Ltd, pg 416
Fuzambo Publishing Co, pg 416
Gakken Co Ltd, pg 416
Hakusui-Sha Co Ltd, pg 417
Hakutei-Sha, pg 417
Hakuyu-Sha, pg 417
Heibonsha Ltd, Publishers, pg 417
Hirokawa Publishing Co, pg 417
Hokuryukan Co Ltd, pg 417
Ishihara Publishing Company Ltd, pg 418
Iwanami Shoten, Publishers, pg 418
Kadokawa Shoten Publishing Co, pg 419
Kaitakusha, pg 419
Maruzen Co Ltd, pg 421
Nagaoka Shoten Company Ltd, pg 421
Nan'un-Do Company Ltd, pg 422
Nigensha Publishing Co Ltd, pg 422
Obunsha Co Ltd, pg 423
Ohmsha Ltd, pg 423
Ongaku No Tomo Sha Corporation, pg 423
Rinsen Book Co Ltd, pg 424
Sanseido Co Ltd, pg 424
Sanshusha Publishing Co, Ltd, pg 424
Shimizu-Shoin, pg 425
Shincho-Sha Co Ltd, pg 425
Toho Book Store, pg 427
Tokyo Shoseki Co Ltd, pg 427

Kenya
Heinemann Kenya Limited (EAEP), pg 431
Kenway Publications Ltd, pg 432
Lake Publishers & Enterprises Ltd, pg 432
Phoenix Publishers, pg 433

Democratic People's Republic of Korea
Grand People's Study House, pg 434
Korea Science and Encyclopedia Publishing House, pg 434

Republic of Korea
Chung Rim Publishing Co Ltd, pg 435
Dong-A Publishing & Printing Co Ltd, pg 436
Hollym Corporation Publishers, pg 437
Kemongsa Publishing Co Ltd, pg 437
Ki Moon Dang, pg 437
Korea Britannica Corp, pg 437
Kukmin Doseo Publishing Co Inc, pg 438
Kukminseokwan Publishing Co Ltd, pg 438
Kyohaksa Publishing Co Ltd, pg 438
Min Jung Seo Rim Publishing Co, pg 438
Panmun Book Co Ltd, pg 439
Samseong Publishing Co Ltd, pg 440
YBM/Si-sa, pg 441

TYPE OF PUBLICATION INDEX

Latvia
Avots, pg 441
Nordik/Tapals Publishers Ltd, pg 442
Preses Nams, pg 442
Vaidelote, pg 442

Lebanon
Darl el-Machreq Sarl, pg 443
Librairie du Liban, pg 443
Librairie Orientale sal, pg 443

Lithuania
Alma Littera, pg 445
Eugrimas, pg 445
Klaipedos Universiteto Leidykla, pg 445
Lietuvos Informacijos Institutas, pg 446
Lithuanian National Museum Publishing House, pg 446
Mokslo ir enciklopediju leidybos institutas, pg 446
Margi Rastai Publishers, pg 446
Sviesa Publishers, pg 446
TEV Leidykla, pg 446
Tyto Alba Publishers, pg 446
Vaga Ltd, pg 446
Victoria Publishers, pg 446

The Former Yugoslav Republic of Macedonia
Detska radost, pg 448
Murgorski Zoze, pg 449
Strk Publishing House, pg 449

Malaysia
S Abdul Majeed & Co, pg 451
Eastview Productions Sdn Bhd, pg 452
Federal Publications Sdn Bhd, pg 452
FEP International Sdn Bhd, pg 452
Mahir Publications Sdn Bhd, pg 452
Minerva Publications, pg 453
Pelanduk Publications (M) Sdn Bhd, pg 453
Penerbit Jayatinta Sdn Bhd, pg 454
Perfect Frontier Sdn Bhd, pg 454
Pustaka Delta Pelajaran Sdn Bhd, pg 454
Times Educational Co Sdn Bhd, pg 455

Mexico
Editora Cientifica Medica Latinoamerican SA de CV, pg 458
Ediciones Culturales Internacionales SA de CV Edicion Compra y Venta de Libros, Casetes, Videos, pg 459
Maria Esther De Fleischmann, pg 459
Editorial Diana SA de CV, pg 459
Entretenlibro SA de CV, pg 460
Editorial Esfinge SA de CV, pg 460
Editorial Fata Morgana SA de CV, pg 461
Fernandez Editores SA de CV, pg 461
Fondo de Cultura Economica, pg 461
Grupo Editorial Iberoamerica, SA de CV, pg 461
Ediciones Larousse SA de CV, pg 462
Libros y Revistas SA de CV, pg 463
Editorial Limusa SA de CV, pg 463

TYPE OF PUBLICATION INDEX BOOK

Naves Internacional de Ediciones SA, pg 464
Nova Grupo Editorial SA de CV, pg 464
Organizacion Cultural LP SA de CV, pg 465
Pangea Editores, Sa de CV, pg 465
Panorama Editorial, SA, pg 465
Plaza y Valdes SA de CV, pg 465
Ediciones Promesa, SA de CV, pg 466
Salvat Editores de Mexico, pg 466
SCRIPTA - Distribucion y Servicios Editoriales, SA de CV, pg 467
Sistemas Tecnicos de Edicion SA de CV, pg 467
Ediciones Suromex SA, pg 467

Republic of Moldova

Lumina Publishing House, pg 468

Morocco

Editions Okad, pg 470

Myanmar

Sarpay Beikman Board, pg 471

Netherlands

APA (Academic Publishers Associated), pg 472
BoekWerk, pg 474
Brill Academic Publishers, pg 475
Elmar BV, pg 476
Kluwer Technische Boeken BV, pg 480
Reed Elsevier Nederland BV, pg 483
Uitgeverij Het Spectrum BV, pg 484
Van Dale Lexicografie BV, pg 486

New Zealand

Auckland University Press, pg 488
David Bateman Ltd, pg 488
HarperCollins Publishers (New Zealand) Ltd, pg 491

Nigeria

Evans Brothers (Nigeria Publishers) Ltd, pg 499
Nigerian Trade Review, pg 500
Riverside Communications, pg 501

Norway

J W Cappelens Forlag A/S, pg 503
N W Damm og Son A/S, pg 503
Elanders Publishing AS, pg 503
Gyldendal Norsk Forlag A/S, pg 503
Egmont Hjemmets Bokforlag AS, pg 504
Kunnskapsforlaget ANS, pg 504

Pakistan

The Book House, pg 506
Ferozsons (Private) Ltd, pg 506
Jang Publishers, pg 507
Maqbool Academy, pg 508
Nashiran-e-Quran Pvt Ltd, pg 508
Sang-e-Meel Publications, pg 509

Peru

Ediciones Brown SA, pg 511

Philippines

Anvil Publishing Inc, pg 512
Encyclopaedia Britannica (Philippines) Inc, pg 513
J C Palabay Enterprises, pg 513

Marren Publishing House, Inc, pg 513
Our Lady of Manaoag Publisher, pg 514
Rex Bookstores & Publishers, pg 514

Poland

Energeia sp zoo Wydawnictwo, pg 516
Instytut Wydawniczy Pax, Inco-Veritas, pg 517
Iskry - Publishing House Ltd spotka zoo, pg 517
Ksiaznica Publishing Ltd, pg 517
Ludowa Spoldzielnia Wydawnicza, pg 518
Magnum Publishing House Ltd, pg 518
Muza SA, pg 518
Ossolineum Zaklad Narodowy im Ossolinskich - Wydawnictwo, pg 518
Polish Scientific Publishers PWN, pg 519
Wydawnictwo Prawnicze Co, pg 519
PZWL Wydawnictwo Lekarskie Ltd, pg 519
Oficyna Wydawnicza Read Me, pg 519
Res Polona, pg 519
Wydawnictwo RTW, pg 520
'Slask' Ltd, pg 520
Videograf II Sp z o o Zaklad Poracy Chronionej, pg 520
'Wiedza Powszechna' Panstwowe Wydawnictwo, pg 521
Wydawnictwo Wilga sp zoo, pg 521
Wydawnictwa Naukowo-Techniczne, pg 521
Wydawnictwo DiG, pg 521

Portugal

Publicacoes Alfa SA, pg 522
Bertrand Editora Lda, pg 522
Editora Classica, pg 523
Editorial Confluencia Lda, pg 524
Constancia Editores, SA, pg 524
Edicoes Cosmos, pg 524
DIFEL - Difusao Editorial SA, pg 524
Dinalivro, pg 524
Edicoes 70, Lda, pg 524
Europress Editores e Distribuidores de Publicacoes Lda, pg 525
Everest Editora, pg 525
Empresa Literaria Fluminense, Lda, pg 525
Latina Livraria, pg 526
Livraria Apostolado da Imprensa, pg 526
McGraw-Hill Editora de Portugal, pg 527
Melhoramentos de Portugal Editora, Lda, pg 527
Editorial Noticias, pg 527
Planeta Editora, LDA, pg 528
Porto Editora Lda, pg 528
Editorial Presenca, pg 528
Quimera Editores, pg 529
Editora Replicacao Lda, pg 529
Edicioes Joao Sa da Costa Lda, pg 529
Teorema, pg 529
Editorial Verbo SA, pg 530

Romania

Editura Academiei Romane, pg 531
Editura Aius, pg 531
Editora All, pg 531
Artemis Verlag, pg 532

The Center for Romanian Studies, pg 532
Editura Clusium, Casa de Editura Atlas-Clusium SRL, pg 532
Coresi SRL, pg 532
Corint Verlag, pg 532
Enzyklopadie Verlag, pg 533
Editura Excelsior, pg 533
FF Press, pg 533
Hasefer, pg 533
Editura Humanitas, pg 533
Humanitas Publishing House, pg 533
Editura Kriterion SA, pg 534
Lider Verlag, pg 534
Editura Meridiane, pg 534
Nemira Verlag, pg 534
Editura Niculescu, pg 534
RAO International Publishing Co, pg 535
RAO Publishing Group, pg 535
Rentrop & Straton Verlagsgruppe und Wirtschaftsconsulting, pg 535
Saeculum IO, pg 535
Editura Stiintifica, pg 536
Editura Stiintifica si Enciclopedica, pg 536
Est-Samuel Tastet Verlag, pg 536
Editura Tehnica, pg 536
Editura Teora, pg 536
Vestala Verlag, pg 536
Vox Verlag und Vertrieb, pg 536

Russian Federation

Airis Press, pg 537
Aspect Press Ltd, pg 537
FGUP Izdatelstvo Mashinostroenie, pg 538
Finansy i Statistika Publishing House, pg 538
Izdatel'stvo Ural' skogo, pg 538
Izdatelstvo Bolshaya Rossiyskaya Entsiklopedia, pg 538
Izdatelstvo Iskusstvo, pg 538
Izdatelskii Dom Kompositor, pg 539
KUbK Publishing House, pg 539
Ladomir Publishing House, pg 539
Publishing House Limbus Press, pg 539
Izdatelstvo Mir, pg 540
Mir Knigi Ltd, pg 540
Izdatelstvo Muzyka, pg 540
Izdatelstvo Prosveshchenie, pg 541
Raduga Publishers, pg 541
Russkij Jazyk, pg 541
Izdatelstvo Sudostroenie, pg 542
Teorija Verojatnostej i ee Primenenija, pg 542
Text Publishers Ltd Too, pg 542
Voronezh State University Publishers, pg 542

Saudi Arabia

King Saud University, pg 543

Senegal

Nouvelles Editions Africaines du Senegal (NEAS), pg 544
Les Nouvelles Editions Africaines du Senegal NEAS, pg 544

Singapore

Archipelago Press, pg 545
Chopsons Pte Ltd, pg 545
Federal Publications (S) Pte Ltd, pg 546
FEP International Private Ltd, pg 546
Shing Lee Group Publishers, pg 548

Slovakia

Priroda, pg 550
Slo Viet, pg 550
Slovenske pedagogicke nakladateistvo, pg 550
Ustav informacii a prognoz skolstva mladeze a telovychovy, pg 551
VEDA (Vydavatel'stvo Slovenskej akademie vied), pg 551

Slovenia

Cankarjeva Zalozba, pg 551
Mladinska Knjiga International, pg 552
Zalozba Mihelac d o o, pg 552
Zalozba Obzorja d d Maribor, pg 552

South Africa

Educum Publishers Ltd, pg 554
New Africa Books (Pty) Ltd, pg 557
Sasavona Publishers & Booksellers, pg 559
Tafelberg Publishers Ltd, pg 560
Witwatersrand University Press, pg 560

Spain

Ediciones Akal SA, pg 562
Anaya Educacion, pg 563
Anglo-Didactica, SL Editorial, pg 563
Arco Libros SL, pg 564
Editorial Argos Vergara SA, pg 564
Calambur Editorial, SL, pg 566
Editorial CISSPRAXIS SA, pg 567
Editorial Claret SA, pg 568
Editora Comercial de Publicaciones, pg 568
Curial Edicions Catalanes SA, pg 569
Ediciones Daly S L, pg 569
Editorial De Vecchi SA, pg 569
Didaco Comunicacion y Didactica, SA, pg 569
Edicions del Drac SA, pg 570
Durvan SA de Ediciones, pg 570
Ediciones l'Isard, S L, pg 571
Edicomunicacion SA, pg 572
Editorial Everest SA, pg 572
El Hogar y la Moda SA, pg 572
Elkar, Euskal Liburu eta Kantuen Argitaldaria, SL, pg 573
Editorial Espasa-Calpe SA, pg 573
EUNSA (Ediciones Universidad de Navarra SA), pg 574
Forum Artis, SA, pg 574
Galaxia SA Editorial, pg 575
Gran Enciclopedia-Asturiana Silverio Canada, pg 576
Editorial Gredos SA, pg 576
Grijalbo Mondadori SA, pg 576
Hercules de Ediciones, SA, pg 577
Ediciones Istmo SA, pg 579
Editorial Juventud SA, pg 579
Editorial Labor SA, pg 579
Larousse Planeta SA, pg 579
Libsa Editorial SA, pg 580
Lid Editorial Empresarial, SL, pg 580
Lynx Edicions, pg 580
Editorial Marin SA, pg 581
Editorial Moll SL, pg 582
Anaya & Mario Muchnik, pg 583
Mundi-Prensa Libros SA, pg 583
Ediciones Norma SA, pg 584
Ediciones Oceano Grupo SA, pg 584
Oikos-Tau SA Ediciones, pg 584
Editorial Alfredo Ortells SL, pg 585

PUBLISHERS

Editorial Paidotribo SL, pg 585
Editorial Paraninfo SA, pg 586
Parramon Ediciones SA, pg 586
Editorial Parthenon Communication, SL, pg 586
Ediciones Piramide SA, pg 586
Pulso Ediciones, SL, pg 588
Ediciones Rialp SA, pg 589
Josep Ruaix Editor, pg 589
San Pablo Ediciones, pg 589
Edicions 62, pg 591
Grup 62, pg 591
Ramon Sopena SA, pg 591
SPES Editorial SL, pg 591
Stanley Editorial, pg 591
Editorial Verbo Divino, pg 595
Editorial Verbum SL, pg 595
Veron Editor, pg 595

Sri Lanka

Lake House Investments Ltd, pg 597
Warna Publishers, pg 598

Sweden

Bokforlaget Bra Bocker AB, pg 600
Bokforlaget Rediviva, Facsimileforlaget, pg 600
Forlagshuset Norden AB, pg 602
Informationsfoerlaget AB, pg 603
Lidman Production AB, pg 604
Mezopotamya Publishing & Distribution, pg 604
Bokfoerlaget Naturoch Kultur, pg 604
Norstedts Ordbok, pg 605
Psykologifoerlaget AB, pg 605

Switzerland

Armenia Editions, pg 608
Cockatoo Press (Schweiz), Thailand-Publikationen, pg 611
Comite international de la Croix-Rouge, pg 612
Marcel Dekker AG, pg 612
Verlag Harri Deutsch, pg 612
Duboux Editions SA, pg 612
Kinderbuchverlag Luzern, pg 617
Kindler Verlag AG, pg 617
Larousse (Suisse) SA, pg 618
Muslim Architecture Research Program (MARP), pg 619
Edition Olms AG, pg 620
Ott Verlag AG, pg 621
Punktum AG, Buchredaktion und Bildarchiv, pg 622
Editiones Roche, pg 623
Schnellmann-Verlag, pg 624
Schwabe & Co AG, pg 624
Weltrundschau Verlag AG, pg 627

Taiwan, Province of China

Chien Chen Bookstore Publishing Company Ltd, pg 629
Chung Hwa Book Co Ltd, pg 629
Far East Book Co Ltd, pg 630
Hsiao Yuan Publication Co, Ltd, pg 630
Kuang Fu Book Co Ltd, pg 630
Laureate Book Co Ltd, pg 631
Linking Publishing Company Ltd, pg 631
San Min Book Co Ltd, pg 631
World Book Co Ltd, pg 632

United Republic of Tanzania

Ben and Company Ltd, pg 633

Thailand

Suksapan Panit (Business Organization of Teachers Council of Thailand), pg 635
Thai Watana Panich Co, Ltd, pg 636

Tunisia

Academie Tunisienne des Sciences, des Lettres et des Arts Beit El Hekma, pg 637
Dar Arabia Lil Kitab, pg 637

Turkey

ABC Kitabevi AS, pg 638
Afa Yayincilik Sanayi Tic AS, pg 638
Altin Kitaplar Yayinevi, pg 638
Arkadas Ltd, pg 639
Ataturk Kultur, Dil ve Tarih, Yusek Kurumu Baskanligi, pg 639
Ezel Erverdi (Dergah Yayinlari AS) Muessese Muduru, pg 640
IKI NOKTA Research Press & Publications Industry & Trade Ltd, pg 640
Iletisim Yayinlari, pg 640
Inkilap Publishers Ltd, pg 640
Pearson Education Turkey, pg 641
Remzi Kitabevi, pg 641
Sabah Kitaplari, pg 641
Yapi-Endustri Merkezi Yayinlari-Yem Yayin, pg 642

Uganda

Fountain Publishers Ltd, pg 642

Ukraine

ASK Ltd, pg 643
Naukova Dumka Publishers, pg 643
Osvita, pg 643

United Kingdom

ABC-CLIO, pg 644
Academic Press Ltd, pg 644
Andromeda Oxford Ltd, pg 647
Arms & Armour Press, pg 648
Art Sales Index Ltd, pg 649
AS Publishing, pg 649
Ashgate Publishing Ltd, pg 649
BCA, pg 653
Berlitz (UK) Ltd, pg 654
Blandford Publishing Ltd, pg 656
Bloomsbury Publishing PLC, pg 656
Blueprint, pg 656
Book Packaging & Marketing, pg 657
Books for Europe Ltd, pg 657
Butterworths Tolley, pg 661
Cambridge University Press, pg 662
Cassell & Co, pg 664
Chambers Harrap Publishers Ltd, pg 666
James Clarke & Co Ltd, pg 668
Peter Collin Publishing Ltd, pg 669
Constable Publishers, pg 670
Leo Cooper, pg 671
CTBI Publications, pg 672
Christopher Davies Publishers Ltd, pg 674
Diagram Visual Information Ltd, pg 675
Encyclopaedia Britannica (UK) International Ltd, pg 679
Facet Publishing, pg 681
Facts On File, pg 681
Fishing News Books Ltd, pg 682
Flicks Books, pg 683
Folens Ltd, pg 683

Gairm Publications, pg 685
Gale Research, pg 685
Geddes & Grosset, pg 686
Graham-Cameron Publishing & Illustration, pg 688
W Green The Scottish Law Publisher, pg 689
Guinness Publishing Ltd, pg 690
Harcourt Publishers Ltd, pg 691
HarperCollins Publishers, pg 692
Helicon Publishing Ltd, pg 694
Hilmarton Manor Press, pg 696
Institute of Physics Publishing, pg 700
International Bee Research Association, pg 701
Irish Texts Society (Cumann Na Scribeann nGaedhilge), pg 701
The Islamic Texts Society, pg 701
Kegan Paul International Ltd, pg 703
Kingfisher Publications Plc, pg 704
Letterbox Library, pg 707
The Lutterworth Press, pg 709
Macmillan Heinemann ELT, pg 710
The Mansk Svenska Publishing Co Ltd, pg 711
Melrose Press Ltd, pg 713
Mirabel Books Ltd, pg 715
Motilal (UK) Books of India, pg 715
Oneworld Publications, pg 721
Orpheus Books Ltd, pg 722
Packard Publishing Ltd, pg 723
Pearson Education, pg 725
Penguin Books Ltd, pg 725
Portland Press Ltd, pg 730
Quartz Editions, pg 732
The Reader's Digest Association Ltd, pg 733
Routledge, pg 736
Routledge Curzon, pg 736
Salamander Books Ltd, pg 738
St Pauls Publishing, pg 744
Stacey International, pg 745
Sweet & Maxwell Ltd, pg 746
I B Tauris & Co Ltd, pg 747
Thoemmes Press, pg 748
University of Wales Press, pg 751
Verbatim, pg 752
Witherby & Co Ltd, pg 758
Wordsworth Editions Ltd, pg 758

Venezuela

Biblioteca Ayacucho, pg 762

Viet Nam

Science & Technics Publishing House, pg 763

Yugoslavia

Alfa-Narodna Knjiga, pg 764
Beogradski Izdavacko-Graficki Zavod, pg 764
Minerva, pg 764
Obod, pg 765
Izdavacko Preduzece Matice Srpske, pg 765
Radnicka Stampa, pg 765
Vuk Karadzic, pg 766

Zimbabwe

The Literature Bureau, pg 768
Zimbabwe Publishing House (Pvt) Ltd, pg 769
ZRD Trust, pg 770

TYPE OF PUBLICATION INDEX

DIRECTORIES, REFERENCE BOOKS

Argentina

Alfagrama SRL ediciones, pg 3
Editorial Atlantida SA, pg 3
Oikos, pg 8

Armenia

Ajstan Publishers, pg 10

Australia

Australasian Medical Publishing Company Ltd (AMPCO), pg 13
Australian Marine Conservation Society Inc (AMCS), pg 14
Australian Scholarly Publishing, pg 14
Board of Studies, pg 15
Bridgeway Publications, pg 16
Cambridge University Press, pg 17
Casket Publications, pg 17
China Books, pg 18
CHOICE Magazine, pg 18
Church Archivists Press, pg 18
Coconut Productions, pg 18
Currency Press Pty Ltd, pg 19
D&B Marketing Pty Ltd, pg 20
Encyclopaedia Britannica (Australia) Inc, pg 22
Flora Publications International Pty Ltd, pg 23
Ginninderra Press, pg 24
Hargreen Publishing Co, pg 25
Hodder Headline Australia, pg 26
The Images Publishing Group Pty Ltd, pg 27
Jesuit Publications, pg 28
Kingsclear Books, pg 29
Kookaburra Technical Publications Pty Ltd, pg 29
Library of Australian History, pg 30
Lowden Publishing Co, pg 31
The Macquarie Library Pty Ltd, pg 31
Magpie Books, pg 31
Magpie Publications, pg 31
Maxwell Macmillan Publishing (Australia) Pty Ltd, pg 32
McDonald-Kirkwood Pty Ltd, pg 32
Melway Publishing Pty Ltd, pg 33
Moonlight Publishing, pg 33
Mulavon Press Pty Ltd, pg 34
National Library of Australia, pg 34
Navarine Publishing, pg 34
Nimrod Publications, pg 35
Anne O'Donovan Pty Ltd, pg 35
Online Information Resources Pty Ltd, pg 35
Pacific Publications (Australia) Pty Ltd, pg 36
Pandani Press, pg 37
Pearson Education Australia, pg 37
Priestley Consulting, pg 39
Queen Victoria Museum & Art Gallery Publications, pg 39
Queensland Art Gallery, pg 39
Rankin Publishers, pg 40
Reader's Digest (Australia) Pty Ltd, pg 40
Saltwater Publications, pg 41
Seanachas Press, pg 42
Shakespeare Head Press Pty Ltd, pg 42
Skills Publishing, pg 42
Standards Association of Australia, pg 43
D W Thorpe, pg 44
Three Sisters Publications Pty Ltd, pg 44
Tudor Australia Press, pg 45

795

TYPE OF PUBLICATION INDEX — BOOK

Turton & Armstrong Publishers Pty Ltd, pg 45
Universal Business Directories, Australia Pty Ltd, pg 46
Universal Press Pty Ltd, pg 46
University of Western Australia Press, pg 46
Villamonta Publishing Service Inc, pg 47
Wileman Publications, pg 47
Winetitles, pg 48
Zoe Publishing Pty Ltd, pg 48

Austria

Autorensolidaritat - Verlag der Interessengemeinschaft osterreichischer Autorinnen und Autoren, pg 49
Buchkultur Verlags GmbH Zeitschrift fuer Literatur & Kunst, pg 50
Compass-Verlag GmbH, pg 50
Cura Verlag GmbH, pg 50
Ferdinand Berger und Sohne, pg 51
Herold Business Data AG, pg 52
Johannes Heyn, Gert und Volkmar Zechner, pg 52
Hollinek Bruder & Co mbH Gesellschaftsdruckerei & Verlagsbuchhandring, pg 53
Thomas Mlakar Verlag, pg 55
Oesterreichischer Bundesverlag GmbH, pg 56
Pinguin-Verlag, Pawlowski GmbH, pg 57
Verlag Styria, pg 59
Zirkular - Verlag der Dokumentationsstelle fuer neuere oesterreichische Literatur, pg 61

Azerbaijan

Sada, Literaturno-Izdatel'skij Centr, pg 61

Bangladesh

The University Press Ltd, pg 62

Belarus

Belaruskaya Encyklapedyya, pg 63
Kavaler Publishers, pg 63
Publishing Center of Belarus State University, pg 63

Belgium

Editions Gerard Blanchart & Cie SA, pg 65
Brepols Publishers NV, pg 65
Editions du CEFAL, pg 66
Editions De Boeck-Larcier SA, pg 67
Editions Delta SA, pg 67
Documenta CV, pg 68
Ediblanchart sprl, pg 68
Girault Gilbert bvba, pg 69
Heideland-Orbis NV, pg 69
Editions Labor, pg 70
La Renaissance du Livre, pg 73
Paul Schiltz, pg 74
Snoeck-Ducaju en Zoon NV, pg 74
Uitgevery Scoop Infotex NV, pg 75

Bosnia and Herzegovina

Veselin Maslesa, pg 77
Svjetlost, pg 77

Brazil

Abril SA, pg 77
Associacao Brasileira de Liverivos Antiquarios, pg 79
Editora do Brasil SA, pg 80
Instituto Brasileiro de Edicoes Pedagogicas (IBEP), pg 80
Editora Campus Ltda, pg 80
Centro de Estudos Juridicosdo Para (CEJUP), pg 80
Ediouro Publicacoes, SA, pg 81
Editora Expressao e Cultura Exped Ltda, pg 83
Editora Globo SA, pg 84
Grafica Editora Primor Ltda, pg 84
Hemus Editora Ltda, pg 85
Livro Ibero-Americano Ltda, pg 85
LISA (Livros Irradiantes SA), pg 86
Editora Melhoramentos Ltda, pg 87
Editora Nova Fronteira SA, pg 88
Editora Rideel Ltda, pg 90
Editora Vecchi SA, pg 93
Editora Verbo Ltda, pg 93

Bulgaria

Abagar Pabloiing, pg 94
Gea-Libris Publishing House, pg 95
LIK IZDANIJA, pg 96
Prozoretz Ltd Publishing House, pg 97
Technica, pg 98

Chile

Publicaciones Lo Castillo SA, pg 101
Editorial Texido Ltda, pg 101

China

Anhui People's Publishing House, pg 102
Beijing Publishing House, pg 102
Chemical Industry Press, pg 102
China Foreign Economic Relations & Trade Publishing House, pg 103
China Machine Press (CMP), pg 103
China Materials Management Publishing House, pg 103
China Ocean Press, pg 103
China Theatre Publishing House, pg 104
China Translation & Publishing Corp, pg 104
Chinese Pedagogics Publishing House, pg 104
CITIC Publishing House, pg 104
Foreign Language Teaching & Research Press, pg 105
Guizhou Education Publishing House, pg 106
Higher Education Press, pg 106
Inner Mongolia Science & Technology Publishing House, pg 106
Jinan Publishing House, pg 107
Knowledge Press, pg 107
Lanzhou University Press, pg 107
Nanjing University Press, pg 107
National Defence Industry Press, pg 107
Patent Documentation Publishing House, pg 107
The People's Communications Publishing House, pg 107
Qingdao Publishing House, pg 108
Science Press, pg 108
Shandong Education Publishing House, pg 108
Shandong Friendship Press, pg 108
Shanghai Educational Publishing House, pg 109
Shanghai Fine Arts Publishers, pg 109
South China University of Science and Technology Press, pg 109
Tsinghua University Press, pg 110
World Affairs Press, pg 110
Xinhua Publishing House, pg 110

Colombia

Centro Regional para el Fomento del Libro en America Latina y el Caribe, pg 111
Instituto Caro y Cuervo, pg 112
Editorial Santillana SA, pg 113

The Democratic Republic of the Congo

Presses Universitaires du Zaiire (PUZ), pg 115

Costa Rica

Editorial Nacional de Salud y Seguridad Social Ednass, pg 116

Cote d'Ivoire

Centre d'Edition et de Diffusion Africaines, pg 117
Heritage Publishing Co, pg 118

Croatia

AGM doo, pg 118
Graficki zavod Hrvatske, pg 118
Masmedia, pg 119
Mladost d d Izdavacku graficku i informaticku djelatnost, pg 119
Nakladni zavod Matice hrvatske, pg 119
Otokar Kersovani, pg 120
Skolska Knjiga, pg 120
Tehnicka Knjiga, pg 120

Cuba

Instituto de Informacion Cientifica y Tecnologica (IDICT), pg 121

Czech Republic

Aleko, Nakladatelska Divize, pg 122
Barrister & Principal, pg 123
Divadelni Ustav, pg 124
Karolinum, nakladatelstvi, pg 125
Mlada fronta, pg 126
Cesky normalizacni institut, pg 127
Omnipress Praha, pg 127
Statisticke a evidencni vydavatelstvi tiskopisu (SEVT), pg 128
SystemConsult, pg 128

Denmark

Aschehoug Dansk Forlag A/S, pg 130
Dansk Historisk Handbogsforlag ApS, pg 131
Gyldendalske Boghandel - Nordisk Forlag A/S, pg 132
Holkenfeldt 3, pg 133
Ingenioeren/Boger, pg 133
Kraks Forlag AS, pg 133
Mellemfolkeligt Samvirke, pg 133
Nyt Nordisk Forlag Arnold Busck A/S, pg 134
Joergen Paludans Forlag ApS, pg 134
Det Schonbergske Forlag, pg 135
Statens Information (Danish State Information Service), pg 135
Systime, pg 136

Dominican Republic

Sociedad Editorial Dominicana SA, pg 137

Egypt (Arab Republic of Egypt)

American University in Cairo Press, pg 138
The Egyptian Society for the Dissemination of Universal Culture and Knowledge (ESDUCK), pg 138

Estonia

Estonian Encyclopaedia Publishers Ltd, pg 140
National Library of Estonia, pg 140
Olion Publishers, pg 140

Finland

Kirja-Leitzinger, pg 143
Schildts Foerlagsaktiebolag, pg 144
Soederstroem et Co Foerlagsaktiebolag, pg 144
Weilin & Goeoes Oy, pg 145
Yritystieto Oy - Foretagsdata AB, pg 145

France

ADPF Publications, pg 146
Agence Bibliographique de L'Enseignement Superieur, pg 146
Editions Aubier-Montaigne SA, pg 149
Beauchesne Editeur, pg 150
Berg International Editeurs, pg 150
Bibliotheque des Arts, pg 150
Bibliotheque Nationale de France, pg 150
Editions Bordas, pg 151
Bureau des Longitudes de France, pg 152
La Decouverte et Syros, pg 158
Editions Denoel Sarl, pg 158
Doin Editeurs, pg 160
Les Dossiers d'Aquitaine, pg 160
Editions Grund, pg 161
Editions Farel, pg 163
Librairie Artheme Fayard, pg 163
Editions Fivedit, pg 164
Folklore Comtois, pg 164
Association Frank, pg 165
Gippe-Marche Du Livre Ancien, pg 166
Editions Jean Paul Gisserot, pg 166
Hachette Livre, pg 167
Hachette Pratiques, pg 167
Fernand Hazan Editeur SA, pg 168
Hermann editeurs des Sciences et des Arts SA, pg 168
INRA Editions (Institut National de la Recherche Agronomique), pg 169
Institut International de la Marionnette, pg 170
Editions Klincksieck, pg 171
Lacour-Olle, pg 171
Librairie Larousse, pg 172
Lavoisier, pg 172
Le Livre de Paris, pg 173
Editions Maritimes et d'Outre-Mer SA, pg 175
Masson-Williams et Wilkins, pg 175
Editions Franck Mercier, pg 176
Fernand Nathan, pg 177
Editions A et J Picard SA, pg 179
Editions Jean Picollec, pg 179
Jean-Michel Place, pg 180
Point Hors Ligne, pg 180
Editions du Point Veterinaire, pg 180
Presence Africaine Editions, pg 180
Presses de la Sorbonne Nouvelle/PSN, pg 181
Presses Universitaires de France (PUF), pg 181

PUBLISHERS

PRODIG UMR 8586 CNRS-Paris 1,4,7 ephe, pg 182
References cf, pg 182
Guide Rosenwald, pg 183
Editions Sand et Tchou SA, pg 183
Editions Scientifiques et Medicales Elsevier, pg 184
Selection du Reader's Digest SA, pg 184
Service Technique pour l'Education, pg 185
Sofiac (Societe Francaise des Imprimeries Administratives Centrales), pg 185
Sofradif Editions Philippe Auzou, pg 185
Editions Louis Soulanges Le Livrer Ouvert, pg 186
Editions Springer France, pg 186
Editions Tallandier, pg 187
Terre Vivante, pg 187
UNESCO Publishing, pg 188
Editions Vilo SA, pg 189
Librairie Philosophique J Vrin, pg 189

Germany

ABC der Deutschen Wirtschaft, Verlagsgesellschaft mbH, pg 191
Angelika und Lothar Binding, pg 193
Antiquariat und Verlag Auvermann Keip GmbH, pg 194
AOL-Verlag Frohmut Menze, pg 194
Arnoldsche Verlagsanstalt GmbH, pg 195
Axel Juncker Verlag Jacobi KG, pg 197
Verlag C H Beck (OHG), pg 200
Beleke KG Verlag, pg 200
Bettendorf'sche Verlagsanstalt GmbH, pg 202
Biblio-Zeller Verlag, pg 202
Bibliographisches Institut & F A Brockhaus AG, pg 203
Bleicher Verlag GmbH, pg 204
Bouvier Verlag, pg 206
R Brockhaus Verlag, pg 206
Verlag C J Bucher GmbH, pg 207
Buchhaendler-Vereinigung GmbH, pg 207
Buchverlage Langen-Mueller/Herbig, pg 207
Bundesanzeiger Verlagsgesellschaft, pg 208
Calwer Verlag Stuttgart eV, pg 209
Compact Verlag GmbH, pg 211
Copress Verlag, pg 211
Verlag Darmstaedter Blaetter Schwarz und Co, pg 212
Verlag Werner Dausien, pg 212
Degener & Co, Manfred Dreiss Verlag, pg 213
Verlag Harri Deutsch, pg 213
Deutsche Blinden-Bibliothek, pg 213
Deutscher Adressbuch-Verlag fuer Wirtschaft und Verkehr GmbH, pg 214
Deutscher Taschenbuch Verlag GmbH & Co KG (dtv), pg 215
Droemersche Verlagsanstalt Th Knaur Nachfolger GmbH & Co, pg 218
Dumjahn Verlag, pg 219
DuMont Buchverlag GmbH & Co KG, pg 219
Dustri-Verlag Dr Karl Feistle, pg 219
Eckardt & Messtorff GmbH, pg 220
Econ Verlag GmbH, pg 220

Europ Export Edition GmbH, pg 224
F Bruckmann Munchen Verlag & Druck GmbH & Co Produkt KG, pg 225
FAB-Verlag, pg 226
Festland Verlag GmbH, pg 227
Fink - Kummerly und Frey Verlag GmbH, pg 227
S Fischer Verlag GmbH, pg 228
Fischer Taschenbuch Verlag GmbH, pg 228
Focus-Verlag Gesellschaft mbH, pg 229
Verlag Franz Vahlen GmbH, pg 229
Fraunhofer IRB Verlag Fraunhofer Informationszentrum Raum und Bau, pg 229
Friedemann von Engel Verlag, pg 230
GeoCenter Touristik Medienservice GmbH, pg 231
Graefe und Unzer Verlag GmbH, pg 233
Gunter Olzog Verlag GmbH, pg 235
Walter Haedecke Verlag, pg 236
Hallwag Verlag GmbH, pg 236
Rudolf Haufe Verlag GmbH & Co KG, pg 238
Dr Ernst Hauswedell & Co Verlag, pg 238
G Henle Verlag, pg 239
F A Herbig Verlagsbuchhandlung GmbH, pg 239
Erika Heydick Sax-Verlag Beucha, pg 240
Anton Hiersemann, Verlag, pg 240
Verlag Hoppenstedt GmbH, pg 242
Humboldt-Taschenbuchverlag Jacobi KG, pg 243
Huss-Verlag GmbH, pg 244
Edition ID-Archiv/ID-Verlag, pg 244
Industrie- und Handelsverlag GmbH & Co KG, pg 244
Industrieschau Verlagsgesellschaft mbH, pg 244
Kastell Verlag GmbH, pg 248
Verlag im Kilian GmbH, pg 249
Kindler Verlag GmbH, pg 249
Unterwegs Verlag, Manfred Klemann, pg 250
Vittorio Klostermann GmbH, pg 250
Verlag Fritz Knapp GmbH, pg 250
Knowledge Media International, pg 251
Franckh-Kosmos Verlags-GmbH & Co, pg 252
Roman Kovar Verlag, pg 253
Alfred Kroner Verlag, pg 253
Verlag Ernst Kuhn, pg 254
Ambro Lacus, Buch- und Bildverlag Walter Kremnitz, pg 255
Leitfadenverlag Verlag Dieter Sudholt, pg 257
Dr Gisela Lermann, pg 257
Verlag Leske plus Budrich GmbH, pg 257
Maeander Verlag GmbH, pg 260
Magnus Verlag, pg 260
Mairs Geographischer Verlag, pg 260
Matthiesen Verlag Ingwert Paulsen Jr, pg 261
Midena Verlag, pg 264
Mitteldeutscher Verlag GmbH, pg 264
Mosaik Verlag GmbH, pg 265
Motorbuch-Verlag, pg 265
Neuer Honos Verlag GmbH, pg 267
Edition Parabolis, pg 271
Pendragon Verlag, pg 272

TYPE OF PUBLICATION INDEX

Jens Peters Publikationen, pg 272
Philipp Reclam Jun Verlag GmbH, pg 273
pmi Verlag, pg 274
Polygraph Verlag GmbH, pg 274
Presse Verlagsgesellschaft mbH, pg 275
Projektion J Buch- und Musikverlag GmbH, pg 275
R Oldenbourg Verlag GmbH, pg 276
R V Reise- und Verkehrsverlag GmbH, pg 276
Dr Josef Raabe-Verlags GmbH, pg 276
Dr Ludwig Reichert Verlag, pg 278
Peter Meyer Reisefuhrer, pg 278
Rombach GmbH Druck und Verlagshaus & Co, pg 280
Verlag Werner Sachon GmbH & Co, pg 281
Eugen Salzer-Verlag GmbH & Co KG, pg 281
K G Saur Verlag GmbH, A Gale/Thomson Learning Company, pg 282
Verlag der Schillerbuchhandlung Hans Banger OHG, pg 283
Max Schmidt-Roemhild Verlag, pg 284
Verlag Schnell und Steiner GmbH, pg 284
Verlag Schulte und Gerth GmbH & Co KG, pg 285
Schwaneberger Verlag GmbH, pg 286
Springer-Verlag GmbH & Co KG, pg 288
Staatsbibliothek zu Berlin - Preussischer Kulturbesitz, pg 288
Stadler Verlagsgesellschaft mbH, pg 288
Verlag Stahleisen GmbH, pg 289
C A Starke Verlag, pg 289
Stattbuch Verlag GmbH, pg 289
Conrad Stein Verlag, pg 289
Stollfuss Verlag Bonn GmbH & Co KG, pg 290
Suedwest Verlag GmbH & Co KG, pg 291
Telex-Verlag Jaeger & Waldmann GmbH, pg 292
B G Teubner GmbH, pg 292
edition Text & Kritik im Richard Boorberg Verlag GmbH & Co, pg 293
Georg Thieme Verlag KG, pg 293
Tipress Dienstleistungen fur das Verlagswesen GmbH, pg 294
Tomus Verlag GmbH, pg 294
Transpress Verlagsgesellschaft mbH, pg 294
Trias-Thieme, Hippokrates Enke, pg 295
Tuebinger Vereinigung fur Volkskunde eV (TVV), pg 295
Ullstein Heyne List GmbH & Co KG, pg 295
Verlag Eugen Ulmer GmbH & Co, pg 295
Urban und Fischer Verlag fur Medizin, pg 296
Dorothea van der Koelen, pg 297
Curt R Vincentz Verlag, pg 298
Voggenreiter-Verlag, pg 299
VS Verlagshaus Stuttgart GmbH, pg 299
W Ludwig Verlag GmbH, pg 300
Weidler Buchverlag Berlin, pg 301
WEKA Firmengruppe GmbH & Co KG, pg 301
Werner Verlag GmbH & Co KG, pg 302

Wiley-VCH Verlag GmbH, pg 302
Gert Wohlfarth GmbH Verlag Fachtechnik & Mercator Verlag, Verlag Puppen & Spielzeug, pg 304
Xenos Verlagsgesellschaft mbH, pg 304
Zeller Verlag GmbH & Co, pg 305
Zweiburgen-Verlag GmbH, pg 305

Ghana

Anowuo Educational Publications, pg 306
Ghana Publishing Corporation, pg 307
Moxon Paperbacks, pg 307
World Literature Project, pg 308

Greece

Alamo Hellas, pg 308
Beta Medical Publishers, pg 309
Chrysi Penna - Golden Pen Books, pg 309
Giovanis Publications, Pangosmios Ekdotikos Organismos, pg 310
Karatzas Charis, pg 312
Logos, pg 312
Minoas SA, pg 313
Nakas Music House, pg 313

Honduras

Editorial Guaymuras, pg 318

Hong Kong

Benefit Publishing Co, pg 318
Chung Hwa Book Co (HK) Ltd, pg 319
Joint Publishing (HK) Co Ltd, pg 320
Peace Book Co Ltd, pg 321
Ta Kung Pao (HK) Ltd, pg 322

Hungary

Akademiai Kiado, pg 323
Greger-Delacroix, pg 324
Kossuth Kiado RT, pg 325
Mezoegazdasagi Koenyvkiado Vallalat, pg 325
Novorg Kiado, pg 326

Iceland

Bokautgafan Orn og Orlygur ehf, pg 327
Frodi Ltd, pg 328
ldunn, pg 328

India

Academic Book Corporation, pg 329
Agam Kala Prakashan, pg 330
Amar Prakashan, pg 330
Asia Pacific Business Press Inc, pg 331
Asian Educational Services, pg 331
Associated Publishing House, pg 331
Atma Ram & Sons, pg 331
Bharat Law House Pvt Ltd, pg 332
Book Circle, pg 333
BR Publishing Corporation, pg 334
BS Publications, pg 334
Chowkhamba Sanskrit Series Office, pg 335
Cosmo Publications, pg 335
DC Books, pg 336
Disha Prakashan, pg 336
DK Printworld (P) Ltd, pg 336
Eastern Book Co, pg 336
Geeta Prakasham, pg 337
General Book Depot, pg 337

797

TYPE OF PUBLICATION INDEX BOOK

Gyan Publishing House, pg 338
Arnold Heinman Publishers (India) Pvt Ltd, pg 338
Heritage Publishers, pg 338
Intertrade Publications, pg 340
Jaico Publishing House, pg 340
Kalyani Publishers, pg 341
Law Publishers, pg 341
Ministry of Information & Broadcasting, pg 342
National Institute of Industrial Research (NIIR), pg 344
Navajivan Trust, pg 344
Nem Chand & Brothers, pg 344
Newspread International, pg 344
Orient Paperbacks, pg 345
Oxford University Press, pg 345
Oxonian Press (P) Ltd, pg 345
Panjab University Publication Bureau, pg 345
Parimal Prakashan, pg 345
Pitambar Publishing Co (P) Ltd, pg 346
Pointer Publishers, pg 346
Promilla and Co, pg 346
Rahul Publishing House, pg 347
Reliance Publishing House, pg 347
Scientific Book Agency, pg 349
Sita Publications, pg 350
Small Industry Research Institute (SIRI), pg 350
Spectrum Publications, pg 350
Sri Satguru Publications, pg 351
Sterling Publishers Pvt Ltd, pg 351
Today & Tomorrow's Printers & Publishers, pg 352
Vidya Puri, pg 352
Vidyarthi Mithram Press, pg 352

Indonesia
CV Angkasa CV (Publishers), pg 354
Lembaga Demografi Fakultas Ekonomi Universitas Indonesia, pg 356
Penerbit Nusa Indah, pg 356
Pustaka Utama Grafiti, PT, pg 357
Tintamas Indonesia PT, pg 357

Ireland
An Gum, pg 358
Ballinakella Press, pg 358
Dee-Jay Publications, pg 359
Flyleaf Press, pg 360
Gill & Macmillan Ltd, pg 361
Institute of Public Administration, pg 361
Irish Management Institute, pg 361
On Stream Publications Ltd, pg 363
Royal Irish Academy, pg 364

Israel
Achiasaf Publishing House Ltd, pg 365
Am Oved Publishers Ltd, pg 365
Amichai Publishing House Ltd, pg 365
The Bialik Institute, pg 365
Carta, The Israel Map & Publishing Co Ltd, pg 366
Dekel Publishing House, pg 366
Edanim Publishers Ltd, pg 367
Encyclopedia Judaica, pg 367
Feldheim Publishers Ltd, pg 367
Intermedia Audio, Video Book Publishing Ltd, pg 368
Israel Exploration Society, pg 368
Israel Universities Press, pg 369
The Jerusalem Publishing House Ltd, pg 369
Karni Publishers Ltd, pg 369
Keter Publishing House Ltd, pg 369

Ma'ariv Book Guild (Sifriat Ma'ariv), pg 370
MAP-Mapping & Publishing Ltd, pg 370
Massada Press Ltd, pg 370
Massada Publishers Ltd, pg 370
Medcom Ltd, pg 370
Saar Publishing House, pg 372
Sadan Publishing Ltd, pg 372
Steimatzky Group Ltd, pg 372
Tcherikover Publishers Ltd, pg 372
Yad Vashem - The Holocaust Martyrs' & Heroes' Remembrance Authority, pg 373
Yedioth Ahronoth Books, pg 373

Italy
Umberto Allemandi & C SRL, pg 375
Arcanta Aries Gruppo Editoriale, pg 376
Gruppo Editoriale Armenia SpA, pg 376
Nuova Casa Editrice Licinio Cappelli GEM srl, pg 379
Casa Editrice Libraria Ulrico Hoepli SpA, pg 380
Centro Di, pg 381
Citta Nuova Editrice, pg 382
Edizioni Cremonese SRL, pg 383
Istituto della Enciclopedia Italiana, pg 384
Direzione Generale Archivi, pg 385
Edagricole - Edizioni Agricole, pg 385
Editrice Bibliografica SpA, pg 386
Editrice Eraclea, pg 388
Giangiacomo Feltrinelli SpA, pg 389
Garzanti Editore, pg 390
Istituto Geografico de Agostini SpA, pg 390
Giunti Publishing Group, pg 391
Gius Laterza e Figli SpA, pg 391
Ernesto Gremese Editore SRL, pg 391
Gremese International Srl, pg 391
Gruppo Editoriale Faenza Editrice SpA, pg 392
Il Saggiatore, pg 393
L'Airone Editrice, pg 395
Edizioni Librex, pg 396
LIM Editrice SRL, pg 396
Arnoldo Mondadori Editore SpA, pg 399
Giorgio Mondadori & Associati, pg 399
Gruppo Ugo Mursia Editore SpA, pg 400
Newton Compton Editori SRL, pg 401
Nuova Alfa Editoriale, pg 401
La Nuova Italia Editrice SpA, pg 401
Leo S Olschki, pg 402
Paravia Bruno Mondadori Editori, pg 402
Pontificio Istituto Orientale, pg 404
RCS Libri SpA, pg 405
RCS Rizzoli Libri SpA, pg 405
Franco Maria Ricci Editore (FMR), pg 405
SAIE Editrice SRL, pg 406
Edizioni San Paolo SRL, pg 407
UTET (Unione Tipografico-Editrice Torinese), pg 411
Societa Editrice Vannini, pg 411
Zanichelli Editore SpA, pg 412

Jamaica
American Chamber of Commerce of Jamaica, pg 412

Japan
The American Chamber of Commerce in Japan, pg 414
GakuseiSha Publishing Co Ltd, pg 416
Heibonsha Ltd, Publishers, pg 417
Hirokawa Publishing Co, pg 417
Hokuryukan Co Ltd, pg 417
Hyoronsha Publishing Co Ltd, pg 417
Iwanami Shoten, Publishers, pg 418
The Japan Times, pg 418
Kaitakusha, pg 419
Kenkyusha Ltd, pg 419
Kinokuniya Co Ltd (Publishing Department), pg 420
Kodansha, pg 420
Kodansha International, pg 420
Kodansha Scientific Ltd, pg 420
Nagaoka Shoten Company Ltd, pg 421
Nanzando Co Ltd, pg 422
Nigensha Publishing Co Ltd, pg 422
Nihon Bunka Kagakusha Co Ltd, pg 422
Nihon Tosho Center Co Ltd, pg 422
Obunsha Co Ltd, pg 423
Rinsen Book Co Ltd, pg 424
Sanseido Co Ltd, pg 424
Sanshusha Publishing Co, Ltd, pg 424
Seibido, pg 424
Seibido Shuppan Company Ltd, pg 424
Shogakukan Inc, pg 426
Tokyo Shoseki Co Ltd, pg 427
Toyo Keizai Inc (The Oriental Economist), pg 428
Tsukiji Shokan Publishing Co, pg 428
University of Tokyo Press, pg 428

Kazakhstan
Kazakh Al-Farabi State National University, pg 430

Kenya
Africa Book Services (EA) Ltd, pg 430
Bookman Consultants Ltd, pg 431
Kenya Energy & Environment Organisation, Kengo, pg 432
Transafrica Press, pg 433

Republic of Korea
DanKook University Press, pg 436
Kemongsa Publishing Co Ltd, pg 437
Korean Publishers Association, pg 437
Maeil Gyeongje, pg 438
Woongjin Media Corporation, pg 440

Latvia
Avots, pg 441

Lebanon
Librairie du Liban, pg 443
Publitec Publications, pg 443

Liechtenstein
Bonafides Verlags-Anstalt, pg 444

Lithuania
Eugrimas, pg 445
Lietuvos Informacijos Institutas, pg 446
Lithuanian National Museum Publishing House, pg 446

Luxembourg
Service Central de la Statistique et des Etudes Economiques (STATEC), pg 448

The Former Yugoslav Republic of Macedonia
Prosvetno Delo, pg 449
St Clement of Ohrid National & University Library, pg 449

Madagascar
Madagascar Print & Press Company, pg 450
Societe Malgache d'Edition, pg 450

Malaysia
Amiza Associate Malaysia Sdn Bhd, pg 451
Berita Publishing Sdn Bhd, pg 451
Dewan Bahasa dan Pustaka, pg 451
Federal Publications Sdn Bhd, pg 452
FEP International Sdn Bhd, pg 452
Geetha Publishers Sdn Bhd, pg 452
MDC Publishers Printers, pg 453
Oscar Book International, pg 453
Pearson Education, pg 453
Penerbit Fajar Bakti Sdn Bhd, pg 454
Pustaka Cipta Sdn Bhd, pg 454
Trix Corporation Sdn Bhd, pg 455
Vinpress Sdn Bhd, pg 455

Maldive Islands
Novelty Printers & Publishers, pg 455

Mexico
Libreria y Ediciones Botas SA, pg 458
Editorial Edicol SA, pg 460
Ibcon SA, pg 462
Informatica Cosmos SA de CV, pg 462
Medios y Medios, Sa de CV, pg 464
Mercametrica Ediciones SA Edicion de Libros, pg 464
Nova Grupo Editorial SA de CV, pg 464
Ediciones Roca, SA, pg 466

Morocco
Access International Services, pg 469
Association de la Recherche Historique et Sociale, pg 469
Office Marocain D'Annonces-OMA, pg 470
Editions Services et Informations pour Etudiants, pg 470

Netherlands
Uitgeversmaatschappij Agon, pg 472
APA (Academic Publishers Associated), pg 472
Ars Scribendi bv Uitgeverij, pg 473
B M Israel BV, pg 473
John Benjamins BV, pg 474
BV Uitgeversbedryf Het Goede Boek, pg 477
De Graaf Publishers, pg 478
Helmond B. V. Uitgeverij, pg 478
HES & De Graaf Publishers BV, pg 478
Holland B V Uitgeversmaatschappij, pg 478

PUBLISHERS

Uitgeefmaatschappij J H Kok BV, pg 480
Nico Israel, pg 482
Pearson Education Netherlands, pg 482
Reed Elsevier Nederland BV, pg 483
A J G Strengholt's Boeken, Anno 1928, BV, pg 484
Unieboek BV, pg 485

New Caledonia
Savannah Editions SARL, pg 488

New Zealand
David Bateman Ltd, pg 488
Brooker's Ltd, pg 489
Current Pacific Limited, pg 490
David's Marine Books, pg 490
Eton Press (Auckland) Ltd, pg 490
Evagean Publishing, pg 491
GCL Publishing (1997) Ltd, pg 491
HarperCollins Publishers (New Zealand) Ltd, pg 491
Landcare Research NZ, pg 492
Learning Guides (Writers & Publishers Ltd), pg 492
Legislation Direct, pg 492
New Zealand Council for Educational Research, pg 494
Oxford University Press, pg 494
Reed Publishing (NZ) Ltd, pg 495
Shoal Bay Press Ltd, pg 495
Statistics New Zealand, pg 496

Nigeria
ABIC Books & Equipment Ltd, pg 497
Adebara Publishers Ltd, pg 497
Ahmadu Bello University Press Ltd, pg 498
Daily Times of Nigeria Ltd (Publication Division), pg 498
Ethiope Publishing Corporation, pg 499
Ibadan University Press, pg 499
Longman Nigeria Plc, pg 500
Obafemi Awolowo University Press Ltd, pg 501
West African Book Publishers Ltd, pg 502
John West Publications Co Ltd, pg 502

Norway
H Aschehoug & Co (W Nygaard) A/S, pg 502
J W Cappelens Forlag A/S, pg 503
Det Norske Samlaget, pg 503
Gyldendal Norsk Forlag A/S, pg 503
Chr Schibsteds Forlag A/S, pg 505
Teknologisk Forlag, pg 505
Tiden Norsk Forlag, pg 505
Universitetsforlaget, pg 505

Oman
Apex Publishing, pg 506

Pakistan
Hamdard Foundation, pg 507
Jang Publishers, pg 507
Publishers United Pvt Ltd, pg 508
Sang-e-Meel Publications, pg 509
Shibil Publications (Pvt) Ltd, pg 509

Panama
Focus Publications International SA, pg 509

Papua New Guinea
IMPS Research Pty Ltd, pg 510
National Research Institute of Papua New Guinea, pg 510

Peru
Editorial Desarrollo SA, pg 511

Philippines
Abiva Publishing House Inc, pg 512
Bright Concepts Printing House, pg 512
Communication Foundation for Asia Media Group (CFAMG), pg 513
J C Palabay Enterprises, pg 513
National Museum of the Philippines, pg 514
New Day Publishers, pg 514
Philippine Baptist Mission SBC FMB Church Growth International, pg 514
SIBS Publishing House Inc, pg 515
Solidaridad Publishing House, pg 515

Poland
Wydawnictwa Normalizacyjne Alfa-Wero, pg 516
Laumann-Polska, pg 517
Wydawnictwo Medyczne Urban & Partner, pg 518
Oficyna Wydawnicza Read Me, pg 519
Wydawnictwo RTW, pg 520
'Slask' Ltd, pg 520
Spotdzielna Anagram, pg 520
Wydawnictwa Przemyslowe WEMA, pg 521

Portugal
Publicacoes Alfa SA, pg 522
Difusao Cultural, pg 524
Edicoes 70, Lda, pg 524
Publicacoes Europa-America Lda, pg 524
Gradiva-Publicacnoes Lda, pg 525
Instituto de Investigacao Cientifica Tropical, pg 526
McGraw-Hill Editora de Portugal, pg 527
Editorial Presenca, pg 528
Publicacoes Dom Quixote Lda, pg 528
Almerinda Teixeira, pg 529

Puerto Rico
University of Puerto Rico Press (EDUPR), pg 531

Romania
Editura Academiei Romane, pg 531
Alcor-Edimpex (Verlag) Ltd, pg 531
The Center for Romanian Studies, pg 532
Editura Cronos SRL, pg 532
Enzyklopadie Verlag, pg 533
Editura Excelsior, pg 533
Hasefer, pg 533
Editura Meridiane, pg 534
Polirom Verlag, pg 535
Editura Stiintifica si Enciclopedica, pg 536
Editura Tehnica, pg 536
Vestala Verlag, pg 536

Russian Federation
N E Bauman Moscow State Technical University Publishers, pg 537
BLIC, russko-Baltijskij informaciionnyj centr, AO, pg 537
FGUP Izdatelstvo Mashinostroenie, pg 538
Izdatelstvo Galart, pg 538
Izdatel 'stvo Ural' skogo, pg 538
Izdatelstvo Bolshaya Rossiyskaya Entsiklopedia, pg 538
Izdatelskii Dom Kompositor, pg 539
KUbK Publishing House, pg 539
Izdatelstvo Mezhdunarodnye Otnosheniа, pg 540
Ministerstvo Kul 'tury RF, pg 540
Moscow University Press, pg 540
Izdatelstvo Muzyka, pg 540
Pedagogika Press, pg 541
Izdatelstvo Prosveshchenie, pg 541
Russkij Jazyk, pg 541
Izdatelstvo Standartov, pg 542
Vsesoyuznii Molodejnii Knizhnii Centre, pg 542

Saudi Arabia
King Saud University, pg 543

Senegal
Agence de Distribution de Presse, pg 544

Singapore
APA Production Pte Ltd, pg 545
Chopsons Pte Ltd, pg 545
Federal Publications (S) Pte Ltd, pg 546
FEP International Private Ltd, pg 546
LexisNexis, pg 547
Reed Elsevier, South East Asia, pg 547
SNP Pan Pacific Publishing Pte Ltd, pg 548

Slovenia
Cankarjeva Zalozba, pg 551

South Africa
Ad Donker (Pty) Ltd, pg 554
Erudita Publications (Pty) Ltd, pg 554
Flesch Financial Publications (Pty) Ltd, pg 554
HarperCollins Religious, pg 554
Human & Rousseau (Pty) Ltd, pg 555
National Botanical Institute, pg 557
New Africa Books (Pty) Ltd, pg 557
Queillerie Publishers, pg 558
Reader's Digest Southern Africa, pg 559
Southern Book Publishers (Pty) Ltd, pg 559
Thomson Publications, pg 560
Unisa Press, pg 560
Van Schaik Publishers, pg 560
Who's Who of Southern Africa, pg 560

Spain
Ediciones Agrotecnicas, SL, pg 562
Aguilar SA de Ediciones, pg 562
Anaya Educacion, pg 563
Anglo-Didactica, SL Editorial, pg 563
Arco Libros SL, pg 564
Carroggio SA de Ediciones, pg 566
Comunidad Autonoma de Madrid, Servicio de Documentacion y Publicaciones, pg 568
Editorial Espasa-Calpe SA, pg 573
Fundacion Marcelino Botin, pg 575
Generalitat de Catalunya Diari Oficial de la Generalitat vern, pg 575
Grijalbo Mondadori SA, pg 576
Editorial Herder SA, pg 577
Idea Books, SA, pg 578
Ediciones Istmo SA, pg 579
Editorial Kairos SA, pg 579
Editorial Marin SA, pg 581
Ediciones Nauta Credito SA, pg 584
Editorial Noray, pg 584
Parramon Ediciones SA, pg 586
Pearson Educacion S A, pg 586
Plastic Comunicacion SL, pg 587
Plaza y Janes Editores SA, pg 587
Polifemo, Ediciones, pg 587
Ediciones Scriba SA, pg 589
Ramon Sopena SA, pg 591
Tesitex, SL, pg 592
Trea Ediciones, SL, pg 593
Veron Editor, pg 595
Vinaches Lopez, Luisa, pg 595
Xunta de Galicia, pg 596

Sri Lanka
Business Directory of Lanka Limited, pg 596
National Library & Documentation Services Board, pg 597
Waruni Publishers, pg 598

Sudan
Al-Ayam Press Co Ltd, pg 598
Khartoum University Press, pg 598

Sweden
Bibliotekstjaenst AB, pg 600
Bokforlaget Spektra AB, pg 601
Forlagshuset Norden AB, pg 602
Informationsfoerlaget AB, pg 603
Klassikerfoerlaget, pg 604
Norstedts Ordbok, pg 605
Psykologifoerlaget AB, pg 605
Richters Egmont, pg 605
Wahlstrom & Widstrand, pg 607

Switzerland
Aare-Verlag, pg 607
Editions de la Baconniere SA, pg 609
U Baer Verlag, pg 609
Bibliographisches Institut und F A Brockhaus AG, pg 610
Verlag Bibliophile Drucke von Josef Stocker AG, pg 610
Bugra Suisse Burchler Grafino AG, pg 610
Cockatoo Press (Schweiz), Thailand-Publikationen, pg 611
Cosa-Verlag, Giusep Condrau SA, pg 611
Editions Delachaux et Niestle SA, pg 612
Larousse (Suisse) SA, pg 618
Maihof Verlag, pg 618
Motovun Book GmbH, pg 619
Presses Polytechniques et Universitaires Romandes, PPUR, pg 622
Rex Verlag, pg 623
Der Universitatsverlag Freiburg, pg 626

Syrian Arab Republic
Damascus University Press, pg 628

TYPE OF PUBLICATION INDEX — BOOK

Taiwan, Province of China
Chien Chen Bookstore Publishing Company Ltd, pg 629
Chung Hwa Book Co Ltd, pg 629
Designer Publisher Inc, pg 629
Kuang Fu Book Co Ltd, pg 630
Petroleum Information Publishing Co, pg 631
San Min Book Co Ltd, pg 631

United Republic of Tanzania
Ben and Company Ltd, pg 633
East African Publishing House, pg 633
Eastern Africa Publications Ltd, pg 633
Kanisa la Biblia Publishers (KLB), pg 633
Oxford University Press, pg 634

Thailand
Ruamsarn (1977) Co Ltd, pg 635
Thai Watana Panich Co, Ltd, pg 636

Trinidad & Tobago
Jett Samm Publishing Ltd, pg 637

Tunisia
Ceres Editions, pg 637
Editions Techniques Specialisees, pg 638

Turkey
ABC Kitabevi AS, pg 638
Arkadas Ltd, pg 639
Arkin Kitabevi, pg 639
Remzi Kitabevi, pg 641
Sabah Kitaplari, pg 641
Yapi-Endustri Merkezi Yayinlari-Yem Yayin, pg 642
Yetkin Printing & Publishing Co Inc, pg 642

Uganda
Fountain Publishers Ltd, pg 642

Ukraine
Naukova Dumka Publishers, pg 643

United Kingdom
A A Publishing, pg 644
ABC-CLIO, pg 644
Act 3 Publishing, pg 645
Adamantine Press Ltd, pg 645
A4 Publications Ltd, pg 645
Aldwych Press Ltd, pg 645
Umberto Allemandi & Co Publishing, pg 646
Anderson Rand Ltd, pg 647
Antique Collectors' Club Ltd, pg 647
Appletree Press Ltd, pg 648
Arms & Armour Press, pg 648
Art Sales Index Ltd, pg 649
The Art Trade Press Ltd, pg 649
Arts Council of England, pg 649
Ashgate Publishing Ltd, pg 649
Aslib, The Association for Information Management, pg 650
Association of Commonwealth Universities (ACU), pg 650
Association for Science Education, pg 650
Barn Dance Publications Ltd, pg 652
BBC Worldwide Publishers, pg 653
Mitchell Beazley, pg 653

BIOS Scientific Publishers Ltd, pg 654
BLA Publishing Ltd, pg 655
A & C Black Publishers Ltd, pg 655
Blackstaff Press, pg 655
Blackwell Publishers, pg 655
Blandford Publishing Ltd, pg 656
Bloomsbury Publishing PLC, pg 656
Blueprint, pg 656
Book Marketing Ltd, pg 657
Books for Europe Ltd, pg 657
Boulevard Books UK/The Babel Guides, pg 657
Bradt Travel Guides Ltd, pg 658
Brassey's UK Ltd, pg 658
Bridge Books, pg 659
British Library Publications, pg 660
British Museum Press, pg 660
Brooklands Books Ltd, pg 660
Business Monitor International, pg 661
Cambridge University Press, pg 662
Canongate Books Ltd, pg 663
Cassell & Co, pg 664
Castlemead Publications, pg 665
Kyle Cathie Ltd, pg 665
Paul Cave Publications Ltd, pg 665
CBD Research Ltd, pg 665
Chadwyck-Healey Ltd, pg 666
Chatham Publishing, pg 667
Cicerone Press, pg 668
James Clarke & Co Ltd, pg 668
E W Classey Ltd, pg 668
Compendium Publishing, pg 670
Computer Step, pg 670
Constable Publishers, pg 670
The Continuum International Publishing Group Ltd, pg 670
Croner CCH Group Ltd, pg 672
CSA (Cambridge Scientific Abstracts), pg 672
CTBI Publications, pg 672
D&B Ltd, pg 673
The C W Daniel Co Ltd, pg 673
David & Charles Ltd, pg 674
Debrett's Peerage Ltd, pg 674
Andre Deutsch Ltd, pg 675
DMG Business Media Ltd, pg 675
Donhead Publishing Ltd, pg 675
East-West Publications (UK) Ltd, pg 677
Editon XII, pg 677
ELC International, pg 678
Edward Elgar Publishing Ltd, pg 678
Elsevier Science Ltd, pg 678
Encyclopaedia Britannica (UK) International Ltd, pg 679
estamp, pg 679
Estates Gazette, pg 679
Euromonitor PLC, pg 680
Europa Publications, pg 680
The Eurospan Group, pg 680
Faber & Faber Ltd, pg 681
Facet Publishing, pg 681
The Factory Shop Guide, pg 681
FHG Publications Ltd, pg 682
Financial World Publishing, pg 682
First & Best in Education Ltd, pg 682
Flicks Books, pg 683
Forbes Publications Ltd, pg 683
Foulsham Publishers, pg 683
Fourth Estate Ltd, pg 683
Francis Balsom Associates, pg 684
Samuel French Ltd, pg 684
Gale Research, pg 685
Geddes & Grosset, pg 686
Stanley Gibbons Publications, pg 687

Greenhill Books/Lionel Leventhal Ltd, pg 689
Guinness Publishing Ltd, pg 690
Robert Hale Ltd, pg 691
Hamlyn, pg 691
Harcourt Publishers Ltd, pg 691
Harden's Ltd, pg 692
Harley Books, pg 692
HarperCollins Publishers, pg 692
Harvard University Press, pg 692
Helicon Publishing Ltd, pg 694
Helm Information Ltd, pg 694
Hendon Publishing Co Ltd, pg 695
Heraldry Today, pg 695
Heritage Press, pg 695
Hilmarton Manor Press, pg 696
Hobsons, pg 696
Hodder & Stoughton Educational, pg 696
Hodder Headline Ltd, pg 696
Hollis Publishing Ltd, pg 697
Hoover's Business Press, pg 697
How To Books Ltd, pg 697
Hugo's Language Books Ltd, pg 697
ICC United Kingdom, pg 698
IFLA International Programme for UAP, pg 698
Institute of Physics Publishing, pg 700
International Communications, pg 701
The Islamic Texts Society, pg 701
James & James (Science Publishers) Ltd, pg 702
Jane's Information Group, pg 702
Michael Joseph Ltd, pg 703
Richard Joseph Publishers Ltd, pg 703
Kegan Paul International Ltd, pg 703
Kelly's, pg 704
Kemps Publishing Ltd, pg 704
Kingfisher Publications Plc, pg 704
Kogan Page Ltd, pg 705
Ladybird Books, pg 705
Law Pack Publishing Ltd, pg 706
Library & Information Statistics Unit, pg 707
Lion Publishing PLC, pg 708
LLP Ltd, pg 708
The Lutterworth Press, pg 709
Lyle Publications Ltd, pg 709
Macmillan Audio Books, pg 710
Macmillan Reference Ltd, pg 710
Management Books 2000 Ltd, pg 711
Peter Marcan Publications, pg 711
Market House Books Ltd, pg 712
Kenneth Mason Publications Ltd, pg 712
Adam Matthew Publications, pg 712
McGraw-Hill Publishing Company, pg 712
Media Research Publishing Ltd, pg 712
Melrose Press Ltd, pg 713
Methodist Publishing House, pg 714
Mirabel Books Ltd, pg 715
Muze UK Ltd, pg 716
NAG Press, pg 716
National Assembly for Wales, pg 717
National Foundation for Educational Research, pg 717
National Library of Scotland, pg 717
National Portrait Gallery Publications, pg 717
NCVO, pg 718
New Leaf Books Ltd, pg 719
Nile & Mackenzie Ltd, pg 719
NTC Publications Ltd, pg 720

Oilfield Publications Ltd, pg 720
The Oleander Press, pg 721
Open University Press, pg 721
Opus Book Publishing Ltd, pg 722
Oxfam, pg 722
Oxford University Press, pg 723
Palgrave Publishers Ltd, pg 723
Panos Institute, pg 723
Pen & Sword Books Ltd, pg 725
Penguin Books Ltd, pg 725
The Penguin Group UK, pg 726
Pharmaceutical Press, pg 726
PIRA Intl, pg 728
Professional Book Supplies Ltd, pg 730
Professional Engineering Publishing Ltd, pg 730
Quarto Publishing plc, pg 731
Queen Anne Press, pg 732
RAC Publishing, pg 732
Ramsay Head Press, pg 732
The Reader's Digest Association Ltd, pg 733
William Reed Directories, pg 734
Retail Entertainment Data Publishing Ltd, pg 735
Rough Guides Ltd, pg 735
Routledge, pg 736
Routledge Curzon, pg 736
The Rutland Press, pg 737
Sage Publications Ltd, pg 737
St Paul's Bibliographies Ltd, pg 738
Salamander Books Ltd, pg 738
Savannah Publications, pg 738
Shaw & Sons Ltd, pg 741
Sheed & Ward Ltd, pg 741
Silver Link Publishing Ltd, pg 742
Charles Skilton Ltd, pg 742
Colin Smythe Ltd, pg 743
Stacey International, pg 745
Harold Starke Publishers Ltd, pg 745
The Stationery Office, pg 745
Sutton Publishing Ltd, pg 746
Sweet & Maxwell Ltd, pg 746
I B Tauris & Co Ltd, pg 747
Telegraph Books, pg 748
Transport Bookman Publications Ltd, pg 750
Trigon Press, pg 750
University of Wales Press, pg 751
Vacation Work Publications, pg 752
Vacher Dod Publishing Ltd, pg 752
Veloce Publishing Ltd, pg 752
Verbatim, pg 752
Verulam Publishing Ltd, pg 753
Virago Press, pg 753
VNU Business Publications, pg 753
Voltaire Foundation Ltd, pg 753
The Watts Publishing Group Ltd, pg 754
Websters International Publishers Ltd, pg 755
Wilmington Business Information Ltd, pg 756
Philip Wilson Publishers, pg 757
Wordsworth Editions Ltd, pg 758

Uruguay
Instituto del Tercer Mundo, pg 760

Viet Nam
Science & Technics Publishing House, pg 763

Yugoslavia
Association of Yugoslav Publishers & Booksellers, pg 764
Narodna Biblioteka Srbije, pg 764
Naucna Knjiga, pg 764
Privredni Pregled, pg 765
Savremena Administracija, pg 765

PUBLISHERS

Turisticka Stampa, pg 766
Vuk Karadzic, pg 766

Zimbabwe
Bold ADS, pg 768
The Bulletin Newspaper, pg 768
Mercury Press Pvt Ltd, pg 769
National Archives of Zimbabwe, pg 769
Thomson Publications Zimbabwe (Pvt) Ltd, pg 769
University of Zimbabwe Publications, pg 769
Vision Publications, pg 769

FINE EDITIONS, ILLUSTRATED BOOKS

Albania
NL SH, pg 1

Argentina
Ediciones de Arte Gaglianone, pg 6
Quetzal-Domingo Cortizo, pg 8

Australia
Aeolian Press, pg 11
Art Gallery of South Australia Bookshop, pg 12
Artmoves, pg 12
Cornford Press, pg 19
Crawford House Publishing, pg 19
Dragon Press, pg 20
Gangan Publishing, pg 23
The Images Publishing Group Pty Ltd, pg 27
Incunabula Press, pg 27
Laurel Press, pg 29
Mountain House Press, pg 33
New Endeavour Press, pg 34
NMA Publications, pg 35
Pandani Press, pg 37
Plantagenet Press, pg 38
Plantain Park, pg 38
Raincloud Productions, pg 39
Random House Australia, pg 40
Rankin Publishers, pg 40
State Library of NSW Press, pg 43
State Publishing Unit of State Print SA, pg 43
Wellington Lane Press Pty Ltd, pg 47
Yanagang Publishing, pg 48

Austria
Annette Betz Verlag im Verlag Carl Ueberreuter, pg 49
Buchkultur Verlags GmbH Zeitschrift fuer Literatur & Kunst, pg 50
Carinthia Verlag, pg 50
Czernin Verlag, pg 50
Development News Ltd, pg 51
Diotima Presse, pg 51
Gangan Verlag, pg 52
Edition Graphischer Zirkel, pg 52
Haymon-Verlag GesmbH, pg 52
Karolinger Verlag GmbH & Co KG, pg 53
Edition Koenigstein, pg 54
Verlag Monte Verita, pg 55
Oesterreichischer Kunst und Kulturverlag, pg 56
E Perlinger Naturprodukte Handelsgesellschaft mbH, pg 57
Verlag Anton Pustet, pg 57
Thanhaeuser Edition, pg 59
Edition Thurnhof KEG, pg 59
Trauner Verlag, pg 59
Tyrolia Verlagsanstalt GmbH, pg 59

Universitaetsverlag Wagner GmbH, pg 60
Herbert Weishaupt Verlag, pg 60

Belarus
Belarus (The Belorussia), pg 63
Interdigets Publishing House, pg 63
Kavaler Publishers, pg 63

Belgium
Alamire vzw, Music Publishers, pg 64
Uitgeverij Clavis, pg 66
Editions De Boeck-Larcier SA, pg 67
Dexia Bank, pg 68
Glenat Benelux SA, pg 69
Groeninghe NV, pg 69
King Baudouin Foundation, pg 70
Uitgeverij Lannoo NV, pg 70
Claude Lefrancq Editeur, pg 71
Mercatorfonds NV, pg 72
La Renaissance du Livre, pg 73

Bermuda
Bermudian Publishing Co, pg 76

Brazil
Abril SA, pg 77
Action Editora Ltda, pg 77
AGIR S/A Editora, pg 78
Conquista, Empresa de Publicacoes Ltda, pg 81
Editora Elevacao, pg 82
Empresa Brasileira de Pesquisa Agropecaria, pg 83
Livraria Martins Fontes Editora Ltda, pg 83
Editora Globo SA, pg 84
Grafica Editora Primor Ltda, pg 84
LDA Editores Ltda, pg 86
Editora Manole Ltda, pg 87
Editora Marco Zero Ltda, pg 87
Editora Nova Fronteira SA, pg 88
Editora Primor Ltda, pg 90
Rede Das Artes (Boccato Editores Collector's), pg 90
Editora Revan Ltda, pg 90
Spala Editora Ltda, pg 92
Talento Publicacoes Editora e Grafica Ltda, pg 92
Editora da Universidade de Sao Paulo, pg 93

Bulgaria
Abagar Pablioing, pg 94
Abagar, Veliko Tarnovo, pg 94
Bulgarski Houdozhnik Publishers, pg 94
Fondacija Zlatno Kljuce, pg 95
Hermes Publishing House, pg 95
Heron Press Publishing House, pg 96
Kibea Publishing Co, pg 96
Publishing House Narodno delo OOD, pg 97

Chile
Editorial Cuarto Propio, pg 100
Museo Chileno de Arte Precolombino, pg 100

China
Beijing Arts & Crafts Publishing House, pg 102
Beijing Juvenile & Children's Books Publishing House, pg 102
Beijing Publishing House, pg 102
China Film Press, pg 103

Cultural Relics Publishing House, pg 105
Dolphin Books, pg 105
Fudan University Press, pg 105
Fujian Science & Technology Publishing House, pg 106
Morning Glory Publishers, pg 107
People's Sports Publishing House, pg 108
Qingdao Publishing House, pg 108
Science Press, pg 108
Shandong Education Publishing House, pg 108

Colombia
Editorial Santillana SA, pg 113

The Democratic Republic of the Congo
Facultes Catoliques de Kinshasa, pg 115

Costa Rica
Litografia Artex, SA, pg 116
Promesa, Ediciones, pg 116
Editorial de la Universidad de Costa Rica, pg 117

Croatia
ALFA dd za izdavacke, graficke i trgovacke poslove, pg 118
ArTresor naklada, pg 118
Matica hrvatska, pg 119

Cuba
Editorial Letras Cubanas, pg 121

Czech Republic
AULOS sro, pg 123
Jiri Chvojka, pg 123
Mariadan, pg 126
Nadace Lyry Pragensis, pg 126

Denmark
Borgens Forlag A/S, pg 130
Carit Andersens Forlag A/S, pg 131
Christian Ejlers' Forlag aps, pg 131
Forlaget Hovedland, pg 133
Mallings ApS, pg 133

Egypt (Arab Republic of Egypt)
Dar El Shorouk, pg 138
Dar El Shorouk Publishing & Distributing House, pg 138

Estonia
Ilmamaa, pg 140
Kunst Publishers Ltd, pg 140
Kupar Publishers, pg 140
National Library of Estonia, pg 140

Finland
Kustannus Oy Kolibri, pg 143
Tammi Publishers, pg 144

France
ACR Edition Internationale (Art Creation Realisation), pg 145
Actes Graphiques, pg 145
Adrian, pg 146
Adverbum SARL, pg 146
Editions Alternatives, pg 146
L'Amitie par le Livre, pg 147
Edition Anthese, pg 147
Art & Metiers Du Livre/Editions, pg 148
Compagnie Francaise des Arts Graphiques SA, pg 148
ATP - Packager, pg 149

TYPE OF PUBLICATION INDEX

Editions A Barthelemy, pg 149
Editions Bertout, pg 150
Bibliotheque des Arts, pg 150
Bibliotheque Nationale de France, pg 150
Societe Nouvelle Adam Biro, pg 150
William Blake & Co, pg 150
Editions Andre Bonne, pg 151
Michele Broutta Oeuvres Graphiques Contemporaines, pg 152
BSI - ELOR Editions Jeunesse, pg 152
Le Cadratin, pg 152
Editions Caracteres, pg 152
Editions Cenomane, pg 153
Chasse Maree-Armen, pg 154
Editions du Chene, pg 154
CPL- La Communication Par le Livre, pg 157
La Delirante, pg 158
Editions Denoel Sarl, pg 158
Editions Dis Voir, pg 159
Du May, pg 160
Edisud, pg 161
Editions Grund, pg 161
EPA SA (Editions Presse Audiovisuel), pg 162
Les Editions de l'Epargne, pg 162
Editions Errance, pg 162
Editions Fanlac, pg 163
Fata Morgana, pg 163
FBT de R Editions/Editions des Limbes d'Or, pg 163
Editions Filipacchi-Sonodip, pg 164
Groupe Fleurus-Mame, pg 164
Folklore Comtois, pg 164
Editions du Garde-Temps, pg 166
Hachette Pratiques, pg 167
Fernand Hazan Editeur SA, pg 168
Herscher, pg 168
Indigo & Cote-Femmes Editions, pg 169
Editions Interferences, pg 169
Interpublications, pg 170
Editions du Jaguar, pg 170
Editions Klincksieck, pg 171
Editions des Limbes d'Or/FBT de R Editions, pg 173
Editions Loubatieres, pg 174
Editions Lyonnaises d'Art et d'Histoire, pg 174
Editions Mango, pg 174
Editions Marie-Noelle, pg 175
Marval, pg 175
Masson-Williams et Wilkins, pg 175
Editions Medianes, pg 175
Editions Memo, pg 175
Editions Memoire des Arts, pg 175
Societe des Editions Menges, pg 175
Nanga, pg 177
Editions Norma, pg 177
Editions J H Paillet et B Drouaud, pg 178
Editions Parentheses, pg 179
Editions Christian Pirot, pg 180
Editions Plume, pg 180
Editions du Centre Pompidou, pg 180
Presses de l'Ecole Nationale des Ponts et Chaussees, pg 181
Editions Ramsay, pg 182
Revue Noire, pg 183
Yves Riviere Editeur, pg 183
Editions Robert Laffont, Nil, Fixot, Seghers, Julliard, pg 183
Editions Scala, pg 184
Nouvelles Editions Seguier, pg 184
Editions du Seuil, pg 185
Societe Nouveaux Loisirs, pg 185

801

TYPE OF PUBLICATION INDEX — BOOK

Sofradif Editions Philippe Auzou, pg 185
Somogy editions d'art, pg 186
Stil, pg 186
Editions Pierre Terrail/Finest SA, pg 187
Thames & Hudson, pg 187
Alain Thomas Editeur, pg 188
Ulisse Edition, pg 188
Editions Unes, pg 188
Publications de l'Universite de Pau, pg 188
La Vague Verte, pg 188
Editions Van de Velde, pg 188
Galerie Lucie Weill-Seligmann, pg 189
Zodiaque, pg 190

Germany

Albert Propster Verlag und Buchhandlung, pg 192
Verlag und Antiquariat Frank Albrecht, pg 192
Arnoldsche Verlagsanstalt GmbH, pg 195
Ars Edition GmbH, pg 195
Babel Verlag Kevin Perryman, pg 197
Dr Bachmaier Verlag GmbH, pg 197
Edition Balance Marion Gunther Bonsack, pg 198
Bartkowiaks Forum Book Art, pg 198
Dr Wolfgang Baur Verlag Kunst & Alltag, pg 199
Verlag C H Beck (OHG), pg 200
Beerenverlag, pg 200
Berliner Handpresse Wolfgang Joerg und Erich Schonig, pg 201
Bibliographisches Institut & F A Brockhaus AG, pg 203
Brigg Verlag Franz-Joset Buchler KG, pg 206
Brunnen-Verlag GmbH, pg 207
Christian Verlag GmbH, pg 210
CTL-Presse Clemens-Tobias Lange, pg 212
Die Deutsche Bibliothek/Deutsche Buecherei Leipzig, pg 213
Deutsche Landwirtschaft-Gesellschaft VerlagsgesGmbH, pg 214
Eugen Diederichs Verlag GmbH & Co KG, pg 216
Dieterichsche Verlagsbuchhandlung Mainz, pg 216
Maximilian Dietrich Verlag, pg 216
Droste Verlag GmbH, pg 218
DuMont Buchverlag GmbH & Co KG, pg 219
DuMont Monte, pg 219
Edition Solitude - Akademie Schloss Solitude, pg 221
Egmont vgs verlagsgesellschaft mbH, pg 221
Ellert & Richter Verlag GmbH, pg 222
Verlag Esoterische Philosophie GmbH, pg 224
Extent Verlag und Service Wolfgang M Flamm, pg 225
F Bruckmann Munchen Verlag & Druck GmbH & Co Produkt KG, pg 225
Fahrner & Fahrner, pg 226
Frederking & Thaler Verlag GmbH, pg 230
Verlag Freies Geistesleben, pg 230
G Braun (vormals G Braun'sche Hofbuchdruckerei und Verlag) Gmbh, pg 231
Gerstenberg Verlag, pg 232

Gondrom Verlag GmbH & Co KG, pg 233
Graefe und Unzer Verlag GmbH, pg 233
Greven Verlag Koeln GmbH, pg 234
Walter Haedecke Verlag, pg 236
Harenberg Kommunikation Verlags- und Medien GmbH & Co KG, pg 237
Hatje Cantz Verlag, pg 238
Dr Ernst Hauswedell & Co Verlag, pg 238
Heigl Verlag, Horst Edition, pg 239
G Henle Verlag, pg 239
Hertenstein, Axel, Hernstein-Presse, pg 240
Hestra-Verlag Hernichel & Dr Strauss GmbH & Co KG, pg 240
Erika Heydick Sax-Verlag Beucha, pg 240
Wilhelm Heyne Verlag, pg 240
Anton Hiersemann, Verlag, pg 240
Hirmer Verlag GmbH, pg 241
Hoffmann und Campe Verlag GmbH, pg 242
Hyperion - Verlag, pg 244
Jan Thorbecke Verlag GmbH & Co, pg 246
Jovis Verlag GmbH, pg 246
Knesebeck Verlag, pg 250
Knowledge Media International, pg 251
W Kohlhammer GmbH, abt Haussortiment, pg 252
KONTEXTverlag, pg 252
Koptisch-Orthodoxes Zentrum, pg 252
Ambro Lacus, Buch- und Bildverlag Walter Kremnitz, pg 255
Karl Robert Langewiesche Nachfolger Hans Koester KG, pg 256
Verlag Laterna magica GmbH & Co KG, pg 256
Verlag fuer Lehrmittel Poessneck GmbH, pg 256
Leipziger Universitaetsverlag GmbH, pg 257
Edition Libri Illustri GmbH, pg 257
Wolfgang Mann-Verlag GmbH, pg 260
Mannerschwarm Skript Verlag Bartholomae & Co OHG, pg 260
Maro Verlag und Druck, Benno Kasmayr, pg 261
Mergus Verlag GmbH Hans A Baensch, pg 263
Merlin Verlag Andreas Meyer Verlags GmbH und Co KG, pg 263
modo verlag GmbH, pg 264
Edition Monika, pg 265
Mueller & Schindler Verlag, pg 265
C W Niemeyer Buchverlage GmbH, pg 268
Nusser Verlag, pg 269
Edition Octopus & Okeanos Presse, pg 269
Verlag Friedrich Oetinger GmbH, pg 270
One Way Medien OHG, pg 270
Pendragon Verlag, pg 272
Pfaffenweiler Presse, pg 272
Podzun-Pallas Verlag GmbH, pg 274
Prasenz Verlag der Jesus Bruderschaft eV, pg 274
Guido Pressler Verlag, pg 275
Verlag fur Regionalgeschichte, pg 277
Regura Verlag, pg 277
Dr Ludwig Reichert Verlag, pg 278

Verlag Th Schaefer im Vicentz Verlag KG, pg 282
Richard Scherpe Verlag GmbH, pg 283
Rudolf Schneider Verlag, pg 284
Verlag Schnell und Steiner GmbH, pg 284
Theodor Schuster, pg 285
Dr Wolfgang Schwarze Verlag, pg 286
Sigloch Edition Helmut Sigloch GmbH & Co KG, pg 286
Silberburg-Verlag Titus Haeussermann GmbH, pg 287
L Staackmann Verlag KG, pg 288
Staatliche Museen Kassel, pg 288
Stapp Verlag Wolfgang Stapp, pg 289
Steiger Verlag, pg 289
Edition Gunter Stoberlein, pg 290
Straelener Manuskripte Verlag, pg 290
Svato Zapletal, pg 291
teNeues Verlag GmbH & Co KG, pg 292
Tiessen, Wolfgang, Moderne, pg 294
Tipress Dienstleistungen fur das Verlagswesen GmbH, pg 294
Titania-Verlag Ferdinand Schroll, pg 294
Dorothea van der Koelen, pg 297
Verein der Benediktiner zu Beuron-Beuroner Kunstverlag, pg 297
Edition Curt Visel, pg 298
VS Verlagshaus Stuttgart GmbH, pg 299
Uwe Warnke Verlag, pg 300
Ziethen-Panorama Verlag GmbH, pg 305
Zweimuehlen Verlag GmbH, pg 305
Zweipunkt Verlag K Kaiser KG, pg 305

Ghana

World Literature Project, pg 308

Greece

Akritas, pg 308
Alexiadou Vefa Editions, pg 309
Apostoliki Diakonia tis Ekklisias tis Hellados, pg 309
Beta Medical Publishers, pg 309
Diachronikes Ekdoseis, pg 309
Ekdotike Athenon SA, pg 310
Evrodiastasi, pg 310
Govostis Publishing SA, pg 311
Hestia's I D Hestia-Kollaros & Co Corporation, pg 311
Editions Kalentis, pg 312
Kastaniotis Editions SA, pg 312
Melissa Publishing House, pg 313
Orfanidis Publications, pg 314
Patakis Publishers, pg 314
To Rodakio, pg 315

Hungary

Aranyhal Konyvkiado Goldfish Publishing, pg 323
Kiiarat Konyvdiado, pg 324
Officina Nova, Koenyv-es Lapkiado/Bertelsmann Media Kft, pg 324

Iceland

Forlagid, pg 327
Frodi Ltd, pg 328
Mal og menning, pg 328
Setberg, pg 328

India

Addison-Wesley (Singapore) Pte Ltd, pg 329
Brijbasi Printers Pvt Ltd, pg 334
India Book House Pvt Ltd, pg 339
Reliance Publishing House, pg 347
Roli Books Pvt Ltd, pg 348

Ireland

Tir Eolas, pg 364

Israel

Bitan Publishers Ltd, pg 365
DAT Publications, pg 366
Dvir Publishing Ltd, pg 366
Inbal Publishers, pg 368

Italy

A & A, pg 374
Adea Edizioni, pg 374
Alberti Libraio Editore, pg 375
Umberto Allemandi & C SRL, pg 375
Gruppo Editoriale Armenia SpA, pg 376
Arsenale Editrice SRL, pg 376
Artema, pg 377
Artioli Editore in Modena, pg 377
Belforte Editore Libraio srl, pg 377
BeMa, pg 377
Biblos srl, pg 378
Giuseppe Bonanno Editore, pg 378
Casa Editrice Bonechi, pg 378
Bonechi-Edizioni Il Turismo Srl, pg 378
Edizioni Bora SNC di E Brandani & C, pg 378
Campanotto, pg 379
Il Castoro, pg 380
Il Cigno Galileo Galilei-Edizioni di Arte e Scienza, pg 381
Citta Nuova Editrice, pg 382
Colonnese Editore, pg 382
Edizioni Dedalo SRL, pg 384
Edizioni del Capricorno, pg 384
Edizioni Della Torre di Salvatore Fozzi & C SAS, pg 384
Di Baio Editore SpA, pg 385
Direzione Generale Archivi, pg 385
EDIFIR SRL, pg 386
Edizioni d'Arte e Moderna, Edam, pg 386
Edizioni Mediterranee SRL, pg 387
Essegi, pg 388
ETR (Editrice Trasporti su Rotaie), pg 388
FEDA SA, pg 388
Federico Motta Editore SpA, pg 389
Fenice 2000, pg 389
Festina Lente Edizioni, pg 389
Folini, pg 389
Edizioni Frassinelli SRL, pg 389
Edizioni Futuro SRL, pg 389
Giunti (Gruppo Editoriale), pg 390
Grafica e Arte SRL, pg 391
Ernesto Gremese Editore SRL, pg 391
Gremese International Srl, pg 391
Idea Books, pg 393
Editoriale Jaca Book SpA, pg 394
Jandi-Sapi Editori, pg 394
Kaos Edizioni SRL, pg 395
L'Airone Editrice, pg 395
Laruffa Editore SRL, pg 395
L'Erma di Bretschneider SRL, pg 395
Levante, pg 395
Lindau, pg 396
Linea d'Ombra Libri, pg 396
Angelo Longo Editore, pg 396
Luni, pg 397
Magnus Edizioni SpA, pg 397

PUBLISHERS

Giorgio Mondadori & Associati, pg 399
Moretti & Vitali editori srl, pg 400
Giorgio Nada Editore SRL, pg 400
NodoLibri, pg 401
OCTAVO Franco Cantini Editore, pg 401
Leo S Olschki, pg 402
Maria Pacini Fazzi Editore, pg 402
Franco Cosimo Panini Editore SpA, pg 402
Amilcare Pizzi SpA, pg 403
Il Pomerio, pg 404
Priuli e Verlucca, Editori, pg 404
RAI.ERI, pg 405
RCS Rizzoli Libri SpA, pg 405
Reverdito Edizioni, pg 405
Rossato, pg 406
Rubbettino Editore, pg 406
Salerno Editrice SRL, pg 406
Fausto Sardini Editrice, pg 407
Scala Group spa, pg 407
SEMAR Publishers SRL, pg 407
Sicania, pg 408
Silvana Editoriale SpA, pg 408
Edizioni Rosminiane Sodalitas, pg 408
Tappeiner, pg 409
Turris, pg 410
Vaccari SRL, pg 411
Vinciana Editrice sas, pg 411
Vivere In SRL, pg 411
Viviani Editore srl, pg 412

Japan
Genko-Sha, pg 416
Hoikusha Publishing Co Ltd, pg 417
Kosei Publishing Co Ltd, pg 420
Nigensha Publishing Co Ltd, pg 422
Seibido Shuppan Company Ltd, pg 424
Shincho-Sha Co Ltd, pg 425
Tankosha Publishing Co Ltd, pg 427

Kenya
Camerapix Publishers International Ltd, pg 431
Kenway Publications Ltd, pg 432

Democratic People's Republic of Korea
Korea Science and Encyclopedia Publishing House, pg 434

Republic of Korea
Youl Hwa Dang Publisher, pg 436
Omun Gak, pg 439

Latvia
Liesma Publishers, pg 442
Madris, pg 442
Preses Nams, pg 442

Liechtenstein
Frank P van Eck Publishers, pg 444

Lithuania
AS Narbuto Leidykla (AS Narbutas' Publishers), pg 445
Lietus Ltd, pg 445
Lithuanian National Museum Publishing House, pg 446

Luxembourg
Editions Emile Borschette, pg 447
Edition Objectif Lune, pg 447
Editions Phi, pg 448

Macau
Livros Do Oriente, pg 448
Museu Maritimo, pg 448

The Former Yugoslav Republic of Macedonia
St Clement of Ohrid National & University Library, pg 449
Zumpres Publishing Firm, pg 449

Mauritius
Editions de l'Ocean Indien Ltd, pg 457
Vizavi Editions, pg 457

Mexico
Editorial AGATA SA de CV, pg 457
Artes de Mexico y del Mundo, SA de CV, pg 458
Ediciones Culturales Internacionales SA de CV Edicion Compra y Venta de Libros, Casetes, Videos, pg 459
Editorial Diana SA de CV, pg 459
Edamex SA de CV, pg 460
Editorial Edicol SA, pg 460
Ediciones Era SA de CV, pg 460
Fondo Editorial de la Plastica Mexicana, pg 461
Editorial Jilguero, SA de CV, pg 462
Editorial Limusa SA de CV, pg 463
Instituto Nacional de Antropologia e Historia, pg 464
Naves Internacional de Ediciones SA, pg 464
Promociones de Mercados Turisticos SA de CV, pg 466
SCRIPTA - Distribucion y Servicios Editoriales, SA de CV, pg 467

Monaco
Editions EGC, pg 468

Morocco
Editions Le Fennec, pg 470
Editions Oum, pg 470

Netherlands
Gaberbocchus Press, pg 477
De Harmonie, pg 478
HES & De Graaf Publishers BV, pg 478
Uitgeverij Heuff Nieuwkoop, pg 478
Hotei Publishing, pg 478
Miland Publishers, pg 481
Mondria Publishers, pg 481
Omega Boek BV, pg 482
The Pepin Press, pg 482
Smeets Illustrated Projects, pg 484
Uitgeverij Het Spectrum BV, pg 484
Stedelijk Van Abbemuseum, pg 484
Steltman Editions, pg 484
Twente University Press, pg 485

New Zealand
The Caxton Press, pg 490
Hazard Press Ltd, pg 491
David Ling Publishing, pg 493

Oman
Apex Publishing, pg 506

Pakistan
Sang-e-Meel Publications, pg 509

TYPE OF PUBLICATION INDEX

Peru
Ediciones Peisa (Promocion Editorial Inca SA), pg 511

Philippines
Cacho Publishing House, Inc, pg 512

Poland
Biblioteka Narodowa, pg 516
BOSZ scp, pg 516
Ludowa Spoldzielnia Wydawnicza, pg 518
Norbertinum, pg 518
Rosikon Press, pg 519
Videograf II Sp z o o Zaklad Poracy Chronionej, pg 520
Wydawnictwo Baturo, pg 521

Portugal
Arvore Coop de Actividades Artisticas, CRL, pg 522
Contexto Editora, pg 524
Difusao Cultural, pg 524
Dinalivro, pg 524
Distri Cultural Lda, pg 524
Distri Editora Lda, pg 524
Edicoes ELO, pg 524
Editorial Estampa, Lda, pg 524
Gradiva-Publicacnoes Lda, pg 525
Imprensa Nacional-Casa da Moeda, pg 526
Latina Livraria, pg 526
Editorial Presenca, pg 528
Quimera Editores, pg 529
Edicioes Joao Sa da Costa Lda, pg 529
Solivros, pg 529
Teorema, pg 529

Romania
Alcor-Edimpex (Verlag) Ltd, pg 531
Enzyklopadie Verlag, pg 533
Editura Humanitas, pg 533
Humanitas Publishing House, pg 533
Mentor Kiado, pg 534
Editura Meridiane, pg 534
Editura Minerva, pg 534
Editura Paideia, pg 535
Saeculum IO, pg 535
Est-Samuel Tastet Verlag, pg 536
Vestala Verlag, pg 536

Russian Federation
Interbook-Business AO, pg 538
Izdatelstvo Iskusstvo, pg 538
Izvestia Sovetov Narodnyh Deputatov Russian Federation (RF), pg 539
Izdatelstvo Khudozhestvennaya Literatura, pg 539
Izdatelstvo Kniga, pg 539
Izdatelstvo Mir, pg 540
Obdeestro Znanie, pg 541
Panorama Publishing House, pg 541
Permskaja Kniga, pg 541
Planeta Publishers, pg 541
Profizdat, pg 541

Singapore
Aquanut Agencies Pte Ltd, pg 545
Archipelago Press, pg 545

Slovenia
Mladinska Knjiga International, pg 552

South Africa
The Brenthurst Press (Pty) Ltd, pg 553
Erudita Publications (Pty) Ltd, pg 554
Fernwood Press (Pty) Ltd, pg 554
Human & Rousseau (Pty) Ltd, pg 555
Janssen Publishers CC, pg 556
Johannesburg Art Gallery, pg 556
New Africa Books (Pty) Ltd, pg 557
Reader's Digest Southern Africa, pg 559
Struik Publishers (Pty) Ltd, pg 559

Spain
Editorial Acanto SA, pg 561
Editorial Algazara, pg 562
Alinco SA - Aura Comunicacio, pg 563
Ambit Serveis Editorials, SA, pg 563
Calambur Editorial, SL, pg 566
Carroggio SA de Ediciones, pg 566
Editorial Casariego, pg 566
Celeste Ediciones, pg 567
Editora Comercial de Publicaciones, pg 568
Compania Literaria, pg 568
Consello da Cultura Galega - CCG, pg 568
Ediciones Daly S L, pg 569
Ediciones Doce Calles SL, pg 570
Ediciones l'Isard, S L, pg 571
Ediles-Ediciones Leonesas SA, pg 572
El Viso, SA Ediciones, pg 572
Ediciones Elfos SL, pg 572
Ediciones Encuentro SA, pg 573
Naipes Heraclio Fournier SA, pg 574
Vicent Garcia Editores, SA, pg 575
Grijalbo Mondadori SA, pg 576
Hercules de Ediciones, SA, pg 577
Idea Books, SA, pg 578
Editorial Juventud SA, pg 579
Editorin Laiovento SL, pg 579
Liber Ediciones, SA, pg 580
Lunwerg Editores, SA, pg 580
Editorial Mediterrania SL, pg 582
M Moleiro Editor, SA, pg 582
Editorial Noray, pg 584
Ediciones del Oriente y del Mediterraneo, pg 585
Plastic Comunicacion SL, pg 587
Instituto Provincial de Investigaciones y Estudios Toledanos, pg 588
Rueda, SL Editorial, pg 589
Universidad de Santiago de Compostela, pg 589
Silex Ediciones, pg 590
Equipo Sirius SA, pg 591
Ediciones Siruela SA, pg 591
Edicions 62, pg 591
Grup 62, pg 591
Tesitex, SL, pg 592
Tf Editores, pg 592
Trea Ediciones, SL, pg 593
Turner Publicaciones, pg 593
Publicacions de la Universitat de Barcelona, pg 594

Sweden
Bokforlaget Atlantis AB, pg 600
Bokforlaget Bra Bocker AB, pg 600
Bokforlaget Settern AB, pg 601
BOOX, pg 601
Byggforlaget, pg 601
Bengt Forsbergs Foerlag AB, pg 602

803

TYPE OF PUBLICATION INDEX   BOOK

Natur och Kultur/LTs foerlag, pg 604
Wahlstrom & Widstrand, pg 607

Switzerland

Ammann Verlag & Co, pg 608
Armenia Editions, pg 608
AT Verlag, pg 608
U Baer Verlag, pg 609
Benteli Verlag, pg 609
Christoph Merian Verlag, pg 611
Diogenes Verlag AG, pg 612
Erker-Verlag, pg 613
Verlag Gachnang & Springer, Bern-Berlin, pg 614
Giampiero Casagrande Editore, pg 614
Pierre Gonin Editions d'Art, pg 615
Junod Nicholas, pg 616
Galerie Kornfeld & Co, pg 617
Kossodo Verlag AG, pg 617
Kranich-Verlag, Dres AG & H R Bosch-Gwalter, pg 617
Bernard Letu Editeur, pg 618
Lars Mueller Publishers, pg 619
Neue Zuercher Zeitung AG Buchverlag, pg 620
Orell Fuessli Verlag, pg 620
Parkett Publishers Inc, pg 621
Editiones Roche, pg 623
Editions Scriptar SA, pg 624
Edition Stemmle AG, pg 625
Versus Verlag AG, pg 627
Verlag im Waldgut AG, pg 627
Werner Druck AG, pg 627
J E Wolfensberger AG, pg 628

Taiwan, Province of China

Art Book Co Ltd, pg 629
Designer Publisher Inc, pg 629
Echo Publishing Company Ltd, pg 629
Highlight Publishing Company Ltd, pg 630
Kuang Fu Book Co Ltd, pg 630

United Republic of Tanzania

Central Tanganyika Press, pg 633

Thailand

Sang Dad Publishing Company Ltd, pg 635

Tunisia

Ceres Editions, pg 637
Maison Tunisienne de l'Edition, pg 638

Turkey

Arkeoloji Ve Sanat Yayinlari, pg 639
Dost Yayinlari San Ve Tic Ltd, pg 639

Ukraine

Mystetstvo Publishers, pg 643

United Arab Emirates

Motivate Publishing, pg 644

United Kingdom

Umberto Allemandi & Co Publishing, pg 646
Architectural Association Publications, pg 648
Art Books International Ltd, pg 649
Ashgate Publishing Ltd, pg 649
Ashmolean Museum Publications, pg 650

Atlas Press, pg 651
Mitchell Beazley, pg 653
Blackstaff Press, pg 655
Blandford Publishing Ltd, pg 656
Book Packaging & Marketing, pg 657
Books for Europe Ltd, pg 657
Books of Zimbabwe Publishing Co (Pvt) Ltd, pg 657
Bridge Books, pg 659
British Library Publications, pg 660
Camerapix Publishers Intl Ltd, pg 662
Canongate Books Ltd, pg 663
Cardinal Publishing Ltd, pg 663
Cockbird Press, pg 669
Conran Octopus, pg 670
Conway Maritime Press, pg 671
Leo Cooper, pg 671
Cottage Publications, pg 671
Defiant Publications, pg 675
Elfande Ltd, pg 678
The Erskine Press, pg 679
Faber & Faber Ltd, pg 681
The Fraser Press, pg 684
Garnet Publishing Ltd, pg 685
Genesis Publications Ltd, pg 686
Hamlyn, pg 691
The Harvill Press Ltd, pg 693
Hawk Books, pg 693
Alan Hutchison Ltd, pg 698
The Islamic Texts Society, pg 701
James & James (Publishers) Ltd, pg 702
Michael Joseph Ltd, pg 703
Kegan Paul International Ltd, pg 703
Mainstream Publishing Co (Edinburgh) Ltd, pg 711
Manchester University Press, pg 711
Maney Publishing, pg 711
Marcham Books, pg 711
Merrell Publishers Ltd, pg 713
Mirabel Books Ltd, pg 715
National Portrait Gallery Publications, pg 717
New Cavendish Books, pg 718
Newpro UK Ltd, pg 719
Octopus Publishing Group, pg 720
Osprey Publishing Ltd, pg 722
Parapress Ltd, pg 724
Pavilion Books Ltd, pg 724
Phaidon Press Ltd, pg 726
Piatkus Books, pg 727
Pickering & Chatto (Publishers) Ltd, pg 727
Plexus Publishing Ltd, pg 728
Prion Books Ltd, pg 730
Quentin Books Ltd, pg 732
Reaktion Books Ltd, pg 733
RotoVision SA, pg 735
Ryland Peters & Small Ltd, pg 737
Salamander Books Ltd, pg 738
Shepheard-Walwyn (Publishers) Ltd, pg 741
The Society for Promoting Christian Knowledge (SPCK), pg 743
Harold Starke Publishers Ltd, pg 745
Sutton Publishing Ltd, pg 746
Taschen UK Ltd, pg 747
I B Tauris & Co Ltd, pg 747
John Taylor Book Ventures, pg 747
Tern Press, pg 748
Textile & Art Publications Ltd, pg 748
Transedition Ltd, pg 749
Trigon Press, pg 750
Veloce Publishing Ltd, pg 752
Webb & Bower (Publishers) Ltd, pg 755

Websters International Publishers Ltd, pg 755
Wordwright Publishing, pg 758

Uzbekistan

Izdatelstvo Literatury i isskustva, pg 761

Yugoslavia

Alfa-Narodna Knjiga, pg 764

Zimbabwe

National Archives of Zimbabwe, pg 769

FOREIGN LANGUAGE & BILINGUAL BOOKS

Afghanistan

Ministry of Education, Department of Educational Publications, pg 1
Pushtu Toulana, Afghan Academy, pg 1

Albania

State Textbook Publishing House, pg 1

Argentina

Editorial Idearium de la Universidad de Mendoza (EDIUM), pg 5
Ediciones Preescolar SA, pg 8

Australia

Bayda Books, pg 14
Boinkie Publishers, pg 15
Boombana Publications, pg 16
China Books, pg 18
CIS Publishers, pg 18
Curriculum Corporation, pg 19
Flora Publications International Pty Ltd, pg 23
Gangan Publishing, pg 23
Hospitality Press Pty Ltd, pg 26
Illert Publications, pg 27
The Images Publishing Group Pty Ltd, pg 27
Institute of Aboriginal Development (IAD Press), pg 28
Int Press, pg 28
Little Red Apple Publishing, pg 30
Lonely Planet Publications Pty Ltd, pg 30
Magabala Books Aboriginal Corporation, pg 31
Mimosa Publications Pty Ltd, pg 33
Pearson Education Australia, pg 37
Stafford Books, pg 43
State Library of NSW Press, pg 43
Tom Publications, pg 45

Austria

Gangan Verlag, pg 52
Langenscheidt-Verlag GmbH, pg 54
Merbod Verlag, pg 55
Thomas Mlakar Verlag, pg 55
oebv & hpt Verlagsgesellschaft mbH & Co KG, pg 56
Osterreichischer Bundesveilag Ges.mbh, pg 57
Richard Pils Publication P, pg 57
Roetzer Druck GmbH & Co KG, pg 58
Andreas Schnider Verlags-Atelier, pg 58
Edition Thurnhof KEG, pg 59
Verlag Mag Wanzenbock, pg 60
Wieser Verlag, pg 61

Azerbaijan

Sada, Literaturno-Izdatel'skij Centr, pg 61

Bangladesh

Ankur Prakashani, pg 62

Belarus

Junactva, Vydavectva, pg 63
Kavaler Publishers, pg 63
Izdatelstvo Mastatskaya Litarutura, pg 63
Narodnaya Asveta, pg 63
Publishing Center of Belarus State University, pg 63

Belgium

Assimil NV, pg 64
Coda, pg 66
Ediblanchart sprl, pg 68
King Baudouin Foundation, pg 70
Marabout, pg 72
Stichting Ons Erfdeel VZW, pg 74
Uitgeverij De Garve, pg 75
Vander Editions, SA, pg 75
Vita, pg 75
Vlaamse Esperantobond VZW, pg 75
Zuid-Nederlandse Uitgeverij NV/ Central Uitgeverij, pg 76

Brazil

Ao Livro Tecnico Industria e Comercio Ltda, pg 78
Ars Poetica Editora Ltda, pg 79
Callis Editora Ltda, pg 80
Editorial Dimensao Ltda, pg 81
E P U Editora Pedagogica e Universitaria Ltd, pg 81
Hemus Editora Ltda, pg 85
Editora Kuarup Ltda, pg 86
Waldyr Lima Editora, pg 86
Editora Mundo Cristao, pg 88
Editora Nova Alexandria Ltda, pg 88
Editora Revan Ltda, pg 90

Bulgaria

Abagar Pablioing, pg 94
Bojko Kacarmazov, pg 94
CHRIKER, pg 94
Factor-Alias, pg 95
Interpres, pg 96
Kibea Publishing Co, pg 96
Naouka i Izkoustvo, Ltd, pg 97
Prosveta Publishers as, pg 97
Prozoretz Ltd Publishing House, pg 97
Seven Hills Publishers, pg 97
Svetra Publishing House, pg 98

Chile

Arrayan Editores, pg 99

China

Beijing Publishing House, pg 102
Beijing University Press, pg 102
Chemical Industry Press, pg 102
China Film Press, pg 103
China Ocean Press, pg 103
China Translation & Publishing Corp, pg 104
Chinese Pedagogics Publishing House, pg 104
CITIC Publishing House, pg 104
Commercial Press (Hong Kong) Ltd, pg 104
Education Science Publishing House, pg 105

PUBLISHERS

Foreign Language Teaching & Research Press, pg 105
Foreign Languages Press, pg 105
Fudan University Press, pg 105
Guizhou Education Publishing House, pg 106
Heilongjiang Science & Technology Press, pg 106
Higher Education Press, pg 106
Inner Mongolia Science & Technology Publishing House, pg 106
Jilin Science & Technology Publishing House, pg 106
Lanzhou University Press, pg 107
Liaoning People's Publishing House, pg 107
Morning Glory Publishers, pg 107
Nanjing University Press, pg 107
The Nationalities Publishing House, pg 107
New Times Press, pg 107
Qingdao Publishing House, pg 108
Science Press, pg 108
Shandong Friendship Press, pg 108
Shandong University Press, pg 109
Shanghai Educational Publishing House, pg 109
Shanghai Foreign Language Education Press, pg 109
Tianjin Science & Technology Publishing House, pg 109
World Affairs Press, pg 110
Wuhan University Press, pg 110
Zhejiang Education Publishing House, pg 110
Zhejiang University Press, pg 110
Zhong Hua Book Co, pg 110

Colombia
Asociacion Instituto Linguistico de Verano, pg 111
Pearson Educacion de Colombia LTDA, pg 113
Editorial Santillana SA, pg 113

The Democratic Republic of the Congo
Centre Protestant d'Editions et de Diffusion (CEDI), pg 115
Facultes Catoliques de Kinshasa, pg 115

Costa Rica
Centro Agronomico Tropical de Investigacion y Ensenanza (CATIE), pg 115
Promesa, Ediciones, pg 116
Scout Interamericana, pg 117
Editorial Texto Ltda, pg 117
Union Mundial para la Naturaleza (UICN), Oficina Regional para Mesoamerica, pg 117

Croatia
ArTresor naklada, pg 118
Durieux d o o, pg 118
Faust Vrani, pg 118
Edit Niro (Novinska-izdavacka radna organizacija), pg 119
Sveucilisna tiskara doo, pg 120
Vitagraf, pg 120

Cuba
Editora Politica, pg 121

Czech Republic
Aventinum Nakladatelstvi, pg 123
Karmelitanske Nakladatelstvi, pg 125
Konias, pg 125

Nadace Lyry Pragensis, pg 126
Votobia sro, pg 129

Denmark
Kaleidoscope Publishers Ltd, pg 133
Samfundslitteratur, pg 135
Systime, pg 136

Egypt (Arab Republic of Egypt)
Al Arab Publishing House, pg 138
Dar Al-Kitab Al-Masri, pg 138
Dar al-Nahda al Arabia, pg 138
Dar El Shorouk Publishing & Distributing House, pg 138
Elias Modern Publishing House, pg 138
Dar Al Maaref, pg 139
Ummah Press for Translation & Publishing, pg 139

Estonia
Perioodika, pg 140

Finland
Kaantopiiri Oy, pg 142
Kirja-Leitzinger, pg 143
Yliopistopaino/Helsinki University Press, pg 145

France
Editions Al Liamm, pg 146
Editions Assimil SA, pg 148
Aubanel SA, pg 149
Editions Bertout, pg 150
William Blake & Co, pg 150
Emgleo Breiz, pg 151
Brud Nevez, pg 152
Editions Caracteres, pg 152
Librairie Jose Corti, pg 156
Counseil International de la Langue Francaise, pg 157
La Delirante, pg 158
Georges-Charles Demay, pg 158
Editions Dis Voir, pg 159
Les Editeurs Reunis, pg 161
Institut d'Etudes Slaves, pg 163
Editions Farel, pg 163
Flammarion SA, pg 164
Association Frank, pg 165
Paul Geuthner Librairie Orientaliste, pg 166
Hachette Livre, pg 167
L'Harmattan, pg 168
Hemma Joven, SA, pg 168
Indigo & Cote-Femmes Editions, pg 169
Langues & Mondes/L'Asiatheque, pg 171
Librairie Larousse, pg 172
Magnard SA, pg 174
Centre National de la Recherche Scientifique, pg 177
Noir Sur Blanc, pg 177
Editions Norma, pg 177
Editions Ophrys, pg 178
Peeters-France, pg 179
Presses de la Sorbonne Nouvelle/PSN, pg 181
Editions Prosveta SA, pg 182
Realisations pour l'Enseignement Multilingue International (REMI), pg 182
Service des Publications Scientifiques du Museum National d'Histoire Naturelle, pg 184
Sofradif Editions Philippe Auzou, pg 185
Editions Pierre Terrail/Finest SA, pg 187

UNESCO Publishing, pg 188
YMCA-Press, pg 189
Pierre Zech Editeur, pg 189

French Polynesia
Scoop/Au Vent des Iles, pg 190

Georgia
Merani Publishing House, pg 190

Germany
A Francke Verlag (Tubingen und Basel), pg 191
AOL-Verlag Frohmut Menze, pg 194
ARCult Media, pg 194
Arnoldsche Verlagsanstalt GmbH, pg 195
Ars Edition GmbH, pg 195
Aschendorffsche Verlagsbuchhandlung GmbH & Co KG, pg 195
Aulis Verlag Deubner & Co KG, pg 197
Babel Verlag Kevin Perryman, pg 197
Bauverlag GmbH, pg 199
Bergverlag Rudolf Rother GmbH, pg 200
C Bertelsmann Verlag GmbH, pg 201
Bertelsmann Lexikon Verlag GmbH, pg 201
Bibliographisches Institut & F A Brockhaus AG, pg 203
Helmut Buske Verlag GmbH, pg 208
Dr Cantz'sche, Druckerei GmbH & Co, Cantz Verlag, pg 209
Compact Verlag GmbH, pg 211
Copress Verlag, pg 211
Cornelsen Verlag GmbH & Co OHG, pg 211
Verlag fuer Deutsch GmbH, pg 213
Deutscher Taschenbuch Verlag GmbH & Co KG (dtv), pg 215
Dieterichsche Verlagsbuchhandlung Mainz, pg 216
Domowina Verlag GmbH, pg 217
Verlag Duerr & Kessler GmbH, pg 219
Edition Solitude - Akademie Schloss Solitude, pg 221
N G Elwert Verlag, pg 222
Festo Didactic GmbH & Co, pg 227
Konkursbuch Verlag Claudia Gehrke, pg 231
Brigitte Grabitz - ikoo Buchverlag, pg 233
Verlag der Stiftung Gralsbotschaft GmbH, pg 234
Walter de Gruyter GmbH & Co KG, pg 234
Haering, Siegfried, Literaten-Verlag Ulm, pg 236
Horlemann Verlag, pg 243
Max Hueber Verlag GmbH & Co KG, pg 243
Hyperion - Verlag, pg 244
IKO Verlag fur Interkulturelle Kommunikation, pg 244
Insel Verlag, pg 245
Klaus Isele, pg 245
ludicium Verlag GmbH, pg 245
Jovis Verlag GmbH, pg 246
Ernst Klett Verlag GmbH, pg 250
Koptisch-Orthodoxes Zentrum, pg 252
Karin Kramer Verlag, pg 253
Kubon Und Sagner, pg 254
Kunstverlag Weingarten GmbH, pg 254

TYPE OF PUBLICATION INDEX

Laaber-Verlag, pg 255
Langenscheidt KG, pg 256
Libertas- Europaeisches Institut GmbH, pg 257
Hildegard Liebaug-Dartmann, pg 258
Logophon Lehrmittelverlag GmbH, pg 258
Karin Mader, pg 260
Monia Verlag, pg 265
Verlag Stephanie Naglschmid, pg 266
Gunter Narr Verlag, pg 266
Neuthor - Verlag, pg 268
Osho Verlag GmbH, pg 271
Erich Roeth-Verlag, pg 279
Romiosini Verlag, pg 280
Ruhland Verlag Gimblt, pg 281
Verlag Schnell und Steiner GmbH, pg 284
Stadler Verlagsgesellschaft mbH, pg 288
Verlag Stahleisen GmbH, pg 289
Stauffenburg Verlag Brigitte Narr GmbH, pg 289
Tipress Dienstleistungen fur das Verlagswesen, pg 294
Turkischer Schulbuchverlag Onel Cengiz, pg 295
Dorothea van der Koelen, pg 297
Vervuert Verlagsgesellschaft, pg 298
Vogel Medien GmbH & Co KG, pg 299
Zambon Verlag, pg 305
Ziethen-Panorama Verlag GmbH, pg 305

Ghana
Anowuo Educational Publications, pg 306
Bureau of Ghana Languages, pg 306
Ghana Institute of Linguistics Literacy & Bible Translation (GILLBT), pg 307
Ghana Publishing Corporation, pg 307
Sedco Publishing Ltd, pg 308

Greece
Akritas, pg 308
Athina, Mary Mavrogiannis, pg 309
Eleftheroudakis, GCSA International Bookstore, pg 310
Hestia-I D Hestia-Kollaros & Co Corporation, pg 311
Michalis Sideris, pg 313
Nakas Music House, pg 313
Pagoulatos G-G P Publications, pg 314
Scripta, pg 315
Spyropoulos A, pg 315
S J Zacharopoulos SA Publishing Co, pg 316

Guadeloupe
Librairie Generale JASOR, pg 316

Hong Kong
The Chinese University Press, pg 319
Chopsticks Publications Ltd, pg 319
The Dharmasthiti Buddist Institute Ltd, pg 319
Hong Kong University Press, pg 320
Island Press, pg 320
Joint Publishing (HK) Co Ltd, pg 320
Ling Kee Publishing Group, pg 320

805

TYPE OF PUBLICATION INDEX   BOOK

Research Centre for Translation, pg 321
Shanghai Book Co Ltd, pg 321

Hungary
Balassi Kiado Kft, pg 323
Corvina Books Ltd, pg 323
Nemzeti Tankoenyvkiado, pg 326

India
Asian Educational Services, pg 331
Bharat Publishing House, pg 332
Bharatiya Vidya Bhavan, pg 333
Bihar Hindi Granth Akademi, pg 333
Brijbasi Printers Pvt Ltd, pg 334
S Chand & Co Ltd, pg 334
Diamond Comics (P) Ltd, pg 336
General Book Depot, pg 337
Gyan Publishing House, pg 338
Kitab Ghar, pg 341
Sri Ramakrishna Math, pg 342
Motilal Banarsidass Publishers Pvt Ltd, pg 343
Neeta Prakashan, pg 344
Sri Satguru Publications, pg 349, 351
Star Publications (P) Ltd, pg 351
Suman Prakashan Pvt Ltd, pg 351
N M Tripathi Pvt Ltd, pg 352

Indonesia
Bina Aksara Parta, pg 354

Iraq
National House for Publishing, Distributing and Advertising, pg 358

Ireland
Ballinakella Press, pg 358
Clo Iar-Chonnachta Teo, pg 359
The Educational Company of Ireland, pg 360
On Stream Publications Ltd, pg 363

Israel
Achiasaf Publishing House Ltd, pg 365
Agudat Sabah, pg 365
Breslov Research Institute, pg 366
Carta, The Israel Map & Publishing Co Ltd, pg 366
Dekel Publishing House, pg 366
Eretz Hemdah Institute for Advanced Jewish Studies, pg 367
Gefen Publishing House Ltd, pg 367
(JDC) Brookdale Institute of Gerontology & Adult Human Development in Israel, pg 369
Prolog Publishing House, pg 371
Rubin Mass Ltd, pg 371
Schlesinger Institute, pg 372
Urim Publications, pg 373
Y L Peretz Publishing Co, pg 374

Italy
Umberto Allemandi & C SRL, pg 375
BeMa, pg 377
Campanotto, pg 379
Edistudio di Brunetto Casini, pg 380
Cideb Editrice SRL, pg 381
Ciranna - Roma, pg 381
Cittadella Editrice, pg 382
CLUEB (Cooperativa Libraria Universitaria Editrice Bologna), pg 382

Costa e Nolan SpA, pg 383
M d'Auria Editore SAS, pg 384
Editrice Edisco, pg 386
Ernesto Gremese Editore SRL, pg 391
Gruppo Editoriale Faenza Editrice SpA, pg 392
Guerra Edizioni Guru Azp, pg 392
Kompass Fleischmann, pg 395
L'Erma di Bretschneider SRL, pg 395
Levante, pg 395
Lybra Immagine, pg 397
Macmillan Heinemann ELT, pg 397
Giorgio Nada Editore SRL, pg 400
Istituto Nazionale di Studi Romani, pg 400
OCTAVO Franco Cantini Editore, pg 401
Pizzicato Edizioni Musicali, pg 403
Pontificio Istituto Orientale, pg 404
Priuli e Verlucca, Editori, pg 404
Psicologica Editrice, pg 404
Riccardo Ricciardi Editore SpA, pg 405
Rossato, pg 406
SEMAR Publishers SRL, pg 407
Vaccari SRL, pg 411
Vianello Libri, pg 411

Japan
Baberu Inc, pg 414
Chuo-Tosho Co Ltd, pg 415
Contex Corporation, pg 415
Hakusui-Sha Co Ltd, pg 417
Hayakawa Publishing Inc, pg 417
Hoikusha Publishing Co Ltd, pg 417
The Hokuseido Press, pg 417
Hyoronsha Publishing Co Ltd, pg 417
Japan Broadcast Publishing Co Ltd, pg 418
The Japan Times, pg 418
Kaitakusha, pg 419
Myrtos Inc, pg 421
Nippon Hoso Shuppan Kyokai (NHK Publishing), pg 422
Nobunkyo (Rural Village Culture Association), pg 423
Obunsha Co Ltd, pg 423
Rinsen Book Co Ltd, pg 424
Sanshusha Publishing Co, Ltd, pg 424
Seibido, pg 424
Shufunotomo sha Co Ltd, pg 426
3A Corporation, pg 427
Toho Book Store, pg 427
Tsukiji Shokan Publishing Co, pg 428
Yakuji Nippo Ltd, pg 429
Yohan Shuppan, pg 429

Kazakstan
Kazakh Al-Farabi State National University, pg 430
Kazakhstan, Izd-Vo, pg 430
Zazusy, pg 430

Kenya
Focus Publications Ltd, pg 431

Democratic People's Republic of Korea
The Foreign Language Press Group, pg 434
Foreign Languages Publishing House, pg 434

Republic of Korea
Gim-Yeong Co, pg 436
Hollym Corporation Publishers, pg 437
Hongik Media Plus Ltd, pg 437
Koreaone Press Inc, pg 438
Kukmin Doseo Publishing Co Inc, pg 438
Moon Jin Media Co Ltd, pg 438
Omun Gak, pg 439
Oriental Books, pg 439
Pyeong-hwa Chulpansa, pg 439
Twenty-First Century Publishers, Inc, pg 440
Word of Life Press, pg 440

Latvia
Nordik/Tapals Publishers Ltd, pg 442

Lebanon
Arab Institute for Research and Publishing, pg 442
Dar Al-Kitab Alloubnani, pg 443
Dar Al-Maaref-Liban Sarl, pg 443
Librairie Orientale sal, pg 443
World Book Publishing, pg 443

Lesotho
Mazenod Book Centre, pg 444

Lithuania
AS Narbuto Leidykla (AS Narbutas' Publishers), pg 445
Dargenis Publishers, pg 445
Lietuvos Informacijos Institutas, pg 446
Lietuvos Rasytoju Sajungos Leidykla, pg 446
Mokslo ir enciklopediju leidybos institutas, pg 446
Margi Rastai Publishers, pg 446
Sviesa Publishers, pg 446
Vaga Ltd, pg 446

Luxembourg
Cahiers Luxembourgeois, pg 447
Varkki Verghese, pg 448

Macau
Museu Maritimo, pg 448

The Former Yugoslav Republic of Macedonia
Detska radost, pg 448
Medis, Skopje, pg 449
Murgorski Zoze, pg 449
St Clement of Ohrid National & University Library, pg 449

Madagascar
Foibe Filan-Kevitry NY Mpampianatra (FOFIPA), pg 450
Librarie Mixte, pg 450
Imprimerie Takariva, pg 450

Malaysia
Penerbit Fajar Bakti Sdn Bhd, pg 454

Martinique
George Lise-Huyghes des Etages, pg 456

Mexico
Centro de Estudios Mexicanos y Centroamericanos, pg 458
Editorial Diana SA de CV, pg 459

Ediciones Euroamericanas, pg 461
Lasser Press Mexicana SA de CV, pg 462
Phillip Richard Conover Lazo, pg 462
Editorial Limusa SA de CV, pg 463
Sistemas Tecnicos de Edicion SA de CV, pg 467

Republic of Moldova
Lumina Publishing House, pg 468

Monaco
Editions EGC, pg 468

Morocco
Editions La Porte, pg 470

Myanmar
Hanthawaddy Book House, pg 471

Namibia
Bureau for Indigenous Languages, pg 471
Gamsberg Macmillan Publishers (Pty) Ltd, pg 471

Netherlands
Uitgeverij Jan van Arkel, pg 473
H W Blok Uitgeverij BV, pg 474
BoekWerk, pg 474
BZZTOH Publishers, pg 475
Prometheus, pg 483
Servire BV Uitgevers, pg 484
Sociaal en Cultureel Planbureau, pg 484
Uitgeverij G A van Oorschot bv, pg 486

New Zealand
Maori Publications Unit, pg 493
Shearwater Associates Ltd, pg 495
Te Reo Publications, pg 496

Nigeria
Alliance West African Publishers & Co, pg 498
Hudanuda Publishing Co Ltd, pg 499
Ilesanmi Press (Educational Publishers) Ltd, pg 499
Longman Nigeria Plc, pg 500
Thomas Nelson (Nigeria) Ltd, pg 500
Northern Nigerian Publishing Co Ltd, pg 500
Nwamife Publishers Ltd, pg 500
Onibon-Oje Publishers, pg 501
Riverside Communications, pg 501
University Publishing Co, pg 502

Norway
NKI Forlaget, pg 504

Pakistan
HMR Publishing Co, pg 507

Panama
Focus Publications International SA, pg 509

Peru
Ediciones Brown SA, pg 511
Ediciones Peisa (Promocion Editorial Inca SA), pg 511

PUBLISHERS

Philippines
De La Salle University, pg 513
Sonny A Mendoza, pg 513

Poland
Energeia sp zoo Wydawnictwo, pg 516
Katolicki Uniwersytet Wydawniczo-Redakcja, pg 517
Wydawnictwo Literackie, pg 517
Wydawnictwo Lodzkie, pg 517
Oficyna Wydawnicza Politechniki Wroclawskiej, pg 519
Rosikon Press, pg 519
'Slask' Ltd, pg 520
Wydawnictwo TPPR Wspolpraca, pg 520
Wydawn Na Sprawa' Wydawniczo-Oswiatowa Spotdzielnia Inwalidow, pg 521
Wydawnictwa Uniwersytetu Warszawskiego, pg 521

Portugal
Atica, SA Editores e Livreiros, pg 522
Bertrand Editora Lda, pg 522
Brasilia Editora (J Carvalho Branco), pg 523
Edicoes Colibri, pg 523
Contexto Editora, pg 524
Didactica Editora, pg 524
DIFEL - Difusao Editorial SA, pg 524
Dinalivro, pg 524
Edicoes ELO, pg 524
Editora Replicacao Lda, pg 529
Solivros, pg 529

Puerto Rico
Editorial Cordillera Inc, pg 530
Ediciones Huracan Inc, pg 530
Piedras Press, Inc, pg 531
Publishing Resources Inc, pg 531
University of Puerto Rico Press (EDUPR), pg 531

Romania
Editura Academiei Romane, pg 531
Alcor-Edimpex (Verlag) Ltd, pg 531
Ars Longa Publishing House, pg 532
Editura Cronos SRL, pg 532
Editura Didactica si Pedagogica, pg 532
Editura Eminescu, pg 533
Enzyklopadie Verlag, pg 533
Editura Excelsior, pg 533
Editura Humanitas, pg 533
Humanitas Publishing House, pg 533
Editura Institutul European, pg 533
Editura Junimea, pg 534
Editura Kriterion SA, pg 534
MAST Verlag, pg 534
Editura Militara, pg 534
Monitorul Oficial, Editura, pg 534
Editura Niculescu, pg 534
Editura Paideia, pg 535
Pandora Publishing House, pg 535
Polirom Verlag, pg 535
Est-Samuel Tastet Verlag, pg 536
Editura Teora, pg 536

Russian Federation
Airis Press, pg 537
BLIC, russko-Baltijskij informaciionnyj centr, AO, pg 537
Finansy i Statistika Publishing House, pg 538
Interbook-Business AO, pg 538
Izdatelstvo Iskusstvo, pg 538
Izdatelstvo Khudozhestvennaya Literatura, pg 539
Izdatelstvo Muzyka, pg 540
Okoshko Ltd Publishers (Izdatelstvo), pg 541
Progress Publishers, pg 541
Raduga Publishers, pg 541
Russkij Jazyk, pg 541
Izdatelstvo Vysshaya Shkola, pg 543

Saudi Arabia
King Saud University, pg 543
Saudi Publishing and Distribution House, pg 543

Senegal
Centre de Linguistique Appliquee, pg 544
CODESRIA (Council for the Development of Social Science Research in Africa), pg 544

Sierra Leone
United Christian Council Literature Bureau, pg 545

Singapore
Aquanut Agencies Pte Ltd, pg 545
Archipelago Press, pg 545
Chopsons Pte Ltd, pg 545
Europhone Language Institute (Pte) Ltd, pg 546
Graham Brash Pte Ltd, pg 546
Pustaka Nasional Pte Ltd, pg 547
World Scientific Publishing Co Pte Ltd, pg 549

Slovakia
Vydavatelstvo Obzor, pg 550
Priroda, pg 550
Slo Viet, pg 550
Slovenske pedagogicke nakladateistvo, pg 550
Sofa, pg 551

Slovenia
Franc-Franc podjetje za promocijo kulture Murska Sobota d o o, pg 551
Zalozba Mihelac d o o, pg 552

South Africa
HAUM - De Jager Publishers, pg 555
HAUM (Hollandsch Afrikaansche Uitgevers Maatschappij), pg 555
Ithemba! Publishing, pg 555
LAPA Publishers (Pty) Ltd, pg 556
Maskew Miller Longman, pg 557
The Methodist Publishing House, pg 557
Nasou Via Afrika, pg 557
Shuter & Shooter (Pty) Ltd, pg 559
Taurus, pg 560
Van Schaik Publishers, pg 560
Vivlia Publishers & Booksellers, pg 560

Spain
Editorial AEDOS SA, pg 561
Anglo-Didactica, SL Editorial, pg 563
Editorial Ariel SA, pg 564
Editorial Barcanova SA, pg 565
Editorial Clie, pg 568
Ediciones Daly S L, pg 569
Didaco Comunicacion y Didactica, SA, pg 569
Ediciones Doce Calles SL, pg 570
Edilux, pg 572
Emece Editores, pg 573
Editorial Gulaab, pg 577
Ediciones Hiperion SL, pg 577
Icaria Editorial SA, pg 577
Idea Books, SA, pg 578
Editorial Incafo SA, pg 578
Larousse Planeta SA, pg 579
Lid Editorial Empresarial, SL, pg 580
Lynx Edicions, pg 580
Macmillan Heinemann ELT, pg 581
Editorial Moll SL, pg 582
Ediciones del Oriente y del Mediterraneo, pg 585
Plastic Comunicacion SL, pg 587
Silex Ediciones, pg 590
Sociedad General Espanola de Libreria SA - SGEL, pg 591
Stanley Editorial, pg 591
Ediciones 29 - Libros Rio Nuevo, pg 594
Universidad de Navarra, Ediciones SA, pg 594
Editorial Verbum SL, pg 595
Vinaches Lopez, Luisa, pg 595

Sri Lanka
Gihan Book Shop, pg 597
Inter-Cultural Book Promoters, pg 597
Lake House Investments Ltd, pg 597

Sudan
Al-Ayam Press Co Ltd, pg 598
Khartoum University Press, pg 598

Sweden
Bokforlaget Rediviva, Facsimileforlaget, pg 600
Ekelunds Forlag AB, pg 601
Folkuniversitetets foerlag, pg 602
Hallgren och Fallgren Studieforlag AB, pg 603
Invandrarfoerlaget, pg 603
Hans Richter Laromedel, pg 604
Frank Stenvalls Forlag, pg 606

Switzerland
Armenia Editions, pg 608
Birkhauser Verlag AG, pg 610
Castle Publications SA, pg 611
Cockatoo Press (Schweiz), Thailand-Publikationen, pg 611
Edizioni Armando Dado, Tipografia Stazione, pg 612
Dimension World Ltd, pg 612
Duboux Editions SA, pg 612
GVA Publishers Ltd, pg 615
Kolumbus-Verlag, pg 617
Lia rumantscha, pg 618
Lars Mueller Publishers, pg 619
Editions du Panorama, pg 621
Parkett Publishers Inc, pg 621
Editions Patino, pg 621
Editions Pro Schola, pg 622
Schweizerisches Jugendschriftenwerk, SJW, pg 624
Editions Scriptar SA, pg 624
Viktoria-Verlag Peter Marti, pg 627

Taiwan, Province of China
Highlight Publishing Company Ltd, pg 630
Hsiao Yuan Publication Co, Ltd, pg 630

TYPE OF PUBLICATION INDEX

Jillion Publishing Co, pg 630
Youth Cultural Publishing Co, pg 632

United Republic of Tanzania
East African Publishing House, pg 633
Eastern Africa Publications Ltd, pg 633
Inland Publishers, pg 633
Institute of Kiswahili Research, pg 633
Oxford University Press, pg 634

Thailand
Bandansan, pg 635
Bannakhan, pg 635
Duang Kamon, pg 635
Graphic Art Publishing, pg 635
Khlang Withaya Pub, pg 635
Non, pg 635
Pikkhanet Kanphim, pg 635
Sang Dad Publishing Company Ltd, pg 635
Soemwit Barwakhan, pg 635
Suksit Siam Co Ltd, pg 635
Sut Phaisan, pg 636
Thai Watana Panich Co, Ltd, pg 636
Viratham, pg 636

Tunisia
Academie Tunisienne des Sciences, des Lettres et des Arts Beit El Hekma, pg 637
Ceres Editions, pg 637
Maison Tunisienne de l'Edition, pg 638

Turkey
ABC Kitabevi AS, pg 638
Inkilap Publishers Ltd, pg 640
Redhouse Press, pg 641
Saray Medikal Yayin Tic Ltd Sti, pg 641
Yapi-Endustri Merkezi Yayinlari-Yem Yayin, pg 642

Uganda
Roce (Consultants) Ltd, pg 642

Ukraine
ASK Ltd, pg 643
Dnipro, pg 643
Osvita, pg 643

United Arab Emirates
Motivate Publishing, pg 644

United Kingdom
Acair Ltd, pg 645
Aris & Phillips Ltd, pg 648
Arnold, pg 648
Atlas Press, pg 651
b small publishing, pg 651
BBC English, pg 652
Berlitz (UK) Ltd, pg 654
Bible Society, pg 654
Bloodaxe Books Ltd, pg 656
Books for Europe Ltd, pg 657
Books International, pg 657
Bridge Books, pg 659
Centre for Information on Language Teaching & Research (CILT), pg 666
Chambers Harrap Publishers Ltd, pg 666
Chapter Two, pg 666
Peter Collin Publishing Ltd, pg 669

TYPE OF PUBLICATION INDEX   BOOK

European Schoolbooks Ltd, pg 680
The Greek Bookshop, pg 689
Gwasg y Dref Wen, pg 690
Gwasg Gwenffrwd, pg 690
HarperCollins Publishers, pg 692
Haynes Publishing, pg 693
Hilmarton Manor Press, pg 696
Angus Hudson Ltd, pg 697
Hugo's Language Books Ltd, pg 697
ICC United Kingdom, pg 698
International Bee Research Association, pg 701
Islam International Publications Ltd, pg 701
Kingfisher Publications Plc, pg 704
Letterbox Library, pg 707
Linguaphone Institute Ltd, pg 708
Y Lolfa Cyf, pg 708
Macmillan Heinemann ELT, pg 710
Magi Publications, pg 710
Willem A Meeuws Publisher, pg 713
Nelson Thornes Ltd, pg 718
Octopus Publishing Group, pg 720
Old Vicarage Publications, pg 720
Packard Publishing Ltd, pg 723
Pathfinder London, pg 724
Pearson Education Europe, Mideast & Africa, pg 725
School of Oriental & African Studies, pg 739
St Pauls Publishing, pg 744
Textile & Art Publications Ltd, pg 748
Verulam Publishing Ltd, pg 753
World Microfilms Publications Ltd, pg 758

Uruguay
EQ Opciones en Educacion, pg 760
A Monteverde y Cia SA, pg 760

Uzbekistan
Izdatelstvo Literatury i isskustva, pg 761

Venezuela
Armitano Editores CA, pg 761

Viet Nam
Science & Technics Publishing House, pg 763

Yugoslavia
Forum, pg 764
Libertatea, pg 764
Sluzbeni List, pg 765

Zambia
Lundula Publishing House, pg 766

Zimbabwe
College Press Publishers (Pvt) Ltd, pg 768

GENERAL TRADE BOOKS - HARDCOVER

Argentina
Colmegna SA, pg 4

Australia
Aerospace Publications, pg 11
Allen & Unwin Pty Ltd, The Australian Newspaper, Vogel Breads, pg 11
Australian Scholarly Publishing, pg 14
Barbara Beckett Publishing Pty Ltd, pg 14
Cookery Book, pg 18
Crawford House Publishing, pg 19
Enterprise Publications, pg 22
Florilegium, pg 23
Hale & Iremonger Pty Ltd, pg 24
Histec Publications, pg 26
Hodder Headline Australia, pg 26
Hyland House Publishing Pty Ltd, pg 27
Institute of Aboriginal Development (IAD Press), pg 28
Joval Publications, pg 29
Gregory Kefalas Publishing, pg 29
Lansdowne Publishing Pty Ltd, pg 29
Life Planning Foundation of Australia, Inc, pg 30
Lightbild PTY Ltd, pg 30
Magabala Books Aboriginal Corporation, pg 31
Melbourne University Press, pg 33
Mulini Press, pg 34
Navarine Publishing, pg 34
New Era Publications Australia Pty Ltd, pg 34
Anne O'Donovan Pty Ltd, pg 35
Off the Shelf Publishing, pg 35
Pascal Press, pg 37
Pearson Education Australia, pg 37
Penguin Books Australia Ltd, pg 37
Queensland Art Gallery, pg 39
R & R Publications Marketing P/L, pg 39
Rams Skull Press, pg 40
Random House Australia, pg 40
Slouch Hat Publications, pg 42
Social Club Books, pg 42
State Library of NSW Press, pg 43
The Text Publishing Company Pty Ltd, pg 44
Thames & Hudson (Australia) Pty Ltd, pg 44
Caroline Thornton, pg 44
Turton & Armstrong Publishers Pty Ltd, pg 45
University of New South Wales Press Ltd, pg 46
University of Western Australia Press, pg 46
Vital Publications, pg 47
Windhorse Books, pg 48

Austria
Christian Brandstatter Verlagsgesellschaft GmbH, pg 50
Buchkultur Verlags GmbH Zeitschrift fuer Literatur & Kunst, pg 50
Carinthia Verlag, pg 50
Czernin Verlag, pg 50
Verlag Harald Denzel, Auto- und Freizeitfuehrer, pg 51
Franz Deuticke Verlagsges mbH, pg 51
Development News Ltd, pg 51
Edition S der OSD, pg 51
Verlag Lynkeus/H Hakel Gesellschaft, pg 52
Herold Business Data AG, pg 52
Kremayr & Scheriau Verlag, pg 54
Leopold Stocker Verlag, pg 54
Linde Verlag Wien GmbH, pg 54
Niederosterreichisches Pressehaus Druck- und Verlagsgesellschaft mbH, pg 55
Verlag Orac im Verlag Kremayr & Scheriau, pg 56
Verlag des Osterr Kneippbundes GmbH, pg 57
Anna Pichler Verlag GmbH, pg 57
Promedia Verlagsges mbH, pg 57
Verlag Anton Pustet, pg 57
Studien Verlag Gmbh, pg 59

Belarus
Interdigets Publishing House, pg 63

Belgium
Altina, pg 64
Coda, pg 66
Claude Lefrancq Editeur, pg 71
Michelin Editions des Voyages, pg 72
Pelckmans NV, De Nederlandsche Boekhandel, pg 73
Prodim SPRL, pg 73

Benin
Les Editions du Flamboyant, pg 76

Brazil
Companhia Editora Forense, pg 82
Forense Universitaria Editora, pg 83
Ordem do Graal na Terra, pg 84
Editora Harbra Ltda, pg 84
LDA Editores Ltda, pg 86
Madras Editora, pg 87
Editora Nova Fronteira SA, pg 88
Pallas Editora e Distribuidora Ltda, pg 89

Bulgaria
Abagar Pabloing, pg 94
Aratron, IK, pg 94
Dolphin Press Group Ltd, pg 95
Kibea Publishing Co, pg 96
Nov Covek Publishing House, pg 97
Reporter, pg 97

Burundi
Editions Intore, pg 98

Chile
Pontificia Universidad Catolica de Chile, pg 101

China
Book Marketing Ltd, pg 102
China Foreign Economic Relations & Trade Publishing House, pg 103
China Materials Management Publishing House, pg 103
Commercial Press (Hong Kong) Ltd, pg 104
Fudan University Press, pg 105
Kunlun Publishing House, pg 107
Qingdao Publishing House, pg 108

The Democratic Republic of the Congo
Centre de Vulgarisation Agricole, pg 115

Costa Rica
Academia de Centro America, pg 115
Litografia Artex, SA, pg 116
Editorial Texto Ltda, pg 117

Cote d'Ivoire
Universite d' Abidjan, pg 118

Croatia
Znaci Vremena, Institut Za Istrazivanje Biblije, pg 120

Czech Republic
Aventinum Nakladatelstvi, pg 123
Granit SRO, pg 124
Jota, pg 125
Pavla Momcilova, pg 126
NLN, Ltd The Lidove noviny Publishing House, pg 127
Paseka, pg 127
Prostor, Ltd, pg 128
Svojtka & Co, pg 128
Zvon, pg 129

Denmark
Atuakkiorfik A/S Det Greenland Publishers, pg 130
Borgens Forlag A/S, pg 130
Christian Ejlers' Forlag aps, pg 131
GEC Gads Forlag Aktieselskab af 1994, pg 132
P Haase & Sons Forlag A/S, pg 132
Forlaget Hjulet, pg 132
Holkenfeldt 3, pg 133
New Era Publications International ApS, pg 134
Politisk Revy, pg 134
Samlerens Forlag A/S, pg 135
Scandinavia Publishing House, pg 135
Det Schonbergske Forlag, pg 135
Unitas Forlag, pg 136

Egypt (Arab Republic of Egypt)
Dar El Shorouk Publishing & Distributing House, pg 138
The Egyptian Society for the Dissemination of Universal Culture and Knowledge (ESDUCK), pg 138

Estonia
Kunst Publishers Ltd, pg 140
Mats Publishers Ltd, pg 140

Finland
Herattaja-yhdistys Ry, pg 142
Karisto Oy, pg 142
Koala-Kustannus/Oy Greenbay House Publishing Ltd, pg 143
Otava Publishing Co Ltd, pg 143
Recallmed Oy, pg 144

France
Editions A M Metailie, pg 145
Actes Graphiques, pg 145
Editions Albin Michel, pg 146
Editions Alternatives, pg 146
L'Amitie par le Livre, pg 147
Editions Amrita SA, pg 147
APRD - Association pour la Recherche et l'Information demographiques, pg 147
ATP - Packager, pg 149
Editions de l'Aube, pg 149
Autrement Editions, pg 149
Editions A Barthelemy, pg 149
Editions Bertout, pg 150
Pierre Bordas et Fils, pg 151
Le Cadratin, pg 152
Editions des Cahiers Bourbonnais, pg 152
Editions Casterman, pg 153
Editions Cenomane, pg 153
Jacqueline Chambon, pg 154
Editions Chiron, pg 154
CPL- La Communication Par le Livre, pg 157
De Vecchi Editions SA, pg 158
Edisud, pg 161
Edition1, pg 161
EPA SA (Editions Presse Audiovisuel), pg 162

L'Esprit Du Temps, pg 162
Editions Fanlac, pg 163
Federation Francaise de la Randonnee Pedestre, pg 164
Editions Filipacchi-Sonodip, pg 164
Flammarion SA, pg 164
Les Editions Franciscaines SA, pg 165
Editions du Garde-Temps, pg 166
L'Harmattan, pg 168
Fernand Hazan Editeur SA, pg 168
Editions du Jaguar, pg 170
Editions Jean-Claude Lattes, pg 170
Editions Universitaires LCF, pg 172
Editions Loubatieres, pg 174
Editions Josette Lyon, pg 174
Editions Mango, pg 174
Editions Medianes, pg 175
Editions Mediaspaul, pg 175
Editions Franck Mercier, pg 176
Nil Editions, pg 177
Editions Norma, pg 177
Editions Odile Jacob, pg 178
Editions Christian Pirot, pg 180
Presses de la Cite, pg 180
Les Presses du Management, pg 181
Editions Robert Laffont, Nil, Fixot, Seghers, Julliard, pg 183
Editions Saint-Michel SA, pg 183
Le Serpent a Plumes, pg 184
Sofradif Editions Philippe Auzou, pg 185
Somogy editions d'art, pg 186
Editions Stock, pg 186
Editions Pierre Terrail/Finest SA, pg 187
Alain Thomas Editeur, pg 188
Editions Tiresias Michel Reynaud, pg 188
Editions Viviane Hamy, pg 189
Pierre Zech Editeur, pg 189

French Polynesia

Scoop/Au Vent des Iles, pg 190

Germany

ADAC Verlag GmBH, pg 191
AOL-Verlag Frohmut Menze, pg 194
Arbeiterpresse Verlag GmbH, pg 194
ARCult Media, pg 194
Ars Edition GmbH, pg 195
Augustus Verlag, pg 196
Autovision Verlag Guther Co, pg 197
Aviatic Verlag GmbH, pg 197
Dr Wolfgang Baur Verlag Kunst & Alltag, pg 199
Beleke KG Verlag, pg 200
Bertelsmann Lexikon Verlag GmbH, pg 201
BLV Verlagsgesellschaft mbH, pg 204
Verlag Georg D W Callwey GmbH & Co, pg 208
Dr Cantz'sche, Druckerei GmbH & Co, Cantz Verlag, pg 209
Verlag Deutsche Unitarier, pg 214
Dharma Edition, Tibetisches Zentrum, pg 216
Dietz Verlag Berlin GmbH, pg 217
Christoph Dohr, pg 217
Donat Verlag, pg 217
Drei Brunnen Verlag GmbH & Co, pg 218
Droemersche Verlagsanstalt Th Knaur Nachfolger GmbH & Co, pg 218
DRW-Verlag Weinbrenner-GmbH & Co, pg 219
Ehrenwirth Verlag, pg 221

Elektor-Verlag GmbH, pg 222
Englisch Verlag GmbH, pg 222
Verlag am Eschbach GmbH, pg 224
Esogetics GmbH, pg 224
Eulenhof-Verlag Wolfgang Ehrhardt Heinold, pg 224
Fabel-Verlag Gudrun Liebchen, pg 226
Fachbuchverlag Pfanneberg & Co, pg 226
Franz Ferzak World & Space Publications, pg 227
Flechsig Buchvertrieb, pg 228
Franz-Sales-Verlag, pg 229
Frederking & Thaler Verlag GmbH, pg 230
Friedrich Kiehl Verlag GmbH, pg 230
Gatzanis Verlags GmbH, pg 231
Genius Verlag, pg 231
H Gietl Verlag & Publikationsservice GmbH, pg 232
GLB Parkland Verlags-und Vertriebs GmbH, pg 232
Graefe und Unzer Verlag GmbH, pg 233
Verlag der Stiftung Gralsbotschaft GmbH, pg 234
Gunter Olzog Verlag GmbH, pg 235
Walter Haedecke Verlag, pg 236
Heel Verlag GmbH, pg 238
Heigl Verlag, Horst Edition, pg 239
Horlemann Verlag, pg 243
Jovis Verlag GmbH, pg 246
SachBuchVerlag Kellner, pg 248
Kleiner Bachmann Verlag fur Kinder und Umwelt, pg 250
Knesebeck Verlag, pg 250
Knowledge Media International, pg 251
Koehler und Amelang Verlagsgesellschaft mbH, pg 251
Adam Kraft Verlag, pg 253
Kunstverlag Weingarten GmbH, pg 254
Karl Robert Langewiesche Nachfolger Hans Koester KG, pg 256
Libertas- Europaeisches Institut GmbH, pg 257
Gustav Luebbe Verlag, pg 259
Verlagsgruppe Luebbe GmbH & Co KG, pg 259
Lusatia Verlag-Dr Stuebner & Co KG, pg 259
Maro Verlag und Druck, Benno Kasmayr, pg 261
Matthias-Gruenewald-Verlag GmbH, pg 261
Metropolis- Verlag fur Okonomie, Gesellschaft und Politik GmbH, pg 263
J B Metzler'sche Verlagsbuchhandlung, pg 263
Meyer & Meyer Fachverlag und Buchhandel GmbH, pg 263
Midena Verlag, pg 264
Verlagsgesellschaft Rudolf Mueller GmbH & Co KG, pg 265
NaturaViva Verlags GmbH, pg 266
New Era Publications Deutschland GmbH, pg 268
Hans-Nietsch-Verlag, pg 269
Nusser Verlag, pg 269
Osho Verlag GmbH, pg 271
Ostfalia-Verlag Jurgen Schierer, pg 271
Palmyra Verlag, pg 271
Verlag Parzeller GmbH & Co KG, pg 271
Pfalzische Verlagsanstalt GmbH, pg 272

Polygraph Verlag GmbH, pg 274
Propylaeen Verlag, Zweigniederlassung Berlin der Ullstein Buchverlage GmbH, pg 275
Rake Verlag GmbH, pg 277
E Reinhold Verlag, pg 278
Rowohlt Berlin Verlag GmbH, pg 280
J D Sauerlaender's Verlag, pg 282
Moritz Schauenburg Verlag, pg 282
Verlag der Schillerbuchhandlung Hans Banger OHG, pg 283
Schoeffling & Co, pg 284
Schwabenverlag Aktiengesellschaft, pg 285
Siedler Verlag, pg 286
Silberburg-Verlag Titus Haeussermann GmbH, pg 287
Springer-Verlag GmbH & Co KG, pg 288
Stadler Verlagsgesellschaft mbH, pg 288
C A Starke Verlag, pg 289
Steidl Verlag, pg 289
Steiger Verlag, pg 289
teNeues Verlag GmbH & Co KG, pg 292
Konrad Theiss Verlag GmbH, pg 293
Tipress Dienstleistungen fur das Verlagswesen GmbH, pg 294
Traditionell Bogenschiessen Verlag Angelika Hornig, pg 294
Verlag Moderne Industrie AG & Co KG, pg 298
Weidlich Verlag, pg 301
Gert Wohlfarth GmbH Verlag Fachtechnik & Mercator Verlag, Verlag Puppen & Spielzeug, pg 304
Verlag im Ziegelhaus Ulrich Gohl, pg 305

Ghana

Afram Publications (Ghana) Ltd, pg 306
Educational Press & Manufacturers Ltd, pg 307
World Literature Project, pg 308

Greece

Kyriakidis, pg 312
Orfanidis Publications, pg 314
Patakis Publishers, pg 314
Proskinio, pg 314
Toubis M, pg 315

Hong Kong

Joint Publishing (HK) Co Ltd, pg 320
Ling Kee Publishing Group, pg 320
Research Centre for Translation, pg 321
Ta Kung Pao (HK) Ltd, pg 322
Unicorn Books Ltd, pg 322
Vista Productions Ltd, pg 322

Hungary

Officina Nova, Koenyv-es Lapkiado/ Bertelsmann Media Kft, pg 324
Novorg Kiado, pg 326
Panem, pg 326

Iceland

Bokaforlag Birtingur, pg 327
Forlagid, pg 327
Frodi Ltd, pg 328
Islendingasagnautgafan, pg 328
Skjaldborg Ltd, pg 328

India

Academic Book Corporation, pg 329
Addison-Wesley (Singapore) Pte Ltd, pg 329
Agam Kala Prakashan, pg 330
Allied Book Centre, pg 330
Bani Mandir, Book-Sellers, Publishers & Educational Suppliers, pg 332
Cosmo Publications, pg 335
Daya Publishing House, pg 336
Eastern Law House Pvt Ltd, pg 336
Frank Brothers & Co (Publishers) Ltd, pg 337
Gyan Publishing House, pg 338
Indus Publishing Co, pg 339
International Book Distributors, pg 340
Kali For Women, pg 341
Konark Publishers, Pvt, Ltd, pg 341
Oxford University Press, pg 345
Rahul Publishing House, pg 347
Rajesh Publications, pg 347
Regency Publications, pg 347
Reliance Publishing House, pg 347
SABDA, pg 348
Scientific Book Agency, pg 349
Somaiya Publications Pvt Ltd, pg 350
Vidya Puri, pg 352
Vision Books Pvt Ltd, pg 353

Indonesia

CV Angkasa CV (Publishers), pg 354
PT BPK Gunung Mulia, pg 355

Ireland

The Collins Press, pg 359
Dee-Jay Publications, pg 359
Gill & Macmillan Ltd, pg 361
The Hannon Press, pg 361
Mount Eagle Publications Ltd, pg 362
New Writers' Press, pg 362
The O'Brien Press Ltd, pg 363
Relay Books, pg 363
Roberts Rinehart Publishers, pg 363
Town House & Country House, pg 364
Wolfhound Press, pg 364

Israel

Classikaletet, pg 366
DAT Publications, pg 366
L B Publishing Co, pg 369
Rubin Mass Ltd, pg 371
Schocken Publishing House Ltd, pg 372
R Sirkis Publishers Ltd, pg 372
Urim Publications, pg 373

Italy

Adea Edizioni, pg 374
Artioli Editore in Modena, pg 377
Casa Editrice Astrolabio-Ubaldini Editore, pg 377
Belforte Editore Libraio srl, pg 377
La Culturale, pg 383
Edizioni Dedalo SRL, pg 384
EDIFIR SRL, pg 386
Edizioni Studio Domenicano (ESD), pg 387
EDT Edizioni di Torino, pg 387
Folini, pg 389
Giunti (Gruppo Editoriale), pg 390
Ernesto Gremese Editore SRL, pg 391
Gremese International Srl, pg 391
Ibis, pg 393

Il Saggiatore, pg 393
Kaos Edizioni SRL, pg 395
L'Airone Editrice, pg 395
Edizioni Piemme SpA, pg 403
Edition Raetia Srl-GmbH, pg 404
Red/Studio Redazionale SpA, pg 405
Rossato, pg 406
Samaya SRL, pg 406
Edizioni Segno SRL, pg 407
Sperling e Kupfer Editori SpA, pg 408
Marco Tropea Editore, pg 410
Turris, pg 410

Jamaica
Institute of Jamaica Publications, pg 413
Kingston Publishers Ltd, pg 413
West Indies Publishing Ltd, pg 414

Japan
Bijutsu Shuppan-Sha, Ltd, pg 415
Chijin Shokan Co Ltd, pg 415
Chikuma Shobo Publishing Co Ltd, pg 415
Diamond Inc, pg 416
Dohosha Publishing Co Ltd, pg 416
Fuzambo Publishing Co, pg 416
Hakuyo-Sha, pg 417
Institute for Financial Affairs Inc-KINZAI, pg 418
Kinokuniya Co Ltd (Publishing Department), pg 420
KINZAI Corporation, pg 420
Kosei Publishing Co Ltd, pg 420
Kyodo-Isho Shuppan Co Ltd, pg 420
Mirai-Sha, pg 421
Nippon Hoso Shuppan Kyokai (NHK Publishing), pg 422
Nippon Jitsugyo Publishing Co, Ltd, pg 423
Nobunkyo (Rural Village Culture Association), pg 423
Ohmsha Ltd, pg 423
Ongaku No Tomo Sha Corporation, pg 423
President Inc, pg 423
Reimei-Shobo Co Ltd, pg 424
Shincho-Sha Co Ltd, pg 425
Shufunotomo sha Co Ltd, pg 426
Soshisha Co Ltd, pg 426
Toho Shuppan, pg 427
Tokyo Shoseki Co Ltd, pg 427

Kenya
Heinemann Kenya Limited (EAEP), pg 431
Kenway Publications Ltd, pg 432

Republic of Korea
Chung Rim Publishing Co Ltd, pg 435
Koreaone Press Inc, pg 438
Minumsa Publishing Co Ltd, pg 438
O Neul Publishing Co, pg 439
Woong Jin Publishing Co Ltd, pg 440
Word of Life Press, pg 440

Latvia
Alberts XII, pg 441
Liesma Publishers, pg 442
Madris, pg 442

Lebanon
Librairie Orientale sal, pg 443
World Book Publishing, pg 443

Luxembourg
Editions Emile Borschette, pg 447
Editions Tousch, pg 448

Malawi
Central Africana Ltd, pg 450

Malaysia
Darulfikir, pg 451
Dewan Bahasa dan Pustaka, pg 451
Federal Publications Sdn Bhd, pg 452
MDC Publishers Printers, pg 453
Pearson Education, pg 453
Penerbit Jayatinta Sdn Bhd, pg 454
Pustaka Cipta Sdn Bhd, pg 454
Pustaka Delta Pelajaran Sdn Bhd, pg 454
Tempo Publishing (M) Sdn Bhd, pg 455
Tropical Press Sdn Bhd, pg 455

Maldive Islands
Novelty Printers & Publishers, pg 455

Malta
Fondazzjoni Patrimonju Malti, pg 456

Martinique
Editions Gondwana, pg 456
George Lise-Huyghes des Etages, pg 456

Mauritius
Editions de l'Ocean Indien Ltd, pg 457

Mexico
Ediciones Eca SA de CV, pg 460
Edamex SA de CV, pg 460
Editorial Limusa SA de CV, pg 463
Pearson Educacion de Mexico, SA de CV, pg 465

Morocco
Dar Nachr Al Maarifa Pour L'Edition et La Distribution, pg 469

Netherlands
Uitgeverij Arena BV, pg 473
Uitgeverij Balans, pg 473
Business Contact BV, pg 475
BZZTOH Publishers, pg 475
Uitgeverij Cantecleer BV, pg 475
BV Uitgeversbedryf Het Goede Boek, pg 477
Mets & Schilt Uitgevers en Distributeurs, pg 481
Uitgeverij Mingus, pg 481
Prometheus, pg 483
Servire BV Uitgevers, pg 484
SWP, BV Uitgeverij, pg 485
Terra Publishing Co, pg 485
Tirion Uitgevers BV, pg 485
Van Buuren Uitgeverij BV, pg 486

New Caledonia
Editions du Santal, pg 488

New Zealand
Auckland University Press, pg 488
David Bateman Ltd, pg 488
Book Data Asia Pacific, pg 488
Bush Press Communications Ltd, pg 489
David's Marine Books, pg 490
Exisle Publishing Ltd, pg 491
Gnostic Press, pg 491
Godwit Publishing Ltd, pg 491
Halcyon Publishing Ltd, pg 491
HarperCollins Publishers (New Zealand) Ltd, pg 491
Hodder Moa Beckett Publishers Ltd, pg 492
Huia Publishers, pg 492
Magari Publishing, pg 493
Otago Heritage Books, pg 494
R P L Books, pg 495
Resource Books Ltd, pg 495
Shoal Bay Press Ltd, pg 495
Southern Press Ltd, pg 496
Tandem Press, pg 496
Bridget Williams Books Ltd, pg 497

Nigeria
Riverside Communications, pg 501

Norway
Ex Libris Forlag A/S, pg 503
Pax Forlag A/S, pg 504

Pakistan
National Book Foundation, pg 508
Sang-e-Meel Publications, pg 509

Panama
Focus Publications International SA, pg 509

Peru
Ediciones Peisa (Promocion Editorial Inca SA), pg 511

Philippines
De La Salle University, pg 513
Rex Bookstores & Publishers, pg 514

Poland
Ksiaznica Publishing Ltd, pg 517
Magnum Publishing House Ltd, pg 518
Muza SA, pg 518

Portugal
Editorial Estampa, Lda, pg 524
Nova Acropole, pg 527
Planeta Editora, LDA, pg 528

Puerto Rico
University of Puerto Rico Press (EDUPR), pg 531

Romania
The Center for Romanian Studies, pg 532
Editura Cronos SRL, pg 532
Editura Humanitas, pg 533
Humanitas Publishing House, pg 533
Editura Meridiane, pg 534
Monitorul Oficial, Editura, pg 534

Russian Federation
Armada Publishing House, pg 537
N E Bauman Moscow State Technical University Publishers, pg 537
Izdatelstvo Mir, pg 540
Izdatelstvo Muzyka, pg 540
Novosti Izdatel 'stvo, pg 541
Obdeestro Znanie, pg 541
Permskaja Kniga, pg 541
Profizdat, pg 541
Russkaya Kniga Izdatelstvo (Publishers), pg 541
Text Publishers Ltd Too, pg 542
Top Secret Collection Publishers, pg 542

Singapore
Aquanut Agencies Pte Ltd, pg 545
Archipelago Press, pg 545
Hillview Publications Pte Ltd, pg 546
Pearson Education Asia, pg 547
Taylor & Francis Asia Pacific, pg 548
World Scientific Publishing Co Pte Ltd, pg 549

Slovakia
Vydavatepstvo Praca spol sro, pg 550
Serafin, pg 550
Sofa, pg 551

South Africa
Bet-El Publishers, pg 553
Fernwood Press (Pty) Ltd, pg 554
Flesch Financial Publications (Pty) Ltd, pg 554
Galago Publishing Pty Ltd, pg 554
Human & Rousseau (Pty) Ltd, pg 555
New Africa Books (Pty) Ltd, pg 557
Southern Book Publishers (Pty) Ltd, pg 559

Spain
Alberdania SL, pg 562
CEAC, Grupo Editorial SA, pg 567
Comunidad Autonoma de Madrid, Servicio de Documentacion y Publicaciones, pg 568
Ediciones Daly S L, pg 569
EDHASA (Editora y Distribuidora Hispano-Americana SA), pg 571
Ediles-Ediciones Leonesas SA, pg 572
Editorial Gustavo Gili SA, pg 576
Grijalbo Mondadori SA, pg 576
Grupo Comunicar, pg 576
Idea Books, SA, pg 578
Ediciones Libertarias/Prodhufi SA, pg 580
Ediciones Maeva, pg 581
Ediciones Medici SA, pg 582
Editorial El Perpetuo Socorro, pg 586
Plastic Comunicacion SL, pg 587
Editorial Presencia Gitana, pg 587
Instituto Provincial de Investigaciones y Estudios Toledanos, pg 588
Grup 62, pg 591
Tursen, SA, pg 593
Tusquets Editores, pg 593
Ediciones Urano, SA, pg 595

Sri Lanka
Buddhist Publication Society Inc, pg 596

Sweden
Allt om Hobby AB, pg 600
Bokforlaget Settern AB, pg 601
Fischer & Co, pg 602
ICA bokforlag, pg 603
Bokforlaget Nya Doxa AB, pg 605
Ordfront Foerlag AB, pg 605
Sjoestrands Foerlag, pg 606

PUBLISHERS

Frank Stenvalls Forlag, pg 606
Tryckeriforlaget AB, pg 607

Switzerland

ADIRA, pg 607
Benziger Verlag AG, pg 609
Bergli Books AG, pg 609
Birkhauser Verlag AG, pg 610
Christoph Merian Verlag, pg 611
Rene Coeckelberghs Editions, pg 611
Diogenes Verlag AG, pg 612
eFeF-Verlag/Edition Ebersbach, pg 613
Edition Exodus, pg 614
Haffmans Verlag AG, pg 615
Oesch Verlag AG, pg 620
Ott Verlag AG, pg 621
Editions du Parvis, pg 621
Editions Payot Lausanne, pg 621
Perret Edition, pg 621
Verlag Die Pforte im Rudolf Steiner Verlag, pg 621
Rudolf Steiner Verlag, pg 625
Verlag im Waldgut AG, pg 627

Taiwan, Province of China

Asian Culture Co, pg 629
Echo Publishing Company Ltd, pg 629
Highlight Publishing Company Ltd, pg 630
Linking Publishing Company Ltd, pg 631

United Republic of Tanzania

Nyota Publishers Ltd, pg 634
Tanzania Publishing House, pg 634

Thailand

Chokechai Thewet Co Ltd, pg 635

Tunisia

Ceres Editions, pg 637
Maison Tunisienne de l'Edition, pg 638

Turkey

Sabah Kitaplari, pg 641

United Arab Emirates

Motivate Publishing, pg 644

United Kingdom

Act 3 Publishing, pg 645
Adamantine Press Ltd, pg 645
Allison & Busby, pg 646
Amber Books Ltd, pg 646
Andromeda Oxford Ltd, pg 647
AP Information Services, pg 648
Apple Press, pg 648
Arms & Armour Press, pg 648
Art Books International Ltd, pg 649
Arthur James Ltd, pg 649
Atlantic Transport Publishers, pg 650
The Banner of Truth Trust, pg 652
Colin Baxter Photography Ltd, pg 652
Bay View Books Ltd, pg 652
Ruth Bean Publishers, pg 653
Black Ace Books, pg 655
Blackstaff Press, pg 655
Blandford Publishing Ltd, pg 656
Bloomsbury Publishing PLC, pg 656
Blueprint, pg 656
The Book Guild Ltd, pg 657

Book Packaging & Marketing, pg 657
Books for Europe Ltd, pg 657
Boxtree Ltd, pg 658
Brassey's UK Ltd, pg 658
Nicholas Brealey Publishing, pg 659
Breedon Books Publishing Company Ltd, pg 659
Breslich & Foss, pg 659
Brewin Books Ltd, pg 659
Bryntirion Press, pg 661
Calder Publications Ltd, pg 662
Cameron & Hollis, pg 663
Canongate Books Ltd, pg 663
Capstone Publishing Ltd, pg 663
Cassell & Co, pg 664
Cockbird Press, pg 669
Colourpoint Books, pg 669
Compass Equestrian Ltd, pg 669
Compendium Publishing, pg 670
Conran Octopus, pg 670
Constable & Robinson Ltd, pg 670
Constable Publishers, pg 670
Conway Maritime Press, pg 671
Leo Cooper, pg 671
Cressrelles Publishing Company Ltd, pg 672
Crossbridge Books, pg 672
The Crowood Press Ltd, pg 672
Dance Books Ltd, The Old Bakery, pg 673
Delectus Books, pg 675
Gerald Duckworth & Co Ltd, pg 676
Aidan Ellis Publishing, pg 678
Eurobook Ltd, pg 679
Exley Publications Ltd, pg 681
Faber & Faber Ltd, pg 681
Forbes Publications Ltd, pg 683
Four Seasons Publishing Ltd, pg 683
Fourth Estate Ltd, pg 683
Frontier Publishing, pg 684
Garden Art Press Ltd, pg 685
Garnet Publishing Ltd, pg 685
George Mann Publications, pg 687
GMC Publications Ltd, pg 687
Gollancz/Witherby, pg 688
Granta Books, pg 689
HarperCollins Publishers, pg 692
Harvard University Press, pg 692
The Harvill Press Ltd, pg 693
Headline Book Publishing Ltd, pg 693
Christopher Helm (Publishers) Ltd, pg 694
Helm Information Ltd, pg 694
Hodder & Stoughton General, pg 696
Hodder & Stoughton Religious, pg 696
Hodder Headline Ltd, pg 696
ICC United Kingdom, pg 698
The Islamic Texts Society, pg 701
Janus Publishing Company Ltd, pg 702
John Blake Publishing Ltd, pg 703
The Kenilworth Press Ltd, pg 704
Law Pack Publishing Ltd, pg 706
Frances Lincoln Ltd, pg 707
Lion Publishing PLC, pg 708
The Littman Library of Jewish Civilization, pg 708
LLP Ltd, pg 708
Luath Press Ltd, pg 709
The Lutterworth Press, pg 709
Management Books 2000 Ltd, pg 711
Marston House, pg 712
Mercat Press, pg 713
Metro Publishing Ltd, pg 714
Middleton Press, pg 714
Mirabel Books Ltd, pg 715

Multilingual Matters Ltd, pg 716
John Murray (Publishers) Ltd, pg 716
National Portrait Gallery Publications, pg 717
New Era Publications UK Ltd, pg 718
New European Publications Ltd, pg 718
New Leaf Books Ltd, pg 719
NMS Publishing Ltd, pg 719
The Octagon Press Ltd, pg 720
Octopus Publishing Group, pg 720
Michael O'Mara Books Ltd, pg 721
Open Gate Press, pg 721
Orion Publishing Group Ltd, pg 722
The Orkney Press Ltd, pg 722
Peter Owen Ltd, pg 722
Parapress Ltd, pg 724
Pavilion Books Ltd, pg 724
Pen & Sword Books Ltd, pg 725
Penguin Books Ltd, pg 725
The Penguin Group UK, pg 726
Plough Publishing House of Bruderhof Communities in the UK, pg 728
Poetry Wales Press Ltd, pg 729
Polybooks Ltd, pg 729
David Porteous Editions, pg 729
Profile Books Ltd, pg 731
Quarto Publishing plc, pg 731
Queen Anne Press, pg 732
Quiller Publishing Ltd, pg 732
Quintet Publishing Ltd, pg 732
Reaktion Books Ltd, pg 733
Regency House Publishing Ltd, pg 734
Roundhouse Publishing Ltd, pg 736
The Rubicon Press, pg 737
Ryland Peters & Small Ltd, pg 737
Sainsbury Publishing Ltd, pg 737
SCM Press, pg 739
Severn House Publishers Ltd, pg 740
Shepheard-Walwyn (Publishers) Ltd, pg 741
Silver Link Publishing Ltd, pg 742
Skoob Russell Square, pg 742
Smith Settle Ltd, pg 743
Rudolf Steiner Press, pg 745
Stobart Davies Ltd, pg 745
Sutton Publishing Ltd, pg 746
Tabb House, pg 746
I B Tauris & Co Ltd, pg 747
John Taylor Book Ventures, pg 747
Telegraph Books, pg 748
Thistle Press, pg 748
Time Warner Books UK, pg 749
Titan Books Ltd, pg 749
Veloce Publishing Ltd, pg 752
Verso, pg 752
Virago Press, pg 753
Ward Lock Ltd, pg 754
White Cockade Publishing, pg 755
White Eagle Publishing Trust, pg 755
Whittet Books Ltd, pg 756
Wiley Europe Ltd, pg 756
Neil Wilson Publishing Ltd, pg 757
Witherby & Co Ltd, pg 758
The Women's Press Ltd, pg 758
Wordwright Publishing, pg 758
Gordon Wright Publishing Ltd, pg 759

Viet Nam

Science & Technics Publishing House, pg 763

Yugoslavia

Alfa-Narodna Knjiga, pg 764

Zimbabwe

Academic Books Pvt Ltd, pg 767
The Graham Publishing Company (Pvt) Ltd, pg 768
Zimbabwe Publishing House (Pvt) Ltd, pg 769
ZRD Trust, pg 770

JUVENILE & YOUNG ADULT BOOKS

Albania

NL SH, pg 1

Algeria

Enterprise Nationale du Livre (ENAL), pg 2

Argentina

Editorial Acme SA, pg 3
Aguilar Altea Taurus Alfaguara SA de Ediciones, pg 3
Editorial Atlantida SA, pg 3
Beas Ediciones SRL, pg 4
Bonum Editorial SACI, pg 4
Centro Editor de America Latina SA, pg 4
Ediciones Don Bosco Argentina, pg 5
Ediciones del Eclipse, pg 5
Editorial Ciudad Nueva de la Sefoma, pg 5
Errepar SA, pg 5
Editorial Guadalupe, pg 6
Kapelusz Editora SA, pg 6
Editorial Norte SA, pg 8
Editora Patria Grande, pg 8
Ediciones Preescolar SA, pg 8
San Pablo, pg 8
Editorial Sigmar SACI, pg 9

Australia

ABC Books (Australian Broadcasting Corporation), pg 10
Access Press, pg 10
Allen & Unwin Pty Ltd, The Australian Newspaper, Vogel Breads, pg 11
Beazer Publishing Company Pty Ltd, pg 14
Boinkie Publishers, pg 15
Louis Braille Audio, pg 16
Cole Publications, pg 18
Coolabah Publishing, pg 18
Crawford House Publishing, pg 19
D'Artagnan Publishing, pg 20
Encyclopaedia Britannica (Australia) Inc, pg 22
Fremantle Arts Centre Press, pg 23
Greater Glider Productions Australia Pty Ltd, pg 24
Hodder Headline Australia, pg 26
Hunter Books, pg 27
Hyland House Publishing Pty Ltd, pg 27
Jarrah Publications, pg 28
Little Red Apple Publishing, pg 30
Magabala Books Aboriginal Corporation, pg 31
Pearson Education Australia, pg 37
Penguin Books Australia Ltd, pg 37
Random House Australia, pg 40
Scholastic Australia Pty Ltd, pg 41
Stafford Books, pg 43
Tarka Publishing, pg 44
Transworld Publishers Pty Ltd, pg 45
University of Queensland Press, pg 46

TYPE OF PUBLICATION INDEX   BOOK

Walker Books Australia Pty Ltd, pg 47
Weather Press, pg 47
Wizard Books Pty Ltd, pg 48

Austria

BSE Verlag Dr Bernhard Schuttengruber, pg 50
Dachs-Verlag GmbH, pg 50
Danubia Werbung und Verlagsservice, pg 50
Denkmayr GmbH Druck & Verlag, pg 51
Development News Ltd, pg 51
Alois Goschl & Co, pg 52
Johannes Heyn, Gert und Volkmar Zechner, pg 52
Verlag Jungbrunnen - Wiener Spielzeugschachtel GesellschaftmbH, pg 53
Verlag Kerle im Verlag Herder & Co, pg 53
Edition Neues Marchen, pg 55
Niederosterreichisches Pressehaus Druck- und Verlagsgesellschaft mbH, pg 55
oebv & hpt Verlagsgesellschaft mbH & Co KG, pg 56
Verlag Oesterreich GmbH, pg 56
Oesterreichischer Bundesverlag GmbH, pg 56
Richard Pils Publication P, pg 57
Pinguin-Verlag, Pawlowski GmbH, pg 57
Andreas Schnider Verlags-Atelier, pg 58
J Steinbrener OHG, pg 59
Tyrolia Verlagsanstalt GmbH, pg 59
Verlag Carl Ueberreuter GmbH, pg 59
Dr Otfried Weise Verlag Tabula Smaragdina, pg 60

Bangladesh

Gatidhara, pg 62

Belarus

Junactva, Vydavectva, pg 63

Belgium

NV Uitgeverij Altiora Averbode, pg 64
Averbode Publishers, pg 64
Maison d'Editions Baha'ies ASBL, pg 64
Editions Gerard Blanchart & Cie SA, pg 65
Uitgeverij Clavis, pg 66
Conservart SA, pg 67
Daphne Diffusion SA, pg 67
Davidsfonds - Infodok NV, pg 67
Davidsfonds VZW, pg 67
Editions Hemma, pg 69
Infoboek NV, pg 69
Uitgeverij J van In, pg 70
Editions Lampe d'Or ASBL, pg 70
Lansman Editeur, pg 70
Claude Lefrancq Editeur, pg 71
Editeurs de Litterature Biblique, pg 71
Les Editions du Lombard SA, pg 71
La Longue Vue, pg 71
Editions Memor, pg 72
Michelin Editions des Voyages, pg 72
Uitgeverij Pelckmans N V, pg 73
Henri Proost & Co, Pvba, pg 73
Standaard Uitgeverij, pg 74
Les Editions Vie ouvriere ASBL, pg 75
Volk NV, Boekandel het, pg 75

C De Vries Brouwers BVBA, pg 75
Zuid-Nederlandse Uitgeverij NV/ Central Uitgeverij, pg 76

Benin

Les Editions du Flamboyant, pg 76

Bosnia and Herzegovina

Veselin Maslesa, pg 77
Svjetlost, pg 77

Brazil

A & A & A Edicoes e Promocoes Internacionais Ltda, pg 77
AGIR S/A Editora, pg 78
Livraria Alema, pg 78
Editora Alfa Omega Ltda, pg 78
Editora Antroposofica Ltda, pg 78
Ao Livro Tecnico Industria e Comercio Ltda, pg 78
Associacao Arvore da Vida, pg 79
Editora do Brasil SA, pg 80
Editora Brasiliense SA, pg 80
Centro de Estudos Juridicosdo Para (CEJUP), pg 80
Concordia Editora Ltda, pg 81
Dumara Distribuidora de Publicacoes Ltda, pg 81
Edicon Editora e Consultorial Ltda, pg 81
Ediouro Publicacoes, SA, pg 81
Editora Brasil-America (EBAL) SA, pg 82
Editora Companhia das Letras/ Editora Schwarcz Ltda, pg 82
Livraria Martins Fontes Editora Ltda, pg 83
Forense Universitaria Editora, pg 83
Formato Editorial ltda, pg 83
Editora Globo SA, pg 84
Editora e Grafica Carisio Ltda, pg 84
Grafica Editora Primor Ltda, pg 84
Hemus Editora Ltda, pg 85
Editora Kuarup Ltda, pg 86
Editora Leitura Ltda, pg 86
Editora Mantiqueira de Ciencia e Arte, pg 87
Editora Marco Zero Ltda, pg 87
Editora Melhoramentos Ltda, pg 87
Memorias Futuras Edicoes Ltda, pg 88
Editora Mercuryo Ltda, pg 88
Editora Moderna Ltda, pg 88
Editora Nova Alexandria Ltda, pg 88
Editora Nova Fronteira SA, pg 88
Olho D'Agua Comercio e Servicos Editoriais Ltda, pg 88
Edit Palavra Magica, pg 89
Paulinas Editorial, pg 89
Livraria Pioneira Editora/Enio Matheus Guazzelli e Cia Ltd, pg 89
Distribuidora Record de Servicos de Imprensa SA, pg 90
Editora Revan Ltda, pg 90
RHJ Livros Ltda, pg 90
Editora Rideel Ltda, pg 90
Editora Rocco Ltda, pg 91
Salamandra Consultoria Editorial SA, pg 91
Editora Santuario, pg 91
Saraiva SA, Livreiros Editores, pg 91
Editora Scipione Ltda, pg 91
Sobrindes Linha Grafica E Editora Ltda, pg 91
Livraria Sulina Editora, pg 92
Thex Editora e Distribuidora Ltda, pg 92
34 Literatura S/C Ltda, pg 92

Editora Vecchi SA, pg 93
Editora Verbo Ltda, pg 93
Editora Vida Crista Ltda, pg 93
Editora Vigilia Ltda, pg 93
Zip Editora Ltda, pg 93

Bulgaria

EA Publishing House, pg 95
Fama, pg 95
Hermes Publishing House, pg 95
Kibea Publishing Co, pg 96
Mladezh, pg 96
Sluntse Publishing House, pg 98

Cameroon

Editions CLE, pg 99

Chile

Arrayan Editores, pg 99
Editorial Andres Bello/Editorial Juridica de Chile, pg 100
Dolmen Ediciones SA, pg 100
Norma de Chile, pg 101
Pehuen Editores Ltda, pg 101
Editorial Texido Ltda, pg 101
Zig-Zag SA, pg 102

China

Anhui People's Publishing House, pg 102
Beijing Juvenile & Children's Books Publishing House, pg 102
Beijing Publishing House, pg 102
China Film Press, pg 103
China Materials Management Publishing House, pg 103
Foreign Language Teaching & Research Press, pg 105
Fujian Science & Technology Publishing House, pg 106
Guizhou Education Publishing House, pg 106
Inner Mongolia Science & Technology Publishing House, pg 106
Jinan Publishing House, pg 107
Lanzhou University Press, pg 107
Morning Glory Publishers, pg 107
People's Literature Publishing House, pg 108
Shandong Education Publishing House, pg 108
Shandong Friendship Press, pg 108
Shanghai Educational Publishing House, pg 109

Colombia

Bedout Editores SA, pg 111
Eurolibros Ltda, pg 111
Editorial Norma SA, pg 113
Editorial Oveja Negra, pg 113
Editorial Santillana SA, pg 113

The Democratic Republic of the Congo

Centre Protestant d'Editions et de Diffusion (CEDI), pg 115
Saint-Paul, pg 115
Editions Saint Paul-Afrique, pg 115

Costa Rica

Scout Interamericana, pg 117
Editorial de la Universidad de Costa Rica, pg 117

Cote d'Ivoire

Centre d'Edition et de Diffusion Africaines, pg 117
Les Nouvelles Editions Africaines, pg 118

Croatia

ALFA dd za izdavacke, graficke i trgovacke poslove, pg 118
Mladost d d Izdavacku graficku i informaticku djelatnost, pg 119
Skolska Knjiga, pg 120
Znaci Vremena, Institut Za Istrazivanje Biblije, pg 120
Znanje d d, pg 120

Cuba

Casa Editora Abril, pg 120
Editorial Gente Nueva, pg 121
Editorial Oriente, pg 121
Editora Politica, pg 121

Czech Republic

Albatros Publishing House, Co Ltd, pg 122
Bakalar spol sro, pg 123
Cesky spisovatel, pg 123
Erika, pg 124
Granit SRO, pg 124
Kalich SRO, pg 125
Lidove noviny Nakladatelstvi, pg 125
Nadace Lyry Pragensis, pg 126
Nakladatelstvi Svoboda, pg 126
Nase vojsko, nakladatelstvi a knizni obchod, pg 126
Nakladatelstvi Olympia AS, pg 127
Panton, pg 127
Portal Ltd, pg 127
Prace, pg 127
Ladislav Vasicek, pg 129
Votobia sro, pg 129
Vysehrad, pg 129

Denmark

Alma, pg 129
Atuakkiorfik A/S Det Greenland Publishers, pg 130
Bogfabrikken Fakta ApS, pg 130
Borgens Forlag A/S, pg 130
Egmont Serieforlaget A/S, pg 131
Forum Publishers, pg 132
Fremad A/S, pg 132
Grevas Forlag, pg 132
Gyldendalske Boghandel - Nordisk Forlag A/S, pg 132
P Haase & Sons Forlag A/S, pg 132
Hernovs Forlag, pg 132
Forlaget Hjulet, pg 132
Holkenfeldt 3, pg 133
Interpresse A/S, pg 133
Kaleidoscope Publishers Ltd, pg 133
Lohses Forlag, pg 133
Mallings ApS, pg 133
Scandinavia Publishing House, pg 135
Sommer og Soerensen Forlag ApS, pg 135
Wisby & Wilkens, pg 136

Dominican Republic

Pontificia Universedad Catolica Madre y Maestra, pg 136

Egypt (Arab Republic of Egypt)

Dar El Shorouk Publishing & Distributing House, pg 138
Elias Modern Publishing House, pg 138

Estonia

Ilmamaa, pg 140
Kunst Publishers Ltd, pg 140
Kupar Publishers, pg 140

PUBLISHERS

Tuum, pg 141
Valgus Publishers, pg 141

Finland

Aika Oy Kristilliset Kirjat, pg 141
Forlagsaktiebolaget Scriptum, pg 142
Karisto Oy, pg 142
Kustannus Oy Semic, pg 143
Lasten Keskus Oy, pg 143
Otava Publishing Co Ltd, pg 143
Schildts Foerlagsaktiebolag, pg 144
Soederstroem et Co Foerlagsaktiebolag, pg 144
SV-Kauppiaskanava Oy, pg 144
Tammi Publishers, pg 144
Werner Soederstroem Osakeyhtioe (WSOY), pg 145

France

Editions Albin Michel, pg 146
L'Amitie par le Livre, pg 147
Editions des Beatitudes, Pneumatheque, pg 150
Editions Belin, pg 150
Berger-Levrault SA, pg 150
Editions Andre Bonne, pg 151
Pierre Bordas et Fils, pg 151
Bragelonne, pg 151
Emgleo Breiz, pg 151
Editions BRGM, pg 152
BSl - ELOR Editions Jeunesse, pg 152
Editions Casterman, pg 153
Chardon Bleu, pg 154
Circonflexe, pg 155
Codes Rousseau, pg 155
Dargaud, pg 157
Delagrave Edition SA, pg 158
Dessain et Tolra SA, pg 159
Les Editions des Deux Coqs d'Or, pg 159
Devenirs Visuels SA, pg 159
Editions J Dupuis, pg 160
L'Ecole/L'Ecole des Loisirs Sarl, pg 160
Editions Grund, pg 161
Editions Tarmeye, pg 161
Editions Farel, pg 163
Des Femmes, pg 164
France-Loisirs, pg 165
Editions Gallimard, pg 165
Editions Gamma, pg 165
Editions Gammaprim, pg 166
Hachette Education, pg 167
Hachette Jeunesse Image, pg 167
Hachette JeunesseRoman, pg 167
Hachette Livre, pg 167
Editions Hatier SA, pg 168
Hemma Joven, SA, pg 168
Pierre Horay Editeur, pg 168
Editions l'Instant Durable (Soprep), pg 169
Librairie Larousse, pg 172
Le Laurier, pg 172
Editions Lito, pg 173
Le Livre de Paris, pg 173
Les Livres du Dragon d'Or, pg 173
LLB France (Ligue pour la Lecture de la Bible), pg 173
Editions Loubatieres, pg 174
Magnard SA, pg 174
Editions Mango, pg 174
Editions MDI (La Maison des Instituteurs), pg 175
Fernand Nathan, pg 177
Editions Ophrys, pg 178
Les Presses d'Ile-de-France Sarl, pg 181
Publi-Fusion, pg 182
Rageot Editeur, pg 182
Editions Le Sarment, pg 184
Editions Scala, pg 184
Selection du Reader's Digest SA, pg 184
Service Technique pour l'Education, pg 185
Editions du Seuil, pg 185
Societe des Editions Grasset et Fasquelle, pg 185
Sofradif Editions Philippe Auzou, pg 185
Association d'Editions Sorg, pg 186
Editions Louis Soulanges Le Livrer Ouvert, pg 186
Librairie Pierre Tequi et Editions Tequi, pg 187
La Vague a l'ame, pg 188
La Vague Verte, pg 188
Les Editions Vaillant-Miroir-Sprint Publications, pg 188
Vents d'Ouest, pg 189

French Polynesia

Simone Sanchez, pg 190

Germany

Abakus Musik Barbara Fietz, pg 191
Agentur des Rauhen Hauses Hamburg GmbH, pg 192
Alibaba Verlag GmbH, pg 193
Anrich Verlag GmbH, pg 193
Arena Verlag GmbH, pg 194
Asso Verlag, pg 196
Aussaat Verlag, pg 197
Baken-Verlag Walter Schnoor, pg 198
Julius Beltz GmbH & Co KG, pg 200
C Bertelsmann Verlag GmbH, pg 201
Bertelsmann Lexikon Verlag GmbH, pg 201
Bibliographisches Institut & F A Brockhaus AG, pg 203
R Brockhaus Verlag, pg 206
Buchverlag Junge Welt GmbH, pg 207
Buchergilde Gutenberg Verlagsgesellschaft mbH, pg 207
Bund-Verlag GmbH, pg 208
Carlsen Verlag GmbH, pg 209
Christliches Verlagshaus GmbH, pg 210
Cornelsen Verlag Scriptor GmbH & Co KG, pg 212
Verlag Werner Dausien, pg 212
Delphin Verlag GmbH, pg 213
Deutsche Bibelgesellschaft, pg 213
Deutscher Literatur-Verlag, pg 215
Deutscher Taschenbuch Verlag GmbH & Co KG (dtv), pg 215
Dingfelder-Verlag Inh Gerd Gmelin, pg 217
Dreisam Ratgeber in der Rutsker Verlag GmbH, pg 218
Cecilie Dressler Verlag, pg 218
Echter Wurzburg Frankische Gesellschaftsdruckerei und Verlag GmbH, pg 219
Egmont EHAPA Verlag GmbH, pg 221
Egmont Franz Schneider Verlag GmbH, pg 221
Egmont Pestalozzi-Verlag, pg 221
Egmont vgs verlagsgesellschaft mbH, pg 221
Elefanten Press Verlag GmbH, pg 222
Verlag Heinrich Ellermann GmbH & Co KG, pg 222
Ensslin und Laiblin Verlag GmbH & Co KG, pg 223
Esslinger Verlag J F Schreiber GmbH, pg 224
Extent Verlag und Service Wolfgang M Flamm, pg 225
Fabel-Verlag Gudrun Liebchen, pg 226
FN-Verlag der Deutschen Reiterlichen Vereinigung GmbH, pg 229
Franz-Sales-Verlag, pg 229
Verlag Freies Geistesleben, pg 230
Margarethe Freudenberger - selbstverlag fur jedermann, pg 230
Garbe Verlag Ellen Vogt, pg 231
Gatzanis Verlags GmbH, pg 231
Verlag Junge Gemeinde E Schwinghammer GmbH & Co KG, pg 231
Gerstenberg Verlag, pg 232
Gondrom Verlag GmbH & Co KG, pg 233
Brigitte Grabitz - ikoo Buchverlag, pg 233
Verlag der Stiftung Gralsbotschaft GmbH, pg 234
Grass-Verlag, pg 234
Guetersloher Verlagshaus Gerd Mohn, pg 235
Verlag des Gustav-Adolf-Werks, pg 235
Carl Hanser Verlag, pg 237
Heinz-Theo Gremme Verlag, pg 239
Edition Hentrich Druck & Verlag Gebr Hentrich und Tank GmbH & Co KG, pg 239
Herold Verlag Dr Wetzel, pg 240
Max Hieber KG, pg 240
Verlag Wolfgang Hoelker, pg 241
Horlemann Verlag, pg 243
J Ch Mellinger Verlag GmbH, pg 246
Julius Klinkhardt Verlagsbuchhandlung, pg 247
Verlag Kerle im Verlag Herder, pg 248
Verlag im Kilian GmbH, pg 249
Der Kinderbuch Verlag GmbH, pg 249
Kleiner Bachmann Verlag fur Kinder und Umwelt, pg 250
Klens Verlag GmbH, pg 250
Erika Klopp Verlag GmbH, pg 250
Knowledge Media International, pg 251
Verlag Knut Reim, Jugendpresseverlag, pg 251
Koptisch-Orthodoxes Zentrum, pg 252
Francksh-Kosmos Verlags-GmbH & Co, pg 252
Roman Kovar Verlag, pg 253
Verlag Antje Kunstmann GmbH, pg 254
Lahn-Verlag GmbH, pg 255
Landbuch-Verlagsgesellschaft mbH, pg 255
Lentz Verlag, pg 257
Loewe Verlag GmbH & Co KG, pg 258
Logos-Verlag Literatur & Layout GmblI, pg 258
Wolfgang Mann-Verlag GmbH, pg 260
Gertraud Middelhauve Verlag GmbH & Co KG, pg 263
Monia Verlag, pg 265
Naumann & Goebel Verlagsgesellschaft mbH, pg 267
Verlag Neue Stadt GmbH, pg 267
Neuer Honos Verlag GmbH, pg 267
Oekotopia Verlag, Wolfgang Hoffman, pg 270

TYPE OF PUBLICATION INDEX

Verlag Friedrich Oetinger GmbH, pg 270
Oncken Verlag KG, pg 270
One Way Medien OHG, pg 270
Pandion-Verlag, Ulrike Schmoll, pg 271
J Pfeiffer Verlag, pg 273
Projektion J Buch- und Musikverlag GmbH, pg 275
Ravensburger Buchverlag Otto Maier GmbH, pg 277
Konrad Reich Verlag GmbH, pg 278
Verlag an der Ruhr GmbH, pg 281
Saatkorn-Verlag GmbH, pg 281
Eugen Salzer-Verlag GmbH & Co KG, pg 281
Verlag der Sankt-Johannis-Druckerei C Schweickhardt, pg 281
Verlag Sauerlaender GmbH, pg 282
Scheffler-Verlag, pg 282
Richard Scherpe Verlag GmbH, pg 283
Agora Verlag Manfred Schlosser, pg 283
Buchverlag Andrea Schmitz, pg 284
Verlag Karl Waldemar Schuetz, pg 285
Verlag Schulte und Gerth GmbH & Co KG, pg 285
Sellier Verlag GmbH, pg 286
Verlag Stendel, pg 290
Steyler Verlag, pg 290
Suedverlag GmbH, pg 291
Druck-und Verlagshans Thiele & Schwarz GmbH, pg 293
K Thienemanns Verlag, pg 293
Tipress Dienstleistungen fur das Verlagswesen GmbH, pg 294
Transpress Verlagsgesellschaft mbH, pg 294
Treves Editions Verein Zur Foerderung der Kuenstlerischen Taetigkeiten, pg 295
Turkischer Schulbuchverlag Onel Cengiz, pg 295
Union-Verlag GmbH, pg 296
Unrast Verlag e V, pg 296
Verlag Beltz & Gelberg, pg 297
Voggenreiter-Verlag, pg 299
A Weichert Verlag GmbH & Co KG, pg 301
The World of Books Literaturverlag, pg 304
Xenos Verlagsgesellschaft mbH, pg 304

Ghana

Afram Publications (Ghana) Ltd, pg 306
Anowuo Educational Publications, pg 306
Beginners Publishers, pg 306
Ghana Publishing Corporation, pg 307
Moxon Paperbacks, pg 307
Waterville Publishing House, pg 308
World Literature Project, pg 308

Greece

Bergadis, pg 309
Chrysi Penna - Golden Pen Books, pg 309
Dodoni Publications, pg 310
Eleftheroudakis, GCSA International Bookstore, pg 310
Elliniki Leschi Tou Vivliou, pg 310
Ekdoseis Filon, pg 310
Hestia-I D Hestia-Kollaros & Co Corporation, pg 311
Editions Kalentis, pg 312
Ilias Kambanas Publishing Organization, SA, pg 312

813

TYPE OF PUBLICATION INDEX — BOOK

Kastaniotis Editions SA, pg 312
Kedros Publishers, pg 312
Mamuth Comix Ltd, pg 313
Minoas SA, pg 313
Pagoulatos G-G P Publications, pg 314
Patakis Publishers, pg 314
Psichogios Publications SA, pg 314
Siamantas Publications, pg 315
J Sideris OE Ekdoseis, pg 315
D & J Vardikos, pg 315

Haiti
Editions Caraiibes SA, pg 317

Hong Kong
Breakthrough Ltd - Breakthrough Publishers, pg 318
Chung Hwa Book Co (HK) Ltd, pg 319
Joint Publishing (HK) Co Ltd, pg 320
Publications (Holdings) Ltd, pg 321
Sun Ya Publications (HK) Ltd, pg 322
Witman Publishing Co (HK) Ltd, pg 322

Hungary
Advent Kiado, pg 323
Aranyhal Konyvkiado Goldfish Publishing, pg 323
Ifjusagi Lap-eskonyvkiado Vallalat, pg 324
Marton Aron Kiado Publishing House, pg 325
Mora Ferenc Ifjusagi Koenyvkiado Rt, pg 325
Park Konyvkiado Kft (Park Publisher), pg 326

Iceland
AEskan, pg 327
Almenna Bokafelagid, pg 327
Bokautgafan Orn og Orlygur ehf, pg 327
Frjals fjolmiolun hf-Urvalsbaekur, pg 327
Frodi Ltd, pg 328
Idunn, pg 328
Islendingasagnautgafan, pg 328
Mal og menning, pg 328
Setberg, pg 328
Skjaldborg Ltd, pg 328

India
Ananda Publishers Pvt Ltd, pg 330
Atma Ram & Sons, pg 331
Bhawan Book Service, Publishers & Distributors, pg 333
Chowkhamba Sanskrit Series Office, pg 335
Dolphin Publications, pg 336
Frank Brothers & Co (Publishers) Ltd, pg 337
Ministry of Information & Broadcasting, pg 342
People's Publishing House (P) Ltd, pg 346
Pitambar Publishing Co (P) Ltd, pg 346
Rajkamal Prakashan Pvt Ltd, pg 347
Rajpal & Sons, pg 347
Regency Publications, pg 347
Shaibya Prakashan Bibhag, pg 349
Shiksha Bharati, pg 350
Vidya Puri, pg 352
Vidyarthi Mithram Press, pg 352

Indonesia
Auroa, pg 354
Bina Rena Pariwara, pg 354
P T Bulan Bintang, pg 354
Djambatan PT, pg 355
Gaya Favorit Press, pg 355
Mizan, pg 356
Mutiara Sumber Widya PT, pg 356
Yayasan Obor Indonesia, pg 357

Ireland
An Gum, pg 358
Attic Press Ltd, pg 358
Ballinakella Press, pg 358
The Children's Press, pg 359
Clo Iar-Chonnachta Teo, pg 359
The O'Brien Press Ltd, pg 363
Roberts Rinehart Publishers, pg 363

Israel
Achiasaf Publishing House Ltd, pg 365
Am Oved Publishers Ltd, pg 365
Amichai Publishing House Ltd, pg 365
Boostan Publishing House, pg 366
Breslov Research Institute, pg 366
Dalia Peled Publishers, Division of Modan, pg 366
DAT Publications, pg 366
Dekel Publishing House, pg 366
Dvir Publishing Ltd, pg 366
Feldheim Publishers Ltd, pg 367
Gefen Publishing House Ltd, pg 367
Hakibbutz Hameuchad Publishing House Ltd, pg 368
The Institute for the Translation of Hebrew Literature, pg 368
Karni Publishers Ltd, pg 369
Keter Publishing House Ltd, pg 369
Kiryat Sefer, pg 369
Ma'ariv Book Guild (Sifriat Ma'ariv), pg 370
Machbarot Lesifrut, pg 370
Massada Press Ltd, pg 370
Massada Publishers Ltd, pg 370
M Mizrahi Publishers, pg 370
Pitspopany Press, pg 371
Rubin Mass Ltd, pg 371
Schocken Publishing House Ltd, pg 372
Sifriat Poalim Ltd, pg 372
Samuel Simson Ltd, pg 372
Y Sreberk, pg 372
Steimatzky Group Ltd, pg 372
Yad Vashem - The Holocaust Martyrs' & Heroes' Remembrance Authority, pg 373
Yavneh Publishing House Ltd, pg 373

Italy
Editrice Ancora, pg 375
Editore Armando Armando SRL, pg 376
Bompiani-RCS Libri, pg 378
Edizioni Borla SRL, pg 378
Edizioni Bresciane, pg 378
Nuova Casa Editrice Licinio Cappelli GEM srl, pg 379
Edizioni Cartedit SRL, pg 379
Casa Editrice Felice Le Monnier, pg 380
Casa Editrice Libraria Ulrico Hoepli SpA, pg 380
Centro Biblico, pg 380
Citta Nuova Editrice, pg 382
Editrice la Scuola SpA, pg 386
Elle Di Ci - Libreria Dottrina Cristiana, pg 388
Feguagiskia' Studios, pg 389
Giangiacomo Feltrinelli SpA, pg 389
Garzanti Editore, pg 390
Istituto Geografico de Agostini SpA, pg 390
Giunti Publishing Group, pg 391
Piero Gribaudi Editore, pg 391
In Dialogo, pg 393
Edizioni Internazionali di Letteratura e Scienze, pg 394
Editoriale Jaca Book SpA, pg 394
Lalli Editore SRL, pg 395
Edizioni Librex, pg 396
Lusva Editrice, pg 397
Editrice Massimo SAS di Crespi Cesare e C, pg 398
Milano Libri, pg 398
Minerva Italica SpA, pg 399
Arnoldo Mondadori Editore SpA, pg 399
Motta Junior Srl, pg 400
Gruppo Ugo Mursia Editore SpA, pg 400
Nardini Editore srl, pg 400
La Nuova Italia Editrice SpA, pg 401
Franco Panini SPA Editore in Bologna, pg 402
Edizioni Piemme SpA, pg 403
Piero Manni srl, pg 403
RCS Libri SpA, pg 405
RCS Rizzoli Libri SpA, pg 405
SAIE Editrice SRL, pg 406
Edizioni San Paolo SRL, pg 407
Edizioni Sonda, pg 408
Nicola Teti e C Editore SRL, pg 409
Transeuropa Libri, pg 410
Editrice Uomini Nuovi, pg 410
UTET (Unione Tipografico-Editrice Torinese), pg 411
Vallardi Industrie Grafiche, pg 411
Zanichelli Editore SpA, pg 412

Jamaica
West Indies Publishing Ltd, pg 414

Japan
Akita Shoten Publishing Co Ltd, pg 414
Bunkasha Publishing Co, Ltd, pg 415
Chikuma Shobo Publishing Co Ltd, pg 415
Child Honsha Co Ltd, pg 415
Dainippon Tosho Publishing Co, Ltd, pg 416
Froebel-Kan Co Ltd, pg 416
Fukuinkan Shoten Publishers Inc, pg 416
Fuzambo Publishing Co, pg 416
Gakken Co Ltd, pg 416
GakuseiSha Publishing Co Ltd, pg 416
Hikarinokuni Ltd, pg 417
Hokuryukan Co Ltd, pg 417
Holp Book Co Ltd, pg 417
Hyoronsha Publishing Co Ltd, pg 417
Iwanami Shoten, Publishers, pg 418
Iwasaki Shoten Publishing Co Ltd, pg 418
Kodansha, pg 420
Komine Shoten Publishing Co Ltd, pg 420
Kosei Publishing Co Ltd, pg 420
Nobunkyo (Rural Village Culture Association), pg 423
Obunsha Co Ltd, pg 423
Seibido Shuppan Company Ltd, pg 424
Seibundo Shinkosha Publishing Co Ltd, pg 425
Sekai Bunka Publishing Inc, pg 425
Shingakusha Co Ltd, pg 425
Akane Shobo Co Ltd, pg 425
Shogakukan Inc, pg 426
Shueisha Inc, pg 426
Shufu-to-Seikatsu Sha Ltd, pg 426
Takahashi Shoten Co Ltd, pg 427
Tokuma-Shoten, pg 427
Tokyo Shoseki Co Ltd, pg 427
Charles E Tuttle Publishing Co Inc, pg 428
Zoshindo JukenKenkyusha, pg 429

Kenya
Focus Publications Ltd, pg 431
Foundation Books, pg 431
Heinemann Kenya Limited (EAEP), pg 431
Kenway Publications Ltd, pg 432
Kenya Quality & Productivity Institute, pg 432
Phoenix Publishers, pg 433
Transafrica Press, pg 433

Democratic People's Republic of Korea
The Foreign Language Press Group, pg 434

Republic of Korea
Chung Rim Publishing Co Ltd, pg 435
Dai Hak Publishing Co, pg 436
Gim-Yeong Co, pg 436
Hanjin Publishing Co, pg 436
Hollym Corporation Publishers, pg 437
Hw Moon Publishing Co, pg 437
Hyein Publishing House, pg 437
Kemongsa Publishing Co Ltd, pg 437
Korea Britannica Corp, pg 437
Koreaone Press Inc, pg 438
Literature Academy, pg 438
Munye Publishing Co, pg 439
Seoul International Publishing House, pg 440
Sohaksa, pg 440
Woong Jin Publishing Co Ltd, pg 440
Woongjin Media Corporation, pg 440

Latvia
Alberts XII, pg 441
Artava Ltd, pg 441
Egmont Latvia Ltd, pg 442
Nordik/Tapals Publishers Ltd, pg 442
Patmos, pg 442
Spriditis Publishers, pg 442

Lebanon
Khayat Book and Publishing Co Sarl, pg 443
Librairie Orientale sal, pg 443

Liechtenstein
Frank P van Eck Publishers, pg 444

Lithuania
Egmont Lietuva, pg 445
Lietus Ltd, pg 445
Sviesa Publishers, pg 446
Tyto Alba Publishers, pg 446
Victoria Publishers, pg 446

PUBLISHERS

The Former Yugoslav Republic of Macedonia
Detska radost, pg 448
Makedonska kniga (Knigoizdatelstvo), pg 449
Prosvetno Delo, pg 449

Madagascar
Maison d'Edition Protestante ANTSO, pg 450

Malawi
Christian Literature Association in Malawi, pg 450

Malaysia
Berita Publishing Sdn Bhd, pg 451
Penerbit Jayatinta Sdn Bhd, pg 454
Penerbitan Tinta, pg 454
Pustaka Cipta Sdn Bhd, pg 454
Pustaka Delta Pelajaran Sdn Bhd, pg 454
Tempo Publishing (M) Sdn Bhd, pg 455
Uni-Text Book Co, pg 455

Maldive Islands
Non-Formal Education Centre, pg 455

Mauritius
Editions de l'Ocean Indien Ltd, pg 457
Vizavi Editions, pg 457

Mexico
Aconcagua Ediciones y Publicaciones SA, pg 457
Ediciones Alpe, pg 458
Ediciones Corunda SA de CV, pg 459
Ediciones Culturales Internacionales SA de CV Edicion Compra y Venta de Libros, Casetes, Videos, pg 459
Editorial Diana SA de CV, pg 459
Edamex SA de CV, pg 460
Entretenlibro SA de CV, pg 460
Editorial Esfinge SA de CV, pg 460
Fernandez Editores SA de CV, pg 461
Fondo de Cultura Economica, pg 461
Libra Editorial SA de CV, pg 463
Editorial Limusa SA de CV, pg 463
Nova Grupo Editorial SA de CV, pg 464
Organizacion Cultural LP SA de CV, pg 465
Pangea Editores, Sa de CV, pg 465
Panorama Editorial, SA, pg 465
Plaza y Valdes SA de CV, pg 465
Ediciones Promesa, SA de CV, pg 466
Salvat Editores de Mexico, pg 466
Sistemas Tecnicos de Edicion SA de CV, pg 467
Ediciones Suromex SA, pg 467
Editorial Trillas SA de CV, pg 467

Morocco
Editions Al-Fourkane, pg 469
Editions Services et Informations pour Etudiants, pg 470

Myanmar
Kyi-Pwar-Ye Book House, pg 471
Smart & Mookerdum, pg 471

Netherlands
Altamira BV, pg 472
Ark Boeken Publishing House, pg 473
Ars Scribendi bv Uitgeverij, pg 473
Uitgeverij A W Bruna en Zoon NV, pg 475
BV Uitgevery NZV (Nederlandse Zondagsschool Vereniging), pg 475
Uitgeverij G F Callenbach BV, pg 475
Casterman NV, pg 475
Uitgeverij Hans Elzenga BV, pg 477
Frank Fehmers Productions, pg 477
Uitgeverij De Fontein BV, pg 477
Gottmer Uitgevers Groop, pg 477
De Harmonie, pg 478
Helmond B. V. Uitgeverij, pg 478
Uitgeverij Heuff Nieuwkoop, pg 478
Holland B V Uitgeversmaatschappij, pg 478
Uitgeverij Kluitman Alkmaar BV, pg 479
Uitgeefmaatschappij J H Kok BV, pg 480
LCG Malmberg BV, pg 480
Lemniscaat, pg 480
Uitgeverij Leopold BV, pg 480
Otto Maier Benelux BV, pg 481
Meander Uitgeverij BV, pg 481
Mulder Holland BV, pg 481
Uitgeverij Ploegsma BV, pg 483
Em Querido's Uitgeverij BV, pg 483
Rebo Productions BV, pg 483
Sjaloom en Wildeboer Publishers, pg 484
Unieboek BV, pg 485
Uitgeverij De Vuurbaak BV, pg 487
Uitgeverij Zwijsen BV, pg 487

Netherlands Antilles
Bredero, pg 488

New Zealand
David Bateman Ltd, pg 488
Cape Catley, pg 489
Wendy Crane Books, pg 490
HarperCollins Publishers (New Zealand) Ltd, pg 491
Hazard Press Ltd, pg 491
Longacre Press, pg 493
Magari Publishing, pg 493
Nelson Price Milburn Ltd, pg 494
Shearwater Associates Ltd, pg 495

Nigeria
Aromolaran Publishing Co Ltd, pg 498
Cross Continent Press Ltd, pg 498
Ethiope Publishing Corporation, pg 499
Evans Brothers (Nigeria Publishers) Ltd, pg 499
Fourth Dimension Publishing Co Ltd, pg 499
Longman Nigeria Plc, pg 500
Nwamife Publishers Ltd, pg 500
Onibon-Oje Publishers, pg 501
Saros International Publishers, pg 501
University Publishing Co, pg 502
West African Book Publishers Ltd, pg 502

Norway
H Aschehoug & Co (W Nygaard) A/S, pg 502
Atheneum Forlag A/S, pg 502
J W Cappelens Forlag A/S, pg 503
N W Damm og Son A/S, pg 503
Det Norske Samlaget, pg 503
J W Eides Forlag A/S, pg 503
Fonna Forlag L/L, pg 503
Egmont Hjemmets Bokforlag AS, pg 504
Lunde Forlag og Bokhandel A/S, pg 504
Luther Forlag A/S, pg 504
Chr Schibsteds Forlag A/S, pg 505
Solum Forlag A/S, pg 505

Pakistan
Sheikh Muhammad Ashraf Publishers, pg 506
Ferozsons (Private) Ltd, pg 506
Maqbool Academy, pg 508
National Book Foundation, pg 508

Papua New Guinea
Kristen Pres, pg 510

Peru
Ediciones Brown SA, pg 511
Asociacion Editorial Bruno, pg 511
Carvajal SA, pg 511
Ediciones Peisa (Promocion Editorial Inca SA), pg 511
Tassorello, SA, pg 511

Philippines
Anvil Publishing Inc, pg 512
Bookman Printing & Publishing House Inc, pg 512
Encyclopaedia Britannica (Philippines) Inc, pg 513
Sonny A Mendoza, pg 513
National Book Store Inc, pg 514
Our Lady of Manaoag Publisher, pg 514

Poland
Wydawnictwo Dolnoslaskie, pg 516
Instytut Wydawniczy Pax, Inco-Veritas, pg 517
Iskry - Publishing House Ltd spotka zoo, pg 517
KAW Krajowa Agencja Wydawnicza, pg 517
Wydawnictwo Lubelskie, pg 518
Wydawnictwo Nasza Ksiegarnia Sp zoo, pg 518
Ossolineum Zaklad Narodowy im Ossolinskich - Wydawnictwo, pg 518
'Slask' Ltd, pg 520
Spotdzielnia Anagram, pg 520
Videograf II Sp z o o Zaklad Poracy Chronionej, pg 520
Wydawn Na Sprawa' Wydawniczo-Oswiatowa Spotdzielnia Inwalidow, pg 521

Portugal
Livraria Arnado Lda, pg 522
Bertrand Editora Lda, pg 522
Editorial Caminho SARL, pg 523
Livraria Civilizacao (Americo Fraga Lamares & Ca Lda), pg 523
Editora Classica, pg 523
DIFEL - Difusao Editorial SA, pg 524
Distri Editora Lda, pg 524
Editorial Estampa, Lda, pg 524
Europress Editores e Distribuidores de Publicacoes Lda, pg 525
Everest Editora, pg 525
Editorial Franciscana, pg 525
Girassol Edicoes, LDA, pg 525

TYPE OF PUBLICATION INDEX

Gradiva-Publicacnoes Lda, pg 525
Editorial Inquerito Lda, pg 526
Edicoes ITAU (Instituto Tecnico de Alimentacao Humana) Lda, pg 526
Livros Horizonte Lda, pg 526
Livraria Tavares Martins, pg 527
Melhoramentos de Portugal Editora, Lda, pg 527
Nova Arrancada Sociedade Editora SA, pg 527
Paulinas, pg 528
Editorial Perpetuo Socorro, pg 528
Platano Editora SA, pg 528
Portugalmundo, pg 528
Editorial Presenca, pg 528
Puma Editora Lda, pg 528
Editora Replicacao Lda, pg 529
Edicoes Salesianas, pg 529
Almerinda Teixeira, pg 529
Vega-Publicacao e Distribuicao de Livros e Revistas, Lda, pg 530
Editorial Verbo SA, pg 530
Livraria Verdade e Vida Editora, pg 530

Romania
Corint Verlag, pg 532
Editura Excelsior, pg 533
Nemira Verlag, pg 534
Editura Niculescu, pg 534
Pandora Publishing House, pg 535
RAO International Publishing Co, pg 535
Saeculum IO, pg 535
Vox Verlag und Vertrieb, pg 536

Russian Federation
Armada Publishing House, pg 537
Izdatelstvo Detskaya Literatura, pg 537
Druzhba Narodov, pg 537
Finansy i Statistika Publishing House, pg 538
Ladomir Publishing House, pg 539
Izdatelstvo Lenizdat, pg 539
Obdeestro Znanie, pg 541
Raduga Publishers, pg 541
Russkaya Kniga Izdatelstvo (Publishers), pg 541

Saudi Arabia
Dar Al-Shareff for Publishing & Distribution, pg 543

Senegal
Centre Africain d'Animation et d'Echanges Culturels Editions Khoudia, pg 544
Les Nouvelles Editions Africaines du Senegal NEAS, pg 544

Singapore
Asiapac Books Pte Ltd, pg 545
Hillview Publications Pte Ltd, pg 546

Slovakia
AV Studio Reklamno-vydavatel'ska agentura, pg 549
Egmont Neografia spol sro, pg 549
Mlade leta Spd sro, pg 550
Vydavatelstvo Obzor, pg 550
Smena Publishing House, pg 550

Slovenia
Zalozba Mihelac d o o, pg 552

815

TYPE OF PUBLICATION INDEX BOOK

South Africa

HAUM (Hollandsch Afrikaansche Uitgevers Maatschappij), pg 555
Heinemann Educational Publishers Southern Africa, pg 555
Human & Rousseau (Pty) Ltd, pg 555
Johannesburg Art Gallery, pg 556
Juventus/Femina Publishers, pg 556
LAPA Publishers (Pty) Ltd, pg 556
New Africa Books (Pty) Ltd, pg 557
Queillerie Publishers, pg 558
Tafelberg Publishers Ltd, pg 560
University Publishers & Booksellers (Pty) Ltd, pg 560

Spain

Publicacions de l'Abadia de Montserrat, pg 561
Acento Editorial, pg 561
Alberdania SL, pg 562
Alinco SA - Aura Comunicacio, pg 563
Anaya Educacion, pg 563
Ediciones Atril, pg 564
Ediciones B, SA, pg 565
Beascoa SA Ediciones, pg 565
Edicions Bromera SL, pg 566
Editorial Cantabrica SA, pg 566
Editorial Casals SA, pg 566
CEAC, Grupo Editorial SA, pg 567
Celeste Ediciones, pg 567
Central Catequistica Salesiana (CCS), pg 567
Editorial Claret SA, pg 568
Editora Comercial de Publicaciones, pg 568
Creaciones Monar Editorial, pg 569
Ediciones Daly S L, pg 569
Ediciones Destino SA, pg 569
Didaco Comunicacion y Didactica, SA, pg 569
Ediciones Diputacion de Salamanca, pg 570
Diseno Editorial SA, pg 570
Ediciones Ebenezer, pg 571
Edebe, pg 571
Edi-Liber Irlan SA, pg 571
Edicions Camacuc, pg 571
Editorial Everest SA, pg 572
Elkar, Euskal Liburu eta Kantuen Argitaldaria, SL, pg 573
Emece Editores, pg 573
Erein, pg 573
Editorial Espasa-Calpe SA, pg 573
Eumo Editorial, pg 574
Galaxia SA Editorial, pg 575
Grijalbo Mondadori SA, pg 576
Grupo Editorial CEAC SA, pg 576
Harlequin Iberica SA, pg 577
Hercules de Ediciones, SA, pg 577
Ibaizabal Edelvives SA, pg 577
Ediciones Internacionales Universitarias SA, pg 578
Ediciones JLA, pg 579
JOC Internacional, SA, pg 579
Editorial Juventud SA, pg 579
Laertes SA de Ediciones, pg 579
LEDA (Las Ediciones de Arte), pg 579
Libsa Editorial SA, pg 580
Llibres del Segle, pg 580
Loguez Ediciones, pg 580
Editorial Luis Vives (Edelvives), pg 580
Editorial Lumen SA, pg 580
Edicions de la Magrana SA, pg 581
Editorial Marfil SA, pg 581
La Mascara, SL Editorial, pg 581
Editorial Mediterrania SL, pg 582
Ediciones Mensajero, pg 582
Editorial Molino, pg 582
Editorial Moll SL, pg 582
Mundo Negro Editorial, pg 583
Narcea SA de Ediciones, pg 583
Ediciones Olimpic, SL, pg 585
Editorial Alfredo Ortells SL, pg 585
Parramon Ediciones SA, pg 586
Editorial El Perpetuo Socorro, pg 586
Pirene Editorial, sal, pg 587
Plastic Comunicacion SL, pg 587
Editorial Playor SA, pg 587
Pre-Textos, pg 587
Edicions Proa, SA, pg 588
San Pablo Ediciones, pg 589
Ediciones San Pio X, pg 589
Signament I Comunicacio, SL Signament Edicions, pg 590
Equipo Sirius SA, pg 591
Ediciones Siruela SA, pg 591
Grup 62, pg 591
Ediciones SM, pg 591
Ramon Sopena SA, pg 591
Ediciones Susaeta SA, pg 592
Editorial Sal Terrae, pg 592
Ediciones Toray SA, pg 593
Gregorio del Toro Editor, pg 593
Ediciones de la Torre, pg 593
Tursen, SA, pg 593
Ultramar Editores SA, pg 594
Xunta de Galicia, pg 596

Sri Lanka

Dayawansa Jayakody & Co, pg 597
Sunera Publishers, pg 598
Warna Publishers, pg 598

Sweden

Akademiforlaget Corona AB, pg 599
Allt om Hobby AB, pg 600
Berghs, pg 600
Bokforlaget Opal AB, pg 600
Bokforlaget Plus AB, pg 600
Egmont Serieforlaget, pg 601
Ekonomibok Forlag AB, pg 601
Gidlunds Bokforlag, pg 602
Gothia Publishing House, pg 603
Bokforlaget Hegas AB, pg 603
Invandrarfoerlaget, pg 603
Libris Bokforlaget, pg 604
Raben och Sjoegren Bokfoerlag, pg 605
Richters Egmont, pg 605
Sjoestrands Foerlag, pg 606
Var Skola Foerlag AB, pg 607
Verbum Foerlag AB, pg 607
B Wahlstroms, pg 607

Switzerland

Aare-Verlag, pg 607
Atrium Verlag AG, pg 609
Basilius Presse AG, pg 609
Bibellesbund Verlag, pg 610
Blaukreuz-Verlag Bern, pg 610
Werner Classen Verlag, pg 611
Editions Delachaux et Niestle SA, pg 612
E Lopfe-Benz AG Rorschach, Graphische Anstalt und Verlag, pg 612
Drei Eidgenossen Verlag, pg 613
Editions Eisele SA, pg 613
Globi Verlag AG, pg 614
Gotthelf-Verlag, pg 615
Junod Nicholas, pg 616
Verlag Walter Keller, Dornach, pg 617
La Maison de la Bible, pg 618
Orell Fuessli Verlag, pg 620
Pharos-Verlag, Hansrudolf Schwabe AG, pg 621
Verlag Friedrich Reinhardt AG, pg 622
Rex Verlag, pg 623
Rodera-Verlag der Cardun AG, pg 623
Sauerlaender AG, pg 623
Schweizerisches Jugendschriftenwerk, SJW, pg 624
Speer -Verlag, pg 625
Editions 24 Heures, pg 626
J E Wolfensberger AG, pg 628

Taiwan, Province of China

Campus Evangelical Fellowship, Literature Department, pg 629
Chien Chen Bookstore Publishing Company Ltd, pg 629
Chung Hwa Book Co Ltd, pg 629
Echo Publishing Company Ltd, pg 629
Grimm Press Ltd, pg 630
Jillion Publishing Co, pg 630
Laureate Book Co Ltd, pg 631
Linking Publishing Company Ltd, pg 631
Morning Star Publisher Inc, pg 631
Youth Cultural Publishing Co, pg 632

United Republic of Tanzania

East African Publishing House, pg 633
Nyota Publishers Ltd, pg 634
Tanzania Publishing House, pg 634

Thailand

Suksapan Panit (Business Organization of Teachers Council of Thailand), pg 635

Togo

Editions Akpagnon, pg 636
Les Nouvelles Editions Africaines du TOGO (NEA-TOGO), pg 636

Tunisia

Les Editions de l'Arbre, pg 638
Maison Tunisienne de l'Edition, pg 638

Turkey

Altin Kitaplar Yayinevi, pg 638
Arkin Kitabevi, pg 639
Inkilap Publishers Ltd, pg 640
Soez Yayin/Oyunajans, pg 641

Uganda

Fountain Publishers Ltd, pg 642

Ukraine

Veselka Publishers, pg 643

United Kingdom

Acair Ltd, pg 645
Act 3 Publishing, pg 645
Aladdin Books Ltd, pg 645
Andersen Press Ltd, pg 647
Andromeda Oxford Ltd, pg 647
Apex Publishing Ltd, pg 648
Appletree Press Ltd, pg 648
AS Publishing, pg 649
Award Publications Ltd, pg 651
BBC Worldwide Publishers, pg 653
Belitha Press Ltd, pg 653
Blackie Children's Books, pg 655
Bloomsbury Publishing PLC, pg 656
The Book Guild Ltd, pg 657
Books for Europe Ltd, pg 657
Boxtree Ltd, pg 658
Cambridge University Press, pg 662
Canongate Books Ltd, pg 663
The Cartoon Cave, pg 664
Cassell & Co, pg 664
Christian Education, pg 667
Church Union, pg 668
Diagram Visual Information Ltd, pg 675
Dramatic Lines Publishers, pg 676
Encyclopaedia Britannica (UK) International Ltd, pg 679
Eurobook Ltd, pg 679
Exley Publications Ltd, pg 681
W H Freeman & Co Ltd, pg 684
Golden Books Publishing Company, Inc, pg 688
Gollancz/Witherby, pg 688
Gomer Press (J D Lewis & Sons Ltd), pg 688
Graham-Cameron Publishing & Illustration, pg 688
Grandreams Ltd, pg 689
Grange Books PLC, pg 689
Gwasg y Dref Wen, pg 690
Hamish Hamilton Ltd, pg 691
HarperCollins Publishers, pg 692
Hodder Children's Books, pg 696
Hodder Headline Ltd, pg 696
Angus Hudson Ltd, pg 697
Islamic Foundation Publications, pg 701
The Islamic Texts Society, pg 701
Janus Publishing Company Ltd, pg 702
Kingfisher Publications Plc, pg 704
Letterbox Library, pg 707
Lion Publishing PLC, pg 708
Y Lolfa Cyf, pg 708
The Lutterworth Press, pg 709
Macmillan Audio Books, pg 710
Macmillan Children's Books, pg 710
Macmillan Heinemann ELT, pg 710
The Medici Society Ltd, pg 713
Mirabel Books Ltd, pg 715
New Era Publications UK Ltd, pg 718
Norwood Publishers, pg 720
Octopus Publishing Group, pg 720
Orion Publishing Group Ltd, pg 722
Orpheus Books Ltd, pg 722
Oxford University Press, pg 723
Parapress Ltd, pg 724
Penguin Books Ltd, pg 725
The Penguin Group UK, pg 726
Piccadilly Press, pg 727
Porthill Publishers, pg 730
Portland Press Ltd, pg 730
Quarto Publishing plc, pg 731
Quartz Editions, pg 732
Ragged Bears Ltd, pg 732
Ravette Publishing Ltd, pg 733
The Salariya Book Co Ltd, pg 738
Salvationist Publishing & Supplies Ltd, pg 738
Scholastic Ltd, pg 739
SchoolPlay Productions Ltd, pg 739
Scripture Union, pg 740
Sherbourne Publications, pg 741
Souvenir Press Ltd, pg 743
Supportive Learning Publications, pg 746
Tabb House, pg 746
Telegraph Books, pg 748
Transedition Ltd, pg 749
Two-Can Publishing Ltd, pg 750
Ward Lock Ltd, pg 754
Wayland Publishers Ltd (Incorporating Macdonald Young Books), pg 754
The Women's Press Ltd, pg 758

PUBLISHERS

Venezuela
Alfadil Ediciones, pg 761
Colegial Bolivariana CA, pg 762
Ediciones Ekare, pg 762
Universidad de los Andes, Consejo de Publicaciones, pg 763

Viet Nam
Science & Technics Publishing House, pg 763

Yugoslavia
Alfa-Narodna Knjiga, pg 764
Beogradski Izdavacko-Graficki Zavod, pg 764
Niro Decje Novine, pg 765
Nolit Publishing House, pg 765
Partenon MAM Sistem, pg 765

Zambia
ZPC Publications, pg 767

LARGE PRINT BOOKS

Australia
Australian Large Print Pty Ltd, pg 14
Pearson Education Australia, pg 37
Veritas Press, pg 46

Belarus
Interdigets Publishing House, pg 63

Belgium
Van Hemeldonck NV, pg 69

Bulgaria
Abagar Pablioing, pg 94
Abagar, Veliko Tarnovo, pg 94

China
China Light Industry Press, pg 103
Cultural Relics Publishing House, pg 105
Foreign Language Teaching & Research Press, pg 105

Czech Republic
Granit SRO, pg 124

Dominican Republic
Editorama SA, pg 136

Ecuador
Corporacion de Estudios y Publicaciones, pg 137

Egypt (Arab Republic of Egypt)
Dar El Shorouk Publishing & Distributing House, pg 138

Estonia
Estonian Academy Publishers, pg 139

France
Editions des Beatitudes, Pneumatheque, pg 150
Chardon Bleu, pg 154
Jean-Michel Place, pg 180
Editions Saint-Michel SA, pg 183

Germany
Agentur des Rauhen Hauses Hamburg GmbH, pg 192
Butzon & Bercker GmbH, pg 208
Deutscher Taschenbuch Verlag GmbH & Co KG (dtv), pg 215
Karl Elser Druck GmbH, pg 218
Econ Verlag GmbH, pg 220
Fabel-Verlag Gudrun Liebchen, pg 226
Margarethe Freudenberger - selbstverlag fur jedermann, pg 230
Verlag der Stiftung Gralsbotschaft GmbH, pg 234
Koptisch-Orthodoxes Zentrum, pg 252
Lahn-Verlag GmbH, pg 255
Verlag der Sankt-Johannis-Druckerei C Schweickhardt, pg 281
K G Saur Verlag GmbH, A Gale/ Thomson Learning Company, pg 282
Steyler Verlag, pg 290
Tipress Dienstleistungen fur das Verlagswesen GmbH, pg 294
Wichern Verlag, pg 302

Ghana
World Literature Project, pg 308

Greece
Akritas, pg 308
Evrodiastasi, pg 310
Zyrichidi Bros, pg 316

Hong Kong
Joint Publishing (HK) Co Ltd, pg 320
Peace Book Co Ltd, pg 321

India
B 1 Publications Pvt Ltd, pg 331
Reliance Publishing House, pg 347
Star Publications (P) Ltd, pg 351
Vidyarthi Mithram Press, pg 352

Italy
Centro Biblico, pg 380
Cittadella Editrice, pg 382
Edizioni Cultura della Pace, pg 383
Effata Editrice, pg 387
Horus, pg 393
Museo Storico in Trento, pg 400
Casa Editrice Roberto Napoleone, pg 400
Piero Manni srl, pg 403
Vianello Libri, pg 411
Vinciana Editrice sas, pg 411

Japan
Bunkasha Publishing Co, Ltd, pg 415
Tankosha Publishing Co Ltd, pg 427

Malaysia
Penerbitan Tinta, pg 454

New Zealand
Taylor Books, pg 496

Pakistan
Islamic Publications (Pvt) Ltd, pg 507
National Book Foundation, pg 508

Poland
'Slask' Ltd, pg 520

Portugal
Planeta Editora, LDA, pg 528
Editora Replicacao Lda, pg 529

Russian Federation
CentrePolygraph Traders & Publishers Co, pg 537

Saudi Arabia
Dar Al-Shareef for Publishing & Distribution, pg 543

South Africa
HAUM - Daan Retief Publishers (Pty) Ltd, pg 555
Jacklin Enterprises (Pty) Ltd, pg 556
Publitoria Publishers, pg 558

Spain
Ediciones Alfar SA, pg 562
CEAC, Grupo Editorial SA, pg 567
Ediciones l'Isard, S L, pg 571
Edicions Camacuc, pg 571
Fundacion Marcelino Botin, pg 575
Plastic Comunicacion SL, pg 587
Instituto Provincial de Investigaciones y Estudios Toledanos, pg 588
Trea Ediciones, SL, pg 593

Switzerland
Comite international de la Croix-Rouge, pg 612

Taiwan, Province of China
National Museum of History, pg 631

United Kingdom
Bible Reading Fellowship, pg 654
Isis Publishing Ltd, pg 701
Magna Large Print Books, pg 710
Ulverscroft Large Print Books Ltd, pg 751

Zimbabwe
Dorothy Duncan Braille & Transcription Library, pg 768

MAPS, ATLASES

Albania
NL SH, pg 1
State Textbook Publishing House, pg 1

Argentina
Aguilar Altea Taurus Alfaguara SA de Ediciones, pg 3
Editorial Ruy Diaz SAEIC, pg 5
Angel Estrada y Cia SA, pg 6
Instituto Nacional de Ciencia y Tecnica Hidrica (INCYTH), pg 7
Oikos, pg 8
Ediciones Preescolar SA, pg 8

Australia
Casket Publications, pg 17
China Books, pg 18
Crawford House Publishing, pg 19
Encyclopaedia Britannica (Australia) Inc, pg 22
Hema Maps Pty Ltd, pg 26
Int Press, pg 28
John Wiley & Sons Australia Ltd, pg 28

TYPE OF PUBLICATION INDEX

Lonely Planet Publications Pty Ltd, pg 30
Melway Publishing Pty Ltd, pg 33
Outdoor Press Pty Ltd, pg 36
Reed Educational Publishing Australia, pg 40
See Australia Guides P/L, pg 42
Universal Press Pty Ltd, pg 46

Austria
Freytag-Berndt und Artaria, Kartographische Anstalt, pg 52
Kuemmerly und Frey Verlags GmbH, pg 54
Oesterreichischer Kunst und Kulturverlag, pg 56
Universitaetsverlag Wagner GmbH, pg 60

Belgium
Abimo, pg 63
Carto BVBA, pg 65
Editions De Boeck-Larcier SA, pg 67
Geocart Uitg Cartogr AG Claus BVBA, pg 68
Girault Gilbert bvba, pg 69
Koepel van de Vlaamse Noord - Zuidbeweging 11.11.11, pg 70
Michelin Editions des Voyages, pg 72
Uitgeverij De Sikkel NV, pg 74
Standaard Uitgeverij, pg 74

Botswana
The Botswana Society, pg 77

Brazil
Fundacao Instituto Brasileiro de Geografia e Estatistica (IBGE - CDDI/DECOP), pg 84
Editora Harbra Ltda, pg 84
Libreria Editora Ltda, pg 86
Editora Scipione Ltda, pg 91
Editora Vigilia Ltda, pg 93

Bulgaria
Abagar Pablioing, pg 94
DATAMAP - Europe, pg 95
Prosveta Publishers as, pg 97
Prozoretz Ltd Publishing House, pg 97

Chile
Instituto Geografico Militar, pg 100
Zig-Zag SA, pg 102

China
Chengdu Maps Publishing House, pg 103
China Cartographic Publishing House, pg 103
China Ocean Press, pg 103
The People's Communications Publishing House, pg 107
Science Press, pg 108
Xi'an Cartography Publishing House, pg 110

Colombia
Eurolibros Ltda, pg 111
Migema Ediciones Ltda, pg 113
Editorial Santillana SA, pg 113

Costa Rica
Litografia Artex, SA, pg 116
Union Mundial para la Naturaleza (UICN), Oficina Regional para Mesoamerica, pg 117

817

TYPE OF PUBLICATION INDEX BOOK

Croatia
ALFA dd za izdavacke, graficke i trgovacke poslove, pg 118
Masmedia, pg 119

Czech Republic
Geodeticky a kartograficky podnik v Praha, sp, pg 124
Karmelitanske Nakladatelstvi, pg 125

Denmark
Kraks Forlag AS, pg 133
Scan-Globe A/S, pg 135

Egypt (Arab Republic of Egypt)
Dar El Shorouk Publishing & Distributing House, pg 138
Lehnert & Landrock Bookshop, pg 139

Estonia
Estonian Bible Society, pg 140
Sinisukk, pg 140

France
Autrement Editions, pg 149
Blay-Foldex, pg 151
Blondel La Rougery SARL, pg 151
Editions BRGM, pg 152
Le Cadratin, pg 152
Cirad, pg 155
Devenirs Visuels SA, pg 159
Encyclopedia Universalis France SA, pg 162
Librairie Artheme Fayard, pg 163
Federation Francaise de la Randonnee Pedestre, pg 164
Editions Jean Paul Gisserot, pg 166
Hachette Education, pg 167
IGN (Institut Geographique National), pg 169
INRA Editions (Institut National de la Recherche Agronomique), pg 169
IRD Editions, pg 170
Editions Marcus, pg 174
Editions MDI (La Maison des Instituteurs), pg 175
Editions Memo, pg 175
Editions Franck Mercier, pg 176
Michelin et Cie (Services de Tourisme), pg 176
Publications de l'Universite de Rouen, pg 182
Selection du Reader's Digest SA, pg 184
Societe Nouveaux Loisirs, pg 185
Sofradif Editions Philippe Auzou, pg 185
Taride Editions, pg 187
Editions Vilo SA, pg 189

Germany
ADAC Verlag GmBH, pg 191
Aufstieg-Verlag GmbH, pg 196
Bayerischer Schulbuch-Verlag GmbH, pg 199
Berndtson & Berndtson GmbH Verlag-Publishing, pg 201
Bertelsmann Lexikon Verlag GmbH, pg 201
Bibliographisches Institut & F A Brockhaus AG, pg 203
Bielefelder Verlagsanstalt GmbH & Co KG Richard Kaselowsky, pg 203
Bollmann-Bildkarten-Verlag GmbH & Co KG, pg 205
Kartographischer Verlag Busche GmbH, pg 208
Columbus Verlag Paul Oestergaard GmbH, pg 211
Cornelsen Verlag GmbH & Co OHG, pg 211
Deutscher Taschenbuch Verlag GmbH & Co KG (dtv), pg 215
Droemersche Verlagsanstalt Th Knaur Nachfolger GmbH & Co, pg 218
E Schweizerbart'sche Verlagsbuchhandlung (Nagele und Obermiller), pg 220
Falk Verlag AG, pg 226
Emil Fink Verlag, pg 227
Gebrueder Borntraeger Science Publishers, pg 231
GeoCenter Touristik Medienservice GmbH, pg 231
Gloatz, Hille GmbH & Co KG fur Mehrfarben und Zellglasdruck, pg 233
Karto + Grafik Verlagsgesellschaft (K & G Verlagsgesellschaft), pg 248
Kartographischer Verlag Reinhard Ryborsch, pg 248
Ernst Klett Verlag GmbH, pg 250
Knowledge Media International, pg 251
Franckh-Kosmos Verlags-GmbH & Co, pg 252
Karin Mader, pg 260
Mairs Geographischer Verlag, pg 260
Verlag Mueller und Kiepenheuer, pg 265
Naumann & Goebel Verlagsgesellschaft mbH, pg 267
Nelles Verlag GmbH, pg 267
Neuer Honos Verlag GmbH, pg 267
Justus Perthes Verlag Gotha GmbH, pg 272
R V Reise- und Verkehrsverlag GmbH, pg 276
Ravenstein Verlag GmbH, pg 277
Dr Ludwig Reichert Verlag, pg 278
E Reinhold Verlag, pg 278
Verlagsgruppe Reise-Know-How, pg 278
Springer-Verlag GmbH & Co KG, pg 288
Staedte-Verlag, E v Wagner und J Mitterhuber GmbH, pg 288
Steiger Verlag, pg 289
Stiefel GmbH Wandkarten Verlag, pg 290
Guenter Albert Ulmer Verlag, pg 295
VS Verlagshaus Stuttgart GmbH, pg 299
Wachholtz Verlag GmbH, pg 300
Weidlich Verlag, pg 301
Westermann Schulbuchverlag GmbH, pg 302
Herbert Wichmann Verlag, pg 302

Ghana
Unimax Macmillan Ltd, pg 308

Greece
Anixis Publications, pg 309
Dodoni Publications, pg 310
Ekdoseis Domi AE, pg 310
Giovanis Publications, Pangosmios Ekdotikos Organismos, pg 310
Hestia-I D Hestia-Kollaros & Co Corporation, pg 311
Ianos, pg 311
Ilias Kambanas Publishing Organization, SA, pg 312
Patakis Publishers, pg 314
Toubis M, pg 315

Haiti
Editions Caraiibes SA, pg 317

Hong Kong
Chung Hwa Book Co (HK) Ltd, pg 319
Geocarto International Centre, pg 320
Ling Kee Publishing Group, pg 320

Hungary
Cartographia Ltd, pg 323
Officina Nova, Koenyv-es Lapkiado/ Bertelsmann Media Kft, pg 324
Szarvas Andras Cartographic Agency, pg 326

Iceland
Mal og menning, pg 328
Namsgagnastofnun, pg 328

India
Addison-Wesley (Singapore) Pte Ltd, pg 329
Indian Book Depot (Map House), pg 339
Kali For Women, pg 341
National Book Organization, pg 343
Rajendra Publishing House Pvt Ltd, pg 347
Scientific Book Agency, pg 349

Indonesia
Bina Aksara Parta, pg 354
Djambatan PT, pg 355
Mutiara Sumber Widya PT, pg 356
PATCO, pg 356

Ireland
An Gum, pg 358
Events of the Week, pg 360
Royal Irish Academy, pg 364
Tir Eolas, pg 364

Israel
Carta, The Israel Map & Publishing Co Ltd, pg 366
Kiryat Sefer, pg 369
MAP-Mapping & Publishing Ltd, pg 370
Steimatzky Group Ltd, pg 372
Steinhart-Katzir Publishers, pg 372
Terra Sancta Arts, pg 373
Yavneh Publishing House Ltd, pg 373

Italy
De Agostini Scolastica, pg 375
Gruppo Editoriale Armenia SpA, pg 376
Verlagsanstalt Athesia, pg 377
Edizioni Bresciane, pg 378
Capone Editore SRL, pg 379
Edizioni Cartografiche Milanesi, pg 379
Centro Biblico, pg 380
Edizioni del Riccio SAS di G Bernardi, pg 384
Editrice Eraclea, pg 388
EuroGeoGrafiche Mencattini SRL, pg 388
Istituto Geografico de Agostini SpA, pg 390
Bruno Ghigi Editore, pg 390
Editoriale Jaca Book SpA, pg 394
Kompass Fleischmann, pg 395
LAC - Litografia Artistica Cartografica Srl, pg 395
Leo S Olschki, pg 402
Red/Studio Redazionale SpA, pg 405
Lo Scarabeo Srl, pg 407
Vallardi Industrie Grafiche, pg 411

Jamaica
American Chamber of Commerce of Jamaica, pg 412
West Indies Publishing Ltd, pg 414

Japan
Japan Travel Bureau Inc, pg 418
Rinsen Book Co Ltd, pg 424
Shobunsha Publications Inc, pg 426
Teikoku-Shoin Co Ltd, pg 427
Tokyo Shoseki Co Ltd, pg 427

Kenya
Heinemann Kenya Limited (EAEP), pg 431
Kenway Publications Ltd, pg 432
Transafrica Press, pg 433

Democratic People's Republic of Korea
Academy of Sciences Publishing House, pg 434
Korea Science and Encyclopedia Publishing House, pg 434

Republic of Korea
Korea Britannica Corp, pg 437

Kuwait
Ministry of Information, pg 441

Latvia
Preses Nams, pg 442

Lebanon
Geoprojects Sarl, pg 443
Khayat Book and Publishing Co Sarl, pg 443

Luxembourg
Service Central de la Statistique et des Etudes Economiques (STATEC), pg 448

Malaysia
Panther Publishing, pg 453
Penerbit Fajar Bakti Sdn Bhd, pg 454

Mexico
Editorial Avante SA de Cv, pg 458
Editorial Diana SA de CV, pg 459
Fernandez Editores SA de CV, pg 461
Fondo de Cultura Economica, pg 461
Organizacion Cultural LP SA de CV, pg 465
Instituto Panamericano de Geografia e Historia, pg 465
Ediciones Suromex SA, pg 467

Morocco
Dar Nachr Al Maarifa Pour L'Edition et La Distribution, pg 469

Namibia
Desert Research Foundation of Namibia (DRFN), pg 471

PUBLISHERS

Netherlands
Buijten en Schipperheijn BV Drukkerij en Uitg Mij v/h, pg 475
Falkplan-Suurland BV, pg 477

New Caledonia
Savannah Editions SARL, pg 488

New Zealand
Hodder Moa Beckett Publishers Ltd, pg 492
Southern Press Ltd, pg 496

Norway
J W Cappelens Forlag A/S, pg 503

Oman
Apex Publishing, pg 506

Pakistan
Sang-e-Meel Publications, pg 509

Peru
Carvajal SA, pg 511
Editorial Lima 2000 SA, pg 511

Philippines
Bookman Printing & Publishing House Inc, pg 512
Encyclopaedia Britannica (Philippines) Inc, pg 513

Poland
Biblioteka Narodowa, pg 516
Panstwowe Przedsiebiorstwo Wydawnictw Kartograficznych, pg 517
Instytut Meteorologii i Gospodarki Wodnej, pg 518
'Slask' Ltd, pg 520

Portugal
Constancia Editores, SA, pg 524
Distri Cultural Lda, pg 524
Everest Editora, pg 525
Imprensa Nacional-Casa da Moeda, pg 526
Instituto de Investigacao Cientifica Tropical, pg 526
Porto Editora Lda, pg 528
Edicioes Joao Sa da Costa Lda, pg 529
Turinta-Turismo Internacional, pg 530

Romania
Editura Academiei Romane, pg 531
Corint Verlag, pg 532
Editura Didactica si Pedagogica, pg 532
Editura Militara, pg 534
Vox Verlag und Vertrieb, pg 536

Russian Federation
Gidrometeoizdat, pg 538

Slovakia
Slovenska kartografia as, pg 550

South Africa
Jacana Education, pg 555
New Africa Books (Pty) Ltd, pg 557

Spain
Aguilar SA de Ediciones, pg 562
Ediciones Akal SA, pg 562
Anaya Educacion, pg 563
Anaya-Touring Club, pg 563
Arco Libros SL, pg 564
Editorial Bruno, pg 566
Comunidad Autonoma de Madrid, Servicio de Documentacion y Publicaciones, pg 568
Ediciones Diputacion de Salamanca, pg 570
Edebe, pg 571
Edigol Ediciones SA, pg 572
Editorial Everest SA, pg 572
Erein, pg 573
Editorial Espasa-Calpe SA, pg 573
Generalitat de Catalunya Diari Oficial de la Generalitat vern, pg 575
Editorial Herder SA, pg 577
Institucion Fernando el Catolico de la Excma Diputacion de Zaragoza, pg 578
Ediciones Istmo SA, pg 579
Larousse Planeta SA, pg 579
Editorial la Muralla SA, pg 583
Ediciones Nauta Credito SA, pg 584
Instituto Provincial de Investigaciones y Estudios Toledanos, pg 588
Grup 62, pg 591
Ramon Sopena SA, pg 591
Tursen, SA, pg 593

Sri Lanka
Colombo Book Association, pg 596

Suriname
Vaco NV Uitgeversmij, pg 599

Sweden
Norstedt, pg 605

Switzerland
Cockatoo Press (Schweiz), Thailand-Publikationen, pg 611
Hallwag AG, pg 615
Kuemmerly & Frey (Geographischer Verlag), pg 617
Schweizerische Stiftung fuer Alpine Forschungen, pg 624
Verlag Stocker-Schmid AG, pg 625

United Republic of Tanzania
Ben and Company Ltd, pg 633
Tanzania Publishing House, pg 634

Thailand
Thai Watana Panich Co, Ltd, pg 636

Trinidad & Tobago
Joan Bacchus-Xavier, pg 636

Turkey
Altin Kitaplar Yayinevi, pg 638
Arkeoloji Ve Sanat Yayinlari, pg 639
Arkin Kitabevi, pg 639
Eren Yayincilik ve Kitapcilik Ltd Sti, pg 639
IKI NOKTA Research Press & Publications Industry & Trade Ltd, pg 640
Iletisim Yayinlari, pg 640
Inkilap Publishers Ltd, pg 640
Remzi Kitabevi, pg 641
Saray Medikal Yayin Tic Ltd Sti, pg 641

Ukraine
Derzhavne Naukovo-Vyrobnyche Pidpryemstro Kartografia, pg 643

United Kingdom
A A Publishing, pg 644
Absolute Press, pg 644
Advisory Unit: Computers in Education, pg 645
Ian Allan Publishing Ltd, pg 646
Andromeda Oxford Ltd, pg 647
AS Publishing, pg 649
BCA, pg 653
Belitha Press Ltd, pg 653
Books for Europe Ltd, pg 657
Books of Zimbabwe Publishing Co (Pvt) Ltd, pg 657
Compass Maps Ltd, pg 670
Leo Cooper, pg 671
Discovery Walking Guides Ltd, pg 675
Dorling Kindersley Ltd, pg 676
Encyclopaedia Britannica (UK) International Ltd, pg 679
Express Newspapers, pg 681
The Factory Shop Guide, pg 681
Forth Naturalist & Historian, pg 683
Garnet Publishing Ltd, pg 685
Geographers' A-Z Map Company Ltd, pg 686
Grange Books PLC, pg 689
The Greek Bookshop, pg 689
Greenhill Books/Lionel Leventhal Ltd, pg 689
HarperCollins Publishers, pg 692
Harvey Map Services Ltd, pg 692
Angus Hudson Ltd, pg 697
Islamic Foundation Publications, pg 701
Kuperard, pg 705
Roger Lascelles, pg 706
Lonely Planet, UK, pg 709
Macmillan Heinemann ELT, pg 710
Michelin Tyre PLC, Tourism Dept, Maps & Guides Division, pg 714
Mirabel Books Ltd, pg 715
National Library of Wales, pg 717
New Holland Publishers (UK) Ltd, pg 718
Octopus Publishing Group, pg 720
Oilfield Publications Ltd, pg 720
Old Vicarage Publications, pg 720
Ordnance Survey, pg 722
Orpheus Books Ltd, pg 722
Oxford University Press, pg 723
Pearson Education, pg 725
Pen & Sword Books Ltd, pg 725
Philip's, pg 727
RAC Publishing, pg 732
The Reader's Digest Association Ltd, pg 733
Rough Guides Ltd, pg 735
Shire Publications Ltd, pg 741
Telegraph Books, pg 748
Wales Tourist Board, pg 754

Uruguay
EQ Opciones en Educacion, pg 760
A Monteverde y Cia SA, pg 760

Venezuela
Armitano Editores CA, pg 761

Yugoslavia
Naucna Knjiga, pg 764
Turisticka Stampa, pg 766

TYPE OF PUBLICATION INDEX

Zimbabwe
The Bulletin Newspaper, pg 768

MICROCOMPUTER SOFTWARE

Australia
Bible Society in Australia National Headquarters, pg 15
R J Cleary Publishing, pg 18
Lightbild PTY Ltd, pg 30

Austria
Osterreichischer Bundesveilag Ges.mbh, pg 57

Belgium
CED-Samsom, pg 66
Easy Computing NV, pg 68
Marabout, pg 72
Uitgeverij De Sikkel NV, pg 74

Brazil
Livraria Alema, pg 78
Editora Campus Ltda, pg 80
Livraria Pioneira Editora/Enio Matheus Guazzelli e Cia Ltd, pg 89

Bulgaria
Aleks Soft, pg 94
Foi-Commerce, pg 95
Makros 2000 - Plovdiv, pg 96
Pensoft Publishers, pg 97

Chile
Edeval (Universidad de Valparaiso), pg 100

China
Aviation Industry Press, pg 102
Beijing University Press, pg 102
China Machine Press (CMP), pg 103
Electronics Industry Publishing House, pg 105
Fudan University Press, pg 105
Guizhou Education Publishing House, pg 106
Jilin Science & Technology Publishing House, pg 106
Shandong University Press, pg 109
Shanghai Educational Publishing House, pg 109
Southwest China Jiaotong University Press, pg 109
Tianjin Science & Technology Publishing House, pg 109
Wuhan University Press, pg 110

Colombia
Pearson Educacion de Colombia LTDA, pg 113

Croatia
Skolska Knjiga, pg 120

Cuba
Apocalipis Digital, pg 120
Instituto de Informacion Cientifica y Tecnologica (IDICT), pg 121
Editora Politica, pg 121

Denmark
J H Schultz Information A/S, pg 135
Systime, pg 136

TYPE OF PUBLICATION INDEX BOOK

Egypt (Arab Republic of Egypt)
Dar El Shorouk Publishing & Distributing House, pg 138

Finland
Teknolit Oy, pg 144

France
Agence Bibliographique de L'Enseignement Superieur, pg 146
IRD Editions, pg 170
Sybex, pg 186

Germany
ARCult Media, pg 194
Data Becker GmbH & Co KG, pg 212
Deutscher Adressbuch-Verlag fuer Wirtschaft und Verkehr GmbH, pg 214
expert verlag GmbH, Fachverlag fur Wirtschaft & Technik, pg 225
Feltron-Elektronik Zeissler & Co GmbH, pg 227
Ferd Dummler's Verlag, pg 227
Verlag Ernst und Werner Gieseking GmbH, pg 232
Ing W Hofacker GmbH Verlag, pg 241
Hans Holzmann Verlag GmbH und Co KG, pg 242
Langenscheidt KG, pg 256
Verlag Laterna magica GmbH & Co KG, pg 256
Verlag Neue Wirtschafts-Briefe GmbH & Co, pg 267
Sybex Verlag GmbH, pg 291
Wiley-VCH Verlag GmbH, pg 302

Greece
Hestia-I D Hestia-Kollaros & Co Corporation, pg 311
Kleidarithmos, pg 312
Scripta, pg 315

Iceland
Namsgagnastofnun, pg 328

India
Affiliated East West Press Pvt Ltd, pg 329
Nem Chand & Brothers, pg 344
Pitambar Publishing Co (P) Ltd, pg 346
Scientific Book Agency, pg 349
Vidyarthi Mithram Press, pg 352

Indonesia
Dinastindo, pg 355
Gramedia, pg 355
PT Indira, pg 355

Israel
Rolnik Publishers, pg 371

Italy
Fausto Sardini Editrice, pg 407
Societa Editrice Internazionale - SEI, pg 408
Societa Stampa Sportiva, pg 408

Japan
Gakken Co Ltd, pg 416
Nippon Jitsugyo Publishing Co, Ltd, pg 423
Shingakusha Co Ltd, pg 425

Republic of Korea
Kemongsa Publishing Co Ltd, pg 437

The Former Yugoslav Republic of Macedonia
Medis, Skopje, pg 449

Mexico
Editora Cientifica Medica Latinoamerican SA de CV, pg 458
Ventura Ediciones, SA de CV, pg 468

Netherlands
Elmar BV, pg 476
Hagen & Stam Uitgeverij Ten, pg 478
LCG Malmberg BV, pg 480

Norway
Kunnskapsforlaget ANS, pg 504

Paraguay
Instituto de Ciencias de la Computacion (NCR), pg 510

Poland
Biblioteka Narodowa, pg 516
Oficyna Wydawnicza Read Me, pg 519

Portugal
FCA Editora de Informatica, pg 525
Lua Viajante-Edicao e Distribuicao de Livros e Material Audiovisual, Lda, pg 527

Romania
Editura Militara, pg 534
Editura Teora, pg 536

Russian Federation
N E Bauman Moscow State Technical University Publishers, pg 537
Izdatelstvo Mir, pg 540

Slovakia
Ustav informacii a prognoz skolstva mladeze a telovychovy, pg 551

Spain
Marcombo SA de Boixareu Editores, pg 581
Pentalfa Ediciones, pg 586
Pulso Ediciones, SL, pg 588

Taiwan, Province of China
Dayi Information Co, pg 629
Lead Wave Publishing Company Ltd, pg 631
Shuttle Multimedia Inc, pg 631

Turkey
Alkim Kitapcilik-Yayimcilik, pg 638
Arkadas Ltd, pg 639
Kok Yayincilik, pg 640

Ukraine
ASK Ltd, pg 643

United Kingdom
Advisory Unit: Computers in Education, pg 645
British Educational Communication & Technology Agency (BECTA), pg 660
Butterworth-Heinemann Ltd, pg 661
Castlemead Publications, pg 665
Computer Step, pg 670
Elm Publications, pg 678
First & Best in Education Ltd, pg 682
The NFER-NELSON Publishing Co Ltd, pg 719
Oxford University Press, pg 723
Telegraph Books, pg 748
Wiley Europe Ltd, pg 756

PAPERBACK BOOKS - MASS MARKET

Algeria
Enterprise Nationale du Livre (ENAL), pg 2

Argentina
Editorial Acme SA, pg 3
Ada Korn Editora SA, pg 3
Alianza Editorial de Argentina SA, pg 3
Argentine Bible Society, pg 3
Beas Ediciones SRL, pg 4
Emece Editores SA, pg 5
Ediciones de la Flor SRL, pg 6
Editorial Galerna SRL, pg 6
Editorial Kier SACIFI, pg 7
Editorial Sopena Argentina SACI e I, pg 9

Australia
Aletheia Publishing, pg 11
Allen & Unwin Pty Ltd, The Australian Newspaper, Vogel Breads, pg 11
Artemis Publishing Pty Ltd, pg 12
Ashling Books, pg 12
Austed Publishing Co, pg 13
Books for Our Times, pg 16
Candlelight Trust T/A Candlelight Farm, pg 17
R J Cleary Publishing, pg 18
Conscious Living Publications, pg 18
Cornford Press, pg 19
Crossroad Distributors Pty Ltd, pg 19
EK Press, pg 21
David Ell Press Pty Ltd, pg 21
Garr Publishing, pg 23
Garradunga Press, pg 23
Hale & Iremonger Pty Ltd, pg 24
Hartys Creek Press, pg 25
Hodder Headline Australia, pg 26
In-Tune Books, pg 27
Joval Publications, pg 29
Levanter Publishing & Associates, pg 30
Little Hills Press, pg 30
Magabala Books Aboriginal Corporation, pg 31
Matthias Media, pg 32
Mayne Publishing, pg 32
Media East Press, pg 33
New Creation Publications Ministries & Resource Centre, pg 34
New Endeavour Press, pg 34
New Era Publications Australia Pty Ltd, pg 34
Nimrod Publications, pg 35
Parabel Place, pg 37
Pascoe Publishing, pg 37
Penguin Books Australia Ltd, pg 37
Pinevale Publications, pg 38
Plantagenet Press, pg 38
Playlab Press, pg 38
Pluto Press Australia, pg 38
Raincloud Productions, pg 39
Rams Skull Press, pg 40
Random House Australia, pg 40
Rankin Publishers, pg 40
St Pauls, pg 41
Scholastic Australia Pty Ltd, pg 41
Scroll Publishers, pg 42
Simon & Schuster Australia Pty Ltd, pg 42
Tarka Publishing, pg 44
Transworld Publishers Pty Ltd, pg 45
Tropicana Press, pg 45
University of Queensland Press, pg 46
The Useful Publishing Co, pg 46
Veritas Press, pg 46
Vista Publications, pg 47

Austria
Dachs-Verlag GmbH, pg 50
Johannes Heyn, Gert und Volkmar Zechner, pg 52
Georg Westermann Verlag GmbH, pg 61

Belarus
Interdigets Publishing House, pg 63

Belgium
EPO Publishers, Printers, Booksellers, pg 68
Claude Lefrancq Editeur, pg 71
Marabout, pg 72
Roularta Books NV, pg 73
Sonneville Press (Uitgeverij) VTW, pg 74
Uitgevery Scoop Infotex NV, pg 75

Bermuda
Bermudian Publishing Co, pg 76

Bolivia
Gisbert y Cia SA, pg 76

Brazil
Editora Agora Ltda, pg 78
Editora Aquariana Ltda, pg 78
Editora Campus Ltda, pg 80
Ediouro Publicacoes, SA, pg 81
Forense Universitaria Editora, pg 83
Editora Melhoramentos Ltda, pg 87
MG Editores Associados Ltda, pg 88
Summus Editorial Ltda, pg 92
Zip Editora Ltda, pg 93

Bulgaria
Aratron, IK, pg 94
DA-Izdatelstvo Publishers, pg 95
EA Publishing House, pg 95
Eurasia Academic Publishers, pg 95
Kibea Publishing Co, pg 96
Kralica MAB, pg 96
Litera Prima, pg 96
Naouka i Izkoustvo, Ltd, pg 97
Prozoretz Ltd Publishing House, pg 97
Sluntse Publishing House, pg 98
Svetra Publishing House, pg 98
TEMTO, pg 98
Trud - Izd kasta, pg 98
Ivan Vazov Publishing House, pg 98

PUBLISHERS

Peyo K Yavorov Publishing House, pg 98
Zunica, pg 98

Cameroon

Centre d'Edition et de Production pour l'Enseignement et la Recherche (CEPER), pg 99
Editions Semences Africaines, pg 99

Chile

Edeval (Universidad de Valparaiso), pg 100
Editorial Texido Ltda, pg 101
Zig-Zag SA, pg 102

China

Anhui People's Publishing House, pg 102
Beijing Publishing House, pg 102
China Materials Management Publishing House, pg 103
CITIC Publishing House, pg 104
Foreign Language Teaching & Research Press, pg 105
Guangdong Science & Technology Press, pg 106
Heilongjiang Science & Technology Press, pg 106
Inner Mongolia Science & Technology Publishing House, pg 106
Jilin Science & Technology Publishing House, pg 106
Language Publishing House, pg 107
Lanzhou University Press, pg 107
Science Press, pg 108
World Affairs Press, pg 110
Writers' Publishing House, pg 110

Colombia

RAM Editores, pg 113

The Democratic Republic of the Congo

Centre Protestant d'Editions et de Diffusion (CEDI), pg 115
Presses Universitaires du Zaiire (PUZ), pg 115
Editions Saint Paul-Afrique, pg 115

Costa Rica

Editorial Universitaria Centroamericana (EDUCA), pg 117

Cote d'Ivoire

Akohi Editions, pg 117
Centre de Publications Evangeliques, pg 117
Centre d'Edition et de Diffusion Africaines, pg 117

Croatia

Skolska Knjiga, pg 120

Cuba

Editora Politica, pg 121

Czech Republic

Lidove noviny Nakladatelstvi, pg 125
Mlada fronta, pg 126
Pavla Momcilova, pg 126
Svoboda Servis GmbH, pg 128

Denmark

Bogan's Forlag, pg 130
Bonnier Publications AS, pg 130
Borgens Forlag A/S, pg 130
Forum Publishers, pg 132
Gyldendalske Boghandel - Nordisk Forlag A/S, pg 132
Hekla Forlag, pg 132
Holkenfeldt 3, pg 133
Interpresse A/S, pg 133
Lindhardt og Ringhof, pg 133
Nyt Nordisk Forlag Arnold Busck A/S, pg 134
Joergen Paludans Forlag ApS, pg 134
Rosenkilde & Bagger, pg 135
Scandinavia Publishing House, pg 135
Det Schonbergske Forlag, pg 135
Forlaget Vindrose A/S, pg 136

Dominican Republic

Pontificia Universidad Catolica Madre y Maestra, pg 136

Egypt (Arab Republic of Egypt)

Dar El Shorouk Publishing & Distributing House, pg 138
Middle East Book Centre, pg 139

Estonia

Kupar Publishers, pg 140
Olion Publishers, pg 140
Sinisukk, pg 140

Finland

Kirja-Leitzinger, pg 143

France

Alsatia SA, pg 146
Berger-Levrault SA, pg 150
Editions du Cerf, pg 153
Editeurs Crepin-Leblond, pg 157
Des Femmes, pg 164
Editions Generales First, pg 166
Editions Gerard de Villiers, pg 166
Editions Jean Paul Gisserot, pg 166
Hachette Livre, pg 167
Harlequin SA, pg 167
Fernand Hazan Editeur SA, pg 168
Hemma Joven, SA, pg 168
Editions J'ai Lu, pg 170
Librairie Larousse, pg 172
Editions Dominique Leroy, pg 172
Editions Lito, pg 173
Le Livre de Poche-L G F (Librairie Generale Francaise), pg 173
Presence Africaine Editions, pg 180
Presses Universitaires de France (PUF), pg 181
Editions Sand et Tchou SA, pg 183
Seghers, pg 184
Editions Andre Silvaire Sarl, pg 185
Editions Tallandier, pg 187
10/18, pg 187

Germany

Anabas-Verlag Guenter Kaempf GmbH & Co KG, pg 193
Arena Verlag GmbH, pg 194
Argument-Verlag, pg 195
Aufbau Taschenbuch Verlag GmbH, pg 196
Aufbau-Verlag GmbH, pg 196
Aussaat Verlag, pg 197
J P Bachem Verlag GmbH, pg 197
Bastei Luebbe Taschenbuecher, pg 199
Bastei Verlag, pg 199
Beerenverlag, pg 200

TYPE OF PUBLICATION INDEX

Bertelsmann Lexikon Verlag GmbH, pg 201
Bock und Herchen Verlag, pg 204
Gustav Bosse GmbH & Co KG, pg 205
R Brockhaus Verlag, pg 206
Catia Monser Eggcup-Verlag, pg 209
CEC-Cosmic Energy Connections, pg 209
Christliches Verlagshaus GmbH, pg 210
Verlag Harri Deutsch, pg 213
Droemersche Verlagsanstalt Th Knaur Nachfolger GmbH & Co, pg 218
DuMont Buchverlag GmbH & Co KG, pg 219
Dustri-Verlag Dr Karl Feistle, pg 219
Econ Verlag GmbH, pg 220
Eremiten-Presse und Verlag GmbH, pg 223
Rita G Fischer Verlag, pg 228
S Fischer Verlag GmbH, pg 228
Verlag Freies Geistesleben, pg 230
Verlag A Fromm im Druck- u Verlagshaus Fromm GmbH & Co KG, pg 230
Grabert-Verlag, pg 233
Gunter Olzog Verlag GmbH, pg 235
Guetersloher Verlagshaus Gerd Mohn, pg 235
Haag und Herchen Verlag GmbH, pg 235
Hohenrain-Verlag GmbH, pg 242
Humboldt-Taschenbuchverlag Jacobi KG, pg 243
KBV-Verlags-und Mediengesellschaft mbH, pg 248
SachBuchVerlag Kellner, pg 248
Kindler Verlag GmbH, pg 249
Koptisch-Orthodoxes Zentrum, pg 252
Verlagsgruppe Luebbe GmbH & Co KG, pg 259
Moench Verlagsgesellschaft mbH, pg 264
Philipp Reclam Jun Verlag GmbH, pg 273
Propylaeen Verlag, Zweigniederlassung Berlin der Ullstein Buchverlage GmbH, pg 275
Radius-Verlag GmbH, pg 276
Rake Verlag GmbH, pg 277
Ravensburger Buchverlag Otto Maier GmbH, pg 277
Rowohlt Verlag GmbH, pg 280
Verlag an der Ruhr GmbH, pg 281
Scheffler-Verlag, pg 282
Steiger Verlag, pg 289
J F Steinkopf Verlag GmbH, pg 289
Tetra Verlag Gmbh, pg 292
B G Teubner GmbH, pg 292
Tipress Dienstleistungen fur das Verlagswesen GmbH, pg 294
Trotzdem-Verlags Genossenschaft eG, pg 295
Tuebinger Vereinigung fur Volkskunde eV (TVV), pg 295
Verlag Eugen Ulmer GmbH & Co, pg 295
VDI-Verlag GmbH, pg 297
Verlag Klaus Wagenbach GmbH, pg 300
Walhalla Fachverlag GmbH & Co KG Praetoria, pg 300
Xenos Verlagsgesellschaft mbH, pg 304

Ghana

Africa Christian Press, pg 306
Anowuo Educational Publications, pg 306
Ghana Publishing Corporation, pg 307
Moxon Paperbacks, pg 307
Waterville Publishing House, pg 308

Greece

Chrysi Penna - Golden Pen Books, pg 309
Harlenic Hellas Publishing SA, pg 311
Kedros Publishers, pg 312
Kyriakidis, pg 312
Logos, pg 312
Proskinio, pg 314
Sigma, pg 315

Guadeloupe

Librairie Generale JASOR, pg 316

Guatemala

Grupo Editorial RIN-78, pg 316

Hong Kong

Design Human Resources Training & Development, pg 319
Joint Publishing (HK) Co Ltd, pg 320
Ming Pao Publications Ltd, pg 321
Publications (Holdings) Ltd, pg 321
Research Centre for Translation, pg 321

Hungary

Agape Ferences Nyomda es Konyvkiado Kft, pg 323
Magveto Koenyvkiado, pg 325
Szepirodalmi Koenyvkiado Kiado, pg 327
Tajak Korok Muzeumok Egyesuelet, pg 327

Iceland

Frjals fjolmiolun hf-Urvalsbaekur, pg 327

India

Addison-Wesley (Singapore) Pte Ltd, pg 329
Amar Prakashan, pg 330
Atma Ram & Sons, pg 331
Diamond Comics (P) Ltd, pg 336
Galgotia Publications Pvt Ltd, pg 337
Geeta Prakasham, pg 337
General Book Depot, pg 337
Arnold Heinman Publishers (India) Pvt Ltd, pg 338
Hindi Pracharak Sansthan, pg 338
Indian Book Depot (Map House), pg 339
Indian Council of Agricultural Research, pg 339
Kali For Women, pg 341
Lancer Publisher's & Distributors, pg 341
Mehta Publishers, pg 342
Natraj Prakashan, pg 344
Orient Paperbacks, pg 345
People's Publishing House (P) Ltd, pg 346
Popular Prakashan Pvt Ltd, pg 346
Rajkamal Prakashan Pvt Ltd, pg 347
Reliance Publishing House, pg 347
SABDA, pg 348
Sasta Sahitya Mandal, pg 349

TYPE OF PUBLICATION INDEX — BOOK

Scientific Book Agency, pg 349
Star Publications (P) Ltd, pg 351
Sterling Publishers Pvt Ltd, pg 351
Sterling Information Technologies, pg 351
Vision Books Pvt Ltd, pg 353

Indonesia
PT Indira, pg 355

Ireland
Ballinakella Press, pg 358
Brandon Book Publishers Ltd, pg 359
The Collins Press, pg 359
Emerald Publications, pg 360
FISH Publishing, pg 360
The Hannon Press, pg 361
Mount Eagle Publications Ltd, pg 362
New Writers' Press, pg 362
The O'Brien Press Ltd, pg 363
On Stream Publications Ltd, pg 363

Israel
Am Oved Publishers Ltd, pg 365
Bitan Publishers Ltd, pg 365
Schocken Publishing House Ltd, pg 372
Sifriat Poalim Ltd, pg 372
Steimatzky Group Ltd, pg 372

Italy
Nuova Casa Editrice Licinio Cappelli GEM srl, pg 379
Casa Editrice Libraria Ulrico Hoepli SpA, pg 380
Crisalide, pg 383
Edizioni del Centro, pg 384
Ediciclo Editore SRL, pg 386
EDT Edizioni di Torino, pg 387
Giulio Einaudi Editore SpA, pg 387
Giangiacomo Feltrinelli SpA, pg 389
Garzanti Editore, pg 390
Gius Laterza e Figli SpA, pg 391
Ernesto Gremese Editore SRL, pg 391
Piero Gribaudi Editore, pg 391
Ugo Guanda Editore, pg 392
Longanesi & C, pg 396
La Luna, pg 397
Macro Edizioni, pg 397
Manifestolibri, pg 397
Editrice Massimo SAS di Crespi Cesare e C, pg 398
Arnoldo Mondadori Editore SpA, pg 399
Franco Muzzio & C Editore SpA, pg 400
NodoLibri, pg 401
La Nuova Italia Editrice SpA, pg 401
Amilcare Pizzi SpA, pg 403
RCS Rizzoli Libri SpA, pg 405
Edizioni San Paolo SRL, pg 407
Edizioni Segno SRL, pg 407
Sperling e Kupfer Editori SpA, pg 408
Studio Bibliografico Adelmo Polla, pg 409
Marco Tropea Editore, pg 410
Edizioni Ubulibri SAS, pg 410
La Vita Felice, pg 411
Zanichelli Editore SpA, pg 412

Jamaica
Institute of Jamaica Publications, pg 413

Japan
Chuo-Koron-Sha Inc, pg 415
Gakken Co Ltd, pg 416
Hayakawa Publishing Inc, pg 417
Iwanami Shoten, Publishers, pg 418
Japan Publications Inc, pg 418
Nanzando Co Ltd, pg 422
Nippon Hoso Shuppan Kyokai (NHK Publishing), pg 422
Nobunkyo (Rural Village Culture Association), pg 423
Sanseido Co Ltd, pg 424
Seibido Shuppan Company Ltd, pg 424
Shincho-Sha Co Ltd, pg 425
Shufunotomo sha Co Ltd, pg 426
Sogensha Publishing Co Ltd, pg 426
Tsukiji Shokan Publishing Co, pg 428
Yohan Shuppan, pg 429

Kenya
Cosmopolitan Publishers Ltd, pg 431
Evangel Publishing House, pg 431
Foundation Books, pg 431
Heinemann Kenya Limited (EAEP), pg 431
Kenway Publications Ltd, pg 432
Kenya Quality & Productivity Institute, pg 432
Life Challenge AFRICA, pg 433

Democratic People's Republic of Korea
Grand People's Study House, pg 434

Republic of Korea
Bum-Woo Publishing Co, pg 435
Chung Rim Publishing Co Ltd, pg 435
Gim-Yeong Co, pg 436
Hakgojae Publishing Inc, pg 436
Hanul Publishing Co, pg 436
Korea Psychological Testing Institute, pg 437
Koreaone Press Inc, pg 438
Woong Jin Publishing Co Ltd, pg 440
Yeha Publishing Co Ltd, pg 441

Latvia
Artava Ltd, pg 441
Liesma Publishers, pg 442
Patmos, pg 442
Preses Nams, pg 442

Lithuania
Egmont Lietuva, pg 445
Mokslo ir enciklopediju leidybos institutas, pg 446

The Former Yugoslav Republic of Macedonia
Macedonia Prima Publishing House, pg 449

Madagascar
Imprimerie Takariva, pg 450
Trano Printy Fiangonana Loterana Malagasy (TPFLM)-(Imprimerie Lutherienne), pg 450

Malawi
Christian Literature Association in Malawi, pg 450
Mzuzu Publishing Co, pg 451

Malaysia
Darulfikir, pg 451
Mahir Publications Sdn Bhd, pg 452
Pustaka Cipta Sdn Bhd, pg 454

Mali
EDIM SA, pg 455

Mauritius
Editions de l'Ocean Indien Ltd, pg 457

Mexico
Aconcagua Ediciones y Publicaciones SA, pg 457
Editorial AGATA SA de CV, pg 457
Ediciones Alpe, pg 458
Colegio de Postgraduados en Ciencias Agricolas, pg 459
Centro de Estudios Monetarios Latinoamericanos (CEMLA), pg 460
Editorial Limusa SA de CV, pg 463
Naves Internacional de Ediciones SA, pg 464
Panorama Editorial, SA, pg 465
Selector SA de CV, pg 467
Sistemas Tecnicos de Edicion SA de CV, pg 467

Netherlands
BoekWerk, pg 474
Bosch & Keuning, pg 474
Uitgeverij A W Bruna en Zoon NV, pg 475
A W Bruna Uitgevers BV, pg 475
BZZTOH Publishers, pg 475
Uitgeverij G F Callenbach BV, pg 475
Uitgeversmaatschappij Ad Donker BV, pg 476
Helmond B. V. Uitgeverij, pg 478
Uitgeverij Homeovisie BV, pg 478
Uitgeefmaatschappij J H Kok BV, pg 480
Meander Uitgeverij BV, pg 481
Mets & Schilt Uitgevers en Distributeurs, pg 481
Uitgeverij Mingus, pg 481
Mirananda Publishers BV, pg 481
Uitgeverij Maarten Muntinga, pg 481
Narratio Theologische Uitgeverij, pg 482
Nijgh & Van Ditmar Amsterdam, pg 482
Prometheus, pg 483
Em Querido's Uitgeverij BV, pg 483

New Zealand
Cape Catley, pg 489
Church Mouse Press, pg 490
David's Marine Books, pg 490
Moss Associates Ltd, pg 493
Orca Publishing Services Ltd, pg 494
River Press, pg 495
RSVP Publishing Company Ltd, pg 495

Nigeria
Cross Continent Press Ltd, pg 498
Ethiope Publishing Corporation, pg 499
Evans Brothers (Nigeria Publishers) Ltd, pg 499
Fourth Dimension Publishing Co Ltd, pg 499
Goldland Business Co Ltd, pg 499
Heritage Books, pg 499
JAD Publishers Ltd, pg 500
Longman Nigeria Plc, pg 500
New Horn Press Ltd, pg 500
Nwamife Publishers Ltd, pg 500
Onibon-Oje Publishers, pg 501
Saros International Publishers, pg 501
Joe-Tolalu & Associates, pg 501
West African Book Publishers Ltd, pg 502
John West Publications Co Ltd, pg 502

Norway
H Aschehoug & Co (W Nygaard) A/S, pg 502
Atheneum Forlag A/S, pg 502
Bladkompaniet A/S, pg 503
J W Cappelens Forlag A/S, pg 503
Det Norske Samlaget, pg 503
Gyldendal Norsk Forlag A/S, pg 503
Tiden Norsk Forlag, pg 505

Pakistan
Islamic Publications (Pvt) Ltd, pg 507
Sang-e-Meel Publications, pg 509

Peru
Ediciones Brown SA, pg 511

Philippines
Anvil Publishing Inc, pg 512
Books for Pleasure Inc, pg 512
Bright Concepts Printing House, pg 512
De La Salle University, pg 513
Estrella Publishing, pg 513
Marren Publishing House, Inc, pg 513
Sonny A Mendoza, pg 513
National Book Store Inc, pg 514
Our Lady of Manaoag Publisher, pg 514

Poland
Arlekin-Wydawnictwo Harlequin Enterprises sp zoo, pg 516
Spoldzielnia Wydawnicza 'Czytelnik', pg 516
Gdanskie Wydawnictwo Psychologiczne SC, pg 516
Ksiaznica Publishing Ltd, pg 517

Portugal
Comissao para Igualdade e Direitos das Mulheres, pg 524
Difusao Cultural, pg 524
Dinalivro, pg 524
Edicoes 70, Lda, pg 524
Publicacoes Europa-America Lda, pg 524
Gradiva-Publicacnoes Lda, pg 525
Planeta Editora, LDA, pg 528
Editorial Presenca, pg 528
Puma Editora Lda, pg 528
Editora Replicacao Lda, pg 529
Edicoes Salesianas, pg 529
Edicoes 70, pg 529
Editora Ulisseia Lda, pg 530

Puerto Rico
University of Puerto Rico Press (EDUPR), pg 531

PUBLISHERS

Romania
Artemis Verlag, pg 532
Editura Clusium, Casa de Editura Atlas-Clusium SRL, pg 532
Editura Institutul European, pg 533
Nemira Verlag, pg 534
Editura Niculescu, pg 534
RAO International Publishing Co, pg 535
RAO Publishing Group, pg 535

Russian Federation
N E Bauman Moscow State Technical University Publishers, pg 537
Izdatel 'stvo Mordovskogo gosudar stvennogo, pg 538
Izdatelstvo Mir, pg 540
Izdatelstvo Muzyka, pg 540
Novosti Izdatel 'stvo, pg 541
Panorama Publishing House, pg 541
Profizdat, pg 541
Raduga Publishers, pg 541

Senegal
Centre Africain d'Animation et d'Echanges Culturels Editions Khoudia, pg 544
Les Nouvelles Editions Africaines du Senegal NEAS, pg 544

Singapore
Tecman Bible House, pg 549

Slovakia
Smena Publishing House, pg 550
Wist, pg 551

South Africa
Bet-El Publishers, pg 553
Educum Publishers Ltd, pg 554
Galago Publishing Pty Ltd, pg 554
HarperCollins Religious, pg 554
The Hippogriff Press CC, pg 555
Institute for Reformational Studies CHE, pg 555
Kima Global Publishers, pg 556
LAPA Publishers (Pty) Ltd, pg 556
Maskew Miller Longman, pg 557
New Africa Books (Pty) Ltd, pg 557

Spain
Acento Editorial, pg 561
Editorial Aguaclara, pg 562
Alberdania SL, pg 562
Amnistia Internacional Editorial SL, pg 563
Anglo-Didactica, SL Editorial, pg 563
Editorial Aranzadi SA, pg 564
Editorial Astri SA, pg 564
Biblioteca de Catalunya, pg 565
Edicions Bromera SL, pg 566
Calambur Editorial, SL, pg 566
Ediciones Catedra SA, pg 566
Complutense, SA Editorial, pg 568
Ediciones de la Universidad Complutense de Madrid, pg 568
Comunidad Autonoma de Madrid, Servicio de Documentacion y Publicaciones, pg 568
Rafael Dalmau, Editor, pg 569
Ediciones Daly S L, pg 569
Didaco Comunicacion y Didactica, SA, pg 569
Ediciones Diputacion de Salamanca, pg 570
Edi-Liber Irlan SA, pg 571

Ediles-Ediciones Leonesas SA, pg 572
Egales (Editorial Gai y Lesbiana), pg 572
Emece Editores, pg 573
Ediciones Encuentro SA, pg 573
Instituto de Estudios Fiscales, pg 574
Fundacion de Estudios Libertarios Anselmo Lorenzo, pg 575
Editorial Fundamentos, pg 575
Galaxia SA Editorial, pg 575
Editorial Gedisa SA, pg 575
Generalitat de Catalunya Diari Oficial de la Generalitat vern, pg 575
Grijalbo Mondadori SA, pg 576
Institucion Fernando el Catolico de la Excma Diputacion de Zaragoza, pg 578
Ediciones Internacionales Universitarias SA, pg 578
JOC Internacional, SA, pg 579
Junta de Castilla y Leon Consejeria de Educacion y Cultura, pg 579
Libsa Editorial SA, pg 580
Editorial Lumen SA, pg 580
Ediciones Maeva, pg 581
Ediciones Martinez-Roca SA, pg 581
La Mascara, SL Editorial, pg 581
Editorial Mediterrania SL, pg 582
Editorial Milenio Arts Grafiques Bobala, SL, pg 582
Editorial Molino, pg 582
Anaya & Mario Muchnik, pg 583
Munoz Moya Editor, pg 583
Naque Editora, pg 583
Noguer y Caralt Editores SA, pg 584
Editorial Noray, pg 584
OASIS, Producciones Generales de Comunicacion, pg 584
Editorial Paidotribo SL, pg 585
Pais Vasco Servicio Central de Publicaciones, pg 585
Editorial El Perpetuo Socorro, pg 586
Plaza y Janes Editores SA, pg 587
Edicions Proa, SA, pg 588
Ediciones San Pio X, pg 589
Servicio de Publicaciones Universidad de Cadiz, pg 590
Ediciones Seyer, pg 590
Ediciones Siruela SA, pg 591
Edicions 62, pg 591
Grup 62, pg 591
Ramon Sopena SA, pg 591
Editorial Thassalia, SA, pg 592
Torremozas SL Ediciones, pg 593
Trotta SA Editorial, pg 593
Tursen, SA, pg 593
Ediciones 29 - Libros Rio Nuevo, pg 594
Ultramar Editores SA, pg 594
Editorial Verbum SL, pg 595

Sri Lanka
Samayawardena Printers Publishers & Booksellers, pg 598
Sunera Publishers, pg 598

Sudan
Al-Ayam Press Co Ltd, pg 598
Khartoum University Press, pg 598

Suriname
Vaco NV Uitgeversmij, pg 599

Sweden
Bokforlaget Settern AB, pg 601
Bokforlaget Nya Doxa AB, pg 605
B Wahlstroms, pg 607

Switzerland
Birkhauser Verlag AG, pg 610
Werner Classen Verlag, pg 611
Scherz Verlag AG, pg 623
Editions D'Art Albert Skira SA, pg 625
Verlag Die Waage, pg 627

Taiwan, Province of China
Chung Hwa Book Co Ltd, pg 629
Morning Star Publisher Inc, pg 631
Shy Chaur Publishing Co Ltd, pg 631
Shy Mau Publishing Company, pg 631
Zen Now Press, pg 632

United Republic of Tanzania
Central Tanganyika Press, pg 633
DUP (1996) Ltd, pg 633
East African Publishing House, pg 633
Inland Publishers, pg 633

Thailand
Bannakit Trading, pg 635
Chokechai Thewet Co Ltd, pg 635
Odeon Store LP, pg 635
Sang Dad Publishing Company Ltd, pg 635

Tunisia
Faculte des Sciences Humaines et Sociales de Tunis, pg 638

Turkey
Ataturk Kultur, Dil ve Tarih, Yusek Kurumu Baskanligi, pg 639
Cep Kitaplari AS, pg 639
Iletisim Yayinlari, pg 640
Inkilap Publishers Ltd, pg 640
Pan Yayincilik, pg 640
Parantez Yayinlari Ltd, pg 640
Varlik Yayinlari AS, pg 641

Uganda
Fountain Publishers Ltd, pg 642

Ukraine
ASK Ltd, pg 643

United Kingdom
Act 3 Publishing, pg 645
Age Concern Books, pg 645
Allison & Busby, pg 646
Appletree Press Ltd, pg 648
Arthur James Ltd, pg 649
Bernard Babani (Publishing) Ltd, pg 651
BBC Worldwide Publishers, pg 653
Berlitz (UK) Ltd, pg 654
Blackstaff Press, pg 655
Blackwell Publishers, pg 655
Bloomsbury Publishing PLC, pg 656
Books for Europe Ltd, pg 657
Boxtree Ltd, pg 658
Breedon Books Publishing Company Ltd, pg 659
Bryntirion Press, pg 661
Canongate Books Ltd, pg 663
Capall Bann Publishing, pg 663
Cassell & Co, pg 664

TYPE OF PUBLICATION INDEX

Compass Equestrian Ltd, pg 669
Computer Step, pg 670
Constable & Robinson Ltd, pg 670
Constable Publishers, pg 670
Leo Cooper, pg 671
The C W Daniel Co Ltd, pg 673
Defiant Publications, pg 675
Discovery Walking Guides Ltd, pg 675
Eagle/Inter Publishing Service (IPS) Ltd, pg 676
Elliot Right Way Books, pg 678
Extraordinary People Press, pg 681
Faber & Faber Ltd, pg 681
Famedram Publishers Ltd, pg 681
Forth Naturalist & Historian, pg 683
Fourth Estate Ltd, pg 683
Geddes & Grosset, pg 686
Gembooks, pg 686
Gollancz/Witherby, pg 688
W F Graham (Northampton) Ltd, pg 688
Robert Hale Ltd, pg 691
HarperCollins Publishers, pg 692
Hawthorn Press, pg 693
Headline Book Publishing Ltd, pg 693
Heartland Publishing Ltd, pg 694
Hobsons, pg 696
Hodder & Stoughton General, pg 696
Hodder Headline Ltd, pg 696
Hutton Press Ltd, pg 698
The Islamic Texts Society, pg 701
John Blake Publishing Ltd, pg 703
Law Pack Publishing Ltd, pg 706
Letterbox Library, pg 707
Lion Publishing PLC, pg 708
Y Lolfa Cyf, pg 708
Lonely Planet, UK, pg 709
Macmillan Children's Books, pg 710
Macmillan Ltd, pg 710
Marston House, pg 712
Kenneth Mason Publications Ltd, pg 712
Meridian Books, pg 713
Metro Publishing Ltd, pg 714
Monarch Books, pg 715
Moorley's Print & Publishing Ltd, pg 715
New Era Publications UK Ltd, pg 718
New Playwrights' Network, pg 719
Octopus Publishing Group, pg 720
Orion Publishing Group Ltd, pg 722
Oxford University Press, pg 723
Pan Macmillan, pg 723
Parapress Ltd, pg 724
Pathfinder London, pg 724
Pearson Education Europe, Mideast & Africa, pg 725
Penguin Books Ltd, pg 725
The Penguin Group UK, pg 726
Pentathol Publishing, pg 726
Polygon, pg 729
Ramakrishna Vedanta Centre, pg 732
Ravette Publishing Ltd, pg 733
Retail Entertainment Data Publishing Ltd, pg 735
George Ronald Publisher Ltd, pg 735
Roundhouse Publishing Ltd, pg 736
Scottish Office Library & Information Services, pg 740
Sheldon Press, pg 741
Sherwood Publishing, pg 741
Shire Publications Ltd, pg 741
Simon & Schuster Ltd, pg 742
SLG Press, pg 742
Rudolf Steiner Press, pg 745
Sunflower Books, pg 746

TYPE OF PUBLICATION INDEX BOOK

Time Warner Books UK, pg 749
Titan Books Ltd, pg 749
Transport Bookman Publications Ltd, pg 750
University Presses of California, Columbia & Princeton Ltd, pg 752
Van Molle Publishing, pg 752
Virago Press, pg 753
Ward Lock Ltd, pg 754
Wild Goose Publications, pg 756
Windhorse Publications, pg 757
Witherby & Co Ltd, pg 758
The Women's Press Ltd, pg 758
Wordsworth Editions Ltd, pg 758

Uruguay
Rosebud Ediciones, pg 761
Editia Uruguay, pg 761

Viet Nam
Science & Technics Publishing House, pg 763

Yugoslavia
Alfa-Narodna Knjiga, pg 764
Izdavacka Organizacija Rad, pg 765

Zimbabwe
Anvil Press, pg 767
The Graham Publishing Company (Pvt) Ltd, pg 768
Longman Zimbabwe (Pvt) Ltd, pg 768
Manhattan Publications, pg 769
Vision Publications, pg 769

PAPERBACK BOOKS - TRADE

Argentina
Colmegna SA, pg 4
Ediciones de la Flor SRL, pg 6

Australia
ABC Books (Australian Broadcasting Corporation), pg 10
Aerospace Publications, pg 11
Allen & Unwin Pty Ltd, The Australian Newspaper, Vogel Breads, pg 11
Artemis Publishing Pty Ltd, pg 12
Ashling Books, pg 12
Assert Publishing, pg 12
Australian Broadcasting Authority, pg 13
The Australian Council for Educational Research Ltd, pg 13
Books for Our Times, pg 16
Boombana Publications, pg 16
CHOICE Magazine, pg 18
R J Cleary Publishing, pg 18
Cookery Book, pg 18
Covenanter Press, pg 19
Crawford House Publishing, pg 19
Crossroad Distributors Pty Ltd, pg 19
Currency Press Pty Ltd, pg 19
Dellasta Publishing, pg 20
Fernfawn Publications, pg 22
Finch Publishing, pg 22
Fraser Publications, pg 23
Fremantle Arts Centre Press, pg 23
Ginninderra Press, pg 24
Hale & Iremonger Pty Ltd, pg 24
Geoffrey Hamlyn-Harris, pg 25
Hampden Press, pg 25
Histec Publications, pg 26
Hodder Headline Australia, pg 26
Hyland House Publishing Pty Ltd, pg 27
Indra Publishing, pg 27
Instauratio Press, pg 27
Institute of Aboriginal Development (IAD Press), pg 28
Jarrah Publications, pg 28
John Wiley & Sons Australia Ltd, pg 28
Gregory Kefalas Publishing, pg 29
Killara Press, pg 29
Kingsclear Books, pg 29
Barry Long Books, pg 30
Melbourne University Press, pg 33
K & Z Mostafanejad, pg 33
Mulini Press, pg 34
National Library of Australia, pg 34
New Endeavour Press, pg 34
New Era Publications Australia Pty Ltd, pg 34
Nimrod Publications, pg 35
NMA Publications, pg 35
Pearson Education Australia, pg 37
Penguin Books Australia Ltd, pg 37
Playbox Theatre Co, pg 38
Pluto Press Australia, pg 38
Pollitecon Publications, pg 38
Quakers Hill Press, pg 39
Random House Australia, pg 40
The Real Estate Institute of Australia, pg 40
Simon & Schuster Australia Pty Ltd, pg 42
Spacevision Publishing, pg 42
Spectrum Publications, pg 43
Spinifex Press, pg 43
State Library of NSW Press, pg 43
Stirling Press, pg 43
Terania Rainforest Publishing, pg 44
The Text Publishing Company Pty Ltd, pg 44
Turton & Armstrong Publishers Pty Ltd, pg 45
University of New South Wales Press Ltd, pg 46
Villamonta Publishing Service Inc, pg 47
Wakefield Press Pty Ltd, pg 47
Windhorse Books, pg 48
Winetitles, pg 48
Women's Health Advisory Service, pg 48
Worsley Press, pg 48
Wrightbooks Pty Ltd, pg 48

Austria
Czernin Verlag, pg 50
Verlag Harald Denzel, Auto- und Freizeitfuehrer, pg 51
Development News Ltd, pg 51
Ennsthaler GesmbH & Co KG, pg 51
Verlag Monte Verita, pg 55
Verlag Anton Pustet, pg 57
Verlag St Gabriel, pg 58
Studien Verlag Gmbh, pg 59

Belarus
Interdigets Publishing House, pg 63

Belgium
Eteblissements Emile Bruylant SA, pg 65
Coda, pg 66
Eenhoorn BVBA, pg 68
Georeto-Geogidsen, pg 68
Claude Lefrancq Editeur, pg 71
Uitgevery Scoop Infotex NV, pg 75

Brazil
Editora Agora Ltda, pg 78
Editora Aquariana Ltda, pg 78
Camara Dos Deputados Coordenacao De Publicacoes, pg 80
Editora Campus Ltda, pg 80
Ediouro Publicacoes, SA, pg 81
Editora Elevacao, pg 82
Companhia Editora Forense, pg 82
EDUSC - Editora da Universidade do Sagrado Coracao, pg 82
Forense Universitaria Editora, pg 83
Fundacao Cultural Avatar, pg 83
Ordem do Graal na Terra, pg 84
LDA Editores Ltda, pg 86
Madras Editora, pg 87
Editora Marco Zero Ltda, pg 87
Editora Melhoramentos Ltda, pg 87
Editora Mercado Aberto Ltda, pg 88
Editora Mercuryo Ltda, pg 88
Editora Mundo Cristao, pg 88
Editora Nova Fronteira SA, pg 88
Editora Objetiva Ltda, pg 88
Pearson Education Do Brasil, pg 89
Summus Editorial Ltda, pg 92

Bulgaria
Antroposofsko Izdatelstvo Dimo R Daskalov OOD, pg 94
Aratron, IK, pg 94
EA Publishing House, pg 95
Hermes Publishing House, pg 95
Kibea Publishing Co, pg 96
Kralica MAB, pg 96
MATEX, pg 96
Nov Covek Publishing House, pg 97
Reporter, pg 97
Ivan Vazov Publishing House, pg 98

Burundi
Editions Intore, pg 98

Chile
Red Internacional Del Libro, pg 101
Editorial Texido Ltda, pg 101

China
Book Marketing Ltd, pg 102
China Foreign Economic Relations & Trade Publishing House, pg 103
China Materials Management Publishing House, pg 103
Chinese Pedagogics Publishing House, pg 104
Foreign Language Teaching & Research Press, pg 105
Guangdong Science & Technology Press, pg 106
Heilongjiang Science & Technology Press, pg 106
Inner Mongolia Science & Technology Publishing House, pg 106
New Times Press, pg 107
Shanghai Fine Arts Publishers, pg 109

Colombia
Fondo Educativo Interamericano SA, pg 112
RAM Editores, pg 113

Costa Rica
Editorial Texto Ltda, pg 117

Cote d'Ivoire
Centre de Publications Evangeliques, pg 117

Croatia
Durieux d o o, pg 118
Skolska Knjiga, pg 120
Znaci Vremena, Institut Za Istrazivanje Biblije, pg 120

Cuba
Editora Politica, pg 121

Czech Republic
Barrister & Principal, pg 123
Melantrich, pg 126
Cesky normalizacni institut, pg 127

Denmark
Akademisk Forlag, pg 129
Borgens Forlag A/S, pg 130
Egmont-Easy Readers, pg 131
Gyldendalske Boghandel - Nordisk Forlag A/S, pg 132
P Haase & Sons Forlag A/S, pg 132
Holkenfeldt 3, pg 133
Forlaget Hovedland, pg 133
Lindhardt og Ringhof, pg 133
Politisk Revy, pg 134
Samfundslitteratur, pg 135
Samlerens Forlag A/S, pg 135
Scandinavia Publishing House, pg 135
Square Dance Partners Forlag, pg 135
Unitas Forlag, pg 136

Egypt (Arab Republic of Egypt)
Dar El Shorouk, pg 138
Dar El Shorouk Publishing & Distributing House, pg 138
The Egyptian Society for the Dissemination of Universal Culture and Knowledge (ESDUCK), pg 138

Estonia
Estonian Academy Publishers, pg 139
Ilmamaa, pg 140
Mats Publishers Ltd, pg 140

Finland
Kaantopiiri Oy, pg 142
Karisto Oy, pg 142
Koala-Kustannus/Oy Greenbay House Publishing Ltd, pg 143
Otava Publishing Co Ltd, pg 143
Tammi Publishers, pg 144

France
ADPF Publications, pg 146
Editions de l'Aube, pg 149
Editions Baleine, pg 149
Bibliotheque des Arts, pg 150
Bragelonne, pg 151
La Decouverte et Syros, pg 158
Georges-Charles Demay, pg 158
L'Ecole/L'Ecole des Loisirs Sarl, pg 160
Ecole Nationale Superieure des Beaux-Arts, pg 160
Edisud, pg 161
Editions Farel, pg 163
Flammarion SA, pg 164
Ganymede, pg 166
Editions Gerard de Villiers, pg 166
Hermann editeurs des Sciences et des Arts SA, pg 168
Pierre Horay Editeur, pg 168
Editions Mediaspaul, pg 175
Mille et Une Nuits, pg 176
Editions Odile Jacob, pg 178

PUBLISHERS

Presses Universitaires de France (PUF), pg 181
Editions Prosveta SA, pg 182
Editions Le Sarment, pg 184
Le Serpent a Plumes, pg 184
Editions Andre Silvaire Sarl, pg 185
Alain Thomas Editeur, pg 188
Editions Trois Fontaines, pg 188
Union Generale d'Editions, pg 188

French Polynesia

Scoop/Au Vent des Iles, pg 190
Haere Po No Tahiti, pg 190

Germany

AOL-Verlag Frohmut Menze, pg 194
ARCult Media, pg 194
Aussaat Verlag, pg 197
Dr Bachmaier Verlag GmbH, pg 197
Bank-Verlag GmbH, pg 198
Bertelsmann Lexikon Verlag GmbH, pg 201
Blaukreuz-Verlag Wuppertal, pg 204
BLV Verlagsgesellschaft mbH, pg 204
Carlsen Verlag GmbH, pg 209
Claudius Verlag, pg 211
Data Becker GmbH & Co KG, pg 212
Deutsche Landwirtschaft-Gesellschaft VerlagsgesGmbH, pg 214
Verlag Deutsche Unitarier, pg 214
Deutscher Taschenbuch Verlag GmbH & Co KG (dtv), pg 215
Donat Verlag, pg 217
Droemersche Verlagsanstalt Th Knaur Nachfolger GmbH & Co, pg 218
Emons Verlag, pg 222
Englisch Verlag GmbH, pg 222
Erlanger Verlag Fuer Mission und Okumene, pg 223
EVT Energy Video Training & Verlag GmbH, pg 225
Karin Fischer Verlag GmbH, pg 228
S Fischer Verlag GmbH, pg 228
Flensburger Hefte Verlag GmbH, pg 228
Focus-Verlag Gesellschaft mbH, pg 229
Franz-Sales-Verlag, pg 229
G Braun (vormals G Braun'sche Hofbuchdruckerei und Verlag) Gmbh, pg 231
Gatzanis Verlags GmbH, pg 231
Genius Verlag, pg 231
Gesellschaft fur Organisationswissenschaft e V, pg 232
Gieck Reiner v Ursel Gieck, pg 232
Graefe und Unzer Verlag GmbH, pg 233
Grafit Verlag GmbH, pg 234
Verlag der Stiftung Gralsbotschaft GmbH, pg 234
Walter Haedecke Verlag, pg 236
Hallwag Verlag GmbH, pg 236
Heel Verlag GmbH, pg 238
Heigl Verlag, Horst Edition, pg 239
Himmelsturmer Verlag, pg 241
Junfermann-Verlag, pg 247
Verlag Kiepenheuer und Witsch GmbH & Co KG, pg 249
Verlag im Kilian GmbH, pg 249
Verlag Kleine Schritte Ursula Dahm & Co, pg 249
Kolibri-Verlags GmbH, pg 252
Karin Kramer Verlag, pg 253

Institut fuer Landes- und Stadtentwicklungsforschung, ILS Nordrhein-Westfalen, pg 255
Karl Robert Langewiesche Nachfolger Hans Koester KG, pg 256
Dr Gisela Lermann, pg 257
LEU-VERLAG Wolfgang Leupelt, pg 257
Matthias-Gruenewald-Verlag GmbH, pg 261
Midena Verlag, pg 264
MM-Verlagsgesellschaft mbH, pg 264
Verlagsgesellschaft Rudolf Mueller GmbH & Co KG, pg 265
NaturaViva Verlags GmbH, pg 266
Neues Literaturkontor, pg 268
Hans-Nietsch-Verlag, pg 269
Oekobuch Verlag & Versand GmbH, pg 269
One Way Medien OHG, pg 270
Verlag Parzeller GmbH & Co KG, pg 271
J Pfeiffer Verlag, pg 273
Piper Verlag GmbH, pg 274
Propylaeen Verlag, Zweigniederlassung Berlin der Ullstein Buchverlage GmbH, pg 275
Psychosozial-Verlag, pg 275
Werner Rau Verlag, pg 277
Regura Verlag, pg 277
E Reinhold Verlag, pg 278
Reise Know-How Verlag Peter Rump GmbH, pg 278
Verlagsgruppe Reise-Know-How, pg 278
Schott Musik International GmbH & Co KG, pg 284
Siegler & Co Verlag fuer Zeitarchive GmbH, pg 286
Silberburg-Verlag Titus Haeussermann GmbH, pg 287
teNeues Verlag GmbH & Co KG, pg 292
Tetra Verlag Gmbh, pg 292
Konrad Theiss Verlag GmbH, pg 293
Tipress Dienstleistungen fur das Verlagswesen GmbH, pg 294
Traditionell Bogenschiessen Verlag Angelika Hornig, pg 294
Treves Editions Verein Zur Foerderung der Kuenstlerischen Taetigkeiten, pg 295
Tuebinger Vereinigung fur Volkskunde eV (TVV), pg 295
Verlag Moderne Industrie AG & Co KG, pg 298
Friedr Vieweg & Sohn Verlagsgesellschaft mbH, pg 298
Wehr & Wissen Verlagsgesellschaft mbH, pg 300
Westdeutscher Verlag GmbH, pg 302

Ghana

Asempa Publishers, pg 306
Educational Press & Manufacturers Ltd, pg 307

Greece

Chrysi Penna - Golden Pen Books, pg 309
Ekdotike Athenon SA, pg 310
Harlenic Hellas Publishing SA, pg 311
Hestia-I D Hestia-Kollaros & Co Corporation, pg 311
Idmon Publications, pg 311
Medusa/Selas, pg 313
Minoas SA, pg 313

Ed Nea Acropolis, pg 313
Opera, pg 314
Patakis Publishers, pg 314

Hong Kong

Design Human Resources Training & Development, pg 319
Joint Publishing (HK) Co Ltd, pg 320
Lea Publications Ltd, pg 320
Sun Mui Press, pg 322

Hungary

Joszoveg Muhely Kiado, pg 324
Kiiarat Konyvdiado, pg 324
Magyar Kemikusok Egyesulete, pg 325
Szepirodalmi Koenyvkiado Kiado, pg 327
Typotex Kft Elektronikus Kiado, pg 327

Iceland

Bokaforlag Birtingur, pg 327
Mal og menning, pg 328

India

Addison-Wesley (Singapore) Pte Ltd, pg 329
Anmol Publications Pvt Ltd, pg 331
BR Publishing Corporation, pg 334
CICC Book House, pg 335
Eastern Law House Pvt Ltd, pg 336
Frank Brothers & Co (Publishers) Ltd, pg 337
Geeta Prakasham, pg 337
Gyan Publishing House, pg 338
India Book House Pvt Ltd, pg 339
Indus Publishing Co, pg 339
Orient Paperbacks, pg 345
Oxford University Press, pg 345
People's Publishing House (P) Ltd, pg 346
Reliance Publishing House, pg 347
Sterling Publishers Pvt Ltd, pg 351
Stree, pg 351
Vidya Puri, pg 352
Vision Books Pvt Ltd, pg 353

Indonesia

Mizan, pg 356
Penerbit Nusa Indah, pg 356
Tintamas Indonesia PT, pg 357

Ireland

A & A Farmar, pg 358
Anvil Books Ltd, pg 358
Brandon Book Publishers Ltd, pg 359
The Children's Press, pg 359
Clo Iar-Chonnachta Teo, pg 359
The Columba Book Service, pg 359
The Columba Press, pg 359
Dee-Jay Publications, pg 359
Estragon Press Ltd, pg 360
Gill & Macmillan Ltd, pg 361
Mercier Press Ltd, pg 362
Mount Eagle Publications Ltd, pg 362
Oak Tree Press, pg 362
The O'Brien Press Ltd, pg 363
On Stream Publications Ltd, pg 363
Roberts Rinehart Publishers, pg 363
Town House & Country House, pg 364
Veritas Co Ltd, pg 364
Wolfhound Press, pg 364

TYPE OF PUBLICATION INDEX

Israel

Bitan Publishers Ltd, pg 365
Boostan Publishing House, pg 366
Breslov Research Institute, pg 366
DAT Publications, pg 366
Dekel Publishing House, pg 366
Hakibbutz Hameuchad Publishing House Ltd, pg 368
The Institute for Israeli Arabs Studies, pg 368
L B Publishing Co, pg 369
Massada Press Ltd, pg 370
Mirkam Publishers, pg 370
Pitspopany Press, pg 371
R Sirkis Publishers Ltd, pg 372
Urim Publications, pg 373

Italy

Adelphi Edizioni SpA, pg 374
Il Castello srl, pg 380
Centro Biblico, pg 380
CIC Edizioni Internazionali, pg 381
Edizioni del Centro, pg 384
Edizioni Della Torre di Salvatore Fozzi & C SAS, pg 384
Ediciclo Editore SRL, pg 386
Edizioni Il Punto d'Incontro SAS, pg 386
Edizioni l'eta Dell'Acquario Di l Bresci & C Sas, pg 387
Edizioni Mediterranee SRL, pg 387
Edizioni Qiqajon, pg 387
Giulio Einaudi Editore SpA, pg 387
Fanucci, pg 388
Folini, pg 389
Garolla, pg 390
Garzanti Editore, pg 390
Giunti (Gruppo Editoriale), pg 390
Piero Gribaudi Editore, pg 391
IHT Gruppo Editoriale SRL, pg 393
Il Saggiatore, pg 393
Kaos Edizioni SRL, pg 395
L'Airone Editrice, pg 395
Lindau, pg 396
Lusva Editrice, pg 397
Arnoldo Mondadori Editore SpA, pg 399
NodoLibri, pg 401
La Nuova Italia Editrice SpA, pg 401
Servitium, pg 408
Edizioni Sorbona Milano, pg 408
TEA Tascabili degli Editori Associati SpA, pg 409
Transeuropa Libri, pg 410
Marco Tropea Editore, pg 410

Japan

AVACO - Christian Mass Communications Center, pg 414
Chikuma Shobo Publishing Co Ltd, pg 415
Dohosha Publishing Co Ltd, pg 416
Hakuyo-Sha, pg 417
Hoikusha Publishing Co Ltd, pg 417
Hyoronsha Publishing Co Ltd, pg 417
International Society for Educational Information (ISEI), pg 418
Japan Publications Inc, pg 418
Kosei Publishing Co Ltd, pg 420
Kyodo-Isho Shuppan Co Ltd, pg 420
Nippon Hoso Shuppan Kyokai (NHK Publishing), pg 422
Shincho-Sha Co Ltd, pg 425
Shufunotomo sha Co Ltd, pg 426
Toho Shuppan, pg 427
Yohan Shuppan, pg 429

TYPE OF PUBLICATION INDEX BOOK

Kenya
Heinemann Kenya Limited (EAEP), pg 431
Phoenix Publishers, pg 433

Republic of Korea
Gim-Yeong Co, pg 436
Hollym Corporation Publishers, pg 437
Koreaone Press Inc, pg 438
Kukmin Doseo Publishing Co Inc, pg 438
O Neul Publishing Co, pg 439
Prompter Publications, pg 439
Woong Jin Publishing Co Ltd, pg 440
Word of Life Press, pg 440
Yeha Publishing Co Ltd, pg 441

Latvia
Alberts XII, pg 441
Artava Ltd, pg 441
Preses Nams, pg 442

Luxembourg
Essay und Zeitgeist Verlag, pg 447
Op der Lay, pg 447

Malaysia
S Abdul Majeed & Co, pg 451
Holograms (M) Sdn Bhd, pg 452
MDC Publishers Printers, pg 453
Pustaka Cipta Sdn Bhd, pg 454

Malta
Fondazzjoni Patrimonju Malti, pg 456

Mauritius
Hemco Publications, pg 457

Mexico
Colegio de Postgraduados en Ciencias Agricolas, pg 459
Del Verbo Emprender SA de CV, pg 459
Editorial Diana SA de CV, pg 459
Ediciones Eca SA de CV, pg 460
Edamex SA de CV, pg 460
Ediciones Era SA de CV, pg 460
Ediciones Euroamericanas, pg 461
Hoja Casa Editorial SA de CV, pg 462
Libra Editorial SA de CV, pg 463
Editorial Limusa SA de CV, pg 463
Editorial Minutiae Mexicana SA, pg 464
Naves Internacional de Ediciones SA, pg 464
Panorama Editorial, SA, pg 465

Monaco
Editions EGC, pg 468

Netherlands
BV Uitgeverij de Arbeiderspers, pg 473
Uitgeverij Arena BV, pg 473
Bosch & Keuning, pg 474
Buijten en Schipperheijn BV Drukkerij en Uitg Mij v/h, pg 475
Business Contact BV, pg 475
BZZTOH Publishers, pg 475
Cadans, pg 475
Uitgeverij G F Callenbach BV, pg 475
Uitgeverij De Fontein BV, pg 477
De Harmonie, pg 478

Hayit Nederland BV, pg 478
Helmond B. V. Uitgeverij, pg 478
Holland B V Uitgeversmaatschappij, pg 478
Uitgeverij De Kern, pg 479
Uitgeefmaatschappij J H Kok BV, pg 480
Uitgeverij Leopold BV, pg 480
Meinema, pg 481
Mets & Schilt Uitgevers en Distributeurs, pg 481
Uitgeverij Mingus, pg 481
Nijgh & Van Ditmar Amsterdam, pg 482
Servire BV Uitgevers, pg 484
A J G Strengholt's Boeken, Anno 1928, BV, pg 484
Telos Boeken, pg 485
Tirion Uitgevers BV, pg 485
Uitgeverij G A van Oorschot bv, pg 486

New Zealand
Aoraki Press Ltd, pg 488
Auckland University Press, pg 488
Brick Row Publishing Co Ltd, pg 489
Bush Press Communications Ltd, pg 489
Canterbury University Press, pg 489
Cape Catley, pg 489
Exisle Publishing Ltd, pg 491
Fraser Books, pg 491
Gondwanaland Press, pg 491
Graphic Educational Publications, pg 491
Halcyon Publishing Ltd, pg 491
HarperCollins Publishers (New Zealand) Ltd, pg 491
Hazard Press Ltd, pg 491
Heritage Press Ltd, pg 492
Hodder Moa Beckett Publishers Ltd, pg 492
Huia Publishers, pg 492
Lincoln University Press, pg 492
David Ling Publishing, pg 493
Longacre Press, pg 493
Magari Publishing, pg 493
Orca Publishing Services Ltd, pg 494
Otago Heritage Books, pg 494
R P L Books, pg 495
Resource Books Ltd, pg 495
Shoal Bay Press Ltd, pg 495
Southern Press Ltd, pg 496
Tandem Press, pg 496
Te Waihora Press, pg 496
Bridget Williams Books Ltd, pg 497

Nigeria
Riverside Communications, pg 501
Joe-Tolalu & Associates, pg 501
University Publishing Co, pg 502
Vantage Publishers International Ltd, pg 502

Norway
J W Cappelens Forlag A/S, pg 503
Ex Libris Forlag A/S, pg 503
Egmont Hjemmets Bokforlag AS, pg 504
Pax Forlag A/S, pg 504

Peru
Ediciones Peisa (Promocion Editorial Inca SA), pg 511

Philippines
Anvil Publishing Inc, pg 512
Bookmark Inc, pg 512

Bright Concepts Printing House, pg 512
De La Salle University, pg 513
Marren Publishing House, Inc, pg 513
New Day Publishers, pg 514
Rex Bookstores & Publishers, pg 514

Poland
Arlekin-Wydawnictwo Harlequin Enterprises sp zoo, pg 516
Gdanskie Wydawnictwo Psychologiczne SC, pg 516
Ksiaznica Publishing Ltd, pg 517
Oficyna Wydawnicza Read Me, pg 519

Portugal
Edicoes 70, Lda, pg 524
Editorial Estampa, Lda, pg 524
Publicacoes Europa-America Lda, pg 524
Gradiva-Publicacnoes Lda, pg 525
Planeta Editora, LDA, pg 528

Puerto Rico
Modern Guides Company, pg 530

Romania
Editora All, pg 531
Editura Clusium, Casa de Editura Atlas-Clusium SRL, pg 532
Editura Humanitas, pg 533
Humanitas Publishing House, pg 533
Lider Verlag, pg 534
Editura Niculescu, pg 534
Polirom Verlag, pg 535
Rentrop & Straton Verlagsgruppe und Wirtschaftsconsulting, pg 535

Russian Federation
N E Bauman Moscow State Technical University Publishers, pg 537
Glas New Russian Writing, pg 538
Izdatel 'stvo Ural' skogo, pg 538
Publishing House Limbus Press, pg 539
Novosti Izdatel 'stvo, pg 541
Obdeestro Znanie, pg 541
Panorama Publishing House, pg 541
Text Publishers Ltd Too, pg 542

Senegal
Centre Africain d'Animation et d'Echanges Culturels Editions Khoudia, pg 544

Singapore
Aquanut Agencies Pte Ltd, pg 545
Chopsons Pte Ltd, pg 545
Pearson Education Asia, pg 547
Taylor & Francis Asia Pacific, pg 548
Tecman Bible House, pg 549

Slovakia
Priroda, pg 550
Serafin, pg 550
Smena Publishing House, pg 550

South Africa
Educum Publishers Ltd, pg 554
Fernwood Press (Pty) Ltd, pg 554
Galago Publishing Pty Ltd, pg 554
Heinemann Educational Publishers Southern Africa, pg 555

Johannesburg Art Gallery, pg 556
Kima Global Publishers, pg 556
Maskew Miller Longman, pg 557
New Africa Books (Pty) Ltd, pg 557
Queillerie Publishers, pg 558
Ravan Press (Pty) Ltd, pg 558
Southern Book Publishers (Pty) Ltd, pg 559

Spain
Alberdania SL, pg 562
Alianza Editorial SA, pg 562
CEAC, Grupo Editorial SA, pg 567
Complutense, SA Editorial, pg 568
Comunidad Autonoma de Madrid, Servicio de Documentacion y Publicaciones, pg 568
Rafael Dalmau, Editor, pg 569
Ediciones Destino SA, pg 569
Ediciones Diaz de Santos SA, pg 569
Didaco Comunicacion y Didactica, SA, pg 569
EDHASA (Editora y Distribuidora Hispano-Americana SA), pg 571
Edicomunicacion SA, pg 572
Ediles-Ediciones Leonesas SA, pg 572
Elkar, Euskal Liburu eta Kantuen Argitaldaria, SL, pg 573
Fundacion Rosacruz, pg 575
Editorial Gustavo Gili SA, pg 576
Grijalbo Mondadori SA, pg 576
Impredisur, SL, pg 578
LEDA (Las Ediciones de Arte), pg 579
Ediciones Libertarias/Prodhufi SA, pg 580
Ediciones Maeva, pg 581
Ediciones Martinez-Roca SA, pg 581
Ediciones Medici SA, pg 582
Editorial Moll SL, pg 582
Naque Editora, pg 583
Noguer y Caralt Editores SA, pg 584
Omnicon, SA, pg 585
Editorial Peregrino SL, pg 586
Editorial El Perpetuo Socorro, pg 586
Polifemo, Ediciones, pg 587
Equipo Sirius SA, pg 591
Grup 62, pg 591
Tirant lo Blanch SL Libreriaa, pg 592
Tursen, SA, pg 593
Tusquets Editores, pg 593
Ediciones 29 - Libros Rio Nuevo, pg 594
Ediciones Urano, SA, pg 595
Vinaches Lopez, Luisa, pg 595

Sri Lanka
Buddhist Publication Society Inc, pg 596
Inter-Cultural Book Promoters, pg 597

Sweden
Allt om Hobby AB, pg 600
Delta Forlags AB, pg 601

Switzerland
ADIRA, pg 607
Bergli Books AG, pg 609
Christoph Merian Verlag, pg 611
Cosmos-Verlag AG, pg 611
Cultur Prospectiv, Edition, pg 612
Diogenes Verlag AG, pg 612
Edition Exodus, pg 614

PUBLISHERS

Oesch Verlag AG, pg 620
Editiones Payot Lausanne, pg 621
Verlag Die Pforte im Rudolf Steiner Verlag, pg 621
PIE-Peter Lang SA, pg 622
Editiones Roche, pg 623
Editions D'Art Albert Skira SA, pg 625
Rudolf Steiner Verlag, pg 625
Verlag im Waldgut AG, pg 627

Taiwan, Province of China

Chung Hwa Book Co Ltd, pg 629
Linking Publishing Company Ltd, pg 631
Petroleum Information Publishing Co, pg 631
Youth Cultural Publishing Co, pg 632
Yuan Liou Publishing Co, Ltd, pg 632

United Republic of Tanzania

Tanzania Publishing House, pg 634

Tunisia

Alyssa Editions, pg 637
Ceres Editions, pg 637
Maison Tunisienne de l'Edition, pg 638

Turkey

Cep Kitaplari AS, pg 639
Inkilap Publishers Ltd, pg 640
Metis Yayinlari, pg 640
Pan Yayincilik, pg 640
Sabah Kitaplari, pg 641
Toros Yayinlari Ltd Co, pg 641
Varlik Yayinlari AS, pg 641

Ukraine

ASK Ltd, pg 643

United Arab Emirates

Motivate Publishing, pg 644

United Kingdom

Act 3 Publishing, pg 645
Adamantine Press Ltd, pg 645
Allison & Busby, pg 646
Andromeda Oxford Ltd, pg 647
Apex Publishing Ltd, pg 648
Arms & Armour Press, pg 648
Art Books International Ltd, pg 649
Arthur James Ltd, pg 649
Aslib, The Association for Information Management, pg 650
Association for Science Education, pg 650
Atlantic Transport Publishers, pg 650
Atlas Press, pg 651
Aulis Publishers, pg 651
The Banner of Truth Trust, pg 652
Colin Baxter Photography Ltd, pg 652
Bay View Books Ltd, pg 652
BBC Worldwide Publishers, pg 653
Ruth Bean Publishers, pg 653
BFI Publishing, pg 654
Bible Reading Fellowship, pg 654
Birlinn Ltd, pg 655
Black Ace Books, pg 655
Blackstaff Press, pg 655
Blandford Publishing Ltd, pg 656
Bloodaxe Books Ltd, pg 656
Bloomsbury Publishing PLC, pg 656
Blorenge Books, pg 656
Blueprint, pg 656

The Book Guild Ltd, pg 657
Book Packaging & Marketing, pg 657
Books for Europe Ltd, pg 657
Boulevard Books UK/The Babel Guides, pg 658
Bowerdean Publishing Co Ltd, pg 658
Nicholas Brealey Publishing, pg 659
Breese Books Ltd, pg 659
Brewin Books Ltd, pg 659
British Cement Association, pg 660
Calder Publications Ltd, pg 662
Canongate Books Ltd, pg 663
Capstone Publishing Ltd, pg 663
Jon Carpenter Publishing, pg 664
Cassell & Co, pg 664
Centre for Alternative Technology, pg 665
Christian Education, pg 667
Cockbird Press, pg 669
Computer Step, pg 670
Constable & Robinson Ltd, pg 670
Constable Publishers, pg 670
Leo Cooper, pg 671
Countyvise Ltd, pg 671
Creation Books, pg 671
Cressrelles Publishing Company Ltd, pg 672
Crossbridge Books, pg 672
The Crowood Press Ltd, pg 672
CTBI Publications, pg 672
Dance Books Ltd, The Old Bakery, pg 673
The C W Daniel Co Ltd, pg 673
Christopher Davies Publishers Ltd, pg 674
Dedalus Ltd, pg 674
Delectus Books, pg 675
DMG Business Media Ltd, pg 675
Eagle/Inter Publishing Service (IPS) Ltd, pg 676
Elliot Right Way Books, pg 678
Aidan Ellis Publishing, pg 678
Eurobook Ltd, pg 679
Express Newspapers, pg 681
Extraordinary People Press, pg 681
Fabian Society, pg 681
Findhorn Press Inc, pg 682
Fourth Estate Ltd, pg 683
George Mann Publications, pg 687
GMC Publications Ltd, pg 687
GMP Publishers Ltd, pg 687
Granta Books, pg 689
W Green The Scottish Law Publisher, pg 689
Harden's Ltd, pg 692
HarperCollins Publishers, pg 692
Harvard University Press, pg 692
The Harvill Press Ltd, pg 693
Haynes Publishing, pg 693
Headline Book Publishing Ltd, pg 693
Health Development Agency, pg 694
Heartland Publishing Ltd, pg 694
Christopher Helm (Publishers) Ltd, pg 694
Heritage Press, pg 695
Hodder & Stoughton General, pg 696
Hodder & Stoughton Religious, pg 696
Hodder Headline Ltd, pg 696
Honno Welsh Women's Press, pg 697
How To Books Ltd, pg 697
The Islamic Texts Society, pg 701
Janus Publishing Company Ltd, pg 702
John Blake Publishing Ltd, pg 703
Michael Joseph, pg 703
Lang Syne Publishers Ltd, pg 706

Lawrence & Wishart, pg 706
Lion Publishing PLC, pg 708
Luath Press Ltd, pg 709
The Lutterworth Press, pg 709
Macmillan Audio Books, pg 710
Management Books 2000 Ltd, pg 711
Mandrake of Oxford, pg 711
Marston House, pg 712
Mercat Press, pg 713
The Merlin Press Ltd, pg 713
Metro Publishing Ltd, pg 714
J Garnet Miller, pg 714
Mirabel Books Ltd, pg 715
Monarch Books, pg 715
Moorley's Print & Publishing Ltd, pg 715
New Era Publications UK Ltd, pg 718
New European Publications Ltd, pg 718
NMS Publishing Ltd, pg 719
The Octagon Press Ltd, pg 720
Octopus Publishing Group, pg 720
The Oleander Press, pg 721
Michael O'Mara Books Ltd, pg 721
Open Gate Press, pg 721
Orion Publishing Group Ltd, pg 722
The Orkney Press Ltd, pg 722
Osprey Publishing Ltd, pg 722
Peter Owen Ltd, pg 722
Pan Macmillan, pg 723
Parthian Books, pg 724
PC Publishing, pg 725
Pearson Education Europe, Mideast & Africa, pg 725
Pen & Sword Books Ltd, pg 725
Penguin Books Ltd, pg 725
The Penguin Group UK, pg 726
Piatkus Books, pg 727
Plexus Publishing Ltd, pg 728
Pluto Press, pg 728
Poetry Wales Press Ltd, pg 729
Police Review Publishing Company Ltd, pg 729
The Policy Press, pg 729
Polybooks Ltd, pg 729
Polygon, pg 729
David Porteous Editions, pg 729
Prion Books Ltd, pg 730
Profile Books Ltd, pg 731
Quartet Books Ltd, pg 731
Quiller Publishing Ltd, pg 732
Quintet Publishing Ltd, pg 732
Reaktion Books Ltd, pg 733
Retail Entertainment Data Publishing Ltd, pg 735
Rooster Books Ltd, pg 735
Rough Guides Ltd, pg 735
The Rubicon Press, pg 737
Sainsbury Publishing Ltd, pg 737
Saint Andrew Press, pg 737
SAWD Publications, pg 738
SCM Press, pg 739
Scottish Cultural Press, pg 739
Seren, pg 740
Serif, pg 740
Serpent's Tail Ltd, pg 740
Sheldon Press, pg 741
Shelfmark Books, pg 741
Sigma Press, pg 742
Silver Link Publishing Ltd, pg 742
Simon & Schuster Ltd, pg 742
Skoob Russell Square, pg 742
Colin Smythe Ltd, pg 743
The Society for Promoting Christian Knowledge (SPCK), pg 743
Spokesman, pg 744
St Pauls Publishing, pg 744
Stenlake Publishing, pg 745
Stobart Davies Ltd, pg 745
Sutton Publishing Ltd, pg 746
Tabb House, pg 746

TYPE OF PUBLICATION INDEX

Take That Ltd, pg 746
Tarragon Press, pg 746
I B Tauris & Co Ltd, pg 747
John Taylor Book Ventures, pg 747
Telegraph Books, pg 748
Thistle Press, pg 748
Time Warner Books UK, pg 749
Titan Books Ltd, pg 749
University of London Careers Service, pg 751
Verso, pg 752
Ward Lock Ltd, pg 754
Wayland Publishers Ltd (Incorporating Macdonald Young Books), pg 754
White Cockade Publishing, pg 755
White Eagle Publishing Trust, pg 755
Neil Wilson Publishing Ltd, pg 757
The Windrush Press Ltd, pg 757
Gordon Wright Publishing Ltd, pg 759

Uruguay

Nordan-Comunidad, pg 760
Editia Uruguay, pg 761

Viet Nam

Science & Technics Publishing House, pg 763

Yugoslavia

AGAPE, pg 764
Alfa-Narodna Knjiga, pg 764

PERIODICALS, JOURNALS

Afghanistan

Government Press, pg 1

Albania

NL SH, pg 1

Argentina

Libreria Akadia Editorial, pg 3
Diario la Voz del Interior, pg 5
Editorial Idearium de la Universidad de Mendoza (EDIUM), pg 5
Polemos SA, pg 8
Editoria Universitaria de la Patagonia, pg 9

Australia

ACHPER Inc (Australian Council for Health, Physical Education & Recreation), pg 10
Aerospace Publications, pg 11
Arabian Focus Pty Ltd, pg 11
Australasian Medical Publishing Company Ltd (AMPCO), pg 13
Australian Academic Press Pty Ltd, pg 13
Australian Institute of Family Studies (AIFS), pg 13
Bernal Publishing, pg 14
Blackwell Science Pty Ltd, pg 15
David Boyce Publishing, pg 16
Bureau of Resource Sciences, pg 16
Butterworths Australia Ltd, pg 16
China Books, pg 18
Covenanter Press, pg 19
CSIRO Publishing (Commonwealth Scientific & Industrial Research Organisation), pg 19
Fernfawn Publications, pg 22
Gangan Publishing, pg 23
Illert Publications, pg 27
Instauratio Press, pg 27

TYPE OF PUBLICATION INDEX

BOOK

James Nicholas Publishers Pty Ltd, pg 28
Jesuit Publications, pg 28
Law Book Co Information Services, pg 29
Magpies Magazine, pg 31
Matthias Media, pg 32
Melbourne Institute of Applied Economic & Social Research, pg 33
Mulini Press, pg 34
National Gallery of Victoria, pg 34
NMA Publications, pg 35
Jill Oxton Publications Pty Ltd, pg 36
Papyrus Publishing, pg 37
Pearson Education Australia, pg 37
Priestley Consulting, pg 39
Queen Victoria Museum & Art Gallery Publications, pg 39
Royal Society of New South Wales, pg 41
Skills Publishing, pg 42
D W Thorpe, pg 44
University of Queensland Press, pg 46
Windhorse Books, pg 48
Winetitles, pg 48

Austria

Autorensolidaritat - Verlag der Interessengemeinschaft osterreichischer Autorinnen und Autoren, pg 49
Boehlau Verlag GmbH & Co KG, pg 50
Bohmann Druck und Verlag GmbH & Co KG, pg 50
Buchkultur Verlags GmbH Zeitschrift fuer Literatur & Kunst, pg 50
Dachs-Verlag GmbH, pg 50
Docker Verlag GmbH & Co KG, pg 51
Ferdinand Berger und Sohne, pg 51
Globus Buchvertrieb, pg 52
Guthmann & Peterson Liber Libri, Edition, pg 52
Horst Knapp Finanznachrichten, pg 54
Linde Verlag Wien GmbH, pg 54
Medien & Recht, pg 55
Verlag der Oesterreichischen Akademie der Wissenschaften (OEAW), pg 56
Verlag des Oesterreichischen Gewerkschaftsbundes GmbH, pg 56
Oesterreichischer Agrarverlag, Druck- und Verlags- GmbH, pg 56
Oesterreichischer Kunst und Kulturverlag, pg 56
Osterreichischer Bundesveilag Ges.mbH, pg 57
Anna Pichler Verlag GmbH, pg 57
Resch Verlag, pg 57
Dr A Schendl GmbH und Co KG, pg 58
Andreas Schnider Verlags-Atelier, pg 58
Signum Verlag GmbH & Co KG, pg 58
Springer-Verlag Wien, pg 59
Studien Verlag Gmbh, pg 59
Edition Thurnhof KEG, pg 59
Universitaetsverlag Wagner GmbH, pg 60
Georg Westermann Verlag GmbH, pg 61

WUV/Facultas Universitaetsverlag, pg 61
Zirkular - Verlag der Dokumentationsstelle fuer neuere oesterreichische Literatur, pg 61

Azerbaijan

Sada, Literaturno-Izdatel'skij Centr, pg 61

Bangladesh

Gono Prakashani, Gono Shasthya Kendra, pg 62
The University Press Ltd, pg 62

Belgium

Centre Aequatoria, pg 64
NV Uitgeverij Altiora Averbode, pg 64
Bourdeaux-Capelle SA, pg 65
Brepols Publishers NV, pg 65
Eteblissements Emile Bruylant SA, pg 65
CED-Samsom, pg 66
Centre d'Action Laique, pg 66
Cremers (Schoollandkaarten) PVBA, pg 67
Documenta CV, pg 68
Editions Dupuis SA, pg 68
Eenhoorn BVBA, pg 68
Huis Van Het Boek, pg 69
Institut Royal des Relations Internationales, pg 69
Intersentia Uitgevers NV, pg 69
Ipis VZW (International Peace Information Service), pg 69
Uitgeverij J van In, pg 70
Koepel van de Vlaamse Noord - Zuidbeweging 11.11.11, pg 70
Koninklijke Vlaamse Academie van Belgie voor Wetenschappen en Kunsten, pg 70
Larcier-Department of De Boeck & Larcier SA, pg 71
Editeurs de Litterature Biblique, pg 71
Maklu, pg 71
La Part de L'Oeil, pg 72
Sonneville Press (Uitgeverij) VTW, pg 74
Stichting Ons Erfdeel VZW, pg 74
UGA Editions (Uitgeverij), pg 74

Benin

Office National d'Edition de Presse et d'Imprimerie (ONEPI), pg 76

Bosnia and Herzegovina

Svjetlost, pg 77

Botswana

The Botswana Society, pg 77

Brazil

Action Editora Ltda, pg 77
Agalma Psicanalise Editora Ltda, pg 78
Editora Alfa Omega Ltda, pg 78
Antenna Edicoes Tecnicas Ltda, pg 78
Concordia Editora Ltda, pg 81
Ediouro Publicacoes, SA, pg 81
Editora Brasil-America (EBAL) SA, pg 82
Companhia Editora Forense, pg 82
EDUC - Editora da PUC-SP, pg 82
EDUSC - Editora da Universidade do Sagrado Coracao, pg 82
Selecoes Eletronicas Editora Ltda, pg 83

Empresa Brasileira de Pesquisa Agropecaria, pg 83
Fundacao Instituto Brasileiro de Geografia e Estatistica (IBGE - CDDI/DECOP), pg 84
Editora Globo SA, pg 84
Editora Kuarup Ltda, pg 86
Edicoes Loyola SA, pg 87
Oliveira Rocha-Comercio e Servics Ltda, pg 89
Qualitymark Editora Ltda, pg 90
Rede Das Artes (Boccato Editores Collector's), pg 90
Editora Sinodal, pg 91
Spala Editora Ltda, pg 92
Editora UNESP, pg 92
Fundacao Getulio Vargas, pg 93
Editora Vecchi SA, pg 93
Editora Vida Crista Ltda, pg 93

Bulgaria

Agencija Za Ikonomicesko Programirane i Razvitie, pg 94
Bojko Kacarmazov, pg 94
CHRIKER, pg 94
Foi-Commerce, pg 95
Gea-Libris Publishing House, pg 95
Interpres, pg 96
LIK IZDANIJA, pg 96
Litera Prima, pg 96
Makros 2000 - Plovdiv, pg 96
Publishing House Narodno delo OOD, pg 97
Pensoft Publishers, pg 97
Sibi, pg 97
Sila & Zivot, pg 98

Burundi

Editions Intore, pg 98

Cameroon

Presses Universitaires d'Afrique, pg 99

Chile

Ediciones Bat, pg 99
Ediciones Universitarias de Valparaiso, pg 101

China

Beijing Publishing House, pg 102
Chemical Industry Press, pg 102
China Film Press, pg 103
China Foreign Economic Relations & Trade Publishing House, pg 103
China Machine Press (CMP), pg 103
China Ocean Press, pg 103
China Oil & Gas Periodical Office, pg 104
China Tibetology Publishing House, pg 104
China Translation & Publishing Corp, pg 104
China Youth Publishing House, pg 104
Foreign Language Teaching & Research Press, pg 105
Higher Education Press, pg 106
Inner Mongolia Science & Technology Publishing House, pg 106
Language Publishing House, pg 107
The People's Communications Publishing House, pg 107
Printing Industry Publishing House, pg 108
Science Press, pg 108
Shanghai Fine Arts Publishers, pg 109

Shanghai Foreign Language Education Press, pg 109
Tianjin Science & Technology Publishing House, pg 109
World Affairs Press, pg 110

Colombia

Centro Regional para el Fomento del Libro en America Latina y el Caribe, pg 111
Consejo Episcopal Latinoamericano Celam, pg 111
Editorial Norma SA, pg 113
Editorial Santillana SA, pg 113
Universidad de los Andes Editorial, pg 114

The Democratic Republic of the Congo

Connaissance et Pratique du Droit Zairos (CDPZ), pg 115
Facultes Catoliques de Kinshasa, pg 115

Costa Rica

Centro Agronomico Tropical de Investigacion y Ensenanza (CATIE), pg 115
Litografia Artex, SA, pg 116

Cote d'Ivoire

Akohi Editions, pg 117
Universite d' Abidjan, pg 118

Croatia

Drzavna Uprava za Zastitu Prirode i Okolisa (State Directorate for the Protection of Nature & Environment), pg 118
Faust Vrani, pg 118
Filozofski Fakultet Sveucilista u Zagrebu, pg 118
Hrvatsko filozofsko drustvo, pg 119
Krscanska sadasnjost, pg 119
Knjizevni Krug Split, pg 119
Matica hrvatska, pg 119
Nasa Djeca Publishing, pg 119
Tehnicka Knjiga, pg 120
Vitagraf, pg 120
Znaci Vremena, Institut Za Istrazivanje Biblije, pg 120

Cuba

Casa Editora Abril, pg 120
Pueblo y Educacion Editorial (PE), pg 121

Cyprus

Omilos Pnevmatikis Ananeoseos, pg 122

Czech Republic

Aleko, Nakladatelska Divize, pg 122
AMA nakladatelstvi, pg 123
Divadelni Ustav, pg 124
Jota, pg 125
Karolinum, nakladatelstvi, pg 125
Labyrint, pg 125
Narodni Knihovna CR, pg 126
Narodni Muzeum, pg 126
Cesky normalizacni institut, pg 127
Nakladatelstvi a vydavatelstvi Panorama, pg 127
Portal Ltd, pg 127
Zvon, pg 129

Denmark
Bonnier Publications AS, pg 130
Borgens Forlag A/S, pg 130
The Danish Literature Centre, pg 131
Dansk Psykologisk Forlag, pg 131
Djof Publishing Jurist-og Okonomforbundets Forlag, pg 131
Egmont Group, pg 131
FADL's Forlag A/S (Foreningen af danske Laegestuderendes Forlag), pg 132
Fremad A/S, pg 132
Interpresse A/S, pg 133
Mellemfolkeligt Samvirke, pg 133
Museum Tusculanum Press, pg 134
A/S Skattekartoteket, pg 135
Syddansk Universitetsforlag, pg 136

Dominican Republic
Pontificia Universidad Catolica Madre y Maestra, pg 136

Ecuador
CEPLAES, pg 137
CIESPAL (Centro Internacional de Estudios Superiores de Comunicacion para America Latina), pg 137
Corporacion Editora Nacional, pg 137

Egypt (Arab Republic of Egypt)
American University in Cairo Press, pg 138
Dar El Shorouk Publishing & Distributing House, pg 138
Dar Al Hilap Publishing Institution, pg 139
Ummah Press for Translation & Publishing, pg 139

El Salvador
Editorial Universitaria de la Universidad de El Salvador, pg 139

Estonia
Estonian Academy Publishers, pg 139
Kunst Publishers Ltd, pg 140
Tael Ltd, pg 140

Finland
Aika Oy Kristilliset Kirjat, pg 141
Foersamlingsfoerbundets Foerlags AB, pg 142
Kustannus Oy Uusi Tie, pg 143

France
Editions Al Liamm, pg 146
Annales de la Recherche Urbaine, pg 147
Editions Arcam, pg 147
Art & Metiers Du Livre/Editions, pg 148
Les Editions de l'Atelier SA, pg 148
Autrement Editions, pg 149
Editions l'Avant-Scene de Prette Technique, pg 149
La Bartavelle, pg 149
Editions Belin, pg 150
Editions Bertout, pg 150
Emgleo Breiz, pg 151
Brud Nevez, pg 152
Editions des Cahiers Bourbonnais, pg 152
Editions Casterman, pg 153

CERDIC-Publications, pg 153
Editions Champ Vallon, pg 154
Cirad, pg 155
CTNERHI - Centre Technique National d'Etudes et de Recherches sur les Handicaps et les Inadaptations, pg 157
Editions Dalloz Sirey, pg 157
La Documentation Francaise, pg 159
Doin Editeurs, pg 160
Les Dossiers d'Aquitaine, pg 160
Dunod Editeur, pg 160
Editions de l'Ecole des Hautes Etudes en Sciences Sociales (EHESS), pg 160
Presses de l'Ecole Normale Superieure, pg 160
Edicef - Editions Classiques d'Expression Francaise, pg 161
Edisud, pg 161
Les Editeurs Reunis, pg 161
Les Editions ESF, pg 161
EDP Sciences, pg 161
Elf Exploration Production, pg 161
Editions Entente, pg 162
EPEL, pg 162
Ere Nouvelle, pg 162
Editions Eres, pg 162
Editions Errance, pg 162
Editions Eska, pg 162
Institut d'Etudes Augustiniennes, pg 163
Folklore Comtois, pg 164
Association Frank, pg 165
Futuribles SARL, pg 165
Ganymede, pg 166
Paul Geuthner Librairie Orientaliste, pg 166
L'Harmattan, pg 168
Hermes Science Publications, pg 168
Editions d'Histoire Sociale (EDHIS), pg 168
INRA Editions (Institut National de la Recherche Agronomique), pg 169
Institut International de la Marionnette, pg 170
IRD Editions, pg 170
Editions Klincksieck, pg 171
Editions Universitaires LCF, pg 172
Editions Legislatives, pg 172
LLB France (Ligue pour la Lecture de la Bible), pg 173
Editions de la Maison des Sciences de l'Homme, Paris, pg 174
Masson SA, pg 175
Editions Medianes, pg 175
Presses Universitaires du Mirail, pg 176
Editions Ophrys, pg 178
Opsys Operating System, pg 178
Ouest Editions, pg 178
Editions du Papyrus, pg 179
Editions Parentheses, pg 179
Editions Pedone, pg 179
Peeters-France, pg 179
Jean-Michel Place, pg 180
Editions du Point Veterinaire, pg 180
Editions du Centre Pompidou, pg 180
Presses Universitaires de Caen, pg 181
Presses Universitaires de France (PUF), pg 181
Presses Universitaires de Grenoble, pg 181
Presses Universitaires de Nancy, pg 181
PRODIG UMR 8586 CNRS-Paris 1,4,7 ephe, pg 182

Editions Publications de l'Ecole Moderne Francaise sa (PEMF), pg 182
Publications de l'Universite de Rouen, pg 182
Editions Revue EPS, pg 183
Revue Espaces et Societes, pg 183
Revue Noire, pg 183
Editions Scientifiques et Medicales Elsevier, pg 184
Sepia, pg 184
Le Serpent a Plumes, pg 184
Service des Publications Scientifiques du Museum National d'Histoire Naturelle, pg 184
Societe Mathematique de France - Institut Henri Poincare, pg 185
Editions Springer France, pg 186
SUD, pg 186
Editions Techniques et Scientifiques Francaises, pg 187
Terre Vivante, pg 187
Transeuropeennes/RCE, pg 188
Publications de l'Universite de Pau, pg 188
La Vague a l'ame, pg 188
La Vague Verte, pg 188
La Voix du Regard, pg 189

Germany
A Francke Verlag (Tubingen und Basel), pg 191
Accedo Verlagsgesellschaft mbH, pg 191
Akademie Verlag GmbH, pg 192
E Albrecht Verlags- Kommanditgesellschaft, pg 192
ALS-Verlag GmbH, pg 193
Andernach Atelier Verlag (AVA), pg 193
Antiqua-Verlag GmbH, pg 194
AOL-Verlag Frohmut Menze, pg 194
Arbeiterpresse Verlag GmbH, pg 194
ARCult Media, pg 194
Ardey-Verlag GmbH, pg 194
Aschendorffsche Verlagsbuchhandlung GmbH & Co KG, pg 195
J J Augustin GmbH Verlag, pg 196
Aussaat Verlag, pg 197
Aviatic Verlag GmbH, pg 197
J P Bachem Verlag GmbH, pg 197
Bank-Verlag GmbH, pg 198
Barenreiter-Verlag Karl-Votterle GmbH & Co KG, pg 198
Verlag Dr Albert Bartens KG, pg 198
Johann Ambrosius Barth GmbH, pg 198
Bastei Verlag, pg 199
Baumann GmbH & Co KG, pg 199
Bauverlag GmbH, pg 199
Beacon Verlag Koerber OHG, pg 199
Ludwig Bechauf Verlag, pg 200
Verlag C H Beck (OHG), pg 200
Beleke KG Verlag, pg 200
Berliner Debatte Wissenschafts Verlag, GSFP-Gesellschaft fur Sozialwissen-schaftliche Forschung und Publizistik mbH &Co KG, pg 201
Bertelsmann Lexikon Verlag GmbH, pg 201
W Bertelsmann Verlag GmbH & Co KG, pg 201
BertelsmannSpringer Science & Business Media GmbH, pg 202
Bibliomed - Medizinische Verlagsgesellschaft mbH, pg 203

Blackwell Wissenschafts-Verlag GmbH, pg 203
Blaukreuz-Verlag Wuppertal, pg 204
BLV Verlagsgesellschaft mbH, pg 204
Verlag Erwin Bochinsky GmbH & Co KG, pg 204
Bock und Herchen Verlag, pg 204
Boehlau-Verlag GmbH & Cie, pg 204
Verlag Hermann Boehlaus Nachfolger Weimar GmbH & Co, pg 205
Born-Verlag, pg 205
Brandes & Apsel Verlag GmbH, pg 206
Buchhaendler-Vereinigung GmbH, pg 207
BuchMarkt Verlag K Werner GmbH, pg 207
Buchverlag Junge Welt GmbH, pg 207
Buechse der Pandora Verlags-GmbH, pg 207
Bund fuer deutsche Schrift und Sprache, pg 208
Bund-Verlag GmbH, pg 208
Bundesanzeiger Verlagsgesellschaft, pg 208
Aenne Burda Verlag, pg 208
Verlag Georg D W Callwey GmbH & Co, pg 208
Calwer Verlag Stuttgart eV, pg 209
campusbooks Medien AG, pg 209
Fachverlag Hans Carl GmbH, pg 209
Carl Link Verlag-Gesellschaft mbH Fachverlag fur Verwaltungsrecht, pg 209
CEC-Cosmic Energy Connections, pg 209
Centaurus-Verlagsgesellschaft GmbH, pg 209
Chmielorz GmbH Verlag, pg 210
Chr Belser AG fur Verlagsgeschaefte und Co KG, pg 210
Christliches Verlagshaus GmbH, pg 210
Marianne Cieslik, pg 210
Charles Coleman Verlag GmbH & Co KG, pg 211
Compact Verlag GmbH, pg 211
Connection Medien GmbH, pg 211
Cornelsen Verlag GmbH & Co OHG, pg 211
J G Cotta'sche Buchhandlung Nachfolger GmbH, pg 212
Data Becker GmbH & Co KG, pg 212
Degener & Co, Manfred Dreiss Verlag, pg 213
Verlag Horst Deike KG, pg 213
Deutsche Landwirtschaft-Gesellschaft VerlagsgesGmbH, pg 214
Verlag Deutsche Unitarier, pg 214
Deutsche Verlags-Anstalt GmbH (DVA), pg 214
Deutscher Apotheker Verlag, pg 214
Deutscher Drucker Verlagsgesellschaft, pg 214
Deutscher EC-Verband, pg 214
Deutscher Fachverlag GmbH, pg 214
Deutscher Gemeindeverlag GmbH, pg 214
Deutscher Instituts-Verlag GmbH, pg 215
Deutscher Kunstverlag GmbH, pg 215
Deutscher Psychologen Verlag GmbH (DPV), pg 215

TYPE OF PUBLICATION INDEX — BOOK

Deutscher Verlag fur Kunstwissenschaft, pg 215
Deutscher Wirtschaftsdienst John von Freyend GmbH, pg 216
Diagonal-Verlag GbR Rink-Schweer, pg 216
Die Verlag H Schafer GmbH, pg 216
Dietrich zu Klampen Verlag, pg 216
Verlag J H W Dietz Nachf GmbH, pg 217
Dietz Verlag Berlin GmbH, pg 217
Edition Diskord, pg 217
Christoph Dohr, pg 217
Domino Verlag, Guenther Brinek GmbH, pg 217
Domowina Verlag GmbH, pg 217
Duncker und Humblot GmbH, pg 219
Dustri-Verlag Dr Karl Feistle, pg 219
E Schweizerbart'sche Verlagsbuchhandlung (Nagele und Obermiller), pg 220
Echter Wurzburg Frankische Gesellschaftsdruckerei und Verlag GmbH, pg 220
Ecomed Verlagsgesellschaft AG & Co KG, pg 220
Egmont EHAPA Verlag GmbH, pg 221
Elektor-Verlag GmbH, pg 222
Verlag Peter Engstler, pg 223
Eppinger-Verlag OHG, pg 223
Erasmus Grasser-Verlag GmbH, pg 223
Ergebnisse Verlag GmbH, pg 223
Ernst, Wilhelm & Sohn, Verlag Architektur und technische Wissenschaft GmbH & Co, pg 224
Verlag Esoterische Philosophie GmbH, pg 224
Eulenhof-Verlag Wolfgang Ehrhardt Heinold, pg 224
Europa Union Verlag GmbH, pg 224
Verlag Europaeische Wehrkunde, pg 225
Evangelische Verlagsanstalt GmbH, pg 225
Evangelischer Presseverband fur Bayern eV, pg 225
Evangelischer Presseverband STET Baden eVerlag, pg 225
F Bruckmann Munchen Verlag & Druck GmbH & Co Produkt KG, pg 225
Fachverlag fur das graphische Gewerbe GmbH, pg 226
Fachverlag Schiele & Schoen GmbH, pg 226
Ferd Dummler's Verlag, pg 227
Ferdinand Enke Verlag, pg 227
Harald Fischer Verlag GmbH, pg 228
Franz-Sales-Verlag, pg 229
Verlag Franz Vahlen GmbH, pg 229
Fraunhofer IRB Verlag Fraunhofer Informationszentrum Raum und Bau, pg 229
Verlag A Fromm im Druck- u Verlagshaus Fromm GmbH & Co KG, pg 230
Friedrich Frommann Verlag, pg 230
G Braun (vormals G Braun'sche Hofbuchdruckerei und Verlag) Gmbh, pg 231
Verlagsbuchhandlung Megapress, Franz-J Gaber, pg 231
Betriebswirtschaftlicher Verlag Dr Th Gabler GmbH, pg 231
Gebrueder Borntraeger Science Publishers, pg 231
Konkursbuch Verlag Claudia Gehrke, pg 231
Verlag Junge Gemeinde E Schwinghammer GmbH & Co KG, pg 231
Alfons W Gentner Verlag GmbH & Co KG, pg 231
Germanisches Nationalmuseum, pg 232
Gesundheits-Dialog Verlag GmbH, pg 232
H Gietl Verlag & Publikationsservice GmbH, pg 232
Gildefachverlag GmbH & Co KG, pg 232
Gilles und Francke Verlag, pg 232
Verlagsgesellschaft R Gloess & Co, pg 233
Govi-Verlag Pharmazeutischer Verlag GmbH, pg 233
Grass-Verlag, pg 234
Walter de Gruyter GmbH & Co KG, pg 234
Verlag des Gustav-Adolf-Werks, pg 235
Dr Curt Haefner-Verlag GmbH, pg 236
Carl Hanser Verlag, pg 237
Harenberg Kommunikation Verlags- und Medien GmbH & Co KG, pg 237
Harrassowitz Verlag, pg 237
Haufe Medien gruppe, pg 238
Rudolf Haufe Verlag GmbH & Co KG, pg 238
Karl F Haug Verlag GmbH & Co, pg 238
Heel Verlag GmbH, pg 238
Verlag Herder GmbH & Co KG, pg 239
Hestra-Verlag Hernichel & Dr Strauss GmbH & Co KG, pg 240
Carl Heymanns Verlag KG, pg 240
F Hirthammer Verlag GmbH, pg 241
S Hirzel Verlag GmbH und Co, pg 241
Verlag Karl Hofmann GmbH & Co, pg 242
Verlag Hoppenstedt GmbH, pg 242
Horlemann Verlag, pg 243
Edition Humanistische Psychologie (EHP), pg 243
Edition Hundertmark, pg 243
Huss-Medien GmbH, pg 243
Huss-Verlag GmbH, pg 244
Huthig GmbH & Co KG, pg 244
IKO Verlag fur Interkulturelle Kommunikation, pg 244
Verlag fuer Internationale Politik GmbH, pg 245
Klaus Isele, pg 245
Iudicium Verlag GmbH, pg 245
Verlag J P Peter, Gebr Holstein GmbH & Co KG, pg 246
Jahreszeiten-Verlag GmbH, pg 246
Jan Thorbecke Verlag GmbH & Co, pg 246
Janus Verlagsgesellschaft, Dr Norbert Meder & Co, pg 246
Junfermann-Verlag, pg 247
Junius Verlag GmbH, pg 247
Jutta Pohl Verlag, pg 247
Juventa Verlag GmbH, pg 247
Kallmeyer'sche Verlagsbuchhandlung GmbH, pg 247
Katzmann Verlag KG, pg 248
Kirschbaum Verlag, pg 249
Vittorio Klostermann GmbH, pg 250
Verlagsgruppe Koehler/Mittler, pg 251
Koehlers Verlagsgesellschaft mbH, pg 251
Koesler Verlag GmbH, pg 252
W Kohlhammer GmbH, abt Haussortiment, pg 252
Kolibri-Verlags GmbH, pg 252
Konradin-Verlagsgruppe, pg 252
kopaed verlagsgmbh, pg 252
Koptisch-Orthodoxes Zentrum, pg 252
Krafthand Verlag Walter Schultz GmbH, pg 253
Verlag Waldemar Kramer, pg 253
Kubon & Sagner Buchexport-Import GmbH, pg 254
Laaber-Verlag, pg 255
Landbuch-Verlagsgesellschaft mbH, pg 255
Peter Lang GmbH Europaeischer Verlag der Wissenschaften, pg 255
Michael Lassleben Verlag, pg 256
J Latka Verlag GmbH, pg 256
Leipziger Universitaetsverlag GmbH, pg 257
Verlag Otto Lembeck, pg 257
Verlag Leske plus Budrich GmbH, pg 257
Logos-Verlag Literatur & Layout GmbH, pg 258
Antiquariat Oskar Loewe, pg 259
Hermann Luchterhand Verlag GmbH, pg 259
Lucius & Lucius Verlagsgesellschaft mbH, pg 259
Verlagsgruppe Luebbe GmbH & Co KG, pg 259
Institut fuer Marxistische Studien und Forschungen eV (IMSF), pg 261
Mattes Verlag GmbH, pg 261
Matthias-Gruenewald-Verlag, pg 261
Medizinisch-Literarische Verlagsgesellschaft mbH, pg 262
Medpharm Scientific Publishers, pg 262
Meisenbach Verlag GmbH, pg 262
Meyer & Meyer Fachverlag und Buchhandel GmbH, pg 263
Missio eV Aachen, pg 264
E S Mittler und Sohn GmbH, pg 264
MMV Medizin Verlag GmbH Munich, pg 264
mode information Heinz Kramer GmbH, pg 264
Modellsport Verlag GmbH, pg 264
Mohr Siebeck, pg 264
C F Mueller Verlag, Huethig Gmb H & Co, pg 265
Norbert Mueller AG & Co KG Verlag, pg 265
Verlagsgesellschaft Rudolf Mueller GmbH & Co KG, pg 265
Munzinger-Archiv GmbH Archiv fuer publizistische Arbeit, pg 266
Gunter Narr Verlag, pg 266
Verlag Natur & Wissenschaft Harro Hieronimus & Dr Jurgen Schmidt, pg 266
Verlag Neue Stadt GmbH, pg 267
Verlag Neue Wirtschafts-Briefe GmbH & Co, pg 267
Max Niemeyer Verlag GmbH, pg 269
Nomos Verlagsgesellschaft mbH und Co KG, pg 269
Oeko-Test Verlag GmbH & Co KG Betriebsgesellschaft, pg 269
Verlag Offene Worte, pg 270
Georg Olms Verlag AG, pg 270
Edition Parabolis, pg 271
Paranus Verlag - Bruecke Neumuenster, pg 271
Justus Perthes Verlag Gotha GmbH, pg 272
Verlag Dr Friedrich Pfeil, pg 273
Richard Pflaum Verlag GmbH & Co KG, pg 273
Physica-Verlag, pg 273
pmi Verlag, pg 274
Podzun-Pallas Verlag GmbH, pg 274
Polygraph Verlag GmbH, pg 274
Possev-Verlag GmbH, pg 274
Premop Verlag GmbH, pg 275
Presse Verlagsgesellschaft mbH, pg 275
Projektion J Buch- und Musikverlag GmbH, pg 275
Psychiatrie-Verlag GmbH, pg 275
Psychosozial-Verlag, pg 275
Verlag Friedrich Pustet GmbH & Co Kg, pg 276
Quintessenz Verlags-GmbH, pg 276
R Oldenbourg Verlag GmbH, pg 276
Dr Josef Raabe-Verlags GmbH, pg 276
Radius-Verlag GmbH, pg 276
Verlag Recht und Wirtschaft GmbH, pg 277
Dr Ludwig Reichert Verlag, pg 278
E Reinhold Verlag, pg 278
Richardi Helmut Verlag GmbH, pg 279
Ritterbach Verlag GmbH, pg 279
Rossipaul Kommunikation GmbH, pg 280
Verlag Roter Morgen, pg 280
Verlag Werner Sachon GmbH & Co, pg 281
J D Sauerlaender's Verlag, pg 282
K G Saur Verlag GmbH, A Gale/Thomson Learning Company, pg 282
M & H Schaper GmbH & Co KG, pg 282
Schiffahrts-Verlag, pg 283
Schild-Verlag GmbH, pg 283
Verlag Dr Otto Schmidt KG, pg 283
Verlag Schnell und Steiner GmbH, pg 284
Verlag Hans Schoener GmbH, pg 284
Schott Musik International GmbH & Co KG, pg 284
Schueren Verlag GmbH, pg 285
Schulz-Kirchner Verlag GmbH, pg 285
R S Schulz Verlag GmbH, pg 285
Otto Schwartz Fachbochhandlung GmbH, pg 286
Siegler & Co Verlag fuer Zeitarchive GmbH, pg 286
Georg Siemens Verlagsbuchhandlung, pg 286
Silberburg-Verlag Titus Haeussermann GmbH, pg 287
Spektrum der Wissenschaft Verlagsgesellschaft mbH, pg 287
Spiegel-Verlag Rudolf Augstein GmbH & Co KG, pg 287
Springer-Verlag GmbH & Co KG, pg 288
Verlag Stahleisen GmbH, pg 289
C A Starke Verlag, pg 289
Stauffenburg Verlag Brigitte Narr GmbH, pg 289

PUBLISHERS

Franz Steiner Verlag Wiesbaden GmbH, pg 289
Dr Dietrich Steinkopff Verlag GmbH & Co, pg 289
Terra-Verlag GmbH, pg 292
Tetra Verlag Gmbh, pg 292
Tetzlaff Verlag, pg 292
edition Text & Kritik im Richard Boorberg Verlag GmbH & Co, pg 293
Druck-und Verlagshans Thiele & Schwarz GmbH, pg 293
Georg Thieme Verlag KG, pg 293
TR - Verlagsunion GmbH, pg 294
Traditionell Bogenschiessen Verlag Angelika Hornig, pg 294
Trans Tech Publications, pg 294
Treves Editions Verein Zur Foerderung der Kuenstlerischen Taetigkeiten, pg 295
Trotzdem-Verlags Genossenschaft eG, pg 295
Verlag Eugen Ulmer GmbH & Co, pg 295
Ulrike Helmer Verlag, pg 296
Urban & Fischer Verlag GmbH & Co KG Niederlassung Jena, pg 296
UVK Universitatsverlag Konstanz GmbH, pg 297
UVK Verlagsgesellschaft mbH, pg 297
Dorothea van der Koelen, pg 297
Vandenhoeck & Ruprecht, pg 297
VDI-Verlag GmbH, pg 297
Verein der Benediktiner zu Beuron-Beuroner Kunstverlag, pg 297
Vereinigte Fachverlage GmbH, pg 297
Verlag fur die Frau GmbH, pg 297
Verlag fur die Rechts- und Anwaltspraxis GmbH & Co, pg 298
Verlag fur Schweissen und Verwandte Verfahren, pg 298
Verlag und Druckkontor Kamp GmbH, pg 298
Friedr Vieweg & Sohn Verlagsgesellschaft mbH, pg 298
Curt R Vincentz Verlag, pg 298
Edition Curt Visel, pg 298
Vogel Medien GmbH & Co KG, pg 299
Dokument und Analyse Verlag Bogislaw von Randow, pg 299
Verlag Philipp von Zabern, pg 299
VVF Verlag V Florentz GmbH, pg 299
VWB-Verlag fur Wissenschaft & Bildung, Amand Aglaster, pg 300
Wachholtz Verlag GmbH, pg 300
Walhalla Fachverlag GmbH & Co KG Praetoria, pg 300
Uwe Warnke Verlag, pg 300
Waxmann Verlag GmbH, pg 300
WEKA Firmengruppe GmbH & Co KG, pg 301
Verlagsgruppe Weltbild GmbH, pg 301
Westdeutscher Verlag GmbH, pg 302
Westholsteinische Verlagsanstalt und Verlagsdruckerei Boyens & Co, pg 302
Wichern Verlag, pg 302
Herbert Wichmann Verlag, pg 302
Wiley-VCH Verlag GmbH, pg 302
Verlag Wissenschaft und Politik/Helker Pflug, pg 303
Wissenschaftliche Verlagsgesellschaft mbH, pg 303
Verlag Konrad Wittwer GmbH, pg 303

Gert Wohlfarth GmbH Verlag Fachtechnik & Mercator Verlag, Verlag Puppen & Spielzeug, pg 304
WRS Verlag Wirtschaft, Recht und Steuern GmbH & Co KG, pg 304
Verlag Zeitschrift fur Naturforschung, pg 305
Zeller Verlag GmbH & Co, pg 305

Ghana
Black Mask Ltd, pg 306
Educational Press & Manufacturers Ltd, pg 307
World Literature Project, pg 308

Greece
Apostoliki Diakonia tis Ekklisias tis Hellados, pg 309
Beta Medical Publishers, pg 309
Ekdoseis Domi AE, pg 310
Govostis Publishing SA, pg 311
Harmi-Press Publications, Haroula D Papadimitriou G P, pg 311
Hestia-I D Hestia-Kollaros & Co Corporation, pg 311
Karatzas Charis, pg 312
Kritiki Publishing, pg 312
Logos, pg 312
Editions Moressopoulos, pg 313
Ed Nea Acropolis, pg 313
M Psaropoulos & Co EE, pg 314
Sakkoulas Publications SA, pg 314
Society for Macedonian Studies, pg 315
Stochastis, pg 315
Technical Chamber of Greece, pg 315

Guatemala
Grupo Editorial RIN-78, pg 316

Guinea-Bissau
Instituto Nacional de Estudos e Pesquisa, pg 316

Guyana
Hamburgh Press, pg 317

Hong Kong
Celeluck Co Ltd, pg 318
The Chinese University Press, pg 319
Electronic Technology Publishing Co Ltd, pg 319
Federal Publications Ltd, pg 319
Friends of the Earth (Charity) Ltd, pg 320
Geocarto International Centre, pg 320
Joint Publishing (HK) Co Ltd, pg 320
Modern Electronic & Computing Publishing Co Ltd, pg 321
Photoart Ltd, pg 321
Research Centre for Translation, pg 321
Technology Exchange Ltd, pg 322
Thomson Corporation, pg 322
Wellday Ltd, pg 322
Yazhou Zhoukan Ltd, pg 322

Hungary
Agape Ferences Nyomda es Konyvkiado Kft, pg 323
Foldmuvelesugyi Miniszterium Muszaki Intezet, pg 323
Ifjusagi Lap-eskonyvkiado Vallalat, pg 324
KJK-Keaszov, pg 324

Officina Nova, Koenyv-es Lapkiado/Bertelsmann Media Kft, pg 324
Marton Aron Kiado Publishing House, pg 325
Mueszaki Koenyvkiado Ltd, pg 325
Mult es Jovo Kiado, pg 325
Nemzetkozi Szinhazi Intezet Magyar Kozpontja, pg 326

Iceland
Frodi Ltd, pg 328
Mal og menning, pg 328
Stofnun Arna Magnussonar a Islandi, pg 329

India
Advaita Ashrama, pg 329
Allied Book Centre, pg 330
Bani Mandir, Book-Sellers, Publishers & Educational Suppliers, pg 332
Bharatiya Samijik Vigyan Auusandhan Parishad, pg 332
Bharatiya Vidya Bhavan, pg 333
Doaba House, pg 336
Eastern Book Co, pg 336
Hindi Pracharak Sansthan, pg 338
Indian Council of Agricultural Research, pg 339
Indian Museum, pg 339
International Book Distributors, pg 340
B Jain Publishers (P) Ltd, pg 340
Sri Ramakrishna Math, pg 342
National Council of Applied Economic Research, Publications Division, pg 344
Publications & Information Directorate, CSIR, pg 346
Reliance Publishing House, pg 347
Research Signpost, pg 348
Sage Publications India Pvt Ltd, pg 348
Satprakashan Sanchar Kendra, pg 349
Scientific Book Agency, pg 349
Shaibya Prakashan Bibhag, pg 349
Sita Publications, pg 350
South Asian Publishers Pvt Ltd, pg 350
Spectrum Publications, pg 350
Theosophical Publishing House, pg 351
Transworld Research Network, pg 352
Vidya Puri, pg 352

Indonesia
PT Dian Rakyat, pg 355
Lembaga Demografi Fakultas Ekonomi Universitas Indonesia, pg 356

Ireland
Cathedral Books Ltd, pg 359
Cork University Press, pg 359
The Economic & Social Research Institute, pg 360
Gandon Editions, pg 360
Government Publications Ireland, pg 361
Institute of Public Administration, pg 361
Round Hall Sweet & Maxwell, pg 363
Royal Irish Academy, pg 364

Israel
Academy of the Hebrew Language, pg 365
Bar Ilan University Press, pg 365

TYPE OF PUBLICATION INDEX

Ben-Zvi Institute, pg 365
Bitan Publishers Ltd, pg 365
Freund Publishing House Ltd, pg 367
Gefen Publishing House Ltd, pg 367
Habermann Institute for Literary Research, pg 367
Haifa University Press, pg 368
Hanitzotz A-Sharara Publishing House, pg 368
The Institute for the Translation of Hebrew Literature, pg 368
Israel Antiquities Authority, pg 368
Israel Exploration Society, pg 368
Israel Music Institute (IMI), pg 369
Jerusalem Center for Public Affairs, pg 369
Maaliyot-Institute for Research Publications, pg 370
Rubin Mass Ltd, pg 371
Schlesinger Publishers, pg 372
Tirosh Communication Ltd, pg 373
Yad Vashem - The Holocaust Martyrs' & Heroes' Remembrance Authority, pg 373
The Zalman Shazar Center, pg 374

Italy
AIB Associazione Italiana Bibliotheche, pg 375
Alba, pg 375
Umberto Allemandi & C SRL, pg 375
All'Insegna del Giglio, pg 375
Editore Armando Armando SRL, pg 376
Verlagsanstalt Athesia, pg 377
Baha'i, pg 377
Belforte Editore Librario srl, pg 377
Giuseppe Bonanno Editore, pg 378
Edizioni Bora SNC di E Brandani & C, pg 378
Edizioni Borla SRL, pg 378
Edizioni Bresciane, pg 378
Edizioni Bucalo SNC, pg 379
Campanotto, pg 379
Edizioni Cantagalli, pg 379
Edizioni Carmelitane, pg 379
Casa Musicale Edizioni Carrara SRL, pg 379
Il Castoro, pg 380
CEDAM (Casa Editrice Dr A Milani), pg 380
Istituto Centrale per il Catalogo Unico delle Biblioteche Italiane e per le Informazioni Bibliografiche, pg 380
Centro Scientifico Int, pg 381
Centro Scientifico Torinese, pg 381
Edizioni Centro Studi Erickson, pg 381
Centro Studi Terzo Mondo, pg 381
CIC Edizioni Internazionali, pg 381
La Culturale, pg 383
Edizioni Dedalo SRL, pg 384
Edizioni Dehoniane Bologna (EDB), pg 384
Edizioni del Centro, pg 384
Diakronia, pg 385
Direzione Generale Archivi, pg 385
Editoriale Domus Spa, pg 385
Edi Ermes SRL, pg 386
Edizioni d'Arte e Moderna, Edam, pg 386
EDT Edizioni di Torino, pg 387
Elle Di Ci - Libreria Dottrina Cristiana, pg 388
ERGA SNC di Carla Ottino Merli & C (Edizioni Realizzazioni Grafiche - Artigiana), pg 388
Etas Libri, pg 388

TYPE OF PUBLICATION INDEX   BOOK

ETR (Editrice Trasporti su Rotaie), pg 388
EuroGeoGrafiche Mencattini SRL, pg 388
Feguagiskia' Studios, pg 389
Folini, pg 389
Arnaldo Forni Editore SRL, pg 389
Edizioni del Girasole srl, pg 390
Giunti (Gruppo Editoriale), pg 390
Giunti Publishing Group, pg 391
Gruppo Editoriale Faenza Editrice SpA, pg 392
Herder Editrice e Libreria, pg 392
IHT Gruppo Editoriale SRL, pg 393
In Dialogo, pg 393
International University Press Srl, pg 394
Jandi-Sapi Editori, pg 394
Il Lavoro Editoriale, pg 395
L'Erma di Bretschneider SRL, pg 395
Casa Editrice Le Lettere SRL, pg 395
Letture Mensile di Informazione Culturale, Letteratura e Spettacolo, pg 395
Liguori Editore SRL, pg 396
LIM Editrice SRL, pg 396
Lybra Immagine, pg 397
Macro Edizioni, pg 397
Giuseppe Maimone Editore, pg 397
Milella di Lecce Spazio Vivo SRL, pg 399
Giorgio Mondadori & Associati, pg 399
Moretti & Vitali editori srl, pg 400
Societa Editrice Il Mulino, pg 400
Museo Storico in Trento, pg 400
Casa Editrice Roberto Napoleone, pg 400
Istituto Nazionale di Archeologia e Storia dell'Arte, pg 400
New Magazine, pg 400
Editoriale Olimpia SpA, pg 401
Leo S Olschki, pg 402
Palatina Editrice, pg 402
Franco Cosimo Panini Editore SpA, pg 402
Piero Manni srl, pg 403
Pitagora Editrice SRL, pg 403
Pontificio Istituto Orientale, pg 404
Priuli e Verlucca, Editori, pg 404
RAI.ERI, pg 405
Franco Maria Ricci Editore (FMR), pg 405
Rirea Casa Editrice della Rivista Italiana di Ragioneria e di Economia Aziendale, pg 405
Rubbettino Editore, pg 406
Fausto Sardini Editrice, pg 407
Salvatore Sciascia Editore, pg 407
Edizioni Segno SRL, pg 407
Segretariato Nazionale Apostolato della Preghiera, pg 407
SEMAR Publishers SRL, pg 407
Servitium, pg 408
Sicania, pg 408
Edizioni Librarie Siciliane, pg 408
Societa Napoletana Storia Patria Napoli, pg 408
Societa Stampa Sportiva, pg 408
Edizioni Rosminiane Sodalitas, pg 408
Edizioni Sorbona Milano, pg 408
Edizioni del Teresianum, pg 409
Tilgher-Genova sas, pg 410
Vaccari SRL, pg 411
Vivalda Editori SRL, pg 411
Vivere In SRL, pg 411
Zanfi Editori SRL, pg 412

Jamaica
American Chamber of Commerce of Jamaica, pg 412
Institute of Jamaica Publications, pg 413
The Jamaica Bauxite Institute, pg 413
UWI Publishers' Association, pg 414

Japan
Akita Shoten Publishing Co Ltd, pg 414
The American Chamber of Commerce in Japan, pg 414
Bijutsu Shuppan-Sha, Ltd, pg 415
Daiichi Shuppan Co Ltd, pg 415
Dobun Shoin, pg 416
Dohosha Publishing Co Ltd, pg 416
Genko-Sha, pg 416
Heibonsha Ltd, Publishers, pg 417
Ie-No-Hikari Association, pg 418
Igaku-Shoin Ltd, pg 418
Iwanami Shoten, Publishers, pg 418
Kodansha, pg 420
Kosei Publishing Co Ltd, pg 420
Maruzen Co Ltd, pg 421
Mejikaru Furendo-sha, pg 421
Minerva Shobo Co Ltd, pg 421
Nigensha Publishing Co Ltd, pg 422
Nihon Rodo Kenkyu Kiko, pg 422
Nippon Jitsugyo Publishing Co, Ltd, pg 423
Obunsha Co Ltd, pg 423
Ohmsha Ltd, pg 423
Ongaku No Tomo Sha Corporation, pg 423
Rinsen Book Co Ltd, pg 424
Shinkenchiku-Sha Co Ltd, pg 425
Shueisha Inc, pg 426
Tankosha Publishing Co Ltd, pg 427
Universal Academy Press, Inc, pg 428
Yohan Shuppan, pg 429
Zeimukeiri-Kyokai, pg 429

Jordan
Al-Tanwir Al Ilmi (Scientific Enlightenment Publishing House), pg 430

Kazakstan
Gylym, Izd-Vo, pg 430
Kazakh Al-Farabi State National University, pg 430

Kenya
Africa Book Services (EA) Ltd, pg 430
British Institute in Eastern Africa, pg 431
Gaba Publications Amecea, Pastoral Institute, pg 431
International Centre for Research in Agroforestry (ICRAF), pg 432
Kenya Energy & Environment Organisation, Kengo, pg 432
Kenya Medical Research Institute (KEMRI), pg 432
Kenya Meteorological Department, pg 432
Shirikon Publishers, pg 433
Space Sellers Ltd, pg 433
Gideon S Were Press, pg 434

Democratic People's Republic of Korea
The Foreign Language Press Group, pg 434
Foreign Languages Publishing House, pg 434
Korea Science and Encyclopedia Publishing House, pg 434

Republic of Korea
Chung Rim Publishing Co Ltd, pg 435
Hak Won Publishing Co, pg 436
Kemongsa Publishing Co Ltd, pg 437
Korean Publishers Association, pg 437
Literature Academy, pg 438
Nanam Publishing House, pg 439
Prompter Publications, pg 439
YBM/Si-sa, pg 441

Latvia
Artava Ltd, pg 441
Egmont Latvia Ltd, pg 442

Lebanon
Darl el-Machreq Sarl, pg 443
Institute for Palestine Studies, Publishing & Research Organization (IPS), pg 443

Liechtenstein
Botanisch-Zoologische Gesellschaft, pg 444
Topos Verlag AG, pg 445

Lithuania
Academia, pg 445
AS Narbuto Leidykla (AS Narbutas' Publishers), pg 445
Baltos Lankos, pg 445
Egmont Lietuva, pg 445
Martynas Mazvydas National Library of Lithuania, pg 446

Luxembourg
Editions APESS ASBL, pg 447
Cahiers Luxembourgeois, pg 447
Editions Saint-Paul, pg 448
Service Central de la Statistique et des Etudes Economiques (STATEC), pg 448

Macau
Livros Do Oriente, pg 448

The Former Yugoslav Republic of Macedonia
Detska radost, pg 448
Medis, Skopje, pg 449
Mi-An Knigoizdatelstvo, pg 449
St Clement of Ohrid National & University Library, pg 449

Madagascar
Maison d'Edition Protestante ANTSO, pg 450
Foibe Filan-Kevitry NY Mpampianatra (FOFIPA), pg 450
JEAG, pg 450
Madagascar Print & Press Company, pg 450
Societe Malgache d'Edition, pg 450

Malawi
Central Africana Ltd, pg 450

Malaysia
Berita Publishing Sdn Bhd, pg 451
Dewan Bahasa dan Pustaka, pg 451
Mahir Publications Sdn Bhd, pg 452
Malayan Law Journal Sdn Bhd, pg 453
Pustaka Cipta Sdn Bhd, pg 454
Tropical Press Sdn Bhd, pg 455
University of Malaya, Department of Publications, pg 455

Maldive Islands
Non-Formal Education Centre, pg 455

Malta
Fondazzjoni Patrimonju Malti, pg 456

Mexico
Editorial AGATA SA de CV, pg 457
Editorial Armonia SA, pg 458
Centro de Estudios Mexicanos y Centroamericanos, pg 458
Colegio de Postgraduados en Ciencias Agricolas, pg 459
Editorial El Manual Moderno SA de CV, pg 460
Ediciones Era SA de CV, pg 460
Centro de Estudios Monetarios Latinoamericanos (CEMLA), pg 460
Fondo de Cultura Economica, pg 461
Instituto Indigenista Interamericano, pg 462
Janibi Editores SA de CV, pg 462
Editorial Jilguero, SA de CV, pg 462
Ediciones Libra, SA de CV, pg 463
Editorial Nova, SA de CV, pg 464
Instituto Panamericano de Geografia e Historia, pg 465
Plaza y Valdes SA de CV, pg 465
Universo Editorial SA de CV Edicion de Libros Revistas y Periodicos, pg 468

Morocco
Access International Services, pg 469
Editions Al-Fourkane, pg 469
Office Marocain D'Annonces-OMA, pg 470

Myanmar
Sarpay Beikman Board, pg 471

Namibia
Desert Research Foundation of Namibia (DRFN), pg 471

Nepal
International Standards Books & Periodicals (P) Ltd, pg 471

Netherlands
Aeolus Press BV, pg 472
John Benjamins BV, pg 474
Boom Uitgeverij, pg 474
Brill Academic Publishers, pg 475
BZZTOH Publishers, pg 475
Castrum Peregrini Presse, pg 475
Delft University Press, pg 476
Historische Uitgeverij, pg 478
IOS Press BV, pg 479
Kluwer Academic Publishers, pg 479

Kluwer Law International, pg 479
Uitgeefmaatschappij J H Kok BV, pg 480
Uitgeverij Lemma BV, pg 480
Narratio Theologische Uitgeverij, pg 482
Nico Israel, pg 482
Nijgh & Van Ditmar Amsterdam, pg 482
Reed Elsevier Nederland BV, pg 483
Segment BV, pg 484
Semic Junior Press, pg 484
Uitgeverij SUN, pg 484
Swets & Zeitlinger Publishers, pg 485
SWP, BV Uitgeverij, pg 485
V S P International Science Publishers, pg 486
Uitgeverij G A van Oorschot bv, pg 486
Uitgeverij Verloren, pg 486

New Zealand

Brick Row Publishing Co Ltd, pg 489
Brooker's Ltd, pg 489
Commonwealth Council for Educational Administration & Management, pg 490
New Zealand Council for Educational Research, pg 494
Outrigger Publishers, pg 494
Paerangi Books, pg 494
Publishing Solutions Ltd, pg 494
Resource Books Ltd, pg 495
SIR Publishing, pg 495
Southern Press Ltd, pg 496
University of Otago Press, pg 496

Nigeria

Aromolaran Publishing Co Ltd, pg 498
Fourth Dimension Publishing Co Ltd, pg 499
Heritage Books, pg 499
JAD Publishers Ltd, pg 500
Nigerian Institute of International Affairs, pg 500
Riverside Communications, pg 501
University Publishing Co, pg 502
Vantage Publishers International Ltd, pg 502

Norway

Bladkompaniet A/S, pg 503
Det Norske Samlaget, pg 503
Gyldendal Norsk Forlag A/S, pg 503
Ernst G Mortensens Forlag A/S, pg 504
Novus Forlag, pg 504
Erik Sandberg, pg 504
Universitetsforlaget, pg 505

Pakistan

Centre for South Asian Studies, pg 506
Hamdard Foundation, pg 507
HMR Publishing Co, pg 507
Islamic Research Institute, pg 507
Pakistan Institute of Development Economics, pg 508
Sh Ghulam Ali & Sons (Pvt) Ltd, pg 509

Panama

Focus Publications International SA, pg 509

Papua New Guinea

Melanesian Institute, pg 510
National Research Institute of Papua New Guinea, pg 510

Peru

Carvajal SA, pg 511
Instituto Frances de Estudios Andinos, IFEA, pg 511
Sur Casa de Estudios del Socialismo, pg 511

Philippines

Bright Concepts Printing House, pg 512
De La Salle University, pg 513
Our Lady of Manaoag Publisher, pg 514
Philippine Baptist Mission SBC FMB Church Growth International, pg 514
San Carlos Publications, pg 515
SIBS Publishing House Inc, pg 515
Solidaridad Publishing House, pg 515
UST Publishing House, pg 515

Poland

Wydawnictwa Normalizacyjne Alfa-Wero, pg 516
Biblioteka Narodowa, pg 516
Drukarnia I Ksiegarnia Swietego Wojciecha, Dziat Wydawniczy, pg 516
Instytut Historii Nauki PAN, pg 516
Wydawnictwo Medyczne Urban & Partner, pg 518
Instytut Meteorologii i Gospodarki Wodnej, pg 518
Wydawnictwo Nasza Ksiegarnia Sp zoo, pg 518
Ossolineum Zaklad Narodowy im Ossolinskich - Wydawnictwo, pg 518
Polish Scientific Publishers PWN, pg 519
Oficyna Wydawnicza Politechniki Wroclawskiej, pg 519
Wydawnictwo Prawnicze Co, pg 519
Panstwowe Wydawnictwo Rolnicze i Lesne, pg 519
Towarzystwo Naukowe w Toruniu, pg 520
Wydawnictwo Uniwersytetu Wroclawskiego SP ZOO, pg 520
Wydawnictwo Szkolne i Pedagogiczne (Polish Educational Publishers-WSiP), pg 521
Wydawnictwa Uniwersytetu Warszawskiego, pg 521
Wydawnictwo DiG, pg 521

Portugal

Biblioteca Geral da Universidade de Coimbra, pg 523
Centro Estudos Geograficos, pg 523
Edicoes Colibri, pg 523
Comissao para Igualdade e Direitos das Mulheres, pg 524
Edicoes Cosmos, pg 524
Difusao Cultural, pg 524
Impala, pg 525
Instituto de Investigacao Cientifica Tropical, pg 526
Latina Livraria, pg 526
Meriberica/Liber, pg 527
Edicoes Ora & Labora, pg 528
Revista Penteados, pg 529
Talento, pg 529

Romania

Editura Academiei Romane, pg 531
Editura Clusium, Casa de Editura Atlas-Clusium SRL, pg 532
Editura Excelsior, pg 533
Editura Gryphon, pg 533
Editura Medicala, pg 534
Editura Univers, pg 536

Russian Federation

ARGO-RISK Publisher, pg 537
N E Bauman Moscow State Technical University Publishers, pg 537
BLIC, russko-Baltijskij informaciionnyj centr, AO, pg 537
Druzhba Narodov, pg 537
FGUP Izdatelstvo Mashinostroenie, pg 538
Izvestia Sovetov Narodnyh Deputatov Russian Federation (RF), pg 539
Izdatelskii Dom Kompositor, pg 539
Nauka Publishers, pg 540
Profizdat, pg 541
Russkaya Kniga Izdatelstvo (Publishers), pg 541
St Andrew's Biblical Theological College, pg 541
Izdatelstvo Standartov, pg 542
Izdatelstvo Sudostroenie, pg 542
Teorija Verojatnostej i ee Primenenija, pg 542

Senegal

Centre Africain d'Animation et d'Echanges Culturels Editions Khoudia, pg 544
Centre de Linguistique Appliquee, pg 544
CODESRIA (Council for the Development of Social Science Research in Africa), pg 544
Societe d'Edition d'Afrique Nouvelle, pg 544

Singapore

Chopsons Pte Ltd, pg 545
LexisNexis, pg 547
Newscom Pte Ltd, pg 547
Reed Elsevier, South East Asia, pg 547
Singapore University Press Pte Ltd, pg 548
World Scientific Publishing Co Pte Ltd, pg 549

Slovakia

Egmont Neografia spol sro, pg 549
Vydavatelstvo Obzor, pg 550
Sofa, pg 551
Ustav informacii a prognoz skolstva mladeze a telovychovy, pg 551

Slovenia

Zalozba Mihelac d o o, pg 552
Zalozba Obzorja d d Maribor, pg 552

South Africa

Cape Provincial Library Service, pg 553
Centre for Conflict Resolution, pg 553
Flesch Financial Publications (Pty) Ltd, pg 554
Institute for Reformational Studies CHE, pg 555
Jacklin Enterprises (Pty) Ltd, pg 556
National Botanical Institute, pg 557
Oceanographic Research Institute, pg 558
Thomson Publications, pg 560
Unisa Press, pg 560

Spain

Publicacions de l'Abadia de Montserrat, pg 561
Editorial AEDOS SA, pg 561
Editorial Afers, SL, pg 561
Editorial 'Alas', pg 562
Ediciones Alfar SA, pg 562
Arco Libros SL, pg 564
Editorial Astri SA, pg 564
Central Catequistica Salesiana (CCS), pg 567
Editorial CISSPRAXIS SA, pg 567
Diputacion Provincial de Malaga, pg 570
Dorleta SA, pg 570
Edicions del Drac SA, pg 570
Ediciones Deusto SA, pg 571
Ediciones El Almendro de Cordoba, pg 571
Edicions Camacuc, pg 571
Erein, pg 573
Instituto de Estudios Riojanos, pg 574
EUNSA (Ediciones Universidad de Navarra SA), pg 574
Fundacion de Estudios Libertarios Anselmo Lorenzo, pg 575
Galaxia SA Editorial, pg 575
Harlequin Iberica SA, pg 577
Editorial Incafo SA, pg 578
Instituto Vasco de Criminologia, pg 578
Ediciones JLA, pg 579
Llibres del Segle, pg 580
Editorial Noray, pg 584
Nueva Acropolis, pg 584
OASIS, Producciones Generales de Comunicacion, pg 584
Omnicon, SA, pg 585
Editorial Peregrino SL, pg 586
Editorial El Perpetuo Socorro, pg 586
Instituto Provincial de Investigaciones y Estudios Toledanos, pg 588
Pulso Ediciones, SL, pg 588
Editorial Revista Agustiniana, pg 589
Ediciones Rialp SA, pg 589
Ediciones ROL SA, pg 589
Universidad de Santiago de Compostela, pg 590
Secretariado Trinitario, pg 590
Servicio de Publicaciones Universidad de Cordoba, pg 590
Equipo Sirius SA, pg 591
Ediciones Siruela SA, pg 591
Ediciones Tecnicas Rede, SA, pg 592
Editorial Sal Terrae, pg 592
Tesitex, SL, pg 592
Vinaches Lopez, Luisa, pg 595

Sri Lanka

Department of National Museums, pg 597
International Centre for Ethnic Studies, pg 597
Swarna Hansa Foundation, pg 598

Sweden

Allt om Hobby AB, pg 600
Almqvist och Wiksell International, pg 600

TYPE OF PUBLICATION INDEX — BOOK

Bibliotekstjaenst AB, pg 600
Iustus Forlag AB, pg 603
Mezopotamya Publishing & Distribution, pg 604
Semic Bokforlaget International AB, pg 606
Var Skola Foerlag AB, pg 607

Switzerland

Birkhauser Verlag AG, pg 610
Blaukreuz-Verlag Bern, pg 610
Marcel Dekker AG, pg 612
E Lopfe-Benz AG Rorschach, Graphische Anstalt und Verlag, pg 612
Verlag ED Emmentaler Druck AG, pg 613
Editions Eisele SA, pg 613
Elsevier Science SA, pg 613
EULAR Publishers, pg 613
G+B Arts International, pg 614
Haffmans Verlag AG, pg 615
Heilpaedagogisches Institut der Universitaet Freiburg, pg 615
Helbing und Lichtenhahn Verlag AG, pg 615
S Karger AG, Medical and Scientific Publishers, pg 617
Lia rumantscha, pg 618
Maihof Verlag, pg 618
Medecine et Hygiene, pg 619
Nebelspalter-Verlag, pg 620
Verlag Arthur Niggli AG, pg 620
Verlag Organisator AG, pg 620
Parkett Publishers Inc, pg 621
Editions du Parvis, pg 621
Pedrazzini Tipografia, pg 621
PIE-Peter Lang SA, pg 622
Promoedition SA, pg 622
Verlag fuer Recht und Gesellschaft AG, pg 622
RECOM Verlag, pg 622
Sauerlaender AG, pg 623
Schulthess Polygraphischer Verlag AG, pg 624
Schwabe & Co AG, pg 624
Schwengeler-Verlag, pg 624
Editions Scriptar SA, pg 624
Staempfli Verlag AG, pg 625
Terra Grischuna Verlag Buch-und Zeitschriftenverlag, pg 625
Trans Tech Publications SA, pg 626
Verlagsbuchhandlung AG, pg 626

Syrian Arab Republic

Damascus University Press, pg 628

Taiwan, Province of China

Designer Publisher Inc, pg 629
Echo Publishing Company Ltd, pg 629
Laureate Book Co Ltd, pg 631
Petroleum Information Publishing Co, pg 631
Torch of Wisdom, pg 632
Yi Hsien Publishing Co Ltd, pg 632
Youth Cultural Publishing Co, pg 632
Zen Now Press, pg 632

Tunisia

Faculte des Sciences Humaines et Sociales de Tunis, pg 638

Turkey

Altin Kitaplar Yayinevi, pg 638
Arkeoloji Ve Sanat Yayinlari, pg 639
Ataturk Kultur, Dil ve Tarih, Yusek Kurumu Baskanligi, pg 639
Iletisim Yayinlari, pg 640
Kok Yayincilik, pg 640
Metis Yayinlari, pg 640
Sabah Kitaplari, pg 641
Varlik Yayinlari AS, pg 641
Yapi-Endustri Merkezi Yayinlari-Yem Yayin, pg 642

Ukraine

Urozaj, pg 643

United Kingdom

Academic Press Ltd, pg 644
A4 Publications Ltd, pg 645
Umberto Allemandi & Co Publishing, pg 646
Architectural Association Publications, pg 648
Arnold, pg 648
Artetech Publishing Co, pg 649
Arthur James Ltd, pg 649
Ashgate Publishing Ltd, pg 649
Aslib, The Association for Information Management, pg 650
Association for Scottish Literary Studies, pg 650
Association for Science Education, pg 650
Berghahn Books Ltd, pg 654
BILD Publications, pg 654
BIOS Scientific Publishers Ltd, pg 654
Blackwell Publishers, pg 655
BAAF: Adoption & Fostering, pg 659
British Cement Association, pg 660
Bryntirion Press, pg 661
Business Monitor International, pg 661
Butterworths Tolley, pg 661
Cambridge University Press, pg 662
Cavendish Publishing Ltd, pg 665
Chadwyck-Healey Ltd, pg 666
Chapman, pg 666
Chapter Two, pg 666
Church Society, pg 668
Church Union, pg 668
E W Classey Ltd, pg 668
Paul H Crompton Ltd, pg 672
CSA (Cambridge Scientific Abstracts), pg 672
CTBI Publications, pg 672
Terence Dalton Ltd, pg 673
Dawson Holdings PLC, pg 674
Donhead Publishing Ltd, pg 675
Martin Dunitz Ltd, pg 676
Electronic Publishing Services Ltd, pg 678
Elsevier Science Ltd, pg 678
The Energy Information Centre, pg 679
English Teaching Professional, pg 679
Estates Gazette, pg 679
Euromonitor PLC, pg 680
European Schoolbooks Ltd, pg 680
The Eurospan Group, pg 680
Fabian Society, pg 681
Famedram Publishers Ltd, pg 681
Forth Naturalist & Historian, pg 683
Freedom Press, pg 684
Geological Society Publishing House, pg 686
W Green The Scottish Law Publisher, pg 689
Greenhill Books/Lionel Leventhal Ltd, pg 689
Gwasg Gwenffrwd, pg 690
Halldale Publishing & Media Ltd, pg 691
Harcourt Publishers Ltd, pg 691
Hawker Publications Ltd, pg 693
Hobsons, pg 696
Hodder Headline Ltd, pg 696
Immediate Publishing, pg 699
Imperial College Press, pg 699
Institute for Fiscal Studies, pg 699
Institute of Development Studies, pg 699
Institute of Physics Publishing, pg 700
Institution of Electrical Engineers, pg 700
Intellect Ltd, pg 700
Intermediate Technology Publications Ltd, pg 700
International Bee Research Association, pg 701
International Communications, pg 701
International Institute for Strategic Studies, pg 701
IOM Communications Ltd, pg 701
Islamic Foundation Publications, pg 701
JAI Press Ltd, pg 702
James & James (Science Publishers) Ltd, pg 702
Jane's Information Group, pg 702
Kluwer Academic/Plenum Publishers, pg 705
Lang Syne Publishers Ltd, pg 706
Lawrence & Wishart, pg 706
Lippincott Williams & Wilkins, pg 708
Liverpool University Press, pg 708
LLP Ltd, pg 708
Manchester University Press, pg 711
Maney Publishing, pg 711
Methodist Publishing House, pg 714
Multilingual Matters Ltd, pg 716
National Foster Care Association, pg 717
National Library of Wales, pg 717
NCVO, pg 718
New European Publications Ltd, pg 718
NTC Publications Ltd, pg 720
Osprey Publishing Ltd, pg 722
Oxfam, pg 722
Oxford University Press, pg 723
Packard Publishing Ltd, pg 723
The Parthenon Publishing Group Ltd, pg 724
Paternoster Publishing, pg 724
Pathfinder London, pg 724
Perpetuity Press, pg 726
Petroc Press, pg 726
Pharmaceutical Press, pg 726
Pion Ltd, pg 728
PIRA Intl, pg 728
Planet, pg 728
Pluto Press, pg 728
Police Review Publishing Company Ltd, pg 729
The Policy Press, pg 729
Portland Press Ltd, pg 730
Professional Engineering Publishing Ltd, pg 730
Quintessence Publishing Co Ltd, pg 732
Radcliffe Medical Press Ltd, pg 732
Ramakrishna Vedanta Centre, pg 732
Random House UK Ltd, pg 733
Royal College of General Practitioners, pg 736
Royal Institute of International Affairs, pg 736
The Royal Society, pg 737
Sage Publications Ltd, pg 737
St Jerome Publishing, pg 738
Scottish Affairs, pg 739
Scottish Braille Press, pg 739
Scottish Office Library & Information Services, pg 740
Scripture Union, pg 740
Sheffield Academic Press Ltd, pg 741
Sherwood Publishing, pg 741
SHU Press, pg 742
SLS Legal Publications (NI), pg 742
The Stationery Office, pg 745
Take That Ltd, pg 746
Taylor Graham Publishing, pg 747
Time Out Group Ltd, pg 749
Trentham Books Ltd, pg 750
Two-Can Publishing Ltd, pg 750
University of Wales Press, pg 751
The Warburg Institute, pg 754
Whiting & Birch Ltd, pg 756
Wiley Europe Ltd, pg 756
Wilmington Business Information Ltd, pg 756
Woodhead Publishing Ltd, pg 758
World Microfilms Publications Ltd, pg 758

Uruguay

Cotidiano Mujer, pg 760
Instituto del Tercer Mundo, pg 760
Nordan-Comunidad, pg 760
Prensa Medica Latinoamericana, pg 761
La Urpila Editores, pg 761

Venezuela

Fundacion Centro Gumilla, pg 762
Editorial Nueva Sociedad, pg 762

Yugoslavia

AGAPE, pg 764
Beogradski Izdavacko-Graficki Zavod, pg 764
Forum, pg 764
Izdavacka preduzece Gradina, pg 764
Jugoslovenska Revija, pg 764
Libertatea, pg 764
Savez Inzenjera i Tehnicara Jugoslavije, pg 765
Sluzbeni List, pg 765
Turisticka Stampa, pg 766
Vuk Karadzic, pg 766

Zambia

Historical Association of Zambia, pg 766

Zimbabwe

The Bulletin Newspaper, pg 768
Journal on Social Change, pg 768
Thomson Publications Zimbabwe (Pvt) Ltd, pg 769
University of Zimbabwe Publications, pg 769
ZRD Trust, pg 770

PROFESSIONAL BOOKS

Albania

State Textbook Publishing House, pg 1

Argentina

Abeledo-Perrot SAE e I, pg 2
Editorial Acme SA, pg 3
Aguilar Altea Taurus Alfaguara SA de Ediciones, pg 3
Editorial Astrea de Alfredo y Ricardo Depalma SRL, pg 3
Editorial Claridad SA, pg 4
Cosmopolita SRL, pg 4
Editorial Ruy Diaz SAEIC, pg 5

PUBLISHERS

Editorial Idearium de la Universidad de Mendoza (EDIUM), pg 5
Errepar SA, pg 5
EUDEBA (Editorial Universitaria de Buenos Aires), pg 6
Editorial Hemisferio Sur SA, pg 6
Juris Editorial, pg 6
Editorial Medica, Panamericana SA, pg 7
Instituto Nacional de Ciencia y Tecnica Hidrica (INCYTH), pg 7
Instituto de Publicaciones Navales, pg 7
Editorial Paidos SAICF, pg 8
Tipografica Editora Argentina, pg 9
Editoria Universitaria de la Patagonia, pg 9
Victor P de Zavalia SA, pg 10
Editorial Zeus SRL, pg 10

Australia

ACER Press, pg 10
ACHPER Inc (Australian Council for Health, Physical Education & Recreation), pg 10
Appropriate Technology Development Group (Inc) WA, pg 11
Art on the Move, pg 12
Ausmed Publications Pty Ltd, pg 12
Australian Academic Press Pty Ltd, pg 13
Australian Broadcasting Authority, pg 13
The Australian Council for Educational Research Ltd, pg 13
Australian Film Television & Radio School, pg 13
Australian Institute of Family Studies (AIFS), pg 13
Blackwell Science Pty Ltd, pg 15
Books for Our Times, pg 16
Bureau of Resource Sciences, pg 16
Butterworths Australia Ltd, pg 16
Candlelight Trust T/A Candlelight Farm, pg 17
Chiron Media, pg 18
Cole Publications, pg 18
Cookery Book, pg 18
Crawford House Publishing, pg 19
Crista International, pg 19
Deakin University Press, pg 20
The Federation Press, pg 22
Fernfawn Publications, pg 22
Flora Publications International Pty Ltd, pg 23
Fraser Publications, pg 23
Ginninderra Press, pg 24
Gnostic Editions, pg 24
Harcourt Australia Pty Ltd, pg 25
Histec Publications, pg 26
Hospitality Press Pty Ltd, pg 26
The Images Publishing Group Pty Ltd, pg 27
Law Book Co Information Services, pg 29
MacLennan & Petty Pty Ltd, pg 31
Macmillan Education Australia, pg 31
McGraw-Hill Australia Pty Ltd, pg 32
National Gallery of Victoria, pg 34
OTEN (Open Training & Education Network), pg 36
Oxfam Community Aid Abroad, pg 36
Pacific Publications (Australia) Pty Ltd, pg 36
Pademelon Press, pg 36
Pearson Education Australia, pg 37
Pluto Press Australia, pg 38
Press for Success, pg 38
Priestley Consulting, pg 39

RMIT Publishing, pg 41
St Clair Press, pg 41
Frank Shepherd, pg 42
Strucmech Publishing, pg 43
Tarka Publishing, pg 44
Tertiary Press, pg 44
Turton & Armstrong Publishers Pty Ltd, pg 45
Veritas Press, pg 46
Villamonta Publishing Service Inc, pg 47
Vista Publications, pg 47
Wildscape Australia, pg 47
Yanagang Publishing, pg 48

Austria

Autorensolidaritat - Verlag der Interessengemeinschaft osterreichischer Autorinnen und Autoren, pg 49
Braintrust Marketing Services Ges mbH Verlag, pg 50
Georg Fromme and Co, pg 52
Edition Helbling Verlags-Gesellschaft mbH, pg 52
IAEA - International Atomic Energy Agency, pg 53
IG Autorinnen Autoren, pg 53
Verlag Lafite, pg 54
Leopold Stocker Verlag, pg 54
Linde Verlag Wien GmbH, pg 54
Verlag des Oesterreichischen Gewerkschaftsbundes GmbH, pg 56
Osterreichischer Bundesveilag Ges.mbh, pg 57
Signum Verlag GmbH & Co KG, pg 58
Studien Verlag Gmbh, pg 59
Verlag Mag Wanzenbock, pg 60
Dr Otfried Weise Verlag Tabula Smaragdina, pg 60

Azerbaijan

Sada, Literaturno-Izdatel'skij Centr, pg 61

Bangladesh

Gatidhara, pg 62
The University Press Ltd, pg 62

Barbados

Business Tutors, pg 63

Belarus

Interdigets Publishing House, pg 63
Kavaler Publishers, pg 63

Belgium

Academia Press, pg 64
Vanden Broele NV, pg 65
CED-Samsom, pg 66
Editions du CEFAL, pg 66
Coda, pg 66
Conservart SA, pg 67
Editions De Boeck-Larcier SA, pg 67
Documenta CV, pg 68
Intersentia Uitgevers NV, pg 69
King Baudouin Foundation, pg 70
Koepel van de Vlaamse Noord - Zuidbeweging 11.11.11, pg 70
Larcier-Department of De Boeck & Larcier SA, pg 71
Maklu, pg 71
Toulon Uitgeverij, pg 74
UGA Editions (Uitgeverij), pg 74
Uitgeverij De Garve, pg 75
Imprimeur - Editeur Vaillant-Carmanne SA, pg 75

Bolivia

Gisbert y Cia SA, pg 76

Brazil

A & A & A Edicoes e Promocoes Internacionais Ltda, pg 77
Editora Agora Ltda, pg 78
Aide Editora e Comercio de Livros Ltda, pg 78
Antenna Edicoes Tecnicas Ltda, pg 78
Editora Antroposofica Ltda, pg 78
ARTMED, pg 79
Berkeley Brasil Editora Ltda, pg 79
Editora Edgard Blucher Ltda, pg 80
Editora Campus Ltda, pg 80
Alzira Chagas Carpigiani, pg 80
Centro de Estudos Juridicosdo Para (CEJUP), pg 80
Editora Contexto (Editora Pinsky Ltda), pg 81
Ediouro Publicacoes, SA, pg 81
Editora Elevacao, pg 82
Companhia Editora Forense, pg 82
EDUC - Editora da PUC-SP, pg 82
Selecoes Eletronicas Editora Ltda, pg 83
Empresa Brasileira de Pesquisa Agropecaria, pg 83
Editora FCO Ltda, pg 83
Editora Forense, pg 83
Forense Universitaria Editora, pg 83
Livraria Freitas Bastos Editora SA, pg 83
Editora Guanabara Koogan SA, pg 84
Editora Harbra Ltda, pg 84
Hemus Editora Ltda, pg 85
Imago Editora Importacao e Exportacao Ltda, pg 85
Livraria Editora Infobook SA, pg 86
LTC-Livros Tecnicos e Cientificos Editora S/A, pg 87
Editora Lucre Comercio e Representacoes, pg 87
Madras Editora, pg 87
Editora Manole Ltda, pg 87
Editora Manuais Tecnicos de Seguros Ltda, pg 87
Medicina Panamericana Editora Do Brasil Ltda, pg 87
Medsi - Editora Medica e Cientifica Ltda, pg 87
Oliveira Rocha-Comercio e Servics Ltda, pg 89
Editora Ortiz SA, pg 89
Pearson Education Do Brasil, pg 89
Qualitymark Editora Ltda, pg 90
Editora Revan Ltda, pg 90
Livraria Editora Revinter Ltda, pg 90
Saraiva SA, Livreiros Editores, pg 91
Editora Scipione Ltda, pg 91
Livraria Sulina Editora, pg 92
Summus Editorial Ltda, pg 92
Talento Publicacoes Editora e Grafica Ltda, pg 92
Editora Universidade Federal do Rio de Janeiro, pg 93

Bulgaria

Ciela Publishing House, pg 94
DA-Izdatelstvo Publishers, pg 95
Dolphin Press Group Ltd, pg 95
EA Publishing House, pg 95
Fondacija Zlatno Kljuce, pg 95
Makros 2000 - Plovdiv, pg 96
MATEX, pg 96
Musica Publishing House Ltd, pg 96
Pensoft Publishers, pg 97

TYPE OF PUBLICATION INDEX

Sibi, pg 97
Sila & Zivot, pg 98
Sita-MB, pg 98
TEMTO, pg 98
WTU Todor Kableskov, pg 98

Cameroon

Presses Universitaires d'Afrique, pg 99

Chile

Edeval (Universidad de Valparaiso), pg 100
Norma de Chile, pg 101
Editorial Universitaria SA, pg 101
Ediciones Universitarias de Valparaiso, pg 101

China

Anhui People's Publishing House, pg 102
Chemical Industry Press, pg 102
China Agriculture Press, pg 103
China Film Press, pg 103
China Foreign Economic Relations & Trade Publishing House, pg 103
China Forestry Publishing House, pg 103
China Machine Press (CMP), pg 103
China Ocean Press, pg 103
China Theatre Publishing House, pg 104
China Tibetology Publishing House, pg 104
CITIC Publishing House, pg 104
Cultural Relics Publishing House, pg 105
Foreign Language Teaching & Research Press, pg 105
Fudan University Press, pg 105
Guangdong Science & Technology Press, pg 106
Heilongjiang Science & Technology Press, pg 106
Wissenschaft und Technik Verlag Henan Henan Scientific & Technological Publishing House, pg 106
Higher Education Press, pg 106
Inner Mongolia Science & Technology Publishing House, pg 106
International Academic Publishers, pg 106
Language Publishing House, pg 107
Lanzhou University Press, pg 107
Nanjing University Press, pg 107
National Defence Industry Press, pg 107
New Times Press, pg 107
Patent Documentation Publishing House, pg 107
Printing Industry Publishing House, pg 108
The Publishing House of Shanghai University of Traditional Chinese Medicine, pg 108
Science Press, pg 108
Shandong University Press, pg 109
Shanghai Fine Arts Publishers, pg 109
Sichuan University Press, pg 109
South China University of Science and Technology Press, pg 109
Tianjin Science & Technology Publishing House, pg 109
Water Resources and Electric Power Press (CWPP), pg 110

TYPE OF PUBLICATION INDEX BOOK

Colombia
Centro Regional para el Fomento del Libro en America Latina y el Caribe, pg 111
Consejo Episcopal Latinoamericano Celam, pg 111
Fundacion Universidad de la Sabana Ediciones Udes, pg 112
Pearson Educacion de Colombia LTDA, pg 113
Tercer Mundo Editores SA, pg 113
Unidad Universitaria del Sur (UNISUR), pg 114

Costa Rica
Academia de Centro America, pg 115
Centro Agronomico Tropical de Investigacion y Ensenanza (CATIE), pg 115
Editorial Nacional de Salud y Seguridad Social Ednass, pg 116
Scout Interamericana, pg 117
Editorial Tecnologica de Costa Rica, pg 117
Union Mundial para la Naturaleza (UICN), Oficina Regional para Mesoamerica, pg 117
Editorial de la Universidad de Costa Rica, pg 117

Cote d'Ivoire
Universite d' Abidjan, pg 118

Croatia
ALFA dd za izdavacke, graficke i trgovacke poslove, pg 118
Izdavacka Delatnost Hrvatske Akademije Znanosti I Umjetnosti, pg 118
Hrvatsko filozofsko drustvo, pg 119
Vitagraf, pg 120

Cuba
Editorial Oriente, pg 121
Editora Politica, pg 121
Pueblo y Educacion Editorial (PE), pg 121

Czech Republic
Grada Publishing sro, pg 124
Jota, pg 125
Libri s r o, pg 125
Pavla Momcilova, pg 126
Narodni Knihovna CR, pg 126
Cesky normalizacni institut, pg 127
Psychoanalyticke Nakladatelstvi, pg 128
Votobia sro, pg 129

Denmark
Dansk Psykologisk Forlag, pg 131
Djof Publishing Jurist-og Okonomforbundets Forlag, pg 131
Christian Ejlers' Forlag aps, pg 131
FADL's Forlag A/S (Foreningen af danske Laegestuderendes Forlag), pg 132
Forlaget FSR A/S (ITID A/S), pg 132
GEC Gads Forlag Aktieselskab af 1994, pg 132
Ingenioeren/Boger, pg 133
Mellemfolkeligt Samvirke, pg 133
Samfundslitteratur, pg 135
J H Schultz Information A/S, pg 135
A/S Skattekartoteket, pg 135
Systime, pg 136

Dominican Republic
Pontificia Universidad Catolica Madre y Maestra, pg 136

Ecuador
CEPLAES, pg 137

Egypt (Arab Republic of Egypt)
Dar El Shorouk Publishing & Distributing House, pg 138

Estonia
Estonian Academic Library, pg 139
Kunst Publishers Ltd, pg 140
National Library of Estonia, pg 140
Olion Publishers, pg 140
Valgus Publishers, pg 141

Finland
Foersamlingsfoerbundets Foerlags AB, pg 142
Kauppakaari Oyj Lakimiesliiton Kustannus, Yrityksen Tietokirjat, pg 142
Kustannus Oy Duodecim, pg 143
Tietoteos Publishing Co, pg 144
Yliopistopaino/Helsinki University Press, pg 145

France
Adverbum SARL, pg 146
Arnette-Blackwell, pg 148
Editions BRGM, pg 152
Cepadues Editions SA, pg 153
Editions Chiron, pg 154
Chotard et Associes Editeurs, pg 154
Codes Rousseau, pg 155
CTIF (Center Technique des Industries de la Fonderie), pg 157
CTNERHI - Centre Technique National d'Etudes et de Recherches sur les Handicaps et les Inadaptations, pg 157
Editions Dalloz Sirey, pg 157
De Vecchi Editions SA, pg 158
Delagrave Edition SA, pg 158
Editions Delmas, pg 158
Institut pour le Developpement Forestier, pg 159
Doin Editeurs, pg 160
Dunod Editeur, pg 160
Editions d'Organisation, pg 161
EDP Sciences, pg 161
Elf Exploration Production, pg 161
Ellipses - Edition Marketing SA, pg 162
Les Editions de l'Epargne, pg 162
Editions Errance, pg 162
Groupe Fleurus-Mame, pg 164
Groupe de Recherche et d'Echanges Technologiques (GRET), pg 167
Groupe Moniteur -L'Argus, pg 167
INRA Editions (Institut National de la Recherche Agronomique), pg 169
IRD Editions, pg 170
Joly Editions, pg 170
LT Editions-J Lanore-H Laurens, pg 172
Lavoisier, pg 172
Editions Legislatives, pg 172
LiTec (Librairies Techniques SA), pg 173
Masson SA, pg 175
Masson-Williams et Wilkins, pg 175
Maxima Laurent du Mesnil Editeur, pg 175
Editions du Papyrus, pg 179
Editions Parentheses, pg 179
Pearson Education France, pg 179
Editions Pedone, pg 179
Peeters-France, pg 179
Editions du Point Veterinaire, pg 180
Polytechnica, pg 180
Presses de l'Ecole Nationale des Ponts et Chaussees, pg 181
Les Presses du Management, pg 181
Editions Revue EPS, pg 183
Editions Saint-Michel SA, pg 183
Societe Mathematique de France - Institut Henri Poincare, pg 185
Sofiac (Societe Francaise des Imprimeries Administratives Centrales), pg 185
Sofradif Editions Philippe Auzou, pg 185
Editions Springer France, pg 186
Sybex, pg 186
Editions Technip SA, pg 187
Editions Techniques et Scientifiques Francaises, pg 187
Top Editions, pg 188
Editions Village Mondial, pg 189

Germany
A Francke Verlag (Tubingen und Basel), pg 191
E Albrecht Verlags-Kommanditgesellschaft, pg 192
Andernach Atelier Verlag (AVA), pg 193
AOL-Verlag Frohmut Menze, pg 194
Verlag APHAIA Svea Haske, Sonja Schumann GbR, pg 194
ARCult Media, pg 194
Bank-Verlag GmbH, pg 198
Verlag Dr Albert Bartens KG, pg 198
Ludwig Bechauf Verlag, pg 200
Verlag C H Beck (OHG), pg 200
Bertelsmann Lexikon Verlag GmbH, pg 201
Verlag Bertelsmann Stiftung, pg 201
W Bertelsmann Verlag GmbH & Co KG, pg 201
BertelsmannSpringer Science & Business Media GmbH, pg 202
Verlag Beruf + Schule Belz KG, pg 202
Bettendorf'sche Verlagsanstalt GmbH, pg 202
BW Bildung und Wissen Verlag und Software GmbH, pg 203
BLV Verlagsgesellschaft mbH, pg 204
Verlag Erwin Bochinsky GmbH & Co KG, pg 204
Adolf Bonz Verlag GmbH, pg 205
Buchhaendler-Vereinigung GmbH, pg 207
Verlag Georg D W Callwey GmbH & Co, pg 208
Christusbruderschaft Selbitz ev, Abt Verlag, pg 210
Marianne Cieslik, pg 210
Charles Coleman Verlag GmbH & Co KG, pg 211
Cornelsen Verlag GmbH & Co OHG, pg 211
J G Cotta'sche Buchhandlung Nachfolger GmbH, pg 212
Deutsche Blinden-Bibliothek, pg 213
Deutsche Gesellschaft fuer Eisenbahngeschichte eV, pg 213
Deutscher Fachverlag GmbH, pg 214
Deutscher Instituts-Verlag GmbH, pg 215
Deutscher Psychologen Verlag GmbH (DPV), pg 215
Deutscher Verlag fur Grundstoffindustrie GmbH, pg 215
Dingfelder-Verlag Inh Gerd Gmelin, pg 217
Christoph Dohr, pg 217
Donat Verlag, pg 217
DRW-Verlag Weinbrenner-GmbH & Co, pg 219
Archibook Verlag Martina Duettmann, pg 219
E Schweizerbart'sche Verlagsbuchhandlung (Nagele und Obermiller), pg 220
Ecomed Verlagsgesellschaft AG & Co KG, pg 220
Econ Verlag GmbH, pg 220
Elektor-Verlag GmbH, pg 222
Emons Verlag, pg 222
Verlag Esoterische Philosophie GmbH, pg 224
expert verlag GmbH, Fachverlag fur Wirtschaft & Technik, pg 225
Extent Verlag und Service Wolfgang M Flamm, pg 225
Fachbuchverlag Pfanneberg & Co, pg 226
Fachverlag fur das graphische Gewerbe GmbH, pg 226
Festo Didactic GmbH & Co, pg 227
FN-Verlag der Deutschen Reiterlichen Vereinigung GmbH, pg 229
Verlag Franz Vahlen GmbH, pg 229
Fraunhofer IRB Verlag Fraunhofer Informationszentrum Raum und Bau, pg 229
Friedrich Kiehl Verlag GmbH, pg 230
Frieling & Partner GmbH, pg 230
Verlag A Fromm im Druck- u Verlagshaus Fromm GmbH & Co KG, pg 230
Friedrich Frommann Verlag, pg 230
Betriebswirtschaftlicher Verlag Dr Th Gabler GmbH, pg 231
Gebrueder Borntraeger Science Publishers, pg 231
Alfons W Gentner Verlag GmbH & Co KG, pg 231
Gesundheits-Dialog Verlag GmbH, pg 232
Gildefachverlag GmbH & Co KG, pg 232
Govi-Verlag Pharmazeutischer Verlag GmbH, pg 233
Wolfgang G Haas - Musikverlag Koeln ek, pg 235
Alfred Hammer, pg 236
Hardt und Worner Marketing fur das Buch, pg 237
Haschemi Edition Cologne Kunstverlag, pg 237
Hestra-Verlag Hernichel & Dr Strauss GmbH & Co KG, pg 240
Carl Heymanns Verlag KG, pg 240
Hans Holzmann Verlag GmbH und Co KG, pg 242
Edition Humanistische Psychologie (EHP), pg 243
Huss-Medien GmbH, pg 243
Huss-Verlag GmbH, pg 244
Idea Verlag GmbH, pg 244
IKO Verlag fur Interkulturelle Kommunikation, pg 244
Informationsstelle Suedliches Afrika eV (ISSA), pg 245
International Thomson Publishing (ITP), pg 245
Iudicium Verlag GmbH, pg 245
Kallmeyer'sche Verlagsbuchhandlung GmbH, pg 247
Katzmann Verlag KG, pg 248

Verlag im Kilian GmbH, pg 249
Klages-Verlag, pg 249
Verlagsanstalt Alexander Koch GmbH, pg 251
R Koenig GmbH, pg 251
W Kohlhammer GmbH, abt Haussortiment, pg 252
Kolibri-Verlags GmbH, pg 252
kopaed verlagsgmbh, pg 252
Krafthand Verlag Walter Schultz GmbH, pg 253
Laaber-Verlag, pg 255
Landbuch-Verlagsgesellschaft mbH, pg 255
Peter Lang GmbH Europaeischer Verlag der Wissenschaften, pg 255
LEU-VERLAG Wolfgang Leupelt, pg 257
Libertas- Europaeisches Institut GmbH, pg 257
Logos-Verlag Literatur & Layout GmbH, pg 258
Hermann Luchterhand Verlag GmbH, pg 259
Edition Maritim GmbH, pg 261
Max Schimmel Verlag, pg 261
Medien-Verlag Bernhard Gregor GmbH, pg 262
Medizinisch-Literarische Verlagsgesellschaft mbH, pg 262
mode information Heinz Kramer GmbH, pg 264
Norbert Mueller AG & Co KG Verlag, pg 265
Verlagsgesellschaft Rudolf Mueller GmbH & Co KG, pg 265
Musikantiquariat und Dr Hans Schneider Verlag GmbH, pg 266
Verlag Stephanie Naglschmid, pg 266
Gunter Narr Verlag, pg 266
Verlag Natur & Wissenschaft Harro Hieronimus & Dr Jurgen Schmidt, pg 266
Neuland-Verlagsgesellschaft mbH, pg 268
Nusser Verlag, pg 269
Edition Parabolis, pg 271
Pearson Education Deutschland GmbH, pg 272
Richard Pflaum Verlag GmbH & Co KG, pg 273
Physica-Verlag, pg 273
pmi Verlag, pg 274
Premop Verlag GmbH, pg 275
Psychologie Verlags Union GmbH, pg 275
Psychosozial-Verlag, pg 275
Quintessenz Verlags-GmbH, pg 276
Verlag Recht und Wirtschaft GmbH, pg 277
Reed Elsevier Deutschland GmbH, pg 277
Ritterbach Verlag GmbH, pg 279
Ruhland Verlag Gimblt, pg 281
Ryvellus Medienagentur Dopfer, pg 281
1 H Sauer Verlag GmbH, pg 282
K G Saur Verlag GmbH, A Gale/ Thomson Learning Company, pg 282
Verlag Th Schaefer im Vicentz Verlag KG, pg 282
Schaeffer-Poeschel Verlag fuer Wirtschaft Steuern Recht, pg 282
Schapen Edition, H W Louis, pg 282
M & H Schaper GmbH & Co KG, pg 282
Schiffahrts-Verlag, pg 283
Verlag Dr Otto Schmidt KG, pg 283

Springer-Verlag GmbH & Co KG, pg 288
Franz Steiner Verlag Wiesbaden GmbH, pg 289
Dr Dietrich Steinkopff Verlag GmbH & Co, pg 289
Sternberg-Verlag bei Ernst Franz, pg 290
Suin Buch-Verlag, pg 291
Tetra Verlag Gmbh, pg 292
Thalacker Medien GmbH Co KG, pg 293
Georg Thieme Verlag KG, pg 293
Tipress Dienstleistungen fur das Verlagswesen GmbH, pg 294
Wirtschaftsverlag Carl Ueberreuter, pg 295
UNO-Verlag mbH, Vertriebs und Verlagsgesellschaft, pg 296
UVK Verlagsgesellschaft mbH, pg 297
Dorothea van der Koelen, pg 297
VAS-Verlag fuer Akademische Schriften, Vas Karl-Heinz Balon, pg 297
Vereinigte Fachverlage GmbH, pg 297
Verlag fur Schweissen und Verwandte Verfahren, pg 298
Friedr Vieweg & Sohn Verlagsgesellschaft mbH, pg 298
Curt R Vincentz Verlag, pg 298
Werner Verlag GmbH & Co KG, pg 302
Westdeutscher Verlag GmbH, pg 302
Dr Dieter Winkler, pg 303
Wison Verlag GmbH, pg 303
Xenos Verlagsgesellschaft mbH, pg 304

Ghana
Black Mask Ltd, pg 306
Building & Road Research Institute (BRRI), pg 306
World Literature Project, pg 308

Greece
Diavlos, pg 309
Govostis Publishing SA, pg 311
Hestia-1 D Hestia-Kollaros & Co Corporation, pg 311
Karatzas Charis, pg 312
Knossos Publications, pg 312
Alex Siokis & Co, pg 315

Haiti
Editions Caraiibes SA, pg 317

Holy See (Vatican City State)
Pontificia Academia Scientiarum, pg 317

Hong Kong
Hong Kong University Press, pg 320
Joint Publishing (HK) Co Ltd, pg 320

Hungary
CEU-Press, pg 323
Kossuth Kiado RT, pg 325
Mezoegazda Kiado, pg 325
Nemzetkozi Szinhazi Intezet Magyar Kozpontja, pg 326
Novorg Kiado, pg 326
Panem, pg 326
Planetas Kiadoi es Kereskedelmi Kft, pg 326

Saldo Penzugyi Tanacsado es Informatikai Rt, pg 326
Szabvanykiado, pg 326

Iceland
Frodi Ltd, pg 328

India
Academic Book Corporation, pg 329
Addison-Wesley (Singapore) Pte Ltd, pg 329
Agricole Publishing Academy, pg 330
B I Publications Pvt Ltd, pg 331
Daya Publishing House, pg 336
Eastern Book Co, pg 336
Eastern Law House Pvt Ltd, pg 336
Galgotia Publications Pvt Ltd, pg 337
B Jain Publishers Overseas, pg 340
Laxmi Publications Pvt Ltd, pg 341
Multitech Publishing Co, pg 343
Munshiram Manoharlal Publishers Pvt Ltd, pg 343
National Council of Applied Economic Research, Publications Division, pg 344
Parimal Prakashan, pg 345
Reliance Publishing House, pg 347
Research Signpost, pg 348
Sage Publications India Pvt Ltd, pg 348
Scientific Book Agency, pg 349
Sita Publications, pg 350
Somaiya Publications Pvt Ltd, pg 350
South Asian Publishers Pvt Ltd, pg 350
Sterling Information Technologies, pg 351
Transworld Research Network, pg 352
Vastu Gyan Publication, pg 352
Vision Books Pvt Ltd, pg 353
A H Wheeler & Co Ltd, pg 353

Indonesia
P T Bulan Bintang, pg 354
PT BPK Gunung Mulia, pg 355
CV Yasaguna, pg 357

Ireland
The Columba Book Service, pg 359
The Columba Press, pg 359
The Economic & Social Research Institute, pg 360
European Foundation for the Improvement of Living & Working Conditions, pg 360
Gandon Editions, pg 360
Gill & Macmillan Ltd, pg 361
Irish Management Institute, pg 361
Oak Tree Press, pg 362
On Stream Publications Ltd, pg 363
Relay Books, pg 363
Round Hall Sweet & Maxwell, pg 363

Israel
Ben-Zvi Institute, pg 365
The Bialik Institute, pg 365
Dekel Publishing House, pg 366
Freund Publishing House Ltd, pg 367
Gefen Publishing House Ltd, pg 367
Hakibbutz Hameuchad Publishing House Ltd, pg 368
Intermedia Audio, Video Book Publishing Ltd, pg 368

Israel Antiquities Authority, pg 368
Israel Exploration Society, pg 368
Israel Music Institute (IMI), pg 369

Italy
Adea Edizioni, pg 374
AIB Associazione Italiana Bibliotheche, pg 375
Umberto Allemandi & C SRL, pg 375
Franco Angeli SRL, pg 375
Apimondia, pg 375
Editore Armando Armando SRL, pg 376
BeMa, pg 377
Editore Giorgio Bretschneider, pg 378
Edizioni Bucalo SNC, pg 379
CEDAM (Casa Editrice Dr A Milani), pg 380
Istituto Centrale per il Catalogo Unico delle Biblioteche Italiane e per le Informazioni Bibliografiche, pg 380
Centro Biblico, pg 380
Centro Scientifico Int, pg 381
Centro Scientifico Torinese, pg 381
CG Ediz Medico-Scientifiche, pg 381
CIC Edizioni Internazionali, pg 381
Edizioni Dedalo SRL, pg 384
DEI Tipographia del Genio Civile, pg 384
Edizioni del Centro, pg 384
Edi Ermes SRL, pg 386
Editrice Bibliografica SpA, pg 386
Etas Libri, pg 388
Folini, pg 389
Gnocchi Editore, pg 391
Casa Editrice Libraria Idelson di G Gnocchi, pg 393
IHT Gruppo Editoriale SRL, pg 393
Edizioni Internazionali di Letteratura e Scienze, pg 394
Ithaca, pg 394
Linea d'Ombra Libri, pg 396
Lybra Immagine, pg 397
Milella di Lecce Spazio Vivo SRL, pg 399
Mucchi Editore SRL, pg 400
New Magazine, pg 400
Edizioni Olivares, pg 402
Franco Cosimo Panini Editore SpA, pg 402
Piccin Nuova Libraria SpA, pg 403
Pitagora Editrice SRL, pg 403
Pizzicato Edizioni Musicali, pg 403
Pontificio Istituto di Archeologia Cristiana, pg 404
Psicologica Editrice, pg 404
Rirea Casa Editrice della Rivista Italiana di Ragioneria e di Economia Aziendale, pg 405
Editrice San Marco SRL, pg 406
Societa Stampa Sportiva, pg 408
Edizioni Sorbona Milano, pg 408
Tomo Edizioni srl, pg 410
Transeuropa Libri, pg 410
Vinciana Editrice sas, pg 411

Japan
The American Chamber of Commerce in Japan, pg 414
Bun-ichi Sogo Shuppan, pg 415
Daiichi Shuppan Co Ltd, pg 415
Dohosha Publishing Co Ltd, pg 416
Fumaido Publishing Company Ltd, pg 416
Hakutei-Sha, pg 417
Igaku-Shoin Ltd, pg 418
Iwanami Shoten, Publishers, pg 418

Kaibundo Publishing Co Ltd, pg 419
Kazama Shobo, pg 419
Keigaku Publishing Co Ltd, pg 419
Kindai Kagaku Sha Co, Ltd, pg 419
Kosei Publishing Co Ltd, pg 420
Maruzen Co Ltd, pg 421
Nakayama Shoten Company Ltd, pg 421
Nikkagiren Shuppan-Sha (JUSE Press Ltd), pg 422
Nippon Jitsugyo Publishing Co, Ltd, pg 423
Nobunkyo (Rural Village Culture Association), pg 423
Ohmsha Ltd, pg 423
Sangyo-Tosho Publishing Co Ltd, pg 424
Seibido, pg 424
Shokoku Publishing Co Ltd, pg 426
Shorin-Sha Co ltd, pg 426
Shufunotomo sha Co Ltd, pg 426
Sobun-Sha, pg 426
Toho Book Store, pg 427
Toho Shuppan, pg 427
Tokyo Kagaku Dozin Co Ltd, pg 427
Toppan Co Ltd, pg 428
Tsukiji Shokan Publishing Co, pg 428
Zeimukeiri-Kyokai, pg 429
Zenkoku Kyodo Shuppan, pg 429

Kenya
Action Publishers, pg 430
African Centre for Technology Studies (ACTS), pg 431
Focus Publications Ltd, pg 431
Heinemann Kenya Limited (EAEP), pg 431
Kenway Publications Ltd, pg 432
Kenya Energy & Environment Organisation, Kengo, pg 432
Lake Publishers & Enterprises Ltd, pg 432
Midi Teki Publishers, pg 433
Shirikon Publishers, pg 433

Democratic People's Republic of Korea
Korea Science and Encyclopedia Publishing House, pg 434

Republic of Korea
Bal-eon, pg 434
Bi-bong Publishing Co, pg 435
Gim-Yeong Co, pg 436
Hakmun Publishing, Co, pg 436
Korea Psychological Testing Institute, pg 437
Koreaone Press Inc, pg 438
Maeil Gyeongje, pg 438
Nanam Publishing House, pg 439
Prompter Publications, pg 439
Pyeong-hwa Chulpansa, pg 439
Samho Music Publishing Co, pg 440
Twenty-First Century Publishers, Inc, pg 440
Yeha Publishing Co Ltd, pg 441

Latvia
Nordik/Tapals Publishers Ltd, pg 442
Preses Nams, pg 442

Lebanon
Institute for Palestine Studies, Publishing & Research Organization (IPS), pg 443

Lithuania
AS Narbuto Leidykla (AS Narbutas' Publishers), pg 445
Centre of Legal Information, pg 445
Eugrimas, pg 445
Lietus Ltd, pg 445
Lithuanian National Museum Publishing House, pg 446
Martynas Mazvydas National Library of Lithuania, pg 446
Mokslo ir enciklopediju leidybos institutas, pg 446
Scena, pg 446
Svietimo ir mokslo ministerijos Leidybos centras, pg 446

Luxembourg
Editions Emile Borschette, pg 447
Editions Promoculture, pg 448
Varkki Verghese, pg 448

The Former Yugoslav Republic of Macedonia
Detska radost, pg 448
Macedonia Prima Publishing House, pg 449
Medis, Skopje, pg 449

Madagascar
Madagascar Print & Press Company, pg 450
Societe Malgache d'Edition, pg 450

Malaysia
IBS Buku Sdn Bhd, pg 452
Malayan Law Journal Sdn Bhd, pg 453
Minerva Publications, pg 453
Oscar Book International, pg 453

Malta
Publishers' Enterprises Group (PEG) Ltd, pg 456

Mauritius
Hemco Publications, pg 457

Mexico
Editorial AGATA SA de CV, pg 457
ALFA OMEGA Grupo Editor, pg 458
Editorial Azteca SA, pg 458
Colegio de Postgraduados en Ciencias Agricolas, pg 459
Ediciones Contables y Administrativas SA, pg 459
Publicaciones Cruz O SA, pg 459
Editorial Diana SA de CV, pg 459
El Colegio de Michoacan A C, pg 460
Editorial El Manual Moderno SA de CV, pg 460
Centro de Estudios Monetarios Latinoamericanos (CEMLA), pg 460
Editorial Fata Morgana SA de CV, pg 461
Editorial Herrero SA, pg 462
Editorial Limusa SA de CV, pg 463
Naves Internacional de Ediciones SA, pg 464
Organizacion Cultural LP SA de CV, pg 465
Panorama Editorial, SA, pg 465
Pearson Educacion de Mexico, SA de CV, pg 465
Editorial Trillas SA de CV, pg 467

Morocco
Dar Nachr Al Maarifa Pour L'Edition et La Distribution, pg 469

Myanmar
Shumawa Publishing House, pg 471

Namibia
Desert Research Foundation of Namibia (DRFN), pg 471

Netherlands
Aeolus Press BV, pg 472
Backhuys Publishers BV, pg 473
Business Contact BV, pg 475
Educatieve Partners Nederland bv, pg 476
Hagen & Stam Uitgeverij Ten, pg 478
Uitgeverij Homeovisie BV, pg 478
IOS Press BV, pg 479
Katholieke Bijbelstichting, pg 479
Kluwer Law International, pg 479
Koninklijk Instituut Voor de Tropen, pg 480
Samsom BedrijfsInformatie BV, pg 483
Scriptum, pg 483
SDU Juridische & Fiscale Uitgeverij, pg 484
Segment BV, pg 484
SMD Educational Publishers (Spruyt, Van Mantgem & De Does), pg 484
Sociaal en Cultureel Planbureau, pg 484
Swets & Zeitlinger Publishers, pg 485
Uitgeverij de Tijdstroom BV, pg 485

New Zealand
Brooker's Ltd, pg 489
Butterworths New Zealand Ltd, pg 489
CCH New Zealand Ltd, pg 490
Fraser Books, pg 491
Learning Media Ltd, pg 492
Legislation Direct, pg 492
Reach Publications, pg 495
Southern Press Ltd, pg 496
Spinal Publications, pg 496

Nigeria
Evans Brothers (Nigeria Publishers) Ltd, pg 499
Fourth Dimension Publishing Co Ltd, pg 499
Goldland Business Co Ltd, pg 499
New Africa Publishing Company Ltd, pg 500
Riverside Communications, pg 501

Norway
Universitetsforlaget, pg 505
Vett & Viten AS, pg 505

Pakistan
Academy of Education Planning & Management (AEPAM), pg 506
The Book House, pg 506
HMR Publishing Co, pg 507
Sang-e-Meel Publications, pg 509
Vanguard Books Ltd, pg 509

Panama
Editorial Universitaria, pg 509

Paraguay
Intercontinental Editora, pg 510

Philippines
Ateneo de Manila University Press, pg 512
Our Lady of Manaoag Publisher, pg 514
Rex Bookstores & Publishers, pg 514
Salesiana Publishers Inc, pg 515
SIBS Publishing House Inc, pg 515
UST Publishing House, pg 515

Poland
Polskie Wydawnictwo Ekonomiczne PWE SA, pg 516
Impuls, pg 517
Instytut Meteorologii i Gospodarki Wodnej, pg 518
Ossolineum Zaklad Narodowy im Ossolinskich - Wydawnictwo, pg 518
Wydawnictwo Prawnicze Co, pg 519
Oficyna Wydawnicza Szkoly Glownej Handlowej w Warszawie Oficyna Wydawnicza SGH, pg 520
Instytut Techniki Budowlanej, Dzial Wydawniczo- Poligraficzny, pg 520
Wydawnictwa Naukowo-Techniczne, pg 521
Wydawnictwa Uniwersytetu Warszawskiego, pg 521
Wydawnictwo DiG, pg 521

Portugal
Edicoes Cetop, pg 523
Edicoes Colibri, pg 523
Difusao Cultural, pg 524
Dinalivro, pg 524
Instituto de Investigacao Cientifica Tropical, pg 526
Livraria Luzo-Espanhola Lda, pg 526
McGraw-Hill Editora de Portugal, pg 527
Monitor, pg 527
Monitor-Projectos e Edicoes, LDA, pg 527
Petrony Livraria, pg 528
Quid Juris - Sociedade editora, pg 529
Edicoes Salesianas, pg 529
Vega-Publicacao e Distribuicao de Livros e Revistas, Lda, pg 530

Puerto Rico
McGraw-Hill Intermericana del Caribe, Inc, pg 530

Romania
Editora All, pg 531
Editura Clusium, Casa de Editura Atlas-Clusium SRL, pg 532
FF Press, pg 533
Editura Gryphon, pg 533
Editura Humanitas, pg 533
Humanitas Publishing House, pg 533
Editura Meridiane, pg 534
Monitorul Oficial, Editura, pg 534
Editura Niculescu, pg 534
Polirom Verlag, pg 535
Editura 'Scrisul Romanesc', pg 536

PUBLISHERS

Russian Federation
FGUP Izdatelstvo Mashinostroenie, pg 538
Finansy i Statistika Publishing House, pg 538
Fizmatlit Publishing Co, pg 538
Gidrometeoizdat, pg 538
Izdatel'stvo Kazanskago Universiteta, pg 538
Izdatel'stvo Mordovskogo gosudar stvennogo, pg 538
Izvestia Sovetov Narodnyh Deputatov Russian Federation (RF), pg 539
Izdatelskii Dom Kompositor, pg 539
Izdatelstvo Metallurgiya, pg 540
Izdatelstvo Mir, pg 540
Izdatelstvo Muzyka, pg 540
Nauka Publishers, pg 540
Profizdat, pg 541
Izdatelstvo Sudostroenie, pg 542
Voyenizdat, pg 542
Izdatelstvo Vysshaya Shkola, pg 543

Senegal
CODESRIA (Council for the Development of Social Science Research in Africa), pg 544

Singapore
APAC Publishers Services, pg 545
LexisNexis, pg 547
Maruzen Asia (Pte) Ltd, pg 547
Singapore University Press Pte Ltd, pg 548
Taylor & Francis Asia Pacific, pg 548

Slovakia
Dom Techniky Zvazu Slovenskych Vedeckotechnickych Spolocnosti Ltd, pg 549
Priroda, pg 550
Slo Viet, pg 550
Sofa, pg 551

Slovenia
Zalozba Obzorja d d Maribor, pg 552

South Africa
Butterworths South Africa, pg 553
Human Sciences Research Council, pg 555
Institute for Reformational Studies CHE, pg 555
Johannesburg Art Gallery, pg 556
Juta & Co, pg 556
National Botanical Institute, pg 557
New Africa Books (Pty) Ltd, pg 557
Oceanographic Research Institute, pg 558
Van Schaik Publishers, pg 560

Spain
Centro de Estudios Adams-Ediciones Valbuena SA, pg 561
Editorial AEDOS SA, pg 561
AENOR (Asociacion Espanola de Normalizacion y Certificacion), pg 561
Ediciones Agrotecnicas, SL, pg 562
AMV Ediciones, pg 563
Arambol, SL, pg 563
Arco Editorial SA, pg 564
Arco Libros SL, pg 564
Bosch Casa Editorial SA, pg 565
J M Bosch Editor, pg 565
CEAC, Grupo Editorial SA, pg 567
Cedel, Ediciones Jose O Avila Monteso ES, pg 567
Celeste Ediciones, pg 567
Editorial CISSPRAXIS SA, pg 567
Civitas SA Editorial, pg 567
Editorial Constitucion y Leyes SA - COLEX, pg 568
Ediciones Daly S L, pg 569
Ediciones Diaz de Santos SA, pg 569
Ediciones Doce Calles SL, pg 570
Editorial Dossat SA, pg 570
Dykinson SL, pg 571
Edebe, pg 571
EDERSA (Editoriales de Derecho Reunidas SA), pg 571
Edex, Centro de Recursos Comunitarios, pg 571
Edika-Med, SA, pg 572
EOS Gabinete de Orientacion Psicologica, pg 573
Instituto de Estudios Fiscales, pg 574
Etu Ediciones SL, pg 574
Fundacion Marcelino Botin, pg 575
Generalitat de Catalunya Diari Oficial de la Generalitat vern, pg 575
Ediciones Gestio 2000 SA, pg 575
Editorial Gustavo Gili SA, pg 576
Grao Editorial, pg 576
Editorial Grupo Cero, pg 576
Grupo Comunicar, pg 576
Idea Books, SA, pg 578
Institut de Recursos I investigacio per a la Formacio SL (IRIF), pg 578
Ediciones Internacionales Universitarias SA, pg 578
LEDA (Las Ediciones de Arte), pg 579
Ediciones Libertarias/Prodhufi SA, pg 580
Lid Editorial Empresarial, SL, pg 580
Mad SL Editorial, pg 581
Marcial Pons Ediciones Juridicas SA, pg 581
Marcombo SA de Boixareu Editores, pg 581
Ediciones Medici SA, pg 582
Ediciones Morata SL, pg 583
Mundi-Prensa Libros SA, pg 583
Editorial la Muralla SA, pg 583
Naque Editora, pg 583
Navarra, Comunidad Autonoma, Servicio de Prensa, Publica Pamplona, pg 584
Editorial Noray, pg 584
Ediciones Norma SA, pg 584
Ediciones Oceano Grupo SA, pg 584
Ediciones Olimpic, SL, pg 585
Omnicon, SA, pg 585
Editorial Paidotribo SL, pg 585
Pais Vasco Servicio Central de Publicaciones, pg 585
Progensa, pg 588
Pulso Ediciones, SL, pg 588
RA-MA, Libreria y Editorial Microinformatica, pg 588
Editorial Reus SA, pg 588
Ediciones ROL SA, pg 589
Rueda, SL Editorial, pg 589
Servicio de Publicaciones Universidad de Cordoba, pg 590
Signament I Comunicacio, SL Signament Edicions, pg 590
Editorial Sintes SA, pg 590
Editorial Sintesis, SA, pg 590
Ediciones Tecnicas Rede, SA, pg 592

TYPE OF PUBLICATION INDEX

Editores Tecnicos Asociados SA, pg 592
Tesitex, SL, pg 592
Tirant lo Blanch SL Libreriaa, pg 592
Ediciones de la Torre, pg 593
Trea Ediciones, SL, pg 593
Xunta de Galicia, pg 596

Sri Lanka
International Centre for Ethnic Studies, pg 597
National Library & Documentation Services Board, pg 597
Sunera Publishers, pg 598

Sweden
Almqvist och Wiksell International, pg 600
Forlagshuset Norden AB, pg 602
Ingenjoersforlaget AB, pg 603
Iustus Forlag AB, pg 603
Norstedts Juridik, pg 605
Studentlitteratur AB, pg 606
Teknografiska Institutet AB, pg 607

Switzerland
Werner Classen Verlag, pg 611
Cockatoo Press (Schweiz), Thailand-Publikationen, pg 611
Marcel Dekker AG, pg 612
Dimension World Ltd, pg 612
EULAR Publishers, pg 613
Helbing und Lichtenhahn Verlag AG, pg 615
Verlag Industrielle Organisation, pg 616
JPM Publications SA, pg 616
S Karger AG, Medical and Scientific Publishers, pg 617
Editiones Roche, pg 623
Editions Scriptar SA, pg 624
Sinwel-Buchhandlung Verlag, pg 624
3 Dimension World (3-D-World), pg 625
Vdf Hochschulverlag AG an der ETH Zurich, pg 626
Versus Verlag AG, pg 627
Vexer Verlag, pg 627

Taiwan, Province of China
Art Book Co Ltd, pg 629
Chien Chen Bookstore Publishing Company Ltd, pg 629
Farseeing Publishing Company Ltd, pg 630
Fuh-Wen Book Co, pg 630
Chu Hai Publishing (Taiwan) Co Ltd, pg 630
Ho-Chi Book Publishing Co, pg 630
Hsiao Yuan Publication Co, Ltd, pg 630
Laureate Book Co Ltd, pg 631
San Min Book Co Ltd, pg 631
Wei-Chuan Publishing Company Ltd, pg 632
Yi Hsien Publishing Co Ltd, pg 632

United Republic of Tanzania
Bureau of Statistics, pg 633
DUP (1996) Ltd, pg 633
Tanzania Publishing House, pg 634

Thailand
Bannakit Trading, pg 635
Niyom Vidhya, pg 635

Tunisia
Maison Tunisienne de l'Edition, pg 638

Turkey
Ataturk Kultur, Dil ve Tarih, Yusek Kurumu Baskanligi, pg 639
Birsen Yayinevi, pg 639
Inkilap Publishers Ltd, pg 640
Seckin Yayinevi, pg 641
Yapi-Endustri Merkezi Yayinlari-Yem Yayin, pg 642
Yetkin Printing & Publishing Co Inc, pg 642

Uganda
Centre for Basic Research, pg 642
Fountain Publishers Ltd, pg 642

Ukraine
ASK Ltd, pg 643
Osnova, Kharkov State University Press, pg 643
Osnovy Publishers, pg 643
Urozaj, pg 643

United Kingdom
ABG Professional Information, pg 644
Act 3 Publishing, pg 645
Actinic Press Ltd, pg 645
Adamantine Press Ltd, pg 645
Arnold, pg 648
Arts Council of England, pg 649
Ashgate Publishing Ltd, pg 649
Aslib, The Association for Information Management, pg 650
Association for Science Education, pg 650
BILD Publications, pg 654
Blackwell Science Ltd, pg 656
Blueprint, pg 656
Books for Europe Ltd, pg 657
BPP Publishing Ltd, pg 658
BPS Books (British Psychological Society), pg 658
Brassey's UK Ltd, pg 658
Nicholas Brealey Publishing, pg 659
Brilliant Publications, pg 659
BAAF: Adoption & Fostering, pg 659
Business Monitor International, pg 661
Butterworths Tolley, pg 661
Capstone Publishing Ltd, pg 663
Cardiff Academic Press, pg 663
Jon Carpenter Publishing, pg 664
Cassell & Co, pg 664
Cavendish Publishing Ltd, pg 665
Centre for Information on Language Teaching & Research (CILT), pg 666
Chancellor Publications, pg 666
Churchill Livingstone, pg 668
Computer Step, pg 670
The Continuum International Publishing Group Ltd, pg 670
CSA (Cambridge Scientific Abstracts), pg 672
Donhead Publishing Ltd, pg 675
Martin Dunitz Ltd, pg 676
Editon XII, pg 677
Elsevier Advanced Technology, pg 678
Elsevier Science Ltd, pg 678
EPER, pg 679
Ernst & Young, pg 679
Estates Gazette, pg 679
The Eurospan Group, pg 680
Extraordinary People Press, pg 681
Facet Publishing, pg 681

TYPE OF PUBLICATION INDEX — BOOK

Financial World Publishing, pg 682
Fishing News Books Ltd, pg 682
Flicks Books, pg 683
Free Association Books Ltd, pg 684
W H Freeman & Co Ltd, pg 684
David Fulton Publishers Ltd, pg 685
Garnet Publishing Ltd, pg 685
The Geographical Association, pg 686
Geological Society Publishing House, pg 686
Gomer Press (J D Lewis & Sons Ltd), pg 688
Gower Publishing Ltd, pg 688
W Green The Scottish Law Publisher, pg 689
Harcourt Publishers Ltd, pg 691
Harley Books, pg 692
Harvard University Press, pg 692
Haynes Publishing, pg 693
Health Development Agency, pg 694
Hobsons, pg 696
Hodder Headline Ltd, pg 696
Horizon Scientific Press, pg 697
ICC United Kingdom, pg 698
IFLA International Programme for UAP, pg 698
Institute for Fiscal Studies, pg 699
Institute of Education, University of London, pg 699
Institution of Electrical Engineers, pg 700
Intellect Ltd, pg 700
Interfisc Publishing, pg 700
Intermediate Technology Publications Ltd, pg 700
IOM Communications Ltd, pg 701
JAI Press Ltd, pg 702
James & James (Science Publishers) Ltd, pg 702
Jane's Information Group, pg 702
Karnac Books Ltd, pg 703
Jessica Kingsley Publishers, pg 704
Kluwer Academic/Plenum Publishers, pg 705
Kogan Page Ltd, pg 705
The Latchmere Press, pg 706
Learning Matters Ltd, pg 706
Legal Action Group, pg 706
Lemos & Crane, pg 707
Library & Information Statistics Unit, pg 707
LLP Ltd, pg 708
Management Books 2000 Ltd, pg 711
Management Pocketbooks Ltd, pg 711
Manchester University Press, pg 711
Manson Publishing Ltd, pg 711
Marcham Books, pg 711
Media Research Publishing Ltd, pg 712
The Merlin Press Ltd, pg 713
Micelle Press, pg 714
Multilingual Matters Ltd, pg 716
National Association for the Teaching of English (NATE), pg 717
National Foster Care Association, pg 717
National Foundation for Educational Research, pg 717
National Institute of Adult Continuing Education, pg 717
NCVO, pg 718
Nelson Thornes Ltd, pg 718
Open University Press, pg 721
Oxfam, pg 722
Parapress Ltd, pg 724
Pavilion Publishing (Brighton) Ltd, pg 725

Pearson Education Europe, Mideast & Africa, pg 725
Pergamon Flexible Learning, pg 726
Perpetuity Press, pg 726
Petroc Press, pg 726
Phaidon Press Ltd, pg 726
Pharmaceutical Press, pg 726
PIRA Intl, pg 728
Pluto Press, pg 728
Police Review Publishing Company Ltd, pg 729
The Policy Press, pg 729
Portland Press Ltd, pg 730
Professional Engineering Publishing Ltd, pg 730
Publishing Training Centre at BookHouse, pg 731
Quiller Publishing Ltd, pg 732
Quintessence Publishing Co Ltd, pg 732
Radcliffe Medical Press Ltd, pg 732
Reading & Language Information Centre, pg 733
Reed Educational & Professional Publishing, pg 734
Research Studies Press Ltd (RSP), pg 734
RIBA Publications, pg 735
RICS Books, pg 735
Rooster Books Ltd, pg 735
Roundhouse Publishing Ltd, pg 736
Royal College of General Practitioners, pg 736
Royal Institute of International Affairs, pg 736
Sage Publications Ltd, pg 737
St Jerome Publishing, pg 738
Science Reviews Ltd, pg 739
Shaw & Sons Ltd, pg 741
Sheldon Press, pg 741
Sherwood Publishing, pg 741
SLS Legal Publications (NI), pg 742
Southgate Publishers, pg 743
Speechmark Publishing Ltd, pg 744
Spon Press, pg 744
Stainer & Bell Ltd, pg 745
The Stationery Office, pg 745
Rudolf Steiner Press, pg 745
Stobart Davies Ltd, pg 745
Take That Ltd, pg 746
I B Tauris & Co Ltd, pg 747
Thistle Press, pg 748
Trentham Books Ltd, pg 750
Whiting & Birch Ltd, pg 756
Whittles Publishing, pg 756
WIT Press, pg 757
Woodhead Publishing Ltd, pg 758

Uruguay
La Flor del Itapebi, pg 760
Editia Uruguay, pg 761

Venezuela
Ediciones Vega SRL, pg 763

Viet Nam
Science & Technics Publishing House, pg 763

Yugoslavia
Partenon MAM Sistem, pg 765
Savez Inzenjera i Tehnicara Jugoslavije, pg 765

Zimbabwe
Longman Zimbabwe (Pvt) Ltd, pg 768

REPRINTS

Argentina
Oikos, pg 8

Australia
Boombana Publications, pg 16
Cookery Book, pg 18
Geoffrey Hamlyn-Harris, pg 25
Harcourt Australia Pty Ltd, pg 25
Instauratio Press, pg 27
Little Red Apple Publishing, pg 30
Navarine Publishing, pg 34
Protestant Publications, pg 39
St Pauls, pg 41
Veritas Press, pg 46
Windhorse Books, pg 48

Austria
Dachs-Verlag GmbH, pg 50
Development News Ltd, pg 51
Ennsthaler GesmbH & Co KG, pg 51
Oesterreichischer Kunst und Kulturverlag, pg 56

Azerbaijan
Sada, Literaturno-Izdatel'skij Centr, pg 61

Belarus
Belaruskaya Encyklapedyya, pg 63
Kavaler Publishers, pg 63

Belgium
Marabout, pg 72

Benin
Office National d'Edition de Presse et d'Imprimerie (ONEPI), pg 76

Brazil
Agalma Psicanalise Editora Ltda, pg 78
Centro de Estudos Juridicosdo Para (CEJUP), pg 80
Concordia Editora Ltda, pg 81
Edicon Editora e Consultorial Ltda, pg 81
EDUC - Editora da PUC-SP, pg 82
Livraria Freitas Bastos Editora SA, pg 83
Fundacao Cultural Avatar, pg 83
Editora Logosofica, pg 86
Pallas Editora e Distribuidora Ltda, pg 89
Qualitymark Editora Ltda, pg 90
Editora Revan Ltda, pg 90
Editora UNESP, pg 92

Bulgaria
Kralica MAB, pg 96
Seven Hills Publishers, pg 97
Svetra Publishing House, pg 98

China
Anhui People's Publishing House, pg 102
Chemical Industry Press, pg 102
China Film Press, pg 103
China Materials Management Publishing House, pg 103
Language Publishing House, pg 107
Lanzhou University Press, pg 107
The People's Communications Publishing House, pg 107
Shandong University Press, pg 109
South China University of Science and Technology Press, pg 109

Croatia
ArTresor naklada, pg 118
Matica hrvatska, pg 119
Znaci Vremena, Institut Za Istrazivanje Biblije, pg 120

Cuba
Editorial Letras Cubanas, pg 121
Editora Politica, pg 121
Pueblo y Educacion Editorial (PE), pg 121

Czech Republic
Cesky normalizacni institut, pg 127
Odeon, nakladatelstvi krasne literatury a umeni, pg 127
Portal Ltd, pg 127

Denmark
Borgens Forlag A/S, pg 130
Dansk Historisk Handbogsforlag ApS, pg 131
Holkenfeldt 3, pg 133
Rosenkilde & Bagger, pg 135
Scandinavia Publishing House, pg 135

Dominican Republic
Pontificia Universidad Catolica Madre y Maestra, pg 136

Ecuador
Corporacion Editora Nacional, pg 137

Egypt (Arab Republic of Egypt)
Dar El Shorouk Publishing & Distributing House, pg 138

El Salvador
Editorial Universitaria de la Universidad de El Salvador, pg 139

Estonia
Estonian Academy Publishers, pg 139

Finland
Suomalaisen Kirjallisuuden Seura, pg 144

France
Editions Philippe Auzou, pg 149
Editions Bertout, pg 150
Bragelonne, pg 151
Editions des Cahiers Bourbonnais, pg 152
Chasse Maree-Armen, pg 154
Delagrave Edition SA, pg 158
Doin Editeurs, pg 160
Editions Jacques Gabay, pg 165
Editions Christian Pirot, pg 180
Jean-Michel Place, pg 180
Presses Universitaires de Caen, pg 181
Editions de Septembre, pg 184
Editions Springer France, pg 186
Editions Trois Fontaines, pg 188

French Polynesia
Scoop/Au Vent des Iles, pg 190
Haere Po No Tahiti, pg 190

Germany
Antiqua-Verlag GmbH, pg 194
Antiquariat und Verlag Auvermann Keip GmbH, pg 194

AOL-Verlag Frohmut Menze, pg 194
Aufstieg-Verlag GmbH, pg 196
Belser Wissenschaftlicher Dienst, pg 200
Biblio-Zeller Verlag, pg 202
Verlag Wolfgang Bleiweis, pg 204
Boehlau-Verlag GmbH & Cie, pg 204
BRUEN-Verlag, Gorenflo, pg 207
Degener & Co, Manfred Dreiss Verlag, pg 213
Deutsche Landwirtschaft-Gesellschaft VerlagsgesGmbH, pg 214
Engelhorn Verlag, pg 222
Verlag Esoterische Philosophie GmbH, pg 224
Harald Fischer Verlag GmbH, pg 228
Friedrich Frommann Verlag, pg 230
GLB Parkland Verlags-und Vertriebs GmbH, pg 232
Liselotte Hamecher, pg 236
Litteraturverlag Karlheinz Hartmann, pg 237
Edition Hentrich Druck & Verlag Gebr Hentrich und Tank GmbH & Co KG, pg 239
Koptisch-Orthodoxes Zentrum, pg 252
Karin Kramer Verlag, pg 253
Laaber-Verlag, pg 255
Karl Robert Langewiesche Nachfolger Hans Koester KG, pg 256
Edition Libri Illustri GmbH, pg 257
Maro Verlag und Druck, Benno Kasmayr, pg 261
Mueller & Schindler Verlag, pg 265
Musikantiquariat und Dr Hans Schneider Verlag GmbH, pg 266
Neuthor - Verlag, pg 268
C W Niemeyer Buchverlage GmbH, pg 268
Georg Olms Verlag AG, pg 270
Orbis Verlag fur Publizistik GmbH, pg 270
Patio, Galerie und Druckwerkstatt, pg 272
Konrad Reich Verlag GmbH, pg 278
E Reinhold Verlag, pg 278
Roehrig Universitaets Verlag Gmbh, pg 279
Sachsenbuch Verlagsgesellschaft Mbh, pg 281
Verlag Th Schaefer im Vicentz Verlag KG, pg 282
Schmidt Periodicals GmbH, pg 284
Verlag Schnell und Steiner GmbH, pg 284
Theodor Schuster, pg 285
Scientia Verlag und Antiquariat, pg 286
Spieth-Verlag Verlag fuer Symbolforschung, pg 288
Stern-Verlag Janssen & Co, pg 290
Druck-und Verlagshans Thiele & Schwarz GmbH, pg 293
Transpress Verlagsgesellschaft mbH, pg 294
Trotzdem-Verlags Genossenschaft eG, pg 295
Ulrich Schiefer bahnVerlag, pg 296
VWB-Verlag fur Wissenschaft & Bildung, Amand Aglaster, pg 300
Wachholtz Verlag GmbH, pg 300
Weidmannsche Verlagsbuchhandlung GmbH, pg 301
Zeller Verlag GmbH & Co, pg 305

Ghana
Building & Road Research Institute (BRRI), pg 306
EPP Books Services, pg 307
World Literature Project, pg 308

Greece
Dionysis Noti Karavias, pg 309
Denise Harvey, pg 311
Ianos, pg 311
Panepistimio Ioanninon, pg 314

Hong Kong
Lea Publications Ltd, pg 320
Philopsychy Press, pg 321

Hungary
Aranyhal Konyvkiado Goldfish Publishing, pg 323
Kossuth Kiado RT, pg 325

India
Affiliated East West Press Pvt Ltd, pg 329
Agam Kala Prakashan, pg 330
Allied Publishers Pvt Ltd, pg 330
Associated Publishing House, pg 331
B I Publications Pvt Ltd, pg 331
Book Faith India, pg 333
BR Publishing Corporation, pg 334
Cosmo Publications, pg 335
Daya Publishing House, pg 336
Dutta Baruah Publishing Co Pvt Ltd, pg 336
Eastern Law House Pvt Ltd, pg 336
Eurasia Publishing House Pvt Ltd, pg 337
General Book Depot, pg 337
Gyan Publishing House, pg 338
B Jain Publishers (P) Ltd, pg 340
Laxmi Publications Pvt Ltd, pg 343
Multitech Publishing Co, pg 343
Munshiram Manoharlal Publishers Pvt Ltd, pg 343
National Council of Applied Economic Research, Publications Division, pg 344
Navrang Booksellers & Publishers, pg 344
Omsons Publications, pg 345
Orient Paperbacks, pg 345
Rahul Publishing House, pg 347
Reliance Publishing House, pg 347
Scientific Book Agency, pg 349
DB Taraporevala Sons & Co Pvt Ltd, pg 351
Theosophical Publishing House, pg 351

Ireland
Ballinakella Press, pg 358
Clo Iar-Chonnachta Teo, pg 359
The Collins Press, pg 359
Irish Times Ltd, pg 361
Mercier Press Ltd, pg 362
Mount Eagle Publications Ltd, pg 362
The O'Brien Press Ltd, pg 363
Ossian Publications, pg 363

Israel
Hakibbutz Hameuchad Publishing House Ltd, pg 368

Italy
Alberti Libraio Editore, pg 375
Umberto Allemandi & C SRL, pg 375
All'Insegna del Giglio, pg 375
Belforte Editore Libraio srl, pg 377
Giuseppe Bonanno Editore, pg 378
Bonsignori Editore SRL, pg 378
Edizioni Brenner, pg 378
Centro Scientifico Int, pg 381
Centro Scientifico Torinese, pg 381
CIC Edizioni Internazionali, pg 381
Cittadella Editrice, pg 382
Colonnese Editore, pg 382
Edizioni Cultura della Pace, pg 383
Edizioni del Centro, pg 384
Festina Lente Edizioni, pg 389
Arnaldo Forni Editore SRL, pg 389
In Dialogo, pg 393
Casa Editrice Le Lettere SRL, pg 395
Maria Pacini Fazzi Editore, pg 402
Pheljna Edizioni d'Arte e Suggestione, pg 403
Priuli e Verlucca, Editori, pg 404
Rara-Ist Editoriale di Bibliofilia e Reprints, pg 405
Fausto Sardini Editrice, pg 407
Societa Napoletana Storia Patria Napoli, pg 408
Studio Bibliografico Adelmo Polla, pg 409
Nicola Teti e C Editore SRL, pg 409
Turris, pg 410
Vaccari SRL, pg 411

Jamaica
Eureka Press Ltd, pg 413

Japan
Hakutei-Sha, pg 417
Holp Book Co Ltd, pg 417
Rinsen Book Co Ltd, pg 424
Sobun-Sha, pg 426
Yohan Shuppan, pg 429

Kenya
Focus Publications Ltd, pg 431
Heinemann Kenya Limited (EAEP), pg 431
Kenway Publications Ltd, pg 432
Life Challenge AFRICA, pg 433
Phoenix Publishers, pg 433
Gideon S Were Press, pg 434

Latvia
Vaidelote, pg 442

Lebanon
The International Documentary Centre of Arab Manuscripts, pg 443

Liechtenstein
Topos Verlag AG, pg 445

Luxembourg
Editions Emile Borschette, pg 447
Varkki Verghese, pg 448

Macau
Universidadede de Macau, Centro de Publicacoes, pg 448

Madagascar
Maison d'Edition Protestante ANTSO, pg 450

Malaysia
S Abdul Majeed & Co, pg 451
Penerbit Jayatinta Sdn Bhd, pg 454
Pustaka Cipta Sdn Bhd, pg 454
Pustaka Delta Pelajaran Sdn Bhd, pg 454
Tempo Publishing (M) Sdn Bhd, pg 455

Mexico
Editorial AGATA SA de CV, pg 457
AGT Editor SA, pg 457
Centro de Estudios Mexicanos y Centroamericanos, pg 458
Editorial Diana SA de CV, pg 459
Fondo de Cultura Economica, pg 461

Netherlands
APA (Academic Publishers Associated), pg 472
John Benjamins BV, pg 474
Philo Press-Van Heusden-Hissink & Co CV (APA), pg 482
Rebo Productions BV, pg 483
Tirion Uitgevers BV, pg 485

New Zealand
Brick Row Publishing Co Ltd, pg 489
CCH New Zealand Ltd, pg 490
Nagare Press, pg 493
River Press, pg 495
Shoal Bay Press Ltd, pg 495

Nigeria
Fourth Dimension Publishing Co Ltd, pg 499
Vantage Publishers International Ltd, pg 502
West African Book Publishers Ltd, pg 502

Pakistan
The Book House, pg 506
National Book Foundation, pg 508
National Institute of Historical & Cultural Research, pg 508
Royal Book Co, pg 509
Sang-e-Meel Publications, pg 509

Philippines
Ateneo de Manila University Press, pg 512
Bright Concepts Printing House, pg 512
De La Salle University, pg 513
J C Palabay Enterprises, pg 513
New Day Publishers, pg 514
UST Publishing House, pg 515

Poland
Wydawnictwa Artystyczne i Filmowe, pg 516
Biblioteka Narodowa, pg 516
Wydawnictwo Prawnicze Co, pg 519

Portugal
Livraria Apostolado da Imprensa, pg 526

Romania
Editura Institutul European, pg 533
Editura Militara, pg 534
Editura Paideia, pg 535
Saeculum IO, pg 535

Russian Federation
Aspect Press Ltd, pg 537
Izdatelstvo Khudozhestvennaya Literatura, pg 539

TYPE OF PUBLICATION INDEX BOOK

Ladomir Publishing House, pg 539
Ministerstvo Kul 'tury RF, pg 540
Panorama Publishing House, pg 541
Planeta Publishers, pg 541

Senegal

CODESRIA (Council for the Development of Social Science Research in Africa), pg 544

Singapore

Archipelago Press, pg 545
Cannon International, pg 545

Slovenia

East West Operation (EWO) Ltd, pg 551
Zalozba Mihelac d o o, pg 552

South Africa

Fernwood Press (Pty) Ltd, pg 554
Galago Publishing Pty Ltd, pg 554
Human Sciences Research Council, pg 555
Institute for Reformational Studies CHE, pg 555
Oceanographic Research Institute, pg 558
University of Natal Press, pg 560

Spain

Editorial Afers, SL, pg 561
Editorial Algazara, pg 562
Ediciones Atril, pg 564
Ediciones Doce Calles SL, pg 570
Emece Editores, pg 573
Vicent Garcia Editores, SA, pg 575
Grijalbo Mondadori SA, pg 576
Institucion Fernando el Catolico de la Excma Diputacion de Zaragoza, pg 578
Ediciones JLA, pg 579
Ediciones Maeva, pg 581
Pentalfa Ediciones, pg 586
Editorial Peregrino SL, pg 586
Editorial El Perpetuo Socorro, pg 586
Instituto Provincial de Investigaciones y Estudios Toledanos, pg 588
Universidad de Santiago de Compostela, pg 589
Tursen, SA, pg 593
Editorial Txertoa, pg 594

Sri Lanka

Dayawansa Jayakody & Co, pg 597
Swarna Hansa Foundation, pg 598

Sweden

Bokforlaget Rediviva, Facsimileforlaget, pg 600
Ordfront Foerlag AB, pg 605

Switzerland

Editions L'Age d'Homme - La Cite, pg 608
Cockatoo Press (Schweiz), Thailand-Publikationen, pg 611
Rene Coeckelberghs Editions, pg 611
Dimension World Ltd, pg 612
Lars Mueller Publishers, pg 619
Edition Olms AG, pg 620
3 Dimension World (3-D-World), pg 625

Taiwan, Province of China

Cheng Wen Publishing Company, pg 629
Laureate Book Co Ltd, pg 631
Yi Hsien Publishing Co Ltd, pg 632

United Republic of Tanzania

Central Tanganyika Press, pg 633
General Publications Ltd, pg 633
Tanzania Publishing House, pg 634

Thailand

Sang Dad Publishing Company Ltd, pg 635

Turkey

Arkeoloji Ve Sanat Yayinlari, pg 639
Ataturk Kultur, Dil ve Tarih, Yusek Kurumu Baskanligi, pg 639
Isis Yayin Tic ve San Ltd, pg 640
Varlik Yayinlari AS, pg 641

Uganda

Fountain Publishers Ltd, pg 642

United Kingdom

Arthur James Ltd, pg 649
Award Publications Ltd, pg 651
BCA, pg 653
Beaver Publishing Ltd, pg 653
Birlinn Ltd, pg 655
Books of Zimbabwe Publishing Co (Pvt) Ltd, pg 657
Breedon Books Publishing Company Ltd, pg 659
Bridge Books, pg 659
Canongate Books Ltd, pg 663
Chadwyck-Healey Ltd, pg 666
Chapter Two, pg 666
Christian Education, pg 667
Christian Focus Publications Ltd, pg 667
E W Classey Ltd, pg 668
Leo Cooper, pg 671
Darf Publishers Ltd, pg 674
John Donald Publishers Ltd, pg 675
Elliot Right Way Books, pg 678
The Erskine Press, pg 679
Flicks Books, pg 683
The Fraser Press, pg 684
Walter H Gardner & Co, pg 685
Garnet Publishing Ltd, pg 685
George Mann Publications, pg 687
GMP Publishers Ltd, pg 687
A H Gordon, pg 688
Grange Books PLC, pg 689
The Greek Bookshop, pg 689
W Green The Scottish Law Publisher, pg 689
Gregg Publishing Co, pg 690
Hilmarton Manor Press, pg 696
Hodder Headline Ltd, pg 696
Institute of Physics Publishing, pg 700
International Bee Research Association, pg 701
The Islamic Texts Society, pg 701
Janus Publishing Company Ltd, pg 702
Karnac Books Ltd, pg 703
Kershaw Publishing Co Ltd, pg 704
Landy Publishing, pg 706
Lang Syne Publishers Ltd, pg 706
The Lutterworth Press, pg 709
Peter Marcan Publications, pg 711
Octopus Publishing Group, pg 720
Oneworld Publications, pg 721
Peter Owen Ltd, pg 722
Packard Publishing Ltd, pg 723

Plough Publishing House of Bruderhof Communities in the UK, pg 728
Pluto Press, pg 728
ProQuest Information & Learning, pg 731
Regency House Publishing Ltd, pg 734
Royal College of General Practitioners, pg 736
The Rubicon Press, pg 737
Skoob Russell Square, pg 742
Smith Settle Ltd, pg 743
The Society of Metaphysicians Ltd, pg 743
I B Tauris & Co Ltd, pg 747
Textile & Art Publications Ltd, pg 748
Thistle Press, pg 748
Thoemmes Press, pg 748
Tiger Books International PLC, pg 748
Transport Bookman Publications Ltd, pg 750
Veloce Publishing Ltd, pg 752
Verso, pg 752
VNU Business Publications, pg 753

Viet Nam

Science & Technics Publishing House, pg 763

Yugoslavia

Alfa-Narodna Knjiga, pg 764
Libertatea, pg 764
Savez Inzenjera i Tehnicara Jugoslavije, pg 765

Zambia

Apple Books, pg 766
Zambia Association for Research & Development, pg 767

Zimbabwe

College Press Publishers (Pvt) Ltd, pg 768
The Literature Bureau, pg 768
Longman Zimbabwe (Pvt) Ltd, pg 768
National Archives of Zimbabwe, pg 769

SCHOLARLY BOOKS

Albania

NL SH, pg 1

Argentina

Alfagrama SRL ediciones, pg 3
Beatriz Viterbo Editora, pg 4
Editorial Claridad SA, pg 4
Editorial Idearium de la Universidad de Mendoza (EDIUM), pg 5
Editorial Hemisferio Sur SA, pg 6
Juris Editorial, pg 6
Oikos, pg 8
Editorial Paidos SAICF, pg 8
Ediciones Preescolar SA, pg 8
Editorial Troquel SA, pg 9
Victor P de Zavalia SA, pg 10

Armenia

Arevik, pg 10

Australia

AHB Publications, pg 11
Aletheia Publishing, pg 11
Art Gallery of Western Australia, pg 12
Artmoves, pg 12
Athena Press, pg 12
Ausmed Publications Pty Ltd, pg 12
Australian Academy of Science, pg 13
The Australian Council for Educational Research Ltd, pg 13
Australian Film Television & Radio School, pg 13
Australian Institute of Family Studies (AIFS), pg 13
Australian Scholarly Publishing, pg 14
Bio Concepts Publishing, pg 15
Blackwell Science Pty Ltd, pg 15
Board of Studies, pg 15
Boombana Publications, pg 16
Community Quarterly, pg 18
Crawford House Publishing, pg 19
Crystal Publishing, pg 19
CSIRO Publishing (Commonwealth Scientific & Industrial Research Organisation), pg 19
Deakin University Press, pg 20
Dragon Press, pg 20
Dryden Press, pg 21
Freshet Press, pg 23
Gnostic Editions, pg 24
Hunter House Publications, pg 27
Illert Publications, pg 27
James Nicholas Publishers Pty Ltd, pg 28
Law Book Co Information Services, pg 29
Lucasville Press, pg 31
Magpie Books, pg 31
Melbourne Institute of Applied Economic & Social Research, pg 33
Melbourne University Press, pg 33
K & Z Mostafanejad, pg 33
National Gallery of Victoria, pg 34
National Library of Australia, pg 34
Navarine Publishing, pg 34
Nimrod Publications, pg 35
OTEN (Open Training & Education Network), pg 36
Pearson Education Australia, pg 37
Pluto Press Australia, pg 38
Pollitecon Publications, pg 38
Power Publications, pg 38
Quakers Hill Press, pg 39
Rumsby Scientific Publishing, pg 41
Ruskin Rowe Press, pg 41
St Joseph Publications, pg 41
Frank Shepherd, pg 42
Spaniel Books, pg 43
Spinifex Press, pg 43
Stafford Books, pg 43
State Library of NSW Press, pg 43
Tarka Publishing, pg 44
Threshold Publishing, pg 44
University of New South Wales Press Ltd, pg 46
University of Queensland Press, pg 46
Veritas Press, pg 46
Wileman Publications, pg 47
Windhorse Books, pg 48

Austria

Boehlau Verlag GmbH & Co KG, pg 50
Buchhandlung WUV Dolmetsch, pg 50
Carinthia Verlag, pg 50
Development News Ltd, pg 51
Docker Verlag GmbH & Co KG, pg 51
Fassbaender Verlag, pg 51
Guthmann & Peterson Liber Libri, Edition, pg 52

PUBLISHERS

Edition Helbling Verlags-Gesellschaft mbH, pg 52
Verlag Hoelder-Pichler-Tempsky, pg 53
Ibera VerlagsgesmbH, pg 53
International Institute for Applied Systems Analysis (IIASA), pg 53
Verlag Monte Verita, pg 55
Mueller-Speiser Wissenschaftlicher Verlag, pg 55
Verlag der Oesterreichischen Akademie der Wissenschaften (OEAW), pg 56
Oesterreichischer Kunst und Kulturverlag, pg 56
Oesterreichisches Katholisches Bibelwerk, pg 56
Verlag des Osterr Kneippbundes GmbH, pg 57
Osterreichischer Bundesveilag Ges.mbH, pg 57
Promedia Verlagsges mbH, pg 57
Resch Verlag, pg 57
Verlag der Salzburger Druckerei, pg 58
Andreas Schnider Verlags-Atelier, pg 58
Springer-Verlag Wien, pg 59
Verband der Wissenschaftlichen Gesellschaften Oesterreichs (VWGOe), pg 60
Verlag Veritas Mediengesellschaft mbH, pg 60
Universitaetsverlag Wagner GmbH, pg 60
WUV/Facultas Universitaetsverlag, pg 61
Zirkular - Verlag der Dokumentationsstelle fuer neuere oesterreichische Literatur, pg 61

Azerbaijan

Sada, Literaturno-Izdatel'skij Centr, pg 61

Bangladesh

Agamee Prakashani, pg 62
The University Press Ltd, pg 62

Belarus

Narodnaya Asveta, pg 63

Belgium

Abimo, pg 63
Alamire vzw, Music Publishers, pg 64
De Boeck et Larcier SA, pg 65
Brepols Publishers NV, pg 65
Editions De Boeck-Larcier SA, pg 67
Dessain - Departement de De Boeck & Larcier SA, pg 68
Editions Hemma, pg 69
Institut Royal des Relations Internationales, pg 69
Koninklijke Vlaamse Academie van Belgie voor Wetenschappen en Kunsten, pg 70
Leuven University Press, pg 71
Licap CVBA, pg 71
La Part de L'Oeil, pg 72
Pelckmans NV, De Nederlandsche Boekhandel, pg 73

Brazil

Agalma Psicanalise Editora Ltda, pg 78
Editora Alfa Omega Ltda, pg 78
Alzira Chagas Carpigiani, pg 80
Concordia Editora Ltda, pg 81
Ediouro Publicacoes, SA, pg 81
Editora Companhia das Letras/Editora Schwarcz Ltda, pg 82
EDUC - Editora da PUC-SP, pg 82
EDUSC - Editora da Universidade do Sagrado Coracao, pg 82
Empresa Brasileira de Pesquisa Agropecaria, pg 83
Editora FCO Ltda, pg 83
Livraria Martins Fontes Editora Ltda, pg 83
Editora Forense, pg 83
Livraria Freitas Bastos Editora SA, pg 83
Editora Harbra Ltda, pg 84
Editora Manole Ltda, pg 87
Editora Moderna Ltda, pg 88
Editora Nova Alexandria Ltda, pg 88
Editora Nova Fronteira SA, pg 88
Editora Revan Ltda, pg 90
Saraiva SA, Livreiros Editores, pg 91
34 Literatura S/C Ltda, pg 92
Editora UNESP, pg 92
Editora da Universidade de Sao Paulo, pg 93
Editora Universidade Federal do Rio de Janeiro, pg 93
Editora Vigilia Ltda, pg 93
Jorge Zahar Editor, pg 93

Bulgaria

Agencija Za Ikonomicesko Programirane i Razvitie, pg 94
Bulvest 2000 Ltd, pg 94
Ciela Publishing House, pg 94
Eurasia Academic Publishers, pg 95
Fondacija Zlatno Kljuce, pg 95
Lettera, pg 96
LIK IZDANIJA, pg 96
Makros 2000 - Plovdiv, pg 96
Musica Publishing House Ltd, pg 96
Naouka i Izkoustvo, Ltd, pg 97
Pensoft Publishers, pg 97
Regalia 6 Publishing House, pg 97
WTU Todor Kableskov, pg 98
Zunica, pg 98

Chile

Ediciones Cieplan, pg 100
Editorial Cuarto Propio, pg 100
Edeval (Universidad de Valparaiso), pg 100
Publicaciones Lo Castillo SA, pg 101
Red Internacional Del Libro, pg 101
Ediciones Universitarias de Valparaiso, pg 101

China

Anhui People's Publishing House, pg 102
Chemical Industry Press, pg 102
China Film Press, pg 103
China Machine Press (CMP), pg 103
China Ocean Press, pg 103
China Theatre Publishing House, pg 104
China Tibetology Publishing House, pg 104
Dalian Maritime University Press, pg 105
Electronics Industry Publishing House, pg 105
Foreign Language Teaching & Research Press, pg 105
Fudan University Press, pg 105
Heilongjiang Science & Technology Press, pg 106
Wissenschaft und Technik Verlag Henan Henan Scientific & Technological Publishing House, pg 106
Higher Education Press, pg 106
Jinan Publishing House, pg 107
Language Publishing House, pg 107
Lanzhou University Press, pg 107
Nanjing University Press, pg 107
National Defence Industry Press, pg 107
The Publishing House of Shanghai University of Traditional Chinese Medicine, pg 108
Science Press, pg 108
Shandong Education Publishing House, pg 108
Shandong University Press, pg 109
Shanghai Foreign Language Education Press, pg 109
Sichuan University Press, pg 109
South China University of Science and Technology Press, pg 109
Southwest China Jiaotong University Press, pg 109
Tsinghua University Press, pg 110
World Affairs Press, pg 110
Wuhan University Press, pg 110
Zhejiang Education Publishing House, pg 110

Colombia

Asociacion Instituto Linguistico de Verano, pg 111
Consejo Episcopal Latinoamericano Celam, pg 111
Fondo Educativo Interamericano SA, pg 112
RAM Editores, pg 113
Editorial Santillana SA, pg 113
Tercer Mundo Editores SA, pg 113
Unidad Universitaria del Sur (UNISUR), pg 114
Universidad de los Andes Editorial, pg 114

The Democratic Republic of the Congo

Facultes Catoliques de Kinshasa, pg 115

Costa Rica

Academia de Centro America, pg 115
Asamblea Legislativa, Biblioteca Monsenor Sanabria, pg 115
Centro Agronomico Tropical de Investigacion y Ensenanza (CATIE), pg 115
Litografia Artex, SA, pg 116
Editorial Porvenir, pg 116
Promesa, Ediciones, pg 116
Editorial Tecnologica de Costa Rica, pg 117
Editorial de la Universidad de Costa Rica, pg 117

Cote d'Ivoire

Universite d' Abidjan, pg 118

Croatia

ALFA dd za izdavacke, graficke i trgovacke poslove, pg 118
ArTresor naklada, pg 118
Knjizevni Krug Split, pg 119

Cuba

Editora Politica, pg 121

Czech Republic

Barrister & Principal, pg 123
Kalich SRO, pg 125
NLN, Ltd The Lidove noviny Publishing House, pg 127
SystemConsult, pg 128
Trizonia, pg 128
Vydavatelstvi Ceskeho Geologickeho Ustavu, pg 129

Denmark

Aarhus Universitetsforlag, pg 129
Dansk Psykologisk Forlag, pg 131
P Haase & Sons Forlag A/S, pg 132
Forlaget Hovedland, pg 133
Mellemfolkeligt Samvirke, pg 133
Museum Tusculanum Press, pg 134
Samfundslitteratur, pg 135
Scandinavia Publishing House, pg 135
Wisby & Wilkens, pg 136

Dominican Republic

Pontificia Universidad Catolica Madre y Maestra, pg 136

Ecuador

CEPLAES, pg 137

Egypt (Arab Republic of Egypt)

Dar El Shorouk, pg 138
Dar El Shorouk Publishing & Distributing House, pg 138
Sphinx Publishing Co, pg 139

El Salvador

UCA Editores, pg 139
Editorial Universitaria de la Universidad de El Salvador, pg 139

Estonia

Estonian Academy Publishers, pg 139
Olion Publishers, pg 140
Tuum, pg 141
Valgus Publishers, pg 141

Finland

Suomalaisen Kirjallisuuden Seura, pg 144
Osuuskunta Vastapaino, pg 145
Yliopistopaino/Helsinki University Press, pg 145

France

Academie Nationale de Reims, pg 145
Adverbum SARL, pg 146
Atelier National de Reproduction des Theses, pg 148
Berg International Editeurs, pg 150
William Blake & Co, pg 150
Editions des Cahiers Bourbonnais, pg 152
Jacqueline Chambon, pg 154
Chasse Maree-Armen, pg 154
Cicero Editeurs, pg 155
Editions de Compostelle, pg 156
De Vecchi Editions SA, pg 158
Delagrave Edition SA, pg 158
Editions de l'Eclat, pg 160
Editions de l'Ecole des Hautes Etudes en Sciences Sociales (EHESS), pg 160
Edisud, pg 161
Editions Recherche sur les Civilisations (ERC), pg 161
Editions Errance, pg 162

843

TYPE OF PUBLICATION INDEX

BOOK

Fac Editions, pg 163
Editions Fanlac, pg 163
Fata Morgana, pg 163
FBT de R Editions/Editions des Limbes d'Or, pg 163
Editions Filipacchi-Sonodip, pg 164
Librairie Fischbacher, International Art Book Distribution (import-export), pg 164
Folklore Comtois, pg 164
Editions Jacques Gabay, pg 165
Paul Geuthner Librairie Orientaliste, pg 166
Hachette Education, pg 167
L'Harmattan, pg 168
Editions Herault, pg 168
Kailash Editions, pg 171
Editions Klincksieck, pg 171
Langues & Mondes/L'Asiatheque, pg 171
P Lethielleux Editions, pg 172
Letouzey et Ane Sarl, pg 172
Lettres Modernes, pg 172
Editions des Limbes d'Or/FBT de R Editions, pg 173
Macula, pg 174
Editions Marie-Noelle, pg 175
Editions Medianes, pg 175
Librairie Minard, pg 176
Presses Universitaires du Mirail, pg 176
Nil Editions, pg 177
Librairie A-G Nizet Sarl, pg 177
Presses Universitaires de Strasbourg, pg 181
Publications de l'Universite de Rouen, pg 182
Publications Orientalistes de France (POF), pg 182
Nouvelles Editions Seguier, pg 184
Sofradif Editions Philippe Auzou, pg 185
Somogy editions d'art, pg 186
Universitas, pg 188
Pierre Zech Editeur, pg 189

French Polynesia

Scoop/Au Vent des Iles, pg 190
Haere Po No Tahiti, pg 190

Germany

A Francke Verlag (Tubingen und Basel), pg 191
Accedo Verlagsgesellschaft mbH, pg 191
Akademie Verlag GmbH, pg 192
Antiquariat und Verlag Auvermann Keip GmbH, pg 194
AOL-Verlag Frohmut Menze, pg 194
Argument-Verlag, pg 195
J J Augustin GmbH Verlag, pg 196
Augustinus-Verlag Wurzburg Inh Augustinerprovinz, pg 196
Bank-Verlag GmbH, pg 198
Barenreiter-Verlag Karl-Votterle GmbH & Co KG, pg 198
Bayerische Akademie der Wissenschaften, pg 199
Beleke KG Verlag, pg 200
Berlin Verlag Arno Spitz GmbH, pg 200
Berliner Debatte Wissenschafts Verlag, GSFP-Gesellschaft fur Sozialwissen-schaftliche Forschung und Publizistik mbH &Co KG, pg 201
W Bertelsmann Verlag GmbH & Co KG, pg 201
Bettendorf'sche Verlagsanstalt GmbH, pg 202
Beuth Verlag GmbH, pg 202

Blackwell Wissenschafts-Verlag GmbH, pg 203
Verlag Die Blaue Eule, pg 204
Boehlau-Verlag GmbH & Cie, pg 204
Verlag Hermann Boehlaus Nachfolger Weimar GmbH & Co, pg 205
Klaus Boer Verlag, pg 205
Verlag Aurel Bongers, pg 205
Breitkopf & Hartel, pg 206
BRUEN-Verlag, Gorenflo, pg 207
Buechse der Pandora Verlags-GmbH, pg 207
Helmut Buske Verlag GmbH, pg 208
Catia Monser Eggcup-Verlag, pg 209
Centaurus-Verlagsgesellschaft GmbH, pg 209
Compact Verlag GmbH, pg 211
Cornelsen Verlag GmbH & Co OHG, pg 211
Das Arsenal, Verlag fuer Kultur und Politik GmbH, pg 212
Data Becker GmbH & Co KG, pg 212
Deutsche Bibelgesellschaft, pg 213
Deutscher Verlag fur Grundstoffindustrie GmbH, pg 215
Diagonal-Verlag GbR Rink-Schweer, pg 216
Verlag J H W Dietz Nachf GmbH, pg 217
Dietz Verlag Berlin GmbH, pg 217
Edition Diskord, pg 217
agenda Verlag Thomas Dominikowski, pg 217
Donat Verlag, pg 217
Duncker und Humblot GmbH, pg 219
E Schweizerbart'sche Verlagsbuchhandlung (Nagele und Obermiller), pg 220
Echo Verlag, pg 220
Edition Klaus Blahak Dr Fredric Kroll, pg 220
Erlanger Verlag Fuer Mission und Okumene, pg 223
Verlagsgesellschaft des Erziehungsvereins GmbH, pg 224
Europa Union Verlag GmbH, pg 224
Evangelische Verlagsanstalt GmbH, pg 225
Evangelischer Presseverband fur Bayern eV, pg 225
Fachbuchverlag Leipzig im Carl Hanser Verlag, pg 226
Karin Fischer Verlag GmbH, pg 228
Flensburger Hefte Verlag GmbH, pg 228
FN-Verlag der Deutschen Reiterlichen Vereinigung GmbH, pg 229
Franz-Sales-Verlag, pg 229
Fraunhofer IRB Verlag Fraunhofer Informationszentrum Raum und Bau, pg 229
Friedrich Kiehl Verlag GmbH, pg 230
Friedrich Frommann Verlag, pg 230
Gebrueder Borntraeger Science Publishers, pg 231
Germanisches Nationalmuseum, pg 232
Verlag fuer Geschichte der Naturwissenschaften und der Technik, pg 232
Gesundheits-Dialog Verlag GmbH, pg 232
Goldschneck Verlag, pg 233

Govi-Verlag Pharmazeutischer Verlag GmbH, pg 233
Grote'sche Verlagsbuchhandlung GmbH & Co KG, pg 234
Walter de Gruyter GmbH & Co KG, pg 234
Gunter Olzog Verlag GmbH, pg 235
Guetersloher Verlagshaus Gerd Mohn, pg 235
Verlag des Gustav-Adolf-Werks, pg 235
Wolfgang G Haas - Musikverlag Koeln ek, pg 235
Liselotte Hamecher, pg 236
Carl Hanser Verlag, pg 237
Harrassowitz Verlag, pg 237
von Hase & Koehler Verlag KG, pg 238
Hellerau-Verlag Dresden GmbH, pg 239
G Henle Verlag, pg 239
Edition Hentrich Druck & Verlag Gebr Hentrich und Tank GmbH & Co KG, pg 239
Verlag Herder GmbH & Co KG, pg 239
Anton Hiersemann, Verlag, pg 240
F Hirthammer Verlag GmbH, pg 241
Verlag Peter Hoell, pg 241
Hofbauer, Christoph und Trojanow Ilia, Akademischer Verlag Muenchen, pg 241
Holos Verlag, pg 242
Horlemann Verlag, pg 243
Edition Humanistische Psychologie (EHP), pg 243
Huss-Medien GmbH, pg 243
Huss-Verlag GmbH, pg 244
Huthig GmbH & Co KG, pg 244
Edition ID-Archiv/ID-Verlag, pg 244
IKO Verlag fur Interkulturelle Kommunikation, pg 244
Klaus Isele, pg 245
ludicium Verlag GmbH, pg 245
Janus Verlagsgesellschaft, Dr Norbert Meder & Co, pg 246
Juventa Verlag GmbH, pg 247
Kirschbaum Verlag GmbH, pg 249
Vittorio Klostermann GmbH, pg 250
W Kohlhammer GmbH, abt Haussortiment, pg 252
KONTEXTverlag, pg 252
kopaed verlagsgmbh, pg 252
Karin Kramer Verlag, pg 253
Alfred Kroner Verlag, pg 253
Kubon & Sagner Buchexport-Import GmbH, pg 254
Verlag Ernst Kuhn, pg 254
Landbuch-Verlagsgesellschaft mbH, pg 255
Institut fuer Landes- und Stadtentwicklungsforschung, ILS Nordrhein-Westfalen, pg 255
Peter Lang GmbH Europaeischer Verlag der Wissenschaften, pg 255
Karl Robert Langewiesche Nachfolger Hans Koester KG, pg 256
Michael Lassleben Verlag, pg 256
Lebenshilfe-Verlag Marburg, Verlag der Bundesvereinigung Lebenshilfe fuer Menschen mit geistiger Behinderung eV, pg 256
Leipziger Universitaetsverlag GmbH, pg 257
Anton G Leitner Verlag (AGLV), pg 257
Verlag Otto Lembeck, pg 257

Verlag Leske plus Budrich GmbH, pg 257
LEU-VERLAG Wolfgang Leupelt, pg 257
Libertas- Europaeisches Institut GmbH, pg 257
Hildegard Liebaug-Dartmann, pg 258
Robert Lienau GmbH & Co KG, pg 258
Luther-Verlag GmbH, pg 259
Verlag Waldemar Lutz, pg 260
Annemarie Maeger, pg 260
Mannerschwarm Skript Verlag Bartholomae & Co OHG, pg 260
Manutius Verlag, pg 260
Margraf Verlag, pg 261
Edition Marhold, pg 261
Mattes Verlag GmbH, pg 261
Medizinisch-Literarische Verlagsgesellschaft mbH, pg 262
Felix Meiner Verlag GmbH, pg 262
Merlin Verlag Andreas Meyer Verlags GmbH und Co KG, pg 263
MMV Medizin Verlag GmbH Munich, pg 264
Mohr Siebeck, pg 264
Verlag Stephanie Naglschmid, pg 266
Gunter Narr Verlag, pg 266
Verlag Neue Wirtschafts-Briefe GmbH & Co, pg 267
Neuer Weg Verlag und Druck GmbH, pg 268
Neuland-Verlagsgesellschaft mbH, pg 268
Neuthor - Verlag, pg 268
Max Niemeyer Verlag GmbH, pg 269
Rainar Nitzsche Verlag, pg 269
Nusser Verlag, pg 269
Oekobuch Verlag & Versand GmbH, pg 269
Georg Olms Verlag AG, pg 270
Pahl-Rugenstein Verlag Nachfolger-GmbH, pg 271
Justus Perthes Verlag Gotha GmbH, pg 272
Philipps-Universitaet Marburg, pg 273
pmi Verlag, pg 274
Premop Verlag GmbH, pg 275
Guido Pressler Verlag, pg 275
Psychologie Verlags Union, pg 275
Verlag Friedrich Pustet GmbH & Co Kg, pg 276
Quintessenz Verlags-GmbH, pg 276
R Oldenbourg Verlag GmbH, pg 276
Verlag Recht und Wirtschaft GmbH, pg 277
REGENSBERG Druck & Verlag GmbH & Co, pg 277
Verlag fur Regionalgeschichte, pg 277
Dr Ludwig Reichert Verlag, pg 278
Roehrig Universitaets Verlag Gmbh, pg 279
Heidi Rogner, pg 279
Romiosini Verlag, pg 280
Verlag Roter Morgen, pg 280
scaneg Verlag, pg 282
Schelzky & Jeep, Verlag fuer Reisen und Wissen, pg 283
Verlag Dr Otto Schmidt KG, pg 283
Verlag Schnell und Steiner GmbH, pg 284
Ferdinand Schoeningh Verlag GmbH, pg 284
Schott Musik International GmbH & Co KG, pg 284

844

PUBLISHERS

Schueren Verlag GmbH, pg 285
Schulz-Kirchner Verlag GmbH, pg 285
Dr Arthur L Sellier & Co-Walter de Gruyter GmbH & Co KG OHG, pg 286
Edition Sigma e.Kfm, pg 287
Springer-Verlag GmbH & Co KG, pg 288
Verlag Stahleisen GmbH, pg 289
Stauffenburg Verlag Brigitte Narr GmbH, pg 289
Franz Steiner Verlag Wiesbaden GmbH, pg 289
Stern-Verlag Janssen & Co, pg 290
Steyler Verlag, pg 290
Edition Temmen, pg 292
edition Text & Kritik im Richard Boorberg Verlag GmbH & Co, pg 293
Tipress Dienstleistungen fur das Verlagswesen GmbH, pg 294
Trautvetter & Fischer Nachf, pg 294
Ulrike Helmer Verlag, pg 296
Universitaetsverlag C Winter Heidelberg GmbH, pg 296
Unrast Verlag e V, pg 296
Urban und Fischer Verlag fur Medizin, pg 296
UVK Universitaetsverlag Konstanz GmbH, pg 297
UVK Verlagsgesellschaft mbH, pg 297
Dorothea van der Koelen, pg 297
Vandenhoeck & Ruprecht, pg 297
VAS-Verlag fuer Akademische Schriften, Vas Karl-Heinz Balon, pg 297
Verlag fur die Rechts- und Anwaltspraxis GmbH & Co, pg 298
Verlag fur Schweissen und Verwandte Verfahren, pg 298
Vervuert Verlagsgesellschaft, pg 298
Verlag Philipp von Zabern, pg 299
Votum Verlag GmbH, pg 299
VWB-Verlag fur Wissenschaft & Bildung, Amand Aglaster, pg 300
Wachholtz Verlag GmbH, pg 300
Waxmann Verlag GmbH, pg 300
Weidler Buchverlag Berlin, pg 301
Weidmannsche Verlagsbuchhandlung GmbH, pg 301
Verlag Westfaelisches Dampfboot, pg 302
Westholsteinische Verlagsanstalt und Verlagsdruckerei Boyens & Co, pg 302
Herbert Wichmann Verlag, pg 302
Wiley-VCH Verlag GmbH, pg 302
Dr Dieter Winkler, pg 303
Wissenschaftliche Buchgesellschaft, pg 303
Verlag Konrad Wittwer GmbH, pg 303
Zeller Verlag GmbH & Co, pg 305

Ghana

Ghana Universities Press (GUP), pg 307
Sedco Publishing Ltd, pg 308
Woeli Publishing Services, pg 308
World Literature Project, pg 308

Greece

Anixis Publications, pg 309
Athina, Mary Mavrogiannis, pg 309
Ecole francaise d'Athenes, pg 310
Etaireia Spoudon Neoellinikou Politismou Kai Genikis Paideias, pg 310
Denise Harvey, pg 311

Hiotellis P, pg 311
Kardamitsa A, pg 312
Mavrogianni Publications, pg 313
Michalis Sideris, pg 313
Nea Thesis - Evrotas, pg 313
Panepistimio Ioanninon, pg 314

Guadeloupe

Librairie Generale JASOR, pg 316

Guatemala

Grupo Editorial RIN-78, pg 316

Guyana

Hamburgh Press, pg 317

Honduras

Editorial Guaymuras, pg 318

Hong Kong

The Chinese University Press, pg 319
Chung Hwa Book Co (HK) Ltd, pg 319
The Dharmasthiti Buddist Institute Ltd, pg 319
Hong Kong University Press, pg 320
Joint Publishing (HK) Co Ltd, pg 320
Philopsychy Press, pg 321
Research Centre for Translation, pg 321

Hungary

Aranyhal Konyvkiado Goldfish Publishing, pg 323
Atlantisz Kiado, pg 323
Balassi Kiado Kft, pg 323
CEU-Press, pg 323
Janus Pannonius Tudomanyegyetem, pg 324
Jelenkor Verlag, pg 324
Marton Aron Kiado Publishing House, pg 325
Mezoegazda Kiado, pg 325
Nemzeti Tankoenyvkiado, pg 326
Planetas Kiadoi es Kereskedelmi Kft, pg 326

Iceland

Frodi Ltd, pg 328
Haskolautgafan - University of Iceland Press, pg 328
Stofnun Arna Magnussonar a Islandi, pg 329

India

Advaita Ashrama, pg 329
Agam Kala Prakashan, pg 330
Agricole Publishing Academy, pg 330
Allied Publishers Pvt Ltd, pg 330
Amar Prakashan, pg 330
Ananda Publishers Pvt Ltd, pg 330
Anmol Publications Pvt Ltd, pg 331
Asian Educational Services, pg 331
BR Publishing Corporation, pg 334
Clarion Books, pg 335
Concept Publishing Co, pg 335
Cosmo Publications, pg 335
Daya Publishing House, pg 336
DK Printworld (P) Ltd, pg 336
Dutta Baruah Publishing Co Pvt Ltd, pg 336
Gyan Publishing House, pg 338
Hindi Pracharak Sansthan, pg 338
Indian Institute of Advanced Study, pg 339

Indus Publishing Co, pg 339
Jaipur Publishing House, pg 340
Kerala University, Department of Publications, pg 341
Minerva Associates (Publications) Pvt Ltd, pg 342
Mudrak Publishers & Distributors, pg 343
Munshiram Manoharlal Publishers Pvt Ltd, pg 343
National Council of Applied Economic Research, Publications Division, pg 344
Oxford & IBH Publishing Co Pvt Ltd, pg 345
Oxford University Press, pg 345
Panchasheel Prakashan, pg 345
Panjab University Publication Bureau, pg 345
Pitambar Publishing Co (P) Ltd, pg 346
Rahul Publishing House, pg 347
Rastogi Publications, pg 347
Regency Publications, pg 347
Rekha Prakashan, pg 347
Reliance Publishing House, pg 347
SABDA, pg 348
Sage Publications India Pvt Ltd, pg 348
Sasta Sahitya Mandal, pg 349
Scientific Book Agency, pg 349
Somaiya Publications Pvt Ltd, pg 350
South Asian Publishers Pvt Ltd, pg 350
Sterling Publishers Pvt Ltd, pg 351
Stree, pg 351

Indonesia

CV Angkasa CV (Publishers), pg 354
Katalis PT Bina Mitra Plaosan, pg 356
Lembaga Demografi Fakultas Ekonomi Universitas Indonesia, pg 356
Mizan, pg 356
Penerbit Nusa Indah, pg 356
PT Pustaka LP3ES Indonesia, pg 357

Ireland

The Columba Press, pg 359
Cork University Press, pg 359
Dee-Jay Publications, pg 359
Flyleaf Press, pg 360
Four Courts Press Ltd, pg 360
Gandon Editions, pg 360
The Goldsmith Press Ltd, pg 361
Herodotus Press, pg 361
Irish Academic Press, pg 361
Irish Management Institute, pg 361
The Lilliput Press Ltd, pg 362
On Stream Publications Ltd, pg 363
Relay Books, pg 363
Round Hall Sweet & Maxwell, pg 363
Tir Eolas, pg 364
Wolfhound Press, pg 364

Israel

Academon Publishing House, pg 365
Academy of the Hebrew Language, pg 365
Bar Ilan University Press, pg 365
Ben-Zvi Institute, pg 365
The Bialik Institute, pg 365
Breslov Research Institute, pg 366
Dekel Publishing House, pg 366
Dyonon/Papyrus Publishing House of the Tel-Aviv, pg 367

TYPE OF PUBLICATION INDEX

Gefen Publishing House Ltd, pg 367
Habermann Institute for Literary Research, pg 367
Haifa University Press, pg 368
Hakibbutz Hameuchad Publishing House Ltd, pg 368
The Institute for Israeli Arabs Studies, pg 368
The Israel Academy of Sciences & Humanities, pg 368
Israel Antiquities Authority, pg 368
Israel Exploration Society, pg 368
(JDC) Brookdale Institute of Gerontology & Adult Human Development in Israel, pg 369
Kivunim-Arsan Publishing House, pg 369
Maaliyot-Institute for Research Publications, pg 370
MAP-Mapping & Publishing Ltd, pg 370
Misgav Yerushalayim, pg 370
The Moshe Dayan Center for Middle Eastern & African Studies, pg 371
Nehora Press, pg 371
Open University of Israel, pg 371
Password Publishers Ltd, pg 371
Schlesinger Institute, pg 372
University Publishing Projects Ltd, pg 373
Urim Publications, pg 373
Yad Izhak Ben-Zvi Press, pg 373
Yad Vashem - The Holocaust Martyrs' & Heroes' Remembrance Authority, pg 373
The Zalman Shazar Center, pg 374

Italy

Editore Armando Armando SRL, pg 376
Verlagsanstalt Athesia, pg 377
Bastogi, pg 377
Bertello Edizioni, pg 377
Bovolenta, pg 378
Edizioni Bucalo SNC, pg 379
Campanotto, pg 379
Edizioni Cantagalli, pg 379
Casa Musicale Edizioni Carrara SRL, pg 379
Casa Editrice Felice Le Monnier, pg 380
Casa Editrice Lint Srl, pg 380
CEDAM (Casa Editrice Dr A Milani), pg 380
Edizioni Centro Studi Erickson, pg 381
Ciranna e Ferrara, pg 381
CPE - Centro Programmazione Editoriale, pg 383
Edizioni Dedalo SRL, pg 384
Edizioni del Centro, pg 384
Direzione Generale Archivi, pg 385
Editrice Edisco, pg 386
Editori Laterza, pg 386
Edizioni Qiqajon, pg 387
Esselibri, pg 388
Arnaldo Forni Editore SRL, pg 389
Istituto Geografico de Agostini SpA, pg 390
Gruppo Calderini Edagricole, pg 392
Editrice Innocenti SNC, pg 393
Editoriale Jaca Book SpA, pg 394
Editrice Janus SpA, pg 394
Jouvence, pg 394
L'Erma di Bretschneider SRL, pg 395
LIM Editrice SRL, pg 396
Angelo Longo Editore, pg 396
Nicola Milano Editore, pg 398
New Magazine, pg 400

845

TYPE OF PUBLICATION INDEX — BOOK

Leo S Olschki, pg 402
G B Palumbo & C Editore SpA, pg 402
G B Paravia & C SpA, pg 402
Pontifico Istituto Orientale, pg 404
G e C Ricordi SpA, pg 405
Editrice San Marco SRL, pg 406
Sansoni Editore, pg 407
Fausto Sardini Editrice, pg 407
SEMAR Publishers SRL, pg 407
Societa Stampa Sportiva, pg 408
Edizioni di Storia e Letteratura, pg 409
Tappeiner, pg 409
Casa Editrice Luigi Trevisini, pg 410
Il Tripode Srl, pg 410

Jamaica
Institute of Jamaica Publications, pg 413
The Jamaica Bauxite Institute, pg 413
The Press, pg 413
Ian Randle Publishers Ltd, pg 413
University of the West Indies Press, pg 414

Japan
Business Center for Academic Societies Japan, pg 415
Chikuma Shobo Publishing Co Ltd, pg 415
Dobun Shoin, pg 416
Eichosha Company Ltd, pg 416
Fumaido Publishing Company Ltd, pg 416
Kaitakusha, pg 419
Kazama Shobo, pg 419
Keisuisha Publishing Company Ltd, pg 419
Kindai Kagaku Sha Co, Ltd, pg 419
Kosei Publishing Co Ltd, pg 420
Koyo Shobo, pg 420
Myrtos Inc, pg 421
Nikkagiren Shuppan-Sha (JUSE Press Ltd), pg 422
Nippon Hoso Shuppan Kyokai (NHK Publishing), pg 422
Rinsen Book Co Ltd, pg 424
Seibido, pg 424
Seibundo Shuppan, pg 425
Sobun-Sha, pg 426
Taimeido Publishing Co Ltd, pg 427
Tamagawa University Press, pg 427
Thomson Learning, pg 427
Toho Book Store, pg 427
Toyo Keizai Inc (The Oriental Economist), pg 428
United Nations University Press, pg 428

Kenya
Academy Science Publishers, pg 430
Action Publishers, pg 430
African Centre for Technology Studies (ACTS), pg 431
British Institute in Eastern Africa, pg 431
Evangel Publishing House, pg 431
Heinemann Kenya Limited (EAEP), pg 431
Kenway Publications Ltd, pg 432
Lake Publishers & Enterprises Ltd, pg 432
Nairobi University Press, pg 433
Phoenix Publishers, pg 433
Shirikon Publishers, pg 433
Gideon S Were Press, pg 434

Republic of Korea
Bi-bong Publishing Co, pg 435
Chung Rim Publishing Co Ltd, pg 435
Gim-Yeong Co, pg 436
Hakmun Publishing, Co, pg 436
Hanul Publishing Co, pg 436
Iljo-gag Publishers, pg 437
Koreaone Press Inc, pg 438
Minjisa Publishing Co, pg 438
Munye Publishing Co, pg 439
Prompter Publications, pg 439
St Pauls, pg 439
Seogwangsa, pg 440
Sohaksa, pg 440
Yonsei University Press, pg 441

Latvia
Nordik/Tapals Publishers Ltd, pg 442

Lebanon
Darl el-Machreq Sarl, pg 443
Librairie Orientale sal, pg 443

Libyan Arab Jamahiriya
Al-Fatah University, General Administration of Libraries, Printing & Publications, pg 444

Liechtenstein
Verlag der Liechtensteinischen Akademischen Gesellschaft, pg 444

Lithuania
Baltos Lankos, pg 445
Mokslo ir enciklopediju leidybos institutas, pg 446
The Publishing House of the Lithuanian Writers' Union, pg 446
Margi Rastai Publishers, pg 446

Luxembourg
Editions APESS ASBL, pg 447
Thesen Verlag Vowinckel, pg 448
Editions Tousch, pg 448
Varkki Verghese, pg 448

Macau
Instituto Portugues Oriente, pg 448
Universidadede de Macau, Centro de Publicacoes, pg 448

The Former Yugoslav Republic of Macedonia
St Clement of Ohrid National & University Library, pg 449

Madagascar
Editions Ambozontany, pg 450

Malaysia
Penerbit Universiti Sains Malaysia, pg 454
Pustaka Cipta Sdn Bhd, pg 454
Pustaka Sistem Pelajaran Sdn Bhd, pg 454
Unit Penerbitan Akademik Cancelori~ Universiti Teknologi Malaysia, pg 455
University of Malaya, Department of Publications, pg 455

Mexico
ALFA OMEGA Grupo Editor, pg 458
Centro de Estudios Mexicanos y Centroamericanos, pg 458
Colegio de Postgraduados en Ciencias Agricolas, pg 459
Publicaciones Cruz O SA, pg 459
Ediciones Eca SA de CV, pg 460
Ediciones Era SA de CV, pg 460
Editorial Esfinge SA de CV, pg 460
Centro de Estudios Monetarios Latinoamericanos (CEMLA), pg 460
Ediciones Euroamericanas, pg 461
Fondo de Cultura Economica, pg 461
Editorial Limusa SA de CV, pg 463
Instituto Nacional de Antropologia e Historia, pg 464
Nova Grupo Editorial SA de CV, pg 464
Pangea Editores, Sa de CV, pg 465
Plaza y Valdes SA de CV, pg 465
Sistemas Tecnicos de Edicion SA de CV, pg 467
Universidad Nacional Autonoma de Mexico (National University of Mexico), pg 467
Universidad Veracruzana Direccion General Editorial y de Publicaciones, pg 468

Republic of Moldova
Lumina Publishing House, pg 468

Monaco
Rondeau Giannipiero a Monaco, pg 469

Namibia
Multi-Disciplinary Research Centre Library, pg 471

Netherlands
Aeolus Press BV, pg 472
APA (Academic Publishers Associated), pg 472
Backhuys Publishers BV, pg 473
A A Balkema, pg 473
Brill Academic Publishers, pg 475
Buijten en Schipperheijn BV Drukkerij en Uitg Mij v/h, pg 475
Delft University Press, pg 476
HES & De Graaf Publishers BV, pg 478
Historische Uitgeverij, pg 478
Holland University Press BV (APA), pg 478
Hotei Publishing, pg 478
IOS Press BV, pg 479
KITLV Press Royal Institute of Linguistics & Anthropology, pg 479
Koninklijke Vermande bv, pg 480
Uitgeverij Lemma BV, pg 480
The Pepin Press, pg 482
Philo Press-Van Heusden-Hissink & Co CV (APA), pg 482
Swets & Zeitlinger Publishers, pg 485
Uitgeverij Verloren, pg 486
VU Boekhandel/Uitgeverij BV, pg 487

New Zealand
Aoraki Press Ltd, pg 488
Auckland University Press, pg 488
Brooker's Ltd, pg 489
Canterbury University Press, pg 489
Clerestory Press, pg 490
Hazard Press Ltd, pg 491
Heritage Press Ltd, pg 492
Outrigger Publishers, pg 494
Paerangi Books, pg 494
Te Waihora Press, pg 496
University of Otago Press, pg 496
Bridget Williams Books Ltd, pg 497

Nigeria
Adebara Publishers Ltd, pg 497
Evans Brothers (Nigeria Publishers) Ltd, pg 499
Fourth Dimension Publishing Co Ltd, pg 499
Goldland Business Co Ltd, pg 499
Heritage Books, pg 499
Ibadan University Press, pg 499
JAD Publishers Ltd, pg 500
New Africa Publishing Company Ltd, pg 500
New Era Publishers, pg 500
Nigerian Institute of International Affairs, pg 500
Riverside Communications, pg 501
Unity Publishing & Research Company Ltd, pg 502
Vantage Publishers International Ltd, pg 502

Norway
Solum Forlag A/S, pg 505
Universitetsforlaget, pg 505

Pakistan
Academy of Education Planning & Management (AEPAM), pg 506
ASR Publications, pg 506
Centre for South Asian Studies, pg 506
Islamic Publications (Pvt) Ltd, pg 507
National Book Foundation, pg 508
Pakistan Institute of Development Economics, pg 508
Sang-e-Meel Publications, pg 509
Vanguard Books Ltd, pg 509

Papua New Guinea
Papua New Guinea Institute of Medical Research, pg 510
Kristen Pres, pg 510
National Research Institute of Papua New Guinea, pg 510

Paraguay
Instituto de Ciencias de la Computacion (NCR), pg 510

Peru
Centro de la Mujer Peruana Flora Tristan, pg 511
Instituto de Estudios Peruanos, pg 511
Instituto Frances de Estudios Andinos, IFEA, pg 511
Sur Casa de Estudios del Socialismo, pg 511
Tarea Asociacion de Publicaciones Educativas, pg 511
Universidad de Lima-Fondo de Desarollo Editorial, pg 512

Philippines
Ateneo de Manila University Press, pg 512
De La Salle University, pg 513
Logos (Divine Word) Publications Inc, pg 513
New Day Publishers, pg 514

PUBLISHERS

Our Lady of Manaoag Publisher, pg 514
San Carlos Publications, pg 515
UST Publishing House, pg 515

Poland

Energeia sp zoo Wydawnictwo, pg 516
Wydawnictwa Geologiczne, pg 516
Instytut Historii Nauki PAN, pg 516
Impuls, pg 517
Iskry - Publishing House Ltd spotka zoo, pg 517
Katolicki Uniwersytet Wydawniczo -Redakcja, pg 517
Wydawnictwo Medyczne Urban & Partner, pg 518
Ossolineum Zaklad Narodowy im Ossolinskich - Wydawnictwo, pg 518
Wydawnictwo Prawnicze Co, pg 519
Przedsiebiorstwo Wydawniczo-Handlowe Wydawnictwo Siedmiorog, pg 519
PZWL Wydawnictwo Lekarskie Ltd, pg 519
Oficyna Wydawnicza Read Me, pg 519
'Slask' Ltd, pg 520
Towarzystwo Naukowe w Toruniu, pg 520
Wydawnictwa Naukowo-Techniczne, pg 521
Wydawnictwa Szkolne i Pedagogiczne (Polish Educational Publishers-WSiP), pg 521
Wydawnictwo DiG, pg 521

Portugal

Livraria Amado Lda, pg 522
Centro Estudos Geograficos, pg 523
Coimbra Editora Lda, pg 523
Edicoes Colibri, pg 523
Empresa Literaria Fluminense, Lda, pg 525
Gradiva-Publicacnoes Lda, pg 525
Imprensa Nacional-Casa da Moeda, pg 526
Instituto de Investigacao Cientifica Tropical, pg 526
Lua Viajante-Edicao e Distribuicao de Livros e Material Audiovisual, Lda, pg 527
Monitor, pg 527
Perspectivas e Realidades, Artes Graficas, Lda, pg 528
Editora Replicacao Lda, pg 529
Silabo, pg 529
Vega-Publicacao e Distribuicao de Livros e Revistas, Lda, pg 530

Puerto Rico

Piedras Press, Inc, pg 531

Romania

Editura Academiei Romane, pg 531
Editura Aius, pg 531
The Center for Romanian Studies, pg 532
Editura Clusium, Casa de Editura Atlas-Clusium SRL, pg 532
Corint Verlag, pg 532
Editura Dacia, pg 532
Editura Humanitas, pg 533
Humanitas Publishing House, pg 533
Editura Institutul European, pg 533
Editura Kriterion SA, pg 534
Mentor Kiado, pg 534
Editura Meridiane, pg 534
Editura Niculescu, pg 534

Petrion Verlag, pg 535
Saeculum IO, pg 535
Editura Stiintifica, pg 536
Editura Teora, pg 536

Russian Federation

Airis Press, pg 537
Aspect Press Ltd, pg 537
N E Bauman Moscow State Technical University Publishers, pg 537
BLIC, russko-Baltijskij informaciionnyj centr, AO, pg 537
FGUP Izdatelstvo Mashinostroenie, pg 538
Finansy i Statistika Publishing House, pg 538
Fizmatlit Publishing Co, pg 538
Izdatel 'stvo Ural' skogo, pg 538
Izdatelstvo Iskusstvo, pg 538
Kabardino-Balkarskoye knizhnoye izdatelstvo, pg 539
Izdatelstvo Khudozhestvennaya Literatura, pg 539
Izdatelskii Dom Kompositor, pg 539
Ministerstvo Kul 'tury RF, pg 540
Izdatelstvo Mir, pg 540
Moscow University Press, pg 540
Izdatelstvo Muzyka, pg 540
Nauka Publishers, pg 540
St Andrew's Biblical Theological College, pg 541
Voronezh State University Publishers, pg 542
Izdatelstvo Vysshaya Shkola, pg 543

Saudi Arabia

King Saud University, pg 543

Singapore

APAC Publishers Services, pg 545
Federal Publications (S) Pte Ltd, pg 546
Graham Brash Pte Ltd, pg 546
Institute of Southeast Asian Studies, pg 546
Pearson Education Asia, pg 547
Select Books Pte Ltd, pg 548
Singapore University Press Pte Ltd, pg 548
Taylor & Francis Asia Pacific, pg 548
World Scientific Publishing Co Pte Ltd, pg 549

Slovakia

ARCHA sro Vydavatel 'stro, pg 549
Dom Techniky Zvazu Slovenskych Vedeckotechnickych Spolocnosti Ltd, pg 549
Priroda, pg 550

Slovenia

Franc-Franc podjetje za promocijo kulture Murska Sobota d o o, pg 551
Zalozba Obzorja d d Maribor, pg 552

South Africa

The Brenthurst Press (Pty) Ltd, pg 553
Centre for Conflict Resolution, pg 553
Educum Publishers Ltd, pg 554
Human Sciences Research Council, pg 555
Institute for Reformational Studies CHE, pg 555

Ivy Publications, pg 555
Johannesburg Art Gallery, pg 556
Maskew Miller Longman, pg 557
Nasionale Boekhandel Ltd, pg 557
Oceanographic Research Institute, pg 558
Ravan Press (Pty) Ltd, pg 558
South African Institute of Race Relations, pg 559
University of Natal Press, pg 560
Witwatersrand University Press, pg 560

Spain

Publicacions de l'Abadia de Montserrat, pg 561
Acantilado, pg 561
Centro de Estudios Adams-Ediciones Valbuena SA, pg 561
Editorial Afers, SL, pg 561
Ediciones Akal SA, pg 562
Ediciones Alfar SA, pg 562
Arco Libros SL, pg 564
Biblioteca de Catalunya, pg 565
Editorial Bruno, pg 566
Ediciones Catedra SA, pg 566
Central Catequistica Salesiana (CCS), pg 567
Civitas SA Editorial, pg 567
Ediciones Colegio De Espana (ECE), pg 568
Compania Literaria, pg 568
Complutense, SA Editorial, pg 568
Ediciones de la Universidad Complutense de Madrid, pg 568
Dinsic Publicacions Musicals, pg 570
Diputacion Provincial de Malaga, pg 570
Ediciones El Almendro de Cordoba, pg 571
Ediciones Encuentro SA, pg 573
Esic Editorial, pg 573
Editorial Espasa-Calpe SA, pg 573
Instituto de Estudios Riojanos, pg 574
Grupo Comunicar, pg 576
Impredisur, SL, pg 578
Institucion Fernando el Catolico de la Excma Diputacion de Zaragoza, pg 578
Joyas Bibliograficas SA, pg 579
Editorial Juventud SA, pg 579
Ediciones Morata SL, pg 583
Editorial la Muralla SA, pg 583
Oikos-Tau SA Ediciones, pg 584
Pages Editors, SL, pg 585
Polifemo, Ediciones, pg 587
Ediciones Pomares-Corredor, pg 587
Publicaciones de la Universidad de Alicante, pg 588
Secretariado Trinitario, pg 590
Servicio de Publicaciones Universidad de Cadiz, pg 590
Ediciones Seyer, pg 590
Editorial Sintesis, SA, pg 590
Ediciones SM, pg 591
Tirant lo Blanch SL Libreriaa, pg 592
Edicioncs de la Torre, pg 593
Trotta SA Editorial, pg 593
Universidad de Malaga, pg 594
Ediciones Universidad de Salamanca, pg 594
Universidad de Valladolid Secretariado de Publicaciones e Intercambio Editorial, pg 594
Edicions de la Universitat Politecnica de Catalunya SL, pg 594
Editorial Verbum SL, pg 595

Sri Lanka

Inter-Cultural Book Promoters, pg 597
International Centre for Ethnic Studies, pg 597
Pradeepa Publishers, pg 598
Samayawardena Printers Publishers & Booksellers, pg 598
Somawathi Hewavitharana Fund, pg 598
Swarna Hansa Foundation, pg 598
Waruni Publishers, pg 598

Suriname

Stichting Wetenschappelijke Informatie, pg 599

Sweden

Carlsson Bokfoerlag AB, pg 601
Dahlia Books, International Publishers & Booksellers, pg 601
Hillelforlaget, pg 603
ITK Laromedel AB, pg 603
Bokforlaget Nya Doxa AB, pg 605
Studentlitteratur AB, pg 606

Switzerland

Armenia Editions, pg 608
Augustin-Verlag, pg 609
Les Editions de la Fondation Martin Bodmer, pg 610
Edizioni Casagrande SA, pg 611
Marcel Dekker AG, pg 612
Librairie Droz SA, pg 612
eFeF-Verlag/Edition Ebersbach, pg 613
Garuda-Verlag, pg 614
Paul Haupt Berne, pg 615
Parkett Publishers Inc, pg 621
Editions Payot Lausanne, pg 621
Pedrazzini Tipografia, pg 621
PIE-Peter Lang SA, pg 622
Staempfli Verlag AG, pg 625
Vdf Hochschulverlag AG an der ETH Zurich, pg 626
Versus Verlag AG, pg 627

Syrian Arab Republic

Damascus University Press, pg 628

Taiwan, Province of China

Asian Culture Co, pg 629
Cheng Wen Publishing Company, pg 629
Chien Chen Bookstore Publishing Company Ltd, pg 629
Chu Liu Book Company, pg 629
Chung Hwa Book Co Ltd, pg 629
Laureate Book Co Ltd, pg 631
Linking Publishing Company Ltd, pg 631
San Min Book Co Ltd, pg 631
SMC Publishing Inc, pg 632
Torch of Wisdom, pg 632
UNITAS Publishing Co Ltd, pg 632
World Book Co Ltd, pg 632
Yee Wen Publishing Co Ltd, pg 632
Yuan Liou Publishing Co, Ltd, pg 632

United Republic of Tanzania

DUP (1996) Ltd, pg 633
Kanisa la Biblia Publishers (KLB), pg 633
Press & Publicity Centre Ltd, pg 634
Tanzania Publishing House, pg 634
Tema Publishers Ltd, pg 634

TYPE OF PUBLICATION INDEX   BOOK

Thailand
Pra Cha Chang & Co Ltd, pg 635
Sang Dad Publishing Company Ltd, pg 635

Tunisia
Ceres Editions, pg 637
Maison Tunisienne de l'Edition, pg 638

Turkey
Arkeoloji Ve Sanat Yayinlari, pg 639
Aydin Yayincilik, pg 639
Isis Yayin Tic ve San Ltd, pg 640
Kubbealti Akademisi Kultur ve Sasat Vakfi, pg 640

Uganda
Centre for Basic Research, pg 642
Fountain Publishers Ltd, pg 642
Roce (Consultants) Ltd, pg 642

Ukraine
ASK Ltd, pg 643
Osnovy Publishers, pg 643
Osvita, pg 643

United Kingdom
Academic Press Ltd, pg 644
Act 3 Publishing, pg 645
Adamantine Press Ltd, pg 645
Umberto Allemandi & Co Publishing, pg 646
Anglo-German Foundation for the Study of Industrial Society, pg 647
Aris & Phillips Ltd, pg 648
Ashgate Publishing Ltd, pg 649
Ashmolean Museum Publications, pg 650
Atlantic Transport Publishers, pg 650
Atlas Press, pg 651
Ruth Bean Publishers, pg 653
Berg Publishers, pg 654
Berghahn Books Ltd, pg 654
BFI Publishing, pg 654
BILD Publications, pg 654
BIOS Scientific Publishers Ltd, pg 654
Birlinn Ltd, pg 655
Black Ace Books, pg 655
Books for Europe Ltd, pg 657
Boydell & Brewer Ltd, pg 658
Bridge Books, pg 659
The British Academy, pg 659
BAAF: Adoption & Fostering, pg 659
Cameron & Hollis, pg 663
Cardiff Academic Press, pg 663
Cassell & Co, pg 664
Cavendish Publishing Ltd, pg 665
Church Union, pg 668
James Clarke & Co Ltd, pg 668
Commonwealth Secretariat, pg 669
The Continuum International Publishing Group Ltd, pg 670
James Currey Ltd, pg 673
John Donald Publishers Ltd, pg 675
Drake Educational Associates Ltd, pg 676
Gerald Duckworth & Co Ltd, pg 676
Dunedin Academic Press, pg 676
Educational Explorers (Publishers) Ltd, pg 677
Edward Elgar Publishing Ltd, pg 678
Elsevier Science Ltd, pg 678

The Erskine Press, pg 679
estamp, pg 679
The Eurospan Group, pg 680
Flicks Books, pg 683
Free Association Books Ltd, pg 684
Garden Art Press Ltd, pg 685
Garnet Publishing Ltd, pg 685
The Geographical Association, pg 686
Geological Society Publishing House, pg 686
GMP Publishers Ltd, pg 687
The Greek Bookshop, pg 689
Gregg Publishing Co, pg 690
Gwasg Prifysgol Cymru, pg 690
Gwasg Gwenffrwd, pg 690
Hakluyt Society, pg 691
Harcourt Publishers Ltd, pg 691
Harley Books, pg 692
Harvard University Press, pg 692
Christopher Helm (Publishers) Ltd, pg 694
Helm Information Ltd, pg 694
Heraldry Today, pg 695
Hodder & Stoughton Educational, pg 696
Horizon Scientific Press, pg 697
Icon Press, pg 698
Immediate Publishing, pg 699
Imperial College Press, pg 699
Independent Writers Publications Ltd, pg 699
Institute of Education, University of London, pg 699
Institute of Irish Studies, The Queens University of Belfast, pg 699
Institute of Physics Publishing, pg 700
Institution of Electrical Engineers, pg 700
Intellect Ltd, pg 700
International Institute for Strategic Studies, pg 701
IOM Communications Ltd, pg 701
JAI Press Ltd, pg 702
James & James (Science Publishers) Ltd, pg 702
Kegan Paul International Ltd, pg 703
Hilda King Educational, pg 704
Jessica Kingsley Publishers, pg 704
KIT Press - Royal Tropical Institute, pg 705
Kluwer Academic/Plenum Publishers, pg 705
Kogan Page Ltd, pg 705
Landy Publishing, pg 706
Lawrence & Wishart, pg 706
The Littman Library of Jewish Civilization, pg 708
Liverpool University Press, pg 708
The Lutterworth Press, pg 709
Macmillan Reference Ltd, pg 710
Manchester University Press, pg 711
Maney Publishing, pg 711
Manson Publishing Ltd, pg 711
Marcham Books, pg 711
Merrow Publishing Co Ltd, pg 714
Micelle Press, pg 714
Motilal (UK) Books of India, pg 715
Multilingual Matters Ltd, pg 716
National Archives of Scotland, pg 716
National Library of Wales, pg 717
National Portrait Gallery Publications, pg 717
New European Publications Ltd, pg 718
NMS Publishing Ltd, pg 719
Northcote House Publishers Ltd, pg 719

Norwood Publishers, pg 720
The Octagon Press Ltd, pg 720
Octopus Publishing Group, pg 720
The Oleander Press, pg 721
Oneworld Publications, pg 721
Open Gate Press, pg 721
Open University Press, pg 721
Oxfam, pg 722
Packard Publishing Ltd, pg 723
Parapress Ltd, pg 724
Peepal Tree Press, pg 725
Perpetuity Press, pg 726
Phaidon Press Ltd, pg 726
Pickering & Chatto (Publishers) Ltd, pg 727
Pion Ltd, pg 728
Pluto Press, pg 728
Poetry Wales Press Ltd, pg 729
The Policy Press, pg 729
Portland Press Ltd, pg 730
Quintessence Publishing Co Ltd, pg 732
Reaktion Books Ltd, pg 733
Research Studies Press Ltd (RSP), pg 734
Rooster Books Ltd, pg 735
Routledge Curzon, pg 736
Royal Institute of International Affairs, pg 736
Sage Publications Ltd, pg 737
St Jerome Publishing, pg 738
SCM Press, pg 739
Scottish Cultural Press, pg 739
Scottish Text Society, pg 740
Sheffield Academic Press Ltd, pg 741
Shepheard-Walwyn (Publishers) Ltd, pg 741
Skoob Russell Square, pg 742
SLS Legal Publications (NI), pg 742
Colin Smythe Ltd, pg 743
Speechmark Publishing Ltd, pg 744
Stacey International, pg 745
Stainer & Bell Ltd, pg 745
The Stationery Office, pg 745
Sutton Publishing Ltd, pg 746
Tate Publishing Ltd, pg 747
I B Tauris & Co Ltd, pg 747
Taylor Graham Publishing, pg 747
John Taylor Book Ventures, pg 747
Textile & Art Publications Ltd, pg 748
Thistle Press, pg 748
Thoemmes Press, pg 748
Trentham Books Ltd, pg 750
Tuckwell Press Ltd, pg 750
UCL Press Ltd, pg 751
University of Exeter Press, pg 751
University Presses of California, Columbia & Princeton Ltd, pg 752
Verso, pg 752
Voltaire Foundation Ltd, pg 753
The Warburg Institute, pg 754
White Cockade Publishing, pg 755
Whiting & Birch Ltd, pg 756
Wimbledon Publishing Company Ltd, pg 757
Windhorse Publications, pg 757
WIT Press, pg 757
World of Islam Altajir Trust, pg 759
Yale University Press London, pg 759
Zed Books Ltd, pg 759

Uruguay
Fundacion de Cultura Universitaria, pg 760
Nordan-Comunidad, pg 760
Ediciones Trilce, pg 761

Venezuela
Biblioteca Ayacucho, pg 762
Editorial Nueva Sociedad, pg 762

Viet Nam
Science & Technics Publishing House, pg 763

Zambia
Historical Association of Zambia, pg 766
MFK Management Consultants Services, pg 766

Zimbabwe
Academic Books Pvt Ltd, pg 767
Anvil Press, pg 767
ZRD Trust, pg 770

SIDELINES

Argentina
Juegos & Co SRL, pg 6

Australia
Dynamo House P/L, pg 21

Brazil
Brinque Book Editora de Livros Ltda, pg 80
Ediouro Publicacoes, SA, pg 81
Rede Das Artes (Boccato Editores Collector's), pg 90

Colombia
Eurolibros Ltda, pg 111
RAM Editores, pg 113
Editorial Santillana SA, pg 113

Cuba
Casa Editora Abril, pg 120

Czech Republic
Cesky normalizacni institut, pg 127

Germany
ARTC/OLOR, pg 195
Coppenrath Verlag, pg 211
Esslinger Verlag J F Schreiber GmbH, pg 224
Margarethe Freudenberger - selbstverlag fur jedermann, pg 230
Edition Hentrich Druck & Verlag Gebr Hentrich und Tank GmbH & Co KG, pg 239
Friedrich W Heye Verlag GmbH, pg 240
Landbuch-Verlagsgesellschaft mbH, pg 255
Lorber-Verlag & Turm-Verlag Otto Zluhan, pg 259
teNeues Verlag GmbH & Co KG, pg 292
Turm-Verlag Lorber-Verlag Otto Zluhan OHG, pg 295
Dorothea van der Koelen, pg 297

Greece
Toubis M, pg 315

Israel
Schocken Publishing House Ltd, pg 372

PUBLISHERS · TYPE OF PUBLICATION INDEX

Mexico
Fernandez Editores SA de CV, pg 461
Ediciones Libra, SA de CV, pg 463
Sayrols Editorial SA de CV, pg 466
Ediciones Suromex SA, pg 467

Singapore
Aquanut Agencies Pte Ltd, pg 545

Spain
Editorial 'Alas', pg 562
Editorial Astri SA, pg 564
Pirene Editorial, sal, pg 587
Editorial Miguel A Salvatella SA, pg 589
Equipo Sirius SA, pg 591
Stanley Editorial, pg 591

United Kingdom
Four Seasons Publishing Ltd, pg 683

SUBSCRIPTION & MAIL ORDER BOOKS

Argentina
Beatriz Viterbo Editora, pg 4
Juris Editorial, pg 6
Instituto de Publicaciones Navales, pg 7

Australia
ACER Press, pg 10
Artmoves, pg 12
Ashling Books, pg 12
Australian Broadcasting Authority, pg 13
The Australian Council for Educational Research Ltd, pg 13
Bernal Publishing, pg 14
Blackwell Science Pty Ltd, pg 15
Board of Studies, pg 15
Bridge To Peace Publications, pg 16
Butterworths Australia Ltd, pg 16
Covenanter Press, pg 19
Crista International, pg 19
Encyclopaedia Britannica (Australia) Inc, pg 22
Gould Books, pg 24
Hartys Creek Press, pg 25
Instauratio Press, pg 27
Jarrah Publications, pg 28
Law Book Co Information Services, pg 29
Barry Long Books, pg 30
Matthias Media, pg 32
Jill Oxton Publications Pty Ltd, pg 36
Papyrus Publishing, pg 37
Pascoe Publishing, pg 37
Pollitecon Publications, pg 38
Priestley Consulting, pg 39
The Real Estate Institute of Australia, pg 40
Skills Publishing, pg 42
Slouch Hat Publications, pg 42
Threshold Publishing, pg 44
Veritas Press, pg 46
Vista Publications, pg 47

Austria
Andreas Schnider Verlags-Atelier, pg 58

Azerbaijan
Sada, Literaturno-Izdatel'skij Centr, pg 61

Belgium
CED-Samsom, pg 66
Editions De Boeck-Larcier SA, pg 67
Koepel van de Vlaamse Noord - Zuidbeweging 11.11.11, pg 70

Brazil
Abril SA, pg 77
Empresa Brasileira de Pesquisa Agropecaria, pg 83
Fundacao Cultural Avatar, pg 83
Talento Publicacoes Editora e Grafica Ltda, pg 92

Bulgaria
CHRIKER, pg 94
Ciela Publishing House, pg 94
Publishing House Narodno delo OOD, pg 97

Chile
Arrayan Editores, pg 99

China
Foreign Language Teaching & Research Press, pg 105
Lanzhou University Press, pg 107
The People's Communications Publishing House, pg 107

Costa Rica
Scout Interamericana, pg 117
Editorial Texto Ltda, pg 117

Croatia
Vitagraf, pg 120

Cuba
Pueblo y Educacion Editorial (PE), pg 121

Czech Republic
Jota, pg 125
Nadace Lyry Pragensis, pg 126
Nase vojsko, nakladatelstvi a knizni obchod, pg 126

Denmark
J H Schultz Information A/S, pg 135

Egypt (Arab Republic of Egypt)
Al Arab Publishing House, pg 138

France
L'Amitie par le Livre, pg 147
Editions Amrita SA, pg 147
BSI - ELOR Editions Jeunesse, pg 152
Editions Canope, pg 152
Editeurs Crepin-Leblond, pg 157
L'Harmattan, pg 168
Le Laurier, pg 172
Muller Edition, pg 176
Jean-Michel Place, pg 180
Association d'Editions Sorg, pg 186
Zodiaque, pg 190

Germany
Data Becker GmbH & Co KG, pg 212
Dietrich zu Klampen Verlag, pg 216
H Gietl Verlag & Publikationsservice GmbH, pg 232
Heel Verlag GmbH, pg 238

Edition Hentrich Druck & Verlag Gebr Hentrich und Tank GmbH & Co KG, pg 239
Kerber Christof Verlag, pg 248
Koptisch-Orthodoxes Zentrum, pg 252
Laaber-Verlag, pg 255
Edition Libri Illustri GmbH, pg 257
mode information Heinz Kramer GmbH, pg 264
Norbert Mueller AG & Co KG Verlag, pg 265
Edition Octopus & Okeanos Presse, pg 269
Springer-Verlag GmbH & Co KG, pg 288
C A Starke Verlag, pg 289
Tipress Dienstleistungen fur das Verlagswesen GmbH, pg 294
Trans Tech Publications, pg 294
Dorothea van der Koelen, pg 297

Ghana
World Literature Project, pg 308

Greece
Beta Medical Publishers, pg 309
Karatzas Charis, pg 312

Hong Kong
Breakthrough Ltd - Breakthrough Publishers, pg 318
Hong Kong China Tourism Press, pg 320
Press Mark Media Ltd, pg 321

Hungary
Novorg Kiado, pg 326

India
Sri Ramakrishna Math, pg 342
Reliance Publishing House, pg 347

Indonesia
PT Indira, pg 355

Ireland
Ballinakella Press, pg 358
Government Publications Ireland, pg 361
Oak Tree Press, pg 362

Israel
Hanitzotz A-Sharara Publishing House, pg 368

Italy
Apimondia, pg 375
BeMa, pg 377
Electa, pg 387
Macro Edizioni, pg 397
Edizioni Piemme SpA, pg 403
Edizioni Sorbona Milano, pg 408

Japan
Shufunotomo sha Co Ltd, pg 426

Kenya
Gideon S Were Press, pg 434

Republic of Korea
Korea Britannica Corp, pg 437

Mexico
Artes de Mexico y del Mundo, SA de CV, pg 458
Editora Cientifica Medica Latinoamerican SA de CV, pg 458
Colegio de Postgraduados en Ciencias Agricolas, pg 459
Instituto Nacional de Estadistica, Geographia e Informatica, pg 464

Netherlands
Hagen & Stam Uitgeverij Ten, pg 478

New Zealand
Aspect Press, pg 488
CCH New Zealand Ltd, pg 490
Southern Press Ltd, pg 496

Nigeria
Goldland Business Co Ltd, pg 499

Pakistan
The Book House, pg 506
International Educational Services, pg 507

Papua New Guinea
Melanesian Institute, pg 510

Paraguay
Intercontinental Editora, pg 510

Philippines
Encyclopaedia Britannica (Philippines) Inc, pg 513
Our Lady of Manaoag Publisher, pg 514

Poland
Wydawnictwo Medyczne Urban & Partner, pg 518
Wydawnictwo Prawnicze Co, pg 519

Portugal
Imprensa Nacional-Casa da Moeda, pg 526
Latina Livraria, pg 526
Revista Penteados, pg 529
Solivros, pg 529

Romania
Editura Humanitas, pg 533
Humanitas Publishing House, pg 533
Editura Militara, pg 534
Editura Niculescu, pg 534
RAO International Publishing Co, pg 535
Rentrop & Straton Verlagsgruppe und Wirtschaftsconsulting, pg 535

Russian Federation
N E Bauman Moscow State Technical University Publishers, pg 537
Finansy i Statistika Publishing House, pg 538
Mir Knigi Ltd, pg 540
Izdatelstvo Muzyka, pg 540
Profizdat, pg 541
St Andrew's Biblical Theological College, pg 541

Singapore
Select Books Pte Ltd, pg 548

849

TYPE OF PUBLICATION INDEX — BOOK

Slovenia
Zalozba Mihelac d o o, pg 552

South Africa
Institute for Reformational Studies CHE, pg 555
Jacklin Enterprises (Pty) Ltd, pg 556
Juta & Co, pg 556
South African Institute of Race Relations, pg 559

Spain
Ediciones Agrotecnicas, SL, pg 562
Editorial Astri SA, pg 564
Editorial CISSPRAXIS SA, pg 567
Ediciones l'Isard, S L, pg 571
Joyas Bibliograficas SA, pg 579
Lynx Edicions, pg 580
Naque Editora, pg 583
Edicions Proa, SA, pg 588
Instituto Provincial de Investigaciones y Estudios Toledanos, pg 588
Secretariado Trinitario, pg 590
Vinaches Lopez, Luisa, pg 595

Sweden
Hans Richter Laromedel, pg 604

Switzerland
Bergli Books AG, pg 609
Cosmos-Verlag AG, pg 611
Parkett Publishers Inc, pg 621
Weltrundschau Verlag AG, pg 627

Taiwan, Province of China
Senate Books Co Ltd, pg 631
Torch of Wisdom, pg 632
Yuan Liou Publishing Co, Ltd, pg 632

United Republic of Tanzania
Bureau of Statistics, pg 633
Emmaus Bible School, pg 633

Thailand
Sang Dad Publishing Company Ltd, pg 635

Turkey
Iletisim Yayinlari, pg 640

Uganda
Centre for Basic Research, pg 642

United Kingdom
ABG Professional Information, pg 644
AK Press & Distribution, pg 645
Ian Allan Publishing Ltd, pg 646
Arts Council of England, pg 649
Association for Science Education, pg 650
Atlas Press, pg 651
BCA, pg 653
Bible Reading Fellowship, pg 654
Bridge Books, pg 659
Business Monitor International, pg 661
Chapman, pg 666
Christian Education, pg 667
E W Classey Ltd, pg 668
Leo Cooper, pg 671
Croner CCH Group Ltd, pg 672
The Energy Information Centre, pg 679
Epworth Press, pg 679
Free Association Books Ltd, pg 684
Freedom Press, pg 684
The Greek Bookshop, pg 689
Greenhill Books/Lionel Leventhal Ltd, pg 689
Hawk Books, pg 693
Hobsons, pg 696
Institute for Fiscal Studies, pg 699
Intermediate Technology Publications Ltd, pg 700
Lang Syne Publishers Ltd, pg 706
Legal Action Group, pg 706
Letterbox Library, pg 707
Kenneth Mason Publications Ltd, pg 712
Moorley's Print & Publishing Ltd, pg 715
National Association for the Teaching of English (NATE), pg 717
Oilfield Publications Ltd, pg 720
Osprey Publishing Ltd, pg 722
Parapress Ltd, pg 724
Perpetuity Press, pg 726
The Policy Press, pg 729
Ramakrishna Vedanta Centre, pg 732
The Reader's Digest Association Ltd, pg 733
Reading & Language Information Centre, pg 733
Royal College of General Practitioners, pg 736
The Royal Society, pg 737
SchoolPlay Productions Ltd, pg 739
Sheffield Academic Press Ltd, pg 741
Spokesman, pg 744
Stainer & Bell Ltd, pg 745
The Stationery Office, pg 745
Take That Ltd, pg 746
VNU Business Publications, pg 753
Wilmington Business Information Ltd, pg 756

Uruguay
Ediciones de Juan Darien, pg 760
Fundacion de Cultura Universitaria, pg 760
La Urpila Editores, pg 761
Vinten Editor, pg 761

Venezuela
Editorial Nueva Sociedad, pg 762

TEXTBOOKS - ELEMENTARY

Afghanistan
Ministry of Education, Department of Educational Publications, pg 1

Albania
NL SH, pg 1

Argentina
Editorial Acme SA, pg 3
AZ Editora SA, pg 3
Bonum Editorial SACI, pg 4
Cesarini Hermanos, pg 4
Ediciones Don Bosco Argentina, pg 5
Edicial SA, pg 5
Angel Estrada y Cia SA, pg 6
Gram Editora, pg 6
Libreria Huemul SA, pg 6
Kapelusz Editora SA, pg 6
Ediciones Preescolar SA, pg 8

Australia
Board of Studies, pg 15
Boinkie Publishers, pg 15
Cambridge University Press, pg 17
China Books, pg 18
R J Cleary Publishing, pg 18
Coolabah Publishing, pg 18
Curriculum Corporation, pg 19
Dabill Publications, pg 20
Dellasta Publishing, pg 20
Department for Education & Children's Services, South Australia, pg 20
Educational Advantage, pg 21
Era Publications, pg 22
Hawker Brownlow, pg 25
Macmillan Education Australia, pg 31
Horwitz Martin Education, pg 32
McGraw-Hill Australia Pty Ltd, pg 32
Mimosa Publications Pty Ltd, pg 33
Pearson Education Australia, pg 37
Ready-Ed Publications, pg 40
Reed Educational Publishing Australia, pg 40
RIC Publications Pty Ltd, pg 40
Scholastic Australia Pty Ltd, pg 41
University of Western Australia Press, pg 46
Windhorse Books, pg 48
Winetitles, pg 48
Wizard Books Pty Ltd, pg 48

Austria
Dachs-Verlag GmbH, pg 50
Development News Ltd, pg 51
Johannes Heyn, Gert und Volkmar Zechner, pg 52
Verlag Hoelder-Pichler-Tempsky, pg 53
Niederosterreichisches Pressehaus Druck- und Verlagsgesellschaft mbH, pg 55
Osterreichischer Bundesveilag Ges.mbh, pg 57
Roetzer Druck GmbH & Co KG, pg 58

Bangladesh
Mullick Bros, pg 62
The University Press Ltd, pg 62

Belarus
Kavaler Publishers, pg 63
Narodnaya Asveta, pg 63

Belgium
Carto BVBA, pg 65
La Charte Editions juridiques, pg 66
Editions De Boeck-Larcier SA, pg 67
Uitgeverij J van In, pg 70
Editions Labor, pg 70
Editions Lumen Vitae ASBL, pg 71
Uitgeverij Pelckmans N V, pg 73
Uitgeverij De Sikkel NV, pg 74
Wolters Plantyn Educatieve Uitgevers, pg 75

Benin
Les Editions du Flamboyant, pg 76

Bolivia
Editorial Don Bosco, pg 76

Bosnia and Herzegovina
Bemust doo Novinsko-Izdavacko stamparsko i trgovacko preduzece, pg 77

Botswana
Maskew Miller Longman, pg 77

Brazil
A & A & A Edicoes e Promocoes Internacionais Ltda, pg 77
Livraria Francisco Alves Editora SA, pg 78
Ao Livro Tecnico Industria e Comercio Ltda, pg 78
Editora Atica SA, pg 79
Centro de Estudos Juridicosdo Para (CEJUP), pg 80
Conquista, Empresa de Publicacoes Ltda, pg 81
Editora Contexto (Editora Pinsky Ltda), pg 81
Ediouro Publicacoes, SA, pg 81
Editora Brasil-America (EBAL) SA, pg 82
Editora Harbra Ltda, pg 84
Livro Ibero-Americano Ltda, pg 85
Waldyr Lima Editora, pg 86
Edicoes Loyola SA, pg 87
Modulo Editora e Desenvolvimento Educacional Ltda, pg 88
Edit Palavra Magica, pg 89
Distribuidora Record de Servicos de Imprensa SA, pg 90
Saraiva SA, Livreiros Editores, pg 91
Editora Scipione Ltda, pg 91
Editora Vigilia Ltda, pg 93

Bulgaria
Bojko Kacarmazov, pg 94
Bulvest 2000 Ltd, pg 94
Eurasia Academic Publishers, pg 95
Gea-Libris Publishing House, pg 95
Makros 2000 - Plovdiv, pg 96
Musica Publishing House Ltd, pg 96
Pensoft Publishers, pg 97
Prosveta Publishers as, pg 97

Burundi
Editions Intore, pg 98

Cameroon
Editions Buma Kor, pg 99
Editions CLE, pg 99
Editions Semences Africaines, pg 99

Chile
Dolmen Ediciones SA, pg 100
Instituto Geografico Militar, pg 100
Zig-Zag SA, pg 102

China
Beijing Education Publishing House, pg 102
Beijing Publishing House, pg 102
Chinese Pedagogics Publishing House, pg 104
Foreign Language Teaching & Research Press, pg 105
Language Publishing House, pg 107
People's Education Press, pg 107
People's Fine Arts Publishing House, pg 108
Shandong Education Publishing House, pg 108
Shanghai Educational Publishing House, pg 109
Shanghai Fine Arts Publishers, pg 109
Shanghai Foreign Language Education Press, pg 109
Tsinghua University Press, pg 110

PUBLISHERS

Zhejiang Education Publishing House, pg 110
Zhejiang University Press, pg 110

Colombia
Ediciones Cultural Colombiana Ltda, pg 111
Eurolibros Ltda, pg 111
Kapelusz Ltda Editorial, pg 112
Editorial Libros y Libres SA, pg 112
Migema Ediciones Ltda, pg 113
Editorial Santillana SA, pg 113
Editorial Voluntad SA, pg 114

The Democratic Republic of the Congo
Centre de Recherche, et Pedagogie Appliquee, pg 114

Costa Rica
Litografia Artex, SA, pg 116
Scout Interamericana, pg 117
Editorial de la Universidad de Costa Rica, pg 117

Cote d'Ivoire
Centre d'Edition et de Diffusion Africaines, pg 117
Les Nouvelles Editions Ivoiriennes (NEI), pg 118

Croatia
ALFA dd za izdavacke, graficke i trgovacke poslove, pg 118
Skolska Knjiga, pg 120

Cuba
Pueblo y Educacion Editorial (PE), pg 121

Denmark
Alinea A/S, pg 129
Forlaget alokke AS, pg 129
Djof Publishing Jurist-og Okonomforbundets Forlag, pg 131
Gyldendalske Boghandel - Nordisk Forlag A/S, pg 132
P Haase & Sons Forlag A/S, pg 132
Holkenfeldt 3, pg 133
Forlaget Hovedland, pg 133
Kaleidoscope Publishers Ltd, pg 133
Forlaget Modtryk AMBA, pg 133
Nyt Nordisk Forlag Arnold Busck A/S, pg 134
Det Schonbergske Forlag, pg 135
Wisby & Wilkens, pg 136

Egypt (Arab Republic of Egypt)
Dar El Shorouk Publishing & Distributing House, pg 138

El Salvador
Clasicos Roxsil Editorial SA de CV, pg 139
Editorial Universitaria de la Universidad de El Salvador, pg 139

Finland
Otava Publishing Co Ltd, pg 143
Soederstroem et Co Foerlagsaktiebolag, pg 144

France
Alsatia SA, pg 146
Editions Belin, pg 150
Cle International, pg 155
Armand Colin, Editeur, pg 155
Decanord, pg 158
Delagrave Edition SA, pg 158
L'Ecole/L'Ecole des Loisirs Sarl, pg 160
Edicef - Editions Classiques d'Expression Francaise, pg 161
Hachette Education, pg 167
Editions Hatier SA, pg 168
Magnard SA, pg 174
Editions MDI (La Maison des Instituteurs), pg 175
Presence Africaine Editions, pg 180
Editions du Seneve, pg 184
Editions Spratbrow, pg 186
Pierre Zech Editeur, pg 189

Germany
ALS-Verlag GmbH, pg 193
AOL-Verlag Frohmut Menze, pg 194
Auer Verlag GmbH, pg 196
C Bange GmbH & Co KG, pg 198
Bayerischer Schulbuch-Verlag GmbH, pg 199
Julius Beltz GmbH & Co KG, pg 200
Gustav Bosse GmbH & Co KG, pg 205
Christliche Verlagsgesellschaft mbH, pg 210
Cornelsen und Oxford University Press GmbH & Co, pg 211
Cornelsen Verlag GmbH & Co OHG, pg 211
Verlag Darmstaedter Blaetter Schwarz und Co, pg 212
Deutscher Taschenbuch Verlag GmbH & Co KG (dtv), pg 215
Diesterweg, Moritz Verlag, pg 216
Verlag Duerr & Kessler GmbH, pg 219
Ferd Dummler's Verlag, pg 227
Finken Verlag GmbH, pg 228
Alfons W Gentner Verlag GmbH & Co KG, pg 231
Lehrmittelverlag Wilhelm Hagemann GmbH, pg 236
Verlag Otto Heinevetter Lehrmittel GmbH, pg 239
Horlemann Verlag, pg 243
Impuls-Theater-Verlag, pg 244
Kallmeyer'sche Verlagsbuchhandlung GmbH, pg 247
Ernst Klett Verlag GmbH, pg 250
Konkordia Verlag GmbH, pg 252
Lahn-Verlag GmbH, pg 255
Verlag Leske plus Budrich GmbH, pg 257
Lucius & Lucius Verlagsgesellschaft mbH, pg 259
Manz G J Verlag und Druckerel, pg 261
Militzke Verlag, pg 264
Karl Heinrich Moeseler Verlag, pg 264
Oekotopia Verlag, Wolfgang Hoffman, pg 270
Patmos Verlag GmbH & Co KG, pg 272
Verlag Sigrid Persen, pg 272
Philipp Reclam Jun Verlag GmbH, pg 273
Quelle und Meyer Verlag GmbH & Co, pg 276
Verlag an der Ruhr GmbH, pg 281
Buchverlag Andrea Schmitz, pg 284
Schott Musik International GmbH & Co KG, pg 284
Tipress Dienstleistungen fur das Verlagswesen GmbH, pg 294

Turkischer Schulbuchverlag Onel Cengiz, pg 295
Verlag und Druckkontor Kamp GmbH, pg 298
Voggenreiter-Verlag, pg 299
Volk und Wissen Verlag GmbH & Co, pg 299
Westermann Schulbuchverlag GmbH, pg 302
Dr Dieter Winkler, pg 303

Ghana
Afram Publications (Ghana) Ltd, pg 306
Asempa Publishers, pg 306
Black Mask Ltd, pg 306
Educational Press & Manufacturers Ltd, pg 307
EPP Books Services, pg 307
Frank Publishing Ltd, pg 307
Ghana Publishing Corporation, pg 307
Sam Woode Ltd, pg 308
Sedco Publishing Ltd, pg 308
Sub-Saharan Publishers, pg 308
Unimax Macmillan Ltd, pg 308
Waterville Publishing House, pg 308

Greece
Athina, Mary Mavrogiannis, pg 309
Etaireia Spoudon Neoellinikou Politismou Kai Genikis Paideias, pg 310
I Prooptiki, pg 311
Ilias Kambanas Publishing Organization, SA, pg 312
Mavrogianni Publications, pg 313
Nakas Music House, pg 313
Patakis Publishers, pg 314
Nikolas I Rossi, pg 314

Guadeloupe
Librairie Generale JASOR, pg 316

Guatemala
Fundacion para la Cultura y el Desarrollo, pg 316

Haiti
Editions Caraiibes SA, pg 317

Hong Kong
Federal Publications Ltd, pg 319
Joint Publishing (HK) Co Ltd, pg 320
Ling Kee Publishing Group, pg 320
Witman Publishing Co (HK) Ltd, pg 322

Hungary
Corvina Books Ltd, pg 323
Mueszaki Koenyvkiado Ltd, pg 325
Nemzeti Tankoenyvkiado, pg 326

Iceland
Mal og menning, pg 328
Namsgagnastofnun, pg 328

India
Addison-Wesley (Singapore) Pte Ltd, pg 329
Ambar Prakashan, pg 330
B I Publications Pvt Ltd, pg 331
The Bangalore Printing & Publishing Co Ltd, pg 332
Bani Mandir, Book-Sellers, Publishers & Educational Suppliers, pg 332
Bharat Publishing House, pg 332

TYPE OF PUBLICATION INDEX

Bhawan Book Service, Publishers & Distributors, pg 333
Chowkhamba Sanskrit Series Office, pg 335
Frank Brothers & Co (Publishers) Ltd, pg 337
General Book Depot, pg 337
Arnold Heinman Publishers (India) Pvt Ltd, pg 338
Hindi Pracharak Sansthan, pg 338
Indian Book Depot (Map House), pg 339
Konark Publishers, Pvt, Ltd, pg 341
Naresh Publishers, pg 343
National Council of Educational Research & Training, Publication Department, pg 344
Omsons Publications, pg 345
Oxford University Press, pg 345
Paico Publishing House, pg 345
Paramount Sales (India) Pvt Ltd, pg 345
Pitambar Publishing Co (P) Ltd, pg 346
Sasta Sahitya Mandal, pg 349
Scientific Book Agency, pg 349
Shaibya Prakashan Bibhag, pg 349
Shiksha Bharati, pg 350
Somaiya Publications Pvt Ltd, pg 350
Sree Rama Publishers, pg 351
Sterling Information Technologies, pg 351
A H Wheeler & Co Ltd, pg 353

Indonesia
Bina Rena Pariwara, pg 354
PT BPK Gunung Mulia, pg 355
PT Pradnya Paramita, pg 357

Ireland
An Gum, pg 358
C J Fallon, pg 360
Veritas Co Ltd, pg 364

Israel
Am Oved Publishers Ltd, pg 365
Classikaletet, pg 366
Karni Publishers Ltd, pg 369
Kiryat Sefer, pg 369
Ma'alot Publishing Company Ltd, pg 370
Modan Publishers Ltd, pg 371
University Publishing Projects Ltd, pg 373

Italy
De Agostini Scolastica, pg 375
Nuova Casa Editrice Licinio Cappelli GEM srl, pg 379
Edizioni Centro Studi Erickson, pg 381
Edizioni Dehoniane Bologna (EDB), pg 384
Organizzazione Didattica Editoriale Ape, pg 385
Editrice la Scuola SpA, pg 386
Garzanti Editore, pg 388
Istituto Geografico de Agostini SpA, pg 390
Ghisetti e Corvi Editori SpA, pg 390
Giunti (Gruppo Editoriale), pg 390
Hora, pg 392
Nicola Milano Editore, pg 398
Minerva Italica SpA, pg 399
RCS Libri SpA, pg 405
Societa Editrice Internazionale - SEI, pg 408
Gruppo Editoriale Le Stelle SpA, pg 409

TYPE OF PUBLICATION INDEX — BOOK

Jamaica
Carlong Publishers (Caribbean) Ltd, pg 412
Ian Randle Publishers Ltd, pg 413
Twin Guinep Ltd, pg 413
West Indies Publishing Ltd, pg 414

Japan
Dainippon Tosho Publishing Co, Ltd, pg 416
Kaitakusha, pg 419
Nihon-Bunkyo Shuppan (Japan Educational Publishing Co Ltd), pg 422
Sanshusha Publishing Co, Ltd, pg 424
Shingakusha Co Ltd, pg 425
Teikoku-Shoin Co Ltd, pg 427
Thomson Learning, pg 427
Tokyo Shoseki Co Ltd, pg 427

Kenya
Africa Book Services (EA) Ltd, pg 430
Cosmopolitan Publishers Ltd, pg 431
Dhillon Publishers Ltd, Paa Crescent, pg 431
Focus Publications Ltd, pg 431
Foundation Books, pg 431
Heinemann Kenya Limited (EAEP), pg 431
Kenya Literature Bureau, pg 432
The Jomo Kenyatta Foundation, pg 432
Phoenix Publishers, pg 433
Shirikon Publishers, pg 433
Sudan Literature Centre, pg 433
Transafrica Press, pg 433
Gideon S Were Press, pg 434

Republic of Korea
Kyohaksa Publishing Co Ltd, pg 438
Moon Jin Media Co Ltd, pg 438

Latvia
Lielvards Ltd, pg 442
Zvaigzne ABC Publishers, Ltd, pg 442

Lebanon
Librairie Orientale sal, pg 443
World Book Publishing, pg 443

Lesotho
Mazenod Book Centre, pg 444
Saint Michael's Mission, pg 444

Lithuania
Margi Rastai Publishers, pg 446
Sviesa Publishers, pg 446
Svietimo ir mokslo ministerijos Leidybos centras, pg 446
Tyto Alba Publishers, pg 446

Luxembourg
Editions Emile Borschette, pg 447
Service Central des Imprimes et des Fournitures de Bureau de l'Etat, pg 448

The Former Yugoslav Republic of Macedonia
St Clement of Ohrid National & University Library, pg 449

Madagascar
Centre National de Production de Materiel Didactique (CNAPMAD), pg 450
Foibe Filan-Kevitry NY Mpampianatra (FOFIPA), pg 450
Librarie Mixte, pg 450
Societe Malgache d'Edition, pg 450
Trano Printy Fiangonana Loterana Malagasy (TPFLM)-(Imprimerie Lutherienne), pg 450

Malawi
Dzuka Publishing Company Ltd, pg 450

Malaysia
Dewan Bahasa dan Pustaka, pg 451
Federal Publications Sdn Bhd, pg 452
FEP International Sdn Bhd, pg 452
Pearson Education, pg 453
Penerbit Fajar Bakti Sdn Bhd, pg 454
Penerbitan Tinta, pg 454
Pustaka Cipta Sdn Bhd, pg 454

Maldive Islands
Non-Formal Education Centre, pg 455

Mali
EDIM SA, pg 455

Malta
Media Centre, pg 456

Mauritius
Golden Publications, pg 457
Editions de l'Ocean Indien Ltd, pg 457
EDITIONS Le Printemps, pg 457

Mexico
Adivinar y Multiplicar, SA de CV, pg 457
Editorial Avante SA de Cv, pg 458
Edamex SA de CV, pg 460
Editorial Esfinge SA de CV, pg 460
Fernandez Editores SA de CV, pg 461
Fondo de Cultura Economica, pg 461
Ediciones Larousse SA de CV, pg 462
Editorial Limusa SA de CV, pg 463
Nova Grupo Editorial SA de CV, pg 464
Palabra Ediciones Verlagsgesellschaft mbH, pg 465
Editorial Patria SA de CV, pg 465
Pearson Educacion de Mexico, SA de CV, pg 465
Plaza y Valdes SA de CV, pg 465
Editorial Progreso SA de C V, pg 466
Ediciones Promesa, SA de CV, pg 466
Publicaciones Cultural SA de CV, pg 466
Sistemas Tecnicos de Edicion SA de CV, pg 467
Ediciones Suromex SA, pg 467
Editorial Trillas SA de CV, pg 467

Republic of Moldova
Lumina Publishing House, pg 468

Morocco
Dar Nachr Al Maarifa Pour L'Edition et La Distribution, pg 469

Namibia
Bureau for Indigenous Languages, pg 471
Desert Research Foundation of Namibia (DRFN), pg 471

Nepal
International Standards Books & Periodicals (P) Ltd, pg 471

Netherlands
Bosch & Keuning, pg 474
Educatieve Partners Nederland bv, pg 476
Katholieke Bijbelstichting, pg 479
LCG Malmberg BV, pg 480
Pearson Education Netherlands, pg 482
Stenvert Systems & Service BV, pg 484
Wolters-Noordhoff B V, pg 487
Uitgeverij Zwijsen BV, pg 487

New Zealand
Wendy Crane Books, pg 490
ESA Publications (NZ) Ltd, pg 490
Eton Press (Auckland) Ltd, pg 490
Huia Publishers, pg 492
Legislation Direct, pg 492
Macmillan Publishers New Zealand Ltd, pg 493
Oxford University Press, pg 494
Pearson Education, pg 494
Nelson Price Milburn Ltd, pg 494
Reed Publishing (NZ) Ltd, pg 495
Sunshine Books International Ltd, pg 496
Te Reo Publications, pg 496

Nigeria
African Universities Press, pg 497
Africana-FEP Publishers Ltd, pg 498
Alliance West African Publishers & Co, pg 498
Aromolaran Publishing Co Ltd, pg 498
Cross Continent Press Ltd, pg 498
CSS Bookshops, Agency & Publishing Division, pg 498
Educational Research & Study Group, pg 499
Evans Brothers (Nigeria Publishers) Ltd, pg 499
Fourth Dimension Publishing Co Ltd, pg 499
JAD Publishers Ltd, pg 500
Kola Sanya Publishing Enterprise, pg 500
Longman Nigeria Plc, pg 500
New Era Publishers, pg 500
Northern Nigerian Publishing Co Ltd, pg 500
Nwamife Publishers Ltd, pg 500
Onibon-Oje Publishers, pg 501
Riverside Communications, pg 501
University Publishing Co, pg 502
Vantage Publishers International Ltd, pg 502
West African Book Publishers Ltd, pg 502

Norway
H Aschehoug & Co (W Nygaard) A/S, pg 502
J W Eides Forlag A/S, pg 503
Forlaget Fag og Kultur, pg 503
Gyldendal Norsk Forlag A/S, pg 503
Universitetsforlaget, pg 505

Pakistan
Sheikh Shaukat Ali & Sons, pg 506
The Book House, pg 506
Islamic Book Centre, pg 507
Islamic Publications (Pvt) Ltd, pg 507
Jang Publishers, pg 507
Maqbool Academy, pg 508

Papua New Guinea
Kristen Pres, pg 510

Peru
Asociacion Editorial Bruno, pg 511
Tarea Asociacion de Publicaciones Educativas, pg 511
Tassorello, SA, pg 511

Philippines
Abiva Publishing House Inc, pg 512
Ateneo de Manila University Press, pg 512
Bookman Printing & Publishing House Inc, pg 512
Bookmark Inc, pg 512
J C Palabay Enterprises, pg 513
Marren Publishing House, Inc, pg 513
National Book Store Inc, pg 514
Our Lady of Manaoag Publisher, pg 514
Rex Bookstores & Publishers, pg 514
Saint Mary's Publishing Corp, pg 515
Salesiana Publishers Inc, pg 515
SIBS Publishing House Inc, pg 515
UST Publishing House, pg 515

Poland
Impuls, pg 517
PZWL Wydawnictwo Lekarskie Ltd, pg 519
Res Polona, pg 519
Wydawn Na Sprawa' Wydawniczo-Oswiatowa Spotdzielnia Inwalidow, pg 521
Wydawnictwa Szkolne i Pedagogiczne (Polish Educational Publishers-WSiP), pg 521

Portugal
Livraria Amado Lda, pg 522
Constancia Editores, SA, pg 524
Dinalivro, pg 524
Europress Editores e Distribuidores de Publicacoes Lda, pg 525
Lua Viajante-Edicao e Distribuicao de Livros e Material Audiovisual, Lda, pg 527
Editorial O Livro Lda, pg 528
Platano Editora SA, pg 528
Porto Editora Lda, pg 528
Editorial Presenca, pg 528
Almerinda Teixeira, pg 529
Texto Editora, pg 529

Puerto Rico
McGraw-Hill Intermericana del Caribe, Inc, pg 530

PUBLISHERS

Romania
Editora All, pg 531
Editura Clusium, Casa de Editura Atlas-Clusium SRL, pg 532
Editura Didactica si Pedagogica, pg 532
Editura Humanitas, pg 533
Humanitas Publishing House, pg 533
Editura Niculescu, pg 534
Polirom Verlag, pg 535
RAO International Publishing Co, pg 535

Russian Federation
Airis Press, pg 537
Izdatelstvo Mir, pg 540
Izdatelstvo Muzyka, pg 540
Okoshko Ltd Publishers (Izdatelstvo), pg 541
Izdatelstvo Prosveshchenie, pg 541

Senegal
Les Nouvelles Editions Africaines du Senegal NEAS, pg 544

Sierra Leone
Njala Educational Publishing Centre, pg 544

Singapore
Federal Publications (S) Pte Ltd, pg 546
Hillview Publications Pte Ltd, pg 546

Slovakia
Slo Viet, pg 550
Slovenske pedagogicke nakladateistvo, pg 550
Ustav informacii a prognoz skolstva mladeze a telovychovy, pg 551

Slovenia
Zalozba Mihelac d o o, pg 552
Zalozba Obzorja d d Maribor, pg 552

South Africa
Educum Publishers Ltd, pg 554
Heinemann Educational Publishers Southern Africa, pg 555
Heinemann Publishers (Pty) Ltd, pg 555
Ivy Publications, pg 555
Maskew Miller Longman, pg 557
Nasou Via Afrika, pg 557
Publitoria Publishers, pg 558
Shuter & Shooter (Pty) Ltd, pg 559
Vivlia Publishers & Booksellers, pg 560

Spain
Publicacions de l'Abadia de Montserrat, pg 561
Ediciones Akal SA, pg 562
Ediciones Anaya SA, pg 563
Anaya Educacion, pg 563
Editorial Bruno, pg 566
Editorial Casals SA, pg 566
CEAC, Grupo Editorial SA, pg 567
Editorial Claret SA, pg 568
Edebe, pg 571
Editorial Everest SA, pg 572
Elkar, Euskal Liburu eta Kantuen Argitaldaria, SL, pg 573
Erein, pg 573
Eumo Editorial, pg 574
Grupo Comunicar, pg 576

Grupo Santillana de Ediciones SA, pg 576
Ibaizabal Edelvives SA, pg 577
Ediciones JJB, pg 579
Editorial Luis Vives (Edelvives), pg 580
Editorial Magisterio Espanol SA, pg 581
Editorial Marfil SA, pg 581
Editorial Moll SL, pg 582
Editorial la Muralla SA, pg 583
Oikos-Tau SA Ediciones, pg 584
Pearson Educacion S A, pg 586
Editorial Playor SA, pg 587
Editorial Miguel A Salvatella SA, pg 589
San Pablo Ediciones, pg 589
Ediciones Seyer, pg 590
Ediciones SM, pg 591
Editorial Teide SA, pg 592
Thales Sociedad Andaluza de Educacion Matematica, pg 592
Editorial Verbum SL, pg 595

Sri Lanka
M D Gunasena & Co Ltd, pg 597
Ministry of Education, pg 597

Suriname
Vaco NV Uitgeversmij, pg 599

Sweden
Ekelunds Forlag AB, pg 601
SK-Gehrmans Musikforlag AB, pg 602
Hillelforlaget, pg 603
Hans Richter Laromedel, pg 604
Liber AB, pg 604
Bokfoerlaget Naturoch Kultur, pg 604

Switzerland
Aare-Verlag, pg 607
Editions Foma SA, pg 614
Sabe AG Verlagsinstitut, pg 623
Sauerlaender AG, pg 623
Tobler Verlag, pg 626
Verlag Alexander Wild, pg 627

Taiwan, Province of China
Chien Chen Bookstore Publishing Company Ltd, pg 629
Chung Hwa Book Co Ltd, pg 629
San Min Book Co Ltd, pg 631

United Republic of Tanzania
Ben and Company Ltd, pg 633
DUP (1996) Ltd, pg 633
East African Publishing House, pg 633
Eastern Africa Publications Ltd, pg 633
General Publications Ltd, pg 633
Nyota Publishers Ltd, pg 634
Oxford University Press, pg 634
Press & Publicity Centre Ltd, pg 634
Readit Books, pg 634
Tanzania Publishing House, pg 634

Thailand
Thai Watana Panich Co, Ltd, pg 636

Togo
Editions Akpagnon, pg 636

Tunisia
Maison Tunisienne de l'Edition, pg 638

Turkey
Altin Kitaplar Yayinevi, pg 638
Arkadas Ltd, pg 639
Arkin Kitabevi, pg 639
Aydin Yayincilik, pg 639
Inkilap Publishers Ltd, pg 640
Pearson Education Turkey, pg 641

Ukraine
ASK Ltd, pg 643
Osvita, pg 643

United Kingdom
Association for Science Education, pg 650
Blackwell Science Ltd, pg 656
Boosey & Hawkes Music Publishers Ltd, pg 657
Cambridge University Press, pg 662
Child's World Education Ltd, pg 667
Colourpoint Books, pg 669
Curiad, pg 672
Educational Explorers (Publishers) Ltd, pg 677
Evans Brothers Ltd, pg 680
First & Best in Education Ltd, pg 682
Folens Ltd, pg 683
Forbes Publications Ltd, pg 683
Francis Balsom Associates, pg 684
W H Freeman & Co Ltd, pg 684
The Geographical Association, pg 686
Ginn & Co Ltd, pg 687
Graham-Cameron Publishing & Illustration, pg 688
Gwasg y Dref Wen, pg 690
HarperCollins Publishers, pg 692
Heinemann Educational Publishing, pg 694
Hodder & Stoughton Educational, pg 696
Hodder Headline Ltd, pg 696
Home Health Education Service, pg 697
LDA-Living & Learning (Cambridge) Ltd, pg 706
Learning Development Aids, pg 706
Learning Together, pg 706
Letterland International Ltd, pg 707
Lion Publishing PLC, pg 708
Macmillan Heinemann ELT, pg 710
McCrimmon Publishing Co Ltd, pg 712
National Association for the Teaching of English (NATE), pg 717
Nelson Thornes Ltd, pg 718
James Nisbet & Co Ltd, pg 719
Oxford University Press, pg 723
Prim-Ed Publishing UK Ltd, pg 730
Quartz Editions, pg 732
Reed Educational & Professional Publishing, pg 734
Sage Publications Ltd, pg 737
Schofield & Sims Ltd, pg 739
Scholastic Ltd, pg 739
Southgate Publishers, pg 743
Supportive Learning Publications, pg 746
Ward Lock Educational Co Ltd, pg 754
Wimbledon Publishing Company Ltd, pg 757

TYPE OF PUBLICATION INDEX

Uruguay
A Monteverde y Cia SA, pg 760

Uzbekistan
Izdatelstvo Uzbekistan, pg 761

Venezuela
Colegial Bolivariana CA, pg 762
Editorial Kapelusz Venezolana SA, pg 762

Yugoslavia
Republicki Zavod za Unapredivanje Vaspitanja i Obrazovanja, pg 765

Zambia
Wilfred Bwalya Chilangwa Publications, pg 766
Multimedia Zambia, pg 767
ZPC Publications, pg 767

Zimbabwe
College Press Publishers (Pvt) Ltd, pg 768
Longman Zimbabwe (Pvt) Ltd, pg 768
Zimbabwe Publishing House (Pvt) Ltd, pg 769

TEXTBOOKS - SECONDARY

Afghanistan
Ministry of Education, Department of Educational Publications, pg 1

Albania
NL SH, pg 1

Algeria
Enterprise Nationale du Livre (ENAL), pg 2

Argentina
Editorial Acme SA, pg 3
AZ Editora SA, pg 3
Cesarini Hermanos, pg 4
Ediciones Don Bosco Argentina, pg 5
Ediciones del Eclipse, pg 5
Edicial SA, pg 5
Angel Estrada y Cia SA, pg 6
Gram Editora, pg 6
Libreria Huemul SA, pg 6
Kapelusz Editora SA, pg 6
Editorial Losada SA, pg 7

Australia
AHB Publications, pg 11
Edward Arnold (Australia) Pty Ltd, pg 12
Artemis Publishing Pty Ltd, pg 12
Austed Publishing Co, pg 13
Beri Publishing, pg 14
Board of Studies, pg 15
Boinkie Publishers, pg 15
Cambridge University Press, pg 17
Candlelight Trust T/A Candlelight Farm, pg 17
Chalkface Press Pty Ltd, pg 17
China Books, pg 18
R J Cleary Publishing, pg 18
Cookery Book, pg 18
Curriculum Corporation, pg 19
Dabill Publications, pg 20
Dellasta Publishing, pg 20

TYPE OF PUBLICATION INDEX

BOOK

Department for Education & Children's Services, South Australia, pg 20
Educational Advantage, pg 21
EK Press, pg 21
Emerald City Books, pg 22
Hospitality Press Pty Ltd, pg 26
Illert Publications, pg 27
Jarrah Publications, pg 28
John Wiley & Sons Australia Ltd, pg 28
Macmillan Education Australia, pg 31
Maxwell Macmillan Publishing (Australia) Pty Ltd, pg 32
McGraw-Hill Australia Pty Ltd, pg 32
Pearson Education Australia, pg 37
Phoenix Education Pty Ltd, pg 38
Plantain Park, pg 38
Reed Educational Publishing Australia, pg 40
Scholastic Australia Pty Ltd, pg 41
Science Press, pg 41
Tarka Publishing, pg 44
Thornbill Press, pg 44
University of Queensland Press, pg 46
Wileman Publications, pg 47
Windhorse Books, pg 48
Winetitles, pg 48
Wizard Books Pty Ltd, pg 48
Woodlands Publications, pg 48

Austria

Dachs-Verlag GmbH, pg 50
Development News Ltd, pg 51
Johannes Heyn, Gert und Volkmar Zechner, pg 52
Verlag Hoelder-Pichler-Tempsky, pg 53
Niederosterreichisches Pressehaus Druck- und Verlagsgesellschaft mbH, pg 55
Oesterreichischer Gewerbeverlag GmbH, pg 56
Verlag Oldenbourg, pg 56
Osterreichischer Bundesveilag Ges.mbH, pg 57
Roetzer Druck GmbH & Co KG, pg 58
Universitaetsverlag Wagner GmbH, pg 60
Verlag Mag Wanzenbock, pg 60

Bangladesh

Bangladesh Publishers, pg 62
Mullick Bros, pg 62
The University Press Ltd, pg 62

Belarus

Kavaler Publishers, pg 63
Narodnaya Asveta, pg 63

Belgium

De Boeck et Larcier SA, pg 65
Carto BVBA, pg 65
La Charte Editions juridiques, pg 66
Editions De Boeck-Larcier SA, pg 67
Uitgeverij J van ln, pg 70
Editions Labor, pg 70
Editions Lumen Vitae ASBL, pg 71
Uitgeverij Pelckmans N V, pg 73
Uitgeverij De Sikkel NV, pg 74
Les Editions Vie ouvriere ASBL, pg 75
Wolters Plantyn Educatieve Uitgevers, pg 75

Benin

Les Editions du Flamboyant, pg 76

Bolivia

Editorial Don Bosco, pg 76

Botswana

Maskew Miller Longman, pg 77

Brazil

Livraria Francisco Alves Editora SA, pg 78
Ao Livro Tecnico Industria e Comercio Ltda, pg 78
Editora Atica SA, pg 79
Centro de Estudos Juridicosdo Para (CEJUP), pg 80
Ediouro Publicacoes, SA, pg 81
Editora Harbra Ltda, pg 84
Livro Ibero-Americano Ltda, pg 85
Waldyr Lima Editora, pg 86
Edicoes Loyola SA, pg 87
Editora Moderna Ltda, pg 88
Olho D'Agua Comercio e Servicos Editoriais Ltda, pg 88
Edit Palavra Magica, pg 89
Saraiva SA, Livreiros Editores, pg 91
Editora Scipione Ltda, pg 91
Editora Vigilia Ltda, pg 93

Bulgaria

Bulvest 2000 Ltd, pg 94
Eurasia Academic Publishers, pg 95
Gea-Libris Publishing House, pg 95
Makros 2000 - Plovdiv, pg 96
Musica Publishing House Ltd, pg 96
Pensoft Publishers, pg 97
Prosveta Publishers as, pg 97

Burundi

Editions Intore, pg 98

Cameroon

Editions Buma Kor, pg 99
Centre d'Edition et de Production pour l'Enseignement et la Recherche (CEPER), pg 99
Editions Semences Africaines, pg 99

Chile

Arrayan Editores, pg 99
Instituto Geografico Militar, pg 100

China

Anhui People's Publishing House, pg 102
Beijing Education Publishing House, pg 102
Beijing Publishing House, pg 102
Book Marketing Ltd, pg 102
Chemical Industry Press, pg 102
China Materials Management Publishing House, pg 103
Chinese Pedagogics Publishing House, pg 104
Electronics Industry Publishing House, pg 105
Foreign Language Teaching & Research Press, pg 105
Language Publishing House, pg 107
People's Education Press, pg 107
People's Fine Arts Publishing House, pg 108
Shandong Education Publishing House, pg 108
Shanghai Educational Publishing House, pg 109
Shanghai Foreign Language Education Press, pg 109
Tsinghua University Press, pg 110
Zhejiang Education Publishing House, pg 110
Zhejiang University Press, pg 110

Colombia

Ediciones Cultural Colombiana Ltda, pg 111
Kapelusz Ltda Editorial, pg 112
Editorial Libros y Libres SA, pg 112
Migema Ediciones Ltda, pg 113
Pearson Educacion de Colombia LTDA, pg 113
Editorial Santillana SA, pg 113
Editorial Voluntad SA, pg 114

The Democratic Republic of the Congo

Centre de Recherche, et Pedagogie Appliquee, pg 114
Facultes Catoliques de Kinshasa, pg 115

Costa Rica

Jose Alfonso Sandoval Nunez, pg 116
Litografia Artex, SA, pg 116
Scout Interamericana, pg 117
Editorial de la Universidad de Costa Rica, pg 117
Editorial Universidad Nacional (EUNA), pg 117

Cote d'Ivoire

Akohi Editions, pg 117
Centre d'Edition et de Diffusion Africaines, pg 117
Les Nouvelles Editions Ivoiriennes (NEI), pg 118

Croatia

ALFA dd za izdavacke, graficke i trgovacke poslove, pg 118
Skolska Knjiga, pg 120

Cuba

Pueblo y Educacion Editorial (PE), pg 121

Czech Republic

Barrister & Principal, pg 123
Nakladatelstvi Svoboda, pg 126
Svoboda Servis GmbH, pg 128
SystemConsult, pg 128

Denmark

Alinea A/S, pg 129
Forlaget alokke AS, pg 129
Dafolo Forlag, pg 131
Gyldendalske Boghandel - Nordisk Forlag A/S, pg 132
P Haase & Sons Forlag A/S, pg 132
Holkenfeldt 3, pg 133
Kaleidoscope Publishers Ltd, pg 133
Forlaget Modtryk AMBA, pg 133
Nyt Nordisk Forlag Arnold Busck A/S, pg 134
Det Schonbergske Forlag, pg 135
Wisby & Wilkens, pg 136

Dominican Republic

Pontificia Universidad Catolica Madre y Maestra, pg 136

Ecuador

Corporacion Editora Nacional, pg 137

Egypt (Arab Republic of Egypt)

Dar El Shorouk Publishing & Distributing House, pg 138
Middle East Book Centre, pg 139

El Salvador

Clasicos Roxsil Editorial SA de CV, pg 139
Editorial Universitaria de la Universidad de El Salvador, pg 139

Finland

Otava Publishing Co Ltd, pg 143
Sairaanhoitajien Koulutussaatio, pg 144
Soederstroem et Co Foerlagsaktiebolag, pg 144

France

Editions Al Liamm, pg 146
Aubanel SA, pg 149
Editions Belin, pg 150
Emgleo Breiz, pg 151
Brud Nevez, pg 152
Cepadues Editions SA, pg 153
Cle International, pg 155
Armand Colin, Editeur, pg 155
Editions Dalloz Sirey, pg 157
Decanord, pg 158
Delagrave Edition SA, pg 158
Georges-Charles Demay, pg 158
Doin Editeurs, pg 160
L'Ecole/L'Ecole des Loisirs Sarl, pg 160
Edicef - Editions Classiques d'Expression Francaise, pg 161
Editions Gammaprim, pg 166
Hachette Education, pg 167
Editions Hatier SA, pg 168
Editions Fernand Lanore Sarl, pg 172
Magnard SA, pg 174
Editions MDI (La Maison des Instituteurs), pg 175
Editions Ophrys, pg 178
Editions Roudil, pg 183
Editions Spratbrow, pg 186

Germany

ALS-Verlag GmbH, pg 193
AOL-Verlag Frohmut Menze, pg 194
Auer Verlag GmbH, pg 196
C Bange GmbH & Co KG, pg 198
Bayerischer Schulbuch-Verlag GmbH, pg 199
C C Buchners Verlag, pg 207
Cornelsen und Oxford University Press GmbH & Co, pg 211
Cornelsen Verlag GmbH & Co OHG, pg 211
Verlag Darmstaedter Blaetter Schwarz und Co, pg 212
Deutscher Taschenbuch Verlag GmbH & Co KG (dtv), pg 215
Diesterweg, Moritz Verlag, pg 216
Verlag Duerr & Kessler GmbH, pg 219
Ferd Dummler's Verlag, pg 227
Festo Didactic GmbH & Co, pg 227
Friedrich Kiehl Verlag GmbH, pg 230
Betriebswirtschaftlicher Verlag Dr Th Gabler GmbH, pg 231
Lehrmittelverlag Wilhelm Hagemann GmbH, pg 236

PUBLISHERS

Verlag Handwerk und Technik GmbH, pg 237
Max Hieber KG, pg 240
Horlemann Verlag, pg 243
Impuls-Theater-Verlag, pg 244
Ernst Klett Verlag GmbH, pg 250
Konkordia Verlag GmbH, pg 252
Lahn-Verlag GmbH, pg 255
Verlag Leske plus Budrich GmbH, pg 257
Hildegard Liebaug-Dartmann, pg 258
Robert Lienau GmbH & Co KG, pg 258
J Lindauer Verlag, pg 258
Lucius & Lucius Verlagsgesellschaft mbH, pg 259
Manz G J Verlag und Druckerel, pg 261
Militzke Verlag, pg 264
Karl Heinrich Moeseler Verlag, pg 264
Verlag Sigrid Persen, pg 272
Philipp Reclam Jun Verlag GmbH, pg 273
Quelle und Meyer Verlag GmbH & Co, pg 276
Verlag an der Ruhr GmbH, pg 281
Schott Musik International GmbH & Co KG, pg 284
B G Teubner GmbH, pg 292
Tipress Dienstleistungen fur das Verlagswesen GmbH, pg 294
Turkischer Schulbuchverlag Onel Cengiz, pg 295
Voggenreiter-Verlag, pg 299
Volk und Wissen Verlag GmbH & Co, pg 299
Westermann Schulbuchverlag GmbH, pg 302
Dr Dieter Winkler, pg 303

Ghana

Afram Publications (Ghana) Ltd, pg 306
Anowuo Educational Publications, pg 306
Asempa Publishers, pg 306
Black Mask Ltd, pg 306
Educational Press & Manufacturers Ltd, pg 307
EPP Books Services, pg 307
Frank Publishing Ltd, pg 307
Ghana Publishing Corporation, pg 307
Sam Woode Ltd, pg 308
Sedco Publishing Ltd, pg 308
Waterville Publishing House, pg 308
World Literature Project, pg 308

Greece

Athina, Mary Mavrogiannis, pg 309
Chrysi Penna - Golden Pen Books, pg 309
Ilias Kambanas Publishing Organization, SA, pg 312
Nakas Music House, pg 313
Patakis Publishers, pg 314
Nikolas I Rossi, pg 314

Guadeloupe

Librairie Generale JASOR, pg 316

Guatemala

Fundacion para la Cultura y el Desarrollo, pg 316

Haiti

Editions Caraiibes SA, pg 317

Hong Kong

Breakthrough Ltd - Breakthrough Publishers, pg 318
Federal Publications Ltd, pg 319
Joint Publishing (HK) Co Ltd, pg 320
Lea Publications Ltd, pg 320
Ling Kee Publishing Group, pg 320
Macmillan Publishers (China) Ltd, pg 321
Shanghai Book Co Ltd, pg 321
Vision Pub Co Ltd, pg 322
Witman Publishing Co (HK) Ltd, pg 322

Hungary

Corvina Books Ltd, pg 323
Mueszaki Koenyvkiado Ltd, pg 325
Nemzeti Tankoenyvkiado, pg 326
Novorg Kiado, pg 326

Iceland

Almenna Bokafelagid, pg 327
Mal og menning, pg 328

India

Addison-Wesley (Singapore) Pte Ltd, pg 329
Ambar Prakashan, pg 330
B l Publications Pvt Ltd, pg 331
The Bangalore Printing & Publishing Co Ltd, pg 332
Bani Mandir, Book-Sellers, Publishers & Educational Suppliers, pg 332
Bhawan Book Service, Publishers & Distributors, pg 333
Chowkhamba Sanskrit Series Office, pg 335
Dastane Ramchandra & Co, pg 335
Frank Brothers & Co (Publishers) Ltd, pg 337
General Book Depot, pg 337
General Printers & Publishers, pg 337
Arnold Heinman Publishers (India) Pvt Ltd, pg 338
Hindi Pracharak Sansthan, pg 338
Konark Publishers, Pvt, Ltd, pg 341
Laxmi Publications Pvt Ltd, pg 341
National Council of Educational Research & Training, Publication Department, pg 344
Oxford University Press, pg 345
Paico Publishing House, pg 345
Pitambar Publishing Co (P) Ltd, pg 346
Rajesh Publications, pg 347
Sasta Sahitya Mandal, pg 349
Scientific Book Agency, pg 349
Shiksha Bharati, pg 350
Somaiya Publications Pvt Ltd, pg 350
Sree Rama Publishers, pg 351
Sultan Chand & Sons Pvt Ltd, pg 351
DB Taraporevala Sons & Co Pvt Ltd, pg 351
A H Wheeler & Co Ltd, pg 353

Indonesia

PT Pustaka Antara Publishing & Printing, pg 354
Bina Rena Pariwara, pg 354
PT BPK Gunung Mulia, pg 355
PT Pradnya Paramita, pg 357

Ireland

An Gum, pg 358
C J Fallon, pg 360
Gill & Macmillan Ltd, pg 361
Veritas Co Ltd, pg 364

Israel

Am Oved Publishers Ltd, pg 365
Karni Publishers Ltd, pg 369
Kernerman Publishing Ltd, pg 369
Kiryat Sefer, pg 369
Ma'alot Publishing Company Ltd, pg 370
MAP-Mapping & Publishing Ltd, pg 370
Modan Publishers Ltd, pg 371
Rubin Mass Ltd, pg 371
University Publishing Projects Ltd, pg 373
Yad Vashem - The Holocaust Martyrs' & Heroes' Remembrance Authority, pg 373

Italy

De Agostini Scolastica, pg 375
Archimede Edizioni, pg 376
Bianco, pg 377
Bonacci editore, pg 378
Nuova Casa Editrice Licinio Cappelli GEM srl, pg 379
Casa Editrice Giuseppe Principato Spa, pg 380
Casa Editrice Libraria Ulrico Hoepli SpA, pg 380
Cideb Editrice SRL, pg 381
Citta Nuova Editrice, pg 382
Edizioni Cremonese SRL, pg 383
D'Anna, pg 383
Edizioni Dehoniane Bologna (EDB), pg 384
Editrice Edisco, pg 386
Editrice la Scuola SpA, pg 386
Garzanti Editore, pg 390
Istituto Geografico de Agostini SpA, pg 390
Ghisetti e Corvi Editori SpA, pg 390
Giunti (Gruppo Editoriale), pg 390
Gius Laterza e Figli SpA, pg 391
Gruppo Calderini Edagricole, pg 392
Loescher Editore SRL, pg 396
Editrice Massimo SAS di Crespi Cesare e C, pg 398
Minerva Italica SpA, pg 399
Arnoldo Mondadori Editore SpA, pg 399
La Nuova Italia Editrice SpA, pg 401
Paravia Bruno Mondadori Editori, pg 402
Principato, pg 404
RCS Libri SpA, pg 405
Editrice San Marco SRL, pg 406
Societa Editrice Internazionale - SEI, pg 408
Gruppo Editoriale Le Stelle SpA, pg 409
Societa Editrice Vannini, pg 411
Zanichelli Editore SpA, pg 412

Jamaica

Carlong Publishers (Caribbean) Ltd, pg 412
Ian Randle Publishers Ltd, pg 413
West Indies Publishing Ltd, pg 414

Japan

Chikuma Shobo Publishing Co Ltd, pg 415
Chuo-Tosho Co Ltd, pg 415
Dainippon Tosho Publishing Co, Ltd, pg 416
Eichosha Company Ltd, pg 416

TYPE OF PUBLICATION INDEX

Gakken Co Ltd, pg 416
Kaitakusha, pg 419
Nihon-Bunkyo Shuppan (Japan Educational Publishing Co Ltd), pg 422
Ongaku No Tomo Sha Corporation, pg 423
Sanshusha Publishing Co, Ltd, pg 424
Shimizu-Shoin, pg 425
Shingakusha Co Ltd, pg 425
Teikoku-Shoin Co Ltd, pg 427
Thomson Learning, pg 427
Tokyo Shoseki Co Ltd, pg 427
Yamaguchi Shoten, pg 429

Jordan

Jordan House for Publication, pg 430

Kenya

Africa Book Services (EA) Ltd, pg 430
Dhillon Publishers Ltd, Paa Crescent, pg 431
Focus Publications Ltd, pg 431
Foundation Books, pg 431
Heinemann Kenya Limited (EAEP), pg 431
Kenya Literature Bureau, pg 432
The Jomo Kenyatta Foundation, pg 432
Phoenix Publishers, pg 433
Shirikon Publishers, pg 433
Transafrica Press, pg 433
Gideon S Were Press, pg 434

Republic of Korea

Cheong-mun-gag Publishing Co, pg 435
Koreaone Press Inc, pg 438
Kyohaksa Publishing Co Ltd, pg 438
Moon Jin Media Co Ltd, pg 438
Sohaksa, pg 440

Latvia

Lielvards Ltd, pg 442
Zvaigzne ABC Publishers, Ltd, pg 442

Lebanon

Librairie Orientale sal, pg 443

Lesotho

Mazenod Book Centre, pg 444
Saint Michael's Mission, pg 444

Lithuania

Alma Littera, pg 445
Baltos Lankos, pg 445
Margi Rastai Publishers, pg 446
Sviesa Publishers, pg 446
Svietimo ir mokslo ministerijos Leidybos centras, pg 446
TEV Leidykla, pg 446
Tyto Alba Publishers, pg 446

Luxembourg

Editions APESS ASBL, pg 447
Editions Emile Borschette, pg 447
Editions Promoculture, pg 448
Service Central des Imprimes et des Fournitures de Bureau de l'Etat, pg 448

Macau

Instituto Portugues Oriente, pg 448
Universidadede de Macau, Centro de Publicacoes, pg 448

855

TYPE OF PUBLICATION INDEX   BOOK

The Former Yugoslav Republic of Macedonia
St Clement of Ohrid National & University Library, pg 449

Madagascar
Centre National de Production de Materiel Didactique (CNAPMAD), pg 450
Foibe Filan-Kevitry NY Mpampianatra (FOFIPA), pg 450
Librarie Mixte, pg 450
Societe Malgache d'Edition, pg 450
Imprimerie Takariva, pg 450
Trano Printy Fiangonana Loterana Malagasy (TPFLM)-(Imprimerie Lutherienne), pg 450

Malawi
Dzuka Publishing Company Ltd, pg 450

Malaysia
Darulfikir, pg 451
Dewan Bahasa dan Pustaka, pg 451
Federal Publications Sdn Bhd, pg 452
FEP International Sdn Bhd, pg 452
Mahir Publications Sdn Bhd, pg 452
Pearson Education, pg 453
Penerbit Fajar Bakti Sdn Bhd, pg 454
Penerbit Jayatinta Sdn Bhd, pg 454
Penerbitan Tinta, pg 454
Pustaka Cipta Sdn Bhd, pg 454
Pustaka Delta Pelajaran Sdn Bhd, pg 454
Times Educational Co Sdn Bhd, pg 455
Tropical Press Sdn Bhd, pg 455

Mali
EDIM SA, pg 455

Malta
Media Centre, pg 456

Mauritius
Editions Capucines, pg 457
Editions de l'Ocean Indien Ltd, pg 457
EDITIONS Le Printemps, pg 457

Mexico
Edamex SA de CV, pg 460
Editorial Esfinge SA de CV, pg 460
Fernandez Editores SA de CV, pg 461
Fondo de Cultura Economica, pg 461
Grupo Editorial Iberoamerica, SA de CV, pg 461
Editorial Jus SA de CV, pg 462
Ediciones Larousse SA de CV, pg 462
Editorial Limusa SA de CV, pg 463
Nova Grupo Editorial SA de CV, pg 464
Palabra Ediciones Verlagsgesellschaft mbH, pg 465
Editorial Patria SA de CV, pg 465
Pearson Educacion de Mexico, SA de CV, pg 465
Editorial Progreso SA de C V, pg 466
Ediciones Promesa, SA de CV, pg 466
Publicaciones Cultural SA de CV, pg 466
Sistemas Tecnicos de Edicion SA de CV, pg 467
Editorial Trillas SA de CV, pg 467

Republic of Moldova
Lumina Publishing House, pg 468

Morocco
Cabinet Conseil CCMLA, pg 469
Dar Nachr Al Maarifa Pour L'Edition et La Distribution, pg 469

Mozambique
Empresa Moderna Lda, pg 470
Editora Minerva Central, pg 470

Namibia
Bureau for Indigenous Languages, pg 471

Nepal
International Standards Books & Periodicals (P) Ltd, pg 471

Netherlands
Educatieve Partners Nederland bv, pg 476
Katholieke Bijbelstichting, pg 479
LCG Malmberg BV, pg 480
Uitgeverij Lemma BV, pg 480
Pearson Education Netherlands, pg 482
BV Uitgeverij en Boekhandel W J Thieme & Cie, pg 485
Twente University Press, pg 485
Wolters-Noordhoff B V, pg 487

New Zealand
ABA Books, pg 488
Aoraki Press Ltd, pg 488
The Caxton Press, pg 490
Wendy Crane Books, pg 490
Dunmore Press Ltd, pg 490
ESA Publications (NZ) Ltd, pg 490
Eton Press (Auckland) Ltd, pg 490
Huia Publishers, pg 492
Learning Guides (Writers & Publishers Ltd), pg 492
Macmillan Publishers New Zealand Ltd, pg 493
New House Publishers Ltd, pg 493
Oxford University Press, pg 494
Pearson Education, pg 494
Nelson Price Milburn Ltd, pg 494
Reed Publishing (NZ) Ltd, pg 495
Resource Books Ltd, pg 495

Nigeria
African Universities Press, pg 497
Africana-FEP Publishers Ltd, pg 498
Alliance West African Publishers & Co, pg 498
Aromolaran Publishing Co Ltd, pg 498
Cross Continent Press Ltd, pg 498
CSS Bookshops, Agency & Publishing Division, pg 498
Educational Research & Study Group, pg 499
Ethiope Publishing Corporation, pg 499
Evans Brothers (Nigeria Publishers) Ltd, pg 499
Fourth Dimension Publishing Co Ltd, pg 499
JAD Publishers Ltd, pg 500
Kola Sanya Publishing Enterprise, pg 500
Longman Nigeria Plc, pg 500
New Africa Publishing Company Ltd, pg 500
New Era Publishers, pg 500
Northern Nigerian Publishing Co Ltd, pg 500
Nwamife Publishers Ltd, pg 500
Onibon-Oje Publishers, pg 501
Riverside Communications, pg 501
University Publishing Co, pg 502
Vantage Publishers International Ltd, pg 502
West African Book Publishers Ltd, pg 502

Norway
H Aschehoug & Co (W Nygaard) A/S, pg 502
J W Eides Forlag A/S, pg 503
Forlaget Fag og Kultur, pg 503
Gyldendal Norsk Forlag A/S, pg 503
NKI Forlaget, pg 504
Universitetsforlaget, pg 505
Vett & Viten AS, pg 505

Pakistan
Sheikh Shaukat Ali & Sons, pg 506
The Book House, pg 506
Islamic Book Centre, pg 507
Jang Publishers, pg 507
Maqbool Academy, pg 508

Peru
Ediciones Brown SA, pg 511
Asociacion Editorial Bruno, pg 511
Tarea Asociacion de Publicaciones Educativas, pg 511
Tassorello, SA, pg 511

Philippines
Abiva Publishing House Inc, pg 512
Ateneo de Manila University Press, pg 512
Bookman Printing & Publishing House Inc, pg 512
Bookmark Inc, pg 512
J C Palabay Enterprises, pg 513
Marren Publishing House, Inc, pg 513
National Book Store Inc, pg 514
Our Lady of Manaoag Publisher, pg 514
Rex Bookstores & Publishers, pg 514
Saint Mary's Publishing Corp, pg 515
Salesiana Publishers Inc, pg 515
SIBS Publishing House Inc, pg 515
UST Publishing House, pg 515

Poland
Impuls, pg 517
Instytut Meteorologii i Gospodarki Wodnej, pg 518
Oficyna Wydawnicza Politechniki Wroclawskiej, pg 519
PZWL Wydawnictwo Lekarskie Ltd, pg 519
Res Polona, pg 519
Wydawnictwa Naukowo-Techniczne, pg 521
Wydawnictwa Szkolne i Pedagogiczne (Polish Educational Publishers-WSiP), pg 521

Portugal
Livraria Arnado Lda, pg 522
Constancia Editores, SA, pg 524
Didactica Editora, pg 524
Dinalivro, pg 524
Europress Editores e Distribuidores de Publicacoes Lda, pg 525
Livraria Minerva Editora, pg 526
Lua Viajante-Edicao e Distribuicao de Livros e Material Audiovisual, Lda, pg 527
McGraw-Hill Editora de Portugal, pg 527
Editorial O Livro Lda, pg 528
Platano Editora SA, pg 528
Porto Editora Lda, pg 528
Editorial Presenca, pg 528
Editora Replicacao Lda, pg 529
Texto Editora, pg 529

Puerto Rico
Editorial Cultural Inc, pg 530
McGraw-Hill Intermericana del Caribe, Inc, pg 530

Romania
Editora All, pg 531
Editura Clusium, Casa de Editura Atlas-Clusium SRL, pg 532
Editura Didactica si Pedagogica, pg 532
Editura Militara, pg 534
Editura Niculescu, pg 534
Polirom Verlag, pg 535

Russian Federation
Airis Press, pg 537
Fizmatlit Publishing Co, pg 538
Izdatelstvo Mir, pg 540
Izdatelstvo Muzyka, pg 540
Okoshko Ltd Publishers (Izdatelstvo), pg 541
Izdatelstvo Prosveshchenie, pg 541

Senegal
Les Nouvelles Editions Africaines du Senegal NEAS, pg 544

Sierra Leone
Njala Educational Publishing Centre, pg 544

Singapore
Chopsons Pte Ltd, pg 545
Federal Publications (S) Pte Ltd, pg 546
Hillview Publications Pte Ltd, pg 546
Shing Lee Group Publishers, pg 548

Slovakia
Priroda, pg 550
Slovenske pedagogicke nakladateistvo, pg 550
Ustav informacii a prognoz skolstva mladeze a telovychovy, pg 551

Slovenia
Zalozba Mihelac d o o, pg 552
Zalozba Obzorja d d Maribor, pg 552

South Africa
Educum Publishers Ltd, pg 554
Heinemann Educational Publishers Southern Africa, pg 555
Heinemann Publishers (Pty) Ltd, pg 555
Ivy Publications, pg 555
Maskew Miller Longman, pg 557
Nasou Via Afrika, pg 557
Publitoria Publishers, pg 558

PUBLISHERS   TYPE OF PUBLICATION INDEX

Ravan Press (Pty) Ltd, pg 558
Shuter & Shooter (Pty) Ltd, pg 559
University Publishers & Booksellers (Pty) Ltd, pg 560
Vivlia Publishers & Booksellers, pg 560

Spain

Editorial Aguaclara, pg 562
Ediciones Akal SA, pg 562
Ediciones Alfar SA, pg 562
Ediciones Anaya SA, pg 563
Anaya Educacion, pg 563
Editorial Bruno, pg 566
Editorial Casals SA, pg 566
Editorial Claret SA, pg 568
Diseno Editorial SA, pg 570
Editorial Donostiarra SA, pg 570
Edebe, pg 571
Editorial Everest SA, pg 572
Elkar, Euskal Liburu eta Kantuen Argitaldaria, SL, pg 573
Erein, pg 573
Eumo Editorial, pg 574
Grupo Comunicar, pg 576
Grupo Santillana de Ediciones SA, pg 576
Hercules de Ediciones, SA, pg 577
Editorial Herder SA, pg 577
Ibaizabal Edelvives SA, pg 577
Ediciones Istmo SA, pg 579
Ediciones JJB, pg 579
Editorial Luis Vives (Edelvives), pg 580
Editorial Magisterio Espanol SA, pg 581
Editorial Marfil SA, pg 581
McGraw-Hill Iberic/Brazil Group, pg 581
Editorial Moll SL, pg 582
Editorial la Muralla SA, pg 583
Naque Editora, pg 583
Oikos-Tau SA Ediciones, pg 584
Editorial Paidotribo SL, pg 585
Editorial Paraninfo SA, pg 586
Pearson Educacion S A, pg 586
Editorial Playor SA, pg 587
Editorial Reverte SA, pg 588
San Pablo Ediciones, pg 589
Ediciones Seyer, pg 590
Ediciones SM, pg 591
Editorial Teide SA, pg 592
Editorial Augusto E Pila Telena SL, pg 592
Thales Sociedad Andaluza de Educacon Matematica, pg 592
Gregorio del Toro Editor, pg 593
Editorial Trivium, SA, pg 593
Editorial Verbum SL, pg 595

Sri Lanka

M D Gunasena & Co Ltd, pg 597
Ministry of Education, pg 597
Warna Publishers, pg 598

Sudan

Khartoum University Press, pg 598

Suriname

Vaco NV Uitgeversmij, pg 599

Sweden

Akademiforlaget Goteborgslitteratur, pg 600
Ekelunds Forlag AB, pg 601
Folkuniversitetets foerlag, pg 602
SK-Gehrmans Musikforlag AB, pg 602
Hans Richter Laromedel, pg 604
Liber AB, pg 604
Studentlitteratur AB, pg 606

Switzerland

Editions Foma SA, pg 614
Paul Haupt Berne, pg 615
Editions du Panorama, pg 621
Editions Payot Lausanne, pg 621
Editions Pro Schola, pg 622
Sabe AG Verlagsinstitut, pg 623
Sauerlaender AG, pg 623
Tobler Verlag, pg 626
Der Universitatsverlag Freiburg, pg 626
Verlag Alexander Wild, pg 627

Taiwan, Province of China

Chien Chen Bookstore Publishing Company Ltd, pg 629
Chung Hwa Book Co Ltd, pg 629
Farseeing Publishing Company Ltd, pg 630
Lead Wave Publishing Company Ltd, pg 631
San Min Book Co Ltd, pg 631
World Book Co Ltd, pg 632
Youth Cultural Publishing Co, pg 632

United Republic of Tanzania

Ben and Company Ltd, pg 633
DUP (1996) Ltd, pg 633
East African Publishing House, pg 633
Eastern Africa Publications Ltd, pg 633
General Publications Ltd, pg 633
Ndanda Mission Press, pg 634
Nyota Publishers Ltd, pg 634
Oxford University Press, pg 634
Press & Publicity Centre Ltd, pg 634
Readit Books, pg 634
Tanzania Publishing House, pg 634

Thailand

Bannakit Trading, pg 635
Thai Watana Panich Co, Ltd, pg 636

Togo

Editions Akpagnon, pg 636
Les Nouvelles Editions Africaines du TOGO (NEA-TOGO), pg 636

Tunisia

Ceres Editions, pg 637
Maison d'Edition Mohamed Ali Hammi, pg 638
Maison Tunisienne de l'Edition, pg 638

Turkey

Altin Kitaplar Yayinevi, pg 638
Arkadas Ltd, pg 639
Arkin Kitabevi, pg 639
Inkilap Publishers Ltd, pg 640
Pearson Education Turkey, pg 641

Uganda

Roce (Consultants) Ltd, pg 642

Ukraine

ASK Ltd, pg 643
Osvita, pg 643

United Kingdom

Association for Science Education, pg 650
BBC Worldwide Publishers, pg 653
Blackwell Science Ltd, pg 656

Boosey & Hawkes Music Publishers Ltd, pg 657
BPS Books (British Psychological Society), pg 658
Cambridge University Press, pg 662
Cassell & Co, pg 664
Causeway Press Ltd, pg 665
Cavendish Publishing Ltd, pg 665
Child's World Education Ltd, pg 667
Colourpoint Books, pg 669
Computer Step, pg 670
CTBI Publications, pg 672
Curiad, pg 672
Educational Explorers (Publishers) Ltd, pg 677
European Schoolbooks Ltd, pg 680
Evans Brothers Ltd, pg 680
First & Best in Education Ltd, pg 682
Folens Ltd, pg 683
Forbes Publications Ltd, pg 683
W H Freeman & Co Ltd, pg 684
The Geographical Association, pg 686
Gomer Press (J D Lewis & Sons Ltd), pg 688
Graham-Cameron Publishing & Illustration, pg 688
HarperCollins Publishers, pg 692
Heinemann Educational Publishing, pg 694
Hobsons, pg 696
Hodder & Stoughton Educational, pg 696
Hodder Headline Ltd, pg 696
Home Health Education Service, pg 697
Hugo's Language Books Ltd, pg 697
Institute of Physics Publishing, pg 700
LDA-Living & Learning (Cambridge) Ltd, pg 706
Learning Development Aids, pg 706
Macmillan Heinemann ELT, pg 710
McCrimmon Publishing Co Ltd, pg 712
McGraw-Hill Publishing Company, pg 712
John Murray (Publishers) Ltd, pg 716
National Association for the Teaching of English (NATE), pg 717
Nelson Thornes Ltd, pg 718
James Nisbet & Co Ltd, pg 719
The Oleander Press, pg 721
Osborne Books Ltd, pg 722
Oxford University Press, pg 723
Packard Publishing Ltd, pg 723
PC Publishing, pg 725
Portland Press Ltd, pg 730
Reed Educational & Professional Publishing, pg 734
Sage Publications Ltd, pg 737
Schofield & Sims Ltd, pg 739
Sigma Press, pg 742
Stokesby House Publications, pg 745
University of Wales Press, pg 751
Verulam Publishing Ltd, pg 753
Ward Lock Educational Co Ltd, pg 754
Wimbledon Publishing Company Ltd, pg 757
Windhorse Publications, pg 757

Uruguay

Ediciones de Juan Darien, pg 760
EQ Opciones en Educacion, pg 760
La Flor del Itapebi, pg 760

A Monteverde y Cia SA, pg 760
Vinten Editor, pg 761

Uzbekistan

Izdatelstvo Uzbekistan, pg 761

Venezuela

Alfadil Ediciones, pg 761
Colegial Bolivariana CA, pg 762
Editorial Kapelusz Venezolana SA, pg 762

Yugoslavia

Republicki Zavod za Unapredivanje Vaspitanja i Obrazovanja, pg 765

Zambia

Wilfred Bwalya Chilangwa Publications, pg 766
Lundula Publishing House, pg 766
Multimedia Zambia, pg 767
ZPC Publications, pg 767

Zimbabwe

Academic Books Pvt Ltd, pg 767
College Press Publishers (Pvt) Ltd, pg 768
Longman Zimbabwe (Pvt) Ltd, pg 768
Mercury Press Pvt Ltd, pg 769
Zimbabwe Publishing House (Pvt) Ltd, pg 769

TEXTBOOKS - COLLEGE

Afghanistan

Government Press, pg 1

Albania

NL SH, pg 1

Algeria

Les Editions Algeriennes En-Nahdha, pg 2

Argentina

Abeledo-Perrot SAE e l, pg 2
Editorial Abril SA, pg 2
Editorial Acme SA, pg 3
Alianza Editorial de Argentina SA, pg 3
Editorial Astrea de Alfredo y Ricardo Depalma SRL, pg 3
Beatriz Viterbo Editora, pg 4
Editorial Cangallo SACI, pg 4
Cesarini Hermanos, pg 4
Editorial Claridad SA, pg 4
Club de Lectores, pg 4
Libreria del Colegio SA, pg 4
Depalma SRL, pg 5
Ediciones del Eclipse, pg 5
Edicial SA, pg 5
Editorial Idearium de la Universidad de Mendoza (EDIUM), pg 5
Editorial Hemisferio Sur SA, pg 6
Libreria Huemul SA, pg 6
Inter-Medica, pg 6
Juris Editorial, pg 6
Kapelusz Editora SA, pg 6
Editorial Medica, Panamericana SA, pg 7
Editorial Paidos SAICF, pg 8
Editorial Plus Ultra SA, pg 8
Editorial Stella, pg 9
Tipografica Editora Argentina, pg 9
Editoria Universitaria de la Patagonia, pg 9

TYPE OF PUBLICATION INDEX — BOOK

Victor P de Zavalia SA, pg 10
Editorial Zeus SRL, pg 10

Australia

AHB Publications, pg 11
Edward Arnold (Australia) Pty Ltd, pg 12
Artemis Publishing Pty Ltd, pg 12
Ausmed Publications Pty Ltd, pg 12
Australasian Medical Publishing Company Ltd (AMPCO), pg 13
Australian Film Television & Radio School, pg 13
Australian Scholarly Publishing, pg 14
Beri Publishing, pg 14
Bio Concepts Publishing, pg 15
Blackwell Science Pty Ltd, pg 15
Boombana Publications, pg 16
Butterworths Australia Ltd, pg 16
Cambridge University Press, pg 17
China Books, pg 18
Cookery Book, pg 18
Crystal Publishing, pg 19
Dellasta Publishing, pg 20
EK Press, pg 21
The Federation Press, pg 22
Kerri Hamer, pg 25
H&H Publishing, pg 25
Harcourt Australia Pty Ltd, pg 25
Hospitality Books, pg 26
Hospitality Press Pty Ltd, pg 26
Illert Publications, pg 27
Institute of Aboriginal Development (IAD Press), pg 28
James Nicholas Publishers Pty Ltd, pg 28
Jarrah Publications, pg 28
John Wiley & Sons Australia Ltd, pg 28
Landarc Publications, pg 29
Law Book Co Information Services, pg 29
MacLennan & Petty Pty Ltd, pg 31
Macmillan Education Australia, pg 31
Maxwell Macmillan Publishing (Australia) Pty Ltd, pg 32
McGraw-Hill Australia Pty Ltd, pg 32
OTEN (Open Training & Education Network), pg 36
Pearson Education Australia, pg 37
Plantain Park, pg 38
Pluto Press Australia, pg 38
Pollitecon Publications, pg 38
Press for Success, pg 38
Quakers Hill Press, pg 39
Regency Publishing, pg 40
RMIT Publishing, pg 41
Rumsby Scientific Publishing, pg 41
Frank Shepherd, pg 42
Spaniel Books, pg 43
Strucmech Publishing, pg 43
Tarka Publishing, pg 44
Tertiary Press, pg 44
University of New South Wales Press Ltd, pg 46
University of Queensland Press, pg 46
University of Western Australia Press, pg 46
Vista Publications, pg 47
Wileman Publications, pg 47
Windhorse Books, pg 48
Winetitles, pg 48
Woodlands Publications, pg 48

Austria

Boehlau Verlag GmbH & Co KG, pg 50
Buchhandlung WUV Dolmetsch, pg 50
Development News Ltd, pg 51
Fassbaender Verlag, pg 51
Georg Fromme und Co, pg 52
Johannes Heyn, Gert und Volkmar Zechner, pg 52
Verlag Hoelder-Pichler-Tempsky, pg 53
Ibera VerlagsgesmbH, pg 53
Inn-Verlag, DrieBlein & Co KG, pg 53
Leopold Stocker Verlag, pg 54
Leykam Buchverlagsges mbH, pg 54
Manz'sche Verlags- und Universitaetsbuchhandlung, pg 54
Niederosterreichisches Pressehaus Druck- und Verlagsgesellschaft mbH, pg 55
Oesterreichischer Bundesverlag GmbH, pg 56
Verlag Oldenbourg, pg 56
Osterreichischer Bundesverlag Ges.mbh, pg 57
Paul Sappl, Schulbuch- und Lehrmittelverlag, pg 58
Springer-Verlag Wien, pg 59
Trauner Verlag, pg 59
Tyrolia Verlagsanstalt GmbH, pg 59
Universitaetsverlag Wagner GmbH, pg 60
WUV/Facultas Universitaetsverlag, pg 61

Bangladesh

Bangladesh Publishers, pg 62
The University Press Ltd, pg 62

Belarus

Publishing Center of Belarus State University, pg 63

Belgium

Academia Press, pg 64
Aurelia Books PVBA, pg 64
De Boeck et Larcier SA, pg 65
Eteblissements Emile Bruylant SA, pg 65
Campinia Media VZW, pg 65
La Charte Editions juridiques, pg 66
Contact NV, pg 67
Cremers (Schoollandkaarten) PVBA, pg 67
Editions De Boeck-Larcier SA, pg 67
Diligentia-Uitgeverij, pg 68
Infoboek NV, pg 69
Uitgeverij J van In, pg 70
Editions Labor, pg 70
Nauwelaerts Edition SA, pg 72
Uitgeverij Peeters Leuven (Belgie), pg 72
Uitgeverij Pelckmans N V, pg 73
Presses Universitaires de Bruxelles ASBL, pg 73
Uitgeverij De Sikkel NV, pg 74
Uitgeverij De Garve, pg 75
Les Editions Vie ouvriere ASBL, pg 75
Wolters Plantyn Educatieve Uitgevers, pg 75

Bolivia

Gisbert y Cia SA, pg 76

Bosnia and Herzegovina

Svjetlost, pg 77

Brazil

Aide Editora e Comercio de Livros Ltda, pg 78
Editora Alfa Omega Ltda, pg 78
Livraria Francisco Alves Editora SA, pg 78
Ao Livro Tecnico Industria e Comercio Ltda, pg 78
Ars Poetica Editora Ltda, pg 79
ARTMED, pg 79
Editora Atica SA, pg 79
Editora Atlas SA, pg 79
Bloch Editores SA, pg 79
Editora Edgard Blucher Ltda, pg 80
Instituto Brasileiro de Edicoes Pedagogicas (IBEP), pg 80
Editora Campus Ltda, pg 80
Alzira Chagas Carpigiani, pg 80
Centro de Estudos Juridicosdo Para (CEJUP), pg 80
CEPA - Centro Editor de Psicologia Aplicada Ltda, pg 81
Conquista, Empresa de Publicacoes Ltda, pg 81
Editora Contexto (Editora Pinsky Ltda), pg 81
Livraria Duas Cidades Ltda, pg 81
Dumara Distribuidora de Publicacoes Ltda, pg 81
E P U Editora Pedagogica e Universitaria Ltd, pg 81
Ediouro Publicacoes, SA, pg 81
Edipro-Edicoes Profissionais Ltda, pg 81
Editora Companhia das Letras/Editora Schwarcz Ltda, pg 82
Companhia Editora Forense, pg 82
Cia Editora Nacional, pg 82
EDUC - Editora da PUC-SP, pg 82
Empresa Brasileira de Pesquisa Agropecaria, pg 83
Editora FCO Ltda, pg 83
Livraria Martins Fontes Editora Ltda, pg 83
Livraria Freitas Bastos Editora SA, pg 83
Editora FTD SA, pg 83
Fundacao de Assistencia ao Estudante, pg 84
Editora Guanabara Koogan SA, pg 84
Editora Harbra Ltda, pg 84
Hemus Editora Ltda, pg 85
Livro Ibero-Americano Ltda, pg 85
Imago Editora Importacao e Exportacao Ltda, pg 85
Waldyr Lima Editora, pg 86
LISA (Livros Irradiantes SA), pg 86
Edicoes Loyola SA, pg 87
LTC-Livros Tecnicos e Cientificos Editora S/A, pg 87
Editora Lucre Comercio e Representacoes, pg 87
Madras Editora, pg 87
Makron Books do Brasil Editora Ltda, pg 87
Editora Manole Ltda, pg 87
Medicina Panamericana Editora Do Brasil Ltda, pg 87
Medsi - Editora Medica e Cientifica Ltda, pg 87
Editora Mercado Aberto Ltda, pg 88
Editora Moderna Ltda, pg 88
Olho D'Agua Comercio e Servicos Editoriais Ltda, pg 88
Editora Ortiz SA, pg 89
Pearson Education Do Brasil, pg 89
Livraria Pioneira Editora/Enio Matheus Guazzelli e Cia Ltd, pg 89
Qualitymark Editora Ltda, pg 90
Editora Revan Ltda, pg 90
Saraiva SA, Livreiros Editores, pg 91
Livraria Sulina Editora, pg 92
Edicoes Tabajara, pg 92
Tempus Editores, pg 92
34 Literatura S/C Ltda, pg 92
Editora da Universidade de Sao Paulo, pg 93
Editora Universidade Federal do Rio de Janeiro, pg 93
Fundacao Getulio Vargas, pg 93
Jorge Zahar Editor, pg 93

Bulgaria

Bulvest 2000 Ltd, pg 94
Darzhavno Izdatelstvo Zemizdat, pg 95
Dolphin Press Group Ltd, pg 95
Eurasia Academic Publishers, pg 95
Gea-Libris Publishing House, pg 95
Heron Press Publishing House, pg 96
Lettera, pg 96
Makros 2000 - Plovdiv, pg 96
MATEX, pg 96
Musica Publishing House Ltd, pg 96
Nov Covek Publishing House, pg 97
Pensoft Publishers, pg 97
Prosveta Publishers as, pg 97
Slavena, pg 98
Technica, pg 98
WTU Todor Kableskov, pg 98

Cameroon

Centre d'Edition et de Production pour l'Enseignement et la Recherche (CEPER), pg 99

Chile

Arrayan Editores, pg 99
Editorial Andres Bello/Editorial Juridica de Chile, pg 100
Dolmen Ediciones SA, pg 100
Edeval (Universidad de Valparaiso), pg 100
Instituto Geografico Militar, pg 100
Pontificia Universidad Catolica de Chile, pg 101
Editorial Universitaria SA, pg 101
Ediciones Universitarias de Valparaiso, pg 101

China

Anhui People's Publishing House, pg 102
Aviation Industry Press, pg 102
Beijing University Press, pg 102
Chemical Industry Press, pg 102
China Film Press, pg 103
China Forestry Publishing House, pg 103
China Machine Press (CMP), pg 103
China Materials Management Publishing House, pg 103
Chinese Pedagogics Publishing House, pg 104
Commercial Press (Hong Kong) Ltd, pg 104
Cultural Relics Publishing House, pg 105
Foreign Language Teaching & Research Press, pg 105
Fudan University Press, pg 105
Higher Education Press, pg 106
Jilin Science & Technology Publishing House, pg 106
Language Publishing House, pg 107
Metallurgical Industry Press (MIP), pg 107
Nanjing University Press, pg 107

PUBLISHERS

The People's Communications Publishing House, pg 107
People's Medical Publishing House (PMPH), pg 108
Printing Industry Publishing House, pg 108
The Publishing House of Shanghai University of Traditional Chinese Medicine, pg 108
Shandong University Press, pg 109
Shanghai Foreign Language Education Press, pg 109
Sichuan University Press, pg 109
South China University of Science and Technology Press, pg 109
Tsinghua University Press, pg 110
Wuhan University Press, pg 110
Zhejiang University Press, pg 110

Colombia
Bedout Editores SA, pg 111
Consejo Episcopal Latinoamericano Celam, pg 111
Universidad Externado de Colombia, pg 112
Fondo Educativo Interamericano SA, pg 112
Kapelusz Ltda Editorial, pg 112
McGraw-Hill InterAmericana SA, pg 113
Migema Ediciones Ltda, pg 113
Editorial Norma SA, pg 113
Pearson Educacion de Colombia LTDA, pg 113
Editorial Santillana SA, pg 113
Tercer Mundo Editores SA, pg 113
Unidad Universitaria del Sur (UNISUR), pg 114
Universidad de los Andes Editorial, pg 114

The Democratic Republic of the Congo
Centre de Recherche, et Pedagogie Appliquee, pg 114
Facultes Catoliques de Kinshasa, pg 115
Presses Universitaires du Zaiire (PUZ), pg 115

Costa Rica
Garcia Hermanos Imprentay Litografia, pg 116
Jose Alfonso Sandoval Nunez, pg 116
Editorial de la Universidad de Costa Rica, pg 117
Editorial Universidad Estatal a Distancia (EUNED), pg 117

Cote d'Ivoire
Akohi Editions, pg 117
Universite d' Abidjan, pg 118
Les Nouvelles Editions Africaines, pg 118

Croatia
Narodne Novine, pg 119
Skolska Knjiga, pg 120
Sveucilisna tiskara doo, pg 120

Cuba
ISCAH Fructuoso Rodriguez, pg 121
Pueblo y Educacion Editorial (PE), pg 121

Czech Republic
Academia, pg 122
Barrister & Principal, pg 123
Karel Janak Amosium Servis, pg 125
Karolinum, nakladatelstvi, pg 125
Melantrich, pg 126
Mendelova zemedelska a lesnicka univerzita v Brne, pg 126
Nakladatelstvi Svoboda, pg 126
NLN, Ltd The Lidove noviny Publishing House, pg 127
Paseka, pg 127
Portal Ltd, pg 127
Slon Sociologicke Nakladatelstvi, pg 128
Votobia sro, pg 129

Denmark
Aarhus Universitetsforlag, pg 129
Akademisk Forlag, pg 129
Borgens Forlag A/S, pg 130
Dansk Psykologisk Forlag, pg 131
FADL's Forlag A/S (Foreningen af danske Laegestuderendes Forlag), pg 132
Fremad A/S, pg 132
GEC Gads Forlag Aktieselskab af 1994, pg 132
Forlaget GMT, pg 132
Gyldendalske Boghandel - Nordisk Forlag A/S, pg 132
Holkenfeldt 3, pg 133
Forlaget Hovedland, pg 133
Kaleidoscope Publishers Ltd, pg 133
Nyt Nordisk Forlag Arnold Busck A/S, pg 134
Polyteknisk Forlag, pg 134
C A Reitzel A/S, pg 134
Samfundslitteratur, pg 135

Dominican Republic
Pontificia Universidad Catolica Madre y Maestra, pg 136

Egypt (Arab Republic of Egypt)
Cairo University Press, pg 138
Dar Al-Kitab Al-Masri, pg 138
Dar Al-Matbo at Al-Gadidah, pg 138
Dar El Shorouk Publishing & Distributing House, pg 138
The Egyptian Society for the Dissemination of Universal Culture and Knowledge (ESDUCK), pg 138
Dar Al Maaref, pg 139
Middle East Book Centre, pg 139

El Salvador
Clasicos Roxsil Editorial SA de CV, pg 139
UCA Editores, pg 139
Editorial Universitaria de la Universidad de El Salvador, pg 139

Estonia
Valgus Publishers, pg 141

Finland
Akateeminen Kustannusliike Oy, pg 141
Kirjayhtymae Oy, pg 143
Kustannuskiila Oy, pg 143
Otava Publishing Co Ltd, pg 143
Schildts Foerlagsaktiebolag, pg 144
Soederstroem et Co Foerlagsaktiebolag, pg 144
Suomalaisen Kirjallisuuden Seura, pg 144
Osuuskunta Vastapaino, pg 145

Werner Soederstroem Osakeyhtioe (WSOY), pg 145
Yliopistopaino/Helsinki University Press, pg 145

France
ABC Editions, pg 145
Adverbum SARL, pg 146
APRD - Association pour la Recherche et l'Information demographiques, pg 147
Atelier National de Reproduction des Theses, pg 148
Editions Aubier-Montaigne SA, pg 149
Editions Belin, pg 150
Societe d'Edition Les Belles Lettres, pg 150
Presses Universitaires de Bordeaux (PUB), pg 151
Breal, pg 151
Editions BRGM, pg 152
Brud Nevez, pg 152
Cepadues Editions SA, pg 153
Editions Chiron, pg 154
Chotard et Associes Editeurs, pg 154
Cle International, pg 155
Armand Colin, Editeur, pg 155
Editions Cujas, pg 157
Editions Dalloz Sirey, pg 157
De Vecchi Editions SA, pg 158
Delagrave Edition SA, pg 158
Editions Desvigne, pg 159
Doin Editeurs, pg 160
Librairie Generale de Droit et de Jurisprudence (LGDJ) - Montchrestien, pg 160
Dunod Editeur, pg 160
L'Ecole/L'Ecole des Loisirs Sarl, pg 160
Presses de l'Ecole Normale Superieure, pg 160
Edicef - Editions Classiques d'Expression Francaise, pg 161
Editions Tarmeye, pg 161
Elf Exploration Production, pg 161
Les Editions de l'Epargne, pg 162
Editions Errance, pg 162
Editions Jacques Gabay, pg 165
Edition Galilee, pg 165
Paul Geuthner Librairie Orientaliste, pg 166
Hachette Education, pg 167
Hachette Livre, pg 167
Editions Hatier SA, pg 168
Hermann editeurs des Sciences et des Arts SA, pg 168
Hermes Science Publications, pg 168
INRA Editions (Institut National de la Recherche Agronomique), pg 169
Editions INSERM, pg 169
Les Introuvables-Editions L'Harmattan, pg 170
IRD Editions, pg 170
Librairie Larousse, pg 172
Editions Universitaires LCF, pg 172
Librairie Scientifique et Technique Albert Blanchard, pg 173
LiTec (Librairies Techniques SA), pg 173
Magnard SA, pg 174
Masson SA, pg 175
Masson-Williams et Wilkins, pg 175
Maxima Laurent du Mesnil Editeur, pg 175
Editions Modernes Media, pg 176
Editions de la Reunion des Musees Nationaux, pg 176
Fernand Nathan, pg 177
Editions Ophrys, pg 178

Pearson Education France, pg 179
Editions Pedone, pg 179
Editions A et J Picard SA, pg 179
Polytechnica, pg 180
Presses de l'Ecole Nationale des Ponts et Chaussees, pg 181
Presses Universitaires de Caen, pg 181
Presses Universitaires de France (PUF), pg 181
Presses Universitaires de Grenoble, pg 181
Editions Roudil, pg 183
Editions du Seuil, pg 185
Editions Spratbrow, pg 186
Librairie Philosophique J Vrin, pg 189
Librairie Vuibert, pg 189

Germany
A Francke Verlag (Tubingen und Basel), pg 191
AOL-Verlag Frohmut Menze, pg 194
Aschendorffsche Verlagsbuchhandlung GmbH & Co KG, pg 195
Auer Verlag GmbH, pg 196
C Bange GmbH & Co KG, pg 198
Baumann GmbH & Co KG, pg 199
Bayerischer Schulbuch-Verlag GmbH, pg 199
Verlag C H Beck (OHG), pg 200
Julius Beltz GmbH & Co KG, pg 200
Berlin Verlag Arno Spitz GmbH, pg 200
Bernard und Graefe Verlag, pg 201
Biblio-Zeller Verlag, pg 202
Blackwell Wissenschafts-Verlag GmbH, pg 203
Verlag Die Blaue Eule, pg 204
Boehlau-Verlag GmbH & Cie, pg 204
Buechse der Pandora Verlags-GmbH, pg 207
Burckhardthaus-Laetare Verlag GmbH, pg 208
Campus Verlag GmbH, pg 209
Fachverlag Hans Carl GmbH, pg 209
Centaurus-Verlagsgesellschaft GmbH, pg 209
Claudius Verlag, pg 211
Compact Verlag GmbH, pg 211
Cornelsen und Oxford University Press GmbH & Co, pg 211
Cornelsen Verlag GmbH & Co OHG, pg 211
Cornelsen Verlag Scriptor GmbH & Co KG, pg 212
Verlag Werner Dausien, pg 212
Verlag fuer Deutsch GmbH, pg 213
Verlag Harri Deutsch, pg 213
Deutscher Verlag fur Grundstoffindustrie GmbH, pg 215
Dipa-Verlag GmbH, pg 217
Verlag Duerr & Kessler GmbH, pg 219
Duncker und Humblot GmbH, pg 219
E Schweizerbart'sche Verlagsbuchhandlung (Nagele und Obermiller), pg 220
Verlag Europa-Lehrmittel, Nourney, Vollmer GmbH & Co, pg 224
Exil Verlag, pg 225
Fachbuchverlag Leipzig im Carl Hanser Verlag, pg 226
Fachbuchverlag Pfanneberg & Co, pg 226
Ferdinand Enke Verlag, pg 227

TYPE OF PUBLICATION INDEX — BOOK

Festo Didactic GmbH & Co, pg 227
Verlag Reinhard Fischer, pg 228
Rita G Fischer Verlag, pg 228
Focus-Verlag Gesellschaft mbH, pg 229
Verlag Franz Vahlen GmbH, pg 229
Friedrich Kiehl Verlag GmbH, pg 230
Betriebswirtschaftlicher Verlag Dr Th Gabler GmbH, pg 231
Gebrueder Borntraeger Science Publishers, pg 231
Govi-Verlag Pharmazeutischer Verlag GmbH, pg 233
Brigitte Grabitz - ikoo Buchverlag, pg 233
Walter de Gruyter GmbH & Co KG, pg 234
Gunter Olzog Verlag GmbH, pg 235
Guetersloher Verlagshaus Gerd Mohn, pg 235
Haag und Herchen Verlag GmbH, pg 235
Hamburger Lesehefte Verlag Iselt & Co Nfl mbH, pg 236
Carl Hanser Verlag, pg 237
Harrassowitz Verlag, pg 237
Rudolf Haufe Verlag GmbH & Co KG, pg 238
Verlag Herder GmbH & Co KG, pg 239
Hippokrates-Verlag GmbH, pg 241
Hogrefe Verlag GmbH & Co Kg, pg 242
Huss-Medien GmbH, pg 243
Huss-Verlag GmbH, pg 244
Huthig GmbH & Co KG, pg 244
IKO Verlag fur Interkulturelle Kommunikation, pg 244
Impuls-Theater-Verlag, pg 244
ITpress Verlag, pg 245
Ernst Klett Verlag GmbH, pg 250
W Kohlhammer GmbH, abt Haussortiment, pg 252
kopaed verlagsgmbh, pg 252
Peter Lang GmbH Europaeischer Verlag der Wissenschaften, pg 255
Langenscheidt-Hachette, pg 255
Langenscheidt KG, pg 256
Verlag fuer Lehrmittel Poessneck GmbH, pg 256
Verlag Leske plus Budrich GmbH, pg 257
Libertas- Europaeisches Institut GmbH, pg 257
Lucius & Lucius Verlagsgesellschaft mbH, pg 259
Manz G J Verlag und Druckerel, pg 261
Margraf Verlag, pg 261
Matthiesen Verlag Ingwert Paulsen Jr, pg 261
mentis Verlag GmbH, pg 262
Meyer & Meyer Fachverlag und Buchhandel GmbH, pg 263
Karl Heinrich Moeseler Verlag, pg 264
Mohr Siebeck, pg 264
Morsak Verlag, pg 265
Gunter Narr Verlag, pg 266
Verlag Neue Wirtschafts-Briefe GmbH & Co, pg 267
Max Niemeyer Verlag GmbH, pg 269
Patmos Verlag GmbH & Co KG, pg 272
Philipp Reclam Jun Verlag GmbH, pg 273
Psychiatrie-Verlag GmbH, pg 275
Psychologie Verlags Union GmbH, pg 275

Quelle und Meyer Verlag GmbH & Co, pg 276
Quintessenz Verlags-GmbH, pg 276
Dr Ludwig Reichert Verlag, pg 278
Ritterbach Verlag GmbH, pg 279
Roehrig Universitaets Verlag Gmbh, pg 279
Rombach GmbH Druck und Verlagshaus & Co, pg 280
Romiosini Verlag, pg 280
Schaeffer-Poeschel Verlag fuer Wirtschaft Steuern Recht, pg 282
Verlag Dr Otto Schmidt KG, pg 283
Ferdinand Schoeningh Verlag GmbH, pg 284
Schott Musik International GmbH & Co KG, pg 284
Schulz-Kirchner Verlag GmbH, pg 285
Otto Schwartz Fachbochhandlung GmbH, pg 286
Springer-Verlag GmbH & Co KG, pg 288
Verlag H Stam GmbH, pg 289
Franz Steiner Verlag Wiesbaden GmbH, pg 289
B G Teubner GmbH, pg 292
Tipress Dienstleistungen fur das Verlagswesen GmbH, pg 294
Tuduv Verlagsgesellschaft mbH, pg 295
Tuebinger Vereinigung fur Volkskunde eV (TVV), pg 295
Wirtschaftsverlag Carl Ueberreuter, pg 295
Verlag Eugen Ulmer GmbH & Co, pg 295
Urban und Fischer Verlag fur Medizin, pg 296
UVK Universitatsverlag Konstanz GmbH, pg 297
UVK Verlagsgesellschaft mbH, pg 297
Vandenhoeck & Ruprecht, pg 297
Verlag fur Schweissen und Verwandte Verfahren, pg 298
Verlag Moderne Industrie AG & Co KG, pg 298
Verlag und Druckkontor Kamp GmbH, pg 298
Friedr Vieweg & Sohn Verlagsgesellschaft mbH, pg 298
Weidler Buchverlag Berlin, pg 301
Werner Verlag GmbH & Co KG, pg 302
Westdeutscher Verlag GmbH, pg 302
Westermann Schulbuchverlag GmbH, pg 302
Herbert Wichmann Verlag, pg 302
Wiley-VCH Verlag GmbH, pg 302
Dr Dieter Winkler, pg 303
Winklers Verlag Gebrueder Grimm, pg 303
Verlag Konrad Wittwer GmbH, pg 303
Wochenschau Verlag, Dr Kurt Debus GmbH, pg 304
Zeller Verlag GmbH & Co, pg 305

Ghana

Afram Publications (Ghana) Ltd, pg 306
Black Mask Ltd, pg 306
Bureau of Ghana Languages, pg 306
Educational Press & Manufacturers Ltd, pg 307
EPP Books Services, pg 307
Ghana Publishing Corporation, pg 307
Ghana Universities Press (GUP), pg 307
Sedco Publishing Ltd, pg 308
Unimax Macmillan Ltd, pg 308

Greece

Diavlos, pg 309
Ilias Kambanas Publishing Organization, SA, pg 312
Kleidarithmos, pg 312
Kritiki Publishing, pg 312
Nakas Music House, pg 313
Panepistimio Ioanninon, pg 314
Papazissis Publishers SA, pg 314
Patakis Publishers, pg 314

Guadeloupe

Librairie Generale JASOR, pg 316

Guatemala

Grupo Editorial RIN-78, pg 316

Haiti

Editions Caraiibes SA, pg 317

Hong Kong

Federal Publications Ltd, pg 319
Good Earth Publishing Co Ltd, pg 320
Hong Kong University Press, pg 320
Joint Publishing (HK) Co Ltd, pg 320
Philopsychy Press, pg 321
Union Press Ltd, pg 322
Witman Publishing Co (HK) Ltd, pg 322

Hungary

Akademiai Kiado, pg 323
Atlantisz Kiado, pg 323
Corvina Books Ltd, pg 323
Greger-Delacroix, pg 324
Janus Pannonius Tudomanyegyetem, pg 324
Joszoveg Muhely Kiado, pg 324
Mezoegazdasagi Koenyvkiado Vallalat, pg 325
Mueszaki Koenyvkiado Ltd, pg 325
Nemzeti Tankoenyvkiado, pg 326
Panem, pg 326
Typotex Kft Elektronikus Kiado, pg 327

Iceland

Haskolautgafan - University of Iceland Press, pg 328
Idunn, pg 328
Namsgagnastofnun, pg 328

India

Academic Publishers, pg 329
Addison-Wesley (Singapore) Pte Ltd, pg 329
Affiliated East West Press Pvt Ltd, pg 329
Anmol Publications Pvt Ltd, pg 331
Arya Medi Publishing House, pg 331
Atma Ram & Sons, pg 331
B I Publications Pvt Ltd, pg 331
The Bangalore Printing & Publishing Co Ltd, pg 332
Bani Mandir, Book-Sellers, Publishers & Educational Suppliers, pg 332
Bhawan Book Service, Publishers & Distributors, pg 333
BS Publications, pg 334
Chowkhamba Sanskrit Series Office, pg 335
The Christian Literature Society, pg 335
Concept Publishing Co, pg 335
Dastane Ramchandra & Co, pg 335
Dutta Baruah Publishing Co Pvt Ltd, pg 336
Eastern Law House Pvt Ltd, pg 336
Eurasia Publishing House Pvt Ltd, pg 337
Geeta Prakasham, pg 337
General Book Depot, pg 337
Goel Prakashen, pg 337
Arnold Heinman Publishers (India) Pvt Ltd, pg 338
Indian Council of Agricultural Research, pg 339
Intertrade Publications, pg 340
Khanna Publishers, pg 341
Konark Publishers, Pvt, Ltd, pg 341
Laxmi Publications Pvt Ltd, pg 341
Omsons Publications, pg 345
Oxford & IBH Publishing Co Pvt Ltd, pg 345
Oxford University Press, pg 345
Oxonian Press (P) Ltd, pg 345
Paico Publishing House, pg 345
Panjab University Publication Bureau, pg 345
People's Publishing House (P) Ltd, pg 346
Pitambar Publishing Co (P) Ltd, pg 346
Rajasthan Hindi Granth Academy, pg 347
Rajesh Publications, pg 347
Rajpal & Sons, pg 347
Rastogi Publications, pg 347
Regency Publications, pg 347
Reliance Publishing House, pg 347
Sasta Sahitya Mandal, pg 349
Scientific Book Agency, pg 349
Selina Publishers, pg 349
South Asian Publishers Pvt Ltd, pg 350
Sterling Publishers Pvt Ltd, pg 351
Sterling Information Technologies, pg 351
Sultan Chand & Sons Pvt Ltd, pg 351
DB Taraporevala Sons & Co Pvt Ltd, pg 351
Today & Tomorrow's Printers & Publishers, pg 352
Vakils Feffer & Simons Ltd, pg 352
S Viswanathan (Printers & Publishers) Pvt Ltd, pg 353
A H Wheeler & Co Ltd, pg 353

Indonesia

Andi Offset, pg 354
CV Angkasa CV (Publishers), pg 354
Balai Pustaka, pg 354
P T Bulan Bintang, pg 354
Bumi Aksara PT, pg 354
Diponegoro CV, pg 355
Djambatan PT, pg 355
Institut Teknologi Bandung, pg 355
Penerbit Nusa Indah, pg 356
PT Bhakti Baru, pg 356
PT Pradnya Paramita, pg 357

Islamic Republic of Iran

Amir Kabir Book Publishing & Distribution Co, pg 357
University of Tehran Publications & Printing Organization, pg 358

Ireland

An Gum, pg 358
The Economic & Social Research Institute, pg 360

PUBLISHERS

Gill & Macmillan Ltd, pg 361
Herodotus Press, pg 361
Institute of Public Administration, pg 361
Irish Management Institute, pg 361
Oak Tree Press, pg 362
On Stream Publications Ltd, pg 363
Ossian Publications, pg 363
Round Hall Sweet & Maxwell, pg 363
Royal Irish Academy, pg 364
Veritas Co Ltd, pg 364

Israel

Achiasaf Publishing House Ltd, pg 365
Am Oved Publishers Ltd, pg 365
Amichai Publishing House Ltd, pg 365
Dvir Publishing Ltd, pg 366
Otzar Hamore, pg 368
Israel Universities Press, pg 369
The Magnes Press, pg 370
Massada Publishers Ltd, pg 370
Open University of Israel, pg 371
Schocken Publishing House Ltd, pg 372
Y Sreberk, pg 372
Steimatzky Group Ltd, pg 372
Tcherikover Publishers Ltd, pg 372
Tel-Aviv University, pg 373
University Publishing Projects Ltd, pg 373
Yad Eliahu Kitov, pg 373
Yavneh Publishing House Ltd, pg 373

Italy

De Agostini Scolastica, pg 375
Libreria Alfani Editrice SRL, pg 375
Archimede Edizioni, pg 376
Editore Armando Armando SRL, pg 376
Bianco, pg 377
Bollati Boringhieri Editore Srl, pg 378
Giuseppe Bonanno Editore, pg 378
Bulzoni Editore SRL (Le Edizioni Universitarie d'Italia), pg 379
Canova SRL, pg 379
Nuova Casa Editrice Licinio Cappelli GEM srl, pg 379
Casa Editrice Giuseppe Principato Spa, pg 380
Celuc Libri, pg 380
CLEUP - Cooperative Libraria Editrice dell 'Universita di Padova, pg 382
Edizioni Cremonese SRL, pg 383
Edizioni Curci SRL, pg 383
G De Bono Editore, pg 384
DEI Tipographia del Genio Civile, pg 384
Edizioni del Centro, pg 384
Casa Editrice Istituto della Santa, pg 384
ECIG, pg 385
Edi Ermes SRL, pg 386
EDIFIR SRL, pg 386
Editrice Edisco, pg 386
Editori Laterza, pg 386
Giulio Einaudi Editore SpA, pg 387
Etas Libri, pg 388
Giangiacomo Feltrinelli SpA, pg 389
Fratelli Conte Editori SRL, pg 389
Istituto Geografico de Agostini SpA, pg 390
Editrice Giannotta di Sebastiano Pace Giannotta, pg 390
Giunti (Gruppo Editoriale), pg 390

Gius Laterza e Figli SpA, pg 391
Gruppo Calderini Edagricole, pg 392
Herbita Editrice di Leonardo Palermo, pg 392
Levante, pg 395
Levrotto e Bella Libreria Editrice Universitaria SAS, pg 395
Liguori Editore SRL, pg 396
Loescher Editore SRL, pg 396
Loffredo Editore Napoli SpA®, pg 396
Masson SpA, pg 398
Minerva Italica SpA, pg 399
Mucchi Editore SRL, pg 400
Societa Editrice Il Mulino, pg 400
Gruppo Ugo Mursia Editore SpA, pg 400
Nagard, pg 400
La Nuova Italia Editrice SpA, pg 401
Paideia Editrice, pg 402
Paravia Bruno Mondadori Editori, pg 402
Piccin Nuova Libraria SpA, pg 403
Principato, pg 404
RCS Rizzoli Libri SpA, pg 405
Edizioni Universitarie Romane, pg 406
Casa Editrice Mariett Scuola SpA, pg 407
Edizioni Librarie Siciliane, pg 408
Societa Editrice Internazionale - SEI, pg 408
Societa Editrice la Goliardica Pavese SRL, pg 408
Edizioni Studium SpA, pg 409
Nicola Teti e C Editore SRL, pg 409
Edizioni Unicopli SpA, pg 410
Unipress, pg 410
UTET (Unione Tipografico-Editrice Torinese), pg 411
Valmartina Editore SRL, pg 411
Zanichelli Editore SpA, pg 412
Edizioni Zara, pg 412

Jamaica

CVM Publications, pg 413
The Press, pg 413
Ian Randle Publishers Ltd, pg 413

Japan

Bun-ichi Sogo Shuppan, pg 415
Dobun Shoin, pg 416
Eichosha Company Ltd, pg 416
The Eihosha Ltd, pg 416
Hakutei-Sha, pg 417
Hirokawa Publishing Co, pg 417
Hokuryukan Co Ltd, pg 417
Hyoronsha Publishing Co Ltd, pg 417
Igaku-Shoin Ltd, pg 418
Iwanami Shoten, Publishers, pg 418
The Japan Times, pg 418
Kaitakusha, pg 419
Kindai Kagaku Sha Co, Ltd, pg 419
Kodansha Scientific Ltd, pg 420
Kyoritsu Shuppan Co Ltd, pg 420
Maruzen Co Ltd, pg 421
Mejikaru Furendo-sha, pg 421
Minerva Shobo Co Ltd, pg 421
Morikita Shuppan Co Ltd, pg 421
Nanzando Co Ltd, pg 422
Nihon-Bunkyo Shuppan (Japan Educational Publishing Co Ltd), pg 422
Nikkagiren Shuppan-Sha (JUSE Press Ltd), pg 422
Nippon Hoso Shuppan Kyokai (NHK Publishing), pg 422
Obunsha Co Ltd, pg 423

Ohmsha Ltd, pg 423
Ongaku No Tomo Sha Corporation, pg 423
Sagano Shoin, pg 424
Sanseido Co Ltd, pg 424
Sanshusha Publishing Co, Ltd, pg 424
Seibido, pg 424
Shokoku Publishing Co Ltd, pg 426
Sobun-Sha, pg 426
Sogensha Publishing Co Ltd, pg 426
Tamagawa University Press, pg 427
Teikoku-Shoin Co Ltd, pg 427
Thomson Learning, pg 427
Toho Book Store, pg 427
Tokyo Kagaku Dozin Co Ltd, pg 427
Tsukiji Shokan Publishing Co, pg 428
University of Tokyo Press, pg 428
Zeimukeiri-Kyokai, pg 429

Jordan

Jordan House for Publication, pg 430

Kenya

Action Publishers, pg 430
Africa Book Services (EA) Ltd, pg 430
African Centre for Technology Studies (ACTS), pg 431
Book Sales (K) Ltd, pg 431
Cosmopolitan Publishers Ltd, pg 431
Focus Publications Ltd, pg 431
Foundation Books, pg 431
Heinemann Kenya Limited (EAEP), pg 431
Kenway Publications Ltd, pg 432
Kenya Literature Bureau, pg 432
Midi Teki Publishers, pg 433
Nairobi University Press, pg 433
Shirikon Publishers, pg 433
Gideon S Were Press, pg 434

Democratic People's Republic of Korea

Educational Books Publishing House, pg 434

Republic of Korea

Bi-bong Publishing Co, pg 435
Bo Moon Dang, pg 435
Cheong-mun-gag Publishing Co, pg 435
Chung Rim Publishing Co Ltd, pg 435
Daeyoung Munhwasa, pg 435
Dong-A Publishing & Printing Co Ltd, pg 436
Hakmun Publishing, Co, pg 436
Hanul Publishing Co, pg 436
Iljo-gag Publishers, pg 437
Jung-ang Munhwa Sa, pg 437
Koreaone Press Inc, pg 438
Kukminseokwan Publishing Co Ltd, pg 438
Kyohaksa Publishing Co Ltd, pg 438
Literature Academy, pg 438
Minjisa Publishing Co, pg 438
Moon Jin Media Co Ltd, pg 438
Nanam Publishing House, pg 439
Omun Gak, pg 439
Panmun Book Co Ltd, pg 439
Pearson Education Korea Ltd, pg 439
Pochinchai Printing Co Ltd, pg 439
Prompter Publications, pg 439

TYPE OF PUBLICATION INDEX

Sohaksa, pg 440
Yearim-dang, pg 441
Yonsei University Press, pg 441

Kuwait

Ministry of Information, pg 441

Latvia

Lielvards Ltd, pg 442
Zvaigzne ABC Publishers, Ltd, pg 442

Lebanon

Dar Al-Kitab Alloubnani, pg 443
Dar Al-Maaref-Liban Sarl, pg 443
Librairie du Liban, pg 443
Librairie Orientale sal, pg 443
World Book Publishing, pg 443

Lithuania

Eugrimas, pg 445
Klaipedos Universiteto Leidykla, pg 445
Mokslo ir enciklopediju leidybos institutas, pg 446
Margi Rastai Publishers, pg 446
Svietimo ir mokslo ministerijos Leidybos centras, pg 446
TEV Leidykla, pg 446

Luxembourg

Editions Promoculture, pg 448

Macau

Instituto Portugues Oriente, pg 448
Universidadede de Macau, Centro de Publicacoes, pg 448

The Former Yugoslav Republic of Macedonia

Detska radost, pg 448
Prosvetno Delo, pg 449
St Clement of Ohrid National & University Library, pg 449

Madagascar

Foibe Filan-Kevitry NY Mpampianatra (FOFIPA), pg 450
Societe Malgache d'Edition, pg 450

Malawi

Dzuka Publishing Company Ltd, pg 450

Malaysia

AMK Interaksi Sdn Bhd, pg 451
Berita Publishing Sdn Bhd, pg 451
Dewan Bahasa dan Pustaka, pg 451
Eastview Productions Sdn Bhd, pg 452
Federal Publications Sdn Bhd, pg 452
Geetha Publishers Sdn Bhd, pg 452
K Publishing & Distributors Sdn Bhd, pg 452
The Malaya Press Sdn Bhd, pg 453
Malayan Law Journal Sdn Bhd, pg 453
Panther Publishing, pg 453
Pearson Education, pg 453
Penerbit Fajar Bakti Sdn Bhd, pg 454
Penerbit Universiti Sains Malaysia, pg 454
Preston Corporation Sdn Bhd, pg 454
Pustaka Cipta Sdn Bhd, pg 454

Text Books Malaysia Sdn Bhd, pg 455
Times Educational Co Sdn Bhd, pg 455

Mali
EDIM SA, pg 455

Martinique
Editions Gondwana, pg 456

Mauritania
Imprimerie Commerciale et Administrative de Mauritanie, pg 456

Mauritius
Editions Capucines, pg 457
EDITIONS Le Printemps, pg 457

Mexico
Aconcagua Ediciones y Publicaciones SA, pg 457
ALFA OMEGA Grupo Editor, pg 458
Colegio de Postgraduados en Ciencias Agricolas, pg 459
Compania Editorial Continental SA de CV, pg 459
Publicaciones Cruz O SA, pg 459
Editorial Diana SA de CV, pg 459
Editorial El Manual Moderno SA de CV, pg 460
Editorial Esfinge SA de CV, pg 460
Centro de Estudios Monetarios Latinoamericanos (CEMLA), pg 460
Fernandez Editores SA de CV, pg 461
Grupo Editorial Iberoamerica, SA de CV, pg 461
Editorial Herrero SA, pg 462
Editorial Jus SA de CV, pg 462
Phillip Richard Conover Lazo, pg 462
Editorial Limusa SA de CV, pg 463
Instituto Nacional de Antropologia e Historia, pg 464
Libreria Patria SA, pg 465
Pearson Educacion de Mexico, SA de CV, pg 465
Plaza y Valdes SA de CV, pg 465
Publicaciones Cultural SA de CV, pg 466
Sistemas Tecnicos de Edicion SA de CV, pg 467
Sistemas Universales, SA, pg 467
Editorial Trillas SA de CV, pg 467
Universidad Nacional Autonoma de Mexico (National University of Mexico), pg 467
Universidad Veracruzana Direccion General Editorial y de Publicaciones, pg 468
Universo Editorial SA de CV Edicion de Libros Revistas y Periodicos, pg 468

Republic of Moldova
Lumina Publishing House, pg 468

Morocco
Cabinet Conseil CCMLA, pg 469
Dar Nachr Al Maarifa Pour L'Edition et La Distribution, pg 469

Mozambique
Empresa Moderna Lda, pg 470
Editora Minerva Central, pg 470

Myanmar
Hanthawaddy Book House, pg 471

Namibia
Desert Research Foundation of Namibia (DRFN), pg 471
Gamsberg Macmillan Publishers (Pty) Ltd, pg 471

Nepal
International Standards Books & Periodicals (P) Ltd, pg 471
Sajha Prakashan, Co-operative Publishing Organization, pg 472

Netherlands
Uitgeverij Jan van Arkel, pg 473
A A Balkema, pg 473
Uitgeverij Coutinho BV, pg 476
De Graaf Publishers, pg 478
Katholieke Bijbelstichting, pg 479
Uitgeefmaatschappij J H Kok BV, pg 480
Uitgeverij Lemma BV, pg 480
Meinema, pg 481
Uitgeverij H Nelissen BV, pg 482
Nico Israel, pg 482
Oriental Press BV (APA), pg 482
A J G Strengholt's Boeken, Anno 1928, BV, pg 484
ThiemeMeulenhoff, pg 485
Twente University Press, pg 485
Van Gorcum & Comp BV, pg 486
Wolters-Noordhoff B V, pg 487

New Zealand
Aoraki Press Ltd, pg 488
Brooker's Ltd, pg 489
Butterworths New Zealand Ltd, pg 489
Dunmore Press Ltd, pg 490
ESA Publications (NZ) Ltd, pg 490
Learning Guides (Writers & Publishers Ltd), pg 492
Legislation Direct, pg 492
Macmillan Publishers New Zealand Ltd, pg 493
Moss Associates Ltd, pg 493
Oxford University Press, pg 494
Pearson Education, pg 494
Reach Publications, pg 495
RSVP Publishing Company Ltd, pg 495
University of Otago Press, pg 496

Nigeria
ABIC Books & Equipment Ltd, pg 497
African Universities Press, pg 497
Africana-FEP Publishers Ltd, pg 498
Albah Publishers, pg 498
Aromolaran Publishing Co Ltd, pg 498
Cross Continent Press Ltd, pg 498
Ethiope Publishing Corporation, pg 499
Evans Brothers (Nigeria Publishers) Ltd, pg 499
Fourth Dimension Publishing Co Ltd, pg 499
Goldland Business Co Ltd, pg 499
Ibadan University Press, pg 499
Longman Nigeria Plc, pg 500
Thomas Nelson (Nigeria) Ltd, pg 500
New Africa Publishing Company Ltd, pg 500
New Horn Press Ltd, pg 500

Northern Nigerian Publishing Co Ltd, pg 500
Nwamife Publishers Ltd, pg 500
Obafemi Awolowo University Press Ltd, pg 501
Onibon-Oje Publishers, pg 501
Riverside Communications, pg 501
University of Lagos Press, pg 502
Vantage Publishers International Ltd, pg 502
West African Book Publishers Ltd, pg 502

Norway
J W Cappelens Forlag A/S, pg 503
Det Norske Samlaget, pg 503
J W Eides Forlag A/S, pg 503
Folhenuniversitetets Forlag, pg 503
Gyldendal Norsk Forlag A/S, pg 503
NKl Forlaget, pg 504
Erik Sandberg, pg 504
Teknologisk Forlag, pg 505
Universitetsforlaget, pg 505
Vett & Viten AS, pg 505

Pakistan
The Book House, pg 506
HMR Publishing Co, pg 507
Islamic Book Centre, pg 507
Jang Publishers, pg 507
National Book Foundation, pg 508
West-Pakistan Publishing Co (Pvt) Ltd, pg 509

Papua New Guinea
Kristen Pres, pg 510

Paraguay
Intercontinental Editora, pg 510

Peru
Ediciones Brown SA, pg 511
Asociacion Editorial Bruno, pg 511
Carvajal SA, pg 511
Instituto de Estudios Peruanos, pg 511
Libreria Studium SA, pg 511
Universidad de Lima-Fondo de Desarollo Editorial, pg 512
Universidad Nacional Mayor de San Marcos, pg 512
Editorial Universo SA, pg 512

Philippines
Ateneo de Manila University Press, pg 512
Bright Concepts Printing House, pg 512
Communication Foundation for Asia Media Group (CFAMG), pg 513
De La Salle University, pg 513
Garotech, pg 513
Marren Publishing House, Inc, pg 513
National Book Store Inc, pg 514
New Day Publishers, pg 514
Our Lady of Manaoag Publisher, pg 514
Philippine Education Co Inc, pg 514
Rex Bookstores & Publishers, pg 514
Salesiana Publishers Inc, pg 515
SIBS Publishing House Inc, pg 515
Sinag-Tala Publishers Inc, pg 515
UST Publishing House, pg 515

Poland
Polskie Wydawnictwo Ekonomiczne PWE SA, pg 516
Gdanskie Wydawnictwo Psychologiczne SC, pg 516
Impuls, pg 517
Katolicki Uniwersytet Wydawniczo-Redakcja, pg 517
Wydawnictwo Medyczne Urban & Partner, pg 518
Polish Scientific Publishers PWN, pg 519
Oficyna Wydawnicza Politechniki Wroclawskiej, pg 519
PZWL Wydawnictwo Lekarskie Ltd, pg 519
Res Polona, pg 519
Panstwowe Wydawnictwo Rolnicze i Lesne, pg 519
Wydawnictwo Uniwersytetu Wroclawskiego SP ZOO, pg 520
Wydawnictwa Naukowo-Techniczne, pg 521
Wydawnictwa Szkolne i Pedagogiczne (Polish Educational Publishers-WSiP), pg 521
Wydawnictwa Uniwersytetu Warszawskiego, pg 521
Wydawnictwo DiG, pg 521

Portugal
Livraria Almedina, pg 522
Livraria Arnado Lda, pg 522
Basica Editora, pg 522
Biblioteca Geral da Universidade de Coimbra, pg 523
Centro Estudos Geograficos, pg 523
Edicoes Colibri, pg 523
Edicoes Cosmos, pg 524
Dinalivro, pg 524
Edicoes 70, Lda, pg 524
Publicacoes Europa-America Lda, pg 524
Europress Editores e Distribuidores de Publicacoes Lda, pg 525
Imprensa Nacional-Casa da Moeda, pg 526
Livraria Apostolado da Imprensa, pg 526
Livraria Luzo-Espanhola Lda, pg 526
Livraria Minerva Editora, pg 526
Livros Horizonte Lda, pg 526
Lua Viajante-Edicao e Distribuicao de Livros e Material Audiovisual, Lda, pg 527
McGraw-Hill Editora de Portugal, pg 527
Monitor, pg 527
Nova Acropole, pg 527
Porto Editora Lda, pg 528
Editorial Presenca, pg 528
Quid Juris - Sociedade editora, pg 529
Quimera Editores, pg 529
Sa da Costa Editora, pg 529
Edicioes Joao Sa da Costa Lda, pg 529
Silabo, pg 529
Almerinda Teixeira, pg 529
Vega-Publicacao e Distribuicao de Livros e Revistas, Lda, pg 530

Puerto Rico
Editorial Cultural Inc, pg 530
Ediciones Huracan Inc, pg 530
Libros-Ediciones Homines, pg 530
McGraw-Hill Intermericana del Caribe, Inc, pg 530
Piedras Press, Inc, pg 531
University of Puerto Rico Press (EDUPR), pg 531

PUBLISHERS

Romania
Editura Academiei Romane, pg 531
Editora All, pg 531
The Center for Romanian Studies, pg 532
Editura Ceres, pg 532
Editura Clusium, Casa de Editura Atlas-Clusium SRL, pg 532
Editura Dacia, pg 532
Editura Didactica si Pedagogica, pg 532
Editura Medicala, pg 534
Editura Niculescu, pg 534
Editura Paideia, pg 535
Polirom Verlag, pg 535
Editura Stiintifica, pg 536

Russian Federation
Airis Press, pg 537
Aspect Press Ltd, pg 537
N E Bauman Moscow State Technical University Publishers, pg 537
Izdatelstvo 'Ekonomika', pg 537
FGUP Izdatelstvo Mashinostroenie, pg 538
Finansy i Statistika Publishing House, pg 538
Fizmatlit Publishing Co, pg 538
Gidrometeoizdat, pg 538
Izdatel 'stvo Kazanskago Universiteta, pg 538
Izdatel 'stvo Mordovskogo gosudar stvennogo, pg 538
Izdatelstvo Medicina, pg 539
Izdatelstvo Metallurgiya, pg 540
Izdatelstvo Mir, pg 540
Izdatelstvo Muzyka, pg 540
Nauka Publishers, pg 540
Planeta Publishers, pg 541
Izdatelstvo Prosveshchenie, pg 541
Russkij Jazyk, pg 541
St Andrew's Biblical Theological College, pg 541
Izdatelstvo Standartov, pg 542
Voronezh State University Publishers, pg 542
Izdatelstvo Vysshaya Shkola, pg 543

Saudi Arabia
King Saud University, pg 543

Senegal
Les Nouvelles Editions Africaines du Senegal NEAS, pg 544

Sierra Leone
Njala Educational Publishing Centre, pg 544
Sierra Leone University Press, pg 544

Singapore
APAC Publishers Services, pg 545
Cannon International, pg 545
Chopsons Pte Ltd, pg 545
FEP International Private Ltd, pg 546
Hillview Publications Pte Ltd, pg 546
Institute of Southeast Asian Studies, pg 546
LexisNexis, pg 547
Pan Pacific Publications (S) Pte Ltd, pg 547
Pearson Education Asia, pg 547
SNP Pan Pacific Publishing Pte Ltd, pg 548
Taylor & Francis Asia Pacific, pg 548
World Scientific Publishing Co Pte Ltd, pg 549

Slovakia
Slo Viet, pg 550
Ustav informacii a prognoz skolstva mladeze a telovychovy, pg 551
Vydavatel'stvo Osveta (Verlag Osveta), pg 551

Slovenia
Zalozba Mihelac d o o, pg 552
Zalozba Obzorja d d Maribor, pg 552

South Africa
Butterworths South Africa, pg 553
Educum Publishers Ltd, pg 554
HAUM - Daan Retief Publishers (Pty) Ltd, pg 555
HAUM - De Jager Publishers, pg 555
HAUM (Hollandsch Afrikaansche Uitgevers Maatschappij), pg 555
Heinemann Educational Publishers Southern Africa, pg 555
Heinemann Publishers (Pty) Ltd, pg 555
Ivy Publications, pg 555
LAPA Publishers (Pty) Ltd, pg 556
Maskew Miller Longman, pg 557
Nasou Via Afrika, pg 557
New Africa Books (Pty) Ltd, pg 557
Publitoria Editions, pg 558
Ravan Press (Pty) Ltd, pg 558
Unisa Press, pg 560
University Publishers & Booksellers (Pty) Ltd, pg 560
Van Schaik Publishers, pg 560
Witwatersrand University Press, pg 560

Spain
Editorial Acribia SA, pg 561
Agora Editorial, pg 562
Editorial Aguaclara, pg 562
Ediciones Akal SA, pg 562
Ediciones Alfar SA, pg 562
AMV Ediciones, pg 563
Ediciones Anaya SA, pg 563
Arco Libros SL, pg 564
Editorial Ariel SA, pg 564
Editorial Barcanova SA, pg 565
Antoni Bosch Editor SA, pg 565
Celeste Ediciones, pg 567
Central Catequistica Salesiana (CCS), pg 567
Civitas SA Editorial, pg 567
Editorial Claret SA, pg 568
Complutense, SA Editorial, pg 568
Ediciones de la Universidad Complutense de Madrid, pg 568
Editorial Constitucion y Leyes SA - COLEX, pg 568
Ediciones Daly S L, pg 569
Editorial Deimos, SL, pg 569
Ediciones Diaz de Santos SA, pg 569
Editorial Don Quijote, pg 570
Editorial Donostiarra SA, pg 570
Editorial Dossat SA, pg 570
Dykinson SL, pg 571
Edebe, pg 571
EDERSA (Editoriales de Derecho Reunidas SA), pg 571
Ediciones Edinford SA, pg 572
Publicaciones Etea, pg 574
Eumo Editorial, pg 574
Grupo Comunicar, pg 576
Grupo Santillana de Ediciones SA, pg 576
Editorial Herder SA, pg 577
Editorial Horsori SL, pg 577
Icaria Editorial SA, pg 577
Ediciones Istmo SA, pg 579
Editorial Labor SA, pg 579
Laertes SA de Ediciones, pg 579
Ediciones Libertarias/Prodhufi SA, pg 580
Editorial Luis Vives (Edelvives), pg 580
Macmillan Heinemann ELT, pg 581
Marcial Pons Ediciones Juridicas SA, pg 581
McGraw-Hill Iberic/Brazil Group, pg 581
Ediciones Morata SL, pg 583
Mundi-Prensa Libros SA, pg 583
Editorial la Muralla SA, pg 583
Naque Editora, pg 583
Narcea SA de Ediciones, pg 583
Ediciones Norma SA, pg 584
Oikos-Tau SA Ediciones, pg 584
Ediciones Omega SA, pg 585
El Paisaje Editorial, pg 585
Editorial Paraninfo SA, pg 586
Ediciones Partenon, pg 586
Pearson Educacion S A, pg 586
Editorial Playor SA, pg 587
Editorial Pliegos, pg 587
Ediciones Pomares-Corredor, pg 587
PPC Editorial y Distribuidora, SA, pg 587
Progensa, pg 588
Publicaciones de la Universidad Pontificia Comillas-Madrid, pg 588
Editorial Reus SA, pg 588
Editorial Reverte SA, pg 588
Rueda, SL Editorial, pg 589
San Pablo Ediciones, pg 589
Universidad de Santiago de Compostela, pg 589
Ediciones Scriba SA, pg 589
Secretariado Trinitario, pg 590
Servicio de Publicaciones Universidad de Cadiz, pg 590
Servicio de Publicaciones Universidad de Cordoba, pg 590
Ediciones Seyer, pg 590
Silex Ediciones, pg 590
Editorial Sintesis, SA, pg 590
Editores Tecnicos Asociados SA, pg 592
Editorial Teide SA, pg 592
Editorial Augusto E Pila Telena SL, pg 592
Editorial Sal Terrae, pg 592
Tirant lo Blanch SL Libreriaa, pg 592
Ediciones Toray SA, pg 593
Editorial Trivium, SA, pg 593
Trotta SA Editorial, pg 593
Universidad de Malaga, pg 594
Universidad de Oviedo Servicio de Publicaciones, pg 594
Ediciones Universidad de Salamanca, pg 594
Universidad de Valladolid Secretariado de Publicaciones e Intercambio Editorial, pg 594
Publicacions de la Universitat de Barcelona, pg 594
Edicions de la Universitat Politecnica de Catalunya SL, pg 594
Urmo SA de Ediciones, pg 595
Editorial Verbo Divino, pg 595
Editorial Verbum SL, pg 595
Editorial Vicens-Vives, pg 595

TYPE OF PUBLICATION INDEX

Sri Lanka
M D Gunasena & Co Ltd, pg 597
Inter-Cultural Book Promoters, pg 597
Ministry of Education, pg 597
Samayawardena Printers Publishers & Booksellers, pg 598
Warna Publishers, pg 598

Sudan
Khartoum University Press, pg 598

Sweden
Akademiforlaget Corona AB, pg 599
Akademiforlaget Goteborgslitteratur, pg 600
Ekelunds Forlag AB, pg 601
Ekonomibok Forlag AB, pg 601
SK-Gehrmans Musikforlag AB, pg 602
Hans Richter Laromedel, pg 604
Liber AB, pg 604
Bokfoerlaget Naturoch Kultur, pg 604
Norstedts Juridik, pg 605
Bokforlaget Nya Doxa AB, pg 605
Studentlitteratur AB, pg 606
Var Skola Foerlag AB, pg 607
Verbum Foerlag AB, pg 607

Switzerland
Augustin-Verlag, pg 609
Editions de la Baconniere SA, pg 609
Birkhauser Verlag AG, pg 610
Verlag Bo Cavefors, pg 611
Marcel Dekker AG, pg 612
Verlag Harri Deutsch, pg 612
Maurice et Pierre Foetisch SA, pg 614
Paul Haupt Berne, pg 615
Helbing und Lichtenhahn Verlag AG, pg 615
Editions Ides et Calendes SA, pg 616
Klett und Balmer & Co Verlag, pg 617
Kolumbus-Verlag, pg 617
Larousse (Suisse) SA, pg 618
Lehrmittelverlag des Kantons Zurich, pg 618
Medecine et Hygiene, pg 619
Editions H Messeiller SA, pg 619
Neue Zuercher Zeitung AG Buchverlag, pg 620
Editions Payot Lausanne, pg 621
PIE-Peter Lang SA, pg 622
Presses Polytechniques et Universitaires Romandes, PPUR, pg 622
Editions Pro Schola, pg 622
RECOM Verlag, pg 622
Sauerlaender AG, pg 623
Schulthess Polygraphischer Verlag AG, pg 624
Staempfli Verlag AG, pg 625
Tobler Verlag, pg 626
Trans Tech Publications SA, pg 626
Der Universitatsverlag Freiburg, pg 626
Vdf Hochschulverlag AG an der ETH Zurich, pg 626

Syrian Arab Republic
Damascus University Press, pg 628

Taiwan, Province of China
Bookman Books, Ltd, pg 629
Chien Chen Bookstore Publishing Company Ltd, pg 629

Chu Liu Book Company, pg 629
Chung Hwa Book Co Ltd, pg 629
Far East Book Co Ltd, pg 630
Farseeing Publishing Company Ltd, pg 630
Fuh-Wen Book Co, pg 630
Great China Book Corporation, pg 630
Chu Hai Publishing (Taiwan) Co Ltd, pg 630
Hsiao Yuan Publication Co, Ltd, pg 630
Laureate Book Co Ltd, pg 631
San Min Book Co Ltd, pg 631
Torch of Wisdom, pg 632
World Book Co Ltd, pg 632
Yee Wen Publishing Co Ltd, pg 632
Yi Hsien Publishing Co Ltd, pg 632
Youth Cultural Publishing Co, pg 632

United Republic of Tanzania
DUP (1996) Ltd, pg 633
East African Publishing House, pg 633
Emmaus Bible School, pg 633
Oxford University Press, pg 634
Press & Publicity Centre Ltd, pg 634
Tanzania Publishing House, pg 634

Thailand
Akson Charerntat (S/B Akson), pg 635
Graphic Art Publishing, pg 635
Odeon Store LP, pg 635
Prasan Mit, pg 635
Ruamsarn (1977) Co Ltd, pg 635
Suksapan Panit (Business Organization of Teachers Council of Thailand), pg 635
Thai Watana Panich Co, Ltd, pg 636
Watthana Phanit, pg 636

Togo
Editions Akpagnon, pg 636

Trinidad & Tobago
Charran Educational Publishers, pg 636

Tunisia
Academie Tunisienne des Sciences, des Lettres et des Arts Beit El Hekma, pg 637
Ceres Editions, pg 637
Maison Tunisienne de l'Edition, pg 638

Turkey
Alkim Kitapcilik-Yayimcilik, pg 638
Altin Kitaplar Yayinevi, pg 638
Arkadas Ltd, pg 639
Caglayan Kitabevi, pg 639
Inkilap Publishers Ltd, pg 640
Pearson Education Turkey, pg 641
Yetkin Printing & Publishing Co Inc, pg 642

Uganda
Fountain Publishers Ltd, pg 642
Roce (Consultants) Ltd, pg 642

Ukraine
ASK Ltd, pg 643
Osnova, Kharkov State University Press, pg 643
Osvita, pg 643

United Kingdom
Aslib, The Association for Information Management, pg 650
Berg Publishers, pg 654
BILD Publications, pg 654
BIOS Scientific Publishers Ltd, pg 654
Blackwell Science Ltd, pg 656
Blueprint, pg 656
Books for Europe Ltd, pg 657
BPS Books (British Psychological Society), pg 658
BAAF: Adoption & Fostering, pg 659
Butterworths Tolley, pg 661
Cambridge University Press, pg 662
Jon Carpenter Publishing, pg 664
Cassell & Co, pg 664
Causeway Press Ltd, pg 665
Cavendish Publishing Ltd, pg 665
Colourpoint Books, pg 669
Computer Step, pg 670
CTBI Publications, pg 672
Curiad, pg 672
Martin Dunitz Ltd, pg 676
Elm Publications, pg 678
Estates Gazette, pg 679
European Schoolbooks Ltd, pg 680
The Eurospan Group, pg 680
Financial Training Co, pg 682
Flicks Books, pg 683
Forbes Publications Ltd, pg 683
W H Freeman & Co Ltd, pg 684
David Fulton Publishers Ltd, pg 685
The Geographical Association, pg 686
W Green The Scottish Law Publisher, pg 689
Harcourt Publishers Ltd, pg 691
HarperCollins Publishers, pg 692
Hodder Headline Ltd, pg 696
Horizon Scientific Press, pg 697
ICC United Kingdom, pg 698
Immediate Publishing, pg 699
Imperial College Press, pg 699
Institute of Physics Publishing, pg 700
Intellect Ltd, pg 700
Intermediate Technology Publications Ltd, pg 700
IOM Communications Ltd, pg 701
Jones & Bartlett International, pg 703
Laurence King Publishing Ltd, pg 704
Kluwer Academic/Plenum Publishers, pg 705
Learning Matters Ltd, pg 706
Liverpool University Press, pg 708
Macmillan Heinemann ELT, pg 710
Management Books 2000 Ltd, pg 711
Manchester University Press, pg 711
Marcham Books, pg 711
Mars Business Associates Ltd, pg 712
McGraw-Hill Publishing Company, pg 712
The Merlin Press Ltd, pg 713
Micelle Press, pg 714
Motilal (UK) Books of India, pg 715
Multilingual Matters Ltd, pg 716
National Association for the Teaching of English (NATE), pg 717
Nelson Thornes Ltd, pg 718
Open University Press, pg 721
Osborne Books Ltd, pg 722
Oxford University Press, pg 723
Packard Publishing Ltd, pg 723
Palgrave Publishers Ltd, pg 723
PC Publishing, pg 725

Pearson Education Europe, Mideast & Africa, pg 725
Pergamon Flexible Learning, pg 726
Pluto Press, pg 728
Portland Press Ltd, pg 730
Professional Engineering Publishing Ltd, pg 730
Ramakrishna Vedanta Centre, pg 732
Reed Educational & Professional Publishing, pg 734
Routledge Curzon, pg 736
SCM Press, pg 739
Seren, pg 740
Colin Smythe Ltd, pg 743
The Society for Promoting Christian Knowledge (SPCK), pg 743
Spon Press, pg 744
Stokesby House Publications, pg 745
Sweet & Maxwell Ltd, pg 746
Tarragon Press, pg 746
I B Tauris & Co Ltd, pg 747
Trentham Books Ltd, pg 750
University of Wales Press, pg 751
Verulam Publishing Ltd, pg 753
Whittles Publishing, pg 756
Windhorse Publications, pg 757
WIT Press, pg 757

Uruguay
Barreiro y Ramos SA, pg 760
Ediciones de Juan Darien, pg 760
EQ Opciones en Educacion, pg 760
Fundacion de Cultura Universitaria, pg 760
Mosca Hermanos, pg 760
Prensa Medica Latinoamericana, pg 761
Vinten Editor, pg 761

Venezuela
Alfadil Ediciones, pg 761
Editorial Biosfera CA, pg 762
Ediciones Vega SRL, pg 763

Viet Nam
Science & Technics Publishing House, pg 763
Trung-Tam San Xuat Hoc-Lieu, pg 763

Yugoslavia
Beogradski Izdavacko-Graficki Zavod, pg 764
Gradevinska Knjiga, pg 764
Libertatea, pg 764
Minerva, pg 764
Naucna Knjiga, pg 764
Obod, pg 765
Izdavacka Organizacija Rad, pg 765
Radnicka Stampa, pg 765
Sluzbeni List, pg 765
Zavod za Izdavanje Udzbenika, pg 766
Zavod za udzbenike i nastavna sredstva, pg 766

Zambia
Historical Association of Zambia, pg 766
Lundula Publishing House, pg 766
ZPC Publications, pg 767

Zimbabwe
Academic Books Pvt Ltd, pg 767
College Press Publishers (Pvt) Ltd, pg 768
Mercury Press Pvt Ltd, pg 769

University of Zimbabwe Publications, pg 769
Zimbabwe Publishing House (Pvt) Ltd, pg 769

TRANSLATIONS

Albania
Botimpex Publications Import-Export Agency, pg 1
NL SH, pg 1
State Textbook Publishing House, pg 1

Argentina
Ada Korn Editora SA, pg 3
Beatriz Viterbo Editora, pg 4
Instituto de Publicaciones Navales, pg 7
Oikos, pg 8

Australia
Aeolian Press, pg 11
Bayda Books, pg 14
Boombana Publications, pg 16
Bridge To Peace Publications, pg 16
Coconut Productions, pg 18
Gangan Publishing, pg 23
Gnostic Editions, pg 24
Illert Publications, pg 27
Papyrus Publishing, pg 37
Pearson Education Australia, pg 37
Pollitecon Publications, pg 38

Austria
Annette Betz Verlag im Verlag Carl Ueberreuter, pg 49
Docker Verlag GmbH & Co KG, pg 51
Literature Verlag Droschl, pg 51
Ennsthaler GesmbH & Co KG, pg 51
Gangan Verlag, pg 52
Haymon-Verlag GesmbH, pg 52
oebv & hpt Verlagsgesellschaft mbH & Co KG, pg 56
Springer-Verlag Wien, pg 59
Dr Otfried Weise Verlag Tabula Smaragdina, pg 60

Bangladesh
Gatidhara, pg 62
Gono Prakashani, Gono Shasthya Kendra, pg 62

Belarus
Interdigets Publishing House, pg 63

Belgium
Coda, pg 66
EPO Publishers, Printers, Booksellers, pg 68
Koepel van de Vlaamse Noord - Zuidbeweging 11.11.11, pg 70
La Longue Vue, pg 71
Zuid-Nederlandse Uitgeverij NV/ Central Uitgeverij, pg 76

Bosnia and Herzegovina
Bemust doo Novinsko-Izdavacko stamparsko i trgovacko preduzece, pg 77

Brazil
Agalma Psicanalise Editora Ltda, pg 78
Editora Agora Ltda, pg 78
Editora Alfa Omega Ltda, pg 78
Editora Antroposofica Ltda, pg 78

Ao Livro Tecnico Industria e Comercio Ltda, pg 78
Editora Campus Ltda, pg 80
Centro de Estudos Juridicosdo Para (CEJUP), pg 80
Dumara Distribuidora de Publicacoes Ltda, pg 81
Ediouro Publicacoes, SA, pg 81
Editora Companhia das Letras/Editora Schwarcz Ltda, pg 82
Companhia Editora Forense, pg 82
EDUC - Editora da PUC-SP, pg 82
EDUSC - Editora da Universidade do Sagrado Coracao, pg 82
Fundacao Cultural Avatar, pg 83
Editora Harbra Ltda, pg 84
Imago Editora Importacao e Exportacao Ltda, pg 85
LDA Editores Ltda, pg 86
Editora Logosofica, pg 86
Editora Marco Zero Ltda, pg 87
Medicina Panamericana Editora Do Brasil Ltda, pg 87
Editora Mercuryo Ltda, pg 88
Editora Mundo Cristao, pg 88
Editora Nova Alexandria Ltda, pg 88
Editora Nova Fronteira SA, pg 88
Paulinas Editorial, pg 89
Pearson Education Do Brasil, pg 89
Qualitymark Editora Ltda, pg 90
Editora Revan Ltda, pg 90
Livraria Editora Revinter Ltda, pg 90
Summus Editorial Ltda, pg 92
Tempus Editores, pg 92
34 Literatura S/C Ltda, pg 92
Triom Centro de Estudos Marina e Martin Hawey Editorial e Comercial Ltda, pg 92
Editora UNESP, pg 92
Editora Universidade Federal do Rio de Janeiro, pg 93
Jorge Zahar Editor, pg 93

Bulgaria

Abagar, Veliko Tarnovo, pg 94
Aratron, IK, pg 94
CHRIKER, pg 94
DA-Izdatelstvo Publishers, pg 95
Darzavno Izdatelstvo Narodna Kultura, pg 95
Dolphin Press Group Ltd, pg 95
EA Publishing House, pg 95
Eurasia Academic Publishers, pg 95
Fama, pg 95
Gea-Libris Publishing House, pg 95
Hermes Publishing House, pg 95
Heron Press Publishing House, pg 96
Kibea Publishing Co, pg 96
Kralica MAB, pg 96
LIK IZDANIJA, pg 96
MATEX, pg 96
Musica Publishing House Ltd, pg 96
Naouka i Izkoustvo, Ltd, pg 97
Nov Covek Publishing House, pg 97
Prosveta Publishers as, pg 97
Prozoretz Ltd Publishing House, pg 97
Seven Hills Publishers, pg 97
Sila & Zivot, pg 98
Peyo K Yavorov Publishing House, pg 98

Chile

Editora Cuatro Vientos, pg 100

China

Beijing Publishing House, pg 102
Beijing University Press, pg 102
Chemical Industry Press, pg 102
China Film Press, pg 103
China Machine Press (CMP), pg 103
China Translation & Publishing Corp, pg 104
Chinese Pedagogics Publishing House, pg 104
Cultural Relics Publishing House, pg 105
Electronics Industry Publishing House, pg 105
Foreign Languages Press, pg 105
Fudan University Press, pg 105
Guizhou Education Publishing House, pg 106
Heilongjiang Science & Technology Press, pg 106
Higher Education Press, pg 106
Inner Mongolia Science & Technology Publishing House, pg 106
Kunlun Publishing House, pg 107
Lanzhou University Press, pg 107
Morning Glory Publishers, pg 107
The Publishing House of Shanghai University of Traditional Chinese Medicine, pg 108
Shandong Friendship Press, pg 108
Shandong University Press, pg 109
Shanghai Foreign Language Education Press, pg 109
South China University of Science and Technology Press, pg 109
Tianjin Science & Technology Publishing House, pg 109
World Affairs Press, pg 110
Writers' Publishing House, pg 110

Colombia

Asociacion Instituto Linguistico de Verano, pg 111
Universidad Externado de Colombia, pg 112
Tercer Mundo Editores SA, pg 113

The Democratic Republic of the Congo

Saint-Paul, pg 115

Costa Rica

Editorial Texto Ltda, pg 117

Cote d'Ivoire

Heritage Publishing Co, pg 118

Croatia

ArTresor naklada, pg 118
Durieux d o o, pg 118
Faust Vrani, pg 118
Matica hrvatska, pg 119
Znaci Vremena, Institut Za Istrazivanje Biblije, pg 120

Czech Republic

Atlantis sro, pg 123
Aurora, pg 123
Barrister & Principal, pg 123
Jiri Chvojka, pg 123
Columbus, pg 123
Jota, pg 125
Kalich SRO, pg 125
Karmelitanske Nakladatelstvi, pg 125
Karolinum, nakladatelstvi, pg 125
Pavla Momcilova, pg 126
Nadace Lyry Pragensis, pg 126
Cesky normalizacni institut, pg 127
Paseka, pg 127
Portal Ltd, pg 127
Prostor, Ltd, pg 128
Psychoanalyticke Nakladatelstvi, pg 128
Slon Sociologicke Nakladatelstvi, pg 128
Svoboda Servis GmbH, pg 128
Votobia sro, pg 129
Zvon, pg 129

Denmark

Forlaget alokke AS, pg 129
Dansk Psykologisk Forlag, pg 131
P Haase & Sons Forlag A/S, pg 132
Holkenfeldt 3, pg 133
Forlaget Hovedland, pg 133
New Era Publications International ApS, pg 134
Samfundslitteratur, pg 135
Samlerens Forlag A/S, pg 135
Wisby & Wilkens, pg 136

Egypt (Arab Republic of Egypt)

Dar El Shorouk, pg 138
Dar El Shorouk Publishing & Distributing House, pg 138
Elias Modern Publishing House, pg 138

Estonia

Estonian Encyclopaedia Publishers Ltd, pg 140
Kunst Publishers Ltd, pg 140
Olion Publishers, pg 140
Perioodika, pg 140
Sinisukk, pg 140
Tuum, pg 141
Valgus Publishers, pg 141

Finland

Aika Oy Kristilliset Kirjat, pg 141
Kaantopiiri Oy, pg 142
Koala-Kustannus/Oy Greenbay House Publishing Ltd, pg 143
Lasten Keskus Oy, pg 143
Otava Publishing Co Ltd, pg 143
Yliopistopaino/Helsinki University Press, pg 145

France

Editions A M Metailie, pg 145
ATP - Packager, pg 149
Editions de l'Aube, pg 149
Editions des Beatitudes, Pneumatheque, pg 150
Editions Andre Bonne, pg 151
Bragelonne, pg 151
Emgleo Breiz, pg 151
Alain Brethe Editions, pg 152
Brud Nevez, pg 152
CERDIC-Publications, pg 153
Librairie Jose Corti, pg 156
La Decouverte et Syros, pg 158
Georges-Charles Demay, pg 158
Doin Editeurs, pg 160
Dunod Editeur, pg 160
Les Editeurs Reunis, pg 161
Association Frank, pg 165
Editions Infrarouge, pg 169
Editions Interferences, pg 169
Langues & Mondes/L'Asiatheque, pg 171
P Lethielleux Editions, pg 172
Macula, pg 174
Masson-Williams et Wilkins, pg 175
Noir Sur Blanc, pg 177
Editions Odile Jacob, pg 178
Presses de la Sorbonne Nouvelle/PSN, pg 181
Les Presses du Management, pg 181
Presses Universitaires de Caen, pg 181
Publications Orientalistes de France (POF), pg 182
Editions de Septembre, pg 184
Sofradif Editions Philippe Auzou, pg 185
Editions Stock, pg 186
Terre Vivante, pg 187
Thames & Hudson, pg 187
Top Editions, pg 188
Editions Trois Fontaines, pg 188
Pierre Zech Editeur, pg 189

French Polynesia

Haere Po No Tahiti, pg 190

Germany

A Francke Verlag (Tubingen und Basel), pg 191
Antiquariat und Verlag Auvermann Keip GmbH, pg 194
ARCult Media, pg 194
Ars Edition GmbH, pg 195
Babel Verlag Kevin Perryman, pg 197
Beck & Gluckler Verlag GmbH & Co KG, pg 200
Blaukreuz-Verlag Wuppertal, pg 204
BLV Verlagsgesellschaft mbH, pg 204
CEC-Cosmic Energy Connections, pg 209
Claudius Verlag, pg 211
ComMedia & Arte Verlag Bernd Mayer, pg 211
J G Cotta'sche Buchhandlung Nachfolger GmbH, pg 212
Deutscher Taschenbuch Verlag GmbH & Co KG (dtv), pg 215
Donat Verlag, pg 217
Egmont vgs verlagsgesellschaft mbH, pg 221
Europa Verlag GmbH, pg 224
Friedrich Frommann Verlag, pg 230
Genius Verlag, pg 231
GLB Parkland Verlags-und Vertriebs GmbH, pg 232
Brigitte Grabitz - ikoo Buchverlag, pg 233
Carl Hanser Verlag, pg 237
Heel Verlag GmbH, pg 238
Edition Hentrich Druck & Verlag Gebr Hentrich und Tank GmbH & Co KG, pg 239
Anton Hiersemann, Verlag, pg 240
Edition Humanistische Psychologie (EHP), pg 243
Huthig GmbH & Co KG, pg 244
Edition ID-Archiv/ID-Verlag, pg 244
Klaus Isele, pg 245
Kolibri-Verlags GmbH, pg 252
KONTEXTverlag, pg 252
Krug & Schadenberg, pg 254
Verlag Ernst Kuhn, pg 254
Landbuch-Verlagsgesellschaft mbH, pg 255
Mannerschwarm Skript Verlag Bartholomae & Co OHG, pg 260
Matthias-Gruenewald-Verlag GmbH, pg 261
mentis Verlag GmbH, pg 262
Merlin Verlag Andreas Meyer Verlags GmbH und Co KG, pg 263
Midena Verlag, pg 264
Mohr Siebeck, pg 264
Gunter Narr Verlag, pg 266
Neuthor - Verlag, pg 268
nymphenburger, pg 269
One Way Medien OHG, pg 270
Palmyra Verlag, pg 271

865

TYPE OF PUBLICATION INDEX — BOOK

Propylaeen Verlag, Zweigniederlassung Berlin der Ullstein Buchverlage GmbH, pg 275
Psychologie Verlags Union GmbH, pg 275
Quintessenz Verlags-GmbH, pg 276
Verlagsgruppe Reise-Know-How, pg 278
Romiosini Verlag, pg 280
Ruetten & Loening Berlin GmbH, pg 281
Schoeffling & Co, pg 284
Springer-Verlag GmbH & Co KG, pg 288
Steiger Verlag, pg 289
Franz Steiner Verlag Wiesbaden GmbH, pg 289
Straelener Manuskripte Verlag, pg 290
Transpress Verlagsgesellschaft mbH, pg 294
Trotzdem-Verlags Genossenschaft eG, pg 295
Unrast Verlag e V, pg 296
Vervuert Verlagsgesellschaft, pg 298
Friedr Vieweg & Sohn Verlagsgesellschaft mbH, pg 298
Wiley-VCH Verlag GmbH, pg 302
Das Wunderhorn Verlag GmbH, pg 304

Ghana
Ghana Institute of Linguistics Literacy & Bible Translation (GILLBT), pg 307

Greece
Beta Medical Publishers, pg 309
Chrysi Penna - Golden Pen Books, pg 309
Diavlos, pg 309
Govostis Publishing SA, pg 311
Denise Harvey, pg 311
Hestia-I D Hestia-Kollaros & Co Corporation, pg 311
Hiotellis P, pg 311
Kastaniotis Editions SA, pg 312
Kedros Publishers, pg 312
Kritiki Publishing, pg 312
Editions Moressopoulos, pg 313
Morfotiko Idryma Ethnikis Trapezas, pg 313
Nakas Music House, pg 313
Odysseas Publications Ltd, pg 313
Opera, pg 314
Patakis Publishers, pg 314
Psichogios Publications SA, pg 314

Hong Kong
The Chinese University Press, pg 319
Peace Book Co Ltd, pg 321
Philopsychy Press, pg 321
Research Centre for Translation, pg 321
Sun Mui Press, pg 322

Hungary
Advent Kiado, pg 323
Aranyhal Konyvkiado Goldfish Publishing, pg 323
Atlantisz Kiado, pg 323
Balassi Kiado Kft, pg 323
CEU-Press, pg 323
Jelenkor Verlag, pg 324
Joszoveg Muhely Kiado, pg 324
Mora Ferenc Ifjusagi Koenyvkiado Rt, pg 325
Panem, pg 326

Park Konyvkiado Kft (Park Publisher), pg 326
Polgar Citizen Press, pg 326

Iceland
Frjals fjolmiolun hf-Urvalsbaekur, pg 327
Frodi Ltd, pg 328
Mal og menning, pg 328

India
Addison-Wesley (Singapore) Pte Ltd, pg 329
Agricole Publishing Academy, pg 330
Bani Mandir, Book-Sellers, Publishers & Educational Suppliers, pg 332
Dutta Baruah Publishing Co Pvt Ltd, pg 336
Islamic Publishing House, pg 340
Kali For Women, pg 341
Oxford University Press, pg 345
Parimal Prakashan, pg 345
Pitambar Publishing Co (P) Ltd, pg 346
Prabhat Prakashan, pg 346
Pratibha Pratishthan, pg 346
Sasta Sahitya Mandal, pg 349

Indonesia
Andi Offset, pg 354
PT Indira, pg 355
Institut Teknologi Bandung, pg 355
Karya Anda, CV, pg 356
Mizan, pg 356
Penerbit Nusa Indah, pg 356
Yayasan Obor Indonesia, pg 357

Ireland
Clo Iar-Chonnachta Teo, pg 359
The Goldsmith Press Ltd, pg 361

Israel
The Bialik Institute, pg 365
Bitan Publishers Ltd, pg 365
Breslov Research Institute, pg 366
DAT Publications, pg 366
Gefen Publishing House Ltd, pg 367
Hakibbutz Hameuchad Publishing House Ltd, pg 368
The Institute for Israeli Arabs Studies, pg 368
The Institute for the Translation of Hebrew Literature, pg 368
Israel Exploration Society, pg 368
Mirkam Publishers, pg 370
Nehora Press, pg 371
Schocken Publishing House Ltd, pg 372
Shalem Press, pg 372
Steinhart-Katzir Publishers, pg 372
Urim Publications, pg 373

Italy
AIB Associazione Italiana Bibliotheche, pg 375
Editore Armando Armando SRL, pg 376
BeMa, pg 377
Edistudio di Brunetto Casini, pg 380
Centro Biblico, pg 380
Edizioni Centro Studi Erickson, pg 381
CIC Edizioni Internazionali, pg 381
Cittadella Editrice, pg 382
Edizioni Dedalo SRL, pg 384
Edizioni Qiqajon, pg 387

ERGA SNC di Carla Ottino Merli & C (Edizioni Realizzazioni Grafiche - Artigiana), pg 388
Folini, pg 389
Jouvence, pg 394
Kaos Edizioni SRL, pg 395
Levante, pg 395
La Luna, pg 397
Luni, pg 397
Pitagora Editrice SRL, pg 403
Rubbettino Editore, pg 406
Societa Stampa Sportiva, pg 408
Transeuropa Libri, pg 410

Japan
Bunkasha Publishing Co, Ltd, pg 415
Chikuma Shobo Publishing Co Ltd, pg 415
Contex Corporation, pg 415
The Hokuseido Press, pg 417
Iwanami Shoten, Publishers, pg 418
Japan Broadcast Publishing Co Ltd, pg 418
Kosei Publishing Co Ltd, pg 420
Myrtos Inc, pg 421
Nigensha Publishing Co Ltd, pg 422
Nippon Hoso Shuppan Kyokai (NHK Publishing), pg 422
Ohmsha Ltd, pg 423
Pearson Education Japan, pg 423
President Inc, pg 423
Sanshusha Publishing Co, Ltd, pg 424
Shincho-Sha Co Ltd, pg 425
Shufunotomo sha Co Ltd, pg 426
Sobun-Sha, pg 426
Tamagawa University Press, pg 427
Toho Book Store, pg 427
Toppan Co Ltd, pg 428
Tsukiji Shokan Publishing Co, pg 428
Yohan Shuppan, pg 429

Jordan
Al-Tanwir Al Ilmi (Scientific Enlightenment Publishing House), pg 430

Kenya
Focus Publications Ltd, pg 431
Heinemann Kenya Limited (EAEP), pg 431
Kenway Publications Ltd, pg 432
Life Challenge AFRICA, pg 433

Democratic People's Republic of Korea
The Foreign Language Press Group, pg 434
Grand People's Study House, pg 434

Republic of Korea
B & B, pg 434
Cheong-mun-gag Publishing Co, pg 435
Chung Rim Publishing Co Ltd, pg 435
Gim-Yeong Co, pg 436
Iljo-gag Publishers, pg 437
Koreaone Press Inc, pg 438
Nanam Publishing House, pg 439
Woong Jin Publishing Co Ltd, pg 440
Yeha Publishing Co Ltd, pg 441

Latvia
Alberts XII, pg 441
Artava Ltd, pg 441

Hermess Ltd, pg 442
Nordik/Tapals Publishers Ltd, pg 442
Patmos, pg 442
Preses Nams, pg 442
Vaidelote, pg 442
Vieda, pg 442

Lebanon
Librairie Orientale sal, pg 443
World Book Publishing, pg 443

Liechtenstein
Frank P van Eck Publishers, pg 444

Lithuania
Andrena Publishers, pg 445
Dargenis Publishers, pg 445
Lietus Ltd, pg 445
Lietuvos Rasytoju Sajungos Leidykla, pg 446
The Publishing House of the Lithuanian Writers' Union, pg 446
Margi Rastai Publishers, pg 446
Scena, pg 446
Sviesa Publishers, pg 446
Svietimo ir mokslo ministerijos Leidybos centras, pg 446
TEV Leidykla, pg 446
Tyto Alba Publishers, pg 446

Luxembourg
Varkki Verghese, pg 448

The Former Yugoslav Republic of Macedonia
Detska radost, pg 448
Mi-An Knigoizdatelstvo, pg 449
Strk Publishing House, pg 449
Zumpres Publishing Firm, pg 449

Malawi
Mzuzu Publishing Co, pg 451

Malaysia
Darulfikir, pg 451
Federal Publications Sdn Bhd, pg 452
Penerbit Jayatinta Sdn Bhd, pg 454
Penerbit Universiti Sains Malaysia, pg 454
Penerbitan Tinta, pg 454
Pustaka Cipta Sdn Bhd, pg 454
Pustaka Delta Pelajaran Sdn Bhd, pg 454
Tempo Publishing (M) Sdn Bhd, pg 455
Tropical Press Sdn Bhd, pg 455

Maldive Islands
Non-Formal Education Centre, pg 455

Malta
Media Centre, pg 456

Mauritius
Editions de l'Ocean Indien Ltd, pg 457

Mexico
AGT Editor SA, pg 457
Centro de Estudios Mexicanos y Centroamericanos, pg 458
Editorial Diana SA de CV, pg 459
Edamex SA de CV, pg 460
Editorial El Manual Moderno SA de CV, pg 460

Ediciones Exclusivas SA, pg 461
Editorial Fata Morgana SA de CV, pg 461
Fondo de Cultura Economica, pg 461
Libra Editorial SA de CV, pg 463
Sistemas Tecnicos de Edicion SA de CV, pg 467
Editorial Trillas SA de CV, pg 467
Universidad Veracruzana Direccion General Editorial y de Publicaciones, pg 468

Morocco

Association de la Recherche Historique et Sociale, pg 469

Namibia

Desert Research Foundation of Namibia (DRFN), pg 471

Netherlands

Aeolus Press BV, pg 472
Uitgeverij Arena BV, pg 473
Uitgeverij Jan van Arkel, pg 473
Erven J Bijleveld, pg 474
Business Contact BV, pg 475
BZZTOH Publishers, pg 475
Cadans, pg 475
De Harmonie, pg 478
Hayit Nederland BV, pg 478
Historische Uitgeverij, pg 478
Katholieke Bijbelstichting, pg 479
Podium Uitgeverij, pg 483
Prometheus, pg 483
Scriptum, pg 483
Swets & Zeitlinger Publishers, pg 485
Telos Boeken, pg 485
Tirion Uitgevers BV, pg 485
Uitgeverij G A van Oorschot bv, pg 486

New Zealand

Spinal Publications, pg 496

Nigeria

Riverside Communications, pg 501

Norway

Pax Forlag A/S, pg 504
Solum Forlag A/S, pg 505

Pakistan

Islamic Publications (Pvt) Ltd, pg 507
Maqbool Academy, pg 508
Sang-e-Meel Publications, pg 509
Vanguard Books Ltd, pg 509

Peru

Instituto de Estudios Peruanos, pg 511

Philippines

Ateneo de Manila University Press, pg 512
De La Salle University, pg 513

Poland

Wydawnictwo Dolnoslaskie, pg 516
Gdanskie Wydawnictwo Psychologiczne SC, pg 516
Ksiaznica Publishing Ltd, pg 517
Wydawnictwo Literackie, pg 517
Magnum Publishing House Ltd, pg 518
Wydawnictwo Medyczne Urban & Partner, pg 518
Ossolineum Zaklad Narodowy im Ossolinskich - Wydawnictwo, pg 518
Wydawnictwo Podsiedlik-Raniowski i Spolka, pg 519
Oficyna Wydawnicza Read Me, pg 519
'Slask' Ltd, pg 520
Videograf II Sp z o o Zaklad Poracy Chronionej, pg 520
Wydawnictwo WAB, pg 520
Wydawnictwa Przemyslowe WEMA, pg 521
Wydawnictwa Naukowo-Techniczne, pg 521

Portugal

Edicoes Cetop, pg 523
Editora Classica, pg 523
Edicoes Colibri, pg 523
Dinalivro, pg 524
Edicoes 70, Lda, pg 524
Editorial Estampa, Lda, pg 524
Europress Editores e Distribuidores de Publicacoes Lda, pg 525
Gradiva-Publicacnoes Lda, pg 525
Livraria Apostolado da Imprensa, pg 526
Livraria Minerva Editora, pg 526
Quimera Editores, pg 529
Editora Replicacao Lda, pg 529
Edicoes 70, pg 529
Talento, pg 529

Romania

Editura Academiei Romane, pg 531
Editura Aius, pg 531
Ars Longa Publishing House, pg 532
Artemis Verlag, pg 532
Editura Clusium, Casa de Editura Atlas-Clusium SRL, pg 532
Editura Dacia, pg 532
Enzyklopadie Verlag, pg 533
Editura Excelsior, pg 533
FF Press, pg 533
Editura Gryphon, pg 533
Editura Humanitas, pg 533
Humanitas Publishing House, pg 533
Editura Institutul European, pg 533
Editura Kriterion SA, pg 534
Lider Verlag, pg 534
Mentor Kiado, pg 534
Editura Meridiane, pg 534
Editura Niculescu, pg 534
Polirom Verlag, pg 535
RAO International Publishing Co, pg 535
RAO Publishing Group, pg 535
Rentrop & Straton Verlagsgruppe und Wirtschaftsconsulting, pg 535
Saeculum IO, pg 535
Editura Stiintifica, pg 536
Editura Teora, pg 536
Editura Univers, pg 536

Russian Federation

Armada Publishing House, pg 537
Aspect Press Ltd, pg 537
BLIC, russko-Baltijskij informaciionnyj centr, AO, pg 537
CentrePolygraph Traders & Publishers Co, pg 537
Finansy i Statistika Publishing House, pg 538
Fizmatlit Publishing Co, pg 538
Glas New Russian Writing, pg 538
Interbook-Business AO, pg 538
Izdatel'stvo Ural'skogo, pg 538
Izdatelskii Dom Kompozitor, pg 539
Ladomir Publishing House, pg 539
Publishing House Limbus Press, pg 539
Izdatelstvo Medicina, pg 539
Izdatelstvo Mir, pg 540
Izdatelstvo Muzyka, pg 540
Nauka Publishers, pg 540
Panorama Publishing House, pg 541
Profizdat, pg 541
Raduga Publishers, pg 541
St Andrew's Biblical Theological College, pg 541
Teorija Verojatnostej i ee Primenenija, pg 542
Text Publishers Ltd Too, pg 542
Top Secret Collection Publishers, pg 542

Saudi Arabia

King Saud University, pg 543

Slovakia

ARCHA sro Vydavatel'stro, pg 549
Vydavatelstvo Obzor, pg 550
Vydavatepstvo Praca spol sro, pg 550
Priroda, pg 550
Serafin, pg 550
Slo Viet, pg 550
Vydavatel'stvo Osveta (Verlag Osveta), pg 551

Slovenia

Zalozba Mihelac d o o, pg 552
Zalozba Obzorja d d Maribor, pg 552

South Africa

Human & Rousseau (Pty) Ltd, pg 555
Institute for Reformational Studies CHE, pg 555

Spain

Editorial Acribia SA, pg 561
Ediciones Akal SA, pg 562
Anglo-Didactica, SL Editorial, pg 563
Ediciones Atril, pg 564
CEAC, Grupo Editorial SA, pg 567
Complutense, SA Editorial, pg 568
Edi-Liber Irlan SA, pg 571
Egales (Editorial Gai y Lesbiana), pg 572
Elkar, Euskal Liburu eta Kantuen Argitaldaria, SL, pg 573
Emece Editores, pg 573
Erein, pg 573
Fundacion de Estudios Libertarios Anselmo Lorenzo, pg 575
Fundacion Rosacruz, pg 575
Galaxia SA Editorial, pg 575
Editorial Gustavo Gili SA, pg 576
Editorial Gulaab, pg 577
Ediciones Hiperion SL, pg 577
Ibaizabal Edelvives SA, pg 577
Llibres del Segle, pg 580
Edicions de la Magrana SA, pg 581
Ediciones Minotauro, pg 582
Anaya & Mario Muchnik, pg 583
Ediciones del Oriente y del Mediterraneo, pg 585
Editorial Peregrino SL, pg 586
Pre-Textos, pg 587
Edicions Proa, SA, pg 588
Universidad de Santiago de Compostela, pg 589
Editorial Thassalia, SA, pg 592
Ediciones de la Torre, pg 593
Trea Ediciones, SL, pg 593
Tursen, SA, pg 593
Publicacions de la Universitat de Barcelona, pg 594
Universitat de Valencia Servei de Publicacions, pg 594
Ediciones Urano, SA, pg 595
Editorial Verbum SL, pg 595
Vinaches Lopez, Luisa, pg 595

Sri Lanka

Dayawansa Jayakody & Co, pg 597
Pradeepa Publishers, pg 598
Swarna Hansa Foundation, pg 598

Sweden

Ellerstroms, pg 602
Hillelforlaget, pg 603
Bokforlaget Nya Doxa AB, pg 605

Switzerland

Ammann Verlag & Co, pg 608
Cockatoo Press (Schweiz), Thailand-Publikationen, pg 611
Edition Epoca, pg 613
Haffmans Verlag AG, pg 615
Kanisius Verlag, pg 616
Verlag Nagel & Kimche AG, Zurich, pg 619
Editions Patino, pg 621
Rodera-Verlag der Cardun AG, pg 623
Rotpunktverlag, pg 623
Verlag im Waldgut AG, pg 627

Syrian Arab Republic

Damascus University Press, pg 628

Taiwan, Province of China

Cheng Wen Publishing Company, pg 629
Chu Liu Book Company, pg 629
Fuh-Wen Book Co, pg 630
Hsiao Yuan Publication Co, Ltd, pg 630
Laureate Book Co Ltd, pg 631
Lead Wave Publishing Company Ltd, pg 631
Lin Pai Press Company Ltd, pg 631
Linking Publishing Company Ltd, pg 631
San Min Book Co Ltd, pg 631
World Book Co Ltd, pg 632
Yee Wen Publishing Co Ltd, pg 632
Yi Hsien Publishing Co Ltd, pg 632
Youth Cultural Publishing Co, pg 632
Yuan Liou Publishing Co, Ltd, pg 632

United Republic of Tanzania

Kanisa la Biblia Publishers (KLB), pg 633
Northwestern Publishers, pg 634
Press & Publicity Centre Ltd, pg 634
Tanzania Publishing House, pg 634

Thailand

Bannakit Trading, pg 635
Sang Dad Publishing Company Ltd, pg 635

Tunisia

Academie Tunisienne des Sciences, des Lettres et des Arts Beit El Hekma, pg 637
Maison Tunisienne de l'Edition, pg 638

TYPE OF PUBLICATION INDEX — BOOK

Turkey
Alkim Kitapcilik-Yayimcilik, pg 638
Arkadas Ltd, pg 639
Arkeoloji Ve Sanat Yayinlari, pg 639
Iletisim Yayinlari, pg 640
Inkilap Publishers Ltd, pg 640
Kubbealti Akademisi Kultur ve Sasat Vakfi, pg 640
Metis Yayinlari, pg 640
Sabah Kitaplari, pg 641
Varlik Yayinlari AS, pg 641

Ukraine
ASK Ltd, pg 643
Osnova, Kharkov State University Press, pg 643
Osnovy Publishers, pg 643
Veselka Publishers, pg 643

United Kingdom
Umberto Allemandi & Co Publishing, pg 646
Aris & Phillips Ltd, pg 648
Atlas Press, pg 651
Boulevard Books UK/The Babel Guides, pg 657
Calder Publications Ltd, pg 662
Canongate Books Ltd, pg 663
Carcanet Press Ltd, pg 663
Dedalus Ltd, pg 674
Discovery Walking Guides Ltd, pg 675
Aidan Ellis Publishing, pg 678
Garnet Publishing Ltd, pg 685
Gomer Press (J D Lewis & Sons Ltd), pg 688
Gwasg y Dref Wen, pg 690
Gwasg Gwenffrwd, pg 690
Peter Halban Publishers Ltd, pg 691
HarperCollins Publishers, pg 692
The Harvill Press Ltd, pg 693
Icon Press, pg 698
Institute of Physics Publishing, pg 700
International Bee Research Association, pg 701
Islam International Publications Ltd, pg 701
Kegan Paul International Ltd, pg 703
The Littman Library of Jewish Civilization, pg 708
Manchester University Press, pg 711
Motilal (UK) Books of India, pg 715
The Octagon Press Ltd, pg 720
The Oleander Press, pg 721
Peter Owen Ltd, pg 722
Planet, pg 728
Poetry Wales Press Ltd, pg 729
Profile Books Ltd, pg 731
Reaktion Books Ltd, pg 733
The Rubicon Press, pg 737
St Jerome Publishing, pg 738
SCM Press, pg 739
Seren, pg 740
Serpent's Tail Ltd, pg 740
Skoob Russell Square, pg 742
University of Wales Press, pg 751
Veloce Publishing Ltd, pg 752
Verso, pg 752
The Women's Press Ltd, pg 758

Uruguay
Ediciones Trilce, pg 761

Viet Nam
Science & Technics Publishing House, pg 763

Yugoslavia
Alfa-Narodna Knjiga, pg 764
Savez Inzenjera i Tehnicara Jugoslavije, pg 765

Zimbabwe
Christian Audio-Visual Action (CAVA), pg 768
The Literature Bureau, pg 768
Zimbabwe Publishing House (Pvt) Ltd, pg 769
Zimbabwe Women Writers, pg 770

UNIVERSITY PRESSES

Albania
NL SH, pg 1

Algeria
Enterprise Nationale du Livre (ENAL), pg 2

Argentina
EUDEBA (Editorial Universitaria de Buenos Aires), pg 6

Australia
AHB Publications, pg 11
Australian Scholarly Publishing, pg 14
Butterworths Australia Ltd, pg 16
Deakin University Press, pg 20
Hayes Publishing, pg 26
Maxwell Macmillan Publishing (Australia) Pty Ltd, pg 32
Melbourne University Press, pg 33
La Trobe University Press, pg 45
University of New South Wales Press Ltd, pg 46

Austria
Abakus Verlag GmbH, pg 49
Buchhandlung WUV Dolmetsch, pg 50
Linde Verlag Wien GmbH, pg 54
Oesterreichischer Kunst und Kulturverlag, pg 56
Andreas Schnider Verlags-Atelier, pg 58
Verband der Wissenschaftlichen Gesellschaften Oesterreichs (VWGOe), pg 60
WUV/Facultas Universitaetsverlag, pg 61

Bangladesh
Bangladesh Publishers, pg 62

Belgium
Academia-Bruylant, pg 63
Academia Press, pg 64
Artel SC, pg 64
Brepols Publishers NV, pg 65
Campinia Media VZW, pg 65
Editions De Boeck-Larcier SA, pg 67
King Baudouin Foundation, pg 70
Editions Lessius ASBL, pg 71
Leuven University Press, pg 71
La Part de L'Oeil, pg 72
Presses agronomiques de Gembloux ASBL, pg 73
Presses Universitaires de Namur ASBL, pg 73
Publications des Facultes Universitaires Saint Louis, pg 73
VUB University Press, pg 75

Bosnia and Herzegovina
Bemust doo Novinsko-Izdavacko stamparsko i trgovacko preduzece, pg 77

Brazil
Alzira Chagas Carpigiani, pg 80
EDUSC - Editora da Universidade do Sagrado Coracao, pg 82
Thex Editora e Distribuidora Ltda, pg 92
Editora UNESP, pg 92
Editora da Universidade de Sao Paulo, pg 93
Editora Universidade Federal do Rio de Janeiro, pg 93

Bulgaria
Abagar, Veliko Tarnovo, pg 94
Ciela Publishing House, pg 94
Heron Press Publishing House, pg 96
Kralica MAB, pg 96
Lettera, pg 96
Sita-MB, pg 98
TEMTO, pg 98
WTU Todor Kableskov, pg 98

Cameroon
Presses Universitaires d'Afrique, pg 99

Chile
Edeval (Universidad de Valparaiso), pg 100
Ediciones Universitarias de Valparaiso, pg 101

China
Beijing Medical Univ Press, pg 102
China Materials Management Publishing House, pg 103
Chongqing University Press, pg 104
East China University of Science & Technology Press, pg 105
Foreign Language Teaching & Research Press, pg 105
Nanjing University Press, pg 107
Shandong University Press, pg 109
Shanghai Foreign Language Education Press, pg 109
South China University of Science and Technology Press, pg 109
Southwest China Jiaotong University Press, pg 109
Tsinghua University Press, pg 110
Wuhan University Press, pg 110
Zhejiang University Press, pg 110

Colombia
Universidad Externado de Colombia, pg 112
Universidad de Antioquia, Division Publicaciones, pg 114

Costa Rica
Editorial Universidad Nacional (EUNA), pg 117
Editorial Universitaria Centroamericana (EDUCA), pg 117

Cote d'Ivoire
Universite d' Abidjan, pg 118

Croatia
Matica hrvatska, pg 119

Cuba
Universidad Central de la Villas, Centro Documentacion e Informacion Cientifica Tecnica, pg 121

Czech Republic
Doplnek, pg 124
Karolinum, nakladatelstvi, pg 125
Mendelova zemedelska a lesnicka univerzita v Brne, pg 126
Psychoanalyticke Nakladatelstvi, pg 128

Denmark
Aarhus Universitetsforlag, pg 129
Dansk Psykologisk Forlag, pg 131
FADL's Forlag A/S (Foreningen af danske Laegestuderendes Forlag), pg 132
Museum Tusculanum Press, pg 134
Samfundslitteratur, pg 135

Dominican Republic
Pontificia Universidad Catolica Madre y Maestra, pg 136

Egypt (Arab Republic of Egypt)
Al Arab Publishing House, pg 138
Dar El Shorouk Publishing & Distributing House, pg 138

Finland
Abo Akademis forlag - Abo Akademi University Press, pg 141
Osuuskunta Vastapaino, pg 145
Yliopistopaino/Helsinki University Press, pg 145

France
APRD - Association pour la Recherche et l'Information demographiques, pg 147
Autrement Editions, pg 149
Presses Universitaires de Bordeaux (PUB), pg 151
Comite National d'Evaluation (CNE), pg 156
Editions Dalloz Sirey, pg 157
Editions de l'Ecole des Hautes Etudes en Sciences Sociales (EHESS), pg 160
Presses de l'Ecole Normale Superieure, pg 160
ELLUG (Editions Litteraires et Linguistiques de l'Universite de Grenoble III), pg 162
L'Esprit Du Temps, pg 162
Institut d'Etudes Slaves, pg 163
Paul Geuthner Librairie Orientaliste, pg 166
Editions Jean Paul Gisserot, pg 166
Hachette Education, pg 167
L'Harmattan, pg 168
Les Introuvables-Editions L'Harmattan, pg 170
Editions de la Maison des Sciences de l'Homme, Paris, pg 174
Presses Universitaires du Mirail, pg 176
Editions Ophrys, pg 178
Editions Paradigme, pg 179
Presses de la Sorbonne Nouvelle/ PSN, pg 181
Presses Universitaires de Caen, pg 181
Presses Universitaires du Septentrion, pg 181
Publications de l'Universite de Rouen, pg 182

PUBLISHERS

Publications Orientalistes de France (POF), pg 182
Publications de la Sorbonne, pg 186
Universitas, pg 188
Publications de l'Universite de Pau, pg 188

French Polynesia

Scoop/Au Vent des Iles, pg 190

Germany

A Francke Verlag (Tubingen und Basel), pg 191
BertelsmannSpringer Science & Business Media GmbH, pg 202
campusbooks Medien AG, pg 209
Degener & Co, Manfred Dreiss Verlag, pg 213
Deutsche Landwirtschaft-Gesellschaft VerlagsgesGmbH, pg 214
Diesterweg, Moritz Verlag, pg 216
Erika Heydick Sax-Verlag Beucha, pg 240
ITpress Verlag, pg 245
Iudicium Verlag GmbH, pg 245
Justus-Liebig-Universitat Giessen, pg 247
kopaed verlagsgmbh, pg 252
Michael Lassleben Verlag, pg 256
Leipziger Universitaetsverlag GmbH, pg 257
Musikantiquariat und Dr Hans Schneider Verlag GmbH, pg 266
Gunter Narr Verlag, pg 266
Nusser Verlag, pg 269
Edition Parabolis, pg 271
Philipps-Universitaet Marburg, pg 273
Roehrig Universitaets Verlag Gmbh, pg 279
Stauffenburg Verlag Brigitte Narr GmbH, pg 289
Trotzdem-Verlags Genossenschaft eG, pg 295
UVK Universitatsverlag Konstanz GmbH, pg 297
Waxmann Verlag GmbH, pg 300
Weidler Buchverlag Berlin, pg 301

Greece

Beta Medical Publishers, pg 309
Hestia-I D Hestia-Kollaros & Co Corporation, pg 311
Kardamitsa A, pg 312
Kritiki Publishing, pg 312
Kyriakidis, pg 312
Panepistimio Ioanninon, pg 314
Sakkoulas Publications SA, pg 314

Hong Kong

The Chinese University Press, pg 319
Hong Kong University Press, pg 320

Hungary

Atlantisz Kiado, pg 323
Balassi Kiado Kft, pg 323
CEU-Press, pg 323
Kiiarat Konyvdiado, pg 324

Iceland

Haskolautgafan - University of Iceland Press, pg 328

India

Oxford University Press, pg 345
Reliance Publishing House, pg 347
Scientific Book Agency, pg 349

Indonesia

Institut Teknologi Bandung, pg 355
Karya Anda, CV, pg 356

Ireland

Cork University Press, pg 359
Gandon Editions, pg 360

Israel

Bar Ilan University Press, pg 365
Bezalel Academy of Arts & Design, pg 365
The Bialik Institute, pg 365
Dekel Publishing House, pg 366
Dyonon/Papyrus Publishing House of the Tel-Aviv, pg 367
Haifa University Press, pg 368
Hakibbutz Hameuchad Publishing House Ltd, pg 368
Open University of Israel, pg 371

Italy

All'Insegna del Giglio, pg 375
Franco Angeli SRL, pg 375
Editore Armando Armando SRL, pg 376
Belforte Editore Libraio srl, pg 377
BeMa, pg 377
Giuseppe Bonanno Editore, pg 378
Bonsignori Editore SRL, pg 378
Book Editore, pg 378
Editore Giorgio Bretschneider, pg 378
Campanotto, pg 379
Edizioni Cantagalli, pg 379
Casa Editrice Libraria Ulrico Hoepli SpA, pg 380
CEDAM (Casa Editrice Dr A Milani), pg 380
CELID, pg 380
Centro Italiano Studi Alto Medioevo, pg 381
Centro Studi Terzo Mondo, pg 381
Il Cigno Galileo Galilei-Edizioni di Arte e Scienza, pg 381
Cittadella Editrice, pg 382
CLUEB (Cooperativa Libraria Universitaria Editrice Bologna), pg 382
CLUT Editrice, pg 382
Nuova Coletti Editore Roma, pg 382
Cooperativa Libraria IULM SCRL, pg 383
La Culturale, pg 383
M d'Auria Editore SAS, pg 384
Edizioni Dedalo SRL, pg 384
Edizioni del Centro, pg 384
Ecole Francaise de Rome, pg 385
Edi Ermes SRL, pg 386
EDIFIR SRL, pg 386
EGEA (Edizioni Giuridiche Economiche Aziendali), pg 387
Etas Libri, pg 388
Festina Lente Edizioni, pg 389
G Giappichelli Editore SRL, pg 390
Giuseppe Laterza Editore Snc, pg 391
Instituti Editoriali E Poligrafici Internazionali SRL, pg 393
Ist Patristico Augustinianum, pg 394
Editoriale Jaca Book SpA, pg 394
Editrice LAS, pg 395
LED - Edizioni Universitarie di Lettere Economia Diritto, pg 395
Lindau, pg 396
Linea d'Ombra Libri, pg 396
Lubrina Editore Srl, pg 397
Milella di Lecce Spazio Vivo SRL, pg 399
Monduzzi Editore SpA, pg 399
Moretti & Vitali editori srl, pg 400

TYPE OF PUBLICATION INDEX

Istituto Nazionale di Archeologia e Storia dell'Arte, pg 400
Maria Pacini Fazzi Editore, pg 402
Palatina Editrice, pg 402
Paravia Bruno Mondadori Editori, pg 402
Pitagora Editrice SRL, pg 403
Rara-Ist Editoriale di Bibliofilia e Reprints, pg 405
Edizioni Universitarie Romane, pg 406
SEMAR Publishers SRL, pg 407
Sicania, pg 408
Edizioni Librarie Siciliane, pg 408
Edizioni Sorbona Milano, pg 408
Istituto Storico Italiano per l'Eta Moderna e Contemporanea, pg 409
Editrice Tirrenia Stampatori SAS, pg 410
Transeuropa Libri, pg 410
Unipress, pg 410
Urbaniana University Press, pg 410
Vita e Pensiero, pg 411

Jamaica

The Press, pg 413

Japan

Hakutei-Sha, pg 417
Tamagawa University Press, pg 427
Waseda University Press, pg 428

Kenya

Nairobi University Press, pg 433

Democratic People's Republic of Korea

Grand People's Study House, pg 434

Republic of Korea

Suhagsa, pg 440
Yonsei University Press, pg 441

Lithuania

Klaipedos Universiteto Leidykla, pg 445
TEV Leidykla, pg 446

Malaysia

Penerbit Universiti Sains Malaysia, pg 454
University of Malaya, Department of Publications, pg 455

Mexico

Colegio de Postgraduados en Ciencias Agricolas, pg 459
Publicaciones Cruz O SA, pg 459
El Colegio de Michoacan A C, pg 460
Instituto Nacional de Antropologia e Historia, pg 464

Republic of Moldova

Lumina Publishing House, pg 468

Morocco

Association de la Recherche Historique et Sociale, pg 469

Namibia

Multi-Disciplinary Research Centre Library, pg 471

Netherlands

Uitgeverij Jan van Arkel, pg 473
Backhuys Publishers BV, pg 473
Delft University Press, pg 476
KITLV Press Royal Institute of Linguistics & Anthropology, pg 479
Koninklijke Vermande bv, pg 480
Pearson Education Netherlands, pg 482
Tilburg University Press, pg 485
Twente University Press, pg 485

New Zealand

Auckland University Press, pg 488
Canterbury University Press, pg 489
Lincoln University Press, pg 492
University of Otago Press, pg 496

Norway

Glydendal Akademisk, pg 503

Peru

Instituto de Estudios Peruanos, pg 511
Universidad de Lima-Fondo de Desarollo Editorial, pg 512

Philippines

Ateneo de Manila University Press, pg 512
De La Salle University, pg 513
UST Publishing House, pg 515

Poland

Gdanskie Wydawnictwo Psychologiczne SC, pg 516
Impuls, pg 517
Katolicki Uniwersytet Wydawniczo-Redakcja, pg 517
'Slask' Ltd, pg 520
Oficyna Wydawnicza Szkoly Glownej Handlowej w Warszawie Oficyna Wydawnicza SGH, pg 520
Wydawnictwa Uniwersytetu Warszawskiego, pg 521

Portugal

Edicoes Colibri, pg 523
Dinalivro, pg 524
Editorial Estampa, Lda, pg 524
Imprensa Nacional-Casa da Moeda, pg 526
Planeta Editora, LDA, pg 528
Silabo, pg 529
Usus Editora, pg 530

Puerto Rico

Libros-Ediciones Homines, pg 530

Romania

Editura Dacia, pg 532
Editura Excelsior, pg 533
Editura Minerva, pg 534
Editura Niculescu, pg 534
Polirom Verlag, pg 535

Russian Federation

N E Bauman Moscow State Technical University Publishers, pg 537
FGUP Izdatelstvo Mashinostroenie, pg 538
Finansy i Statistika Publishing House, pg 538
Izdatel'stvo Kazanskago Universiteta, pg 538

TYPE OF PUBLICATION INDEX

Izdatel'stvo Mordovskogo gosudar stvennogo, pg 538
Izdatel'stvo Ural' skogo, pg 538
Izdatel'stvo Nizhegorodskogo Gosudarstvennogo Univ, pg 540
St Andrew's Biblical Theological College, pg 541
Teorija Verojatnostej i ee Primenenija, pg 542
Voronezh State University Publishers, pg 542

Singapore
Institute of Southeast Asian Studies, pg 546
Select Books Pte Ltd, pg 548
Singapore University Press Pte Ltd, pg 548
Taylor & Francis Asia Pacific, pg 548

Slovakia
Priroda, pg 550
Ustav informacii a prognoz skolstva mladeze a telovychovy, pg 551
Zilinska Univerzita, pg 551

South Africa
Human Sciences Research Council, pg 555
Institute for Reformational Studies CHE, pg 555
Unisa Press, pg 560
University of Natal Press, pg 560
Witwatersrand University Press, pg 560

Spain
Ediciones Akal SA, pg 562
Editorial Deimos, SL, pg 569
Dykinson SL, pg 571
Publicaciones Etea, pg 574
Grupo Comunicar, pg 576
Editorial Horsori SL, pg 577
Idea Books, SA, pg 578
Ediciones Libertarias/Prodhufi SA, pg 580
Ediciones Morata SL, pg 583
Prensas Universitarias de Zaragoza, pg 587
Servicio de Publicaciones Universidad de Cadiz, pg 590
Servicio de Publicaciones Universidad de Cordoba, pg 590
Tesitex, SL, pg 592
Trea Ediciones, SL, pg 593
Universidad de Malaga, pg 594
Universidad de Oviedo Servicio de Publicaciones, pg 594
Universidad de Valladolid Secretariado de Publicaciones e Intercambio Editorial, pg 594

Sweden
Acta Universitatis Gothoburgensis, pg 599

Switzerland
Birkhauser Verlag AG, pg 610
Helbing und Lichtenhahn Verlag AG, pg 615
Verlag Industrielle Organisation, pg 616
Editions Payot Lausanne, pg 621
Trans Tech Publications SA, pg 626
Vdf Hochschulverlag AG an der ETH Zurich, pg 626

Syrian Arab Republic
Institut Francais d'Etudes Arabes de Damas, pg 628

Taiwan, Province of China
World Book Co Ltd, pg 632

United Republic of Tanzania
DUP (1996) Ltd, pg 633

Tunisia
Faculte des Sciences Humaines et Sociales de Tunis, pg 638

Turkey
Alkim Kitapcilik-Yayimcilik, pg 638
Soez Yayin/Oyunajans, pg 641

Ukraine
Osnova, Kharkov State University Press, pg 643

United Kingdom
The Athlone Press Ltd, pg 650
Books for Europe Ltd, pg 657
Commonwealth Secretariat, pg 669
Harvard University Press, pg 692
Imperial College Press, pg 699
Institute of Irish Studies, The Queens University of Belfast, pg 699
Liverpool University Press, pg 708
Manchester University Press, pg 711
Marcham Books, pg 711
McGraw-Hill Publishing Company, pg 712
Motilal (UK) Books of India, pg 715
Open University Press, pg 721
Pearson Education Europe, Mideast & Africa, pg 725
The Policy Press, pg 729
St Jerome Publishing, pg 738
University of Exeter Press, pg 751
University of Wales Press, pg 751
Voltaire Foundation Ltd, pg 753
Yale University Press London, pg 759

VIDEO CASSETTES

Argentina
San Pablo, pg 8

Australia
Australian Large Print Pty Ltd, pg 14
Bridge To Peace Publications, pg 16
Deakin University Press, pg 20
Department for Education & Children's Services, South Australia, pg 20
Encyclopaedia Britannica (Australia) Inc, pg 22
Fraser Publications, pg 23
Hampden Press, pg 25
Lonely Planet Publications Pty Ltd, pg 30
Barry Long Books, pg 30
New Creation Publications Ministries & Resource Centre, pg 34
OTEN (Open Training & Education Network), pg 36
Oxfam Community Aid Abroad, pg 36
RMIT Publishing, pg 41

Austria
Edition S der OSD, pg 51
Oesterreichischer Kunst und Kulturverlag, pg 56
Verlag des Osterr Kneippbundes GmbH, pg 57
Osterreichischer Bundesveilag Ges.mbh, pg 57

Belgium
Uitgeverij De Sikkel NV, pg 74

Brazil
A & A & A Edicoes e Promocoes Internacionais Ltda, pg 77
Horus Editora Ltda, pg 85

China
Beijing Publishing House, pg 102
Beijing University Press, pg 102
China Film Press, pg 103
China Machine Press (CMP), pg 103
Foreign Language Teaching & Research Press, pg 105
Fudan University Press, pg 105
People's Education Press, pg 107
Shanghai Educational Publishing House, pg 109
Southwest China Jiaotong University Press, pg 109
Tsinghua University Press, pg 110

Colombia
Consejo Episcopal Latinoamericano Celam, pg 111

Costa Rica
Centro Agronomico Tropical de Investigacion y Ensenanza (CATIE), pg 115
Promesa, Ediciones, pg 116

Cuba
Casa Editora Abril, pg 120

Czech Republic
Karmelitanske Nakladatelstvi, pg 125

Denmark
Forlaget alokke AS, pg 129
Kaleidoscope Publishers Ltd, pg 133
Kraks Forlag AS, pg 133
Mellemfolkeligt Samvirke, pg 133
Scandinavia Publishing House, pg 135
Systime, pg 136

Fiji
University of the South Pacific, pg 141

Finland
Aika Oy Kristilliset Kirjat, pg 141

France
Editions Amrita SA, pg 147
Cirad, pg 155
Institut d'Etudes Augustiniennes, pg 163
Folklore Comtois, pg 164
INRA Editions (Institut National de la Recherche Agronomique), pg 169
Le Livre de Paris, pg 173
Editions Memoire des Arts, pg 175
Editions de la Reunion des Musees Nationaux, pg 176
Editions du Centre Pompidou, pg 180
Editions Prosveta SA, pg 182
Sofradif Editions Philippe Auzou, pg 185

Germany
Alouette Verlag, pg 193
AOL-Verlag Frohmut Menze, pg 194
Beleke KG Verlag, pg 200
Bibliographisches Institut & F A Brockhaus AG, pg 203
Buechse der Pandora Verlags-GmbH, pg 207
Carl-Auer-Systeme Verlag, pg 209
CEC-Cosmic Energy Connections, pg 209
Datacom Buchverlag GmbH, pg 212
Falken-Verlag GmbH, pg 227
FN-Verlag der Deutschen Reiterlichen Vereinigung GmbH, pg 229
Lehrmittelverlag Wilhelm Hagemann GmbH, pg 236
Happy Mental Buch- und Musik Verlag, pg 237
Hayit Reisefuhrer in der Rutsker Verlag GmbH, pg 238
Huss-Medien GmbH, pg 243
Knowledge Media International, pg 251
Verlagsgruppe Koehler/Mittler, pg 251
kopaed verlagsgmbh, pg 252
Koptisch-Orthodoxes Zentrum, pg 252
Franckh-Kosmos Verlags-GmbH & Co, pg 252
Lahn-Verlag GmbH, pg 255
Medizinisch-Literarische Verlagsgesellschaft mbH, pg 262
Naumann & Goebel Verlagsgesellschaft mbH, pg 267
Nusser Verlag, pg 269
Georg Olms Verlag AG, pg 270
Osho Verlag GmbH, pg 271
Pollner Verlag, pg 274
Polyband Gesellschaft fur Bild Tontraeger mbH & Co Betriebs KG, pg 274
Quintessenz Verlags-GmbH, pg 276
Schulz-Kirchner Verlag GmbH, pg 285
Silberburg-Verlag Titus Haeussermann GmbH, pg 287
Springer-Verlag GmbH & Co KG, pg 288
TR - Verlagsunion GmbH, pg 294
Turkischer Schulbuchverlag Onel Cengiz, pg 295
Ulrich Schiefer bahnVerlag, pg 296
Verlag fur Schweissen und Verwandte Verfahren, pg 298
Curt R Vincentz Verlag, pg 298
Vista Point Verlag GmbH, pg 299
Voggenreiter-Verlag, pg 299
Verlagsgruppe Weltbild GmbH, pg 301

Greece
Apostoliki Diakonia tis Ekklisias tis Hellados, pg 309

Guyana
Community Based Rehabilitation Progeamme, pg 317

PUBLISHERS

Hong Kong
Christian Communications Ltd, pg 319

Hungary
Nemzeti Tankoenyvkiado, pg 326
Polgar Citizen Press, pg 326

Iceland
Namsgagnastofnun, pg 328

India
Nem Chand & Brothers, pg 344
Spectrum Publications, pg 350
Theosophical Publishing House, pg 351

Ireland
Cathedral Books Ltd, pg 359
Ossian Publications, pg 363

Israel
Doko Video Ltd, pg 366
Hanitzotz A-Sharara Publishing House, pg 368
Prolog Publishing House, pg 371
R Sirkis Publishers Ltd, pg 372

Italy
Umberto Allemandi & C SRL, pg 375
Baha'i, pg 377
CIC Edizioni Internazionali, pg 381
Edi Ermes SRL, pg 386
Elle Di Ci - Libreria Dottrina Cristiana, pg 388
Istituto Geografico de Agostini SpA, pg 390
Ernesto Gremese Editore SRL, pg 391
IHT Gruppo Editoriale SRL, pg 393
Museo Storico in Trento, pg 400
RAI.ERI, pg 405
Red/Studio Redazionale SpA, pg 405
Societa Stampa Sportiva, pg 408
Editrice Uomini Nuovi, pg 410
Vivalda Editori SRL, pg 411

Jamaica
Association of Development Agencies, pg 412
Institute of Jamaica Publications, pg 413

Japan
AVACO - Christian Mass Communications Center, pg 414
Iwanami Shoten, Publishers, pg 418
Myrtos Inc, pg 421
Nigensha Publishing Co Ltd, pg 422
Nobunkyo (Rural Village Culture Association), pg 423
Ongaku No Tomo Sha Corporation, pg 423
Seibido, pg 424
Tokyo Shoseki Co Ltd, pg 427
Yohan Shuppan, pg 429

Kenya
Jacaranda Designs Ltd, pg 432
Life Challenge AFRICA, pg 433

Republic of Korea
Korea Britannica Corp, pg 437
Moon Jin Media Co Ltd, pg 438

Maldive Islands
Non-Formal Education Centre, pg 455

Mexico
Ediciones Culturales Internacionales SA de CV Edicion Compra y Venta de Libros, Casetes, Videos, pg 459
Editorial Jilguero, SA de CV, pg 462
Organizacion Cultural LP SA de CV, pg 465
SCRIPTA - Distribucion y Servicios Editoriales, SA de CV, pg 467

Namibia
Desert Research Foundation of Namibia (DRFN), pg 471

Netherlands
Elmar BV, pg 476
Hayit Nederland BV, pg 478
Uitgeverij Lemma BV, pg 480

New Zealand
Learning Media Ltd, pg 492

Philippines
Communication Foundation for Asia Media Group (CFAMG), pg 513
Encyclopaedia Britannica (Philippines) Inc, pg 513
Rex Bookstores & Publishers, pg 514

Poland
Polish Scientific Publishers PWN, pg 519

Romania
Editura Minerva, pg 534

Slovenia
Mladinska Knjiga International, pg 552
Zalozba Obzorja d d Maribor, pg 552

South Africa
Bet-El Publishers, pg 553
Reader's Digest Southern Africa, pg 559

Spain
Alinco SA - Aura Comunicacio, pg 563
Editorial Astri SA, pg 564
Editorial Casals SA, pg 566
Editorial Claret SA, pg 568
Didaco Comunicacion y Didactica, SA, pg 569
Edilux, pg 572
Fundacion de Estudios Libertarios Anselmo Lorenzo, pg 575
Editorial la Muralla SA, pg 583
Pulso Ediciones, SL, pg 588
San Pablo Ediciones, pg 589
Publicacions de la Universitat de Barcelona, pg 594

TYPE OF PUBLICATION INDEX

Sweden
Folkuniversitetets foerlag, pg 602
Hans Richter Laromedel, pg 604

Switzerland
Vexer Verlag, pg 627
Editions Vivez Soleil SA, pg 627

Taiwan, Province of China
Echo Publishing Company Ltd, pg 629

Thailand
Thai Watana Panich Co, Ltd, pg 636

Turkey
Soez Yayin/Oyunajans, pg 641

United Kingdom
Ian Allan Publishing Ltd, pg 646
Umberto Allemandi & Co Publishing, pg 646
BBC English, pg 652
BCA, pg 653
Chorion IP, pg 667
E W Classey Ltd, pg 668
Coachwise Ltd, pg 668
Dorling Kindersley Ltd, pg 676
Encyclopaedia Britannica (UK) International Ltd, pg 679
GMC Publications Ltd, pg 687
Imperial College Press, pg 699
Linguaphone Institute Ltd, pg 708
New Era Publications UK Ltd, pg 718
Pavilion Publishing (Brighton) Ltd, pg 725
Phaidon Press Ltd, pg 726
Plough Publishing House of Bruderhof Communities in the UK, pg 728
Portland Press Ltd, pg 730
The Reader's Digest Association Ltd, pg 733
Sage Publications Ltd, pg 737
Telegraph Books, pg 748
World Microfilms Publications Ltd, pg 758
World of Islam Altajir Trust, pg 759

Subject Index

ACCOUNTING

Albania
NL SH, pg 1
State Textbook Publishing House, pg 1

Argentina
Ediciones Don Bosco Argentina, pg 5
EUDEBA (Editorial Universitaria de Buenos Aires), pg 6

Australia
Edward Arnold (Australia) Pty Ltd, pg 12
Austed Publishing Co, pg 13
Butterworths Australia Ltd, pg 16
Hospitality Press Pty Ltd, pg 26
The Images Publishing Group Pty Ltd, pg 27
Law Book Co Information Services, pg 29
Macmillan Education Australia, pg 31
McGraw-Hill Australia Pty Ltd, pg 32
OTEN (Open Training & Education Network), pg 36
Pearson Education Australia, pg 37
Prospect Media Pty Ltd, pg 39
The Real Estate Institute of Australia, pg 40
RMIT Publishing, pg 41
Tertiary Press, pg 44
VCTA Publishing, pg 46

Austria
Buchhandlung WUV Dolmetsch, pg 50
Linde Verlag Wien GmbH, pg 54

Azerbaijan
Sada, Literaturno-Izdatel'skij Centr, pg 61

Bangladesh
Bangladesh Publishers, pg 62

Belgium
Academia-Bruylant, pg 63
CED-Samsom, pg 66
Editions de la Chambre de Commerce et d'Industrie SA, pg 66
Editions De Boeck-Larcier SA, pg 67
Intersentia Uitgevers NV, pg 69

Brazil
Editora Atlas SA, pg 79
Livraria Freitas Bastos Editora SA, pg 83
Editora Ortiz SA, pg 89
Pearson Education Do Brasil, pg 89
Livraria Pioneira Editora/Enio Matheus Guazzelli e Cia Ltd, pg 89
Saraiva SA, Livreiros Editores, pg 91
Fundacao Getulio Vargas, pg 93

Bulgaria
Ciela Publishing House, pg 94
Foi-Commerce, pg 95

Chile
Arrayan Editores, pg 99

China
Anhui People's Publishing House, pg 102
China Foreign Economic Relations & Trade Publishing House, pg 103
CITIC Publishing House, pg 104
Fudan University Press, pg 105
Jilin Science & Technology Publishing House, pg 106
Qingdao Publishing House, pg 108
Shandong University Press, pg 109
Sichuan University Press, pg 109
Zhejiang University Press, pg 110

Colombia
McGraw-Hill InterAmericana SA, pg 113
Unidad Universitaria del Sur (UNISUR), pg 114

The Democratic Republic of the Congo
Centre de Recherche, et Pedagogie Appliquee, pg 114

Denmark
Forlaget FSR A/S (ITID A/S), pg 132
Samfundslitteratur, pg 135
Systime, pg 136

Dominican Republic
Pontificia Universidad Catolica Madre y Maestra, pg 136

France
Editions Bertrandl-Lacoste, pg 150
Breal, pg 151
Centre de Librairie et d'Editions Techniques (CLET), pg 153
Editions Delmas, pg 158
Les Editions Foucher SA, pg 164
LiTec (Librairies Techniques SA), pg 173
Ouest Editions, pg 178
Presses Universitaires de Caen, pg 181
Presses Universitaires de Grenoble, pg 181
Sofiac (Societe Francaise des Imprimeries Administratives Centrales), pg 185
Top Editions, pg 188

Germany
Cornelsen Verlag GmbH & Co OHG, pg 211
Betriebswirtschaftlicher Verlag Dr Th Gabler GmbH, pg 231
Rudolf Haufe Verlag GmbH & Co KG, pg 238
IDW-Verlag GmbH, pg 244
Industria-Verlagsbuchhandlung GmbH, pg 244
Verlag Neue Wirtschafts-Briefe GmbH & Co, pg 267
Schaeffer-Poeschel Verlag fuer Wirtschaft Steuern Recht, pg 282
Erich Schmidt Verlag GmbH & Co, pg 284
Stollfuss Verlag Bonn GmbH & Co KG, pg 290
TF Fachverlag Gmbh, pg 293
Wirtschaftsverlag Carl Ueberreuter, pg 295
WRS Verlag Wirtschaft, Recht und Steuern GmbH & Co KG, pg 304

Ghana
EPP Books Services, pg 307

Greece
Kyriakidis, pg 312

Hong Kong
Publications (Holdings) Ltd, pg 321

Hungary
Saldo Penzugyi Tanacsado es Informatikai Rt, pg 326

India
Academic Publishers, pg 329
APH Publishing Corp, pg 331
Eastern Law House Pvt Ltd, pg 336
Frank Brothers & Co (Publishers) Ltd, pg 337
Pitambar Publishing Co (P) Ltd, pg 346
Pointer Publishers, pg 346
Reliance Publishing House, pg 347
Scientific Book Agency, pg 349
Sita Publications, pg 350
Sultan Chand & Sons Pvt Ltd, pg 351
Vidya Puri, pg 352
A H Wheeler & Co Ltd, pg 353

Indonesia
Andi Offset, pg 354
Bumi Aksara PT, pg 354
Gramedia, pg 355

Ireland
Irish Management Institute, pg 361
Oak Tree Press, pg 362

Israel
Open University of Israel, pg 371

Italy
CLUEB (Cooperativa Libraria Universitaria Editrice Bologna), pg 382
Rirea Casa Editrice della Rivista Italiana di Ragioneria e di Economia Aziendale, pg 405

Jamaica
CVM Publications, pg 413

Japan
Institute for Financial Affairs Inc-KINZAI, pg 418
Nippon Jitsugyo Publishing Co, Ltd, pg 423
Zeimukeiri-Kyokai, pg 429

Kenya
Africa Book Services (EA) Ltd, pg 430
Focus Publications Ltd, pg 431
Heinemann Kenya Limited (EAEP), pg 431
Midi Teki Publishers, pg 433
Nairobi University Press, pg 433
Shirikon Publishers, pg 433

Republic of Korea
Chung Rim Publishing Co Ltd, pg 435

Liechtenstein
Bonafides Verlags-Anstalt, pg 444

Luxembourg
Editions Emile Borschette, pg 447
Editions Promoculture, pg 448

Madagascar
Foibe Filan-Kevitry NY Mpampianatra (FOFIPA), pg 450

Malaysia
Professional Publications, pg 454

Mauritius
Editions de l'Ocean Indien Ltd, pg 457

Mexico
Ediciones Contables y Administrativas SA, pg 459
Ediciones Eca SA de CV, pg 460
Editorial Esfinge SA de CV, pg 460
Editorial Limusa SA de CV, pg 463
Organizacion Cultural LP SA de CV, pg 465
Sistemas Universales, SA, pg 467

Morocco
Cabinet Conseil CCMLA, pg 469

Netherlands
Business Contact BV, pg 475
Koninklijke Vermande bv, pg 480

New Zealand
CCH New Zealand Ltd, pg 490
Dunmore Press Ltd, pg 490
ESA Publications (NZ) Ltd, pg 490
New House Publishers Ltd, pg 493
Nelson Price Milburn Ltd, pg 494

Nigeria
Abisega Publishers (Nigeria) Ltd, pg 497
Evans Brothers (Nigeria Publishers) Ltd, pg 499

873

SUBJECT INDEX

Norway
Glydendal Akademisk, pg 503

Pakistan
National Book Foundation, pg 508

Peru
Editorial Desarrollo SA, pg 511
Tassorello, SA, pg 511

Philippines
Mutual Books Inc, pg 513
Rex Bookstores & Publishers, pg 514

Poland
Polskie Wydawnictwo Ekonomiczne PWE SA, pg 516

Portugal
Dinalivro, pg 524

Romania
Nemira Verlag, pg 534
Editura Niculescu, pg 534

Russian Federation
Finansy i Statistika Publishing House, pg 538
INFRA-M Izdatel'skij dom, pg 538

Singapore
Hillview Publications Pte Ltd, pg 546

Slovenia
Univerza v Ljubljani Ekonomska Fakulteta, pg 552

South Africa
Educum Publishers Ltd, pg 554
Juta & Co, pg 556

Spain
Centro de Estudios Adams-Ediciones Valbuena SA, pg 561
Editorial CISSPRAXIS SA, pg 567
Editorial Donostiarra SA, pg 570
Ediciones Deusto SA, pg 571
Esic Editorial, pg 573
Instituto de Estudios Fiscales, pg 574
Ediciones Gestio 2000 SA, pg 575
Editorial Juventud SA, pg 579
Universidad de Valladolid Secretariado de Publicaciones e Intercambio Editorial, pg 594

Sri Lanka
Ministry of Education, pg 597

Sweden
Studentlitteratur AB, pg 606

Switzerland
Cosmos-Verlag AG, pg 611
Verlag Organisator AG, pg 620
Verlag fuer Recht und Gesellschaft AG, pg 622
Versus Verlag AG, pg 627

Syrian Arab Republic
Damascus University Press, pg 628

Taiwan, Province of China
Chien Chen Bookstore Publishing Company Ltd, pg 629
Fuh-Wen Book Co, pg 630

United Republic of Tanzania
DUP (1996) Ltd, pg 633
Nyota Publishers Ltd, pg 634
Tanzania Publishing House, pg 634

Turkey
Seckin Yayinevi, pg 641
Yetkin Printing & Publishing Co Inc, pg 642

Ukraine
ASK Ltd, pg 643

United Kingdom
ABG Professional Information, pg 644
Books for Europe Ltd, pg 657
BPP Publishing Ltd, pg 658
Butterworths Tolley, pg 661
Cassell & Co, pg 664
Ernst & Young, pg 679
Financial Training Co, pg 682
HB Publications, pg 693
JAI Press Ltd, pg 702
Jordan Publishing Ltd, pg 703
Letts Educational, pg 707
Mars Business Associates Ltd, pg 712
Media Research Publishing Ltd, pg 712
John Murray (Publishers) Ltd, pg 716
National Extension College, pg 717
Osborne Books Ltd, pg 722
Pearson Education, pg 725
Professional Book Supplies Ltd, pg 730
SHU Press, pg 742
VNU Business Publications, pg 753
Wiley Europe Ltd, pg 756

Uruguay
Fundacion de Cultura Universitaria, pg 760

Viet Nam
Science & Technics Publishing House, pg 763

Zimbabwe
College Press Publishers (Pvt) Ltd, pg 768
HarperCollins Publishers Zimbabwe Pvt Ltd, pg 768
Longman Zimbabwe (Pvt) Ltd, pg 768
Thomson Publications Zimbabwe (Pvt) Ltd, pg 769

ADVERTISING

Albania
NL SH, pg 1

Australia
Books for Our Times, pg 16
The Images Publishing Group Pty Ltd, pg 27
McGraw-Hill Australia Pty Ltd, pg 32
Priestley Consulting, pg 39
The Real Estate Institute of Australia, pg 40

Belarus
Kavaler Publishers, pg 63

Brazil
Livraria Nobel S/A, pg 86
Livraria Pioneira Editora/Enio Matheus Guazzelli e Cia Ltd, pg 89
Summus Editorial Ltda, pg 92
Talento Publicacoes Editora e Grafica Ltda, pg 92

Bulgaria
Global Kontakts Balgarija, pg 95
Interpres, pg 96
Publishing House Narodno delo OOD, pg 97
Reporter, pg 97
Svetra Publishing House, pg 98
TEMTO, pg 98
WTU Todor Kableskov, pg 98

China
Anhui People's Publishing House, pg 102
Chengdu Maps Publishing House, pg 103
China Film Press, pg 103
Fudan University Press, pg 105
Heilongjiang Science & Technology Press, pg 106
Jilin Science & Technology Publishing House, pg 106
Qingdao Publishing House, pg 108

Costa Rica
Litografia Artex, SA, pg 116

Cuba
Casa Editora Abril, pg 120

Czech Republic
Press Art, pg 127

Denmark
Forlaget alokke AS, pg 129
Samfundslitteratur, pg 135

France
Blondel La Rougery SARL, pg 151
Breal, pg 151
CPL- La Communication Par le Livre, pg 157
Editions Dalloz Sirey, pg 157
Institute, pg 169

Germany
AOL-Verlag Frohmut Menze, pg 194
Art Directors Club Verlag GmbH, pg 195
Cornelsen Verlag GmbH & Co OHG, pg 211
Deutscher Fachverlag GmbH, pg 214
Friedrich Kiehl Verlag GmbH, pg 230
Heinze GmbH, pg 239
Rossipaul Kommunikation GmbH, pg 280
Siegmund Publishing, pg 286
Verlag Moderne Industrie AG & Co KG, pg 298
WRS Verlag Wirtschaft, Recht und Steuern GmbH & Co KG, pg 304

Ghana
World Literature Project, pg 308

Greece
Vivliothiki Eftychia Galeou, pg 315

Hong Kong
Publications (Holdings) Ltd, pg 321
Wellday Ltd, pg 322

India
Reliance Publishing House, pg 347
Sita Publications, pg 350
South Asia Publications, pg 350
A H Wheeler & Co Ltd, pg 353

Indonesia
Yayasan Obor Indonesia, pg 357

Italy
EGEA (Edizioni Giuridiche Economiche Aziendali), pg 387
Gruppo Editoriale Faenza Editrice SpA, pg 392

Republic of Korea
Chung Rim Publishing Co Ltd, pg 435
Nanam Publishing House, pg 439

Latvia
Egmont Latvia Ltd, pg 442

Lithuania
Algarve, pg 445
Lietuvos Informacijos Institutas, pg 446

Mexico
Editorial Diana SA de CV, pg 459
Fondo de Cultura Economica, pg 461
Editorial Limusa SA de CV, pg 463
Medios Publicitarios Mexicanos SA de CV Editora de Directorios de Medios, pg 464
Medios y Medios, Sa de CV, pg 464
Naves Internacional de Ediciones SA, pg 464
Editorial Nova, SA de CV, pg 464

Morocco
Access International Services, pg 469

Netherlands
Samsom BedrijfsInformatie BV, pg 483

Nigeria
West African Book Publishers Ltd, pg 502

Pakistan
International Educational Services, pg 507

Poland
Polskie Wydawnictwo Ekonomiczne PWE SA, pg 516
'Slask' Ltd, pg 520

Portugal
Edicoes Cetop, pg 523

Romania
Editura Cronos SRL, pg 532
Nemira Verlag, pg 534

PUBLISHERS

Russian Federation
Izdatelstvo Standartov, pg 542
Izdatelstvo Sudostroenie, pg 542

Slovenia
Univerza v Ljubljani Ekonomska Fakulteta, pg 552

Spain
Celeste Ediciones, pg 567
Fragua Editorial, pg 574
Ediciones Gestio 2000 SA, pg 575
LEDA (Las Ediciones de Arte), pg 579
Ediciones de la Torre, pg 593
Tursen, SA, pg 593

Turkey
Soez Yayin/Oyunajans, pg 641

United Kingdom
Books for Europe Ltd, pg 657
Cassell & Co, pg 664
ICC United Kingdom, pg 698
Johnson Publications Ltd, pg 703
NTC Publications Ltd, pg 720
RotoVision SA, pg 735
Vacation Work Publications, pg 752
Verulam Publishing Ltd, pg 753

Viet Nam
Science & Technics Publishing House, pg 763

AERONAUTICS, AVIATION

Albania
NL SH, pg 1

Australia
Aerospace Publications, pg 11
Chingchic Publishers, pg 18
Kookaburra Technical Publications Pty Ltd, pg 29
McGraw-Hill Australia Pty Ltd, pg 32
OTEN (Open Training & Education Network), pg 36
Turton & Armstrong Publishers Pty Ltd, pg 45

Austria
Herbert Weishaupt Verlag, pg 60

Belgium
Coda, pg 66

Brazil
Action Editora Ltda, pg 77

China
Aviation Industry Press, pg 102
National Defence Industry Press, pg 107
Qingdao Publishing House, pg 108

Czech Republic
Svet Kridel, pg 125

Finland
Koala-Kustannus/Oy Greenbay House Publishing Ltd, pg 143

France
ATP - Packager, pg 149
Cepadues Editions SA, pg 153
Editions Chiron, pg 154
Editions Delville, pg 158
EPA SA (Editions Presse Audiovisuel), pg 162
Editions Eska, pg 162
Editions Jean Paul Gisserot, pg 166
Association d'Editions Sorg, pg 186

Germany
Air Gallery Edition, Helmut Kreuzer, pg 192
Aviatic Verlag GmbH, pg 197
Bettendorf'sche Verlagsanstalt GmbH, pg 202
Flugzeug Publikations GmbH, pg 229
Alfred Hammer, pg 236
Heel Verlag GmbH, pg 238
Kartographischer Verlag Reinhard Ryborsch, pg 248
Verlagsgruppe Koehler/Mittler, pg 251
Nara Verlag Josef Krauthaeuser, pg 253
E S Mittler und Sohn GmbH, pg 264
Motorbuch-Verlag, pg 265
Neckar Verlag GmbH, pg 267
Palazzi Verlag GmbH, pg 271
Paul Pietsch Verlage GmbH & Co, pg 273
Herbert Wichmann Verlag, pg 302

Greece
D & J Vardikos, pg 315

India
Affiliated East West Press Pvt Ltd, pg 329
Heritage Publishers, pg 338
Himalayan Books, pg 338
Sita Publications, pg 350

Ireland
Avoca Publications, pg 358

Israel
Bitan Publishers Ltd, pg 365
Freund Publishing House Ltd, pg 367

Italy
Edizioni Cremonese SRL, pg 383
Editoriale Domus Spa, pg 385
Fenice 2000, pg 389
Editoriale Olimpia SpA, pg 401

Mexico
Editorial Limusa SA de CV, pg 463

Netherlands
BV Uitgeversbedryf Het Goede Boek, pg 477

New Zealand
Craig Printing Company Ltd, pg 490
David Ling Publishing, pg 493
Southern Press Ltd, pg 496

Poland
Iskry - Publishing House Ltd spotka zoo, pg 517
Wydawnictwa Komunikacji i Lacznosci Co Ltd, pg 517

Portugal
Dinalivro, pg 524
Latina Livraria, pg 526

Russian Federation
FGUP Izdatelstvo Mashinostroenie, pg 538
Izdatelstvo Mir, pg 540
Nauka Publishers, pg 540
Izdatelstvo Transport, pg 542

Singapore
Taylor & Francis Asia Pacific, pg 548

South Africa
Flesch Financial Publications (Pty) Ltd, pg 554
Galago Publishing Pty Ltd, pg 554

Spain
Ediciones Doce Calles SL, pg 570
Editorial Juventud SA, pg 579
Editorial San Martin, pg 589
Silex Ediciones, pg 590

Sweden
Allt om Hobby AB, pg 600
Frank Stenvalls Forlag, pg 606

Switzerland
Editions 24 Heures, pg 626

Ukraine
Osnova, Kharkov State University Press, pg 643

United Kingdom
Airlife Publishing Ltd, pg 645
Ian Allan Publishing Ltd, pg 646
Amber Books Ltd, pg 646
Arms & Armour Press, pg 648
BCA, pg 653
BLA Publishing Ltd, pg 655
Books for Europe Ltd, pg 657
Books International, pg 657
Brassey's UK Ltd, pg 658
Bridge Books, pg 659
Castlemead Publications, pg 665
Compendium Publishing, pg 670
The Crowood Press Ltd, pg 672
Terence Dalton Ltd, pg 673
ERA Technology Ltd, pg 679
Grange Books PLC, pg 689
Greenhill Books/Lionel Leventhal Ltd, pg 689
Halldale Publishing & Media Ltd, pg 691
Haynes Publishing, pg 693
Institution of Electrical Engineers, pg 700
Jane's Information Group, pg 702
Midland Publishing, pg 714
New European Publications Ltd, pg 718
Octopus Publishing Group, pg 720
Osprey Publishing Ltd, pg 722
Pearson Education, pg 725
T & AD Poyser Ltd, pg 730
Salamander Books Ltd, pg 738

Viet Nam
Science & Technics Publishing House, pg 763

SUBJECT INDEX

AFRICAN AMERICAN STUDIES

Brazil
Francisco J Laissue Livraria, pg 86
Pallas Editora e Distribuidora Ltda, pg 89

Cuba
Editorial Oriente, pg 121

France
Les Introuvables-Editions L'Harmattan, pg 170
Revue Noire, pg 183

Germany
Franz Steiner Verlag Wiesbaden GmbH, pg 289

Kenya
Nairobi University Press, pg 433

Poland
Wydawnictwa Uniwersytetu Warszawskiego, pg 521

South Africa
Galago Publishing Pty Ltd, pg 554

Spain
Ediciones Doce Calles SL, pg 570

United Kingdom
Compendium Publishing, pg 670
Adam Matthew Publications, pg 712
Serpent's Tail Ltd, pg 740

AGRICULTURE

Albania
NL SH, pg 1

Argentina
Editorial Albatros SACI, pg 3
Cosmopolita SRL, pg 4
Editorial Hemisferio Sur SA, pg 6
Editoria Universitaria de la Patagonia, pg 9

Armenia
Ajstan Publishers, pg 10

Australia
Bernal Publishing, pg 14
Bureau of Resource Sciences, pg 16
Candlelight Trust T/A Candlelight Farm, pg 17
Cornucopia Press, pg 19
CSIRO Publishing (Commonwealth Scientific & Industrial Research Organisation), pg 19
Department of Primary Industries, Queensland, pg 20
OTEN (Open Training & Education Network), pg 36
Pacific Publications (Australia) Pty Ltd, pg 36
Stafford Books, pg 43
Transpareon Press, pg 45
Winetitles, pg 48

Austria
CEEBA Publications Antenne d'Autriche, pg 50
Development News Ltd, pg 51

875

SUBJECT INDEX

IAEA - International Atomic Energy Agency, pg 53
Leopold Stocker Verlag, pg 54
Oesterreichischer Agrarverlag, Druck- und Verlags- GmbH, pg 56
Georg Prachner KG, pg 57

Azerbaijan
AZernesr, pg 61

Bangladesh
The University Press Ltd, pg 62

Belgium
Campinia Media VZW, pg 65
King Baudouin Foundation, pg 70
Leuven University Press, pg 71
Presses agronomiques de Gembloux ASBL, pg 73

Brazil
Editora Antroposofica Ltda, pg 78
Instituto Campineiro de Ensino Agricola Ltda, pg 80
Empresa Brasileira de Pesquisa Agropecaria, pg 83
Livro Ibero-Americano Ltda, pg 85
Icone Editora Ltda, pg 85
Livraria Nobel S/A, pg 86
Editora Ortiz SA, pg 89
Livraria Pioneira Editora/Enio Matheus Guazzelli e Cia Ltd, pg 89

Bulgaria
Darzhavno Izdatelstvo Zemizdat, pg 95
Pensoft Publishers, pg 97
TEMTO, pg 98

China
Beijing Publishing House, pg 102
Chemical Industry Press, pg 102
China Agriculture Press, pg 103
China Forestry Publishing House, pg 103
East China University of Science & Technology Press, pg 105
Fujian Science & Technology Publishing House, pg 106
Guangdong Science & Technology Press, pg 106
Heilongjiang Science & Technology Press, pg 106
Higher Education Press, pg 106
Inner Mongolia Science & Technology Publishing House, pg 106
International Academic Publishers, pg 106
Jilin Science & Technology Publishing House, pg 106
Jinan Publishing House, pg 107
Qingdao Publishing House, pg 108
Shandong Science & Technology Press, pg 109
Shanghai Science & Technology Publishers, pg 109
Shanghai Scientific & Technological Literature Publishing House, pg 109
Sichuan Science & Technology Publishing House, pg 109
South China University of Science and Technology Press, pg 109
Tianjin Science & Technology Publishing House, pg 109
Zhejiang University Press, pg 110

Colombia
Unidad Universitaria del Sur (UNISUR), pg 114

The Democratic Republic of the Congo
Centre de Vulgarisation Agricole, pg 115

Costa Rica
Academia de Centro America, pg 115
Centro Agronomico Tropical de Investigacion y Ensenanza (CATIE), pg 115
Instituto Interamericano de Cooperacion para la Agricultura (IICA), pg 116
Editorial de la Universidad de Costa Rica, pg 117
Editorial Universidad Estatal a Distancia (EUNED), pg 117

Croatia
Matica hrvatska, pg 119

Cuba
ISCAH Fructuoso Rodriguez, pg 121
Universidad Central de la Villas, Centro Documentacion e Informacion Cientifica Tecnica, pg 121

Czech Republic
Mendelova zemedelska a lesnicka univerzita v Brne, pg 126

Dominican Republic
Pontificia Universidad Catolica Madre y Maestra, pg 136

Ecuador
CEPLAES, pg 137
SECAP, pg 137

Egypt (Arab Republic of Egypt)
Dar Al-Matbo at Al-Gadidah, pg 138

Estonia
Estonian Encyclopaedia Publishers Ltd, pg 140
Valgus Publishers, pg 141

France
Editions J B Bailliere, pg 149
Bottin SA, pg 151
Editions des Cahiers Bourbonnais, pg 152
Cemagref Editions, pg 153
Cirad, pg 155
Counseil International de la Langue Francaise, pg 157
Institut pour le Developpement Forestier, pg 159
Edisud, pg 161
Folklore Comtois, pg 164
Groupe de Recherche et d'Echanges Technologiques (GRET), pg 167
INRA Editions (Institut National de la Recherche Agronomique), pg 169
Lavoisier, pg 172
Editions Legislatives, pg 172
John Libbey Eurotext, pg 173
Editions G P Maisonneuve et Larose, pg 174
Editions Pedone, pg 179

Polytechnica, pg 180
Editions Sang de la Terre, pg 183
Terre Vivante, pg 187

Georgia
Izdatelstvo Sabtchota Sakartvelo, pg 190

Germany
Badischer Landwirtschafts-Verlag GmbH, pg 197
Verlag Dr Albert Bartens KG, pg 198
Blackwell Wissenschafts-Verlag GmbH, pg 203
BLV Verlagsgesellschaft mbH, pg 204
Deutsche Landwirtschaft- Gesellschaft VerlagsgesGmbH, pg 214
Deutscher Fachverlag GmbH, pg 214
DLV Deutscher Landwirtschaftsverlag Berlin, pg 217
Hessisches Ministerium fuer Umwelt, Landwirtschaft und Forsten, pg 240
Justus-Liebig-Universitat Giessen, pg 247
Landbuch-Verlagsgesellschaft mbH, pg 255
Margraf Verlag, pg 261
Nusser Verlag, pg 269
J D Sauerlaender's Verlag, pg 282
Springer-Verlag GmbH & Co KG, pg 288
Thalacker Medien GmbH Co KG, pg 293
Verlag Eugen Ulmer GmbH & Co, pg 295
UNO-Verlag mbH, Vertriebs und Verlagsgesellschaft, pg 296
UTB fuer Wissenschaft Uni-Taschenbuecher GmbH, pg 297

Ghana
Ghana Universities Press (GUP), pg 307
Sam Woode Ltd, pg 308
Sedco Publishing Ltd, pg 308
Unimax Macmillan Ltd, pg 308

Greece
Gartaganis D, pg 310

Guinea-Bissau
Instituto Nacional de Estudos e Pesquisa, pg 316

Haiti
Editions Caraiibes SA, pg 317

Hong Kong
Friends of the Earth (Charity) Ltd, pg 320

Hungary
Foldmuvelesugyi Miniszterium Muszaki Intezet, pg 323
Mezoegazda Kiado, pg 325
Mezoegazdasagi Koenyvkiado Vallalat, pg 325

India
Affiliated East West Press Pvt Ltd, pg 329
Agricole Publishing Academy, pg 330
Allied Book Centre, pg 330
Allied Publishers Pvt Ltd, pg 330
APH Publishing Corp, pg 331
Avinash Reference Publications, pg 331
The Bangalore Printing & Publishing Co Ltd, pg 332
Bhawan Book Service, Publishers & Distributors, pg 333
BR Publishing Corporation, pg 334
BS Publications, pg 334
BSMPS - M/s Bishen Singh Mahendra Pal Singh, pg 334
Cosmo Publications, pg 335
Daya Publishing House, pg 336
Gyan Publishing House, pg 338
Heritage Publishers, pg 338
Indian Council of Agricultural Research, pg 339
Indus Publishing Co, pg 339
Inter-India Publications, pg 340
International Book Distributors, pg 340
Mehta Publishers, pg 342
Minerva Associates (Publications) Pvt Ltd, pg 342
National Book Organization, pg 343
National Council of Applied Economic Research, Publications Division, pg 344
Naya Prokash, pg 344
Nem Chand & Brothers, pg 344
Omsons Publications, pg 345
Oxford & IBH Publishing Co Pvt Ltd, pg 345
Pointer Publishers, pg 346
Rajasthan Hindi Granth Academy, pg 347
Rastogi Publications, pg 347
Regency Publications, pg 347
Reliance Publishing House, pg 347
Research Signpost, pg 348
Sasta Sahitya Mandal, pg 349
Scientific Book Agency, pg 349
Scientific Publishers India, pg 349
Sita Publications, pg 350
Somaiya Publications Pvt Ltd, pg 350
South Asia Publications, pg 350
Sterling Publishers Pvt Ltd, pg 351
Today & Tomorrow's Printers & Publishers, pg 352
Transworld Research Network, pg 352
Vikas Publishing House Pvt Ltd, pg 353

Indonesia
Bhratara Karya Aksara, pg 354
Bumi Aksara PT, pg 354
Karya Anda, CV, pg 356
CV Yasaguna, pg 357

Iraq
National House for Publishing, Distributing and Advertising, pg 358

Ireland
On Stream Publications Ltd, pg 363

Israel
Hakibbutz Hameuchad Publishing House Ltd, pg 368

PUBLISHERS

Italy
Apimondia, pg 375
CLUEB (Cooperativa Libraria Universitaria Editrice Bologna), pg 382
Giovanni De Vecchi Editore SpA, pg 384
Demetra SRL, pg 385
Edagricole - Edizioni Agricole, pg 385
Gangemi Editore, pg 390
Laruffa Editore SRL, pg 395
Patron Editore SrL, pg 403
Red/Studio Redazionale SpA, pg 405
Editrice San Marco SRL, pg 406
Unipress, pg 410

Japan
Ie-No-Hikari Association, pg 418
Japan Publications Inc, pg 418
Nobunkyo (Rural Village Culture Association), pg 423
Seibido Shuppan Company Ltd, pg 424
Taimeido Publishing Co Ltd, pg 427
Yokendo Ltd, pg 429
Zenkoku Kyodo Shuppan, pg 429

Kenya
African Centre for Technology Studies (ACTS), pg 431
Heinemann Kenya Limited (EAEP), pg 431
International Centre for Research in Agroforestry (ICRAF), pg 432
Kenya Energy & Environment Organisation, Kengo, pg 432
Kenya Literature Bureau, pg 432

Democratic People's Republic of Korea
Korea Science and Encyclopedia Publishing House, pg 434

Republic of Korea
Hyangmunsa Publishing Co, pg 437
Korea University Press, pg 437

Latvia
Avots, pg 441
Preses Nams, pg 442

Lithuania
Academia, pg 445
Mokslo ir enciklopediju leidybos institutas, pg 446
Margi Rastai Publishers, pg 446

Luxembourg
Service Central de la Statistique et des Etudes Economiques (STATEC), pg 448

Madagascar
Foibe Filan-Kevitry NY Mpampianatra (FOFIPA), pg 450

Malawi
Dzuka Publishing Company Ltd, pg 450

Maldive Islands
Non-Formal Education Centre, pg 455

Martinique
Editions Gondwana, pg 456

Mauritius
Editions de l'Ocean Indien Ltd, pg 457

Mexico
AGT Editor SA, pg 457
Colegio de Postgraduados en Ciencias Agricolas, pg 459
Fondo de Cultura Economica, pg 461
Grupo Editorial Iberoamerica, SA de CV, pg 461
Editorial Limusa SA de CV, pg 463
Plaza y Valdes SA de CV, pg 465

Republic of Moldova
Izdatelstvo Kartia Moldoveniaske, pg 468

Myanmar
Sarpay Beikman Board, pg 471

Namibia
Desert Research Foundation of Namibia (DRFN), pg 471
Multi-Disciplinary Research Centre Library, pg 471

Nepal
International Standards Books & Periodicals (P) Ltd, pg 471

Netherlands
Koninklijk Instituut Voor de Tropen, pg 480
Wageningen Pers, pg 487

New Zealand
Fraser Books, pg 491
Oxford University Press, pg 494
SIR Publishing, pg 495
Statistics New Zealand, pg 496

Nigeria
Evans Brothers (Nigeria Publishers) Ltd, pg 499
Ibadan University Press, pg 499
West African Book Publishers Ltd, pg 502

Pakistan
National Book Foundation, pg 508
Pakistan Institute of Development Economics, pg 508
Sang-e-Meel Publications, pg 509

Papua New Guinea
Kristen Pres, pg 510

Peru
Instituto Frances de Estudios Andinos, IFEA, pg 511

Philippines
Communication Foundation for Asia Media Group (CFAMG), pg 513
International Rice Research Institute (IRRI), pg 513
Rex Bookstores & Publishers, pg 514

Poland
Ludowa Spoldzielnia Wydawnicza, pg 518
Panstwowe Wydawnictwo Rolnicze i Lesne, pg 519

Portugal
Publicacoes Ciencia e Vida Lda, pg 523
Instituto de Investigacao Cientifica Tropical, pg 526
McGraw-Hill Editora de Portugal, pg 527
Almerinda Teixeira, pg 529

Romania
Editura Ceres, pg 532
MAST Verlag, pg 534

Russian Federation
Izdatelstvo 'Ekonomika', pg 537
Gidrometeoizdat, pg 538
Izdatel 'stvo Mordovskogo gosudar stvennogo, pg 538
Izvestia Sovetov Narodnyh Deputatov Russian Federation (RF), pg 539
Izdatelstvo Lenizdat, pg 539

Saudi Arabia
King Saud University, pg 543

Slovakia
Technicka Univerzita, pg 551

South Africa
Educum Publishers Ltd, pg 554
Erudita Publications (Pty) Ltd, pg 554
New Africa Books (Pty) Ltd, pg 557
South African Institute of Race Relations, pg 559

Spain
Editorial Acribia SA, pg 561
Editorial AEDOS SA, pg 561
Ediciones Agrotecnicas, SL, pg 562
AMV Ediciones, pg 563
Cedel, Ediciones Jose O Avila Monteso ES, pg 567
Comunidad Autonoma de Madrid, Servicio de Documentacion y Publicaciones, pg 568
Editorial De Vecchi SA, pg 569
Dilagro SA, pg 569
Edicions del Drac SA, pg 570
Idea Books, SA, pg 578
Institucion Fernando el Catolico de la Excma Diputacion de Zaragoza, pg 578
Mundi-Prensa Libros SA, pg 583
Oikos-Tau SA Ediciones, pg 584
Ediciones Omega SA, pg 585
Pages Editors, SL, pg 585
Pais Vasco Servicio Central de Publicaciones, pg 585
Publicaciones de la Universidad de Alicante, pg 588
Riquelme y Vargas Ediciones SL, pg 589
Rueda, SL Editorial, pg 589
Servicio de Publicaciones Universidad de Cordoba, pg 590
Editorial Rudolf Steiner, pg 591
Universidad de Malaga, pg 594
Ediciones A Madrid Vicente, pg 595
Xunta de Galicia, pg 596

Sri Lanka
Ministry of Education, pg 597
Swarna Hansa Foundation, pg 598
Waruni Publishers, pg 598

SUBJECT INDEX

Sweden
Natur och Kultur/LTs foerlag, pg 604

Switzerland
Verlag Huber & Co AG, pg 616
SAB Schweiz Arbeitsgemeinschaft fuer die Berggebiete, pg 623
Vdf Hochschulverlag AG an der ETH Zurich, pg 626
Verbandsdruckerei AG, pg 626

Syrian Arab Republic
Damascus University Press, pg 628

Taiwan, Province of China
Chien Chen Bookstore Publishing Company Ltd, pg 629
Fuh-Wen Book Co, pg 630
Chu Hai Publishing (Taiwan) Co Ltd, pg 630
San Min Book Co Ltd, pg 631
Yi Hsien Publishing Co Ltd, pg 632

Tajikistan
Irfon, pg 632

United Republic of Tanzania
Bureau of Statistics, pg 633
General Publications Ltd, pg 633
Peramiho Publications, pg 634
Press & Publicity Centre Ltd, pg 634
Tanzania Publishing House, pg 634

Thailand
Bannakit Trading, pg 635
Thai Watana Panich Co, Ltd, pg 636

Tunisia
Ceres Editions, pg 637
Maison Tunisienne de l'Edition, pg 638

Turkmenistan
Izdatelstvo Turkmenistan, pg 642

Uganda
Centre for Basic Research, pg 642
Fountain Publishers Ltd, pg 642

Ukraine
Naukova Dumka Publishers, pg 643
Osnova, Kharkov State University Press, pg 643
Urozaj, pg 643

United Kingdom
Batsford Ltd, pg 652
BIOS Scientific Publishers Ltd, pg 654
Butterworth-Heinemann Ltd, pg 661
Cambridge University Press, pg 662
Commonwealth Secretariat, pg 669
James Currey Ltd, pg 673
Elsevier Science Ltd, pg 678
The Eurospan Group, pg 680
Green Books Ltd, pg 689
Hyden House Ltd, pg 698
Institute of Development Studies, pg 699
Intercept Ltd, pg 700
Intermediate Technology Publications Ltd, pg 700
International Bee Research Association, pg 701
The Islamic Texts Society, pg 701

KIT Press - Royal Tropical Institute, pg 705
Manson Publishing Ltd, pg 711
Packard Publishing Ltd, pg 723
Pearson Education, pg 725
Scottish Office Library & Information Services, pg 740
The Stationery Office, pg 745
Rudolf Steiner Press, pg 745
Sutton Publishing Ltd, pg 746
Timber Press Inc, pg 749
Westview Press, pg 755

Uruguay
Nordan-Comunidad, pg 760

Venezuela
Fundacion Servicio para el Agricultor, pg 762

Viet Nam
Science & Technics Publishing House, pg 763

Yugoslavia
Nolit Publishing House, pg 765
Partenon MAM Sistem, pg 765

Zambia
Historical Association of Zambia, pg 766
Zambia Educational Publishing House, pg 767
ZPC Publications, pg 767

Zimbabwe
College Press Publishers (Pvt) Ltd, pg 768
Farmesa Regional Prog on Farm Research Methods, pg 768
Longman Zimbabwe (Pvt) Ltd, pg 768
Standards Association of Zimbabwe (SAZ), pg 769
Thomson Publications Zimbabwe (Pvt) Ltd, pg 769
Zimbabwe Women's Bureau, pg 770

ALTERNATIVE

Australia
Allen & Unwin Pty Ltd, The Australian Newspaper, Vogel Breads, pg 11
Appropriate Technology Development Group (Inc) WA, pg 11
Assert Publishing, pg 12
Bio Concepts Publishing, pg 15
Bridge To Peace Publications, pg 16
Gnostic Editions, pg 24
Hihorse Publishing Pty Ltd, pg 26
In-Tune Books, pg 27
Scroll Publishers, pg 42
Simon & Schuster Australia Pty Ltd, pg 42
Tomorrow Publications, pg 45

Austria
Verlag des Osterr Kneippbundes GmbH, pg 57

Belgium
Altina, pg 64
Vita, pg 75

Brazil
Editora Aquariana Ltda, pg 78
Triom Centro de Estudos Marina e Martin Hawey Editorial e Comercial Ltda, pg 92

Bulgaria
Kibea Publishing Co, pg 96

China
Qingdao Publishing House, pg 108

Cuba
ISCAH Fructuoso Rodriguez, pg 121

Czech Republic
Jiri Chvojka, pg 123
Jota, pg 125
Votobia sro, pg 129

Denmark
Borgens Forlag A/S, pg 130
Olivia - det gronne forlag, pg 134

France
Editions Alternatives, pg 146

Germany
EVT Energy Video Training & Verlag GmbH, pg 225
IKO Verlag fur Interkulturelle Kommunikation, pg 244
Karin Kramer Verlag, pg 253
Medizinisch-Literarische Verlagsgesellschaft mbH, pg 262
Die Silberschnur Verlag GmbH, pg 287
Suin Buch-Verlag, pg 291
Trotzdem-Verlags Genossenschaft eG, pg 295
Weber Zucht & Co, pg 300

India
Concept Publishing Co, pg 335
Firma KLM Privatee Ltd, Publishers & International Booksellers, pg 337
B Jain Publishers Overseas, pg 340

Italy
Edizioni Mediterranee SRL, pg 387
Edizioni GB, pg 390
Macro Edizioni, pg 397
Il Punto D Incontro, pg 404

Democratic People's Republic of Korea
Grand People's Study House, pg 434

Luxembourg
Varkki Verghese, pg 448

Netherlands
Servire BV Uitgevers, pg 484

New Zealand
RSVP Publishing Company Ltd, pg 495

Norway
Ex Libris Forlag A/S, pg 503
Hilt & Hansteen A/S, pg 504

South Africa
Kima Global Publishers, pg 556

Spain
Baile del Sol, Colectivo Cultural, pg 565
Editorial Fundamentos, pg 575
Ediciones Norma SA, pg 584
OASIS, Producciones Generales de Comunicacion, pg 584
Ediciones Urano, SA, pg 595

Switzerland
Rotpunktverlag, pg 623

Turkey
Ruh ve Madde Yayinlari ve Saglik Hizmetleri AS, pg 641
Soez Yayin/Oyunajans, pg 641

United Kingdom
Act 3 Publishing, pg 645
Atlas Press, pg 651
Beaconsfield Publishers Ltd, pg 653
Bloomsbury Publishing PLC, pg 656
Capall Bann Publishing, pg 663
Foulsham Publishers, pg 683
Janus Publishing Company Ltd, pg 702
Quarto Publishing plc, pg 731
The Women's Press Ltd, pg 758

Uruguay
Nordan-Comunidad, pg 760

AMERICANA, REGIONAL

Albania
NL SH, pg 1

Mexico
El Colegio de Michoacan A C, pg 460
Instituto Nacional de Antropologia e Historia, pg 464

New Zealand
Barkfire Press, pg 488

Poland
Wydawnictwa Uniwersytetu Warszawskiego, pg 521

ANIMALS, PETS

Albania
NL SH, pg 1
State Textbook Publishing House, pg 1

Argentina
Editorial Albatros SACI, pg 3
Editorial Caymi SACI, pg 4
Editorial Hemisferio Sur SA, pg 6
Ediciones Lidiun, pg 7

Australia
Austed Publishing Co, pg 13
Bandicoot Books, pg 14
Chiron Media, pg 18
D'Artagnan Publishing, pg 20
Department of Primary Industries, Queensland, pg 20
Egan Publishing Pty Ltd, pg 21
Hyland House Publishing Pty Ltd, pg 27
Kingsclear Books, pg 29
Lansdowne Publishing Pty Ltd, pg 29
Tom Roberts (Pat Roberts), pg 41
Simon & Schuster Australia Pty Ltd, pg 42
Stafford Books, pg 43
The Watermark Press, pg 47

Austria
Development News Ltd, pg 51
Verlag Carl Ueberreuter GmbH, pg 59

Belarus
Interdigets Publishing House, pg 63

Belgium
Editions Gerard Blanchart & Cie SA, pg 65
Ediblanchart sprl, pg 68
Marabout, pg 72
Zuid-Nederlandse Uitgeverij NV/ Central Uitgeverij, pg 76

Brazil
Ediouro Publicacoes, SA, pg 81
Editora Mantiqueira de Ciencia e Arte, pg 87

Bulgaria
Gea-Libris Publishing House, pg 95

China
China Agriculture Press, pg 103
China Braille Press, pg 103
China Forestry Publishing House, pg 103
Jilin Science & Technology Publishing House, pg 106
Qingdao Publishing House, pg 108
Science Press, pg 108

Colombia
Editorial Santillana SA, pg 113

Costa Rica
Editorial Texto Ltda, pg 117

Czech Republic
Aventinum Nakladatelstvi, pg 123
Granit SRO, pg 124
Mendelova zemedelska a lesnicka univerzita v Brne, pg 126
Narodni Muzeum, pg 126
Svojtka & Co, pg 128

Denmark
Borgens Forlag A/S, pg 130

Egypt (Arab Republic of Egypt)
Dar Al-Matbo at Al-Gadidah, pg 138

Estonia
Sinisukk, pg 140
Valgus Publishers, pg 141

Finland
Weilin & Goeoes Oy, pg 145

France
Editions d'Annabelle, pg 147
Les Ateliers d'Orion, pg 148
ATP - Packager, pg 149

PUBLISHERS

Editions Bornemann, pg 151
Editeurs Crepin-Leblond, pg 157
De Vecchi Editions SA, pg 158
Les Editions des Deux Coqs d'Or, pg 159
Editions Grund, pg 161
Editions Jean Paul Gisserot, pg 166
Hachette Pratiques, pg 167
Le Jour, Editeur, pg 170
Librairie Larousse, pg 172
Editions G P Maisonneuve et Larose, pg 174
Editions du Point Veterinaire, pg 180
Editions Sang de la Terre, pg 183
Sofradif Editions Philippe Auzou, pg 185

Germany
Augustus Verlag, pg 196
Blackwell Wissenschafts-Verlag GmbH, pg 203
BLV Verlagsgesellschaft mbH, pg 204
Beate Danker-Verlag, pg 212
DLV Deutscher Landwirtschaftsverlag Berlin, pg 217
Echo Verlag, pg 220
Egmont vgs verlagsgesellschaft mbH, pg 221
Engel & Bengel Verlag, pg 222
Graefe und Unzer Verlag GmbH, pg 233
F Hirthammer Verlag GmbH, pg 241
Knowledge Media International, pg 251
Franckh-Kosmos Verlags-GmbH & Co, pg 252
Kunstverlag Weingarten GmbH, pg 254
Kynos Verlag Dr Dieter Fleig GmbH, pg 254
Landbuch-Verlagsgesellschaft mbH, pg 255
Mergus Verlag GmbH Hans A Baensch, pg 263
Karl-Heinz Metz, pg 263
Mosaik Verlag GmbH, pg 265
Verlag Natur & Wissenschaft Harro Hieronimus & Dr Jurgen Schmidt, pg 266
Naumann & Goebel Verlagsgesellschaft mbH, pg 267
Neuer Honos Verlag GmbH, pg 267
Neumann Verlag, pg 268
Oertel & Sporer GmbH & Co, pg 270
Orbis Verlag fur Publizistik GmbH, pg 270
Heidi Rogner, pg 279
M & H Schaper GmbH & Co KG, pg 282
Adolf Sponholtz Verlag, pg 288
Tetra Verlag Gmbh, pg 292
Tomus Verlag GmbH, pg 294
Verlag Eugen Ulmer GmbH & Co, pg 295
Verlagsgruppe Weltbild GmbH, pg 301

Greece
Chrysi Penna - Golden Pen Books, pg 309
Hestia-l D Hestia-Kollaros & Co Corporation, pg 311
Editions Moressopoulos, pg 313

Hong Kong
Publications (Holdings) Ltd, pg 321
Sesame Publication Co, pg 321

Hungary
Aranyhal Konyvkiado Goldfish Publishing, pg 323
Mezoegazda Kiado, pg 325

Iceland
Skjaldborg Ltd, pg 328

India
Dolphin Publications, pg 336
Indian Council of Agricultural Research, pg 339
International Book Distributors, pg 340
Rastogi Publications, pg 347
Sasta Sahitya Mandal, pg 349
Vidya Puri, pg 352
Vikas Publishing House Pvt Ltd, pg 353

Indonesia
Gramedia, pg 355

Italy
Edizioni Arka SRL, pg 376
Gruppo Editoriale Armenia SpA, pg 376
Dami Editore SRL, pg 383
Giovanni De Vecchi Editore SpA, pg 384
Edagricole - Edizioni Agricole, pg 385
Fatatrac, pg 388
Fenice 2000, pg 389
Kompass Fleischmann, pg 395
Editoriale Olimpia SpA, pg 401
Editoriale Scienza, pg 407

Japan
Froebel-Kan Co Ltd, pg 416
Hakuyo-Sha, pg 417
Kaisei-Sha Publishing Co Ltd, pg 419
Nagaoka Shoten Company Ltd, pg 421
Seibido Shuppan Company Ltd, pg 424

Kenya
Kenway Publications Ltd, pg 432
Kenya Literature Bureau, pg 432

Democratic People's Republic of Korea
Korea Science and Encyclopedia Publishing House, pg 434

Republic of Korea
Borim Publishing Co, pg 435

Latvia
Nordik/Tapals Publishers Ltd, pg 442
Preses Nams, pg 442
Vaidelote, pg 442

Liechtenstein
Botanisch-Zoologische Gesellschaft, pg 444

Lithuania
Victoria Publishers, pg 446

Maldive Islands
Novelty Printers & Publishers, pg 455

Mexico
Editorial Diana SA de CV, pg 459
Fernandez Editores SA de CV, pg 461
Editorial Jilguero, SA de CV, pg 462
Sistemas Tecnicos de Edicion SA de CV, pg 467
Ediciones Suromex SA, pg 467

Netherlands
BZZTOH Publishers, pg 475
Littera Scripta Manet, pg 480
Rebo Productions BV, pg 483
Tirion Uitgevers BV, pg 485
Wageningen Pers, pg 487
Zuid Boekprodukties BV, pg 487

Poland
'Ksiazka i Wiedza' Spotdzielnia Wydawniczo-Handlowa, pg 517
Wydawnictwo RTW, pg 520
Wydawnictwo Baturo, pg 521

Portugal
Publicacoes Ciencia e Vida Lda, pg 523
Edicoes 70, Lda, pg 524
Editorial Presenca, pg 528

Romania
Editura Ceres, pg 532
MAST Verlag, pg 534

Russian Federation
Armada Publishing House, pg 537
Gidrometeoizdat, pg 538
KUbK Publishing House, pg 539
Izdatelstvo Mir, pg 540
Scorpion Publishers, pg 541

Saudi Arabia
Dar Al-Shareff for Publishing & Distribution, pg 543

Slovakia
Technicka Univerzita, pg 551

South Africa
Flesch Financial Publications (Pty) Ltd, pg 554
Southern Book Publishers (Pty) Ltd, pg 559

Spain
Editorial AEDOS SA, pg 561
Comunidad Autonoma de Madrid, Servicio de Documentacion y Publicaciones, pg 568
Editorial De Vecchi SA, pg 569
Edicions del Drac SA, pg 570
Editorial Everest SA, pg 572
Editorial Hispano Europea SA, pg 577
Editorial Juventud SA, pg 579
Lynx Edicions, pg 580
Ediciones Martinez-Roca SA, pg 581
Mundi-Prensa Libros SA, pg 583
Pulso Ediciones, SL, pg 588
Ediciones Tutor SA, pg 594

Sweden
Bengt Forsbergs Foerlag AB, pg 602
ICA bokforlag, pg 603
Johnston & Streiffert Editions, pg 604
Natur och Kultur/LTs foerlag, pg 604
Bokforlaget Semic AB, pg 606
Svenska Foerlaget liv & ledarskap ab, pg 607

Switzerland
Bohem Press Kinderbuchverlag, pg 610
Hallwag AG, pg 615
Kinderbuchverlag Luzern, pg 617
Mueller Rueschlikon Verlags AG, pg 619
Editions 24 Heures, pg 626

Taiwan, Province of China
Chien Chen Bookstore Publishing Company Ltd, pg 629
HYS Culture Co Ltd, pg 630
Yi Hsien Publishing Co Ltd, pg 632

United Republic of Tanzania
Tanzania Publishing House, pg 634

Thailand
New Generation Publishing Co Ltd, pg 635

Tunisia
Les Editions de l'Arbre, pg 638

Turkey
Arkadas Ltd, pg 639
Inkilap Publishers Ltd, pg 640
Kok Yayincilik, pg 640

United Kingdom
Academic Press Ltd, pg 644
Andromeda Oxford Ltd, pg 647
BCA, pg 653
Blaketon Hall Ltd, pg 656
Blandford Publishing Ltd, pg 656
Capall Bann Publishing, pg 663
Jon Carpenter Publishing, pg 664
Colour Library Direct, pg 669
The Crowood Press Ltd, pg 672
The C W Daniel Co Ltd, pg 673
David & Charles Ltd, pg 674
Elliot Right Way Books, pg 678
Eurobook Ltd, pg 679
Grange Books PLC, pg 689
HarperCollins Publishers, pg 692
Interpet Publishing, pg 701
The Kenilworth Press Ltd, pg 704
Lorenz Books, pg 709
Mirabel Books Ltd, pg 715
Orpheus Books Ltd, pg 722
Parapress Ltd, pg 724
Primrose Hill Press Ltd, pg 730
Quarto Publishing plc, pg 731
Ravette Publishing Ltd, pg 733
The Reader's Digest Association Ltd, pg 733
Regency House Publishing Ltd, pg 734
Salamander Books Ltd, pg 738
Sherbourne Publications, pg 741
Silver Link Publishing Ltd, pg 742
Two-Can Publishing Ltd, pg 750
Verulam Publishing Ltd, pg 753
Weatherbys Allen Ltd, pg 754
Whittet Books Ltd, pg 756

Viet Nam
Science & Technics Publishing House, pg 763

Zimbabwe
The Literature Bureau, pg 768

SUBJECT INDEX

ANTHROPOLOGY

Albania
NL SH, pg 1

Argentina
Alianza Editorial de Argentina SA, pg 3
Amorrortu Editores SA, pg 3
Editorial Guadalupe, pg 6
Editorial Kier SACIFI, pg 7
Theoria SRL Distribuidora y Editora, pg 9
Tipografica Editora Argentina, pg 9
Ediciones Tres Tiempos SRL, pg 9

Australia
Aboriginal Studies Press, pg 10
Archaeological Publications, pg 12
Crawford House Publishing, pg 19
Deakin University Press, pg 20
Emperor Publishing, pg 22
Gnostic Editions, pg 24
Illert Publications, pg 27
Institute of Aboriginal Development (IAD Press), pg 28
Magabala Books Aboriginal Corporation, pg 31
McGraw-Hill Australia Pty Ltd, pg 32
New Endeavour Press, pg 34
Pearson Education Australia, pg 37
Pollitecon Publications, pg 38
Queen Victoria Museum & Art Gallery Publications, pg 39
Simon & Schuster Australia Pty Ltd, pg 42
Summer Institute of Linguistics, Australian Aborigines Branch, pg 43
Transpareon Press, pg 45
La Trobe University Press, pg 45
Unity Press, pg 46
Veritas Press, pg 46

Austria
Akademische Druck-u Verlagsanstalt Dr Paul Struzl GmbH, pg 49
CEEBA Publications Antenne d'Autriche, pg 50
Development News Ltd, pg 51
Ferdinand Berger und Sohne, pg 51
Promedia Verlagsges mbH, pg 57
Springer-Verlag Wien, pg 59
Edition Va Bene, pg 60

Bangladesh
Ankur Prakashani, pg 62
The University Press Ltd, pg 62

Belgium
Academia-Bruylant, pg 63
Centre Aequatoria, pg 64
Editions De Boeck-Larcier SA, pg 67
EPO Publishers, Printers, Booksellers, pg 68
Koepel van de Vlaamse Noord - Zuidbeweging 11.11.11, pg 70
Claude Lefrancq Editeur, pg 71

Brazil
Agalma Psicanalise Editora Ltda, pg 78
Editora Alfa Omega Ltda, pg 78
Ars Poetica Editora Ltda, pg 79
Associacao Palas Athena do Brasil, pg 79
Editora Bertrand Brasil Ltda, pg 79
Dumara Distribuidora de Publicacoes Ltda, pg 81
Editora Companhia das Letras/ Editora Schwarcz Ltda, pg 82
EDUC - Editora da PUC-SP, pg 82
Fundacao Joaquim Nabuco Editora, pg 84
Global Editora e Distribuidora Ltda, pg 84
Francisco J Laissue Livraria, pg 86
Editora Mercado Aberto Ltda, pg 88
Pallas Editora e Distribuidora Ltda, pg 89
Editora Revan Ltda, pg 90
Editora Rocco Ltda, pg 91
34 Literatura S/C Ltda, pg 92
Editora UNESP, pg 92
Editora da Universidade de Sao Paulo, pg 93
Editora Universidade Federal do Rio de Janeiro, pg 93
Jorge Zahar Editor, pg 93

Bulgaria
Kibea Publishing Co, pg 96
LIK IZDANIJA, pg 96
Litera Prima, pg 96

Chile
Arrayan Editores, pg 99
Ediciones Mil Hojas Ltda, pg 100

China
China Tibetology Publishing House, pg 104
Cultural Relics Publishing House, pg 105
Foreign Languages Press, pg 105
Jilin Science & Technology Publishing House, pg 106
Qingdao Publishing House, pg 108

Colombia
Siglo XXI Editores de Colombia Ltda, pg 113
Tercer Mundo Editores SA, pg 113

The Democratic Republic of the Congo
Facultes Catoliques de Kinshasa, pg 115

Costa Rica
Promesa, Ediciones, pg 116
Editorial de la Universidad de Costa Rica, pg 117

Czech Republic
Narodni Muzeum, pg 126
Slon Sociologicke Nakladatelstvi, pg 128

Denmark
Aarhus Universitetsforlag, pg 129
Museum Tusculanum Press, pg 134

Ecuador
Ediciones Abya-Yala, pg 137
CEPLAES, pg 137
Pontificia Universidad Catolica de Ecuador, Centro de Publicaciones, pg 137

Egypt (Arab Republic of Egypt)
American University in Cairo Press, pg 138

Finland
Suomalaisen Kirjallisuuden Seura, pg 144

France
Editions A M Metailie, pg 145
Adverbum SARL, pg 146
Anako Editions, pg 147
Editions Anthropos Sarl, pg 147
Autrement Editions, pg 149
Berg International Editeurs, pg 150
Presses Universitaires de Bordeaux (PUB), pg 151
Editions de l'Ecole des Hautes Etudes en Sciences Sociales (EHESS), pg 160
Edisud, pg 161
Editions Recherche sur les Civilisations (ERC), pg 161
Paul Geuthner Librairie Orientaliste, pg 166
Editions Jean Paul Gisserot, pg 166
Groupe de Recherche et d'Echanges Technologiques (GRET), pg 167
Editions Imago, pg 169
Indigo & Cote-Femmes Editions, pg 169
Kailash Editions, pg 171
Karthala Editions-Diffusion, pg 171
Editions de la Maison des Sciences de l'Homme, Paris, pg 174
Editions Parentheses, pg 179
Editions Payot & Rivages, pg 179
Peeters-France, pg 179
Jean-Michel Place, pg 180
Revue Espaces et Societes, pg 183

French Polynesia
Haere Po No Tahiti, pg 190

Germany
Verlag C H Beck (OHG), pg 200
Bertelsmann Lexikon Verlag GmbH, pg 201
Boehlau-Verlag GmbH & Cie, pg 204
Brandes & Apsel Verlag GmbH, pg 206
E Schweizerbart'sche Verlagsbuchhandlung (Nagele und Obermiller), pg 220
Verlag Esoterische Philosophie GmbH, pg 224
Europaeische Verlagsanstalt GmbH & Rotbuch Verlag GmbH & Co KG, pg 225
Guetersloher Verlagshaus Gerd Mohn, pg 235
Verlag Peter Hoell, pg 241
Hofbauer, Christoph und Trojanow Ilia, Akademischer Verlag Muenchen, pg 241
Holos Verlag, pg 242
Human Wissenschafilicher Verlag, pg 243
IKO Verlag fur Interkulturelle Kommunikation, pg 244
Iudicium Verlag GmbH, pg 245
Dr Anton Kovac Slavica Verlag, pg 253
Idime Verlag Inge Melzer, pg 262
Merlin Verlag Andreas Meyer Verlags GmbH und Co KG, pg 263
Preubmpassling Verlag Gisela Meussling, pg 263
Palmyra Verlag, pg 271
Edition Parabolis, pg 271
Philipps-Universitaet Marburg, pg 273
Dietrich Reimer Verlag GmbH, pg 278
Renate Schenk Verlag, pg 283
Spieth-Verlag Verlag fuer Symbolforschung, pg 288
Steyler Verlag, pg 290
Suin Buch-Verlag, pg 291
VWB-Verlag fur Wissenschaft & Bildung, Amand Aglaster, pg 300
Verlag Clemens Zerling, pg 305

Ghana
Ghana Institute of Linguistics Literacy & Bible Translation (GILLBT), pg 307

Greece
Hestia-I D Hestia-Kollaros & Co Corporation, pg 311
Kastaniotis Editions SA, pg 312
Ed Nea Acropolis, pg 313
Panepistimio Ioanninon, pg 314
Patakis Publishers, pg 314
Society for Macedonian Studies, pg 315

Guinea-Bissau
Instituto Nacional de Estudos e Pesquisa, pg 316

Guyana
Hamburgh Press, pg 317

Honduras
Editorial Guaymuras, pg 318

Hong Kong
Hong Kong University Press, pg 320

Hungary
Osiris Kiado, pg 326

India
Affiliated East West Press Pvt Ltd, pg 329
Agam Kala Prakashan, pg 330
Ajanta Publications (India), pg 330
Ananda Publishers Pvt Ltd, pg 330
Asian Educational Services, pg 331
K P Bagchi & Co, pg 332
Bani Mandir, Book-Sellers, Publishers & Educational Suppliers, pg 332
Bharatiya Samijik Vigyan Auusandhan Parishad, pg 332
Books & Books, pg 334
BR Publishing Corporation, pg 334
Chowkhamba Sanskrit Series Office, pg 335
Concept Publishing Co, pg 335
Cosmo Publications, pg 335
Gyan Publishing House, pg 338
Indian Museum, pg 339
Inter-India Publications, pg 340
Minerva Associates (Publications) Pvt Ltd, pg 342
Munshiram Manoharlal Publishers Pvt Ltd, pg 343
National Book Organization, pg 343
Omsons Publications, pg 345
Popular Prakashan Pvt Ltd, pg 346
Rahul Publishing House, pg 347
Regency Publications, pg 347
Reliance Publishing House, pg 347
Sage Publications India Pvt Ltd, pg 348
Scientific Book Agency, pg 349
Somaiya Publications Pvt Ltd, pg 350

South Asia Publications, pg 350
South Asian Publishers Pvt Ltd, pg 350
Spectrum Publications, pg 350
Vikas Publishing House Pvt Ltd, pg 353
Vision Books Pvt Ltd, pg 353

Indonesia
Karya Anda, CV, pg 356
Pustaka Utama Grafiti, PT, pg 357

Ireland
Roberts Rinehart Publishers, pg 363
Tir Eolas, pg 364

Israel
Agudat Sabah, pg 365
The Institute for Israeli Arabs Studies, pg 368
Schocken Publishing House Ltd, pg 372
Zmora-Bitan, Publishers Ltd, pg 374

Italy
Adelphi Edizioni SpA, pg 374
Franco Angeli SRL, pg 375
Editore Armando Armando SRL, pg 376
Edizioni Borla SRL, pg 378
Centro Studi Terzo Mondo, pg 381
Le Cerchio Imigiative Editoriali, pg 381
Edizioni Cultura della Pace, pg 383
Edizioni Dedalo SRL, pg 384
Edizioni del Centro, pg 384
Editori Laterza, pg 386
Essegi, pg 388
Gangemi Editore, pg 390
Edizioni GB, pg 390
Grafo Edizioni, pg 391
Edizioni Guerini e Associati SpA, pg 392
Hermes Edizioni SRL, pg 392
Ibis, pg 393
Il Saggiatore, pg 393
Instituti Editoriali E Poligrafici Internazionali SRL, pg 393
Editoriale Jaca Book SpA, pg 394
Liguori Editore SRL, pg 396
La Luna, pg 397
Editrice Missionaria Italiana (EMI), pg 399
Newton Compton Editori SRL, pg 401
Leo S Olschki, pg 402
Priuli e Verlucca, Editori, pg 404
Rubbettino Editore, pg 406
Sellerio Editore, pg 407
Servitium, pg 408
Edizioni Librarie Siciliane, pg 408
Urbaniana University Press, pg 410
Zanichelli Editore SpA, pg 412

Jamaica
University of the West Indies Press, pg 414

Japan
Tosui Shobo Publishers, pg 428
Tsukiji Shokan Publishing Co, pg 428
Waseda University Press, pg 428

Kenya
Gaba Publications Amecea, Pastoral Institute, pg 431
Kenway Publications Ltd, pg 432
Shirikon Publishers, pg 433
Gideon S Were Press, pg 434

Republic of Korea
Iljo-gag Publishers, pg 437
Seogwangsa, pg 440
Sohaksa, pg 440

Lesotho
Saint Michael's Mission, pg 444

Lithuania
Lithuanian National Museum Publishing House, pg 446

Macau
Livros Do Oriente, pg 448

The Former Yugoslav Republic of Macedonia
Zumpres Publishing Firm, pg 449

Malaysia
Forum Publications, pg 452

Mexico
Centro de Estudios Mexicanos y Centroamericanos, pg 458
El Colegio de Michoacan A C, pg 460
Ediciones Euroamericanas, pg 461
Editorial Extemporaneos SA, pg 461
Fondo de Cultura Economica, pg 461
Instituto Indigenista Interamericano, pg 462
Editorial Jilguero, SA de CV, pg 462
Phillip Richard Conover Lazo, pg 462
Editorial Minutiae Mexicana SA, pg 464
Instituto Nacional de Antropologia e Historia, pg 464
Editorial Nueva Imagen SA, pg 464
Instituto Panamericano de Geografia e Historia, pg 465
Pangea Editores, Sa de CV, pg 465
Plaza y Valdes SA de CV, pg 465
Siglo XXI Editores SA de CV, pg 467
Universidad Nacional Autonoma de Mexico (National University of Mexico), pg 467
Universidad Veracruzana Direccion General Editorial y de Publicaciones, pg 468

Morocco
Societe Ennewrasse Service Librairie et Imprimerie, pg 470

Nepal
International Standards Books & Periodicals (P) Ltd, pg 471

Netherlands
KITLV Press Royal Institute of Linguistics & Anthropology, pg 479
Koninklijk Instituut Voor de Tropen, pg 480
Uniepers BV, pg 486
Van Gorcum & Comp BV, pg 486

New Zealand
Outrigger Publishers, pg 494
University of Otago Press, pg 496
Victoria University Press, pg 496

Nigeria
Riverside Communications, pg 501

Pakistan
Pakistan Institute of Development Economics, pg 508
Sang-e-Meel Publications, pg 509

Papua New Guinea
Papua New Guinea Institute of Medical Research, pg 510
Melanesian Institute, pg 510
National Research Institute of Papua New Guinea, pg 510

Peru
Instituto de Estudios Peruanos, pg 511
Fondo Editorial de la Pontificia Universidad Catolica del Peru, pg 511
Instituto Frances de Estudios Andinos, IFEA, pg 511
Editorial Horizonte, pg 511
Sur Casa de Estudios del Socialismo, pg 511

Philippines
Ateneo de Manila University Press, pg 512
Heritage Publishing House, pg 513
National Museum of the Philippines, pg 514
New Day Publishers, pg 514
Our Lady of Manaoag Publisher, pg 514
Rex Bookstores & Publishers, pg 514
San Carlos Publications, pg 515

Poland
Wydawnictwa Uniwersytetu Warszawskiego, pg 521

Portugal
Edicoes Cosmos, pg 524
Edicoes 70, Lda, pg 524
Editorial Estampa, Lda, pg 524
Gradiva-Publicacnoes Lda, pg 525
Imprensa Nacional-Casa da Moeda, pg 526
Instituto de Investigacao Cientifica Tropical, pg 526
Nova Acropole, pg 527
Edicoes Ora & Labora, pg 528
Edicoes 70, pg 529
Teorema, pg 529
Vega-Publicacao e Distribuicao de Livros e Revistas, Lda, pg 530

Puerto Rico
Instituto de Cultura Puertorriquena, pg 530

Romania
Editura Academiei Romane, pg 531
Aion Verlag, pg 531
Editura Excelsior, pg 533
Editura Meridiane, pg 534
Polirom Verlag, pg 535
Saeculum IO, pg 535

Senegal
Centre Africain d'Animation et d'Echanges Culturels Editions Khoudia, pg 544

South Africa
Human & Rousseau (Pty) Ltd, pg 555
Institute for Reformational Studies CHE, pg 555
New Africa Books (Pty) Ltd, pg 557
Ravan Press (Pty) Ltd, pg 558
Witwatersrand University Press, pg 560

Spain
Academia de la Llingua Asturiana, pg 561
Ediciones Akal SA, pg 562
Alberdania SL, pg 562
Ediciones Alfar SA, pg 562
Alta Fulla Editorial, pg 563
Altea, Taurus, Alfaguara SA, pg 563
Editorial Anagrama, pg 563
Compania Literaria, pg 568
Complutense, SA Editorial, pg 568
Ediciones de la Universidad Complutense de Madrid, pg 568
Consello da Cultura Galega - CCG, pg 568
Rafael Dalmau, Editor, pg 569
Diputacion Provincial de Malaga, pg 570
Ediciones Doce Calles SL, pg 570
Ediciones Encuentro SA, pg 573
Fondo de Cultura Economica de Espana, SL, pg 574
Hercules de Ediciones, SA, pg 577
Icaria Editorial SA, pg 577
Iralka Editorial SL, pg 578
Ediciones Istmo SA, pg 579
Laertes SA de Ediciones, pg 579
Ediciones Maeva, pg 581
Marcombo SA de Boixareu Editores, pg 581
Mundo Negro Editorial, pg 583
Munoz Moya Editor, pg 583
Nueva Acropolis, pg 584
Oikos-Tau SA Ediciones, pg 584
Pages Editors, SL, pg 585
Pentalfa Ediciones, pg 586
Polifemo, Ediciones, pg 587
Editorial Presencia Gitana, pg 587
Editora Regional de Murcia - ERM, pg 588
Siglo XXI de Espana Editores SA, pg 590
Editorial Sal Terrae, pg 592
Editorial Txertoa, pg 594
Universidad de Granada, pg 594
Vinaches Lopez, Luisa, pg 595

Sri Lanka
Department of National Museums, pg 597

Suriname
Stichting Wetenschappelijke Informatie, pg 599

Sweden
Carlsson Bokfoerlag AB, pg 601

Switzerland
Les Editions Camphill, pg 610
Helbing und Lichtenhahn Verlag AG, pg 615
Kindler Verlag AG, pg 617
Novalis Media AG, pg 620
Editions Payot Lausanne, pg 621
Verlag Die Pforte im Rudolf Steiner Verlag, pg 621
Zbinden Druck und Verlag AG, pg 628

SUBJECT INDEX   BOOK

Syrian Arab Republic
Damascus University Press, pg 628
Institut Francais d'Etudes Arabes de Damas, pg 628

Taiwan, Province of China
Echo Publishing Company Ltd, pg 629
Laureate Book Co Ltd, pg 631
San Min Book Co Ltd, pg 631
SMC Publishing Inc, pg 632

Trinidad & Tobago
Joan Bacchus-Xavier, pg 636

Tunisia
Maison Tunisienne de l'Edition, pg 638

Turkey
Arkeoloji Ve Sanat Yayinlari, pg 639
Kabalci Yayinevi, pg 642

Uganda
Fountain Publishers Ltd, pg 642

United Kingdom
ABC-CLIO, pg 644
Aris & Phillips Ltd, pg 648
The Athlone Press Ltd, pg 650
Ruth Bean Publishers, pg 653
Berg Publishers, pg 654
Berghahn Books Ltd, pg 654
Cambridge University Press, pg 662
Compendium Publishing, pg 670
James Currey Ltd, pg 673
Delectus Books, pg 675
Edinburgh University Press Ltd, pg 677
The Eurospan Group, pg 680
Garnet Publishing Ltd, pg 685
Gateway Books, pg 686
Gwasg Gwenffrwd, pg 690
HarperCollins Publishers, pg 692
Harvard University Press, pg 692
The Harvill Press Ltd, pg 693
Institute of Irish Studies, The Queens University of Belfast, pg 699
Intermediate Technology Publications Ltd, pg 700
Irish Texts Society (Cumann Na Scribeann nGaedhilge), pg 701
Karnak House, pg 703
KIT Press - Royal Tropical Institute, pg 705
Mirabel Books Ltd, pg 715
The Octagon Press Ltd, pg 720
Oneworld Publications, pg 721
Open Gate Press, pg 721
The Orkney Press Ltd, pg 722
Pearson Education, pg 725
Pluto Press, pg 728
Routledge Curzon, pg 736
Sage Publications Ltd, pg 737
Skoob Russell Square, pg 742
Yale University Press London, pg 759

Uruguay
Editorial Arca SRL, pg 760
Nordan-Comunidad, pg 760
Luis A Retta Libros, pg 761

Venezuela
Armitano Editores CA, pg 761
Monte Avila Editores Latinoamericana CA, pg 762
Biblioteca Ayacucho, pg 762

Yugoslavia
Svetovi, pg 766

Zambia
Historical Association of Zambia, pg 766

ANTIQUES

Albania
NL SH, pg 1

Australia
Carter's Publications, pg 17
Oriental Publications, pg 36

Austria
Oesterreichischer Kunst und Kulturverlag, pg 56

Belgium
Editions Chanlis, pg 66
Glenat Benelux SA, pg 69

Brazil
Edicon Editora e Consultorial Ltda, pg 81

China
Beijing Publishing House, pg 102
Cultural Relics Publishing House, pg 105
Qingdao Publishing House, pg 108
Shanghai Fine Arts Publishers, pg 109
Sichuan University Press, pg 109

Colombia
Editorial Santillana SA, pg 113

Denmark
Museum Tusculanum Press, pg 134

France
Societe Nouvelle Rene Baudouin, pg 149
Societe Nouvelle Adam Biro, pg 150
Editions Casterman, pg 153
ELLUG (Editions Litteraires et Linguistiques de l'Universite de Grenoble III), pg 162
Institut d'Etudes Augustiniennes, pg 163
Paul Geuthner Librairie Orientaliste, pg 166
Macula, pg 174
Editions de la Reunion des Musees Nationaux, pg 176
Editions A et J Picard SA, pg 179
Presses Universitaires de Caen, pg 181
Editions Scala, pg 184
Somogy editions d'art, pg 186

Germany
Arnoldsche Verlagsanstalt GmbH, pg 195
Battenberg Verlag, pg 199
GLB Parkland Verlags-und Vertriebs GmbH, pg 232

Dr Ernst Hauswedell & Co Verlag, pg 238
Klinkhardt & Biermann Verlagsbuchhandlung GmbH, pg 250
Kunstverlag Weingarten GmbH, pg 254
Karl Robert Langewiesche Nachfolger Hans Koester KG, pg 256
J B Metzler'sche Verlagsbuchhandlung, pg 263
Mosaik Verlag GmbH, pg 265
Musikantiquariat und Dr Hans Schneider Verlag GmbH, pg 266
Georg Olms Verlag AG, pg 270
Patmos Verlag GmbH & Co KG, pg 272
Saarbrucker Druckerei und Verlag GmbH (SDV), pg 281
Schild-Verlag GmbH, pg 283
Dr Wolfgang Schwarze Verlag, pg 286
Staatliche Museen Kassel, pg 288
Weidmannsche Verlagsbuchhandlung GmbH, pg 301

Greece
D Papadimas, pg 314

Hong Kong
Chung Hwa Book Co (HK) Ltd, pg 319
Ling Kee Publishing Group, pg 320
Publications (Holdings) Ltd, pg 321
Unicorn Books Ltd, pg 322

Hungary
Officina Nova, Koenyv-es Lapkiado/Bertelsmann Media Kft, pg 324

India
Agam Kala Prakashan, pg 330
Rahul Publishing House, pg 347

Indonesia
Gramedia, pg 355

Italy
Umberto Allemandi & C SRL, pg 375
Artioli Editore in Modena, pg 377
Bardi Editore srl, pg 377
Belforte Editore Libraio srl, pg 377
BeMa, pg 377
M d'Auria Editore SAS, pg 384
Giovanni De Vecchi Editore SpA, pg 384
Edizioni del Centro, pg 384
Edipuglia, pg 386
Edizioni d'Arte e Moderna, Edam, pg 386
Essegi, pg 388
Arnaldo Forni Editore SRL, pg 389
1st Patristico Augustinianum, pg 394
Giorgio Mondadori & Associati, pg 399
OCTAVO Franco Cantini Editore, pg 401
Pontifico Istituto Orientale, pg 404
Priuli e Verlucca, Editori, pg 404
Edizioni Librarie Siciliane, pg 408
Il Tripode Srl, pg 410

Japan
Tankosha Publishing Co Ltd, pg 427

Republic of Korea
Dae Won Sa Co Ltd, pg 435
Youl Hwa Dang Publisher, pg 436

Lithuania
Lithuanian National Museum Publishing House, pg 446

Malta
Fondazzjoni Patrimonju Malti, pg 456

Mexico
Editorial Jilguero, SA de CV, pg 462
Instituto Nacional de Antropologia e Historia, pg 464

Monaco
Les Editions du Rocher, pg 469

Morocco
Association de la Recherche Historique et Sociale, pg 469
Societe Ennewrasse Service Librairie et Imprimerie, pg 470

Netherlands
Castrum Peregrini Presse, pg 475
The Pepin Press, pg 482
Scriptum, pg 483
Tirion Uitgevers BV, pg 485
Uniepers BV, pg 486
Uitgeverij Waanders BV, pg 487

Pakistan
The Book House, pg 506

Poland
Wydawnictwo Arkady, pg 516
Wydawnictwo DiG, pg 521

Portugal
Camara Municipal de Castelo, pg 523
Editorial Estampa, Lda, pg 524

Romania
Enzyklopadie Verlag, pg 533
MAST Verlag, pg 534

Russian Federation
Ladomir Publishing House, pg 539

Singapore
Select Books Pte Ltd, pg 548

Spain
Vicent Garcia Editores, SA, pg 575

Sri Lanka
Department of National Museums, pg 597

Sweden
Tryckeriforlaget AB, pg 607

Switzerland
Cockatoo Press (Schweiz), Thailand-Publikationen, pg 611
Librairie Droz SA, pg 612
Hans Rohr Verlag, pg 623

PUBLISHERS

Taiwan, Province of China
Art Book Co Ltd, pg 629
Echo Publishing Company Ltd, pg 629
Highlight Publishing Company Ltd, pg 630
Lee & Lee Communications, pg 631
National Museum of History, pg 631
National Palace Museum, pg 631

Tunisia
Ceres Editions, pg 637

Turkey
Arkeoloji Ve Sanat Yayinlari, pg 639

United Kingdom
Antique Collectors' Club Ltd, pg 647
Antiques & Collectors Guides Ltd, pg 647
Apple Press, pg 648
Art Books International Ltd, pg 649
BCA, pg 653
Mitchell Beazley, pg 653
BLA Publishing Ltd, pg 655
Books for Europe Ltd, pg 657
Carlton Publishing Group, pg 664
Marshall Cavendish Partworks Ltd, pg 665
Compendium Publishing, pg 670
Constable Publishers, pg 670
Foulsham Publishers, pg 683
Hilmarton Manor Press, pg 696
Lyle Publications Ltd, pg 709
Maney Publishing, pg 711
Miller's Publications, pg 715
Mirabel Books Ltd, pg 715
New Leaf Books Ltd, pg 719
Octopus Publishing Group, pg 720
Quarto Publishing plc, pg 731
The Reader's Digest Association Ltd, pg 733
The Rubicon Press, pg 737
Shire Publications Ltd, pg 741
Charles Skilton Ltd, pg 742
Skoob Russell Square, pg 742
Stenlake Publishing, pg 745
Studio Editions Ltd, pg 746
Towy Publishing, pg 749
White Cockade Publishing, pg 755
Philip Wilson Publishers, pg 757

ARCHAEOLOGY

Albania
NL SH, pg 1

Argentina
EUDEBA (Editorial Universitaria de Buenos Aires), pg 6
Tipografica Editora Argentina, pg 9

Australia
Aboriginal Studies Press, pg 10
Archaeological Publications, pg 12
Gnostic Editions, pg 24
Queen Victoria Museum & Art Gallery Publications, pg 39
Thames & Hudson (Australia) Pty Ltd, pg 44
Three Sisters Publications Pty Ltd, pg 44
Veritas Press, pg 46

Austria
Akademische Druck-u Verlagsanstalt Dr Paul Struzl GmbH, pg 49
Carinthia Verlag, pg 50
Docker Verlag GmbH & Co KG, pg 51
Ferdinand Berger und Sohne, pg 51
Verlag der Oesterreichischen Akademie der Wissenschaften (OEAW), pg 56
Andreas Schnider Verlags-Atelier, pg 58
Verband der Wissenschaftlichen Gesellschaften Oesterreichs (VWGOe), pg 60
Universitaetsverlag Wagner GmbH, pg 60

Bangladesh
The University Press Ltd, pg 62

Belarus
Belaruskaya Encyklapedyya, pg 63

Belgium
Brepols Publishers NV, pg 65
Editions Chanlis, pg 66
Groeninghe NV, pg 69
Leuven University Press, pg 71
Uitgeverij Peeters Leuven (Belgie), pg 72

Botswana
The Botswana Society, pg 77

Brazil
Ars Poetica Editora Ltda, pg 79
Hemus Editora Ltda, pg 85
Francisco J Laissue Livraria, pg 86
Editora Melhoramentos Ltda, pg 87

Bulgaria
Litera Prima, pg 96
Pensoft Publishers, pg 97

Chile
Arrayan Editores, pg 99
Museo Chileno de Arte Precolombino, pg 100

China
China Tibetology Publishing House, pg 104
Cultural Relics Publishing House, pg 105
Foreign Languages Press, pg 105
Qingdao Publishing House, pg 108
Science Press, pg 108

Colombia
Amazonas Editores Ltda, pg 111

Costa Rica
Editorial de la Universidad de Costa Rica, pg 117

Croatia
Knjizevni Krug Split, pg 119
Matica hrvatska, pg 119
Znaci Vremena, Institut Za Istrazivanje Biblije, pg 120

Cyprus
A G Leventis Foundation, pg 122

SUBJECT INDEX

Czech Republic
Academia, pg 122
Barrister & Principal, pg 123
Libri s r o, pg 125
Mariadan, pg 126
Narodni Muzeum, pg 126
NLN, Ltd The Lidove noviny Publishing House, pg 127
Nakladatelstvi a vydavatelstvi Panorama, pg 127

Denmark
Aarhus Universitetsforlag, pg 129
Museum Tusculanum Press, pg 134
Syddansk Universitetsforlag, pg 136

Dominican Republic
Pontificia Universidad Catolica Madre y Maestra, pg 136

Ecuador
Corporacion Editora Nacional, pg 137
Pontificia Universidad Catolica de Ecuador, Centro de Publicaciones, pg 137

Egypt (Arab Republic of Egypt)
Dar El Shorouk Publishing & Distributing House, pg 138
Lehnert & Landrock Bookshop, pg 139

Estonia
Tael Ltd, pg 140
Valgus Publishers, pg 141

Finland
Forlagsaktiebolaget Scriptum, pg 142

France
ATP - Packager, pg 149
De Boccard Edition-Diffusion, pg 151
Editions des Cahiers Bourbonnais, pg 152
Editions Casterman, pg 153
CNRS Editions, pg 155
Editions du Comite des Travaux Historiques et Scientifiques (CTHS), pg 156
Editions du Demi-Cercle, pg 158
Presses de l'Ecole Normale Superieure, pg 160
Edisud, pg 161
Editions Recherche sur les Civilisations (ERC), pg 161
Editions Errance, pg 162
Institut d'Ethnologie du Museum National d'Histoire Naturelle, pg 163
Institut d'Etudes Augustiniennes, pg 163
Editions Jean Paul Gisserot, pg 166
Kailash Editions, pg 171
Editions Klincksieck, pg 171
LLB France (Ligue pour la Lecture de la Bible), pg 173
Editions Lyonnaises d'Art et d'Histoire, pg 174
Editions de la Maison des Sciences de l'Homme, Paris, pg 174
Muller Edition, pg 176
Editions de la Reunion des Musees Nationaux, pg 176
Pardes, pg 179
Peeters-France, pg 179
Editions A et J Picard SA, pg 179
Editions Pygmalion - Gerard Watelet, pg 182
Sepia, pg 184
Somogy editions d'art, pg 186
Publications de la Sorbonne, pg 186
Editions Pierre Terrail/Finest SA, pg 187
Thames & Hudson, pg 187

Germany
Verlag C H Beck (OHG), pg 200
Bettendorf'sche Verlagsanstalt GmbH, pg 202
Biblio-Zeller Verlag, pg 202
Boehlau-Verlag GmbH & Cie, pg 204
DuMont Buchverlag GmbH & Co KG, pg 219
E Schweizerbart'sche Verlagsbuchhandlung (Nagele und Obermiller), pg 220
Wilhelm Fink GmbH & Co Verlags-KG, pg 228
Frederking & Thaler Verlag GmbH, pg 230
Germanisches Nationalmuseum, pg 232
Walter de Gruyter GmbH & Co KG, pg 234
Dr Rudolf Habelt GmbH, pg 235
Hirmer Verlag GmbH, pg 241
Holos Verlag, pg 242
Ikarus - Buchverlag, pg 244
Jan Thorbecke Verlag GmbH & Co, pg 246
Verlag Koenigshausen und Neumann GmbH, pg 251
Karl Robert Langewiesche Nachfolger Hans Koester KG, pg 256
Michael Lassleben Verlag, pg 256
Gustav Luebbe Verlag, pg 259
Lukas Verlag fur Kunst- und Geistesgeschichte, pg 259
Maeander Verlag GmbH, pg 260
Gebr Mann Verlag GmbH & Co, pg 260
Orbis Verlag fur Publizistik GmbH, pg 270
Philipps-Universitaet Marburg, pg 273
Verlag Friedrich Pustet GmbH & Co Kg, pg 276
Dr Ludwig Reichert Verlag, pg 278
RVBG Rheinland-Verlag-und Betriebsgesellschaft des Landschaftsverbandes Rheinland mbH, pg 279
Rowohlt Taschenbuch Verlag GmbH, pg 280
Saarbrucker Druckerei und Verlag GmbH (SDV), pg 281
Verlag Schnell und Steiner GmbH, pg 284
Scientia Verlag und Antiquariat, pg 286
Franz Steiner Verlag Wiesbaden GmbH, pg 289
Konrad Theiss Verlag GmbH, pg 293
Traditionell Bogenschiessen Verlag Angelika Hornig, pg 294
UVK Universitatsverlag Konstanz GmbH, pg 297
Verlag Philipp von Zabern, pg 299
Wachholtz Verlag GmbH, pg 300
Ernst Wasmuth Verlag GmbH & Co, pg 300
Wissenschaftliche Buchgesellschaft, pg 303
Zeller Verlag GmbH & Co, pg 305

Greece
Ecole francaise d'Athenes, pg 310
Ekdotike Athenon SA, pg 310
Evrodiastasi, pg 310
Hestia-I D Hestia-Kollaros & Co Corporation, pg 311
Kardamitsa A, pg 312
Morfotiko Idryma Ethnikis Trapezas, pg 313
Ed Nea Acropolis, pg 313
Nea Thesis - Evrotas, pg 313
Panepistimio Ioanninon, pg 314
D Papadimas, pg 314
Society for Macedonian Studies, pg 315

Guatemala
Grupo Editorial RIN-78, pg 316

Guyana
Hamburgh Press, pg 317

Hong Kong
Hong Kong University Press, pg 320

Hungary
Akademiai Kiado, pg 323
Osiris Kiado, pg 326
Tajak Korok Muzeumok Egyesuelet, pg 327

India
Abhinav Publications, pg 329
Agam Kala Prakashan, pg 330
Ajanta Publications (India), pg 330
APH Publishing Corp, pg 331
Asian Educational Services, pg 331
Books & Books, pg 334
BR Publishing Corporation, pg 334
Chowkhamba Sanskrit Series Office, pg 335
Clarion Books, pg 335
Cosmo Publications, pg 335
DK Printworld (P) Ltd, pg 336
Gyan Publishing House, pg 338
Indian Museum, pg 339
Indus Publishing Co, pg 339
Intellectual Publishing House, pg 339
Inter-India Publications, pg 340
Mapin Publishing Pvt Ltd, pg 342
Munshiram Manoharlal Publishers Pvt Ltd, pg 343
National Book Organization, pg 343
Navrang Booksellers & Publishers, pg 344
Parimal Prakashan, pg 345
Rahul Publishing House, pg 347
Regency Publications, pg 347
Reliance Publishing House, pg 347
Scientific Book Agency, pg 349
Somaiya Publications Pvt Ltd, pg 350

Ireland
The Collins Press, pg 359
Cork University Press, pg 359
Gandon Editions, pg 360
Herodotus Press, pg 361
Morrigan Book Co, pg 362
Royal Irish Academy, pg 364
Tir Eolas, pg 364
Town House & Country House, pg 364

Israel
Bar Ilan University Press, pg 365
The Bialik Institute, pg 365
Carta, The Israel Map & Publishing Co Ltd, pg 366
Gefen Publishing House Ltd, pg 367
Haifa University Press, pg 368
Hakibbutz Hameuchad Publishing House Ltd, pg 368
Israel Antiquities Authority, pg 368
Israel Exploration Society, pg 368
The Jerusalem Publishing House Ltd, pg 369
The Magnes Press, pg 370
Sadan Publishing Ltd, pg 372
R Sirkis Publishers Ltd, pg 372

Italy
Mario Adda Editore SNC, pg 374
Umberto Allemandi & C SRL, pg 375
All'Insegna del Giglio, pg 375
Bardi Editore srl, pg 377
Bibliopolis - Edizioni di Filosofia e Scienze Srl, pg 377
Bonechi-Edizioni Il Turismo Srl, pg 378
Bonsignori Editore SRL, pg 378
Editore Giorgio Bretschneider, pg 378
Calosci, pg 379
Campanotto, pg 379
Colonnese Editore, pg 382
M d'Auria Editore SAS, pg 384
Edizioni del Centro, pg 384
Edizioni Della Torre di Salvatore Fozzi & C SAS, pg 384
Ecole Francaise de Rome, pg 385
Edipuglia, pg 386
Editori Laterza, pg 386
Edizioni Mediterranee SRL, pg 387
Essegi, pg 388
FEDA SA, pg 388
Flaccovio Editore, pg 389
Arnaldo Forni Editore SRL, pg 389
Adriano Gallina Editore sas, pg 389
Gangemi Editore, pg 390
Garolla, pg 390
Edizioni del Girasole srl, pg 390
Giunti (Gruppo Editoriale), pg 390
Gius Laterza e Figli SpA, pg 391
Grafo Edizioni, pg 391
Herbita Editrice di Leonardo Palermo, pg 392
Herder Editrice e Libreria, pg 392
Ila - Palma, Tea Nova, pg 393
Istituti Editoriali E Poligrafici Internazionali SRL, pg 393
ISAL (Ist Storia Arte Lombarda), pg 394
Editoriale Jaca Book SpA, pg 394
Jouvence, pg 394
Laruffa Editore SRL, pg 395
L'Erma di Bretschneider SRL, pg 395
Angelo Longo Editore, pg 396
Edizioni de Luca SRL, pg 397
Macro Edizioni, pg 397
Accademia Naz dei Lincei, pg 400
Istituto Nazionale di Archeologia e Storia dell'Arte, pg 400
Newton Compton Editori SRL, pg 401
OCTAVO Franco Cantini Editore, pg 401
Leo S Olschki, pg 402
Osanna Venosa, pg 402
Franco Cosimo Panini Editore SpA, pg 402
Pontificio Istituto di Archeologia Cristiana, pg 404
Pontifico Istituto Orientale, pg 404
Edizioni Quasar di Severino Tognon SRL, pg 404
Edizioni Quattroventi SNC, pg 404
Scala Group spa, pg 407
Schena Editore, pg 407
Sellerio Editore, pg 407
Edizioni Librarie Siciliane, pg 408
Studio Bibliografico Adelmo Polla, pg 409
Tappeiner, pg 409

Japan
GakuseiSha Publishing Co Ltd, pg 416
Koyo Shobo, pg 420
Myrtos Inc, pg 421
Toho Book Store, pg 427
Tsukiji Shokan Publishing Co, pg 428
Waseda University Press, pg 428

Kenya
British Institute in Eastern Africa, pg 431

Democratic People's Republic of Korea
The Foreign Language Press Group, pg 434

Republic of Korea
Hakgojae Publishing Inc, pg 436
Iljisa Publishing House, pg 437
Sohaksa, pg 440

Lebanon
Librairie Orientale sal, pg 443

Liechtenstein
Historischer Verein fur das Furstentum Liechtenstein, pg 444

Lithuania
Lithuanian National Museum Publishing House, pg 446

Luxembourg
Service Central des Imprimes et des Fournitures de Bureau de l'Etat, pg 448

The Former Yugoslav Republic of Macedonia
Macedonia Prima Publishing House, pg 449
Zumpres Publishing Firm, pg 449

Malta
Fondazzjoni Patrimonju Malti, pg 456

Martinique
Editions Gondwana, pg 456

Mexico
Centro de Estudios Mexicanos y Centroamericanos, pg 458
Editorial Diana SA de CV, pg 459
El Colegio de Michoacan A C, pg 460
Ediciones Euroamericanas, pg 461
Fondo de Cultura Economica, pg 461
Editorial Jilguero, SA de CV, pg 462
Editorial Minutiae Mexicana SA, pg 464
Instituto Nacional de Antropologia e Historia, pg 464
Instituto Panamericano de Geografia e Historia, pg 465
Pangea Editores, Sa de CV, pg 465
Plaza y Valdes SA de CV, pg 465
Universidad Nacional Autonoma de Mexico (National University of Mexico), pg 467

Morocco
Association de la Recherche Historique et Sociale, pg 469
Editions Eddif Maroc, pg 469

Nepal
International Standards Books & Periodicals (P) Ltd, pg 471

Netherlands
A A Balkema, pg 473
Brill Academic Publishers, pg 475
The Pepin Press, pg 482
Unieboek BV, pg 485
Uniepers BV, pg 486

New Zealand
Auckland University Press, pg 488
Bush Press Communications Ltd, pg 489
Clerestory Press, pg 490
Outrigger Publishers, pg 494
Southern Press Ltd, pg 496

Peru
Librerias ABC SA, pg 511
Instituto de Estudios Peruanos, pg 511
Fondo Editorial de la Pontificia Universidad Catolica del Peru, pg 511
Instituto Frances de Estudios Andinos, IFEA, pg 511

Philippines
National Museum of the Philippines, pg 514
Rex Bookstores & Publishers, pg 514
San Carlos Publications, pg 515

Poland
Ossolineum Zaklad Narodowy im Ossolinskich - Wydawnictwo, pg 518
Towarzystwo Naukowe w Toruniu, pg 520
Wydawnictwa Uniwersytetu Warszawskiego, pg 521
Wydawnictwo DiG, pg 521

Portugal
Camara Municipal de Castelo, pg 523
Edicoes Colibri, pg 523
Imprensa Nacional-Casa da Moeda, pg 526
Instituto de Investigacao Cientifica Tropical, pg 526
Nova Acropole, pg 527

Romania
Editura Academiei Romane, pg 531
Enzyklopadie Verlag, pg 533
Editura Excelsior, pg 533
Editura Meridiane, pg 534

Russian Federation
Nauka Publishers, pg 540
Izdatel'stvo Nizhegorodskogo Gosudarstvennogo Univ, pg 540
St Andrew's Biblical Theological College, pg 541

PUBLISHERS

Slovakia
Vydavatelstvo Obzor, pg 550
VEDA (Vydavatel'stvo Slovenskej akademie vied), pg 551

South Africa
New Africa Books (Pty) Ltd, pg 557
Witwatersrand University Press, pg 560

Spain
Ediciones Akal SA, pg 562
Ediciones Alfar SA, pg 562
Casa de Velazquez, pg 566
Comunidad Autonoma de Madrid, Servicio de Documentacion y Publicaciones, pg 568
Diputacion Provincial de Malaga, pg 570
Instituto de Estudios Riojanos, pg 574
Institut d'Estudis Vallencs (IEV), pg 574
Eumo Editorial, pg 574
Fundacion Marcelino Botin, pg 575
Ediciones Garriga SA, pg 575
Institucion Fernando el Catolico de la Excma Diputacion de Zaragoza, pg 578
Junta de Castilla y Leon Consejeria de Educacion y Cultura, pg 579
Laertes SA de Ediciones, pg 579
Lunwerg Editores, SA, pg 580
Nueva Acropolis, pg 584
Polifemo, Ediciones, pg 587
Instituto Provincial de Investigaciones y Estudios Toledanos, pg 588
Editora Regional de Murcia - ERM, pg 588
Servicio de Publicaciones Universidad de Cordoba, pg 590
Silex Ediciones, pg 590
Equipo Sirius SA, pg 591
Universidad de Granada, pg 594
Universidad de Valladolid Secretariado de Publicaciones e Intercambio Editorial, pg 594

Sri Lanka
Karunaratne & Sons Ltd, pg 597

Switzerland
Cockatoo Press (Schweiz), Thailand-Publikationen, pg 611
Les Editions la Matze, pg 618
Motovun Book GmbH, pg 619
Muslim Architecture Research Program (MARP), pg 619
Les Editions Nagel SA (Paris), pg 619
Editions Payot Lausanne, pg 621
Schwabe & Co AG, pg 624

Syrian Arab Republic
Damascus University Press, pg 628
Institut Francais d'Etudes Arabes de Damas, pg 628

Taiwan, Province of China
Asian Culture Co, pg 629
Echo Publishing Company Ltd, pg 629
National Palace Museum, pg 631
Yee Wen Publishing Co Ltd, pg 632

Tunisia
Alyssa Editions, pg 637
Ceres Editions, pg 637
Faculte des Sciences Humaines et Sociales de Tunis, pg 638
Les Editions de l'Arbre, pg 638
Maison Tunisienne de l'Edition, pg 638
Publications de la Fondation Temimi pour la Recherche Scientifique et L'Information, pg 638

Turkey
Arkeoloji Ve Sanat Yayinlari, pg 639
Ataturk Kultur, Dil ve Tarih, Yusek Kurumu Baskanligi, pg 639
IKI NOKTA Research Press & Publications Industry & Trade Ltd, pg 640
Inkilap Publishers Ltd, pg 640
Payel Yayinevi, pg 641
Turkish Republic - Ministry of Culture, pg 641

Ukraine
Osnova, Kharkov State University Press, pg 643

United Kingdom
Andromeda Oxford Ltd, pg 647
Aris & Phillips Ltd, pg 648
Artetech Publishing Co, pg 649
Ashmolean Museum Publications, pg 650
The Athlone Press Ltd, pg 650
Batsford Ltd, pg 652
BCA, pg 653
Books for Europe Ltd, pg 657
The British Academy, pg 659
British Museum Press, pg 660
Cambridge University Press, pg 662
Capall Bann Publishing, pg 663
Constable Publishers, pg 670
Council for British Archaeology, pg 671
James Currey Ltd, pg 673
Darf Publishers Ltd, pg 674
Edinburgh University Press Ltd, pg 677
The Eurospan Group, pg 680
Forth Naturalist & Historian, pg 683
Garnet Publishing Ltd, pg 685
The Greek Bookshop, pg 689
Herbert Press Ltd, pg 695
Institute of Irish Studies, The Queens University of Belfast, pg 699
Kegan Paul International Ltd, pg 703
Liverpool University Press, pg 708
The Lutterworth Press, pg 709
Maney Publishing, pg 711
Methuen Publishing Ltd, pg 714
Mirabel Books Ltd, pg 715
Motilal (UK) Books of India, pg 715
NMS Publishing Ltd, pg 719
Open Gate Press, pg 721
Orion Publishing Group Ltd, pg 722
The Orkney Press Ltd, pg 722
Phillimore & Co Ltd, pg 727
The Reader's Digest Association Ltd, pg 733
Routledge, pg 736
The Rubicon Press, pg 737
Scottish Cultural Press, pg 739
Sheffield Academic Press Ltd, pg 741
Shire Publications Ltd, pg 741
Sidgwick & Jackson Ltd, pg 742
Stacey International, pg 745
The Stationery Office, pg 745
Sutton Publishing Ltd, pg 746
Thames & Hudson Ltd, pg 748
Thistle Press, pg 748
Tuckwell Press Ltd, pg 750
UCL Press Ltd, pg 751
University of Exeter Press, pg 751
University of Wales Press, pg 751
Philip Wilson Publishers, pg 757
World of Islam Altajir Trust, pg 759

Viet Nam
Science & Technics Publishing House, pg 763

SUBJECT INDEX

ARCHITECTURE & INTERIOR DESIGN

Albania
NL SH, pg 1

Argentina
Fundacion Editorial de Belgrano, pg 4
Editorial Idearium de la Universidad de Mendoza (EDIUM), pg 5
EUDEBA (Editorial Universitaria de Buenos Aires), pg 6
Marymar Ediciones SA, pg 7
Ediciones Nueva Vision SAIC, pg 8
Ediciones Tres Tiempos SRL, pg 9

Australia
Art on the Move, pg 12
CHOICE Magazine, pg 18
The Images Publishing Group Pty Ltd, pg 27
McGraw-Hill Australia Pty Ltd, pg 32
Press for Success, pg 38
Ruskin Rowe Press, pg 41
Thames & Hudson (Australia) Pty Ltd, pg 44
University of New South Wales Press Ltd, pg 46
The Watermark Press, pg 47

Austria
Aritbus et Historiae, Rivista Internationale di arti visive ecinema, Institut IRSA - Verlagsanstatt, pg 49
Christian Brandstatter Verlagsgesellschaft GmbH, pg 50
Haymon-Verlag GesmbH, pg 52
Loecker Verlag, pg 54
Modulverlag, pg 55
Oesterreichischer Kunst und Kulturverlag, pg 56
Passagen Verlag GmbH, pg 57
Promedia Verlagsges mbH, pg 57
Verlag Anton Pustet, pg 57
Residenz Verlag GmbH, pg 58
Ritter Verlag, pg 58
Andreas Schnider Verlags-Atelier, pg 58
SN-Verlag, Salzburger Nachrichten Verlags GmbH & Co KG, pg 59
Springer-Verlag Wien, pg 59
Edition Tusch, pg 59

Bangladesh
The University Press Ltd, pg 62

Belarus
Belaruskaya Encyklapedyya, pg 63

Belgium
Brepols Publishers NV, pg 65
Coda, pg 66
Conservart SA, pg 67
King Baudouin Foundation, pg 70
Uitgeverij Lannoo NV, pg 70
Mardaga, Pierre 12, pg 72
Mercatorfonds NV, pg 72
Presses Universitaires de Bruxelles ASBL, pg 73
Editions Racine, pg 73
Roularta Books NV, pg 73
Stichting Kunstboek bvba, pg 74

Brazil
AGIR S/A Editora, pg 78
ARTMED, pg 79
Hemus Editora Ltda, pg 85
LDA Editores Ltda, pg 86
Livraria Nobel S/A, pg 86
Livraria Pioneira Editora/Enio Matheus Guazzelli e Cia Ltd, pg 89
Spala Editora Ltda, pg 92
Editora Universidade Federal do Rio de Janeiro, pg 93

Bulgaria
TEMTO, pg 98

China
Beijing Publishing House, pg 102
Guangdong Science & Technology Press, pg 106
Heilongjiang Science & Technology Press, pg 106
Wissenschaft und Technik Verlag Henan Henan Scientific & Technological Publishing House, pg 106
Higher Education Press, pg 106
Jilin Science & Technology Publishing House, pg 106
Qingdao Publishing House, pg 108
Shandong Science & Technology Press, pg 109
Shandong University Press, pg 109
Tianjin Science & Technology Publishing House, pg 109
Tsinghua University Press, pg 110

Colombia
Amazonas Editores Ltda, pg 111
Escala Ltda, pg 111
Siglo XXI Editores de Colombia Ltda, pg 113

Costa Rica
Editorial de la Universidad de Costa Rica, pg 117

Czech Republic
Karolinum, nakladatelstvi, pg 125
Libri s r o, pg 125
Moravska Galerie v Brne, pg 126

Denmark
Arkitektens Forlag, pg 130
Christian Ejlers' Forlag aps, pg 131

Dominican Republic
Pontificia Universidad Catolica Madre y Maestra, pg 136

Egypt (Arab Republic of Egypt)
American University in Cairo Press, pg 138

Estonia
Kunst Publishers Ltd, pg 140
Valgus Publishers, pg 141

SUBJECT INDEX

Finland
Rakentajain Kustannus Oy (Building Publications Ltd), pg 143
Rakennustieto Oy - Building Information Ltd, pg 144

France
Action Artistique de la Ville de Paris, pg 146
Editions Alternatives, pg 146
Edition Anthese, pg 147
Berger-Levrault SA, pg 150
Bibliotheque des Arts, pg 150
Societe Nouvelle Adam Biro, pg 150
William Blake & Co, pg 150
Editions Casterman, pg 153
CEP Editions, pg 153
Editions du Chene, pg 154
Editions Citadelles & Mazenod, pg 155
CLD, pg 155
Counseil International de la Langue Francaise, pg 157
CPL- La Communication Par le Livre, pg 157
Editions du Demi-Cercle, pg 158
Dessain et Tolra SA, pg 159
Editions Dis Voir, pg 159
Edisud, pg 161
EPA SA (Editions Presse Audiovisuel), pg 162
Les Editions de l'Epargne, pg 162
Editions Eyrolles, pg 163
Flammarion SA, pg 164
Groupe Fleurus-Mame, pg 164
Folklore Comtois, pg 164
Editions Jean Paul Gisserot, pg 166
Groupe Expansion, pg 167
Hachette Livre, pg 167
Editions Hatier SA, pg 168
Fernand Hazan Editeur SA, pg 168
Editions l'Instant Durable (Soprep), pg 169
Institute, pg 169
Librairie Leonce Laget, pg 171
LT Editions-J Lanore-H Laurens, pg 172
Editions Charles Massin et Cie, pg 175
Editions du Moniteur, pg 176
Editions de la Reunion des Musees Nationaux, pg 176
Editions Norma, pg 177
Editions Parentheses, pg 179
Paris Musees, pg 179
Editions A et J Picard SA, pg 179
Editions du Centre Pompidou, pg 180
Revue Noire, pg 183
Selection du Reader's Digest SA, pg 184
Societe Nouveaux Loisirs, pg 185
Sofradif Editions Philippe Auzou, pg 185
Somogy editions d'art, pg 186
Editions Pierre Terrail/Finest SA, pg 187
Thames & Hudson, pg 187
Ulisse Edition, pg 188
Editions Vilo SA, pg 189
Zodiaque, pg 190

Germany
Ardey-Verlag GmbH, pg 194
Aries-Verlag Paul Johannes Muller, pg 195
Arnoldsche Verlagsanstalt GmbH, pg 195
Augustus Verlag, pg 196
Bauverlag GmbH, pg 199
be.bra verlag GmbH, pg 199
BertelsmannSpringer Science & Business Media GmbH, pg 202
Beuth Verlag GmbH, pg 202
Eberhargd Blottner Verlag, pg 204
Verlag Hermann Boehlaus Nachfolger Weimar GmbH & Co, pg 205
Verlag Busse und Seewald GmbH, pg 208
Verlag Georg D W Callwey GmbH & Co, pg 208
Dr Cantz'sche, Druckerei GmbH & Co, Cantz Verlag, pg 209
Christian Verlag GmbH, pg 210
Hans Christians Druckerei und Verlag GmbH & Co, pg 210
Coppenrath Verlag, pg 211
Deutsche Verlags-Anstalt GmbH (DVA), pg 214
Eugen Diederichs Verlag GmbH & Co KG, pg 216
Dolling und Galitz Verlag GmbH, pg 217
Archibook Verlag Martina Duettmann, pg 219
DuMont Monte, pg 219
Edition Solitude - Akademie Schloss Solitude, pg 221
Ellert & Richter Verlag GmbH, pg 222
Ernst, Wilhelm & Sohn, Verlag Architektur und technische Wissenschaft GmbH & Co, pg 224
Europaeische Verlagsanstalt GmbH & Rotbuch Verlag GmbH & Co KG, pg 225
FAB-Verlag, pg 226
Forum Verlag GmbH & Co, pg 229
Fraunhofer IRB Verlag Fraunhofer Informationszentrum Raum und Bau, pg 229
Gerstenberg Verlag, pg 232
GLB Parkland Verlags-und Vertriebs GmbH, pg 232
Heinz-Jurgen Hausser, pg 236
Harenberg Kommunikation Verlags- und Medien GmbH & Co KG, pg 237
Hatje Cantz Verlag, pg 238
Edition Hoffmann & Co, pg 242
Huthig GmbH & Co KG, pg 244
Jahreszeiten-Verlag GmbH, pg 246
Junius Verlag GmbH, pg 247
Kerber Christof Verlag, pg 248
Knesebeck Verlag, pg 250
Knowledge Media International, pg 251
Verlagsanstalt Alexander Koch GmbH, pg 251
Koehler und Amelang Verlagsgesellschaft mbH, pg 251
Koenemann Verlagesellschaft mbH, pg 251
W Kohlhammer GmbH, abt Haussortiment, pg 252
Karl Kraemer Verlag GmbH und Co, pg 253
Kunstverlag Weingarten GmbH, pg 254
Institut fuer Landes- und Stadtentwicklungsforschung, ILS Nordrhein-Westfalen, pg 255
Karl Robert Langewiesche Nachfolger Hans Koester KG, pg 256
Edition Lidiarte, pg 258
Gebr Mann Verlag GmbH & Co, pg 260
Edition Axel Menges, pg 262
mode information Heinz Kramer GmbH, pg 264
modo verlag GmbH, pg 264
Mosaik Verlag GmbH, pg 265
C F Mueller Verlag, Huethig GmbH & Co, pg 265
Neuthor - Verlag, pg 268
Nicolaische Verlagsbuchhandlung Beuermann GmbH, pg 268
C W Niemeyer Buchverlage GmbH, pg 268
Oekobuch Verlag & Versand GmbH, pg 269
Oktagon Verlagsgesellschaft mbH, pg 270
Prestel Verlag, pg 275
Propylaeen Verlag, Zweigniederlassung Berlin der Ullstein Buchverlage GmbH, pg 275
Ritterbach Verlag GmbH, pg 279
Verlag Th Schaefer im Vicentz Verlag KG, pg 282
Schelzky & Jeep, Verlag fuer Reisen und Wissen, pg 283
R S Schulz Verlag GmbH, pg 285
Dr Wolfgang Schwarze Verlag, pg 286
Siegmund Publishing, pg 286
Springer-Verlag GmbH & Co KG, pg 288
Staatliche Museen Kassel, pg 288
TASCHEN GmbH, pg 292
teNeues Verlag GmbH & Co KG, pg 292
TR - Verlagsunion GmbH, pg 294
Verlag Dr Alfons Uhl, pg 295
Vice Versa Verlag, pg 298
Ernst Wasmuth Verlag GmbH & Co, pg 300
WEKA Firmengruppe GmbH & Co KG, pg 301
Verlag fuer Wirtschaft & Verwaltung Hubert Wingen GmbH & Co KG, pg 303
Gert Wohlfarth GmbH Verlag Fachtechnik & Mercator Verlag, Verlag Puppen & Spielzeug, pg 304

Ghana
Building & Road Research Institute (BRRI), pg 306

Greece
Ecole francaise d'Athenes, pg 310
Forma Publications Ltd, pg 310
Giourdas Moschos, pg 310
Hestia-1 D Hestia-Kollaros & Co Corporation, pg 311
Kleidarithmos, pg 312
Melissa Publishing House, pg 313

Hong Kong
Hong Kong University Press, pg 320
Joint Publishing (HK) Co Ltd, pg 320
Press Mark Media Ltd, pg 321

Hungary
Kiiarat Konyvdiado, pg 324
Mueszaki Koenyvkiado Ltd, pg 325
Tajak Korok Muzeumok Egyesuelet, pg 327

Iceland
Frodi Ltd, pg 328

India
Abhinav Publications, pg 329
APH Publishing Corp, pg 331
Books & Books, pg 334
Chowkhamba Sanskrit Series Office, pg 335
Heritage Publishers, pg 338
Himalayan Books, pg 338
India Book House Pvt Ltd, pg 339
Mapin Publishing Pvt Ltd, pg 342
Mudgala Trust, pg 343
Munshiram Manoharlal Publishers Pvt Ltd, pg 343
National Book Organization, pg 343
Nem Chand & Brothers, pg 344
Pustak Mahal, pg 346
Reliance Publishing House, pg 347
Scientific Book Agency, pg 349
Sita Publications, pg 350
Vastu Gyan Publication, pg 352
Vikas Publishing House Pvt Ltd, pg 353

Ireland
Ballinakella Press, pg 358
Gandon Editions, pg 360
The Lilliput Press Ltd, pg 362
The O'Brien Press Ltd, pg 363

Israel
Bezalel Academy of Arts & Design, pg 365

Italy
Mario Adda Editore SNC, pg 374
Alinea, pg 375
Umberto Allemandi & C SRL, pg 375
Arcadia Edizioni Srl, pg 376
L'Archivolto, pg 376
Edizioni ARES, pg 376
Arsenale Editrice SRL, pg 376
Artioli Editore in Modena, pg 377
Automobilia srl, pg 377
Bardi Editore srl, pg 377
Casa Editrice Luigi Battei, pg 377
BeMa, pg 377
Biblos srl, pg 378
Giuseppe Bonanno Editore, pg 378
Bonsignori Editore SRL, pg 378
Calosci, pg 379
CELID, pg 380
CLUEB (Cooperativa Libraria Universitaria Editrice Bologna), pg 382
Edizioni di Comunita SpA, pg 382
Edizioni Dedalo SRL, pg 384
DEI Tipographia del Genio Civile, pg 384
Di Baio Editore SpA, pg 385
Diakronia, pg 385
Editoriale Domus Spa, pg 385
EDIFIR SRL, pg 386
Edizioni d'Arte e Moderna, Edam, pg 386
Electa, pg 387
Essegi, pg 388
FEDA SA, pg 388
Federico Motta Editore SpA, pg 389
Festina Lente Edizioni, pg 389
Flaccovio Editore, pg 389
Arnaldo Forni Editore SRL, pg 389
Gangemi Editore, pg 390
Edizioni GB, pg 390
Gius Laterza e Figli SpA, pg 391
Grafis Edizioni, pg 391
Gruppo Calderini Edagricole, pg 392
Gruppo Editoriale Faenza Editrice SpA, pg 392
Idea Books, pg 393
Editoriale Jaca Book SpA, pg 394
Laruffa Editore SRL, pg 395
L'Erma di Bretschneider SRL, pg 395
Lybra Immagine, pg 397

PUBLISHERS

Magnus Edizioni SpA, pg 397
Giuseppe Maimone Editore, pg 397
Edizioni Gabriele Mazzotta SRL, pg 398
Edizioni Medicea SRL, pg 398
Giorgio Mondadori & Associati, pg 399
Moretti & Vitali editori srl, pg 400
Istituto Nazionale di Studi Romani, pg 400
OCTAVO Franco Cantini Editore, pg 401
Officina Edizioni di Aldo Quinti, pg 401
Leo S Olschki, pg 402
Franco Cosimo Panini Editore SpA, pg 402
Pirola, pg 403
Il Pomerio, pg 404
Edizioni Ripostes, pg 405
SAGEP, pg 406
Sapere 2000 SRL, pg 407
Schena Editore, pg 407
Edizioni Scientifiche Italiane, pg 407
Edizioni Librarie Siciliane, pg 408
Silvana Editoriale SpA, pg 408
Tappeiner, pg 409
Tranchida, pg 410
Transeuropa Libri, pg 410
UTET (Unione Tipografico-Editrice Torinese), pg 411
Vianello Libri, pg 411
Zanichelli Editore SpA, pg 412

Japan

ADA Edita Tokyo Co Ltd, pg 414
Bijutsu Shuppan-Sha, Ltd, pg 415
Dohosha Publishing Co Ltd, pg 416
Kajima Institute Publishing Co Ltd, pg 419
Maruzen Co Ltd, pg 421
Shakai Shiso-Sha, pg 425
Shinkenchiku-Sha Co Ltd, pg 425
Mitsumura Suiko Shoin, pg 426
Shokoku Publishing Co Ltd, pg 426
Shufunotomo sha Co Ltd, pg 426
Tankosha Publishing Co Ltd, pg 427

Democratic People's Republic of Korea

Korea Science and Encyclopedia Publishing House, pg 434

Republic of Korea

Bal-eon, pg 434
Bo Moon Dang, pg 435
Dae Won Sa Co Ltd, pg 435
Youl Hwa Dang Publisher, pg 436
Hakgojae Publishing Inc, pg 436

The Former Yugoslav Republic of Macedonia

Zumpres Publishing Firm, pg 449

Mexico

Artes de Mexico y del Mundo, SA de CV, pg 458
Edamex SA de CV, pg 460
Editorial Edicol SA, pg 460
Editorial Extemporaneos SA, pg 461
Fondo de Cultura Economica, pg 461
Editorial Jilguero, SA de CV, pg 462
Editorial Limusa SA de CV, pg 463
Naves Internacional de Ediciones SA, pg 464
Servicios Especiales Maciel SA de CV, pg 467

Siglo XXI Editores SA de CV, pg 467
Editorial Trillas SA de CV, pg 467
Universidad Nacional Autonoma de Mexico (National University of Mexico), pg 467

Nepal

International Standards Books & Periodicals (P) Ltd, pg 471

Netherlands

BIS Publishers, pg 474
De Walburg Pers, pg 476
Delft University Press, pg 476
Hagen & Stam Uitgeverij Ten, pg 478
Otto Maier Benelux BV, pg 481
Nai Publishers, pg 481
The Pepin Press, pg 482
Uitgeverij SUN, pg 484
Terra Publishing Co, pg 485
Thoth Publishers, pg 485
Unieboek BV, pg 485
Uniepers BV, pg 486
Uitgeverij 010, pg 487

New Zealand

Barkfire Press, pg 488
Craig Potton Publishing, pg 490
Te Waihora Press, pg 496
Victoria University Press, pg 496

Panama

Editorial Universitaria, pg 509

Philippines

Ateneo de Manila University Press, pg 512
UST Publishing House, pg 515

Poland

Wydawnictwo Arkady, pg 516
BOSZ scp, pg 516
Ossolineum Zaklad Narodowy im Ossolinskich - Wydawnictwo, pg 518
Oficyna Wydawnicza Politechniki Wroclawskiej, pg 519
Wydawnictwo Baturo, pg 521

Portugal

Armenio Amado Editora de Simoes, Beirao & Ca Lda, pg 522
Arvore Coop de Actividades Artisticas, CRL, pg 522
Camara Municipal de Castelo, pg 523
Dinalivro, pg 524
Distri Cultural Lda, pg 524
Edicoes 70, Lda, pg 524
Editorial Estampa, Lda, pg 524
Latina Livraria, pg 526
McGraw-Hill Editora de Portugal, pg 527
Meriberica/Liber, pg 527
Editorial Presenca, pg 528
Edicoes 70, pg 529
Vega-Publicacao e Distribuicao de Livros e Revistas, Lda, pg 530

Puerto Rico

McGraw-Hill Intermericana del Caribe, Inc, pg 530

Romania

Editura Meridiane, pg 534

Russian Federation

Izdatelstvo Iskusstvo, pg 538
Planeta Publishers, pg 541
Stroyizdat Publishing House, pg 542

Singapore

APAC Publishers Services, pg 545
Archipelago Press, pg 545
Select Books Pte Ltd, pg 548
Taylor & Francis Asia Pacific, pg 548

Slovakia

Technicka Univerzita, pg 551

South Africa

Human & Rousseau (Pty) Ltd, pg 555
New Africa Books (Pty) Ltd, pg 557

Spain

Ediciones Akal SA, pg 562
Alta Fulla Editorial, pg 563
Arco Editorial SA, pg 564
CEAC, Grupo Editorial SA, pg 567
Celeste Ediciones, pg 567
Comunidad Autonoma de Madrid, Servicio de Documentacion y Publicaciones, pg 568
Consello da Cultura Galega - CCG, pg 568
Ediciones Daly S L, pg 569
Ediciones Destino SA, pg 569
Ediciones Doce Calles SL, pg 570
Editorial Dossat SA, pg 570
Ediciones l'Isard, S L, pg 571
EUNSA (Ediciones Universidad de Navarra SA), pg 574
Editorial Gustavo Gili SA, pg 576
Grijalbo Mondadori SA, pg 576
Editorial Juventud SA, pg 579
LEDA (Las Ediciones de Arte), pg 579
Lunwerg Editores, SA, pg 580
Antonio Machado, SA, pg 580
Mandala Ediciones, pg 581
Editorial Nerea SA, pg 584
Oikos-Tau SA Ediciones, pg 584
Editorial Parthenon Communication, SL, pg 586
Pronaos, SA Ediciones, pg 588
Pulso Ediciones, SL, pg 588
Editora Regional de Murcia - ERM, pg 588
Rueda, SL Editorial, pg 589
Editores Tecnicos Asociados SA, pg 592
Tf Editores, pg 592
Instituto Eduardo Torroja, pg 593
Turner Publicaciones, pg 593
Tursen, SA, pg 593
Universidad de Valladolid Secretariado de Publicaciones e Intercambio Editorial, pg 594
Edicions de la Universitat Politecnica de Catalunya SL, pg 594
Xarait Libros SA, pg 596

Sweden

Arkitektur Forlag AB, pg 600
Byggforlaget, pg 601
Bokforlaget Semic AB, pg 606

Switzerland

Armenia Editions, pg 608
Birkhauser Verlag AG, pg 610
Carre d'Art Edition Archigraphie, pg 610

SUBJECT INDEX

Editions Andre Delcourt & Cie, pg 612
G+B Arts International, pg 614
Giampiero Casagrande Editore, pg 614
Verlag Karl Kraemer & Co, pg 617
Lars Mueller Publishers, pg 619
Muslim Architecture Research Program (MARP), pg 619
Verlag Arthur Niggli AG, pg 620
Office du Livre SA (Buchhaus AG), pg 620
Editions Payot Lausanne, pg 621
Presses Polytechniques et Universitaires Romandes, PPUR, pg 622
SAB Schweiz Arbeitsgemeinschaft fuer die Berggebiete, pg 623
Edition Stemmle AG, pg 625
Vdf Hochschulverlag AG an der ETH Zurich, pg 626
Vogt-Schild Ag, Druck und Verlag, pg 627
Weber SA d'Editions, pg 627
Wepf & Co AG, pg 627
Wiese Verlag AG, pg 627

Syrian Arab Republic

Damascus University Press, pg 628

Taiwan, Province of China

Echo Publishing Company Ltd, pg 629
Chu Hai Publishing (Taiwan) Co Ltd, pg 630

Turkey

Arkeoloji Ve Sanat Yayinlari, pg 639
Kubbealti Akademisi Kultur ve Sasat Vakfi, pg 640
Yapi-Endustri Merkezi Yayinlari-Yem Yayin, pg 642

Ukraine

Osnova, Kharkov State University Press, pg 643

United Kingdom

Ian Allan Publishing Ltd, pg 646
Umberto Allemandi & Co Publishing, pg 646
Antique Collectors' Club Ltd, pg 647
Architectural Association Publications, pg 648
Art Books International Ltd, pg 649
Ashgate Publishing Ltd, pg 649
Batsford Ltd, pg 652
BCA, pg 653
Bellew Publishing Co Ltd, pg 653
Blackwell Science Ltd, pg 656
Bloomsbury Publishing PLC, pg 656
Books for Europe Ltd, pg 657
Breslich & Foss, pg 659
Butterworth-Heinemann Ltd, pg 661
Cambridge University Press, pg 662
Cameron & Hollis, pg 663
Carlton Publishing Group, pg 664
Cassell & Co, pg 664
The Chartered Institute of Building, pg 666
Compendium Publishing, pg 670
Conran Octopus, pg 670
Donhead Publishing Ltd, pg 675
Edinburgh University Press Ltd, pg 677
Elfande Ltd, pg 678
Elsevier Science Ltd, pg 678
The Erskine Press, pg 679

Fourth Estate Ltd, pg 683
The Fraser Press, pg 684
Gaia Books Ltd, pg 685
Gale Research, pg 685
Garnet Publishing Ltd, pg 685
Golden Cockerel Press Ltd, pg 688
Gollancz/Witherby, pg 688
Grange Books PLC, pg 689
Hamlyn, pg 691
Herbert Press Ltd, pg 695
Heritage Press, pg 695
Hilmarton Manor Press, pg 696
James & James (Science Publishers) Ltd, pg 702
Kegan Paul International Ltd, pg 703
Laurence King Publishing Ltd, pg 704
Frances Lincoln Ltd, pg 707
Liverpool University Press, pg 708
Lund Humphries, pg 709
Maney Publishing, pg 711
Marston House, pg 712
Merrell Publishers Ltd, pg 713
Miller's Publications, pg 715
MIT Press Ltd, pg 715
Motilal (UK) Books of India, pg 715
W W Norton & Company Ltd, pg 720
Octopus Publishing Group, pg 720
Open University Worldwide, pg 721
Packard Publishing Ltd, pg 723
Phaidon Press Ltd, pg 726
Phillimore & Co Ltd, pg 727
Pomegranate Europe Ltd, pg 729
PRC Publishing Ltd, pg 730
Ramsay Head Press, pg 732
The Reader's Digest Association Ltd, pg 733
Reaktion Books Ltd, pg 733
Regency House Publishing Ltd, pg 734
RIBA Publications, pg 735
RICS Books, pg 735
RotoVision SA, pg 735
The Rutland Press, pg 737
Ryland Peters & Small Ltd, pg 737
The Salariya Book Co Ltd, pg 738
Shire Publications Ltd, pg 741
Spon Press, pg 744
Stacey International, pg 745
The Stationery Office, pg 745
Studio Editions Ltd, pg 746
Sutton Publishing Ltd, pg 746
Tate Publishing Ltd, pg 747
I B Tauris & Co Ltd, pg 747
Thames & Hudson Ltd, pg 748
Tuckwell Press Ltd, pg 750
University of Wales Press, pg 751
White Cockade Publishing, pg 755
Wiley Europe Ltd, pg 756
Philip Wilson Publishers, pg 757
Windsor Books International, pg 757
WIT Press, pg 757
World Microfilms Publications Ltd, pg 758
Yale University Press London, pg 759
Zwemmer Holdings Co Ltd, pg 759

Uruguay

Nordan-Comunidad, pg 760

Venezuela

Armitano Editores CA, pg 761
Biblioteca Ayacucho, pg 762

Viet Nam

Science & Technics Publishing House, pg 763

ART

Albania

NL SH, pg 1
State Textbook Publishing House, pg 1

Argentina

Centro Editor de America Latina SA, pg 4
Emece Editores SA, pg 5
EUDEBA (Editorial Universitaria de Buenos Aires), pg 6
Laffont Ediciones Electronicas SA, pg 7
Ediciones Nueva Vision SAIC, pg 8
Quetzal-Domingo Cortizo, pg 8
Ediciones Tres Tiempos SRL, pg 9
Manrique Zago Ediciones SRL, pg 10

Australia

Aboriginal Studies Press, pg 10
Aeolian Press, pg 11
Allen & Unwin Pty Ltd, The Australian Newspaper, Vogel Breads, pg 11
Archaeological Publications, pg 12
Art Gallery of South Australia Bookshop, pg 12
Art Gallery of Western Australia, pg 12
Art on the Move, pg 12
Artmoves, pg 12
Barbara Beckett Publishing Pty Ltd, pg 14
Boolarong Press, pg 16
Dangaroo Press, pg 20
D'Artagnan Publishing, pg 20
Edwina Publishing, pg 21
David Ell Press Pty Ltd, pg 21
Encyclopaedia Britannica (Australia) Inc, pg 22
Experimental Art Foundation, pg 22
Fine Arts Press Pty Ltd, pg 23
Fremantle Arts Centre Press, pg 23
Granrott Press, pg 24
Hahndorf Academy Foundation Inc, pg 24
Hartys Creek Press, pg 25
The Images Publishing Group Pty Ltd, pg 27
In-Tune Books, pg 27
Incunabula Press, pg 27
Institute of Aboriginal Development (IAD Press), pg 28
Island Press, pg 28
Magabala Books Aboriginal Corporation, pg 31
McGraw-Hill Australia Pty Ltd, pg 32
Mountain House Press, pg 33
National Gallery of Australia, pg 34
National Gallery of Victoria, pg 34
New Endeavour Press, pg 34
Oriental Publications, pg 36
Oz Publishing Co Pty Ltd, pg 36
Pandani Press, pg 37
Power Publications, pg 38
Press for Success, pg 38
Queen Victoria Museum & Art Gallery Publications, pg 39
Queensland Art Gallery, pg 39
Reed Educational Publishing Australia, pg 40
Ruskin Rowe Press, pg 41
Spinifex Press, pg 43
Stafford Books, pg 43
State Library of NSW Press, pg 43
Thames & Hudson (Australia) Pty Ltd, pg 44
Unity Press, pg 46
Wellington Lane Press Pty Ltd, pg 47
Wileman Publications, pg 47
Yanagang Publishing, pg 48

Austria

Akademische Druck-u Verlagsanstalt Dr Paul Struzl GmbH, pg 49
Amalthea-Verlag, pg 49
Verlag der Apfel, pg 49
Aritbus et Historiae, Rivista Internationale di arti visive ecinema, Institut IRSA - Verlagsanstalt, pg 49
Boehlau Verlag GmbH & Co KG, pg 50
Christian Brandstatter Verlagsgesellschaft GmbH, pg 50
Camera Austria, pg 50
Carinthia Verlag, pg 50
CEEBA Publications Antenne d'Autriche, pg 50
Dachs-Verlag GmbH, pg 50
Danubia Werbung und Verlagsservice, pg 50
Literature Verlag Droschl, pg 51
Ferdinand Berger und Sohne, pg 51
Edition Dr Heinrich Fuchs, pg 52
Edition Graphischer Zirkel, pg 52
Graz Stadtmuseum, pg 52
Haymon-Verlag GesmbH, pg 52
Herold Druck-und Verlagsgesellschaft mbH, pg 52
Johannes Heyn, Gert und Volkmar Zechner, pg 52
Edition E Hilger, pg 53
Edition Koenigstein, pg 54
Kremayr & Scheriau Verlag, pg 54
Leykam Buchverlagsges mbH, pg 54
Loecker Verlag, pg 54
LOG-Internationale Zeitschrift fuer Literatur, pg 54
Modulverlag, pg 55
Paul Neff Verlag KG, pg 55
Oesterreichischer Bundesverlag GmbH, pg 56
Passagen Verlag GmbH, pg 57
Verlag Sankt Peter, pg 57
Richard Pils Publication P, pg 57
Pinguin-Verlag, Pawlowski GmbH, pg 57
Georg Prachner KG, pg 57
Verlag Anton Pustet, pg 57
Residenz Verlag GmbH, pg 58
Ritter Verlag, pg 58
Verlag fuer Sammler, pg 58
Andreas Schnider Verlags-Atelier, pg 58
Springer-Verlag Wien, pg 59
Edition Thurnhof KEG, pg 59
Edition Tusch, pg 59
Verlag Carl Ueberreuter GmbH, pg 59
Verlag Anton Schroll & Co, pg 60
Weilburg Verlag, pg 60
Verlag Galerie Welz Salzburg, pg 60
Kunstverlag Wolfrum, pg 61
WUV/Facultas Universitaetsverlag, pg 61

Bangladesh

The University Press Ltd, pg 62

Belarus

Belarus (The Belorussia), pg 63
Belaruskaya Encyklopedyya, pg 63

Belgium

Libraire Ancienne Noel Anselot, pg 64
SA Artis-Historia, pg 64
Bartleby & Co, pg 65
Editions Gerard Blanchart & Cie SA, pg 65
Brepols Publishers NV, pg 65
Editions Casterman SA, pg 66
Centre International de Recherches 'Primitifs Flamands' ASBL, pg 66
Editions Chanlis, pg 66
Conservart SA, pg 67
Contact NV, pg 67
Le Daily-Bul, pg 67
Davidsfonds VZW, pg 67
Editions De Boeck-Larcier SA, pg 67
Maison d'Editions Cl Dejaie, pg 67
Editions Delta SA, pg 67
Dexia Bank, pg 68
Glenat Benelux SA, pg 69
Groeninghe NV, pg 69
Koninklijke Vlaamse Academie van Belgie voor Wetenschappen en Kunsten, pg 70
Uitgeverij Lannoo NV, pg 70
Lansman Editeur, pg 70
Editions Lessius ASBL, pg 71
Mercatorfonds NV, pg 72
Pandora, pg 72
La Part de L'Oeil, pg 72
Editions Racine, pg 73
La Renaissance du Livre, pg 73
Roularta Books NV, pg 73
Sonneville Press (Uitgeverij) VTW, pg 74
Stichting Kunstboek bvba, pg 74
Stichting Ons Erfdeel VZW, pg 74
Marc Van de Wiele bvba, pg 75
Editions Luce Wilquin, pg 75

Botswana

The Botswana Society, pg 77

Brazil

AGIR S/A Editora, pg 78
Callis Editora Ltda, pg 80
Editora Campus Ltda, pg 80
Conquista, Empresa de Publicacoes Ltda, pg 81
Edicon Editora e Consultorial Ltda, pg 81
Livraria Martins Fontes Editora Ltda, pg 83
Grafica Editora Primor Ltda, pg 84
Livro Ibero-Americano Ltda, pg 85
Editora Index Ltda, pg 85
Edicoes Loyola SA, pg 87
Editora Mantiqueira de Ciencia e Arte, pg 87
Editora Melhoramentos Ltda, pg 87
Editora Mercuryo Ltda, pg 88
Editora Nova Fronteira SA, pg 88
Pallas Editora e Distribuidora Ltda, pg 89
Rede Das Artes (Boccato Editores Collector's), pg 90
Editora Revan Ltda, pg 90
Salamandra Consultoria Editorial SA, pg 91
Spala Editora Ltda, pg 92
Totalidade Editora Ltda, pg 92
Editora da Universidade de Sao Paulo, pg 93
Editora Universidade Federal do Rio de Janeiro, pg 93
Editora Verbo Ltda, pg 93
Jorge Zahar Editor, pg 93

Bulgaria
Abagar Pablioing, pg 94
Abagar, Veliko Tarnovo, pg 94
CHRIKER, pg 94
Fondacija Zlatno Kljuce, pg 95
Kibea Publishing Co, pg 96
Makros 2000 - Plovdiv, pg 96
Musica Publishing House Ltd, pg 96
Naouka i Izkoustvo, Ltd, pg 97
Seven Hills Publishers, pg 97
Slavena, pg 98
Svetra Publishing House, pg 98
Zunica, pg 98

Chile
Arrayan Editores, pg 99
Editorial Andres Bello/Editorial Juridica de Chile, pg 100
Ediciones Mil Hojas Ltda, pg 100
Museo Chileno de Arte Precolombino, pg 100
Norma de Chile, pg 101
Pontificia Universidad Catolica de Chile, pg 101
Ediciones Universitarias de Valparaiso, pg 101

China
Asia 2000 Ltd, pg 102
Beijing Arts & Crafts Publishing House, pg 102
Beijing Publishing House, pg 102
China Braille Press, pg 103
China Film Press, pg 103
China Light Industry Press, pg 103
Chinese Literature Press, pg 104
Commercial Press (Hong Kong) Ltd, pg 104
Cultural Relics Publishing House, pg 105
Encyclopedia of China Publishing House, pg 105
Foreign Languages Press, pg 105
Fudan University Press, pg 105
Fujian Children's Publishing House, pg 106
Guizhou Education Publishing House, pg 106
Morning Glory Publishers, pg 107
People's Fine Arts Publishing House, pg 108
Qingdao Publishing House, pg 108
Shanghai Fine Arts Publishers, pg 109
Zhejiang University Press, pg 110

Colombia
Amazonas Editores Ltda, pg 111
El Ancora Editores, pg 111
Dosmil Editora, pg 111
Escala Ltda, pg 111
Editorial Santillana SA, pg 113
Siglo XXI Editores de Colombia Ltda, pg 113
Universidad de Antioquia, Division Publicaciones, pg 114
Carlos Valencia Editores, pg 114
Villegas Editores Ltda, pg 114
Editorial Voluntad SA, pg 114

The Democratic Republic of the Congo
Facultes Catoliques de Kinshasa, pg 115

Costa Rica
Promesa, Ediciones, pg 116
Editorial de la Universidad de Costa Rica, pg 117

Cote d'Ivoire
Les Nouvelles Editions Africaines, pg 118
Les Nouvelles Editions Ivoiriennes (NEI), pg 118

Croatia
AGM doo, pg 118
Globus-Nakladni zavod, pg 118
Graficki zavod Hrvatske, pg 118
Krscanska sadasnjost, pg 119
Matica hrvatska, pg 119
Mladost d d Izdavacku graficku i informaticku djelatnost, pg 119
Nakladni zavod Matice hrvatske, pg 119
Naprijed d d Naklada, pg 119
Skolska Knjiga, pg 120

Cuba
Casa de las Americas, pg 120
Holguin, Ediciones, pg 121
Editorial Letras Cubanas, pg 121
Ediciones Union, pg 121

Cyprus
A G Leventis Foundation, pg 122

Czech Republic
Aurora, pg 123
Aventinum Nakladatelstvi, pg 123
Nakladatelstvi Blok, pg 123
Brody, pg 123
Karolinum, nakladatelstvi, pg 125
Labyrint, pg 125
Mariadan, pg 126
Maxdorf Ltd, pg 126
Mlada fronta, pg 126
Moravska Galerie v Brne, pg 126
Narodni Muzeum, pg 126
NLN, Ltd The Lidove noviny Publishing House, pg 127
Odeon, nakladatelstvi krasne literatury a umeni, pg 127
Paseka, pg 127
Prazske nakladatelstvi Pluto, pg 127
Votobia sro, pg 129

Denmark
Arnkrone Forlaget A/S, pg 130
Atuakkiorfik A/S Det Greenland Publishers, pg 130
Borgens Forlag A/S, pg 130
Christian Ejlers' Forlag aps, pg 131
Grevas Forlag, pg 132
Gyldendalske Boghandel - Nordisk Forlag A/S, pg 132
Edition Wilhelm Hansen AS, pg 132
Museum Tusculanum Press, pg 134
New Era Publications International ApS, pg 134
Nyt Nordisk Forlag Arnold Busck A/S, pg 134
Det Schonbergske Forlag, pg 135

Ecuador
CIDAP, pg 137
Pontificia Universidad Catolica de Ecuador, Centro de Publicaciones, pg 137

Egypt (Arab Republic of Egypt)
American University in Cairo Press, pg 138
Dar El Shorouk Publishing & Distributing House, pg 138

Estonia
Estonian Encyclopaedia Publishers Ltd, pg 140
Kunst Publishers Ltd, pg 140
National Library of Estonia, pg 140

Finland
Schildts Foerlagsaktiebolag, pg 144
Soederstroem et Co Foerlagsaktiebolag, pg 144
Weilin & Goeoes Oy, pg 145

France
ACR Edition Internationale (Art Creation Realisation), pg 145
Action Artistique de la Ville de Paris, pg 146
ADPF Publications, pg 146
Editions Albin Michel, pg 146
Editions Alternatives, pg 146
Editions de l'Amateur, pg 147
Editions d'Amerique et d'Orient, Adrien Maisonneuve, pg 147
Editions Amez, pg 147
Editions Amrita SA, pg 147
Edition Anthese, pg 147
L'Arbalete, pg 147
Editions Arcam, pg 147
L'Arche Editeur, pg 147
Editions de l'Armancon, pg 148
Art & Metiers Du Livre/Editions, pg 148
Compagnie Francaise des Arts Graphiques SA, pg 148
Atelier National de Reproduction des Theses, pg 148
Editions Philippe Auzou, pg 149
Societe Nouvelle Rene Baudouin, pg 149
Bayard Presse - Department Livre, pg 149
Editions Belfond, pg 150
Editions Belin, pg 150
Berger-Levrault SA, pg 150
Bibliotheque des Arts, pg 150
Societe Nouvelle Adam Biro, pg 150
William Blake & Co, pg 150
De Boccard Edition-Diffusion, pg 151
Editions Andre Bonne, pg 151
Bookmaker, pg 151
Pierre Bordas et Fils, pg 151
Editions Bornemann, pg 151
Michele Broutta Oeuvres Graphiques Contemporaines, pg 152
Editions du Buot, pg 152
Le Cadratin, pg 152
Editions des Cahiers Bourbonnais, pg 152
Editions Cahiers d'Art, pg 152
Editions Canope, pg 152
Editions Casteilla, pg 153
Editions Casterman, pg 153
Editions Cenomane, pg 153
Editions Cercle d'Art SA, pg 153
Jacqueline Chambon, pg 154
Chasse Maree-Armen, pg 154
Editions du Chene, pg 154
Cicero Editeurs, pg 155
Circonflexe, pg 155
Editions Citadelles & Mazenod, pg 155
CNRS Editions, pg 155
Editions du Comite des Travaux Historiques et Scientifiques (CTHS), pg 156
CPL- La Communication Par le Livre, pg 157
Editions Denoel Sarl, pg 158
Dessain et Tolra SA, pg 159
Editions de la Difference, pg 159
Editions Dis Voir, pg 159
La Documentation Francaise, pg 159
Dreamland Editeur, pg 160
Ecole Nationale Superieure des Beaux-Arts, pg 160
Edisud, pg 161
Editions Grund, pg 161
Les Editions de l'Epargne, pg 162
Editions Fanlac, pg 163
Fata Morgana, pg 163
FBT de R Editions/Editions des Limbes d'Or, pg 163
Des Femmes, pg 164
Librairie Fischbacher, International Art Book Distribution (import-export), pg 164
Flammarion SA, pg 164
Groupe Fleurus-Mame, pg 164
Editions Fragments, pg 164
France-Loisirs, pg 165
Edition Galilee, pg 165
Editions Gallimard, pg 165
Imprimerie Librairie Gardet, pg 166
Paul Geuthner Librairie Orientaliste, pg 166
Editions Jean Paul Gisserot, pg 166
Editions Grandir, pg 166
Editions d'Art Albert Guillot, pg 167
Hachette Livre, pg 167
Pierre Hautot SA, pg 168
Fernand Hazan Editeur SA, pg 168
Hermann editeurs des Sciences et des Arts SA, pg 168
Editions de l'Herne, pg 168
Herscher, pg 168
Editions Hoebeke, pg 168
Pierre Horay Editeur, pg 168
Image/Magie, pg 169
Indigo & Cote-Femmes Editions, pg 169
Editions l'Instant Durable (Soprep), pg 169
Institut International de la Marionnette, pg 170
Editions du Jaguar, pg 170
Editions Jannink, pg 170
Editions du Jeu de Paume, pg 170
Kailash Editions, pg 171
Editions Klincksieck, pg 171
Librairie Leonce Laget, pg 171
Editions du Laquet, pg 172
Librairie Larousse, pg 172
Editions Dominique Leroy, pg 172
Editions Liana Levi Sarl, pg 173
Editions des Limbes d'Or/FBT de R Editions, pg 173
Le Livre de Paris, pg 173
Editions Loubatieres, pg 174
Macula, pg 174
Editions Mango, pg 174
Marval, pg 175
Editions Charles Massin et Cie, pg 175
Editions Medianes, pg 175
Editions Memo, pg 175
Editions Memoire des Arts, pg 175
Gerard Monfort Editeur Sarl, pg 176
Editions de la Reunion des Musees Nationaux, pg 176
Nanga, pg 177
F De Nobele, pg 177
Editions Norma, pg 177
Nouvelles Editions Francaises, pg 178
Editions Parentheses, pg 179
Paris Musees, pg 179
Editions Phebus, pg 179
Editions A et J Picard SA, pg 179
Jean-Michel Place, pg 180

SUBJECT INDEX — BOOK

Editions du Centre Pompidou, pg 180
Presses Universitaires de France (PUF), pg 181
Presses Universitaires de Strasbourg, pg 181
Propos de Campagne, pg 182
Editions Pygmalion - Gerard Watelet, pg 182
References cf, pg 182
Revue Noire, pg 183
Yves Riviere Editeur, pg 183
Editions Scala, pg 184
Nouvelles Editions Seguier, pg 184
Selection du Reader's Digest SA, pg 184
Editions Selection J Jacobs SA, pg 184
Sepia, pg 184
Service Technique pour l'Education, pg 185
Editions du Seuil, pg 185
Societe Nouveaux Loisirs, pg 185
Sofradif Editions Philippe Auzou, pg 185
Somogy editions d'art, pg 186
Publications de la Sorbonne, pg 186
Stil, pg 186
Editions Tallandier, pg 187
Editions Pierre Terrail/Finest SA, pg 187
Thames & Hudson, pg 187
Transedition ASBL, pg 188
Transeuropeennes/RCE, pg 188
Ulisse Edition, pg 188
UNESCO Publishing, pg 188
Publications de l'Universite de Pau, pg 188
La Vague Verte, pg 188
Editions Van Wilder, pg 188
Editions de Vergeures, pg 189
Editions Vilo SA, pg 189
La Voix du Regard, pg 189
Pierre Zech Editeur, pg 189
Zodiaque, pg 190

Germany

Accedo Verlagsgesellschaft mbH, pg 191
F A Ackermanns Kunstverlag GmbH, pg 191
Agis Verlag GmbH, pg 192
Aisthesis Verlag Dr Detlev Kopp und Dr Michael Vogt, pg 192
ALS-Verlag GmbH, pg 193
Anabas-Verlag Guenter Kaempf GmbH & Co KG, pg 193
AOL-Verlag Frohmut Menze, pg 194
Verlag APHAIA Svea Haske, Sonja Schumann GbR, pg 194
Aquamarin Verlag, pg 194
ARCult Media, pg 194
Ardey-Verlag GmbH, pg 194
Aries-Verlag Paul Johannes Muller, pg 195
Arkana Verlag Tete Bottger Rainer Wunderlich GmbH, pg 195
Arnoldsche Verlagsanstalt GmbH, pg 195
Ars Edition GmbH, pg 195
ARTC/OLOR, pg 195
Arts & Antiques Edition Munich Verlag, Buch & Kunsthandel GmbH, pg 195
Verlag Atelier im Bauernhaus, pg 196
Atelier Verlag Andernach (AVA), pg 196
AvivA Britta Jurgs GmbH, pg 197
Edition Balance Marion Gunther Bonsack, pg 198

Bartkowiaks Forum Book Art, pg 198
Basilisken-Presse, pg 198
Dr Wolfgang Baur Verlag Kunst & Alltag, pg 199
Verlag C H Beck (OHG), pg 200
Bergstadtverlag Wilhelm Gottlieb Korn GmbH Wuerzburg, pg 200
Berliner Handpresse Wolfgang Joerg und Erich Schonig, pg 201
C Bertelsmann Verlag GmbH, pg 201
Bertelsmann Lexikon Verlag GmbH, pg 201
Betzel Verlag GmbH, pg 202
Biblio-Zeller Verlag, pg 202
Verlag Die Blaue Eule, pg 204
Boehlau-Verlag GmbH & Cie, pg 204
Verlag Hermann Boehlaus Nachfolger Weimar GmbH & Co, pg 205
Klaus Boer Verlag, pg 205
Bonifatius GmbH Druck-Buch-Verlag, pg 205
BrennGlas Verlag Assenheim Juergen Seuss, pg 206
BRUEN-Verlag, Gorenflo, pg 207
Buch- und Kunstverlag Kleinheinrich, pg 207
Verlag C J Bucher GmbH, pg 207
Buchheim-Verlag, pg 207
Buchergilde Gutenberg Verlagsgesellschaft mbH, pg 207
Buechse der Pandora Verlags-GmbH, pg 207
Dr Cantz'sche, Druckerei GmbH & Co, Cantz Verlag, pg 209
Fachverlag Hans Carl GmbH, pg 209
Chorus-Verlag, pg 210
Chr Belser AG fur Verlagsgeschaefte und Co KG, pg 210
Hans Christians Druckerei und Verlag GmbH & Co, pg 210
Christusbruderschaft Selbitz ev, Abt Verlag, pg 210
Coppenrath Verlag, pg 211
CTL-Presse Clemens-Tobias Lange, pg 212
D & D Kommunikation Verlug Dirk Nishen Gmbh & Co KG, pg 212
Daco Verlag Guenter Blase oHG, pg 212
Das Arsenal, Verlag fuer Kultur und Politik GmbH, pg 212
Verlag Werner Dausien, pg 212
Verlag Horst Deike KG, pg 213
Delp'sche Verlagsbuchhandlung, pg 213
Deutscher Kunstverlag GmbH, pg 215
Deutscher Taschenbuch Verlag GmbH & Co KG (dtv), pg 215
Deutscher Verlag fur Kunstwissenschaft GmbH, pg 215
Dieterichsche Verlagsbuchhandlung Mainz, pg 216
Dolling und Galitz Verlag GmbH, pg 217
Donat Verlag, pg 217
Droste Verlag GmbH, pg 218
DuMont Buchverlag GmbH & Co KG, pg 219
DuMont Monte, pg 219
Echter Wurzburg Frankische Gesellschaftsdruckerei und Verlag GmbH, pg 220
Edition Aragon-Verlagsgesellschaft mbH, pg 220

edition q Berlin Edition in der Quintessenz Verlags-GmbH, pg 221
Edition Solitude - Akademie Schloss Solitude, pg 221
Egmont vgs verlagsgesellschaft mbH, pg 221
EinfallsReich Verlagsgesellschaft MbH, pg 222
Elefanten Press Verlag GmbH, pg 222
Ellert & Richter Verlag GmbH, pg 222
Englisch Verlag GmbH, pg 222
Verlag Peter Engstler, pg 223
EOS Verlag der Benefiktiner der Erzabtei St. Ottilien, pg 223
Eremiten-Presse und Verlag GmbH, pg 223
Verlag am Eschbach GmbH, pg 224
Eulen Verlag, pg 224
Extent Verlag und Service Wolfgang M Flamm, pg 225
F Bruckmann Munchen Verlag & Druck GmbH & Co Produkt KG, pg 225
Fackeltrager-Verlag GmbH, pg 226
Fahrner & Fahrner, pg 226
Ferdinand Enke Verlag, pg 227
Emil Fink Verlag, pg 227
Wilhelm Fink GmbH & Co Verlags-KG, pg 228
Franz-Sales-Verlag, pg 229
Frederking & Thaler Verlag GmbH, pg 230
Verlag Freies Geistesleben, pg 230
Margarethe Freudenberger - selbstverlag fur jedermann, pg 230
Erhard Friedrich Verlag, pg 230
G Braun (vormals G Braun'sche Hofbuchdruckerei und Verlag) Gmbh, pg 231
Galerie Der Spiegel-Dr E Stunke Nachfolge GmbH, pg 231
Gatzanis Verlags GmbH, pg 231
Germanisches Nationalmuseum, pg 232
GLB Parkland Verlags-und Vertriebs GmbH, pg 232
Wilhelm Goldmann Verlag GmbH, pg 233
Gondrom Verlag GmbH & Co KG, pg 233
Grabert-Verlag, pg 233
Greven Verlag Koeln GmbH, pg 234
Guenther Butkus, pg 235
Verlag Klaus Guhl, pg 235
Verlag H M Hauschild GmbH, pg 235
Hachmeister Verlag, pg 236
Haenssler Verlag GmbH, pg 236
Heinz-Jurgen Hausser, pg 236
Harenberg Kommunikation Verlags- und Medien GmbH & Co KG, pg 237
Hatje Cantz Verlag, pg 238
Heigl Verlag, Horst Edition, pg 239
Edition Hentrich Druck & Verlag Gebr Hentrich und Tank GmbH & Co KG, pg 239
F A Herbig Verlagsbuchhandlung GmbH, pg 239
Anton Hiersemann, Verlag, pg 240
Hirmer Verlag GmbH, pg 241
Edition Hoffmann & Co, pg 242
Hoffmann und Campe Verlag GmbH, pg 242
Hohenrain-Verlag GmbH, pg 242
Volker Huber Edition & Galerie, pg 243
Edition Hundertmark, pg 243
Insel Verlag, pg 245

Klaus Isele, pg 245
ludicium Verlag GmbH, pg 245
Jan Thorbecke Verlag GmbH & Co, pg 246
Jonas Verlag fuer Kunst und Literatur GmbH, pg 246
Jovis Verlag GmbH, pg 246
Katzmann Verlag KG, pg 248
Kerber Christof Verlag, pg 248
Klinkhardt & Biermann Verlagsbuchhandlung GmbH, pg 250
Albrecht Knaus Verlag GmbH, pg 250
Koehler und Amelang Verlagsgesellschaft mbH, pg 251
Koenemann Verlagesellschaft mbH, pg 251
Verlag Valentin Koerner GmbH, pg 252
Anton H Konrad Verlag, pg 252
KONTEXTverlag, pg 252
Roman Kovar Verlag, pg 253
Karin Kramer Verlag, pg 253
Verlag Waldemar Kramer, pg 253
Kretschmar Hubert Leipziger Verlagsgesellschaft, pg 253
Verlag Hubert Kretschmer, pg 253
Alfred Kroner Verlag, pg 253
Kulturstiftung der deutschen Vertriebenen, pg 254
Archiv fur Kunst & Geschichte Bilderdienst & Verlagsgesellschaft mbH, pg 254
Verlag der Kunst/G+B Fine Arts Verlag GmbH, pg 254
Kunstverlag Weingarten GmbH, pg 254
Kupfergraben Verlagsgesellschaft mbH, pg 254
Karl Robert Langewiesche Nachfolger Hans Koester KG, pg 256
LIT Verlag, pg 258
Lusatia Verlag-Dr Stuebner & Co KG, pg 259
Maeander Verlag GmbH, pg 260
Gebr Mann Verlag GmbH & Co, pg 260
Manutius Verlag, pg 260
Matthes und Seitz Verlag GmbH, pg 261
Matzker Verlag DiA, pg 261
Edition Axel Menges, pg 262
Merlin Verlag Andreas Meyer Verlags GmbH und Co KG, pg 263
J B Metzler'sche Verlagsbuchhandlung, pg 263
Mitteldeutscher Verlag GmbH, pg 264
modo verlag GmbH, pg 264
Mueller & Schindler Verlag, pg 265
Verlag Mueller und Kiepenheuer, pg 265
Multi Media Kunst Verlag Dresden, pg 266
Naumann & Goebel Verlagsgesellschaft mbH, pg 267
Edition Nautilus Verlag, pg 267
Verlag Neue Kritik KG, pg 267
Verlag Neue Musikzeitung GmbH, pg 267
Nicolaische Verlagsbuchhandlung Beuermann GmbH, pg 268
C W Niemeyer Buchverlage GmbH, pg 268
Nieswand-Verlag GmbH, pg 269
Nusser Verlag, pg 269
nymphenburger, pg 269
Edition Octopus & Okeanos Presse, pg 269

PUBLISHERS SUBJECT INDEX

Oekumenischer Verlag Dr R-F Edel, pg 270
Oktagon Verlagsgesellschaft mbH, pg 270
Pandion-Verlag, Ulrike Schmoll, pg 271
Paranus Verlag - Bruecke Neumuenster GmbH, pg 271
Patmos Verlag GmbH & Co KG, pg 272
Pawel Panpresse, pg 272
Pendragon Verlag, pg 272
Pfalzische Verlagsanstalt GmbH, pg 272
Philipp Reclam Jun Verlag GmbH, pg 273
Galerie Eva Poll, pg 274
Portikus, pg 274
Prasenz Verlag der Jesus Bruderschaft eV, pg 274
Guido Pressler Verlag, pg 275
Prestel Verlag, pg 275
Propylaeen Verlag, Zweigniederlassung Berlin der Ullstein Buchverlage GmbH, pg 275
Verlag Friedrich Pustet GmbH & Co Kg, pg 276
Ravensburger Buchverlag Otto Maier GmbH, pg 277
Verlag fur Regionalgeschichte, pg 277
Regura Verlag, pg 277
Konrad Reich Verlag GmbH, pg 278
Dr Ludwig Reichert Verlag, pg 278
Dietrich Reimer Verlag GmbH, pg 278
Ritterbach Verlag GmbH, pg 279
Erich Roeth-Verlag, pg 279
Rogner und Bernhard GmbH & Co Verlags KG, pg 279
Rombach GmbH Druck und Verlagshaus & Co, pg 280
Rosenheimer Verlagshaus GmbH & Co KG, pg 280
Rowohlt Taschenbuch Verlag GmbH, pg 280
Verlag an der Ruhr GmbH, pg 281
Saarbrucker Druckerei und Verlag GmbH (SDV), pg 281
Sachsenbuch Verlagsgesellschaft Mbh, pg 281
Verlag der Sankt-Johannis-Druckerei C Schweickhardt, pg 281
K G Saur Verlag GmbH, A Gale/ Thomson Learning Company, pg 282
scaneg Verlag, pg 282
Verlag Th Schaefer im Vicentz Verlag KG, pg 282
Schillinger Verlag GmbH, pg 283
Schirmer/Mosel Verlag GmbH, pg 283
Verlag Hermann Schmidt Universitatsdruckerei GmbH & Co, pg 284
Wilhelm Schmitz Verlag, pg 284
Verlag Schnell und Steiner GmbH, pg 284
Verlag Silke Schreiber, pg 285
Carl Ed Schuenemann KG, pg 285
H O Schulze KG, pg 285
Schwabenverlag Aktiengesellschaft, pg 285
Dr Wolfgang Schwarze Verlag, pg 286
Siebenberg-Verlag, pg 286
Rudolf G Smend, pg 287
SMG Stiebner Medien gmbh, pg 287
Societaets-Verlag, pg 287
Spee Buchverlag GmbH, pg 287

Springer-Verlag GmbH & Co KG, pg 288
Staatliche Museen Kassel, pg 288
Stadler Verlagsgesellschaft mbH, pg 288
Steidl Verlag, pg 289
Franz Steiner Verlag Wiesbaden GmbH, pg 289
J F Steinkopf Verlag GmbH, pg 289
Steintor Verlag, Rudolf Juedes, pg 290
Steinweg-Verlag, Jurgen romHoff, pg 290
Edition Gunter Stoberlein, pg 290
Sueddeutsche Verlagsgesellschaft mbH, pg 291
Svato Zapletal, pg 291
Systhema Verlag GmbH, pg 291
TASCHEN GmbH, pg 292
teNeues Verlag GmbH & Co KG, pg 292
Konrad Theiss Verlag GmbH, pg 293
Hans Thoma Verlag GmbH Kunst und Buchverlag, pg 294
Treves Editions Verein Zur Foerderung der Kuenstlerischen Taetigkeiten, pg 295
Tuduv Verlagsgesellschaft mbH, pg 295
Verlag Dr Alfons Uhl, pg 295
Ullstein Heyne List GmbH & Co KG, pg 295
Dorothea van der Koelen, pg 297
Verein der Benediktiner zu Beuron-Beuroner Kunstverlag, pg 297
Vice Versa Verlag, pg 298
Edition Curt Visel, pg 298
Verlag Philipp von Zabern, pg 299
VS Verlagshaus Stuttgart GmbH, pg 299
VWB-Verlag fur Wissenschaft & Bildung, Amand Aglaster, pg 300
W Ludwig Verlag GmbH, pg 300
Wachholtz Verlag GmbH, pg 300
Uwe Warnke Verlag, pg 300
Wartburg Verlag GmbH, pg 300
Ernst Wasmuth Verlag GmbH & Co, pg 300
WB Verlag, pg 300
Verlagsgruppe Weltbild GmbH, pg 301
Weltkunst Verlag GmbH, pg 301
Wissenschaftliche Buchgesellschaft, pg 303
Verlag Claus Wittal, pg 303
Friedrich Wittig Verlag GmbH, pg 303
Das Wunderhorn Verlag GmbH, pg 304
Wunderlich Verlag, pg 304
Zeller Verlag GmbH & Co, pg 305

Ghana
Ghana Academy of Arts & Sciences, pg 307

Greece
Akritas, pg 308
Atlantis M Pechlivanides & Co SA, pg 309
Chryssos Typos AE Ekodeis, pg 309
Ecole francaise d'Athenes, pg 310
Ekdotike Athenon SA, pg 310
Evrodiastasi, pg 310
Exandas Publishers, pg 310
Govostis Publishing SA, pg 311
Gutenberg Publications, pg 311
Hestia-I D Hestia-Kollaros & Co Corporation, pg 311
Idryma Meleton Chersonisou tou Aimou, pg 311

Medusa/Selas, pg 313
Melissa Publishing House, pg 313
Minoas SA, pg 313
Okeanida, pg 313
Patakis Publishers, pg 314

Holy See (Vatican City State)
Biblioteca Apostolica Vaticana, pg 317
Libreria Editrice Vaticana, pg 317

Hong Kong
Benefit Publishing Co, pg 318
The Chinese University Press, pg 319
Chung Hwa Book Co (HK) Ltd, pg 319
FormAsia Books Ltd, pg 320
Hong Kong University Press, pg 320
Joint Publishing (HK) Co Ltd, pg 320
Steve Lu Publishing Ltd, pg 320
Press Mark Media Ltd, pg 321
Tai Yip Co, pg 322

Hungary
Akademiai Kiado, pg 323
Balassi Kiado Kft, pg 323
Corvina Books Ltd, pg 323
Helikon Kiado, pg 324
Jelenkor Verlag, pg 324
Officina Nova, Koenyv-es Lapkiado/Bertelsmann Media Kft, pg 324
Kulturtrade, pg 325
Magveto Koenyvkiado, pg 325
Park Konyvkiado Kft (Park Publisher), pg 326
Planetas Kiadoi es Kereskedelmi Kft, pg 326
Tajak Korok Muzeumok Egyesuelet, pg 327

Iceland
Hid Islenzka Bokmenntafelag, pg 328
Iceland Review, pg 328
Idunn, pg 328

India
Abhinav Publications, pg 329
Advaita Ashrama, pg 329
Agam Kala Prakashan, pg 330
Ajanta Publications (India), pg 330
Ananda Publishers Pvt Ltd, pg 330
Associated Publishing House, pg 331
Atma Ram & Sons, pg 331
Bharatiya Vidya Bhavan, pg 333
Books & Books, pg 334
BR Publishing Corporation, pg 334
Brijbasi Printers Pvt Ltd, pg 334
S Chand & Co Ltd, pg 334
Chowkhamba Sanskrit Series Office, pg 335
Cosmo Publications, pg 335
DK Printworld (P) Ltd, pg 336
Dutta Baruah Publishing Co Pvt Ltd, pg 336
Frank Brothers & Co (Publishers) Ltd, pg 337
Goel Prakashen, pg 337
Gyan Publishing House, pg 338
Arnold Heinman Publishers (India) Pvt Ltd, pg 338
Heritage Publishers, pg 338
Himalaya Publishing House, pg 338
India Book House Pvt Ltd, pg 339
Indian Council for Cultural Relations, pg 339
Indian Museum, pg 339

Intellectual Publishing House, pg 339
Inter-India Publications, pg 340
Kali For Women, pg 341
Lalit Kala Akademi, pg 341
Mapin Publishing Pvt Ltd, pg 342
Ministry of Information & Broadcasting, pg 342
Mudgala Trust, pg 343
Munshiram Manoharlal Publishers Pvt Ltd, pg 343
National Museum, pg 344
Navrang Booksellers & Publishers, pg 344
Paramount Sales (India) Pvt Ltd, pg 345
Prabhat Prakashan, pg 346
Pratibha Pratishthan, pg 346
Promilla and Co, pg 346
Rahul Publishing House, pg 347
Rajasthan Hindi Granth Academy, pg 347
Regency Publications, pg 347
Rekha Prakashan, pg 347
Reliance Publishing House, pg 347
Roli Books Pvt Ltd, pg 348
Rupa & Co, pg 348
Samkaleen Prakashan, pg 349
Sat Sahitya Prakashan, pg 349
Sri Satguru Publications, pg 349
South Asia Publications, pg 350
Sterling Publishers Pvt Ltd, pg 351
Suman Prakashan Pvt Ltd, pg 351
DB Taraporevala Sons & Co Pvt Ltd, pg 351
Vakils Feffer & Simons Ltd, pg 352
Vikas Publishing House Pvt Ltd, pg 353

Indonesia
P T Bulan Bintang, pg 354
Djambatan PT, pg 355
Dunia Pustaka Jaya, pg 355
Pustaka Utama Grafiti, PT, pg 357
Yayasan Lontar, pg 357

Ireland
An Gum, pg 358
The Columba Press, pg 359
Four Courts Press Ltd, pg 360
Gandon Editions, pg 360
The Goldsmith Press Ltd, pg 361
Irish Academic Press, pg 361
O'Brien Educational, pg 363
Roberts Rinehart Publishers, pg 363
Town House & Country House, pg 364

Israel
Bezalel Academy of Arts & Design, pg 365
The Bialik Institute, pg 365
Gefen Publishing House Ltd, pg 367
Hakibbutz Hameuchad Publishing House Ltd, pg 368
Keter Publishing House Ltd, pg 369
The Magnes Press, pg 370
Massada Press Ltd, pg 370
Massada Publishers Ltd, pg 370
Misgav Yerushalayim, pg 370
Rolnik Publishers, pg 371
Sifriat Poalim Ltd, pg 372
R Sirkis Publishers Ltd, pg 372
Steimatzky Group Ltd, pg 372
Tcherikover Publishers Ltd, pg 372
Y L Peretz Publishing Co, pg 374

Italy
Mario Adda Editore SNC, pg 374
Aesthetica, pg 374

891

SUBJECT INDEX

BOOK

Alba, pg 375
Alinari Fratelli SpA Istituto di Edizioni Artistiche, pg 375
Alinea, pg 375
Umberto Allemandi & C SRL, pg 375
Amalthea srl, pg 375
Arcadia Edizioni Srl, pg 376
Archivio Guido Izzi Edizioni, pg 376
Edizioni Arka SRL, pg 376
Arnaud Editore SRL, pg 376
Arsenale Editrice SRL, pg 376
Artema, pg 377
Edizioni Artes, pg 377
Artioli Editore in Modena, pg 377
Verlagsanstalt Athesia, pg 377
Automobilia srl, pg 377
Belforte Editore Libraio srl, pg 377
Bianco, pg 377
Biblos srl, pg 378
Bompiani-RCS Libri, pg 378
Giuseppe Bonanno Editore, pg 378
Casa Editrice Bonechi, pg 378
Bonechi-Edizioni Il Turismo Srl, pg 378
Bonsignori Editore SRL, pg 378
Edizioni Bora SNC di E Brandani & C, pg 378
Bulzoni Editore SRL (Le Edizioni Universitarie d'Italia), pg 379
Edizioni Cadmo SRL, pg 379
Calosci, pg 379
Campanotto, pg 379
Canova SRL, pg 379
Capone Editore SRL, pg 379
Nuova Casa Editrice Licinio Cappelli GEM srl, pg 379
Casa Editrice Libraria Ulrico Hoepli SpA, pg 380
Casa Editrice Lint Srl, pg 380
Edizioni Castello di Antonio Careddu, pg 380
Il Castello srl, pg 380
Centro Di, pg 381
Centro Italiano Studi Alto Medioevo, pg 381
Il Cigno Galileo Galilei-Edizioni di Arte e Scienza, pg 381
Ciranna - Roma, pg 381
CLUEB (Cooperativa Libraria Universitaria Editrice Bologna), pg 382
Edizioni di Comunita SpA, pg 382
Costa e Nolan SpA, pg 383
D'Anna, pg 383
Edizioni Dedalo SRL, pg 384
Edizioni del Centro, pg 384
Istituto della Enciclopedia Italiana, pg 384
Edizioni Della Torre di Salvatore Fozzi & C SAS, pg 384
Diakronia, pg 385
Editoriale Domus Spa, pg 385
Ecole Francaise de Rome, pg 385
Edi Ermes SRL, pg 386
Editalia (Edizioni d'Italia), pg 386
Edizioni d'Arte e Moderna, Edam, pg 386
Edizioni l'Arciere SRL, pg 387
Edizioni Mediterranee SRL, pg 387
Giulio Einaudi Editore SpA, pg 387
Electa, pg 387
Edizioni dell'Elefante, pg 388
ERGA SNC di Carla Ottino Merli & C (Edizioni Realizzazioni Grafiche - Artigiana), pg 388
Essegi, pg 388
Edizioni Europa, pg 388
Fatatrac, pg 388
FEDA SA, pg 388
Federico Motta Editore SpA, pg 389

Giangiacomo Feltrinelli SpA, pg 389
Fenice 2000, pg 389
Festina Lente Edizioni, pg 389
Flaccovio Editore, pg 389
Arnaldo Forni Editore SRL, pg 389
Edizioni Frassinelli SRL, pg 389
Edizioni Futuro SRL, pg 389
Adriano Gallina Editore sas, pg 389
Gangemi Editore, pg 390
Garolla, pg 390
Garzanti Editore, pg 390
Istituto Geografico de Agostini SpA, pg 390
Giancarlo Politi Editore, pg 390
Edizioni del Girasole srl, pg 390
Giunti (Gruppo Editoriale), pg 390
Giunti Publishing Group, pg 391
Gius Laterza e Figli SpA, pg 391
Grafica e Arte SRL, pg 391
Grafis Edizioni, pg 391
Grafo Edizioni, pg 391
Ernesto Gremese Editore SRL, pg 391
Gremese International Srl, pg 391
Gruppo Calderini Edagricole, pg 392
Gruppo Editoriale Faenza Editrice SpA, pg 392
Ugo Guanda Editore, pg 392
Herbita Editrice di Leonardo Palermo, pg 392
Hopeful Monster Editore, pg 392
Idea Books, pg 393
IHT Gruppo Editoriale SRL, pg 393
Il Quadrante SRL, pg 393
Il Saggiatore, pg 393
Ila - Palma, Tea Nova, pg 393
ISAL (Ist Storia Arte Lombarda), pg 394
Editoriale Jaca Book SpA, pg 394
Jandi-Sapi Editori, pg 394
L Japadre Editore, pg 394
Lalli Editore SRL, pg 395
Il Lavoro Editoriale, pg 395
L'Erma di Bretschneider SRL, pg 395
Editrice Liguria SNC di Norberto Sabatelli & C, pg 396
Linea d'Ombra Libri, pg 396
Vincenzo Lo Faro Editore, pg 396
Longanesi & C, pg 396
Angelo Longo Editore, pg 396
Edizioni de Luca SRL, pg 397
La Luna, pg 397
Magnus Edizioni SpA, pg 397
Giuseppe Maimone Editore, pg 397
Manfrini Editori, pg 397
Tommaso Marotta Editore Srl, pg 398
Marsilio Editori SpA, pg 398
Edizioni Gabriele Mazzotta SRL, pg 398
McRae Books, pg 398
Minerva Italica SpA, pg 399
Arnoldo Mondadori Editore SpA, pg 399
Giorgio Mondadori & Associati, pg 399
Mondolibro Editore SNC, pg 399
Moretti & Vitali editori srl, pg 400
Gruppo Ugo Mursia Editore SpA, pg 400
Nardini Editore srl, pg 400
Accademia Naz dei Lincei, pg 400
Istituto Nazionale di Archeologia e Storia dell'Arte, pg 400
Istituto Nazionale di Studi Romani, pg 400
NodoLibri, pg 401
Novecento Editrice Srl, pg 401
Nuova Alfa Editoriale, pg 401

La Nuova Italia Editrice SpA, pg 401
Nuovi Sentieri Editore, pg 401
OCTAVO Franco Cantini Editore, pg 401
Officina Edizioni di Aldo Quinti, pg 401
Leo S Olschki, pg 402
Maria Pacini Fazzi Editore, pg 402
Paideia Editrice, pg 402
Palatina Editrice, pg 402
Fratelli Palombi SRL, pg 402
Franco Cosimo Panini Editore SpA, pg 402
Patron Editore SrL, pg 403
Pheljna Edizioni d'Arte e Suggestione, pg 403
Daniela Piazza Editore, pg 403
Francesco Pirella Editore, pg 403
Amilcare Pizzi SpA, pg 403
Istituto Poligrafico e Zecca dello Stato, pg 404
Il Pomerio, pg 404
Neri Pozza Editore, pg 404
Priuli e Verlucca, Editori, pg 404
Psicologica Editrice, pg 404
Edizioni Quasar di Severino Tognon SRL, pg 404
Edizioni Quattroventi SNC, pg 404
Edition Raetia Srl-GmbH, pg 404
RAI.ERI, pg 405
RCS Libri SpA, pg 405
RCS Rizzoli Libri SpA, pg 405
Franco Maria Ricci Editore (FMR), pg 405
G e C Ricordi SpA, pg 405
Edizioni Ripostes, pg 405
Editori Riuniti, pg 405
Rubbettino Editore, pg 406
SAGEP, pg 406
SAIE Editrice SRL, pg 406
Edizioni San Paolo SRL, pg 407
Fausto Sardini Editrice, pg 407
Scala Group spa, pg 407
Lo Scarabeo Srl, pg 407
Schena Editore, pg 407
Salvatore Sciascia Editore, pg 407
Edizioni Scientifiche Italiane, pg 407
Sellerio Editore, pg 407
SEMAR Publishers SRL, pg 407
Sicania, pg 408
Edizioni Librarie Siciliane, pg 408
Silvana Editoriale SpA, pg 408
Spirali Edizioni, pg 408
Stampa Alternativa - Nuovi Equilibri, pg 409
Studio Editoriale Programma, pg 409
Tappeiner, pg 409
Tassotti Editore, pg 409
TEA Tascabili degli Editori Associati SpA, pg 409
Tema Celeste, pg 409
Tomo Edizioni srl, pg 410
Trainer International SRL, pg 410
Turris, pg 410
Editoriale Umbra SAS di Carnevali e, pg 410
UTET (Unione Tipografico-Editrice Torinese), pg 411
Vinciana Editrice sas, pg 411
Viviani Editore srl, pg 412

Japan

Bijutsu Shuppan-Sha, Ltd, pg 415
Chuo-Koron-Sha Inc, pg 415
Dohosha Publishing Co Ltd, pg 416
Fuzambo Publishing Co, pg 416
Genko-Sha, pg 416
Hakusui-Sha Co Ltd, pg 417
Hayakawa Publishing Inc, pg 417

Heibonsha Ltd, Publishers, pg 417
Hoikusha Publishing Co Ltd, pg 417
Holp Book Co Ltd, pg 417
International Society for Educational Information (ISEI), pg 418
Iwanami Shoten, Publishers, pg 418
Iwasaki Shoten Publishing Co Ltd, pg 418
Kadokawa Shoten Publishing Co, pg 419
Kaisei-Sha Publishing Co Ltd, pg 419
Kawade Shobo Shinsha, pg 419
Kinokuniya Co Ltd (Publishing Department), pg 420
Kodansha, pg 420
Kodansha International, pg 420
Kosei Publishing Co Ltd, pg 420
Koyo Shobo, pg 420
Mejikaru Furendo-sha, pg 421
Misuzu Shobo Ltd, pg 421
Nigensha Publishing Co Ltd, pg 422
Nihon-Bunkyo Shuppan (Japan Educational Publishing Co Ltd), pg 422
Nishimura Co Ltd, pg 423
Sekai Bunka Publishing Inc, pg 425
Shakai Shiso-Sha, pg 425
Shibundo Co Ltd, pg 425
Shogakukan Inc, pg 426
Mitsumura Suiko Shoin, pg 426
Shokoku Publishing Co Ltd, pg 426
Shueisha Inc, pg 426
Shufu-to-Seikatsu Sha Ltd, pg 426
Sogensha Publishing Co Ltd, pg 426
Tankosha Publishing Co Ltd, pg 427
Toho Book Store, pg 427
Toho Shuppan, pg 427
Tokai University Press, pg 427
Tokuma-Shoten, pg 427
Tokyo Shoseki Co Ltd, pg 427
Charles E Tuttle Publishing Co Inc, pg 428
Yohan Shuppan, pg 429

Kenya

Camerapix Publishers International Ltd, pg 431
Heinemann Kenya Limited (EAEP), pg 431

Democratic People's Republic of Korea

The Foreign Language Press Group, pg 434
Korea Science and Encyclopedia Publishing House, pg 434
Literature and Art Publishing House, pg 434

Republic of Korea

Ahn Graphics, pg 434
Bal-eon, pg 434
Chung Rim Publishing Co Ltd, pg 435
Dae Won Sa Co Ltd, pg 435
Youl Hwa Dang Publisher, pg 436
Dong Hwa Publishing Co, pg 436
Ewha Womans University Press, pg 436
Hak Won Publishing Co, pg 436
Hakgojae Publishing Inc, pg 436
Hanjin Publishing Co, pg 436
Haseo Publishing Co, pg 436
Hollym Corporation Publishers, pg 437
Ki Moon Dang, pg 437
Korea Textbook Co Ltd, pg 437
Kwangmyong Publishing Co, pg 438

PUBLISHERS

Literature Academy, pg 438
Munhag-gwan, pg 438
Munye Publishing Co, pg 439
Nanam Publishing House, pg 439
Pochinchai Printing Co Ltd, pg 439
Samho Music Publishing Co, pg 440
Samhwa Publishing Co, pg 440
Samseong Publishing Co Ltd, pg 440
Seoul International Publishing House, pg 440
Seoul National University Press, pg 440
Yonsei University Press, pg 441

Kuwait
Ministry of Information, pg 441

Laos People's Democratic Republic
Lao-phanit, pg 441

Latvia
Liesma Publishers, pg 442
Preses Nams, pg 442

Lebanon
Khayat Book and Publishing Co Sarl, pg 443

Liechtenstein
Frank P van Eck Publishers, pg 444
Verlag HP Gassner AG, pg 444
Kliemand Verlag, pg 444
Megatrade AG, pg 445
Saendig Reprint Verlag, Hans-Rainer Wohlwend, pg 445

Lithuania
Academia, pg 445
AS Narbuto Leidykla (AS Narbutas' Publishers), pg 445
Baltos Lankos, pg 445
Lithuanian National Museum Publishing House, pg 446
Scena, pg 446
Tyto Alba Publishers, pg 446
Vaga Ltd, pg 446

Luxembourg
Editions APESS ASBL, pg 447
Galerie Editions Kutter, pg 447
Editions Phi, pg 448
Service Central des Imprimes et des Fournitures de Bureau de l'Etat, pg 448
Editions Tousch, pg 448

Macau
Universidadede de Macau, Centro de Publicacoes, pg 448

The Former Yugoslav Republic of Macedonia
Macedonia Prima Publishing House, pg 449
Makedonska kniga (Knigoizdatelstvo), pg 449
Nov svet (New World), pg 449
Zumpres Publishing Firm, pg 449

Malaysia
Pustaka Cipta Sdn Bhd, pg 454

Malta
Fondazzjoni Patrimonju Malti, pg 456

Mauritius
Editions de l'Ocean Indien Ltd, pg 457

Mexico
Artes de Mexico y del Mundo, SA de CV, pg 458
Libreria y Ediciones Botas SA, pg 458
Cuernavaca Editorial S A, pg 459
Ediciones Culturales Internacionales SA de CV Edicion Compra y Venta de Libros, Casetes, Videos, pg 459
Edamex SA de CV, pg 460
Ediciones Era SA de CV, pg 460
Editorial Extemporaneos SA, pg 461
Fondo de Cultura Economica, pg 461
Fondo Editorial de la Plastica Mexicana, pg 461
Editorial Hermes SA, pg 461
Editorial Herrero SA, pg 462
Editorial Limusa SA de CV, pg 463
Galeria de Arte Misrachi SA, pg 464
Instituto Nacional de Antropologia e Historia, pg 464
Naves Internacional de Ediciones SA, pg 464
Editorial Nueva Imagen SA, pg 464
Pearson Educacion de Mexico, SA de CV, pg 465
SCRIPTA - Distribucion y Servicios Editoriales, SA de CV, pg 467
Servicios Especiales Maciel SA de CV, pg 467
Siglo XXI Editores SA de CV, pg 467
Ediciones Suromex SA, pg 467
Universidad Veracruzana Direccion General Editorial y de Publicaciones, pg 468

Republic of Moldova
Editura Hyperion, pg 468

Monaco
Rondeau Giannipiero a Monaco, pg 469
Editions Andre Sauret SA, pg 469

Morocco
Access International Services, pg 469
Association de la Recherche Historique et Sociale, pg 469
Editions Eddif Maroc, pg 469
Editions Oum, pg 470

Myanmar
Knowledge Printing & Publishing House, pg 471
Kyi-Pwar-Ye Book House, pg 471
Smart & Mookerdum, pg 471

Nepal
International Standards Books & Periodicals (P) Ltd, pg 471
Royal Nepal Academy, pg 472

Netherlands
APA (Academic Publishers Associated), pg 472
B M Israel BV, pg 473
John Benjamins BV, pg 474
BoekWerk, pg 474
Bosch & Keuning, pg 474
Uitgeverij Cantecleer BV, pg 475

Davaco Publishers, pg 476
Fragment Cooperatieve Vereniging UA, Uitgeverij, pg 477
Uitgeverij Vrij Geesteslleven, pg 477
Van Gennep Ltd, pg 477
Uitgeverij Heuff Nieuwkoop, pg 478
Hotei Publishing, pg 478
Mets & Schilt Uitgevers en Distributeurs, pg 481
Mirananda Publishers BV, pg 481
Nai Publishers, pg 481
Omega Boek BV, pg 482
The Pepin Press, pg 482
Philo Press-Van Heusden-Hissink & Co CV (APA), pg 482
Picaron Editions, pg 482
Em Querido's Uitgeverij BV, pg 483
Scriptum, pg 483
Smeets Illustrated Projects, pg 484
Stedelijk Van Abbemuseum, pg 484
Steltman Editions, pg 484
Thoth Publishers, pg 485
Uniepers BV, pg 486
Uitgeverij Waanders BV, pg 487
Uitgeverij 010, pg 487

New Zealand
Auckland University Press, pg 488
Barkfire Press, pg 488
David Bateman Ltd, pg 488
Bush Press Communications Ltd, pg 489
Cicada Press, pg 490
Craig Potton Publishing, pg 490
Godwit Publishing Ltd, pg 491
HarperCollins Publishers (New Zealand) Ltd, pg 491
Hazard Press Ltd, pg 491
David Ling Publishing, pg 493
Oxford University Press, pg 494
Resource Books Ltd, pg 495
Saint Publishing, pg 495
University of Otago Press, pg 496

Nigeria
Aromolaran Publishing Co Ltd, pg 498
New Africa Publishing Company Ltd, pg 500

Norway
Atheneum Forlag A/S, pg 502
J W Eides Forlag A/S, pg 503
Gyldendal Norsk Forlag A/S, pg 503
Tell Forlag, pg 505

Oman
Apex Publishing, pg 506

Pakistan
Classic, pg 506
Sang-e-Meel Publications, pg 509

Panama
Editorial Universitaria, pg 509

Peru
Librerias ABC SA, pg 511
Editorial Horizonte, pg 511

Philippines
Heritage Publishing House, pg 513
National Book Store Inc, pg 514
National Museum of the Philippines, pg 514
Our Lady of Manaoag Publisher, pg 514
Philippine Education Co Inc, pg 514

SUBJECT INDEX

SIBS Publishing House Inc, pg 515
University of the Philippines Press, pg 515
Vera-Reyes Inc, pg 515

Poland
Wydawnictwo Arkady, pg 516
Wydawnictwa Artystyczne i Filmowe, pg 516
BOSZ scp, pg 516
Wydawnictwo Dolnoslaskie, pg 516
Wydawnictwo Literackie, pg 517
Muza SA, pg 518
Ossolineum Zaklad Narodowy im Ossolinskich - Wydawnictwo, pg 518
Rosikon Press, pg 519
Towarzystwo Naukowe w Toruniu, pg 520
Wydawnictwo DiG, pg 521

Portugal
Arvore Coop de Actividades Artisticas, CRL, pg 522
Assirio & Alvim, pg 522
Bertrand Editora Lda, pg 522
Camara Municipal de Castelo, pg 523
Chaves Ferreira Publicacoes SA, pg 523
Livraria Civilizacao (Americo Fraga Lamares & Ca Lda), pg 523
Constancia Editores, SA, pg 524
Difusao Cultural, pg 524
Dinalivro, pg 524
Distri Cultural Lda, pg 524
Edicoes 70, Lda, pg 524
Edicoes ELO, pg 524
Editorial Estampa, Lda, pg 524
Publicacoes Europa-America Lda, pg 524
Editorial Franciscana, pg 525
Imprensa Nacional-Casa da Moeda, pg 526
Latina Livraria, pg 526
Livros Horizonte Lda, pg 526
Livraria Tavares Martins, pg 527
Editora Pergaminho Lda, pg 528
Editorial Presenca, pg 528
Quatro Elementos Editores, pg 529
Quetzal Editores, pg 529
Quimera Editores, pg 529
Realizacoes Artis, pg 529
Edicoes 70, pg 529
Solivros, pg 529
Sociedade Tipografica, SA (Editora Soctip/Livraria Soctip), pg 530
Vega-Publicacao e Distribuicao de Livros e Revistas, Lda, pg 530

Puerto Rico
University of Puerto Rico Press (EDUPR), pg 531

Romania
Editura Academiei Romane, pg 531
Alcor-Edimpex (Verlag) Ltd, pg 531
Artemis Verlag, pg 532
Casa Editoriala Independenta Europa, pg 532
Editura Clusium, Casa de Editura Atlas-Clusium SRL, pg 532
Editure Ion Creanga, pg 532
Editura Gryphon, pg 533
Editura Kriterion SA, pg 534
Lider Verlag, pg 534
Mentor Kiado, pg 534
Editura Meridiane, pg 534
Saeculum IO, pg 535
Est-Samuel Tastet Verlag, pg 536
Editura de Vest, pg 536
Vestala Verlag, pg 536

SUBJECT INDEX

BOOK

Russian Federation
Aurora Art Publishers, pg 537
Izdatelstvo Detskaya Literatura, pg 537
Izdatelstvo Galart, pg 538
Interbook-Business AO, pg 538
Izdatelstvo Iskusstvo, pg 538
Izdatelstvo Lenizdat, pg 539
Izdatelstvo Molodaya Gvardia, pg 540
Nauka Publishers, pg 540
Novosti Izdatel'stvo, pg 541
Panorama Publishing House, pg 541
Profizdat, pg 541
Russkaya Kniga Izdatelstvo (Publishers), pg 541
St Andrew's Biblical Theological College, pg 541
Izdatelstvo Sovetskii Pisatel, pg 542

Singapore
Archipelago Press, pg 545
International Publishers Distributor (S) Pte Ltd, pg 546
Select Books Pte Ltd, pg 548
Taylor & Francis Asia Pacific, pg 548
Times Media Pte Ltd, pg 549

Slovakia
Kalligram Kiado spol sro, pg 549
Vydavatelstvo Obzor, pg 550
Vydavatel'stvo SFVU Pallas, pg 550
Slovansky Tatran, Vydavatel 'stro spoi sro, pg 550

Slovenia
East West Operation (EWO) Ltd, pg 551
Mladinska Knjiga International, pg 552
Moderna galerija Ljubljana/Museum of Modern Art, pg 552
Zalozba Mihelac d o o, pg 552

South Africa
Educum Publishers Ltd, pg 554
Fernwood Press (Pty) Ltd, pg 554
Human & Rousseau (Pty) Ltd, pg 555
Institute for Reformational Studies CHE, pg 555
Janssen Publishers CC, pg 556
Johannesburg Art Gallery, pg 556

Spain
Acantilado, pg 561
Agencia Espanola de Cooperacion, pg 562
Aguilar SA de Ediciones, pg 562
Ediciones Akal SA, pg 562
Alberdania SL, pg 562
Alianza Editorial SA, pg 562
Altea, Taurus, Alfaguara SA, pg 563
Ambit Serveis Editorials, SA, pg 563
Editorial Astri SA, pg 564
Biblioteca de Catalunya, pg 565
Carroggio SA de Ediciones, pg 566
Editorial Casals SA, pg 566
Editorial Casariego, pg 566
Edicios do Castro, pg 566
Ediciones Catedra SA, pg 566
Celeste Ediciones, pg 567
Ediciones Colegio De Espana (ECE), pg 568
Complutense, SA Editorial, pg 568
Comunidad Autonoma de Madrid, Servicio de Documentacion y Publicaciones, pg 568
Consello da Cultura Galega - CCG, pg 568
Curial Edicions Catalanes SA, pg 569
Ediciones Daly S L, pg 569
Ediciones Destino SA, pg 569
Diputacion Provincial de Malaga, pg 570
Ediciones l'Isard, S L, pg 571
Ediciones y Distribuciones Universitarias SA, pg 571
Ediles-Ediciones Leonesas SA, pg 572
Edilux, pg 572
El Viso, SA Ediciones, pg 572
Ediciones Encuentro SA, pg 573
Editorial Espasa-Calpe SA, pg 573
Instituto de Estudios Riojanos, pg 574
Forum Artis, SA, pg 574
Fundacion Coleccion Thyssen-Bornemisza, pg 575
Fundacion Marcelino Botin, pg 575
Galaxia SA Editorial, pg 575
Vicent Garcia Editores, SA, pg 575
Ediciones Garriga SA, pg 575
Generalitat de Catalunya Diari Oficial de la Generalitat vern, pg 575
Instituto de Cultura Juan Gil-Albert, pg 576
Editorial Gustavo Gili SA, pg 576
Guadalquivir SL Ediciones, pg 576
Iberico Europea de Ediciones SA, pg 577
Editorial Incafo SA, pg 578
Institucion Fernando el Catolico de la Excma Diputacion de Zaragoza, pg 578
Ediciones Istmo SA, pg 579
Junta de Castilla y Leon Consejeria de Educacion y Cultura, pg 579
Editorial Juventud SA, pg 579
Editorial Labor SA, pg 579
LEDA (Las Ediciones de Arte), pg 579
Liber Ediciones, SA, pg 580
Libsa Editorial SA, pg 580
Llibres del Segle, pg 580
Loguez Ediciones, pg 580
Editorial Lumen SA, pg 580
Lunwerg Editores, SA, pg 580
Antonio Machado, SA, pg 580
Editorial Marin SA, pg 581
Editorial Mediterrania SL, pg 582
M Moleiro Editor, SA, pg 582
Editorial Moll SL, pg 582
Mundo Negro Editorial, pg 583
Editorial la Muralla SA, pg 583
Naque Editora, pg 583
Ediciones Nauta Credito SA, pg 584
Editorial Nerea SA, pg 584
Noguer y Caralt Editores SA, pg 584
Ediciones Oceano Grupo SA, pg 584
Pais Vasco Servicio Central de Publicaciones, pg 585
Parramon Ediciones SA, pg 586
Pearson Educacion S A, pg 586
Pronaos SA Ediciones, pg 588
Instituto Provincial de Investigaciones y Estudios Toledanos, pg 588
Editora Regional de Murcia - ERM, pg 588
Riquelme y Vargas Ediciones SL, pg 589
Editorial Roasa SL, pg 589
Universidad de Santiago de Compostela, pg 589
Ediciones Scriba SA, pg 589
Ediciones Seyer, pg 590
Silex Ediciones, pg 590
Ediciones Siruela SA, pg 591
Edicions 62, pg 591
Ramon Sopena SA, pg 591
Axel Springer Publicaciones, pg 591
Ediciones Tabapress, SA, pg 592
Ediciones Tarraco, pg 592
Editorial Tecnos SA, pg 592
Tf Editores, pg 592
Trea Ediciones, SL, pg 593
Turner Publicaciones, pg 593
Tursen, SA, pg 593
Editorial Txertoa, pg 594
Universidad de Granada, pg 594
Universidad de Malaga, pg 594
Universidad de Navarra, Ediciones SA, pg 594
Universidad de Valladolid Secretariado de Publicaciones e Intercambio Editorial, pg 594
Publicacions de la Universitat de Barcelona, pg 594
Visor Distribuciones, SA, pg 596
Xarait Libros SA, pg 596
Xunta de Galicia, pg 596

Sri Lanka
Ministry of Cultural Affairs, pg 597

Sweden
Acta Universitatis Gothoburgensis, pg 599
Alfabeta Bokforlag AB, pg 600
Bokforlaget Atlantis AB, pg 600
Albert Bonniers Forlag, pg 601
BOOX, pg 601
Carlsson Bokfoerlag AB, pg 601
Bengt Forsbergs Foerlag AB, pg 602
Gidlunds Bokforlag, pg 602
Hanse Production AB, pg 603
Bokforlaget Nya Doxa AB, pg 605
Schultz Forlag AB, pg 606
Stroemberg B&T Forlag AB, pg 606
Wahlstrom & Widstrand, pg 607

Switzerland
Editions L'Age d'Homme - La Cite, pg 608
Ammann Verlag & Co, pg 608
Archivio Storico Ticinese, pg 608
Armenia Editions, pg 608
Athenaeum Verlag AG, pg 608
Atlantis-Verlag AG, pg 608
Editions de la Baconniere SA, pg 609
U Baer Verlag, pg 609
Basilius Presse AG, pg 609
Benteli Verlag, pg 609
Benziger Verlag AG, pg 609
Editions Beyeler, pg 610
La Bibliotheque des Arts, pg 610
Bugra Suisse Burchler Grafino AG, pg 610
Edizioni Casagrande SA, pg 611
Christoph Merian Verlag, pg 611
Cosa-Verlag, Giusep Condrau SA, pg 611
Edizioni Armando Dado, Tipografia Stazione, pg 612
Editions Andre Delcourt & Cie, pg 612
Dimension World Ltd, pg 612
Diogenes Verlag AG, pg 612
Editions Edita, pg 613
Erker-Verlag, pg 613
Europa Verlag AG, pg 614
G+B Arts International, pg 614
Verlag Gachnang & Springer, Bern-Berlin, pg 614
Giampiero Casagrande Editore, pg 614
Editions du Griffon (Neuchatel), pg 615
GVA Publishers Ltd, pg 615
Haffmans Verlag AG, pg 615
Hallwag AG, pg 615
Paul Haupt Berne, pg 615
Verlag Huber & Co AG, pg 616
Editions Ides et Calendes SA, pg 616
Junod Nicholas, pg 616
Verlag Walter Keller, Dornach, pg 617
Kinderbuchverlag Luzern, pg 617
Galerie Kornfeld & Co, pg 617
Kossodo Verlag AG, pg 617
Kranich-Verlag, Dres AG & H R Bosch-Gwalter, pg 617
Bernard Letu Editeur, pg 618
Limmat Verlag, pg 618
Les Editions la Matze, pg 618
Memory/Cage Editions, pg 619
Editions H Messeiller SA, pg 619
Editions Minkoff, pg 619
Motovun Book GmbH, pg 619
Lars Mueller Publishers, pg 619
Muslim Architecture Research Program (MARP), pg 619
Les Editions Nagel SA (Paris), pg 619
Verlag Arthur Niggli AG, pg 620
Novalis Media AG, pg 620
Office du Livre SA (Buchhaus AG), pg 620
Edition Olms AG, pg 620
Orell Fuessli Verlag, pg 620
Ostschweiz Druck und Verlag, pg 621
Parkett Publishers Inc, pg 621
Perret Edition, pg 621
Philosophisch-Anthroposophischer Verlag am Goetheanum, pg 621
PIE-Peter Lang AG, pg 622
Punktum AG, Buchredaktion und Bildarchiv, pg 622
Rabe Verlag AG Zuerich, pg 622
Regenbogen Verlag, pg 622
Rhein-Trio, Edition/Editions du Fou, pg 623
Roth et Sauter SA, pg 623
Verlag fuer Schoene Wissenschaften, pg 624
Schwabe & Co AG, pg 624
Editions D'Art Albert Skira SA, pg 625
Edition Stemmle AG, pg 625
Theseus - Verlag AG, pg 625
3 Dimension World (3-D-World), pg 625
Editions du Tricorne, pg 626
Editions des Trois Collines Francois Lachenal, pg 626
Editions 24 Heures, pg 626
Der Universitatsverlag Freiburg, pg 626
Versus Verlag AG, pg 627
Vexer Verlag, pg 627
Weber SA d'Editions, pg 627
Weltwoche ABC-Verlag, pg 627
Werner Druck AG, pg 627
Wiese Verlag AG, pg 627
J E Wolfensberger AG, pg 628
Wyss Verlag AG Bern, pg 628

Syrian Arab Republic
Damascus University Press, pg 628

Taiwan, Province of China
Art Book Co Ltd, pg 629
The Artist Publishing Co, pg 629
Chung Hwa Book Co Ltd, pg 629

PUBLISHERS

Echo Publishing Company Ltd, pg 629
Far East Book Co Ltd, pg 630
Chu Hai Publishing (Taiwan) Co Ltd, pg 630
Highlight Publishing Company Ltd, pg 630
Kuang Fu Book Co Ltd, pg 630
Lee & Lee Communications, pg 631
Linking Publishing Company Ltd, pg 631
National Museum of History, pg 631
National Palace Museum, pg 631
San Min Book Co Ltd, pg 631
SMC Publishing Inc, pg 632
World Book Co Ltd, pg 632
Yuan Liou Publishing Co, Ltd, pg 632

United Republic of Tanzania

Tanzania Publishing House, pg 634

Thailand

New Generation Publishing Co Ltd, pg 635
Sang Dad Publishing Company Ltd, pg 635
Thai Watana Panich Co, Ltd, pg 636
White Lotus Co Ltd, pg 636

Tunisia

Academie Tunisienne des Sciences, des Lettres et des Arts Beit El Hekma, pg 637
Ceres Editions, pg 637
Sud Editions, pg 638

Turkey

Arkeoloji Ve Sanat Yayinlari, pg 639
Dost Yayinlari San Ve Tic Ltd, pg 639
Inkilap Publishers Ltd, pg 640
Kubbealti Akademisi Kultur ve Sasat Vakfi, pg 640
Remzi Kitabevi, pg 641
Soez Yayin/Oyunajans, pg 641
Turkish Republic - Ministry of Culture, pg 641
Yapi-Endustri Merkezi Yayinlari-Yem Yayin, pg 642
Kabalci Yayinevi, pg 642

Ukraine

Mystetstvo Publishers, pg 643

United Kingdom

Umberto Allemandi & Co Publishing, pg 646
Alpine Fine Arts Books Ltd, pg 646
Andromeda Oxford Ltd, pg 647
Antique Collectors' Club Ltd, pg 647
Apple Press, pg 648
Appletree Press Ltd, pg 648
Art Books International Ltd, pg 649
Art Sales Index Ltd, pg 649
The Art Trade Press Ltd, pg 649
Arts Council of England, pg 649
Ashgate Publishing Ltd, pg 649
Ashmolean Museum Publications, pg 650
The Athlone Press Ltd, pg 650
Atlas Press, pg 651
Aurum Press Ltd, pg 651
Batsford Ltd, pg 652
BCA, pg 653
Belitha Press Ltd, pg 653

Bellew Publishing Co Ltd, pg 653
A & C Black Publishers Ltd, pg 655
Blackstaff Press, pg 655
Bloomsbury Publishing PLC, pg 656
The Book Guild Ltd, pg 657
Books for Europe Ltd, pg 657
Breslich & Foss, pg 659
The British Academy, pg 659
British Library Publications, pg 660
British Museum Press, pg 660
Calder Publications Ltd, pg 662
Cambridge University Press, pg 662
Camden Press Ltd, pg 662
Cameron & Hollis, pg 663
Canongate Books Ltd, pg 663
Carlton Publishing Group, pg 664
Cassell & Co, pg 664
Marshall Cavendish Partworks Ltd, pg 665
Chadwyck-Healey Ltd, pg 666
Clematis Press Ltd, pg 668
Colour Library Direct, pg 669
Compendium Publishing, pg 670
Constable Publishers, pg 670
Cottage Publications, pg 671
David & Charles Ltd, pg 674
Andre Deutsch Ltd, pg 675
Diagram Visual Information Ltd, pg 675
Dorling Kindersley Ltd, pg 676
Eaglemoss Publications Ltd, pg 676
Edinburgh University Press Ltd, pg 677
Element Books Ltd, pg 678
Elfande Ltd, pg 678
Aidan Ellis Publishing, pg 678
The Erskine Press, pg 679
The Eurospan Group, pg 680
Evans Brothers Ltd, pg 680
Faber & Faber Ltd, pg 681
Francis Balsom Associates, pg 684
The Fraser Press, pg 684
Frontier Publishing, pg 684
The FruitMarket Gallery, pg 685
Gale Research, pg 685
Garnet Publishing Ltd, pg 685
Genesis Publications Ltd, pg 686
GMP Publishers Ltd, pg 687
Golden Cockerel Press Ltd, pg 688
Grange Books PLC, pg 689
The Greek Bookshop, pg 689
Robert Hale Ltd, pg 691
Hamish Hamilton Ltd, pg 691
HarperCollins Publishers, pg 692
Hawk Books, pg 693
Helicon Publishing Ltd, pg 694
Heraldry Today, pg 695
Herbert Press Ltd, pg 695
Heritage Press, pg 695
Hilmarton Manor Press, pg 696
Alan Hutchison Ltd, pg 698
Icon Press, pg 698
Institute of Irish Studies, The Queens University of Belfast, pg 699
International Communications, pg 701
The Islamic Texts Society, pg 701
Kegan Paul International Ltd, pg 703
Laurence King Publishing Ltd, pg 704
KIT Press - Royal Tropical Institute, pg 705
Letterbox Library, pg 707
Liverpool University Press, pg 708
Lund Humphries, pg 709
The Lutterworth Press, pg 709
Lyle Publications Ltd, pg 709
Macmillan Audio Books, pg 710
Macmillan Reference Ltd, pg 710

Mainstream Publishing Co (Edinburgh) Ltd, pg 711
Manchester University Press, pg 711
Mandrake of Oxford, pg 711
Maney Publishing, pg 711
Peter Marcan Publications, pg 711
Marston House, pg 712
The Medici Society Ltd, pg 713
Merrell Publishers Ltd, pg 713
Merrion Press, pg 713
Harvey Miller Publishers, pg 714
Mirabel Books Ltd, pg 715
MIT Press Ltd, pg 715
Motilal (UK) Books of India, pg 715
National Galleries of Scotland, pg 717
National Library of Wales, pg 717
National Portrait Gallery Publications, pg 717
National Trust, pg 717
NMS Publishing Ltd, pg 719
W W Norton & Company Ltd, pg 720
Orion Publishing Group Ltd, pg 722
Peter Owen Ltd, pg 722
Oxford University Press, pg 723
Pallas Athene, pg 723
Pavilion Books Ltd, pg 724
Pearson Education, pg 725
Pearson Education Europe, Mideast & Africa, pg 725
Phaidon Press Ltd, pg 726
Planet, pg 728
Poetry Wales Press Ltd, pg 729
Policy Studies Institute, pg 729
Polybooks, pg 729
Pomegranate Europe Ltd, pg 729
David Porteous Editions, pg 729
Porthill Publishers, pg 730
PRC Publishing Ltd, pg 730
Primrose Hill Press Ltd, pg 730
Quarto Publishing plc, pg 731
Ramboro Books Plc, pg 732
Ramsay Head Press, pg 732
Random House UK Ltd, pg 733
Reaktion Books Ltd, pg 733
Redcliffe Press Ltd, pg 734
Redstone Press, pg 734
Regency House Publishing Ltd, pg 734
School of Oriental & African Studies, pg 739
Search Press Ltd, pg 740
Seren, pg 740
Serindia Publications, pg 740
Shearwater Press Ltd, pg 741
Charles Skilton Ltd, pg 742
Skoob Russell Square, pg 742
Smith Settle Ltd, pg 743
Souvenir Press Ltd, pg 743
SPA Books Ltd, pg 744
Stacey International, pg 745
Rudolf Steiner Press, pg 745
Studio Editions Ltd, pg 746
Sutton Publishing Ltd, pg 746
Taschen UK Ltd, pg 747
Tate Publishing Ltd, pg 747
John Taylor Book Ventures, pg 747
Textile & Art Publications Ltd, pg 748
Thames & Hudson Ltd, pg 748
Time Out Group Ltd, pg 749
Titan Books Ltd, pg 749
Trigon Press, pg 750
UCL Press Ltd, pg 751
University of Wales Press, pg 751
Viking, pg 753
The Warburg Institute, pg 754
Westview Press, pg 755
Philip Wilson Publishers, pg 757
Windsor Books International, pg 757

SUBJECT INDEX

The Women's Press Ltd, pg 758
Wordwright Publishing, pg 758
World Microfilms Publications Ltd, pg 758
World of Islam Altajir Trust, pg 759
Yale University Press London, pg 759
Zwemmer Holdings Co Ltd, pg 759

Uruguay

Ediciones de Juan Darien, pg 760
Punto de Encuentro Ediciones, pg 761
Vinten Editor, pg 761

Uzbekistan

Izdatelstvo Uzbekistan, pg 761

Venezuela

Armitano Editores CA, pg 761
Editorial Ateneo de Caracas, pg 762
Monte Avila Editores Latinoamericana CA, pg 762
Biblioteca Ayacucho, pg 762
Editorial Biosfera CA, pg 762

Yugoslavia

Alfa-Narodna Knjiga, pg 764
Izdavacka preduzece Gradina, pg 764
Jugoslovenska Revija, pg 764
Nolit Publishing House, pg 765
Svetovi, pg 766
Turisticka Stampa, pg 766
Vuk Karadzic, pg 766

Zimbabwe

Academic Books Pvt Ltd, pg 767
Journal on Social Change, pg 768

ASIAN STUDIES

Australia

Allen & Unwin Pty Ltd, The Australian Newspaper, Vogel Breads, pg 11
Edward Arnold (Australia) Pty Ltd, pg 12
China Books, pg 18
Coconut Productions, pg 18
Crawford House Publishing, pg 19
Gerald Griffin Press, pg 24
Hale & Iremonger Pty Ltd, pg 24
Hawker Brownlow, pg 25
Hyland House Publishing Pty Ltd, pg 27
Illert Publications, pg 27
Indra Publishing, pg 27
On The Stone, pg 35
Oriental Publications, pg 36
Queensland Art Gallery, pg 39
Spinifex Press, pg 43
Stafford Books, pg 43
La Trobe University Press, pg 45
Wakefield Press Pty Ltd, pg 47
Windhorse Books, pg 48

Austria

Verlag der Oesterreichischen Akademie der Wissenschaften (OEAW), pg 56
Edition Va Bene, pg 60

Azerbaijan

Sada, Literaturno-Izdatel'skij Centr, pg 61

Bangladesh

Ankur Prakashani, pg 62

SUBJECT INDEX — BOOK

Belgium
Brepols Publishers NV, pg 65
Uitgeverij Peeters Leuven (Belgie), pg 72

Brazil
Fundacao Cultural Avatar, pg 83
Editora Ground Ltda, pg 84
Francisco J Laissue Livraria, pg 86

Bulgaria
Eurasia Academic Publishers, pg 95

China
Asia 2000 Ltd, pg 102
China Tibetology Publishing House, pg 104
Cultural Relics Publishing House, pg 105
Fudan University Press, pg 105
The Publishing House of Shanghai University of Traditional Chinese Medicine, pg 108
Qingdao Publishing House, pg 108

Czech Republic
Narodni Muzeum, pg 126
Nakladatelstvi a vydavatelstvi Panorama, pg 127

Denmark
Aarhus Universitetsforlag, pg 129
Mellemfolkeligt Samvirke, pg 133
Museum Tusculanum Press, pg 134

Finland
Kirja-Leitzinger, pg 143

France
De Boccard Edition-Diffusion, pg 151
Editions de l'Ecole des Hautes Etudes en Sciences Sociales (EHESS), pg 160
Fata Morgana, pg 163
Les Introuvables-Editions L'Harmattan, pg 170
Kailash Editions, pg 171
Karthala Editions-Diffusion, pg 171
Langues & Mondes/L'Asiatheque, pg 171

Germany
J J Augustin GmbH Verlag, pg 196
Dieterichsche Verlagsbuchhandlung Mainz, pg 216
Duncker und Humblot GmbH, pg 219
Egmont vgs verlagsgesellschaft mbH, pg 221
Erlanger Verlag Fuer Mission und Okumene, pg 223
Harrassowitz Verlag, pg 237
Horlemann Verlag, pg 243
IKO Verlag fur Interkulturelle Kommunikation, pg 244
Iudicium Verlag GmbH, pg 245
Kolibri-Verlags GmbH, pg 252
Landbuch-Verlagsgesellschaft mbH, pg 255
LIT Verlag, pg 258
Nusser Verlag, pg 269
Dr Ludwig Reichert Verlag, pg 278
Schillinger Verlag GmbH, pg 283
Siebenberg-Verlag, pg 286
Gerd Simon & Claudia Magiera, Verlagsbuero, pg 287
Rudolf G Smend, pg 287

Franz Steiner Verlag Wiesbaden GmbH, pg 289
Verlag Wissenschaft und Politik/Helker Pflug, pg 303
Wolfgang Arlt u Ute Schiller, pg 304

Hong Kong
Celeluck Co Ltd, pg 318
The Chinese University Press, pg 319
Chung Hwa Book Co (HK) Ltd, pg 319
Hong Kong Publishing Co Ltd, pg 320
Hong Kong University Press, pg 320
Joint Publishing (HK) Co Ltd, pg 320
Peace Book Co Ltd, pg 321
Research Centre for Translation, pg 321
South China Morning Post Ltd, pg 322
Yazhou Zhoukan Ltd, pg 322

India
Agam Kala Prakashan, pg 330
Asian Educational Services, pg 331
Book Faith India, pg 333
Chowkhamba Sanskrit Series Office, pg 335
Concept Publishing Co, pg 335
Cosmo Publications, pg 335
DK Printworld (P) Ltd, pg 336
Gyan Publishing House, pg 338
Inter-India Publications, pg 340
Lancer Publisher's & Distributors, pg 341
Mehta Publishers, pg 342
Minerva Associates (Publications) Pvt Ltd, pg 342
Munshiram Manoharlal Publishers Pvt Ltd, pg 343
Oxford & IBH Publishing Co Pvt Ltd, pg 345
Rahul Publishing House, pg 347
Reliance Publishing House, pg 347
SABDA, pg 348
Sage Publications India Pvt Ltd, pg 348
Somaiya Publications Pvt Ltd, pg 350
South Asian Publishers Pvt Ltd, pg 350
Spectrum Publications, pg 350
Sri Satguru Publications, pg 351
Sterling Publishers Pvt Ltd, pg 351

Indonesia
Auroa, pg 354
Mizan, pg 356
Yayasan Obor Indonesia, pg 357

Italy
Editrice Atanor SRL, pg 377
Herder Editrice e Libreria, pg 392
Il Saggiatore, pg 393
Editoriale Jaca Book SpA, pg 394
Jouvence, pg 394
Paideia Editrice, pg 402
Pontifico Istituto Orientale, pg 404

Japan
Dohosha Publishing Co Ltd, pg 416
Japan Publications Inc, pg 418
The Japan Times, pg 418
Keisuisha Publishing Company Ltd, pg 419
Kokusho Kankokai Co Ltd, pg 420
Rinsen Book Co Ltd, pg 424

Shibundo Co Ltd, pg 425
Sobun-Sha, pg 426
Toho Book Store, pg 427
Toho Shuppan, pg 427
Charles E Tuttle Publishing Co Inc, pg 428
United Nations University Press, pg 428
Yohan Shuppan, pg 429
Yushodo Co Ltd, pg 429

Democratic People's Republic of Korea
Foreign Languages Publishing House, pg 434
Grand People's Study House, pg 434

Republic of Korea
Hakgogjae Publishing Inc, pg 436
Hanul Publishing Co, pg 436
Oruem Publishing House, pg 439
Seogwangsa, pg 440

Luxembourg
Varkki Verghese, pg 448

Macau
Museu Maritimo, pg 448
Instituto Portugues Oriente, pg 448

Malaysia
S Abdul Majeed & Co, pg 451

Mauritius
Editions Capucines, pg 457

Mexico
El Colegio de Mexico AC, pg 459

Netherlands
APA (Academic Publishers Associated), pg 472
Brill Academic Publishers, pg 475
De Driehoek BV, pg 476
Hotei Publishing, pg 478
KITLV Press Royal Institute of Linguistics & Anthropology, pg 479
Oriental Press BV (APA), pg 482
The Pepin Press, pg 482
Philo Press-Van Heusden-Hissink & Co CV (APA), pg 482

New Zealand
Barkfire Press, pg 488
Graphic Educational Publications, pg 491

Pakistan
Centre for South Asian Studies, pg 506
Maqbool Academy, pg 508
Sang-e-Meel Publications, pg 509
Vanguard Books Ltd, pg 509

Philippines
Ateneo de Manila University Press, pg 512
De La Salle University, pg 513
New Day Publishers, pg 514
Our Lady of Manaoag Publisher, pg 514
UST Publishing House, pg 515

Poland
Wydawnictwa Uniwersytetu Warszawskiego, pg 521

Portugal
Gradiva-Publicacnoes Lda, pg 525
Edicoes Manuel Lencastre, pg 526

Russian Federation
Ladomir Publishing House, pg 539
Nauka Publishers, pg 540

Singapore
Aquanut Agencies Pte Ltd, pg 545
Archipelago Press, pg 545
Asiapac Books Pte Ltd, pg 545
Chopsons Pte Ltd, pg 545
Institute of Southeast Asian Studies, pg 546
Maruzen Asia (Pte) Ltd, pg 547
Select Books Pte Ltd, pg 548
Singapore University Press Pte Ltd, pg 548
Taylor & Francis Asia Pacific, pg 548

Slovakia
Slo Viet, pg 550

Spain
Ediciones Akal SA, pg 562
Ediciones del Oriente y del Mediterraneo, pg 585
Polifemo, Ediciones, pg 587

Sweden
Mezopotamya Publishing & Distribution, pg 604

Switzerland
Cockatoo Press (Schweiz), Thailand-Publikationen, pg 611
Office du Livre SA (Buchhaus AG), pg 620

Taiwan, Province of China
Asian Culture Co, pg 629
Echo Publishing Company Ltd, pg 629
Highlight Publishing Company Ltd, pg 630
Linking Publishing Company Ltd, pg 631
National Museum of History, pg 631
SMC Publishing Inc, pg 632
Torch of Wisdom, pg 632
Yee Wen Publishing Co Ltd, pg 632

Thailand
Silkworm Books, pg 635

United Kingdom
Aris & Phillips Ltd, pg 648
Ashmolean Museum Publications, pg 650
The Athlone Press Ltd, pg 650
Books for Europe Ltd, pg 657
British Museum Press, pg 660
Compendium Publishing, pg 670
The Eurospan Group, pg 680
Harvard University Press, pg 692
Marcham Books, pg 711
Adam Matthew Publications, pg 712
Mirabel Books Ltd, pg 715
Motilal (UK) Books of India, pg 715
The Octagon Press Ltd, pg 720
Reaktion Books Ltd, pg 733
Routledge Curzon, pg 736
Royal Institute of International Affairs, pg 736
Serindia Publications, pg 740

PUBLISHERS

Serpent's Tail Ltd, pg 740
Skoob Russell Square, pg 742
I B Tauris & Co Ltd, pg 747
Textile & Art Publications Ltd, pg 748
Yale University Press London, pg 759

ASTROLOGY, OCCULT

Argentina

Editorial Albatros SACl, pg 3
Editorial Caymi SACl, pg 4
Errepar SA, pg 5
EUDEBA (Editorial Universitaria de Buenos Aires), pg 6
Editorial Kier SAClFl, pg 7

Australia

Angel Publications, pg 11
Dynamo House P/L, pg 21
Gnostic Editions, pg 24
Hihorse Publishing Pty Ltd, pg 26
Thomas C Lothian Pty Ltd, pg 30
Social Club Books, pg 42
Unity Press, pg 46
Veritas Press, pg 46

Austria

E Perlinger Naturprodukte Handelsgesellschaft mbH, pg 57
Pinguin-Verlag, Pawlowski GmbH, pg 57
Verlag Carl Ueberreuter GmbH, pg 59
Dr Otfried Weise Verlag Tabula Smaragdina, pg 60

Azerbaijan

Sada, Literaturno-Izdatel'skij Centr, pg 61

Barbados

Business Tutors, pg 63

Belgium

Altina, pg 64
Marabout, pg 72
Parsifal BVBA, pg 72

Brazil

Editora Agora Ltda, pg 78
Livraria Francisco Alves Editora SA, pg 78
Editora Bertrand Brasil Ltda, pg 79
Edicon Editora e Consultorial Ltda, pg 81
Fundacao Cultural Avatar, pg 83
Editora Ground Ltda, pg 84
Hemus Editora Ltda, pg 85
Horus Editora Ltda, pg 85
Icone Editora Ltda, pg 85
Editora Kuarup Ltda, pg 86
Francisco J Laissue Livraria, pg 86
Editora Lidador Ltda, pg 86
Madras Editora, pg 87
Editora Nova Fronteira SA, pg 88
Livraria Pioneira Editora/Enio Matheus Guazzelli e Cia Ltd, pg 89
Totalidade Editora Ltda, pg 92
Triom Centro de Estudos Marina e Martin Hawey Editorial e Comercial Ltda, pg 92
Editora Vecchi SA, pg 93

Bulgaria

Antroposofsko Izdatelstvo Dimo R Daskalov OOD, pg 94
Aratron, IK, pg 94
Kibea Publishing Co, pg 96
Kralica MAB, pg 96
Sila & Zivot, pg 98
Sluntse Publishing House, pg 98

Chile

Ediciones Mil Hojas Ltda, pg 100

China

Qingdao Publishing House, pg 108

Colombia

RAM Editores, pg 113
Tercer Mundo Editores SA, pg 113

Czech Republic

Aventinum Nakladatelstvi, pg 123
Jiri Chvojka, pg 123
Vodnar, pg 129
Votobia sro, pg 129

Denmark

Bogan's Forlag, pg 130
Borgens Forlag A/S, pg 130

Estonia

Perioodika, pg 140
Sinisukk, pg 140

France

Editions Amrita SA, pg 147
Alain Brethe Editions, pg 152
Le Chariot, pg 154
CNRS Editions, pg 155
De Vecchi Editions SA, pg 158
Nouvelles Editions Debresse, pg 158
Editions Grancher, pg 166
Hachette Pratiques, pg 167
Harlequin SA, pg 167
Le Jour, Editeur, pg 170
Lacour-Olle, pg 171
Editions G P Maisonneuve et Larose, pg 174
Mercure de France SA, pg 176
Pardes, pg 179
Editions Saint-Michel SA, pg 183
Editions Sand et Tchou SA, pg 183

Germany

Aquamarin Verlag, pg 194
Arun-Verlag, pg 195
Otto Wilhelm Barth-Verlag KG, pg 198
Verlag Hermann Bauer KG, pg 199
Chiron-Verlag Reinhardt Stiehle, pg 210
Connection Medien GmbH, pg 211
Verlag Esoterische Philosophie GmbH, pg 224
EVT Energy Video Training & Verlag GmbH, pg 225
Extent Verlag und Service Wolfgang M Flamm, pg 225
Wilhelm Goldmann Verlag GmbH, pg 233
Heigl Verlag, Horst Edition, pg 239
Wilhelm Heyne Verlag, pg 240
AIG I Hilbinger Verlag GmbH, pg 241
F Hirthammer Verlag GmbH, pg 241
Verlag Peter Hoell, pg 241
Heinrich Hugendubel Verlag GmbH, pg 243
Verlag Kleine Schritte Ursula Dahm & Co, pg 249
Koenigsfurt Verlag, Evelin Burger et Johannes Fiebig, pg 251
Edition Octopus & Okeanos Presse, pg 269
Reichl Verlag Der Leuchter, pg 278
Dieter Ruggeberg Verlagsbuchhandlung, pg 280
Die Silberschnur Verlag GmbH, pg 287
Spieth-Verlag Verlag fuer Symbolforschung, pg 288
Thauros Verlag GmbH, pg 293
Verlag Clemens Zerling, pg 305

Greece

Chrysi Penna - Golden Pen Books, pg 309
Govostis Publishing SA, pg 311
Hestia-I D Hestia-Kollaros & Co Corporation, pg 311
Orfanidis Publications, pg 314

Hong Kong

Publications (Holdings) Ltd, pg 321

Hungary

Advent Kiado, pg 323

Iceland

Bokaforlag Birtingur, pg 327
Skjaldborg Ltd, pg 328

India

Asian Educational Services, pg 331
Chowkhamba Sanskrit Series Office, pg 335
DK Printworld (P) Ltd, pg 336
Gyan Publishing House, pg 338
Jaico Publishing House, pg 340
Munshiram Manoharlal Publishers Pvt Ltd, pg 343
Orient Paperbacks, pg 345
Parimal Prakashan, pg 345
Pustak Mahal, pg 346
Reliance Publishing House, pg 347
Somaiya Publications Pvt Ltd, pg 350
Sterling Publishers Pvt Ltd, pg 351

Italy

Adea Edizioni, pg 374
Arcanta Aries Gruppo Editoriale, pg 376
Arktos, pg 376
Gruppo Editoriale Armenia SpA, pg 376
Editrice Atanor SRL, pg 377
Crisalide, pg 383
Giovanni De Vecchi Editore SpA, pg 384
Edizioni Il Punto d'Incontro SAS, pg 386
Edizioni Mediterranee SRL, pg 387
Arnaldo Forni Editore SRL, pg 389
Ernesto Gremese Editore SRL, pg 391
Gremese International Srl, pg 391
Horus, pg 393
L'Airone Editrice, pg 395
Mundici & Zanetti srl, pg 400
Il Punto D Incontro, pg 404

Japan

Gakken Co Ltd, pg 416
Koseisha-Koseikaku Co Ltd, pg 420
Seibido Shuppan Company Ltd, pg 424

SUBJECT INDEX

Latvia

Alberts XII, pg 441
Nordik/Tapals Publishers Ltd, pg 442
Preses Nams, pg 442
Vieda, pg 442

Lithuania

AS Narbuto Leidykla (AS Narbutas' Publishers), pg 445

The Former Yugoslav Republic of Macedonia

Strk Publishing House, pg 449
Zumpres Publishing Firm, pg 449

Mexico

Centro Editorial Mexicano Osiris SA, pg 458
Ediciones CUPSA, Centro de Comunicacion Cultural CUPSA, AC, pg 459
Editorial Diana SA de CV, pg 459
Hoja Casa Editorial SA de CV, pg 462
Libra Editorial SA de CV, pg 463
Editorial Orion, pg 465
Pangea Editores, Sa de CV, pg 465
Sayrols Editorial SA de CV, pg 466
Ediciones Suromex SA, pg 467

Monaco

Les Editions du Rocher, pg 469

Netherlands

Ankh-Hermes BV, pg 472
BZZTOH Publishers, pg 475
Mirananda Publishers BV, pg 481
Semic Junior Press, pg 484
Servire BV Uitgevers, pg 484
Uitgeverij Het Spectrum BV, pg 484

New Zealand

Brookfield Press, pg 489
RSVP Publishing Company Ltd, pg 495

Portugal

Brasilia Editora (J Carvalho Branco), pg 523
Edicoes 70, Lda, pg 524
Editorial Estampa, Lda, pg 524
Edicoes Manuel Lencastre, pg 526
Nova Acropole, pg 527
Planeta Editora, LDA, pg 528
Editorial Presenca, pg 528
Editora Replicacao Lda, pg 529
Edicoes 70, pg 529
Vega-Publicacao e Distribuicao de Livros e Revistas, Lda, pg 530

Romania

Editura Dacia, pg 532
MAST Verlag, pg 534
Editura Minerva, pg 534
Vremea Publishers Ltd, pg 536

Russian Federation

CentrePolygraph Traders & Publishers Co, pg 537

Slovenia

Mladinska Knjiga International, pg 552
Zalozba Mihelac d o o, pg 552

897

SUBJECT INDEX — BOOK

South Africa
Bet-El Publishers, pg 553
Kima Global Publishers, pg 556

Spain
Editorial Astri SA, pg 564
Biblioteca de Autores Cristianos, pg 564
Editorial Barath SA, pg 565
Editorial EDAF SA, pg 571
Edicomunicacion SA, pg 572
Editorial Everest SA, pg 572
Etu Ediciones SL, pg 574
Mandala Ediciones, pg 581
Ediciones Martinez-Roca SA, pg 581
Munoz Moya Editor, pg 583
Noguer y Caralt Editores SA, pg 584
Nueva Acropolis, pg 584
Perea Ediciones, pg 586
Ediciones 29 - Libros Rio Nuevo, pg 594
Ediciones Urano, SA, pg 595

Sweden
Sjoestrands Foerlag, pg 606

Switzerland
Astrodata AG, pg 608
Govinda-Verlag, pg 615
Natura-Verlag Arlesheim, pg 619
Psychosophische Gesellschaft, pg 622
Rhein-Trio, Edition/Editions du Fou, pg 623
Sphinx Verlag AG, pg 625

United Republic of Tanzania
Kajura Publications, pg 633
Press & Publicity Centre Ltd, pg 634

Turkey
Alkim Kitapcilik-Yayimcilik, pg 638
Ruh ve Madde Yayinlari ve Saglik Hizmetleri AS, pg 641

Ukraine
ASK Ltd, pg 643

United Kingdom
Ashgrove Press, pg 650
BCA, pg 653
Blandford Publishing Ltd, pg 656
Bloomsbury Publishing PLC, pg 656
Capall Bann Publishing, pg 663
Marshall Cavendish Partworks Ltd, pg 665
Constable Publishers, pg 670
The C W Daniel Co Ltd, pg 673
Element Books Ltd, pg 678
Foulsham Publishers, pg 683
George Mann Publications, pg 687
HarperCollins Publishers, pg 692
Janus Publishing Company Ltd, pg 702
Lucis Press Ltd, pg 709
Mandrake of Oxford, pg 711
Kenneth Mason Publications Ltd, pg 712
Mirabel Books Ltd, pg 715
Piatkus Books, pg 727
Pomegranate Europe Ltd, pg 729
Prism Press Book Publishers Ltd, pg 730
Quarto Publishing plc, pg 731
Quartz Editions, pg 732
Random House UK Ltd, pg 733
Skoob Russell Square, pg 742
The Society of Metaphysicians Ltd, pg 743
Virgin Publishing Ltd, pg 753
White Eagle Publishing Trust, pg 755

Venezuela
Alfadil Ediciones, pg 761

Yugoslavia
Alfa-Narodna Knjiga, pg 764

ASTRONOMY

Albania
NL SH, pg 1

Brazil
Editora Lidador Ltda, pg 86
Editora Nova Fronteira SA, pg 88
Editora Scipione Ltda, pg 91

Bulgaria
Litera Prima, pg 96
Makros 2000 - Plovdiv, pg 96

Chile
Arrayan Editores, pg 99

China
Inner Mongolia Science & Technology Publishing House, pg 106
Jilin Science & Technology Publishing House, pg 106
Qingdao Publishing House, pg 108

Czech Republic
Mlada fronta, pg 126

France
Bookmaker, pg 151
EDP Sciences, pg 161
Editions Jacques Gabay, pg 165
Editions Jean Paul Gisserot, pg 166
Librairie Scientifique et Technique Albert Blanchard, pg 173
Editions Springer France, pg 186

Germany
Bettendorf'sche Verlagsanstalt GmbH, pg 202
BLV Verlagsgesellschaft mbH, pg 204
Columbus Verlag Paul Oestergaard GmbH, pg 211
Deutsche Verlags-Anstalt GmbH (DVA), pg 214
Deutscher Taschenbuch Verlag GmbH & Co KG (dtv), pg 215
Franz Ferzak World & Space Publications, pg 227
F A Herbig Verlagsbuchhandlung GmbH, pg 239
Anton Hiersemann, Verlag, pg 240
Franckh-Kosmos Verlags-GmbH & Co, pg 252
Springer-Verlag GmbH & Co KG, pg 288
Steiger Verlag, pg 289

Greece
Diavlos, pg 309

India
Chowkhamba Sanskrit Series Office, pg 335
Gyan Publishing House, pg 338
Heritage Publishers, pg 338
Rajendra Publishing House Pvt Ltd, pg 347
Reliance Publishing House, pg 347
Scientific Book Agency, pg 349

Italy
Il Castello srl, pg 380
Essegi, pg 388
Arnaldo Forni Editore SRL, pg 389
Editrice Massimo SAS di Crespi Cesare e C, pg 398
Leo S Olschki, pg 402
Editoriale Scienza, pg 407

Japan
Mita Press, Mita Industrial Co, Ltd, pg 421
Nippon Hoso Shuppan Kyokai (NHK Publishing), pg 422

The Former Yugoslav Republic of Macedonia
Zumpres Publishing Firm, pg 449

Malaysia
Federal Publications Sdn Bhd, pg 452

Mexico
Editorial Limusa SA de CV, pg 463
Organizacion Cultural LP SA de CV, pg 465
Pangea Editores, Sa de CV, pg 465
Ediciones Suromex SA, pg 467

Poland
Instytut Historii Nauki PAN, pg 516

Portugal
Constancia Editores, SA, pg 524
Dinalivro, pg 524
Gradiva-Publicacnoes Lda, pg 525
Impala, pg 525
Planeta Editora, LDA, pg 528

Romania
Editura Academiei Romane, pg 531

Russian Federation
Fizmatlit Publishing Co, pg 538
Izdatelstvo Mir, pg 540
Nauka Publishers, pg 540

Saudi Arabia
Dar Al-Shareff for Publishing & Distribution, pg 543

Slovenia
Zalozba Mihelac d o o, pg 552

Spain
Nueva Acropolis, pg 584

Switzerland
Verlag Harri Deutsch, pg 612

United Republic of Tanzania
Readit Books, pg 634

United Kingdom
The Erskine Press, pg 679
Grange Books PLC, pg 689
Institute of Physics Publishing, pg 700
Open University Worldwide, pg 721
Orpheus Books Ltd, pg 722
Philip's, pg 727
Springer-Verlag London Ltd, pg 744

Uruguay
EQ Opciones en Educacion, pg 760
A Monteverde y Cia SA, pg 760

Viet Nam
Science & Technics Publishing House, pg 763

AUTOMOTIVE

Argentina
Editorial Caymi SACI, pg 4

Australia
David Boyce Publishing, pg 16
CHOICE Magazine, pg 18
Graffiti Publications, pg 24
Gregory Kefalas Publishing, pg 29
McGraw-Hill Australia Pty Ltd, pg 32
OTEN (Open Training & Education Network), pg 36
Turton & Armstrong Publishers Pty Ltd, pg 45
Universal Press Pty Ltd, pg 46

Austria
Bohmann Druck und Verlag GmbH & Co KG, pg 50
Universitaetsverlag Wagner GmbH, pg 60

Belarus
Interdigets Publishing House, pg 63

Belgium
Uitgevery Gelbis NV, pg 68
Glenat Benelux SA, pg 69

China
China Machine Press (CMP), pg 103
China Materials Management Publishing House, pg 103
Jilin Science & Technology Publishing House, pg 106
National Defence Industry Press, pg 107
The People's Communications Publishing House, pg 107
Qingdao Publishing House, pg 108

Czech Republic
Cesky normalizacni institut, pg 127

Ecuador
SECAP, pg 137

Estonia
Mats Publishers Ltd, pg 140

France
ATP - Packager, pg 149
Editions Chiron, pg 154
Editions Delville, pg 158
EPA SA (Editions Presse Audiovisuel), pg 162

PUBLISHERS

Publi-Fusion, pg 182
Soline, pg 186
Editions Technip SA, pg 187
Editions Vilo SA, pg 189

Germany

ADAC Verlag GmBH, pg 191
Autovision Verlag Guther Co, pg 197
Verlag Wolfgang Bleiweis, pg 204
Delius, Klasing und Co, pg 213
Verlag Europa-Lehrmittel, Nourney, Vollmer GmbH & Co, pg 224
Alfons W Gentner Verlag GmbH & Co KG, pg 231
Heel Verlag GmbH, pg 238
Huss-Verlag GmbH, pg 244
Jahreszeiten-Verlag GmbH, pg 246
Kirschbaum Verlag GmbH, pg 249
Moby Dick Verlag, pg 264
Motorbuch-Verlag, pg 265
Paul Pietsch Verlage GmbH & Co, pg 273
Verlag Walter Podszun Burobedarf-Bucher Abt, pg 274
Transpress Verlagsgesellschaft mbH, pg 294
Vogel Medien GmbH & Co KG, pg 299

Greece

Kleidarithmos, pg 312
Orfanidis Publications, pg 314

India

Heritage Publishers, pg 338
Sita Publications, pg 350

Indonesia

PT Indira, pg 355
Karya Anda, CV, pg 356

Italy

Automobilia srl, pg 377
Editoriale Domus Spa, pg 385
Giorgio Nada Editore SRL, pg 400

Japan

Gakken Co Ltd, pg 416
Nigensha Publishing Co Ltd, pg 422
Seibido Shuppan Company Ltd, pg 424

Kenya

Heinemann Kenya Limited (EAEP), pg 431
Space Sellers Ltd, pg 433

Lebanon

Arab Scientific Publishers BP, pg 442

Mexico

Editorial Limusa SA de CV, pg 463
Sayrols Editorial SA de CV, pg 466
Sistemas Universales, SA, pg 467

New Zealand

GCL Publishing (1997) Ltd, pg 491

Russian Federation

FGUP Izdatelstvo Mashinostroenie, pg 538
Izdatelstvo Transport, pg 542

Spain

Editorial Dossat SA, pg 570
Marcombo SA de Boixareu Editores, pg 581

Sweden

Johnston & Streiffert Editions, pg 604

Switzerland

Verlag Bucheli, pg 610
Editions 24 Heures, pg 626

Taiwan, Province of China

Fuh-Wen Book Co, pg 630

United Kingdom

Ian Allan Publishing Ltd, pg 646
Amber Books Ltd, pg 646
Bay View Books Ltd, pg 652
BCA, pg 653
Books International, pg 657
Brooklands Books Ltd, pg 660
Compendium Publishing, pg 670
The Crowood Press Ltd, pg 672
The Economist Intelligence Unit, pg 677
ERA Technology Ltd, pg 679
Grange Books PLC, pg 689
Greenhill Books/Lionel Leventhal Ltd, pg 689
Haynes Publishing, pg 693
Ian Henry Publications Ltd, pg 695
Motor Racing Publications Ltd, pg 716
Octopus Publishing Group, pg 720
RAC Publishing, pg 732
Regency House Publishing Ltd, pg 734
Roadmaster Publishing, pg 735
Telegraph Books, pg 748
Veloce Publishing Ltd, pg 752
WIT Press, pg 757

Viet Nam

Science & Technics Publishing House, pg 763

Zimbabwe

Standards Association of Zimbabwe (SAZ), pg 769
Thomson Publications Zimbabwe (Pvt) Ltd, pg 769

BEHAVIORAL SCIENCES

Argentina

Polemos SA, pg 8

Australia

Allen & Unwin Pty Ltd, The Australian Newspaper, Vogel Breads, pg 11
Edward Arnold (Australia) Pty Ltd, pg 12
Artemis Publishing Pty Ltd, pg 12
Ausmed Publications Pty Ltd, pg 12
Australian Academic Press Pty Ltd, pg 13
Australian Institute of Family Studies (AIFS), pg 13
Kerri Hamer, pg 25
Macmillan Education Australia, pg 31
Mayne Publishing, pg 32
McGraw-Hill Australia Pty Ltd, pg 32
Mouse House Press, pg 34

Pearson Education Australia, pg 37
Jurriaan Plesman, pg 38
Stafford Books, pg 43
Wileman Publications, pg 47

Austria

WUV/Facultas Universitaetsverlag, pg 61

Bangladesh

Gatidhara, pg 62

Belgium

Campinia Media VZW, pg 65
Editions De Boeck-Larcier SA, pg 67
Marabout, pg 72

Brazil

Editora Alfa Omega Ltda, pg 78
ARTMED, pg 79
Editora Bertrand Brasil Ltda, pg 79
Editora Harbra Ltda, pg 84
Editora Logosofica, pg 86
MG Editores Associados Ltda, pg 88
Editora Objetiva Ltda, pg 88
Olho D'Agua Comercio e Servicos Editoriais Ltda, pg 88
Edit Palavra Magica, pg 89
Pearson Education Do Brasil, pg 89
Livraria Pioneira Editora/Enio Matheus Guazzelli e Cia Ltd, pg 89
Editora Revan Ltda, pg 90
Summus Editorial Ltda, pg 92
Jorge Zahar Editor, pg 93

Bulgaria

EA Publishing House, pg 95
WTU Todor Kableskov, pg 98

China

Anhui People's Publishing House, pg 102
Beijing Publishing House, pg 102
China Materials Management Publishing House, pg 103
Fudan University Press, pg 105
Lanzhou University Press, pg 107
The Publishing House of Shanghai University of Traditional Chinese Medicine, pg 108
Qingdao Publishing House, pg 108
Shandong University Press, pg 109

Colombia

Editorial Libros y Libres SA, pg 112

Costa Rica

Editorial Nacional de Salud y Seguridad Social Ednass, pg 116
Promesa, Ediciones, pg 116
Editorial de la Universidad de Costa Rica, pg 117

Denmark

Borgens Forlag A/S, pg 130
Tiderne Skifter Forlag A/S, pg 136

Egypt (Arab Republic of Egypt)

Dar El Shorouk, pg 138

Finland

Osuuskunta Vastapaino, pg 145
Ylipistopaino/Helsinki University Press, pg 145

SUBJECT INDEX

France

Adverbum SARL, pg 146
Autrement Editions, pg 149
Editions Saint-Michel SA, pg 183

Germany

Deutscher Taschenbuch Verlag GmbH & Co KG (dtv), pg 215
Landbuch-Verlagsgesellschaft mbH, pg 255
Rainar Nitzsche Verlag, pg 269
Osho Verlag GmbH, pg 271
Psychologie Verlags Union GmbH, pg 275
Springer-Verlag GmbH & Co KG, pg 288
WEKA Firmengruppe GmbH & Co KG, pg 301

Greece

Hestia-I D Hestia-Kollaros & Co Corporation, pg 311

Hong Kong

Hong Kong University Press, pg 320

India

Agricole Publishing Academy, pg 330
Concept Publishing Co, pg 335
Jaico Publishing House, pg 340
National Book Organization, pg 343
Omsons Publications, pg 345
Reliance Publishing House, pg 347
Sage Publications India Pvt Ltd, pg 348
Scientific Book Agency, pg 349
Somaiya Publications Pvt Ltd, pg 350
Sultan Chand & Sons Pvt Ltd, pg 351
A H Wheeler & Co Ltd, pg 353

Indonesia

Karya Anda, CV, pg 356

Ireland

On Stream Publications Ltd, pg 363

Israel

Ach Publishing House, pg 365
Bar Ilan University Press, pg 365
Dyonon/Papyrus Publishing House of the Tel-Aviv, pg 367
Freund Publishing House Ltd, pg 367
Schocken Publishing House Ltd, pg 372

Italy

Editore Armando Armando SRL, pg 376
Belforte Editore Libraio srl, pg 377
Giuseppe Bonanno Editore, pg 378
Edizioni Centro Studi Erickson, pg 381
Piero Gribaudi Editore, pg 391

Japan

Zeimukeiri-Kyokai, pg 429

Kenya

Nairobi University Press, pg 433

Republic of Korea

Chung Rim Publishing Co Ltd, pg 435

Latvia
Preses Nams, pg 442

The Former Yugoslav Republic of Macedonia
Strk Publishing House, pg 449
Zumpres Publishing Firm, pg 449

Martinique
George Lise-Huyghes des Etages, pg 456

Mexico
El Colegio de Michoacan A C, pg 460
Fondo de Cultura Economica, pg 461
Editorial Limusa SA de CV, pg 463
Sistemas Tecnicos de Edicion SA de CV, pg 467

Namibia
Desert Research Foundation of Namibia (DRFN), pg 471

Netherlands
Boom Uitgeverij, pg 474
Brill Academic Publishers, pg 475
Kluwer Academic Publishers, pg 479
Tilburg University Press, pg 485
Uitgeverij De Toorts, pg 485

Nigeria
JAD Publishers Ltd, pg 500

Norway
Universitetsforlaget, pg 505

Pakistan
National Book Foundation, pg 508

Philippines
Ateneo de Manila University Press, pg 512
New Day Publishers, pg 514
Our Lady of Manaoag Publisher, pg 514
Rex Bookstores & Publishers, pg 514

Portugal
Editora Classica, pg 523
Difusao Cultural, pg 524
Gradiva-Publicacnoes Lda, pg 525
Vega-Publicacao e Distribuicao de Livros e Revistas, Lda, pg 530

Puerto Rico
Libros-Ediciones Homines, pg 530

Saudi Arabia
Dar Al-Shareff for Publishing & Distribution, pg 543
King Saud University, pg 543

Senegal
CODESRIA (Council for the Development of Social Science Research in Africa), pg 544

Singapore
Aquanut Agencies Pte Ltd, pg 545

South Africa
Bet-El Publishers, pg 553
Human Sciences Research Council, pg 555
Kima Global Publishers, pg 556

Spain
Ediciones Akal SA, pg 562
Ediciones Alfar SA, pg 562
Mandala Ediciones, pg 581
Ediciones Morata SL, pg 583
Oikos-Tau SA Ediciones, pg 584
Editorial El Perpetuo Socorro, pg 586
Pulso Ediciones, SL, pg 588
Universidad de Oviedo Servicio de Publicaciones, pg 594

Sweden
Akademiforlaget Goteborgslitteratur, pg 600
Studentlitteratur AB, pg 606

Switzerland
Bergli Books AG, pg 609

Syrian Arab Republic
Damascus University Press, pg 628

Taiwan, Province of China
Chien Chen Bookstore Publishing Company Ltd, pg 629
Ho-Chi Book Publishing Co, pg 630
Laureate Book Co Ltd, pg 631

Turkey
Saray Medikal Yayin Tic Ltd Sti, pg 641

United Kingdom
Andromeda Oxford Ltd, pg 647
BILD Publications, pg 654
Blackwell Science Ltd, pg 656
BPS Books (British Psychological Society), pg 658
Constable Publishers, pg 670
Elsevier Science Ltd, pg 678
The Eurospan Group, pg 680
Extraordinary People Press, pg 681
Free Association Books Ltd, pg 684
W H Freeman & Co Ltd, pg 684
HarperCollins Publishers, pg 692
Harvard University Press, pg 692
Hawthorn Press, pg 693
JAI Press Ltd, pg 702
Jessica Kingsley Publishers, pg 704
MIT Press Ltd, pg 715
The Octagon Press Ltd, pg 720
Open University Press, pg 721
Sage Publications Ltd, pg 737
Sherwood Publishing, pg 741
Speechmark Publishing Ltd, pg 744

Viet Nam
Science & Technics Publishing House, pg 763

BIBLICAL STUDIES

Albania
NL SH, pg 1

Argentina
Argentine Bible Society, pg 3
San Pablo, pg 8

Australia
Aletheia Publishing, pg 11
Aquila Press, pg 11
Bible Society in Australia National Headquarters, pg 15
Bridgeway Publications, pg 16
Catholic Institute of Sydney, pg 17
Crossroad Distributors Pty Ltd, pg 19
New Creation Publications Ministries & Resource Centre, pg 34
St Pauls, pg 41
Vital Publications, pg 47

Belgium
Editions Gerard Blanchart & Cie SA, pg 65
Brepols Publishers NV, pg 65
Editions Lessius ASBL, pg 71
La Longue Vue, pg 71
Editions Lumen Vitae ASBL, pg 71
Uitgeverij Peeters Leuven (Belgie), pg 72

Brazil
Associacao Arvore da Vida, pg 79
Editora Cidade Nova Socieda de Movimentodos Focolari, pg 82
Editora Companhia das Letras/ Editora Schwarcz Ltda, pg 82
Editora Elevacao, pg 82
Imago Editora Importacao e Exportacao Ltda, pg 85
Koinonia Comunidade Edicoes Ltda (Editora Koinonia Ltda), pg 86
Edicoes Loyola SA, pg 87
Editora Mercuryo Ltda, pg 88
Editora Mundo Cristao, pg 88
Paulinas Editorial, pg 89
Paulus Editora, pg 89

Bulgaria
Antroposofsko Izdatelstvo Dimo R Daskalov OOD, pg 94
Nov Covek Publishing House, pg 97
Sila & Zivot, pg 98
Svetra Publishing House, pg 98

China
Qingdao Publishing House, pg 108

Colombia
Consejo Episcopal Latinoamericano Celam, pg 111

The Democratic Republic of the Congo
Facultes Catoliques de Kinshasa, pg 115

Cote d'Ivoire
Centre de Publications Evangeliques, pg 117

Croatia
Krscanska sadasnjost, pg 119
Znaci Vremena, Institut Za Istrazivanje Biblije, pg 120

Czech Republic
Karmelitanske Nakladatelstvi, pg 125

Denmark
Aarhus Universitetsforlag, pg 129
Lohses Forlag, pg 133

Scandinavia Publishing House, pg 135
Unitas Forlag, pg 136

Dominican Republic
Pontificia Universidad Catolica Madre y Maestra, pg 136

Estonia
Estonian Bible Society, pg 140

Finland
Foersamlingsfoerbundets Foerlags AB, pg 142
Herattaja-yhdistys Ry, pg 142
Lasten Keskus Oy, pg 143
Suomen pipliaseura RY, pg 144

France
Adverbum SARL, pg 146
Les Editions de l'Atelier SA, pg 148
Editions du Cerf, pg 153
Editions du Chalet, pg 154
Paul Geuthner Librairie Orientaliste, pg 166
P Lethielleux Editions, pg 172
Letouzey et Ane Sarl, pg 172
Editions Mediaspaul, pg 175
Peeters-France, pg 179
Les Editions de la Source Sarl, pg 186
Pierre Zech Editeur, pg 189

Germany
Aussaat Verlag, pg 197
Deutsche Bibelgesellschaft, pg 213
Echter Wurzburg Frankische Gesellschaftsdruckerei und Verlag GmbH, pg 220
Evangelische Verlagsanstalt GmbH, pg 225
Genius Verlag, pg 231
Guetersloher Verlagshaus Gerd Mohn, pg 235
Verlag Herder GmbH & Co KG, pg 239
Johannis, pg 246
Verlag Katholisches Bibelwerk GmbH, pg 248
Naumann & Goebel Verlagsgesellschaft mbH, pg 267
Verlag Neue Stadt GmbH, pg 267
Neuer Honos Verlag GmbH, pg 267
Oekumenischer Verlag Dr R-F Edel, pg 270
One Way Medien OHG, pg 270
Verlag Schnell und Steiner GmbH, pg 284
J F Steinkopf Verlag GmbH, pg 289
Sternberg-Verlag bei Ernst Franz, pg 290
Thauros Verlag GmbH, pg 293
Verein der Benediktiner zu Beuron-Beuroner Kunstverlag, pg 297
Verlag und Studio fuer Hoerbuchproduktionen, pg 298
Friedrich Wittig Verlag GmbH, pg 303

Ghana
Asempa Publishers, pg 306
Ghana Institute of Linguistics Literacy & Bible Translation (GILLBT), pg 307
World Literature Project, pg 308

PUBLISHERS

Greece
Alamo Hellas, pg 308
Apostoliki Diakonia tis Ekklisias tis Hellados, pg 309
Hestia-I D Hestia-Kollaros & Co Corporation, pg 311

Hong Kong
Christian Communications Ltd, pg 319
Federal Publications Ltd, pg 319
Philopsychy Press, pg 321

Hungary
Advent Kiado, pg 323

India
Dolphin Publications, pg 336
Indian Society for Promoting Christian Knowledge (ISPCK), pg 339
Satprakashan Sanchar Kendra, pg 349

Indonesia
Auroa, pg 354
Penerbit Nusa Indah, pg 356

Ireland
Cathedral Books Ltd, pg 359

Israel
Bar Ilan University Press, pg 365
The Bialik Institute, pg 365
Breslov Research Institute, pg 366
DAT Publications, pg 366
Gefen Publishing House Ltd, pg 367
Haifa University Press, pg 368
Hakibbutz Hameuchad Publishing House Ltd, pg 368
Israel Exploration Society, pg 368
Koren Publishers Jerusalem Ltd, pg 369
Open University of Israel, pg 371
Rolnik Publishers, pg 371
Rubin Mass Ltd, pg 371
Sadan Publishing Ltd, pg 372
Terra Sancta Arts, pg 373
Urim Publications, pg 373

Italy
Edizioni Cantagalli, pg 379
Centro Biblico, pg 380
Citta Nuova Editrice, pg 382
Cittadella Editrice, pg 382
Claudiana Editrice, pg 382
Nuova Coletti Editore Roma, pg 382
Edizioni Dehoniane Bologna (EDB), pg 384
Edizioni del Centro, pg 384
Elle Di Ci - Libreria Dottrina Cristiana, pg 388
Piero Gribaudi Editore, pg 391
In Dialogo, pg 393
Editrice LAS, pg 395
Lubrina Editore Srl, pg 397
Macro Edizioni, pg 397
Casa Editrice Marietti SpA, pg 397
Editrice Massimo SAS di Crespi Cesare e C, pg 398
Leo S Olschki, pg 402
Paideia Editrice, pg 402
Edizioni Piemme SpA, pg 403
Pontificio Istituto Orientale, pg 404
Editrice Queriniana, pg 404
Edizioni Segno SRL, pg 407
Edizioni del Teresianum, pg 409
Editrice Uomini Nuovi, pg 410

Urbaniana University Press, pg 410
Vivere In SRL, pg 411
Voce della Bibbia, pg 412

Japan
Sobun-Sha, pg 426

Kenya
Gaba Publications Amecea, Pastoral Institute, pg 431
Paulines Publications-Africa, pg 433
Shirikon Publishers, pg 433

Democratic People's Republic of Korea
Grand People's Study House, pg 434

Republic of Korea
St Pauls, pg 439

Latvia
Patmos, pg 442
Spriditis Publishers, pg 442

Lebanon
Darl el-Machreq Sarl, pg 443

The Former Yugoslav Republic of Macedonia
Zumpres Publishing Firm, pg 449

Madagascar
Maison d'Edition Protestante ANTSO, pg 450

Malawi
Popular Publications, pg 451

Malta
Media Centre, pg 456

Mexico
Ediciones CUPSA, Centro de Comunicacion Cultural CUPSA, AC, pg 459
Editorial Jus SA de CV, pg 462
Ediciones Promesa, SA de CV, pg 466

Netherlands
Buijten en Schipperheijn BV Drukkerij en Uitg Mij v/h, pg 475
Uitgeverij G F Callenbach BV, pg 475
Katholieke Bijbelstichting, pg 479
Philo Press-Van Heusden-Hissink & Co CV (APA), pg 482
Tilburg University Press, pg 485

New Zealand
Church Mouse Press, pg 490
Outrigger Publishers, pg 494

Nigeria
Vantage Publishers International Ltd, pg 502

Papua New Guinea
Kristen Pres, pg 510

Philippines
Claretian Communications Inc, pg 513
Communication Foundation for Asia Media Group (CFAMG), pg 513
New Day Publishers, pg 514
Our Lady of Manaoag Publisher, pg 514
Philippine Baptist Mission SBC FMB Church Growth International, pg 514
UST Publishing House, pg 515

Poland
Drukarnia I Ksiegarnia Swietego Wojciecha, Dziat Wydawniczy, pg 516
Instytut Wydawniczy Pax, Inco-Veritas, pg 517
Katolicki Uniwersytet Wydawniczo-Redakcja, pg 517
Pallottinum Wydawnictwo Stowarzyszenia Apostolstwa Katolickiego, pg 518
Vocatio Publishing House, pg 520

Portugal
Paulinas, pg 528
Planeta Editora, LDA, pg 528

Puerto Rico
Publicaciones Voz de Gracia, pg 531

Romania
Editura Excelsior, pg 533
Hasefer, pg 533

Russian Federation
N E Bauman Moscow State Technical University Publishers, pg 537
St Andrew's Biblical Theological College, pg 541

Singapore
Tecman Bible House, pg 549

Slovenia
Zalozba Mihelac d o o, pg 552

South Africa
Bet-El Publishers, pg 553
Bible Society of South Africa, pg 553
Educum Publishers Ltd, pg 554
HarperCollins Religious, pg 554
Institute for Reformational Studies CHE, pg 555

Spain
Central Catequistica Salesiana (CCS), pg 567
Editora Comercial de Publicaciones, pg 568
Creaciones Monar Editorial, pg 569
Ediciones Cristiandad, pg 569
Espanola Desclee De Brouwer SA, pg 569
Ediciones El Almendro de Cordoba, pg 571
Editorial Peregrino SL, pg 586
Editorial El Perpetuo Socorro, pg 586
Editorial Revista Agustiniana, pg 589
Ediciones San Pio X, pg 589
Ediciones Sigueme SA, pg 590
Editorial Verbo Divino, pg 595

SUBJECT INDEX

Sweden
Bokforlaget Nya Doxa AB, pg 605

Switzerland
Beroa-Verlag, pg 609
Jordanverlag AG, pg 616
Jugend mit einer Mission Verlag, pg 616
Kanisius Verlag, pg 616
Kranich-Verlag, Dres AG & H R Bosch-Gwalter, pg 617
La Maison de la Bible, pg 618

Taiwan, Province of China
Campus Evangelical Fellowship, Literature Department, pg 629

United Republic of Tanzania
Central Tanganyika Press, pg 633
Emmaus Bible School, pg 633
Kanisa la Biblia Publishers (KLB), pg 633

Ukraine
ASK Ltd, pg 643

United Kingdom
Bible Reading Fellowship, pg 654
Bible Society, pg 654
Bryntirion Press, pg 661
Cambridge University Press, pg 662
Cassell & Co, pg 664
Christian Education, pg 667
James Clarke & Co Ltd, pg 668
CTBI Publications, pg 672
Cyhoeddiadau'r Gair, pg 673
Darton, Longman & Todd Ltd, pg 674
Epworth Press, pg 679
The Eurospan Group, pg 680
Evangelical Press & Services Ltd, pg 680
The Foundational Book Company for the John W Doorly Trust, pg 683
HarperCollins Publishers, pg 692
Hodder & Stoughton Educational, pg 696
Lion Publishing PLC, pg 708
The Lutterworth Press, pg 709
Marcham Books, pg 711
McCrimmon Publishing Co Ltd, pg 712
Methodist Publishing House, pg 714
Monarch Books, pg 715
Moorley's Print & Publishing Ltd, pg 715
SCM Press, pg 739
Scripture Union, pg 740
Sheffield Academic Press Ltd, pg 741
The Society for Promoting Christian Knowledge (SPCK), pg 743
Tern Press, pg 748
University of Wales Press, pg 751
Wild Goose Publications, pg 756

Zimbabwe
Christian Audio-Visual Action (CAVA), pg 768
College Press Publishers (Pvt) Ltd, pg 768

BIOGRAPHY

Albania
Botimpex Publications Import-Export Agency, pg 1
NL SH, pg 1

SUBJECT INDEX

Algeria
Enterprise Nationale du Livre (ENAL), pg 2

Argentina
Editorial Acme SA, pg 3
Centro Editor de America Latina SA, pg 4
Editorial Claridad SA, pg 4
Editorial Ciudad Nueva de la Sefoma, pg 5
Emece Editores SA, pg 5
Ediciones de la Flor SRL, pg 6
Editorial Losada SA, pg 7
Editorial Planeta Argentina SAIC, pg 8
Quetzal-Domingo Cortizo, pg 8
Editorial Sudamericana SA, pg 9
Theoria SRL Distribuidora y Editora, pg 9
Javier Vergara Editor SA, pg 9

Australia
Aboriginal Studies Press, pg 10
Access Press, pg 10
Artemis Publishing Pty Ltd, pg 12
Athena Press, pg 12
R G Bahnsen, pg 14
Bernal Publishing, pg 14
Boolarong Press, pg 16
Louis Braille Audio, pg 16
Casket Publications, pg 17
Church Archivists Press, pg 18
Cornford Press, pg 19
Crawford House Publishing, pg 19
Emperor Publishing, pg 22
Fremantle Arts Centre Press, pg 23
Ginninderra Press, pg 24
Hale & Iremonger Pty Ltd, pg 24
Histec Publications, pg 26
Hyland House Publishing Pty Ltd, pg 27
The Images Publishing Group Pty Ltd, pg 27
Indra Publishing, pg 27
Institute of Aboriginal Development (IAD Press), pg 28
Kangaroo Press, pg 29
Little Red Apple Publishing, pg 30
Lowden Publishing Co, pg 31
Lucasville Press, pg 31
Magabala Books Aboriginal Corporation, pg 31
Melbourne University Press, pg 33
Mulini Press, pg 34
Ocean Press, pg 35
Ollif Publishing, pg 35
Outback Books - CQU Press, pg 36
Pan Macmillan Australia Pty Ltd, pg 36
Penguin Books Australia Ltd, pg 37
Pinevale Publications, pg 38
The Polding Press, pg 38
Quakers Hill Press, pg 39
Ruskin Rowe Press, pg 41
St Pauls, pg 41
Single X Publications, pg 42
Spectrum Publications, pg 43
State Library of NSW Press, pg 43
The Text Publishing Company Pty Ltd, pg 44
Transpareon Press, pg 45
Turton & Armstrong Publishers Pty Ltd, pg 45
University of New South Wales Press Ltd, pg 46
University of Queensland Press, pg 46
University of Western Australia Press, pg 46
Vista Publications, pg 47

Austria
Akademische Druck-u Verlagsanstalt Dr Paul Struzl GmbH, pg 49
Astor-Verlag, Willibald Schlager, pg 49
Christian Brandstatter Verlagsgesellschaft GmbH, pg 50
Docker Verlag GmbH & Co KG, pg 51
Verlag Lynkeus/H Hakel Gesellschaft, pg 52
Haymon-Verlag GesmbH, pg 52
Johannes Heyn, Gert und Volkmar Zechner, pg 52
Milena Verlag, pg 55
Paul Neff Verlag KG, pg 55
Verlag Neues Leben, pg 55
Niederosterreichisches Pressehaus Druck- und Verlagsgesellschaft mbH, pg 55
Verlag der Oesterreichischen Akademie der Wissenschaften (OEAW), pg 56
Promedia Verlagsges mbH, pg 57
Verlag Styria, pg 59
Edition Tau u Tau Type Druck Verlags-und Handels GmbH, pg 59
Verlag Carl Ueberreuter GmbH, pg 59
Wieser Verlag, pg 61
Zirkular - Verlag der Dokumentationsstelle fuer neuere oesterreichische Literatur, pg 61
Paul Zsolnay Verlag GmbH, pg 61

Bangladesh
The University Press Ltd, pg 62

Belarus
Belaruskaya Encyklapedyya, pg 63
Interdigets Publishing House, pg 63

Belgium
Centre Aequatoria, pg 64
Libraire Ancienne Noel Anselot, pg 64
Maison d'Editions Baha'ies ASBL, pg 64
Centre d'Action Laique, pg 66
Coda, pg 66
Le Cri Editions, pg 67
Editions Delta SA, pg 67
EPO Publishers, Printers, Booksellers, pg 68
Editions Labor, pg 70
Uitgeverij Lannoo NV, pg 70
Claude Lefrancq Editeur, pg 71
Editions Lessius ASBL, pg 71
Standaard Uitgeverij, pg 74
Uitgeverij De Garve, pg 75
Uitgevery Scoop Infotex NV, pg 75
Zuid En Noord VZW, pg 76

Brazil
AGIR S/A Editora, pg 78
Editora Alfa Omega Ltda, pg 78
Ars Poetica Editora Ltda, pg 79
Artes e Oficios Editora Ltda, pg 79
Editora Bertrand Brasil Ltda, pg 79
Ediouro Publicacoes, SA, pg 81
Editora Companhia das Letras/Editora Schwarcz Ltda, pg 82
Editora Elevacao, pg 82
Companhia Editora Forense, pg 82
Editora Forense, pg 83
Fundacao Cultural Avatar, pg 83
Global Editora e Distribuidora Ltda, pg 84
Editora Globo SA, pg 84
Editora Harbra Ltda, pg 84
Icone Editora Ltda, pg 85
Imago Editora Importacao e Exportacao Ltda, pg 85
LDA Editores Ltda, pg 86
Livraria Nobel S/A, pg 86
Editora Marco Zero Ltda, pg 87
Editora Mercuryo Ltda, pg 88
Editora Mundo Cristao, pg 88
Editora Nova Alexandria Ltda, pg 88
Editora Nova Fronteira SA, pg 88
Editora Objetiva Ltda, pg 88
Pallas Editora e Distribuidora Ltda, pg 89
Paulinas Editorial, pg 89
Distribuidora Record de Servicos de Imprensa SA, pg 90
Editora Revan Ltda, pg 90
Editora Rocco Ltda, pg 91
Spala Editora Ltda, pg 92
Editora Vecchi SA, pg 93
Jorge Zahar Editor, pg 93

Bulgaria
EA Publishing House, pg 95
Publishing House Hristo Botev, pg 96
Kibea Publishing Co, pg 96
Makros 2000 - Plovdiv, pg 96
Musica Publishing House Ltd, pg 96
Pet Plus, pg 97
Reporter, pg 97
Sluntse Publishing House, pg 98
Trud - Izd kasta, pg 98
Ivan Vazov Publishing House, pg 98

Chile
Arrayan Editores, pg 99
Ediciones Bat, pg 99
Pehuen Editores Ltda, pg 101

China
Beijing Publishing House, pg 102
China Film Press, pg 103
China Ocean Press, pg 103
Foreign Languages Press, pg 105
Fudan University Press, pg 105
Jilin Science & Technology Publishing House, pg 106
Kunlun Publishing House, pg 107
Nanjing University Press, pg 107
People's Fine Arts Publishing House, pg 108
Qingdao Publishing House, pg 108
SDX (Shenghuo-Dushu-Xinzhi) Joint Publishing Co, pg 108
Shanghai Fine Arts Publishers, pg 109
World Affairs Press, pg 110
Xinhua Publishing House, pg 110

Colombia
Editorial Oveja Negra, pg 113

The Democratic Republic of the Congo
Centre Protestant d'Editions et de Diffusion (CEDI), pg 115
Presses Universitaires du Zaiire (PUZ), pg 115

Costa Rica
Promesa, Ediciones, pg 116

Cote d'Ivoire
Centre d'Edition et de Diffusion Africaines, pg 117
Universite d' Abidjan, pg 118
Heritage Publishing Co, pg 118

Croatia
Graficki zavod Hrvatske, pg 118
Nakladni zavod Matice hrvatske, pg 119
Otokar Kersovani, pg 120
Skolska Knjiga, pg 120

Cuba
Holguin, Ediciones, pg 121
Editora Politica, pg 121

Cyprus
AndreouChr- Publishers, pg 122

Czech Republic
Atlantis sro, pg 123
Cesky spisovatel, pg 123
Columbus, pg 123
Doplnek, pg 124
Jota, pg 125
Jan Kanzelsberger, pg 125
Karmelitanske Nakladatelstvi, pg 125
Knihovna A Tiskarna Pro Nevidome, pg 125
Melantrich, pg 126
Mlada fronta, pg 126
NLN, Ltd The Lidove noviny Publishing House, pg 127
Odeon, nakladatelstvi krasne literatury a umeni, pg 127
Nakladatelstvi a vydavatelstvi Panorama, pg 127
Paseka, pg 127
Prostor, Ltd, pg 128
Vitalis SRO, pg 129
Votobia sro, pg 129

Denmark
Aschehoug Dansk Forlag A/S, pg 130
Dansk Historisk Handbogsforlag ApS, pg 130
Christian Ejlers' Forlag aps, pg 131
Grevas Forlag, pg 132
Gyldendalske Boghandel - Nordisk Forlag A/S, pg 132
Forlaget Hovedland, pg 133
Nyt Nordisk Forlag Arnold Busck A/S, pg 134
Scandinavia Publishing House, pg 135
Det Schonbergske Forlag, pg 135
Unitas Forlag, pg 136

Dominican Republic
Pontificia Universidad Catolica Madre y Maestra, pg 136

Ecuador
CIESPAL (Centro Internacional de Estudios Superiores de Comunicacion para America Latina), pg 137
Corporacion Editora Nacional, pg 137

Egypt (Arab Republic of Egypt)
Dar El Shorouk, pg 138
Dar El Shorouk Publishing & Distributing House, pg 138
Middle East Book Centre, pg 139

El Salvador
Clasicos Roxsil Editorial SA de CV, pg 139

PUBLISHERS

SUBJECT INDEX

Estonia
Oue Eesti Raamat, pg 139
Estonian Encyclopaedia Publishers Ltd, pg 140
Kunst Publishers Ltd, pg 140
Olion Publishers, pg 140
Sinisukk, pg 140

Finland
Recallmed Oy, pg 144
Schildts Foerlagsaktiebolag, pg 144
Soederstroem et Co Foerlagsaktiebolag, pg 144

France
Academie Nationale de Reims, pg 145
Editions Actes Sud, pg 146
ADPF Publications, pg 146
Editions Albin Michel, pg 146
Alsatia SA, pg 146
ALTESS Editions Argel, pg 146
L'Amitie par le Livre, pg 147
Edition Anthese, pg 147
L'Arche Editeur, pg 147
L'Archipel, pg 148
Editions de l'Armancon, pg 148
Les Editions de l'Atelier SA, pg 148
Editions Balland, pg 149
Beauchesne Editeur, pg 150
Editions Belfond, pg 150
Editions Andre Bonne, pg 151
Editions Buchet/Chastel, pg 152
Editions Calmann-Levy SA, pg 152
Editions Canope, pg 152
Editions Champ Vallon, pg 154
Corsaire Editions, pg 156
Editions Criterion, pg 157
Culture et Bibliotheque pour Tous, pg 157
Les Dossiers d'Aquitaine, pg 160
Edition1, pg 161
Librairie Artheme Fayard, pg 163
Des Femmes, pg 164
Editions Gallimard, pg 165
Paul Geuthner Librairie Orientaliste, pg 166
Editions Jean Paul Gisserot, pg 166
Librairie Guenegaud Sarl, pg 167
Hachette Pratiques, pg 167
Editions Herault, pg 168
Pierre Horay Editeur, pg 168
Indigo & Cote-Femmes Editions, pg 169
Kailash Editions, pg 171
Editions Michel Lafon SA, pg 171
Letouzey et Ane Sarl, pg 172
Le Livre de Poche-L G F (Librairie Generale Francaise), pg 173
Editions Lyonnaises d'Art et d'Histoire, pg 174
Editions Medianes, pg 175
Mercure de France SA, pg 176
Nil Editions, pg 177
Noir Sur Blanc, pg 177
Editions Odile Jacob, pg 178
Editions Payot & Rivages, pg 179
Editions Jean Picollec, pg 179
Editions Christian Pirot, pg 180
Presses de la Cite, pg 180
Presses de la Renaissance, pg 180
Presses Universitaires de France (PUF), pg 181
Editions Pygmalion - Gerard Watelet, pg 182
Les Editions du Sagittaire, pg 183
Editions Sand et Tchou SA, pg 183
Nouvelles Editions Seguier, pg 184
Editions de Septembre, pg 184
Service Technique pour l'Education, pg 185
Editions du Seuil, pg 185
Sofradif Editions Philippe Auzou, pg 185
Somogy editions d'art, pg 186
Editions Stock, pg 186
Les Editions de la Table Ronde, pg 187
Editions Tiresias Michel Reynaud, pg 188
La Vague Verte, pg 188

French Polynesia
Scoop/Au Vent des Iles, pg 190

Germany
Asclepios Edition Lothar Baus, pg 196
Bechtle Graphische Betriebe und Verlagsgesellschaft mbH und Co KG, pg 200
Beleke KG Verlag, pg 200
Bergstadtverlag Wilhelm Gottlieb Korn GmbH Wuerzburg, pg 200
C Bertelsmann Verlag GmbH, pg 201
Bertelsmann Lexikon Verlag GmbH, pg 201
Blanvalet VerlagGmbH, pg 204
Verlag Wolfgang Bleiweis, pg 204
Brandenburgisches Verlagshaus in der Dornier Medienholding GmbH, pg 206
R Brockhaus Verlag, pg 206
Hans Christians Druckerei und Verlag GmbH & Co, pg 210
Claassen Verlag GmbH, pg 210
CMA Edition, pg 211
Deutsche Verlags-Anstalt GmbH (DVA), pg 214
Deutscher Taschenbuch Verlag GmbH & Co KG (dtv), pg 215
Edition Dia, pg 216
Eugen Diederichs Verlag GmbH & Co KG, pg 216
Maximilian Dietrich Verlag, pg 216
Dietz Verlag Berlin GmbH, pg 217
Edition Diskord, pg 217
Drei Ulmen Verlag GmbH, pg 218
Droemersche Verlagsanstalt Th Knaur Nachfolger GmbH & Co, pg 218
Karl Elser Druck GmbH, pg 218
Duncker und Humblot GmbH, pg 219
Edition Klaus Blahak Dr Fredric Kroll, pg 220
Egmont vgs verlagsgesellschaft mbH, pg 221
Ehrenwirth Verlag GmbH, pg 221
Engelhorn Verlag, pg 222
Ernst Kabel Verlag GmbH, pg 223
Europa Verlag GmbH, pg 224
Europaeische Verlagsanstalt GmbH & Rotbuch Verlag GmbH & Co KG, pg 225
Evangelische Verlagsanstalt GmbH, pg 225
Fischer Taschenbuch Verlag GmbH, pg 228
FVA-Frankfurter Verlagsanstalt GmbH, pg 229
Franz-Sales-Verlag, pg 229
Verlag Freies Geistesleben, pg 230
Gatzanis Verlags GmbH, pg 231
Genius Verlag, pg 231
Verlagsgesellschaft R Gloess & Co, pg 233
Wilhelm Goldmann Verlag GmbH, pg 233
Grabert-Verlag, pg 233
Brigitte Grabitz - ikoo Buchverlag, pg 233
Guetersloher Verlagshaus Gerd Mohn, pg 235
von Hase & Koehler Verlag KG, pg 238
Edition Hentrich Druck & Verlag Gebr Hentrich und Tank GmbH & Co KG, pg 239
F A Herbig Verlagsbuchhandlung GmbH, pg 239
Erika Heydick Sax-Verlag Beucha, pg 240
Wilhelm Heyne Verlag, pg 240
Anton Hiersemann, Verlag, pg 240
Hoffmann und Campe Verlag GmbH, pg 242
Hohenrain-Verlag GmbH, pg 242
ludicium Verlag GmbH, pg 245
J Ch Mellinger Verlag GmbH, pg 246
JKL Publikationen GmbH, pg 246
Gustav Kiepenheuer Verlag GmbH, pg 249
Verlag Kiepenheuer und Witsch GmbH & Co KG, pg 249
Kindler Verlag GmbH, pg 249
Verlag Kleine Schritte Ursula Dahm & Co, pg 249
Albrecht Knaus Verlag GmbH, pg 250
Knesebeck Verlag, pg 250
K F Koehler Verlag, pg 251
Koehler und Amelang Verlagsgesellschaft mbH, pg 251
Anton H Konrad Verlag, pg 252
Karin Kramer Verlag, pg 253
Verlag Ernst Kuhn, pg 254
Dr Gisela Lermann, pg 257
Liebenzeller Mission, GmbH, Abt. Verlag, pg 258
Christoph Links Verlag - LinksDruck GmbH, pg 258
Gustav Luebbe Verlag, pg 259
Verlagsgruppe Luebbe GmbH & Co KG, pg 259
Matthias-Gruenewald-Verlag GmbH, pg 261
Medien-Verlag Bernhard Gregor GmbH, pg 262
Merlin Verlag Andreas Meyer Verlags GmbH und Co KG, pg 263
Militzke Verlag, pg 264
Miranda-Verlag Stefan Ehlert, pg 264
Monia Verlag, pg 265
Munzinger-Archiv GmbH Archiv fuer publizistische Arbeit, pg 266
Musikantiquariat und Dr Hans Schneider Verlag GmbH, pg 266
Muster-Schmidt Verlag, pg 266
Edition Nautilus Verlag, pg 267
Verlag Neue Stadt GmbH, pg 267
Verlag Neues Leben GmbH, pg 268
Neuthor - Verlag, pg 268
Nicolaische Verlagsbuchhandlung Beuermann GmbH, pg 268
nymphenburger, pg 269
Georg Olms Verlag AG, pg 270
Oreos Verlag, pg 270
Pahl-Rugenstein Verlag Nachfolger-GmbH, pg 271
Pal Verlagsgesellschaft mbH, pg 271
Pfalzische Verlagsanstalt GmbH, pg 272
Piper Verlag GmbH, pg 274
Propylaeen Verlag, Zweigniederlassung Berlin der Ullstein Buchverlage GmbH, pg 275
Verlag Friedrich Pustet GmbH & Co Kg, pg 276
Quell Verlag, pg 276
Quintessenz Verlags-GmbH, pg 276
Reclam Verlag Leipzig, pg 277
E Reinhold Verlag, pg 278
Eugen Salzer-Verlag GmbH & Co KG, pg 281
Verlag der Sankt-Johannis-Druckerei C Schweickhardt, pg 281
K G Saur Verlag GmbH, A Gale/Thomson Learning Company, pg 282
Verlag Schnell und Steiner GmbH, pg 284
Schoeffling & Co, pg 284
Ferdinand Schoeningh Verlag GmbH, pg 284
Schott Musik International GmbH & Co KG, pg 284
Schueren Verlag GmbH, pg 285
Verlag Schulte und Gerth GmbH & Co KG, pg 285
Siedler Verlag, pg 286
Sonnentanz-Verlag Roland Kron, pg 287
Springer-Verlag GmbH & Co KG, pg 288
Stapp Verlag Wolfgang Stapp, pg 288
C A Starke Verlag, pg 289
Steidl Verlag, pg 289
Stern-Verlag Janssen & Co, pg 290
Sternberg-Verlag bei Ernst Franz, pg 290
Steyler Verlag, pg 290
Suedverlag GmbH, pg 291
Suhrkamp Verlag, pg 291
Thauros Verlag GmbH, pg 293
Toleranz Verlag, Nielsen Frederic W, pg 294
Trotzdem-Verlags Genossenschaft eG, pg 295
Tuduv Verlagsgesellschaft mbH, pg 295
Ullstein Heyne List GmbH & Co KG, pg 295
Edition Curt Visel, pg 298
Weber Zucht & Co, pg 300
Wichern Verlag, pg 302
Verlag Wissenschaft und Politik/Helker Pflug, pg 303
Das Wunderhorn Verlag GmbH, pg 304
Wunderlich Verlag, pg 304
Verlag Clemens Zerling, pg 305

Ghana
Africa Christian Press, pg 306
Asempa Publishers, pg 306
Bureau of Ghana Languages, pg 306
Ghana Publishing Corporation, pg 307
Waterville Publishing House, pg 308

Greece
D I Arsenidis Publications, pg 309
Dorikos Publishing House, pg 310
Govostis Publishing SA, pg 311
Denise Harvey, pg 311
Hestia-I D Hestia-Kollaros & Co Corporation, pg 311
Ianos, pg 311
Irini Publishing House - Vassilis G Katsikeas SA, pg 311
Knossos Publications, pg 312
Minoas SA, pg 313
Odysseas Publications Ltd, pg 313
Patakis Publishers, pg 314
Vlassis, pg 316

903

Hong Kong
Hong Kong University Press, pg 320
Ming Pao Publications Ltd, pg 321

Hungary
Europa Konyvkiado, pg 323
Zenemukiado Vallalat, pg 327

Iceland
Almenna Bokafelagid, pg 327
Bokautgafan Orn og Orlygur ehf, pg 327
Frodi Ltd, pg 328
Skjaldborg Ltd, pg 328

India
Ananda Publishers Pvt Ltd, pg 330
APH Publishing Corp, pg 331
Asian Educational Services, pg 331
The Bangalore Printing & Publishing Co Ltd, pg 332
Bharatiya Vidya Bhavan, pg 333
Chowkhamba Sanskrit Series Office, pg 335
Disha Prakashan, pg 336
Enkay Publishers Pvt Ltd, pg 336
Geeta Prakasham, pg 337
Gyan Publishing House, pg 338
HarperCollins Publishers India Pty Ltd, pg 338
Heritage Publishers, pg 338
Hind Pocket Books Private Ltd, pg 338
Indian Society for Promoting Christian Knowledge (ISPCK), pg 339
Intertrade Publications, pg 340
Islamic Publishing House, pg 340
Jaico Publishing House, pg 340
Kairali Children's Book Trust, pg 340
Kairalee Mudralayam, pg 341
Kali For Women, pg 341
Kitab Ghar, pg 341
Sri Ramakrishna Math, pg 342
Ministry of Information & Broadcasting, pg 342
Natraj Prakashan, pg 344
Navajivan Trust, pg 344
Omsons Publications, pg 345
Oxford University Press, pg 345
Panjab University Publication Bureau, pg 345
People's Publishing House (P) Ltd, pg 346
Popular Prakashan Pvt Ltd, pg 346
Prabhat Prakashan, pg 346
Pratibha Pratishthan, pg 346
Promilla and Co, pg 346
Pustak Mahal, pg 346
Reliance Publishing House, pg 347
Sasta Sahitya Mandal, pg 349
Sat Sahitya Prakashan, pg 349
Shaibya Prakashan Bibhag, pg 349
Sharda Prakashan, pg 350
Sterling Publishers Pvt Ltd, pg 351
Theosophical Publishing House, pg 351
Vidya Puri, pg 352
Vidyarthi Mithram Press, pg 352
Vikas Publishing House Pvt Ltd, pg 353

Indonesia
Pustaka Utama Grafiti, PT, pg 357
Tintamas Indonesia PT, pg 357

Ireland
Anvil Books Ltd, pg 358
Attic Press Ltd, pg 358
Ballinakella Press, pg 358
Brandon Book Publishers Ltd, pg 359
The Children's Press, pg 359
The Collins Press, pg 359
Dee-Jay Publications, pg 359
Gill & Macmillan Ltd, pg 361
The Hannon Press, pg 361
The Lilliput Press Ltd, pg 362
Mercier Press Ltd, pg 362
Mount Eagle Publications Ltd, pg 362
The O'Brien Press Ltd, pg 363
On Stream Publications Ltd, pg 363
Roberts Rinehart Publishers, pg 363
Tir Eolas, pg 364
Town House & Country House, pg 364
Wolfhound Press, pg 364

Israel
Am Oved Publishers Ltd, pg 365
Bitan Publishers Ltd, pg 365
Boostan Publishing House, pg 366
Breslov Research Institute, pg 366
Edanim Publishers Ltd, pg 367
Feldheim Publishers Ltd, pg 367
Freund Publishing House Ltd, pg 367
Gefen Publishing House Ltd, pg 367
Hakibbutz Hameuchad Publishing House Ltd, pg 368
Karni Publishers Ltd, pg 369
Ma'ariv Book Guild (Sifriat Ma'ariv), pg 370
The Magnes Press, pg 370
Massada Press Ltd, pg 370
Rav Kook Institute, pg 371
Rubin Mass Ltd, pg 371
Steimatzky Group Ltd, pg 372
Urim Publications, pg 373
Yad Vashem - The Holocaust Martyrs' & Heroes' Remembrance Authority, pg 373
Zmora-Bitan, Publishers Ltd, pg 374

Italy
Adea Edizioni, pg 374
Adelphi Edizioni SpA, pg 374
Archinto snc, pg 376
Baha'i, pg 377
Belforte Editore Libraio srl, pg 377
Edizioni Bora SNC di E Brandani & C, pg 378
Nuova Casa Editrice Licinio Cappelli GEM srl, pg 379
Casa Editrice Felice Le Monnier, pg 380
Il Castoro, pg 380
Cittadella Editrice, pg 382
Edizioni Cultura della Pace, pg 383
Edizioni la Scala, pg 387
Edizioni l'Arciere SRL, pg 387
Edizioni Mediterranee SRL, pg 387
Arnaldo Forni Editore SRL, pg 389
Edizioni Frassinelli SRL, pg 389
Edizioni Futuro SRL, pg 389
Galzerano Editore, pg 390
Garzanti Editore, pg 390
Gius Laterza e Figli SpA, pg 391
Piero Gribaudi Editore, pg 391
Il Quadrante SRL, pg 393
Kaos Edizioni SRL, pg 395
Lalli Editore SRL, pg 395
Longanesi & C, pg 396
Lubrina Editore Srl, pg 397
Giuseppe Maimone Editore, pg 397
Tommaso Marotta Editore Srl, pg 398
Editrice Massimo SAS di Crespi Cesare e C, pg 398
Messaggero di San Antonio, pg 398
Arnoldo Mondadori Editore SpA, pg 399
Moretti & Vitali editori srl, pg 400
Gruppo Ugo Mursia Editore SpA, pg 400
Nardini Editore srl, pg 400
La Nuova Italia Editrice SpA, pg 401
Editrice Nuovi Autori, pg 401
Passigli Editori srl, pg 403
Daniela Piazza Editore, pg 403
Pizzicato Edizioni Musicali, pg 403
RCS Rizzoli Libri SpA, pg 405
Archinto Rosellina, pg 406
Rusconi Libri Srl, pg 406
Salerno Editrice SRL, pg 406
Edizioni San Paolo SRL, pg 407
Sperling e Kupfer Editori SpA, pg 408
Sugarco Edizioni SRL, pg 409
Edizioni del Teresianum, pg 409
Editrice Uomini Nuovi, pg 410
Vivere In SRL, pg 411
Viviani Editore srl, pg 412
Who's Who In Italy SRL, pg 412

Jamaica
Eureka Press Ltd, pg 413
Jamaica Publishing House Ltd, pg 413
Ian Randle Publishers Ltd, pg 413

Japan
Chikuma Shobo Publishing Co Ltd, pg 415
Hayakawa Publishing Inc, pg 417
Hoikusha Publishing Co Ltd, pg 417
The Hokuseido Press, pg 417
Iwanami Shoten, Publishers, pg 418
Kaisei-Sha Publishing Co Ltd, pg 419
Kinokuniya Co Ltd (Publishing Department), pg 420
Poplar Publishing Co Ltd, pg 423
Shimizu-Shoin, pg 425
Shincho-Sha Co Ltd, pg 425
Tokyo Tosho Co Ltd, pg 428

Kenya
Foundation Books, pg 431
Kenway Publications Ltd, pg 432
Paulines Publications-Africa, pg 433
Transafrica Press, pg 433

Democratic People's Republic of Korea
The Foreign Language Press Group, pg 434
Grand People's Study House, pg 434

Republic of Korea
Chung Rim Publishing Co Ltd, pg 435
Hongik Media Plus Ltd, pg 437
Hw Moon Publishing Co, pg 437
Kemongsa Publishing Co Ltd, pg 437
Koreaone Press Inc, pg 438

Latvia
Artava Ltd, pg 441
Nordik/Tapals Publishers Ltd, pg 442
Preses Nams, pg 442

Lesotho
Saint Michael's Mission, pg 444

Lithuania
Baltos Lankos, pg 445
Tyto Alba Publishers, pg 446
Vaga Ltd, pg 446

Macau
Livros Do Oriente, pg 448

The Former Yugoslav Republic of Macedonia
Strk Publishing House, pg 449
Zumpres Publishing Firm, pg 449

Malawi
Christian Literature Association in Malawi, pg 450
Mzuzu Publishing Co, pg 451

Malaysia
Pelanduk Publications (M) Sdn Bhd, pg 453
Pustaka Cipta Sdn Bhd, pg 454
University of Malaya, Department of Publications, pg 455

Mali
EDIM SA, pg 455

Malta
Fondazzjoni Patrimonju Malti, pg 456

Mauritius
Editions de l'Ocean Indien Ltd, pg 457
EDITIONS Le Printemps, pg 457
Vizavi Editions, pg 457

Mexico
Editorial Avante SA de Cv, pg 458
Publicaciones Cruz O SA, pg 459
Editorial Diana SA de CV, pg 459
Edamex SA de CV, pg 460
Lasser Press Mexicana SA de CV, pg 462
Pangea Editores, Sa de CV, pg 465
Editorial Patria SA de CV, pg 465
Ediciones Promesa, SA de CV, pg 466
Ediciones Suromex SA, pg 467
Javier Vergara Editor SA de CV, pg 468

Monaco
Les Editions du Rocher, pg 469

Morocco
Editions Al-Fourkane, pg 469
Association de la Recherche Historique et Sociale, pg 469

Myanmar
Sarpay Beikman Board, pg 471

Netherlands
Uitgeverij Anthos, pg 472
BV Uitgeverij de Arbeiderspers, pg 473
Uitgeverij Arena BV, pg 473
Uitgeverij Balans, pg 473
De Boekerij BV, pg 474
Bohn Stafleu Van Loghum BV, pg 474
Bosch & Keuning, pg 474
BZZTOH Publishers, pg 475
Castrum Peregrini Presse, pg 475
Uitgeverij Conserve, pg 475

PUBLISHERS SUBJECT INDEX

Uitgeversmaatschappij Ad Donker BV, pg 476
Elmar BV, pg 476
Uitgeverij Vrij Geestesleven, pg 477
Mets & Schilt Uitgevers en Distributeurs, pg 481
Em Querido's Uitgeverij BV, pg 483
A J G Strengholt's Boeken, Anno 1928, BV, pg 484
Tirion Uitgevers BV, pg 485
Uitgeverij Verloren, pg 486

New Zealand

Auckland University Press, pg 488
Brick Row Publishing Co Ltd, pg 489
Canterbury University Press, pg 489
Cape Catley, pg 489
The Caxton Press, pg 490
Clerestory Press, pg 490
Exisle Publishing Ltd, pg 491
Fraser Books, pg 491
Graphic Educational Publications, pg 491
HarperCollins Publishers (New Zealand) Ltd, pg 491
Heritage Press Ltd, pg 492
Hodder Moa Beckett Publishers Ltd, pg 492
Huia Publishers, pg 492
David Ling Publishing, pg 493
Longacre Press, pg 493
Nestegg Books, pg 493
Oxford University Press, pg 494
R P L Books, pg 495
Reed Publishing (NZ) Ltd, pg 495
University of Otago Press, pg 496
Bridget Williams Books Ltd, pg 497

Nigeria

Adebara Publishers Ltd, pg 497
Alliance West African Publishers & Co, pg 498
Aromolaran Publishing Co Ltd, pg 498
Black Academy Press, pg 498
Cross Continent Press Ltd, pg 498
CSS Bookshops, Agency & Publishing Division, pg 498
Delta Publications (Nigeria) Ltd, pg 498
Educational Research & Study Group, pg 499
Ethiope Publishing Corporation, pg 499
Fourth Dimension Publishing Co Ltd, pg 499
Ilesanmi Press (Educational Publishers) Ltd, pg 499
JAD Publishers Ltd, pg 500
Longman Nigeria Plc, pg 500
New Africa Publishing Company Ltd, pg 500
Nwamife Publishers Ltd, pg 500
Obafemi Awolowo University Press Ltd, pg 501
Obobo Books, pg 501
Onibon-Oje Publishers, pg 501
Joe-Tolalu & Associates, pg 501
University of Lagos Press, pg 502
University Publishing Co, pg 502
Vantage Publishers International Ltd, pg 502
John West Publications Co Ltd, pg 502

Norway

Atheneum Forlag A/S, pg 502
Det Norske Samlaget, pg 503
Fonna Forlag L/L, pg 503
Genesis Forlag, pg 503

Gyldendal Norsk Forlag A/S, pg 503
Lunde Forlag og Bokhandel A/S, pg 504
Luther Forlag A/S, pg 504
Chr Schibsteds Forlag A/S, pg 505
Snofugl Forlag, pg 505

Pakistan

Sheikh Muhammad Ashraf Publishers, pg 506
East & West Publishing Co, pg 506
Hamdard Foundation, pg 507
Malik Sirajuddin & Sons, pg 507
National Institute of Historical & Cultural Research, pg 508

Papua New Guinea

Kristen Pres, pg 510

Philippines

Communication Foundation for Asia Media Group (CFAMG), pg 513
Galleon Publications, pg 513
New Day Publishers, pg 514
Solidaridad Publishing House, pg 515

Poland

Spoldzielnia Wydawnicza 'Czytelnik', pg 516
Instytut Historii Nauki PAN, pg 516
Iskry - Publishing House Ltd spotka zoo, pg 517
'Ksiazka i Wiedza' Spotdzielnia Wydawniczo-Handlowa, pg 517
Wydawnictwo Literackie, pg 517
Wydawnictwo Lodzkie, pg 517
Ludowa Spoldzielnia Wydawnicza, pg 518
Magnum Publishing House Ltd, pg 518
Norbertinum, pg 518
Ossolineum Zaklad Narodowy im Ossolinskich - Wydawnictwo, pg 518
Panstwowy Instytut Wydawniczy (PIW), pg 518
Videograf II Sp z o o Zaklad Poracy Chronionej, pg 520
Wydawnictwa Uniwersytetu Warszawskiego, pg 521
Wydawnictwo DiG, pg 521

Portugal

Apostolado da Oracao Secretariado Nacional, pg 522
Brasilia Editora (J Carvalho Branco), pg 523
Publicacoes Europa-America Lda, pg 524
Editorial Franciscana, pg 525
Impala, pg 525
Imprensa Nacional-Casa da Moeda, pg 526
Livraria Apostolado da Imprensa, pg 526
Editora Livros do Brasil Sarl, pg 526
Livraria Tavares Martins, pg 527
Edicoes Ora & Labora, pg 528
Paulinas, pg 528
Editorial Presenca, pg 528
Quimera Editores, pg 529
Realizacoes Artis, pg 529
Edicoes Salesianas, pg 529
Talento, pg 529
Vega-Publicacao e Distribuicao de Livros e Revistas, Lda, pg 530
Livraria Verdade e Vida Editora, pg 530

Puerto Rico

Editorial Cultural Inc, pg 530

Romania

Artemis Verlag, pg 532
The Center for Romanian Studies, pg 532
Editure Ion Creanga, pg 532
Editura DOINA SRL, pg 533
Enzyklopadie Verlag, pg 533
Editura Excelsior, pg 533
Editura Humanitas, pg 533
Humanitas Publishing House, pg 533
Editura Meridiane, pg 534
Editura Minerva, pg 534
Editura Muzicala, pg 534
Editura Niculescu, pg 534
Pallas-Akademia Koenyvkiadoes Koenyvkereskedes, pg 535
Pandora Publishing House, pg 535
RAO International Publishing Co, pg 535
RAO Publishing Group, pg 535
Saeculum IO, pg 535
Est-Samuel Tastet Verlag, pg 536
Editura Univers, pg 536
Vestala Verlag, pg 536

Russian Federation

BLIC, russko-Baltijskij informaciionnyj centr, AO, pg 537
FGUP Izdatelstvo Mashinostroenie, pg 538
Izdatelskii Dom Kompozitor, pg 539
Publishing House Limbus Press, pg 539
Izdatelstvo Mezhdunarodnye Otnoshenia, pg 540
Izdatelstvo Molodaya Gvardia, pg 540
Progress Publishers, pg 541
Raduga Publishers, pg 541
Top Secret Collection Publishers, pg 542
Voyenizdat, pg 542

Saudi Arabia

Dar Al-Shareff for Publishing & Distribution, pg 543

Senegal

Les Nouvelles Editions Africaines du Senegal NEAS, pg 544

Slovakia

Danubiaprint, pg 549
Luc vydavatelske druzstvo, pg 550
Vydavatel'stvo SFVU Pallas, pg 550
Smena Publishing House, pg 550
Vydavatel' Sky odbor, pg 551

Slovenia

Cankarjeva Zalozba, pg 551
Zalozba Obzorja d d Maribor, pg 552

South Africa

Jonathan Ball Publishers, pg 552
Galago Publishing Pty Ltd, pg 554
HAUM (Hollandsch Afrikaansche Uitgevers Maatschappij), pg 555
Human & Rousseau (Pty) Ltd, pg 555
Ithemba! Publishing, pg 555
Mayibuye Books, pg 557
New Africa Books (Pty) Ltd, pg 557
Queillerie Publishers, pg 558

Ravan Press (Pty) Ltd, pg 558
Shuter & Shooter (Pty) Ltd, pg 559

Spain

Publicacions de l'Abadia de Montserrat, pg 561
Agencia Espanola de Cooperacion, pg 562
Altea, Taurus, Alfaguara SA, pg 563
Sociedad de Educacion Atenas SA, pg 564
Ediciones B, SA, pg 565
Editorial Biblioteca Nueva SL, pg 565
Central Catequistica Salesiana (CCS), pg 567
Circe Ediciones, SA, pg 567
Compania Literaria, pg 568
Complutense, SA Editorial, pg 568
Rafael Dalmau, Editor, pg 569
EDERSA (Editoriales de Derecho Reunidas SA), pg 571
Editorial Espasa-Calpe SA, pg 573
Fundacion de Estudios Libertarios Anselmo Lorenzo, pg 575
Editorial Gedisa SA, pg 575
Hogar del Libro, SA, pg 577
Iberico Europea de Ediciones SA, pg 577
Ediciones Internacionales Universitarias SA, pg 578
Junta de Castilla y Leon Consejeria de Educacion y Cultura, pg 579
Editorial Juventud SA, pg 579
Laertes SA de Ediciones, pg 579
Lid Editorial Empresarial, SL, pg 580
Ediciones Maeva, pg 581
Edicions de la Magrana SA, pg 581
Ediciones Martinez-Roca SA, pg 581
La Mascara, SL Editorial, pg 581
Ediciones Minotauro, pg 582
Editorial Moll SL, pg 582
Mundo Negro Editorial, pg 583
Noguer y Caralt Editores SA, pg 584
Oikos-Tau SA Ediciones, pg 584
Ediciones del Oriente y del Mediterraneo, pg 585
El Paisaje Editorial, pg 585
Ediciones Palabra SA, pg 585
Editorial Parthenon Communication, SL, pg 586
Editorial Peregrino SL, pg 586
Editorial El Perpetuo Socorro, pg 586
Pirene Editorial, sal, pg 587
Plaza y Janes Editores SA, pg 587
Editorial Portic SA, pg 587
Pre-Textos, pg 587
Editorial Presencia Gitana, pg 587
San Pablo Ediciones, pg 589
Ediciones Sigueme SA, pg 590
Silex Ediciones, pg 590
Editorial Sintesis, SA, pg 590
Ediciones Siruela SA, pg 591
Edicions 62, pg 591
Grup 62, pg 591
Ediciones SM, pg 591
Ediciones Temas de Hoy, SA, pg 592
Editorial Sal Terrae, pg 592
Tusquets Editores, pg 593
Editorial Txertoa, pg 594
Ultramar Editores SA, pg 594
Javier Vergara Editor SA, pg 595
Ediciones Versal SA, pg 595
Vinaches Lopez, Luisa, pg 595

905

SUBJECT INDEX

BOOK

Sri Lanka
Law Publishers Association, pg 597
Waruni Publishers, pg 598

Sudan
Khartoum University Press, pg 598

Sweden
Fischer & Co, pg 602
Gidlunds Bokforlag, pg 602
Bokfoerlaget Naturoch Kultur, pg 604
Svenska Foerlaget liv & ledarskap ab, pg 607
Wahlstrom & Widstrand, pg 607
Zindermans AB, pg 607

Switzerland
Editions L'Age d'Homme - La Cite, pg 608
Arche Verlag AG, Raabe und Vitali, pg 608
Armenia Editions, pg 608
Athenaeum Verlag AG, pg 608
Editions de la Baconniere SA, pg 609
Blaukreuz-Verlag Bern, pg 610
Caux Books, pg 611
Caux Edition SA, pg 611
Editions l'Eau Vive, pg 613
eFeF-Verlag/Edition Ebersbach, pg 613
Kanisius Verlag, pg 616
Limmat Verlag, pg 618
Maihof Verlag, pg 618
La Maison de la Bible, pg 618
Les Editions Noir sur Blanc, pg 620
Orell Fuessli Verlag, pg 620
Verlag Friedrich Reinhardt AG, pg 622
Rodera-Verlag der Cardun AG, pg 623
Scherz Verlag AG, pg 623
3 Dimension World (3-D-World), pg 625
Zbinden Druck und Verlag AG, pg 628

Taiwan, Province of China
Campus Evangelical Fellowship, Literature Department, pg 629
Chung Hwa Book Co Ltd, pg 629
Commonwealth Publishing Company Ltd, pg 629
Linking Publishing Company Ltd, pg 631
Newton Publishing Company Ltd, pg 631

United Republic of Tanzania
Central Tanganyika Press, pg 633
East African Publishing House, pg 633
Eastern Africa Publications Ltd, pg 633

Thailand
Bannakit Trading, pg 635
Thai Watana Panich Co, Ltd, pg 636

Togo
Editions Akpagnon, pg 636

Tunisia
Academie Tunisienne des Sciences, des Lettres et des Arts Beit El Hekma, pg 637
Ceres Editions, pg 637
Dar Arabia Lil Kitab, pg 637
Maison Tunisienne de l'Edition, pg 638

Turkey
Afa Yayincilik Sanayi Tic AS, pg 638
Kubbealti Akademisi Kultur ve Sasat Vakfi, pg 640
Parantez Yayinlari Ltd, pg 640
Remzi Kitabevi, pg 641
Sabah Kitaplari, pg 641

Uganda
Fountain Publishers Ltd, pg 642

United Arab Emirates
Motivate Publishing, pg 644

United Kingdom
Absolute Press, pg 644
Acair Ltd, pg 645
Allison & Busby, pg 646
Alun Books, pg 646
Amber Lane Press Ltd, pg 646
Argyll Publishing, pg 648
Atlas Press, pg 651
Aurum Press Ltd, pg 651
Avero Publications Ltd, pg 651
BBC Audiobooks, pg 652
Belitha Press Ltd, pg 653
Bishopsgate Press Ltd, pg 655
Blackstaff Press, pg 655
Bloomsbury Publishing PLC, pg 656
The Book Guild Ltd, pg 657
Books of Zimbabwe Publishing Co (Pvt) Ltd, pg 657
Breedon Books Publishing Company Ltd, pg 659
Brewin Books Ltd, pg 659
Bryntirion Press, pg 661
Calder Publications Ltd, pg 662
Cambridge University Press, pg 662
Camden Press Ltd, pg 662
Canongate Books Ltd, pg 663
Cardiff Academic Press, pg 663
Carlton Publishing Group, pg 664
Cassell & Co, pg 664
Kyle Cathie Ltd, pg 665
The Chrysalis Press, pg 667
James Clarke & Co Ltd, pg 668
Cockbird Press, pg 669
Colourpoint Books, pg 669
Constable & Robinson Ltd, pg 670
Leo Cooper, pg 671
Countyvise Ltd, pg 671
Creation Books, pg 671
Crossbridge Books, pg 672
CTBI Publications, pg 672
James Currey Ltd, pg 673
Debrett's Peerage Ltd, pg 674
Andre Deutsch Ltd, pg 675
Dunedin Academic Press, pg 676
Eland, pg 677
Element Books Ltd, pg 678
Aidan Ellis Publishing, pg 678
The Eurospan Group, pg 680
Ex Libris Press, pg 680
Faber & Faber Ltd, pg 681
Forth Naturalist & Historian, pg 683
Fourth Estate Ltd, pg 683
Gairm Publications, pg 685
Gale Research, pg 685
Garnet Publishing Ltd, pg 685
George Mann Publications, pg 687
Gollancz/Witherby, pg 688
Granta Books, pg 689
Gwasg Gwenffrwd, pg 690
Peter Halban Publishers Ltd, pg 691
Robert Hale Ltd, pg 691
Hamish Hamilton Ltd, pg 691
HarperCollins Publishers, pg 692
The Harvill Press Ltd, pg 693
Hawthorns Publications Ltd, pg 693
Headline Book Publishing Ltd, pg 693
William Heinemann Ltd, pg 694
Helicon Publishing Ltd, pg 694
Helion & Co, pg 694
Highland Books Ltd, pg 695
Hodder & Stoughton General, pg 696
Hodder & Stoughton Religious, pg 696
Honeyglen Publishing Ltd, pg 697
Honno Welsh Women's Press, pg 697
Institute of Irish Studies, The Queens University of Belfast, pg 699
Institute of Physics Publishing, pg 700
Isis Publishing Ltd, pg 701
The Islamic Texts Society, pg 701
Janus Publishing Company Ltd, pg 702
John Blake Publishing Ltd, pg 703
Johnson Publications Ltd, pg 703
John Jones Publishing Ltd, pg 703
Michael Joseph Ltd, pg 703
Knight Features, pg 705
Jay Landesman, pg 706
Libris Ltd, pg 707
Linen Hall Library, pg 707
The Littman Library of Jewish Civilization, pg 708
Luath Press Ltd, pg 709
The Lutterworth Press, pg 709
Macmillan Audio Books, pg 710
Mainstream Publishing Co (Edinburgh) Ltd, pg 711
Mango Publishing, pg 711
The Mansk Svenska Publishing Co Ltd, pg 711
Marcham Books, pg 711
Melrose Press Ltd, pg 713
Methuen Publishing Ltd, pg 714
Metro Publishing Ltd, pg 714
Monarch Books, pg 715
John Murray (Publishers) Ltd, pg 716
Muze UK Ltd, pg 716
National Portrait Gallery Publications, pg 717
NMS Publishing Ltd, pg 719
W W Norton & Company Ltd, pg 720
The Oleander Press, pg 721
Oliver Books, pg 721
Michael O'Mara Books Ltd, pg 721
Omnibus Press, pg 721
Orion Publishing Group Ltd, pg 722
Peter Owen Ltd, pg 722
Owl Books, pg 722
Oxford University Press, pg 723
Parapress Ltd, pg 724
Pavilion Books Ltd, pg 724
Phaidon Press Ltd, pg 726
Piatkus Books, pg 727
Pitkin Unichrome Ltd, pg 728
Plantin Publishers, pg 728
Plexus Publishing Ltd, pg 728
Pluto Press, pg 728
Poetry Wales Press Ltd, pg 729
Polybooks Ltd, pg 729
Profile Books Ltd, pg 731
Quartet Books Ltd, pg 731
Quiller Publishing Ltd, pg 732
Ramsay Head Press, pg 732
Random House UK Ltd, pg 733
Robson Books, pg 735
Roundhouse Publishing Ltd, pg 736
Routledge, pg 736
The Rubicon Press, pg 737
Scottish Cultural Press, pg 739
Seren, pg 740
Serpent's Tail Ltd, pg 740
Shire Publications Ltd, pg 741
Sidgwick & Jackson Ltd, pg 742
Silver Link Publishing Ltd, pg 742
Simon & Schuster Ltd, pg 742
Charles Skilton Ltd, pg 742
Smith Settle Ltd, pg 743
Colin Smythe Ltd, pg 743
The Society for Promoting Christian Knowledge (SPCK), pg 743
Souvenir Press Ltd, pg 743
SPA Books Ltd, pg 744
Spellmount Ltd Publishers, pg 744
Rudolf Steiner Press, pg 745
Sutton Publishing Ltd, pg 746
Sydney Jary Ltd, pg 746
Tabb House, pg 746
Thistle Press, pg 748
Titan Books Ltd, pg 749
Transworld Publishers Ltd, pg 750
Tuckwell Press Ltd, pg 750
Ulverscroft Large Print Books Ltd, pg 751
United Writers Publications Ltd, pg 751
Veloce Publishing Ltd, pg 752
Viking, pg 753
Virago Press, pg 753
Virgin Publishing Ltd, pg 753
Welsh Academic Press, pg 755
Neil Wilson Publishing Ltd, pg 757
Wimbledon Publishing Company Ltd, pg 757
The Windrush Press Ltd, pg 757
The Women's Press Ltd, pg 758
Yale University Press London, pg 759

Uruguay
Rosebud Ediciones, pg 761

Yugoslavia
Izdavacka Organizacija Rad, pg 765

Zambia
Aafzam Ltd, pg 766
Apple Books, pg 766
Multimedia Zambia, pg 767
Zambia Educational Publishing House, pg 767

Zimbabwe
College Press Publishers (Pvt) Ltd, pg 768

BIOLOGICAL SCIENCES

Albania
NL SH, pg 1
State Textbook Publishing House, pg 1

Argentina
Editorial Hemisferio Sur SA, pg 6
Editorial Medica Panamericana, pg 7
Editorial Medica, Panamericana SA, pg 7
Editoria Universitaria de la Patagonia, pg 9

Australia
Aboriginal Studies Press, pg 10
Australian Academy of Science, pg 13

PUBLISHERS SUBJECT INDEX

Australian Marine Conservation Society Inc (AMCS), pg 14
Robert Berthold Photography, pg 14
Bureau of Resource Sciences, pg 16
CSIRO Publishing (Commonwealth Scientific & Industrial Research Organisation), pg 19
Emerald City Books, pg 22
Encyclopaedia Britannica (Australia) Inc, pg 22
Illert Publications, pg 27
McGraw-Hill Australia Pty Ltd, pg 32
Pearson Education Australia, pg 37
Queen Victoria Museum & Art Gallery Publications, pg 39
Frank Shepherd, pg 42
Three Sisters Publications Pty Ltd, pg 44
La Trobe University Press, pg 45
University of New South Wales Press Ltd, pg 46

Austria
Bethania Verlag, pg 49
IAEA - International Atomic Energy Agency, pg 53
Verlag der Oesterreichischen Akademie der Wissenschaften (OEAW), pg 56
Osterreichischer Bundesveilag Ges.mbh, pg 57
Springer-Verlag Wien, pg 59

Belarus
Belaruskaya Encyklapedyya, pg 63
Narodnaya Asveta, pg 63

Belgium
Artel SC, pg 64
Campinia Media VZW, pg 65
Editions De Boeck-Larcier SA, pg 67
Leuven University Press, pg 71
Presses agronomiques de Gembloux ASBL, pg 73

Brazil
ARTMED, pg 79
Editora Edgard Blucher Ltda, pg 80
Centro de Estudos Juridicosdo Para (CEJUP), pg 80
EDUC - Editora da PUC-SP, pg 82
EDUSC - Editora da Universidade do Sagrado Coracao, pg 82
Empresa Brasileira de Pesquisa Agropecaria, pg 83
Editora Guanabara Koogan SA, pg 84
Editora Harbra Ltda, pg 84
Interlivros Edicoes Ltda, pg 85
Editora Nova Fronteira SA, pg 88
Pearson Education Do Brasil, pg 89
Editora Scipione Ltda, pg 91

Bulgaria
Gea-Libris Publishing House, pg 95
Makros 2000 - Plovdiv, pg 96
Medicina i Fizkultura EOOD, pg 96
Pensoft Publishers, pg 97

Chile
Arrayan Editores, pg 99
Pontificia Universidad Catolica de Chile, pg 101

China
Beijing Medical Univ Press, pg 102
Beijing University Press, pg 102
Chemical Industry Press, pg 102
China Agriculture Press, pg 103
China Forestry Publishing House, pg 103
China Ocean Press, pg 103
Fudan University Press, pg 105
Wissenschaft und Technik Verlag Henan Henan Scientific & Technological Publishing House, pg 106
Higher Education Press, pg 106
International Academic Publishers, pg 106
Jilin Science & Technology Publishing House, pg 106
Nanjing University Press, pg 107
Qingdao Publishing House, pg 108
Science Press, pg 108
South China University of Science and Technology Press, pg 109
Tianjin Science & Technology Publishing House, pg 109
Wuhan University Press, pg 110
Zhejiang University Press, pg 110

Colombia
Fundacion Universidad de la Sabana Ediciones Udes, pg 112
Editorial Libros y Libres SA, pg 112
McGraw-Hill InterAmericana SA, pg 113
Unidad Universitaria del Sur (UNISUR), pg 114

Costa Rica
Centro Agronomico Tropical de Investigacion y Ensenanza (CATIE), pg 115
Editorial Nacional de Salud y Seguridad Social Ednass, pg 116
Union Mundial para la Naturaleza (UICN), Oficina Regional para Mesoamerica, pg 117
Editorial de la Universidad de Costa Rica, pg 117

Czech Republic
Aventinum Nakladatelstvi, pg 123
Granit SRO, pg 124
Mendelova zemedelska a lesnicka univerzita v Brne, pg 126
Narodni Muzeum, pg 126
Nakladatelstvi a vydavatelstvi Panorama, pg 127

Denmark
FADL's Forlag A/S (Foreningen af danske Laegestuderendes Forlag), pg 132
GEC Gads Forlag Aktieselskab af 1994, pg 132

Dominican Republic
Pontificia Universidad Catolica Madre y Maestra, pg 136

Estonia
Estonian Academic Library, pg 139
Valgus Publishers, pg 141

Finland
Yliopistopaino/Helsinki University Press, pg 145

France
Breal, pg 151
CNRS Editions, pg 155
Corsaire Editions, pg 156
Doin Editeurs, pg 160
Editions Espaces 34, pg 162
L'Expansion Scientifique Francaise, pg 163
Editions Gammaprim, pg 166
Editions Hatier SA, pg 168
INRA Editions (Institut National de la Recherche Agronomique), pg 169
Editions INSERM, pg 169
InterEditions Paris, pg 169
Lavoisier, pg 172
Masson-Williams et Wilkins, pg 175
Ouest Editions, pg 178
Polytechnica, pg 180
Presses Universitaires de Caen, pg 181
Sofradif Editions Philippe Auzou, pg 185
Librairie Vuibert, pg 189

Germany
AOL-Verlag Frohmut Menze, pg 194
Aulis Verlag Deubner & Co KG, pg 197
Bayerischer Schulbuch-Verlag GmbH, pg 199
Blackwell Wissenschafts-Verlag GmbH, pg 203
Cornelsen Verlag GmbH & Co OHG, pg 211
Verlag Harri Deutsch, pg 213
Dreisam Ratgeber in der Rutsker Verlag GmbH, pg 218
E Schweizerbart'sche Verlagsbuchhandlung (Nagele und Obermiller), pg 220
Ecomed Verlagsgesellschaft AG & Co KG, pg 220
Fachverlag Schiele & Schoen GmbH, pg 226
Gebrueder Borntraeger Science Publishers, pg 231
Walter de Gruyter GmbH & Co KG, pg 234
Lehrmittelverlag Wilhelm Hagemann GmbH, pg 236
Human Wissenschafilicher Verlag, pg 243
Franckh-Kosmos Verlags-GmbH & Co, pg 252
Verlag Waldemar Kramer, pg 253
Landbuch-Verlagsgesellschaft mbH, pg 255
Logos-Verlag Literatur & Layout GmbH, pg 258
Margraf Verlag, pg 261
Verlag Stephanie Naglschmid, pg 266
Verlag Natur & Wissenschaft Harro Hieronimus & Dr Jurgen Schmidt, pg 266
Neumann Verlag, pg 268
Rainar Nitzsche Verlag, pg 269
Nusser Verlag, pg 272
Verlag Dr Friedrich Pfeil, pg 273
pmi Verlag, pg 274
Psychologie Verlags Union GmbH, pg 275
Quelle und Meyer Verlag GmbH & Co, pg 276
Springer-Verlag GmbH & Co KG, pg 288
Stiefel GmbH Wandkarten Verlag, pg 290
Georg Thieme Verlag KG, pg 293
Urania Verlag mit Ravensburger Ratgebern, pg 296
Urban & Fischer Verlag GmbH & Co KG Niederlassung Jena, pg 296
UTB fuer Wissenschaft Uni-Taschenbuecher GmbH, pg 297
Volk und Wissen Verlag GmbH & Co, pg 299
VS Verlagshaus Stuttgart GmbH, pg 299
VWB-Verlag fur Wissenschaft & Bildung, Amand Aglaster, pg 300
Wiley-VCH Verlag GmbH, pg 302
Wissenschaftliche Verlagsgesellschaft mbH, pg 303
Verlag Zeitschrift fur Naturforschung, pg 305

Ghana
Ghana Universities Press (GUP), pg 307
Sedco Publishing Ltd, pg 308

Greece
Athina, Mary Mavrogiannis, pg 309

Holy See (Vatican City State)
Pontificia Academia Scientiarum, pg 317

Hong Kong
Federal Publications Ltd, pg 319
Hong Kong University Press, pg 320

Hungary
Akademiai Kiado, pg 323
Nemzeti Tankoenyvkiado, pg 326

India
Addison-Wesley (Singapore) Pte Ltd, pg 329
Affiliated East West Press Pvt Ltd, pg 329
Agricole Publishing Academy, pg 330
Arihant Publishers, pg 331
B I Publications Pvt Ltd, pg 331
Bani Mandir, Book-Sellers, Publishers & Educational Suppliers, pg 332
BSMPS - M/s Bishen Singh Mahendra Pal Singh, pg 334
Daya Publishing House, pg 336
Frank Brothers & Co (Publishers) Ltd, pg 337
International Book Distributors, pg 340
Narosa Publishing House, pg 343
Oxford & IBH Publishing Co Pvt Ltd, pg 345
Pointer Publishers, pg 346
Publications & Information Directorate, CSIR, pg 346
Rastogi Publications, pg 347
Regency Publications, pg 347
Reliance Publishing House, pg 347
Scientific Book Agency, pg 349
Scientific Publishers India, pg 349
Sita Publications, pg 350
South Asian Publishers Pvt Ltd, pg 350
Sultan Chand & Sons Pvt Ltd, pg 351
Vidya Puri, pg 352
Vidyarthi Mithram Press, pg 352
S Viswanathan (Printers & Publishers) Pvt Ltd, pg 353

Ireland
Royal Dublin Society, pg 364
Royal Irish Academy, pg 364

907

Israel
Hakibbutz Hameuchad Publishing House Ltd, pg 368
The Israel Academy of Sciences & Humanities, pg 368
Open University of Israel, pg 371

Italy
Apimondia, pg 375
Archimede Edizioni, pg 376
Casa Editrice Giuseppe Principato Spa, pg 380
CEDAM (Casa Editrice Dr A Milani), pg 380
CG Ediz Medico-Scientifiche, pg 381
La Culturale, pg 383
Demetra SRL, pg 385
Edagricole - Edizioni Agricole, pg 385
Edi Ermes SRL, pg 386
Folini, pg 389
Edizioni GB, pg 390
Ibis, pg 393
Casa Editrice Libraria Idelson di G Gnocchi, pg 393
Casa Editrice Maccari (CEM), pg 397
Monduzzi Editore SpA, pg 399
Accademia Naz dei Lincei, pg 400
Editoriale Olimpia SpA, pg 401
Paravia Bruno Mondadori Editori, pg 402
Piccin Nuova Libraria SpA, pg 403
Edizioni Universitarie Romane, pg 406
Editrice San Marco SRL, pg 406
Editoriale Scienza, pg 407
Societa Editrice la Goliardica Pavese SRL, pg 408
Tilgher-Genova sas, pg 410
Transeuropa Libri, pg 410
Unipress, pg 410
Zanichelli Editore SpA, pg 412

Japan
Baifukan Co Ltd, pg 414
Bun-ichi Sogo Shuppan, pg 415
CMC Co Ltd, pg 415
Hirokawa Publishing Co, pg 417
Kyoritsu Shuppan Co Ltd, pg 420
Maruzen Co Ltd, pg 421
Mita Press, Mita Industrial Co, Ltd, pg 421
Nakayama Shoten Company Ltd, pg 421
Nippon Hoso Shuppan Kyokai (NHK Publishing), pg 422
Sangyo-Tosho Publishing Co Ltd, pg 424
Tokai University Press, pg 427
Toppan Co Ltd, pg 428
Tsukiji Shokan Publishing Co, pg 428

Kazakstan
Gylym, Izd-Vo, pg 430
Kazakh Al-Farabi State National University, pg 430

Kenya
African Centre for Technology Studies (ACTS), pg 431
Heinemann Kenya Limited (EAEP), pg 431
Kenya Medical Research Institute (KEMRI), pg 432
Lake Publishers & Enterprises Ltd, pg 432

Democratic People's Republic of Korea
Academy of Sciences Publishing House, pg 434
Korea Science and Encyclopedia Publishing House, pg 434

Latvia
Lielvards Ltd, pg 442
Preses Nams, pg 442

Lebanon
Arab Scientific Publishers BP, pg 442

Lithuania
Academia, pg 445
Klaipedos Universiteto Leidykla, pg 445
Mokslo ir enciklopediju leidybos institutas, pg 446

The Former Yugoslav Republic of Macedonia
Medis, Skopje, pg 449

Malaysia
Penerbit Universiti Sains Malaysia, pg 454

Mexico
AGT Editor SA, pg 457
Centro de Estudios Mexicanos y Centroamericanos, pg 458
Colegio de Postgraduados en Ciencias Agricolas, pg 459
Editorial El Manual Moderno SA de CV, pg 460
Fondo de Cultura Economica, pg 461
Editorial Limusa SA de CV, pg 463
Editorial Minutiae Mexicana SA, pg 464
Organizacion Cultural LP SA de CV, pg 465
Pangea Editores, Sa de CV, pg 465
Pearson Educacion de Mexico, SA de CV, pg 465
Ediciones Cientificas La Prensa Medica Mexicana SA de CV, pg 466
Sistemas Tecnicos de Edicion SA de CV, pg 467
Universo Editorial SA de CV Edicion de Libros Revistas y Periodicos, pg 468

Republic of Moldova
Lumina Publishing House, pg 468

Namibia
Desert Research Foundation of Namibia (DRFN), pg 471

Netherlands
Backhuys Publishers BV, pg 473
A A Balkema, pg 473
Brill Academic Publishers, pg 475
Elsevier Science BV, pg 477
Hagen & Stam Uitgeverij Ten, pg 478
IOS Press BV, pg 479
LCG Malmberg BV, pg 480
VU Boekhandel/Uitgeverij BV, pg 487

New Zealand
Canterbury University Press, pg 489
Craig Potton Publishing, pg 490
Wendy Crane Books, pg 490
ESA Publications (NZ) Ltd, pg 490
Landcare Research NZ, pg 492
Nelson Price Milburn Ltd, pg 494
SIR Publishing, pg 495

Nigeria
JAD Publishers Ltd, pg 500
Riverside Communications, pg 501
Vantage Publishers International Ltd, pg 502

Pakistan
HMR Publishing Co, pg 507
National Book Foundation, pg 508
Publishers United Pvt Ltd, pg 508

Philippines
National Museum of the Philippines, pg 514
Rex Bookstores & Publishers, pg 514
San Carlos Publications, pg 515
SIBS Publishing House Inc, pg 515
UST Publishing House, pg 515

Poland
Instytut Historii Nauki PAN, pg 516
Ossolineum Zaklad Narodowy im Ossolinskich - Wydawnictwo, pg 518
PZWL Wydawnictwo Lekarskie Ltd, pg 519
Towarzystwo Naukowe w Toruniu, pg 520
Wydawnictwa Uniwersytetu Warszawskiego, pg 521

Portugal
Constancia Editores, SA, pg 524
Dinalivro, pg 524
Gradiva-Publicacnoes Lda, pg 525
Instituto de Investigacao Cientifica Tropical, pg 526
McGraw-Hill Editora de Portugal, pg 527
Editora Replicacao Lda, pg 529

Romania
Editura Academiei Romane, pg 531
Editura Dacia, pg 532
Enzyklopadie Verlag, pg 533
Editura Niculescu, pg 534
Editura Stiintifica, pg 536

Russian Federation
Izdatelstvo Mir, pg 540
Nauka Publishers, pg 540
Izdatel'stvo Nizhegorodskogo Gosudarstvennogo Univ, pg 540
Voronezh State University Publishers, pg 542
Izdatelstvo Vysshaya Shkola, pg 543

Saudi Arabia
King Saud University, pg 543

Singapore
Reed Elsevier, South East Asia, pg 547
Taylor & Francis Asia Pacific, pg 548
World Scientific Publishing Co Pte Ltd, pg 549

South Africa
Clever Books, pg 553
Educum Publishers Ltd, pg 554
National Botanical Institute, pg 557
Oceanographic Research Institute, pg 558

Spain
Editorial AEDOS SA, pg 561
Cedel, Ediciones Jose O Avila Monteso ES, pg 567
Ediciones de la Universidad Complutense de Madrid, pg 568
Comunidad Autonoma de Madrid, Servicio de Documentacion y Publicaciones, pg 568
Consello da Cultura Galega - CCG, pg 568
Didaco Comunicacion y Didactica, SA, pg 569
Instituto de Estudios Riojanos, pg 574
EUNSA (Ediciones Universidad de Navarra SA), pg 574
Idea Books, SA, pg 578
McGraw-Hill Iberic/Brazil Group, pg 581
Mundi-Prensa Libros SA, pg 583
Editorial la Muralla SA, pg 583
Oikos-Tau SA Ediciones, pg 584
Ediciones Omega SA, pg 585
Editorial Paraninfo SA, pg 586
Instituto Provincial de Investigaciones y Estudios Toledanos, pg 588
Rueda, SL Editorial, pg 589
Servicio de Publicaciones Universidad de Cordoba, pg 590
Editorial Sintesis, SA, pg 590
Trea Ediciones, SL, pg 593
Universidad de Granada, pg 594
Universitat de Valencia Servei de Publicacions, pg 594

Sweden
Studentlitteratur AB, pg 606

Switzerland
Birkhauser Verlag AG, pg 610
Christiana-Verlag, pg 611
Verlag Harri Deutsch, pg 612
S Karger AG, Medical and Scientific Publishers, pg 617
Presses Polytechniques et Universitaires Romandes, PPUR, pg 622
Sabe AG Verlagsinstitut, pg 623

Taiwan, Province of China
Chien Chen Bookstore Publishing Company Ltd, pg 629
Ho-Chi Book Publishing Co, pg 630
SMC Publishing Inc, pg 632
Yi Hsien Publishing Co Ltd, pg 632

United Republic of Tanzania
DUP (1996) Ltd, pg 633

Thailand
Graphic Art Publishing, pg 635

Tunisia
Ceres Editions, pg 637

Ukraine
Naukova Dumka Publishers, pg 643
Osnova, Kharkov State University Press, pg 643
Osvita, pg 643

PUBLISHERS   SUBJECT INDEX

United Kingdom
Academic Press Ltd, pg 644
Association for Science Education, pg 650
BIOS Scientific Publishers Ltd, pg 654
BLA Publishing Ltd, pg 655
Cambridge University Press, pg 662
E W Classey Ltd, pg 668
Current Science Group, pg 672
Elsevier Science Ltd, pg 678
The Eurospan Group, pg 680
Forth Naturalist & Historian, pg 683
W H Freeman & Co Ltd, pg 684
Harley Books, pg 692
Harvard University Press, pg 692
Hodder & Stoughton Educational, pg 696
Horizon Scientific Press, pg 697
Imperial College Press, pg 699
Intercept Ltd, pg 700
International Bee Research Association, pg 701
JAI Press Ltd, pg 702
Jones & Bartlett International, pg 703
Kluwer Academic/Plenum Publishers, pg 705
Manson Publishing Ltd, pg 711
Micelle Press, pg 714
John Murray (Publishers) Ltd, pg 716
Open University Worldwide, pg 721
Orion Publishing Group Ltd, pg 722
Packard Publishing Ltd, pg 723
Pearson Education, pg 725
Portland Press Ltd, pg 730
Research Studies Press Ltd (RSP), pg 734
Sage Publications Ltd, pg 737
Sheffield Academic Press Ltd, pg 741
Stokesby House Publications, pg 745
Tarragon Press, pg 746
Wiley Europe Ltd, pg 756
Wimbledon Publishing Company Ltd, pg 757
WIT Press, pg 757

Uruguay
A Monteverde y Cia SA, pg 760

Venezuela
Editorial Biosfera CA, pg 762
Sociedad Fondo Editorial Cenamec, pg 762

Viet Nam
Science & Technics Publishing House, pg 763

Zimbabwe
College Press Publishers (Pvt) Ltd, pg 768

BUSINESS

Albania
NL SH, pg 1
State Textbook Publishing House, pg 1

Argentina
Editorial Cangallo SACI, pg 4
Depalma SRL, pg 5
Javier Vergara Editor SA, pg 9

Australia
Allen & Unwin Pty Ltd, The Australian Newspaper, Vogel Breads, pg 11
Books for Our Times, pg 16
Boolarong Press, pg 16
Butterworths Australia Ltd, pg 16
Crista International, pg 19
D&B Marketing Pty Ltd, pg 20
Deakin University Press, pg 20
Dryden Press, pg 21
Emerald City Books, pg 22
The Federation Press, pg 22
Hale & Iremonger Pty Ltd, pg 24
Harcourt Australia Pty Ltd, pg 25
Hospitality Press Pty Ltd, pg 26
James Nicholas Publishers Pty Ltd, pg 28
Laams Publications, pg 29
Law Book Co Information Services, pg 29
Thomas C Lothian Pty Ltd, pg 30
Marketing Focus, pg 31
Mosby Lifeline, pg 33
Network Promotions P/L, pg 34
Nimaroo Publishers, pg 35
OTEN (Open Training & Education Network), pg 36
Pearson Education Australia, pg 37
Press for Success, pg 38
Prospect Media Pty Ltd, pg 39
The Real Estate Institute of Australia, pg 40
RMIT Publishing, pg 41
Stirling Press, pg 43
Tertiary Press, pg 44
D W Thorpe, pg 44
Universal Business Directories, Australia Pty Ltd, pg 46
VCTA Publishing, pg 46
Woodlands Publications, pg 48
Worsley Press, pg 48
Wrightbooks Pty Ltd, pg 48

Austria
Bohmann Druck und Verlag GmbH & Co KG, pg 50
Buchhandlung WUV Dolmetsch, pg 50
Compass-Verlag GmbH, pg 50
Horst Knapp Finanznachrichten, pg 54
Linde Verlag Wien GmbH, pg 54
Signum Verlag GmbH & Co KG, pg 58
Springer-Verlag Wien, pg 59
Verband der Wissenschaftlichen Gesellschaften Oesterreichs (VWGOe), pg 60

Azerbaijan
Sada, Literaturno-Izdatel'skij Centr, pg 61

Barbados
Business Tutors, pg 63

Belarus
Kavaler Publishers, pg 63

Belgium
Academia Press, pg 64
CED-Samsom, pg 66
Editions de la Chambre de Commerce et d'Industrie SA, pg 66
Coda, pg 66
Creadif, pg 67
Editions De Boeck-Larcier SA, pg 67
Documenta CV, pg 68

Roularta Books NV, pg 73
Uitgevery Scoop Infotex NV, pg 75

Bermuda
Bermudian Publishing Co, pg 76

Bosnia and Herzegovina
Svjetlost, pg 77

Botswana
Morula Press, Business School of Botswana, pg 77

Brazil
Editora Atlas SA, pg 79
Berkeley Brasil Editora Ltda, pg 79
Editora Elevacao, pg 82
Cia Editora Nacional, pg 82
Editora Globo SA, pg 84
Livraria Nobel S/A, pg 86
Makron Books do Brasil Editora Ltda, pg 87
Editora Nova Fronteira SA, pg 88
Editora Ortiz SA, pg 89
Pearson Education Do Brasil, pg 89
Livraria Pioneira Editora/Enio Matheus Guazzelli e Cia Ltd, pg 89
Distribuidora Record de Servicos de Imprensa SA, pg 90
Saraiva SA, Livreiros Editores, pg 91
Summus Editorial Ltda, pg 92
Fundacao Getulio Vargas, pg 93

Bulgaria
Aratron, IK, pg 94
Ciela Publishing House, pg 94
Dolphin Press Group Ltd, pg 95
Foi-Commerce, pg 95
Interpres, pg 96
Makros 2000 - Plovdiv, pg 96
Naouka i Izkoustvo, Ltd, pg 97
Pensoft Publishers, pg 97
Seven Hills Publishers, pg 97
WTU Todor Kableskov, pg 98

China
Beijing Publishing House, pg 102
China Foreign Economic Relations & Trade Publishing House, pg 103
China Labour Publishing House, pg 103
China Machine Press (CMP), pg 103
China Materials Management Publishing House, pg 103
CITIC Publishing House, pg 104
Fudan University Press, pg 105
Heilongjiang Science & Technology Press, pg 106
Jilin Science & Technology Publishing House, pg 106
Qingdao Publishing House, pg 108
Shandong Science & Technology Press, pg 109
Shandong University Press, pg 109
Shanghai Foreign Language Education Press, pg 109
Zhejiang University Press, pg 110

Colombia
McGraw-Hill InterAmericana SA, pg 113
Unidad Universitaria del Sur (UNISUR), pg 114

Costa Rica
Academia de Centro America, pg 115

Croatia
Masmedia, pg 119
Prosvjeta, pg 120

Czech Republic
Karolinum, nakladatelstvi, pg 125
Pragma 4, pg 127
Press Art, pg 127
Svoboda Servis GmbH, pg 128
SystemConsult, pg 128

Denmark
Fremad A/S, pg 132
Forlaget FSR A/S (ITID A/S), pg 132
Ingenioeren/Boger, pg 133
Samfundslitteratur, pg 135
J H Schultz Information A/S, pg 135

Dominican Republic
Pontificia Universidad Catolica Madre y Maestra, pg 136

Egypt (Arab Republic of Egypt)
Dar El Shorouk, pg 138

Estonia
Olion Publishers, pg 140

Finland
Kauppakaari Oyj Lakimiesliiton Kustannus, Yrityksen Tietokirjat, pg 142
Yritystieto Oy - Foretagsdata AB, pg 145

France
Bottin SA, pg 151
Editions des Cahiers Bourbonnais, pg 152
De Vecchi Editions SA, pg 158
Editions d'Organisation, pg 161
Les Editions ESF, pg 161
InterEditions Paris, pg 169
Editions Legislatives, pg 172
Maxima Laurent du Mesnil Editeur, pg 175
Pearson Education France, pg 179
Les Presses du Management, pg 181
Sofiac (Societe Francaise des Imprimeries Administratives Centrales), pg 185

Germany
AZ Bertelsmann Direct GmbH, pg 197
Bank-Verlag GmbH, pg 198
Bayerischer Schulbuch-Verlag GmbH, pg 199
Beleke KG Verlag, pg 200
Berlin Verlag Arno Spitz GmbH, pg 200
Bertelsmann Lexikon Verlag GmbH, pg 201
Campus Verlag GmbH, pg 209
Compact Verlag GmbH, pg 211
Deutscher Adressbuch-Verlag fuer Wirtschaft und Verkehr GmbH, pg 214
Deutscher Betriebswirte-Verlag GmbH, pg 214
Deutscher Fachverlag GmbH, pg 214

SUBJECT INDEX

Deutscher Wirtschaftsdienst John von Freyend GmbH, pg 216
Droemersche Verlagsanstalt Th Knaur Nachfolger GmbH & Co, pg 218
Eppinger-Verlag OHG, pg 223
Fachbuchverlag Pfanneberg & Co, pg 226
Fachverlag fur das graphische Gewerbe GmbH, pg 226
Friedrich Kiehl Verlag GmbH, pg 230
Betriebswirtschaftlicher Verlag Dr Th Gabler GmbH, pg 231
Alfons W Gentner Verlag GmbH & Co KG, pg 231
Graefe und Unzer Verlag GmbH, pg 233
Walter de Gruyter GmbH & Co KG, pg 234
Dr Curt Haefner-Verlag GmbH, pg 236
Haufe Mediengruppe, pg 238
Rudolf Haufe Verlag GmbH & Co KG, pg 238
Hofbauer, Christoph und Trojanow Ilia, Akademischer Verlag Muenchen, pg 241
Hans Holzmann Verlag GmbH und Co KG, pg 242
Huss-Verlag GmbH, pg 244
Huthig GmbH & Co KG, pg 244
IDW-Verlag GmbH, pg 244
IKO Verlag fur Interkulturelle Kommunikation, pg 244
Inno Vatio Verlags AG, pg 245
Koelner Universitaets-Verlag GmbH, pg 251
W Kohlhammer GmbH, abt Haussortiment, pg 252
Leitfadenverlag Verlag Dieter Sudholt, pg 257
Libertas- Europaeisches Institut GmbH, pg 257
Logophon Lehrmittelverlag GmbH, pg 258
Hermann Luchterhand Verlag GmbH, pg 259
Metropolis- Verlag fur Okonomie, Gesellschaft und Politik GmbH, pg 263
Verlag Neue Wirtschafts-Briefe GmbH & Co, pg 267
Nomos Verlagsgesellschaft mbH und Co KG, pg 269
Physica-Verlag, pg 273
Psychologie Verlags Union GmbH, pg 275
Rationalisierungs-Kuratorium der Deutschen Wirtschaft eV (RKW), pg 277
Verlag Norman Rentrop, pg 279
Ruhland Verlag Gimblt, pg 281
Schaeffer-Poeschel Verlag fuer Wirtschaft Steuern Recht, pg 282
Verlag Dr Otto Schmidt KG, pg 283
Erich Schmidt Verlag GmbH & Co, pg 284
Schulz-Kirchner Verlag GmbH, pg 285
Societaets-Verlag, pg 287
Springer-Verlag GmbH & Co KG, pg 288
Telex-Verlag Jaeger & Waldmann GmbH, pg 292
TF Fachverlag Gmbh, pg 293
Wirtschaftsverlag Carl Ueberreuter, pg 295
UTB fuer Wissenschaft Uni-Taschenbuecher GmbH, pg 297
Verlag Moderne Industrie AG & Co KG, pg 298
Verlagsgruppe Jehle-Rehm GmbH, pg 298
Walhalla Fachverlag GmbH & Co KG Praetoria, pg 300
WEKA Firmengruppe GmbH & Co KG, pg 301
Wer liefert was? GmbH, pg 301
WRS Verlag Wirtschaft, Recht und Steuern GmbH & Co KG, pg 304
Fachbuchverlag Armin W Wuth, pg 304

Greece

Hestia-I D Hestia-Kollaros & Co Corporation, pg 311
Patakis Publishers, pg 314
Sakkoulas Publications SA, pg 314
Vivliothiki Eftychia Galeou, pg 315

Haiti

Editions Caraiibes SA, pg 317

Hong Kong

The Chinese University Press, pg 319
Chung Hwa Book Co (HK) Ltd, pg 319
Joint Publishing (HK) Co Ltd, pg 320
Ming Pao Publications Ltd, pg 321
Publications (Holdings) Ltd, pg 321
Wellday Ltd, pg 322
Yazhou Zhoukan Ltd, pg 322

Hungary

KJK-Keaszov, pg 324
Kossuth Kiado RT, pg 325
Lang Kiado, pg 325
Novorg Kiado, pg 326

India

Academic Publishers, pg 329
Addison-Wesley (Singapore) Pte Ltd, pg 329
Asia Pacific Business Press Inc, pg 331
Associated Publishing House, pg 331
Bharatiya Samijik Vigyan Auusandhan Parishad, pg 332
S Chand & Co Ltd, pg 334
Frank Brothers & Co (Publishers) Ltd, pg 337
General Book Depot, pg 337
Himalaya Publishing House, pg 338
National Council of Applied Economic Research, Publications Division, pg 344
National Institute of Industrial Research (NIIR), pg 344
Omsons Publications, pg 345
Orient Paperbacks, pg 345
Oxford University Press, pg 345
Reliance Publishing House, pg 347
Roli Books Pvt Ltd, pg 348
Sage Publications India Pvt Ltd, pg 348
Scientific Book Agency, pg 349
Sita Publications, pg 350
Somaiya Publications Pvt Ltd, pg 350
South Asia Publications, pg 350
Sultan Chand & Sons Pvt Ltd, pg 351
N M Tripathi Pvt Ltd, pg 352
Vidya Puri, pg 352
A H Wheeler & Co Ltd, pg 353

Indonesia

P T Bulan Bintang, pg 354
Bumi Aksara PT, pg 354
Dinastindo, pg 355
PT Indira, pg 355
Pustaka Utama Grafiti, PT, pg 357
Yayasan Obor Indonesia, pg 357

Iraq

National House for Publishing, Distributing and Advertising, pg 358

Ireland

A & A Farmar, pg 358
The Educational Company of Ireland, pg 360
Gill & Macmillan Ltd, pg 361
The Hannon Press, pg 361
Irish Management Institute, pg 361
Oak Tree Press, pg 362
O'Brien Educational, pg 363
The O'Brien Press Ltd, pg 363

Israel

Dyonon/Papyrus Publishing House of the Tel-Aviv, pg 367
Intermedia Audio, Video Book Publishing Ltd, pg 368

Italy

Franco Angeli SRL, pg 375
Bancaria Editrice SpA, pg 377
Ciranna - Roma, pg 381
CLUEB (Cooperativa Libraria Universitaria Editrice Bologna), pg 382
Giovanni De Vecchi Editore SpA, pg 384
Casa Editrice Istituto della Santa, pg 384
Etas Libri, pg 388
Isper SRL, pg 394
Ithaca, pg 394
Edizioni Olivares, pg 402
Pirola, pg 403
RCS Libri SpA, pg 405
Edizioni Universitarie Romane, pg 406
Tecniche Nuove SpA, pg 409
Who's Who In Italy SRL, pg 412

Jamaica

Carlong Publishers (Caribbean) Ltd, pg 412

Japan

The American Chamber of Commerce in Japan, pg 414
CMC Co Ltd, pg 415
Diamond Inc, pg 416
Dobun Shoin, pg 416
Gakken Co Ltd, pg 416
Kaibundo Publishing Co Ltd, pg 419
Koyo Shobo, pg 420
Nikkagiren Shuppan-Sha (JUSE Press Ltd), pg 422
The Nikkan Kogyo Shimbun Ltd, pg 422
Nippon Hoso Shuppan Kyokai (NHK Publishing), pg 422
Nippon Jitsugyo Publishing Co, Ltd, pg 423
Pearson Education Japan, pg 423
PHP Kenkyujo, pg 423
President Inc, pg 423
Sagano Shoin, pg 424
Seibido Shuppan Company Ltd, pg 424
Seibundo Shinkosha Publishing Co Ltd, pg 425
Shincho-Sha Co Ltd, pg 425

BOOK

The Simul Press Inc, pg 426
Sobun-Sha, pg 426
Zeimukeiri-Kyokai, pg 429

Jordan

Jordan Book Centre Co Ltd, pg 430

Kenya

Focus Publications Ltd, pg 431
Heinemann Kenya Limited (EAEP), pg 431
Midi Teki Publishers, pg 433
Shirikon Publishers, pg 433
Space Sellers Ltd, pg 433

Democratic People's Republic of Korea

Industrial Publishing House, pg 434

Republic of Korea

Bi-bong Publishing Co, pg 435
Chung Rim Publishing Co Ltd, pg 435
Gim-Yeong Co, pg 436
Hakmun Publishing, Co, pg 436
Koreaone Press Inc, pg 438
Kyohaksa Publishing Co Ltd, pg 438
Maeil Gyeongje, pg 438
Oruem Publishing House, pg 439
Samseong Publishing Co Ltd, pg 440
Twenty-First Century Publishers, Inc, pg 440
Woong Jin Publishing Co Ltd, pg 440
Woongjin Media Corporation, pg 440
Yeha Publishing Co Ltd, pg 441

Latvia

Preses Nams, pg 442

Liechtenstein

Megatrade AG, pg 445

Lithuania

Lietuvos Informacijos Institutas, pg 446
Tyto Alba Publishers, pg 446

Luxembourg

Service Central de la Statistique et des Etudes Economiques (STATEC), pg 448

Malaysia

Amiza Associate Malaysia Sdn Bhd, pg 451
Berita Publishing Sdn Bhd, pg 451
Minerva Publications, pg 453
Pelanduk Publications (M) Sdn Bhd, pg 453
Penerbitan Tinta, pg 454

Mauritius

Editions de l'Ocean Indien Ltd, pg 457

Mexico

Editorial Banca y Comercio SA de CV, pg 458
Ediciones Contables y Administrativas SA, pg 459
Ediciones Eca SA de CV, pg 460
Ibcon SA, pg 462
Editorial Limusa SA de CV, pg 463

PUBLISHERS

McGraw-Hill Interamericana de Mexico, SA de CV, pg 463
Panorama Editorial, SA, pg 465
Editorial Pax Mexico, pg 465
Pearson Educacion de Mexico, SA de CV, pg 465
Sayrols Editorial SA de CV, pg 466
SCRIPTA - Distribucion y Servicios Editoriales, SA de CV, pg 467
Editorial Trillas SA de CV, pg 467
Javier Vergara Editor SA de CV, pg 468

Morocco
Access International Services, pg 469
Societe Ennewrasse Service Librairie et Imprimerie, pg 470

Nepal
International Standards Books & Periodicals (P) Ltd, pg 471

Netherlands
BoekWerk, pg 474
Business Contact BV, pg 475
Frank Fehmers Productions, pg 477
Kluwer Bedrijfswetenschappen, pg 479
Uitgeverij Lemma BV, pg 480
Mets & Schilt Uitgevers en Distributeurs, pg 481
Pearson Education Netherlands, pg 482
Samsom BedrijfsInformatie BV, pg 483
Scriptum, pg 483
VNU Business Press Group BV, pg 487

New Zealand
David Bateman Ltd, pg 488
Brooker's Ltd, pg 489
Current Pacific Limited, pg 490
Dunmore Press Ltd, pg 490
Exisle Publishing Ltd, pg 491
Learning Guides (Writers & Publishers Ltd), pg 492
Moss Associates Ltd, pg 493
Nahanni Publishing Ltd, pg 493
Nelson Price Milburn Ltd, pg 494
Pursuit Publishing, pg 494
Shoal Bay Press Ltd, pg 495
Statistics New Zealand, pg 496
Tandem Press, pg 496

Nigeria
Adebara Publishers Ltd, pg 497
Fourth Dimension Publishing Co Ltd, pg 499
Goldland Business Co Ltd, pg 499
New Africa Publishing Company Ltd, pg 500
Vantage Publishers International Ltd, pg 502

Norway
Glydendal Akademisk, pg 503
Universitetsforlaget, pg 505

Oman
Apex Publishing, pg 506

Pakistan
International Educational Services, pg 507
National Book Foundation, pg 508

Papua New Guinea
Kristen Pres, pg 510

Peru
Editorial Desarrollo SA, pg 511

Philippines
Bright Concepts Printing House, pg 512
De La Salle University, pg 513
Garotech, pg 513
Logos (Divine Word) Publications Inc, pg 513
Mutual Books Inc, pg 513
New Day Publishers, pg 514
Our Lady of Manaoag Publisher, pg 514
Rex Bookstores & Publishers, pg 514
Sinag-Tala Publishers Inc, pg 515
University of the Philippines Press, pg 515
UST Publishing House, pg 515

Poland
Polskie Wydawnictwo Ekonomiczne PWE SA, pg 516
Polish Scientific Publishers PWN, pg 519

Portugal
Edicoes Cetop, pg 523
Editora Classica, pg 523
GECTI (Gabinete de Especializacao e Cooperacao Tecnica Internacional L), pg 525
McGraw-Hill Editora de Portugal, pg 527
Editorial Presenca, pg 528

Puerto Rico
McGraw-Hill Intermericana del Caribe, Inc, pg 530

Romania
Editura Cronos SRL, pg 532
Editura Excelsior, pg 533
Editura Niculescu, pg 534
Rentrop & Straton Verlagsgruppe und Wirtschaftsconsulting, pg 535

Russian Federation
Airis Press, pg 537
N E Bauman Moscow State Technical University Publishers, pg 537
Izdatelstvo 'Ekonomika', pg 537
Finansy i Statistika Publishing House, pg 538
INFRA-M Izdatel'skij dom, pg 538
Izvestia Sovetov Narodnyh Deputatov Russian Federation (RF), pg 539
Legprombytizdat, pg 539
Obdeestro Znanie, pg 541
Vsesoyuznoe Obyedineniye Vneshtorgizdat, pg 542

Singapore
APAC Publishers Services, pg 545
Pearson Education Asia, pg 547
Taylor & Francis Asia Pacific, pg 548

Slovakia
Dom Techniky Zvazu Slovenskych Vedeckotechnickych Spolocnosti Ltd, pg 549
Priroda, pg 550

Slovenia
Univerza v Ljubljani Ekonomska Fakulteta, pg 552

South Africa
Educum Publishers Ltd, pg 554
Flesch Financial Publications (Pty) Ltd, pg 554
Human & Rousseau (Pty) Ltd, pg 555
Juta & Co, pg 556
Queillerie Publishers, pg 558
Ravan Press (Pty) Ltd, pg 558
South African Institute of Race Relations, pg 559
Van Schaik Publishers, pg 560
Witwatersrand University Press, pg 560

Spain
Asociacion para el Progreso de la Direccion (APD), pg 564
Editorial CISSPRAXIS SA, pg 567
Comunidad Autonoma de Madrid, Servicio de Documentacion y Publicaciones, pg 568
CTE-Centro de Tecnologia Educativa SA, pg 569
Ediciones Diaz de Santos SA, pg 569
Eumo Editorial, pg 574
EUNSA (Ediciones Universidad de Navarra SA), pg 574
Editorial Hispano Europea SA, pg 577
Iberico Europea de Ediciones SA, pg 577
Editorial Labor SA, pg 579
Lid Editorial Empresarial, SL, pg 580
Marcombo SA de Boixareu Editores, pg 581
Pais Vasco Servicio Central de Publicaciones, pg 585
Editorial Paraninfo SA, pg 586
Ediciones Piramide SA, pg 586
Editorial Tecnos SA, pg 592
Universidad de Valladolid Secretariado de Publicaciones e Intercambio Editorial, pg 594
Ediciones Urano, SA, pg 595
Javier Vergara Editor SA, pg 595
Xunta de Galicia, pg 596

Sweden
Ekonomibok Forlag AB, pg 601
Iustus Forlag AB, pg 603
Liber AB, pg 604
Studentlitteratur AB, pg 606
Svenska Foerlaget liv & ledarskap ab, pg 607
Tryckeriforlaget AB, pg 607

Switzerland
Cockatoo Press (Schweiz), Thailand-Publikationen, pg 611
Cosmos-Verlag AG, pg 611
Marcel Dekker AG, pg 612
Dimension World Ltd, pg 612
Ott Verlag AG, pg 621
Editions du Panorama, pg 621
Promoedition SA, pg 622
Editiones Roche, pg 623
Schulthess Polygraphischer Verlag AG, pg 624
Versus Verlag AG, pg 627

Syrian Arab Republic
Damascus University Press, pg 628

Taiwan, Province of China
Asian Culture Co, pg 629
Chien Chen Bookstore Publishing Company Ltd, pg 629
Commonwealth Publishing Company Ltd, pg 629
Dayi Information Co, pg 629
Chu Hai Publishing (Taiwan) Co Ltd, pg 630
Hsiao Yuan Publication Co, Ltd, pg 630
Laureate Book Co Ltd, pg 631
Linking Publishing Company Ltd, pg 631
Shy Mau Publishing Company, pg 631
Yuan Liou Publishing Co, Ltd, pg 632

United Republic of Tanzania
General Publications Ltd, pg 633
Nyota Publishers Ltd, pg 634

Tunisia
Ceres Editions, pg 637

Turkey
Alkim Kitapcilik-Yayimcilik, pg 638
Inkilap Publishers Ltd, pg 640
Sabah Kitaplari, pg 641
Soez Yayin/Oyunajans, pg 641

Ukraine
ASK Ltd, pg 643
Osnova, Kharkov State University Press, pg 643
Osnovy Publishers, pg 643

United Arab Emirates
Motivate Publishing, pg 644

United Kingdom
ABG Professional Information, pg 644
Academic Press Ltd, pg 644
Adamantine Press Ltd, pg 645
AP Information Services, pg 648
Ashgate Publishing Ltd, pg 649
Ashton & Denton Publishing Co (CI) Ltd, pg 650
Aslib, The Association for Information Management, pg 650
Blackwell Publishers, pg 655
BPP Publishing Ltd, pg 658
Nicholas Brealey Publishing, pg 659
Business Monitor International, pg 661
Capstone Publishing Ltd, pg 663
Cassell & Co, pg 664
Causeway Press Ltd, pg 665
CCH Editions Ltd, pg 665
Chartered Institute of Personnel & Development, pg 667
Computer Step, pg 670
The Continuum International Publishing Group Ltd, pg 670
Croner CCH Group Ltd, pg 672
The Economist Intelligence Unit, pg 677
Editon XII, pg 677
Edward Elgar Publishing Ltd, pg 678
Elliot Right Way Books, pg 678
Elm Publications, pg 678
Elsevier Advanced Technology, pg 678
Elsevier Science Ltd, pg 678
Euromonitor PLC, pg 680
The Eurospan Group, pg 680
Express Newspapers, pg 681

SUBJECT INDEX BOOK

Facts On File, pg 681
Financial World Publishing, pg 682
First & Best in Education Ltd, pg 682
Forbes Publications Ltd, pg 683
Gale Research, pg 685
Gower Publishing Ltd, pg 688
HarperCollins Publishers, pg 692
Harvard University Press, pg 692
HB Publications, pg 693
HLT Publications, pg 696
Hobsons, pg 696
Hodder & Stoughton Educational, pg 696
How To Books Ltd, pg 697
ICC United Kingdom, pg 698
Institution of Electrical Engineers, pg 700
Interfisc Publishing, pg 700
International Communications, pg 701
JAI Press Ltd, pg 702
James & James (Publishers) Ltd, pg 702
Jordan Publishing Ltd, pg 703
Kelly's, pg 704
Kogan Page Ltd, pg 705
Lang Syne Publishers Ltd, pg 706
Law Pack Publishing Ltd, pg 706
Learning Matters Ltd, pg 706
London Chamber of Commerce & Industry Examinations Board, pg 709
Management Books 2000 Ltd, pg 711
Management Pocketbooks Ltd, pg 711
Marshall Editions Ltd, pg 712
MCB University Press Ltd, pg 712
Media Research Publishing Ltd, pg 712
National Assembly for Wales, pg 717
National Extension College, pg 717
Nelson Thornes Ltd, pg 718
New Era Publications UK Ltd, pg 718
The NFER-NELSON Publishing Co Ltd, pg 719
Orion Publishing Group Ltd, pg 722
Osborne Books Ltd, pg 722
Palgrave Publishers Ltd, pg 723
PasTest, pg 724
Pearson Education, pg 725
Pearson Education Europe, Mideast & Africa, pg 725
Pergamon Flexible Learning, pg 726
Perpetuity Press, pg 726
Piatkus Books, pg 727
Policy Studies Institute, pg 729
Profile Books Ltd, pg 731
ProQuest Information & Learning, pg 731
Quiller Publishing Ltd, pg 732
William Reed Directories, pg 734
Rooster Books Ltd, pg 735
Roundhouse Publishing Ltd, pg 736
Routledge, pg 736
Routledge Curzon, pg 736
Royal Institute of International Affairs, pg 736
Sage Publications Ltd, pg 737
SHU Press, pg 742
Silver Link Publishing Ltd, pg 742
Simon & Schuster Ltd, pg 742
Spokesman, pg 744
Stacey International, pg 745
The Stationery Office, pg 745
Sutton Publishing Ltd, pg 746
Sydney Jary Ltd, pg 746
Take That Ltd, pg 746
Thoemmes Press, pg 748
Time Warner Books UK, pg 749

Verulam Publishing Ltd, pg 753
VNU Business Publications, pg 753
Which? Ltd, pg 755
Whurr Publishers Ltd, pg 756
Wiley Europe Ltd, pg 756
Wilmington Business Information Ltd, pg 756
Wimbledon Publishing Company Ltd, pg 757
Witherby & Co Ltd, pg 758
World of Information, pg 759

Viet Nam
Science & Technics Publishing House, pg 763

Zambia
Aafzam Ltd, pg 766
MFK Management Consultants Services, pg 766

Zimbabwe
College Press Publishers (Pvt) Ltd, pg 768
HarperCollins Publishers Zimbabwe Pvt Ltd, pg 768
Longman Zimbabwe (Pvt) Ltd, pg 768
Manhattan Publications, pg 769
Thomson Publications Zimbabwe (Pvt) Ltd, pg 769

CAREER DEVELOPMENT

Albania
NL SH, pg 1

Australia
Edward Arnold (Australia) Pty Ltd, pg 12
Artemis Publishing Pty Ltd, pg 12
Hale & Iremonger Pty Ltd, pg 24
Hospitality Press Pty Ltd, pg 26
The Useful Publishing Co, pg 46
VCTA Publishing, pg 46
Woodlands Publications, pg 48
Wrightbooks Pty Ltd, pg 48

Austria
Braintrust Marketing Services Ges mbH Verlag, pg 50
Buchhandlung WUV Dolmetsch, pg 50
Verlag des Oesterreichischen Gewerkschaftsbundes GmbH, pg 56
Oesterreichischer Gewerbeverlag GmbH, pg 56
Osterreichischer Bundesveilag Ges.mbh, pg 57

Belarus
Interdigets Publishing House, pg 63

Belgium
Marabout, pg 72
Uitgevery Scoop Infotex NV, pg 75

Brazil
Hemus Editora Ltda, pg 85
Editora Lucre Comercio e Representacoes, pg 87
Qualitymark Editora Ltda, pg 90

Bulgaria
Dolphin Press Group Ltd, pg 95
Regalia 6 Publishing House, pg 97

China
China Film Press, pg 103
Jilin Science & Technology Publishing House, pg 106

Costa Rica
Scout Interamericana, pg 117
Editorial de la Universidad de Costa Rica, pg 117

Croatia
Narodne Novine, pg 119

Cuba
Instituto de Informacion Cientifica y Tecnologica (IDICT), pg 121

Denmark
Det Schonbergske Forlag, pg 135

Dominican Republic
Pontificia Universidad Catolica Madre y Maestra, pg 136

France
Le Jour, Editeur, pg 170
Librairie Leonce Laget, pg 171
LT Editions-J Lanore-H Laurens, pg 172
Editions Legislatives, pg 172
Maxima Laurent du Mesnil Editeur, pg 175
Les Presses du Management, pg 181
Sofradif Editions Philippe Auzou, pg 185
Top Editions, pg 188

Germany
E Albrecht Verlags-Kommanditgesellschaft, pg 192
AOL-Verlag Frohmut Menze, pg 194
Bertelsmann Lexikon Verlag GmbH, pg 201
W Bertelsmann Verlag GmbH & Co KG, pg 201
Verlag Beruf + Schule Belz KG, pg 202
BW Bildung und Wissen Verlag und Software GmbH, pg 203
Charles Coleman Verlag GmbH & Co KG, pg 211
Cornelsen Verlag GmbH & Co OHG, pg 211
Deutscher Wirtschaftsdienst John von Freyend GmbH, pg 216
Dreisam Ratgeber in der Rutsker Verlag GmbH, pg 218
Econ Taschenbuchverlag, pg 220
Eppinger-Verlag OHG, pg 223
Fachbuchverlag Pfanneberg & Co, pg 226
Festo Didactic GmbH & Co, pg 227
Friedrich Kiehl Verlag GmbH, pg 230
Genius Verlag, pg 231
Alfons W Gentner Verlag GmbH & Co KG, pg 231
Verlag Gruppenpaedagogischer Literatur, pg 234
Verlag Handwerk und Technik GmbH, pg 237
Heckners Verlag, pg 238
HelfRecht Verlag und Druck, pg 239
Max Hueber Verlag GmbH & Co KG, pg 243
Huss-Medien GmbH, pg 243

Kallmeyer'sche Verlagsbuchhandlung GmbH, pg 247
Landbuch-Verlagsgesellschaft mbH, pg 255
Verlag Leske plus Budrich GmbH, pg 257
Mosaik Verlag GmbH, pg 265
Verlag Neue Wirtschafts-Briefe GmbH & Co, pg 267
Polygraph Verlag GmbH, pg 274
Quintessenz Verlags-GmbH, pg 276
Ritterbach Verlag GmbH, pg 279
Rossipaul Kommunikation GmbH, pg 280
1 H Sauer Verlag GmbH, pg 282
Verlag Moderne Industrie AG & Co KG, pg 298
Verlag und Studio fuer Hoerbuchproduktionen, pg 298
Walhalla Fachverlag GmbH & Co KG Praetoria, pg 300
WEKA Firmengruppe GmbH & Co KG, pg 301
Winklers Verlag Gebrueder Grimm, pg 303

Ghana
Sam Woode Ltd, pg 308

Greece
Hestia-I D Hestia-Kollaros & Co Corporation, pg 311

Hong Kong
Chung Hwa Book Co (HK) Ltd, pg 319
Publications (Holdings) Ltd, pg 321

Hungary
Mueszaki Koenyvkiado Ltd, pg 325

India
Dastane Ramchandra & Co, pg 335
General Book Depot, pg 337
Gyan Publishing House, pg 338
Nem Chand & Brothers, pg 344
Omsons Publications, pg 345
Orient Paperbacks, pg 345
Parimal Prakashan, pg 345
Reliance Publishing House, pg 347
Sultan Chand & Sons Pvt Ltd, pg 351
A H Wheeler & Co Ltd, pg 353

Indonesia
Dinastindo, pg 355
PT Indira, pg 355
Katalis PT Bina Mitra Plaosan, pg 356

Ireland
Careers & Educational Publishers Ltd, pg 359
The Educational Company of Ireland, pg 360
Oak Tree Press, pg 362
O'Brien Educational, pg 363

Italy
Giovanni De Vecchi Editore SpA, pg 384
EGEA (Edizioni Giuridiche Economiche Aziendali), pg 387

PUBLISHERS

Japan
Diamond Inc, pg 416
Seibido Shuppan Company Ltd, pg 424
Shufunotomo sha Co Ltd, pg 426

Kenya
Action Publishers, pg 430
Space Sellers Ltd, pg 433

Republic of Korea
Anam Publishing Co, pg 434
Ario Company Ltd, pg 434
Chung Rim Publishing Co Ltd, pg 435
Hongik Media Plus Ltd, pg 437
Koreaone Press Inc, pg 438

Liechtenstein
Rheintal Handelsgesellschaft Anstalt, pg 445

Lithuania
Sviesa Publishers, pg 446

Luxembourg
Editions Emile Borschette, pg 447

Malaysia
Federal Publications Sdn Bhd, pg 452
IBS Buku Sdn Bhd, pg 452
Minerva Publications, pg 453
Trix Corporation Sdn Bhd, pg 455

Mauritius
Editions de l'Ocean Indien Ltd, pg 457

Mexico
Editorial Diana SA de CV, pg 459
Grupo Editorial Iberoamerica, SA de CV, pg 461
Editorial Limusa SA de CV, pg 463
Editorial Pax Mexico, pg 465

Morocco
Office Marocain D'Annonces-OMA, pg 470

Nepal
International Standards Books & Periodicals (P) Ltd, pg 471

Netherlands
Business Contact BV, pg 475
Twente University Press, pg 485
VNU Business Press Group BV, pg 487

New Zealand
Legislation Direct, pg 492
Moss Associates Ltd, pg 493

Pakistan
National Book Foundation, pg 508

Philippines
New Day Publishers, pg 514
Our Lady of Manaoag Publisher, pg 514

Portugal
Edicoes Cetop, pg 523
Impala, pg 525
Monitor-Projectos e Edicoes, LDA, pg 527

Romania
Coresi SRL, pg 532
Editura Niculescu, pg 534

Russian Federation
Airis Press, pg 537
Finansy i Statistika Publishing House, pg 538

Slovakia
Ustav informacii a prognoz skolstva mladeze a telovychovy, pg 551

South Africa
Erudita Publications (Pty) Ltd, pg 554
Human Sciences Research Council, pg 555

Spain
Centro de Estudios Adams-Ediciones Valbuena SA, pg 561
Ediciones Gestio 2000 SA, pg 575
Lid Editorial Empresarial, SL, pg 580
Ediciones Norma SA, pg 584
Ediciones Tutor SA, pg 594

Sri Lanka
Sunera Publishers, pg 598

Sweden
Svenska Foerlaget liv & ledarskap ab, pg 607

Switzerland
Oesch Verlag AG, pg 620

Taiwan, Province of China
Chien Chen Bookstore Publishing Company Ltd, pg 629
Jillion Publishing Co, pg 630
Linking Publishing Company Ltd, pg 631
Shy Mau Publishing Company, pg 631

Turkey
Soez Yayin/Oyunajans, pg 641

Uganda
Fountain Publishers Ltd, pg 642

Ukraine
ASK Ltd, pg 643

United Kingdom
Bloomsbury Publishing PLC, pg 656
Nicholas Brealey Publishing, pg 659
Careers & Occupational Information Centre (COIC), pg 663
Cassell & Co, pg 664
Elliot Right Way Books, pg 678
Elm Publications, pg 678
Facts On File, pg 681
Hobsons, pg 696
Hodder & Stoughton Educational, pg 696
Hospitality Training Foundation, pg 697
How To Books Ltd, pg 697
Kogan Page Ltd, pg 705
Management Books 2000 Ltd, pg 711
McGraw-Hill Publishing Company, pg 712
National Extension College, pg 717
Pearson Education, pg 725
Piatkus Books, pg 727
Publishing Training Centre at BookHouse, pg 731
Sherwood Publishing, pg 741
Telegraph Books, pg 748
Trotman Publishing, pg 750
University of London Careers Service, pg 751
Vacation Work Publications, pg 752

Viet Nam
Science & Technics Publishing House, pg 763

CHEMISTRY, CHEMICAL ENGINEERING

Albania
NL SH, pg 1

Argentina
EUDEBA (Editorial Universitaria de Buenos Aires), pg 6

Australia
Australian Academy of Science, pg 13
CSIRO Publishing (Commonwealth Scientific & Industrial Research Organisation), pg 19
EA Books, pg 21
Emerald City Books, pg 22
McGraw-Hill Australia Pty Ltd, pg 32
Reed Educational Publishing Australia, pg 40
Royal Society of New South Wales, pg 41
Standards Association of Australia, pg 43
La Trobe University Press, pg 45

Austria
Bethania Verlag, pg 49
IAEA - International Atomic Energy Agency, pg 53
Osterreichischer Bundesverlag Ges.mbh, pg 57
Springer-Verlag Wien, pg 59

Belarus
Belaruskaya Encyklapedyya, pg 63

Belgium
Conservart SA, pg 67
Editions De Boeck-Larcier SA, pg 67

Bolivia
Editorial Don Bosco, pg 76

Brazil
LTC-Livros Tecnicos e Cientificos Editora S/A, pg 87
Editora Scipione Ltda, pg 91

Bulgaria
Gea-Libris Publishing House, pg 95
Makros 2000 - Plovdiv, pg 96

SUBJECT INDEX

Chile
Arrayan Editores, pg 99

China
Beijing University Press, pg 102
Chemical Industry Press, pg 102
China Forestry Publishing House, pg 103
China Ocean Press, pg 103
Fudan University Press, pg 105
Guizhou Education Publishing House, pg 106
Wissenschaft und Technik Verlag Henan Henan Scientific & Technological Publishing House, pg 106
International Academic Publishers, pg 106
Jiangsu Science & Technology Publishing House, pg 106
Jilin Science & Technology Publishing House, pg 106
Metallurgical Industry Press (MIP), pg 107
Nanjing University Press, pg 107
Printing Industry Publishing House, pg 108
Science Press, pg 108
Shandong University Press, pg 109
South China University of Science and Technology Press, pg 109
Tianjin Science & Technology Publishing House, pg 109
Tsinghua University Press, pg 110
Wuhan University Press, pg 110
Zhejiang University Press, pg 110

Colombia
McGraw-Hill InterAmericana SA, pg 113
Unidad Universitaria del Sur (UNISUR), pg 114

Czech Republic
Academia, pg 122
Cesky normalizacni institut, pg 127
Vydavatelstvi Ceskeho Geologickeho Ustavu, pg 129

Denmark
Systime, pg 136

Dominican Republic
Pontificia Universidad Catolica Madre y Maestra, pg 136

France
CNRS Editions, pg 155
Doin Editeurs, pg 160
Editions Jacques Gabay, pg 165
Editions Gammaprim, pg 166
Hermann editeurs des Sciences et des Arts SA, pg 168
Hermes Science Publications, pg 168
InterEditions Paris, pg 169
Lavoisier, pg 172
Librairie Scientifique et Technique Albert Blanchard, pg 173
Ouest Editions, pg 178
Polytechnica, pg 180
Presses Universitaires de Grenoble, pg 181
Editions Springer France, pg 186
Editions Technip SA, pg 187
Librairie Vuibert, pg 189

Germany

Aol-Verlag Frohmut Menze, pg 194
Aulis Verlag Deubner & Co KG, pg 197
Johann Ambrosius Barth GmbH, pg 198
Bayerischer Schulbuch-Verlag GmbH, pg 199
Verlag Beruf + Schule Belz KG, pg 202
Beuth Verlag GmbH, pg 202
Oscar Brandstetter Verlag GmbH & Co KG, pg 206
Fachverlag Hans Carl GmbH, pg 209
Cornelsen Verlag GmbH & Co OHG, pg 211
Verlag Harri Deutsch, pg 213
Deutscher Verlag fur Grundstoffindustrie GmbH, pg 215
Ecomed Verlagsgesellschaft AG & Co KG, pg 220
Fachbuchverlag Leipzig im Carl Hanser Verlag, pg 226
Ferd Dummler's Verlag, pg 227
S Hirzel Verlag GmbH und Co, pg 241
Huthig GmbH & Co KG, pg 244
Franckh-Kosmos Verlags-GmbH & Co, pg 252
Springer-Verlag GmbH & Co KG, pg 288
Verlag Stahleisen GmbH, pg 289
B G Teubner GmbH, pg 292
Georg Thieme Verlag KG, pg 293
Trans Tech Publications, pg 294
UTB fuer Wissenschaft Uni-Taschenbuecher GmbH, pg 297
Curt R Vincentz Verlag, pg 298
Vogel Medien GmbH & Co KG, pg 299
Volk und Wissen Verlag GmbH & Co, pg 299
Vulkan-Verlag GmbH, pg 299
Wiley-VCH Verlag GmbH, pg 302
Verlag Zeitschrift fur Naturforschung, pg 305

Ghana

Sedco Publishing Ltd, pg 308

Greece

Kyriakidis, pg 312
Panepistimio Ioanninon, pg 314

Holy See (Vatican City State)

Pontificia Academia Scientiarum, pg 317

Hungary

Magyar Tudomanyos Akademia Koezponti Fizikai Kutato Intezet Koenyvtara, pg 325
Mueszaki Koenyvkiado Ltd, pg 325

India

Addison-Wesley (Singapore) Pte Ltd, pg 329
Affiliated East West Press Pvt Ltd, pg 329
APH Publishing Corp, pg 331
Asia Pacific Business Press Inc, pg 331
B I Publications Pvt Ltd, pg 331
Bani Mandir, Book-Sellers, Publishers & Educational Suppliers, pg 332
Bhawan Book Service, Publishers & Distributors, pg 333
Goel Prakashen, pg 337
Heritage Publishers, pg 338
Multitech Publishing Co, pg 343
Narosa Publishing House, pg 343
National Institute of Industrial Research (NIIR), pg 344
Pitambar Publishing Co (P) Ltd, pg 346
Publications & Information Directorate, CSIR, pg 346
Rajasthan Hindi Granth Academy, pg 347
Scientific Book Agency, pg 349
Sita Publications, pg 350
South Asian Publishers Pvt Ltd, pg 350
Sultan Chand & Sons Pvt Ltd, pg 351
Vidya Puri, pg 352
Vidyarthi Mithram Press, pg 352
Vikas Publishing House Pvt Ltd, pg 353
S Viswanathan (Printers & Publishers) Pvt Ltd, pg 353

Indonesia

Andi Offset, pg 354
Institut Teknologi Bandung, pg 355

Israel

Dyonon/Papyrus Publishing House of the Tel-Aviv, pg 367
Freund Publishing House Ltd, pg 367
Medcom Ltd, pg 370
Open University of Israel, pg 371

Italy

Casa Editrice Giuseppe Principato Spa, pg 380
D'Anna, pg 383
Editrice Edisco, pg 386
Giunti Publishing Group, pg 391
Gruppo Editoriale Faenza Editrice SpA, pg 392
Loescher Editore SRL, pg 396
Masson SpA, pg 398
Monduzzi Editore SpA, pg 399
Nagard, pg 400
Principato, pg 404
Edizioni Universitarie Romane, pg 406
Societa Editrice la Goliardica Pavese SRL, pg 408
Edizioni Sorbona Milano, pg 408
Unipress, pg 410
Zanichelli Editore SpA, pg 412

Japan

Baifukan Co Ltd, pg 414
Dainippon Tosho Publishing Co, Ltd, pg 416
Hirokawa Publishing Co, pg 417
Kyoritsu Shuppan Co Ltd, pg 420
Maruzen Co Ltd, pg 421
Nippon Hoso Shuppan Kyokai (NHK Publishing), pg 422
Sangyo-Tosho Publishing Co Ltd, pg 424
Sankyo Publishing Company Ltd, pg 424
Sanyo Shuppan Boeki Co Inc, pg 424
Tokyo Kagaku Dozin Co Ltd, pg 427

Kazakstan

Gylym, Izd-Vo, pg 430
Kazakh Al-Farabi State National University, pg 430

Democratic People's Republic of Korea

Academy of Sciences Publishing House, pg 434
Korea Science and Encyclopedia Publishing House, pg 434

Republic of Korea

Bo Moon Dang, pg 435
Prompter Publications, pg 439

Latvia

Lielvards Ltd, pg 442

Lithuania

Academia, pg 445

Malaysia

Penerbit Universiti Sains Malaysia, pg 454
Unit Penerbitan Akademik Cancelori~ Universiti Teknologi Malaysia, pg 455

Mexico

Editorial Esfinge SA de CV, pg 460
Grupo Editorial Iberoamerica, SA de CV, pg 461
Editorial Limusa SA de CV, pg 463
Pearson Educacion de Mexico, SA de CV, pg 465
Universidad Nacional Autonoma de Mexico (National University of Mexico), pg 467

Republic of Moldova

Lumina Publishing House, pg 468

Nepal

International Standards Books & Periodicals (P) Ltd, pg 471

Netherlands

Baltzer Science Publishers, pg 474
Delft University Press, pg 476
Elsevier Science BV, pg 477
Hagen & Stam Uitgeverij Ten, pg 478
IOS Press BV, pg 479
LCG Malmberg BV, pg 480
V S P International Science Publishers, pg 486

New Zealand

ABA Books, pg 488
ESA Publications (NZ) Ltd, pg 490
New House Publishers Ltd, pg 493
Nelson Price Milburn Ltd, pg 494

Nigeria

Ilesanmi Press (Educational Publishers) Ltd, pg 499
Riverside Communications, pg 501
West African Book Publishers Ltd, pg 502

Norway

Elanders Publishing AS, pg 503
NKI Forlaget, pg 504

Pakistan

National Book Foundation, pg 508
Publishers United Pvt Ltd, pg 508
Quaid-i-Azam University Department of Biological Sciences, pg 508

Philippines

UST Publishing House, pg 515

Poland

Instytut Historii Nauki PAN, pg 516
PZWL Wydawnictwo Lekarskie Ltd, pg 519
Wydawnictwa Naukowo-Techniczne, pg 521

Portugal

Constancia Editores, SA, pg 524
Europress Editores e Distribuidores de Publicacoes Lda, pg 525
McGraw-Hill Editora de Portugal, pg 527

Romania

Editura Academiei Romane, pg 531
Editura Dacia, pg 532

Russian Federation

Izdatel'stvo Kazanskago Universiteta, pg 538
Izdatelstvo Mir, pg 540
Nauka Publishers, pg 540
Izdatel'stvo Nizhegorodskogo Gosudarstvennogo Univ, pg 540
Voronezh State University Publishers, pg 542
Izdatelstvo Vysshaya Shkola, pg 543

Saudi Arabia

King Saud University, pg 543

Singapore

APAC Publishers Services, pg 545
Reed Elsevier, South East Asia, pg 547
World Scientific Publishing Co Pte Ltd, pg 549

South Africa

Educum Publishers Ltd, pg 554

Spain

Ediciones y Distribuciones Universitarias SA, pg 571
Instituto de Estudios Riojanos, pg 574
Ediciones Omega SA, pg 585
Publicaciones de la Universidad de Alicante, pg 588
Servicio de Publicaciones Universidad de Cadiz, pg 590
Editorial Sintesis, SA, pg 590
Universidad de Valladolid Secretariado de Publicaciones e Intercambio Editorial, pg 594
Edicions de la Universitat Politecnica de Catalunya SL, pg 594

Sri Lanka

Ministry of Education, pg 597
Warna Publishers, pg 598

Sweden

Studentlitteratur AB, pg 606

Switzerland

Marcel Dekker AG, pg 612
Verlag Harri Deutsch, pg 612
Elsevier Science SA, pg 613
Verlag Helvetica Chimica Acta, pg 615

Presses Polytechniques et Universitaires Romandes, PPUR, pg 622
Editiones Roche, pg 623
Trans Tech Publications SA, pg 626
Vogt-Schild Ag, Druck und Verlag, pg 627

Syrian Arab Republic
Damascus University Press, pg 628

Taiwan, Province of China
Fuh-Wen Book Co, pg 630
Hsiao Yuan Publication Co, Ltd, pg 630
Petroleum Information Publishing Co, pg 631
Yi Hsien Publishing Co Ltd, pg 632

United Republic of Tanzania
DUP (1996) Ltd, pg 633

Thailand
Graphic Art Publishing, pg 635

Tunisia
Ceres Editions, pg 637

Turkey
Caglayan Kitabevi, pg 639

Ukraine
Naukova Dumka Publishers, pg 643
Osnova, Kharkov State University Press, pg 643
Osvita, pg 643

United Kingdom
Academic Press Ltd, pg 644
Association for Science Education, pg 650
Blackwell Science Ltd, pg 656
Business Monitor International, pg 661
Cambridge University Press, pg 662
DMG Business Media Ltd, pg 675
Elsevier Science Ltd, pg 678
The Eurospan Group, pg 680
W H Freeman & Co Ltd, pg 684
Hodder & Stoughton Educational, pg 696
Imperial College Press, pg 699
Institution of Chemical Engineers, pg 700
IOM Communications Ltd, pg 701
JAI Press Ltd, pg 702
Kluwer Academic/Plenum Publishers, pg 705
Manson Publishing Ltd, pg 711
Micelle Press, pg 714
John Murray (Publishers) Ltd, pg 716
Open University Worldwide, pg 721
Pearson Education, pg 725
Pharmaceutical Press, pg 726
Portland Press Ltd, pg 730
Research Studies Press Ltd (RSP), pg 734
The Royal Society of Chemistry, pg 737
Science Reviews Ltd, pg 739
Sheffield Academic Press Ltd, pg 741
Wiley Europe Ltd, pg 756

Uruguay
A Monteverde y Cia SA, pg 760

Venezuela
Sociedad Fondo Editorial Cenamec, pg 762

Viet Nam
Science & Technics Publishing House, pg 763

Zimbabwe
College Press Publishers (Pvt) Ltd, pg 768
Standards Association of Zimbabwe (SAZ), pg 769

CHILD CARE & DEVELOPMENT

Albania
NL SH, pg 1

Argentina
Editorial Paidos SAICF, pg 8

Australia
The Australian Council for Educational Research Ltd, pg 13
Chase Just Publishing, pg 17
Crossroad Distributors Pty Ltd, pg 19
Finch Publishing, pg 22
Hale & Iremonger Pty Ltd, pg 24
Hampden Press, pg 25
Little Red Apple Publishing, pg 30
McGraw-Hill Australia Pty Ltd, pg 32
OTEN (Open Training & Education Network), pg 36
Pademelon Press, pg 36
Pearson Education Australia, pg 37
Priestley Consulting, pg 39
RMIT Publishing, pg 41
Simon & Schuster Australia Pty Ltd, pg 42
Tertiary Press, pg 44
Zoe Publishing Pty Ltd, pg 48

Austria
Development News Ltd, pg 51
Verlag des Osterr Kneippbundes GmbH, pg 57

Azerbaijan
Sada, Literaturno-Izdatel'skij Centr, pg 61

Bangladesh
Gatidhara, pg 62
Gono Prakashani, Gono Shasthya Kendra, pg 62

Belarus
Interdigets Publishing House, pg 63

Belgium
Davidsfonds - Infodok NV, pg 67
Koepel van de Vlaamse Noord - Zuidbeweging 11.11.11, pg 70
Marabout, pg 72
Zuid-Nederlandse Uitgeverij NV/ Central Uitgeverij, pg 76

Brazil
A & A & A Edicoes e Promocoes Internacionais Ltda, pg 77
Agalma Psicanalise Editora Ltda, pg 78
Editora Antroposofica Ltda, pg 78
ARTMED, pg 79
EDUSC - Editora da Universidade do Sagrado Coracao, pg 82
Editora Marco Zero Ltda, pg 87
Editora Mundo Cristao, pg 88
Paulinas Editorial, pg 89

Bulgaria
Fondacija Zlatno Kljuce, pg 95
Musica Publishing House Ltd, pg 96
Nov Covek Publishing House, pg 97
Reporter, pg 97
Sila & Zivot, pg 98
Sluntse Publishing House, pg 98

China
Beijing Juvenile & Children's Books Publishing House, pg 102
Beijing Publishing House, pg 102
China Braille Press, pg 103
Guizhou Education Publishing House, pg 106
Jilin Science & Technology Publishing House, pg 106
Shandong Education Publishing House, pg 108
Shanghai Educational Publishing House, pg 109
Tianjin Science & Technology Publishing House, pg 109

Colombia
Consejo Episcopal Latinoamericano Celam, pg 111

Costa Rica
Promesa, Ediciones, pg 116

Czech Republic
Pavla Momcilova, pg 126
Portal Ltd, pg 127

Denmark
Borgens Forlag A/S, pg 130
Fremad A/S, pg 132

Ecuador
CEPLAES, pg 137

Egypt (Arab Republic of Egypt)
Dar El Shorouk Publishing & Distributing House, pg 138

Estonia
Sinisukk, pg 140
Valgus Publishers, pg 141

Finland
Lasten Keskus Oy, pg 143

France
Editions Albin Michel, pg 146
Disney Hachette Edition, pg 159
LT Editions-J Lanore-H Laurens, pg 172
Librairie Larousse, pg 172
Editions Mango, pg 174
Editions Stock, pg 186

Germany
AOL-Verlag Frohmut Menze, pg 194
Ars Edition GmbH, pg 195
Beust Verlag GmbH, pg 202
Carl-Auer-Systeme Verlag, pg 209
J G Cotta'sche Buchhandlung Nachfolger GmbH, pg 212
Deutscher Taschenbuch Verlag GmbH & Co KG (dtv), pg 215
Gatzanis Verlags GmbH, pg 231
Gesundheits-Dialog Verlag GmbH, pg 232
Verlag Gruppenpaedagogischer Literatur, pg 234
Dr Curt Haefner-Verlag GmbH, pg 236
Verlag im Kilian GmbH, pg 249
Knowledge Media International, pg 251
Midena Verlag, pg 264
Mosaik Verlag GmbH, pg 265
nymphenburger, pg 269
Psychologie Verlags Union GmbH, pg 275
Ernst Reinhardt GmbH & Co KG Verlag, pg 278
Springer-Verlag GmbH & Co KG, pg 288

Ghana
World Literature Project, pg 308

Greece
Akritas, pg 308
Anixis Publications, pg 309
Chrysi Penna - Golden Pen Books, pg 309
Govostis Publishing SA, pg 311
Hestia-I D Hestia-Kollaros & Co Corporation, pg 311
Kastaniotis Editions SA, pg 312
Odysseas Publications Ltd, pg 313
Patakis Publishers, pg 314

Guyana
Community Based Rehabilitation Progeamme, pg 317

Hong Kong
The Chinese University Press, pg 319
Hong Kong University Press, pg 320
Ming Pao Publications Ltd, pg 321
Publications (Holdings) Ltd, pg 321
Sesame Publication Co, pg 321
Unicorn Books Ltd, pg 322

Hungary
Aranyhal Konyvkiado Goldfish Publishing, pg 323
Kossuth Kiado RT, pg 325
Park Konyvkiado Kft (Park Publisher), pg 326

Iceland
Idunn, pg 328

India
Gyan Publishing House, pg 338
National Book Organization, pg 343
Pointer Publishers, pg 346
Reliance Publishing House, pg 347
Sita Publications, pg 350
Vidyarthi Mithram Press, pg 352

Indonesia
Advent Indonesia Publishing, pg 353
Gramedia, pg 355
Lembaga Demografi Fakultas Ekonomi Universitas Indonesia, pg 356
Yayasan Obor Indonesia, pg 357

SUBJECT INDEX

Ireland
A & A Farmar, pg 358
Gill & Macmillan Ltd, pg 361
Irish YouthWork Press, pg 362
Tivenan Publications, pg 364

Israel
Bitan Publishers Ltd, pg 365
Classikaletet, pg 366
Dyonon/Papyrus Publishing House of the Tel-Aviv, pg 367
Schocken Publishing House Ltd, pg 372
R Sirkis Publishers Ltd, pg 372

Italy
Gruppo Abele, pg 374
Editore Armando Armando SRL, pg 376
Belforte Editore Libraio srl, pg 377
Edizioni Centro Studi Erickson, pg 381
Elle Di Ci - Libreria Dottrina Cristiana, pg 388
Fatatrac, pg 388
Feguagiskia' Studios, pg 389
In Dialogo, pg 393
Red/Studio Redazionale SpA, pg 405
Samaya SRL, pg 406

Japan
Alice-Kan, pg 414
Gakken Co Ltd, pg 416
Japan Publications Inc, pg 418
Kokudo-Sha, pg 420
Kosei Publishing Co Ltd, pg 420
Minerva Shobo Co Ltd, pg 421
Reimei-Shobo Co Ltd, pg 424
Seibido Shuppan Company Ltd, pg 424
Shufunotomo sha Co Ltd, pg 426
Tsukiji Shokan Publishing Co, pg 428

Kenya
Paulines Publications-Africa, pg 433

Democratic People's Republic of Korea
The Foreign Language Press Group, pg 434
Grand People's Study House, pg 434

Republic of Korea
Bo Ri, pg 435
Chung Rim Publishing Co Ltd, pg 435
Hak Won Publishing Co, pg 436
Hakmun Publishing, Co, pg 436
Minjisa Publishing Co, pg 438
O Neul Publishing Co, pg 439

Latvia
Preses Nams, pg 442

Lithuania
Sviesa Publishers, pg 446
Victoria Publishers, pg 446

Malaysia
S Abdul Majeed & Co, pg 451
Federal Publications Sdn Bhd, pg 452
Tropical Press Sdn Bhd, pg 455

Maldive Islands
Non-Formal Education Centre, pg 455

Mexico
Ediciones Culturales Internacionales SA de CV Edicion Compra y Venta de Libros, Casetes, Videos, pg 459
Del Verbo Emprender SA de CV, pg 459
Editorial Diana SA de CV, pg 459
Fernandez Editores SA de CV, pg 461
Libra Editorial SA de CV, pg 463
Editorial Limusa SA de CV, pg 463
Organizacion Cultural LP SA de CV, pg 465
Selector SA de CV, pg 467
Editorial Trillas SA de CV, pg 467

Republic of Moldova
Lumina Publishing House, pg 468

Netherlands
Erven J Bijleveld, pg 474
De Boekerij BV, pg 474
Boom Uitgeverij, pg 474
Uitgeverij Ploegsma BV, pg 483
Sociaal en Cultureel Planbureau, pg 484
SWP, BV Uitgeverij, pg 485
Tirion Uitgevers BV, pg 485
Uitgeverij De Toorts, pg 485

New Zealand
Nagare Press, pg 493
Nelson Price Milburn Ltd, pg 494
Reach Publications, pg 495
Shoal Bay Press Ltd, pg 495
Words Work, pg 497

Nigeria
Evans Brothers (Nigeria Publishers) Ltd, pg 499
West African Book Publishers Ltd, pg 502

Philippines
Bookmark Inc, pg 512
Our Lady of Manaoag Publisher, pg 514
Rex Bookstores & Publishers, pg 514

Poland
PZWL Wydawnictwo Lekarskie Ltd, pg 519

Portugal
Difusao Cultural, pg 524
Direccao Geral Familia, pg 524
Impala, pg 525
Editorial Presenca, pg 528
Vega-Publicacao e Distribuicao de Livros e Revistas, Lda, pg 530

Romania
Editura Niculescu, pg 534

Russian Federation
Airis Press, pg 537
Dom, Izdatel'stvo sovetskogo deskkogo fonda im & 1 Lenina, pg 537
Obdeestro Znanie, pg 541
Panorama Publishing House, pg 541
St Andrew's Biblical Theological College, pg 541

Singapore
Taylor & Francis Asia Pacific, pg 548

Slovakia
Sofa, pg 551

Slovenia
Zalozba Mihelac d o o, pg 552

South Africa
Bet-El Publishers, pg 553
Human & Rousseau (Pty) Ltd, pg 555
Jacana Education, pg 555
New Africa Books (Pty) Ltd, pg 557
Struik Publishers (Pty) Ltd, pg 559

Spain
Edex, Centro de Recursos Comunitarios, pg 571
Editorial Editex SA, pg 572
Emece Editores, pg 573
Editorial Espasa-Calpe SA, pg 573
Hercules de Ediciones, SA, pg 577
Idea Books, SA, pg 578
LEDA (Las Ediciones de Arte), pg 579
Ediciones Medici SA, pg 582
Ediciones Morata SL, pg 583
Ediciones Norma SA, pg 584
Ediciones de la Torre, pg 593
Tursen, SA, pg 593

Sweden
Eriksson & Lindgren Bokforlag, pg 602
Gothia Publishing House, pg 603

Switzerland
Bohem Press Kinderbuchverlag, pg 610
Editions Jouvence, pg 616

Taiwan, Province of China
Ai Chih Book Co Ltd, pg 629
Campus Evangelical Fellowship, Literature Department, pg 629
Chu Liu Book Company, pg 629
Commonwealth Publishing Company Ltd, pg 629
Echo Publishing Company Ltd, pg 629
Ho-Chi Book Publishing Co, pg 630
Laureate Book Co Ltd, pg 631
Linking Publishing Company Ltd, pg 631
Shy Mau Publishing Company, pg 631
Wei-Chuan Publishing Company Ltd, pg 632

United Republic of Tanzania
Central Tanganyika Press, pg 633
Tanzania Publishing House, pg 634

Thailand
Sang Dad Publishing Company Ltd, pg 635

Turkey
Afa Yayincilik Sanayi Tic AS, pg 638
Alkim Kitapcilik-Yayimcilik, pg 638
Inkilap Publishers Ltd, pg 640
Kok Yayincilik, pg 640
Saray Medikal Yayin Tic Ltd Sti, pg 641

Ukraine
ASK Ltd, pg 643
Osvita, pg 643

United Kingdom
Act 3 Publishing, pg 645
BILD Publications, pg 654
Blackwell Science Ltd, pg 656
Bloomsbury Publishing PLC, pg 656
BAAF: Adoption & Fostering, pg 659
Castlemead Publications, pg 665
Constable Publishers, pg 670
Dorling Kindersley Ltd, pg 676
Elsevier Science Ltd, pg 678
The Eurospan Group, pg 680
Free Association Books Ltd, pg 684
W H Freeman & Co Ltd, pg 684
Gale Research, pg 685
HarperCollins Publishers, pg 692
Hawker Publications Ltd, pg 693
Hawthorn Press, pg 693
Health Development Agency, pg 694
Hodder & Stoughton General, pg 696
Hodder & Stoughton Religious, pg 696
JAI Press Ltd, pg 702
Jessica Kingsley Publishers, pg 704
LDA-Living & Learning (Cambridge) Ltd, pg 706
Frances Lincoln Ltd, pg 707
Kenneth Mason Publications Ltd, pg 712
Metro Publishing Ltd, pg 714
John Murray (Publishers) Ltd, pg 716
National Foster Care Association, pg 717
Nelson Thornes Ltd, pg 718
The NFER-NELSON Publishing Co Ltd, pg 719
Speechmark Publishing Ltd, pg 744
Trentham Books Ltd, pg 750
Virgin Publishing Ltd, pg 753
Whiting & Birch Ltd, pg 756

Uruguay
Prensa Medica Latinoamericana, pg 761

Yugoslavia
Alfa-Narodna Knjiga, pg 764

Zambia
ZPC Publications, pg 767

Zimbabwe
College Press Publishers (Pvt) Ltd, pg 768

CIVIL ENGINEERING

Australia
EA Books, pg 21
H&H Publishing, pg 25
The Images Publishing Group Pty Ltd, pg 27
OTEN (Open Training & Education Network), pg 36
Standards Association of Australia, pg 43
Strucmech Publishing, pg 43

PUBLISHERS

Austria
Springer-Verlag Wien, pg 59

Brazil
ARTMED, pg 79
Editora Campus Ltda, pg 80
Editora FCO Ltda, pg 83
Hemus Editora Ltda, pg 85

Bulgaria
WTU Todor Kableskov, pg 98

China
Chemical Industry Press, pg 102
China Ocean Press, pg 103
Higher Education Press, pg 106
Jilin Science & Technology Publishing House, pg 106
Knowledge Press, pg 107
The People's Communications Publishing House, pg 107
South China University of Science and Technology Press, pg 109
Southwest China Jiaotong University Press, pg 109
Tsinghua University Press, pg 110
Water Resources and Electric Power Press (CWPP), pg 110
Zhejiang University Press, pg 110

Costa Rica
Editorial de la Universidad de Costa Rica, pg 117

Dominican Republic
Pontificia Universidad Catolica Madre y Maestra, pg 136

Finland
Teknolit Oy, pg 144

France
Hermes Science Publications, pg 168
Ouest Editions, pg 178
Presses de l'Ecole Nationale des Ponts et Chaussees, pg 181
Editions Springer France, pg 186

Germany
Institut fuer Baustoffe, Massivbau und Brandschutz/Bibliothek, pg 199
Bauverlag GmbH, pg 199
Ernst, Wilhelm & Sohn, Verlag Architektur und technische Wissenschaft GmbH & Co, pg 224
Ferd Dummler's Verlag, pg 227
Fraunhofer IRB Verlag Fraunhofer Informationszentrum Raum und Bau, pg 229
Hestra-Verlag Hernichel & Dr Strauss GmbH & Co KG, pg 240
Huthig GmbH & Co KG, pg 244
Kirschbaum Verlag GmbH, pg 249
Krafthand Verlag Walter Schultz GmbH, pg 253
Verlagsgesellschaft Rudolf Mueller GmbH & Co KG, pg 265
Oekobuch Verlag & Versand GmbH, pg 269
Springer-Verlag GmbH & Co KG, pg 288
Verlag Stahleisen GmbH, pg 289
Suin Buch-Verlag, pg 291
B G Teubner GmbH, pg 292
Trans Tech Publications, pg 294

Friedr Vieweg & Sohn Verlagsgesellschaft mbH, pg 298
Vogel Medien GmbH & Co KG, pg 299
WEKA Firmengruppe GmbH & Co KG, pg 301
Verlag fuer Wirtschaft & Verwaltung Hubert Wingen GmbH & Co KG, pg 303

Ghana
Building & Road Research Institute (BRRI), pg 306

Greece
Kleidarithmos, pg 312

India
Addison-Wesley (Singapore) Pte Ltd, pg 329
Affiliated East West Press Pvt Ltd, pg 329
Charotar Publishing House, pg 334
Heritage Publishers, pg 338
Khanna Publishers, pg 341
Laxmi Publications Pvt Ltd, pg 341
Oxford & IBH Publishing Co Pvt Ltd, pg 345
Scientific Book Agency, pg 349
Sita Publications, pg 350
South Asian Publishers Pvt Ltd, pg 350
A H Wheeler & Co Ltd, pg 353

Italy
Edizioni Cremonese SRL, pg 383
DEI Tipographia del Genio Civile, pg 384
New Magazine, pg 400

Japan
Kajima Institute Publishing Co Ltd, pg 419
Maruzen Co Ltd, pg 421

Democratic People's Republic of Korea
Korea Science and Encyclopedia Publishing House, pg 434

Republic of Korea
Bo Moon Dang, pg 435

Latvia
Preses Nams, pg 442

Malaysia
Unit Penerbitan Akademik Cancelori~ Universiti Teknologi Malaysia, pg 455

Mexico
Editorial Limusa SA de CV, pg 463

Netherlands
A A Balkema, pg 473
Delft University Press, pg 476
Hagen & Stam Uitgeverij Ten, pg 478

New Zealand
Southern Press Ltd, pg 496

Nigeria
Evans Brothers (Nigeria Publishers) Ltd, pg 499

Pakistan
National Book Foundation, pg 508

Poland
Instytut Techniki Budowlanej, Dzial Wydawniczo- Poligraficzny, pg 520

Portugal
McGraw-Hill Editora de Portugal, pg 527

Romania
Editura Gryphon, pg 533

Russian Federation
Izdatel 'stvo Mordovskogo gosudar stvennogo, pg 538

Singapore
APAC Publishers Services, pg 545

Spain
Ediciones Agrotecnicas, SL, pg 562
Ediciones Doce Calles SL, pg 570
Editorial Dossat SA, pg 570
Marcombo SA de Boixareu Editores, pg 581
Rueda, SL Editorial, pg 589
Edicions de la Universitat Politecnica de Catalunya SL, pg 594

Switzerland
Marcel Dekker AG, pg 612
Presses Polytechniques et Universitaires Romandes, PPUR, pg 622

Syrian Arab Republic
Damascus University Press, pg 628

Taiwan, Province of China
Fuh-Wen Book Co, pg 630
Chu Hai Publishing (Taiwan) Co Ltd, pg 630

United Republic of Tanzania
DUP (1996) Ltd, pg 633

Turkey
Caglayan Kitabevi, pg 639
Yapi-Endustri Merkezi Yayinlari-Yem Yayin, pg 642

United Kingdom
British Cement Association, pg 660
DMG Business Media Ltd, pg 675
Elsevier Science Ltd, pg 678
Geological Society Publishing House, pg 686
The Policy Press, pg 729
Research Studies Press Ltd (RSP), pg 734
RICS Books, pg 735
Spon Press, pg 744
Whittles Publishing, pg 756
WIT Press, pg 757

Viet Nam
Science & Technics Publishing House, pg 763

Yugoslavia
Savez Inzenjera i Tehnicara Jugoslavije, pg 765

SUBJECT INDEX

Zimbabwe
Standards Association of Zimbabwe (SAZ), pg 769

COMMUNICATIONS

Albania
State Textbook Publishing House, pg 1

Argentina
Edicial SA, pg 5
Editorial Paidos SAICF, pg 8

Australia
Australian Broadcasting Authority, pg 13
Finch Publishing, pg 22
Kerri Hamer, pg 25
Hospitality Press Pty Ltd, pg 26
James Nicholas Publishers Pty Ltd, pg 28
Pearson Education Australia, pg 37
Standards Association of Australia, pg 43
VCTA Publishing, pg 46
Woodlands Publications, pg 48

Austria
Buchkultur Verlags GmbH Zeitschrift fuer Literatur & Kunst, pg 50
Development News Ltd, pg 51
Dr Verena Hofstaetter, pg 53
Linde Verlag Wien GmbH, pg 54
Medien & Recht, pg 55
Oesterreichischer Kunst und Kulturverlag, pg 56
Springer-Verlag Wien, pg 59
Studien Verlag Gmbh, pg 59
Edition Va Bene, pg 60
WUV/Facultas Universitaetsverlag, pg 61

Belgium
Editions De Boeck-Larcier SA, pg 67
EPO Publishers, Printers, Booksellers, pg 68
VUB University Press, pg 75

Brazil
AGIR S/A Editora, pg 78
Editora Campus Ltda, pg 80
Editora Elevacao, pg 82
EDUC - Editora da PUC-SP, pg 82
Editora Lidador Ltda, pg 86
Edicoes Loyola SA, pg 87
Editora Mantiqueira de Ciencia e Arte, pg 87
Paulinas Editorial, pg 89
Editora Rocco Ltda, pg 91
Summus Editorial Ltda, pg 92
Talento Publicacoes Editora e Grafica Ltda, pg 92
Vozes Editora Ltda, pg 93

Bulgaria
Sita-MB, pg 98
WTU Todor Kableskov, pg 98

Chile
Arrayan Editores, pg 99

China
Chemical Industry Press, pg 102
Chengdu Maps Publishing House, pg 103

Dalian Maritime University Press, pg 105
Electronics Industry Publishing House, pg 105
Fudan University Press, pg 105
Fujian Science & Technology Publishing House, pg 106
Heilongjiang Science & Technology Press, pg 106
Language Publishing House, pg 107
The People's Communications Publishing House, pg 107
The People's Posts & Telecommunication Publishing House, pg 108
Shandong University Press, pg 109

Colombia
Instituto Misionerao Hijas De San Pablo, pg 113
Unidad Universitaria del Sur (UNISUR), pg 114
Editorial Voluntad SA, pg 114

The Democratic Republic of the Congo
Facultes Catoliques de Kinshasa, pg 115
Saint-Paul, pg 115

Cote d'Ivoire
Universite d' Abidjan, pg 118

Czech Republic
Omnipress Praha, pg 127
Portal Ltd, pg 127

Denmark
Samfundslitteratur, pg 135

Dominican Republic
Pontificia Universidad Catolica Madre y Maestra, pg 136

Ecuador
Centro De Educacion Popular, pg 137
CIESPAL (Centro Internacional de Estudios Superiores de Comunicacion para America Latina), pg 137

Finland
Yliopistopaino/Helsinki University Press, pg 145

France
ABC Editions, pg 145
Academie Nationale de Reims, pg 145
Breal, pg 151
Les Editions du CFPJ (Centre de Formation et de Perfectionnement des Journalistes) - Sarl Presse et Formation, pg 154
CNRS Editions, pg 155
La Decouverte et Syros, pg 158
Les Editions ESF, pg 161
ELLUG (Editions Litteraires et Linguistiques de l'Universite de Grenoble III), pg 162
Editions Juris Service, pg 171
Presses Universitaires de Grenoble, pg 181
Presses Universitaires de Nancy, pg 181
Top Editions, pg 188
UNESCO Publishing, pg 188

Germany
Verlag Karl Alber GmbH, pg 192
Art Directors Club Verlag GmbH, pg 195
Bertelsmann Lexikon Verlag GmbH, pg 201
Beuth Verlag GmbH, pg 202
Oscar Brandstetter Verlag GmbH & Co KG, pg 206
Hans Christians Druckerei und Verlag GmbH & Co, pg 210
Cornelsen Verlag GmbH & Co OHG, pg 211
Daedalus Verlag, pg 212
Datacom Buchverlag GmbH, pg 212
Deutscher Fachverlag GmbH, pg 214
Deutscher Wirtschaftsdienst John von Freyend GmbH, pg 216
Deutsches Bucharchiv Muenchen, Institut fur Buchwissenschaften, pg 216
Extent Verlag und Service Wolfgang M Flamm, pg 225
FAB-Verlag, pg 226
Fachverlag Schiele & Schoen GmbH, pg 226
Feltron-Elektronik Zeissler & Co GmbH, pg 227
Festland Verlag GmbH, pg 227
Verlag Reinhard Fischer, pg 228
Franzis-Verlag GmbH, pg 229
von Hase & Koehler Verlag KG, pg 238
Huthig GmbH & Co KG, pg 244
Edition ID-Archiv/ID-Verlag, pg 244
Iudicium Verlag GmbH, pg 245
Kriebel Verlag GmbH, pg 253
Leipziger Universitaetsverlag GmbH, pg 257
Gunter Narr Verlag, pg 266
Richard Pflaum Verlag GmbH & Co KG, pg 273
Psychologie Verlags Union GmbH, pg 275
Quintessenz Verlags-GmbH, pg 276
Verlag an der Ruhr GmbH, pg 281
1 H Sauer Verlag GmbH, pg 282
K G Saur Verlag GmbH, A Gale/Thomson Learning Company, pg 282
Schueren Verlag GmbH, pg 285
Spiess Volker Wissenschaftsverlag GmbH, pg 287
Stauffenburg Verlag Brigitte Narr GmbH, pg 289
Telex-Verlag Jaeger & Waldmann GmbH, pg 292
Tuduv Verlagsgesellschaft mbH, pg 295
UVK Verlagsgesellschaft mbH, pg 297
VDE-Verlag GmbH, pg 297
Verlag Moderne Industrie AG & Co KG, pg 298
Vogel Medien GmbH & Co KG, pg 299
WEKA Firmengruppe GmbH & Co KG, pg 301
Westdeutscher Verlag GmbH, pg 302
Herbert Wichmann Verlag, pg 302

Ghana
Ghana Universities Press (GUP), pg 307

Greece
Hestia-I D Hestia-Kollaros & Co Corporation, pg 311

Hong Kong
Electronic Technology Publishing Co Ltd, pg 319
Hong Kong University Press, pg 320
Modern Electronic & Computing Publishing Co Ltd, pg 321
Technology Exchange Ltd, pg 322

Hungary
Kossuth Kiado RT, pg 325

India
Asian Trading Corporation, pg 331
Concept Publishing Co, pg 335
Gyan Publishing House, pg 338
Khanna Publishers, pg 341
Reliance Publishing House, pg 347
Sage Publications India Pvt Ltd, pg 348
Satprakashan Sanchar Kendra, pg 349
Scientific Book Agency, pg 349
Somaiya Publications Pvt Ltd, pg 350
Sterling Publishers Pvt Ltd, pg 351
A H Wheeler & Co Ltd, pg 353

Indonesia
Bina Rena Pariwara, pg 354

Ireland
Events of the Week, pg 360
Irish Management Institute, pg 361

Italy
Gruppo Abele, pg 374
Editore Armando Armando SRL, pg 376
Capone Editore SRL, pg 379
Edizioni Cultura della Pace, pg 383
Editori Laterza, pg 386
In Dialogo, pg 393
Ithaca, pg 394
RAI.ERI, pg 405

Jamaica
Association of Development Agencies, pg 412

Japan
Chikuma Shobo Publishing Co Ltd, pg 415
Nippon Hoso Shuppan Kyokai (NHK Publishing), pg 422
Thomson Learning, pg 427

Kenya
Paulines Publications-Africa, pg 433

Democratic People's Republic of Korea
Grand People's Study House, pg 434
Korea Science and Encyclopedia Publishing House, pg 434

Republic of Korea
Bum-Woo Publishing Co, pg 435
Chung Rim Publishing Co Ltd, pg 435
Nanam Publishing House, pg 439
Oruem Publishing House, pg 439

Latvia
Nordik/Tapals Publishers Ltd, pg 442

The Former Yugoslav Republic of Macedonia
Medis, Skopje, pg 449

Madagascar
Societe Malgache d'Edition, pg 450

Malaysia
Pustaka Cipta Sdn Bhd, pg 454

Malta
Media Centre, pg 456

Mexico
Editorial Edicol SA, pg 460
Fondo de Cultura Economica, pg 461
Editorial Limusa SA de CV, pg 463
Nova Grupo Editorial SA de CV, pg 464
Plaza y Valdes SA de CV, pg 465

Morocco
Access International Services, pg 469
Societe Ennewrasse Service Librairie et Imprimerie, pg 470

Netherlands
Baltzer Science Publishers, pg 474
BIS Publishers, pg 474
Boom Uitgeverij, pg 474
Otto Cramwinckel Uitgever, pg 476
Educatieve Uitgeverij Edu'Actief BV, pg 476
Uitgeverij Lemma BV, pg 480

New Zealand
Moss Associates Ltd, pg 493
Nelson Price Milburn Ltd, pg 494

Peru
Ediciones Brown SA, pg 511
Universidad de Lima-Fondo de Desarollo Editorial, pg 512

Philippines
Communication Foundation for Asia Media Group (CFAMG), pg 513
Logos (Divine Word) Publications Inc, pg 513
New Day Publishers, pg 514
Our Lady of Manaoag Publisher, pg 514
Salesiana Publishers Inc, pg 515

Poland
Wydawnictwa Komunikacji i Lacznosci Co Ltd, pg 517

Portugal
Editora Classica, pg 523
Gradiva-Publicacnoes Lda, pg 525
Vega-Publicacao e Distribuicao de Livros e Revistas, Lda, pg 530

Romania
Aion Verlag, pg 531
Editura Excelsior, pg 533
Polirom Verlag, pg 535

Russian Federation
N E Bauman Moscow State Technical University Publishers, pg 537
Fizmatlit Publishing Co, pg 538
Izdatelstvo Mir, pg 540

PUBLISHERS

Nauka Publishers, pg 540
Izdatelstvo Radio i Svyaz, pg 541
Teorija Verojatnostej i ee Primenenija, pg 542

Slovenia

Zalozba Mihelac d o o, pg 552

South Africa

Erudita Publications (Pty) Ltd, pg 554
Human & Rousseau (Pty) Ltd, pg 555

Spain

Editorial Bruno, pg 566
Comunidad Autonoma de Madrid, Servicio de Documentacion y Publicaciones, pg 568
Fragua Editorial, pg 574
Editorial Gustavo Gili SA, pg 576
Grupo Comunicar, pg 576
Marcombo SA de Boixareu Editores, pg 581
Ediciones Paidos Iberica SA, pg 585
Editorial Sintesis, SA, pg 590
Ediciones de la Torre, pg 593

Sri Lanka

National Library & Documentation Services Board, pg 597

Sweden

Allt om Hobby AB, pg 600
Bokforlaget Nya Doxa AB, pg 605
Samsprak Forlags AB, pg 606

Switzerland

Castle Publications SA, pg 611
Dimension World Ltd, pg 612
Promoedition SA, pg 622
Verkehrshaus der Schweiz, pg 626

Syrian Arab Republic

Damascus University Press, pg 628

Turkey

IKI NOKTA Research Press & Publications Industry & Trade Ltd, pg 640

United Kingdom

Adamantine Press Ltd, pg 645
Artech House, pg 649
Bloomsbury Publishing PLC, pg 656
DMG Business Media Ltd, pg 675
Elsevier Science Ltd, pg 678
ERA Technology Ltd, pg 679
The Eurospan Group, pg 680
ICC United Kingdom, pg 698
Institution of Electrical Engineers, pg 700
Kluwer Academic/Plenum Publishers, pg 705
John Murray (Publishers) Ltd, pg 716
Pearson Education Europe, Mideast & Africa, pg 725
Polybooks Ltd, pg 729
Routledge, pg 736
Sage Publications Ltd, pg 737
John Taylor Book Ventures, pg 747
VNU Business Publications, pg 753

Uruguay

Nordan-Comunidad, pg 760

Viet Nam

Science & Technics Publishing House, pg 763

Yugoslavia

Savez Inzenjera i Tehnicara Jugoslavije, pg 765

Zambia

Multimedia Zambia, pg 767

Zimbabwe

Thomson Publications Zimbabwe (Pvt) Ltd, pg 769

COMPUTER SCIENCE

Argentina

Gram Editora, pg 6
Instituto Nacional de Ciencia y Tecnica Hidrica (INCYTH), pg 7

Australia

Edward Arnold (Australia) Pty Ltd, pg 12
Blackwell Science Pty Ltd, pg 15
Church Archivists Press, pg 18
Emerald City Books, pg 22
Illert Publications, pg 27
McGraw-Hill Australia Pty Ltd, pg 32
OTEN (Open Training & Education Network), pg 36
Pearson Education Australia, pg 37
Prospect Media Pty Ltd, pg 39
Tertiary Press, pg 44

Austria

Bohmann Druck und Verlag GmbH & Co KG, pg 50
International Institute for Applied Systems Analysis (IIASA), pg 53
Medien & Recht, pg 55
Andreas Schnider Verlags-Atelier, pg 58
Springer-Verlag Wien, pg 59

Belarus

Publishing Center of Belarus State University, pg 63

Belgium

Campinia Media VZW, pg 65
Easy Computing NV, pg 68
Marabout, pg 72
Wolters Plantyn Educatieve Uitgevers, pg 75

Brazil

Antenna Edicoes Tecnicas Ltda, pg 78
ARTMED, pg 79
Berkeley Brasil Editora Ltda, pg 79
Callis Editora Ltda, pg 80
Editora Campus Ltda, pg 80
Selecoes Eletronicas Editora Ltda, pg 83
Editora Harbra Ltda, pg 84
Livraria Editora Infobook SA, pg 86
Edicoes Loyola SA, pg 87
LTC-Livros Tecnicos e Cientificos Editora S/A, pg 87
Makron Books do Brasil Editora Ltda, pg 87
Livraria Pioneira Editora/Enio Matheus Guazzelli e Cia Ltd, pg 89
Editora Revan Ltda, pg 90

SUBJECT INDEX

Bulgaria

Aleks Soft, pg 94
Foi-Commerce, pg 95
Makros 2000 - Plovdiv, pg 96
Regalia 6 Publishing House, pg 97
TEMTO, pg 98

Chile

Arrayan Editores, pg 99

China

Aviation Industry Press, pg 102
Beijing Publishing House, pg 102
Beijing University Press, pg 102
Chengdu Maps Publishing House, pg 103
China Machine Press (CMP), pg 103
China Ocean Press, pg 103
Dalian Maritime University Press, pg 105
East China University of Science & Technology Press, pg 105
Electronics Industry Publishing House, pg 105
Fudan University Press, pg 105
Fujian Science & Technology Publishing House, pg 106
Guangdong Science & Technology Press, pg 106
Higher Education Press, pg 106
International Academic Publishers, pg 106
Jiangsu Science & Technology Publishing House, pg 106
Jilin Science & Technology Publishing House, pg 106
Metallurgical Industry Press (MIP), pg 107
Nanjing University Press, pg 107
National Defence Industry Press, pg 107
The People's Posts & Telecommunication Publishing House, pg 108
Science Press, pg 108
Shandong University Press, pg 109
Sichuan University Press, pg 109
South China University of Science and Technology Press, pg 109
Southwest China Jiaotong University Press, pg 109
Tianjin Science & Technology Publishing House, pg 109
Tsinghua University Press, pg 110
Wuhan University Press, pg 110
Zhejiang University Press, pg 110

Colombia

Pearson Educacion de Colombia LTDA, pg 113
Unidad Universitaria del Sur (UNISUR), pg 114

The Democratic Republic of the Congo

Facultes Catoliques de Kinshasa, pg 115

Costa Rica

Instituto Interamericano de Cooperacion para la Agricultura (IICA), pg 116
Editorial de la Universidad de Costa Rica, pg 117

Cuba

Apocalipis Digital, pg 120
Pueblo y Educacion Editorial (PE), pg 121

Czech Republic

Grada Publishing sro, pg 124
SystemConsult, pg 128
Votobia sro, pg 129

Denmark

Ingenioeren/Boger, pg 133
Systime, pg 136

Egypt (Arab Republic of Egypt)

Dar El Shorouk, pg 138

Finland

Teknolit Oy, pg 144

France

Editions Bertrandl-Lacoste, pg 150
Breal, pg 151
Cepadues Editions SA, pg 153
Dunod Editeur, pg 160
Editions d'Organisation, pg 161
Editions Eyrolles, pg 163
Editions Generales First, pg 166
InterEditions Paris, pg 169
Microsoft Press France, pg 176
Pearson Education France, pg 179
Presses de l'Ecole Nationale des Ponts et Chaussees, pg 181
Editions Springer France, pg 186
Editions Technip SA, pg 187
Editions Weka, pg 189

Germany

AOL-Verlag Frohmut Menze, pg 194
Verlag Beruf + Schule Belz KG, pg 202
Oscar Brandstetter Verlag GmbH & Co KG, pg 206
Data Becker GmbH & Co KG, pg 212
Deutscher Taschenbuch Verlag GmbH & Co KG (dtv), pg 215
Econ Taschenbuchverlag, pg 220
Verlag Europa-Lehrmittel, Nourney, Vollmer GmbH & Co, pg 224
Fachbuchverlag Leipzig im Carl Hanser Verlag, pg 226
Feltron-Elektronik Zeissler & Co GmbH, pg 227
Ferd Dummler's Verlag, pg 227
Franzis-Verlag GmbH, pg 229
Friedrich Kiehl Verlag GmbH, pg 230
Carl Hanser Verlag, pg 237
Rudolf Haufe Verlag GmbH & Co KG, pg 238
Ing W Hofacker GmbH Verlag, pg 241
Huthig GmbH & Co KG, pg 244
International Thomson Publishing (ITP), pg 245
ITpress Verlag, pg 245
Verlag Laterna magica GmbH & Co KG, pg 256
Naumann & Goebel Verlagsgesellschaft mbH, pg 267
Neuer Honos Verlag GmbH, pg 267
Pearson Education Deutschland GmbH, pg 272
Rossipaul Kommunikation GmbH, pg 280
Rowohlt Taschenbuch Verlag GmbH, pg 280
Springer-Verlag GmbH & Co KG, pg 288
Sybex Verlag GmbH, pg 291
Systhema Verlag GmbH, pg 291
Tangens Systemverlag GmbH, pg 291

919

SUBJECT INDEX

Te-Wi Verlag Unternehmensbereich Buch der Ziff Verlag GmbH, pg 292
B G Teubner GmbH, pg 292
TF Fachverlag Gmbh, pg 293
UTB fuer Wissenschaft Uni-Taschenbuecher GmbH, pg 297
Verlag Moderne Industrie AG & Co KG, pg 298
Friedr Vieweg & Sohn Verlagsgesellschaft mbH, pg 298
Vogel Medien GmbH & Co KG, pg 299
WRS Verlag Wirtschaft, Recht und Steuern GmbH & Co KG, pg 304
Fachbuchverlag Armin W Wuth, pg 304

Ghana
Building & Road Research Institute (BRRI), pg 306

Greece
Diavlos, pg 309
Epikerotita, pg 310
Giourdas Moschos, pg 310
Govostis Publishing SA, pg 311
Kleidarithmos, pg 312

Hong Kong
Chung Hwa Book Co (HK) Ltd, pg 319
Electronic Technology Publishing Co Ltd, pg 319
Federal Publications Ltd, pg 319
Logical Products (HK) Ltd, pg 320
Modern Electronic & Computing Publishing Co Ltd, pg 321

Hungary
Magyar Tudomanyos Akademia Koezponti Fizikai Kutato Intezet Koenyvtara, pg 325
Mueszaki Koenyvkiado Ltd, pg 325
Panem, pg 326
Statiqum Kiado es Nyomda Kft, pg 326

India
Addison-Wesley (Singapore) Pte Ltd, pg 329
Affiliated East West Press Pvt Ltd, pg 329
Allied Book Centre, pg 330
Bhawan Book Service, Publishers & Distributors, pg 333
Bookionics, pg 333
BPB Publications, pg 334
Frank Brothers & Co (Publishers) Ltd, pg 337
Galgotia Publications Pvt Ltd, pg 337
Heritage Publishers, pg 338
Khanna Publishers, pg 341
Laxmi Publications Pvt Ltd, pg 341
Mehta Publishers, pg 342
Narosa Publishing House, pg 343
Pitambar Publishing Co (P) Ltd, pg 346
Popular Prakashan Pvt Ltd, pg 346
Pustak Mahal, pg 346
Scientific Book Agency, pg 349
Shaibya Prakashan Bibhag, pg 349
Sita Publications, pg 350
Sterling Information Technologies, pg 351
Sultan Chand & Sons Pvt Ltd, pg 351
Vidya Puri, pg 352
Vidyarthi Mithram Press, pg 352
Vikas Publishing House Pvt Ltd, pg 353
S Viswanathan (Printers & Publishers) Pvt Ltd, pg 353
A H Wheeler & Co Ltd, pg 353

Indonesia
Andi Offset, pg 354
Dinastindo, pg 355
Gramedia, pg 355
PT Indira, pg 355

Ireland
The Educational Company of Ireland, pg 360

Israel
Dalia Peled Publishers, Division of Modan, pg 366
Hod-Ami, Computer Books Ltd, pg 368
Open University of Israel, pg 371

Italy
Edizioni di Comunita SpA, pg 382
Giuseppe Laterza Editore Snc, pg 391
Gruppo Calderini Edagricole, pg 392
Herbita Editrice di Leonardo Palermo, pg 392
Marsilio Editori SpA, pg 398
Franco Muzzio & C Editore SpA, pg 400
Editoriale Scienza, pg 407
Tecniche Nuove SpA, pg 409
Zanichelli Editore SpA, pg 412

Japan
Baifukan Co Ltd, pg 414
Dobun Shoin, pg 416
Gakken Co Ltd, pg 416
Keigaku Publishing Co Ltd, pg 419
Kindai Kagaku Sha Co, Ltd, pg 419
Kyoritsu Shuppan Co Ltd, pg 420
Maruzen Co Ltd, pg 421
Nikkagiren Shuppan-Sha (JUSE Press Ltd), pg 422
Nippon Jitsugyo Publishing Co, Ltd, pg 423
Obunsha Co Ltd, pg 423
Pearson Education Japan, pg 423
Sagano Shoin, pg 424
Sangyo-Tosho Publishing Co Ltd, pg 424
Seibido Shuppan Company Ltd, pg 424
Toppan Co Ltd, pg 428

Jordan
Jordan Book Centre Co Ltd, pg 430

Republic of Korea
Ahn Graphics, pg 434
B & B, pg 434
Bo Moon Dang, pg 435
Chung Rim Publishing Co Ltd, pg 435
Hakmun Publishing, Co, pg 436
Hongik Media Plus Ltd, pg 437
Ohmsa, pg 439
Pearson Education Korea Ltd, pg 439
Prompter Publications, pg 439

Latvia
Lielvards Ltd, pg 442

Lebanon
Arab Scientific Publishers BP, pg 442

Lithuania
TEV Leidykla, pg 446

The Former Yugoslav Republic of Macedonia
Medis, Skopje, pg 449
Seizmoloska Opservatorija, pg 449
Zumpres Publishing Firm, pg 449

Malaysia
Federal Publications Sdn Bhd, pg 452
Penerbit Universiti Sains Malaysia, pg 454
Pustaka Cipta Sdn Bhd, pg 454
Unit Penerbitan Akademik Cancelori~ Universiti Teknologi Malaysia, pg 455

Mauritius
Editions de l'Ocean Indien Ltd, pg 457

Mexico
ALFA OMEGA Grupo Editor, pg 458
Editora Cientifica Medica Latinoamerican SA de CV, pg 458
Centro de Estudios Monetarios Latinoamericanos (CEMLA), pg 460
Grupo Editorial Iberoamerica, SA de CV, pg 461
Editorial Limusa SA de CV, pg 463
Organizacion Cultural LP SA de CV, pg 465
Pearson Educacion de Mexico, SA de CV, pg 465
Sayrols Editorial SA de CV, pg 466
Ventura Ediciones, SA de CV, pg 468

Netherlands
Baltzer Science Publishers, pg 474
Erven J Bijleveld, pg 474
BoekWerk, pg 474
A W Bruna Uitgevers BV, pg 475
Elsevier Science BV, pg 477
Hagen & Stam Uitgeverij Ten, pg 478
IOS Press BV, pg 479
De Muiderkring BV, pg 481
Pearson Education Netherlands, pg 482
Uitgeverij Het Spectrum BV, pg 484
Sybex BV, pg 485
Twente University Press, pg 485
VNU Business Press Group BV, pg 487

New Zealand
ESA Publications (NZ) Ltd, pg 490
Learning Guides (Writers & Publishers Ltd), pg 492
Nelson Price Milburn Ltd, pg 494

Norway
Vett & Viten AS, pg 505

Paraguay
Instituto de Ciencias de la Computacion (NCR), pg 510

Peru
Fondo Editorial de la Pontificia Universidad Catolica del Peru, pg 511
Universidad de Lima-Fondo de Desarollo Editorial, pg 512

Philippines
Mutual Books Inc, pg 513
Salesiana Publishers Inc, pg 515

Poland
Komputerowa Oficyna Wydawnicza Help, pg 517
Oficyna Wydawnicza Read Me, pg 519
Wydawnictwa Naukowo-Techniczne, pg 521

Portugal
Edicoes Cetop, pg 523
Dinalivro, pg 524
FCA Editora de Informatica, pg 525
Gradiva-Publicacnoes Lda, pg 525
Lidel Edicoes Tecnicas, Lda, pg 526
Livraria Minerva Editora, pg 526
Lua Viajante-Edicao e Distribuicao de Livros e Material Audiovisual, Lda, pg 527
McGraw-Hill Editora de Portugal, pg 527
Editorial Presenca, pg 528
Silabo, pg 529
Vega-Publicacao e Distribuicao de Livros e Revistas, Lda, pg 530

Romania
Editura Academiei Romane, pg 531
Editora All, pg 531
Editura Minerva, pg 534
Editura Teora, pg 536

Russian Federation
N E Bauman Moscow State Technical University Publishers, pg 537
Energoatomizdat, pg 537
FGUP Izdatelstvo Mashinostroenie, pg 538
Finansy i Statistika Publishing House, pg 538
Fizmatlit Publishing Co, pg 538
KUbK Publishing House, pg 539
Izdatelstvo Mir, pg 540
Nauka Publishers, pg 540
Izdatel'stvo Nizhegorodskogo Gosudarstvennogo Univ, pg 540
Izdatelstvo Radio i Svyaz, pg 541

Singapore
APAC Publishers Services, pg 545
Tech Publications Pte Ltd, pg 548
World Scientific Publishing Co Pte Ltd, pg 549

Slovakia
Ustav informacii a prognoz skolstva mladeze a telovychovy, pg 551

South Africa
Educum Publishers Ltd, pg 554
Heinemann Publishers (Pty) Ltd, pg 555
Reader's Digest Southern Africa, pg 559

PUBLISHERS

Spain
Centro de Estudios Adams-Ediciones Valbuena SA, pg 561
Ediciones Diaz de Santos SA, pg 569
Ediciones Gestio 2000 SA, pg 575
Marcombo SA de Boixareu Editores, pg 581
Editorial Paraninfo SA, pg 586
Pulso Ediciones, SL, pg 588
RA-MA, Libreria y Editorial Microinformatica, pg 588
Servicio de Publicaciones Universidad de Cordoba, pg 590
Editorial Sintesis, SA, pg 590
Editores Tecnicos Asociados SA, pg 592
Universidad de Valladolid Secretariado de Publicaciones e Intercambio Editorial, pg 594
Edicions de la Universitat Politecnica de Catalunya SL, pg 594
Editorial Zendrera Zariquiey, SA, pg 596

Sri Lanka
Ministry of Education, pg 597
National Library & Documentation Services Board, pg 597

Sweden
Bokforlaget Spektra AB, pg 601
Pagina Forlags AB, pg 605
Studentlitteratur AB, pg 606

Switzerland
Verlag Harri Deutsch, pg 612
Pearson Education, pg 621
Presses Polytechniques et Universitaires Romandes, PPUR, pg 622
Vdf Hochschulverlag AG an der ETH Zurich, pg 626
Weka Informations Schriften Verlag AG, pg 627

Syrian Arab Republic
Damascus University Press, pg 628

Taiwan, Province of China
Fuh-Wen Book Co, pg 630
Chu Hai Publishing (Taiwan) Co Ltd, pg 630
Hsiao Yuan Publication Co, Ltd, pg 630
Lead Wave Publishing Company Ltd, pg 631
San Min Book Co Ltd, pg 631

United Republic of Tanzania
Press & Publicity Centre Ltd, pg 634

Turkey
Alkim Kitapcilik-Yayimcilik, pg 638
Arkadas Ltd, pg 639
Saray Medikal Yayin Tic Ltd Sti, pg 641
Seckin Yayinevi, pg 641
Yetkin Printing & Publishing Co Inc, pg 642
Yuce Reklam Yay Dagt AS, pg 642

Ukraine
ASK Ltd, pg 643
Naukova Dumka Publishers, pg 643

United Kingdom
Academic Press Ltd, pg 644
Advisory Unit: Computers in Education, pg 645
Artech House, pg 649
Association for Science Education, pg 650
Bernard Babani (Publishing) Ltd, pg 651
Blackwell Publishers, pg 655
Butterworth-Heinemann Ltd, pg 661
Cambridge University Press, pg 662
Dickson Price Publishers Ltd, pg 675
Eaglemoss Publications Ltd, pg 676
Edinburgh University Press Ltd, pg 677
Editon XII, pg 677
Elsevier Science Ltd, pg 678
ERA Technology Ltd, pg 679
The Eurospan Group, pg 680
Facet Publishing, pg 681
W H Freeman & Co Ltd, pg 684
Haynes Publishing, pg 693
Helicon Publishing Ltd, pg 694
Hodder & Stoughton Educational, pg 696
Immediate Publishing, pg 699
Institute of Physics Publishing, pg 700
Institution of Electrical Engineers, pg 700
Intellect Ltd, pg 700
Jones & Bartlett International, pg 703
Kluwer Academic/Plenum Publishers, pg 705
Learning Matters Ltd, pg 706
Letts Educational, pg 707
McGraw-Hill Publishing Company, pg 712
MIT Press Ltd, pg 715
Open University Worldwide, pg 721
Palgrave Publishers Ltd, pg 723
PC Publishing, pg 725
Pearson Education, pg 725
Research Studies Press Ltd (RSP), pg 734
Rooster Books Ltd, pg 735
Sage Publications Ltd, pg 737
Skoob Russell Square, pg 742
Springer-Verlag London Ltd, pg 744
The Stationery Office, pg 745
Take That Ltd, pg 746
Taylor Graham Publishing, pg 747
TFPL, pg 748
Transworld Publishers Ltd, pg 750
VNU Business Publications, pg 753
Ward Lock Educational Co Ltd, pg 754
Which? Ltd, pg 755
Wiley Europe Ltd, pg 756
WIT Press, pg 757

Uruguay
La Flor del Itapebi, pg 760
Editia Uruguay, pg 761

Viet Nam
Science & Technics Publishing House, pg 763

Yugoslavia
Tehnicka Knjiga, pg 764

COOKERY

Albania
NL SH, pg 1

Argentina
Editorial Caymi SACI, pg 4
Editorial Ruy Diaz SAEIC, pg 5
Errepar SA, pg 5
Librograf, pg 7
Ediciones Preescolar SA, pg 8

Australia
ACP Publishing Pty Ltd, pg 10
Allen & Unwin Pty Ltd, The Australian Newspaper, Vogel Breads, pg 11
Edward Arnold (Australia) Pty Ltd, pg 12
Barbara Beckett Publishing Pty Ltd, pg 14
Blackhead Ink Publishing, pg 15
Cookery Book, pg 18
Egan Publishing Pty Ltd, pg 21
Horan Wall & Walker, pg 26
Hospitality Press Pty Ltd, pg 26
Hyland House Publishing Pty Ltd, pg 27
Lansdowne Publishing Pty Ltd, pg 29
Sandra Lee Agencies, pg 29
Mayne Publishing, pg 32
McDonald-Kirkwood Pty Ltd, pg 32
Anne O'Donovan Pty Ltd, pg 35
Oriental Publications, pg 36
Parabel Place, pg 37
Penguin Books Australia Ltd, pg 37
R & R Publications Marketing P/L, pg 39
Regency Publishing, pg 40
Simon & Schuster Australia Pty Ltd, pg 42
Social Club Books, pg 42
Stafford Books, pg 43
Wakefield Press Pty Ltd, pg 47
The Watermark Press, pg 47

Austria
Carinthia Verlag, pg 50
Ennsthaler GesmbH & Co KG, pg 51
Leopold Stocker Verlag, pg 54
Niederosterreichisches Pressehaus Druck- und Verlagsgesellschaft mbH, pg 55
Verlag Orac im Verlag Kremayr & Scheriau, pg 56
Verlag des Osterr Kneippbundes GmbH, pg 57
Richard Pils Publication P, pg 57
Pinguin-Verlag, Pawlowski GmbH, pg 57
Verlag Anton Pustet, pg 57
Trauner Verlag, pg 59
Verlag Veritas Mediengesellschaft mbH, pg 60

Belarus
Belaruskaya Encyklapedyya, pg 63

Belgium
SA Artis-Historia, pg 64
Coda, pg 66
Editions Delta SA, pg 67
Koepel van de Vlaamse Noord - Zuidbeweging 11.11.11, pg 70
Uitgeverij Lannoo NV, pg 70
Marabout, pg 72
Henri Proost & Co, Pvba, pg 73

Brazil
A & A & A Edicoes e Promocoes Internacionais Ltda, pg 77
Abril SA, pg 77
AGIR S/A Editora, pg 78
Editora Antroposofica Ltda, pg 78

SUBJECT INDEX

Editora Bertrand Brasil Ltda, pg 79
Brinque Book Editora de Livros Ltda, pg 80
Callis Editora Ltda, pg 80
Conquista, Empresa de Publicacoes Ltda, pg 81
Editora Companhia das Letras/Editora Schwarcz Ltda, pg 82
Companhia Editora Forense, pg 82
Editora Gaia Ltda, pg 84
Editora Globo SA, pg 84
LDA Editores Ltda, pg 86
Libreria Editora Ltda, pg 86
Livraria Nobel S/A, pg 86
Editora Manole Ltda, pg 87
Editora Marco Zero Ltda, pg 87
Editora Melhoramentos Ltda, pg 87
Editora Nova Alexandria Ltda, pg 88
Rede Das Artes (Boccato Editores Collector's), pg 90
Editora Rideel Ltda, pg 90
Editora Vecchi SA, pg 93

Bulgaria
Darzhavno Izdatelstvo Zemizdat, pg 95
Kibea Publishing Co, pg 96
Kralica MAB, pg 96
MATEX, pg 96
Rakla, pg 97
Peyo K Yavorov Publishing House, pg 98

Chile
Editora Nueva Generacion, pg 101

China
Beijing Publishing House, pg 102
China Light Industry Press, pg 103
Foreign Languages Press, pg 105
Guangdong Science & Technology Press, pg 106
Higher Education Press, pg 106
Jilin Science & Technology Publishing House, pg 106
Jinan Publishing House, pg 107
Morning Glory Publishers, pg 107
Tianjin Science & Technology Publishing House, pg 109

Colombia
Editorial Santillana SA, pg 113
Villegas Editores Ltda, pg 114
Editorial Voluntad SA, pg 114

Costa Rica
Editorial de la Universidad de Costa Rica, pg 117

Croatia
ALFA dd za izdavacke, graficke i trgovacke poslove, pg 118
Vitagraf, pg 120

Cuba
Editorial Oriente, pg 121

Czech Republic
Jan Vasut Publishing, pg 124
Pavla Momcilova, pg 126
Svojtka & Co, pg 128
Vitalis SRO, pg 129
Votobia sro, pg 129

Denmark
Aschehoug Dansk Forlag A/S, pg 130
Christian Ejlers' Forlag aps, pg 131

SUBJECT INDEX

BOOK

GEC Gads Forlag Aktieselskab af 1994, pg 132
Forlaget Hjulet, pg 132
Olivia - det gronne forlag, pg 134

Estonia
Perioodika, pg 140
Sinisukk, pg 140
Valgus Publishers, pg 141

Fiji
Lotu Pacifika Productions, pg 141

Finland
SV-Kauppiaskanava Oy, pg 144

France
Editions Albin Michel, pg 146
Editions de l'Armancon, pg 148
ATP - Packager, pg 149
Editions de l'Aube, pg 149
Editions A Barthelemy, pg 149
Societe Nouvelle Rene Baudouin, pg 149
Editions Bertout, pg 150
Pierre Bordas et Fils, pg 151
Editions Casterman, pg 153
Editions du Chene, pg 154
Editions Delville, pg 158
Edisud, pg 161
Editions Entente, pg 162
EPA SA (Editions Presse Audiovisuel), pg 162
Editions Fanlac, pg 163
Editions Filipacchi-Sonodip, pg 164
Editions Jean Paul Gisserot, pg 166
Editions J Glenat SA, pg 166
Editions Grancher, pg 166
Hachette Pratiques, pg 167
Editions du Jaguar, pg 170
Lacour-Olle, pg 171
Editions Michel Lafon SA, pg 171
Langues & Mondes/L'Asiatheque, pg 171
LT Editions-J Lanore-H Laurens, pg 172
Editions du Laquet, pg 172
Librairie Larousse, pg 172
Lavoisier, pg 172
Societe des Editions Menges, pg 175
Noir Sur Blanc, pg 177
Editions Payot & Rivages, pg 179
Editions Christian Pirot, pg 180
Editions Rombaldi SA, pg 183
Editions du Rouergue, pg 183
Editions Sang de la Terre, pg 183
Sofradif Editions Philippe Auzou, pg 185
Editions Sud Ouest, pg 186
Taride Editions, pg 187
Terre Vivante, pg 187
La Vague a l'ame, pg 188

French Polynesia
Scoop/Au Vent des Iles, pg 190

Germany
R van Acken GmbH Druckerei und Verlag, pg 191
Albert Propster Verlag und Buchhandlung, pg 192
Arcus-Medien Wolfgang Steinhardt, pg 194
Ars Edition GmbH, pg 195
Ars Vivendi Verlag, pg 195
ARTC/OLOR, pg 195
Aufstieg-Verlag GmbH, pg 196
Bassermann Verlag, pg 198
BBT Bhaktivedanta Book Trust, pg 202
Buchverlage Langen-Mueller/Herbig, pg 207
Aenne Burda Verlag, pg 208
Chmielorz GmbH Verlag, pg 210
Christian Verlag GmbH, pg 210
Hans Christians Druckerei und Verlag GmbH & Co, pg 210
Compact Verlag GmbH, pg 211
Deutscher Taschenbuch Verlag GmbH & Co KG (dtv), pg 215
Edition Dia, pg 216
Dr Oetker Verlag KG, pg 218
Dreisam Ratgeber in der Rutsker Verlag GmbH, pg 218
Droemersche Verlagsanstalt Th Knaur Nachfolger GmbH & Co, pg 218
DuMont Buchverlag GmbH & Co KG, pg 219
DuMont Monte, pg 219
Fachbuchverlag Pfanneberg & Co, pg 226
Falken-Verlag GmbH, pg 227
Gildefachverlag GmbH & Co KG, pg 232
Graefe und Unzer Verlag GmbH, pg 233
Walter Haedecke Verlag, pg 236
Mary Hahn's Kochbuchverlag, pg 236
Hallwag Verlag GmbH, pg 236
Heel Verlag GmbH, pg 238
F A Herbig Verlagsbuchhandlung GmbH, pg 239
Wilhelm Heyne Verlag, pg 240
Verlag Wolfgang Hoelker, pg 241
Jahreszeiten-Verlag GmbH, pg 246
Kochbuch Verlag Olga Leeb, pg 251
Koenemann Verlagesellschaft mbH, pg 251
Kunstverlag Weingarten GmbH, pg 254
Landbuch-Verlagsgesellschaft mbH, pg 255
Hugo Matthaes Druckerei und Verlag GmbH & Co KG, pg 261
Medizinisch-Literarische Verlagsgesellschaft mbH, pg 262
Midena Verlag, pg 264
Mosaik Verlag GmbH, pg 265
Naumann & Goebel Verlagsgesellschaft mbH, pg 267
Nebel Verlag GmbH, pg 267
Neuer Honos Verlag GmbH, pg 267
Verlag Neues Leben GmbH, pg 268
Oertel & Sporer GmbH & Co, pg 270
Orbis Verlag fur Publizistik GmbH, pg 270
Pala-Verlag GmbH, pg 271
Walter Rau Verlag GmbH & Co KG, pg 277
Regura Verlag, pg 277
Romiosini Verlag, pg 280
Schangrila Verlags und Vertriebs GmbH, pg 282
Moritz Schauenburg Verlag, pg 282
Sigloch Edition Helmut Sigloch GmbH & Co KG, pg 286
Springer-Verlag GmbH & Co KG, pg 288
Suedwest Verlag GmbH & Co KG, pg 291
Tipress Dienstleistungen fur das Verlagswesen GmbH, pg 294
Tomus Verlag GmbH, pg 294
VS Verlagshaus Stuttgart GmbH, pg 299
Verlagsgruppe Weltbild GmbH, pg 301
Westholsteinische Verlagsanstalt und Verlagsdruckerei Boyens & Co, pg 302
Zambon Verlag, pg 305
ZS Verlag Zabert Sandmann GmbH, pg 305

Ghana
Adaex Educational Publications Ltd, pg 306
Black Mask Ltd, pg 306
World Literature Project, pg 308

Greece
Akritas, pg 308
Alamo Hellas, pg 308
Alexiadou Vefa Editions, pg 309
Chrysi Penna - Golden Pen Books, pg 309
Ekdoseis Domi AE, pg 310
Exandas Publishers, pg 310
Orfanidis Publications, pg 314
Patakis Publishers, pg 314

Hong Kong
CFW Publications Ltd, pg 318
Chopsticks Publications Ltd, pg 319
Ming Pao Publications Ltd, pg 321
Publications (Holdings) Ltd, pg 321

Hungary
Advent Kiado, pg 323
Aranyhal Konyvkiado Goldfish Publishing, pg 323
Corvina Books Ltd, pg 323
Officina Nova, Koenyv-es Lapkiado/Bertelsmann Media Kft, pg 324
Novorg Kiado, pg 326

Iceland
Bokautgafan Orn og Orlygur ehf, pg 327
Frodi Ltd, pg 328
Setberg, pg 328

India
Ananda Publishers Pvt Ltd, pg 330
Bani Mandir, Book-Sellers, Publishers & Educational Suppliers, pg 332
Brijbasi Printers Pvt Ltd, pg 334
Diamond Comics (P) Ltd, pg 336
Dutta Baruah Publishing Co Pvt Ltd, pg 336
Frank Brothers & Co (Publishers) Ltd, pg 337
Gyan Publishing House, pg 338
Jaico Publishing House, pg 340
Orient Paperbacks, pg 345
Popular Prakashan Pvt Ltd, pg 346
Prabhat Prakashan, pg 346
Pratibha Pratishthan, pg 346
Pustak Mahal, pg 346
Roli Books Pvt Ltd, pg 348
Sat Sahitya Prakashan, pg 349
Scientific Book Agency, pg 349
Vakils Feffer & Simons Ltd, pg 352
Vidyarthi Mithram Press, pg 352
Vikas Publishing House Pvt Ltd, pg 353
Vision Books Pvt Ltd, pg 353

Indonesia
PT Dian Rakyat, pg 355
Gramedia, pg 355

Ireland
A & A Farmar, pg 358
An Gum, pg 358
Careers & Educational Publishers Ltd, pg 359
Estragon Press Ltd, pg 360
Gill & Macmillan Ltd, pg 361
The Goldsmith Press Ltd, pg 361
The O'Brien Press Ltd, pg 363
On Stream Publications Ltd, pg 363

Israel
Classikaletet, pg 366
Dekel Publishing House, pg 366
Gefen Publishing House Ltd, pg 367
Massada Press Ltd, pg 370
Massada Publishers Ltd, pg 370
Modan Publishers Ltd, pg 371
Pitspopany Press, pg 371
R Sirkis Publishers Ltd, pg 372
Zmora-Bitan, Publishers Ltd, pg 374

Italy
Verlagsanstalt Athesia, pg 377
Giuseppe Bonanno Editore, pg 378
Casa Editrice Bonechi, pg 378
Il Castello srl, pg 380
Edizioni del Riccio SAS di G Bernardi, pg 384
Di Baio Editore SpA, pg 385
Diakronia, pg 385
Editoriale Domus Spa, pg 385
ERGA SNC di Carla Ottino Merli & C (Edizioni Realizzazioni Grafiche - Artigiana), pg 388
Fenice 2000, pg 389
Arnaldo Forni Editore SRL, pg 389
Adriano Gallina Editore sas, pg 389
Ernesto Gremese Editore SRL, pg 391
Gremese International Srl, pg 391
Gruppo Calderini Edagricole, pg 392
Macro Edizioni, pg 397
McRae Books, pg 398
Mundici & Zanetti srl, pg 400
Maria Pacini Fazzi Editore, pg 402
Pheljna Edizioni d'Arte e Suggestione, pg 403
Daniela Piazza Editore, pg 403
Edizioni Piemme SpA, pg 403
Priuli e Verlucca, Editori, pg 404
Rara-lst Editoriale di Bibliofilia e Reprints, pg 405
Reverdito Edizioni, pg 405
Edizioni Scientifiche Italiane, pg 407
Tappeiner, pg 409
La Tartaruga Edizioni SAS, pg 409
TEA Tascabili degli Editori Associati SpA, pg 409
Zanfi Editori SRL, pg 412

Jamaica
Kingston Publishers Ltd, pg 413
Ian Randle Publishers Ltd, pg 413
West Indies Publishing Ltd, pg 414

Japan
Contex Corporation, pg 415
Dohosha Publishing Co Ltd, pg 416
Japan Publications Inc, pg 418
Kodansha International, pg 420
Nagaoka Shoten Company Ltd, pg 421
Nihon Vogue Co Ltd, pg 422
Nippon Hoso Shuppan Kyokai (NHK Publishing), pg 422
President Inc, pg 423
Sanyo Shuppan Boeki Co Inc, pg 424
Seibido Shuppan Company Ltd, pg 424

PUBLISHERS — SUBJECT INDEX

Shufunotomo sha Co Ltd, pg 426
Tankosha Publishing Co Ltd, pg 427
Charles E Tuttle Publishing Co Inc, pg 428

Kenya
Heinemann Kenya Limited (EAEP), pg 431
Kenway Publications Ltd, pg 432

Democratic People's Republic of Korea
The Foreign Language Press Group, pg 434

Republic of Korea
Hak Won Publishing Co, pg 436
Hollym Corporation Publishers, pg 437
Seoul International Publishing House, pg 440
Shinkwang Publishing Co, pg 440
Yearim-dang, pg 441

Laos People's Democratic Republic
Lao-phanit, pg 441

Latvia
Alberts XII, pg 441
Avots, pg 441

Lebanon
Arab Scientific Publishers BP, pg 442

Luxembourg
Editions Emile Borschette, pg 447

Madagascar
Foibe Filan-Kevitry NY Mpampianatra (FOFIPA), pg 450

Malaysia
S Abdul Majeed & Co, pg 451
Berita Publishing Sdn Bhd, pg 451
Times Educational Co Sdn Bhd, pg 455

Malta
Publishers' Enterprises Group (PEG) Ltd, pg 456

Mauritius
Editions de l'Ocean Indien Ltd, pg 457
Vizavi Editions, pg 457

Mexico
Ediciones Alpe, pg 458
Editorial Armonia SA, pg 458
Centro Editorial Mexicano Osiris SA, pg 458
Editorial Diana SA de CV, pg 459
Editorial Iztaccihuatl SA, pg 462
Editorial Jilguero, SA de CV, pg 462
Libra Editorial SA de CV, pg 463
Editorial Limusa SA de CV, pg 463
Editorial Minutiae Mexicana SA, pg 464
Naves Internacional de Ediciones SA, pg 464
Organizacion Cultural LP SA de CV, pg 465
Salvat Editores de Mexico, pg 466
Sayrols Editorial SA de CV, pg 466

Servicios Especiales Maciel SA de CV, pg 467
Sistemas Tecnicos de Edicion SA de CV, pg 467
Ediciones Suromex SA, pg 467

Myanmar
Smart & Mookerdum, pg 471

Netherlands
BZZTOH Publishers, pg 475
Mets & Schilt Uitgevers en Distributeurs, pg 481
Terra Publishing Co, pg 485
Tirion Uitgevers BV, pg 485
Uitgeverij De Toorts, pg 485
Unieboek BV, pg 485
Zuid Boekprodukties BV, pg 487

New Zealand
ABA Books, pg 488
Barkfire Press, pg 488
David Bateman Ltd, pg 488
Bush Press Communications Ltd, pg 489
Concept Publishing Ltd, pg 490
Halcyon Publishing Ltd, pg 491
HarperCollins Publishers (New Zealand) Ltd, pg 491
Hazard Press Ltd, pg 491
Reed Publishing (NZ) Ltd, pg 495
Tandem Press, pg 496

Nigeria
Fourth Dimension Publishing Co Ltd, pg 499
Riverside Communications, pg 501

Norway
Ex Libris Forlag A/S, pg 503

Pakistan
Jang Publishers, pg 507
Maqbool Academy, pg 508

Philippines
Anvil Publishing Inc, pg 512
Bookmark Inc, pg 512
Books for Pleasure Inc, pg 512
Marren Publishing House, Inc, pg 513
New Day Publishers, pg 514
Rex Bookstores & Publishers, pg 514

Poland
Iskry - Publishing House Ltd spotka zoo, pg 517
Muza SA, pg 518

Portugal
Difusao Cultural, pg 524
Editorial Estampa, Lda, pg 524
Everest Editora, pg 525
Meriberica/Liber, pg 527
Editorial Noticias, pg 527
Editorial Presenca, pg 528
Texto Editora, pg 529
Vega-Publicacao e Distribuicao de Livros e Revistas, Lda, pg 530

Romania
Editura Excelsior, pg 533
Editura Niculescu, pg 534

Russian Federation
Airis Press, pg 537
Dom, Izdatel'stvo sovetskogo deskkogo fonda im & I Lenina, pg 537
Izdatelstvo 'Ekonomika', pg 537
KUbK Publishing House, pg 539
Permskaja Kniga, pg 541
Profizdat, pg 541
Raduga Publishers, pg 541
Russkaya Kniga Izdatelstvo (Publishers), pg 541

Singapore
Archipelago Press, pg 545
Shing Lee Group Publishers, pg 548
Times Media Pte Ltd, pg 549

Slovakia
Vydavatepstvo Praca spol sro, pg 550

Slovenia
Zalozba Obzorja d d Maribor, pg 552

South Africa
Educum Publishers Ltd, pg 554
Human & Rousseau (Pty) Ltd, pg 555
New Africa Books (Pty) Ltd, pg 557
Queillerie Publishers, pg 558
Reader's Digest Southern Africa, pg 559
Struik Publishers (Pty) Ltd, pg 559
Tafelberg Publishers Ltd, pg 560

Spain
Editorial Acanto SA, pg 561
Alta Fulla Editorial, pg 563
Ambit Serveis Editorials, SA, pg 563
Editorial Astri SA, pg 564
Editorial Cantabrica SA, pg 566
Comunidad Autonoma de Madrid, Servicio de Documentacion y Publicaciones, pg 568
Ediciones Daly S L, pg 569
Editorial De Vecchi SA, pg 569
Edicions del Drac SA, pg 570
Edi-Liber Irlan SA, pg 571
Ediciones l'Isard, S L, pg 571
Ediles-Ediciones Leonesas SA, pg 572
Editorial Everest SA, pg 572
Ediciones Elfos SL, pg 572
Editorial Espasa-Calpe SA, pg 573
Icaria Editorial SA, pg 577
Ediciones Irusa, pg 578
Ediciones Libertarias/Prodhufi SA, pg 580
Libsa Editorial SA, pg 580
Lunwerg Editores, SA, pg 580
Edicions de la Magrana SA, pg 581
Mandala Ediciones, pg 581
Ediciones Medici SA, pg 582
Noguer y Caralt Editores SA, pg 584
Ediciones Norma SA, pg 584
OASIS, Producciones Generales de Comunicacion, pg 584
Instituto Provincial de Investigaciones y Estudios Toledanos, pg 588
Editora Regional de Murcia - ERM, pg 588
Ediciones Rialp SA, pg 589
Axel Springer Publicaciones, pg 591
Ediciones Susaeta SA, pg 592

Trea Ediciones, SL, pg 593
Tursen, SA, pg 593
Ediciones Tutor SA, pg 594
Ediciones 29 - Libros Rio Nuevo, pg 594
Editorial Zendrera Zariquiey, SA, pg 596

Sweden
Akademiforlaget Goteborgslitteratur, pg 600
Albert Bonniers Forlag, pg 601
BOOX, pg 601
ICA bokforlag, pg 603
Informationsfoerlaget AB, pg 603
Natur och Kultur/LTs foerlag, pg 604
Bokforlaget Prisma, pg 605
Bokforlaget Semic AB, pg 606
Semic Bokforlaget International AB, pg 606
Stromberg, pg 606
Wahlstrom & Widstrand, pg 607

Switzerland
Armenia Editions, pg 608
AT Verlag, pg 608
Cockatoo Press (Schweiz), Thailand-Publikationen, pg 611
Duboux Editions SA, pg 612
Hallwag AG, pg 615
Junod Nicholas, pg 616
Kanisius Verlag, pg 616
Verlag Rene Kramer AG, pg 617
Mueller Rueschlikon Verlags AG, pg 619
Les Editions Noir sur Blanc, pg 620

Taiwan, Province of China
Highlight Publishing Company Ltd, pg 630
Hilit Publishing Co Ltd, pg 630
Linking Publishing Company Ltd, pg 631
Shy Mau Publishing Company, pg 631
Wei-Chuan Publishing Company Ltd, pg 632
Youth Cultural Publishing Co, pg 632

Thailand
Sang Dad Publishing Company Ltd, pg 635

Turkey
Alkim Kitapcilik-Yayimcilik, pg 638
Arkadas Ltd, pg 639
Inkilap Publishers Ltd, pg 640

Uganda
Fountain Publishers Ltd, pg 642

Ukraine
ASK Ltd, pg 643

United Arab Emirates
Motivate Publishing, pg 644

United Kingdom
Absolute Press, pg 644
Ian Allan Publishing Ltd, pg 646
Apple Press, pg 648
Appletree Press Ltd, pg 648
Ashgrove Press, pg 650
BBC Worldwide Publishers, pg 653
BCA, pg 653
Mitchell Beazley, pg 653
Blackstaff Press, pg 655

SUBJECT INDEX

Bloomsbury Publishing PLC, pg 656
Breslich & Foss, pg 659
The Brown Reference Group PLC, pg 660
Cardinal Publishing Ltd, pg 663
Jon Carpenter Publishing, pg 664
Cassell & Co, pg 664
Kyle Cathie Ltd, pg 665
Marshall Cavendish Partworks Ltd, pg 665
Colour Library Direct, pg 669
Compendium Publishing, pg 670
Paul H Crompton Ltd, pg 672
David & Charles Ltd, pg 674
Christopher Davies Publishers Ltd, pg 674
Andre Deutsch Ltd, pg 675
Dorling Kindersley Ltd, pg 676
Eaglemoss Publications Ltd, pg 676
Elliot Right Way Books, pg 678
The Erskine Press, pg 679
Express Newspapers, pg 681
Foulsham Publishers, pg 683
Fourth Estate Ltd, pg 683
Garnet Publishing Ltd, pg 685
Grange Books PLC, pg 689
The Greek Bookshop, pg 689
Grub Street, pg 690
Robert Hale Ltd, pg 691
Hamlyn, pg 691
HarperCollins Publishers, pg 692
Headline Book Publishing Ltd, pg 693
Hemming Information Services, pg 695
Hendon Publishing Co Ltd, pg 695
Hodder & Stoughton General, pg 696
Angus Hudson Ltd, pg 697
Y Lolfa Cyf, pg 708
Lorenz Books, pg 709
Macmillan Audio Books, pg 710
Kenneth Mason Publications Ltd, pg 712
Mercat Press, pg 713
Merehurst Publishers, pg 713
Metro Publishing Ltd, pg 714
MQ Publications Ltd, pg 716
National Trust, pg 717
New Holland Publishers (UK) Ltd, pg 718
New Leaf Books Ltd, pg 719
NMS Publishing Ltd, pg 719
Octopus Publishing Group, pg 720
Pavilion Books Ltd, pg 724
Piatkus Books, pg 727
PRC Publishing Ltd, pg 730
Prism Press Book Publishers Ltd, pg 730
Quarto Publishing plc, pg 731
Ramboro Books Plc, pg 732
Random House UK Ltd, pg 733
The Reader's Digest Association Ltd, pg 733
Regency House Publishing Ltd, pg 734
Robson Books, pg 735
Rosendale Press Ltd, pg 735
Ryland Peters & Small Ltd, pg 737
Salamander Books Ltd, pg 738
SAWD Publications, pg 738
Serif, pg 742
Sidgwick & Jackson Ltd, pg 742
Charles Skilton Ltd, pg 742
Stacey International, pg 745
Telegraph Books, pg 748
Transedition Ltd, pg 749
Vallentine, Mitchell & Co Ltd, pg 752
The Vegetarian Society, pg 752
Verulam Publishing Ltd, pg 753
Viking, pg 753
Ward Lock Ltd, pg 754
Websters International Publishers Ltd, pg 755
WI Enterprises Ltd, pg 756
Wiley Europe Ltd, pg 756
Neil Wilson Publishing Ltd, pg 757
Wordwright Publishing, pg 758

Uruguay
Ediciones de Juan Darien, pg 760

Yugoslavia
Alfa-Narodna Knjiga, pg 764

Zambia
Multimedia Zambia, pg 767

Zimbabwe
College Press Publishers (Pvt) Ltd, pg 768
Longman Zimbabwe (Pvt) Ltd, pg 768
Zimbabwe Publishing House (Pvt) Ltd, pg 769

CRAFTS, GAMES, HOBBIES

Albania
NL SH, pg 1

Australia
Books for Our Times, pg 16
Egan Publishing Pty Ltd, pg 21
David Ell Press Pty Ltd, pg 21
Graffiti Publications, pg 24
Horan Wall & Walker, pg 26
Kangaroo Press, pg 29
Little Hills Press, pg 30
Tracy Marsh Publications Pty Ltd, pg 32
Mayne Publishing, pg 32
J M McGregor Pty Ltd, pg 32
Off the Shelf Publishing, pg 35
Jill Oxton Publications Pty Ltd, pg 36
R & R Publications Marketing P/L, pg 39
Rams Skull Press, pg 40
Simon & Schuster Australia Pty Ltd, pg 42
Skills Publishing, pg 42
Stafford Books, pg 43
Turton & Armstrong Publishers Pty Ltd, pg 45
The Watermark Press, pg 47

Belarus
Belaruskaya Encyklapedyya, pg 63

Belgium
SA Artis-Historia, pg 64
Caramel SA, pg 65
Editions Chanlis, pg 66
Contact NV, pg 67
Glenat Benelux SA, pg 69
Infoboek NV, pg 69
Editeurs de Litterature Biblique, pg 71
Marabout, pg 72
Stichting Kunstboek bvba, pg 74
Vita, pg 75
Zuid-Nederlandse Uitgeverij NV/ Central Uitgeverij, pg 76

Brazil
Icone Editora Ltda, pg 85
Editora Manole Ltda, pg 87

Bulgaria
Darzhavno Izdatelstvo Zemizdat, pg 95
Interpres, pg 96
Regalia 6 Publishing House, pg 97
Slavena, pg 98

China
China Braille Press, pg 103
China Film Press, pg 103
China Theatre Publishing House, pg 104
The People's Posts & Telecommunication Publishing House, pg 108
People's Sports Publishing House, pg 108
Sichuan Science & Technology Publishing House, pg 109

Colombia
RAM Editores, pg 113
Editorial Voluntad SA, pg 114

Costa Rica
Scout Interamericana, pg 117

Croatia
Mladost d d Izdavacku graficku i informaticku djelatnost, pg 119
Vitagraf, pg 120

Cuba
Editorial Oriente, pg 121

Cyprus
James Bendon Ltd, pg 122

Czech Republic
Granit SRO, pg 124
Jan Vasut Publishing, pg 124
Jota, pg 125
Svojtka & Co, pg 128

Denmark
Bogfabrikken Fakta ApS, pg 130
Borgens Forlag A/S, pg 130
Dansk Teknologisk Institut, Forlaget, pg 131
GEC Gads Forlag Aktieselskab af 1994, pg 132
Host & Son Publishers Ltd, pg 133
Forlaget Hovedland, pg 133
Forlaget Klematis A/S, pg 133
Olivia - det gronne forlag, pg 134
Square Dance Partners Forlag, pg 135
Wisby & Wilkens, pg 136

Ecuador
CIDAP, pg 137

Estonia
Sinisukk, pg 140
Valgus Publishers, pg 141

Finland
Lasten Keskus Oy, pg 143
SV-Kauppiaskanava Oy, pg 144

France
Editions Amphora SA, pg 147
Editions Andre Bonne, pg 151
Pierre Bordas et Fils, pg 151
Bragelonne, pg 151
BSI - ELOR Editions Jeunesse, pg 152
Editions Didier Carpentier, pg 152
Philippe Chancerel Editeur, pg 154
Chasse Maree-Armen, pg 154
Dessain et Tolra SA, pg 159
Editions Eyrolles, pg 163
Groupe Fleurus-Mame, pg 164
Imprimerie Librairie Gardet, pg 166
Hachette Pratiques, pg 167
Hemma Joven, SA, pg 168
Librairie Leonce Laget, pg 171
Editions Lito, pg 173
Editions Mango, pg 174
Les Presses d'Ile-de-France Sarl, pg 181
Editions Rombaldi SA, pg 183
Editions Sang de la Terre, pg 183
Sofradif Editions Philippe Auzou, pg 185
Ulisse Edition, pg 188
Pierre Zech Editeur, pg 189

Germany
Alba Fachverlag GmbH und Co KG, pg 192
ALS-Verlag GmbH, pg 193
Ars Edition GmbH, pg 195
AUE-Verlag GmbH, pg 196
Augustus Verlag, pg 196
Bassermann Verlag, pg 198
Joachim Beyer Verlag, pg 202
Eberhargd Blottner Verlag, pg 204
Aenne Burda Verlag, pg 208
Verlag Georg D W Callwey GmbH & Co, pg 208
Hans Christians Druckerei und Verlag GmbH & Co, pg 210
Christophorus-Verlag GmbH, pg 210
Marianne Cieslik, pg 210
Compact Verlag GmbH, pg 211
DuMont Monte, pg 219
Egmont Pestalozzi-Verlag, pg 221
Egmont vgs verlagsgesellschaft mbH, pg 221
Ehrenwirth Verlag GmbH, pg 221
Englisch Verlag GmbH, pg 222
Eulen Verlag, pg 224
Fachbuchverlag Leipzig im Carl Hanser Verlag, pg 226
Fachverlag Schiele & Schoen GmbH, pg 226
Falken-Verlag GmbH, pg 227
Ferd Dummler's Verlag, pg 227
Frech-Verlag GmbH und Co Druck KG, pg 229
H Gietl Verlag & Publikationsservice GmbH, pg 232
Gildefachverlag GmbH & Co KG, pg 232
Verlag Gruppenpaedagogischer Literatur, pg 234
Heel Verlag GmbH, pg 238
Idea Verlag GmbH, pg 244
Jahreszeiten-Verlag GmbH, pg 246
Kallmeyer'sche Verlagsbuchhandlung GmbH, pg 247
Franckh-Kosmos Verlags-GmbH & Co, pg 252
Landbuch-Verlagsgesellschaft mbH, pg 255
Gebr Mann Verlag GmbH & Co, pg 260
Edition Maritim GmbH, pg 261
Otto Meissner Verlag, pg 262
Moby Dick Verlag, pg 264
Mosaik Verlag GmbH, pg 265
Naumann & Goebel Verlagsgesellschaft mbH, pg 267
nymphenburger, pg 269
Oekobuch Verlag & Versand GmbH, pg 269

Oertel & Sporer GmbH & Co, pg 270
Ravensburger Buchverlag Otto Maier GmbH, pg 277
Ritterbach Verlag GmbH, pg 279
Rosenheimer Verlagshaus GmbH & Co KG, pg 280
Rowohlt Taschenbuch Verlag GmbH, pg 280
Verlag Th Schaefer im Vicentz Verlag KG, pg 282
M & H Schaper GmbH & Co KG, pg 282
Schwaneberger Verlag GmbH, pg 286
Siebert und Engelbert Dessart Verlag GmbH, pg 286
Tipress Dienstleistungen fur das Verlagswesen GmbH, pg 294
Tomus Verlag GmbH, pg 294
Mario Truant Verlag, pg 295
Ulrich Schiefer bahnVerlag, pg 296
VS Verlagshaus Stuttgart GmbH, pg 299
Verlagsgruppe Weltbild GmbH, pg 301
Gert Wohlfarth GmbH Verlag Fachtechnik & Mercator Verlag, Verlag Puppen & Spielzeug, pg 304
Zweipunkt Verlag K Kaiser KG, pg 305

Greece
Dorikos Publishing House, pg 310
Ilias Kambanas Publishing Organization, SA, pg 312
Editions Moressopoulos, pg 313

Hong Kong
Publications (Holdings) Ltd, pg 321
Unicorn Books Ltd, pg 322

Hungary
Aranyhal Konyvkiado Goldfish Publishing, pg 323
Ifjusagi Lap-eskonyvkiado Vallalat, pg 324

Iceland
Skjaldborg Ltd, pg 328

India
Diamond Comics (P) Ltd, pg 336
Dolphin Publications, pg 336
Gyan Publishing House, pg 338
Heritage Publishers, pg 338
Inter-India Publications, pg 340
Mapin Publishing Pvt Ltd, pg 342
Orient Paperbacks, pg 345
Pankaj Publications, pg 345
Pustak Mahal, pg 346
Rupa & Co, pg 348
Vikas Publishing House Pvt Ltd, pg 353

Indonesia
Gaya Favorit Press, pg 355
Gramedia, pg 355
PT Indira, pg 355

Ireland
Careers & Educational Publishers Ltd, pg 359

Israel
Dekel Publishing House, pg 366
R Sirkis Publishers Ltd, pg 372

Italy
Mario Adda Editore SNC, pg 374
Gruppo Editoriale Armenia SpA, pg 376
Il Castello srl, pg 380
La Coccinella Editrice SRL, pg 382
Giovanni De Vecchi Editore SpA, pg 384
Di Baio Editore SpA, pg 385
ETR (Editrice Trasporti su Rotaie), pg 388
Fenice 2000, pg 389
Ernesto Gremese Editore SRL, pg 391
Gremese International Srl, pg 391
Gruppo Calderini Edagricole, pg 392
Idea Books, pg 393
L'Airone Editrice, pg 395
Mucchi Editore SRL, pg 400
Franco Panini SPA Editore in Bologna, pg 402
RCS Libri SpA, pg 405
RCS Rizzoli Libri SpA, pg 405
Editoriale Scienza, pg 407
Vaccari SRL, pg 411
Vinciana Editrice sas, pg 411

Japan
Bijutsu Shuppan-Sha, Ltd, pg 415
Hoikusha Publishing Co Ltd, pg 417
International Society for Educational Information (ISEI), pg 418
Japan Publications Inc, pg 418
Kaisei-Sha Publishing Co Ltd, pg 419
Kodansha International, pg 420
Nagaoka Shoten Company Ltd, pg 421
Nihon Vogue Co Ltd, pg 422
Nippon Hoso Shuppan Kyokai (NHK Publishing), pg 422
Ondorisha Publishers Ltd, pg 423
Seibido Shuppan Company Ltd, pg 424
Seibundo Shinkosha Publishing Co Ltd, pg 425
Shufunotomo sha Co Ltd, pg 426
Tankosha Publishing Co Ltd, pg 427
Toho Book Store, pg 427
Toho Shuppan, pg 427
Tokuma-Shoten, pg 427
Charles E Tuttle Publishing Co Inc, pg 428

Republic of Korea
Chung Rim Publishing Co Ltd, pg 435
Dae Won Sa Co Ltd, pg 435
Youl Hwa Dang Publisher, pg 436
Prompter Publications, pg 439
Pyeong-hwa Chulpansa, pg 439
Samho Music Publishing Co, pg 440

Latvia
Alberts XII, pg 441
Nordik/Tapals Publishers Ltd, pg 442
Preses Nams, pg 442

Lebanon
Khayat Book and Publishing Co Sarl, pg 443

Lithuania
Sviesa Publishers, pg 446
Victoria Publishers, pg 446

Malta
Gozo Press, pg 456
Publishers' Enterprises Group (PEG) Ltd, pg 456

Mexico
Editorial Jilguero, SA de CV, pg 462
Ediciones Libra, SA de CV, pg 463
Libros y Revistas SA de CV, pg 463
Editorial Limusa SA de CV, pg 463
Editorial Minutiae Mexicana SA, pg 464
Sayrols Editorial SA de CV, pg 466
Selector SA de CV, pg 467
Editorial Trillas SA de CV, pg 467

Monaco
Les Editions du Rocher, pg 469

Netherlands
BV Uitgevery NZV (Nederlandse Zondagsschool Vereniging), pg 475
Uitgeverij Cantecleer BV, pg 475
Gottmer Uitgevers Groop, pg 477
Otto Maier Benelux BV, pg 481
De Muiderkring BV, pg 481
Rebo Productions BV, pg 483
Terra Publishing Co, pg 485
Tirion Uitgevers BV, pg 485
Zuid Boekprodukties BV, pg 487

New Zealand
Bush Press Communications Ltd, pg 489
Craig Potton Publishing, pg 490
David's Marine Books, pg 490
Halcyon Publishing Ltd, pg 491
Shoal Bay Press Ltd, pg 495

Norway
Tell Forlag, pg 505

Philippines
Anvil Publishing Inc, pg 512
Bright Concepts Printing House, pg 512
Sonny A Mendoza, pg 513

Poland
Wydawnictwa Normalizacyjne Alfa-Wero, pg 516
Wydawnictwo Arkady, pg 516
Wydawnictwo Podsiedlik-Raniowski i Spolka, pg 519
Wydawn Na Sprawa' Wydawniczo-Oswiatowa Spotdzielnia Inwalidow, pg 521

Portugal
Gradiva-Publicacnoes Lda, pg 525
Editorial Presenca, pg 528

Reunion
Editions Ocean, pg 531

Romania
Alcor-Edimpex (Verlag) Ltd, pg 531
Editura Excelsior, pg 533

Russian Federation
Airis Press, pg 537
Dom, Izdatel'stvo sovetskogo desskogo fonda im & I Lenina, pg 537
Druzhba Narodov, pg 537
Permskaja Kniga, pg 541
Scorpion Publishers, pg 541

Singapore
Archipelago Press, pg 545

Slovakia
Vydavatepstvo Praca spol sro, pg 550
Smena Publishing House, pg 550

South Africa
Human & Rousseau (Pty) Ltd, pg 555
Tafelberg Publishers Ltd, pg 560

Spain
Editorial Acanto SA, pg 561
Alta Fulla Editorial, pg 563
Editorial Astri SA, pg 564
Central Catequistica Salesiana (CCS), pg 567
Comunidad Autonoma de Madrid, Servicio de Documentacion y Publicaciones, pg 568
Ediciones Daly S L, pg 569
Editorial De Vecchi SA, pg 569
Editorial Everest SA, pg 572
Editorial Fundamentos, pg 575
Idea Books, SA, pg 578
JOC Internacional, SA, pg 579
LEDA (Las Ediciones de Arte), pg 579
Libsa Editorial SA, pg 580
Ediciones Martinez-Roca SA, pg 581
Editorial Noray, pg 584
Parramon Ediciones SA, pg 586
Pleniluni Edicions, pg 587
Editora Regional de Murcia - ERM, pg 588
Equipo Sirius SA, pg 591
Axel Springer Publicaciones, pg 591
Ediciones Susaeta SA, pg 592
Tursen, SA, pg 593
Ediciones Tutor SA, pg 594

Sweden
Allt om Hobby AB, pg 600
Berghs, pg 600
Bokforlaget Spektra AB, pg 601
BOOX, pg 601
ICA bokforlag, pg 603
Jannersten Forlag AB, pg 604
Johnston & Streiffert Editions, pg 604
Natur och Kultur/LTs foerlag, pg 604
Bokforlaget Semic AB, pg 606
Semic Bokforlaget International AB, pg 606

Switzerland
Verlag Eisenbahn, pg 613
Paul Haupt Berne, pg 615
Motovun Book GmbH, pg 619
Mueller Rueschlikon Verlags AG, pg 619
Office du Livre SA (Buchhaus AG), pg 620
Sinwel-Buchhandlung Verlag, pg 624
Editions du Tricorne, pg 626
Verlagsbuchhandlung AG, pg 626
Wiese Verlag AG, pg 627
Zumstein & Cie, pg 628

SUBJECT INDEX

Taiwan, Province of China
Echo Publishing Company Ltd, pg 629
Highlight Publishing Company Ltd, pg 630
Wei-Chuan Publishing Company Ltd, pg 632

Turkey
Alkim Kitapcilik-Yayimcilik, pg 638
Soez Yayin/Oyunajans, pg 641

United Kingdom
Amber Books Ltd, pg 646
Apple Press, pg 648
Appletree Press Ltd, pg 648
Arms & Armour Press, pg 648
Art Books International Ltd, pg 649
Ashmolean Museum Publications, pg 650
Batsford Ltd, pg 652
BCA, pg 653
Ruth Bean Publishers, pg 653
Belitha Press Ltd, pg 653
Bellew Publishing Co Ltd, pg 653
Bishopsgate Press Ltd, pg 655
BLA Publishing Ltd, pg 655
A & C Black Publishers Ltd, pg 655
Blaketon Hall Ltd, pg 656
Blandford Publishing Ltd, pg 656
Bloomsbury Publishing PLC, pg 656
Books International, pg 657
Breslich & Foss, pg 659
British Museum Press, pg 660
The Brown Reference Group PLC, pg 660
Cassell & Co, pg 664
Marshall Cavendish Partworks Ltd, pg 665
Christian Education, pg 667
Compendium Publishing, pg 670
Conran Octopus, pg 670
Paul H Crompton Ltd, pg 672
The Crowood Press Ltd, pg 672
David & Charles Ltd, pg 674
Diagram Visual Information Ltd, pg 675
Dorling Kindersley Ltd, pg 676
Eaglemoss Publications Ltd, pg 676
Elliot Right Way Books, pg 678
Floris Books, pg 683
Foulsham Publishers, pg 683
Stanley Gibbons Publications, pg 687
GMC Publications Ltd, pg 687
Grange Books PLC, pg 689
Hamlyn, pg 691
HarperCollins Publishers, pg 692
Hawthorn Press, pg 693
Hodder & Stoughton Educational, pg 696
Jade Publishers, pg 702
Frances Lincoln Ltd, pg 707
Y Lolfa Cyf, pg 708
Lorenz Books, pg 709
The Lutterworth Press, pg 709
Marshall Editions Ltd, pg 712
Merehurst Publishers, pg 713
MQ Publications Ltd, pg 716
New Holland Publishers (UK) Ltd, pg 718
Newpro UK Ltd, pg 719
Nexus Special Interests, pg 719
Nicholas Enterprises Ltd, pg 719
Octopus Publishing Group, pg 720
Oldcastle Books Ltd, pg 720
Michael O'Mara Books Ltd, pg 721
Orion Publishing Group Ltd, pg 722
Osprey Publishing Ltd, pg 722

Parapress Ltd, pg 724
Picton Publishing (Chippenham) Ltd, pg 727
David Porteous Editions, pg 729
PRC Publishing Ltd, pg 730
Quarto Publishing plc, pg 731
Quintet Publishing Ltd, pg 732
The Reader's Digest Association Ltd, pg 733
Regency House Publishing Ltd, pg 734
Salamander Books Ltd, pg 738
Savitri Books, pg 738
Search Press Ltd, pg 740
Shire Publications Ltd, pg 741
Sigma Press, pg 742
Silver Link Publishing Ltd, pg 742
Spon Press, pg 744
Stobart Davies Ltd, pg 745
Thames & Hudson Ltd, pg 748
Time Warner Books UK, pg 749
Vacation Work Publications, pg 752
White Cockade Publishing, pg 755
WI Enterprises Ltd, pg 756

Viet Nam
Science & Technics Publishing House, pg 763

CRIMINOLOGY

Argentina
Abeledo-Perrot SAE e l, pg 2
Juris Editorial, pg 6

Australia
Artemis Publishing Pty Ltd, pg 12
Australian Institute of Criminology, pg 13
Australian Institute of Family Studies (AIFS), pg 13
Kingsclear Books, pg 29
Law Book Co Information Services, pg 29
McGraw-Hill Australia Pty Ltd, pg 32
Pearson Education Australia, pg 37
Jurriaan Plesman, pg 38
Wileman Publications, pg 47

Austria
Edition S der OSD, pg 51

Belarus
Interdigets Publishing House, pg 63

Belgium
Acco CV, pg 64
Leuven University Press, pg 71

Brazil
Livraria Francisco Alves Editora SA, pg 78
Centro de Estudos Juridicosdo Para (CEJUP), pg 80
Editora Forense, pg 83
Editora Revan Ltda, pg 90

Chile
Edeval (Universidad de Valparaiso), pg 100

Colombia
Universidad Externado de Colombia, pg 112

Denmark
Bonnier Publications AS, pg 130

France
Librairie des Champs-Elysees SA, pg 154
Editions Eres, pg 162
FBT de R Editions/Editions des Limbes d'Or, pg 163
Editions Jean-Claude Lattes, pg 170
Editions des Limbes d'Or/FBT de R Editions, pg 173

Germany
Beleke KG Verlag, pg 200
Centaurus-Verlagsgesellschaft GmbH, pg 209
Duncker und Humblot GmbH, pg 219
Europaeische Verlagsanstalt GmbH & Rotbuch Verlag GmbH & Co KG, pg 225
Wilhelm Goldmann Verlag GmbH, pg 233
Huthig GmbH & Co KG, pg 244
Juventa Verlag GmbH, pg 247
KBV-Verlags-und Mediengesellschaft mbH, pg 248
Pendragon Verlag, pg 272
Max Schmidt-Roemhild Verlag, pg 284
Springer-Verlag GmbH & Co KG, pg 288
Zebulon Verlag GmbH & Co KG, pg 305

Hong Kong
Hong Kong University Press, pg 320

India
Abhinav Publications, pg 329
APH Publishing Corp, pg 331
Bharatiya Samijik Vigyan Auusandhan Parishad, pg 332
Diamond Comics (P) Ltd, pg 336
Jaico Publishing House, pg 340
Law Publishers, pg 341
Reliance Publishing House, pg 347

Ireland
Emerald Publications, pg 360
The O'Brien Press Ltd, pg 363
Round Hall Sweet & Maxwell, pg 363

Israel
Dyonon/Papyrus Publishing House of the Tel-Aviv, pg 367
Schocken Publishing House Ltd, pg 372
Tcherikover Publishers Ltd, pg 372

Italy
CEDAM (Casa Editrice Dr A Milani), pg 380
Levante, pg 395

Latvia
Nordik/Tapals Publishers Ltd, pg 442

Lithuania
Eugrimas, pg 445

Mexico
Editorial Limusa SA de CV, pg 463
Siglo XXI Editores SA de CV, pg 467

Morocco
Societe Ennewrasse Service Librairie et Imprimerie, pg 470

Netherlands
Koninklijke Vermande bv, pg 480
Kugler Publications, pg 480
Sociaal en Cultureel Planbureau, pg 484
Uitgeverij Het Spectrum BV, pg 484
SWP, BV Uitgeverij, pg 485

Pakistan
Sang-e-Meel Publications, pg 509

Papua New Guinea
National Research Institute of Papua New Guinea, pg 510

Philippines
Rex Bookstores & Publishers, pg 514

Poland
Wydawnictwo Prawnicze Co, pg 519

Portugal
Quid Juris - Sociedade editora, pg 529

Russian Federation
Izdatel'stvo Kazanskago Universiteta, pg 538

Singapore
Taylor & Francis Asia Pacific, pg 548

South Africa
Human Sciences Research Council, pg 555

Spain
Bosch Casa Editorial SA, pg 565
Editorial M J Bosch, SL, pg 565
Instituto Vasco de Criminologia, pg 578
Tirant lo Blanch SL Libreriaa, pg 592

Turkey
Altin Kitaplar Yayinevi, pg 638
Sabah Kitaplari, pg 641

United Kingdom
Amber Books Ltd, pg 646
Ashgate Publishing Ltd, pg 649
Blandford Publishing Ltd, pg 656
Breedon Books Publishing Company Ltd, pg 659
Carlton Publishing Group, pg 664
Cavendish Publishing Ltd, pg 665
Constable & Robinson Ltd, pg 670
Delectus Books, pg 675
Eaglemoss Publications Ltd, pg 676
Farsight Press, pg 682
Gembooks, pg 686
John Blake Publishing Ltd, pg 703
Jessica Kingsley Publishers, pg 704
Open University Press, pg 721
Pearson Education, pg 725
Perpetuity Press, pg 726
Piatkus Books, pg 727
Police Review Publishing Company Ltd, pg 729

PUBLISHERS

Profile Books Ltd, pg 731
Ravette Publishing Ltd, pg 733
Sage Publications Ltd, pg 737
Scottish Office Library & Information Services, pg 740
Serpent's Tail Ltd, pg 740
SHU Press, pg 742
Transworld Publishers Ltd, pg 750
Virgin Publishing Ltd, pg 753
Whiting & Birch Ltd, pg 756

Uruguay
Fundacion de Cultura Universitaria, pg 760

Yugoslavia
Alfa-Narodna Knjiga, pg 764

DEVELOPING COUNTRIES

Albania
NL SH, pg 1

Australia
Ocean Press, pg 35
Spinifex Press, pg 43
Stafford Books, pg 43

Austria
Development News Ltd, pg 51
Guthmann & Peterson Liber Libri, Edition, pg 52
Verlag Jungbrunnen - Wiener Spielzeugschachtel GesellschaftmbH, pg 53
Promedia Verlagsges mbH, pg 57
Edition Va Bene, pg 60

Belgium
EPO Publishers, Printers, Booksellers, pg 68
Institut Royal des Relations Internationales, pg 69
Ipis VZW (International Peace Information Service), pg 69
Koepel van de Vlaamse Noord - Zuidbeweging 11.11.11, pg 70
Wereldwijd Vzw, pg 75

Burundi
Editions Intore, pg 98

Chile
Ediciones Cieplan, pg 100

China
World Affairs Press, pg 110

Costa Rica
Centro Agronomico Tropical de Investigacion y Ensenanza (CATIE), pg 115
Instituto Interamericano de Cooperacion para la Agricultura (IICA), pg 116
Union Mundial para la Naturaleza (UICN), Oficina Regional para Mesoamerica, pg 117

Cote d'Ivoire
Universite d' Abidjan, pg 118
Heritage Publishing Co, pg 118

Denmark
Forlaget Hjulet, pg 132
Mellemfolkeligt Samvirke, pg 133
Samfundslitteratur, pg 135

Dominican Republic
Pontificia Universidad Catolica Madre y Maestra, pg 136

Egypt (Arab Republic of Egypt)
Al Arab Publishing House, pg 138
Dar El Shorouk Publishing & Distributing House, pg 138

France
Annales de la Recherche Urbaine, pg 147
La Decouverte et Syros, pg 158
Editions Entente, pg 162
Futuribles SARL, pg 165
Groupe de Recherche et d'Echanges Technologiques (GRET), pg 167
L'Harmattan, pg 168
Les Introuvables-Editions L'Harmattan, pg 170
IRD Editions, pg 170
Karthala Editions-Diffusion, pg 171

Germany
Altberliner Verlag GmbH, pg 193
ARCult Media, pg 194
Brandes & Apsel Verlag GmbH, pg 206
Claudius Verlag, pg 211
Deutscher Instituts-Verlag GmbH, pg 215
Verlag J H W Dietz Nachf GmbH, pg 217
agenda Verlag Thomas Dominikowski, pg 217
Duncker und Humblot GmbH, pg 219
Elefanten Press Verlag GmbH, pg 222
Eppinger-Verlag OHG, pg 223
Erlanger Verlag Fuer Mission und Okumene, pg 223
Verlag des Gustav-Adolf-Werks, pg 235
Peter Hammer Verlag GmbH, pg 237
Horlemann Verlag, pg 243
Edition ID-Archiv/ID-Verlag, pg 244
IKO Verlag fur Interkulturelle Kommunikation, pg 244
Informationsstelle Suedliches Afrika eV (ISSA), pg 245
K L V Konkret Literatur Verlag GmbH, pg 247
Lamuv Verlag GmbH, pg 255
Libertas- Europaeisches Institut GmbH, pg 257
Margraf Verlag, pg 261
Missio eV Aachen, pg 264
Neuer Weg Verlag und Druck GmbH, pg 268
Nusser Verlag, pg 269
Orlanda Frauenverlag, pg 270
Pahl-Rugenstein Verlag Nachfolger-GmbH, pg 271
PapyRossa Verlags GmbH & Co Kommanditgesellschaft KG, pg 271
Verlag Roter Morgen, pg 280
Verlag an der Ruhr GmbH, pg 281
Franz Steiner Verlag Wiesbaden GmbH, pg 289
Steyler Verlag, pg 290
UNO-Verlag mbH, Vertriebs und Verlagsgesellschaft, pg 296

Unrast Verlag e V, pg 296
Vervuert Verlagsgesellschaft, pg 298
Weltforum Verlag GmbH, pg 301
Zambon Verlag, pg 305

Ghana
World Literature Project, pg 308

Guinea-Bissau
Instituto Nacional de Estudos e Pesquisa, pg 316

Guyana
Community Based Rehabilitation Progeamme, pg 317

Hungary
CEU-Press, pg 323

India
Cosmo Publications, pg 335
Gyan Publishing House, pg 338
National Book Organization, pg 343
Navrang Booksellers & Publishers, pg 344
Oxford University Press, pg 345
Reliance Publishing House, pg 347
Sage Publications India Pvt Ltd, pg 348
Scientific Book Agency, pg 349
South Asian Publishers Pvt Ltd, pg 350
Sterling Publishers Pvt Ltd, pg 351

Indonesia
Lembaga Demografi Fakultas Ekonomi Universitas Indonesia, pg 356
Yayasan Obor Indonesia, pg 357

Ireland
On Stream Publications Ltd, pg 363

Israel
Hanitzotz A-Sharara Publishing House, pg 368

Italy
Edizioni Cultura della Pace, pg 383
Fatatrac, pg 388

Jamaica
Association of Development Agencies, pg 412

Japan
Koyo Shobo, pg 420
Sobun-Sha, pg 426
United Nations University Press, pg 428

Kenya
Academy Science Publishers, pg 430
Action Publishers, pg 430
African Centre for Technology Studies (ACTS), pg 431
Kenya Quality & Productivity Institute, pg 432
Midi Teki Publishers, pg 433
Nairobi University Press, pg 433
Shirikon Publishers, pg 433

Madagascar
Maison d'Edition Protestante ANTSO, pg 450

SUBJECT INDEX

Malaysia
Forum Publications, pg 452
Holograms (M) Sdn Bhd, pg 452

Mexico
El Colegio de Michoacan A C, pg 460
Fondo de Cultura Economica, pg 461
Instituto Nacional de Estadistica, Geographia e Informatica, pg 464

Morocco
Cabinet Conseil CCMLA, pg 469

Namibia
Desert Research Foundation of Namibia (DRFN), pg 471
Multi-Disciplinary Research Centre Library, pg 471

Netherlands
Koninklijk Instituut Voor de Tropen, pg 480
Mets & Schilt Uitgevers en Distributeurs, pg 481

Nigeria
JAD Publishers Ltd, pg 500
Riverside Communications, pg 501
Unity Publishing & Research Company Ltd, pg 502

Pakistan
Pakistan Institute of Development Economics, pg 508

Papua New Guinea
National Research Institute of Papua New Guinea, pg 510

Peru
Instituto de Estudios Peruanos, pg 511
Sur Casa de Estudios del Socialismo, pg 511

Philippines
Our Lady of Manaoag Publisher, pg 514

Poland
Verbinum Wydawnictwo Ksiezy Werbistow, pg 520

Senegal
CODESRIA (Council for the Development of Social Science Research in Africa), pg 544

Singapore
Select Books Pte Ltd, pg 548

South Africa
Institute for Reformational Studies CHE, pg 555
New Africa Books (Pty) Ltd, pg 557

Spain
Editorial AEDOS SA, pg 561
Amnistia Internacional Editorial SL, pg 563
Icaria Editorial SA, pg 577

SUBJECT INDEX

Mundo Negro Editorial, pg 583
Ediciones del Oriente y del Mediterraneo, pg 585

Suriname
Stichting Wetenschappelijke Informatie, pg 599

Switzerland
Rotpunktverlag, pg 623
Verlag im Waldgut AG, pg 627

United Republic of Tanzania
DUP (1996) Ltd, pg 633

Togo
Editions Akpagnon, pg 636

Tunisia
Ceres Editions, pg 637

United Kingdom
Association of Commonwealth Universities (ACU), pg 650
Business Monitor International, pg 661
Jon Carpenter Publishing, pg 664
Frank Cass Publishers, pg 664
Cassell & Co, pg 664
Catholic Institute for International Relations, pg 665
Commonwealth Secretariat, pg 669
James Currey Ltd, pg 673
Earthscan Publications Ltd, pg 677
The Economist Intelligence Unit, pg 677
Edward Elgar Publishing Ltd, pg 678
Europa Publications, pg 680
The Eurospan Group, pg 680
Institute of Development Studies, pg 699
Intermediate Technology Publications Ltd, pg 700
KIT Press - Royal Tropical Institute, pg 705
Letterbox Library, pg 707
Open University Press, pg 721
Open University Worldwide, pg 721
Oxfam, pg 722
Panos Institute, pg 723
Pathfinder London, pg 724
Pluto Press, pg 728
Profile Books Ltd, pg 731
Rough Guides Ltd, pg 735
Routledge, pg 736
Routledge Curzon, pg 736
Royal Institute of International Affairs, pg 736
Serif, pg 740
I B Tauris & Co Ltd, pg 747
Vacation Work Publications, pg 752

Uruguay
Nordan-Comunidad, pg 760
Ediciones Trilce, pg 761

Venezuela
Biblioteca Ayacucho, pg 762
Editorial Nueva Sociedad, pg 762

Zambia
Aafzam Ltd, pg 766
MFK Management Consultants Services, pg 766

Zimbabwe
Journal on Social Change, pg 768
Sapes Trust Ltd, pg 769
Zimbabwe International Book Fair, pg 769

DISABILITY, SPECIAL NEEDS

Argentina
Alfagrama SRL ediciones, pg 3

Australia
The Australian Council for Educational Research Ltd, pg 13
Australian Institute of Family Studies (AIFS), pg 13
Australian Large Print Pty Ltd, pg 14
Chase Just Publishing, pg 17
Ginninderra Press, pg 24
Indra Publishing, pg 27
Killara Press, pg 29
Little Red Apple Publishing, pg 30
MacLennan & Petty Pty Ltd, pg 31
McGraw-Hill Australia Pty Ltd, pg 32
OTEN (Open Training & Education Network), pg 36
Spinifex Press, pg 43
Stafford Books, pg 43
Villamonta Publishing Service Inc, pg 47

Azerbaijan
Sada, Literaturno-Izdatel'skij Centr, pg 61

Barbados
Business Tutors, pg 63

Brazil
Editora Antroposofica Ltda, pg 78
EDUC - Editora da PUC-SP, pg 82

China
China Braille Press, pg 103
People's Education Press, pg 107

Czech Republic
Portal Ltd, pg 127

France
CTNERHI - Centre Technique National d'Etudes et de Recherches sur les Handicaps et les Inadaptations, pg 157

Germany
Catia Monser Eggcup-Verlag, pg 209
Engel & Bengel Verlag, pg 222
Harald Fischer Verlag GmbH, pg 228
Lebenshilfe-Verlag Marburg, Verlag der Bundesvereinigung Lebenshilfe fuer Menschen mit geistiger Behinderung eV, pg 256
Edition Marhold, pg 261
Meyer & Meyer Fachverlag und Buchhandel GmbH, pg 263

Guyana
Community Based Rehabilitation Progeamme, pg 317

Hong Kong
Hong Kong University Press, pg 320

Iceland
Namsgagnastofnun, pg 328

India
Reliance Publishing House, pg 347
Somaiya Publications Pvt Ltd, pg 350

Italy
Editore Armando Armando SRL, pg 376
Edizioni Cantagalli, pg 379
Gangemi Editore, pg 390
Lecce Spazio Vivo Srl, pg 395
Milella di Lecce Spazio Vivo SRL, pg 399

Jamaica
Alice J M Rhodd, pg 413

Japan
Kaisei-Sha Publishing Co Ltd, pg 419
Minerva Shobo Co Ltd, pg 421
Tokyo Shoseki Co Ltd, pg 427

Latvia
Preses Nams, pg 442

Mexico
Maria Esther De Fleischmann, pg 459

New Zealand
Reach Publications, pg 495

Norway
Solum Forlag A/S, pg 505

Spain
Editorial Dossat SA, pg 570
Tursen, SA, pg 593

Switzerland
Heilpaedagogisches Institut der Universitaet Freiburg, pg 615
Editiones Roche, pg 623

United Kingdom
Advisory Unit: Computers in Education, pg 645
Association for Science Education, pg 650
BILD Publications, pg 654
Colourpoint Books, pg 669
Drake Educational Associates Ltd, pg 676
The Eurospan Group, pg 680
David Fulton Publishers Ltd, pg 685
Jessica Kingsley Publishers, pg 704
Letterbox Library, pg 707
NCVO, pg 718
Open University Worldwide, pg 721
The Policy Press, pg 729
Psychological Corporation Ltd, pg 731
Scottish Office Library & Information Services, pg 740
Speechmark Publishing Ltd, pg 744
Supportive Learning Publications, pg 746
Wilmington Business Information Ltd, pg 756

BOOK

The Women's Press Ltd, pg 758
Anglia Young Books, pg 759

DRAMA, THEATER

Albania
NL SH, pg 1

Argentina
Ada Korn Editora SA, pg 3
Beatriz Viterbo Editora, pg 4
Bonum Editorial SACI, pg 4
Ediciones Corregidor SAICI y E, pg 4
Ediciones Don Bosco Argentina, pg 5
EUDEBA (Editorial Universitaria de Buenos Aires), pg 6
Ediciones de la Flor SRL, pg 6
Editorial Galerna SRL, pg 6
Editorial Losada SA, pg 7
Ediciones Nueva Vision SAIC, pg 8
Quetzal-Domingo Cortizo, pg 8
Ediciones Tres Tiempos SRL, pg 9

Australia
Currency Press Pty Ltd, pg 19
EK Press, pg 21
Geoffrey Hamlyn-Harris, pg 25
Jika Publishing, pg 28
Magabala Books Aboriginal Corporation, pg 31
Plantain Park, pg 38
Playbox Theatre Co, pg 38
Playlab Press, pg 38
Sydney Studies In English, pg 43
Wizard Books Pty Ltd, pg 48

Austria
Aarachne Verlag, pg 49
Literature Verlag Droschl, pg 51
Gerda Leber Buch-Kunst-und Musikverlag Proscenium Edition, pg 54
Mueller-Speiser Wissenschaftlicher Verlag, pg 55
Verlag Neues Leben, pg 55
Richard Pils Publication P, pg 57
SN-Verlag, Salzburger Nachrichten Verlags GmbH & Co KG, pg 59
Wieser Verlag, pg 61

Azerbaijan
Sada, Literaturno-Izdatel'skij Centr, pg 61

Bangladesh
Bangladesh Publishers, pg 62
Gatidhara, pg 62

Belgium
Abimo, pg 63
Lansman Editeur, pg 70
Toneelfonds J Janssens BVBA, pg 74

Brazil
AGIR S/A Editora, pg 78
Editora Bertrand Brasil Ltda, pg 79
Centro de Estudos Juridicosdo Para (CEJUP), pg 80
Dumara Distribuidora de Publicacoes Ltda, pg 81
Edicon Editora e Consultorial Ltda, pg 81
Editora Globo SA, pg 84
Edicoes Loyola SA, pg 87
Editora Paz e Terra, pg 89
Editora Perspectiva, pg 89

PUBLISHERS SUBJECT INDEX

Edicoes Tabajara, pg 92
34 Literatura S/C Ltda, pg 92

Bulgaria
Fondacija Zlatno Kljuce, pg 95
Zunica, pg 98

Cameroon
Editions Buma Kor, pg 99
Editions CLE, pg 99
Editions Semences Africaines, pg 99

Chile
Arrayan Editores, pg 99

China
Beijing Publishing House, pg 102
China Film Press, pg 103
China Theatre Publishing House, pg 104
Foreign Languages Press, pg 105
Shandong Literature & Art Publishing House, pg 109

Colombia
Universidad de Antioquia, Division Publicaciones, pg 114

The Democratic Republic of the Congo
Saint-Paul, pg 115

Costa Rica
Promesa, Ediciones, pg 116

Cote d'Ivoire
Akohi Editions, pg 117
Les Nouvelles Editions Africaines, pg 118

Croatia
AGM doo, pg 118
Durieux d o o, pg 118
Knjizevni Krug Split, pg 119
Matica hrvatska, pg 119

Cuba
Holguin, Ediciones, pg 121
Editorial Letras Cubanas, pg 121

Cyprus
Chrysopolitissa Publishers, pg 122

Czech Republic
Divadelni Ustav, pg 124
Nadace Lyry Pragensis, pg 126
Narodni Muzeum, pg 126
Press Art, pg 127

Denmark
Aarhus Universitetsforlag, pg 129
The Danish Literature Centre, pg 131
Teaterforlaget Drama, pg 136

Dominican Republic
Pontificia Universidad Catolica Madre y Maestra, pg 136

Egypt (Arab Republic of Egypt)
Dar El Shorouk Publishing & Distributing House, pg 138

Finland
Yliopistopaino/Helsinki University Press, pg 145

France
Editions Actes Sud, pg 146
Editions Al Liamm, pg 146
L'Arche Editeur, pg 147
Compagnie Francaise des Arts Graphiques SA, pg 148
Editions d'Aujourd'hui (Les Introuvables), pg 149
Editions l'Avant-Scene de Prette Technique, pg 149
Editions Jacques Bremond, pg 151
Cicero Editeurs, pg 155
Circe, pg 155
La Delirante, pg 158
Georges-Charles Demay, pg 158
Editions Espaces 34, pg 162
L'Esprit Du Temps, pg 162
L'Etoile/Cahiers du Cinema, pg 163
Des Femmes, pg 164
Association Frank, pg 165
Editions Infrarouge, pg 169
Institut International de la Marionnette, pg 170
Editions Michel Lafon SA, pg 171
Editions du Laquet, pg 172
Le Livre de Poche-L G F (Librairie Generale Francaise), pg 173
Editions Medianes, pg 175
Librairie A-G Nizet Sarl, pg 177
Noir Sur Blanc, pg 177
Editions Norma, pg 177
Editions Plume, pg 180
POL Editeur, pg 180
Presses de la Sorbonne Nouvelle/PSN, pg 181
Presses Universitaires de Nancy, pg 181
Publications Orientalistes de France (POF), pg 182
Editions Ramsay, pg 182
Editions Andre Silvaire Sarl, pg 185
Editions Theatrales, pg 187
Transeuropeennes/RCE, pg 188
La Vague a l'ame, pg 188
La Voix du Regard, pg 189

Germany
A Francke Verlag (Tubingen und Basel), pg 191
Alexander Verlag Berlin, pg 192
Alpha Literatur Verlag/Alpha Presse, pg 193
AOL-Verlag Frohmut Menze, pg 194
Arcadia Verlag GmbH, pg 194
ARCult Media, pg 194
Verlag der Autoren GmbH & Co KG, pg 197
Belser Wissenschaftlicher Dienst, pg 200
Betzel Verlag GmbH, pg 202
Das Arsenal, Verlag fuer Kultur und Politik GmbH, pg 212
Domino Verlag, Guenther Brinek GmbH, pg 217
Edition Aragon-Verlagsgesellschaft mbH, pg 220
Edition Solitude - Akademie Schloss Solitude, pg 221
Fabel-Verlag Gudrun Liebchen, pg 226
Erhard Friedrich Verlag, pg 230
Haering, Siegfried, Literaten-Verlag Ulm, pg 236
Edition Hentrich Druck & Verlag Gebr Hentrich und Tank GmbH & Co KG, pg 239
Anton Hiersemann, Verlag, pg 240
Impuls-Theater-Verlag, pg 244
ludicium Verlag GmbH, pg 245
Alfred Kroner Verlag, pg 253
Verlag Antje Kunstmann GmbH, pg 254
Robert Lienau GmbH & Co KG, pg 258
Annemarie Maeger, pg 260
Merlin Verlag Andreas Meyer Verlags GmbH und Co KG, pg 263
Meyer & Meyer Fachverlag und Buchhandel GmbH, pg 263
Gunter Narr Verlag, pg 266
Edition Octopus & Okeanos Presse, pg 269
Oekotopia Verlag, Wolfgang Hoffman, pg 270
Georg Olms Verlag AG, pg 270
Gerhard Rautenberg Druckerei und Verlag GmbH & Co KG, pg 277
Otto Teich, pg 292
Trotzdem-Verlags Genossenschaft eG, pg 295
Vervuert Verlagsgesellschaft, pg 298
Weidler Buchverlag Berlin, pg 301

Ghana
Black Mask Ltd, pg 306
Bureau of Ghana Languages, pg 306
Woeli Publishing Services, pg 308

Greece
Dorikos Publishing House, pg 310
Ekdoseis Kazantzaki (Kazantzakis Publications), pg 310
Etaireia Spoudon Neoellinikou Politismou Kai Genikis Paideias, pg 310
Govostis Publishing SA, pg 311
Hestia-1 D Hestia-Kollaros & Co Corporation, pg 311
Kastaniotis Editions SA, pg 312
Kedros Publishers, pg 312
Ed Nea Acropolis, pg 313
Patakis Publishers, pg 314
To Rodakio, pg 315
S J Zacharopoulos SA Publishing Co, pg 316

Hungary
Jelenkor Verlag, pg 324
Nemzetkozi Szinhazi Intezet Magyar Kozpontja, pg 326

India
Abhinav Publications, pg 329
Ananda Publishers Pvt Ltd, pg 330
CICC Book House, pg 335
Cosmo Publications, pg 335
DK Printworld (P) Ltd, pg 336
Gyan Publishing House, pg 338
Indian Council for Cultural Relations, pg 339
Kali for Women, pg 341
Kitab Ghar, pg 341
Mudgala Trust, pg 343
Munshiram Manoharlal Publishers Pvt Ltd, pg 343
Omsons Publications, pg 345
Orient Paperbacks, pg 345
Reliance Publishing House, pg 347
Sharda Prakashan, pg 350
Vidyarthi Mithram Press, pg 352

Indonesia
Dunia Pustaka Jaya, pg 355

Ireland
Campus Publishing Ltd, pg 359
Clo Iar-Chonnachta Teo, pg 359
Gallery Books, Ireland, pg 360
Mercier Press Ltd, pg 362

Israel
Hakibbutz Hameuchad Publishing House Ltd, pg 368
Schocken Publishing House Ltd, pg 372

Italy
Edizioni Abete, pg 374
Argalia Editore delle Arti Grafiche Editoriali SRL, pg 376
Artioli Editore in Modena, pg 377
Bompiani-RCS Libri, pg 378
Bulzoni Editore SRL (Le Edizioni Universitarie d'Italia), pg 379
Nuova Casa Editrice Licinio Cappelli GEM srl, pg 379
Edistudio di Brunetto Casini, pg 380
Colonnese Editore, pg 382
Costa e Nolan SpA, pg 383
Effata Editrice, pg 387
Essegi, pg 388
Arnaldo Forni Editore SRL, pg 389
Ernesto Gremese Editore SRL, pg 391
Kaos Edizioni SRL, pg 395
Lalli Editore SRL, pg 395
Letture Mensile di Informazione Culturale, Letteratura e Spettacolo, pg 395
Levante, pg 395
Editrice Liguria SNC di Norberto Sabatelli & C, pg 396
Vincenzo Lo Faro Editore, pg 396
Angelo Longo Editore, pg 396
Editrice Massimo SAS di Crespi Cesare e C, pg 398
Casa Editrice Menna di Sinisgalli Menna Giuseppina, pg 398
Mondolibro Editore SNC, pg 399
Officina Edizioni di Aldo Quinti, pg 401
Maria Pacini Fazzi Editore, pg 402
Luigi Pellegrini Editore, pg 403
Pratiche Editrice, pg 404
G e C Ricordi SpA, pg 405
Rubbettino Editore, pg 406
Edizioni Scientifiche Italiane, pg 407
SEMAR Publishers SRL, pg 407
Sicania, pg 408
La Tartaruga Edizioni SAS, pg 409
Edizioni Ubulibri SAS, pg 410
Viviani Editore srl, pg 412
Edizioni Zara, pg 412

Jamaica
Carlong Publishers (Caribbean) Ltd, pg 412

Japan
Hakusui-Sha Co Ltd, pg 417
Hayakawa Publishing Inc, pg 417
Koyo Shobo, pg 420
Nippon Hoso Shuppan Kyokai (NHK Publishing), pg 422
Shakai Shiso-Sha, pg 425

Kenya
Heinemann Kenya Limited (EAEP), pg 431
Lake Publishers & Enterprises Ltd, pg 432

SUBJECT INDEX — BOOK

Republic of Korea
Bum-Woo Publishing Co, pg 435

Latvia
Preses Nams, pg 442

Lithuania
The Publishing House of the Lithuanian Writers' Union, pg 446
Scena, pg 446

Luxembourg
Editions Emile Borschette, pg 447
Edition Objectif Lune, pg 447
Editions Phi, pg 448

The Former Yugoslav Republic of Macedonia
Ktitor, pg 449

Mauritius
De l'edition Bukie Banane, pg 457

Mexico
Editorial AGATA SA de CV, pg 457
Arbol Editorial SA de CV, pg 458
Editorial Avante SA de Cv, pg 458
Editorial Extemporaneos SA, pg 461
Editorial Limusa SA de CV, pg 463
Universidad Nacional Autonoma de Mexico (National University of Mexico), pg 467
Universidad Veracruzana Direccion General Editorial y de Publicaciones, pg 468

Monaco
Les Editions du Rocher, pg 469

Morocco
Editions Eddif Maroc, pg 469
Editions Le Fennec, pg 470

Netherlands
De Walburg Pers, pg 476
Uitgevery International Theatre & Film Books, pg 479

New Zealand
Aoraki Press Ltd, pg 488
Clerestory Press, pg 490
Hazard Press Ltd, pg 491
Huia Publishers, pg 492
Nelson Price Milburn Ltd, pg 494
Victoria University Press, pg 496

Nigeria
Evans Brothers (Nigeria Publishers) Ltd, pg 499
Saros International Publishers, pg 501
Vantage Publishers International Ltd, pg 502

Pakistan
Maqbool Academy, pg 508
Sang-e-Meel Publications, pg 509

Philippines
Ateneo de Manila University Press, pg 512

Poland
Wydawnictwa Artystyczne i Filmowe, pg 516
Energeia sp zoo Wydawnictwo, pg 516
Wydawnictwo Literackie, pg 517
Panstwowy Instytut Wydawniczy (PIW), pg 518

Portugal
Atica, SA Editores e Livreiros, pg 522
Bezerr-Editorae e Distribuidora de Abel Antonio Bezerra, pg 522
Editora Classica, pg 523
Editorial Estampa, Lda, pg 524
Europress Editores e Distribuidores de Publicacoes Lda, pg 525
Guimaraes Editores, Lda, pg 525
Livraria Minerva Editora, pg 526
Livraria Tavares Martins, pg 527
Nova Arrancada Sociedade Editora SA, pg 527
Platano Editora SA, pg 528
Quimera Editores, pg 529
Vega-Publicacao e Distribuicao de Livros e Revistas, Lda, pg 530

Romania
Editura Cartea Romaneasca, pg 532
Editura Excelsior, pg 533
Mentor Kiado, pg 534
Editura Meridiane, pg 534
Est-Samuel Tastet Verlag, pg 536

Russian Federation
BLIC, russko-Baltijskij informaciionnyj centr, AO, pg 537
Izdatelstvo Iskusstvo, pg 538
Sovremennik Publishers Too, pg 542

Saudi Arabia
Dar Al-Shareff for Publishing & Distribution, pg 543

Senegal
Centre Africain d'Animation et d'Echanges Culturels Editions Khoudia, pg 544

Singapore
Select Books Pte Ltd, pg 548

Slovenia
Zalozba Mihelac d o o, pg 552

South Africa
Bet-El Publishers, pg 553
Human & Rousseau (Pty) Ltd, pg 555
New Africa Books (Pty) Ltd, pg 557
Witwatersrand University Press, pg 560

Spain
Agencia Espanola de Cooperacion, pg 562
Edicios do Castro, pg 566
Central Catequistica Salesiana (CCS), pg 567
Diputacion Provincial de Malaga, pg 570
Editorial Don Quijote, pg 570
Edi-Liber Irlan SA, pg 571
Editorial Fundamentos, pg 575
Lunwerg Editores, SA, pg 580

Antonio Machado, SA, pg 580
MK Ediciones y Publicaciones, pg 582
Naque Editora, pg 583
Pages Editors, SL, pg 585
El Paisaje Editorial, pg 585
Editorial Pliegos, pg 587
Instituto Provincial de Investigaciones y Estudios Toledanos, pg 588
Edicions 62, pg 591
Grup 62, pg 591
Ediciones de la Torre, pg 593
Editorial Verbum SL, pg 595
Vinaches Lopez, Luisa, pg 595

Sri Lanka
Dayawansa Jayakody & Co, pg 597

Switzerland
Editions L'Age d'Homme - La Cite, pg 608
Caux Edition SA, pg 611
Diogenes Verlag AG, pg 612
G+B Arts International, pg 614
Editions Minkoff, pg 619
Les Editions Noir sur Blanc, pg 620

Taiwan, Province of China
World Book Co Ltd, pg 632

United Republic of Tanzania
DUP (1996) Ltd, pg 633
Tanzania Publishing House, pg 634

Tunisia
Academie Tunisienne des Sciences, des Lettres et des Arts Beit El Hekma, pg 637
Maison Tunisienne de l'Edition, pg 638

Turkey
Afa Yayincilik Sanayi Tic AS, pg 638
Alkim Kitapcilik-Yayimcilik, pg 638
Inkilap Publishers Ltd, pg 640
Turkish Republic - Ministry of Culture, pg 641
Kabalci Yayinevi, pg 642

Ukraine
Mystetstvo Publishers, pg 643

United Kingdom
Amber Lane Press Ltd, pg 646
Aris & Phillips Ltd, pg 648
Art Books International Ltd, pg 649
Atlas Press, pg 651
Ruth Bean Publishers, pg 653
A & C Black Publishers Ltd, pg 655
Blackstaff Press, pg 655
Bloomsbury Publishing PLC, pg 656
Marion Boyars Publishers Ltd, pg 658
Brown, Son & Ferguson, Ltd, pg 661
Calder Publications Ltd, pg 662
Cambridge University Press, pg 662
Chadwyck-Healey Ltd, pg 666
Chapman, pg 666
Christian Education, pg 667
The Continuum International Publishing Group Ltd, pg 670
Cressrelles Publishing Company Ltd, pg 672
James Currey Ltd, pg 673

Dramatic Lines Publishers, pg 676
The Eurospan Group, pg 680
Faber & Faber Ltd, pg 681
Samuel French Ltd, pg 684
Gale Research, pg 685
Golden Cockerel Press Ltd, pg 688
Ian Henry Publications Ltd, pg 695
Nick Hern Books Ltd, pg 695
Intellect Ltd, pg 700
Kenyon-Deane, pg 704
The Littman Library of Jewish Civilization, pg 708
Maney Publishing, pg 711
Methuen Publishing Ltd, pg 714
J Garnet Miller, pg 714
Moorley's Print & Publishing Ltd, pg 715
National Association for the Teaching of English (NATE), pg 717
New Playwrights' Network, pg 719
Northcote House Publishers Ltd, pg 719
Octopus Publishing Group, pg 720
The Oleander Press, pg 721
Peter Owen Ltd, pg 722
Parthian Books, pg 724
Pearson Education Europe, Mideast & Africa, pg 725
Phaidon Press Ltd, pg 726
Picton Publishing (Chippenham) Ltd, pg 727
Plexus Publishing Ltd, pg 728
Poetry Wales Press Ltd, pg 729
Polygon, pg 729
Quarto Publishing plc, pg 731
SchoolPlay Productions Ltd, pg 739
Seren, pg 740
Sheffield Academic Press Ltd, pg 741
Colin Smythe Ltd, pg 743
Supportive Learning Publications, pg 746
Time Out Group Ltd, pg 749
Trentham Books Ltd, pg 750
University of Exeter Press, pg 751
Wilmington Business Information Ltd, pg 756
World Microfilms Publications Ltd, pg 758

Uruguay
Editorial Arca SRL, pg 760

Venezuela
Biblioteca Ayacucho, pg 762

Zambia
Zambia Educational Publishing House, pg 767
ZPC Publications, pg 767

Zimbabwe
Anvil Press, pg 767
College Press Publishers (Pvt) Ltd, pg 768
The Literature Bureau, pg 768
Zimbabwe Foundation for Education with Production (ZIMFEP), pg 769

EARTH SCIENCES

Albania
NL SH, pg 1
State Textbook Publishing House, pg 1

PUBLISHERS

Argentina
Instituto Nacional de Ciencia y Tecnica Hidrica (INCYTH), pg 7
Oikos, pg 8

Australia
Allen & Unwin Pty Ltd, The Australian Newspaper, Vogel Breads, pg 11
Aussie Books, pg 12
Australian Marine Conservation Society Inc (AMCS), pg 14
Beazer Publishing Company Pty Ltd, pg 14
Blackwell Science Pty Ltd, pg 15
Brookfield Press, pg 16
Department of Energy (NSW), pg 20
McGraw-Hill Australia Pty Ltd, pg 32
Queen Victoria Museum & Art Gallery Publications, pg 39
University of New South Wales Press Ltd, pg 46

Azerbaijan
Sada, Literaturno-Izdatel'skij Centr, pg 61

Belgium
Abimo, pg 63

Botswana
The Botswana Society, pg 77

Brazil
Editora Edgard Blucher Ltda, pg 80
Edicon Editora e Consultorial Ltda, pg 81
Empresa Brasileira de Pesquisa Agropecaria, pg 83
Editora Harbra Ltda, pg 84
Edit Palavra Magica, pg 89
Thex Editora e Distribuidora Ltda, pg 92

Bulgaria
Pensoft Publishers, pg 97

Chile
Instituto Geografico Militar, pg 100

China
Chengdu Maps Publishing House, pg 103
China Cartographic Publishing House, pg 103
China Ocean Press, pg 103
Jiangsu Science & Technology Publishing House, pg 106
Metallurgical Industry Press (MIP), pg 107
Nanjing University Press, pg 107
Science Press, pg 108
Shandong Science & Technology Press, pg 109
Xi'an Cartography Publishing House, pg 110

Colombia
Editorial Libros y Libres SA, pg 112

Costa Rica
Instituto Interamericano de Cooperacion para la Agricultura (IICA), pg 116
Editorial de la Universidad de Costa Rica, pg 117

Czech Republic
Mariadan, pg 126
Mendelova zemedelska a lesnicka univerzita v Brne, pg 126
Narodni Muzeum, pg 126
Vydavatelstvi Ceskeho Geologickeho Ustavu, pg 129

Egypt (Arab Republic of Egypt)
American University in Cairo Press, pg 138

Finland
Ursa ry, pg 145

France
ATP - Packager, pg 149
Editions BRGM, pg 152
Bureau des Longitudes de France, pg 152
Cemagref Editions, pg 153
Corsaire Editions, pg 156
Doin Editeurs, pg 160
Elf Exploration Production, pg 161
Editions Eyrolles, pg 163
INRA Editions (Institut National de la Recherche Agronomique), pg 169
IRD Editions, pg 170
Librairie Scientifique et Technique Albert Blanchard, pg 173
Nanga, pg 177
Editions Ophrys, pg 178
Ouest Editions, pg 178
Editions Pedone, pg 179
Presses de l'Ecole Nationale des Ponts et Chaussees, pg 181
Service des Publications Scientifiques du Museum National d'Histoire Naturelle, pg 184
Editions Springer France, pg 186
Editions Technip SA, pg 187
Editions Trois Fontaines, pg 188
La Vague Verte, pg 188
Librairie Vuibert, pg 189

French Polynesia
Haere Po No Tahiti, pg 190

Germany
Aluminium-Verlag Marketing & Kommunikation GmbH, pg 193
Eberhargd Blottner Verlag, pg 204
C C Buchners Verlag, pg 207
Chmielorz GmbH Verlag, pg 210
Verlag Harri Deutsch, pg 213
Deutsche Verlags-Anstalt GmbH (DVA), pg 214
Deutscher Verlag fur Grundstoffindustrie GmbH, pg 215
E Schweizerbart'sche Verlagsbuchhandlung (Nagele und Obermiller), pg 220
Ferd Dummler's Verlag, pg 227
Fraunhofer IRB Verlag Fraunhofer Informationszentrum Raum und Bau, pg 229
Gebrueder Borntraeger Science Publishers, pg 231
Verlag Glueckauf GmbH, pg 233
Walter de Gruyter GmbH & Co KG, pg 234
Huthig GmbH & Co KG, pg 244
Ambro Lacus, Buch- und Bildverlag Walter Kremnitz, pg 255
Landbuch-Verlagsgesellschaft mbH, pg 255
Verlag Natur & Wissenschaft Harro Hieronimus & Dr Jurgen Schmidt, pg 266
Palazzi Verlag GmbH, pg 271
Renate Schenk Verlag, pg 283
Springer-Verlag GmbH & Co KG, pg 288
Steiger Verlag, pg 289
Franz Steiner Verlag Wiesbaden GmbH, pg 289
Trans Tech Publications, pg 294
Guenter Albert Ulmer Verlag, pg 295
Weidler Buchverlag Berlin, pg 301
Herbert Wichmann Verlag, pg 302
Verlag Konrad Wittwer GmbH, pg 303

Ghana
Building & Road Research Institute (BRRI), pg 306

Greece
Michalis Sideris, pg 313

Holy See (Vatican City State)
Pontificia Academia Scientiarum, pg 317

Hong Kong
Geocarto International Centre, pg 320

Hungary
Akademiai Kiado, pg 323
Janus Pannonius Tudomanyegyetem, pg 324
Springer Hungarica Kiado Kft, pg 326
Szarvas Andras Cartographic Agency, pg 326

India
Agam Kala Prakashan, pg 330
Bhawan Book Service, Publishers & Distributors, pg 333
BSMPS - M/s Bishen Singh Mahendra Pal Singh, pg 334
Concept Publishing Co, pg 335
Daya Publishing House, pg 336
Gyan Publishing House, pg 338
Nem Chand & Brothers, pg 344
Oxford & IBH Publishing Co Pvt Ltd, pg 345
Rahul Publishing House, pg 347
Rastogi Publications, pg 347
Reliance Publishing House, pg 347
Scientific Book Agency, pg 349

Indonesia
Yayasan Obor Indonesia, pg 357

Ireland
Royal Irish Academy, pg 364

Italy
Archimede Edizioni, pg 376
BeMa, pg 377
Casa Editrice Giuseppe Principato Spa, pg 380
Arnaldo Forni Editore SRL, pg 389
Horus, pg 393
Editoriale Jaca Book SpA, pg 394
Paravia Bruno Mondadori Editori, pg 402
Principato, pg 404
Red/Studio Redazionale SpA, pg 405
SAIE Editrice SRL, pg 406

SUBJECT INDEX

Editoriale Scienza, pg 407
Zanichelli Editore SpA, pg 412

Jamaica
The Jamaica Bauxite Institute, pg 413

Japan
Nippon Hoso Shuppan Kyokai (NHK Publishing), pg 422
Sanseido Co Ltd, pg 424
Shogakukan Inc, pg 426
Tokai University Press, pg 427
Tsukiji Shokan Publishing Co, pg 428
Yama-Kei Publishers Co Ltd, pg 429

Kazakstan
Gylym, Izd-Vo, pg 430

Kenya
African Centre for Technology Studies (ACTS), pg 431

Republic of Korea
Korea University Press, pg 437
Seoul National University Press, pg 440

Latvia
Nordik/Tapals Publishers Ltd, pg 442

Liechtenstein
Botanisch-Zoologische Gesellschaft, pg 444

The Former Yugoslav Republic of Macedonia
Seizmoloska Opservatorija, pg 449

Mexico
Centro de Estudios Mexicanos y Centroamericanos, pg 458
Fondo de Cultura Economica, pg 461
Editorial Limusa SA de CV, pg 463
Instituto Nacional de Estadistica, Geographia e Informatica, pg 464
Sistemas Tecnicos de Edicion SA de CV, pg 467
Ediciones Suromex SA, pg 467

Namibia
Desert Research Foundation of Namibia (DRFN), pg 471

Nepal
International Standards Books & Periodicals (P) Ltd, pg 471

Netherlands
Backhuys Publishers BV, pg 473
A A Balkema, pg 473
Elsevier Science BV, pg 477
V S P International Science Publishers, pg 486

New Zealand
Bush Press Communications Ltd, pg 489
Wendy Crane Books, pg 490
Landcare Research NZ, pg 492
New House Publishers Ltd, pg 493
SIR Publishing, pg 495

SUBJECT INDEX

Norway
Chr Schibsteds Forlag A/S, pg 505
Vett & Viten AS, pg 505

Peru
Instituto Frances de Estudios Andinos, IFEA, pg 511

Philippines
Salesiana Publishers Inc, pg 515

Poland
Instytut Historii Nauki PAN, pg 516
Instytut Meteorologii i Gospodarki Wodnej, pg 518

Portugal
Constancia Editores, SA, pg 524
Gradiva-Publicacnoes Lda, pg 525
Instituto de Investigacao Cientifica Tropical, pg 526
Planeta Editora, LDA, pg 528

Romania
Editura Academiei Romane, pg 531

Russian Federation
N E Bauman Moscow State Technical University Publishers, pg 537
Gidrometeoizdat, pg 538
Izdatelstvo Metallurgiya, pg 540
Izdatelstvo Mir, pg 540
Nauka Publishers, pg 540
Izdatelstvo Nedra, pg 540
Pressa Publishing House, pg 541

Slovakia
VEDA (Vydavatel'stvo Slovenskej akademie vied), pg 551

South Africa
Bet-El Publishers, pg 553

Spain
Editorial AEDOS SA, pg 561
Instituto de Estudios Riojanos, pg 574
Idea Books, SA, pg 578
Loguez Ediciones, pg 580
Mandala Ediciones, pg 581
OASIS, Producciones Generales de Comunicacion, pg 584
Oikos-Tau SA Ediciones, pg 584
Rueda, SL Editorial, pg 589
Editorial Sintesis, SA, pg 590
Universidad de Malaga, pg 594

Switzerland
Marcel Dekker AG, pg 612
Editions Delachaux et Niestle SA, pg 612
Ott Verlag AG, pg 621
Presses Polytechniques et Universitaires Romandes, PPUR, pg 622
Schweizerische Stiftung fuer Alpine Forschungen, pg 624
Wepf & Co AG, pg 627

Syrian Arab Republic
Damascus University Press, pg 628

Taiwan, Province of China
Yi Hsien Publishing Co Ltd, pg 632

Turkey
Ruh ve Madde Yayinlari ve Saglik Hizmetleri AS, pg 641

Ukraine
Naukova Dumka Publishers, pg 643

United Kingdom
Academic Press Ltd, pg 644
Andromeda Oxford Ltd, pg 647
Artetech Publishing Co, pg 649
Blackwell Science Ltd, pg 656
Bloomsbury Publishing PLC, pg 656
Cambridge University Press, pg 662
E W Classey Ltd, pg 668
Commonwealth Secretariat, pg 669
Dunedin Academic Press, pg 676
Elsevier Science Ltd, pg 678
The Eurospan Group, pg 680
Forth Naturalist & Historian, pg 683
W H Freeman & Co Ltd, pg 684
Gateway Books, pg 686
Geological Society Publishing House, pg 686
Harvard University Press, pg 692
Hyden House Ltd, pg 698
Jones & Bartlett International, pg 703
Manson Publishing Ltd, pg 711
Mirabel Books Ltd, pg 715
MIT Press Ltd, pg 715
Open University Worldwide, pg 721
Orpheus Books Ltd, pg 722
The Reader's Digest Association Ltd, pg 733
RICS Books, pg 735
The Society of Metaphysicians Ltd, pg 743
The Stationery Office, pg 745
Thistle Press, pg 748
Wiley Europe Ltd, pg 756
WIT Press, pg 757

Uruguay
A Monteverde y Cia SA, pg 760

Viet Nam
Science & Technics Publishing House, pg 763

ECONOMICS

Albania
NL SH, pg 1

Argentina
Editorial Abaco de Rodolfo Depalma SRL, pg 2
Aguilar Altea Taurus Alfaguara SA de Ediciones, pg 3
Editorial Albatros SACI, pg 3
Amorrortu Editores SA, pg 3
Editorial Astrea de Alfredo y Ricardo Depalma SRL, pg 3
AZ Editora SA, pg 3
Fundacion Editorial de Belgrano, pg 4
Editorial Cangallo SACI, pg 4
Ediciones Corregidor SAICI y E, pg 4
Errepar SA, pg 5
EUDEBA (Editorial Universitaria de Buenos Aires), pg 6
La Ley SA Editora e Impresora, pg 7
Marymar Ediciones SA, pg 7
Editorial Plus Ultra SA, pg 8
Instituto Torcuato Di Tella, pg 9

Ediciones Tres Tiempos SRL, pg 9
Editorial Universidad SRL, pg 9

Australia
Allen & Unwin Pty Ltd, The Australian Newspaper, Vogel Breads, pg 11
Australian Institute of Family Studies (AIFS), pg 13
Crystal Publishing, pg 19
Dabill Publications, pg 20
Emerald City Books, pg 22
Macmillan Education Australia, pg 31
McGraw-Hill Australia Pty Ltd, pg 32
Melbourne Institute of Applied Economic & Social Research, pg 33
Oxfam Community Aid Abroad, pg 36
Pearson Education Australia, pg 37
Tertiary Press, pg 44
VCTA Publishing, pg 46

Austria
Buchhandlung WUV Dolmetsch, pg 50
Compass-Verlag GmbH, pg 50
Verlag fuer Geschichte und Politik, pg 52
Horst Knapp Finanznachrichten, pg 54
Linde Verlag Wien GmbH, pg 54
Manz'sche Verlags- und Universitaetsbuchhandlung, pg 54
Verlag Neues Leben, pg 55
Verlag Orac im Verlag Kremayr & Scheriau, pg 56
Passagen Verlag GmbH, pg 57
Dr A Schendl GmbH und Co KG, pg 58
Signum Verlag GmbH & Co KG, pg 58
Springer-Verlag Wien, pg 59
Verlag Carl Ueberreuter GmbH, pg 59

Azerbaijan
Sada, Literaturno-Izdatel'skij Centr, pg 61

Bangladesh
Ankur Prakashani, pg 62
Bangladesh Publishers, pg 62
The University Press Ltd, pg 62

Belarus
Belarus (The Belorussia), pg 63
Narodnaya Asveta, pg 63

Belgium
Academia Press, pg 64
Acco CV, pg 64
CED-Samsom, pg 66
Creadif, pg 67
Editions De Boeck-Larcier SA, pg 67
Documenta CV, pg 68
Institut Royal des Relations Internationales, pg 69
King Baudouin Foundation, pg 70
Editions Juridiques Kluwer a Deurne Anvers, pg 70
Koepel van de Vlaamse Noord - Zuidbeweging 11.11.11, pg 70
Editions Labor, pg 70
Uitgeverij Lannoo NV, pg 70
Leuven University Press, pg 71
Maklu, pg 71

Nauwelaerts Edition SA, pg 72
Presses Universitaires de Bruxelles ASBL, pg 73
Publications des Facultes Universitaires Saint Louis, pg 73
Roularta Books NV, pg 73
Uitgevery Scoop Infotex NV, pg 75
Editions de l'Universite de Bruxelles, pg 75
Vander Editions, SA, pg 75
Les Editions Vie ouvriere ASBL, pg 75
Wolters Plantyn Educatieve Uitgevers, pg 75

Brazil
Editora Alfa Omega Ltda, pg 78
Editora Antroposofica Ltda, pg 78
ARTMED, pg 79
Editora Atlas SA, pg 79
Editora Campus Ltda, pg 80
Editora Contexto (Editora Pinsky Ltda), pg 81
EDUC - Editora da PUC-SP, pg 82
Empresa Brasileira de Pesquisa Agropecaria, pg 83
Forense Universitaria Editora, pg 83
Fundacao Instituto Brasileiro de Geografia e Estatistica (IBGE - CDDI/DECOP), pg 84
Fundacao Joaquim Nabuco Editora, pg 84
Editora Globo SA, pg 84
Edicoes Graal Ltda, pg 84
IBRASA (Instituicao Brasileira de Difusao Cultural Ltda), pg 85
Editora Lidador Ltda, pg 86
Edicoes Loyola SA, pg 87
LTC-Livros Tecnicos e Cientificos Editora S/A, pg 87
Editora Lucre Comercio e Representacoes, pg 87
Editora Ortiz SA, pg 89
Pearson Education Do Brasil, pg 89
Editora Perspectiva, pg 89
Livraria Pioneira Editora/Enio Matheus Guazzelli e Cia Ltd, pg 89
Pool Editorial Ltda, pg 90
Qualitymark Editora Ltda, pg 90
Saraiva SA, Livreiros Editores, pg 91
Thex Editora e Distribuidora Ltda, pg 92
Editora Universidade Federal do Rio de Janeiro, pg 93
Fundacao Getulio Vargas, pg 93
Jorge Zahar Editor, pg 93

Bulgaria
Agencija Za Ikonomicesko Programirane i Razvitie, pg 94
Ciela Publishing House, pg 94
Dolphin Press Group Ltd, pg 95
Galaktika Publishing House, pg 95
Gea-Libris Publishing House, pg 95
Makros 2000 - Plovdiv, pg 96
Naouka i Izkoustvo, Ltd, pg 97
Slavena, pg 98
WTU Todor Kableskov, pg 98

Cameroon
Editions Buma Kor, pg 99
Presses Universitaires d'Afrique, pg 99

Chile
Arrayan Editores, pg 99
Ediciones Cieplan, pg 100

Edeval (Universidad de Valparaiso), pg 100
Pontificia Universidad Catolica de Chile, pg 101

China
Anhui People's Publishing House, pg 102
Aviation Industry Press, pg 102
Beijing Publishing House, pg 102
Beijing University Press, pg 102
China Braille Press, pg 103
China Foreign Economic Relations & Trade Publishing House, pg 103
China Forestry Publishing House, pg 103
China Materials Management Publishing House, pg 103
China Tibetology Publishing House, pg 104
China Translation & Publishing Corp, pg 104
CITIC Publishing House, pg 104
Dalian Maritime University Press, pg 105
Foreign Languages Press, pg 105
Fudan University Press, pg 105
Guizhou Education Publishing House, pg 106
Heilongjiang Science & Technology Press, pg 106
Jinan Publishing House, pg 107
Lanzhou University Press, pg 107
Liaoning People's Publishing House, pg 107
Nanjing University Press, pg 107
SDX (Shenghuo-Dushu-Xinzhi) Joint Publishing Co, pg 108
Shandong People's Publishing House, pg 109
Shandong Science & Technology Press, pg 109
Shandong University Press, pg 109
Sichuan University Press, pg 109
South China University of Science and Technology Press, pg 109
Wuhan University Press, pg 110
Xinhua Publishing House, pg 110

Colombia
El Ancora Editores, pg 111
Fundacion Centro de Investigacion y Educacion Popular (CINEP), pg 112
Fundacion Universidad de la Sabana Ediciones Udes, pg 112
LEGIS - Editores SA, pg 112
McGraw-Hill InterAmericana SA, pg 113
Procultura SA, pg 113
Tercer Mundo Editores SA, pg 113
Unidad Universitaria del Sur (UNISUR), pg 114
Universidad de los Andes Editorial, pg 114
Carlos Valencia Editores, pg 114

The Democratic Republic of the Congo
Facultes Catoliques de Kinshasa, pg 115
Presses Universitaires du Zaire (PUZ), pg 115

Costa Rica
Academia de Centro America, pg 115
Asamblea Legislativa, Biblioteca Monsenor Sanabria, pg 115
Centro Agronomico Tropical de Investigacion y Ensenanza (CATIE), pg 115
Editorial DEI (Departamento Ecumenico de Investigaciones), pg 116
Editorial Porvenir, pg 116
Editorial de la Universidad de Costa Rica, pg 117
Editorial Universidad Estatal a Distancia (EUNED), pg 117

Cote d'Ivoire
Universite d' Abidjan, pg 118

Croatia
Informator dd, pg 119
Masmedia, pg 119
Nakladni zavod Matice hrvatske, pg 119
Naprijed d d Naklada, pg 119

Cuba
ISCAH Fructuoso Rodriguez, pg 121
Editora Politica, pg 121
Universidad Central de la Villas, Centro Documentacion e Informacion Cientifica Tecnica, pg 121

Czech Republic
Academia, pg 122
Aleko, Nakladatelska Divize, pg 122
Babtext Nakladatelska Spolecnost, pg 123
Barrister & Principal, pg 123
Doplnek, pg 124
Grada Publishing sro, pg 124
Nakladatelstvi Josef Hribal, pg 124
Karolinum, nakladatelstvi, pg 125
Libri s r o, pg 125
Mendelova zemedelska a lesnicka univerzita v Brne, pg 126
Trizonia, pg 128

Denmark
Akademisk Forlag, pg 129
Djof Publishing Jurist-og Okonomforbundets Forlag, pg 131
Fremad A/S, pg 132
GEC Gads Forlag Aktieselskab af 1994, pg 132
Forlaget Hovedland, pg 133
Mellemfolkeligt Samvirke, pg 133
Joergen Paludans Forlag ApS, pg 134
Samfundslitteratur, pg 135
Systime, pg 136

Dominican Republic
Pontificia Universidad Catolica Madre y Maestra, pg 136
Sociedad Editorial Dominicana SA, pg 137
Editora Taller, pg 137

Ecuador
Centro De Educacion Popular, pg 137
Corporacion Editora Nacional, pg 137
Pontificia Universidad Catolica de Ecuador, Centro de Publicaciones, pg 137

Egypt (Arab Republic of Egypt)
Al Arab Publishing House, pg 138
Ummah Press for Translation & Publishing, pg 139

Estonia
Olion Publishers, pg 140

Finland
Tietoteos Publishing Co, pg 144

France
Editions Anthropos Sarl, pg 147
Les Editions de l'Atelier SA, pg 148
Editions de l'Aube, pg 149
Editions Bertrandl-Lacoste, pg 150
Breal, pg 151
Les Cahiers Fiscaux Europeens Sarl, pg 152
Editions Calmann-Levy SA, pg 152
Editions Casteilla, pg 153
Centre de Librairie et d'Editions Techniques (CLET), pg 153
Chotard et Associes Editeurs, pg 154
CNRS Editions, pg 155
Editions Cujas, pg 157
DAFSA, pg 157
Editions Dalloz Sirey, pg 157
La Decouverte et Syros, pg 158
Editions Delmas, pg 158
Editions Denoel Sarl, pg 158
Devenirs Visuels SA, pg 159
La Documentation Francaise, pg 159
Librairie Generale de Droit et de Jurisprudence (LGDJ) - Montchrestien, pg 160
Dunod Editeur, pg 160
Editions de l'Ecole des Hautes Etudes en Sciences Sociales (EHESS), pg 160
Presses de l'Ecole Normale Superieure, pg 160
Edicef - Editions Classiques d'Expression Francaise, pg 161
Les Editions ESF, pg 161
Editions Entente, pg 162
Les Editions de l'Epargne, pg 162
Editions Eska, pg 162
FBT de R Editions/Editions des Limbes d'Or, pg 163
Presses de la Fondation Nationale des Sciences Politiques, pg 164
Les Editions Foucher SA, pg 164
Futuribles SARL, pg 165
Editions Jacques Gabay, pg 165
Editions Gammaprim, pg 166
Groupe Expansion, pg 167
Groupe Moniteur -L'Argus, pg 167
Hachette Livre, pg 167
Editions Hatier SA, pg 168
Editions d'Histoire Sociale (EDHIS), pg 168
INRA Editions (Institut National de la Recherche Agronomique), pg 169
Editions Juridiques Associees - LGDJ/Montchrestien, pg 170
Karthala Editions-Diffusion, pg 171
Editions Legislatives, pg 172
John Libbey Eurotext, pg 173
Editions des Limbes d'Or/FBT de R Editions, pg 173
Editions de la Maison des Sciences de l'Homme, Paris, pg 174
Maxima Laurent du Mesnil Editeur, pg 175
Editions du Moniteur, pg 176
Nouvelles Editions Fiduciaires, pg 178
Editions Odile Jacob, pg 178
OECD, pg 178
Ouest Editions, pg 178
Editions Pedone, pg 179
Les Presses du Management, pg 181
Presses Universitaires de Grenoble, pg 181
Presses Universitaires de Lyon, pg 181
Presses Universitaires de Nancy, pg 181
Selection du Reader's Digest SA, pg 184
Publications de la Sorbonne, pg 186
Editions Springer France, pg 186
Editions Village Mondial, pg 189
Librairie Vuibert, pg 189

Germany
A Francke Verlag (Tubingen und Basel), pg 191
Accedo Verlagsgesellschaft mbH, pg 191
Antiquariat und Verlag Auvermann Keip GmbH, pg 194
Bank-Verlag GmbH, pg 198
Verlag Dr Albert Bartens KG, pg 198
Bayerische Verlagsanstalt GmbH, pg 199
Verlag C H Beck (OHG), pg 200
Berlin Verlag Arno Spitz GmbH, pg 200
Bertelsmann Lexikon Verlag GmbH, pg 201
BertelsmannSpringer Science & Business Media GmbH, pg 202
Oscar Brandstetter Verlag GmbH & Co KG, pg 206
Buchverlage Langen-Mueller/ Herbig, pg 207
Bund-Verlag GmbH, pg 208
Campus Verlag GmbH, pg 209
Cornelsen Verlag GmbH & Co OHG, pg 211
Verlag Harri Deutsch, pg 213
Deutscher Betriebswirte-Verlag GmbH, pg 214
Deutscher Instituts-Verlag GmbH, pg 215
Deutscher Universitats-Verlag, pg 215
Die Verlag H Schafer GmbH, pg 216
Dreisam Ratgeber in der Rutsker Verlag GmbH, pg 218
Droste Verlag GmbH, pg 218
DSI Data Service & Information, pg 219
Duncker und Humblot GmbH, pg 219
Econ Taschenbuchverlag, pg 220
Econ Verlag GmbH, pg 220
Eppinger-Verlag OHG, pg 223
Verlag Europa-Lehrmittel, Nourney, Vollmer GmbH & Co, pg 224
Festland Verlag GmbH, pg 227
Verlag Franz Vahlen GmbH, pg 229
Friedrich Kiehl Verlag GmbH, pg 230
Verlag A Fromm im Druck- u Verlagshaus Fromm GmbH & Co KG, pg 230
Betriebswirtschaftlicher Verlag Dr Th Gabler GmbH, pg 231
Griese Ingolf Wipe Griese, pg 234
Gunter Olzog Verlag GmbH, pg 235
Carl Hanser Verlag, pg 237
Rudolf Haufe Verlag GmbH & Co KG, pg 238
Heckners Verlag, pg 238
Joh Heider Verlag GmbH, pg 239

SUBJECT INDEX

HelfRecht Verlag und Druck, pg 239
Carl Heymanns Verlag KG, pg 240
Hofbauer, Christoph und Trojanow Ilia, Akademischer Verlag Muenchen, pg 241
Klages-Verlag, pg 249
Verlag Fritz Knapp GmbH, pg 250
Verlag Knut Reim, Jugendpresseverlag, pg 251
Koelner Universitaets-Verlag GmbH, pg 251
Verlag Koenigshausen und Neumann GmbH, pg 251
W Kohlhammer GmbH, abt Haussortiment, pg 252
Leitfadenverlag Verlag Dieter Sudholt, pg 257
Libertas- Europaeisches Institut GmbH, pg 257
LIT Verlag, pg 258
Lucius & Lucius Verlagsgesellschaft mbH, pg 259
Marketing & Wirtschaft Verlagsges, Flade & Partner mbH, pg 261
Metropolis- Verlag fur Okonomie, Gesellschaft und Politik GmbH, pg 263
Metropolitan Verlag, pg 263
Mohr Siebeck, pg 264
Mosaik Verlag GmbH, pg 265
Munzinger-Archiv GmbH Archiv fuer publizistische Arbeit, pg 266
Neuer ISP Verlag GmbH, pg 268
Nomos Verlagsgesellschaft mbH und Co KG, pg 269
Nusser Verlag, pg 269
Georg Olms Verlag AG, pg 270
Philosophia Verlag GmbH, pg 273
Physica-Verlag, pg 273
Rationalisierungs-Kuratorium der Deutschen Wirtschaft eV (RKW), pg 277
Verlag Recht und Wirtschaft GmbH, pg 277
I H Sauer Verlag GmbH, pg 282
Schaeffer-Poeschel Verlag fuer Wirtschaft Steuern Recht, pg 282
Erich Schmidt Verlag GmbH & Co, pg 283
Schueren Verlag GmbH, pg 285
Schulz-Kirchner Verlag GmbH, pg 285
Scientia Verlag und Antiquariat, pg 286
Societaets-Verlag, pg 287
Springer-Verlag GmbH & Co KG, pg 288
Verlag H Stam GmbH, pg 289
Stollfuss Verlag Bonn GmbH & Co KG, pg 290
TF Fachverlag Gmbh, pg 293
S Toeche-Mittler Verlag GmbH, pg 294
UNO-Verlag mbH, Vertriebs und Verlagsgesellschaft, pg 296
UTB fuer Wissenschaft Uni-Taschenbuecher GmbH, pg 297
Vandenhoeck & Ruprecht, pg 297
Verlag Moderne Industrie AG & Co KG, pg 298
Verlagsgruppe Jehle-Rehm GmbH, pg 298
Dokument und Analyse Verlag Bogislaw von Randow, pg 299
Werner Verlag GmbH & Co KG, pg 302
Wison Verlag GmbH, pg 303
Verlag Wissenschaft und Politik/ Helker Pflug, pg 303
Wissenschaftliche Buchgesellschaft, pg 303

WRS Verlag Wirtschaft, Recht und Steuern GmbH & Co KG, pg 304
Fachbuchverlag Armin W Wuth, pg 304

Ghana

Black Mask Ltd, pg 306
Frank Publishing Ltd, pg 307
Kwamfori Publishing Enterprise, pg 307

Greece

Exandas Publishers, pg 310
Forma Publications Ltd, pg 310
Gutenberg Publications, pg 311
Idryma Meleton Chersonisou tou Aimou, pg 311
Irini Publishing House - Vassilis G Katsikeas SA, pg 311
Karatzas Charis, pg 312
Kritiki Publishing, pg 312
Kyriakidis, pg 312
Papazissis Publishers SA, pg 314
Sakkoulas Publications SA, pg 314

Hong Kong

Ming Pao Publications Ltd, pg 321
Sun Mui Press, pg 322
Yazhou Zhoukan Ltd, pg 322

Hungary

Akademiai Kiado, pg 323
Central European University Press, pg 323
CEU-Press, pg 323
KJK-Keaszov, pg 324
Novorg Kiado, pg 326
Osiris Kiado, pg 326
Panem, pg 326
Saldo Penzugyi Tanacsado es Informatikai Rt, pg 326
Statiqum Kiado es Nyomda Kft, pg 326

India

Addison-Wesley (Singapore) Pte Ltd, pg 329
Affiliated East West Press Pvt Ltd, pg 329
Agricole Publishing Academy, pg 330
Allied Publishers Pvt Ltd, pg 330
Amar Prakashan, pg 330
Ananda Publishers Pvt Ltd, pg 330
APH Publishing Corp, pg 331
Associated Publishing House, pg 331
Avinash Reference Publications, pg 331
K P Bagchi & Co, pg 332
Bani Mandir, Book-Sellers, Publishers & Educational Suppliers, pg 332
Bharatiya Samijik Vigyan Auusandhan Parishad, pg 332
Bhawan Book Service, Publishers & Distributors, pg 333
BIG Database Publishing Pvt Ltd, pg 333
BR Publishing Corporation, pg 334
S Chand & Co Ltd, pg 334
Chowkhamba Sanskrit Series Office, pg 335
Concept Publishing Co, pg 335
Cosmo Publications, pg 335
Dastane Ramchandra & Co, pg 335
Disha Prakashan, pg 336
Ess Ess Publications, pg 337
Frank Brothers & Co (Publishers) Ltd, pg 337
Gitanjali Publishing House, pg 337

Goel Prakashen, pg 337
Gyan Publishing House, pg 338
Heritage Publishers, pg 338
Inter-India Publications, pg 340
Jaico Publishing House, pg 340
Minerva Associates (Publications) Pvt Ltd, pg 342
National Book Organization, pg 343
National Council of Applied Economic Research, Publications Division, pg 344
Omsons Publications, pg 345
Oxford University Press, pg 345
Pitambar Publishing Co (P) Ltd, pg 346
Pointer Publishers, pg 346
Popular Prakashan Pvt Ltd, pg 346
Promilla and Co, pg 346
Radiant Publishers, pg 347
Rajasthan Hindi Granth Academy, pg 347
Rajesh Publications, pg 347
Reliance Publishing House, pg 347
Sage Publications India Pvt Ltd, pg 348
Sasta Sahitya Mandal, pg 349
Scientific Book Agency, pg 349
Sita Publications, pg 350
Somaiya Publications Pvt Ltd, pg 350
South Asia Publications, pg 350
Sterling Publishers Pvt Ltd, pg 351
Sultan Chand & Sons Pvt Ltd, pg 351
Vidyarthi Mithram Press, pg 352
Vikas Publishing House Pvt Ltd, pg 353
Vivek Prakashan, pg 353

Indonesia

Alumni PT, pg 353
Bhratara Karya Aksara, pg 354
Bina Rena Pariwara, pg 354
P T Bulan Bintang, pg 354
Bumi Aksara PT, pg 354
PT Dian Rakyat, pg 355
Eresco PT, pg 355
Lembaga Demografi Fakultas Ekonomi Universitas Indonesia, pg 356
Mutiara Sumber Widya PT, pg 356
Pustaka Utama Grafiti, PT, pg 357
Yayasan Obor Indonesia, pg 357

Iraq

National House for Publishing, Distributing and Advertising, pg 358

Ireland

The Economic & Social Research Institute, pg 360
Gill & Macmillan Ltd, pg 361
Institute of Public Administration, pg 361
Irish Management Institute, pg 361
New Books/Connolly Books, pg 362

Israel

Bar Ilan University Press, pg 365
Dyonon/Papyrus Publishing House of the Tel-Aviv, pg 367
Hakibbutz Hameuchad Publishing House Ltd, pg 368
Hanitzotz A-Sharara Publishing House, pg 368
The Institute for Israeli Arabs Studies, pg 368
Open University of Israel, pg 371
Schocken Publishing House Ltd, pg 372

Shalem Press, pg 372
Tcherikover Publishers Ltd, pg 372
Zmora-Bitan, Publishers Ltd, pg 374

Italy

Edizioni Abete, pg 374
Edizioni della Fondazione Giovanni Agnelli, pg 375
Franco Angeli SRL, pg 375
Apimondia, pg 375
Argalia Editore delle Arti Grafiche Editoriali SRL, pg 376
Baha'i, pg 377
Bancaria Editrice SpA, pg 377
Bollati Boringhieri Editore Srl, pg 378
Giuseppe Bonanno Editore, pg 378
Buffetti, pg 379
Cacucci Editore, pg 379
Camera dei Deputati Ufficio Pubblicazioni Informazione Parlamentare, pg 379
CEDAM (Casa Editrice Dr A Milani), pg 380
Celuc Libri, pg 380
Centro Studi Terzo Mondo, pg 381
Cisalpino - Monduzzi, pg 382
CLUEB (Cooperativa Libraria Universitaria Editrice Bologna), pg 382
Edizioni di Comunita SpA, pg 382
Costa e Nolan SpA, pg 383
La Culturale, pg 383
Datanews, pg 384
Edi Ermes SRL, pg 386
Ediciclo Editore SRL, pg 386
EGEA (Edizioni Giuridiche Economiche Aziendali), pg 387
Etas Libri, pg 388
Edizioni Europa, pg 388
Arnaldo Forni Editore SRL, pg 389
G Giappichelli Editore SRL, pg 390
A Giuffre Editore SpA, pg 390
Gius Laterza e Figli SpA, pg 391
Herbita Editrice di Leonardo Palermo, pg 392
Ila - Palma, Tea Nova, pg 393
Editoriale Jaca Book SpA, pg 394
L Japadre Editore, pg 394
Casa Editrice Dott Eugenio Jovene SpA, pg 394
LED - Edizioni Universitarie di Lettere Economia Diritto, pg 395
Liguori Editore SRL, pg 396
Monduzzi Editore SpA, pg 399
Societa Editrice Il Mulino, pg 400
Nardini Editore srl, pg 400
Accademia Naz dei Lincei, pg 400
Pirola, pg 403
Psicologica Editrice, pg 404
RCS Rizzoli Libri SpA, pg 405
Rirea Casa Editrice della Rivista Italiana di Ragioneria e di Economia Aziendale, pg 405
Editori Riuniti, pg 405
Rubbettino Editore, pg 406
SAGEP, pg 406
SAIE Editrice SRL, pg 406
Edizioni Scientifiche Italiane, pg 407
SIPI (Servizio Italiano Pubblicazioni Internazionali) Srl, pg 408
Edizioni del Sole 24 Ore, pg 408
Sperling & Kupfer Editori SpA, pg 408
Edizioni di Storia e Letteratura, pg 409
Edizioni Studio Tesi SRL, pg 409
Il Tripode Srl, pg 410
Zanichelli Editore SpA, pg 412

PUBLISHERS

Jamaica
The Jamaica Bauxite Institute, pg 413

Japan
Chikuma Shobo Publishing Co Ltd, pg 415
Chuo-Koron-Sha Inc, pg 415
Diamond Inc, pg 416
International Society for Educational Information (ISEI), pg 418
Iwanami Shoten, Publishers, pg 418
Keisuisha Publishing Company Ltd, pg 419
Kodansha, pg 420
Koyo Shobo, pg 420
Minerva Shobo Co Ltd, pg 421
Nippon Hoso Shuppan Kyokai (NHK Publishing), pg 422
Nippon Jitsugyo Publishing Co, Ltd, pg 423
Otsuki Shoten Publishers, pg 423
Pearson Education Japan, pg 423
President Inc, pg 423
Sagano Shoin, pg 424
The Simul Press Inc, pg 426
Sobun-Sha, pg 426
Springer-Verlag Tokyo, pg 426
Taimeido Publishing Co Ltd, pg 427
Toho Book Store, pg 427
Toyo Keizai Inc (The Oriental Economist), pg 428
United Nations University Press, pg 428
Waseda University Press, pg 428
Yuhikaku Publishing Co Ltd, pg 429
Yushodo Co Ltd, pg 429
Zeimukeiri-Kyokai, pg 429

Jordan
Jordan Book Centre Co Ltd, pg 430

Kazakstan
Gylym, Izd-Vo, pg 430
Kazakh Al-Farabi State National University, pg 430
Kazakhstan, Izd-Vo, pg 430

Kenya
Heinemann Kenya Limited (EAEP), pg 431
Kenya Quality & Productivity Institute, pg 432
Shirikon Publishers, pg 433

Democratic People's Republic of Korea
Academy of Sciences Publishing House, pg 434
Korea Science and Encyclopedia Publishing House, pg 434

Republic of Korea
Bi-bong Publishing Co, pg 435
Chung Rim Publishing Co Ltd, pg 435
Hanul Publishing Co, pg 436
Hollym Corporation Publishers, pg 437
Hyangmunsa Publishing Co, pg 437
Koreaone Press Inc, pg 438
Maeil Gyeongje, pg 438
Oruem Publishing House, pg 439
Twenty-First Century Publishers, Inc, pg 440
YBM/Si-sa, pg 441

Laos People's Democratic Republic
Lao-phanit, pg 441

Liechtenstein
Verlag der Liechtensteinischen Akademischen Gesellschaft, pg 444
Megatrade AG, pg 445
Topos Verlag AG, pg 445

Lithuania
Eugrimas, pg 445
Margi Rastai Publishers, pg 446

Luxembourg
Editions Promoculture, pg 448
Service Central de la Statistique et des Etudes Economiques (STATEC), pg 448
Varkki Verghese, pg 448

Macau
Universidadede de Macau, Centro de Publicacoes, pg 448

The Former Yugoslav Republic of Macedonia
Strk Publishing House, pg 449

Madagascar
Societe Malgache d'Edition, pg 450

Malaysia
Forum Publications, pg 452
Pelanduk Publications (M) Sdn Bhd, pg 453
Penerbit Jayatinta Sdn Bhd, pg 454
Pustaka Delta Pelajaran Sdn Bhd, pg 454
University of Malaya, Department of Publications, pg 455

Mauritius
Editions de l'Ocean Indien Ltd, pg 457

Mexico
Editores Asociados Mexicanos SA de CV (EDAMEX), pg 458
Libreria y Ediciones Botas SA, pg 458
Ediciones el Caballito SA, pg 458
Centro de Estudios Mexicanos y Centroamericanos, pg 458
El Colegio de Mexico AC, pg 459
Colegio de Postgraduados en Ciencias Agricolas, pg 459
Publicaciones Cruz O SA, pg 459
Editorial Diana SA de CV, pg 459
Ediciones Era SA de CV, pg 460
Centro de Estudios Monetarios Latinoamericanos (CEMLA), pg 460
Editorial Extemporaneos SA, pg 461
Fondo de Cultura Economica, pg 461
Grupo Editorial Iberoamerica, SA de CV, pg 462
Editorial Jus SA de CV, pg 462
Editorial Limusa SA de CV, pg 463
Mercametrica Ediciones SA Edicion de Libros, pg 464
Instituto Nacional de Estadistica, Geographia e Informatica, pg 464
Editorial Nueva Imagen SA, pg 464
Pearson Educacion de Mexico, SA de CV, pg 465
Siglo XXI Editores SA de CV, pg 467
Universidad Nacional Autonoma de Mexico (National University of Mexico), pg 467

Republic of Moldova
Izdatelstvo Kartia Moldoveniaske, pg 468

Monaco
Editions EGC, pg 468

Morocco
Access International Services, pg 469
Cabinet Conseil CCMLA, pg 469
Dar Nachr Al Maarifa Pour L'Edition et La Distribution, pg 469
Editions Le Fennec, pg 470
Les Editions du Journal L' Unite Maghrebine, pg 470
Editions Okad, pg 470
Editions La Porte, pg 470

Mozambique
Centro De Estudos Africanos, pg 470

Namibia
Multi-Disciplinary Research Centre Library, pg 471

Nepal
International Standards Books & Periodicals (P) Ltd, pg 471

Netherlands
Uitgeverij Jan van Arkel, pg 473
Business Contact BV, pg 475
Educatieve Uitgeverij Edu'Actief BV, pg 476
Elsevier Science BV, pg 477
KITLV Press Royal Institute of Linguistics & Anthropology, pg 479
Kluwer Bedrijfswetenschappen, pg 479
Uitgeverij Lemma BV, pg 480
Pearson Education Netherlands, pg 482
Tilburg University Press, pg 485
Van Gorcum & Comp BV, pg 486
VU Boekhandel/Uitgeverij BV, pg 487

New Zealand
Dunmore Press Ltd, pg 490
ESA Publications (NZ) Ltd, pg 490
Fraser Books, pg 491
New House Publishers Ltd, pg 493
Oxford University Press, pg 494
Nelson Price Milburn Ltd, pg 494
Statistics New Zealand, pg 496

Nigeria
Evans Brothers (Nigeria Publishers) Ltd, pg 499
JAD Publishers Ltd, pg 500
Nigerian Institute of International Affairs, pg 500
West African Book Publishers Ltd, pg 502

Norway
Bedriftsokonomens Forlag A/S, pg 502
Glydendal Akademisk, pg 503

SUBJECT INDEX

Pakistan
Academy of Education Planning & Management (AEPAM), pg 506
Pakistan Institute of Development Economics, pg 508
Publishers United Pvt Ltd, pg 508
Royal Book Co, pg 509
Vanguard Books Ltd, pg 509

Papua New Guinea
National Research Institute of Papua New Guinea, pg 510

Peru
Instituto de Estudios Peruanos, pg 511
Fondo Editorial de la Pontificia Universidad Catolica del Peru, pg 511
Editorial Horizonte, pg 511
Sur Casa de Estudios del Socialismo, pg 511
Universidad de Lima-Fondo de Desarollo Editorial, pg 512

Philippines
Ateneo de Manila University Press, pg 512
Mutual Books Inc, pg 513
New Day Publishers, pg 514
Rex Bookstores & Publishers, pg 514
Saint Mary's Publishing Corp, pg 515
SIBS Publishing House Inc, pg 515
Sinag-Tala Publishers Inc, pg 515
UST Publishing House, pg 515

Poland
Polskie Wydawnictwo Ekonomiczne PWE SA, pg 516
Polish Scientific Publishers PWN, pg 519
Oficyna Wydawnicza Read Me, pg 519
Zaklad Wydawnictw Statystycznych, pg 520
Oficyna Wydawnicza Szkoly Glownej Handlowej w Warszawie Oficyna Wydawnicza SGH, pg 520
Wydawnictwa Uniwersytetu Warszawskiego, pg 521

Portugal
Editorial 'Avante!', pg 522
Livraria Civilizacao (Americo Fraga Lamares & Ca Lda), pg 523
Constancia Editores, SA, pg 524
Edicoes Cosmos, pg 524
Difusao Cultural, pg 524
Editorial Estampa, Lda, pg 524
Gradiva-Publicacnoes Lda, pg 525
Impala, pg 525
Imprensa Nacional-Casa da Moeda, pg 526
Editorial Inquerito Lda, pg 526
Livraria Luzo-Espanhola Lda, pg 526
McGraw-Hill Editora de Portugal, pg 527
Nova Arrancada Sociedade Editora SA, pg 527
Quid Juris - Sociedade editora, pg 527
Silabo, pg 529
Almerinda Teixeira, pg 529
Teorema, pg 529
Vega-Publicacao e Distribuicao de Livros e Revistas, Lda, pg 530

Romania
Editura Aius, pg 531
Enzyklopadie Verlag, pg 533
Editura Excelsior, pg 533
Casa de editura Globus, pg 533
Nemira Verlag, pg 534
Editura Niculescu, pg 534
Rentrop & Straton Verlagsgruppe und Wirtschaftsconsulting, pg 535

Russian Federation
Aspect Press Ltd, pg 537
N E Bauman Moscow State Technical University Publishers, pg 537
Izdatelstvo 'Ekonomika', pg 537
FGUP Izdatelstvo Mashinostroenie, pg 538
Finansy i Statistika Publishing House, pg 538
INFRA-M Izdatel 'skij dom, pg 538
Izdatel 'stvo Kazanskago Universiteta, pg 538
Izdatel 'stvo Mordovskogo gosudar stvennogo, pg 538
Izvestia Sovetov Narodnyh Deputatov Russian Federation (RF), pg 539
Mezdunarodnye Otno Denija, pg 540
Izdatelstvo Mysl, pg 540
Nauka Publishers, pg 540
Izdatel'stvo Nizhegorodskogo Gosudarstvennogo Univ, pg 540
Novosti Izdatel 'stvo, pg 541
Progress Publishers, pg 541
Teorija Verojatnostej i ee Primenenija, pg 542
Voronezh State University Publishers, pg 542
Izdatelstvo Vysshaya Shkola, pg 543

Senegal
CODESRIA (Council for the Development of Social Science Research in Africa), pg 544
Societe Africaine d'Edition, pg 544

Singapore
APAC Publishers Services, pg 545
Hillview Publications Pte Ltd, pg 546
Institute of Southeast Asian Studies, pg 546
Singapore University Press Pte Ltd, pg 548
Taylor & Francis Asia Pacific, pg 548

Slovakia
Danubiaprint, pg 549
Sofa, pg 551
Technicka Univerzita, pg 551

Slovenia
East West Operation (EWO) Ltd, pg 551
Univerza v Ljubljani Ekonomska Fakulteta, pg 552

South Africa
Butterworths South Africa, pg 553
Educum Publishers Ltd, pg 554
Heinemann Educational Publishers Southern Africa, pg 555
Human & Rousseau (Pty) Ltd, pg 555
New Africa Books (Pty) Ltd, pg 557
Ravan Press (Pty) Ltd, pg 558
South African Institute of International Affairs, pg 559
Unisa Press, pg 560
Van Schaik Publishers, pg 560

Spain
Editorial AEDOS SA, pg 561
Agencia Espanola de Cooperacion, pg 562
Ediciones Akal SA, pg 562
Alta Fulla Editorial, pg 563
Editorial Ariel SA, pg 564
Editorial Biblioteca Nueva SL, pg 565
Antoni Bosch Editor SA, pg 565
Edicios do Castro, pg 566
Celeste Ediciones, pg 567
Editorial CISSPRAXIS SA, pg 567
Civitas SA Editorial, pg 567
Ediciones de la Universidad Complutense de Madrid, pg 568
Comunidad Autonoma de Madrid, Servicio de Documentacion y Publicaciones, pg 568
Editorial Constitucion y Leyes SA - COLEX, pg 568
Ediciones Diaz de Santos SA, pg 569
Edicions del Drac SA, pg 570
Dykinson SL, pg 571
Ediciones Encuentro SA, pg 573
Esic Editorial, pg 573
Instituto de Estudios Fiscales, pg 574
Publicaciones Etea, pg 574
Eumo Editorial, pg 574
EUNSA (Ediciones Universidad de Navarra SA), pg 574
Fondo de Cultura Economica de Espana, SL, pg 574
Fundacion de Estudios Libertarios Anselmo Lorenzo, pg 575
Ediciones Gestio 2000 SA, pg 575
Editorial Gredos SA, pg 576
Editorial Herder SA, pg 577
Icaria Editorial SA, pg 577
Instituto de Estudios Economicos, pg 578
Ediciones Internacionales Universitarias SA, pg 578
Editorin Laiovento SL, pg 579
Lid Editorial Empresarial, SL, pg 580
Marcombo SA de Boixareu Editores, pg 581
Mundi-Prensa Libros SA, pg 583
Oikos-Tau SA Ediciones, pg 584
Ediciones Piramide SA, pg 586
Publicaciones de la Universidad de Alicante, pg 588
Publicaciones de la Universidad Pontificia Comillas-Madrid, pg 588
Editora Regional de Murcia - ERM, pg 588
Ediciones Rialp SA, pg 589
Servicio de Publicaciones Universidad de Cordoba, pg 590
Editorial Sintesis, SA, pg 590
Editorial Tecnos SA, pg 592
Editorial Trivium, SA, pg 593
Universidad de Malaga, pg 594
Universidad de Valladolid Secretariado de Publicaciones e Intercambio Editorial, pg 594
Publicacions de la Universitat de Barcelona, pg 594
Universitat de Valencia Servei de Publicacions, pg 594
Xunta de Galicia, pg 596

Sri Lanka
Karunaratne & Sons Ltd, pg 597
Sunera Publishers, pg 598

Sweden
Iustus Forlag AB, pg 603
SNS Foerlag, pg 606
Stromberg, pg 606
AB Timbro, pg 607

Switzerland
Archivio Storico Ticinese, pg 608
Verlag Harri Deutsch, pg 612
Gottlieb Duttweiler Institute for Trends & Futures, pg 612
Elsevier Science SA, pg 613
Elvetica Edizioni SA, pg 613
Georg Editeur SA, pg 614
Graduate Institute of International Studies, pg 615
Paul Haupt Berne, pg 615
Helbing und Lichtenhahn Verlag AG, pg 615
Interfrom AG Editions, pg 616
Orell Fuessli Verlag, pg 620
Ott Verlag AG, pg 621
SAB Schweiz Arbeitsgemeinschaft fuer die Berggebiete, pg 623
Editions du Tricorne, pg 626
Der Universitatsverlag Freiburg, pg 626
Vdf Hochschulverlag AG an der ETH Zurich, pg 626
Versus Verlag AG, pg 627

Syrian Arab Republic
Damascus University Press, pg 628

Taiwan, Province of China
Commonwealth Publishing Company Ltd, pg 629
Fuh-Wen Book Co, pg 630
Linking Publishing Company Ltd, pg 631
San Min Book Co Ltd, pg 631

Tajikistan
Irfon, pg 632

United Republic of Tanzania
Bureau of Statistics, pg 633

Trinidad & Tobago
Inprint Caribbean Ltd, pg 637

Tunisia
Ceres Editions, pg 637
Dar Arabia Lil Kitab, pg 637

Turkey
Alkim Kitapcilik-Yayimcilik, pg 638
Altin Kitaplar Yayinevi, pg 638
Inkilap Publishers Ltd, pg 640
Seckin Yayinevi, pg 641

Uganda
Fountain Publishers Ltd, pg 642

Ukraine
ASK Ltd, pg 643
Naukova Dumka Publishers, pg 643
Osnovy Publishers, pg 643

United Kingdom
Academic Press Ltd, pg 644
Advisory Unit: Computers in Education, pg 645
Aldwych Press Ltd, pg 645
Anglo-German Foundation for the Study of Industrial Society, pg 647
Ashgate Publishing Ltd, pg 649
The Athlone Press Ltd, pg 650
Berghahn Books Ltd, pg 654
Blackwell Publishers, pg 655
Bloomsbury Publishing PLC, pg 656
Bookmarks Publications, pg 657
BPP Publishing Ltd, pg 658
Dr Barry Bracewell-Milnes, pg 658
Nicholas Brealey Publishing, pg 659
Business Monitor International, pg 661
Cambridge University Press, pg 662
Capstone Publishing Ltd, pg 663
Jon Carpenter Publishing, pg 664
Frank Cass Publishers, pg 664
Catholic Institute for International Relations, pg 665
Causeway Press Ltd, pg 665
Chadwyck-Healey Ltd, pg 666
Commonwealth Secretariat, pg 669
Conservative Policy Forum, pg 670
James Currey Ltd, pg 673
Dunedin Academic Press, pg 676
The Economist Intelligence Unit, pg 677
Edinburgh University Press Ltd, pg 677
Editon XII, pg 677
Edward Elgar Publishing Ltd, pg 678
Elsevier Science Ltd, pg 678
Europa Publications, pg 680
European Schoolbooks Ltd, pg 680
The Eurospan Group, pg 680
Fabian Society, pg 681
Forbes Publications Ltd, pg 683
Freedom Press, pg 684
W H Freeman & Co Ltd, pg 684
Green Books Ltd, pg 689
Harvard University Press, pg 692
C Hurst & Co (Publishers) Ltd, pg 698
ICC United Kingdom, pg 698
Institute for Fiscal Studies, pg 699
Institute of Development Studies, pg 699
Institute of Economic Affairs, pg 699
Islamic Foundation Publications, pg 701
JAI Press Ltd, pg 702
Lawrence & Wishart, pg 706
Letts Educational, pg 707
Macmillan Reference Ltd, pg 710
Manchester University Press, pg 711
Adam Matthew Publications, pg 712
The Merlin Press Ltd, pg 713
MIT Press Ltd, pg 715
John Murray (Publishers) Ltd, pg 716
National Assembly for Wales, pg 717
W W Norton & Company Ltd, pg 720
NTC Publications Ltd, pg 720
Open Gate Press, pg 721
Open University Worldwide, pg 721
Oxfam, pg 722
Oxford University Press, pg 723
Palgrave Publishers Ltd, pg 723
Pathfinder London, pg 724
Pearson Education, pg 725
Pearson Education Europe, Mideast & Africa, pg 725
Pluto Press, pg 728
The Policy Press, pg 729
Policy Studies Institute, pg 729
Profile Books Ltd, pg 731

ProQuest Information & Learning, pg 731
Rooster Books Ltd, pg 735
Routledge, pg 736
Routledge Curzon, pg 736
Royal Institute of International Affairs, pg 736
Sage Publications Ltd, pg 737
Scottish Office Library & Information Services, pg 740
Shepheard-Walwyn (Publishers) Ltd, pg 741
Sidgwick & Jackson Ltd, pg 742
Skoob Russell Square, pg 742
Spokesman, pg 744
The Stationery Office, pg 745
Telegraph Books, pg 748
University of Wales Press, pg 751
Verso, pg 752
VNU Business Publications, pg 753
Westview Press, pg 755
WI Enterprises Ltd, pg 756
Wiley Europe Ltd, pg 756
Wimbledon Publishing Company Ltd, pg 757
Witherby & Co Ltd, pg 758
World Microfilms Publications Ltd, pg 758
World of Information, pg 759

Uruguay
Editorial Arca SRL, pg 760
Arpoador, pg 760
Ediciones de Juan Darien, pg 760
Fundacion de Cultura Universitaria, pg 760
Nordan-Comunidad, pg 760
Vinten Editor, pg 761

Uzbekistan
Izdatelstvo Uzbekistan, pg 761

Venezuela
Alfadil Ediciones, pg 761
Monte Avila Editores Latinoamericana CA, pg 762
Fundacion Centro Gumilla, pg 762
Editorial Nueva Sociedad, pg 762

Viet Nam
Science & Technics Publishing House, pg 763

Yugoslavia
Izdavacka Organizacija Rad, pg 765
Radnicka Stampa, pg 765
Savez Inzenjera i Tehnicara Jugoslavije, pg 765
Savremena Administracija, pg 765

Zambia
MFK Management Consultants Services, pg 766

Zimbabwe
College Press Publishers (Pvt) Ltd, pg 768
Journal on Social Change, pg 768
Longman Zimbabwe (Pvt) Ltd, pg 768
Manhattan Publications, pg 769
Nehanda Publishers, pg 769
Sapes Trust Ltd, pg 769
Thomson Publications Zimbabwe (Pvt) Ltd, pg 769

EDUCATION

Albania
NL SH, pg 1
State Textbook Publishing House, pg 1

Argentina
Amorrortu Editores SA, pg 3
Bonum Editorial SACI, pg 4
Centro Editor de America Latina SA, pg 4
Libreria del Colegio SA, pg 4
Editorial Ruy Diaz SAEIC, pg 5
Ediciones Don Bosco Argentina, pg 5
ECA (Ediciones Culturales Argentinas), pg 5
Editorial Ciudad Nueva de la Sefoma, pg 5
Errepar SA, pg 5
Angel Estrada y Cia SA, pg 6
EUDEBA (Editorial Universitaria de Buenos Aires), pg 6
Gram Editora, pg 6
Editorial Guadalupe, pg 6
Kapelusz Editora SA, pg 6
Laffont Ediciones Electronicas SA, pg 7
Librograf, pg 7
Editorial Losada SA, pg 7
Marymar Ediciones SA, pg 7
Editorial Norte SA, pg 8
Editorial Paidos SAICF, pg 8
Editorial Plus Ultra SA, pg 8
Ediciones Preescolar SA, pg 8
Ricordi Americana SAEC, pg 8
San Pablo, pg 8
Ediciones Tres Tiempos SRL, pg 9

Australia
Aboriginal Studies Press, pg 10
ACER Press, pg 10
ACHPER Inc (Australian Council for Health, Physical Education & Recreation), pg 10
The Advancement Centre, pg 11
Allen & Unwin Pty Ltd, The Australian Newspaper, Vogel Breads, pg 11
Robert Andersen & Associates Pty Ltd, pg 11
Ansay Pty Ltd, pg 11
Artemis Publishing Pty Ltd, pg 12
Auslib Press Pty Ltd, pg 12
Austed Publishing Co, pg 13
The Australian Council for Educational Research Ltd, pg 13
Beri Publishing, pg 14
Board of Studies, pg 15
Cambridge University Press, pg 17
Candlelight Trust T/A Candlelight Farm, pg 17
Centre Publications, pg 17
CIS Publishers, pg 18
Coolabah Publishing, pg 18
Curriculum Corporation, pg 19
Eleanor Curtain Publishing, pg 19
Dabill Publications, pg 20
Dellasta Publishing, pg 20
Department for Education & Children's Services, South Australia, pg 20
Educational Advantage, pg 21
Era Publications, pg 22
Fernfawn Publications, pg 22
Finch Publishing, pg 22
Fremantle Arts Centre Press, pg 23
Gerald Griffin Press, pg 24
Ginninderra Press, pg 24
Greater Glider Productions Australia Pty Ltd, pg 24
Kerri Hamer, pg 25
Harcourt Australia Pty Ltd, pg 25
Hargreen Publishing Co, pg 25
Illert Publications, pg 27
Institute of Aboriginal Development (IAD Press), pg 28
James Nicholas Publishers Pty Ltd, pg 28
Jenelle Press, pg 28
John Wiley & Sons Australia Ltd, pg 28
Little Red Apple Publishing, pg 30
MacLennan & Petty Pty Ltd, pg 31
Macmillan Education Australia, pg 31
Horwitz Martin Education, pg 32
Matthias Media, pg 32
Maxwell Macmillan Publishing (Australia) Pty Ltd, pg 32
McGraw-Hill Australia Pty Ltd, pg 32
J M McGregor Pty Ltd, pg 32
Museum of Victoria, pg 34
Newman Centre Publications, pg 35
Openbook Publishers, pg 35
Oxfam Community Aid Abroad, pg 36
Pascal Press, pg 37
Pearson Education Australia, pg 37
Price Publishing, pg 39
Priestley Consulting, pg 39
Reader's Digest (Australia) Pty Ltd, pg 40
Ready-Ed Publications, pg 40
RIC Publications Pty Ltd, pg 40
Ruskin Rowe Press, pg 41
St Clair Press, pg 41
St Joseph Publications, pg 41
St Pauls, pg 41
Scholastic Australia Pty Ltd, pg 41
Science Press, pg 41
Shakespeare Head Press Pty Ltd, pg 42
Social Science Press, pg 42
Spectrum Publications, pg 43
Spinifex Press, pg 43
Summer Institute of Linguistics, Australian Aborigines Branch, pg 43
Tirian Publications, pg 45
La Trobe University Press, pg 45
Uniting Education, pg 45
Vista Publications, pg 47
Vital Publications, pg 47
Walker Books Australia Pty Ltd, pg 47
Wileman Publications, pg 47
Wizard Books Pty Ltd, pg 48
Woodlands Publications, pg 48

Austria
Braintrust Marketing Services Ges mbH Verlag, pg 50
Cura Verlag GmbH, pg 50
Dachs-Verlag GmbH, pg 50
Development News Ltd, pg 51
Docker Verlag GmbH & Co KG, pg 51
Edition Helbling Verlags-Gesellschaft mbH, pg 52
Ferdinand Hirt mbH & Co KG, pg 53
NOI - Verlag, pg 55
oebv & hpt Verlagsgesellschaft mbH & Co KG, pg 56
Oesterreichischer Bundesverlag GmbH, pg 56
Osterreichischer Bundesverlag Ges.mbh, pg 57
Andreas Schnider Verlags-Atelier, pg 58
Springer-Verlag Wien, pg 59
Studien Verlag Gmbh, pg 59
Verlag Styria, pg 59
Verband der Wissenschaftlichen Gesellschaften Oesterreichs (VWGOe), pg 60
Verlag Veritas Mediengesellschaft mbH, pg 60

Azerbaijan
Sada, Literaturno-Izdatel'skij Centr, pg 61

Bangladesh
Ankur Prakashani, pg 62
Gatidhara, pg 62
Mullick Bros, pg 62
The University Press Ltd, pg 62

Belarus
Belaruskaya Encyklapedyya, pg 63
Publishing Center of Belarus State University, pg 63

Belgium
Abimo, pg 63
Acco CV, pg 64
Actualquarto, pg 64
NV Uitgeverij Altiora Averbode, pg 64
De Boeck et Larcier SA, pg 65
Carto BVBA, pg 65
Contact NV, pg 67
Davidsfonds VZW, pg 67
Editions De Boeck-Larcier SA, pg 67
Dessain - Departement de De Boeck & Larcier SA, pg 68
Infoboek NV, pg 69
Uitgeverij J van In, pg 70
Die Keure, pg 70
Editions Labor, pg 70
Lansman Editeur, pg 70
Leuven University Press, pg 71
Licap CVBA, pg 71
Editeurs de Litterature Biblique, pg 71
Editions Lumen Vitae ASBL, pg 71
Mardaga, Pierre 12, pg 72
Reader's Digest SA, pg 73
Uitgeverij De Sikkel NV, pg 74
Sonneville Press (Uitgeverij) VTW, pg 74
Toulon Uitgeverij, pg 74
Imprimeur - Editeur Vaillant-Carmanne SA, pg 75
Vlaamse Esperantobond VZW, pg 75
Wolters Plantyn Educatieve Uitgevers, pg 75

Bosnia and Herzegovina
Bemust doo Novinsko-Izdavacko stamparsko i trgovacko preduzece, pg 77

Brazil
A & A & A Edicoes e Promocoes Internacionais Ltda, pg 77
AGIR S/A Editora, pg 78
Editora Antroposofica Ltda, pg 78
Ao Livro Tecnico Industria e Comercio Ltda, pg 78
ARTMED, pg 79
Editora Bertrand Brasil Ltda, pg 79
Editora do Brasil SA, pg 80
Editora Brasiliense SA, pg 80
Centro de Estudos Juridicosdo Para (CEJUP), pg 80
Consultor Assessoria de Planejamento Ltda, pg 81

Editora Contexto (Editora Pinsky Ltda), pg 81
E P U Editora Pedagogica e Universitaria Ltd, pg 81
Edicon Editora e Consultorial Ltda, pg 81
Editora Elevacao, pg 82
Companhia Editora Forense, pg 82
Cia Editora Nacional, pg 82
EDUC - Editora da PUC-SP, pg 82
EDUSC - Editora da Universidade do Sagrado Coracao, pg 82
Editora Expressao e Cultura Exped Ltda, pg 83
Editora FCO Ltda, pg 83
Livraria Martins Fontes Editora Ltda, pg 83
Formato Editorial ltda, pg 83
Fundacao Cultural Avatar, pg 83
Fundacao Joaquim Nabuco Editora, pg 84
Global Editora e Distribuidora Ltda, pg 84
Editora Globo SA, pg 84
Edicoes Graal Ltda, pg 84
Grafica Editora Primor Ltda, pg 84
IBRASA (Instituicao Brasileira de Difusao Cultural Ltda), pg 85
Iglu Editora Ltda, pg 85
Editora Kuarup Ltda, pg 86
Editora Leitura Ltda, pg 86
Editora Lidador Ltda, pg 86
Waldyr Lima Editora, pg 86
LISA (Livros Irradiantes SA), pg 86
Editora Logosofica, pg 86
Edicoes Loyola SA, pg 87
Editora Mercado Aberto Ltda, pg 88
MG Editores Associados Ltda, pg 88
Editora Moderna Ltda, pg 88
Modulo Editora e Desenvolvimento Educacional Ltda, pg 88
Editora Nova Alexandria Ltda, pg 88
Editora Nova Fronteira SA, pg 88
Olho D'Agua Editora Comercio e Servicos Editoriais Ltda, pg 88
Paulinas Editorial, pg 89
Paulus Editora, pg 89
Editora Perspectiva, pg 89
Livraria Pioneira Editora/Enio Matheus Guazzelli e Cia Ltd, pg 89
Qualitymark Editora Ltda, pg 90
Editora Resenha Tributaria Ltda, pg 90
Saraiva SA, Livreiros Editores, pg 91
Editora Scipione Ltda, pg 91
Editora Sinodal, pg 91
Summus Editorial Ltda, pg 92
Edicoes Tabajara, pg 92
Thex Editora e Distribuidora Ltda, pg 92
Editora UNESP, pg 92
Editora Universidade Federal do Rio de Janeiro, pg 93
Fundacao Getulio Vargas, pg 93
Editora Verbo Ltda, pg 93
Editora Vigilia Ltda, pg 93
Jorge Zahar Editor, pg 93

Bulgaria

Abagar, Veliko Tarnovo, pg 94
Antroposofsko Izdatelstvo Dimo R Daskalov OOD, pg 94
Bojko Kacarmazov, pg 94
Bulvest 2000 Ltd, pg 94
Ciela Publishing House, pg 94
Eurasia Academic Publishers, pg 95
Factor-Alias, pg 95
Fondacija Zlatno Kljuce, pg 95
Hermes Publishing House, pg 95
Interpres, pg 96
Lettera, pg 96
LIK IZDANIJA, pg 96
Makros 2000 - Plovdiv, pg 96
MATEX, pg 96
Musica Publishing House Ltd, pg 96
Prosveta Publishers as, pg 97
Regalia 6 Publishing House, pg 97
Sila & Zivot, pg 98
Slavena, pg 98
Sluntse Publishing House, pg 98

Cameroon

Presses Universitaires d'Afrique, pg 99

Chile

Arrayan Editores, pg 99
Editorial Andres Bello/Editorial Juridica de Chile, pg 100
Dolmen Ediciones SA, pg 100
Ediciones Mil Hojas Ltda, pg 100
Pontificia Universidad Catolica de Chile, pg 101
Publicaciones Lo Castillo SA, pg 101
Red Internacional Del Libro, pg 101
Ediciones Universitarias de Valparaiso, pg 101

China

Beijing Education Publishing House, pg 102
Beijing Juvenile & Children's Books Publishing House, pg 102
Beijing Publishing House, pg 102
Beijing University Press, pg 102
Chemical Industry Press, pg 102
Chengdu Maps Publishing House, pg 103
China Braille Press, pg 103
China Theatre Publishing House, pg 104
China Tibetology Publishing House, pg 104
China Translation & Publishing Corp, pg 104
China Youth Publishing House, pg 104
Chinese Pedagogics Publishing House, pg 104
Commercial Press (Hong Kong) Ltd, pg 104
East China University of Science & Technology Press, pg 105
Education Science Publishing House, pg 105
Encyclopedia of China Publishing House, pg 105
Fudan University Press, pg 105
Fujian Children's Publishing House, pg 106
Guizhou Education Publishing House, pg 106
Higher Education Press, pg 106
Jinan Publishing House, pg 107
Lanzhou University Press, pg 107
New Times Press, pg 107
Shandong Education Publishing House, pg 108
Shandong Science & Technology Press, pg 109
Shanghai Educational Publishing House, pg 109
Shanghai Foreign Language Education Press, pg 109
South China University of Science and Technology Press, pg 109
Tsinghua University Press, pg 110
Zhejiang Education Publishing House, pg 110
Zhejiang University Press, pg 110

Colombia

Bedout Editores SA, pg 111
Consejo Episcopal Latinoamericano Celam, pg 111
Ediciones Culturales Ver Ltda, pg 111
Eurolibros Ltda, pg 111
Universidad Externado de Colombia, pg 112
Instituto Caro y Cuervo, pg 112
Kapelusz Ltda Editorial, pg 112
Editorial Libros y Libres SA, pg 112
Instituto Misionerao Hijas De San Pablo, pg 113
Pearson Educacion de Colombia LTDA, pg 113
Tercer Mundo Editores SA, pg 113
Universidad de Antioquia, Division Publicaciones, pg 114

The Democratic Republic of the Congo

Centre de Recherche, et Pedagogie Appliquee, pg 114
Presses Universitaires du Zaiire (PUZ), pg 115

Costa Rica

Asamblea Legislativa, Biblioteca Monsenor Sanabria, pg 115
Centro Agronomico Tropical de Investigacion y Ensenanza (CATIE), pg 115
Jose Alfonso Sandoval Nunez, pg 116
Promesa, Ediciones, pg 116
Scout Interamericana, pg 117
Editorial de la Universidad de Costa Rica, pg 117
Editorial Universidad Estatal a Distancia (EUNED), pg 117
Editorial Universidad Nacional (EUNA), pg 117

Croatia

ALFA dd za izdavacke, graficke i trgovacke poslove, pg 118
Izdavacka Delatnost Hrvatske Akademije Znanosti I Umjetnosti, pg 118
Skolska Knjiga, pg 120

Cuba

ISCAH Fructuoso Rodriguez, pg 121
Editora Politica, pg 121
Pueblo y Educacion Editorial (PE), pg 121

Czech Republic

Barrister & Principal, pg 123
Doplnek, pg 124
Galaxie, vydavatelelstvi a nakladatelstvi, pg 124
Granit SRO, pg 124
Karolinum, nakladatelstvi, pg 125
Pavla Momcilova, pg 126
Editio Moravia-Moravske hudebni vydavatelstvi, pg 126
Panton, pg 127
Portal Ltd, pg 127
Psychoanalyticke Nakladatelstvi, pg 128

Denmark

Akademisk Forlag, pg 129
Atuakkiorfik A/S Det Greenland Publishers, pg 130
Borgens Forlag A/S, pg 130
Dafolo Forlag, pg 131
Christian Ejlers' Forlag aps, pg 131
Forlaget FSR A/S (ITID A/S), pg 132
GEC Gads Forlag Aktieselskab af 1994, pg 132
Forlaget GMT, pg 132
Gyldendalske Boghandel - Nordisk Forlag A/S, pg 132
P Haase & Sons Forlag A/S, pg 132
Edition Wilhelm Hansen AS, pg 132
Kaleidoscope Publishers Ltd, pg 133
Mallings ApS, pg 133
New Era Publications International ApS, pg 134
Joergen Paludans Forlag ApS, pg 134
Hans Reitzel Publishers Ltd, pg 134
Samfundslitteratur, pg 135
Scandinavia Publishing House, pg 135

Dominican Republic

Pontificia Universidad Catolica Madre y Maestra, pg 136

Ecuador

CEPLAES, pg 137
Corporacion Editora Nacional, pg 137
Libresa S A, pg 137
SECAP, pg 137

Egypt (Arab Republic of Egypt)

Dar Al-Kitab Al-Masri, pg 138
Dar El Shorouk, pg 138
Dar El Shorouk Publishing & Distributing House, pg 138
Dar Al Maaref, pg 139
Sphinx Publishing Co, pg 139

Estonia

Olion Publishers, pg 140

Fiji

Lotu Pacifika Productions, pg 141
University of the South Pacific, pg 141

Finland

AB Svenska Laromedel-Editum, pg 141
Lasten Keskus Oy, pg 143
Osuuskunta Vastapaino, pg 145
Werner Soederstroem Osakeyhtioe (WSOY), pg 145
Yliopistopaino/Helsinki University Press, pg 145

France

ABC Editions, pg 145
Editions Al Liamm, pg 146
Alsatia SA, pg 146
L'Amitie par le Livre, pg 147
Les Ateliers d'Orion, pg 148
Editions Aubier-Montaigne SA, pg 149
Bayard Presse - Department Livre, pg 149
Editions Belin, pg 150
Societe d'Edition Les Belles Lettres, pg 150
Editions Bordas, pg 151

PUBLISHERS

Pierre Bordas et Fils, pg 151
Presses Universitaires de Bordeaux (PUB), pg 151
Brud Nevez, pg 152
Centre National de Documentation Pedagogique (CNDP), pg 153
Cepadues Editions SA, pg 153
Circonflexe, pg 155
Cle International, pg 155
CNRS Editions, pg 155
Codes Rousseau, pg 155
Armand Colin, Editeur, pg 155
Comite National d'Evaluation (CNE), pg 156
Editions Cujas, pg 157
Delagrave Édition SA, pg 158
Editions Desvigne, pg 159
Doin Editeurs, pg 160
Dunod Editeur, pg 160
L'Ecole/L'Ecole des Loisirs Sarl, pg 160
Edicef - Editions Classiques d'Expression Francaise, pg 161
Les Editions ESF, pg 161
Editions Entente, pg 162
Les Editions Foucher SA, pg 164
Imprimerie Librairie Gardet, pg 166
Editions Jean Paul Gisserot, pg 166
Groupe Expansion, pg 167
Hachette Education, pg 167
Hachette Livre, pg 167
Editions Hatier SA, pg 168
Karthala Editions-Diffusion, pg 171
Langues & Mondes/L'Asiatheque, pg 171
Editions Fernand Lanore Sarl, pg 172
Magnard SA, pg 174
Editions MDI (La Maison des Instituteurs), pg 175
Editions Modernes Media, pg 176
Fernand Nathan, pg 177
Institut National de Recherche Pedagogique, pg 177
Librairie A-G Nizet Sarl, pg 177
Nouvelle Cite, pg 178
Editions Ophrys, pg 178
Pearson Education France, pg 179
Editions A et J Picard SA, pg 179
Editions Pierron, pg 180
Presses Universitaires de Nancy, pg 181
Editions Prosveta SA, pg 182
Editions Revue EPS, pg 183
Editions du Scarabée, pg 184
Editions du Seneve, pg 184
Service Technique pour l'Education, pg 185
Editions Spratbrow, pg 186
Librairie Pierre Tequi et Editions Tequi, pg 187
UNESCO Publishing, pg 188
Pierre Zech Editeur, pg 189

Germany

ALS-Verlag GmbH, pg 193
AOL-Verlag Frohmut Menze, pg 194
AUE-Verlag GmbH, pg 196
Auer Verlag GmbH, pg 196
Aussaat Verlag, pg 197
C Bange GmbH & Co KG, pg 198
Verlag Bertelsmann Stiftung, pg 201
W Bertelsmann Verlag GmbH & Co KG, pg 201
BW Bildung und Wissen Verlag und Software GmbH, pg 203
Verlag Die Blaue Eule, pg 204
Boehlau-Verlag GmbH & Cie, pg 204
Adolf Bonz Verlag GmbH, pg 205
Gustav Bosse GmbH & Co KG, pg 205
Brandes & Apsel Verlag GmbH, pg 206
Buchverlag Junge Welt GmbH, pg 207
Buechse der Pandora Verlags-GmbH, pg 207
Burckhardthaus-Laetare Verlag GmbH, pg 208
Calwer Verlag Stuttgart eV, pg 209
CEC-Cosmic Energy Connections, pg 209
Centaurus-Verlagsgesellschaft GmbH, pg 209
Hans Christians Druckerei und Verlag GmbH & Co, pg 210
Compact Verlag GmbH, pg 211
Cornelsen und Oxford University Press GmbH & Co, pg 211
Cornelsen Verlag GmbH & Co OHG, pg 211
Cornelsen Verlag Scriptor GmbH & Co KG, pg 212
J G Cotta'sche Buchhandlung Nachfolger GmbH, pg 212
Verlag CSA Rosemarie Schneider, pg 212
Verlag fuer Deutsch GmbH, pg 213
Deutscher Taschenbuch Verlag GmbH & Co KG (dtv), pg 215
Deutsches Jugendinstitut (DJI), pg 216
Diesterweg, Moritz Verlag, pg 216
Dipa-Verlag GmbH, pg 217
Don Bosco Verlag, pg 217
Dreisam Ratgeber in der Rutsker Verlag GmbH, pg 218
Verlag Duerr & Kessler GmbH, pg 219
Ensslin und Laiblin Verlag GmbH & Co KG, pg 223
Falken-Verlag GmbH, pg 227
Festland Verlag, pg 227
Festo Didactic GmbH & Co, pg 227
Finken Verlag GmbH, pg 228
Flensburger Hefte Verlag GmbH, pg 228
Verlag Freies Geistesleben, pg 230
Erhard Friedrich Verlag, pg 230
Friedrich Kiehl Verlag GmbH, pg 230
Verlag A Fromm im Druck- u Verlagshaus Fromm GmbH & Co KG, pg 230
Verlag Junge Gemeinde E Schwinghammer GmbH & Co KG, pg 231
Wilhelm Goldmann Verlag GmbH, pg 233
Verlag Gruppenpaedagogischer Literatur, pg 234
Dr Curt Haefner-Verlag GmbH, pg 236
Hahnsche Buchhandlung, pg 236
Verlag Handwerk und Technik GmbH, pg 237
von Hase & Koehler Verlag KG, pg 238
Haufe Mediengruppe, pg 238
Verlag Herder GmbH & Co KG, pg 239
Erika Heydick Sax-Verlag Beucha, pg 240
Holland & Josenhans GmbH & Co, pg 242
Hans Holzmann Verlag GmbH und Co KG, pg 242
Horlemann Verlag, pg 243
Hans Huber, pg 243
IKO Verlag fur Interkulturelle Kommunikation, pg 244
Iudicium Verlag GmbH, pg 245
J Ch Mellinger Verlag GmbH, pg 246
Julius Klinkhardt Verlagsbuchhandlung, pg 247
Juventa Verlag GmbH, pg 247
Kallmeyer'sche Verlagsbuchhandlung GmbH, pg 247
Katzmann Verlag KG, pg 248
Klens Verlag GmbH, pg 250
Ernst Klett Verlag GmbH, pg 250
Koelner Universitaets-Verlag GmbH, pg 251
Verlag Koenigshausen und Neumann GmbH, pg 251
Koesel-Verlag GmbH & Co, pg 252
W Kohlhammer GmbH, abt Haussortiment, pg 252
Konkordia Verlag GmbH, pg 252
kopaed verlagsgmbh, pg 252
Verlag Waldemar Kramer, pg 253
Verlag Antje Kunstmann GmbH, pg 254
Peter Lang GmbH Europaeischer Verlag der Wissenschaften, pg 255
Langenscheidt-Hachette, pg 255
Anton G Leitner Verlag (AGLV), pg 257
Verlag Leske plus Budrich GmbH, pg 257
LEU-VERLAG Wolfgang Leupelt, pg 257
Hermann Luchterhand Verlag GmbH, pg 259
Manz G J Verlag und Druckerel, pg 261
Matzker Verlag DiA, pg 261
Midena Verlag, pg 264
Naumann & Goebel Verlagsgesellschaft mbH, pg 267
Neuer Weg Verlag und Druck GmbH, pg 268
Nusser Verlag, pg 269
Oekotopia Verlag, Wolfgang Hoffman, pg 270
Georg Olms Verlag AG, pg 270
Propylaeen Verlag, Zweigniederlassung Berlin der Ullstein Buchverlage GmbH, pg 275
Psychologie Verlags Union GmbH, pg 275
Quelle und Meyer Verlag GmbH & Co, pg 276
R Oldenbourg Verlag GmbH, pg 276
Dr Josef Raabe-Verlags GmbH, pg 276
Raethgloben Verlagsgesellschaft mbH, pg 276
Ravensburger Buchverlag Otto Maier GmbH, pg 277
Ernst Reinhardt GmbH & Co KG Verlag, pg 278
Ritterbach Verlag GmbH, pg 279
Rot-Gelb-Gruen Lehrmittel GmbH & Co Verlagsgesellschaft, pg 280
Rowohlt Taschenbuch Verlag GmbH, pg 280
Verlag an der Ruhr GmbH, pg 281
Richard Scherpe Verlag GmbH, pg 283
Schott Musik International GmbH & Co KG, pg 284
Scientia Verlag und Antiquariat, pg 286
Stadt Duisburg - Amt Fuer Statistik, Stadtforschung und Europaangelegenheiten, pg 288
Franz Steiner Verlag Wiesbaden GmbH, pg 289
Suin Buch-Verlag, pg 291
TR - Verlagsunion GmbH, pg 294
Trotzdem-Verlags Genossenschaft eG, pg 295
UNO-Verlag mbH, Vertriebs und Verlagsgesellschaft, pg 296
Vandenhoeck & Ruprecht, pg 297
VAS-Verlag fuer Akademische Schriften, Vas Karl-Heinz Balon, pg 297
Verlag und Druckkontor Kamp GmbH, pg 298
Volk und Wissen Verlag GmbH & Co, pg 299
Verlagsgruppe Georg von Holtzbrinck GmbH, pg 299
VWB-Verlag fur Wissenschaft & Bildung, Amand Aglaster, pg 300
Waxmann Verlag GmbH, pg 300
Weber Zucht & Co, pg 300
Weidler Buchverlag Berlin, pg 301
Westermann Schulbuchverlag GmbH, pg 302
Windmuehle GmbH Verlag und Vertrieb von Medien, pg 303
Dr Dieter Winkler, pg 303
Wissenschaftliche Buchgesellschaft, pg 303
Wochenschau Verlag, Dr Kurt Debus GmbH, pg 304

Ghana

Black Mask Ltd, pg 306
Ekab Business Ltd, pg 307
Quick Service Books Ltd, pg 308
Sedco Publishing Ltd, pg 308
Sub-Saharan Publishers, pg 308

Greece

Athina, Mary Mavrogiannis, pg 309
Atlantis M Pechlivanides & Co SA, pg 309
Axiotelis G, pg 309
Boukoumanis' Editions, pg 309
Chrysi Penna - Golden Pen Books, pg 309
Etaireia Spoudon Neoellinikou Politismou Kai Genikis Paideias, pg 310
Gutenberg Publications, pg 311
Hestia-I D Hestia-Kollaros & Co Corporation, pg 311
I Prooptiki, pg 311
Idryma Meleton Chersonisou tou Aimou, pg 311
Institute of Neohellenic Studies, Manolis Triantaphyllidis Foundation, pg 311
Kastaniotis Editions SA, pg 312
Mavrogianni Publications, pg 313
Michalis Sideris, pg 313
Panepistimio Ioanninon, pg 314
Papazissis Publishers SA, pg 314
Patakis Publishers, pg 314
Nikolas I Rossi, pg 314

Guyana

Community Based Rehabilitation Progeamme, pg 317

Haiti

Deschamps Imprimerie, pg 317
Editions du Soleil, pg 317

Honduras

Editorial Guaymuras, pg 318

Hong Kong

The Chinese University Press, pg 319
The Dharmasthiti Buddist Institute Ltd, pg 319

SUBJECT INDEX

Hong Kong University Press, pg 320
Island Press, pg 320
Ling Kee Publishing Group, pg 320
Modern Electronic & Computing Publishing Co Ltd, pg 321
Vista Productions Ltd, pg 322

Hungary

Advent Kiado, pg 323
Aranyhal Konyvkiado Goldfish Publishing, pg 323
KJK-Keaszov, pg 324
Kossuth Kiado RT, pg 325
Marton Aron Kiado Publishing House, pg 325
Nemzeti Tankoenyvkiado, pg 326
Szepirodalmi Koenyvkiado Kiado, pg 327

Iceland

Bokaverslun Sigfusar Eymundssonar, pg 327
Forlagid, pg 327
Frodi Ltd, pg 328
Isafoldarprentsmidja hf, pg 328
Mal og menning, pg 328
Namsgagnastofnun, pg 328

India

Agricole Publishing Academy, pg 330
Allied Publishers Pvt Ltd, pg 330
Ambar Prakashan, pg 330
Anmol Publications Pvt Ltd, pg 331
APH Publishing Corp, pg 331
Atma Ram & Sons, pg 331
Baha'i Publishing Trust of India, pg 332
Bani Mandir, Book-Sellers, Publishers & Educational Suppliers, pg 332
Bharatiya Samijik Vigyan Auusandhan Parishad, pg 332
Bhawan Book Service, Publishers & Distributors, pg 333
Concept Publishing Co, pg 335
Cosmo Publications, pg 335
Doaba House, pg 336
Era Book Enterprises, pg 336
Eurasia Publishing House Pvt Ltd, pg 337
Frank Brothers & Co (Publishers) Ltd, pg 337
General Printers & Publishers, pg 337
Gyan Publishing House, pg 338
HarperCollins Publishers India Pty Ltd, pg 338
Heritage Publishers, pg 338
Kalyani Publishers, pg 341
Mehta Publishers, pg 342
Minerva Associates (Publications) Pvt Ltd, pg 342
A Mukherjee & Co Pvt Ltd, pg 343
National Book Organization, pg 343
National Council of Educational Research & Training, Publication Department, pg 344
Navrang Booksellers & Publishers, pg 344
Neeta Prakashan, pg 344
Omsons Publications, pg 345
Parimal Prakashan, pg 345
Pointer Publishers, pg 346
Radiant Publishers, pg 347
Rajasthan Hindi Granth Academy, pg 347
Rajesh Publications, pg 347
Rajkamal Prakashan Pvt Ltd, pg 347
Rastogi Publications, pg 347
Regency Publications, pg 347
Reliance Publishing House, pg 347
Rupa & Co, pg 348
SABDA, pg 348
Sasta Sahitya Mandal, pg 349
Scientific Book Agency, pg 349
Selina Publishers, pg 349
Shiksha Bharati, pg 350
Sita Publications, pg 350
Somaiya Publications Pvt Ltd, pg 350
Sterling Publishers Pvt Ltd, pg 351
Sultan Chand & Sons Pvt Ltd, pg 351
Vikas Publishing House Pvt Ltd, pg 353
Vision Books Pvt Ltd, pg 353

Indonesia

Auroa, pg 354
Balai Pustaka, pg 354
Bhratara Karya Aksara, pg 354
Bina Rena Pariwara, pg 354
P T Bulan Bintang, pg 354
Institut Teknologi Bandung, pg 355
Karya Anda, CV, pg 356
Lembaga Demografi Fakultas Ekonomi Universitas Indonesia, pg 356
Mutiara Sumber Widya PT, pg 356
Yayasan Obor Indonesia, pg 357

Iraq

National House for Publishing, Distributing and Advertising, pg 358

Ireland

An Gum, pg 358
Campus Publishing Ltd, pg 359
Careers & Educational Publishers Ltd, pg 359
The Economic & Social Research Institute, pg 360
Fitzwilliam Publishing Co Ltd, pg 360
Folens Publishers, pg 360
Gill & Macmillan Ltd, pg 361
Irish YouthWork Press, pg 362

Israel

Ach Publishing House, pg 365
Bar Ilan University Press, pg 365
Boostan Publishing House, pg 366
Breslov Research Institute, pg 366
Carta, The Israel Map & Publishing Co Ltd, pg 366
Dyonon/Papyrus Publishing House of the Tel-Aviv, pg 367
Haifa University Press, pg 368
Hakibbutz Hameuchad Publishing House Ltd, pg 368
Otzar Hamore, pg 368
Hanitzotz A-Sharara Publishing House, pg 368
Intermedia Audio, Video Book Publishing Ltd, pg 368
Kernerman Publishing Ltd, pg 369
Ma'ariv Book Guild (Sifriat Ma'ariv), pg 370
Massada Press Ltd, pg 370
Open University of Israel, pg 371
Rubin Mass Ltd, pg 371
Schocken Publishing House Ltd, pg 372
Tcherikover Publishers Ltd, pg 372
Yad Vashem - The Holocaust Martyrs' & Heroes' Remembrance Authority, pg 373

Italy

Gruppo Abele, pg 374
De Agostini Scolastica, pg 375
Alinari Fratelli SpA Istituto di Edizioni Artistiche, pg 375
Archimede Edizioni, pg 376
Argalia Editore delle Arti Grafiche Editoriali SRL, pg 376
Editore Armando Armando SRL, pg 376
Baha'i, pg 377
Belforte Editore Libraio srl, pg 377
Edizioni Borla SRL, pg 378
Casa Editrice Felice Le Monnier, pg 380
Edistudio di Brunetto Casini, pg 380
Edizioni Centro Studi Erickson, pg 381
Ciranna - Roma, pg 381
Citta Nuova Editrice, pg 382
CLUEB (Cooperativa Libraria Universitaria Editrice Bologna), pg 382
La Coccinella Editrice SRL, pg 382
Nuova Coletti Editore Roma, pg 382
Continental SRL Editrice, pg 383
CPE - Centro Programmazione Editoriale, pg 383
Edizioni Cultura della Pace, pg 383
D'Anna, pg 383
G De Bono Editore, pg 384
Edizioni Dehoniane, pg 384
Edizioni Dehoniane Bologna (EDB), pg 384
Editrice Edisco, pg 386
Editrice la Scuola SpA, pg 386
Effata Editrice, pg 387
Elle Di Ci - Libreria Dottrina Cristiana, pg 388
Fatatrac, pg 388
Libreria Editrice Fiorentina di Vittorio Zani e C SAS, pg 389
Editrice Garigliano SRL, pg 390
Giunti (Gruppo Editoriale), pg 390
Giunti Publishing Group, pg 391
Piero Gribaudi Editore, pg 391
Gruppo Calderini Edagricole, pg 392
Guerra Edizioni Guru Azp, pg 392
Il Pensiero Scientifico Editore SRL, pg 393
In Dialogo, pg 393
Lalli Editore SRL, pg 395
Laruffa Editore SRL, pg 395
Editrice LAS, pg 395
Lecce Spazio Vivo Srl, pg 395
Vincenzo Lo Faro Editore, pg 396
Lusva Editrice, pg 397
Macro Edizioni, pg 397
Milella di Lecce Spazio Vivo SRL, pg 399
Minerva Italica SpA, pg 399
Arnoldo Mondadori Editore SpA, pg 399
Mucchi Editore SRL, pg 400
Gruppo Ugo Mursia Editore SpA, pg 400
Nagard, pg 400
Nardini Editore srl, pg 400
OCTAVO Franco Cantini Editore, pg 401
Franco Panini SPA Editore in Bologna, pg 402
Edizioni Panini SpA, pg 402
Paravia Bruno Mondadori Editori, pg 402
Psicologica Editrice, pg 404
Editori Riuniti, pg 405
SAIE Editrice SRL, pg 406
Editrice San Marco SRL, pg 406
Scala Group spa, pg 407
Societa Editrice Internazionale - SEI, pg 408
Gruppo Editoriale Le Stelle SpA, pg 409
Nicola Teti e C Editore SRL, pg 409
Edizioni Thyrus SRL, pg 409
Casa Musicale G Zanibon SRL, pg 412
Zanichelli Editore SpA, pg 412

Jamaica

Eureka Press Ltd, pg 413
Jamaica Publishing House Ltd, pg 413
West Indies Publishing Ltd, pg 414

Japan

AVACO - Christian Mass Communications Center, pg 414
Chikuma Shobo Publishing Co Ltd, pg 415
Child Honsha Co Ltd, pg 415
Froebel-Kan Co Ltd, pg 416
Fumaido Publishing Company Ltd, pg 416
Gakken Co Ltd, pg 416
Heibonsha Ltd, Publishers, pg 417
Hikarinokuni Ltd, pg 417
Holp Book Co Ltd, pg 417
Hyoronsha Publishing Co Ltd, pg 417
Kaitakusha, pg 419
Kazama Shobo, pg 419
Keisuisha Publishing Company Ltd, pg 419
Kin no Hoshi-Sha Co Ltd, pg 419
Kodansha, pg 420
Kokudo-Sha, pg 420
Kokusho Kankokai Co Ltd, pg 420
Komine Shoten Publishing Co Ltd, pg 420
Kosei Publishing Co Ltd, pg 420
Koyo Shobo, pg 420
Minerva Shobo Co Ltd, pg 421
Myrtos Inc, pg 421
Nihon Bunka Kagakusha Co Ltd, pg 422
Nihon-Bunkyo Shuppan (Japan Educational Publishing Co Ltd), pg 422
Nihon Tosho Center Co Ltd, pg 422
Nippon Hoso Shuppan Kyokai (NHK Publishing), pg 422
Nobunkyo (Rural Village Culture Association), pg 423
Ongaku No Tomo Sha Corporation, pg 423
Reimei-Shobo Co Ltd, pg 424
Riso-Sha, pg 424
Sagano Shoin, pg 424
Sanseido Co Ltd, pg 424
Sanshusha Publishing Co, Ltd, pg 424
Sekai Bunka Publishing Inc, pg 425
Shingakusha Co Ltd, pg 425
Shogakukan Inc, pg 426
Shokoku Publishing Co Ltd, pg 426
Shufunotomo sha Co Ltd, pg 426
The Simul Press Inc, pg 426
Sobun-Sha, pg 426
Sogensha Publishing Co Ltd, pg 426
Takahashi Shoten Co Ltd, pg 427
Tamagawa University Press, pg 427
Tokyo Shoseki Co Ltd, pg 427
Waseda University Press, pg 428
Yuhikaku Publishing Co Ltd, pg 429
Zoshindo JukenKenkyusha, pg 429

PUBLISHERS

Jordan
Al-Tanwir Al Ilmi (Scientific Enlightenment Publishing House), pg 430

Kenya
Action Publishers, pg 430
African Centre for Technology Studies (ACTS), pg 431
Focus Publications Ltd, pg 431
Heinemann Kenya Limited (EAEP), pg 431
Kenya Literature Bureau, pg 432
Lake Publishers & Enterprises Ltd, pg 432
Paulines Publications-Africa, pg 433
Phoenix Publishers, pg 433
Shirikon Publishers, pg 433
Sudan Literature Centre, pg 433
Transafrica Press, pg 433
Vipopremo Agencies, pg 433

Democratic People's Republic of Korea
Academy of Sciences Publishing House, pg 434
Educational Books Publishing House, pg 434
The Foreign Language Press Group, pg 434
Grand People's Study House, pg 434
Korea Science and Encyclopedia Publishing House, pg 434

Republic of Korea
BCM Media Inc, pg 434
Bo Ri, pg 435
Chung Rim Publishing Co Ltd, pg 435
Ewha Womans University Press, pg 436
Hainaim Publishing Co Ltd, pg 436
Hakmun Publishing, Co, pg 436
Hongik Media Plus Ltd, pg 437
Hyein Publishing House, pg 437
Iljo-gag Publishers, pg 437
Korea Britannica Corp, pg 437
Korea Textbook Co Ltd, pg 437
Korea University Press, pg 437
Koreaone Press Inc, pg 438
Minjisa Publishing Co, pg 438
Oruem Publishing House, pg 439
Seogwangsa, pg 440
Woong Jin Publishing Co Ltd, pg 440

Kuwait
Ministry of Information, pg 441

Laos People's Democratic Republic
Lao-phanit, pg 441

Latvia
Preses Nams, pg 442
Zvaigzne ABC Publishers, Ltd, pg 442

Lebanon
Khayat Book and Publishing Co Sarl, pg 443
Librairie Orientale sal, pg 443
World Book Publishing, pg 443

Liechtenstein
Rheintal Handelsgesellschaft Anstalt, pg 445
Topos Verlag AG, pg 445

Lithuania
Klaipedos Universiteto Leidykla, pg 445
Lietus Ltd, pg 445
Sviesa Publishers, pg 446
Svietimo ir mokslo ministerijos Leidybos centras, pg 446
TEV Leidykla, pg 446
Tyto Alba Publishers, pg 446

Luxembourg
Editions APESS ASBL, pg 447
Editions Emile Borschette, pg 447
Keyware sarl, pg 447
Editions Promoculture, pg 448

Macau
Universidadede de Macau, Centro de Publicacoes, pg 448

The Former Yugoslav Republic of Macedonia
Medis, Skopje, pg 449
Murgorski Zoze, pg 449
Prosvetno Delo, pg 449

Madagascar
Maison d'Edition Protestante ANTSO, pg 450
Societe Malgache d'Edition, pg 450

Malawi
Dzuka Publishing Company Ltd, pg 450

Malaysia
Amiza Associate Malaysia Sdn Bhd, pg 451
Berita Publishing Sdn Bhd, pg 451
Darulfikir, pg 451
Federal Publications Sdn Bhd, pg 452
Geetha Publishers Sdn Bhd, pg 452
Mahir Publications Sdn Bhd, pg 452
Malaya Educational Supplies Sdn Bhd, pg 453
The Malaya Press Sdn Bhd, pg 453
Penerbit Universiti Sains Malaysia, pg 454
Penerbitan Tinta, pg 454
Preston Corporation Sdn Bhd, pg 454
Pustaka Cipta Sdn Bhd, pg 454
Syarikat Cultural Supplies Sdn Bhd, pg 454
Trix Corporation Sdn Bhd, pg 455
Uni-Text Book Co, pg 455
Unit Penerbitan Akademik Cancelori~ Universiti Teknologi Malaysia, pg 455

Maldive Islands
Non-Formal Education Centre, pg 455

Malta
Media Centre, pg 456
Publishers' Enterprises Group (PEG) Ltd, pg 456

Martinique
George Lise-Huyghes des Etages, pg 456

Mauritania
Imprimerie Commerciale et Administrative de Mauritanie, pg 456

Mauritius
Editions Capucines, pg 457
Hemco Publications, pg 457
Editions de l'Ocean Indien Ltd, pg 457

Mexico
Aconcagua Ediciones y Publicaciones SA, pg 457
Adivinar y Multiplicar, SA de CV, pg 457
Editorial Avante SA de Cv, pg 458
Colegio de Postgraduados en Ciencias Agricolas, pg 459
Editorial Diana SA de CV, pg 459
Editorial Edicol SA, pg 460
El Colegio de Michoacan A C, pg 460
Entretenlibro SA de CV, pg 460
Editorial Extemporaneos SA, pg 461
Fernandez Editores SA de CV, pg 461
Fondo de Cultura Economica, pg 461
Editorial Jus SA de CV, pg 462
Libra Editorial SA de CV, pg 463
Libros y Revistas SA de CV, pg 463
Editorial Limusa SA de CV, pg 463
Nova Grupo Editorial SA de CV, pg 464
Editorial Pax Mexico, pg 465
Pearson Educacion de Mexico, SA de CV, pg 465
Ediciones Cientificas La Prensa Medica Mexicana SA de CV, pg 466
Editorial Progreso SA de C V, pg 466
Ediciones Promesa, SA de CV, pg 466
Ediciones Roca, SA, pg 466
Sayrols Editorial SA de CV, pg 466
Siglo XXI Editores SA de CV, pg 467
Editorial Trillas SA de CV, pg 467
Universidad Nacional Autonoma de Mexico (National University of Mexico), pg 467
Universidad Veracruzana Direccion General Editorial y de Publicaciones, pg 468
Editorial Varazen SA, pg 468

Morocco
Dar Nachr Al Maarifa Pour L'Edition et La Distribution, pg 469
Editions Eddif Maroc, pg 469

Mozambique
Empresa Moderna Lda, pg 470

Myanmar
Knowledge Printing & Publishing House, pg 471

Namibia
Desert Research Foundation of Namibia (DRFN), pg 471

Nepal
International Standards Books & Periodicals (P) Ltd, pg 471

Netherlands
John Benjamins BV, pg 474
Boekencentrum BV, pg 474
Boom Uitgeverij, pg 474

Bosch & Keuning, pg 474
Uitgeversmaatschappij Ad Donker BV, pg 476
Educatieve Uitgeverij Edu'Actief BV, pg 476
Uitgeverij Vrij Geestesleven, pg 477
LCG Malmberg BV, pg 480
Uitgeverij Lemma BV, pg 480
Mirananda Publishers BV, pg 481
Uitgeverij H Nelissen BV, pg 482
Partners Training & Innovatie, pg 482
Pearson Education Netherlands, pg 482
SMD Educational Publishers (Spruyt, Van Mantgem & De Does), pg 484
Sociaal en Cultureel Planbureau, pg 484
Stichting IVIO, pg 484
Swets & Zeitlinger Publishers, pg 485
ThiemeMeulenhoff, pg 485
Twente University Press, pg 485
Van Gorcum & Comp BV, pg 486

New Zealand
Catholic Supplies (NZ) LTD, pg 489
Clerestory Press, pg 490
Commonwealth Council for Educational Administration & Management, pg 490
Dunmore Press Ltd, pg 490
Gondwanaland Press, pg 491
Huia Publishers, pg 492
Learning Media Ltd, pg 492
Magari Publishing, pg 493
Nagare Press, pg 493
New Zealand Council for Educational Research, pg 494
Nelson Price Milburn Ltd, pg 494
Reach Publications, pg 495
Resource Books Ltd, pg 495
Shearwater Associates Ltd, pg 495
Statistics New Zealand, pg 496
University of Otago Press, pg 496

Nigeria
Adebara Publishers Ltd, pg 497
Ahmadu Bello University Press Ltd, pg 498
Albah Publishers, pg 498
Book Representation & Publishing Co Ltd, pg 498
ECWA Productions Ltd, pg 498
Evans Brothers (Nigeria Publishers) Ltd, pg 499
Olaiya Fagbamigbe Ltd (Publishers), pg 499
Fourth Dimension Publishing Co Ltd, pg 499
Gbabeks Publishers Ltd, pg 499
Literamed Publications Nigeria Ltd, pg 500
New Africa Publishing Company Ltd, pg 500
Nwamife Publishers Ltd, pg 500
Obafemi Awolowo University Press Ltd, pg 501
Paperback Publishers Ltd, pg 501
Spectrum Books Ltd, pg 501
University of Lagos Press, pg 502
Vantage Publishers International Ltd, pg 502

Norway
Ariel Lydbokforlag, pg 502
J W Eides Forlag A/S, pg 503
Folhenuniversitetets Forlag, pg 503
Fono Forlag, pg 503

Glydendal Akademisk, pg 503
Lunde Forlag og Bokhandel A/S, pg 504
Novus Forlag, pg 504
Skolebokforlaget A/S, pg 505
Universitetsforlaget, pg 505

Pakistan

Academy of Education Planning & Management (AEPAM), pg 506
The Book House, pg 506
Hamdard Foundation, pg 507
International Educational Services, pg 507
Maqbool Academy, pg 508
Nafees Academy, pg 508
Sh Ghulam Ali & Sons (Pvt) Ltd, pg 509
Urdu Academy Sind, pg 509

Panama

Editorial Universitaria, pg 509

Papua New Guinea

Kristen Pres, pg 510
National Research Institute of Papua New Guinea, pg 510

Peru

Asociacion Editorial Bruno, pg 511
Instituto de Estudios Peruanos, pg 511
Fondo Editorial de la Pontificia Universidad Catolica del Peru, pg 511
Editorial Horizonte, pg 511
Tarea Asociacion de Publicaciones Educativas, pg 511
Tassorello, SA, pg 511

Philippines

Abiva Publishing House Inc, pg 512
Ateneo de Manila University Press, pg 512
Bookman Printing & Publishing House Inc, pg 512
De La Salle University, pg 513
Garotech, pg 513
Logos (Divine Word) Publications Inc, pg 513
New Day Publishers, pg 514
Our Lady of Manaoag Publisher, pg 514
Philippine Education Co Inc, pg 514
Rex Bookstores & Publishers, pg 514
Saint Mary's Publishing Corp, pg 515
SIBS Publishing House Inc, pg 515
University of the Philippines Press, pg 515
UST Publishing House, pg 515

Poland

Instytut Historii Nauki PAN, pg 516
Impuls, pg 517
Instytut Wydawniczy Pax, Inco-Veritas, pg 517
KAW Krajowa Agencja Wydawnicza, pg 517
Muza SA, pg 518
Wydawnictwo Nasza Ksiegarnia Sp zoo, pg 518
Wydawnictwo Podsiedlik-Raniowski i Spolka, pg 519
Wydawnictwa Radia i Telewizji, pg 519
Oficyna Wydawnicza Read Me, pg 519
Res Polona, pg 519
Wydawnictwo RTW, pg 520

Videograf Il Sp z o o Zaklad Poracy Chronionej, pg 520
Wydawnictwo Wilga sp zoo, pg 521
Wydawnictwa Szkolne i Pedagogiczne (Polish Educational Publishers-WSiP), pg 521
Wydawnictwa Uniwersytetu Warszawskiego, pg 521

Portugal

Livraria Almedina, pg 522
Basica Editora, pg 522
Bezerr-Editorae e Distribuidora de Abel Antonio Bezerra, pg 522
Biblioteca Geral da Universidade de Coimbra, pg 523
Coimbra Editora Lda, pg 523
Constancia Editores, SA, pg 524
Dinalivro, pg 524
Distri Editora Lda, pg 524
Edicoes 70, Lda, pg 524
Edicoes ELO, pg 524
Editorial Estampa, Lda, pg 524
Publicacoes Europa-America Lda, pg 524
Gradiva-Publicacnoes Lda, pg 525
Impala, pg 525
Edicoes ITAU (Instituto Tecnico de Alimentacao Humana) Lda, pg 526
Livros Horizonte Lda, pg 526
McGraw-Hill Editora de Portugal, pg 527
Palas Editores Lda, pg 528
Editorial Perpetuo Socorro, pg 528
Porto Editora Lda, pg 528
Editorial Presenca, pg 528
Publicacoes Dom Quixote Lda, pg 528
Edicoes Salesianas, pg 529
Texto Editora, pg 529
Vega-Publicacao e Distribuicao de Livros e Revistas, Lda, pg 530
Editorial Verbo SA, pg 530
Livraria Verdade e Vida Editora, pg 530

Puerto Rico

McGraw-Hill Intermericana del Caribe, Inc, pg 530
University of Puerto Rico Press (EDUPR), pg 531

Romania

Editora All, pg 531
Editura Excelsior, pg 533
Hasefer, pg 533
Editura Institutul European, pg 533
Editura Militara, pg 534
Editura Minerva, pg 534
Nemira Verlag, pg 534
Editura Niculescu, pg 534
Petrion Verlag, pg 535
RAO Publishing Group, pg 535
Realitatea Casa de Edituri Productie Audio-Video Film, pg 535
Editura Univers, pg 536
Universal Dalsi, pg 536

Russian Federation

Airis Press, pg 537
N E Bauman Moscow State Technical University Publishers, pg 537
Dom, Izdatel'stvo sovetskogo deskkogo fonda im & I Lenina, pg 537
INFRA-M Izdatel'skij dom, pg 538
Izdatel'stvo Mordovskogo gosudar stvennogo, pg 538
Izdatelskii Dom Kompositor, pg 539
Moscow University Press, pg 540

Izdatelstvo Muzyka, pg 540
Nauka Publishers, pg 540
Izdatel'stvo Nizhegorodskogo Gosudarstvennogo Univ, pg 540
Okoshko Ltd Publishers (Izdatelstvo), pg 541
Pedagogika Press, pg 541
Izdatelstvo Prosveshchenie, pg 541
St Andrew's Biblical Theological College, pg 541
Izdatelstvo Sudostroenie, pg 542

Senegal

Centre Africain d'Animation et d'Echanges Culturels Editions Khoudia, pg 544
CODESRIA (Council for the Development of Social Science Research in Africa), pg 544
Les Nouvelles Editions Africaines du Senegal NEAS, pg 544

Singapore

Cannon International, pg 545
Chopsons Pte Ltd, pg 545
EPB Publishers Pte Ltd, pg 546
Federal Publications (S) Pte Ltd, pg 546
Graham Brash Pte Ltd, pg 546
Hillview Publications Pte Ltd, pg 546
Pan Pacific Publications (S) Pte Ltd, pg 547
SNP Pan Pacific Publishing Pte Ltd, pg 548
Stamford College Publishers/Authors-Publishers, pg 548
Success Publications Pte Ltd, pg 548
Taylor & Francis Asia Pacific, pg 548

Slovakia

Luc vydavatelske druzstvo, pg 550
Slovenske pedagogicke nakladateistvo, pg 550
Technicka Univerzita, pg 551
Ustav informacii a prognoz skolstva mladeze a telovychovy, pg 551
Vydavatel'stvo Osveta (Verlag Osveta), pg 551

South Africa

Butterworths South Africa, pg 553
Clever Books, pg 553
College of Careers (Pty) Ltd, pg 553
Educum Publishers Ltd, pg 554
Government Printer, pg 554
HAUM - Daan Retief Publishers (Pty) Ltd, pg 555
HAUM (Hollandsch Afrikaansche Uitgevers Maatschappij), pg 555
Heinemann Educational Publishers Southern Africa, pg 555
Human Sciences Research Council, pg 555
Institute for Reformational Studies CHE, pg 555
Ivy Publications, pg 555
Jacana Education, pg 555
Johannesburg Art Gallery, pg 556
Juta & Co, pg 556
Maskew Miller Longman, pg 557
Nasionale Boekhandel Ltd, pg 557
Nasou - Oudiovista, pg 557
New Africa Books (Pty) Ltd, pg 557
Pearson Education (Prentice Hall), pg 558
Perskor Books (Pty) Ltd, pg 558

Publitoria Publishers, pg 558
Publitoria Editions, pg 558
Ravan Press (Pty) Ltd, pg 558
Sasavona Publishers & Booksellers, pg 559
Unisa Press, pg 560
Van Schaik Publishers, pg 560
Vivlia Publishers & Booksellers, pg 560

Spain

Agencia Espanola de Cooperacion, pg 562
Ediciones Akal SA, pg 562
Altea, Taurus, Alfaguara SA, pg 563
Amnistia Internacional Editorial SL, pg 563
Ediciones Anaya SA, pg 563
Anglo-Didactica, SL Editorial, pg 563
Sociedad de Educacion Atenas SA, pg 564
Editorial Barcanova SA, pg 565
Editorial Bruno, pg 566
Editorial Castalia, pg 566
CEAC, Grupo Editorial SA, pg 567
Central Catequistica Salesiana (CCS), pg 567
Centro UNESCO de San Sebastian, pg 567
Comunidad Autonoma de Madrid, Servicio de Documentacion y Publicaciones, pg 568
CTE-Centro de Tecnologia Educativa SA, pg 569
Ediciones Daly S L, pg 569
Diseno Editorial SA, pg 570
Dykinson SL, pg 571
Edebe, pg 571
Edex, Centro de Recursos Comunitarios, pg 571
Edigol Ediciones SA, pg 572
Elkar, Euskal Liburu eta Kantuen Argitaldaria, SL, pg 573
Erein, pg 573
Editorial Esin, SA, pg 573
Eumo Editorial, pg 574
EUNSA (Ediciones Universidad de Navarra SA), pg 574
La Galera, SA Editorial, pg 575
Editorial Gedisa SA, pg 575
Generalitat de Catalunya Diari Oficial de la Generalitat vern, pg 575
Grao Editorial, pg 576
Editorial Gredos SA, pg 576
Grupo Comunicar, pg 576
Grupo Editorial CEAC SA, pg 576
Grupo Santillana de Ediciones SA, pg 576
Hercules de Ediciones, SA, pg 577
Editorial Herder SA, pg 577
Hogar del Libro, SA, pg 577
Editorial Horsori SL, pg 577
Ibaizabal Edelvives SA, pg 577
Publicaciones ICCE, pg 577
Idea Books, SA, pg 578
Imagen y Deporte, SL, pg 578
Institut de Recursos I investigacio per a la Formacio SL (IRIF), pg 578
Laertes SA de Ediciones, pg 579
Editorin Laiovento SL, pg 579
Llibres del Segle, pg 580
Loguez Ediciones, pg 580
Editorial Luis Vives (Edelvives), pg 580
Editorial Magisterio Espanol SA, pg 581
Editorial Marfil SA, pg 581
Ediciones Marova SL, pg 581
McGraw-Hill Iberic/Brazil Group, pg 581

Ediciones Medici SA, pg 582
Ediciones Mensajero, pg 582
Editorial Molino, pg 582
Ediciones Morata SL, pg 583
Editorial la Muralla SA, pg 583
Naque Editora, pg 583
Narcea SA de Ediciones, pg 583
Ediciones Oceano Grupo SA, pg 584
Oikos-Tau SA Ediciones, pg 584
Ediciones del Oriente y del Mediterraneo, pg 585
Oxford University Press Espana SA, pg 585
Editorial Paidotribo SL, pg 585
Pais Vasco Servicio Central de Publicaciones, pg 585
Ediciones Palabra SA, pg 585
Parramon Ediciones SA, pg 586
Pearson Educacion S A, pg 586
Pirene Editorial, sal, pg 587
Editorial Playor SA, pg 587
Ediciones Pomares-Corredor, pg 587
Editorial Popular SA, pg 587
PPC Editorial y Distribuidora, SA, pg 587
Editorial Presencia Gitana, pg 587
Editora Regional de Murcia - ERM, pg 588
Ediciones Rialp SA, pg 589
Editorial Miguel A Salvatella SA, pg 589
San Pablo Ediciones, pg 589
Ediciones San Pio X, pg 589
Universidad de Santiago de Compostela, pg 589
Editorial Sintesis, SA, pg 590
Equipo Sirius SA, pg 591
Ediciones SM, pg 591
Editorial Rudolf Steiner, pg 591
Ediciones Tarraco, pg 592
Editorial Tecnos SA, pg 592
Editorial Teide SA, pg 592
Thales Sociedad Andaluza de Educacion Matematica, pg 592
Tirant lo Blanch SL Libreriaa, pg 592
Ediciones de la Torre, pg 593
Trea Ediciones, SL, pg 593
Universidad de Granada, pg 594
Universidad de Malaga, pg 594
Ediciones Universidad de Salamanca, pg 594
Universidad de Valladolid Secretariado de Publicaciones e Intercambio Editorial, pg 594
Publicacions de la Universitat de Barcelona, pg 594
Universitat de Valencia Servei de Publicacions, pg 594
Editorial Vicens-Vives, pg 595
Visor Distribuciones, SA, pg 596
Edicions Xerais de Galicia, pg 596
Xunta de Galicia, pg 596

Sri Lanka
Colombo Book Association, pg 596
Karunaratne & Sons Ltd, pg 597
Lake House Investments Ltd, pg 597
Samayawardena Printers Publishers & Booksellers, pg 598
Swarna Hansa Foundation, pg 598

Swaziland
Macmillan Boleswa Publishers (Pty) Ltd, pg 599

Sweden
Acta Universitatis Gothoburgensis, pg 599
Akademiforlaget Corona AB, pg 599
Akademiforlaget Goteborgslitteratur, pg 600
Ekelunds Forlag AB, pg 601
Folkuniversitetets foerlag, pg 602
Gothia AB, Forlagshuset, pg 603
Gothia Publishing House, pg 603
Hallgren och Fallgren Studieforlag AB, pg 603
Invandrarfoerlaget, pg 603
Hans Richter Laromedel, pg 604
Lidman Production AB, pg 604
Psykologifoerlaget AB, pg 605
Samsprak Forlags AB, pg 606
Stromberg, pg 606
Studentlitteratur AB, pg 606

Switzerland
Aare-Verlag, pg 607
Antonius-Verlag, pg 608
Bugra Suisse Burchler Grafino AG, pg 610
Les Editions Camphill, pg 610
Christiana-Verlag, pg 611
Editions Delachaux et Niestle SA, pg 612
Editions Eisele SA, pg 613
Maurice et Pierre Foetisch SA, pg 614
Paul Haupt Berne, pg 615
Heilpaedagogisches Institut der Universitaet Freiburg, pg 615
Interfrom AG Editions, pg 616
Jugend mit einer Mission Verlag, pg 616
Klett und Balmer & Co Verlag, pg 617
Editions H Messeiller SA, pg 619
Natura-Verlag Arlesheim, pg 619
Novalis Media AG, pg 620
Orell Fuessli Verlag, pg 620
Editions Payot Lausanne, pg 621
Pedrazzini Tipografia, pg 621
Editions Pro Schola, pg 622
Psychosophische Gesellschaft, pg 622
Rex Verlag, pg 623
Sabe AG Verlagsinstitut, pg 623
Editions Saint-Paul, pg 623
Sauerlaender AG, pg 623
Verlag fuer Schoene Wissenschaften, pg 624
Schweizer Spiegel Verlag Mit, pg 624
Editions D'Art Albert Skira SA, pg 625
Editions 24 Heures, pg 626
Verlag im Waldgut AG, pg 627
Zbinden Druck und Verlag AG, pg 628

Syrian Arab Republic
Damascus University Press, pg 628

Taiwan, Province of China
Cheng Chung Book Co, Ltd, pg 629
Chu Liu Book Company, pg 629
Chung Hwa Book Co Ltd, pg 629
Far East Book Co Ltd, pg 630
Kuang Fu Book Co Ltd, pg 630
Laureate Book Co Ltd, pg 631
San Min Book Co Ltd, pg 631
Shuttle Multimedia Inc, pg 631
Youth Cultural Publishing Co, pg 632

United Republic of Tanzania
Bureau of Statistics, pg 633
East African Publishing House, pg 633
Nyota Publishers Ltd, pg 634
Press & Publicity Centre Ltd, pg 634
Tema Publishers Ltd, pg 634

Thailand
Pra Cha Chang & Co Ltd, pg 635
Thai Watana Panich Co, Ltd, pg 636

Togo
Editions Akpagnon, pg 636
Editogo, pg 636

Trinidad & Tobago
Inprint Caribbean Ltd, pg 637

Tunisia
Ceres Editions, pg 637
Dar Arabia Lil Kitab, pg 637
Maison Tunisienne de l'Edition, pg 638

Turkey
ABC Kitabevi AS, pg 638
Arkin Kitabevi, pg 639
Bilden Bilgisayar, pg 639
Ezel Erverdi (Dergah Yayinlari AS) Muessese Muduru, pg 640
Kok Yayincilik, pg 640
Redhouse Press, pg 641
Remzi Kitabevi, pg 641

Uganda
Centenary Publishing House Ltd, pg 642
Fountain Publishers Ltd, pg 642

Ukraine
Osvita, pg 643

United Kingdom
AP Information Services, pg 648
Apex Publishing Ltd, pg 648
Association of Commonwealth Universities (ACU), pg 650
Association for Science Education, pg 650
Bible Reading Fellowship, pg 654
A & C Black Publishers Ltd, pg 655
Books of Zimbabwe Publishing Co (Pvt) Ltd, pg 657
BPS Books (British Psychological Society), pg 658
Brewin Books Ltd, pg 659
Brilliant Publications, pg 659
British Educational Communication & Technology Agency (BECTA), pg 660
Cambridge University Press, pg 662
Canongate Books Ltd, pg 663
Capall Bann Publishing, pg 663
Cardiff Academic Press, pg 663
Cassell & Co, pg 664
Centaur Press (1954), pg 665
Centre for Information on Language Teaching & Research (CILT), pg 666
Chancerel International Publishers Ltd, pg 666
Child's World Education Ltd, pg 667
Christian Education, pg 667
Colourpoint Books, pg 669
Commonwealth Secretariat, pg 669
The Continuum International Publishing Group Ltd, pg 670
Council for British Archaeology, pg 671
Crown House Publishing Ltd, pg 672
CTBI Publications, pg 672
James Currey Ltd, pg 673
Drake Educational Associates Ltd, pg 676
Dunedin Academic Press, pg 676
Edinburgh University Press Ltd, pg 677
Editon XII, pg 677
Elm Publications, pg 678
Elsevier Science Ltd, pg 678
Europa Publications, pg 680
The Eurospan Group, pg 680
Facts On File, pg 681
First & Best in Education Ltd, pg 682
Folens Ltd, pg 683
Forbes Publications Ltd, pg 683
Foulsham Publishers, pg 683
David Fulton Publishers Ltd, pg 685
Ginn & Co Ltd, pg 687
Gomer Press (J D Lewis & Sons Ltd), pg 688
Graham-Cameron Publishing & Illustration, pg 688
Harcourt Publishers Ltd, pg 691
Harvard University Press, pg 692
Harvey Map Services Ltd, pg 692
Hawthorn Press, pg 693
Hawthorns Publications Ltd, pg 693
Heinemann Educational Publishing, pg 694
Hobsons, pg 696
Iaith Cyf, pg 698
Incorporated Catholic Truth Society, pg 699
Institute of Development Studies, pg 699
Institute of Economic Affairs, pg 699
Institute of Education, University of London, pg 699
Inter-Varsity Press, pg 700
International Bee Research Association, pg 701
Islamic Foundation Publications, pg 701
JAI Press Ltd, pg 702
Janus Publishing Company Ltd, pg 702
Karnak House, pg 703
Jessica Kingsley Publishers, pg 704
Kogan Page Ltd, pg 705
Kuperard, pg 705
Ladybird Books, pg 705
The Latchmere Press, pg 706
Lawrence & Wishart, pg 706
LDA-Living & Learning (Cambridge) Ltd, pg 706
Learning Matters Ltd, pg 706
Learning Together, pg 706
Letterland International Ltd, pg 707
Liverpool University Press, pg 708
Lucis Press Ltd, pg 709
The Lutterworth Press, pg 709
McCrimmon Publishing Co Ltd, pg 712
Monarch Books, pg 715
Motilal (UK) Books of India, pg 715
Multilingual Matters Ltd, pg 716
National Assembly for Wales, pg 717
National Association for the Teaching of English (NATE), pg 717
National Extension College, pg 717

National Foundation for Educational Research, pg 717
National Institute of Adult Continuing Education, pg 717
Nelson Thornes Ltd, pg 718
New Era Publications UK Ltd, pg 718
The NFER-NELSON Publishing Co Ltd, pg 719
Nile & Mackenzie Ltd, pg 719
James Nisbet & Co Ltd, pg 719
Northcote House Publishers Ltd, pg 719
Norwood Publishers, pg 720
The Octagon Press Ltd, pg 720
Oneworld Publications, pg 721
Open University Press, pg 721
Open University Worldwide, pg 721
Oxford University Press, pg 723
Pan Macmillan, pg 723
Parapress Ltd, pg 724
Pearson Education, pg 725
Pearson Education Europe, Mideast & Africa, pg 725
Peepal Tree Press, pg 725
Pergamon Flexible Learning, pg 726
Philip & Tacey Ltd, pg 726
The Policy Press, pg 729
Policy Studies Institute, pg 729
Prim-Ed Publishing UK Ltd, pg 730
Qualum Publishing, pg 731
Ravette Publishing Ltd, pg 733
Reader's Digest Children's Books, pg 733
Reading & Language Information Centre, pg 733
Reed Educational & Professional Publishing, pg 734
Routledge, pg 736
Royal College of General Practitioners, pg 736
The Royal Society, pg 737
Sage Publications Ltd, pg 737
Scottish Office Library & Information Services, pg 740
Scripture Union, pg 740
Sherwood Publishing, pg 741
SHU Press, pg 742
Southgate Publishers, pg 743
Speechmark Publishing Ltd, pg 744
SRHE, pg 744
Stacey International, pg 745
Stainer & Bell Ltd, pg 745
The Stationery Office, pg 745
Rudolf Steiner Press, pg 745
Supportive Learning Publications, pg 746
Tarquin Publications, pg 746
Tate Publishing Ltd, pg 747
Taylor & Francis Group, pg 747
Telegraph Books, pg 748
Thoemmes Press, pg 748
Trentham Books Ltd, pg 750
Trotman Publishing, pg 750
Ulster Historical Foundation, pg 751
University of Exeter Press, pg 751
University of Wales Press, pg 751
The Vegetarian Society, pg 752
Veritas Foundation Publication Centre, pg 752
Virago Press, pg 753
Whiting & Birch Ltd, pg 756
Whurr Publishers Ltd, pg 756
The Woburn Press, pg 758

Uruguay
Ediciones de Juan Darien, pg 760
EQ Opciones en Educacion, pg 760
Nordan-Comunidad, pg 760
Vinten Editor, pg 761

Venezuela
Monte Avila Editores Latinoamericana CA, pg 762
Fundacion Centro Gumilla, pg 762
Teduca, Tecnicas Educativas, CA, pg 763
Vadell Hermanos Editores CA, pg 763

Viet Nam
Giao Duc Publishing House, pg 763
Science & Technics Publishing House, pg 763

Yugoslavia
Naucna Knjiga, pg 764
Niro Decje Novine, pg 765
Republicki Zavod za Unapredivanje Vaspitanja i Obrazovanja, pg 765
Zavod za Izdavanje Udzbenika, pg 766
Zavod za udzbenike i nastavna sredstva, pg 766

Zambia
Wilfred Bwalya Chilangwa Publications, pg 766
Lundula Publishing House, pg 766
University of Zambia Press (UNZA Press), pg 767
Zambia Educational Publishing House, pg 767
ZPC Publications, pg 767

Zimbabwe
Academic Books Pvt Ltd, pg 767
The Bulletin Newspaper, pg 768
HarperCollins Publishers Zimbabwe Pvt Ltd, pg 768
Longman Zimbabwe (Pvt) Ltd, pg 768
Mercury Press Pvt Ltd, pg 769
Vision Publications, pg 769
Zimbabwe Foundation for Education with Production (ZIMFEP), pg 769
Zimbabwe Publishing House (Pvt) Ltd, pg 769

ELECTRONICS, ELECTRICAL ENGINEERING

Albania
NL SH, pg 1
State Textbook Publishing House, pg 1

Argentina
Editorial Albatros SACI, pg 3
Editorial Idearium de la Universidad de Mendoza (EDIUM), pg 5

Australia
EA Books, pg 21
McGraw-Hill Australia Pty Ltd, pg 32
OTEN (Open Training & Education Network), pg 36
Standards Association of Australia, pg 43

Austria
Andreas Schnider Verlags-Atelier, pg 58
Springer-Verlag Wien, pg 59

Belgium
Documenta CV, pg 68
Easy Computing NV, pg 68

Brazil
Antenna Edicoes Tecnicas Ltda, pg 78
Editora Edgard Blucher Ltda, pg 80
Editora Campus Ltda, pg 80
Selecoes Eletronicas Editora Ltda, pg 83
Hemus Editora Ltda, pg 85
Livro Ibero-Americano Ltda, pg 85

Bulgaria
Makros 2000 - Plovdiv, pg 96
MATEX, pg 96
WTU Todor Kableskov, pg 98

China
Chemical Industry Press, pg 102
China Machine Press (CMP), pg 103
Dalian Maritime University Press, pg 105
Electronics Industry Publishing House, pg 105
Fudan University Press, pg 105
Fujian Science & Technology Publishing House, pg 106
Heilongjiang Science & Technology Press, pg 106
Inner Mongolia Science & Technology Publishing House, pg 106
International Academic Publishers, pg 106
Jilin Science & Technology Publishing House, pg 106
Metallurgical Industry Press (MIP), pg 107
National Defence Industry Press, pg 107
New Times Press, pg 107
The People's Posts & Telecommunication Publishing House, pg 108
Printing Industry Publishing House, pg 108
Science Press, pg 108
Shandong Science & Technology Press, pg 109
Shandong University Press, pg 109
South China University of Science and Technology Press, pg 109
Southwest China Jiaotong University Press, pg 109
Tianjin Science & Technology Publishing House, pg 109
Tsinghua University Press, pg 110
Water Resources and Electric Power Press (CWPP), pg 110

Colombia
Cekit SA, pg 111

Czech Republic
Cesky normalizacni institut, pg 127

Dominican Republic
Pontificia Universidad Catolica Madre y Maestra, pg 136

Estonia
Valgus Publishers, pg 141

France
Breal, pg 151
Codes Rousseau, pg 155
Dunod Editeur, pg 160
Editions d'Organisation, pg 161
Editions Eyrolles, pg 163
Hermes Science Publications, pg 168
Institute, pg 169
Lavoisier, pg 172
Polytechnica, pg 180
Editions Springer France, pg 186
Editions Technip SA, pg 187
Editions Weka, pg 189

Germany
Beuth Verlag GmbH, pg 202
Verlag Erwin Bochinsky GmbH & Co KG, pg 204
Oscar Brandstetter Verlag GmbH & Co KG, pg 206
Verlag Harri Deutsch, pg 213
Elektor-Verlag GmbH, pg 222
Verlag Europa-Lehrmittel, Nourney, Vollmer GmbH & Co, pg 224
expert verlag GmbH, Fachverlag fur Wirtschaft & Technik, pg 225
Fachbuchverlag Leipzig im Carl Hanser Verlag, pg 226
Feltron-Elektronik Zeissler & Co GmbH, pg 227
Franz Ferzak World & Space Publications, pg 227
Festo Didactic GmbH & Co, pg 227
Franzis-Verlag GmbH, pg 229
Frech-Verlag GmbH und Co Druck KG, pg 229
Carl Hanser Verlag, pg 237
Ing W Hofacker GmbH Verlag, pg 241
Huss-Medien GmbH, pg 243
Huss-Verlag GmbH, pg 244
Huthig GmbH & Co KG, pg 244
ITpress Verlag, pg 245
Franckh-Kosmos Verlags-GmbH & Co, pg 252
Richard Pflaum Verlag GmbH & Co KG, pg 273
R Oldenbourg Verlag GmbH, pg 276
Springer-Verlag GmbH & Co KG, pg 288
B G Teubner GmbH, pg 292
UTB fuer Wissenschaft Uni-Taschenbuecher GmbH, pg 297
VDE-Verlag GmbH, pg 297
Friedr Vieweg & Sohn Verlagsgesellschaft mbH, pg 298
Vogel Medien GmbH & Co KG, pg 299
WEKA Firmengruppe GmbH & Co KG, pg 301

Greece
Hiotellis P, pg 311
Kleidarithmos, pg 312

Hong Kong
Electronic Technology Publishing Co Ltd, pg 319
Nam Hing Holdings Limited, pg 321
Technology Exchange Ltd, pg 322

Hungary
Foldmuvelesugyi Miniszterium Muszaki Intezet, pg 323
Magyar Tudomanyos Akademia Koezponti Fizikai Kutato Intezet Koenyvtara, pg 325
Mueszaki Koenyvkiado Ltd, pg 325

PUBLISHERS

India
Addison-Wesley (Singapore) Pte Ltd, pg 329
Affiliated East West Press Pvt Ltd, pg 329
B I Publications Pvt Ltd, pg 331
BPB Publications, pg 334
Heritage Publishers, pg 338
Khanna Publishers, pg 341
Laxmi Publications Pvt Ltd, pg 341
Pitambar Publishing Co (P) Ltd, pg 346
Scientific Book Agency, pg 349
Shaibya Prakashan Bibhag, pg 349
Sita Publications, pg 350
South Asian Publishers Pvt Ltd, pg 350
Sultan Chand & Sons Pvt Ltd, pg 351

Indonesia
Andi Offset, pg 354
Gramedia, pg 355
Institut Teknologi Bandung, pg 355

Italy
Edizioni Cremonese SRL, pg 383
DEI Tipographia del Genio Civile, pg 384
Editrice Edisco, pg 386
Giuseppe Laterza Editore Snc, pg 391
Gruppo Calderini Edagricole, pg 392
Gruppo Editoriale Faenza Editrice SpA, pg 392
Franco Muzzio & C Editore SpA, pg 400
Tecniche Nuove SpA, pg 409
Zanichelli Editore SpA, pg 412

Japan
Bun-ichi Sogo Shuppan, pg 415
CMC Co Ltd, pg 415
Fuji Keizai Company Ltd, pg 416
Gakken Co Ltd, pg 416
Iwanami Shoten, Publishers, pg 418
Keigaku Publishing Co Ltd, pg 419
Kindai Kagaku Sha Co, Ltd, pg 419
Maruzen Co Ltd, pg 421
Nippon Hoso Shuppan Kyokai (NHK Publishing), pg 422
Sangyo-Tosho Publishing Co Ltd, pg 424
Seibundo Shinkosha Publishing Co Ltd, pg 425

Jordan
Al-Tanwir Al Ilmi (Scientific Enlightenment Publishing House), pg 430

Kenya
Kenya Meteorological Department, pg 432

Democratic People's Republic of Korea
Grand People's Study House, pg 434
Korea Science and Encyclopedia Publishing House, pg 434

Republic of Korea
Bo Moon Dang, pg 435
Chung Rim Publishing Co Ltd, pg 435

The Former Yugoslav Republic of Macedonia
Medis, Skopje, pg 449
Seizmoloska Opservatorija, pg 449

Malaysia
Penerbit Universiti Sains Malaysia, pg 454
Unit Penerbitan Akademik Cancelori~ Universiti Teknologi Malaysia, pg 455

Mexico
ALFA OMEGA Grupo Editor, pg 458
Editorial Limusa SA de CV, pg 463
Sistemas Universales, SA, pg 467

Netherlands
Delft University Press, pg 476
Hagen & Stam Uitgeverij Ten, pg 478
IOS Press BV, pg 479
De Muiderkring BV, pg 481
Segment BV, pg 484

New Zealand
David's Marine Books, pg 490
Nelson Price Milburn Ltd, pg 494

Nigeria
Evans Brothers (Nigeria Publishers) Ltd, pg 499

Norway
NKI Forlaget, pg 504
Vett & Viten AS, pg 505

Poland
Wydawnictwa Komunikacji i Lacznosci Co Ltd, pg 517
Wydawnictwa Przemyslowe WEMA, pg 521
Wydawnictwa Naukowo-Techniczne, pg 521

Portugal
Dinalivro, pg 524
McGraw-Hill Editora de Portugal, pg 527
Almerinda Teixeira, pg 529

Romania
Editura Academiei Romane, pg 531
Editura Dacia, pg 532
Editura Militara, pg 534
Editura Teora, pg 536

Russian Federation
N E Bauman Moscow State Technical University Publishers, pg 537
Energoatomizdat, pg 537
Izdatelstvo Mir, pg 540
Nauka Publishers, pg 540
Izdatel'stvo Nizhegorodskogo Gosudarstvennogo Univ, pg 540
Izdatelstvo Radio i Svyaz, pg 541

Singapore
Reed Elsevier, South East Asia, pg 547
Tech Publications Pte Ltd, pg 548
World Scientific Publishing Co Pte Ltd, pg 549

Spain
AMV Ediciones, pg 563
CEAC, Grupo Editorial SA, pg 567
Editorial Dossat SA, pg 570
Eumo Editorial, pg 574
Marcombo SA de Boixareu Editores, pg 581
Progensa, pg 588
Universidad de Santiago de Compostela, pg 589
Ediciones Tecnicas Rede, SA, pg 592
Universidad de Valladolid Secretariado de Publicaciones e Intercambio Editorial, pg 594
Edicions de la Universitat Politecnica de Catalunya SL, pg 594
Ediciones A Madrid Vicente, pg 595

Sweden
Allt om Hobby AB, pg 600

Switzerland
Marcel Dekker AG, pg 612
Verlag Harri Deutsch, pg 612
Elektrowirtschaft Verlag, pg 613
Verlag Industrielle Organisation, pg 616
Presses Polytechniques et Universitaires Romandes, PPUR, pg 622
Vogt-Schild Ag, Druck und Verlag, pg 627

Syrian Arab Republic
Damascus University Press, pg 628

Taiwan, Province of China
Fuh-Wen Book Co, pg 630
Hsiao Yuan Publication Co, Ltd, pg 630

United Republic of Tanzania
DUP (1996) Ltd, pg 633

Thailand
Graphic Art Publishing, pg 635

Trinidad & Tobago
Caribbean Telecommunications Union, pg 636

Turkey
Caglayan Kitabevi, pg 639
Inkilap Publishers Ltd, pg 640
Yuce Reklam Yay Dagt AS, pg 642

United Kingdom
Artech House, pg 649
Bernard Babani (Publishing) Ltd, pg 651
Butterworth-Heinemann Ltd, pg 661
Dickson Price Publishers Ltd, pg 675
Elsevier Science Ltd, pg 678
ERA Technology Ltd, pg 679
W H Freeman & Co Ltd, pg 684
Imperial College Press, pg 699
Institute of Physics Publishing, pg 700
Institution of Electrical Engineers, pg 700
James & James (Science Publishers) Ltd, pg 702
Kluwer Academic/Plenum Publishers, pg 705

SUBJECT INDEX

John Murray (Publishers) Ltd, pg 716
Open University Worldwide, pg 721
PC Publishing, pg 725
ProQuest Information & Learning, pg 731
Research Studies Press Ltd (RSP), pg 734
Shire Publications Ltd, pg 741
The Society of Metaphysicians Ltd, pg 743
WIT Press, pg 757

Viet Nam
Science & Technics Publishing House, pg 763

Yugoslavia
Tehnicka Knjiga, pg 764
Savez Inzenjera i Tehnicara Jugoslavije, pg 765

Zimbabwe
Standards Association of Zimbabwe (SAZ), pg 769

ENERGY

Albania
NL SH, pg 1
State Textbook Publishing House, pg 1

Austria
IAEA - International Atomic Energy Agency, pg 53
International Institute for Applied Systems Analysis (IIASA), pg 53
Metrica Fachverlag u Versandbuchhandlung Ing Bartak, pg 55

Brazil
Comissao Nacional de Energia Nuclear, pg 81

Bulgaria
EnEffect, Center for Energy Efficiency, pg 95

China
Chemical Industry Press, pg 102
China Oil & Gas Periodical Office, pg 104
Shandong Science & Technology Press, pg 109
Shandong University Press, pg 109
Water Resources and Electric Power Press (CWPP), pg 110

Costa Rica
Editorial de la Universidad de Costa Rica, pg 117

Denmark
Mellemfolkeligt Samvirke, pg 133

Dominican Republic
Pontificia Universidad Catolica Madre y Maestra, pg 136

Egypt (Arab Republic of Egypt)
Dar El Shorouk Publishing & Distributing House, pg 138

SUBJECT INDEX

France
Edisud, pg 161
Editions Entente, pg 162
Ere Nouvelle, pg 162
Editions Paradigme, pg 179
Polytechnica, pg 180
PYC Edition, pg 182
Editions Technip SA, pg 187
Terre Vivante, pg 187

Germany
Aerogie-Verlag, pg 191
AOL-Verlag Frohmut Menze, pg 194
Verlag Dr Albert Bartens KG, pg 198
Bauverlag GmbH, pg 199
Beuth Verlag GmbH, pg 202
Deutscher Verlag fur Grundstoffindustrie GmbH, pg 215
Deutscher Wirtschaftsdienst John von Freyend GmbH, pg 216
expert verlag GmbH, Fachverlag fur Wirtschaft & Technik, pg 225
Franz Ferzak World & Space Publications, pg 227
Verlag Glueckauf GmbH, pg 233
Hessisches Ministerium fuer Umwelt, Landwirtschaft und Forsten, pg 240
Huthig GmbH & Co KG, pg 244
Institut fuer Landes- und Stadtentwicklungsforschung, ILS Nordrhein-Westfalen, pg 255
Marketing & Wirtschaft Verlagsges, Flade & Partner mbH, pg 261
C F Mueller Verlag, Huethig Gmb H & Co, pg 265
Oekobuch Verlag & Versand GmbH, pg 269
Schulz-Kirchner Verlag GmbH, pg 285
Adolf Sponholtz Verlag, pg 288
Springer-Verlag GmbH & Co KG, pg 288
TUeV-Verlag GmbH, pg 295
UNO-Verlag mbH, Vertriebs und Verlagsgesellschaft, pg 296
Vulkan-Verlag GmbH, pg 299
WEKA Firmengruppe GmbH & Co KG, pg 301

Greece
Hestia-I D Hestia-Kollaros & Co Corporation, pg 311
Michalis Sideris, pg 313

Hong Kong
Friends of the Earth (Charity) Ltd, pg 320

Hungary
Foldmuvelesugyi Miniszterium Muszaki Intezet, pg 323

India
Agricole Publishing Academy, pg 330
Allied Publishers Pvt Ltd, pg 330
APH Publishing Corp, pg 331
Concept Publishing Co, pg 335
Khanna Publishers, pg 341
Reliance Publishing House, pg 347
Scientific Book Agency, pg 349
Sita Publications, pg 350

Indonesia
PT Indira, pg 355

Italy
Franco Muzzio & C Editore SpA, pg 400
Editrice San Marco SRL, pg 406
Tecniche Nuove SpA, pg 409

Kenya
Kenya Energy & Environment Organisation, Kengo, pg 432

Lithuania
Academia, pg 445

Mexico
Fondo de Cultura Economica, pg 461
Editorial Limusa SA de CV, pg 463

Namibia
Desert Research Foundation of Namibia (DRFN), pg 471

Netherlands
Hagen & Stam Uitgeverij Ten, pg 478

Portugal
Constancia Editores, SA, pg 524

Romania
Editura Academiei Romane, pg 531

Russian Federation
N E Bauman Moscow State Technical University Publishers, pg 537
Nauka Publishers, pg 540
Izdatelstvo Nedra, pg 540

Singapore
Institute of Southeast Asian Studies, pg 546

Spain
Editorial AEDOS SA, pg 561
Icaria Editorial SA, pg 577
Marcombo SA de Boixareu Editores, pg 581
Progensa, pg 588

Switzerland
SAB Schweiz Arbeitsgemeinschaft fuer die Berggebiete, pg 623

United Kingdom
Association for Science Education, pg 650
Business Monitor International, pg 661
Centre for Alternative Technology, pg 665
Commonwealth Secretariat, pg 669
Elsevier Science Ltd, pg 678
The Energy Information Centre, pg 679
The Eurospan Group, pg 680
Institution of Electrical Engineers, pg 700
James & James (Science Publishers) Ltd, pg 702
Oilfield Publications Ltd, pg 720
Professional Engineering Publishing Ltd, pg 730
Research Studies Press Ltd (RSP), pg 734
Royal Institute of International Affairs, pg 736
The Royal Society, pg 737
Scottish Office Library & Information Services, pg 740
The Stationery Office, pg 745
Woodhead Publishing Ltd, pg 758

Viet Nam
Science & Technics Publishing House, pg 763

ENGINEERING (GENERAL)

Albania
NL SH, pg 1
State Textbook Publishing House, pg 1

Argentina
Editorial Idearium de la Universidad de Mendoza (EDIUM), pg 5

Australia
Blackwell Science Pty Ltd, pg 15
Hayes Publishing, pg 26
Histec Publications, pg 26
The Images Publishing Group Pty Ltd, pg 27
Maxwell Macmillan Publishing (Australia) Pty Ltd, pg 32
McGraw-Hill Australia Pty Ltd, pg 32
Pearson Education Australia, pg 37
Regency Publishing, pg 40
RMIT Publishing, pg 41
Standards Association of Australia, pg 43
University of New South Wales Press Ltd, pg 46

Austria
Metrica Fachverlag u Versandbuchhandlung Ing Bartak, pg 55
Oesterreichischer Kunst und Kulturverlag, pg 56
Verlag Oldenbourg, pg 56
Springer-Verlag Wien, pg 59

Belgium
Presses Universitaires de Bruxelles ASBL, pg 73

Brazil
Associacao Brasileira de Liverivos Antiquarios, pg 79
Editora Edgard Blucher Ltda, pg 80
Editora Campus Ltda, pg 80
Comissao Nacional de Energia Nuclear, pg 81
Editora FCO Ltda, pg 83
LTC-Livros Tecnicos e Cientificos Editora S/A, pg 87
Pearson Education Do Brasil, pg 89

Bulgaria
WTU Todor Kableskov, pg 98

Chile
Arrayan Editores, pg 99
Pontificia Universidad Catolica de Chile, pg 101
Ediciones Universitarias de Valparaiso, pg 101

China
Beijing Publishing House, pg 102
Chemical Industry Press, pg 102
East China University of Science & Technology Press, pg 105
Higher Education Press, pg 106
International Academic Publishers, pg 106
Jiangsu Science & Technology Publishing House, pg 106
Jilin Science & Technology Publishing House, pg 106
Metallurgical Industry Press (MIP), pg 107
Printing Industry Publishing House, pg 108
Shandong Science & Technology Press, pg 109
Shandong University Press, pg 109
Shanghai Science & Technology Publishers, pg 109
Shanghai Scientific & Technological Literature Publishing House, pg 109
Southwest China Jiaotong University Press, pg 109
Tianjin Science & Technology Publishing House, pg 109
Tsinghua University Press, pg 110
Water Resources and Electric Power Press (CWPP), pg 110

Colombia
Escala Ltda, pg 111
McGraw-Hill InterAmericana SA, pg 113

Costa Rica
Centro Agronomico Tropical de Investigacion y Ensenanza (CATIE), pg 115
Editorial de la Universidad de Costa Rica, pg 117

Croatia
Skolska Knjiga, pg 120
Tehnicka Knjiga, pg 120

Cuba
Editorial Cientifico Tecnica, pg 121
Universidad Central de la Villas, Centro Documentacion e Informacion Cientifica Tecnica, pg 121

Czech Republic
Academia, pg 122
Aleko, Nakladatelska Divize, pg 122
Cesky normalizacni institut, pg 127
Prace, pg 127

Denmark
Akademisk Forlag, pg 129
Ingenioeren/Boger, pg 133
Polyteknisk Forlag, pg 134

Dominican Republic
Pontificia Universidad Catolica Madre y Maestra, pg 136

Egypt (Arab Republic of Egypt)
Dar El Shorouk Publishing & Distributing House, pg 138

Estonia
Valgus Publishers, pg 141

Finland
Teknolit Oy, pg 144

PUBLISHERS

France
Cemagref Editions, pg 153
Chotard et Associes Editeurs, pg 154
Editions d'Organisation, pg 161
EDP Sciences, pg 161
Editions Eska, pg 162
Hachette Livre, pg 167
Hermes Science Publications, pg 168
Lavoisier, pg 172
Editions Pedone, pg 179
Polytechnica, pg 180
Presses Universitaires de France (PUF), pg 181
Editions Springer France, pg 186
Editions Technip SA, pg 187

Germany
Aerogie-Verlag, pg 191
BertelsmannSpringer Science & Business Media GmbH, pg 202
Beuth Verlag GmbH, pg 202
Bibliographisches Institut & F A Brockhaus AG, pg 203
Verlag Wolfgang Bleiweis, pg 204
Brandenburgisches Verlagshaus in der Dornier Medienholding GmbH, pg 206
Oscar Brandstetter Verlag GmbH & Co KG, pg 206
Charles Coleman Verlag GmbH & Co KG, pg 211
Verlag Harri Deutsch, pg 213
Deutscher Fachverlag GmbH, pg 214
Deutscher Verlag fur Grundstoffindustrie GmbH, pg 215
Ecomed Verlagsgesellschaft AG & Co KG, pg 220
Elektor-Verlag GmbH, pg 222
Fachbuchverlag Leipzig im Carl Hanser Verlag, pg 226
Fachverlag Schiele & Schoen GmbH, pg 226
Franz Ferzak World & Space Publications, pg 227
Festo Didactic GmbH & Co, pg 227
Harald Fischer Verlag GmbH, pg 228
Rita G Fischer Verlag, pg 228
Alfons W Gentner Verlag GmbH & Co KG, pg 231
Gieck Reiner v Ursel Gieck, pg 232
Gloatz, Hille GmbH & Co KG fur Mehrfarben und Zellglasdruck, pg 233
Haag und Herchen Verlag GmbH, pg 235
Carl Hanser Verlag, pg 237
Hestra-Verlag Hernichel & Dr Strauss GmbH & Co KG, pg 240
Carl Heymanns Verlag KG, pg 240
S Hirzel Verlag GmbH und Co, pg 241
Huss-Verlag GmbH, pg 244
Kallmeyer'sche Verlagsbuchhandlung GmbH, pg 247
W Kohlhammer GmbH, abt Haussortiment, pg 252
Franckh-Kosmos Verlags-GmbH & Co, pg 252
Moench Verlagsgesellschaft mbH, pg 264
C F Mueller Verlag, Huethig GmbH & Co, pg 265
Verlag Walter Podszun Burobedarf-Bucher Abt, pg 274
R Oldenbourg Verlag GmbH, pg 276
Rationalisierungs-Kuratorium der Deutschen Wirtschaft eV (RKW), pg 277
Verlag Werner Sachon GmbH & Co, pg 281
Springer-Verlag GmbH & Co KG, pg 288
Verlag Stahleisen GmbH, pg 289
UTB fuer Wissenschaft Uni-Taschenbuecher GmbH, pg 297
VDI-Verlag GmbH, pg 297
Verlag fur Schweissen und Verwandte Verfahren, pg 298
Vulkan-Verlag GmbH, pg 299
WEKA Firmengruppe GmbH & Co KG, pg 301
Werner Verlag GmbH & Co KG, pg 302
Wison Verlag GmbH, pg 303

Greece
Giourdas Moschos, pg 310

Hungary
Akademiai Kiado, pg 323
Foldmuvelesugyi Miniszterium Muszaki Intezet, pg 323
Panem, pg 326
Springer Hungarica Kiado Kft, pg 326

India
Agricole Publishing Academy, pg 330
Atma Ram & Sons, pg 331
B I Publications Pvt Ltd, pg 331
Bookionics, pg 333
BS Publications, pg 334
Eurasia Publishing House Pvt Ltd, pg 337
Galgotia Publications Pvt Ltd, pg 337
Arnold Heinman Publishers (India) Pvt Ltd, pg 338
Jaico Publishing House, pg 340
Khanna Publishers, pg 341
Law Publishers, pg 341
Multitech Publishing Co, pg 343
Narosa Publishing House, pg 343
Oxford & IBH Publishing Co Pvt Ltd, pg 345
Oxonian Press (P) Ltd, pg 345
People's Publishing House (P) Ltd, pg 346
Scientific Book Agency, pg 349
Scientific Publishers India, pg 349
Sita Publications, pg 350
Somaiya Publications Pvt Ltd, pg 350
South Asian Publishers Pvt Ltd, pg 350
Sultan Chand & Sons Pvt Ltd, pg 351
Vikas Publishing House Pvt Ltd, pg 353

Indonesia
P T Bulan Bintang, pg 354
Institut Teknologi Bandung, pg 355

Israel
Freund Publishing House Ltd, pg 367

Italy
Alinea, pg 375
BeMa, pg 377
Bianco, pg 377
Editoriale Bios, pg 378
Bulzoni Editore SRL (Le Edizioni Universitarie d'Italia), pg 379
Casa Editrice Libraria Ulrico Hoepli SpA, pg 380
CELID, pg 380
CLEUP - Cooperative Libraria Editrice dell 'Universita di Padova, pg 382
Edizioni Cremonese SRL, pg 383
Etas Libri, pg 388
Monduzzi Editore SpA, pg 399
Patron Editore SrL, pg 403
Pirola, pg 403
Pitagora Editrice SRL, pg 403
Zanichelli Editore SpA, pg 412

Japan
Baifukan Co Ltd, pg 414
Chijin Shokan Co Ltd, pg 415
Kaibundo Publishing Co Ltd, pg 419
Kajima Institute Publishing Co Ltd, pg 419
Kyoritsu Shuppan Co Ltd, pg 420
Ohmsha Ltd, pg 423
Sangyo-Tosho Publishing Co Ltd, pg 424
Shokoku Publishing Co Ltd, pg 426
Universal Academy Press, Inc, pg 428
University of Tokyo Press, pg 428
Yokendo Ltd, pg 429

Jordan
Jordan Book Centre Co Ltd, pg 430

Kazakstan
Gylym, Izd-Vo, pg 430

Democratic People's Republic of Korea
Korea Science and Encyclopedia Publishing House, pg 434

Republic of Korea
Bo Moon Dang, pg 435
Hakmun Publishing, Co, pg 436
Hyangmunsa Publishing Co, pg 437
Iljo-gag Publishers, pg 437
Ki Moon Dang, pg 437
Korea University Press, pg 437
Mun Un Dang, pg 438
Pearson Education Korea Ltd, pg 439

Lithuania
TEV Leidykla, pg 446

Mexico
ALFA OMEGA Grupo Editor, pg 458
Compania Editorial Continental SA de CV, pg 459
Grupo Editorial Iberoamerica, SA de CV, pg 461
Editorial Limusa SA de CV, pg 463
McGraw-Hill Interamericana de Mexico, SA de CV, pg 463
Universidad Nacional Autonoma de Mexico (National University of Mexico), pg 467

Nepal
International Standards Books & Periodicals (P) Ltd, pg 471

Netherlands
A A Balkema, pg 473
Delft University Press, pg 476
Elsevier Science BV, pg 477

SUBJECT INDEX

Hagen & Stam Uitgeverij Ten, pg 478
Swets & Zeitlinger Publishers, pg 485

Nigeria
Ilesanmi Press (Educational Publishers) Ltd, pg 499

Norway
Teknologisk Forlag, pg 505
Vett & Viten AS, pg 505

Peru
Universidad de Lima-Fondo de Desarollo Editorial, pg 512
Universidad Nacional Mayor de San Marcos, pg 512

Poland
Oficyna Wydawnicza Politechniki Wroclawskiej, pg 519

Portugal
Dinalivro, pg 524
Publicacoes Europa-America Lda, pg 524
Gradiva-Publicacnoes Lda, pg 525
McGraw-Hill Editora de Portugal, pg 527
Monitor, pg 527
Monitor-Projectos e Edicoes, LDA, pg 527

Puerto Rico
McGraw-Hill Intermericana del Caribe, Inc, pg 530

Romania
Editura Militara, pg 534
Editura Niculescu, pg 534
Editura Tehnica, pg 536

Russian Federation
N E Bauman Moscow State Technical University Publishers, pg 537
FGUP Izdatelstvo Mashinostroenie, pg 538
Izdatel'stvo Mordovskogo gosudar stvennogo, pg 538
Izdatelstvo Metallurgiya, pg 540
Izdatelstvo Mir, pg 540
Nauka Publishers, pg 540
Izdatel'stvo Nizhegorodskogo Gosudarstvennogo Univ, pg 540
Izdatelstvo Sudostroenie, pg 542

Singapore
APAC Publishers Services, pg 545
Taylor & Francis Asia Pacific, pg 548
World Scientific Publishing Co Pte Ltd, pg 549

South Africa
Educum Publishers Ltd, pg 554

Spain
AMV Ediciones, pg 563
CEAC, Grupo Editorial SA, pg 567
Ediciones Daly S L, pg 569
Editorial Donostiarra SA, pg 570
Editorial Dossat SA, pg 570
EUNSA (Ediciones Universidad de Navarra SA), pg 574
Editorial Labor SA, pg 579
Editorial Reverte SA, pg 588

SUBJECT INDEX

Servicio de Publicaciones Universidad de Cadiz, pg 590
Editorial Sintesis, SA, pg 590
Editores Tecnicos Asociados SA, pg 592
Instituto Eduardo Torroja, pg 593
Universidad de Valladolid Secretariado de Publicaciones e Intercambio Editorial, pg 594
Edicions de la Universitat Politecnica de Catalunya SL, pg 594
Urmo SA de Ediciones, pg 595

Sweden
Studentlitteratur AB, pg 606

Switzerland
Birkhauser Verlag AG, pg 610
Elsevier Science SA, pg 613
Presses Polytechniques et Universitaires Romandes, PPUR, pg 622
Vdf Hochschulverlag AG an der ETH Zurich, pg 626

Syrian Arab Republic
Damascus University Press, pg 628

Taiwan, Province of China
Chung Hwa Book Co Ltd, pg 629
Fuh-Wen Book Co, pg 630
Chu Hai Publishing (Taiwan) Co Ltd, pg 630

Turkey
Caglayan Kitabevi, pg 639
Eren Yayincilik ve Kitapcilik Ltd Sti, pg 639
Saray Medikal Yayin Tic Ltd Sti, pg 641

United Kingdom
Artech House, pg 649
British Cement Association, pg 660
Business Monitor International, pg 661
Butterworth-Heinemann Ltd, pg 661
Cambridge University Press, pg 662
DMG Business Media Ltd, pg 675
Editon XII, pg 677
The Eurospan Group, pg 680
Hodder & Stoughton Educational, pg 696
Imperial College Press, pg 699
Intermediate Technology Publications Ltd, pg 700
IOM Communications Ltd, pg 701
McGraw-Hill Publishing Company, pg 712
Nexus Special Interests, pg 719
Oxford University Press, pg 723
Palgrave Publishers Ltd, pg 723
Pearson Education, pg 725
Professional Engineering Publishing Ltd, pg 730
Research Studies Press Ltd (RSP), pg 734
The Royal Society, pg 737
The Royal Society of Chemistry, pg 737
Sage Publications Ltd, pg 737
SHU Press, pg 742
Springer-Verlag London Ltd, pg 744
Sutton Publishing Ltd, pg 746
Taylor & Francis Group, pg 747
Training Publications Ltd, pg 749
WIT Press, pg 757
Woodhead Publishing Ltd, pg 758

Viet Nam
Science & Technics Publishing House, pg 763

Yugoslavia
Gradevinska Knjiga, pg 764
Tehnicka Knjiga, pg 764
Naucna Knjiga, pg 764
Izdavacka Organizacija Rad, pg 765
Savez Inzenjera i Tehnicara Jugoslavije, pg 765

Zimbabwe
Standards Association of Zimbabwe (SAZ), pg 769

ENGLISH AS A SECOND LANGUAGE

Albania
NL SH, pg 1
State Textbook Publishing House, pg 1

Australia
Int Press, pg 28
McGraw-Hill Australia Pty Ltd, pg 32
Melting Pot Press, pg 33
OTEN (Open Training & Education Network), pg 36
Wileman Publications, pg 47

Austria
Development News Ltd, pg 51
Edition Helbling Verlags-Gesellschaft mbH, pg 52
Oesterreichischer Gewerbeverlag GmbH, pg 56
Osterreichischer Bundesveilag Ges.mbh, pg 57
Verlag Mag Wanzenbock, pg 60

Azerbaijan
Sada, Literaturno-Izdatel'skij Centr, pg 61

Belarus
Kavaler Publishers, pg 63

Belgium
De Boeck et Larcier SA, pg 65
Editions De Boeck-Larcier SA, pg 67
Marabout, pg 72
Uitgeverij De Sikkel NV, pg 74
Zuid-Nederlandse Uitgeverij NV/ Central Uitgeverij, pg 76

Botswana
Maskew Miller Longman, pg 77

Brazil
EDUC - Editora da PUC-SP, pg 82
Livraria Martins Fontes Editora Ltda, pg 83
Libreria Editora Ltda, pg 86
Waldyr Lima Editora, pg 86
Editora Meca Ltda, pg 87
Editora Melhoramentos Ltda, pg 87

Bulgaria
Factor-Alias, pg 95
Lettera, pg 96
Prozoretz Ltd Publishing House, pg 97
Regalia 6 Publishing House, pg 97

Sanra Book Trust, pg 97
Seven Hills Publishers, pg 97

China
Aviation Industry Press, pg 102
Beijing Publishing House, pg 102
Beijing University Press, pg 102
Book Marketing Ltd, pg 102
China Braille Press, pg 103
China Foreign Economic Relations & Trade Publishing House, pg 103
Dalian Maritime University Press, pg 105
East China University of Science & Technology Press, pg 105
Education Science Publishing House, pg 105
Foreign Language Teaching & Research Press, pg 105
Fudan University Press, pg 105
Guangdong Science & Technology Press, pg 106
Higher Education Press, pg 106
Jilin Science & Technology Publishing House, pg 106
Nanjing University Press, pg 107
New Times Press, pg 107
Shandong Science & Technology Press, pg 109
Shandong University Press, pg 109
Shanghai Educational Publishing House, pg 109
Shanghai Foreign Language Education Press, pg 109
Tianjin Science & Technology Publishing House, pg 109
Tsinghua University Press, pg 110
Wuhan University Press, pg 110
Zhejiang Education Publishing House, pg 110

Costa Rica
Editorial de la Universidad de Costa Rica, pg 117

Denmark
Forlaget alokke AS, pg 129
GEC Gads Forlag Aktieselskab af 1994, pg 132
Kaleidoscope Publishers Ltd, pg 133
Samfundslitteratur, pg 135
Systime, pg 136

Dominican Republic
Pontificia Universidad Catolica Madre y Maestra, pg 136

Egypt (Arab Republic of Egypt)
Dar El Shorouk, pg 138
Dar El Shorouk Publishing & Distributing House, pg 138

Estonia
Valgus Publishers, pg 141

France
Edicef - Editions Classiques d'Expression Francaise, pg 161
Editions Jean Paul Gisserot, pg 166
Editions Hatier SA, pg 168
Editions Ophrys, pg 178
Sofradif Editions Philippe Auzou, pg 185
Editions Spratbrow, pg 186

Germany
AOL-Verlag Frohmut Menze, pg 194
Bayerischer Schulbuch-Verlag GmbH, pg 199
Compact Verlag GmbH, pg 211
Cornelsen Verlag GmbH & Co OHG, pg 211
Finken Verlag GmbH, pg 228
Logophon Lehrmittelverlag GmbH, pg 258
Orbis Verlag fur Publizistik GmbH, pg 270
Verlag Sigrid Persen, pg 272
Verlag an der Ruhr GmbH, pg 281
Stauffenburg Verlag Brigitte Narr GmbH, pg 289
Stiefel GmbH Wandkarten Verlag, pg 290
TR - Verlagsunion GmbH, pg 294

Ghana
Beginners Publishers, pg 306
Frank Publishing Ltd, pg 307
Ghana Institute of Linguistics Literacy & Bible Translation (GILLBT), pg 307
Kwamfori Publishing Enterprise, pg 307
Paul Ntem Maanoh, pg 307
Sam Woode Ltd, pg 308
Sedco Publishing Ltd, pg 308

Greece
Alamo Hellas, pg 308
Macmillan Heinemann ELT, pg 313
Michalis Sideris, pg 313
Pagoulatos G-G P Publications, pg 314
Scripta, pg 315

Haiti
Editions Caraiibes SA, pg 317

Hong Kong
Chung Hwa Book Co (HK) Ltd, pg 319
Hong Kong University Press, pg 320
Lea Publications Ltd, pg 320
Ling Kee Publishing Group, pg 320
Sesame Publication Co, pg 321

India
Addison-Wesley (Singapore) Pte Ltd, pg 329
Ambar Prakashan, pg 330
Bhawan Book Service, Publishers & Distributors, pg 333
Doaba House, pg 336
Frank Brothers & Co (Publishers) Ltd, pg 337
General Book Depot, pg 337
Shaibya Prakashan Bibhag, pg 349
Somaiya Publications Pvt Ltd, pg 350
Star Publications (P) Ltd, pg 351
Sterling Publishers Pvt Ltd, pg 351
Sultan Chand & Sons Pvt Ltd, pg 351
S Viswanathan (Printers & Publishers) Pvt Ltd, pg 353

Indonesia
PT Indira, pg 355

PUBLISHERS SUBJECT INDEX

Israel
Gefen Publishing House Ltd, pg 367
Intermedia Audio, Video Book Publishing Ltd, pg 368
Kernerman Publishing Ltd, pg 369
Password Publishers Ltd, pg 371
University Publishing Projects Ltd, pg 373

Italy
Archimede Edizioni, pg 376
BeMa, pg 377
Casa Editrice Giuseppe Principato Spa, pg 380
Cooperativa Libraria IULM SCRL, pg 383
Editrice Edisco, pg 386
Hora, pg 392
Lecce Spazio Vivo Srl, pg 395
Loescher Editore SRL, pg 396
Macmillan Heinemann ELT, pg 397
Milella di Lecce Spazio Vivo SRL, pg 399
Paravia Bruno Mondadori Editori, pg 402
Principato, pg 404
Il Tripode Srl, pg 410
Zanichelli Editore SpA, pg 412

Japan
Eichosha Company Ltd, pg 416
Kaitakusha, pg 419
Nihon-Bunkyo Shuppan (Japan Educational Publishing Co Ltd), pg 422
Nippon Hoso Shuppan Kyokai (NHK Publishing), pg 422
Pearson Education Japan, pg 423
Sanshusha Publishing Co, Ltd, pg 424
Seibido, pg 424
Thomson Learning, pg 427
Tokyo Shoseki Co Ltd, pg 427
Yamaguchi Shoten, pg 429
Yohan Shuppan, pg 429

Kenya
Danmar Publishers, pg 431
Dhillon Publishers Ltd, Paa Crescent, pg 431
Focus Publications Ltd, pg 431

Republic of Korea
Chung Rim Publishing Co Ltd, pg 435
Hakmun Publishing, Co, pg 436
Hongik Media Plus Ltd, pg 437
Kemongsa Publishing Co Ltd, pg 437
Koreaone Press Inc, pg 438
Moon Jin Media Co Ltd, pg 438
Pyeong-hwa Chulpansa, pg 439
Sohaksa, pg 440
Woong Jin Publishing Co Ltd, pg 440

Latvia
Avots, pg 441
Zvaigzne ABC Publishers, Ltd, pg 442

Lebanon
Librairie Orientale sal, pg 443

Lithuania
Alma Littera, pg 445
Dargenis Publishers, pg 445
Sviesa Publishers, pg 446
Svietimo ir mokslo ministerijos Leidybos centras, pg 446

Luxembourg
Eiffes Romain, pg 447

The Former Yugoslav Republic of Macedonia
Murgorski Zoze, pg 449

Madagascar
Foibe Filan-Kevitry NY Mpampianatra (FOFIPA), pg 450

Malaysia
S Abdul Majeed & Co, pg 451
Federal Publications Sdn Bhd, pg 452
Mahir Publications Sdn Bhd, pg 452
Minerva Publications, pg 453
Penerbit Jayatinta Sdn Bhd, pg 454
Penerbitan Tinta, pg 454
Pustaka Cipta Sdn Bhd, pg 454
Pustaka Delta Pelajaran Sdn Bhd, pg 454

Maldive Islands
Non-Formal Education Centre, pg 455

Mexico
Ediciones Larousse SA de CV, pg 462
Selector SA de CV, pg 467
Sistemas Universales, SA, pg 467
Editorial Trillas SA de CV, pg 467

Netherlands
Uitgeverij Coutinho BV, pg 476

New Zealand
ESA Publications (NZ) Ltd, pg 490
Maori Publications Unit, pg 493
New House Publishers Ltd, pg 493
Taylor Books, pg 496

Nigeria
Vantage Publishers International Ltd, pg 502

Norway
NKI Forlaget, pg 504

Pakistan
Academy of Education Planning & Management (AEPAM), pg 506
International Educational Services, pg 507

Peru
Ediciones Brown SA, pg 511

Philippines
Bookman Printing & Publishing House Inc, pg 512
Saint Mary's Publishing Corp, pg 515
SIBS Publishing House Inc, pg 515
UST Publishing House, pg 515

Poland
Energeia sp zoo Wydawnictwo, pg 516
'Slask' Ltd, pg 520
Oficyna Wydawnicza Szkoly Glownej Handlowej w Warszawie Oficyna Wydawnicza SGH, pg 520
Wydawnictwa Uniwersytetu Warszawskiego, pg 521

Portugal
Constancia Editores, SA, pg 524
Editora Replicacao Lda, pg 529
Solivros, pg 529

Puerto Rico
McGraw-Hill Intermericana del Caribe, Inc, pg 530

Romania
Coresi SRL, pg 532
Editura Gryphon, pg 533
Editura Institutul European, pg 533
Editura Niculescu, pg 534

Russian Federation
Airis Press, pg 537
Izdatel'stvo Nizhegorodskogo Gosudarstvennogo Univ, pg 540
Okoshko Ltd Publishers (Izdatel'stvo), pg 541
Izdatelstvo Prosveshchenie, pg 541
Russkij Jazyk, pg 541

Singapore
Hillview Publications Pte Ltd, pg 546
Success Publications Pte Ltd, pg 548

Slovakia
Slovenske pedagogicke nakladateistvo, pg 550

Slovenia
Zalozba Mihelac d o o, pg 552
Zalozba Obzorja d d Maribor, pg 552

South Africa
Clever Books, pg 553
Heinemann Educational Publishers Southern Africa, pg 555
Ivy Publications, pg 555
Jacana Education, pg 555
New Africa Books (Pty) Ltd, pg 557

Spain
Ediciones Akal SA, pg 562
Anglo-Didactica, SL Editorial, pg 563
Didacta Comunicacion y Didactica, SA, pg 569
Editorial Espasa-Calpe SA, pg 573
Sociedad General Espanola de Libreria SA - SGEL, pg 591

Sri Lanka
Colombo Book Association, pg 596
Samayawardena Printers Publishers & Booksellers, pg 598

Sweden
Akademiforlaget Goteborgslitteratur, pg 600
Ekelunds Forlag AB, pg 601
Hans Richter Laromedel, pg 604
Liber AB, pg 604

Switzerland
Editions Pro Schola, pg 622

Syrian Arab Republic
Damascus University Press, pg 628

Taiwan, Province of China
Farseeing Publishing Company Ltd, pg 630
Hsiao Yuan Publication Co, Ltd, pg 630
Jillion Publishing Co, pg 630
Linking Publishing Company Ltd, pg 631
Shuttle Multimedia Inc, pg 631

United Republic of Tanzania
Ben and Company Ltd, pg 633
Nyota Publishers Ltd, pg 634
Tanzania Publishing House, pg 634

Thailand
New Generation Publishing Co Ltd, pg 635

Tunisia
Ceres Editions, pg 637

Turkey
Arkadas Ltd, pg 639
Pearson Education Turkey, pg 641

Ukraine
ASK Ltd, pg 643
Osvita, pg 643

United Kingdom
BBC English, pg 652
The British Council, Design, Publishing & Print Department, pg 660
Cambridge University Press, pg 662
English Teaching Professional, pg 679
EPER, pg 679
Evans Brothers Ltd, pg 680
Garnet Publishing Ltd, pg 685
Graham-Cameron Publishing & Illustration, pg 688
HarperCollins Publishers, pg 692
Hugo's Language Books Ltd, pg 697
Ladybird Books, pg 705
Language Teaching Publications, pg 706
Letterbox Library, pg 707
Magi Publications, pg 710
National Association for the Teaching of English (NATE), pg 717
National Extension College, pg 717
Reading & Language Information Centre, pg 733
Reed Educational & Professional Publishing, pg 734
Supportive Learning Publications, pg 746

Viet Nam
Science & Technics Publishing House, pg 763

Zambia
Lundula Publishing House, pg 766

SUBJECT INDEX

Zimbabwe
College Press Publishers (Pvt) Ltd, pg 768
HarperCollins Publishers Zimbabwe Pvt Ltd, pg 768
Longman Zimbabwe (Pvt) Ltd, pg 768
Mercury Press Pvt Ltd, pg 769

ENVIRONMENTAL STUDIES

Argentina
Editorial Albatros SACI, pg 3
Cesarini Hermanos, pg 4
Editorial Idearium de la Universidad de Mendoza (EDIUM), pg 5
Marymar Ediciones SA, pg 7
Editorial Paidos SAICF, pg 8
Editorial Planeta Argentina SAIC, pg 8
Ediciones Tres Tiempos SRL, pg 9

Australia
Appropriate Technology Development Group (Inc) WA, pg 11
Australian Academy of Science, pg 13
Australian Marine Conservation Society Inc (AMCS), pg 14
Australian Scholarly Publishing, pg 14
Beazer Publishing Company Pty Ltd, pg 14
Robert Berthold Photography, pg 14
Candlelight Trust T/A Candlelight Farm, pg 17
Chiron Media, pg 18
CSIRO Publishing (Commonwealth Scientific & Industrial Research Organisation), pg 19
Dabill Publications, pg 20
Deakin University Press, pg 20
Dellasta Publishing, pg 20
Envirobook, pg 22
The Federation Press, pg 22
Hartys Creek Press, pg 25
Illert Publications, pg 27
Law Book Co Information Services, pg 29
McGraw-Hill Australia Pty Ltd, pg 32
Mulavon Press Pty Ltd, pg 34
Ocean Press, pg 35
Oxfam Community Aid Abroad, pg 36
Palms Press, pg 36
Pioneer Design Studio Pty Ltd, pg 38
Pluto Press Australia, pg 38
Prospect Media Pty Ltd, pg 39
The Pythagorean Press, pg 39
Rainforest Publishing, pg 39
Reed Educational Publishing Australia, pg 40
Royal Society of New South Wales, pg 41
Spinifex Press, pg 43
Terania Rainforest Publishing, pg 44
University of New South Wales Press Ltd, pg 46
Vista Publications, pg 47
Wakefield Press Pty Ltd, pg 47
Yanagang Publishing, pg 48

Austria
Abakus Verlag GmbH, pg 49
Bohmann Druck und Verlag GmbH & Co KG, pg 50
IAEA - International Atomic Energy Agency, pg 53
International Institute for Applied Systems Analysis (IIASA), pg 53
NOI - Verlag, pg 55
Oesterreichischer Agrarverlag, Druck- und Verlags- GmbH, pg 56
Verlag Orac im Verlag Kremayr & Scheriau, pg 56
Anna Pichler Verlag GmbH, pg 57
Springer-Verlag Wien, pg 59

Bangladesh
The University Press Ltd, pg 62

Belarus
Narodnaya Asveta, pg 63

Belgium
Artel SC, pg 64
Editions De Boeck-Larcier SA, pg 67
Leuven University Press, pg 71
Presses agronomiques de Gembloux ASBL, pg 73
VUB University Press, pg 75

Botswana
The Botswana Society, pg 77

Brazil
Editora Aquariana Ltda, pg 78
Editora Campus Ltda, pg 80
Comissao Nacional de Energia Nuclear, pg 81
Editora Gaia Ltda, pg 84
Editora Globo SA, pg 84
Editora Ground Ltda, pg 84
Editora Guanabara Koogan SA, pg 84
Editora Index Ltda, pg 85
Qualitymark Editora Ltda, pg 90
Editora Scipione Ltda, pg 91

Bulgaria
Darzhavno Izdatelstvo Zemizdat, pg 95
EnEffect, Center for Energy Efficiency, pg 95
Gea-Libris Publishing House, pg 95
Pensoft Publishers, pg 97

Chile
Arrayan Editores, pg 99
Cetal Ediciones, pg 100

China
Beijing Medical Univ Press, pg 102
Chemical Industry Press, pg 102
China Ocean Press, pg 103
East China University of Science & Technology Press, pg 105
Jiangsu Science & Technology Publishing House, pg 106
Jilin Science & Technology Publishing House, pg 106
Metallurgical Industry Press (MIP), pg 107
Nanjing University Press, pg 107
Science Press, pg 108
Shandong Science & Technology Press, pg 109
Shandong University Press, pg 109
Water Resources and Electric Power Press (CWPP), pg 110
Xi'an Cartography Publishing House, pg 110

Colombia
Amazonas Editores Ltda, pg 111
Tercer Mundo Editores SA, pg 113
Unidad Universitaria del Sur (UNISUR), pg 114

The Democratic Republic of the Congo
Centre de Vulgarisation Agricole, pg 115

Costa Rica
Academia de Centro America, pg 115
Centro Agronomico Tropical de Investigacion y Ensenanza (CATIE), pg 115
Instituto Interamericano de Cooperacion para la Agricultura (IICA), pg 116
Scout Interamericana, pg 117
Union Mundial para la Naturaleza (UICN), Oficina Regional para Mesoamerica, pg 117
Editorial de la Universidad de Costa Rica, pg 117

Cote d'Ivoire
Universite d' Abidjan, pg 118

Croatia
Drzavna Uprava za Zastitu Prirode i Okolisa (State Directorate for the Protection of Nature & Environment), pg 118

Cuba
ISCAH Fructuoso Rodriguez, pg 121

Czech Republic
Doplnek, pg 124
Cesky normalizacni institut, pg 127

Denmark
Bogfabrikken Fakta ApS, pg 130
Borgens Forlag A/S, pg 130
GEC Gads Forlag Aktieselskab af 1994, pg 132
Host & Son Publishers Ltd, pg 133
Forlaget Hovedland, pg 133
Mellemfolkeligt Samvirke, pg 133
Samfundslitteratur, pg 135
J H Schultz Information A/S, pg 135
Statens Information (Danish State Information Service), pg 135

Dominican Republic
Pontificia Universidad Catolica Madre y Maestra, pg 136

Ecuador
Ediciones Abya-Yala, pg 137

Fiji
University of the South Pacific, pg 141

Finland
Yliopistopaino/Helsinki University Press, pg 145

France
Annales de la Recherche Urbaine, pg 147
Editions de l'Aube, pg 149
Pierre Bordas et Fils, pg 151
Presses Universitaires de Bordeaux (PUB), pg 151
Editions Bornemann, pg 151
Editions BRGM, pg 152
Cemagref Editions, pg 153
CNRS Editions, pg 155
Courrier du Livre Sarl, pg 157
Editeurs Crepin-Leblond, pg 157
Editions du Demi-Cercle, pg 158
Institut pour le Developpement Forestier, pg 159
La Documentation Francaise, pg 159
Edicef - Editions Classiques d'Expression Francaise, pg 161
Edisud, pg 161
Editions Grund, pg 161
Editions Entente, pg 162
Institut Francais de Recherche pour l'Exploitation de la Mer (IFREMER), pg 165
Futuribles SARL, pg 165
Editions Hatier SA, pg 168
INRA Editions (Institut National de la Recherche Agronomique), pg 169
IRD Editions, pg 170
Lavoisier, pg 172
Editions Legislatives, pg 172
John Libbey Eurotext, pg 173
Le Livre de Poche-L G F (Librairie Generale Francaise), pg 173
Revue Espaces et Societes, pg 183
Editions Sang de la Terre, pg 183
Selection du Reader's Digest SA, pg 184
Service des Publications Scientifiques du Museum National d 'Histoire Naturelle, pg 184
Societe Nouveaux Loisirs, pg 185
La Vague Verte, pg 188

Germany
Aerogie-Verlag, pg 191
ALS-Verlag GmbH, pg 193
AOL-Verlag Frohmut Menze, pg 194
Roland Asanger Verlag GmbH, pg 195
Baken-Verlag Walter Schnoor, pg 198
Dr Wolfgang Baur Verlag Kunst & Alltag, pg 199
Bauverlag GmbH, pg 199
Bayerischer Schulbuch-Verlag GmbH, pg 199
Berlin Verlag Arno Spitz GmbH, pg 200
Bettendorf'sche Verlagsanstalt GmbH, pg 202
Beuth Verlag GmbH, pg 202
Blackwell Wissenschafts-Verlag GmbH, pg 203
Eberhargd Blottner Verlag, pg 204
Deutscher Verlag fur Grundstoffindustrie GmbH, pg 215
Deutscher Wirtschaftsdienst John von Freyend GmbH, pg 216
Verlag J H W Dietz Nachf GmbH, pg 217
DLV
Deutscher Landwirtschaftsverlag Berlin, pg 217
agenda Verlag Thomas Dominikowski, pg 217
Dreisam Ratgeber in der Rutsker Verlag GmbH, pg 218
Duncker und Humblot GmbH, pg 219

E Schweizerbart'sche Verlagsbuchhandlung (Nagele und Obermiller), pg 220
Echo Verlag, pg 220
Ecomed Verlagsgesellschaft AG & Co KG, pg 220
EinfallsReich Verlagsgesellschaft MbH, pg 222
Elektor-Verlag GmbH, pg 222
expert verlag GmbH, Fachverlag fur Wirtschaft & Technik, pg 225
Fabel-Verlag Gudrun Liebchen, pg 226
Fachbuchverlag Leipzig im Carl Hanser Verlag, pg 226
Focus-Verlag Gesellschaft mbH, pg 229
Fraunhofer IRB Verlag Fraunhofer Informationszentrum Raum und Bau, pg 229
Verlag A Fromm im Druck- u Verlagshaus Fromm GmbH & Co KG, pg 230
Garbe Verlag Ellen Vogt, pg 231
Alfons W Gentner Verlag GmbH & Co KG, pg 231
Verlag Glueckauf GmbH, pg 233
Lehrmittelverlag Wilhelm Hagemann GmbH, pg 236
Carl Hanser Verlag, pg 237
Hessisches Ministerium fuer Umwelt, Landwirtschaft und Forsten, pg 240
F Hirthammer Verlag GmbH, pg 241
Horlemann Verlag, pg 243
IKO Verlag fur Interkulturelle Kommunikation, pg 244
Justus-Liebig-Universitat Giessen, pg 247
Kallmeyer'sche Verlagsbuchhandlung GmbH, pg 247
Kleiner Bachmann Verlag fur Kinder und Umwelt, pg 250
Franckh-Kosmos Verlags-GmbH & Co, pg 252
Verlag Waldemar Kramer, pg 253
Kulturbuch-Verlag GmbH, pg 254
Landbuch-Verlagsgesellschaft mbH, pg 255
Institut fuer Landes- und Stadtentwicklungsforschung, ILS Nordrhein-Westfalen, pg 255
Verlag Leske plus Budrich GmbH, pg 257
Libertas- Europaeisches Institut GmbH, pg 257
Margraf Verlag, pg 261
Metropolis- Verlag fur Okonomie, Gesellschaft und Politik GmbH, pg 263
Verlag Stephanie Naglschmid, pg 266
Verlag Natur & Wissenschaft Harro Hieronimus & Dr Jurgen Schmidt, pg 266
Neue Erde Verlags GmbH, pg 267
Neuer Weg Verlag und Druck GmbH, pg 268
Neumann Verlag, pg 268
Nusscr Verlag, pg 269
Oeko-Test Verlag GmbH & Co KG Betriebsgesellschaft, pg 269
Oekobuch Verlag & Versand GmbH, pg 269
Oekotopia Verlag, Wolfgang Hoffman, pg 270
Pala-Verlag GmbH, pg 271
Palazzi Verlags GmbH, pg 271
Pollner Verlag, pg 274
Pro Natur Verlag GmbH, pg 275

Psychologie Verlags Union GmbH, pg 275
Dr Josef Raabe-Verlags GmbH, pg 276
Reed Elsevier Deutschland GmbH, pg 277
Verlag an der Ruhr GmbH, pg 281
Ryvellus Medienagentur Dopfer, pg 281
Schapen Edition, H W Louis, pg 282
Schillinger Verlag GmbH, pg 283
Erich Schmidt Verlag GmbH & Co, pg 283
Heinrich Schwab Verlag, pg 285
Seibt Verlag GmbH, pg 286
Adolf Sponholtz Verlag, pg 288
Springer-Verlag GmbH & Co KG, pg 288
Stiefel GmbH Wandkarten Verlag, pg 290
TUeV-Verlag GmbH, pg 295
Guenter Albert Ulmer Verlag, pg 295
Verlag Eugen Ulmer GmbH & Co, pg 295
UNO-Verlag mbH, Vertriebs und Verlagsgesellschaft, pg 296
VAS-Verlag fuer Akademische Schriften, Vas Karl-Heinz Balon, pg 297
Vogel Medien GmbH & Co KG, pg 299
Vulkan-Verlag GmbH, pg 299
Weber Zucht & Co, pg 300
WEKA Firmengruppe GmbH & Co KG, pg 301
Verlagsgruppe Weltbild GmbH, pg 301
Zebulon Verlag GmbH & Co KG, pg 305

Ghana
Ghana Institute of Linguistics Literacy & Bible Translation (GILLBT), pg 307
Sub-Saharan Publishers, pg 308
Unimax Macmillan Ltd, pg 308

Greece
Boukoumanis' Editions, pg 309
Exandas Publishers, pg 310
Papazissis Publishers SA, pg 314

Guinea-Bissau
Instituto Nacional de Estudos e Pesquisa, pg 316

Holy See (Vatican City State)
Pontificia Academia Scientiarum, pg 317

Honduras
Editorial Guaymuras, pg 318

Hong Kong
Friends of the Earth (Charity) Ltd, pg 320
Hong Kong University Press, pg 320
Island Press, pg 320
Joint Publishing (HK) Co Ltd, pg 320

Hungary
CEU-Press, pg 323
Foldmuvelesugyi Miniszterium Muszaki Intezet, pg 323
Mezoegazda Kiado, pg 325

India
Agricole Publishing Academy, pg 330
Anmol Publications Pvt Ltd, pg 331
APH Publishing Corp, pg 331
Bani Mandir, Book-Sellers, Publishers & Educational Suppliers, pg 332
BS Publications, pg 334
BSMPS - M/s Bishen Singh Mahendra Pal Singh, pg 334
Concept Publishing Co, pg 335
Daya Publishing House, pg 336
Frank Brothers & Co (Publishers) Ltd, pg 337
Gyan Publishing House, pg 338
Indus Publishing Co, pg 339
International Book Distributors, pg 340
Kali For Women, pg 341
Khanna Publishers, pg 341
Law Publishers, pg 341
Ministry of Information & Broadcasting, pg 342
Narosa Publishing House, pg 343
National Book Organization, pg 343
Naya Prokash, pg 344
Omsons Publications, pg 345
Pointer Publishers, pg 346
Radiant Publishers, pg 347
Regency Publications, pg 347
Reliance Publishing House, pg 347
Sage Publications India Pvt Ltd, pg 348
Scientific Book Agency, pg 349
Sita Publications, pg 350
South Asian Publishers Pvt Ltd, pg 350

Indonesia
Karya Anda, CV, pg 356
Lembaga Demografi Fakultas Ekonomi Universitas Indonesia, pg 356
Yayasan Obor Indonesia, pg 357

Ireland
The Economic & Social Research Institute, pg 360
Environmental Research Unit, pg 360
Gandon Editions, pg 360
O'Brien Educational, pg 363
Roberts Rinehart Publishers, pg 363
Royal Irish Academy, pg 364
Tir Eolas, pg 364

Israel
Freund Publishing House Ltd, pg 367
The Israel Academy of Sciences & Humanities, pg 368

Italy
Gruppo Abele, pg 374
Edizioni Abete, pg 374
Arcadia Edizioni Srl, pg 376
Edizioni Cultura della Pace, pg 383
Datanews, pg 384
Ediciclo Editore SRL, pg 386
Folini, pg 389
Edizioni Futuro SRL, pg 389
Edizioni GB, pg 390
Vincenzo Lo Faro Editore, pg 396
Macro Edizioni, pg 397
Pitagora Editrice SRL, pg 403
Priuli e Verlucca, Editori, pg 404
Red/Studio Redazionale SpA, pg 405
SEMAR Publishers SRL, pg 407
Edizioni Zara, pg 412

Jamaica
American Chamber of Commerce of Jamaica, pg 412
University of the West Indies Press, pg 414

Japan
Bun-ichi Sogo Shuppan, pg 415
Diamond Inc, pg 416
Gakken Co Ltd, pg 416
Kaisei-Sha Publishing Co Ltd, pg 419
Koyo Shobo, pg 420
Nippon Hoso Shuppan Kyokai (NHK Publishing), pg 422
Nobunkyo (Rural Village Culture Association), pg 423
Toppan Co Ltd, pg 428
Tsukiji Shokan Publishing Co, pg 428
United Nations University Press, pg 428

Kazakstan
Kazakh Al-Farabi State National University, pg 430

Kenya
Academy Science Publishers, pg 430
African Centre for Technology Studies (ACTS), pg 431
International Centre for Research in Agroforestry (ICRAF), pg 432
Kenya Energy & Environment Organisation, Kengo, pg 432
Kenya Medical Research Institute (KEMRI), pg 432
Kenya Meteorological Department, pg 432
Phoenix Publishers, pg 433
Tree Shade Technical Services, pg 433

Republic of Korea
Dae Won Sa Co Ltd, pg 435
Gim-Yeong Co, pg 436
Koreaone Press Inc, pg 438

Latvia
Nordik/Tapals Publishers Ltd, pg 442
Preses Nams, pg 442

Madagascar
Tsipika Edition, pg 450

Malaysia
Penerbit Jayatinta Sdn Bhd, pg 454
Pustaka Delta Pelajaran Sdn Bhd, pg 454

Maldive Islands
Non-Formal Education Centre, pg 455

Mexico
Arbol Editorial SA de CV, pg 458
Centro de Estudios Mexicanos y Centroamericanos, pg 458
El Colegio de Mexico AC, pg 459
El Colegio de Michoacan A C, pg 460
Fernandez Editores SA de CV, pg 461
Grupo Editorial Iberoamerica, SA de CV, pg 461
Ediciones Roca, SA, pg 466

SUBJECT INDEX

Namibia
Desert Research Foundation of Namibia (DRFN), pg 471
Multi-Disciplinary Research Centre Library, pg 471

Netherlands
Uitgeverij Jan van Arkel, pg 473
A A Balkema, pg 473
Boom Uitgeverij, pg 474
Hagen & Stam Uitgeverij Ten, pg 478
IOS Press BV, pg 479
KITLV Press Royal Institute of Linguistics & Anthropology, pg 479
Koninklijk Instituut Voor de Tropen, pg 480
Koninklijke Vermande bv, pg 480
Uitgeverij Het Spectrum BV, pg 484
Twente University Press, pg 485

New Zealand
Lincoln College Centre for Resource Management, pg 492
RSVP Publishing Company Ltd, pg 495
SIR Publishing, pg 495
University of Otago Press, pg 496

Nigeria
Evans Brothers (Nigeria Publishers) Ltd, pg 499
JAD Publishers Ltd, pg 500
Riverside Communications, pg 501

Norway
NKI Forlaget, pg 504
Vett & Viten AS, pg 505

Pakistan
Pakistan Institute of Development Economics, pg 508

Papua New Guinea
National Research Institute of Papua New Guinea, pg 510

Philippines
Ateneo de Manila University Press, pg 512
Claretian Communications Inc, pg 513
Communication Foundation for Asia Media Group (CFAMG), pg 513
Rex Bookstores & Publishers, pg 514
SIBS Publishing House Inc, pg 515

Poland
Wydawnictwo Arkady, pg 516
Polskie Wydawnictwo Ekonomiczne PWE SA, pg 516
Impuls, pg 517
Instytut Meteorologii i Gospodarki Wodnej, pg 518
Ossolineum Zaklad Narodowy im Ossolinskich - Wydawnictwo, pg 518
Oficyna Wydawnicza Politechniki Wroclawskiej, pg 519
Panstwowe Wydawnictwo Rolnicze i Lesne, pg 519

Portugal
Publicacoes Ciencia e Vida Lda, pg 523
Edicoes Colibri, pg 523
Difusao Cultural, pg 524
Gradiva-Publicacnoes Lda, pg 525
Instituto de Investigacao Cientifica Tropical, pg 526
McGraw-Hill Editora de Portugal, pg 527

Romania
Editura Ceres, pg 532

Russian Federation
Izdatelstvo Ekologija, pg 537
Energoatomizdat, pg 537
FGUP Izdatelstvo Mashinostroenie, pg 538
Finansy i Statistika Publishing House, pg 538
Gidrometeoizdat, pg 538
Izdatel 'stvo Kazanskago Universiteta, pg 538
Izdatelstvo Mir, pg 540
Nauka Publishers, pg 540
Izdatel'stvo Nizhegorodskogo Gosudarstvennogo Univ, pg 540

Senegal
CODESRIA (Council for the Development of Social Science Research in Africa), pg 544

Singapore
APAC Publishers Services, pg 545
Institute of Southeast Asian Studies, pg 546
Singapore University Press Pte Ltd, pg 548
Taylor & Francis Asia Pacific, pg 548

Slovakia
Technicka Univerzita, pg 551

South Africa
Ashanti Publishing, pg 552
Jacana Education, pg 555
National Botanical Institute, pg 557
New Africa Books (Pty) Ltd, pg 557
Oceanographic Research Institute, pg 558
Ravan Press (Pty) Ltd, pg 558
Struik Publishers (Pty) Ltd, pg 559

Spain
Editorial AEDOS SA, pg 561
Cedel, Ediciones Jose O Avila Monteso ES, pg 567
Institut d'Estudis Vallencs (IEV), pg 574
Fundacion Marcelino Botin, pg 575
Icaria Editorial SA, pg 577
Editorial Incafo SA, pg 578
Mandala Ediciones, pg 581
OASIS, Producciones Generales de Comunicacion, pg 584
Editorial Parthenon Communication, SL, pg 586
Editora Regional de Murcia - ERM, pg 588
Rueda, SL Editorial, pg 589
Tursen, SA, pg 593

Sri Lanka
Swarna Hansa Foundation, pg 598

Switzerland
Birkhauser Verlag AG, pg 610
Daimon Verlag AG, pg 612
Georg Editeur SA, pg 614
Helbing und Lichtenhahn Verlag AG, pg 615
Verlag Huber & Co AG, pg 616
Interfrom AG Editions, pg 616
Editions Jouvence, pg 616
Verlag Friedrich Reinhardt AG, pg 622
SAB Schweiz Arbeitsgemeinschaft fuer die Berggebiete, pg 623
Vdf Hochschulverlag AG an der ETH Zurich, pg 626
Buchverlag der Druckerei Wetzikon AG, pg 627

Syrian Arab Republic
Damascus University Press, pg 628

Taiwan, Province of China
Fuh-Wen Book Co, pg 630
Chu Hai Publishing (Taiwan) Co Ltd, pg 630
Morning Star Publisher Inc, pg 631
Petroleum Information Publishing Co, pg 631

United Republic of Tanzania
Press & Publicity Centre Ltd, pg 634
Tema Publishers Ltd, pg 634

Tunisia
Ceres Editions, pg 637

Turkey
Arkadas Ltd, pg 639
Kubbealti Akademisi Kultur ve Sasat Vakfi, pg 640

Uganda
Centre for Basic Research, pg 642

Ukraine
Naukova Dumka Publishers, pg 643
Urozaj, pg 643

United Kingdom
Academic Press Ltd, pg 644
Acair Ltd, pg 645
Anglo-German Foundation for the Study of Industrial Society, pg 647
Arnold, pg 648
Artetech Publishing Co, pg 649
Ashgate Publishing Ltd, pg 649
Banson, pg 652
Belitha Press Ltd, pg 653
Bellew Publishing Co Ltd, pg 653
Cambridge University Press, pg 662
Cameron & Hollis, pg 663
Capall Bann Publishing, pg 663
Jon Carpenter Publishing, pg 664
Cassell & Co, pg 664
Centaur Press (1954), pg 665
The Chartered Institute of Building, pg 666
E W Classey Ltd, pg 668
Colour Library Direct, pg 669
Commonwealth Secretariat, pg 669
CTBI Publications, pg 672
James Currey Ltd, pg 673
Terence Dalton Ltd, pg 673
Earthscan Publications Ltd, pg 677
Edinburgh University Press Ltd, pg 677
Element Books Ltd, pg 678
Edward Elgar Publishing Ltd, pg 678
Elsevier Science Ltd, pg 678
ERA Technology Ltd, pg 679
European Schoolbooks Ltd, pg 680
The Eurospan Group, pg 680
Forth Naturalist & Historian, pg 683
W H Freeman & Co Ltd, pg 684
Gaia Books Ltd, pg 685
Gateway Books, pg 686
Green Books Ltd, pg 689
Harley Books, pg 692
Heretic Books Ltd, pg 695
Hyden House Ltd, pg 698
ICC United Kingdom, pg 698
Institute of Development Studies, pg 699
Intercept Ltd, pg 700
Intermediate Technology Publications Ltd, pg 700
James & James (Publishers) Ltd, pg 702
James & James (Science Publishers) Ltd, pg 702
Lawrence & Wishart, pg 706
Letterbox Library, pg 707
Liverpool University Press, pg 708
MIT Press Ltd, pg 715
Multilingual Matters Ltd, pg 716
National Extension College, pg 717
Nelson Thornes Ltd, pg 718
Packard Publishing Ltd, pg 723
Panos Institute, pg 723
The Parthenon Publishing Group Ltd, pg 724
Pearson Education, pg 725
Pluto Press, pg 728
Pomegranate Europe Ltd, pg 729
T & AD Poyser Ltd, pg 730
Prism Press Book Publishers Ltd, pg 730
Profile Books Ltd, pg 731
Ravette Publishing Ltd, pg 733
Regency Press CP Ltd, pg 734
The Richmond Publishing Co Ltd, pg 735
Roadmaster Publishing, pg 735
Royal Institute of International Affairs, pg 736
Sage Publications Ltd, pg 737
Science Reviews Ltd, pg 739
Scottish Cultural Press, pg 739
Scottish Office Library & Information Services, pg 740
The Society of Metaphysicians Ltd, pg 743
Southgate Publishers, pg 743
Spokesman, pg 744
Spon Press, pg 744
The Stationery Office, pg 745
Stokesby House Publications, pg 745
Tarragon Press, pg 746
Thistle Press, pg 748
Tuckwell Press Ltd, pg 750
UCL Press Ltd, pg 751
Westview Press, pg 755
WIT Press, pg 757
The Women's Press Ltd, pg 758
Yale University Press London, pg 759
Zed Books Ltd, pg 759

Uruguay
Nordan-Comunidad, pg 760

Venezuela
Armitano Editores CA, pg 761
Editorial Nueva Sociedad, pg 762

Viet Nam
Science & Technics Publishing House, pg 763

Zambia
ZPC Publications, pg 767

Zimbabwe
Action Magazine, pg 767
Anvil Press, pg 767
College Press Publishers (Pvt) Ltd, pg 768
Longman Zimbabwe (Pvt) Ltd, pg 768
Nehanda Publishers, pg 769
Sapes Trust Ltd, pg 769

EROTICA

Brazil
Editora Lidador Ltda, pg 86

France
Editions Dominique Leroy, pg 172

Germany
Droemersche Verlagsanstalt Th Knaur Nachfolger GmbH & Co, pg 218
Hyperion - Verlag, pg 244
TASCHEN GmbH, pg 292
Treves Editions Verein Zur Foerderung der Kuenstlerischen Taetigkeiten, pg 295

Greece
Exandas Publishers, pg 310

Iceland
Frodi Ltd, pg 328

India
Roli Books Pvt Ltd, pg 348

Italy
Ernesto Gremese Editore SRL, pg 391

South Africa
Janssen Publishers CC, pg 556

Spain
Ediciones 29 - Libros Rio Nuevo, pg 594

United Kingdom
Atlas Press, pg 651
Carlton Publishing Group, pg 664
Compendium Publishing, pg 670
Constable Publishers, pg 670
Creation Books, pg 671
Delectus Books, pg 675
Polybooks Ltd, pg 729
Charles Skilton Ltd, pg 742
Virgin Publishing Ltd, pg 753

ETHNICITY

Afghanistan
Government Press, pg 1
Historical Society of Afghanistan, pg 1

Argentina
ECA (Ediciones Culturales Argentinas), pg 5
Editorial Sopena Argentina SACI e I, pg 9
Manrique Zago Ediciones SRL, pg 10

Australia
Aboriginal Studies Press, pg 10
Allen & Unwin Pty Ltd, The Australian Newspaper, Vogel Breads, pg 11
Artemis Publishing Pty Ltd, pg 12
Athena Press, pg 12
Ausmed Publications Pty Ltd, pg 12
Centre for Comparative Literature & Cultural Studies, pg 17
Dangaroo Press, pg 20
Indra Publishing, pg 27
Int Press, pg 28
Papyrus Publishing, pg 37
Polliteicon Publications, pg 38
State Library of NSW Press, pg 43
Tom Publications, pg 45

Austria
Aarachne Verlag, pg 49
CEEBA Publications Antenne d'Autriche, pg 50
Dachs-Verlag GmbH, pg 50
Development News Ltd, pg 51
NOI - Verlag, pg 55
E Perlinger Naturprodukte Handelsgesellschaft mbH, pg 57
Dr A Schendl GmbH und Co KG, pg 58
Edition Tusch, pg 59
Edition Va Bene, pg 60

Belgium
Centre Aequatoria, pg 64
Creadif, pg 67
Cremers (Schoollandkaarten) PVBA, pg 67
Sonneville Press (Uitgeverij) VTW, pg 74
Stichting Ons Erfdeel VZW, pg 74
Editions Techniques et Scientifiques SPRL, pg 74

Brazil
Pallas Editora e Distribuidora Ltda, pg 89

Bulgaria
Bilblioteka Nov den - Sajuz na Svobodnite Demokrati (Union of Free Democrats), pg 94
CHRIKER, pg 94

Burundi
Editions Intore, pg 98

Chile
Arrayan Editores, pg 99

China
Commercial Press (Hong Kong) Ltd, pg 104
Xinhua Publishing House, pg 110

The Democratic Republic of the Congo
Presses Universitaires du Zaiire (PUZ), pg 115

Croatia
Hrvatsko filozofsko drustvo, pg 119
Sveucilisna tiskara doo, pg 120

Cuba
Casa de las Americas, pg 120

Cyprus
MAM (The House of the Cyprus & Cyprological Publications), pg 122
Nikoklis Publishers, pg 122

Czech Republic
Nakladatelstvi Blok, pg 123
Galaxie, vydavatelelstvi a nakladatelstvi, pg 124
Vysehrad, pg 129

Denmark
Arnkrone Forlaget A/S, pg 130
Dansk Historisk Handbogsforlag ApS, pg 131
Mellemfolkeligt Samvirke, pg 133
Strandbergs Forlag, pg 135
Tiderne Skifter Forlag A/S, pg 136

Estonia
Estonian Academic Library, pg 139

Fiji
Lotu Pacifika Productions, pg 141

Finland
Kirja-Leitzinger, pg 143

France
Editions d'Amerique et d'Orient, Adrien Maisonneuve, pg 147
Annales de la Recherche Urbaine, pg 147
Editions d'Aujourd'hui (Les Introuvables), pg 149
Berger-Levrault SA, pg 150
CLD, pg 155
CNRS Editions, pg 155
Editions du Comite des Travaux Historiques et Scientifiques (CTHS), pg 156
Edisud, pg 161
Editions Recherche sur les Civilisations (ERC), pg 161
Institut d'Ethnologie du Museum National d'Histoire Naturelle, pg 163
Laffitte Reprints, pg 171
Editions de la Reunion des Musees Nationaux, pg 176
Editions Parentheses, pg 179
Editions A et J Picard SA, pg 179
Editions Jean Picollec, pg 179
Sepia, pg 184

French Polynesia
Haere Po No Tahiti, pg 190

Germany
Dr Wolfgang Baur Verlag Kunst & Alltag, pg 199
BKV-Brasilienkunde Verlag GmbH, pg 203
Brandes & Apsel Verlag GmbH, pg 206
Hans Christians Druckerei und Verlag GmbH & Co, pg 210
Eugen Diederichs Verlag GmbH & Co KG, pg 216
Domowina Verlag GmbH, pg 217
Verlag A Fromm im Druck- u Verlagshaus Fromm GmbH & Co KG, pg 230
IKO Verlag fur Interkulturelle Kommunikation, pg 244
Insel Verlag, pg 245
Verlag Koenigshausen und Neumann GmbH, pg 251

Dr Anton Kovac Slavica Verlag, pg 253
Lettre International Kulturzeitung, pg 257
LIT Verlag, pg 258
Verlag Neue Musikzeitung GmbH, pg 267
Oekumenischer Verlag Dr R-F Edel, pg 270
Orlanda Frauenverlag, pg 270
Edition Parabolis, pg 271
Propylaeen Verlag, Zweigniederlassung Berlin der Ullstein Buchverlage GmbH, pg 275
Dr Mohan Krischke Ramaswamy Edition RE, pg 277
Konrad Reich Verlag GmbH, pg 278
Dietrich Reimer Verlag GmbH, pg 278
Wilhelm Schmitz Verlag, pg 284
Otto Schwartz Fachbochhandlung GmbH, pg 286
Tuduv Verlagsgesellschaft mbH, pg 295
Tuebinger Vereinigung fur Volkskunde eV (TVV), pg 295
Vervuert Verlagsgesellschaft, pg 298
VS Verlagshaus Stuttgart GmbH, pg 299
VWB-Verlag fur Wissenschaft & Bildung, Amand Aglaster, pg 300
Waxmann Verlag GmbH, pg 300
Verlagsgruppe Weltbild GmbH, pg 301
Verlag Wissenschaft und Politik/Helker Pflug, pg 303

Ghana
Ghana Publishing Corporation, pg 307
Moxon Paperbacks, pg 307
Waterville Publishing House, pg 308

Greece
Denise Harvey, pg 311
Ianos, pg 311
Idryma Meleton Chersonisou tou Aimou, pg 311
Nea Thesis - Evrotas, pg 313
Stochastis, pg 315

Honduras
Editorial Guaymuras, pg 318

Hong Kong
The Dharmasthiti Buddist Institute Ltd, pg 319

India
Abhinav Publications, pg 329
Ajanta Publications (India), pg 330
Amar Prakashan, pg 330
APH Publishing Corp, pg 331
Asian Educational Services, pg 331
Bani Mandir, Book-Sellers, Publishers & Educational Suppliers, pg 332
Bharatiya Vidya Bhavan, pg 333
Central Tibetan Secretariat, pg 334
Chanakya Publications, pg 334
Concept Publishing Co, pg 335
Cosmo Publications, pg 335
Indian Council for Cultural Relations, pg 339
Indian Institute of World Culture, pg 339
Inter-India Publications, pg 340
Jaico Publishing House, pg 340
Lalit Kala Akademi, pg 341

Manohar Publishers & Distributors, pg 342
Minerva Associates (Publications) Pvt Ltd, pg 342
Ministry of Information & Broadcasting, pg 342
Mudgala Trust, pg 343
National Museum, pg 344
National Publishing House, pg 344
Navrang Booksellers & Publishers, pg 344
Navyug Publishers, pg 344
Pankaj Publications, pg 345
Parimal Prakashan, pg 345
Regency Publications, pg 347
Reliance Publishing House, pg 347
Sasta Sahitya Mandal, pg 349
DB Taraporevala Sons & Co Pvt Ltd, pg 351
N M Tripathi Pvt Ltd, pg 352
Vani Prakashan, pg 352
Vikas Publishing House Pvt Ltd, pg 353

Indonesia
Balai Pustaka, pg 354
Dunia Pustaka Jaya, pg 355
Lembaga Demografi Fakultas Ekonomi Universitas Indonesia, pg 356
Yayasan Lontar, pg 357

Ireland
Dublin Institute for Advanced Studies, pg 360
The Educational Company of Ireland, pg 360
Fitzwilliam Publishing Co Ltd, pg 360
Mercier Press Ltd, pg 362
Ossian Publications, pg 363
Raven Arts Press, pg 363
Roberts Rinehart Publishers, pg 363
Royal Irish Academy, pg 364

Israel
Ben-Zvi Institute, pg 365
Habermann Institute for Literary Research, pg 367
The Institute for Israeli Arabs Studies, pg 368
Misgav Yerushalayim, pg 370
Urim Publications, pg 373

Italy
Gruppo Abele, pg 374
Adriatica Editrice, pg 374
Edizioni Brenner, pg 378
Capone Editore SRL, pg 379
Centro Studi Terzo Mondo, pg 381
Edizioni Cultura della Pace, pg 383
La Culturale, pg 383
Datanews, pg 384
Edizioni del Centro, pg 384
Editalia (Edizioni d'Italia), pg 386
Edizioni Il Punto d'Incontro SAS, pg 386
ERGA SNC di Carla Ottino Merli & C (Edizioni Realizzazioni Grafiche - Artigiana), pg 388
Adriano Gallina Editore sas, pg 389
Galzerano Editore, pg 390
Grafica e Arte SRL, pg 391
Grafo Edizioni, pg 391
L Japadre Editore, pg 394
Lalli Editore SRL, pg 395
Officina Edizioni di Aldo Quinti, pg 401
Pizzicato Edizioni Musicali, pg 403
Priuli e Verlucca, Editori, pg 404

SAGEP, pg 406
Sapere 2000 SRL, pg 407

Jamaica
Institute of Jamaica Publications, pg 413
The Press, pg 413
University of the West Indies Press, pg 414

Japan
Koyo Shobo, pg 420
Sagano Shoin, pg 424
Sobun-Sha, pg 426
Tankosha Publishing Co Ltd, pg 427
United Nations University Press, pg 428

Kenya
British Institute in Eastern Africa, pg 431

Luxembourg
Centre Culturel De Differdange, pg 447

Madagascar
Editions Ambozontany, pg 450

Malaysia
Holograms (M) Sdn Bhd, pg 452
Vinpress Sdn Bhd, pg 455

Malta
The University of Malta Publications Section, pg 456

Mexico
Centro de Estudios Mexicanos y Centroamericanos, pg 458
Ediciones Culturales Internacionales SA de CV Edicion Compra y Venta de Libros, Casetes, Videos, pg 459
Fondo de Cultura Economica, pg 461
Instituto Panamericano de Geografia e Historia, pg 465
Universidad Nacional Autonoma de Mexico (National University of Mexico), pg 467
Editorial Varazen SA, pg 468

Morocco
Les Editions du Journal L' Unite Maghrebine, pg 470

Myanmar
Sarpay Beikman Board, pg 471

Netherlands
De Walburg Pers, pg 476
Sociaal en Cultureel Planbureau, pg 484
Uitgeverij SUN, pg 484
Uitgeverij Waanders BV, pg 487

New Zealand
Barkfire Press, pg 488
Dunmore Press Ltd, pg 490
Huia Publishers, pg 492
Tandem Press, pg 496
Te Reo Publications, pg 496
Viking Sevenseas NZ Ltd, pg 496

Nicaragua
Editorial Nueva Nicaragua, pg 497

Nigeria
Adebara Publishers Ltd, pg 497
Ahmadu Bello University Press Ltd, pg 498
Alliance West African Publishers & Co, pg 498
CSS Bookshops, Agency & Publishing Division, pg 498
Daystar Press (Publishers), pg 498
Educational Research & Study Group, pg 499
Ethiope Publishing Corporation, pg 499
Heritage Books, pg 499
Ibadan University Press, pg 499
Ilesanmi Press (Educational Publishers) Ltd, pg 499
Institute of African Studies, Onyeka, A, pg 500
Longman Nigeria Plc, pg 500
Nwamife Publishers Ltd, pg 500
Obafemi Awolowo University Press Ltd, pg 501
Onibon-Oje Publishers, pg 501
University of Lagos Press, pg 502
University Publishing Co, pg 502

Norway
Hjemmenes Forlag, pg 504

Pakistan
Centre for South Asian Studies, pg 506
International Institute of Islamic Thought, pg 507
National Institute of Historical & Cultural Research, pg 508

Peru
Instituto de Estudios Peruanos, pg 511
Fondo Editorial de la Pontificia Universidad Catolica del Peru, pg 511
Libreria Studium SA, pg 511

Philippines
Garotech, pg 513
New Day Publishers, pg 514
Our Lady of Manaoag Publisher, pg 514
Vibal Publishing House Inc (VPHI), pg 515

Poland
KAW Krajowa Agencja Wydawnicza, pg 517
Panstwowy Instytut Wydawniczy (PIW), pg 518
Spotdzielna Anagram, pg 520
Wydawnictwa Uniwersytetu Warszawskiego, pg 521

Portugal
Bezerr-Editorae e Distribuidora de Abel Antonio Bezerra, pg 522
Imprensa Nacional-Casa da Moeda, pg 526
Instituto de Investigacao Cientifica Tropical, pg 526

Puerto Rico
Publishing Resources Inc, pg 531

Romania
Editura Excelsior, pg 533
Editura Kriterion SA, pg 534

Mentor Kiado, pg 534
Pallas-Akademia Koenyvkiadoes Koenyvkereskedes, pg 535

Russian Federation
Kabardino-Balkarskoye knizhnoye izdatelstvo, pg 539

Senegal
Centre Africain d'Animation et d'Echanges Culturels Editions Khoudia, pg 544
CODESRIA (Council for the Development of Social Science Research in Africa), pg 544
Les Nouvelles Editions Africaines du Senegal NEAS, pg 544

Sierra Leone
Sierra Leone University Press, pg 544

Singapore
Select Books Pte Ltd, pg 548
Taylor & Francis Asia Pacific, pg 548

Slovakia
Slo Viet, pg 550
Slovenske pedagogicke nakladateistvo, pg 550
Vydavatel' Sky odbor, pg 551

South Africa
Bet-El Publishers, pg 553
HAUM (Hollandsch Afrikaansche Uitgevers Maatschappij), pg 555
Ravan Press (Pty) Ltd, pg 558
Shuter & Shooter (Pty) Ltd, pg 559
South African Institute of Race Relations, pg 559

Spain
Edicions Alfons el Magnanim, Institucio Valenciana d'Estudis i Investigacio, pg 562
Curial Edicions Catalanes SA, pg 569
Rafael Dalmau, Editor, pg 569
Dilagro SA, pg 569
Mundo Negro Editorial, pg 583
OASIS, Producciones Generales de Comunicacion, pg 584
Ediciones del Oriente y del Mediterraneo, pg 585
Pages Editors, SL, pg 585
Editorial Presencia Gitana, pg 587
Instituto Provincial de Investigaciones y Estudios Toledanos, pg 588
Selecta-Catalonia Ed, pg 590
Editorial Txertoa, pg 594
Editorial Vicens-Vives, pg 595

Sri Lanka
International Centre for Ethnic Studies, pg 597
Karunaratne & Sons Ltd, pg 597
Ministry of Cultural Affairs, pg 597
National Library & Documentation Services Board, pg 597

Sudan
Khartoum University Press, pg 598

Suriname
Stichting Wetenschappelijke Informatie, pg 599

PUBLISHERS SUBJECT INDEX

Sweden
Alfabeta Bokforlag AB, pg 600
Industrilitteratur Vindex, Forlags AB, pg 603
Invandrarfoerlaget, pg 603
Mezopotamya Publishing & Distribution, pg 604
Bokforlaget Nya Doxa AB, pg 605

Switzerland
Bergli Books AG, pg 609
Dimension World Ltd, pg 612
Georg Editeur SA, pg 614
Th Gut Verlag, pg 615
Verlag Huber & Co AG, pg 616
Interfrom AG Editions, pg 616
ISIOM Verlag fur Tondokumente, Weinreb Tonarchiv, pg 616
Librairie-Editions J Marguerat, pg 618
Editions Olizane, pg 620
Punktum AG, Buchredaktion und Bildarchiv, pg 622
Verlag fuer Schoene Wissenschaften, pg 624
Strom-Verlag Luzern, pg 625
Der Universitatsverlag Freiburg, pg 626
Verlagsbuchhandlung AG, pg 626
Verlag im Waldgut AG, pg 627
Wepf & Co AG, pg 627

Taiwan, Province of China
Yee Wen Publishing Co Ltd, pg 632

Thailand
Suriyaban Publishers, pg 635
White Lotus Co Ltd, pg 636

Tunisia
Ceres Editions, pg 637
Faculte des Sciences Humaines et Sociales de Tunis, pg 638

Turkey
Ataturk Kultur, Dil ve Tarih, Yusek Kurumu Baskanligi, pg 639
Ezel Erverdi (Dergah Yayinlari AS) Muessese Muduru, pg 640
Iletisim Yayinlari, pg 640
Toker Yayinlari, pg 641
Alev Yayinlari, pg 642

Uganda
Centre for Basic Research, pg 642

Ukraine
Mystetstvo Publishers, pg 643

United Kingdom
Berg Publishers, pg 654
Bridge Books, pg 659
British Museum Press, pg 660
James Currey Ltd, pg 673
The Eurospan Group, pg 680
Free Association Books Ltd, pg 684
Institute of Irish Studies, The Queens University of Belfast, pg 699
Lawrence & Wishart, pg 706
Letterbox Library, pg 707
The Littman Library of Jewish Civilization, pg 708
Maney Publishing, pg 711
Adam Matthew Publications, pg 712
Old Vicarage Publications, pg 720
The Policy Press, pg 729
Pomegranate Europe Ltd, pg 729
Profile Books Ltd, pg 731

Routledge Curzon, pg 736
Sage Publications Ltd, pg 737
Serpent's Tail Ltd, pg 740
Shire Publications Ltd, pg 741
Thames & Hudson Ltd, pg 748
Trentham Books Ltd, pg 750
Verso, pg 752
Whiting & Birch Ltd, pg 756
The Women's Press Ltd, pg 758

Uruguay
Rosebud Ediciones, pg 761

Venezuela
Editorial Nueva Sociedad, pg 762

Zambia
Zambia Educational Publishing House, pg 767

FASHION

Australia
Australasian Textiles Publishers, pg 13
The Images Publishing Group Pty Ltd, pg 27
Little Hills Press, pg 30
National Gallery of Victoria, pg 34
OTEN (Open Training & Education Network), pg 36
RMIT Publishing, pg 41
Thames & Hudson (Australia) Pty Ltd, pg 44

Austria
Thomas Mlakar Verlag, pg 55

Brazil
Global Editora e Distribuidora Ltda, pg 84

China
China Film Press, pg 103
China Light Industry Press, pg 103
Shandong Friendship Press, pg 108
Shanghai Fine Arts Publishers, pg 109
Sichuan Science & Technology Publishing House, pg 109

Colombia
RAM Editores, pg 113

Costa Rica
Promesa, Ediciones, pg 116

Denmark
Bogfabrikken Fakta ApS, pg 130

France
Societe Nouvelle Adam Biro, pg 150
Georges-Charles Demay, pg 158
Association Frank, pg 165
Hachette Pratiques, pg 167
Paris Musees, pg 179
Editions Plume, pg 180
Revue Noire, pg 183
Soline, pg 186
Thames & Hudson, pg 187

Germany
Arnoldsche Verlagsanstalt GmbH, pg 195
Deutscher Fachverlag GmbH, pg 214

Extent Verlag und Service Wolfgang M Flamm, pg 225
Jahreszeiten-Verlag GmbH, pg 246
LIT Verlag, pg 258
mode information Heinz Kramer GmbH, pg 264
Naumann & Goebel Verlagsgesellschaft mbH, pg 267
Verlag Hans Schoener GmbH, pg 284
teNeues Verlag GmbH & Co KG, pg 292
Verlag fur die Frau GmbH, pg 297
Verlagsgruppe Weltbild GmbH, pg 301

Hungary
Szabad Ter Kiado, pg 326

Iceland
Frodi Ltd, pg 328

India
Nem Chand & Brothers, pg 344
Sita Publications, pg 350

Israel
R Sirkis Publishers Ltd, pg 372

Italy
Essegi, pg 388
Ernesto Gremese Editore SRL, pg 391
Idea Books, pg 393
Lybra Immagine, pg 397
Zanfi Editori SRL, pg 412

Japan
Bunkasha Publishing Co, Ltd, pg 415
Nippon Hoso Shuppan Kyokai (NHK Publishing), pg 422
Shufunotomo sha Co Ltd, pg 426

Kenya
Heinemann Kenya Limited (EAEP), pg 431

Republic of Korea
Suhagsa, pg 440

Mexico
Editorial Armonia SA, pg 458
Janibi Editores SA de CV, pg 462
Ediciones Libra, SA de CV, pg 463
Libros y Revistas SA de CV, pg 463
Sayrols Editorial SA de CV, pg 466

Netherlands
The Pepin Press, pg 482

Pakistan
Maqbool Academy, pg 508

Portugal
Impala, pg 525
Vega-Publicacao e Distribuicao de Livros e Revistas, Lda, pg 530

Romania
Editura Meridiane, pg 534

Spain
Editorial Astri SA, pg 564

Taiwan, Province of China
Youth Cultural Publishing Co, pg 632

United Kingdom
Apple Press, pg 648
Art Books International Ltd, pg 649
Batsford Ltd, pg 652
Ruth Bean Publishers, pg 653
Berg Publishers, pg 654
Blackwell Science Ltd, pg 656
Bloomsbury Publishing PLC, pg 656
Carlton Publishing Group, pg 664
Gale Research, pg 685
Hamlyn, pg 691
Laurence King Publishing Ltd, pg 704
Piatkus Books, pg 727
Plexus Publishing Ltd, pg 728
Quarto Publishing plc, pg 731
Quintet Publishing Ltd, pg 732
Random House UK Ltd, pg 733
Taschen UK Ltd, pg 747
Thames & Hudson Ltd, pg 748
Time Out Group Ltd, pg 749
Philip Wilson Publishers, pg 757

FICTION

Afghanistan
Book Publishing Institute, pg 1

Albania
Botimpex Publications Import-Export Agency, pg 1
Fan Noli Verlag Rexhep Hida, pg 1

Algeria
Enterprise Nationale du Livre (ENAL), pg 2

Argentina
Editorial Abril SA, pg 2
Editorial Acme SA, pg 3
Ada Korn Editora SA, pg 3
Alianza Editorial de Argentina SA, pg 3
Editorial Argentina Plaza y Janes SA, pg 3
Editorial Atlantida SA, pg 3
Beas Ediciones SRL, pg 4
Beatriz Viterbo Editora, pg 4
Critica, pg 4
Emece Editores SA, pg 5
Ediciones de la Flor SRL, pg 6
Editorial Losada SA, pg 7
Marymar Ediciones SA, pg 7
Editorial Planeta Argentina SAIC, pg 8
Editorial Sudamericana SA, pg 9
Ediciones Tres Tiempos SRL, pg 9
Editoria Universitaria de la Patagonia, pg 9
Javier Vergara Editor SA, pg 9

Australia
ABC Books (Australian Broadcasting Corporation), pg 10
Allen & Unwin Pty Ltd, The Australian Newspaper, Vogel Breads, pg 11
Angel Publications, pg 11
Ansay Pty Ltd, pg 11
Artemis Publishing Pty Ltd, pg 12
Ashling Books, pg 12
Austed Publishing Co, pg 13
Australian Large Print Pty Ltd, pg 14

955

SUBJECT INDEX

Bandicoot Books, pg 14
Louis Braille Audio, pg 16
Egan Publishing Pty Ltd, pg 21
EK Press, pg 21
Fremantle Arts Centre Press, pg 23
Galley Press Publishing, pg 23
Gangan Publishing, pg 23
Garr Publishing, pg 23
Ginninderra Press, pg 24
Geoffrey Hamlyn-Harris, pg 25
Hat Box Press, pg 25
Hunter Books, pg 27
Hyland House Publishing Pty Ltd, pg 27
Indra Publishing, pg 27
Jarrah Publications, pg 28
Killara Press, pg 29
Levanter Publishing & Associates, pg 30
Little Red Apple Publishing, pg 30
Magabala Books Aboriginal Corporation, pg 31
Mayne Publishing, pg 32
Moggy Publications, pg 33
Narkaling Inc, pg 34
New Creation Publications Ministries & Resource Centre, pg 34
New Endeavour Press, pg 34
New Era Publications Australia Pty Ltd, pg 34
Newman Centre Publications, pg 35
Ollif Publishing, pg 35
Omnibus Books, pg 35
Pan Macmillan Australia Pty Ltd, pg 36
Papyrus Publishing, pg 37
Pascoe Publishing, pg 37
Pearson Education Australia, pg 37
Penguin Books Australia Ltd, pg 37
Plantagenet Press, pg 38
Quakers Hill Press, pg 39
Random House Australia, pg 40
Spinifex Press, pg 43
The Text Publishing Company Pty Ltd, pg 44
Tom Publications, pg 45
Tomorrow Publications, pg 45
Transworld Publishers Pty Ltd, pg 45
Troll Books of Australia, pg 45
Tropicana Press, pg 45
University of Queensland Press, pg 46
University of Western Australia Press, pg 46
Wakefield Press Pty Ltd, pg 47
Walker Books Australia Pty Ltd, pg 47
Weather Press, pg 47

Austria
Aarachne Verlag, pg 49
Amalthea-Verlag, pg 49
Andreas und Andreas Verlagsbuchhandel, pg 49
Astor-Verlag, Willibald Schlager, pg 49
Danubia Werbung und Verlagsservice, pg 50
Development News Ltd, pg 51
Docker Verlag GmbH & Co KG, pg 51
Edition S der OSD, pg 51
Verlag Lynkeus/H Hakel Gesellschaft, pg 52
Edition Graphischer Zirkel, pg 52
Haymon-Verlag GesmbH, pg 52
Johannes Heyn, Gert und Volkmar Zechner, pg 52
Verlag Jungbrunnen - Wiener Spielzeugschachtel GesellschaftmbH, pg 53

Karolinger Verlag GmbH & Co KG, pg 53
Leykam Buchverlagsges mbH, pg 54
Merbod Verlag, pg 55
Milena Verlag, pg 55
Paul Neff Verlag KG, pg 55
Oesterreichischer Agrarverlag, Druck- und Verlags- GmbH, pg 56
Oesterreichischer Bundesverlag GmbH, pg 56
Anna Pichler Verlag GmbH, pg 57
Richard Pils Publication P, pg 57
Georg Prachner KG, pg 57
Andreas Schnider Verlags-Atelier, pg 58
Verlag Carl Ueberreuter GmbH, pg 59
Waren-Erzeungungs-und Handelsgesellschaft GmbH, pg 60
Wieser Verlag, pg 61
Paul Zsolnay Verlag GmbH, pg 61

Azerbaijan
AZernesr, pg 61

Bangladesh
Ankur Prakashani, pg 62
Gatidhara, pg 62
Agamee Prakashani, pg 62

Belarus
Belaruskaya Encyklapedyya, pg 63
Interdigets Publishing House, pg 63
Kavaler Publishers, pg 63
Izdatelstvo Mastatskaya Litaratura, pg 63

Belgium
Caramel SA, pg 65
Editions Chantecler, pg 66
Uitgeverij Clavis, pg 66
Davidsfonds - Infodok NV, pg 67
Eenhoorn BVBA, pg 68
EPO Publishers, Printers, Booksellers, pg 68
Helyode Editions (SA-ADN), pg 69
Les Editions du Lombard SA, pg 71
La Longue Vue, pg 71
Editions Memor, pg 72
Paradox Pers vzw, pg 72
Scissors Books, pg 74
Standaard Uitgeverij, pg 74
Vlaamse Esperantobond VZW, pg 75
Editions Luce Wilquin, pg 75

Bermuda
Bermudian Publishing Co, pg 76

Bosnia and Herzegovina
Veselin Maslesa, pg 77

Botswana
Maskew Miller Longman, pg 77

Brazil
AGIR S/A Editora, pg 78
Livraria Francisco Alves Editora SA, pg 78
Artes e Oficios Editora Ltda, pg 79
Editora Bertrand Brasil Ltda, pg 79
Centro de Estudos Juridicosdo Para (CEJUP), pg 80
Dumara Distribuidora de Publicacoes Ltda, pg 81
Editora Companhia das Letras/ Editora Schwarcz Ltda, pg 82

Cia Editora Nacional, pg 82
Editora Globo SA, pg 84
Editora e Grafica Carisio Ltda, pg 84
Imago Editora Importacao e Exportacao Ltda, pg 85
Editora Lidador Ltda, pg 86
Editora Mantiqueira de Ciencia e Arte, pg 87
Memorias Futuras Edicoes Ltda, pg 88
Editora Mercado Aberto Ltda, pg 88
Editora Mercuryo Ltda, pg 88
Editora Moderna Ltda, pg 88
Editora Mundo Cristao, pg 88
Editora Nova Alexandria Ltda, pg 88
Editora Nova Fronteira SA, pg 88
Editora Objetiva Ltda, pg 88
Editora Primor Ltda, pg 90
Distribuidora Record de Servicos de Imprensa SA, pg 90
Editora Revan Ltda, pg 90
Editora Scipione Ltda, pg 91
Sobrindes Linha Grafica E Editora Ltda, pg 91
Thex Editora e Distribuidora Ltda, pg 92
34 Literatura S/C Ltda, pg 92

Bulgaria
Abagar Pablioing, pg 94
Abagar, Veliko Tarnovo, pg 94
Bulgarski Pissatel, pg 94
Ciela Publishing House, pg 94
DA-Izdatelstvo Publishers, pg 95
Hristo G Danov State Publishing House, pg 95
EA Publishing House, pg 95
Factor-Alias, pg 95
Hermes Publishing House, pg 95
Heron Press Publishing House, pg 96
Publishing House Hristo Botev, pg 96
Kibea Publishing Co, pg 96
Kolibri Publishing Group, pg 96
Lettera, pg 96
MATEX, pg 96
Mladezh, pg 96
Prozoretz Ltd Publishing House, pg 97
Reporter, pg 97
Sluntse Publishing House, pg 98
Svetra Publishing House, pg 98
Trud - Izd kasta, pg 98
Ivan Vazov Publishing House, pg 98
Peyo K Yavorov Publishing House, pg 98
Zunica, pg 98

Cameroon
Editions Buma Kor, pg 99
Editions CLE, pg 99
Editions Semences Africaines, pg 99

Chile
Editorial Cuarto Propio, pg 100

China
Asia 2000 Ltd, pg 102
Beijing Publishing House, pg 102
China Film Press, pg 103
China Theatre Publishing House, pg 104
Chinese Literature Press, pg 104
Encyclopedia of China Publishing House, pg 105
Shandong Education Publishing House, pg 108

Shandong Friendship Press, pg 108
World Affairs Press, pg 110
Writers' Publishing House, pg 110

Colombia
Siglo XXI Editores de Colombia Ltda, pg 113

The Democratic Republic of the Congo
Centre Protestant d'Editions et de Diffusion (CEDI), pg 115
Saint-Paul, pg 115
Editions Saint Paul-Afrique, pg 115

Costa Rica
Libreria Imprenta y Litografia Lehmann SA, pg 116

Cote d'Ivoire
Heritage Publishing Co, pg 118

Croatia
ALFA dd za izdavacke, graficke i trgovacke poslove, pg 118
Durieux d o o, pg 118
Faust Vrani, pg 118
Globus-Nakladni zavod, pg 118
Graficki zavod Hrvatske, pg 118
Mladost d d Izdavacku graficku i informaticku djelatnost, pg 119
Nakladni zavod Matice hrvatske, pg 119
Naprijed d d Naklada, pg 119
Otokar Kersovani, pg 120

Cuba
Editorial Letras Cubanas, pg 121
Editorial Oriente, pg 121

Czech Republic
AULOS sro, pg 123
Aurora, pg 123
Baronet, pg 123
Nakladatelstvi Blok, pg 123
Brody, pg 123
Cesky spisovatel, pg 123
Galaxie, vydavatelstvi a nakladatelstvi, pg 124
Karolinum, nakladatelstvi, pg 125
Knihovna A Tiskarna Pro Nevidome, pg 125
Labyrint, pg 125
Lidove noviny Nakladatelstvi, pg 125
Mariadan, pg 126
Mlada fronta, pg 126
Nadace Lyry Pragensis, pg 126
Nava, pg 127
Odeon, nakladatelstvi krasne literatury a umeni, pg 127
Paseka, pg 127
Prace, pg 127
Prostor, Ltd, pg 128
Vitalis SRO, pg 129

Denmark
Alma, pg 129
Aschehoug Dansk Forlag A/S, pg 130
Atuakkiorfik A/S Det Greenland Publishers, pg 130
Bonnier Publications AS, pg 130
Bonniers Specialmagasiner A/S Bogdivisionen, pg 130
Borgens Forlag A/S, pg 130
Carit Andersens Forlag A/S, pg 131
Forlaget Centrum, pg 131
Cicero-Chr Erichsens, pg 131

PUBLISHERS   SUBJECT INDEX

The Danish Literature Centre, pg 131
Forum Publishers, pg 132
Fremad A/S, pg 132
J Frimodts Forlag, pg 132
Forlaget GMT, pg 132
Grevas Forlag, pg 132
Gyldendalske Boghandel - Nordisk Forlag A/S, pg 132
P Haase & Sons Forlag A/S, pg 132
Hekla Forlag, pg 132
Hernovs Forlag, pg 132
Forlaget Hjulet, pg 132
Host & Son Publishers Ltd, pg 133
Forlaget Hovedland, pg 133
Interpresse A/S, pg 133
Forlaget Klematis A/S, pg 133
Lindhardt og Ringhof, pg 133
Lohses Forlag, pg 133
Forlaget Modtryk AMBA, pg 133
Nyt Nordisk Forlag Arnold Busck A/S, pg 134
Politisk Revy, pg 134
Samlerens Forlag A/S, pg 135
Det Schonbergske Forlag, pg 135
Sommer og Soerensen Forlag ApS, pg 135
Syddansk Universitetsforlag, pg 136
Tiderne Skifter Forlag A/S, pg 136
Unitas Forlag, pg 136
Forlaget Vindrose A/S, pg 136
Wisby & Wilkens, pg 136
Forlaget Woldike K/S, pg 136

Egypt (Arab Republic of Egypt)
Al Arab Publishing House, pg 138
Dar El Shorouk, pg 138
Dar El Shorouk Publishing & Distributing House, pg 138
Dar Al Hilap Publishing Institution, pg 139
Middle East Book Centre, pg 139

Estonia
Oue Eesti Raamat, pg 139
Ilmamaa, pg 140
Kunst Publishers Ltd, pg 140
Kupar Publishers, pg 140
Olion Publishers, pg 140
Sinisukk, pg 140

Finland
AB Svenska Laromedel-Editum, pg 141
Basam Books Oy, pg 142
Forlagsaktiebolaget Scriptum, pg 142
Gummerus Publishers, pg 142
Kaantopiiri Oy, pg 142
Karisto Oy, pg 142
Kirjayhtymae Oy, pg 143
Kustannus Oy Uusi Tie, pg 143
Otava Publishing Co Ltd, pg 143
Oy LIKE Kustannus Ltd, pg 144
Schildts Foerlagsaktiebolag, pg 144
Soederstroem et Co Foerlagsaktiebolag, pg 144
Tammi Publishers, pg 144
Werner Soederstroem Osakeyhtioe (WSOY), pg 145

France
Editions A M Metailie, pg 145
Editions Al Liamm, pg 146
Editions Albin Michel, pg 146
L'Archipel, pg 148
Publications Aredit, pg 148
Aubanel SA, pg 149
Editions d'Aujourd'hui (Les Introuvables), pg 149
Autrement Editions, pg 149

Editions Baleine, pg 149
Editions Balland, pg 149
Editions Belfond, pg 150
Societe d'Edition Les Belles Lettres, pg 150
Bragelonne, pg 151
Brud Nevez, pg 152
Editions Buchet/Chastel, pg 152
Editions Calmann-Levy SA, pg 152
Editions Casterman, pg 153
Editions Champ Vallon, pg 154
Christian Bourgois Editeur, pg 155
Circe, pg 155
Circonflexe, pg 155
Librairie Jose Corti, pg 156
Culture et Bibliotheque pour Tous, pg 157
Dargaud, pg 157
Editions du Dauphin, pg 158
Nouvelles Editions Debresse, pg 158
La Decouverte et Syros, pg 158
Georges-Charles Demay, pg 158
Editions Denoel Sarl, pg 158
Les Editions des Deux Coqs d'Or, pg 159
Editions Dis Voir, pg 159
Librairie Artheme Fayard, pg 163
FBT de R Editions/Editions des Limbes d'Or, pg 163
Des Femmes, pg 164
Fixot, pg 164
Flammarion SA, pg 164
Groupe Fleurus-Mame, pg 164
Association Frank, pg 165
Editions Gallimard, pg 165
Editions Gerard de Villiers, pg 166
Editions J Glenat SA, pg 166
Editions Grandir, pg 166
Hachette Livre, pg 167
Hemma Joven, SA, pg 168
Editions de l'Herne, pg 168
Editions Hoebeke, pg 168
Pierre Horay Editeur, pg 168
Editions Infrarouge, pg 169
Editions J'ai Lu, pg 170
Editions Jean-Claude Lattes, pg 170
Editions Michel Lafon SA, pg 171
Editions du Laquet, pg 172
Editions Dominique Leroy, pg 172
Editions Liana Levi Sarl, pg 173
Editions des Limbes d'Or/FBT de R Editions, pg 173
Le Livre de Poche-L G F (Librairie Generale Francaise), pg 173
Editions Marie-Noelle, pg 175
Mercure de France SA, pg 176
Les Editions de Minuit SA, pg 176
Gabriel Mony, pg 176
Naufal Group Sarl, pg 177
Nil Editions, pg 177
Noir Sur Blanc, pg 177
Nouvelles Editions Latines, pg 178
Editions Odile Jacob, pg 178
Editions Payot & Rivages, pg 179
Editions Jean Picollec, pg 179
Editions Christian Pirot, pg 180
POL Editeur, pg 180
Presence Africaine Editions, pg 180
Presses de la Cite, pg 180
Editions Pygmalion - Gerard Watelet, pg 182
Editions Ramsay, pg 182
Editions Robert Laffont, Nil, Fixot, Seghers, Julliard, pg 183
Editions Roudil, pg 183
Editions du Rouergue, pg 183
Les Editions du Sagittaire, pg 183
Editions Sand et Tchou SA, pg 183
Nouvelles Editions Seguier, pg 184
Selection du Reader's Digest SA, pg 184
Maren Sell, pg 184

Sepia, pg 184
Editions de Septembre, pg 184
Le Serpent a Plumes, pg 184
Service Technique pour l'Education, pg 185
Editions du Seuil, pg 185
Editions Andre Silvaire Sarl, pg 185
Societe des Editions Grasset et Fasquelle, pg 185
Association d'Editions Sorg, pg 186
Editions Louis Soulanges Le Livrer Ouvert, pg 186
Spengler Editeur, pg 186
Editions Stock, pg 186
Les Editions de la Table Ronde, pg 187
Editions Tallandier, pg 187
10/18, pg 187
TF 1 Editions, pg 187
Union Generale d'Editions, pg 188
La Voix du Regard, pg 189

French Polynesia
Scoop/Au Vent des Iles, pg 190
Simone Sanchez, pg 190

Germany
Acbrecht Kraus Verlag GmbH, pg 191
Altberliner Verlag GmbH, pg 193
AOL-Verlag Frohmut Menze, pg 194
Arena Verlag GmbH, pg 194
Argon Verlag GmbH, pg 195
Argument-Verlag, pg 195
Ars Edition GmbH, pg 195
Verlag Atelier im Bauernhaus, pg 196
Aufbau Taschenbuch Verlag GmbH, pg 196
Aufbau-Verlag GmbH, pg 196
Aufstieg-Verlag GmbH, pg 196
Aussaat Verlag GmbH, pg 197
C Bange GmbH & Co KG, pg 198
Bastei Luebbe Taschenbuecher, pg 199
Bastei Verlag GmbH, pg 199
Beerenverlag, pg 200
Berliner Handpresse Wolfgang Joerg und Erich Schonig, pg 201
C Bertelsmann Verlag GmbH, pg 201
Bertelsmann Lexikon Verlag GmbH, pg 201
Betzel Verlag GmbH, pg 202
Bleicher Verlag GmbH, pg 204
C Bosendahl, pg 205
Brandes & Apsel Verlag GmbH, pg 206
R Brockhaus Verlag, pg 206
BRUEN-Verlag, Gorenflo, pg 207
Buchverlage Langen-Mueller/Herbig, pg 207
Bund-Verlag GmbH, pg 208
Fachverlag Hans Carl GmbH, pg 209
Carlsen Verlag GmbH, pg 209
Claassen Verlag GmbH, pg 210
ComMedia & Arte Verlag Bernd Mayer, pg 211
J G Cotta'sche Buchhandlung Nachfolger GmbH, pg 212
Das Arsenal, Verlag fuer Kultur und Politik GmbH, pg 212
Deutsche Verlags-Anstalt GmbH (DVA), pg 214
Deutscher Taschenbuch Verlag GmbH & Co KG (dtv), pg 215
Dingfelder-Verlag Inh Gerd Gmelin, pg 217
Dipa-Verlag GmbH, pg 217
Cecilie Dressler Verlag, pg 218

Droemersche Verlagsanstalt Th Knaur Nachfolger GmbH & Co, pg 218
Karl Elser Druck GmbH, pg 218
Echter Wurzburg Frankische Gesellschaftsdruckerei und Verlag GmbH, pg 220
Econ Verlag GmbH, pg 220
Edition Solitude - Akademie Schloss Solitude, pg 221
Egmont Franz Schneider Verlag GmbH, pg 221
Egmont vgs verlagsgesellschaft mbH, pg 221
Ehrenwirth Verlag, pg 221
Ehrenwirth Verlag GmbH, pg 221
Eichborn AG, pg 222
EinfallsReich Verlagsgesellschaft MbH, pg 222
Engel & Bengel Verlag, pg 222
Verlag Peter Engstler, pg 223
Ensslin und Laiblin Verlag GmbH & Co KG, pg 223
EOS Verlag der Benefiktiner der Erzabtei St. Ottilien, pg 223
Eremiten-Presse und Verlag GmbH, pg 223
Ernst Kabel Verlag GmbH, pg 223
Europa Verlag GmbH, pg 224
Evangelische Verlagsanstalt GmbH, pg 225
Fahrner & Fahrner, pg 226
Fannei & Walz Verlag, pg 227
Karin Fischer Verlag GmbH, pg 228
Rita G Fischer Verlag, pg 228
S Fischer Verlag GmbH, pg 228
Margarethe Freudenberger - selbstverlag fur jedermann, pg 230
Gilles und Francke Verlag, pg 232
Wilhelm Goldmann Verlag GmbH, pg 233
Brigitte Grabitz - ikoo Buchverlag, pg 233
Grafit Verlag GmbH, pg 234
Guenther Butkus, pg 235
Carl Hanser Verlag, pg 237
Heinz-Theo Gremme Verlag, pg 239
Hellerau-Verlag Dresden GmbH, pg 239
Wilhelm Heyne Verlag, pg 240
Hoffmann und Campe Verlag GmbH, pg 242
Hohenrain-Verlag GmbH, pg 242
Holos Verlag, pg 242
Horlemann Verlag, pg 243
Hyperion - Verlag, pg 244
Klaus Isele, pg 245
ludicium Verlag GmbH, pg 245
J Ch Mellinger Verlag GmbH, pg 246
Karl-May-Verlag Lothar Schmid GmbH, pg 248
KBV-Verlags-und Mediengesellschaft mbH, pg 248
Verlag Kiepenheuer und Witsch GmbH & Co KG, pg 249
Kindler Verlag GmbH, pg 249
Ingrid Klein Verlag GmbH, pg 249
Verlag Kleine Schritte Ursula Dahm & Co, pg 249
Kleiner Bachmann Verlag fur Kinder und Umwelt, pg 250
Klink, Vincent, Edition, Stecknadel, pg 250
Albrecht Knaus Verlag GmbH, pg 250
Verlag Knut Reim, Jugendpresseverlag, pg 251
Koehlers Verlagsgesellschaft mbH, pg 251
Lucy Koerner Verlag, pg 252
Franckh-Kosmos Verlags-GmbH & Co, pg 252

957

SUBJECT INDEX

Dr Anton Kovac Slavica Verlag, pg 253
Wolfgang Krueger Verlag GmbH, pg 254
Krug & Schadenberg, pg 254
Verlag Antje Kunstmann GmbH, pg 254
Lambda Edition GmbH, pg 255
Landbuch-Verlagsgesellschaft mbH, pg 255
Ingrid Langner, pg 256
Lentz Verlag, pg 257
Dr Gisela Lermann, pg 257
Libertas- Europaeisches Institut GmbH, pg 257
Liebenzeller Mission, GmbH, Abt. Verlag, pg 258
Logos-Verlag Literatur & Layout GmbH, pg 258
Luchterhand Literaturverlag GmbH/ Verlag Volk & Welt GmbH, pg 259
Gustav Luebbe Verlag, pg 259
Verlagsgruppe Luebbe GmbH & Co KG, pg 259
Lusatia Verlag-Dr Stuebner & Co KG, pg 259
Edition Maritim GmbH, pg 261
Maro Verlag und Druck, Benno Kasmayr, pg 261
Matthes und Seitz Verlag GmbH, pg 261
Matzker Verlag DiA, pg 261
Merlin Verlag Andreas Meyer Verlags GmbH und Co KG, pg 263
Mitteldeutscher Verlag GmbH, pg 264
Monia Verlag, pg 265
Verlag Mueller und Kiepenheuer, pg 265
Naumann & Goebel Verlagsgesellschaft mbH, pg 267
Verlag Neue Kritik KG, pg 267
Verlag Neue Stadt GmbH, pg 267
Neuer Honos Verlag GmbH, pg 267
Verlag Neues Leben GmbH, pg 268
Neuthor - Verlag, pg 268
C W Niemeyer Buchverlage GmbH, pg 268
nymphenburger, pg 269
Oekotopia Verlag, Wolfgang Hoffman, pg 270
Verlag Friedrich Oetinger GmbH, pg 270
Oncken Verlag KG, pg 270
One Way Medien OHG, pg 270
Ostfalia-Verlag Jurgen Schierer, pg 271
Pandion-Verlag, Ulrike Schmoll, pg 271
Passavia Druckerei GmbH, Verlag, pg 271
Pelikan Vertriebsgesellschaft mbH & Co KG, pg 272
Pendragon Verlag, pg 272
Pfalzische Verlagsanstalt GmbH, pg 272
Philipp Reclam Jun Verlag GmbH, pg 273
Piper Verlag GmbH, pg 274
Projektion J Buch- und Musikverlag GmbH, pg 275
Propylaeen Verlag, Zweigniederlassung Berlin der Ullstein Buchverlage GmbH, pg 275
Pulp Master Frank Nowatzki Verlag, pg 276
Quell Verlag, pg 276
Querverlag GmbH, pg 276
Quintessenz Verlags-GmbH, pg 276
Radius-Verlag GmbH, pg 276

Rake Verlag GmbH, pg 277
Gerhard Rautenberg Druckerei und Verlag GmbH & Co KG, pg 277
Ravensburger Buchverlag Otto Maier GmbH, pg 277
Regura Verlag, pg 277
Konrad Reich Verlag GmbH, pg 278
Rogner und Bernhard GmbH & Co Verlags KG, pg 279
Romiosini Verlag, pg 280
Rosenheimer Verlagshaus GmbH & Co KG, pg 280
Rowohlt Berlin Verlag GmbH, pg 280
Rowohlt Taschenbuch Verlag GmbH, pg 280
Ruetten & Loening Berlin GmbH, pg 281
Eugen Salzer-Verlag GmbH & Co KG, pg 281
Verlag der Sankt-Johannis-Druckerei C Schweickhardt, pg 281
Verlag Sauerlaender GmbH, pg 282
Richard Scherpe Verlag GmbH, pg 283
Schillinger Verlag GmbH, pg 283
Agora Verlag Manfred Schlosser, pg 283
Buchverlag Andrea Schmitz, pg 284
Schoeffling & Co, pg 284
Verlag Schulte und Gerth GmbH & Co KG, pg 285
R S Schulz Verlag GmbH, pg 285
H O Schulze KG, pg 285
Theodor Schuster, pg 285
Gerd Simon & Claudia Magiera, Verlagsbuero, pg 287
Snayder Verlag Gunter VOB & Jurgen Schroder OHG, pg 287
Adolf Sponholtz Verlag, pg 288
L Staackmann Verlag KG, pg 288
Steidl Verlag, pg 289
Verlag Stendel, pg 290
Suhrkamp Verlag, pg 291
Svato Zapletal, pg 291
Tangens Systemverlag GmbH, pg 291
K Thienemanns Verlag, pg 293
Titania-Verlag Ferdinand Schroll, pg 294
Treves Editions Verein Zur Foerderung der Kuenstlerischen Taetigkeiten, pg 295
Mario Truant Verlag, pg 295
Ullstein Heyne List GmbH & Co KG, pg 295
Ulrike Helmer Verlag, pg 296
Unrast Verlag e V, pg 296
Verlagsgruppe Georg von Holtzbrinck GmbH, pg 299
W Ludwig Verlag GmbH, pg 300
Verlag Klaus Wagenbach GmbH, pg 300
A Weichert Verlag GmbH & Co KG, pg 301
Weidler Buchverlag Berlin, pg 301
Verlagsgruppe Weltbild GmbH, pg 301
Wolf's-Verlag Berlin, pg 304
Das Wunderhorn Verlag GmbH, pg 304
Wunderlich Verlag, pg 304
Verlag Andreas Zettner KG, pg 305

Ghana

Adaex Educational Publications Ltd, pg 306
Afram Publications (Ghana) Ltd, pg 306
Africa Christian Press, pg 306
Anowuo Educational Publications, pg 306
Asempa Publishers, pg 306

Beginners Publishers, pg 306
Bureau of Ghana Languages, pg 306
Educational Press & Manufacturers Ltd, pg 307
Ghana Publishing Corporation, pg 307
Moxon Paperbacks, pg 307
Paul Ntem Maanoh, pg 307
Sedco Publishing Ltd, pg 308
Waterville Publishing House, pg 308
Woeli Publishing Services, pg 308

Greece

Atlantis M Pechlivanides & Co SA, pg 309
Chrysi Penna - Golden Pen Books, pg 309
Dodoni Publications, pg 310
Dorikos Publishing House, pg 310
Ekdoseis Kazantzaki (Kazantzakis Publications), pg 310
Eleftheroudakis, GCSA International Bookstore, pg 310
Elliniki Leschi Tou Vivliou, pg 310
Exandas Publishers, pg 310
Govostis Publishing SA, pg 311
Harlenic Hellas Publishing SA, pg 311
Hestia-1 D Hestia-Kollaros & Co Corporation, pg 311
Irini Publishing House - Vassilis G Katsikeas SA, pg 311
Editions Kalentis, pg 312
Kastaniotis Editions SA, pg 312
Medusa/Selas, pg 313
Minoas SA, pg 313
Patakis Publishers, pg 314
M Psaropoulos & Co EE, pg 314
Psichogios Publications SA, pg 314
Siamantas Publications, pg 315
Sigma, pg 315
J Vassiliou Bibliopolein, pg 315
Vlassis, pg 316

Guatemala

Grupo Editorial RIN-78, pg 316

Guyana

Roraima Publishers Ltd, pg 317

Haiti

Deschamps Imprimerie, pg 317
Theodor (Imprimerie), pg 317

Hong Kong

Breakthrough Ltd - Breakthrough Publishers, pg 318
Hong Kong Publishing Co Ltd, pg 320
Lea Publications Ltd, pg 320
Ming Pao Publications Ltd, pg 321
Publications (Holdings) Ltd, pg 321
Research Centre for Translation, pg 321
Sesame Publication Co, pg 321
Sun Ya Publications (HK) Ltd, pg 322
Witman Publishing Co (HK) Ltd, pg 322

Hungary

Corvina Books Ltd, pg 323
Europa Konyvkiado, pg 323
Ifjusagi Lap-eskonyvkiado Vallalat, pg 324
Jelenkor Verlag, pg 324
Magveto Koenyvkiado, pg 325

BOOK

Szepirodalmi Koenyvkiado Kiado, pg 327
Tevan Kiado Vallalat, pg 327

Iceland

Almenna Bokafelagid, pg 327
Fjolvi, pg 327
Forlagid, pg 327
Frjals fjolmiolun hf-Urvalsbaekur, pg 327
Frodi Ltd, pg 328
Idunn, pg 328
Isafoldarprentsmidja hf, pg 328
Islendingasagnautgafan, pg 328
Mal og menning, pg 328
Setberg, pg 328
Skjaldborg Ltd, pg 328
Skuggsja bokaforlag, pg 329

India

Ananda Publishers Pvt Ltd, pg 330
APH Publishing Corp, pg 331
The Bangalore Printing & Publishing Co Ltd, pg 332
Bharatiya Vidya Bhavan, pg 333
Chanakya Publications, pg 334
CICC Book House, pg 335
Current Books, pg 335
DC Books, pg 336
Diamond Comics (P) Ltd, pg 336
Frank Brothers & Co (Publishers) Ltd, pg 337
Hans Prakashan, pg 338
HarperCollins Publishers India Pty Ltd, pg 338
Arnold Heinman Publishers (India) Pvt Ltd, pg 338
Hind Pocket Books Private Ltd, pg 338
Hindi Pracharak Sansthan, pg 338
Kairali Children's Book Trust, pg 340
Kairalee Mudralayam, pg 341
Kali For Women, pg 341
Kitab Ghar, pg 341
M/S Gulshan Nanda Publications, pg 343
Natraj Prakashan, pg 344
Omsons Publications, pg 345
Orient Paperbacks, pg 345
Paico Publishing House, pg 345
Panchasheel Prakashan, pg 345
Pitambar Publishing Co (P) Ltd, pg 346
Prabhat Prakashan, pg 346
Pratibha Pratishthan, pg 346
Rajpal & Sons, pg 347
Regency Publications, pg 347
Reliance Publishing House, pg 347
Roli Books Pvt Ltd, pg 348
Rupa & Co, pg 348
M C Sarkar & Sons (P) Ltd, pg 349
Sat Sahitya Prakashan, pg 349
Scientific Book Agency, pg 349
Sharda Prakashan, pg 350
R R Sheth & Co, pg 350
Somaiya Publications Pvt Ltd, pg 350
Sterling Publishers Pvt Ltd, pg 351
Vani Prakashan, pg 352
Vikas Publishing House Pvt Ltd, pg 353
Vision Books Pvt Ltd, pg 353
Vivek Prakashan, pg 353

Indonesia

CV Angkasa CV (Publishers), pg 354
Bina Aksara Parta, pg 354
P T Bulan Bintang, pg 354
Dunia Pustaka Jaya, pg 355
Gaya Favorit Press, pg 355

Gramedia, pg 355
Karya Anda, CV, pg 356

Ireland
Attic Press Ltd, pg 358
Brandon Book Publishers Ltd, pg 359
The Children's Press, pg 359
Clo lar-Chonnachta Teo, pg 359
FISH Publishing, pg 360
Gill & Macmillan Ltd, pg 361
The Goldsmith Press Ltd, pg 361
Irish Times Ltd, pg 361
The Lilliput Press Ltd, pg 362
Mercier Press Ltd, pg 362
Mount Eagle Publications Ltd, pg 362
The O'Brien Press Ltd, pg 363
Poolbeg Press Ltd, pg 363
Publishers Group South West (Ireland), pg 363
Roberts Rinehart Publishers, pg 363
Town House & Country House, pg 364
Wolfhound Press, pg 364

Israel
Achiasaf Publishing House Ltd, pg 365
Am Oved Publishers Ltd, pg 365
Amichai Publishing House Ltd, pg 365
Bitan Publishers Ltd, pg 365
Boostan Publishing House, pg 366
DAT Publications, pg 366
Gefen Publishing House Ltd, pg 367
Gvanim Publishing House, pg 367
Hakibbutz Hameuchad Publishing House Ltd, pg 368
Karni Publishers Ltd, pg 369
Keter Publishing House Ltd, pg 369
Kiryat Sefer, pg 369
Ma'ariv Book Guild (Sifriat Ma'ariv), pg 370
Machbarot Lesifrut, pg 370
Massada Publishers Ltd, pg 370
M Mizrahi Publishers, pg 370
Pitspopany Press, pg 371
Saar Publishing House, pg 372
Schocken Publishing House Ltd, pg 372
Sifriat Poalim Ltd, pg 372
Steimatzky Group Ltd, pg 372
Urim Publications, pg 373
Yavneh Publishing House Ltd, pg 373
Yedioth Ahronoth Books, pg 373
Zmora-Bitan, Publishers Ltd, pg 374

Italy
Adelphi Edizioni SpA, pg 374
Edizioni Anabasi SpA, pg 375
Archimede Edizioni, pg 376
Argalia Editore delle Arti Grafiche Editoriali SRL, pg 376
Gruppo Editoriale Armenia SpA, pg 376
Belforte Editore Libraio srl, pg 377
Bompiani-RCS Libri, pg 378
Giuseppe Bonanno Editore, pg 378
Bulzoni Editore SRL (Le Edizioni Universitarie d'Italia), pg 379
Campanotto, pg 379
Nuova Casa Editrice Licinio Cappelli GEM srl, pg 379
Edistudio di Brunetto Casini, pg 380
Edizioni Castello di Antonio Careddu, pg 380
Il Castoro, pg 380
Colonnese Editore, pg 382

Costa e Nolan SpA, pg 383
Dami Editore SRL, pg 383
G De Bono Editore, pg 384
Organizzazione Didattica Editoriale Ape, pg 385
Edizioni E/O, pg 385
Edizioni l'Arciere SRL, pg 387
Effata Editrice, pg 387
Giulio Einaudi Editore SpA, pg 387
Giangiacomo Feltrinelli SpA, pg 389
Fogola Editore in Torino, pg 389
Edizioni Frassinelli SRL, pg 389
Fratelli Conte Editori SRL, pg 389
Galzerano Editore, pg 390
Gamberetti Editrice SRL, pg 390
Garzanti Editore, pg 390
Giunti (Gruppo Editoriale), pg 390
Giunti Publishing Group, pg 391
Ernesto Gremese Editore SRL, pg 391
Ibis, pg 393
Il Minotauro, pg 393
Il Quadrante SRL, pg 393
Il Saggiatore, pg 393
Editoriale Jaca Book SpA, pg 394
L Japadre Editore, pg 394
Lalli Editore SRL, pg 395
Edizioni Lavoro SRL, pg 395
Editrice Liguria SNC di Norberto Sabatelli & C, pg 396
Lindau, pg 396
Vincenzo Lo Faro Editore, pg 396
Longanesi & C, pg 396
Angelo Longo Editore, pg 396
Lorenzo Editore, pg 397
La Luna, pg 397
Lusva Editrice, pg 397
Tommaso Marotta Editore Srl, pg 398
Marsilio Editori SpA, pg 398
Editrice Massimo SAS di Crespi Cesare e C, pg 398
Il Melangolo, pg 398
Milano Libri, pg 398
Minerva Italica SpA, pg 399
Arnoldo Mondadori Editore SpA, pg 399
Mondolibro Editore SNC, pg 399
Gruppo Ugo Mursia Editore SpA, pg 400
Newton Compton Editori SRL, pg 401
OCTAVO Franco Cantini Editore, pg 401
Luigi Pellegrini Editore, pg 403
Edizioni Piemme SpA, pg 403
La Pilotta Editrice Coop RL, pg 403
Francesco Pirella Editore, pg 403
RAI.ERI, pg 405
RCS Rizzoli Libri SpA, pg 405
Editori Riuniti, pg 405
Adriano Salani Editore srl, pg 406
Salerno Editrice SRL, pg 406
Edizioni San Paolo SRL, pg 407
Sansoni Editore, pg 407
Fausto Sardini Editrice, pg 407
Sonzogno, pg 408
Sperling e Kupfer Editori SpA, pg 408
Gruppo Editoriale Le Stelle SpA, pg 409
Edizioni Studio Tesi SRL, pg 409
Sugarco Edizioni SRL, pg 409
TEA Tascabili degli Editori Associati SpA, pg 409
Edizioni Thyrus SRL, pg 409
Todariana Editrice, pg 410
Tranchida, pg 410
Transeuropa Libri, pg 410
Marco Tropea Editore, pg 410
La Vita Felice, pg 411

Jamaica
Institute of Jamaica Publications, pg 413
Kingston Publishers Ltd, pg 413
West Indies Publishing Ltd, pg 414

Japan
Bunkasha Publishing Co, Ltd, pg 415
Chikuma Shobo Publishing Co Ltd, pg 415
Dainippon Tosho Publishing Co, Ltd, pg 416
Fukuinkan Shoten Publishers Inc, pg 416
Hakusui-Sha Co Ltd, pg 417
Hayakawa Publishing Inc, pg 417
Kadokawa Shoten Publishing Co, pg 419
Kawade Shobo Shinsha, pg 419
Kodansha, pg 420
Kodansha International, pg 420
Kokusho Kankokai Co Ltd, pg 420
Nippon Hoso Shuppan Kyokai (NHK Publishing), pg 422
Poplar Publishing Co Ltd, pg 423
Saera Shobo (Librairie Ca et La), pg 424
Seibu Time Co Ltd, pg 425
Shakai Shiso-Sha, pg 425
Shincho-Sha Co Ltd, pg 425
Akane Shobo Co Ltd, pg 425
Shueisha Inc, pg 426
Shufunotomo sha Co Ltd, pg 426
Tokuma-Shoten, pg 427
Tokyo Shoseki Co Ltd, pg 427
Charles E Tuttle Publishing Co Inc, pg 428

Jordan
Jordan Book Centre Co Ltd, pg 430

Kenya
Focus Publications Ltd, pg 431
Heinemann Kenya Limited (EAEP), pg 431
Jacaranda Designs Ltd, pg 432
Lake Publishers & Enterprises Ltd, pg 432
Transafrica Press, pg 433
Uzima Press, pg 433

Democratic People's Republic of Korea
Literature and Art Publishing House, pg 434
Working People's Organization Publishing House, pg 434

Republic of Korea
Big Tree Publishing, pg 435
Borim Publishing Co, pg 435
Bum-Woo Publishing Co, pg 435
Chung Rim Publishing Co Ltd, pg 435
Gim-Yeong Co, pg 436
Hainaim Publishing Co Ltd, pg 436
Hollym Corporation Publishers, pg 437
Hw Moon Publishing Co, pg 437
Iljisa Publishing House, pg 437
Jeong-eum Munhwasa, pg 437
Jigyungsa Ltd, pg 437
Kemongsa Publishing Co Ltd, pg 437
Koreaone Press Inc, pg 438
Kum Sung Publishing Co Ltd, pg 438
Minumsa Publishing Co Ltd, pg 438
Munye Publishing Co, pg 439

O Neul Publishing Co, pg 439
St Pauls, pg 439
Woongjin Media Corporation, pg 440

Laos People's Democratic Republic
Lao-phanit, pg 441

Latvia
Artava Ltd, pg 441
Egmont Latvia Ltd, pg 442
Liesma Publishers, pg 442
Madris, pg 442
Nordik/Tapals Publishers Ltd, pg 442
Preses Nams, pg 442
Spriditis Publishers, pg 442
Vaidelote, pg 442

Lebanon
Khayat Book and Publishing Co Sarl, pg 443
Librairie du Liban, pg 443

Lithuania
Algarve, pg 445
Alma Littera, pg 445
Baltos Lankos, pg 445
Lietus Ltd, pg 445
Lietuvos Rasytoju Sajungos Leidykla, pg 446
The Publishing House of the Lithuanian Writers' Union, pg 446
Margi Rastai Publishers, pg 446
Tyto Alba Publishers, pg 446
Vaga Ltd, pg 446

The Former Yugoslav Republic of Macedonia
Detska radost, pg 448
Makedonska kniga (Knigoizdatelstvo), pg 449
Zumpres Publishing Firm, pg 449

Madagascar
Imprimerie Takariva, pg 450
Trano Printy Fiangonana Loterana Malagasy (TPFLM)-(Imprimerie Lutherienne), pg 450

Malawi
Christian Literature Association in Malawi, pg 450
Dzuka Publishing Company Ltd, pg 450
Mzuzu Publishing Co, pg 451
Popular Publications, pg 451

Malaysia
Associated Educational Distributors (M) Sdn Bhd, pg 451
Berita Publishing Sdn Bhd, pg 451
Holograms (M) Sdn Bhd, pg 452
K Publishing & Distributors Sdn Bhd, pg 452
Pustaka Cipta Sdn Bhd, pg 454
Tempo Publishing (M) Sdn Bhd, pg 455
University of Malaya, Department of Publications, pg 455

Mali
EDIM SA, pg 455

Mauritius
Editions de l'Ocean Indien Ltd, pg 457

SUBJECT INDEX

Mexico
Ediciones Alpe, pg 458
Libreria y Ediciones Botas SA, pg 458
Editorial Diana SA de CV, pg 459
Empresas Editoriales SA, pg 460
Ediciones Era SA de CV, pg 460
Editorial Grijalbo SA de CV, pg 461
Editorial Hermes SA, pg 461
Hoja Casa Editorial SA de CV, pg 462
Editorial Joaquin Mortiz SA de CV, pg 462
Editores Mexicanos Unidos SA, pg 464
Editorial Nueva Imagen SA, pg 464
Grupo Editorial Planeta, pg 465
Ediciones Roca, SA, pg 466
Salvat Editores de Mexico, pg 466
Universidad Veracruzana Direccion General Editorial y de Publicaciones, pg 468
Universo Editorial SA de CV Edicion de Libros Revistas y Periodicos, pg 468
Editorial Universo SA de CV, pg 468
Javier Vergara Editor SA de CV, pg 468

Republic of Moldova
Editura Hyperion, pg 468

Monaco
Les Editions du Rocher, pg 469
Rondeau Giannipiero a Monaco, pg 469
Editions Andre Sauret SA, pg 469

Morocco
Editions Eddif Maroc, pg 469
Editions Le Fennec, pg 470

Mozambique
Empresa Moderna Lda, pg 470

Netherlands
Uitgeverij Anthos, pg 472
BV Uitgeverij de Arbeiderspers, pg 473
Uitgeverij Aristos, pg 473
Uitgeverij Balans, pg 473
De Bezige Bij, pg 474
De Boekerij BV, pg 474
A W Bruna Uitgevers BV, pg 475
BZZTOH Publishers, pg 475
Cadans, pg 475
Uitgeverij G F Callenbach BV, pg 475
Uitgeverij Conserve, pg 475
Uitgeversmaatschappij Ad Donker BV, pg 476
ECI voor Boeken en Grammofoonplaten BV, pg 476
Uitgeverij De Fontein BV, pg 477
Uitgeverij De Geus BV, pg 477
Gottmer Uitgevers Groop, pg 477
Uitgeverij Heuff Nieuwkoop, pg 478
Holland B V Uitgeversmaatschappij, pg 478
Uitgeverij Hollandia BV, pg 478
Uitgeefmaatschappij J H Kok BV, pg 480
Uitgeverij Leopold BV, pg 480
J M Meulenhoff BV, pg 481
Uitgeverij Mingus, pg 481
Omega Boek BV, pg 482
Prometheus, pg 483
Em Querido's Uitgeverij BV, pg 483

Sjaloom en Wildeboer Publishers, pg 484
Unieboek BV, pg 485
Van Buuren Uitgeverij BV, pg 486
Uitgeverij Vassallucci, pg 486
Wereldbibliotheek, pg 487
Uitgeverij Westers, pg 487

New Zealand
Brick Row Publishing Co Ltd, pg 489
Cape Catley, pg 489
Church Mouse Press, pg 490
Cicada Press, pg 490
David's Marine Books, pg 490
HarperCollins Publishers (New Zealand) Ltd, pg 491
Hodder Moa Beckett Publishers Ltd, pg 492
Huia Publishers, pg 492
Lincoln University Press, pg 492
David Ling Publishing, pg 493
Nagare Press, pg 493
Orca Publishing Services Ltd, pg 494
Reed Publishing (NZ) Ltd, pg 495
RSVP Publishing Company Ltd, pg 495
Shearwater Associates Ltd, pg 495
Tandem Press, pg 496
Te Reo Publications, pg 496
University of Otago Press, pg 496
Words Work, pg 497

Nicaragua
Editorial Nueva Nicaragua, pg 497

Nigeria
Adebara Publishers Ltd, pg 497
Cross Continent Press Ltd, pg 498
Delta Publications (Nigeria) Ltd, pg 498
Ethiope Publishing Corporation, pg 499
Evans Brothers (Nigeria Publishers) Ltd, pg 499
Fourth Dimension Publishing Co Ltd, pg 499
Heritage Books, pg 499
Longman Nigeria Plc, pg 500
Thomas Nelson (Nigeria) Ltd, pg 500
New Era Publishers, pg 500
New Horn Press Ltd, pg 500
Nwamife Publishers Ltd, pg 500
Obobo Books, pg 501
Onibon-Oje Publishers, pg 501
Paperback Publishers Ltd, pg 501
Saros International Publishers, pg 501
Spectrum Books Ltd, pg 501
Tana Press Ltd & Flora Nwapa Books Ltd, pg 501
Vantage Publishers International Ltd, pg 502

Norway
Ariel Lydbokforlag, pg 502
H Aschehoug & Co (W Nygaard) A/S, pg 502
Atheneum Forlag A/S, pg 502
Bladkompaniet A/S, pg 503
J W Cappelens Forlag A/S, pg 503
N W Damm og Son A/S, pg 503
Det Norske Samlaget, pg 503
Fonna Forlag L/L, pg 503
Fono Forlag, pg 503
John Grieg Forlag AS, pg 503
Gyldendal Norsk Forlag A/S, pg 503

Egmont Hjemmets Bokforlag AS, pg 504
Lunde Forlag og Bokhandel A/S, pg 504
Luther Forlag A/S, pg 504
Norsk Bokreidingslag L/L, pg 504
Pax Forlag A/S, pg 504
Erik Sandberg, pg 504
Snofugl Forlag, pg 505
Solum Forlag A/S, pg 505
Stabenfeldt A/S, pg 505
Tiden Norsk Forlag, pg 505

Pakistan
Classic, pg 506
Malik Sirajuddin & Sons, pg 507
Maqbool Academy, pg 508
Sang-e-Meel Publications, pg 509

Papua New Guinea
Kristen Pres, pg 510

Philippines
Anvil Publishing Inc, pg 512
Ateneo de Manila University Press, pg 512
De La Salle University, pg 513
Estrella Publishing, pg 513
Kadena Press, pg 513
Marren Publishing House, Inc, pg 513
National Book Store Inc, pg 514
New Day Publishers, pg 514
Philippine Education Co Inc, pg 514
Solidaridad Publishing House, pg 515
University of the Philippines Press, pg 515

Poland
Albatros, pg 516
Wydawnictwa Normalizacyjne Alfa-Wero, pg 516
Spoldzielnia Wydawnicza 'Czytelnik', pg 516
Ksiaznica Publishing Ltd, pg 517
Muza SA, pg 518
Wydawnictwo Nasza Ksiegarnia Sp zoo, pg 518
Norbertinum, pg 518
Panstwowy Instytut Wydawniczy (PIW), pg 518
Wydawnictwa Radia i Telewizji, pg 519
Videograf II Sp z o o Zaklad Poracy Chronionej, pg 520
Wydawnictwo WAB, pg 520
Wydawnictwo Wilga sp zoo, pg 521

Portugal
Edicoes Antigona, pg 522
Editorial 'Avante!', pg 522
Bezerr-Editorae e Distribuidora de Abel Antonio Bezerra, pg 522
Brasilia Editora (J Carvalho Branco), pg 523
Editorial Caminho SARL, pg 523
Livraria Civilizacao (Americo Fraga Lamares & Ca Lda), pg 523
Editora Classica, pg 523
Contexto Editora, pg 524
DIFEL - Difusao Editorial SA, pg 524
Difusao Cultural, pg 524
Editorial Estampa, Lda, pg 524
Publicacoes Europa-America Lda, pg 524
Europress Editores e Distribuidores de Publicacoes Lda, pg 525
Gradiva-Publicacnoes Lda, pg 525
Guimaraes Editores, Lda, pg 525

BOOK

Editorial Minerva, pg 527
Editorial Noticias, pg 527
Planeta Editora, LDA, pg 528
Editorial Presenca, pg 528
Publicacoes Dom Quixote Lda, pg 528
Puma Editora Lda, pg 528
Quatro Elementos Editores, pg 529
Quimera Editores, pg 529
Almerinda Teixeira, pg 529
Teorema, pg 529
Texto Editora, pg 529
Vega-Publicacao e Distribuicao de Livros e Revistas, Lda, pg 530
Livraria Verdade e Vida Editora, pg 530

Puerto Rico
Modern Guides Company, pg 530

Romania
Editora All, pg 531
Ars Longa Publishing House, pg 532
Editura Cartea Romaneasca, pg 532
Corint Verlag, pg 532
Editure Ion Creanga, pg 532
Editura Dacia, pg 532
Editura Excelsior, pg 533
Editura Kriterion SA, pg 534
Editura Niculescu, pg 534
Pallas-Akademia Koenyvkiadoes Koenyvkereskedes, pg 535
Pandora Publishing House, pg 535
RAO International Publishing Co, pg 535
RAO Publishing Group, pg 535
Saeculum IO, pg 535
Est-Samuel Tastet Verlag, pg 536
Editura Univers, pg 536
Universal Dalsi, pg 536
Editura de Vest, pg 536
Vremea Publishers Ltd, pg 536

Russian Federation
Armada Publishing House, pg 537
BLIC, russko-Baltijskij informaciionnyj centr, AO, pg 537
CentrePolygraph Traders & Publishers Co, pg 537
Izdatelstvo Detskaya Literatura, pg 537
Dom, Izdatel'stvo sovetskogo deskkogo fonda im & I Lenina, pg 537
Glas New Russian Writing, pg 538
Izdatelstvo Moskovskii Rabochii, pg 539
Kavkazskaya Biblioteka Publishing House, pg 539
Izdatelstvo Khudozhestvennaya Literatura, pg 539
Izdatelstvo Knizhnaya Palata, pg 539
Ladomir Publishing House, pg 539
Izdatelstvo Lenizdat, pg 539
Publishing House Limbus Press, pg 539
Izdatelstvo Mir, pg 540
Mir Knigi Ltd, pg 540
Novosti Izdatel 'stvo, pg 541
Obdeestvo Znanie, pg 541
Panorama Publishing House, pg 541
Permskaja Kniga, pg 541
Pressa Publishing House, pg 541
Profizdat, pg 541
Progress Publishers, pg 541
Raduga Publishers, pg 541
Russkaya Kniga Izdatelstvo (Publishers), pg 541
Sovremennik Publishers Too, pg 542

PUBLISHERS SUBJECT INDEX

Sredne-Uralskoye knizhnoye izatelstve (Middle Urals Publishing House), pg 542
Top Secret Collection Publishers, pg 542
Voyenizdat, pg 542
Vsesoyuznii Molodejnii Knizhnii Centre, pg 542

Senegal

Centre Africain d'Animation et d'Echanges Culturels Editions Khoudia, pg 544
Les Nouvelles Editions Africaines du Senegal NEAS, pg 544

Singapore

Chopsons Pte Ltd, pg 545

Slovakia

Danubiaprint, pg 549
Slovensky Spisovatel Ltd as, pg 550
Smena Publishing House, pg 550
Sport Publishing House Ltd, pg 551
Vydavatel'stvo Osveta (Verlag Osveta), pg 551
Wist, pg 551

Slovenia

Cankarjeva Zalozba, pg 551
Franc-Franc podjetje za promocijo kulture Murska Sobota d o o, pg 551
Pomurska zalozba, pg 552
Zalozba Mihelac d o o, pg 552

South Africa

HarperCollins Religious, pg 554
HAUM (Hollandsch Afrikaansche Uitgevers Maatschappij), pg 555
The Hippogriff Press CC, pg 555
Human & Rousseau (Pty) Ltd, pg 555
Ithemba! Publishing, pg 555
Jacklin Enterprises (Pty) Ltd, pg 556
Juventus/Femina Publishers, pg 556
LAPA Publishers (Pty) Ltd, pg 556
Nasou Via Afrika, pg 557
New Africa Books (Pty) Ltd, pg 557
Queillerie Publishers, pg 558
Ravan Press (Pty) Ltd, pg 558
Tafelberg Publishers Ltd, pg 560

Spain

Acantilado, pg 561
Acento Editorial, pg 561
Editorial Aguaclara, pg 562
Aguilar SA de Ediciones, pg 562
Alfaguara Ediciones SA - Grupo Santillana, pg 562
Ediciones Alfar SA, pg 562
Alianza Editorial SA, pg 562
Ediciones B, SA, pg 565
Calambur Editorial, SL, pg 566
Calamo Editorial, pg 566
CEAC, Grupo Editorial SA, pg 567
Circe Ediciones, SA, pg 567
Columna Edicions, Libres i Comunicacio, SA, pg 568
Ediciones Destino SA, pg 569
Editorial Don Quijote, pg 570
Edebe, pg 571
EDHASA (Editora y Distribuidora Hispano-Americana SA), pg 571
Edi-Liber Irlan SA, pg 571
Emece Editores, pg 573
Editorial Empeno 14, pg 573
Editorial Esin, SA, pg 573
Editorial Espasa-Calpe SA, pg 573
Editorial Fundamentos, pg 575
Grijalbo Mondadori SA, pg 576
Hogar del Libro, SA, pg 577
Ediciones Jucar, pg 579
Editorial Juventud SA, pg 579
Laertes SA de Ediciones, pg 579
Edicions de l'Eixample, SA, pg 580
Loguez Ediciones, pg 580
Editorial Lumen SA, pg 580
Editorial Magisterio Espanol SA, pg 581
Edicions de la Magrana SA, pg 581
Ediciones Martinez-Roca SA, pg 581
Ediciones Minotauro, pg 582
Editorial Molino, pg 582
Editorial Moll SL, pg 582
Noguer y Caralt Editores SA, pg 584
Editorial Noray, pg 584
Ediciones Oceano Grupo SA, pg 584
Ediciones Olimpic, SL, pg 585
Ediciones del Oriente y del Mediterraneo, pg 585
Pages Editors, SL, pg 585
El Paisaje Editorial, pg 585
Pirene Editorial, sal, pg 587
Editorial Planeta SA, pg 587
Plaza y Janes Editores SA, pg 587
Editorial Pliegos, pg 587
Pre-Textos, pg 587
Editorial Prensa Espanola, pg 587
Edicions Proa, SA, pg 588
Editorial Seix Barral SA, pg 590
Ediciones Siruela SA, pg 591
Edicions 62, pg 591
Grup 62, pg 591
Anna Soler-Pont Literary Agecy, pg 591
Ediciones Susaeta SA, pg 592
Editorial Thassalia, SA, pg 592
Ediciones Toray SA, pg 593
Gregorio del Toro Editor, pg 593
Trea Ediciones, SL, pg 593
Tusquets Editores, pg 593
Ultramar Editores SA, pg 594
Ediciones Urano, SA, pg 595
Editorial Verbum SL, pg 595
Javier Vergara Editor SA, pg 595
Editorial Vicens-Vives, pg 595
Vinaches Lopez, Luisa, pg 595
Edicions Xerais de Galicia, pg 596
Xunta de Galicia, pg 596

Sri Lanka

Dayawansa Jayakody & Co, pg 597
Lake House Investments Ltd, pg 597
Pradeepa Publishers, pg 598
Saman & Madara Publishers, pg 598

Sudan

Al-Ayam Press Co Ltd, pg 598
Khartoum University Press, pg 598

Suriname

Lutchman, Drs LFS, pg 599

Sweden

Akademiforlaget Corona AB, pg 599
Albert Bonniers Forlag, pg 600
Alfabeta Bokforlag AB, pg 600
Bokforlaget Atlantis AB, pg 600
Bokforlaget Bra Bocker AB, pg 600
Bokforlaget Plus AB, pg 600
Bokforlaget Spektra AB, pg 601
Bonnier Audio, pg 601
Albert Bonniers Forlag, pg 601
Brombergs Bokforlag AB, pg 601
Rene Coeckelberghs Bokfoerlag AB, pg 601
Delta Forlags AB, pg 601
Egmont Serieforlaget, pg 601
Ekonomibok Forlag AB, pg 601
Ellerstroms, pg 602
Bokforlaget Fingraf AB, pg 602
Fischer & Co, pg 602
Bokforlaget Forum AB, pg 602
Gedins Forlag, pg 602
Lars Hoekerbergs Bokfoerlag, pg 603
Interculture, pg 603
Libris Bokforlaget, pg 604
Bokfoerlaget Naturoch Kultur, pg 604
Norstedts Foerlag, pg 605
Ordfront Foerlag AB, pg 605
Bokforlaget Prisma, pg 605
Richters Egmont, pg 605
Sjoestrands Foerlag, pg 606
AB Wahlstrom & Widstrand, pg 607
Wahlstrom & Widstrand, pg 607
B Wahlstroms, pg 607
Zindermans AB, pg 607

Switzerland

Editions L'Age d'Homme - La Cite, pg 608
Ammann Verlag & Co, pg 608
Arche Verlag AG, Raabe und Vitali, pg 608
Bohem Press Kinderbuchverlag, pg 610
Verlag Bo Cavefors, pg 611
Chronos Verlag, pg 611
Cosmos-Verlag AG, pg 611
Diogenes Verlag AG, pg 612
Verlag ED Emmentaler Druck AG, pg 613
Edition Epoca, pg 613
eFeF-Verlag/Edition Ebersbach, pg 613
Haffmans Verlag AG, pg 615
Limmat Verlag, pg 618
Les Editions la Matze, pg 618
Mueller Rueschlikon Verlags AG, pg 619
Verlag Nagel & Kimche AG, Zurich, pg 619
Oesch Verlag AG, pg 620
Editions du Panorama, pg 621
Editions Patino, pg 621
Robert Raeber, Buchhandlung am Schweizerhof, pg 622
Verlag Friedrich Reinhardt AG, pg 622
Rex Verlag, pg 623
Rotpunktverlag, pg 623
Speer -Verlag, pg 625
Sphinx Verlag AG, pg 625
Strom-Verlag Luzern, pg 625
Theseus - Verlag AG, pg 625
Istituto Editoriale Ticinese (IET) SA, pg 626
Verlag Die Waage, pg 627

Taiwan, Province of China

Asian Culture Co, pg 629
Chung Hwa Book Co Ltd, pg 629
Commonwealth Publishing Company Ltd, pg 629
Grimm Press Ltd, pg 630
Highlight Publishing Company Ltd, pg 630
Kuang Fu Book Co Ltd, pg 630
Lin Pai Press Company Ltd, pg 631
Linking Publishing Company Ltd, pg 631
Morning Star Publisher Inc, pg 631
UNITAS Publishing Co Ltd, pg 632
Yuan Liou Publishing Co, Ltd, pg 632

Tajikistan

Irfon, pg 632

United Republic of Tanzania

Akajase Enterprises, pg 633
East African Publishing House, pg 633
Ndanda Mission Press, pg 634
Nyota Publishers Ltd, pg 634
Press & Publicity Centre Ltd, pg 634
Readit Books, pg 634
Tanzania Publishing House, pg 634
Tema Publishers Ltd, pg 634

Thailand

Bannakit Trading, pg 635
Chokechai Thewet Co Ltd, pg 635
New Generation Publishing Co Ltd, pg 635
Ruamsarn (1977) Co Ltd, pg 635

Togo

Les Nouvelles Editions Africaines du TOGO (NEA-TOGO), pg 636

Tunisia

Alyssa Editions, pg 637
Ceres Editions, pg 637

Turkey

Altin Kitaplar Yayinevi, pg 638
Cep Kitaplari AS, pg 639
Iletisim Yayinlari, pg 640
Inkilap Publishers Ltd, pg 640
Pan Yayincilik, pg 640
Parantez Yayinlari Ltd, pg 640
Remzi Kitabevi, pg 641
Soez Yayin/Oyunajans, pg 641
Varlik Yayinlari AS, pg 641

Turkmenistan

Izdatelstvo Turkmenistan, pg 642

Uganda

Fountain Publishers Ltd, pg 642

Ukraine

ASK Ltd, pg 643
Veselka Publishers, pg 643

United Kingdom

Acair Ltd, pg 645
Act 3 Publishing, pg 645
AK Press & Distribution, pg 645
Allied Mouse Ltd, pg 646
Alun Books, pg 646
Andersen Press Ltd, pg 647
Apex Publishing Ltd, pg 648
Atlas Press, pg 651
BBC Audiobooks, pg 652
BCA, pg 653
Beaver Publishing Ltd, pg 653
Bellew Publishing Co Ltd, pg 653
Birlinn Ltd, pg 655
Black Ace Books, pg 655
Black Spring Press Ltd, pg 655
Blackstaff Press, pg 655
Bloomsbury Publishing PLC, pg 656
Blorenge Books, pg 656
The Book Guild Ltd, pg 657
Books of Zimbabwe Publishing Co (Pvt) Ltd, pg 657

961

SUBJECT INDEX

Boulevard Books UK/The Babel Guides, pg 657
Marion Boyars Publishers Ltd, pg 658
Breese Books Ltd, pg 659
Brewin Books Ltd, pg 659
Brimax Books, pg 659
Calder Publications Ltd, pg 662
Canongate Books Ltd, pg 663
Carcanet Press Ltd, pg 663
Cassell & Co, pg 664
Chorion IP, pg 667
Christian Focus Publications Ltd, pg 667
The Chrysalis Press, pg 667
Constable & Robinson Ltd, pg 670
Constable Publishers, pg 670
Creation Books, pg 671
Dedalus Ltd, pg 674
Denor Press, pg 675
Andre Deutsch Ltd, pg 675
Gerald Duckworth & Co Ltd, pg 676
Eland, pg 677
Faber & Faber Ltd, pg 681
Fourth Estate Ltd, pg 683
Gairm Publications, pg 685
Geiser Productions, pg 686
Gembooks, pg 686
George Mann Publications, pg 687
GMP Publishers Ltd, pg 687
Gollancz/Witherby, pg 688
Gomer Press (J D Lewis & Sons Ltd), pg 688
Grandreams Ltd, pg 689
Granta Books, pg 689
Robert Hale Ltd, pg 691
Hamish Hamilton Ltd, pg 691
Patrick Hardy Books, pg 692
HarperCollins Publishers, pg 692
The Harvill Press Ltd, pg 693
Headline Book Publishing Ltd, pg 693
Heinemann Educational Publishing, pg 694
William Heinemann Ltd, pg 694
Hodder & Stoughton General, pg 696
Hodder Children's Books, pg 696
Honeyglen Publishing Ltd, pg 697
Honno Welsh Women's Press, pg 697
Independent Writers Publications Ltd, pg 699
Isis Publishing Ltd, pg 701
The Islamic Texts Society, pg 701
Jade Publishers, pg 702
Janus Publishing Company Ltd, pg 702
John Blake Publishing Ltd, pg 703
Michael Joseph Ltd, pg 703
Ladybird Books, pg 705
Letterbox Library, pg 707
Libris Ltd, pg 707
Y Lolfa Cyf, pg 708
Luath Press Ltd, pg 709
Macmillan Audio Books, pg 710
Macmillan Children's Books, pg 710
Macmillan Ltd, pg 710
Magi Publications, pg 710
Mandrake of Oxford, pg 711
The Mansk Svenska Publishing Co Ltd, pg 711
Methuen Publishing Ltd, pg 714
New Era Publications UK Ltd, pg 718
Octopus Publishing Group, pg 720
Oldcastle Books Ltd, pg 720
Orion Publishing Group Ltd, pg 722
Peter Owen Ltd, pg 722
Oyster Books, pg 723
Parthian Books, pg 724

Peepal Tree Press, pg 725
Piatkus Books, pg 727
Plough Publishing House of Bruderhof Communities in the UK, pg 728
Poetry Wales Press Ltd, pg 729
Polybooks Ltd, pg 729
Polygon, pg 729
Pookie Productions Ltd, pg 729
Quartet Books Ltd, pg 731
Ramsay Head Press, pg 732
Random House UK Ltd, pg 733
Ravette Publishing Ltd, pg 733
The Reader's Digest Association Ltd, pg 733
The Rubicon Press, pg 737
St George's Press, pg 737
The Salariya Book Co Ltd, pg 738
Sangam Books Ltd, pg 738
Scholastic Ltd, pg 739
Martin Secker & Warburg, pg 740
Seren, pg 740
Serpent's Tail Ltd, pg 740
Severn House Publishers Ltd, pg 740
Shearwater Press Ltd, pg 741
Sidgwick & Jackson Ltd, pg 742
Simon & Schuster Ltd, pg 742
Skoob Russell Square, pg 742
Souvenir Press Ltd, pg 743
Sutton Publishing Ltd, pg 746
Tabb House, pg 746
Telegraph Books, pg 748
Tiger Books International PLC, pg 748
Time Warner Books UK, pg 749
Transworld Publishers Ltd, pg 750
Tuba Press, pg 750
Ulverscroft Large Print Books Ltd, pg 751
United Writers Publications Ltd, pg 751
Van Molle Publishing, pg 752
Viking, pg 753
Virago Press, pg 753
Walker Books Ltd, pg 754
The Watts Publishing Group Ltd, pg 754
Wayland Publishers Ltd (Incorporating Macdonald Young Books), pg 754
Wilmington Business Information Ltd, pg 756
Neil Wilson Publishing Ltd, pg 757
The Women's Press Ltd, pg 758
Gordon Wright Publishing Ltd, pg 759
Anglia Young Books, pg 759

Uruguay
La Flor del Itapebi, pg 760
Rosebud Ediciones, pg 761
Ediciones Trilce, pg 761

Venezuela
Alfadil Ediciones, pg 761
Monte Avila Editores Latinoamericana CA, pg 762
Biblioteca Ayacucho, pg 762
Ediciones Ekare, pg 762

Yugoslavia
Alfa-Narodna Knjiga, pg 764
Forum, pg 764
Nolit Publishing House, pg 765
Obod, pg 765
Partenon MAM Sistem, pg 765
Svetovi, pg 766

Zambia
Apple Books, pg 766
Multimedia Zambia, pg 767
Zambia Educational Publishing House, pg 767

Zimbabwe
Academic Books Pvt Ltd, pg 767
College Press Publishers (Pvt) Ltd, pg 768
The Graham Publishing Company (Pvt) Ltd, pg 768
Mambo Press, pg 768
Vision Publications, pg 769

FILM, VIDEO

Argentina
Marymar Ediciones SA, pg 7

Australia
Australian Film Television & Radio School, pg 13
R J Cleary Publishing, pg 18
Currency Press Pty Ltd, pg 19
McGraw-Hill Australia Pty Ltd, pg 32
Power Publications, pg 38

Austria
Docker Verlag GmbH & Co KG, pg 51
Edition S der OSD, pg 51
Dr Verena Hofstaetter, pg 53

Belgium
Graton Editeur SA, pg 69
Claude Lefrancq Editeur, pg 71

Brazil
Editora Brasil-America (EBAL) SA, pg 82
Summus Editorial Ltda, pg 92

China
China Film Press, pg 103
China Light Industry Press, pg 103
The People's Communications Publishing House, pg 107

Colombia
Unidad Universitaria del Sur (UNISUR), pg 114

Costa Rica
Promesa, Ediciones, pg 116

Cuba
Casa Editora Abril, pg 120

Czech Republic
Cesky Filmovy ustav, pg 123
Cinema, pg 123
Nakladatelstvi a vydavatelstvi Panorama, pg 127

Denmark
Interpresse A/S, pg 133
Kaleidoscope Publishers Ltd, pg 133
Systime, pg 136

Estonia
Sinisukk, pg 140

Finland
Koala-Kustannus/Oy Greenbay House Publishing Ltd, pg 143

France
Editions d'Aujourd'hui (Les Introuvables), pg 149
Editions l'Avant-Scene de Prette Technique, pg 149
Editions Balland, pg 149
Bragelonne, pg 151
Climats, pg 155
Copernic, pg 156
Editions Dis Voir, pg 159
Dreamland Editeur, pg 160
Dunod Editeur, pg 160
Editions du Jeu de Paume, pg 170
Editions Michel Lafon SA, pg 171
Lettres Modernes, pg 172
Macula, pg 174
Librairie Minard, pg 176
Editions Paul Montel, pg 176
Editions Plume, pg 180
Editions du Centre Pompidou, pg 180
Sofradif Editions Philippe Auzou, pg 185
Editions Stock, pg 186
La Voix du Regard, pg 189

Germany
Alba Fachverlag GmbH und Co KG, pg 192
Alexander Verlag Berlin, pg 192
AOL-Verlag Frohmut Menze, pg 194
Aufbau Taschenbuch Verlag GmbH, pg 196
Aufbau-Verlag GmbH, pg 196
Verlag der Autoren GmbH & Co KG, pg 197
Bertelsmann Lexikon Verlag GmbH, pg 201
Chmielorz GmbH Verlag, pg 210
Corian-Verlag Heinrich Wimmer, pg 211
Klaus D Dutz, pg 219
Egmont Franz Schneider Verlag GmbH, pg 221
Egmont vgs verlagsgesellschaft mbH, pg 221
EK-Verlag GmbH, pg 222
Emons Verlag, pg 222
F Bruckmann Munchen Verlag & Druck GmbH & Co Produkt KG, pg 225
FN-Verlag der Deutschen Reiterlichen Vereinigung GmbH, pg 229
Wilhelm Goldmann Verlag GmbH, pg 233
Gunter Olzog Verlag GmbH, pg 235
Haenssler Verlag GmbH, pg 236
Litteraturverlag Karlheinz Hartmann, pg 237
Heel Verlag GmbH, pg 238
Wilhelm Heyne Verlag, pg 240
Huebner Felicitas Verlag, pg 243
Huthig GmbH & Co KG, pg 244
Impuls-Theater-Verlag, pg 244
Jovis Verlag GmbH, pg 246
Kino Verlag GmbH, pg 249
Verlagsgruppe Koehler/Mittler, pg 251
kopaed verlagsgmbh, pg 252
Verlag Laterna magica GmbH & Co KG, pg 256
Edition Axel Menges, pg 262
J B Metzler'sche Verlagsbuchhandlung, pg 263
Mosaik Verlag GmbH, pg 265

PUBLISHERS

Verlag Stephanie Naglschmid, pg 266
Philipp Reclam Jun Verlag GmbH, pg 273
Polyband Gesellschaft fur Bild Tontraeger mbH & Co Betriebs KG, pg 274
Propylaeen Verlag, Zweigniederlassung Berlin der Ullstein Buchverlage GmbH, pg 275
Quintessenz Verlags-GmbH, pg 276
Schueren Verlag GmbH, pg 285
Schulz-Kirchner Verlag GmbH, pg 285
Spiess Volker Wissenschaftsverlag GmbH, pg 287
edition Text & Kritik im Richard Boorberg Verlag GmbH & Co, pg 293
TR - Verlagsunion GmbH, pg 294
Trescher Verlag GmbH, pg 295
Tuebinger Vereinigung fur Volkskunde eV (TVV), pg 295
Ulrich Schiefer bahnVerlag, pg 296
Das Wunderhorn Verlag GmbH, pg 304

Ghana
World Literature Project, pg 308

Greece
Apostoliki Diakonia tis Ekklisias tis Hellados, pg 309
Kastaniotis Editions SA, pg 312
Medusa/Selas, pg 313

Hong Kong
Benefit Publishing Co, pg 318
Joint Publishing (HK) Co Ltd, pg 320

Hungary
Jelenkor Verlag, pg 324
Osiris Kiado, pg 326

Indonesia
PT Indira, pg 355

Israel
Hanitzotz A-Sharara Publishing House, pg 368
The Harry Karren Institute for the Analysis of Propaganda, Yad Labanim, pg 369
Rolnik Publishers, pg 371

Italy
Bulzoni Editore SRL (Le Edizioni Universitarie d'Italia), pg 379
Nuova Casa Editrice Licinio Cappelli GEM srl, pg 379
Il Castoro, pg 380
Cooperativa Libraria IULM SCRL, pg 383
Edizioni Dedalo SRL, pg 384
Ernesto Gremese Editore SRL, pg 391
Gremese International Srl, pg 391
IHT Gruppo Editoriale SRL, pg 393
Kaos Edizioni SRL, pg 395
Lalli Editore SRL, pg 395
Letture Mensile di Informazione Culturale, Letteratura e Spettacolo, pg 395
Lindau, pg 396
Angelo Longo Editore, pg 396
Giuseppe Maimone Editore, pg 397
Marsilio Editori SpA, pg 398

Edizioni Gabriele Mazzotta SRL, pg 398
Mondolibro Editore SNC, pg 399
Officina Edizioni di Aldo Quinti, pg 401
RAI.ERI, pg 405
SAIE Editrice SRL, pg 406
Scala Group spa, pg 407
Transeuropa Libri, pg 410
Edizioni Ubulibri SAS, pg 410

Japan
Bunkasha Publishing Co, Ltd, pg 415
Genko-Sha, pg 416
Shincho-Sha Co Ltd, pg 425
Waseda University Press, pg 428

Republic of Korea
Youl Hwa Dang Publisher, pg 436

Latvia
Egmont Latvia Ltd, pg 442
Preses Nams, pg 442

Luxembourg
Edition Objectif Lune, pg 447

Mexico
SCRIPTA - Distribucion y Servicios Editoriales, SA de CV, pg 467

Netherlands
Uitgeverij Cantecleer BV, pg 475
Frank Fehmers Productions, pg 477
Uitgevery International Theatre & Film Books, pg 479
Rostrum Publishing, pg 483
Tirion Uitgevers BV, pg 485

Norway
J W Eides Forlag A/S, pg 503
Vett & Viten AS, pg 505

Peru
Universidad de Lima-Fondo de Desarollo Editorial, pg 512

Philippines
Communication Foundation for Asia Media Group (CFAMG), pg 513
Our Lady of Manaoag Publisher, pg 514

Poland
Wydawnictwa Artystyczne i Filmowe, pg 516
Wydawnictwo Literackie, pg 517
Videograf II Sp z o o Zaklad Poracy Chronionej, pg 520

Portugal
Edicoes Afrontamento, pg 522

Romania
Editura Meridiane, pg 534
Editura Minerva, pg 534
Editura Niculescu, pg 534

Russian Federation
Izdatelstvo Iskusstvo, pg 538

South Africa
Bet-El Publishers, pg 553

Spain
Ediciones Akal SA, pg 562
Editorial Astri SA, pg 564
Ediciones Catedra SA, pg 566
Comunidad Autonoma de Madrid, Servicio de Documentacion y Publicaciones, pg 568
Editorial Donostiarra SA, pg 570
Edicions del Drac SA, pg 570
Ediciones Ebenezer, pg 571
Editorial Fundamentos, pg 575
Laertes SA de Ediciones, pg 579
Mandala Ediciones, pg 581
Ediciones Omega SA, pg 585
Ultramar Editores SA, pg 594

Sweden
Alfabeta Bokforlag AB, pg 600
Interculture, pg 603
Schultz Forlag AB, pg 606

Switzerland
Editions L'Age d'Homme - La Cite, pg 608
Chronos Verlag, pg 611
Editions Esprit Ouvert, pg 613
Editions Foma SA, pg 614
Lehrmittelverlag des Kantons Zurich, pg 618
Edition Olms AG, pg 620
Promoedition SA, pg 622
Hans Rohr Verlag, pg 623
3 Dimension World (3-D-World), pg 625
Vexer Verlag, pg 627

Turkey
Afa Yayincilik Sanayi Tic AS, pg 638
Parantez Yayinlari Ltd, pg 640
Payel Yayinevi, pg 641
Soez Yayin/Oyunajans, pg 641

Ukraine
Mystetstvo Publishers, pg 643

United Kingdom
Act 3 Publishing, pg 645
The Athlone Press Ltd, pg 650
Aurum Press Ltd, pg 651
Batsford Ltd, pg 652
BCA, pg 653
BFI Publishing, pg 654
Bishopsgate Press Ltd, pg 655
Bloomsbury Publishing PLC, pg 656
Boxtree Ltd, pg 658
Butterworth-Heinemann Ltd, pg 661
Cameron & Hollis, pg 663
Carlton Publishing Group, pg 664
Cassell & Co, pg 664
Chadwyck-Healey Ltd, pg 666
Chorion IP, pg 667
Creation Books, pg 671
Edinburgh University Press Ltd, pg 677
The Eurospan Group, pg 680
Faber & Faber Ltd, pg 681
Flicks Books, pg 683
Foulsham Publishers, pg 683
Golden Cockerel Press Ltd, pg 688
Hamlyn, pg 691
HarperCollins Publishers, pg 692
Harvard University Press, pg 692
Institute of Irish Studies, The Queens University of Belfast, pg 699
Intellect Ltd, pg 700
Janus Publishing Company Ltd, pg 702

SUBJECT INDEX

Laurence King Publishing Ltd, pg 704
Lawrence & Wishart, pg 706
John Libbey & Co Ltd, pg 707
Manchester University Press, pg 711
National Association for the Teaching of English (NATE), pg 717
Octopus Publishing Group, pg 720
Old Vicarage Publications, pg 720
Oliver Books Ltd, pg 721
Orion Publishing Group Ltd, pg 722
Pavilion Books Ltd, pg 724
Plexus Publishing Ltd, pg 728
Polygon, pg 729
The Reader's Digest Association Ltd, pg 733
Reaktion Books Ltd, pg 733
Roundhouse Publishing Ltd, pg 736
Routledge, pg 736
I B Tauris & Co Ltd, pg 747
Time Out Group Ltd, pg 749
Titan Books Ltd, pg 749
Transworld Publishers Ltd, pg 750
University of Exeter Press, pg 751
Verso, pg 752
Virgin Publishing Ltd, pg 753
World Microfilms Publications Ltd, pg 758
Zwemmer Holdings Co Ltd, pg 759

Zimbabwe
Africa Film & TV t/a Z Promotions, pg 767

FINANCE

Albania
NL SH, pg 1

Australia
D&B Marketing Pty Ltd, pg 20
Horan Wall & Walker, pg 26
Law Book Co Information Services, pg 29
Life Planning Foundation of Australia, Inc, pg 30
Anne O'Donovan Pty Ltd, pg 35
OTEN (Open Training & Education Network), pg 36
Prospect Media Pty Ltd, pg 39
The Real Estate Institute of Australia, pg 40
The Useful Publishing Co, pg 46
VCTA Publishing, pg 46
Woodlands Publications, pg 48
Wrightbooks Pty Ltd, pg 48

Austria
Buchhandlung WUV Dolmetsch, pg 50
Compass-Verlag GmbH, pg 50
Horst Knapp Finanznachrichten, pg 54

Azerbaijan
Sada, Literaturno-Izdatel'skij Centr, pg 61

Bangladesh
The University Press Ltd, pg 62

Belarus
Belaruskaya Encyklapedyya, pg 63

Belgium
Editions De Boeck-Larcier SA, pg 67
Intersentia Uitgevers NV, pg 69

SUBJECT INDEX

Brazil
Editora Atlas SA, pg 79
Editora Lucre Comercio e Representacoes, pg 87
Editora Ortiz SA, pg 89
Qualitymark Editora Ltda, pg 90
Saraiva SA, Livreiros Editores, pg 91
Jorge Zahar Editor, pg 93

Bulgaria
Ciela Publishing House, pg 94
Dolphin Press Group Ltd, pg 95
Pensoft Publishers, pg 97

Cameroon
Presses Universitaires d'Afrique, pg 99

China
Beijing Publishing House, pg 102
Beijing University Press, pg 102
China Foreign Economic Relations & Trade Publishing House, pg 103
CITIC Publishing House, pg 104
East China University of Science & Technology Press, pg 105
Fudan University Press, pg 105
Higher Education Press, pg 106
Shandong University Press, pg 109

Colombia
Universidad Externado de Colombia, pg 112
Unidad Universitaria del Sur (UNISUR), pg 114

Costa Rica
Academia de Centro America, pg 115
Confederacion de Cooperativas del Caribe y Centro America, pg 115

Croatia
Informator dd, pg 119
Masmedia, pg 119

Czech Republic
Nakladatelstvi Svoboda, pg 126

Denmark
Djof Publishing Jurist-og Okonomforbundets Forlag, pg 131
Samfundslitteratur, pg 135

France
Bottin SA, pg 151
Centre de Librairie et d'Editions Techniques (CLET), pg 153
DAFSA, pg 157
Editions Dalloz Sirey, pg 157
Les Editions ESF, pg 161
Les Editions de l'Epargne, pg 162
Groupe de Recherche et d'Echanges Technologiques (GRET), pg 167
Groupe Moniteur -L'Argus, pg 167
Maxima Laurent du Mesnil Editeur, pg 175
Pearson Education France, pg 179
Top Editions, pg 188
Editions Village Mondial, pg 189

Germany
Bank-Verlag GmbH, pg 198
Bund-Verlag GmbH, pg 208
Deutscher Wirtschaftsdienst John von Freyend GmbH, pg 216
Duncker und Humblot GmbH, pg 219
Verlag Franz Vahlen GmbH, pg 229
Friedrich Kiehl Verlag GmbH, pg 230
Betriebswirtschaftlicher Verlag Dr Th Gabler GmbH, pg 231
von Hase & Koehler Verlag KG, pg 238
Rudolf Haufe Verlag GmbH & Co KG, pg 238
Verlag Hoppenstedt GmbH, pg 242
IDW-Verlag GmbH, pg 244
Verlag Fritz Knapp GmbH, pg 250
Libertas- Europaeisches Institut GmbH, pg 257
Mosaik Verlag GmbH, pg 265
Norbert Mueller AG & Co KG Verlag, pg 265
Physica-Verlag, pg 273
pmi Verlag, pg 274
Verlag Norman Rentrop, pg 279
Richardi Helmut Verlag GmbH, pg 279
Rossipaul Kommunikation GmbH, pg 280
Schaeffer-Poeschel Verlag fuer Wirtschaft Steuern Recht, pg 282
Verlag Dr Otto Schmidt KG, pg 283
Erich Schmidt Verlag GmbH & Co, pg 284
Schulz-Kirchner Verlag GmbH, pg 285
Springer-Verlag GmbH & Co KG, pg 288
Stollfuss Verlag Bonn GmbH & Co KG, pg 290

Greece
Kritiki Publishing, pg 312
Vivliothiki Eftychia Galeou, pg 315

Hong Kong
Asia Pacific Communications Ltd, pg 318
Joint Publishing (HK) Co Ltd, pg 320
Publications (Holdings) Ltd, pg 321
Thomson Corporation, pg 322
Yazhou Zhoukan Ltd, pg 322

Hungary
Kossuth Kiado RT, pg 325
Novorg Kiado, pg 326
Saldo Penzugyi Tanacsado es Informatikai Rt, pg 326

India
Ananda Publishers Pvt Ltd, pg 330
Reliance Publishing House, pg 347
Scientific Book Agency, pg 349
Sita Publications, pg 350
South Asia Publications, pg 350
Sultan Chand & Sons Pvt Ltd, pg 351

Indonesia
Bina Rena Pariwara, pg 354
P T Bulan Bintang, pg 354

Ireland
The Economic & Social Research Institute, pg 360
Irish Management Institute, pg 361
Oak Tree Press, pg 362
Round Hall Sweet & Maxwell, pg 363

Israel
Dyonon/Papyrus Publishing House of the Tel-Aviv, pg 367

Italy
Bancaria Editrice SpA, pg 377
CEDAM (Casa Editrice Dr A Milani), pg 380
EGEA (Edizioni Giuridiche Economiche Aziendali), pg 387

Japan
Institute for Financial Affairs Inc-KINZAI, pg 418
KINZAI Corporation, pg 420
Nikkagiren Shuppan-Sha (JUSE Press Ltd), pg 422
President Inc, pg 423
Sobun-Sha, pg 426
Waseda University Press, pg 428

Kenya
Focus Publications Ltd, pg 431
Heinemann Kenya Limited (EAEP), pg 431

Republic of Korea
Chung Rim Publishing Co Ltd, pg 435

Liechtenstein
Bonafides Verlags-Anstalt, pg 444
Liechtenstein Verlag AG, pg 444

Luxembourg
Editions Promoculture, pg 448
Service Central de la Statistique et des Etudes Economiques (STATEC), pg 448

Madagascar
Societe Malgache d'Edition, pg 450

Mexico
Centro de Estudios Monetarios Latinoamericanos (CEMLA), pg 460
Grupo Editorial Iberoamerica, SA de CV, pg 461
Editorial Limusa SA de CV, pg 463

Netherlands
Business Contact BV, pg 475
BZZTOH Publishers, pg 475
Samsom BedrijfsInformatie BV, pg 483
SDU Juridische & Fiscale Uitgeverij, pg 484

New Zealand
Business Bureau Christchurch, pg 489
Legislation Direct, pg 492
Nelson Price Milburn Ltd, pg 494
Shoal Bay Press Ltd, pg 495
Statistics New Zealand, pg 496

Nigeria
Goldland Business Co Ltd, pg 499
New Africa Publishing Company Ltd, pg 500

Norway
Glydendal Akademisk, pg 503

Pakistan
Royal Book Co, pg 509

Peru
Universidad de Lima-Fondo de Desarollo Editorial, pg 512

Philippines
Rex Bookstores & Publishers, pg 514

Poland
Polskie Wydawnictwo Ekonomiczne PWE SA, pg 516
Oficyna Wydawnicza Szkoly Glownej Handlowej w Warszawie Oficyna Wydawnicza SGH, pg 520

Portugal
Edicoes Cetop, pg 523
Livraria Minerva Editora, pg 526

Romania
Editura Dacia, pg 532
FF Press, pg 533
Editura Minerva, pg 534

Russian Federation
Finansy i Statistika Publishing House, pg 538

Singapore
Institute of Southeast Asian Studies, pg 546
Singapore University Press Pte Ltd, pg 548

Slovakia
Dom Techniky Zvazu Slovenskych Vedeckotechnickych Spolocnosti Ltd, pg 549
Vydavatepstvo Praca spol sro, pg 550

Slovenia
Univerza v Ljubljani Ekonomska Fakulteta, pg 552

Spain
Editorial Aranzadi SA, pg 564
Editorial Donostiarra SA, pg 570
Ediciones Deusto SA, pg 571
Ediciones Gestio 2000 SA, pg 575
Lid Editorial Empresarial, SL, pg 580
Marcombo SA de Boixareu Editores, pg 581
Xunta de Galicia, pg 596

Sweden
Ekonomibok Forlag AB, pg 601
Iustus Forlag AB, pg 603

Switzerland
Cosmos-Verlag AG, pg 611
Fortuna Finanz-Verlag AG, pg 614
Promoedition SA, pg 622
Versus Verlag AG, pg 627

Syrian Arab Republic
Damascus University Press, pg 628

Taiwan, Province of China
Fuh-Wen Book Co, pg 630

Turkey
Alkim Kitapcilik-Yayimcilik, pg 638
Soez Yayin/Oyunajans, pg 641

PUBLISHERS SUBJECT INDEX

Ukraine
Osnovy Publishers, pg 643

United Kingdom
ABG Professional Information, pg 644
Academic Press Ltd, pg 644
Age Concern Books, pg 645
AP Information Services, pg 648
Ashton & Denton Publishing Co (CI) Ltd, pg 650
Bishopsgate Press Ltd, pg 655
Blackwell Publishers, pg 655
Bloomsbury Publishing PLC, pg 656
Dr Barry Bracewell-Milnes, pg 658
Nicholas Brealey Publishing, pg 659
Business Monitor International, pg 661
Butterworth-Heinemann Ltd, pg 661
Butterworths Tolley, pg 661
Chorion IP, pg 667
Commonwealth Secretariat, pg 669
Croner CCH Group Ltd, pg 672
The Economist Intelligence Unit, pg 677
Edward Elgar Publishing Ltd, pg 678
Elliot Right Way Books, pg 678
The Eurospan Group, pg 680
Financial World Publishing, pg 682
Foulsham Publishers, pg 683
HarperCollins Publishers, pg 692
HB Publications, pg 693
How To Books Ltd, pg 697
ICC United Kingdom, pg 698
Institute for Fiscal Studies, pg 699
Kogan Page Ltd, pg 705
Letts Educational, pg 707
LLP Ltd, pg 708
London Chamber of Commerce & Industry Examinations Board, pg 709
Macmillan Reference Ltd, pg 710
Mars Business Associates Ltd, pg 712
MIT Press Ltd, pg 715
NCVO, pg 718
Profile Books Ltd, pg 731
Sage Publications Ltd, pg 737
Scottish Office Library & Information Services, pg 740
The Stationery Office, pg 745
Take That Ltd, pg 746
VNU Business Publications, pg 753
Which? Ltd, pg 755
Wiley Europe Ltd, pg 756
Wilmington Business Information Ltd, pg 756
Woodhead Publishing Ltd, pg 758

Uruguay
Fundacion de Cultura Universitaria, pg 760

Viet Nam
Science & Technics Publishing House, pg 763

Zambia
MFK Management Consultants Services, pg 766

FOREIGN COUNTRIES

Albania
NL SH, pg 1

Australia
AHB Publications, pg 11
Bandicoot Books, pg 14
Emperor Publishing, pg 22
Indra Publishing, pg 27
Oxfam Community Aid Abroad, pg 36
Pollitecon Publications, pg 38
Stafford Books, pg 43
Thames & Hudson (Australia) Pty Ltd, pg 44

Austria
Pinguin-Verlag, Pawlowski GmbH, pg 57
Promedia Verlagsges mbH, pg 57
Verlag Josef Otto Slezak, pg 58
Edition Va Bene, pg 60

Belgium
Abimo, pg 63
Institut Royal des Relations Internationales, pg 69
Ipis VZW (International Peace Information Service), pg 69

Bulgaria
Kibea Publishing Co, pg 96
Sluntse Publishing House, pg 98

China
Chengdu Maps Publishing House, pg 103
Foreign Language Teaching & Research Press, pg 105
World Affairs Press, pg 110

The Democratic Republic of the Congo
Presses Universitaires du Zaiire (PUZ), pg 115

Czech Republic
Karolinum, nakladatelstvi, pg 125
Mariadan, pg 126
Vitalis SRO, pg 129

Denmark
Dafolo Forlag, pg 131
Mellemfolkeligt Samvirke, pg 133
Museum Tusculanum Press, pg 134

Egypt (Arab Republic of Egypt)
Dar El Shorouk Publishing & Distributing House, pg 138

Finland
Kaantopiiri Oy, pg 142
Kirja-Leitzinger, pg 143

France
Editions de l'Aube, pg 149
Autrement Editions, pg 149
Blondel La Rougery SARL, pg 151
La Decouverte et Syros, pg 158
FBT de R Editions/Editions des Limbes d'Or, pg 163
Paul Geuthner Librairie Orientaliste, pg 166
Editions Jean Paul Gisserot, pg 166
L'Harmattan, pg 168
Editions d'Histoire Sociale (EDHIS), pg 168
Les Introuvables-Editions L'Harmattan, pg 170
Editions Juridiques Africaines, pg 171
Langues & Mondes/L'Asiatheque, pg 171
Editions des Limbes d'Or/FBT de R Editions, pg 173
Editions Norma, pg 177
Sepia, pg 184
Le Serpent a Plumes, pg 184
Sofradif Editions Philippe Auzou, pg 185
Transeuropeennes/RCE, pg 188

Germany
AOL-Verlag Frohmut Menze, pg 194
Aufstieg-Verlag GmbH, pg 196
Bertelsmann Lexikon Verlag GmbH, pg 201
W Bertelsmann Verlag GmbH & Co KG, pg 201
BKV-Brasilienkunde Verlag GmbH, pg 203
Verlag Hermann Boehlaus Nachfolger Weimar GmbH & Co, pg 205
Brandenburgisches Verlagshaus in der Dornier Medienholding GmbH, pg 206
Egmont vgs verlagsgesellschaft mbH, pg 221
Ellert & Richter Verlag GmbH, pg 222
Eppinger-Verlag OHG, pg 223
Frederking & Thaler Verlag GmbH, pg 230
Gunter Olzog Verlag GmbH, pg 235
Peter Hammer Verlag GmbH, pg 237
Horlemann Verlag, pg 243
Iudicium Verlag GmbH, pg 245
Jahreszeiten-Verlag GmbH, pg 246
Jan Thorbecke Verlag GmbH & Co, pg 246
Knowledge Media International, pg 251
Dr Anton Kovac Slavica Verlag, pg 253
Adam Kraft Verlag, pg 253
Landbuch-Verlagsgesellschaft mbH, pg 255
Idime Verlag Inge Melzer, pg 262
Munzinger-Archiv GmbH Archiv fuer publizistische Arbeit, pg 266
Neuthor - Verlag, pg 268
Nusser Verlag, pg 269
Palazzi Verlag GmbH, pg 271
Palmyra Verlag, pg 271
Pfalzische Verlagsanstalt GmbH, pg 272
Reise Know-How Verlag Peter Rump GmbH, pg 278
Schillinger Verlag GmbH, pg 283
Wilhelm Schmitz Verlag, pg 284
Gerd Simon & Claudia Magiera, Verlagsbuero, pg 287
Steiger Verlag, pg 289
Franz Steiner Verlag Wiesbaden GmbH, pg 289
Vervuert Verlagsgesellschaft, pg 298
VS Verlagshaus Stuttgart GmbH, pg 299
Weidlich Verlag, pg 301
Ziethen-Panorama Verlag GmbH, pg 305

Hong Kong
Macmillan Publishers (China) Ltd, pg 321

India
Kairali Children's Book Trust, pg 340
National Book Trust India, pg 343
Omsons Publications, pg 345
Scientific Book Agency, pg 349

Israel
Ben-Zvi Institute, pg 365
Hakibbutz Hameuchad Publishing House Ltd, pg 368
Hanitzotz A-Sharara Publishing House, pg 368
Ministry of Defence Publishing House, pg 370
Tel-Aviv University, pg 373
The Van Leer Jerusalem Institute, pg 373

Italy
Giuseppe Bonanno Editore, pg 378
Edizioni Cultura della Pace, pg 383
Giorgio Mondadori & Associati, pg 399

Jamaica
Carlong Publishers (Caribbean) Ltd, pg 412

Japan
The American Chamber of Commerce in Japan, pg 414
Kaisei-Sha Publishing Co Ltd, pg 419
Nippon Hoso Shuppan Kyokai (NHK Publishing), pg 422
Sobun-Sha, pg 426

Republic of Korea
Hakgojae Publishing Inc, pg 436

Malaysia
University of Malaya, Department of Publications, pg 455

Maldive Islands
Novelty Printers & Publishers, pg 455

Mexico
Centro de Estudios Mexicanos y Centroamericanos, pg 458

Mozambique
Centro De Estudos Africanos, pg 470

Namibia
Agrivet Publishers, pg 471

Netherlands
Educatieve Uitgeverij Edu'Actief BV, pg 476
Mets & Schilt Uitgevers en Distributeurs, pg 481

Netherlands Antilles
Bredero, pg 488

New Zealand
Aoraki Press Ltd, pg 488
Millwood Press Ltd, pg 493

Nigeria
Adebara Publishers Ltd, pg 497
Ahmadu Bello University Press Ltd, pg 498
Alliance West African Publishers & Co, pg 498
CSS Bookshops, Agency & Publishing Division, pg 498

Daily Times of Nigeria Ltd (Publication Division), pg 498
Educational Research & Study Group, pg 499
Ethiope Publishing Corporation, pg 499
Ibadan University Press, pg 499
Ilesanmi Press (Educational Publishers) Ltd, pg 499
Onibon-Oje Publishers, pg 501
University of Lagos Press, pg 502
University Publishing Co, pg 502

Peru
Ediciones Peisa (Promocion Editorial Inca SA), pg 511

Philippines
Garotech, pg 513
Vibal Publishing House Inc (VPHI), pg 515

Poland
Instytut Meteorologii i Gospodarki Wodnej, pg 518

Romania
Editura Academiei Romane, pg 531
The Center for Romanian Studies, pg 532

Senegal
Societe Africaine d'Edition, pg 544
Societe d'Edition d'Afrique Nouvelle, pg 544

Singapore
Institute of Southeast Asian Studies, pg 546
Masagung Books Pte Ltd, pg 547
Pustaka Nasional Pte Ltd, pg 547

Slovakia
Serafin, pg 550

Slovenia
Zalozba Mihelac d o o, pg 552

South Africa
Ashanti Publishing, pg 552
Galago Publishing Pty Ltd, pg 554
South African Institute of International Affairs, pg 559
Struik Publishers (Pty) Ltd, pg 559

Spain
Editorial AEDOS SA, pg 561
Amnistia Internacional Editorial SL, pg 563
Ediciones Maeva, pg 581
Mundo Negro Editorial, pg 583
Ediciones del Oriente y del Mediterraneo, pg 585
Ediciones Jose Porrua Turanzas SA, pg 593

Switzerland
Bergli Books AG, pg 609
Cockatoo Press (Schweiz), Thailand-Publikationen, pg 611
Dimension World Ltd, pg 612
Verlag im Waldgut AG, pg 627

United Arab Emirates
Motivate Publishing, pg 644

United Kingdom
ABC-CLIO, pg 644
Belitha Press Ltd, pg 653
Books of Zimbabwe Publishing Co (Pvt) Ltd, pg 657
Nicholas Brealey Publishing, pg 659
Business Monitor International, pg 661
James Currey Ltd, pg 673
Ernst & Young, pg 679
Europa Publications, pg 680
European Schoolbooks Ltd, pg 680
The Eurospan Group, pg 680
Garnet Publishing Ltd, pg 685
Grant & Cutler Ltd, pg 689
Gwasg Gwenffrwd, pg 690
Harden's Ltd, pg 692
HarperCollins Publishers, pg 692
Icon Press, pg 698
Jane's Information Group, pg 702
Letterbox Library, pg 707
Ravette Publishing Ltd, pg 733
Rough Guides Ltd, pg 735
Routledge Curzon, pg 736
Royal Institute of International Affairs, pg 736
The Salariya Book Co Ltd, pg 738
Serif, pg 740
Sheffield Academic Press Ltd, pg 741
Stacey International, pg 745
Vacation Work Publications, pg 752
Vacher Dod Publishing Ltd, pg 752

Uruguay
Nordan-Comunidad, pg 760

Zimbabwe
Bold ADS, pg 768
Nehanda Publishers, pg 769

GARDENING, PLANTS

Albania
NL SH, pg 1

Argentina
Editorial Albatros SACI, pg 3
Editorial Caymi SACI, pg 4
Editorial Hemisferio Sur SA, pg 6

Australia
Bloomings Books, pg 15
Candlelight Trust T/A Candlelight Farm, pg 17
Cornucopia Press, pg 19
Department of Primary Industries, Queensland, pg 20
Egan Publishing Pty Ltd, pg 21
Flora Publications International Pty Ltd, pg 23
Florilegium, pg 23
Freshet Press, pg 23
Hyland House Publishing Pty Ltd, pg 27
Kangaroo Press, pg 29
Landarc Publications, pg 29
Lansdowne Publishing Pty Ltd, pg 29
Mulini Press, pg 34
Pioneer Design Studio Pty Ltd, pg 38
R & R Publications Marketing P/L, pg 39
Frank Shepherd, pg 42
Social Club Books, pg 42
Terania Rainforest Publishing, pg 44
Three Sisters Publications Pty Ltd, pg 44
University of New South Wales Press Ltd, pg 46
The Watermark Press, pg 47

Austria
Leopold Stocker Verlag, pg 54

Belgium
Uitgeverij Lannoo NV, pg 70
Marabout, pg 72
Henri Proost & Co, Pvba, pg 73
Roularta Books NV, pg 73
Stichting Kunstboek bvba, pg 74
Zuid-Nederlandse Uitgeverij NV/ Central Uitgeverij, pg 76

Brazil
Livraria Nobel S/A, pg 86
Rede Das Artes (Boccato Editores Collector's), pg 90

Bulgaria
Gea-Libris Publishing House, pg 95
Rakla, pg 97
Sluntse Publishing House, pg 98

Chile
Editorial Texido Ltda, pg 101

China
China Agriculture Press, pg 103
China Forestry Publishing House, pg 103
Guangdong Science & Technology Press, pg 106
Guizhou Education Publishing House, pg 106
Wissenschaft und Technik Verlag Henan Henan Scientific & Technological Publishing House, pg 106
Higher Education Press, pg 106
Science Press, pg 108
Tianjin Science & Technology Publishing House, pg 109

The Democratic Republic of the Congo
Centre de Vulgarisation Agricole, pg 115

Costa Rica
Centro Agronomico Tropical de Investigacion y Ensenanza (CATIE), pg 115

Croatia
ALFA dd za izdavacke, graficke i trgovacke poslove, pg 118

Czech Republic
Aventinum Nakladatelstvi, pg 123
Granit SRO, pg 124
Svojtka & Co, pg 128

Denmark
GEC Gads Forlag Aktieselskab af 1994, pg 132

El Salvador
Editorial Universitaria de la Universidad de El Salvador, pg 139

Estonia
Sinisukk, pg 140

France
ATP - Packager, pg 149
Editions Belin, pg 150
Bookmaker, pg 151
Courrier du Livre Sarl, pg 157
Edisud, pg 161
Flammarion SA, pg 164
Editions Jean Paul Gisserot, pg 166
Hachette Pratiques, pg 167
Librairie Larousse, pg 172
Editions Mango, pg 174
Societe des Editions Menges, pg 175
Editions du Rouergue, pg 183
Editions Sang de la Terre, pg 183
Sofradif Editions Philippe Auzou, pg 185
Soline, pg 186
Terre Vivante, pg 187

Germany
August Guse Verlag GmbH, pg 196
Augustus Verlag, pg 196
Bassermann Verlag, pg 198
Blackwell Wissenschafts-Verlag GmbH, pg 203
BLV Verlagsgesellschaft mbH, pg 204
Bonsai-Centrum, pg 205
Verlag Georg D W Callwey GmbH & Co, pg 208
Christian Verlag GmbH, pg 210
Hans Christians Druckerei und Verlag GmbH & Co, pg 210
Compact Verlag GmbH, pg 211
DLV Deutscher Landwirtschaftsverlag Berlin, pg 217
DuMont Buchverlag GmbH & Co KG, pg 219
DuMont Monte, pg 219
Ecomed Verlagsgesellschaft AG & Co KG, pg 220
Egmont vgs verlagsgesellschaft mbH, pg 221
Ellert & Richter Verlag GmbH, pg 222
F Bruckmann Munchen Verlag & Druck GmbH & Co Produkt KG, pg 225
Falken-Verlag GmbH, pg 227
Gerstenberg Verlag, pg 232
GLB Parkland Verlags-und Vertriebs GmbH, pg 232
Graefe und Unzer Verlag GmbH, pg 233
Heel Verlag GmbH, pg 238
Jahreszeiten-Verlag GmbH, pg 246
Knowledge Media International, pg 251
Franckh-Kosmos Verlags-GmbH & Co, pg 252
Ambro Lacus, Buch- und Bildverlag Walter Kremnitz, pg 255
Landbuch-Verlagsgesellschaft mbH, pg 255
Mosaik Verlag GmbH, pg 265
Verlag Natur & Wissenschaft Harro Hieronimus & Dr Jurgen Schmidt, pg 266
Naumann & Goebel Verlagsgesellschaft mbH, pg 267
Nebel Verlag GmbH, pg 267
Neumann Verlag, pg 268
Georg Olms Verlag AG, pg 270
Orbis Verlag fur Publizistik GmbH, pg 270
Pala-Verlag GmbH, pg 271
Heinrich Schwab Verlag, pg 285
Thalacker Medien GmbH Co KG, pg 293

PUBLISHERS

Guenter Albert Ulmer Verlag, pg 295
Verlag Eugen Ulmer GmbH & Co, pg 295
VS Verlagshaus Stuttgart GmbH, pg 299
Verlagsgruppe Weltbild GmbH, pg 301

Greece
Alamo Hellas, pg 308
Orfanidis Publications, pg 314

Hong Kong
Publications (Holdings) Ltd, pg 321
Unicorn Books Ltd, pg 322

Hungary
Officina Nova, Koenyv-es Lapkiado/Bertelsmann Media Kft, pg 324
Mezoegazda Kiado, pg 325
Park Konyvkiado Kft (Park Publisher), pg 326

Iceland
Bokautgafan Orn og Orlygur ehf, pg 327
Frodi Ltd, pg 328
Skjaldborg Ltd, pg 328

India
Ananda Publishers Pvt Ltd, pg 330
International Book Distributors, pg 340
Naya Prokash, pg 344
Nem Chand & Brothers, pg 344
Sterling Publishers Pvt Ltd, pg 351
Vakils Feffer & Simons Ltd, pg 352

Indonesia
Gramedia, pg 355

Israel
R Sirkis Publishers Ltd, pg 372

Italy
L'Archivolto, pg 376
Giovanni De Vecchi Editore SpA, pg 384
Di Baio Editore SpA, pg 385
Edagricole - Edizioni Agricole, pg 385
Edizioni Mediterranee SRL, pg 387
Fenice 2000, pg 389
Arnaldo Forni Editore SRL, pg 389
Istituto Geografico de Agostini SpA, pg 390
Giorgio Mondadori & Associati, pg 399
Edizioni Piemme SpA, pg 403
Zanfi Editori SRL, pg 412

Japan
Gakken Co Ltd, pg 416
Nagaoka Shoten Company Ltd, pg 421
Nihon Vogue Co Ltd, pg 422
Nippon Hoso Shuppan Kyokai (NHK Publishing), pg 422
Seibido Shuppan Company Ltd, pg 424
Seibundo Shinkosha Publishing Co Ltd, pg 425
Shufunotomo sha Co Ltd, pg 426
Tankosha Publishing Co Ltd, pg 427

Kenya
Space Sellers Ltd, pg 433

Republic of Korea
Pyeong-hwa Chulpansa, pg 439

Latvia
Avots, pg 441
Preses Nams, pg 442

Liechtenstein
Botanisch-Zoologische Gesellschaft, pg 444

Luxembourg
Editions Emile Borschette, pg 447

Malaysia
Federal Publications Sdn Bhd, pg 452

Martinique
Editions Gondwana, pg 456

Mexico
Ediciones Suromex SA, pg 467

Nepal
International Standards Books & Periodicals (P) Ltd, pg 471

Netherlands
Ankh-Hermes BV, pg 472
Hotei Publishing, pg 478
Rebo Productions BV, pg 483
Terra Publishing Co, pg 485
Tirion Uitgevers BV, pg 485
Zuid Boekprodukties BV, pg 487

Netherlands Antilles
De Wit Stores NV, pg 488

New Zealand
David Bateman Ltd, pg 488
Bush Press Communications Ltd, pg 489
Business Bureau Christchurch, pg 489
The Caxton Press, pg 490
Godwit Publishing Ltd, pg 491
HarperCollins Publishers (New Zealand) Ltd, pg 491
Longacre Press, pg 493
Shoal Bay Press Ltd, pg 495

Norway
Forlaget Fag og Kultur, pg 503

Oman
Apex Publishing, pg 506

Pakistan
Maqbool Academy, pg 508

Philippines
Anvil Publishing Inc, pg 512
Bookmark Inc, pg 512

Poland
Videograf II Sp z o o Zaklad Poracy Chronionej, pg 520
Wydawnictwo Baturo, pg 521

Portugal
Dinalivro, pg 524
Impala, pg 525
Editorial Presenca, pg 528

Romania
MAST Verlag, pg 534
Editura Niculescu, pg 534
Vox Verlag und Vertrieb, pg 536

Russian Federation
Airis Press, pg 537
Interbook-Business AO, pg 538
Permskaja Kniga, pg 541
Profizdat, pg 541

Singapore
Times Media Pte Ltd, pg 549

Slovakia
Priroda, pg 550

Slovenia
East West Operation (EWO) Ltd, pg 551

South Africa
Human & Rousseau (Pty) Ltd, pg 555
Jacana Education, pg 555
National Botanical Institute, pg 557
Reader's Digest Southern Africa, pg 559
Southern Book Publishers (Pty) Ltd, pg 559
Struik Publishers (Pty) Ltd, pg 559
Tafelberg Publishers Ltd, pg 560

Spain
Editorial Acanto SA, pg 561
AMV Ediciones, pg 563
Editorial Astri SA, pg 564
Comunidad Autonoma de Madrid, Servicio de Documentacion y Publicaciones, pg 568
Ediciones Daly S L, pg 569
Edicions del Drac SA, pg 570
Editorial Everest SA, pg 572
Vicent Garcia Editores, SA, pg 575
Grijalbo Mondadori SA, pg 576
Editorial Hispano Europea SA, pg 577
Libsa Editorial SA, pg 580
Mundi-Prensa Libros SA, pg 583
Pronaos, SA Ediciones, pg 588
Editora Regional de Murcia - ERM, pg 588
Ediciones Rialp SA, pg 589
Rueda, SL Editorial, pg 589
Axel Springer Publicaciones, pg 591
Tursen, SA, pg 593
Ediciones Tutor SA, pg 594

Sweden
BOOX, pg 601
Hagaberg AB, pg 603
ICA bokforlag, pg 603
Natur och Kultur/LTs foerlag, pg 604
Bokforlaget Prisma, pg 605
Bokforlaget Semic AB, pg 606

Switzerland
Ott Verlag AG, pg 621

Taiwan, Province of China
Chu Hai Publishing (Taiwan) Co Ltd, pg 630
Highlight Publishing Company Ltd, pg 630

United Republic of Tanzania
Tanzania Publishing House, pg 634

Tunisia
Les Editions de l'Arbre, pg 638

Turkey
Inkilap Publishers Ltd, pg 640

Ukraine
ASK Ltd, pg 643
Urozaj, pg 643

United Kingdom
Ian Allan Publishing Ltd, pg 646
Umberto Allemandi & Co Publishing, pg 646
Andromeda Oxford Ltd, pg 647
Antique Collectors' Club Ltd, pg 647
Batsford Ltd, pg 652
BBC Worldwide Publishers, pg 653
BCA, pg 653
Mitchell Beazley, pg 653
Bloomsbury Publishing PLC, pg 656
Breslich & Foss, pg 659
Capall Bann Publishing, pg 663
Cardinal Publishing Ltd, pg 663
Cassell & Co, pg 664
Kyle Cathie Ltd, pg 665
Marshall Cavendish Partworks Ltd, pg 665
Centre for Alternative Technology, pg 665
Conran Octopus, pg 670
The Crowood Press Ltd, pg 672
David & Charles Ltd, pg 674
Discovery Walking Guides Ltd, pg 675
Dorling Kindersley Ltd, pg 676
Aidan Ellis Publishing, pg 678
Eurobook Ltd, pg 679
The Factory Shop Guide, pg 681
Foulsham Publishers, pg 683
Gaia Books Ltd, pg 685
Garden Art Press Ltd, pg 685
GMC Publications Ltd, pg 687
Grange Books PLC, pg 689
Hamlyn, pg 691
HarperCollins Publishers, pg 692
The Harvill Press Ltd, pg 693
Headline Book Publishing Ltd, pg 693
Hyden House Ltd, pg 698
Intercept Ltd, pg 700
Interpet Publishing, pg 701
Knockabout Comics, pg 705
Frances Lincoln Ltd, pg 707
Lorenz Books, pg 709
Marshall Editions Ltd, pg 712
Marston House, pg 712
Mercat Press, pg 713
Merehurst Publishers, pg 713
Metro Publishing Ltd, pg 714
Mirabel Books Ltd, pg 715
National Trust, pg 717
New Leaf Books Ltd, pg 719
Nexus Special Interests, pg 719
Octopus Publishing Group, pg 720
Open Books Publishing Ltd, pg 721
Packard Publishing Ltd, pg 723
Pavilion Books Ltd, pg 724
Picton Publishing (Chippenham) Ltd, pg 727
PRC Publishing Ltd, pg 730
Primrose Hill Press Ltd, pg 730
Quarto Publishing plc, pg 731
Quintet Publishing Ltd, pg 732
The Reader's Digest Association Ltd, pg 733
Ryland Peters & Small Ltd, pg 737
Salamander Books Ltd, pg 738
SAWD Publications, pg 738
Search Press Ltd, pg 740

Shire Publications Ltd, pg 741
Stacey International, pg 745
Telegraph Books, pg 748
Timber Press Inc, pg 749
Transedition Ltd, pg 749
Ward Lock Ltd, pg 754
Which? Ltd, pg 755
WI Enterprises Ltd, pg 756
Wordwright Publishing, pg 758

Viet Nam
Science & Technics Publishing House, pg 763

Zambia
ZPC Publications, pg 767

GAY & LESBIAN

Argentina
Alfagrama SRL ediciones, pg 3

Australia
Allen & Unwin Pty Ltd, The Australian Newspaper, Vogel Breads, pg 11
Artemis Publishing Pty Ltd, pg 12
Spinifex Press, pg 43

Austria
Milena Verlag, pg 55

Brazil
Edicon Editora e Consultorial Ltda, pg 81

Finland
Yliopistopaino/Helsinki University Press, pg 145

France
Editions du Centre Pompidou, pg 180

Germany
Argument-Verlag, pg 195
ComMedia & Arte Verlag Bernd Mayer, pg 211
Edition Dia, pg 216
FVerlag Anke Schaefer, pg 231
Gatzanis Verlags GmbH, pg 231
Bruno Gmuender Verlag GmbH, pg 233
Himmelsturmer Verlag, pg 241
Holos Verlag, pg 242
Verlag Kleine Schritte Ursula Dahm & Co, pg 249
Krug & Schadenberg, pg 254
Mannerschwarm Skript Verlag Bartholomae & Co OHG, pg 260
Merlin Verlag Andreas Meyer Verlags GmbH und Co KG, pg 263
Verlag Neues Leben GmbH, pg 268
Orlanda Frauenverlag, pg 270
Querverlag GmbH, pg 276
Ulrike Helmer Verlag, pg 296
Rosa Winkel Verlag GmbH, pg 303

Ireland
Clo Iar-Chonnachta Teo, pg 359

Mexico
Libra Editorial SA de CV, pg 463

Netherlands
Prometheus, pg 483

New Zealand
Lincoln University Press, pg 492
Longacre Press, pg 493

Portugal
Vega-Publicacao e Distribuicao de Livros e Revistas, Lda, pg 530

Russian Federation
ARGO-RISK Publisher, pg 537

South Africa
Bet-El Publishers, pg 553
Janssen Publishers CC, pg 556
Queillerie Publishers, pg 558

Spain
Egales (Editorial Gai y Lesbiana), pg 572
Laertes SA de Ediciones, pg 579
Loguez Ediciones, pg 580

Turkey
Parantez Yayinlari Ltd, pg 640

United Kingdom
Absolute Press, pg 644
Bloomsbury Publishing PLC, pg 656
Cassell & Co, pg 664
Constable Publishers, pg 670
Delectus Books, pg 675
The Eurospan Group, pg 680
Extraordinary People Press, pg 681
Fourth Estate Ltd, pg 683
GMP Publishers Ltd, pg 687
HarperCollins Publishers, pg 692
Heretic Books Ltd, pg 695
Lawrence & Wishart, pg 706
Letterbox Library, pg 707
Monarch Books, pg 715
Peter Owen Ltd, pg 722
Quarto Publishing plc, pg 731
Serpent's Tail Ltd, pg 740
Time Out Group Ltd, pg 749
The Women's Press Ltd, pg 758

GENEALOGY

Argentina
Theoria SRL Distribuidora y Editora, pg 9

Australia
Access Press, pg 10
Assert Publishing, pg 12
Church Archivists Press, pg 18
Gould Books, pg 24
Hahndorf Academy Foundation Inc, pg 24
Hale & Iremonger Pty Ltd, pg 24
Illert Publications, pg 27
Library of Australian History, pg 30
Lucasville Press, pg 31
Navarine Publishing, pg 34
Oxfam Community Aid Abroad, pg 36
Seanachas Press, pg 42
State Library of NSW Press, pg 43

Belgium
Dexia Bank, pg 68
Marabout, pg 72

China
Fudan University Press, pg 105

Costa Rica
Museo Historico Cultural Juan Santamaria, pg 116

Denmark
Dansk Historisk Handbogsforlag ApS, pg 131

Finland
Kirja-Leitzinger, pg 143

France
Editions Bertout, pg 150
Editions Jean Paul Gisserot, pg 166
Librairie Guenegaud Sarl, pg 167
Editions Herault, pg 168
Editions Lyonnaises d'Art et d'Histoire, pg 174
Editions Ophrys, pg 178
References cf, pg 182

Germany
Bettendorf'sche Verlagsanstalt GmbH, pg 202
Verlag Ekkehard & Ulrich Brockhaus GmbH & Co KG, pg 206
Degener & Co, Manfred Dreiss Verlag, pg 213
Anton Hiersemann, Verlag, pg 240
Vittorio Klostermann GmbH, pg 250
Landbuch-Verlagsgesellschaft mbH, pg 255
C A Starke Verlag, pg 289

Ireland
Ballinakella Press, pg 358
Dee-Jay Publications, pg 359
Flyleaf Press, pg 360
Herodotus Press, pg 361
History House Publishing, pg 361
Irish Times Ltd, pg 361
Sean Ros Press, pg 364

Israel
Agudat Sabah, pg 365
Dyonon/Papyrus Publishing House of the Tel-Aviv, pg 367

Italy
Arnaldo Forni Editore SRL, pg 389
Palatina Editrice, pg 402

Netherlands
Uitgeverij Verloren, pg 486

New Zealand
Bush Press Communications Ltd, pg 489
Clerestory Press, pg 490
Evagean Publishing, pg 491
Godwit Publishing Ltd, pg 491
Graphic Educational Publications, pg 491
Heritage Press Ltd, pg 492

Poland
Wydawnictwa Uniwersytetu Warszawskiego, pg 521
Wydawnictwo DiG, pg 521

Russian Federation
Ministerstvo Kul'tury RF, pg 540

Sri Lanka
Waruni Publishers, pg 598

United Kingdom
Breedon Books Publishing Company Ltd, pg 659
Brewin Books Ltd, pg 659
Bridge Books, pg 659
Countryside Books, pg 671
Debrett's Peerage Ltd, pg 674
Elliot Right Way Books, pg 678
The Eurospan Group, pg 680
Gale Research, pg 685
Gwasg Gwenffrwd, pg 690
Ian Henry Publications Ltd, pg 695
Heraldry Today, pg 695
Luath Press Ltd, pg 709
National Library of Wales, pg 717
Scottish Text Society, pg 740
Shire Publications Ltd, pg 741
Stacey International, pg 745
Sutton Publishing Ltd, pg 746
Ulster Historical Foundation, pg 751

GEOGRAPHY, GEOLOGY

Albania
NL SH, pg 1

Argentina
EUDEBA (Editorial Universitaria de Buenos Aires), pg 6
Laffont Ediciones Electronicas SA, pg 7
Instituto Nacional de Ciencia y Tecnica Hidrica (INCYTH), pg 7
Oikos, pg 8
Editoria Universitaria de la Patagonia, pg 9

Australia
Edward Arnold (Australia) Pty Ltd, pg 12
Aussie Books, pg 12
Australian Academy of Science, pg 13
Australian Marine Conservation Society Inc (AMCS), pg 14
Australian Scholarly Publishing, pg 14
Brookfield Press, pg 16
Dabill Publications, pg 20
Dellasta Publishing, pg 20
Encyclopaedia Britannica (Australia) Inc, pg 22
Fortune Publications, pg 23
Hartys Creek Press, pg 25
Macmillan Education Australia, pg 31
McGraw-Hill Australia Pty Ltd, pg 32
Reed Educational Publishing Australia, pg 40
Royal Society of New South Wales, pg 41
Stafford Books, pg 43
Tabletop Press, pg 44
Three Sisters Publications Pty Ltd, pg 44
Tudor Australia Press, pg 45

Austria
Verlag Harald Denzel, Auto- und Freizeitfuehrer, pg 51
Freytag-Berndt und Artaria, Kartographische Anstalt, pg 52
Ferdinand Hirt mbH & Co KG, pg 53
IAEA - International Atomic Energy Agency, pg 53
Pinguin-Verlag, Pawlowski GmbH, pg 57

PUBLISHERS

Dr A Schendl GmbH und Co KG, pg 58
Vorarlberger Verlagsanstalt Aktiengesellschaft, pg 60
Universitaetsverlag Wagner GmbH, pg 60

Bangladesh

The University Press Ltd, pg 62

Belarus

Narodnaya Asveta, pg 63

Belgium

SA Artis-Historia, pg 64
Carto BVBA, pg 65
Creadif, pg 67
Cremers (Schoollandkaarten) PVBA, pg 67
Editions De Boeck-Larcier SA, pg 67
Dessain - Departement de De Boeck & Larcier SA, pg 68
Dexia Bank, pg 68
Georeto-Geogidsen, pg 68
Koepel van de Vlaamse Noord - Zuidbeweging 11.11.11, pg 70
Leuven University Press, pg 71
Pelckmans NV, De Nederlandsche Boekhandel, pg 73
Reader's Digest SA, pg 73
Sonneville Press (Uitgeverij) VTW, pg 74
Editions Techniques et Scientifiques SPRL, pg 74

Bosnia and Herzegovina

Bemust doo Novinsko-Izdavacko stamparsko i trgovacko preduzece, pg 77

Botswana

Maskew Miller Longman, pg 77

Brazil

Editora Bertrand Brasil Ltda, pg 79
EDUC - Editora da PUC-SP, pg 82
Fundacao Instituto Brasileiro de Geografia e Estatistica (IBGE - CDDI/DECOP), pg 84
Libreria Editora Ltda, pg 86
Modulo Editora e Desenvolvimento Educacional Ltda, pg 88
Editora Scipione Ltda, pg 91
Editora Verbo Ltda, pg 93

Bulgaria

Gea-Libris Publishing House, pg 95
Heron Press Publishing House, pg 96
Makros 2000 - Plovdiv, pg 96
Medicina i Fizkultura EOOD, pg 96

Chile

Arrayan Editores, pg 99
Instituto Geografico Militar, pg 100

China

Chengdu Maps Publishing House, pg 103
China Cartographic Publishing House, pg 103
China Ocean Press, pg 103
Foreign Languages Press, pg 105
Fudan University Press, pg 105
Geological Publishing House, pg 106
Higher Education Press, pg 106
Jiangsu Science & Technology Publishing House, pg 106
Metallurgical Industry Press (MIP), pg 107
Shandong University Press, pg 109
Xi'an Cartography Publishing House, pg 110

The Democratic Republic of the Congo

Centre de Recherche, et Pedagogie Appliquee, pg 114

Czech Republic

Academia, pg 122
Columbus, pg 123
Granit SRO, pg 124
Libri s r o, pg 125
Vydavatelstvi Ceskeho Geologickeho Ustavu, pg 129

Denmark

Scan-Globe A/S, pg 135
Systime, pg 136

Dominican Republic

Pontificia Universidad Catolica Madre y Maestra, pg 136

Ecuador

Corporacion Editora Nacional, pg 137

Egypt (Arab Republic of Egypt)

Dar El Shorouk Publishing & Distributing House, pg 138

Estonia

Estonian Academic Library, pg 139
Valgus Publishers, pg 141

Ethiopia

Addis Ababa University Press, pg 141

France

Actes Graphiques, pg 145
Atelier National de Reproduction des Theses, pg 148
Blondel La Rougery SARL, pg 151
Presses Universitaires de Bordeaux (PUB), pg 151
Editions BRGM, pg 152
Brud Nevez, pg 152
CNRS Editions, pg 155
Armand Colin, Editeur, pg 155
Editions du Comite des Travaux Historiques et Scientifiques (CTHS), pg 156
Devenirs Visuels SA, pg 159
Edisud, pg 161
Elf Exploration Production, pg 161
Editions Gammaprim, pg 166
Paul Geuthner Librairie Orientaliste, pg 166
Hermes Science Publications, pg 168
INRA Editions (Institut National de la Recherche Agronomique), pg 169
IRD Editions, pg 170
Editions du Jaguar, pg 170
Karthala Editions-Diffusion, pg 171
Lavoisier, pg 172
Editions Loubatieres, pg 174
Editions MDI (La Maison des Instituteurs), pg 175
Editions Franck Mercier, pg 176
Presses Universitaires du Mirail, pg 176
Editions Ophrys, pg 178
Ouest Editions, pg 178
Editions Paradigme, pg 179
Presses Universitaires de Caen, pg 181
Presses Universitaires de France (PUF), pg 181
Presses Universitaires de Nancy, pg 181
PRODIG UMR 8586 CNRS-Paris 1,4,7 ephe, pg 182
Publications de l'Universite de Rouen, pg 182
Siloe - Kerdore, pg 185
Societe Nouveaux Loisirs, pg 185
Sofradif Editions Philippe Auzou, pg 185
Publications de la Sorbonne, pg 186
Editions Tallandier, pg 187
Taride Editions, pg 187
Publications de l'Universite de Pau, pg 188

French Polynesia

Scoop/Au Vent des Iles, pg 190

Germany

Antiqua-Verlag GmbH, pg 194
Ardey-Verlag GmbH, pg 194
Aulis Verlag Deubner & Co KG, pg 197
Bayerischer Schulbuch-Verlag GmbH, pg 199
Berndtson & Berndtson GmbH Verlag-Publishing, pg 201
Bibliographisches Institut & F A Brockhaus AG, pg 203
Brockhaus/Kommission GmbH, pg 206
Hans Christians Druckerei und Verlag GmbH & Co, pg 210
Columbus Verlag Paul Oestergaard GmbH, pg 211
Cornelsen Verlag GmbH & Co OHG, pg 211
Deutscher Verlag fur Grundstoffindustrie GmbH, pg 215
E Schweizerbart'sche Verlagsbuchhandlung (Nagele und Obermiller), pg 220
Verlag Europa-Lehrmittel, Nourney, Vollmer GmbH & Co, pg 224
Ferdinand Enke Verlag, pg 227
Gebruder Borntraeger Science Publishers, pg 231
GeoCenter Touristik Medienservice GmbH, pg 231
Gloatz, Hille GmbH & Co KG fur Mehrfarben und Zellglasdruck, pg 233
Goldschneck Verlag, pg 233
Walter de Gruyter GmbH & Co KG, pg 234
Holos Verlag, pg 242
Kartographischer Verlag Reinhard Ryborsch, pg 248
Kirschbaum Verlag GmbH, pg 249
Ernst Klett Verlag GmbH, pg 250
Knowledge Media International, pg 251
K F Koehler Verlag, pg 251
Anton H Konrad Verlag, pg 252
Franckh-Kosmos Verlags-GmbH & Co, pg 252
Verlag Waldemar Kramer, pg 253
Landbuch-Verlagsgesellschaft mbH, pg 255
Michael Lassleben Verlag, pg 256
Siegbert Linnemann Verlag, pg 258

SUBJECT INDEX

Logos-Verlag Literatur & Layout GmbH, pg 258
Margraf Verlag, pg 261
Verlag Natur & Wissenschaft Harro Hieronimus & Dr Jurgen Schmidt, pg 266
Nusser Verlag, pg 269
Georg Olms Verlag AG, pg 270
Palazzi Verlag GmbH, pg 271
Justus Perthes Verlag Gotha GmbH, pg 272
Propylaeen Verlag, Zweigniederlassung Berlin der Ullstein Buchverlage GmbH, pg 275
Raethgloben Verlagsgesellschaft mbH, pg 276
Konrad Reich Verlag GmbH, pg 278
Dr Ludwig Reichert Verlag, pg 278
Reise Know-How Verlag Peter Rump GmbH, pg 278
Verlag an der Ruhr GmbH, pg 281
H O Schulze KG, pg 285
Springer-Verlag GmbH & Co KG, pg 288
Stadler Verlagsgesellschaft mbH, pg 288
Staedte-Verlag, E v Wagner und J Mitterhuber GmbH, pg 288
Stapp Verlag Wolfgang Stapp, pg 289
Steiger Verlag, pg 289
Franz Steiner Verlag Wiesbaden GmbH, pg 289
Verlag Dr Alfons Uhl, pg 295
Volk und Wissen Verlag GmbH & Co, pg 299
VWB-Verlag fur Wissenschaft & Bildung, Amand Aglaster, pg 300
Weidler Buchverlag Berlin, pg 301
Herbert Wichmann Verlag, pg 302
Wochenschau Verlag, Dr Kurt Debus GmbH, pg 304

Greece

Anixis Publications, pg 309
Ekdoseis Domi AE, pg 310
Giovanis Publications, Pangosmios Ekdotikos Organismos, pg 310
Hestia-I D Hestia-Kollaros & Co Corporation, pg 311
Orfanidis Publications, pg 314
D Papadimas, pg 314

Hong Kong

The Chinese University Press, pg 319
Federal Publications Ltd, pg 319
Geocarto International Centre, pg 320
Hong Kong University Press, pg 320

Hungary

Kossuth Kiado RT, pg 325
Nemzeti Tankoenyvkiado, pg 326
Szarvas Andras Cartographic Agency, pg 326

India

Anmol Publications Pvt Ltd, pg 331
APH Publishing Corp, pg 331
Bharat Publishing House, pg 332
Bharatiya Samijik Vigyan Ausandhan Parishad, pg 332
Bhawan Book Service, Publishers & Distributors, pg 333
BSMPS - M/s Bishen Singh Mahendra Pal Singh, pg 334
Chowkhamba Sanskrit Series Office, pg 335

969

Concept Publishing Co, pg 335
Daya Publishing House, pg 336
Frank Brothers & Co (Publishers) Ltd, pg 337
Gyan Publishing House, pg 338
Indian Museum, pg 339
Inter-India Publications, pg 340
National Book Organization, pg 343
Omsons Publications, pg 345
Pointer Publishers, pg 346
Rajendra Publishing House Pvt Ltd, pg 347
Rajesh Publications, pg 347
Regency Publications, pg 347
Reliance Publishing House, pg 347
Scientific Book Agency, pg 349
Sultan Chand & Sons Pvt Ltd, pg 351
Vikas Publishing House Pvt Ltd, pg 353

Ireland
An Gum, pg 358
Ballinakella Press, pg 358
Cork University Press, pg 359
The Educational Company of Ireland, pg 360
Royal Irish Academy, pg 364

Israel
Ariel Publishing House, pg 365
Bar Ilan University Press, pg 365
Hakibbutz Hameuchad Publishing House Ltd, pg 368
The Israel Academy of Sciences & Humanities, pg 368
Israel Exploration Society, pg 368
Ma'ariv Book Guild (Sifriat Ma'ariv), pg 370
Tcherikover Publishers Ltd, pg 372
Yad Izhak Ben-Zvi Press, pg 373

Italy
Edizioni della Fondazione Giovanni Agnelli, pg 375
De Agostini Scolastica, pg 375
Verlagsanstalt Athesia, pg 377
BeMa, pg 377
Edizioni Cartografiche Milanesi, pg 379
Casa Editrice Giuseppe Principato Spa, pg 380
Edistudio di Brunetto Casini, pg 380
Centro Documentazione Alpina, pg 381
Centro Studi Terzo Mondo, pg 381
Ciranna - Roma, pg 381
Edizioni Della Torre di Salvatore Fozzi & C SAS, pg 384
Edizioni l'Arciere SRL, pg 387
EuroGeoGrafiche Mencattini, pg 388
Arnaldo Forni Editore SRL, pg 389
Istituto Geografico de Agostini SpA, pg 390
Bruno Ghigi Editore, pg 390
Herbita Editrice di Leonardo Palermo, pg 392
Editoriale Jaca Book SpA, pg 394
Kompass Fleischmann, pg 395
LAC - Litografia Artistica Cartografica Srl, pg 395
Loescher Editore SRL, pg 396
Marzorati Editore SRL, pg 398
McRae Books, pg 398
Leo S Olschki, pg 402
Paravia Bruno Mondadori Editori, pg 402
Pitagora Editrice SRL, pg 403
Principato, pg 404

Edizioni Scientifiche Italiane, pg 407
Editoriale Scienza, pg 407
Societa Editrice Internazionale - SEI, pg 408
Gruppo Editoriale Le Stelle SpA, pg 409
Tappeiner, pg 409
Editrice Tirrenia Stampatori SAS, pg 410
Zanichelli Editore SpA, pg 412
Edizioni Zara, pg 412

Jamaica
Carlong Publishers (Caribbean) Ltd, pg 412
Jamaica Publishing House Ltd, pg 413
West Indies Publishing Ltd, pg 414

Japan
Fuzambo Publishing Co, pg 416
GakuseiSha Publishing Co Ltd, pg 416
Holp Book Co Ltd, pg 417
International Society for Educational Information (ISEI), pg 418
Japan Travel Bureau Inc, pg 418
Kodansha, pg 420
Poplar Publishing Co Ltd, pg 423
Sekai Bunka Publishing Inc, pg 425
Shogakukan Inc, pg 426
Taimeido Publishing Co Ltd, pg 427
Teikoku-Shoin Co Ltd, pg 427
Toho Book Store, pg 427
United Nations University Press, pg 428
Yama-Kei Publishers Co Ltd, pg 429

Kenya
Heinemann Kenya Limited (EAEP), pg 431
Nairobi University Press, pg 433
Phoenix Publishers, pg 433

Democratic People's Republic of Korea
Academy of Sciences Publishing House, pg 434
Korea Science and Encyclopedia Publishing House, pg 434

Republic of Korea
Hanul Publishing Co, pg 436
Kemongsa Publishing Co Ltd, pg 437

Kuwait
Ministry of Information, pg 441

Laos People's Democratic Republic
Lao-phanit, pg 441

Latvia
Lielvards Ltd, pg 442

Lithuania
Academia, pg 445
Victoria Publishers, pg 446

The Former Yugoslav Republic of Macedonia
Seizmoloska Opservatorija, pg 449

Malawi
Dzuka Publishing Company Ltd, pg 450

Malaysia
Penerbit Jayatinta Sdn Bhd, pg 454
Pustaka Delta Pelajaran Sdn Bhd, pg 454

Mauritius
Editions de l'Ocean Indien Ltd, pg 457

Mexico
Editorial Esfinge SA de CV, pg 460
Editorial Limusa SA de CV, pg 463
Instituto Nacional de Estadistica, Geographia e Informatica, pg 464
Instituto Panamericano de Geografia e Historia, pg 465
Salvat Editores de Mexico, pg 466
Universidad Nacional Autonoma de Mexico (National University of Mexico), pg 467

Republic of Moldova
Lumina Publishing House, pg 468

Mongolia
State Press, pg 469

Namibia
Desert Research Foundation of Namibia (DRFN), pg 471
Multi-Disciplinary Research Centre Library, pg 471

Nepal
International Standards Books & Periodicals (P) Ltd, pg 471

Netherlands
Uitgeverij Jan van Arkel, pg 473
Backhuys Publishers BV, pg 473
A A Balkema, pg 473
Educatieve Uitgeverij Edu'Actief BV, pg 476
Nico Israel, pg 482
Van Gorcum & Comp BV, pg 486

New Zealand
Barkfire Press, pg 488
Bush Press Communications Ltd, pg 489
Wendy Crane Books, pg 490
ESA Publications (NZ) Ltd, pg 490
New House Publishers Ltd, pg 493
Nelson Price Milburn Ltd, pg 494

Nigeria
Evans Brothers (Nigeria Publishers) Ltd, pg 499
Ogunsanya Press, Publishers and Bookstores Ltd, pg 501
West African Book Publishers Ltd, pg 502

Norway
Vett & Viten AS, pg 505

Pakistan
Sheikh Muhammad Ashraf Publishers, pg 506
Publishers United Pvt Ltd, pg 508

Panama
Editorial Universitaria, pg 509

Peru
Instituto Frances de Estudios Andinos, IFEA, pg 511

Philippines
National Museum of the Philippines, pg 514
Saint Mary's Publishing Corp, pg 515

Poland
Wydawnictwa Geologiczne, pg 516
Instytut Historii Nauki PAN, pg 516
Instytut Meteorologii i Gospodarki Wodnej, pg 518
Polish Scientific Publishers PWN, pg 519
Wydawnictwo RTW, pg 520
Towarzystwo Naukowe w Toruniu, pg 520
Wydawnictwa Uniwersytetu Warszawskiego, pg 521

Portugal
Centro Estudos Geograficos, pg 523
Edicoes Colibri, pg 523
Constancia Editores, SA, pg 524
Edicoes Cosmos, pg 524
Editorial Estampa, Lda, pg 524
Gradiva-Publicacnoes Lda, pg 525
Impala, pg 525
Instituto de Investigacao Cientifica Tropical, pg 526

Romania
Corint Verlag, pg 532
Editura Dacia, pg 532
Editura Niculescu, pg 534
Editura Stiintifica, pg 536

Russian Federation
Gidrometeoizdat, pg 538
Izdatel 'stvo Mordovskogo gosudar stvennogo, pg 538
Izdatelstvo Mir, pg 540
Izdatelstvo Mysl, pg 540
Nauka Publishers, pg 540
Izdatelstvo Nedra, pg 540
Stroyizdat Publishing House, pg 542
Voronezh State University Publishers, pg 542

Saudi Arabia
King Saud University, pg 543

Singapore
Hillview Publications Pte Ltd, pg 546

South Africa
Educum Publishers Ltd, pg 554
Government Printer, pg 554

Spain
Aguilar SA de Ediciones, pg 562
Ambit Serveis Editorials, SA, pg 563
Editorial Ariel SA, pg 564
Cabildo Insular de Gran Canaria Departamento de Ediciones, pg 566
Casa de Velazquez, pg 566
Edicios do Castro, pg 566
Curial Edicions Catalanes SA, pg 569
Rafael Dalmau, Editor, pg 569
Ediciones Diputacion de Salamanca, pg 570

Diputacion Provincial de Malaga, pg 570
Edigol Ediciones SA, pg 572
Instituto de Estudios Riojanos, pg 574
Institut d'Estudis Vallencs (IEV), pg 574
Eumo Editorial, pg 574
Idea Books, SA, pg 578
Institucion Fernando el Catolico de la Excma Diputacion de Zaragoza, pg 578
Editorial la Muralla SA, pg 583
Editorial 92 SA, pg 584
Noguer y Caralt Editores SA, pg 584
Ediciones Oceano Grupo SA, pg 584
Oikos-Tau SA Ediciones, pg 584
Ediciones Omega SA, pg 585
Instituto Provincial de Investigaciones y Estudios Toledanos, pg 588
Editora Regional de Murcia - ERM, pg 588
Rueda, SL Editorial, pg 589
Universidad de Santiago de Compostela, pg 589
Servicio de Publicaciones Universidad de Cordoba, pg 590
Editorial Sintesis, SA, pg 590
Ediciones de la Torre, pg 593
Trea Ediciones, SL, pg 593
Editorial Txertoa, pg 594
Universidad de Granada, pg 594
Universidad de Valladolid Secretariado de Publicaciones e Intercambio Editorial, pg 594
Xunta de Galicia, pg 596

Sri Lanka
Ministry of Education, pg 597

Sweden
Bokforlaget Bra Bocker AB, pg 600
Bokforlaget Rediviva, Facsimileforlaget, pg 600
Liber AB, pg 604

Switzerland
Atlantis-Verlag AG, pg 608
Augustin-Verlag, pg 609
Kuemmerly & Frey (Geographischer Verlag), pg 617
Librairie-Editions J Marguerat, pg 618
Motovun Book GmbH, pg 619
Orell Fuessli Verlag, pg 620
Ott Verlag AG, pg 621
Sabe AG Verlagsinstitut, pg 623
Schweizerische Stiftung fuer Alpine Forschungen, pg 624
Terra Grischuna Verlag Buch-und Zeitschriftenverlag, pg 625
3 Dimension World (3-D-World), pg 625
Wepf & Co AG, pg 627

Syrian Arab Republic
Damascus University Press, pg 628
Institut Francais d'Etudes Arabes de Damas, pg 628

Taiwan, Province of China
Hilit Publishing Co Ltd, pg 630

United Republic of Tanzania
Eastern Africa Publications Ltd, pg 633
General Publications Ltd, pg 633
Press & Publicity Centre Ltd, pg 634
Tanzania Publishing House, pg 634

Tunisia
Academie Tunisienne des Sciences, des Lettres et des Arts Beit El Hekma, pg 637
Ceres Editions, pg 637
Faculte des Sciences Humaines et Sociales de Tunis, pg 638

Turkey
IKI NOKTA Research Press & Publications Industry & Trade Ltd, pg 640

Uganda
Centre for Basic Research, pg 642

Ukraine
Derzhavne Naukovo-Vyrobnyche Pidpryemstro Kartografia, pg 643
Naukova Dumka Publishers, pg 643

United Kingdom
Advisory Unit: Computers in Education, pg 645
Andromeda Oxford Ltd, pg 647
Arnold, pg 648
BCA, pg 653
Belitha Press Ltd, pg 653
Blackwell Publishers, pg 655
Blackwell Science Ltd, pg 656
Cambridge University Press, pg 662
Cassell & Co, pg 664
Causeway Press Ltd, pg 665
Dunedin Academic Press, pg 676
European Schoolbooks Ltd, pg 680
The Eurospan Group, pg 680
Evans Brothers Ltd, pg 680
Ex Libris Press, pg 680
Forth Naturalist & Historian, pg 683
W H Freeman & Co Ltd, pg 684
The Geographical Association, pg 686
Geological Society Publishing House, pg 686
Hakluyt Society, pg 691
Robert Hale Ltd, pg 691
Hodder & Stoughton Educational, pg 696
Institute of Irish Studies, The Queens University of Belfast, pg 699
Intercept Ltd, pg 700
Jones & Bartlett International, pg 703
Hilda King Educational, pg 704
Letterbox Library, pg 707
Liverpool University Press, pg 708
Marshall Editions Ltd, pg 712
Mirabel Books Ltd, pg 715
Multilingual Matters Ltd, pg 716
John Murray (Publishers) Ltd, pg 716
Nelson Thornes Ltd, pg 718
NMS Publishing Ltd, pg 719
Octopus Publishing Group, pg 720
Orpheus Books Ltd, pg 722
Packard Publishing Ltd, pg 723
Pearson Education, pg 725
Philip's, pg 727
Pion Ltd, pg 728
The Policy Press, pg 729
Quartz Editions, pg 732
Quentin Books Ltd, pg 732
Quintet Publishing Ltd, pg 732
Reaktion Books Ltd, pg 733
Roadmaster Publishing, pg 735
Rough Guides Ltd, pg 735
Routledge, pg 736
The Royal Society, pg 737
The Salariya Book Co Ltd, pg 738
Shearwater Press Ltd, pg 741
Stacey International, pg 745
Supportive Learning Publications, pg 746
Thoemmes Press, pg 748
Two-Can Publishing Ltd, pg 750
UCL Press Ltd, pg 751
University of Wales Press, pg 751
Ward Lock Educational Co Ltd, pg 754
Wordwright Publishing, pg 758

Uruguay
Editorial Arca SRL, pg 760
A Monteverde y Cia SA, pg 760

Venezuela
Alfadil Ediciones, pg 761
Monte Avila Editores Latinoamericana CA, pg 762

Viet Nam
Science & Technics Publishing House, pg 763

Zimbabwe
Academic Books Pvt Ltd, pg 767
College Press Publishers (Pvt) Ltd, pg 768
Geological Survey Department, pg 768
Zimbabwe Publishing House (Pvt) Ltd, pg 769

GOVERNMENT, POLITICAL SCIENCE

Albania
NL SH, pg 1
State Textbook Publishing House, pg 1

Argentina
Editorial Astrea de Alfredo y Ricardo Depalma SRL, pg 3
Fundacion Editorial de Belgrano, pg 4
Editorial Claridad SA, pg 4
Marymar Ediciones SA, pg 7
Editorial Paidos SAICF, pg 8
Editorial Pleamar, pg 8
Editorial Plus Ultra SA, pg 8
Editorial Sopena Argentina SACI e I, pg 9
Theoria SRL Distribuidora y Editora, pg 9
Instituto Torcuato Di Tella, pg 9
Ediciones Tres Tiempos SRL, pg 9

Armenia
Ajstan Publishers, pg 10

Australia
Allen & Unwin Pty Ltd, The Australian Newspaper, Vogel Breads, pg 11
Edward Arnold (Australia) Pty Ltd, pg 12
Artemis Publishing Pty Ltd, pg 12
Australian Scholarly Publishing, pg 14
Chiron Media, pg 18
Crawford House Publishing, pg 19
Crystal Publishing, pg 19
Hale & Iremonger Pty Ltd, pg 24
James Nicholas Publishers Pty Ltd, pg 28
Macmillan Education Australia, pg 31
Mayne Publishing, pg 32
Ocean Press, pg 35
Oxfam Community Aid Abroad, pg 36
Pearson Education Australia, pg 37
Pluto Press Australia, pg 38
Shakespeare Head Press Pty Ltd, pg 42
University of New South Wales Press Ltd, pg 46
Vista Publications, pg 47

Austria
Boehlau Verlag GmbH & Co KG, pg 50
Development News Ltd, pg 51
Verlag fuer Geschichte und Politik, pg 52
Globus Buchvertrieb, pg 52
Guthmann & Peterson Liber Libri, Edition, pg 52
Karolinger Verlag GmbH & Co KG, pg 53
Horst Knapp Finanznachrichten, pg 54
Leopold Stocker Verlag, pg 54
Verlag des Oesterreichischen Gewerkschaftsbundes GmbH, pg 56
Verlag Orac im Verlag Kremayr & Scheriau, pg 56
Passagen Verlag GmbH, pg 57
Promedia Verlagsges mbH, pg 57
Andreas Schnider Verlags-Atelier, pg 58
Signum Verlag GmbH & Co KG, pg 58
Suedwind - Buchwelt GmbH, pg 59
Verlag Carl Ueberreuter GmbH, pg 59
Wieser Verlag, pg 61

Azerbaijan
AZernesr, pg 61

Bangladesh
Ankur Prakashani, pg 62
Agamee Prakashani, pg 62
The University Press Ltd, pg 62

Belarus
Belarus (The Belorussia), pg 63

Belgium
Artel SC, pg 64
Vanden Broele NV, pg 65
Eteblissements Emile Bruylant SA, pg 65
Centre d'Action Laique, pg 66
La Charte Editions juridiques, pg 66
Davidsfonds VZW, pg 67
Editions De Boeck-Larcier SA, pg 67
Institut Royal des Relations Internationales, pg 69
Ipis VZW (International Peace Information Service), pg 69
Koepel van de Vlaamse Noord - Zuidbeweging 11.11.11, pg 70
Kritak Uitgeverij, pg 70
Uitgeverij Lannoo NV, pg 70
Leuven University Press, pg 71
Maklu, pg 71
Presses Universitaires de Liege, pg 73
Sonneville Press (Uitgeverij) VTW, pg 74

Uitgeverij De Garve, pg 75
Uitgevery Scoop Infotex NV, pg 75
Editions de l'Universite de Bruxelles, pg 75
Imprimeur - Editeur Vaillant-Carmanne SA, pg 75
Vander Editions, SA, pg 75
VUB University Press, pg 75

Bosnia and Herzegovina
Veselin Maslesa, pg 77

Botswana
The Botswana Society, pg 77

Brazil
Editora Bertrand Brasil Ltda, pg 79
Camara Dos Deputados Coordenacao De Publicacoes, pg 80
Editora Campus Ltda, pg 80
EDUC - Editora da PUC-SP, pg 82
Forense Universitaria Editora, pg 83
IBRASA (Instituicao Brasileira de Difusao Cultural Ltda), pg 85
Editora Paz e Terra, pg 89
Pool Editorial Ltda, pg 90
Editora UNESP, pg 92
Editora Universidade de Brasilia, pg 92

Bulgaria
Publishing House Hristo Botev, pg 96
Mladezh, pg 96
Ivan Vazov Publishing House, pg 98

Chile
Edeval (Universidad de Valparaiso), pg 100
Ediciones y Publicidad Melquiades, pg 100

China
Anhui People's Publishing House, pg 102
Asia 2000 Ltd, pg 102
China Foreign Economic Relations & Trade Publishing House, pg 103
Foreign Languages Press, pg 105
Fudan University Press, pg 105
Lanzhou University Press, pg 107
SDX (Shenghuo-Dushu-Xinzhi) Joint Publishing Co, pg 108
Shandong People's Publishing House, pg 109
World Affairs Press, pg 110
Wuhan University Press, pg 110
Xinhua Publishing House, pg 110

Colombia
Amazonas Editores Ltda, pg 111
Universidad Externado de Colombia, pg 112
Siglo XXI Editores de Colombia Ltda, pg 113
Tercer Mundo Editores SA, pg 113
Carlos Valencia Editores, pg 114

The Democratic Republic of the Congo
Facultes Catolicas de Kinshasa, pg 115

Costa Rica
Editorial DEI (Departamento Ecumenico de Investigaciones), pg 116
Editorial de la Universidad de Costa Rica, pg 117
Editorial Universidad Estatal a Distancia (EUNED), pg 117

Cote d'Ivoire
Heritage Publishing Co, pg 118

Croatia
ALFA dd za izdavacke, graficke i trgovacke poslove, pg 118
Globus-Nakladni zavod, pg 118
Izdavacka Delatnost Hrvatske Akademije Znanosti I Umjetnosti, pg 118
Informator dd, pg 119
Nakladni zavod Matice hrvatske, pg 119
Naprijed d d Naklada, pg 119

Cuba
Editorial Capitan San Luis, pg 120
Editora Politica, pg 121

Czech Republic
Barrister & Principal, pg 123
Iuventus, pg 124
Konsultace, pg 125
Prace, pg 127
Prostor, Ltd, pg 128
Slon Sociologicke Nakladatelstvi, pg 128

Denmark
Forlaget GMT, pg 132
Mellemfolkeligt Samvirke, pg 133
Joergen Paludans Forlag ApS, pg 134
Politisk Revy, pg 134
Samlerens Forlag A/S, pg 135
Statens Information (Danish State Information Service), pg 135

Dominican Republic
Pontificia Universidad Catolica Madre y Maestra, pg 136

Ecuador
Corporacion Editora Nacional, pg 137
Pontificia Universidad Catolica de Ecuador, Centro de Publicaciones, pg 137

Egypt (Arab Republic of Egypt)
Al Arab Publishing House, pg 138
Dar El Shorouk Publishing & Distributing House, pg 138
Ummah Press for Translation & Publishing, pg 139

El Salvador
Editorial Universitaria de la Universidad de El Salvador, pg 139

Finland
Ekenas Tryckeri AB, pg 142
Kirja-Leitzinger, pg 143
Kuva ja Sana, pg 143

France
Actes Graphiques, pg 145
Annales de la Recherche Urbaine, pg 147
Editions Anthropos Sarl, pg 147
Les Editions de l'Atelier SA, pg 148
Beauchesne Editeur, pg 150
Editions Cujas, pg 157
Editions Denoel Sarl, pg 158
La Documentation Francaise, pg 159
FBT de R Editions/Editions des Limbes d'Or, pg 163
Presses de la Fondation Nationale des Sciences Politiques, pg 164
Futuribles SARL, pg 165
Groupe Expansion, pg 167
Hachette Livre, pg 167
Editions de l'Herne, pg 168
Editions du Jaguar, pg 170
Editions Juridiques Associees - LGDJ/Montchrestien, pg 170
Editions des Limbes d'Or/FBT de R Editions, pg 173
LiTec (Librairies Techniques SA), pg 173
Le Livre de Poche-L G F (Librairie Generale Francaise), pg 173
Editions Odile Jacob, pg 178
Editions Jean Picollec, pg 179
Presses Universitaires de France (PUF), pg 181
Presses Universitaires de Lyon, pg 181
Presses Universitaires de Nancy, pg 181
Editions du Seuil, pg 185
Publications de la Sorbonne, pg 186
10/18, pg 187

Georgia
Izdatelstvo Sabtchota Sakartvelo, pg 190

Germany
A Francke Verlag (Tubingen und Basel), pg 191
Accedo Verlagsgesellschaft mbH, pg 191
Ahriman-Verlag GmbH, pg 192
Verlag Karl Alber GmbH, pg 192
Verlag und Antiquariat Frank Albrecht, pg 192
Andernach Atelier Verlag (AVA), pg 193
AOL-Verlag Frohmut Menze, pg 194
Arbeiterpresse Verlag GmbH, pg 194
Argument-Verlag, pg 195
Aufbau Taschenbuch Verlag GmbH, pg 196
Aufbau-Verlag GmbH, pg 196
BasisDruck Verlag GmbH, pg 198
be.bra verlag GmbH, pg 199
Berlin Verlag Arno Spitz GmbH, pg 200
Berliner Debatte Wissenschafts Verlag, GSFP-Gesellschaft fur Sozialwissen-schaftliche Forschung und Publizistik mbH &Co KG, pg 201
C Bertelsmann Verlag GmbH, pg 201
Verlag Bertelsmann Stiftung, pg 201
Bleicher Verlag GmbH, pg 204
Bouvier Verlag, pg 206
Verlag Brandenburger Tor GmbH, pg 206
Brandes & Apsel Verlag GmbH, pg 206
C C Buchners Verlag, pg 207
Buchergilde Gutenberg Verlagsgesellschaft mbH, pg 207
Bund demokratischer Wissenschaftlerinnen und Wissenschafler eV (BdWi), pg 207
Bund-Verlag GmbH, pg 208
Bundesanzeiger Verlagsgesellschaft, pg 208
Campus Verlag GmbH, pg 209
Daedalus Verlag, pg 212
Deutsche Verlags-Anstalt GmbH (DVA), pg 214
Deutscher Gemeindeverlag GmbH, pg 214
Deutscher Taschenbuch Verlag GmbH & Co KG (dtv), pg 215
Die Verlag H Schafer GmbH, pg 216
Dietrich zu Klampen Verlag, pg 216
Verlag J H W Dietz Nachf GmbH, pg 217
Dietz Verlag Berlin GmbH, pg 217
Dipa-Verlag GmbH, pg 217
agenda Verlag Thomas Dominikowski, pg 217
Donat Verlag, pg 217
Droste Verlag GmbH, pg 218
Druffel-Verlag, pg 219
Duncker und Humblot GmbH, pg 219
DVG-Deutsche Verlagsgesellschaft mbH, pg 219
Elefanten Press Verlag GmbH, pg 222
Verlag Peter Engstler, pg 223
Europa Union Verlag GmbH, pg 224
Europa Verlag GmbH, pg 224
Europaeische Verlagsanstalt GmbH & Rotbuch Verlag GmbH & Co KG, pg 225
Ferd Dummler's Verlag, pg 227
Festland Verlag GmbH, pg 227
Rita G Fischer Verlag, pg 228
Forum Verlag Leipzig Buch-Gesellschaft, pg 229
Verlag A Fromm im Druck- u Verlagshaus Fromm GmbH & Co KG, pg 230
Verlagsbuchhandlung Megapress, Franz-J Gaber, pg 231
Verlagsgesellschaft R Gloess & Co, pg 233
Goll Bruno Verlag fur Aussergewoehnliche Perspektiven (VAP), pg 233
Walter de Gruyter GmbH & Co KG, pg 234
Gunter Olzog Verlag GmbH, pg 235
Guetersloher Verlagshaus Gerd Mohn, pg 235
Verlag Klaus Guhl, pg 235
Haag und Herchen Verlag GmbH, pg 235
Edition Hentrich Druck & Verlag Gebr Hentrich und Tank GmbH & Co KG, pg 239
Hans-Alfred Herchen & Co Verlag KG, pg 239
Verlag Herder GmbH & Co KG, pg 239
Carl Heymanns Verlag KG, pg 240
Hohenrain-Verlag GmbH, pg 242
Horlemann Verlag, pg 243
Edition ID-Archiv/ID-Verlag, pg 244
Verlag fuer Internationale Politik GmbH, pg 245
Junius Verlag GmbH, pg 247
K L V Konkret Literatur Verlag GmbH, pg 247
KBV-Verlags-und Mediengesellschaft mbH, pg 248
SachBuchVerlag Kellner, pg 248

PUBLISHERS SUBJECT INDEX

Kindler Verlag GmbH, pg 249
Klartext Verlagsgesellschaft mbH, pg 249
Druckerei & Verlag Ernst Knoth GmbH, pg 251
K F Koehler Verlag, pg 251
Koelner Universitaets-Verlag GmbH, pg 251
W Kohlhammer GmbH, abt Haussortiment, pg 252
KONTEXTverlag, pg 252
Dr Anton Kovac Slavica Verlag, pg 253
Karin Kramer Verlag, pg 253
Kulturstiftung der deutschen Vertriebenen, pg 254
Verlag Antje Kunstmann GmbH, pg 254
Lamuv Verlag GmbH, pg 255
Peter Lang GmbH Europaeischer Verlag der Wissenschaften, pg 255
Dr Gisela Lermann, pg 257
Verlag Leske plus Budrich GmbH, pg 257
Lettre International Kulturzeitung, pg 257
Libertas- Europaeisches Institut GmbH, pg 257
Christoph Links Verlag - LinksDruck GmbH, pg 258
Merlin Verlag Andreas Meyer Verlags GmbH und Co KG, pg 263
Metropolis- Verlag fur Okonomie, Gesellschaft und Politik GmbH, pg 263
Militzke Verlag, pg 264
E S Mittler und Sohn GmbH, pg 264
Munzinger-Archiv GmbH Archiv fuer publizistische Arbeit, pg 266
MUT Verlag, pg 266
Edition Nautilus Verlag, pg 267
NDV Neue Darmstadter Verlagsanstalt, pg 267
Neuer ISP Verlag GmbH, pg 268
Neuer Weg Verlag und Druck GmbH, pg 268
Nomos Verlagsgesellschaft mbH und Co KG, pg 269
Nusser Verlag, pg 269
Oberbaum Verlag GmbH, pg 269
Verlag Offene Worte, pg 270
Georg Olms Verlag AG, pg 270
Pahl-Rugenstein Verlag Nachfolger-GmbH, pg 271
Palmyra Verlag, pg 271
PapyRossa Verlags GmbH & Co Kommanditgesellschaft KG, pg 271
Propylaeen Verlag, Zweigniederlassung Berlin der Ullstein Buchverlage GmbH, pg 275
Roehrig Universitaets Verlag Gmbh, pg 279
Rombach GmbH Druck und Verlagshaus & Co, pg 280
Verlag Roter Morgen, pg 280
Rowohlt Taschenbuch Verlag GmbH, pg 280
Dieter Ruggeberg Verlagsbuchhandlung, pg 280
Ruetten & Loening Berlin GmbH, pg 281
Richard Scherpe Verlag GmbH, pg 283
Ferdinand Schoeningh Verlag GmbH, pg 284
Schueren Verlag GmbH, pg 285
Siedler Verlag, pg 286

Siegler & Co Verlag fuer Zeitarchive GmbH, pg 286
Springer-Verlag GmbH & Co KG, pg 288
Edition Temmen, pg 292
Toleranz Verlag, Nielsen Frederic W, pg 294
Trotzdem- Verlags Genossenschaft eG, pg 295
Tuduv Verlagsgesellschaft mbH, pg 295
UNO-Verlag mbH, Vertriebs und Verlagsgesellschaft, pg 296
Unrast Verlag e V, pg 296
UTB fuer Wissenschaft Uni-Taschenbuecher GmbH, pg 297
VAS-Verlag fuer Akademische Schriften, Vas Karl-Heinz Balon, pg 297
Dokument und Analyse Verlag Bogislaw von Randow, pg 299
VVF Verlag V Florentz GmbH, pg 299
Verlag Klaus Wagenbach GmbH, pg 300
Weber Zucht & Co, pg 300
Verlag Wissenschaft und Politik/ Helker Pflug, pg 303
Wochenschau Verlag, Dr Kurt Debus GmbH, pg 304
Zambon Verlag, pg 305
Zebulon Verlag GmbH & Co KG, pg 305

Ghana
Frank Publishing Ltd, pg 307
Ghana Universities Press (GUP), pg 307

Greece
Axiotelis G, pg 309
Boukoumanis' Editions, pg 309
Dorikos Publishing House, pg 310
Exandas Publishers, pg 310
Govostis Publishing SA, pg 311
Gutenberg Publications, pg 311
Irini Publishing House - Vassilis G Katsikeas SA, pg 311
Kritiki Publishing, pg 312
Nea Thesis - Evrotas, pg 313
Papazissis Publishers SA, pg 314
Pontiki Publications SA, pg 314
Proskinio, pg 314

Honduras
Editorial Guaymuras, pg 318

Hong Kong
Celeluck Co Ltd, pg 318
The Chinese University Press, pg 319
Friends of the Earth (Charity) Ltd, pg 320
Hong Kong University Press, pg 320
Sun Mui Press, pg 322

Hungary
Central European University Press, pg 323
CEU-Press, pg 323
Joszoveg Muhely Kiado, pg 324
KJK-Keaszov, pg 324
Szabad Ter Kiado, pg 326

Iceland
Hid Islenzka Bokmenntafelag, pg 328

India
Abhinav Publications, pg 329
Abhishek Publications, pg 329
Ajanta Publications (India), pg 330
Allied Publishers Pvt Ltd, pg 330
Amar Prakashan, pg 330
Ankur Publishing House, pg 330
APH Publishing Corp, pg 331
K P Bagchi & Co, pg 332
BR Publishing Corporation, pg 334
S Chand & Co Ltd, pg 334
Cosmo Publications, pg 335
Eastern Law House Pvt Ltd, pg 336
Frank Brothers & Co (Publishers) Ltd, pg 337
Gitanjali Publishing House, pg 337
Goel Prakashen, pg 337
Gyan Publishing House, pg 338
Arnold Heinman Publishers (India) Pvt Ltd, pg 338
Indian Society for Promoting Christian Knowledge (ISPCK), pg 339
Intellectual Publishing House, pg 339
Inter-India Publications, pg 340
Islamic Publishing House, pg 340
Jaico Publishing House, pg 340
Konark Publishers, Pvt, Ltd, pg 341
Manohar Publishers & Distributors, pg 342
Minerva Associates (Publications) Pvt Ltd, pg 342
A Mukherjee & Co Pvt Ltd, pg 343
National Book Organization, pg 343
Naya Prokash, pg 344
Omsons Publications, pg 345
Pointer Publishers, pg 346
Popular Prakashan Pvt Ltd, pg 346
Promilla and Co, pg 346
Radiant Publishers, pg 347
Rastogi Publications, pg 347
Regency Publications, pg 347
Reliance Publishing House, pg 347
SABDA, pg 348
Sage Publications India Pvt Ltd, pg 348
Scientific Book Agency, pg 349
Somaiya Publications Pvt Ltd, pg 350
South Asian Publishers Pvt Ltd, pg 350
Sterling Publishers Pvt Ltd, pg 351
Sultan Chand & Sons Pvt Ltd, pg 351
Vikas Publishing House Pvt Ltd, pg 353

Indonesia
Bina Rena Pariwara, pg 354
P T Bulan Bintang, pg 354
Pustaka Utama Grafiti, PT, pg 357
Yayasan Obor Indonesia, pg 357

Iraq
National House for Publishing, Distributing and Advertising, pg 358

Ireland
Attic Press Ltd, pg 358
Emerald Publications, pg 360
Gill & Macmillan Ltd, pg 361
Government Publications Ireland, pg 361
Institute of Public Administration, pg 361
New Books/Connolly Books, pg 362
Royal Irish Academy, pg 364

Israel
Gefen Publishing House Ltd, pg 367
Hakibbutz Hameuchad Publishing House Ltd, pg 368
The Institute for Israeli Arabs Studies, pg 368
Israel Universities Press, pg 369
Jabotinsky Institute in Israel, pg 369
Ma'ariv Book Guild (Sifriat Ma'ariv), pg 370
Machbarot Lesifrut, pg 370
Open University of Israel, pg 371
Rubin Mass Ltd, pg 371
Shalem Press, pg 372
Tel-Aviv University, pg 373
The Van Leer Jerusalem Institute, pg 373
Zmora-Bitan, Publishers Ltd, pg 374

Italy
Edizioni della Fondazione Giovanni Agnelli, pg 375
Arnaud Editore SRL, pg 376
Giuseppe Bonanno Editore, pg 378
Edizioni Borla SRL, pg 378
Nuova Casa Editrice Licinio Cappelli GEM srl, pg 379
CEDAM (Casa Editrice Dr A Milani), pg 380
Celuc Libri, pg 380
Centro Studi Terzo Mondo, pg 381
CLEUP - Cooperativa Libraria Editrice dell 'Universita di Padova, pg 382
Edizioni di Comunita SpA, pg 382
Edizioni Cultura della Pace, pg 383
La Culturale, pg 383
Datanews, pg 384
Edizioni Dedalo SRL, pg 384
Edizioni EBE, pg 385
Edizioni Associate/Editrice Internazionale Srl, pg 386
Edizioni Europa, pg 388
Galzerano Editore, pg 390
Garzanti Editore, pg 390
Edizioni GB, pg 390
G Giappichelli Editore SRL, pg 390
A Giuffre Editore SpA, pg 390
Giuseppe Laterza Editore Snc, pg 391
Herbita Editrice di Leonardo Palermo, pg 392
Il Minotauro, pg 393
In Dialogo, pg 393
Editoriale Jaca Book SpA, pg 394
Kaos Edizioni SRL, pg 395
Lalli Editore SRL, pg 395
Edizioni Lavoro SRL, pg 395
Manifestolibri, pg 397
Edizioni Medicea SRL, pg 398
Societa Editrice Il Mulino, pg 400
Newton Compton Editori SRL, pg 401
Nuove Autonomie, pg 401
Leo S Olschki, pg 402
Istituto Poligrafico e Zecca dello Stato, pg 404
Edition Raetia Srl-GmbH, pg 404
Editori Riuniti, pg 405
Rubbettino Editore, pg 406
Editrice San Marco SRL, pg 406
Sapere 2000 SRL, pg 407
SIPI (Servizio Italiano Pubblicazioni Internazionali) Srl, pg 408
Edizioni di Storia e Letteratura, pg 409
Nicola Teti e C Editore SRL, pg 409

Jamaica
The Press, pg 413

SUBJECT INDEX

Japan
Chuo-Koron-Sha Inc, pg 415
Hayakawa Publishing Inc, pg 417
Koyo Shobo, pg 420
Minerva Shobo Co Ltd, pg 421
Nippon Hoso Shuppan Kyokai (NHK Publishing), pg 422
President Inc, pg 423
Ryosho-Fukyu-Kai Co Ltd, pg 424
Waseda University Press, pg 428

Kazakhstan
Kazakh Al-Farabi State National University, pg 430
Kazakhstan, Izd-Vo, pg 430

Kenya
Cosmopolitan Publishers Ltd, pg 431
Heinemann Kenya Limited (EAEP), pg 431
Kenway Publications Ltd, pg 432
Lake Publishers & Enterprises Ltd, pg 432
Midi Teki Publishers, pg 433
Nairobi University Press, pg 433
Gideon S Were Press, pg 434

Democratic People's Republic of Korea
Korea Science and Encyclopedia Publishing House, pg 434
Working People's Organization Publishing House, pg 434

Republic of Korea
Korea Textbook Co Ltd, pg 437
Kyobo Book Centre, pg 438
Oruem Publishing House, pg 439

Lebanon
Institute for Palestine Studies, Publishing & Research Organization (IPS), pg 443

Liechtenstein
Bonafides Verlags-Anstalt, pg 444
Liechtenstein Verlag AG, pg 444
Verlag der Liechtensteinischen Akademischen Gesellschaft, pg 444

Lithuania
Eugrimas, pg 445
Lietuvos Informacijos Institutas, pg 446

Luxembourg
Varkki Verghese, pg 448

Macau
Universidadede de Macau, Centro de Publicacoes, pg 448

Malaysia
Forum Publications, pg 452
University of Malaya, Department of Publications, pg 455

Mauritius
Vizavi Editions, pg 457

Mexico
Editores Asociados Mexicanos SA de CV (EDAMEX), pg 458
Centro de Estudios Mexicanos y Centroamericanos, pg 458
El Colegio de Mexico AC, pg 459
Comision Nacional Forestal, pg 459
El Colegio de Michoacan A C, pg 460
Ediciones Era SA de CV, pg 460
Editorial Extemporaneos SA, pg 461
Fondo de Cultura Economica, pg 461
Editorial Jus SA de CV, pg 462
Editorial Limusa SA de CV, pg 463
Siglo XXI Editores SA de CV, pg 467

Republic of Moldova
Izdatelstvo Kartia Moldoveniaske, pg 468

Mongolia
State Press, pg 469

Morocco
Editions Al-Fourkane, pg 469
Les Editions du Journal L' Unite Maghrebine, pg 470
Editions La Porte, pg 470

Mozambique
Centro De Estudos Africanos, pg 470

Myanmar
Knowledge Printing & Publishing House, pg 471
Shwepyidan Printing & Publishing House, pg 471

Namibia
Multi-Disciplinary Research Centre Library, pg 471

Nepal
International Standards Books & Periodicals (P) Ltd, pg 471

Netherlands
Uitgeverij Jan van Arkel, pg 473
Boom Uitgeverij, pg 474
Van Gennep Ltd, pg 477
Heureka Uitgeverij, pg 478
Uitgeverij H Nelissen BV, pg 482
Sociaal en Cultureel Planbureau, pg 484
Staatsdrukkerij en Uitgeverijbedrijf, pg 484
Unieboek BV, pg 485
Uitgeverij Van Wijnen, pg 486

New Zealand
Auckland University Press, pg 488
Fraser Books, pg 491
Gondwanaland Press, pg 491
Hazard Press Ltd, pg 491
Legislation Direct, pg 492
University of Otago Press, pg 496
Victoria University Press, pg 496
Bridget Williams Books Ltd, pg 497

Nicaragua
Editorial Nueva Nicaragua, pg 497

Nigeria
Evans Brothers (Nigeria Publishers) Ltd, pg 499
Fourth Dimension Publishing Co Ltd, pg 499
Goldland Business Co Ltd, pg 499
JAD Publishers Ltd, pg 500
Literamed Publications Nigeria Ltd, pg 500
Unity Publishing & Research Company Ltd, pg 502
Vantage Publishers International Ltd, pg 502
West African Book Publishers Ltd, pg 502

Norway
Glydendal Akademisk, pg 503
Gyldendal Norsk Forlag A/S, pg 503
Snofugl Forlag, pg 505

Pakistan
Sheikh Muhammad Ashraf Publishers, pg 506
Centre for South Asian Studies, pg 506
Jang Publishers, pg 507
Maqbool Academy, pg 508
Pak American Commercial (Pvt) Ltd, pg 508
Royal Book Co, pg 509
Shibil Publications (Pvt) Ltd, pg 509

Papua New Guinea
National Research Institute of Papua New Guinea, pg 510

Paraguay
Intercontinental Editora, pg 510

Peru
Centro de la Mujer Peruana Flora Tristan, pg 511
Instituto de Estudios Peruanos, pg 511

Philippines
Ateneo de Manila University Press, pg 512
Garotech, pg 513
Heritage Publishing House, pg 513
University of the Philippines Press, pg 515

Poland
KAW Krajowa Agencja Wydawnicza, pg 517
'Ksiazka i Wiedza' Spotdzielnia Wydawniczo-Handlowa, pg 517
Wydawnictwo Lubelskie, pg 518
Magnum Publishing House Ltd, pg 518
Spotdzielna Anagram, pg 520
Wydawnictwo TPPR Wspolpraca, pg 520
Wydawnictwa Uniwersytetu Warszawskiego, pg 521

Portugal
Edicoes Afrontamento, pg 522
Armenio Amado Editora de Simoes, Beirao & Ca Lda, pg 522
Edicoes Antigona, pg 522
Editorial 'Avante!', pg 522
Brasilia Editora (J Carvalho Branco), pg 523
Editorial Caminho SARL, pg 523
Livraria Civilizacao (Americo Fraga Lamares & Ca Lda), pg 523
Gradiva-Publicacnoes Lda, pg 525
Imprensa Nacional-Casa da Moeda, pg 526
Editora Livros do Brasil Sarl, pg 526
McGraw-Hill Editora de Portugal, pg 527
Nova Arrancada Sociedade Editora SA, pg 527
Perspectivas e Realidades, Artes Graficas, Lda, pg 528
Editorial Presenca, pg 528
Edicoes Rolim Lda, pg 529

Puerto Rico
Libros-Ediciones Homines, pg 530

Romania
Casa de editura Globus, pg 533
Humanitas Publishing House, pg 533
Editura Institutul European, pg 533
Nemira Verlag, pg 534
Editura Niculescu, pg 534
Realitatea Casa de Edituri Productie Audio-Video Film, pg 535
Editura 'Scrisul Romanesc', pg 536

Russian Federation
Aspect Press Ltd, pg 537
INFRA-M Izdatel 'skij dom, pg 538
Izvestia Sovetov Narodnyh Deputatov Russian Federation (RF), pg 539
Ladomir Publishing House, pg 539
Izdatelstvo Lenizdat, pg 539
Mezdunarodnye Otno Denija, pg 540
Izdatelstvo Mezhdunarodnye Otnoshenia, pg 540
Izdatelstvo Molodaya Gvardia, pg 540
Nauka Publishers, pg 540
Izdatel'stvo Nizhegorodskogo Gosudarstvennogo Univ, pg 540
Novosti Izdatel 'stvo, pg 541
Progress Publishers, pg 541
Respublika, pg 541
Russkaya Kniga Izdatelstvo (Publishers), pg 541
Voyenizdat, pg 542

Saudi Arabia
Al Jazirah Organization for Press, Printing, Publishing, pg 543

Senegal
CODESRIA (Council for the Development of Social Science Research in Africa), pg 544
Societe Africaine d'Edition, pg 544

Singapore
Chopsons Pte Ltd, pg 545
Institute of Southeast Asian Studies, pg 546
Select Books Pte Ltd, pg 548
Singapore University Press Pte Ltd, pg 548
Taylor & Francis Asia Pacific, pg 548
Times Media Pte Ltd, pg 549

Slovakia
ARCHA sro Vydavatel 'stro, pg 549
Danubiaprint, pg 549

Slovenia
Univerza v Ljubljani Ekonomska Fakulteta, pg 552
Zalozba Mihelac d o o, pg 552

PUBLISHERS

South Africa
Ashanti Publishing, pg 552
Jonathan Ball Publishers, pg 552
Educum Publishers Ltd, pg 554
Human Sciences Research Council, pg 555
Institute for Reformational Studies CHE, pg 555
New Africa Books (Pty) Ltd, pg 557
Ravan Press (Pty) Ltd, pg 558
South African Institute of International Affairs, pg 559
South African Institute of Race Relations, pg 559
Van Schaik Publishers, pg 560

Spain
Edicions Alfons el Magnanim, Institucio Valenciana d'Estudis i Investigacio, pg 562
Alianza Editorial SA, pg 562
Altea, Taurus, Alfaguara SA, pg 563
Amnistia Internacional Editorial SL, pg 563
Centro de Estudios Politicos Y Constitucionales, pg 567
Editorial Constitucion y Leyes SA - COLEX, pg 568
Edicions del Drac SA, pg 570
Fondo de Cultura Economica de Espana, SL, pg 574
Editorial Fundamentos, pg 575
Ediciones Jucar, pg 579
Ediciones Libertarias/Prodhufi SA, pg 580
Ediciones Morata SL, pg 583
Siglo XXI de Espana Editores SA, pg 590
Universidad de Valladolid Secretariado de Publicaciones e Intercambio Editorial, pg 594

Sri Lanka
Warna Publishers, pg 598

Suriname
Stichting Wetenschappelijke Informatie, pg 599

Sweden
Carlsson Bokfoerlag AB, pg 601
Forlaget By och Bygd, pg 602
Iustus Forlag AB, pg 603
AB Timbro, pg 607
Zindermans AB, pg 607

Switzerland
Athenaeum Verlag AG, pg 608
Cahiers de la Renaissance Vaudoise, pg 610
Europa Verlag AG, pg 614
Georg Editeur SA, pg 614
Editions Francois Grounauer, pg 615
Th Gut Verlag, pg 615
Helbing und Lichtenhahn Verlag AG, pg 615
Verlag Huber & Co AG, pg 616
Interfrom AG Editions, pg 616
Junod Nicholas, pg 616
Klett und Balmer & Co Verlag, pg 617
Lenos Verlag, pg 618
Limmat Verlag, pg 618
Peter Meili & Co, Buchhandluna, pg 619
Les Editions Nagel SA (Paris), pg 619
Verlag Organisator AG, pg 620
Pendo Verlag GmbH, pg 621
Rotpunktverlag, pg 623
Verlag SOI (Schweizerisches Ost-Institut), pg 625
Staempfli Verlag AG, pg 625
Editions des Trois Collines Francois Lachenal, pg 626
Der Universitatsverlag Freiburg, pg 626
Weltrundschau Verlag AG, pg 627

Syrian Arab Republic
Damascus University Press, pg 628

Taiwan, Province of China
Laureate Book Co Ltd, pg 631
San Min Book Co Ltd, pg 631

Tajikistan
Irfon, pg 632

United Republic of Tanzania
Eastern Africa Publications Ltd, pg 633
Kajura Publications, pg 633
Tanzania Publishing House, pg 634

Thailand
Suksit Siam Co Ltd, pg 635
Thai Watana Panich Co, Ltd, pg 636

Trinidad & Tobago
Inprint Caribbean Ltd, pg 637

Tunisia
Ceres Editions, pg 637
Dar El Afaq, pg 637

Turkey
Afa Yayincilik Sanayi Tic AS, pg 638
Ezel Erverdi (Dergah Yayinlari AS) Muessese Muduru, pg 640
Iletisim Yayinlari, pg 640
Alev Yayinlari, pg 642

Turkmenistan
Izdatelstvo Turkmenistan, pg 642

Uganda
Centre for Basic Research, pg 642
Fountain Publishers Ltd, pg 642

Ukraine
Osnovy Publishers, pg 643

United Kingdom
Aldwych Press Ltd, pg 645
Anglo-German Foundation for the Study of Industrial Society, pg 647
Arms & Armour Press, pg 648
Ashgate Publishing Ltd, pg 649
Baha'i Publishing Trust, pg 651
Berg Publishers, pg 654
Berghahn Books Ltd, pg 654
Blackwell Publishers, pg 655
Bookmarks Publications, pg 657
British Educational Communication & Technology Agency (BECTA), pg 660
Business Monitor International, pg 661
Cambridge University Press, pg 662
Jon Carpenter Publishing, pg 664
Catholic Institute for International Relations, pg 665
Causeway Press Ltd, pg 665
Colourpoint Books, pg 669
Commonwealth Secretariat, pg 669
Conservative Policy Forum, pg 670
The Continuum International Publishing Group Ltd, pg 670
James Currey Ltd, pg 673
Andre Deutsch Ltd, pg 675
Edinburgh University Press Ltd, pg 677
Edward Elgar Publishing Ltd, pg 678
Europa Publications, pg 680
The Eurospan Group, pg 680
Fabian Society, pg 681
Facts On File, pg 681
Francis Balsom Associates, pg 684
Freedom Press, pg 684
Geiser Productions, pg 686
Golden Cockerel Press Ltd, pg 688
HarperCollins Publishers, pg 692
Harvard University Press, pg 692
William Heinemann Ltd, pg 694
Helicon Publishing Ltd, pg 694
Hemming Information Services, pg 695
C Hurst & Co (Publishers) Ltd, pg 698
ICC United Kingdom, pg 698
Institute of Development Studies, pg 699
Institute of Irish Studies, The Queens University of Belfast, pg 699
International Institute for Strategic Studies, pg 701
Islamic Foundation Publications, pg 701
JAI Press Ltd, pg 702
Macmillan Reference Ltd, pg 710
Mainstream Publishing Co (Edinburgh) Ltd, pg 711
Manchester University Press, pg 711
The Merlin Press Ltd, pg 713
National Assembly for Wales, pg 717
National Library of Wales, pg 717
NCLC Publishing Society Ltd, pg 718
New European Publications Ltd, pg 718
W W Norton & Company Ltd, pg 720
NTC Publications Ltd, pg 720
Open Gate Press, pg 721
Open University Press, pg 721
Oxfam, pg 722
Oxford University Press, pg 723
Pathfinder London, pg 724
Pearson Education, pg 725
Pearson Education Europe, Mideast & Africa, pg 725
Pluto Press, pg 728
The Policy Press, pg 729
Policy Studies Institute, pg 729
Prism Press Book Publishers Ltd, pg 730
Random House UK Ltd, pg 733
Reaktion Books Ltd, pg 733
Robson Books, pg 735
Routledge, pg 736
Royal Institute of International Affairs, pg 736
Sage Publications Ltd, pg 737
Scottish Affairs, pg 739
Scottish Office Library & Information Services, pg 740
Seren, pg 740
Serif, pg 740
Shaw & Sons Ltd, pg 741
Shepheard-Walwyn (Publishers) Ltd, pg 741
SHU Press, pg 742

SUBJECT INDEX

Sidgwick & Jackson Ltd, pg 742
Skoob Russell Square, pg 742
The Society of Metaphysicians Ltd, pg 743
Spokesman, pg 744
The Stationery Office, pg 745
I B Tauris & Co Ltd, pg 747
Transworld Publishers Ltd, pg 750
UCL Press Ltd, pg 751
Vacher Dod Publishing Ltd, pg 752
Verso, pg 752
Virago Press, pg 753
Welsh Academic Press, pg 755
Westview Press, pg 755
Wild Goose Publications, pg 756
Wimbledon Publishing Company Ltd, pg 757
The Women's Press Ltd, pg 758
World of Information, pg 759
Yale University Press London, pg 759

Uruguay
Fundacion de Cultura Universitaria, pg 760
Linardi y Risso Libreria, pg 760
Nordan-Comunidad, pg 760
Ediciones Trilce, pg 761

Uzbekistan
Izdatelstvo Uzbekistan, pg 761

Venezuela
Editorial Ateneo de Caracas, pg 762
Monte Avila Editores Latinoamericana CA, pg 762
Fundacion Centro Gumilla, pg 762
Editorial Nueva Sociedad, pg 762

Viet Nam
Su Hoc (Historical) Publishing House, pg 763
Su That (Truth) Publishing House, pg 763

Yugoslavia
Alfa-Narodna Knjiga, pg 764
Forum, pg 764
Izdavacka Organizacija Rad, pg 765
Panorama NIJP/ID Grigorije Bozovic, pg 765
Radnicka Stampa, pg 765

Zambia
Aafzam Ltd, pg 766
MFK Management Consultants Services, pg 766
Movement for Multi-Party Democracy, pg 767
Zambia Association for Research & Development, pg 767
Zambia Educational Publishing House, pg 767

Zimbabwe
Journal on Social Change, pg 768
Nehanda Publishers, pg 769
Sapes Trust Ltd, pg 769

HEALTH, NUTRITION

Argentina
Libreria Akadia Editorial, pg 3
Editorial Albatros SACI, pg 3
Editorial Kier SACIFI, pg 7
Ediciones Lidiun, pg 7
Editorial Planeta Argentina SAIC, pg 8
Ediciones Preescolar SA, pg 8

San Pablo, pg 8
Editorial Sopena Argentina SACI e I, pg 9

Australia

Allen & Unwin Pty Ltd, The Australian Newspaper, Vogel Breads, pg 11
Michelle Anderson Publishing Pty Ltd, pg 11
Edward Arnold (Australia) Pty Ltd, pg 12
Assert Publishing, pg 12
Ausmed Publications Pty Ltd, pg 12
Bio Concepts Publishing, pg 15
Blackhead Ink Publishing, pg 15
Centre Publications, pg 17
CHOICE Magazine, pg 18
Dynamo House P/L, pg 21
Family Health Publications, pg 22
Fraser Publications, pg 23
Ginninderra Press, pg 24
Greater Glider Productions Australia Pty Ltd, pg 24
Hale & Iremonger Pty Ltd, pg 24
James Nicholas Publishers Pty Ltd, pg 28
Kingsclear Books, pg 29
Lansdowne Publishing Pty Ltd, pg 29
Life Planning Foundation of Australia, Inc, pg 30
Thomas C Lothian Pty Ltd, pg 30
MacLennan & Petty Pty Ltd, pg 31
Mayne Publishing, pg 32
McGraw-Hill Australia Pty Ltd, pg 32
Moon-Ta-Gu Books, pg 33
Mosby Lifeline, pg 33
Mouse House Press, pg 34
Anne O'Donovan Pty Ltd, pg 35
Oidium Books, pg 35
Oxfam Community Aid Abroad, pg 36
Pan Macmillan Australia Pty Ltd, pg 36
Pearson Education Australia, pg 37
Jurriaan Plesman, pg 38
The Pythagorean Press, pg 39
R & R Publications Marketing P/L, pg 39
Reed Educational Publishing Australia, pg 40
Regency Publishing, pg 40
Shakespeare Head Press Pty Ltd, pg 42
Simon & Schuster Australia Pty Ltd, pg 42
Spinifex Press, pg 43
Stirling Press, pg 43
Tomorrow Publications, pg 45
Transworld Publishers Pty Ltd, pg 45
Unity Press, pg 46
Veritas Press, pg 46
Vista Publications, pg 47
Wellness Australia, pg 47
Women's Health Advisory Service, pg 48
Zoe Publishing Pty Ltd, pg 48

Austria

CEEBA Publications Antenne d'Autriche, pg 50
Ennsthaler GesmbH & Co KG, pg 51
Alois Goschl & Co, pg 52
IAEA - International Atomic Energy Agency, pg 53
Niederosterreichisches Pressehaus Druck- und Verlagsgesellschaft mbH, pg 55

NO1 - Verlag, pg 55
Verlag Orac im Verlag Kremayr & Scheriau, pg 56
Verlag des Osterr Kneippbundes GmbH, pg 57
Verlag Carl Ueberreuter GmbH, pg 59
Edition Va Bene, pg 60
Verlag Veritas Mediengesellschaft mbH, pg 60
Dr Otfried Weise Verlag Tabula Smaragdina, pg 60

Bangladesh

Gatidhara, pg 62
Gono Prakashani, Gono Shasthya Kendra, pg 62

Belarus

Interdigets Publishing House, pg 63

Belgium

Altina, pg 64
Coda, pg 66
Editions De Boeck-Larcier SA, pg 67
Eenhoorn BVBA, pg 68
Koepel van de Vlaamse Noord - Zuidbeweging 11.11.11, pg 70
Uitgeverij Lannoo NV, pg 70
Marabout, pg 72
Vita, pg 75

Brazil

Editora Agora Ltda, pg 78
Editora Antroposofica Ltda, pg 78
ARTMED, pg 79
Editora Campus Ltda, pg 80
Editora Contexto (Editora Pinsky Ltda), pg 81
Editora Elevacao, pg 82
EDUSC - Editora da Universidade do Sagrado Coracao, pg 82
Editora Forense, pg 83
Editora Gaia Ltda, pg 84
Global Editora e Distribuidora Ltda, pg 84
Editora Ground Ltda, pg 84
IBRASA (Instituicao Brasileira de Difusao Cultural Ltda), pg 85
Iglu Editora Ltda, pg 85
Interlivros Edicoes Ltda, pg 85
Editora Manole Ltda, pg 87
Editora Mercado Aberto Ltda, pg 88
Editora Nova Fronteira SA, pg 88
Rede Das Artes (Boccato Editores Collector's), pg 90

Bulgaria

Abagar, Veliko Tarnovo, pg 94
Aratron, IK, pg 94
Gea-Libris Publishing House, pg 95
Hermes Publishing House, pg 95
Kibea Publishing Co, pg 96
LIK IZDANIJA, pg 96
MATEX, pg 96
Medicina i Fizkultura EOOD, pg 96
Prozoretz Ltd Publishing House, pg 97
Reporter, pg 97
Sluntse Publishing House, pg 98
TEMTO, pg 98

China

Beijing Medical Univ Press, pg 102
Chemical Industry Press, pg 102
Fudan University Press, pg 105
Fujian Science & Technology Publishing House, pg 106

Heilongjiang Science & Technology Press, pg 106
Jiangsu Science & Technology Publishing House, pg 106
Jilin Science & Technology Publishing House, pg 106
Knowledge Press, pg 107
People's Medical Publishing House (PMPH), pg 108
The Publishing House of Shanghai University of Traditional Chinese Medicine, pg 108
Sichuan Science & Technology Publishing House, pg 109
Tianjin Science & Technology Publishing House, pg 109

Colombia

RAM Editores, pg 113

The Democratic Republic of the Congo

Centre de Vulgarisation Agricole, pg 115

Costa Rica

Academia de Centro America, pg 115
Editorial Nacional de Salud y Seguridad Social Ednass, pg 116
Scout Interamericana, pg 117
Editorial de la Universidad de Costa Rica, pg 117

Croatia

Znaci Vremena, Institut Za Istrazivanje Biblije, pg 120

Cuba

Editorial Oriente, pg 121
Editora Politica, pg 121

Czech Republic

Dimenze 2 Plus 2 Praha, pg 124
Erika, pg 124
Granit SRO, pg 124
Jota, pg 125
Luxpress VOS, pg 126
Maxdorf Ltd, pg 126
Pavla Momcilova, pg 126
Nakladatelstvi a vydavatelstvi Panorama, pg 127
Pragma 4, pg 127
Svojtka & Co, pg 128

Denmark

Aschehoug Dansk Forlag A/S, pg 130
Bogan's Forlag, pg 130
Borgens Forlag A/S, pg 130
Fremad A/S, pg 132
P Haase & Sons Forlag A/S, pg 132
Olivia - det gronne forlag, pg 134

Dominican Republic

Pontificia Universidad Catolica Madre y Maestra, pg 136

Ecuador

CEPLAES, pg 137

Estonia

Valgus Publishers, pg 141

Ethiopia

Addis Ababa University Press, pg 141

Finland

Kirjatoimi, pg 143
Weilin & Goeoes Oy, pg 145
Yliopistopaino/Helsinki University Press, pg 145

France

Adverbum SARL, pg 146
ALTESS Editions Argel, pg 146
Editions Amrita SA, pg 147
ATP - Packager, pg 149
Editions A Barthelemy, pg 149
Editions Belfond, pg 150
Alain Brethe Editions, pg 152
Editions Chiron, pg 154
Courrier du Livre Sarl, pg 157
De Vecchi Editions SA, pg 158
Doin Editeurs, pg 160
Ellebore, pg 161
Ere Nouvelle, pg 162
Editions Generales First, pg 166
Editions Grancher, pg 166
Hachette Pratiques, pg 167
Hermes Science Publications, pg 168
INRA Editions (Institut National de la Recherche Agronomique), pg 169
Editions INSERM, pg 169
IRD Editions, pg 170
Editions du Jaguar, pg 170
Le Jour, Editeur, pg 170
LT Editions-J Lanore-H Laurens, pg 172
Editions Universitaires LCF, pg 172
Editions Josette Lyon, pg 174
Maisonneuve, pg 174
Editions Mango, pg 174
Societe des Editions Menges, pg 175
Pardes, pg 179
Polytechnica, pg 180
Guide Rosenwald, pg 183
Editions du Rouergue, pg 183
Editions Sand et Tchou SA, pg 183
Editions Sang de la Terre, pg 183
Sofradif Editions Philippe Auzou, pg 185
Terre Vivante, pg 187
Editions Trois Fontaines, pg 188

Germany

Andernach Atelier Verlag (AVA), pg 193
AOL-Verlag Frohmut Menze, pg 194
Roland Asanger Verlag GmbH, pg 195
Aurum Verlag GmbH, pg 197
Verlag Hermann Bauer KG, pg 199
Beuth Verlag GmbH, pg 202
Blaukreuz-Verlag Wuppertal, pg 204
Buchverlage Langen-Mueller/Herbig, pg 207
Catia Monser Eggcup-Verlag, pg 209
Chmielorz GmbH Verlag, pg 210
Compact Verlag GmbH, pg 211
Copress Verlag, pg 211
Dingfelder-Verlag Inh Gerd Gmelin, pg 217
Dreisam Ratgeber in der Rutsker Verlag GmbH, pg 218
Econ Taschenbuchverlag, pg 220
Egmont vgs verlagsgesellschaft mbH, pg 221
Verlag Peter Erd GmbH, pg 223
Ergebnisse Verlag GmbH, pg 223
Esogetics GmbH, pg 224
Fachbuchverlag Pfanneberg & Co, pg 226
Falken-Verlag GmbH, pg 227

PUBLISHERS

Fink - Kummerly und Frey Verlag GmbH, pg 227
Flensburger Hefte Verlag GmbH, pg 228
Gesundheits-Dialog Verlag GmbH, pg 232
Gildefachverlag GmbH & Co KG, pg 232
Verlagsgesellschaft R Gloess & Co, pg 233
Graefe und Unzer Verlag GmbH, pg 233
Verlag der Stiftung Gralsbotschaft GmbH, pg 234
Walter Haedecke Verlag, pg 236
Dr Curt Haefner-Verlag GmbH, pg 236
Lehrmittelverlag Wilhelm Hagemann GmbH, pg 236
Happy Mental Buch- und Musik Verlag, pg 237
Karl F Haug Verlag GmbH & Co, pg 238
F A Herbig Verlagsbuchhandlung GmbH, pg 239
F Hirthammer Verlag GmbH, pg 241
Huebner Felicitas Verlag, pg 243
Heinrich Hugendubel Verlag GmbH, pg 243
Huthig GmbH & Co KG, pg 244
Jahreszeiten-Verlag GmbH, pg 246
Dr Werner Jopp Verlag, pg 246
Joy Verlag GmbH, pg 247
Jutta Pohl Verlag, pg 247
Juventa Verlag GmbH, pg 247
K L V Konkret Literatur Verlag GmbH, pg 247
Verlag im Kilian GmbH, pg 249
Knowledge Media International, pg 251
Kolibri-Verlags GmbH, pg 252
Kunstverlag Weingarten GmbH, pg 254
Landbuch-Verlagsgesellschaft mbH, pg 255
Lebensbaum Verlags-GmbH, pg 256
Lebenshilfe-Verlag Marburg, Verlag der Bundesvereinigung Lebenshilfe fuer Menschen mit geistiger Behinderung eV, pg 256
Medizinisch-Literarische Verlagsgesellschaft mbH, pg 262
Meyer & Meyer Fachverlag und Buchhandel GmbH, pg 263
Midena Verlag, pg 264
Mosaik Verlag GmbH, pg 265
NaturaViva Verlags GmbH, pg 266
Naumann & Goebel Verlagsgesellschaft mbH, pg 267
Neue Dimension Buch-und Musik-Verlag, pg 267
Neuer Honos Verlag GmbH, pg 267
Neuer Weg Verlag und Druck GmbH, pg 268
Neuland-Verlagsgesellschaft mbH, pg 268
nymphenburger, pg 269
Oeko-Test Verlag GmbH & Co KG Betriebsgesellschaft, pg 269
Orbis Verlag fur Publizistik GmbH, pg 270
Orlanda Frauenverlag, pg 270
Pala-Verlag GmbH, pg 271
pmi Verlag, pg 274
Propylaeen Verlag, Zweigniederlassung Berlin der Ullstein Buchverlage GmbH, pg 275
Psychiatrie-Verlag GmbH, pg 275
Quintessenz Verlags-GmbH, pg 276
Rossipaul Kommunikation GmbH, pg 280
Ryvellus Medienagentur Dopfer, pg 281
Saatkorn-Verlag GmbH, pg 281
Verlag Werner Sachon GmbH & Co, pg 281
Moritz Schauenburg Verlag, pg 282
Schnitzer GmbH & Co KG, pg 284
Schulz-Kirchner Verlag GmbH, pg 285
R S Schulz Verlag GmbH, pg 285
Heinrich Schwab Verlag, pg 285
Spiridon-Verlags GmbH, pg 288
Springer-Verlag GmbH & Co KG, pg 288
Dr Dietrich Steinkopff Verlag GmbH & Co, pg 289
Suedwest Verlag GmbH & Co KG, pg 291
Synthesis Verlag, pg 291
Georg Thieme Verlag KG, pg 293
Tipress Dienstleistungen fur das Verlagswesen GmbH, pg 294
TR - Verlagsunion GmbH, pg 294
Treves Editions Verein Zur Foerderung der Kuenstlerischen Taetigkeiten, pg 295
Trias-Thieme, Hippokrates Enke, pg 295
Turm-Verlag Lorber-Verlag Otto Zluhan OHG, pg 295
Guenter Albert Ulmer Verlag, pg 295
Umschau Buchverlag Breidenstein GmbH, pg 296
UNO-Verlag mbH, Vertriebs und Verlagsgesellschaft, pg 296
UTB fuer Wissenschaft Uni-Taschenbuecher GmbH, pg 297
WDV Wirtschaftsdienst Gesellschaft fur Medien & Kommunikation mbH & Co OHG, pg 300
Verlagsgruppe Weltbild GmbH, pg 301
Verlag DAS WORT GmbH, pg 304
Zebulon Verlag GmbH & Co KG, pg 305
ZS Verlag Zabert Sandmann GmbH, pg 305

Ghana
Adaex Educational Publications Ltd, pg 306
Ghana Institute of Linguistics Literacy & Bible Translation (GILLBT), pg 307
World Literature Project, pg 308

Greece
Chrysi Penna - Golden Pen Books, pg 309
Patakis Publishers, pg 314

Guinea-Bissau
Instituto Nacional de Estudos e Pesquisa, pg 316

Hong Kong
Federal Publications Ltd, pg 319
Friends of the Earth (Charity) Ltd, pg 320
Joint Publishing (HK) Co Ltd, pg 320
Ming Pao Publications Ltd, pg 321
Peace Book Co Ltd, pg 321
Publications (Holdings) Ltd, pg 321

Hungary
Advent Kiado, pg 323
Officina Nova, Koenyv-es Lapkiado/Bertelsmann Media Kft, pg 324
Kossuth Kiado RT, pg 325
Kulturtrade, pg 325

Iceland
Bokaforlag Birtingur, pg 327
Bokautgafan Orn og Orlygur ehf, pg 327
Frodi Ltd, pg 328
Idunn, pg 328

India
Agricole Publishing Academy, pg 330
APH Publishing Corp, pg 331
B l Publications Pvt Ltd, pg 331
The Bangalore Printing & Publishing Co Ltd, pg 332
BR Publishing Corporation, pg 334
Chowkhamba Sanskrit Series Office, pg 335
Diamond Comics (P) Ltd, pg 336
Frank Brothers & Co (Publishers) Ltd, pg 337
Islamic Publishing House, pg 340
Jaico Publishing House, pg 340
B Jain Publishers Overseas, pg 340
B Jain Publishers (P) Ltd, pg 340
Kali For Women, pg 341
Orient Paperbacks, pg 345
Popular Prakashan Pvt Ltd, pg 346
Pustak Mahal, pg 346
Rajendra Publishing House Pvt Ltd, pg 347
Scientific Book Agency, pg 349
Sultan Chand & Sons Pvt Ltd, pg 351
Vision Books Pvt Ltd, pg 353

Indonesia
Advent Indonesia Publishing, pg 353
Bhratara Karya Aksara, pg 354
Institut Teknologi Bandung, pg 355
Lembaga Demografi Fakultas Ekonomi Universitas Indonesia, pg 356

Ireland
Attic Press Ltd, pg 358
The Economic & Social Research Institute, pg 360
Emerald Publications, pg 360
Gill & Macmillan Ltd, pg 361
On Stream Publications Ltd, pg 363
Tivenan Publications, pg 364

Israel
Books in the Attic Publishers Ltd, pg 366
Breslov Research Institute, pg 366
Carta, The Israel Map & Publishing Co Ltd, pg 366
Gefen Publishing House Ltd, pg 367
Hakibbutz Hameuchad Publishing House Ltd, pg 368
Intermedia Audio, Video Book Publishing Ltd, pg 368
(JDC) Brookdale Institute of Gerontology & Adult Human Development in Israel, pg 369
Pitspopany Press, pg 371
Schocken Publishing House Ltd, pg 372
R Sirkis Publishers Ltd, pg 372
Yedioth Ahronoth Books, pg 373

Italy
Gruppo Abele, pg 374
Arcanta Aries Gruppo Editoriale, pg 376

SUBJECT INDEX

Editore Armando Armando SRL, pg 376
Gruppo Editoriale Armenia SpA, pg 376
Centro Scientifico Torinese, pg 381
CIC Edizioni Internazionali, pg 381
Giovanni De Vecchi Editore SpA, pg 384
Demetra SRL, pg 385
Edagricole - Edizioni Agricole, pg 385
Edizioni Il Punto d'Incontro SAS, pg 386
Edizioni Mediterranee SRL, pg 387
Folini, pg 389
Ernesto Gremese Editore SRL, pg 391
Hermes Edizioni SRL, pg 392
Il Pensiero Scientifico Editore SRL, pg 393
Lyra Libri SAS, pg 397
Macro Edizioni, pg 397
Nuove Autonomie, pg 401
Il Punto D Incontro, pg 404
Red/Studio Redazionale SpA, pg 405
Reverdito Edizioni, pg 405
Samaya SRL, pg 406
Editoriale Scienza, pg 407
Sperling e Kupfer Editori SpA, pg 408
Stampa Alternativa - Nuovi Equilibri, pg 409
TEA Tascabili degli Editori Associati SpA, pg 409
Tecniche Nuove SpA, pg 409
Voce della Bibbia, pg 412
Zanfi Editori SRL, pg 412

Japan
Daiichi Shuppan Co Ltd, pg 415
Fumaido Publishing Company Ltd, pg 416
Hakutei-Sha, pg 417
Ishiyaku Publishers Inc, pg 418
Japan Publications Inc, pg 418
Mejikaru Furendo-sha, pg 421
Nagaoka Shoten Company Ltd, pg 421
Nippon Hoso Shuppan Kyokai (NHK Publishing), pg 422
Nobunkyo (Rural Village Culture Association), pg 423
Seibido Shuppan Company Ltd, pg 424
Shufunotomo sha Co Ltd, pg 426
United Nations University Press, pg 428

Kenya
African Centre for Technology Studies (ACTS), pg 431
Kenya Literature Bureau, pg 432
Kenya Medical Research Institute (KEMRI), pg 432
Sudan Literature Centre, pg 433

Republic of Korea
Hanul Publishing Co, pg 436
Hyein Publishing House, pg 437
Minjisa Publishing Co, pg 438
Suhagsa, pg 440

Latvia
Alberts XII, pg 441
Lielvards Ltd, pg 442
Patmos, pg 442
Preses Nams, pg 442

Lithuania
Algarve, pg 445

SUBJECT INDEX

Malaysia
S Abdul Majeed & Co, pg 451
Vinpress Sdn Bhd, pg 455

Maldive Islands
Non-Formal Education Centre, pg 455

Mauritius
Editions de l'Ocean Indien Ltd, pg 457

Mexico
Ediciones Alpe, pg 458
Arbol Editorial SA de CV, pg 458
Editorial Armonia SA, pg 458
Editorial Diana SA de CV, pg 459
Editorial El Manual Moderno SA de CV, pg 460
Ediciones Exclusivas SA, pg 461
Libros y Revistas SA de CV, pg 463
Editorial Limusa SA de CV, pg 463
Nova Grupo Editorial SA de CV, pg 464
Editorial Nueva Imagen SA, pg 464
Panorama Editorial, SA, pg 465
Editorial Pax Mexico, pg 465
Selector SA de CV, pg 467
Siglo XXI Editores SA de CV, pg 467

Monaco
Les Editions du Rocher, pg 469

Morocco
Editions Le Fennec, pg 470

Netherlands
Aeolus Press BV, pg 472
Ankh-Hermes BV, pg 472
De Boekerij BV, pg 474
BZZTOH Publishers, pg 475
De Driehoek BV, pg 476
Elmar BV, pg 476
Uitgeverij Vrij Geestesleven, pg 477
Uitgeverij Homeovisie BV, pg 478
IOS Press BV, pg 479
Koninklijk Instituut Voor de Tropen, pg 480
Uitgeverij Lemma BV, pg 480
Servire BV Uitgevers, pg 484
Sjaloom en Wildeboer Publishers, pg 484
Sociaal en Cultureel Planbureau, pg 484
A J G Strengholt's Boeken, Anno 1928, BV, pg 484
Swets & Zeitlinger Publishers, pg 485
Terra Publishing Co, pg 485
Uitgeverij de Tijdstroom BV, pg 485
Tirion Uitgevers BV, pg 485
Uitgeverij De Toorts, pg 485

Netherlands Antilles
De Wit Stores NV, pg 488

New Zealand
Barkfire Press, pg 488
ESA Publications (NZ) Ltd, pg 490
Nelson Price Milburn Ltd, pg 494
Spinal Publications, pg 496
Tandem Press, pg 496

Nigeria
Daystar Press (Publishers), pg 498

Norway
Ex Libris Forlag A/S, pg 503
Genesis Forlag, pg 503
Glydendal Akademisk, pg 503
Hilt & Hansteen A/S, pg 504
Sandviks Bokforlag, pg 505

Pakistan
HMR Publishing Co, pg 507
Sang-e-Meel Publications, pg 509

Papua New Guinea
Kristen Pres, pg 510

Peru
Centro de la Mujer Peruana Flora Tristan, pg 511
Instituto de Estudios Peruanos, pg 511

Philippines
Anvil Publishing Inc, pg 512
UST Publishing House, pg 515

Poland
Ksiaznica Publishing Ltd, pg 517
PZWL Wydawnictwo Lekarskie Ltd, pg 519
Oficyna Wydawnicza Read Me, pg 519
Panstwowe Wydawnictwo Rolnicze i Lesne, pg 519
Wydawnictwo WAB, pg 520

Portugal
Brasilia Editora (J Carvalho Branco), pg 523
Dinalivro, pg 524
Editorial Estampa, Lda, pg 524
Europress Editores e Distribuidores de Publicacoes Lda, pg 525
Edicoes ITAU (Instituto Tecnico de Alimentacao Humana) Lda, pg 526
Edicoes Manuel Lencastre, pg 526
McGraw-Hill Editora de Portugal, pg 527
Paz-Editora de Multimedia, LDA, pg 528
Editorial Presenca, pg 528
Editora Replicacao Lda, pg 529
Texto Editora, pg 529

Romania
Editura Excelsior, pg 533
Editura Gryphon, pg 533
Editura Niculescu, pg 534
Vremea Publishers Ltd, pg 536

Russian Federation
Airis Press, pg 537
Izdatelstvo Medicina, pg 539
Izdatelstvo Mir, pg 540
Nauka Publishers, pg 540
Panorama Publishing House, pg 541
Russkaya Kniga Izdatelstvo (Publishers), pg 541
Scorpion Publishers, pg 541

Singapore
Times Media Pte Ltd, pg 549

Slovakia
AV Studio Reklamno-vydavatel 'ska agentura, pg 549
Sofa, pg 551

Slovenia
East West Operation (EWO) Ltd, pg 551

South Africa
Erudita Publications (Pty) Ltd, pg 554
Jacana Education, pg 555
Reader's Digest Southern Africa, pg 559
Southern Book Publishers (Pty) Ltd, pg 559

Spain
Editorial Acanto SA, pg 561
Editorial 'Alas', pg 562
AMV Ediciones, pg 563
Editorial Astri SA, pg 564
Ediciones Atril, pg 564
CEAC, Grupo Editorial SA, pg 567
Cedel, Ediciones Jose O Avila Monteso ES, pg 567
Didaco Comunicacion y Didactica, SA, pg 569
Ediciones Doce Calles SL, pg 570
Editorial Donostiarra SA, pg 570
Editorial EDAF SA, pg 571
Ediciones l'Isard, S L, pg 571
Editorial Editex SA, pg 572
Ediciones Elfos SL, pg 572
Eumo Editorial, pg 574
Generalitat de Catalunya Diari Oficial de la Generalitat vern, pg 575
Editorial Hispano Europea SA, pg 577
Editorial Iberia, SA, pg 577
Ediciones Libertarias/Prodhufi SA, pg 580
Libsa Editorial SA, pg 580
Ediciones Martinez-Roca SA, pg 581
McGraw-Hill Iberic/Brazil Group, pg 581
Ediciones Medici SA, pg 582
Editorial Mediterrania SL, pg 582
Instituto Nacional de la Salud, pg 583
OASIS, Producciones Generales de Comunicacion, pg 584
Editorial Paidotribo SL, pg 585
Pais Vasco Servicio Central de Publicaciones, pg 585
Parramon Ediciones SA, pg 586
Pulso Ediciones, SL, pg 588
Ediciones Rialp SA, pg 589
Ediciones ROL SA, pg 589
Editorial Sintes SA, pg 590
Ediciones Tutor SA, pg 594
Ediciones Urano, SA, pg 595
Xunta de Galicia, pg 596

Sri Lanka
Swarna Hansa Foundation, pg 598

Sweden
Energica Foerlags AB/Halsabocker, pg 602
Gothia AB, Forlagshuset, pg 603
Gothia Publishing House, pg 603
ICA bokforlag, pg 603
Liber AB, pg 604
Natur och Kultur/LTs foerlag, pg 604
Sober Foerlags AB, pg 606
AB Wahlstrom & Widstrand, pg 607

Switzerland
AT Verlag, pg 608
Blaukreuz-Verlag Bern, pg 610
EULAR Publishers, pg 613
Editions Jouvence, pg 616
Junod Nicholas, pg 616
Oesch Verlag AG, pg 620
Editions du Parvis, pg 621
Editiones Roche, pg 623
Verlag fuer Schoene Wissenschaften, pg 624
Sphinx Verlag AG, pg 625
Tobler Verlag, pg 626
Editions Vivez Soleil SA, pg 627
Weber SA d'Editions, pg 627

Syrian Arab Republic
Damascus University Press, pg 628

Taiwan, Province of China
Asian Culture Co, pg 629
Commonwealth Publishing Company Ltd, pg 629
Farseeing Publishing Company Ltd, pg 630
Chu Hai Publishing (Taiwan) Co Ltd, pg 630
Ho-Chi Book Publishing Co, pg 630
Kuang Fu Book Co Ltd, pg 630
Linking Publishing Company Ltd, pg 631
Morning Star Publisher Inc, pg 631
Shy Chaur Publishing Co Ltd, pg 631
Torch of Wisdom, pg 632
Yi Hsien Publishing Co Ltd, pg 632
Yuan Liou Publishing Co, Ltd, pg 632

United Republic of Tanzania
Press & Publicity Centre Ltd, pg 634
Tanzania Publishing House, pg 634

Thailand
Thai Watana Panich Co, Ltd, pg 636

Turkey
Kok Yayincilik, pg 640
Soez Yayin/Oyunajans, pg 641

Uganda
Fountain Publishers Ltd, pg 642

Ukraine
Naukova Dumka Publishers, pg 643

United Kingdom
Age Concern Books, pg 645
Amberwood Publishing Ltd, pg 646
Anglo-German Foundation for the Study of Industrial Society, pg 647
Apex Publishing Ltd, pg 648
Apple Press, pg 648
Ashgrove Press, pg 650
Beaconsfield Publishers Ltd, pg 653
BILD Publications, pg 654
Blackwell Science Ltd, pg 656
Bloomsbury Publishing PLC, pg 656
Breslich & Foss, pg 659
Brewin Books Ltd, pg 659
Camden Press Ltd, pg 662
Cardinal Publishing Ltd, pg 663
Carlton Publishing Group, pg 664
Jon Carpenter Publishing, pg 664
Kyle Cathie Ltd, pg 665
Causeway Press Ltd, pg 665
Marshall Cavendish Partworks Ltd, pg 665

PUBLISHERS

Class Publishing, pg 668
Coachwise Ltd, pg 668
Constable & Robinson Ltd, pg 670
Constable Publishers, pg 670
Paul H Crompton Ltd, pg 672
Croner CCH Group Ltd, pg 672
The C W Daniel Co Ltd, pg 673
David & Charles Ltd, pg 674
Christopher Davies Publishers Ltd, pg 674
Denor Press, pg 675
Dobro Publishing, pg 675
Dorling Kindersley Ltd, pg 676
Element Books Ltd, pg 678
Elliot Right Way Books, pg 678
Aidan Ellis Publishing, pg 678
Elsevier Science Ltd, pg 678
The Eurospan Group, pg 680
Extraordinary People Press, pg 681
Forbes Publications, pg 683
Foulsham Publishers, pg 683
Francis Balsom Associates, pg 684
Gaia Books Ltd, pg 685
Gateway Books, pg 686
Global Books Ltd, pg 687
Godsfield Press Ltd, pg 688
Grub Street, pg 690
Hamlyn, pg 691
HarperCollins Publishers, pg 692
Health Development Agency, pg 694
Isis Publishing Ltd, pg 701
Janus Publishing Company Ltd, pg 702
Jones & Bartlett International, pg 703
King's Fund Publishing, pg 704
KIT Press - Royal Tropical Institute, pg 705
Knockabout Comics, pg 705
Learning Development Aids, pg 706
Letterbox Library, pg 707
Frances Lincoln Ltd, pg 707
Lorenz Books, pg 709
Mandrake of Oxford, pg 711
Marshall Editions Ltd, pg 712
Kenneth Mason Publications Ltd, pg 712
Metro Publishing Ltd, pg 714
Micelle Press, pg 714
National Assembly for Wales, pg 717
New Era Publications UK Ltd, pg 718
New Leaf Books Ltd, pg 719
The NFER-NELSON Publishing Co Ltd, pg 719
Norwood Publishers, pg 720
Octopus Publishing Group, pg 720
Open University Press, pg 721
Parapress Ltd, pg 724
Pearson Education, pg 725
Pharmaceutical Press, pg 726
Piatkus Books, pg 727
The Policy Press, pg 729
Portland Press Ltd, pg 730
Quarto Publishing plc, pg 731
Quartz Editions, pg 732
Quintet Publishing Ltd, pg 732
Random House UK Ltd, pg 733
The Reader's Digest Association Ltd, pg 733
Rosendale Press Ltd, pg 735
Roundhouse Publishing Ltd, pg 736
Royal College of General Practitioners, pg 736
The Royal Society of Chemistry, pg 737
Sage Publications Ltd, pg 737
Salamander Books Ltd, pg 738
Scottish Office Library & Information Services, pg 740
Sheldon Press, pg 741
SHU Press, pg 742
Silver Link Publishing Ltd, pg 742
Smith-Gordon, pg 743
The Stationery Office, pg 745
Rudolf Steiner Press, pg 745
Tarragon Press, pg 746
Transworld Publishers Ltd, pg 750
Virago Press, pg 753
Ward Lock Ltd, pg 754
Websters International Publishers Ltd, pg 755
Which? Ltd, pg 755
Wimbledon Publishing Company Ltd, pg 757
The Women's Press Ltd, pg 758
Woodhead Publishing Ltd, pg 758

Uruguay
Editorial Arca SRL, pg 760
Nordan-Comunidad, pg 760
Prensa Medica Latinoamericana, pg 761

Viet Nam
Science & Technics Publishing House, pg 763

Yugoslavia
Alfa-Narodna Knjiga, pg 764

Zambia
Zambia Association for Research & Development, pg 767

Zimbabwe
Action Magazine, pg 767

HISTORY

Afghanistan
Book Publishing Institute, pg 1
Government Press, pg 1
Historical Society of Afghanistan, pg 1

Albania
Botimpex Publications Import-Export Agency, pg 1
NL SH, pg 1
State Textbook Publishing House, pg 1

Algeria
Les Editions Algeriennes En-Nahdha, pg 2
Enterprise Nationale du Livre (ENAL), pg 2

Argentina
Editorial Abaco de Rodolfo Depalma SRL, pg 2
Alianza Editorial de Argentina SA, pg 3
Editorial Astrea de Alfredo y Ricardo Depalma SRL, pg 3
AZ Editora SA, pg 3
Centro Editor de America Latina SA, pg 4
Editorial Claridad SA, pg 4
Club de Lectores, pg 4
Depalma SRL, pg 5
Ediciones Don Bosco Argentina, pg 5
Emece Editores SA, pg 5
EUDEBA (Editorial Universitaria de Buenos Aires), pg 6
Ediciones de la Flor SRL, pg 6
Editorial Galerna SRL, pg 6
Editorial Guadalupe, pg 6
Laffont Ediciones Electronicas SA, pg 7
La Ley SA Editora e Impresora, pg 7
Editorial Losada SA, pg 7
Marymar Ediciones SA, pg 7
Editorial Planeta Argentina SAIC, pg 8
Editorial Plus Ultra SA, pg 8
Editorial Sopena Argentina SACI e I, pg 9
Editorial Sudamericana SA, pg 9
Theoria SRL Distribuidora y Editora, pg 9
Tipografica Editora Argentina, pg 9
Instituto Torcuato Di Tella, pg 9
Editoria Universitaria de la Patagonia, pg 9
Javier Vergara Editor SA, pg 9

Australia
Aboriginal Studies Press, pg 10
Access Press, pg 10
Aletheia Publishing, pg 11
Allen & Unwin Pty Ltd, The Australian Newspaper, Vogel Breads, pg 11
Artemis Publishing Pty Ltd, pg 12
Artmoves, pg 12
Athena Press, pg 12
Aussie Books, pg 12
Australasian Medical Publishing Company Ltd (AMPCO), pg 13
Australian Scholarly Publishing, pg 14
Bandicoot Books, pg 14
Joycelyn Bayne, pg 14
Bellcourt Books, pg 14
Bernal Publishing, pg 14
Blubber Head Press, pg 15
Boolarong Press, pg 16
Louis Braille Audio, pg 16
Bridge To Peace Publications, pg 16
Casket Publications, pg 17
Catholic Institute of Sydney, pg 17
Centenary of Technical Education in Bairnsdale Group, pg 17
Chase Just Publishing, pg 17
Church Archivists Press, pg 18
Covenanter Press, pg 19
Crawford House Publishing, pg 19
Dryden Press, pg 21
Elton Publications, pg 21
Enterprise Publications, pg 22
Fremantle Arts Centre Press, pg 23
Gerald Griffin Press, pg 24
Ginninderra Press, pg 24
Gould Books, pg 24
Hahndorf Academy Foundation Inc, pg 24
Hale & Iremonger Pty Ltd, pg 24
F H Halpern, pg 25
Hargreen Publishing Co, pg 25
Hat Box Press, pg 25
Histec Publications, pg 26
Hunter House Publications, pg 27
Hyland House Publishing Pty Ltd, pg 27
Illert Publications, pg 27
Institute of Aboriginal Development (IAD Press), pg 28
Joval Publications, pg 29
Kangaroo Press, pg 29
Kingsclear Books, pg 29
Lachlan Publishing, pg 29
Lansdowne Publishing Pty Ltd, pg 29
Library of Australian History, pg 30
Little Red Apple Publishing, pg 30
Lowden Publishing Co, pg 31
Lucasville Press, pg 31

SUBJECT INDEX

Macmillan Education Australia, pg 31
Yvonne McBurney, pg 32
Melbourne University Press, pg 33
Mostly Unsung, pg 33
Mulini Press, pg 34
Museum of Victoria, pg 34
Navarine Publishing, pg 34
Ocean Press, pg 35
Oceans Enterprises, pg 35
Ollif Publishing, pg 35
Outback Books - CQU Press, pg 36
Palms Press, pg 36
Pascoe Publishing, pg 37
Pearson Education Australia, pg 37
Pinevale Publications, pg 38
Pioneer Design Studio Pty Ltd, pg 38
Plantagenet Press, pg 38
Playlab Press, pg 38
Pluto Press Australia, pg 38
The Polding Press, pg 38
Pollitecon Publications, pg 38
Protestant Publications, pg 39
Quakers Hill Press, pg 39
Queen Victoria Museum & Art Gallery Publications, pg 39
Rainforest Publishing, pg 39
Reed Educational Publishing Australia, pg 40
Ruskin Rowe Press, pg 41
St Joseph Publications, pg 41
Seanachas Press, pg 42
Shearwater Press, pg 42
Frank Shepherd, pg 42
The Sheringa Book Committee, pg 42
Simon & Schuster Australia Pty Ltd, pg 42
Slouch Hat Publications, pg 42
Spectrum Publications, pg 43
State Library of NSW Press, pg 43
State Publishing Unit of State Print SA, pg 43
Tabletop Press, pg 44
Tarka Publishing, pg 44
The Text Publishing Company Pty Ltd, pg 44
Thames & Hudson (Australia) Pty Ltd, pg 44
Caroline Thornton, pg 44
Three Sisters Publications Pty Ltd, pg 44
Transpareon Press, pg 45
La Trobe University Press, pg 45
Tudor Australia Press, pg 45
Turton & Armstrong Publishers Pty Ltd, pg 45
University of New South Wales Press Ltd, pg 46
University of Queensland Press, pg 46
University of Western Australia Press, pg 46
Vista Publications, pg 47
Wakefield Press Pty Ltd, pg 47

Austria
Alekto Verlag GmbH, pg 49
Aritbus et Historiae, Rivista Internationale di arti visive ecinema, Institut IRSA - Verlagsanstatt, pg 49
Boehlau Verlag GmbH & Co KG, pg 50
BSE Verlag Dr Bernhard Schuttengruber, pg 50
Carinthia Verlag, pg 50
CEEBA Publications Antenne d'Autriche, pg 50
Development News Ltd, pg 51
Docker Verlag GmbH & Co KG, pg 51

SUBJECT INDEX

Edition S der OSD, pg 51
Ennsthaler GesmbH & Co KG, pg 51
Fassbaender Verlag, pg 51
Verlag fuer Geschichte und Politik, pg 52
Graz Stadtmuseum, pg 52
Haymon-Verlag GesmbH, pg 52
Herold Druck-und Verlagsgesellschaft mbH, pg 52
Johannes Heyn, Gert und Volkmar Zechner, pg 52
Inn-Verlag, DrieBlein & Co KG, pg 53
Karolinger Verlag GmbH & Co KG, pg 53
Kremayr & Scheriau Verlag, pg 54
Leopold Stocker Verlag, pg 54
Loecker Verlag, pg 54
Merbod Verlag, pg 55
Milena Verlag, pg 55
Thomas Mlakar Verlag, pg 55
Verlag Monte Verita, pg 55
Otto Mueller Verlag GesmbH & Co KG, pg 55
Wolfgang Neugebauer Verlag GmbH, pg 55
Niederosterreichisches Pressehaus Druck- und Verlagsgesellschaft mbH, pg 55
NOI - Verlag, pg 55
Verlag der Oesterreichischen Akademie der Wissenschaften (OEAW), pg 56
Verlag des Oesterreichischen Gewerkschaftsbundes GmbH, pg 56
Oesterreichischer Bundesverlag GmbH, pg 56
Oesterreichischer Kunst und Kulturverlag, pg 56
Verlag Oldenbourg, pg 56
Osterreichischer Bundesveilag Ges.mbH, pg 57
Georg Prachner KG, pg 57
Promedia Verlagsges mbH, pg 57
Verlag Anton Pustet, pg 57
Verlag fuer Sammler, pg 58
Dr A Schendl GmbH und Co KG, pg 58
Andreas Schnider Verlags-Atelier, pg 58
Verlag Josef Otto Slezak, pg 58
SN-Verlag, Salzburger Nachrichten Verlags GmbH & Co KG, pg 59
Studien Verlag Gmbh, pg 59
Verlag Styria, pg 59
Verlag Carl Ueberreuter GmbH, pg 59
Verband der Wissenschaftlichen Gesellschaften Oesterreichs (VWGOe), pg 60
Verlag Anton Schroll & Co, pg 60
Vorarlberger Verlagsanstalt Aktiengesellschaft, pg 60
Universitaetsverlag Wagner GmbH, pg 60
Waren-Erzeungungs-und Handelsgesellschaft GmbH, pg 60
WUV/Facultas Universitaetsverlag, pg 61
Paul Zsolnay Verlag GmbH, pg 61

Azerbaijan

Sada, Literaturno-Izdatel'skij Centr, pg 61

Bangladesh

The University Press Ltd, pg 62

Belarus

Belaruskaya Encyklapedyya, pg 63
Kavaler Publishers, pg 63
Narodnaya Asveta, pg 63

Belgium

Acco CV, pg 64
Centre Aequatoria, pg 64
Artel SC, pg 64
SA Artis-Historia, pg 64
Maison d'Editions Baha'ies ASBL, pg 64
Brepols Publishers NV, pg 65
Carto BVBA, pg 65
Editions Casterman SA, pg 66
Centre d'Action Laique, pg 66
Editions Chanlis, pg 66
Creadif, pg 67
Cremers (Schoollandkaarten) PVBA, pg 67
Le Cri Editions, pg 67
Dexia Bank, pg 68
EPO Publishers, Printers, Booksellers, pg 68
Georeto-Geogidsen, pg 68
Groeningn NV, pg 69
Imprimerie Hayez SPRL, pg 69
Helyode Editions (SA-ADN), pg 69
Editions Labor, pg 70
Uitgeverij Lannoo NV, pg 70
Leuven University Press, pg 71
Les Editions du Lombard SA, pg 71
Marabout, pg 72
Mercatorfonds NV, pg 72
Nauwelaerts Edition SA, pg 72
Uitgeverij Peeters Leuven (Belgie), pg 72
Pelckmans NV, De Nederlandsche Boekhandel, pg 73
Uitgeverij Pelckmans N V, pg 73
Le Pole Nord ASBL, pg 73
Henri Proost & Co, Pvba, pg 73
Publications des Facultes Universitaires Saint Louis, pg 73
Editions Racine, pg 73
Reader's Digest SA, pg 73
La Renaissance du Livre, pg 73
Editions Scaillet, SA, pg 74
Sonneville Press (Uitgeverij) VTW, pg 74
Stichting Kunstboek bvba, pg 74
Editions Techniques et Scientifiques SPRL, pg 74
UGA Editions (Uitgeverij), pg 74
Uitgevery Scoop Infotex NV, pg 75
Editions de l'Université de Bruxelles, pg 75
Imprimeur - Editeur Vaillant-Carmanne SA, pg 75
Marc Van de Wiele bvba, pg 75
Les Editions Vie ouvriere ASBL, pg 75
C De Vries Brouwers BVBA, pg 75
VUB University Press, pg 75
Editions Luce Wilquin, pg 75

Bolivia

Editorial Don Bosco, pg 76
Gisbert y Cia SA, pg 76
Universidad Autonoma Tomas Frias, Div de Extension Universitaria, pg 76

Bosnia and Herzegovina

Bemust doo Novinsko-Izdavacko stamparsko i trgovacko preduzece, pg 77

Botswana

The Botswana Society, pg 77
Maskew Miller Longman, pg 77

Brazil

Action Editora Ltda, pg 77
AGIR S/A Editora, pg 78
Editora Alfa Omega Ltda, pg 78
Associacao Brasileira de Liverivos Antiquarios, pg 79
Editora do Brasil SA, pg 80
Editora Campus Ltda, pg 80
Editora Contexto (Editora Pinsky Ltda), pg 81
Editora Companhia das Letras/Editora Schwarcz Ltda, pg 82
Companhia Editora Forense, pg 82
Cia Editora Nacional, pg 82
EDUC - Editora da PUC-SP, pg 82
EDUSC - Editora da Universidade do Sagrado Coracao, pg 82
Livraria Martins Fontes Editora Ltda, pg 83
Fundacao Joaquim Nabuco Editora, pg 84
Global Editora e Distribuidora Ltda, pg 84
Editora Globo SA, pg 84
Edicoes Graal Ltda, pg 84
Livro Ibero-Americano Ltda, pg 85
IBRASA (Instituicao Brasileira de Difusao Cultural Ltda), pg 85
Imago Editora Importacao e Exportacao Ltda, pg 85
Editora Index Ltda, pg 85
LDA Editores Ltda, pg 86
Edicoes Loyola SA, pg 87
Editora Mantiqueira de Ciencia e Arte, pg 87
Editora Melhoramentos Ltda, pg 87
Editora Mercado Aberto Ltda, pg 88
Editora Mercuryo Ltda, pg 88
Editora Moderna Ltda, pg 88
Modulo Editora e Desenvolvimento Educacional Ltda, pg 88
Editora Nova Alexandria Ltda, pg 88
Editora Nova Fronteira SA, pg 88
Editora Perspectiva, pg 89
Livraria Pioneira Editora/Enio Matheus Guazzelli e Cia Ltd, pg 89
Pool Editorial Ltda, pg 90
Casa Editora Presbiteriana S.C., pg 90
Distribuidora Record de Servicos de Imprensa SA, pg 90
Editora Rideel Ltda, pg 90
Editora Scipione Ltda, pg 91
Sobrindes Linha Grafica E Editora Ltda, pg 91
Editora UNESP, pg 92
Editora Universidade Federal do Rio de Janeiro, pg 93
Editora Verbo Ltda, pg 93
Jorge Zahar Editor, pg 93

Bulgaria

Abagar Pablioing, pg 94
Abagar, Veliko Tarnovo, pg 94
Bilblioteka Nov den - Sajuz na Svobodnite Demokrati (Union of Free Democrats), pg 94
DA-Izdatelstvo Publishers, pg 95
Eurasia Academic Publishers, pg 95
Heron Press Publishing House, pg 96
Publishing House Hristo Botev, pg 96
Kibea Publishing Co, pg 96
LIK IZDANIJA, pg 96
Makros 2000 - Plovdiv, pg 96
Izdatelstvo na Ministerstvoto na Otbranata, pg 96
Naouka i Izkoustvo, Ltd, pg 97
Nov Covek Publishing House, pg 97
Pensoft Publishers, pg 97
Rakla, pg 97
Slavena, pg 98
Trud - Izd kasta, pg 98
Ivan Vazov Publishing House, pg 98
Peyo K Yavorov Publishing House, pg 98

Burundi

Editions Intore, pg 98

Cameroon

Centre d'Edition et de Production pour l'Enseignement et la Recherche (CEPER), pg 99
Editions Semences Africaines, pg 99

Chile

Arrayan Editores, pg 99
Ediciones Bat, pg 99
Editorial Andres Bello/Editorial Juridica de Chile, pg 100
Edeval (Universidad de Valparaiso), pg 100
Pontificia Universidad Catolica de Chile, pg 101
Ediciones Universitarias de Valparaiso, pg 101

China

Anhui People's Publishing House, pg 102
Beijing Publishing House, pg 102
China Film Press, pg 103
China Theatre Publishing House, pg 104
Cultural Relics Publishing House, pg 105
Foreign Language Teaching & Research Press, pg 105
Foreign Languages Press, pg 105
Fudan University Press, pg 105
Guizhou Education Publishing House, pg 106
Higher Education Press, pg 106
Lanzhou University Press, pg 107
Liaoning People's Publishing House, pg 107
Morning Glory Publishers, pg 107
People's Fine Arts Publishing House, pg 108
SDX (Shenghuo-Dushu-Xinzhi) Joint Publishing Co, pg 108
Shandong People's Publishing House, pg 109
Shandong University Press, pg 109
Shanghai Educational Publishing House, pg 109
Sichuan University Press, pg 109
World Affairs Press, pg 110
Wuhan University Press, pg 110
Zhejiang University Press, pg 110

Colombia

Amazonas Editores Ltda, pg 111
El Ancora Editores, pg 111
Lerner Limitada, pg 112
Procultura SA, pg 113
Siglo XXI Editores de Colombia Ltda, pg 113
Tercer Mundo Editores SA, pg 113
Universidad de Antioquia, Division Publicaciones, pg 114

The Democratic Republic of the Congo

Facultes Catoliques de Kinshasa, pg 115
Presses Universitaires du Zaiire (PUZ), pg 115

PUBLISHERS

Costa Rica
Editorial DEI (Departamento Ecumenico de Investigaciones), pg 116
Museo Historico Cultural Juan Santamaria, pg 116
Editorial Porvenir, pg 116
Promesa, Ediciones, pg 116
Editorial de la Universidad de Costa Rica, pg 117
Editorial Universidad Estatal a Distancia (EUNED), pg 117
Editorial Universidad Nacional (EUNA), pg 117
Editorial Universitaria Centroamericana (EDUCA), pg 117

Cote d'Ivoire
Centre d'Edition et de Diffusion Africaines, pg 117
Les Nouvelles Editions Africaines, pg 118

Croatia
AGM doo, pg 118
ArTresor naklada, pg 118
Durieux d o o, pg 118
Filozofski Fakultet Sveucilista u Zagrebu, pg 118
Globus-Nakladni zavod, pg 118
Izdavacka Delatnost Hrvatske Akademije Znanosti I Umjetnosti, pg 118
Knjizevni Krug Split, pg 119
Matica hrvatska, pg 119
Mladost d d Izdavacku graficku i informaticku djelatnost, pg 119
Nakladni zavod Matice hrvatske, pg 119
Naprijed d d Naklada, pg 119
Skolska Knjiga, pg 120
Vitagraf, pg 120

Cuba
Casa Editora Abril, pg 120
Holguin, Ediciones, pg 121
Editorial Oriente, pg 121
Editora Politica, pg 121

Cyprus
AndreouChr- Publishers, pg 122
James Bendon Ltd, pg 122
A G Leventis Foundation, pg 122

Czech Republic
Academia, pg 122
Atlantis sro, pg 123
Barrister & Principal, pg 123
Nakladatelstvi Blok, pg 123
Ceska Expedice, pg 123
Jiri Chvojka, pg 123
Columbus, pg 123
Doplnek, pg 124
Historicky ustav Akademie ved Ceske republiky, pg 124
Jota, pg 125
Kalich SRO, pg 125
Karmelitanske Nakladatelstvi, pg 125
Karolinum, nakladatelstvi, pg 125
Konsultace, pg 125
Libri s r o, pg 125
Mariadan, pg 126
Maxdorf Ltd, pg 126
Mlada fronta, pg 126
Nakladatelstvi Svoboda, pg 126
Narodni Muzeum, pg 126
Nase vojsko, nakladatelstvi a knizni obchod, pg 126
Nava, pg 127

NLN, Ltd The Lidove noviny Publishing House, pg 127
Nakladatelstvi a vydavatelstvi Panorama, pg 127
Paseka, pg 127
Prazske nakladatelstvi Pluto, pg 127
Pressfoto Vydavatelstvi Ceske Tiskove Kancelare, pg 128
Prostor, Ltd, pg 128
Slon Sociologicke Nakladatelstvi, pg 128
SystemConsult, pg 128
Votobia sro, pg 129
Zvon, pg 129

Denmark
Akademisk Forlag, pg 129
Dafolo Forlag, pg 131
Dansk Historisk Handbogsforlag ApS, pg 131
Christian Ejlers' Forlag aps, pg 131
Forum Publishers, pg 132
Fremad A/S, pg 132
GEC Gads Forlag Aktieselskab af 1994, pg 132
Forlaget GMT, pg 132
Gyldendalske Boghandel - Nordisk Forlag A/S, pg 132
Host & Son Publishers Ltd, pg 133
Forlaget Hovedland, pg 133
Museum Tusculanum Press, pg 134
Nyt Nordisk Forlag Arnold Busck A/S, pg 134
Joergen Paludans Forlag ApS, pg 134
Samfundslitteratur, pg 135
Samlerens Forlag A/S, pg 135
Det Schonbergske Forlag, pg 135
Syddansk Universitetsforlag, pg 136
Systime, pg 136

Dominican Republic
Pontificia Universidad Catolica Madre y Maestra, pg 136
Sociedad Editorial Dominicana SA, pg 137
Editora Taller, pg 137

Ecuador
Corporacion Editora Nacional, pg 137
Pontificia Universidad Catolica de Ecuador, Centro de Publicaciones, pg 137

Egypt (Arab Republic of Egypt)
American University in Cairo Press, pg 138
Al Arab Publishing House, pg 138
Dar El Shorouk, pg 138
Dar El Shorouk Publishing & Distributing House, pg 138
Lehnert & Landrock Bookshop, pg 139
Middle East Book Centre, pg 139
Senouhy Publishers, pg 139

Estonia
Estonian Academic Library, pg 139
Estonian Bible Society, pg 140
Estonian Encyclopaedia Publishers Ltd, pg 140
Ilmamaa, pg 140
Kunst Publishers Ltd, pg 140
Mats Publishers Ltd, pg 140
National Library of Estonia, pg 140
Olion Publishers, pg 140

Ethiopia
Addis Ababa University Press, pg 141

Finland
Akateeminen Kustannusliike Oy, pg 141
Atena Kustannus Oy, pg 142
Ekenas Tryckeri AB, pg 142
Herattaja-yhdistys Ry, pg 142
Kirja-Leitzinger, pg 143
Koala-Kustannus/Oy Greenbay House Publishing Ltd, pg 143
Kustannuskiila Oy, pg 143
Schildts Foerlagsaktiebolag, pg 144
Soederstroem et Co Foerlagsaktiebolag, pg 144
Suomalaisen Kirjallisuuden Seura, pg 144
Osuuskunta Vastapaino, pg 145
Weilin & Goeoes Oy, pg 145
Yliopistopaino/Helsinki University Press, pg 145

France
Academie Nationale de Reims, pg 145
Action Artistique de la Ville de Paris, pg 146
Editions Albin Michel, pg 146
Alsatia SA, pg 146
Editions d'Amerique et d'Orient, Adrien Maisonneuve, pg 147
Editions l'Ancre de Marine, pg 147
Editions Anthropos Sarl, pg 147
Editions de l'Armancon, pg 148
Les Editions de l'Atelier SA, pg 148
Atelier National de Reproduction des Theses, pg 148
ATP - Packager, pg 149
Editions Aubier-Montaigne SA, pg 149
Autrement Editions, pg 149
Beauchesne Editeur, pg 150
Editions Belfond, pg 150
Societe d'Edition Les Belles Lettres, pg 150
Berg International Editeurs, pg 150
Berger-Levrault SA, pg 150
Editions Bertout, pg 150
Bibliotheque Nationale de France, pg 150
De Boccard Edition-Diffusion, pg 151
Editions Andre Bonne, pg 151
Presses Universitaires de Bordeaux (PUB), pg 151
Bragelonne, pg 151
Breal, pg 151
Editions Buchet/Chastel, pg 152
Le Cadratin, pg 152
Editions des Cahiers Bourbonnais, pg 152
Editions Calmann-Levy SA, pg 152
Editions Canope, pg 152
Editions Casterman, pg 153
Editions Cenomane, pg 153
CERDIC-Publications, pg 153
Editions du Cerf, pg 153
Editions Champ Vallon, pg 154
Editions Honore Champion, pg 154
Chasse Maree-Armen, pg 154
Circonflexe, pg 155
CLD, pg 155
CNRS Editions, pg 155
Armand Colin, Editeur, pg 155
Editions du Comite des Travaux Historiques et Scientifiques (CTHS), pg 156
Editions Complexe SPRL, pg 156
Copernic, pg 156

Editions Coprur, pg 156
Corsaire Editions, pg 156
CPL- La Communication Par le Livre, pg 157
Editions Criterion, pg 157
Editions Cujas, pg 157
Culture et Bibliotheque pour Tous, pg 157
Nouvelles Editions Debresse, pg 158
La Decouverte et Syros, pg 158
Editions Delville, pg 158
Georges-Charles Demay, pg 158
Editions Denoel Sarl, pg 158
Dervy-Livres, pg 158
Desclee de Brouwer SA, pg 158
Les Editions des Deux Coqs d'Or, pg 159
Les Dossiers d'Aquitaine, pg 160
Editions de l'Ecole des Hautes Etudes en Sciences Sociales (EHESS), pg 160
Presses de l'Ecole Normale Superieure, pg 160
Edisud, pg 161
Editions Recherche sur les Civilisations (ERC), pg 161
EPA SA (Editions Presse Audiovisuel), pg 162
Les Editions de l'Epargne, pg 162
Editions Errance, pg 162
Institut d'Etudes Augustiniennes, pg 163
Institut d'Etudes Slaves, pg 163
Librairie Artheme Fayard, pg 163
Des Femmes, pg 164
Librairie Fischbacher, International Art Book Distribution (import-export), pg 164
Folklore Comtois, pg 164
Presses de la Fondation Nationale des Sciences Politiques, pg 164
Edition Galilee, pg 165
Editions Gallimard, pg 165
Editions Gammaprim, pg 166
Imprimerie Librairie Gardet, pg 166
Paul Geuthner Librairie Orientaliste, pg 166
Editions Jean Paul Gisserot, pg 166
Sarl Editions Jean Grassin, pg 167
Librairie Guenegaud Sarl, pg 167
Hachette Livre, pg 167
Editions Herault, pg 168
Editions d'Histoire Sociale (EDHIS), pg 168
Pierre Horay Editeur, pg 168
Editions Imago, pg 169
Institute, pg 169
Les Introuvables-Editions L'Harmattan, pg 170
Isoete, pg 170
Editions Ivrea, pg 170
Editions du Jaguar, pg 170
Editions Jannink, pg 170
Editions Juridiques Associees - LGDJ/Montchrestien, pg 170
Kailash Editions, pg 171
Editions Klincksieck, pg 171
L'Adret editions, pg 171
Laffitte Reprints, pg 171
Editions Michel Lafon SA, pg 171
Librairie Leonce Laget, pg 171
Editions Fernand Lanore Sarl, pg 172
Librairie Larousse, pg 172
Editions Universitaires LCF, pg 172
Letouzey et Ane Sarl, pg 172
Editions Liana Levi Sarl, pg 173
Le Livre de Poche-L G F (Librairie Generale Francaise), pg 173
Editions Loubatieres, pg 174
Editions Lyonnaises d'Art et d'Histoire, pg 174

Macula, pg 174
Editions de la Maison des Sciences de l'Homme, Paris, pg 174
Editions MDI (La Maison des Instituteurs), pg 175
Editions Medianes, pg 175
Mercure de France SA, pg 176
Presses Universitaires du Mirail, pg 176
Gerard Monfort Editeur Sarl, pg 176
Muller Edition, pg 176
Editions de la Reunion des Musees Nationaux, pg 176
Fernand Nathan, pg 177
Naufal Group Sarl, pg 177
Editions Norma, pg 177
Nouvelles Editions Francaises, pg 178
Nouvelles Editions Latines, pg 178
Editions Odile Jacob, pg 178
Editions Ophrys, pg 178
Editions de l'Orante, pg 178
Ouest Editions, pg 178
Editions Ouest-France, pg 178
Editions Paradigme, pg 179
Pardes, pg 179
Paris Musees, pg 179
Editions Payot & Rivages, pg 179
Peeters-France, pg 179
Editions A et J Picard SA, pg 179
Editions Jean Picollec, pg 179
Editions Pierron, pg 180
Presence Africaine Editions, pg 180
Presses de la Cite, pg 180
Presses de la Sorbonne Nouvelle/PSN, pg 181
Presses Universitaires de Caen, pg 181
Presses Universitaires de France (PUF), pg 181
Presses Universitaires de Grenoble, pg 181
Presses Universitaires de Lyon, pg 181
Presses Universitaires de Nancy, pg 181
Presses Universitaires de Strasbourg, pg 181
Presses Universitaires du Septentrion, pg 181
Publications de l'Universite de Rouen, pg 182
Publications Orientalistes de France (POF), pg 182
Editions Pygmalion - Gerard Watelet, pg 182
Editions Ramsay, pg 182
References cf, pg 182
Editions Roudil, pg 183
Les Editions du Sagittaire, pg 183
Selection du Reader's Digest SA, pg 184
Maren Sell, pg 184
Service Technique pour l'Education, pg 185
Editions du Seuil, pg 185
Siloe - Kerdore, pg 185
Societe Nouveaux Loisirs, pg 185
Sofradif Editions Philippe Auzou, pg 185
Publications de la Sorbonne, pg 186
Association d'Editions Sorg, pg 186
Editions SOS (Editions du Secours Catholique), pg 186
Editions Sud Ouest, pg 186
Les Editions de la Table Ronde, pg 187
Editions Tallandier, pg 187
Editions Tiresias Michel Reynaud, pg 188
Transeuropeennes/RCE, pg 188
Universitas, pg 188

La Vague Verte, pg 188
Editions Vilo SA, pg 189
Librairie Philosophique J Vrin, pg 189
Zodiaque, pg 190

French Polynesia

Scoop/Au Vent des Iles, pg 190
Haere Po No Tahiti, pg 190
Simone Sanchez, pg 190

Germany

Aisthesis Verlag Dr Detlev Kopp und Dr Michael Vogt, pg 192
Akademie Verlag GmbH, pg 192
Verlag Karl Alber GmbH, pg 192
Verlag und Antiquariat Frank Albrecht, pg 192
Anabas-Verlag Guenter Kaempf GmbH & Co KG, pg 193
Antiquariat und Verlag Auvermann Keip GmbH, pg 194
AOL-Verlag Frohmut Menze, pg 194
arani-Verlag GmbH, pg 194
Arbeiterpresse Verlag GmbH, pg 194
Ardey-Verlag GmbH, pg 194
Arkana Verlag Tete Bottger Rainer Wunderlich GmbH, pg 195
Aschendorffsche Verlagsbuchhandlung GmbH & Co KG, pg 195
Auer Verlag GmbH, pg 196
Aufstieg-Verlag GmbH, pg 196
Aulis Verlag Deubner & Co KG, pg 197
Dr Bachmaier Verlag GmbH, pg 197
Baken-Verlag Walter Schnoor, pg 198
Basilisken-Presse, pg 198
BasisDruck Verlag GmbH, pg 198
Bayerischer Schulbuch-Verlag GmbH, pg 199
Verlag C H Beck (OHG), pg 200
Bergstadtverlag Wilhelm Gottlieb Korn GmbH Wuerzburg, pg 200
Berlin Verlag Arno Spitz GmbH, pg 200
Berliner Debatte Wissenschafts Verlag, GSFP-Gesellschaft fur Sozialwissen-schaftliche Forschung und Publizistik mbH &Co KG, pg 201
Bertelsmann Lexikon Verlag GmbH, pg 201
Bettendorf'sche Verlagsanstalt GmbH, pg 202
Biblio-Zeller Verlag, pg 202
Verlag Die Blaue Eule, pg 204
Bleicher Verlag GmbH, pg 204
Verlag Wolfgang Bleiweis, pg 204
Boehlau-Verlag GmbH & Cie, pg 204
Verlag Hermann Boehlaus Nachfolger Weimar GmbH & Co, pg 205
Klaus Boer Verlag, pg 205
Brandenburgisches Verlagshaus in der Dornier Medienholding GmbH, pg 206
BRUEN-Verlag, Gorenflo, pg 207
C C Buchners Verlag, pg 207
Buchergilde Gutenberg Verlagsgesellschaft mbH, pg 207
Bundesanzeiger Verlagsgesellschaft, pg 208
Campus Verlag GmbH, pg 209
Fachverlag Hans Carl GmbH, pg 209

Centaurus-Verlagsgesellschaft GmbH, pg 209
Chr Belser AG fur Verlagsgeschaefte und Co KG, pg 210
Hans Christians Druckerei und Verlag GmbH & Co, pg 210
Compact Verlag GmbH, pg 211
Copress Verlag, pg 211
Cornelsen Verlag GmbH & Co OHG, pg 211
J G Cotta'sche Buchhandlung Nachfolger GmbH, pg 212
D & D Kommunikation Verlug Dirk Nishen Gmbh & Co KG, pg 212
Das Arsenal, Verlag fuer Kultur und Politik GmbH, pg 212
Degener & Co, Manfred Dreiss Verlag, pg 213
Deutsche Verlags-Anstalt GmbH (DVA), pg 214
Deutscher Taschenbuch Verlag GmbH & Co KG (dtv), pg 215
Eugen Diederichs Verlag GmbH & Co KG, pg 216
Dieterichsche Verlagsbuchhandlung Mainz, pg 216
Verlag J H W Dietz Nachf GmbH, pg 217
Dietz Verlag Berlin GmbH, pg 217
Dipa-Verlag, pg 217
Edition Diskord, pg 217
Dolling und Galitz Verlag GmbH, pg 217
agenda Verlag Thomas Dominikowski, pg 217
Donat Verlag, pg 217
Droste Verlag GmbH, pg 218
Druffel-Verlag, pg 219
Duncker und Humblot GmbH, pg 219
DVG-Deutsche Verlagsgesellschaft mbH, pg 219
Echter Wurzburg Frankische Gesellschaftsdruckerei und Verlag GmbH, pg 220
edition q Berlin Edition in der Quintessenz Verlags-GmbH, pg 221
Egmont Franz Schneider Verlag GmbH, pg 221
Egmont vgs verlagsgesellschaft mbH, pg 221
Ehrenwirth Verlag GmbH, pg 221
Eichborn AG, pg 222
Eironeia-Verlag, pg 222
Elefanten Press Verlag GmbH, pg 222
N G Elwert Verlag, pg 222
EOS Verlag der Benefiktiner der Erzabtei St. Ottilien, pg 223
Ergebnisse Verlag GmbH, pg 223
Europaeische Verlagsanstalt GmbH & Rotbuch Verlag GmbH & Co KG, pg 225
F Bruckmann Munchen Verlag & Druck GmbH & Co Produkt KG, pg 225
FAB-Verlag, pg 226
Fackeltrager-Verlag GmbH, pg 226
Falken-Verlag GmbH, pg 227
Ferd Dummler's Verlag, pg 227
Wilhelm Fink GmbH & Co Verlags-KG, pg 228
Harald Fischer Verlag GmbH, pg 228
Fischer Taschenbuch Verlag GmbH, pg 228
Fleischhauer & Spohn GmbH & Co, pg 228
Flensburger Hefte Verlag GmbH, pg 228

Flugzeug Publikations GmbH, pg 229
Focus-Verlag Gesellschaft mbH, pg 229
Forum Verlag Leipzig Buch-Gesellschaft, pg 229
Verlag Freies Geistesleben, pg 230
Verlag A Fromm im Druck- u Verlagshaus Fromm GmbH & Co KG, pg 230
G Braun (vormals G Braun'sche Hofbuchdruckerei und Verlag) Gmbh, pg 231
Georgi GmbH, pg 232
Germanisches Nationalmuseum, pg 232
Verlag fuer Geschichte der Naturwissenschaften und der Technik, pg 232
H Gietl Verlag & Publikationsservice GmbH, pg 232
Wilhelm Goldmann Verlag GmbH, pg 233
Gondrom Verlag GmbH & Co KG, pg 233
Grabert-Verlag, pg 233
Grote'sche Verlagsbuchhandlung GmbH & Co KG, pg 234
Walter de Gruyter GmbH & Co KG, pg 234
Gunter Olzog Verlag GmbH, pg 235
Dr Rudolf Habelt GmbH, pg 235
Hahnsche Buchhandlung, pg 236
Liselotte Hamecher, pg 236
Harenberg Kommunikation Verlags- und Medien GmbH & Co KG, pg 237
Haude und Spenersche Verlagsbuchhandlung, pg 238
Hellerau-Verlag Dresden GmbH, pg 239
Edition Hentrich Druck & Verlag Gebr Hentrich und Tank GmbH & Co KG, pg 239
F A Herbig Verlagsbuchhandlung GmbH, pg 239
Verlag Herder GmbH & Co KG, pg 239
Erika Heydick Sax-Verlag Beucha, pg 240
Wilhelm Heyne Verlag, pg 240
Anton Hiersemann, Verlag, pg 240
Verlag Hinder und Deelmann, pg 241
Dieter Hoffmann Verlag, pg 242
Hoffmann und Campe Verlag GmbH, pg 242
Hohenrain-Verlag GmbH, pg 242
Holos Verlag, pg 242
Edition ID-Archiv/ID-Verlag, pg 244
Ikarus - Buchverlag, pg 244
Inno Vatio Verlags AG, pg 245
Iudicium Verlag GmbH, pg 245
Jan Thorbecke Verlag GmbH & Co, pg 246
Janus Verlagsgesellschaft, Dr Norbert Meder & Co, pg 246
JKL Publikationen GmbH, pg 246
Jonas Verlag fuer Kunst und Literatur GmbH, pg 246
Jovis Verlag GmbH, pg 246
Juventa Verlag GmbH, pg 247
K L V Konkret Literatur Verlag GmbH, pg 247
Kastell Verlag GmbH, pg 248
Kerber Christof Verlag, pg 248
Verlag Kiepenheuer und Witsch GmbH & Co KG, pg 249
Kindler Verlag GmbH, pg 249
Klartext Verlagsgesellschaft mbH, pg 249

PUBLISHERS

Klosterhaus-Verlagsbuchhandlung Dr Grimm KG, pg 250
Vittorio Klostermann GmbH, pg 250
Albrecht Knaus Verlag GmbH, pg 250
Knowledge Media International, pg 251
K F Koehler Verlag, pg 251
Verlagsgruppe Koehler/Mittler, pg 251
Koehler und Amelang Verlagsgesellschaft mbH, pg 251
Koenemann Verlagesellschaft mbH, pg 251
Verlag Valentin Koerner GmbH, pg 252
W Kohlhammer GmbH, abt Haussortiment, pg 252
Anton H Konrad Verlag, pg 252
Dr Anton Kovac Slavica Verlag, pg 253
Karin Kramer Verlag, pg 253
Verlag Waldemar Kramer, pg 253
Kretschmar Hubert Leipziger Verlagsgesellschaft, pg 253
Alfred Kroner Verlag, pg 253
Verlag Ernst Kuhn, pg 254
Kulturstiftung der deutschen Vertriebenen, pg 254
Archiv fur Kunst & Geschichte Bilderdienst & Verlagsgesellschaft mbH, pg 254
Landbuch-Verlagsgesellschaft mbH, pg 255
Peter Lang GmbH Europaeischer Verlag der Wissenschaften, pg 255
Karl Robert Langewiesche Nachfolger Hans Koester KG, pg 256
Michael Lasslaben Verlag, pg 256
J Latka Verlag GmbH, pg 256
Leipziger Universitaetsverlag GmbH, pg 257
Libertas- Europaeisches Institut GmbH, pg 257
Edition Libri Illustri GmbH, pg 257
Christoph Links Verlag - LinksDruck GmbH, pg 258
Logos Verlag GmbH, pg 258
Gustav Luebbe Verlag, pg 259
Lukas Verlag fur Kunst- und Geistesgeschichte, pg 259
Annemarie Maeger, pg 260
Gebr Mann Verlag GmbH & Co, pg 260
Manutius Verlag, pg 260
Matthes und Seitz Verlag GmbH, pg 261
Karl-Heinz Metz, pg 263
J B Metzler'sche Verlagsbuchhandlung, pg 263
Preubmpassling Verlag Gisela Meussling, pg 263
Mitteldeutscher Verlag GmbH, pg 264
Moench Verlagsgesellschaft mbH, pg 264
Mohr Siebeck, pg 264
Motorbuch-Verlag, pg 265
Mueller & Schindler Verlag, pg 265
Munzinger-Archiv GmbH Archiv fuer publizistische Arbeit, pg 266
Musikantiquariat und Dr Hans Schneider Verlag GmbH, pg 266
Muster-Schmidt Verlag, pg 266
MUT Verlag, pg 266
Naumann & Goebel Verlagsgesellschaft mbH, pg 267
Nebel Verlag GmbH, pg 267
Neuer ISP Verlag GmbH, pg 268

Neuer Weg Verlag und Druck GmbH, pg 268
Verlag Neues Leben GmbH, pg 268
Neuthor - Verlag, pg 268
Niederland-Verlag Helmut Michel, pg 268
C W Niemeyer Buchverlage GmbH, pg 268
Max Niemeyer Verlag GmbH, pg 269
Nusser Verlag, pg 269
Oberbaum Verlag GmbH, pg 269
Oekotopia Verlag, Wolfgang Hoffman, pg 270
Oekumenischer Verlag Dr R-F Edel, pg 270
Georg Olms Verlag AG, pg 270
Orbis Verlag fur Publizistik GmbH, pg 270
Pahl-Rugenstein Verlag Nachfolger-GmbH, pg 271
PapyRossa Verlags GmbH & Co Kommanditgesellschaft KG, pg 271
Patmos Verlag GmbH & Co KG, pg 272
Pendragon Verlag, pg 272
Justus Perthes Verlag Gotha GmbH, pg 272
Philipps-Universitaet Marburg, pg 273
Piper Verlag GmbH, pg 274
Guido Pressler Verlag, pg 275
Propylaeen Verlag, Zweigniederlassung Berlin der Ullstein Buchverlage GmbH, pg 275
Psychosozial-Verlag, pg 275
Verlag Friedrich Pustet GmbH & Co Kg, pg 276
Quell Verlag, pg 276
Quelle und Meyer Verlag GmbH & Co, pg 276
R Oldenbourg Verlag GmbH, pg 276
Reclam Verlag Leipzig, pg 277
Verlag fur Regionalgeschichte, pg 277
Dr Ludwig Reichert Verlag, pg 278
E Reinhold Verlag, pg 278
RVBG Rheinland-Verlag-und Betriebsgesellschaft des Landschaftsverbandes Rheinland mbH, pg 279
Ritzau KG Verlag Zeit und Eisenbahn, pg 279
Roehrig Universitaets Verlag Gmbh, pg 279
Rombach GmbH Druck und Verlagshaus & Co, pg 280
Romiosini Verlag, pg 280
Rosenheimer Verlagshaus GmbH & Co KG, pg 280
Verlag Roter Morgen, pg 280
Rowohlt Taschenbuch Verlag GmbH, pg 280
Ruetten & Loening Berlin GmbH, pg 281
Verlag an der Ruhr GmbH, pg 281
Saarbrucker Druckerei und Verlag GmbH (SDV), pg 281
K G Saur Verlag GmbH, A Gale/ Thomson Learning Company, pg 282
scaneg Verlag, pg 282
Moritz Schauenburg Verlag, pg 282
Schild-Verlag GmbH, pg 283
Schillinger Verlag GmbH, pg 283
Max Schmidt-Roemhild Verlag, pg 284
Verlag Schnell und Steiner GmbH, pg 284

Ferdinand Schoeningh Verlag GmbH, pg 284
Verlag Karl Waldemar Schuetz, pg 285
Schulz-Kirchner Verlag GmbH, pg 285
H O Schulze KG, pg 285
Scientia Verlag und Antiquariat, pg 286
Siedler Verlag, pg 286
Siegler & Co Verlag fuer Zeitarchive GmbH, pg 286
Societaets-Verlag, pg 287
Spee Buchverlag GmbH, pg 287
Spiess Volker Wissenschaftsverlag GmbH, pg 287
Adolf Sponholtz Verlag, pg 288
Springer-Verlag GmbH & Co KG, pg 288
Staatliche Museen Kassel, pg 288
Stadler Verlagsgesellschaft mbH, pg 288
Stapp Verlag Wolfgang Stapp, pg 289
C A Starke Verlag, pg 289
Steidl Verlag, pg 289
Franz Steiner Verlag Wiesbaden GmbH, pg 289
J F Steinkopf Verlag GmbH, pg 289
Steinweg-Verlag, Jurgen romHoff, pg 290
Stern-Verlag Janssen & Co, pg 290
Sternberg-Verlag bei Ernst Franz, pg 290
Stiefel GmbH Wandkarten Verlag, pg 290
Sueddeutsche Verlagsgesellschaft mbH, pg 291
Suin Buch-Verlag, pg 291
Systhema Verlag GmbH, pg 291
Edition Temmen, pg 292
Konrad Theiss Verlag GmbH, pg 293
Toleranz Verlag, Nielsen Frederic W, pg 294
Traditionell Bogenschiessen Verlag Angelika Hornig, pg 294
Trautvetter & Fischer Nachf, pg 294
Trees Wolfgang Triangel Verlag, pg 294
Treves Editions Verein Zur Foerderung der Kuenstlerischen Taetigkeiten, pg 295
Trotzdem-Verlags Genossenschaft eG, pg 295
Tuduv Verlagsgesellschaft mbH, pg 295
Tuebinger Vereinigung fur Volkskunde eV (TVV), pg 295
Ullstein Heyne List GmbH & Co KG, pg 295
Ulrike Helmer Verlag, pg 296
UTB fuer Wissenschaft Uni-Taschenbuecher GmbH, pg 297
UVK Universitatsverlag Konstanz GmbH, pg 297
UVK Verlagsgesellschaft mbH, pg 297
Vandenhoeck & Ruprecht, pg 297
VAS-Verlag fuer Akademische Schriften, Vas Karl-Heinz Balon, pg 297
Verlag Philipp von Zabern, pg 299
VS Verlagshaus Stuttgart GmbH, pg 299
W Ludwig Verlag GmbH, pg 300
Wachholtz Verlag GmbH, pg 300
Verlag Klaus Wagenbach GmbH, pg 300
Waxmann Verlag GmbH, pg 300
Weber Zucht & Co, pg 300
Wehr & Wissen Verlagsgesellschaft mbH, pg 300

SUBJECT INDEX

Weidmannsche Verlagsbuchhandlung GmbH, pg 301
Verlagsgruppe Weltbild GmbH, pg 301
Westermann Schulbuchverlag GmbH, pg 302
Wichern Verlag, pg 302
Wichern-Verlag GmbH, pg 302
Dr Dieter Winkler, pg 303
Verlag Wissenschaft und Politik/ Helker Pflug, pg 303
Wissenschaftliche Buchgesellschaft, pg 303
Friedrich Wittig Verlag GmbH, pg 303
Wochenschau Verlag, Dr Kurt Debus GmbH, pg 304
Wolfgang Arlt u Ute Schiller, pg 304
Das Wunderhorn Verlag GmbH, pg 304
Wunderlich Verlag, pg 304
Zambon Verlag, pg 305
Zeller Verlag GmbH & Co, pg 305
Verlag Clemens Zerling, pg 305
Verlag im Ziegelhaus Ulrich Gohl, pg 305
Zweimuehlen Verlag GmbH, pg 305

Ghana

Adaex Educational Publications Ltd, pg 306
Anowuo Educational Publications, pg 306
Ghana Publishing Corporation, pg 307
Ghana Universities Press (GUP), pg 307
Moxon Paperbacks, pg 307
Sedco Publishing Ltd, pg 308
Waterville Publishing House, pg 308

Greece

Akritas, pg 308
Anixis Publications, pg 309
Apostoliki Diakonia tis Ekklisias tis Hellados, pg 309
D I Arsenidis Publications, pg 309
Bergadis, pg 309
Boukoumanis' Editions, pg 309
Chryssos Typos AE Ekodeis, pg 309
Dionysis Noti Karavias, pg 309
Dodoni Publications, pg 310
Dorikos Publishing House, pg 310
Ecole francaise d'Athenes, pg 310
Ekdotike Athenon SA, pg 310
Elliniki Leschi Tou Vivliou, pg 310
Etaireia Spoudon Neoellinikou Politismou Kai Genikis Paideias, pg 310
Evrodiastasi, pg 310
Exandas Publishers, pg 310
Forma Publications Ltd, pg 310
Giovanis Publications, Pangosmios Ekdotikos Organismos, pg 310
Govostis Publishing SA, pg 311
Gutenberg Publications, pg 311
Hestia-I D Hestia-Kollaros & Co Corporation, pg 311
Hiotellis P, pg 311
Ianos, pg 311
Idmon Publications, pg 311
Idryma Meleton Chersonisou tou Aimou, pg 311
Irini Publishing House - Vassilis G Katsikeas SA, pg 311
Editions Kalentis, pg 312
Kardamitsa A, pg 312
Knossos Publications, pg 312
Kritiki Publishing, pg 312
Kyriakidis, pg 312

983

Kyriakidis Vasileios, pg 312
Melissa Publishing House, pg 313
Minoas SA, pg 313
Morfotiko Idryma Ethnikis Trapezas, pg 313
Ed Nea Acropolis, pg 313
Nea Thesis - Evrotas, pg 313
Odysseas Publications Ltd, pg 313
Okeanida, pg 313
Panepistimio Ioanninon, pg 314
D Papadimas, pg 314
Papazissis Publishers SA, pg 314
Patakis Publishers, pg 314
Pontiki Publications SA, pg 314
Proskinio, pg 314
Siamantas Publications, pg 315
Society for Macedonian Studies, pg 315
Stochastis, pg 315
Thetili Publications, pg 315
J Vassiliou Bibliopolein, pg 315
S J Zacharopoulos SA Publishing Co, pg 316
Har Zolindakis, pg 316

Guatemala
Fundacion para la Cultura y el Desarrollo, pg 316
Grupo Editorial RIN-78, pg 316

Guinea-Bissau
Instituto Nacional de Estudos e Pesquisa, pg 316

Haiti
Editions Caraiibes SA, pg 317
Theodor (Imprimerie), pg 317

Holy See (Vatican City State)
Biblioteca Apostolica Vaticana, pg 317
Libreria Editrice Vaticana, pg 317

Honduras
Editorial Guaymuras, pg 318

Hong Kong
Celeluck Co Ltd, pg 318
The Chinese University Press, pg 319
Chung Hwa Book Co (HK) Ltd, pg 319
FormAsia Books Ltd, pg 320
Hong Kong University Press, pg 320
Joint Publishing (HK) Co Ltd, pg 320
Ling Kee Publishing Group, pg 320
Sun Mui Press, pg 322
Witman Publishing Co (HK) Ltd, pg 322

Hungary
Akademiai Kiado, pg 323
Atlantisz Kiado, pg 323
Balassi Kiado Kft, pg 323
Central European University Press, pg 323
CEU-Press, pg 323
Helikon Kiado, pg 324
Janus Pannonius Tudomanyegyetem, pg 324
Jelenkor Verlag, pg 324
Officina Nova, Koenyv-es Lapkiado/ Bertelsmann Media Kft, pg 324
Magveto Koenyvkiado, pg 325
Mult es Jovo Kiado, pg 325
Nemzeti Tankoenyvkiado, pg 326
Osiris Kiado, pg 326

Park Konyvkiado Kft (Park Publisher), pg 326
Tajak Korok Muzeumok Egyesuelet, pg 327

Iceland
Almenna Bokafelagid, pg 327
Fjolvi, pg 327
Frodi Ltd, pg 328
Hid Islenzka Bokmenntafelag, pg 328
Idunn, pg 328
Stofnun Arna Magnussonar a Islandi, pg 329

India
Abhinav Publications, pg 329
Abhishek Publications, pg 329
The Academic Press, pg 329
Agam Kala Prakashan, pg 330
Amar Prakashan, pg 330
Ananda Publishers Pvt Ltd, pg 330
APH Publishing Corp, pg 331
Asian Educational Services, pg 331
Associated Publishing House, pg 331
Atma Ram & Sons, pg 331
K P Bagchi & Co, pg 332
Bharatiya Samijik Vigyan Auusandhan Parishad, pg 332
Bharatiya Vidya Bhavan, pg 333
Books & Books, pg 334
BR Publishing Corporation, pg 334
Chowkhamba Sanskrit Series Office, pg 335
Concept Publishing Co, pg 335
Cosmo Publications, pg 335
Dastane Ramchandra & Co, pg 335
Disha Prakashan, pg 336
DK Printworld (P) Ltd, pg 336
Dolphin Publications, pg 336
Enkay Publishers Pvt Ltd, pg 336
Ess Ess Publications, pg 337
Frank Brothers & Co (Publishers) Ltd, pg 337
Geeta Prakasham, pg 337
Gitanjali Publishing House, pg 337
Goel Prakashen, pg 337
Gyan Publishing House, pg 338
Heritage Publishers, pg 338
Indus Publishing Co, pg 339
Intellectual Publishing House, pg 339
Inter-India Publications, pg 340
Intertrade Publications, pg 340
Islamic Publishing House, pg 340
Jaico Publishing House, pg 340
Kali For Women, pg 341
Law Publishers, pg 341
Manohar Publishers & Distributors, pg 342
Minerva Associates (Publications) Pvt Ltd, pg 342
Ministry of Information & Broadcasting, pg 342
Motilal Banarsidass Publishers Pvt Ltd, pg 343
Munshiram Manoharlal Publishers Pvt Ltd, pg 343
National Book Organization, pg 343
Navajivan Trust, pg 344
Navrang Booksellers & Publishers, pg 344
Naya Prokash, pg 344
Omsons Publications, pg 345
Oxford University Press, pg 345
Paico Publishing House, pg 345
Panjab University Publication Bureau, pg 345
People's Publishing House (P) Ltd, pg 346

Pitambar Publishing Co (P) Ltd, pg 346
Pointer Publishers, pg 346
Popular Prakashan Pvt Ltd, pg 346
Promilla and Co, pg 346
Pustak Mahal, pg 346
Rahul Publishing House, pg 347
Rajendra Publishing House Pvt Ltd, pg 347
Rajesh Publications, pg 347
Regency Publications, pg 347
Reliance Publishing House, pg 347
Roli Books Pvt Ltd, pg 348
Rupa & Co, pg 348
Sasta Sahitya Mandal, pg 349
Sri Satguru Publications, pg 349
Scientific Book Agency, pg 349
Somaiya Publications Pvt Ltd, pg 350
South Asia Publications, pg 350
Star Publications (P) Ltd, pg 351
Sterling Publishers Pvt Ltd, pg 351
Sultan Chand & Sons Pvt Ltd, pg 351
Suman Prakashan Pvt Ltd, pg 351
DB Taraporevala Sons & Co Pvt Ltd, pg 351
Theosophical Publishing House, pg 351
Vani Prakashan, pg 352
Vikas Publishing House Pvt Ltd, pg 353
Vision Books Pvt Ltd, pg 353
S Viswanathan (Printers & Publishers) Pvt Ltd, pg 353

Indonesia
Bhratara Karya Aksara, pg 354
P T Bulan Bintang, pg 354
Pustaka Utama Grafiti, PT, pg 357
Tintamas Indonesia PT, pg 357
Yayasan Obor Indonesia, pg 357

Islamic Republic of Iran
Scientific and Cultural Publications, pg 358

Ireland
Anvil Books Ltd, pg 358
Attic Press Ltd, pg 358
Ballinakella Press, pg 358
Edmund Burke Publisher, pg 359
The Children's Press, pg 359
Clo Iar-Chonnachta Teo, pg 359
The Collins Press, pg 359
The Columba Press, pg 359
Cork University Press, pg 359
Dee-Jay Publications, pg 359
The Educational Company of Ireland, pg 360
Four Courts Press Ltd, pg 360
Gandon Editions, pg 360
Gill & Macmillan Ltd, pg 361
The Goldsmith Press Ltd, pg 361
Herodotus Press, pg 361
History House Publishing, pg 361
Institute of Public Administration, pg 361
Irish Academic Press, pg 361
Kerryman Ltd, pg 362
The Lilliput Press Ltd, pg 362
Mercier Press Ltd, pg 362
Mount Eagle Publications Ltd, pg 362
New Books/Connolly Books, pg 362
O'Brien Educational, pg 363
The O'Brien Press Ltd, pg 363
On Stream Publications Ltd, pg 363
Poolbeg Press Ltd, pg 363
Relay Books, pg 363
Roberts Rinehart Publishers, pg 363
Royal Irish Academy, pg 364

Sean Ros Press, pg 364
Tir Eolas, pg 364
Tomar Publishing Ltd, pg 364

Israel
Agudat Sabah, pg 365
Am Oved Publishers Ltd, pg 365
Ariel Publishing House, pg 365
Bar Ilan University Press, pg 365
Ben-Zvi Institute, pg 365
The Bialik Institute, pg 365
Boostan Publishing House, pg 366
Breslov Research Institute, pg 366
Carta, The Israel Map & Publishing Co Ltd, pg 366
DAT Publications, pg 366
Dyonon/Papyrus Publishing House of the Tel-Aviv, pg 367
Edanim Publishers Ltd, pg 367
Feldheim Publishers Ltd, pg 367
The Arnold & Leona Finkler Institute of Holocaust Research, pg 367
Gefen Publishing House Ltd, pg 367
Hadar Publishing House Ltd, pg 367
Haifa University Press, pg 368
Hakibbutz Hameuchad Publishing House Ltd, pg 368
The Israel Academy of Sciences & Humanities, pg 368
Israel Exploration Society, pg 368
Jabotinsky Institute in Israel, pg 369
The Jerusalem Publishing House Ltd, pg 369
L B Publishing Co, pg 369
Ma'ariv Book Guild (Sifriat Ma'ariv), pg 370
Machbarot Lesifrut, pg 370
The Magnes Press, pg 370
MAP-Mapping & Publishing Ltd, pg 370
Massada Press Ltd, pg 370
Massada Publishers Ltd, pg 370
Ministry of Defence Publishing House, pg 370
Misgav Yerushalayim, pg 370
M Mizrahi Publishers, pg 370
The Moshe Dayan Center for Middle Eastern & African Studies, pg 371
Open University of Israel, pg 371
Schocken Publishing House Ltd, pg 372
Shalem Press, pg 372
Sifriat Poalim Ltd, pg 372
Tcherikover Publishers Ltd, pg 372
Tel-Aviv University, pg 373
Yad Izhak Ben-Zvi Press, pg 373
Yad Vashem - The Holocaust Martyrs' & Heroes' Remembrance Authority, pg 373
Y L Peretz Publishing Co, pg 374
The Zalman Shazar Center, pg 374
Zmora-Bitan, Publishers Ltd, pg 374

Italy
Mario Adda Editore SNC, pg 374
Adelphi Edizioni SpA, pg 374
De Agostini Scolastica, pg 375
Alberti Libraio Editore, pg 375
All'Insegna del Giglio, pg 375
Franco Angeli SRL, pg 375
Archimede Edizioni, pg 376
Archivio Guido Izzi Edizioni, pg 376
Argalia Editore delle Arti Grafiche Editoriali SRL, pg 376
Arnaud Editore SRL, pg 376
Verlagsanstalt Athesia, pg 377
Bardi Editore srl, pg 377

PUBLISHERS SUBJECT INDEX

Bastogi, pg 377
Bianco, pg 377
Bibliotheca di Gabriele Chiusano, pg 378
Bollati Boringhieri Editore Srl, pg 378
Bonacci editore, pg 378
Giuseppe Bonanno Editore, pg 378
Bonsignori Editore SRL, pg 378
Edizioni Borla SRL, pg 378
Bovolenta, pg 378
Edizioni Brenner, pg 378
Edizioni Bresciane, pg 378
Editore Giorgio Bretschneider, pg 378
Edizioni Cadmo SRL, pg 379
Calosci, pg 379
Camera dei Deputati Ufficio Pubblicazioni Informazione Parlamentare, pg 379
Campanotto, pg 379
Canova SRL, pg 379
Edizioni Cantagalli, pg 379
Capone Editore SRL, pg 379
Nuova Casa Editrice Licinio Cappelli GEM srl, pg 379
Edizioni Carmelitane, pg 379
Casa Editrice Felice Le Monnier, pg 380
Casa Editrice Giuseppe Principato Spa, pg 380
CELID, pg 380
Celuc Libri, pg 380
Centro Ambrosiano di Documentazione e Studi Religiosi, pg 380
Centro Italiano Studi Alto Medioevo, pg 381
Centro Studi Terzo Mondo, pg 381
Le Cerchio Imigiative Editoriali, pg 381
Ciranna - Roma, pg 381
Cisalpino - Monduzzi, pg 382
Claudiana Editrice, pg 382
CLUEB (Cooperativa Libraria Universitaria Editrice Bologna), pg 382
Nuova Coletti Editore Roma, pg 382
Colonnese Editore, pg 382
Edizioni di Comunita SpA, pg 382
Edizioni Cultura della Pace, pg 383
La Culturale, pg 383
D'Anna, pg 383
Datanews, pg 384
M d'Auria Editore SAS, pg 384
Edizioni Dedalo SRL, pg 384
Edizioni del Centro, pg 384
Edizioni Della Torre di Salvatore Fozzi & C SAS, pg 384
Edizioni dell'Orso SAS, pg 385
Diakronia, pg 385
Direzione Generale Archivi, pg 385
Edizioni EBE, pg 385
Ecole Francaise de Rome, pg 385
Ediciclo Editore SRL, pg 386
EDIFIR SRL, pg 386
Edipuglia, pg 386
Editalia (Edizioni d'Italia), pg 386
Editori Laterza, pg 386
Edizioni l'Arciere SRL, pg 387
EGEA (Edizioni Giuridiche Economiche Aziendali), pg 387
Giulio Einaudi Editore SpA, pg 387
ERGA SNC di Carla Ottino Merli & C (Edizioni Realizzazioni Grafiche - Artigiana), pg 388
Essegi, pg 388
Edizioni Europa, pg 388
Giangiacomo Feltrinelli SpA, pg 388
La Fenice SRL, pg 389
Festina Lente Edizioni, pg 389
Flaccovio Editore, pg 389
Fogola Editore in Torino, pg 389
Arnaldo Forni Editore SRL, pg 389
Biblioteca Francescana, pg 389
Galzerano Editore, pg 390
Gangemi Editore, pg 390
Garzanti Editore, pg 390
Istituto Geografico de Agostini SpA, pg 390
Bruno Ghigi Editore, pg 390
Edizioni del Girasole srl, pg 390
A Giuffre Editore SpA, pg 390
Giunti (Gruppo Editoriale), pg 390
Giunti Publishing Group, pg 391
Gius Laterza e Figli SpA, pg 391
Grafica e Arte SRL, pg 391
Grafis Edizioni, pg 391
Grafo Edizioni, pg 391
Herder Editrice e Libreria, pg 392
Institutum Historicum S l, pg 392
Hopeful Monster Editore, pg 392
Ibis, pg 393
Il Poligrafo, pg 393
Il Saggiatore, pg 393
Ila - Palma, Tea Nova, pg 393
Edizioni Internazionali di Letteratura e Scienze, pg 394
Editoriale Jaca Book SpA, pg 394
L Japadre Editore, pg 394
Jouvence, pg 394
Kaos Edizioni SRL, pg 395
Laruffa Editore SRL, pg 395
Edizioni Lavoro SRL, pg 395
Il Lavoro Editoriale, pg 395
Lecce Spazio Vivo Srl, pg 395
LED - Edizioni Universitarie di Lettere Economia Diritto, pg 395
L'Erma di Bretschneider SRL, pg 395
Casa Editrice Le Lettere SRL, pg 395
Liguori Editore SRL, pg 396
Editrice Liguria SNC di Norberto Sabatelli & C, pg 396
Editrice la Locusta, pg 396
Loescher Editore SRL, pg 396
Loffredo Editore Napoli SpA®, pg 396
Longanesi & C, pg 396
Angelo Longo Editore, pg 396
Edizioni di Luca SRL, pg 397
Giuseppe Maimone Editore, pg 397
Manfrini Editori, pg 397
Casa Editrice Marietti SpA, pg 397
Tommaso Marotta Editore Srl, pg 398
Marzorati Editore SRL, pg 398
Editrice Massimo SAS di Crespi Cesare e C, pg 398
McRae Books, pg 398
Memorie Domenicane, pg 398
Casa Editrice Menna di Sinisgalli Menna Giuseppina, pg 398
Messaggero di San Antonio, pg 398
Arnoldo Mondadori Editore SpA, pg 399
Editrice Morcelliana SpA, pg 399
Mucchi Editore SRL, pg 400
Societa Editrice Il Mulino, pg 400
Gruppo Ugo Mursia Editore SpA, pg 400
Museo Storico in Trento, pg 400
Giorgio Nada Editore SRL, pg 400
Accademia Naz dei Lincei, pg 400
Istituto Nazionale di Studi Romani, pg 400
Newton Compton Editori SRL, pg 401
NodoLibri, pg 401
La Nuova Italia Editrice SpA, pg 401
Editrice Nuovi Autori, pg 401
Nuovi Sentieri Editore, pg 401
OCTAVO Franco Cantini Editore, pg 401
Leo S Olschki, pg 402
Osanna Venosa, pg 402
Maria Pacini Fazzi Editore, pg 402
Pagano Editore, pg 402
Palatina Editrice, pg 402
Fratelli Palombi SRL, pg 402
Paravia Bruno Mondadori Editori, pg 402
Passigli Editori srl, pg 403
Patron Editore SrL, pg 403
Luigi Pellegrini Editore, pg 403
Daniela Piazza Editore, pg 403
Piero Lacaita Editore, pg 403
Francesco Pirella Editore, pg 403
Il Pomerio, pg 404
Pontificio Istituto di Archeologia Cristiana, pg 404
Neri Pozza Editore, pg 404
Pratiche Editrice, pg 404
Principato, pg 404
Edizioni Quasar di Severino Tognon SRL, pg 404
Edizioni Quattroventi SNC, pg 404
Edition Raetia Srl-GmbH, pg 404
Rara-Ist Editoriale di Bibliofilia e Reprints, pg 405
RCS Libri SpA, pg 405
RCS Rizzoli Libri SpA, pg 405
Reverdito Edizioni, pg 405
Riccardo Ricciardi Editore SpA, pg 405
Edizioni Ripostes, pg 405
Editori Riuniti, pg 405
Rossato, pg 406
Rubbettino Editore, pg 406
Rusconi Libri Srl, pg 406
SAGEP, pg 406
Salerno Editrice SRL, pg 406
Collegio San Bonaventura di Grottaferrata, pg 406
Edizioni San Paolo SRL, pg 407
Fausto Sardini Editrice, pg 407
Salvatore Sciascia Editore, pg 407
Edizioni Scientifiche Italiane, pg 407
Sellerio Editore, pg 407
Sicania, pg 408
Edizioni Librarie Siciliane, pg 408
Societa Editrice Internazionale - SEI, pg 408
Societa Napoletana Storia Patria Napoli, pg 408
Societa Storica Catanese, pg 408
Gruppo Editoriale Le Stelle SpA, pg 409
Edizioni di Storia e Letteratura, pg 409
Istituto Storico Italiano per l'Eta Moderna e Contemporanea, pg 409
Studio Bibliografico Adelmo Polla, pg 409
Studio Editoriale Programma, pg 409
Edizioni Studio Tesi SRL, pg 409
Edizioni Studium SpA, pg 409
Sugarco Edizioni SRL, pg 409
Tappeiner, pg 409
Tassotti Editore, pg 409
TEA Tascabili degli Editori Associati SpA, pg 409
Edizioni del Teresianum, pg 409
Nicola Teti e C Editore SRL, pg 409
Edizioni Thyrus SRL, pg 409
Editrice Tirrenia Stampatori SAS, pg 410
Trainer International SRL, pg 410
Transeuropa Libri, pg 410
Editoriale Umbra SAS di Carnevali e, pg 410
UTET (Unione Tipografico-Editrice Torinese), pg 411
Vita e Pensiero, pg 411
Zanichelli Editore SpA, pg 412

Jamaica

Carlong Publishers (Caribbean) Ltd, pg 412
Institute of Jamaica Publications, pg 413
Jamaica Publishing House Ltd, pg 413
The Press, pg 413
Ian Randle Publishers Ltd, pg 413
University of the West Indies Press, pg 414
West Indies Publishing Ltd, pg 414

Japan

Akita Shoten Publishing Co Ltd, pg 414
Baseball Magazine-Sha Co Ltd, pg 415
Chikuma Shobo Publishing Co Ltd, pg 415
Chuo-Koron-Sha Inc, pg 415
Dohosha Publishing Co Ltd, pg 416
Fuzambo Publishing Co, pg 416
GakuseiSha Publishing Co Ltd, pg 416
Hayakawa Publishing Inc, pg 417
Heibonsha Ltd, Publishers, pg 417
Hoikusha Publishing Co Ltd, pg 417
Hyoronsha Publishing Co Ltd, pg 417
International Society for Educational Information (ISEI), pg 418
Iwanami Shoten, Publishers, pg 418
Japan Travel Bureau Inc, pg 418
Kadokawa Shoten Publishing Co, pg 419
Kaisei-Sha Publishing Co Ltd, pg 419
Kawade Shobo Shinsha, pg 419
Kazama Shobo, pg 419
Keisuisha Publishing Company Ltd, pg 419
Kinokuniya Co Ltd (Publishing Department), pg 420
Kodansha, pg 420
Kodansha International, pg 420
Kokusho Kankokai Co Ltd, pg 420
Kosei Publishing Co Ltd, pg 420
Koyo Shobo, pg 420
Minerva Shobo Co Ltd, pg 421
Mirai-Sha, pg 421
Myrtos Inc, pg 421
Nigensha Publishing Co Ltd, pg 422
Nihon Tosho Center Co Ltd, pg 422
Obunsha Co Ltd, pg 423
Otsuki Shoten Publishers, pg 423
Poplar Publishing Co Ltd, pg 423
Rinsen Book Co Ltd, pg 424
Sanseido Co Ltd, pg 424
Seibundo Shuppan, pg 425
Sekai Bunka Publishing Inc, pg 425
Shakai Shiso-Sha, pg 425
Shimizu-Shoin, pg 425
Shogakukan Inc, pg 426
Shufu-to-Seikatsu Sha Ltd, pg 426
The Simul Press Inc, pg 426
Sogensha Publishing Co Ltd, pg 426
Taimeido Publishing Co Ltd, pg 427
Tankosha Publishing Co Ltd, pg 427
Teikoku-Shoin Co Ltd, pg 427
Toho Book Store, pg 427
Toho Shuppan, pg 427
Tokai University Press, pg 427
Tokyo Shoseki Co Ltd, pg 427
Tosui Shobo Publishers, pg 428
University of Tokyo Press, pg 428

Waseda University Press, pg 428
Yuhikaku Publishing Co Ltd, pg 429

Jordan

Jordan Distribution Agency Co Ltd, pg 430

Kazakstan

Kazakh Al-Farabi State National University, pg 430

Kenya

British Institute in Eastern Africa, pg 431
Heinemann Kenya Limited (EAEP), pg 431
Kenway Publications Ltd, pg 432
Nairobi University Press, pg 433
Paulines Publications-Africa, pg 433
Phoenix Publishers, pg 433
Shirikon Publishers, pg 433
Transafrica Press, pg 433
Gideon S Were Press, pg 434

Democratic People's Republic of Korea

Academy of Sciences Publishing House, pg 434
The Foreign Language Press Group, pg 434
Korea Science and Encyclopedia Publishing House, pg 434

Republic of Korea

Ba-reunsa Publishing Co, pg 434
Borim Publishing Co, pg 435
Bum-Woo Publishing Co, pg 435
Chang-josa Publishing Co, pg 435
Chong No Books Publishing Co Ltd, pg 435
Chung Rim Publishing Co Ltd, pg 435
DanKook University Press, pg 436
Dong Hwa Publishing Co, pg 436
Eulyu Publishing Co Ltd, pg 436
Hainaim Publishing Co Ltd, pg 436
Hakgojae Publishing Inc, pg 436
Hangil Art Vision, pg 436
Hanul Publishing Co, pg 436
Hollym Corporation Publishers, pg 437
Hw Moon Publishing Co, pg 437
Hyangmunsa Publishing Co, pg 437
Iljisa Publishing House, pg 437
Iljo-gag Publishers, pg 437
Korea University Press, pg 437
Minjisa Publishing Co, pg 438
Minumsa Publishing Co Ltd, pg 438
Munhag-gwan, pg 438
Munye Publishing Co, pg 439
O Neul Publishing Co, pg 439
Pochinchai Printing Co Ltd, pg 439
Samseong Publishing Co Ltd, pg 440
Sejong Daewang Kinyom Saophoe, pg 440
Seoul International Publishing House, pg 440
Seoul National University Press, pg 440
Sogang University Press, pg 440
Sohaksa, pg 440
Woongjin Media Corporation, pg 440
Yonsei University Press, pg 441

Kuwait

Ministry of Information, pg 441

Laos People's Democratic Republic

Lao-phanit, pg 441

Latvia

Lielvards Ltd, pg 442
Nordik/Tapals Publishers Ltd, pg 442
Preses Nams, pg 442
Spriditis Publishers, pg 442
Vieda, pg 442

Lebanon

Darl el-Machreq Sarl, pg 443
Khayat Book and Publishing Co Sarl, pg 443
Librairie Orientale sal, pg 443

Lesotho

Mazenod Book Centre, pg 444
Saint Michael's Mission, pg 444

Liechtenstein

Verlag HP Gassner AG, pg 444
Historischer Verein fur das Furstentum Liechtenstein, pg 444
Liechtenstein Verlag AG, pg 444
Saendig Reprint Verlag, Hans-Rainer Wohlwend, pg 445

Lithuania

Baltos Lankos, pg 445
Eugrimas, pg 445
Klaipedos Universiteto Leidykla, pg 445
Lithuanian National Museum Publishing House, pg 446
Mokslo ir enciklopediju leidybos institutas, pg 446
Margi Rastai Publishers, pg 446
Svietimo ir mokslo ministerijos Leidybos centras, pg 446

Luxembourg

Editions APESS ASBL, pg 447
Editions Emile Borschette, pg 447
Cahiers Luxembourgeois, pg 447
Editions Saint-Paul, pg 448
Editions Tousch, pg 448

Macau

Museu Maritimo, pg 448
Instituto Portugues Oriente, pg 448
Universidadede de Macau, Centro de Publicacoes, pg 448

The Former Yugoslav Republic of Macedonia

Macedonia Prima Publishing House, pg 449
Strk Publishing House, pg 449
Zumpres Publishing Firm, pg 449

Madagascar

Editions Ambozontany, pg 450
Madagascar Print & Press Company, pg 450
Tsipika Edition, pg 450

Malawi

Central Africana Ltd, pg 450
Christian Literature Association in Malawi, pg 450
Dzuka Publishing Company Ltd, pg 450
Mzuzu Publishing Co, pg 451

Malaysia

Forum Publications, pg 452
Geetha Publishers Sdn Bhd, pg 452
Penerbit Jayatinta Sdn Bhd, pg 454
Pustaka Delta Pelajaran Sdn Bhd, pg 454
Uni-Text Book Co, pg 455
University of Malaya, Department of Publications, pg 455

Mali

EDIM SA, pg 455

Malta

Gaulitana, pg 456
Gozo Press, pg 456

Mauritius

Editions Capucines, pg 457
Vizavi Editions, pg 457

Mexico

Aconcagua Ediciones y Publicaciones SA, pg 457
Libreria y Ediciones Botas SA, pg 458
Ediciones el Caballito SA, pg 458
Centro de Estudios Mexicanos y Centroamericanos, pg 458
El Colegio de Mexico AC, pg 459
Comision Nacional Forestal, pg 459
Editorial Diana SA de CV, pg 459
Editorial Edicol SA, pg 460
El Colegio de Michoacan A C, pg 460
Ediciones Era SA de CV, pg 460
Editorial Esfinge SA de CV, pg 460
Ediciones Euroamericanas, pg 461
Fernandez Editores SA de CV, pg 461
Fondo de Cultura Economica, pg 461
Editorial Hermes SA, pg 461
Instituto Indigenista Interamericano, pg 462
Editorial Jilguero, SA de CV, pg 462
Editorial Joaquin Mortiz SA de CV, pg 462
Editorial Jus SA de CV, pg 462
Phillip Richard Conover Lazo, pg 462
Editorial Minutiae Mexicana SA, pg 464
Instituto Nacional de Antropologia e Historia, pg 464
Editorial Nueva Imagen SA, pg 464
Instituto Panamericano de Geografia e Historia, pg 465
Panorama Editorial, SA, pg 465
Editorial Patria SA de CV, pg 465
Pearson Educacion de Mexico, SA de CV, pg 465
Grupo Editorial Planeta, pg 465
Ediciones Roca, SA, pg 466
Salvat Editores de Mexico, pg 466
SCRIPTA - Distribucion y Servicios Editoriales, SA de CV, pg 467
Siglo XXI Editores SA de CV, pg 467
Sistemas Tecnicos de Edicion SA de CV, pg 467
Universidad Nacional Autonoma de Mexico (National University of Mexico), pg 467
Universidad Veracruzana Direccion General Editorial y de Publicaciones, pg 468
Javier Vergara Editor SA de CV, pg 468

Republic of Moldova

Lumina Publishing House, pg 468

Monaco

Editions EGC, pg 468
Les Editions du Rocher, pg 469
Rondeau Giannipiero a Monaco, pg 469

Morocco

Association de la Recherche Historique et Sociale, pg 469
Dar El Kitab, pg 469
Dar Nachr Al Maarifa Pour L'Edition et La Distribution, pg 469
Editions Eddif Maroc, pg 469
Editions Okad, pg 470
Societe Ennewrasse Service Librairie et Imprimerie, pg 470

Mozambique

Empresa Moderna Lda, pg 470
Centro De Estudos Africanos, pg 470

Myanmar

Sarpay Beikman Board, pg 471

Nepal

International Standards Books & Periodicals (P) Ltd, pg 471
Royal Nepal Academy, pg 472

Netherlands

Uitgeversmaatschappij Agon, pg 472
Uitgeverij Ambo BV, pg 472
APA (Academic Publishers Associated), pg 472
BV Uitgeverij de Arbeiderspers, pg 473
Uitgeverij Balans, pg 473
Erven J Bijleveld, pg 474
De Boekerij BV, pg 474
Boom Uitgeverij, pg 474
Bosch & Keuning, pg 474
Brill Academic Publishers, pg 475
A W Bruna Uitgevers BV, pg 475
Uitgeverij Conserve, pg 475
Uitgeverij Coutinho BV, pg 476
De Walburg Pers, pg 476
Uitgeversmaatschappij Ad Donker BV, pg 476
Elmar BV, pg 476
Van Gennep Ltd, pg 477
HES & De Graaf Publishers BV, pg 478
Uitgeverij Heuff Nieuwkoop, pg 478
Heureka Uitgeverij, pg 478
Uitgeverij Heureka, pg 478
Historische Uitgeverij, pg 478
Holland University Press BV (APA), pg 478
Hotei Publishing, pg 478
KITLV Press Royal Institute of Linguistics & Anthropology, pg 479
Uitgeefmaatschappij J H Kok BV, pg 480
Mets & Schilt Uitgevers en Distributeurs, pg 481
Nico Israel, pg 482
The Pepin Press, pg 482
Philo Press-Van Heusden-Hissink & Co CV (APA), pg 482
Prometheus, pg 483
Uitgeverij Het Spectrum BV, pg 484

PUBLISHERS

A J G Strengholt's Boeken, Anno 1928, BV, pg 484
Uitgeverij SUN, pg 484
Unieboek BV, pg 485
Uniepers BV, pg 486
Van Gorcum & Comp BV, pg 486
Uitgeverij Van Wijnen, pg 486
Uitgeverij Verloren, pg 486
VU Boekhandel/Uitgeverij BV, pg 487
Uitgeverij Waanders BV, pg 487

Netherlands Antilles
Bredero, pg 488

New Caledonia
Editions du Santal, pg 488

New Zealand
Aoraki Press Ltd, pg 488
Aspect Press, pg 488
Auckland University Press, pg 488
Bush Press Communications Ltd, pg 489
C&S Publications, pg 489
Canterbury University Press, pg 489
Cape Catley, pg 489
Clerestory Press, pg 490
Craig Printing Company Ltd, pg 490
Dunmore Press Ltd, pg 490
ESA Publications (NZ) Ltd, pg 490
Fraser Books, pg 491
Gondwanaland Press, pg 491
Grantham House Publishing, pg 491
HarperCollins Publishers (New Zealand) Ltd, pg 491
Heritage Press Ltd, pg 492
Huia Publishers, pg 492
IPL Publishing Group, pg 492
David Ling Publishing, pg 493
Nestegg Books, pg 493
Northland Historical Publications Society, pg 494
Otago Heritage Books, pg 494
Outrigger Publishers, pg 494
Oxford University Press, pg 494
Nelson Price Milburn Ltd, pg 494
Reed Publishing (NZ) Ltd, pg 495
River Press, pg 495
Shearwater Associates Ltd, pg 495
Shoal Bay Press Ltd, pg 495
Te Waihora Press, pg 496
University of Otago Press, pg 496
Victoria University Press, pg 496
Bridget Williams Books Ltd, pg 497

Nigeria
ABIC Books & Equipment Ltd, pg 497
Ahmadu Bello University Press Ltd, pg 498
Alliance West African Publishers & Co, pg 498
Black Academy Press, pg 498
CSS Bookshops, Agency & Publishing Division, pg 498
Educational Research & Study Group, pg 499
Ethiope Publishing Corporation, pg 499
Evans Brothers (Nigeria Publishers) Ltd, pg 499
Ibadan University Press, pg 499
Ilesanmi Press (Educational Publishers) Ltd, pg 499
JAD Publishers Ltd, pg 500
Longman Nigeria Plc, pg 500
Nwamife Publishers Ltd, pg 500
Obafemi Awolowo University Press Ltd, pg 501
Obobo Books, pg 501
Ogunsanya Press, Publishers and Bookstores Ltd, pg 501
Onibon-Oje Publishers, pg 501
Riverside Communications, pg 501
University Publishing Co, pg 502

Norway
Det Norske Samlaget, pg 503
J W Eides Forlag A/S, pg 503
Gyldendal Norsk Forlag A/S, pg 503
Hjemmenes Forlag, pg 504
Norsk Bokreidingslag L/L, pg 504
Snofugl Forlag, pg 505

Oman
Apex Publishing, pg 506

Pakistan
Sheikh Muhammad Ashraf Publishers, pg 506
H I Jaffari & Co Publishers, pg 506
Hamdard Foundation, pg 507
Islamic Research Institute, pg 507
Jang Publishers, pg 507
Maqbool Academy, pg 508
Nafees Academy, pg 508
National Institute of Historical & Cultural Research, pg 508
Pak American Commercial (Pvt) Ltd, pg 508
Pakistan Publishing House, pg 508
Publishers United Pvt Ltd, pg 508
Royal Book Co, pg 509
Sang-e-Meel Publications, pg 509

Panama
Editorial Universitaria, pg 509

Peru
Librerias ABC SA, pg 511
Instituto de Estudios Peruanos, pg 511
Fondo Editorial de la Pontificia Universidad Catolica del Peru, pg 511
Instituto Frances de Estudios Andinos, IFEA, pg 511
Editorial Horizonte, pg 511
Sur Casa de Estudios del Socialismo, pg 511

Philippines
Abiva Publishing House Inc, pg 512
Ateneo de Manila University Press, pg 512
Bookmark Inc, pg 512
Galleon Publications, pg 513
Garotech, pg 513
Heritage Publishing House, pg 513
J C Palabay Enterprises, pg 513
New Day Publishers, pg 514
Our Lady of Manaoag Publisher, pg 514
Philippine Baptist Mission SBC FMB Church Growth International, pg 514
Rex Bookstores & Publishers, pg 514
Saint Mary's Publishing Corp, pg 515
San Carlos Publications, pg 515
SIBS Publishing House Inc, pg 515
Solidaridad Publishing House, pg 515
UST Publishing House, pg 515
Vera-Reyes Inc, pg 515

SUBJECT INDEX

Poland
Wydawnictwo Dolnoslaskie, pg 516
Instytut Historii Nauki PAN, pg 516
Instytut Wydawniczy Pax, Inco-Veritas, pg 517
Interpress, pg 517
Iskry - Publishing House Ltd spotka zoo, pg 517
Katolicki Uniwersytet Wydawniczo-Redakcja, pg 517
'Ksiazka i Wiedza' Spotdzielnia Wydawniczo-Handlowa, pg 517
Wydawnictwo Literackie, pg 517
Ludowa Spoldzielnia Wydawnicza, pg 518
Magnum Publishing House Ltd, pg 518
Norbertinum, pg 518
Ossolineum Zaklad Narodowy im Ossolinskich - Wydawnictwo, pg 518
Panstwowy Instytut Wydawniczy (PIW), pg 518
Wydawnictwo Podsiedlik-Raniowski i Spolka, pg 519
Rosikon Press, pg 519
Wydawnictwo RTW, pg 520
'Slask' Ltd, pg 520
Spoleczny Instytut Wydawniczy Znak, pg 520
Oficyna Wydawnicza Szkoly Glownej Handlowej w Warszawie Oficyna Wydawnicza SGH, pg 520
Towarzystwo Naukowe w Toruniu, pg 520
Wydawnictwo DiG, pg 521

Portugal
Publicacoes Alfa SA, pg 522
Armenio Amado Editora de Simoes, Beirao & Ca Lda, pg 522
Edicoes Antigona, pg 522
Assirio & Alvim, pg 522
Bezerr-Editorae e Distribuidora de Abel Antonio Bezerra, pg 522
Biblioteca Geral da Universidade de Coimbra, pg 523
Camara Municipal de Castelo, pg 523
Chaves Ferreira Publicacoes SA, pg 523
Livraria Civilizacao (Americo Fraga Lamares & Ca Lda), pg 523
Editora Classica, pg 523
Edicoes Colibri, pg 523
Constancia Editores, SA, pg 524
Edicoes Cosmos, pg 524
Dinalivro, pg 524
Edicoes 70, Lda, pg 524
Edicoes ELO, pg 524
Editorial Estampa, Lda, pg 524
Publicacoes Europa-America Lda, pg 524
Europress Editores e Distribuidores de Publicacoes Lda, pg 525
Editorial Franciscana, pg 525
Gradiva-Publicacnoes Lda, pg 525
Guimaraes Editores, Lda, pg 525
Imprensa Nacional-Casa da Moeda, pg 526
Editorial Inquerito Lda, pg 526
Instituto de Investigacao Cientifica Tropical, pg 526
Latina Livraria, pg 526
Editora Livros do Brasil Sarl, pg 526
Livros Horizonte Lda, pg 526
Livraria Tavares Martins, pg 527
Editorial Noticias, pg 527
Nova Acropole, pg 527
Nova Arrancada Sociedade Editora SA, pg 527
Palas Editores Lda, pg 528
Editorial Presenca, pg 528
Publicacoes Dom Quixote Lda, pg 528
Quimera Editores, pg 529
Edicoes Rolim Lda, pg 529
Sa da Costa Editora, pg 529
Edicoes 70, pg 529
Almerinda Teixeira, pg 529
Teorema, pg 529
Vega-Publicacao e Distribuicao de Livros e Revistas, Lda, pg 530
Editorial Verbo SA, pg 530
Livraria Verdade e Vida Editora, pg 530

Puerto Rico
Instituto de Cultura Puertorriquena, pg 530
Editorial Cultural Inc, pg 530
Ediciones Huracan Inc, pg 530
University of Puerto Rico Press (EDUPR), pg 531

Reunion
Editions Ocean, pg 531

Romania
Editura Academiei Romane, pg 531
Editura Aius, pg 531
Editura Albatros, pg 531
Alcor-Edimpex (Verlag) Ltd, pg 531
Editora All, pg 531
Ararat Verlag und Druckerei, pg 532
Ars Longa Publishing House, pg 532
Artemis Verlag, pg 532
Casa Editoriala Independenta Europa, pg 532
The Center for Romanian Studies, pg 532
Editura Clusium, Casa de Editura Atlas-Clusium SRL, pg 532
Corint Verlag, pg 532
Editure Ion Creanga, pg 532
Editura Eminescu, pg 533
Enzyklopadie Verlag, pg 533
Editura Excelsior, pg 533
FF Press, pg 533
Casa de editura Globus, pg 533
Hasefer, pg 533
Editura Humanitas, pg 533
Humanitas Publishing House, pg 533
Editura Institutul European, pg 533
Editura Kriterion SA, pg 534
Lider Verlag, pg 534
Mentor Kiado, pg 534
Editura Meridiane, pg 534
Editura Militara, pg 534
Editura Niculescu, pg 534
Polirom Verlag, pg 535
RAO Publishing Group, pg 535
Saeculum IO, pg 535
Editura Stiintifica, pg 536
Vestala Verlag, pg 536
Vremea Publishers Ltd, pg 536

Russian Federation
Agni Publishing House, pg 537
Aspect Press Ltd, pg 537
BLIC, russko-Baltijskij informaciionnyj centr, AO, pg 537
Izdatelstvo Detskaya Literatura, pg 537
Izdatel'stvo Mordovskogo gosudar stvennogo, pg 538
Izdatelstvo Iskusstvo, pg 538

987

Ladomir Publishing House, pg 539
Ministerstvo Kul 'tury RF, pg 540
Izdatelstvo Molodaya Gvardia, pg 540
Izdatelstvo Mysl, pg 540
Nauka Publishers, pg 540
Izdatel'stvo Nizhegorodskogo Gosudarstvennogo Univ, pg 540
Novosti Izdatel 'stvo, pg 541
Panorama Publishing House, pg 541
Progress Publishers, pg 541
Raduga Publishers, pg 541
Respublika, pg 541
Russkaya Kniga Izdatelstvo (Publishers), pg 541
St Andrew's Biblical Theological College, pg 541
Izdatelstvo Sudostroenie, pg 542
Voyenizdat, pg 542
Izdatelstvo Vysshaya Shkola, pg 543

Saudi Arabia
Dar Al-Shareff for Publishing & Distribution, pg 543

Senegal
CODESRIA (Council for the Development of Social Science Research in Africa), pg 544
Les Nouvelles Editions Africaines du Senegal NEAS, pg 544

Sierra Leone
Sierra Leone University Press, pg 544

Singapore
Archipelago Press, pg 545
Singapore University Press Pte Ltd, pg 548
Taylor & Francis Asia Pacific, pg 548

Slovakia
ARCHA sro Vydavatel 'stro, pg 549
Danubiaprint, pg 549
Luc vydavatelske druzstvo, pg 550
Slo Viet, pg 550
Slovenske pedagogicke nakladateistvo, pg 550
Smena Publishing House, pg 550
VEDA (Vydavatel'stvo Slovenskej akademie vied), pg 551

Slovenia
Cankarjeva Zalozba, pg 551
East West Operation (EWO) Ltd, pg 551
Zalozba Mihelac d o o, pg 552
Zalozba Obzorja d d Maribor, pg 552

South Africa
Jonathan Ball Publishers, pg 552
Bet-El Publishers, pg 553
The Brenthurst Press (Pty) Ltd, pg 553
Educum Publishers Ltd, pg 554
Fernwood Press (Pty) Ltd, pg 554
Galago Publishing Pty Ltd, pg 554
HAUM (Hollandsch Afrikaansche Uitgevers Maatschappij), pg 555
Human & Rousseau (Pty) Ltd, pg 555
Maybuye Books, pg 557
New Africa Books (Pty) Ltd, pg 557
Ravan Press (Pty) Ltd, pg 558
Shuter & Shooter (Pty) Ltd, pg 559

Unisa Press, pg 560
University of Natal Press, pg 560
Van Schaik Publishers, pg 560
Witwatersrand University Press, pg 560

Spain
Publicacions de l'Abadia de Montserrat, pg 561
Acantilado, pg 561
Editorial Acervo SL, pg 561
Editorial Afers, SL, pg 561
Agencia Espanola de Cooperacion, pg 562
Aguilar SA de Ediciones, pg 562
Ediciones Alfar SA, pg 562
Edicions Alfons el Magnanim, Institucio Valenciana d'Estudis i Investigacio, pg 562
Editorial Algazara, pg 562
Alianza Editorial SA, pg 562
Altea, Taurus, Alfaguara SA, pg 563
Arco Libros SL, pg 564
Editorial Ariel SA, pg 564
Biblioteca de Autores Cristianos, pg 564
Baile del Sol, Colectivo Cultural, pg 565
Biblioteca de Catalunya, pg 565
Editorial Biblioteca Nueva SL, pg 565
Cabildo Insular de Gran Canaria Departamento de Ediciones, pg 566
Carroggio SA de Ediciones, pg 566
Casa de Velazquez, pg 566
Edicios do Castro, pg 566
Ediciones Catedra SA, pg 566
Celeste Ediciones, pg 567
Centro de Estudios Politicos Y Constitucionales, pg 567
Editora Comercial de Publicaciones, pg 568
Compania Literaria, pg 568
Complutense, SA Editorial, pg 568
Ediciones de la Universidad Complutense de Madrid, pg 568
Comunidad Autonoma de Madrid, Servicio de Documentacion y Publicaciones, pg 568
Ediciones Cristiandad, pg 569
Curial Edicions Catalanes SA, pg 569
Rafael Dalmau, Editor, pg 569
Editorial Deimos, SL, pg 569
Ediciones Destino SA, pg 569
Dilagro SA, pg 569
Ediciones Diputacion de Salamanca, pg 570
Diputacion Provincial de Malaga, pg 570
Diputacion Provincial de Sevilla, Servicio de Publicaciones, pg 570
Ediciones Doce Calles SL, pg 570
Editorial Don Quijote, pg 570
Editorial EDAF SA, pg 571
EDERSA (Editoriales de Derecho Reunidas SA), pg 571
EDHASA (Editora y Distribuidora Hispano-Americana SA), pg 571
Edicins Camacuc, pg 571
Editorial Everest SA, pg 572
Emece Editores, pg 573
Ediciones Encuentro SA, pg 573
Editorial Espasa-Calpe SA, pg 573
Instituto de Estudios Riojanos, pg 574
Institut d'Estudis Vallencs (IEV), pg 574
Eumo Editorial, pg 574
EUNSA (Ediciones Universidad de Navarra SA), pg 574

Fondo de Cultura Economica de Espana, SL, pg 574
Fundacion de Estudios Libertarios Anselmo Lorenzo, pg 575
Fundacion Marcelino Botin, pg 575
Galaxia SA Editorial, pg 575
Vicent Garcia Editores, SA, pg 575
Ediciones Garriga SA, pg 575
Generalitat de Catalunya Diari Oficial de la Generalitat vern, pg 575
Editorial Gredos SA, pg 576
Guadalquivir SL Ediciones, pg 576
Ibaizabal Edelvives SA, pg 577
Publicaciones ICCE, pg 577
Institucion Fernando el Catolico de la Excma Diputacion de Zaragoza, pg 578
Ediciones Istmo SA, pg 579
Joyas Bibliograficas SA, pg 579
Junta de Castilla y Leon Consejeria de Educacion y Cultura, pg 579
Editorial Juventud SA, pg 579
Editorial Labor SA, pg 579
Editorin Laiovento SL, pg 579
Ediciones Libertarias/Prodhufi SA, pg 580
Llibres del Segle, pg 580
Lunwerg Editores, SA, pg 580
Antonio Machado, SA, pg 580
Ediciones Maeva, pg 581
Editorial Mediterrania SL, pg 582
Editorial Moll SL, pg 582
Mundo Negro Editorial, pg 583
Munoz Moya Editor, pg 583
Editorial la Muralla SA, pg 583
Editorial Nerea SA, pg 584
Editorial 92 SA, pg 584
Noguer y Caralt Editores SA, pg 584
Nueva Acropolis, pg 584
Ediciones Oceano Grupo SA, pg 584
Oikos-Tau SA Ediciones, pg 584
Ediciones del Oriente y del Mediterraneo, pg 585
Pages Editors, SL, pg 585
Pais Vasco Servicio Central de Publicaciones, pg 585
Ediciones Palabra SA, pg 585
Pearson Educacion S A, pg 586
Editorial Playor SA, pg 587
Plaza y Janes Editores SA, pg 587
Polifemo, Ediciones, pg 587
Prensas Universitarias de Zaragoza, pg 587
Editorial Presencia Gitana, pg 587
Instituto Provincial de Investigaciones y Estudios Toledanos, pg 588
Publicaciones de la Universidad Pontificia Comillas-Madrid, pg 588
Quaderns Crema SA, pg 588
Editora Regional de Murcia - ERM, pg 588
Ediciones Rialp SA, pg 589
Riquelme y Vargas Ediciones SL, pg 589
Editorial Roasa SL, pg 589
Editorial San Martin, pg 589
Universidad de Santiago de Compostela, pg 589
Servicio de Publicaciones Universidad de Cadiz, pg 590
Siglo XXI de Espana Editores SA, pg 590
Signament I Comunicacio, SL Signament Edicions, pg 590
Ediciones Siguemo SA, pg 590
Silex Ediciones, pg 590
Editorial Sintesis, SA, pg 590
Edicions 62, pg 591

Grup 62, pg 591
Ramon Sopena SA, pg 591
Axel Springer Publicaciones, pg 591
Stanley Editorial, pg 591
Ediciones Tabapress, SA, pg 592
Editorial Tecnos SA, pg 592
Ediciones Temas de Hoy, SA, pg 592
Editorial Sal Terrae, pg 592
Editorial Thassalia, SA, pg 592
Ediciones de la Torre, pg 593
Trea Ediciones, SL, pg 593
Trotta SA Editorial, pg 593
Turner Publicaciones, pg 593
Tusquets Editores, pg 593
Universidad de Granada, pg 594
Universidad de Malaga, pg 594
Ediciones Universidad de Salamanca, pg 594
Universidad de Valladolid Secretariado de Publicaciones e Intercambio Editorial, pg 594
Publicacions de la Universitat de Barcelona, pg 594
Universitat de Valencia Servei de Publicacions, pg 594
Parlamento Vasco, pg 595
Javier Vergara Editor SA, pg 595
Editorial Vicens-Vives, pg 595
Edicions Xerais de Galicia, pg 596
Xunta de Galicia, pg 596

Sri Lanka
Karunaratne & Sons Ltd, pg 597
KVG de Silva & Sons, pg 597
Lake House Investments Ltd, pg 597
Swarna Hansa Foundation, pg 598

Sudan
Khartoum University Press, pg 598

Suriname
Stichting Wetenschappelijke Informatie, pg 599
Vaco NV Uitgeversmij, pg 599

Sweden
Allt om Hobby AB, pg 600
Bokforlaget Bra Bocker AB, pg 600
Bokforlaget Cordia AB, pg 600
Carlsson Bokfoerlag AB, pg 601
Fischer & Co, pg 602
Bengt Forsbergs Foerlag AB, pg 602
Gidlunds Bokforlag, pg 602
Liber AB, pg 604
Mezopotamya Publishing & Distribution, pg 604
Bokfoerlaget Naturoch Kultur, pg 604
Bokforlaget Nya Doxa AB, pg 605
Ordfront Foerlag AB, pg 605
Bokforlaget Prisma, pg 605
Stroemberg B&T Forlag AB, pg 606
Svenska Foerlaget liv & ledarskap ab, pg 607
Wahlstrom & Widstrand, pg 607
Zindermans AB, pg 607

Switzerland
Archivio Storico Ticinese, pg 608
Armenia Editions, pg 608
Athenaeum Verlag AG, pg 608
Augustin-Verlag, pg 608
Editions de la Baconniere SA, pg 609
H R Balmer AG Verlag, pg 609
Berichthaus Verlag, Dr Conrad Ulrich, pg 609

PUBLISHERS

Cahiers de la Renaissance Vaudoise, pg 610
Edizioni Casagrande SA, pg 611
Christoph Merian Verlag, pg 611
Chronos Verlag, pg 611
Edizioni Armando Dado, Tipografia Stazione, pg 612
Daimon Verlag AG, pg 612
Librairie Droz SA, pg 612
E Lopfe-Benz AG Rorschach, Graphische Anstalt und Verlag, pg 612
Editions Edita, pg 613
Editions Eisele SA, pg 613
Europa Verlag AG, pg 614
Fondation de l'Encyclopedie de Geneve, pg 614
Frobenius AG, pg 614
G+B Arts International, pg 614
Georg Editeur SA, pg 614
Giampiero Casagrande Editore, pg 614
Graduate Institute of International Studies, pg 615
Editions Francois Grounauer, pg 615
Hallwag AG, pg 615
Helbing und Lichtenhahn Verlag AG, pg 615
Verlag Huber & Co AG, pg 616
Interfrom AG Editions, pg 616
Junod Nicholas, pg 616
Juris Druck & Verlag AG, pg 616
Editions Ketty & Alexandre, pg 617
Kranich-Verlag, Dres AG & H R Bosch-Gwalter, pg 617
Lia rumantscha, pg 618
Maihof Verlag, pg 618
Manesse Verlag GmbH, pg 618
Librairie-Editions J Marguerat, pg 618
Les Editions la Matze, pg 618
Peter Meili & Co, Buchhandluna, pg 619
Editions Minkoff, pg 619
Motovun Book GmbH, pg 619
Neptun-Verlag, pg 620
Les Editions Noir sur Blanc, pg 620
Orell Fuessli Verlag, pg 620
Ostschweiz Druck und Verlag, pg 621
Editions Payot Lausanne, pg 621
Pedrazzini Tipografia, pg 621
Pendo Verlag GmbH, pg 621
PIE-Peter Lang SA, pg 622
Punktum AG, Buchredaktion und Bildarchiv, pg 622
Verlag Friedrich Reinhardt AG, pg 622
Editiones Roche, pg 623
Rodera-Verlag der Cardun AG, pg 623
Rotpunktverlag, pg 623
Sabe AG Verlagsinstitut, pg 623
Scherz Verlag AG, pg 623
Schwabe & Co AG, pg 624
Verlag SOI (Schweizerisches Ost-Institut), pg 625
Editions 24 Heures, pg 626
Der Universitatsverlag Freiburg, pg 626
Wyss Verlag AG Bern, pg 628
Editions Zoe, pg 628

Syrian Arab Republic

Damascus University Press, pg 628
Institut Francais d'Etudes Arabes de Damas, pg 628

Taiwan, Province of China

Art Book Co Ltd, pg 629
Asian Culture Co, pg 629
Chu Liu Book Company, pg 629
Chung Hwa Book Co Ltd, pg 629
Far East Book Co Ltd, pg 630
Kuang Fu Book Co Ltd, pg 630
Laureate Book Co Ltd, pg 631
Linking Publishing Company Ltd, pg 631
National Museum of History, pg 631
National Palace Museum, pg 631
SMC Publishing Inc, pg 632
World Book Co Ltd, pg 632
Yuan Liou Publishing Co, Ltd, pg 632

United Republic of Tanzania

DUP (1996) Ltd, pg 633
Eastern Africa Publications Ltd, pg 633
Ndanda Mission Press, pg 634
Tanzania Publishing House, pg 634

Thailand

New Generation Publishing Co Ltd, pg 635
Ruamsarn (1977) Co Ltd, pg 635
Sang Dad Publishing Company Ltd, pg 635
Thai Watana Panich Co, Ltd, pg 636

Trinidad & Tobago

Joan Bacchus-Xavier, pg 636
Inprint Caribbean Ltd, pg 637

Tunisia

Alyssa Editions, pg 637
Arcs Editions, pg 637
Academie Tunisienne des Sciences, des Lettres et des Arts Beit El Hekma, pg 637
Editions Bouslama, pg 637
Dar Arabia Lil Kitab, pg 637
Faculte des Sciences Humaines et Sociales de Tunis, pg 638
Maison d'Edition Mohamed Ali Hammi, pg 638
Les Editions de l'Arbre, pg 638
Maison Tunisienne de l'Edition, pg 638
Publications de la Fondation Temimi pour la Recherche Scientifique et L'Information, pg 638

Turkey

Altin Kitaplar Yayinevi, pg 638
Arkeoloji Ve Sanat Yayinlari, pg 639
Ataturk Kultur, Dil ve Tarih, Yusek Kurumu Baskanligi, pg 639
Dost Kitabevi Yayinlari, pg 639
Ezel Erverdi (Dergah Yayinlari AS) Muessese Muduru, pg 640
IKI NOKTA Research Press & Publications Industry & Trade Ltd, pg 640
Iletisim Yayinlari, pg 640
Isis Yayin Tic ve San Ltd, pg 640
Kubbealti Akademisi Kultur ve Sasat Vakfi, pg 640
Payel Yayinevi, pg 641
Remzi Kitabevi, pg 641
Sabah Kitaplari, pg 641
Toker Yayinlari, pg 641
Turkish Republic - Ministry of Culture, pg 641
Kabalci Yayinevi, pg 642

Uganda

Centre for Basic Research, pg 642
Fountain Publishers Ltd, pg 642

Ukraine

Naukova Dumka Publishers, pg 643
Osnovy Publishers, pg 643
Osvita, pg 643

United Arab Emirates

Motivate Publishing, pg 644

United Kingdom

ABC-CLIO, pg 644
Acair Ltd, pg 645
Alun Books, pg 646
The Ampersand Press (Cl) Ltd, pg 647
Andromeda Oxford Ltd, pg 647
Appletree Press Ltd, pg 648
Argyll Publishing, pg 648
Aris & Phillips Ltd, pg 648
Arms & Armour Press, pg 648
Arnold, pg 648
Ashgate Publishing Ltd, pg 649
Ashmolean Museum Publications, pg 650
The Athlone Press Ltd, pg 650
Atlantic Transport Publishers, pg 650
Aulis Publishers, pg 651
Avero Publications Ltd, pg 651
Batsford Ltd, pg 652
BBC Worldwide Publishers, pg 653
BCA, pg 653
Bellew Publishing Co Ltd, pg 653
Berg Publishers, pg 654
Berghahn Books Ltd, pg 654
Birlinn Ltd, pg 655
Black Ace Books, pg 655
Blackstaff Press, pg 655
Blackwell Publishers, pg 655
Blandford Publishing Ltd, pg 656
Bloomsbury Publishing PLC, pg 656
Blorenge Books, pg 656
The Book Guild Ltd, pg 657
Book Packaging & Marketing, pg 657
Bookmarks Publications, pg 657
Books International, pg 657
Books of Zimbabwe Publishing Co (Pvt) Ltd, pg 657
Boydell & Brewer Ltd, pg 658
Brassey's UK Ltd, pg 658
Breedon Books Publishing Company Ltd, pg 659
Brewin Books Ltd, pg 659
Bridge Books, pg 659
The British Academy, pg 659
British Library Publications, pg 660
The Brown Reference Group PLC, pg 660
Bryntirion Press, pg 661
Cambridge University Press, pg 662
Canongate Books Ltd, pg 663
Carlton Publishing Group, pg 664
Jon Carpenter Publishing, pg 664
Frank Cass Publishers, pg 664
Cassell & Co, pg 664
Kyle Cathie Ltd, pg 665
Causeway Press Ltd, pg 665
Chadwyck-Healey Ltd, pg 666
Chartered Institute of Library & Information Professionals in Scotland, pg 666
James Clarke & Co Ltd, pg 668
Cockbird Press, pg 669
Colourpoint Books, pg 669
Compendium Publishing, pg 670
Constable & Robinson Ltd, pg 670
Constable Publishers, pg 670
The Continuum International Publishing Group Ltd, pg 670
Leo Cooper, pg 671
Cottage Publications, pg 671
Countryside Books, pg 671
Countyvise Ltd, pg 671
CTBI Publications, pg 672
James Currey Ltd, pg 673
Darf Publishers Ltd, pg 674
Christopher Davies Publishers Ltd, pg 674
Andre Deutsch Ltd, pg 675
John Donald Publishers Ltd, pg 675
Dorling Kindersley Ltd, pg 676
Dunedin Academic Press, pg 676
Edinburgh University Press Ltd, pg 677
Elm Publications, pg 678
The Erskine Press, pg 679
The Eurospan Group, pg 680
Evans Brothers Ltd, pg 680
Ex Libris Press, pg 680
Faber & Faber Ltd, pg 681
Facts On File, pg 681
Firebird Books Ltd, pg 682
Forth Naturalist & Historian, pg 683
Fourth Estate Ltd, pg 683
Freedom Press, pg 684
Frontier Publishing, pg 684
Gale Research, pg 685
Garnet Publishing Ltd, pg 685
Genesis Publications Ltd, pg 686
E J W Gibb Memorial Trust, pg 687
Glasgow City Libraries Publications, pg 687
GMP Publishers Ltd, pg 687
Golden Cockerel Press Ltd, pg 688
Gollancz/Witherby, pg 688
Granta Books, pg 689
The Greek Bookshop, pg 689
Greenhill Books/Lionel Leventhal Ltd, pg 689
Gresham Books Ltd, pg 690
Gwasg Prifysgol Cymru, pg 690
Gwasg Gwenffrwd, pg 690
Hakluyt Society, pg 691
Peter Halban Publishers Ltd, pg 691
Robert Hale Ltd, pg 691
The Hambledon Press, pg 691
Hamish Hamilton Ltd, pg 691
Hamlyn, pg 691
HarperCollins Publishers, pg 692
Harvard University Press, pg 692
The Harvill Press Ltd, pg 693
Hawthorns Publications Ltd, pg 693
Haynes Publishing, pg 693
Headline Book Publishing Ltd, pg 693
William Heinemann Ltd, pg 694
Helicon Publishing Ltd, pg 694
Helion & Co, pg 694
Helm Information Ltd, pg 694
Hendon Publishing Co Ltd, pg 695
Ian Henry Publications Ltd, pg 695
Heraldry Today, pg 695
Hodder & Stoughton General, pg 696
Honeyglen Publishing Ltd, pg 697
C Hurst & Co (Publishers) Ltd, pg 698
Hutton Press Ltd, pg 698
Icon Press, pg 698
Institute of Irish Studies, The Queens University of Belfast, pg 699
Institution of Electrical Engineers, pg 700
Irish Texts Society (Cumann Na Scribeann nGaedhilge), pg 701
Islamic Foundation Publications, pg 701
The Islamic Texts Society, pg 701

SUBJECT INDEX

James & James (Publishers) Ltd, pg 702
John Jones Publishing Ltd, pg 703
Michael Joseph Ltd, pg 703
Karnak House, pg 703
Hilda King Educational, pg 704
Ladybird Books, pg 705
Landy Publishing, pg 706
Lang Syne Publishers Ltd, pg 706
Letterbox Library, pg 707
Libris Ltd, pg 707
Linen Hall Library, pg 707
The Littman Library of Jewish Civilization, pg 708
Liverpool University Press, pg 708
Luath Press Ltd, pg 709
The Lutterworth Press, pg 709
Macmillan Audio Books, pg 710
Macmillan Reference Ltd, pg 710
Mainstream Publishing Co (Edinburgh) Ltd, pg 711
Manchester University Press, pg 711
Maney Publishing, pg 711
The Mansk Svenska Publishing Co Ltd, pg 711
Peter Marcan Publications, pg 711
Marcham Books, pg 711
Marshall Editions Ltd, pg 712
Adam Matthew Publications, pg 712
Willem A Meeuws Publisher, pg 713
The Merlin Press Ltd, pg 713
Methuen Publishing Ltd, pg 714
Harvey Miller Publishers, pg 714
Mirabel Books Ltd, pg 715
E J Morten (Publishers), pg 715
Motilal (UK) Books of India, pg 715
MQ Publications Ltd, pg 716
Murchison's Pantheon Ltd, pg 716
John Murray (Publishers) Ltd, pg 716
National Archives of Scotland, pg 716
National Library of Scotland, pg 717
National Portrait Gallery Publications, pg 717
National Trust, pg 717
Nelson Thornes Ltd, pg 718
Newpro UK Ltd, pg 719
NMS Publishing Ltd, pg 719
W W Norton & Company Ltd, pg 720
Oakwood Press, pg 720
Michael O'Mara Books Ltd, pg 721
Oneworld Publications, pg 721
Orion Publishing Group Ltd, pg 722
The Orkney Press Ltd, pg 722
Orpheus Books Ltd, pg 722
Osborne Books Ltd, pg 722
Osprey Publishing Ltd, pg 722
Owl Books, pg 722
Oxford University Press, pg 723
Palgrave Publishers Ltd, pg 723
Parapress Ltd, pg 724
Paternoster Publishing, pg 724
Pathfinder London, pg 724
Pearson Education, pg 725
Pearson Education Europe, Mideast & Africa, pg 725
Peepal Tree Press, pg 725
Pen & Sword Books Ltd, pg 725
Phaidon Press Ltd, pg 726
Pickering & Chatto (Publishers) Ltd, pg 727
Pitkin Unichrome Ltd, pg 728
Pluto Press, pg 728
Poetry Wales Press Ltd, pg 729
Polo Publishing, pg 729
Polybooks Ltd, pg 729
Polygon, pg 729
Porthill Publishers, pg 730

Prim-Ed Publishing UK Ltd, pg 730
Profile Books Ltd, pg 731
Quartet Books Ltd, pg 731
Quartz Editions, pg 732
Quentin Books Ltd, pg 732
Quiller Publishing Ltd, pg 732
Quintet Publishing Ltd, pg 732
Ramboro Books Plc, pg 732
Ramsay Head Press, pg 732
Reaktion Books Ltd, pg 733
Roadmaster Publishing, pg 735
Rough Guides Ltd, pg 735
Roundhouse Publishing Ltd, pg 736
Routledge, pg 736
Routledge Curzon, pg 736
The Rubicon Press, pg 737
Sage Publications Ltd, pg 737
Saint Andrew Press, pg 737
The Salariya Book Co Ltd, pg 738
The Saltire Society, pg 738
SB Publications, pg 738
Scarthin Books, pg 738
School of Oriental & African Studies, pg 739
Scottish Cultural Press, pg 739
Scottish Text Society, pg 740
Seren, pg 740
Serif, pg 740
Shearwater Press Ltd, pg 741
Sheed & Ward Ltd, pg 741
Shelfmark Books, pg 741
Shepheard-Walwyn (Publishers) Ltd, pg 741
Shire Publications Ltd, pg 741
SHU Press, pg 742
Sidgwick & Jackson Ltd, pg 742
Silver Link Publishing Ltd, pg 742
Charles Skilton Ltd, pg 742
Skoob Russell Square, pg 742
Smith Settle Ltd, pg 743
Souvenir Press Ltd, pg 743
SPA Books Ltd, pg 744
Spellmount Ltd Publishers, pg 744
Stacey International, pg 745
The Stationery Office, pg 745
Stenlake Publishing, pg 745
Supportive Learning Publications, pg 746
Sutton Publishing Ltd, pg 746
Sydney Jary Ltd, pg 746
I B Tauris & Co Ltd, pg 747
Thames & Hudson Ltd, pg 748
Thistle Press, pg 748
Thoemmes Press, pg 748
Toucan Press, pg 749
Transedition Ltd, pg 749
Tuckwell Press Ltd, pg 749
Two-Can Publishing Ltd, pg 750
UCL Press Ltd, pg 751
Ulster Historical Foundation, pg 751
University of Exeter Press, pg 751
University of Wales Press, pg 751
Vallentine, Mitchell & Co Ltd, pg 752
Verso, pg 752
Viking, pg 753
Virago Press, pg 753
Virgin Publishing Ltd, pg 753
Voltaire Foundation Ltd, pg 753
The Warburg Institute, pg 754
Ward Lock Educational Co Ltd, pg 754
Welsh Academic Press, pg 755
Westview Press, pg 755
Wharncliffe Publishing Ltd, pg 755
White Cockade Publishing, pg 755
Neil Wilson Publishing Ltd, pg 757
Wimbledon Publishing Company Ltd, pg 757
The Windrush Press Ltd, pg 757
Wordsworth Editions Ltd, pg 758
Wordwright Publishing, pg 758

World Microfilms Publications Ltd, pg 758
Yale University Press London, pg 759
Anglia Young Books, pg 759

Uruguay
Editorial Arca SRL, pg 760
Arpoador, pg 760
Ediciones de Juan Darien, pg 760
Fundacion de Cultura Universitaria, pg 760
Linardi y Risso Libreria, pg 760
A Monteverde y Cia SA, pg 760
Luis A Retta Libros, pg 761
Rosebud Ediciones, pg 761
Ediciones Sol del Sur, pg 761
Ediciones Trilce, pg 761

Uzbekistan
Izdatelstvo Uzbekistan, pg 761

Venezuela
Alfadil Ediciones, pg 761
Armitano Editores CA, pg 761
Editorial Ateneo de Caracas, pg 762
Monte Avila Editores Latinoamericana CA, pg 762
Biblioteca Ayacucho, pg 762

Yugoslavia
Alfa-Narodna Knjiga, pg 764
Jugoslavijapublik, pg 764
Narodna Biblioteka Srbije, pg 764
Nolit Publishing House, pg 765
Panorama NIJP/ID Grigorije Bozovic, pg 765
Izdavacko Preduzece Matice Srpske, pg 765
Srpska Knjizevna Zadruga, pg 765
Vuk Karadzic, pg 766

Zambia
Apple Books, pg 766
Historical Association of Zambia, pg 766
Zambia Educational Publishing House, pg 767
ZPC Publications, pg 767

Zimbabwe
Academic Books Pvt Ltd, pg 767
College Press Publishers (Pvt) Ltd, pg 768
The Graham Publishing Company (Pvt) Ltd, pg 768
Longman Zimbabwe (Pvt) Ltd, pg 768
Mambo Press, pg 768
National Archives of Zimbabwe, pg 769
University of Zimbabwe Publications, pg 769
Zimbabwe Publishing House (Pvt) Ltd, pg 769
ZRD Trust, pg 770

HOUSE & HOME

Australia
CHOICE Magazine, pg 18
Simon & Schuster Australia Pty Ltd, pg 42
Skills Publishing, pg 42

Belarus
Belaruskaya Encyklapedyya, pg 63

Belgium
Coda, pg 66
Uitgeverij Lannoo NV, pg 70

Bulgaria
Sluntse Publishing House, pg 98

Chile
Publicaciones Lo Castillo SA, pg 101

China
China Light Industry Press, pg 103
Jilin Science & Technology Publishing House, pg 106

Cuba
Editorial Oriente, pg 121

Estonia
Mats Publishers Ltd, pg 140
Sinisukk, pg 140

Finland
SV-Kauppiaskanava Oy, pg 144

France
Editions Alternatives, pg 146
ATP - Packager, pg 149
Editions Didier Carpentier, pg 152
Editions d'Organisation, pg 161
Editions Filipacchi-Sonodip, pg 164
Flammarion SA, pg 164
Folklore Comtois, pg 164
LT Editions-J Lanore-H Laurens, pg 172
Editions Mango, pg 174
Editions Charles Massin et Cie, pg 175
Editions Norma, pg 177
Nouvelles Editions Francaises, pg 178
Sofradif Editions Philippe Auzou, pg 185
Soline, pg 186
Terre Vivante, pg 187
Ulisse Edition, pg 188

Germany
Ars Edition GmbH, pg 195
Eberhargd Blottner Verlag, pg 204
Verlag Georg D W Callwey GmbH & Co, pg 208
Columbus Verlag Paul Oestergaard GmbH, pg 211
Compact Verlag GmbH, pg 211
DuMont Monte, pg 219
Egmont vgs verlagsgesellschaft mbH, pg 221
Fraunhofer IRB Verlag Fraunhofer Informationszentrum Raum und Bau, pg 229
Mary Hahn's Kochbuchverlag, pg 236
Hammonia-Verlag GmbH Fachverlag der Wohnungswirtschaft, pg 237
Jahreszeiten-Verlag GmbH, pg 246
Franckh-Kosmos Verlags-GmbH & Co, pg 252
Landbuch-Verlagsgesellschaft mbH, pg 255
Mosaik Verlag GmbH, pg 265
Naumann & Goebel Verlagsgesellschaft mbH, pg 267
Neumann Verlag, pg 268
Oekobuch Verlag & Versand GmbH, pg 269

PUBLISHERS

Passavia Druckerei GmbH, Verlag, pg 271
Verlag Th Schaefer im Vicentz Verlag KG, pg 282
Dr Wolfgang Schwarze Verlag, pg 286
Verlag Deutsches Volksheimstaettenwerk GmbH, pg 299
Gert Wohlfarth GmbH Verlag Fachtechnik & Mercator Verlag, Verlag Puppen & Spielzeug, pg 304
WRS Verlag Wirtschaft, Recht und Steuern GmbH & Co KG, pg 304

Hong Kong
Press Mark Media Ltd, pg 321

Hungary
Ifjusagi Lap-eskonyvkiado Vallalat, pg 324
Park Konyvkiado Kft (Park Publisher), pg 326

Iceland
Frodi Ltd, pg 328

India
Nem Chand & Brothers, pg 344
Pustak Mahal, pg 346

Israel
Classikaletet, pg 366

Italy
Umberto Allemandi & C SRL, pg 375
Di Baio Editore SpA, pg 385
Ernesto Gremese Editore SRL, pg 391
Macro Edizioni, pg 397
Giorgio Mondadori & Associati, pg 399
Mundici & Zanetti srl, pg 400

Jamaica
Association of Development Agencies, pg 412
Jamaica Publishing House Ltd, pg 413

Japan
Gakken Co Ltd, pg 416
Kodansha, pg 420
Nagaoka Shoten Company Ltd, pg 421
Seibido Shuppan Company Ltd, pg 424
Shufunotomo sha Co Ltd, pg 426

Republic of Korea
O Neul Publishing Co, pg 439
Suhagsa, pg 440

Latvia
Avots, pg 441
Preses Nams, pg 442

Lithuania
Sviesa Publishers, pg 446

Mexico
Editorial Armonia SA, pg 458
Editorial Limusa SA de CV, pg 463
Ediciones Suromex SA, pg 467
Editorial Trillas SA de CV, pg 467

Netherlands
Uitgeverij Cantecleer BV, pg 475
Gottmer Uitgevers Groop, pg 477

New Zealand
Barkfire Press, pg 488

Nigeria
Daystar Press (Publishers), pg 498

Poland
Muza SA, pg 518

Portugal
Edicoes ELO, pg 524
Latina Livraria, pg 526
Meriberica/Liber, pg 527

Romania
Editura Niculescu, pg 534

Russian Federation
Dom, Izdatel'stvo sovetskogo deskkogo fonda im & 1 Lenina, pg 537
Panorama Publishing House, pg 541
Permskaja Kniga, pg 541

Slovakia
Priroda, pg 550

South Africa
Human & Rousseau (Pty) Ltd, pg 555

Spain
Editorial Astri SA, pg 564
Libsa Editorial SA, pg 580

Sweden
ICA bokforlag, pg 603
Natur och Kultur/LTs foerlag, pg 604
Bokforlaget Prisma, pg 605
Bokforlaget Semic AB, pg 606

Tunisia
Les Editions de l'Arbre, pg 638

Turkey
Kok Yayincilik, pg 640

Ukraine
Urozaj, pg 643

United Kingdom
Apple Press, pg 648
Batsford Ltd, pg 652
Mitchell Beazley, pg 653
Bloomsbury Publishing PLC, pg 656
Cassell & Co, pg 664
Dorling Kindersley Ltd, pg 676
Elliot Right Way Books, pg 678
Foulsham Publishers, pg 683
HarperCollins Publishers, pg 692
Haynes Publishing, pg 693
Laurence King Publishing Ltd, pg 704
Frances Lincoln Ltd, pg 707
Kenneth Mason Publications Ltd, pg 712
Merehurst Publishers, pg 713
New Holland Publishers (UK) Ltd, pg 718
New Leaf Books Ltd, pg 719
Pavilion Books Ltd, pg 724
Quarto Publishing plc, pg 731
Quiller Publishing Ltd, pg 732
Quintet Publishing Ltd, pg 732
The Reader's Digest Association Ltd, pg 733
Ryland Peters & Small Ltd, pg 737
Salamander Books Ltd, pg 738
Shire Publications Ltd, pg 741
Sutton Publishing Ltd, pg 746
Ward Lock Ltd, pg 754

HOW-TO

Argentina
Editorial Acme SA, pg 3
Centro Editor de America Latina SA, pg 4
Angel Estrada y Cia SA, pg 6
Editorial Planeta Argentina SAIC, pg 8
Editorial Sopena Argentina SACI e I, pg 9

Australia
Ashling Books, pg 12
Books for Our Times, pg 16
Bridge To Peace Publications, pg 16
Crista International, pg 19
Elephas Books Pty Ltd, pg 21
Great Western Press Pty Ltd, pg 24
Kerri Hamer, pg 25
Hospitality Books, pg 26
Mayne Publishing, pg 32
Palms Press, pg 36
Jurriaan Plesman, pg 38
Press for Success, pg 38
R & R Publications Marketing P/L, pg 39
Simon & Schuster Australia Pty Ltd, pg 42
Skills Publishing, pg 42
Tomorrow Publications, pg 45
Vista Publications, pg 47
Wileman Publications, pg 47
Worsley Press, pg 48

Austria
Johannes Heyn, Gert und Volkmar Zechner, pg 52
Linde Verlag Wien GmbH, pg 54

Brazil
Ediouro Publicacoes, SA, pg 81
Editora Globo SA, pg 84
Editora Marco Zero Ltda, pg 87

Bulgaria
Aratron, IK, pg 94
Kibea Publishing Co, pg 96

Cameroon
Editions CLE, pg 99

China
Beijing Publishing House, pg 102
CITIC Publishing House, pg 104
Commercial Press (Hong Kong) Ltd, pg 104
Fudan University Press, pg 105
Heilongjiang Science & Technology Press, pg 106
Jilin Science & Technology Publishing House, pg 106
Zhejiang University Press, pg 110

Costa Rica
Centro Agronomico Tropical de Investigacion y Ensenanza (CATIE), pg 115

SUBJECT INDEX

Croatia
Mladost d d Izdavacku graficku i informaticku djelatnost, pg 119
Skolska Knjiga, pg 120

Czech Republic
Prace, pg 127
Svojtka & Co, pg 128

Denmark
Aschehoug Dansk Forlag A/S, pg 130
Borgens Forlag A/S, pg 130
Cicero-Chr Erichsens, pg 131
Gyldendalske Boghandel - Nordisk Forlag A/S, pg 132
Nyt Nordisk Forlag Arnold Busck A/S, pg 134
Square Dance Partners Forlag, pg 135

Estonia
Sinisukk, pg 140

Finland
Rakentajain Kustannus Oy (Building Publications Ltd), pg 143
Otava Publishing Co Ltd, pg 143
Soederstroem et Co Foerlagsaktiebolag, pg 144

France
Adverbum SARL, pg 146
Editions Albin Michel, pg 146
Alsatia SA, pg 146
Editions Alternatives, pg 146
Editions Amrita SA, pg 147
Editions Belfond, pg 150
Blay-Foldex, pg 151
Blondel La Rougery SARL, pg 151
Editions Bornemann, pg 151
Editions Casterman, pg 153
Chasse Maree-Armen, pg 154
Le Cherche Midi Editeur, pg 154
Editions Chiron, pg 154
Editions du Dauphin, pg 158
De Vecchi Editions SA, pg 158
Editions Delville, pg 158
Georges-Charles Demay, pg 158
Dessain et Tolra SA, pg 159
Doin Editeurs, pg 160
Les Dossiers d'Aquitaine, pg 160
Edisud, pg 161
Editions d'Organisation, pg 161
Editions Grund, pg 161
Les Editions de l'Epargne, pg 162
Editions Fivedit, pg 164
Association Frank, pg 165
Editions Jean Paul Gisserot, pg 166
Editions Grancher, pg 166
Pierre Horay Editeur, pg 168
Editions du Jaguar, pg 170
Le Jour, Editeur, pg 170
Le Livre de Paris, pg 173
LLB France (Ligue pour la Lecture de la Bible), pg 173
Editions Lyonnaises d'Art et d'Histoire, pg 174
Editions Mango, pg 174
Editions Franck Mercier, pg 176
Muller Edition, pg 176
Editions Odile Jacob, pg 178
Les Presses du Management, pg 181
Editions du Puits Fleuri, pg 182
Guide Rosenwald, pg 183
Editions du Rouergue, pg 183
Editions Sand et Tchou SA, pg 183
Editions Sang de la Terre, pg 183
Selection du Reader's Digest SA, pg 184

991

SUBJECT INDEX

Editions Selection J Jacobs SA, pg 184
Editions du Seuil, pg 185
Siloe - Kerdore, pg 185
Societe Nouveaux Loisirs, pg 185
Sofradif Editions Philippe Auzou, pg 185
Editions Sud Ouest, pg 186
Top Editions, pg 188
Editions Trois Fontaines, pg 188
Editions de Vergeures, pg 189

French Polynesia

Scoop/Au Vent des Iles, pg 190

Germany

ALS-Verlag GmbH, pg 193
Arcus-Medien Wolfgang Steinhardt, pg 194
Bertelsmann Lexikon Verlag GmbH, pg 201
Bielefelder Verlagsanstalt GmbH & Co KG Richard Kaselowsky, pg 203
Verlag Georg D W Callwey GmbH & Co, pg 208
Christophorus-Verlag GmbH, pg 210
Compact Verlag GmbH, pg 211
Verlag Werner Dausien, pg 212
Deutscher Taschenbuch Verlag GmbH & Co KG (dtv), pg 215
Droemersche Verlagsanstalt Th Knaur Nachfolger GmbH & Co, pg 218
DuMont Monte, pg 219
Ehrenwirth Verlag, pg 221
Ehrenwirth Verlag GmbH, pg 221
Engel & Bengel Verlag, pg 222
Englisch Verlag GmbH, pg 222
Falken-Verlag GmbH, pg 227
Rita G Fischer Verlag, pg 228
Verlag Freies Geistesleben, pg 230
Margarethe Freudenberger - selbstverlag fur jedermann, pg 230
Gabal-Verlag GmbH, pg 231
Georgi GmbH, pg 232
Wilhelm Goldmann Verlag GmbH, pg 233
Haag und Herchen Verlag GmbH, pg 235
Wilhelm Heyne Verlag, pg 240
Jahreszeiten-Verlag GmbH, pg 246
Karl Robert Langewiesche Nachfolger Hans Koester KG, pg 256
Verlag Gerald Leue, pg 257
Gustav Luebbe Verlag, pg 259
Moench Verlagsgesellschaft mbH, pg 264
Naumann & Goebel Verlagsgesellschaft mbH, pg 267
Verlag Neue Stadt GmbH, pg 267
Neuer Honos Verlag GmbH, pg 267
Paul Pietsch Verlage GmbH & Co, pg 273
Projektion J Buch- und Musikverlag GmbH, pg 275
Propylaeen Verlag, Zweigniederlassung Berlin der Ullstein Buchverlage GmbH, pg 275
Eugen Salzer-Verlag GmbH & Co KG, pg 281
Sportverlag Berlin GmbH SVB, pg 288
J F Steinkopf Verlag GmbH, pg 289
Traditionell Bogenschiessen Verlag Angelika Hornig, pg 294
Verlag Eugen Ulmer GmbH & Co, pg 295

Wehr & Wissen Verlagsgesellschaft mbH, pg 300
WEKA Firmengruppe GmbH & Co KG, pg 301

Ghana

Adaex Educational Publications Ltd, pg 306
Anowuo Educational Publications, pg 306
World Literature Project, pg 308

Greece

Diavlos, pg 309
Editions Moressopoulos, pg 313

Hong Kong

Breakthrough Ltd - Breakthrough Publishers, pg 318
Electronic Technology Publishing Co Ltd, pg 319
Ling Kee Publishing Group, pg 320
Modern Electronic & Computing Publishing Co Ltd, pg 338
Publications (Holdings) Ltd, pg 321
Unicorn Books Ltd, pg 322

Hungary

Kulturtrade, pg 325
Novorg Kiado, pg 326

Iceland

Bokautgafan Orn og Orlygur ehf, pg 327
Frodi Ltd, pg 328
Skjaldborg Ltd, pg 328

India

Atma Ram & Sons, pg 331
Diamond Comics (P) Ltd, pg 336
General Book Depot, pg 337
Hind Pocket Books Private Ltd, pg 338
Orient Paperbacks, pg 345
Rajendra Publishing House Pvt Ltd, pg 347
Sultan Chand & Sons Pvt Ltd, pg 351
Vision Books Pvt Ltd, pg 353

Indonesia

Gramedia, pg 355
Katalis PT Bina Mitra Plaosan, pg 356

Ireland

The Hannon Press, pg 361
On Stream Publications Ltd, pg 363
Ossian Publications, pg 363

Israel

Bitan Publishers Ltd, pg 365
Boostan Publishing House, pg 366
Classikaletet, pg 366
Dekel Publishing House, pg 366
Gefen Publishing House Ltd, pg 367
Karni Publishers Ltd, pg 369
Keter Publishing House Ltd, pg 369
Massada Press Ltd, pg 370
Massada Publishers Ltd, pg 370
Prolog Publishing House, pg 371
R Sirkis Publishers Ltd, pg 372
Yedioth Ahronoth Books, pg 373

Italy

Franco Angeli SRL, pg 375
Gruppo Editoriale Armenia SpA, pg 376

Verlagsanstalt Athesia, pg 377
Casa Editrice Libraria Ulrico Hoepli SpA, pg 380
Giovanni De Vecchi Editore SpA, pg 384
Edizioni Mediterranee SRL, pg 387
Edizioni Futuro SRL, pg 389
Giunti Publishing Group, pg 391
Ernesto Gremese Editore SRL, pg 391
Hermes Edizioni SRL, pg 392
Longanesi & C, pg 396
Macro Edizioni, pg 397
Arnoldo Mondadori Editore SpA, pg 399
Newton Compton Editori SRL, pg 401
Edizioni San Paolo SRL, pg 407
Sperling e Kupfer Editori SpA, pg 408
Sugarco Edizioni SRL, pg 409
TEA Tascabili degli Editori Associati SpA, pg 409
Vinciana Editrice sas, pg 411

Japan

Bijutsu Shuppan-Sha, Ltd, pg 415
Dobun Shoin, pg 416
Dohosha Publishing Co Ltd, pg 416
Genko-Sha, pg 416
Hoikusha Publishing Co Ltd, pg 417
Japan Broadcast Publishing Co Ltd, pg 418
Kodansha International, pg 420
Nagaoka Shoten Company Ltd, pg 421
Seibido Shuppan Company Ltd, pg 424
Shufunotomo sha Co Ltd, pg 426
Soryusha, pg 426
Tokuma-Shoten, pg 427

Kenya

Action Publishers, pg 430
Space Sellers Ltd, pg 433
Transafrica Press, pg 433
Vipopremo Agencies, pg 433

Republic of Korea

Chung Rim Publishing Co Ltd, pg 435
Gim-Yeong Co, pg 436
Pyeong-hwa Chulpansa, pg 439
Woong Jin Publishing Co Ltd, pg 440

Latvia

Artava Ltd, pg 441
Avots, pg 441

Lebanon

Librairie Orientale sal, pg 443

Lithuania

Tyto Alba Publishers, pg 446

Luxembourg

Guy Binsfeld & Co Sarl, pg 447
Editions Emile Borschette, pg 447

Malaysia

Geetha Publishers Sdn Bhd, pg 452

Mexico

Aconcagua Ediciones y Publicaciones SA, pg 457
Libra Editorial SA de CV, pg 463

Editorial Patria SA de CV, pg 465
Editorial Pax Mexico, pg 465

Monaco

Les Editions du Rocher, pg 469

Morocco

Access International Services, pg 469
Editions Eddif Maroc, pg 469
Editions Oum, pg 470
Editions Services et Informations pour Etudiants, pg 470

Netherlands

Business Contact BV, pg 475
Elmar BV, pg 476
Helmond B. V. Uitgeverij, pg 478
Uitgeverij Ploegsma BV, pg 483
A J G Strengholt's Boeken, Anno 1928, BV, pg 484

New Caledonia

Savannah Editions SARL, pg 488

New Zealand

Barkfire Press, pg 488
Bush Press Communications Ltd, pg 489
David's Marine Books, pg 490
Learning Guides (Writers & Publishers Ltd), pg 492
Words Work, pg 497

Nigeria

Africana-FEP Publishers Ltd, pg 498
Alliance West African Publishers & Co, pg 498
Aromolaran Publishing Co Ltd, pg 498
Cross Continent Press Ltd, pg 498
Educational Research & Study Group, pg 499
Ethiope Publishing Corporation, pg 499
Goldland Business Co Ltd, pg 499
Ilesanmi Press (Educational Publishers) Ltd, pg 499
Kola Sanya Publishing Enterprise, pg 500
New Horn Press Ltd, pg 500
Nwamife Publishers Ltd, pg 500
Onibon-Oje Publishers, pg 501
John West Publications Co Ltd, pg 502

Norway

Gyldendal Norsk Forlag A/S, pg 503
Chr Schibsteds Forlag A/S, pg 505
Teknologisk Forlag, pg 505

Pakistan

Malik Sirajuddin & Sons, pg 507

Peru

Ediciones Brown SA, pg 511

Philippines

Anvil Publishing Inc, pg 512
National Book Store Inc, pg 514
New Day Publishers, pg 514
University of the Philippines Press, pg 515

PUBLISHERS

Poland
Wydawnictwo Podsiedlik-Raniowski i Spolka, pg 519
Wydawnictwo Baturo, pg 521

Portugal
Brasilia Editora (J Carvalho Branco), pg 523
Publicacoes Europa-America Lda, pg 524
Impala, pg 525
Editorial Presenca, pg 528

Puerto Rico
Piedras Press, Inc, pg 531

Romania
Aion Verlag, pg 531
Rentrop & Straton Verlagsgruppe und Wirtschaftsconsulting, pg 535

Russian Federation
Airis Press, pg 537
Dom, Izdatel'stvo sovetskogo deskkogo fonda im & 1 Lenina, pg 537

Singapore
Aquanut Agencies Pte Ltd, pg 545

Slovakia
Priroda, pg 550

Slovenia
Cankarjeva Zalozba, pg 551
Mladinska Knjiga International, pg 552

South Africa
Human & Rousseau (Pty) Ltd, pg 555
Kima Global Publishers, pg 556
Southern Book Publishers (Pty) Ltd, pg 559

Spain
Acento Editorial, pg 561
Aguilar SA de Ediciones, pg 562
Editorial Astri SA, pg 564
Iberico Europea de Ediciones SA, pg 577
Ediciones Martinez-Roca SA, pg 581
Ediciones Mensajero, pg 582
Ediciones Norma SA, pg 584
Ediciones El Pais SA, pg 585
Editorial Paraninfo SA, pg 586
Parramon Ediciones SA, pg 586
Progensa, pg 588
Editores Tecnicos Asociados SA, pg 592
Ediciones Urano, SA, pg 595

Sweden
Bokforlaget Spektra AB, pg 601
ICA bokforlag, pg 603
Informationsfoerlaget AB, pg 603
Johnston & Streiffert Editions, pg 604
Zindermans AB, pg 607

Switzerland
Ariston Editions, pg 608
AT Verlag, pg 608
Dimension World Ltd, pg 612
Hallwag AG, pg 615
Paul Haupt Berne, pg 615
Leonis Verlag, pg 618

Mueller Rueschlikon Verlags AG, pg 619
Orell Fuessli Verlag, pg 620
Verlag Friedrich Reinhardt AG, pg 622

Taiwan, Province of China
Art Book Co Ltd, pg 629
Highlight Publishing Company Ltd, pg 630
Jillion Publishing Co, pg 630
Morning Star Publisher Inc, pg 631
Wei-Chuan Publishing Company Ltd, pg 632
Yuan Liou Publishing Co, Ltd, pg 632

United Republic of Tanzania
East African Publishing House, pg 633

Tunisia
Ceres Editions, pg 637

Turkey
Alkim Kitapcilik-Yayimcilik, pg 638
Soez Yayin/Oyunajans, pg 641

United Kingdom
Amber Books Ltd, pg 646
BCA, pg 653
Blaketon Hall Ltd, pg 656
Bloomsbury Publishing PLC, pg 656
Cardinal Publishing Ltd, pg 663
Cassell & Co, pg 664
Compendium Publishing, pg 670
Computer Step, pg 670
David & Charles Ltd, pg 674
Elliot Right Way Books, pg 678
Faber & Faber Ltd, pg 681
Foulsham Publishers, pg 683
GMC Publications Ltd, pg 687
Green Books Ltd, pg 689
Robert Hale Ltd, pg 691
HarperCollins Publishers, pg 692
Haynes Publishing, pg 693
How To Books Ltd, pg 697
Hugo's Language Books Ltd, pg 697
Law Pack Publishing Ltd, pg 706
Lorenz Books, pg 709
New Holland Publishers (UK) Ltd, pg 718
New Leaf Books Ltd, pg 719
Parapress Ltd, pg 724
David Porteous Editions, pg 729
PRC Publishing Ltd, pg 730
Quarto Publishing plc, pg 731
Quintet Publishing Ltd, pg 732
The Reader's Digest Association Ltd, pg 733
Savitri Books, pg 738
Search Press Ltd, pg 740
Souvenir Press Ltd, pg 743
Stobart Davies Ltd, pg 745
Telegraph Books, pg 748
Ward Lock Ltd, pg 754

Viet Nam
Science & Technics Publishing House, pg 763

Yugoslavia
Alfa-Narodna Knjiga, pg 764
Tehnicka Knjiga, pg 764

SUBJECT INDEX

HUMAN RELATIONS

Argentina
San Pablo, pg 8

Australia
ACER Press, pg 10
Australian Institute of Family Studies (AIFS), pg 13
Joan Blair, pg 15
Bridge To Peace Publications, pg 16
Community Quarterly, pg 18
Crossroad Distributors Pty Ltd, pg 19
Deva Wings Publications, pg 20
Finch Publishing, pg 22
Gnostic Editions, pg 24
Kerri Hamer, pg 25
Hawker Brownlow, pg 25
Jarrah Publications, pg 28
Killara Press, pg 29
Life Planning Foundation of Australia, Inc, pg 30
Little Red Apple Publishing, pg 30
Magabala Books Aboriginal Corporation, pg 31
New Creation Publications Ministries & Resource Centre, pg 34
St Pauls, pg 41
Tertiary Press, pg 44
Thin Rich Press, pg 44
Uniting Education, pg 45
Wileman Publications, pg 47
Windhorse Books, pg 48

Austria
Aarachne Verlag, pg 49
Edition S der OSD, pg 51
Verlag Jungbrunnen - Wiener Spielzeugschachtel GesellschaftmbH, pg 53
Niederosterreichisches Pressehaus Druck- und Verlagsgesellschaft mbH, pg 55

Belgium
Editions De Boeck-Larcier SA, pg 67
Marabout, pg 72
Mardaga, Pierre 12, pg 72
Scissors Books, pg 74

Brazil
Artes e Oficios Editora Ltda, pg 79
Editora Crescer Ltda, pg 81
Editora Elevacao, pg 82
Editora Lidador Ltda, pg 86
Editora Mercuryo Ltda, pg 88
Editora Objetiva Ltda, pg 88
Edit Palavra Magica, pg 89
Pallas Editora e Distribuidora Ltda, pg 89
Paulinas Editorial, pg 89
Editora Perspectiva, pg 89
Summus Editorial Ltda, pg 92
Thex Editora e Distribuidora Ltda, pg 92
Editora Universidade de Brasilia, pg 92
Jorge Zahar Editor, pg 93

Bulgaria
Interpres, pg 96
Kibea Publishing Co, pg 96
Nov Covek Publishing House, pg 97
Sita-MB, pg 98
Sluntse Publishing House, pg 98

Chile
Edeval (Universidad de Valparaiso), pg 100
Editora Nueva Generacion, pg 101
Editorial Texido Ltda, pg 101

China
Beijing Publishing House, pg 102
China Materials Management Publishing House, pg 103
Education Science Publishing House, pg 105
Fudan University Press, pg 105
Guizhou Education Publishing House, pg 106
Knowledge Press, pg 107
Shandong University Press, pg 109

Costa Rica
Promesa, Ediciones, pg 116

Cote d'Ivoire
Akohi Editions, pg 117

Croatia
Znaci Vremena, Institut Za Istrazivanje Biblije, pg 120

Cuba
Editora Politica, pg 121

Czech Republic
Luxpress VOS, pg 126
Portal Ltd, pg 127
Zvon, pg 129

Denmark
Borgens Forlag A/S, pg 130
C A Reitzel A/S, pg 134

Egypt (Arab Republic of Egypt)
Al Ahram Establishment, pg 138

Estonia
Kupar Publishers, pg 140
Tuum, pg 141

Finland
Karas-Sana Oy, pg 142
Lasten Keskus Oy, pg 143

France
Editions d'Aujourd'hui (Les Introuvables), pg 149
Beauchesne Editeur, pg 150
Editions Belfond, pg 150
Bottin SA, pg 151
Alain Brethe Editions, pg 152
Chronique Sociale, pg 155
Editions de Compostelle, pg 156
Culture et Bibliotheque pour Tous, pg 157
Dervy-Livres, pg 158
Editions Entente, pg 162
FBT de R Editions/Editions des Limbes d'Or, pg 163
Les Introuvables-Editions L'Harmattan, pg 170
Editions du Jaguar, pg 170
Editions des Limbes d'Or/FBT de R Editions, pg 173
Matrice, pg 175
Maxima Laurent du Mesnil Editeur, pg 175
Presses Universitaires de France (PUF), pg 181
Presses Universitaires de Lyon, pg 181
Editions Salvator Sarl, pg 183

993

Tacor International, pg 187
Editions Trois Fontaines, pg 188
UNESCO Publishing, pg 188
Editions Village Mondial, pg 189

Germany
Blaukreuz-Verlag Wuppertal, pg 204
Brandes & Apsel Verlag GmbH, pg 206
Carl-Auer-Systeme Verlag, pg 209
Catia Monser Eggcup-Verlag, pg 209
CEC-Cosmic Energy Connections, pg 209
Connection Medien GmbH, pg 211
J G Cotta'sche Buchhandlung Nachfolger GmbH, pg 212
Maximilian Dietrich Verlag, pg 216
Dreisam Ratgeber in der Rutsker Verlag GmbH, pg 218
Eironeia-Verlag, pg 222
Engel & Bengel Verlag, pg 222
Verlag Peter Erd GmbH, pg 223
Extent Verlag und Service Wolfgang M Flamm, pg 225
Flensburger Hefte Verlag GmbH, pg 228
Margarethe Freudenberger - selbstverlag fur jedermann, pg 230
Gatzanis Verlags GmbH, pg 231
Genius Verlag, pg 231
Brigitte Grabitz - ikoo Buchverlag, pg 233
Verlag der Stiftung Gralsbotschaft GmbH, pg 234
Gruner + Jahr AG & Co, pg 234
Dr Curt Haefner-Verlag GmbH, pg 236
Heinz-Theo Gremme Verlag, pg 239
Verlag Peter Hoell, pg 241
Heinrich Hugendubel Verlag GmbH, pg 243
Edition Humanistische Psychologie (EHP), pg 243
Verlag Kleine Schritte Ursula Dahm & Co, pg 249
Kleiner Bachmann Verlag fur Kinder und Umwelt, pg 250
Krug & Schadenberg, pg 254
Leibniz Verlag, pg 256
Dr Gisela Lermann, pg 257
Logophon Lehrmittelverlag GmbH, pg 258
Medico International eV, pg 262
Otto Meissner Verlag, pg 262
Midena Verlag, pg 264
Mosaik Verlag GmbH, pg 265
Verlag Neues Leben GmbH, pg 268
Oekotopia Verlag, Wolfgang Hoffman, pg 270
One Way Medien OHG, pg 270
Osho Verlag GmbH, pg 271
PapyRossa Verlags GmbH & Co Kommanditgesellschaft KG, pg 271
Projektion J Buch- und Musikverlag GmbH, pg 275
Verlag an der Ruhr GmbH, pg 281
Heinrich Schwab Verlag, pg 285
Suin Buch-Verlag, pg 291
Guenter Albert Ulmer Verlag, pg 295
VAS-Verlag fuer Akademische Schriften, Vas Karl-Heinz Balon, pg 297
Verlag DAS WORT GmbH, pg 304
Zeitgeist Media GmbH, pg 305

Ghana
World Literature Project, pg 308

Greece
Akritas, pg 308
Elliniki Leschi Tou Vivliou, pg 310
Hestia-I D Hestia-Kollaros & Co Corporation, pg 311
Odysseas Publications Ltd, pg 313
Thymari Publications, pg 315

Holy See (Vatican City State)
Scuola Vaticana Paleografia - Scuola Vaticana di Paleografia Diplomatica e Archivistica, pg 317

Hong Kong
Breakthrough Ltd - Breakthrough Publishers, pg 318

Hungary
Marton Aron Kiado Publishing House, pg 325

Iceland
Frodi Ltd, pg 328

India
Abhinav Publications, pg 329
The Academic Press, pg 329
Arihant Publishers, pg 331
Bihar Hindi Granth Akademi, pg 333
Chanakya Publications, pg 334
Chugh Publications, pg 335
Ess Ess Publications, pg 337
Firma KLM Privatee Ltd, Publishers & International Booksellers, pg 337
Gitanjali Publishing House, pg 337
Gyan Publishing House, pg 338
Islamic Publishing House, pg 340
Konark Publishers, Pvt, Ltd, pg 341
National Book Organization, pg 343
National Book Trust India, pg 343
National Publishing House, pg 344
Parimal Prakashan, pg 345
Rajasthan Hindi Granth Academy, pg 347
Rajpal & Sons, pg 347
Reliance Publishing House, pg 347
Scientific Book Agency, pg 349
Sultan Chand & Sons Pvt Ltd, pg 351
Theosophical Publishing House, pg 351
Lok Vangamaya Griha Pvt Ltd, pg 352

Indonesia
Advent Indonesia Publishing, pg 353
Penerbit Nusa Indah, pg 356

Ireland
The Collins Press, pg 359

Israel
Bitan Publishers Ltd, pg 365
Hakibbutz Hameuchad Publishing House Ltd, pg 368
Urim Publications, pg 373

Italy
Gruppo Abele, pg 374
Adea Edizioni, pg 374
Belforte Editore Libraio srl, pg 377
Centro Scientifico Torinese, pg 381
CLUEB (Cooperativa Libraria Universitaria Editrice Bologna), pg 382
CLUT Editrice, pg 382
Edizioni Cultura della Pace, pg 383
Effata Editrice, pg 387
Piero Gribaudi Editore, pg 391
In Dialogo, pg 393
Editoriale Jaca Book SpA, pg 394
Il Lavoro Editoriale, pg 395
Lecce Spazio Vivo Srl, pg 395
Milella di Lecce Spazio Vivo SRL, pg 399
Moretti & Vitali editori srl, pg 400
Piero Manni srl, pg 403
Edizioni Universitarie Romane, pg 406
Edizioni Librarie Siciliane, pg 408
Editrice Uomini Nuovi, pg 410

Jamaica
Carlong Publishers (Caribbean) Ltd, pg 412

Japan
Chikuma Shobo Publishing Co Ltd, pg 415
Kosei Publishing Co Ltd, pg 420
Mirai-Sha, pg 421
Misuzu Shobo Ltd, pg 421
Nikkagiren Shuppan-Sha (JUSE Press Ltd), pg 422
Zeimukeiri-Kyokai, pg 429

Kazakhstan
Kazakh Al-Farabi State National University, pg 430

Republic of Korea
Chung Rim Publishing Co Ltd, pg 435
Ewha Womans University Press, pg 436
St Pauls, pg 439

Latvia
Nordik/Tapals Publishers Ltd, pg 442
Preses Nams, pg 442

Lithuania
Dargenis Publishers, pg 445
Tyto Alba Publishers, pg 446

The Former Yugoslav Republic of Macedonia
Zumpres Publishing Firm, pg 449

Martinique
George Lise-Huyghes des Etages, pg 456

Mexico
Del Verbo Emprender SA de CV, pg 459
Editorial Diana SA de CV, pg 459
Ediciones Exclusivas SA, pg 461
Editorial Limusa SA de CV, pg 463
Panorama Editorial, SA, pg 465
Selector SA de CV, pg 467

Republic of Moldova
Izdatelstvo Kartia Moldoveniaske, pg 468

Morocco
Access International Services, pg 469
Societe Ennewrasse Service Librairie et Imprimerie, pg 470

Nepal
International Standards Books & Periodicals (P) Ltd, pg 471

Netherlands
APA (Academic Publishers Associated), pg 472
Bohn Stafleu Van Loghum BV, pg 474
Buijten en Schipperheijn BV Drukkerij en Uitg Mij v/h, pg 475
Uitgeverij Coutinho BV, pg 476
Holland University Press BV (APA), pg 478
Philo Press-Van Heusden-Hissink & Co CV (APA), pg 482
Rodopi, pg 483
Servire BV Uitgevers, pg 484
Telos Boeken, pg 485
Uitgeverij De Toorts, pg 485

New Zealand
Moss Associates Ltd, pg 493
Nagare Press, pg 493

Nigeria
New Africa Publishing Company Ltd, pg 500
University of Lagos Press, pg 502
West African Book Publishers Ltd, pg 502

Norway
Ex Libris Forlag A/S, pg 503
Genesis Forlag, pg 503
Hilt & Hansteen A/S, pg 504

Peru
Tassorello, SA, pg 511

Philippines
New Day Publishers, pg 514
Rex Bookstores & Publishers, pg 514
Salesiana Publishers Inc, pg 515

Poland
Wydawnictwo Lodzkie, pg 517
Wydawnictwo Lubelskie, pg 518
Wydawnictwo SIC, pg 520
Wydawnictwo WAB, pg 520

Portugal
Gradiva-Publicacnoes Lda, pg 525
McGraw-Hill Editora de Portugal, pg 527
Monitor, pg 527
Monitor-Projectos e Edicoes, LDA, pg 527
Paulinas, pg 528
Editorial Presenca, pg 528

Romania
Aion Verlag, pg 531
Editura Excelsior, pg 533

Russian Federation
Finansy i Statistika Publishing House, pg 538
Izdatel'stovo Dal'nevostonogo Gosudarstvennogo Universite, pg 538
Kavkazskaya Biblioteka Publishing House, pg 539

Singapore
Aquanut Agencies Pte Ltd, pg 545

PUBLISHERS

Slovakia
Sofa, pg 551

South Africa
Bet-El Publishers, pg 553
Centre for Conflict Resolution, pg 553
Human Sciences Research Council, pg 555
Kima Global Publishers, pg 556
Queillerie Publishers, pg 558
South African Institute of Race Relations, pg 559

Spain
Editorial AEDOS SA, pg 561
Editorial Barath SA, pg 565
Calamo Editorial, pg 566
Ediciones Catedra SA, pg 566
Fundacion Marcelino Botin, pg 575
Editorial Gedisa SA, pg 575
Ediciones Gestio 2000 SA, pg 575
Grijalbo Mondadori SA, pg 576
Editorial Gulaab, pg 577
Idea Books, SA, pg 578
Editorial Labor SA, pg 579
Ediciones Medici SA, pg 582
Ediciones ROL SA, pg 589
Ediciones de la Torre, pg 593

Sri Lanka
National Library & Documentation Services Board, pg 597

Sweden
Akademiforlaget Goteborgslitteratur, pg 600
Bokforlaget Cordia AB, pg 600
Egmont Serieforlaget, pg 601
Svenska Foerlaget liv & ledarskap ab, pg 607

Switzerland
Bergli Books AG, pg 609
Verlag Industrielle Organisation, pg 616
La Maison de la Bible, pg 618
Editions Du Signal Rene Gaillard, pg 624
Versus Verlag AG, pg 627
Editions Vivez Soleil SA, pg 627

Taiwan, Province of China
Campus Evangelical Fellowship, Literature Department, pg 629
Chu Liu Book Company, pg 629
Linking Publishing Company Ltd, pg 631
Morning Star Publisher Inc, pg 631

Turkey
Kok Yayincilik, pg 640

United Kingdom
Act 3 Publishing, pg 645
Andromeda Oxford Ltd, pg 647
Arnold, pg 648
Baha'i Publishing Trust, pg 651
Bloomsbury Publishing PLC, pg 656
The British Council, Design, Publishing & Print Department, pg 660
Chartered Institute of Personnel & Development, pg 667
Commission for Racial Equality, pg 669
The Eurospan Group, pg 680
Extraordinary People Press, pg 681

Forbes Publications Ltd, pg 683
Free Association Books Ltd, pg 684
George Mann Publications, pg 687
HarperCollins Publishers, pg 692
Hodder & Stoughton Religious, pg 696
Holyoake Books, pg 697
Lawrence & Wishart, pg 706
Letterbox Library, pg 707
Macmillan Reference Ltd, pg 710
MCB University Press Ltd, pg 712
Palgrave Publishers Ltd, pg 723
RELATE, pg 734
Rosendale Press Ltd, pg 735
Sage Publications Ltd, pg 737
Sherwood Publishing, pg 741
The Society of Metaphysicians Ltd, pg 743
St Pauls Publishing, pg 744
Sutton Publishing Ltd, pg 746
UCL Press Ltd, pg 751

Uruguay
Instituto del Tercer Mundo, pg 760

Yugoslavia
Izdavacko Preduzece Matice Srpske, pg 765
Prosveta, pg 765

Zambia
Wilfred Bwalya Chilangwa Publications, pg 766
M & M Management & Labour Consultants Ltd, pg 766

HUMOR

Albania
NL SH, pg 1

Argentina
Beas Ediciones SRL, pg 4
Ediciones de la Flor SRL, pg 6

Australia
Aussies Afire Publishing, pg 13
Cole Publications, pg 18
Dynamo House P/L, pg 21
Emperor Publishing, pg 22
Fernfawn Publications, pg 22
Hartys Creek Press, pg 25
Little Red Apple Publishing, pg 30
Moggy Publications, pg 33
New Endeavour Press, pg 34
Orin Books, pg 36
Palms Press, pg 36
Pan Macmillan Australia Pty Ltd, pg 36
Penguin Books Australia Ltd, pg 37
Plantagenet Press, pg 38
Plantain Park, pg 38
Playlab Press, pg 38
The Text Publishing Company Pty Ltd, pg 44
Thin Rich Press, pg 44
Transworld Publishers Pty Ltd, pg 45
The Watermark Press, pg 47

Austria
Astor-Verlag, Willibald Schlager, pg 49
Verlag Lynkeus/H Hakel Gesellschaft, pg 52
Merbod Verlag, pg 55
Niederosterreichisches Pressehaus Druck- und Verlagsgesellschaft mbH, pg 55

SUBJECT INDEX

Azerbaijan
Sada, Literaturno-Izdatel'skij Centr, pg 61

Bangladesh
Gatidhara, pg 62

Belgium
Editions Casterman SA, pg 66
Editions Dupuis SA, pg 68
Glenat Benelux SA, pg 69
Helyode Editions (SA-ADN), pg 69
Kritak Uitgeverij, pg 70
Claude Lefrancq Editeur, pg 71
Les Editions du Lombard SA, pg 71
Marabout, pg 72
Scissors Books, pg 74
Standaard Uitgeverij, pg 74
Zuid-Nederlandse Uitgeverij NV/ Central Uitgeverij, pg 76

Brazil
Artes e Oficios Editora Ltda, pg 79
Editora Companhia das Letras/ Editora Schwarcz Ltda, pg 82
EDUC - Editora da PUC-SP, pg 82
Editora Globo SA, pg 84
Editora Objetiva Ltda, pg 88
Editora Primor Ltda, pg 90

Bulgaria
Interpres, pg 96
Lettera, pg 96
Trud - Izd kasta, pg 98
Ivan Vazov Publishing House, pg 98
Peyo K Yavorov Publishing House, pg 98
Zunica, pg 98

Chile
Editora Nueva Generacion, pg 101

China
Fujian Children's Publishing House, pg 106

Colombia
El Ancora Editores, pg 111
Editorial Oveja Negra, pg 113

Cuba
Casa Editora Abril, pg 120

Czech Republic
Aurora, pg 123
Doplnek, pg 124
Jan Vasut Publishing, pg 124
Knihovna A Tiskarna Pro Nevidome, pg 125
Konsultace, pg 125
Josef Lukasik A Spol, pg 125
Nase vojsko, nakladatelstvi a knizni obchod, pg 126
Nava, pg 127

Denmark
Bogan's Forlag, pg 130
Borgens Forlag A/S, pg 130
Forlaget Carlsen A/S, pg 131
Forum Publishers, pg 132
P Haase & Sons Forlag A/S, pg 132
Forlaget Hovedland, pg 133
Interpresse A/S, pg 133
Det Schonbergske Forlag, pg 135
Strandbergs Forlag, pg 135
Wisby & Wilkens, pg 136

France
Actes Graphiques, pg 145
Editions Albin Michel, pg 146
L'Amitie par le Livre, pg 147
Editions Balland, pg 149
Bragelonne, pg 151
Editions Calmann-Levy SA, pg 152
Editions Canal, pg 152
Philippe Chancerel Editeur, pg 154
Le Cherche Midi Editeur, pg 154
Circonflexe, pg 155
Corsaire Editions, pg 156
Dargaud, pg 157
Georges-Charles Demay, pg 158
Editions J Dupuis, pg 160
Editions Tarmeye, pg 161
Editions Generales First, pg 166
Editions Jean Paul Gisserot, pg 166
Editions J Glenat SA, pg 166
Editions Grancher, pg 166
Editions Hoebeke, pg 168
Editions Hors Collection, pg 168
Editions Infrarouge, pg 169
Editions Dominique Leroy, pg 172
Editions Payot & Rivages, pg 179
Les Editions Albert Rene, pg 182
Editions Rombaldi SA, pg 183
Editions de Septembre, pg 184
Association d'Editions Sorg, pg 186
La Vague a l'ame, pg 188
Les Editions Vaillant-Miroir-Sprint Publications, pg 188
Vents d'Ouest, pg 189

Germany
Achterbahn AG Buch, pg 191
Aufstieg-Verlag GmbH, pg 196
Dr Wolfgang Baur Verlag Kunst & Alltag, pg 199
Beerenverlag, pg 200
Verlag Beruf + Schule Belz KG, pg 202
Carlsen Verlag GmbH, pg 209
Claudius Verlag, pg 211
Deutscher Taschenbuch Verlag GmbH & Co KG (dtv), pg 215
Droemersche Verlagsanstalt Th Knaur Nachfolger GmbH & Co, pg 218
Droste Verlag GmbH, pg 218
Egmont EHAPA Verlag GmbH, pg 221
Eichborn AG, pg 222
EinfallsReich Verlagsgesellschaft MbH, pg 222
Elefanten Press Verlag GmbH, pg 222
F Bruckmann Munchen Verlag & Druck GmbH & Co Produkt KG, pg 225
Fackeltrager-Verlag GmbH, pg 226
Falken-Verlag GmbH, pg 227
Forum Verlag Leipzig Buch-Gesellschaft, pg 229
Margarethe Freudenberger - selbstverlag fur jedermann, pg 230
Garbe Verlag Ellen Vogt, pg 231
Gatzanis Verlags GmbH, pg 231
Heel Verlag GmbH, pg 238
Wilhelm Heyne Verlag, pg 240
Wolfgang Krueger Verlag GmbH, pg 254
Verlag Antje Kunstmann GmbH, pg 254
Landbuch-Verlagsgesellschaft mbH, pg 255
Verlag Gerald Leue, pg 257
C W Niemeyer Buchverlage GmbH, pg 268
Oekotopia Verlag, Wolfgang Hoffman, pg 270

Passavia Druckerei GmbH, Verlag, pg 271
Verlag Walter Podszun Burobedarf-Bucher Abt, pg 274
Pollner Verlag, pg 274
Propylaeen Verlag, Zweigniederlassung Berlin der Ullstein Buchverlage GmbH, pg 275
Rake Verlag GmbH, pg 277
Gerhard Rautenberg Druckerei und Verlag GmbH & Co KG, pg 277
Moritz Schauenburg Verlag, pg 282
Buchverlag Andrea Schmitz, pg 284
Theodor Schuster, pg 285
Suedverlag GmbH, pg 291
Otto Teich, pg 292
Tomus Verlag GmbH, pg 294
Verein der Benediktiner zu Beuron-Beuroner Kunstverlag, pg 297
Verlag W Weinmann, pg 301
Zeitgeist Media GmbH, pg 305

Ghana
Kwamfori Publishing Enterprise, pg 307
World Literature Project, pg 308

Greece
Diavlos, pg 309
Kastaniotis Editions SA, pg 312
Mamuth Comix Ltd, pg 313

Hong Kong
Breakthrough Ltd - Breakthrough Publishers, pg 318

Hungary
Aranyhal Konyvkiado Goldfish Publishing, pg 323
Officina Nova, Koenyv-es Lapkiado/Bertelsmann Media Kft, pg 324

Iceland
Frodi Ltd, pg 328
Skjaldborg Ltd, pg 328

India
Jaico Publishing House, pg 340
Kairalee Mudralayam, pg 341
Omsons Publications, pg 345
Orient Paperbacks, pg 345
Prabhat Prakashan, pg 346
Pratibha Pratishthan, pg 346
Reliance Publishing House, pg 347
Sat Sahitya Prakashan, pg 349
Scientific Book Agency, pg 349

Indonesia
Karya Anda, CV, pg 356
Pustaka Utama Grafiti, PT, pg 357

Ireland
Attic Press Ltd, pg 358
Mercier Press Ltd, pg 362
The O'Brien Press Ltd, pg 363

Israel
Classikaletet, pg 366
Dalia Peled Publishers, Division of Modan, pg 366
DAT Publications, pg 366
Kivunim-Arsan Publishing House, pg 369
Pitspopany Press, pg 371
Saar Publishing House, pg 372

Italy
Gruppo Editoriale Armenia SpA, pg 376
Verlagsanstalt Athesia, pg 377
Colonnese Editore, pg 382
Giovanni De Vecchi Editore SpA, pg 384
Piero Gribaudi Editore, pg 391
L'Airone Editrice, pg 395
Lalli Editore SRL, pg 395
Mundici & Zanetti srl, pg 400
Edition Raetia Srl-GmbH, pg 404
TEA Tascabili degli Editori Associati SpA, pg 409

Japan
Kodansha, pg 420

Kenya
Kenway Publications Ltd, pg 432

Republic of Korea
Chung Rim Publishing Co Ltd, pg 435

Latvia
Preses Nams, pg 442

Lithuania
AS Narbuto Leidykla (AS Narbutas' Publishers), pg 445

Luxembourg
Editions Emile Borschette, pg 447
Hubsch, pg 447
Editions Tousch, pg 448

Mexico
Ediciones Alpe, pg 458
Editores Asociados Mexicanos SA de CV (EDAMEX), pg 458
Editorial Extemporaneos SA, pg 461
Libra Editorial SA de CV, pg 463
Editorial Nueva Imagen SA, pg 464
Panorama Editorial, SA, pg 465
Selector SA de CV, pg 467

Monaco
Rondeau Giannipiero a Monaco, pg 469

Morocco
Editions Eddif Maroc, pg 469

Netherlands
BZZTOH Publishers, pg 475
Elmar BV, pg 476
De Harmonie, pg 478
Kartoen, pg 479
Mondria Publishers, pg 481

New Zealand
HarperCollins Publishers (New Zealand) Ltd, pg 491
Magari Publishing, pg 493
Saint Publishing, pg 495

Nigeria
New Africa Publishing Company Ltd, pg 500
Joe-Tolalu & Associates, pg 501

Norway
Ex Libris Forlag A/S, pg 503
Fono Forlag, pg 503

Pakistan
Jang Publishers, pg 507
Maqbool Academy, pg 508

Philippines
Anvil Publishing Inc, pg 512
Sonny A Mendoza, pg 513
New Day Publishers, pg 514
Our Lady of Manaoag Publisher, pg 514

Portugal
Europress Editores e Distribuidores de Publicacoes Lda, pg 525
Editorial Futura, pg 525
Gradiva-Publicacnoes Lda, pg 525
Impala, pg 525
Meriberica/Liber, pg 527
Editora Replicacao Lda, pg 529
Edicoes Salesianas, pg 529
Vega-Publicacao e Distribuicao de Livros e Revistas, Lda, pg 530

Romania
Editura Clusium, Casa de Editura Atlas-Clusium SRL, pg 532
Editura Excelsior, pg 533
Editura Niculescu, pg 534
Pandora Publishing House, pg 535

Saudi Arabia
Dar Al-Shareff for Publishing & Distribution, pg 543

Singapore
Aquanut Agencies Pte Ltd, pg 545
Asiapac Books Pte Ltd, pg 545

Slovakia
Egmont Neografia spol sro, pg 549

South Africa
Bet-El Publishers, pg 553
Media House Publications, pg 557
New Africa Books (Pty) Ltd, pg 557

Spain
Aguilar SA de Ediciones, pg 562
Ediciones B, SA, pg 565
Calambur Editorial, SL, pg 566
Editorial Cantabrica SA, pg 566
Casset Ediciones SL, pg 566
Ediciones la Cupula SL, pg 569
Edicomunicacion SA, pg 572
Ediciones Elfos SL, pg 572
Grijalbo Mondadori SA, pg 576
Ediciones Irusa, pg 578
Ediciones Junior SA, pg 579
Editorial Lumen SA, pg 580
Pirene Editorial, sal, pg 587
Editorial Presencia Gitana, pg 587
Ediciones SM, pg 591
Ediciones Temas de Hoy, SA, pg 592
Ediciones Tutor SA, pg 594

Sweden
Bonnier Carlsen Bokforlag AB, pg 601
Bokforlaget Fingraf AB, pg 602
Semic Bokforlaget International AB, pg 606

Switzerland
Werner Classen Verlag, pg 611
E Lopfe-Benz AG Rorschach, Graphische Anstalt und Verlag, pg 612
Edition Hans Erpf Verlagsgenossenschaft, pg 613
Globi Verlag AG, pg 614
Haffmans Verlag AG, pg 615
Junod Nicholas, pg 616
Nebelspalter-Verlag, pg 620
Les Editions Noir sur Blanc, pg 620
Edition Olms AG, pg 620
Rhein-Trio, Edition/Editions du Fou, pg 623
Satyr-Verlag Dr Humbel, pg 623
Viktoria-Verlag Peter Marti, pg 627

Tunisia
Les Editions de l'Arbre, pg 638

Turkey
Dost Yayinlari San Ve Tic Ltd, pg 639
Inkilap Publishers Ltd, pg 640
Parantez Yayinlari Ltd, pg 640

Uganda
Fountain Publishers Ltd, pg 642

United Kingdom
Act 3 Publishing, pg 645
BCA, pg 653
Beaver Publishing Ltd, pg 653
Blackstaff Press, pg 655
Bloomsbury Publishing PLC, pg 656
Boxtree Ltd, pg 658
Canongate Books Ltd, pg 663
Carlton Publishing Group, pg 664
Cassell & Co, pg 664
Constable Publishers, pg 670
Defiant Publications, pg 675
Andre Deutsch Ltd, pg 675
Elliot Right Way Books, pg 678
Exley Publications Ltd, pg 681
Express Newspapers, pg 681
Foulsham Publishers, pg 683
Fourth Estate Ltd, pg 683
Hawk Books, pg 693
Hodder & Stoughton General, pg 696
Hodder & Stoughton Religious, pg 696
Icon Press, pg 698
The Islamic Texts Society, pg 701
Knight Features, pg 705
Knockabout Comics, pg 705
Jay Landesman, pg 706
Lang Syne Publishers Ltd, pg 706
Methuen Publishing Ltd, pg 714
Monarch Books, pg 715
Michael O'Mara Books Ltd, pg 721
Parapress Ltd, pg 724
Piatkus Books, pg 727
Piccadilly Press, pg 727
Polygon, pg 729
Random House UK Ltd, pg 733
Ravette Publishing Ltd, pg 733
Robson Books, pg 735
Sainsbury Publishing Ltd, pg 737
SAWD Publications, pg 738
Silver Link Publishing Ltd, pg 742
Smith Settle Ltd, pg 743
The Sportsman's Press, pg 744
St Pauls Publishing, pg 744
Supportive Learning Publications, pg 746
Telegraph Books, pg 748
Transworld Publishers Ltd, pg 750
Trentham Books Ltd, pg 750

PUBLISHERS

Verulam Publishing Ltd, pg 753
Virgin Publishing Ltd, pg 753
Neil Wilson Publishing Ltd, pg 757
Wimbledon Publishing Company Ltd, pg 757
The Windrush Press Ltd, pg 757
Wordwright Publishing, pg 758
Gordon Wright Publishing Ltd, pg 759

Uruguay
Editorial Arca SRL, pg 760
Rosebud Ediciones, pg 761

Zambia
Apple Books, pg 766

JOURNALISM

Argentina
Editorial Abaco de Rodolfo Depalma SRL, pg 2
Ediciones Don Bosco Argentina, pg 5

Australia
McGraw-Hill Australia Pty Ltd, pg 32
New Endeavour Press, pg 34
Pearson Education Australia, pg 37
Plantagenet Press, pg 38

Austria
Aarachne Verlag, pg 49
Buchkultur Verlags GmbH Zeitschrift fuer Literatur & Kunst, pg 50
Development News Ltd, pg 51
Docker Verlag GmbH & Co KG, pg 51
Verlag Lafite, pg 54
Medien & Recht, pg 55
Studien Verlag Gmbh, pg 59
Verlag Styria, pg 59

Bangladesh
Agamee Prakashani, pg 62

Belgium
Academia-Bruylant, pg 63
Academia Press, pg 64
EPO Publishers, Printers, Booksellers, pg 68
Graton Editeur SA, pg 69
Koepel van de Vlaamse Noord - Zuidbeweging 11.11.11, pg 70
Uitgevery Scoop Infotex NV, pg 75

Brazil
Artes e Oficios Editora Ltda, pg 79
Ediouro Publicacoes, SA, pg 81
EDUSC - Editora da Universidade do Sagrado Coracao, pg 82
Empresa Brasileira de Pesquisa Agropecaria, pg 83
Editora Globo SA, pg 84
LDA Editores Ltda, pg 86
Editora Mantiqueira de Ciencia e Arte, pg 87
Olho D'Agua Comercio e Servicos Editoriais Ltda, pg 88
Sobrindes Linha Grafica E Editora Ltda, pg 91
Summus Editorial Ltda, pg 92

Burundi
Editions Intore, pg 98

Chile
Arrayan Editores, pg 99
Publicaciones Lo Castillo SA, pg 101

China
World Affairs Press, pg 110
Xinhua Publishing House, pg 110

Colombia
El Ancora Editores, pg 111
Universidad de Antioquia, Division Publicaciones, pg 114
Editorial Voluntad SA, pg 114

Croatia
Faust Vrani, pg 118
Prosvjeta, pg 120

Cuba
Casa Editora Abril, pg 120

Czech Republic
Barrister & Principal, pg 123
Doplnek, pg 124

Denmark
Samfundslitteratur, pg 135

Ecuador
CIESPAL (Centro Internacional de Estudios Superiores de Comunicacion para America Latina), pg 137

Egypt (Arab Republic of Egypt)
Al Arab Publishing House, pg 138
Ummah Press for Translation & Publishing, pg 139

Finland
Osuuskunta Vastapaino, pg 145
Yliopistopaino/Helsinki University Press, pg 145

France
Beauchesne Editeur, pg 150
Les Editions du CFPJ (Centre de Formation et de Perfectionnement des Journalistes) - Sarl Presse et Formation, pg 154
Groupe de Recherche et d'Echanges Technologiques (GRET), pg 167
Editions de Septembre, pg 184

Germany
Verlag Karl Alber GmbH, pg 192
ARCult Media, pg 194
Boehlau-Verlag GmbH & Cie, pg 204
Deutsches Bucharchiv Muenchen, Institut fur Buchwissenschaften, pg 216
agenda Verlag Thomas Dominikowski, pg 217
Verlag Reinhard Fischer, pg 228
Walter de Gruyter GmbH & Co KG, pg 234
Gunter Olzog Verlag GmbH, pg 235
Jahreszeiten-Verlag GmbH, pg 246
Siedler Verlag, pg 286
Spiess Volker Wissenschaftsverlag GmbH, pg 287
UVK Verlagsgesellschaft mbH, pg 297

Greece
Hestia-1 D Hestia-Kollaros & Co Corporation, pg 311

Hong Kong
Celeluck Co Ltd, pg 318
The Chinese University Press, pg 319
Island Press, pg 320

Hungary
KJK-Keaszov, pg 324

India
Central Tibetan Secretariat, pg 334
Concept Publishing Co, pg 335
Gyan Publishing House, pg 338
Minerva Associates (Publications) Pvt Ltd, pg 342
Reliance Publishing House, pg 347
Scientific Book Agency, pg 349
Somaiya Publications Pvt Ltd, pg 350
Sterling Publishers Pvt Ltd, pg 351
Vikas Publishing House Pvt Ltd, pg 353

Israel
Intermedia Audio, Video Book Publishing Ltd, pg 368
The Harry Karren Institute for the Analysis of Propaganda, Yad Labanim, pg 369
Open University of Israel, pg 371

Italy
Editore Armando Armando SRL, pg 376
Edizioni Bresciane, pg 378
La Luna, pg 397
Messaggero di San Antonio, pg 398
RAI.ERI, pg 405

Kazakstan
Kazakh Al-Farabi State National University, pg 430

Republic of Korea
Chung Rim Publishing Co Ltd, pg 435
Hanul Publishing Co, pg 436
Nanam Publishing House, pg 439

The Former Yugoslav Republic of Macedonia
Mi-An Knigoizdatelstvo, pg 449
Nov svet (New World), pg 449

Madagascar
Maison d'Edition Protestante ANTSO, pg 450
Societe Malgache d'Edition, pg 450

Malaysia
Pustaka Cipta Sdn Bhd, pg 454

Mexico
Editorial AGATA SA de CV, pg 457
Editorial Diana SA de CV, pg 459
Edamex SA de CV, pg 460
Editorial Limusa SA de CV, pg 463
Universidad Nacional Autonoma de Mexico (National University of Mexico), pg 467
Universo Editorial SA de CV Edicion de Libros Revistas y Periodicos, pg 468

SUBJECT INDEX

Netherlands
Uitgeverij Balans, pg 473
Historische Uitgeverij, pg 478
Mets & Schilt Uitgevers en Distributeurs, pg 481

New Zealand
Barkfire Press, pg 488

Nigeria
Evans Brothers (Nigeria Publishers) Ltd, pg 499

Pakistan
Sang-e-Meel Publications, pg 509

Peru
Universidad de Lima-Fondo de Desarollo Editorial, pg 512

Philippines
SIBS Publishing House Inc, pg 515

Poland
Spoldzielnia Wydawnicza 'Czytelnik', pg 516

Portugal
Gradiva-Publicacnoes Lda, pg 525
Editorial Noticias, pg 527
Quid Juris - Sociedade editora, pg 529

Romania
Aion Verlag, pg 531
Editura Excelsior, pg 533
Pallas-Akademia Koenyvkiadoes Koenyvkereskedes, pg 535
Polirom Verlag, pg 535

Slovenia
Franc-Franc podjetje za promocijo kulture Murska Sobota d o o, pg 551
Zalozba Mihelac d o o, pg 552
Zalozba Obzorja d d Maribor, pg 552

South Africa
Ivy Publications, pg 555

Spain
Aguilar SA de Ediciones, pg 562
Bosch Casa Editorial SA, pg 565
Compania Literaria, pg 568
Consello da Cultura Galega - CCG, pg 568
Editorial Dossat SA, pg 570
EUNSA (Ediciones Universidad de Navarra SA), pg 574
Fragua Editorial, pg 574
Ediciones Internacionales Universitarias SA, pg 578
Editorial Pliegos, pg 587
Editorial Portic SA, pg 587
Editorial Sintesis, SA, pg 590
Ediciones de la Torre, pg 593

Sri Lanka
Swarna Hansa Foundation, pg 598

Sweden
Carlsson Bokfoerlag AB, pg 601
Ordfront Foerlag AB, pg 605

Switzerland
Lenos Verlag, pg 618

SUBJECT INDEX

Syrian Arab Republic
Damascus University Press, pg 628

Taiwan, Province of China
Lin Pai Press Company Ltd, pg 631
UNITAS Publishing Co Ltd, pg 632

United Republic of Tanzania
Tanzania Publishing House, pg 634

Tunisia
Academie Tunisienne des Sciences, des Lettres et des Arts Beit El Hekma, pg 637

United Kingdom
Business Monitor International, pg 661
Butterworth-Heinemann Ltd, pg 661
The Eurospan Group, pg 680
Geiser Productions, pg 686
Telegraph Books, pg 748

Uruguay
Cotidiano Mujer, pg 760
Editorial Dismar, pg 760

Venezuela
Alfadil Ediciones, pg 761

Yugoslavia
Alfa-Narodna Knjiga, pg 764

LABOR, INDUSTRIAL RELATIONS

Albania
Encyclopaedia Publishing House, pg 1
NL SH, pg 1

Australia
Allen & Unwin Pty Ltd, The Australian Newspaper, Vogel Breads, pg 11
Histec Publications, pg 26
Law Book Co Information Services, pg 29
McGraw-Hill Australia Pty Ltd, pg 32
Pearson Education Australia, pg 37
Pluto Press Australia, pg 38

Austria
Docker Verlag GmbH & Co KG, pg 51
Linde Verlag Wien GmbH, pg 54
Verlag des Oesterreichischen Gewerkschaftsbundes GmbH, pg 56

Belgium
CED-Samsom, pg 66
King Baudouin Foundation, pg 70
Koepel van de Vlaamse Noord - Zuidbeweging 11.11.11, pg 70

Brazil
Qualitymark Editora Ltda, pg 90

Bulgaria
Sibi, pg 97
Sita-MB, pg 98

Chile
Edeval (Universidad de Valparaiso), pg 100

China
China Labour Publishing House, pg 103

Costa Rica
Academia de Centro America, pg 115

Denmark
Dansk Teknologisk Institut, Forlaget, pg 131

France
Editions J B Bailliere, pg 149
Editions Eska, pg 162
Association Frank, pg 165
Futuribles SARL, pg 165
Lavoisier, pg 172
Editions Legislatives, pg 172
LiTec (Librairies Techniques SA), pg 173
Editions Weka, pg 189

Germany
Arbeiterpresse Verlag GmbH, pg 194
Asso Verlag, pg 196
Belser Wissenschaftlicher Dienst, pg 200
W Bertelsmann Verlag GmbH & Co KG, pg 201
Deutscher Instituts-Verlag GmbH, pg 215
Ecomed Verlagsgesellschaft AG & Co KG, pg 220
Verlag Handwerk und Technik GmbH, pg 237
IKO Verlag fur Interkulturelle Kommunikation, pg 244
SachBuchVerlag Kellner, pg 248
Nusser Verlag, pg 269
Rationalisierungs-Kuratorium der Deutschen Wirtschaft eV (RKW), pg 277
Verlag Roter Morgen, pg 280
I H Sauer Verlag GmbH, pg 282
Schueren Verlag GmbH, pg 285
Schulz-Kirchner Verlag GmbH, pg 285
UNO-Verlag mbH, Vertriebs und Verlagsgesellschaft, pg 296
VVF Verlag V Florentz GmbH, pg 299
Verlag Westfaelisches Dampfboot, pg 302

Greece
Karatzas Charis, pg 312
Sakkoulas Publications SA, pg 314

Hong Kong
Hong Kong University Press, pg 320

India
Agricole Publishing Academy, pg 330
APH Publishing Corp, pg 331
Konark Publishers, Pvt, Ltd, pg 341
Minerva Associates (Publications) Pvt Ltd, pg 342
National Book Organization, pg 343
Reliance Publishing House, pg 347
Scientific Book Agency, pg 349
Sita Publications, pg 350

Somaiya Publications Pvt Ltd, pg 350
South Asian Publishers Pvt Ltd, pg 350
Sultan Chand & Sons Pvt Ltd, pg 351

Indonesia
Lembaga Demografi Fakultas Ekonomi Universitas Indonesia, pg 356

Ireland
Irish Management Institute, pg 361
Libra House Ltd, pg 362
Oak Tree Press, pg 362
Round Hall Sweet & Maxwell, pg 363

Israel
Hanitzotz A-Sharara Publishing House, pg 368
The Institute for Israeli Arabs Studies, pg 368
Sifriat Poalim Ltd, pg 372

Italy
Editrice San Marco SRL, pg 406
SIPI (Servizio Italiano Pubblicazioni Internazionali) Srl, pg 408

Japan
Hakuyu-Sha, pg 417
Kanehara & Co Ltd, pg 419
Koseisha-Koseikaku Co Ltd, pg 420
Nihon Rodo Kenkyu Kiko, pg 422
Toyo Keizai Inc (The Oriental Economist), pg 428

Kenya
Lake Publishers & Enterprises Ltd, pg 432

Republic of Korea
Bo Ri, pg 435
Chung Rim Publishing Co Ltd, pg 435

Lithuania
Lietuvos Informacijos Institutas, pg 446

Luxembourg
Service Central de la Statistique et des Etudes Economiques (STATEC), pg 448

Malaysia
Forum Publications, pg 452

Mexico
Editorial Limusa SA de CV, pg 463

Netherlands
Aeolus Press BV, pg 472
Hagen & Stam Uitgeverij Ten, pg 478
Uitgeverij Lemma BV, pg 480
Samsom BedrijfsInformatie BV, pg 483
Swets & Zeitlinger Publishers, pg 485

Pakistan
Pakistan Institute of Development Economics, pg 508

Philippines
New Day Publishers, pg 514
Rex Bookstores & Publishers, pg 514

Poland
Instytut Wydawniczy Zwiazkow Zawodowych, pg 521

Portugal
Lidel Edicoes Tecnicas, Lda, pg 526

Russian Federation
Legprombytizdat, pg 539
Profizdat, pg 541

Senegal
CODESRIA (Council for the Development of Social Science Research in Africa), pg 544

Slovakia
Ustav informacii a prognoz skolstva mladeze a telovychovy, pg 551

South Africa
Queillerie Publishers, pg 558
Ravan Press (Pty) Ltd, pg 558
Van Schaik Publishers, pg 560

Spain
Centro de Estudios Adams-Ediciones Valbuena SA, pg 561
Editorial AEDOS SA, pg 561
Editorial CISSPRAXIS SA, pg 567
Publicaciones Etea, pg 574
Fundacion de Estudios Libertarios Anselmo Lorenzo, pg 575
Tirant lo Blanch SL Libreriaa, pg 592

Suriname
Stichting Wetenschappelijke Informatie, pg 599

Switzerland
Verlag Organisator AG, pg 620
SAB Schweiz Arbeitsgemeinschaft fuer die Berggebiete, pg 623
Versus Verlag AG, pg 627

United Republic of Tanzania
Tanzania Publishing House, pg 634

Uganda
Centre for Basic Research, pg 642

United Kingdom
Anglo-German Foundation for the Study of Industrial Society, pg 647
Barmarick Publications, pg 652
Blackwell Publishers, pg 655
Bookmarks Publications, pg 657
Cassell & Co, pg 664
Croner CCH Group Ltd, pg 672
Edward Elgar Publishing Ltd, pg 678
The Eurospan Group, pg 680
Lawrence & Wishart, pg 706
Letts Educational, pg 707
The Merlin Press Ltd, pg 713
Pathfinder London, pg 724
Pluto Press, pg 728
The Policy Press, pg 729
Policy Studies Institute, pg 729
Shire Publications Ltd, pg 741

PUBLISHERS

SHU Press, pg 742
Spokesman, pg 744
Sutton Publishing Ltd, pg 746

Venezuela
Fundacion Centro Gumilla, pg 762

Zambia
M & M Management & Labour Consultants Ltd, pg 766

Zimbabwe
Journal on Social Change, pg 768

LANGUAGE ARTS, LINGUISTICS

Albania
NL SH, pg 1

Argentina
Academia Argentina de Letras, pg 2
Edicial SA, pg 5
Editorial Guadalupe, pg 6
San Pablo, pg 8
Editorial Sopena Argentina SACI e I, pg 9

Australia
Aboriginal Studies Press, pg 10
Bandicoot Books, pg 14
Boombana Publications, pg 16
China Books, pg 18
Dellasta Publishing, pg 20
Illert Publications, pg 27
Institute of Aboriginal Development (IAD Press), pg 28
McGraw-Hill Australia Pty Ltd, pg 32
Mimosa Publications Pty Ltd, pg 33
New Endeavour Press, pg 34
Nimrod Publications, pg 35
Oriental Publications, pg 36
Pearson Education Australia, pg 37
Phoenix Education Pty Ltd, pg 38
RMIT Publishing, pg 41
Summer Institute of Linguistics, Australian Aborigines Branch, pg 43
Wileman Publications, pg 47

Austria
Abakus Verlag GmbH, pg 49
Akademische Druck-u Verlagsanstalt Dr Paul Struzl GmbH, pg 49
Boehlau Verlag GmbH & Co KG, pg 50
CEEBA Publications Antenne d'Autriche, pg 50
Fassbaender Verlag, pg 51
Gerold & Co, pg 52
LOG-Internationale Zeitschrift fuer Literatur, pg 54
Wolfgang Neugebauer Verlag GmbH, pg 55
Verlag der Oesterreichischen Akademie der Wissenschaften (OEAW), pg 56
Osterreichischer Bundesverlag Ges.mbh, pg 57
Studien Verlag Gmbh, pg 59
Universitaetsverlag Wagner GmbH, pg 60
WUV/Facultas Universitaetsverlag, pg 61

Azerbaijan
Sada, Literaturno-Izdatel'skij Centr, pg 61

Belgium
Acco CV, pg 64
Centre Aequatoria, pg 64
Assimil NV, pg 64
De Boeck et Larcier SA, pg 65
Bourdeaux-Capelle SA, pg 65
Brepols Publishers NV, pg 65
Campinia Media VZW, pg 65
La Charte Editions juridiques, pg 66
Editions De Boeck-Larcier SA, pg 67
Infoboek NV, pg 69
Uitgeverij J van In, pg 70
Editions Lessius ASBL, pg 71
Leuven University Press, pg 71
Mardaga, Pierre 12, pg 72
La Part de L'Oeil, pg 72
Uitgeverij Peeters Leuven (Belgie), pg 72
Pelckmans NV, De Nederlandsche Boekhandel, pg 73
Sonneville Press (Uitgeverij) VTW, pg 74
Stichting Ons Erfdeel VZW, pg 74
UGA Editions (Uitgeverij), pg 74
Uitgeverij De Garve, pg 75
Vlaamse Esperantobond VZW, pg 75
Wolters Plantyn Educatieve Uitgevers, pg 75

Botswana
The Botswana Society, pg 77
Maskew Miller Longman, pg 77

Brazil
Ao Livro Tecnico Industria e Comercio Ltda, pg 78
Ars Poetica Editora Ltda, pg 79
Associacao Brasileira de Liverivos Antiquarios, pg 79
EDUC - Editora da PUC-SP, pg 82
Forense Universitaria Editora, pg 83
Editora Globo SA, pg 84
Livro Ibero-Americano Ltda, pg 85
Libreria Editora Ltda, pg 86
Waldyr Lima Editora, pg 86
Editora Nova Fronteira SA, pg 88
Livraria Pioneira Editora/Enio Matheus Guazzelli e Cia Ltd, pg 89
Editora Rideel Ltda, pg 90
Edicoes Tabajara, pg 92
Editora Universidade Federal do Rio de Janeiro, pg 93
Vozes Editora Ltda, pg 93

Bulgaria
Bojko Kacarmazov, pg 94
Interpres, pg 96
Lettera, pg 96
Pensoft Publishers, pg 97
Seven Hills Publishers, pg 97

Chile
Arrayan Editores, pg 99

China
Beijing Publishing House, pg 102
China Light Industry Press, pg 103
China Youth Publishing House, pg 104
Chinese Pedagogics Publishing House, pg 104
Chongqing University Press, pg 104
Foreign Language Teaching & Research Press, pg 105
Fudan University Press, pg 105
Higher Education Press, pg 106
Shanghai Foreign Language Education Press, pg 109

SUBJECT INDEX

Colombia
Asociacion Instituto Linguistico de Verano, pg 111
Instituto Caro y Cuervo, pg 112
Siglo XXI Editores de Colombia Ltda, pg 113
Editorial Voluntad SA, pg 114

The Democratic Republic of the Congo
Centre de Recherche, et Pedagogie Appliquee, pg 114

Costa Rica
Promesa, Ediciones, pg 116
Editorial de la Universidad de Costa Rica, pg 117

Cote d'Ivoire
Heritage Publishing Co, pg 118

Croatia
ArTresor naklada, pg 118
Filozofski Fakultet Sveucilista u Zagrebu, pg 118
Knjizevni Krug Split, pg 119
Matica hrvatska, pg 119
Sveucilisna tiskara doo, pg 120

Czech Republic
Academia, pg 122
Barrister & Principal, pg 123
Jan Kanzelsberger, pg 125
Karolinum, nakladatelstvi, pg 125
NLN, Ltd The Lidove noviny Publishing House, pg 127
Pop Plus Rock Centrum, pg 127
Verlag Harry Putz, pg 128

Denmark
Aarhus Universitetsforlag, pg 129
Akademisk Forlag, pg 129
Egmont-Easy Readers, pg 131
Fremad A/S, pg 132
Kaleidoscope Publishers Ltd, pg 133
Museum Tusculanum Press, pg 134
Samfundslitteratur, pg 135

Dominican Republic
Pontificia Universidad Catolica Madre y Maestra, pg 136

Ecuador
Ediciones Abya-Yala, pg 137

Egypt (Arab Republic of Egypt)
American University in Cairo Press, pg 138
Al Arab Publishing House, pg 138
Dar El Shorouk Publishing & Distributing House, pg 138
Elias Modern Publishing House, pg 138
Middle East Book Centre, pg 139

Ethiopia
Addis Ababa University Press, pg 141

Finland
Akateeminen Kustannusliike Oy, pg 141
Suomalaisen Kirjallisuuden Seura, pg 144
Yliopistopaino/Helsinki University Press, pg 145

France
ABC Editions, pg 145
Editions Assimil SA, pg 148
Atelier National de Reproduction des Theses, pg 148
Editions Aubier-Montaigne SA, pg 149
Societe d'Edition Les Belles Lettres, pg 150
Breal, pg 151
Brud Nevez, pg 152
Circonflexe, pg 155
Cle International, pg 155
CNRS Editions, pg 155
Counseil International de la Langue Francaise, pg 157
Dunod Editeur, pg 160
ELLUG (Editions Litteraires et Linguistiques de l'Universite de Grenoble III), pg 162
Institut d'Ethnologie du Museum National d'Histoire Naturelle, pg 163
Institut d'Etudes Slaves, pg 163
Hachette Livre, pg 167
L'Harmattan, pg 168
Hermes Science Publications, pg 168
Editions Klincksieck, pg 171
Langues & Mondes/L'Asiatheque, pg 171
Editions Fernand Lanore Sarl, pg 172
Librairie Larousse, pg 172
Le Livre de Poche-L G F (Librairie Generale Francaise), pg 173
Editions G P Maisonneuve et Larose, pg 174
Presses Universitaires du Mirail, pg 176
Editions Modernes Media, pg 176
Editions Ophrys, pg 178
Editions Payot & Rivages, pg 179
Peeters-France, pg 179
Editions A et J Picard SA, pg 179
Presses de la Sorbonne Nouvelle/PSN, pg 181
Presses Universitaires de Caen, pg 181
Presses Universitaires de Grenoble, pg 181
Presses Universitaires de Lyon, pg 181
Presses Universitaires de Nancy, pg 181
Presses Universitaires du Septentrion, pg 181
Publications Orientalistes de France (POF), pg 182
Sofradif Editions Philippe Auzou, pg 185
Editions Spratbrow, pg 186
Universitas, pg 188
Publications de l'Universite de Pau, pg 188
Editions Vilo SA, pg 189

French Polynesia
Haere Po No Tahiti, pg 190

Germany
Akademie Verlag GmbH, pg 192
Aschendorffsche Verlagsbuchhandlung GmbH & Co KG, pg 195
Assimil GmbH, pg 196
Beacon Verlag Koerber OHG, pg 199
Verlag C H Beck (OHG), pg 200
Biblio-Zeller Verlag, pg 202

999

Bibliographisches Institut & F A Brockhaus AG, pg 203
Verlag Die Blaue Eule, pg 204
Boehlau-Verlag GmbH & Cie, pg 204
Oscar Brandstetter Verlag GmbH & Co KG, pg 206
Helmut Buske Verlag GmbH, pg 208
Verlag Darmstaedter Blaetter Schwarz und Co, pg 212
Diesterweg, Moritz Verlag, pg 216
Verlag Duerr & Kessler GmbH, pg 219
Klaus D Dutz, pg 219
Ein Fach-Verlag, pg 222
Ferd Dummler's Verlag, pg 227
Wilhelm Fink GmbH & Co Verlags-KG, pg 228
Harald Fischer Verlag GmbH, pg 228
Friedrich Frommann Verlag, pg 230
Graf Editions, pg 234
Verlag Grundlagen und Praxis GmbH & Co, pg 234
Walter de Gruyter GmbH & Co KG, pg 234
Harrassowitz Verlag, pg 237
S Hirzel Verlag GmbH und Co, pg 241
Holos Verlag, pg 242
Intertrans-Verlag GmbH, pg 245
ludicium Verlag GmbH, pg 245
Janus Verlagsgesellschaft, Dr Norbert Meder & Co, pg 246
Karl Knoll Verlag Alte Uni, pg 250
W Kohlhammer GmbH, abt Haussortiment, pg 252
Dr Anton Kovac Slavica Verlag, pg 253
Alfred Kroner Verlag, pg 253
Kubon Und Sagner, pg 254
Peter Lang GmbH Europaeischer Verlag der Wissenschaften, pg 255
Langenscheidt-Hachette, pg 255
Ingrid Langner, pg 256
Leibniz Verlag, pg 256
Logophon Lehrmittelverlag GmbH, pg 258
mentis Verlag GmbH, pg 262
J B Metzler'sche Verlagsbuchhandlung, pg 263
Gunter Narr Verlag, pg 266
Neuer Honos Verlag GmbH, pg 267
Max Niemeyer Verlag GmbH, pg 269
Oekumenischer Verlag Dr R-F Edel, pg 270
Georg Olms Verlag AG, pg 270
Orbis Verlag fur Publizistik GmbH, pg 270
Verlag Sigrid Persen, pg 272
Quelle und Meyer Verlag GmbH & Co, pg 276
Dr Ludwig Reichert Verlag, pg 278
Reise Know-How Verlag Peter Rump GmbH, pg 278
Verlagsgruppe Reise-Know-How, pg 278
Peter Meyer Reisefuhrer, pg 278
Roehrig Universitaets Verlag Gmbh, pg 279
Rossipaul Kommunikation GmbH, pg 280
Saarbrucker Druckerei und Verlag GmbH (SDV), pg 281
J D Sauerlaender's Verlag, pg 282
Erich Schmidt Verlag GmbH & Co, pg 283
Wilhelm Schmitz Verlag, pg 284
Ferdinand Schoeningh Verlag GmbH, pg 284

Schulz-Kirchner Verlag GmbH, pg 285
Spiess Volker Wissenschaftsverlag GmbH, pg 287
Stauffenburg Verlag Brigitte Narr GmbH, pg 289
Franz Steiner Verlag Wiesbaden GmbH, pg 289
Stern-Verlag Janssen & Co, pg 290
Steyler Verlag, pg 290
Stiefel GmbH Wandkarten Verlag, pg 290
Systhema Verlag GmbH, pg 291
Tuduv Verlagsgesellschaft mbH, pg 295
Tuebinger Vereinigung fur Volkskunde eV (TVV), pg 295
Universitaetsverlag C Winter Heidelberg GmbH, pg 296
UTB fuer Wissenschaft Uni-Taschenbuecher GmbH, pg 297
Vandenhoeck & Ruprecht, pg 297
VAS-Verlag fuer Akademische Schriften, Vas Karl-Heinz Balon, pg 297
Vervuert Verlagsgesellschaft, pg 298
Wachholtz Verlag GmbH, pg 300
Weidler Buchverlag Berlin, pg 301
Weidmannsche Verlagsbuchhandlung GmbH, pg 301
Verlag Wissenschaft und Politik/Helker Pflug, pg 303
Wissenschaftliche Buchgesellschaft, pg 303
Zeller Verlag GmbH & Co, pg 305

Ghana

Beginners Publishers, pg 306
Ghana Institute of Linguistics Literacy & Bible Translation (GILLBT), pg 307
Ghana Publishing Corporation, pg 307
Ghana Universities Press (GUP), pg 307

Greece

Hestia-1 D Hestia-Kollaros & Co Corporation, pg 311
Institute of Neohellenic Studies, Manolis Triantaphyllidis Foundation, pg 311
Mavrogianni Publications, pg 313
Morfotiko Idryma Ethnikis Trapezas, pg 313
Patakis Publishers, pg 314
J Sideris OE Ekdoseis, pg 315

Guadeloupe

Librairie Generale JASOR, pg 316

Holy See (Vatican City State)

Biblioteca Apostolica Vaticana, pg 317
Scuola Vaticana Paleografia - Scuola Vaticana di Paleografia Diplomatica e Archivistica, pg 317

Honduras

Editorial Guaymuras, pg 318

Hong Kong

The Chinese University Press, pg 319
Chung Hwa Book Co (HK) Ltd, pg 319
Hong Kong University Press, pg 320

Joint Publishing (HK) Co Ltd, pg 320
Witman Publishing Co (HK) Ltd, pg 322

Hungary

Akademiai Kiado, pg 323
Aranyhal Konyvkiado Goldfish Publishing, pg 323
Balassi Kiado Kft, pg 323
Nemzeti Tankoenyvkiado, pg 326

Iceland

Hid Islenzka Bokmenntafelag, pg 328
Stofnun Arna Magnussonar a Islandi, pg 329

India

Agam Kala Prakashan, pg 330
Ajanta Publications (India), pg 330
Asian Educational Services, pg 331
K P Bagchi & Co, pg 332
Bharat Publishing House, pg 332
Cosmo Publications, pg 335
Disha Prakashan, pg 336
Dutta Baruah Publishing Co Pvt Ltd, pg 336
General Book Depot, pg 337
Gyan Publishing House, pg 338
Heritage Publishers, pg 338
Jaico Publishing House, pg 340
Motilal Banarsidass Publishers Pvt Ltd, pg 343
Munshiram Manoharlal Publishers Pvt Ltd, pg 343
Naya Prokash, pg 344
New Light Publishers, pg 344
Paramount Sales (India) Pvt Ltd, pg 345
Pustak Mahal, pg 346
Rahul Publishing House, pg 347
Rajasthan Hindi Granth Academy, pg 347
Regency Publications, pg 347
Samkaleen Prakashan, pg 349
Sri Satguru Publications, pg 349
Somaiya Publications Pvt Ltd, pg 350
Star Publications (P) Ltd, pg 351

Indonesia

Bhratara Karya Aksara, pg 354
Penerbit Nusa Indah, pg 356

Israel

Agudat Sabah, pg 365
Amichai Publishing House Ltd, pg 365
Bar Ilan University Press, pg 365
Ben-Zvi Institute, pg 365
Dekel Publishing House, pg 366
Gefen Publishing House Ltd, pg 367
Haifa University Press, pg 368
Machbarot Lesifrut, pg 370
Misgav Yerushalayim, pg 370
Password Publishers Ltd, pg 371
Prolog Publishing House, pg 371
Tcherikover Publishers Ltd, pg 372

Italy

Editore Armando Armando SRL, pg 376
Atlantica Editrice SARL, pg 377
Book Editore, pg 378
Bulzoni Editore SRL (Le Edizioni Universitarie d'Italia), pg 379
Edizioni Cadmo SRL, pg 379
Casa Editrice Felice Le Monnier, pg 380

Edistudio di Brunetto Casini, pg 380
Ciranna - Roma, pg 381
Cisalpino - Monduzzi, pg 382
CLEUP - Cooperative Libraria Editrice dell 'Universita di Padova, pg 382
CLUEB (Cooperativa Libraria Universitaria Editrice Bologna), pg 382
Colonnese Editore, pg 382
Edizioni Della Torre di Salvatore Fozzi & C SAS, pg 384
Edizioni dell'Orso SAS, pg 385
Essegi, pg 388
Arnaldo Forni Editore SRL, pg 389
Giunti Publishing Group, pg 391
Guerra Edizioni Guru Azp, pg 392
Herder Editrice e Libreria, pg 392
Editrice Innocenti SNC, pg 393
Instituti Editoriali E Poligrafici Internazionali SRL, pg 393
Edizioni Internazionali di Letterature e Scienze, pg 394
L Japadre Editore, pg 394
L'Erma di Bretschneider SRL, pg 395
Casa Editrice Le Lettere SRL, pg 395
Liguori Editore SRL, pg 396
Loescher Editore SRL, pg 396
Loffredo Editore Napoli SpA®, pg 396
Angelo Longo Editore, pg 396
Macmillan Heinemann ELT, pg 397
Mucchi Editore SRL, pg 400
Societa Editrice Il Mulino, pg 400
Officina Edizioni di Aldo Quinti, pg 401
Leo S Olschki, pg 402
Palatina Editrice, pg 402
G B Palumbo & C Editore SpA, pg 402
Patron Editore SrL, pg 403
Pitagora Editrice SRL, pg 403
Istituto Poligrafico e Zecca dello Stato, pg 404
Riccardo Ricciardi Editore SpA, pg 405
Editori Riuniti, pg 405
Rosenberg e Sellier Editori in Torino, pg 406
SAIE Editrice SRL, pg 406
Salerno Editrice SRL, pg 406
Schena Editore, pg 407
Sicania, pg 408
Studio Bibliografico Adelmo Polla, pg 409
Editrice Tirrenia Stampatori SAS, pg 410
Todariana Editrice, pg 410
Unipress, pg 410
Valmartina Editore SRL, pg 411
Zanichelli Editore SpA, pg 412
Edizioni Zara, pg 412

Jamaica

Carlong Publishers (Caribbean) Ltd, pg 412
Jamaica Publishing House Ltd, pg 413

Japan

Eichosha Company Ltd, pg 416
Fuzambo Publishing Co, pg 416
GakuseiSha Publishing Co Ltd, pg 416
Hakutei-Sha, pg 417
Hyoronsha Publishing Co Ltd, pg 417
Japan Broadcast Publishing Co Ltd, pg 418

PUBLISHERS

Japan Travel Bureau Inc, pg 418
Kaitakusha, pg 419
Keisuisha Publishing Company Ltd, pg 419
Kenkyusha Ltd, pg 419
Kodansha, pg 420
Kodansha International, pg 420
Kokusho Kankokai Co Ltd, pg 420
Nankodo Co Ltd, pg 421
Nan'un-Do Company Ltd, pg 422
Nippon Hoso Shuppan Kyokai (NHK Publishing), pg 422
Sanseido Co Ltd, pg 424
Sanshusha Publishing Co, Ltd, pg 424
Seibido, pg 424
Seibundo Shuppan, pg 425
Seiwa Shoten Co Ltd, pg 425
Shueisha Inc, pg 426
The Simul Press Inc, pg 426
Takahashi Shoten Co Ltd, pg 427
Thomson Learning, pg 427
3A Corporation, pg 427
Toho Book Store, pg 427
Tokai University Press, pg 427
Charles E Tuttle Publishing Co Inc, pg 428
Yamaguchi Shoten, pg 429
Yohan Shuppan, pg 429

Kenya
British Institute in Eastern Africa, pg 431
Kenway Publications Ltd, pg 432

Republic of Korea
Bakyoung Publishing Co, pg 434
BCM Media Inc, pg 434
Chang-josa Publishing Co, pg 435
Chong No Books Publishing Co Ltd, pg 435
Eulyu Publishing Co Ltd, pg 436
Ewha Womans University Press, pg 436
Iljisa Publishing House, pg 437
Korea University Press, pg 437
Koreaone Press Inc, pg 438
Literature Academy, pg 438
Pan Korea Book Corporation, pg 439
Samhwa Publishing Co, pg 440
Seoul International Publishing House, pg 440
Seoul National University Press, pg 440
Sogang University Press, pg 440

Kuwait
Ministry of Information, pg 441

Latvia
Avots, pg 441

Lebanon
Darl el-Machreq Sarl, pg 443
Librairie du Liban, pg 443
Librairie Orientale sal, pg 443

Liechtenstein
Saendig Reprint Verlag, Hans-Rainer Wohlwend, pg 445

Lithuania
Academia, pg 445
AS Narbuto Leidykla (AS Narbutas' Publishers), pg 445
Baltos Lankos, pg 445
Mokslo ir enciklopediju leidybos institutas, pg 446

Luxembourg
Editions Emile Borschette, pg 447

Macau
Instituto Portugues Oriente, pg 448

The Former Yugoslav Republic of Macedonia
Murgorski Zoze, pg 449
Zumpres Publishing Firm, pg 449

Malaysia
Darulfikir, pg 451
Oscar Book International, pg 453
Pelanduk Publications (M) Sdn Bhd, pg 453

Malta
The University of Malta Publications Section, pg 456

Mexico
Editorial Avante SA de Cv, pg 458
El Colegio de Mexico AC, pg 459
Editorial Edicol SA, pg 460
El Colegio de Michoacan A C, pg 460
Libra Editorial SA de CV, pg 463
Instituto Nacional de Antropologia e Historia, pg 464
Nova Grupo Editorial SA de CV, pg 464
Editorial Nueva Imagen SA, pg 464
Pearson Educacion de Mexico, SA de CV, pg 465
Siglo XXI Editores SA de CV, pg 467
Sistemas Tecnicos de Edicion SA de CV, pg 467
Universidad Nacional Autonoma de Mexico (National University of Mexico), pg 467

Republic of Moldova
Lumina Publishing House, pg 468

Morocco
Editions Le Fennec, pg 470
Editions Okad, pg 470
Editions La Porte, pg 470

Nepal
International Standards Books & Periodicals (P) Ltd, pg 471

Netherlands
APA (Academic Publishers Associated), pg 472
John Benjamins BV, pg 474
Boom Uitgeverij, pg 474
Uitgeverij Coutinho BV, pg 476
HES & De Graaf Publishers BV, pg 478
Holland University Press BV (APA), pg 478
ICG Publications Holland, pg 479
Uitgeverij Intertaal BV, pg 479
IOS Press BV, pg 479
KITLV Press Royal Institute of Linguistics & Anthropology, pg 479
Mirananda Publishers BV, pg 481
Prometheus, pg 483
Swets & Zeitlinger Publishers, pg 485
Tilburg University Press, pg 485
Van Gorcum & Comp BV, pg 486
VU Boekhandel/Uitgeverij BV, pg 487

New Zealand
ABA Books, pg 488
New House Publishers Ltd, pg 493
Outrigger Publishers, pg 494
Nelson Price Milburn Ltd, pg 494
Victoria University Press, pg 496

Nicaragua
Academia Nicaraguense de la Lengua, pg 497

Nigeria
Gbabeks Publishers Ltd, pg 499
Ilesanmi Press (Educational Publishers) Ltd, pg 499
Ogunsanya Press, Publishers and Bookstores Ltd, pg 501
Riverside Communications, pg 501
Vantage Publishers International Ltd, pg 502

Norway
Forlaget Fag og Kultur, pg 503
Folhenuniversitetets Forlag, pg 503
Norsk Bokreidingslag L/L, pg 504
Universitetsforlaget, pg 505

Pakistan
International Educational Services, pg 507

Papua New Guinea
Summer Institute of Linguistics, pg 510

Peru
Ediciones Brown SA, pg 511
Fondo Editorial de la Pontificia Universidad Catolica del Peru, pg 511
Instituto Frances de Estudios Andinos, IFEA, pg 511
Editorial Horizonte, pg 511

Philippines
Anvil Publishing Inc, pg 512
Saint Mary's Publishing Corp, pg 515
Salesiana Publishers Inc, pg 515
SIBS Publishing House Inc, pg 515
Vibal Publishing House Inc (VPHI), pg 515

Poland
Energeia sp zoo Wydawnictwo, pg 516
Ossolineum Zaklad Narodowy im Ossolinskich - Wydawnictwo, pg 518
Polish Scientific Publishers PWN, pg 519
Towarzystwo Naukowe w Toruniu, pg 520
'Wiedza Powszechna' Panstwowe Wydawnictwo, pg 521
Wydawnictwo DiG, pg 521

Portugal
Armenio Amado Editora de Simoes, Beirao & Ca Lda, pg 522
Coimbra Editora Lda, pg 523
Constancia Editores, SA, pg 524
Edicoes Cosmos, pg 524
Edicoes 70, Lda, pg 524
Imprensa Nacional-Casa da Moeda, pg 526
Lidel Edicoes Tecnicas, Lda, pg 526
Porto Editora Lda, pg 528

SUBJECT INDEX

Editorial Presenca, pg 528
Edicoes Rolim Lda, pg 529
Almerinda Teixeira, pg 529

Puerto Rico
Piedras Press, Inc, pg 531

Romania
Editura Academiei Romane, pg 531
Ars Longa Publishing House, pg 532
The Center for Romanian Studies, pg 532
Coresi SRL, pg 532
Editura Excelsior, pg 533
Lider Verlag, pg 534
Editura Meridiane, pg 534
Editura Niculescu, pg 534
Editura Stiintifica si Enciclopedica, pg 536

Russian Federation
Airis Press, pg 537
Izdatel'stvo Mordovskogo gosudar stvennogo, pg 538
Nauka Publishers, pg 540
Okoshko Ltd Publishers (Izdatelstvo), pg 541
Progress Publishers, pg 541
Voronezh State University Publishers, pg 542
Izdatelstvo Vysshaya Shkola, pg 543

Saudi Arabia
King Saud University, pg 543

Senegal
Centre de Linguistique Appliquee, pg 544

Singapore
Cannon International, pg 545
Celebrity Educational Publishers, pg 545
Global Educational Services Pte Ltd, pg 546
Intellectual Publishing Co, pg 546
Singapore University Press Pte Ltd, pg 548

Slovakia
Slo Viet, pg 550
Slovenske pedagogicke nakladateistvo, pg 550
VEDA (Vydavatel'stvo Slovenskej akademie vied), pg 551

Slovenia
Franc-Franc podjetje za promocijo kulture Murska Sobota d o o, pg 551
Univerza v Ljubljani Ekonomska Fakulteta, pg 552
Zalozba Mihelac d o o, pg 552
Zalozba Obzorja d d Maribor, pg 552

South Africa
Clever Books, pg 553
Human & Rousseau (Pty) Ltd, pg 555
Ivy Publications, pg 555
Maskew Miller Longman, pg 557
Unisa Press, pg 560
Van Schaik Publishers, pg 560

1001

SUBJECT INDEX

Spain

Academia de la Llingua Asturiana, pg 561
Altea, Taurus, Alfaguara SA, pg 563
Anglo-Didactica, SL Editorial, pg 563
Arco Libros SL, pg 564
Bosch Casa Editorial SA, pg 565
Calesa SA Editorial La, pg 566
Editorial Cantabrica SA, pg 566
Casa de Velazquez, pg 566
Ediciones Catedra SA, pg 566
Ediciones Colegio De Espana (ECE), pg 568
Didaco Comunicacion y Didactica, SA, pg 569
Ediciones y Distribuciones Universitarias SA, pg 571
Editorial Ediseis SA, pg 572
Editorial Empeno 14, pg 573
Instituto de Estudios Riojanos, pg 574
EUNSA (Ediciones Universidad de Navarra SA), pg 574
Fondo de Cultura Economica de Espana, SL, pg 574
Fragua Editorial, pg 574
Vicent Garcia Editores, SA, pg 575
Editorial Herder SA, pg 577
Ediciones Hiperion SL, pg 577
Ediciones Istmo SA, pg 579
Editorial Juventud SA, pg 579
Libsa Editorial SA, pg 580
Lid Editorial Empresarial, SL, pg 580
Antonio Machado, SA, pg 580
Editorial Moll SL, pg 582
Editorial la Muralla SA, pg 583
Oikos-Tau SA Ediciones, pg 584
Oxford University Press Espana SA, pg 585
Ediciones Partenon, pg 586
Pearson Educacion S A, pg 586
Editorial Playor SA, pg 587
Pre-Textos, pg 587
Josep Ruaix Editor, pg 589
Universidad de Santiago de Compostela, pg 589
Editorial Sintesis, SA, pg 590
Grup 62, pg 591
Ramon Sopena SA, pg 591
SPES Editorial SL, pg 591
Axel Springer Publicaciones, pg 591
Stanley Editorial, pg 591
Editorial Txertoa, pg 594
Universidad de Oviedo Servicio de Publicaciones, pg 594
Editorial Verbum SL, pg 595
Visor Libros, pg 596
Edicions Xerais de Galicia, pg 596

Sri Lanka

Inter-Cultural Book Promoters, pg 597

Sweden

Acta Universitatis Gothoburgensis, pg 599
Akademiforlaget Goteborgslitteratur, pg 600
Folkuniversitetets foerlag, pg 602
Hans Richter Laromedel, pg 604
Liber AB, pg 604
Mezopotamya Publishing & Distribution, pg 604
Studentlitteratur AB, pg 606

Switzerland

Armenia Editions, pg 608
Bibliographisches Institut und F A Brockhaus AG, pg 610
Les Editions de la Fondation Martin Bodmer, pg 610
Castle Publications SA, pg 611
Cockatoo Press (Schweiz), Thailand-Publikationen, pg 611
Georg Editeur SA, pg 614
Helbing und Lichtenhahn Verlag AG, pg 615
Verlag Huber & Co AG, pg 616
Kolumbus-Verlag, pg 617
Langenscheidt AG Zuerich-Zug, pg 618
Lia rumantscha, pg 618
Peter Meili & Co, Buchhandluna, pg 619
PIE-Peter Lang SA, pg 622
Editions Pro Schola, pg 622
Hans Rohr Verlag, pg 623
Sabe AG Verlagsinstitut, pg 623

Syrian Arab Republic

Damascus University Press, pg 628
Institut Francais d'Etudes Arabes de Damas, pg 628

Taiwan, Province of China

Jillion Publishing Co, pg 630

United Republic of Tanzania

DUP (1996) Ltd, pg 633
Institute of Kiswahili Research, pg 633
Northwestern Publishers, pg 634
Press & Publicity Centre Ltd, pg 634
Tanzania Publishing House, pg 634

Thailand

Graphic Art Publishing, pg 635
Thai Watana Panich Co, Ltd, pg 636

Tunisia

Academie Tunisienne des Sciences, des Lettres et des Arts Beit El Hekma, pg 637
Dar Arabia Lil Kitab, pg 637
Faculte des Sciences Humaines et Sociales de Tunis, pg 638
Maison d'Edition Mohamed Ali Hammi, pg 638
Les Editions de l'Arbre, pg 638

Turkey

Ataturk Kultur, Dil ve Tarih, Yusek Kurumu Baskanligi, pg 639
Bilden Bilgisayar, pg 639

Uganda

Fountain Publishers Ltd, pg 642

Ukraine

Naukova Dumka Publishers, pg 643

United Kingdom

Aris & Phillips Ltd, pg 648
Arnold, pg 648
BBC Worldwide Publishers, pg 653
Blackwell Publishers, pg 655
Cambridge University Press, pg 662
Centre for Information on Language Teaching & Research (CILT), pg 666
Chancerel International Publishers Ltd, pg 666
Chapter Two, pg 666
Gerald Duckworth & Co Ltd, pg 676

Educational Explorers (Publishers) Ltd, pg 677
Elm Publications, pg 678
EPER, pg 679
European Schoolbooks Ltd, pg 680
The Eurospan Group, pg 680
Facts On File, pg 681
Global Books Ltd, pg 687
Gomer Press (J D Lewis & Sons Ltd), pg 688
Graham-Cameron Publishing & Illustration, pg 688
Gwasg Prifysgol Cymru, pg 690
Gwasg Gwenffrwd, pg 690
Helicon Publishing Ltd, pg 694
Hodder & Stoughton Educational, pg 696
Hugo's Language Books Ltd, pg 697
Institute of Irish Studies, The Queens University of Belfast, pg 699
Intellect Ltd, pg 700
Karnak House, pg 703
Letterland International Ltd, pg 707
Linguaphone Institute Ltd, pg 708
Y Lolfa Cyf, pg 708
Maney Publishing, pg 711
MIT Press Ltd, pg 715
Motilal (UK) Books of India, pg 715
Multilingual Matters Ltd, pg 716
Nelson Thornes Ltd, pg 718
The Oleander Press, pg 721
Peter Owen Ltd, pg 722
Oxford University Press, pg 723
Pearson Education, pg 725
Pearson Education Europe, Mideast & Africa, pg 725
Prim-Ed Publishing UK Ltd, pg 730
Psychological Corporation Ltd, pg 731
Reading & Language Information Centre, pg 733
Reaktion Books Ltd, pg 733
Roundhouse Publishing Ltd, pg 736
Routledge, pg 736
Routledge Curzon, pg 736
Sage Publications Ltd, pg 737
St Jerome Publishing, pg 738
School of Oriental & African Studies, pg 739
Sheffield Academic Press Ltd, pg 741
Speechmark Publishing Ltd, pg 744
Thoemmes Press, pg 748
University of Exeter Press, pg 751
University of Wales Press, pg 751
Verbatim, pg 752
Voltaire Foundation Ltd, pg 753
Whiting & Birch Ltd, pg 756
Wimbledon Publishing Company Ltd, pg 757
Yale University Press London, pg 759

Uruguay

Nordan-Comunidad, pg 760

Venezuela

Editorial Biosfera CA, pg 762

Yugoslavia

Alfa-Narodna Knjiga, pg 764

Zambia

Lundula Publishing House, pg 766
Zambia Educational Publishing House, pg 767

Zimbabwe

Mercury Press Pvt Ltd, pg 769
University of Zimbabwe Publications, pg 769
Vision Publications, pg 769

LAW

Albania

NL SH, pg 1

Argentina

Editorial Abaco de Rodolfo Depalma, pg 2
Abeledo-Perrot SAE e l, pg 2
Editorial Astrea de Alfredo y Ricardo Depalma SRL, pg 3
AZ Editora SA, pg 3
Fundacion Editorial de Belgrano, pg 4
Editorial Cangallo SACl, pg 4
Editorial Claridad SA, pg 4
Depalma SRL, pg 5
Editorial Ruy Diaz SAEIC, pg 5
Editorial Idearium de la Universidad de Mendoza (EDIUM), pg 5
EUDEBA (Editorial Universitaria de Buenos Aires), pg 6
Juris Editorial, pg 6
La Ley SA Editora e Impresora, pg 7
Editorial Losada SA, pg 7
Instituto Nacional de Ciencia y Tecnica Hidrica (INCYTH), pg 7
Editorial Plus Ultra SA, pg 8
Ediciones La Rocca, pg 8
Tipografica Editora Argentina, pg 9
Editorial Universidad SRL, pg 9
Victor P de Zavalia SA, pg 10
Editorial Zeus SRL, pg 10

Armenia

Ajstan Publishers, pg 10

Australia

Edward Arnold (Australia) Pty Ltd, pg 12
Artemis Publishing Pty Ltd, pg 12
Beazer Publishing Company Pty Ltd, pg 14
Blackstone Press Pty Ltd, pg 15
Butterworths Australia Ltd, pg 16
The Federation Press, pg 22
Fernfawn Publications, pg 22
Laams Publications, pg 29
Law Book Co Information Services, pg 29
Pearson Education Australia, pg 37
Prospect Media Pty Ltd, pg 39
Thornbill Press, pg 44
La Trobe University Press, pg 45
VCTA Publishing, pg 46
Villamonta Publishing Service Inc, pg 47
Wileman Publications, pg 47

Austria

Boehlau Verlag GmbH & Co KG, pg 50
Buchhandlung WUV Dolmetsch, pg 50
Hollinek Bruder & Co mbH Gesellschaftsdruckerei & Verlagsbuchhandring, pg 53
IAEA - International Atomic Energy Agency, pg 53
Linde Verlag Wien GmbH, pg 54
Manz'sche Verlags- und Universitaetsbuchhandlung, pg 54
Medien & Recht, pg 55

Verlag der Oesterreichischen Akademie der Wissenschaften (OEAW), pg 56
Verlag des Oesterreichischen Gewerkschaftsbundes GmbH, pg 56
Andreas Schnider Verlags-Atelier, pg 58
Signum Verlag GmbH & Co KG, pg 58
Springer-Verlag Wien, pg 59
WUV/Facultas Universitaetsverlag, pg 61

Belarus
Belaruskaya Encyklapedyya, pg 63
Publishing Center of Belarus State University, pg 63

Belgium
Academia-Bruylant, pg 63
Acco CV, pg 64
Maison d'Editions Baha'ies ASBL, pg 64
Vanden Broele NV, pg 65
Eteblissements Emile Bruylant SA, pg 65
CED-Samsom, pg 66
Editions de la Chambre de Commerce et d'Industrie SA, pg 66
La Charte Editions juridiques, pg 66
Creadif, pg 67
Davidsfonds VZW, pg 67
Editions De Boeck-Larcier SA, pg 67
Institut Royal des Relations Internationales, pg 69
Intersentia Uitgevers NV, pg 69
Uitgeverij J van ln, pg 70
Editions Juridiques Kluwer a Deurne Anvers, pg 70
Larcier-Department of De Boeck & Larcier SA, pg 71
Editions Lessius ASBL, pg 71
Leuven University Press, pg 71
Maklu, pg 71
Presses Universitaires de Liege, pg 73
Publications des Facultes Universitaires Saint Louis, pg 73
Sonneville Press (Uitgeverij) VTW, pg 74
Editions Techniques et Scientifiques SPRL, pg 74
UGA Editions (Uitgeverij), pg 74
Uitgeverij De Garve, pg 75
Editions de l'Universite de Bruxelles, pg 75
Imprimeur - Editeur Vaillant-Carmanne SA, pg 75
Vander Editions, SA, pg 75

Bolivia
Gisbert y Cia SA, pg 76

Bosnia and Herzegovina
Bemust doo Novinsko-Izdavacko stamparsko i trgovacko preduzece, pg 77

Botswana
The Botswana Society, pg 77
Morula Press, Business School of Botswana, pg 77

Brazil
Aide Editora e Comercio de Livros Ltda, pg 78
Editora Alfa Omega Ltda, pg 78
Editora Atlas SA, pg 79

Centro de Estudos Juridicosdo Para (CEJUP), pg 80
Editorial Dimensao Ltda, pg 81
Edipro-Edicoes Profissionais Ltda, pg 81
Companhia Editora Forense, pg 82
EDUC - Editora da PUC-SP, pg 82
EDUSC - Editora da Universidade do Sagrado Coracao, pg 82
Livraria Martins Fontes Editora Ltda, pg 83
Editora Forense, pg 83
Forense Universitaria Editora, pg 83
Livraria Freitas Bastos Editora SA, pg 83
Editora Globo SA, pg 84
Hemus Editora Ltda, pg 85
Icone Editora Ltda, pg 85
Iglu Editora Ltda, pg 85
Livraria Dos Advogados Editora Ltda, pg 86
Edicoes Loyola SA, pg 87
LTR Editora Ltda, pg 87
Oliveira Rocha-Comercio e Servics Ltda, pg 89
Editora Resenha Tributaria Ltda, pg 90
Saraiva SA, Livreiros Editores, pg 91
Livraria Sulina Editora, pg 92
Tempus Editores, pg 92
Livraria e Editora Universitaria de Direito Ltda, pg 93

Bulgaria
Ciela Publishing House, pg 94
Dolphin Press Group Ltd, pg 95
Naouka i Izkoustvo, Ltd, pg 97
Seven Hills Publishers, pg 97
Sibi, pg 97
Slavena, pg 98

Cameroon
Presses Universitaires d'Afrique, pg 99

Chile
Editorial Andres Bello/Editorial Juridica de Chile, pg 100
Edeval (Universidad de Valparaiso), pg 100
Ediciones Universitarias de Valparaiso, pg 101

China
Anhui People's Publishing House, pg 102
Beijing Publishing House, pg 102
China Film Press, pg 103
CITIC Publishing House, pg 104
Foreign Languages Press, pg 105
Fudan University Press, pg 105
Lanzhou University Press, pg 107
The Law Publishing House, pg 107
Patent Documentation Publishing House, pg 107
Science Press, pg 108
Shandong People's Publishing House, pg 109
Wuhan University Press, pg 110

Colombia
Centro Regional para el Fomento del Libro en America Latina y el Caribe, pg 111
Universidad Externado de Colombia, pg 112
LEGIS - Editores SA, pg 112
Ediciones Monserrate, pg 113

The Democratic Republic of the Congo
Connaissance et Pratique du Droit Zairos (CDPZ), pg 115
Presses Universitaires du Zaiire (PUZ), pg 115

Costa Rica
Juricom, pg 116
Editorial Porvenir, pg 116
Editorial de la Universidad de Costa Rica, pg 117

Cote d'Ivoire
Centre d'Edition et de Diffusion Africaines, pg 117
Universite d' Abidjan, pg 118

Croatia
Informator dd, pg 119
Knjizevni Krug Split, pg 119
Narodne Novine, pg 119

Cuba
Editora Politica, pg 121
Universidad Central de la Villas, Centro Documentacion e Informacion Cientifica Tecnica, pg 121

Czech Republic
Babtext Nakladatelska Spolecnost, pg 123
Doplnek, pg 124
Grada Publishing sro, pg 124
Nakladatelstvi Josef Hribal, pg 124
Karolinum, nakladatelstvi, pg 125
Prace, pg 127
Trizonia, pg 128

Denmark
Akademisk Forlag, pg 129
Dansk Historisk Handbogsforlag ApS, pg 131
Djof Publishing Jurist-og Okonomforbundets Forlag, pg 131
Christian Ejlers' Forlag aps, pg 131
Forlaget FSR A/S (ITID A/S), pg 132
J H Schultz Information A/S, pg 135

Dominican Republic
Pontificia Universidad Catolica Madre y Maestra, pg 136
Sociedad Editorial Dominicana SA, pg 137

Ecuador
Corporacion de Estudios y Publicaciones, pg 137
Corporacion Editora Nacional, pg 137
Ediciones Legales SA, pg 137
Pontificia Universidad Catolica de Ecuador, Centro de Publicaciones, pg 137

Egypt (Arab Republic of Egypt)
Al Arab Publishing House, pg 138
Dar al-Nahda al Arabia, pg 138
Dar El Shorouk, pg 138
Dar El Shorouk Publishing & Distributing House, pg 138

Estonia
National Library of Estonia, pg 140
Olion Publishers, pg 140

Finland
Kauppakaari Oyj Lakimiesliiton Kustannus, Yrityksen Tietokirjat, pg 142

France
Atelier National de Reproduction des Theses, pg 148
Les Ateliers d'Orion, pg 148
Editions Bertrandl-Lacoste, pg 150
Presses Universitaires de Bordeaux (PUB), pg 151
Breal, pg 151
Editions Casteilla, pg 153
Centre de Librairie et d'Editions Techniques (CLET), pg 153
CERDIC-Publications, pg 153
Editions Charles-Lavauzelle SA, pg 154
CNRS Editions, pg 155
Codes Rousseau, pg 155
Council of Europe Publishing, pg 156
Editions Cujas, pg 157
Editions Dalloz Sirey, pg 157
Editions Delmas, pg 158
La Documentation Francaise, pg 159
Librairie Generale de Droit et de Jurisprudence (LGDJ) - Montchrestien, pg 160
Edicef - Editions Classiques d'Expression Francaise, pg 161
Editions d'Organisation, pg 161
Les Editions ESF, pg 161
Les Editions de l'Epargne, pg 162
Editions Eres, pg 162
Editions Eska, pg 162
Paul Geuthner Librairie Orientaliste, pg 166
Groupe Expansion, pg 167
Groupe Moniteur -L'Argus, pg 167
Hermes Science Publications, pg 168
Joly Editions, pg 170
Editions Juridiques Associees - LGDJ/Montchrestien, pg 170
Editions Juridiques Africaines, pg 171
Editions Juridiques et Techniques Lamy SA, pg 171
Editions du Juris-Classeur, pg 171
Editions Juris Service, pg 171
LT Editions-J Lanore-H Laurens, pg 172
Editions Universitaires LCF, pg 172
Editions Francis Lefebvre, pg 172
Editions Legislatives, pg 172
LiTec (Librairies Techniques SA), pg 173
Maxima Laurent du Mesnil Editeur, pg 175
Editions du Moniteur, pg 176
Naufal Group Sarl, pg 177
Nouvelles Editions Fiduciaires, pg 178
Editions Odile Jacob, pg 178
Editions du Papyrus, pg 179
Editions Pedone, pg 179
Presses Universitaires de France (PUF), pg 181
Presses Universitaires de Grenoble, pg 181
Presses Universitaires de Lyon, pg 181
Presses Universitaires de Nancy, pg 181
Presses Universitaires du Septentrion, pg 181
Publications de l'Universite de Rouen, pg 182
Editions du Puits Fleuri, pg 182

Sofiac (Societe Francaise des Imprimeries Administratives Centrales), pg 185
Sofradif Editions Philippe Auzou, pg 185
Publications de la Sorbonne, pg 186
Publications de l'Universite de Pau, pg 188
Librairie Vuibert, pg 189
Editions Weka, pg 189

Germany

Verlag Karl Alber GmbH, pg 192
Antiquariat und Verlag Auvermann Keip GmbH, pg 194
Bank-Verlag GmbH, pg 198
Verlag C H Beck (OHG), pg 200
Berlin Verlag Arno Spitz GmbH, pg 200
Bertelsmann Lexikon Verlag GmbH, pg 201
W Bertelsmann Verlag GmbH & Co KG, pg 201
Biblio-Zeller Verlag, pg 202
Verlag Hermann Boehlaus Nachfolger Weimar GmbH & Co, pg 205
Richard Boorberg Verlag GmbH & Co, pg 205
Oscar Brandstetter Verlag GmbH & Co KG, pg 206
Bund-Verlag GmbH, pg 208
Bundesanzeiger Verlagsgesellschaft, pg 208
Carl Link Verlag-Gesellschaft mbH Fachverlag fur Verwaltungsrecht, pg 209
Centaurus-Verlagsgesellschaft GmbH, pg 209
Compact Verlag GmbH, pg 211
Die Verlag H Schafer GmbH, pg 216
Dreisam Ratgeber in der Rutsker Verlag GmbH, pg 218
Duncker und Humblot GmbH, pg 219
N G Elwert Verlag, pg 222
Erich Fleischer Verlag, pg 228
Verlag Franz Vahlen GmbH, pg 229
Friedrich Kiehl Verlag GmbH, pg 230
Friedrich Frommann Verlag, pg 230
Verlag Ernst und Werner Gieseking GmbH, pg 232
Wilhelm Goldmann Verlag GmbH, pg 233
Walter de Gruyter GmbH & Co KG, pg 234
Alfred Hammer, pg 236
Haufe Mediengruppe, pg 238
Rudolf Haufe Verlag GmbH & Co KG, pg 238
Joh Heider Verlag GmbH, pg 239
Hestra-Verlag Hernichel & Dr Strauss GmbH & Co KG, pg 240
Carl Heymanns Verlag KG, pg 240
Hans Holzmann Verlag GmbH und Co KG, pg 242
Huthig GmbH & Co KG, pg 244
Industria-Verlagsbuchhandlung GmbH, pg 244
SachBuchVerlag Kellner, pg 248
Kirschbaum Verlag GmbH, pg 249
Klages-Verlag, pg 249
Vittorio Klostermann GmbH, pg 250
Verlag Knut Reim, Jugendpresseverlag, pg 251
K F Koehler Verlag, pg 251
Verlagsgruppe Koehler/Mittler, pg 251
Verlag Koenigshausen und Neumann GmbH, pg 251

W Kohlhammer GmbH, abt Haussortiment, pg 252
Kulturbuch-Verlag GmbH, pg 254
Kulturstiftung der deutschen Vertriebenen, pg 254
Ambro Lacus, Buch- und Bildverlag Walter Kremnitz, pg 255
Institut fuer Landes- und Stadtentwicklungsforschung, ILS Nordrhein-Westfalen, pg 255
Peter Lang GmbH Europaeischer Verlag der Wissenschaften, pg 255
Lebenshilfe-Verlag Marburg, Verlag der Bundesvereinigung Lebenshilfe fuer Menschen mit geistiger Behinderung eV, pg 256
Leipziger Universitaetsverlag GmbH, pg 257
Leitfadenverlag Verlag Dieter Sudholt, pg 257
Libertas- Europaeisches Institut GmbH, pg 257
Hermann Luchterhand Verlag GmbH, pg 259
Mohr Siebeck, pg 264
Verlag Neue Wirtschafts-Briefe GmbH & Co KG, pg 267
Nomos Verlagsgesellschaft mbH und Co KG, pg 269
Georg Olms Verlag AG, pg 270
pmi Verlag, pg 274
PIAG Presse Informations AG, pg 275
Verlag Recht und Wirtschaft GmbH, pg 277
Rossipaul Kommunikation GmbH, pg 280
Schapen Edition, H W Louis, pg 282
Verlag Dr Otto Schmidt KG, pg 283
Erich Schmidt Verlag GmbH & Co, pg 283, 284
Max Schmidt-Roemhild Verlag, pg 284
R S Schulz Verlag GmbH, pg 285
Otto Schwartz Fachbochhandlung GmbH, pg 286
Scientia Verlag und Antiquariat, pg 286
Dr Arthur L Sellier & Co-Walter de Gruyter GmbH & Co KG OHG, pg 286
Springer-Verlag GmbH & Co KG, pg 288
Verlag fuer Standesamtswesen GmbH, pg 289
Franz Steiner Verlag Wiesbaden GmbH, pg 289
Stollfuss Verlag Bonn GmbH & Co KG, pg 290
TF Fachverlag Gmbh, pg 293
S Toeche-Mittler Verlag GmbH, pg 294
Wirtschaftsverlag Carl Ueberreuter, pg 295
Verlag fur die Rechts- und Anwaltspraxis GmbH & Co, pg 298
Verlagsgruppe Jehle-Rehm GmbH, pg 298
Verlag Deutsches Volksheimstaettenwerk GmbH, pg 299
Dokument und Analyse Verlag Bogislaw von Randow, pg 299
Votum Verlag, pg 299
VVF Verlag V Florentz GmbH, pg 299
Walhalla Fachverlag GmbH & Co KG Praetoria, pg 300
WEKA Firmengruppe GmbH & Co KG, pg 301

Werner Verlag GmbH & Co KG, pg 302
Verlag Westfaelisches Dampfboot, pg 302
Wiley-VCH Verlag GmbH, pg 302
Verlag fuer Wirtschaft & Verwaltung Hubert Wingen GmbH & Co KG, pg 303
Verlag Wissenschaft und Politik/ Helker Pflug, pg 303
Wissenschaftliche Buchgesellschaft, pg 303
WRS Verlag Wirtschaft, Recht und Steuern GmbH & Co KG, pg 304
Zeller Verlag GmbH & Co, pg 305

Ghana

Sedco Publishing Ltd, pg 308

Greece

Alamo Hellas, pg 308
Hestia-I D Hestia-Kollaros & Co Corporation, pg 311
Karatzas Charis, pg 312
Papazissis Publishers SA, pg 314
Sakkoulas Publications SA, pg 314

Holy See (Vatican City State)

Biblioteca Apostolica Vaticana, pg 317

Hong Kong

Butterworths Hong Kong, pg 318
The Chinese University Press, pg 319
Hong Kong University Press, pg 320
Joint Publishing (HK) Co Ltd, pg 320

Hungary

Akademiai Kiado, pg 323
Janus Pannonius Tudomanyegyetem, pg 324
KJK-Keaszov, pg 324
Nemzeti Tankoenyvkiado, pg 326
Novorg Kiado, pg 326
Osiris Kiado, pg 326
Saldo Penzugyi Tanacsado es Informatikai Rt, pg 326

India

Academic Book Corporation, pg 329
APH Publishing Corp, pg 331
Bharat Law House Pvt Ltd, pg 332
Bharatiya Samijik Vigyan Auusandhan Parishad, pg 332
Eastern Book Co, pg 336
Eastern Law House Pvt Ltd, pg 336
Gyan Publishing House, pg 338
Himalaya Publishing House, pg 338
Islamic Publishing House, pg 340
Jaico Publishing House, pg 340
Kali For Women, pg 341
Law Publishers, pg 341
National Book Organization, pg 343
Rajasthan Hindi Granth Academy, pg 347
Regency Publications, pg 347
Samkaleen Prakashan, pg 349
Scientific Book Agency, pg 349
Sultan Chand & Sons Pvt Ltd, pg 351
Vidhi, pg 352

Indonesia

Alumni PT, pg 353
P T Bulan Bintang, pg 354
Bumi Aksara PT, pg 354

Eresco PT, pg 355
Tintamas Indonesia PT, pg 357

Ireland

Emerald Publications, pg 360
Four Courts Press Ltd, pg 360
Gill & Macmillan Ltd, pg 361
Institute of Public Administration, pg 361
Oak Tree Press, pg 362
Round Hall Sweet & Maxwell, pg 363
Topaz Publications, pg 364

Israel

Bar Ilan University Press, pg 365
Eretz Hemdah Institute for Advanced Jewish Studies, pg 367
Gefen Publishing House Ltd, pg 367
The Magnes Press, pg 370
Sadan Publishing Ltd, pg 372
Schlesinger Institute, pg 372
Schocken Publishing House Ltd, pg 372

Italy

Verlagsanstalt Athesia, pg 377
Bancaria Editrice SpA, pg 377
Giuseppe Bonanno Editore, pg 378
Edizioni Bucalo SNC, pg 379
Buffetti, pg 379
Bulzoni Editore SRL (Le Edizioni Universitarie d'Italia), pg 379
Cacucci Editore, pg 379
Camera dei Deputati Ufficio Pubblicazioni Informazione Parlamentare, pg 379
Casa Editrice Libraria Ulrico Hoepli SpA, pg 380
CEDAM (Casa Editrice Dr A Milani), pg 380
Celuc Libri, pg 380
Il Cigno Galileo Galilei-Edizioni di Arte e Scienza, pg 381
Ciranna - Roma, pg 381
Cisalpino - Monduzzi, pg 382
Edizioni di Comunita SpA, pg 382
Giovanni De Vecchi Editore SpA, pg 384
DEI Tipographia del Genio Civile, pg 384
Direzione Generale Archivi, pg 385
Ecole Francaise de Rome, pg 385
Editori Laterza, pg 386
EGEA (Edizioni Giuridiche Economiche Aziendali), pg 387
ERGA SNC di Carla Ottino Merli & C (Edizioni Realizzazioni Grafiche - Artigiana), pg 388
Arnaldo Forni Editore SRL, pg 389
Editrice Giannotta di Sebastiano Pace Giannotta, pg 390
G Giappichelli Editore SRL, pg 390
A Giuffre Editore SpA, pg 390
Giuseppe Laterza Editore Snc, pg 391
Herbita Editrice di Leonardo Palermo, pg 392
Jandi-Sapi Editori, pg 394
Casa Editrice Dott Eugenio Jovene SpA, pg 394
LED - Edizioni Universitarie di Lettere Economia Diritto, pg 395
Liguori Editore SRL, pg 396
Vincenzo Lo Faro Editore, pg 396
Casa Editrice Menna di Sinisgalli Menna Giuseppina, pg 398
Edizioni del Mondo Giudiziario, pg 399
Monduzzi Editore SpA, pg 399
Mucchi Editore SRL, pg 400

PUBLISHERS — SUBJECT INDEX

Societa Editrice Il Mulino, pg 400
Patron Editore SrL, pg 403
Piccin Nuova Libraria SpA, pg 403
Pirola, pg 403
Istituto Poligrafico e Zecca dello Stato, pg 404
Editori Riuniti, pg 405
Laurus Robuffo Edizioni, pg 405
Rubbettino Editore, pg 406
Edizioni Scientifiche Italiane, pg 407
Societa Storica Catanese, pg 408
Edizioni del Sole 24 Ore, pg 408
Spirali Edizioni, pg 408
Urbaniana University Press, pg 410
UTET (Unione Tipografico-Editrice Torinese), pg 411
Zanichelli Editore SpA, pg 412

Jamaica
The Caribbean Law Publishing Co Ltd, pg 412
Jamaica Printing Services, pg 413

Japan
Fuzambo Publishing Co, pg 416
GakuseiSha Publishing Co Ltd, pg 416
Hyoronsha Publishing Co Ltd, pg 417
Ichiryu-Sha, pg 417
Koyo Shobo, pg 420
Nippon Hoso Shuppan Kyokai (NHK Publishing), pg 422
Ryosho-Fukyu-Kai Co Ltd, pg 424
Sagano Shoin, pg 424
Sanseido Co Ltd, pg 424
Takahashi Shoten Co Ltd, pg 427
Waseda University Press, pg 428
Yuhikaku Publishing Co Ltd, pg 429
Zeimukeiri-Kyokai, pg 429
Zenkoku Kyodo Shuppan, pg 429

Kenya
African Centre for Technology Studies (ACTS), pg 431
Focus Publications Ltd, pg 431
Kenya Literature Bureau, pg 432
Nairobi University Press, pg 433

Democratic People's Republic of Korea
Korea Science and Encyclopedia Publishing House, pg 434

Republic of Korea
Chung Rim Publishing Co Ltd, pg 435
Hanul Publishing Co, pg 436
Iljo-gag Publishers, pg 437
Kyobo Book Centre, pg 438

Latvia
Nordik/Tapals Publishers Ltd, pg 442
S/A Tiesiskas informacijas cerfus, pg 442

Liechtenstein
Liechtenstein Verlag AG, pg 444
Verlag der Liechtensteinischen Akademischen Gesellschaft, pg 444
Megatrade AG, pg 445
Topos Verlag AG, pg 445

Lithuania
Centre of Legal Information, pg 445
Eugrimas, pg 445
Lietuvos Informacijos Institutas, pg 446

Luxembourg
Guy Binsfeld & Co Sarl, pg 447
Editions Promoculture, pg 448
Service Central des Imprimes et des Fournitures de Bureau de l'Etat, pg 448

Madagascar
Societe Malgache d'Edition, pg 450

Malaysia
International Law Book Services, pg 452
Malayan Law Journal Sdn Bhd, pg 453
The Malaysian Current Law Journal Sdn Bhd, pg 453
MDC Publishers Printers, pg 453

Malta
The University of Malta Publications Section, pg 456

Mexico
Editorial Banca y Comercio SA de CV, pg 458
Libreria y Ediciones Botas SA, pg 458
Publicaciones Cruz O SA, pg 459
Editorial Esfinge SA de CV, pg 460
Editorial Jus SA de CV, pg 462
Editorial Limusa SA de CV, pg 463
Siglo XXI Editores SA de CV, pg 467
Editorial Trillas SA de CV, pg 467
Universidad Nacional Autonoma de Mexico (National University of Mexico), pg 467

Mongolia
State Press, pg 469

Morocco
Access International Services, pg 469
Dar Nachr Al Maarifa Pour L'Edition et La Distribution, pg 469
Editions Eddif Maroc, pg 469
Editions La Porte, pg 470
Societe Ennewrasse Service Librairie et Imprimerie, pg 470

Myanmar
Sarpay Beikman Board, pg 471
Shwepyidan Printing & Publishing House, pg 471

Nepal
International Standards Books & Periodicals (P) Ltd, pg 471

Netherlands
APA (Academic Publishers Associated), pg 472
Boom Uitgeverij, pg 474
Holland University Press BV (APA), pg 478
Kluwer Academic Publishers, pg 479
Koninklijke Vermande bv, pg 480
Uitgeverij Lemma BV, pg 480

SDU Juridische & Fiscale Uitgeverij, pg 484
W E J Tjeenk Willink BV, pg 485
Van Gorcum & Comp BV, pg 486
VU Boekhandel/Uitgeverij BV, pg 487

Netherlands Antilles
Drukkerij Scherpenheuvel Haseth, pg 488

New Zealand
Aoraki Press Ltd, pg 488
Brooker's Ltd, pg 489
Butterworths New Zealand Ltd, pg 489
CCH New Zealand Ltd, pg 490
Clerestory Press, pg 490
Legislation Direct, pg 492
Oxford University Press, pg 494
Nelson Price Milburn Ltd, pg 494
RSVP Publishing Company Ltd, pg 495
Victoria University Press, pg 496

Nigeria
CSS Bookshops, Agency & Publishing Division, pg 498
Ethiope Publishing Corporation, pg 499
Evans Brothers (Nigeria Publishers) Ltd, pg 499
Fourth Dimension Publishing Co Ltd, pg 499
Ibadan University Press, pg 499
JAD Publishers Ltd, pg 500
New Africa Publishing Company Ltd, pg 500
Nigerian Institute of Advanced Legal Studies, pg 500
Nigerian Institute of International Affairs, pg 500
Nwamife Publishers Ltd, pg 500
Obafemi Awolowo University Press Ltd, pg 501
University of Lagos Press, pg 502

Norway
Elanders Publishing AS, pg 503
Glydendal Akademisk, pg 503
Universitetsforlaget, pg 505

Pakistan
Sheikh Muhammad Ashraf Publishers, pg 506
Islamic Research Institute, pg 507
Pakistan Publishing House, pg 508

Panama
Editorial Universitaria, pg 509

Paraguay
Intercontinental Editora, pg 510

Peru
Fondo Editorial de la Pontificia Universidad Catolica del Peru, pg 511
Universidad de Lima-Fondo de Desarollo Editorial, pg 512
Universidad Nacional Mayor de San Marcos, pg 512

Philippines
Claretian Communications Inc, pg 513
Rex Bookstores & Publishers, pg 514
University of the Philippines Press, pg 515

Poland
Katolicki Uniwersytet Wydawniczo -Redakcja, pg 517
Wydawnictwo Prawnicze Co, pg 519
Oficyna Wydawnicza Szkoly Glownej Handlowej w Warszawie Oficyna Wydawnicza SGH, pg 520
Towarzystwo Naukowe w Toruniu, pg 520

Portugal
Livraria Almedina, pg 522
Armenio Amado Editora de Simoes, Beirao & Ca Lda, pg 522
Livraria Arnado Lda, pg 522
Coimbra Editora Lda, pg 523
Edicoes Cosmos, pg 524
Editorial Estampa, Lda, pg 524
Europress Editores e Distribuidores de Publicacoes Lda, pg 525
Imprensa Nacional-Casa da Moeda, pg 526
Editorial Inquerito Lda, pg 526
Livraria Tavares Martins, pg 527
McGraw-Hill Editora de Portugal, pg 527
Editorial Noticias, pg 527
Petrony Livraria, pg 528
Portugalmundo, pg 528
Quid Juris - Sociedade editora, pg 529
Usus Editora, pg 530
Vega-Publicacao e Distribuicao de Livros e Revistas, Lda, pg 530

Romania
Editura Academiei Romane, pg 531
Monitorul Oficial, Editura, pg 534
Editura Niculescu, pg 534
Rentrop & Straton Verlagsgruppe und Wirtschaftsconsulting, pg 535

Russian Federation
N E Bauman Moscow State Technical University Publishers, pg 537
Finansy i Statistika Publishing House, pg 538
INFRA-M Izdatel'skij dom, pg 538
Izvestia Sovetov Narodnyh Deputatov Russian Federation (RF), pg 539
Mezdunarodnye Otno Denija, pg 540
Nauka Publishers, pg 540
Izdatel'stvo Nizhegorodskogo Gosudarstvennogo Univ, pg 540
Progress Publishers, pg 541
Izdatelstvo Standartov, pg 542

Saudi Arabia
Al Jazirah Organization for Press, Printing, Publishing, pg 543

Singapore
LexisNexis, pg 547
Reed Elsevier, South East Asia, pg 547
Singapore University Press Pte Ltd, pg 548

SUBJECT INDEX

Slovakia
ARCHA sro Vydavatel 'stro, pg 549
Danubiaprint, pg 549
Vydavatelstvo Obzor, pg 550
Vydavatepstvo Praca spol sro, pg 550

Slovenia
Casopisni zavod Uradni list Republike Slovenije, pg 551
Univerza v Ljubljani Ekonomska Fakulteta, pg 552

South Africa
Butterworths South Africa, pg 553
Digma Publications, pg 554
Juta & Co, pg 556
LAPA Publishers (Pty) Ltd, pg 556
Perskor Books (Pty) Ltd, pg 558
South African Institute of Race Relations, pg 559
Unisa Press, pg 560

Spain
Editorial Acervo SL, pg 561
Agencia Espanola de Cooperacion, pg 562
Ediciones Akal SA, pg 562
Amnistia Internacional Editorial SL, pg 563
Editorial Aranzadi SA, pg 564
Boletin Oficial del Estado, pg 565
Bosch Casa Editorial SA, pg 565
J M Bosch Editor, pg 565
Editorial M J Bosch, SL, pg 565
Centro de Estudios Politicos Y Constitucionales, pg 567
Editorial CISSPRAXIS SA, pg 567
Civitas SA Editorial, pg 567
Editora Comercial de Publicaciones, pg 568
Comunidad Autonoma de Madrid, Servicio de Documentacion y Publicaciones, pg 568
Consello da Cultura Galega - CCG, pg 568
Editorial Constitucion y Leyes SA - COLEX, pg 568
Dykinson SL, pg 571
EDERSA (Editoriales de Derecho Reunidas SA), pg 571
Instituto de Estudios Fiscales, pg 574
EUNSA (Ediciones Universidad de Navarra SA), pg 574
Fondo de Cultura Economica de Espana, SL, pg 574
Vicent Garcia Editores, SA, pg 575
Generalitat de Catalunya Diari Oficial de la Generalitat vern, pg 575
Impredisur, SL, pg 578
Institucion Fernando el Catolico de la Excma Diputacion de Zaragoza, pg 578
Mad SL Editorial, pg 581
Marcial Pons Ediciones Juridicas SA, pg 581
Ministerio de Justicia e Interior, Centro de Publicaciones, pg 582
Pais Vasco Servicio Central de Publicaciones, pg 585
Ediciones Piramide SA, pg 586
Publicaciones de la Universidad Pontificia Comillas-Madrid, pg 588
Editorial Reus SA, pg 588
Riquelme y Vargas Ediciones SL, pg 589
Universidad de Santiago de Compostela, pg 589
Servicio de Publicaciones Universidad de Cadiz, pg 590
Servicio de Publicaciones Universidad de Cordoba, pg 590
Editorial Tecnos SA, pg 592
Tirant lo Blanch SL Libreriaa, pg 592
Editorial Trivium, SA, pg 593
Trotta SA Editorial, pg 593
Universidad de Granada, pg 594
Universidad de Malaga, pg 594
Universidad de Valladolid Secretariado de Publicaciones e Intercambio Editorial, pg 594
Publicacions de la Universitat de Barcelona, pg 594
Parlamento Vasco, pg 595
Xunta de Galicia, pg 596

Sri Lanka
Lake House Investments Ltd, pg 597
Law Publishers Association, pg 597
Sunera Publishers, pg 598

Sweden
Iustus Forlag AB, pg 603
Norstedts Juridik, pg 605
Stromberg, pg 606
Studentlitteratur AB, pg 606

Switzerland
Comite international de la Croix-Rouge, pg 612
Editions Francois Feij, pg 614
Frobenius AG, pg 614
Georg Editeur SA, pg 614
Graduate Institute of International Studies, pg 615
Helbing und Lichtenhahn Verlag AG, pg 615
Editions Ides et Calendes SA, pg 616
Juris Druck & Verlag AG, pg 616
Editions H Messeiller SA, pg 619
Editions Payot Lausanne, pg 621
PIE-Peter Lang SA, pg 622
Verlag fuer Recht und Gesellschaft AG, pg 622
Schulthess Polygraphischer Verlag AG, pg 624
Staempfli Verlag AG, pg 625
Tobler Verlag, pg 626
Der Universitatsverlag Freiburg, pg 626
Versus Verlag AG, pg 627
Weka Informations Schriften Verlag AG, pg 627
Wyss Verlag AG Bern, pg 628

Syrian Arab Republic
Damascus University Press, pg 628

Taiwan, Province of China
San Min Book Co Ltd, pg 631
Senate Books Co Ltd, pg 631
Shy Chaur Publishing Co Ltd, pg 631

United Republic of Tanzania
Tanzania Publishing House, pg 634

Thailand
Sut Phaisan, pg 636

Tunisia
Academie Tunisienne des Sciences, des Lettres et des Arts Beit El Hekma, pg 637
Ceres Editions, pg 637

Turkey
Alkim Kitapcilik-Yayimcilik, pg 638
Seckin Yayinevi, pg 641
Yetkin Printing & Publishing Co Inc, pg 642

Uganda
Centre for Basic Research, pg 642

Ukraine
ASK Ltd, pg 643
Naukova Dumka Publishers, pg 643
Osnovy Publishers, pg 643

United Kingdom
Aldwych Press Ltd, pg 645
Ashgate Publishing Ltd, pg 649
Aslib, The Association for Information Management, pg 650
The Athlone Press Ltd, pg 650
Blackwell Publishers, pg 655
Blackwell Science Ltd, pg 656
Butterworths Tolley, pg 661
Cambridge University Press, pg 662
Frank Cass Publishers, pg 664
Cavendish Publishing Ltd, pg 665
CCH Editions Ltd, pg 665
Chancellor Publications, pg 666
Deborah Charles Publications, pg 666
The Chartered Institute of Building, pg 666
Class Publishing, pg 668
Commonwealth Secretariat, pg 669
Croner CCH Group Ltd, pg 672
James Currey Ltd, pg 673
CyberClub, pg 673
Dunedin Academic Press, pg 676
Editon XII, pg 677
Elm Publications, pg 678
The Eurospan Group, pg 680
Financial World Publishing, pg 682
W Green The Scottish Law Publisher, pg 689
Hart Publishing, pg 692
Harvard University Press, pg 692
HLT Publications, pg 696
ICC United Kingdom, pg 698
Jordan Publishing Ltd, pg 703
Law Pack Publishing Ltd, pg 706
Legal Action Group, pg 706
Lemos & Crane, pg 707
Letts Educational, pg 707
Liberty, pg 707
LLP Ltd, pg 708
Kenneth Mason Publications Ltd, pg 712
Oxford University Press, pg 723
Pearson Education, pg 725
Perpetuity Press, pg 726
Pharmaceutical Press, pg 726
Pluto Press, pg 728
Police Review Publishing Company Ltd, pg 729
Professional Book Supplies Ltd, pg 730
Routledge, pg 736
Shaw & Sons Ltd, pg 741
SLS Legal Publications (NI), pg 742
The Stationery Office, pg 745
Sweet & Maxwell Ltd, pg 746
Telegraph Books, pg 748
Trentham Books Ltd, pg 750
Which? Ltd, pg 755
Wilmington Business Information Ltd, pg 756
Yale University Press London, pg 759

Uruguay
Libreria Amalio M Fernandez, Editorial, pg 760
Fundacion de Cultura Universitaria, pg 760

Uzbekistan
Izdatelstvo Uzbekistan, pg 761

Yugoslavia
Savremena Administracija, pg 765
Sluzbeni List, pg 765

Zimbabwe
HarperCollins Publishers Zimbabwe Pvt Ltd, pg 768
Legal Resources Foundation Publications Unit, pg 768

LIBRARY & INFORMATION SCIENCES

Albania
NL SH, pg 1

Argentina
Alfagrama SRL ediciones, pg 3
Marymar Ediciones SA, pg 7
Instituto Nacional de Ciencia y Tecnica Hidrica (INCYTH), pg 7

Australia
Auslib Press Pty Ltd, pg 12
Elephas Books Pty Ltd, pg 21
Ginninderra Press, pg 24
Magpies Magazine, pg 31
Online Information Resources Pty Ltd, pg 35
Pearson Education Australia, pg 37
D W Thorpe, pg 44

Austria
Milena Verlag, pg 55

Belgium
Alamire vzw, Music Publishers, pg 64
Editions du CEFAL, pg 66

Brazil
A & A & A Edicoes e Promocoes Internacionais Ltda, pg 77
Editora Universidade Federal do Rio de Janeiro, pg 93

Bulgaria
Foi-Commerce, pg 95

China
Fudan University Press, pg 105
Shandong University Press, pg 109
Wuhan University Press, pg 110

Cuba
Instituto de Informacion Cientifica y Tecnologica (IDICT), pg 121

Czech Republic
Labyrint, pg 125
Statni Vedecka Knihovna Usti Nad Labem, pg 128

PUBLISHERS

Denmark
Danish National Library Authority, pg 131
Statens Information (Danish State Information Service), pg 135

Dominican Republic
Pontificia Universidad Catolica Madre y Maestra, pg 136

Ecuador
SECAP, pg 137

Egypt (Arab Republic of Egypt)
Dar Al-Matbo at Al-Gadidah, pg 138
Dar El Shorouk Publishing & Distributing House, pg 138

Estonia
Estonian Academic Library, pg 139
National Library of Estonia, pg 140

France
Agence Bibliographique de L'Enseignement Superieur, pg 146
Bibliotheque Nationale de France, pg 150
Michele Broutta Oeuvres Graphiques Contemporaines, pg 152
Electre Editions du Cercle de la Librairie, pg 161
Editions Legislatives, pg 172
Opsys Operating System, pg 178
PRODIG UMR 8586 CNRS-Paris 1,4,7 ephe, pg 182
References cf, pg 182
Editions Unes, pg 188

Germany
Belser Wissenschaftlicher Dienst, pg 200
Berlin Verlag Arno Spitz GmbH, pg 200
Bock und Herchen Verlag, pg 204
Deutsches Bucharchiv Muenchen, Institut fur Buchwissenschaften, pg 216
Eulenhof-Verlag Wolfgang Ehrhardt Heinold, pg 224
Harald Fischer Verlag GmbH, pg 228
Friedrich Frommann Verlag, pg 230
Harrassowitz Verlag, pg 237
Dr Ernst Hauswedell & Co Verlag, pg 238
Anton Hiersemann, Verlag, pg 240
Iudicium Verlag GmbH, pg 245
Vittorio Klostermann GmbH, pg 250
Roman Kovar Verlag, pg 253
C W Niemeyer Buchverlage GmbH, pg 268
Georg Olms Verlag AG, pg 270
Philipps-Universitaet Marburg, pg 273
Dr Ludwig Reichert Verlag, pg 278
K G Saur Verlag GmbH, A Gale/Thomson Learning Company, pg 282
Staatsbibliothek zu Berlin - Preussischer Kulturbesitz, pg 288
UTB fuer Wissenschaft Uni-Taschenbuecher GmbH, pg 297

Greece
Hestia-I D Hestia-Kollaros & Co Corporation, pg 311

Holy See (Vatican City State)
Scuola Vaticana Paleografia - Scuola Vaticana di Paleografia Diplomatica e Archivistica, pg 317

Hong Kong
Hong Kong University Press, pg 320

Hungary
Osiris Kiado, pg 326

India
Anmol Publications Pvt Ltd, pg 331
APH Publishing Corp, pg 331
Concept Publishing Co, pg 335
Cosmo Publications, pg 335
Dastane Ramchandra & Co, pg 335
Ess Ess Publications, pg 337
Gyan Publishing House, pg 338
Law Publishers, pg 341
Omsons Publications, pg 345
Pointer Publishers, pg 346
Prabhat Prakashan, pg 346
Pratibha Pratishthan, pg 346
Rajasthan Hindi Granth Academy, pg 347
Reliance Publishing House, pg 347
Sat Sahitya Prakashan, pg 349
Sita Publications, pg 350
Sterling Publishers Pvt Ltd, pg 351
Vikas Publishing House Pvt Ltd, pg 353

Indonesia
Lembaga Demografi Fakultas Ekonomi Universitas Indonesia, pg 356

Israel
University of Haifa Library, pg 373

Italy
AIB Associazione Italiana Bibliotheche, pg 375
Belforte Editore Libraio srl, pg 377
Istituto Centrale per il Catalogo Unico delle Biblioteche Italiane e per le Informazioni Bibliografiche, pg 380
Direzione Generale Archivi, pg 385
Editrice Bibliografica SpA, pg 386
Edizioni GB, pg 390
Leo S Olschki, pg 402

Japan
Nikkagiren Shuppan-Sha (JUSE Press Ltd), pg 422
Toppan Co Ltd, pg 428

Kazakhstan
Kazakh Al-Farabi State National University, pg 430

Kenya
Africa Book Services (EA) Ltd, pg 430

Republic of Korea
Prompter Publications, pg 439

Lithuania
Lietuvos Informacijos Institutas, pg 446
Lithuanian National Museum Publishing House, pg 446
Martynas Mazvydas National Library of Lithuania, pg 446

Luxembourg
Service Central de la Statistique et des Etudes Economiques (STATEC), pg 448

The Former Yugoslav Republic of Macedonia
St Clement of Ohrid National & University Library, pg 449

Mexico
El Colegio de Mexico AC, pg 459

Monaco
Editions Andre Sauret SA, pg 469

Netherlands
APA (Academic Publishers Associated), pg 472
Stedelijk Van Abbemuseum, pg 484
Tilburg University Press, pg 485
VNU Business Press Group BV, pg 487

Pakistan
Academy of Education Planning & Management (AEPAM), pg 506
Hamdard Foundation, pg 507
Library Promotion Bureau, pg 507
Pakistan Institute of Development Economics, pg 508

Poland
Biblioteka Narodowa, pg 516
Instytut Meteorologii i Gospodarki Wodnej, pg 518
Wydawnictwo DiG, pg 521

Portugal
Biblioteca Geral da Universidade de Coimbra, pg 523

Romania
Editura Excelsior, pg 533
Editura Minerva, pg 534

Russian Federation
Finansy i Statistika Publishing House, pg 538
Izdatelstvo Kniga, pg 539
Ministerstvo Kul'tury RF, pg 540
Nauka Publishers, pg 540

Singapore
Taylor & Francis Asia Pacific, pg 548

Slovakia
Sofa, pg 551
Ustav informacii a prognoz skolstva mladeze a telovychovy, pg 551

South Africa
Cape Provincial Library Service, pg 553

Spain
Arco Libros SL, pg 564
Biblioteca de Catalunya, pg 565

SUBJECT INDEX

Eumo Editorial, pg 574
EUNSA (Ediciones Universidad de Navarra SA), pg 574
Fragua Editorial, pg 574
Editorial Sintesis, SA, pg 590
Trea Ediciones, SL, pg 593

Sri Lanka
National Library & Documentation Services Board, pg 597

Sweden
Bibliotekstjaenst AB, pg 600

Switzerland
Verlag Stocker-Schmid AG, pg 625
Weber SA d'Editions, pg 627

Syrian Arab Republic
Damascus University Press, pg 628

Taiwan, Province of China
Hilit Publishing Co Ltd, pg 630

United Republic of Tanzania
Tanzania Library Services Board, pg 634

Tunisia
Publications de la Fondation Temimi pour la Recherche Scientifique et L'Information, pg 638

United Kingdom
Aldwych Press Ltd, pg 645
Anderson Rand Ltd, pg 647
Ashgate Publishing Ltd, pg 649
Aslib, The Association for Information Management, pg 650
Book Data, pg 657
Cassell & Co, pg 664
Chartered Institute of Library & Information Professionals in Scotland, pg 666
James Clarke & Co Ltd, pg 668
CSA (Cambridge Scientific Abstracts), pg 672
Electronic Publishing Services Ltd, pg 678
Elm Publications, pg 678
Elsevier Science Ltd, pg 678
The Eurospan Group, pg 680
Evans Brothers Ltd, pg 680
Facet Publishing, pg 681
IFLA International Programme for UAP, pg 698
JAI Press Ltd, pg 702
Letts Educational, pg 707
Library & Information Statistics Unit, pg 707
Linen Hall Library, pg 707
Maney Publishing, pg 711
MCB University Press Ltd, pg 712
National Library of Wales, pg 717
SHU Press, pg 742
The Stationery Office, pg 745
Taylor Graham Publishing, pg 747
TFPL, pg 748
Trigon Press, pg 750

LITERATURE, LITERARY CRITICISM, ESSAYS

Albania
Botimpex Publications Import-Export Agency, pg 1
NL SH, pg 1
State Textbook Publishing House, pg 1

Argentina
Academia Argentina de Letras, pg 2
Aguilar Altea Taurus Alfaguara SA de Ediciones, pg 3
Alianza Editorial de Argentina SA, pg 3
Beatriz Viterbo Editora, pg 4
Fundacion Editorial de Belgrano, pg 4
Bonum Editorial SACI, pg 4
Centro Editor de America Latina SA, pg 4
Colmegna SA, pg 4
Ediciones Corregidor SAICI y E, pg 4
Ediciones del Eclipse, pg 5
Edicial SA, pg 5
Emece Editores SA, pg 5
EUDEBA (Editorial Universitaria de Buenos Aires), pg 6
Ediciones de la Flor SRL, pg 6
Editorial Galerna SRL, pg 6
Editorial Guadalupe, pg 6
Editorial Planeta Argentina SAIC, pg 8
Editorial Plus Ultra SA, pg 8
Quetzal-Domingo Cortizo, pg 8
Editorial Santiago Rueda, pg 9
Seix Barral, pg 9
Editorial Sopena Argentina SACI e I, pg 9
Editorial Sudamericana SA, pg 9
Theoria SRL Distribuidora y Editora, pg 9
Editorial Troquel SA, pg 9

Armenia
Ajstan Publishers, pg 10

Australia
Access Press, pg 10
Allen & Unwin Pty Ltd, The Australian Newspaper, Vogel Breads, pg 11
Assert Publishing, pg 12
Boombana Publications, pg 16
Centre for Comparative Literature & Cultural Studies, pg 17
Eleanor Curtain Publishing, pg 19
Dangaroo Press, pg 20
Dragon Press, pg 20
Experimental Art Foundation, pg 22
Fremantle Arts Centre Press, pg 23
Freshet Press, pg 23
Gangan Publishing, pg 23
Hat Box Press, pg 25
Hudson Publishing, pg 27
Hyland House Publishing Pty Ltd, pg 27
Indra Publishing, pg 27
Institute of Aboriginal Development (IAD Press), pg 28
Magabala Books Aboriginal Corporation, pg 31
Horwitz Martin Education, pg 32
Maxwell Macmillan Publishing (Australia) Pty Ltd, pg 32
Melbourne University Press, pg 33
Mulini Press, pg 34
Nimrod Publications, pg 35
NMA Publications, pg 35
Pan Macmillan Australia Pty Ltd, pg 36
Papyrus Publishing, pg 37
Pascoe Publishing, pg 37
Penguin Books Australia Ltd, pg 37
Playlab Press, pg 38
Pollitecon Publications, pg 38
Spaniel Books, pg 43
Spinifex Press, pg 43
State Library of NSW Press, pg 43
Sydney Studies In English, pg 43
The Text Publishing Company Pty Ltd, pg 44
Thames & Hudson (Australia) Pty Ltd, pg 44
Thornbill Press, pg 44
University of Queensland Press, pg 46
University of Western Australia Press, pg 46
Wakefield Press Pty Ltd, pg 47
Wizard Books Pty Ltd, pg 48

Austria
Aarachne Verlag, pg 49
Verlag der Apfel, pg 49
Astor-Verlag, Willibald Schlager, pg 49
Der Baum Wolfgang Biedermann Verlag, pg 49
Buchkultur Verlags GmbH Zeitschrift fuer Literatur & Kunst, pg 50
CEEBA Publications Antenne d'Autriche, pg 50
Dachs-Verlag GmbH, pg 50
Franz Deuticke Verlagsges mbH, pg 51
Development News Ltd, pg 51
Literature Verlag Droschl, pg 51
Edition S der OSD, pg 51
Gangan Verlag, pg 52
Verlag Lynkeus/H Hakel Gesellschaft, pg 52
Edition Graphischer Zirkel, pg 52
Guthmann & Peterson Liber Libri, Edition, pg 52
Haymon-Verlag GesmbH, pg 52
Karolinger Verlag GmbH & Co KG, pg 53
Loecker Verlag, pg 54
LOG-Internationale Zeitschrift fuer Literatur, pg 54
Merbod Verlag, pg 55
Milena Verlag, pg 55
Thomas Mlakar Verlag, pg 55
Verlag Monte Verita, pg 55
Otto Mueller Verlag GesmbH & Co KG, pg 55
Wolfgang Neugebauer Verlag GmbH, pg 55
Passagen Verlag GmbH, pg 57
Richard Pils Publication P, pg 57
Ritter Verlag, pg 58
Dr A Schendl GmbH und Co KG, pg 58
Andreas Schnider Verlags-Atelier, pg 58
Studien Verlag Gmbh, pg 59
Edition Va Bene, pg 60
Wespennest - Zeitschrift fuer brauchbare Texte und Bilder, pg 61
Wieser Verlag, pg 61
Zirkular - Verlag der Dokumentationsstelle fuer neuere oesterreichische Literatur, pg 61

Bangladesh
Ankur Prakashani, pg 62
Gatidhara, pg 62
Agamee Prakashani, pg 62

Belarus
Belaruskaya Encyklapedyya, pg 63
Izdatelstvo Mastatskaya Litaratura, pg 63

Belgium
Bartleby & Co, pg 65
De Boeck et Larcier SA, pg 65
Brepols Publishers NV, pg 65
De Clauwaert VZW, pg 66
Conservart SA, pg 67
Contact NV, pg 67
Le Cri Editions, pg 67
Le Daily-Bul, pg 67
Davidsfonds VZW, pg 67
Maison d'Editions Cl Dejaie, pg 67
Editions les eperonniers, pg 68
EPO Publishers, Printers, Booksellers, pg 68
Huis Van Het Boek, pg 69
Infoboek NV, pg 69
Koepel van de Vlaamse Noord - Zuidbeweging 11.11.11, pg 70
Kritak Uitgeverij, pg 70
Lansman Editeur, pg 70
Claude Lefrancq Editeur, pg 71
Editions Lessius ASBL, pg 71
Leuven University Press, pg 71
La Longue Vue, pg 71
Editions Memor, pg 72
Nauwelaerts Edition SA, pg 72
La Part de L'Oeil, pg 72
Pelckmans NV, De Nederlandsche Boekhandel, pg 73
Roularta Books NV, pg 73
Snoeck-Ducaju en Zoon NV, pg 74
Sonneville Press (Uitgeverij) VTW, pg 74
Stichting Ons Erfdeel VZW, pg 74
Uitgevery Scoop Infotex NV, pg 75
Vita, pg 75
Editions Luce Wilquin, pg 75
Zuid En Noord VZW, pg 76

Bolivia
Editorial Don Bosco, pg 76
Universidad Autonoma Tomas Frias, Div de Extension Universitaria, pg 76

Botswana
Maskew Miller Longman, pg 77

Brazil
AGIR S/A Editora, pg 78
Livraria Francisco Alves Editora SA, pg 78
Editora Atica SA, pg 79
Editora Bertrand Brasil Ltda, pg 79
Editora Brasiliense SA, pg 80
Alzira Chagas Carpigiani, pg 80
Conquista, Empresa de Publicacoes Ltda, pg 81
Consultor Assessoria de Planejamento Ltda, pg 81
Livraria Duas Cidades Ltda, pg 81
Ediouro Publicacoes, SA, pg 81
Editora Companhia das Letras/ Editora Schwarcz Ltda, pg 82
EDUC - Editora da PUC-SP, pg 82
EDUSC - Editora da Universidade do Sagrado Coracao, pg 82
Editora Expressao e Cultura Exped Ltda, pg 83
Formato Editorial ltda, pg 83
Editora Globo SA, pg 84
IBRASA (Instituicao Brasileira de Difusao Cultural Ltda), pg 85
Imago Editora Importacao e Exportacao Ltda, pg 85
LDA Editores Ltda, pg 86
Oficina de Livros Ltda, pg 86
Edicoes Loyola SA, pg 87
Editora Marco Zero Ltda, pg 87
Editora Melhoramentos Ltda, pg 87
Editora Mercado Aberto Ltda, pg 88
Editora Moderna Ltda, pg 88
Editora Nova Alexandria Ltda, pg 88
Editora Nova Fronteira SA, pg 88
Olho D'Agua Comercio e Servicos Editoriais Ltda, pg 88
Editora Paz e Terra, pg 89
RHJ Livros Ltda, pg 90
Editora Santuario, pg 91
Editora Scipione Ltda, pg 91
Selinunte Editora Ltda, pg 91
Agencia Siciliano de Livros Jornais e Rivistas Ltda, pg 91
Tempus Editores, pg 92
Thex Editora e Distribuidora Ltda, pg 92
34 Literatura S/C Ltda, pg 92
Editora da Universidade de Sao Paulo, pg 93
Jorge Zahar Editor, pg 93

Bulgaria
Bojko Kacarmazov, pg 94
CHRIKER, pg 94
EA Publishing House, pg 95
Fama, pg 95
Galaktika Publishing House, pg 95
Publishing House Hristo Botev, pg 96
Interpres, pg 96
Kolibri Publishing Group, pg 96
Kralica MAB, pg 96
LIK IZDANIJA, pg 96
Makros 2000 - Plovdiv, pg 96
Narodna Kultura, pg 97
Pet Plus, pg 97
Slavena, pg 98
Srebaren lav, pg 98
Svetra Publishing House, pg 98
Ivan Vazov Publishing House, pg 98

Burundi
Editions Intore, pg 98

Cameroon
Editions CLE, pg 99
Presses Universitaires d'Afrique, pg 99

Chile
Arrayan Editores, pg 99
Ediciones Bat, pg 99
Editorial Andres Bello/Editorial Juridica de Chile, pg 100
Dolmen Ediciones SA, pg 100
Ediciones y Publicidad Melquiades, pg 100
Norma de Chile, pg 101
Pehuen Editores Ltda, pg 101
Pontificia Universidad Catolica de Chile, pg 101
Red Internacional Del Libro, pg 101
Editorial Universitaria SA, pg 101
Ediciones Universitarias de Valparaiso, pg 101
Zig-Zag SA, pg 102

China
Beijing Publishing House, pg 102
China Film Press, pg 103

PUBLISHERS SUBJECT INDEX

China Theatre Publishing House, pg 104
China Youth Publishing House, pg 104
Foreign Language Teaching & Research Press, pg 105
Foreign Languages Press, pg 105
Fudan University Press, pg 105
Fujian Children's Publishing House, pg 106
Kunlun Publishing House, pg 107
People's Literature Publishing House, pg 108
SDX (Shenghuo-Dushu-Xinzhi) Joint Publishing Co, pg 108
Shandong Literature & Art Publishing House, pg 109
Shanghai Foreign Language Education Press, pg 109

Colombia
El Ancora Editores, pg 111
Bedout Editores SA, pg 111
Centro Regional para el Fomento del Libro en America Latina y el Caribe, pg 111
Dosmil Editora, pg 111
Editora Guadalupe Ltda, pg 112
Lerner Limitada, pg 112
Editorial Oveja Negra, pg 113
Procultura SA, pg 113
Tercer Mundo Editores SA, pg 113
Universidad de Antioquia, Division Publicaciones, pg 114

The Democratic Republic of the Congo
Presses Universitaires du Zaiire (PUZ), pg 115
Saint-Paul, pg 115

Costa Rica
Promesa, Ediciones, pg 116
Editorial Universidad Nacional (EUNA), pg 117

Cote d'Ivoire
Akohi Editions, pg 117
Les Nouvelles Editions Africaines, pg 118
Les Nouvelles Editions Ivoiriennes (NEI), pg 118

Croatia
AGM doo, pg 118
ALFA dd za izdavacke, graficke i trgovacke poslove, pg 118
ArTresor naklada, pg 118
Durieux d o o, pg 118
Faust Vrani, pg 118
Filozofski Fakultet Sveucilista u Zagrebu, pg 118
Knjizevni Krug Split, pg 119
Matica hrvatska, pg 119
Nakladni zavod Matice hrvatske, pg 119
Nasa Djeca Publishing, pg 119
Sveucilisna tiskara doo, pg 120
Tehnicka Knjiga, pg 120

Cuba
Editorial Capitan San Luis, pg 120
Casa Editora Abril, pg 120
Holguin, Ediciones, pg 121
Editorial Letras Cubanas, pg 121
Editorial Oriente, pg 121
Pueblo y Educacion Editorial (PE), pg 121
Ediciones Union, pg 121

Cyprus
AndreouChr- Publishers, pg 122
Chrysopolitissa Publishers, pg 122
Omilos Pnevmatikis Ananeoseos, pg 122

Czech Republic
Atlantis sro, pg 123
AULOS sro, pg 123
Nakladatelstvi Blok, pg 123
Brody, pg 123
Ceska Expedice, pg 123
Concordia, pg 124
Doplnek, pg 124
Galaxie, vydavatelstvi a nakladatelstvi, pg 124
Paseka, pg 127
Pop Plus Rock Centrum, pg 127
Votobia sro, pg 129

Denmark
Aarhus Universitetsforlag, pg 129
Borgens Forlag A/S, pg 130
The Danish Literature Centre, pg 131
Forlaget Hjulet, pg 132
Forlaget Hovedland, pg 133
Kaleidoscope Publishers Ltd, pg 133
Museum Tusculanum Press, pg 134
Politisk Revy, pg 134
C A Reitzel A/S, pg 134
Samlerens Forlag A/S, pg 135
Syddansk Universitetsforlag, pg 136
Tiderne Skifter Forlag A/S, pg 136
Wisby & Wilkens, pg 136

Dominican Republic
Pontificia Universidad Catolica Madre y Maestra, pg 136
Sociedad Editorial Dominicana SA, pg 137
Editora Taller, pg 137

Ecuador
Corporacion Editora Nacional, pg 137
Libresa S A, pg 137
Pontificia Universidad Catolica de Ecuador, Centro de Publicaciones, pg 137

Egypt (Arab Republic of Egypt)
American University in Cairo Press, pg 138
Al Arab Publishing House, pg 138
Dar al-Nahda al Arabia, pg 138
Dar El Shorouk, pg 138
Dar El Shorouk Publishing & Distributing House, pg 138
Elias Modern Publishing House, pg 138
Middle East Book Centre, pg 139

El Salvador
Clasicos Roxsil Editorial SA de CV, pg 139
Editorial Universitaria de la Universidad de El Salvador, pg 139

Estonia
Ilmamaa, pg 140
Tuum, pg 141

Ethiopia
Addis Ababa University Press, pg 141

Finland
Basam Books Oy, pg 142
Herattaja-yhdistys Ry, pg 142
Kaantopiiri Oy, pg 142
Suomalaisen Kirjallisuuden Seura, pg 144
Osuuskunta Vastapaino, pg 145
Yliopistopaino/Helsinki University Press, pg 145

France
Editions A M Metailie, pg 145
ABC Editions, pg 145
Actes Graphiques, pg 145
Editions Actes Sud, pg 146
ADPF Publications, pg 146
Editions Al Liamm, pg 146
Editions Albin Michel, pg 146
L'Amitie par le Livre, pg 147
L'Anabase, pg 147
L'Arbalete, pg 147
L'Arche Editeur, pg 147
L'Archipel, pg 148
Editions de l'Armancon, pg 148
Atelier National de Reproduction des Theses, pg 148
Editions de l'Aube, pg 149
Editions d'Aujourd'hui (Les Introuvables), pg 149
Autrement Editions, pg 149
Autres Temps, pg 149
La Bartavelle, pg 149
Beauchesne Editeur, pg 150
Editions Belfond, pg 150
Editions Belin, pg 150
Societe d'Edition Les Belles Lettres, pg 150
Berg International Editeurs, pg 150
Bibliotheque des Arts, pg 150
Bibliotheque Nationale de France, pg 150
William Blake & Co, pg 150
Editions Andre Bonne, pg 151
Pierre Bordas et Fils, pg 151
Presses Universitaires de Bordeaux (PUB), pg 151
Bragelonne, pg 151
Editions Jacques Bremond, pg 151
Brud Nevez, pg 152
Le Cadratin, pg 152
Editions des Cahiers Bourbonnais, pg 152
Le Castor Astral, pg 153
Editions Cenomane, pg 153
Jacqueline Chambon, pg 154
Editions Champ Vallon, pg 154
Le Cherche Midi Editeur, pg 154
Cicero Editeurs, pg 155
Circe, pg 155
Climats, pg 155
CNRS Editions, pg 155
Armand Colin, Editeur, pg 155
COMP'ACT, pg 156
Editions Complexe SPRL, pg 156
Corsaire Editions, pg 156
Librairie Jose Corti, pg 156
Editions Criterion, pg 157
Culture et Bibliotheque pour Tous, pg 157
La Delirante, pg 158
Georges-Charles Demay, pg 158
Desclee de Brouwer SA, pg 158
Desclee et Cie, Editeurs, pg 159
Editions de la Difference, pg 159
Le Dilettante, pg 159
Editions Dis Voir, pg 159
Les Dossiers d'Aquitaine, pg 160
Dunod Editeur, pg 160
Presses de l'Ecole Normale Superieure, pg 160
Edicef - Editions Classiques d'Expression Francaise, pg 161

Les Editeurs Reunis, pg 161
Edition1, pg 161
ELLUG (Editions Litteraires et Linguistiques de l'Universite de Grenoble III), pg 162
Editions Entente, pg 162
Editions Espaces 34, pg 162
L'Esprit Du Temps, pg 162
Institut d'Etudes Slaves, pg 163
Bernard de Fallois, pg 163
Editions Fanlac, pg 163
Fata Morgana, pg 163
FBT de R Editions/Editions des Limbes d'Or, pg 163
Des Femmes, pg 164
Editions du Feu Nouveau, pg 164
Flammarion SA, pg 164
France-Loisirs, pg 165
Association Frank, pg 165
Edition Galilee, pg 165
Editions Gammaprim, pg 166
Gippe-Marche Du Livre Ancien, pg 166
Sarl Editions Jean Grassin, pg 167
Groupe Expansion, pg 167
L'Harmattan, pg 168
Ici et Ailleurs-Vents des Iles, pg 169
Editions Imago, pg 169
Indigo & Cote-Femmes Editions, pg 169
Editions Infrarouge, pg 169
Editions Interferences, pg 169
Interpublications, pg 170
Isoete, pg 170
Editions Ivrea, pg 170
Kailash Editions, pg 171
Karthala Editions-Diffusion, pg 171
Editions Klincksieck, pg 171
Langues & Mondes/L'Asiatheque, pg 171
Editions du Laquet, pg 172
Editions Dominique Leroy, pg 172
Lettres Modernes, pg 172
Lettres Vives, pg 173
Editions des Limbes d'Or/FBT de R Editions, pg 173
Le Livre de Poche-L G F (Librairie Generale Francaise), pg 173
Editions Lyonnaises d'Art et d'Histoire, pg 174
Macula, pg 174
Editions Marie-Noelle, pg 175
Editions Medianes, pg 175
Mercure de France SA, pg 176
Mille et Une Nuits, pg 176
Librairie Minard, pg 176
Les Editions de Minuit SA, pg 176
Presses Universitaires du Mirail, pg 176
Editions Modernes Media, pg 176
Gerard Monfort Editeur Sarl, pg 176
Gabriel Mony, pg 176
Editions Maurice Nadeau, Les Lettres Nouvelles, pg 177
Nanga, pg 177
Naufal Group Sarl, pg 177
Nil Editions, pg 177
Librairie A-G Nizet Sarl, pg 177
Noir Sur Blanc, pg 177
Mare Nostrum, pg 177
Nouvelle Cite, pg 178
Editions Obsidiane, pg 178
Editions J H Paillet et B Drouaud, pg 178
Editions Paradigme, pg 179
Editions Payot & Rivages, pg 179
Peeters-France, pg 179
Editions Phebus, pg 179
Editions A et J Picard SA, pg 179
Editions Jean Picollec, pg 179
Editions Philippe Picquier, pg 180

1009

SUBJECT INDEX

Editions Christian Pirot, pg 180
Jean-Michel Place, pg 180
POL Editeur, pg 180
Presses de la Sorbonne Nouvelle/PSN, pg 181
Presses Universitaires de Caen, pg 181
Presses Universitaires de Grenoble, pg 181
Presses Universitaires de Lyon, pg 181
Presses Universitaires de Nancy, pg 181
Presses Universitaires de Strasbourg, pg 181
Presses Universitaires du Septentrion, pg 181
Publi-Fusion, pg 182
Publications de l'Universite de Rouen, pg 182
Publications Orientalistes de France (POF), pg 182
Editions Pygmalion - Gerard Watelet, pg 182
Editions Ramsay, pg 182
Revue Noire, pg 183
Editions Robert Laffont, Nil, Fixot, Seghers, Julliard, pg 183
Les Editions du Sagittaire, pg 183
Salvy Editeur, pg 183
Nouvelles Editions Seguier, pg 184
Maren Sell, pg 184
Editions de Septembre, pg 184
Le Serpent a Plumes, pg 184
Editions du Seuil, pg 185
Siloe - Kerdore, pg 185
Editions Andre Silvaire Sarl, pg 185
Societe des Editions Grasset et Fasquelle, pg 185
Publications de la Sorbonne, pg 186
Spectres Familiers, pg 186
Spengler Editeur, pg 186
Stil, pg 186
Editions Stock, pg 186
SUD, pg 186
10/18, pg 187
Editions Tiresias Michel Reynaud, pg 188
Transedition ASBL, pg 188
Transeuropeennes/RCE, pg 188
Editions Unes, pg 188
Universitas, pg 188
Publications de l'Universite de Pau, pg 188
La Vague Verte, pg 188
Editions Verdier, pg 189
Editions Vilo SA, pg 189
Editions Viviane Hamy, pg 189
La Voix du Regard, pg 189
YMCA-Press, pg 189

French Polynesia

Scoop/Au Vent des Iles, pg 190

Germany

A Francke Verlag (Tubingen und Basel), pg 191
R van Acken GmbH Druckerei und Verlag, pg 191
Aisthesis Verlag Dr Detlev Kopp und Dr Michael Vogt, pg 192
Akademie Verlag GmbH, pg 192
M Akselrad, pg 192
Verlag und Antiquariat Frank Albrecht, pg 192
Alexander Verlag Berlin, pg 192
Altberliner Verlag GmbH, pg 193
AOL-Verlag Frohmut Menze, pg 194
Verlag APHAIA Svea Haske, Sonja Schumann GbR, pg 194
Ardey-Verlag GmbH, pg 194

Asclepios Edition Lothar Baus, pg 196
Aufbau Taschenbuch Verlag GmbH, pg 196
Aufbau-Verlag GmbH, pg 196
J J Augustin GmbH Verlag, pg 196
AvivA Britta Jurgs GmbH, pg 197
Dr Bachmaier Verlag GmbH, pg 197
Bayerische Verlagsanstalt GmbH, pg 199
Bayerischer Schulbuch-Verlag GmbH, pg 199
Verlag C H Beck (OHG), pg 200
Bergstadtverlag Wilhelm Gottlieb Korn GmbH Wuerzburg, pg 200
Blaukreuz-Verlag Wuppertal, pg 204
Verlag Hermann Boehlaus Nachfolger Weimar GmbH & Co, pg 205
Klaus Boer Verlag, pg 205
Bonifatius GmbH Druck-Buch-Verlag, pg 205
Brandes & Apsel Verlag GmbH, pg 206
BrennGlas Verlag Assenheim Juergen Seuss, pg 206
Buch- und Kunstverlag Kleinheinrich, pg 207
Buchergilde Gutenberg Verlagsgesellschaft mbH, pg 207
Buechse der Pandora Verlags-GmbH, pg 207
Christliches Verlagshaus GmbH, pg 210
Claassen Verlag GmbH, pg 210
J G Cotta'sche Buchhandlung Nachfolger GmbH, pg 212
Verlag Horst Deike KG, pg 213
Die Deutsche Bibliothek/Deutsche Buecherei Leipzig, pg 213
Deutsche Verlags-Anstalt GmbH (DVA), pg 214
Deutscher Taschenbuch Verlag GmbH & Co KG (dtv), pg 215
Diagonal-Verlag GbR Rink-Schweer, pg 216
Eugen Diederichs Verlag GmbH & Co KG, pg 216
Sammlung Dieterich Verlagsgesellschaft mbH, pg 216
Dieterichsche Verlagsbuchhandlung Mainz, pg 216
Dingfelder-Verlag Inh Gerd Gmelin, pg 217
Dolling und Galitz Verlag GmbH, pg 217
Drei Ulmen Verlag GmbH, pg 218
Duncker und Humblot GmbH, pg 219
Edition Klaus Blahak Dr Fredric Kroll, pg 220
edition q Berlin Edition in der Quintessenz Verlags-GmbH, pg 221
Eichborn AG, pg 222
EinfallsReich Verlagsgesellschaft MbH, pg 222
Eironeia-Verlag, pg 222
Elefanten Press Verlag GmbH, pg 222
N G Elwert Verlag, pg 222
Verlag Peter Engstler, pg 223
Ensslin und Laiblin Verlag GmbH & Co KG, pg 223
Europa Verlag GmbH, pg 224
Europaeische Verlagsanstalt GmbH & Rotbuch Verlag GmbH & Co KG, pg 225
Evangelische Haupt-Bibelgesellschaft und von Cansteinsche Bibelanstalt, pg 225

Extent Verlag und Service Wolfgang M Flamm, pg 225
Fabel-Verlag Gudrun Liebchen, pg 226
Fahrner & Fahrner, pg 226
Fannei & Walz Verlag, pg 227
Wilhelm Fink GmbH & Co Verlags-KG, pg 228
Karin Fischer Verlag GmbH, pg 228
S Fischer Verlag GmbH, pg 228
Fischer Taschenbuch Verlag GmbH, pg 228
Friedrich Frommann Verlag, pg 230
Gabal-Verlag GmbH, pg 231
Konkursbuch Verlag Claudia Gehrke, pg 231
Gilles und Francke Verlag, pg 232
Gondrom Verlag GmbH & Co KG, pg 233
Walter de Gruyter GmbH & Co KG, pg 234
Verlag Klaus Guhl, pg 235
Haenssler Verlag GmbH, pg 236
Heinz-Jurgen Hausser, pg 236
Peter Hammer Verlag GmbH, pg 237
Hannibal-Verlag, pg 237
Hansa Verlag Ingwert Paulsen Jr, pg 237
Litteraturverlag Karlheinz Hartmann, pg 237
von Hase & Koehler Verlag KG, pg 238
Anton Hiersemann, Verlag, pg 240
Hinstorff Verlag GmbH, pg 241
Verlag Peter Hoell, pg 241
Hofbauer, Christoph und Trojanow Ilia, Akademischer Verlag Muenchen, pg 241
Horlemann Verlag, pg 243
Max Hueber Verlag GmbH & Co KG, pg 243
Edition Humanistische Psychologie (EHP), pg 243
Edition Hundertmark, pg 243
Hyperion - Verlag, pg 244
Edition ID-Archiv/ID-Verlag, pg 244
Idea Verlag GmbH, pg 244
Ikarus - Buchverlag, pg 244
Informationsstelle Suedliches Afrika eV (ISSA), pg 245
Insel Verlag, pg 245
Klaus Isele, pg 245
Iudicium Verlag GmbH, pg 245
Jan Thorbecke Verlag GmbH & Co, pg 246
Peter Kirchheim Verlag, pg 249
Vittorio Klostermann GmbH, pg 250
Koenemann Verlagesellschaft mbH, pg 251
Verlag Koenigshausen und Neumann GmbH, pg 251
KONTEXTverlag, pg 252
Dr Anton Kovac Slavica Verlag, pg 253
Roman Kovar Verlag, pg 253
Karin Kramer Verlag, pg 253
Kretschmar Hubert Leipziger Verlagsgesellschaft, pg 253
Alfred Kroner Verlag, pg 253
Kubon Und Sagner, pg 254
Kulturstiftung der deutschen Vertriebenen, pg 254
Verlag Antje Kunstmann GmbH, pg 254
Kunstverlag Weingarten GmbH, pg 254
Kupfergraben Verlagsgesellschaft mbH, pg 254
Lamuv Verlag GmbH, pg 255

Peter Lang GmbH Europaeischer Verlag der Wissenschaften, pg 255
Ingrid Langner, pg 256
Michael Lassleben Verlag, pg 256
Leibniz-Buecherwarte, pg 257
Anton G Leitner Verlag (AGLV), pg 257
Dr Gisela Lermann, pg 257
Lettre International Kulturzeitung, pg 257
Lienhard Pallast Verlag, pg 258
Logos-Verlag Literatur & Layout GmbH, pg 258
Luchterhand Literaturverlag GmbH/Verlag Volk & Welt GmbH, pg 259
Verlag Waldemar Lutz, pg 260
Manutius Verlag, pg 260
Mattes Verlag GmbH, pg 261
Matthes und Seitz Verlag GmbH, pg 261
mentis Verlag GmbH, pg 262
Merlin Verlag Andreas Meyer Verlags GmbH und Co KG, pg 263
J B Metzler'sche Verlagsbuchhandlung, pg 263
Miranda-Verlag Stefan Ehlert, pg 264
Mitteldeutscher Verlag GmbH, pg 264
Monia Verlag, pg 265
Multi Media Kunst Verlag Dresden, pg 266
Gunter Narr Verlag, pg 266
Edition Nautilus Verlag, pg 267
Nebel Verlag GmbH, pg 267
Neckar Verlag GmbH, pg 267
Nie/Nie/Sagen-Verlag, pg 268
C W Niemeyer Buchverlage GmbH, pg 268
Max Niemeyer Verlag GmbH, pg 269
Oberbaum Verlag GmbH, pg 269
Edition Octopus & Okeanos Presse, pg 269
Georg Olms Verlag AG, pg 270
Orlanda Frauenverlag, pg 270
Oros Verlag, pg 271
Paranus Verlag - Bruecke Neumuenster GmbH, pg 271
Patmos Verlag GmbH & Co KG, pg 272
Pawel Panpresse, pg 272
Pendragon Verlag, pg 272
Guido Pressler Verlag, pg 275
Propylaeen Verlag, Zweigniederlassung Berlin der Ullstein Buchverlage GmbH, pg 275
Quelle und Meyer Verlag GmbH & Co, pg 276
Quintessenz Verlags-GmbH, pg 276
Reclam Verlag Leipzig, pg 277
Rigodon-Verlag Norbert Wehr, pg 279
Rimbaud Verlagsgesellschaft mbH, pg 279
Roehrig Universitaets Verlag Gmbh, pg 279
Rombach GmbH Druck und Verlagshaus & Co, pg 280
Romiosini Verlag, pg 280
ROSPO Verlag, pg 280
Rowohlt Taschenbuch Verlag GmbH, pg 280
Ruetten & Loening Berlin GmbH, pg 281
Verlag an der Ruhr GmbH, pg 281
Sassafras Verlag, pg 281

PUBLISHERS

K G Saur Verlag GmbH, A Gale/ Thomson Learning Company, pg 282
scaneg Verlag, pg 282
Schild-Verlag GmbH, pg 283
Agora Verlag Manfred Schlosser, pg 283
Wilhelm Schmitz Verlag, pg 284
Schoeffling & Co, pg 284
Ferdinand Schoeningh Verlag GmbH, pg 284
Verlag und Schriftenmission der Evangelischen Gesellschaft Wuppertal, pg 285
Societaets-Verlag, pg 287
Adolf Sponholtz Verlag, pg 288
Stapp Verlag Wolfgang Stapp, pg 289
Stattbuch Verlag GmbH, pg 289
Stauffenburg Verlag Brigitte Narr GmbH, pg 289
Steidl Verlag, pg 289
J F Steinkopf Verlag GmbH, pg 289
Verlag Stendel, pg 290
Edition Gunter Stoberlein, pg 290
Straelener Manuskripte Verlag, pg 290
Stroemfeld Verlag, pg 290
Edition Temmen, pg 292
edition Text & Kritik im Richard Boorberg Verlag GmbH & Co, pg 293
Treves Editions Verein Zur Foerderung der Kuenstlerischen Taetigkeiten, pg 295
Tuduv Verlagsgesellschaft mbH, pg 295
Ullstein Heyne List GmbH & Co KG, pg 295
Ulrike Helmer Verlag, pg 296
Universitaetsverlag C Winter Heidelberg GmbH, pg 296
UTB fuer Wissenschaft Uni-Taschenbuecher GmbH, pg 297
UVK Universitatsverlag Konstanz GmbH, pg 297
Vervuert Verlagsgesellschaft, pg 298
Verlag Klaus Wagenbach GmbH, pg 300
Friedenauer Presse Katharina Wagenbach-Wolff, pg 300
Uwe Warnke Verlag, pg 300
Wartburg Verlag GmbH, pg 300
Waxmann Verlag GmbH, pg 300
Weidler Buchverlag Berlin, pg 301
Westholsteinische Verlagsanstalt und Verlagsdruckerei Boyens & Co, pg 302
Wissenschaftliche Buchgesellschaft, pg 303
Wolf's-Verlag Berlin, pg 304
Wolgang Fietkau, pg 304
Das Wunderhorn Verlag GmbH, pg 304

Ghana

Ghana Academy of Arts & Sciences, pg 307
Paul Ntem Maanoh, pg 307

Greece

Difros Publications, pg 309
Dioptra Publishing, pg 309
Dorikos Publishing House, pg 310
Ekdoseis Kazantzaki (Kazantzakis Publications), pg 310
Etaireia Spoudon Neoellinikou Politismou Kai Genikis Paideias, pg 310
Exandas Publishers, pg 310
Ekdoseis Filon, pg 310
Forma Publications Ltd, pg 310
Gutenberg Publications, pg 311
Harlenic Hellas Publishing SA, pg 311
Denise Harvey, pg 311
Hestia-1 D Hestia-Kollaros & Co Corporation, pg 311
Hiotellis P, pg 311
Ianos, pg 311
Idmon Publications, pg 311
Ikaros Ekdotiki, pg 311
Kardamitsa A, pg 312
Kastaniotis Editions SA, pg 312
Kedros Publishers, pg 312
Knossos Publications, pg 312
Kritiki Publishing, pg 312
Kyriakidis Vasileios, pg 312
Morfotiko Idryma Ethnikis Trapezas, pg 313
Okeanida, pg 313
Patakis Publishers, pg 314
J Sideris OE Ekdoseis, pg 315
Stochastis, pg 315
To Rodakio, pg 315
Vlassis, pg 316
Zyrichidi Bros, pg 316

Guadeloupe

Librairie Generale JASOR, pg 316

Guatemala

Grupo Editorial RIN-78, pg 316

Haiti

Deschamps Imprimerie, pg 317
Theodor (Imprimerie), pg 317

Holy See (Vatican City State)

Libreria Editrice Vaticana, pg 317

Hong Kong

Breakthrough Ltd - Breakthrough Publishers, pg 318
Chinese Christian Literature Council Ltd, pg 318
The Chinese University Press, pg 319
Chung Hwa Book Co (HK) Ltd, pg 319
Island Press, pg 320
Joint Publishing (HK) Co Ltd, pg 320
Research Centre for Translation, pg 321

Hungary

Akademiai Kiado, pg 323
Aranyhal Konyvkiado Goldfish Publishing, pg 323
Balassi Kiado Kft, pg 323
Central European University Press, pg 323
CEU-Press, pg 323
Jelenkor Verlag, pg 324
Kiiarat Konyvdiado, pg 324
Lang Kiado, pg 325
Mult es Jovo Kiado, pg 325
Nemzeti Tankoenyvkiado, pg 326
Nemzetkozi Szinhazi Intezet Magyar Kozpontja, pg 326
Osiris Kiado, pg 326
Polgar Citizen Press, pg 326
Szabad Ter Kiado, pg 326

Iceland

Frodi Ltd, pg 328
Hid Islenzka Bokmenntafelag, pg 328
Iceland Review, pg 328
Mal og menning, pg 328
Stofnun Arna Magnussonar a Islandi, pg 329

India

Abhinav Publications, pg 329
Ajanta Publications (India), pg 330
Ankur Publishing House, pg 330
K P Bagchi & Co, pg 332
Bharatiya Vidya Bhavan, pg 333
BR Publishing Corporation, pg 334
CICC Book House, pg 335
Cosmo Publications, pg 335
Dastane Ramchandra & Co, pg 335
DC Books, pg 336
Disha Prakashan, pg 336
Doaba House, pg 336
Dutta Baruah Publishing Co Pvt Ltd, pg 336
Geeta Prakasham, pg 337
Arnold Heinman Publishers (India) Pvt Ltd, pg 338
Heritage Publishers, pg 338
Indian Council for Cultural Relations, pg 339
Intellectual Publishing House, pg 339
Minerva Associates (Publications) Pvt Ltd, pg 342
Motilal Banarsidass Publishers Pvt Ltd, pg 343
Natraj Prakashan, pg 344
Omsons Publications, pg 345
Oxford University Press, pg 345
Parimal Prakashan, pg 345
Pointer Publishers, pg 346
Rajpal & Sons, pg 347
Reliance Publishing House, pg 347
Rupa & Co, pg 348
SABDA, pg 348
Sahitya Akademi, pg 348
Sahitya Pravarthaka Co-operative Society Ltd, pg 348
Sasta Sahitya Mandal, pg 349
Sri Satguru Publications, pg 349
Sharda Prakashan, pg 350
R R Sheth & Co, pg 350
Sita Publications, pg 350
Star Publications (P) Ltd, pg 351
Sterling Publishers Pvt Ltd, pg 351
Surjeet Publications, pg 351
Vani Prakashan, pg 352
Vidya Puri, pg 352
Vikas Publishing House Pvt Ltd, pg 353
Vivek Prakashan, pg 353

Indonesia

P T Bulan Bintang, pg 354
PT Dian Rakyat, pg 355
Djambatan PT, pg 355
Dunia Pustaka Jaya, pg 355
Katalis PT Bina Mitra Plaosan, pg 356
Penerbit Nusa Indah, pg 356
Pustaka Utama Grafiti, PT, pg 357
Yayasan Lontar, pg 357
Yayasan Obor Indonesia, pg 357

Ireland

A & A Farmar, pg 358
Attic Press Ltd, pg 358
Brandon Book Publishers Ltd, pg 359
Campus Publishing Ltd, pg 359
FISH Publishing, pg 360
Four Courts Press Ltd, pg 360
Gill & Macmillan Ltd, pg 361
The Goldsmith Press Ltd, pg 361
Irish Academic Press, pg 361
Irish Times Ltd, pg 361
The Lilliput Press Ltd, pg 362

SUBJECT INDEX

Mount Eagle Publications Ltd, pg 362
New Writers' Press, pg 362
Raven Arts Press, pg 363
Relay Books, pg 363

Israel

Bar Ilan University Press, pg 365
Ben-Zvi Institute, pg 365
The Bialik Institute, pg 365
Bitan Publishers Ltd, pg 365
Breslov Research Institute, pg 366
DAT Publications, pg 366
Dvir Publishing Ltd, pg 366
Habermann Institute for Literary Research, pg 367
Hadar Publishing House Ltd, pg 367
Haifa University Press, pg 368
Hakibbutz Hameuchad Publishing House Ltd, pg 368
The Institute for the Translation of Hebrew Literature, pg 368
Machbarot Lesifrut, pg 370
Misgav Yerushalayim, pg 370
Open University of Israel, pg 371
Schocken Publishing House Ltd, pg 372
Y Sreberk, pg 372
Tcherikover Publishers Ltd, pg 372
Urim Publications, pg 373
Y L Peretz Publishing Co, pg 374

Italy

Edizioni Abete, pg 374
Accademia (Milano), pg 374
Mario Adda Editore SNC, pg 374
Adea Edizioni, pg 374
Adelphi Edizioni SpA, pg 374
Adriatica Editrice, pg 374
Alba, pg 375
Edizioni Anabasi SpA, pg 375
Archinto snc, pg 376
Archivio Guido Izzi Edizioni, pg 376
Argalia Editore delle Arti Grafiche Editoriali SRL, pg 376
Bastogi, pg 377
Casa Editrice Luigi Battei, pg 377
Belforte Editore Libraio srl, pg 377
Bibliopolis - Edizioni di Filosofia e Scienze Srl, pg 377
Bibliotheca di Gabriele Chiusano, pg 378
Bollati Boringhieri Editore Srl, pg 378
Giuseppe Bonanno Editore, pg 378
Book Editore, pg 378
Bovolenta, pg 378
Edizioni Bresciane, pg 378
Bulzoni Editore SRL (Le Edizioni Universitarie d'Italia), pg 379
Calosci, pg 379
Campanotto, pg 379
Capone Editore SRL, pg 379
Casa Editrice Giuseppe Principato Spa, pg 380
Edistudio di Brunetto Casini, pg 380
Celuc Libri, pg 380
Centro Italiano Studi Alto Medioevo, pg 381
Centro Studi Terzo Mondo, pg 381
Cideb Editrice SRL, pg 381
Ciranna - Roma, pg 381
Cisalpino - Monduzzi, pg 382
CLUEB (Cooperativa Libraria Universitaria Editrice Bologna), pg 382
Nuova Coletti Editore Roma, pg 382
Colonnese Editore, pg 382

SUBJECT INDEX

Cooperativa Libraria IULM SCRL, pg 383
Costa e Nolan SpA, pg 383
D'Anna, pg 383
M d'Auria Editore SAS, pg 384
Demetra SRL, pg 385
ECIG, pg 385
Editrice Edisco, pg 386
Edizioni Associate/Editrice Internazionale Srl, pg 386
Edizioni l'Arciere SRL, pg 387
ERGA SNC di Carla Ottino Merli & C (Edizioni Realizzazioni Grafiche - Artigiana), pg 388
Essegi, pg 388
Fatatrac, pg 388
Feguagiskia' Studios, pg 389
Festina Lente Edizioni, pg 389
Fogola Editore in Torino, pg 389
Arnaldo Forni Editore SRL, pg 389
Gamberetti Editrice SRL, pg 390
Gangemi Editore, pg 390
Editrice Garigliano SRL, pg 390
Garzanti Editore, pg 390
Istituto Geografico de Agostini SpA, pg 390
Editrice Giannotta di Sebastiano Pace Giannotta, pg 390
Giunti Publishing Group, pg 391
Giuseppe Laterza Editore Snc, pg 391
Ernesto Gremese Editore SRL, pg 391
Herbita Editrice di Leonardo Palermo, pg 392
Ibis, pg 393
Il Minotauro, pg 393
Il Poligrafo, pg 393
Il Quadrante SRL, pg 393
Il Saggiatore, pg 393
Ila - Palma, Tea Nova, pg 393
Edizioni Internazionali di Letteratura e Scienze, pg 394
Iperborea, pg 394
Ist Patristico Augustinianum, pg 394
Editoriale Jaca Book SpA, pg 394
Editrice Janus SpA, pg 394
L Japadre Editore, pg 394
Jouvence, pg 394
Il Lavoro Editoriale, pg 395
Lecce Spazio Vivo Srl, pg 395
LED - Edizioni Universitarie di Lettere Economia Diritto, pg 395
Casa Editrice Le Lettere SRL, pg 395
Letture Mensile di Informazione Culturale, Letteratura e Spettacolo, pg 395
Liguori Editore SRL, pg 396
Editrice Liguria SNC di Norberto Sabatelli & C, pg 396
Editrice la Locusta, pg 396
Loescher Editore SRL, pg 396
Loffredo Editore Napoli SpA®, pg 396
Angelo Longo Editore, pg 396
Lorenzo Editore, pg 397
Lubrina Editore Srl, pg 397
La Luna, pg 397
Luni, pg 397
Casa Editrice Maccari (CEM), pg 397
Giuseppe Maimone Editore, pg 397
Manfrini Editori, pg 397
Casa Editrice Marietti SpA, pg 397
Aldo Marino Editore, pg 398
Marsilio Editori SpA, pg 398
Marzorati Editore SRL, pg 398
Editrice Massimo SAS di Crespi Cesare e C, pg 398
Il Melangolo, pg 398
Casa Editrice Menna di Sinisgalli Menna Giuseppina, pg 398

Milano Libri, pg 398
Milella di Lecce Spazio Vivo SRL, pg 399
Mondolibro Editore SNC, pg 399
Monduzzi Editore SpA, pg 399
Moretti & Vitali editori srl, pg 400
Mucchi Editore SRL, pg 400
Museo Storico in Trento, pg 400
Nardini Editore srl, pg 400
Istituto Nazionale di Studi Romani, pg 400
New Magazine, pg 400
Nistri - Lischi Editori, pg 401
Novecento Editrice Srl, pg 401
Nuova Alfa Editoriale, pg 401
Editrice Nuovi Autori, pg 401
Nuovi Sentieri Editore, pg 401
Leo S Olschki, pg 402
Osanna Venosa, pg 402
Maria Pacini Fazzi Editore, pg 402
Pagano Editore, pg 402
Palatina Editrice, pg 402
G B Palumbo & C Editore SpA, pg 402
Franco Cosimo Panini Editore SpA, pg 402
Paravia Bruno Mondadori Editori, pg 402
Passigli Editori srl, pg 403
Patron Editore SrL, pg 403
Luigi Pellegrini Editore, pg 403
Piccin Nuova Libraria SpA, pg 403
Piero Lacaita Editore, pg 403
Piero Manni srl, pg 403
La Pilotta Editrice Coop RL, pg 403
Francesco Pirella Editore, pg 403
Istituto Poligrafico e Zecca dello Stato, pg 404
Neri Pozza Editore, pg 404
Principato, pg 404
Edizioni Quattroventi SNC, pg 404
Rara-Ist Editoriale di Bibliofilia e Reprints, pg 405
Riccardo Ricciardi Editore SpA, pg 405
Edizioni Ripostes, pg 405
Editori Riuniti, pg 405
Archinto Rosellina, pg 406
Rubbettino Editore, pg 406
Rusconi Libri Srl, pg 406
SAIE Editrice SRL, pg 406
Salerno Editrice SRL, pg 406
Schena Editore, pg 407
Salvatore Sciascia Editore, pg 407
Edizioni Scientifiche Italiane, pg 407
Sellerio Editore, pg 407
SEMAR Publishers SRL, pg 407
Sicania, pg 408
Societa Editrice Internazionale - SEI, pg 408
Societa Storica Catanese, pg 408
Spirali Edizioni, pg 408
Stampa Alternativa - Nuovi Equilibri, pg 408
Edizioni di Storia e Letteratura, pg 409
Studio Bibliografico Adelmo Polla, pg 409
Studio Editoriale Programma, pg 409
Edizioni Studio Tesi SRL, pg 409
Edizioni Studium SpA, pg 409
La Tartaruga Edizioni SAS, pg 409
Edizioni Thyrus SRL, pg 409
Tilgher-Genova sas, pg 410
Editrice Tirrenia Stampatori SAS, pg 410
Todariana Editrice, pg 410
Tranchida, pg 410
Transeuropa Libri, pg 410
Editoriale Umbra SAS di Carnevale, pg 410

Edizioni Unicopli SpA, pg 410
Unipress, pg 410
Vita e Pensiero, pg 411
La Vita Felice, pg 411
Viviani Editore srl, pg 412
Zanichelli Editore SpA, pg 412
Edizioni Zara, pg 412

Jamaica
Carlong Publishers (Caribbean) Ltd, pg 412
Jamaica Publishing House Ltd, pg 413
University of the West Indies Press, pg 414
UWI Publishers' Association, pg 414

Japan
Akita Shoten Publishing Co Ltd, pg 414
Eichosha Company Ltd, pg 416
The Eihosha Ltd, pg 416
Fukuinkan Shoten Publishers Inc, pg 416
Fuzambo Publishing Co, pg 416
GakuseiSha Publishing Co Ltd, pg 416
Hakusui-Sha Co Ltd, pg 417
Hakutei-Sha, pg 417
Hayakawa Publishing Inc, pg 417
Holp Book Co Ltd, pg 417
Japan Broadcast Publishing Co Ltd, pg 418
Kadokawa Shoten Publishing Co, pg 419
Kaitakusha, pg 419
Kazama Shobo, pg 419
Keisuisha Publishing Company Ltd, pg 419
Kinokuniya Co Ltd (Publishing Department), pg 420
Kodansha, pg 420
Kokudo-Sha, pg 420
Kokusho Kankokai Co Ltd, pg 420
Kosei Publishing Co Ltd, pg 420
Mirai-Sha, pg 421
Misuzu Shobo Ltd, pg 421
Myrtos Inc, pg 421
Nihon Tosho Center Co Ltd, pg 422
Nippon Hoso Shuppan Kyokai (NHK Publishing), pg 422
Otsuki Shoten Publishers, pg 423
Rinsen Book Co Ltd, pg 424
Sagano Shoin, pg 424
Sanseido Co Ltd, pg 424
Sanshusha Publishing Co, Ltd, pg 424
Seibundo Shuppan, pg 425
Shibundo Co Ltd, pg 425
Shincho-Sha Co Ltd, pg 425
Akane Shobo Co Ltd, pg 425
Shueisha Inc, pg 426
Shufu-to-Seikatsu Sha Ltd, pg 426
The Simul Press Inc, pg 426
Soshisha Co Ltd, pg 426
Toho Book Store, pg 427
Tokai University Press, pg 427
Tokuma-Shoten, pg 427
Tokyo Sogensha Co Ltd, pg 428
Charles E Tuttle Publishing Co Inc, pg 428
Waseda University Press, pg 428
Yamaguchi Shoten, pg 429

Kazakstan
Zazusy, pg 430

Kenya
Heinemann Kenya Limited (EAEP), pg 431
Lake Publishers & Enterprises Ltd, pg 432
Shirikon Publishers, pg 433
Sudan Literature Centre, pg 433

Democratic People's Republic of Korea
Korea Science and Encyclopedia Publishing House, pg 434

Republic of Korea
Bakyoung Publishing Co, pg 434
Bo Ri, pg 435
Bum-Woo Publishing Co, pg 435
Chang-josa Publishing Co, pg 435
Chong No Books Publishing Co Ltd, pg 435
Chung Rim Publishing Co Ltd, pg 435
DanKook University Press, pg 436
Dong Hwa Publishing Co, pg 436
Eulyu Publishing Co Ltd, pg 436
Hak Won Publishing Co, pg 436
Hakgojae Publishing Inc, pg 436
Hanjin Publishing Co, pg 436
Hangil Art Vision, pg 436
Hanul Publishing Co, pg 436
Haseo Publishing Co, pg 436
Hyun Am Publishing Co, pg 437
Korea University Press, pg 437
Koreaone Press Inc, pg 438
Kyobo Book Centre, pg 438
Literature Academy, pg 438
Minjisa Publishing Co, pg 438
Minumsa Publishing Co Ltd, pg 438
Mirinae, pg 438
Munhag-gwan, pg 438
Munye Publishing Co, pg 439
Nanam Publishing House, pg 439
Omun Gak, pg 439
Pan Korea Book Corporation, pg 439
Pyeong-hwa Chulpansa, pg 439
Samseong Publishing Co Ltd, pg 440
Seoul National University Press, pg 440
Sogang University Press, pg 440
Woong Jin Publishing Co Ltd, pg 440
YBM/Si-sa, pg 441
Yeha Publishing Co Ltd, pg 441

Kuwait
Ministry of Information, pg 441

Latvia
Preses Nams, pg 442

Lebanon
Darl el-Machreq Sarl, pg 443
Librairie du Liban, pg 443
Librairie Orientale sal, pg 443
World Book Publishing, pg 443

Lesotho
Mazenod Book Centre, pg 444

Liechtenstein
Verlag HP Gassner AG, pg 444

Lithuania
AS Narbuto Leidykla (AS Narbutas' Publishers), pg 445
Baltos Lankos, pg 445
Lietuvos Rasytoju Sajungos Leidykla, pg 446

PUBLISHERS

Mokslo ir enciklopediju leidybos institutas, pg 446
The Publishing House of the Lithuanian Writers' Union, pg 446
Vaga Ltd, pg 446

Luxembourg

Editions APESS ASBL, pg 447
Editions Emile Borschette, pg 447
Cahiers Luxembourgeois, pg 447
Centre Culturel De Differdange, pg 447
Essay und Zeitgeist Verlag, pg 447
Editions Phi, pg 448
Editions Saint-Paul, pg 448

Macau

Universidadede de Macau, Centro de Publicacoes, pg 448

The Former Yugoslav Republic of Macedonia

Detska radost, pg 448
Ktitor, pg 449
Macedonia Prima Publishing House, pg 449
Mi-An Knigoizdatelstvo, pg 449
Nov svet (New World), pg 449
Strk Publishing House, pg 449
Zumpres Publishing Firm, pg 449

Madagascar

Maison d'Edition Protestante ANTSO, pg 450
Madagascar Print & Press Company, pg 450

Malaysia

Pearson Education, pg 453
Pustaka Cipta Sdn Bhd, pg 454
Tempo Publishing (M) Sdn Bhd, pg 455
Uni-Text Book Co, pg 455

Malta

Gozo Press, pg 456
Progress Press Co Ltd, pg 456

Mauritius

Editions de l'Ocean Indien Ltd, pg 457
Vizavi Editions, pg 457

Mexico

Aconcagua Ediciones y Publicaciones SA, pg 457
Editorial AGATA SA de CV, pg 457
Editores Asociados Mexicanos SA de CV (EDAMEX), pg 458
Editorial Azteca SA, pg 458
Centro Editorial Mexicano Osiris SA, pg 458
El Colegio de Mexico AC, pg 459
Ediciones Corunda SA de CV, pg 459
Editorial Diana SA de CV, pg 459
Ediciones Era SA de CV, pg 460
Editorial Esfinge SA de CV, pg 460
Editorial Extemporaneos SA, pg 461
Fernandez Editores SA de CV, pg 461
Hoja Casa Editorial SA de CV, pg 462
Editorial Iztaccihuatl SA, pg 462
Editorial Jus SA de CV, pg 462
Lasser Press Mexicana SA de CV, pg 462

Phillip Richard Conover Lazo, pg 462
Editorial Orion, pg 465
Editorial Patria SA de CV, pg 465
Libreria Patria SA, pg 465
Editorial Porrua SA, pg 466
Ediciones Roca, SA, pg 466
Siglo XXI Editores SA de CV, pg 467
Universidad Nacional Autonoma de Mexico (National University of Mexico), pg 467
Universo Editorial SA de CV Edicion de Libros Revistas y Periodicos, pg 468

Republic of Moldova

Editura Hyperion, pg 468
Izdatelstvo Kartia Moldoveniaske, pg 468
Lumina Publishing House, pg 468

Monaco

Editions EGC, pg 468
Les Editions du Rocher, pg 469
Rondeau Giannipiero a Monaco, pg 469

Morocco

Dar Nachr Al Maarifa Pour L'Edition et La Distribution, pg 469
Editions Eddif Maroc, pg 469
Editions Le Fennec, pg 470
Societe Ennewrasse Service Librairie et Imprimerie, pg 470

Myanmar

Sarpay Beikman Board, pg 471

Namibia

Gamsberg Macmillan Publishers (Pty) Ltd, pg 471

Nepal

International Standards Books & Periodicals (P) Ltd, pg 471
Royal Nepal Academy, pg 472
Sajha Prakashan, Co-operative Publishing Organization, pg 472

Netherlands

Altamira BV, pg 472
Uitgeverij Ambo BV, pg 472
Uitgeverij Arena BV, pg 473
Uitgeverij Aristos, pg 473
Uitgeverij Balans, pg 473
John Benjamins BV, pg 474
De Bezige Bij, pg 474
Uitgeverij A W Bruna en Zoon NV, pg 475
BZZTOH Publishers, pg 475
Cadans, pg 475
Castrum Peregrini Presse, pg 475
Uitgeverij Conserve, pg 475
Uitgeverij Coutinho BV, pg 476
Fragment Cooperatieve Vereniging UA, Uitgeverij, pg 477
Gaberbocchus Press, pg 477
Uitgeverij Vrij Geestesleven, pg 477
Uitgeverij CJ Goossens BV, pg 477
De Harmonie, pg 478
HES & De Graaf Publishers BV, pg 478
Historische Uitgeverij, pg 478
J M Meulenhoff BV, pg 481
Uitgeverij Maarten Muntinga, pg 481
Nijgh & Van Ditmar Amsterdam, pg 482

SUBJECT INDEX

Podium Uitgeverij, pg 483
Prometheus, pg 483
Uitgeverij Het Spectrum BV, pg 484
Thoth Publishers, pg 485
Unieboek BV, pg 485
Van Gorcum & Comp BV, pg 486
Uitgeverij G A van Oorschot bv, pg 486
Uitgeverij Vassallucci, pg 486
West-Friesland/Boekproject-ontwikkeling, pg 487

New Zealand

Auckland University Press, pg 488
Brick Row Publishing Co Ltd, pg 489
Cape Catley, pg 489
Clerestory Press, pg 490
Hazard Press Ltd, pg 491
Lincoln University Press, pg 492
Outrigger Publishers, pg 494
Oxford University Press, pg 494
Te Ropu Kahurangi, pg 496
University of Otago Press, pg 496
Victoria University Press, pg 496

Nicaragua

Editorial Nueva Nicaragua, pg 497

Nigeria

Evans Brothers (Nigeria Publishers) Ltd, pg 499
Hudanuda Publishing Co Ltd, pg 499
Saros International Publishers, pg 501
Vantage Publishers International Ltd, pg 502

Norway

Fono Forlag, pg 503
Snofugl Forlag, pg 505
Tiden Norsk Forlag, pg 505

Pakistan

Fazlee Sons (Pvt) Ltd, pg 506
Hamdard Foundation, pg 507
Jang Publishers, pg 507
Maqbool Academy, pg 508
Nashiran-e-Quran Pvt Ltd, pg 508
Pakistan Publishing House, pg 508
Publishers United Pvt Ltd, pg 508
Sang-e-Meel Publications, pg 509
Urdu Academy Sind, pg 509

Panama

Editorial Universitaria, pg 509

Papua New Guinea

The Christian Book Centre, pg 510

Paraguay

Intercontinental Editora, pg 510

Peru

Centro de la Mujer Peruana Flora Tristan, pg 511
Fondo Editorial de la Pontificia Universidad Catolica del Peru, pg 511
Editorial Horizonte, pg 511
Lluvia Editores Srl, pg 511
Sur Casa de Estudios del Socialismo, pg 511
Universidad Nacional Mayor de San Marcos, pg 512

Philippines

Anvil Publishing Inc, pg 512
Ateneo de Manila University Press, pg 512
De La Salle University, pg 513
New Day Publishers, pg 514
Salesiana Publishers Inc, pg 515
SIBS Publishing House Inc, pg 515
UST Publishing House, pg 515

Poland

Wydawnictwo Dolnoslaskie, pg 516
Energeia sp zoo Wydawnictwo, pg 516
Impuls, pg 517
Instytut Wydawniczy Pax, Inco-Veritas, pg 517
Iskry - Publishing House Ltd spotka zoo, pg 517
Wydawnictwo Literackie, pg 517
Ludowa Spoldzielnia Wydawnicza, pg 518
Norbertinum, pg 518
Ossolineum Zaklad Narodowy im Ossolinskich - Wydawnictwo, pg 518
Panstwowy Instytut Wydawniczy (PIW), pg 518
'Slask' Ltd, pg 520
Wydawnictwo TPPR Wspolpraca, pg 520
Wydawnictwo DiG, pg 521

Portugal

Edicoes Afrontamento, pg 522
Edicoes Antigona, pg 522
Apaginastantas - Cooperativa de Servicos Culturais, pg 522
Livraria Arnado Lda, pg 522
Assirio & Alvim, pg 522
Atica, SA Editores e Livreiros, pg 522
Bertrand Editora Lda, pg 522
Biblioteca Geral da Universidade de Coimbra, pg 523
Coimbra Editora Lda, pg 523
Edicoes Colibri, pg 523
Edicoes Cosmos, pg 524
Dinalivro, pg 524
Edicoes 70, Lda, pg 524
Editorial Estampa, Lda, pg 524
Europress Editores e Distribuidores de Publicacoes Lda, pg 525
Fenda Edicoes, pg 525
Livraria Editora Figueirinhas Lda, pg 525
Editorial Futura, pg 525
Gradiva-Publicacnoes Lda, pg 525
Impala, pg 525
Imprensa Nacional-Casa da Moeda, pg 526
Edicoes ITAU (Instituto Tecnico de Alimentacao Humana) Lda, pg 526
Latina Livraria, pg 526
Livraria Minerva Editora, pg 526
Melhoramentos de Portugal Editora, Lda, pg 527
Nova Arrancada Sociedade Editora SA, pg 527
Paulinas, pg 528
Perspectivas e Realidades, Artes Graficas, Lda, pg 528
Quatro Elementos Editores, pg 529
Quetzal Editores, pg 529
Edicoes Rolim Lda, pg 529
Sa da Costa Editora, pg 529
Edicoes 70, pg 529
Solivros, pg 529
Teorema, pg 529
Editora Ulisseia Lda, pg 530

Usus Editora, pg 530
Vega-Publicacao e Distribuicao de Livros e Revistas, Lda, pg 530

Puerto Rico
Editorial Cordillera Inc, pg 530
Instituto de Cultura Puertorriquena, pg 530
Editorial Cultural Inc, pg 530
Ediciones Huracan Inc, pg 530

Romania
Editura Aius, pg 531
Editura Albatros, pg 531
Ararat Verlag und Druckerei, pg 532
Ars Longa Publishing House, pg 532
Editura Cartea Romaneasca, pg 532
Casa Editoriala Independenta Europa, pg 532
The Center for Romanian Studies, pg 532
Editura Clusium, Casa de Editura Atlas-Clusium SRL, pg 532
Editure Ion Creanga, pg 532
Editura DOINA SRL, pg 533
Editura Excelsior, pg 533
FF Press, pg 533
Hasefer, pg 533
Editura Humanitas, pg 533
Humanitas Publishing House, pg 533
Editura Institutul European, pg 533
Editura Junimea, pg 534
Editura Kriterion SA, pg 534
Lider Verlag, pg 534
Litera Publishing House, pg 534
Mentor Kiado, pg 534
Editura Meridiane, pg 534
Nemira Verlag, pg 534
Editura Paideia, pg 535
Pallas-Akademia Koenyvkiadoes Koenyvkereskedes, pg 535
Pandora Publishing House, pg 535
Polirom Verlag, pg 535
RAO International Publishing Co, pg 535
Realitatea Casa de Edituri Productie Audio-Video Film, pg 535
Rentrop & Straton Verlagsgruppe und Wirtschaftsconsulting, pg 535
Saeculum IO, pg 535
Editura 'Scrisul Romanesc', pg 536
Editura Stiintifica si Enciclopedica, pg 536
Est-Samuel Tastet Verlag, pg 536
Editura Univers, pg 536
Universal Dalsi, pg 536
Vestala Verlag, pg 536
Vremea Publishers Ltd, pg 536

Russian Federation
ARGO-RISK Publisher, pg 537
Izdatelstvo Detskaya Literatura, pg 537
Energoatomizdat, pg 537
Glas New Russian Writing, pg 538
Izdatel 'stvo Mordovskogo gosudar stvennogo, pg 538
Izdatel 'stvo Ural' skogo, pg 538
Kavkazskaya Biblioteka Publishing House, pg 539
Izdatelstvo Khudozhestvennaya Literatura, pg 539
Izdatelstvo Molodaya Gvardia, pg 540
Nauka Publishers, pg 540
Pressa Publishing House, pg 541
Progress Publishers, pg 541
Raduga Publishers, pg 541
Izdatelstvo Sovetskii Pisatel, pg 542

Sovremennik Publishers Too, pg 542
Sredne-Uralskoye knizhnoye izatelstve (Middle Urals Publishing House), pg 542
Voronezh State University Publishers, pg 542
Vsesoyuznii Molodejnii Knizhnii Centre, pg 542
Izdatelstvo Vysshaya Shkola, pg 543

Rwanda
INADES (Institut Africain pour le Developpment Economique et Social), pg 543

Saudi Arabia
Dar Al-Shareff for Publishing & Distribution, pg 543
Saudi Publishing and Distribution House, pg 543

Senegal
Nouvelles Editions Africaines du Senegal (NEAS), pg 544
Centre Africain d'Animation et d'Echanges Culturels Editions Khoudia, pg 544
Centre de Linguistique Appliquee, pg 544

Singapore
Cannon International, pg 545
Singapore University Press Pte Ltd, pg 548
Times Media Pte Ltd, pg 549

Slovakia
Vydavatelstvo Obzor, pg 550
Vydavatel'stvo SFVU Pallas, pg 550
Slovansky Tatran, Vydavatel 'stro spoi sro, pg 550
Slovenske pedagogicke nakladateistvo, pg 550
Slovensky Spisovatel Ltd as, pg 550

Slovenia
Franc-Franc podjetje za promocijo kulture Murska Sobota d o o, pg 551
Pomurska zalozba, pg 552
Slovenska matica, pg 552
Zalozba Mihelac d o o, pg 552
Zalozba Obzorja d d Maribor, pg 552

South Africa
Jonathan Ball Publishers, pg 552
Educum Publishers Ltd, pg 554
HAUM - De Jager Publishers, pg 555
Human & Rousseau (Pty) Ltd, pg 555
Ivy Publications, pg 555
Maskew Miller Longman, pg 557
Mayibuye Books, pg 557
New Africa Books (Pty) Ltd, pg 557
Sasavona Publishers & Booksellers, pg 559
University of Natal Press, pg 560
Vivlia Publishers & Booksellers, pg 560
Witwatersrand University Press, pg 560

Spain
A-Z Ediciones y Publications, pg 561
Publicacions de l'Abadia de Montserrat, pg 561
Academia de la Llingua Asturiana, pg 561
Acantilado, pg 561
Editorial Acervo SL, pg 561
Agencia Espanola de Cooperacion, pg 562
Agora Editorial, pg 562
Editorial Aguaclara, pg 562
Alberdania SL, pg 562
Alfaguara Ediciones SA - Grupo Santillana, pg 562
Ediciones Alfar SA, pg 562
Editorial Algazara, pg 562
Altea, Taurus, Alfaguara SA, pg 563
Ediciones Altera SL, pg 563
Editorial Anagrama, pg 563
Arco Libros SL, pg 564
Editorial Ariel SA, pg 564
Editorial Barcino SA, pg 565
Biblioteca de Catalunya, pg 565
Bosch Casa Editorial SA, pg 565
Edicions Bromera SL, pg 566
Calamo Editorial, pg 566
Carroggio SA de Ediciones, pg 566
Casa de Velazquez, pg 566
Editorial Casals SA, pg 566
Editorial Castalia, pg 566
Edicios do Castro, pg 566
Ediciones Catedra SA, pg 566
Circe Ediciones, SA, pg 567
Ediciones Colegio De Espana (ECE), pg 568
Compania Literaria, pg 568
Curial Edicions Catalanes SA, pg 569
Ediciones Destino SA, pg 569
Diputacion Provincial de Malaga, pg 570
Diputacion Provincial de Sevilla, Servicio de Publicaciones, pg 570
Diseno Editorial SA, pg 570
Editorial Don Quijote, pg 570
Editorial EDAF SA, pg 571
Edebe, pg 571
EDHASA (Editora y Distribuidora Hispano-Americana SA), pg 571
Edi-Liber Irlan SA, pg 571
Edicions Camacuc, pg 571
Ediles-Ediciones Leonesas SA, pg 572
Ediciones Encuentro SA, pg 573
Erein, pg 573
Editorial Espasa-Calpe SA, pg 573
Instituto de Estudios Riojanos, pg 574
Eumo Editorial, pg 574
EUNSA (Ediciones Universidad de Navarra SA), pg 574
Fondo de Cultura Economica de Espana, SL, pg 574
Fundacion de Estudios Libertarios Anselmo Lorenzo, pg 575
Fundacion Rosacruz, pg 575
Editorial Fundamentos, pg 575
Galaxia SA Editorial, pg 575
Editorial Gredos SA, pg 576
Grijalbo Mondadori SA, pg 576
Editorial Grupo Cero, pg 576
Guadalquivir SL Ediciones, pg 576
Ediciones Hiperion SL, pg 577
Hogar del Libro, SA, pg 577
Ibaizabal Edelvives SA, pg 577
Editorial Iberia, SA, pg 577
Icaria Editorial SA, pg 577
Institucion Fernando el Catolico de la Excma Diputacion de Zaragoza, pg 578
Iralka Editorial SL, pg 578

Ediciones Istmo SA, pg 579
Joyas Bibliograficas SA, pg 579
Ediciones Jucar, pg 579
Junta de Castilla y Leon Consejeria de Educacion y Cultura, pg 579
Laertes SA de Ediciones, pg 579
Editorin Laiovento SL, pg 579
Ediciones Libertarias/Prodhufi SA, pg 580
Libsa Editorial SA, pg 580
Llibres del Segle, pg 580
Loguez Ediciones, pg 580
Editorial Lumen SA, pg 580
Antonio Machado, SA, pg 580
Ediciones Maeva, pg 581
Editorial Magisterio Espanol SA, pg 581
Edicins de la Magrana SA, pg 581
Editorial Marfil SA, pg 581
Ediciones Martinez-Roca SA, pg 581
Editorial Mediterrania SL, pg 582
Ediciones Minotauro, pg 582
Editorial Moll SL, pg 582
Anaya & Mario Muchnik, pg 583
Munoz Moya Editor, pg 583
Editorial la Muralla SA, pg 583
Naque Editora, pg 583
Noguer y Caralt Editores SA, pg 584
Ediciones Oceano Grupo SA, pg 584
Oikos-Tau SA Ediciones, pg 584
Ediciones del Oriente y del Mediterraneo, pg 585
El Paisaje Editorial, pg 585
Ediciones Partenon, pg 586
Centre de Pastoral Liturgica, pg 586
Perea Ediciones, pg 586
Editorial Playor SA, pg 587
Editorial Pliegos, pg 587
Editorial Popular SA, pg 587
Editorial Portic SA, pg 587
Pre-Textos, pg 587
Prensas Universitarias de Zaragoza, pg 587
Edicions Proa, SA, pg 588
Publicaciones de la Universidad de Alicante, pg 588
Quaderns Crema SA, pg 588
Editora Regional de Murcia - ERM, pg 588
Ediciones Rialp SA, pg 589
Riquelme y Vargas Ediciones SL, pg 589
Selecta-Catalonia Ed, pg 590
Servicio de Publicaciones Universidad de Cadiz, pg 590
Ediciones Seyer, pg 590
Siglo XXI de Espana Editores SA, pg 590
Editorial Sintesis, SA, pg 590
Edicions 62, pg 591
Grup 62, pg 591
Ediciones SM, pg 591
Editorial Tecnos SA, pg 592
Ediciones Temas de Hoy, SA, pg 592
Editorial Sal Terrae, pg 592
Tf Editores, pg 592
Ediciones de la Torre, pg 593
Torremozas SL Ediciones, pg 593
Trea Ediciones, SL, pg 593
Trotta SA Editorial, pg 593
Ediciones Jose Porrua Turanzas SA, pg 593
Turner Publicaciones, pg 593
Tusquets Editores, pg 593
Ediciones 29 - Libros Rio Nuevo, pg 594
Editorial Txertoa, pg 594
Ultramar Editores SA, pg 594
Universidad de Granada, pg 594

PUBLISHERS

Ediciones Universidad de Salamanca, pg 594
Universidad de Valladolid Secretariado de Publicaciones e Intercambio Editorial, pg 594
Universitat de Valencia Servei de Publicacions, pg 594
Editorial Verbum SL, pg 595
Veron Editor, pg 595
Ediciones Versal SA, pg 595
Vinaches Lopez, Luisa, pg 595
Visor Distribuciones, SA, pg 596
Visor Libros, pg 596
Ediciones Vulcano, pg 596
Xunta de Galicia, pg 596

Sri Lanka

Danuma Prakashakayo, pg 596
Dayawansa Jayakody & Co, pg 597
Ministry of Cultural Affairs, pg 597
National Library & Documentation Services Board, pg 597
Pradeepa Publishers, pg 598
Saman & Madara Publishers, pg 598
Swarna Hansa Foundation, pg 598

Suriname

Stichting Wetenschappelijke Informatie, pg 599

Sweden

Acta Universitatis Gothoburgensis, pg 599
Bokforlaget Fabel AB, pg 600
Carlsson Bokfoerlag AB, pg 601
Ellerstroms, pg 602
Klassikerfoerlaget, pg 604
Bokforlaget Nya Doxa AB, pg 605
Schultz Forlag AB, pg 606

Switzerland

Editions L'Age d'Homme - La Cite, pg 608
Ammann Verlag & Co, pg 608
Arche Verlag AG, Raabe und Vitali, pg 608
Archivio Storico Ticinese, pg 608
Armenia Editions, pg 608
Athenaeum Verlag AG, pg 608
H R Balmer AG Verlag, pg 609
Bargezzi-Verlag AG, pg 609
Bartschi Publishing, pg 609
Bergli Books AG, pg 609
Edizioni Casagrande SA, pg 611
Christoph Merian Verlag, pg 611
Edizioni Armando Dado, Tipografia Stazione, pg 612
Editions Andre Delcourt & Cie, pg 612
Diogenes Verlag AG, pg 612
Librairie Droz SA, pg 612
Eboris-Coda-Bompiani, pg 613
Eco Verlags AG, pg 613
Edition Epoca, pg 613
Erker-Verlag, pg 613
Edition Hans Erpf Verlagsgenossenschaft, pg 613
Editions Esprit Ouvert, pg 613
Editions Foma SA, pg 614
Frobenius AG, pg 614
Haffmans Verlag AG, pg 615
Kranich-Verlag, Dres AG & H R Bosch-Gwalter, pg 617
Lia rumantscha, pg 618
Limmat Verlag, pg 618
Manesse Verlag GmbH, pg 618
Memory/Cage Editions, pg 619
Les Editions Noir sur Blanc, pg 620
Editions Payot Lausanne, pg 621
Pedrazzini Tipografia, pg 621

Philosophisch-Anthroposophischer Verlag am Goetheanum, pg 621
PIE-Peter Lang SA, pg 622
Editions Pourquoi Pas, pg 622
Raphael, Editions, pg 622
Rauhreif Verlag, pg 622
Rodera-Verlag der Cardun AG, pg 623
Satyr-Verlag Dr Humbel, pg 623
Verlag fuer Schoene Wissenschaften, pg 624
Schwabe & Co AG, pg 624
Schwengeler-Verlag, pg 624
Istituto Editoriale Ticinese (IET) SA, pg 626
Der Universitatsverlag Freiburg, pg 626
Vexer Verlag, pg 627
Verlag Die Waage, pg 627
Verlag Alexander Wild, pg 627
Editions Zoe, pg 628

Syrian Arab Republic

Institut Francais d'Etudes Arabes de Damas, pg 628

Taiwan, Province of China

Ai Chih Book Co Ltd, pg 629
Asian Culture Co, pg 629
Bookman Books, Ltd, pg 629
Chu Liu Book Company, pg 629
Chung Hwa Book Co Ltd, pg 629
Far East Book Co Ltd, pg 630
Hilit Publishing Co Ltd, pg 630
Hsiao Yuan Publication Co, Ltd, pg 630
Kuang Fu Book Co Ltd, pg 630
Laureate Book Co Ltd, pg 631
Lin Pai Press Company Ltd, pg 631
Linking Publishing Company Ltd, pg 631
UNITAS Publishing Co Ltd, pg 632
World Book Co Ltd, pg 632
Youth Cultural Publishing Co, pg 632

United Republic of Tanzania

Bilal Muslim Mission of Tanzania, pg 633
Institute of Kiswahili Research, pg 633
Oxford University Press, pg 634
Press & Publicity Centre Ltd, pg 634

Thailand

Suriyaban Publishers, pg 635

Togo

Editions Akpagnon, pg 636

Tunisia

Academie Tunisienne des Sciences, des Lettres et des Arts Beit El Hekma, pg 637
Ceres Editions, pg 637
Dar Arabia Lil Kitab, pg 637
Dar El Afaq, pg 637
Faculte des Sciences Humaines et Sociales de Tunis, pg 638
Maison d'Edition Mohamed Ali Hammi, pg 638
Les Editions de l'Arbre, pg 638
Maison Tunisienne de l'Edition, pg 638
Sud Editions, pg 638

Turkey

Dost Yayinlari San Ve Tic Ltd, pg 639
Ezel Erverdi (Dergah Yayinlari AS) Muessese Muduru, pg 640
Iletisim Yayinlari, pg 640
Kiyi Yayinlari, pg 640
Kubbealti Akademisi Kultur ve Sasat Vakfi, pg 640
Metis Yayinlari, pg 640
Payel Yayinevi, pg 641
Toker Yayinlari, pg 641
Toros Yayinlari Ltd Co, pg 641
Turkish Republic - Ministry of Culture, pg 641
Kabalci Yayinevi, pg 642
Alev Yayinlari, pg 642

Ukraine

Dnipro, pg 643
Naukova Dumka Publishers, pg 643
Osvita, pg 643

United Kingdom

ABC-CLIO, pg 644
Appletree Press Ltd, pg 648
Aris & Phillips Ltd, pg 648
Arnold, pg 648
Ashgate Publishing Ltd, pg 649
Association for Scottish Literary Studies, pg 650
BCA, pg 653
Berghahn Books Ltd, pg 654
Blackstaff Press, pg 655
Blackwell Publishers, pg 655
Bloomsbury Publishing PLC, pg 656
The Book Guild Ltd, pg 657
Boulevard Books UK/The Babel Guides, pg 657
Marion Boyars Publishers Ltd, pg 658
Boydell & Brewer Ltd, pg 658
The British Academy, pg 659
Calder Publications Ltd, pg 662
Cambridge University Press, pg 662
Canongate Books Ltd, pg 663
Carcanet Press Ltd, pg 663
Cardiff Academic Press, pg 663
Frank Cass Publishers, pg 664
Chadwyck-Healey Ltd, pg 666
Chapman, pg 666
The Chrysalis Press, pg 667
James Clarke & Co Ltd, pg 668
The Continuum International Publishing Group Ltd, pg 670
Cyhoeddiadau Barddas, pg 673
Dedalus Ltd, pg 674
Gerald Duckworth & Co Ltd, pg 676
Dunedin Academic Press, pg 676
Edinburgh University Press Ltd, pg 677
Element Books Ltd, pg 678
Aidan Ellis Publishing, pg 678
The Eurospan Group, pg 680
Ex Libris Press, pg 680
Faber & Faber Ltd, pg 681
Facts On File, pg 681
Fourth Estate Ltd, pg 683
Gale Research, pg 685
Garnet Publishing Ltd, pg 685
Genesis Publications Ltd, pg 686
E J W Gibb Memorial Trust, pg 687
Golden Cockerel Press Ltd, pg 688
Grant & Cutler Ltd, pg 689
Granta Books, pg 689
The Greek Bookshop, pg 689
Gwasg Prifysgol Cymru, pg 690
HarperCollins Publishers, pg 692
Harvard University Press, pg 692
The Harvill Press Ltd, pg 693

SUBJECT INDEX

Helm Information Ltd, pg 694
Hodder & Stoughton Educational, pg 696
Libris Ltd, pg 707
Linen Hall Library, pg 707
The Littman Library of Jewish Civilization, pg 708
Liverpool University Press, pg 708
Luath Press Ltd, pg 709
Mainstream Publishing Co (Edinburgh) Ltd, pg 711
Manchester University Press, pg 711
Maney Publishing, pg 711
Mango Publishing, pg 711
Mercat Press, pg 713
Merrion Press, pg 713
Motilal (UK) Books of India, pg 715
National Association for the Teaching of English (NATE), pg 717
National Library of Wales, pg 717
Northcote House Publishers Ltd, pg 719
W W Norton & Company Ltd, pg 720
Octopus Publishing Group, pg 720
The Oleander Press, pg 721
Osborne Books Ltd, pg 722
Peter Owen Ltd, pg 722
Oxford University Press, pg 723
Parapress Ltd, pg 724
Pearson Education, pg 725
Peepal Tree Press, pg 725
Pickering & Chatto (Publishers) Ltd, pg 727
Planet, pg 728
Plantin Publishers, pg 728
Poetry Wales Press Ltd, pg 729
Polybooks Ltd, pg 729
Polygon, pg 729
Ramsay Head Press, pg 732
Rationalist Press Association, pg 733
Reaktion Books Ltd, pg 733
Redcliffe Press Ltd, pg 734
Roundhouse Publishing Ltd, pg 736
Routledge, pg 736
The Rubicon Press, pg 737
St George's Press, pg 737
School of Oriental & African Studies, pg 739
Scottish Cultural Press, pg 739
Scottish Text Society, pg 740
Seren, pg 740
Serpent's Tail Ltd, pg 740
Sheffield Academic Press Ltd, pg 741
Shelfmark Books, pg 741
Skoob Russell Square, pg 742
Colin Smythe Ltd, pg 743
Sutton Publishing Ltd, pg 746
Tabb House, pg 746
Tern Press, pg 748
Toucan Press, pg 749
Trigon Press, pg 750
Tuckwell Press Ltd, pg 750
Ulverscroft Large Print Books Ltd, pg 751
University of Exeter Press, pg 751
University of Wales Press, pg 751
Vallentine, Mitchell & Co Ltd, pg 752
Verso, pg 752
Voltaire Foundation Ltd, pg 753
Welsh Academic Press, pg 755
Whiting & Birch Ltd, pg 756
Wimbledon Publishing Company Ltd, pg 757
The Women's Press Ltd, pg 758
Wordsworth Editions Ltd, pg 758

SUBJECT INDEX

Gordon Wright Publishing Ltd, pg 759
Yale University Press London, pg 759

Uruguay

Arpoador, pg 760
Barreiro y Ramos SA, pg 760
Ediciones de Juan Darien, pg 760
Linardi y Risso Libreria, pg 760
A Monteverde y Cia SA, pg 760
Mosca Hermanos, pg 760
Nordan-Comunidad, pg 760
Punto de Encuentro Ediciones, pg 761
Luis A Retta Libros, pg 761
Ediciones Sol del Sur, pg 761
Ediciones Trilce, pg 761
La Urpila Editores, pg 761
Vinten Editor, pg 761

Uzbekistan

Izdatelstvo Literatury i isskustva, pg 761

Venezuela

Alfadil Ediciones, pg 761
Editorial Ateneo de Caracas, pg 762
Monte Avila Editores Latinoamericana CA, pg 762
Biblioteca Ayacucho, pg 762

Yugoslavia

Alfa-Narodna Knjiga, pg 764
Izdavacko Preduzece Matice Srpske, pg 765

Zambia

Zambia Educational Publishing House, pg 767

Zimbabwe

Academic Books Pvt Ltd, pg 767
Anvil Press, pg 767
The Literature Bureau, pg 768
Nehanda Publishers, pg 769
University of Zimbabwe Publications, pg 769
Vision Publications, pg 769
Zimbabwe Publishing House (Pvt) Ltd, pg 769

MANAGEMENT

Albania

NL SH, pg 1

Argentina

Ediciones Tres Tiempos SRL, pg 9

Australia

Boolarong Press, pg 16
Fernfawn Publications, pg 22
Hale & Iremonger Pty Ltd, pg 24
Hospitality Press Pty Ltd, pg 26
James Nicholas Publishers Pty Ltd, pg 28
Macmillan Education Australia, pg 31
McGraw-Hill Australia Pty Ltd, pg 32
OTEN (Open Training & Education Network), pg 36
Pearson Education Australia, pg 37
Plum Press, pg 38
The Real Estate Institute of Australia, pg 40
RMIT Publishing, pg 41

Simon & Schuster Australia Pty Ltd, pg 42
Tertiary Press, pg 44
Wellness Australia, pg 47
Wrightbooks Pty Ltd, pg 48

Austria

Braintrust Marketing Services Ges mbH Verlag, pg 50
Buchhandlung WUV Dolmetsch, pg 50
International Institute for Applied Systems Analysis (IIASA), pg 53
Linde Verlag Wien GmbH, pg 54
Verlag Orac im Verlag Kremayr & Scheriau, pg 56
Signum Verlag GmbH & Co KG, pg 58

Azerbaijan

Sada, Literaturno-Izdatel'skij Centr, pg 61

Bangladesh

The University Press Ltd, pg 62

Barbados

Business Tutors, pg 63

Belgium

Editions De Boeck-Larcier SA, pg 67
Documenta CV, pg 68
Uitgeverij Lannoo NV, pg 70
Maklu, pg 71
Roularta Books NV, pg 73
Uitgevery Scoop Infotex NV, pg 75

Brazil

Editora Alfa Omega Ltda, pg 78
Editora Aquariana Ltda, pg 78
ARTMED, pg 79
Editora Atlas SA, pg 79
Editora Edgard Blucher Ltda, pg 80
Editora FCO Ltda, pg 83
Editora Harbra Ltda, pg 84
Livraria Editora Infobook SA, pg 86
Edicoes Loyola SA, pg 87
LTC-Livros Tecnicos e Cientificos Editora S/A, pg 87
Editora Lucre Comercio e Representacoes, pg 87
Editora Ortiz SA, pg 89
Livraria Pioneira Editora/Enio Matheus Guazzelli e Cia Ltd, pg 89
Qualitymark Editora Ltda, pg 90
Editora Rocco Ltda, pg 91
Saraiva SA, Livreiros Editores, pg 91
Editora Universidade Federal do Rio de Janeiro, pg 93
Jorge Zahar Editor, pg 93

Bulgaria

Dolphin Press Group Ltd, pg 95
Makros 2000 - Plovdiv, pg 96
Sita-MB, pg 98

Chile

Norma de Chile, pg 101

China

Beijing Publishing House, pg 102
China Foreign Economic Relations & Trade Publishing House, pg 103
China Machine Press (CMP), pg 103

China Materials Management Publishing House, pg 103
China Ocean Press, pg 103
China Translation & Publishing Corp, pg 104
Chongqing University Press, pg 104
CITIC Publishing House, pg 104
Dalian Maritime University Press, pg 105
Fudan University Press, pg 105
Heilongjiang Science & Technology Press, pg 106
Higher Education Press, pg 106
Jilin Science & Technology Publishing House, pg 106
Metallurgical Industry Press (MIP), pg 107
Printing Industry Publishing House, pg 108
SDX (Shenghuo-Dushu-Xinzhi) Joint Publishing Co, pg 108
Shandong University Press, pg 109
Southwest China Jiaotong University Press, pg 109

Colombia

Universidad Externado de Colombia, pg 112
Fundacion Universidad de la Sabana Ediciones Udes, pg 112
LEGIS - Editores SA, pg 112
Editorial Santillana SA, pg 113
Unidad Universitaria del Sur (UNISUR), pg 114

Costa Rica

Editorial de la Universidad de Costa Rica, pg 117

Croatia

Masmedia, pg 119

Cuba

ISCAH Fructuoso Rodriguez, pg 121

Czech Republic

Nakladatelstvi Svoboda, pg 126
Svoboda Servis GmbH, pg 128

Denmark

Bierman og Bierman I/S, pg 130
Borsens Forlag, pg 130
New Era Publications International ApS, pg 134
Samfundslitteratur, pg 135

Dominican Republic

Pontificia Universidad Catolica Madre y Maestra, pg 136

Egypt (Arab Republic of Egypt)

Dar El Shorouk, pg 138

France

Association Francaise de Normalisation, pg 148
Breal, pg 151
Centre de Librairie et d'Editions Techniques (CLET), pg 153
Chotard et Associes Editeurs, pg 154
La Documentation Francaise, pg 159
Dunod Editeur, pg 160
Editions d'Organisation, pg 161
Les Editions ESF, pg 161
Editions Eska, pg 162
Editions Eyrolles, pg 163

Futuribles SARL, pg 165
Hachette Pratiques, pg 167
Institute, pg 169
InterEditions Paris, pg 169
Editions Juris Service, pg 171
Maxima Laurent du Mesnil Editeur, pg 175
Nouvelles Editions Fiduciaires, pg 178
Editions Pedone, pg 179
Les Presses du Management, pg 181
Presses Universitaires de Grenoble, pg 181
Presses Universitaires de Lyon, pg 181
Top Editions, pg 188
Editions Village Mondial, pg 189
Editions Weka, pg 189

Germany

Accedo Verlagsgesellschaft mbH, pg 191
AOL-Verlag Frohmut Menze, pg 194
ARCult Media, pg 194
Bank-Verlag GmbH, pg 198
Verlag C H Beck (OHG), pg 200
Berlin Verlag Arno Spitz GmbH, pg 200
Bertelsmann Lexikon Verlag GmbH, pg 201
W Bertelsmann Verlag GmbH & Co KG, pg 201
Beuth Verlag GmbH, pg 202
Brandenburgisches Verlagshaus in der Dornier Medienholding GmbH, pg 206
Carl-Auer-Systeme Verlag, pg 209
Cornelsen Verlag GmbH & Co OHG, pg 211
J G Cotta'sche Buchhandlung Nachfolger GmbH, pg 212
Deutscher Wirtschaftsdienst John von Freyend GmbH, pg 216
Die Verlag H Schafer GmbH, pg 216
Eppinger-Verlag OHG, pg 223
expert verlag GmbH, Fachverlag fur Wirtschaft & Technik, pg 225
Verlag Franz Vahlen GmbH, pg 229
Gabal-Verlag GmbH, pg 231
Betriebswirtschaftlicher Verlag Dr Th Gabler GmbH, pg 231
Walter de Gruyter GmbH & Co KG, pg 234
Gunter Olzog Verlag GmbH, pg 235
Alfred Hammer, pg 236
Carl Hanser Verlag, pg 237
Rudolf Haufe Verlag GmbH & Co KG, pg 238
Carl Heymanns Verlag KG, pg 240
Heinrich Hugendubel Verlag GmbH, pg 243
Edition Humanistische Psychologie (EHP), pg 243
Junfermann-Verlag, pg 247
W Kohlhammer GmbH, abt Haussortiment, pg 252
Libertas- Europaeisches Institut GmbH, pg 257
Hermann Luchterhand Verlag GmbH, pg 259
mode information Heinz Kramer GmbH, pg 264
Norbert Mueller AG & Co KG Verlag, pg 265
Projektion J Buch- und Musikverlag GmbH, pg 275
Quintessenz Verlags-GmbH, pg 276
Dr Josef Raabe-Verlags GmbH, pg 276

PUBLISHERS SUBJECT INDEX

Rationalisierungs-Kuratorium der Deutschen Wirtschaft eV (RKW), pg 277
Ernst Reinhardt GmbH & Co KG Verlag, pg 278
Rossipaul Kommunikation GmbH, pg 280
Ruhland Verlag Gimblt, pg 281
Verlag Werner Sachon GmbH & Co, pg 281
I H Sauer Verlag GmbH, pg 282
Schaeffer-Poeschel Verlag fuer Wirtschaft Steuern Recht, pg 282
Erich Schmidt Verlag GmbH & Co, pg 283
Springer-Verlag GmbH & Co KG, pg 288
Wirtschaftsverlag Carl Ueberreuter, pg 295
Verlag Moderne Industrie AG & Co KG, pg 298
Verlag und Studio fuer Hoerbuchproduktionen, pg 298
Vogel Medien GmbH & Co KG, pg 299
Weidler Buchverlag Berlin, pg 301
WEKA Firmengruppe GmbH & Co KG, pg 301
Windmuehle GmbH Verlag und Vertrieb von Medien, pg 303
WRS Verlag Wirtschaft, Recht und Steuern GmbH & Co KG, pg 304

Greece
Hestia-I D Hestia-Kollaros & Co Corporation, pg 311
Kleidarithmos, pg 312
Patakis Publishers, pg 314
Sakkoulas Publications SA, pg 314
Vivliothiki Eftychia Galeou, pg 315

Hong Kong
Chung Hwa Book Co (HK) Ltd, pg 319
Design Human Resources Training & Development, pg 319
Joint Publishing (HK) Co Ltd, pg 320
Ming Pao Publications Ltd, pg 321
Publications (Holdings) Ltd, pg 321

Hungary
Janus Pannonius Tudomanyegyetem, pg 324
Kossuth Kiado RT, pg 325
Mueszaki Koenyvkiado Ltd, pg 325
Novorg Kiado, pg 326
Park Konyvkiado Kft (Park Publisher), pg 326

India
Academic Book Corporation, pg 329
Academic Publishers, pg 329
Addison-Wesley (Singapore) Pte Ltd, pg 329
Affiliated East West Press Pvt Ltd, pg 329
Ajanta Publications (India), pg 330
Allied Publishers Pvt Ltd, pg 330
Amar Prakashan, pg 330
Anmol Publications Pvt Ltd, pg 331
APH Publishing Corp, pg 331
Bharatiya Samijik Vigyan Auusandhan Parishad, pg 332
Bookionics, pg 333
Concept Publishing Co, pg 335
Ess Ess Publications, pg 337
Frank Brothers & Co (Publishers) Ltd, pg 337

Galgotia Publications Pvt Ltd, pg 337
Gyan Publishing House, pg 338
Himalaya Publishing House, pg 338
Jaico Publishing House, pg 340
Khanna Publishers, pg 341
Multitech Publishing Co, pg 343
National Book Organization, pg 343
Naya Prokash, pg 344
Omsons Publications, pg 345
Pointer Publishers, pg 346
Popular Prakashan Pvt Ltd, pg 346
Rajendra Publishing House Pvt Ltd, pg 347
Rajesh Publications, pg 347
Reliance Publishing House, pg 347
Roli Books Pvt Ltd, pg 348
Sage Publications India Pvt Ltd, pg 348
Scientific Book Agency, pg 349
Sita Publications, pg 350
Somaiya Publications Pvt Ltd, pg 350
South Asia Publications, pg 350
Sterling Publishers Pvt Ltd, pg 351
Sterling Information Technologies, pg 351
Sultan Chand & Sons Pvt Ltd, pg 351
Vakils Feffer & Simons Ltd, pg 352
Vikas Publishing House Pvt Ltd, pg 353
Vision Books Pvt Ltd, pg 353

Indonesia
Andi Offset, pg 354
Bumi Aksara PT, pg 354
Dinastindo, pg 355
Gramedia, pg 355

Ireland
Irish Management Institute, pg 361
Oak Tree Press, pg 362

Israel
Agudat Sabah, pg 365
Kivunim-Arsan Publishing House, pg 369
Open University of Israel, pg 371
Tcherikover Publishers Ltd, pg 372

Italy
Franco Angeli SRL, pg 375
Bancaria Editrice SpA, pg 377
Buffetti, pg 379
CEDAM (Casa Editrice Dr A Milani), pg 380
Cisalpino - Monduzzi, pg 382
Cooperativa Libraria IULM SCRL, pg 383
EGEA (Edizioni Giuridiche Economiche Aziendali), pg 387
Etas Libri, pg 388
Edizioni Guerini e Associati SpA, pg 392
Ila - Palma, Tea Nova, pg 393
Isper SRL, pg 394
Ithaca, pg 394
Accademia Naz dei Lincei, pg 400
Edizioni Olivares, pg 402
Pirola, pg 403
Rirea Casa Editrice della Rivista Italiana di Ragioneria e di Economia Aziendale, pg 405
Edizioni del Sole 24 Ore, pg 408
Sperling e Kupfer Editori SpA, pg 408
Who's Who In Italy SRL, pg 412

Jamaica
American Chamber of Commerce of Jamaica, pg 412
CVM Publications, pg 413

Japan
Diamond Inc, pg 416
Koyo Shobo, pg 420
Nikkagiren Shuppan-Sha (JUSE Press Ltd), pg 422
Nippon Hoso Shuppan Kyokai (NHK Publishing), pg 422
Nippon Jitsugyo Publishing Co, Ltd, pg 423
President Inc, pg 423
Seibundo Shinkosha Publishing Co Ltd, pg 425
3A Corporation, pg 427
Zeimukeiri-Kyokai, pg 429
Zenkoku Kyodo Shuppan, pg 429

Kazakstan
Kazakh Al-Farabi State National University, pg 430

Kenya
Cosmopolitan Publishers Ltd, pg 431
Heinemann Kenya Limited (EAEP), pg 431
Kenya Quality & Productivity Institute, pg 432
Shirikon Publishers, pg 433

Republic of Korea
Bi-bong Publishing Co, pg 435
Chung Rim Publishing Co Ltd, pg 435
Gim-Yeong Co, pg 436
Koreaone Press Inc, pg 438
Sohaksa, pg 440
Twenty-First Century Publishers, Inc, pg 440

Lithuania
Lietuvos Informacijos Institutas, pg 446

Macau
Universidadede de Macau, Centro de Publicacoes, pg 448

Malaysia
S Abdul Majeed & Co, pg 451
Glad Sounds Sdn Bhd, pg 452
MDC Publishers Printers, pg 453
Pelanduk Publications (M) Sdn Bhd, pg 453
Penerbit Universiti Sains Malaysia, pg 454
Penerbitan Tinta, pg 454

Mauritius
Editions de l'Ocean Indien Ltd, pg 457

Mexico
ALFA OMEGA Grupo Editor, pg 458
Compania Editorial Continental SA de CV, pg 459
Del Verbo Emprender SA de CV, pg 459
Editorial Diana SA de CV, pg 459
Edamex SA de CV, pg 460
Grupo Editorial Iberoamerica, SA de CV, pg 461
Editorial Limusa SA de CV, pg 463

Mercametrica Ediciones SA Edicion de Libros, pg 464
Organizacion Cultural LP SA de CV, pg 465
Panorama Editorial, SA, pg 465
Pearson Educacion de Mexico, SA de CV, pg 465
Sistemas Tecnicos de Edicion SA de CV, pg 467

Netherlands
Uitgeverij Aristos, pg 473
BoekWerk, pg 474
Business Contact BV, pg 475
Educatieve Uitgeverij Edu'Actief BV, pg 476
Hagen & Stam Uitgeverij Ten, pg 478
IOS Press BV, pg 479
Kluwer Technische Boeken BV, pg 480
Koninklijke Vermande bv, pg 480
Uitgeverij Lemma BV, pg 480
Uitgeverij H Nelissen BV, pg 482
Omega Boek BV, pg 482
Pearson Education Netherlands, pg 482
Samsom BedrijfsInformatie BV, pg 483
Scriptum, pg 483
Uitgeverij Het Spectrum BV, pg 484
SWP, BV Uitgeverij, pg 485
Uitgeverij de Tijdstroom BV, pg 485
Twente University Press, pg 485

New Zealand
Commonwealth Council for Educational Administration & Management, pg 490
Learning Guides (Writers & Publishers Ltd), pg 492
Moss Associates Ltd, pg 493
New House Publishers Ltd, pg 493
Nelson Price Milburn Ltd, pg 494
Shoal Bay Press Ltd, pg 495

Nigeria
Evans Brothers (Nigeria Publishers) Ltd, pg 499
Goldland Business Co Ltd, pg 499
New Africa Publishing Company Ltd, pg 500

Norway
Bedriftsokonomens Forlag A/S, pg 502
Tiden Norsk Forlag, pg 505

Pakistan
Academy of Education Planning & Management (AEPAM), pg 506
International Educational Services, pg 507

Peru
Universidad de Lima-Fondo de Desarrollo Editorial, pg 512

Philippines
Mutual Books Inc, pg 513
New Day Publishers, pg 514
Our Lady of Manaoag Publisher, pg 514

Poland
Polskie Wydawnictwo Ekonomiczne PWE SA, pg 516

1017

SUBJECT INDEX

Portugal
Edicoes Cetop, pg 523
Editora Classica, pg 523
Difusao Cultural, pg 524
Gradiva-Publicacnoes Lda, pg 525
McGraw-Hill Editora de Portugal, pg 527
Monitor, pg 527
Monitor-Projectos e Edicoes, LDA, pg 527
Editorial Presenca, pg 528
Silabo, pg 529
Almerinda Teixeira, pg 529
Texto Editora, pg 529

Romania
Editura Niculescu, pg 534
Polirom Verlag, pg 535
Rentrop & Straton Verlagsgruppe und Wirtschaftsconsulting, pg 535

Russian Federation
N E Bauman Moscow State Technical University Publishers, pg 537
Izdatelstvo 'Ekonomika', pg 537
Finansy i Statistika Publishing House, pg 538
INFRA-M Izdatel 'skij dom, pg 538
Nauka Publishers, pg 540

Singapore
APAC Publishers Services, pg 545
Pearson Education Asia, pg 547
Singapore University Press Pte Ltd, pg 548
Taylor & Francis Asia Pacific, pg 548
World Scientific Publishing Co Pte Ltd, pg 549

Slovakia
Dom Techniky Zvazu Slovenskych Vedeckotechnickych Spolocnosti Ltd, pg 549
Priroda, pg 550
Ustav informacii a prognoz skolstva mladeze a telovychovy, pg 551

Slovenia
Univerza v Ljubljani Ekonomska Fakulteta, pg 552
Zalozba Obzorja d d Maribor, pg 552

South Africa
Human & Rousseau (Pty) Ltd, pg 555
Ivy Publications, pg 555
Ravan Press (Pty) Ltd, pg 558
Van Schaik Publishers, pg 560

Spain
Editorial AEDOS SA, pg 561
Editorial Aranzadi SA, pg 564
Editorial CISSPRAXIS SA, pg 567
Comunidad Autonoma de Madrid, Servicio de Documentacion y Publicaciones, pg 568
Editorial Constitucion y Leyes SA - COLEX, pg 568
Espanola Desclee De Brouwer SA, pg 569
Ediciones Diaz de Santos SA, pg 569
Ediciones Deusto SA, pg 571
Editorial Editex SA, pg 572
Ediciones Gestio 2000 SA, pg 575
Marcombo SA de Boixareu Editores, pg 581

Ediciones Oceano Grupo SA, pg 584
Editorial Paraninfo SA, pg 586
Editorial Sintesis, SA, pg 590
Tirant lo Blanch SL Libreriaa, pg 592
Ediciones Urano, SA, pg 595
Xunta de Galicia, pg 596

Sri Lanka
Sunera Publishers, pg 598

Sweden
Iustus Forlag AB, pg 603
Kungl Ingenjoersvetenskapsakademien (IVA), pg 604
Studentlitteratur AB, pg 606
Svenska Foerlaget liv & ledarskap ab, pg 607

Switzerland
Cosmos-Verlag AG, pg 611
Gottlieb Duttweiler Institute for Trends & Futures, pg 612
Helbing und Lichtenhahn Verlag AG, pg 615
Verlag Industrielle Organisation, pg 616
Oesch Verlag AG, pg 620
Ott Verlag AG, pg 621
Presses Polytechniques et Universitaires Romandes, PPUR, pg 622
Editiones Roche, pg 623
Tobler Verlag, pg 626
Editions du Tricorne, pg 626
Vdf Hochschulverlag AG an der ETH Zurich, pg 626
Versus Verlag AG, pg 627
Weka Informations Schriften Verlag AG, pg 627

Taiwan, Province of China
Commonwealth Publishing Company Ltd, pg 629
Laureate Book Co Ltd, pg 631
Linking Publishing Company Ltd, pg 631
Morning Star Publisher Inc, pg 631
Newton Publishing Company Ltd, pg 631
Shy Mau Publishing Company, pg 631

United Republic of Tanzania
Tanzania Publishing House, pg 634

Thailand
Thai Watana Panich Co, Ltd, pg 636

Turkey
Alkim Kitapcilik-Yayimcilik, pg 638
Caglayan Kitabevi, pg 639
Inkilap Publishers Ltd, pg 640
Sabah Kitaplari, pg 641
Soez Yayin/Oyunajans, pg 641
Yetkin Printing & Publishing Co Inc, pg 642

Uganda
Roce (Consultants) Ltd, pg 642

Ukraine
Osnovy Publishers, pg 643

United Kingdom
ABG Professional Information, pg 644
Anglo-German Foundation for the Study of Industrial Society, pg 647
Artech House, pg 649
Ashgate Publishing Ltd, pg 649
Aslib, The Association for Information Management, pg 650
Barmarick Publications, pg 652
Bloomsbury Publishing PLC, pg 656
Bowerdean Publishing Co Ltd, pg 658
BPS Books (British Psychological Society), pg 658
Nicholas Brealey Publishing, pg 659
Butterworth-Heinemann Ltd, pg 661
Capstone Publishing Ltd, pg 663
Cassell & Co, pg 664
The Chartered Institute of Building, pg 666
Chartered Institute of Personnel & Development, pg 667
Commonwealth Secretariat, pg 669
The Economist Intelligence Unit, pg 677
Element Books Ltd, pg 678
Elm Publications, pg 678
Ernst & Young, pg 679
The Eurospan Group, pg 680
Express Newspapers, pg 681
Facet Publishing, pg 681
Financial World Publishing, pg 682
Gower Publishing Ltd, pg 688
HarperCollins Publishers, pg 692
HB Publications, pg 693
How To Books Ltd, pg 697
Institution of Electrical Engineers, pg 700
JAI Press Ltd, pg 702
Kogan Page Ltd, pg 705
Law Pack Publishing Ltd, pg 706
Lemos & Crane, pg 707
Letts Educational, pg 707
Library & Information Statistics Unit, pg 707
Management Books 2000 Ltd, pg 711
Management Pocketbooks Ltd, pg 711
Marshall Editions Ltd, pg 712
MCB University Press Ltd, pg 712
McGraw-Hill Publishing Company, pg 712
Monarch Books, pg 715
NCVO, pg 718
New Era Publications UK Ltd, pg 718
Open University Press, pg 721
Orion Publishing Group Ltd, pg 722
Palgrave Publishers Ltd, pg 723
Pearson Education, pg 725
Pergamon Flexible Learning, pg 726
Perpetuity Press, pg 726
Piatkus Books, pg 727
The Policy Press, pg 729
Professional Engineering Publishing Ltd, pg 730
Profile Books Ltd, pg 731
ProQuest Information & Learning, pg 731
Sage Publications Ltd, pg 737
Sherwood Publishing, pg 741
SHU Press, pg 742
Sydney Jary Ltd, pg 746
Taylor Graham Publishing, pg 747
Thoemmes Press, pg 748
VNU Business Publications, pg 753
Wiley Europe Ltd, pg 756
Witherby & Co Ltd, pg 758

Viet Nam
Science & Technics Publishing House, pg 763

Zambia
M & M Management & Labour Consultants Ltd, pg 766
MFK Management Consultants Services, pg 766

MARITIME

Argentina
Instituto de Publicaciones Navales, pg 7

Australia
Australian Marine Conservation Society Inc (AMCS), pg 14
Robert Berthold Photography, pg 14
Crawford House Publishing, pg 19
Dragon Press, pg 20
Enterprise Publications, pg 22
Kingfisher Books, pg 29
McGraw-Hill Australia Pty Ltd, pg 32
Navarine Publishing, pg 34
Oceans Enterprises, pg 35
OTEN (Open Training & Education Network), pg 36
Saltwater Publications, pg 41
Ian Stewart Marine Publications, pg 43
Turton & Armstrong Publishers Pty Ltd, pg 45
Windward Publications, pg 48

Austria
Edition S der OSD, pg 51
Herbert Weishaupt Verlag, pg 60

Bulgaria
Publishing House Narodno delo OOD, pg 97

Chile
Edeval (Universidad de Valparaiso), pg 100

China
China Ocean Press, pg 103
Dalian Maritime University Press, pg 105

Costa Rica
Scout Interamericana, pg 117

Croatia
Knjizevni Krug Split, pg 119

Czech Republic
Nase vojsko, nakladatelstvi a knizni obchod, pg 126

Denmark
Aschehoug Dansk Forlag A/S, pg 130
P Haase & Sons Forlag A/S, pg 132

Finland
Koala-Kustannus/Oy Greenbay House Publishing Ltd, pg 143

France
Editions l'Ancre de Marine, pg 147
Brud Nevez, pg 152
Chasse Maree-Armen, pg 154

PUBLISHERS

EPA SA (Editions Presse Audiovisuel), pg 162
Institut Francais de Recherche pour l'Exploitation de la Mer (IFREMER), pg 165
Editions Jean Paul Gisserot, pg 166
Lavoisier, pg 172
Editions Maritimes et d'Outre-Mer SA, pg 175
Editions Paradigme, pg 179
Editions Pedone, pg 179

Germany
Brandenburgisches Verlagshaus in der Dornier Medienholding GmbH, pg 206
Verlag Busse und Seewald GmbH, pg 208
Delius, Klasing und Co, pg 213
Delius Klasing Verlag, pg 213
E Schweizerbart'sche Verlagsbuchhandlung (Nagele und Obermiller), pg 220
Eckardt & Messtorff GmbH, pg 220
Gebrueder Borntraeger Science Publishers, pg 231
Liselotte Hamecher, pg 236
Heel Verlag GmbH, pg 238
Verlagsgruppe Koehler/Mittler, pg 251
Koehlers Verlagsgesellschaft mbH, pg 251
Edition Maritim GmbH, pg 261
E S Mittler und Sohn GmbH, pg 264
Paul Pietsch Verlage GmbH & Co, pg 273
Propylaeen Verlag, Zweigniederlassung Berlin der Ullstein Buchverlage GmbH, pg 275
Stadler Verlagsgesellschaft mbH, pg 288
Edition Temmen, pg 292
Tetra Verlag Gmbh, pg 292

Greece
Melissa Publishing House, pg 313
Sakkoulas Publications SA, pg 314

India
Sita Publications, pg 350

Ireland
Dee-Jay Publications, pg 359
Herodotus Press, pg 361

Italy
Automobilia srl, pg 377
Istituto Idrografico della Marina, pg 393
Gruppo Ugo Mursia Editore SpA, pg 400

Japan
Kaibundo Publishing Co Ltd, pg 419
Seizando-Shoten Publishing Co Ltd, pg 425

Lithuania
Klaipedos Universiteto Leidykla, pg 445

Macau
Museu Maritimo, pg 448

Netherlands
BV Uitgeversbedryf Het Goede Boek, pg 477
Uitgeverij Hollandia BV, pg 478

Netherlands Antilles
Bredero, pg 488

New Caledonia
Savannah Editions SARL, pg 488

New Zealand
Exisle Publishing Ltd, pg 491
Halcyon Publishing Ltd, pg 491
David Ling Publishing, pg 493
Publishing Solutions Ltd, pg 494
River Press, pg 495
Southern Press Ltd, pg 496

Norway
Elanders Publishing AS, pg 503
Sandviks Bokforlag, pg 505

Philippines
Rex Bookstores & Publishers, pg 514

Poland
Iskry - Publishing House Ltd spotka zoo, pg 517

Russian Federation
BLIC, russko-Baltijskij informaciionnyj centr, AO, pg 537
Izdatelstvo Sudostroenie, pg 542
Izdatelstvo Transport, pg 542

Singapore
Singapore University Press Pte Ltd, pg 548

South Africa
Flesch Financial Publications (Pty) Ltd, pg 554

Spain
Ediciones Garriga SA, pg 575
Lunwerg Editores, SA, pg 580
Editorial Noray, pg 584
Ediciones Seyer, pg 590
Silex Ediciones, pg 590
Xunta de Galicia, pg 596

Sweden
Allt om Hobby AB, pg 600
Johnston & Streiffert Editions, pg 604
Nautiska Foerlaget AB, pg 605
Frank Stenvalls Forlag, pg 606

Switzerland
Verlag Eisenbahn, pg 613
Maihof Verlag, pg 618

United Kingdom
Ian Allan Publishing Ltd, pg 646
Amber Books Ltd, pg 646
Arms & Armour Press, pg 648
BLA Publishing Ltd, pg 655
A & C Black Publishers Ltd, pg 655
Books International, pg 657
Brassey's UK Ltd, pg 658
Brown, Son & Ferguson, Ltd, pg 661
Capall Bann Publishing, pg 663
Chatham Publishing, pg 667
Colourpoint Books, pg 669
Compendium Publishing, pg 670
Conway Maritime Press, pg 671
Leo Cooper, pg 671
Countyvise Ltd, pg 671
The Crowood Press Ltd, pg 672
Terence Dalton Ltd, pg 673
David & Charles Ltd, pg 674
DMG Business Media Ltd, pg 675
Gerald Duckworth & Co Ltd, pg 676
Aidan Ellis Publishing, pg 678
The Eurospan Group, pg 680
Facts On File, pg 681
Fernhurst Books, pg 682
Fishing News Books Ltd, pg 682
Greenhill Books/Lionel Leventhal Ltd, pg 689
Halldale Publishing & Media Ltd, pg 691
Haynes Publishing, pg 693
Hutton Press Ltd, pg 698
Jane's Information Group, pg 702
LLP Ltd, pg 708
Maritime Books, pg 712
Kenneth Mason Publications Ltd, pg 712
Mirabel Books Ltd, pg 715
James Munro & Co, pg 716
W W Norton & Company Ltd, pg 720
Oilfield Publications Ltd, pg 720
Opus Book Publishing Ltd, pg 722
The Orkney Press Ltd, pg 722
Parapress Ltd, pg 724
Pen & Sword Books Ltd, pg 725
Perpetuity Press, pg 726
Quintet Publishing Ltd, pg 732
SB Publications, pg 738
Shire Publications Ltd, pg 741
Silver Link Publishing Ltd, pg 742
Stenlake Publishing, pg 745
Sutton Publishing Ltd, pg 746
University of Exeter Press, pg 751
Whittles Publishing, pg 756
WIT Press, pg 757
Witherby & Co Ltd, pg 758

Viet Nam
Science & Technics Publishing House, pg 763

MARKETING

Albania
NL SH, pg 1

Australia
Art on the Move, pg 12
Assert Publishing, pg 12
Books for Our Times, pg 16
Crista International, pg 19
E J Dwyer (Australia) Pty Ltd, pg 21
Hospitality Press Pty Ltd, pg 26
James Nicholas Publishers Pty Ltd, pg 28
Marketing Focus, pg 31
McGraw-Hill Australia Pty Ltd, pg 32
OTEN (Open Training & Education Network), pg 36
Priestley Consulting, pg 39
The Real Estate Institute of Australia, pg 40
Tertiary Press, pg 44

SUBJECT INDEX

Austria
Buchhandlung WUV Dolmetsch, pg 50
Herold Business Data AG, pg 52
Dr Verena Hofstaetter, pg 53
Linde Verlag Wien GmbH, pg 54
Modulverlag, pg 55

Azerbaijan
Sada, Literaturno-Izdatel'skij Centr, pg 61

Belgium
Editions De Boeck-Larcier SA, pg 67
Roularta Books NV, pg 73
Uitgevery Scoop Infotex NV, pg 75

Brazil
Editora Aquariana Ltda, pg 78
ARTMED, pg 79
Editora Atlas SA, pg 79
Editora Ortiz SA, pg 89
Pearson Education Do Brasil, pg 89
Saraiva SA, Livreiros Editores, pg 91
Summus Editorial Ltda, pg 92
Thex Editora e Distribuidora Ltda, pg 92
Fundacao Getulio Vargas, pg 93
Jorge Zahar Editor, pg 93

Bulgaria
Dolphin Press Group Ltd, pg 95
Sluntse Publishing House, pg 98

Chile
Arrayan Editores, pg 99
Norma de Chile, pg 101

China
Beijing Publishing House, pg 102
China Film Press, pg 103
China Foreign Economic Relations & Trade Publishing House, pg 103
China Materials Management Publishing House, pg 103
CITIC Publishing House, pg 104
Fudan University Press, pg 105
Heilongjiang Science & Technology Press, pg 106
Jilin Science & Technology Publishing House, pg 106
Sichuan University Press, pg 109

Colombia
LEGIS - Editores SA, pg 112

Costa Rica
Instituto Interamericano de Cooperacion para la Agricultura (IICA), pg 116

Croatia
Informator dd, pg 119
Masmedia, pg 119

Czech Republic
Nakladatelstvi Svoboda, pg 126

Denmark
Samfundslitteratur, pg 135

Dominican Republic
Pontificia Universidad Catolica Madre y Maestra, pg 136

1019

SUBJECT INDEX

France
ABC Editions, pg 145
Breal, pg 151
Chotard et Associes Editeurs, pg 154
Editions Dalloz Sirey, pg 157
Les Editions ESF, pg 161
Editions Generales First, pg 166
Maxima Laurent du Mesnil Editeur, pg 175
Les Presses du Management, pg 181
Presses Universitaires de Grenoble, pg 181
Top Editions, pg 188
Editions Village Mondial, pg 189

Germany
AZ Bertelsmann Direct GmbH, pg 197
Berlin Verlag Arno Spitz GmbH, pg 200
Bertelsmann Lexikon Verlag GmbH, pg 201
Cornelsen Verlag GmbH & Co OHG, pg 211
Deutscher Fachverlag GmbH, pg 214
Duncker und Humblot GmbH, pg 219
FAB-Verlag, pg 226
Verlag Reinhard Fischer, pg 228
Verlag Franz Vahlen GmbH, pg 229
Friedrich Kiehl Verlag GmbH, pg 230
Betriebswirtschaftlicher Verlag Dr Th Gabler GmbH, pg 231
Walter de Gruyter GmbH & Co KG, pg 234
Gunter Olzog Verlag GmbH, pg 235
Rudolf Haufe Verlag GmbH & Co KG, pg 238
Hans Holzmann Verlag GmbH und Co KG, pg 242
Verlag Hoppenstedt GmbH, pg 242
W Kohlhammer GmbH, abt Haussortiment, pg 252
Max Schimmel Verlag, pg 261
mode information Heinz Kramer GmbH, pg 264
Norbert Mueller AG & Co KG Verlag, pg 265
Verlag Werner Sachon GmbH & Co, pg 281
I H Sauer Verlag GmbH, pg 282
Schaeffer-Poeschel Verlag fuer Wirtschaft Steuern Recht, pg 282
Schulz-Kirchner Verlag GmbH, pg 285
Springer-Verlag GmbH & Co KG, pg 288
Steidl Verlag, pg 289
Tangens Systemverlag GmbH, pg 291
Verlag Moderne Industrie AG & Co KG, pg 298
Verlag und Studio fuer Hoerbuchproduktionen, pg 298
Weidler Buchverlag Berlin, pg 301
Wer liefert was? GmbH, pg 301
WRS Verlag Wirtschaft, Recht und Steuern GmbH & Co KG, pg 304

Ghana
World Literature Project, pg 308

Greece
Kleidarithmos, pg 312
Vivliothiki Eftychia Galeou, pg 315

Haiti
Editions Caraiibes SA, pg 317

Hong Kong
Chung Hwa Book Co (HK) Ltd, pg 319
Electronic Technology Publishing Co Ltd, pg 319
Joint Publishing (HK) Co Ltd, pg 320
Publications (Holdings) Ltd, pg 321

Hungary
Janus Pannonius Tudomanyegyetem, pg 324
KJK-Keaszov, pg 324
Nemzeti Tankoenyvkiado, pg 326
Novorg Kiado, pg 326

India
APH Publishing Corp, pg 331
Omsons Publications, pg 345
Reliance Publishing House, pg 347
Scientific Book Agency, pg 349
Sita Publications, pg 350
Somaiya Publications Pvt Ltd, pg 350
Sterling Information Technologies, pg 351
Sultan Chand & Sons Pvt Ltd, pg 351

Indonesia
Andi Offset, pg 354
Bumi Aksara PT, pg 354

Ireland
Events of the Week, pg 360
Oak Tree Press, pg 362

Italy
Franco Angeli SRL, pg 375
Apimondia, pg 375
Bancaria Editrice SpA, pg 377
CEDAM (Casa Editrice Dr A Milani), pg 380
Cooperativa Libraria IULM SCRL, pg 383
EGEA (Edizioni Giuridiche Economiche Aziendali), pg 387
Ithaca, pg 394
Lybra Immagine, pg 397
Editrice San Marco SRL, pg 406

Jamaica
American Chamber of Commerce of Jamaica, pg 412

Japan
The American Chamber of Commerce in Japan, pg 414
Diamond Inc, pg 416
Koyo Shobo, pg 420
Nippon Jitsugyo Publishing Co, Ltd, pg 423
President Inc, pg 423
Sagano Shoin, pg 424
Zeimukeiri-Kyokai, pg 429

Kazakstan
Kazakh Al-Farabi State National University, pg 430

Republic of Korea
Chung Rim Publishing Co Ltd, pg 435
Gim-Yeong Co, pg 436

Lithuania
Lietuvos Informacijos Institutas, pg 446

Malaysia
S Abdul Majeed & Co, pg 451
Penerbitan Tinta, pg 454

Mauritius
Editions de l'Ocean Indien Ltd, pg 457

Mexico
Editorial Limusa SA de CV, pg 463
Mercametrica Ediciones SA Edicion de Libros, pg 464

Netherlands
BoekWerk, pg 474
Business Contact BV, pg 475
Educatieve Uitgeverij Edu'Actief BV, pg 476
Uitgeverij Lemma BV, pg 480
Samsom BedrijfsInformatie BV, pg 483
Scriptum, pg 483
VNU Business Press Group BV, pg 487

New Zealand
Nelson Price Milburn Ltd, pg 494
Shoal Bay Press Ltd, pg 495

Nigeria
Goldland Business Co Ltd, pg 499

Pakistan
International Educational Services, pg 507

Panama
Focus Publications International SA, pg 509

Peru
Universidad de Lima-Fondo de Desarollo Editorial, pg 512

Philippines
New Day Publishers, pg 514
Rex Bookstores & Publishers, pg 514

Poland
Polskie Wydawnictwo Ekonomiczne PWE SA, pg 516
Polish Scientific Publishers PWN, pg 519
Wydawnictwo Prawnicze Co, pg 519

Portugal
GECTI (Gabinete de Especializacao e Cooperacao Tecnica Internacional L), pg 525
McGraw-Hill Editora de Portugal, pg 527
Editorial Presenca, pg 528

Romania
Nemira Verlag, pg 534
Editura Niculescu, pg 534
Polirom Verlag, pg 535
Rentrop & Straton Verlagsgruppe und Wirtschaftsconsulting, pg 535

Russian Federation
Finansy i Statistika Publishing House, pg 538
INFRA-M Izdatel'skij dom, pg 538
Nauka Publishers, pg 540
Izdatel'stvo Nizhegorodskogo Gosudarstvennogo Univ, pg 540

Slovakia
Dom Techniky Zvazu Slovenskych Vedeckotechnickych Spolocnosti Ltd, pg 549

Slovenia
Univerza v Ljubljani Ekonomska Fakulteta, pg 552
Zalozba Obzorja d d Maribor, pg 552

South Africa
Bet-El Publishers, pg 553
Human & Rousseau (Pty) Ltd, pg 555

Spain
Editorial CISSPRAXIS SA, pg 567
Ediciones y Distribuciones Universitarias SA, pg 571
Ediciones Gestio 2000 SA, pg 575
Lid Editorial Empresarial, SL, pg 580
Marcombo SA de Boixareu Editores, pg 581
Oikos-Tau SA Ediciones, pg 584
Xunta de Galicia, pg 596

Sweden
Industrilitteratur Vindex, Forlags AB, pg 603

Switzerland
Dimension World Ltd, pg 612
Gottlieb Duttweiler Institute for Trends & Futures, pg 612
Verlag Industrielle Organisation, pg 616
Oesch Verlag AG, pg 620
3 Dimension World (3-D-World), pg 625
Tobler Verlag, pg 626
Versus Verlag AG, pg 627

Syrian Arab Republic
Damascus University Press, pg 628

Taiwan, Province of China
Fuh-Wen Book Co, pg 630
Newton Publishing Company Ltd, pg 631

Thailand
Thai Watana Panich Co, Ltd, pg 636

Turkey
Alkim Kitapcilik-Yayimcilik, pg 638

Uganda
Roce (Consultants) Ltd, pg 642

Ukraine
ASK Ltd, pg 643

United Kingdom
Ashgate Publishing Ltd, pg 649
Bloomsbury Publishing PLC, pg 656
BPP Publishing Ltd, pg 658
Butterworth-Heinemann Ltd, pg 661
Cassell & Co, pg 664
Euromonitor PLC, pg 680

PUBLISHERS

The Eurospan Group, pg 680
HB Publications, pg 693
Hemming Information Services, pg 695
ICC United Kingdom, pg 698
Johnson Publications Ltd, pg 703
Kogan Page Ltd, pg 705
Letts Educational, pg 707
Management Books 2000 Ltd, pg 711
MCB University Press Ltd, pg 712
John Murray (Publishers) Ltd, pg 716
NTC Publications Ltd, pg 720
Pergamon Flexible Learning, pg 726
Profile Books Ltd, pg 731
ProQuest Information & Learning, pg 731
Sage Publications Ltd, pg 737
Verulam Publishing Ltd, pg 753
Wiley Europe Ltd, pg 756

Viet Nam
Science & Technics Publishing House, pg 763

MATHEMATICS

Albania
NL SH, pg 1
State Textbook Publishing House, pg 1

Argentina
EUDEBA (Editorial Universitaria de Buenos Aires), pg 6
Juegos & Co SRL, pg 6
Instituto Nacional de Ciencia y Tecnica Hidrica (INCYTH), pg 7

Australia
Edward Arnold (Australia) Pty Ltd, pg 12
Austed Publishing Co, pg 13
Australian Academy of Science, pg 13
Blackwell Science Pty Ltd, pg 15
Deakin University Press, pg 20
Dellasta Publishing, pg 20
Dubois Publishing, pg 21
Educational Advantage, pg 21
Emerald City Books, pg 22
Harcourt Australia Pty Ltd, pg 25
Hawker Brownlow, pg 25
Illert Publications, pg 27
Macmillan Education Australia, pg 31
McGraw-Hill Australia Pty Ltd, pg 32
Mimosa Publications Pty Ltd, pg 33
K & Z Mostafanejad, pg 33
Pearson Education Australia, pg 37
Phoenix Education Pty Ltd, pg 38
Quakers Hill Press, pg 39
Reed Educational Publishing Australia, pg 40
Royal Society of New South Wales, pg 41
Rumsby Scientific Publishing, pg 41

Austria
Abakus Verlag GmbH, pg 49
Verlag Hoelder-Pichler-Tempsky, pg 53
International Institute for Applied Systems Analysis (IIASA), pg 53
Springer-Verlag Wien, pg 59
Verband der Wissenschaftlichen Gesellschaften Oesterreichs (VWGOe), pg 60

Belarus
Belaruskaya Encyklapedyya, pg 63
Narodnaya Asveta, pg 63
Publishing Center of Belarus State University, pg 63

Belgium
Acco CV, pg 64
Artel SC, pg 64
Editions De Boeck-Larcier SA, pg 67
Dessain - Departement de De Boeck & Larcier SA, pg 68
Leuven University Press, pg 71
Pelckmans NV, De Nederlandsche Boekhandel, pg 73
Presses agronomiques de Gembloux ASBL, pg 73
Publications des Facultes Universitaires Saint Louis, pg 73
Editions Techniques et Scientifiques SPRL, pg 74
Uitgeverij De Garve, pg 75
Editions de l'Universite de Bruxelles, pg 75
Wolters Plantyn Educatieve Uitgevers, pg 75

Bolivia
Editorial Don Bosco, pg 76

Brazil
Editora Edgard Blucher Ltda, pg 80
Edicon Editora e Consultorial Ltda, pg 81
EDUC - Editora da PUC-SP, pg 82
Fundacao Instituto Brasileiro de Geografia e Estatistica (IBGE - CDDI/DECOP), pg 84
LTC-Livros Tecnicos e Cientificos Editora S/A, pg 87
Editora Moderna Ltda, pg 88
Modulo Editora e Desenvolvimento Educacional Ltda, pg 88
Saraiva SA, Livreiros Editores, pg 91
Editora Scipione Ltda, pg 91
Edicoes Tabajara, pg 92

Bulgaria
Abagar Pablioing, pg 94
Foi-Commerce, pg 95
Gea-Libris Publishing House, pg 95
Heron Press Publishing House, pg 96
Lettera, pg 96
LIK IZDANIJA, pg 96
Makros 2000 - Plovdiv, pg 96
MATEX, pg 96
Naouka i Izkoustvo, Ltd, pg 97
Pensoft Publishers, pg 97
Regalia 6 Publishing House, pg 97
TEMTO, pg 98

Cameroon
Editions Buma Kor, pg 99

Chile
Arrayan Editores, pg 99

China
Fudan University Press, pg 105
Guangdong Science & Technology Press, pg 106
Inner Mongolia Science & Technology Publishing House, pg 106
Jilin Science & Technology Publishing House, pg 106
Metallurgical Industry Press (MIP), pg 107
Science Press, pg 108
Shandong University Press, pg 109
Sichuan University Press, pg 109
Southwest China Jiaotong University Press, pg 109
Tianjin Science & Technology Publishing House, pg 109
Tsinghua University Press, pg 110
Wuhan University Press, pg 110

Colombia
Universidad Externado de Colombia, pg 112
Unidad Universitaria del Sur (UNISUR), pg 114

The Democratic Republic of the Congo
Centre de Recherche, et Pedagogie Appliquee, pg 114

Costa Rica
Jose Alfonso Sandoval Nunez, pg 116

Czech Republic
Academia, pg 122
Karolinum, nakladatelstvi, pg 125

Denmark
Fremad A/S, pg 132
GEC Gads Forlag Aktieselskab af 1994, pg 132
Systime, pg 136

Dominican Republic
Pontificia Universidad Catolica Madre y Maestra, pg 136

Finland
Yliopistopaino/Helsinki University Press, pg 145

France
Breal, pg 151
Cepadues Editions SA, pg 153
CNRS Editions, pg 155
Edicef - Editions Classiques d'Expression Francaise, pg 161
EDP Sciences, pg 161
Editions Espaces 34, pg 162
Editions Jacques Gabay, pg 165
Editions Gammaprim, pg 166
Hermann editeurs des Sciences et des Arts SA, pg 168
InterEditions Paris, pg 169
Librairie Scientifique et Technique Albert Blanchard, pg 173
Presses Universitaires de Grenoble, pg 181
Editions Scientifiques et Medicales Elsevier, pg 184
Societe Mathematique de France - Institut Henri Poincare, pg 185
Sofradif Editions Philippe Auzou, pg 185
Editions Springer France, pg 186
Editions Technip SA, pg 187
Librairie Vuibert, pg 189

Germany
AOL-Verlag Frohmut Menze, pg 194
Aulis Verlag Deubner & Co KG, pg 197
Johann Ambrosius Barth GmbH, pg 198

Bayerischer Schulbuch-Verlag GmbH, pg 199
Berlin Verlag Arno Spitz GmbH, pg 200
Verlag Beruf + Schule Belz KG, pg 202
Beuth Verlag GmbH, pg 202
Cornelsen Verlag GmbH & Co OHG, pg 211
Verlag Harri Deutsch, pg 213
Fachbuchverlag Leipzig im Carl Hanser Verlag, pg 226
Ferd Dummler's Verlag, pg 227
Finken Verlag GmbH, pg 228
Walter de Gruyter GmbH & Co KG, pg 234
Carl Hanser Verlag, pg 237
Konkordia Verlag GmbH, pg 252
Anton G Leitner Verlag (AGLV), pg 257
Annemarie Maeger, pg 260
Naumann & Goebel Verlagsgesellschaft mbH, pg 267
Verlag Sigrid Persen, pg 272
Verlag an der Ruhr GmbH, pg 281
Springer-Verlag GmbH & Co KG, pg 288
Stiefel GmbH Wandkarten Verlag, pg 290
B G Teubner GmbH, pg 292
Friedr Vieweg & Sohn Verlagsgesellschaft mbH, pg 298
Volk und Wissen Verlag GmbH & Co, pg 299
Wissenschaftliche Buchgesellschaft, pg 303
Verlag Konrad Wittwer GmbH, pg 303
Zentralantiquariat Leipzig GmbH Buchhandlung, pg 305

Ghana
Beginners Publishers, pg 306
EPP Books Services, pg 307
Sam Woode Ltd, pg 308
Sedco Publishing Ltd, pg 308
Unimax Macmillan Ltd, pg 308

Greece
Athina, Mary Mavrogiannis, pg 309
Diavlos, pg 309
Kyriakidis, pg 312
Mavrogianni Publications, pg 313
Michalis Sideris, pg 313

Holy See (Vatican City State)
Pontificia Academia Scientiarum, pg 317

Hong Kong
Federal Publications Ltd, pg 319
Vision Pub Co Ltd, pg 322
Witman Publishing Co (HK) Ltd, pg 322

Hungary
Magyar Tudomanyos Akademia Koezponti Fizikai Kutato Intezet Koenyvtara, pg 325
Mueszaki Koenyvkiado Ltd, pg 325
Nemzeti Tankoenyvkiado, pg 326
Statiqum Kiado es Nyomda Kft, pg 326
Typotex Kft Elektronikus Kiado, pg 327

India
Addison-Wesley (Singapore) Pte Ltd, pg 329
Affiliated East West Press Pvt Ltd, pg 329

Ambar Prakashan, pg 330
Bharat Publishing House, pg 332
Dolphin Publications, pg 336
Era Book Enterprises, pg 336
Frank Brothers & Co (Publishers) Ltd, pg 337
Goel Prakashen, pg 337
Indian Book Depot (Map House), pg 339
Khanna Publishers, pg 341
Laxmi Publications Pvt Ltd, pg 341
Narosa Publishing House, pg 343
Pitambar Publishing Co (P) Ltd, pg 346
Scientific Book Agency, pg 349
Sita Publications, pg 350
South Asian Publishers Pvt Ltd, pg 350
Sultan Chand & Sons Pvt Ltd, pg 351
Suman Prakashan Pvt Ltd, pg 351
Vikas Publishing House Pvt Ltd, pg 353
S Viswanathan (Printers & Publishers) Pvt Ltd, pg 353

Indonesia
Institut Teknologi Bandung, pg 355
Mutiara Sumber Widya PT, pg 356

Ireland
An Gum, pg 358
The Educational Company of Ireland, pg 360
Royal Irish Academy, pg 364

Israel
Dekel Publishing House, pg 366
Freund Publishing House Ltd, pg 367
Otzar Hamore, pg 368
Intermedia Audio, Video Book Publishing Ltd, pg 368
Open University of Israel, pg 371

Italy
Adelphi Edizioni SpA, pg 374
Archimede Edizioni, pg 376
Bibliopolis - Edizioni di Filosofia e Scienze Srl, pg 377
Cacucci Editore, pg 379
Casa Editrice Giuseppe Principato Spa, pg 380
CEDAM (Casa Editrice Dr A Milani), pg 380
Celuc Libri, pg 380
Il Cigno Galileo Galilei-Edizioni di Arte e Scienza, pg 381
Ciranna - Roma, pg 381
CLEUP - Cooperativa Libraria Editrice dell 'Universita di Padova, pg 382
CPE - Centro Programmazione Editoriale, pg 383
Edizioni Cremonese SRL, pg 383
Etas Libri, pg 388
Arnaldo Forni Editore SRL, pg 389
Giunti Publishing Group, pg 391
Herbita Editrice di Leonardo Palermo, pg 392
Liguori Editore SRL, pg 396
Accademia Naz dei Lincei, pg 400
Newton Compton Editori SRL, pg 401
Paravia Bruno Mondadori Editori, pg 402
Pitagora Editrice SRL, pg 403
Principato, pg 404
Edizioni Universitarie Romane, pg 406
Editoriale Scienza, pg 407

Societa Editrice Internazionale - SEI, pg 408
Editrice Tirrenia Stampatori SAS, pg 410
Vita e Pensiero, pg 411

Jamaica
Carlong Publishers (Caribbean) Ltd, pg 412
Jamaica Publishing House Ltd, pg 413
Packer-Evans and Associates Ltd, pg 413
West Indies Publishing Ltd, pg 414

Japan
Baifukan Co Ltd, pg 414
Holp Book Co Ltd, pg 417
Kindai Kagaku Sha Co, Ltd, pg 419
Kyoritsu Shuppan Co Ltd, pg 420
Nikkagiren Shuppan-Sha (JUSE Press Ltd), pg 422
Nippon Hoso Shuppan Kyokai (NHK Publishing), pg 422
Saera Shobo (Librairie Ca et La), pg 424
Sangyo-Tosho Publishing Co Ltd, pg 424
Shokabo Publishing Co Ltd, pg 426
Soryusha, pg 426
Tokyo Shoseki Co Ltd, pg 427

Kazakstan
Gylym, Izd-Vo, pg 430
Kazakh Al-Farabi State National University, pg 430

Kenya
Cosmopolitan Publishers Ltd, pg 431
Guru Publishers Ltd, pg 431
Kenya Literature Bureau, pg 432
Kenya Quality & Productivity Institute, pg 432
Lake Publishers & Enterprises Ltd, pg 432
Nairobi University Press, pg 433
Phoenix Publishers, pg 433

Democratic People's Republic of Korea
Korea Science and Encyclopedia Publishing House, pg 434

Republic of Korea
Prompter Publications, pg 439

Kuwait
Ministry of Information, pg 441

Liechtenstein
Saendig Reprint Verlag, Hans-Rainer Wohlwend, pg 445

Lithuania
Klaipedos Universiteto Leidykla, pg 445
Mokslo ir enciklopediju leidybos institutas, pg 446
Svietimo ir mokslo ministerijos Leidybos centras, pg 446
TEV Leidykla, pg 446

Luxembourg
Editions Emile Borschette, pg 447
Editions Promoculture, pg 448

The Former Yugoslav Republic of Macedonia
Medis, Skopje, pg 449

Malawi
Dzuka Publishing Company Ltd, pg 450

Malaysia
Federal Publications Sdn Bhd, pg 452
Pearson Education, pg 453
Penerbit Universiti Sains Malaysia, pg 454
Pustaka Delta Pelajaran Sdn Bhd, pg 454
Tropical Press Sdn Bhd, pg 455
Unit Penerbitan Akademik Cancelori~ Universiti Teknologi Malaysia, pg 455

Mexico
Adivinar y Multiplicar, SA de CV, pg 457
Editorial Banca y Comercio SA de CV, pg 458
Colegio de Postgraduados en Ciencias Agricolas, pg 459
Compania Editorial Continental SA de CV, pg 459
Editorial Esfinge SA de CV, pg 460
Fernandez Editores SA de CV, pg 461
Grupo Editorial Iberoamerica, SA de CV, pg 461
Editorial Limusa SA de CV, pg 463
McGraw-Hill Interamericana de Mexico, SA de CV, pg 463
Nova Grupo Editorial SA de CV, pg 464
Pearson Educacion de Mexico, SA de CV, pg 465
Sistemas Tecnicos de Edicion SA de CV, pg 467
Editorial Trillas SA de CV, pg 467
Universidad Nacional Autonoma de Mexico (National University of Mexico), pg 467

Republic of Moldova
Lumina Publishing House, pg 468

Morocco
Dar Nachr Al Maarifa Pour L'Edition et La Distribution, pg 469

Nepal
International Standards Books & Periodicals (P) Ltd, pg 471

Netherlands
Baltzer Science Publishers, pg 474
Elsevier Science BV, pg 477
IOS Press BV, pg 479
Em Querido's Uitgeverij BV, pg 483
A J G Strengholt's Boeken, Anno 1928, BV, pg 484
V S P International Science Publishers, pg 486

New Zealand
ABA Books, pg 488
ESA Publications (NZ) Ltd, pg 490
Eton Press (Auckland) Ltd, pg 490
New House Publishers Ltd, pg 493
Nelson Price Milburn Ltd, pg 494
Statistics New Zealand, pg 496

Nigeria
Evans Brothers (Nigeria Publishers) Ltd, pg 499
JAD Publishers Ltd, pg 500
Ogunsanya Press, Publishers and Bookstores Ltd, pg 501
Riverside Communications, pg 501
West African Book Publishers Ltd, pg 502

Norway
NKI Forlaget, pg 504

Pakistan
Publishers United Pvt Ltd, pg 508

Philippines
Bookman Printing & Publishing House Inc, pg 512
Mutual Books Inc, pg 513
Rex Bookstores & Publishers, pg 514
Saint Mary's Publishing Corp, pg 515
Salesiana Publishers Inc, pg 515
SIBS Publishing House Inc, pg 515
Vibal Publishing House Inc (VPHI), pg 515

Poland
Wydawnictwa Geologiczne, pg 516
Polish Scientific Publishers PWN, pg 519
Zaklad Wydawnictw Statystycznych, pg 520
Oficyna Wydawnicza Szkoly Glownej Handlowej w Warszawie Oficyna Wydawnicza SGH, pg 520
Wydawnictwa Naukowo-Techniczne, pg 521

Portugal
Livraria Arnado Lda, pg 522
Constancia Editores, SA, pg 524
Didactica Editora, pg 524
Gradiva-Publicacnoes Lda, pg 525
McGraw-Hill Editora de Portugal, pg 527
Editora Replicacao Lda, pg 529
Silabo, pg 529

Romania
Editura Academiei Romane, pg 531
Corint Verlag, pg 532
Editura Niculescu, pg 534
Petrion Verlag, pg 535
Editura Stiintifica, pg 536

Russian Federation
N E Bauman Moscow State Technical University Publishers, pg 537
FGUP Izdatelstvo Mashinostroenie, pg 538
Finansy i Statistika Publishing House, pg 538
Fizmatlit Publishing Co, pg 538
Izdatel'stvo Kazanskago Universiteta, pg 538
Izdatel'stvo Mordovskogo gosudar stvennogo, pg 538
Izdatel'stvo Ural'skogo, pg 538
Izdatel'stvo Dal'nevostonogo Gosudarstvennogo Universite, pg 538
Izdatelstvo Mir, pg 540
Nauka Publishers, pg 540
Izdatel'stvo Nizhegorodskogo Gosudarstvennogo Univ, pg 540

PUBLISHERS

Teorija Verojatnostej i ee Primenenija, pg 542
Voronezh State University Publishers, pg 542

Saudi Arabia
King Saud University, pg 543

Singapore
Global Educational Services Pte Ltd, pg 546
Hillview Publications Pte Ltd, pg 546
Success Publications Pte Ltd, pg 548
World Scientific Publishing Co Pte Ltd, pg 549

Slovakia
Slovenske pedagogicke nakladateistvo, pg 550

Slovenia
Univerza v Ljubljani Ekonomska Fakulteta, pg 552

South Africa
Clever Books, pg 553
Educum Publishers Ltd, pg 554
Heinemann Educational Publishers Southern Africa, pg 555
Vivlia Publishers & Booksellers, pg 560

Spain
Agora Editorial, pg 562
Ediciones Alfar SA, pg 562
Alianza Editorial SA, pg 562
Calesa SA Editorial La, pg 566
Editorial Casals SA, pg 566
Celeste Ediciones, pg 567
Editorial Deimos, SL, pg 569
Ediciones y Distribuciones Universitarias SA, pg 571
Instituto de Estudios Riojanos, pg 574
Ibaizabal Edelvives SA, pg 577
Instituto Nacional de Estadistica, pg 578
Marcombo SA de Boixareu Editores, pg 581
Ediciones Morata SL, pg 583
Editorial la Muralla SA, pg 583
Editorial Playor SA, pg 587
Editorial Sintesis, SA, pg 590
Thales Sociedad Andaluza de Educacion Matematica, pg 592
Publicacions de la Universitat de Barcelona, pg 594
Editorial Vicens-Vives, pg 595

Sri Lanka
Gihan Book Shop, pg 597
Ministry of Education, pg 597
Warna Publishers, pg 598

Sweden
Akademiforlaget Goteborgslitteratur, pg 600
Liber AB, pg 604
Studentlitteratur AB, pg 606

Switzerland
Birkhauser Verlag AG, pg 610
Marcel Dekker AG, pg 612
Verlag Harri Deutsch, pg 612
Presses Polytechniques et Universitaires Romandes, PPUR, pg 622

Sabe AG Verlagsinstitut, pg 623
Editions du Tricorne, pg 626
Vdf Hochschulverlag AG an der ETH Zurich, pg 626

Syrian Arab Republic
Damascus University Press, pg 628

Taiwan, Province of China
Fuh-Wen Book Co, pg 630
Hsiao Yuan Publication Co, Ltd, pg 630
Newton Publishing Company Ltd, pg 631
San Min Book Co Ltd, pg 631

United Republic of Tanzania
Ben and Company Ltd, pg 633
DUP (1996) Ltd, pg 633
General Publications Ltd, pg 633
Tanzania Publishing House, pg 634

Thailand
Thai Watana Panich Co, Ltd, pg 636

Tunisia
Academie Tunisienne des Sciences, des Lettres et des Arts Beit El Hekma, pg 637
Ceres Editions, pg 637
Maison d'Edition Mohamed Ali Hammi, pg 638

Turkey
Arkadas Ltd, pg 639
Aydin Yayincilik, pg 639
Bilden Bilgisayar, pg 639
Caglayan Kitabevi, pg 639
Inkilap Publishers Ltd, pg 640
Kok Yayincilik, pg 640

Uganda
Fountain Publishers Ltd, pg 642

Ukraine
Naukova Dumka Publishers, pg 643
Osvita, pg 643

United Kingdom
Advisory Unit: Computers in Education, pg 645
Belitha Press Ltd, pg 653
Cambridge University Press, pg 662
Causeway Press Ltd, pg 665
Educational Explorers (Publishers) Ltd, pg 677
The Eurospan Group, pg 680
Evans Brothers Ltd, pg 680
W H Freeman & Co Ltd, pg 684
The Harvill Press Ltd, pg 693
Hodder & Stoughton Educational, pg 696
Imperial College Press, pg 699
Institute of Physics Publishing, pg 700
Jones & Bartlett International, pg 703
Kershaw Publishing Co Ltd, pg 704
Hilda King Educational, pg 704
Kluwer Academic/Plenum Publishers, pg 705
Learning Together, pg 706
Letts Educational, pg 707
McGraw-Hill Publishing Company, pg 712
John Murray (Publishers) Ltd, pg 716
Nelson Thornes Ltd, pg 718

Oxford University Press, pg 723
Pearson Education, pg 725
Pion Ltd, pg 728
Prim-Ed Publishing UK Ltd, pg 730
Research Studies Press Ltd (RSP), pg 734
The Royal Society, pg 737
SHU Press, pg 742
Skoob Russell Square, pg 742
Southgate Publishers, pg 743
Springer-Verlag London Ltd, pg 744
Supportive Learning Publications, pg 746
Tarquin Publications, pg 746
Ward Lock Educational Co Ltd, pg 754
Wiley Europe Ltd, pg 756
WIT Press, pg 757

Uruguay
La Flor del Itapebi, pg 760
A Monteverde y Cia SA, pg 760

Venezuela
Editorial Biosfera CA, pg 762
Sociedad Fondo Editorial Cenamec, pg 762

Viet Nam
Science & Technics Publishing House, pg 763

Zimbabwe
College Press Publishers (Pvt) Ltd, pg 768
Longman Zimbabwe (Pvt) Ltd, pg 768
Zimbabwe Publishing House (Pvt) Ltd, pg 769

MECHANICAL ENGINEERING

Albania
NL SH, pg 1

Australia
EA Books, pg 21
H&H Publishing, pg 25
McGraw-Hill Australia Pty Ltd, pg 32
Standards Association of Australia, pg 43

Austria
Springer-Verlag Wien, pg 59

Bulgaria
WTU Todor Kableskov, pg 98

China
Aviation Industry Press, pg 102
Chemical Industry Press, pg 102
China Machine Press (CMP), pg 103
China Ocean Press, pg 103
Wissenschaft und Technik Verlag Henan Henan Scientific & Technological Publishing House, pg 106
Jilin Science & Technology Publishing House, pg 106
Metallurgical Industry Press (MIP), pg 107
Printing Industry Publishing House, pg 108
Shandong Science & Technology Press, pg 109

SUBJECT INDEX

Shandong University Press, pg 109
Southwest China Jiaotong University Press, pg 109

Czech Republic
Cesky normalizacni institut, pg 127

Dominican Republic
Pontificia Universidad Catolica Madre y Maestra, pg 136

Egypt (Arab Republic of Egypt)
Dar El Shorouk Publishing & Distributing House, pg 138

France
Cemagref Editions, pg 153
Cepadues Editions SA, pg 153
EDP Sciences, pg 161
Editions Eyrolles, pg 163
Polytechnica, pg 180
PYC Edition, pg 182
Editions Springer France, pg 186

Germany
Beuth Verlag GmbH, pg 202
Charles Coleman Verlag GmbH & Co KG, pg 211
Deutscher Verlag fur Grundstoffindustrie GmbH, pg 215
expert verlag GmbH, Fachverlag fur Wirtschaft & Technik, pg 225
Fachbuchverlag Leipzig im Carl Hanser Verlag, pg 226
Ferd Dummler's Verlag, pg 227
Gieck Reiner v Ursel Gieck, pg 232
Carl Hanser Verlag, pg 237
Huss-Medien GmbH, pg 243
Verlag Werner Sachon GmbH & Co, pg 281
Seibt Verlag GmbH, pg 286
Springer-Verlag GmbH & Co KG, pg 288
Verlag Stahleisen GmbH, pg 289
B G Teubner GmbH, pg 292
Trans Tech Publications, pg 294
Verlag fur Schweissen und Verwandte Verfahren, pg 298
Friedr Vieweg & Sohn Verlagsgesellschaft mbH, pg 298
Vogel Medien GmbH & Co KG, pg 299
Vulkan-Verlag GmbH, pg 299
WEKA Firmengruppe GmbH & Co KG, pg 301

Greece
Kleidarithmos, pg 312

Hong Kong
Business & Industrial Publication Co Ltd, pg 318
Nam Hing Holdings Limited, pg 321

Hungary
Foldmuvelesugyi Miniszterium Muszaki Intezet, pg 323
Nemzeti Tankoenyvkiado, pg 326

India
Affiliated East West Press Pvt Ltd, pg 329
B I Publications Pvt Ltd, pg 331
Khanna Publishers, pg 341
Law Publishers, pg 341
Laxmi Publications Pvt Ltd, pg 341
Multitech Publishing Co, pg 343

1023

SUBJECT INDEX

Oxford & IBH Publishing Co Pvt Ltd, pg 345
Scientific Book Agency, pg 349
Sita Publications, pg 350
Somaiya Publications Pvt Ltd, pg 350

Israel
Freund Publishing House Ltd, pg 367

Italy
Edizioni Cremonese SRL, pg 383
Editrice Edisco, pg 386
Gruppo Calderini Edagricole, pg 392
Zanichelli Editore SpA, pg 412

Japan
Maruzen Co Ltd, pg 421
Nippon Hoso Shuppan Kyokai (NHK Publishing), pg 422
Sangyo-Tosho Publishing Co Ltd, pg 424

Democratic People's Republic of Korea
Korea Science and Encyclopedia Publishing House, pg 434

Republic of Korea
Bo Moon Dang, pg 435

Malaysia
Unit Penerbitan Akademik Cancelori~ Universiti Teknologi Malaysia, pg 455

Mexico
Grupo Editorial Iberoamerica, SA de CV, pg 461
Editorial Limusa SA de CV, pg 463

Myanmar
Shumawa Publishing House, pg 471

Netherlands
A A Balkema, pg 473
Delft University Press, pg 476
Hagen & Stam Uitgeverij Ten, pg 478
IOS Press BV, pg 479
Kluwer Technische Boeken BV, pg 480
Twente University Press, pg 485

New Zealand
Southern Press Ltd, pg 496

Norway
NKl Forlaget, pg 504
Universitetsforlaget, pg 505

Poland
Wydawnictwa Komunikacji i Lacznosci Co Ltd, pg 517
Wydawnictwa Przemyslowe WEMA, pg 521
Wydawnictwa Naukowo-Techniczne, pg 521

Portugal
McGraw-Hill Editora de Portugal, pg 527

Romania
Editura Excelsior, pg 533

Russian Federation
N E Bauman Moscow State Technical University Publishers, pg 537
FGUP Izdatelstvo Mashinostroenie, pg 538
Fizmatlit Publishing Co, pg 538
Izdatelstvo Mir, pg 540
Nauka Publishers, pg 540
Izdatel'stvo Nizhegorodskogo Gosudarstvennogo Univ, pg 540
Stroyizdat Publishing House, pg 542
Izdatelstvo Sudostroenie, pg 542

Slovakia
Dom Techniky Zvazu Slovenskych Vedeckotechnickych Spolocnosti Ltd, pg 549

South Africa
Heinemann Educational Publishers Southern Africa, pg 555

Spain
Mundi-Prensa Libros SA, pg 583
Editorial Sintesis, SA, pg 590

Switzerland
Presses Polytechniques et Universitaires Romandes, PPUR, pg 622
Trans Tech Publications SA, pg 626

Syrian Arab Republic
Damascus University Press, pg 628

Taiwan, Province of China
Fuh-Wen Book Co, pg 630

United Republic of Tanzania
DUP (1996) Ltd, pg 633

Turkey
Caglayan Kitabevi, pg 639

Ukraine
Naukova Dumka Publishers, pg 643

United Kingdom
Atlantic Transport Publishers, pg 650
Elsevier Science Ltd, pg 678
Merrow Publishing Co Ltd, pg 714
Professional Engineering Publishing Ltd, pg 730
Research Studies Press Ltd (RSP), pg 734
The Royal Society, pg 737
The Royal Society of Chemistry, pg 737
Veloce Publishing Ltd, pg 752
Wiley Europe Ltd, pg 756
WIT Press, pg 757

Viet Nam
Science & Technics Publishing House, pg 763

Yugoslavia
Savez Inzenjera i Tehnicara Jugoslavije, pg 765

Zimbabwe
Standards Association of Zimbabwe (SAZ), pg 769

MEDICINE, NURSING, DENTISTRY

Albania
NL SH, pg 1
State Textbook Publishing House, pg 1

Argentina
Libreria Akadia Editorial, pg 3
Editorial Albatros SACI, pg 3
Editorial Caymi SACI, pg 4
EUDEBA (Editorial Universitaria de Buenos Aires), pg 6
Lopez Libreros Editores S R L, pg 7
Editorial Medica Panamericana, pg 7
Editorial Medica, Panamericana SA, pg 7
Polemos SA, pg 8

Australia
Ausmed Publications Pty Ltd, pg 12
Australasian Medical Publishing Company Ltd (AMPCO), pg 13
Blackwell Science Pty Ltd, pg 15
Chase Just Publishing, pg 17
Deakin University Press, pg 20
Fraser Publications, pg 23
Hampden Press, pg 25
Harcourt Australia Pty Ltd, pg 25
James Nicholas Publishers Pty Ltd, pg 28
Law Book Co Information Services, pg 29
MacLennan & Petty Pty Ltd, pg 31
McGraw-Hill Australia Pty Ltd, pg 32
Mosby Lifeline, pg 33
Pearson Education Australia, pg 37
Jurriaan Plesman, pg 38
Royal Society of New South Wales, pg 41
La Trobe University Press, pg 45
Veritas Press, pg 46

Austria
Ennsthaler GesmbH & Co KG, pg 51
Verlag Wilhelm Maudrich, pg 54
Verlag Neues Leben, pg 55
Verlag des Osterr Kneippbundes GmbH, pg 57
E Perlinger Naturprodukte Handelsgesellschaft mbH, pg 57
Springer-Verlag Wien, pg 59
Trauner Verlag, pg 59
Urban und Schwarzenberg GmbH, pg 60
WUV/Facultas Universitaetsverlag, pg 61

Bangladesh
Gono Prakashani, Gono Shasthya Kendra, pg 62

Belarus
Belarus (The Belorussia), pg 63
Belaruskaya Encyklapedyya, pg 63

Belgium
Acco CV, pg 64
Aurelia Books PVBA, pg 64
Editions De Boeck-Larcier SA, pg 67
Imprimerie Hayez SPRL, pg 69
Leuven University Press, pg 71
Marabout, pg 72
Nauwelaerts Edition SA, pg 72

Presses Universitaires de Bruxelles ASBL, pg 73
Presses Universitaires de Liege, pg 73
Prodim SPRL, pg 73
Paul Schiltz, pg 74
Editions de l'Universite de Bruxelles, pg 75
Imprimeur - Editeur Vaillant-Carmanne SA, pg 75

Brazil
Editora Antroposofica Ltda, pg 78
ARTMED, pg 79
Editora Atheneu Ltda, pg 79
Editora Cultura Medica Ltda, pg 81
E P U Editora Pedagogica e Universitaria Ltd, pg 81
Editora Artes Medicas Ltda, pg 82
EDUC - Editora da PUC-SP, pg 82
Editora Globo SA, pg 84
Edicoes Graal Ltda, pg 84
Editora Guanabara Koogan SA, pg 84
IBRASA (Instituicao Brasileira de Difusao Cultural Ltda), pg 85
Icone Editora Ltda, pg 85
Interlivros Edicoes Ltda, pg 85
Editora Manole Ltda, pg 87
Medicina Panamericana Editora Do Brasil Ltda, pg 87
Medsi - Editora Medica e Cientifica Ltda, pg 87
Organizacao Andrei Editora Ltda, pg 89
Proton Editora Ltda, pg 90
Editora de Publicacoes Medicas Ltda, pg 90
Qualitymark Editora Ltda, pg 90
Livraria Editora Revinter Ltda, pg 90
Editora Rideel Ltda, pg 90
Livraria Roca Ltda, pg 90
Livraria Santos Editora Comercio e Importacao Ltda, pg 91
Sarvier - Editora de Livros Medicos Ltda, pg 91
Editora da Universidade de Sao Paulo, pg 93

Bulgaria
Ciela Publishing House, pg 94
DA-Izdatelstvo Publishers, pg 95
Heron Press Publishing House, pg 96
Makros 2000 - Plovdiv, pg 96
Medicina i Fizkultura EOOD, pg 96
Seven Hills Publishers, pg 97

Chile
Arrayan Editores, pg 99
Editorial Andres Bello/Editorial Juridica de Chile, pg 100
Publicaciones Tecnicas Mediterraneo, pg 101

China
Beijing Medical Univ Press, pg 102
Beijing Publishing House, pg 102
Chemical Industry Press, pg 102
Commercial Press (Hong Kong) Ltd, pg 104
Foreign Languages Press, pg 105
Fujian Science & Technology Publishing House, pg 106
Guangdong Science & Technology Press, pg 106
Heilongjiang Science & Technology Press, pg 106

PUBLISHERS

Wissenschaft und Technik Verlag Henan Henan Scientific & Technological Publishing House, pg 106
International Academic Publishers, pg 106
Jilin Science & Technology Publishing House, pg 106
Jinan Publishing House, pg 107
People's Medical Publishing House (PMPH), pg 108
Science Press, pg 108
Shandong Science & Technology Press, pg 109
Shanghai Science & Technology Publishers, pg 109
Shanghai Scientific & Technological Literature Publishing House, pg 109
Sichuan Science & Technology Publishing House, pg 109
Tianjin Science & Technology Publishing House, pg 109

Colombia
Lerner Limitada, pg 112
Universidad de Antioquia, Division Publicaciones, pg 114

The Democratic Republic of the Congo
Centre de Recherche, et Pedagogie Appliquee, pg 114
Presses Universitaires du Zaiire (PUZ), pg 115

Costa Rica
Litografia Artex, SA, pg 116
Editorial Nacional de Salud y Seguridad Social Ednass, pg 116
Editorial Universidad Estatal a Distancia (EUNED), pg 117

Croatia
Izdavacka Delatnost Hrvatske Akademije Znanosti 1 Umjetnosti, pg 118
Matica hrvatska, pg 119
Skolska Knjiga, pg 120

Czech Republic
Karolinum, nakladatelstvi, pg 125
Maxdorf Ltd, pg 126
Pavla Momcilova, pg 126
Cesky normalizacni institut, pg 127
Omnipress Praha, pg 127
Psychoanalyticke Nakladatelstvi, pg 128

Denmark
Akademisk Forlag, pg 129
Arnkrone Forlaget A/S, pg 130
FADL's Forlag A/S (Foreningen af danske Laegestuderendes Forlag), pg 132
Forlaget for Faglitteratur A/S, pg 132
Gyldendalske Boghandel - Nordisk Forlag A/S, pg 132
Nyt Nordisk Forlag Arnold Busck A/S, pg 134
Syddansk Universitetsforlag, pg 136

Dominican Republic
Pontificia Universidad Catolica Madre y Maestra, pg 136

Estonia
AS Medicina, pg 140
Valgus Publishers, pg 141

Finland
Kustannus Oy Duodecim, pg 143
Recallmed Oy, pg 144
Sairaanhoitajien Koulutussaatio, pg 144
Yliopistopaino/Helsinki University Press, pg 145

France
Adverbum SARL, pg 146
Alsatia SA, pg 146
Arnette-Blackwell, pg 148
Editions J B Bailliere, pg 149
Bottin SA, pg 151
Editions Buchet/Chastel, pg 152
Counseil International de la Langue Francaise, pg 157
Les Editions Roger Dacosta, pg 157
Editions Dangles SA, pg 157
Doin Editeurs, pg 160
Ellipses - Edition Marketing SA, pg 162
Editions Eska, pg 162
Editions Espaces 34, pg 162
L'Esprit Du Temps, pg 162
L'Expansion Scientifique Francaise, pg 163
Flammarion SA, pg 164
Les Editions Foucher SA, pg 164
Hermann editeurs des Sciences et des Arts SA, pg 168
Editions INSERM, pg 169
InterEditions Paris, pg 169
Le Jour, Editeur, pg 170
Editions Lamarre SA, pg 171
Librairie Larousse, pg 172
Lavoisier, pg 172
Editions Legislatives, pg 172
John Libbey Eurotext, pg 173
Librairie Luginbuhl, pg 173
Maisonneuve, pg 174
Editions Maloine, pg 174
Masson SA, pg 175
Masson-Williams et Wilkins, pg 175
Presses Universitaires de France (PUF), pg 181
Guide Rosenwald, pg 183
Editions Saint-Michel SA, pg 183
Sauramps Medical, pg 184
Editions Scientifiques et Medicales Elsevier, pg 184
Selection du Reader's Digest SA, pg 184
Sofradif Editions Philippe Auzou, pg 185
Editions Springer France, pg 186
Editions Trois Fontaines, pg 188
Editions Vigot Freres, pg 189

Germany
Andernach Atelier Verlag (AVA), pg 193
Antiqua-Verlag GmbH, pg 194
Johann Ambrosius Barth GmbH, pg 198
Beleke KG Verlag, pg 200
Berlin Verlag Arno Spitz GmbH, pg 200
Bertelsmann Lexikon Verlag GmbH, pg 201
BertelsmannSpringer Science & Business Media GmbH, pg 202
Bettendorf'sche Verlagsanstalt GmbH, pg 202
Bibliographisches Institut & F A Brockhaus AG, pg 203
Bibliomed - Medizinische Verlagsgesellschaft mbH, pg 203
Biermann Verlag GmbH, pg 203
Blackwell Wissenschafts-Verlag GmbH, pg 203

SUBJECT INDEX

Oscar Brandstetter Verlag GmbH & Co KG, pg 206
Catia Monser Eggcup-Verlag, pg 209
Deutscher Aerzte-Verlag GmbH, pg 214
Deutscher Apotheker Verlag, pg 214
Deutscher Taschenbuch Verlag GmbH & Co KG (dtv), pg 215
Dingfelder-Verlag Inh Gerd Gmelin, pg 217
Dreisam Ratgeber in der Rutsker Verlag GmbH, pg 218
Dustri-Verlag Dr Karl Feistle, pg 219
Ecomed Verlagsgesellschaft AG & Co KG, pg 220
Ergebnisse Verlag GmbH, pg 223
Esogetics GmbH, pg 224
EVT Energy Video Training & Verlag GmbH, pg 225
Fachverlag Schiele & Schoen GmbH, pg 226
Ferdinand Enke Verlag, pg 227
Harald Fischer Verlag GmbH, pg 228
Rita G Fischer Verlag, pg 228
Verlag Freies Geistesleben, pg 230
Friedrich Kiehl Verlag GmbH, pg 230
Alfons W Gentner Verlag GmbH & Co KG, pg 231
Gesundheits-Dialog Verlag GmbH, pg 232
Gloatz, Hille GmbH & Co KG fur Mehrfarben und Zellglasdruck, pg 233
Wilhelm Goldmann Verlag GmbH, pg 233
Verlag Grundlagen und Praxis GmbH & Co, pg 234
Walter de Gruyter GmbH & Co KG, pg 234
Haag und Herchen Verlag GmbH, pg 235
Dr Curt Haefner-Verlag GmbH, pg 236
Karl F Haug Verlag GmbH & Co, pg 238
Hippokrates-Verlag GmbH, pg 241
F Hirthammer Verlag GmbH, pg 241
Hogrefe Verlag GmbH & Co Kg, pg 242
Hans Huber, pg 243
Human Wissenschafilicher Verlag, pg 243
Huthig GmbH & Co KG, pg 244
Mediteg-Gesellschaft fuer Informatik Technik und Systeme Verlag, pg 245
K L V Konkret Literatur Verlag GmbH, pg 247
S Karger GmbH Verlag fuer Medizin und Naturwissenschaften, pg 247
Verlag im Kilian GmbH, pg 249
W Kohlhammer GmbH, abt Haussortiment, pg 252
Lebensbaum Verlags-GmbH, pg 256
Lebenshilfe-Verlag Marburg, Verlag der Bundesvereinigung Lebenshilfe fuer Menschen mit geistiger Behinderung eV, pg 256
Leipziger Universitaetsverlag GmbH, pg 257
Mattes Verlag GmbH, pg 261
Medizinisch-Literarische Verlagsgesellschaft mbH, pg 262
Medpharm Scientific Publishers, pg 262
Midena Verlag, pg 264

MMV Medizin Verlag GmbH Munich, pg 264
Mueller und Steinicke Verlag, pg 266
Naumann & Goebel Verlagsgesellschaft mbH, pg 267
Neuland-Verlagsgesellschaft mbH, pg 268
Nusser Verlag, pg 269
Pala-Verlag GmbH, pg 271
Richard Pflaum Verlag GmbH & Co KG, pg 273
pmi Verlag, pg 274
Quintessenz Verlags-GmbH, pg 276
Reed Elsevier Deutschland GmbH, pg 277
Reichl Verlag Der Leuchter, pg 278
Ernst Reinhardt GmbH & Co KG Verlag, pg 278
Schangrila Verlags und Vertriebs GmbH, pg 282
F K Schattauer Verlagsgesellschaft mbH, pg 282
Max Schmidt-Roemhild Verlag, pg 284
Buchverlag Andrea Schmitz, pg 284
Wilhelm Schmitz Verlag, pg 284
Schulz-Kirchner Verlag GmbH, pg 285
Seibt Verlag GmbH, pg 286
Springer-Verlag GmbH & Co KG, pg 288
Dr Dietrich Steinkopff Verlag GmbH & Co, pg 289
Georg Thieme Verlag KG, pg 293
Trias-Thieme, Hippokrates Enke, pg 295
Tuduv Verlagsgesellschaft mbH, pg 295
Universitatsverlag Ulm GmbH, pg 296
Urban & Fischer Verlag GmbH & Co KG Niederlassung Jena, pg 296
Urban und Fischer Verlag fur Medizin, pg 296
UTB fuer Wissenschaft Uni-Taschenbuecher GmbH, pg 297
Curt R Vincentz Verlag, pg 298
VWB-Verlag fur Wissenschaft & Bildung, Amand Aglaster, pg 300
WEKA Firmengruppe GmbH & Co KG, pg 301
Wissenschaftliche Buchgesellschaft, pg 303
Wissenschaftliche Verlagsgesellschaft mbH, pg 303
Fachbuchverlag Armin W Wuth, pg 304

Ghana
Ghana Universities Press (GUP), pg 307
World Literature Project, pg 308

Greece
Beta Medical Publishers, pg 309
Chryssos Typos AE Ekodeis, pg 309
Giovanis Publications, Pangosmios Ekdotikos Organismos, pg 310
M Psaropoulos & Co EE, pg 314
Alex Siokis & Co, pg 315

Holy See (Vatican City State)
Pontificia Academia Scientiarum, pg 317

Hong Kong
Hong Kong University Press, pg 320
Joint Publishing (HK) Co Ltd, pg 320

1025

SUBJECT INDEX

Hungary
Advent Kiado, pg 323
Akademiai Kiado, pg 323
Medicina Koenyvkiado, pg 325
Springer Hungarica Kiado Kft, pg 326

India
Academic Publishers, pg 329
AL Publishers, pg 330
Atma Ram & Sons, pg 331
B 1 Publications Pvt Ltd, pg 331
S Chand & Co Ltd, pg 334
Galgotia Publications Pvt Ltd, pg 337
Arnold Heinman Publishers (India) Pvt Ltd, pg 338
Intertrade Publications, pg 340
B Jain Publishers Overseas, pg 340
B Jain Publishers (P) Ltd, pg 340
Jaypee Brothers Medical Publishers Pvt Ltd, pg 340
Mehta Publications, pg 342
Motilal Banarsidass Publishers Pvt Ltd, pg 343
Narosa Publishing House, pg 343
Parimal Prakashan, pg 345
Popular Prakashan Pvt Ltd, pg 346
Pustak Mahal, pg 346
Rajasthan Hindi Granth Academy, pg 347
Reliance Publishing House, pg 347
Research Signpost, pg 348
Sri Satguru Publications, pg 349
Scientific Book Agency, pg 349
Sterling Publishers Pvt Ltd, pg 351
Transworld Research Network, pg 352
Vikas Publishing House Pvt Ltd, pg 353
Vision Books Pvt Ltd, pg 353
S Viswanathan (Printers & Publishers) Pvt Ltd, pg 353

Indonesia
Alumni PT, pg 353
PT Dian Rakyat, pg 355

Ireland
On Stream Publications Ltd, pg 363

Israel
Books in the Attic Publishers Ltd, pg 366
Boostan Publishing House, pg 366
Dyonon/Papyrus Publishing House of the Tel-Aviv, pg 367
Freund Publishing House Ltd, pg 367
Gefen Publishing House Ltd, pg 367
Intermedia Audio, Video Book Publishing Ltd, pg 368
Medcom Ltd, pg 370
M Mizrahi Publishers, pg 370
Rubin Mass Ltd, pg 371
Schlesinger Institute, pg 372

Italy
Editore Armando Armando SRL, pg 376
Editoriale Bios, pg 378
Edizioni Brenner, pg 378
Calosci, pg 379
Nuova Casa Editrice Licinio Cappelli GEM srl, pg 379
CEDAM (Casa Editrice Dr A Milani), pg 380
Centro Scientifico Int, pg 381
Centro Scientifico Torinese, pg 381
CG Ediz Medico-Scientifiche, pg 381
CIC Edizioni Internazionali, pg 381
CLEUP - Cooperative Libraria Editrice dell 'Universita di Padova, pg 382
Libreria Cortina Editrice SRL, pg 383
Giovanni De Vecchi Editore SpA, pg 384
Edizioni del Riccio SAS di G Bernardi, pg 384
Edi Ermes SRL, pg 386
Edizioni Mediterranee SRL, pg 387
EDT Edizioni di Torino, pg 387
Festina Lente Edizioni, pg 389
Folini, pg 389
Arnaldo Forni Editore SRL, pg 389
Gangemi Editore, pg 390
Edizioni GB, pg 390
Gnocchi Editore, pg 391
Gruppo Editoriale Faenza Editrice SpA, pg 392
Hermes Edizioni SRL, pg 392
Casa Editrice Libraria Idelson di G Gnocchi, pg 393
International University Press Srl, pg 394
Liguori Editore SRL, pg 396
Vincenzo Lo Faro Editore, pg 396
Longanesi & C, pg 396
Casa Editrice Maccari (CEM), pg 397
Masson SpA, pg 398
Mediserve SRL, pg 398
Arnoldo Mondadori Editore SpA, pg 399
Monduzzi Editore SpA, pg 399
Nardini Editore srl, pg 400
New Magazine, pg 400
Novartis Edizioni - Novartis Farma SpA, pg 401
OEMF srl International, pg 401
Patron Editore SrL, pg 403
Piccin Nuova Libraria SpA, pg 403
Edizioni Luigi Pozzi SRL, pg 404
Rara-Ist Editoriale di Bibliofilia e Reprints, pg 405
RCS Libri SpA, pg 405
RCS Rizzoli Libri SpA, pg 405
Red/Studio Redazionale SpA, pg 405
Edizioni Universitarie Romane, pg 406
SAIE Editrice SRL, pg 406
Edizioni San Paolo SRL, pg 407
Edizioni Scientifiche Italiane, pg 407
Societa Editrice la Goliardica Pavese SRL, pg 408
Edizioni Sorbona Milano, pg 408
Stampa Alternativa - Nuovi Equilibri, pg 409
Transeuropa Libri, pg 410
UTET Periodici Scientifici, pg 411
Vita e Pensiero, pg 411
Zanichelli Editore SpA, pg 412

Japan
Chijin Shokan Co Ltd, pg 415
Daiichi Shuppan Co Ltd, pg 415
Dobun Shoin, pg 416
Dohosha Publishing Co Ltd, pg 416
Hirokawa Publishing Co, pg 417
Igaku-Shoin Ltd, pg 418
Ishiyaku Publishers Inc, pg 418
Kanehara & Co Ltd, pg 419
Kinpodo, pg 420
Kodansha, pg 420
Kosei Publishing Co Ltd, pg 420
Kyodo-Isho Shuppan Co Ltd, pg 420
Kyoritsu Shuppan Co Ltd, pg 420
Medical Sciences International Ltd, pg 421
Mejikaru Furendo-sha, pg 421
Minerva Shobo Co Ltd, pg 421
Mita Press, Mita Industrial Co, Ltd, pg 421
Nagai Shoten Co Ltd, pg 421
Nakayama Shoten Company Ltd, pg 421
Nankodo Co Ltd, pg 421
Nanzando Co Ltd, pg 422
Nihon Bunka Kagakusha Co Ltd, pg 422
Nishimura Co Ltd, pg 423
Nobunkyo (Rural Village Culture Association), pg 423
Pearson Education Japan, pg 423
Seibido Shuppan Company Ltd, pg 424
Seiwa Shoten Co Ltd, pg 425
Shorin-Sha Co ltd, pg 426
Shufu-to-Seikatsu Sha Ltd, pg 426
Sogensha Publishing Co Ltd, pg 426
Takahashi Shoten Co Ltd, pg 427
Toho Book Store, pg 427
Tokyo Kagaku Dozin Co Ltd, pg 427
Universal Academy Press, Inc, pg 428
University of Tokyo Press, pg 428
Yakuji Nippo Ltd, pg 429

Jordan
Jordan Book Centre Co Ltd, pg 430
Jordan House for Publication, pg 430

Kazakstan
Kazakhstan, Izd-Vo, pg 430

Kenya
Kenya Literature Bureau, pg 432
Kenya Medical Research Institute (KEMRI), pg 432

Democratic People's Republic of Korea
Korea Science and Encyclopedia Publishing House, pg 434

Republic of Korea
Hanul Publishing Co, pg 436
Iljo-gag Publishers, pg 437
Panmun Book Co Ltd, pg 439
Seoul National University Press, pg 440
Shinkwang Publishing Co, pg 440
Yonsei University Press, pg 441

Lebanon
Khayat Book and Publishing Co Sarl, pg 443

Lithuania
Academia, pg 445
AS Narbuto Leidykla (AS Narbutas' Publishers), pg 445
Mokslo ir enciklopediju leidybos institutas, pg 446

The Former Yugoslav Republic of Macedonia
Medis, Skopje, pg 449

Malaysia
University of Malaya, Department of Publications, pg 455

Mauritius
Hemco Publications, pg 457

Mexico
Libreria y Ediciones Botas SA, pg 458
Editora Cientifica Medica Latinoamerican SA de CV, pg 458
Comision Nacional Forestal, pg 459
Editorial El Manual Moderno SA de CV, pg 460
Ediciones Exclusivas SA, pg 461
Intersistemas SA de CV, pg 462
Editorial Limusa SA de CV, pg 463
Mundo Medico SA de CV Edicion y Distribucion de Revistas Medicas, pg 464
Ediciones Cientificas La Prensa Medica Mexicana SA de CV, pg 466
Salvat Editores de Mexico, pg 466
Editorial Trillas SA de CV, pg 467
Universidad Nacional Autonoma de Mexico (National University of Mexico), pg 467
Universo Editorial SA de CV Edicion de Libros Revistas y Periodicos, pg 468

Republic of Moldova
Lumina Publishing House, pg 468

Morocco
Editions Eddif Maroc, pg 469
Editions Oum, pg 470

Mozambique
Editora Minerva Central, pg 470

Nepal
International Standards Books & Periodicals (P) Ltd, pg 471

Netherlands
Aeolus Press BV, pg 472
B M Israel BV, pg 473
Bohn Stafleu Van Loghum BV, pg 474
Bosch & Keuning, pg 474
De Driehoek BV, pg 476
Elsevier Science BV, pg 477
Uitgeverij Homeovisie BV, pg 478
ICG Publications Holland, pg 479
IOS Press BV, pg 479
Kluwer Academic Publishers, pg 479
Kugler Publications, pg 480
SMD Educational Publishers (Spruyt, Van Mantgem & De Does), pg 484
Swets & Zeitlinger Publishers, pg 485
Uitgeverij de Tijdstroom BV, pg 485
Twente University Press, pg 485
V S P International Science Publishers, pg 486
Van Gorcum & Comp BV, pg 486
VU Boekhandel/Uitgeverij BV, pg 487

New Zealand
Resource Books Ltd, pg 495

PUBLISHERS

Nigeria
CSS Bookshops, Agency & Publishing Division, pg 498
Evans Brothers (Nigeria Publishers) Ltd, pg 499
Ibadan University Press, pg 499
Obafemi Awolowo University Press Ltd, pg 501
Riverside Communications, pg 501
University of Lagos Press, pg 502

Norway
Elanders Publishing AS, pg 503
Glydendal Akademisk, pg 503
Sandviks Bokforlag, pg 505
Universitetsforlaget, pg 505
Vett & Viten AS, pg 505

Pakistan
Hamdard Foundation, pg 507
HMR Publishing Co, pg 507

Papua New Guinea
Papua New Guinea Institute of Medical Research, pg 510

Peru
Universidad Nacional Mayor de San Marcos, pg 512

Philippines
University of the Philippines Press, pg 515
UST Publishing House, pg 515
Vera-Reyes Inc, pg 515

Poland
Wydawnictwo Medyczne Urban & Partner, pg 518
Ossolineum Zaklad Narodowy im Ossolinskich - Wydawnictwo, pg 518
Polish Scientific Publishers PWN, pg 519
PZWL Wydawnictwo Lekarskie Ltd, pg 519
Towarzystwo Naukowe w Toruniu, pg 520

Portugal
Publicacoes Ciencia e Vida Lda, pg 523
Dinalivro, pg 524
Editorial Estampa, Lda, pg 524
Publicacoes Europa-America Lda, pg 524
Europress Editores e Distribuidores de Publicacoes Lda, pg 525
Imprensa Nacional-Casa da Moeda, pg 526
Livraria Luzo-Espanhola Lda, pg 526
Livraria Minerva Editora, pg 526
Livraria Lopes Da Silva-Editora de M Moreira Soares Rocha Lda, pg 527
McGraw-Hill Editora de Portugal, pg 527

Puerto Rico
McGraw-Hill Intermericana del Caribe, Inc, pg 530

Romania
Editura Academiei Romane, pg 531
Editura Aius, pg 531
Editora All, pg 531
Editura Clusium, Casa de Editura Atlas-Clusium SRL, pg 532
Editura Excelsior, pg 533
Editura Institutul European, pg 533
Lider Verlag, pg 534
MAST Verlag, pg 534
Editura Medicala, pg 534
Editura Meridiane, pg 534
Polirom Verlag, pg 535
Vremea Publishers Ltd, pg 536

Russian Federation
Airis Press, pg 537
Izdatel 'stvo Mordovskogo gosudar stvennogo, pg 538
Izdatelstvo Medicina, pg 539
Nauka Publishers, pg 540

Saudi Arabia
Dar Al-Shareff for Publishing & Distribution, pg 543
King Saud University, pg 543

Singapore
APAC Publishers Services, pg 545
Maruzen Asia (Pte) Ltd, pg 547
PG Publishing Pte Ltd, pg 547
Taylor & Francis Asia Pacific, pg 548
World Scientific Publishing Co Pte Ltd, pg 549

Slovakia
Vydavatel'stvo Osveta (Verlag Osveta), pg 551

Slovenia
Zalozba Mihelac d o o, pg 552

South Africa
Bet-El Publishers, pg 553
Butterworths South Africa, pg 553
Heinemann Publishers (Pty) Ltd, pg 555
Jacana Education, pg 555
Juta & Co, pg 556
Nasionale Boekhandel Ltd, pg 557
Reader's Digest Southern Africa, pg 559
Van Schaik Publishers, pg 560
Witwatersrand University Press, pg 560

Spain
Editorial Acribia SA, pg 561
Aguilar SA de Ediciones, pg 562
Ediciones Alfar SA, pg 562
AMV Ediciones, pg 563
Ediciones Atril, pg 564
Comunidad Autonoma de Madrid, Servicio de Documentacion y Publicaciones, pg 568
Ediciones Diaz de Santos SA, pg 569
Ediciones Doce Calles SL, pg 570
Editorial Dossat SA, pg 570
Ediciones Doyma SA, pg 570
Edika-Med, SA, pg 572
Editorial Espaxs SA, pg 573
EUNSA (Ediciones Universidad de Navarra SA), pg 574
Editorial Grupo Cero, pg 576
Editorial Herder SA, pg 577
Editorial Labor SA, pg 579
Mandala Ediciones, pg 581
Editorial Marin SA, pg 581
McGraw-Hill Iberic/Brazil Group, pg 581
Editorial Medica JIMS, SL, pg 582
Ediciones Medici SA, pg 582
Ediciones Morata SL, pg 583
Ediciones Norma SA, pg 584
Oikos-Tau SA Ediciones, pg 584
Pearson Educacion S A, pg 586
Permanyer Publications, pg 586
Publicaciones de la Universidad de Alicante, pg 588
Publicaciones de la Universidad Pontificia Comillas-Madrid, pg 588
Pulso Ediciones, SL, pg 588
Ediciones ROL SA, pg 589
Ediciones Scriba SA, pg 589
Servicio de Publicaciones Universidad de Cadiz, pg 590
Signament I Comunicacio, SL Signament Edicions, pg 590
Axel Springer Publicaciones, pg 591
Ediciones Toray SA, pg 593
Universidad de Granada, pg 594
Universidad de Malaga, pg 594
Universidad de Valladolid Secretariado de Publicaciones e Intercambio Editorial, pg 594
Universitat de Valencia Servei de Publicacions, pg 594

Sri Lanka
Lake House Investments Ltd, pg 597

Sweden
Akademiforlaget Goteborgslitteratur, pg 600
AB Arcanum, pg 600
Bokforlaget Fingraf AB, pg 602
Bengt Forsbergs Foerlag AB, pg 602
Gothia Publishing House, pg 603
Liber AB, pg 604
Studentlitteratur AB, pg 606

Switzerland
Antonius-Verlag, pg 608
Ariston Editions, pg 608
Marcel Dekker AG, pg 612
Editions Delachaux et Niestle SA, pg 612
Editions Andre Delcourt & Cie, pg 612
EULAR Publishers, pg 613
S Karger AG, Medical and Scientific Publishers, pg 617
Medecine et Hygiene, pg 619
Editions Payot Lausanne, pg 621
Philosophisch-Anthroposophischer Verlag am Goetheanum, pg 621
RECOM Verlag, pg 622
Schwabe & Co AG, pg 624
Sciamed Verlag AG, pg 624
Der Universitatsverlag Freiburg, pg 626

Syrian Arab Republic
Damascus University Press, pg 628

Taiwan, Province of China
Chung Hwa Book Co Ltd, pg 629
Farseeing Publishing Company Ltd, pg 630
Chu Hai Publishing (Taiwan) Co Ltd, pg 630
Ho-Chi Book Publishing Co, pg 630
Kuang Fu Book Co Ltd, pg 630
Newton Publishing Company Ltd, pg 631
Shy Mau Publishing Company, pg 631
SMC Publishing Inc, pg 632
World Book Co Ltd, pg 632
Yi Hsien Publishing Co Ltd, pg 632

SUBJECT INDEX

Tajikistan
Irfon, pg 632

United Republic of Tanzania
DUP (1996) Ltd, pg 633
Ndanda Mission Press, pg 634
Nyota Publishers Ltd, pg 634

Tunisia
Academie Tunisienne des Sciences, des Lettres et des Arts Beit El Hekma, pg 637

Turkey
Saray Medikal Yayin Tic Ltd Sti, pg 641
Yuce Reklam Yay Dagt AS, pg 642

Ukraine
Naukova Dumka Publishers, pg 643

United Kingdom
Ai Interactive Ltd, pg 645
Arnold, pg 648
Ashgrove Press, pg 650
Bailliere Tindall Limited, pg 652
Beaconsfield Publishers Ltd, pg 653
BIOS Scientific Publishers Ltd, pg 654
Blackwell Science Ltd, pg 656
Bloomsbury Publishing PLC, pg 656
BMJ Publishing Group, pg 656
Butterworth-Heinemann Ltd, pg 661
Cambridge University Press, pg 662
Castlemead Publications, pg 665
Cavendish Publishing Ltd, pg 665
Churchill Livingstone, pg 668
Class Publishing, pg 668
Current Science Group, pg 672
Denor Press, pg 675
Dobro Publishing, pg 675
Martin Dunitz Ltd, pg 676
Elsevier Science Ltd, pg 678
The Eurospan Group, pg 680
Facts On File, pg 681
W H Freeman & Co Ltd, pg 684
Harcourt Publishers Ltd, pg 691
Harvard University Press, pg 692
Hawker Publications Ltd, pg 693
Health Development Agency, pg 694
Horizon Scientific Press, pg 697
Intercept Ltd, pg 700
Jones & Bartlett International, pg 703
Jessica Kingsley Publishers, pg 704
John Libbey & Co Ltd, pg 707
Lippincott Williams & Wilkins, pg 708
Liverpool University Press, pg 708
Manson Publishing Ltd, pg 711
McGraw-Hill Publishing Company, pg 712
Nelson Thornes Ltd, pg 718
Oxford University Press, pg 723
The Parthenon Publishing Group Ltd, pg 724
PasTest, pg 724
Pearson Education Europe, Mideast & Africa, pg 725
Petroc Press, pg 726
Pharmaceutical Press, pg 726
Portland Press Ltd, pg 730
Quintessence Publishing Co Ltd, pg 732
Radcliffe Medical Press Ltd, pg 732
Royal College of General Practitioners, pg 736
Sage Publications Ltd, pg 737

1027

Sangam Books Ltd, pg 738
W B Saunders & Co Ltd, pg 738
Science Reviews Ltd, pg 739
Sheffield Academic Press Ltd, pg 741
Smith-Gordon, pg 743
Souvenir Press Ltd, pg 743
Speechmark Publishing Ltd, pg 744
Springer-Verlag London Ltd, pg 744
Harold Starke Publishers Ltd, pg 745
The Stationery Office, pg 745
Tarragon Press, pg 746
Taylor & Francis Group, pg 747
Telegraph Books, pg 748
Whurr Publishers Ltd, pg 756
Wiley Europe Ltd, pg 756

Uruguay
Editorial Dismar, pg 760
Prensa Medica Latinoamericana, pg 761

Venezuela
Universidad de los Andes, Consejo de Publicaciones, pg 763

Viet Nam
Science & Technics Publishing House, pg 763
Y Hoc Publishing House, pg 763

Yugoslavia
Alfa-Narodna Knjiga, pg 764
Naucna Knjiga, pg 764
Panorama NIJP/ID Grigorije Bozovic, pg 765

Zimbabwe
University of Zimbabwe Publications, pg 769

MICROCOMPUTERS

Albania
NL SH, pg 1

Australia
OTEN (Open Training & Education Network), pg 36
Price Publishing, pg 39
Tertiary Press, pg 44

Barbados
Business Tutors, pg 63

Belgium
Easy Computing NV, pg 68

Brazil
Antenna Edicoes Tecnicas Ltda, pg 78
Berkeley Brasil Editora Ltda, pg 79
Callis Editora Ltda, pg 80
Editora Campus Ltda, pg 80
Selecoes Eletronicas Editora Ltda, pg 83

Bulgaria
Aleks Soft, pg 94
Makros 2000 - Plovdiv, pg 96
TEMTO, pg 98

China
China Machine Press (CMP), pg 103
Electronics Industry Publishing House, pg 105
Fudan University Press, pg 105
Inner Mongolia Science & Technology Publishing House, pg 106
Jilin Science & Technology Publishing House, pg 106
National Defence Industry Press, pg 107
Shandong University Press, pg 109
Shanghai Educational Publishing House, pg 109
Tianjin Science & Technology Publishing House, pg 109

Cote d'Ivoire
Universite d' Abidjan, pg 118

Cuba
Apocalipis Digital, pg 120
Casa Editora Abril, pg 120

Finland
Teknolit Oy, pg 144

France
Dunod Editeur, pg 160
Les Editions ESF, pg 161
Editions Mango, pg 174
Pearson Education France, pg 179
Sybex, pg 186

Germany
Data Becker GmbH & Co KG, pg 212
Elektor-Verlag GmbH, pg 222
Fachbuchverlag Leipzig im Carl Hanser Verlag, pg 226
Feltron-Elektronik Zeissler & Co GmbH, pg 227
Carl Hanser Verlag, pg 237
Ing W Hofacker GmbH Verlag, pg 241
ITpress Verlag, pg 245

Greece
Kleidarithmos, pg 312

Hong Kong
Modern Electronic & Computing Publishing Co Ltd, pg 321

Hungary
Magyar Tudomanyos Akademia Koezponti Fizikai Kutato Intezet Koenyvtara, pg 325

India
Affiliated East West Press Pvt Ltd, pg 329
Pitambar Publishing Co (P) Ltd, pg 346
Scientific Book Agency, pg 349
Sita Publications, pg 350
Sterling Information Technologies, pg 351

Indonesia
Gramedia, pg 355

Italy
IHT Gruppo Editoriale SRL, pg 393

Japan
Dobun Shoin, pg 416
Kaibundo Publishing Co Ltd, pg 419
Pearson Education Japan, pg 423

Republic of Korea
Ohmsa, pg 439

The Former Yugoslav Republic of Macedonia
Medis, Skopje, pg 449

Mexico
ALFA OMEGA Grupo Editor, pg 458
Editorial Limusa SA de CV, pg 463
Pearson Educacion de Mexico, SA de CV, pg 465
Sistemas Universales, SA, pg 467
Ventura Ediciones, SA de CV, pg 468

Netherlands
Erven J Bijleveld, pg 474
BoekWerk, pg 474
BV Uitgeversbedryf Het Goede Boek, pg 477
Hagen & Stam Uitgeverij Ten, pg 478

Pakistan
Academy of Education Planning & Management (AEPAM), pg 506

Paraguay
Instituto de Ciencias de la Computacion (NCR), pg 510

Poland
Oficyna Wydawnicza Politechniki Wroclawskiej, pg 519
Oficyna Wydawnicza Read Me, pg 519
Wydawnictwa Naukowo-Techniczne, pg 521

Portugal
Edicoes Cetop, pg 523
Impala, pg 525

Romania
Petrion Verlag, pg 535

Russian Federation
N E Bauman Moscow State Technical University Publishers, pg 537
Finansy i Statistika Publishing House, pg 538
Fizmatlit Publishing Co, pg 538
Izdatelstvo Mir, pg 540
Nauka Publishers, pg 540
Izdatel'stvo Nizhegorodskogo Gosudarstvennogo Univ, pg 540

Slovakia
Ustav informacii a prognoz skolstva mladeze a telovychovy, pg 551

Spain
Marcombo SA de Boixareu Editores, pg 581
RA-MA, Libreria y Editorial Microinformatica, pg 588
Urmo SA de Ediciones, pg 595

Taiwan, Province of China
Lead Wave Publishing Company Ltd, pg 631

Turkey
Alkim Kitapcilik-Yayimcilik, pg 638

Ukraine
ASK Ltd, pg 643

United Kingdom
Advisory Unit: Computers in Education, pg 645
BCA, pg 653
CTBl Publications, pg 672
The Eurospan Group, pg 680

Viet Nam
Science & Technics Publishing House, pg 763

MILITARY SCIENCE

Albania
Ndermarrja e Botimeve Ushtarake, pg 1
NL SH, pg 1

Argentina
Instituto de Publicaciones Navales, pg 7
Theoria SRL Distribuidora y Editora, pg 9

Armenia
Ajstan Publishers, pg 10

Australia
Gerald Griffin Press, pg 24
Maxwell Macmillan Publishing (Australia) Pty Ltd, pg 32
Mostly Unsung, pg 33
Oceans Enterprises, pg 35
Slouch Hat Publications, pg 42
The Watermark Press, pg 47

Austria
Akademische Druck-u Verlagsanstalt Dr Paul Struzl GmbH, pg 49
Leopold Stocker Verlag, pg 54
Oesterreichischer Bundesverlag GmbH, pg 56
Herbert Weishaupt Verlag, pg 60

Bangladesh
The University Press Ltd, pg 62

Belgium
Editions Chanlis, pg 66
Ipis VZW (International Peace Information Service), pg 69
De Krijger, pg 70

Brazil
Action Editora Ltda, pg 77
Callis Editora Ltda, pg 80
Editora Revan Ltda, pg 90

Bulgaria
Izdatelstvo na Ministerstvoto na Otbranata, pg 96

PUBLISHERS

China
Education Science Publishing House, pg 105
Kunlun Publishing House, pg 107
National Defence Industry Press, pg 107

Czech Republic
Aurora, pg 123
Baronet, pg 123
Jota, pg 125
Nase vojsko, nakladatelstvi a knizni obchod, pg 126

Denmark
Bonnier Publications AS, pg 130

Finland
Koala-Kustannus/Oy Greenbay House Publishing Ltd, pg 143

France
Editions Anthropos Sarl, pg 147
Publications Aredit, pg 148
Editions Cenomane, pg 153
Editions Charles-Lavauzelle SA, pg 154
EPA SA (Editions Presse Audiovisuel), pg 162
Editions Grancher, pg 166
Editions Ivrea, pg 170
Muller Edition, pg 176

Germany
Bernard und Graefe Verlag, pg 201
Biblio-Zeller Verlag, pg 202
Brandenburgisches Verlagshaus in der Dornier Medienholding GmbH, pg 206
Degener & Co, Manfred Dreiss Verlag, pg 213
Duncker und Humblot GmbH, pg 219
DVG-Deutsche Verlagsgesellschaft mbH, pg 219
Liselotte Hamecher, pg 236
Verlagsgruppe Koehler/Mittler, pg 251
E S Mittler und Sohn GmbH, pg 264
Motorbuch-Verlag, pg 265
Nusser Verlag, pg 269
Verlag Offene Worte, pg 270
Paul Pietsch Verlage GmbH & Co, pg 273
Podzun-Pallas Verlag GmbH, pg 274
Propylaeen Verlag, Zweigniederlassung Berlin der Ullstein Buchverlage GmbH, pg 275
Schild-Verlag GmbH, pg 283
Verlag Karl Waldemar Schuetz, pg 285
Edition Temmen, pg 292
Trees Wolfgang Triangel Verlag, pg 294
Weber Zucht & Co, pg 300
Zeller Verlag GmbH & Co, pg 305

Guatemala
Grupo Editorial RIN-78, pg 316

Hungary
Zrinyi Kiado, pg 327

India
Asian Educational Services, pg 331
Himalayan Books, pg 338
Lancer Publisher's & Distributors, pg 341
National Book Organization, pg 343
Naya Prokash, pg 344
Reliance Publishing House, pg 347
Scientific Book Agency, pg 349
Vikas Publishing House Pvt Ltd, pg 353
Vision Books Pvt Ltd, pg 353

Indonesia
Yayasan Obor Indonesia, pg 357

Ireland
Irish Academic Press, pg 361

Israel
Dekel Publishing House, pg 366
Gefen Publishing House Ltd, pg 367
Ministry of Defence Publishing House, pg 370
Tel-Aviv University, pg 373

Italy
Gruppo Abele, pg 374
Ermanno Albertelli Editore, pg 375
Verlagsanstalt Athesia, pg 377
Edizioni l'Arciere SRL, pg 387
Edizioni Mediterranee SRL, pg 387
La Fenice SRL, pg 389
IHT Gruppo Editoriale SRL, pg 393
Rossato, pg 406

Japan
Kokusho Kankokai Co Ltd, pg 420

Monaco
Les Editions du Rocher, pg 469

Namibia
McGregor Publishers, pg 471

Netherlands
Omega Boek BV, pg 482

Romania
Editura Militara, pg 534

Russian Federation
Izdatel'stvo Patriot, pg 541
Izdatelstvo Sudostroenie, pg 542
Teorija Verojatnostei i ee Primenenija, pg 542
Voyenizdat, pg 542

South Africa
Ashanti Publishing, pg 552
Galago Publishing Pty Ltd, pg 554
South African Institute of International Affairs, pg 559

Spain
Ediciones Rialp SA, pg 589
Editorial San Martin, pg 589
Axel Springer Publicaciones, pg 591

Sweden
Allt om Hobby AB, pg 600

Switzerland
Les Editions la Matze, pg 618
Ott Verlag AG, pg 621
Verlag Stocker-Schmid AG, pg 625
Editions 24 Heures, pg 626

United Kingdom
Airlife Publishing Ltd, pg 645
Aldwych Press Ltd, pg 645
Amber Books Ltd, pg 646
The Ampersand Press (Cl) Ltd, pg 647
Arms & Armour Press, pg 648
Aurum Press Ltd, pg 651
BCA, pg 653
Berghahn Books Ltd, pg 654
The Book Guild Ltd, pg 657
Book Packaging & Marketing, pg 657
Books International, pg 657
Brassey's UK Ltd, pg 658
Brewin Books Ltd, pg 659
Bridge Books, pg 659
Frank Cass Publishers, pg 664
Cassell & Co, pg 664
Compendium Publishing, pg 670
Constable & Robinson Ltd, pg 670
Constable Publishers, pg 670
Leo Cooper, pg 671
The Eurospan Group, pg 680
Facts On File, pg 681
Firebird Books Ltd, pg 682
Greenhill Books/Lionel Leventhal Ltd, pg 689
Guinness Publishing Ltd, pg 690
Hodder & Stoughton General, pg 696
International Institute for Strategic Studies, pg 701
Jane's Information Group, pg 702
Macmillan Audio Books, pg 710
Marshall Editions Ltd, pg 712
Middleton Press, pg 714
Midland Publishing, pg 714
Mirabel Books Ltd, pg 715
Osprey Publishing Ltd, pg 722
Oxford University Press, pg 723
Parapress Ltd, pg 724
Pen & Sword Books Ltd, pg 725
Picton Publishing (Chippenham) Ltd, pg 727
PRC Publishing Ltd, pg 730
Quintet Publishing Ltd, pg 732
Robson Books, pg 735
Shire Publications Ltd, pg 741
Sidgwick & Jackson Ltd, pg 742
SPA Books Ltd, pg 744
Spellmount Ltd Publishers, pg 744
Sutton Publishing Ltd, pg 746
Sydney Jary Ltd, pg 746
Unicorn Books, pg 751

Viet Nam
Popular Army Publishing House, pg 763

Yugoslavia
Vojnoizdavacki i novinski centar, pg 766

MUSIC, DANCE

Albania
NL SH, pg 1

Argentina
Bonum Editorial SACI, pg 4
Cesarini Hermanos, pg 4
Ediciones Corregidor SAICI y E, pg 4
EUDEBA (Editorial Universitaria de Buenos Aires), pg 6
Ediciones de Arte Gaglianone, pg 6
Editorial Guadalupe, pg 6
Marymar Ediciones SA, pg 7
Quetzal-Domingo Cortizo, pg 8

Ricordi Americana SAEC, pg 8
Javier Vergara Editor SA, pg 9

Australia
Aboriginal Studies Press, pg 10
Currency Press Pty Ltd, pg 19
Ginninderra Press, pg 24
Grainger Museum, pg 24
Moonlight Publishing, pg 33
NMA Publications, pg 35
Anne O'Donovan Pty Ltd, pg 35
Playlab Press, pg 38
St Joseph Publications, pg 41
Spectrum Publications, pg 43
Thames & Hudson (Australia) Pty Ltd, pg 44
Turton & Armstrong Publishers Pty Ltd, pg 45
Unity Press, pg 46
Yanagang Publishing, pg 48

Austria
Akademische Druck-u Verlagsanstalt Dr Paul Struzl GmbH, pg 49
Amalthea-Verlag, pg 49
Dachs-Verlag GmbH, pg 50
Ludwig Doblinger (Bernhard Herzmansky) Musikverlag KG, pg 51
Edition Helbling Verlags-Gesellschaft mbH, pg 52
Johannes Heyn, Gert und Volkmar Zechner, pg 52
Kremayr & Scheriau Verlag, pg 54
Verlag Lafite, pg 54
Gerda Leber Buch-Kunst-und Musikverlag Proscenium Edition, pg 54
Mueller-Speiser Wissenschaftlicher Verlag, pg 55
Paul Neff Verlag KG, pg 55
Oesterreichischer Bundesverlag GmbH, pg 56
Osterreichischer Bundesverlag Ges.mbH, pg 57
Residenz Verlag GmbH, pg 58
Ritter Verlag, pg 58
Salzburger Kulturvereinigung, pg 58
Dr A Schendl GmbH und Co KG, pg 58
SN-Verlag, Salzburger Nachrichten Verlags GmbH & Co KG, pg 59
Studien Verlag Gmbh, pg 59
Verlag Carl Ueberreuter GmbH, pg 59
Universal Edition AG, pg 60
Verband der Wissenschaftlichen Gesellschaften Oesterreichs (VWGOe), pg 60

Azerbaijan
Sada, Literaturno-Izdatel'skij Centr, pg 61

Bangladesh
Agamee Prakashani, pg 62

Belarus
Belarus (The Belorussia), pg 63
Interdigets Publishing House, pg 63

Belgium
Alamire vzw, Music Publishers, pg 64
Altina, pg 64
SA Artis-Historia, pg 64
Dexia Bank, pg 68
Infoboek NV, pg 69

SUBJECT INDEX

Koninklijke Vlaamse Academie van Belgie voor Wetenschappen en Kunsten, pg 70
Leuven University Press, pg 71
Editeurs de Litterature Biblique, pg 71
Mardaga, Pierre 12, pg 72
Schott Freres SA (Editeurs de Musique), pg 74
Sonneville Press (Uitgeverij) VTW, pg 74
Stichting Kunstboek bvba, pg 74
Uitgeverij De Garve, pg 75

Botswana
The Botswana Society, pg 77

Brazil
Associacao Brasileira de Liverivos Antiquarios, pg 79
Brinque Book Editora de Livros Ltda, pg 80
Concordia Editora Ltda, pg 81
Companhia Editora Forense, pg 82
EDUC - Editora da PUC-SP, pg 82
Editora Forense, pg 83
Global Editora e Distribuidora Ltda, pg 84
Editora Globo SA, pg 84
Horus Editora Ltda, pg 85
Editora Lidador Ltda, pg 86
Musimed Edicoes Musicais Importacao E Exportacao Ltda, pg 88
Pallas Editora e Distribuidora Ltda, pg 89
Editora Perspectiva, pg 89
Editora Sinodal, pg 91
Summus Editorial Ltda, pg 92
34 Literatura S/C Ltda, pg 92
Triom Centro de Estudos Marina e Martin Hawey Editorial e Comercial Ltda, pg 92
Jorge Zahar Editor, pg 93

Bulgaria
Makros 2000 - Plovdiv, pg 96
Musica Publishing House Ltd, pg 96
Sila & Zivot, pg 98

Chile
Arrayan Editores, pg 99
Ediciones Universitarias de Valparaiso, pg 101

China
Shandong Literature & Art Publishing House, pg 109

Colombia
Universidad de Antioquia, Division Publicaciones, pg 114
Editorial Voluntad SA, pg 114

Costa Rica
Promesa, Ediciones, pg 116

Cote d'Ivoire
Akohi Editions, pg 117

Croatia
Faust Vrani, pg 118
Mladost d d Izdavacku graficku i informaticku djelatnost, pg 119
Muzicka Naklada, pg 119
Skolska Knjiga, pg 120

Czech Republic
Editio Moravia-Moravske hudebni vydavatelstvi, pg 126
Nadace Lyry Pragensis, pg 126
Narodni Muzeum, pg 126
Panton, pg 127
Pop Plus Rock Centrum, pg 127
Supraphon, pg 128
Svojtka & Co, pg 128
Evzen Uher, Musikverlag UHER, pg 129
Votobia sro, pg 129

Denmark
Borgens Forlag A/S, pg 130
Gyldendalske Boghandel - Nordisk Forlag A/S, pg 132
Edition Wilhelm Hansen AS, pg 132
Nyt Nordisk Forlag Arnold Busck A/S, pg 134
Square Dance Partners Forlag, pg 135

Egypt (Arab Republic of Egypt)
Dar El Shorouk Publishing & Distributing House, pg 138

Estonia
National Library of Estonia, pg 140

Finland
Kirja-Leitzinger, pg 143
Koala-Kustannus/Oy Greenbay House Publishing Ltd, pg 143
Recallmed Oy, pg 144
Schildts Foerlagsaktiebolag, pg 144
Yliopistopaino/Helsinki University Press, pg 145

France
Editions Albin Michel, pg 146
Editions Alternatives, pg 146
L'Arche Editeur, pg 147
Compagnie Francaise des Arts Graphiques SA, pg 148
Editions d'Aujourd'hui (Les Introuvables), pg 149
Editions l'Avant-Scene de Prette Technique, pg 149
Editions Belfond, pg 150
Editions Buchet/Chastel, pg 152
Chasse Maree-Armen, pg 154
Editions Chiron, pg 154
Cicero Editeurs, pg 155
Climats, pg 155
CNRS Editions, pg 155
Editions Dis Voir, pg 159
Edisud, pg 161
Librairie Artheme Fayard, pg 163
Librairie Fischbacher, International Art Book Distribution (import-export), pg 164
Editions Gallimard, pg 165
Paul Geuthner Librairie Orientaliste, pg 166
Editions Jean Paul Gisserot, pg 166
Pierre Horay Editeur, pg 168
Editions Klincksieck, pg 171
Librairie Larousse, pg 172
Editions de la Maison des Sciences de l'Homme, Paris, pg 174
Editions Parentheses, pg 179
Editions A et J Picard SA, pg 179
Editions Christian Pirot, pg 180
Editions Plume, pg 180
Les Presses d'Ile-de-France Sarl, pg 181
Presses Universitaires de France (PUF), pg 181
Publications Orientalistes de France (POF), pg 182
Revue Noire, pg 183
Editions Sand et Tchou SA, pg 183
Service Technique pour l'Education, pg 185
Editions du Seuil, pg 185
Stil, pg 186
Editions Van de Velde, pg 188

Germany
Abakus Musik Barbara Fietz, pg 191
Alexander Verlag Berlin, pg 192
Alkor-Edition Kassel GmbH, pg 193
Angelika und Lothar Binding, pg 193
Verlag APHAIA Svea Haske, Sonja Schumann GbR, pg 194
Apollo-Verlag Paul Lincke GmbH, pg 194
Arcadia Verlag GmbH, pg 194
ARCult Media, pg 194
Atlantis Musikbuch, pg 196
Barenreiter-Verlag Karl-Votterle GmbH & Co KG, pg 198
Bayerischer Schulbuch-Verlag GmbH, pg 199
Verlag C H Beck (OHG), pg 200
Berlin Verlag Arno Spitz GmbH, pg 200
BBT Bhaktivedanta Book Trust, pg 202
Verlag Die Blaue Eule, pg 204
Verlag Erwin Bochinsky GmbH & Co KG, pg 204
Bonifatius GmbH Druck-Buch-Verlag, pg 205
Boosey & Hawkes Music Publishers LTD, London, pg 205
Gustav Bosse GmbH & Co KG, pg 205
Bote & Bock Musikalienhandelsgesellschaft mbH, pg 206
Breitkopf & Hartel, pg 206
R Brockhaus Verlag, pg 206
Chr Belser AG fur Verlagsgeschaefte und Co KG, pg 210
Hans Christians Druckerei und Verlag GmbH & Co, pg 210
Verlag Werner Dausien, pg 212
Verlag Horst Deike KG, pg 213
Deutsche Verlags-Anstalt GmbH (DVA), pg 214
Deutscher Taschenbuch Verlag GmbH & Co KG (dtv), pg 215
Christoph Dohr, pg 217
Dolling und Galitz Verlag GmbH, pg 217
Edition Solitude - Akademie Schloss Solitude, pg 221
Egmont vgs verlagsgesellschaft mbH, pg 221
EinfallsReich Verlagsgesellschaft MbH, pg 222
Eres Editions-Horst Schubert Musikverlag, pg 223
ERF-Verlag GmbH, pg 223
EVT Energy Video Training & Verlag GmbH, pg 225
Extent Verlag und Service Wolfgang M Flamm, pg 225
FAB-Verlag, pg 226
Wilhelm Fink GmbH & Co Verlags-KG, pg 228
Verlag Freies Geistesleben, pg 230
Genius Verlag, pg 231
Georgi GmbH, pg 232
Gerth, Klaus, Verlag GmbH, pg 232
Verlag Ernst und Werner Gieseking GmbH, pg 232
Verlag Gruppenpaedagogischer Literatur, pg 234
Wolfgang G Haas - Musikverlag Koeln ek, pg 235
Haenssler Verlag GmbH, pg 236
Happy Mental Buch- und Musik Verlag, pg 237
Harenberg Kommunikation Verlags- und Medien GmbH & Co KG, pg 237
Harth Musik Verlag-Pro musica Verlag GmbH, pg 237
Heel Verlag GmbH, pg 238
G Henle Verlag, pg 239
Max Hieber KG, pg 240
Hoffmann und Campe Verlag GmbH, pg 242
Friedrich Hofmeister Musikverlag GmbH, pg 242
Impuls-Theater-Verlag, pg 244
Iudicium Verlag GmbH, pg 245
Jutta Pohl Verlag, pg 247
Kallmeyer'sche Verlagsbuchhandlung GmbH, pg 247
Kastell Verlag GmbH, pg 248
Klink, Vincent, Edition, Stecknadel, pg 250
Koenemann Verlagesellschaft mbH, pg 251
Verlag Valentin Koerner GmbH, pg 252
Alfred Kroner Verlag, pg 253
Verlag Ernst Kuhn, pg 254
Kunstverlag Weingarten GmbH, pg 254
Laaber-Verlag, pg 255
LEU-VERLAG Wolfgang Leupelt, pg 257
Robert Lienau GmbH & Co KG, pg 258
Martha Lindner Verlags-GmbH, pg 258
Manutius Verlag, pg 260
Matthes und Seitz Verlag GmbH, pg 261
Medium-Buchmarkt, pg 262
Menschenkinder Verlag und Vertrieb GmbH, pg 262
J B Metzler'sche Verlagsbuchhandlung, pg 263
Meyer & Meyer Fachverlag und Buchhandel GmbH, pg 263
Karl Heinrich Moeseler Verlag, pg 264
Munzinger-Archiv GmbH Archiv fuer publizistische Arbeit, pg 266
Musikantiquariat und Dr Hans Schneider Verlag GmbH, pg 266
Musikverlag Zimmermann, pg 266
Neue Dimension Buch-und Musik-Verlag, pg 267
Verlag Neue Musik GmbH, pg 267
Verlag Neue Musikzeitung GmbH, pg 267
Verlag Neue Stadt GmbH, pg 267
Nieswand-Verlag GmbH, pg 269
Florian Noetzel Verlag, pg 269
Oekotopia Verlag, Wolfgang Hoffman, pg 270
Georg Olms Verlag AG, pg 270
Oreos Verlag GmbH, pg 270
Palmyra Verlag, pg 271
Verlag Sigrid Persen, pg 272
C F Peters Musikverlag GmbH & Co KG, pg 272
Philipp Reclam Jun Verlag GmbH, pg 273
Piper Verlag GmbH, pg 274
Premop Verlag GmbH, pg 275
Projektion J Buch- und Musikverlag GmbH, pg 275

Propylaeen Verlag, Zweigniederlassung Berlin der Ullstein Buchverlage GmbH, pg 275
Dr Mohan Krischke Ramaswamy Edition RE, pg 277
Dr Ludwig Reichert Verlag, pg 278
Ernst Reinhardt GmbH & Co KG Verlag, pg 278
Respublica Verlag, pg 279
Rimbaud Verlagsgesellschaft mbH, pg 279
Erich Roeth-Verlag, pg 279
Romiosini Verlag, pg 280
Sattva Kunst Verlag, pg 281
K G Saur Verlag GmbH, A Gale/Thomson Learning Company, pg 282
Agora Verlag Manfred Schlosser, pg 283
Verlag Schnell und Steiner GmbH, pg 284
Verlag Hans Schoener GmbH, pg 284
Schott Musik International GmbH & Co KG, pg 284
Verlag Schulte und Gerth GmbH & Co KG, pg 285
Sonnentanz-Verlag Roland Kron, pg 287
Stadler Verlagsgesellschaft mbH, pg 288
Stapp Verlag Wolfgang Stapp, pg 289
Franz Steiner Verlag Wiesbaden GmbH, pg 289
edition Text & Kritik im Richard Boorberg Verlag GmbH & Co, pg 293
Treves Editions Verein Zur Foerderung der Kuenstlerischen Taetigkeiten, pg 295
Voggenreiter-Verlag, pg 299
VS Verlagshaus Stuttgart GmbH, pg 299
VWB-Verlag fur Wissenschaft & Bildung, Amand Aglaster, pg 300
Wissenschaftliche Buchgesellschaft, pg 303
Wolke Verlags GmbH, pg 304

Ghana
Asempa Publishers, pg 306
Ghana Academy of Arts & Sciences, pg 307

Greece
Apostoliki Diakonia tis Ekklisias tis Hellados, pg 309
Hestia-I D Hestia-Kollaros & Co Corporation, pg 311
Medusa/Selas, pg 313
Minoas SA, pg 313
Editions Moressopoulos, pg 313
Nakas Music House, pg 313
Ed Nea Acropolis, pg 313

Hong Kong
Benefit Publishing Co, pg 318
Chinese Christian Literature Council Ltd, pg 318
Shanghai Book Co Ltd, pg 321

Hungary
Akademiai Kiado, pg 323
Magveto Koenyvkiado, pg 325
Nemzeti Tankoenyvkiado, pg 326
Planetas Kiadoi es Kereskedelmi Kft, pg 326
Zenemukiado Vallalat, pg 327

Iceland
Stofnun Arna Magnussonar a Islandi, pg 329

India
Abhinav Publications, pg 329
Asian Educational Services, pg 331
Chowkhamba Sanskrit Series Office, pg 335
Cosmo Publications, pg 335
DK Printworld (P) Ltd, pg 336
Gyan Publishing House, pg 338
Mudgala Trust, pg 343
Munshiram Manoharlal Publishers Pvt Ltd, pg 343
Oxonian Press (P) Ltd, pg 345
Pankaj Publications, pg 345
Popular Prakashan Pvt Ltd, pg 346
Pustak Mahal, pg 346
Reliance Publishing House, pg 347
Roli Books Pvt Ltd, pg 348
Sri Satguru Publications, pg 349
Somaiya Publications Pvt Ltd, pg 350
Sri Satguru Publications, pg 351

Indonesia
Bina Aksara Parta, pg 354
Mutiara Sumber Widya PT, pg 356

Ireland
Clo Iar-Chonnachta Teo, pg 359
The O'Brien Press Ltd, pg 363
Ossian Publications, pg 363

Israel
Classikaletet, pg 366
Doko Video Ltd, pg 366
Hakibbutz Hameuchad Publishing House Ltd, pg 368
Israel Music Institute (IMI), pg 369
Israeli Music Publications Ltd, pg 369
The Magnes Press, pg 370
Massada Press Ltd, pg 370
Y Sreberk, pg 372
Steimatzky Group Ltd, pg 372
Yavneh Publishing House Ltd, pg 373
Yedioth Ahronoth Books, pg 373

Italy
Mario Adda Editore SNC, pg 374
Bardi Editore srl, pg 377
Ditta F Bongiovanni SAS, pg 378
Edizioni Cadmo SRL, pg 379
Calosci, pg 379
Campanotto, pg 379
Edizioni Cantagalli, pg 379
Nuova Casa Editrice Licinio Cappelli GEM srl, pg 379
Casa Musicale Edizioni Carrara SRL, pg 379
Edistudio di Brunetto Casini, pg 380
CLUEB (Cooperativa Libraria Universitaria Editrice Bologna), pg 382
Edizioni Curci SRL, pg 383
Edizioni la Scala, pg 387
EDT Edizioni di Torino, pg 387
Giulio Einaudi Editore SpA, pg 387
Elle Di Ci - Libreria Dottrina Cristiana, pg 388
ERGA SNC di Carla Ottino Merli & C (Edizioni Realizzazioni Grafiche - Artigiana), pg 388
Edizioni Europa, pg 388
Arnaldo Forni Editore SRL, pg 389
Adriano Gallina Editore sas, pg 389
Ernesto Gremese Editore SRL, pg 391
Gremese International Srl, pg 391
Il Saggiatore, pg 393
Editoriale Jaca Book SpA, pg 394
Kaos Edizioni SRL, pg 395
Letture Mensile di Informazione Culturale, Letteratura e Spettacolo, pg 395
LIM Editrice SRL, pg 396
Longanesi & C, pg 396
Angelo Longo Editore, pg 396
Tommaso Marotta Editore Srl, pg 398
mnemes - Alfieri & Ranieri Publishing, pg 399
Arnoldo Mondadori Editore SpA, pg 399
Franco Muzzio & C Editore SpA, pg 400
Leo S Olschki, pg 402
Pagano Editore, pg 402
Paideia Editrice, pg 402
Palatina Editrice, pg 402
Passigli Editori srl, pg 403
Pizzicato Edizioni Musicali, pg 403
RCS Libri SpA, pg 405
RCS Rizzoli Libri SpA, pg 405
G e C Ricordi SpA, pg 405
Rugginenti Editore, pg 406
Rusconi Libri Srl, pg 406
Edizioni San Paolo SRL, pg 407
Edizioni Scientifiche Italiane, pg 407
SEMAR Publishers SRL, pg 407
Spirali Edizioni, pg 408
Stampa Alternativa - Nuovi Equilibri, pg 409
Gruppo Editoriale Le Stelle SpA, pg 409
Edizioni Studio Tesi SRL, pg 409
Turris, pg 410
Edizioni Ubulibri SAS, pg 410
UT Orpheus Edizioni, pg 411
UTET (Unione Tipografico-Editrice Torinese), pg 411
Voce della Bibbia, pg 412
Casa Musicale G Zanibon SRL, pg 412

Jamaica
Kingston Publishers Ltd, pg 413

Japan
Hakusui-Sha Co Ltd, pg 417
Hoikusha Publishing Co Ltd, pg 417
Kosei Publishing Co Ltd, pg 420
Nippon Hoso Shuppan Kyokai (NHK Publishing), pg 422
Ongaku No Tomo Sha Corporation, pg 423
Seibido Shuppan Company Ltd, pg 424
Shakai Shiso-Sha, pg 425

Kenya
Action Publishers, pg 430
Heinemann Kenya Limited (EAEP), pg 431
Kenway Publications Ltd, pg 432
Lake Publishers & Enterprises Ltd, pg 432

Republic of Korea
Chung Rim Publishing Co Ltd, pg 435
Youl Hwa Dang Publisher, pg 436
Ewha Womans University Press, pg 436
Samho Music Publishing Co, pg 440
Se-Kwang Music Publishing Co, pg 440
Yeha Publishing Co Ltd, pg 441

Laos People's Democratic Republic
Lao-phanit, pg 441

Latvia
Preses Nams, pg 442

Liechtenstein
Saendig Reprint Verlag, Hans-Rainer Wohlwend, pg 445

Lithuania
Svietimo ir mokslo ministerijos Leidybos centras, pg 446

Luxembourg
Editions Emile Borschette, pg 447
Eiffes Romain, pg 447
Op der Lay, pg 447
Varkki Verghese, pg 448

The Former Yugoslav Republic of Macedonia
Ktitor, pg 449

Mexico
Centro de Estudios Mexicanos y Centroamericanos, pg 458
Janibi Editores SA de CV, pg 462
Editorial Jilguero, SA de CV, pg 462
Ediciones Libra, SA de CV, pg 463
Instituto Nacional de Antropologia e Historia, pg 464
Universidad Nacional Autonoma de Mexico (National University of Mexico), pg 467
Universidad Veracruzana Direccion General Editorial y de Publicaciones, pg 468
Javier Vergara Editor SA de CV, pg 468

Republic of Moldova
Editura Hyperion, pg 468

Monaco
Editions de l'Oiseau-Lyre SAM, pg 469

Morocco
Editions Eddif Maroc, pg 469

Nepal
International Standards Books & Periodicals (P) Ltd, pg 471

Netherlands
Bosch & Keuning, pg 474
BZZTOH Publishers, pg 475
East-West Publications Fonds BV, pg 476
Uitgeverij Heuff Nieuwkoop, pg 478
Uitgevery International Theatre & Film Books, pg 479
Swets & Zeitlinger Publishers, pg 485
Uitgeverij De Toorts, pg 485
Uniepers BV, pg 486

SUBJECT INDEX

BOOK

New Zealand
Aoraki Press Ltd, pg 488
Barkfire Press, pg 488

Nigeria
Ilesanmi Press (Educational Publishers) Ltd, pg 499

Norway
J W Eides Forlag A/S, pg 503
Gyldendal Norsk Forlag A/S, pg 503

Philippines
National Book Store Inc, pg 514
University of the Philippines Press, pg 515

Poland
Polskie Wydawnictwo Muzyczne, pg 518

Portugal
Biblioteca Geral da Universidade de Coimbra, pg 523
Constancia Editores, SA, pg 524
Edicoes Cosmos, pg 524
Edicoes 70, Lda, pg 524
Publicacoes Europa-America Lda, pg 524
Editorial Franciscana, pg 525
Impala, pg 525
Latina Livraria, pg 526
Meriberica/Liber, pg 527
Musicoteca Lda, pg 527
Editora Pergaminho Lda, pg 528
Talento, pg 529

Puerto Rico
Instituto de Cultura Puertorriquena, pg 530
Publicaciones Voz de Gracia, pg 531

Romania
Editure Ion Creanga, pg 532
Editura Meridiane, pg 534
Editura Muzicala, pg 534

Russian Federation
Izdatelstvo Khudozhestvennaya Literatura, pg 539
Izdatelskii Dom Kompozitor, pg 539
Izdatelstvo Muzyka, pg 540

Slovakia
Opus Records & Publishing House, pg 550
Slovenske pedagogicke nakladateistvo, pg 550

Slovenia
Zalozba Obzorja d d Maribor, pg 552

South Africa
Educum Publishers Ltd, pg 554
Human & Rousseau (Pty) Ltd, pg 555
Ravan Press (Pty) Ltd, pg 558

Spain
Acento Editorial, pg 561
Alianza Editorial SA, pg 562
Altea, Taurus, Alfaguara SA, pg 563
Arambol, SL, pg 563
Biblioteca de Catalunya, pg 565
Antoni Bosch Editor SA, pg 565
Editorial Casals SA, pg 566
Ediciones Catedra SA, pg 566
Celeste Ediciones, pg 567
Comunidad Autonoma de Madrid, Servicio de Documentacion y Publicaciones, pg 568
Dinsic Publicacions Musicals, pg 570
Edicions del Drac SA, pg 570
Ediciones Ebenezer, pg 571
Editorial Fundamentos, pg 575
Iberico Europea de Ediciones SA, pg 577
Idea Books, SA, pg 578
Institucion Fernando el Catolico de la Excma Diputacion de Zaragoza, pg 578
Ediciones Jucar, pg 579
Loguez Ediciones, pg 580
Antonio Machado, SA, pg 580
Mandala Ediciones, pg 581
La Mascara, SL Editorial, pg 581
Editorial la Muralla SA, pg 583
Editorial Musica Moderna, pg 583
Opera Tres Ediciones Musicales, pg 585
El Paisaje Editorial, pg 585
Editorial El Perpetuo Socorro, pg 586
Pre-Textos, pg 587
Editora Regional de Murcia - ERM, pg 588
Ediciones Rialp SA, pg 589
Ediciones Seyer, pg 590
Edicions 62, pg 591
Axel Springer Publicaciones, pg 591
Universidad de Granada, pg 594
Editorial Verbum SL, pg 595
Javier Vergara Editor SA, pg 595

Sri Lanka
J K Publications, pg 597
Lake House Investments Ltd, pg 597

Sweden
Akademiforlaget Goteborgslitteratur, pg 600
Alfabeta Bokforlag AB, pg 600
SK-Gehrmans Musikforlag AB, pg 602
Hans Richter Laromedel, pg 604
Verbum Foerlag AB, pg 607

Switzerland
Editions L'Age d'Homme - La Cite, pg 608
Arche Verlag AG, Raabe und Vitali, pg 608
Armenia Editions, pg 608
Editions de la Baconniere SA, pg 609
Barenreiter Verlag Basel AG, pg 609
Benziger Verlag AG, pg 609
Werner Classen Verlag, pg 611
Maurice et Pierre Foetisch SA, pg 614
Georg Editeur SA, pg 614
Hug & Co, pg 616
Edition Kunzelmann GmbH, pg 617
Lia rumantscha, pg 618
Librairie-Editions J Marguerat, pg 618
Editions Minkoff, pg 619
Edition Olms AG, pg 620
Ostschweiz Druck und Verlag, pg 621
Editions Payot Lausanne, pg 621
Editions Musicales de la Schola Cantorum, pg 624
Editions 24 Heures, pg 626
Der Universitatsverlag Freiburg, pg 626
Verlagsbuchhandling AG, pg 626

Taiwan, Province of China
Chung Hwa Book Co Ltd, pg 629

Thailand
Thai Watana Panich Co, Ltd, pg 636

Trinidad & Tobago
Jett Samm Publishing Ltd, pg 637

Tunisia
Academie Tunisienne des Sciences, des Lettres et des Arts Beit El Hekma, pg 637

Turkey
Arkadas Ltd, pg 639
Inkilap Publishers Ltd, pg 640
Kok Yayincilik, pg 640
Kubbealti Akademisi Kultur ve Sasat Vakfi, pg 640
Pan Yayincilik, pg 640

Ukraine
Osvita, pg 643

United Kingdom
Amber Lane Press Ltd, pg 646
Appletree Press Ltd, pg 648
Art Books International Ltd, pg 649
Ashgate Publishing Ltd, pg 649
Barn Dance Publications Ltd, pg 652
BCA, pg 653
Belitha Press Ltd, pg 653
A & C Black Publishers Ltd, pg 655
Black Spring Press Ltd, pg 655
Blackstaff Press, pg 655
Blandford Publishing Ltd, pg 656
Bloomsbury Publishing PLC, pg 656
Boosey & Hawkes Music Publishers Ltd, pg 657
Marion Boyars Publishers Ltd, pg 658
The Brown Reference Group PLC, pg 660
Calder Publications Ltd, pg 662
Cambridge University Press, pg 662
Capall Bann Publishing, pg 663
Carlton Publishing Group, pg 664
Cassell & Co, pg 664
Chadwyck-Healey Ltd, pg 666
Coachwise Ltd, pg 668
Curiad, pg 672
Dance Books Ltd, The Old Bakery, pg 673
Denor Press, pg 675
Andre Deutsch Ltd, pg 675
Dorling Kindersley Ltd, pg 676
East-West Publications (UK) Ltd, pg 677
Edinburgh University Press Ltd, pg 677
Element Books Ltd, pg 678
The Eurospan Group, pg 680
Evans Brothers Ltd, pg 680
Faber & Faber Ltd, pg 681
Facts On File, pg 681
Gairm Publications, pg 685
Gale Research, pg 685
Golden Cockerel Press Ltd, pg 688
Gollancz/Witherby, pg 688
Gresham Books Ltd, pg 690
Guinness Publishing Ltd, pg 690
Robert Hale Ltd, pg 691
Hamish Hamilton Ltd, pg 691
Hamlyn, pg 691
Heartland Publishing Ltd, pg 694
Helicon Publishing Ltd, pg 694
The Islamic Texts Society, pg 701
Kahn & Averill, pg 703
Lang Syne Publishers Ltd, pg 706
Y Lolfa Cyf, pg 708
Macmillan Reference Ltd, pg 710
Peter Marcan Publications, pg 711
Marcham Books, pg 711
Adam Matthew Publications, pg 712
McCrimmon Publishing Co Ltd, pg 712
Media Research Publishing Ltd, pg 712
Mercat Press, pg 713
Methuen Publishing Ltd, pg 714
Mirabel Books Ltd, pg 715
Moorley's Print & Publishing Ltd, pg 715
Muze UK Ltd, pg 716
Nelson Thornes Ltd, pg 718
Northcote House Publishers Ltd, pg 719
W W Norton & Company Ltd, pg 720
Novello & Co Ltd, pg 720
Octopus Publishing Group, pg 720
Oliver Books Ltd, pg 721
Omnibus Press, pg 721
Peter Owen Ltd, pg 722
Oxford University Press, pg 723
Parapress Ltd, pg 724
PC Publishing, pg 725
Pearson Education, pg 725
Pearson Education Europe, Mideast & Africa, pg 725
Peartree Publications, pg 725
Plexus Publishing Ltd, pg 728
Polygon, pg 729
PRC Publishing Ltd, pg 730
ProQuest Information & Learning, pg 731
Quartet Books Ltd, pg 731
Quintet Publishing Ltd, pg 732
Retail Entertainment Data Publishing Ltd, pg 735
Rough Guides Ltd, pg 735
Salvationist Publishing & Supplies Ltd, pg 738
SchoolPlay Productions Ltd, pg 739
Seren, pg 740
Serpent's Tail Ltd, pg 740
Shire Publications Ltd, pg 741
Sidgwick & Jackson Ltd, pg 742
Sigma Press, pg 742
Southgate Publishers, pg 743
Souvenir Press Ltd, pg 743
Stainer & Bell Ltd, pg 745
Rudolf Steiner Press, pg 745
Thames & Hudson Ltd, pg 748
Timber Press Inc, pg 749
Unicorn Books, pg 751
Virgin Publishing Ltd, pg 753
Ward Lock Educational Co Ltd, pg 754
Wild Goose Publications, pg 756
Wilmington Business Information Ltd, pg 756
Windsor Books International, pg 757
The Women's Press Ltd, pg 758
World Microfilms Publications Ltd, pg 758
Yale University Press London, pg 759

Uruguay
Editorial Arca SRL, pg 760
A Monteverde y Cia SA, pg 760

PUBLISHERS

Venezuela
Alfadil Ediciones, pg 761
Monte Avila Editores Latinoamericana CA, pg 762

Zambia
Aafzam Ltd, pg 766

MYSTERIES

Albania
NL SH, pg 1

Argentina
Emece Editores SA, pg 5

Australia
Bandicoot Books, pg 14
Gnostic Editions, pg 24
Spacevision Publishing, pg 42
Unity Press, pg 46
Wakefield Press Pty Ltd, pg 47

Austria
Aarachne Verlag, pg 49
Franz Deuticke Verlagsges mbH, pg 51
Haymon-Verlag GesmbH, pg 52
oebv & hpt Verlagsgesellschaft mbH & Co KG, pg 56

Azerbaijan
Sada, Literaturno-Izdatel'skij Centr, pg 61

Belgium
Claude Lefrancq Editeur, pg 71
Scissors Books, pg 74

Brazil
Ediouro Publicacoes, SA, pg 81
Editora Globo SA, pg 84
Editora Marco Zero Ltda, pg 87
Editora Mercuryo Ltda, pg 88
Editora Nova Fronteira SA, pg 88
Livraria Pioneira Editora/Enio Matheus Guazzelli e Cia Ltd, pg 89
Editora Scipione Ltda, pg 91
Thex Editora e Distribuidora Ltda, pg 92

Bulgaria
Abagar Pablioing, pg 94
Kralica MAB, pg 96
Litera Prima, pg 96
Trud - Izd kasta, pg 98
Zunica, pg 98

Czech Republic
Knihovna A Tiskarna Pro Nevidome, pg 125
Josef Lukasik A Spol, pg 125
Nakladatelstvi Svoboda, pg 126
Nase vojsko, nakladatelstvi a knizni obchod, pg 126
Svoboda Servis GmbH, pg 128

Denmark
Cicero-Chr Erichsens, pg 131
Forum Publishers, pg 132
Forlaget Hovedland, pg 133
Forlaget Modtryk AMBA, pg 133

Egypt (Arab Republic of Egypt)
Dar El Shorouk, pg 138
Dar El Shorouk Publishing & Distributing House, pg 138

France
Editions A M Metailie, pg 145
Actes Graphiques, pg 145
Editions de l'Aube, pg 149
Editions Baleine, pg 149
Editions Belfond, pg 150
Bragelonne, pg 151
Le Cherche Midi Editeur, pg 154
Climats, pg 155
Culture et Bibliotheque pour Tous, pg 157
Dargaud, pg 157
Georges-Charles Demay, pg 158
Editions Gerard de Villiers, pg 166
Hemma Joven, SA, pg 168
Librairie des Champs-Elysees, Groupe Hachette, pg 173
Editions Payot & Rivages, pg 179
Presses de la Cite, pg 180
10/18, pg 187
Union Generale d'Editions, pg 188
La Vague Verte, pg 188

French Polynesia
Scoop/Au Vent des Iles, pg 190

Germany
Altberliner Verlag GmbH, pg 193
Aufbau-Verlag GmbH, pg 196
Catia Monser Eggcup-Verlag, pg 209
Dagmar Dreves Verlag, pg 212
Droemersche Verlagsanstalt Th Knaur Nachfolger GmbH & Co, pg 218
Econ Taschenbuchverlag, pg 220
Egmont vgs verlagsgesellschaft mbH, pg 221
Eichborn AG, pg 222
Elefanten Press Verlag GmbH, pg 222
Emons Verlag, pg 222
Europa Verlag GmbH, pg 224
Fabylon-Verlag, pg 226
Grafit Verlag GmbH, pg 234
Wilhelm Heyne Verlag, pg 240
KBV-Verlags-und Mediengesellschaft mbH, pg 248
Knowledge Media International, pg 251
Dr Gisela Lermann, pg 257
Logos-Verlag Literatur & Layout GmbH, pg 258
Karl-Heinz Metz, pg 263
Moby Dick Verlag, pg 264
Gunter Narr Verlag, pg 266
Neuthor - Verlag, pg 268
C W Niemeyer Buchverlage GmbH, pg 268
Propylaeen Verlag, Zweigniederlassung Berlin der Ullstein Buchverlage GmbH, pg 275
Pulp Master Frank Nowatzki Verlag, pg 276
Quintessenz Verlags-GmbH, pg 276
Ruetten & Loening Berlin GmbH, pg 281
Buchverlag Andrea Schmitz, pg 284
Treves Editions Verein Zur Foerderung der Kuenstlerischen Taetigkeiten, pg 295
Verlag und Studio fuer Hoerbuchproduktionen, pg 298

SUBJECT INDEX

Ghana
World Literature Project, pg 308

Greece
Exandas Publishers, pg 310
Hestia-I D Hestia-Kollaros & Co Corporation, pg 311
Ed Nea Acropolis, pg 313
Orfanidis Publications, pg 314

Hong Kong
Publications (Holdings) Ltd, pg 321

Hungary
Ifjusagi Lap-eskonyvkiado Vallalat, pg 324
Szabad Ter Kiado, pg 326

Iceland
Bokaforlag Birtingur, pg 327
Frjals fjolmiolun hf-Urvalsbaekur, pg 327
Frodi Ltd, pg 328

India
Ananda Publishers Pvt Ltd, pg 330
Reliance Publishing House, pg 347
Scientific Book Agency, pg 349
Theosophical Publishing House, pg 351

Indonesia
Gramedia, pg 355

Israel
Bitan Publishers Ltd, pg 365
Pitspopany Press, pg 371

Italy
Adelphi Edizioni SpA, pg 374
Horus, pg 393
L'Airone Editrice, pg 395
Levante, pg 395
Arnoldo Mondadori Editore SpA, pg 399
Edizioni Segno SRL, pg 407
Sonzogno, pg 408

Japan
Hayakawa Publishing Inc, pg 417
Nippon Hoso Shuppan Kyokai (NHK Publishing), pg 422
Shincho-Sha Co Ltd, pg 425
Tokyo Sogensha Co Ltd, pg 428

Republic of Korea
Gim-Yeong Co, pg 436
Koreaone Press Inc, pg 438
O Neul Publishing Co, pg 439
Woong Jin Publishing Co Ltd, pg 440

The Former Yugoslav Republic of Macedonia
Zumpres Publishing Firm, pg 449

Monaco
Les Editions du Rocher, pg 469

Morocco
Editions Le Fennec, pg 470

Netherlands
De Boekerij BV, pg 474
A W Bruna Uitgevers BV, pg 475
BZZTOH Publishers, pg 475

Uitgeverij Conserve, pg 475
Uitgeverij Het Spectrum BV, pg 484

New Zealand
Cape Catley, pg 489
River Press, pg 495

Norway
Fono Forlag, pg 503
Hilt & Hansteen A/S, pg 504

Pakistan
Jang Publishers, pg 507

Philippines
Anvil Publishing Inc, pg 512
Books for Pleasure Inc, pg 512

Poland
Wydawnictwo Dolnoslaskie, pg 516
Iskry - Publishing House Ltd spotka zoo, pg 517
Videograf II Sp z o o Zaklad Poracy Chronionej, pg 520

Portugal
Planeta Editora, LDA, pg 528
Editorial Presenca, pg 528

Romania
Editura Excelsior, pg 533
Editura Militara, pg 534
Editura Niculescu, pg 534
RAO International Publishing Co, pg 535
Saeculum IO, pg 535
Vestala Verlag, pg 536

Russian Federation
Armada Publishing House, pg 537
CentrePolygraph Traders & Publishers Co, pg 537

Slovakia
Vydavatelstvo Obzor, pg 550

Spain
Edicions del Drac SA, pg 570
Fundacion Rosacruz, pg 575
Munoz Moya Editor, pg 583
Ediciones Urano, SA, pg 595

Switzerland
AT Verlag, pg 608
Cockatoo Press (Schweiz), Thailand-Publikationen, pg 611
Diogenes Verlag AG, pg 612
Govinda-Verlag, pg 615
Haffmans Verlag AG, pg 615
Origo Verlag, pg 621
Rhein-Trio, Edition/Editions du Fou, pg 623

Taiwan, Province of China
Lin Pai Press Company Ltd, pg 631

Tunisia
Alyssa Editions, pg 637

United Kingdom
BBC Audiobooks, pg 652
BCA, pg 653
Blorenge Books, pg 656
Capall Bann Publishing, pg 663
Gateway Books, pg 686
Gembooks, pg 686

SUBJECT INDEX

Gollancz/Witherby, pg 688
HarperCollins Publishers, pg 692
Hodder & Stoughton General, pg 696
Isis Publishing Ltd, pg 701
Lang Syne Publishers Ltd, pg 706
Macmillan Audio Books, pg 710
Octopus Publishing Group, pg 720
Oldcastle Books Ltd, pg 720
Orion Publishing Group Ltd, pg 722
Quintet Publishing Ltd, pg 732
The Reader's Digest Association Ltd, pg 733
Serpent's Tail Ltd, pg 740
Time Warner Books UK, pg 749
Ulverscroft Large Print Books Ltd, pg 751
The Windrush Press Ltd, pg 757

Yugoslavia
Alfa-Narodna Knjiga, pg 764

MYTHOLOGY

Chile
Arrayan Editores, pg 99

Germany
Verlag Die Blaue Eule, pg 204

Greece
Sigma, pg 315

India
Reliance Publishing House, pg 347

Spain
Alta Fulla Editorial, pg 563

United Kingdom
The Harvill Press Ltd, pg 693

NATIVE AMERICAN STUDIES

Albania
NL SH, pg 1

Belgium
Brepols Publishers NV, pg 65

Bulgaria
Sluntse Publishing House, pg 98

Germany
Arun-Verlag, pg 195

Italy
Editoriale Jaca Book SpA, pg 394

Mexico
El Colegio de Michoacan A C, pg 460
Instituto Nacional de Antropologia e Historia, pg 464

New Zealand
Barkfire Press, pg 488

NATURAL HISTORY

Australia
Australian Marine Conservation Society Inc (AMCS), pg 14
Robert Berthold Photography, pg 14
Bloomings Books, pg 15
Robert Brown & Associates Australia Pty Ltd, pg 16
Crawford House Publishing, pg 19
CSIRO Publishing (Commonwealth Scientific & Industrial Research Organisation), pg 19
Enterprise Publications, pg 22
Envirobook, pg 22
Greater Glider Productions Australia Pty Ltd, pg 24
Illert Publications, pg 27
Institute of Aboriginal Development (IAD Press), pg 28
Kangaroo Press, pg 29
Laurel Press, pg 29
Magabala Books Aboriginal Corporation, pg 31
Melbourne University Press, pg 33
Mulavon Press Pty Ltd, pg 34
Oz Publishing Co Pty Ltd, pg 36
Pandani Press, pg 37
Queen Victoria Museum & Art Gallery Publications, pg 39
Simon & Schuster Australia Pty Ltd, pg 42
State Library of NSW Press, pg 43
Terania Rainforest Publishing, pg 44
Thames & Hudson (Australia) Pty Ltd, pg 44
Three Sisters Publications Pty Ltd, pg 44
University of New South Wales Press Ltd, pg 46
University of Western Australia Press, pg 46

Austria
Ferdinand Berger und Sohne, pg 51
Thomas Mlakar Verlag, pg 55
Verlag fuer Sammler, pg 58
Dr A Schendl GmbH und Co KG, pg 58
Herbert Weishaupt Verlag, pg 60

Azerbaijan
Sada, Literaturno-Izdatel'skij Centr, pg 61

Belarus
Belaruskaya Encyklapedyya, pg 63

Belgium
SA Artis-Historia, pg 64
Dessain - Departement de De Boeck & Larcier SA, pg 68

Botswana
The Botswana Society, pg 77

Brazil
Libreria Editora Ltda, pg 86
Editora Nova Fronteira SA, pg 88

Bulgaria
Eurasia Academic Publishers, pg 95
Heron Press Publishing House, pg 96
Litera Prima, pg 96
Pensoft Publishers, pg 97

China
Education Science Publishing House, pg 105
Fudan University Press, pg 105
Science Press, pg 108

Costa Rica
Centro Agronomico Tropical de Investigacion y Ensenanza (CATIE), pg 115
Editorial de la Universidad de Costa Rica, pg 117

Croatia
Matica hrvatska, pg 119

Czech Republic
Aventinum Nakladatelstvi, pg 123
Granit SRO, pg 124
Narodni Muzeum, pg 126

Denmark
GEC Gads Forlag Aktieselskab af 1994, pg 132

Estonia
Tuum, pg 141

Fiji
University of the South Pacific, pg 141

France
L'Amitie par le Livre, pg 147
ATP - Packager, pg 149
Autrement Editions, pg 149
Editions Coprur, pg 156
Editions Jean Paul Gisserot, pg 166
Librairie Scientifique et Technique Albert Blanchard, pg 173
Service des Publications Scientifiques du Museum National d'Histoire Naturelle, pg 184
Sofradif Editions Philippe Auzou, pg 185
La Vague Verte, pg 188

French Polynesia
Haere Po No Tahiti, pg 190

Germany
Alouette Verlag, pg 193
AOL-Verlag Frohmut Menze, pg 194
Blackwell Wissenschafts-Verlag GmbH, pg 203
BLV Verlagsgesellschaft mbH, pg 204
Hans Christians Druckerei und Verlag GmbH & Co, pg 210
Verlag Harri Deutsch, pg 213
Egmont vgs verlagsgesellschaft mbH, pg 221
Finken Verlag GmbH, pg 228
Graefe und Unzer Verlag GmbH, pg 233
Knowledge Media International, pg 251
Franckh-Kosmos Verlags-GmbH & Co, pg 252
Verlag Waldemar Kramer, pg 253
Landbuch-Verlagsgesellschaft mbH, pg 255
Johannes Loriz Verlag der Kooperative Duernau, pg 259
Mergus Verlag GmbH Hans A Baensch, pg 263

Verlag Stephanie Naglschmid, pg 266
Verlag Natur & Wissenschaft Harro Hieronimus & Dr Jurgen Schmidt, pg 266
Neumann Verlag, pg 268
Palazzi Verlag GmbH, pg 271
Renate Schenk Verlag, pg 283
Stapp Verlag Wolfgang Stapp, pg 289
Systhema Verlag GmbH, pg 291
Guenter Albert Ulmer Verlag, pg 295
VS Verlagshaus Stuttgart GmbH, pg 299

Greece
Hestia-I D Hestia-Kollaros & Co Corporation, pg 311

Hong Kong
Hong Kong University Press, pg 320
Steve Lu Publishing Ltd, pg 320

Hungary
Kossuth Kiado RT, pg 325
Tajak Korok Muzeumok Egyesuelet, pg 327

Iceland
Fjolvi, pg 327
Hid Islenzka Bokmenntafelag, pg 328

India
APH Publishing Corp, pg 331
Asian Educational Services, pg 331
Brijbasi Printers Pvt Ltd, pg 334
BSMPS - M/s Bishen Singh Mahendra Pal Singh, pg 334
Cosmo Publications, pg 335
Daya Publishing House, pg 336
Dolphin Publications, pg 336
Gyan Publishing House, pg 338
Indus Publishing Co, pg 339
International Book Distributors, pg 340
Minerva Associates (Publications) Pvt Ltd, pg 342
Oxford & IBH Publishing Co Pvt Ltd, pg 345
Oxford University Press, pg 345
Scientific Book Agency, pg 349
Scientific Publishers India, pg 349
Today & Tomorrow's Printers & Publishers, pg 352

Indonesia
Yayasan Obor Indonesia, pg 357

Ireland
The Collins Press, pg 359
Flyleaf Press, pg 360
The Lilliput Press Ltd, pg 362
Roberts Rinehart Publishers, pg 363
Sean Ros Press, pg 364
Tir Eolas, pg 364

Israel
Hakibbutz Hameuchad Publishing House Ltd, pg 368

Italy
Alberti Libraio Editore, pg 375
Edizioni Della Torre di Salvatore Fozzi & C SAS, pg 384
Editoriale Jaca Book SpA, pg 394
Kompass Fleischmann, pg 395

PUBLISHERS

Leo S Olschki, pg 402
Edizioni Librarie Siciliane, pg 408
Nicola Teti e C Editore SRL, pg 409
Edizioni Zara, pg 412

Jamaica
Institute of Jamaica Publications, pg 413
University of the West Indies Press, pg 414

Japan
Bun-ichi Sogo Shuppan, pg 415
Hoikusha Publishing Co Ltd, pg 417
Kyoritsu Shuppan Co Ltd, pg 420

Kenya
Kenway Publications Ltd, pg 432

Democratic People's Republic of Korea
Korea Science and Encyclopedia Publishing House, pg 434

Luxembourg
Service Central des Imprimes et des Fournitures de Bureau de l'Etat, pg 448

Malaysia
Tropical Press Sdn Bhd, pg 455

Malta
The University of Malta Publications Section, pg 456

Mexico
Editorial Minutiae Mexicana SA, pg 464

Morocco
Association de la Recherche Historique et Sociale, pg 469

Namibia
Desert Research Foundation of Namibia (DRFN), pg 471

Nepal
International Standards Books & Periodicals (P) Ltd, pg 471

Netherlands
Backhuys Publishers BV, pg 473
A A Balkema, pg 473
Uniepers BV, pg 486

New Zealand
Barkfire Press, pg 488
David Bateman Ltd, pg 488
Bush Press Communications Ltd, pg 489
Canterbury University Press, pg 489
Craig Potton Publishing, pg 490
Exisle Publishing Ltd, pg 491
Godwit Publishing Ltd, pg 491
HarperCollins Publishers (New Zealand) Ltd, pg 491
Landcare Research NZ, pg 492
Longacre Press, pg 493
Nestegg Books, pg 493
Otago Heritage Books, pg 494
Oxford University Press, pg 494
Reed Publishing (NZ) Ltd, pg 495
Shearwater Associates Ltd, pg 495
Shoal Bay Press Ltd, pg 495

University of Otago Press, pg 496
Viking Sevenseas NZ Ltd, pg 496

Philippines
National Museum of the Philippines, pg 514

Portugal
Constancia Editores, SA, pg 524
Gradiva-Publicacnoes Lda, pg 525

Romania
Editura Niculescu, pg 534

Russian Federation
Nauka Publishers, pg 540

Singapore
Archipelago Press, pg 545

South Africa
Acorn Books, pg 552
The Brenthurst Press (Pty) Ltd, pg 553
Educum Publishers Ltd, pg 554
Fernwood Press (Pty) Ltd, pg 554
Russel Friedman Books, pg 554
Human & Rousseau (Pty) Ltd, pg 555
National Botanical Institute, pg 557
New Africa Books (Pty) Ltd, pg 557
Oceanographic Research Institute, pg 558
Southern Book Publishers (Pty) Ltd, pg 559
Struik Publishers (Pty) Ltd, pg 559
University of Natal Press, pg 560
Witwatersrand University Press, pg 560

Spain
Editorial Acribia SA, pg 561
Cabildo Insular de Gran Canaria Departamento de Ediciones, pg 566
Carroggio SA de Ediciones, pg 566
Comunidad Autonoma de Madrid, Servicio de Documentacion y Publicaciones, pg 568
Ediciones Doce Calles SL, pg 570
Editorial Incafo SA, pg 578
Lynx Edicions, pg 580
Editorial Moll SL, pg 582

Sri Lanka
Department of National Museums, pg 597

Switzerland
Kinderbuchverlag Luzern, pg 617
Sabe AG Verlagsinstitut, pg 623
Strom-Verlag Luzern, pg 625
Terra Grischuna Verlag Buch-und Zeitschriftenverlag, pg 625

Syrian Arab Republic
Damascus University Press, pg 628

Thailand
New Generation Publishing Co Ltd, pg 635

Tunisia
Les Editions de l'Arbre, pg 638

Uganda
T & E Publishers, pg 642

Ukraine
Naukova Dumka Publishers, pg 643

United Arab Emirates
Motivate Publishing, pg 644

United Kingdom
Andromeda Oxford Ltd, pg 647
Colin Baxter Photography Ltd, pg 652
BBC Worldwide Publishers, pg 653
BCA, pg 653
Beaver Publishing Ltd, pg 653
Belitha Press Ltd, pg 653
A & C Black Publishers Ltd, pg 655
Blackstaff Press, pg 655
Blandford Publishing Ltd, pg 656
Bloomsbury Publishing PLC, pg 656
The Brown Reference Group PLC, pg 660
Cameron & Hollis, pg 663
Cardinal Publishing Ltd, pg 663
Carlton Publishing Group, pg 664
Cassell & Co, pg 664
Castlemead Publications, pg 665
Kyle Cathie Ltd, pg 665
E W Classey Ltd, pg 668
The Crowood Press Ltd, pg 672
Christopher Davies Publishers Ltd, pg 674
Edinburgh University Press Ltd, pg 677
Eurobook Ltd, pg 679
The Eurospan Group, pg 680
Facts On File, pg 681
Forth Naturalist & Historian, pg 683
Genesis Publications Ltd, pg 686
Gollancz/Witherby, pg 688
Grange Books PLC, pg 689
Hamlyn, pg 691
Harley Books, pg 692
HarperCollins Publishers, pg 692
Harvard University Press, pg 692
The Harvill Press Ltd, pg 693
Christopher Helm (Publishers) Ltd, pg 694
Helm Information Ltd, pg 694
Hodder & Stoughton Educational, pg 696
Intercept Ltd, pg 700
International Bee Research Association, pg 701
The Islamic Texts Society, pg 701
The Kenilworth Press Ltd, pg 704
Ladybird Books, pg 705
Luath Press Ltd, pg 709
The Lutterworth Press, pg 709
Macmillan Audio Books, pg 710
Maney Publishing, pg 711
Marshall Editions Ltd, pg 712
Mercat Press, pg 713
Micelle Press, pg 714
Mirabel Books Ltd, pg 715
New Holland Publishers (UK) Ltd, pg 718
New Leaf Books Ltd, pg 719
NMS Publishing Ltd, pg 719
Octopus Publishing Group, pg 720
The Orkney Press Ltd, pg 722
Orpheus Books Ltd, pg 722
Packard Publishing Ltd, pg 723
Pearson Education, pg 725
T & AD Poyser Ltd, pg 730
PRC Publishing Ltd, pg 730
Quarto Publishing plc, pg 731
Quartz Editions, pg 732

SUBJECT INDEX

Quintet Publishing Ltd, pg 732
The Richmond Publishing Co Ltd, pg 735
Roadmaster Publishing, pg 735
Sainsbury Publishing Ltd, pg 737
Salamander Books Ltd, pg 738
The Salariya Book Co Ltd, pg 738
Savitri Books, pg 738
Shire Publications Ltd, pg 741
Stacey International, pg 745
Stobart Davies Ltd, pg 745
Telegraph Books, pg 748
Tern Press, pg 748
Two-Can Publishing Ltd, pg 750
Whittet Books Ltd, pg 756
Whittles Publishing, pg 756
Wordwright Publishing, pg 758
Yale University Press London, pg 759

Uruguay
A Monteverde y Cia SA, pg 760

Viet Nam
Science & Technics Publishing House, pg 763

Zambia
Zambian Ornithological Society, pg 767

Zimbabwe
Longman Zimbabwe (Pvt) Ltd, pg 768
Mambo Press, pg 768
Zimbabwe Publishing House (Pvt) Ltd, pg 769

NONFICTION (GENERAL)

Albania
Fan Noli Verlag Rexhep Hida, pg 1
NL SH, pg 1

Algeria
Enterprise Nationale du Livre (ENAL), pg 2

Argentina
Editorial Abril SA, pg 2
Ada Korn Editora SA, pg 3
Editorial Argentina Plaza y Janes SA, pg 3
Editorial Atlantida SA, pg 3
Beas Ediciones SRL, pg 4
Beatriz Viterbo Editora, pg 4
Bonum Editorial SACI, pg 4
Cesarini Hermanos, pg 4
Critica, pg 4
Emece Editores SA, pg 5
Editorial Planeta Argentina SAIC, pg 8
Editorial Stella, pg 9
Editorial Sudamericana SA, pg 9
Javier Vergara Editor SA, pg 9

Australia
ABC Books (Australian Broadcasting Corporation), pg 10
Access Press, pg 10
Allen & Unwin Pty Ltd, The Australian Newspaper, Vogel Breads, pg 11
Edward Arnold (Australia) Pty Ltd, pg 12
Assert Publishing, pg 12
Australian Large Print Pty Ltd, pg 14

1035

SUBJECT INDEX

Australian Scholarly Publishing, pg 14
Bernal Publishing, pg 14
Books for Our Times, pg 16
Boolarong Press, pg 16
Boombana Publications, pg 16
Bridge To Peace Publications, pg 16
Coconut Productions, pg 18
Dangaroo Press, pg 20
Deva Wings Publications, pg 20
Emperor Publishing, pg 22
Era Publications, pg 22
Finch Publishing, pg 22
Hale & Iremonger Pty Ltd, pg 24
Geoffrey Hamlyn-Harris, pg 25
Hargreen Publishing Co, pg 25
Hudson Publishing, pg 27
Hyland House Publishing Pty Ltd, pg 27
Institute of Aboriginal Development (IAD Press), pg 28
John Wiley & Sons Australia Ltd, pg 28
Kangaroo Press, pg 29
Life Planning Foundation of Australia, Inc, pg 30
Little Hills Press, pg 30
Little Red Apple Publishing, pg 30
Thomas C Lothian Pty Ltd, pg 30
Magabala Books Aboriginal Corporation, pg 31
Media East Press, pg 33
Melbourne University Press, pg 33
Mulavon Press Pty Ltd, pg 34
Narkaling Inc, pg 34
Navarine Publishing, pg 34
Anne O'Donovan Pty Ltd, pg 35
Omnibus Books, pg 35
Outback Books - CQU Press, pg 36
Pan Macmillan Australia Pty Ltd, pg 36
Penguin Books Australia Ltd, pg 37
Plantagenet Press, pg 38
Quakers Hill Press, pg 39
Random House Australia, pg 40
Ruskin Rowe Press, pg 41
St George Books, pg 41
St Pauls, pg 41
Simon & Schuster Australia Pty Ltd, pg 42
Spectrum Publications, pg 43
Spinifex Press, pg 43
Stafford Books, pg 43
State Library of NSW Press, pg 43
The Text Publishing Company Pty Ltd, pg 44
Tom Publications, pg 45
Transworld Publishers Pty Ltd, pg 45
Troll Books of Australia, pg 45
Turton & Armstrong Publishers Pty Ltd, pg 45
University of New South Wales Press Ltd, pg 46
University of Queensland Press, pg 46
University of Western Australia Press, pg 46
The Useful Publishing Co, pg 46
Vista Publications, pg 47
The Watermark Press, pg 47

Austria

Czernin Verlag, pg 50
Franz Deuticke Verlagsges mbH, pg 51
Development News Ltd, pg 51
Ibera VerlagsgesmbH, pg 53
Kremayr & Scheriau Verlag, pg 54
Merbod Verlag, pg 55
Milena Verlag, pg 55

Niederosterreichisches Pressehaus Druck- und Verlagsgesellschaft mbH, pg 55
oebv & hpt Verlagsgesellschaft mbH & Co KG, pg 56
Oesterreichischer Kunst und Kulturverlag, pg 56
Verlag Orac im Verlag Kremayr & Scheriau, pg 56
Osterreichischer Bundesveilag Ges.mbh, pg 57
Anna Pichler Verlag GmbH, pg 57
Pinguin-Verlag, Pawlowski GmbH, pg 57
Promedia Verlagsges mbH, pg 57
Signum Verlag GmbH & Co KG, pg 58
Suedwind - Buchwelt GmbH, pg 59
Edition Tau u Tau Type Druck Verlags-und Handels GmbH, pg 59
Tyrolia Verlagsanstalt GmbH, pg 59
Verlag Carl Ueberreuter GmbH, pg 59
Dr Otfried Weise Verlag Tabula Smaragdina, pg 60
Herbert Weishaupt Verlag, pg 60
Georg Westermann Verlag GmbH, pg 61
WUV/Facultas Universitaetsverlag, pg 61
Paul Zsolnay Verlag GmbH, pg 61

Bangladesh

Ankur Prakashani, pg 62

Belarus

Interdigets Publishing House, pg 63
Kavaler Publishers, pg 63

Belgium

Altina, pg 64
Editions Chantecler, pg 66
Uitgeverij Clavis, pg 66
EPO Publishers, Printers, Booksellers, pg 68
Ipis VZW (International Peace Information Service), pg 69
Uitgeverij Lannoo NV, pg 70
Editions Racine, pg 73
Roularta Books NV, pg 73

Brazil

Agalma Psicanalise Editora Ltda, pg 78
Livraria Francisco Alves Editora SA, pg 78
Editora Bertrand Brasil Ltda, pg 79
Callis Editora Ltda, pg 80
Editora Campus Ltda, pg 80
Companhia Editora Forense, pg 82
Livraria Martins Fontes Editora Ltda, pg 83
Imago Editora Importacao e Exportacao Ltda, pg 85
Editora Marco Zero Ltda, pg 87
Editora Mercuryo Ltda, pg 88
Editora Nova Fronteira SA, pg 88
Editora Objetiva Ltda, pg 88
Editora Primor Ltda, pg 90
Qualitymark Editora Ltda, pg 90
Distribuidora Record de Servicos de Imprensa SA, pg 90
Editora Scipione Ltda, pg 91

Bulgaria

Aratron, IK, pg 94
Ciela Publishing House, pg 94
Darzhavno Izdatelstvo Zemizdat, pg 95
Hermes Publishing House, pg 95

Heron Press Publishing House, pg 96
Kibea Publishing Co, pg 96
Kolibri Publishing Group, pg 96
MATEX, pg 96
Reporter, pg 97
Sluntse Publishing House, pg 98
Ivan Vazov Publishing House, pg 98
Peyo K Yavorov Publishing House, pg 98

Cameroon

Editions Buma Kor, pg 99
Centre d'Edition et de Production pour l'Enseignement et la Recherche (CEPER), pg 99

Chile

Editorial Cuarto Propio, pg 100
Editora Cuatro Vientos, pg 100
Editorial Texido Ltda, pg 101

China

Beijing Publishing House, pg 102
China Theatre Publishing House, pg 104
CITIC Publishing House, pg 104
Jinan Publishing House, pg 107
Kunlun Publishing House, pg 107
People's Literature Publishing House, pg 108
Xi'an Cartography Publishing House, pg 110

Colombia

Consejo Episcopal Latinoamericano Celam, pg 111

The Democratic Republic of the Congo

Editions Saint Paul-Afrique, pg 115

Costa Rica

Libreria Imprenta y Litografia Lehmann SA, pg 116

Cote d'Ivoire

Centre de Publications Evangeliques, pg 117
Centre d'Edition et de Diffusion Africaines, pg 117
Heritage Publishing Co, pg 118

Croatia

AGM doo, pg 118
Matica hrvatska, pg 119

Czech Republic

Aurora, pg 123
Baronet, pg 123
Brody, pg 123
Erika, pg 124
Nakladatelstvi Josef Hribal, pg 124
Lidove noviny Nakladatelstvi, pg 125
Josef Lukasik A Spol, pg 125
Mlada fronta, pg 126
Nakladatelstvi Svoboda, pg 126
Nase vojsko, nakladatelstvi a knizni obchod, pg 126
NLN, Ltd The Lidove noviny Publishing House, pg 127
Prace, pg 127
Prostor, Ltd, pg 128

Denmark

Atuakkiorfik A/S Det Greenland Publishers, pg 130
Bogan's Forlag, pg 130

Bogfabrikken Fakta ApS, pg 130
Bonniers Specialmagasiner A/S Bogdivisionen, pg 130
Borgens Forlag A/S, pg 130
Carit Andersens Forlag A/S, pg 131
Forlaget Centrum, pg 131
Christian Ejlers' Forlag aps, pg 131
GEC Gads Forlag Aktieselskab af 1994, pg 132
P Haase & Sons Forlag A/S, pg 132
Hekla Forlag, pg 132
Hernovs Forlag, pg 132
Holkenfeldt 3, pg 133
Forlaget Hovedland, pg 133
Forlaget Klematis A/S, pg 133
Lindhardt og Ringhof, pg 133
Forlaget Modtryk AMBA, pg 133
Joergen Paludans Forlag ApS, pg 134
Politisk Revy, pg 134
C A Reitzel A/S, pg 134
J H Schultz Information A/S, pg 135
Spektrum Forlagsaktieselskab, pg 135
Wisby & Wilkens, pg 136
Forlaget Woldike K/S, pg 136

Egypt (Arab Republic of Egypt)

Dar El Shorouk, pg 138
Dar El Shorouk Publishing & Distributing House, pg 138
Dar Al Hilap Publishing Institution, pg 139
Senouhy Publishers, pg 139

Estonia

Estonian Encyclopaedia Publishers Ltd, pg 140
Ilmamaa, pg 140
Olion Publishers, pg 140
Sinisukk, pg 140

Finland

AB Svenska Laromedel-Editum, pg 141
Atena Kustannus Oy, pg 142
Fenix-Kustannus Oy, pg 142
Gummerus Publishers, pg 142
Kaantopiiri Oy, pg 142
Karisto Oy, pg 142
Kirjayhtymae Oy, pg 143
Koala-Kustannus/Oy Greenbay House Publishing Ltd, pg 143
Kustannus Oy Kolibri, pg 143
Otava Publishing Co Ltd, pg 143
Oy LIKE Kustannus Ltd, pg 144
Tammi Publishers, pg 144
Weilin & Goeoes Oy, pg 145
Werner Soederstroem Osakeyhtioe (WSOY), pg 145

France

Editions Albin Michel, pg 146
Autrement Editions, pg 149
Editions Belfond, pg 150
Editions Bordas, pg 151
Editions Canal, pg 152
Circe, pg 155
Edition1, pg 161
Flammarion SA, pg 164
Editions Grancher, pg 166
Hachette Jeunesse Image, pg 167
Hachette Livre, pg 167
Editions Jean-Claude Lattes, pg 170
Editions Liana Levi Sarl, pg 173
Editions Lito, pg 173
Editions Payot & Rivages, pg 179
Editions Jean Picollec, pg 179
Presses de la Cite, pg 180
Editions Ramsay, pg 182

Editions Robert Laffont, Nil, Fixot, Seghers, Julliard, pg 183
Maren Sell, pg 184
Societe des Editions Grasset et Fasquelle, pg 185
Sofradif Editions Philippe Auzou, pg 185
Editions Stock, pg 186
Les Editions de la Table Ronde, pg 187
Editions Vilo SA, pg 189

Germany

M Akselrad, pg 192
AOL-Verlag Frohmut Menze, pg 194
Arcus-Medien Wolfgang Steinhardt, pg 194
Ardey-Verlag GmbH, pg 194
Arena Verlag GmbH, pg 194
Argon Verlag GmbH, pg 195
Ars Edition GmbH, pg 195
Ars Vivendi Verlag, pg 195
Aulis Verlag Deubner & Co KG, pg 197
Bassermann Verlag, pg 198
Bastei Luebbe Taschenbuecher, pg 199
Verlag C H Beck (OHG), pg 200
Beleke KG Verlag, pg 200
Bergverlag Rudolf Rother GmbH, pg 200
C Bertelsmann Verlag GmbH, pg 201
Bettendorf'sche Verlagsanstalt GmbH, pg 202
Blackwell Wissenschafts-Verlag GmbH, pg 203
Verlag Erwin Bochinsky GmbH & Co KG, pg 204
Brandenburgisches Verlagshaus in der Dornier Medienholding GmbH, pg 206
BRUEN-Verlag, Gorenflo, pg 207
Verlag C J Bucher GmbH, pg 207
Verlag Busse und Seewald GmbH, pg 208
Caann Verlag, Klaus Wagner, pg 208
Chr Belser AG fur Verlagsgeschaefte und Co KG, pg 210
Christian Verlag GmbH, pg 210
Hans Christians Druckerei und Verlag GmbH & Co, pg 210
Claassen Verlag GmbH, pg 210
Compact Verlag GmbH, pg 211
Coppenrath Verlag, pg 211
J G Cotta'sche Buchhandlung Nachfolger GmbH, pg 212
Daedalus Verlag, pg 212
Dagmar Dreves Verlag, pg 212
Deutscher Fachverlag GmbH, pg 214
Deutscher Taschenbuch Verlag GmbH & Co KG (dtv), pg 215
Deutscher Verlag fur Grundstoffindustrie GmbH, pg 215
Edition Dia, pg 216
Verlag J H W Dietz Nachf GmbH, pg 217
Dingfelder-Verlag Inh Gerd Gmelin, pg 217
Dipa-Verlag GmbH, pg 217
Droemersche Verlagsanstalt Th Knaur Nachfolger GmbH & Co, pg 218
DRW-Verlag Weinbrenner-GmbH & Co, pg 219
Econ Taschenbuchverlag, pg 220
Econ Verlag GmbH, pg 220

Egmont Franz Schneider Verlag GmbH, pg 221
Egmont vgs verlagsgesellschaft mbH, pg 221
Ehrenwirth Verlag, pg 221
Eichborn AG, pg 221
EinfallsReich Verlagsgesellschaft MbH, pg 222
Elektor-Verlag GmbH, pg 222
Ellert & Richter Verlag GmbH, pg 222
Ensslin und Laiblin Verlag GmbH & Co KG, pg 223
Ernst Kabel Verlag GmbH, pg 223
Europa Verlag GmbH, pg 224
FAB-Verlag, pg 226
Fabel-Verlag Gudrun Liebchen, pg 226
Fink - Kummerly und Frey Verlag GmbH, pg 227
Karin Fischer Verlag GmbH, pg 228
S Fischer Verlag GmbH, pg 228
Fischer Taschenbuch Verlag GmbH, pg 228
Forum Verlag Leipzig Buch-Gesellschaft, pg 229
Gerstenberg Verlag, pg 232
Gondrom Verlag GmbH & Co KG, pg 233
Verlag der Stiftung Gralsbotschaft GmbH, pg 234
Carl Hanser Verlag, pg 237
Haude und Spenersche Verlagsbuchhandlung, pg 238
Heel Verlag GmbH, pg 238
Edition Hentrich Druck & Verlag Gebr Hentrich und Tank GmbH & Co KG, pg 239
F A Herbig Verlagsbuchhandlung GmbH, pg 239
Verlag Herder GmbH & Co KG, pg 239
Erika Heydick Sax-Verlag Beucha, pg 240
Hoffmann und Campe Verlag GmbH, pg 242
Horlemann Verlag, pg 243
Heinrich Hugendubel Verlag GmbH, pg 243
Edition Humanistische Psychologie (EHP), pg 243
Humboldt-Taschenbuchverlag Jacobi KG, pg 243
Verlag der Islam, pg 245
ITpress Verlag, pg 245
Jovis Verlag GmbH, pg 246
K L V Konkret Literatur Verlag GmbH, pg 247
Kallmeyer'sche Verlagsbuchhandlung GmbH, pg 247
KBV-Verlags-und Mediengesellschaft mbH, pg 248
SachBuchVerlag Kellner, pg 248
Gustav Kiepenheuer Verlag GmbH, pg 249
Verlag Kiepenheuer und Witsch GmbH & Co KG, pg 249
Der Kinderbuch Verlag GmbH, pg 249
Kindler Verlag GmbH, pg 249
Klartext Verlagsgesellschaft mbH, pg 249
Ingrid Klein Verlag GmbH, pg 249
Verlag Kleine Schritte Ursula Dahm & Co, pg 249
Albrecht Knaus Verlag GmbH, pg 250
Knowledge Media International, pg 251
Koehlers Verlagsgesellschaft mbH, pg 251

Koenigsfurt Verlag, Evelin Burger et Johannes Fiebig, pg 251
Koesler Verlag GmbH, pg 252
Kolibri-Verlags GmbH, pg 252
kopaed verlagsgmbh, pg 252
Koptisch-Orthodoxes Zentrum, pg 252
Franckh-Kosmos Verlags-GmbH & Co, pg 252
Karin Kramer Verlag, pg 253
Wolfgang Krueger Verlag GmbH, pg 254
Verlag Antje Kunstmann GmbH, pg 254
Ambro Lacus, Buch- und Bildverlag Walter Kremnitz, pg 255
Landbuch-Verlagsgesellschaft mbH, pg 255
Lebenshilfe-Verlag Marburg, Verlag der Bundesvereinigung Lebenshilfe fuer Menschen mit geistiger Behinderung eV, pg 256
Lentz Verlag, pg 257
Dr Gisela Lermann, pg 257
Libertas- Europaeisches Institut GmbH, pg 257
Logos-Verlag Literatur & Layout GmbH, pg 258
Luchterhand Literaturverlag GmbH/Verlag Volk & Welt GmbH, pg 259
Gustav Luebbe Verlag, pg 259
Verlagsgruppe Luebbe GmbH & Co KG, pg 259
Wolfgang Mann-Verlag GmbH, pg 260
Otto Meissner Verlag, pg 262
Meyer & Meyer Fachverlag und Buchhandel GmbH, pg 263
Mitteldeutscher Verlag GmbH, pg 264
Motorbuch-Verlag, pg 265
Neuer Honos Verlag GmbH, pg 267
Verlag Neues Leben GmbH, pg 268
nymphenburger, pg 269
Oekotopia Verlag, Wolfgang Hoffmann, pg 270
Oertel & Sporer GmbH & Co, pg 270
One Way Medien OHG, pg 270
Palmyra Verlag, pg 271
Edition Parabolis, pg 271
Pattloch Verlag GmbH & Co KG, pg 272
Projektion J Buch- und Musikverlag GmbH, pg 275
Propylaeen Verlag, Zweigniederlassung Berlin der Ullstein Buchverlage GmbH, pg 275
Querverlag GmbH, pg 276
Ravensburger Buchverlag Otto Maier GmbH, pg 277
Rossipaul Kommunikation GmbH, pg 280
Rowohlt Berlin Verlag GmbH, pg 280
Rowohlt Taschenbuch Verlag GmbH, pg 280
Rowohlt Verlag GmbH, pg 280
Ryvellus Medienagentur Dopfer, pg 281
Buchverlag Andrea Schmitz, pg 284
Schueren Verlag GmbH, pg 285
Verlag Schulte und Gerth GmbH & Co KG, pg 285
H O Schulze KG, pg 285
Theodor Schuster, pg 285
Heinrich Schwab Verlag, pg 285
Siedler Verlag, pg 286
Snayder Verlag Gunter VOB & Jurgen Schroder OHG, pg 287
Adolf Sponholtz Verlag, pg 288

Springer-Verlag GmbH & Co KG, pg 288
Stadler Verlagsgesellschaft mbH, pg 288
Stapp Verlag Wolfgang Stapp, pg 289
C A Starke Verlag, pg 289
Steidl Verlag, pg 289
Stern-Verlag Janssen & Co, pg 290
Sueddeutsche Verlagsgesellschaft mbH, pg 291
Suedwest Verlag GmbH & Co KG, pg 291
Tangens Systemverlag GmbH, pg 291
Edition Temmen, pg 292
Konrad Theiss Verlag GmbH, pg 293
K Thienemanns Verlag, pg 293
S Toeche-Mittler Verlag GmbH, pg 294
Trescher Verlag GmbH, pg 295
Treves Editions Verein Zur Foerderung der Kuenstlerischen Taetigkeiten, pg 295
Trias-Thieme, Hippokrates Enke, pg 295
Guenter Albert Ulmer Verlag, pg 295
Umschau Buchverlag Breidenstein GmbH, pg 296
Union-Verlag GmbH, pg 296
Urania Verlag mit Ravensburger Ratgebern, pg 296
Verlagsgruppe Georg von Holtzbrinck GmbH, pg 299
VS Verlagshaus Stuttgart GmbH, pg 299
W Ludwig Verlag GmbH, pg 300
Weber Zucht & Co, pg 300
Weidler Buchverlag Berlin, pg 301
Verlagsgruppe Weltbild GmbH, pg 301
Rosa Winkel Verlag GmbH, pg 303
Dr Dieter Winkler, pg 303
Verlag Konrad Wittwer GmbH, pg 303
WRS Verlag Wirtschaft, Recht und Steuern GmbH & Co KG, pg 304
Wunderlich Verlag, pg 304
Xenos Verlagsgesellschaft mbH, pg 304
Zebulon Verlag GmbH & Co KG, pg 305
Zweimuehlen Verlag GmbH, pg 305

Ghana

Afram Publications (Ghana) Ltd, pg 306
Africa Christian Press, pg 306
Asempa Publishers, pg 306
Ghana Publishing Corporation, pg 307
Moxon Paperbacks, pg 307
Waterville Publishing House, pg 308

Greece

Atlantis M Pechlivanides & Co SA, pg 309
Chrysi Penna - Golden Pen Books, pg 309
Diavlos, pg 309
Dodoni Publications, pg 310
Elliniki Leschi Tou Vivliou, pg 310
Govostis Publishing SA, pg 311
Medusa/Selas, pg 313
Minoas SA, pg 313
Morfotiko Idryma Ethnikis Trapezas, pg 313
Patakis Publishers, pg 314
Siamantas Publications, pg 315

SUBJECT INDEX

Guyana
Roraima Publishers Ltd, pg 317

Hong Kong
Ling Kee Publishing Group, pg 320
Ming Pao Publications Ltd, pg 321
Publications (Holdings) Ltd, pg 321
Sun Ya Publications (HK) Ltd, pg 322

Hungary
Aranyhal Konyvkiado Goldfish Publishing, pg 323
Balassi Kiado Kft, pg 323
CEU-Press, pg 323
Gondolat Kiado, pg 324
Park Konyvkiado Kft (Park Publisher), pg 326
Szabvanykiado, pg 326

Iceland
Almenna Bokafelagid, pg 327
Forlagid, pg 327
Frodi Ltd, pg 328
Idunn, pg 328
Islendingasagnautgafan, pg 328
Mal og menning, pg 328
Setberg, pg 328
Skjaldborg Ltd, pg 328

India
Cosmo Publications, pg 335
Current Books, pg 335
Dolphin Publications, pg 336
Frank Brothers & Co (Publishers) Ltd, pg 337
General Book Depot, pg 337
Hind Pocket Books Private Ltd, pg 338
Kali For Women, pg 341
A Mukherjee & Co Pvt Ltd, pg 343
Orient Paperbacks, pg 345
Prabhat Prakashan, pg 346
Pratibha Pratishthan, pg 346
Reliance Publishing House, pg 347
M C Sarkar & Sons (P) Ltd, pg 349
Sat Sahitya Prakashan, pg 349
Somaiya Publications Pvt Ltd, pg 350

Indonesia
CV Angkasa CV (Publishers), pg 354
Bina Rena Pariwara, pg 354
P T Bulan Bintang, pg 354
Gaya Favorit Press, pg 355
Katalis PT Bina Mitra Plaosan, pg 356
Yayasan Obor Indonesia, pg 357

Ireland
Brandon Book Publishers Ltd, pg 359
Dee-Jay Publications, pg 359
Gandon Editions, pg 360
Mount Eagle Publications Ltd, pg 362
The O'Brien Press Ltd, pg 363
Poolbeg Press Ltd, pg 363

Israel
Achiasaf Publishing House Ltd, pg 365
Astrolog Publishing House, pg 365
Bitan Publishers Ltd, pg 365
Breslov Research Institute, pg 366
Classikaletet, pg 366
DAT Publications, pg 366
Dyonon/Papyrus Publishing House of the Tel-Aviv, pg 367
Gefen Publishing House Ltd, pg 367
Hakibbutz Hameuchad Publishing House Ltd, pg 368
MAP-Mapping & Publishing Ltd, pg 370
Schocken Publishing House Ltd, pg 372
Tcherikover Publishers Ltd, pg 372
Yad Vashem - The Holocaust Martyrs' & Heroes' Remembrance Authority, pg 373
Yedioth Ahronoth Books, pg 373
Zmora-Bitan, Publishers Ltd, pg 374

Italy
Archinto snc, pg 376
Gruppo Editoriale Armenia SpA, pg 376
Belforte Editore Libraio srl, pg 377
Bompiani-RCS Libri, pg 378
Edizioni Cantagalli, pg 379
Edizioni Centro Studi Erickson, pg 381
Edizioni l'eta Dell'Acquario Di I Bresci & C Sas, pg 387
Edizioni Frassinelli SRL, pg 389
Gremese International Srl, pg 391
Il Saggiatore, pg 393
Editoriale Jaca Book SpA, pg 394
Kaos Edizioni SRL, pg 395
L'Airone Editrice, pg 395
La Luna, pg 397
Manfrini Editori, pg 397
Marsilio Editori SpA, pg 398
McRae Books, pg 398
Mondolibro Editore SNC, pg 399
Franco Muzzio & C Editore SpA, pg 400
Edizioni Piemme SpA, pg 403
RAI.ERI, pg 405
Rusconi Libri Srl, pg 406
Editoriale Scienza, pg 407
Edizioni Segno SRL, pg 407
Sonzogno, pg 408
Sperling e Kupfer Editori SpA, pg 408
TEA Tascabili degli Editori Associati SpA, pg 409
Marco Tropea Editore, pg 410

Jamaica
Institute of Jamaica Publications, pg 413
Kingston Publishers Ltd, pg 413

Japan
Chikuma Shobo Publishing Co Ltd, pg 415
Diamond Inc, pg 416
Dobun Shoin, pg 416
Fukuinkan Shoten Publishers Inc, pg 416
Gakken Co Ltd, pg 416
Hakusui-Sha Co Ltd, pg 417
Hakuyo-Sha, pg 417
Hayakawa Publishing Inc, pg 417
Heibonsha Ltd, Publishers, pg 417
The Japan Times, pg 418
Kawade Shobo Shinsha, pg 419
Kodansha, pg 420
Kosei Publishing Co Ltd, pg 420
Mita Press, Mita Industrial Co, Ltd, pg 421
Seibu Time Co Ltd, pg 425
Shimizu-Shoin, pg 425
Shincho-Sha Co Ltd, pg 425
Akane Shobo Co Ltd, pg 425
Shueisha Inc, pg 426
Shufunotomo sha Co Ltd, pg 426
Soshisha Co Ltd, pg 426
Toho Book Store, pg 427
Tokuma-Shoten, pg 427
Toyo Keizai Inc (The Oriental Economist), pg 428

Jordan
Jordan Book Centre Co Ltd, pg 430

Kenya
Africa Book Services (EA) Ltd, pg 430
Heinemann Kenya Limited (EAEP), pg 431
Jacaranda Designs Ltd, pg 432
Kenway Publications Ltd, pg 432
Paulines Publications-Africa, pg 433
Transafrica Press, pg 433
Uzima Press, pg 433

Republic of Korea
Big Tree Publishing, pg 435
Borim Publishing Co, pg 435
Chung Rim Publishing Co Ltd, pg 435
Hainaim Publishing Co Ltd, pg 436
Jigyungsa Ltd, pg 437
Kemongsa Publishing Co Ltd, pg 437
Koreaone Press Inc, pg 438
Kum Sung Publishing Co Ltd, pg 438
Kyohaksa Publishing Co Ltd, pg 438
Minumsa Publishing Co Ltd, pg 438
Munye Publishing Co, pg 439
O Neul Publishing Co, pg 439
Woong Jin Publishing Co Ltd, pg 440
Woongjin Media Corporation, pg 440

Latvia
Alberts XII, pg 441
Avots, pg 441
Nordik/Tapals Publishers Ltd, pg 442
Zvaigzne ABC Publishers, Ltd, pg 442

Lebanon
Librairie Orientale sal, pg 443

Liechtenstein
Bonafides Verlags-Anstalt, pg 444

Lithuania
Lietus Ltd, pg 445
Tyto Alba Publishers, pg 446

Luxembourg
Guy Binsfeld & Co Sarl, pg 447

The Former Yugoslav Republic of Macedonia
Detska radost, pg 448

Malaysia
Pustaka Cipta Sdn Bhd, pg 454
Tempo Publishing (M) Sdn Bhd, pg 455

Mali
EDIM SA, pg 455

Mauritius
Vizavi Editions, pg 457

Mexico
Ediciones el Caballito SA, pg 458
Editorial Diana SA de CV, pg 459
Fernandez Editores SA de CV, pg 461
Fondo de Cultura Economica, pg 461
Editorial Grijalbo SA de CV, pg 461
Editorial Joaquin Mortiz SA de CV, pg 462
Lasser Press Mexicana SA de CV, pg 462
Libra Editorial SA de CV, pg 463
Editores Mexicanos Unidos SA, pg 464
Nova Grupo Editorial SA de CV, pg 464
Grupo Editorial Planeta, pg 465
Selector SA de CV, pg 467
Time-Life Internacional de Mexico, pg 467
Editorial Universo SA de CV, pg 468
Javier Vergara Editor SA de CV, pg 468

Netherlands
Uitgeverij Arena BV, pg 473
Uitgevirj Aristos, pg 473
Uitgeverij Balans, pg 473
De Bezige Bij, pg 474
De Boekerij BV, pg 474
A W Bruna Uitgevers BV, pg 475
BZZTOH Publishers, pg 475
Cadans, pg 475
Uitgeverij Cantecleer BV, pg 475
ECI voor Boeken en Grammofoonplaten BV, pg 476
Educatieve Uitgeverij Edu'Actief BV, pg 476
Elmar BV, pg 476
Uitgeverij De Fontein BV, pg 477
Uitgeverij De Geus BV, pg 477
Gottmer Uitgevers Groep, pg 477
Historische Uitgeverij, pg 478
M & P Publishing House, pg 480
Otto Maier Benelux BV, pg 481
Mets & Schilt Uitgevers en Distributeurs, pg 481
J M Meulenhoff BV, pg 481
Uitgeverij Mingus, pg 481
Uitgeverij Maarten Muntinga, pg 481
Omega Boek BV, pg 482
Podium Uitgeverij, pg 483
Prometheus, pg 483
Rostrum Publishing, pg 483
Uitgeverij Het Spectrum BV, pg 484
A J G Strengholt's Boeken, Anno 1928, BV, pg 484
Thoth Publishers, pg 485
Unieboek BV, pg 485
Van Buuren Uitgeverij BV, pg 486
Uitgeverij G A van Oorschot bv, pg 486
Uitgeverij Vassallucci, pg 486
Wereldbibliotheek, pg 487
West-Friesland/Boekproject-ontwikkeling, pg 487

Netherlands Antilles
Bredero, pg 488

New Zealand
Brick Row Publishing Co Ltd, pg 489
Bush Press Communications Ltd, pg 489
Canterbury University Press, pg 489

PUBLISHERS

Cape Catley, pg 489
The Caxton Press, pg 490
Craig Potton Publishing, pg 490
Craig Printing Company Ltd, pg 490
Dunmore Press Ltd, pg 490
Exisle Publishing Ltd, pg 491
Godwit Publishing Ltd, pg 491
Hazard Press Ltd, pg 491
Hodder Moa Beckett Publishers Ltd, pg 492
Legislation Direct, pg 492
Longacre Press, pg 493
Mills Group, pg 493
Orca Publishing Services Ltd, pg 494
Reed Publishing (NZ) Ltd, pg 495
RIMU Publishing Co Ltd, pg 495
River Press, pg 495
RSVP Publishing Company Ltd, pg 495
Shearwater Associates Ltd, pg 495
Shoal Bay Press Ltd, pg 495
Tandem Press, pg 496
Bridget Williams Books Ltd, pg 497

Nicaragua

Editorial Nueva Nicaragua, pg 497

Nigeria

Black Academy Press, pg 498
Cross Continent Press Ltd, pg 498
CSS Bookshops, Agency & Publishing Division, pg 498
Educational Research & Study Group, pg 499
Ethiope Publishing Corporation, pg 499
Heritage Books, pg 499
Kola Sanya Publishing Enterprise, pg 500
Longman Nigeria Plc, pg 500
Thomas Nelson (Nigeria) Ltd, pg 500
New Horn Press Ltd, pg 500
Northern Nigerian Publishing Co Ltd, pg 500
Nwamife Publishers Ltd, pg 500
Onibon-Oje Publishers, pg 501
Riverside Communications, pg 501
University Publishing Co, pg 502
Vantage Publishers International Ltd, pg 502
John West Publications Co Ltd, pg 502

Norway

H Aschehoug & Co (W Nygaard) A/S, pg 502
Bedriftsokonomens Forlag A/S, pg 502
J W Cappelens Forlag A/S, pg 503
N W Damm og Son A/S, pg 503
Fono Forlag, pg 503
Genesis Forlag, pg 503
John Grieg Forlag AS, pg 503
Egmont Hjemmets Bokforlag AS, pg 504
Pax Forlag A/S, pg 504
Erik Sandberg, pg 504
Snofugl Forlag, pg 505
Stabenfeldt A/S, pg 505
Tiden Norsk Forlag, pg 505

Pakistan

Jang Publishers, pg 507

Peru

Ediciones Brown SA, pg 511

Philippines

Bookman Printing & Publishing House Inc, pg 512
National Book Store Inc, pg 514
New Day Publishers, pg 514
SIBS Publishing House Inc, pg 515

Poland

Albatros, pg 516
Ksiaznica Publishing Ltd, pg 517
Muza SA, pg 518
'Slask' Ltd, pg 520
Wydawnictwo WAB, pg 520

Portugal

DIFEL - Difusao Editorial SA, pg 524
Distri Cultural Lda, pg 524
Distri Editora Lda, pg 524
Edicoes 70, Lda, pg 524
Editorial Estampa, Lda, pg 524
Europress Editores e Distribuidores de Publicacoes Lda, pg 525
Gradiva-Publicacnoes Lda, pg 525
Porto Editora Lda, pg 528
Editorial Presenca, pg 528
Puma Editora Lda, pg 528
Teorema, pg 529

Puerto Rico

McGraw-Hill Intermericana del Caribe, Inc, pg 530
University of Puerto Rico Press (EDUPR), pg 531

Romania

Editora All, pg 531
Artemis Verlag, pg 532
Editura Clusium, Casa de Editura Atlas-Clusium SRL, pg 532
Editura Excelsior, pg 533
Editura Meridiane, pg 534
Editura Niculescu, pg 534
Pandora Publishing House, pg 535
RAO International Publishing Co, pg 535
RAO Publishing Group, pg 535
Realitatea Casa de Edituri Productie Audio-Video Film, pg 535
Editura Stiintifica, pg 536

Russian Federation

BLIC, russko-Baltijskij informaciionnyj centr, AO, pg 537
Izdatelstvo Moskovskii Rabochii, pg 539
Publishing House Limbus Press, pg 539
Mir Knigi Ltd, pg 540
Novosti Izdatel 'stvo, pg 541
Profizdat, pg 541
Top Secret Collection Publishers, pg 542

Saudi Arabia

Dar Al-Shareff for Publishing & Distribution, pg 543

Senegal

Les Nouvelles Editions Africaines du Senegal NEAS, pg 544

Sierra Leone

Sierra Leone University Press, pg 544

Singapore

Aquanut Agencies Pte Ltd, pg 545

Slovakia

Vydavatel'stvo Osveta (Verlag Osveta), pg 551

Slovenia

Mladinska Knjiga International, pg 552
Zalozba Obzorja d d Maribor, pg 552

South Africa

Delta Books (Pty) Ltd, pg 553
Ad Donker (Pty) Ltd, pg 554
Fernwood Press (Pty) Ltd, pg 554
Galago Publishing Pty Ltd, pg 554
HarperCollins Religious, pg 554
HAUM (Hollandsch Afrikaansche Uitgevers Maatschappij), pg 555
Heinemann Publishers (Pty) Ltd, pg 555
Human & Rousseau (Pty) Ltd, pg 555
Ivy Publications, pg 555
Juventus/Femina Publishers, pg 556
LAPA Publishers (Pty) Ltd, pg 556
Media House Publications, pg 557
New Africa Books (Pty) Ltd, pg 557
Queillerie Publishers, pg 558
Ravan Press (Pty) Ltd, pg 558
Reader's Digest Southern Africa, pg 559
Shuter & Shooter (Pty) Ltd, pg 559
Southern Book Publishers (Pty) Ltd, pg 559
Tafelberg Publishers Ltd, pg 560
Unisa Press, pg 560
University Publishers & Booksellers (Pty) Ltd, pg 560

Spain

Acento Editorial, pg 561
Aguilar SA de Ediciones, pg 562
Amnistia Internacional Editorial SL, pg 563
Editorial Astri SA, pg 564
Ediciones B, SA, pg 565
Circe Ediciones, SA, pg 567
Compania Literaria, pg 568
Ediciones Destino SA, pg 569
Didaco Comunicacion y Didactica, SA, pg 572
Edicomunicacion SA, pg 572
Editorial Espasa-Calpe SA, pg 573
Eumo Editorial, pg 574
Editorial Gedisa SA, pg 575
Grijalbo Mondadori SA, pg 576
Ediciones Internacionales Universitarias SA, pg 578
Libsa Editorial SA, pg 580
Llibres del Segle, pg 580
Ediciones Maeva, pg 581
Editorial Marin SA, pg 581
Ediciones Martinez-Roca SA, pg 581
Ediciones Medici SA, pg 582
Ediciones Nauta Credito SA, pg 584
Noguer y Caralt Editores SA, pg 584
Ediciones del Oriente y del Mediterraneo, pg 585
Pages Editors, SL, pg 585
Ediciones El Pais SA, pg 585
Editorial Planeta SA, pg 587
Plaza y Janes Editores SA, pg 587
Pre-Textos, pg 587
Editorial Prensa Espanola, pg 587
Editorial Sintesis, SA, pg 590
Ediciones Siruela SA, pg 591
Edicions 62, pg 591
Grup 62, pg 591

Tesitex, SL, pg 592
Editorial Thassalia, SA, pg 592
Gregorio del Toro Editor, pg 593
Ediciones de la Torre, pg 593
Trea Ediciones, SL, pg 593
Turner Publicaciones, pg 593
Javier Vergara Editor SA, pg 595
Veron Editor, pg 595
Ediciones Versal SA, pg 595
Vinaches Lopez, Luisa, pg 595

Sri Lanka

Samayawardena Printers Publishers & Booksellers, pg 598

Sudan

Al-Ayam Press Co Ltd, pg 598
Khartoum University Press, pg 598

Sweden

Akademiforlaget Corona AB, pg 599
Albert Bonniers Forlag, pg 600
Alfabeta Bokforlag AB, pg 600
Berghs, pg 600
Bokforlaget Atlantis AB, pg 600
Bokforlaget Cordia AB, pg 600
Bokforlaget Plus AB, pg 600
Bokforlaget Settern AB, pg 601
Albert Bonniers Forlag, pg 601
BOOX, pg 601
Brombergs Bokforlag AB, pg 601
Rene Coeckelberghs Bokfoerlag AB, pg 601
Delta Forlags AB, pg 601
Fischer & Co, pg 602
Bokforlaget Forum AB, pg 602
Gedins Forlag, pg 602
Lars Hoekerbergs Bokfoerlag, pg 603
Bokforlaget Robert Larson AB, pg 604
Bokfoerlaget Naturoch Kultur, pg 604
Norstedts Foerlag, pg 605
Bokforlaget Nya Doxa AB, pg 605
Raben och Sjoegren Bokfoerlag, pg 605
Sjoestrands Foerlag, pg 606
Stromberg, pg 606
Svenska Foerlaget liv & ledarskap ab, pg 607
AB Timbro, pg 607
Var Skola Foerlag AB, pg 607
AB Wahlstrom & Widstrand, pg 607
Wahlstrom & Widstrand, pg 607
B Wahlstroms, pg 607
Zindermans AB, pg 607

Switzerland

Ariston Editions, pg 608
Athenaeum Verlag AG, pg 608
Basilius Presse AG, pg 609
Bergli Books AG, pg 609
Birkhauser Verlag AG, pg 610
Chronos Verlag, pg 611
Rene Coeckelberghs Editions, pg 611
Eco Verlags AG, pg 613
Hallwag AG, pg 615
Kinderbuchverlag Luzern, pg 617
Lenos Verlag, pg 618
Oesch Verlag AG, pg 620
Ott Verlag AG, pg 621
Editions Payot Lausanne, pg 621
Rotpunktverlag, pg 623
Sauerlaender AG, pg 623
Tobler Verlag, pg 626
Uranium Verlag Zug, pg 626
Verbandsdruckerei AG, pg 626
Weltwoche ABC-Verlag, pg 627

SUBJECT INDEX — BOOK

Taiwan, Province of China
Commonwealth Publishing Company Ltd, pg 629
Linking Publishing Company Ltd, pg 631
Newton Publishing Company Ltd, pg 631
UNITAS Publishing Co Ltd, pg 632

United Republic of Tanzania
East African Publishing House, pg 633
Eastern Africa Publications Ltd, pg 633
Inland Publishers, pg 633
Tanzania Publishing House, pg 634
Tema Publishers Ltd, pg 634

Thailand
Odeon Store LP, pg 635

Turkey
Afa Yayincilik Sanayi Tic AS, pg 638
Alkim Kitapcilik-Yayimcilik, pg 638
Altin Kitaplar Yayinevi, pg 638
Cep Kitaplari AS, pg 639
Iletisim Yayinlari, pg 640
Kiyi Yayinlari, pg 640
Metis Yayinlari, pg 640
Remzi Kitabevi, pg 641
Ruh ve Madde Yayinlari ve Saglik Hizmetleri AS, pg 641
Sabah Kitaplari, pg 641
Varlik Yayinlari AS, pg 641

Uganda
Fountain Publishers Ltd, pg 642

Ukraine
ASK Ltd, pg 643

United Kingdom
Act 3 Publishing, pg 645
Aladdin Books Ltd, pg 645
Amber Books Ltd, pg 646
Apex Publishing Ltd, pg 648
Apple Press, pg 648
Argo Spoken Word, pg 648
Aurum Press Ltd, pg 651
Batsford Ltd, pg 652
BBC Audiobooks, pg 652
BCA, pg 653
Beaver Publishing Ltd, pg 653
Belitha Press Ltd, pg 653
A & C Black Publishers Ltd, pg 655
Blackstaff Press, pg 655
Blaketon Hall Ltd, pg 656
Bloomsbury Publishing PLC, pg 656
Books of Zimbabwe Publishing Co (Pvt) Ltd, pg 657
Brewin Books Ltd, pg 659
Brimax Books, pg 659
Brown Wells & Jacobs Ltd, pg 661
Calder Publications Ltd, pg 662
Canongate Books Ltd, pg 663
Cassell & Co, pg 664
Centre for Alternative Technology, pg 665
Chatham Publishing, pg 667
James Clarke & Co Ltd, pg 668
Compass Equestrian Ltd, pg 669
Compendium Publishing, pg 670
Constable & Robinson Ltd, pg 670
Constable Publishers, pg 670
The Continuum International Publishing Group Ltd, pg 670
Leo Cooper, pg 671
Creation Books, pg 671
Denor Press, pg 675
Dorling Kindersley Ltd, pg 676
Gerald Duckworth & Co Ltd, pg 676
Gwasg Dwyfor, pg 676
Eddison Sadd Editions Ltd, pg 677
Aidan Ellis Publishing, pg 678
Eurobook Ltd, pg 679
The Eurospan Group, pg 680
Exley Publications Ltd, pg 681
Extraordinary People Press, pg 681
Frontier Publishing, pg 684
George Mann Publications, pg 687
GMP Publishers Ltd, pg 687
Gollancz/Witherby, pg 688
Gomer Press (J D Lewis & Sons Ltd), pg 688
Grandreams Ltd, pg 689
Grange Books PLC, pg 689
Granta Books, pg 689
Grub Street, pg 690
Hamlyn, pg 691
Patrick Hardy Books, pg 692
HarperCollins Publishers, pg 692
Harvard University Press, pg 692
The Harvill Press Ltd, pg 693
Headline Book Publishing Ltd, pg 693
Heinemann Educational Publishing, pg 694
William Heinemann Ltd, pg 694
Helion & Co, pg 694
Heritage Press, pg 695
Hodder Children's Books, pg 696
Honno Welsh Women's Press, pg 697
Isis Publishing Ltd, pg 701
The Islamic Texts Society, pg 701
Janus Publishing Company Ltd, pg 702
John Blake Publishing Ltd, pg 703
Karnak House, pg 703
Knight Features, pg 705
Ladybird Books, pg 705
Letterbox Library, pg 707
Lion Publishing PLC, pg 708
Luath Press Ltd, pg 709
The Lutterworth Press, pg 709
Macmillan Children's Books, pg 710
Macmillan Ltd, pg 710
Marston House, pg 712
Mercat Press, pg 713
Merehurst Publishers, pg 713
Metro Publishing Ltd, pg 714
Mirabel Books Ltd, pg 715
Moonlight Publishing Ltd, pg 715
John Murray (Publishers) Ltd, pg 716
New Cavendish Books, pg 718
New Era Publications UK Ltd, pg 718
Nicholas Enterprises Ltd, pg 719
NMS Publishing Ltd, pg 719
Octopus Publishing Group, pg 720
Michael O'Mara Books Ltd, pg 721
Open Books Publishing Ltd, pg 721
Orion Publishing Group Ltd, pg 722
Oyster Books, pg 723
Pan Macmillan, pg 723
Parapress Ltd, pg 724
Piatkus Books, pg 727
Piccadilly Press, pg 727
Polybooks Ltd, pg 729
Polygon, pg 729
PRC Publishing Ltd, pg 730
Profile Books Ltd, pg 731
Quarto Publishing plc, pg 731
Quartz Editions, pg 732
Random House UK Ltd, pg 733
Ravette Publishing Ltd, pg 733
The Reader's Digest Association Ltd, pg 733
Reaktion Books Ltd, pg 733
Michael Russell Publishing Ltd, pg 737
Sangam Books Ltd, pg 738
SAWD Publications, pg 738
Scholastic Ltd, pg 739
Scottish Cultural Press, pg 739
Martin Secker & Warburg, pg 740
Serpent's Tail Ltd, pg 740
Shaw & Sons Ltd, pg 741
Shepheard-Walwyn (Publishers) Ltd, pg 741
Silver Link Publishing Ltd, pg 742
Simon & Schuster Ltd, pg 742
Smith Settle Ltd, pg 743
SPA Books Ltd, pg 744
Spellmount Ltd Publishers, pg 744
Sutton Publishing Ltd, pg 746
Tabb House, pg 746
I B Tauris & Co Ltd, pg 747
Tiger Books International PLC, pg 748
Time Warner Books UK, pg 749
Transworld Publishers Ltd, pg 750
Ulverscroft Large Print Books Ltd, pg 751
Verso, pg 752
Viking, pg 753
Virgin Publishing Ltd, pg 753
John Waite Ltd, pg 754
Walker Books Ltd, pg 754
Ward Lock Ltd, pg 754
The Watts Publishing Group Ltd, pg 754
Wayland Publishers Ltd (Incorporating Macdonald Young Books), pg 754
Webb & Bower (Publishers) Ltd, pg 755
The Windrush Press Ltd, pg 757
The Women's Press Ltd, pg 758
Wordwright Publishing, pg 758
Gordon Wright Publishing Ltd, pg 759
Yale University Press London, pg 759

Uruguay
Ediciones de Juan Darien, pg 760
Rosebud Ediciones, pg 761
Vinten Editor, pg 761

Venezuela
Alfadil Ediciones, pg 761
Editorial Biosfera CA, pg 762

Yugoslavia
Alfa-Narodna Knjiga, pg 764

Zimbabwe
Academic Books Pvt Ltd, pg 767
The Graham Publishing Company (Pvt) Ltd, pg 768
Mambo Press, pg 768
Vision Publications, pg 769
Zimbabwe Women Writers, pg 770

OUTDOOR RECREATION

Argentina
Ediciones Lidium, pg 7

Australia
Robert Berthold Photography, pg 14
Enterprise Publications, pg 22
Envirobook, pg 22
Flora Publications International Pty Ltd, pg 23
Kingsclear Books, pg 29
Mulavon Press Pty Ltd, pg 34
Rankin Publishers, pg 40
Saltwater Publications, pg 41
Frank Shepherd, pg 42
Simon & Schuster Australia Pty Ltd, pg 42

Austria
Verlag Harald Denzel, Auto- und Freizeitfuehrer, pg 51
Docker Verlag GmbH & Co KG, pg 51
Niederosterreichisches Pressehaus Druck- und Verlagsgesellschaft mbH, pg 55
Verlag des Osterr Kneippbundes GmbH, pg 57
Verlag Veritas Mediengesellschaft mbH, pg 60

Belgium
Georeto-Geogidsen, pg 68

China
China Film Press, pg 103
Jilin Science & Technology Publishing House, pg 106

Colombia
Eurolibros Ltda, pg 111

Costa Rica
Scout Interamericana, pg 117

Czech Republic
Aurora, pg 123
Jota, pg 125

Denmark
Wisby & Wilkens, pg 136

France
ATP - Packager, pg 149
Editions Chiron, pg 154
De Vecchi Editions SA, pg 158
Edisud, pg 161
Federation Francaise de la Randonnee Pedestre, pg 164
Institut Francais de Recherche pour l'Exploitation de la Mer (IFREMER), pg 165
Librairie Guenegaud Sarl, pg 167
Editions Fernand Lanore Sarl, pg 172
Editions Mango, pg 174
Editions Franck Mercier, pg 176
Les Presses d'Ile-de-France Sarl, pg 181
Sofradif Editions Philippe Auzou, pg 185
Editions Sud Ouest, pg 186

Germany
Alba Fachverlag GmbH und Co KG, pg 192
ALS-Verlag GmbH, pg 193
AOL-Verlag Frohmut Menze, pg 194
ARCult Media, pg 194
Bassermann Verlag, pg 198
Bergverlag Rudolf Rother GmbH, pg 200
Bielefelder Verlagsanstalt GmbH & Co KG Richard Kaselowsky, pg 203

PUBLISHERS

BLV Verlagsgesellschaft mbH, pg 204
Verlag Busse und Seewald GmbH, pg 208
Fachverlag Hans Carl GmbH, pg 209
Hans Christians Druckerei und Verlag GmbH & Co, pg 210
Christophorus-Verlag GmbH, pg 210
Copress Verlag, pg 211
Delius, Klasing und Co, pg 213
Deutscher Wanderverlag Dr Mair & Schnabel & Co, pg 215
Drei Brunnen Verlag GmbH & Co, pg 218
Egmont vgs verlagsgesellschaft mbH, pg 221
Eulen Verlag, pg 224
F Bruckmann Munchen Verlag & Druck GmbH & Co Produkt KG, pg 225
Fink - Kummerly und Frey Verlag GmbH, pg 227
Fraunhofer IRB Verlag Fraunhofer Informationszentrum Raum und Bau, pg 229
Verlag Gruppenpaedagogischer Literatur, pg 234
Heel Verlag GmbH, pg 238
Dieter Hoffmann Verlag, pg 242
Jutta Pohl Verlag, pg 247
SachBuchVerlag Kellner, pg 248
Franckh-Kosmos Verlags-GmbH & Co, pg 252
Landbuch-Verlagsgesellschaft mbH, pg 255
Institut fuer Landes- und Stadtentwicklungsforschung, ILS Nordrhein-Westfalen, pg 255
Moby Dick Verlag, pg 264
Verlag Stephanie Naglschmid, pg 266
Verlag J Neumann-Neudamm GmbH & Co KG, pg 268
nymphenburger, pg 269
Oekotopia Verlag, Wolfgang Hoffmann, pg 270
Pollner Verlag, pg 274
Rossipaul Kommunikation GmbH, pg 280
Buchverlag Andrea Schmitz, pg 284
Adolf Sponholtz Verlag, pg 288
Stadler Verlagsgesellschaft mbH, pg 288
Staedte-Verlag, E v Wagner und J Mitterhuber GmbH, pg 288
Stapp Verlag Wolfgang Stapp, pg 289
Steiger Verlag, pg 289
Conrad Stein Verlag, pg 289
Stoeppel Verlag-Buchvertrieb KG, pg 290
Traditionell Bogenschiessen Verlag Angelika Hornig, pg 294
Trescher Verlag GmbH, pg 295
VS Verlagshaus Stuttgart GmbH, pg 299
WEKA Firmengruppe GmbH & Co KG, pg 301
Zeitgeist Media GmbH, pg 305

Ghana
World Literature Project, pg 308

Hungary
Aranyhal Konyvkiado Goldfish Publishing, pg 323

Iceland
Frodi Ltd, pg 328

Ireland
Tir Eolas, pg 364

Israel
Bitan Publishers Ltd, pg 365

Italy
Verlagsanstalt Athesia, pg 377
Il Castello srl, pg 380
Giovanni De Vecchi Editore SpA, pg 384
Ediciclo Editore SRL, pg 386
RCS Libri SpA, pg 405
Tappeiner, pg 409
Zanfi Editori SRL, pg 412

Japan
Gakken Co Ltd, pg 416
Seibido Shuppan Company Ltd, pg 424

Republic of Korea
Pyeong-hwa Chulpansa, pg 439
Samho Music Publishing Co, pg 440

Malta
Publishers' Enterprises Group (PEG) Ltd, pg 456

Mexico
Editorial Jilguero, SA de CV, pg 462

New Caledonia
Savannah Editions SARL, pg 488

New Zealand
Barkfire Press, pg 488
Bush Press Communications Ltd, pg 489
Craig Potton Publishing, pg 490
Exisle Publishing Ltd, pg 491
Halcyon Publishing Ltd, pg 491
Nelson Price Milburn Ltd, pg 494
Reed Publishing (NZ) Ltd, pg 495
Shoal Bay Press Ltd, pg 495
Tandem Press, pg 496

Oman
Apex Publishing, pg 506

Poland
Oficyna Wydawnicza Read Me, pg 519

Romania
Corint Verlag, pg 532
Editura Niculescu, pg 534

Russian Federation
Izdatelstvo Fizkultura i Sport, pg 538

Slovakia
Vydavatepstvo Praca spol sro, pg 550
Priroda, pg 550
Ustav informacii a prognoz skolstva mladeze a telovychovy, pg 551

South Africa
Erudita Publications (Pty) Ltd, pg 554

Spain
Editorial Mediterrania SL, pg 582
Noguer y Caralt Editores SA, pg 584
OASIS, Producciones Generales de Comunicacion, pg 584
Editora Regional de Murcia - ERM, pg 588
Tursen, SA, pg 593
Ediciones Tutor SA, pg 594

Switzerland
Mueller Rueschlikon Verlags AG, pg 619
Rotpunktverlag, pg 623
Sinwel-Buchhandlung Verlag, pg 624

Trinidad & Tobago
Joan Bacchus-Xavier, pg 636

Tunisia
Les Editions de l'Arbre, pg 638

United Kingdom
Adlard Coles Nautical, pg 645
Batsford Ltd, pg 652
BCA, pg 653
Blandford Publishing Ltd, pg 656
Bloomsbury Publishing PLC, pg 656
Blorenge Books, pg 656
Bradt Travel Guides Ltd, pg 658
Cassell & Co, pg 664
Cicerone Press, pg 668
Coachwise Ltd, pg 668
Constable & Robinson Ltd, pg 670
Constable Publishers, pg 670
Cordee Ltd, pg 671
The Crowood Press Ltd, pg 672
David & Charles Ltd, pg 674
Eaglemoss Publications Ltd, pg 676
Geiser Productions, pg 686
Gollancz/Witherby, pg 688
HarperCollins Publishers, pg 692
Haynes Publishing, pg 693
Luath Press Ltd, pg 709
Mercat Press, pg 713
Parapress Ltd, pg 724
Quarto Publishing plc, pg 731
Quiller Publishing Ltd, pg 732
Quintet Publishing Ltd, pg 732
Rough Guides Ltd, pg 735
Scarthin Books, pg 738
Sigma Press, pg 742
Thistle Press, pg 748
Vacation Work Publications, pg 752
Veloce Publishing Ltd, pg 752
Ward Lock Ltd, pg 754
Wharncliffe Publishing Ltd, pg 755
Neil Wilson Publishing Ltd, pg 757

PARAPSYCHOLOGY

Argentina
Editorial Kier SACIFI, pg 7
Editorial Planeta Argentina SAIC, pg 8

Australia
Angel Publications, pg 11
Blackhead Ink Publishing, pg 15
Gnostic Editions, pg 24
Hihorse Publishing Pty Ltd, pg 26
The Pythagorean Press, pg 39
Unity Press, pg 46
Wileman Publications, pg 47

SUBJECT INDEX

Austria
Edition S der OSD, pg 51
Resch Verlag, pg 57

Belarus
Belaruskaya Encyklapedyya, pg 63

Belgium
Parsifal BVBA, pg 72

Brazil
Editora Elevacao, pg 82
IBRASA (Instituicao Brasileira de Difusao Cultural Ltda), pg 85
Editora Lidador Ltda, pg 86
Editora Meca Ltda, pg 87
Editora Mercuryo Ltda, pg 88

Bulgaria
Aratron, 1K, pg 94
Kibea Publishing Co, pg 96
Kralica MAB, pg 96
Litera Prima, pg 96
Sila & Zivot, pg 98

Czech Republic
Jiri Chvojka, pg 123
Columbus, pg 123

Estonia
Kupar Publishers, pg 140

France
Editions Amrita SA, pg 147
Le Chariot, pg 154
Editions de Compostelle, pg 156
Editions Dangles SA, pg 157
De Vecchi Editions SA, pg 158
Editions Grancher, pg 166
Lacour-Olle, pg 171
Editions Pygmalion - Gerard Watelet, pg 182
Editions Saint-Michel SA, pg 183

Germany
Aquamarin Verlag, pg 194
Verlag Hermann Bauer KG, pg 199
Buchverlage Langen-Mueller/Herbig, pg 207
Connection Medien GmbH, pg 211
Dagmar Dreves Verlag, pg 212
Divyanand Verlags GmbH, pg 217
Verlag Peter Erd GmbH, pg 223
Verlag Esoterische Philosophie GmbH, pg 224
EVT Energy Video Training & Verlag GmbH, pg 225
Verlag der Stiftung Gralsbotschaft GmbH, pg 234
AIG 1 Hilbinger Verlag GmbH, pg 241
F Hirthammer Verlag GmbH, pg 241
Lorber-Verlag & Turm-Verlag Otto Zluhan, pg 259
Merlin Verlag Andreas Meyer Verlags GmbH und Co KG, pg 263
Neue Erde Verlags GmbH, pg 267
Reichl Verlag Der Leuchter, pg 278
Heinrich Schwab Verlag, pg 285
Die Silberschnur Verlag GmbH, pg 287
Spieth-Verlag Verlag fuer Symbolforschung, pg 288
Mario Truant Verlag, pg 295
Turm-Verlag Lorber-Verlag Otto Zluhan OHG, pg 295

SUBJECT INDEX

Greece
Ed Nea Acropolis, pg 313

Iceland
Bokaforlag Birtingur, pg 327

India
Pustak Mahal, pg 346
Scientific Book Agency, pg 349
Somaiya Publications Pvt Ltd, pg 350
Theosophical Publishing House, pg 351

Italy
Gruppo Editoriale Armenia SpA, pg 376
Crisalide, pg 383
Edizioni l'eta Dell'Acquario Di 1 Bresci & C Sas, pg 387
Edizioni Mediterranee SRL, pg 387
Hermes Edizioni SRL, pg 392
L'Airone Editrice, pg 395
Reverdito Edizioni, pg 405

Latvia
Vieda, pg 442

Lithuania
AS Narbuto Leidykla (AS Narbutas' Publishers), pg 445

The Former Yugoslav Republic of Macedonia
Zumpres Publishing Firm, pg 449

Mexico
Centro Editorial Mexicano Osiris SA, pg 458
Editorial Diana SA de CV, pg 459
Edamex SA de CV, pg 460
Editorial Orion, pg 465

Netherlands
Ankh-Hermes BV, pg 472

Norway
Hilt & Hansteen A/S, pg 504

Paraguay
Intercontinental Editora, pg 510

Philippines
Rex Bookstores & Publishers, pg 514

Poland
Iskry - Publishing House Ltd spotka zoo, pg 517

Portugal
Edicoes 70, Lda, pg 524
Editorial Estampa, Lda, pg 524

Romania
Editura Excelsior, pg 533
Saeculum IO, pg 535
Vestala Verlag, pg 536
Vremea Publishers Ltd, pg 536

Slovakia
Vydavatelstvo Obzor, pg 550

Slovenia
Zalozba Mihelac d o o, pg 552

South Africa
Bet-El Publishers, pg 553

Spain
Editorial 'Alas', pg 562
Casset Ediciones SL, pg 566
Edicomunicacion SA, pg 572
Ediciones Morata SL, pg 583
Nueva Acropolis, pg 584
Grup 62, pg 591

Switzerland
Ariston Editions, pg 608
Govinda-Verlag, pg 615
Origo Verlag, pg 621
Scherz Verlag AG, pg 623
Tobler Verlag, pg 626
Editions Vivez Soleil SA, pg 627

Togo
Editions Akpagnon, pg 636

Turkey
Ruh ve Madde Yayinlari ve Saglik Hizmetleri AS, pg 641

Ukraine
ASK Ltd, pg 643

United Kingdom
Amber Books Ltd, pg 646
Bloomsbury Publishing PLC, pg 656
Capall Bann Publishing, pg 663
Mandrake of Oxford, pg 711
Quartz Editions, pg 732
The Society of Metaphysicians Ltd, pg 743

PHILOSOPHY

Albania
NL SH, pg 1

Algeria
Enterprise Nationale du Livre (ENAL), pg 2

Argentina
Editorial Abaco de Rodolfo Depalma SRL, pg 2
Abeledo-Perrot SAE e I, pg 2
Aguilar Altea Taurus Alfaguara SA de Ediciones, pg 3
Alianza Editorial de Argentina SA, pg 3
Amorrortu Editores SA, pg 3
Editorial Astrea de Alfredo y Ricardo Depalma SRL, pg 3
Bonum Editorial SACI, pg 4
Editorial Claridad SA, pg 4
Club de Lectores, pg 4
Edicial SA, pg 5
EUDEBA (Editorial Universitaria de Buenos Aires), pg 6
Ediciones de la Flor SRL, pg 6
Editorial Guadalupe, pg 6
La Ley SA Editora e Impresora, pg 7
Editorial Losada SA, pg 7
Marymar Ediciones SA, pg 7
Editorial Paidos SAICF, pg 8
Editorial Plus Ultra SA, pg 8
Editorial Sudamericana SA, pg 9
Ediciones Tres Tiempos SRL, pg 9
Editoria Universitaria de la Patagonia, pg 9

Australia
Michelle Anderson Publishing Pty Ltd, pg 11
Angel Publications, pg 11
Bridge To Peace Publications, pg 16
Catholic Institute of Sydney, pg 17
Coconut Productions, pg 18
Crystal Publishing, pg 19
Experimental Art Foundation, pg 22
Freshet Press, pg 23
Gnostic Editions, pg 24
Hale & Iremonger Pty Ltd, pg 24
In-Tune Books, pg 27
Inwardpath Publishers, pg 28
Magabala Books Aboriginal Corporation, pg 31
McGraw-Hill Australia Pty Ltd, pg 32
Newman Centre Publications, pg 35
Quakers Hill Press, pg 39
Shakespeare Head Press Pty Ltd, pg 42
Tamarind Publications, pg 44
Thin Rich Press, pg 44
Unity Press, pg 46

Austria
Verlag Alexander Bernhardt, pg 49
Bethania Verlag, pg 49
Franz Deuticke Verlagsges mbH, pg 51
Diotima Presse, pg 51
Gerold & Co, pg 52
Haymon-Verlag GesmbH, pg 52
Verlag Hoelder-Pichler-Tempsky, pg 53
Milena Verlag, pg 55
Verlag Monte Verita, pg 55
Mueller-Speiser Wissenschaftlicher Verlag, pg 55
Verlag Oldenbourg, pg 56
Verlag des Osterr Kneippbundes GmbH, pg 57
Osterreichischer Bundesveilag Ges.mbh, pg 57
Passagen Verlag GmbH, pg 57
Anna Pichler Verlag GmbH, pg 57
Verlag Anton Pustet, pg 57
Springer-Verlag Wien, pg 59
Studien Verlag Gmbh, pg 59
Verlag Styria, pg 59
Edition Va Bene, pg 60
Verband der Wissenschaftlichen Gesellschaften Oesterreichs (VWGOe), pg 60
WUV/Facultas Universitaetsverlag, pg 61

Bangladesh
Agamee Prakashani, pg 62

Belgium
Acco CV, pg 64
Altina, pg 64
Maison d'Editions Baha'ies ASBL, pg 64
Brepols Publishers NV, pg 65
Centre d'Action Laique, pg 66
Davidsfonds VZW, pg 67
Editions De Boeck-Larcier SA, pg 67
Maison d'Editions Cl Dejaie, pg 67
Editions les eperonniers, pg 68
Imprimerie Hayez SPRL, pg 69
Infoboek NV, pg 69
Koninklijke Vlaamse Academie van Belgie voor Wetenschappen en Kunsten, pg 70
Editions Labor, pg 70
Editions Lessius ASBL, pg 71
Leuven University Press, pg 71

Editeurs de Litterature Biblique, pg 71
La Longue Vue, pg 71
Mardaga, Pierre 12, pg 72
Nauwelaerts Edition SA, pg 72
Paradox Pers vzw, pg 72
Parsifal BVBA, pg 72
La Part de L'Oeil, pg 72
Uitgeverij Peeters Leuven (Belgie), pg 72
Pelckmans NV, De Nederlandsche Boekhandel, pg 73
Uitgeverij Pelckmans N V, pg 73
Presses Universitaires de Bruxelles ASBL, pg 73
Publications des Facultes Universitaires Saint Louis, pg 73
Sonneville Press (Uitgeverij) VTW, pg 74
Editions de l'Universite de Bruxelles, pg 75
Vita, pg 75
VUB University Press, pg 75

Bolivia
Editorial Don Bosco, pg 76

Bosnia and Herzegovina
Bemust doo Novinsko-Izdavacko stamparsko i trgovacko preduzece, pg 77
Veselin Maslesa, pg 77

Brazil
Agalma Psicanalise Editora Ltda, pg 78
AGIR S/A Editora, pg 78
Editora Alfa Omega Ltda, pg 78
Editora Antroposofica Ltda, pg 78
Associacao Palas Athena do Brasil, pg 79
Livraria Duas Cidades Ltda, pg 81
E P U Editora Pedagogica e Universitaria Ltd, pg 81
Edicon Editora e Consultorial Ltda, pg 81
Editora Companhia das Letras/ Editora Schwarcz Ltda, pg 82
Editora Elevacao, pg 82
Companhia Editora Forense, pg 82
Cia Editora Nacional, pg 82
EDUC - Editora da PUC-SP, pg 82
EDUSC - Editora da Universidade do Sagrado Coracao, pg 82
Livraria Martins Fontes Editora Ltda, pg 83
Forense Universitaria Editora, pg 83
Fundacao Cultural Avatar, pg 83
Editora Gente Livraria e Editora Ltda, pg 84
Edicoes Graal Ltda, pg 84
Ordem do Graal na Terra, pg 84
Editora Ground Ltda, pg 84
Hemus Editora Ltda, pg 85
Livro Ibero-Americano Ltda, pg 85
IBRASA (Instituicao Brasileira de Difusao Cultural Ltda), pg 85
Imago Editora Importacao e Exportacao Ltda, pg 85
LDA Editores Ltda, pg 86
Editora Logosofica, pg 86
Edicoes Loyola SA, pg 87
Editora Nova Alexandria Ltda, pg 88
Editora Nova Fronteira SA, pg 88
Pallas Editora e Distribuidora Ltda, pg 89
Paulus Editora, pg 89
Editora Paz e Terra, pg 89
Editora Perspectiva, pg 89
Distribuidora Record de Servicos de Imprensa SA, pg 90

PUBLISHERS SUBJECT INDEX

Saraiva SA, Livreiros Editores, pg 91
34 Literatura S/C Ltda, pg 92
Editora UNESP, pg 92
Editora da Universidade de Sao Paulo, pg 93
Editora Vecchi SA, pg 93
Editora Vigilia Ltda, pg 93
Vozes Editora Ltda, pg 93
Jorge Zahar Editor, pg 93

Bulgaria

Antroposofsko Izdatelstvo Dimo R Daskalov OOD, pg 94
Bilblioteka Nov den - Sajuz na Svobodnite Demokrati (Union of Free Democrats), pg 94
CHRIKER, pg 94
EA Publishing House, pg 95
Eurasia Academic Publishers, pg 95
Publishing House Hristo Botev, pg 96
Kibea Publishing Co, pg 96
Kralica MAB, pg 96
LIK IZDANIJA, pg 96
Makros 2000 - Plovdiv, pg 96
Mladezh, pg 96
Naouka i Izkoustvo, Ltd, pg 97
Nov Covek Publishing House, pg 97
Prozoretz Ltd Publishing House, pg 97
Sila & Zivot, pg 98

Burundi

Editions Intore, pg 98

Chile

Arrayan Editores, pg 99
Edeval (Universidad de Valparaiso), pg 100
Pehuen Editores Ltda, pg 101
Pontificia Universidad Catolica de Chile, pg 101
Ediciones Universitarias de Valparaiso, pg 101

China

Anhui People's Publishing House, pg 102
Beijing Publishing House, pg 102
Foreign Languages Press, pg 105
Fudan University Press, pg 105
Lanzhou University Press, pg 107
SDX (Shenghuo-Dushu-Xinzhi) Joint Publishing Co, pg 108
Shandong People's Publishing House, pg 109
Shandong University Press, pg 109

Colombia

Consejo Episcopal Latinoamericano Celam, pg 111
Fundacion Universidad de la Sabana Ediciones Udes, pg 112
Instituto Misionerao Hijas De San Pablo, pg 113
Siglo XXI Editores de Colombia Ltda, pg 113
Unidad Universitaria del Sur (UNISUR), pg 114
Universidad de Antioquia, Division Publicaciones, pg 114

The Democratic Republic of the Congo

Presses Universitaires du Zaiire (PUZ), pg 115

Costa Rica

Promesa, Ediciones, pg 116
Editorial Universidad Estatal a Distancia (EUNED), pg 117

Cote d'Ivoire

Centre d'Edition et de Diffusion Africaines, pg 117

Croatia

AGM doo, pg 118
ArTresor naklada, pg 118
Durieux d o o, pg 118
Faust Vrani, pg 118
Globus-Nakladni zavod, pg 118
Izdavacka Delatnost Hrvatske Akademije Znanosti I Umjetnosti, pg 118
Hrvatsko filozofsko drustvo, pg 119
Matica hrvatska, pg 119
Mladost d d Izdavacku grafiku i informaticku djelatnost, pg 119
Naprijed d d Naklada, pg 119
Skolska Knjiga, pg 120

Cuba

Casa Editora Abril, pg 120
Editora Politica, pg 121

Czech Republic

Academia, pg 122
AULOS sro, pg 123
Aurora, pg 123
Barrister & Principal, pg 123
Brody, pg 123
Cesky spisovatel, pg 123
Dimenze 2 Plus 2 Praha, pg 124
Inspirace, pg 124
Kalich SRO, pg 125
Karolinum, nakladatelstvi, pg 125
Konsultace, pg 125
Melantrich, pg 126
Mlada fronta, pg 126
Nadace Lyry Pragensis, pg 126
Nase vojsko, nakladatelstvi a knizni obchod, pg 126
Omnipress Praha, pg 127
Pragma 4, pg 127
Prostor, Ltd, pg 128
Slon Sociologicke Nakladatelstvi, pg 128
Svoboda Servis GmbH, pg 128
Vodnar, pg 129
Votobia sro, pg 129
Vysehrad, pg 129
Zvon, pg 129

Denmark

Aarhus Universitetsforlag, pg 129
Akademisk Forlag, pg 129
Borgens Forlag A/S, pg 130
Forlaget GMT, pg 132
Gyldendalske Boghandel - Nordisk Forlag A/S, pg 132
Forlaget Hovedland, pg 133
Museum Tusculanum Press, pg 134
New Era Publications International ApS, pg 134
Nyt Nordisk Forlag Arnold Busck A/S, pg 134
Politisk Revy, pg 134
C A Reitzel A/S, pg 134
Hans Reitzel Publishers Ltd, pg 134
Det Schonbergske Forlag, pg 135
Syddansk Universitetsforlag, pg 136
Systime, pg 136

Dominican Republic

Pontificia Universidad Catolica Madre y Maestra, pg 136
Sociedad Editorial Dominicana SA, pg 137

Ecuador

Corporacion Editora Nacional, pg 137
Libresa S A, pg 137
Pontificia Universidad Catolica de Ecuador, Centro de Publicaciones, pg 137

Egypt (Arab Republic of Egypt)

Al Arab Publishing House, pg 138
Dar El Shorouk Publishing & Distributing House, pg 138
Middle East Book Centre, pg 139

El Salvador

UCA Editores, pg 139
Editorial Universitaria de la Universidad de El Salvador, pg 139

Estonia

Ilmamaa, pg 140
Olion Publishers, pg 140
Tuum, pg 141

Finland

Basam Books Oy, pg 142
Schildts Foerlagsaktiebolag, pg 144
Soederstroem et Co Foerlagsaktiebolag, pg 144
Osuuskunta Vastapaino, pg 145

France

ABC Editions, pg 145
ADPF Publications, pg 146
Editions Albin Michel, pg 146
Editions d'Amerique et d'Orient, Adrien Maisonneuve, pg 147
Editions Amrita SA, pg 147
L'Anabase, pg 147
Editions Anthropos Sarl, pg 147
L'Arche Editeur, pg 147
Atelier National de Reproduction des Theses, pg 148
Editions de l'Aube, pg 149
Editions Aubier-Montaigne SA, pg 149
Autrement Editions, pg 149
Societe d'Edition Les Belles Lettres, pg 150
Berg International Editeurs, pg 150
William Blake & Co, pg 150
Presses Universitaires de Bordeaux (PUB), pg 151
Breal, pg 151
Alain Brethe Editions, pg 152
Editions Buchet/Chastel, pg 152
Editions Calmann-Levy SA, pg 152
Editions Caracteres, pg 152
Editions du Cerf, pg 153
Jacqueline Chambon, pg 154
Editions Champ Vallon, pg 154
Chronique Sociale, pg 155
Circe, pg 155
CNRS Editions, pg 155
Armand Colin, Editeur, pg 155
Editions de Compostelle, pg 156
Copernic, pg 156
Courrier du Livre Sarl, pg 157
La Decouverte et Syros, pg 158
Editions Denoel Sarl, pg 158
Desclee et Cie, Editeurs, pg 159
Editions Dis Voir, pg 159
Editions de l'Eclat, pg 160

Presses de l'Ecole Normale Superieure, pg 160
EPEL, pg 162
Ere Nouvelle, pg 162
Editions Eres, pg 162
Institut d'Etudes Augustiniennes, pg 163
Fac Editions, pg 163
Fata Morgana, pg 163
Librairie Artheme Fayard, pg 163
Librairie Fischbacher, International Art Book Distribution (import-export), pg 164
Editions Jacques Gabay, pg 165
Edition Galilee, pg 165
Editions Gallimard, pg 165
Editions Gammaprim, pg 166
Ganymede, pg 166
Paul Geuthner Librairie Orientaliste, pg 166
Hachette Livre, pg 167
Editions de l'Herne, pg 168
Editions Imago, pg 169
Editions Fernand Lanore Sarl, pg 172
Librairie Scientifique et Technique Albert Blanchard, pg 173
Le Livre de Poche-L G F (Librairie Generale Francaise), pg 173
Maison de la Revelation, pg 174
Mercure de France SA, pg 176
Les Editions de Minuit SA, pg 176
Presses Universitaires du Mirail, pg 176
Editions Modernes Media, pg 176
Gabriel Mony, pg 176
Fernand Nathan, pg 177
Nil Editions, pg 177
Mare Nostrum, pg 177
Editions Odile Jacob, pg 178
Editions de l'Orante, pg 178
L'Originel - Editions Accarias, pg 178
Editions Paradigme, pg 179
Editions Payot & Rivages, pg 179
Peeters-France, pg 179
Jean-Michel Place, pg 180
Presence Africaine Editions, pg 180
Presses de la Renaissance, pg 180
Presses Universitaires de Caen, pg 181
Presses Universitaires de France (PUF), pg 181
Presses Universitaires de Nancy, pg 181
Presses Universitaires de Strasbourg, pg 181
Presses Universitaires du Septentrion, pg 181
Editions Prosveta SA, pg 182
Editions Robert Laffont, Nil, Fixot, Seghers, Julliard, pg 183
Editions Roudil, pg 183
Editions Saint-Paul SA, pg 183
Maren Sell, pg 184
Service Technique pour l'Education, pg 185
Editions du Seuil, pg 185
Editions Andre Silvaire Sarl, pg 185
Societe des Editions Grasset et Fasquelle, pg 185
Publications de la Sorbonne, pg 186
Association d'Editions Sorg, pg 186
Editions SOS (Editions du Secours Catholique), pg 186
Editions Louis Soulanges Le Livrer Ouvert, pg 186
Librairie Pierre Tequi et Editions Tequi, pg 187
Transeuropeennes/RCE, pg 188
Editions Trois Fontaines, pg 188
Universitas, pg 188

1043

SUBJECT INDEX

Editions Verdier, pg 189
Librairie Philosophique J Vrin, pg 189

Germany

A Francke Verlag (Tubingen und Basel), pg 191
Accedo Verlagsgesellschaft mbH, pg 191
Agis Verlag GmbH, pg 192
Aisthesis Verlag Dr Detlev Kopp und Dr Michael Vogt, pg 192
Akademie Verlag GmbH, pg 192
Verlag Karl Alber GmbH, pg 192
Aquamarin Verlag, pg 194
Argument-Verlag, pg 195
Arun-Verlag, pg 195
Aschendorffsche Verlagsbuchhandlung GmbH & Co KG, pg 195
Asclepios Edition Lothar Baus, pg 196
Otto Wilhelm Barth-Verlag KG, pg 198
Verlag Hermann Bauer KG, pg 199
Dr Wolfgang Baur Verlag Kunst & Alltag, pg 199
Bayerischer Schulbuch-Verlag GmbH, pg 199
Verlag C H Beck (OHG), pg 200
Berlin Verlag Arno Spitz GmbH, pg 200
Berliner Debatte Wissenschafts Verlag, GSFP-Gesellschaft fur Sozialwissen-schaftliche Forschung und Publizistik mbH &Co KG, pg 201
Betzel Verlag GmbH, pg 202
BBT Bhaktivedanta Book Trust, pg 202
Biblio-Zeller Verlag, pg 202
Verlag Die Blaue Eule, pg 204
Klaus Boer Verlag, pg 205
Buechse der Pandora Verlags-GmbH, pg 207
Ulrich Burgdorf/Homeopathic Publishing House, pg 208
Caann Verlag, Klaus Wagner, pg 208
Campus Verlag GmbH, pg 209
Carl-Auer-Systeme Verlag, pg 209
Fachverlag Hans Carl GmbH, pg 209
CEC-Cosmic Energy Connections, pg 209
J G Cotta'sche Buchhandlung Nachfolger GmbH, pg 212
Verlag Darmstaedter Blaetter Schwarz und Co, pg 212
Das Arsenal, Verlag fuer Kultur und Politik GmbH, pg 212
Verlag Deutsche Unitarier, pg 214
Deutsche Verlags-Anstalt GmbH (DVA), pg 214
Deutscher Taschenbuch Verlag GmbH & Co KG (dtv), pg 215
Eugen Diederichs Verlag GmbH & Co KG, pg 216
Sammlung Dieterich Verlagsgesellschaft mbH, pg 216
Dieterichsche Verlagsbuchhandlung Mainz, pg 216
Dietrich zu Klampen Verlag, pg 216
Dingfelder-Verlag Inh Gerd Gmelin, pg 217
Edition Diskord, pg 217
Divyanand Verlags GmbH, pg 217
Drei Eichen Verlag Manuel Kissener, pg 218
Duncker und Humblot GmbH, pg 219
Klaus D Dutz, pg 219
Ein Fach-Verlag, pg 222

Eironeia-Verlag, pg 222
Elpis Verlag GmbH, pg 222
Verlag Esoterische Philosophie GmbH, pg 224
Europa Verlag GmbH, pg 224
Europaeische Verlagsanstalt GmbH & Rotbuch Verlag GmbH & Co KG, pg 225
Evangelischer Presseverband fur Bayern eV, pg 225
Wilhelm Fink GmbH & Co Verlags-KG, pg 228
Harald Fischer Verlag GmbH, pg 228
Karin Fischer Verlag GmbH, pg 228
Flensburger Hefte Verlag GmbH, pg 228
Verlag Freies Geistesleben, pg 230
Friedrich Frommann Verlag, pg 230
Garbe Verlag Ellen Vogt, pg 231
Genius Verlag, pg 231
Verlag der Stiftung Gralsbotschaft GmbH, pg 234
Walter de Gruyter GmbH & Co KG, pg 234
Guetersloher Verlagshaus Gerd Mohn, pg 235
Dr Haensel-Hohenhausen AG, pg 236
Carl Hanser Verlag, pg 237
Verlag Hinder und Deelmann, pg 241
F Hirthammer Verlag GmbH, pg 241
S Hirzel Verlag GmbH und Co, pg 241
Hoffmann und Campe Verlag GmbH, pg 242
Holos Verlag, pg 242
Horlemann Verlag, pg 243
Hyperion - Verlag, pg 244
Iudicium Verlag GmbH, pg 245
Johannes Verlag Einsiedeln, Freiburg, pg 246
Junius Verlag GmbH, pg 247
Vittorio Klostermann GmbH, pg 250
Verlagsgruppe Koehler/Mittler, pg 251
Verlag Koenigshausen und Neumann GmbH, pg 251
Koesel-Verlag GmbH & Co, pg 252
W Kohlhammer GmbH, abt Haussortiment, pg 252
Kolibri-Verlags GmbH, pg 252
Anton H Konrad Verlag, pg 252
KONTEXTverlag, pg 252
Dr Anton Kovac Slavica Verlag, pg 253
Karin Kramer Verlag, pg 253
Alfred Kroner Verlag, pg 253
Peter Lang GmbH Europaeischer Verlag der Wissenschaften, pg 255
Leibniz Verlag, pg 256
Leibniz-Buecherwarte, pg 257
Leipziger Universitaetsverlag GmbH, pg 257
Dr Gisela Lermann, pg 257
Verlag Leske plus Budrich GmbH, pg 257
Libertas- Europaeisches Institut GmbH, pg 257
Lukas Verlag fur Kunst- und Geistesgeschichte, pg 259
Maeander Verlag GmbH, pg 260
Annemarie Maeger, pg 260
Manutius Verlag, pg 260
Matthes und Seitz Verlag GmbH, pg 261
Felix Meiner Verlag GmbH, pg 262
mentis Verlag GmbH, pg 262

Merlin Verlag Andreas Meyer Verlags GmbH und Co KG, pg 263
Metropolis- Verlag fur Okonomie, Gesellschaft und Politik GmbH, pg 263
J B Metzler'sche Verlagsbuchhandlung, pg 263
Preubmpassling Verlag Gisela Meussling, pg 263
Mohr Siebeck, pg 264
Verlag Neue Kritik KG, pg 267
Neuer ISP Verlag GmbH, pg 268
Max Niemeyer Verlag GmbH, pg 269
nymphenburger, pg 269
Oekumenischer Verlag Dr R-F Edel, pg 270
Georg Olms Verlag AG, pg 270
Oros Verlag, pg 271
Osho Verlag GmbH, pg 271
Pahl-Rugenstein Verlag Nachfolger-GmbH, pg 271
Verlag Dr Friedrich Pfeil, pg 273
Philipp Reclam Jun Verlag GmbH, pg 273
Philosophia Verlag GmbH, pg 273
Piper Verlag GmbH, pg 274
Guido Pressler Verlag, pg 275
Quell Verlag, pg 276
Quelle und Meyer Verlag GmbH & Co, pg 276
Radius-Verlag GmbH, pg 276
Reclam Verlag Leipzig, pg 277
Ernst Reinhardt GmbH & Co KG Verlag, pg 278
Verlag Roter Morgen, pg 280
Rowohlt Taschenbuch Verlag GmbH, pg 280
Verlag an der Ruhr GmbH, pg 281
K G Saur Verlag GmbH, A Gale/ Thomson Learning Company, pg 282
Schangrila Verlags und Vertriebs GmbH, pg 282
Ferdinand Schoeningh Verlag GmbH, pg 284
Schulz-Kirchner Verlag GmbH, pg 285
Heinrich Schwab Verlag, pg 285
Scientia Verlag und Antiquariat, pg 286
Spieth-Verlag Verlag fuer Symbolforschung, pg 288
Springer-Verlag GmbH & Co KG, pg 288
Steidl Verlag, pg 289
Franz Steiner Verlag Wiesbaden GmbH, pg 289
Stern-Verlag Janssen & Co, pg 290
Suhrkamp Verlag, pg 291
Suin Buch-Verlag, pg 291
Ullstein Heyne List GmbH & Co KG, pg 295
Ulrike Helmer Verlag, pg 296
UTB fuer Wissenschaft Uni-Taschenbuecher GmbH, pg 297
UVK Universitatsverlag Konstanz GmbH, pg 297
Vandenhoeck & Ruprecht, pg 297
VJK Verlag Josef Knecht, pg 299
Weber Zucht & Co, pg 300
Weidler Buchverlag Berlin, pg 301
Weidmannsche Verlagsbuchhandlung, pg 301
Verlagsgruppe Weltbild GmbH, pg 301
Erich Wewel Verlag, pg 302
Wissenschaftliche Buchgesellschaft, pg 303
Verlag DAS WORT GmbH, pg 304

Zeller Verlag GmbH & Co, pg 305
Zentralantiquariat Leipzig GmbH Buchhandlung, pg 305

Greece

Alamo Hellas, pg 308
D I Arsenidis Publications, pg 309
Boukoumanis' Editions, pg 309
Dorikos Publishing House, pg 310
Ekdoseis Kazantzaki (Kazantzakis Publications), pg 310
Elliniki Leschi Tou Vivliou, pg 310
Ekdoseis Filon, pg 310
Gutenberg Publications, pg 311
Denise Harvey, pg 311
Hestia-I D Hestia-Kollaros & Co Corporation, pg 311
Ianos, pg 311
Kardamitsa A, pg 312
Kastaniotis Editions SA, pg 312
Kedros Publishers, pg 312
Kritiki Publishing, pg 312
Morfotiko Idryma Ethnikis Trapezas, pg 313
Ed Nea Acropolis, pg 313
Nea Thesis - Evrotas, pg 313
Odysseas Publications Ltd, pg 313
Orfanidis Publications, pg 314
Patakis Publishers, pg 314
Psichogios Publications SA, pg 314
Society for Macedonian Studies, pg 315
Stochastis, pg 315
J Vassiliou Bibliopolein, pg 315

Guatemala

Grupo Editorial RIN-78, pg 316

Holy See (Vatican City State)

Biblioteca Apostolica Vaticana, pg 317
Libreria Editrice Vaticana, pg 317

Hong Kong

The Chinese University Press, pg 319
Chung Hwa Book Co (HK) Ltd, pg 319
The Dharmasthiti Buddist Institute Ltd, pg 319
Hong Kong University Press, pg 320
Logical Products (HK) Ltd, pg 320
Ming Pao Publications Ltd, pg 321
Philopsychy Press, pg 321

Hungary

Akademiai Kiado, pg 323
Atlantisz Kiado, pg 323
Balassi Kiado Kft, pg 323
Europa Konyvkiado, pg 323
Janus Pannonius Tudomanyegyetem, pg 324
Jelenkor Verlag, pg 324
Joszoveg Muhely Kiado, pg 324
Kiiarat Konyvdiado, pg 324
Kossuth Kiado RT, pg 325
Magveto Koenyvkiado, pg 325
Nemzeti Tankoenyvkiado, pg 326
Osiris Kiado, pg 326
Typotex Kft Elektronikus Kiado, pg 327

Iceland

Bokaforlag Birtingur, pg 327

India

Abhinav Publications, pg 329
Abhishek Publications, pg 329
The Academic Press, pg 329

PUBLISHERS

Ajanta Publications (India), pg 330
APH Publishing Corp, pg 331
Asian Educational Services, pg 331
Asian Trading Corporation, pg 331
Associated Publishing House, pg 331
Atma Ram & Sons, pg 331
The Bangalore Printing & Publishing Co Ltd, pg 332
Bharatiya Vidya Bhavan, pg 333
Books & Books, pg 334
S Chand & Co Ltd, pg 334
Chetana Private Ltd, pg 334
Chowkhamba Sanskrit Series Office, pg 335
Concept Publishing Co, pg 335
Cosmo Publications, pg 335
Disha Prakashan, pg 336
DK Printworld (P) Ltd, pg 336
Ess Ess Publications, pg 337
Ganesh & Co, pg 337
Geeta Prakasham, pg 337
Gyan Publishing House, pg 338
Arnold Heinman Publishers (India) Pvt Ltd, pg 338
Heritage Publishers, pg 338
Intellectual Publishing House, pg 339
Inter-India Publications, pg 340
Intertrade Publications, pg 340
Islamic Publishing House, pg 340
Jaico Publishing House, pg 340
Law Publishers, pg 341
Sri Ramakrishna Math, pg 342
Minerva Associates (Publications) Pvt Ltd, pg 342
Motilal Banarsidass Publishers Pvt Ltd, pg 343
Mudgala Trust, pg 343
Munshiram Manoharlal Publishers Pvt Ltd, pg 343
Narosa Publishing House, pg 343
Navajivan Trust, pg 344
Navrang Booksellers & Publishers, pg 344
Omsons Publications, pg 345
Oxford University Press, pg 345
Panjab University Publication Bureau, pg 345
People's Publishing House (P) Ltd, pg 346
Rajasthan Hindi Granth Academy, pg 347
Rajesh Publications, pg 347
Rebel Publishing House Pvt Ltd, pg 347
Regency Publications, pg 347
Reliance Publishing House, pg 347
Rupa & Co, pg 348
SABDA, pg 348
Sasta Sahitya Mandal, pg 349
Sri Satguru Publications, pg 349
SBW Publishers, pg 349
Scientific Book Agency, pg 349
Somaiya Publications Pvt Ltd, pg 350
Sterling Publishers Pvt Ltd, pg 351
Theosophical Publishing House, pg 351
Vikas Publishing House Pvt Ltd, pg 353

Indonesia

P T Bulan Bintang, pg 354
Djambatan PT, pg 355
Dunia Pustaka Jaya, pg 355
Eresco PT, pg 355
Pustaka Utama Grafiti, PT, pg 357
Tintamas Indonesia PT, pg 357
Yayasan Obor Indonesia, pg 357

Islamic Republic of Iran

Scientific and Cultural Publications, pg 358

Ireland

Cathedral Books Ltd, pg 359
Four Courts Press Ltd, pg 360
New Books/Connolly Books, pg 362
Publishers Group South West (Ireland), pg 363
Runa Press, pg 364

Israel

Am Oved Publishers Ltd, pg 365
Bar Ilan University Press, pg 365
The Bialik Institute, pg 365
Breslov Research Institute, pg 366
DAT Publications, pg 366
Dyonon/Papyrus Publishing House of the Tel-Aviv, pg 367
Feldheim Publishers Ltd, pg 367
Haifa University Press, pg 368
Hakibbutz Hameuchad Publishing House Ltd, pg 368
Intermedia Audio, Video Book Publishing Ltd, pg 368
The Israel Academy of Sciences & Humanities, pg 368
Keter Publishing House Ltd, pg 369
The Magnes Press, pg 370
Massada Press Ltd, pg 370
Misgav Yerushalayim, pg 370
Nehora Press, pg 371
Rav Kook Institute, pg 371
Rubin Mass Ltd, pg 371
Schocken Publishing House Ltd, pg 372
Shalem Press, pg 372
Sifriat Poalim Ltd, pg 372
Yachdav, United Publishers Co Ltd, pg 373
Y L Peretz Publishing Co, pg 374

Italy

Edizioni Abete, pg 374
Mario Adda Editore SNC, pg 374
Adea Edizioni, pg 374
Adelphi Edizioni SpA, pg 374
Aesthetica, pg 374
Edizioni Anabasi SpA, pg 375
Edizioni ARES, pg 376
Argalia Editore delle Arti Grafiche Editoriali SRL, pg 376
Arktos, pg 376
Editore Armando Armando SRL, pg 376
Casa Editrice Astrolabio-Ubaldini Editore, pg 377
Belforte Editore Libraio srl, pg 377
Bibliopolis - Edizioni di Filosofia e Scienze Srl, pg 377
Bibliotheca di Gabriele Chiusano, pg 378
Bollati Boringhieri Editore Srl, pg 378
Book Editore, pg 378
Edizioni Borla SRL, pg 378
Bovolenta, pg 378
Edizioni Bresciane, pg 378
Bulzoni Editore SRL (Le Edizioni Universitarie d'Italia), pg 379
Edizioni Cadmo SRL, pg 379
Campanotto, pg 379
Edizioni Cantagalli, pg 379
Capone Editore SRL, pg 379
Nuova Casa Editrice Licinio Cappelli GEM srl, pg 379
Casa Editrice Felice Le Monnier, pg 380
Casa Editrice Giuseppe Principato Spa, pg 380
Edizioni Castello di Antonio Careddu, pg 380
CEDAM (Casa Editrice Dr A Milani), pg 380
Celuc Libri, pg 380
Centro Italiano Studi Alto Medioevo, pg 381
Le Cerchio Imigiative Editoriali, pg 381
Ciranna - Roma, pg 381
Citta Nuova Editrice, pg 382
CLUEB (Cooperativa Libraria Universitaria Editrice Bologna), pg 382
Nuova Coletti Editore Roma, pg 382
Edizioni Cultura della Pace, pg 383
La Culturale, pg 383
G De Bono Editore, pg 384
Edizioni Dedalo SRL, pg 384
Edizioni Dehoniane, pg 384
ECIG, pg 385
Editori Laterza, pg 386
Editrice la Scuola SpA, pg 386
Edizioni Il Punto d'Incontro SAS, pg 386
Edizioni la Scala, pg 387
Edizioni Mediterranee SRL, pg 387
Edizioni Studio Domenicano (ESD), pg 387
EGEA (Edizioni Giuridiche Economiche Aziendali), pg 387
Giulio Einaudi Editore SpA, pg 387
Esselibri, pg 388
Giangiacomo Feltrinelli SpA, pg 389
La Fenice SRL, pg 389
Arnaldo Forni Editore SRL, pg 389
Gangemi Editore, pg 390
Editrice Garigliano SRL, pg 390
Edizioni GB, pg 390
Editrice Giannotta di Sebastiano Pace Giannotta, pg 390
G Giappichelli Editore SRL, pg 390
Gius Laterza e Figli SpA, pg 391
Libreria Editrice Gregoriana, pg 391
Edizioni Guerini e Associati SpA, pg 392
Herbita Editrice di Leonardo Palermo, pg 392
Herder Editrice e Libreria, pg 392
Hopeful Monster Editore, pg 392
Ibis, pg 393
Il Minotauro, pg 393
Il Poligrafo, pg 393
Il Saggiatore, pg 393
Ila - Palma, Tea Nova, pg 393
Instituti Editoriali E Poligrafici Internazionali SRL, pg 393
Editoriale Jaca Book SpA, pg 394
L Japadre Editore, pg 394
Jouvence, pg 394
Lalli Editore SRL, pg 395
Editrice LAS, pg 395
Edizioni Lavoro SRL, pg 395
Lecce Spazio Vivo Srl, pg 395
LED - Edizioni Universitarie di Lettere Economia Diritto, pg 395
Casa Editrice Le Lettere SRL, pg 395
Levante, pg 395
Liguori Editore SRL, pg 396
Vincenzo Lo Faro Editore, pg 396
Loescher Editore SRL, pg 396
Loffredo Editore Napoli SpA®, pg 396
Longanesi & C, pg 396
Angelo Longo Editore, pg 396
Lubrina Editore Srl, pg 397
Luni, pg 397
Macro Edizioni, pg 397
Manifestolibri, pg 397
Casa Editrice Marietti SpA, pg 397
Marzorati Editore SRL, pg 398
Editrice Massimo SAS di Crespi Cesare e C, pg 398
Il Melangolo, pg 398
Milella di Lecce Spazio Vivo SRL, pg 399
Arnoldo Mondadori Editore SpA, pg 399
Editrice Morcelliana SpA, pg 399
Mucchi Editore SRL, pg 400
Societa Editrice Il Mulino, pg 400
Gruppo Ugo Mursia Editore SpA, pg 400
Nardini Editore srl, pg 400
Newton Compton Editori SRL, pg 401
La Nuova Italia Editrice SpA, pg 401
Leo S Olschki, pg 402
Maria Pacini Fazzi Editore, pg 402
Paideia Editrice, pg 402
Paravia Bruno Mondadori Editori, pg 402
Patron Editore SrL, pg 403
Pratiche Editrice, pg 404
Psicologica Editrice, pg 404
Il Punto D Incontro, pg 404
Edizioni Quattroventi SNC, pg 404
Editrice Queriniana, pg 404
Riccardo Ricciardi Editore SpA, pg 405
Edizioni Riposte, pg 405
Editori Riuniti, pg 405
Rosenberg e Sellier Editori in Torino, pg 406
Rubbettino Editore, pg 406
Rusconi Libri Srl, pg 406
SAIE Editrice SRL, pg 406
Edizioni San Paolo SRL, pg 407
Edizioni Scientifiche Italiane, pg 407
SEMAR Publishers SRL, pg 407
Sicania, pg 408
Edizioni Librarie Siciliane, pg 408
Societa Editrice Internazionale - SEI, pg 408
Edizioni Rosminiane Sodalitas, pg 408
Spirali Edizioni, pg 408
Edizioni di Storia e Letteratura, pg 409
Edizioni Studium SpA, pg 409
Sugarco Edizioni SRL, pg 409
TEA Tascabili degli Editori Associati SpA, pg 409
Tilgher-Genova sas, pg 410
Editrice Tirrenia Stampatori SAS, pg 410
Tranchida, pg 410
Transeuropa Libri, pg 410
Il Tripode Srl, pg 410
Unipress, pg 410
Urbaniana University Press, pg 410
UTET (Unione Tipografico-Editrice Torinese), pg 411
Vita e Pensiero, pg 411
Vivere In SRL, pg 411
Zanichelli Editore SpA, pg 412
Edizioni Zara, pg 412

Japan

Chikuma Shobo Publishing Co Ltd, pg 415
Chuo-Koron-Sha Inc, pg 415
Fuzambo Publishing Co, pg 416
GakuseiSha Publishing Co Ltd, pg 416
Hakusui-Sha Co Ltd, pg 417
Hayakawa Publishing Inc, pg 417
Heibonsha Ltd, Publishers, pg 417
The Hokuseido Press, pg 417
Hyoronsha Publishing Co Ltd, pg 417

Iwanami Shoten, Publishers, pg 418
Kawade Shobo Shinsha, pg 419
Kazama Shobo, pg 419
Keisuisha Publishing Company Ltd, pg 419
Kinokuniya Co Ltd (Publishing Department), pg 420
Kodansha, pg 420
Kodansha International, pg 420
Kosei Publishing Co Ltd, pg 420
Koseisha-Koseikaku Co Ltd, pg 420
Koyo Shobo, pg 420
Minerva Shobo Co Ltd, pg 421
Mirai-Sha, pg 421
Otsuki Shoten Publishers, pg 423
President Inc, pg 423
Riso-Sha, pg 424
Sangyo-Tosho Publishing Co Ltd, pg 424
Sanshusha Publishing Co, Ltd, pg 424
Shimizu-Shoin, pg 425
Mitsumura Suiko Shoin, pg 426
Shufu-to-Seikatsu Sha Ltd, pg 426
The Simul Press Inc, pg 426
Sogensha Publishing Co Ltd, pg 426
Taimeido Publishing Co Ltd, pg 427
Tankosha Publishing Co Ltd, pg 427
Toho Book Store, pg 427
Toho Shuppan, pg 427
Tokai University Press, pg 427
University of Tokyo Press, pg 428
Waseda University Press, pg 428

Jordan

Al-Tanwir Al Ilmi (Scientific Enlightenment Publishing House), pg 430

Kazakstan

Kazakh Al-Farabi State National University, pg 430

Kenya

Action Publishers, pg 430
Heinemann Kenya Limited (EAEP), pg 431
Nairobi University Press, pg 433
Shirikon Publishers, pg 433

Democratic People's Republic of Korea

Academy of Sciences Publishing House, pg 434
The Foreign Language Press Group, pg 434
Korea Science and Encyclopedia Publishing House, pg 434

Republic of Korea

Bakyoung Publishing Co, pg 434
Bum-Woo Publishing Co, pg 435
Chong No Books Publishing Co Ltd, pg 435
Chung Rim Publishing Co Ltd, pg 435
Dae Won Sa Co Ltd, pg 435
Dong Hwa Publishing Co, pg 436
Eulyu Publishing Co Ltd, pg 436
Ewha Womans University Press, pg 436
Gim-Yeong Co, pg 436
Hangil Art Vision, pg 436
Hanul Publishing Co, pg 436
Hw Moon Publishing Co, pg 437
Hyun Am Publishing Co, pg 437
Iljisa Publishing House, pg 437
Jeong-eum Munhwasa, pg 437
Korea University Press, pg 437
Koreaone Press Inc, pg 438
Kyungnam University Press, pg 438
Minumsa Publishing Co Ltd, pg 438
Munhag-gwan, pg 438
Munye Publishing Co, pg 439
Prompter Publications, pg 439
St Pauls, pg 439
Seogwangsa, pg 440
Seoul National University Press, pg 440
Sohaksa, pg 440
Yonsei University Press, pg 441

Latvia

Preses Nams, pg 442
Vieda, pg 442

Lebanon

Darl el-Machreq Sarl, pg 443
Librairie Orientale sal, pg 443
World Book Publishing, pg 443

Lithuania

Academia, pg 445
Baltos Lankos, pg 445
Eugrimas, pg 445
Tyto Alba Publishers, pg 446

Luxembourg

Editions APESS ASBL, pg 447
Essay und Zeitgeist Verlag, pg 447

The Former Yugoslav Republic of Macedonia

Ktitor, pg 449
Nov svet (New World), pg 449
Zumpres Publishing Firm, pg 449

Malaysia

Penerbit Jayatinta Sdn Bhd, pg 454
Vinpress Sdn Bhd, pg 455

Mauritius

Editions de l'Ocean Indien Ltd, pg 457

Mexico

Libreria y Ediciones Botas SA, pg 458
Publicaciones Cruz O SA, pg 459
Editorial Diana SA de CV, pg 459
El Colegio de Michoacan A C, pg 460
Editorial Extemporaneos SA, pg 461
Fondo de Cultura Economica, pg 461
Editorial Jus SA de CV, pg 462
Phillip Richard Conover Lazo, pg 462
Editorial Orion, pg 465
Editorial Patria SA de CV, pg 465
Ediciones Promesa, SA de CV, pg 466
Siglo XXI Editores SA de CV, pg 467
Universidad Nacional Autonoma de Mexico (National University of Mexico), pg 467
Universidad Veracruzana Direccion General Editorial y de Publicaciones, pg 468

Morocco

Dar El Kitab, pg 469
Editions Eddif Maroc, pg 469

Nepal

International Standards Books & Periodicals (P) Ltd, pg 471

Netherlands

Uitgeverij Ambo BV, pg 472
Ankh-Hermes BV, pg 472
John Benjamins BV, pg 474
Erven J Bijleveld, pg 474
Boom Uitgeverij, pg 474
A W Bruna Uitgevers BV, pg 475
Buijten en Schipperheijn BV Drukkerij en Uitg Mij v/h, pg 475
BZZTOH Publishers, pg 475
Uitgeverij Coutinho BV, pg 476
HES & De Graaf Publishers BV, pg 478
Historische Uitgeverij, pg 478
Mirananda Publishers BV, pg 481
Uitgeverij H Nelissen BV, pg 482
Picaron Editions, pg 482
Prometheus, pg 483
Segment BV, pg 484
Uitgeverij SUN, pg 484
Telos Boeken, pg 485
Tilburg University Press, pg 485
Van Gorcum & Comp BV, pg 486
Uitgeverij Van Wijnen, pg 486
VU Boekhandel/Uitgeverij BV, pg 487

New Zealand

Brookfield Press, pg 489
Gnostic Press, pg 491

Nigeria

Ethiope Publishing Corporation, pg 499
Evans Brothers (Nigeria Publishers) Ltd, pg 499
Ibadan University Press, pg 499
Ilesanmi Press (Educational Publishers) Ltd, pg 499
Obafemi Awolowo University Press Ltd, pg 501
Unity Publishing & Research Company Ltd, pg 502
University Publishing Co, pg 502

Norway

Det Norske Samlaget, pg 503
Glydendal Akademisk, pg 503
Gyldendal Norsk Forlag A/S, pg 503
Pax Forlag A/S, pg 504
Teknologisk Forlag, pg 505
Universitetsforlaget, pg 505

Pakistan

Hamdard Foundation, pg 507
Publishers United Pvt Ltd, pg 508

Panama

Editorial Universitaria, pg 509

Peru

Fondo Editorial de la Pontificia Universidad Catolica del Peru, pg 511
Editorial Horizonte, pg 511
Sur Casa de Estudios del Socialismo, pg 511

Philippines

Communication Foundation for Asia Media Group (CFAMG), pg 513
De La Salle University, pg 513
New Day Publishers, pg 514
Our Lady of Manaoag Publisher, pg 514
University of the Philippines Press, pg 515
UST Publishing House, pg 515
Vera-Reyes Inc, pg 515

Poland

Impuls, pg 517
Instytut Wydawniczy Pax, Inco-Veritas, pg 517
Iskry - Publishing House Ltd spotka zoo, pg 517
Katolicki Uniwersytet Wydawniczo-Redakcja, pg 517
'Ksiazka i Wiedza' Spotdzielnia Wydawniczo-Handlowa, pg 517
Ossolineum Zaklad Narodowy im Ossolinskich - Wydawnictwo, pg 518
Pallottinum Wydawnictwo Stowarzyszenia Apostolstwa Katolickiego, pg 518
Przedsiebiorstwo Wydawniczo-Handlowe Wydawnictwo Siedmiorog, pg 519
Spoleczny Instytut Wydawniczy Znak, pg 520
Oficyna Wydawnicza Szkoly Glownej Handlowej w Warszawie Oficyna Wydawnicza SGH, pg 520

Portugal

Armenio Amado Editora de Simoes, Beirao & Ca Lda, pg 522
Editorial 'Avante!', pg 522
Brasilia Editora (J Carvalho Branco), pg 523
Edicoes Colibri, pg 523
Constancia Editores, SA, pg 524
Edicoes Cosmos, pg 524
Edicoes 70, Lda, pg 524
Editorial Estampa, Lda, pg 524
Publicacoes Europa-America Lda, pg 524
Editorial Franciscana, pg 525
Gradiva-Publicacnoes Lda, pg 525
Guimaraes Editores, Lda, pg 525
Imprensa Nacional-Casa da Moeda, pg 526
Editorial Inquerito Lda, pg 526
Edicoes Manuel Lencastre, pg 526
Livraria Apostolado da Imprensa, pg 526
Livraria Minerva Editora, pg 526
Editora Livros do Brasil Sarl, pg 526
Livraria Tavares Martins, pg 527
Nova Acropole, pg 527
Editorial Presenca, pg 528
Publicacoes Dom Quixote Lda, pg 528
Sa da Costa Editora, pg 529
Edicoes 70, pg 529
Silabo, pg 529
Teorema, pg 529
Usus Editora, pg 530
Vega-Publicacao e Distribuicao de Livros e Revistas, Lda, pg 530
Livraria Verdade e Vida Editora, pg 530

Puerto Rico

University of Puerto Rico Press (EDUPR), pg 531

Romania

Editura Academiei Romane, pg 531
Aion Verlag, pg 531
Ararat Verlag und Druckerei, pg 532
Ars Longa Publishing House, pg 532
Editura Clusium, Casa de Editura Atlas-Clusium SRL, pg 532

PUBLISHERS

Editura Excelsior, pg 533
Editura Humanitas, pg 533
Humanitas Publishing House, pg 533
Editura Institutul European, pg 533
Lider Verlag, pg 534
Mentor Kiado, pg 534
Editura Niculescu, pg 534
Editura Paideia, pg 535
Polirom Verlag, pg 535
Realitatea Casa de Edituri Productie Audio-Video Film, pg 535
Saeculum IO, pg 535
Editura Stiintifica, pg 536
Editura Univers, pg 536
Universal Dalsi, pg 536
Vestala Verlag, pg 536
Vremea Publishers Ltd, pg 536

Russian Federation

Agni Publishing House, pg 537
Aspect Press Ltd, pg 537
Izdatel 'stvo Mordovskogo gosudar stvennogo, pg 538
Izdatel 'stvo Ural' skogo, pg 538
Izdatelstvo Iskusstvo, pg 538
Ladomir Publishing House, pg 539
Izdatelstvo Mysl, pg 540
Nauka Publishers, pg 540
Izdatel'stvo Nizhegorodskogo Gosudarstvennogo Univ, pg 540
Novosti Izdatel 'stvo, pg 541
Progress Publishers, pg 541
Raduga Publishers, pg 541
St Andrew's Biblical Theological College, pg 541
Scorpion Publishers, pg 541
Izdatelstvo Vysshaya Shkola, pg 543

Saudi Arabia

Dar Al-Shareff for Publishing & Distribution, pg 543

Senegal

Les Nouvelles Editions Africaines du Senegal NEAS, pg 544

Singapore

Asiapac Books Pte Ltd, pg 545
Taylor & Francis Asia Pacific, pg 548

Slovakia

ARCHA sro Vydavatel 'stro, pg 549
Danubiaprint, pg 549
Kalligram Kiado spol sro, pg 549
Luc vydavatelske druzstvo, pg 550
Smena Publishing House, pg 550
Sofa, pg 551
VEDA (Vydavatel'stvo Slovenskej akademie vied), pg 551

Slovenia

Cankarjeva Zalozba, pg 551
Slovenska matica, pg 552
Zalozba Mihelac d o o, pg 552

South Africa

Human & Rousseau (Pty) Ltd, pg 555
Human Sciences Research Council, pg 555
LAPA Publishers (Pty) Ltd, pg 556

Spain

Publicacions de l' Abadia de Montserrat, pg 561
Acantilado, pg 561
Aguilar SA de Ediciones, pg 562
Ediciones Akal SA, pg 562
Ediciones Alfar SA, pg 562
Alianza Editorial SA, pg 562
Altea, Taurus, Alfaguara SA, pg 563
Editorial Anagrama, pg 563
Editorial Ariel SA, pg 564
Biblioteca de Autores Cristianos, pg 564
Editorial Casals SA, pg 566
Ediciones Catedra SA, pg 566
Centro de Estudios Politicos Y Constitucionales, pg 567
Editora Comercial de Publicaciones, pg 568
Complutense, SA Editorial, pg 568
Ediciones Cristiandad, pg 569
EDERSA (Editoriales de Derecho Reunidas SA), pg 571
Ediciones Encuentro SA, pg 573
EUNSA (Ediciones Universidad de Navarra SA), pg 574
Fondo de Cultura Economica de Espana, SL, pg 574
Fragua Editorial, pg 574
Fundacion Rosacruz, pg 575
Editorial Fundamentos, pg 575
Galaxia SA Editorial, pg 575
Editorial Gedisa SA, pg 575
Editorial Gredos SA, pg 576
Editorial Gulaab, pg 577
Editorial Herder SA, pg 577
Editorial Horsori SL, pg 577
Ibaizabal Edelvives SA, pg 577
Idea Books, SA, pg 578
Ediciones Internacionales Universitarias SA, pg 578
Iralka Editorial SL, pg 578
Ediciones Istmo SA, pg 579
Editorial Kairos SA, pg 579
Laertes SA de Ediciones, pg 579
Antonio Machado, SA, pg 580
Editorial Magisterio Espanol SA, pg 581
Edicions de la Magrana SA, pg 581
Ediciones Mensajero, pg 582
Ediciones Morata SL, pg 583
Nueva Acropolis, pg 584
Ediciones del Oriente y del Mediterraneo, pg 585
Pages Editors, SL, pg 585
Pearson Educacion S A, pg 586
Pentalfa Ediciones, pg 586
PPC Editorial y Distribuidora, SA, pg 587
Pre-Textos, pg 587
Publicaciones de la Universidad Pontificia Comillas-Madrid, pg 588
Editora Regional de Murcia - ERM, pg 588
Editorial Revista Agustiniana, pg 589
Ediciones Rialp SA, pg 589
Ediciones San Pio X, pg 589
Universidad de Santiago de Compostela, pg 589
Siglo XXI de Espana Editores SA, pg 590
Ediciones Sigueme SA, pg 590
Editorial Sintesis, SA, pg 590
Ediciones Siruela SA, pg 591
Edicions 62, pg 591
Grup 62, pg 591
Ediciones SM, pg 591
Editorial Rudolf Steiner, pg 591
Editorial Tecnos SA, pg 592
Editorial Sal Terrae, pg 592
Ediciones de la Torre, pg 593
Trotta SA Editorial, pg 593
Turner Publicaciones, pg 593
Universidad de Granada, pg 594
Universidad de Malaga, pg 594
Ediciones Universidad de Salamanca, pg 594
Universidad de Valladolid Secretariado de Publicaciones e Intercambio Editorial, pg 594
Universitat de Valencia Servei de Publicacions, pg 594
Editorial Verbum SL, pg 595
Visor Distribuciones, SA, pg 596

Sri Lanka

Inter-Cultural Book Promoters, pg 597
Karunaratne & Sons Ltd, pg 597
Samayawardena Printers Publishers & Booksellers, pg 598

Sudan

Khartoum University Press, pg 598

Sweden

Akademiforlaget Goteborgslitteratur, pg 600
Gidlunds Bokforlag, pg 602
Hagaberg AB, pg 603
Bokforlaget Nya Doxa AB, pg 605
Studentlitteratur AB, pg 606
Svenska Foerlaget liv & ledarskap ab, pg 607

Switzerland

ADIRA, pg 607
Editions L'Age d'Homme - La Cite, pg 608
Editions de la Baconniere SA, pg 609
Bibliographisches Institut und F A Brockhaus AG, pg 610
Christiana-Verlag, pg 611
Diogenes Verlag AG, pg 612
Edition Epoca, pg 613
Erker-Verlag, pg 613
Europa Verlag AG, pg 614
Verlag Gachnang & Springer, Bern-Berlin, pg 614
Georg Editeur SA, pg 614
Govinda-Verlag, pg 615
Klett und Balmer & Co Verlag, pg 617
Kober Verlag AG, pg 617
Kolumbus-Verlag, pg 617
Les Editions Nagel SA (Paris), pg 619
Natura-Verlag Arlesheim, pg 619
Novalis Media AG, pg 620
Origo Verlag, pg 621
Editions Patino, pg 621
Editions Payot Lausanne, pg 621
Verlag Die Pforte im Rudolf Steiner Verlag, pg 621
Philosophisch-Anthroposophischer Verlag am Goetheanum, pg 621
PIE-Peter Lang SA, pg 622
Psychosophische Gesellschaft, pg 622
Editions Saint-Paul, pg 623
Scherz Verlag AG, pg 623
Verlag fuer Schoene Wissenschaften, pg 624
Schwabe & Co AG, pg 624
Speer -Verlag, pg 625
Sphinx Verlag AG, pg 625
Rudolf Steiner Verlag, pg 625
Theseus - Verlag AG, pg 625
Tobler Verlag, pg 626
Editions du Tricorne, pg 626
Editions des Trois Collines Francois Lachenal, pg 626
Der Universitatsverlag Freiburg, pg 626
Verlag Die Waage, pg 627

SUBJECT INDEX

Syrian Arab Republic

Damascus University Press, pg 628
Institut Francais d'Etudes Arabes de Damas, pg 628

Taiwan, Province of China

Asian Culture Co, pg 629
Chung Hwa Book Co Ltd, pg 629
Laureate Book Co Ltd, pg 631
San Min Book Co Ltd, pg 631
World Book Co Ltd, pg 632
Yee Wen Publishing Co Ltd, pg 632

Tajikistan

Irfon, pg 632

Thailand

Graphic Art Publishing, pg 635
Thai Watana Panich Co, Ltd, pg 636

Togo

Editions Akpagnon, pg 636

Tunisia

Academie Tunisienne des Sciences, des Lettres et des Arts Beit El Hekma, pg 637
Ceres Editions, pg 637
Faculte des Sciences Humaines et Sociales de Tunis, pg 638
Maison d'Edition Mohamed Ali Hammi, pg 638
Maison Tunisienne de l'Edition, pg 638

Turkey

Altin Kitaplar Yayinevi, pg 638
Ezel Erverdi (Dergah Yayinlari AS) Muessese Muduru, pg 640
Iletisim Yayinlari, pg 640
Inkilap Publishers Ltd, pg 640
Metis Yayinlari, pg 640
Remzi Kitabevi, pg 641
Ruh ve Madde Yayinlari ve Saglik Hizmetleri AS, pg 641
Saray Medikal Yayin Tic Ltd Sti, pg 641
Kabalci Yayinevi, pg 642

Ukraine

Naukova Dumka Publishers, pg 643
Osnovy Publishers, pg 643

United Kingdom

AK Press & Distribution, pg 645
Aldwych Press Ltd, pg 645
Apex Publishing Ltd, pg 648
Aris & Phillips Ltd, pg 648
Arthur James Ltd, pg 649
Ashgate Publishing Ltd, pg 649
The Athlone Press Ltd, pg 650
Baha'i Publishing Trust, pg 651
Black Ace Books, pg 655
Blackwell Publishers, pg 655
Marion Boyars Publishers Ltd, pg 658
The British Academy, pg 659
Calder Publications Ltd, pg 662
Cambridge University Press, pg 662
Capall Bann Publishing, pg 663
Kyle Cathie Ltd, pg 665
Deborah Charles Publications, pg 666
James Clarke & Co Ltd, pg 668
James Currey Ltd, pg 673
Gerald Duckworth & Co Ltd, pg 676

1047

SUBJECT INDEX

Edinburgh University Press Ltd, pg 677
Element Books Ltd, pg 678
The Eurospan Group, pg 680
Faber & Faber Ltd, pg 681
Free Association Books Ltd, pg 684
Freedom Press, pg 684
Gateway Books, pg 686
George Mann Publications, pg 687
E J W Gibb Memorial Trust, pg 687
Golden Cockerel Press Ltd, pg 688
The Greek Bookshop, pg 689
Green Books Ltd, pg 689
Peter Halban Publishers Ltd, pg 691
Robert Hale Ltd, pg 691
HarperCollins Publishers, pg 692
Harvard University Press, pg 692
The Harvill Press Ltd, pg 693
Janus Publishing Company Ltd, pg 702
Karnak House, pg 703
Kershaw Publishing Co Ltd, pg 704
The Littman Library of Jewish Civilization, pg 708
Lucis Press Ltd, pg 709
Marcham Books, pg 711
The Merlin Press Ltd, pg 713
MIT Press Ltd, pg 715
Motilal (UK) Books of India, pg 715
New Era Publications UK Ltd, pg 718
The Octagon Press Ltd, pg 720
Oneworld Publications, pg 721
Open Gate Press, pg 721
The Orkney Press Ltd, pg 722
Oxford University Press, pg 723
Paternoster Publishing, pg 724
Pearson Education, pg 725
Pearson Education Europe, Mideast & Africa, pg 725
Pickering & Chatto (Publishers) Ltd, pg 727
Polygon, pg 729
Prism Press Book Publishers Ltd, pg 730
Quartet Books Ltd, pg 731
Ramakrishna Vedanta Centre, pg 732
Random House UK Ltd, pg 733
Rationalist Press Association, pg 733
Routledge, pg 736
Routledge Curzon, pg 736
Sage Publications Ltd, pg 737
Sheed & Ward Ltd, pg 741
Sheppeard-Walwyn (Publishers) Ltd, pg 741
Skoob Russell Square, pg 742
The Society of Metaphysicians Ltd, pg 743
Souvenir Press Ltd, pg 743
St Pauls Publishing, pg 744
Rudolf Steiner Press, pg 745
Thames & Hudson Ltd, pg 748
Thoemmes Press, pg 748
UCL Press Ltd, pg 751
University of Exeter Press, pg 751
University of Wales Press, pg 751
Verso, pg 752
Virago Press, pg 753
Voltaire Foundation Ltd, pg 753
The Warburg Institute, pg 754
Yale University Press London, pg 759

Uruguay
A Monteverde y Cia SA, pg 760
Nordan-Comunidad, pg 760

Venezuela
Alfadil Ediciones, pg 761
Monte Avila Editores Latinoamericana CA, pg 762
Biblioteca Ayacucho, pg 762

Viet Nam
Su Hoc (Historical) Publishing House, pg 763
Su That (Truth) Publishing House, pg 763

Yugoslavia
Alfa-Narodna Knjiga, pg 764
Beogradski Izdavacko-Graficki Zavod, pg 764
Jugoslavijapublik, pg 764
Nolit Publishing House, pg 765
Izdavacka Organizacija Rad, pg 765
Panorama NIJP/ID Grigorije Bozovic, pg 765
Svetovi, pg 766
Vuk Karadzic, pg 766

Zambia
MFK Management Consultants Services, pg 766

Zimbabwe
University of Zimbabwe Publications, pg 769

PHOTOGRAPHY

Albania
NL SH, pg 1

Australia
Robert Berthold Photography, pg 14
Emperor Publishing, pg 22
Enterprise Publications, pg 22
Joval Publications, pg 29
Kingsclear Books, pg 29
Laurel Press, pg 29
Lightbild PTY Ltd, pg 30
McGraw-Hill Australia Pty Ltd, pg 32
J M McGregor Pty Ltd, pg 32
Mountain House Press, pg 33
Raincloud Productions, pg 39
Rankin Publishers, pg 40
Tabletop Press, pg 44
Thames & Hudson (Australia) Pty Ltd, pg 44
Wellington Lane Press Pty Ltd, pg 47

Austria
Christian Brandstatter Verlagsgesellschaft GmbH, pg 50
Camera Austria, pg 50
Loecker Verlag, pg 54
Richard Pils Publication P, pg 57
Andreas Schnider Verlags-Atelier, pg 58

Belgium
Editions Gerard Blanchart & Cie SA, pg 65
Conservart SA, pg 67
Dexia Bank, pg 68
Graton Editeur SA, pg 69
Uitgeverij Lannoo NV, pg 70
Les Editions Vie ouvriere ASBL, pg 75

Brazil
Editora Companhia das Letras/Editora Schwarcz Ltda, pg 82
Livro Ibero-Americano Ltda, pg 85
Livraria Pioneira Editora/Enio Matheus Guazzelli e Cia Ltd, pg 89
Rede Das Artes (Boccato Editores Collector's), pg 90

China
Asia 2000 Ltd, pg 102
China Film Press, pg 103
Fudan University Press, pg 105
Heilongjiang Science & Technology Press, pg 106
Jilin Science & Technology Publishing House, pg 106
Morning Glory Publishers, pg 107
People's Fine Arts Publishing House, pg 108
Printing Industry Publishing House, pg 108
Shanghai Fine Arts Publishers, pg 109

Colombia
Villegas Editores Ltda, pg 114

Czech Republic
Moravska Galerie v Brne, pg 126
Prostor, Ltd, pg 128

Denmark
Politisk Revy, pg 134
Tiderne Skifter Forlag A/S, pg 136

France
Actes Graphiques, pg 145
ADPF Publications, pg 146
Editions Alternatives, pg 146
L'Amitie par le Livre, pg 147
Anako Editions, pg 147
Editions de l'Armancon, pg 148
La Bartavelle, pg 149
Societe Nouvelle Adam Biro, pg 150
William Blake & Co, pg 150
Jacqueline Chambon, pg 154
COMP'ACT, pg 156
Dunod Editeur, pg 160
Editions Fanlac, pg 163
Des Femmes, pg 164
Editions Filipacchi-Sonodip, pg 164
Editions Fragments, pg 164
Editions Hoebeke, pg 168
Image/Magie, pg 169
Isoete, pg 170
Eric Koehler, pg 171
Macula, pg 174
Marval, pg 175
Editions Medianes, pg 175
Editions Paul Montel, pg 176
Centre National de la Photographie, pg 177
Paris Musees, pg 179
Jean-Michel Place, pg 180
Editions Plume, pg 180
Revue Noire, pg 183
Editions du Seuil, pg 185
Siloe - Kerdore, pg 185
Somogy editions d'art, pg 186
Thames & Hudson, pg 187
Alain Thomas Editeur, pg 188
Transeuropeennes/RCE, pg 188
Publications de l'Universite de Pau, pg 188
La Vague a l'ame, pg 188
Editions VM, pg 189
La Voix du Regard, pg 189
Pierre Zech Editeur, pg 189

Germany
F A Ackermanns Kunstverlag GmbH, pg 191
Arnoldsche Verlagsanstalt GmbH, pg 195
ARTC/OLOR, pg 195
Augustus Verlag, pg 196
Bildarchiv Preussischer Kulturbesitz bpk, pg 203
Verlag C J Bucher GmbH, pg 207
Ulrich Burgdorf/Homeopathic Publishing House, pg 208
Verlag Georg D W Callwey GmbH & Co, pg 208
Dr Cantz'sche, Druckerei GmbH & Co, Cantz Verlag, pg 209
Christian Verlag GmbH, pg 210
Hans Christians Druckerei und Verlag GmbH & Co, pg 210
CTL-Presse Clemens-Tobias Lange, pg 212
D & D Kommunikation Verlug Dirk Nishen Gmbh & Co KG, pg 212
Dolling und Galitz Verlag GmbH, pg 217
Edition Solitude - Akademie Schloss Solitude, pg 221
Elefanten Press Verlag GmbH, pg 222
Eulen Verlag, pg 224
Falken-Verlag GmbH, pg 227
Frederking & Thaler Verlag GmbH, pg 230
Brigitte Grabitz - ikoo Buchverlag, pg 233
Gruner + Jahr AG & Co, pg 234
Haschemi Edition Cologne Kunstverlag, pg 237
Hatje Cantz Verlag, pg 238
Heel Verlag GmbH, pg 238
Helmut Hermann, pg 240
Johannis, pg 246
Jovis Verlag GmbH, pg 246
Knesebeck Verlag, pg 250
Koenemann Verlagesellschaft mbH, pg 251
Verlag Hubert Kretschmer, pg 253
Verlag der Kunst/G+B Fine Arts Verlag GmbH, pg 254
Kunstverlag Weingarten GmbH, pg 254
Karl Robert Langewiesche Nachfolger Hans Koester KG, pg 256
Verlag Laterna magica GmbH & Co KG, pg 256
Edition Axel Menges, pg 262
Mitteldeutscher Verlag GmbH, pg 264
Verlag Stephanie Naglschmid, pg 266
Nicolaische Verlagsbuchhandlung Beuermann GmbH, pg 268
Nieswand-Verlag GmbH, pg 269
nymphenburger, pg 269
Edition Octopus & Okeanos Presse, pg 269
Prestel Verlag, pg 275
E Reinhold Verlag, pg 278
Rimbaud Verlagsgesellschaft mbH, pg 279
Rogner und Bernhard GmbH & Co Verlags KG, pg 279
Schirmer/Mosel Verlag GmbH, pg 283
Verlag Hans Schoener GmbH, pg 284
Steidl Verlag, pg 289
Steinweg-Verlag, Jurgen romHoff, pg 290
TASCHEN GmbH, pg 292
teNeues Verlag GmbH & Co KG, pg 292

PUBLISHERS SUBJECT INDEX

Trotzdem-Verlags Genossenschaft eG, pg 295
Uwe Warnke Verlag, pg 300

Greece
Chryssos Typos AE Ekodeis, pg 309
Giovanis Publications, Pangosmios Ekdotikos Organismos, pg 310
Hestia-1 D Hestia-Kollaros & Co Corporation, pg 311
Editions Moressopoulos, pg 313

Hong Kong
Steve Lu Publishing Ltd, pg 320
Photoart Ltd, pg 321

India
Ananda Publishers Pvt Ltd, pg 330
Mapin Publishing Pvt Ltd, pg 342

Ireland
The Collins Press, pg 359
Real Ireland Design, pg 363
Roberts Rinehart Publishers, pg 363
Wolfhound Press, pg 364

Israel
Bezalel Academy of Arts & Design, pg 365
Gefen Publishing House Ltd, pg 367

Italy
A & A, pg 374
Mario Adda Editore SNC, pg 374
Alinari Fratelli SpA Istituto di Edizioni Artistiche, pg 375
Umberto Allemandi & C SRL, pg 375
L'Archivolto, pg 376
Artioli Editore in Modena, pg 377
Campanotto, pg 379
Casa Editrice Castalia, pg 380
Il Castello srl, pg 380
Colonnese Editore, pg 382
Edizioni del Capricorno, pg 384
Electa, pg 387
Essegi, pg 388
Fatatrac, pg 388
FEDA SA, pg 388
Federico Motta Editore SpA, pg 389
Fenice 2000, pg 389
Edizioni del Girasole srl, pg 390
Grafica e Arte SRL, pg 391
Grafis Edizioni, pg 391
Gremese International Srl, pg 391
Hopeful Monster Editore, pg 392
Idea Books, pg 393
Editoriale Jaca Book SpA, pg 394
L'Airone Editrice, pg 395
Linea d'Ombra Libri, pg 396
Angelo Longo Editore, pg 396
Lybra Immagine, pg 397
Magnus Edizioni SpA, pg 397
Edizioni Gabriele Mazzotta SRL, pg 398
NodoLibri, pg 401
Novecento Editrice Srl, pg 401
Nuovi Sentieri Editore, pg 401
OCTAVO Franco Cantini Editore, pg 401
Pheljna Edizioni d'Arte e Suggestione, pg 403
Priuli e Verlucca, Editori, pg 404
Edition Raetia Srl-GmbH, pg 404
Edizioni Ripostes, pg 405
Scala Group spa, pg 407
Sellerio Editore, pg 407
Sicania, pg 408
Silvana Editoriale SpA, pg 408
TEA Tascabili degli Editori Associati SpA, pg 409
Tomo Edizioni srl, pg 410
Vianello Libri, pg 411
Zanichelli Editore SpA, pg 412

Japan
Bun-ichi Sogo Shuppan, pg 415
Genko-Sha, pg 416
Iwanami Shoten, Publishers, pg 418
Seibido Shuppan Company Ltd, pg 424
Shincho-Sha Co Ltd, pg 425
Shufunotomo sha Co Ltd, pg 426
Tankosha Publishing Co Ltd, pg 427
Toho Shuppan, pg 427

Kazakstan
Kramds-reklama Publishing & Advertising, pg 430

Republic of Korea
Youl Hwa Dang Publisher, pg 436
Hakgojae Publishing Inc, pg 436
Seoul International Publishing House, pg 440

Latvia
Preses Nams, pg 442

Lithuania
Lithuanian National Museum Publishing House, pg 446

Luxembourg
Guy Binsfeld & Co Sarl, pg 447
Editions Emile Borschette, pg 447
Galerie Editions Kutter, pg 447
Edition Objectif Lune, pg 447
Editions Tousch, pg 448

Macau
Livros Do Oriente, pg 448

The Former Yugoslav Republic of Macedonia
Macedonia Prima Publishing House, pg 449

Mexico
Instituto Nacional de Antropologia e Historia, pg 464
Naves Internacional de Ediciones SA, pg 464
Servicios Especiales Maciel SA de CV, pg 467

Morocco
Editions Oum, pg 470

Netherlands
Uitgeverij Cantecleer BV, pg 475
Fragment Cooperatieve Vereniging UA, Uitgeverij, pg 477
Hotei Publishing, pg 478

New Zealand
Barkfire Press, pg 488
Bush Press Communications Ltd, pg 489
Craig Potton Publishing, pg 490
RSVP Publishing Company Ltd, pg 495
Shoal Bay Press Ltd, pg 495
Tandem Press, pg 496
University of Otago Press, pg 496

Peru
Universidad de Lima-Fondo de Desarollo Editorial, pg 512

Poland
Wydawnictwo Arkady, pg 516
Wydawnictwa Artystyczne i Filmowe, pg 516
BOSZ scp, pg 516
Rosikon Press, pg 519
Videograf II Sp z o o Zaklad Poracy Chronionej, pg 520
Wydawnictwo Baturo, pg 521

Portugal
Assirio & Alvim, pg 522
Dinalivro, pg 524
Edicoes 70, Lda, pg 524
Impala, pg 525
Latina Livraria, pg 526
Quatro Elementos Editores, pg 529
Vega-Publicacao e Distribuicao de Livros e Revistas, Lda, pg 530

Singapore
Archipelago Press, pg 545

Slovenia
Zalozba Mihelac d o o, pg 552

South Africa
Janssen Publishers CC, pg 556
Johannesburg Art Gallery, pg 556
New Africa Books (Pty) Ltd, pg 557

Spain
Ambit Serveis Editorials, SA, pg 563
CEAC, Grupo Editorial SA, pg 567
Celeste Ediciones, pg 567
Consello da Cultura Galega - CCG, pg 568
Edicions del Drac SA, pg 570
Edilux, pg 572
El Viso, SA Ediciones, pg 572
Fragua Editorial, pg 574
Editorial Gustavo Gili SA, pg 576
Lunwerg Editores, SA, pg 580
Editorial Mediterrania SL, pg 582
Ediciones Omega SA, pg 585
Omnicon, SA, pg 585
Silex Ediciones, pg 590
Equipo Sirius SA, pg 591
Tf Editores, pg 592
Trea Ediciones, SL, pg 593
Turner Publicaciones, pg 593
Tursen, SA, pg 593

Sweden
Allt om Hobby AB, pg 600
BOOX, pg 601
Bengt Forsbergs Foerlag AB, pg 602
Natur och Kultur/LTs foerlag, pg 604
Schultz Forlag AB, pg 606

Switzerland
U Baer Verlag, pg 609
Benteli Verlag, pg 609
Christoph Merian Verlag, pg 611
Edizioni Armando Dado, Tipografia Stazione, pg 612
Editions Andre Delcourt & Cie, pg 612
Dimension World Ltd, pg 612
Eboris-Coda-Bompiani, pg 613
Verlag ED Emmentaler Druck AG, pg 613
Editions Foma SA, pg 614
G+B Arts International, pg 614
Giampiero Casagrande Editore, pg 614
Bernard Letu Editeur, pg 618
Memory/Cage Editions, pg 619
Lars Mueller Publishers, pg 619
Editions Olizane, pg 620
Edition Olms AG, pg 620
Perret Edition, pg 621
Reich Verlag AG, pg 622
Schwabe & Co AG, pg 624
Edition Stemmle AG, pg 625
Strom-Verlag Luzern, pg 625
Tobler Verlag, pg 626
Weber SA d'Editions, pg 627

United Republic of Tanzania
Tanzania Publishing House, pg 634

Thailand
Graphic Art Publishing, pg 635

Turkey
Arkeoloji Ve Sanat Yayinlari, pg 639
Inkilap Publishers Ltd, pg 640

Ukraine
Naukova Dumka Publishers, pg 643

United Kingdom
Ian Allan Publishing Ltd, pg 646
Appletree Press Ltd, pg 648
Art Books International Ltd, pg 649
Arts Council of England, pg 649
Aurum Press Ltd, pg 651
Batsford Ltd, pg 652
Colin Baxter Photography Ltd, pg 652
BCA, pg 653
Blackstaff Press, pg 655
Bloomsbury Publishing PLC, pg 656
Blueprint, pg 656
Book Packaging & Marketing, pg 657
Butterworth-Heinemann Ltd, pg 661
Canongate Books Ltd, pg 663
Cassell & Co, pg 664
Colour Library Direct, pg 669
Constable Publishers, pg 670
Creation Books, pg 671
Creative Monochrome Ltd, pg 672
David & Charles Ltd, pg 674
Andre Deutsch Ltd, pg 675
Dorling Kindersley Ltd, pg 676
Eaglemoss Publications Ltd, pg 676
Elfande Ltd, pg 678
Frontier Publishing, pg 684
Garnet Publishing Ltd, pg 685
GMC Publications Ltd, pg 687
The Harvill Press Ltd, pg 693
Hilmarton Manor Press, pg 696
Hodder & Stoughton Educational, pg 696
The Islamic Texts Society, pg 701
Kegan Paul International Ltd, pg 703
Lund Humphries, pg 709
Mainstream Publishing Co (Edinburgh) Ltd, pg 711
Merrell Publishers Ltd, pg 713
National Galleries of Scotland, pg 717
National Library of Wales, pg 717
National Portrait Gallery Publications, pg 717
National Trust, pg 717

SUBJECT INDEX

New Leaf Books Ltd, pg 719
Newpro UK Ltd, pg 719
W W Norton & Company Ltd, pg 720
Octopus Publishing Group, pg 720
Osborne Books Ltd, pg 722
Pavilion Books Ltd, pg 724
Phaidon Press Ltd, pg 726
Plexus Publishing Ltd, pg 728
Pomegranate Europe Ltd, pg 729
Quintet Publishing Ltd, pg 732
Reaktion Books Ltd, pg 733
Regency House Publishing Ltd, pg 734
RotoVision SA, pg 735
Seren, pg 740
Shire Publications Ltd, pg 741
Sutton Publishing Ltd, pg 746
Taschen UK Ltd, pg 747
Thames & Hudson Ltd, pg 748
Verulam Publishing Ltd, pg 753
Yale University Press London, pg 759
Zwemmer Holdings Co Ltd, pg 759

Venezuela
Biblioteca Ayacucho, pg 762

PHYSICAL SCIENCES

Albania
NL SH, pg 1

Australia
Blackwell Science Pty Ltd, pg 15
CSIRO Publishing (Commonwealth Scientific & Industrial Research Organisation), pg 19
McGraw-Hill Australia Pty Ltd, pg 32
Queen Victoria Museum & Art Gallery Publications, pg 39

Austria
Bethania Verlag, pg 49
IAEA - International Atomic Energy Agency, pg 53
Verlag der Oesterreichischen Akademie der Wissenschaften (OEAW), pg 56
Pinguin-Verlag, Pawlowski GmbH, pg 57
Edition Va Bene, pg 60
Verband der Wissenschaftlichen Gesellschaften Oesterreichs (VWGOe), pg 60

Belgium
Academia-Bruylant, pg 63
Editions De Boeck-Larcier SA, pg 67
Leuven University Press, pg 71

Brazil
Editora Harbra Ltda, pg 84
Editora Universidade de Brasilia, pg 92
Editora Universidade Federal do Rio de Janeiro, pg 93

Bulgaria
Abagar Pablioing, pg 94
Gea-Libris Publishing House, pg 95
Heron Press Publishing House, pg 96
Litera Prima, pg 96
Makros 2000 - Plovdiv, pg 96

Chile
Arrayan Editores, pg 99

China
China Ocean Press, pg 103
Fudan University Press, pg 105
Heilongjiang Science & Technology Press, pg 106
Wissenschaft und Technik Verlag Henan Henan Scientific & Technological Publishing House, pg 106
Jiangsu Science & Technology Publishing House, pg 106
Jilin Science & Technology Publishing House, pg 106
Shandong University Press, pg 109
Tianjin Science & Technology Publishing House, pg 109

The Democratic Republic of the Congo
Centre de Recherche, et Pedagogie Appliquee, pg 114

Costa Rica
Editorial de la Universidad de Costa Rica, pg 117

Czech Republic
Karolinum, nakladatelstvi, pg 125
Mendelova zemedelska a lesnicka univerzita v Brne, pg 126
Vydavatelstvi Ceskeho Geologickeho Ustavu, pg 129

Dominican Republic
Pontificia Universidad Catolica Madre y Maestra, pg 136

Finland
Ursa ry, pg 145

France
Breal, pg 151
Devenirs Visuels SA, pg 159
Editions Eyrolles, pg 163
Editions Jacques Gabay, pg 165
Editions Grandir, pg 166
Polytechnica, pg 180
Editions du Scarabee, pg 184

Germany
AOL-Verlag Frohmut Menze, pg 194
Johann Ambrosius Barth GmbH, pg 198
Blackwell Wissenschafts-Verlag GmbH, pg 203
Oscar Brandstetter Verlag GmbH & Co KG, pg 206
Cornelsen Verlag GmbH & Co OHG, pg 211
Verlag Harri Deutsch, pg 213
Dingfelder-Verlag Inh Gerd Gmelin, pg 217
DRW-Verlag Weinbrenner-GmbH & Co, pg 219
Elektor-Verlag GmbH, pg 222
Fachbuchverlag Leipzig im Carl Hanser Verlag, pg 226
Ferd Dummler's Verlag, pg 227
Franz Ferzak World & Space Publications, pg 227
Walter de Gruyter GmbH & Co KG, pg 234
Lehrmittelverlag Wilhelm Hagemann GmbH, pg 236
Hallwag Verlag GmbH, pg 236

Heigl Verlag, Horst Edition, pg 239
F A Herbig Verlagsbuchhandlung GmbH, pg 239
Hofbauer, Christoph und Trojanow Ilia, Akademischer Verlag Muenchen, pg 241
Landbuch-Verlagsgesellschaft mbH, pg 255
Institut fuer Landes- und Stadtentwicklungsforschung, ILS Nordrhein-Westfalen, pg 255
Preubmpassling Verlag Gisela Meussling, pg 263
Verlag Stephanie Naglschmid, pg 266
Neuer Weg Verlag und Druck GmbH, pg 268
Palazzi Verlag GmbH, pg 271
Verlag an der Ruhr GmbH, pg 281
Springer-Verlag GmbH & Co KG, pg 288
Universitatsverlag Ulm GmbH, pg 296
Volk und Wissen Verlag GmbH & Co, pg 299
Wiley-VCH Verlag GmbH, pg 302
Verlag Zeitschrift fur Naturforschung, pg 305

Ghana
Sam Woode Ltd, pg 308

Greece
Diavlos, pg 309

Hungary
Janus Pannonius Tudomanyegyetem, pg 324
Magyar Tudomanyos Akademia Koezponti Fizikai Kutato Intezet Koenyvtara, pg 325
Kulturtrade, pg 325

India
Affiliated East West Press Pvt Ltd, pg 329
Chowkhamba Sanskrit Series Office, pg 335
Law Publishers, pg 341
Scientific Book Agency, pg 349

Ireland
Royal Irish Academy, pg 364

Italy
Adea Edizioni, pg 374
Bibliopolis - Edizioni di Filosofia e Scienze Srl, pg 377
Edizioni Dedalo SRL, pg 384
Edizioni GB, pg 390
Leo S Olschki, pg 402
Editoriale Scienza, pg 407
Societa Editrice la Goliardica Pavese SRL, pg 408
Societa Stampa Sportiva, pg 408

Japan
Chijin Shokan Co Ltd, pg 415
Mita Press, Mita Industrial Co, Ltd, pg 421
Sangyo-Tosho Publishing Co Ltd, pg 424

Kazakstan
Gylym, Izd-Vo, pg 430
Kazakh Al-Farabi State National University, pg 430

BOOK

Kenya
Heinemann Kenya Limited (EAEP), pg 431
Nairobi University Press, pg 433
Phoenix Publishers, pg 433

Democratic People's Republic of Korea
Korea Science and Encyclopedia Publishing House, pg 434

Liechtenstein
Botanisch-Zoologische Gesellschaft, pg 444
Saendig Reprint Verlag, Hans-Rainer Wohlwend, pg 445

Malaysia
Tropical Press Sdn Bhd, pg 455

Mexico
Editorial Limusa SA de CV, pg 463

Namibia
Desert Research Foundation of Namibia (DRFN), pg 471

Netherlands
Uitgeverij Lemma BV, pg 480

New Zealand
ABA Books, pg 488
Wendy Crane Books, pg 490
Nelson Price Milburn Ltd, pg 494

Peru
Fondo Editorial de la Pontificia Universidad Catolica del Peru, pg 511

Poland
Instytut Meteorologii i Gospodarki Wodnej, pg 518
Oficyna Wydawnicza Politechniki Wroclawskiej, pg 519
Towarzystwo Naukowe w Toruniu, pg 520

Portugal
Constancia Editores, SA, pg 524
Didactica Editora, pg 524

Romania
Editura Academiei Romane, pg 531

Russian Federation
Fizmatlit Publishing Co, pg 538
Izdatelstvo Mir, pg 540
Izdatel'stvo Nizhegorodskogo Gosudarstvennogo Univ, pg 540

Singapore
Reed Elsevier, South East Asia, pg 547
Taylor & Francis Asia Pacific, pg 548

South Africa
Clever Books, pg 553
Educum Publishers Ltd, pg 554

Spain
Instituto de Estudios Riojanos, pg 574
Editorial la Muralla SA, pg 583
Editorial Paraninfo SA, pg 586

PUBLISHERS

Editorial Sintesis, SA, pg 590
Equipo Sirius SA, pg 591
Universidad de Oviedo Servicio de Publicaciones, pg 594

Sweden
Studentlitteratur AB, pg 606

Switzerland
Elsevier Science SA, pg 613

Taiwan, Province of China
Fuh-Wen Book Co, pg 630
Hsiao Yuan Publication Co, Ltd, pg 630
Newton Publishing Company Ltd, pg 631

United Republic of Tanzania
DUP (1996) Ltd, pg 633

Tunisia
Ceres Editions, pg 637

Uganda
Fountain Publishers Ltd, pg 642

Ukraine
Naukova Dumka Publishers, pg 643
Osvita, pg 643

United Kingdom
Academic Press Ltd, pg 644
Aulis Publishers, pg 651
Butterworth-Heinemann Ltd, pg 661
Cambridge University Press, pg 662
W H Freeman & Co Ltd, pg 684
Imperial College Press, pg 699
Institute of Physics Publishing, pg 700
Institution of Electrical Engineers, pg 700
Kluwer Academic/Plenum Publishers, pg 705
Micelle Press, pg 714
Pion Ltd, pg 728
Portland Press Ltd, pg 730
The Royal Society, pg 737
The Society of Metaphysicians Ltd, pg 743
Tarragon Press, pg 746
Yale University Press London, pg 759

Uruguay
A Monteverde y Cia SA, pg 760

Viet Nam
Science & Technics Publishing House, pg 763

PHYSICS

Albania
NL SH, pg 1

Argentina
EUDEBA (Editorial Universitaria de Buenos Aires), pg 6

Australia
Robert Berthold Photography, pg 14
Blackwell Science Pty Ltd, pg 15
Brookfield Press, pg 16
CSIRO Publishing (Commonwealth Scientific & Industrial Research Organisation), pg 19
Emerald City Books, pg 22
Illert Publications, pg 27
Macmillan Education Australia, pg 31
McGraw-Hill Australia Pty Ltd, pg 32
Rankin Publishers, pg 40
Reed Educational Publishing Australia, pg 40
Royal Society of New South Wales, pg 41

Austria
Verlag Hoelder-Pichler-Tempsky, pg 53
IAEA - International Atomic Energy Agency, pg 53
Resch Verlag, pg 57
Roetzer Druck GmbH & Co KG, pg 58
Springer-Verlag Wien, pg 59
Urban und Schwarzenberg GmbH, pg 60

Bangladesh
Bangladesh Publishers, pg 62

Belarus
Belaruskaya Encyklapedyya, pg 63
Publishing Center of Belarus State University, pg 63

Belgium
Campinia Media VZW, pg 65
Dessain - Departement de De Boeck & Larcier SA, pg 68
Leuven University Press, pg 71
Uitgeverij De Garve, pg 75
Wolters Plantyn Educatieve Uitgevers, pg 75

Bolivia
Editorial Don Bosco, pg 76

Brazil
Editora Edgard Blucher Ltda, pg 80
Editora Campus Ltda, pg 80
Edicon Editora e Consultorial Ltda, pg 81
LTC-Livros Tecnicos e Cientificos Editora S/A, pg 87
Editora Scipione Ltda, pg 91

Bulgaria
Heron Press Publishing House, pg 96
Makros 2000 - Plovdiv, pg 96
Naouka i Izkoustvo, Ltd, pg 97
Pensoft Publishers, pg 97

China
Beijing Publishing House, pg 102
China Ocean Press, pg 103
Fudan University Press, pg 105
Inner Mongolia Science & Technology Publishing House, pg 106
Jilin Science & Technology Publishing House, pg 106
Lanzhou University Press, pg 107
Science Press, pg 108
Shandong University Press, pg 109
Shanghai Educational Publishing House, pg 109

Colombia
Kapelusz Ltda Editorial, pg 112
McGraw-Hill InterAmericana SA, pg 113
Unidad Universitaria del Sur (UNISUR), pg 114

Czech Republic
Academia, pg 122

Denmark
GEC Gads Forlag Aktieselskab af 1994, pg 132
Systime, pg 136

Dominican Republic
Pontificia Universidad Catolica Madre y Maestra, pg 136

France
Breal, pg 151
CNRS Editions, pg 155
Edicef - Editions Classiques d'Expression Francaise, pg 161
EDP Sciences, pg 161
Editions Jacques Gabay, pg 165
Editions Gammaprim, pg 166
Ganymede, pg 166
Hermann editeurs des Sciences et des Arts SA, pg 168
InterEditions Paris, pg 169
Librairie Scientifique et Technique Albert Blanchard, pg 173
Polytechnica, pg 180
Editions Scientifiques et Medicales Elsevier, pg 184
Editions Springer France, pg 186
Librairie Vuibert, pg 189

Germany
AOL-Verlag Frohmut Menze, pg 194
Aulis Verlag Deubner & Co KG, pg 197
Johann Ambrosius Barth GmbH, pg 198
Bayerischer Schulbuch-Verlag GmbH, pg 199
Beuth Verlag GmbH, pg 202
Cornelsen Verlag GmbH & Co OHG, pg 211
Verlag Harri Deutsch, pg 213
Verlag Europa-Lehrmittel, Nourney, Vollmer GmbH & Co, pg 224
Fachbuchverlag Leipzig im Carl Hanser Verlag, pg 226
Ferd Dummler's Verlag, pg 227
Franz Ferzak World & Space Publications, pg 227
Walter de Gruyter GmbH & Co KG, pg 234
Carl Hanser Verlag, pg 237
Franckh-Kosmos Verlags-GmbH & Co, pg 252
Hildegard Liebaug-Dartmann, pg 258
Springer-Verlag GmbH & Co KG, pg 288
B G Teubner GmbH, pg 292
UTB fuer Wissenschaft Uni-Taschenbuecher GmbH, pg 297
Volk und Wissen Verlag GmbH & Co, pg 299
Wiley-VCH Verlag GmbH, pg 302

Ghana
Sedco Publishing Ltd, pg 308

SUBJECT INDEX

Greece
Diavlos, pg 309
Govostis Publishing SA, pg 311
Mavrogianni Publications, pg 313
Michalis Sideris, pg 313
Panepistimio Ioanninon, pg 314

Haiti
Editions Caraiibes SA, pg 317

Holy See (Vatican City State)
Pontificia Academia Scientiarum, pg 317

Hungary
Aranyhal Konyvkiado Goldfish Publishing, pg 323
Magyar Tudomanyos Akademia Koezponti Fizikai Kutato Intezet Koenyvtara, pg 325
Mueszaki Koenyvkiado Ltd, pg 325
Nemzeti Tankoenyvkiado, pg 326
Typotex Kft Elektronikus Kiado, pg 327

India
Addison-Wesley (Singapore) Pte Ltd, pg 329
Affiliated East West Press Pvt Ltd, pg 329
B I Publications Pvt Ltd, pg 331
Bharat Publishing House, pg 332
Frank Brothers & Co (Publishers) Ltd, pg 337
Narosa Publishing House, pg 343
Publications & Information Directorate, CSIR, pg 346
Rajasthan Hindi Granth Academy, pg 347
Scientific Book Agency, pg 349
Sita Publications, pg 350
South Asian Publishers Pvt Ltd, pg 350
Sultan Chand & Sons Pvt Ltd, pg 351
Vikas Publishing House Pvt Ltd, pg 353
S Viswanathan (Printers & Publishers) Pvt Ltd, pg 353

Indonesia
Mutiara Sumber Widya PT, pg 356

Ireland
Dublin Institute for Advanced Studies, pg 360

Israel
Open University of Israel, pg 371

Italy
Adelphi Edizioni SpA, pg 374
Bibliopolis - Edizioni di Filosofia e Scienze Srl, pg 377
Casa Editrice Giuseppe Principato Spa, pg 380
Edizioni Dedalo SRL, pg 384
Editrice Edisco, pg 386
Editoriale Jaca Book SpA, pg 394
Masson SpA, pg 398
Monduzzi Editore SpA, pg 399
Principato, pg 404
Societa Editrice Internazionale - SEI, pg 408
Societa Editrice la Goliardica Pavese SRL, pg 408
Edizioni Sorbona Milano, pg 408
Zanichelli Editore SpA, pg 412

1051

SUBJECT INDEX

Japan
Baifukan Co Ltd, pg 414
Kindai Kagaku Sha Co, Ltd, pg 419
Kyoritsu Shuppan Co Ltd, pg 420
Maruzen Co Ltd, pg 421
Mita Press, Mita Industrial Co, Ltd, pg 421
Sangyo-Tosho Publishing Co Ltd, pg 424

Kenya
Heinemann Kenya Limited (EAEP), pg 431
Nairobi University Press, pg 433

Democratic People's Republic of Korea
Academy of Sciences Publishing House, pg 434
Korea Science and Encyclopedia Publishing House, pg 434

Republic of Korea
Prompter Publications, pg 439

Kuwait
Ministry of Information, pg 441

Laos People's Democratic Republic
Lao-phanit, pg 441

Latvia
Lielvards Ltd, pg 442

Lithuania
Mokslo ir enciklopediju leidybos institutas, pg 446
TEV Leidykla, pg 446

Malaysia
Pearson Education, pg 453

Mexico
Editorial Esfinge SA de CV, pg 460
Fernandez Editores SA de CV, pg 461
Editorial Limusa SA de CV, pg 463
Pearson Educacion de Mexico, SA de CV, pg 465
Universidad Nacional Autonoma de Mexico (National University of Mexico), pg 467

Republic of Moldova
Lumina Publishing House, pg 468

Nepal
International Standards Books & Periodicals (P) Ltd, pg 471

Netherlands
A A Balkema, pg 473
Baltzer Science Publishers, pg 474
Delft University Press, pg 476
Elsevier Science BV, pg 477
IOS Press BV, pg 479
LCG Malmberg BV, pg 480
Uitgeverij de Tijdstroom BV, pg 485
V S P International Science Publishers, pg 486

New Zealand
ABA Books, pg 488
ESA Publications (NZ) Ltd, pg 490

New House Publishers Ltd, pg 493
Nelson Price Milburn Ltd, pg 494

Nigeria
Ilesanmi Press (Educational Publishers) Ltd, pg 499

Norway
NKI Forlaget, pg 504

Pakistan
Publishers United Pvt Ltd, pg 508

Philippines
Rex Bookstores & Publishers, pg 514
Salesiana Publishers Inc, pg 515

Poland
Oficyna Wydawnicza Politechniki Wroclawskiej, pg 519
Wydawnictwa Naukowo-Techniczne, pg 521

Portugal
Dinalivro, pg 524
Gradiva-Publicacnoes Lda, pg 525
McGraw-Hill Editora de Portugal, pg 527
Silabo, pg 529

Romania
Editura Academiei Romane, pg 531
Corint Verlag, pg 532
Editura Niculescu, pg 534
Petrion Verlag, pg 535

Russian Federation
Energoatomizdat, pg 537
Fizmatlit Publishing Co, pg 538
Izdatelstvo Mir, pg 540
Nauka Publishers, pg 540
Izdatel'stvo Nizhegorodskogo Gosudarstvennogo Univ, pg 540
Teorija Verojatnostej i ee Primenenija, pg 542
Izdatelstvo Vysshaya Shkola, pg 543

Singapore
Hillview Publications Pte Ltd, pg 546
Reed Elsevier, South East Asia, pg 547
World Scientific Publishing Co Pte Ltd, pg 549

Slovakia
Slovenske pedagogicke nakladateistvo, pg 550
Sofa, pg 551

South Africa
Educum Publishers Ltd, pg 554

Spain
Editorial Everest SA, pg 572
Editorial Iberia, SA, pg 577
Idea Books, SA, pg 578
Editorial la Muralla SA, pg 583
Universidad de Santiago de Compostela, pg 589
Ediciones de la Torre, pg 593
Universidad de Valladolid Secretariado de Publicaciones e Intercambio Editorial, pg 594

Sri Lanka
Ministry of Education, pg 597

Switzerland
Birkhauser Verlag AG, pg 610
Verlag Harri Deutsch, pg 612
Presses Polytechniques et Universitaires Romandes, PPUR, pg 622
Trans Tech Publications SA, pg 626
Vdf Hochschulverlag AG an der ETH Zurich, pg 626

Syrian Arab Republic
Damascus University Press, pg 628

Taiwan, Province of China
Far East Book Co Ltd, pg 630
Fuh-Wen Book Co, pg 630

United Republic of Tanzania
DUP (1996) Ltd, pg 633
Tanzania Publishing House, pg 634

Thailand
Graphic Art Publishing, pg 635

Tunisia
Academie Tunisienne des Sciences, des Lettres et des Arts Beit El Hekma, pg 637

Turkey
Arkadas Ltd, pg 639
Caglayan Kitabevi, pg 639
Inkilap Publishers Ltd, pg 640

Ukraine
Osvita, pg 643

United Kingdom
Association for Science Education, pg 650
The Eurospan Group, pg 680
Hodder & Stoughton Educational, pg 696
Institute of Physics Publishing, pg 700
James & James (Science Publishers) Ltd, pg 702
Kluwer Academic/Plenum Publishers, pg 705
John Murray (Publishers) Ltd, pg 716
Nelson Thornes Ltd, pg 718
Pearson Education, pg 725
ProQuest Information & Learning, pg 731
The Royal Society, pg 737
The Society of Metaphysicians Ltd, pg 743
Taylor & Francis Group, pg 747
Two-Can Publishing Ltd, pg 750
Wiley Europe Ltd, pg 756

Uruguay
A Monteverde y Cia SA, pg 760

Venezuela
Sociedad Fondo Editorial Cenamec, pg 762

Viet Nam
Science & Technics Publishing House, pg 763

Zimbabwe
College Press Publishers (Pvt) Ltd, pg 768

POETRY

Albania
Botimpex Publications Import-Export Agency, pg 1
NL SH, pg 1

Algeria
Enterprise Nationale du Livre (ENAL), pg 2

Argentina
Beatriz Viterbo Editora, pg 4
Editorial Claridad SA, pg 4
Colmegna SA, pg 4
Ediciones Corregidor SAICI y E, pg 4
Editorial Losada SA, pg 7
Editora Patria Grande, pg 8
Quetzal-Domingo Cortizo, pg 8
Ediciones Tres Tiempos SRL, pg 9

Australia
Access Press, pg 10
Aeolian Press, pg 11
Ashling Books, pg 12
Assert Publishing, pg 12
Bandicoot Books, pg 14
Church Archivists Press, pg 18
Cornford Press, pg 19
Eleanor Curtain Publishing, pg 19
Dangaroo Press, pg 20
Dragon Press, pg 20
EK Press, pg 21
Feakle Press, pg 22
Fremantle Arts Centre Press, pg 23
Freshet Press, pg 23
Galley Press Publishing, pg 23
Gangan Publishing, pg 23
Ginninderra Press, pg 24
Geoffrey Hamlyn-Harris, pg 25
Incunabula Press, pg 27
Island Press, pg 28
Jesuit Publications, pg 28
Jika Publishing, pg 28
Joval Publications, pg 29
Lightbild PTY Ltd, pg 30
Little Red Apple Publishing, pg 30
Mimosa Publications Pty Ltd, pg 33
Mountain House Press, pg 33
Mulini Press, pg 34
New Albion Press, pg 34
New Endeavour Press, pg 34
Nimrod Publications, pg 35
Omnibus Books, pg 35
Papyrus Publishing, pg 37
Pinchgut Press, pg 38
Plantain Park, pg 38
Raincloud Productions, pg 39
South Head Press, pg 42
Spinifex Press, pg 43
Tamarind Publications, pg 44
Tarka Publishing, pg 44
Thin Rich Press, pg 44
Tom Publications, pg 45
Unity Press, pg 46
University of Queensland Press, pg 46
Veritas Press, pg 46
Vista Publications, pg 47
Windhorse Books, pg 48
Yanagang Publishing, pg 48

PUBLISHERS

Austria
Alekto Verlag GmbH, pg 49
BSE Verlag Dr Bernhard Schuttengruber, pg 50
Denkmayr GmbH Druck & Verlag, pg 51
Development News Ltd, pg 51
Diotima Presse, pg 51
Literature Verlag Droschl, pg 51
Ennsthaler GesmbH & Co KG, pg 51
Verlag Lynkeus/H Hakel Gesellschaft, pg 52
Edition Graphischer Zirkel, pg 52
Johannes Heyn, Gert und Volkmar Zechner, pg 52
Edition Koenigstein, pg 54
LOG-Internationale Zeitschrift fuer Literatur, pg 54
Merbod Verlag, pg 55
Otto Mueller Verlag GesmbH & Co KG, pg 55
Edition Neues Marchen, pg 55
Anna Pichler Verlag GmbH, pg 57
Richard Pils Publication P, pg 57
Residenz Verlag GmbH, pg 58
Verlag Roeschnar, pg 58
Andreas Schnider Verlags-Atelier, pg 58
Thanhaeuser Edition, pg 59
Edition Thurnhof KEG, pg 59
Edition Va Bene, pg 60
Weilburg Verlag, pg 60
Wieser Verlag, pg 61
Paul Zsolnay Verlag GmbH, pg 61

Bangladesh
Gatidhara, pg 62
Agamee Prakashani, pg 62

Belarus
Junactva, Vydavectva, pg 63
Kavaler Publishers, pg 63

Belgium
Libraire Ancienne Noel Anselot, pg 64
Le Daily-Bul, pg 67
Davidsfonds - Infodok NV, pg 67
Imprimerie Hayez SPRL, pg 69
Editions Labor, pg 70
Uitgeverij Lannoo NV, pg 70
La Longue Vue, pg 71
Paradox Pers vzw, pg 72
La Part de L'Oeil, pg 72
Poeziecentrum, pg 73
Standaard Uitgeverij, pg 74
Vita, pg 75
Vlaamse Esperantobond VZW, pg 75
Zuid En Noord VZW, pg 76

Bosnia and Herzegovina
Bemust doo Novinsko-Izdavacko stamparsko i trgovacko preduzece, pg 77

Botswana
Maskew Miller Longman, pg 77

Brazil
Ars Poetica Editora Ltda, pg 79
Editora Bertrand Brasil Ltda, pg 79
Edicon Editora e Consultorial Ltda, pg 81
Editora Companhia das Letras/ Editora Schwarcz Ltda, pg 82
Editora Elevacao, pg 82
Global Editora e Distribuidora Ltda, pg 84
Editora Globo SA, pg 84
Editora Mantiqueira de Ciencia e Arte, pg 87
Editora Nova Alexandria Ltda, pg 88
Editora Nova Fronteira SA, pg 88
Pool Editorial Ltda, pg 90
Thex Editora e Distribuidora Ltda, pg 92
34 Literatura S/C Ltda, pg 92

Bulgaria
Bojko Kacarmazov, pg 94
CHRIKER, pg 94
Hristo G Danov State Publishing House, pg 95
EA Publishing House, pg 95
Kibea Publishing Co, pg 96
Musica Publishing House Ltd, pg 96
Narodna Kultura, pg 97
Pet Plus, pg 97
Prozoretz Ltd Publishing House, pg 97
Svetra Publishing House, pg 98
TEMTO, pg 98
Ivan Vazov Publishing House, pg 98
Peyo K Yavorov Publishing House, pg 98
Zunica, pg 98

Cameroon
Editions Buma Kor, pg 99
Editions CLE, pg 99
Editions Semences Africaines, pg 99

Chile
Editorial Cuarto Propio, pg 100
Pehuen Editores Ltda, pg 101
Red Internacional Del Libro, pg 101

China
Beijing Publishing House, pg 102
Chinese Literature Press, pg 104
Fudan University Press, pg 105
People's Literature Publishing House, pg 108
Writers' Publishing House, pg 110

Colombia
Amazonas Editores Ltda, pg 111
El Ancora Editores, pg 111
Procultura SA, pg 113
Universidad de Antioquia, Division Publicaciones, pg 114

The Democratic Republic of the Congo
Centre Protestant d'Editions et de Diffusion (CEDI), pg 115
Presses Universitaires du Zaiire (PUZ), pg 115
Editions Saint Paul-Afrique, pg 115

Costa Rica
Litografia Artex, SA, pg 116
Promesa, Ediciones, pg 116
Editorial de la Universidad de Costa Rica, pg 117
Editorial Universidad Nacional (EUNA), pg 117
Editorial Universitaria Centroamericana (EDUCA), pg 117

Cote d'Ivoire
Akohi Editions, pg 117
Les Nouvelles Editions Ivoiriennes (NEI), pg 118

Croatia
ALFA dd za izdavacke, graficke i trgovacke poslove, pg 118
ArTresor naklada, pg 118
Durieux d o o, pg 118
Faust Vrani, pg 118
Knjizevni Krug Split, pg 119
Matica hrvatska, pg 119
Mladost d d Izdavacku graficku i informaticku djelatnost, pg 119
Nasa Djeca Publishing, pg 119
Skolska Knjiga, pg 120

Cuba
Casa Editora Abril, pg 120
Holguin, Ediciones, pg 121
Editorial Letras Cubanas, pg 121
Editorial Oriente, pg 121
Editora Politica, pg 121

Czech Republic
AULOS sro, pg 123
Aurora, pg 123
Barrister & Principal, pg 123
Nakladatelstvi Blok, pg 123
Ceska Expedice, pg 123
Cesky spisovatel, pg 123
Karmelitanske Nakladatelstvi, pg 125
Knihovna A Tiskarna Pro Nevidome, pg 125
Konsultace, pg 125
Labyrint, pg 125
Lidove noviny Nakladatelstvi, pg 125
Melantrich, pg 126
Mlada fronta, pg 126
Pavla Momcilova, pg 126
Nadace Lyry Pragensis, pg 126
Odeon, nakladatelstvi krasne literatury a umeni, pg 127
Paseka, pg 127
Ladislav Vasicek, pg 129
Vitalis SRO, pg 129
Votobia sro, pg 129
Vysehrad, pg 129

Denmark
Borgens Forlag A/S, pg 130
The Danish Literature Centre, pg 131
Grevas Forlag, pg 132
Gyldendalske Boghandel - Nordisk Forlag A/S, pg 132
Politisk Revy, pg 134
Det Schonbergske Forlag, pg 135
Forlaget Vindrose A/S, pg 136

Dominican Republic
Pontificia Universidad Catolica Madre y Maestra, pg 136

Egypt (Arab Republic of Egypt)
Al Arab Publishing House, pg 138
Dar El Shorouk, pg 138
Dar El Shorouk Publishing & Distributing House, pg 138
Elias Modern Publishing House, pg 138
Middle East Book Centre, pg 139
Senouhy Publishers, pg 139

El Salvador
Clasicos Roxsil Editorial SA de CV, pg 139
Editorial Universitaria de la Universidad de El Salvador, pg 139

SUBJECT INDEX

Estonia
Oue Eesti Raamat, pg 139
Ilmamaa, pg 140
Tuum, pg 141

Fiji
Lotu Pacifika Productions, pg 141

Finland
Basam Books Oy, pg 142
Forlagsaktiebolaget Scriptum, pg 142
Herattaja-yhdistys Ry, pg 142
Schildts Foerlagsaktiebolag, pg 144
Soederstroem et Co Foerlagsaktiebolag, pg 144
Svenska Oesterbottens Litteraturfoerening, pg 144

France
Editions Actes Sud, pg 146
ADPF Publications, pg 146
Editions Al Liamm, pg 146
Alsatia SA, pg 146
ALTESS Editions Argel, pg 146
L'Amitie par le Livre, pg 147
Editions Arcam, pg 147
Editions Aubier-Montaigne SA, pg 149
Editions d'Aujourd'hui (Les Introuvables), pg 149
Editions Belfond, pg 150
Editions Belin, pg 150
Bibliotheque des Arts, pg 150
William Blake & Co, pg 150
Editions Andre Bonne, pg 151
Pierre Bordas et Fils, pg 151
Editions Jacques Bremond, pg 151
Brud Nevez, pg 152
Editions des Cahiers Bourbonnais, pg 152
Editions Caracteres, pg 152
Editions Champ Vallon, pg 154
Le Cherche Midi Editeur, pg 154
Circe, pg 155
COMP'ACT, pg 156
Corsaire Editions, pg 156
Librairie Jose Corti, pg 156
Nouvelles Editions Debresse, pg 158
La Delirante, pg 158
Georges-Charles Demay, pg 158
Editions de la Difference, pg 159
Les Dossiers d'Aquitaine, pg 160
Encres Vives, pg 162
Editions Entente, pg 162
Editions Fanlac, pg 163
Des Femmes, pg 164
Association Frank, pg 165
Edition Galilee, pg 165
Editions Gallimard, pg 165
Sarl Editions Jean Grassin, pg 167
Editions de l'Herne, pg 168
Editions Ivrea, pg 170
Lettres Vives, pg 173
Le Livre de Poche-L G F (Librairie Generale Francaise), pg 173
Mercure de France SA, pg 176
Gabriel Mony, pg 176
Nanga, pg 177
Mare Nostrum, pg 177
Nouvelles Editions Latines, pg 178
Editions Obsidiane, pg 178
Editions de l'Orante, pg 178
Editions Christian Pirot, pg 180
POL Editeur, pg 180
Presence Africaine Editions, pg 180
Propos de Campagne, pg 182
Publications Orientalistes de France (POF), pg 182
Revue Noire, pg 183

1053

SUBJECT INDEX

Editions Robert Laffont, Nil, Fixot, Seghers, Julliard, pg 183
Editions Saint-Germain-des-Pres SA, pg 183
Seghers, pg 184
Service Technique pour l'Education, pg 185
Editions du Seuil, pg 185
Editions Andre Silvaire Sarl, pg 185
Spectres Familiers, pg 186
Editions Stock, pg 186
SUD, pg 186
Editions Unes, pg 188
Publications de l'Universite de Pau, pg 188
La Vague a l'ame, pg 188
La Vague Verte, pg 188
La Voix du Regard, pg 189

Germany

Alpha Literatur Verlag/Alpha Presse, pg 193
Anabas-Verlag Guenter Kaempf GmbH & Co KG, pg 193
Verlag APHAlA Svea Haske, Sonja Schumann GbR, pg 194
Asso Verlag, pg 196
Atelier Verlag Andernach (AVA), pg 196
Aufbau Taschenbuch Verlag GmbH, pg 196
Aufbau-Verlag GmbH, pg 196
Babel Verlag Kevin Perryman, pg 197
Dr Bachmaier Verlag GmbH, pg 197
Dr Wolfgang Baur Verlag Kunst & Alltag, pg 199
Beerenverlag, pg 200
Belser Wissenschaftlicher Dienst, pg 200
Bergstadtverlag Wilhelm Gottlieb Korn GmbH Wuerzburg, pg 200
Verlag Beruf + Schule Belz KG, pg 202
Betzel Verlag GmbH, pg 202
Blaukreuz-Verlag Wuppertal, pg 204
Verlag Hermann Boehlaus Nachfolger Weimar GmbH & Co, pg 205
Brandes & Apsel Verlag GmbH, pg 206
Brigg Verlag Franz-Joset Buchler KG, pg 206
BRUEN-Verlag, Gorenflo, pg 207
Bund-Verlag GmbH, pg 208
Fachverlag Hans Carl GmbH, pg 209
Christusbruderschaft Selbitz ev, Abt Verlag, pg 210
CMA Edition, pg 211
J G Cotta'sche Buchhandlung Nachfolger GmbH, pg 212
CTL-Presse Clemens-Tobias Lange, pg 212
Deutsche Verlags-Anstalt GmbH (DVA), pg 214
Deutscher Taschenbuch Verlag GmbH & Co KG (dtv), pg 215
Diagonal-Verlag GbR Rink-Schweer, pg 216
Dieterichsche Verlagsbuchhandlung Mainz, pg 216
Dietrich zu Klampen Verlag, pg 216
Ehrenwirth Verlag GmbH, pg 221
Elpis Verlag GmbH, pg 222
Verlag Peter Engstler, pg 223
Eremiten-Presse und Verlag GmbH, pg 223
Fabel-Verlag Gudrun Liebchen, pg 226
Wolfgang Fietkau Verlag, pg 227
Karin Fischer Verlag GmbH, pg 228
Rita G Fischer Verlag, pg 228
Margarethe Freudenberger - selbstverlag fur jedermann, pg 230
Galrev Druck-und Verlagsgesellschaft Hesse & Partner OHG, pg 231
Garbe Verlag Ellen Vogt, pg 231
Gilles und Francke Verlag, pg 232
GLB Parkland Verlags-und Vertriebs GmbH, pg 232
Guenther Butkus, pg 235
Carl Hanser Verlag, pg 237
Litteraturverlag Karlheinz Hartmann, pg 237
von Hase & Koehler Verlag KG, pg 238
Heinz-Theo Gremme Verlag, pg 239
Hertenstein, Axel, Hernstein-Presse, pg 240
Hoffmann und Campe Verlag GmbH, pg 242
Horlemann Verlag, pg 243
Klaus Isele, pg 245
ludicium Verlag GmbH, pg 245
Verlag J P Peter, Gebr Holstein GmbH & Co KG, pg 246
K L V Konkret Literatur Verlag GmbH, pg 247
Verlag Kleine Schritte Ursula Dahm & Co, pg 249
Klink, Vincent, Edition, Stecknadel, pg 250
Dr Anton Kovac Slavica Verlag, pg 253
Karin Kramer Verlag, pg 253
Lahn-Verlag GmbH, pg 255
Verlag Langewiesche-Brandt KG, pg 256
Anton G Leitner Verlag (AGLV), pg 257
Dr Gisela Lermann, pg 257
Lienhard Pallast Verlag, pg 258
Logos-Verlag Literatur & Layout GmbH, pg 258
Maro Verlag und Druck, Benno Kasmayr, pg 261
Matthes und Seitz Verlag GmbH, pg 261
Matzker Verlag DiA, pg 261
Merlin Verlag Andreas Meyer Verlags GmbH und Co KG, pg 263
Mitteldeutscher Verlag GmbH, pg 264
Monia Verlag, pg 265
Verlag Neue Kritik KG, pg 267
Neues Literaturkontor, pg 268
Nie/Nie/Sagen-Verlag, pg 268
Edition Octopus & Okeanos Presse, pg 269
Ostfalia-Verlag Jurgen Schierer, pg 271
Pandion-Verlag, Ulrike Schmoll, pg 271
Pawel Panpresse, pg 272
Pendragon Verlag, pg 272
Philipp Reclam Jun Verlag GmbH, pg 273
Prasenz Verlag der Jesus Bruderschaft eV, pg 274
Propylaeen Verlag, Zweigniederlassung Berlin der Ullstein Buchverlage GmbH, pg 275
Rimbaud Verlagsgesellschaft mbH, pg 279
Romiosini Verlag, pg 280
ROSPO Verlag, pg 280
Ruetten & Loening Berlin GmbH, pg 281
Sassafras Verlag, pg 281
scaneg Verlag, pg 282
Agora Verlag Manfred Schlosser, pg 283
Buchverlag Andrea Schmitz, pg 284
Theodor Schuster, pg 285
Heinrich Schwab Verlag, pg 285
Siebenberg-Verlag, pg 286
Snayder Verlag Gunter VOB & Jurgen Schroder OHG, pg 287
Steidl Verlag, pg 289
Edition Gunter Stoberlein, pg 290
Straelener Manuskripte Verlag, pg 290
Suhrkamp Verlag, pg 291
Svato Zapletal, pg 291
Tangens Systemverlag GmbH, pg 291
Toleranz Verlag, Nielsen Frederic W, pg 294
Treves Editions Verein Zur Foerderung der Kuenstlerischen Taetigkeiten, pg 295
Guenter Albert Ulmer Verlag, pg 295
Verlag und Studio fuer Hoerbuchproduktionen, pg 298
Verlag Klaus Wagenbach GmbH, pg 300
Uwe Warnke Verlag, pg 300
Weidler Buchverlag Berlin, pg 301
Wolgang Fietkau, pg 304
Das Wunderhorn Verlag GmbH, pg 304
Zambon Verlag, pg 305

Ghana

Anowuo Educational Publications, pg 306
Asempa Publishers, pg 306
Bureau of Ghana Languages, pg 306
Ghana Publishing Corporation, pg 307
Moxon Paperbacks, pg 307
Waterville Publishing House, pg 308
Woeli Publishing Services, pg 308

Greece

Athina, Mary Mavrogiannis, pg 309
Dorikos Publishing House, pg 310
Ekdoseis Kazantzaki (Kazantzakis Publications), pg 310
Elliniki Leschi Tou Vivliou, pg 310
Etaireia Spoudon Neoellinikou Politismou Kai Genikis Paideias, pg 310
Ekdoseis Filon, pg 310
Forma Publications Ltd, pg 310
Govostis Publishing SA, pg 311
Denise Harvey, pg 311
Hestia-I D Hestia-Kollaros & Co Corporation, pg 311
Hiotellis P, pg 311
Idmon Publications, pg 311
Irini Publishing House - Vassilis G Katsikeas SA, pg 311
Kedros Publishers, pg 312
Knossos Publications, pg 312
Patakis Publishers, pg 314
To Rodakio, pg 315
S J Zacharopoulos SA Publishing Co, pg 316

Guatemala

Grupo Editorial RIN-78, pg 316

Hong Kong

Breakthrough Ltd - Breakthrough Publishers, pg 318
Research Centre for Translation, pg 321

Hungary

Advent Kiado, pg 323
Europa Konyvkiado, pg 323
Jelenkor Verlag, pg 324
Magveto Koenyvkiado, pg 325
Szepirodalmi Koenyvkiado Kiado, pg 327
Tevan Kiado Vallalat, pg 327

Iceland

Almenna Bokafelagid, pg 327
Fjolvi, pg 327
Frodi Ltd, pg 328
Godord, pg 328
Idunn, pg 328
Islendingasagnautgafan, pg 328
Mal og menning, pg 328
Stofnun Arna Magnussonar a Islandi, pg 329

India

Ananda Publishers Pvt Ltd, pg 330
Associated Publishing House, pg 331
Chanakya Publications, pg 334
Chowkhamba Sanskrit Series Office, pg 335
DC Books, pg 336
Dutta Baruah Publishing Co Pvt Ltd, pg 336
Geeta Prakasham, pg 337
HarperCollins Publishers India Pty Ltd, pg 338
Arnold Heinman Publishers (India) Pvt Ltd, pg 338
Intertrade Publications, pg 340
Kitab Ghar, pg 341
Natraj Prakashan, pg 344
Orient Paperbacks, pg 345
Panjab University Publication Bureau, pg 345
People's Publishing House (P) Ltd, pg 346
Prabhat Prakashan, pg 346
Pratibha Pratishthan, pg 346
Reliance Publishing House, pg 347
SABDA, pg 348
Samkaleen Prakashan, pg 349
Sat Sahitya Prakashan, pg 349
Vani Prakashan, pg 352

Indonesia

Dunia Pustaka Jaya, pg 355
Penerbit Nusa Indah, pg 356

Ireland

Clo Iar-Chonnachta Teo, pg 359
Gallery Books, Ireland, pg 360
The Goldsmith Press Ltd, pg 361
The Lilliput Press Ltd, pg 362
New Writers' Press, pg 362
Publishers Group South West (Ireland), pg 363
Raven Arts Press, pg 363
Runa Press, pg 364
Salmon Publishing, pg 364

Israel

Am Oved Publishers Ltd, pg 365
The Bialik Institute, pg 365
Bitan Publishers Ltd, pg 365
Boostan Publishing House, pg 366
Dvir Publishing Ltd, pg 366
Gefen Publishing House Ltd, pg 367
Gvanim Publishing House, pg 367
Habermann Institute for Literary Research, pg 367
Hakibbutz Hameuchad Publishing House Ltd, pg 368

The Institute for the Translation of Hebrew Literature, pg 368
Karni Publishers Ltd, pg 369
Kiryat Sefer, pg 369
Schocken Publishing House Ltd, pg 372
Y L Peretz Publishing Co, pg 374

Italy
Mario Adda Editore SNC, pg 374
Adelphi Edizioni SpA, pg 374
Adriatica Editrice, pg 374
Alba, pg 375
Archinto snc, pg 376
Argalia Editore delle Arti Grafiche Editoriali SRL, pg 376
Verlagsanstalt Athesia, pg 377
Belforte Editore Libraio srl, pg 377
Bibliotheca di Gabriele Chiusano, pg 378
Book Editore, pg 378
Edizioni Bresciane, pg 378
Campanotto, pg 379
Nuova Casa Editrice Licinio Cappelli GEM srl, pg 379
Edistudio di Brunetto Casini, pg 380
Edizioni Castello di Antonio Careddu, pg 380
Centro Studi Terzo Mondo, pg 381
Colonnese Editore, pg 382
Edizioni Della Torre di Salvatore Fozzi & C SAS, pg 384
Edizioni dell'Orso SAS, pg 385
Edizioni l'Arciere SRL, pg 387
Giulio Einaudi Editore SpA, pg 387
ERGA SNC di Carla Ottino Merli & C (Edizioni Realizzazioni Grafiche - Artigiana), pg 388
Giangiacomo Feltrinelli SpA, pg 389
Adriano Gallina Editore sas, pg 389
Galzerano Editore, pg 390
Garzanti Editore, pg 390
Edizioni del Girasole srl, pg 390
Giuseppe Laterza Editore Snc, pg 391
Ugo Guanda Editore, pg 392
Il Saggiatore, pg 393
Editoriale Jaca Book SpA, pg 394
L Japadre Editore, pg 394
Lalli Editore SRL, pg 395
Letture Mensile di Informazione Culturale, Letteratura e Spettacolo, pg 395
Editrice Liguria SNC di Norberto Sabatelli & C, pg 396
Linea d'Ombra Libri, pg 396
Vincenzo Lo Faro Editore, pg 396
Editrice la Locusta, pg 396
Angelo Longo Editore, pg 396
Lorenzo Editore, pg 397
Lusva Editrice, pg 397
Tommaso Marotta Editore Srl, pg 398
Il Melangolo, pg 398
Casa Editrice Menna di Sinisgalli Menna Giuseppina, pg 398
Arnoldo Mondadori Editore SpA, pg 399
Gruppo Ugo Mursia Editore SpA, pg 400
Nardini Editore srl, pg 400
Newton Compton Editori SRL, pg 401
Editrice Nuovi Autori, pg 401
Nuovi Sentieri Editore, pg 401
Paideia Editrice, pg 402
Franco Cosimo Panini Editore SpA, pg 402
Passigli Editori srl, pg 403
Luigi Pellegrini Editore, pg 403
Daniela Piazza Editore, pg 403

Piero Manni srl, pg 403
La Pilotta Editrice Coop RL, pg 403
Francesco Pirella Editore, pg 403
Edizioni Quasar di Severino Tognon SRL, pg 404
Reverdito Edizioni, pg 405
Riccardo Ricciardi Editore SpA, pg 405
Edizioni Ripostes, pg 405
Rubbettino Editore, pg 406
Fausto Sardini Editrice, pg 407
Salvatore Sciascia Editore, pg 407
SEMAR Publishers SRL, pg 407
Societa Storica Catanese, pg 408
Spirali Edizioni, pg 408
TEA Tascabili degli Editori Associati SpA, pg 409
Todariana Editrice, pg 410
Il Tripode Srl, pg 410
La Vita Felice, pg 411
Vivere In SRL, pg 411

Japan
Hoikusha Publishing Co Ltd, pg 417
The Hokuseido Press, pg 417
Shakai Shiso-Sha, pg 425
Charles E Tuttle Publishing Co Inc, pg 428

Kazakhstan
Zazusy, pg 430

Kenya
Foundation Books, pg 431
Heinemann Kenya Limited (EAEP), pg 431
Lake Publishers & Enterprises Ltd, pg 432
Phoenix Publishers, pg 433
Transafrica Press, pg 433

Republic of Korea
Ba-reunsa Publishing Co, pg 434
Haedong, pg 436
Hollym Corporation Publishers, pg 437
Hw Moon Publishing Co, pg 437
Iljisa Publishing House, pg 437
Literature Academy, pg 438
Mirinae, pg 438
Nanam Publishing House, pg 439
O Neul Publishing Co, pg 439
St Pauls, pg 439

Latvia
Artava Ltd, pg 441
Liesma Publishers, pg 442
Madris, pg 442
Nordik/Tapals Publishers Ltd, pg 442
Preses Nams, pg 442

Lebanon
World Book Publishing, pg 443

Liechtenstein
Kliemand Verlag, pg 444

Lithuania
Andrena Publishers, pg 445
Baltos Lankos, pg 445
Lietuvos Rasytoju Sajungos Leidykla, pg 446
The Publishing House of the Lithuanian Writers' Union, pg 446

Luxembourg
Editions APESS ASBL, pg 447
Editions Emile Borschette, pg 447
Eiffes Romain, pg 447
Op der Lay, pg 447
Editions Tousch, pg 448
Varkki Verghese, pg 448

The Former Yugoslav Republic of Macedonia
Detska radost, pg 448
Ktitor, pg 449
Macedonia Prima Publishing House, pg 449
Mi-An Knigoizdatelstvo, pg 449
Nov svet (New World), pg 449
Strk Publishing House, pg 449
Zumpres Publishing Firm, pg 449

Malawi
Christian Literature Association in Malawi, pg 450

Malaysia
Pustaka Cipta Sdn Bhd, pg 454
University of Malaya, Department of Publications, pg 455

Mali
EDIM SA, pg 455

Mauritius
De l'edition Bukie Banane, pg 457
Editions de l'Ocean Indien Ltd, pg 457

Mexico
Editorial AGATA SA de CV, pg 457
Ediciones Alpe, pg 458
Artes de Mexico y del Mundo, SA de CV, pg 458
Editorial Avante SA de Cv, pg 458
Centro Editorial Mexicano Osiris SA, pg 458
Ediciones CUPSA, Centro de Comunicacion Cultural CUPSA, AC, pg 459
Fondo de Cultura Economica, pg 461
Phillip Richard Conover Lazo, pg 462
Universo Editorial SA de CV Edicion de Libros Revistas y Periodicos, pg 468

Morocco
Association de la Recherche Historique et Sociale, pg 469
Editions Le Fennec, pg 470
Editions Okad, pg 470

Netherlands
BV Uitgeverij de Arbeiderspers, pg 473
De Bezige Bij, pg 474
Buijten en Schipperheijn BV Drukkerij en Uitg Mij v/h, pg 475
Cadans, pg 475
Uitgeverij G F Callenbach BV, pg 475
Castrum Peregrini Presse, pg 475
De Harmonie, pg 478
Historische Uitgeverij, pg 478
Holland B V Uitgeversmaatschappij, pg 478
Uitgeefmaatschappij J H Kok BV, pg 480

Prometheus, pg 483
Em Querido's Uitgeverij BV, pg 483
Uitgeverij G A van Oorschot bv, pg 486

New Zealand
Auckland University Press, pg 488
Brick Row Publishing Co Ltd, pg 489
Cape Catley, pg 489
Cicada Press, pg 490
Hazard Press Ltd, pg 491
John Martin Press, pg 493
Nagare Press, pg 493
Orca Publishing Services Ltd, pg 494
Oxford University Press, pg 494
Nelson Price Milburn Ltd, pg 494
Seagull Press, pg 495
University of Otago Press, pg 496
Victoria University Press, pg 496
Words Work, pg 497

Nicaragua
Editorial Nueva Nicaragua, pg 497

Nigeria
ABIC Books & Equipment Ltd, pg 497
Aromolaran Publishing Co Ltd, pg 498
Black Academy Press, pg 498
Cross Continent Press Ltd, pg 498
Ethiope Publishing Corporation, pg 499
Heritage Books, pg 499
Longman Nigeria Plc, pg 500
New Horn Press Ltd, pg 500
Northern Nigerian Publishing Co Ltd, pg 500
Nwamife Publishers Ltd, pg 500
Onibon-Oje Publishers, pg 501
Saros International Publishers, pg 501
University Publishing Co, pg 502
Vantage Publishers International Ltd, pg 502

Norway
Ariel Lydbokforlag, pg 502
Atheneum Forlag A/S, pg 502
Det Norske Samlaget, pg 503
Fonna Forlag L/L, pg 503
Gyldendal Norsk Forlag A/S, pg 503
Lunde Forlag og Bokhandel A/S, pg 504
Norsk Bokreidingslag L/L, pg 504
Snofugl Forlag, pg 505
Solum Forlag A/S, pg 505

Pakistan
Sheikh Shaukat Ali & Sons, pg 506
H I Jaffari & Co Publishers, pg 506
Jang Publishers, pg 507
Maqbool Academy, pg 508
Sang-e-Meel Publications, pg 509

Paraguay
Intercontinental Editora, pg 510

Philippines
Ateneo de Manila University Press, pg 512
De La Salle University, pg 513
New Day Publishers, pg 514
UST Publishing House, pg 515

SUBJECT INDEX

Poland
Spoldzielnia Wydawnicza 'Czytelnik', pg 516
Wydawnictwo Dolnoslaskie, pg 516
Instytut Wydawniczy Pax, Inco-Veritas, pg 517
Wydawnictwo Lubelskie, pg 518
Ludowa Spoldzielnia Wydawnicza, pg 518
Norbertinum, pg 518
Ossolineum Zaklad Narodowy im Ossolinskich - Wydawnictwo, pg 518
Panstwowy Instytut Wydawniczy (PIW), pg 518
Wydawnictwo Podsiedlik-Raniowski i Spolka, pg 519
'Slask' Ltd, pg 520

Portugal
Apostolado da Oracao Secretariado Nacional, pg 522
Atica, SA Editores e Livreiros, pg 522
Bezerr-Editorae e Distribuidora de Abel Antonio Bezerra, pg 522
Brasilia Editora (J Carvalho Branco), pg 523
Camara Municipal de Castelo, pg 523
Contexto Editora, pg 524
Publicacoes Europa-America Lda, pg 524
Europress Editores e Distribuidores de Publicacoes Lda, pg 525
Fenda Edicoes, pg 525
Guimaraes Editores, Lda, pg 525
Imprensa Nacional-Casa da Moeda, pg 526
Edicoes ITAU (Instituto Tecnico de Alimentacao Humana) Lda, pg 526
Livraria Minerva Editora, pg 526
Livraria Tavares Martins, pg 527
Perspectivas e Realidades, Artes Graficas, Lda, pg 528
Platano Editora SA, pg 528
Editorial Presenca, pg 528
Publicacoes Dom Quixote Lda, pg 528
Quatro Elementos Editores, pg 529
Quetzal Editores, pg 529
Realizacoes Artis, pg 529
Solivros, pg 529
Almerinda Teixeira, pg 529
Usus Editora, pg 530
Vega-Publicacao e Distribuicao de Livros e Revistas, Lda, pg 530

Puerto Rico
Instituto de Cultura Puertorriquena, pg 530
Ediciones Puerto, pg 531
University of Puerto Rico Press (EDUPR), pg 531

Romania
Ars Longa Publishing House, pg 532
Editura Cartea Romaneasca, pg 532
The Center for Romanian Studies, pg 532
Editura Clusium, Casa de Editura Atlas-Clusium SRL, pg 532
Editure Ion Creanga, pg 532
Editura Eminescu, pg 533
Editura Excelsior, pg 533
FF Press, pg 533
Editura Kriterion SA, pg 534
Mentor Kiado, pg 534
Pandora Publishing House, pg 535
Saeculum lO, pg 535

Est-Samuel Tastet Verlag, pg 536
Editura Univers, pg 536
Universal Dalsi, pg 536
Vremea Publishers Ltd, pg 536

Russian Federation
ARGO-RISK Publisher, pg 537
BLIC, russko-Baltijskij informaciionnyj centr, AO, pg 537
Izdatelstvo Detskaya Literatura, pg 537
Kavkazskaya Biblioteka Publishing House, pg 539
Izdatelstvo Khudozhestvennaya Literatura, pg 539
Izdatelstvo Molodaya Gvardia, pg 540
Permskaja Kniga, pg 541
Profizdat, pg 541
Raduga Publishers, pg 541
Izdatelstvo Sovetskii Pisatel, pg 542

Senegal
Centre Africain d'Animation et d'Echanges Culturels Editions Khoudia, pg 544
Les Nouvelles Editions Africaines du Senegal NEAS, pg 544

Singapore
Chopsons Pte Ltd, pg 545

Slovakia
Luc vydavatelske druzstvo, pg 550
Serafin, pg 550
Slo Viet, pg 550
Slovansky Tatran, Vydavatel 'stro spoi sro, pg 550
Slovensky Spisovatel Ltd as, pg 550
Smena Publishing House, pg 550

Slovenia
Cankarjeva Zalozba, pg 551
Franc-Franc podjetje za promocijo kulture Murska Sobota d o o, pg 551
Pomurska zalozba, pg 552
Zalozba Obzorja d d Maribor, pg 552

South Africa
Educum Publishers Ltd, pg 554
HAUM (Hollandsch Afrikaansche Uitgevers Maatschappij), pg 555
The Hippogriff Press CC, pg 555
Human & Rousseau (Pty) Ltd, pg 555
Nasou Via Afrika, pg 557
New Africa Books (Pty) Ltd, pg 557
Publitoria Publishers, pg 558

Spain
Acantilado, pg 561
Agencia Espanola de Cooperacion, pg 562
Editorial Aguaclara, pg 562
Alianza Editorial SA, pg 562
Baile del Sol, Colectivo Cultural, pg 565
Editorial Biblioteca Nueva SL, pg 565
Calambur Editorial, SL, pg 566
Edicios do Castro, pg 566
Ediciones Catedra SA, pg 566
Columna Edicions, Libres i Comunicacio, SA, pg 568

Comunidad Autonoma de Madrid, Servicio de Documentacion y Publicaciones, pg 568
Diputacion Provincial de Malaga, pg 570
Editorial Don Quijote, pg 570
Edi-Liber Irlan SA, pg 571
Edicomunicacion SA, pg 572
Editorial Empeno 14, pg 573
Ediciones Endymion, pg 573
Erein, pg 573
Eumo Editorial, pg 574
Galaxia SA Editorial, pg 575
Instituto de Cultura Juan Gil-Albert, pg 576
Grijalbo Mondadori SA, pg 576
Editorial Grupo Cero, pg 576
Ediciones Hiperion SL, pg 577
Icaria Editorial SA, pg 577
Iralka Editorial SL, pg 578
Joyas Bibliograficas SA, pg 579
Ediciones Jucar, pg 579
Junta de Castilla y Leon Consejeria de Educacion y Cultura, pg 579
Editorin Laiovento SL, pg 579
Ediciones Libertarias/Prodhufi SA, pg 580
Llibres del Segle, pg 580
Editorial Lumen SA, pg 580
La Mascara, SL Editorial, pg 581
Editorial Moll SL, pg 582
Munoz Moya Editor, pg 583
Oikos-Tau SA Ediciones, pg 584
Ediciones del Oriente y del Mediterraneo, pg 585
El Paisaje Editorial, pg 585
Editorial Pliegos, pg 587
Pre-Textos, pg 587
Edicions Proa, SA, pg 588
Instituto Provincial de Investigaciones y Estudios Toledanos, pg 588
Quaderns Crema SA, pg 588
Editora Regional de Murcia - ERM, pg 588
Ediciones Rialp SA, pg 589
Editorial Seix Barral SA, pg 590
Ediciones Seyer, pg 590
Ediciones Siruela SA, pg 591
Edicions 62, pg 591
Grup 62, pg 591
Suaver, Javier Presa Suarez, pg 591
Ediciones de la Torre, pg 593
Torremozas SL Ediciones, pg 593
Trea Ediciones, SL, pg 593
Turner Publicaciones, pg 593
Ediciones 29 - Libros Rio Nuevo, pg 594
Editorial Verbum SL, pg 595
Vinaches Lopez, Luisa, pg 595
Visor Libros, pg 596
Ediciones Vulcano, pg 596
Edicions Xerais de Galicia, pg 596

Sri Lanka
Danuma Prakashakayo, pg 596
Dayawansa Jayakody & Co, pg 597
Swarna Hansa Foundation, pg 598

Sudan
Al-Ayam Press Co Ltd, pg 598
Khartoum University Press, pg 598

Suriname
Lutchman, Drs LFS, pg 599

Sweden
Rene Coeckelberghs Bokfoerlag AB, pg 601
Ellerstroms, pg 602

Schultz Forlag AB, pg 606
AB Wahlstrom & Widstrand, pg 607

Switzerland
Adonia-Verlag, pg 608
Editions L'Age d'Homme - La Cite, pg 608
Ammann Verlag & Co, pg 608
Arche Verlag AG, Raabe und Vitali, pg 608
Armenia Editions, pg 608
Editions de la Baconniere SA, pg 609
Bartschi Publishing, pg 609
Verlag Bibliophile Drucke von Josef Stocker AG, pg 610
Verlag Bo Cavefors, pg 611
Werner Classen Verlag, pg 611
Daimon Verlag AG, pg 612
Daphnis-Verlag, pg 612
E Lopfe-Benz AG Rorschach, Graphische Anstalt und Verlag, pg 612
Erker-Verlag, pg 613
Govinda-Verlag, pg 615
Haffmans Verlag AG, pg 615
Kranich-Verlag, Dres AG & H R Bosch-Gwalter, pg 617
Lia rumantscha, pg 618
Manesse Verlag GmbH, pg 618
Orte-Verlag, pg 621
Ostschweiz Druck und Verlag, pg 621
Pendo Verlag GmbH, pg 621
Rhein-Trio, Edition/Editions du Fou, pg 623
Verlag fuer Schoene Wissenschaften, pg 624
Speer -Verlag, pg 625
Istituto Editoriale Ticinese (IET) SA, pg 626
Editions du Tricorne, pg 626
Editions Eliane Vernay, pg 626
Verlag im Waldgut AG, pg 627
Zbinden Druck und Verlag AG, pg 628

Syrian Arab Republic
Damascus University Press, pg 628

Taiwan, Province of China
Chung Hwa Book Co Ltd, pg 629
Far East Book Co Ltd, pg 630
UNITAS Publishing Co Ltd, pg 632
World Book Co Ltd, pg 632

United Republic of Tanzania
East African Publishing House, pg 633
Eastern Africa Publications Ltd, pg 633
Oxford University Press, pg 634
Tanzania Publishing House, pg 634

Togo
Editions Akpagnon, pg 636
Les Nouvelles Editions Africaines du TOGO (NEA-TOGO), pg 636

Tunisia
Academie Tunisienne des Sciences, des Lettres et des Arts Beit El Hekma, pg 637
Ceres Editions, pg 637
Les Editions de l'Arbre, pg 638
Maison Tunisienne de l'Edition, pg 638

PUBLISHERS

Turkey
Inkilap Publishers Ltd, pg 640
Metis Yayinlari, pg 640
Varlik Yayinlari AS, pg 641
Kabalci Yayinevi, pg 642

Uganda
Fountain Publishers Ltd, pg 642
Roce (Consultants) Ltd, pg 642

Ukraine
Osnovy Publishers, pg 643

United Kingdom
Abbotsford Publishing, pg 644
Acair Ltd, pg 645
Act 3 Publishing, pg 645
AK Press & Distribution, pg 645
Alun Books, pg 646
Anvil Press Poetry Ltd, pg 648
Apex Publishing Ltd, pg 648
Argo Spoken Word, pg 648
Argyll Publishing, pg 648
Aris & Phillips Ltd, pg 648
BCA, pg 653
Blackstaff Press, pg 655
Bloodaxe Books Ltd, pg 656
Calder Publications Ltd, pg 662
Canongate Books Ltd, pg 663
Carcanet Press Ltd, pg 663
Cassell & Co, pg 664
Chapman, pg 666
Cyhoeddiadau Barddas, pg 673
The Eurospan Group, pg 680
Faber & Faber Ltd, pg 681
Famedram Publishers Ltd, pg 681
Frontier Publishing, pg 684
Gairm Publications, pg 685
Genesis Publications Ltd, pg 686
Gomer Press (J D Lewis & Sons Ltd), pg 688
The Greek Bookshop, pg 689
Gwasg Gwenffrwd, pg 690
Robert Hale Ltd, pg 691
The Harvill Press Ltd, pg 693
Heartland Publishing Ltd, pg 694
Honno Welsh Women's Press, pg 697
Icon Press, pg 698
Irish Texts Society (Cumann Na Scribeann nGaedhilge), pg 701
The Islamic Texts Society, pg 701
Janus Publishing Company Ltd, pg 702
Jay Landesman, pg 706
Libris Ltd, pg 707
The Littman Library of Jewish Civilization, pg 708
Y Lolfa Cyf, pg 708
Luath Press Ltd, pg 709
Macmillan Audio Books, pg 710
Mango Publishing, pg 711
The Medici Society Ltd, pg 713
MGM, pg 714
Moorley's Print & Publishing Ltd, pg 715
National Association for the Teaching of English (NATE), pg 717
NMS Publishing Ltd, pg 719
The Octagon Press Ltd, pg 720
Octopus Publishing Group, pg 720
The Oleander Press, pg 721
Orion Publishing Group Ltd, pg 722
Oxford University Press, pg 723
PARAS, pg 724
Pearson Education, pg 725
Peepal Tree Press, pg 725
Pentathol Publishing, pg 726
Planet, pg 728
Plough Publishing House of Bruderhof Communities in the UK, pg 728
Poetry Wales Press Ltd, pg 729
Polygon, pg 729
Primrose Hill Press Ltd, pg 730
Ramsay Head Press, pg 732
Random House UK Ltd, pg 733
Regency House Publishing Ltd, pg 734
The Saltire Society, pg 738
Scottish Cultural Press, pg 739
Scottish Text Society, pg 740
Seren, pg 740
Sherbourne Publications, pg 741
Charles Skilton Ltd, pg 742
Skoob Russell Square, pg 742
Souvenir Press Ltd, pg 743
Supportive Learning Publications, pg 746
Tabb House, pg 746
Telegraph Books, pg 748
Tern Press, pg 748
Time Out Group Ltd, pg 749
Tuba Press, pg 750
University of Exeter Press, pg 751
Ward Lock Educational Co Ltd, pg 754
Wayland Publishers Ltd (Incorporating Macdonald Young Books), pg 754
Wordsworth Editions Ltd, pg 758

Uruguay
Editorial Arca SRL, pg 760
Ediciones de Juan Darien, pg 760
Nordan-Comunidad, pg 760
Luis A Retta Libros, pg 761
Rosebud Ediciones, pg 761
La Urpila Editores, pg 761
Vinten Editor, pg 761

Venezuela
Alfadil Ediciones, pg 761
Editorial Ateneo de Caracas, pg 762
Monte Avila Editores Latinoamericana CA, pg 762
Biblioteca Ayacucho, pg 762

Yugoslavia
Alfa-Narodna Knjiga, pg 764
Beogradski Izdavacko-Graficki Zavod, pg 764
Izdavacka Organizacija Rad, pg 765
Svetovi, pg 766

Zambia
Zambia Educational Publishing House, pg 767

Zimbabwe
College Press Publishers (Pvt) Ltd, pg 768
The Literature Bureau, pg 768
Longman Zimbabwe (Pvt) Ltd, pg 768
Mambo Press, pg 768
Mercury Press Pvt Ltd, pg 769
Phantom Publishers, pg 769
Vision Publications, pg 769

PSYCHOLOGY, PSYCHIATRY

Albania
NL SH, pg 1
State Textbook Publishing House, pg 1

Argentina
Editorial Abaco de Rodolfo Depalma SRL, pg 2
Alianza Editorial de Argentina SA, pg 3
Amorrortu Editores SA, pg 3
AZ Editora SA, pg 3
Fundacion Editorial de Belgrano, pg 4
Bonum Editorial SACI, pg 4
Centro Editor de America Latina SA, pg 4
Club de Lectores, pg 4
Ediciones del Eclipse, pg 5
EUDEBA (Editorial Universitaria de Buenos Aires), pg 6
Ediciones de la Flor SRL, pg 6
Editorial Guadalupe, pg 6
Kapelusz Editora SA, pg 6
Ediciones Lidium, pg 7
Editorial Losada SA, pg 7
Marymar Ediciones SA, pg 7
Editorial Medica Panamericana, pg 7
Editorial Medica, Panamericana SA, pg 7
Ediciones Nueva Vision SAIC, pg 8
Editorial Paidos SAICF, pg 8
Editorial Planeta Argentina SAIC, pg 8
Editorial Plus Ultra SA, pg 8
Polemos SA, pg 8
San Pablo, pg 8
Editorial Sudamericana SA, pg 9
Ediciones Tres Tiempos SRL, pg 9
Editorial Troquel SA, pg 9
Javier Vergara Editor SA, pg 9

Australia
ACER Press, pg 10
The Advancement Centre, pg 11
Michelle Anderson Publishing Pty Ltd, pg 11
Edward Arnold (Australia) Pty Ltd, pg 12
Australian Academic Press Pty Ltd, pg 13
The Australian Council for Educational Research Ltd, pg 13
Blackwell Science Pty Ltd, pg 15
Bridge To Peace Publications, pg 16
Chase Just Publishing, pg 17
Conscious Living Publications, pg 18
Deva Wings Publications, pg 20
Finch Publishing, pg 22
Freshet Press, pg 23
Gnostic Editions, pg 24
Hale & Iremonger Pty Ltd, pg 24
Kerri Hamer, pg 25
Hampden Press, pg 25
Harcourt Australia Pty Ltd, pg 25
Kurlana Publishing, pg 29
Linking Up Publishing, pg 30
Maxwell Macmillan Publishing (Australia) Pty Ltd, pg 32
McGraw-Hill Australia Pty Ltd, pg 32
Melbourne University Press, pg 33
Jurriaan Plesman, pg 38
Spectrum Publications, pg 43
Unity Press, pg 46
Wellness Australia, pg 47
Wileman Publications, pg 47
Windhorse Books, pg 48

Austria
CEEBA Publications Antenne d'Autriche, pg 50
Dachs-Verlag GmbH, pg 50
Alois Goschl & Co, pg 52
Literas-Verlag GmbH, pg 54
Verlag Wilhelm Maudrich, pg 54
Otto Mueller Verlag GesmbH & Co KG, pg 55
Verlag des Osterr Kneippbundes GmbH, pg 57
Verlag Anton Pustet, pg 57
Andreas Schnider Verlags-Atelier, pg 58
Springer-Verlag Wien, pg 59
Urban und Schwarzenberg GmbH, pg 60
WUV/Facultas Universitaetsverlag, pg 61

Belgium
Academia Press, pg 64
Acco CV, pg 64
Altina, pg 64
Editions De Boeck-Larcier SA, pg 67
EPO Publishers, Printers, Booksellers, pg 68
Editions Labor, pg 70
Leuven University Press, pg 71
Mardaga, Pierre 12, pg 72
Nauwelaerts Edition SA, pg 72
La Part de L'Oeil, pg 72
Publications des Facultes Universitaires Saint Louis, pg 73
Vander Editions, SA, pg 75
Les Editions Vie ouvriere ASBL, pg 75
Wolters Plantyn Educatieve Uitgevers, pg 75

Brazil
Agalma Psicanalise Editora Ltda, pg 78
Editora Agora Ltda, pg 78
Editora Antroposofica Ltda, pg 78
Ars Poetica Editora Ltda, pg 79
Artes e Oficios Editora Ltda, pg 79
ARTMED, pg 79
Associacao Palas Athena do Brasil, pg 79
Editora Atheneu Ltda, pg 79
Editora do Brasil SA, pg 80
Editora Campus Ltda, pg 80
CEPA - Centro Editor de Psicologia Aplicada Ltda, pg 81
Editorial Dimensao Ltda, pg 81
Livraria Duas Cidades Ltda, pg 81
E P U Editora Pedagogica e Universitaria Ltd, pg 81
Companhia Editora Forense, pg 82
Cia Editora Nacional, pg 82
EDUC - Editora da PUC-SP, pg 82
EDUSC - Editora da Universidade do Sagrado Coracao, pg 82
Livraria Martins Fontes Editora Ltda, pg 83
Editora Forense, pg 83
Forense Universitaria Editora, pg 83
Fundacao Cultural Avatar, pg 83
Editora Gente Livraria e Editora Ltda, pg 84
Edicoes Graal Ltda, pg 84
Horus Editora Ltda, pg 85
Livro Ibero-Americano Ltda, pg 85
IBRASA (Instituicao Brasileira de Difusao Cultural Ltda), pg 85
Imago Editora Importacao e Exportacao Ltda, pg 85
Interlivros Edicoes Ltda, pg 85
Edicoes Loyola SA, pg 87
Editora Mercuryo Ltda, pg 88
Editora Nova Fronteira SA, pg 88
Olho D'Agua Comercio e Servicos Editoriais Ltda, pg 88
Paulinas Editorial, pg 89
Paulus Editora, pg 89
Editora Perspectiva, pg 89

1057

SUBJECT INDEX

Livraria Pioneira Editora/Enio Matheus Guazzelli e Cia Ltd, pg 89
Proton Editora Ltda, pg 90
Saraiva SA, Livreiros Editores, pg 91
Livraria Sulina Editora, pg 92
Summus Editorial Ltda, pg 92
Totalidade Editora Ltda, pg 92
Editora UNESP, pg 92
Fundacao Getulio Vargas, pg 93
Editora Verbo Ltda, pg 93
Vozes Editora Ltda, pg 93
Jorge Zahar Editor, pg 93

Bulgaria

Ciela Publishing House, pg 94
DA-Izdatelstvo Publishers, pg 95
EA Publishing House, pg 95
Eurasia Academic Publishers, pg 95
Kibea Publishing Co, pg 96
Kralica MAB, pg 96
LIK IZDANIJA, pg 96
Makros 2000 - Plovdiv, pg 96
Naouka i Izkoustvo, Ltd, pg 97
Nov Covek Publishing House, pg 97
Seven Hills Publishers, pg 97
TEMTO, pg 98

Chile

Arrayan Editores, pg 99
Editora Cuatro Vientos, pg 100
Pontificia Universidad Catolica de Chile, pg 101

China

Beijing Medical Univ Press, pg 102
Fudan University Press, pg 105
Higher Education Press, pg 106
Lanzhou University Press, pg 107
SDX (Shenghuo-Dushu-Xinzhi) Joint Publishing Co, pg 108

Colombia

Kapelusz Ltda Editorial, pg 112
McGraw-Hill InterAmericana SA, pg 113
Siglo XXI Editores de Colombia Ltda, pg 113
Tercer Mundo Editores SA, pg 113

The Democratic Republic of the Congo

Presses Universitaires du Zaiire (PUZ), pg 115

Costa Rica

Editorial Porvenir, pg 116
Promesa, Ediciones, pg 116

Croatia

Hrvatsko filozofsko drustvo, pg 119
Naprijed d d Naklada, pg 119
Skolska Knjiga, pg 120

Cuba

Editora Politica, pg 121
Pueblo y Educacion Editorial (PE), pg 121

Czech Republic

Barrister & Principal, pg 123
Jiri Chvojka, pg 123
Doplnek, pg 124
Knihovna A Tiskarna Pro Nevidome, pg 125
Portal Ltd, pg 127
Psychoanalyticke Nakladatelstvi, pg 128
Slon Sociologicke Nakladatelstvi, pg 128
Zvon, pg 129

Denmark

Aarhus Universitetsforlag, pg 129
Akademisk Forlag, pg 129
Borgens Forlag A/S, pg 130
Dansk Psykologisk Forlag, pg 131
Forlaget GMT, pg 132
Gyldendalske Boghandel - Nordisk Forlag A/S, pg 132
Nyt Nordisk Forlag Arnold Busck A/S, pg 134
Olivia - det gronne forlag, pg 134
Joergen Paludans Forlag ApS, pg 134
Politisk Revy, pg 134
Hans Reitzel Publishers Ltd, pg 134
Det Schonbergske Forlag, pg 135

Egypt (Arab Republic of Egypt)

Al Arab Publishing House, pg 138
Dar El Shorouk, pg 138
Dar El Shorouk Publishing & Distributing House, pg 138

Estonia

Sinisukk, pg 140
Tuum, pg 141

Finland

Basam Books Oy, pg 142
Foersamlingsfoerbundets Foerlags AB, pg 142
Kustannus Oy Duodecim, pg 143
Soederstroem et Co Foerlagsaktiebolag, pg 144
Yliopistopaino/Helsinki University Press, pg 145

France

ALTESS Editions Argel, pg 146
L'Anabase, pg 147
L'Arche Editeur, pg 147
Atelier National de Reproduction des Theses, pg 148
Aubanel SA, pg 149
Editions Aubier-Montaigne SA, pg 149
Autremont Editions, pg 149
Alain Brethe Editions, pg 152
Editions Calmann-Levy SA, pg 152
Editions Champ Vallon, pg 154
Editions Chiron, pg 154
Chotard et Associes Editeurs, pg 154
Chronique Sociale, pg 155
CNRS Editions, pg 155
Armand Colin, Editeur, pg 155
CTNERHI - Centre Technique National d'Etudes et de Recherches sur les Handicaps et les Inadaptations, pg 157
Editions Dangles SA, pg 157
Editions du Dauphin, pg 158
Editions Denoel Sarl, pg 158
Dervy-Livres, pg 158
Doin Editeurs, pg 160
Dunod Editeur, pg 160
Les Editions ESF, pg 161
Ellebore, pg 161
EPEL, pg 162
Ere Nouvelle, pg 162
Editions Eres, pg 162
Groupe Fleurus-Mame, pg 164
Edition Galilee, pg 165
Ganymede, pg 166
Editions Grancher, pg 166
Editions Imago, pg 169
InterEditions Paris, pg 169
Le Jour, Editeur, pg 170
Librairie Larousse, pg 172
Macula, pg 174
Editions de la Maison des Sciences de l'Homme, Paris, pg 174
Masson SA, pg 175
Presses Universitaires du Mirail, pg 176
Fernand Nathan, pg 177
Editions Odile Jacob, pg 178
Point Hors Ligne, pg 180
Les Presses du Management, pg 181
Presses Universitaires de France (PUF), pg 181
Presses Universitaires de Grenoble, pg 181
Presses Universitaires de Nancy, pg 181
Presses Universitaires du Septentrion, pg 181
Publications de l'Universite de Rouen, pg 182
Editions Robert Laffont, Nil, Fixot, Seghers, Julliard, pg 183
Editions Sand et Tchou SA, pg 183
Editions du Scarabee, pg 184
Maren Sell, pg 184
Editions du Seuil, pg 185
Sofradif Editions Philippe Auzou, pg 185
Editions Springer France, pg 186
Les Editions de la Table Ronde, pg 187
Editions Trois Fontaines, pg 188
Librairie Philosophique J Vrin, pg 189

Germany

A Francke Verlag (Tubingen und Basel), pg 191
Ahriman-Verlag GmbH, pg 192
Roland Asanger Verlag GmbH, pg 195
Aschendorffsche Verlagsbuchhandlung GmbH & Co KG, pg 195
Auer Verlag GmbH, pg 196
Aurum Verlag GmbH, pg 197
Johann Ambrosius Barth GmbH, pg 198
Belser Wissenschaftlicher Dienst, pg 200
Beust Verlag GmbH, pg 202
Verlag Die Blaue Eule, pg 204
Adolf Bonz Verlag GmbH, pg 205
Brandes & Apsel Verlag GmbH, pg 206
R Brockhaus Verlag, pg 206
Bund demokratischer Wissenschafterlnnen und Wissenschafler eV (BdWi), pg 207
Burckhardthaus-Laetare Verlag GmbH, pg 208
Ulrich Burgdorf/Homeopathic Publishing House, pg 208
Carl-Auer-Systeme Verlag, pg 209
CEC-Cosmic Energy Connections, pg 209
Centaurus-Verlagsgesellschaft GmbH, pg 209
J G Cotta'sche Buchhandlung Nachfolger GmbH, pg 212
Verlag CSA Rosemarie Schneider, pg 212
Daedalus Verlag, pg 212
Verlag Darmstaedter Blaetter Schwarz und Co, pg 212
Deutsche Verlags-Anstalt GmbH (DVA), pg 214
Deutscher Psychologen Verlag GmbH (DPV), pg 215
Deutscher Studien Verlag, pg 215
Deutscher Taschenbuch Verlag GmbH & Co KG (dtv), pg 215
Dietrich zu Klampen Verlag, pg 216
Edition Diskord, pg 217
Dreisam Ratgeber in der Rutsker Verlag GmbH, pg 218
Ehrenwirth Verlag GmbH, pg 221
Ergebnisse Verlag GmbH, pg 223
Ernst Kabel Verlag GmbH, pg 223
EVT Energy Video Training & Verlag GmbH, pg 225
Ferdinand Enke Verlag, pg 227
Wilhelm Fink GmbH & Co Verlags-KG, pg 228
Rita G Fischer Verlag, pg 228
Fischer Taschenbuch Verlag GmbH, pg 229
Focus-Verlag Gesellschaft mbH, pg 229
Verlag Freies Geistesleben, pg 230
Friedrich Frommann Verlag, pg 230
Wilhelm Goldmann Verlag GmbH, pg 233
Haag und Herchen Verlag GmbH, pg 235
Wilhelm Heyne Verlag, pg 240
S Hirzel Verlag GmbH und Co, pg 241
Hoffmann und Campe Verlag GmbH, pg 242
Hogrefe Verlag GmbH & Co Kg, pg 242
Holos Verlag, pg 242
Hans Huber, pg 243
Heinrich Hugendubel Verlag GmbH, pg 243
Human Wissenschafilicher Verlag, pg 243
Edition Humanistische Psychologie (EHP), pg 243
Julius Klinkhardt Verlagsbuchhandlung, pg 247
Junfermann-Verlag, pg 247
Juventa Verlag GmbH, pg 247
S Karger GmbH Verlag fuer Medizin und Naturwissenschaften, pg 247
Kindler Verlag GmbH, pg 249
Ingrid Klein Verlag GmbH, pg 249
Verlag Kleine Schritte Ursula Dahm & Co, pg 249
Koenigsfurt Verlag, Evelin Burger et Johannes Fiebig, pg 251
Verlag Koenigshausen und Neumann GmbH, pg 251
Koesel-Verlag GmbH & Co, pg 252
W Kohlhammer GmbH, abt Haussortiment, pg 252
Dr Gisela Lermann, pg 257
Verlag Leske plus Budrich GmbH, pg 257
Mattes Verlag GmbH, pg 261
Matthias-Gruenewald-Verlag GmbH, pg 261
Midena Verlag, pg 264
Gunter Narr Verlag, pg 266
Neuland-Verlagsgesellschaft mbH, pg 268
Oekotopia Verlag, Wolfgang Hoffman, pg 270
Orlanda Frauenverlag, pg 270
Osho Verlag GmbH, pg 271
Pal Verlagsgesellschaft mbH, pg 271
Paranus Verlag - Bruecke Neumuenster GmbH, pg 271
J Pfeiffer Verlag, pg 273
Philipps-Universitaet Marburg, pg 273
Piper Verlag GmbH, pg 274
Guido Pressler Verlag, pg 275
Psychiatrie-Verlag GmbH, pg 275

PUBLISHERS

Psychologie Verlags Union GmbH, pg 275
Psychosozial-Verlag, pg 275
Quelle und Meyer Verlag GmbH & Co, pg 276
R Oldenbourg Verlag GmbH, pg 276
Radius-Verlag GmbH, pg 276
Ernst Reinhardt GmbH & Co KG Verlag, pg 278
Rowohlt Taschenbuch Verlag GmbH, pg 280
Ryvellus Medienagentur Dopfer, pg 281
I H Sauer Verlag GmbH, pg 282
Heinrich Schwab Verlag, pg 285
Spieth-Verlag Verlag fuer Symbolforschung, pg 288
Springer-Verlag GmbH & Co KG, pg 288
Steidl Verlag, pg 289
Dr Dietrich Steinkopff Verlag GmbH & Co, pg 289
Verlag Stendel, pg 290
Stroemfeld Verlag, pg 290
Suhrkamp Verlag, pg 291
Georg Thieme Verlag KG, pg 293
Ullstein Heyne List GmbH & Co KG, pg 295
UTB fuer Wissenschaft Uni-Taschenbuecher GmbH, pg 297
Vandenhoeck & Ruprecht, pg 297
VAS-Verlag fuer Akademische Schriften, Vas Karl-Heinz Balon, pg 297
Votum Verlag GmbH, pg 299
VWB-Verlag fur Wissenschaft & Bildung, Amand Aglaster, pg 300
Waxmann Verlag GmbH, pg 300
Weidler Buchverlag Berlin, pg 301
Windpferd Verlagsgesellschaft mbH, pg 303
Wissenschaftliche Buchgesellschaft, pg 303

Ghana
World Literature Project, pg 308

Greece
Akritas, pg 308
Boukoumanis' Editions, pg 309
Dioptra Publishing, pg 309
Dorikos Publishing House, pg 310
Exandas Publishers, pg 310
Gutenberg Publications, pg 311
Hestia-I D Hestia-Kollaros & Co Corporation, pg 311
Kastaniotis Editions SA, pg 312
Kyriakidis Vasileios, pg 312
Odysseas Publications Ltd, pg 313
Panepistimio Ioanninon, pg 314
Patakis Publishers, pg 314
Thetili Publications, pg 315
Thymari Publications, pg 315

Hong Kong
The Chinese University Press, pg 319
Ming Pao Publications Ltd, pg 321
Philopsychy Press, pg 321
Publications (Holdings) Ltd, pg 321

Hungary
Joszoveg Muhely Kiado, pg 324
KJK-Keaszov, pg 324
Kossuth Kiado RT, pg 325
Nemzeti Tankoenyvkiado, pg 326
Osiris Kiado, pg 326

Iceland
Bokaforlag Birtingur, pg 327
Hid Islenzka Bokmenntafelag, pg 328

India
Ananda Publishers Pvt Ltd, pg 330
The Bangalore Printing & Publishing Co Ltd, pg 332
Bharatiya Samijik Vigyan Auusandhan Parishad, pg 332
Concept Publishing Co, pg 335
Eurasia Publishing House Pvt Ltd, pg 337
Gyan Publishing House, pg 338
Himalaya Publishing House, pg 338
Jaico Publishing House, pg 340
Minerva Associates (Publications) Pvt Ltd, pg 342
Narosa Publishing House, pg 343
Omsons Publications, pg 345
Oxford & IBH Publishing Co Pvt Ltd, pg 345
Reliance Publishing House, pg 347
SABDA, pg 348
Sage Publications India Pvt Ltd, pg 348
Scientific Book Agency, pg 349
Sita Publications, pg 350
Somaiya Publications Pvt Ltd, pg 350
Vikas Publishing House Pvt Ltd, pg 353

Indonesia
Alumni PT, pg 353
P T Bulan Bintang, pg 354
Eresco PT, pg 355

Ireland
Cathedral Books Ltd, pg 359
Gill & Macmillan Ltd, pg 361

Israel
Am Oved Publishers Ltd, pg 365
Bar Ilan University Press, pg 365
Boostan Publishing House, pg 366
Breslov Research Institute, pg 366
Classikaletet, pg 366
Gefen Publishing House Ltd, pg 367
Hakibbutz Hameuchad Publishing House Ltd, pg 368
Otzar Hamore, pg 368
Keter Publishing House Ltd, pg 369
The Magnes Press, pg 370
Massada Press Ltd, pg 370
Open University of Israel, pg 371
Rubin Mass Ltd, pg 371
Schocken Publishing House Ltd, pg 372
R Sirkis Publishers Ltd, pg 372
Tcherikover Publishers Ltd, pg 372
The Van Leer Jerusalem Institute, pg 373
Yachdav, United Publishers Co Ltd, pg 373

Italy
Franco Angeli SRL, pg 375
Apostolato della Preghiera, pg 376
Arcanta Aries Gruppo Editoriale, pg 376
Edizioni ARES, pg 376
Editore Armando Armando SRL, pg 376
Casa Editrice Astrolabio-Ubaldini Editore, pg 377
Belforte Editore Libraio srl, pg 377
Edizioni Borla SRL, pg 378
Nuova Casa Editrice Licinio Cappelli GEM srl, pg 379
CEDAM (Casa Editrice Dr A Milani), pg 380
Centro Scientifico Int, pg 381
Centro Scientifico Torinese, pg 381
Edizioni Centro Studi Erickson, pg 381
CIC Edizioni Internazionali, pg 381
Ciranna - Roma, pg 381
Citta Nuova Editrice, pg 382
Cittadella Editrice, pg 382
CLEUP - Cooperative Libraria Editrice dell 'Universita di Padova, pg 382
CLUEB (Cooperativa Libraria Universitaria Editrice Bologna), pg 382
CPE - Centro Programmazione Editoriale, pg 383
Crisalide, pg 383
Edizioni Dedalo SRL, pg 384
Edizioni Dehoniane, pg 384
Edizioni del Riccio SAS di G Bernardi, pg 384
ECIG, pg 385
Editrice la Scuola SpA, pg 386
Edizioni Mediterranee SRL, pg 387
Effata Editrice, pg 387
Giulio Einaudi Editore SpA, pg 387
Festina Lente Edizioni, pg 389
Arnaldo Forni Editore SRL, pg 389
Editrice Garigliano SRL, pg 390
Giunti Publishing Group, pg 391
Gius Laterza e Figli SpA, pg 391
Giuseppe Laterza Editore Snc, pg 391
Libreria Editrice Gregoriana, pg 391
Edizioni Guerini e Associati SpA, pg 392
Hermes Edizioni SRL, pg 392
Il Pensiero Scientifico Editore SRL, pg 393
Il Poligrafo, pg 393
L Japadre Editore, pg 394
Editrice LAS, pg 395
Lecce Spazio Vivo Srl, pg 395
LED - Edizioni Universitarie di Lettere Economia Diritto, pg 395
Levante, pg 395
Longanesi & C, pg 396
Lubrina Editore Srl, pg 397
Lyra Libri SAS, pg 397
Macro Edizioni, pg 397
Marsilio Editori SpA, pg 398
Editrice Massimo SAS di Crespi Cesare e C, pg 398
Milella di Lecce Spazio Vivo SRL, pg 399
Arnoldo Mondadori Editore SpA, pg 399
Monduzzi Editore SpA, pg 399
Moretti & Vitali editori srl, pg 400
Societa Editrice Il Mulino, pg 400
Newton Compton Editori SRL, pg 401
La Nuova Italia Editrice SpA, pg 401
OS (Organizzazioni Speciali SRL), pg 402
Patron Editore SrL, pg 403
Psicologica Editrice, pg 404
Red/Studio Redazionale SpA, pg 405
Edizioni Ripostes, pg 405
Editori Riuniti, pg 405
Edizioni Universitarie Romane, pg 406
Rusconi Libri Srl, pg 406
Edizioni San Paolo SRL, pg 407
Edizioni Scientifiche Italiane, pg 407

SUBJECT INDEX

Societa Editrice Internazionale - SEI, pg 408
Spirali Edizioni, pg 408
TEA Tascabili degli Editori Associati SpA, pg 409
Edizioni Thyrus SRL, pg 409
Editrice Tirrenia Stampatori SAS, pg 410
Todariana Editrice, pg 410
Tranchida, pg 410
Unipress, pg 410
Editrice Uomini Nuovi, pg 410
Urbaniana University Press, pg 410
UTET (Unione Tipografico-Editrice Torinese), pg 411
Vita e Pensiero, pg 411
Zanichelli Editore SpA, pg 412

Jamaica
Jamaica Publishing House Ltd, pg 413

Japan
Baifukan Co Ltd, pg 414
Baseball Magazine-Sha Co Ltd, pg 415
Dainippon Tosho Publishing Co, Ltd, pg 416
Diamond Inc, pg 416
Hakuyo-Sha, pg 417
Iwanami Shoten, Publishers, pg 418
Kazama Shobo, pg 419
Kinokuniya Co Ltd (Publishing Department), pg 420
Kokudo-Sha, pg 420
Kosei Publishing Co Ltd, pg 420
Koyo Shobo, pg 420
Minerva Shobo Co Ltd, pg 421
Misuzu Shobo Ltd, pg 421
Mita Press, Mita Industrial Co, Ltd, pg 421
Nippon Jitsugyo Publishing Co, Ltd, pg 423
Reimei-Shobo Co Ltd, pg 424
Riso-Sha, pg 424
Sangyo-Tosho Publishing Co Ltd, pg 424
Seiwa Shoten Co Ltd, pg 425
Sogensha Publishing Co Ltd, pg 426
University of Tokyo Press, pg 428
Waseda University Press, pg 428
Yuhikaku Publishing Co Ltd, pg 429

Kenya
Cosmopolitan Publishers Ltd, pg 431
Paulines Publications-Africa, pg 433

Republic of Korea
Chung Rim Publishing Co Ltd, pg 435
Iljo-gag Publishers, pg 437
Korea Psychological Testing Institute, pg 437
Korea University Press, pg 437
Minjisa Publishing Co, pg 438
Sohaksa, pg 440

Latvia
Preses Nams, pg 442

Lithuania
Andrena Publishers, pg 445
Dargenis Publishers, pg 445

The Former Yugoslav Republic of Macedonia
Zumpres Publishing Firm, pg 449

1059

SUBJECT INDEX

Martinique
George Lise-Huyghes des Etages, pg 456

Mexico
Publicaciones Cruz O SA, pg 459
Editorial El Manual Moderno SA de CV, pg 460
Ediciones Exclusivas SA, pg 461
Editorial Fata Morgana SA de CV, pg 461
Fondo de Cultura Economica, pg 461
Editorial Joaquin Mortiz SA de CV, pg 462
Editorial Limusa SA de CV, pg 463
Editorial Orion, pg 465
Editorial Pax Mexico, pg 465
Pearson Educacion de Mexico, SA de CV, pg 465
Grupo Editorial Planeta, pg 465
Siglo XXI Editores SA de CV, pg 467
Editorial Trillas SA de CV, pg 467
Universidad Nacional Autonoma de Mexico (National University of Mexico), pg 467
Universidad Veracruzana Direccion General Editorial y de Publicaciones, pg 468
Javier Vergara Editor SA de CV, pg 468

Republic of Moldova
Lumina Publishing House, pg 468

Morocco
Editions Eddif Maroc, pg 469
Editions Le Fennec, pg 470

Nepal
International Standards Books & Periodicals (P) Ltd, pg 471

Netherlands
Uitgeverij Ambo BV, pg 472
John Benjamins BV, pg 474
Erven J Bijleveld, pg 474
Boom Uitgeverij, pg 474
A W Bruna Uitgevers BV, pg 475
Buijten en Schipperheijn BV Drukkerij en Uitg Mij v/h, pg 475
Uitgeversmaatschappij Ad Donker BV, pg 476
Uitgeverij Vrij Geestesleven, pg 477
Historische Uitgeverij, pg 478
Uitgeverij Lemma BV, pg 480
Lemniscaat, pg 480
Mirananda Publishers BV, pg 481
Prometheus, pg 483
Servire BV Uitgevers, pg 484
Swets & Zeitlinger Publishers, pg 485
SWP, BV Uitgeverij, pg 485
Uitgeverij de Tijdstroom BV, pg 485
Tilburg University Press, pg 485
Uitgeverij De Toorts, pg 485
Van Gorcum & Comp BV, pg 486
VU Boekhandel/Uitgeverij BV, pg 487

New Zealand
Outrigger Publishers, pg 494
Tandem Press, pg 496
University of Otago Press, pg 496

Nigeria
Ibadan University Press, pg 499
Longman Nigeria Plc, pg 500

Norway
Atheneum Forlag A/S, pg 502
Genesis Forlag, pg 503
Glydendal Akademisk, pg 503
Gyldendal Norsk Forlag A/S, pg 503
Pax Forlag A/S, pg 504

Pakistan
Malik Sirajuddin & Sons, pg 507
Publishers United Pvt Ltd, pg 508

Peru
Fondo Editorial de la Pontificia Universidad Catolica del Peru, pg 511
Universidad de Lima-Fondo de Desarollo Editorial, pg 512

Philippines
Ateneo de Manila University Press, pg 512
Rex Bookstores & Publishers, pg 514
University of the Philippines Press, pg 515

Poland
Gdanskie Wydawnictwo Psychologiczne SC, pg 516
Katolicki Uniwersytet Wydawniczo-Redakcja, pg 517
PZWL Wydawnictwo Lekarskie Ltd, pg 519
Wydawnictwa Szkolne i Pedagogiczne (Polish Educational Publishers-WSiP), pg 521

Portugal
Armenio Amado Editora de Simoes, Beirao & Ca Lda, pg 522
Brasilia Editora (J Carvalho Branco), pg 523
Coimbra Editora Lda, pg 523
Dinalivro, pg 524
Editorial Estampa, Lda, pg 524
Publicacoes Europa-America Lda, pg 524
Fenda Edicoes, pg 525
Gradiva-Publicacnoes Lda, pg 525
Livros Horizonte Lda, pg 526
McGraw-Hill Editora de Portugal, pg 527
Editorial Presenca, pg 528
Edicoes Salesianas, pg 529
Almerinda Teixeira, pg 529
Teorema, pg 529
Livraria Verdade e Vida Editora, pg 530

Puerto Rico
University of Puerto Rico Press (EDUPR), pg 531

Romania
Editura Academiei Romane, pg 531
Aion Verlag, pg 531
Editura Excelsior, pg 533
Editura Humanitas, pg 533
Humanitas Publishing House, pg 533
Polirom Verlag, pg 535
Editura Stiintifica, pg 536

Russian Federation
Izdatelstvo Medicina, pg 539
Izdatelstvo Mir, pg 540
Nauka Publishers, pg 540
Izdatel'stvo Nizhegorodskogo Gosudarstvennogo Univ, pg 540

Senegal
Les Nouvelles Editions Africaines du Senegal NEAS, pg 544

Singapore
Singapore University Press Pte Ltd, pg 548
Taylor & Francis Asia Pacific, pg 548

Slovakia
Slovenske pedagogicke nakladateistvo, pg 550
Smena Publishing House, pg 550
Sofa, pg 551
Ustav informacii a prognoz skolstva mladeze a telovychovy, pg 551
VEDA (Vydavatel'stvo Slovenskej akademie vied), pg 551

Slovenia
Cankarjeva Zalozba, pg 551
Zalozba Mihelac d o o, pg 552

South Africa
Bet-El Publishers, pg 553
Human Sciences Research Council, pg 555
Unisa Press, pg 560

Spain
Centro de Estudios Adams-Ediciones Valbuena SA, pg 561
Ediciones Akal SA, pg 562
Editorial Anagrama, pg 563
Editorial Ariel SA, pg 564
Sociedad de Educacion Atenas SA, pg 564
Editorial Biblioteca Nueva SL, pg 565
Ediciones de la Universidad Complutense de Madrid, pg 568
Espanola Desclee De Brouwer SA, pg 569
Edicions del Drac SA, pg 570
Dykinson SL, pg 571
Edika-Med, SA, pg 572
EOS Gabinete de Orientacion Psicologica, pg 573
Estudio de Bioinformacion, S L, pg 574
Fondo de Cultura Economica de Espana, SL, pg 574
Editorial Fundamentos, pg 575
Editorial Gedisa SA, pg 575
Editorial Gredos SA, pg 576
Editorial Grupo Cero, pg 576
Editorial Herder SA, pg 577
Editorial Iberia, SA, pg 577
Publicaciones ICCE, pg 577
Editorial Kairos SA, pg 579
Ediciones Libertarias/Prodhufi SA, pg 580
Antonio Machado, SA, pg 580
Mandala Ediciones, pg 581
Editorial Marfil SA, pg 581
Ediciones Marova SL, pg 581
Ediciones Martinez-Roca SA, pg 581
Ediciones Mensajero, pg 582
Ediciones Morata SL, pg 583
Narcea SA de Ediciones, pg 583

OASIS, Producciones Generales de Comunicacion, pg 584
Oikos-Tau SA Ediciones, pg 584
Pages Editors, SL, pg 585
Ediciones Paidos Iberica SA, pg 585
Pearson Educacion S A, pg 586
Ediciones Piramide SA, pg 586
Ediciones Pomares-Corredor, pg 587
Pulso Ediciones, SL, pg 588
Ediciones ROL SA, pg 589
Siglo XXI de Espana Editores SA, pg 590
Editorial Sintesis, SA, pg 590
Grup 62, pg 591
Editorial Rudolf Steiner, pg 591
TEA Ediciones SA, pg 592
Editorial Tecnos SA, pg 592
Editorial Sal Terrae, pg 592
Trotta SA Editorial, pg 593
Universidad de Valladolid Secretariado de Publicaciones e Intercambio Editorial, pg 594
Ediciones Urano, pg 595
Javier Vergara Editor SA, pg 595
Visor Distribuciones, SA, pg 596
Ediciones Xandro, pg 596

Sweden
Alfabeta Bokforlag AB, pg 600
Energica Foerlags AB/Halsabocker, pg 602
Hagaberg AB, pg 603
Bokfoerlaget Naturoch Kultur, pg 604
Psykologfoerlaget AB, pg 605
Studentlitteratur AB, pg 606
Svenska Foerlaget liv & ledarskap ab, pg 607
AB Wahlstrom & Widstrand, pg 607
Zindermans AB, pg 607

Switzerland
Editions L'Age d'Homme - La Cite, pg 608
Antonius-Verlag, pg 608
Ariston Editions, pg 608
Astrodata AG, pg 608
H R Balmer AG Verlag, pg 609
Bartschi Publishing, pg 609
Werner Classen Verlag, pg 611
Daimon Verlag AG, pg 612
Editions Delachaux et Niestle SA, pg 612
Editions Foma SA, pg 614
Georg Editeur SA, pg 614
Editions Jouvence, pg 616
S Karger AG, Medical and Scientific Publishers, pg 617
Kindler Verlag AG, pg 617
Medecine et Hygiene, pg 619
Editions H Messeiller SA, pg 619
Psychosophische Gesellschaft, pg 622
Raphael, Editions, pg 622
Editions Saint-Paul, pg 623
Scherz Verlag AG, pg 623
Schwabe & Co AG, pg 624
Schweizer Spiegel Verlag Mit, pg 624
Sphinx Verlag AG, pg 625
Tobler Verlag, pg 626
Editions du Tricorne, pg 626
Editions des Trois Collines Francois Lachenal, pg 626
Der Universitatsverlag Freiburg, pg 626
Editions Vivez Soleil SA, pg 627
Walter Verlag AG, pg 627

PUBLISHERS

Syrian Arab Republic
Damascus University Press, pg 628

Taiwan, Province of China
Chu Liu Book Company, pg 629
Chung Hwa Book Co Ltd, pg 629
Ho-Chi Book Publishing Co, pg 630
Laureate Book Co Ltd, pg 631
Shy Mau Publishing Company, pg 631
Yi Hsien Publishing Co Ltd, pg 632
Youth Cultural Publishing Co, pg 632
Yuan Liou Publishing Co, Ltd, pg 632

Thailand
Thai Watana Panich Co, Ltd, pg 636

Tunisia
Faculte des Sciences Humaines et Sociales de Tunis, pg 638

Turkey
Alkim Kitapcilik-Yayimcilik, pg 638
Altin Kitaplar Yayinevi, pg 638
Inkilap Publishers Ltd, pg 640
Metis Yayinlari, pg 640
Payel Yayinevi, pg 641
Remzi Kitabevi, pg 641
Soez Yayin/Oyunajans, pg 641

Uganda
Fountain Publishers Ltd, pg 642

Ukraine
Naukova Dumka Publishers, pg 643

United Kingdom
Act 3 Publishing, pg 645
Arnold, pg 648
Arthur James Ltd, pg 649
Blackwell Publishers, pg 655
Blackwell Science Ltd, pg 656
Bloomsbury Publishing PLC, pg 656
BAAF: Adoption & Fostering, pg 659
Cambridge University Press, pg 662
Capall Bann Publishing, pg 663
Causeway Press Ltd, pg 665
Constable & Robinson Ltd, pg 670
Constable Publishers, pg 670
The Continuum International Publishing Group Ltd, pg 670
Crown House Publishing Ltd, pg 672
Delectus Books, pg 675
Dobro Publishing, pg 675
Gerald Duckworth & Co Ltd, pg 676
Martin Dunitz Ltd, pg 676
Educational Explorers (Publishers) Ltd, pg 677
Element Books Ltd, pg 678
The Eurospan Group, pg 680
Extraordinary People Press, pg 681
Faber & Faber Ltd, pg 681
Free Association Books Ltd, pg 684
W H Freeman & Co Ltd, pg 684
Gateway Books, pg 686
Harcourt Publishers Ltd, pg 691
HarperCollins Publishers, pg 692
Harvard University Press, pg 692
Hawthorn Press, pg 693
JAI Press Ltd, pg 702
Karnac Books Ltd, pg 703
Jessica Kingsley Publishers, pg 704
Learning Matters Ltd, pg 706
McGraw-Hill Publishing Company, pg 712
Metro Publishing Ltd, pg 714
MGM, pg 714
MIND Publications, pg 715
MIT Press Ltd, pg 715
Monarch Books, pg 715
The NFER-NELSON Publishing Co Ltd, pg 719
W W Norton & Company Ltd, pg 720
The Octagon Press Ltd, pg 720
Oneworld Publications, pg 721
Open Gate Press, pg 721
Open University Press, pg 721
Oxford University Press, pg 723
Pearson Education, pg 725
Pearson Education Europe, Mideast & Africa, pg 725
Piatkus Books, pg 727
Profile Books Ltd, pg 731
Psychological Corporation Ltd, pg 731
Rationalist Press Association, pg 733
RELATE, pg 734
Routledge, pg 736
Royal College of General Practitioners, pg 736
The Royal Society, pg 737
Sage Publications Ltd, pg 737
Sheldon Press, pg 741
Sherwood Publishing, pg 741
The Society of Metaphysicians Ltd, pg 743
Souvenir Press Ltd, pg 743
Speechmark Publishing Ltd, pg 744
Taylor & Francis Group, pg 747
Thames & Hudson Ltd, pg 748
Trentham Books Ltd, pg 750
Verso, pg 752
Whurr Publishers Ltd, pg 756
Wiley Europe Ltd, pg 756
The Women's Press Ltd, pg 758
Yale University Press London, pg 759

Uruguay
Editorial Dismar, pg 760
Nordan-Comunidad, pg 760
Prensa Medica Latinoamericana, pg 761
Ediciones Trilce, pg 761

Venezuela
Editorial Ateneo de Caracas, pg 762
Monte Avila Editores Latinoamericana CA, pg 762

Yugoslavia
Alfa-Narodna Knjiga, pg 764
Nolit Publishing House, pg 765
Vuk Karadzic, pg 766

PUBLIC ADMINISTRATION

Albania
NL SH, pg 1

Argentina
Editorial Abaco de Rodolfo Depalma SRL, pg 2
Abeledo-Perrot SAE e I, pg 2

SUBJECT INDEX

Australia
Chiron Media, pg 18
Hale & Iremonger Pty Ltd, pg 24
Palms Press, pg 36

Austria
Fachverlag fur Burgerinformation, Eigenvelag, pg 50
Czernin Verlag, pg 50
Inn-Verlag, DrieBlein & Co KG, pg 53

Bangladesh
Bangladesh Publishers, pg 62
The University Press Ltd, pg 62

Belgium
Vanden Broele NV, pg 65
Editions Delta SA, pg 67
UGA Editions (Uitgeverij), pg 74

Brazil
A & A & A Edicoes e Promocoes Internacionais Ltda, pg 77
Camara Dos Deputados Coordenacao De Publicacoes, pg 80
Editora Ortiz SA, pg 89
Qualitymark Editora Ltda, pg 90
Fundacao Getulio Vargas, pg 93
Vozes Editora Ltda, pg 93

Bulgaria
Dolphin Press Group Ltd, pg 95

Cameroon
Presses Universitaires d'Afrique, pg 99

Chile
Ediciones Cieplan, pg 100

China
Fudan University Press, pg 105
Shandong University Press, pg 109

Costa Rica
Confederacion de Cooperativas del Caribe y Centro America, pg 115
Editorial Nacional de Salud y Seguridad Social Ednass, pg 116
Editorial de la Universidad de Costa Rica, pg 117

Cote d'Ivoire
Universite d' Abidjan, pg 118

Czech Republic
Vysehrad, pg 129

Denmark
Samfundslitteratur, pg 135
A/S Skattekartoteket, pg 135
Statens Information (Danish State Information Service), pg 135

Ecuador
Corporacion de Estudios y Publicaciones, pg 137
SECAP, pg 137

France
Annales de la Recherche Urbaine, pg 147
Les Ateliers d'Orion, pg 148
Blondel La Rougery SARL, pg 151
Counseil International de la Langue Francaise, pg 157
Editions Delmas, pg 158
Les Editions Foucher SA, pg 164
Editions Juridiques Associees - LGDJ/Montchrestien, pg 170
Sofiac (Societe Francaise des Imprimeries Administratives Centrales), pg 185

Germany
Andernach Atelier Verlag (AVA), pg 193
Berlin Verlag Arno Spitz GmbH, pg 200
W Bertelsmann Verlag GmbH & Co KG, pg 201
Deutscher Betriebswirte-Verlag GmbH, pg 214
Dr Curt Haefner-Verlag GmbH, pg 236
Carl Heymanns Verlag KG, pg 240
ITpress Verlag, pg 245
SachBuchVerlag Kellner, pg 248
Klages-Verlag, pg 249
Verlagsgruppe Koehler/Mittler, pg 251
W Kohlhammer GmbH, abt Haussortiment, pg 252
Institut fuer Landes- und Stadtentwicklungsforschung, ILS Nordrhein-Westfalen, pg 255
LIT Verlag, pg 258
Dr Josef Raabe-Verlags GmbH, pg 276
Verlag Norman Rentrop, pg 279
Otto Schwartz Fachbochhandlung GmbH, pg 286
Stollfuss Verlag Bonn GmbH & Co KG, pg 290
Walhalla Fachverlag GmbH & Co KG Praetoria, pg 300
Verlag fuer Wirtschaft & Verwaltung Hubert Wingen GmbH & Co KG, pg 303
Das Wunderhorn Verlag GmbH, pg 304

Greece
Exandas Publishers, pg 310
Hestia-I D Hestia-Kollaros & Co Corporation, pg 311
Sakkoulas Publications SA, pg 314

Hong Kong
Hong Kong University Press, pg 320

Hungary
Lang Kiado, pg 325
Novorg Kiado, pg 326
Saldo Penzugyi Tanacsado es Informatikai Rt, pg 326

India
Ajanta Publications (India), pg 330
APH Publishing Corp, pg 331
Associated Publishing House, pg 331
Bharatiya Samijik Vigyan Auusandhan Parishad, pg 332
Concept Publishing Co, pg 335
Gyan Publishing House, pg 338
Minerva Associates (Publications) Pvt Ltd, pg 342
Reliance Publishing House, pg 347
Sage Publications India Pvt Ltd, pg 348
Scientific Book Agency, pg 349

1061

SUBJECT INDEX

Sterling Publishers Pvt Ltd, pg 351
Sultan Chand & Sons Pvt Ltd, pg 351

Ireland
Institute of Public Administration, pg 361

Israel
Haifa University Press, pg 368
Yachdav, United Publishers Co Ltd, pg 373

Italy
Cacucci Editore, pg 379
CEDAM (Casa Editrice Dr A Milani), pg 380
Ciranna - Roma, pg 381
Direzione Generale Archivi, pg 385
EGEA (Edizioni Giuridiche Economiche Aziendali), pg 387
Rubbettino Editore, pg 406

Japan
Ryosho-Fukyu-Kai Co Ltd, pg 424
Charles E Tuttle Publishing Co Inc, pg 428

Kenya
Heinemann Kenya Limited (EAEP), pg 431
Midi Teki Publishers, pg 433

Republic of Korea
Daeyoung Munhwasa, pg 435
Korea Local Authorities Foundation for International Relations, pg 437
Oruem Publishing House, pg 439

Luxembourg
Service Central de la Statistique et des Etudes Economiques (STATEC), pg 448
Service Central des Imprimes et des Fournitures de Bureau de l'Etat, pg 448

Macau
Universidadede de Macau, Centro de Publicacoes, pg 448

Mexico
Edamex SA de CV, pg 460
Fondo de Cultura Economica, pg 461
Editorial Limusa SA de CV, pg 463
McGraw-Hill Interamericana de Mexico, SA de CV, pg 463
Plaza y Valdes SA de CV, pg 465

Netherlands
Samsom BedrijfsInformatie BV, pg 483
Twente University Press, pg 485
VU Boekhandel/Uitgeverij BV, pg 487

New Zealand
Gondwanaland Press, pg 491

Nigeria
Vantage Publishers International Ltd, pg 502

Poland
Wydawnictwo Prawnicze Co, pg 519
Oficyna Wydawnicza Szkoly Glownej Handlowej w Warszawie Oficyna Wydawnicza SGH, pg 520

Portugal
Edicoes Cosmos, pg 524
GECTI (Gabinete de Especializacao e Cooperacao Tecnica Internacional L), pg 525
Imprensa Nacional-Casa da Moeda, pg 526

Russian Federation
Finansy i Statistika Publishing House, pg 538
Izvestia Sovetov Narodnyh Deputatov Russian Federation (RF), pg 539

South Africa
South African Institute of Race Relations, pg 559
Van Schaik Publishers, pg 560

Spain
Centro de Estudios Adams-Ediciones Valbuena SA, pg 561
Boletin Oficial del Estado, pg 565
Bosch Casa Editorial SA, pg 565
Civitas SA Editorial, pg 567
Instituto de Estudios Fiscales, pg 574
Generalitat de Catalunya Diari Oficial de la Generalitat vern, pg 575
Marcial Pons Ediciones Juridicas SA, pg 581
Pais Vasco Servicio Central de Publicaciones, pg 585
Trea Ediciones, SL, pg 593
Xunta de Galicia, pg 596

Sweden
Industrilitteratur Vindex, Forlags AB, pg 603
Iustus Forlag AB, pg 603

Switzerland
Editions H Messeiller SA, pg 619
Versus Verlag AG, pg 627

Syrian Arab Republic
Damascus University Press, pg 628

United Republic of Tanzania
Tanzania Publishing House, pg 634

Trinidad & Tobago
Caribbean Telecommunications Union, pg 636

Tunisia
Maison Tunisienne de l'Edition, pg 638

Ukraine
Osnovy Publishers, pg 643

United Kingdom
Anglo-German Foundation for the Study of Industrial Society, pg 647
Ashgate Publishing Ltd, pg 649

Commonwealth Secretariat, pg 669
Edinburgh University Press Ltd, pg 677
The Eurospan Group, pg 680
Institute for Fiscal Studies, pg 699
Institute of Development Studies, pg 699
Library & Information Statistics Unit, pg 707
National Assembly for Wales, pg 717
NCVO, pg 718
Open University Press, pg 721
The Policy Press, pg 729
Policy Studies Institute, pg 729
SHU Press, pg 742
Virago Press, pg 753

Zambia
Movement for Multi-Party Democracy, pg 767

Zimbabwe
Sapes Trust Ltd, pg 769

PUBLISHING & BOOK TRADE REFERENCE

Albania
NL SH, pg 1

Argentina
Alfagrama SRL ediciones, pg 3

Australia
Australian Scholarly Publishing, pg 14
Magpie Books, pg 31
Melway Publishing Pty Ltd, pg 33
D W Thorpe, pg 44
Worsley Press, pg 48

Austria
Autorensolidaritat - Verlag der Interessengemeinschaft osterreichischer Autorinnen und Autoren, pg 49
Buchkultur Verlags GmbH Zeitschrift fuer Literatur & Kunst, pg 50
IG Autorinnen Autoren, pg 53

Bangladesh
The University Press Ltd, pg 62

Belgium
Coda, pg 66
Huis Van Het Boek, pg 69

Brazil
Editora Nova Fronteira SA, pg 88

Bulgaria
Abagar Pablioing, pg 94
Ciela Publishing House, pg 94
Musica Publishing House Ltd, pg 96
Sluntse Publishing House, pg 98

Chile
Edeval (Universidad de Valparaiso), pg 100

China
Inner Mongolia Science & Technology Publishing House, pg 106
Southwest China Jiaotong University Press, pg 109

Czech Republic
Studio Dobre Nalady Spol SRO, pg 128

Ecuador
CIESPAL (Centro Internacional de Estudios Superiores de Comunicacion para America Latina), pg 137

France
Editions des Cahiers Bourbonnais, pg 152
Culture et Bibliotheque pour Tous, pg 157
Les Dossiers d'Aquitaine, pg 160
Jean-Michel Place, pg 180
References cf, pg 182

Germany
ARCult Media, pg 194
Berlin Verlag Arno Spitz GmbH, pg 200
Verlag Beruf + Schule Belz KG, pg 202
Buchhaendler-Vereinigung GmbH, pg 207
BuchMarkt Verlag K Werner GmbH, pg 207
Deutsches Bucharchiv Muenchen, Institut fur Buchwissenschaften, pg 216
Dumjahn Verlag, pg 219
Harald Fischer Verlag GmbH, pg 228
Gunter Olzog Verlag GmbH, pg 235
Gutenberg-Gesellschaft eV, pg 235
Hardt und Worner Marketing fur das Buch, pg 237
Dr Ernst Hauswedell & Co Verlag, pg 238
Edition ID-Archiv/ID-Verlag, pg 244
Vittorio Klostermann GmbH, pg 250
K F Koehler Verlag, pg 251
Polygraph Verlag GmbH, pg 274
K G Saur Verlag GmbH, A Gale/Thomson Learning Company, pg 282
Buchverlag Andrea Schmitz, pg 284

Ghana
World Literature Project, pg 308

Greece
Karatzas Charis, pg 312

Hong Kong
Benefit Publishing Co, pg 318
Island Press, pg 320
Photoart Ltd, pg 321
Press Mark Media Ltd, pg 321

India
Reliance Publishing House, pg 347
Shaibya Prakashan Bibhag, pg 349
Sita Publications, pg 350

Indonesia
Yayasan Obor Indonesia, pg 357

PUBLISHERS

Israel
Rubin Mass Ltd, pg 371

Kenya
Bookman Consultants Ltd, pg 431

Republic of Korea
Bum-Woo Publishing Co, pg 435
Korean Publishers Association, pg 437
Samho Music Publishing Co, pg 440

Latvia
Bibliography Institute of the National Library of Latvia, pg 441

The Former Yugoslav Republic of Macedonia
Mi-An Knigoizdatelstvo, pg 449

Malaysia
Geetha Publishers Sdn Bhd, pg 452
Pustaka Cipta Sdn Bhd, pg 454

Morocco
Access International Services, pg 469

Netherlands
Frank Fehmers Productions, pg 477

Nigeria
Unity Publishing & Research Company Ltd, pg 502

Norway
Ex Libris Forlag A/S, pg 503

Pakistan
International Educational Services, pg 507

Romania
Editura Excelsior, pg 533

Russian Federation
Izdatelstvo Kniga, pg 539
Izdatelstvo Knizhnaya Palata, pg 539
St Andrew's Biblical Theological College, pg 541

Singapore
Newscom Pte Ltd, pg 547

Slovakia
Sofa, pg 551

South Africa
Bet-El Publishers, pg 553
New Africa Books (Pty) Ltd, pg 557

Spain
Antonio Machado, SA, pg 580
Tesitex, SL, pg 592

Sweden
Bokforlaget Spektra AB, pg 601
Ordfront Foerlag AB, pg 605

Switzerland
Pedrazzini Tipografia, pg 621

Taiwan, Province of China
Yi Hsien Publishing Co Ltd, pg 632

Tunisia
Les Editions de l'Arbre, pg 638

United Kingdom
Anderson Rand Ltd, pg 647
Blueprint, pg 656
Book Data, pg 657
Book Marketing Ltd, pg 657
Books International, pg 657
Cassell & Co, pg 664
James Clarke & Co Ltd, pg 668
CSA (Cambridge Scientific Abstracts), pg 672
DMG Business Media Ltd, pg 675
Electronic Publishing Services Ltd, pg 678
Euromonitor PLC, pg 680
Europa Publications, pg 680
The Robert Gordon University, pg 688
J Whitaker & Sons Ltd, pg 702
Merchiston Publishing, pg 713
National Library of Wales, pg 717
Peter Owen Ltd, pg 722
Oxford University Press, pg 723
PIRA Intl, pg 728
Publishing Training Centre at BookHouse, pg 731
Skoob Russell Square, pg 742
John Taylor Book Ventures, pg 747

RADIO, TV

Albania
NL SH, pg 1
State Textbook Publishing House, pg 1

Argentina
Fundacion Editorial de Belgrano, pg 4
Ediciones Don Bosco Argentina, pg 5

Australia
Australian Film Television & Radio School, pg 13

Brazil
Summus Editorial Ltda, pg 92

Chile
Arrayan Editores, pg 99

China
Electronics Industry Publishing House, pg 105

Croatia
Vitagraf, pg 120

Czech Republic
AMA nakladatelstvi, pg 123

Ecuador
CIESPAL (Centro Internacional de Estudios Superiores de Comunicacion para America Latina), pg 137

France
Bragelonne, pg 151
Dreamland Editeur, pg 160
La Voix du Regard, pg 189

Germany
ARCult Media, pg 194
Bertelsmann Lexikon Verlag GmbH, pg 201
Die Verlag H Schafer GmbH, pg 216
Egmont vgs verlagsgesellschaft mbH, pg 221
Verlag Reinhard Fischer, pg 228
von Hase & Koehler Verlag KG, pg 238
Huss-Medien GmbH, pg 243
kopaed verlagsgmbh, pg 252
Schueren Verlag GmbH, pg 285
TR - Verlagsunion GmbH, pg 294
UVK Verlagsgesellschaft mbH, pg 297

Hong Kong
Electronic Technology Publishing Co Ltd, pg 319
South China Morning Post Ltd, pg 322
Technology Exchange Ltd, pg 322

Italy
Editore Armando Armando SRL, pg 376
Campanotto, pg 379
Ernesto Gremese Editore SRL, pg 391
Edizioni Medicea SRL, pg 398
RAI.ERI, pg 405
SAIE Editrice SRL, pg 406

Jamaica
Alice J M Rhodd, pg 413

Japan
Gakken Co Ltd, pg 416

Mexico
Ediciones Alpe, pg 458
Editorial Limusa SA de CV, pg 463
Medios y Medios, Sa de CV, pg 464

Netherlands
Otto Cramwinckel Uitgever, pg 476
Frank Fehmers Productions, pg 477
Sociaal en Cultureel Planbureau, pg 484

Norway
J W Eides Forlag A/S, pg 503
Vett & Viten AS, pg 505

Peru
Universidad de Lima-Fondo de Desarollo Editorial, pg 512

Poland
Wydawnictwa Komunikacji i Lacznosci Co Ltd, pg 517
Wydawnictwa Radia i Telewizji, pg 519

Portugal
Impala, pg 525
Editora Pergaminho Lda, pg 528

Russian Federation
Nauka Publishers, pg 540
Izdatelstvo Radio i Svyaz, pg 541

South Africa
Bet-El Publishers, pg 553

SUBJECT INDEX

Spain
Bosch Casa Editorial SA, pg 565
Fragua Editorial, pg 574
Ediciones JLA, pg 579
Marcombo SA de Boixareu Editores, pg 581
Ediciones de la Torre, pg 593

Switzerland
Maurice et Pierre Foetisch SA, pg 614
Junod Nicholas, pg 616
Lehrmittelverlag des Kantons Zurich, pg 618

United Kingdom
Artech House, pg 649
Bernard Babani (Publishing) Ltd, pg 651
BBC Television Training, pg 653
BFI Publishing, pg 654
Boxtree Ltd, pg 658
Carlton Publishing Group, pg 664
Chadwyck-Healey Ltd, pg 666
DMG Business Media Ltd, pg 675
The Eurospan Group, pg 680
Faber & Faber Ltd, pg 681
Fourth Estate Ltd, pg 683
John Blake Publishing Ltd, pg 703
Manchester University Press, pg 711
NTC Publications Ltd, pg 720
Plexus Publishing Ltd, pg 728
Roundhouse Publishing Ltd, pg 736
Time Out Group Ltd, pg 749
Titan Books Ltd, pg 749
Virgin Publishing Ltd, pg 753
Windsor Books International, pg 757

Uruguay
Nordan-Comunidad, pg 760

Viet Nam
Science & Technics Publishing House, pg 763

Zimbabwe
Africa Film & TV t/a Z Promotions, pg 767

REAL ESTATE

Australia
Coconut Productions, pg 18
Horan Wall & Walker, pg 26
Law Book Co Information Services, pg 29
OTEN (Open Training & Education Network), pg 36
The Real Estate Institute of Australia, pg 40
Wrightbooks Pty Ltd, pg 48

China
China Ocean Press, pg 103

Costa Rica
Editorial Texto Ltda, pg 117

France
CPL- La Communication Par le Livre, pg 157
Editions Delmas, pg 158
Editions Juris Service, pg 171

SUBJECT INDEX

Editions Legislatives, pg 172
Presses de l'Ecole Nationale des Ponts et Chaussees, pg 181

Germany
Berlin Verlag Arno Spitz GmbH, pg 200
Compact Verlag GmbH, pg 211
Rudolf Haufe Verlag GmbH & Co KG, pg 238
Norbert Mueller AG & Co KG Verlag, pg 265
Verlag Norman Rentrop, pg 279
Richardi Helmut Verlag GmbH, pg 279
WEKA Firmengruppe GmbH & Co KG, pg 301
Verlag fuer Wirtschaft & Verwaltung Hubert Wingen GmbH & Co KG, pg 303

Ghana
Building & Road Research Institute (BRRI), pg 306

Hong Kong
Hong Kong University Press, pg 320

Hungary
Novorg Kiado, pg 326

India
Agricole Publishing Academy, pg 330

Kenya
Nairobi University Press, pg 433

Republic of Korea
Chung Rim Publishing Co Ltd, pg 435

Mexico
Editorial Limusa SA de CV, pg 463

Netherlands
BZZTOH Publishers, pg 475
Hagen & Stam Uitgeverij Ten, pg 478
Sociaal en Cultureel Planbureau, pg 484

Russian Federation
Finansy i Statistika Publishing House, pg 538

Switzerland
Dimension World Ltd, pg 612

Taiwan, Province of China
Shy Chaur Publishing Co Ltd, pg 631

United Kingdom
Management Books 2000 Ltd, pg 711
RICS Books, pg 735
Spon Press, pg 744

REGIONAL INTERESTS

Afghanistan
Government Press, pg 1
Historical Society of Afghanistan, pg 1

Albania
Encyclopaedia Publishing House, pg 1

Algeria
Enterprise Nationale du Livre (ENAL), pg 2

Argentina
Amorrortu Editores SA, pg 3
ECA (Ediciones Culturales Argentinas), pg 5
Edicial SA, pg 5

Australia
Aboriginal Studies Press, pg 10
Arabian Focus Pty Ltd, pg 11
Aussies Afire Publishing, pg 13
Blubber Head Press, pg 15
Book Agencies of Tasmania, pg 16
R J Cleary Publishing, pg 18
Enterprise Publications, pg 22
The Five Mile Press Pty Ltd, pg 23
Gangan Publishing, pg 23
Histec Publications, pg 26
Institute of Aboriginal Development (IAD Press), pg 28
Kangaroo Press, pg 29
Lachlan Publishing, pg 29
Library of Australian History, pg 30
Yvonne McBurney, pg 32
Mostly Unsung, pg 33
Navarine Publishing, pg 34
On The Stone, pg 35
Outback Books - CQU Press, pg 36
Oz Publishing Co Pty Ltd, pg 36
Pacific Publications (Australia) Pty Ltd, pg 36
Pollitecon Publications, pg 38
Ruskin Rowe Press, pg 41
St George Books, pg 41
State Publishing Unit of State Print SA, pg 43
Tabletop Press, pg 44
Transpareon Press, pg 45
University of Western Australia Press, pg 46
VCTA Publishing, pg 46
Wellington Lane Press Pty Ltd, pg 47

Austria
Akademische Druck-u Verlagsanstalt Dr Paul Struzl GmbH, pg 49
Astor-Verlag, Willibald Schlager, pg 49
Christian Brandstatter Verlagsgesellschaft GmbH, pg 50
Buchkultur Verlags GmbH Zeitschrift fuer Literatur & Kunst, pg 50
Cura Verlag GmbH, pg 50
Denkmayr GmbH Druck & Verlag, pg 51
Franz Deuticke Verlagsges mbH, pg 51
Development News Ltd, pg 51
Ennsthaler GesmbH & Co KG, pg 51
Graz Stadtmuseum, pg 52
Oesterreichischer Kunst und Kulturverlag, pg 56
Verlag Sankt Peter, pg 57
SN-Verlag, Salzburger Nachrichten Verlags GmbH & Co KG, pg 59
Verlag Veritas Mediengesellschaft mbH, pg 60
Vorarlberger Verlagsanstalt Aktiengesellschaft, pg 60
Waren-Erzeugungs-und Handelsgesellschaft GmbH, pg 60
Herbert Weishaupt Verlag, pg 60

Barbados
Carib Research & Publications Inc, pg 63

Belgium
Centre Aequatoria, pg 64
Aurelia Books PVBA, pg 64
Editions Delta SA, pg 67
Glenat Benelux SA, pg 69
Stichting Ons Erfdeel VZW, pg 74

Bolivia
Los Amigos del Libro Ediciones, pg 76

Bosnia and Herzegovina
Bemust doo Novinsko-Izdavacko stamparsko i trgovacko preduzece, pg 77

Botswana
The Botswana Society, pg 77

Brazil
Editora Atica SA, pg 79
Editora Nova Fronteira SA, pg 88
Edit Palavra Magica, pg 89
Editora Paz e Terra, pg 89

Bulgaria
Publishing House Narodno delo OOD, pg 97

Cameroon
Editions Semences Africaines, pg 99

Chile
Arrayan Editores, pg 99

China
Asia 2000 Ltd, pg 102
Fudan University Press, pg 105

Colombia
Consejo Episcopal Latinoamericano Celam, pg 111
Dosmil Editora, pg 111
Fundacion Centro de Investigacion y Educacion Popular (CINEP), pg 112
RAM Editores, pg 113
Carlos Valencia Editores, pg 114

Costa Rica
Editorial Costa Rica, pg 115
Editorial Texto Ltda, pg 117
Editorial Universitaria Centroamericana (EDUCA), pg 117

Cote d'Ivoire
Centre d'Edition et de Diffusion Africaines, pg 117

Croatia
Matica hrvatska, pg 119

Cuba
Ediciones Union, pg 121

Cyprus
AndreouChr- Publishers, pg 122

Czech Republic
Nakladatelstvi Blok, pg 123
Pressfoto Vydavatelstvi Ceske Tiskove Kancelare, pg 128

Denmark
Borgens Forlag A/S, pg 130
Dansk Historisk Handbogsforlag ApS, pg 131
Host & Son Publishers Ltd, pg 133
Kraks Forlag AS, pg 133

Dominican Republic
Pontificia Universidad Catolica Madre y Maestra, pg 136

Egypt (Arab Republic of Egypt)
Dar Al-Kitab Al-Masri, pg 138
Dar Al Maaref, pg 139
Middle East Book Centre, pg 139
Senouhy Publishers, pg 139
Ummah Press for Translation & Publishing, pg 139

El Salvador
Editorial Universitaria de la Universidad de El Salvador, pg 139

Fiji
University of the South Pacific, pg 141

France
Actes Graphiques, pg 145
Editions l'Ancre de Marine, pg 147
Annales de la Recherche Urbaine, pg 147
Editions de l'Armancon, pg 148
Aubanel SA, pg 149
Autrement Editions, pg 149
Editions A Barthelemy, pg 149
Editions Bertout, pg 150
Editions Canope, pg 152
Editions Cenomane, pg 153
CLD, pg 155
Editions Coprur, pg 156
Edisud, pg 161
Editions Fanlac, pg 163
Imprimerie Librairie Gardet, pg 166
Editions Jean Paul Gisserot, pg 166
Librairie Guenegaud Sarl, pg 167
Editions Herault, pg 168
Isoete, pg 170
Editions du Jaguar, pg 170
Lacour-Olle, pg 171
L'Adret editions, pg 171
Laffitte Reprints, pg 171
Librairie Larousse, pg 172
Editions Loubatieres, pg 174
Editions G P Maisonneuve et Larose, pg 174
Martelle, pg 175
Editions Medianes, pg 175
Editions Norma, pg 177
Editions Ophrys, pg 178
Ouest Editions, pg 178
Editions Jean Picollec, pg 179
Siloe - Kerdore, pg 185
Societe des Editions Privat SA, pg 185
Societe Nouveaux Loisirs, pg 185
Editions Sud Ouest, pg 186
La Vague Verte, pg 188

French Polynesia
Simone Sanchez, pg 190

PUBLISHERS

Georgia
Merani Publishing House, pg 190

Germany
Joh van Acken GmbH & Co KG, pg 191
R van Acken GmbH Druckerei und Verlag, pg 191
arani-Verlag GmbH, pg 194
Ardey-Verlag GmbH, pg 194
ARTC/OLOR, pg 195
Aschendorffsche Verlagsbuchhandlung GmbH & Co KG, pg 195
Asso Verlag, pg 196
Verlag Atelier im Bauernhaus, pg 196
J P Bachem Verlag GmbH, pg 197
Badenia Verlag und Druckerei GmbH, pg 197
Baken-Verlag Walter Schnoor, pg 198
Bautz Traugott, pg 199
Bayerische Verlagsanstalt GmbH, pg 199
be.bra verlag GmbH, pg 199
Beleke KG Verlag, pg 200
Bergstadtverlag Wilhelm Gottlieb Korn GmbH Wuerzburg, pg 200
Bindernagelsche Buchhandlung, pg 203
BKV-Brasilienkunde Verlag GmbH, pg 203
C Bosendahl, pg 205
Bouvier Verlag, pg 206
Brandenburgisches Verlagshaus in der Dornier Medienholding GmbH, pg 206
Brigg Verlag Franz-Joset Buchler KG, pg 206
BRUEN-Verlag, Gorenflo, pg 207
C C Buchners Verlag, pg 207
Bundesanzeiger Verlagsgesellschaft, pg 208
Verlag Busse und Seewald GmbH, pg 208
Fachverlag Hans Carl GmbH, pg 209
Hans Christians Druckerei und Verlag GmbH & Co, pg 210
D & D Kommunikation Verlug Dirk Nishen Gmbh & Co KG, pg 212
Degener & Co, Manfred Dreiss Verlag, pg 213
Delp'sche Verlagsbuchhandlung, pg 213
Dialog-Verlag GmbH, pg 216
Maximilian Dietrich Verlag, pg 216
agenda Verlag Thomas Dominikowski, pg 217
Donat Verlag, pg 217
Karl Elser Druck GmbH, pg 218
DRW-Verlag Weinbrenner-GmbH & Co, pg 219
Echter Wurzburg Frankische Gesellschaftsdruckerei und Verlag GmbH, pg 220
Eppinger-Verlag OHG, pg 223
Ergebnisse Verlag GmbH, pg 223
Eulen Verlag, pg 224
F Bruckmann Munchen Verlag & Druck GmbH & Co Produkt KG, pg 225
FAB-Verlag, pg 226
Fannei & Walz Verlag, pg 227
Fleischhauer & Spohn GmbH & Co, pg 228
Forum Verlag Leipzig Buch-Gesellschaft, pg 229
Fraunhofer IRB Verlag Fraunhofer Informationszentrum Raum und Bau, pg 229
G Braun (vormals G Braun'sche Hofbuchdruckerei und Verlag) Gmbh, pg 231
Brigitte Grabitz - ikoo Buchverlag, pg 233
Greven Verlag Koeln GmbH, pg 234
H L Schlapp Buch- und Antiquariatshandlung GmbH und Co KG Abt Verlag, pg 235
Verlag H M Hauschild GmbH, pg 235
Dr Rudolf Habelt GmbH, pg 235
Hahnsche Buchhandlung, pg 236
Haude und Spenersche Verlagsbuchhandlung, pg 238
Hellerau-Verlag Dresden GmbH, pg 239
Erika Heydick Sax-Verlag Beucha, pg 240
Harro V Hirschheydt, pg 241
S Hirzel Verlag GmbH und Co, pg 241
Husum Druck- und Verlagsgesellschaft mbH Co KG, pg 244
Jan Thorbecke Verlag GmbH & Co, pg 246
Gustav Kiepenheuer Verlag GmbH, pg 249
Klartext Verlagsgesellschaft mbH, pg 249
Karl Knoll Verlag Alte Uni, pg 250
Koehler und Amelang Verlagsgesellschaft mbH, pg 251
Konkordia Verlag GmbH, pg 252
Anton H Konrad Verlag, pg 252
Adam Kraft Verlag, pg 253
Kretschmar Hubert Leipziger Verlagsgesellschaft, pg 253
Kubon & Sagner Buchexport-Import GmbH, pg 254
Kulturbuch-Verlag GmbH, pg 254
Verlag der Kunst/G+B Fine Arts Verlag GmbH, pg 254
Lamuv Verlag GmbH, pg 255
Landbuch-Verlagsgesellschaft mbH, pg 255
Institut fuer Landes- und Stadtentwicklungsforschung, ILS Nordrhein-Westfalen, pg 255
Libertas- Europaeisches Institut GmbH, pg 257
Logos-Verlag Literatur & Layout GmbH, pg 258
Lusatia Verlag-Dr Stuebner & Co KG, pg 259
Lutherische Verlagsgesellschaft mbH, pg 259
Verlag Waldemar Lutz, pg 260
Mairs Geographischer Verlag, pg 260
J A Mayersche Buchhandlung GmbH & Co KG Abt Verlag, pg 261
Missionshandlung, pg 264
Mitteldeutscher Verlag GmbH, pg 264
Morsak Verlag, pg 265
Nicolaische Verlagsbuchhandlung Beuermann GmbH, pg 268
Niederland-Verlag Helmut Michel, pg 268
Oberbaum Verlag GmbH, pg 269
Oreos Verlag GmbH, pg 270
Ostfalia-Verlag Jurgen Schierer, pg 271
Pandion-Verlag, Ulrike Schmoll, pg 271
Verlag Parzeller GmbH & Co KG, pg 271
Physica-Verlag, pg 273
Presse Verlagsgesellschaft mbH, pg 275
Gerhard Rautenberg Druckerei und Verlag GmbH & Co KG, pg 277
REGENSBERG Druck & Verlag GmbH & Co, pg 277
Verlag fur Regionalgeschichte, pg 277
E Reinhold Verlag, pg 278
Respublica Verlag, pg 279
RVBG Rheinland-Verlag-und Betriebsgesellschaft des Landschaftsverbandes Rheinland mbH, pg 279
Rombach GmbH Druck und Verlagshaus & Co, pg 280
Rosenheimer Verlagshaus GmbH & Co KG, pg 280
Sachsenbuch Verlagsgesellschaft Mbh, pg 281
Schelzky & Jeep, Verlag fuer Reisen und Wissen, pg 283
Schillinger Verlag GmbH, pg 283
Max Schmidt-Roemhild Verlag, pg 284
Carl Ed Schuenemann KG, pg 285
Schueren Verlag GmbH, pg 285
Schwabenverlag Aktiengesellschaft, pg 285
Silberburg-Verlag Titus Haeussermann GmbH, pg 287
Stadler Verlagsgesellschaft mbH, pg 288
Stapp Verlag Wolfgang Stapp, pg 289
Steiger Verlag, pg 289
Steinweg-Verlag, Jurgen romHoff, pg 290
Sueddeutsche Verlagsgesellschaft mbH, pg 291
Suedverlag GmbH, pg 291
Verlag Theodor Thoben, pg 293
Trautvetter & Fischer Nachf, pg 294
Trees Wolfgang Triangel Verlag, pg 294
Tuebinger Vereinigung fur Volkskunde eV (TVV), pg 295
TUeV-Verlag GmbH, pg 295
Guenter Albert Ulmer Verlag, pg 295
Verlag Philipp von Zabern, pg 299
VVF Verlag V Florentz GmbH, pg 299
Wartburg Verlag GmbH, pg 300
Weidler Buchverlag Berlin, pg 301
Westholsteinische Verlagsanstalt und Verlagsdruckerei Boyens & Co, pg 302
Dr Dieter Winkler, pg 303
Gert Wohlfarth GmbH Verlag Fachtechnik & Mercator Verlag, Verlag Puppen & Spielzeug, pg 304
Zambon Verlag, pg 305
Ziethen-Panorama Verlag GmbH, pg 305

Ghana
Anowuo Educational Publications, pg 306

Greece
D Papadimas, pg 314
Papazissis Publishers SA, pg 314
Costas Spanos, pg 315

Hong Kong
The Dharmasthiti Buddist Institute Ltd, pg 319
Ming Pao Publications Ltd, pg 321
Press Mark Media Ltd, pg 321
Yazhou Zhoukan Ltd, pg 322

SUBJECT INDEX

Hungary
Szarvas Andras Cartographic Agency, pg 326

Iceland
Iceland Review, pg 328
Stofnun Arna Magnussonar a Islandi, pg 329

India
Himalayan Books, pg 338
Rahul Publishing House, pg 347
Regency Publications, pg 347
Rekha Prakashan, pg 347
Reliance Publishing House, pg 347
Sahasrara Publications, pg 348
SBW Publishers, pg 349
Sri Satguru Publications, pg 351

Indonesia
PATCO, pg 356

Ireland
Ballinakella Press, pg 358
Edmund Burke Publisher, pg 359
Clo Iar-Chonnachta Teo, pg 359
Eason & Son Ltd, pg 360
Gill & Macmillan Ltd, pg 361
The Goldsmith Press Ltd, pg 361
The Lilliput Press Ltd, pg 362
National Library of Ireland, pg 362
Relay Books, pg 363
Roberts Rinehart Publishers, pg 363

Israel
Agudat Sabah, pg 365
Ariel Publishing House, pg 365
Ben-Zvi Institute, pg 365
Edanim Publishers Ltd, pg 367
Hakibbutz Hameuchad Publishing House Ltd, pg 368
The Institute for Israeli Arabs Studies, pg 368
Israel Universities Press, pg 369
L B Publishing Co, pg 369
Tel-Aviv University, pg 373
Yad Izhak Ben-Zvi Press, pg 373

Italy
Mario Adda Editore SNC, pg 374
Alberti Libraio Editore, pg 375
Artioli Editore in Modena, pg 377
Atlantica Editrice SARL, pg 377
Casa Editrice Luigi Battei, pg 377
Belforte Editore Libraio srl, pg 377
Edizioni Brenner, pg 378
Calosci, pg 379
Edizioni Cantagalli, pg 379
Capone Editore SRL, pg 379
Edizioni Della Torre di Salvatore Fozzi & C SAS, pg 384
Edizioni dell'Orso SAS, pg 385
Organizzazione Didattica Editoriale Ape, pg 385
Edizioni l'Arciere SRL, pg 387
ERGA SNC di Carla Ottino Merli & C (Edizioni Realizzazioni Grafiche - Artigiana), pg 388
Libreria Editrice Fiorentina di Vittorio Zani e C SAS, pg 389
Flaccovio Editore, pg 389
Arnaldo Forni Editore SRL, pg 389
Adriano Gallina Editore sas, pg 389
Istituto Geografico de Agostini SpA, pg 390
Grafis Edizioni, pg 391
Grafo Edizioni, pg 391
Il Poligrafo, pg 393
Lalli Editore SRL, pg 395
Giuseppe Maimone Editore, pg 397

SUBJECT INDEX — BOOK

Tommaso Marotta Editore Srl, pg 398
NodoLibri, pg 401
Nuovi Sentieri Editore, pg 401
Palatina Editrice, pg 402
Fratelli Palombi SRL, pg 402
Daniela Piazza Editore, pg 403
Francesco Pirella Editore, pg 403
Priuli e Verlucca, Editori, pg 404
Edition Raetia Srl-GmbH, pg 404
Fausto Sardini Editrice, pg 407
Sicania, pg 408
SIPI (Servizio Italiano Pubblicazioni Internazionali) Srl, pg 408
Societa Storica Catanese, pg 408
Edizioni Thyrus SRL, pg 409
Editoriale Umbra SAS di Carnevali e, pg 410
Vivere In SRL, pg 411

Jamaica
Association of Development Agencies, pg 412

Japan
Nippon Hoso Shuppan Kyokai (NHK Publishing), pg 422
Seibundo Shuppan, pg 425
Shibundo Co Ltd, pg 425
The Simul Press Inc, pg 426
Toho Book Store, pg 427
Yushodo Co Ltd, pg 429

Kenya
Camerapix Publishers International Ltd, pg 431
Kenway Publications Ltd, pg 432
Transafrica Press, pg 433

Republic of Korea
Kwangmyong Publishing Co, pg 438
Seoul International Publishing House, pg 440

Lebanon
Geoprojects Sarl, pg 443
Librairie Orientale sal, pg 443

Lesotho
Mazenod Book Centre, pg 444
Saint Michael's Mission, pg 444

Luxembourg
Editions Emile Borschette, pg 447
Galerie Editions Kutter, pg 447
Editions Promoculture, pg 448

Malawi
Christian Literature Association in Malawi, pg 450

Malaysia
Forum Publications, pg 452
Uni-Text Book Co, pg 455
Vinpress Sdn Bhd, pg 455

Maldive Islands
Novelty Printers & Publishers, pg 455

Malta
The University of Malta Publications Section, pg 456

Mauritius
De l'edition Bukie Banane, pg 457

Mexico
Editorial AGATA SA de CV, pg 457
Ediciones el Caballito SA, pg 458
Ediciones Euroamericanas, pg 461
Fondo Editorial de la Plastica Mexicana, pg 461
Editorial Nueva Imagen SA, pg 464
Instituto Panamericano de Geografia e Historia, pg 465
Panorama Editorial, SA, pg 465
Siglo XXI Editores SA de CV, pg 467

Morocco
Dar El Kitab, pg 469

Mozambique
Empresa Moderna Lda, pg 470
Centro De Estudos Africanos, pg 470

Namibia
Desert Research Foundation of Namibia (DRFN), pg 471

Netherlands
Uitgeverij Balans, pg 473
East-West Publications Fonds BV, pg 476
Twente University Press, pg 485
West-Friesland/Boekproject-ontwikkeling, pg 487

Netherlands Antilles
De Wit Stores NV, pg 488

New Zealand
Aoraki Press Ltd, pg 488
Bush Press Communications Ltd, pg 489
Clerestory Press, pg 490
Craig Printing Company Ltd, pg 490
Fraser Books, pg 491
Grantham House Publishing, pg 491
HarperCollins Publishers (New Zealand) Ltd, pg 491
Heritage Press Ltd, pg 492
Kotuku Media Ltd, pg 492
Nestegg Books, pg 493
Otago Heritage Books, pg 494
Paerangi Books, pg 494
Reed Publishing (NZ) Ltd, pg 495
Te Ropu Kahurangi, pg 496

Nigeria
Northern Nigerian Publishing Co Ltd, pg 500

Pakistan
East & West Publishing Co, pg 506
Ferozsons (Private) Ltd, pg 506
Jang Publishers, pg 507
National Institute of Historical & Cultural Research, pg 508
Vanguard Books Ltd, pg 509

Poland
Interpress, pg 517
Iskry - Publishing House Ltd spotka zoo, pg 517
Laumann-Polska, pg 517
'Slask' Ltd, pg 520
Towarzystwo Naukowe w Toruniu, pg 520

Portugal
Solivros, pg 529

Puerto Rico
Libros-Ediciones Homines, pg 530
Publishing Resources Inc, pg 531

Romania
Editura Excelsior, pg 533
Pallas-Akademia Koenyvkiadoes Koenyvkereskedes, pg 535

Rwanda
INADES (Institut Africain pour le Developpment Economique et Social), pg 543

Saudi Arabia
International Publications Agency (IPA), pg 543

Slovenia
Franc-Franc podjetje za promocijo kulture Murska Sobota d o o, pg 551
Zalozba Mihelac d o o, pg 552

South Africa
The Brenthurst Press (Pty) Ltd, pg 553
Fernwood Press (Pty) Ltd, pg 554
HAUM - Daan Retief Publishers (Pty) Ltd, pg 555
Human Sciences Research Council, pg 555
Ithemba! Publishing, pg 555
New Africa Books (Pty) Ltd, pg 557
University of Natal Press, pg 560

Spain
Editorial Afers, SL, pg 561
Amnistia Internacional Editorial SL, pg 563
Ayalga Ediciones SA, pg 564
Cabildo Insular de Gran Canaria Departamento de Ediciones, pg 566
Dilagro SA, pg 569
Ediciones Diputacion de Salamanca, pg 570
Instituto de Estudios Riojanos, pg 574
Generalitat de Catalunya Diari Oficial de la Generalitat vern, pg 575
Gran Enciclopedia-Asturiana Silverio Canada, pg 576
Impredisur, SL, pg 578
Junta de Castilla y Leon Consejeria de Educacion y Cultura, pg 579
Ediciones Maeva, pg 581
Editorial Moll SL, pg 582
Publicaciones de la Universidad de Alicante, pg 588
Editora Regional de Murcia - ERM, pg 588
Selecta-Catalonia Ed, pg 590
Turner Publicaciones, pg 593
Editorial Txertoa, pg 594

Sri Lanka
KVG de Silva & Sons, pg 597
National Library & Documentation Services Board, pg 597

Suriname
Drs F H R Oedayrajsingh Varma, pg 599
Vaco NV Uitgeversmij, pg 599

Sweden
Gothia Publishing House, pg 603
Hanse Production AB, pg 603
Hillelforlaget, pg 603
Stromberg, pg 606

Switzerland
Editions L'Age d'Homme - La Cite, pg 608
Armenia Editions, pg 608
AT Verlag, pg 608
Bugra Suisse Burchler Grafino AG, pg 610
Christoph Merian Verlag, pg 611
Cosmos-Verlag AG, pg 611
Verlag ED Emmentaler Druck AG, pg 613
Frobenius AG, pg 614
Th Gut Verlag, pg 615
Verlag Huber & Co AG, pg 616
Lia rumantscha, pg 618
Peter Meili & Co, Buchhandluna, pg 619
Editions Payot Lausanne, pg 621
Hans Rohr Verlag, pg 623
SAB Schweiz Arbeitsgemeinschaft fuer die Berggebiete, pg 623
Verlag Stocker-Schmid AG, pg 625
Terra Grischuna Verlag Buch-und Zeitschriftenverlag, pg 625
Editions du Tricorne, pg 626
Verbandsdruckerei AG, pg 626
Verlagsbuchhandlung AG, pg 626
Viktoria-Verlag Peter Marti, pg 627
Walter Verlag AG, pg 627

Taiwan, Province of China
Morning Star Publisher Inc, pg 631
Yee Wen Publishing Co Ltd, pg 632

United Republic of Tanzania
East African Publishing House, pg 633

Thailand
Graphic Art Publishing, pg 635
White Lotus Co Ltd, pg 636

Tunisia
Alyssa Editions, pg 637

Turkey
Altin Kitaplar Yayinevi, pg 638

United Kingdom
The Ampersand Press (CI) Ltd, pg 647
Appletree Press Ltd, pg 648
Ashmolean Museum Publications, pg 650
Ashton & Denton Publishing Co (CI) Ltd, pg 650
Birlinn Ltd, pg 655
Blackstaff Press, pg 655
Brewin Books Ltd, pg 659
Bridge Books, pg 659
The British Council, Design, Publishing & Print Department, pg 660
Canongate Books Ltd, pg 663
Cardiff Academic Press, pg 663
Castlemead Publications, pg 665
Paul Cave Publications Ltd, pg 665

PUBLISHERS SUBJECT INDEX

The Chartered Institute of Building, pg 666
Chartered Institute of Library & Information Professionals in Scotland, pg 666
Cottage Publications, pg 671
Countryside Books, pg 671
Countyvise Ltd, pg 671
Terence Dalton Ltd, pg 673
John Donald Publishers Ltd, pg 675
The Eurospan Group, pg 680
Forth Naturalist & Historian, pg 683
Gairm Publications, pg 685
Glasgow City Libraries Publications, pg 687
Gomer Press (J D Lewis & Sons Ltd), pg 688
Gwasg Gwenffrwd, pg 690
Ian Henry Publications Ltd, pg 695
C Hurst & Co (Publishers) Ltd, pg 698
Hutton Press Ltd, pg 698
Icon Press, pg 698
Institute of Irish Studies, The Queens University of Belfast, pg 699
Intellect Ltd, pg 700
Jarrold Publishing, pg 703
Kingfisher Publications Plc, pg 704
Landy Publishing, pg 706
Liverpool University Press, pg 708
Lodenek Press, pg 708
Y Lolfa Cyf, pg 708
Luath Press Ltd, pg 709
Mercat Press, pg 713
Merchiston Publishing, pg 713
Meresborough Books, pg 713
Middleton Press, pg 714
E J Morten (Publishers), pg 715
MWH London Publishers, pg 716
National Library of Scotland, pg 717
NCLC Publishing Society Ltd, pg 718
Old Vicarage Publications, pg 720
The Oleander Press, pg 721
Phillimore & Co Ltd, pg 727
Quentin Books Ltd, pg 732
Redcliffe Press Ltd, pg 734
Regency House Publishing Ltd, pg 734
Roadmaster Publishing, pg 735
Routledge Curzon, pg 736
Saint Andrew Press, pg 737
SB Publications, pg 738
Scottish Cultural Press, pg 739
Shearwater Press Ltd, pg 741
SHU Press, pg 742
Sigma Press, pg 742
Smith Settle Ltd, pg 743
SPA Books Ltd, pg 744
Stenlake Publishing, pg 745
Sutton Publishing Ltd, pg 746
Thistle Press, pg 748
Ulster Historical Foundation, pg 751
University of Exeter Press, pg 751
Wharncliffe Publishing Ltd, pg 755
White Cockade Publishing, pg 755
Whittles Publishing, pg 756
Neil Wilson Publishing Ltd, pg 757

Uruguay
Editorial Arca SRL, pg 760
Fundacion de Cultura Universitaria, pg 760
Ediciones Sol del Sur, pg 761

Venezuela
Monte Avila Editores Latinoamericana CA, pg 762
Universidad de los Andes, Consejo de Publicaciones, pg 763

Zimbabwe
Nehanda Publishers, pg 769

RELIGION - BUDDHIST

Argentina
Editorial Kier SACIFI, pg 7

Australia
Oriental Publications, pg 36
Spectrum Publications, pg 43
Tamarind Publications, pg 44
Thin Rich Press, pg 44
Unity Press, pg 46
Windhorse Books, pg 48

Brazil
Editora Bertrand Brasil Ltda, pg 79
Companhia Editora Forense, pg 82
Horus Editora Ltda, pg 85
Francisco J Laissue Livraria, pg 86

Bulgaria
Eurasia Academic Publishers, pg 95
Kibea Publishing Co, pg 96

China
China Ocean Press, pg 103
China Tibetology Publishing House, pg 104
Fudan University Press, pg 105

Czech Republic
Nadace Lyry Pragensis, pg 126
Votobia sro, pg 129

France
Paul Geuthner Librairie Orientaliste, pg 166
Langues & Mondes/L'Asiatheque, pg 171
L'Originel - Editions Accarias, pg 178
Pardes, pg 179

Germany
Adyar-Verlag, pg 191
Aquamarin Verlag, pg 194
Connection Medien GmbH, pg 211
Dharma Edition, Tibetisches Zentrum, pg 216
Eugen Diederichs Verlag GmbH & Co KG, pg 216
Verlag Esoterische Philosophie GmbH, pg 224
Happy Mental Buch- und Musik Verlag, pg 237
Verlag Herder GmbH & Co KG, pg 239
Anton Hiersemann, Verlag, pg 240
F Hirthammer Verlag GmbH, pg 241
Klaus Isele, pg 245
Joy Verlag GmbH, pg 247
Klink, Vincent, Edition, Stecknadel, pg 250
Knowledge Media International, pg 251
Kolibri-Verlags GmbH, pg 252
Nie/Nie/Sagen-Verlag, pg 268
Nusser Verlag, pg 269
nymphenburger, pg 269
Osho Verlag GmbH, pg 271
Franz Steiner Verlag Wiesbaden GmbH, pg 289

Hong Kong
Chung Hwa Book Co (HK) Ltd, pg 319
The Dharmasthiti Buddist Institute Ltd, pg 319
Hong Kong University Press, pg 320

India
Asian Educational Services, pg 331
Book Faith India, pg 333
Books & Books, pg 334
Cosmo Publications, pg 335
DK Printworld (P) Ltd, pg 336
Gyan Publishing House, pg 338
Indus Publishing Co, pg 339
B Jain Publishers (P) Ltd, pg 340
Law Publishers, pg 341
Minerva Associates (Publications) Pvt Ltd, pg 342
Munshiram Manoharlal Publishers Pvt Ltd, pg 343
Navrang Booksellers & Publishers, pg 344
Pitambar Publishing Co (P) Ltd, pg 346
Reliance Publishing House, pg 347
Roli Books Pvt Ltd, pg 348
Sri Satguru Publications, pg 349
Somaiya Publications Pvt Ltd, pg 350
South Asian Publishers Pvt Ltd, pg 350
Sri Satguru Publications, pg 351

Italy
Adea Edizioni, pg 374
Adelphi Edizioni SpA, pg 374
Crisalide, pg 383
Edizioni Cultura della Pace, pg 383
Edizioni Il Punto d'Incontro SAS, pg 386
Hermes Edizioni SRL, pg 392
Luni, pg 397
Il Melangolo, pg 398
Il Punto D Incontro, pg 404
TEA Tascabili degli Editori Associati SpA, pg 409
Zanfi Editori SRL, pg 412

Japan
Chikuma Shobo Publishing Co Ltd, pg 415
Dohosha Publishing Co Ltd, pg 416
Hakutei-Sha, pg 417
Hyoronsha Publishing Co Ltd, pg 417
Kokusho Kankokai Co Ltd, pg 420
Kosei Publishing Co Ltd, pg 420
Nippon Hoso Shuppan Kyokai (NHK Publishing), pg 422
Rinsen Book Co Ltd, pg 424
Riso-Sha, pg 424
Sanshusha Publishing Co, Ltd, pg 424
Mitsumura Suiko Shoin, pg 426
Shufunotomo sha Co Ltd, pg 426
Toho Shuppan, pg 427
Tokyo Shoseki Co Ltd, pg 427

Republic of Korea
Koreaone Press Inc, pg 438
Seogwangsa, pg 440

Mauritius
Hemco Publications, pg 457

Mexico
Publicaciones Cruz O SA, pg 459
Phillip Richard Conover Lazo, pg 462
Plaza y Valdes SA de CV, pg 465

Netherlands
BZZTOH Publishers, pg 475
De Driehoek BV, pg 476
Hotei Publishing, pg 478
Servire BV Uitgevers, pg 484

New Zealand
Aspect Press, pg 488
Gnostic Press, pg 491

Portugal
Edicoes Manuel Lencastre, pg 526
Editorial Presenca, pg 528
Vega-Publicacao e Distribuicao de Livros e Revistas, Lda, pg 530

Romania
Editura Humanitas, pg 533
Humanitas Publishing House, pg 533

Russian Federation
Ladomir Publishing House, pg 539

Slovenia
Zalozba Mihelac d o o, pg 552

South Africa
Bet-El Publishers, pg 553

Spain
Editorial 'Alas', pg 562
Editorial Gulaab, pg 577
Mandala Ediciones, pg 581
Munoz Moya Editor, pg 583
Ediciones Siruela SA, pg 591
Editorial Thassalia, SA, pg 592

Sri Lanka
Buddhist Publication Society Inc, pg 596
Inter-Cultural Book Promoters, pg 597
Karunaratne & Sons Ltd, pg 597
Pradeepa Publishers, pg 598
Samayawardena Printers Publishers & Booksellers, pg 598
Somawathi Hewavitharana Fund, pg 598
Swarna Hansa Foundation, pg 598

Switzerland
Cockatoo Press (Schweiz), Thailand-Publikationen, pg 611
Garuda-Verlag, pg 614
Origo Verlag, pg 621
Theseus - Verlag AG, pg 625

Taiwan, Province of China
SMC Publishing Inc, pg 632
Torch of Wisdom, pg 632
Zen Now Press, pg 632

Thailand
Thai Watana Panich Co, Ltd, pg 636

United Kingdom
Arthur James Ltd, pg 649
Blackstaff Press, pg 655
The Eurospan Group, pg 680

1067

Janus Publishing Company Ltd, pg 702
Motilal (UK) Books of India, pg 715
Oneworld Publications, pg 721
Routledge Curzon, pg 736
Textile & Art Publications Ltd, pg 748
Tharpa Publications, pg 748
Windhorse Publications, pg 757

RELIGION - CATHOLIC

Argentina
Bonum Editorial SACl, pg 4
Editorial Claretiana, pg 4
Ediciones Don Bosco Argentina, pg 5
Editorial Ciudad Nueva de la Sefoma, pg 5
Errepar SA, pg 5
Gram Editora, pg 6
Editorial Guadalupe, pg 6
San Pablo, pg 8
Theoria SRL Distribuidora y Editora, pg 9

Australia
Ashling Books, pg 12
Bible Society in Australia National Headquarters, pg 15
Catholic Institute of Sydney, pg 17
Instauratio Press, pg 27
Jesuit Publications, pg 28
Little Red Apple Publishing, pg 30
Newman Centre Publications, pg 35
Protestant Publications, pg 39
St Joseph Publications, pg 41
St Pauls, pg 41
Shakespeare Head Press Pty Ltd, pg 42
Spectrum Publications, pg 43

Austria
Ennsthaler GesmbH & Co KG, pg 51
Herold Druck-und Verlagsgesellschaft mbH, pg 52
Verlag St Gabriel, pg 58
Andreas Schnider Verlags-Atelier, pg 58
Edition Va Bene, pg 60
Wiener Dom-Verlag GmbH, pg 61

Belgium
Artel SC, pg 64
Averbode Publishers, pg 64
Editions Gerard Blanchart & Cie SA, pg 65
Dessain - Departement de De Boeck & Larcier SA, pg 68
Editions Lessius ASBL, pg 71
Licap CVBA, pg 71
Editions Lumen Vitae ASBL, pg 71
Pelckmans NV, De Nederlandsche Boekhandel, pg 73

Bolivia
Editorial Don Bosco, pg 76

Brazil
Editora Cidade Nova Societa de Movimentodos Focolari, pg 82
EDUSC - Editora da Universidade do Sagrado Coracao, pg 82
Horus Editora Ltda, pg 85
Edit Palavra Magica, pg 89
Pallas Editora e Distribuidora Ltda, pg 89
Paulinas Editorial, pg 89
Paulus Editora, pg 89
Raboni Editora Ltda, pg 90
Editora Santuario, pg 91

Chile
Congregacion Paulinas - Hijas de San Pablo, pg 100

Colombia
Consejo Episcopal Latinoamericano Celam, pg 111
Eurolibros Ltda, pg 111
Fundacion Universidad de la Sabana Ediciones Udes, pg 112

Costa Rica
Litografia Artex, SA, pg 116
Promesa, Ediciones, pg 116
Scout Interamericana, pg 117

Croatia
ALFA dd za izdavacke, graficke i trgovacke poslove, pg 118

Cuba
Editora Politica, pg 121

Czech Republic
Barrister & Principal, pg 123
Kalich SRO, pg 125
Karmelitanske Nakladatelstvi, pg 125
Portal Ltd, pg 127
Zvon, pg 129

Dominican Republic
Pontificia Universidad Catolica Madre y Maestra, pg 136

France
Actes Graphiques, pg 145
Adverbum SARL, pg 146
Les Editions de l'Atelier SA, pg 148
Les Ateliers d'Orion, pg 148
Editions des Beatitudes, Pneumatheque, pg 150
Societe Biblique Francaise, pg 150
BSI - ELOR Editions Jeunesse, pg 152
CERDIC-Publications, pg 153
Editions du Chalet, pg 154
Decanord, pg 158
Les Editions des Deux Coqs d'Or, pg 159
Droguet et Ardant, pg 160
Institut d'Etudes Augustiniennes, pg 163
Fac Editions, pg 163
Fata Morgana, pg 163
Editions du Feu Nouveau, pg 164
Les Editions Franciscaines SA, pg 165
Paul Geuthner Librairie Orientaliste, pg 166
Editions Jean Paul Gisserot, pg 166
Editions Grancher, pg 166
Editions Infrarouge, pg 169
Karthala Editions-Diffusion, pg 171
Lacour-Olle, pg 171
Le Laurier, pg 172
P Lethielleux Editions, pg 172
Letouzey et Ane Sarl, pg 172
Editions Mediaspaul, pg 175
Les Presses d'Ile-de-France Sarl, pg 181
Editions Le Sarment, pg 184
Editions du Seneve, pg 184
Siloe - Kerdore, pg 185
Editions Tardy SA, pg 187
Librairie Pierre Tequi et Editions Tequi, pg 187
La Vague a l'ame, pg 188
Pierre Zech Editeur, pg 189

Germany
Auer Verlag GmbH, pg 196
Belser Wissenschaftlicher Dienst, pg 200
Born-Verlag, pg 205
Bundes-Verlag GmbH, pg 208
Butzon & Bercker GmbH, pg 208
Deutscher EC-Verband, pg 214
Echter Wurzburg Frankische Gesellschaftsdruckerei und Verlag GmbH, pg 220
Verlag am Eschbach GmbH, pg 224
Franz-Sales-Verlag, pg 229
Verlag Herder GmbH & Co KG, pg 239
Anton Hiersemann, Verlag, pg 240
Human Wissenschafilicher Verlag, pg 243
ludicium Verlag GmbH, pg 245
Johannes Verlag Einsiedeln, Freiburg, pg 246
Verlag Katholisches Bibelwerk GmbH, pg 248
Knowledge Media International, pg 251
W Kohlhammer GmbH, abt Haussortiment, pg 252
Lahn-Verlag GmbH, pg 255
Medien-Verlag Bernhard Gregor GmbH, pg 262
Missio eV Aachen, pg 264
Nusser Verlag, pg 269
Osho Verlag GmbH, pg 271
Verlag Parzeller GmbH & Co KG, pg 271
Verlag Friedrich Pustet GmbH & Co Kg, pg 276
Sankt Otto Verlag GmbH, pg 281
Verlag Schnell und Steiner GmbH, pg 284
Ferdinand Schoeningh Verlag GmbH, pg 284
Schwabenverlag Aktiengesellschaft, pg 285
Steyler Verlag, pg 290
Sueddeutsche Verlagsgesellschaft mbH, pg 291
Suin Buch-Verlag, pg 291
Verein der Benediktiner zu Beuron-Beuroner Kunstverlag, pg 297
Verlag fuer Wirtschaft & Verwaltung Hubert Wingen GmbH & Co KG, pg 303

Ghana
Frank Publishing Ltd, pg 307

Greece
Alamo Hellas, pg 308

Hungary
Agape Ferences Nyomda es Konyvkiado Kft, pg 323
Kossuth Kiado RT, pg 325
Marton Aron Kiado Publishing House, pg 325
Osiris Kiado, pg 326

Iceland
Katholska kirkjan a Islandi - Landakot Publishers Thorlakssjodur, pg 328

India
Asian Trading Corporation, pg 331
Satprakashan Sanchar Kendra, pg 349

Indonesia
Auroa, pg 354
Penerbit Nusa Indah, pg 356

Ireland
Campus Publishing Ltd, pg 359
Cathedral Books Ltd, pg 359
The Columba Book Service, pg 359
The Columba Press, pg 359
Dominican Publications, pg 359
Four Courts Press Ltd, pg 360
Mercier Press Ltd, pg 362

Italy
Verlagsanstalt Athesia, pg 377
Edizioni Bresciane, pg 378
Campanotto, pg 379
Edizioni Cantagalli, pg 379
Edizioni Carmelitane, pg 379
Casa Musicale Edizioni Carrara SRL, pg 379
Edizioni Carroccio, pg 379
Casa Editrice Felice Le Monnier, pg 380
Centro Editoriale Valtortiano SRL, pg 381
Cittadella Editrice, pg 382
Nuova Coletti Editore Roma, pg 382
Edizioni Cultura della Pace, pg 383
Edizioni Dehoniane Bologna (EDB), pg 384
Edizioni Il Punto d'Incontro SAS, pg 386
Edizioni la Scala, pg 387
Edizioni Qiqajon, pg 387
Edizioni Studio Domenicano (ESD), pg 387
Effata Editrice, pg 387
EFR-Editrici Francescane, pg 387
Elle Di Ci - Libreria Dottrina Cristiana, pg 388
Arnaldo Forni Editore SRL, pg 389
Biblioteca Francescana, pg 389
Piero Gribaudi Editore, pg 391
Herbita Editrice di Leonardo Palermo, pg 392
In Dialogo, pg 393
Ist Patristico Augustinianum, pg 394
Editoriale Jaca Book SpA, pg 394
Laruffa Editore SRL, pg 395
Editrice LAS, pg 395
Letture Mensile di Informazione Culturale, Letteratura e Spettacolo, pg 395
Casa Editrice Marietti SpA, pg 397
Editrice Massimo SAS di Crespi Cesare e C, pg 398
Il Melangolo, pg 398
Leo S Olschki, pg 402
Paideia Editrice, pg 402
Edizioni Piemme SpA, pg 403
Pontifico Istituto Orientale, pg 404
Editrice Queriniana, pg 404
Reverdito Edizioni, pg 405
Fausto Sardini Editrice, pg 407
Edizioni Segno SRL, pg 407
Segretariato Nazionale Apostolato della Preghiera, pg 407
Servitium, pg 408
Societa Editrice Internazionale - SEI, pg 408
TEA Tascabili degli Editori Associati SpA, pg 409
Edizioni del Teresianum, pg 409
Urbaniana University Press, pg 410

PUBLISHERS

Vivere In SRL, pg 411
Edizioni Zara, pg 412

Japan
Nippon Hoso Shuppan Kyokai (NHK Publishing), pg 422
Riso-Sha, pg 424
Salesian Press/Don Bosco Sha, pg 424
Shiko-Sha Co Ltd, pg 425

Kenya
Focus Publications Ltd, pg 431
Gaba Publications Amecea, Pastoral Institute, pg 431
Paulines Publications-Africa, pg 433
Shirikon Publishers, pg 433

Republic of Korea
St Pauls, pg 439
Seogwangsa, pg 440

Latvia
Spriditis Publishers, pg 442

Lebanon
Darl el-Machreq Sarl, pg 443
Librairie Orientale sal, pg 443

Lithuania
Andrena Publishers, pg 445
Vaga Ltd, pg 446

Malta
Gaulitana, pg 456
Media Centre, pg 456

Mauritius
Hemco Publications, pg 457

Mexico
Publicaciones Cruz O SA, pg 459
Editorial Diana SA de CV, pg 459
El Colegio de Michoacan A C, pg 460
Fernandez Editores SA de CV, pg 461
Editorial Jus SA de CV, pg 462
Editorial Limusa SA de CV, pg 463
Editorial Minutiae Mexicana SA, pg 464
Palabra Ediciones Verlagsgesellschaft mbH, pg 465
Editorial Progreso SA de C V, pg 466
Ediciones Promesa, SA de CV, pg 466

Netherlands
Katholieke Bijbelstichting, pg 479
Meinema, pg 481
Narratio Theologische Uitgeverij, pg 482

New Zealand
Catholic Supplies (NZ) LTD, pg 489

Nigeria
Riverside Communications, pg 501

Papua New Guinea
Melanesian Institute, pg 510

Peru
Asociacion Editorial Bruno, pg 511

Philippines
Anvil Publishing Inc, pg 512
Ateneo de Manila University Press, pg 512
De La Salle University, pg 513
New Day Publishers, pg 514
Our Lady of Manaoag Publisher, pg 514
Salesiana Publishers Inc, pg 515
Sinag-Tala Publishers Inc, pg 515
UST Publishing House, pg 515

Poland
Drukarnia I Ksiegarnia Swietego Wojciecha, Dziat Wydawniczy, pg 516
Impuls, pg 517
Instytut Wydawniczy Pax, Inco-Veritas, pg 517
Katolicki Uniwersytet Wydawniczo-Redakcja, pg 517
Norbertinum, pg 518
Pallottinum Wydawnictwo Stowarzyszenia Apostolstwa Katolickiego, pg 518
Rosikon Press, pg 519
Vocatio Publishing House, pg 520

Portugal
Biblioteca Geral da Universidade de Coimbra, pg 523
Edicoes Manuel Lencastre, pg 526
Nova Arrancada Sociedade Editora SA, pg 527
Edicoes Ora & Labora, pg 528
Paulinas, pg 528
Solivros, pg 529

Romania
Ars Longa Publishing House, pg 532
Editura Humanitas, pg 533
Humanitas Publishing House, pg 533
Pallas-Akademia Koenyvkiadoes Koenyvkereskedes, pg 535

Slovakia
Luc vydavatelske druzstvo, pg 550
Serafin, pg 550

Slovenia
Zalozba Mihelac d o o, pg 552

South Africa
Bet-El Publishers, pg 553

Spain
Publicacions de l'Abadia de Montserrat, pg 561
Editorial Aguaclara, pg 562
Editorial Bruno, pg 566
Editorial Casals SA, pg 566
Central Catequistica Salesiana (CCS), pg 567
Editora Comercial de Publicaciones, pg 568
Ediciones Cristiandad, pg 569
Editorial Deimos, SL, pg 569
Ediciones El Almendro de Cordoba, pg 571
Editorial Everest SA, pg 572
Editorial Esin, SA, pg 573
Vicent Garcia Editores, SA, pg 575
Ibaizabal Edelvives SA, pg 577
Loguez Ediciones, pg 580
Editorial Magisterio Espanol SA, pg 581
Editorial Mediterrania SL, pg 582
Editorial Monte Carmelo, pg 583
Mundo Negro Editorial, pg 583
Munoz Moya Editor, pg 583
Pages Editors, SL, pg 585
Editorial El Perpetuo Socorro, pg 586
Editorial Revista Agustiniana, pg 589
Ediciones San Pio X, pg 589
Secretariado Trinitario, pg 590
Ediciones Sigueme SA, pg 590
Ediciones Siruela SA, pg 591
Trotta SA Editorial, pg 593
Ediciones 29 - Libros Rio Nuevo, pg 594
Editorial Verbo Divino, pg 595

Sri Lanka
Inter-Cultural Book Promoters, pg 597

Switzerland
Benziger Verlag AG, pg 609
Verlag Bo Cavefors, pg 611
Christiana-Verlag, pg 611
Edition Exodus, pg 614
Jordanverlag AG, pg 616
Kanisius Verlag, pg 616
Kranich-Verlag, Dres AG & H R Bosch-Gwalter, pg 617
Neue Zeitschrift Missionswissenschaft Verlag, pg 620
NZN Buchverlag AG, pg 620
Editions du Parvis, pg 621
Rex Verlag, pg 623
Editions Saint Augustin, pg 623
Verlag Schweizerisches Katholisches Bibelwerk, pg 624

United Republic of Tanzania
Ndanda Mission Press, pg 634

United Kingdom
Arthur James Ltd, pg 649
Blackstaff Press, pg 655
Cassell & Co, pg 664
Church Union, pg 668
James Clarke & Co Ltd, pg 668
CTBI Publications, pg 672
Darton, Longman & Todd Ltd, pg 674
Eagle/Inter Publishing Service (IPS) Ltd, pg 676
The Eurospan Group, pg 680
Gresham Books Ltd, pg 690
Hodder & Stoughton Religious, pg 696
Incorporated Catholic Truth Society, pg 699
Institute of Irish Studies, The Queens University of Belfast, pg 699
Lion Publishing PLC, pg 708
Marcham Books, pg 711
McCrimmon Publishing Co Ltd, pg 712
Oneworld Publications, pg 721
SCM Press, pg 739
Colin Smythe Ltd, pg 743
The Society for Promoting Christian Knowledge (SPCK), pg 743
St Pauls Publishing, pg 744
Wild Goose Publications, pg 756

Venezuela
Fundacion Centro Gumilla, pg 762
Ediciones Tripode, pg 763

Yugoslavia
AGAPE, pg 764

SUBJECT INDEX

RELIGION - HINDU

Argentina
Errepar SA, pg 5
Editorial Kier SACIFI, pg 7

Australia
Oriental Publications, pg 36
Spectrum Publications, pg 43

Bangladesh
Bangladesh Publishers, pg 62

Belgium
Editions Lessius ASBL, pg 71

Brazil
Editora Bertrand Brasil Ltda, pg 79
Horus Editora Ltda, pg 85
Francisco J Laissue Livraria, pg 86

Bulgaria
Eurasia Academic Publishers, pg 95

France
Fata Morgana, pg 163
Paul Geuthner Librairie Orientaliste, pg 166
Langues & Mondes/L'Asiatheque, pg 171
L'Originel - Editions Accarias, pg 178
Pardes, pg 179

Germany
Adyar-Verlag, pg 191
Aquamarin Verlag, pg 194
BBT Bhaktivedanta Book Trust, pg 202
Eugen Diederichs Verlag GmbH & Co KG, pg 216
Ein Fach-Verlag, pg 222
Happy Mental Buch- und Musik Verlag, pg 237
Anton Hiersemann, Verlag, pg 240
F Hirthammer Verlag GmbH, pg 241
Nusser Verlag, pg 269
Osho Verlag GmbH, pg 271
Franz Steiner Verlag Wiesbaden GmbH, pg 289

India
Advaita Ashrama, pg 329
APH Publishing Corp, pg 331
Asian Educational Services, pg 331
Book Faith India, pg 333
Books & Books, pg 334
Brijbasi Printers Pvt Ltd, pg 334
Cosmo Publications, pg 335
Diamond Comics (P) Ltd, pg 336
DK Printworld (P) Ltd, pg 336
Dutta Baruah Publishing Co Pvt Ltd, pg 336
Ess Ess Publications, pg 337
Gyan Publishing House, pg 338
Indus Publishing Co, pg 339
B Jain Publishers (P) Ltd, pg 340
Law Publishers, pg 341
Sri Ramakrishna Math, pg 342
Minerva Associates (Publications) Pvt Ltd, pg 342
Munshiram Manoharlal Publishers Pvt Ltd, pg 343
Natraj Prakashan, pg 344
Navrang Booksellers & Publishers, pg 344
Oxford University Press, pg 345

Pitambar Publishing Co (P) Ltd, pg 346
Reliance Publishing House, pg 347
Roli Books Pvt Ltd, pg 348
SABDA, pg 348
Shaibya Prakashan Bibhag, pg 349
Somaiya Publications Pvt Ltd, pg 350
South Asian Publishers Pvt Ltd, pg 350
Star Publications (P) Ltd, pg 351
Sterling Publishers Pvt Ltd, pg 351
N M Tripathi Pvt Ltd, pg 352
Vakils Feffer & Simons Ltd, pg 352
S Viswanathan (Printers & Publishers) Pvt Ltd, pg 353

Indonesia
Bina Aksara Parta, pg 354

Italy
Adelphi Edizioni SpA, pg 374
Edizioni Cultura della Pace, pg 383
Edizioni Il Punto d'Incontro SAS, pg 386
Hermes Edizioni SRL, pg 392
Il Punto D Incontro, pg 404
TEA Tascabili degli Editori Associati SpA, pg 409

Japan
Nippon Hoso Shuppan Kyokai (NHK Publishing), pg 422

Republic of Korea
Seogwangsa, pg 440

Mauritius
Editions Capucines, pg 457
Hemco Publications, pg 457

Mexico
Ediciones Alpe, pg 458
Phillip Richard Conover Lazo, pg 462

Netherlands
BZZTOH Publishers, pg 475
Servire BV Uitgevers, pg 484

New Zealand
Gnostic Press, pg 491

Portugal
Edicoes Manuel Lencastre, pg 526

Romania
Editura Humanitas, pg 533
Humanitas Publishing House, pg 533

Russian Federation
Ladomir Publishing House, pg 539

South Africa
Bet-El Publishers, pg 553

Spain
Editorial Gulaab, pg 577
Mandala Ediciones, pg 581
Ediciones Siruela SA, pg 591
Editorial Thassalia, SA, pg 592

Sri Lanka
Inter-Cultural Book Promoters, pg 597

Switzerland
Govinda-Verlag, pg 615

United Kingdom
Arthur James Ltd, pg 649
Blackstaff Press, pg 655
The Eurospan Group, pg 680
Letterbox Library, pg 707
Mandrake of Oxford, pg 711
Motilal (UK) Books of India, pg 715
Oneworld Publications, pg 721
Ramakrishna Vedanta Centre, pg 732
Routledge Curzon, pg 736

RELIGION - ISLAMIC

Argentina
Editorial Kier SACIFI, pg 7

Australia
Oriental Publications, pg 36
Spectrum Publications, pg 43

Bangladesh
Gatidhara, pg 62
The University Press Ltd, pg 62

Belgium
Academia-Bruylant, pg 63

Bosnia and Herzegovina
Bemust doo Novinsko-Izdavacko stamparsko i trgovacko preduzece, pg 77

Brazil
Horus Editora Ltda, pg 85
Francisco J Laissue Livraria, pg 86

China
China Ocean Press, pg 103

Egypt (Arab Republic of Egypt)
Al Arab Publishing House, pg 138
Dar El Shorouk, pg 138
Dar El Shorouk Publishing & Distributing House, pg 138
Ummah Press for Translation & Publishing, pg 139

France
Berg International Editeurs, pg 150
CERDIC-Publications, pg 153
Editions de l'Eclat, pg 160
Fata Morgana, pg 163
Paul Geuthner Librairie Orientaliste, pg 166
Editions Grancher, pg 166
Editions du Jaguar, pg 170
Karthala Editions-Diffusion, pg 171
Letouzey et Ane Sarl, pg 172
Editions Verdier, pg 189

Germany
J J Augustin GmbH Verlag, pg 196
Dreisam Ratgeber in der Rutsker Verlag GmbH, pg 218
Erlanger Verlag Fuer Mission und Okumene, pg 223
Verlag Herder GmbH & Co KG, pg 239
Anton Hiersemann, Verlag, pg 240
Horlemann Verlag, pg 243
Verlag der Islam, pg 245
W Kohlhammer GmbH, abt Haussortiment, pg 252
Nusser Verlag, pg 269
Georg Olms Verlag AG, pg 270
Osho Verlag GmbH, pg 271
Franz Steiner Verlag Wiesbaden GmbH, pg 289

Greece
Alamo Hellas, pg 308

India
APH Publishing Corp, pg 331
Asian Educational Services, pg 331
Books & Books, pg 334
Cosmo Publications, pg 335
DK Printworld (P) Ltd, pg 336
Gyan Publishing House, pg 338
Islamic Publishing House, pg 340
Law Publishers, pg 341
Munshiram Manoharlal Publishers Pvt Ltd, pg 343
Roli Books Pvt Ltd, pg 348
Sterling Publishers Pvt Ltd, pg 351
Vakils Feffer & Simons Ltd, pg 352

Indonesia
PT Pustaka Antara Publishing & Printing, pg 354
Bina Rena Pariwara, pg 354
P T Bulan Bintang, pg 354
Bumi Aksara PT, pg 354
Mizan, pg 356

Israel
The Institute for Israeli Arabs Studies, pg 368

Italy
Arktos, pg 376
Edizioni Cultura della Pace, pg 383
Edizioni Il Punto d'Incontro SAS, pg 386
Jouvence, pg 394
Luni, pg 397
Casa Editrice Marietti SpA, pg 397
TEA Tascabili degli Editori Associati SpA, pg 409

Japan
Nippon Hoso Shuppan Kyokai (NHK Publishing), pg 422

Kenya
Life Challenge AFRICA, pg 433

Lebanon
Darl el-Machreq Sarl, pg 443
World Book Publishing, pg 443

Malaysia
S Abdul Majeed & Co, pg 451
Darulfikir, pg 451
Dewan Pustaka Islam, pg 451
Forum Publications, pg 452
Minerva Publications, pg 453
Pelanduk Publications (M) Sdn Bhd, pg 453
Penerbit Jayatinta Sdn Bhd, pg 454
Pustaka Cipta Sdn Bhd, pg 454
Pustaka Delta Pelajaran Sdn Bhd, pg 454

Maldive Islands
Non-Formal Education Centre, pg 455

Mauritius
Hemco Publications, pg 457

Morocco
Access International Services, pg 469
Editions Al-Fourkane, pg 469
Editions Le Fennec, pg 470
Editions La Porte, pg 470
Societe Ennewrasse Service Librairie et Imprimerie, pg 470

Netherlands
Brill Academic Publishers, pg 475
Oriental Press BV (APA), pg 482
Philo Press-Van Heusden-Hissink & Co CV (APA), pg 482
Servire BV Uitgevers, pg 484

New Zealand
Gnostic Press, pg 491

Pakistan
Sheikh Shaukat Ali & Sons, pg 506
Ferozsons (Private) Ltd, pg 506
H I Jaffari & Co Publishers, pg 506
Hamdard Foundation, pg 507
HMR Publishing Co, pg 507
Institute of Islamic Culture, pg 507
International Institute of Islamic Thought, pg 507
Islamic Publications (Pvt) Ltd, pg 507
Jang Publishers, pg 507
Malik Sirajuddin & Sons, pg 507
Maqbool Academy, pg 508
Nashiran-e-Quran Pvt Ltd, pg 508
National Book Foundation, pg 508
Pakistan Institute of Development Economics, pg 508
Sh Ghulam Ali & Sons (Pvt) Ltd, pg 509
Vanguard Books Ltd, pg 509
West-Pakistan Publishing Co (Pvt) Ltd, pg 509

Portugal
Edicoes Manuel Lencastre, pg 526

Romania
Editura Humanitas, pg 533
Humanitas Publishing House, pg 533

Russian Federation
Ladomir Publishing House, pg 539

Saudi Arabia
Asam Establishment for Publishing & Distribution, pg 543
Dar Al-Shareff for Publishing & Distribution, pg 543

Singapore
Pustaka Nasional Pte Ltd, pg 547

South Africa
Bet-El Publishers, pg 553

Spain
Calamo Editorial, pg 566
Ediciones Hiperion SL, pg 577
Mandala Ediciones, pg 581
Ediciones del Oriente y del Mediterraneo, pg 585
Editora Regional de Murcia - ERM, pg 588
Ediciones Siruela SA, pg 591

Editorial Thassalia, SA, pg 592
Trotta SA Editorial, pg 593

Sri Lanka
Inter-Cultural Book Promoters, pg 597

Syrian Arab Republic
Damascus University Press, pg 628
Institut Francais d'Etudes Arabes de Damas, pg 628

Tunisia
Academie Tunisienne des Sciences, des Lettres et des Arts Beit El Hekma, pg 637
Ceres Editions, pg 637
Dar El Afaq, pg 637
Maison Tunisienne de l'Edition, pg 638

Turkey
Cep Kitaplari AS, pg 639
Inkilap Publishers Ltd, pg 640
Kubbealti Akademisi Kultur ve Sasat Vakfi, pg 640
Oguz Yayinlari, pg 640
Ruh ve Madde Yayinlari ve Saglik Hizmetleri AS, pg 641

United Kingdom
Andromeda Oxford Ltd, pg 647
Blackstaff Press, pg 655
Darf Publishers Ltd, pg 674
Edinburgh University Press Ltd, pg 677
The Eurospan Group, pg 680
Garnet Publishing Ltd, pg 685
Islam International Publications Ltd, pg 701
Islamic Foundation Publications, pg 701
Letterbox Library, pg 707
Motilal (UK) Books of India, pg 715
The Octagon Press Ltd, pg 720
Oneworld Publications, pg 721
Routledge Curzon, pg 736
Stacey International, pg 745
I B Tauris & Co Ltd, pg 747
World of Islam Altajir Trust, pg 759

RELIGION - JEWISH

Argentina
Editorial Kier SACIFI, pg 7

Australia
Spectrum Publications, pg 43

Austria
Czernin Verlag, pg 50

Belgium
Editions Lessius ASBL, pg 71

Brazil
Editora Bertrand Brasil Ltda, pg 79
Horus Editora Ltda, pg 85
Francisco J Laissue Livraria, pg 86

China
China Ocean Press, pg 103

Czech Republic
Kalich SRO, pg 125
Zvon, pg 129

France
Les Ateliers d'Orion, pg 148
Berg International Editeurs, pg 150
CERDIC-Publications, pg 153
Editions de l'Eclat, pg 160
Fata Morgana, pg 163
Paul Geuthner Librairie Orientaliste, pg 166
Editions Grancher, pg 166
Editions G P Maisonneuve et Larose, pg 174
Mare Nostrum, pg 177
Service Technique pour l'Education, pg 185
Thames & Hudson, pg 187
Editions Verdier, pg 189

Germany
arani-Verlag GmbH, pg 194
Hans Christians Druckerei und Verlag GmbH & Co, pg 210
Verlag Darmstaedter Blaetter Schwarz und Co, pg 212
Dolling und Galitz Verlag GmbH, pg 217
Donat Verlag, pg 217
Harald Fischer Verlag GmbH, pg 228
Haude und Spenersche Verlagsbuchhandlung, pg 238
Edition Hentrich Druck & Verlag Gebr Hentrich und Tank GmbH & Co KG, pg 239
Anton Hiersemann, Verlag, pg 240
Juedischer Verlag GmbH, pg 247
W Kohlhammer GmbH, abt Haussortiment, pg 252
Roman Kovar Verlag, pg 253
Verlag Neues Leben GmbH, pg 268
Nusser Verlag, pg 269
Georg Olms Verlag AG, pg 270
Osho Verlag GmbH, pg 271
Prasenz Verlag der Jesus Bruderschaft eV, pg 274
Dr Ludwig Reichert Verlag, pg 278
Agora Verlag Manfred Schlosser, pg 283
Thauros Verlag GmbH, pg 293

Greece
Alamo Hellas, pg 308

India
Roli Books Pvt Ltd, pg 348

Israel
Agudat Sabah, pg 365
Bar Ilan University Press, pg 365
Ben-Zvi Institute, pg 365
The Bialik Institute, pg 365
Breslov Research Institute, pg 366
Dvir Publishing Ltd, pg 366
Eretz Hemdah Institute for Advanced Jewish Studies, pg 367
Eshkol Books Publishers & Printing Ltd, pg 367
The Arnold & Leona Finkler Institute of Holocaust Research, pg 367
Gefen Publishing House Ltd, pg 367
Habermann Institute for Literary Research, pg 367
Hakibbutz Hameuchad Publishing House Ltd, pg 368
The Israel Academy of Sciences & Humanities, pg 368
The Jerusalem Publishing House Ltd, pg 369
Koren Publishers Jerusalem Ltd, pg 369
L B Publishing Co, pg 369
Maaliyot-Institute for Research Publications, pg 370
Massada Press Ltd, pg 370
Misgav Yerushalayim, pg 370
Modan Publishers Ltd, pg 371
Nehora Press, pg 371
Open University of Israel, pg 371
Pitspopany Press, pg 371
Rav Kook Institute, pg 371
Rubin Mass Ltd, pg 371
Schlesinger Institute, pg 372
Schocken Publishing House Ltd, pg 372
Sinai Publishing Co, pg 372
Talmudic Encyclopedia Publications, pg 372
University Publishing Projects Ltd, pg 373
Urim Publications, pg 373
Yad Izhak Ben-Zvi Press, pg 373
Yavneh Publishing House Ltd, pg 373
Yedioth Ahronoth Books, pg 373
Y L Peretz Publishing Co, pg 374
The Zalman Shazar Center, pg 374

Italy
Belforte Editore Libraio srl, pg 377
Edizioni Cultura della Pace, pg 383
Editrice la Giuntina, pg 386
Edizioni Qiqajon, pg 387
Piero Gribaudi Editore, pg 391
Casa Editrice Marietti SpA, pg 397
Il Melangolo, pg 398
Leo S Olschki, pg 402
Paideia Editrice, pg 402
TEA Tascabili degli Editori Associati SpA, pg 409

Japan
Myrtos Inc, pg 421
Nippon Hoso Shuppan Kyokai (NHK Publishing), pg 422

Mexico
Publicaciones Cruz O SA, pg 459

Netherlands
Erven J Bijleveld, pg 474
Brill Academic Publishers, pg 475
BZZTOH Publishers, pg 475
Philo Press-Van Heusden-Hissink & Co CV (APA), pg 482
Servire BV Uitgevers, pg 484

New Zealand
Barkfire Press, pg 488
Outrigger Publishers, pg 494

Romania
Editura Humanitas, pg 533
Humanitas Publishing House, pg 533

South Africa
Bet-El Publishers, pg 553
Witwatersrand University Press, pg 560

Spain
Ediciones El Almendro de Cordoba, pg 571
Ediciones Hiperion SL, pg 577
Munoz Moya Editor, pg 583
Ediciones Siruela SA, pg 591
Trotta SA Editorial, pg 593

Sri Lanka
Inter-Cultural Book Promoters, pg 597

Sweden
Hillelforlaget, pg 603

Switzerland
Victor Goldschmidt Verlagsbuchhandlung, pg 615
ISIOM Verlag fur Tondokumente, Weinreb Tonarchiv, pg 616
Origo Verlag, pg 621

United Kingdom
Andromeda Oxford Ltd, pg 647
Arthur James Ltd, pg 649
Berghahn Books Ltd, pg 654
Blackstaff Press, pg 655
The Eurospan Group, pg 680
Peter Halban Publishers Ltd, pg 691
Harvard University Press, pg 692
Janus Publishing Company Ltd, pg 702
Letterbox Library, pg 707
The Littman Library of Jewish Civilization, pg 708
Oneworld Publications, pg 721
Polo Publishing, pg 729
Routledge Curzon, pg 736
SCM Press, pg 739
Sheffield Academic Press Ltd, pg 741
Vallentine, Mitchell & Co Ltd, pg 752
Yale University Press London, pg 759

RELIGION - PROTESTANT

Australia
Aletheia Publishing, pg 11
Aquila Press, pg 11
Aussies Afire Publishing, pg 13
Bible Society in Australia National Headquarters, pg 15
Bridgeway Publications, pg 16
Covenanter Press, pg 19
Crossroad Distributors Pty Ltd, pg 19
Jesuit Publications, pg 28
Matthias Media, pg 32
Openbook Publishers, pg 35
PCE Press, pg 37
Protestant Publications, pg 39
Spectrum Publications, pg 43
Uniting Education, pg 45

Belgium
Editions Gerard Blanchart & Cie SA, pg 65

Brazil
Ars Poetica Editora Ltda, pg 79
Alzira Chagas Carpigiani, pg 80
Koinonia Comunidade Edicoes Ltda (Editora Koinonia Ltda), pg 86
Editora Mundo Cristao, pg 88
Editora Vida Crista Ltda, pg 93

Cameroon
Editions Buma Kor, pg 99
Editions CLE, pg 99

Costa Rica
Scout Interamericana, pg 117

SUBJECT INDEX

Cote d'Ivoire
Centre de Publications Evangeliques, pg 117

Croatia
Znaci Vremena, Institut Za Istrazivanje Biblije, pg 120

Czech Republic
Kalich SRO, pg 125

Denmark
J Frimodts Forlag, pg 132
Samfundslitteratur, pg 135
Unitas Forlag, pg 136

Finland
Aika Oy Kristilliset Kirjat, pg 141
Akateeminen Kustannusliike Oy, pg 141
Foersamlingsfoerbundets Foerlags AB, pg 142
Herattaja-yhdistys Ry, pg 142
Karas-Sana Oy, pg 142
Kirjatoimi, pg 143
Lasten Keskus Oy, pg 143
Paiva Osakeyhtio, pg 144

France
Societe Biblique Francaise, pg 150
CERDIC-Publications, pg 153
Editions Farel, pg 163
Librairie Fischbacher, International Art Book Distribution (import-export), pg 164
Paul Geuthner Librairie Orientaliste, pg 166
Editions Jean Paul Gisserot, pg 166
Editions Grancher, pg 166
Karthala Editions-Diffusion, pg 171
Lacour-Olle, pg 171
LLB France (Ligue pour la Lecture de la Bible), pg 173

Germany
Agentur des Rauhen Hauses Hamburg GmbH, pg 192
AUE-Verlag GmbH, pg 196
Aussaat Verlag, pg 197
Born-Verlag, pg 205
Christusbruderschaft Selbitz ev, Abt Verlag, pg 210
Claudius Verlag, pg 211
Deutscher EC-Verband, pg 214
Verlagsgesellschaft des Erziehungsvereins GmbH, pg 224
Verlag am Eschbach, pg 224
Evangelische Verlagsanstalt GmbH, pg 225
Evangelischer Presseverband STET Baden eVerlag, pg 225
Friedrich Frommann Verlag, pg 230
Verlag Junge Gemeinde E Schwinghammer GmbH & Co KG, pg 231
Grass-Verlag, pg 234
Guetersloher Verlagshaus Gerd Mohn, pg 235
Verlag des Gustav-Adolf-Werks, pg 235
Anton Hiersemann, Verlag, pg 240
Human Wissenschafilicher Verlag, pg 243
Johannis, pg 246
Verlag Ernst Kaufmann GmbH, pg 248
Knowledge Media International, pg 251
W Kohlhammer GmbH, abt Haussortiment, pg 252

Verlag Otto Lembeck, pg 257
Logos Verlag GmbH, pg 258
Luther-Verlag GmbH, pg 259
Mohr Siebeck, pg 264
Nusser Verlag, pg 269
Georg Olms Verlag AG, pg 270
One Way Medien OHG, pg 270
Osho Verlag GmbH, pg 271
Pahl-Rugenstein Verlag Nachfolger-GmbH, pg 271
Verlag Parzeller GmbH & Co KG, pg 271
Verlag der Sankt-Johannis-Druckerei C Schweickhardt, pg 281
Verlag Schnell und Steiner GmbH, pg 284
Sternberg-Verlag bei Ernst Franz, pg 290
Suin Buch-Verlag, pg 291
Guenter Albert Ulmer Verlag, pg 295
Verein der Benediktiner zu Beuron-Beuroner Kunstverlag, pg 297

Ghana
Asempa Publishers, pg 306
Frank Publishing Ltd, pg 307
Ghana Institute of Linguistics Literacy & Bible Translation (GILLBT), pg 307

Greece
Alamo Hellas, pg 308
Logos, pg 312

Hong Kong
Chinese Christian Literature Council Ltd, pg 318
Christian Communications Ltd, pg 319
Federal Publications Ltd, pg 319
Philopsychy Press, pg 321

Hungary
Advent Kiado, pg 323
Osiris Kiado, pg 326

Indonesia
Advent Indonesia Publishing, pg 353
Auroa, pg 354

Ireland
Campus Publishing Ltd, pg 359
The Columba Book Service, pg 359
The Columba Press, pg 359

Italy
Centro Biblico, pg 380
Claudiana Editrice, pg 382
Edizioni Cultura della Pace, pg 383
Edizioni Qiqajon, pg 387
Paideia Editrice, pg 402

Japan
AVACO - Christian Mass Communications Center, pg 414
Myrtos Inc, pg 421
Nippon Hoso Shuppan Kyokai (NHK Publishing), pg 422
Shiko-Sha Co Ltd, pg 425

Kenya
Evangel Publishing House, pg 431
Lake Publishers & Enterprises Ltd, pg 432
Nairobi University Press, pg 433
Shirikon Publishers, pg 433

Sudan Literature Centre, pg 433
Uzima Press, pg 433

Republic of Korea
Chung Rim Publishing Co Ltd, pg 435
Kukmin Doseo Publishing Co Inc, pg 438
Word of Life Press, pg 440

Latvia
Patmos, pg 442
Spriditis Publishers, pg 442

Lithuania
Svietimo ir mokslo ministerijos Leidybos centras, pg 446

Madagascar
Maison d'Edition Protestante ANTSO, pg 450

Mexico
Ediciones CUPSA, Centro de Comunicacion Cultural CUPSA, AC, pg 459

Netherlands
Ark Boeken Publishing House, pg 473
Boekencentrum BV, pg 474
Uitgeverij G F Callenbach BV, pg 475
Meinema, pg 481
Narratio Theologische Uitgeverij, pg 482
Servire BV Uitgevers, pg 484
Telos Boeken, pg 485
Uitgeverij De Vuurbaak BV, pg 487

New Zealand
Words Work, pg 497

Nigeria
Riverside Communications, pg 501
Vantage Publishers International Ltd, pg 502

Norway
Genesis Forlag, pg 503
Luther Forlag A/S, pg 504

Papua New Guinea
Kristen Pres, pg 510
Melanesian Institute, pg 510
Nazarene Publications, pg 510

Philippines
New Day Publishers, pg 514
Philippine Baptist Mission SBC FMB Church Growth International, pg 514

Poland
Vocatio Publishing House, pg 520

Singapore
Tecman Bible House, pg 549

South Africa
Bet-El Publishers, pg 553
Educum Publishers Ltd, pg 554
Human & Rousseau (Pty) Ltd, pg 555

Institute for Reformational Studies CHE, pg 555
The Methodist Publishing House, pg 557

Spain
Editorial Clie, pg 568
Editorial Peregrino SL, pg 586
Ediciones Sigueme SA, pg 590

Sri Lanka
Calvary Press, pg 596
Inter-Cultural Book Promoters, pg 597

Sweden
Forlaget Sanctus (Metodistkyrkans Forlag), pg 602

Switzerland
Benziger Verlag AG, pg 609
Berchtold Haller Verlag, pg 609
Bibellesbund Verlag, pg 610
Blaukreuz-Verlag Bern, pg 610
Edition Exodus, pg 614
Jordanverlag AG, pg 614
Jugend mit einer Mission Verlag, pg 616
Kranich-Verlag, Dres AG & H R Bosch-Gwalter, pg 617
La Maison de la Bible, pg 618
Raphael, Editions, pg 622

Taiwan, Province of China
Campus Evangelical Fellowship, Literature Department, pg 629

United Republic of Tanzania
Central Tanganyika Press, pg 633
Kanisa la Biblia Publishers (KLB), pg 633
Northwestern Publishers, pg 634

United Kingdom
Arthur James Ltd, pg 649
The Banner of Truth Trust, pg 652
McCall Barbour, pg 652
Bible Reading Fellowship, pg 654
Blackstaff Press, pg 655
Bryntirion Press, pg 661
Cassell & Co, pg 664
Chapter Two, pg 666
Christian Education, pg 667
Christian Focus Publications Ltd, pg 667
Church Society, pg 668
Church Union, pg 668
James Clarke & Co Ltd, pg 668
Crossbridge Books, pg 672
CTBI Publications, pg 672
Cyhoeddiadau'r Gair, pg 673
Darton, Longman & Todd Ltd, pg 674
Eagle/Inter Publishing Service (IPS) Ltd, pg 676
The Eurospan Group, pg 680
Evangelical Press & Services Ltd, pg 680
Gresham Books Ltd, pg 690
Highland Books Ltd, pg 695
Hodder & Stoughton Religious, pg 696
Angus Hudson Ltd, pg 697
Institute of Irish Studies, The Queens University of Belfast, pg 699
Kingsway Publications, pg 705
Letterbox Library, pg 707
Lion Publishing PLC, pg 708
The Lutterworth Press, pg 709

PUBLISHERS   SUBJECT INDEX

Marcham Books, pg 711
Methodist Publishing House, pg 714
Monarch Books, pg 715
Moorley's Print & Publishing Ltd, pg 715
Oneworld Publications, pg 721
Sage Publications Ltd, pg 737
Saint Andrew Press, pg 737
SCM Press, pg 739
Scottish Text Society, pg 740
Scripture Union, pg 740
The Society for Promoting Christian Knowledge (SPCK), pg 743
Sovereign World Ltd, pg 744
Sutton Publishing Ltd, pg 746
Tuckwell Press Ltd, pg 750
Wild Goose Publications, pg 756

Zimbabwe
Vision Publications, pg 769

RELIGION - OTHER

Afghanistan
Book Publishing Institute, pg 1

Algeria
Enterprise Nationale du Livre (ENAL), pg 2

Argentina
Amorrortu Editores SA, pg 3
Asociacion Bautista Argentina de Publicaciones, pg 3
Bonum Editorial SACI, pg 4
Club de Lectores, pg 4
Errepar SA, pg 5
Gram Editora, pg 6
Editorial Kier SACIFI, pg 7
Ediciones Lidiun, pg 7
Editora Patria Grande, pg 8
Editorial Planeta Argentina SAIC, pg 8
Editorial Troquel SA, pg 9

Australia
Aletheia Publishing, pg 11
Anzea Publishers Ltd, pg 11
Desbooks Pty Ltd, pg 20
E J Dwyer (Australia) Pty Ltd, pg 21
Freshet Press, pg 23
John Garratt Publishing, pg 24
Gnostic Editions, pg 24
Hahndorf Academy Foundation Inc, pg 24
Jesuit Publications, pg 28
Kingsclear Books, pg 29
Little Red Apple Publishing, pg 30
Barry Long Books, pg 30
Lowden Publishing Co, pg 31
Magabala Books Aboriginal Corporation, pg 31
Mission Publications of Australia, pg 33
Openbook Publishers, pg 35
Pan Pacific Publications, pg 37
Plantain Park, pg 38
The Polding Press, pg 38
Rainbow Book Agencies Pty Ltd, pg 39
Shakespeare Head Press Pty Ltd, pg 42
Unity Press, pg 46
Vital Publications, pg 47

Austria
Carinthia Verlag, pg 50
CEEBA Publications Antenne d'Autriche, pg 50

Cura Verlag GmbH, pg 50
Development News Ltd, pg 51
Otto Mueller Verlag GesmbH & Co KG, pg 55
Mueller-Speiser Wissenschaftlicher Verlag, pg 55
Oesterreichisches Katholisches Bibelwerk, pg 56
Verlag Sankt Peter, pg 57
Andreas Schnider Verlags-Atelier, pg 58
J Steinbrener OHG, pg 59
Verlag Styria, pg 59
Edition Tau u Tau Type Druck Verlags-und Handels GmbH, pg 59
Tyrolia Verlagsanstalt GmbH, pg 59

Belarus
Belaruskaya Encyklapedyya, pg 63

Belgium
Acco CV, pg 64
Aurelia Books PVBA, pg 64
NV Uitgeverij Altiora Averbode, pg 64
Maison d'Editions Baha'ies ASBL, pg 64
Editions Gerard Blanchart & Cie SA, pg 65
Brepols Publishers NV, pg 65
Carmelitana VZW, pg 65
Centre d'Action Laique, pg 66
Davidsfonds VZW, pg 67
Imprimerie Hayez SPRL, pg 69
Infoboek NV, pg 69
Editions Lampe d'Or ASBL, pg 70
Uitgeverij Lannoo NV, pg 70
Editeurs de Litterature Biblique, pg 71
Uitgeverij Peeters Leuven (Belgie), pg 72
Uitgeverij Pelckmans N V, pg 73
Henri Proost & Co, Pvba, pg 73
Sonneville Press (Uitgeverij) VTW, pg 74
Unistad Verspreiding CV, pg 75
Imprimeur - Editeur Vaillant-Carmanne SA, pg 75
Les Editions Vie ouvriere ASBL, pg 75

Brazil
Associacao Palas Athena do Brasil, pg 79
Editora Betania S/C, pg 79
Concordia Editora Ltda, pg 81
Livraria Duas Cidades Ltda, pg 81
Editora Elevacao, pg 82
Fundacao Cultural Avatar, pg 83
Ordem do Graal na Terra, pg 84
Editora e Grafica Carisio Ltda, pg 84
Horus Editora Ltda, pg 85
Livro Ibero-Americano Ltda, pg 85
Junta de Educacao Religiosa e Publicacoes da Convencao Batista Brasileira (JUERP), pg 85
Editora Kuarup Ltda, pg 86
Edicoes Loyola SA, pg 87
Editora Mercuryo Ltda, pg 88
Edit Palavra Magica, pg 89
Pallas Editora e Distribuidora Ltda, pg 89
Editora Perspectiva, pg 89
Petit Editora e Distribuidora Ltda, pg 89
Casa Editora Presbiteriana S.C., pg 90
Editora Rideel Ltda, pg 90
Editora Scipione Ltda, pg 91
Editora Sinodal, pg 91

Sobrindes Linha Grafica E Editora Ltda, pg 91
Editora Vecchi SA, pg 93
Editora Verbo Ltda, pg 93
Vozes Editora Ltda, pg 93

Bulgaria
Bilblioteka Nov den - Sajuz na Svobodnite Demokrati (Union of Free Democrats), pg 94
Kibea Publishing Co, pg 96
Pensoft Publishers, pg 97
Pet Plus, pg 97
Prozoretz Ltd Publishing House, pg 97
Sinodalno Izdatelstvo, pg 98

Cameroon
Editions Semences Africaines, pg 99

Chile
Editorial Patris SA, pg 101
Pontificia Universidad Catolica de Chile, pg 101

The Democratic Republic of the Congo
Centre Protestant d'Editions et de Diffusion (CEDI), pg 115
Presses Universitaires du Zaiire (PUZ), pg 115
Editions Saint Paul-Afrique, pg 115

Cote d'Ivoire
Centre de Publications Evangeliques, pg 117
Les Nouvelles Editions Africaines, pg 118

Croatia
Krscanska sadasnjost, pg 119

Cuba
Editora Politica, pg 121

Czech Republic
Inspirace, pg 124
Kalich SRO, pg 125
Karolinum, nakladatelstvi, pg 125
Knihovna A Tiskarna Pro Nevidome, pg 125
Luxpress VOS, pg 126
Vysehrad, pg 129
Zvon, pg 129

Denmark
Aarhus Universitetsforlag, pg 129
Borgens Forlag A/S, pg 130
Lohses Forlag, pg 133
Museum Tusculanum Press, pg 134
Nyt Nordisk Forlag Arnold Busck A/S, pg 134
Systime, pg 136

Egypt (Arab Republic of Egypt)
Al Arab Publishing House, pg 138
Middle East Book Centre, pg 139
Senouhy Publishers, pg 139

El Salvador
UCA Editores, pg 139

Fiji
Lotu Pacifika Productions, pg 141

Finland
Kustannus Oy Uusi Tie, pg 143
Kuva ja Sana, pg 143
Paiva Osakeyhtio, pg 144
Soederstroem et Co Foerlagsaktiebolag, pg 144

France
Actes Graphiques, pg 145
Editions Albin Michel, pg 146
Alsatia SA, pg 146
ALTESS Editions Argel, pg 146
Editions d'Amerique et d'Orient, Adrien Maisonneuve, pg 147
Editions Amrita SA, pg 147
Ateliers et Presses de Taize, pg 148
Editions Aubier-Montaigne SA, pg 149
Bayard Presse - Department Livre, pg 149
Beauchesne Editeur, pg 150
Societe d'Edition Les Belles Lettres, pg 150
Berg International Editeurs, pg 150
De Boccard Edition-Diffusion, pg 151
Editions Buchet/Chastel, pg 152
CERDIC-Publications, pg 153
Editions du Cerf, pg 153
Editions du Chalet, pg 154
Chronique Sociale, pg 155
CLD, pg 155
CNRS Editions, pg 155
Editions de Compostelle, pg 156
Cooperative Regionale de l'Enseignement Religieux (CRER), pg 156
Copernic, pg 156
Courrier du Livre Sarl, pg 157
Nouvelles Editions Debresse, pg 158
Dervy-Livres, pg 158
Desclee de Brouwer SA, pg 158
Desclee et Cie, Editeurs, pg 159
Les Editions des Deux Coqs d'Or, pg 159
Les Editeurs Reunis, pg 161
Fata Morgana, pg 163
Librairie Artheme Fayard, pg 163
Editions du Feu Nouveau, pg 164
Groupe Fleurus-Mame, pg 164
J Gabalda et Cie (Librairie Lecoffre) SA, pg 165
Editions Grancher, pg 166
Lacour-Olle, pg 171
Editions Fernand Lanore Sarl, pg 172
Letouzey et Ane Sarl, pg 172
Maison de la Revelation, pg 174
Nouvelle Cite, pg 178
Nouvelles Editions Latines, pg 178
Editions de l'Orante, pg 178
L'Originel - Editions Accarias, pg 178
Editions Payot & Rivages, pg 179
Editions A et J Picard SA, pg 179
Presence Africaine Editions, pg 180
Presses Universitaires de France (PUF), pg 181
Presses Universitaires de Nancy, pg 181
Editions Prosveta SA, pg 182
Editions Saint-Paul SA, pg 183
Editions Salvator Sarl, pg 183
Maren Sell, pg 184
Service Technique pour l'Education, pg 185
Editions du Seuil, pg 185
Editions SOS (Editions du Secours Catholique), pg 186
Editions Louis Soulanges Le Livrer Ouvert, pg 186

1073

SUBJECT INDEX

Les Editions de la Source Sarl, pg 186
Les Editions de la Table Ronde, pg 187
Tacor International, pg 187
Editions Tardy SA, pg 187
Editions Vilo SA, pg 189
Librairie Philosophique J Vrin, pg 189
YMCA-Press, pg 189

Germany

Abakus Musik Barbara Fietz, pg 191
Agentur des Rauhen Hauses Hamburg GmbH, pg 192
Ardey-Verlag GmbH, pg 194
Arun-Verlag, pg 195
Aschendorffsche Verlagsbuchhandlung GmbH & Co KG, pg 195
AUE-Verlag GmbH, pg 196
Augustinus-Verlag Wurzburg Inh Augustinerprovinz, pg 196
Aurum Verlag GmbH, pg 197
Aussaat Verlag, pg 197
Baha'i Verlag GmbH, pg 198
Otto Wilhelm Barth-Verlag KG, pg 198
Bettendorf'sche Verlagsanstalt GmbH, pg 202
BBT Bhaktivedanta Book Trust, pg 202
Biblio-Zeller Verlag, pg 202
BKV-Brasilienkunde Verlag GmbH, pg 203
Breklumer Buchhandlung und Verlag, pg 206
Joh & Sohn Brendow Verlag GmbH, pg 206
R Brockhaus Verlag, pg 206
Brunnen-Verlag GmbH, pg 207
Burckhardthaus-Laetare Verlag GmbH, pg 208
Calwer Verlag Stuttgart eV, pg 209
Centaurus-Verlagsgesellschaft GmbH, pg 209
Chr Belser AG fur Verlagsgeschaefte und Co KG, pg 210
Christliche Verlagsgesellschaft mbH, pg 210
Christliches Verlagshaus GmbH, pg 210
Claudius Verlag, pg 211
Concordia-Buchhandlung & Verlag, pg 211
Connection Medien GmbH, pg 211
Verlag CSA Rosemarie Schneider, pg 212
Verlag Deutsche Unitarier, pg 214
Deutscher Taschenbuch Verlag GmbH & Co KG (dtv), pg 215
Diagonal-Verlag GbR Rink-Schweer, pg 216
Eugen Diederichs Verlag GmbH & Co KG, pg 216
Dieterichsche Verlagsbuchhandlung Mainz, pg 216
Divyanand Verlags GmbH, pg 217
Dolling und Galitz Verlag GmbH, pg 217
Don Bosco Verlag, pg 217
Echter Wurzburg Frankische Gesellschaftsdruckerei und Verlag GmbH, pg 220
N G Elwert Verlag, pg 222
EOS Verlag der Benefiktiner der Erzabtei St. Ottilien, pg 223
ERF-Verlag GmbH, pg 223
Erlanger Verlag Fuer Mission und Okumene, pg 223

Verlag Esoterische Philosophie GmbH, pg 224
Evangelische Verlagsanstalt GmbH, pg 225
Flensburger Hefte Verlag GmbH, pg 228
Verlag Freies Geistesleben, pg 230
Freimund-Verlag der Gesellschaft fur Innere und Aeussere Mission im Sinne der Lutherischen Kirche eV, pg 230
Gerth, Klaus, Verlag GmbH, pg 232
Verlag der Stiftung Gralsbotschaft GmbH, pg 234
Guetersloher Verlagshaus Gerd Mohn, pg 235
Gutersloher Verlaghaus GmbH /Chr Kaiser/Kiefel/Quell, pg 235
Haenssler Verlag GmbH, pg 236
Heigl Verlag, Horst Edition, pg 239
Verlag Herder GmbH & Co KG, pg 239
Anton Hiersemann, Verlag, pg 240
Verlag Hinder und Deelmann, pg 241
F Hirthammer Verlag GmbH, pg 241
Heinrich Hugendubel Verlag GmbH, pg 243
Verlag J P Peter, Gebr Holstein GmbH & Co KG, pg 246
Katzmann Verlag KG, pg 248
Verlag Ernst Kaufmann GmbH, pg 248
Kindler Verlag GmbH, pg 249
Klens Verlag GmbH, pg 250
Knowledge Media International, pg 251
Koesel-Verlag GmbH & Co, pg 252
W Kohlhammer GmbH, abt Haussortiment, pg 252
Koptisch-Orthodoxes Zentrum, pg 252
Dr Anton Kovac Slavica Verlag, pg 253
Alfred Kroner Verlag, pg 253
Leibniz-Buecherwarte, pg 257
Verlag Otto Lembeck, pg 257
Leuchter-Verlag EG, pg 257
Edition Libri Illustri GmbH, pg 257
Lorber-Verlag & Turm-Verlag Otto Zluhan, pg 259
Lutherisches Verlagshaus GmbH, pg 260
Matthias-Gruenewald-Verlag GmbH, pg 261
Missio eV Aachen, pg 264
Mohr Siebeck, pg 264
Morus-Verlag GmbH, pg 265
Mueller & Schindler Verlag, pg 265
Neue Dimension Buch-und Musik-Verlag, pg 267
Verlag Neue Stadt GmbH, pg 267
New Era Publications Deutschland GmbH, pg 268
Nie/Nie/Sagen-Verlag, pg 268
Hans-Nietsch-Verlag, pg 269
Edition Octopus & Okeanos Presse, pg 269
Oekumenischer Verlag Dr R-F Edel, pg 270
Oncken Verlag KG, pg 270
Osho Verlag GmbH, pg 271
Pandion-Verlag, Ulrike Schmoll, pg 271
Verlag Parzeller GmbH & Co KG, pg 271
Patmos Verlag GmbH & Co KG, pg 272
Paulinus Verlag GmbH, pg 272
J Pfeiffer Verlag, pg 273
Philipp Reclam Jun Verlag GmbH, pg 273

Projektion J Buch- und Musikverlag GmbH, pg 275
Quell Verlag, pg 276
Quelle und Meyer Verlag GmbH & Co, pg 276
Radius-Verlag GmbH, pg 276
Reichl Verlag Der Leuchter, pg 278
Ernst Reinhardt GmbH & Co KG Verlag, pg 278
Rowohlt Taschenbuch Verlag GmbH, pg 280
Dieter Ruggeberg Verlagsbuchhandlung, pg 280
Verlag an der Ruhr GmbH, pg 281
Verlag und Schriftenmission der Evangelischen Gesellschaft Wuppertal, pg 285
Verlag Schulte und Gerth GmbH & Co KG, pg 285
Heinrich Schwab Verlag, pg 285
Schwabenverlag Aktiengesellschaft, pg 285
Scientia Verlag und Antiquariat, pg 286
Spieth-Verlag Verlag fuer Symbolforschung, pg 288
J F Steinkopf Verlag GmbH, pg 289
Stephanus Edition Verlags GmbH, pg 290
Stiefel GmbH Wandkarten Verlag, pg 290
Suin Buch-Verlag, pg 291
Thauros Verlag GmbH, pg 293
TR - Verlagsunion GmbH, pg 294
Turm-Verlag Lorber-Verlag Otto Zluhan OHG, pg 295
Ullstein Heyne List GmbH & Co KG, pg 295
UTB fuer Wissenschaft Uni-Taschenbuecher GmbH, pg 297
Vandenhoeck & Ruprecht, pg 297
Verein der Benediktiner zu Beuron-Beuroner Kunstverlag, pg 297
Vier Tuerme GmbH Verlag Klosterbetriebe, pg 298
VJK Verlag Josef Knecht, pg 299
Erich Wewel Verlag, pg 302
Wichern Verlag, pg 302
Wichern-Verlag GmbH, pg 302
Wissenschaftliche Buchgesellschaft, pg 303
Friedrich Wittig Verlag GmbH, pg 303
Verlag DAS WORT GmbH, pg 304
Zeller Verlag GmbH & Co, pg 305
Verlag Clemens Zerling, pg 305

Ghana

The Advent Press, pg 306
Africa Christian Press, pg 306
Asempa Publishers, pg 306
Frank Publishing Ltd, pg 307
Waterville Publishing House, pg 308
World Literature Project, pg 308

Greece

Akritas, pg 308
Apostoliki Diakonia tis Ekklisias tis Hellados, pg 309
Giovanis Publications, Pangosmios Ekdotikos Organismos, pg 310
ZOI, pg 316

Haiti

Deschamps Imprimerie, pg 317

Holy See (Vatican City State)

Libreria Editrice Vaticana, pg 317

Hungary

Atlantisz Kiado, pg 323

Iceland

Bokaforlag Birtingur, pg 327

India

Abhinav Publications, pg 329
The Academic Press, pg 329
Ajanta Publications (India), pg 330
APH Publishing Corp, pg 331
Asian Educational Services, pg 331
Asian Trading Corporation, pg 331
Associated Publishing House, pg 331
Baha'i Publishing Trust of India, pg 332
The Bangalore Printing & Publishing Co Ltd, pg 332
Bharatiya Vidya Bhavan, pg 333
Central Tibetan Secretariat, pg 334
Chetana Private Ltd, pg 334
Chowkhamba Sanskrit Series Office, pg 335
The Christian Literature Society, pg 335
Disha Prakashan, pg 336
Dutta Baruah Publishing Co Pvt Ltd, pg 336
Enkay Publishers Pvt Ltd, pg 336
Ganesh & Co, pg 337
Geeta Prakasham, pg 337
Arnold Heinman Publishers (India) Pvt Ltd, pg 338
Heritage Publishers, pg 338
Himalayan Books, pg 338
Indian Society for Promoting Christian Knowledge (ISPCK), pg 339
Intellectual Publishing House, pg 339
Inter-India Publications, pg 340
Intertrade Publications, pg 340
Jaico Publishing House, pg 340
Motilal Banarsidass Publishers Pvt Ltd, pg 343
Mudgala Trust, pg 343
A Mukherjee & Co Pvt Ltd, pg 343
Munshiram Manoharlal Publishers Pvt Ltd, pg 343
Narosa Publishing House, pg 343
National Book Organization, pg 343
Navajivan Trust, pg 344
Panjab University Publication Bureau, pg 345
Promilla and Co, pg 346
Radiant Publishers, pg 347
Rajesh Publications, pg 347
Rebel Publishing House Pvt Ltd, pg 347
Regency Publications, pg 347
Rupa & Co, pg 348
SABDA, pg 348
Samkaleen Prakashan, pg 349
Sasta Sahitya Mandal, pg 349
Sri Satguru Publications, pg 349
Sawan Kirpal Publications, pg 349
SBW Publishers, pg 349
South Asia Publications, pg 350
Sterling Publishers Pvt Ltd, pg 351
Theosophical Publishing House, pg 351
Vakils Feffer & Simons Ltd, pg 352
Vision Books Pvt Ltd, pg 353

Indonesia

Advent Indonesia Publishing, pg 353
CV Angkasa CV (Publishers), pg 354
Diponegoro CV, pg 355
Djambatan PT, pg 355
PT BPK Gunung Mulia, pg 355
Mutiara Sumber Widya PT, pg 356
PT Bhakti Baru, pg 356

PUBLISHERS — SUBJECT INDEX

Pustaka Utama Grafiti, PT, pg 357
Tintamas Indonesia PT, pg 357

Islamic Republic of Iran
Scientific and Cultural Publications, pg 358

Ireland
Campus Publishing Ltd, pg 359
The Columba Book Service, pg 359
The Educational Company of Ireland, pg 360
Kerryman Ltd, pg 362
Veritas Co Ltd, pg 364

Israel
Ariel Publishing House, pg 365
DAT Publications, pg 366
Doko Video Ltd, pg 366
Feldheim Publishers Ltd, pg 367
Kiryat Sefer, pg 369
Ma'ariv Book Guild (Sifriat Ma'ariv), pg 370
Massada Press Ltd, pg 370
Rav Kook Institute, pg 371
Rubin Mass Ltd, pg 371
Steimatzky Group Ltd, pg 372
Terra Sancta Arts, pg 373
Yad Eliahu Kitov, pg 373
Yavneh Publishing House Ltd, pg 373

Italy
Editrice Ancora, pg 375
Editrice Antroposofica SRL, pg 375
Apostolato della Preghiera, pg 376
Baha'i, pg 377
Bastogi, pg 377
Edizioni Borla SRL, pg 378
Campanotto, pg 379
Nuova Casa Editrice Licinio Cappelli GEM srl, pg 379
Edizioni Carroccio, pg 379
Celuc Libri, pg 380
Centro Ambrosiano di Documentazione e Studi Religiosi, pg 380
Le Cerchio Imigiative Editoriali, pg 381
Citta Nuova Editrice, pg 382
Cittadella Editrice, pg 382
Edizioni Cultura della Pace, pg 383
M d'Auria Editore SAS, pg 384
Edizioni Dehoniane, pg 384
Edizioni Dehoniane Bologna (EDB), pg 384
Edizioni del Centro, pg 384
Editori Laterza, pg 386
Editrice la Scuola SpA, pg 386
Edizioni Il Punto d'Incontro SAS, pg 386
Edizioni l'eta Dell'Acquario Di I Bresci & C Sas, pg 387
Edizioni Mediterranee SRL, pg 387
ERGA SNC di Carla Ottino Merli & C (Edizioni Realizzazioni Grafiche - Artigiana), pg 388
Libreria Editrice Fiorentina di Vittorio Zani e C SAS, pg 389
Arnaldo Forni Editore SRL, pg 389
Istituto Geografico de Agostini SpA, pg 390
Gius Laterza e Figli SpA, pg 391
Libreria Editrice Gregoriana, pg 391
Herder Editrice e Libreria, pg 392
Hermes Edizioni SRL, pg 392
Editoriale Jaca Book SpA, pg 394
L Japadre Editore, pg 394
Lalli Editore SRL, pg 395
L'Erma di Bretschneider SRL, pg 395
Vincenzo Lo Faro Editore, pg 396
Loffredo Editore Napoli SpA®, pg 396
Longanesi & C, pg 396
Luni, pg 397
Macro Edizioni, pg 397
Editrice Massimo SAS di Crespi Cesare e C, pg 398
McRae Books, pg 398
Il Melangolo, pg 398
Messaggero di San Antonio, pg 398
Editrice Missionaria Italiana (EMI), pg 399
Arnoldo Mondadori Editore SpA, pg 399
Editrice Morcelliana SpA, pg 399
Gruppo Ugo Mursia Editore SpA, pg 400
Nardini Editore srl, pg 400
Paideia Editrice, pg 402
Palatina Editrice, pg 402
Pontificio Istituto di Archeologia Cristiana, pg 404
Pontifico Istituto Orientale, pg 404
Editrice Queriniana, pg 404
RCS Rizzoli Libri SpA, pg 405
Libreria Editrice Rogate (LER), pg 406
Rubbettino Editore, pg 406
Rusconi Libri Srl, pg 406
SAIE Editrice SRL, pg 406
Collegio San Bonaventura di Grottaferrata, pg 406
Edizioni San Paolo SRL, pg 407
Sapere 2000 SRL, pg 407
Gruppo Editoriale Le Stelle SpA, pg 409
Edizioni Studium SpA, pg 409
Editrice Uomini Nuovi, pg 410
UTET (Unione Tipografico-Editrice Torinese), pg 411
Vita e Pensiero, pg 411

Jamaica
Eureka Press Ltd, pg 413

Japan
Chuo-Koron-Sha Inc, pg 415
Fuzambo Publishing Co, pg 416
GakuseiSha Publishing Co Ltd, pg 416
Hayakawa Publishing Inc, pg 417
The Hokuseido Press, pg 417
Hyoronsha Publishing Co Ltd, pg 417
Kadokawa Shoten Publishing Co, pg 419
Kodansha, pg 420
Nippon Hoso Shuppan Kyokai (NHK Publishing), pg 422
Shufu-to-Seikatsu Sha Ltd, pg 426
The Simul Press Inc, pg 426
Sogensha Publishing Co Ltd, pg 426
Taimeido Publishing Co Ltd, pg 427
Tankosha Publishing Co Ltd, pg 427
Toho Book Store, pg 427
Tokai University Press, pg 427
University of Tokyo Press, pg 428

Kenya
Action Publishers, pg 430
Evangel Publishing House, pg 431
Gaba Publications Amecea, Pastoral Institute, pg 431
Heinemann Kenya Limited (EAEP), pg 431
Life Challenge AFRICA, pg 433
Paulines Publications-Africa, pg 433
Transafrica Press, pg 433
Uzima Press, pg 433

Republic of Korea
Chong No Books Publishing Co Ltd, pg 435
Ewha Womans University Press, pg 436
Gim-Yeong Co, pg 436
Hanjin Publishing Co, pg 436
Hw Moon Publishing Co, pg 437
Hyun Am Publishing Co, pg 437
Sejong Daewang Kinyom Saophoe, pg 440
Seogwangsa, pg 440
Yonsei University Press, pg 441

Lebanon
Khayat Book and Publishing Co Sarl, pg 443

Lesotho
Mazenod Book Centre, pg 444
Saint Michael's Mission, pg 444

Liechtenstein
Saendig Reprint Verlag, Hans-Rainer Wohlwend, pg 445

The Former Yugoslav Republic of Macedonia
Ktitor, pg 449

Madagascar
Editions Ambozontany, pg 450
Trano Printy Fiangonana Loterana Malagasy (TPFLM)-(Imprimerie Lutherienne), pg 450

Malawi
Christian Literature Association in Malawi, pg 450

Malaysia
Glad Sounds Sdn Bhd, pg 452
Uni-Text Book Co, pg 455
Vinpress Sdn Bhd, pg 455

Mali
EDIM SA, pg 455

Malta
Gozo Press, pg 456

Mauritius
Editions Capucines, pg 457
Hemco Publications, pg 457

Mexico
Aconcagua Ediciones y Publicaciones SA, pg 457
Arbol Editorial SA de CV, pg 458
Ediciones CUPSA, Centro de Comunicacion Cultural CUPSA, AC, pg 459
Ediciones Dabar, SA de CV, pg 459
Ediciones Don Bosco SA de C, pg 460
Editorial Orion, pg 465
Ediciones Roca, SA, pg 466
Ediciones Suromex SA, pg 467

Morocco
Editions Eddif Maroc, pg 469
Editions La Porte, pg 470

Myanmar
Knowledge Printing & Publishing House, pg 471
Kyi-Pwar-Ye Book House, pg 471
Shwepyidan Printing & Publishing House, pg 471
Thudhammawaddy Press, pg 471

Netherlands
Uitgeverij Ambo BV, pg 472
Uitgeverij Arbor, pg 473
Uitgeverij Balans, pg 473
Erven J Bijleveld, pg 474
Bosch & Keuning, pg 474
Brill Academic Publishers, pg 475
Buijten en Schipperheijn BV Drukkerij en Uitg Mij v/h, pg 475
BV Uitgevery NZV (Nederlandse Zondagsschool Vereniging), pg 475
Uitgeverij G F Callenbach BV, pg 475
East-West Publications Fonds BV, pg 476
Gottmer Uitgevers Groop, pg 477
De Graaf Publishers, pg 478
Uitgeverij Ten Have, pg 478
Uitgeefmaatschappij J H Kok BV, pg 480
Mirananda Publishers BV, pg 481
Uitgeverij H Nelissen BV, pg 482
Servire BV Uitgevers, pg 484
Van Gorcum & Comp BV, pg 486
Uitgeverij Van Wijnen, pg 486

New Zealand
Cicada Press, pg 490
Gnostic Press, pg 491

Nicaragua
Editorial Nueva Nicaragua, pg 497

Nigeria
Adebara Publishers Ltd, pg 497
Aromolaran Publishing Co Ltd, pg 498
CSS Bookshops, Agency & Publishing Division, pg 498
Daystar Press (Publishers), pg 498
ECWA Productions Ltd, pg 498
Educational Research & Study Group, pg 499
Longman Nigeria Plc, pg 500
Northern Nigerian Publishing Co Ltd, pg 500
Obafemi Awolowo University Press Ltd, pg 501
Onibon-Oje Publishers, pg 501
Joe-Tolalu & Associates, pg 501
University Publishing Co, pg 502

Norway
Atheneum Forlag A/S, pg 502
J W Cappelens Forlag A/S, pg 503
Det Norske Samlaget, pg 503
Gyldendal Norsk Forlag A/S, pg 503
Lunde Forlag og Bokhandel A/S, pg 504
Luther Forlag A/S, pg 504
Sambandet Forlag, pg 504

Pakistan
Sheikh Muhammad Ashraf Publishers, pg 506
Fazlee Sons (Pvt) Ltd, pg 506
Islamic Book Centre, pg 507
Islamic Research Institute, pg 507
Maqbool Academy, pg 508
Publishers United Pvt Ltd, pg 508
Taj Co Ltd, pg 509

Papua New Guinea
Assemblies of God Mission, pg 510
The Christian Book Centre, pg 510
Melanesian Institute, pg 510

Philippines
Abiva Publishing House Inc, pg 512
Bookmark Inc, pg 512
Communication Foundation for Asia Media Group (CFAMG), pg 513
Logos (Divine Word) Publications Inc, pg 513
SIBS Publishing House Inc, pg 515
University of the Philippines Press, pg 515
Vera-Reyes Inc, pg 515
Vibal Publishing House Inc (VPHI), pg 515

Poland
Spoleczny Instytut Wydawniczy Znak, pg 520
Verbinum Wydawnictwo Ksiezy Werbistow, pg 520
Wydawnictwa Uniwersytetu Warszawskiego, pg 521

Portugal
Armenio Amado Editora de Simoes, Beirao & Ca Lda, pg 522
Apostolado da Oracao Secretariado Nacional, pg 522
Brasilia Editora (J Carvalho Branco), pg 523
Editorial Estampa, Lda, pg 524
Europress Editores e Distribuidores de Publicacoes Lda, pg 525
Editorial Franciscana, pg 525
Edicoes Manuel Lencastre, pg 526
Livraria Tavares Martins, pg 527
Editorial Noticias, pg 527
Editorial Perpetuo Socorro, pg 528
Edicoes Salesianas, pg 529
Almerinda Teixeira, pg 529
Vega-Publicacao e Distribuicao de Livros e Revistas, Lda, pg 530
Livraria Verdade e Vida Editora, pg 530

Romania
Aion Verlag, pg 531
Editura Albatros, pg 531
Alcor-Edimpex (Verlag) Ltd, pg 531
Artemis Verlag, pg 532
Enzyklopadie Verlag, pg 533
Editura Excelsior, pg 533
Hasefer, pg 533
Editura Institutul European, pg 533
Editura Meridiane, pg 534
Editura Paideia, pg 535
RAO International Publishing Co, pg 535

Russian Federation
BLIC, russko-Baltijskij informaciionnyj centr, AO, pg 537
St Andrew's Biblical Theological College, pg 541

Rwanda
INADES (Institut Africain pour le Developpment Economique et Social), pg 543

Saudi Arabia
Saudi Publishing and Distribution House, pg 543

Senegal
Les Nouvelles Editions Africaines du Senegal NEAS, pg 544
Societe d'Edition d'Afrique Nouvelle, pg 544

Sierra Leone
Sierra Leone University Press, pg 544

Singapore
Chopsons Pte Ltd, pg 545
Taylor & Francis Asia Pacific, pg 548

Slovakia
AV Studio Reklamno-vydavatel 'ska agentura, pg 549

South Africa
Bet-El Publishers, pg 553
Bible Society of South Africa, pg 553
Digma Publications, pg 554
HAUM - De Jager Publishers, pg 555
Kima Global Publishers, pg 556
LAPA Publishers (Pty) Ltd, pg 556
Lux Verbi (Pty) Ltd, pg 556
Sasavona Publishers & Booksellers, pg 559
Waterkant-Uitgewers (Edms) Bpk, pg 560

Spain
Aguilar SA de Ediciones, pg 562
Sociedad de Educacion Atenas SA, pg 564
Biblioteca de Autores Cristianos, pg 564
Editorial Ciudad Nueva, pg 567
Editorial Claret SA, pg 568
Espanola Desclee De Brouwer SA, pg 569
Ediciones Ega, pg 572
Etu Ediciones SL, pg 574
EUNSA (Ediciones Universidad de Navarra SA), pg 574
Fundacion Rosacruz, pg 575
Ediciones Garriga SA, pg 575
Editorial Gulaab, pg 577
Editorial Herder SA, pg 577
Publicaciones ICCE, pg 577
Idea Books, SA, pg 578
Editorial Kairos SA, pg 579
Loguez Ediciones, pg 580
Ediciones Marova SL, pg 581
Ediciones Mensajero, pg 582
Mundo Negro Editorial, pg 583
Narcea SA de Ediciones, pg 583
Nueva Acropolis, pg 584
Ediciones Palabra SA, pg 585
Centre de Pastoral Liturgica, pg 586
PPC Editorial y Distribuidora, SA, pg 587
Ediciones Rialp SA, pg 589
San Pablo Ediciones, pg 589
Secretariado Trinitario, pg 590
Ediciones Siruela SA, pg 591
Ediciones SM, pg 591
Editorial Rudolf Steiner, pg 591
Editorial Sal Terrae, pg 592
Trotta SA Editorial, pg 593
Editorial Txertoa, pg 594

Sri Lanka
Inter-Cultural Book Promoters, pg 597
KVG de Silva & Sons, pg 597
Ministry of Cultural Affairs, pg 597

Sudan
Khartoum University Press, pg 598

Sweden
Stroemberg B&T Forlag AB, pg 606
Svenska alliansmissionens (SAM) foerlage, pg 606
Verbum Foerlag AB, pg 607

Switzerland
ADIRA, pg 607
Editions L'Age d'Homme - La Cite, pg 608
Armenia Editions, pg 608
Bargezzi-Verlag AG, pg 609
Basileia Verlag, pg 609
Blaukreuz-Verlag Bern, pg 610
Brunnen-Verlag Basel, pg 610
Caux Books, pg 611
Caux Edition SA, pg 611
Editions l'Eau Vive, pg 613
Georg Editeur SA, pg 614
Gotthelf-Verlag, pg 615
Govinda-Verlag, pg 615
Kober Verlag AG, pg 617
Labor et Fides SA, pg 618
Leonis Verlag, pg 618
Lia rumantscha, pg 618
Editions H Messeiller SA, pg 619
Motovun Book GmbH, pg 619
Origo Verlag, pg 621
Pedrazzini Tipografia, pg 621
Pendo Verlag GmbH, pg 621
Verlag Friedrich Reinhardt AG, pg 622
Verlag fuer Schoene Wissenschaften, pg 624
Schwengeler-Verlag, pg 624
Theologischer Verlag und Buchhandlungen AG, pg 625
Trachsel - Verlag AG, pg 626
Editions du Tricorne, pg 626
Der Universitatsverlag Freiburg, pg 626
Walter Verlag AG, pg 627
World Council of Churches (WCC Publications), pg 628

Taiwan, Province of China
Chung Hwa Book Co Ltd, pg 629
Heavenly Lotus Publishing Co, Ltd, pg 630
Yee Wen Publishing Co Ltd, pg 632

United Republic of Tanzania
East African Publishing House, pg 633
Inland Publishers, pg 633
Ndanda Mission Press, pg 634
Peramiho Publications, pg 634

Thailand
Suriyaban Publishers, pg 635

Tunisia
Dar Arabia Lil Kitab, pg 637

Turkey
Ruh ve Madde Yayinlari ve Saglik Hizmetleri AS, pg 641

Uganda
Centenary Publishing House Ltd, pg 642

United Kingdom
Apex Publishing Ltd, pg 648
Ashgrove Press, pg 650
Baha'i Publishing Trust, pg 651
Bishopsgate Press Ltd, pg 655
BLA Publishing Ltd, pg 655
Blackstaff Press, pg 655
Blackwell Publishers, pg 655
Bloomsbury Publishing PLC, pg 656
Capall Bann Publishing, pg 663
Cardiff Academic Press, pg 663
Church House Publishing, pg 668
Church Union, pg 668
Colourpoint Books, pg 669
Covenant Publishing Co Ltd, pg 671
CTBI Publications, pg 672
Darton, Longman & Todd Ltd, pg 674
Gerald Duckworth & Co Ltd, pg 676
Eagle/Inter Publishing Service (IPS) Ltd, pg 676
East-West Publications (UK) Ltd, pg 677
Element Books Ltd, pg 678
Epworth Press, pg 679
The Eurospan Group, pg 680
Evans Brothers Ltd, pg 680
Faber & Faber Ltd, pg 681
Floris Books, pg 683
The Foundational Book Company for the John W Doorly Trust, pg 683
Gateway Books, pg 686
E J W Gibb Memorial Trust, pg 687
Global Books Ltd, pg 687
Gracewing Publishing, pg 688
Patrick Hardy Books, pg 692
Hodder & Stoughton Religious, pg 696
Home Health Education Service, pg 697
John Hunt Publishing Ltd, pg 698
C Hurst & Co (Publishers) Ltd, pg 698
Hymns Ancient & Modern Ltd, pg 698
Inter-Varsity Press, pg 700
The Islamic Texts Society, pg 701
Karnak House, pg 703
Laurence King Publishing Ltd, pg 704
Kingsway Publications, pg 705
Letterbox Library, pg 707
Lucis Press Ltd, pg 709
Mandrake of Oxford, pg 711
Marshall Editions Ltd, pg 712
Adam Matthew Publications, pg 712
McCrimmon Publishing Co Ltd, pg 712
Nelson Thornes Ltd, pg 718
New Era Publications UK Ltd, pg 718
The Octagon Press Ltd, pg 720
Oneworld Publications, pg 721
Orion Publishing Group Ltd, pg 722
Oxford University Press, pg 723
Paternoster Publishing, pg 724
Pearson Education, pg 725
Pearson Education Europe, Mideast & Africa, pg 725
Plough Publishing House of Bruderhof Communities in the UK, pg 728
Prim-Ed Publishing UK Ltd, pg 730
Quaker Home Service, pg 731
Rationalist Press Association, pg 733
George Ronald Publisher Ltd, pg 735
Routledge, pg 736
Routledge Curzon, pg 736
Saint Andrew Press, pg 737
Salvationist Publishing & Supplies Ltd, pg 738

PUBLISHERS

School of Oriental & African Studies, pg 739
SCM Press, pg 739
Sheed & Ward Ltd, pg 741
Shepheard-Walwyn (Publishers) Ltd, pg 741
SLG Press, pg 742
Souvenir Press Ltd, pg 743
St Pauls Publishing, pg 744
Stainer & Bell Ltd, pg 745
Thames & Hudson Ltd, pg 748
Transedition Ltd, pg 749
Veritas Foundation Publication Centre, pg 752
Ward Lock Educational Co Ltd, pg 754
White Eagle Publishing Trust, pg 755
Wiley Europe Ltd, pg 756
World Microfilms Publications Ltd, pg 758
Anglia Young Books, pg 759

Uruguay

Editorial Arca SRL, pg 760
Barreiro y Ramos SA, pg 760
Mosca Hermanos, pg 760

Venezuela

Ediciones Tripode, pg 763

Yugoslavia

Alfa-Narodna Knjiga, pg 764
Jugoslavijapublik, pg 764

Zambia

Multimedia Zambia, pg 767

Zimbabwe

Longman Zimbabwe (Pvt) Ltd, pg 768
Mambo Press, pg 768
University of Zimbabwe Publications, pg 769

ROMANCE

Australia

D'Artagnan Publishing, pg 20
Great Western Press Pty Ltd, pg 24
Indra Publishing, pg 27
Jarrah Publications, pg 28
Levanter Publishing & Associates, pg 30
Little Red Apple Publishing, pg 30
Tom Publications, pg 45
Transworld Publishers Pty Ltd, pg 45

Austria

oebv & hpt Verlagsgesellschaft mbH & Co KG, pg 56
Edition Va Bene, pg 60

Belgium

Claude Lefrancq Editeur, pg 71
Editions Luce Wilquin, pg 75
Zuid En Noord VZW, pg 76

Brazil

Agalma Psicanalise Editora Ltda, pg 78
Artes e Oficios Editora Ltda, pg 79
Editora Bertrand Brasil Ltda, pg 79
Alzira Chagas Carpigiani, pg 80
Edicon Editora e Consultorial Ltda, pg 81
Editora Elevacao, pg 82
Companhia Editora Forense, pg 82
Global Editora e Distribuidora Ltda, pg 84
Livraria Nobel S/A, pg 86
Editora Mercado Aberto Ltda, pg 88
Editora Nova Alexandria Ltda, pg 88
Editora Nova Fronteira SA, pg 88
Edit Palavra Magica, pg 89
Editora Scipione Ltda, pg 91
Tempus Editores, pg 92
34 Literatura S/C Ltda, pg 92

Bulgaria

Aleks Print Publishing House, pg 94
EA Publishing House, pg 95
Hermes Publishing House, pg 95
Zunica, pg 98

China

Writers' Publishing House, pg 110

Costa Rica

Editorial Universitaria Centroamericana (EDUCA), pg 117

Cuba

Editorial Letras Cubanas, pg 121

Czech Republic

Baronet, pg 123
Josef Lukasik A Spol, pg 125

Estonia

Perioodika, pg 140

France

Publications Aredit, pg 148
Editions Belfond, pg 150
Culture et Bibliotheque pour Tous, pg 157
Georges-Charles Demay, pg 158
Librairie Guenegaud Sarl, pg 167
Harlequin SA, pg 167
Presses de la Cite, pg 180
Editions du Rouergue, pg 183

Germany

Ars Edition GmbH, pg 195
Aufbau Taschenbuch Verlag GmbH, pg 196
Aufbau-Verlag GmbH, pg 196
Wilhelm Heyne Verlag, pg 240
Dr Gisela Lermann, pg 257
Verlagsgruppe Luebbe GmbH & Co KG, pg 259
Nebel Verlag GmbH, pg 267
Georg Olms Verlag AG, pg 270
Propylaeen Verlag, Zweigniederlassung Berlin der Ullstein Buchverlage GmbH, pg 275
Ruetten & Loening Berlin GmbH, pg 281
Weidmannsche Verlagsbuchhandlung GmbH, pg 301

Ghana

Beginners Publishers, pg 306

Greece

Elliniki Leschi Tou Vivliou, pg 310
Exandas Publishers, pg 310
Harlenic Hellas Publishing SA, pg 311
Hestia-1 D Hestia-Kollaros & Co Corporation, pg 311
Odysseas Publications Ltd, pg 313

Hungary

Ifjusagi Lap-eskonyvkiado Vallalat, pg 324

Iceland

Frjals fjolmiolun hf-Urvalsbaekur, pg 327
Frodi Ltd, pg 328

Ireland

Town House & Country House, pg 364

Italy

Edizioni Bresciane, pg 378
ERGA SNC di Carla Ottino Merli & C (Edizioni Realizzazioni Grafiche - Artigiana), pg 388
Gangemi Editore, pg 390
Edizioni del Girasole srl, pg 390
Il Saggiatore, pg 393
Edizioni Internazionali di Letteratura e Scienze, pg 394
La Luna, pg 397
Editrice Massimo SAS di Crespi Cesare e C, pg 398
Arnoldo Mondadori Editore SpA, pg 399
Edizioni Piemme SpA, pg 403
Rubbettino Editore, pg 406
Servitium, pg 408
Il Tripode Srl, pg 410

Jamaica

Kingston Publishers Ltd, pg 413

Japan

Shincho-Sha Co Ltd, pg 425

Republic of Korea

Big Tree Publishing, pg 435
Chung Rim Publishing Co Ltd, pg 435
Koreaone Press Inc, pg 438
Woong Jin Publishing Co Ltd, pg 440

Latvia

Alberts XII, pg 441
Artava Ltd, pg 441

Lithuania

Andrena Publishers, pg 445
The Publishing House of the Lithuanian Writers' Union, pg 446
Victoria Publishers, pg 446

Luxembourg

Hubsch, pg 447

Macau

Livros Do Oriente, pg 448

The Former Yugoslav Republic of Macedonia

Strk Publishing House, pg 449

Mexico

Ediciones Alpe, pg 458

Monaco

Les Editions du Rocher, pg 469

SUBJECT INDEX

Netherlands

De Boekerij BV, pg 474
BZZTOH Publishers, pg 475

New Zealand

River Press, pg 495

Nigeria

Evans Brothers (Nigeria Publishers) Ltd, pg 499

Pakistan

Maqbool Academy, pg 508

Philippines

Anvil Publishing Inc, pg 512
Books for Pleasure Inc, pg 512
Estrella Publishing, pg 513
Sonny A Mendoza, pg 513
New Day Publishers, pg 514

Poland

Arlekin-Wydawnictwo Harlequin Enterprises sp zoo, pg 516
Ksiaznica Publishing Ltd, pg 517

Portugal

Editorial Estampa, Lda, pg 524
Europress Editores e Distribuidores de Publicacoes Lda, pg 525
Gradiva-Publicacnoes Lda, pg 525
Latina Livraria, pg 526
Livraria Minerva Editora, pg 526
Paulinas, pg 528
Quetzal Editores, pg 529
Teorema, pg 529
Vega-Publicacao e Distribuicao de Livros e Revistas, Lda, pg 530

Romania

Lider Verlag, pg 534
Mentor Kiado, pg 534
RAO International Publishing Co, pg 535
Realitatea Casa de Edituri Productie Audio-Video Film, pg 535
Saeculum IO, pg 535
Editura Univers, pg 536

Russian Federation

Armada Publishing House, pg 537
BLIC, russko-Baltijskij informaciionnyj centr, AO, pg 537
KUbK Publishing House, pg 539
Permskaja Kniga, pg 541
Raduga Publishers, pg 541

Saudi Arabia

Dar Al-Shareff for Publishing & Distribution, pg 543

Slovakia

Vydavatepstvo Praca spol sro, pg 550
Wist, pg 551

South Africa

Human & Rousseau (Pty) Ltd, pg 555
Ivy Publications, pg 555
Jacklin Enterprises (Pty) Ltd, pg 556
Tafelberg Publishers Ltd, pg 560

Spain

Emece Editores, pg 573
Harlequin Iberica SA, pg 577

SUBJECT INDEX

Ediciones Martinez-Roca SA, pg 581
Ediciones Urano, SA, pg 595

Switzerland

Armenia Editions, pg 608
Berchtold Haller Verlag, pg 609
Terra Grischuna Verlag Buch-und Zeitschriftenverlag, pg 625

Taiwan, Province of China

Lin Pai Press Company Ltd, pg 631
Morning Star Publisher Inc, pg 631
UNITAS Publishing Co Ltd, pg 632

Thailand

Chokechai Thewet Co Ltd, pg 635

United Kingdom

BBC Audiobooks, pg 652
BCA, pg 653
The Greek Bookshop, pg 689
HarperCollins Publishers, pg 692
Motilal (UK) Books of India, pg 715
Orion Publishing Group Ltd, pg 722
Pan Macmillan, pg 723
Time Warner Books UK, pg 749
Ulverscroft Large Print Books Ltd, pg 751

Uruguay

Fundacion de Cultura Universitaria, pg 760

SCIENCE (GENERAL)

Albania

NL SH, pg 1
State Textbook Publishing House, pg 1

Algeria

Enterprise Nationale du Livre (ENAL), pg 2

Argentina

Ada Korn Editora SA, pg 3
Alfagrama SRL ediciones, pg 3
Centro Editor de America Latina SA, pg 4
EUDEBA (Editorial Universitaria de Buenos Aires), pg 6
Editorial Hemisferio Sur SA, pg 6
Laffont Ediciones Electronicas SA, pg 7
Marymar Ediciones SA, pg 7
Polemos SA, pg 8
Ediciones Tres Tiempos SRL, pg 9

Armenia

Ajstan Publishers, pg 10

Australia

Allen & Unwin Pty Ltd, The Australian Newspaper, Vogel Breads, pg 11
Beazer Publishing Company Pty Ltd, pg 14
Robert Berthold Photography, pg 14
Blackwell Science Pty Ltd, pg 15
Books for Our Times, pg 16
Bureau of Resource Sciences, pg 16
Clunies Ross Press, pg 18
CSIRO Publishing (Commonwealth Scientific & Industrial Research Organisation), pg 19
Dellasta Publishing, pg 20

Emerald City Books, pg 22
Encyclopaedia Britannica (Australia) Inc, pg 22
Great Western Press Pty Ltd, pg 24
Greater Glider Productions Australia Pty Ltd, pg 24
Harcourt Australia Pty Ltd, pg 25
Illert Publications, pg 27
Macmillan Education Australia, pg 31
Maxwell Macmillan Publishing (Australia) Pty Ltd, pg 32
Mimosa Publications Pty Ltd, pg 33
K & Z Mostafanejad, pg 33
Nimaroo Publishers, pg 35
Pearson Education Australia, pg 37
Rankin Publishers, pg 40
Royal Society of New South Wales, pg 41
Royal Society of Victoria Inc, pg 41
Transpareon Press, pg 45
Troll Books of Australia, pg 45
University of New South Wales Press Ltd, pg 46
Veritas Press, pg 46
Wizard Books Pty Ltd, pg 48

Austria

Bethania Verlag, pg 49
Boehlau Verlag GmbH & Co KG, pg 50
Czernin Verlag, pg 50
Danubia Werbung und Verlagsservice, pg 50
Franz Deuticke Verlagsges mbH, pg 51
Fassbaender Verlag, pg 51
Georg Fromme und Co, pg 52
Guthmann & Peterson Liber Libri, Edition, pg 52
Johannes Heyn, Gert und Volkmar Zechner, pg 52
Ferdinand Hirt mbH & Co KG, pg 53
International Institute for Applied Systems Analysis (IIASA), pg 53
Verlag der Oesterreichischen Akademie der Wissenschaften (OEAW), pg 56
Oesterreichischer Bundesverlag GmbH, pg 56
Verlag Oldenbourg, pg 56
Resch Verlag, pg 57
Springer-Verlag Wien, pg 59
Studien Verlag Gmbh, pg 59
Trauner Verlag, pg 59
Verlag Carl Ueberreuter GmbH, pg 59
Edition Va Bene, pg 60
Universitaetsverlag Wagner GmbH, pg 60
Waren-Erzeungungs-und Handelsgesellschaft GmbH, pg 60
WUV/Facultas Universitaetsverlag, pg 61

Azerbaijan

AZernesr, pg 61

Bangladesh

Agamee Prakashani, pg 62

Belarus

Publishing Center of Belarus State University, pg 63

Belgium

Academia Press, pg 64
Acco CV, pg 64
Campinia Media VZW, pg 65

Editions De Boeck-Larcier SA, pg 67
Dessain - Departement de De Boeck & Larcier SA, pg 68
Editions les eperonniers, pg 68
Imprimerie Hayez SPRL, pg 69
Koninklijke Vlaamse Academie van Belgie voor Wetenschappen en Kunsten, pg 70
Editions Labor, pg 70
Leuven University Press, pg 71
Presses Universitaires de Bruxelles ASBL, pg 73
Editions Techniques et Scientifiques SPRL, pg 74
Presses Universitaires de Louvain-UCL, pg 75
Imprimeur - Editeur Vaillant-Carmanne SA, pg 75
Vander Editions, SA, pg 75
VUB University Press, pg 75
Wolters Plantyn Educatieve Uitgevers, pg 75

Bolivia

Editorial Don Bosco, pg 76

Bosnia and Herzegovina

Veselin Maslesa, pg 77
Svjetlost, pg 77

Brazil

Abril SA, pg 77
Livraria Francisco Alves Editora SA, pg 78
ARTMED, pg 79
Editora Edgard Blucher Ltda, pg 80
Cadence Publicacoes Internacionais Ltda, pg 80
Editora Campus Ltda, pg 80
Cia Editora Nacional, pg 82
EDUSC - Editora da Universidade do Sagrado Coracao, pg 82
Editora Globo SA, pg 84
Editora Harbra Ltda, pg 84
IBRASA (Instituicao Brasileira de Difusao Cultural Ltda), pg 85
Icone Editora Ltda, pg 85
Editora Interciencia Ltda, pg 85
Modulo Editora e Desenvolvimento Educacional Ltda, pg 88
Editora Nova Fronteira SA, pg 88
Editora Objetiva Ltda, pg 88
Proton Editora Ltda, pg 90
Editora Revan Ltda, pg 90
Editora Rocco Ltda, pg 91
Editora Scipione Ltda, pg 91
Livraria Sulina Editora, pg 92
Edicoes Tabajara, pg 92
Editora da Universidade de Sao Paulo, pg 93
Jorge Zahar Editor, pg 93

Bulgaria

Abagar Pablioing, pg 94
Abagar, Veliko Tarnovo, pg 94
Aleks Print Publishing House, pg 94
Antroposofsko Izdatelstvo Dimo R Daskalov OOD, pg 94
Izdatelstvo na Balgarskata Akademija na Naukite, pg 94
Darzhavno Izdatelstvo Zemizdat, pg 95
Foi-Commerce, pg 95
Gea-Libris Publishing House, pg 95
Heron Press Publishing House, pg 96
Litera Prima, pg 96
Makros 2000 - Plovdiv, pg 96
Naouka i Izkoustvo, Ltd, pg 97

BOOK

Universitetsko Izdatelstvo 'Kliment Ochridski', pg 97
Pensoft Publishers, pg 97
Regalia 6 Publishing House, pg 97
Slavena, pg 98
Technica, pg 98
Ivan Vazov Publishing House, pg 98

Cameroon

Centre d'Edition et de Production pour l'Enseignement et la Recherche (CEPER), pg 99

Chile

Editorial Universitaria SA, pg 101
Ediciones Universitarias de Valparaiso, pg 101

China

Beijing Publishing House, pg 102
China Ocean Press, pg 103
China Youth Publishing House, pg 104
Chongqing University Press, pg 104
Dalian Maritime University Press, pg 105
Foreign Languages Press, pg 105
Fudan University Press, pg 105
Fujian Science & Technology Publishing House, pg 106
Heilongjiang Science & Technology Press, pg 106
Higher Education Press, pg 106
Inner Mongolia Science & Technology Publishing House, pg 106
Jiangsu Science & Technology Publishing House, pg 106
Jilin Science & Technology Publishing House, pg 106
Knowledge Press, pg 107
National Defence Industry Press, pg 107
New Times Press, pg 107
Patent Documentation Publishing House, pg 107
The Publishing House of Shanghai University of Traditional Chinese Medicine, pg 108
Science Press, pg 108
Shandong University Press, pg 109
Shanghai Educational Publishing House, pg 109
Shanghai Science & Technology Publishers, pg 109
Shanghai Scientific & Technological Literature Publishing House, pg 109
Sichuan Science & Technology Publishing House, pg 109
Southwest China Jiaotong University Press, pg 109
Tianjin Science & Technology Publishing House, pg 109
Zhejiang University Press, pg 110

Colombia

Editora Guadalupe Ltda, pg 112
Editorial Libros y Libres SA, pg 112
Unidad Universitaria del Sur (UNISUR), pg 114

The Democratic Republic of the Congo

Presses Universitaires du Zaiire (PUZ), pg 115

Costa Rica
Editorial Tecnologica de Costa Rica, pg 117
Editorial de la Universidad de Costa Rica, pg 117

Cote d'Ivoire
Centre d'Edition et de Diffusion Africaines, pg 117

Croatia
Izdavacka Delatnost Hrvatske Akademije Znanosti I Umjetnosti, pg 118
Matica hrvatska, pg 119
Mladost d d Izdavacku graficku i informaticku djelatnost, pg 119
Nakladni zavod Matice hrvatske, pg 119
Naprijed d d Naklada, pg 119
Narodne Novine, pg 119
Skolska Knjiga, pg 120
Sveucilisna tiskara doo, pg 120
Tehnicka Knjiga, pg 120

Cuba
Editorial Cientifico Tecnica, pg 121
Editora Politica, pg 121
Pueblo y Educacion Editorial (PE), pg 121

Czech Republic
Aleko, Nakladatelska Divize, pg 122
Granit SRO, pg 124
Karolinum, nakladatelstvi, pg 125
Maxdorf Ltd, pg 126
Narodni Muzeum, pg 126
NLN, Ltd The Lidove noviny Publishing House, pg 127
Omnipress Praha, pg 127
Vysehrad, pg 129

Denmark
Akademisk Forlag, pg 129
Bogan's Forlag, pg 130
Bogfabrikken Fakta ApS, pg 130
Fremad A/S, pg 132
Gyldendalske Boghandel - Nordisk Forlag A/S, pg 132
Nyt Nordisk Forlag Arnold Busck A/S, pg 134
Polyteknisk Forlag, pg 134
C A Reitzel A/S, pg 134
Rosenkilde & Bagger, pg 135
Forlaget Vindrose A/S, pg 136

Ecuador
Pontificia Universidad Catolica de Ecuador, Centro de Publicaciones, pg 137

Egypt (Arab Republic of Egypt)
Al Ahram Establishment, pg 138
Dar El Shorouk Publishing & Distributing House, pg 138
Dar Al Maaref, pg 139
Middle East Book Centre, pg 139

Estonia
Estonian Academy Publishers, pg 139
Estonian Encyclopaedia Publishers Ltd, pg 140
Valgus Publishers, pg 141

Ethiopia
Addis Ababa University Press, pg 141

Finland
Abo Akademis forlag - Abo Akademi University Press, pg 141
Soederstroem et Co Foerlagsaktiebolag, pg 144
Ursa ry, pg 145

France
Editions Belin, pg 150
Bureau des Longitudes de France, pg 152
Cepadues Editions SA, pg 153
CNRS Editions, pg 155
Editions Complexe SPRL, pg 156
Delagrave Edition SA, pg 158
Le Dilettante, pg 159
Doin Editeurs, pg 160
Dunod Editeur, pg 160
Presses de l'Ecole Normale Superieure, pg 160
EDP Sciences, pg 161
Ellipses - Edition Marketing SA, pg 162
Editions Entente, pg 162
Librairie Artheme Fayard, pg 163
Editions Jacques Gabay, pg 165
Ganymede, pg 166
Groupe Expansion, pg 167
Hachette Livre, pg 167
L'Harmattan, pg 168
Hermann editeurs des Sciences et des Arts SA, pg 168
IRD Editions, pg 170
Editions Klincksieck, pg 171
Librairie Larousse, pg 172
Librairie Scientifique et Technique Albert Blanchard, pg 173
Le Livre de Poche-L G F (Librairie Generale Francaise), pg 173
Editions MDI (La Maison des Instituteurs), pg 175
Gabriel Mony, pg 176
Fernand Nathan, pg 177
Editions Odile Jacob, pg 178
Editions Ouest-France, pg 178
Polytechnica, pg 180
Editions Robert Laffont, Nil, Fixot, Seghers, Julliard, pg 183
Selection du Reader's Digest SA, pg 184
Maren Sell, pg 184
Editions de Septembre, pg 184
Editions du Seuil, pg 185
Sofradif Editions Philippe Auzou, pg 185
UNESCO Publishing, pg 188

Georgia
Izdatelstvo Sabtchota Sakartvelo, pg 190

Germany
Accedo Verlagsgesellschaft mbH, pg 191
Aerogie-Verlag, pg 191
Agis Verlag GmbH, pg 192
Ahriman-Verlag GmbH, pg 192
Aisthesis Verlag Dr Detlev Kopp und Dr Michael Vogt, pg 192
Verlag Karl Alber GmbH, pg 192
AOL-Verlag Frohmut Menze, pg 194
Aquamarin Verlag, pg 194
Arkana Verlag Tete Bottger Rainer Wunderlich GmbH, pg 195
J J Augustin GmbH Verlag, pg 196
Aulis Verlag Deubner & Co KG, pg 197
Dr Bachmaier Verlag GmbH, pg 197
Dr Wolfgang Baur Verlag Kunst & Alltag, pg 199
Bayerische Akademie der Wissenschaften, pg 199
Julius Beltz GmbH & Co KG, pg 200
W Bertelsmann Verlag GmbH & Co KG, pg 201
BertelsmannSpringer Science & Business Media GmbH, pg 202
Bibliographisches Institut & F A Brockhaus AG, pg 203
Verlag Die Blaue Eule, pg 204
Bock und Herchen Verlag, pg 204
Verlag Hermann Boehlaus Nachfolger Weimar GmbH & Co, pg 205
Bouvier Verlag, pg 206
Buchverlag Junge Welt GmbH, pg 207
Fachverlag Hans Carl GmbH, pg 209
J G Cotta'sche Buchhandlung Nachfolger GmbH, pg 212
Deutsche Verlags-Anstalt GmbH (DVA), pg 214
Deutscher Universitats-Verlag, pg 215
Diagonal-Verlag GbR Rink-Schweer, pg 216
Dietrich zu Klampen Verlag, pg 216
Dingfelder-Verlag Inh Gerd Gmelin, pg 217
Droemersche Verlagsanstalt Th Knaur Nachfolger GmbH & Co, pg 218
Duncker und Humblot GmbH, pg 219
Klaus D Dutz, pg 219
E Schweizerbart'sche Verlagsbuchhandlung (Nagele und Obermiller), pg 220
Econ Verlag GmbH, pg 220
Ein Fach-Verlag, pg 222
Esogetics GmbH, pg 224
Verlag Esoterische Philosophie GmbH, pg 224
F Bruckmann Munchen Verlag & Druck GmbH & Co Produkt KG, pg 225
Ferdinand Enke Verlag, pg 227
Franz Ferzak World & Space Publications, pg 227
Harald Fischer Verlag GmbH, pg 228
Verlag Freies Geistesleben, pg 230
Verlag A Fromm im Druck- u Verlagshaus Fromm GmbH & Co KG, pg 230
Genius Verlag, pg 231
Georgi GmbH, pg 232
Verlagsgesellschaft R Gloess & Co, pg 233
Wilhelm Goldmann Verlag GmbH, pg 233
Walter de Gruyter GmbH & Co KG, pg 234
Haag und Herchen Verlag GmbH, pg 235
Dr Curt Haefner-Verlag GmbH, pg 236
Hahner Verlagsgesellschaft mbH, pg 236
Dr Ernst Hauswedell & Co Verlag, pg 238
Erika Heydick Sax-Verlag Beucha, pg 240
Anton Hiersemann, Verlag, pg 240
S Hirzel Verlag GmbH und Co, pg 241
Hoffmann und Campe Verlag GmbH, pg 242
Heinrich Hugendubel Verlag GmbH, pg 243
Edition Humanistische Psychologie (EHP), pg 243
Huthig GmbH & Co KG, pg 244
Idea Verlag GmbH, pg 244
IKO Verlag fur Interkulturelle Kommunikation, pg 244
Janus Verlagsgesellschaft, Dr Norbert Meder & Co, pg 246
Johann Wolfgang Goethe Universitat, pg 246
S Karger GmbH Verlag fuer Medizin und Naturwissenschaften, pg 247
Keysersche Verlagsbuchhandlung GmbH, pg 248
Kindler Verlag GmbH, pg 249
Vittorio Klostermann GmbH, pg 250
Franckh-Kosmos Verlags-GmbH & Co, pg 252
Reinhold Kraemer Verlag, pg 253
Verlag Waldemar Kramer, pg 253
Ambro Lacus, Buch- und Bildverlag Walter Kremnitz, pg 255
Peter Lang GmbH Europaeischer Verlag der Wissenschaften, pg 255
Leibniz Verlag, pg 256
Leipziger Universitaetsverlag GmbH, pg 257
Martha Lindner Verlags-GmbH, pg 258
LIT Verlag, pg 258
Verlag an der Lottbek, pg 259
Annemarie Maeger, pg 260
Matthiesen Verlag Ingwert Paulsen Jr, pg 261
Moench Verlagsgesellschaft mbH, pg 264
Musikantiquariat und Dr Hans Schneider Verlag GmbH, pg 266
Naumann & Goebel Verlagsgesellschaft mbH, pg 267
Neumann Verlag, pg 268
Verlag J Neumann-Neudamm GmbH & Co KG, pg 268
Nusser Verlag, pg 269
Georg Olms Verlag AG, pg 270
Passavia Universitaetsverlag und -Druck GmbH, pg 272
Philipps-Universitaet Marburg, pg 273
Physica-Verlag, pg 273
Piper Verlag GmbH, pg 274
Propylaeen Verlag, Zweigniederlassung Berlin der Ullstein Buchverlage GmbH, pg 275
R Oldenbourg Verlag GmbH, pg 276
Dr Josef Raabe-Verlags GmbH, pg 276
Raethgloben Verlagsgesellschaft mbH, pg 276
Dr Ludwig Reichert Verlag, pg 278
Ernst Reinhardt GmbH & Co KG Verlag, pg 278
Roehrig Universitaets Verlag Gmbh, pg 279
Rowohlt Taschenbuch Verlag GmbH, pg 280
Verlag Sauerlaender GmbH, pg 282
F K Schattauer Verlagsgesellschaft mbH, pg 282
Schmidt Periodicals GmbH, pg 284
Schueren Verlag GmbH, pg 285
Schulz-Kirchner Verlag GmbH, pg 285
Spektrum der Wissenschaft Verlagsgesellschaft mbH, pg 287

1079

SUBJECT INDEX — BOOK

Springer-Verlag GmbH & Co KG, pg 288
Steyler Verlag, pg 290
Suhrkamp Verlag, pg 291
Synthesis Verlag, pg 291
Tomus Verlag GmbH, pg 294
Ullstein Heyne List GmbH & Co KG, pg 295
Verlag Eugen Ulmer GmbH & Co, pg 295
Umschau Buchverlag Breidenstein GmbH, pg 296
Urban & Fischer Verlag GmbH & Co KG Niederlassung Jena, pg 296
UVK Universitatsverlag Konstanz GmbH, pg 297
Dorothea van der Koelen, pg 297
VDI-Verlag GmbH, pg 297
Verlag fur die Frau GmbH, pg 297
VJK Verlag Josef Knecht, pg 299
Verlagsgruppe Georg von Holtzbrinck GmbH, pg 299
Dokument und Analyse Verlag Bogislaw von Randow, pg 299
VWB-Verlag fur Wissenschaft & Bildung, Amand Aglaster, pg 300
Waxmann Verlag GmbH, pg 300
Weber Zucht & Co, pg 300
Weidler Buchverlag Berlin, pg 301
Wiley-VCH Verlag GmbH, pg 302
Dr Dieter Winkler, pg 303
Wissenschaftliche Buchgesellschaft, pg 303
Wissenschaftliche Verlagsgesellschaft mbH, pg 303
Verlag Konrad Wittwer GmbH, pg 303
Das Wunderhorn Verlag GmbH, pg 304

Ghana
Anowuo Educational Publications, pg 306
Bureau of Ghana Languages, pg 306
Ghana Academy of Arts & Sciences, pg 307
Ghana Publishing Corporation, pg 307
Sam Woode Ltd, pg 308
Sedco Publishing Ltd, pg 308
Unimax Macmillan Ltd, pg 308
Waterville Publishing House, pg 308

Greece
Chryssos Typos AE Ekodeis, pg 309
Diavlos, pg 309
Giovanis Publications, Pangosmios Ekdotikos Organismos, pg 310
Morfotiko Idryma Ethnikis Trapezas, pg 313
J Sideris OE Ekdoseis, pg 315
Technical Chamber of Greece, pg 315
S J Zacharopoulos SA Publishing Co, pg 316

Holy See (Vatican City State)
Pontificia Academia Scientiarum, pg 317

Hong Kong
The Chinese University Press, pg 319
Federal Publications Ltd, pg 319

Hungary
Akademiai Kiado, pg 323
Foldmuvelesugyi Miniszterium Muszaki Intezet, pg 323
Hatter Lap- es Konyvkiado Kft, pg 324
Idegenforgalmi Propaganda es Kiado Vallalat, pg 324
Mezoegazda Kiado, pg 325
Mezoegazdasagi Koenyvkiado Vallalat, pg 325
Mueszaki Koenyvkiado Ltd, pg 325
Panem, pg 326
Polgar Citizen Press, pg 326
Zrinyi Kiado, pg 327

Iceland
Fjolvi, pg 327

India
Addison-Wesley (Singapore) Pte Ltd, pg 329
Affiliated East West Press Pvt Ltd, pg 329
Allied Book Centre, pg 330
Ambar Prakashan, pg 330
Ananda Publishers Pvt Ltd, pg 330
Ankur Publishing House, pg 330
Anmol Publications Pvt Ltd, pg 331
APH Publishing Corp, pg 331
Arya Medi Publishing House, pg 331
Asia Pacific Business Press Inc, pg 331
Atma Ram & Sons, pg 331
Bharat Publishing House, pg 332
Bihar Hindi Granth Akademi, pg 333
S Chand & Co Ltd, pg 334
Dastane Ramchandra & Co, pg 335
Eurasia Publishing House Pvt Ltd, pg 337
Frank Brothers & Co (Publishers) Ltd, pg 337
Geeta Prakasham, pg 337
Himalaya Publishing House, pg 338
IBD Publisher & Distributors, pg 338
Indian Museum, pg 339
International Book Distributors, pg 340
Kitab Ghar, pg 341
Ministry of Information & Broadcasting, pg 342
National Institute of Industrial Research (NIIR), pg 344
Naya Prokash, pg 344
Oxford & IBH Publishing Co Pvt Ltd, pg 345
Oxonian Press (P) Ltd, pg 345
Paico Publishing House, pg 345
Publications & Information Directorate, CSIR, pg 346
Pustak Mahal, pg 346
Rajasthan Hindi Granth Academy, pg 347
Rajendra Publishing House Pvt Ltd, pg 347
Rajpal & Sons, pg 347
Rastogi Publications, pg 347
Research Signpost, pg 348
Researchco Reprints, pg 348
Scientific Book Agency, pg 349
Shaibya Prakashan Bibhag, pg 349
South Asian Publishers Pvt Ltd, pg 350
Sterling Publishers Pvt Ltd, pg 351
Suman Prakashan Pvt Ltd, pg 351
Theosophical Publishing House, pg 351
Today & Tomorrow's Printers & Publishers, pg 352
Transworld Research Network, pg 352
Vikas Publishing House Pvt Ltd, pg 353
Vision Books Pvt Ltd, pg 353
S Viswanathan (Printers & Publishers) Pvt Ltd, pg 353

Indonesia
Andi Offset, pg 354
Bhratara Karya Aksara, pg 354
P T Bulan Bintang, pg 354
Institut Teknologi Bandung, pg 355
Katalis PT Bina Mitra Plaosan, pg 356
PT Pustaka LP3ES Indonesia, pg 357
Yayasan Obor Indonesia, pg 357

Islamic Republic of Iran
Scientific and Cultural Publications, pg 358

Iraq
National House for Publishing, Distributing and Advertising, pg 358

Ireland
An Gum, pg 358
The Educational Company of Ireland, pg 360
O'Brien Educational, pg 363
Royal Dublin Society, pg 364

Israel
Achiasaf Publishing House Ltd, pg 365
Amichai Publishing House Ltd, pg 365
Freund Publishing House Ltd, pg 367
Ma'ariv Book Guild (Sifriat Ma'ariv), pg 370
The Magnes Press, pg 370
Massada Press Ltd, pg 370
M Mizrahi Publishers, pg 370
The Van Leer Jerusalem Institute, pg 373
Yavneh Publishing House Ltd, pg 373

Italy
Adelphi Edizioni SpA, pg 374
De Agostini Scolastica, pg 375
Umberto Allemandi & C SRL, pg 375
Argalia Editore delle Arti Grafiche Editoriali SRL, pg 376
Editrice Atanor SRL, pg 377
Atlantica Editrice SARL, pg 377
Bianco, pg 377
Bibliopolis - Edizioni di Filosofia e Scienze Srl, pg 377
Bollati Boringhieri Editore Srl, pg 378
Bompiani-RCS Libri, pg 378
Bulzoni Editore SRL (Le Edizioni Universitarie d'Italia), pg 379
Edizioni Cantagalli, pg 379
Nuova Casa Editrice Licinio Cappelli GEM srl, pg 379
Casa Editrice Lint Srl, pg 380
Edistudio di Brunetto Casini, pg 380
Celuc Libri, pg 380
Il Cigno Galileo Galilei-Edizioni di Arte e Scienza, pg 381
Ciranna - Roma, pg 381
CLEUP - Cooperative Libraria Editrice dell 'Universita di Padova, pg 382
CLUEB (Cooperativa Libraria Universitaria Editrice Bologna), pg 382
CLUT Editrice, pg 382
Edizioni di Comunita SpA, pg 382
Libreria Cortina Editrice SRL, pg 383
Edizioni Cremonese SRL, pg 383
Edizioni Dedalo SRL, pg 384
Edagricole - Edizioni Agricole, pg 385
Ediciclo Editore SRL, pg 386
Editrice Edisco, pg 386
ERGA SNC di Carla Ottino Merli & C (Edizioni Realizzazioni Grafiche - Artigiana), pg 388
Giangiacomo Feltrinelli SpA, pg 389
Flaccovio Editore, pg 389
Edizioni GB, pg 390
Editrice Giannotta di Sebastiano Pace Giannotta, pg 390
Giunti (Gruppo Editoriale), pg 390
Giunti Publishing Group, pg 391
Gius Laterza e Figli SpA, pg 391
Gruppo Calderini Edagricole, pg 392
Hopeful Monster Editore, pg 392
IHT Gruppo Editoriale SRL, pg 393
Il Poligrafo, pg 393
Il Saggiatore, pg 393
Editoriale Jaca Book SpA, pg 394
L Japadre Editore, pg 394
Lalli Editore SRL, pg 394
Levrotto e Bella Libreria Editrice Universitaria SAS, pg 395
Liguori Editore SRL, pg 396
Loffredo Editore Napoli SpA®, pg 396
Longanesi & C, pg 396
Macro Edizioni, pg 397
Manfrini Editori, pg 397
Aldo Marino Editore, pg 398
Editrice Massimo SAS di Crespi Cesare e C, pg 398
Masson SpA, pg 398
McRae Books, pg 398
Edizioni Medicea SRL, pg 398
Mediserve SRL, pg 398
Arnoldo Mondadori Editore SpA, pg 399
Mucchi Editore SRL, pg 400
Gruppo Ugo Mursia Editore SpA, pg 400
Franco Muzzio & C Editore SpA, pg 400
Newton Compton Editori SRL, pg 401
Novartis Edizioni - Novartis Farma SpA, pg 401
Leo S Olschki, pg 402
Piccin Nuova Libraria SpA, pg 403
Psicologica Editrice, pg 404
RCS Libri SpA, pg 405
Editori Riuniti, pg 405
Edizioni Universitarie Romane, pg 406
SAGEP, pg 406
Fausto Sardini Editrice, pg 407
Edizioni Scientifiche Italiane, pg 407
Editoriale Scienza, pg 407
Societa Editrice la Goliardica Pavese SRL, pg 408
Edizioni Sorbona Milano, pg 408
Sperling e Kupfer Editori SpA, pg 408
Gruppo Editoriale Le Stelle SpA, pg 409
Edizioni Studio Tesi SRL, pg 409
Edizioni Studium SpA, pg 409
UTET (Unione Tipografico-Editrice Torinese), pg 411
Zanichelli Editore SpA, pg 412

PUBLISHERS

Jamaica
Carlong Publishers (Caribbean) Ltd, pg 412
Institute of Jamaica Publications, pg 413
West Indies Publishing Ltd, pg 414

Japan
Business Center for Academic Societies Japan, pg 415
Chijin Shokan Co Ltd, pg 415
Chuo-Koron-Sha Inc, pg 415
Corona Publishing Co Ltd, pg 415
Diamond Inc, pg 416
Dobun Shoin, pg 416
Fukuinkan Shoten Publishers Inc, pg 416
Hakuyo-Sha, pg 417
Hakuyu-Sha, pg 417
Hayakawa Publishing Inc, pg 417
Hirokawa Publishing Co, pg 417
Hoikusha Publishing Co Ltd, pg 417
Hokuryukan Co Ltd, pg 417
Holp Book Co Ltd, pg 417
Iwanami Shoten, Publishers, pg 418
Japan Broadcast Publishing Co Ltd, pg 418
Kawade Shobo Shinsha, pg 419
Keigaku Publishing Co Ltd, pg 419
Kinokuniya Co Ltd (Publishing Department), pg 420
Kodansha Scientific Ltd, pg 420
Koseisha-Koseikaku Co Ltd, pg 420
Maruzen Co Ltd, pg 421
Misuzu Shobo Ltd, pg 421
Mita Press, Mita Industrial Co, Ltd, pg 421
Morikita Shuppan Co Ltd, pg 421
Nakayama Shoten Company Ltd, pg 421
Nankodo Co Ltd, pg 421
Nippon Hoso Shuppan Kyokai (NHK Publishing), pg 422
Nippon Jitsugyo Publishing Co, Ltd, pg 423
Obunsha Co Ltd, pg 423
Ohmsha Ltd, pg 423
Poplar Publishing Co Ltd, pg 423
Saera Shobo (Librairie Ca et La), pg 424
Sangyo-Tosho Publishing Co Ltd, pg 424
Sanseido Co Ltd, pg 424
Sanshusha Publishing Co, Ltd, pg 424
Sanyo Shuppan Boeki Co Inc, pg 424
Seibundo Shinkosha Publishing Co Ltd, pg 425
Shincho-Sha Co Ltd, pg 425
Akane Shobo Co Ltd, pg 425
Shokabo Publishing Co Ltd, pg 426
Shokoku Publishing Co Ltd, pg 426
Soshisha Co Ltd, pg 426
Tokyo Kagaku Dozin Co Ltd, pg 427
Tokyo Shoseki Co Ltd, pg 427
Tokyo Tosho Co Ltd, pg 428
Universal Academy Press, Inc, pg 428
University of Tokyo Press, pg 428
Yokendo Ltd, pg 429

Jordan
Al-Tanwir Al Ilmi (Scientific Enlightenment Publishing House), pg 430

Kazakstan
Gylym, Izd-Vo, pg 430
Kazakhstan, Izd-Vo, pg 430

Kenya
Academy Science Publishers, pg 430
African Centre for Technology Studies (ACTS), pg 431
Kenya Literature Bureau, pg 432

Democratic People's Republic of Korea
Academy of Sciences Publishing House, pg 434
Korea Science and Encyclopedia Publishing House, pg 434

Republic of Korea
Ba-reunsa Publishing Co, pg 434
Bakyoung Publishing Co, pg 434
Bo Moon Dang, pg 435
Borim Publishing Co, pg 435
Cheong-mun-gag Publishing Co, pg 435
Chung Rim Publishing Co Ltd, pg 435
Dae Won Sa Co Ltd, pg 435
Ewha Womans University Press, pg 436
Gim-Yeong Co, pg 436
Gyeom-jisa, pg 436
Hainaim Publishing Co Ltd, pg 436
Hakmun Publishing, Co, pg 436
Hyangmunsa Publishing Co, pg 437
Hyein Publishing House, pg 437
Iljo-gag Publishers, pg 437
Kemongsa Publishing Co Ltd, pg 437
Koreaone Press Inc, pg 438
Minumsa Publishing Co Ltd, pg 438
Mun Un Dang, pg 438
Panmun Book Co Ltd, pg 439
Prompter Publications, pg 439
Seoul National University Press, pg 440
Shinkwang Publishing Co, pg 440
Sogang University Press, pg 440
Woongjin Media Corporation, pg 440
Yonsei University Press, pg 441

Latvia
Madris, pg 442

Liechtenstein
Saendig Reprint Verlag, Hans-Rainer Wohlwend, pg 445

Lithuania
Algarve, pg 445
Klaipedos Universiteto Leidykla, pg 445
Mokslo ir enciklopediju leidybos institutas, pg 446

Luxembourg
Editions APESS ASBL, pg 447

The Former Yugoslav Republic of Macedonia
Ktitor, pg 449
Menora Publishing House, pg 449
Nov svet (New World), pg 449

Malaysia
Federal Publications Sdn Bhd, pg 452
Pearson Education, pg 453
Penerbit Jayatinta Sdn Bhd, pg 454
Pustaka Cipta Sdn Bhd, pg 454
Pustaka Delta Pelajaran Sdn Bhd, pg 454
Tropical Press Sdn Bhd, pg 455
Unit Penerbitan Akademik Cancelori~ Universiti Teknologi Malaysia, pg 455
University of Malaya, Department of Publications, pg 455

Maldive Islands
Non-Formal Education Centre, pg 455

Mauritius
Editions de l'Ocean Indien Ltd, pg 457

Mexico
Editorial Azteca SA, pg 458
Libreria y Ediciones Botas SA, pg 458
Centro de Estudios Mexicanos y Centroamericanos, pg 458
Colegio de Postgraduados en Ciencias Agricolas, pg 459
Compania Editorial Continental SA de CV, pg 459
Fernandez Editores SA de CV, pg 461
Fondo de Cultura Economica, pg 461
Editorial Limusa SA de CV, pg 463
Nova Grupo Editorial SA de CV, pg 464
Editorial Nueva Imagen SA, pg 464
Pearson Educacion de Mexico, SA de CV, pg 465
Plaza y Valdes SA de CV, pg 465
Editorial Trillas SA de CV, pg 467
Universidad Nacional Autonoma de Mexico (National University of Mexico), pg 467

Morocco
Dar El Kitab, pg 469
Dar Nachr Al Maarifa Pour L'Edition et La Distribution, pg 469
Les Editions du Journal L' Unite Maghrebine, pg 470

Mozambique
Editora Minerva Central, pg 470

Myanmar
Sarpay Beikman Board, pg 471
Smart & Mookerdum, pg 471

Namibia
Desert Research Foundation of Namibia (DRFN), pg 471
Multi-Disciplinary Research Centre Library, pg 471

Nepal
Royal Nepal Academy, pg 472

Netherlands
Uitgeverij Anthos, pg 472
APA (Academic Publishers Associated), pg 472
B M Israel BV, pg 473
Bosch & Keuning, pg 474
Brill Academic Publishers, pg 475
A W Bruna Uitgevers BV, pg 475
Delft University Press, pg 476
Educatieve Partners Nederland bv, pg 476
Elsevier Science BV, pg 477
Gottmer Uitgevers Groop, pg 477

SUBJECT INDEX

Hagen & Stam Uitgeverij Ten, pg 478
Holland B V Uitgeversmaatschappij, pg 478
Kluwer Academic Publishers, pg 479
Kluwer Technische Boeken BV, pg 480
Uitgeefmaatschappij J H Kok BV, pg 480
Koninklijke Vermande bv, pg 480
Littera Scripta Manet, pg 480
Mirananda Publishers BV, pg 481
Philo Press-Van Heusden-Hissink & Co CV (APA), pg 482
Uitgeverij Ploegsma BV, pg 483
Prometheus, pg 483
Reed Elsevier Nederland BV, pg 483
Segment BV, pg 484
Swets & Zeitlinger Publishers, pg 485
BV Uitgeverij en Boekhandel W J Thieme & Cie, pg 485
V S P International Science Publishers, pg 486
VU Boekhandel/Uitgeverij BV, pg 487

New Zealand
ABA Books, pg 488
Brick Row Publishing Co Ltd, pg 489
ESA Publications (NZ) Ltd, pg 490
Landcare Research NZ, pg 492
Learning Guides (Writers & Publishers) Ltd, pg 492
New House Publishers Ltd, pg 493
Nelson Price Milburn Ltd, pg 494
SIR Publishing, pg 495

Nigeria
Africana-FEP Publishers Ltd, pg 498
Alliance West African Publishers & Co, pg 498
Aromolaran Publishing Co Ltd, pg 498
CSS Bookshops, Agency & Publishing Division, pg 498
Educational Research & Study Group, pg 499
Ethiope Publishing Corporation, pg 499
Evans Brothers (Nigeria Publishers) Ltd, pg 499
Gbabeks Publishers Ltd, pg 499
Ibadan University Press, pg 499
Ilesanmi Press (Educational Publishers) Ltd, pg 499
Kola Sanya Publishing Enterprise, pg 500
Longman Nigeria Plc, pg 500
Thomas Nelson (Nigeria) Ltd, pg 500
New Era Publishers, pg 500
Nwamife Publishers Ltd, pg 500
Ogunsanya Press, Publishers and Bookstores Ltd, pg 501
Onibon-Oje Publishers, pg 501
Riverside Communications, pg 501
West African Book Publishers Ltd, pg 502

Norway
H Aschehoug & Co (W Nygaard) A/S, pg 502
F Bruns Bokhandel og Forlag A/S, pg 503
Forlaget Fag og Kultur, pg 503
Novus Forlag, pg 504
Solum Forlag A/S, pg 505

SUBJECT INDEX

Teknologisk Forlag, pg 505
Universitetsforlaget, pg 505

Pakistan
Hamdard Foundation, pg 507
HMR Publishing Co, pg 507
Maqbool Academy, pg 508
Urdu Academy Sind, pg 509

Panama
Editorial Universitaria, pg 509

Peru
Centro de la Mujer Peruana Flora Tristan, pg 511
Fondo Editorial de la Pontificia Universidad Catolica del Peru, pg 511
Universidad de Lima-Fondo de Desarollo Editorial, pg 512
Universidad Nacional Mayor de San Marcos, pg 512

Philippines
Abiva Publishing House Inc, pg 512
Bookman Printing & Publishing House Inc, pg 512
Rex Bookstores & Publishers, pg 514
Saint Mary's Publishing Corp, pg 515
Salesiana Publishers Inc, pg 515
SIBS Publishing House Inc, pg 515
University of the Philippines Press, pg 515
Vibal Publishing House Inc (VPHI), pg 515

Poland
Wydawnictwa Normalizacyjne Alfa-Wero, pg 516
Interpress, pg 517
KAW Krajowa Agencja Wydawnicza, pg 517
Wydawnictwo Lubelskie, pg 518
Wydawnictwo Nasza Ksiegarnia Sp zoo, pg 518
Norbertinum, pg 518
Ossolineum Zaklad Narodowy im Ossolinskich - Wydawnictwo, pg 518
Panstwowy Instytut Wydawniczy (PIW), pg 518
Oficyna Wydawnicza Politechniki Wroclawskiej, pg 519
Wydawnictwa Radia i Telewizji, pg 519
Wydawnictwo RTW, pg 520
'Slask' Ltd, pg 520
Spotdzielna Anagram, pg 520
'Wiedza Powszechna' Panstwowe Wydawnictwo, pg 521

Portugal
Didactica Editora, pg 524
Dinalivro, pg 524
Publicacoes Europa-America Lda, pg 524
Europress Editores e Distribuidores de Publicacoes Lda, pg 525
Gradiva-Publicacnoes Lda, pg 525
Editora Livros do Brasil Sarl, pg 526
Livraria Lopes Da Silva-Editora de M Moreira Soares Rocha Lda, pg 527
McGraw-Hill Editora de Portugal, pg 527
Editorial Presenca, pg 528
Publicacoes Dom Quixote Lda, pg 528

Editora Replicacao Lda, pg 529
Silabo, pg 529
Almerinda Teixeira, pg 529
Teorema, pg 529
Editorial Verbo SA, pg 530

Puerto Rico
Publishing Resources Inc, pg 531

Romania
Editora All, pg 531
Casa Editoriala Independenta Europa, pg 532
Editura Excelsior, pg 533
FF Press, pg 533
Editura Gryphon, pg 533
Humanitas Publishing House, pg 533
Editura Niculescu, pg 534
Pandora Publishing House, pg 535
Editura Stiintifica, pg 536
Editura Stiintifica si Enciclopedica, pg 536
Editura Tehnica, pg 536
Universal Dalsi, pg 536
Editura de Vest, pg 536

Russian Federation
N E Bauman Moscow State Technical University Publishers, pg 537
BLIC, russko-Baltijskij informaciionnyj centr, AO, pg 537
Energoatomizdat, pg 537
Gidrometeoizdat, pg 538
Izdatelstvo Lenizdat, pg 539
Izdatelstvo Medicina, pg 539
Izdatelstvo Mir, pg 540
Izdatelstvo Mysl, pg 540
Nauka Publishers, pg 540
Obdeestro Znanie, pg 541
Pedagogika Press, pg 541
Izdatelstvo Sudostroenie, pg 542
Vsesoyuznii Molodejnii Knizhnii Centre, pg 542

Saudi Arabia
Saudi Publishing and Distribution House, pg 543

Senegal
Les Nouvelles Editions Africaines du Senegal NEAS, pg 544

Singapore
APAC Publishers Services, pg 545
Celebrity Educational Publishers, pg 545
Chopsons Pte Ltd, pg 545
Global Educational Services Pte Ltd, pg 546
Reed Elsevier, South East Asia, pg 547
Singapore University Press Pte Ltd, pg 548
Success Publications Pte Ltd, pg 548
Taylor & Francis Asia Pacific, pg 548

Slovakia
ARCHA sro Vydavatel 'stro, pg 549
Technicka Univerzita, pg 551
Vydavatel'stvo Osveta (Verlag Osveta), pg 551

Slovenia
Zalozba Obzorja d d Maribor, pg 552

South Africa
Butterworths South Africa, pg 553
Clever Books, pg 553
Educum Publishers Ltd, pg 554
Erudita Publications (Pty) Ltd, pg 554
Heinemann Publishers (Pty) Ltd, pg 555
Nasou Via Afrika, pg 557
National Botanical Institute, pg 557
Oceanographic Research Institute, pg 558
Shuter & Shooter (Pty) Ltd, pg 559
Vivlia Publishers & Booksellers, pg 560

Spain
Acento Editorial, pg 561
Editorial Acribia SA, pg 561
Aguilar SA de Ediciones, pg 562
Alianza Editorial SA, pg 562
AMV Ediciones, pg 563
Editorial Ariel SA, pg 564
Ediciones Bellaterra SA, pg 565
Editorial Casals SA, pg 566
Edicios do Castro, pg 566
Celeste Ediciones, pg 567
Complutense, SA Editorial, pg 568
Comunidad Autonoma de Madrid, Servicio de Documentacion y Publicaciones, pg 568
Consejo Superior de Investigaciones Cientificas, pg 568
Ediciones Diaz de Santos SA, pg 569
Editorial Dossat SA, pg 570
Editorial Empeno 14, pg 573
Fondo de Cultura Economica de Espana, SL, pg 574
Fundacion Marcelino Botin, pg 575
Idea Books, SA, pg 578
Junta de Castilla y Leon Consejeria de Educacion y Cultura, pg 579
Editorial Labor SA, pg 579
Edicions de la Magrana SA, pg 581
McGraw-Hill Iberic/Brazil Group, pg 581
Ediciones Oceano Grupo SA, pg 584
Ediciones Omega SA, pg 585
Editorial Paraninfo SA, pg 586
Pearson Educacion S A, pg 586
Ediciones Piramide, pg 586
Editorial Playor SA, pg 587
Prensas Universitarias de Zaragoza, pg 587
Publicaciones de la Universidad de Alicante, pg 588
Pulso Ediciones, SL, pg 588
Editorial Reverte SA, pg 588
Ediciones Rialp SA, pg 589
Ediciones ROL SA, pg 589
Universidad de Santiago de Compostela, pg 589
Ediciones Scriba SA, pg 589
Servicio de Publicaciones Universidad de Cadiz, pg 590
Editorial Sintesis, SA, pg 590
Equipo Sirius SA, pg 591
Grup 62, pg 591
Ramon Sopena SA, pg 591
Axel Springer Publicaciones, pg 591
Editorial Tecnos SA, pg 592
Ediciones de la Torre, pg 593
Tusquets Editores, pg 593
Universidad de Granada, pg 594
Universidad de Oviedo Servicio de Publicaciones, pg 594
Ediciones Universidad de Salamanca, pg 594

Universidad de Valladolid Secretariado de Publicaciones e Intercambio Editorial, pg 594
Publicacions de la Universitat de Barcelona, pg 594
Edicions de la Universitat Politecnica de Catalunya SL, pg 594
Urmo SA de Ediciones, pg 595
Editorial Vicens-Vives, pg 595
Xunta de Galicia, pg 596

Sri Lanka
Lake House Investments Ltd, pg 597
Ministry of Education, pg 597
Vidura Science Publishers, pg 598
Warna Publishers, pg 598

Sudan
Khartoum University Press, pg 598

Suriname
Stichting Wetenschappelijke Informatie, pg 599

Sweden
Almqvist och Wiksell International, pg 600
Bokforlaget Spektra AB, pg 601
Delta Forlags AB, pg 601
Hallgren och Fallgren Studieforlag AB, pg 603
Ingenjoersforlaget AB, pg 603
ITK Laromedel AB, pg 603
Kungl Ingenjoersvetenskapsakademien (IVA), pg 604
Liber AB, pg 604
Natur och Kultur/LTs foerlag, pg 604
Bokfoerlaget Naturoch Kultur, pg 604
Bokforlaget Nya Doxa AB, pg 605

Switzerland
Ammann Verlag & Co, pg 608
Athenaeum Verlag AG, pg 608
Basilius Presse AG, pg 609
Bibliographisches Institut und F A Brockhaus AG, pg 610
Birkhauser Verlag AG, pg 610
Editions Delachaux et Niestle SA, pg 612
Verlag Harri Deutsch, pg 612
Editions Eisele SA, pg 613
Georg Editeur SA, pg 614
Hallwag AG, pg 615
Paul Haupt Berne, pg 615
Interfrom AG Editions, pg 616
Klett und Balmer & Co Verlag, pg 617
Herbert Lang & Cie AG, Buchhandlung, Antiquariat, pg 618
Medecine et Hygiene, pg 619
Editions Payot Lausanne, pg 621
Philosophisch-Anthroposophischer Verlag am Goetheanum, pg 621
Presses Polytechniques et Universitaires Romandes, PPUR, pg 622
Editiones Roche, pg 623
Schwengeler-Verlag, pg 624
Sphinx Verlag AG, pg 625
Strom-Verlag Luzern, pg 625
Vdf Hochschulverlag AG an der ETH Zurich, pg 626

Syrian Arab Republic
Damascus University Press, pg 628

PUBLISHERS   SUBJECT INDEX

Taiwan, Province of China
Chung Hwa Book Co Ltd, pg 629
Commonwealth Publishing Company Ltd, pg 629
Fuh-Wen Book Co, pg 630
Kuang Fu Book Co Ltd, pg 630
Newton Publishing Company Ltd, pg 631
Petroleum Information Publishing Co, pg 631
San Min Book Co Ltd, pg 631
Shy Chaur Publishing Co Ltd, pg 631
Yi Hsien Publishing Co Ltd, pg 632
Youth Cultural Publishing Co, pg 632

United Republic of Tanzania
Ben and Company Ltd, pg 633
East African Publishing House, pg 633
Eastern Africa Publications Ltd, pg 633
General Publications Ltd, pg 633
Press & Publicity Centre Ltd, pg 634
Readit Books, pg 634
Tanzania Publishing House, pg 634

Thailand
New Generation Publishing Co Ltd, pg 635
Thai Watana Panich Co, Ltd, pg 636

Turkey
Arkin Kitabevi, pg 639
Aydin Yayincilik, pg 639
Bilden Bilgisayar, pg 639
Cep Kitaplari AS, pg 639
Pan Yayincilik, pg 640
Payel Yayinevi, pg 641
Remzi Kitabevi, pg 641
Varlik Yayinlari AS, pg 641

Turkmenistan
Izdatelstvo Turkmenistan, pg 642

Uganda
Fountain Publishers Ltd, pg 642

United Kingdom
Academic Press Ltd, pg 644
Andromeda Oxford Ltd, pg 647
Artech House, pg 649
Association for Science Education, pg 650
The Athlone Press Ltd, pg 650
BCA, pg 653
Blackwell Science Ltd, pg 656
Bloomsbury Publishing PLC, pg 656
The Brown Reference Group PLC, pg 660
Cardinal Publishing Ltd, pg 663
Cassell & Co, pg 664
Chadwyck-Healey Ltd, pg 666
E W Classey Ltd, pg 668
Current Science Group, pg 672
Gerald Duckworth & Co Ltd, pg 676
Edinburgh University Press Ltd, pg 677
Element Books Ltd, pg 678
Eurobook Ltd, pg 679
The Eurospan Group, pg 680
Evans Brothers Ltd, pg 680
Floris Books, pg 683
Forbes Publications Ltd, pg 683
W H Freeman & Co Ltd, pg 684

Genesis Publications Ltd, pg 686
Geological Society Publishing House, pg 686
Gollancz/Witherby, pg 688
Harcourt Publishers Ltd, pg 691
Harvard University Press, pg 692
Headline Book Publishing Ltd, pg 693
Helicon Publishing Ltd, pg 694
Hobsons, pg 696
Hodder & Stoughton Educational, pg 696
Horizon Scientific Press, pg 697
Imperial College Press, pg 699
Institute of Physics Publishing, pg 700
Intercept Ltd, pg 700
Karnak House, pg 703
Learning Together, pg 706
Liverpool University Press, pg 708
Macmillan Reference Ltd, pg 710
Mandrake of Oxford, pg 711
Marshall Editions Ltd, pg 712
Adam Matthew Publications, pg 712
McGraw-Hill Publishing Company, pg 712
Merrow Publishing Co Ltd, pg 714
Micelle Press, pg 714
Mirabel Books Ltd, pg 715
MIT Press Ltd, pg 715
John Murray (Publishers) Ltd, pg 716
Nelson Thornes Ltd, pg 718
New Leaf Books Ltd, pg 719
NMS Publishing Ltd, pg 719
Orion Publishing Group Ltd, pg 722
The Orkney Press Ltd, pg 722
Orpheus Books Ltd, pg 722
Oxford University Press, pg 723
Palgrave Publishers Ltd, pg 723
Pearson Education, pg 725
Pearson Education Europe, Mideast & Africa, pg 725
Portland Press Ltd, pg 730
Prim-Ed Publishing UK Ltd, pg 730
ProQuest Information & Learning, pg 731
Quarto Publishing plc, pg 731
Rationalist Press Association, pg 733
The Reader's Digest Association Ltd, pg 733
The Royal Society, pg 737
The Salariya Book Co Ltd, pg 738
Sangam Books Ltd, pg 738
Science Reviews Ltd, pg 739
Sheffield Academic Press Ltd, pg 741
Simon & Schuster Ltd, pg 742
Skoob Russell Square, pg 742
Smith-Gordon, pg 743
The Society of Metaphysicians Ltd, pg 743
Southgate Publishers, pg 743
Supportive Learning Publications, pg 746
Tarquin Publications, pg 746
Tarragon Press, pg 746
Taylor & Francis Group, pg 747
Thames & Hudson Ltd, pg 748
Thoemmes Press, pg 748
Two-Can Publishing Ltd, pg 750
University of Wales Press, pg 751
The Warburg Institute, pg 754
Ward Lock Educational Co Ltd, pg 754
World Microfilms Publications Ltd, pg 758

Venezuela
Editorial Ateneo de Caracas, pg 762
Monte Avila Editores Latinoamericana CA, pg 762

Editorial Biosfera CA, pg 762
Universidad de los Andes, Consejo de Publicaciones, pg 763
Vadell Hermanos Editores CA, pg 763

Viet Nam
Science & Technics Publishing House, pg 763

Yugoslavia
Alfa-Narodna Knjiga, pg 764
Izdavacka preduzece Gradina, pg 764
Tehnicka Knjiga, pg 764
Minerva, pg 764
Naucna Knjiga, pg 764
Nio Pobjeda - Oour Izdavacko-Publicisticka Djelatnost, pg 765
Partenon MAM Sistem, pg 765
Savez Inzenjera i Tehnicara Jugoslavije, pg 765
Vuk Karadzic, pg 766

Zimbabwe
Academic Books Pvt Ltd, pg 767
College Press Publishers (Pvt) Ltd, pg 768
Longman Zimbabwe (Pvt) Ltd, pg 768
University of Zimbabwe Publications, pg 769
Zimbabwe Publishing House (Pvt) Ltd, pg 769

SCIENCE FICTION, FANTASY

Albania
NL SH, pg 1

Argentina
Editorial Caymi SACI, pg 4

Australia
Crawford House Publishing, pg 19
Geoffrey Hamlyn-Harris, pg 25
Jarrah Publications, pg 28
K & Z Mostafanejad, pg 33
Nimrod Publications, pg 35
Penguin Books Australia Ltd, pg 37
Tomorrow Publications, pg 45
Transworld Publishers Pty Ltd, pg 45
University of Western Australia Press, pg 46

Austria
Aarachne Verlag, pg 49
Verlag Carl Ueberreuter GmbH, pg 59

Belarus
Yunatstva, pg 63

Belgium
Les Editions du Lombard SA, pg 71
Scissors Books, pg 74

Brazil
A & A & A Edicoes e Promocoes Internacionais Ltda, pg 77
Livraria Francisco Alves Editora SA, pg 78
Centro de Estudos Juridicosdo Para (CEJUP), pg 80
Edicon Editora e Consultorial Ltda, pg 81

Ediouro Publicacoes, SA, pg 81
Imago Editora Importacao e Exportacao Ltda, pg 85
Editora Mercuryo Ltda, pg 88
34 Literatura S/C Ltda, pg 92

Bulgaria
Abagar Pablioing, pg 94
Aleks Print Publishing House, pg 94
Galaktika Publishing House, pg 95
MATEX, pg 96
Svetra Publishing House, pg 98
Zunica, pg 98

Chile
Norma de Chile, pg 101

China
Education Science Publishing House, pg 105
Jilin Science & Technology Publishing House, pg 106

Colombia
Editorial Santillana SA, pg 113
Tercer Mundo Editores SA, pg 113

Croatia
Faust Vrani, pg 118

Cuba
Casa Editora Abril, pg 120
Editorial Letras Cubanas, pg 121

Czech Republic
Baronet, pg 123
Doplnek, pg 124
Jota, pg 125
Knihovna A Tiskarna Pro Nevidome, pg 125
Mariadan, pg 126
Mlada fronta, pg 126
Svoboda Servis GmbH, pg 128
Touzimsky & Moravec, pg 128

Denmark
New Era Publications International ApS, pg 134
Wisby & Wilkens, pg 136

Egypt (Arab Republic of Egypt)
Dar El Shorouk Publishing & Distributing House, pg 138

Estonia
Tuum, pg 141

Finland
Oy LIKE Kustannus Ltd, pg 144

France
Publications Aredit, pg 148
Editions Baleine, pg 149
Bragelonne, pg 151
Editions Calmann-Levy SA, pg 152
Copernic, pg 156
Dargaud, pg 157
Georges-Charles Demay, pg 158
Editions Denoel Sarl, pg 158
Editions J Glenat SA, pg 166
Hemma Joven, SA, pg 168
Editions Infrarouge, pg 169
Editions J'ai Lu, pg 170
Le Livre de Poche-L G F (Librairie Generale Francaise), pg 173
Editions Marie-Noelle, pg 175
Editions Payot & Rivages, pg 179
Presses de la Cite, pg 180

1083

SUBJECT INDEX

Editions Robert Laffont, Nil, Fixot, Seghers, Julliard, pg 183
Vents d'Ouest, pg 189

Germany
Argument-Verlag, pg 195
Dr Bachmaier Verlag GmbH, pg 197
Bastei Verlag, pg 199
Corian-Verlag Heinrich Wimmer, pg 211
Dana Verlag, pg 212
Drei Eichen Verlag Manuel Kissener, pg 218
Egmont Franz Schneider Verlag GmbH, pg 221
Egmont vgs verlagsgesellschaft mbH, pg 221
Ensslin und Laiblin Verlag GmbH & Co KG, pg 223
Fabylon-Verlag, pg 226
Wilhelm Goldmann Verlag GmbH, pg 233
Heel Verlag GmbH, pg 238
Heinz-Theo Gremme Verlag, pg 239
Wilhelm Heyne Verlag, pg 240
Karin Kramer Verlag, pg 253
Logos-Verlag Literatur & Layout GmbH, pg 258
New Era Publications Deutschland GmbH, pg 268
Rainar Nitzsche Verlag, pg 269
Buchverlag Andrea Schmitz, pg 284
Verlag Stendel, pg 290
Mario Truant Verlag, pg 295
VS Verlagshaus Stuttgart GmbH, pg 299

Greece
Diavlos, pg 309
Elliniki Leschi Tou Vivliou, pg 310
Exandas Publishers, pg 310
Hestia-I D Hestia-Kollaros & Co Corporation, pg 311

Guatemala
Grupo Editorial RIN-78, pg 316

Hungary
Ifjusagi Lap-eskonyvkiado Vallalat, pg 324
Mora Ferenc Ifjusagi Koenyvkiado Rt, pg 325

India
Ananda Publishers Pvt Ltd, pg 330
Dastane Ramchandra & Co, pg 335
Reliance Publishing House, pg 347
Shaibya Prakashan Bibhag, pg 349

Israel
Pitspopany Press, pg 371

Italy
Fanucci, pg 388
Fatatrac, pg 388
Edizioni Internazionali di Letteratura e Scienze, pg 394
Letture Mensile di Informazione Culturale, Letteratura e Spettacolo, pg 395
Casa Editrice Nord SRL, pg 401
Editoriale Scienza, pg 407
TEA Tascabili degli Editori Associati SpA, pg 409
Todariana Editrice, pg 410

Japan
Fukuinkan Shoten Publishers Inc, pg 416
Hayakawa Publishing Inc, pg 417
Shincho-Sha Co Ltd, pg 425
Tokyo Sogensha Co Ltd, pg 428

Kenya
Kenya Literature Bureau, pg 432

Republic of Korea
Chung Rim Publishing Co Ltd, pg 435
Koreaone Press Inc, pg 438

Latvia
Alberts XII, pg 441
Artava Ltd, pg 441
Hermess Ltd, pg 442

Luxembourg
Hubsch, pg 447

The Former Yugoslav Republic of Macedonia
Detska radost, pg 448
Macedonia Prima Publishing House, pg 449

Malaysia
Pustaka Cipta Sdn Bhd, pg 454

Mexico
Ediciones Corunda SA de CV, pg 459
Fernandez Editores SA de CV, pg 461
Fondo de Cultura Economica, pg 461
Pangea Editores, Sa de CV, pg 465
Plaza y Valdes SA de CV, pg 465
Selector SA de CV, pg 467

Netherlands
Uitgeverij Het Spectrum BV, pg 484

Norway
Gyldendal Norsk Forlag A/S, pg 503
Tiden Norsk Forlag, pg 505

Philippines
Anvil Publishing Inc, pg 512
New Day Publishers, pg 514

Poland
Wydawnictwa Normalizacyjne Alfa-Wero, pg 516
Iskry - Publishing House Ltd spotka zoo, pg 517
Przedsiebiorstwo Wydawniczo-Handlowe Wydawnictwo Siedmiorog, pg 519

Portugal
Editora Classica, pg 523
Gradiva-Publicacnoes Lda, pg 525
Editora Livros do Brasil Sarl, pg 526
Paulinas, pg 528
Planeta Editora, LDA, pg 528
Vega-Publicacao e Distribuicao de Livros e Revistas, Lda, pg 530

Romania
Editura Excelsior, pg 533
Nemira Verlag, pg 534
Pandora Publishing House, pg 535
RAO International Publishing Co, pg 535
RAO Publishing Group, pg 535
Editura Teora, pg 536
Editura Univers, pg 536
Vremea Publishers Ltd, pg 536

Russian Federation
Armada Publishing House, pg 537
BLIC, russko-Baltijskij informaciionnyj centr, AO, pg 537
CentrePolygraph Traders & Publishers Co, pg 537
Kavkazskaya Biblioteka Publishing House, pg 539
Ladomir Publishing House, pg 539
Izdatelstvo Lenizdat, pg 539
Izdatelstvo Mir, pg 540
Obdeestro Znanie, pg 541
Raduga Publishers, pg 541

Slovakia
Sport Publishing House Ltd, pg 551

Slovenia
Mladinska Knjiga International, pg 552

Spain
Editorial Acervo SL, pg 561
Editorial Astri SA, pg 564
CEAC, Grupo Editorial SA, pg 567
Edicions Camacuc, pg 571
Editorial Espasa-Calpe SA, pg 573
Grupo Editorial CEAC SA, pg 576
Editorin Laioyento SL, pg 579
Ediciones Libertarias/Prodhufi SA, pg 580
Ediciones Martinez-Roca SA, pg 581
Ediciones Minotauro, pg 582
Ediciones Olimpic, SL, pg 585
Pleniluni Edicions, pg 587
Ediciones Seyer, pg 590
Ultramar Editores SA, pg 594

Sri Lanka
Danuma Prakashakayo, pg 596
Warna Publishers, pg 598

Sweden
Sjoestrands Foerlag, pg 606

Switzerland
Editions L'Age d'Homme - La Cite, pg 608
Haffmans Verlag AG, pg 615

United Republic of Tanzania
Kajura Publications, pg 633

Thailand
Chokechai Thewet Co Ltd, pg 635
Graphic Art Publishing, pg 635

Turkey
Altin Kitaplar Yayinevi, pg 638
Cep Kitaplari AS, pg 639
Iletisim Yayinlari, pg 640
Metis Yayinlari, pg 640

Ukraine
ASK Ltd, pg 643

United Kingdom
Apex Publishing Ltd, pg 648
BCA, pg 653
Boxtree Ltd, pg 658
Cassell & Co, pg 664
Constable & Robinson Ltd, pg 670
Constable Publishers, pg 670
The Eurospan Group, pg 680
Gollancz/Witherby, pg 688
HarperCollins Publishers, pg 692
Hodder Children's Books, pg 696
Janus Publishing Company Ltd, pg 702
Liverpool University Press, pg 708
Y Lolfa Cyf, pg 708
Luath Press Ltd, pg 709
Mandrake of Oxford, pg 711
New Era Publications UK Ltd, pg 718
Octopus Publishing Group, pg 720
Orion Publishing Group Ltd, pg 722
Time Warner Books UK, pg 749
Titan Books Ltd, pg 749
Transworld Publishers Ltd, pg 750
Trigon Press, pg 750
Virgin Publishing Ltd, pg 753

SECURITIES

Albania
NL SH, pg 1

Argentina
Bonum Editorial SACl, pg 4
Editorial Ciudad Nueva de la Sefoma, pg 5

Brazil
Editora Manuais Tecnicos de Seguros Ltda, pg 87
Saraiva SA, Livreiros Editores, pg 91

China
Fudan University Press, pg 105

France
Editions Delmas, pg 158
Joly Editions, pg 170
Top Editions, pg 188

Germany
Bank-Verlag GmbH, pg 198
Beuth Verlag GmbH, pg 202
Verlag Hoppenstedt GmbH, pg 242

Ghana
World Literature Project, pg 308

Israel
Dekel Publishing House, pg 366

Malaysia
Trix Corporation Sdn Bhd, pg 455

Mexico
Pearson Educacion de Mexico, SA de CV, pg 465
Ediciones Promesa, SA de CV, pg 466

Poland
Wydawnictwo Prawnicze Co, pg 519

Portugal
Paulinas, pg 528

PUBLISHERS

Russian Federation
Finansy i Statistika Publishing House, pg 538
Teorija Verojatnostej i ee Primenenija, pg 542

Slovenia
Univerza v Ljubljani Ekonomska Fakulteta, pg 552

United Kingdom
Business Monitor International, pg 661
Cavendish Publishing Ltd, pg 665
DMG Business Media Ltd, pg 675

Viet Nam
Science & Technics Publishing House, pg 763

SELF-HELP

Albania
NL SH, pg 1

Argentina
Beas Ediciones SRL, pg 4
Bonum Editorial SACI, pg 4
Editorial Caymi SACI, pg 4
Errepar SA, pg 5
Editorial Kier SACIFI, pg 7
Editorial Paidos SAICF, pg 8
San Pablo, pg 8
Javier Vergara Editor SA, pg 9

Australia
Angel Publications, pg 11
Ashling Books, pg 12
Bio Concepts Publishing, pg 15
Blackhead Ink Publishing, pg 15
Joan Blair, pg 15
Bridge To Peace Publications, pg 16
CHOICE Magazine, pg 18
Coconut Productions, pg 18
Community Quarterly, pg 18
Crawford House Publishing, pg 19
Crista International, pg 19
Crossroad Distributors Pty Ltd, pg 19
Deva Wings Publications, pg 20
E J Dwyer (Australia) Pty Ltd, pg 21
Finch Publishing, pg 22
Fraser Publications, pg 23
Gnostic Editions, pg 24
Hale & Iremonger Pty Ltd, pg 24
Kerri Hamer, pg 25
Hihorse Publishing Pty Ltd, pg 26
In-Tune Books, pg 27
Life Planning Foundation of Australia, Inc, pg 30
Barry Long Books, pg 30
Thomas C Lothian Pty Ltd, pg 30
Mayne Publishing, pg 32
Moon-Ta-Gu Books, pg 33
New Era Publications Australia Pty Ltd, pg 34
Anne O'Donovan Pty Ltd, pg 35
Pan Macmillan Australia Pty Ltd, pg 36
Penguin Books Australia Ltd, pg 37
Pinchgut Press, pg 38
Jurriaan Plesman, pg 38
Priestley Consulting, pg 39
The Real Estate Institute of Australia, pg 40
Shakespeare Head Press Pty Ltd, pg 42
Simon & Schuster Australia Pty Ltd, pg 42
Single X Publications, pg 42
Stirling Press, pg 43
Thin Rich Press, pg 44
Tomorrow Publications, pg 45
Transworld Publishers Pty Ltd, pg 45
Unity Press, pg 46
Wileman Publications, pg 47
Windhorse Books, pg 48
Wrightbooks Pty Ltd, pg 48

Austria
Denkmayr GmbH Druck & Verlag, pg 51

Bangladesh
Gono Prakashani, Gono Shasthya Kendra, pg 62

Barbados
Business Tutors, pg 63

Belgium
Altina, pg 64
Uitgeverij Lannoo NV, pg 70
Marabout, pg 72

Brazil
Editora Agora Ltda, pg 78
Editora Aquariana Ltda, pg 78
Editora Bertrand Brasil Ltda, pg 79
Editora Crescer Ltda, pg 81
Editora Elevacao, pg 82
Companhia Editora Forense, pg 82
Editora Gaia Ltda, pg 84
Editora Globo SA, pg 84
Ordem do Graal na Terra, pg 84
Editora e Grafica Carisio Ltda, pg 84
Editora Harbra Ltda, pg 84
Imago Editora Importacao e Exportacao Ltda, pg 85
Livraria Nobel S/A, pg 86
Edicoes Loyola SA, pg 87
Madras Editora, pg 87
Editora Mercuryo Ltda, pg 88
Editora Nova Fronteira SA, pg 88
Editora Objetiva Ltda, pg 88
Pallas Editora e Distribuidora Ltda, pg 89
Paulinas Editorial, pg 89
Paulus Editora, pg 89
Qualitymark Editora Ltda, pg 90
Editora Revan Ltda, pg 90
Editora Rocco Ltda, pg 91
Summus Editorial Ltda, pg 92
Thex Editora e Distribuidora Ltda, pg 92
Totalidade Editora Ltda, pg 92

Bulgaria
Aratron, IK, pg 94
Kibea Publishing Co, pg 96
Prozoretz Ltd Publishing House, pg 97
Sila & Zivot, pg 98

Cameroon
Editions Buma Kor, pg 99

Chile
Arrayan Editores, pg 99
Ediciones Mil Hojas Ltda, pg 100
Norma de Chile, pg 101

China
Beijing Juvenile & Children's Books Publishing House, pg 102
Beijing Publishing House, pg 102
Book Marketing Ltd, pg 102

Colombia
RAM Editores, pg 113
Editorial Santillana SA, pg 113
Tercer Mundo Editores SA, pg 113

Costa Rica
Promesa, Ediciones, pg 116
Scout Interamericana, pg 117

Cuba
Editorial Oriente, pg 121

Czech Republic
Pavla Momcilova, pg 126
Pragma 4, pg 127

Denmark
Borgens Forlag A/S, pg 130
Forlaget Hovedland, pg 133
New Era Publications International ApS, pg 134
Olivia - det gronne forlag, pg 134

Estonia
Sinisukk, pg 140

Finland
Karas-Sana Oy, pg 142

France
Chronique Sociale, pg 155
Edition1, pg 161
Hachette Livre, pg 167
Editions Hatier SA, pg 168
Langues & Mondes/L'Asiatheque, pg 171
Librairie Larousse, pg 172
Editions Ophrys, pg 178
Les Presses du Management, pg 181
Editions Robert Laffont, Nil, Fixot, Seghers, Julliard, pg 183
Sofradif Editions Philippe Auzou, pg 185
Editions Spratbrow, pg 186
Editions Trois Fontaines, pg 188

Germany
Blaukreuz-Verlag Wuppertal, pg 204
Buchverlage Langen-Mueller/Herbig, pg 207
CEC-Cosmic Energy Connections, pg 209
Claudius Verlag, pg 211
Connection Medien GmbH, pg 211
Verlag CSA Rosemarie Schneider, pg 212
Divyanand Verlags GmbH, pg 217
Drei Eichen Verlag Manuel Kissener, pg 218
Droemersche Verlagsanstalt Th Knaur Nachfolger GmbH & Co, pg 218
Econ Taschenbuchverlag, pg 220
Ernst Kabel Verlag GmbH, pg 223
EVT Energy Video Training & Verlag GmbH, pg 225
Gatzanis Verlags GmbH, pg 231
Genius Verlag, pg 231
Graefe und Unzer Verlag GmbH, pg 233
Verlag der Stiftung Gralsbotschaft GmbH, pg 234
Walter Haedecke Verlag, pg 236

SUBJECT INDEX

Heinz-Theo Gremme Verlag, pg 239
Verlag Herder GmbH & Co KG, pg 239
AIG 1 Hilbinger Verlag GmbH, pg 241
Heinrich Hugendubel Verlag GmbH, pg 243
Joy Verlag GmbH, pg 247
Junfermann-Verlag, pg 247
Klartext Verlagsgesellschaft mbH, pg 249
Verlag Kleine Schritte Ursula Dahm & Co, pg 249
Koenigsfurt Verlag, Evelin Burger et Johannes Fiebig, pg 251
Krug & Schadenberg, pg 254
Lebenshilfe-Verlag Marburg, Verlag der Bundesvereinigung Lebenshilfe fuer Menschen mit geistiger Behinderung eV, pg 256
Midena Verlag, pg 264
Mosaik Verlag GmbH, pg 265
Neue Erde Verlags GmbH, pg 267
Neuland-Verlagsgesellschaft mbH, pg 268
New Era Publications Deutschland GmbH, pg 268
Nie/Nie/Sagen-Verlag, pg 268
nymphenburger, pg 269
Orlanda Frauenverlag, pg 270
Osho Verlag GmbH, pg 271
Projektion J Buch- und Musikverlag GmbH, pg 275
Rake Verlag GmbH, pg 277
Reichl Verlag Der Leuchter, pg 278
Schueren Verlag GmbH, pg 285
Heinrich Schwab Verlag, pg 285
Spieth-Verlag Verlag fuer Symbolforschung, pg 288
Suin Buch-Verlag, pg 291
Weber Zucht & Co, pg 300
Verlag DAS WORT GmbH, pg 304

Ghana
World Literature Project, pg 308

Greece
Kedros Publishers, pg 312

Hong Kong
Chung Hwa Book Co (HK) Ltd, pg 319
Design Human Resources Training & Development, pg 319
Philopsychy Press, pg 321
Unicorn Books Ltd, pg 322

Hungary
Park Konyvkiado Kft (Park Publisher), pg 326

Iceland
Idunn, pg 328
Islendingasagnautgafan, pg 328

India
Concept Publishing Co, pg 335
Dastane Ramchandra & Co, pg 335
General Book Depot, pg 337
Gyan Publishing House, pg 338
Hind Pocket Books Private Ltd, pg 338
Jaico Publishing House, pg 340
B Jain Publishers Overseas, pg 340
Lancer Publisher's & Distributors, pg 341
New Light Publishers, pg 344
Orient Paperbacks, pg 345

1085

Rajendra Publishing House Pvt Ltd, pg 347
Sultan Chand & Sons Pvt Ltd, pg 351

Indonesia
Dinastindo, pg 355

Ireland
Campus Publishing Ltd, pg 359
Cathedral Books Ltd, pg 359
The Columba Book Service, pg 359
The Columba Press, pg 359
Gill & Macmillan Ltd, pg 361
The O'Brien Press Ltd, pg 363
Tivenan Publications, pg 364

Israel
Bitan Publishers Ltd, pg 365
Breslov Research Institute, pg 366
DAT Publications, pg 366
Dekel Publishing House, pg 366
Intermedia Audio, Video Book Publishing Ltd, pg 368
Pitspopany Press, pg 371
R Sirkis Publishers Ltd, pg 372
Zmora-Bitan, Publishers Ltd, pg 374

Italy
Editore Armando Armando SRL, pg 376
Gruppo Editoriale Armenia SpA, pg 376
Edizioni Centro Studi Erickson, pg 381
Effata Editrice, pg 387
ERGA SNC di Carla Ottino Merli & C (Edizioni Realizzazioni Grafiche - Artigiana), pg 388
Folini, pg 389
Piero Gribaudi Editore, pg 391
Gruppo Calderini Edagricole, pg 392
Lyra Libri SAS, pg 397
Edizioni Piemme SpA, pg 403
Il Punto D Incontro, pg 404
TEA Tascabili degli Editori Associati SpA, pg 409
Editrice Uomini Nuovi, pg 410

Jamaica
Association of Development Agencies, pg 412

Japan
Diamond Inc, pg 416
Kosei Publishing Co Ltd, pg 420
Nikkagiren Shuppan-Sha (JUSE Press Ltd), pg 422

Kenya
Action Publishers, pg 430
Kenya Quality & Productivity Institute, pg 432
Space Sellers Ltd, pg 433

Republic of Korea
Gim-Yeong Co, pg 436

Latvia
Artava Ltd, pg 441

Lithuania
Dargenis Publishers, pg 445
Tyto Alba Publishers, pg 446

Malaysia
Federal Publications Sdn Bhd, pg 452
Glad Sounds Sdn Bhd, pg 452
Minerva Publications, pg 453

Mexico
Ediciones Alpe, pg 458
Del Verbo Emprender SA de CV, pg 459
Editorial Diana SA de CV, pg 459
Edamex SA de CV, pg 460
Editorial El Manual Moderno SA de CV, pg 460
Hoja Casa Editorial SA de CV, pg 462
Editorial Jus SA de CV, pg 462
Libra Editorial SA de CV, pg 463
Nova Grupo Editorial SA de CV, pg 464
Pangea Editores, Sa de CV, pg 465
Panorama Editorial, SA, pg 465
Ediciones Promesa, SA de CV, pg 466
Selector SA de CV, pg 467
Sistemas Tecnicos de Edicion SA de CV, pg 467
Ediciones Suromex SA, pg 467
Javier Vergara Editor SA de CV, pg 468

Netherlands
BZZTOH Publishers, pg 475
Kartoen, pg 479
Servire BV Uitgevers, pg 484
Uitgeverij De Toorts, pg 485

Netherlands Antilles
De Wit Stores NV, pg 488

New Zealand
Gnostic Press, pg 491
HarperCollins Publishers (New Zealand) Ltd, pg 491
Magari Publishing, pg 493
Spinal Publications, pg 496
Tandem Press, pg 496
Taylor Books, pg 496

Nigeria
Evans Brothers (Nigeria Publishers) Ltd, pg 499

Norway
Hilt & Hansteen A/S, pg 504

Philippines
New Day Publishers, pg 514

Poland
Gdanskie Wydawnictwo Psychologiczne SC, pg 516
Iskry - Publishing House Ltd spotka zoo, pg 517
Oficyna Wydawnicza Read Me, pg 519
Wydawnictwo SIC, pg 520

Portugal
Gradiva-Publicacnoes Lda, pg 525
Monitor-Projectos e Edicoes, LDA, pg 527
Editorial Noticias, pg 527
Editorial Presenca, pg 528

Puerto Rico
Piedras Press, Inc, pg 531

Romania
Editura Niculescu, pg 534
RAO Publishing Group, pg 535

Russian Federation
Finansy i Statistika Publishing House, pg 538
Izdatelstvo Mir, pg 540
Obdeestro Znanie, pg 541

Singapore
Aquanut Agencies Pte Ltd, pg 545

Slovakia
Priroda, pg 550

Slovenia
Zalozba Mihelac d o o, pg 552

South Africa
Human & Rousseau (Pty) Ltd, pg 555
Kima Global Publishers, pg 556

Spain
Acento Editorial, pg 561
Aguilar SA de Ediciones, pg 562
Editorial Astri SA, pg 564
Baile del Sol, Colectivo Cultural, pg 565
Los Libros del Comienzo, pg 568
Editorial EDAF SA, pg 571
Editorial Espasa-Calpe SA, pg 573
Libsa Editorial SA, pg 580
Lid Editorial Empresarial, SL, pg 580
Loguez Ediciones, pg 580
Antonio Machado, SA, pg 580
Ediciones Martinez-Roca SA, pg 581
Ediciones Norma SA, pg 584
OASIS, Producciones Generales de Comunicacion, pg 584
Obelisco Ediciones S, pg 584
Ediciones Paidos Iberica SA, pg 585
Ediciones Temas de Hoy, SA, pg 592
Tursen, SA, pg 593
Ediciones 29 - Libros Rio Nuevo, pg 594
Ediciones Urano, SA, pg 595
Javier Vergara Editor SA, pg 595

Sweden
ICA bokforlag, pg 603
Svenska Foerlaget liv & ledarskap ab, pg 607

Switzerland
Ariston Editions, pg 608
Editions Jouvence, pg 616
Kanisius Verlag, pg 616
Leonis Verlag, pg 618
Oesch Verlag AG, pg 620

Taiwan, Province of China
Asian Culture Co, pg 629
Commonwealth Publishing Company Ltd, pg 629
Linking Publishing Company Ltd, pg 631
Morning Star Publisher Inc, pg 631
Shy Chaur Publishing Co Ltd, pg 631
Shy Mau Publishing Company, pg 631
Yuan Liou Publishing Co, Ltd, pg 632

Togo
Editions Akpagnon, pg 636

Tunisia
Les Editions de l'Arbre, pg 638

Turkey
Ruh ve Madde Yayinlari ve Saglik Hizmetleri AS, pg 641
Saray Medikal Yayin Tic Ltd Sti, pg 641
Soez Yayin/Oyunajans, pg 641
Varlik Yayinlari AS, pg 641

United Kingdom
Act 3 Publishing, pg 645
Apex Publishing Ltd, pg 648
Ashgrove Press, pg 650
BCA, pg 653
Bloomsbury Publishing PLC, pg 656
Nicholas Brealey Publishing, pg 659
Capall Bann Publishing, pg 663
Constable & Robinson Ltd, pg 670
Crossbridge Books, pg 672
The C W Daniel Co Ltd, pg 673
Dorling Kindersley Ltd, pg 676
Element Books Ltd, pg 678
Elliot Right Way Books, pg 678
Extraordinary People Press, pg 681
Facts On File, pg 681
Findhorn Press Inc, pg 682
Foulsham Publishers, pg 683
Gateway Books, pg 686
Green Books Ltd, pg 689
HarperCollins Publishers, pg 692
The Harvill Press Ltd, pg 693
Hawthorn Press, pg 693
Highland Books Ltd, pg 695
Hodder & Stoughton General, pg 696
Hodder & Stoughton Religious, pg 696
How To Books Ltd, pg 697
Isis Publishing Ltd, pg 701
Kogan Page Ltd, pg 705
Law Pack Publishing Ltd, pg 706
Lion Publishing PLC, pg 708
Kenneth Mason Publications Ltd, pg 712
MIND Publications, pg 715
National Extension College, pg 717
New Era Publications UK Ltd, pg 718
Michael O'Mara Books Ltd, pg 721
Oneworld Publications, pg 721
Orion Publishing Group Ltd, pg 722
Pan Macmillan, pg 723
Parapress Ltd, pg 724
Piatkus Books, pg 727
Plough Publishing House of Bruderhof Communities in the UK, pg 728
Prism Press Book Publishers Ltd, pg 730
Quarto Publishing plc, pg 731
Ravette Publishing Ltd, pg 733
Rosendale Press Ltd, pg 735
Roundhouse Publishing Ltd, pg 736
Sheldon Press, pg 741
Sherwood Publishing, pg 741
The Society for Promoting Christian Knowledge (SPCK), pg 743
Rudolf Steiner Press, pg 745
Telegraph Books, pg 748
Ward Lock Ltd, pg 754
Which? Ltd, pg 755
Wimbledon Publishing Company Ltd, pg 757
The Women's Press Ltd, pg 758
World Microfilms Publications Ltd, pg 758

PUBLISHERS SUBJECT INDEX

Uruguay
Rosebud Ediciones, pg 761

Venezuela
Alfadil Ediciones, pg 761

Yugoslavia
Alfa-Narodna Knjiga, pg 764

SOCIAL SCIENCES, SOCIOLOGY

Albania
NL SH, pg 1
State Textbook Publishing House, pg 1

Algeria
Enterprise Nationale du Livre (ENAL), pg 2

Argentina
Editorial Abaco de Rodolfo Depalma SRL, pg 2
Editorial Albatros SACI, pg 3
Alianza Editorial de Argentina SA, pg 3
Amorrortu Editores SA, pg 3
Editorial Astrea de Alfredo y Ricardo Depalma SRL, pg 3
Fundacion Editorial de Belgrano, pg 4
Centro Editor de America Latina SA, pg 4
Club de Lectores, pg 4
Depalma SRL, pg 5
Editorial Idearium de la Universidad de Mendoza (EDIUM), pg 5
Ediciones de la Flor SRL, pg 6
Editorial Galerna SRL, pg 6
Editorial Guadalupe, pg 6
Marymar Ediciones SA, pg 7
Editorial Medica Panamericana, pg 7
Ediciones Nueva Vision SAIC, pg 8
Oikos, pg 8
Editorial Paidos SAICF, pg 8
Editorial Pleamar, pg 8
Editorial Plus Ultra SA, pg 8
Polemos SA, pg 8
Instituto Torcuato Di Tella, pg 9
Ediciones Tres Tiempos SRL, pg 9
Editorial Universidad SRL, pg 9

Australia
Artemis Publishing Pty Ltd, pg 12
Ausmed Publications Pty Ltd, pg 12
Australian Institute of Family Studies (AIFS), pg 13
Australian Scholarly Publishing, pg 14
Community Quarterly, pg 18
Crawford House Publishing, pg 19
Crystal Publishing, pg 19
Dabill Publications, pg 20
Dangaroo Press, pg 20
E J Dwyer (Australia) Pty Ltd, pg 21
Finch Publishing, pg 22
Freshet Press, pg 23
Gerald Griffin Press, pg 24
Kerri Hamer, pg 25
Harcourt Australia Pty Ltd, pg 25
Histec Publications, pg 26
James Nicholas Publishers Pty Ltd, pg 28
Macmillan Education Australia, pg 31
Maxwell Macmillan Publishing (Australia) Pty Ltd, pg 32
McGraw-Hill Australia Pty Ltd, pg 32
Melbourne Institute of Applied Economic & Social Research, pg 33
Ocean Press, pg 35
Pascoe Publishing, pg 37
Pearson Education Australia, pg 37
Jurriaan Plesman, pg 38
Pluto Press Australia, pg 38
Pollitecon Publications, pg 38
Priestley Consulting, pg 39
St Pauls, pg 41
Spinifex Press, pg 43
State Library of NSW Press, pg 43
La Trobe University Press, pg 45
University of New South Wales Press Ltd, pg 46
University of Western Australia Press, pg 46
Vista Publications, pg 47
Wileman Publications, pg 47

Austria
Boehlau Verlag GmbH & Co KG, pg 50
CEEBA Publications Antenne d'Autriche, pg 50
Dachs-Verlag GmbH, pg 50
Development News Ltd, pg 51
Verlag fuer Geschichte und Politik, pg 52
Guthmann & Peterson Liber Libri, Edition, pg 52
Haymon-Verlag GesmbH, pg 52
Dr Verena Hofstaetter, pg 53
Milena Verlag, pg 55
NOI - Verlag, pg 55
Verlag der Oesterreichischen Akademie der Wissenschaften (OEAW), pg 56
Oesterreichischer Kunst und Kulturverlag, pg 56
Verlag Oldenbourg, pg 56
Verlag fuer Sammler, pg 58
WUV/Facultasuniversitaetsverlag, pg 61

Bangladesh
Academic Publishers, pg 62
Gono Prakashani, Gono Shasthya Kendra, pg 62
Agamee Prakashani, pg 62

Belgium
Academia-Bruylant, pg 63
Academia Press, pg 64
Acco CV, pg 64
Centre Aequatoria, pg 64
Artel SC, pg 64
Vanden Broele NV, pg 65
Campinia Media VZW, pg 65
CED-Samsom, pg 66
Centre d'Action Laique, pg 66
La Charte Editions juridiques, pg 66
Davidsfonds VZW, pg 67
Editions De Boeck-Larcier SA, pg 67
EPO Publishers, Printers, Booksellers, pg 68
King Baudouin Foundation, pg 70
Kritak Uitgeverij, pg 70
Editions Labor, pg 70
Editions Lessius ASBL, pg 71
Leuven University Press, pg 71
Maklu, pg 71
Nauwelaerts Edition SA, pg 72
Uitgeverij Pelckmans N V, pg 73
Presses Universitaires de Liege, pg 73
Publications des Facultes Universitaires Saint Louis, pg 73
Sonneville Press (Uitgeverij) VTW, pg 74
UGA Editions (Uitgeverij), pg 74
Uitgeverij De Garve, pg 75
Editions de l'Universite de Bruxelles, pg 75
Vander Editions, SA, pg 75
Les Editions Vie ouvriere ASBL, pg 75
VUB University Press, pg 75

Bermuda
Bermudian Publishing Co, pg 76

Brazil
AGIR S/A Editora, pg 78
Editora Alfa Omega Ltda, pg 78
Editora do Brasil SA, pg 80
Editora Brasiliense SA, pg 80
Editora Campus Ltda, pg 80
Centro de Estudos Juridicosdo Para (CEJUP), pg 80
Livraria Duas Cidades Ltda, pg 81
Dumara Distribuidora de Publicacoes Ltda, pg 81
Editora Cidade Nova Socieda de Movimentodos Focolari, pg 82
Cia Editora Nacional, pg 82
EDUC - Editora da PUC-SP, pg 82
EDUSC - Editora da Universidade do Sagrado Coracao, pg 82
Empresa Brasileira de Pesquisa Agropecaria, pg 83
Livraria Martins Fontes Editora Ltda, pg 83
Editora Forense, pg 83
Forense Universitaria Editora, pg 83
Fundacao Joaquim Nabuco Editora, pg 84
Global Editora e Distribuidora Ltda, pg 84
Edicoes Graal Ltda, pg 84
Editora Harbra Ltda, pg 84
IBRASA (Instituicao Brasileira de Difusao Cultural Ltda), pg 85
Editora Lidador Ltda, pg 86
Oficina de Livros Ltda, pg 86
Edicoes Loyola SA, pg 87
Editora Moderna Ltda, pg 88
Editora Nova Fronteira SA, pg 88
Olho D'Agua Comercio e Servicos Editoriais Ltda, pg 88
Edit Palavra Magica, pg 89
Pallas Editora e Distribuidora Ltda, pg 89
Paulinas Editorial, pg 89
Paulus Editora, pg 89
Editora Paz e Terra, pg 89
Editora Perspectiva, pg 89
Livraria Pioneira Editora/Enio Matheus Guazzelli e Cia Ltd, pg 89
Editora Revan Ltda, pg 90
Editora Rocco Ltda, pg 91
Editora Sinodal, pg 91
Edicoes Tabajara, pg 92
Thex Editora e Distribuidora Ltda, pg 92
Editora UNESP, pg 92
Editora Universidade de Brasilia, pg 92
Editora da Universidade de Sao Paulo, pg 93
Editora Universidade Federal do Rio de Janeiro, pg 93
Fundacao Getulio Vargas, pg 93
Editora Verbo Ltda, pg 93
Vozes Editora Ltda, pg 93
Jorge Zahar Editor, pg 93

Bulgaria
Antroposofsko Izdatelstvo Dimo R Daskalov OOD, pg 94
Bojko Kacarmazov, pg 94
Darzavno Izdatelstvo Narodna Kultura, pg 95
Publishing House Hristo Botev, pg 96
LIK IZDANIJA, pg 96
Makros 2000 - Plovdiv, pg 96
Izdatelstvo na Ministervstoto na Otbranata, pg 96
Mladezh, pg 96
Naouka i Izkoustvo, Ltd, pg 97
Nov Covek Publishing House, pg 97

Burundi
Editions Intore, pg 98

Cameroon
Centre d'Edition et de Production pour l'Enseignement et la Recherche (CEPER), pg 99
Editions CLE, pg 99
Presses Universitaires d'Afrique, pg 99

Chile
Arrayan Editores, pg 99
Edeval (Universidad de Valparaiso), pg 100
Ediciones y Publicidad Melquiades, pg 100
Editora Nueva Generacion, pg 101
Pehuen Editores Ltda, pg 101
Editorial Universitaria SA, pg 101
Ediciones Universitarias de Valparaiso, pg 101

China
Anhui People's Publishing House, pg 102
Beijing Publishing House, pg 102
China Ocean Press, pg 103
China Social Sciences Publishing House, pg 104
China Tibetology Publishing House, pg 104
China Youth Publishing House, pg 104
Chongqing University Press, pg 104
Foreign Language Teaching & Research Press, pg 105
Fudan University Press, pg 105
Higher Education Press, pg 106
Jinan Publishing House, pg 107
Knowledge Press, pg 107
Kunlun Publishing House, pg 107
Lanzhou University Press, pg 107
SDX (Shenghuo-Dushu-Xinzhi) Joint Publishing Co, pg 108
Shandong People's Publishing House, pg 109
Shanghai Educational Publishing House, pg 109
World Affairs Press, pg 110
Wuhan University Press, pg 110
Xinhua Publishing House, pg 110

Colombia
El Ancora Editores, pg 111
Bedout Editores SA, pg 111
Dosmil Editora, pg 111
Universidad Externado de Colombia, pg 112
Fundacion Centro de Investigacion y Educacion Popular (CINEP), pg 112
Editorial Libros y Libres SA, pg 112

SUBJECT INDEX

McGraw-Hill InterAmericana SA, pg 113
Editorial Oveja Negra, pg 113
Siglo XXI Editores de Colombia Ltda, pg 113
Tercer Mundo Editores SA, pg 113
Unidad Universitaria del Sur (UNISUR), pg 114
Universidad de Antioquia, Division Publicaciones, pg 114
Carlos Valencia Editores, pg 114

The Democratic Republic of the Congo

Presses Universitaires du Zaiire (PUZ), pg 115

Costa Rica

Asamblea Legislativa, Biblioteca Monsenor Sanabria, pg 115
Centro Agronomico Tropical de Investigacion y Ensenanza (CATIE), pg 115
Editorial Nacional de Salud y Seguridad Social Ednass, pg 116
Editorial Porvenir, pg 116
Promesa, Ediciones, pg 116
Editorial de la Universidad de Costa Rica, pg 117
Editorial Universitaria Centroamericana (EDUCA), pg 117

Cote d'Ivoire

Centre d'Edition et de Diffusion Africaines, pg 117
Universite d' Abidjan, pg 118

Croatia

AGM doo, pg 118
Filozofski Fakultet Sveucilista u Zagrebu, pg 118
Globus-Nakladni zavod, pg 118
Hrvatsko filozofsko drustvo, pg 119
Informator dd, pg 119
Matica hrvatska, pg 119
Mladost d d Izdavacku graficku i informaticku djelatnost, pg 119
Nakladni zavod Matice hrvatske, pg 119
Naprijed d d Naklada, pg 119
Skolska Knjiga, pg 120

Cuba

Casa de las Americas, pg 120
Editorial de Ciencias Sociales, pg 121
Editora Politica, pg 121
Pueblo y Educacion Editorial (PE), pg 121
Universidad Central de la Villas, Centro Documentacion e Informacion Cientifica Tecnica, pg 121

Czech Republic

Barrister & Principal, pg 123
Doplnek, pg 124
Kalich SRO, pg 125
Karolinum, nakladatelstvi, pg 125
Libri s r o, pg 125
Lidove noviny Nakladatelstvi, pg 125
Slon Sociologicke Nakladatelstvi, pg 128

Denmark

Aarhus Universitetsforlag, pg 129
Akademisk Forlag, pg 129
Djof Publishing Jurist-og Okonomforbundets Forlag, pg 131
Fremad A/S, pg 132
Forlaget GMT, pg 132
Gyldendalske Boghandel - Nordisk Forlag A/S, pg 132
Forlaget Hovedland, pg 133
Museum Tusculanum Press, pg 134
Nyt Nordisk Forlag Arnold Busck A/S, pg 134
Politisk Revy, pg 134
Hans Reitzel Publishers Ltd, pg 134
Samfundslitteratur, pg 135
Forlaget Vindrose A/S, pg 136

Dominican Republic

Pontificia Universidad Catolica Madre y Maestra, pg 136
Sociedad Editorial Dominicana SA, pg 137

Ecuador

CEPLAES, pg 137
Corporacion Editora Nacional, pg 137
Pontificia Universidad Catolica de Ecuador, Centro de Publicaciones, pg 137

Egypt (Arab Republic of Egypt)

American University in Cairo Press, pg 138
Al Arab Publishing House, pg 138
Dar Al-Matbo at Al-Gadidah, pg 138
Dar El Shorouk Publishing & Distributing House, pg 138
Middle East Book Centre, pg 139

El Salvador

UCA Editores, pg 139
Editorial Universitaria de la Universidad de El Salvador, pg 139

Estonia

Kupar Publishers, pg 140
Olion Publishers, pg 140

Finland

Kuva ja Sana, pg 143
Osuuskunta Vastapaino, pg 145
Yliopistopaino/Helsinki University Press, pg 145

France

Editions A M Metailie, pg 145
Editions Albin Michel, pg 146
Editions d'Amerique et d'Orient, Adrien Maisonneuve, pg 147
L'Anabase, pg 147
Annales de la Recherche Urbaine, pg 147
Editions - Anthropos Sarl, pg 147
APRD - Association pour la Recherche et l'Information demographiques, pg 147
L'Arche Editeur, pg 147
Les Editions de l'Atelier SA, pg 148
Atelier National de Reproduction des Theses, pg 148
Editions de l'Aube, pg 149
Editions Aubier-Montaigne SA, pg 149
Autrement Editions, pg 149
Beauchesne Editeur, pg 150
Berger-Levrault SA, pg 150
Editions Buchet/Chastel, pg 152
Editions Calmann-Levy SA, pg 152
CERDIC-Publications, pg 153
Editions du Cerf, pg 153
Editions Champ Vallon, pg 154
Chotard et Associes Editeurs, pg 154
Chronique Sociale, pg 155
CNRS Editions, pg 155
Armand Colin, Editeur, pg 155
Corsaire Editions, pg 156
Council of Europe Publishing, pg 156
Editions Criterion, pg 157
CTNERHI - Centre Technique National d'Etudes et de Recherches sur les Handicaps et les Inadaptations, pg 157
Editions Cujas, pg 157
Nouvelles Editions Debresse, pg 158
La Decouverte et Syros, pg 158
Dervy-Livres, pg 158
Desclee de Brouwer SA, pg 158
Doin Editeurs, pg 160
Librairie Generale de Droit et de Jurisprudence (LGDJ) - Montchrestien, pg 160
Editions de l'Ecole des Hautes Etudes en Sciences Sociales (EHESS), pg 160
Presses de l'Ecole Normale Superieure, pg 160
Editions d'Organisation, pg 161
Editions Recherche sur les Civilisations (ERC), pg 161
EDP Sciences, pg 161
Ere Nouvelle, pg 162
Editions Eres, pg 162
Editions Espaces 34, pg 162
Librairie Artheme Fayard, pg 163
Librairie Fischbacher, International Art Book Distribution (import-export), pg 164
Groupe Fleurus-Mame, pg 164
Presses de la Fondation Nationale des Sciences Politiques, pg 164
Futuribles SARL, pg 165
Edition Galilee, pg 165
Editions Gamma, pg 165
Paul Geuthner Librairie Orientaliste, pg 166
Groupe Expansion, pg 167
Hachette Livre, pg 167
L'Harmattan, pg 168
Editions de l'Herne, pg 168
Editions d'Histoire Sociale (EDHIS), pg 168
Editions Imago, pg 169
Editions Infrarouge, pg 169
INRA Editions (Institut National de la Recherche Agronomique), pg 169
Editions INSERM, pg 169
Les Introuvables-Editions L'Harmattan, pg 170
IRD Editions, pg 170
Editions Ivrea, pg 170
Editions du Jaguar, pg 170
Editions Juridiques et Techniques Lamy SA, pg 171
Karthala Editions-Diffusion, pg 171
Editions Klincksieck, pg 171
Librairie Larousse, pg 172
Le Livre de Poche-L G F (Librairie Generale Francaise), pg 173
Editions de la Maison des Sciences de l'Homme, Paris, pg 174
Les Editions de Minuit SA, pg 176
Presses Universitaires du Mirail, pg 176
Fernand Nathan, pg 177
Editions Odile Jacob, pg 178
Editions Ophrys, pg 178
L'Originel - Editions Accarias, pg 178
Pardes, pg 179
Editions Payot & Rivages, pg 179
Presses Universitaires de Caen, pg 181
Presses Universitaires de France (PUF), pg 181
Presses Universitaires de Grenoble, pg 181
Presses Universitaires de Nancy, pg 181
Presses Universitaires de Strasbourg, pg 181
Presses Universitaires du Septentrion, pg 181
Publications Orientalistes de France (POF), pg 182
Revue Espaces et Societes, pg 183
Editions Robert Laffont, Nil, Fixot, Seghers, Julliard, pg 183
Editions Sand et Tchou SA, pg 183
Selection du Reader's Digest SA, pg 184
Maren Sell, pg 184
Sepia, pg 184
Editions de Septembre, pg 184
Editions du Seuil, pg 185
Editions Andre Silvaire Sarl, pg 185
Publications de la Sorbonne, pg 186
Editions SOS (Editions du Secours Catholique), pg 186
Editions Stock, pg 186
Tacor International, pg 187
Librairie Pierre Tequi et Editions Tequi, pg 187
Transeuropeennes/RCE, pg 188
UNESCO Publishing, pg 188
Publications de l'Universite de Pau, pg 188
Editions Weka, pg 189

Georgia

Izdatelstvo Sabtchota Sakartvelo, pg 190

Germany

A Francke Verlag (Tubingen und Basel), pg 191
Accedo Verlagsgesellschaft mbH, pg 191
Akademie Verlag GmbH, pg 192
Andernach Atelier Verlag (AVA), pg 193
Antiquariat und Verlag Auvermann Keip GmbH, pg 194
Arbeiterpresse Verlag GmbH, pg 194
ARCult Media, pg 194
Argument-Verlag, pg 195
Roland Asanger Verlag GmbH, pg 195
Asso Verlag, pg 196
Verlag C H Beck (OHG), pg 200
Belser Wissenschaftlicher Dienst, pg 200
Berliner Debatte Wissenschafts Verlag, GSFP-Gesellschaft fur Sozialwissen-schaftliche Forschung und Publizistik mbH &Co KG, pg 201
W Bertelsmann Verlag GmbH & Co KG, pg 201
BKV-Brasilienkunde Verlag GmbH, pg 203
Verlag Die Blaue Eule, pg 204
Bleicher Verlag GmbH, pg 204
Boehlau-Verlag GmbH & Cie, pg 204
Brandes & Apsel Verlag GmbH, pg 206

PUBLISHERS SUBJECT INDEX

Bund demokratischer Wissenschaftlerinnen und Wissenschafler eV (BdWi), pg 207
Caann Verlag, Klaus Wagner, pg 208
Campus Verlag GmbH, pg 209
Centaurus-Verlagsgesellschaft GmbH, pg 209
Chmielorz GmbH Verlag, pg 210
Hans Christians Druckerei und Verlag GmbH & Co, pg 210
Daedalus Verlag, pg 212
Verlag Darmstaedter Blaetter Schwarz und Co, pg 212
Deutscher Studien Verlag, pg 215
Deutscher Taschenbuch Verlag GmbH & Co KG (dtv), pg 215
Deutscher Universitats-Verlag, pg 215
Deutsches Jugendinstitut (DJI), pg 216
Eugen Diederichs Verlag GmbH & Co KG, pg 216
Diesterweg, Moritz Verlag, pg 216
Dietrich zu Klampen Verlag, pg 216
Verlag J H W Dietz Nachf GmbH, pg 217
Dietz Verlag Berlin GmbH, pg 217
Edition Diskord, pg 217
agenda Verlag Thomas Dominikowski, pg 217
Droste Verlag GmbH, pg 218
DSI Data Service & Information, pg 219
Duncker und Humblot GmbH, pg 219
Ehrenwirth Verlag GmbH, pg 221
Elefanten Press Verlag GmbH, pg 222
N G Elwert Verlag, pg 222
Ferdinand Enke Verlag, pg 227
Festland Verlag GmbH, pg 227
Wilhelm Fink GmbH & Co Verlags-KG, pg 228
Karin Fischer Verlag GmbH, pg 228
Rita G Fischer Verlag, pg 228
Flensburger Hefte Verlag GmbH, pg 228
Focus-Verlag Gesellschaft mbH, pg 229
Verlag Freies Geistesleben, pg 230
Verlag A Fromm im Druck- u Verlagshaus Fromm GmbH & Co KG, pg 230
Friedrich Frommann Verlag, pg 230
Gesellschaft fur Organisationswissenschaft e V, pg 232
Wilhelm Goldmann Verlag GmbH, pg 233
Walter de Gruyter GmbH & Co KG, pg 234
Gunter Olzog Verlag GmbH, pg 235
Haag und Herchen Verlag GmbH, pg 235
Dr Curt Haefner-Verlag GmbH, pg 236
Joh Heider Verlag GmbH, pg 239
Edition Hentrich Druck & Verlag Gebr Hentrich und Tank GmbH & Co KG, pg 239
Hans-Alfred Herchen & Co Verlag KG, pg 239
Erika Heydick Sax-Verlag Beucha, pg 240
Verlag Hinder und Deelmann, pg 241
Hoffmann und Campe Verlag GmbH, pg 242
Holos Verlag, pg 242
Horlemann Verlag, pg 243

Human Wissenschafilicher Verlag, pg 243
Edition Humanistische Psychologie (EHP), pg 243
ludicium Verlag GmbH, pg 245
Janus Verlagsgesellschaft, Dr Norbert Meder & Co, pg 246
Junius Verlag GmbH, pg 247
Juventa Verlag GmbH, pg 247
K L V Konkret Literatur Verlag GmbH, pg 247
Katzmann Verlag KG, pg 248
Verlag Kiepenheuer und Witsch GmbH & Co KG, pg 249
Kindler Verlag GmbH, pg 249
Klartext Verlagsgesellschaft mbH, pg 249
K F Koehler Verlag, pg 251
Verlagsgruppe Koehler/Mittler, pg 251
Koelner Universitaets-Verlag GmbH, pg 251
Verlag Koenigshausen und Neumann GmbH, pg 251
W Kohlhammer GmbH, abt Haussortiment, pg 252
Karin Kramer Verlag, pg 253
Institut fuer Landes- und Stadtentwicklungsforschung, ILS Nordrhein-Westfalen, pg 255
Lebenshilfe-Verlag Marburg, Verlag der Bundesvereinigung Lebenshilfe fuer Menschen mit geistiger Behinderung eV, pg 256
Verlag Leske plus Budrich GmbH, pg 257
Libertas- Europaeisches Institut GmbH, pg 257
LIT Verlag, pg 258
Logos-Verlag Literatur & Layout GmbH, pg 258
Lucius & Lucius Verlagsgesellschaft mbH, pg 259
Lukas Verlag fur Kunst- und Geistesgeschichte, pg 259
Metropolis- Verlag fur Okonomie, Gesellschaft und Politik GmbH, pg 263
Karl-Heinz Metz, pg 263
Mohr Siebeck, pg 264
Gunter Narr Verlag, pg 266
Neuer ISP Verlag GmbH, pg 268
Neuland-Verlagsgesellschaft mbH, pg 268
Georg Olms Verlag AG, pg 270
Orlanda Frauenverlag, pg 270
Pahl-Rugenstein Verlag Nachfolger-GmbH, pg 271
PapyRossa Verlags GmbH & Co Kommanditgesellschaft KG, pg 271
Edition Parabolis, pg 271
Propylaeen Verlag, Zweigniederlassung Berlin der Ullstein Buchverlage GmbH, pg 275
Psychologie Verlags Union GmbH, pg 275
Psychosozial-Verlag, pg 275
Quelle und Meyer Verlag GmbH & Co, pg 276
R Oldenbourg Verlag GmbH, pg 276
Dr Mohan Krischke Ramaswamy Edition RE, pg 277
Verlag Recht und Wirtschaft GmbH, pg 277
Verlag fur Regionalgeschichte, pg 277
Ernst Reinhardt GmbH & Co KG Verlag, pg 278
Rombach GmbH Druck und Verlagshaus & Co, pg 280

Rowohlt Taschenbuch Verlag GmbH, pg 280
K G Saur Verlag GmbH, A Gale/Thomson Learning Company, pg 282
Schelzky & Jeep, Verlag fuer Reisen und Wissen, pg 283
Max Schmidt-Roemhild Verlag, pg 284
Schueren Verlag GmbH, pg 285
Schulz-Kirchner Verlag GmbH, pg 285
R S Schulz Verlag GmbH, pg 285
Otto Schwartz Fachbochhandlung GmbH, pg 286
Scientia Verlag und Antiquariat, pg 286
Edition Sigma e.Kfm, pg 287
Spiess Volker Wissenschaftsverlag GmbH, pg 287
Springer-Verlag GmbH & Co KG, pg 288
J F Steinkopf Verlag GmbH, pg 289
Steinweg-Verlag, Jurgen romHoff, pg 290
Suin Buch-Verlag, pg 291
Edition Temmen, pg 292
Trotzdem-Verlags Genosenschaft eG, pg 295
Tuduv Verlagsgesellschaft mbH, pg 295
Tuebinger Vereinigung fur Volkskunde eV (TVV), pg 295
Ullstein Heyne List GmbH & Co KG, pg 295
Ulrike Helmer Verlag, pg 296
UNO-Verlag mbH, Vertriebs und Verlagsgesellschaft, pg 296
UTB fuer Wissenschaft Uni-Taschenbuecher GmbH, pg 297
UVK Verlagsgesellschaft mbH, pg 297
VAS-Verlag fuer Akademische Schriften, Vas Karl-Heinz Balon, pg 297
VJK Verlag Josef Knecht, pg 299
Dokument und Analyse Verlag Bogislaw von Randow, pg 299
Votum Verlag GmbH, pg 299
VWB-Verlag fur Wissenschaft & Bildung, Amand Aglaster, pg 300
Wachholtz Verlag GmbH, pg 300
Waxmann Verlag GmbH, pg 300
Weber Zucht & Co, pg 300
Verlag Klaus Wagenbach GmbH, pg 300
Weidler Buchverlag Berlin, pg 301
Westdeutscher Verlag GmbH, pg 302
Verlag Westfaelisches Dampfboot, pg 302
Dr Dieter Winkler, pg 303
Verlag Wissenschaft und Politik/Helker Pflug, pg 303
Wissenschaftliche Buchgesellschaft, pg 303

Ghana

Asempa Publishers, pg 306
Black Mask Ltd, pg 306
EPP Books Services, pg 307
Ghana Publishing Corporation, pg 307
Ghana Universities Press (GUP), pg 307
Waterville Publishing House, pg 308

Greece

Apostoliki Diakonia tis Ekklisias tis Hellados, pg 309
D l Arsenidis Publications, pg 309
Bergadis, pg 309
Boukoumanis' Editions, pg 309

Ecole francaise d'Athenes, pg 310
Etaireia Spoudon Neoellinikou Politismou Kai Genikis Paideias, pg 310
Exandas Publishers, pg 310
Gutenberg Publications, pg 311
Hestia-I D Hestia-Kollaros & Co Corporation, pg 311
ldryma Meleton Chersonisou tou Aimou, pg 311
Irini Publishing House - Vassilis G Katsikeas SA, pg 311
Kritiki Publishing, pg 312
Kyriakidis Vasileios, pg 312
Panepistimio Ioanninon, pg 314
Papazissis Publishers SA, pg 314
Patakis Publishers, pg 314
Sakkoulas Publications SA, pg 314
Stochastis, pg 315
Thymari Publications, pg 315

Guatemala

Grupo Editorial RIN-78, pg 316

Guinea-Bissau

Instituto Nacional de Estudos e Pesquisa, pg 316

Honduras

Editorial Guaymuras, pg 318

Hong Kong

The Chinese University Press, pg 319
Chung Hwa Book Co (HK) Ltd, pg 319
Hong Kong University Press, pg 320

Hungary

Akademiai Kiado, pg 323
Atlantisz Kiado, pg 323
Balassi Kiado Kft, pg 323
Central European University Press, pg 323
CEU-Press, pg 323
Janus Pannonius Tudomanyegyetem, pg 324
Joszoveg Muhely Kiado, pg 324
KJK-Keaszov, pg 324
Mult es Jovo Kiado, pg 325
Osiris Kiado, pg 326
Statiqum Kiado es Nyomda Kft, pg 326

Iceland

Hid Islenzka Bokmenntafelag, pg 328

India

Abhinav Publications, pg 329
The Academic Press, pg 329
Addison-Wesley (Singapore) Pte Ltd, pg 329
Agricole Publishing Academy, pg 330
Ajanta Publications (India), pg 330
Amar Prakashan, pg 330
Ananda Publishers Pvt Ltd, pg 330
Anmol Publications Pvt Ltd, pg 331
APH Publishing Corp, pg 331
Arihant Publishers, pg 331
Arya Medi Publishing House, pg 331
Asian Educational Services, pg 331
Asian Trading Corporation, pg 331
Associated Publishing House, pg 331
Atma Ram & Sons, pg 331

1089

SUBJECT INDEX

Avinash Reference Publications, pg 331
K P Bagchi & Co, pg 332
Baha'i Publishing Trust of India, pg 332
The Bangalore Printing & Publishing Co Ltd, pg 332
Bharatiya Samijik Vigyan Auusandhan Parishad, pg 332
Bharatiya Vidya Bhavan, pg 333
Booklinks Corporation, pg 334
BR Publishing Corporation, pg 334
Chanakya Publications, pg 334
S Chand & Co Ltd, pg 334
Chugh Publications, pg 335
Classical Publishing Co, pg 335
Concept Publishing Co, pg 335
Cosmo Publications, pg 335
Dastane Ramchandra & Co, pg 335
Disha Prakashan, pg 336
Eastern Book Centre, pg 336
Eastern Law House Pvt Ltd, pg 336
Enkay Publishers Pvt Ltd, pg 336
Ess Ess Publications, pg 337
Eurasia Publishing House Pvt Ltd, pg 337
Firma KLM Privatee Ltd, Publishers & International Booksellers, pg 337
Geeta Prakasham, pg 337
Gitanjali Publishing House, pg 337
Gyan Publishing House, pg 338
Arnold Heinman Publishers (India) Pvt Ltd, pg 338
Heritage Publishers, pg 338
Himalaya Publishing House, pg 338
Indian Institute of Advanced Study, pg 339
Indian Society for Promoting Christian Knowledge (ISPCK), pg 339
Indus Publishing Co, pg 339
Intellectual Publishing House, pg 339
Inter-India Publications, pg 340
Kali For Women, pg 341
Kitab Ghar, pg 341
Konark Publishers, Pvt, Ltd, pg 341
Manohar Publishers & Distributors, pg 342
Minerva Associates (Publications) Pvt Ltd, pg 342
Ministry of Information & Broadcasting, pg 342
Mittal Publications, pg 343
National Book Organization, pg 343
National Publishing House, pg 344
Naya Prokash, pg 344
Omsons Publications, pg 345
Panjab University Publication Bureau, pg 345
Parimal Prakashan, pg 345
People's Publishing House (P) Ltd, pg 346
Pointer Publishers, pg 346
Popular Prakashan Pvt Ltd, pg 346
Promilla and Co, pg 346
Radiant Publishers, pg 347
Rajasthan Hindi Granth Academy, pg 347
Rajendra Publishing House Pvt Ltd, pg 347
Regency Publications, pg 347
Reliance Publishing House, pg 347
SABDA, pg 348
Sage Publications India Pvt Ltd, pg 348
SBW Publishers, pg 349
Scientific Book Agency, pg 349
Scientific Publishers India, pg 349
Somaiya Publications Pvt Ltd, pg 350
South Asian Publishers Pvt Ltd, pg 350
Spectrum Publications, pg 350
Sterling Publishers Pvt Ltd, pg 351
Sultan Chand & Sons Pvt Ltd, pg 351
Surjeet Publications, pg 351
DB Taraporevala Sons & Co Pvt Ltd, pg 351
Lok Vangamaya Griha Pvt Ltd, pg 352
Vivek Prakashan, pg 353

Indonesia
Alumni PT, pg 353
Bhratara Karya Aksara, pg 354
P T Bulan Bintang, pg 354
Djambatan PT, pg 355
Lembaga Demografi Fakultas Ekonomi Universitas Indonesia, pg 356
Pustaka Utama Grafiti, PT, pg 357
Yayasan Obor Indonesia, pg 357

Iraq
National House for Publishing, Distributing and Advertising, pg 358

Ireland
Attic Press Ltd, pg 358
Campus Publishing Ltd, pg 359
Cork University Press, pg 359
The Economic & Social Research Institute, pg 360
Institute of Public Administration, pg 361
Irish YouthWork Press, pg 362

Israel
Am Oved Publishers Ltd, pg 365
Bar Ilan University Press, pg 365
Dyonon/Papyrus Publishing House of the Tel-Aviv, pg 367
Freund Publishing House Ltd, pg 367
Hakibbutz Hameuchad Publishing House Ltd, pg 368
Hanitzotz A-Sharara Publishing House, pg 368
The Institute for Israeli Arabs Studies, pg 368
Israel Universities Press, pg 369
(JDC) Brookdale Institute of Gerontology & Adult Human Development in Israel, pg 369
Keter Publishing House Ltd, pg 369
Massada Press Ltd, pg 370
Open University of Israel, pg 371
Sifriat Poalim Ltd, pg 372
Steimatzky Group Ltd, pg 372
Tel-Aviv University, pg 373
The Van Leer Jerusalem Institute, pg 373
Yachdav, United Publishers Co Ltd, pg 373
Y L Peretz Publishing Co, pg 374

Italy
Mario Adda Editore SNC, pg 374
Edizioni della Fondazione Giovanni Agnelli, pg 375
Edizioni Anabasi SpA, pg 375
Editrice Ancora, pg 375
Franco Angeli SRL, pg 375
Editore Armando Armando SRL, pg 376
Casa Editrice Astrolabio-Ubaldini Editore, pg 377
Baha'i, pg 377
Bibliotheca di Gabriele Chiusano, pg 378
Bollati Boringhieri Editore Srl, pg 378
Edizioni Borla SRL, pg 378
Bulzoni Editore SRL (Le Edizioni Universitarie d'Italia), pg 379
Edizioni Cadmo SRL, pg 379
Nuova Casa Editrice Licinio Cappelli GEM srl, pg 379
Casa Editrice Libraria Ulrico Hoepli SpA, pg 380
CEDAM (Casa Editrice Dr A Milani), pg 380
Celuc Libri, pg 380
Edizioni Centro Studi Erickson, pg 381
Centro Studi Terzo Mondo, pg 381
Citta Nuova Editrice, pg 382
Cittadella Editrice, pg 382
Edizioni di Comunita SpA, pg 382
Cooperativa Libraria IULM SCRL, pg 383
Edizioni Cultura della Pace, pg 383
La Culturale, pg 383
Edizioni Dedalo SRL, pg 384
Edizioni Dehoniane, pg 384
Ediciclo Editore SRL, pg 386
Edizioni Studio Domenicano (ESD), pg 387
Giulio Einaudi Editore SpA, pg 387
Libreria Editrice Fiorentina di Vittorio Zani e C SAS, pg 389
Gangemi Editore, pg 390
Edizioni GB, pg 390
Editrice Giannotta di Sebastiano Pace Giannotta, pg 390
G Giappichelli Editore SRL, pg 390
A Giuffre Editore SpA, pg 390
Gius Laterza e Figli SpA, pg 391
Libreria Editrice Gregoriana, pg 391
Edizioni Guerini e Associati SpA, pg 392
Horus, pg 393
Ibis, pg 393
Il Saggiatore, pg 393
Instituti Editoriali E Poligrafici Internazionali SRL, pg 393
Edizioni Internazionali di Letteratura e Scienze, pg 394
Editoriale Jaca Book SpA, pg 394
L Japadre Editore, pg 394
Kaos Edizioni SRL, pg 395
Lalli Editore SRL, pg 395
Laruffa Editore SRL, pg 395
Editrice LAS, pg 395
Edizioni Lavoro SRL, pg 395
Lecce Spazio Vivo Srl, pg 395
Liguori Editore SRL, pg 396
Vincenzo Lo Faro Editore, pg 396
Longanesi & C, pg 396
Manifestolibri, pg 397
Marsilio Editori SpA, pg 398
Editrice Massimo SAS di Crespi Cesare e C, pg 398
Edizioni Medicea SRL, pg 398
Milella di Lecce Spazio Vivo SRL, pg 399
Editrice Missionaria Italiana (EMI), pg 399
Monduzzi Editore SpA, pg 399
Editrice Morcelliana SpA, pg 399
Societa Editrice Il Mulino, pg 400
Gruppo Ugo Mursia Editore SpA, pg 400
Museo Storico in Trento, pg 400
Newton Compton Editori SRL, pg 401
La Nuova Italia Editrice SpA, pg 401
Officina Edizioni di Aldo Quinti, pg 401
Leo S Olschki, pg 402
Maria Pacini Fazzi Editore, pg 402
Patron Editore SrL, pg 403
Piero Manni srl, pg 403
Pirola, pg 403
RAI.ERI, pg 405
RCS Rizzoli Libri SpA, pg 405
Editori Riuniti, pg 405
Edizioni Universitarie Romane, pg 406
Rosenberg e Sellier Editori in Torino, pg 406
Rubbettino Editore, pg 406
Salerno Editrice SRL, pg 406
Sapere 2000 SRL, pg 407
Edizioni Scientifiche Italiane, pg 407
Sellerio Editore, pg 407
Societa Storica Catanese, pg 408
Edizioni Studium SpA, pg 409
Nicola Teti e C Editore SRL, pg 409
Edizioni Thyrus SRL, pg 409
Editrice Tirrenia Stampatori SAS, pg 410
Todariana Editrice, pg 410
UTET (Unione Tipografico-Editrice Torinese), pg 411
Vivere In SRL, pg 411
Zanichelli Editore SpA, pg 412

Jamaica
Carlong Publishers (Caribbean) Ltd, pg 412
Institute of Jamaica Publications, pg 413
Jamaica Publishing House Ltd, pg 413
University of the West Indies Press, pg 414

Japan
Akita Shoten Publishing Co Ltd, pg 414
Aoki Shoten Co Ltd, pg 414
Baifukan Co Ltd, pg 414
Chikuma Shobo Publishing Co Ltd, pg 415
Chuo-Koron-Sha Inc, pg 415
Fuzambo Publishing Co, pg 416
GakuseiSha Publishing Co Ltd, pg 416
Hayakawa Publishing Inc, pg 417
Heibonsha Ltd, Publishers, pg 417
Hyoronsha Publishing Co Ltd, pg 417
Ichiryu-Sha, pg 417
Ie-No-Hikari Association, pg 418
Iwanami Shoten, Publishers, pg 418
Japan Broadcast Publishing Co Ltd, pg 418
Kawade Shobo Shinsha, pg 419
Kazama Shobo, pg 419
Keisuisha Publishing Company Ltd, pg 419
Kinokuniya Co Ltd (Publishing Department), pg 420
Kodansha, pg 420
Kokudo-Sha, pg 420
Koseisha-Koseikaku Co Ltd, pg 420
Koyo Shobo, pg 420
Minerva Shobo Co Ltd, pg 421
Mirai-Sha, pg 421
Misuzu Shobo Ltd, pg 421
Nihon Bunka Kagakusha Co Ltd, pg 422
Nihon-Bunkyo Shuppan (Japan Educational Publishing Co Ltd), pg 422
Nihon Tosho Center Co Ltd, pg 422
Nippon Hoso Shuppan Kyokai (NHK Publishing), pg 422
Otsuki Shoten Publishers, pg 423

PHP Kenkyujo, pg 423
Riso-Sha, pg 424
Ryosho-Fukyu-Kai Co Ltd, pg 424
Sanseido Co Ltd, pg 424
Shakai Shiso-Sha, pg 425
The Simul Press Inc, pg 426
Tamagawa University Press, pg 427
Tokai University Press, pg 427
Tokuma-Shoten, pg 427
Tokyo Sogensha Co Ltd, pg 428
Toyo Keizai Inc (The Oriental Economist), pg 428
Tsukiji Shokan Publishing Co, pg 428
Charles E Tuttle Publishing Co Inc, pg 428
United Nations University Press, pg 428
University of Tokyo Press, pg 428
Waseda University Press, pg 428
Yuhikaku Publishing Co Ltd, pg 429

Jordan
Al-Tanwir Al Ilmi (Scientific Enlightenment Publishing House), pg 430

Kazakstan
Gylym, Izd-Vo, pg 430
Kazakh Al-Farabi State National University, pg 430
Kazakhstan, Izd-Vo, pg 430

Kenya
African Centre for Technology Studies (ACTS), pg 431
Heinemann Kenya Limited (EAEP), pg 431
Midi Teki Publishers, pg 433
Nairobi University Press, pg 433
Phoenix Publishers, pg 433
Shirikon Publishers, pg 433
Transafrica Press, pg 433
Uzima Press, pg 433
Gideon S Were Press, pg 434

Democratic People's Republic of Korea
Korea Science and Encyclopedia Publishing House, pg 434

Republic of Korea
Bakyoung Publishing Co, pg 434
Bum-Woo Publishing Co, pg 435
Chung Rim Publishing Co Ltd, pg 435
Ewha Womans University Press, pg 436
Hak Won Publishing Co, pg 436
Hakmun Publishing, Co, pg 436
Hangil Art Vision, pg 436
Hanul Publishing Co, pg 436
Haseo Publishing Co, pg 436
Iljisa Publishing House, pg 437
Iljo-gag Publishers, pg 437
Jeong-eum Munhwasa, pg 437
Korea University Press, pg 437
Koreaone Press Inc, pg 438
Kukminseokwan Publishing Co Ltd, pg 438
Kyungnam University Press, pg 438
Minumsa Publishing Co Ltd, pg 438
Munhag-gwan, pg 438
Munye Publishing Co, pg 439
Nanam Publishing House, pg 439
Omun Gak, pg 439
Oruem Publishing House, pg 439
Panmun Book Co Ltd, pg 439
Pochinchai Printing Co Ltd, pg 439
Samhwa Publishing Co, pg 440
Samkwang Publishing Co, pg 440
Seoul National University Press, pg 440
Sogang University Press, pg 440
Sohaksa, pg 440
Yonsei University Press, pg 441

Kuwait
Ministry of Information, pg 441

Laos People's Democratic Republic
Lao-phanit, pg 441

Latvia
Lielvards Ltd, pg 442

Lebanon
Institute for Palestine Studies, Publishing & Research Organization (IPS), pg 443
Khayat Book and Publishing Co Sarl, pg 443

Lesotho
Saint Michael's Mission, pg 444

Liechtenstein
Topos Verlag AG, pg 445

Lithuania
Academia, pg 445
Klaipedos Universiteto Leidykla, pg 445

Luxembourg
Essay und Zeitgeist Verlag, pg 447
Service Central de la Statistique et des Etudes Economiques (STATEC), pg 448

Macau
Livros Do Oriente, pg 448
Universidadede de Macau, Centro de Publicacoes, pg 448

The Former Yugoslav Republic of Macedonia
Macedonia Prima Publishing House, pg 449

Madagascar
Editions Ambozontany, pg 450

Malaysia
Pelanduk Publications (M) Sdn Bhd, pg 453
Penerbit Universiti Sains Malaysia, pg 454
University of Malaya, Department of Publications, pg 455

Maldive Islands
Non-Formal Education Centre, pg 455

Mali
EDIM SA, pg 455

Malta
Media Centre, pg 456

Mexico
Editores Asociados Mexicanos SA de CV (EDAMEX), pg 458
Editorial Avante SA de Cv, pg 458
Ediciones el Caballito SA, pg 458
Centro de Estudios Mexicanos y Centroamericanos, pg 458
El Colegio de Mexico AC, pg 459
Colegio de Postgraduados en Ciencias Agricolas, pg 459
Comision Nacional Forestal, pg 459
Publicaciones Cruz O SA, pg 459
Edamex SA de CV, pg 460
Editorial Edicol SA, pg 460
El Colegio de Michoacan A C, pg 460
Ediciones Era SA de CV, pg 460
Editorial Extemporaneos SA, pg 461
Fernandez Editores SA de CV, pg 461
Fondo de Cultura Economica, pg 461
Editorial Joaquin Mortiz SA de CV, pg 462
Editorial Jus SA de CV, pg 462
Editorial Limusa SA de CV, pg 463
McGraw-Hill Interamericana de Mexico, SA de CV, pg 463
Instituto Nacional de Antropologia e Historia, pg 464
Instituto Nacional de Estadistica, Geographia e Informatica, pg 464
Editorial Nuestro Tiempo SA, pg 464
Editorial Nueva Imagen SA, pg 464
Grupo Editorial Planeta, pg 465
Plaza y Valdes SA de CV, pg 465
Ediciones Cientificas La Prensa Medica Mexicana SA de CV, pg 466
Siglo XXI Editores SA de CV, pg 467
Editorial Trillas SA de CV, pg 467
Universidad Nacional Autonoma de Mexico (National University of Mexico), pg 467
Universidad Veracruzana Direccion General Editorial y de Publicaciones, pg 468

Republic of Moldova
Izdatelstvo Kartia Moldoveniaske, pg 468

Morocco
Editions Al-Fourkane, pg 469
Dar El Kitab, pg 469
Dar Nachr Al Maarifa Pour L'Edition et La Distribution, pg 469
Editions Eddif Maroc, pg 469
Editions Le Fennec, pg 470

Myanmar
Knowledge Printing & Publishing House, pg 471

Namibia
Multi-Disciplinary Research Centre Library, pg 471

Nepal
International Standards Books & Periodicals (P) Ltd, pg 471
Royal Nepal Academy, pg 472

Netherlands
Uitgeverij Ambo BV, pg 472
APA (Academic Publishers Associated), pg 472
Uitgeverij Jan van Arkel, pg 473
John Benjamins BV, pg 474
Erven J Bijleveld, pg 474
Bohn Stafleu Van Loghum BV, pg 474
Boom Uitgeverij, pg 474
Brill Academic Publishers, pg 475
A W Bruna Uitgevers BV, pg 475
Uitgeversmaatschappij Ad Donker BV, pg 476
KITLV Press Royal Institute of Linguistics & Anthropology, pg 479
Kluwer Academic Publishers, pg 479
Uitgeefmaatschappij J H Kok BV, pg 480
Uitgeverij Lemma BV, pg 480
Lemniscaat, pg 480
Mets & Schilt Uitgevers en Distributeurs, pg 481
Uitgeverij H Nelissen BV, pg 482
Nijgh & Van Ditmar Amsterdam, pg 482
Prometheus, pg 483
Samsom BedrijfsInformatie BV, pg 483
Sociaal en Cultureel Planbureau, pg 484
Uitgeverij de Tijdstroom BV, pg 485
Twente University Press, pg 485
Van Gorcum & Comp BV, pg 486
VU Boekhandel/Uitgeverij BV, pg 487

New Zealand
Aoraki Press Ltd, pg 488
Auckland University Press, pg 488
ESA Publications (NZ) Ltd, pg 490
Fraser Books, pg 491
Nelson Price Milburn Ltd, pg 494
RSVP Publishing Company Ltd, pg 495
Victoria University Press, pg 496

Nicaragua
Editorial Nueva Nicaragua, pg 497

Nigeria
Ahmadu Bello University Press Ltd, pg 498
Educational Research & Study Group, pg 499
Ethiope Publishing Corporation, pg 499
Evans Brothers (Nigeria Publishers) Ltd, pg 499
Fourth Dimension Publishing Co Ltd, pg 499
Gbabeks Publishers Ltd, pg 499
Ibadan University Press, pg 499
Ilesanmi Press (Educational Publishers) Ltd, pg 499
JAD Publishers Ltd, pg 500
Literamed Publications Nigeria Ltd, pg 500
Longman Nigeria Plc, pg 500
Thomas Nelson (Nigeria) Ltd, pg 500
Obafemi Awolowo University Press Ltd, pg 501
Ogunsanya Press, Publishers and Bookstores Ltd, pg 501
Onibon-Oje Publishers, pg 501
Unity Publishing & Research Company Ltd, pg 502
University of Lagos Press, pg 502
Vantage Publishers International Ltd, pg 502

Norway
H Aschehoug & Co (W Nygaard) A/S, pg 502
Glydendal Akademisk, pg 503

Gyldendal Norsk Forlag A/S, pg 503
Pax Forlag A/S, pg 504

Pakistan
Hamdard Foundation, pg 507
Pakistan Institute of Development Economics, pg 508
Quaid-i-Azam University Department of Biological Sciences, pg 508

Panama
Editorial Universitaria, pg 509

Papua New Guinea
Papua New Guinea Institute of Medical Research, pg 510
Melanesian Institute, pg 510
National Research Institute of Papua New Guinea, pg 510

Peru
Centro de la Mujer Peruana Flora Tristan, pg 511
Instituto de Estudios Peruanos, pg 511
Fondo Editorial de la Pontificia Universidad Catolica del Peru, pg 511
Instituto Frances de Estudios Andinos, IFEA, pg 511
Editorial Horizonte, pg 511
Sur Casa de Estudios del Socialismo, pg 511
Editorial Universo SA, pg 512

Philippines
Ateneo de Manila University Press, pg 512
Philippine Education Co Inc, pg 514
Rex Bookstores & Publishers, pg 514
Saint Mary's Publishing Corp, pg 515
Salesiana Publishers Inc, pg 515
San Carlos Publications, pg 515
SIBS Publishing House Inc, pg 515
University of the Philippines Press, pg 515
UST Publishing House, pg 515
Vibal Publishing House Inc (VPHI), pg 515

Poland
Spoldzielnia Wydawnicza 'Czytelnik', pg 516
Impuls, pg 517
Katolicki Uniwersytet Wydawniczo -Redakcja, pg 517
'Ksiazka i Wiedza' Spotdzielnia Wydawniczo-Handlowa, pg 517
Wydawnictwo Lubelskie, pg 518
Muza SA, pg 518
Norbertinum, pg 518
Ossolineum Zaklad Narodowy im Ossolinskich - Wydawnictwo, pg 518
Spotdzielnia Anagram, pg 520
Zaklad Wydawnictw Statystycznych, pg 520
Oficyna Wydawnicza Szkoly Glownej Handlowej w Warszawie Oficyna Wydawnicza SGH, pg 520
Wydawnictwa Uniwersytetu Warszawskiego, pg 521

Portugal
Edicoes Afrontamento, pg 522
Armenio Amado Editora de Simoes, Beirao & Ca Lda, pg 522
Edicoes Antigona, pg 522
Apaginastantas - Cooperativa de Servicos Culturais, pg 522
Atica, SA Editores e Livreiros, pg 522
Bertrand Editora Lda, pg 522
Brasilia Editora (J Carvalho Branco), pg 523
Centro Estudos Geograficos, pg 523
Livraria Civilizacao (Americo Fraga Lamares & Ca Lda), pg 523
Editora Classica, pg 523
Edicoes Colibri, pg 523
Constancia Editores, SA, pg 524
Edicoes Cosmos, pg 524
Dinalivro, pg 524
Direccao Geral Familia, pg 524
Edicoes 70, Lda, pg 524
Editorial Estampa, Lda, pg 524
Publicacoes Europa-America Lda, pg 524
Gradiva-Publicacnoes Lda, pg 525
Guimaraes Editores, Lda, pg 525
Imprensa Nacional-Casa da Moeda, pg 526
Editorial Inquerito Lda, pg 526
Instituto de Investigacao Cientifica Tropical, pg 526
Edicoes ITAU (Instituto Tecnico de Alimentacao Humana) Lda, pg 526
Livros Horizonte Lda, pg 526
McGraw-Hill Editora de Portugal, pg 527
Nova Arrancada Sociedade Editora SA, pg 527
Editorial Presenca, pg 528
Publicacoes Dom Quixote Lda, pg 528
Quid Juris - Sociedade editora, pg 529
Edicoes Rolim Lda, pg 529
Edicoes 70, pg 529
Almerinda Teixeira, pg 529
Teorema, pg 529
Vega-Publicacao e Distribuicao de Livros e Revistas, Lda, pg 530

Puerto Rico
Editorial Cordillera Inc, pg 530
Ediciones Huracan Inc, pg 530
Libros-Ediciones Homines, pg 530
Ediciones Puerto, pg 531
University of Puerto Rico Press (EDUPR), pg 531

Reunion
Editions Ocean, pg 531

Romania
Editura Academiei Romane, pg 531
Aion Verlag, pg 531
Ararat Verlag und Druckerei, pg 532
Editura Excelsior, pg 533
Editura Humanitas, pg 533
Humanitas Publishing House, pg 533
Mentor Kiado, pg 534
Editura Meridiane, pg 534
Editura Militara, pg 534
Editura Niculescu, pg 534
Editura Paideia, pg 535
Polirom Verlag, pg 535
Editura 'Scrisul Romanesc', pg 536
Editura Stiintifica si Enciclopedica, pg 536
Universal Dalsi, pg 536

Russian Federation
Aspect Press Ltd, pg 537
Izdatel 'stvo Mordovskogo gosudar stvennogo, pg 538
Izvestia Sovetov Narodnyh Deputatov Russian Federation (RF), pg 539
Legprombytizdat, pg 539
Ministerstvo Kul 'tury RF, pg 540
Izdatelstvo Molodaya Gvardia, pg 540
Nauka Publishers, pg 540
Izdatel'stvo Nizhegorodskogo Gosudarstvennogo Univ, pg 540
Novosti Izdatel 'stvo, pg 541
Progress Publishers, pg 541
Stroyizdat Publishing House, pg 542
Voronezh State University Publishers, pg 542

Rwanda
INADES (Institut Africain pour le Developpment Economique et Social), pg 543

Senegal
Nouvelles Editions Africaines du Senegal (NEAS), pg 544
CODESRIA (Council for the Development of Social Science Research in Africa), pg 544
Les Nouvelles Editions Africaines du Senegal NEAS, pg 544

Sierra Leone
Sierra Leone University Press, pg 544

Singapore
APAC Publishers Services, pg 545
Aquanut Agencies Pte Ltd, pg 545
Chopsons Pte Ltd, pg 545
Hillview Publications Pte Ltd, pg 546
Institute of Southeast Asian Studies, pg 546
Maruzen Asia (Pte) Ltd, pg 547
Reed Elsevier, South East Asia, pg 547
Singapore University Press Pte Ltd, pg 548
Taylor & Francis Asia Pacific, pg 548

Slovakia
ARCHA sro Vydavatel 'stro, pg 549
Danubiaprint, pg 549
Kalligram Kiado spol sro, pg 549
Slovenske pedagogicke nakladateistvo, pg 550
Smena Publishing House, pg 550
Sofa, pg 551
Ustav informacii a prognoz skolstva mladeze a telovychovy, pg 551

Slovenia
Cankarjeva Zalozba, pg 551
Zalozba Mihelac d o o, pg 552

South Africa
Centre for Conflict Resolution, pg 553
Educum Publishers Ltd, pg 554
Human Sciences Research Council, pg 555
Juventus/Femina Publishers, pg 556
Nasou Via Afrika, pg 557
Ravan Press (Pty) Ltd, pg 558
Shuter & Shooter (Pty) Ltd, pg 559
South African Institute of Race Relations, pg 559
Van Schaik Publishers, pg 560

Spain
Editorial Afers, SL, pg 561
Agencia Espanola de Cooperacion, pg 562
Ediciones Akal SA, pg 562
Ediciones Alfar SA, pg 562
Edicions Alfons el Magnanim, Institucio Valenciana d'Estudis i Investigacio, pg 562
Alianza Editorial SA, pg 562
Alta Fulla Editorial, pg 563
Amnistia Internacional Editorial SL, pg 563
Editorial Anagrama, pg 563
Editorial Ariel SA, pg 564
Editorial Ayuso, pg 564
Ediciones Bellaterra SA, pg 565
Casa de Velazquez, pg 566
Editorial Casals SA, pg 566
Edicios do Castro, pg 566
Centro de Estudios Politicos Y Constitucionales, pg 567
Compania Literaria, pg 568
Complutense, SA Editorial, pg 568
Ediciones de la Universidad Complutense de Madrid, pg 568
Ediciones Cristiandad, pg 569
Diputacion Provincial de Sevilla, Servicio de Publicaciones, pg 570
EDERSA (Editoriales de Derecho Reunidas SA), pg 571
Editorial Empeno 14, pg 573
Ediciones Encuentro SA, pg 573
Editorial Espasa-Calpe SA, pg 573
Instituto de Estudios Riojanos, pg 574
Fondo de Cultura Economica de Espana, SL, pg 574
Fundacion de Estudios Libertarios Anselmo Lorenzo, pg 575
Editorial Fundamentos, pg 575
Galaxia SA Editorial, pg 575
Editorial Gedisa SA, pg 575
Instituto de Cultura Juan Gil-Albert, pg 576
Editorial Grupo Cero, pg 576
Editorial Herder SA, pg 577
Iberico Europea de Ediciones SA, pg 577
Icaria Editorial SA, pg 577
Publicaciones ICCE, pg 577
Instituto de Estudios Economicos, pg 578
Iralka Editorial SL, pg 578
Ediciones Istmo SA, pg 579
Editorial Kairos SA, pg 579
Editorin Laiovento SL, pg 579
Ediciones Libertarias/Prodhufi SA, pg 580
Llibres del Segle, pg 580
Editorial Lumen SA, pg 580
Edicions de la Magrana SA, pg 581
Ediciones Marova SL, pg 581
Ediciones Mensajero, pg 582
Editorial Moll SL, pg 582
Ediciones Morata SL, pg 583
Narcea SA de Ediciones, pg 583
Oikos-Tau SA Ediciones, pg 584
Ediciones Olimpic, SL, pg 585
Ediciones del Oriente y del Mediterraneo, pg 585
Pages Editors, SL, pg 585
Ediciones Paidos Iberica SA, pg 585
Pais Vasco Servicio Central de Publicaciones, pg 585
Ediciones Partenon, pg 586
Ediciones Pomares-Corredor, pg 587

PUBLISHERS — SUBJECT INDEX

Editorial Popular SA, pg 587
Prensas Universitarias de Zaragoza, pg 587
Editorial Presencia Gitana, pg 587
Edicions Proa, SA, pg 588
Instituto Provincial de Investigaciones y Estudios Toledanos, pg 588
Publicaciones de la Universidad de Alicante, pg 588
Publicaciones de la Universidad Pontificia Comillas-Madrid, pg 588
Ediciones ROL SA, pg 589
Ediciones San Pio X, pg 589
Universidad de Santiago de Compostela, pg 589
Siglo XXI de Espana Editores SA, pg 590
Editorial Sintesis, SA, pg 590
Edicions 62, pg 591
Ediciones SM, pg 591
Editorial Tecnos SA, pg 592
Tirant lo Blanch SL Libreriaa, pg 592
Ediciones de la Torre, pg 593
Trotta SA Editorial, pg 593
Editorial Txertoa, pg 594
Universidad de Granada, pg 594
Universidad de Malaga, pg 594
Universidad de Oviedo Servicio de Publicaciones, pg 594
Universidad de Valladolid Secretariado de Publicaciones e Intercambio Editorial, pg 594
Publicacions de la Universitat de Barcelona, pg 594
Parlamento Vasco, pg 595
Editorial Verbo Divino, pg 595
Edicions Xerais de Galicia, pg 596

Sri Lanka

Karunaratne & Sons Ltd, pg 597
National Library & Documentation Services Board, pg 597
Swarna Hansa Foundation, pg 598

Sudan

Khartoum University Press, pg 598

Suriname

Stichting Wetenschappelijke Informatie, pg 599

Sweden

Acta Universitatis Gothoburgensis, pg 599
Forlaget By och Bygd, pg 602
Gidlunds Bokforlag, pg 602
Liber AB, pg 604
Bokforlaget Nya Doxa AB, pg 605
Ordfront Foerlag AB, pg 605
SNS Foerlag, pg 606
Sober Foerlags AB, pg 606
Studentlitteratur AB, pg 606
AB Timbro, pg 607
Zindermans AB, pg 607

Switzerland

Editions L'Age d'Homme - La Cite, pg 608
Editions de la Baconniere SA, pg 609
Basileia Verlag, pg 609
Les Editions Camphill, pg 610
Caux Books, pg 611
Caux Edition SA, pg 611
Chronos Verlag, pg 611
Cockatoo Press (Schweiz), Thailand-Publikationen, pg 611
Cultur Prospectiv, Edition, pg 612

Editions Delachaux et Niestle SA, pg 612
Librairie Droz SA, pg 612
Gottlieb Duttweiler Institute for Trends & Futures, pg 612
Edition Epoca, pg 613
Edition Exodus, pg 614
Georg Editeur SA, pg 614
Editions Francois Grounauer, pg 615
Paul Haupt Berne, pg 615
Interfrom AG Editions, pg 616
Editions Jouvence, pg 616
Labor et Fides SA, pg 618
Limmat Verlag, pg 618
Novalis Media AG, pg 620
Ostschweiz Druck und Verlag, pg 621
Editions Payot Lausanne, pg 621
PIE-Peter Lang SA, pg 622
SAB Schweiz Arbeitsgemeinschaft fuer die Berggebiete, pg 623
Schulthess Polygraphischer Verlag AG, pg 624
Verlag SOI (Schweizerisches Ost-Institut), pg 625
Editions du Tricorne, pg 626
Editions Zoe, pg 628

Syrian Arab Republic

Damascus University Press, pg 628
Institut Francais d'Etudes Arabes de Damas, pg 628

Taiwan, Province of China

Bookman Books, Ltd, pg 629
Chu Liu Book Company, pg 629
Chung Hwa Book Co Ltd, pg 629
Chu Hai Publishing (Taiwan) Co Ltd, pg 630
Laureate Book Co Ltd, pg 631
Newton Publishing Company Ltd, pg 631

Tajikistan

Irfon, pg 632

United Republic of Tanzania

East African Publishing House, pg 633
Kisambo Publishers Ltd, pg 633
Ndanda Mission Press, pg 634

Thailand

Suksit Siam Co Ltd, pg 635
Thai Watana Panich Co, Ltd, pg 636

Togo

Editions Akpagnon, pg 636

Trinidad & Tobago

Inprint Caribbean Ltd, pg 637

Tunisia

Academie Tunisienne des Sciences, des Lettres et des Arts Beit El Hekma, pg 637
Ceres Editions, pg 637
Faculte des Sciences Humaines et Sociales de Tunis, pg 638
Publications de la Fondation Temimi pour la Recherche Scientifique et L'Information, pg 638

Turkey

Bilden Bilgisayar, pg 639
Dost Kitabevi Yayinlari, pg 639

Iletisim Yayinlari, pg 640
Isis Yayin Tic ve San Ltd, pg 640
Metis Yayinlari, pg 640
Payel Yayinevi, pg 641
Remzi Kitabevi, pg 641
Saray Medikal Yayin Tic Ltd Sti, pg 641
Varlik Yayinlari AS, pg 641
Kabalci Yayinevi, pg 642

Turkmenistan

Izdatelstvo Turkmenistan, pg 642

Uganda

Centre for Basic Research, pg 642
Fountain Publishers Ltd, pg 642

Ukraine

ASK Ltd, pg 643
Osnovy Publishers, pg 643

United Kingdom

AK Press & Distribution, pg 645
Aldwych Press Ltd, pg 645
Anglo-German Foundation for the Study of Industrial Society, pg 647
Appletree Press Ltd, pg 648
Arnold, pg 648
Arthur James Ltd, pg 649
Ashgate Publishing Ltd, pg 649
The Athlone Press Ltd, pg 650
Baha'i Publishing Trust, pg 651
Barmarick Publications, pg 652
Batsford Ltd, pg 652
Berg Publishers, pg 654
Berghahn Books Ltd, pg 654
BFI Publishing, pg 654
Blackwell Publishers, pg 655
Bloomsbury Publishing PLC, pg 656
Bowerdean Publishing Co Ltd, pg 658
The British Academy, pg 659
BAAF: Adoption & Fostering, pg 659
The Brown Reference Group PLC, pg 660
Business Monitor International, pg 661
Cambridge University Press, pg 662
Camden Press Ltd, pg 662
Cardiff Academic Press, pg 663
Jon Carpenter Publishing, pg 664
Cassell & Co, pg 664
Causeway Press Ltd, pg 665
Cavendish Publishing Ltd, pg 665
Chadwyck-Healey Ltd, pg 666
Deborah Charles Publications, pg 666
Commonwealth Secretariat, pg 669
James Currey Ltd, pg 673
Dunedin Academic Press, pg 676
Edinburgh University Press Ltd, pg 677
Editon XII, pg 677
European Schoolbooks Ltd, pg 680
The Eurospan Group, pg 680
Extraordinary People Press, pg 681
Faber & Faber Ltd, pg 681
Free Association Books Ltd, pg 684
Freedom Press, pg 684
Golden Cockerel Press Ltd, pg 688
Gregg Publishing Co, pg 690
Harcourt Publishers Ltd, pg 691
Harvard University Press, pg 692
Holyoake Books, pg 697
JAI Press Ltd, pg 702
Karnac Books Ltd, pg 703
Kershaw Publishing Co Ltd, pg 704
King's Fund Publishing, pg 704

Jessica Kingsley Publishers, pg 704
Kluwer Academic/Plenum Publishers, pg 705
Knockabout Comics, pg 705
Lawrence & Wishart, pg 706
Liverpool University Press, pg 708
Lucis Press Ltd, pg 709
Macmillan Reference Ltd, pg 710
Manchester University Press, pg 711
Adam Matthew Publications, pg 712
McGraw-Hill Publishing Company, pg 712
The Merlin Press Ltd, pg 713
MIT Press Ltd, pg 715
Motilal (UK) Books of India, pg 715
Multilingual Matters Ltd, pg 716
National Assembly for Wales, pg 717
National Trust, pg 717
Nelson Thornes Ltd, pg 718
Norwood Publishers, pg 720
Open Gate Press, pg 721
Open University Press, pg 721
Peter Owen Ltd, pg 722
Oxfam, pg 722
Oxford University Press, pg 723
Palgrave Publishers Ltd, pg 723
Pathfinder London, pg 724
Pavilion Publishing (Brighton) Ltd, pg 725
Pearson Education, pg 725
Pearson Education Europe, Mideast & Africa, pg 725
Peepal Tree Press, pg 725
Pluto Press, pg 728
The Policy Press, pg 729
Policy Studies Institute, pg 729
Profile Books Ltd, pg 731
ProQuest Information & Learning, pg 731
Rationalist Press Association, pg 733
RELATE, pg 734
Routledge, pg 736
Routledge Curzon, pg 736
Sage Publications Ltd, pg 737
Sangam Books Ltd, pg 738
Scottish Cultural Press, pg 739
Scottish Office Library & Information Services, pg 740
Shire Publications Ltd, pg 741
SHU Press, pg 742
The Society of Metaphysicians Ltd, pg 743
Souvenir Press Ltd, pg 743
Speechmark Publishing Ltd, pg 744
Spokesman, pg 744
St Pauls Publishing, pg 744
The Stationery Office, pg 745
Sutton Publishing Ltd, pg 746
Taylor & Francis Group, pg 747
Thoemmes Press, pg 748
Trentham Books Ltd, pg 750
UCL Press Ltd, pg 751
University of Wales Press, pg 751
University Presses of California, Columbia & Princeton Ltd, pg 752
Verso, pg 752
Viking, pg 753
Virago Press, pg 753
Westview Press, pg 755
White Cockade Publishing, pg 755
Whiting & Birch Ltd, pg 756
Wordwright Publishing, pg 758
Yale University Press London, pg 759
Zed Books Ltd, pg 759

SUBJECT INDEX

Uruguay
Ediciones de Juan Darien, pg 760
Libreria Amalio M Fernandez, Editorial, pg 760
Fundacion de Cultura Universitaria, pg 760
Nordan-Comunidad, pg 760
Ediciones Trilce, pg 761
Vinten Editor, pg 761

Venezuela
Alfadil Ediciones, pg 761
Monte Avila Editores Latinoamericana CA, pg 762
Fundacion Centro Gumilla, pg 762
Editorial Nueva Sociedad, pg 762
Universidad de los Andes, Consejo de Publicaciones, pg 763

Viet Nam
Su That (Truth) Publishing House, pg 763

Yugoslavia
Beogradski Izdavacko-Graficki Zavod, pg 764
Nolit Publishing House, pg 765
Izdavacka Organizacija Rad, pg 765
Panorama NIJP/ID Grigorije Bozovic, pg 765
Radnicka Stampa, pg 765
Vuk Karadzic, pg 766

Zambia
Lundula Publishing House, pg 766
MFK Management Consultants Services, pg 766
Multimedia Zambia, pg 767
University of Zambia Press (UNZA Press), pg 767
Zambia Association for Research & Development, pg 767
Zambia Educational Publishing House, pg 767

Zimbabwe
Anvil Press, pg 767
Journal on Social Change, pg 768
Sapes Trust Ltd, pg 769
University of Zimbabwe Publications, pg 769

SPORTS, ATHLETICS

Albania
NL SH, pg 1
State Textbook Publishing House, pg 1

Algeria
Enterprise Nationale du Livre (ENAL), pg 2

Argentina
Editorial Albatros SACI, pg 3
Editorial Caymi SACI, pg 4
Ediciones Lidiun, pg 7
Instituto de Publicaciones Navales, pg 7
Ediciones Preescolar SA, pg 8

Australia
ACHPER Inc (Australian Council for Health, Physical Education & Recreation), pg 10
Robert Berthold Photography, pg 14
Bio Concepts Publishing, pg 15
Boobook Publications, pg 15
Coconut Productions, pg 18
Galley Press Publishing, pg 23
Kangaroo Press, pg 29
McGraw-Hill Australia Pty Ltd, pg 32
Oceans Enterprises, pg 35
R & R Publications Marketing P/L, pg 39
Single X Publications, pg 42
University of Queensland Press, pg 46
Wild Publications, pg 47

Austria
Inn-Verlag, DrieBlein & Co KG, pg 53
Verlag des Osterr Kneippbundes GmbH, pg 57
Osterreichischer Bundesveilag Ges.mbH, pg 57

Belarus
Belaruskaya Encyklapedyya, pg 63

Belgium
Contact NV, pg 67
Graton Editeur SA, pg 69
Imprimerie Hayez SPRL, pg 69
Infoboek NV, pg 69
Editeurs de Litterature Bibliique, pg 71
Reader's Digest SA, pg 73
Roularta Books NV, pg 73
Sonneville Press (Uitgeverij) VTW, pg 74

Bermuda
Bermudian Publishing Co, pg 76

Brazil
Action Editora Ltda, pg 77
Ao Livro Tecnico Industria e Comercio Ltda, pg 78
Ars Poetica Editora Ltda, pg 79
ARTMED, pg 79
Editora Elevacao, pg 82
Companhia Editora Forense, pg 82
Editora Globo SA, pg 84
IBRASA (Instituicao Brasileira de Difusao Cultural Ltda), pg 85
Icone Editora Ltda, pg 85
Livraria Nobel S/A, pg 86
Editora Manole Ltda, pg 87
Modulo Editora e Desenvolvimento Educacional Ltda, pg 88
Editora Nova Alexandria Ltda, pg 88
Rede Das Artes (Boccato Editores Collector's), pg 90
Summus Editorial Ltda, pg 92

Bulgaria
Medicina i Fizkultura EOOD, pg 96

Chile
Arrayan Editores, pg 99
Ediciones Mil Hojas Ltda, pg 100

China
Foreign Languages Press, pg 105
Jilin Science & Technology Publishing House, pg 106
People's Sports Publishing House, pg 108

Colombia
Editorial Voluntad SA, pg 114

Costa Rica
Scout Interamericana, pg 117
Editorial de la Universidad de Costa Rica, pg 117

Croatia
Mladost d d Izdavacku graficku i informaticku djelatnost, pg 119

Cuba
ISCAH Fructuoso Rodriguez, pg 121
Editorial Oriente, pg 121
Pueblo y Educacion Editorial (PE), pg 121

Czech Republic
Jan Vasut Publishing, pg 124
Narodni Muzeum, pg 126
Nakladatelstvi Olympia AS, pg 127
Svojtka & Co, pg 128

Denmark
Forlaget Hovedland, pg 133

Egypt (Arab Republic of Egypt)
Dar El Shorouk Publishing & Distributing House, pg 138

Finland
Koala-Kustannus/Oy Greenbay House Publishing Ltd, pg 143
Recallmed Oy, pg 144

France
Editions Amphora SA, pg 147
Editions Bornemann, pg 151
Bottin SA, pg 151
Editions Calmann-Levy SA, pg 152
Editions Canal, pg 152
Philippe Chancerel Editeur, pg 154
Editions Charles-Lavauzelle SA, pg 154
Editions Chiron, pg 154
Courrier du Livre Sarl, pg 157
Editeurs Crepin-Leblond, pg 157
De Vecchi Editions SA, pg 158
Edisud, pg 161
Edition1, pg 161
EPA SA (Editions Presse Audiovisuel), pg 162
EPLS - ACLA Edition, pg 162
Federation Francaise de la Randonnee Pedestre, pg 164
Editions J Glenat SA, pg 166
Hachette Livre, pg 167
Hachette Pratiques, pg 167
Editions Michel Lafon SA, pg 171
Librairie Larousse, pg 172
Editions Mango, pg 174
Editions Maritimes et d'Outre-Mer SA, pg 175
Societe des Editions Menges, pg 175
Editions Franck Mercier, pg 176
Presses Universitaires de Grenoble, pg 181
Editions Revue EPS, pg 183
Editions Trois Fontaines, pg 188
Ulisse Edition, pg 188
Les Editions Vaillant-Miroir-Sprint Publications, pg 188
Editions Vigot Freres, pg 189
Editions Vilo SA, pg 189
Editions Philateliques Yvert et Tellier, pg 189

Germany
E Albrecht Verlags-Kommanditgesellschaft, pg 192
AOL-Verlag Frohmut Menze, pg 194
Bergverlag Rudolf Rother GmbH, pg 200
BLV Verlagsgesellschaft mbH, pg 204
CEC-Cosmic Energy Connections, pg 209
Chmielorz GmbH Verlag, pg 210
Copress Verlag, pg 211
Beate Danker-Verlag, pg 212
Verlag Harri Deutsch, pg 213
Falken-Verlag GmbH, pg 227
Ferd Dummler's Verlag, pg 227
Fink - Kummerly und Frey Verlag GmbH, pg 227
Gesundheits-Dialog Verlag GmbH, pg 232
Griese Ingolf Wipe Griese, pg 234
Verlag Gruppenpaedagogischer Literatur, pg 234
Heel Verlag GmbH, pg 238
Verlag Karl Hofmann GmbH & Co, pg 242
Huebner Felicitas Verlag, pg 243
Idea Verlag GmbH, pg 244
Jutta Pohl Verlag, pg 247
Kallmeyer'sche Verlagsbuchhandlung GmbH, pg 247
Klartext Verlagsgesellschaft mbH, pg 249
Knowledge Media International, pg 251
Koesler Verlag GmbH, pg 252
Kolibri-Verlags GmbH, pg 252
Limpert Verlag, pg 258
Edition Maritim GmbH, pg 261
Medizinisch-Literarische Verlagsgesellschaft mbH, pg 262
Meyer & Meyer Fachverlag und Buchhandel GmbH, pg 263
Moby Dick Verlag, pg 264
Mosaik Verlag, pg 265
Munzinger-Archiv GmbH Archiv fuer publizistische Arbeit, pg 266
Verlag Stephanie Naglschmid, pg 266
Verlag J Neumann-Neudamm GmbH & Co KG, pg 268
nymphenburger, pg 269
Pala-Verlag GmbH, pg 271
Philippka-Sportverlag, pg 273
Walter Rau Verlag GmbH & Co KG, pg 277
Max Schmidt-Roemhild Verlag, pg 284
SMG Stiebner Medien gmbh, pg 287
Spiridon-Verlags GmbH, pg 288
Sportverlag Berlin GmbH SVB, pg 288
Steiger Verlag, pg 289
S Toeche-Mittler Verlag GmbH, pg 294
Traditionell Bogenschiessen Verlag Angelika Hornig, pg 294
von Stengel oHG Verlag, pg 299
Verlag W Weinmann, pg 301
Wolfgang Arlt u Ute Schiller, pg 304

Greece
Editions Moressopoulos, pg 313

Hong Kong
Courseguides International Ltd, pg 319
Press Mark Media Ltd, pg 321

PUBLISHERS SUBJECT INDEX

Hungary
Medicina Koenyvkiado, pg 325

Iceland
Frodi Ltd, pg 328

India
Ananda Publishers Pvt Ltd, pg 330
Dastane Ramchandra & Co, pg 335
Dutta Baruah Publishing Co Pvt Ltd, pg 336
Gyan Publishing House, pg 338
Orient Paperbacks, pg 345
Regency Publications, pg 347
Reliance Publishing House, pg 347
Rupa & Co, pg 348

Indonesia
P T Bulan Bintang, pg 354

Ireland
The O'Brien Press Ltd, pg 363

Israel
Dekel Publishing House, pg 366

Italy
Arcadia Edizioni Srl, pg 376
Arcanta Aries Gruppo Editoriale, pg 376
Edistudio di Brunetto Casini, pg 380
Giovanni De Vecchi Editore SpA, pg 384
Edi Ermes SRL, pg 386
Ediciclo Editore SRL, pg 386
Edizioni Mediterranee SRL, pg 387
ERGA SNC di Carla Ottino Merli & C (Edizioni Realizzazioni Grafiche - Artigiana), pg 388
Edizioni GB, pg 390
Ernesto Gremese Editore SRL, pg 391
Gruppo Calderini Edagricole, pg 392
Hermes Edizioni SRL, pg 392
L'Airone Editrice, pg 395
Luni, pg 397
Gruppo Ugo Mursia Editore SpA, pg 400
Editoriale Olimpia SpA, pg 401
Edizioni Panini SpA, pg 402
Edizioni Quattroventi SNC, pg 404
Societa Stampa Sportiva, pg 408
Sperling e Kupfer Editori SpA, pg 408
Vivalda Editori SRL, pg 411

Jamaica
Ian Randle Publishers Ltd, pg 413

Japan
Aiki News, pg 414
Baseball Magazine-Sha Co Ltd, pg 415
Bunkasha Publishing Co, Ltd, pg 415
Dobun Shoin, pg 416
Fumaido Publishing Company Ltd, pg 416
Hakutei-Sha, pg 417
Kodansha International, pg 420
Nihon Vogue Co Ltd, pg 422
Nippon Hoso Shuppan Kyokai (NHK Publishing), pg 422
Obunsha Co Ltd, pg 423
Sagano Shoin, pg 424
Seibido Shuppan Company Ltd, pg 424

Tokuma-Shoten, pg 427
Tsukiji Shokan Publishing Co, pg 428
Charles E Tuttle Publishing Co Inc, pg 428
Waseda University Press, pg 428
Yama-Kei Publishers Co Ltd, pg 429

Kenya
Kenway Publications Ltd, pg 432

Republic of Korea
Pyeong-hwa Chulpansa, pg 439
Samho Music Publishing Co, pg 440

Latvia
Egmont Latvia Ltd, pg 442
Preses Nams, pg 442

Lebanon
Khayat Book and Publishing Co Sarl, pg 443

Liechtenstein
Frank P van Eck Publishers, pg 444

Lithuania
Margi Rastai Publishers, pg 446
Sviesa Publishers, pg 446

Malaysia
Federal Publications Sdn Bhd, pg 452

Maldive Islands
Non-Formal Education Centre, pg 455

Mexico
Editorial Diana SA de CV, pg 459
Edamex SA de CV, pg 460
Editorial Limusa SA de CV, pg 463
Organizacion Cultural LP SA de CV, pg 465
Pearson Educacion de Mexico, SA de CV, pg 465
Sayrols Editorial SA de CV, pg 466
Ediciones Suromex SA, pg 467

Monaco
Les Editions du Rocher, pg 469

Morocco
Les Editions du Journal L' Unite Maghrebine, pg 470

Netherlands
BZZTOH Publishers, pg 475
Elmar BV, pg 476
BV Uitgeversbedryf Het Goede Boek, pg 477
Rostrum Publishing, pg 483
Tirion Uitgevers BV, pg 485

New Caledonia
Savannah Editions SARL, pg 488

New Zealand
David's Marine Books, pg 490
Halcyon Publishing Ltd, pg 491
HarperCollins Publishers (New Zealand) Ltd, pg 491
Longacre Press, pg 493
Nelson Price Milburn Ltd, pg 494
R P L Books, pg 495
Saint Publishing, pg 495

Shoal Bay Press Ltd, pg 495
Shortland Publications Ltd, pg 495

Nigeria
Evans Brothers (Nigeria Publishers) Ltd, pg 499

Norway
John Grieg Forlag AS, pg 503

Pakistan
H I Jaffari & Co Publishers, pg 506
Jang Publishers, pg 507

Portugal
Editorial Estampa, Lda, pg 524
Europress Editores e Distribuidores de Publicacoes Lda, pg 525
Impala, pg 525
Editorial Presenca, pg 528
Editora Replicacao Lda, pg 529
Talento, pg 529

Romania
The Center for Romanian Studies, pg 532

Russian Federation
BLIC, russko-Baltijskij informaciionnyj centr, AO, pg 537
Izdatelstvo Fizkultura i Sport, pg 538
Interbook-Business AO, pg 538
Izvestia Sovetov Narodnyh Deputatov Russian Federation (RF), pg 539
Ladomir Publishing House, pg 539
Izdatelstvo Molodaya Gvardia, pg 540
Profizdat, pg 541

Saudi Arabia
Dar Al-Shareff for Publishing & Distribution, pg 543

Slovakia
Slovenske pedagogicke nakladateistvo, pg 550
Sport Publishing House Ltd, pg 551

South Africa
Ashanti Publishing, pg 552
Jonathan Ball Publishers, pg 552
Human & Rousseau (Pty) Ltd, pg 555

Spain
Editorial Acanto SA, pg 561
Editorial 'Alas', pg 562
Editorial Cantabrica SA, pg 566
Comunidad Autonoma de Madrid, Servicio de Documentacion y Publicaciones, pg 568
Editorial De Vecchi SA, pg 569
Dorleta SA, pg 570
Edicions del Drac SA, pg 570
Editorial Gedisa SA, pg 575
Editorial Hispano Europea SA, pg 577
Imagen y Deporte, SL, pg 578
Editorial Juventud SA, pg 579
Ediciones Martinez-Roca SA, pg 581
Editorial Mediterrania SL, pg 582
Editorial Molino, pg 582
Editorial Noray, pg 584
OASIS, Producciones Generales de Comunicacion, pg 584

Editorial Paidotribo SL, pg 585
Pleniluni Edicions, pg 587
Ediciones Seyer, pg 590
Editorial Sintes SA, pg 590
Axel Springer Publicaciones, pg 591
Editorial Augusto E Pila Telena SL, pg 592
Trazo Editorial, SL, pg 593
Tursen, SA, pg 593
Ediciones Tutor SA, pg 594

Sri Lanka
Lake House Investments Ltd, pg 597

Sweden
Johnston & Streiffert Editions, pg 604
Bokforlaget Semic AB, pg 606
Semic Bokforlaget International AB, pg 606
Stroemberg B&T Forlag AB, pg 606

Switzerland
Verlag Harri Deutsch, pg 612
Editions Foma SA, pg 614
Office du Livre SA (Buchhaus AG), pg 620
Ott Verlag AG, pg 621
Weltrundschau Verlag AG, pg 627

United Republic of Tanzania
Tanzania Publishing House, pg 634

Turkey
Alkim Kitapcilik-Yayimcilik, pg 638

United Kingdom
ABC-CLIO, pg 644
Adlard Coles Nautical, pg 645
Amber Books Ltd, pg 646
Aurum Press Ltd, pg 651
BCA, pg 653
A & C Black Publishers Ltd, pg 655
Blackwell Science Ltd, pg 656
Blandford Publishing Ltd, pg 656
Breedon Books Publishing Company Ltd, pg 659
Carlton Publishing Group, pg 664
Cassell & Co, pg 664
Coachwise Ltd, pg 668
Compendium Publishing, pg 670
Countyvise Ltd, pg 671
The Crowood Press Ltd, pg 672
Andre Deutsch Ltd, pg 675
John Donald Publishers Ltd, pg 675
Dorling Kindersley Ltd, pg 676
Eaglemoss Publications Ltd, pg 676
Elliot Right Way Books, pg 678
Express Newspapers, pg 681
Francis Balsom Associates, pg 684
Geiser Productions, pg 686
Gollancz/Witherby, pg 688
Guinness Publishing Ltd, pg 690
Robert Hale Ltd, pg 691
Hamlyn, pg 691
HarperCollins Publishers, pg 692
Harvey Map Services Ltd, pg 692
Headline Book Publishing Ltd, pg 693
Health Development Agency, pg 694
Hodder & Stoughton Educational, pg 696
International Communications, pg 701
The Islamic Texts Society, pg 701
The Kenilworth Press Ltd, pg 704
Knight Features, pg 705

SUBJECT INDEX

Luath Press Ltd, pg 709
Mainstream Publishing Co (Edinburgh) Ltd, pg 711
Octopus Publishing Group, pg 720
Orion Publishing Group Ltd, pg 722
Owl Books, pg 722
Parapress Ltd, pg 724
Queen Anne Press, pg 732
Quintet Publishing Ltd, pg 732
Robson Books, pg 735
Salamander Books Ltd, pg 738
Seren, pg 740
Shire Publications Ltd, pg 741
SHU Press, pg 742
Sidgwick & Jackson Ltd, pg 742
Sigma Press, pg 742
Souvenir Press Ltd, pg 743
Spon Press, pg 744
The Sportsman's Press, pg 744
Sutton Publishing Ltd, pg 746
Telegraph Books, pg 748
Transworld Publishers Ltd, pg 750
United Writers Publications Ltd, pg 751
Verulam Publishing Ltd, pg 753
Virgin Publishing Ltd, pg 753
Ward Lock Ltd, pg 754
Weatherbys Allen Ltd, pg 754
Neil Wilson Publishing Ltd, pg 757
Wordwright Publishing, pg 758

Yugoslavia

Sportska Knjiga, pg 765

TECHNOLOGY

Albania

Ndermarrja e Botimeve Ushtarake, pg 1
NL SH, pg 1
State Textbook Publishing House, pg 1

Argentina

Alfagrama SRL ediciones, pg 3
Cesarini Hermanos, pg 4
Editorial Idearium de la Universidad de Mendoza (EDIUM), pg 5
Marymar Ediciones SA, pg 7
Instituto Nacional de Ciencia y Tecnica Hidrica (INCYTH), pg 7
Ediciones Tres Tiempos SRL, pg 9
Editorial Troquel SA, pg 9

Australia

Appropriate Technology Development Group (Inc) WA, pg 11
Edward Arnold (Australia) Pty Ltd, pg 12
Books for Our Times, pg 16
David Boyce Publishing, pg 16
Clunies Ross Press, pg 18
CSIRO Publishing (Commonwealth Scientific & Industrial Research Organisation), pg 19
Hawker Brownlow, pg 25
Illert Publications, pg 27
Lightbild PTY Ltd, pg 30
Spinifex Press, pg 43
Standards Association of Australia, pg 43
Tertiary Press, pg 44
University of New South Wales Press Ltd, pg 46

Austria

IAEA - International Atomic Energy Agency, pg 53
Metrica Fachverlag u Versandbuchhandlung Ing Bartak, pg 55
Springer-Verlag Wien, pg 59

Azerbaijan

AZernesr, pg 61

Bangladesh

The University Press Ltd, pg 62

Belgium

Documenta CV, pg 68
Presses agronomiques de Gembloux ASBL, pg 73
Editions Techniques et Scientifiques SPRL, pg 74

Bosnia and Herzegovina

Bemust doo Novinsko-Izdavacko stamparsko i trgovacko preduzece, pg 77

Brazil

Antenna Edicoes Tecnicas Ltda, pg 78
ARTMED, pg 79
Berkeley Brasil Editora Ltda, pg 79
Editora Edgard Blucher Ltda, pg 80
Cadence Publicacoes Internacionais Ltda, pg 80
Cia Editora Nacional, pg 82
Selecoes Eletronicas Editora Ltda, pg 83
Empresa Brasileira de Pesquisa Agropecaria, pg 83
Icone Editora Ltda, pg 85
Livraria Nobel S/A, pg 86
LTC-Livros Tecnicos e Cientificos Editora S/A, pg 87
Pearson Education Do Brasil, pg 89
34 Literatura S/C Ltda, pg 92

Bulgaria

Ciela Publishing House, pg 94

Cameroon

Centre d'Edition et de Production pour l'Enseignement et la Recherche (CEPER), pg 99

Chile

Arrayan Editores, pg 99
Ediciones Cieplan, pg 100
Ediciones Universitarias de Valparaiso, pg 101

China

Chemical Industry Press, pg 102
China Agriculture Press, pg 103
China Machine Press (CMP), pg 103
China Ocean Press, pg 103
Chongqing University Press, pg 104
East China University of Science & Technology Press, pg 105
Encyclopedia of China Publishing House, pg 105
Fudan University Press, pg 105
Fujian Science & Technology Publishing House, pg 106
Heilongjiang Science & Technology Press, pg 106
Higher Education Press, pg 106
International Academic Publishers, pg 106

Jiangsu Science & Technology Publishing House, pg 106
Jilin Science & Technology Publishing House, pg 106
Metallurgical Industry Press (MIP), pg 107
National Defence Industry Press, pg 107
New Times Press, pg 107
Patent Documentation Publishing House, pg 107
Printing Industry Publishing House, pg 108
Science Press, pg 108
Shandong Science & Technology Press, pg 109
Shandong University Press, pg 109
Shanghai Science & Technology Publishers, pg 109
Sichuan Science & Technology Publishing House, pg 109
Tianjin Science & Technology Publishing House, pg 109
Tsinghua University Press, pg 110
Zhejiang University Press, pg 110

Colombia

Editora Guadalupe Ltda, pg 112
McGraw-Hill InterAmericana SA, pg 113
Tercer Mundo Editores SA, pg 113

The Democratic Republic of the Congo

Presses Universitaires du Zaiire (PUZ), pg 115

Costa Rica

Centro Agronomico Tropical de Investigacion y Ensenanza (CATIE), pg 115
Instituto Interamericano de Cooperacion para la Agricultura (IICA), pg 116
Editorial Tecnologica de Costa Rica, pg 117

Cuba

Instituto de Informacion Cientifica y Tecnologica (IDICT), pg 121
Pueblo y Educacion Editorial (PE), pg 121

Czech Republic

Grada Publishing sro, pg 124

Denmark

Forlaget for Faglitteratur A/S, pg 132
Syddansk Universitetsforlag, pg 136
Systime, pg 136

Dominican Republic

Pontificia Universidad Catolica Madre y Maestra, pg 136

Ecuador

CIESPAL (Centro Internacional de Estudios Superiores de Comunicacion para America Latina), pg 137

Ethiopia

Addis Ababa University Press, pg 141

France

Editions J B Bailliere, pg 149
CEP Editions, pg 153

Cepadues Editions SA, pg 153
CTIF (Center Technique des Industries de la Fonderie), pg 157
Delagrave Edition SA, pg 158
La Documentation Francaise, pg 159
Les Editions ESF, pg 161
EDP Sciences, pg 161
Editions Entente, pg 162
Librairie Artheme Fayard, pg 163
Institut Francais de Recherche pour l'Exploitation de la Mer (IFREMER), pg 165
Futuribles SARL, pg 165
Groupe de Recherche et d'Echanges Technologiques (GRET), pg 167
Groupe Expansion, pg 167
Hermann editeurs des Sciences et des Arts SA, pg 168
IRD Editions, pg 170
LT Editions-J Lanore-H Laurens, pg 172
Librairie Larousse, pg 172
Lavoisier, pg 172
Editions du Moniteur, pg 176
Editions Payot & Rivages, pg 179
Polytechnica, pg 180
Selection du Reader's Digest SA, pg 184
Editions Selection J Jacobs SA, pg 184
Editions Technip SA, pg 187
Terre Vivante, pg 187

Germany

Autovision Verlag Guther Co, pg 197
Verlag Dr Albert Bartens KG, pg 198
Bertelsmann Lexikon Verlag GmbH, pg 201
Beuth Verlag GmbH, pg 202
Oscar Brandstetter Verlag GmbH & Co KG, pg 206
Buchverlag Junge Welt GmbH, pg 207
Cornelsen Verlag GmbH & Co OHG, pg 211
Deutscher Verlag fur Grundstoffindustrie GmbH, pg 215
Deutscher Wirtschaftsdienst John von Freyend GmbH, pg 216
Ecomed Verlagsgesellschaft AG & Co KG, pg 220
Elektor-Verlag GmbH, pg 222
Eppinger-Verlag OHG, pg 223
Ernst, Wilhelm & Sohn, Verlag Architektur und technische Wissenschaft GmbH & Co, pg 224
Fachbuchverlag Leipzig im Carl Hanser Verlag, pg 226
Fachverlag Schiele & Schoen GmbH, pg 226
Franz Ferzak World & Space Publications, pg 227
Huss-Medien GmbH, pg 243
Huthig GmbH & Co KG, pg 244
Idea Verlag GmbH, pg 244
Konradin-Verlagsgruppe, pg 252
Franckh-Kosmos Verlags-GmbH & Co, pg 252
Institut fuer Landes- und Stadtentwicklungsforschung, ILS Nordrhein-Westfalen, pg 255
Meisenbach Verlag GmbH, pg 262
Moby Dick Verlag, pg 264
C F Mueller Verlag, Huethig Gmb H & Co, pg 265
Polygraph Verlag GmbH, pg 274
R Oldenbourg Verlag GmbH, pg 276

PUBLISHERS SUBJECT INDEX

Rationalisierungs-Kuratorium der Deutschen Wirtschaft eV (RKW), pg 277
Sigloch Edition Helmut Sigloch GmbH & Co KG, pg 286
Spektrum der Wissenschaft Verlagsgesellschaft mbH, pg 287
Springer-Verlag GmbH & Co KG, pg 288
Verlag Stahleisen GmbH, pg 289
Verlag H Stam GmbH, pg 289
B G Teubner GmbH, pg 292
Tuduv Verlagsgesellschaft mbH, pg 295
TUeV-Verlag GmbH, pg 295
Urban & Fischer Verlag GmbH & Co KG Niederlassung Jena, pg 296
VDI-Verlag GmbH, pg 297
Verlag fur Schweissen und Verwandte Verfahren, pg 298
Verlag Moderne Industrie AG & Co KG, pg 298
Friedr Vieweg & Sohn Verlagsgesellschaft mbH, pg 298
WEKA Firmengruppe GmbH & Co KG, pg 301

Ghana
Building & Road Research Institute (BRRI), pg 306
Ghana Publishing Corporation, pg 307

Greece
Chrysi Penna - Golden Pen Books, pg 309
Technical Chamber of Greece, pg 315

Guinea-Bissau
Instituto Nacional de Estudos e Pesquisa, pg 316

Hong Kong
Business & Industrial Publication Co Ltd, pg 318
Electronic Technology Publishing Co Ltd, pg 319
Hong Kong University Press, pg 320
Modern Electronic & Computing Publishing Co Ltd, pg 321
Vision Pub Co Ltd, pg 322

Hungary
Foldmuvelesugyi Miniszterium Muszaki Intezet, pg 323
Mueszaki Koenyvkiado Ltd, pg 325

India
Agricole Publishing Academy, pg 330
Allied Book Centre, pg 330
Asia Pacific Business Press Inc, pg 331
Atma Ram & Sons, pg 331
S Chand & Co Ltd, pg 334
IBD Publisher & Distributors, pg 338
International Book Distributors, pg 340
Khanna Publishers, pg 341
Law Publishers, pg 341
Multitech Publishing Co, pg 343
National Institute of Industrial Research (NIIR), pg 344
Publications & Information Directorate, CSIR, pg 346
Reliance Publishing House, pg 347
Researchco Reprints, pg 348

Samkaleen Prakashan, pg 349
Scientific Book Agency, pg 349
Sita Publications, pg 350
Small Industry Research Institute (SIRI), pg 350
Somaiya Publications Pvt Ltd, pg 350
South Asian Publishers Pvt Ltd, pg 350
Sterling Publishers Pvt Ltd, pg 351
Sterling Information Technologies, pg 351
Sultan Chand & Sons Pvt Ltd, pg 351
Vikas Publishing House Pvt Ltd, pg 353

Indonesia
Andi Offset, pg 354
Bhratara Karya Aksara, pg 354
P T Bulan Bintang, pg 354
Gramedia, pg 355
Institut Teknologi Bandung, pg 355
Yayasan Obor Indonesia, pg 357

Italy
Apimondia, pg 375
BeMa, pg 377
Casa Editrice Libraria Ulrico Hoepli SpA, pg 380
Ciranna - Roma, pg 381
CLUT Editrice, pg 382
Edizioni Cremonese SRL, pg 383
DEI Tipographia del Genio Civile, pg 384
Di Baio Editore SpA, pg 385
IHT Gruppo Editoriale SRL, pg 393
L Japadre Editore, pg 394
Levrotto e Bella Libreria Editrice Universitaria SAS, pg 395
Editrice Liguria SNC di Norberto Sabatelli & C, pg 396
Masson SpA, pg 398
Pitagora Editrice SRL, pg 403
Rara-Ist Editoriale di Bibliofilia e Reprints, pg 405
Red/Studio Redazionale SpA, pg 405
Editrice San Marco SRL, pg 406
Edizioni Scientifiche Italiane, pg 407
Editoriale Scienza, pg 407
Tecniche Nuove SpA, pg 409

Jamaica
Alice J M Rhodd, pg 413

Japan
Chijin Shokan Co Ltd, pg 415
Corona Publishing Co Ltd, pg 415
Kaibundo Publishing Co Ltd, pg 419
Kanehara & Co Ltd, pg 419
Koseisha-Koseikaku Co Ltd, pg 420
Kyoritsu Shuppan Co Ltd, pg 420
Mita Press, Mita Industrial Co, Ltd, pg 421
Morikita Shuppan Co Ltd, pg 421
Nankodo Co Ltd, pg 421
Nikkagiren Shuppan-Sha (JUSE Press Ltd), pg 422
The Nikkan Kogyo Shimbun Ltd, pg 422
Nippon Hoso Shuppan Kyokai (NHK Publishing), pg 422
Saera Shobo (Librairie Ca et La), pg 424
Sangyo-Tosho Publishing Co Ltd, pg 424
Seibundo Shinkosha Publishing Co Ltd, pg 425

Seizando-Shoten Publishing Co Ltd, pg 425
Shokabo Publishing Co Ltd, pg 426
Shufu-to-Seikatsu Sha Ltd, pg 426
Takahashi Shoten Co Ltd, pg 427
Tokai University Press, pg 427
Universal Academy Press, Inc, pg 428

Kenya
Academy Science Publishers, pg 430
African Centre for Technology Studies (ACTS), pg 431

Democratic People's Republic of Korea
Korea Science and Encyclopedia Publishing House, pg 434

Republic of Korea
Cheong-mun-gag Publishing Co, pg 435
Chung Rim Publishing Co Ltd, pg 435
Dai Hak Publishing Co, pg 436
Pan Korea Book Corporation, pg 439
Pochinchai Printing Co Ltd, pg 439
Yonsei University Press, pg 441

Macau
Museu Maritimo, pg 448

Malaysia
Pustaka Cipta Sdn Bhd, pg 454
Tropical Press Sdn Bhd, pg 455

Mexico
Aconcagua Ediciones y Publicaciones SA, pg 457
ALFA OMEGA Grupo Editor, pg 458
Colegio de Postgraduados en Ciencias Agricolas, pg 459
Compania Editorial Continental SA de CV, pg 459
Editorial Limusa SA de CV, pg 463
Pearson Educacion de Mexico, SA de CV, pg 465
Universidad Nacional Autonoma de Mexico (National University of Mexico), pg 467

Netherlands
Delft University Press, pg 476
Elsevier Science BV, pg 477
Hagen & Stam Uitgeverij Ten, pg 478
IOS Press BV, pg 479
Kluwer Academic Publishers, pg 479
Kluwer Bedrijfswetenschappen, pg 479
Kluwer Technische Boeken BV, pg 480
Uitgeverij Lemma BV, pg 480
Pearson Education Netherlands, pg 482
Samsom BedrijfsInformatie BV, pg 483
Swets & Zeitlinger Publishers, pg 485
Twente University Press, pg 485
V S P International Science Publishers, pg 486

New Zealand
New House Publishers Ltd, pg 493
Nelson Price Milburn Ltd, pg 494
Southern Press Ltd, pg 496

Nigeria
Ethiope Publishing Corporation, pg 499
Evans Brothers (Nigeria Publishers) Ltd, pg 499
Goldland Business Co Ltd, pg 499
Ibadan University Press, pg 499
Longman Nigeria Plc, pg 500

Norway
F Bruns Bokhandel og Forlag A/S, pg 503
Forlaget Fag og Kultur, pg 503
Vett & Viten AS, pg 505

Pakistan
Publishers United Pvt Ltd, pg 508

Paraguay
Instituto de Ciencias de la Computacion (NCR), pg 510

Peru
Instituto de Estudios Peruanos, pg 511

Philippines
Salesiana Publishers Inc, pg 515
University of the Philippines Press, pg 515

Poland
Oficyna Wydawnicza Politechniki Wroclawskiej, pg 519
Wydawnictwa Naukowo-Techniczne, pg 521

Portugal
Edicoes Cetop, pg 523
Chaves Ferreira Publicacoes SA, pg 523
Constancia Editores, SA, pg 524
Publicacoes Europa-America Lda, pg 524
Livraria Lopes Da Silva-Editora de M Moreira Soares Rocha Lda, pg 527
Monitor, pg 527

Puerto Rico
McGraw-Hill Intermericana del Caribe, Inc, pg 530

Romania
Editura Excelsior, pg 533
Editura Gryphon, pg 533
Editura Junimea, pg 534
Editura Signata, pg 536
Editura Tehnica, pg 536
Editura de Vest, pg 536

Russian Federation
N E Bauman Moscow State Technical University Publishers, pg 537
Energoatomizdat, pg 537
FGUP Izdatelstvo Mashinostroenie, pg 538
Izdatelstvo Lenizdat, pg 539
Izdatelstvo Metallurgiya, pg 540
Izdatelstvo Mir, pg 540
Nauka Publishers, pg 540

SUBJECT INDEX

Izdatelstvo Sudostroenie, pg 542
Izdatelstvo Vysshaya Shkola, pg 543

Saudi Arabia
King Saud University, pg 543

Singapore
APAC Publishers Services, pg 545
Maruzen Asia (Pte) Ltd, pg 547
Newscom Pte Ltd, pg 547
Reed Elsevier, South East Asia, pg 547

Slovakia
Technicka Univerzita, pg 551
VEDA (Vydavatel'stvo Slovenskej akademie vied), pg 551

South Africa
Educum Publishers Ltd, pg 554
Erudita Publications (Pty) Ltd, pg 554
Heinemann Publishers (Pty) Ltd, pg 555
Jacklin Enterprises (Pty) Ltd, pg 556
Nasou Via Afrika, pg 557
Shuter & Shooter (Pty) Ltd, pg 559

Spain
AMV Ediciones, pg 563
Ediciones Bellaterra SA, pg 565
Ediciones Daly S L, pg 569
Editorial Donostiarra SA, pg 570
Edebe, pg 571
Editorial Empeno 14, pg 573
Fondo de Cultura Economica de Espana, SL, pg 574
Fragua Editorial, pg 574
Ediciones Gestio 2000 SA, pg 575
Editorial Gustavo Gili SA, pg 576
Grupo Editorial CEAC SA, pg 576
Ibaizabal Edelvives SA, pg 577
Editorial Labor SA, pg 579
Editorin Laiovento SL, pg 579
McGraw-Hill Iberic/Brazil Group, pg 581
Mundi-Prensa Libros SA, pg 583
Editorial la Muralla SA, pg 583
Ediciones Omega SA, pg 585
Editorial Paraninfo SA, pg 586
Ediciones Piramide SA, pg 586
Progensa, pg 588
Editorial Tecnos SA, pg 592
Ediciones A Madrid Vicente, pg 595
Ediciones Vulcano, pg 596

Sudan
Khartoum University Press, pg 598

Sweden
Akademiforlaget Goteborgslitteratur, pg 600
ITK Laromedel AB, pg 603
Kungl Ingenjoersvetenskapsakademien (IVA), pg 604
Liber AB, pg 604
Studentlitteratur AB, pg 606

Switzerland
Verlag Harri Deutsch, pg 612
Presses Polytechniques et Universitaires Romandes, PPUR, pg 622
Vogt-Schild Ag, Druck und Verlag, pg 627

Taiwan, Province of China
Hsiao Yuan Publication Co, Ltd, pg 630
Petroleum Information Publishing Co, pg 631
San Min Book Co Ltd, pg 631

Tajikistan
Irfon, pg 632

Trinidad & Tobago
Caribbean Telecommunications Union, pg 636

Turkey
Caglayan Kitabevi, pg 639

Ukraine
Urozaj, pg 643

United Kingdom
Academic Press Ltd, pg 644
Advisory Unit: Computers in Education, pg 645
Artech House, pg 649
Aslib, The Association for Information Management, pg 650
British Educational Communication & Technology Agency (BECTA), pg 660
Butterworth-Heinemann Ltd, pg 661
Causeway Press Ltd, pg 665
Centre for Alternative Technology, pg 665
Commonwealth Secretariat, pg 669
Computer Step, pg 670
Elsevier Science Ltd, pg 678
ERA Technology Ltd, pg 679
The Eurospan Group, pg 680
Facet Publishing, pg 681
Forbes Publications Ltd, pg 683
Foulsham Publishers, pg 683
Haynes Publishing, pg 693
Hobsons, pg 696
Institute of Physics Publishing, pg 700
Institution of Electrical Engineers, pg 700
Intercept Ltd, pg 700
Intermediate Technology Publications Ltd, pg 700
Adam Matthew Publications, pg 712
Merrow Publishing Co Ltd, pg 714
Micelle Press, pg 714
MIT Press Ltd, pg 715
Motor Racing Publications Ltd, pg 716
Nelson Thornes Ltd, pg 718
New Cavendish Books, pg 718
New Leaf Books Ltd, pg 719
NMS Publishing Ltd, pg 719
Palgrave Publishers Ltd, pg 723
Pearson Education Europe, Mideast & Africa, pg 725
PIRA Intl, pg 728
Prism Press Book Publishers Ltd, pg 730
Professional Engineering Publishing Ltd, pg 730
Qualum Publishing, pg 731
Quintet Publishing Ltd, pg 732
Research Studies Press Ltd (RSP), pg 734
The Salariya Book Co Ltd, pg 738
Sangam Books Ltd, pg 738
Sheffield Academic Press Ltd, pg 741
SHU Press, pg 742
Skoob Russell Square, pg 742
Smith-Gordon, pg 743
The Stationery Office, pg 745
Sutton Publishing Ltd, pg 746
Taylor Graham Publishing, pg 747
Telegraph Books, pg 748
Thames & Hudson Ltd, pg 748
Trentham Books Ltd, pg 750
Two-Can Publishing Ltd, pg 750
UCL Press Ltd, pg 751
VNU Business Publications, pg 753
Wiley Europe Ltd, pg 756
WIT Press, pg 757
Witherby & Co Ltd, pg 758
Woodhead Publishing Ltd, pg 758

Uruguay
Editorial Arca SRL, pg 760

Venezuela
Editorial Nueva Sociedad, pg 762
Universidad de los Andes, Consejo de Publicaciones, pg 763

Viet Nam
Science & Technics Publishing House, pg 763

Yugoslavia
Savez Inzenjera i Tehnicara Jugoslavije, pg 765

Zimbabwe
University of Zimbabwe Publications, pg 769

THEOLOGY

Albania
NL SH, pg 1

Argentina
Bonum Editorial SACI, pg 4
Editorial Claretiana, pg 4
Editorial Ciudad Nueva de la Sefoma, pg 5
EUDEBA (Editorial Universitaria de Buenos Aires), pg 6
Editorial Galerna SRL, pg 6
Editorial Guadalupe, pg 6
San Pablo, pg 8

Australia
Aletheia Publishing, pg 11
Bible Society in Australia National Headquarters, pg 15
Bridgeway Publications, pg 16
Catholic Institute of Sydney, pg 17
Church Archivists Press, pg 18
Covenanter Press, pg 19
Crossroad Distributors Pty Ltd, pg 19
Desbooks Pty Ltd, pg 20
E J Dwyer (Australia) Pty Ltd, pg 21
Gnostic Editions, pg 24
Granrott Press, pg 24
Jesuit Publications, pg 28
New Creation Publications Ministries & Resource Centre, pg 34
Pan Pacific Publications, pg 37
Plantain Park, pg 38
St Pauls, pg 41
Spaniel Books, pg 43
Spectrum Publications, pg 43
Uniting Education, pg 45

Austria
Ennsthaler GesmbH & Co KG, pg 51
Otto Mueller Verlag GesmbH & Co KG, pg 55
Mueller-Speiser Wissenschaftlicher Verlag, pg 55
Wolfgang Neugebauer Verlag GmbH, pg 55
Passagen Verlag GmbH, pg 57
Verlag Anton Pustet, pg 57
Resch Verlag, pg 57
Verlag St Gabriel, pg 58
Andreas Schnider Verlags-Atelier, pg 58
Edition Va Bene, pg 60

Belgium
Artel SC, pg 64
Editions Lessius ASBL, pg 71
Leuven University Press, pg 71
Licap CVBA, pg 71
Editions Lumen Vitae ASBL, pg 71
Nauwelaerts Edition SA, pg 72
Uitgeverij Peeters Leuven (Belgie), pg 72
Publications des Facultes Universitaires Saint Louis, pg 73
Vita, pg 75

Brazil
Ars Poetica Editora Ltda, pg 79
Concordia Editora Ltda, pg 81
Editora Cidade Nova Socieda de Movimentodos Focolari, pg 82
Editora Elevacao, pg 82
EDUC - Editora da PUC-SP, pg 82
Horus Editora Ltda, pg 85
Editora Mundo Cristao, pg 88
Editora Nova Fronteira SA, pg 88
Olho D'Agua Comercio e Servicos Editoriais Ltda, pg 88
Pallas Editora e Distribuidora Ltda, pg 89
Paulinas Editorial, pg 89
Paulus Editora, pg 89
Editora Sinodal, pg 91

Bulgaria
Kralica MAB, pg 96
Nov Covek Publishing House, pg 97
Sila & Zivot, pg 98

Cameroon
Presses Universitaires d'Afrique, pg 99

Chile
Congregacion Paulinas - Hijas de San Pablo, pg 100

Colombia
Consejo Episcopal Latinoamericano Celam, pg 111

Costa Rica
Editorial DEI (Departamento Ecumenico de Investigaciones), pg 116
Promesa, Ediciones, pg 116

Croatia
Krscanska sadasnjost, pg 119
Znaci Vremena, Institut Za Istrazivanje Biblije, pg 120

Czech Republic
Barrister & Principal, pg 123
Kalich SRO, pg 125

PUBLISHERS SUBJECT INDEX

Karmelitanske Nakladatelstvi, pg 125
Zvon, pg 129

Denmark
Aarhus Universitetsforlag, pg 129
Forlaget Hovedland, pg 133
Scandinavia Publishing House, pg 135
Unitas Forlag, pg 136

Dominican Republic
Pontificia Universidad Catolica Madre y Maestra, pg 136

Ecuador
Ediciones Abya-Yala, pg 137
Pontificia Universidad Catolica de Ecuador, Centro de Publicaciones, pg 137

Egypt (Arab Republic of Egypt)
Dar El Shorouk Publishing & Distributing House, pg 138

El Salvador
UCA Editores, pg 139

Finland
Herattaja-yhdistys Ry, pg 142
Kustannus Oy Uusi Tie, pg 143
Yliopistopaino/Helsinki University Press, pg 145

France
Beauchesne Editeur, pg 150
Editions du Chalet, pg 154
Editions de Compostelle, pg 156
Desclee de Brouwer SA, pg 158
Institut d'Etudes Augustiniennes, pg 163
Fac Editions, pg 163
Librairie Fischbacher, International Art Book Distribution (import-export), pg 164
Les Editions Franciscaines SA, pg 165
J Gabalda et Cie (Librairie Lecoffre) SA, pg 165
P Lethielleux Editions, pg 172
LLB France (Ligue pour la Lecture de la Bible), pg 173
Editions Mediaspaul, pg 175
Peeters-France, pg 179
Editions Saint-Paul SA, pg 183
Maren Sell, pg 184
Editions du Seneve, pg 184
Les Editions de la Source Sarl, pg 186
Librairie Pierre Tequi et Editions Tequi, pg 187
Pierre Zech Editeur, pg 189

Germany
A Francke Verlag (Tubingen und Basel), pg 191
Adyar-Verlag, pg 191
Agentur des Rauhen Hauses Hamburg GmbH, pg 192
Aschendorffsche Verlagsbuchhandlung GmbH & Co KG, pg 195
Aussaat Verlag, pg 197
Bautz Traugott, pg 199
Ludwig Bechauf Verlag, pg 200
Verlag C H Beck (OHG), pg 200
Berlin Verlag Arno Spitz GmbH, pg 200
Beuth Verlag GmbH, pg 202
Verlag Die Blaue Eule, pg 204

Verlag Hermann Boehlaus Nachfolger Weimar GmbH & Co, pg 205
Bonifatius GmbH Druck-Buch-Verlag, pg 205
R Brockhaus Verlag, pg 206
Brunnen-Verlag GmbH, pg 207
Butzon & Bercker GmbH, pg 208
Calwer Verlag Stuttgart eV, pg 209
Chr Belser AG fur Verlagsgeschaefte und Co KG, pg 210
Christusbruderschaft Selbitz ev, Abt Verlag, pg 210
Claudius Verlag, pg 211
Concordia-Buchhandlung & Verlag, pg 211
Duncker und Humblot GmbH, pg 219
Echter Wurzburg Frankische Gesellschaftsdruckerei und Verlag GmbH, pg 220
EOS Verlag der Benefiktiner der Erzabtei St. Ottilien, pg 223
Erlanger Verlag Fuer Mission und Okumene, pg 223
Verlagsgesellschaft des Erziehungsvereins GmbH, pg 224
Evangelische Verlagsanstalt GmbH, pg 225
Evangelischer Presseverband fur Bayern eV, pg 225
Verlag der Francke Buchhandlung GmbH, pg 229
Franz-Sales-Verlag, pg 229
Friedrich Frommann Verlag, pg 230
Genius Verlag, pg 231
Gerth, Klaus, Verlag GmbH, pg 232
Walter de Gruyter GmbH & Co KG, pg 234
Guetersloher Verlagshaus Gerd Mohn, pg 235
Verlag des Gustav-Adolf-Werks, pg 235
Gutersloher Verlagshaus GmbH /Chr Kaiser/Kiefel/Quell, pg 235
Dr Haensel-Hohenhausen AG, pg 236
Verlag Herder GmbH & Co KG, pg 239
Anton Hiersemann, Verlag, pg 240
Iudicium Verlag, pg 245
Jan Thorbecke Verlag GmbH & Co, pg 246
Johannes Verlag Einsiedeln, Freiburg, pg 246
Johannis, pg 246
Katzmann Verlag KG, pg 248
Verlag Valentin Koerner GmbH, pg 252
W Kohlhammer GmbH, abt Haussortiment, pg 252
Lahn-Verlag GmbH, pg 255
Peter Lang GmbH Europaeischer Verlag der Wissenschaften, pg 255
Liebenzeller Mission, GmbH, Abt. Verlag, pg 258
Martha Lindner Verlags-GmbH, pg 258
Logos Verlag GmbH, pg 258
Lutherische Verlagsgesellschaft mbH, pg 259
Lutherisches Verlagshaus GmbH, pg 260
Annemarie Maeger, pg 260
Matthes und Seitz Verlag GmbH, pg 261
Matthias-Gruenewald-Verlag GmbH, pg 261
Medien-Verlag Bernhard Gregor GmbH, pg 262
Mohr Siebeck, pg 264

Verlag Neue Stadt GmbH, pg 267
Oekumenischer Verlag Dr R-F Edel, pg 270
Georg Olms Verlag AG, pg 270
One Way Medien OHG, pg 270
Oros Verlag, pg 271
Pahl-Rugenstein Verlag Nachfolger-GmbH, pg 271
Patmos Verlag GmbH & Co KG, pg 272
Paulinus Verlag GmbH, pg 272
Piper Verlag GmbH, pg 274
Projektion J Buch- und Musikverlag GmbH, pg 275
Verlag Friedrich Pustet GmbH & Co Kg, pg 276
Saatkorn-Verlag GmbH, pg 281
Verlag Schnell und Steiner GmbH, pg 284
Ferdinand Schoeningh Verlag GmbH, pg 284
Schwabenverlag Aktiengesellschaft, pg 285
Scientia Verlag und Antiquariat, pg 286
Sternberg-Verlag bei Ernst Franz, pg 290
Suin Buch-Verlag, pg 291
Guenter Albert Ulmer Verlag, pg 295
Vandenhoeck & Ruprecht, pg 297
Vereinte Evangelische Mission, Abt Verlag, pg 297
Vier Tuerme GmbH Verlag Klosterbetriebe, pg 298
Waxmann Verlag GmbH, pg 300
Erich Wewel Verlag, pg 302
Wichern Verlag, pg 302
Wolgang Fietkau, pg 304

Ghana
Asempa Publishers, pg 306

Greece
Akritas, pg 308
Alamo Hellas, pg 308
Apostoliki Diakonia tis Ekklisias tis Hellados, pg 309
Denise Harvey, pg 311
Kyriakidis, pg 312
D Papadimas, pg 314

Holy See (Vatican City State)
Biblioteca Apostolica Vaticana, pg 317
Libreria Editrice Vaticana, pg 317

Hong Kong
Chinese Christian Literature Council Ltd, pg 318
Philopsychy Press, pg 321

Hungary
Atlantisz Kiado, pg 323
Marton Aron Kiado Publishing House, pg 325
Osiris Kiado, pg 326

India
Asian Educational Services, pg 331
Asian Trading Corporation, pg 331
Indian Society for Promoting Christian Knowledge (ISPCK), pg 339
Rebel Publishing House Pvt Ltd, pg 347
Sree Rama Publishers, pg 351
Theosophical Publishing House, pg 351

Indonesia
Penerbit Nusa Indah, pg 356

Ireland
Cathedral Books Ltd, pg 359
The Columba Book Service, pg 359
The Columba Press, pg 359
Emerald Publications, pg 360
Four Courts Press Ltd, pg 360

Israel
Breslov Research Institute, pg 366
DAT Publications, pg 366
Gefen Publishing House Ltd, pg 367
Hakibbutz Hameuchad Publishing House Ltd, pg 368
Rav Kook Institute, pg 371

Italy
Adea Edizioni, pg 374
Edizioni ARES, pg 376
Edizioni Cantagalli, pg 379
Centro Biblico, pg 380
Centro Editoriale Valtortiano SRL, pg 381
Citta Nuova Editrice, pg 382
Cittadella Editrice, pg 382
Claudiana Editrice, pg 382
Nuova Coletti Editore Roma, pg 382
Edizioni Cultura della Pace, pg 383
Edizioni Dehoniane, pg 384
Edizioni Dehoniane Bologna (EDB), pg 384
Edizioni Qiqajon, pg 387
Edizioni Studio Domenicano (ESD), pg 387
Elle Di Ci - Libreria Dottrina Cristiana, pg 388
Biblioteca Francescana, pg 389
Glossa, pg 391
Piero Gribaudi Editore, pg 391
In Dialogo, pg 393
Editoriale Jaca Book SpA, pg 394
Editrice LAS, pg 395
Letture Mensile di Informazione Culturale, Letteratura e Spettacolo, pg 395
Liguori Editore SRL, pg 396
Casa Editrice Marietti SpA, pg 397
Editrice Massimo SAS di Crespi Cesare e C, pg 398
Il Melangolo, pg 398
Memorie Domenicane, pg 398
Leo S Olschki, pg 402
Edizioni Piemme SpA, pg 403
Editrice Queriniana, pg 404
Libreria Editrice Rogate (LER), pg 406
Rubbettino Editore, pg 406
Collegio San Bonaventura di Grottaferrata, pg 406
Fausto Sardini Editrice, pg 407
Edizioni Segno SRL, pg 407
Servitium, pg 408
Edizioni Rosminiane Sodalitas, pg 408
Edizioni del Teresianum, pg 409
Edizioni Thyrus SRL, pg 409
Urbaniana University Press, pg 410
Vivere In SRL, pg 411

Jamaica
Eureka Press Ltd, pg 413

Kenya
Action Publishers, pg 430
Evangel Publishing House, pg 431
Gaba Publications Amecea, Pastoral Institute, pg 431

SUBJECT INDEX

Heinemann Kenya Limited (EAEP), pg 431
Paulines Publications-Africa, pg 433
Shirikon Publishers, pg 433
Uzima Press, pg 433

Republic of Korea
Hanul Publishing Co, pg 436
Kukmin Doseo Publishing Co Inc, pg 438
St Pauls, pg 439

Latvia
Patmos, pg 442

Lebanon
Darl el-Machreq Sarl, pg 443

Luxembourg
Varkki Verghese, pg 448

Mexico
Ediciones CUPSA, Centro de Comunicacion Cultural CUPSA, AC, pg 459
El Colegio de Michoacan A C, pg 460
Editorial Jus SA de CV, pg 462
Phillip Richard Conover Lazo, pg 462
Ediciones Promesa, SA de CV, pg 466

Netherlands
APA (Academic Publishers Associated), pg 472
Erven J Bijleveld, pg 474
Boekencentrum BV, pg 474
Brill Academic Publishers, pg 475
Buijten en Schipperheijn BV Drukkerij en Uitg Mij v/h, pg 475
Uitgeverij G F Callenbach BV, pg 475
HES & De Graaf Publishers BV, pg 478
Holland University Press BV (APA), pg 478
Meinema, pg 481
Narratio Theologische Uitgeverij, pg 482
Philo Press-Van Heusden-Hissink & Co CV (APA), pg 482
Servire BV Uitgevers, pg 484
Telos Boeken, pg 485
Tilburg University Press, pg 485
Uitgeverij Van Wijnen, pg 486
VU Boekhandel/Uitgeverij BV, pg 487
Uitgeverij De Vuurbaak BV, pg 487

New Zealand
Church Mouse Press, pg 490

Norway
Genesis Forlag, pg 503
Lunde Forlag og Bokhandel A/S, pg 504

Papua New Guinea
Kristen Pres, pg 510
Nazarene Publications, pg 510

Peru
Fondo Editorial de la Pontificia Universidad Catolica del Peru, pg 511

Philippines
Ateneo de Manila University Press, pg 512
Claretian Communications Inc, pg 513
Communication Foundation for Asia Media Group (CFAMG), pg 513
New Day Publishers, pg 514
Philippine Baptist Mission SBC FMB Church Growth International, pg 514
Rex Bookstores & Publishers, pg 514
UST Publishing House, pg 515

Poland
Drukarnia I Ksiegarnia Swietego Wojciecha, Dziat Wydawniczy, pg 516
Instytut Wydawniczy Pax, Inco-Veritas, pg 517
Katolicki Uniwersytet Wydawniczo-Redakcja, pg 517
Norbertinum, pg 518
Pallottinum Wydawnictwo Stowarzyszenia Apostolstwa Katolickiego, pg 518
Vocatio Publishing House, pg 520

Portugal
Apostolado da Oracao Secretariado Nacional, pg 522
Editorial Franciscana, pg 525
Edicoes Ora & Labora, pg 528
Editorial Perpetuo Socorro, pg 528
Usus Editora, pg 530
Livraria Verdade e Vida Editora, pg 530

Romania
Ars Longa Publishing House, pg 532
Humanitas Publishing House, pg 533
Editura Institutul European, pg 533
Saeculum IO, pg 535
Universal Dalsi, pg 536

Russian Federation
Druzhba Narodov, pg 537
St Andrew's Biblical Theological College, pg 541
Scorpion Publishers, pg 541

Singapore
Tecman Bible House, pg 549

Slovakia
Luc vydavatelske druzstvo, pg 550

Slovenia
Zalozba Mihelac d o o, pg 552

South Africa
Institute for Reformational Studies CHE, pg 555
Lux Verbi (Pty) Ltd, pg 556
Unisa Press, pg 560

Spain
Publicacions de l'Abadia de Montserrat, pg 561
Biblioteca de Autores Cristianos, pg 564
Avgvstinvs, pg 564
Ediciones Encuentro SA, pg 573
EUNSA (Ediciones Universidad de Navarra SA), pg 574
Editorial Herder SA, pg 577

Ediciones Internacionales Universitarias SA, pg 578
Loguez Ediciones, pg 580
Mundo Negro Editorial, pg 583
Centre de Pastoral Liturgica, pg 586
Editorial El Perpetuo Socorro, pg 586
Publicaciones de la Universidad Pontificia Comillas-Madrid, pg 588
San Pablo Ediciones, pg 589
Ediciones San Pio X, pg 589
Secretariado Trinitario, pg 590
Ediciones Sigueme SA, pg 590
Ediciones Siruela SA, pg 591
Ediciones SM, pg 591
Editorial Sal Terrae, pg 592
Trotta SA Editorial, pg 593
Editorial Verbo Divino, pg 595

Sweden
Forlaget Sanctus (Metodistkyrkans Forlag), pg 602
Hagaberg AB, pg 603
Libris Bokforlaget, pg 604
Bokforlaget Nya Doxa AB, pg 605
Verbum Foerlag AB, pg 607

Switzerland
Armenia Editions, pg 608
Benziger Verlag AG, pg 609
Edition Exodus, pg 614
Jugend mit einer Mission Verlag, pg 616
Kanisius Verlag, pg 616
Labor et Fides SA, pg 618
La Maison de la Bible, pg 618
Neue Zeitschrift Missionswissenschaft Verlag, pg 620
PIE-Peter Lang SA, pg 622
Psychosophische Gesellschaft, pg 622
Rodera-Verlag der Cardun AG, pg 623
Editions Saint Augustin, pg 623
Schwabe & Co AG, pg 624
Swedenborg - Verlag, pg 625
Theologischer Verlag und Buchhandlungen AG, pg 625
Der Universitatsverlag Freiburg, pg 626
World Council of Churches (WCC Publications), pg 628

United Republic of Tanzania
Kanisa la Biblia Publishers (KLB), pg 633
Kisambo Publishers Ltd, pg 633
Ndanda Mission Press, pg 634
Northwestern Publishers, pg 634

Turkey
Oguz Yayinlari, pg 640

United Kingdom
Arthur James Ltd, pg 649
Ashgate Publishing Ltd, pg 649
Bible Reading Fellowship, pg 654
Bloomsbury Publishing PLC, pg 656
Bryntirion Press, pg 661
Cambridge University Press, pg 662
Cassell & Co, pg 664
Catholic Institute for International Relations, pg 665
Chapter Two, pg 666
Christian Focus Publications Ltd, pg 667
Church Society, pg 668
James Clarke & Co Ltd, pg 668

CTBI Publications, pg 672
Darton, Longman & Todd Ltd, pg 674
Dunedin Academic Press, pg 676
Edinburgh University Press Ltd, pg 677
Epworth Press, pg 679
The Eurospan Group, pg 680
Evangelical Press & Services Ltd, pg 680
Golden Cockerel Press Ltd, pg 688
Gracewing Publishing, pg 688
The Handsel Press, pg 691
HarperCollins Publishers, pg 692
Hodder & Stoughton Educational, pg 696
Hodder & Stoughton Religious, pg 696
Angus Hudson Ltd, pg 697
Islam International Publications Ltd, pg 701
Janus Publishing Company Ltd, pg 702
Kingsway Publications, pg 705
Lion Publishing PLC, pg 708
The Littman Library of Jewish Civilization, pg 708
The Lutterworth Press, pg 709
Maney Publishing, pg 711
Marcham Books, pg 711
Methodist Publishing House, pg 714
Monarch Books, pg 715
Moorley's Print & Publishing Ltd, pg 715
Plough Publishing House of Bruderhof Communities in the UK, pg 728
Saint Andrew Press, pg 737
SCM Press, pg 739
Scottish Text Society, pg 740
Scripture Union, pg 740
Sheffield Academic Press Ltd, pg 741
SLG Press, pg 742
The Society for Promoting Christian Knowledge (SPCK), pg 743
St Pauls Publishing, pg 744
Thoemmes Press, pg 748
Transedition Ltd, pg 749
University of Wales Press, pg 751
Vallentine, Mitchell & Co Ltd, pg 752
Wild Goose Publications, pg 756
World of Islam Altajir Trust, pg 759
Yale University Press London, pg 759

Venezuela
Fundacion Centro Gumilla, pg 762

Yugoslavia
AGAPE, pg 764

Zimbabwe
Christian Audio-Visual Action (CAVA), pg 768
Vision Publications, pg 769

TRANSPORTATION

Australia
Kangaroo Press, pg 29
Kingsclear Books, pg 29
Lowden Publishing Co, pg 31
Marque Publishing, pg 31
Navarine Publishing, pg 34
Turton & Armstrong Publishers Pty Ltd, pg 45

PUBLISHERS

Austria
Bohmann Druck und Verlag GmbH & Co KG, pg 50
Verlag Josef Otto Slezak, pg 58

Belgium
Editions Gerard Blanchart & Cie SA, pg 65
Ediblanchart sprl, pg 68

Bulgaria
DA-Izdatelstvo Publishers, pg 95
WTU Todor Kableskov, pg 98

China
Chemical Industry Press, pg 102
China Cartographic Publishing House, pg 103
Fujian Science & Technology Publishing House, pg 106
Heilongjiang Science & Technology Press, pg 106
The People's Communications Publishing House, pg 107
Southwest China Jiaotong University Press, pg 109

Czech Republic
SystemConsult, pg 128

Denmark
Bogfabrikken Fakta ApS, pg 130
Mercantila Publishers A/S, pg 133

Estonia
Mats Publishers Ltd, pg 140

France
Annales de la Recherche Urbaine, pg 147
Blondel La Rougery SARL, pg 151
CELSE (Compagnie d'Editions Libres, Sociales et Economiques SA), pg 153
Editions Cenomane, pg 153
Cepadues Editions SA, pg 153
Le Cherche Midi Editeur, pg 154
Codes Rousseau, pg 155
EPA SA (Editions Presse Audiovisuel), pg 162
Institut Francais de Recherche pour l'Exploitation de la Mer (IFREMER), pg 165
Editions Payot & Rivages, pg 179
Presses de l'Ecole Nationale des Ponts et Chaussees, pg 181

Germany
Aerogie-Verlag, pg 191
AOL-Verlag Frohmut Menze, pg 194
BertelsmannSpringer Science & Business Media GmbH, pg 202
Beuth Verlag GmbH, pg 202
Verlag Wolfgang Bleiweis, pg 204
Deutsche Gesellschaft fuer Eisenbahngeschichte eV, pg 213
Dumjahn Verlag, pg 219
Ecomed Verlagsgesellschaft AG & Co KG, pg 220
EK-Verlag GmbH, pg 222
Verkehrs-Verlag J Fischer GmbH & Co KG, pg 228
Heel Verlag GmbH, pg 238
Hestra-Verlag Hernichel & Dr Strauss GmbH & Co KG, pg 240
Huss-Verlag GmbH, pg 244
Kirschbaum Verlag GmbH, pg 249

Koenemann Verlagesellschaft mbH, pg 251
Institut fuer Landes- und Stadtentwicklungsforschung, ILS Nordrhein-Westfalen, pg 255
Libertas- Europaeisches Institut GmbH, pg 257
Edition Maritim GmbH, pg 261
Moby Dick Verlag, pg 264
Verlag Walter Podszun Burobedarf-Bucher Abt, pg 274
Ritzau KG Verlag Zeit und Eisenbahn, pg 279
Schweers + Wall GmbH Verlag, pg 286
Tetzlaff Verlag, pg 292
Transpress Verlagsgesellschaft mbH, pg 294
TUeV-Verlag GmbH, pg 295
Ulrich Schiefer bahnVerlag, pg 296

Ghana
Building & Road Research Institute (BRRI), pg 306

Hungary
Hatter Lap- es Konyvkiado Kft, pg 324
Szarvas Andras Cartographic Agency, pg 326

India
Inter-India Publications, pg 340

Ireland
Libra House Ltd, pg 362

Italy
Ermanno Albertelli Editore, pg 375
Automobilia srl, pg 377
Calosci, pg 379
Editoriale Domus Spa, pg 385
ETR (Editrice Trasporti su Rotaie), pg 388
Instituti Editoriali E Poligrafici Internazionali SRL, pg 393
Giorgio Nada Editore SRL, pg 400

Japan
Seizando-Shoten Publishing Co Ltd, pg 425

Macau
Museu Maritimo, pg 448

Mexico
Editorial Limusa SA de CV, pg 463

Netherlands
Hagen & Stam Uitgeverij Ten, pg 478
Ministerie van Verkeer en Waterstaat, pg 481
V S P International Science Publishers, pg 486

New Zealand
Grantham House Publishing, pg 491
IPL Publishing Group, pg 492
Southern Press Ltd, pg 496

Norway
Elanders Publishing AS, pg 503
NKI Forlaget, pg 504

Poland
Wydawnictwa Komunikacji i Lacznosci Co Ltd, pg 517

Russian Federation
Izdatelstvo Sudostroenie, pg 542
Izdatelstvo Transport, pg 542

South Africa
Jacklin Enterprises (Pty) Ltd, pg 556

Spain
Centro de Estudios Adams-Ediciones Valbuena SA, pg 561
Comunidad Autonoma de Madrid, Servicio de Documentacion y Publicaciones, pg 568
Axel Springer Publicaciones, pg 591

Sweden
Allt om Hobby AB, pg 600
Frank Stenvalls Forlag, pg 606

Switzerland
Verlag Eisenbahn, pg 613
Pharos-Verlag, Hansrudolf Schwabe AG, pg 621
Editions 24 Heures, pg 626
Verkehrshaus der Schweiz, pg 626
Vogt-Schild Ag, Druck und Verlag, pg 627

Syrian Arab Republic
Damascus University Press, pg 628

United Kingdom
Airlife Publishing Ltd, pg 645
Ian Allan Publishing Ltd, pg 646
Amber Books Ltd, pg 646
Apple Press, pg 648
Arms & Armour Press, pg 648
Artech House, pg 649
Ashgate Publishing Ltd, pg 649
Atlantic Transport Publishers, pg 650
Books International, pg 657
Brewin Books Ltd, pg 659
Castlemead Publications, pg 665
Colourpoint Books, pg 669
Compendium Publishing, pg 670
Countyvise Ltd, pg 671
Croner CCH Group Ltd, pg 672
David & Charles Ltd, pg 674
Defiant Publications, pg 675
DMG Business Media Ltd, pg 675
Eaglemoss Publications Ltd, pg 676
Elliot Right Way Books, pg 678
A H Gordon, pg 688
Grange Books PLC, pg 689
Greenhill Books/Lionel Leventhal Ltd, pg 689
Haynes Publishing, pg 693
Jane's Information Group, pg 702
Kogan Page Ltd, pg 705
Middleton Press, pg 714
Midland Publishing, pg 714
Motor Racing Publications Ltd, pg 716
Oakwood Press, pg 720
Orpheus Books Ltd, pg 722
Platform 5 Publishing Ltd, pg 728
PRC Publishing Ltd, pg 730
Professional Engineering Publishing Ltd, pg 730
Quintet Publishing Ltd, pg 732
Ramboro Books Plc, pg 732
Regency House Publishing Ltd, pg 734
Roadmaster Publishing, pg 735
Salamander Books Ltd, pg 738
SB Publications, pg 738
Scottish Office Library & Information Services, pg 740

SUBJECT INDEX

Shire Publications Ltd, pg 741
Sigma Press, pg 742
Silver Link Publishing Ltd, pg 742
Spon Press, pg 744
The Stationery Office, pg 745
Sutton Publishing Ltd, pg 746
Transport Bookman Publications Ltd, pg 750
Unicorn Books, pg 751
Veloce Publishing Ltd, pg 752
WIT Press, pg 757
Witherby & Co Ltd, pg 758

Viet Nam
Science & Technics Publishing House, pg 763

TRAVEL

Algeria
Enterprise Nationale du Livre (ENAL), pg 2

Australia
Blubber Head Press, pg 15
Louis Braille Audio, pg 16
Robert Brown & Associates Australia Pty Ltd, pg 16
CHOICE Magazine, pg 18
Companion Travel Guide Books, pg 18
Cornford Press, pg 19
Crawford House Publishing, pg 19
Dryden Press, pg 21
Emperor Publishing, pg 22
Garradunga Press, pg 23
F H Halpern, pg 25
Hartys Creek Press, pg 25
Hema Maps Pty Ltd, pg 26
Horan Wall & Walker, pg 26
Hospitality Press Pty Ltd, pg 26
Kangaroo Press, pg 29
Kingsclear Books, pg 29
Lightbild PTY Ltd, pg 30
Little Hills Press, pg 30
Lonely Planet Publications Pty Ltd, pg 30
Tracy Marsh Publications Pty Ltd, pg 32
Media East Press, pg 33
Melbourne University Press, pg 33
Oceans Enterprises, pg 35
Off the Shelf Publishing, pg 35
Pan Macmillan Australia Pty Ltd, pg 36
Penguin Books Australia Ltd, pg 37
Pinevale Publications, pg 38
RMIT Publishing, pg 41
See Australia Guides P/L, pg 42
Single X Publications, pg 42
Spinifex Press, pg 43
Thames & Hudson (Australia) Pty Ltd, pg 44
Universal Press Pty Ltd, pg 46
University of Queensland Press, pg 46
Wakefield Press Pty Ltd, pg 47
The Watermark Press, pg 47
Windward Publications, pg 48
Woodlands Publications, pg 48

Austria
Bohmann Druck und Verlag GmbH & Co KG, pg 50
Verlag Harald Denzel, Auto- und Freizeitfuehrer, pg 51
Edition Graphischer Zirkel, pg 52
Kuemmerly und Frey Verlags GmbH, pg 54

1101

SUBJECT INDEX

Niederosterreichisches Pressehaus Druck- und Verlagsgesellschaft mbH, pg 55
Osterreichischer Alpenverein Sektion Weiner Lehrer, pg 57
Pinguin-Verlag, Pawlowski GmbH, pg 57
Promedia Verlagsges mbH, pg 57
Verlag Anton Pustet, pg 57
Tyrolia Verlagsanstalt GmbH, pg 59
Edition Va Bene, pg 60
Verlag Anton Schroll & Co, pg 60
Herbert Weishaupt Verlag, pg 60

Bangladesh
The University Press Ltd, pg 62

Belgium
SA Artis-Historia, pg 64
Carto BVBA, pg 65
Cartoeristiek (Federatie van Belgische Autobus- en Autocarondernemers) (BAAV), pg 66
Creadif, pg 67
Cremers (Schoollandkaarten) PVBA, pg 67
Daphne Diffusion SA, pg 67
DEF (De Blauwe Vogel) NV/SA, pg 67
Uitgevery Gelbis NV, pg 68
Koepel van de Vlaamse Noord - Zuidbeweging 11.11.11, pg 70
Uitgeverij Lannoo NV, pg 70
Michelin Editions des Voyages, pg 72
Henri Proost & Co, Pvba, pg 73
Reader's Digest SA, pg 73
Roularta Books NV, pg 73
Sonneville Press (Uitgeverij) VTW, pg 74
Editions Techniques et Scientifiques SPRL, pg 74
Uitgevery Scoop Infotex NV, pg 75

Botswana
Maskew Miller Longman, pg 77

Brazil
Artes e Oficios Editora Ltda, pg 79
Associacao Brasileira de Liverivos Antiquarios, pg 79
Editora Campus Ltda, pg 80
Companhia Editora Forense, pg 82
Editora Forense, pg 83
Editora Globo SA, pg 84
LDA Editores Ltda, pg 86
Livraria Nobel S/A, pg 86
Editora Mantiqueira de Ciencia e Arte, pg 87
Editora Marco Zero Ltda, pg 87
Rede Das Artes (Boccato Editores Collector's), pg 90

Bulgaria
Aleks Print Publishing House, pg 94
Publishing House Narodno delo OOD, pg 97

Chile
Arrayan Editores, pg 99
Ediciones Mil Hojas Ltda, pg 100
Publicaciones Lo Castillo SA, pg 101

China
Chengdu Maps Publishing House, pg 103
China Cartographic Publishing House, pg 103
Foreign Languages Press, pg 105
Higher Education Press, pg 106
Jilin Science & Technology Publishing House, pg 106
Shandong Friendship Press, pg 108

Colombia
Ediciones Gamma, pg 112

Cyprus
Action Publications, pg 121
Nikoklis Publishers, pg 122

Czech Republic
Konias, pg 125
Mlada fronta, pg 126
NLN, Ltd The Lidove noviny Publishing House, pg 127
Nakladatelstvi Olympia AS, pg 127
Prazske nakladatelstvi Pluto, pg 127
Svojtka & Co, pg 128
SystemConsult, pg 128

Denmark
GEC Gads Forlag Aktieselskab af 1994, pg 132
Forlaget Hjulet, pg 132
Det Schonbergske Forlag, pg 135

Egypt (Arab Republic of Egypt)
Lehnert & Landrock Bookshop, pg 139

Finland
Kirja-Leitzinger, pg 143
Suomen Matkailuliitto ry (The Finish Travel Association), pg 144
Tietoteos Publishing Co, pg 144
Yliopistopaino/Helsinki University Press, pg 145

France
Anako Editions, pg 147
Aubanel SA, pg 149
Autrement Editions, pg 149
Editions A Barthelemy, pg 149
Bibliotheque des Arts, pg 150
Editions Andre Bonne, pg 151
Pierre Bordas et Fils, pg 151
Brud Nevez, pg 152
Editions du Buot, pg 152
Editions du Chene, pg 154
CLD, pg 155
Editions Grund, pg 161
Editions Fanlac, pg 163
FBT de R Editions/Editions des Limbes d'Or, pg 163
Editions Filipacchi-Sonodip, pg 164
Editions Fivedit, pg 164
Editions du Garde-Temps, pg 166
Editions Jean Paul Gisserot, pg 166
Editions J Glenat SA, pg 166
Editions Grancher, pg 166
Hachette Livre, pg 167
Image/Magie, pg 169
Editions du Jaguar, pg 170
Kailash Editions, pg 171
Karthala Editions-Diffusion, pg 171
Editions Fernand Lanore Sarl, pg 172
LT Editions-J Lanore-H Laurens, pg 172
Editions du Laquet, pg 172
Editions des Limbes d'Or/FBT de R Editions, pg 173
Lonely Planet, pg 174
Editions Loubatieres, pg 174
Editions Marcus, pg 174
Editions Franck Mercier, pg 176
Michelin et Cie (Services de Tourisme), pg 176
Nouvelles Editions Latines, pg 178
Editions Ophrys, pg 178
Editions Ouest-France, pg 178
Editions Payot & Rivages, pg 179
Editions Jean Picollec, pg 179
Editions Christian Pirot, pg 180
Selection du Reader's Digest SA, pg 184
Siloe - Kerdore, pg 185
Taride Editions, pg 187
Alain Thomas Editeur, pg 188
Ulisse Edition, pg 188
La Vague a l'ame, pg 188
La Vague Verte, pg 188
Editions Vilo SA, pg 189
Zodiaque, pg 190

French Polynesia
Haere Po No Tahiti, pg 190

Germany
ADAC Verlag GmbH, pg 191
Alouette Verlag, pg 193
Anabas-Verlag Guenter Kaempf GmbH & Co KG, pg 193
Arcus-Medien Wolfgang Steinhardt, pg 194
Ars Vivendi Verlag, pg 195
ARTC/OLOR, pg 195
Badenia Verlag und Druckerei GmbH, pg 197
Beerenverlag, pg 200
Bergstadtverlag Wilhelm Gottlieb Korn GmbH Wuerzburg, pg 200
Berndtson & Berndtson GmbH Verlag-Publishing, pg 201
Bertelsmann Lexikon Verlag GmbH, pg 201
Bielefelder Verlagsanstalt GmbH & Co KG Richard Kaselowsky, pg 203
BLV Verlagsgesellschaft mbH, pg 204
Brandenburgisches Verlagshaus in der Dornier Medienholding GmbH, pg 206
Verlag C J Bucher GmbH, pg 207
Kartographischer Verlag Busche GmbH, pg 208
Verlag Busse und Seewald GmbH, pg 208
Chr Belser AG fur Verlagsgeschaefte und Co KG, pg 210
Hans Christians Druckerei und Verlag GmbH & Co, pg 210
Compact Verlag GmbH, pg 211
Deutscher Taschenbuch Verlag GmbH & Co KG (dtv), pg 215
Deutscher Wanderverlag Dr Mair & Schnabel & Co, pg 215
Dialog-Verlag GmbH, pg 216
Drei Brunnen Verlag GmbH & Co, pg 218
Drei Ulmen Verlag GmbH, pg 218
Dumjahn Verlag, pg 219
DuMont Buchverlag GmbH & Co KG, pg 219
Edition Aragon-Verlagsgesellschaft mbH, pg 220
Egmont vgs verlagsgesellschaft mbH, pg 221
EinfallsReich Verlagsgesellschaft MbH, pg 222
Elektor-Verlag GmbH, pg 222
Ellert & Richter Verlag GmbH, pg 222
Eulen Verlag, pg 224
F Bruckmann Munchen Verlag & Druck GmbH & Co Produkt KG, pg 225
Flechsig Buchvertrieb, pg 228
Fleischhauer & Spohn GmbH & Co, pg 228
Frederking & Thaler Verlag GmbH, pg 230
Friedemann von Engel Verlag, pg 230
G Braun (vormals G Braun'sche Hofbuchdruckerei und Verlag) Gmbh, pg 231
Konkursbuch Verlag Claudia Gehrke, pg 231
GLB Parkland Verlags-und Vertriebs GmbH, pg 232
Verlagsgesellschaft R Gloess & Co, pg 233
Graefe und Unzer Verlag GmbH, pg 233
Graf Editions, pg 234
Harenberg Kommunikation Verlags- und Medien GmbH & Co KG, pg 237
Haschemi Edition Cologne Kunstverlag, pg 237
Haude und Spenersche Verlagsbuchhandlung, pg 238
Hayit Reisefuhrer in der Rutsker Verlag GmbH, pg 238
Heel Verlag GmbH, pg 238
F A Herbig Verlagsbuchhandlung GmbH, pg 239
Helmut Hermann, pg 240
Humboldt-Taschenbuchverlag Jacobi KG, pg 243
Ikarus - Buchverlag, pg 244
Interconnections Reisen und Arbeiten Georg Beckmann, pg 245
Klaus Isele, pg 245
Reisebuchverlag Iwanowski GmbH, pg 246
Jahreszeiten-Verlag GmbH, pg 246
Jan Thorbecke Verlag GmbH & Co, pg 246
KaJo Verlag, pg 247
Verlag Karl Baedeker GmbH, pg 248
Karto + Grafik Verlagsgesellschaft (K & G Verlagsgesellschaft), pg 248
Kartographischer Verlag Reinhard Ryborsch, pg 248
SachBuchVerlag Kellner, pg 248
Kleiner Bachmann Verlag fur Kinder und Umwelt, pg 250
Doris Knop-Verlag, pg 251
Knowledge Media International, pg 251
Adam Kraft Verlag, pg 253
Ambro Lacus, Buch- und Bildverlag Walter Kremnitz, pg 255
Landbuch-Verlagsgesellschaft mbH, pg 255
J Latka Verlag GmbH, pg 256
Siegbert Linnemann Verlag, pg 258
Stefan Loose Verlag, pg 259
Lusatia Verlag-Dr Stuebner & Co KG, pg 259
Karin Mader, pg 260
Mairs Geographischer Verlag, pg 260
Mais Verlag GmbH und Reisefuehrer, pg 260
Edition Maritim GmbH, pg 261
Edition Axel Menges, pg 262
Meyer & Meyer Fachverlag und Buchhandel GmbH, pg 263
Mitteldeutscher Verlag GmbH, pg 264
Moby Dick Verlag, pg 264

PUBLISHERS

Mundo Verlag GmbH, pg 266
Verlag Stephanie Naglschmid, pg 266
Naumann & Goebel Verlagsgesellschaft mbH, pg 267
Nebel Verlag GmbH, pg 267
Nelles Verlag GmbH, pg 267
Neuer Honos Verlag GmbH, pg 267
Neumann Verlag, pg 268
Neuthor - Verlag, pg 268
Georg Olms Verlag AG, pg 270
Palazzi Verlag GmbH, pg 271
Passavia Druckerei GmbH, Verlag, pg 271
Jens Peters Publikationen, pg 272
Paul Pietsch Verlage GmbH & Co, pg 273
Pollner Verlag, pg 274
Polyglott-Verlag, pg 274
Prestel Verlag, pg 275
Propylaeen Verlag, Zweigniederlassung Berlin der Ullstein Buchverlage GmbH, pg 275
Werner Rau Verlag, pg 277
Konrad Reich Verlag GmbH, pg 278
E Reinhold Verlag, pg 278
Reise Know-How, pg 278
Reise-Know-How Verlag-Daerr GmbH, pg 278
Reise Know-How Verlag Peter Rump GmbH, pg 278
Reise Know-How Verlag Tondok, pg 278
Verlagsgruppe Reise-Know-How, pg 278
Peter Meyer Reisefuhrer, pg 278
Romiosini Verlag, pg 280
Moritz Schauenburg Verlag, pg 282
Schelzky & Jeep, Verlag fuer Reisen und Wissen, pg 283
Renate Schenk Verlag, pg 283
Schillinger Verlag GmbH, pg 283
Schmid Verlag GmbH, pg 283
Verlag Schnell und Steiner GmbH, pg 284
Schoeffling & Co, pg 284
H O Schulze KG, pg 285
Schweers + Wall GmbH Verlag, pg 286
Gerd Simon & Claudia Magiera, Verlagsbuero, pg 287
Stapp Verlag Wolfgang Stapp, pg 289
Stattbuch Verlag GmbH, pg 289
Steiger Verlag, pg 289
Conrad Stein Verlag, pg 289
Stoeppel Verlag-Buchvertrieb KG, pg 290
Sturtz Verlag GmbH, pg 291
Suedwest Verlag GmbH & Co KG, pg 291
Edition Temmen, pg 292
teNeues Verlag GmbH & Co KG, pg 292
Tomus Verlag GmbH, pg 294
TR - Verlagsunion GmbH, pg 294
Trees Wolfgang Triangel Verlag, pg 294
Trescher Verlag GmbH, pg 295
Treves Editions Verein Zur Foerderung der Kuenstlerischen Taetigkeiten, pg 295
Turkischer Schulbuchverlag Onel Cengiz, pg 295
Vista Point Verlag GmbH, pg 299
VS Verlagshaus Stuttgart GmbH, pg 299
W Ludwig Verlag GmbH, pg 300
WDV Wirtschaftsdienst Gesellschaft fur Medien & Kommunikation mbH & Co OHG, pg 300
Weidlich Verlag, pg 301
Wolfgang Arlt u Ute Schiller, pg 304
Wolf's-Verlag Berlin, pg 304
Zambon Verlag, pg 305
Zeitgeist Media GmbH, pg 305
Ziethen-Panorama Verlag GmbH, pg 305
Zweimuehlen Verlag GmbH, pg 305

Ghana
Moxon Paperbacks, pg 307

Greece
Alamo Hellas, pg 308
Ekdoseis Kazantzaki (Kazantzakis Publications), pg 310
Ekdotike Athenon SA, pg 310
Evrodiastasi, pg 310
Hestia-I D Hestia-Kollaros & Co Corporation, pg 311
Kedros Publishers, pg 312
Knossos Publications, pg 312
Editions Moressopoulos, pg 313
Patakis Publishers, pg 314
Stochastis, pg 315

Hong Kong
Business Traveller Asia Pacific, pg 318
CFW Publications Ltd, pg 318
Hong Kong China Tourism Press, pg 320
Hong Kong Publishing Co Ltd, pg 320
Island Press, pg 320
Steve Lu Publishing Ltd, pg 320
Press Mark Media Ltd, pg 321
Publications (Holdings) Ltd, pg 321

Hungary
Corvina Books Ltd, pg 323
Idegenforgalmi Propaganda es Kiado Vallalat, pg 324
Officina Nova, Koenyv-es Lapkiado/ Bertelsmann Media Kft, pg 324
Kossuth Kiado RT, pg 325
Magyar Kemikusok Egyesulete, pg 325
Medicina Koenyvkiado, pg 325
Szarvas Andras Cartographic Agency, pg 326

Iceland
Forlagid, pg 327
Mal og menning, pg 328

India
APH Publishing Corp, pg 331
Asian Educational Services, pg 331
Associated Publishing House, pg 331
Brijbasi Printers Pvt Ltd, pg 334
General Book Depot, pg 337
Gyan Publishing House, pg 338
Himalayan Books, pg 338
Indian Book Depot (Map House), pg 339
Indus Publishing Co, pg 339
Islamic Publishing House, pg 340
A Mukherjee & Co Pvt Ltd, pg 343
Omsons Publications, pg 345
Reliance Publishing House, pg 347
Roli Books Pvt Ltd, pg 348
Spectrum Publications, pg 350
Vakils Feffer & Simons Ltd, pg 352
Vision Books Pvt Ltd, pg 353

Indonesia
Bina Aksara Parta, pg 354
Bina Rena Pariwara, pg 354

Ireland
Ballinakella Press, pg 358
Dee-Jay Publications, pg 359
Estragon Press Ltd, pg 360
Events of the Week, pg 360
Gill & Macmillan Ltd, pg 361
Libra House Ltd, pg 362
The O'Brien Press Ltd, pg 363
On Stream Publications Ltd, pg 363
Real Ireland Design, pg 363
Roberts Rinehart Publishers, pg 363

Israel
Bitan Publishers Ltd, pg 365
Classikaletet, pg 366
Gefen Publishing House Ltd, pg 367
Hakibbutz Hameuchad Publishing House Ltd, pg 368
Inbal Travel Information, pg 368
Ma'ariv Book Guild (Sifriat Ma'ariv), pg 370
MAP-Mapping & Publishing Ltd, pg 370
Saar Publishing House, pg 372
Schocken Publishing House Ltd, pg 372
R Sirkis Publishers Ltd, pg 372
Steinhart-Katzir Publishers, pg 372

Italy
Arcadia Edizioni Srl, pg 376
Verlagsanstalt Athesia, pg 377
Casa Editrice Bonechi, pg 378
Bonechi-Edizioni Il Turismo Srl, pg 378
Edizioni Castello di Antonio Careddu, pg 380
Edizioni del Riccio SAS di G Bernardi, pg 384
Diakronia, pg 385
Editoriale Domus Spa, pg 385
Ediciclo Editore SRL, pg 386
Edizioni l'Arciere SRL, pg 387
EDT Edizioni di Torino, pg 387
ETR (Editrice Trasporti su Rotaie), pg 388
Adriano Gallina Editore sas, pg 389
Edizioni GB, pg 390
Giunti (Gruppo Editoriale), pg 390
Ernesto Gremese Editore SRL, pg 391
Gremese International Srl, pg 391
Gruppo Calderini Edagricole, pg 392
Hopeful Monster Editore, pg 392
Ibis, pg 393
Il Minotauro, pg 393
Kompass Fleischmann, pg 395
L'Airone Editrice, pg 395
LAC - Litografia Artistica Cartografica Srl, pg 395
Laruffa Editore SRL, pg 395
Levante, pg 395
Editrice Liguria SNC di Norberto Sabatelli & C, pg 396
Manfrini Editori, pg 397
Mondolibro Editore SNC, pg 399
Palatina Editrice, pg 402
Passigli Editori srl, pg 403
Daniela Piazza Editore, pg 403
Plurigraf SPA, pg 404
Edizioni Primavera SRL, pg 404
Priuli e Verlucca, Editori, pg 404
Edizioni Quasar di Severino Tognon SRL, pg 404
Rossato, pg 406
SAGEP, pg 406
Scala Group spa, pg 407
Sperling e Kupfer Editori SpA, pg 408

SUBJECT INDEX

Studio Bibliografico Adelmo Polla, pg 409
Studio Editoriale Programma, pg 409
Tassotti Editore, pg 409
Todariana Editrice, pg 410
Trainer International SRL, pg 410
Valmartina Editore SRL, pg 411
Zanfi Editori SRL, pg 412

Jamaica
Kingston Publishers Ltd, pg 413

Japan
The American Chamber of Commerce in Japan, pg 414
Contex Corporation, pg 415
Japan Travel Bureau Inc, pg 418
Kosei Publishing Co Ltd, pg 420
Nagaoka Shoten Company Ltd, pg 421
Nippon Hoso Shuppan Kyokai (NHK Publishing), pg 422
Sanshusha Publishing Co, Ltd, pg 424
Seibido Shuppan Company Ltd, pg 424
Shakai Shiso-Sha, pg 425
Shobunsha Publications Inc, pg 426
Shufunotomo sha Co Ltd, pg 426
Tokyo Shoseki Co Ltd, pg 427
Charles E Tuttle Publishing Co Inc, pg 428
Yama-Kei Publishers Co Ltd, pg 429

Kenya
Camerapix Publishers International Ltd, pg 431
Kenway Publications Ltd, pg 432
Space Sellers Ltd, pg 433

Democratic People's Republic of Korea
Transportation Publishing House, pg 434

Republic of Korea
Chung Rim Publishing Co Ltd, pg 435
Dae Won Sa Co Ltd, pg 435
Hollym Corporation Publishers, pg 437
Hyein Publishing House, pg 437
Pyeong-hwa Chulpansa, pg 439
Seoul International Publishing House, pg 440
Woong Jin Publishing Co Ltd, pg 440

Latvia
Liesma Publishers, pg 442
Madris, pg 442
Preses Nams, pg 442
Spriditis Publishers, pg 442

Lebanon
Arab Scientific Publishers BP, pg 442
Geoprojects Sarl, pg 443
Librairie du Liban, pg 443

Lithuania
Sviesa Publishers, pg 446

Luxembourg
Op der Lay, pg 447

SUBJECT INDEX

BOOK

Macau
Livros Do Oriente, pg 448

Madagascar
Musee d'Art et d'Archaeologie, pg 450

Malawi
Central Africana Ltd, pg 450

Malaysia
S Abdul Majeed & Co, pg 451
Panther Publishing, pg 453
Pustaka Cipta Sdn Bhd, pg 454

Maldive Islands
Novelty Printers & Publishers, pg 455

Malta
Gaulitana, pg 456
Publishers' Enterprises Group (PEG) Ltd, pg 456

Mauritius
Editions de l'Ocean Indien Ltd, pg 457

Mexico
Editorial AGATA SA de CV, pg 457
Editorial Jilguero, SA de CV, pg 462
Editorial Minutiae Mexicana SA, pg 464
Panorama Editorial, SA, pg 465
Promociones de Mercados Turisticos SA de CV, pg 466

Morocco
Editions Eddif Maroc, pg 469
Editions La Porte, pg 470

Myanmar
Kyi-Pwar-Ye Book House, pg 471

Namibia
Agrivet Publishers, pg 471

Netherlands
Buijten en Schipperheijn BV Drukkerij en Uitg Mij v/h, pg 475
BZZTOH Publishers, pg 475
Cadans, pg 475
Elmar BV, pg 476
Gottmer Uitgevers Groep, pg 477
Hayit Nederland BV, pg 478
Uitgeverij Hollandia BV, pg 478
Mets & Schilt Uitgevers en Distributeurs, pg 481
Nico Israel, pg 482
Uitgeverij Het Spectrum BV, pg 484
Telos Boeken, pg 485

Netherlands Antilles
Bredero, pg 488
De Wit Stores NV, pg 488

New Caledonia
Editions du Santal, pg 488
Savannah Editions SARL, pg 488

New Zealand
Barkfire Press, pg 488
David Bateman Ltd, pg 488
Craig Printing Company Ltd, pg 490
David's Marine Books, pg 490
HarperCollins Publishers (New Zealand) Ltd, pg 491
Kowhai Publishing Ltd, pg 492
Reed Publishing (NZ) Ltd, pg 495
River Press, pg 495
RSVP Publishing Company Ltd, pg 495
Shoal Bay Press Ltd, pg 495
Tandem Press, pg 496

Nigeria
Joe-Tolalu & Associates, pg 501

Oman
Apex Publishing, pg 506

Pakistan
Jang Publishers, pg 507
Sang-e-Meel Publications, pg 509

Panama
Focus Publications International SA, pg 509

Philippines
Bookmark Inc, pg 512
Galleon Publications, pg 513
Rex Bookstores & Publishers, pg 514

Poland
BOSZ scp, pg 516
Iskry - Publishing House Ltd spotka zoo, pg 517
KAW Krajowa Agencja Wydawnicza, pg 517
'Ksiazka i Wiedza' Spotdzielnia Wydawniczo-Handlowa, pg 517
Laumann-Polska, pg 517
Muza SA, pg 518
Oficyna Wydawnicza Read Me, pg 519

Portugal
Bezerr-Editorae e Distribuidora de Abel Antonio Bezerra, pg 522
Edicoes Cetop, pg 523
Distri Cultural Lda, pg 524
Distri Editora Lda, pg 524
Edicoes ELO, pg 524
Everest Editora, pg 525
Latina Livraria, pg 526
Editorial Presenca, pg 528
Quetzal Editores, pg 529

Puerto Rico
Modern Guides Company, pg 530
Publishing Resources Inc, pg 531

Romania
Alcor-Edimpex (Verlag) Ltd, pg 531
Editura Cronos SRL, pg 532
Editura Meridiane, pg 534

Russian Federation
Top Secret Collection Publishers, pg 542

Singapore
APA Production Pte Ltd, pg 545
Archipelago Press, pg 545
Reed Elsevier, South East Asia, pg 547
Times Media Pte Ltd, pg 549

Slovakia
Priroda, pg 550
Slovenske pedagogicke nakladateistvo, pg 550
Sport Publishing House Ltd, pg 551
Vydavatel'stvo Osveta (Verlag Osveta), pg 551

Slovenia
Zalozba Mihelac d o o, pg 552

South Africa
Acorn Books, pg 552
Erudita Publications (Pty) Ltd, pg 554
Fernwood Press (Pty) Ltd, pg 554
Jacana Education, pg 555
Reader's Digest Southern Africa, pg 559
Southern Book Publishers (Pty) Ltd, pg 559

Spain
Acento Editorial, pg 561
Aguilar SA de Ediciones, pg 562
Alfaguara Ediciones SA - Grupo Santillana, pg 562
Anaya-Touring Club, pg 563
Calamo Editorial, pg 566
Celeste Ediciones, pg 567
Compania Literaria, pg 568
Comunidad Autonoma de Madrid, Servicio de Documentacion y Publicaciones, pg 568
Ediles-Ediciones Leonesas SA, pg 572
Edilux, pg 572
Galaxia SA Editorial, pg 575
Vicent Garcia Editores, SA, pg 575
Editorial Gustavo Gili SA, pg 576
Junta de Castilla y Leon Consejeria de Educacion y Cultura, pg 579
Editorial Juventud SA, pg 579
Laertes SA de Ediciones, pg 579
Lunwerg Editores, SA, pg 580
Ediciones Maeva, pg 581
Editorial Mediterrania SL, pg 582
Editorial Moll SL, pg 582
Ediciones El Pais SA, pg 585
Polifemo, Ediciones, pg 587
Silex Ediciones, pg 590
Editorial Sintesis, SA, pg 590
Edicions 62, pg 591
Grup 62, pg 591
Ediciones Susaeta SA, pg 592
Trazo Editorial, SL, pg 593
Trea Ediciones, SL, pg 593
Tursen, SA, pg 593
Ediciones Vulcano, pg 596
Editorial Zendrera Zariquiey, SA, pg 596

Sweden
Alfabeta Bokforlag AB, pg 600
Carlsson Bokfoerlag AB, pg 601
Streiffert Forlag AB, pg 606

Switzerland
Arche Verlag AG, Raabe und Vitali, pg 608
Armenia Editions, pg 608
Bergli Books AG, pg 609
Cockatoo Press (Schweiz), Thailand-Publikationen, pg 611
Dimension World Ltd, pg 612
Duboux Editions SA, pg 612
GVA Publishers Ltd, pg 615
Hallwag AG, pg 615
JPM Publications SA, pg 616
Kuemmerly & Frey (Geographischer Verlag), pg 617
Librairie-Editions J Marguerat, pg 618
Motovun Book GmbH, pg 619
Les Editions Nagel SA (Paris), pg 619
Neptun-Verlag, pg 620
Editions Olizane, pg 620
Punktum AG, Buchredaktion und Bildarchiv, pg 622
Robert Raeber, Buchhandlung am Schweizerhof, pg 622
Regenbogen Verlag, pg 622
Hans Rohr Verlag, pg 623
Rotpunktverlag, pg 623
Strom-Verlag Luzern, pg 625
Terra Grischuna Verlag Buch-und Zeitschriftenverlag, pg 625
3 Dimension World (3-D-World), pg 625

Taiwan, Province of China
Chu Hai Publishing (Taiwan) Co Ltd, pg 630
Linking Publishing Company Ltd, pg 631
Shy Chaur Publishing Co Ltd, pg 631
Youth Cultural Publishing Co, pg 632

Thailand
Sang Dad Publishing Company Ltd, pg 635

Trinidad & Tobago
Joan Bacchus-Xavier, pg 636
Jett Samm Publishing Ltd, pg 637

Turkey
Arkeoloji Ve Sanat Yayinlari, pg 639
Dost Kitabevi Yayinlari, pg 639

Uganda
Fountain Publishers Ltd, pg 642

Ukraine
Mystetstvo Publishers, pg 643

United Arab Emirates
Motivate Publishing, pg 644

United Kingdom
A A Publishing, pg 644
Absolute Press, pg 644
Alun Books, pg 646
Chris Andrews Publications, pg 647
Ashmolean Museum Publications, pg 650
Aurum Press Ltd, pg 651
Colin Baxter Photography Ltd, pg 652
BCA, pg 653
Bellew Publishing Co Ltd, pg 653
A & C Black Publishers Ltd, pg 655
Blackstaff Press, pg 655
Bloomsbury Publishing PLC, pg 656
Blorenge Books, pg 656
The Book Guild Ltd, pg 657
Book Packaging & Marketing, pg 657
Bradt Travel Guides Ltd, pg 658
Brewin Books Ltd, pg 659
British Tourist Authority, pg 660
Butterworth-Heinemann Ltd, pg 661
Cadogan Guides, pg 662

Camerapix Publishers Intl Ltd, pg 662
Canongate Books Ltd, pg 663
Cicerone Press, pg 668
Cockbird Press, pg 669
Colour Library Direct, pg 669
Compendium Publishing, pg 670
Constable & Robinson Ltd, pg 670
Constable Publishers, pg 670
Leo Cooper, pg 671
Cordee Ltd, pg 671
Dalesman Publishing Co Ltd, pg 673
Darf Publishers Ltd, pg 674
David & Charles Ltd, pg 674
Andre Deutsch Ltd, pg 675
Discovery Walking Guides Ltd, pg 675
John Donald Publishers Ltd, pg 675
The Economist Intelligence Unit, pg 677
Eland, pg 677
Element Books Ltd, pg 678
Elm Publications, pg 678
The Erskine Press, pg 679
The Factory Shop Guide, pg 681
Famedram Publishers Ltd, pg 681
FHG Publications Ltd, pg 682
Foulsham Publishers, pg 683
Frontier Publishing, pg 684
Garnet Publishing Ltd, pg 685
Global Books Ltd, pg 687
Gollancz/Witherby, pg 688
Grange Books PLC, pg 689
Granta Books, pg 689
The Greek Bookshop, pg 689
Hakluyt Society, pg 691
Harden's Ltd, pg 692
HarperCollins Publishers, pg 692
The Harvill Press Ltd, pg 693
Heartland Publishing Ltd, pg 694
William Heinemann Ltd, pg 694
How To Books Ltd, pg 697
Angus Hudson Ltd, pg 697
Icon Press, pg 698
Jarrold Publishing, pg 703
John Jones Publishing Ltd, pg 703
Kegan Paul International Ltd, pg 703
Kuperard, pg 705
Roger Lascelles, pg 706
Lonely Planet, UK, pg 709
Luath Press Ltd, pg 709
Marshall Editions Ltd, pg 712
Meridian Books, pg 713
Methuen Publishing Ltd, pg 714
Metro Publishing Ltd, pg 714
Michelin Tyre PLC, Tourism Dept, Maps & Guides Division, pg 714
Multilingual Matters Ltd, pg 716
Murchison's Pantheon Ltd, pg 716
National Trust, pg 717
New European Publications Ltd, pg 718
New Holland Publishers (UK) Ltd, pg 718
New Leaf Books Ltd, pg 719
The Octagon Press Ltd, pg 720
Octopus Publishing Group, pg 720
Old Vicarage Publications, pg 720
The Oleander Press, pg 721
Pallas Athene, pg 723
Pavilion Books Ltd, pg 724
Philip's, pg 727
Pitkin Unichrome Ltd, pg 728
Profile Books Ltd, pg 731
Quiller Publishing Ltd, pg 732
Quintet Publishing Ltd, pg 732
Random House UK Ltd, pg 733
The Reader's Digest Association Ltd, pg 733
Reaktion Books Ltd, pg 733
Robson Books, pg 735

Rooster Books Ltd, pg 735
Rough Guides Ltd, pg 735
Roundhouse Publishing Ltd, pg 736
Routledge Curzon, pg 736
The Rubicon Press, pg 737
The Rutland Press, pg 737
SB Publications, pg 738
Sidgwick & Jackson Ltd, pg 742
SPA Books Ltd, pg 744
Stacey International, pg 745
Sunflower Books, pg 746
Sutton Publishing Ltd, pg 746
Thames & Hudson Ltd, pg 748
Thistle Press, pg 748
Time Out Group Ltd, pg 749
Time Warner Books UK, pg 749
Ulverscroft Large Print Books Ltd, pg 751
United Writers Publications Ltd, pg 751
Vacation Work Publications, pg 752
Viking, pg 753
Virago Press, pg 753
Virgin Publishing Ltd, pg 753
Wales Tourist Board, pg 754
Websters International Publishers Ltd, pg 755
Which? Ltd, pg 755
The Windrush Press Ltd, pg 757
Windsor Books International, pg 757

Yugoslavia
Jugoslovenska Revija, pg 764

Zimbabwe
The Graham Publishing Company (Pvt) Ltd, pg 768

VETERINARY SCIENCE

Albania
NL SH, pg 1

Argentina
Editorial Albatros SACI, pg 3
EUDEBA (Editorial Universitaria de Buenos Aires), pg 6
Editorial Hemisferio Sur SA, pg 6
Inter-Medica, pg 6

Australia
Bureau of Resource Sciences, pg 16
Chiron Media, pg 18
Harcourt Australia Pty Ltd, pg 25
Mosby Lifeline, pg 33

Austria
Alois Goschl & Co, pg 52
IAEA - International Atomic Energy Agency, pg 53
Andreas Schnider Verlags-Atelier, pg 58

Brazil
ARTMED, pg 79
Empresa Brasileira de Pesquisa Agropecaria, pg 83
Editora Guanabara Koogan SA, pg 84
Editora Manole Ltda, pg 87
Organizacao Andrei Editora Ltda, pg 89
Livraria Roca Ltda, pg 90
Livraria Santos Editora Comercio e Importacao Ltda, pg 91

Chile
Arrayan Editores, pg 99

China
China Agriculture Press, pg 103
Heilongjiang Science & Technology Press, pg 106
Inner Mongolia Science & Technology Publishing House, pg 106
Jilin Science & Technology Publishing House, pg 106

Costa Rica
Instituto Interamericano de Cooperacion para la Agricultura (IICA), pg 116

Cuba
ISCAH Fructuoso Rodriguez, pg 121

France
Cirad, pg 155
INRA Editions (Institut National de la Recherche Agronomique), pg 169
Editions Maloine, pg 174
Masson SA, pg 175
Editions du Point Veterinaire, pg 180
Editions Vigot Freres, pg 189

Germany
Blackwell Wissenschafts-Verlag GmbH, pg 203
Ferdinand Enke Verlag, pg 227
Landbuch-Verlagsgesellschaft mbH, pg 255
M & H Schaper GmbH & Co KG, pg 282
R S Schulz Verlag GmbH, pg 285
Verlag Eugen Ulmer GmbH & Co, pg 295
UTB fuer Wissenschaft Uni-Taschenbuecher GmbH, pg 297

Greece
Beta Medical Publishers, pg 309
Gartaganis D, pg 310
Hestia-I D Hestia-Kollaros & Co Corporation, pg 311

Hungary
Akademiai Kiado, pg 323
Mezoegazda Kiado, pg 325

India
Affiliated East West Press Pvt Ltd, pg 329
Cosmo Publications, pg 335
Daya Publishing House, pg 336
International Book Distributors, pg 340
Omsons Publications, pg 345
Scientific Book Agency, pg 349

Italy
Apimondia, pg 375
CG Ediz Medico-Scientifiche, pg 381
Edagricole - Edizioni Agricole, pg 385
Edi Ermes SRL, pg 386
Giuseppe Laterza Editore Snc, pg 391
OEMF srl International, pg 401
UTET (Unione Tipografico-Editrice Torinese), pg 411
Vinciana Editrice sas, pg 411

Japan
Ishiyaku Publishers Inc, pg 418
Nishimura Co Ltd, pg 423

Kenya
Kenya Literature Bureau, pg 432
Nairobi University Press, pg 433

Democratic People's Republic of Korea
Korea Science and Encyclopedia Publishing House, pg 434

Mexico
AGT Editor SA, pg 457
Colegio de Postgraduados en Ciencias Agricolas, pg 459
Editorial El Manual Moderno SA de CV, pg 460
Editorial Limusa SA de CV, pg 463
Ediciones Cientificas La Prensa Medica Mexicana SA de CV, pg 466
Editorial Trillas SA de CV, pg 467
Universidad Nacional Autonoma de Mexico (National University of Mexico), pg 467

Namibia
Agrivet Publishers, pg 471

New Zealand
Publishing Solutions Ltd, pg 494

Nigeria
Ahmadu Bello University Press Ltd, pg 498
Riverside Communications, pg 501

Poland
PZWL Wydawnictwo Lekarskie Ltd, pg 519
Panstwowe Wydawnictwo Rolnicze i Lesne, pg 519

Portugal
Instituto de Investigacao Cientifica Tropical, pg 526

Romania
Editura Ceres, pg 532
MAST Verlag, pg 534

Russian Federation
Scorpion Publishers, pg 541

Saudi Arabia
Dar Al-Shareff for Publishing & Distribution, pg 543

Slovakia
Priroda, pg 550

Spain
Editorial Acribia SA, pg 561
Editorial AEDOS SA, pg 561
Mundi-Prensa Libros SA, pg 583
Permanyer Publications, pg 586
Pulso Ediciones, SL, pg 588
Servicio de Publicaciones Universidad de Cordoba, pg 590

Switzerland
S Karger AG, Medical and Scientific Publishers, pg 617

SUBJECT INDEX

Taiwan, Province of China
Ho-Chi Book Publishing Co, pg 630
Yi Hsien Publishing Co Ltd, pg 632

Tunisia
Academie Tunisienne des Sciences, des Lettres et des Arts Beit El Hekma, pg 637

Ukraine
Urozaj, pg 643

United Kingdom
Bailliere Tindall Limited, pg 652
Blackwell Science Ltd, pg 656
Butterworth-Heinemann Ltd, pg 661
The Eurospan Group, pg 680
Harcourt Publishers Ltd, pg 691
Interpet Publishing, pg 701
The Kenilworth Press Ltd, pg 704
Lippincott Williams & Wilkins, pg 708
Liverpool University Press, pg 708
Manson Publishing Ltd, pg 711
New Leaf Books Ltd, pg 719
Pearson Education, pg 725
Pharmaceutical Press, pg 726
W B Saunders & Co Ltd, pg 738

Viet Nam
Science & Technics Publishing House, pg 763

WESTERN FICTION

Bulgaria
Factor-Alias, pg 95
Trud - Izd kasta, pg 98

China
Beijing Publishing House, pg 102
Foreign Language Teaching & Research Press, pg 105

Czech Republic
Touzimsky & Moravec, pg 128

Denmark
Bonnier Publications AS, pg 130

Estonia
Kupar Publishers, pg 140
Olion Publishers, pg 140

France
Publications Aredit, pg 148
Dargaud, pg 157
Alain Thomas Editeur, pg 188

Germany
Bastei Verlag, pg 199
Karl-May-Verlag Lothar Schmid GmbH, pg 248
Projektion J Buch- und Musikverlag GmbH, pg 275

Israel
Schocken Publishing House Ltd, pg 372

Japan
Kokusho Kankokai Co Ltd, pg 420
Nippon Hoso Shuppan Kyokai (NHK Publishing), pg 422

Republic of Korea
Koreaone Press Inc, pg 438

Latvia
Egmont Latvia Ltd, pg 442

Monaco
Les Editions du Rocher, pg 469

Philippines
Anvil Publishing Inc, pg 512

Portugal
Europress Editores e Distribuidores de Publicacoes Lda, pg 525

Romania
Editura Excelsior, pg 533

Russian Federation
CentrePolygraph Traders & Publishers Co, pg 537

Slovakia
Sport Publishing House Ltd, pg 551

Spain
Editorial Astri SA, pg 564
Ediciones Olimpic, SL, pg 585

Turkey
Metis Yayinlari, pg 640

Ukraine
ASK Ltd, pg 643

United Kingdom
BBC Audiobooks, pg 652
Isis Publishing Ltd, pg 701
New Era Publications UK Ltd, pg 718
Orion Publishing Group Ltd, pg 722
Ulverscroft Large Print Books Ltd, pg 751

WINE & SPIRITS

Argentina
Editorial Hemisferio Sur SA, pg 6

Australia
Australian Scholarly Publishing, pg 14
Cookery Book, pg 18
Crawford House Publishing, pg 19
Hospitality Books, pg 26
Hospitality Press Pty Ltd, pg 26
R & R Publications Marketing P/L, pg 39
The Watermark Press, pg 47
Winetitles, pg 48

Austria
Leopold Stocker Verlag, pg 54
Niederosterreichisches Pressehaus Druck- und Verlagsgesellschaft mbH, pg 55

Belarus
Kavaler Publishers, pg 63

Belgium
Glenat Benelux SA, pg 69

Brazil
Rede Das Artes (Boccato Editores Collector's), pg 90

China
China Light Industry Press, pg 103

Croatia
Vitagraf, pg 120

Finland
Kustannus Oy Kolibri, pg 143

France
Editions de l'Armancon, pg 148
ATP - Packager, pg 149
Presses Universitaires de Bordeaux (PUB), pg 151
Edisud, pg 161
EPA SA (Editions Presse Audiovisuel), pg 162
Flammarion SA, pg 164
Editions Jean Paul Gisserot, pg 166
Hachette Pratiques, pg 167
Editions Universitaires LCF, pg 172
Editions Mango, pg 174
Editions du Rouergue, pg 183
Siloe - Kerdore, pg 185
Soline, pg 186

Germany
Arcus-Medien Wolfgang Steinhardt, pg 194
Arts & Antiques Edition Munich Verlag, Buch & Kunsthandel GmbH, pg 195
Verlag Busse und Seewald GmbH, pg 208
Fachverlag Hans Carl GmbH, pg 209
Christian Verlag GmbH, pg 210
Droemersche Verlagsanstalt Th Knaur Nachfolger GmbH & Co, pg 218
Echter Wurzburg Frankische Gesellschaftsdruckerei und Verlag GmbH, pg 220
Walter Haedecke Verlag, pg 236
Hallwag Verlag GmbH, pg 236
Jahreszeiten-Verlag GmbH, pg 246
Mosaik Verlag GmbH, pg 265
Pfalzische Verlagsanstalt GmbH, pg 272
Verlag Werner Sachon GmbH & Co, pg 281
Moritz Schauenburg Verlag, pg 282

Greece
Editions Moressopoulos, pg 313

Hong Kong
Press Mark Media Ltd, pg 321

Hungary
Kossuth Kiado RT, pg 325
Mezoegazda Kiado, pg 325

Ireland
A & A Farmar, pg 358
Estragon Press Ltd, pg 360
The O'Brien Press Ltd, pg 363
On Stream Publications Ltd, pg 363

Israel
Gefen Publishing House Ltd, pg 367

Italy
Belforte Editore Libraio srl, pg 377
Ernesto Gremese Editore SRL, pg 391
Trainer International SRL, pg 410

Mexico
Editorial Iztaccihuatl SA, pg 462

Netherlands
Uitgeverij Cantecleer BV, pg 475
Uitgeverij De Toorts, pg 485

New Zealand
Barkfire Press, pg 488
Nagare Press, pg 493

Portugal
Editora Classica, pg 523
Latina Livraria, pg 526

Romania
Editura Niculescu, pg 534

Slovenia
East West Operation (EWO) Ltd, pg 551

South Africa
Fernwood Press (Pty) Ltd, pg 554

Spain
AMV Ediciones, pg 563
Comunidad Autonoma de Madrid, Servicio de Documentacion y Publicaciones, pg 568
Ediciones l'Isard, S L, pg 571

Sweden
BOOX, pg 601
Informationsfoerlaget AB, pg 603
Tryckeriforlaget AB, pg 607

Switzerland
Mueller Rueschlikon Verlags AG, pg 619
Pharos-Verlag, Hansrudolf Schwabe AG, pg 621

Taiwan, Province of China
Linking Publishing Company Ltd, pg 631

United Kingdom
Absolute Press, pg 644
BCA, pg 653
Mitchell Beazley, pg 653
Bloomsbury Publishing PLC, pg 656
Breslich & Foss, pg 659
Carlton Publishing Group, pg 664
Dorling Kindersley Ltd, pg 676
Faber & Faber Ltd, pg 681
Famedram Publishers Ltd, pg 681
Foulsham Publishers, pg 683
Grange Books PLC, pg 689
Grub Street, pg 690
HarperCollins Publishers, pg 692
Headline Book Publishing Ltd, pg 693
Hilmarton Manor Press, pg 696
Luath Press Ltd, pg 709
Marshall Editions Ltd, pg 712
Mirabel Books Ltd, pg 715
New Leaf Books Ltd, pg 719
Nexus Special Interests, pg 719
Octopus Publishing Group, pg 720

PUBLISHERS SUBJECT INDEX

Polybooks Ltd, pg 729
PRC Publishing Ltd, pg 730
Prism Press Book Publishers Ltd, pg 730
Quarto Publishing plc, pg 731
Quintet Publishing Ltd, pg 732
Ryland Peters & Small Ltd, pg 737
Websters International Publishers Ltd, pg 755
Neil Wilson Publishing Ltd, pg 757

Zambia

Aafzam Ltd, pg 766

WOMEN'S STUDIES

Albania

NL SH, pg 1

Argentina

Alfagrama SRL ediciones, pg 3
Editorial Paidos SAICF, pg 8

Australia

Artemis Publishing Pty Ltd, pg 12
Artmoves, pg 12
Australian Institute of Family Studies (AIFS), pg 13
Dangaroo Press, pg 20
Deakin University Press, pg 20
Finch Publishing, pg 22
Granrott Press, pg 24
Hale & Iremonger Pty Ltd, pg 24
Indra Publishing, pg 27
Network Promotions P/L, pg 34
Ocean Press, pg 35
Oxfam Community Aid Abroad, pg 36
Parabel Place, pg 37
Playlab Press, pg 38
Pluto Press Australia, pg 38
Ruskin Rowe Press, pg 41
Spinifex Press, pg 43
State Library of NSW Press, pg 43
Tarka Publishing, pg 44
Transpareon Press, pg 45
Unity Press, pg 46
University of New South Wales Press Ltd, pg 46
University of Western Australia Press, pg 46
Wakefield Press Pty Ltd, pg 47
Windhorse Books, pg 48
Women's Health Advisory Service, pg 48

Austria

Boehlau Verlag GmbH & Co KG, pg 50
Development News Ltd, pg 51
Docker Verlag GmbH & Co KG, pg 51
Milena Verlag, pg 55
Promedia Verlagsges mbH, pg 57
Studien Verlag Gmbh, pg 59
WUV/Facultas Universitaetsverlag, pg 61

Bangladesh

Agamee Prakashani, pg 62
The University Press Ltd, pg 62

Belarus

Interdigets Publishing House, pg 63

Belgium

VUB University Press, pg 75

Brazil

Editora Bertrand Brasil Ltda, pg 79
Companhia Editora Forense, pg 82
Editora Rocco Ltda, pg 91
Summus Editorial Ltda, pg 92
Triom Centro de Estudos Marina e Martin Hawey Editorial e Comercial Ltda, pg 92

Chile

Editorial Cuarto Propio, pg 100

China

Beijing Publishing House, pg 102
Fudan University Press, pg 105
Higher Education Press, pg 106

Colombia

Instituto Misionerao Hijas De San Pablo, pg 113
Tercer Mundo Editores SA, pg 113

Costa Rica

Editorial DEI (Departamento Ecumenico de Investigaciones), pg 116
Instituto Interamericano de Cooperacion para la Agricultura (IICA), pg 116
Promesa, Ediciones, pg 116

Denmark

Museum Tusculanum Press, pg 134

Ecuador

CEPLAES, pg 137

Estonia

Perioodika, pg 140

Finland

Kaantopiiri Oy, pg 142
Osuuskunta Vastapaino, pg 145
Yliopistopaino/Helsinki University Press, pg 145

France

CERDIC-Publications, pg 153
Indigo & Cote-Femmes Editions, pg 169
Le Jour, Editeur, pg 170
Presses Universitaires du Mirail, pg 176

Germany

ARCult Media, pg 194
Argument-Verlag, pg 195
AvivA Britta Jurgs GmbH, pg 197
Belser Wissenschaftlicher Dienst, pg 200
Boehlau-Verlag GmbH & Cie, pg 204
Bund demokratischer Wissenschaftlerinnen und Wissenschafler eV (BdWi), pg 207
Campus Verlag GmbH, pg 209
Centaurus-Verlagsgesellschaft GmbH, pg 209
Edition Diskord, pg 217
agenda Verlag Thomas Dominikowski, pg 217
Ein Fach-Verlag, pg 222
Elefanten Press Verlag GmbH, pg 222
Harald Fischer Verlag GmbH, pg 228
Fischer Taschenbuch Verlag GmbH, pg 228

Frauenoffensive Verlagsgesellschaft MbH, pg 229
FVerlag Anke Schaefer, pg 231
Konkursbuch Verlag Claudia Gehrke, pg 231
Human Wissenschafilicher Verlag, pg 243
IKO Verlag fur Interkulturelle Kommunikation, pg 244
Iudicium Verlag GmbH, pg 245
Jahreszeiten-Verlag GmbH, pg 246
K L V Konkret Literatur Verlag GmbH, pg 247
Ingrid Klein Verlag GmbH, pg 249
Verlag Kleine Schritte Ursula Dahm & Co, pg 249
Krug & Schadenberg, pg 254
Institut fuer Landes- und Stadtentwicklungsforschung, ILS Nordrhein-Westfalen, pg 255
Leipziger Universitaetsverlag GmbH, pg 257
Dr Gisela Lermann, pg 257
Verlag Leske plus Budrich GmbH, pg 257
Annemarie Maeger, pg 260
Preubmpassling Verlag Gisela Meussling, pg 263
Mosaik Verlag GmbH, pg 265
Verlag Neue Kritik KG, pg 267
Neuer Weg Verlag und Druck GmbH, pg 268
PapyRossa Verlags GmbH & Co Kommanditgesellschaft KG, pg 271
Stauffenburg Verlag Brigitte Narr GmbH, pg 289
Tuebinger Vereinigung fur Volkskunde eV (TVV), pg 295
Ulrike Helmer Verlag, pg 296
Unrast Verlag e V, pg 296
VAS-Verlag fuer Akademische Schriften, Vas Karl-Heinz Balon, pg 297
Votum Verlag GmbH, pg 299
VWB-Verlag fur Wissenschaft & Bildung, Amand Aglaster, pg 300
Waxmann Verlag GmbH, pg 300
Verlag Westfaelisches Dampfboot, pg 302
Das Wunderhorn Verlag GmbH, pg 304
Zebulon Verlag GmbH & Co KG, pg 305

Ghana

Ghana Institute of Linguistics Literacy & Bible Translation (GILLBT), pg 307
Woeli Publishing Services, pg 308
World Literature Project, pg 308

Greece

Hestia-I D Hestia-Kollaros & Co Corporation, pg 311
Odysseas Publications Ltd, pg 313
Thetili Publications, pg 315

Hong Kong

Hong Kong University Press, pg 320

India

Affiliated East West Press Pvt Ltd, pg 329
Anmol Publications Pvt Ltd, pg 331
APH Publishing Corp, pg 331
Concept Publishing Co, pg 335
Dastane Ramchandra & Co, pg 335
Gyan Publishing House, pg 338
Inter-India Publications, pg 340
Kali For Women, pg 341

Law Publishers, pg 341
National Book Organization, pg 343
Nem Chand & Brothers, pg 344
Omsons Publications, pg 345
Pointer Publishers, pg 345
Popular Prakashan Pvt Ltd, pg 346
Promilla and Co, pg 346
Radiant Publishers, pg 347
Regency Publications, pg 347
Reliance Publishing House, pg 347
Sage Publications India Pvt Ltd, pg 348
Somaiya Publications Pvt Ltd, pg 350
Sterling Publishers Pvt Ltd, pg 351
Stree, pg 351

Indonesia

Lembaga Demografi Fakultas Ekonomi Universitas Indonesia, pg 356

Ireland

Attic Press Ltd, pg 358
Cathedral Books Ltd, pg 359
Cork University Press, pg 359
The O'Brien Press Ltd, pg 363

Israel

Bitan Publishers Ltd, pg 365
Hakibbutz Hameuchad Publishing House Ltd, pg 368
The Institute for Israeli Arabs Studies, pg 368
Schocken Publishing House Ltd, pg 372
Urim Publications, pg 373

Italy

Belforte Editore Libraio srl, pg 377
Colonnese Editore, pg 382
Edizioni Cultura della Pace, pg 383
Angelo Longo Editore, pg 396
La Luna, pg 397
Lyra Libri SAS, pg 397
Edizioni Olivares, pg 402
Psicologica Editrice, pg 404
Rosenberg e Sellier Editori in Torino, pg 406
Rubbettino Editore, pg 406
La Tartaruga Edizioni SAS, pg 409
Transeuropa Libri, pg 410

Jamaica

Association of Development Agencies, pg 412
University of the West Indies Press, pg 414

Japan

Chikuma Shobo Publishing Co Ltd, pg 415
Sagano Shoin, pg 424

Kenya

Paulines Publications-Africa, pg 433
Phoenix Publishers, pg 433
Shirikon Publishers, pg 433
Gideon S Were Press, pg 434

Republic of Korea

Chung Rim Publishing Co Ltd, pg 435
Hanul Publishing Co, pg 436
Munye Publishing Co, pg 439
O Neul Publishing Co, pg 439
Samseong Publishing Co Ltd, pg 440

SUBJECT INDEX

Latvia
Preses Nams, pg 442

Lithuania
Victoria Publishers, pg 446

Luxembourg
Varkki Verghese, pg 448

Malaysia
Pustaka Cipta Sdn Bhd, pg 454

Mexico
El Colegio de Mexico AC, pg 459
Fondo de Cultura Economica, pg 461
Libra Editorial SA de CV, pg 463
Sayrols Editorial SA de CV, pg 466

Morocco
Editions Eddif Maroc, pg 469
Editions Le Fennec, pg 470
Societe Ennewrasse Service Librairie et Imprimerie, pg 470

Netherlands
Uitgeverij Jan van Arkel, pg 473
BZZTOH Publishers, pg 475
KITLV Press Royal Institute of Linguistics & Anthropology, pg 479
Koninklijk Instituut Voor de Tropen, pg 480
Servire BV Uitgevers, pg 484
Sociaal en Cultureel Planbureau, pg 484

Netherlands Antilles
De Wit Stores NV, pg 488

New Zealand
Auckland University Press, pg 488
Barkfire Press, pg 488
Clerestory Press, pg 490
Lincoln University Press, pg 492
New Women's Press Ltd, pg 494
Statistics New Zealand, pg 496
Tandem Press, pg 496
Bridget Williams Books Ltd, pg 497

Nigeria
Unity Publishing & Research Company Ltd, pg 502

Norway
Pax Forlag A/S, pg 504

Pakistan
ASR Publications, pg 506
Pakistan Institute of Development Economics, pg 508

Papua New Guinea
Kristen Pres, pg 510

Peru
Instituto de Estudios Peruanos, pg 511

Philippines
Anvil Publishing Inc, pg 512
Ateneo de Manila University Press, pg 512
Claretian Communications Inc, pg 513

Poland
Wydawnictwa Uniwersytetu Warszawskiego, pg 521

Portugal
Comissao para Igualdade e Direitos das Mulheres, pg 524
Impala, pg 525

Puerto Rico
Libros-Ediciones Homines, pg 530

Russian Federation
Dom, Izdatel'stvo sovetskogo deskkogo fonda im & 1 Lenina, pg 537

Saudi Arabia
Dar Al-Shareff for Publishing & Distribution, pg 543

Senegal
CODESRIA (Council for the Development of Social Science Research in Africa), pg 544

South Africa
Human Sciences Research Council, pg 555
Institute for Reformational Studies CHE, pg 555
Juventus/Femina Publishers, pg 556
New Africa Books (Pty) Ltd, pg 557
Ravan Press (Pty) Ltd, pg 558
University of Natal Press, pg 560

Spain
Ediciones Catedra SA, pg 566
Complutense, SA Editorial, pg 568
El Hogar y la Moda SA, pg 572
Eumo Editorial, pg 574
Editorial Gulaab, pg 577
Icaria Editorial SA, pg 577
Ediciones Morata SL, pg 583
Editorial Nerea SA, pg 584
Ediciones del Oriente y del Mediterraneo, pg 585
Publicaciones de la Universidad Pontificia Comillas-Madrid, pg 588
Torremozas SL Ediciones, pg 593
Vinaches Lopez, Luisa, pg 595

Sri Lanka
International Centre for Ethnic Studies, pg 597
Karunaratne & Sons Ltd, pg 597
Swarna Hansa Foundation, pg 598

Suriname
Stichting Wetenschappelijke Informatie, pg 599

Sweden
Acta Universitatis Gothoburgensis, pg 599
Carlsson Bokfoerlag AB, pg 601
Bokforlaget Nya Doxa AB, pg 605

Switzerland
Adonia-Verlag, pg 608
Bergli Books AG, pg 609
eFeF-Verlag/Edition Ebersbach, pg 613
Limmat Verlag, pg 618

Taiwan, Province of China
Asian Culture Co, pg 629
Hilit Publishing Co Ltd, pg 630
Laureate Book Co Ltd, pg 631
Linking Publishing Company Ltd, pg 631
UNITAS Publishing Co Ltd, pg 632

United Republic of Tanzania
DUP (1996) Ltd, pg 633
Tema Publishers Ltd, pg 634

Tunisia
Ceres Editions, pg 637

Turkey
Cep Kitaplari AS, pg 639
Metis Yayinlari, pg 640
Payel Yayinevi, pg 641
Varlik Yayinlari AS, pg 641

Uganda
Centre for Basic Research, pg 642
Fountain Publishers Ltd, pg 642

Ukraine
Osnovy Publishers, pg 643

United Kingdom
Berg Publishers, pg 654
Berghahn Books Ltd, pg 654
BFI Publishing, pg 654
Blackwell Publishers, pg 655
Bloomsbury Publishing PLC, pg 656
Camden Press Ltd, pg 662
Capall Bann Publishing, pg 663
Cardiff Academic Press, pg 663
Chapman, pg 666
Commonwealth Secretariat, pg 669
The Continuum International Publishing Group Ltd, pg 670
CTBI Publications, pg 672
Edinburgh University Press Ltd, pg 677
Element Books Ltd, pg 678
The Eurospan Group, pg 680
Gale Research, pg 685
Robert Hale Ltd, pg 691
HarperCollins Publishers, pg 692
Harvard University Press, pg 692
Hawthorn Press, pg 693
Health Development Agency, pg 694
Institute of Development Studies, pg 699
Intellect Ltd, pg 700
Adam Matthew Publications, pg 712
MIND Publications, pg 715
Motilal (UK) Books of India, pg 715
Open University Press, pg 721
Peter Owen Ltd, pg 722
Oxfam, pg 722
Parapress Ltd, pg 724
Pathfinder London, pg 724
Pearson Education, pg 725
Pickering & Chatto (Publishers) Ltd, pg 727
Pluto Press, pg 728
The Policy Press, pg 729
Polygon, pg 729
Pomegranate Europe Ltd, pg 729
Routledge, pg 736
Routledge Curzon, pg 736
The Rubicon Press, pg 737
Sage Publications Ltd, pg 737
Seren, pg 740
Serpent's Tail Ltd, pg 740
SHU Press, pg 742
Trentham Books Ltd, pg 750
University of Wales Press, pg 751
Verso, pg 752
Virago Press, pg 753
White Cockade Publishing, pg 755
WI Enterprises Ltd, pg 756
Wimbledon Publishing Company Ltd, pg 757
The Women's Press Ltd, pg 758
Wordwright Publishing, pg 758
Yale University Press London, pg 759
Zed Books Ltd, pg 759

Uruguay
Cotidiano Mujer, pg 760
Nordan-Comunidad, pg 760
Luis A Retta Libros, pg 761
Ediciones Trilce, pg 761

Venezuela
Editorial Nueva Sociedad, pg 762

Zambia
Zambia Association for Research & Development, pg 767
ZPC Publications, pg 767

Literary Agents

Argentina

International Editors' Co
Ave Cabildo 1156 - 1 A, 1426 Buenos Aires
Tel: (011) 4788-2992; (011) 4786-0888
Fax: (011) 4786-0888
E-mail: costa@lvd.com.ar
Founded: 1939
Agencia Literaria; Subsidiaries in Spain & Brazil.

Guillermo Schavelzon
Rodriguez Pena 2067, C1021ABQ Buenos Aires
Tel: (011) 48 13 84 20 *Fax:* (011) 48 13 28 76
E-mail: info@schavelzon.com
Key Personnel
Main Agent: Guillermo Schavelzon
Foreign Rights: Monica Herrero
  E-mail: monicaherrero@schavelzon.com
Licensing: Hugo Princ
Founded: 1998
Specialize in Latin American writers (fiction & nonfiction). No unsolicited mss, query first; submit a brief author's biblio-biography (2-3 pgs), a summary of the work that the author intends to submit (2-3 pgs), a sample reading of the work consisting of 2-3 chapters; no reading fees, online content providers.

Australia

Curtis Brown (Australia) Pty Ltd
27 Union St, Paddington, Sydney, NSW 2021
Mailing Address: PO Box 19, Paddington, NSW 2021
Tel: (02) 93315301; (02) 93616161 *Fax:* (02) 93603935
E-mail: info@curtisbrown.com.au
Key Personnel
Man Dir: Fiona Inglis
Dir: Tim Curnow *E-mail:* tim@curtisbrown.com.au
Contact: Garth Nix
Founded: 1967

Bryson Agency Australia Pty Ltd Fran Bryson
313-315 Flinders Lane, 1st floor, 226, Flinders Lane, Melbourne 8009

The Mary Cunnane Agency Pty Ltd
28 Dover Rd, Wamberal, NSW 2260
Mailing Address: PO Box 781, Terrigal, NSW 2260
Tel: (02) 43859911 *Fax:* (02) 43859922
Key Personnel
Director: Mary Cunnane
Founded: 1999
Entire mss & sample chapters in hard copy only after query which may be by mail, phone or email. Adult fiction & nonfiction.

Diversity Management
PO Box 1449, Darlinghurst, NSW 1300
Tel: (02) 9130 4305 *Fax:* (02) 9365 1426
Key Personnel
Agent: Bill Tikos *E-mail:* bill@diversitym.com.au
Specialize in adult nonfiction. Contact via e-mail.

The Drummond Agency
PO Box 572, Woodend, Victoria 3442
Tel: (03) 5427 3644 *Fax:* (03) 5427 3655
Key Personnel
Dir: Sheila Drummond *E-mail:* sheilad@ozemail.com.au
Founded: 1995
Also offers international rights consultancy to publishers.

Austria

Literarische Agentur Diana Voigt
Hoher Markt 1, 1010 Vienna
Tel: (01) 5333191 *Fax:* (01) 5333192
E-mail: voigt@literaturagentur.at
Web Site: www.literaturagentur.at
Key Personnel
Dir & Owner: Diana Voigt
Agent: Andreas Brunner *E-mail:* brunner@literaturagentur.at
Founded: 1996
Covering the German language market for US, UK & Canadian publishers & international authors.
Specializes in High quality fiction, psychology, self help, history, politics, spirituality, theatre, film.

Barbados

Barbados National Trust
Wildey House, Wildey St, St Michael
Tel: 426-2421 *Fax:* 429-9055
E-mail: natrust@sunbeach.net
Key Personnel
Executive Dir: Penelope Hynam Roach
President: John Cole
Founded: 1961
Specializes in Heritage & Environmental Conservation.

Belgium

Toneelfonds J Janssens BVBA
Te Boelaerlei 107, B-2140 Borgerhout, Antwerp
Tel: (03) 366.44.00 *Fax:* (03) 3664501
E-mail: info@toneelfonds.be
Web Site: www.toneelfonds.be
Key Personnel
Dir: Jessica Janssens *E-mail:* jessica.janssens@toneelfonds.be
Founded: 1880
Publisher of plays & literary agent for playwrights.
Specializes in Plays.

Brazil

Agencia Literaria Balcells Mello e Souza Riff S/C Ltda (Balcells Mello & Souza Riff Literary Agency)
Rua Visconde de Piraja 414/s 1108, 22410-002 Rio de Janeiro RJ
Tel: (021) 22876299 *Fax:* (021) 22676393
Key Personnel
Literary Agent & Executive: Lucia Riff
  E-mail: lucia@bmsr.com.br
Founded: 1991
Specialize in foreign authors for the Brazilian/Portuguese language market & Brazilian authors for Brazil & abroad; co-agenting of foreign publishers & literary agencies.

BMSR Literary Agency, see Agencia Literaria Balcells Mello e Souza Riff S/C Ltda

Pagina da Cultura Agencia Literaria Ideias sobre Linhas Ltda (Pagina da Cultura Literary Agency Ideas over Liens Ltda)
Affiliate of Camara Brasileira do Livro
Av Paulista, 2076, Horsa 1 - sala 1524, 01311-940 Sao Paulo
Tel: (011) 3266 4299 *Fax:* (011) 3266 4299
E-mail: paginadacultura@pobox.com
Web Site: www.pagina-da-cultura.com.br
Key Personnel
Contact: Marisa Moura *E-mail:* marisa.moura@paginadacultura.com.br
Founded: 1994
Specializes in Business, Essays, Fiction, History, Religions, Self-Help, Children & Juvenile books.

Karin Schindler
CP 19051, 04505-970 Sao Paulo
Tel: (011) 50419177 *Fax:* (011) 2419077
Key Personnel
Contact: Karin Schindler *E-mail:* kschind@terra.com.br

China

Big Apple Tuttle-Mori Agency Inc
8 Alley 19, 1 Tung St, Taipei 10431
Tel: (010) 64020119; (02) 25067828 *Fax:* (010) 64020119
E-mail: 76540.101@compuserve.com
Key Personnel
President: Lily Chen
Executive Vice President: Dr Luc Kwanten
US Representative: Chandler Crawford *Tel:* (212) 206-5600
European Representative: Anne Martyn *Tel:* (071) 2868701
Specializes in Rights & Authors Agent.
Branch Office(s)
Chinan
Shanghai
Nanking
Bangkok, Thailand
Big Apple Tuttle-Mori Beijing, Beijing *Tel:* (010) 6401 6276

Czech Republic

Agence de l'Est (French Literary Agency)
Tachovske Nam 2, 13000 Prague
Tel: (02) 602 978 281 *Fax:* (02) 2278 1937
E-mail: agencedelest@mbox.vol.cz
Key Personnel
Agent: Patricia Pasqualini
Founded: 1999
Represents French authors in central & eastern Europe.
Specializes in Negotiating between France & Eastern Europe (from Estonia to Albania & from the Czech Republic to Russia) for non-illustrated & illustrated books.

DILIA
Kratkeho 1, 19003 Prague 9
Tel: (02) 826444; (02) 8268418 *Fax:* (02) 824009
Cable: DILIA PRAG
Key Personnel
Man Dir: Ladislav Simon
Contact: Dr Vera Stranska
Theatrical and Literary Agency, Society for Protection of Authors' Rights.

Denmark

Bookman Literary Agency
Bastager 3, DK-2950 Vedbaek Copenhagen
Tel: 45892520 *Fax:* 45892501
E-mail: IHL@bookman.dk *Cable:* BOOKMAN; COPENHAGEN
Key Personnel
Agent: Ib H Lauritzen *E-mail:* ihl@bookman.dk; Mrs Bebbe Lauritzen
Founded: 1912
Also acts as a literary agent in Denmark, Sweden, Norway, Finland & Iceland for foreign authors.
Specializes in Business books, general fiction, quality novels, sales to magazines, sport books (golf, tennis).

ICBS, see ICBS/IBIS ApS

ICBS/IBIS ApS
Kvaesthusgade 3F, 1251 Copenhagen K
Tel: 33114255 *Fax:* 33911167
E-mail: icbs@get2net.dk
Key Personnel
Contact: Virginia Allen Jensen; Johan Broensted
Founded: 1962
Specializes in Children's Books, Co-productions, Adult Fiction & Nonfiction.

Leonhardt & Hoier Literary Agency aps
Studiestr 35, DK-1455 Copenhagen K
Tel: 33132523 *Fax:* 33134992
Key Personnel
Dir: Anneli Hoier *E-mail:* anneli@leonhardt-hoier.dk
Contact: Monica Gram *E-mail:* monica@leonhardt-hoier.dk
Representing international publishers & agents in Scandinavia & Scandinavian authors worldwide.
Specializes in Specialize modern fiction.

Licht & Licht Literary Agency
Maglemosevej 46, DK-2920 Charlottenlund
Tel: 39610908 *Fax:* 39611105
Key Personnel
Chief Executive: Ole Licht; Agnes Licht
Representing American, Australian, British and Canadian agents & publishers in Denmark, Finland, Iceland, Norway & Sweden & representing Scandanavian authors worldwide.

Ulla Lohren Literary Agency
89 Vaerebrovej, DK-2880 Bagsvaerd
Tel: 44494515 *Fax:* 44493515

Rights Promotion Distribution Translation
Oresundsvej 22, 1 TV 2300, DK-2300 Copenhagen S
Tel: 32591556 *Fax:* 32591556
Key Personnel
Dir: Elisabeth Neel
Founded: 1994
Specializes in Books on Cassette, Children's Books, Juvenile & Young Adult Books, Disability-Special Needs, Education, English as Second Language, Religion-Catholic.

Scanvik Books Import ApS
Esplanaden 8 B, 1263 Copenhagen
Tel: 33127766 *Fax:* 33912882
E-mail: scanvik@bog.dk
Key Personnel
Dir: John Roberts; Uwe Schultheiss
Founded: 1980
Wholesaler, distributor & agent.
Specializes in Maps & Travel Guides.

Egypt (Arab Republic of Egypt)

The Egyptian Society for the Dissemination of Universal Culture and Knowledge (ESDUCK)
1081 Corniche El Nil St, Garden City, Cairo
Mailing Address: PO Box 21, Cairo
Tel: (02) 3545079 *Fax:* (02) 3540295 *Cable:* ESDUCK
Key Personnel
Executive Manager: Dr Amin El-Gamal

ESDUCK, see The Egyptian Society for the Dissemination of Universal Culture and Knowledge (ESDUCK)

Finland

Werner Soederstroem Osakeyhtioe (WSOY)
Bulevardi 12, 00120 Helsinki
Mailing Address: PO Box 222, 00121 Helsinki
Tel: (00) 61681 *Fax:* (90) 61683566
Telex: 122644 Wsoy *Cable:* WSOY HELSINKI
Key Personnel
Rights & Permissions: Sirkku Klemola
Founded: 1878
Also Publisher.
Parent Company: Sanoma WSOY

WSOY, see Werner Soederstroem Osakeyhtioe (WSOY)

France

Eliane Benisti Literary Agency
80 rue des Sts-Peres, F-75007 Paris
Tel: (01) 42228533 *Fax:* (01) 45441817
E-mail: benisti@compuserve.com
Key Personnel
Dir: Eliane Benisti

EAIS Literary Agents
10/12 rue de l'Abreuvoir, F-92400 Courbevoie
Tel: (01) 47880840 *Fax:* (01) 47880840
Key Personnel
Vice President: Vera le Marie *E-mail:* vera.le.marie@wanadoo.fr
Founded: 1983
Representation of American publishers & writers in France, & French publishers & writers in the USA & Russia. Specialize in foreign languages: English, German, French, Dutch, & Polish.
Ultimate Parent Company: EAIS - France
U.S. Office(s): European American Information Services Inc, Sarasota, FL 34236, United States, Contact: Dr Allan M Chyrtowski
Tel: 941-955-3472 *Fax:* 941-955-5365

European American Information Services Inc, see EAIS Literary Agents

Lora Fountain & Associates Literary Agency
(Agence Litteraire Lora Fountain & Associates)
7 rue de Belfort, F-75011 Paris
Tel: (01) 43562196 *Fax:* (01) 43482272
E-mail: FountLit@aol.com
Key Personnel
Man Dir: Lora Fountain
Associate Agent: Alexandre Civico
 E-mail: acivicolf@aol.com; Svetlana Ramon *E-mail:* svetlana.ramon@wanadoo.fr; Helene Raude *E-mail:* lnraude@aol.com
Founded: 1985
No unsolicited manuscripts. Also sale of children's books to Italy, Holland, Spain & Russia.
Specializes in French rights sales for English-language publishers (UK, Ireland, USA, Canada, Australia & New Zealand). Quality Adult Fiction & Nonfiction, Children's Literature.

Agence Hoffman
77 blvd St-Michel, F-75005 Paris
Tel: (01) 43265694 *Fax:* (01) 43263407
Telex: 203605 F *Cable:* AGHOFF PARIS
Key Personnel
Contact: Boris Hoffman; Ursula Veit; Georges Hoffman
Branch Office(s)
Munich, Germany

Michelle Lapautre
6 rue Jean Carries, F-75007 Paris
Tel: (01) 47348241 *Fax:* (01) 47340090
E-mail: lapautre@club_internet.fr
Parent Company: Agence Michelle Lapautre

Montreal-Contacts/The Rights Agency
20, rue du Telegraphe, 75020 Paris
Tel: (01) 43 40 06 10 *Fax:* (01) 43 40 02 12
Key Personnel
Owner: Luc Jutras *Tel:* 450-461-1575 (Canada)
 E-mail: ljutras@montreal-contacts.com
Dir: Anne Confuron *E-mail:* aconfuron@montreal-contacts.com
Represents American, Canadian & other foreign publishers &/or literary exclusively. No author representation.

AGENTS

La Nouvelle Agence
7 rue Corneille, F-75006 Paris
Tel: (01) 43258560 *Fax:* (01) 43254798
Telex: 250303 F (Paris Bourse)
Key Personnel
Contact: Mary Kling

Frederique Porretta
70 rue d'Assas, F-75006 Paris
Tel: (01) 45448868 *Fax:* (01) 45446936
Founded: 1992

Shelley Power Literary Agency Ltd
13 rue du Pre Saint Gervais, 75019 Paris
Tel: (01) 42383649 *Fax:* (01) 40407008
E-mail: shelley.power@wanadoo.fr
Key Personnel
Dir: Shelley Power
Founded: 1976

Promotion Litteraire
12 rue Pergolese, F-75116 Paris
Tel: (01) 45004210 *Fax:* (01) 45001018
E-mail: promolit@club-internet.fr
Key Personnel
Dir: Mariella Giannetti
Specializes in Literary Translations, Book & Article Translations.

Germany

Agence Hoffman
Bechsteinstr 2, 80804 Munich
Tel: (089) 3084807 *Fax:* (089) 3082108
Cable: AGHOFF MUNICH
Key Personnel
Contact: Ursula Bender
Literary agents & publishers from UK & USA.
Branch Office(s)
Blvd St Michel, 77, 75005 Paris, France

Agency for Literature, Arts & Communication,
see LITkom Elisabeth Falk Agentur fur Literatur und Kommunikation

AVA-Autoren- und Verlags-Agentur GmbH
Seeblickstr 46, 82211 Herrsching-Breitbrunn, Bavaria
Tel: (08152) 925883 *Fax:* (08152) 3076
E-mail: avagmbh@aol.com
Founded: 1989
Specializes in Fiction & Nonfiction.

Dr Ivana Beil, Internationale Handelsvermittlung im Medien- und Verlagswesen
Schollstrasse 1, 69469 Weinheim
Tel: (06201) 14611 *Fax:* (06201) 17280
Founded: 1984
Specializes in Copyright Intervention, Co-Productions, Representation of Publishing Houses, Authors, Illustrators, Children's & Young Readers' Books (Also on Film & television productions), Marketing.
Branch Office(s)
Theodor Heuss Str 14, 69469 Weinheim

The Berlin Agency
Mommsenstr 2, 10629 Berlin
Tel: (030) 88677000 *Fax:* (030) 88677011
E-mail: junglindemann@berlinagency.de
Key Personnel
Contact: Ms Franke Jung-Lindemann
E-mail: jung-lindemann@berlinagency.de

Cartoon-Caricature-Contor Arno Koch-CCC
Rosmarinstr 4, 80939 Munich
Tel: (089) 3233669 *Fax:* (089) 3226859
E-mail: ccc@c5.net
Web Site: www.c5.net
Founded: 1977
Acts as agents for Cartoons & Karikaturen, Illustrations.
Specializes in Stock with about 100,000 cartoons.

Mo Cohen
Wentzelstr 15, 22301 Hamburg
Tel: (040) 273814
Rights between publishers in Germany, UK & USA.

Copyright International Agency Corina GmbH
Beerenstr 22A, 14163 Berlin
Tel: (030) 80902386 *Fax:* (030) 80902388
E-mail: info@corina.com
Web Site: www.corina.com
Founded: 1998
Internet Literary Agency.
Specializes in Literature from & for Middle & Eastern European countries.

DMK-Verlag
Hutergasse 4, 90403 Nuernberg
Tel: (0911) 203946; (0911) 227698 *Fax:* (0911) 208897 *Cable:* KLINGERKUNST
Key Personnel
Contact: D M Klinger
Specializes in Art, Photography, The Arts.

Gesellschaft zur Foerderung der Literatur aus Afrika, Asien und Lateinamerika eV, see Society for the Promotion of African, Asian & Latin American Literature

Gina Schlenz Literatur-Agentur Koln
Gruenenborn 49, 53797 Lohmar 53797
Tel: (02206) 81125 *Fax:* (02206) 81125
E-mail: litschleuz@aol.com
Founded: 1989
Specializes in Children & young adults.

IBA International Book Agency Schmidt-Braul & Partner
Friedberger Landstr 86, D-60316 Frankfurt am Main
Mailing Address: Postfach 18 24 05, D-60085 Frankfurt am Main
Tel: (069) 9441 4744 *Fax:* (069) 9441 4746
E-mail: iba.media@t-online.de
Key Personnel
President & Executive Dir: Ingo-Eric M Schmidt-Braul
Founded: 1991
Specializes in Fiction, Nonfiction, Economics; Also acts as representative of authors & publishing houses.
Branch Office(s)
Moscow, Russian Federation
Kharkov, Russian Federation

Keil & Keil Literary Agency
Schulterblatt 58, 20357 Hamburg
Tel: (040) 27166892 *Fax:* (040) 27166896
E-mail: anfragen@keil-keil.com
Web Site: www.keil-keil.com
Key Personnel
Agent: Anya Keil *Tel:* (040) 27166894; Bettina Keil *Tel:* (040) 27166893 *E-mail:* bk@keil-keil.com
Founded: 1995
Specializes in General trade fiction & nonfiction. No fantasy, sci-fi and Children's & young adult. Have representatives in all major international markets. No unsol mss, query first; provide outline with SASE.

GERMANY

Ingrid Anna Kleihues Verlags und Autorenagentur
Weinbergweg 62A, 70569 Stuttgart
Tel: (0711) 6788800 *Fax:* (0711) 6788801
E-mail: info@agentur-kleihues.de
Founded: 1990
Specializes in Non-fiction.

Libresso Berlin
Michael Hinze Goerschstr 6, 13187 Berlin
Tel: (030) 2826346 *Fax:* (030) 2834494
Key Personnel
Manager: Michael Hinze
Founded: 1990
Specializes in Belles Lettres, Nonfiction.

LITkom Elisabeth Falk Agentur fur Literatur und Kommunikation
Formerly Agency for Literature, Arts & Communication
Regentenstr 82, 51063 Cologne
Mailing Address: PO Box 800648, 51006 Cologne
Tel: (221) 885413 *Fax:* (221) 885433
Web Site: www.litkom.de *Cable:* LITKOM E.FALK
Key Personnel
Agent: Elisabeth Falk *E-mail:* falk@litkom.de
Founded: 1993
a) Represent authors & handle their manuscripts.
b) Exhibit international book art objects.
c) Organize literary events.
Specializes in Art Books, Exhibitions, Literary Functions.

MBMS-Bibliography and Management Service
Postfach 1206, 57271 Hilchenbach
Tel: (02733) 7657 *Fax:* (02733) 8492
E-mail: iurlea@wolnet.de
Key Personnel
Contact: Christiane Urlea-Schoen
Founded: 1989
Specializes in Literature, Medicine, Management, Business.

Medienbuero Muenchen
Division of Philosophia Verlag GmbH
Gundelindenstr 4, 80805 Munich
Tel: (089) 299975 *Fax:* (089) 299975
E-mail: info@philosophiaverlag.com
Web Site: www.philosophiaverlag.com
Key Personnel
Publisher: Ulrich Standinger *E-mail:* ulrich.standinger@philosophiaverlag.com
Founded: 2000
Agency for authors & publishers in print, TV, film & new media.
Specializes in Non-Fiction, Science Fiction.

Merchandising Muenchen KG
Gutenbergstrasse 1, 85774 Unterfohring
Tel: (089) 95078600 *Fax:* (089) 95078600
E-mail: jens.puppe@pro-sieben.de
Key Personnel
Contact: Patrick Hoare; Katarina Dietrich
Specializes in Sales, Marketing, Business Licenses.

Dr Ray-Gude Mertin Literarische Agentur
Friedrichstr 1, 61348 Bad Homburg
Tel: (06172) 29842 *Fax:* (06172) 29771
E-mail: mertin@em.uni-frankfurt.de
Key Personnel
Contact: Mrs Ray-Guede Mertin
Worldwide representation of authors from Brazil, Portugal, Africa, Latin America & Spain.
Specializes in Fiction & Nonfiction.

Literaturbetreuung Klaus Middendorf (LKM)
Averbergweg 8, 86836 Gvaben
Tel: (08232) 78463 *Fax:* (08232) 78468

GERMANY

E-mail: lkm@compuserve.com
Founded: 1986
Author & Publisher Representation.

Martina M Oepping Literary Agency
Wolfsgangstr 34, 60322 Frankfurt
Tel: (069) 59790011 *Fax:* (069) 59790012
E-mail: litag@oepping.de
Key Personnel
Literary Agent: Martina M Oepping
Founded: 1996
Specializes in Children's & Juvenile Books, Authors & Illustrators.

Literatur-Agentur Axel Poldner-Verlagsbuero
Rauheckstr 11 und Gruentenstr 22a, 80686 Munich
Tel: (089) 574824 *Fax:* (089) 5707640
Key Personnel
Contact: Axel Poldner
Founded: 1970
Specializes in Multimedia Projects.

Quelle Press
Postfach 1314, 79013 Freiburg/Br
Tel: (07664) 7016 *Fax:* (07664) 60979
E-mail: qu.pre.frei@lycosmail.com *Cable:* QUELLEPRESS
Key Personnel
President: Friedrich-Wilhelm Koenig
Founded: 1948
Services include editing advice, reading, translation and international activities; global licensing since 50 years; 18,900 copyrights sold.
Specializes in Mass Market, Business Books, Esoteric, Holistic, New Age, Romances, Anthologies, Newspaper (serials), books for young readers, trade books, alternative medicine, basic business books, self counsel books, self improvement books, life style books, psychology, religion, human science, sports, self help books for young readers.
Branch Office(s)
Australia
Bulgaria
China
Croatia
Czech Republic
France
Hungary
India
Indonesia
Italy
Japan
Republic of Korea
Poland
Portugal
Russian Federation (East European Market)
Slovakia
Spain
Taiwan, Province of China

Thomas Schlueck GmbH
Hinter der Worth 12, 30827 Garbsen
Tel: (05131) 497560 *Fax:* (05131) 497589
E-mail: mail@schlueckagent.com
Key Personnel
Contact: Joachim Jessen; Bastian Schlueck; Thomas Schlueck
Founded: 1970
Full representation of Anglo-American authors, agents & publishers in German language areas, as well as representation of German authors. Handle second rights of cover illustrations, Europe wide.

Skandinavia Verlag
Ithweg 31, 14163 Berlin
Tel: (030) 8137006 *Fax:* (030) 8141029
Key Personnel
Contact: Marianne Weno
Founded: 1969
Specializes in Scandinavian Stage, Radio & TV plays.

Society for the Promotion of African, Asian & Latin American Literature
Reineckstr 3, 60313 Frankfurt
Mailing Address: Postfach 10 01 16, 60001 Frankfurt
Tel: (069) 2102247 *Fax:* (069) 2102227
E-mail: litprom@book-fair.com
Web Site: www.litprom.de
Key Personnel
President: Peter Weidhaas
Dir: Peter Ripken
Founded: 1980
The Society seeks to promote German translations of creative writing from Africa, Asia & Latin America. It works as a non-profit agency & as a consultant for German language publishers & for "Third World" publishers & authors who have German translation rights to offer. Publishes LiteraturNachrichten (Literary News).

Corry Theegarten-Schlotterer
Kulmerstr 3, 81927 Munich
Tel: (089) 932566 *Fax:* (089) 9303992
Founded: 1981
Specializes in Co-production.

Tipress Deutschland GmbH, see Tipress Dienstleistungen fur das Verlagswesen GmbH

Tipress Dienstleistungen fur das Verlagswesen GmbH
Johannes-Fecht-Str 2, 79295 Sulzburg
Tel: (011) 533487 *Fax:* (011) 535283
E-mail: tipress@t-online.de *Cable:* TIPRESS
Key Personnel
Chief Executive: Roberto Toso
Assistant: Claudia Robert
Founded: 1980
Specializes in Co-editions, Illustrated Books, Handbooks, Encyclopedias, Children's Books.
Branch Office(s)
Tipress Deutschland GmbH, via Cernaia 34, I-10122 Turino, Italy, Contact: Ms Claudia Robert *Tel:* (011) 533487 *Fax:* (011) 535283 *E-mail:* tipress@fileita.it

Hungary

Artisjus
PO Box 593, H-1539 Budapest
Tel: (01) 2121553 *Fax:* (01) 2121552 *Cable:* ARTISJUS
Key Personnel
Contact: Anita Kenedi
Agency for Theater & Literature of the Hungarian Bureau for Copyright Protection.

Katai & Bolza Irodalmi Ugynokseg (Katai & Bolza Literary Agents)
Vamhaz Krt 15, H-1093 Budapest
Mailing Address: PO Box 1666, Budapest H-1965
Tel: (01) 456-0313 *Fax:* (01) 215-4420
Web Site: www.kataibolza.hu
Key Personnel
Agent: Peter Bolza *E-mail:* peter@kataibolza.hu; Katalin Katai *E-mail:* katalin@kataibolza.hu
Founded: 1995
Represents mainly US & British publishers & agents in the Hungarian market.

India

Ajanta Books International
One U B Jawahar Nagar, Bangalow Rd, Delhi 110007
Tel: (011) 3926182 *Fax:* (011) 7415016
  Fax on Demand: (011) 7415016
E-mail: ajantabi@ndf.vsnl.net.in; ajantabi@id.erh.net
Key Personnel
Proprietor: Mr S Balwant
Founded: 1975
Specializes in Social Sciences & Humanities, Children, Paperbook.

Dipak Kumar Guha
PO Box 3205, New Delhi 110013
Tel: (011) 5500998 *Fax:* (011) 6880198; (011) 6117058
E-mail: dkginfo@bol.net.in
Founded: 1986
Activities also include Market Evaluation, Promotion & PR, special sales, excess inventory sales, Specializing in East/West Rights, Co-editions, English & Regional Languages, wire services syndication/hook-ups, magazine syndication & reprint consulting, seek multi-media rights on CDs, Multimedia OEM & distribution marketing consulting service.
Specializes in Syndication from wire services.

Ireland

The Government Supplies Agency, Publications Branch
51 St Stephens Green, Dublin 2
Tel: (01) 6476000 *Fax:* (01) 6476843
E-mail: opw@iol.ie
Web Site: www.opw.ie
Key Personnel
Assistant Dir: Fintan Butler *Tel:* (01) 6476877
  E-mail: fintan.butler@opw.ie
Irish Government Publications.
Specializes in Government Publications.

Jonathan Williams Literary Agency
Ferrybank House, 6 Park Rd, Dun Laoghaire, County Dublin
Tel: (01) 2803482 *Fax:* (01) 2803482
Key Personnel
Contact: Jonathan Williams
Founded: 1980
International coupons, return postage appreciated.
Specializes in Works by Irish writers or of Irish interest.
Branch Office(s)
Loecher & Lawrence, Munich, Germany
Lora Fountain, Paris, France
Jan Michael, Amsterdam, Netherlands
Piergiorgio Nicolazzini Literary Agency, Milan, Italy

Israel

The Book Publishers' Association of Israel, International Promotion and Literary Rights Department
29 Carlebach St, Tel Aviv 67132
Mailing Address: PO Box 20123, Tel Aviv 61201
Tel: (03) 5614121 *Fax:* (03) 5611996
E-mail: rights@tbpai.co.il
Web Site: www.tbpai.co.il
Founded: 1939

Harris-Elon Agency
9 Yael St, Jerusalem
Mailing Address: PO Box 8528, Jerusalem 91083
Tel: (02) 672 2143/5 *Fax:* (02) 672 5797
E-mail: litagent@netvision.net.il
Key Personnel
Dir: Deborah Harris *E-mail:* d_harris@netvision.net.il; Beth Elon *E-mail:* b_elon@netvision.net.il
Foreign Rights Dir: Efrat Lev *E-mail:* litagent@netvision.net.il
Managing Editor: Ines Austern *E-mail:* iaustern@netvision.net.il
Founded: 1991
Branch Office(s)
43 Emek Refa'im St, Jerusalem *Tel:* (02) 563 3237 *Fax:* (02) 561 8711 (foreign rights)

The Institute for the Translation of Hebrew Literature
23 Baruch Hirsch St, Bnei Brak
Mailing Address: PO Box 10051, Ramat Gan 52001
Tel: (03) 5796830 *Fax:* (03) 5796832
E-mail: litscene@ithl.org.il
Web Site: www.ithl.org.il
Key Personnel
Dir: Mrs Nilli Cohen
Founded: 1962
Main activities include promotion of modern Hebrew literature & children's literature in translation & serves as literary agent for a large number of Israeli writers & assists in the preparation of anthologies of Hebrew literature.
Specializes in Hebrew literature in translation.

Italy

Agenzia Letteraria Internazionale
Via Fratelli Gabba 3, I-20121 Milan
Tel: (02) 86463418; (02) 865445; (02) 861572 *Fax:* (02) 876222
Key Personnel
President: Dr Donatella Barbieri
Founded: 1898
Right's Representative.

Luigi Bernabo Associates SRL
Via Bianca di Savoia 4, I 20122 Milan
Tel: (02) 58306332; (02) 58306378 *Fax:* (02) 58306312
Key Personnel
Contact: Luigi Bernabo; Daniela Bernabo

Daniel Doglioli
Via Lomonaco 15/B, 27100 Pavia
Tel: (0382) 529317 *Fax:* (0382) 529317
Web Site: www.filastrocche.it/contempo/daniele/daniele.asp
Key Personnel
Contact: Daniel Doglioli *E-mail:* daniel.doglioli@iol.it
Founded: 1994

Eulama Literary Agencies
Via Guido de Ruggiero 28/2, Int 6, I-00142 Rome
Tel: (06) 5407309 *Fax:* (06) 5408772 *Cable:* EULAROM
Key Personnel
President: Harald Kahnemann
Founded: 1967
Also Translation Agency.
Specializes in Social sciences, politics, psychology, education, philosophy, religion, linguistics & literature, mass-media, technology, computer science, architecture, urban studies, Spanish & Latin-American literature & books for young readers, quality fiction.
Branch Office(s)
Eulama SA, Germany

Grandi & Associati SRL
Via Caradosso 12, I-20123 Milan
Tel: (02) 4695541; (02) 4818962 *Fax:* (02) 48195108
E-mail: agenzia@grandieassociati.it
Key Personnel
Contact: Chiara Ferrari *E-mail:* chiaraferrari@grandieassociati.it; Laura Grandi; Stefano Tettamanti
Represents writers & acts as a subagent for selected publishing houses & agencies outside Italy. Sells foreign rights & acts as a consultant for various Italian publishing houses.

ILA (International Literary Agency) USA
I-18010 Terzorio (IM)
Tel: (0184) 484048; (0347) 9334966 *Fax:* (0184) 487292
E-mail: libri.gg@dmw.it
Key Personnel
Contact: Tomas D W Friedmann
Founded: 1970
An American agency headquartered in Europe. Specialize in handling of foreign language translation rights to multi-volume book & magazine projects, children's books, encyclopedias, bestsellers, illustrated books on antiques & collectibles (in all European languages).
Specializes in Mass Market, Antiques & Collectibles, Nonfiction, Fiction.

International Literary Agency, see ILA (International Literary Agency) USA

Living Literary Agency
Via Poliziano 8, I-20154 Milan
Tel: (02) 33100584 *Fax:* (02) 33100618
E-mail: living@galactica.it
Key Personnel
Contact: Elfriede Pexa
Founded: 1976
Specializes in Italian translation rights in books in English & German.

Pietro Missorini & Co - Libreria Commissionaria
Via Abbeveratoia 63, CP 326, 43100 Parma
Tel: (0521) 993919 *Fax:* (0521) 993929
Web Site: www.rsadvnet.it/missorini/
Key Personnel
Administration: Pietro Missorini *E-mail:* missorini@rsadvnet.it
Contact: Lucia Missorini
Founded: 1972
Vat nr IT01514140340.
Specializes in Food Service & Technology.

Natoli Stefan & Oliva Literary Agency
Corso Plebisciti 12, 20129 Milan
Tel: (02) 7000 1645 *Fax:* (02) 741277
E-mail: natoli.oliva@tiscalinet.it
Key Personnel
Partner: Roberta Oliva
Founded: 1962
Literary agency handling foreign publishers, agents authors in Italy & Italian authors in Italy & worldwide.

Piergiorgio Nicolazzini Literary Agency
Via G B Moroni 22, 20146 Milan
Tel: (02) 48713365 *Fax:* (02) 48713365
Key Personnel
Owner: Piergiorgio Nicolazzini *E-mail:* piergiorgio.nicolazzini@tin.it
Founded: 1994
Represents foreign publishers, agents & authors in Italy.
Specializes in Fiction & Nonfiction.

RCS Rizzoli Libri SpA
Via Mecenate 91, 20138 Milan
Tel: (02) 50951 *Fax:* (02) 5065361
Telex: 333543
Key Personnel
President: Giorgio Fattori
Dir General: Giovanni Ungarelli
Editorial Dirs: Rosaria Carpinelli; Evaldo Violo
Also Publisher & Major Bookseller.
Specializes in Literature, Fiction, Essays, Art, History.

Susanna Zevi Agenzia Letteraria
Via G Marcora 6, 20121 Milan
Tel: (02) 6570863; (02) 6570867 *Fax:* (02) 6570915

Japan

The Asano Agency, Inc
Tokuda Bldg 302, 44-8 Sengoku 4-chome, Bunkyo-ku, Tokyo 112
Tel: (03) 39434171 *Fax:* (03) 39437637
Telex: 272-2436 ASANO K
Key Personnel
President: Kiyoshi Asano
Founded: 1988

The English Agency (Japan) Ltd
Sakuragi Bldg 4F, 6-7-3 Minami Aoyama, Minato-ku, Tokyo 107-0062
Tel: (03) 34065385 *Fax:* (03) 34065387
E-mail: info@eaj.co.jp
Key Personnel
Man Dir: William Miller *E-mail:* willmill@eaj.co.jp
Executive Dir: Junzo Sawa
Dir: Desmond Briggs; Peter Thompson
Adult Books: Yoshinori Kaba; Kaori Shibayama
Academic Books: Takako Murakami
Children's Books: Noriko Hasegawa
Sports Books & Accountant: Tadashi Onitsuka
London Representative: Louise Allen-Jones *Tel:* (020) 7720-2453
New York Representative: Aram Fox *Tel:* 212-989-8805
Founded: 1979
Sales of book & ancillary rights for translation mainly into Japanese; author's agent for books with international appeal by writers living in or frequently visiting Japan.

Japan Foreign-Rights Centre (JFC)
27-18-804 Naka Ochiai 2-chome, Shinjuku-ku, Tokyo 161-0032
Tel: (03) 59960321 *Fax:* (03) 59960323
Key Personnel
Man Dir: Akiko Kurita
Manager, General Books: Harumi Sakai
Manager, Children's Books: Yurika Yokota Yoshida
Founded: 1981 (as Kurita-Bando Literary Agency)
Specializes in Foreign rights to Japanese books, co-production, packaging.

Japan UNI Agency Inc
Tokyodo-Jinbocho, No 2 Bldg, 1-27 Kanda Jinbocho, Chiyoda-ku, Tokyo 101-0051
Tel: (03) 32950301 *Fax:* (03) 32945173
E-mail: info@japanuni.co.jp
Telex: J27260 Unilit *Cable:* UNILITERARY

Key Personnel
Chairman: Noboru Miyata
President: Yoshio Taketomi
Dir: Tatsuko Nagasawa; Okimitsu Ohishi
Founded: 1967

Motovun Co Ltd, Tokyo
Coop Nomura Ichibancho 103, 15-6 Ichibancho, Chiyoda-ku, Tokyo 102 0082
Tel: (03) 32614002 *Fax:* (03) 32641443
Key Personnel
President: Mari Koga *E-mail:* koga_motovun@mbd.sphere.ne.jp
Dir: Norio Irie
Founded: 1983
Firm sells rights & co-production between foreign publishers & Japanese publishers.

The Sakai Agency Inc
1-7-12-4F Kanda-Jimbocho, Chiyoda-ku Tokyo 101-0051
Tel: (03) 32951405; (03) 32951406 *Fax:* (03) 32954366
E-mail: sakai@sakaiagency.com
Key Personnel
Contact: Tatemi Sakai
Founded: 1952
Specializes in Book rights, serial rights, co-editions, theatrical performing rights, motion picture rights, TV & radio broadcasting rights, video rights, merchandising rights; both rights for export/import market, representing Japanese authors.

Tuttle-Mori Agency Inc
2-15 Kanda-Jimbocho, Chiyoda-ku, Tokyo 101-0051
Tel: (03) 3230-4081 *Fax:* (03) 3234-5249
Key Personnel
President: Ken Mori
Managing Dir: Yuji Takeda *E-mail:* yuji@tuttlemori.com
Executive Dir: Yoshikazu Iwasaki
Financial Dir: Sakae Mino
Specializes in Book rights, serial rights, co-productions, motion picture, TV, radio & stage rights, merchandising rights.
Branch Office(s)
Tuttle-Mori Agency Inc, 5F, No 8, Wu-Chuan Third Rd, Shin-Juang, Taipei County 242, Taiwan, Province of China *Tel:* (02) 3234-4255 *Fax:* (02) 3234-4244
Siam Inter Comics Bldg, 6th floor 459 Soi Piboonopathum Ladprao 48, Samsen Nok, Huay Kwang, Bangkok 10310, Thailand *Tel:* (02) 694-3026 *Fax:* (02) 694-3027 (Affiliate)
58 Clifton Gardens, London W9 1AU, United Kingdom, Contact: Anne Martyn *Tel:* (020) 7286-8701 *Fax:* (020) 7286-8629
U.S. Office(s): Sanford J Greenburger Associates Inc, 55 Fifth Ave, New York, NY 10003, United States, Contact: Carol Frederick *Tel:* 212-206-5610 *Fax:* 212-627-9281

Republic of Korea

DRT International
Garden Tower Bldg 6F, 98-78, Unni-dong, Chongno-gu, Seoul 110-350
Tel: (02) 7453350 *Fax:* (02) 7453612
E-mail: drt@chollian.dacom.co.kr *Cable:* DEEP ROOTED TREE
Key Personnel
President: Changgi Hahn
Executive Vice President: So Jin Kwak
Agent: Mi-Sook Hong; Jeong-Hwa Kim; Seung-Won Han; Marie Lee
Founded: 1990
Specializes in Book rights (fiction, nonfiction, juvenile, academic etc), serial rights, TV/radio rights, merchandising rights, co-productions, CD-ROM & video rights.

Imprima Korea Agency
2A Sisa Bldg, 274 Yongkang-Dong, Mapo-Ku, Seoul 121-070
Tel: (02) 714 9154 *Fax:* (02) 714 9150
E-mail: imprima@bora.dacom.co.kr; imprima@chollian.net
Key Personnel
President: Hong Sung-Il
Dir: Duram Kim *E-mail:* duramkim@hnc.net
Founded: 1993
Specializes in Publishing Newspaper.

IPS Copyright Agency (International Publications Service
YBM/Si-sa Bldg 9F, 48-1, Chongro 2-ga, Chongro-gu, Seoul 110-772
Tel: (02) 7342666 *Fax:* (02) 7336936
E-mail: copyright@ips-korea.com
Founded: 1986
Promoting foreign rights to Korean publishers.

Mediabank
Kwanghwamoon, Seoul 110-605
Mailing Address: PO Box 530, Seoul 110-605
Tel: (02) 7420425 *Fax:* (02) 7452174
Web Site: mediabank.pe.kr
Key Personnel
President: Jay Sung Rhee *E-mail:* jaysrhee@nownuri.net
Founded: 1985
Also deals in video rights for home & educational markets.
Specializes in Children's Books, El-Hi Reference Books, Instructional Multi-media.

Shin Won Agency Co
147-44, Dongkyo-dong, Mapo-ku, Seoul 121-220
Tel: (02) 3356388; (02) 3356833 *Fax:* (02) 3356389
E-mail: main@shinwonagency.co.kr
Web Site: www.shinwonagency.co.kr
Key Personnel
Chairman: Sang Hyung Kim
Dir: Cheol Eung Kim
President: Soon Eung Kim
Founded: 1986
Literary Agency & Editorial Production.
Branch Office(s)
Shin Won Planning Co, 250-4, Towha-dong, Mapo-ku, Seoul *Tel:* (02) 7184829 *Fax:* (02) 7186620

Time-Space Inc
Hanyeong Bldg 4F, 57-8 Ch'ungmuro 3-ga, Jung-gu, Seoul 100-013
Tel: (02) 2272-2381 *Fax:* (02) 2632380; (02) 2273 8900
E-mail: tspace@timespace.co.kr
Web Site: www.fotato.com
Key Personnel
Contact: Hyang-Ja Yim
Founded: 1984
Specialize in stock photography & royalty free CD-ROM.
Specializes in Photography, Arts.

Universal Publications Agency Press
54 Gyeonji-dong, Jongro-gu, Seoul 110-170
Tel: (02) 328175 *Fax:* (02) 328176
Telex: K 22702 *Cable:* CHANGHOSHIN SEOUL
Key Personnel
Chairman: Chang-Ho Shin
President: Kwang-Hoon Cow
Founded: 1958
Also publisher & distributor.
Specializes in Advertising, Media Representation.
Branch Office(s)
Will Academia, No 1, Jangkyo-dong, Ste 2613, Chung-ku, Seoul 100-760

Eric Yang Agency
3F Shangjery Bldg, 50-10 Banpo-Dong, Seocho-ku, Seoul
Tel: (02) 5923356 *Fax:* (02) 5923359
Key Personnel
President: Eric Yang *E-mail:* ericyang@chollian.dacom.co.kr; ericyang@ericyangagency.co.kr
Contact: Danny Hong *E-mail:* dannyhong@ericyangagency.co.kr
Founded: 1994

Yeong Mun Copyright Agency
69-1 Samsong Dong, Gangnam-gu, Seoul 135-090
Tel: (02) 7568944 *Fax:* (02) 7568943
Key Personnel
President: Pyong-Cho Park
Copyright agent & publishing company for both reprinting & translation of foreign medical books and architecture & design.

Liechtenstein

Liechtenstein Verlag AG
Schwefelstr 33, 9490 Vaduz
Mailing Address: PO Box 133, 9490 Vaduz
Tel: (00423) 2322414 *Fax:* (00423) 2324340
E-mail: flbooks@verlag_ag.LOL.li
Key Personnel
Man Dir: Albart Piet Schiks
Founded: 1945
Firm is also a publisher.

Lithuania

Penki Kontinentai
Stulginskio St 5, LT-2001 Vilnius 2001
Tel: (02) 1481; (02) 221482 *Fax:* (02) 226115
E-mail: info@post.5ci.lt
Web Site: www.5ci.lt
Key Personnel
Contact: Irena Juskauskaite
Founded: 1992
Represents Nordic Council of Ministers, Oxford University Press & Cambridge University Press.

Netherlands

Auteursbureau Greta Baars-Jelgersma
Maasstaete 40, 6585 CB Mook
Tel: (024) 6963336 *Fax:* (024) 6963293
Web Site: home.hetnet.nl/~jelgersma696
Founded: 1951
Literary agent & sworn translator-interpreter.
Specializes in International co-printing of illustrated books, mediation of copyrights, translations from Scandinavian & German languages into Dutch, sworn interpreter/translator Danish, Norwegian, Swedish.

Caroline van Gelderen Literary Agency
Bachlaan 34, 1217 BX Hilversum

Tel: (035) 6241336 *Fax:* (035) 6232740
E-mail: mail@carvang.nl
Key Personnel
Dir: Caroline van Gelderen
Founded: 1979
Representative of American & English publishers & agents for the Dutch territories.
Specializes in Translation rights.

Foundation for the Production & Translation of Dutch Literature
Singel 464, 1017 AW Amsterdam
Tel: (020) 6206261 *Fax:* (020) 6207179
E-mail: bp@nlpvf.xs4all.nl
Web Site: www.nlpvf.nl
Key Personnel
Dir: Frank Ligtvoet; Rudi Wester
Founded: 1991

International Literatuur Bureau BV
Koninginneweg 2A, 1217 KW Hilversum
Mailing Address: Postbus 10014, 1201 DA Hilversum
Tel: (035) 6213500 *Fax:* (035) 6215771
Web Site: www.ilb.nu *Cable:* ILB
Key Personnel
Chief Executive: Menno Kohn *E-mail:* mkohn@planet.nl

Lijnkamp Literary Agents
Johannes Verhulststraat 153-B, 1075 GW Amsterdam
Tel: (020) 6207742 *Fax:* (020) 6385298
E-mail: lijnkamp@xs4all.nl
Web Site: www.lijnkamp.nl
Key Personnel
Dir: Marijke Lijnkamp
Assistant Literary Agent: Liz Waters
Founded: 1989
Represents foreign literary agencies & publishing houses in Netherlands. Represents Dutch authors worldwide.
Specializes in The Netherlands & Flemish Belgium as representative areas.

De Lindenboom/INOR Publikaties
M A de Ruyterstraat 20A, 7480 AE Haaksbergen
Mailing Address: PO Box 202, 7480 AE Haaksbergen
Tel: (05427) 40004 *Fax:* (05427) 29296
E-mail: lindeboo@worldonline.nl
Represents Nordic Council of Ministers Publications.

Servire BV Uitgevers
Postbus 14095, 3511 BP Utrecht
Tel: (030) 2349211 *Fax:* (030) 2349247
E-mail: servire@pi.net
Key Personnel
Chief Executive: Felix Erkelens
Founded: 1921
Also Publisher.
Specializes in Psychology, Health, Spirituality.

Alice Toledo, see Toledo Creative Management

Toledo Creative Management
Binnenkant 20, 1011 BH Amsterdam
Tel: (020) 6226873 *Fax:* (020) 6276720
E-mail: agency@toledo-cm.nl
Founded: 1991
Specializes in Dutch & American Writers, Literary, TV & Films.

New Zealand

John Bentley Book Agencies
Milford, Auckland 9
Mailing Address: PO Box 31-328, Auckland 9
Tel: (09) 4736920 *Fax:* (09) 4736920
E-mail: sjsb@connected.net.nzed
Key Personnel
Contact: John Bentley
Founded: 1982
Commission agent acting for publishers on a representation only basis.

Michael Gifkins & Associates
PO Box 6496, Auckland 1
Tel: (09) 5235032 *Fax:* (09) 5235033
Key Personnel
Principal: Michael Gifkins *E-mail:* michael.gifkins@xtra.co.nz
Founded: 1983
Specializes in General, Adult Fiction, Juvenile, Film, Television, Co-publications.

Playmarket
PO Box 9767, Wellington
Tel: (04) 3828461 *Fax:* (04) 3854279
Key Personnel
Executive Officer: John Mc Davitt
Script Advisor: Susan Wilson
Administrative Assistant: Stephanie Creed
Playwrights Agency & Script Advisory Service.

Nigeria

University Publishing Co/Varsity Press & Bookshop
11, Central School Rd, Onitsha
Mailing Address: PO Box 386, Onitsha
Tel: (046) 230013
Key Personnel
Chairman, Author & Publisher: F C Ogbalu
Specializes in Writing, Editing, Printing & Publishing Primary and Secondary School Books.
Branch Office(s)
Varsity Bookshops
Abagana
Awka
Ogidi
Owerri Amawbia
IMO State Branch, 14 Owerri-Orluroad Owerr, IMO

Norway

June Heggenhougen
Brannpostveien 5, 3014 Drammen
Tel: 32832125 *Fax:* 32832125
Key Personnel
International Consultant: Gudbrand Heggenhougen *E-mail:* gudbrand@online.no
Publishing Consultant: June Heggenhougen

Pakistan

Mirza Book Agency
65 Shahrah-e-Quaid-e-Azam, 54000 Lahore
Mailing Address: PO Box 729, 54000 Lahore
Tel: (042) 7353601 *Fax:* (042) 5763714
Cable: KNOWLEDGE
Key Personnel
Proprietor: Mirza Mahmud
Founded: 1949
Deals with foreign publication & government publication; Subscription Agent.
Specializes in Educational & Professional Books, Developing Countries, Dictionaries, Reference, Social Science, Scientific, Medical.
Branch Office(s)
Mirza Book Corporation, 247/A-3, Gulberg-3, Lahore 54660 *Tel:* (042) 5714653 *Fax:* (042) 5763714 *E-mail:* merchant@brain.net.pk

Romania

Simona Kessler International Copyright Agency Ltd
Str Banul Antonache 37, 70 000 Bucharest 1
Tel: (01) 2318150 *Fax:* (01) 2314522
Key Personnel
President: Simona Kessler *E-mail:* skessler@fx.ro
Founded: 1995
Specializes in Subsidiary Rights.

Russian Federation

Permission & Rights, Moscow
Bolshaya Bronnaya St, 6A, Moscow 103006
Tel: (095) 2092263 *Fax:* (095) 8836050
Key Personnel
Literary Agent: Mr Konstantin Palchikov
Founded: 1992
Representation of American, British & French authors in Russia 1993.
Subsidiary of P&R Permissions & Rights Ltd.

RAO, see Rossijskoye avtorskoye obshestvo

Rossijskoye avtorskoye obshestvo (Russian Author's Society)
6-A Bolshaya Bronnaya, Moscow, K-104 GSP-9, 101999
Tel: (095) 2034991 *Fax:* (095) 2001263
E-mail: rao@smtp.cnt.ru
Telex: 411327 Avtor SU *Cable:* Moscow Avtor
Key Personnel
Chairman: V Tverdovsky
Vice Chairman: A Alabiev
Dir, Rights & Permissions Dept: G Zareev
Tel: (095) 203-06-95
Literary & big rights, internet, mechanical & musical rights; licensing of TV & radio stations.

Slovakia

LITA Ochranna Autorska Spolocnost' Agentura
Mozartova 9, CS-81530 Bratislava
Tel: (07) 313623; (07) 580 2248; (07) 580 2251
Fax: (07) 580 2246
Key Personnel
Contact: Yvona Vlasata
Slovak Literary Agency: the copyright organization representing Slovak authors in foreign transactions & foreign authors in the territory of Slovakia; Member of CISAC.

South Africa

Frances Bond Literary Services
32B Stanley Teale Rd, Westville, Kwazulu Natal 3630
Mailing Address: PO Box 223, Westville 3630, Kwazulu Natal
Tel: (031) 2624532 *Fax:* (031) 2622620
E-mail: fbond@mweb.com.za
Key Personnel
Chief Executive: Frances Bond
Chief Editor: Eileen Molver
Founded: 1983
Specializes in Adult Fiction & Nonfiction, Children's Books.

Cherokee Literary Agency
3 Blythwood Rd, Rondebosch, Cape Province 7700
Tel: (021) 6714508 *Fax:* (021) 761-4329
Key Personnel
Dir: DonnaKay Lee *E-mail:* dklee@mweb.co.sa
Founded: 1988
Specializes in Children's Picture Books.

The International Press Agency (Pty) Ltd
56 Morningside, Ndabeni 7405
Mailing Address: PO Box 67, Howard Place 7450
Tel: (021) 5311926 *Fax:* (021) 5318789
E-mail: inpra@iafrica.com
Key Personnel
Dir: Dr Ursula A Barnett
Manager & Dir: Terry Temple
Founded: 1934
Specializes in Literary Agents & Press.

Literary Dynamics
Suite 222, Musgrave 4062
Mailing Address: PO Box 51037, Musgrave 4062
Tel: (031) 2016919 *Fax:* (031) 2016919
E-mail: literary@saol.com
Web Site: www.enterest.co.za/literarydynamics
Key Personnel
Man Editor: Isabel Cooke
Founded: 1985
Writing Tuition, Public Speaking Consultant also.
Specializes in Nonfiction, Novels, Scripts.

Spain

ACER Agencia Literaria
Amor de Dios, 1, 28014 Madrid
Tel: (091) 3692061 *Fax:* (091) 3692052
Key Personnel
Contact: Elizbeth Atkins *E-mail:* eatkins@ctvies.es; Laure Merle d'Aubigne *E-mail:* laurette@teleline.es
Founded: 1959

Carmen Balcells Agencia Literaria SA (The Balcells Agency)
Diagonal 580, 08021 Barcelona
Tel: (093) 2008933 *Fax:* (093) 2007041
E-mail: ag-balcells@ag-balcells.com *Cable:* COPYRIGHT BARCELONA
Key Personnel
President: Carmen Balcells
Contact: Gloria Gutierrez

Bookbank SL
Rafael Calvo 13, 28010 Madrid
Mailing Address: San Martin De Porres, TY, 28035 Madrid
Tel: (091) 3733539 *Fax:* (091) 3165591
Key Personnel
Contact: Angela Gonzalez
Correspondence in Spanish and English.

International Editors' Co SL
Rambla de Cataluna 63 - 3 1a, 08007 Barcelona
Tel: (093) 2158812 *Fax:* (093) 4873583
E-mail: ieco@internationaleditors.com
Key Personnel
Manager: Isabel Monteagudo
Branch Office(s)
Buenos Aires, Argentina

Ute Koerner Literary Agent
Ronda Guinardo 32 - 5 5a, 08025 Barcelona
Tel: (093) 4550414 *Fax:* (093) 4365548
Key Personnel
Agents: Ute Koerner; Guenter G Rodewald
Representing foreign publishers, authors & agents in Spanish & Portuguese-speaking countries.

Marcombo SA
Gran Via de les Corts Catalanes 594, Barcelona 08007
Tel: (093) 3180079 *Fax:* (093) 3189339
E-mail: marcombo.boixareu@marcombo.es
Key Personnel
Contact: Josep M Boixareu Vilaplana
Founded: 1945
Specializes in Technical Books.

RDC Agencia Literaria
Plaza de Las Salesas 9, E-28004 Madrid
Tel: (091) 3085585 *Fax:* (091) 3085600
Key Personnel
Contact: Raquel de la Concha
Representing Spanish writers & Foreign publishers, fiction & nonfiction.

Mercedes Ros Literary Agency
Castell 38, 08329 Teia (Barcelona)
Tel: (093) 5401353 *Fax:* (093) 5401346
E-mail: info@mercedesros.com
Web Site: www.mercedesros.com
Key Personnel
Dir: Mercedes Ros
Founded: 1996
Represents publishers, packagers & authors all over the world. Specializes in illustrated, reference, craft & hobby, religious, children's fiction & nonfiction books.

Lennart Sane Agency AB
Paseo de Mejico 65, Las Cumbres-Elviria, E-29600 Marbella Malaga
Tel: (0952) 834180 *Fax:* (0952) 833196
Key Personnel
Dir: Elisabeth Sane; Lennart Sane
E-mail: lennart.sane@telia.com
Branch Office(s)
Lennart Sane Agency AB, Hollaendareplan 9, S-374 34 Karlshamn, Sweden *Tel:* (0454) 123 56 *Fax:* (0454) 149 20 *E-mail:* lennart.sane@telia.com

Sant Jordi Asociados Agencia
C/Llull, 84 1o, 1a, 08005 Barcelona
Tel: (093) 3091159 *Fax:* (093) 3091160
E-mail: santjo@corecta.es
Key Personnel
Contact: Monica Antunes
Founded: 1994
Specializes in Latin America Authors & Spanish.

Cristina Vizcaino Literary Agency
Juan de Austria 31, 1-B, 28010 Madrid
Tel: (091) 5944992 *Fax:* (091) 5944992
E-mail: vizcaino@infornet.es
Web Site: www.vizcaino.com
Key Personnel
Manager: Cristina Vizcaino
Associate: Paula Serraller
Founded: 1997
Specializes in Education, Gay & Lesbian, Children & Juvenile titles, literature & reference.

Julio F Yanez, Agencia Literaria S L
Via Augusta 139 - 6 2a, 08021 Barcelona
Tel: (093) 2007107; (093) 2005443 *Fax:* (093) 2094865
E-mail: yanezag@retemail.es *Cable:* AGENLITER
Key Personnel
Dir: Julio F Yanez; Montse F Yanez
Founded: 1960
Covering all Spanish and Portuguese speaking countries.
Specializes in Modern Literature, Documents & Memoirs; Educational: History, Art, Sociology; Topical Books on Modern Facts; Co-productions.

Sweden

Ann-Christine Danielsson Agency
Haeggstigen 17, 24013 Genarpe
Tel: (040) 482380 *Fax:* (040) 482190
E-mail: acd.agency@swipnet.se

Monica Heyum Agency
Vendelsoe, Box 3300, S-136 03 Haninge
Tel: (08) 7451934 *Fax:* (08) 7771470
Key Personnel
Dir & Literary Agent: Monica Heyum
E-mail: monica@heum-agency.a.se
Founded: 1985

Kerstin Kvint Literary & Co-Production Agency
PO Box 45164, S-104 30 Stockholm
Tel: (08) 107014 *Fax:* (08) 107606
Handles foreign rights' sales for individual writers & Scandinavian publishers. Co-productions arranged for children's picture books.

Bengt Nordin Agency
PO Box 2101, S-130 13 Stockholm
Tel: (08) 57168525 *Fax:* (08) 57168524
E-mail: info@nordinagency.se
Web Site: www.nordinagency.se
Key Personnel
President: Bengt Nordin *E-mail:* bengt.nordin@nordinagency.se
Founded: 1990
Specializes in Film, TV & Literary Agency.

Lennart Sane Agency AB
Hollaendareplan 9, S-374 34 Karlshamn
Tel: (0454) 123 56 *Fax:* (0454) 149 20
Key Personnel
Dir: Lennart Sane *E-mail:* lennart.sane@telia.com
Assistant Dir: Elisabeth Sane; Ann-Mari Selander; Ulf Toregard *E-mail:* ulf.toregard@sanetoeregard.se
Founded: 1969
Branch Office(s)
Paseo de Mejico 65, Las Cumbres-Elviria, E-296 00 Marbella, Spain *Tel:* (0952) 83 41 80; (0908) 15 56 75 *Fax:* (0952) 83 31 96 *E-mail:* lennart.sane@telia.com (Malaga)

Sane Toregard Agency
Hollaendareplan 9, S-374 34 Karlshamn
Tel: (0454) 123 56 *Fax:* (0454) 149 20
Key Personnel
Dir: Ulf Toregard *E-mail:* ulf.toregard@sanetoregard.se

Founded: 1995
Representing publishers in Scandinavia & Holland for rights in fiction & non-fiction.

Switzerland

Paul und Peter Fritz AG Literary Agency
Jupiterstr 1, CH-8032 Zurich
Mailing Address: Postfach 1773
Tel: (01) 3884140 *Fax:* (01) 3884130
E-mail: info@fritzagency.com
Web Site: www.fritzagency.com
Key Personnel
Man Dir: Peter S Fritz
Founded: 1962
Representation of American & English authors, agents & publishers in German-language areas, German-language authors worldwide.

Gaia Media AG/Literary & Media Agency
Spalenvorstadt 13, CH 4003 Basel
Tel: (061) 2619119 *Fax:* (061) 2619117
E-mail: gaiamediaag@access.ch
Key Personnel
President: Dieter A Hagenbach
Founded: 1990

Liepman AG
Maienburgweg 23, CH-8044 Zurich
Tel: (01) 2617660 *Fax:* (01) 2610124
E-mail: info@liepmanagency.com
Key Personnel
Dir: Eva Koralnik; Ruth Weibel *E-mail:* ruth.weibel@liepmanagency.com
Contact: AG Liepman
Founded: 1949
Represent authors, publishers & agents for the German language publication rights, & authors from manuscript on throughout the world.

MOHRBOOKS AG, Literary Agency
Klosbachstr 110, CH-8032 Zurich
Tel: (01) 2511610 *Fax:* (01) 2625213
Key Personnel
Contact: Sabine Ibach

Neue Presse Agentur, see NPA (Neue Presse Agentur)

Niedieck Linder AG
Zollikerstr 87, CH-8034 Zurich
Tel: (01) 3816592 *Fax:* (01) 3816513
E-mail: info@nlagency.ch
Key Personnel
Contact: Antoinette Matejka
Agent: Leonardo LaRosa *E-mail:* larosa@nlagency.ch
Founded: 1975
Representation of German-language authors (including major authors' estates) as well as Italian publishers & agencies on the German language market.
Specializes in Giulio Einaudi, Bollati Boringhieri, Rusconi Libri, Edizioni EL, Sellerio Editore, Avagliano Editore, Agenzia Letteraria Internazionale, Agenzia Letteraria Agnese Incisa for German speaking countries.

NPA (Neue Presse Agentur)
Haldenstr 5, Haus am Herterberg, CH-8500 Frauenfeld-Herten
Tel: (052) 7214374 *Cable:* NPA, CH-8500 FRAUENFELD
Key Personnel
Contact: Rene Marti
Founded: 1950
Specializes in Serialization in newspapers & magazines, especially women's & educational interest, fiction, exclusives.

Syrian Arab Republic

Nour E-Sham Book Centre
BP 249, Damascus
Tel: (11) 4457458 *Fax:* (11) 3324913
E-mail: nouresham@mail.sy
Web Site: www.nouresham.com
Telex: 412432 NOSHAM
Key Personnel
Manager: Mr Maher Abul-Zahab
Founded: 1983
Represents the following publishers in Syria: Oxford University Press UK, Cambridge University Press UK, BBC UK, Macmillan UK, Wiley USA, McGraw-Hill USA.
Branch Office(s)
Aleppo
Homs

Taiwan, Province of China

Bardon-Chinese Media Agency
4F, No 230, Hsin-Yi Rd, Sec 2, Taipei
Tel: (02) 23655753 *Fax:* (02) 23658148; (02) 23652615
Web Site: www.bardonchinese.com
Key Personnel
President: Phillip C Chen *E-mail:* phillip@bardon.com.tw
Contact: Yiwen Chen; Jian-mei Wang; Ming Ming Lu
Founded: 1988
Literary & Rights agency covering Taiwan, Hong Kong, Singapore & China.
Specializes in Chinese Language, simplified & complex.

Thailand

Silkroad Publishers Agency, Ltd
32/3 Sukhumvit 31 Rd, Bangkok 10110
Tel: (02) 2584798; (02) 2588266 *Fax:* (02) 6620553
E-mail: silkroad@ksc15.th.com
Key Personnel
Man Dir: Jane Ngarmpun Vejjajiva
Founded: 1994
Specializes in General Trade Fiction & Nonfiction, Juvenile.

Turkey

Akcali Copyright Agency
Bahariye Cad 8/6, 81300 Kadikoy, Istanbul
Tel: (0216) 3388771; (0216) 3485160 *Fax:* (0216) 3490778
E-mail: akcali@attglobal.net
Key Personnel
President & Dir: Ms Kezban Akcali

Gamma Medya Agency
Eceler Sok, No 6/1, Florya, 34810 Istanbul
Tel: (212) 663 96 80 *Fax:* (212) 663 96 81
E-mail: web@gammamedya.net
Web Site: www.gammamedya.net
Key Personnel
Man Dir: Zeynep Ataman *E-mail:* zeynep@gammamedya.net
Founded: 1991
Publishing, press & licensing agency.

Nurcihan Kesim Literary Agency, Inc
Nuruosmaniye Cad, Kardesler Han No 3/4, Sirkeci, Istanbul
Mailing Address: PO Box 868, 34410 Istanbul
Tel: (0212) 5111078; (0212) 5285797 *Fax:* (0212) 5285791
E-mail: kesim@superonline.com
Web Site: www.nurcihankesim.com
Key Personnel
Man Dir & Executive President: Nurcihan Kesim
Rights & Permissions: Karasuil Asli
Founded: 1971
Specializes in Fiction, Nonfiction, Art Works, Serials, Encyclopedias, Licensing, Merchandising, Music Rights, Children's Books.

ONK Agency Ltd
Inoenue caddesi 31/7 Taksim, 80090 Istanbul
Mailing Address: PO Box 983, Sirkeci, 34436 Istanbul
Tel: (0212) 2498602; (0212) 2498603 *Fax:* (0212) 2525153
E-mail: info@onkagency.com
Web Site: www.onkagency.com *Cable:* COPYRIGHT ISTANBUL
Key Personnel
President: Osman N Karaca *E-mail:* karaca@onkagency.com
Man Dir: Ms Nimet Tuna
Rights: Ms Hatice Goek
Founded: 1959
Representing Turkish writers, illustrators, playwriters, SACD, many major foreign publishers & agents. Syndicated materials, Sipa press. Literary, dramatic & TV rights.
Specializes in Books, (Adult/Young Adult & Children Books), Serials, Encyclopedias, Comics & Cartoons, Plays, Dia Positive.

United Kingdom

A & B Personal Management Ltd
4th Floor, Plaza Suite 114, Jermyn St, London SW1Y 6HJ
Tel: (020) 7839 4433 *Fax:* (020) 7930 5738
Key Personnel
Dir: R W Ellis

The Agency (London) Ltd
24 Pottery Lane, Holland Park, London W11 4LZ
Tel: (020) 7727 1346 *Fax:* (020) 7727 9037
E-mail: info@theagency.co.uk
Web Site: www.agentsassoc.co.uk
Key Personnel
Dir: Stephen Durbridge
Contact: Kris Forbes *E-mail:* kris.forbes@theagency.co.uk

Works in conjunction with agents in USA & all foreign countries.
Specializes in Theater, Film, TV, Radio, Novels, Children's Fiction.

Gillon Aitken Associates Ltd
Formerly Aitken Stone Ltd
29 Fernshaw Rd, London SW10 0TG
Tel: (020) 7351 7561 *Fax:* (020) 7352 9105
E-mail: 100303.1765@compuserve.com
Key Personnel
Dir & Chairman: Gillon Aitken
Dir: Sally Riley; Brian Stone; Anthony Harwood

Aitken Stone Ltd, see Gillon Aitken Associates Ltd

Darley Anderson Literary TV & Film Agency
Estelle House, 11 Eustace Rd, London SW6 1JB
Tel: (020) 7385 6652 *Fax:* (020) 7386 5571
E-mail: dander6652@aol.comm
Key Personnel
President: Darley Anderson
Foreign Rights Associate: Kerith Biggs
Founded: 1988
Commercial fiction of all genres, sexy, psychological thrillers & adventure thrillers, sagas, contemporary romantic fiction, all types of crime & horror.
Specializes in General Trade Fiction & Nonfiction.
Branch Office(s)
Darley Anderson Books

Aquarius Library
136 Emmanuel Rd, Hastings TN34 3LF
Mailing Address: PO Box 5, Hastings, E Sussex TN34 1HR
Tel: (01424) 721196 *Fax:* (01424) 717704
E-mail: aquarius.lib@clara.net
Web Site: www.aquariuscollection.com
Key Personnel
Man Dir: Gilbert Gibson
Contact: David P Corkill
Founded: 1962
Showbusiness picture library (Films, stage, pop, TV, etc)
Membership: British Association of Picture Libraries.
Specializes in Film & TV stills, current & vintage.
Parent Company: Sun-Pacific Music Ltd, London

David Bolt Associates
12 Heath Dr, Send, Surrey GU23 7EP
Tel: (01483) 721118 *Fax:* (01483) 721118
Key Personnel
Dir: David Bolt

Book Production Consultants PLC
25-27 High St, Chesterton, Cambridge CB4 1ND
Tel: (01223) 352790 *Fax:* (01223) 460718
E-mail: cw@bpccam.co.uk
Web Site: www.bpccam.co.uk
Key Personnel
Joint Dir: Tony Littlechild; Colin Walsh
Editorial, Rights: Roz Williams
Founded: 1974
Organization includes international publishing, production & involvement in all media. Joint ventures with London Tourist Board, & National Childbirth Trust.
Specializes in Book & Magazine Publishing Services.
Branch Office(s)
c/o Bank of Bermuda, London Representative Office, Austin Friars House, 2-6 Austin Friars, London EC2N 2HE

Booklink
43 Maycock Grove, Northwood, Middlesex HA6 3PU
Tel: (01923) 828612 *Fax:* (01923) 828455
E-mail: booklink@aol.com
Key Personnel
President: Evelyne Duval
Founded: 1978
International Rights Agency.
Specializes in Foreign Rights, Co-editions.

Curtis Brown
4th floor, Haymarket House, 28-29 Haymarket, London SW1Y 4SP
Tel: (020) 7396 6600 *Fax:* (020) 7396 0110
E-mail: cb@curtisbrown.co.uk
Key Personnel
Group Man Dir: Jonathan Lloyd *E-mail:* jlloyd@curtisbrown.co.uk
Man Dir, Media: Nick Marston
Foreign Rights Dir: Diana Mackay
Founded: 1899
Representation of directors, writers, designers & presenters in theater, film & television & a wide range of authors of fiction & nonfiction.
Branch Office(s)
Curtis Brown Pty Ltd, 27 Union St, Paddington NSW 2021 Sydney, Australia, Contact: Fiona Inglis *Tel:* (00612) 9331 5301 *Fax:* (00612) 9360 3935 *E-mail:* fiona@curtisbrown.can.au

Felicity Bryan
2a N Parade Banbury Rd, Oxford OX2 6LX
Tel: (01865) 513816 *Fax:* (01865) 310055
Key Personnel
Dir: Felicity Bryan *E-mail:* agency@felicitybryan.com
Associate, Europe: Andrew Nurnberg

The Buckman Agency
Ryman's Cottage, Little Tew, Oxford OX7 4JJ
Tel: (01608) 683677 *Fax:* (01608) 683449
Key Personnel
Contact: Rosemarie Buckman *E-mail:* r.buckman@talk21.com; Jessica Buckman *Tel:* (020) 7385 3135 *Fax:* (020) 7385 3137 *E-mail:* j.buckman@talk21.com
Representing American & UK publishers & agents for the handling of all translation rights.
Specializes in Translation rights.

Bycornute Books
76a Ashford Rd, Eastbourne BN21 3TE
Tel: (01323) 649053
Key Personnel
Contact: Asia Haleem *E-mail:* asia.haleem@chq.alstom.com
Founded: 1986
Specializes in Illustrated books on Art History, Religion, Cosmology, Ancient History, Mythology, Archaeology.

Campbell Thomson & McLaughlin Ltd
One King's Mews, London WC1N 2JA
Tel: (020) 7242 0958 *Fax:* (020) 7242 2408
Key Personnel
Man Dir: John McLaughlin

Carnell Literary Agency
Danescroft, Goose Lane, Little Hallingbury, Bishop's Stortford, Herts CM22 7RG
Tel: (01279) 723626 *Fax:* (01279) 600308
Key Personnel
Contact: Pamela Buckmaster
Specializes in Science Fiction, Fantasy, Horror.

Casarotto Ramsay & Associates Ltd
National House 60-66 Wardour St, London W1V 4ND
Tel: (020) 7287 4450 *Fax:* (020) 7287 9128
E-mail: agents@casarotto.uk.com

Web Site: www.casarotto.uk.com
Key Personnel
Man Dir: Giorgio Casarotto
Dir (Film & TV): Jenne Casarotto; Tracey Hyde; Charlotte Kelly
Dir (Theatre): Tom Erhardt; Mel Kenyon
Also represent writers, producers, directors & key technical staff in film, TV & theater.

Jonathan Clowes Ltd
10 Iron Bridge House, Bridge Approach, London NW1 8BD
Tel: (020) 7722 7674 *Fax:* (020) 7722 7677
Key Personnel
Dir: Jonathan Clowes *E-mail:* jonathanclowes@aol.com; Ann Evans
Founded: 1960

Elspeth Cochrane Agency
Southbank Commercial Centre, 140 Battersea Park Rd, London SW11 4NB
Tel: (020) 7622 0314 *Fax:* (020) 7622 5815
Key Personnel
Manager: Elspeth Cochrane
Founded: 1960

Rosica Colin Ltd
One Clareville Grove Mews, London SW7 5AH
Tel: (020) 7370 1080 *Fax:* (020) 7244 6441

Jane Conway-Gordon
One Old Compton St, London W19 5JA
Tel: (020) 7494 0148 *Fax:* (020) 7287 9264

Copytrain
Pitts, Great Milton, Oxford OX44 7NF
Tel: (01844) 279345 *Fax:* (01844) 279345
Key Personnel
Proprietor: Richard Balkwill *E-mail:* rbalkwill@aol.com
Founded: 1992
Specializes in Co-publishing, copyright & training consultancy.

Rupert Crew Ltd
One A King's Mews, London WC1N 2JA
Tel: (020) 7242 8586 *Fax:* (020) 7831 7914
E-mail: rupertcrew@compuserve.com
Key Personnel
Chairman & Man Dir: Doreen Montgomery
Dir: Caroline Montgomery
Founded: 1927
Specializes in Fiction, Nonfiction, Major Book Projects with International Appeal.

David Godwin Associates
55 Monmouth St, London WC2H 9DG
Tel: (020) 7240 9992 *Fax:* (020) 7395 6110
Web Site: www.davidgodwinassociates.co.uk
Founded: 1995
Specializes in Fiction & general nonfiction.

Diagram Visual Information Ltd
195 Kentish Town Rd, London NW5 2JU
Tel: (020) 74823633 *Fax:* (020) 74824932
E-mail: diagramuis@aol.com
Key Personnel
Dir: Bruce Robertson
Secretary: Carole Dease
Founded: 1967

Drake Educational Associates Ltd
Saint Fagans Rd, Fairwater, Cardiff CF5 3AE
Tel: (01222) 2056 0333 *Fax:* (01222) 29 20554909
E-mail: drakegroup@btinternet.com
Web Site: www.drakegroup.co.uk
Key Personnel
Man Dir: Mr R G Drake
Children's books.
Specializes in Education.

AGENTS

UNITED KINGDOM

Toby Eady Associates Ltd
9 Orme Court, London W2 4RL
Tel: (020) 7792 0092 *Fax:* (020) 7792 0879
E-mail: toby@tobyeady.demon.co.uk
Key Personnel
Dir: Toby Eady; Jessica Woollard
    E-mail: jessica@tobyeady.demon.co.uk
Founded: 1968

Ebury Press
Division of Random House Group Ltd
Random House, 20 Vauxhall Bridge Rd, London SW1V 2SA
Tel: (020) 7840 8400 *Fax:* (020) 7233 7398
Web Site: www.randomhouse.co.uk
Key Personnel
Deputy Rights Dir: Rae Shirvington
Rights Dir: Maria White
Rights Assistant: Jan Clementson *Tel:* (020) 78408761 *E-mail:* jclementson@randomhouse.co.uk

Faith Evans Associates
27 Park Ave North, London N8 7RV
Tel: (020) 8340 9920 *Fax:* (020) 8340 9410
Key Personnel
Contact: Faith Evans
Founded: 1987

Anne-Louise Fisher
46 Lexington St, London W1F OLP
Tel: (020) 7494 4609 *Fax:* (020) 7494 4611
Key Personnel
Publisher's Scout: Anne-Louise Fisher
    E-mail: annelouise@alfisher.co.uk
Literary scout representing Doubleday, Nan Talese & Broadnay books in America; editions Plon & Poruet in France; Karl Blessing Verlag, Knaus Verlag, Berlin Verlag & Siedler Verlag in Germany; Arnoldo Mondadori Editore in Italy; Albert Bonniers Bokporlag in Sweden; Otave in Finland; Giloendal Norsk Forlag in Norway; De Boekerij in Holland; Plaza y Janes, Debate & Lumen in Spain; Patakis Publications in Greece.

French's
78 Loudoun Rd, London NW8 ONA
Tel: (020) 74834269 *Fax:* (020) 77220574
Key Personnel
Contact: Mark Taylor
Founded: 1975
A reading service is available on all mss. Send SASE for details.

Blake Friedmann Literary Agency Ltd
122 Arlington Rd, London NW1 7HP
Tel: (020) 7284 0408 *Fax:* (020) 7284 0442
Web Site: www.blakefriedmann.co.uk
Key Personnel
Joint Man Dir: Carole Blake *E-mail:* carole@blakefriedmann.co.uk; Julian Friedmann
Finance Dir: Barbara Jones
Dir: Isobel Dixon; Conrad William
Founded: 1977
Specializes in Literary & Commercial Fiction & Nonfiction, Film & TV Development.

Vernon Futerman Associates
Accounts & Administration, 159A Goldhurst Terr, London NW6 3EU
Mailing Address: Editorial Submissions Dept, 17 Deanhill Rd, London SW14 7DQ
Tel: (020) 7625 9601 *Fax:* (020) 7625 9601
Key Personnel
Man Dir: Vernon Futerman
Dir: Guy Rose; Alexandra Groom
Founded: 1984
Mobile: 0410 224680.
Specializes in Fiction & Academic Nonfiction, TV Film & Theatre Scripts.

Eric Glass Ltd
25 Ladbroke Crescent, Notting Hill, London W11 1PS
Tel: (020) 7229 9500 *Fax:* (020) 7229 6220
Key Personnel
Dir: Janet Glass; Daniela Szmigielska
Founded: 1932
Represents Societe des Auteurs et Compositeurs Dramatiques (SACD), Paris & Societi Civil des Auteurs Multimedia (SCAM) (formerly Societe des Gens de Lettres).
Specializes in Books (fiction & nonfiction), Plays & Screenplays.

Christine Green Authors' Agent
6 Whitehorse Mews, Westminster Bridge Road, London SE1 7QD
Tel: (020) 7401 8844 *Fax:* (020) 7401 8860
Key Personnel
Dir: Christine Green
Founded: 1984
Specializes in Fiction & General Nonfiction.

Greene & Heaton Ltd
37 Goldhawk Rd, London W12 8QQ
Tel: (020) 8749 0315 *Fax:* (020) 8749 0318
Key Personnel
Contact: Carol Heaton; Judith Murray; Antony Topping
Rights Assistant: Julia Jordan

Gregory & Radice Authors' Agents
3 Barb Mews, Hammersmith, London W6 7PA
Tel: (020) 7610 4676 *Fax:* (020) 7610 4686
E-mail: info@gregoryradice.co.uk
Web Site: www.gregoryradice.co.uk
Key Personnel
Partner: Jane Gregory *E-mail:* jane@gregoryradice.co.uk
Editorial Partner: Dr Lisanne Radice
Rights Executive: Jane Barlow *E-mail:* janeb@gregoryradice.co.uk
Founded: 1987
Deals with full-length mss, fiction & nonfiction. Particularly interested in books with potential for sales abroad and/or film & TV (home 15%, articles, USA & translation 20%, film/TV rights 15%). No short stories, plays, film scripts, science fiction, fantasy, horror, poetry, academic or children's books. Represented in all foreign markets. No reading fees, editorial advice given to our authors. No unsolicited unrestricted mss: preliminary letter, synopsis & first three chapters essential plus return postage.
Specializes in Commercial & literary fiction, crime fiction, thrillers & politics.

David Grossman Literary Agency Ltd
118B Holland Park Ave, London W11 4UA
Tel: (020) 7221 2770 *Fax:* (020) 7221 1445

Gunnar Lie & Associates Ltd
Roebuck House, 3rd floor, 288 Upper Richmond Rd W, London SW14 7JG
Tel: (020) 8487 9020 *Fax:* (020) 8878 2832
Key Personnel
Man Dir: Gunnar Lie *E-mail:* gunnarlie@compuserve.com
Export Manager: Frances Buequet; John Edgeler *Tel:* (020) 8487 9021 *E-mail:* johnedgeler@compuserve.com
Founded: 1995
Specializes in International Sales & Marketing.

A M Heath & Co Ltd
79 St Martin's Lane, London WC2N 4AA
Tel: (020) 7836 4271 *Fax:* (020) 7497 2561
E-mail: amheath@demon.co.uk *Cable:* SCRIPT LONDON WC2
Key Personnel
Chairman: Michael Thomas
Dir: Sara Fisher; William Hamilton; Victoria Hobbs; Sarah Molloy
Founded: 1919

David Higham Associates Ltd
5-8 Lower John St, Golden Sq, London W1F 9HA
Tel: (020) 7434 5900 *Fax:* (020) 7437 1072
E-mail: dha@davidhigham.co.uk
Key Personnel
Contact: Ania Corless; Anthony Goff; Bruce Hunter; Jacqueline Korn; Caroline Walsh
Founded: 1935
Incorporating Murray Pollinger Agency.

Vanessa Holt Ltd
59 Crescent Rd, Leigh-on-Sea, Essex SS9 2PF
Tel: (01702) 473787 *Fax:* (01702) 471890
Founded: 1989
No unsolicited material.
Specializes in Fiction.

Kate Hordern
18 Mortimer Rd, Clifton, Bristol BS8 4EY

Hutton-Williams Agency
58 Melbury Gardens, London SW20 0DJ
Tel: (020) 8879 0237 *Fax:* (020) 8879 3831
Key Personnel
Contact: Mr C Huttin Williams
    E-mail: hwagency@email.com
Founded: 1988
Syndication & foreign rights of newspapers, magazines & books throughout the world.
Specializes in Annuals, special issues, supplements & partworks.

Imrie & Dervis Literary Agency
7 Carlton Mansions, London N16 5PX
Tel: (020) 8809 3282 *Fax:* (020) 8880 2086
E-mail: info@imriedervis.com
Key Personnel
Agent: Martina Dervis; Malcolm Imrie
    E-mail: malcolm@imriedervis.com

Information Agents Ltd
26 Rosebery Ave, London EC1R 4SX
Tel: (020) 7837 3345 *Fax:* (020) 7837 8901
E-mail: eps@epsltd.com
Web Site: www.epsltd.com
Key Personnel
Chairman: David Worlock
Dir: D J Powell
Founded: 1989
Specializes in Negotiating Electronic Rights.

Intercontinental Literary Agency, see The Peters Fraser & Dunlop Group Ltd

Intercontinental Literary Agency
The Chambers, 5th floor, Chelsea Harbour, London SW10 0XF
Tel: (020) 7351 4763 *Fax:* (020) 7351 4809
E-mail: mesdaile@pfd.co.uk
Key Personnel
Dir: Anthony Gornall; Nicki Kennedy
Founded: 1965
Specializes in Translation Rights.

The International Press Agency
19 Ave South, Surbiton KT5 8JP
Tel: (0181) 3904414 *Fax:* (0181) 3904414
Key Personnel
Man Editor: U A Barnett
Founded: 1934 (Abroad, 1989 UK)
Specializes in Children's Books.
Branch Office(s)
Cape Town, South Africa

UNITED KINGDOM

International Scripts Ltd
1A Kidbrooke Park Rd, Blackheath, London SE3 0LR
Tel: (020) 8319 8666 *Fax:* (020) 8319 0801
Key Personnel
Man Dir: Bob Tanner
Dir: Jill Lawson
Founded: 1978
Literary Agency involved in selling UK & Commonwealth, translation & US rights & subsidiary rights. Also involved in film & TV scripts.
Specializes in contemporary & women's fiction, biographies, business & general nonfiction.

Jane Judd Literary Agency
18 Belitha Villas, London N1 1PD
Tel: (020) 7607 0273 *Fax:* (020) 7607 0623
Key Personnel
Contact: Jane Judd
Founded: 1986
Also represents US companies Avon Books & Mercury House & US agents Marian Young & Penguin Canada.
Specializes in General Fiction & Nonfiction.

Jennifer Kavanagh
44 Langham St, London W1M 5RG
Tel: (020) 7636 2477 *Fax:* (020) 7636 2479
Founded: 1984

The Frances Kelly Agency
111 Clifton Rd, Kingston-upon-Thames, Surrey KT2 6PL
Tel: (0181) 5497830 *Fax:* (0181) 5470051
Founded: 1978
Specializes in Nonfiction, Trade, Reference, Academic.

Knight Features
20 Crescent Grove, London SW4 7AH
Tel: (020) 7622 1522 *Fax:* (020) 7622 1522
Key Personnel
Dir, Proprietor: Peter Knight *E-mail:* peter@knightfeatures.co.uk
Founded: 1985
Full unsolicited mss not accepted; outline & sample chapters to be accompanied by a self-addressed envelope; no cookery or science fiction books.
Specializes in Strip Cartoons, Major Features, Serializations.
Branch Office(s)
Peter Knight Literary Agency

Lenz-Mulligan Rights & Co-editions
15 Sandbourne Ave, Merton Park, London SW19 3EW
Tel: (020) 8543 7846 *Fax:* (020) 8543 8909
Key Personnel
Contact: Gundhild Lenz-Mulligan *E-mail:* glenzmulligan@dial.pipex.com
Founded: 1998
Specializes in Children's books.

Barbara Levy Literary Agency
64 Greenhill, Hampstead High St, London NW3 5TZ
Tel: (020) 7435 9046 *Fax:* (020) 7431 2063
E-mail: blevy@dircon.co.uk
Key Personnel
Dir: Barbara Levy
Associate: John F Selby
Founded: 1986

Litopia Corp Ltd
186 Bickenhall Mansions, London W1V 6RX
Tel: (020) 7224 1748 *Fax:* (020) 7224 1802; 212-202-4236 (N.Y.)
E-mail: info@litopia.com
Web Site: www.litopia.com

Key Personnel
CEO: Peter Cox *E-mail:* peter@litopia.com
Contact: Peggy Brusseau *E-mail:* peggy@litopia.com; Jane Mountbatten *E-mail:* jane@litopia.com
Founded: 1986
Require all submissions to follow the guidelines on website.
Specializes in General, no children's or poetry.

Christopher Little Literary Agency
10 Eel Brook Studios, 125 Moore Park Rd, London SW6 4PS
Tel: (020) 7736 4455 *Fax:* (020) 7736 4490
Key Personnel
Proprietor: Christopher J Little
  E-mail: christopher@christopherlittle.net
Contact: Jeanine Berigliano *E-mail:* jeanine@christopherlittle.net; Kellee Nunley
  E-mail: kellee@christopherlittle.net
Founded: 1979
Commercial & literary full-length fiction & nonfiction (home 15%, US, Canada, translation, audio, motion picture 20%). No reading fee; no unsol mss. No poetry, plays, science fiction, fantasy, textbooks, illustrated children's or short stories. Film scripts for established clients only.

London Independent Books
26 Chalcot Crescent, London NW1 8YD
Tel: (020) 7706 0486 *Fax:* (020) 7724 3122
Key Personnel
Literary Agent: Carolyn Whitaker
Founded: 1972
All subjects considered except young children's & computer books.
Specializes in Fantasy fiction, Crime fiction, Travel, Young adult fiction.

Andrew Lownie Literary Agency
17 Sutherland St, London SW1V 4JU
Tel: (020) 7828 1274 *Fax:* (020) 7828 7608
E-mail: lownie@globalnet.co.uk
Web Site: www.andrewlownie.co.uk
Key Personnel
Chief Executive: Andrew Lownie
  E-mail: lowrie@globalnet.co.uk
Founded: 1988
Specializes in Nonfiction, History, Biography, Current Affairs.

Lucas, Alexander, Whitley
Elsinore House, 77 Fulham, Palace Rd, London W6 8JA
Tel: (020) 7471 7900 *Fax:* (020) 7471 7910
Key Personnel
Contact: Mark Lucas; Araminta Whitley
Representing British authors for fiction & nonfiction.

Lutyens & Rubinstein
231 Westbourne Park Rd, London W11 1EB
Tel: (020) 7792 4855 *Fax:* (020) 7792 4833
E-mail: name@lutyensrubinstein.co.uk
Key Personnel
Partner: Sarah Lutyens; Felicity Rubinstein
Founded: 1993
Membership: Association of Authors' Agents.

MacLean Dubois Ltd (Writers & Agents)
Hillend House, Hillend, Edinburgh EH10 7DX
Tel: (0131) 4455885 *Fax:* (0131) 4455898
E-mail: whisteymac@clearut.com
Key Personnel
Dir: Charles MacLean
Founded: 1976
Literary Agents & professional writers, providing a range of editorial services. Main activity is writing of promotional & marketing materials.
Specializes in Scottish Fiction & Nonfiction.

The Marsh Agency
11-12 Dover St, London W1X 3PH
Tel: (020) 7399 2800 *Fax:* (020) 7399 2801
E-mail: enquiries@marsh-agency.co.uk
Web Site: www.marsh-agency.co.uk
Key Personnel
Partner: Paul Marsh; Susanna Nicklin
Contact: Juliet Matthews
Founded: 1994
Specializes in International Rights.

Blanche Marvin Agency
21a St Johns Wood High St, London NW8 7NG
Tel: (020) 7722 2313 *Fax:* (020) 7722 2313
Key Personnel
Editor & Publisher: Blanche Marvin
  E-mail: blanchemarvin@madasafish.com
Founded: 1968
Established work only.
Specializes in Theater & Drama.

MBA Literary Agents Ltd
62 Grafton Way, London W1P 5LD
Tel: (020) 7387 2076 *Fax:* (020) 7387 2042
E-mail: agent@mbalit.co.uk
Key Personnel
Man Dir: Diana Tyler
Dir: Meg Davis; John Richard Parker; Tim Webb

Cathy Miller Foreign Rights Agency
18 The Quadrangle, 49 Atalanta St, London SW6 6TU
Tel: (020) 7386 5473 *Fax:* (020) 7385 1774
Key Personnel
Managing Dir: Cathy Miller *E-mail:* cathy@millerrightsagency.com
Founded: 1981
Consultants to publishers worldwide in the field of translation rights, worldwide market research for publishers interested in European potential, help with negotiating rights contracts and representation.
Specializes in foreign rights.

Richard Milne Ltd
15 Summerlee Gardens, London N2 9QN
Tel: (020) 8883 3987 *Fax:* (020) 8883 0323
E-mail: dsharp121@aol.com
Key Personnel
Dir: R M Sharples; K N Sharples
Founded: 1956
Presently not undertaking additional representation.
Specializes in Television & film scripts.

William Morris Agency (UK) Ltd
52/53 Poland St, London W1F 7LX
Tel: (020) 7534 6800 *Fax:* (020) 7534 6900
Key Personnel
Man Dir: Stephanie Cabot
Literary Agent, Books: Eugenie Furniss
Literary Agent, TV: Holly Pie; Hans Schiff
Founded: 1965

Michael Motley Ltd
Flat 4, 42 Craven Hill Gardens, London W2 3EA
Tel: (020) 7723 2973 *Fax:* (020) 7262 4566
Key Personnel
Dir: Michael Motley
Founded: 1973

Negotiate Ltd
99 Caiyside, Edinburgh EH10 7HR
Tel: (0131) 445 7571 *Fax:* (0131) 445 7572
E-mail: gavin@neg1.demon.co.uk
Web Site: www.negotiate.co.uk
Key Personnel
Man Dir: Gavin Kennedy
Founded: 1986

AGENTS UNITED KINGDOM

Negotiation of authors, publishers, agents & contracts.
Specializes in Contract Negotiation.

The Maggie Noach Literary Agency
22 Dorville Crescent, London W6 0HJ
Tel: (020) 8748 2926 *Fax:* (020) 8748 8057
E-mail: m-noach@dircon.co.uk
Founded: 1982

Andrew Nurnberg Associates Ltd
Clerkenwell House, 45-47 Clerkenwell Green, London EC1R 0HT
Tel: (020) 7417 8800 *Fax:* (020) 7417 8812
E-mail: 100663.727@compuserve.com
Telex: 23353 *Cable:* NURNBOOKS LONDON
Key Personnel
Man Dir: Andrew Nurnberg
Dir: Klaasje Mul; Sarah Nundy
Contact: Sam Edenborough
 E-mail: sedenborough@nurnberg.co.uk
Specializes in Translation Rights.
Branch Office(s)
Andrew Nurnberg Associates Sofia, 11 Slaveikov Sq, PO Box 453, 1000 Sofia, Bulgaria *Tel:* (02) 803854 *Fax:* (02) 803854
Andrew Nurnberg Associates Prague, Seifertova 81, Prague 3, Czech Republic *Tel:* (02) 227 82041 *Fax:* (02) 227 82308
Andrew Nurnberg Associates Budapest, Hold u 29, 1054 Budapest, Hungary *Tel:* (01) 3026451 *Fax:* (01) 1113948
Andrew Nurnberg Associates Baltic, PO Box 77, Riga 1011, Latvia *Tel:* 7289759 *Fax:* 7821241
Andrew Nurnberg Associates Warsaw, UL Milobedzka 10/2, 02-634 Warsaw, Poland *Tel:* (022) 441393 *Fax:* (022) 441393
Andrew Nurnberg Associates Bucharest, Bdul Averescu 3, Bloc 2, Apt 6, Sector 1, Bucharest, Romania *Tel:* (01) 6665118 *Fax:* (01) 6665118
Andrew Nurnberg Literary Agency (Moscow), Voprosy Literatury, Bolshoi Gnezdnikovsky 10, Moscow 103009, Russian Federation *Tel:* (095) 229-5281 *Fax:* (095) 883-6403

David O'Leary Literary Agents
10 Lansdowne Court, Lansdowne Rise, London W11 2NR
Tel: (020) 7229 1623 *Fax:* (020) 7727 9624
E-mail: d.o'leary@virgin.net
Key Personnel
Dir: David O'Leary
Founded: 1986
Include brief synopsis of subject of novel with initial correspondence. Include SAE if return requested.
Specializes in Fiction & Nonfiction (both Literary & Commercial), History, Popular Science & Irish subjects.

Deborah Owen Ltd
78 Narrow St, Limehouse, London E14 8BP
Tel: (020) 7987 5119; (020) 7987 5441
Fax: (020) 7538 4004
E-mail: debowen@dial.pipex.com
Founded: 1971

Mark Paterson & Associates, Authors & Publishers Literary Agents
10 Brook Street, Wivenhoe, Essex CO7 9DS
Tel: (01206) 825433 *Fax:* (01206) 822990
E-mail: info@markpaterson.co.uk
Key Personnel
Proprietor: Mark Paterson
Associate: Mary Swinney *E-mail:* mary@markpaterson.co.uk
Founded: 1961
Specializes in Psychology, Psychotherapy, Psychoanalysis, History.

John Pawsey
60 Tarring High St, Worthing, West Sussex BN14 7NR
Tel: (01903) 205167 *Fax:* (01903) 205167
Founded: 1981
Represents American publishers & literary agencies in the UK.
Specializes in Popular & Contemporary Fiction, Biography, Politics & Current Affairs, Sports, Popular Culture.
Branch Office(s)
Europe
Far East
Latin America

Peake Associates Tony Peake
14 Grafton Crescent, London NW1 8SL
Tel: (020) 7267 8033 *Fax:* (020) 7284 1876

Maggie Pearlstine Associates Limited
31 Ashley Gardens, Ambrosden Ave, London SW1P 1QE
Tel: (020) 7828-4212 *Fax:* (020) 7834-5546
E-mail: post@pearlstine.co.uk
Key Personnel
Dir: Maggie Pearlstine
Associate: John Oates *E-mail:* john@pearlstine.co.uk
Founded: 1989
Small, selective agency. UK based authors only.
Specializes in Commercial Fiction, General Nonfiction, History, Current Affairs, Biography, Health.

The Penman Literary Service-Agency Department
185 Daws Heath Rd, Benfleet, Essex SS7 2TF
Tel: (01702) 557431
Key Personnel
Dir: Mark Sorrell

A D Peters & Co, see The Peters Fraser & Dunlop Group Ltd

The Peters Fraser & Dunlop Group Ltd
Drury House, 34-43 Russell St, London WC2B 5HA
Tel: (020) 7344 1000 *Fax:* (020) 7836 9541
E-mail: rscoular@pfd.co.uk
Key Personnel
Joint Chair: Tim Corrie; Anthony Jones
Man Dir: Anthony Baring
Agent: Annabel Hardman *Tel:* (020) 7344 1054
 E-mail: ahardman@pfd.co.uk
Founded: 1924
Specializes in Literary, Film & Actors Agency.

Pollinger Ltd
Goldsmiths' House, 137-141 Regent St, London W1B 4HZ
Tel: (020) 7025 7820 *Fax:* (020) 7025 7829
Web Site: www.pollingerltd.com
Key Personnel
Man Dir: Lesley Hadcroft
Foreign Rights: Heather Chalcroft
 E-mail: heatherchalcroft@pollingerltd.com
Branch Office(s)
Micheline Steinberg, 409 Triumph House, 187-191 Regent St, London W1R 7WF

Polygon
22 George Sq, Edinburgh EH8 9LF
Tel: (0131) 6504223 *Fax:* (0131) 662053
E-mail: editorial@eup.ed.ac.uk
Key Personnel
Editorial Dir: Jackie Jones

Quest-Meridien Ltd
420 Vale Rd, Tonbridge, Kent TN9 1TD
Tel: (0802) 470283 *Fax:* (01732) 770620

Key Personnel
Financial Dir: Betty M Skippon
Supplier of anatomical charts.
Specializes in Medical.

Rogers, Coleridge & White Ltd
20 Powis Mews, London W11 1JN
Tel: (020) 7221 3717 *Fax:* (020) 7229 9084
 Cable: DEBROGERS LONDON W11
Key Personnel
Dir: Gill Coleridge; Deborah Rogers
Dir, USA: Patricia White
Dir: David Miller
Consultant: Ann Warnford-Davis
Foreign Rights: Stephen Edwards; Laurence Laluyaux
Founded: 1967

Elizabeth Roy Literary Agency
White Cottage, Greatford, Near Stamford, Lincs PE9 4PR
Tel: (01778) 560672 *Fax:* (01778) 560672
Key Personnel
Contact: Elizabeth Roy
Founded: 1990
Specializes in Children's Books (fiction & nonfiction), Children's Books Illustrators.

Hilary Rubinstein Books
32 Ladbroke Grove, London W11 3BQ
Tel: (020) 7792 4282 *Fax:* (020) 7221 5291
E-mail: hrubinstein@beeb.net
Key Personnel
Dir: Hilary Rubinstein
Founded: 1978

Tessa Sayle Agency
11 Jubilee Pl, London SW3 3TD
Tel: (020) 7823 3883 *Fax:* (020) 7823 3363
E-mail: info@thesayleagency.co.uk
Key Personnel
Contact: Rachel Calder
Contact, Film & TV: Matthew Bates; Jane Villiers
Specializes in Fiction, Nonfiction, Film & TV.

Search Press Ltd
Wellwood, North Farm Rd, Tunbridge Wells, Kent TN2 3DR
Tel: (01892) 510850 *Fax:* (01892) 515903
E-mail: searchpress@searchpress.com
Key Personnel
Chairman: Lottie de la Bedoyere
Man Dir: Martin de la Bedoyere
 E-mail: martind@searchpress.com
Foreign Rights Dir: Caroline de la Bedoyere
Founded: 1970

Sheil Land Associates Ltd Rights Department
43 Doughty St, London WC1N 2LF
Tel: (020) 7405 9351 *Fax:* (020) 7831 2127
Key Personnel
Rights Dir: Laura Susijn
Contact: Talya Boston
Founded: 1985
Specializes in US & translation rights.

Sheil Land Associates Ltd
43 Doughty St, London WC1N 2LF
Tel: (020) 7405 9351 *Fax:* (020) 7831 2127
Key Personnel
Chairman: Anthony Sheil
Chief Executive: Sonia Land
Founded: 1962
Specializes in Literary, Theatre & Film Agents.
U.S. Office(s): Sheil Land Associates in association with George Borchart Inc, 136 E 57 St, New York, NY 10022, United States *Tel:* 212-753-5785

Caroline Sheldon Literary Agency
Thorley Manor Farm, Thorley, Yarmouth PO41 0S1

UNITED KINGDOM

Tel: (01983) 760205
Key Personnel
Literary Agent & Proprietor: Caroline Sheldon
Founded: 1985
Specializes in Fiction, Children's Books.

Jeffrey Simmons
10 Lowndes Sq, London SW1X 9HA
Tel: (020) 7235 8852 *Fax:* (020) 7235 9733
Key Personnel
Contact: Jeffrey Simmons
Specializes in adult fiction, personality books, biography, autobiography, show business, law, crime, politics, world affairs.

The Stationery Office
Publications Centre, 51 Nine Elms Lane, London SW8 5DR
Mailing Address: PO Box 29, Norwich NR3 1GN
Tel: (020) 7600 5522 *Fax:* (020) 7873 8200 (orders)
E-mail: book.order@theso.co.uk
Web Site: www.the-stationery-office.co.uk
Key Personnel
Chief Executive: Fred J Perkins
Man Dir: Robert McKay
Founded: 1996

Abner Stein
10 Roland Gardens, London SW7 3PH
Tel: (020) 7373 0456 *Fax:* (020) 7370 6316
E-mail: abnerstein@compuserve.com
Key Personnel
Dir: Abner Stein
Specializes in Nonfiction, Fiction, Children's Books.

Micheline Steinberg Playwrights' Agent
110 Frognal, London NW3 6XU
Tel: (020) 7287 4383 *Fax:* (020) 7794 4011
E-mail: steinbergplaywright@freeserve.co.uk
Key Personnel
Contact: Micheline Steinberg
Founded: 1987
In association with Laurence Pollinger Ltd.
Specializes in Dramatic Works.

Tanja Howarth Literary Agency
19 New Row, London WC2N 4LA
Tel: (020) 7240 5553; (020) 7836 4142
Fax: (020) 7379 0969
Key Personnel
Contact: Tanja Howarth *E-mail:* tanja.howarth@virgin.net
Specializes in Full length mss. General fiction & nonfiction, thrillers, contemporary & historical women's novels & sagas & general nonfiction. Represented in the USA by Writers House Inc. Submit preliminary letter, synopsis & three sample chapters with return postage. No reading fee.

J M Thurley
30 Cambridge Rd, Teddington, Middlesex TW11 8DR
Tel: (0208) 9773176 *Fax:* (0208) 9432678

Key Personnel
Proprietor: J M Thurley *E-mail:* jmthurley@aol.com
Specialize in literary & commercial fiction & nonfiction.

Lavinia Trevor
7 The Glasshouse 49A Goldhawk Rd, London W12 8QP
Tel: (020) 8749 8481 *Fax:* (020) 8749 7377
Key Personnel
Agent: Lavinia Trevor

Turnaround Publisher Services Ltd
Unit 3, Olympia Trading Estate, Coburg Rd, London N22 6TZ
Tel: (020) 8829 3009 *Fax:* (020) 8881 5088
E-mail: sales@turnaround-uk.com
Key Personnel
Pres & Man Dir: Bill Godber
Marketing Dir: Claire Thompson *E-mail:* claire@turnaround-uk.com
Founded: 1984
Sales Agent & distributor to the UK & continental European Booktrade for a wide variety of quality US & UK publishers.
Specializes in Black Interest, Gay Interest, American Imports.

Jane Turnbull
13 Wendell Rd, London W12 9RS
Tel: (020) 8743 9580 *Fax:* (020) 8749 6079
E-mail: agents@cwcom.net
Key Personnel
Proprietor: Jane Tornbull
Founded: 1986
Literary agency, member of association of authors agents.
Specializes in Nonfiction of all kinds literary fiction. No children's books or film scripts.

Kelvin van Hasselt Publishing Services
Corner Cottage, Mayflower Close, Lymington, Hants SO41 3SN
Tel: (01590) 671695 *Fax:* (01590) 671533
E-mail: kvhbooks@aol.com
Key Personnel
Man Dir: Kevin van Hasselt
Order Processing: Gill Hinds
Representing Book Publishers in Africa, Asia & the Caribbean.
Specializes in Academic & Professional.

Van Lear Associates
Parsons Green, Fulham, London SW6 5ZU
Mailing Address: PO Box 21816, Fulham, London SW6 5ZU
Tel: (020) 7610 6165 *Fax:* (020) 7610 6045
E-mail: 100700.3266@compuserve.com
Key Personnel
Scout: John Toba
Contact: Elizabeth van Lear
Assistant: Eugenie Furniss
International publishers representative literary scout.

Ed Victor Ltd
6 Bayley St, Bedford Square, London WC1B 3HB

Tel: (020) 7304 4100 *Fax:* (020) 7304 4111
Key Personnel
Man Dir: Ed Victor
Dir: Graham Greene; Maggie Phillips; Sophie Hicks; Carol Ryan; Leon Morgan

S Walker Literary Agency
11 Clare Rd, Putnoe, Bedford MK41 8QX
Tel: (01234) 216229
Key Personnel
Partner: Alan Oldfield; Cora-Louise Oldfield
Founded: 1939
Specializes in Full-length Novels.

Peter Ward Book Exports
Taylors Yard, Unit 3, 67 Alderbrook Rd, London SW12 8AD
Tel: (020) 8772 3300 *Fax:* (020) 8772 3309
E-mail: pwbookex@dircon.co.uk
Key Personnel
Partner: Peter Ward *E-mail:* peter@pwbookex.dircon.co.uk; Richard Ward *E-mail:* richard@pwbookex.dircon.co.uk
Founded: 1974
Freelance representatives of UK & US publishers.
Specializes in Middle East, Cyprus, Turkey, Iran, Greece & Malta.

Warner Chappell Plays Ltd
Griffin House, 161 Hammersmith Rd, London W6 8BS
Tel: (020) 8563 5800 *Fax:* (020) 8563 5801
E-mail: warner.chappell@dial.pipex.com
Key Personnel
Manager: Michael Callahan
Specializes in Drama Playscripts.

Watson, Little Ltd
Capo Di Monte, Windmill Hill, London NW3 6RJ
Tel: (020) 7431 0770 *Fax:* (020) 7431 7225
Key Personnel
Dir: Sheila Watson; Amanda Little; Sugra Zaman *E-mail:* sz@watsonlittle.com
Specializes in Business, popular science, psychology & culture, history, fiction, children's fiction/non-fiction.

A P Watt Ltd
20 John St, London WC1N 2DR
Tel: (020) 7405 6774 *Fax:* (020) 7831 2154
E-mail: apwatt@apwatt.co.uk
Web Site: www.apwatt.co.uk
Key Personnel
Man Dir: Caradoc King
Foreign Rights Dir: Linda Shaughnessy
Joint Manager: Derek Johns
Founded: 1875
Literary, film & television agents.

Dinah Wiener Ltd
Cornwall Grove, Chiswick, London W4 2LB
Tel: (020) 8994 6011 *Fax:* (020) 8994 6044
Key Personnel
Contact: Dinah Wiener *E-mail:* dinahwiener@enterprise.net
Founded: 1985

International Publishing Services

Listed within this section are U.S. and Canadian companies offering services to the book publishing industry internationally.

MapQuest
Formerly MapQuest.com
Subsidiary of AOL Time Warner
3710 Hempland Rd, Box 601, Mountville, PA 17554
Tel: 717-285-8500 *Fax:* 717-285-8456
E-mail: infodms@mapquest.com
Web Site: www.oneworldmapping.com
Key Personnel
VP: Jim Hilliard *Tel:* 717-285-8412
 Fax: jhilliard@mapquest.com
Mktg Mgr: Ed Kladky *Tel:* 717-285-8480
 E-mail: ekladky@mapquest.com
Sales Dir: Bennett Moe *Tel:* 443-367-3046
 E-mail: bmoe@mapquest.com
Founded: 1967
Serves the world's leading publishers with creative mapping solutions in any media. Develop exciting map products & create custom mapping content for reference books, travel guides, directories & textbooks.
ISBN Prefix(es): 1-57262; 1-879856
Branch Office(s)
6450-C Dobbin Rd, Columbia, MD 21045
 Tel: 443-367-3042
Membership(s): Association of Directory Publishers; International Map Trade Association; YPPA (Yellow Pages Publishers Association)
See ad in this section

Translation Agencies & Associations

Austria

Oesterreichischer Uebersetzer- und Dolmetscherverband Universitas
Gymnasiumstr 50, A-1190 Vienna
Tel: (01) 3686060 *Fax:* (01) 3686008
E-mail: info@universitas.org
Web Site: www.univeritas.org
Key Personnel
President: Elisabeth Schwarz
Austrian Association of Interpreters & Translators.

Uebersetzergemeinschaft Interessengemeinschaft von Uebersetzerinnen und Uebersetzern literarischer und wissenschaftlicher Werke
Seidengasse 13, A-1070 Vienna
Tel: (01) 526204418 *Fax:* (01) 526204430
E-mail: ueg@literaturhaus.at
Web Site: www.translators.at
Key Personnel
Chairman: Werner Richter
Secretary General: Brigitte Rapp *E-mail:* br@literaturhaus.at
Austrian Association of Literary & Scientific Translators.
Publication(s): *Literature Infonet* (handbook); *The Translators' Companion*; *Uebersetzerverzeichnis* (directory)

Bulgaria

Union of Translators of Bulgaria, Magazin Panorama
16, Graf Ignatiev Str, 1000 Sofia
Mailing Address: PO Box 161, 1000 Sofia
Tel: (02) 655190 *Fax:* (02) 656187
Key Personnel
Editor: Gancho Savov
Publication(s): *Panorama* (magazine)
Branch Office(s)
Magazine & Publishing House

China

CIPG Editorial & Translation Research Center
24 Baiwanzhuang Rd, Wa Wen Bldg, Beijing 10037
Tel: (010) 68326681
E-mail: ftrchina@public3.bta.net.cn
Key Personnel
Dir: Sun Chengtang
Publication(s): *Chinese Translators Journal*

Polyglot Translation
Office Tower Central Hotel, Suite 968, 33 Airport Rd, Guangzhou
Tel: (020) 8657-3608 *Fax:* (020) 8657-3965
E-mail: info@polyglot.com.cn
Web Site: www.polyglot.com.cn; www.chinapolyglot.com
A professional translation organization that provides translation, interpretation & simultaneous meeting interpretation in all fields. In addition, we provide localization of websites into Chinese, writing articles in multi-languages, foreign languages recording, proofreading, interpreters/translators recommending, website designing & making & so on. We can provide a large variety of languages translating services such as English, Japanese, French, German, Russian, Korean, Italian, Spanish, Dutch, Swedish, Finnish, Portuguese, Czechish, Slovak, Romanian, Polish, Hungarian, Bulgarian, Arabic, Turkish, Cambodian, Malay, Indonesian, Thai, Vietnamese, Nepali, Laotian, Burmese, Mongolian, Indic, Bengalese, Tamil etc. Altogether, we can provide more than 30-languages translation service fast & accurately. For details please visit our website.

Translator's Association of China (TAC), see CIPG Editorial & Translation Research Center

Cuba

Centro de Traducciones y Terminologia Especializada (CTTE)
Industry & Barcelona, Apdo Postal 2014, 10200 La Habana
Tel: (07) 626531 *Fax:* (07) 626501; (07) 338237
E-mail: ctte@ceniai.inf.cu
Web Site: www.Z.cuba.cu/ciencia/idict/ctte/inicio.html
Key Personnel
Dir: Luis Alberto Gonzalez Moreno
Translation & Specialized Terminology Center (CTTE).
Publication(s): *Catalogo de Cubalingua*

Czech Republic

Jednota Tlumocniku a Prekladatelu (JTP - Union of Interpreters and Translators)
Senovazne Namesti 23, 11000 Prague 1
Tel: (02) 24142517 *Fax:* (02) 24142312
E-mail: JTP@4u.net
Web Site: www.JTPunion.org
Key Personnel
President: Dr Andrej Ra'dy
Dir: Peter Kautsky
Press Officer: Jiri Eichler
Glossaries, dictionaries, terminology, proceedings of specialised conferences.
Publication(s): *ToP* (quarterly, bulletin)

Translators Guild
Pod nuselskymi schody 3, 12000 Prague 2
Tel: (02) 6911908 ext 30 *Fax:* (02) 3117224
Key Personnel
President: Jarmila Emmerova

Egypt (Arab Republic of Egypt)

Al Ahram Establishment
6 Al-Galaa' St, Cairo
Tel: (02) 748248 *Fax:* (02) 745888
Telex: 20185-92544

The Egyptian Society for the Dissemination of Universal Culture and Knowledge (ESDUCK)
1081 Corniche el Nil St, Garden City, Cairo
Mailing Address: PO Box 21, Garden City, Cairo
Tel: (02) 3545079; (02) 3540295
Telex: 92548

ESDUCK, see The Egyptian Society for the Dissemination of Universal Culture and Knowledge (ESDUCK)

France

Ecole de Traducteurs et d'Interpretes de Beyrouth-Universite Saint-Joseph (ETIB)
Bureau Administratif, 42 Rue de Grenelle, F-75343 Paris Cedex 07
Mailing Address: BP 175-208, Beyrouth-Liban
Tel: (01) 201617 *Fax:* (01) 423369; (01) 200631
Web Site: www.usj.edu.1b/ecolede
Key Personnel
Contact: M Henri Awaiss

Societe Francaise des Traducteurs
Affiliate of Federation Internationale der Traducteurs (FIT)
22 Rue des Martyrs, 75009 Paris
Tel: (01) 48784332 *Fax:* (01) 44530114
E-mail: sft@sft.fr
Web Site: www.sft.fr
Key Personnel
President: Suzanne Boizard
Vice President: Marie-Christine Garcin
Secretary General: Mirella Lamolie
Editor-in-Chief: Maurice Morvillez *Tel:* (01) 47750625 *E-mail:* morvillez@aol.com
French Union of Translators.
Publication(s): *Traduire* (quarterly)

Germany

BDU, see Bundesverband der Dolmetscher und Ubersetzer eV (BDU)

Bundesverband der Dolmetscher und Ubersetzer eV (BDU) (German Association of Interpreters & Translators)
Kurfuerstendamm 170, 10707 Berlin
Tel: (030) 88712830 *Fax:* (030) 88712840

GERMANY

E-mail: bdue-bgs@t-online.de
Web Site: www.bdue.de
Key Personnel
President: Prof Dr Ulrich Daum
Secretary-General: Mary Hoecker
Publication(s): *Mitteilungsblatt fuer Dolmetscher und Uebersetzer - MDU*

VDU, see Verband deutschsprachiger Uebersetzer literarischer und wissenschaftlicher Werke eV (VDUe)

Verband deutschsprachiger Uebersetzer literarischer und wissenschaftlicher Werke eV (VDUe) (Association of German-speaking Translators of Literary & Scientific Works)
Chausseestr 111 (Raum 230), 10115 Berlin
Tel: (030) 2829331 *Fax:* (030) 2829331
E-mail: kvschweder@aol.com
Key Personnel
Dir: Dr Burkhart Kroeber

Ghana

Bureau of Ghana Languages
PO Box 1851, Accra
Tel: (021) 64130; (021) 65194; (021) 65461 ext 514
Also Publisher.
Branch Office(s)
PO Box 177, Tamale, Northern Region

Greece

EEML, see Elliniki Etaireia Metafraston Logotechnias

Elliniki Etaireia Metafraston Logotechnias (Hellenic Society of Translators of Literature)
Tsakona 7, Pal Psychico, 154 52 Athens
Tel: (01) 6717466 *Fax:* (01) 6776912
Key Personnel
President: Dr Vassilis Vitsaxis
General Secretary: Costas Assimekopoulos
Founded: 1983
Also publish Greek Letters Yearbook containing translations in English, French, German, Italian & Spanish of contemporary Greek literature.
Publication(s): *Greek Letters Yearly* (in English, French, Spanish Italian & German)
Membership(s): Federation of International Translators

Hong Kong

KAMS Information & Publishing Ltd
PO Box 72050, Kowloon Central Post Office, Kowloon
Tel: 23889172 *Fax:* 27716403
E-mail: kamsinfo@hkstar.com
Web Site: kamsinfo.com
Key Personnel
Project Dir: Kam-sun Yiu
Founded: 1989
Specialize in editing translation & publishing services in more than 20 languages.

KCL Language Consultancy Ltd
18/F Grand View Commercial Centre, 29-31 Sugar St, Causeway Bay
Tel: (02) 8811368 *Fax:* (02) 8080389
E-mail: kcl@iohk.com
Key Personnel
Dir: Karen Chan

Hungary

Magyar Iroszoevetseg Koenyvtara
Bajza u 18, Budapest 1062
Tel: (01) 3228840 *Fax:* (01) 213419
Key Personnel
President: Bela Pomogats
Library of Hungarian Writers' Union.

India

Amerind Publishing Co (P) Ltd
66 Janpath, 2nd floor, New Delhi 110001
Tel: (011) 3324578; (011) 3320518 *Cable:* INDAMER
Key Personnel
Dir: Mohan Primlani; Raju Primlani; Vijay Primlani
Translating Russian, German, Japanese, French.

Indian National Scientific Documentation Centre (INSDOC)
14 Satsang Vihar Marg, New Delhi 110067
Tel: (011) 660141 *Fax:* (011) 6862228
E-mail: mcs@sirnet.ernet.in
Web Site: www.insdoc.org
Telex: 031-73099 *Cable:* INSDOC, NEW DELHI
Key Personnel
Dir: Prof T Vishwanathan
Group Head: Mr D N Gupta; Mr J M Bhardwaj; Mr On Chaddha
Translating European & Asian languages into English; specializes in library automation, computer networking & database design; national member of FID.
Publication(s): *Annals of Library Science & Documentation*; *Database on Indian Patents (IN-PAT)*; *Databases - Current Contents of Indian Journals*; *Directory of Indian Scientific Periodicals*; *Directory of Scientific Research Institutions in India*; *Indian Science Abstracts*; *Medical & Aromatic Plants Abstracts (MAPA)*; *Metallurgy Index*; *National Union Catalogue of Scientific Serials in India (NUCSSI)*; *Polymer Science Database*
Branch Office(s)
Bangalore
Calcutta
Madras

National Social Science Documentation Centre
35 Ferozeshah Rd, New Delhi 110001
Tel: (011) 3383091; (011) 3385959; (011) 3073437; (011) 3073438; (011) 3073563
Fax: (011) 3381571
E-mail: nassdocigss@hotmail.com
Web Site: www.icssr.org/nassdoc.htm *Cable:* ICSORES
Key Personnel
Chief Executive: K G Tyagi
Deputy Dir: Mrs O K Choudhry *Tel:* (011) 3381987
Founded: 1970
Specializing in serving the information needs of social scientists in India. Provides library & references services, literature search from digital databases & from CD-ROMs in social sciences. Compile short bibliographies on demand for scholars on the topic of their research interest; provides photocopies of documents available in the library as well as from documents procured on interlibrary loan. Gives grant for bibliographical & documentation projects. Study grant is given to doctoral students for collection of material pertaining to their research work from various libraries located anywhere in India. Grant/financial assistance is provided in the form of bulk purchase of bibliographies, directories & reference sources in social sciences & also in the acquisition of theses. Maintains a depository of periodicals & unpublished dissertations & reports for reference purposes. Organizes short term training courses to expose research scholars, social scientists, librarians & information professionals with the latest information technology to access digital, social science information.
Specializes in Documentation & information support to social scientists.
Publication(s): *Aged in India: An Annotated Bibliography*; *Agriculture*; *Aquisition Update* (journal); *Banks & Banking*; *Bibliographical Reprints*; *Bibliography on India in 2000 AD (with abstracts)*; *Conference Alert* (4 times/yr, journal); *Annotated Index of Indian Social Science Journals* (4 times/yr, journal); *Directory of Indian Social Science Periodicals*; *Directory of Social Science Libraries & Information Centres in India*; *Documents in Micro Form: A List of Resources at SSDC, JNU, University of Bombay, ICSSR Regional Centre, Calcutta*; *Family Welfare Education in India: A Bibliography*; *Foreign Collaboration*; *ICSSR Directory of Asian Social Science Research & Training Institutions/Organisations in India*; *ICSSR Directory of Social Science Research & Training Institutions in India*; *Index to Indian Periodicals: Sociology & Psychology 1886-1970*; *Indian Education Index (1947-1978)*; *Indian Tribes*; *Labour & Labouring Class*; *Mohandas Karamchand Gandhi: Bibliography*; *Poverty*; *Public Finance*; *Rural Development*; *Silver Generation in India: A Bibliographical Study*; *Social Science Research*; *Union Catalogue of CD-ROM Databases in Social Science Libraries in India* (catalog); *Union Catalogue of Library Science & Information Publications: Delhi Libraries* (catalog); *Union Catalogue of Reference Books in Delhi Libraries* (catalog); *Union Catalogue of Social Science Periodicals in 32 vols* (catalog); *Women*
Parent Company: Indian Council of Social Science Research, PO Box 10528, Aruna Asaf Ali Marg, New Delhi 11067
Ultimate Parent Company: Government of India, Ministry of Human Resource Development

Ireland

Cumann Aistritheoiri nahEireann, see Irish Translators' Association

Ireland Literature Exchange (Idirmhalartan Litriocht Eireann)
Irish Writers Centre, 19 Parnell Sq, Dublin 1
Tel: (01) 8727900 *Fax:* (01) 8727875
E-mail: info@irelandliterature.com
Web Site: www.irelandliterature.com
Key Personnel
Dir: Dara O'Hare *E-mail:* dara@irelandliterature.com
Administrator: Maire N Dhonnchadha
Founded: 1994

Not-for-profit organization founded to fund translations of literature from Ireland into foreign languages & foreign literature into English & Irish.

Irish Translators' Association
The Irish Writers' Centre, 19 Parnell Sq, Dublin 1
Tel: (01) 8721302 *Fax:* (01) 8726282
E-mail: translation@eircom.net
Web Site: www.homepage.eircom.net/~translation; www.translatorsassociation.ie
Key Personnel
Honorary Secretary: Ms Miriam Lee *Tel:* (01) 2859137
Publication(s): *Transverse*; *Transverse II*

Israel

Freund Publishing House Ltd
PO Box 35010, Tel Aviv 61350
Tel: (03) 562-8540 *Fax:* (03) 562-8538
E-mail: h_freund@netvision.net.il
Web Site: www.angelfire.com/il/feund/
Key Personnel
Man Dir & Publisher: Edmund Freund
Founded: 1968

The Institute for the Translation of Hebrew Literature
23 Baruch Hirsch St, Bnei Brak
Mailing Address: PO Box 10051, Ramat Gan 52001
Tel: (03) 5796830 *Fax:* (03) 5796832
E-mail: litscene@ithl.org.il
Web Site: www.ithl.org.il
Key Personnel
Chairman: Prof Ory Bernstein
Man Dir: Mrs Nilli Cohen
Office Manager: Debbie Dagan
Founded: 1962
Main activities include promotion of modern Hebrew literature & children's literature in translation & serves as literary agent for a large number of Israeli writers & assists in the preparation of anthologies of Hebrew literature. Specializes in Hebrew literature in translation.

Israel Translators' Association
c/o Mrs Ophira Rahat, PO Box 9082, Jerusalem 91090
Tel: (02) 412821
Key Personnel
Chairperson: Ms Ophira Rahat
Association of some 500 translators, mostly freelance. Detailed database of members, with languages & specialties.
Publication(s): *Targima*

Italy

AITI (Associazione Italiana Traduttoried Interpreti)
Mue Vittoria Lo Faro, Via dei Prati, Fiscali 158, 00141 Rome
Tel: (06) 88327535 *Fax:* (06) 88327535
E-mail: aiti@maix.it
Web Site: www.mix.it/AITI
Key Personnel
Chairman: Furio Incolto
Secretary General: Prof Gustavo Dresbach
National Association for Translators and Interpreters.

Mexico

Gibson Golubov & Associates, Translation Services
Minatitlan 68-A, San Jeromino Aculco, Magdalena Contreras, Mexico DF 10400
Tel: (05) 5686240
E-mail: mexlon@compuserve.com
Key Personnel
Contact: Charlotte Broad
English/Spanish translations. Specialize in the area of the humanities, particularly in gender studies, literary theory & criticism, translations theory, post-colonial studies, politics, history, etc. However, consideration will be given to other sources.
Branch Office(s)
46a Stoke Newington Church St, London N16 0LU, United Kingdom, Contact: Nattie Golubov *Tel:* (020) 7241 6101 *E-mail:* n.l.golubov@qmw.ac.uk

Nigeria

Igbo Language Translation Agency
c/o University Publishing Co Ltd, 11 Central Schools Rd, Onitsha
Mailing Address: PO Box 386, Onitsha
Tel: (046) 230013
Key Personnel
Dir-General: F Chidozie Ogbalu
Publication(s): *M B E D I O G U-La-Tortue* (published in Igbo)

Norway

The Norwegian Association of Literary Translators
Raadhusgaten 7, Postboks 579 Sentrum, N-0150 Oslo
Tel: 22478090 *Fax:* 22420356
Web Site: www.boknett.no/no
Key Personnel
Contact: Hilde Sveinsson *E-mail:* hilde@translators.no
Founded: 1948

Poland

Stowarzyszenie Tlumaczy Polskich (Association of Polish Translators & Interpreters)
ul Hoza 29/31 m 92, 00-521 Warsaw
Tel: (02) 6215678; (02) 6212772 *Fax:* (02) 6215678
Key Personnel
President: Wojciech Gilewski
Vice President: Ewa Karska
Association of Polish Translators & Interpreters.
Branch Office(s)
Oddzial Warszawski, OO-684 Warsaw *Fax:* 00-21-217376

STP, see Stowarzyszenie Tlumaczy Polskich

Spain

Tek Translation International SA
OneWorld Localization Center, Centro Empresarial El Plantio Ochandiano, 10, 28023 Madrid
Tel: (091) 4141111 *Fax:* (091) 4144444
E-mail: sales@tektrans.com
Web Site: www.tektrans.com
Key Personnel
Group Head: Alba Guix
Account Manager: Veit Gunther
Technical specialists in over 100 languages, including Chinese, Arabic, Japanese, Russian.

Sweden

Exportradet Spraktjanst AB
Storgatan 19, S-114 85 Stockholm
Mailing Address: Box 5513, S-114 85 Stockholm
Tel: (08) 7838500 *Fax:* (08) 7838550
E-mail: sed@swedishtrade.se
Web Site: www.swedishtrade.com
Telex: 15679
Key Personnel
President: Gunnar Lindberg
Translating & Interpreting Service of the Swedish Trade Council (See Sveriges Exportrad under Publishers).

Foereningen Auktoriserade Translatorer
Rimbogatan 19, S-753 24 Uppsala
Tel: (018) 858 355869 *Fax:* (018) 858 355869
Key Personnel
President: Adolf Dahl
Secretary: Paula Ehrnebo; Gerda Billig *Fax:* (08) 7788205
The Federation of Authorized Translators in Sweden.
Publication(s): *FATaburen* (in Swedish, 4 issues annually)

Switzerland

Association Suisse des Traducteurs Terminologues et Interpretes (ASTTI)
Postgasse 17, 3011 Bern
Tel: (031) 3123303 *Fax:* (031) 3121250
Key Personnel
President: Doris Schmidt
Vice President: Henry Braun; David Fuhruann
Swiss Association of Translators and Interpreters.

Taiwan, Province of China

National Institute for Compilation and Translation
247 Choushan Rd, Taipei
Fax: (02) 23629256
Key Personnel
Dir: Nancy Chao Li-Yun
Publication(s): *Counter Attack*

United Republic of Tanzania

Baraza la Kiswahili la Taifa
SLP 4766, Dar Es Salaam
Tel: (051) 23452; (051) 24139
Key Personnel
Chief Editor: Mastidia Kailembo Mbeo
Translations in English, Kiswahili, Arabic, French, Portuguese and Spanish.

United Kingdom

Ad-Ex Translations Ltd
296 Kingston Rd, London SW20 8LZ
Mailing Address: PO Box 428, London SW20 8LZ
Tel: (020) 8542 7809 *Fax:* (020) 8543 1253
E-mail: adx@cable.inet.co.uk
Key Personnel
President: Mr W Brodnicki
Business Manager: George M Dudzinski
Service includes medical & pharmaceutical translations in English, German, French, Spanish & Italian.

Deborah Adlam
Member of Edinburgh University & Oxford Universities
41 West Savile Terrace, Edinburgh EH9 3DP
Tel: (0131) 6676048
Key Personnel
Contact: Deborah Adlam
E-mail: deborah_adlam@hotmail.com
Founded: 1982
Translation into English carried out from Russian, French, Latin & Classical Ancient Greek. Academic, literary, medical, legal & theological texts. Research work also carried out.
Specializes in 12th-19th century Latin documents, theses & books, Classical Greek & Latin texts.

AE Technical Translation Services
Ty Coch, Betws Garmon, Caernarfon, Gwynedd LL54 7AQ
Tel: (01286) 650667 *Fax:* (01286) 650500
Key Personnel
Contact: Debra Lockett
Services include interpreting, laser printing, typesetting, color printing, & translations in over 100 language combinations, specializing in rare languages.

Alpnet UK
Centre Tower, Whitgift Centre, Croydon CR9 3QJ
Tel: (0181) 6883852 *Fax:* (0181) 6888888
E-mail: croydon@alpnet.com
Key Personnel
Dir: Ray King
Member of the Alpnet Translation Services Network.
Specializes in Services include foreign language publishing, translating & interpreting.
Branch Office(s)
Birmingham
Manchester
Newcastle
Nottingham
Leeds

Amigo Translations Ltd
136 Dove House Lane, Solihull, West Midlands B91 2EW
Tel: (0121) 7426905 *Fax:* (0121) 7420583
Key Personnel
Man Dir: Dr Arthur Rothwell
Translations in English, Portuguese, Brazilian or Lusitanian, & Spanish only.

ARADCO VSI Ltd
132 Cleveland St, London W1P 6AB
Tel: (020) 7692 7700 *Fax:* (020) 7692 7711
Key Personnel
Contact: R Dawood

Asgard Publishing Services
1a Headingley Mount, Leeds LS6 3EL
Tel: (0113) 2741037 *Fax:* (0113) 2741037
E-mail: info@asgardpublishing.co.uk
Web Site: www.asgardpublishing.co.uk
Key Personnel
Partner: Philip Gardner *E-mail:* philip.gardner@asgardpublishing.co.uk; Allan Scott *E-mail:* allan.scott@asgardpublishing.co.uk; Andrew Shaddeton *E-mail:* allan.scott@asgardpublishing.co.uk
Services include editorial, translation, audio-visual & multimedia.

Associated Translation & Typesetting
Alexander House, 64 Robin Hood Lane, Hall Green, Birmingham B28 0JT
Tel: (0121) 603 6344 *Fax:* (0121) 603 6399
E-mail: ATTEuro@aol.com (European translation); ATTAsia@aol.com (Eastern/Asian translation); ATTgraphic@jaure.demon.com (web design/graphics)
Key Personnel
Dir: Mr S Ahmed
Specialize in translation & typesetting into five popular Indian Languages. Also typesetting of European, Russian, Vietnamese, Chinese & other Indian languages.

Castle Translations
11a Castle Hill, Lancaster LA1 1YS
Tel: (01524) 841169 *Fax:* (01524) 381721
E-mail: info@castletranslations.co.uk
Web Site: www.castletranslations.co.uk
Key Personnel
Owner: Lynda Burke
Founded: 1986
Translating & interpreting of all languages; language training.

CBA Translations
Straightway Head, Whimple Mr, Exeter EX5 2QT
Tel: (01) 1404822284 *Fax:* (01) 1404823136
E-mail: enquires@cbatranslations.freeserve.co.uk
Web Site: www.cbatranslations.freeserve.co.uk
Key Personnel
Off Manager, Bristol: Anna Swoboda
Man Dir, Basingstoke: Gerd Ziemer
Branch Office(s)
CBA Translations, 20 Kingsclere Rd, Basingstoke RG21 2UQ

Chinese Marketing & Communications
16 Nicholas St, 5th Floor, Manchester M1 4EJ
Tel: (0161) 2373821 *Fax:* (0161) 2367558
E-mail: info@chinese-marketing.com
Web Site: www.chinese-marketing.com
Key Personnel
Editor: Shen Yan; Jamie Kenny
Project Manager: David Starway
Marketing materials in Chinese language, market research & advertising agency.

Publication(s): *Chinese Business Impact* (English, monthly); *Siyu Chinese Times* (Chinese, monthly)
Branch Office(s)
First Floor West, 90-98 Shaftesbury Ave, London W1V 7DM

Colrick & Associates Ltd
Hethe Pl, Hartfield Rd, Cowden near Edenbridge, Kent TN8 7DZ
Tel: (07000) 265742 *Fax:* (07000) 265741
Telex: 885798
Key Personnel
Dir: J Gigney *E-mail:* jg@colrick.demon.co.uk

Conference Interpreters Group
10 Barley Mow Passage, Chiswick, London W4 4PH
Tel: (0208) 9950801 *Fax:* (0208) 7421066
E-mail: cig@clara.net
Key Personnel
Executive Secretary: Andrew Brock
E-mail: abrock3650@aol.com

Deutschklub
64 Ventnor Rd, Linthorpe, Middlesbrough TS5 6DU
Tel: (01642) 813467 *Fax:* (01642) 865943
Key Personnel
Contact: Rosie O'Hara *E-mail:* rosie.ohara@deutschklub.onyxnet.co.uk
Provide translation, interpreting & tuition into & out of German only.

Dutch Connection
196 Prestbury Rd, Macclesfield SK10 3BS
Tel: (01625) 610613 *Fax:* (01625) 610613
E-mail: 100345.14@compuserve.com
Key Personnel
Contact: M Kuik
Founded: 1982

East Word
170a Kennington Park Rd, London SE11 4BT
Tel: (020) 7582 9349 *Fax:* (020) 7793 0474
E-mail: info@eastword.uk.com
Key Personnel
Dir: Gladys Ko
Oriental language translation including Chinese, Japanese, Korean, Thai & Vietnamese.

Esperanto Translating Service
Kebbell House, Watford WD1 5BE
Mailing Address: 137 Penrose Ave, Watford WD1 5AA
Tel: (0181) 4282829 *Fax:* (0181) 4282829
E-mail: espero@moose.co.uk
Key Personnel
Owner & Manager: Peter W Miles
Also provides guide lecturers in approximately 35 languages.

Euro Translations
6 Field End, Coulsdon, Surrey CR5 2AY
Tel: (0208) 6686133 *Fax:* (0208) 6686133
E-mail: eurotrans@lineone.net
Key Personnel
Owner: Mrs P Kain

First Edition Translations Ltd
6 Wellington Court, Wellington St, Cambridge CB1 1HZ
Tel: (01223) 356733 *Fax:* (01223) 321488
E-mail: info@firstedit.co.uk
Key Personnel
Dir: Sheila Waller *E-mail:* sheila@firstedit.co.uk
Specializing in translations of all material for publication. Services include copy-editing, proof-reading, indexing, interpreting, voice-overs, typesetting.

& ASSOCIATIONS

Franco-English Bureau
32 Stanwick Mansions, Stanwick Rd, London W14 8TP
Tel: (020) 7603 5390 *Fax:* (020) 7602 1592
Key Personnel
Proprietor: Anne Marie Richardson
  E-mail: amrichardson1@compuserve.com
Specializes in Translations into & from French & English.

Michael Fulton Partners
The Chase, Behoes Lane, Woodcote, Reading, Berks RG8 0PP
Tel: (01491) 680042 *Fax:* (01491) 680085
Key Personnel
Senior Partner: Dr Michael Fulton
  E-mail: mike@fultonm.fsngt.co.uk
Founded: 1968
Translations from Spanish & Portuguese (technical, scientific, commercial & patents subject matter); Spanish interpreting.

Gibson Golubov & Associates, Translation Services
46a Stoke Newington Church St, London N16 0LU
Tel: (020) 7241 6101
Key Personnel
Contact: Nattie Golubov *E-mail:* n.l.golubov@qmw.ac.uk
English/Spanish translations. Specialize in the area of the humanities, particularly in gender studies, literary theory & criticism, translations theory, post-colonial studies, politics, history, etc. However, consideration will be given to other sources.
Branch Office(s)
Minatitlan 68-A, San Jeromino Aculco, Magdalena Contreras, Mexico DF 10400, Mexico, Contact: Charlotte Broad *Tel:* (05) 5686240
  E-mail: mexlon@compuserve.com

GLS Language Services
The Pentagon Centre, 36 Washington St, Glasgow G3 8AZ
Tel: (0141) 2268440 *Fax:* (0141) 2268441
E-mail: glslanguageservices@compuserve.com
Key Personnel
Partner: Dagmar Fortsch

Greek Institute
34 Bush Hill Rd, London N21 2DS
Tel: (020) 8360 7968 *Fax:* (020) 8360 7968
Key Personnel
Dir: Dr Kypros Tofallis
Publication(s): *Greek Institute Review* (journal, quarterly)

Greek Translations
31 Athenaeum Rd, London N20 9AL
Tel: (020) 8445 3324 *Fax:* (020) 8446 1448
Key Personnel
Manager: Zannetos Tofallis

Hook & Hatton Ltd
34 Central Ave, Whitehills, Northampton NN2 8DZ
Tel: (01604) 847278 *Fax:* (01604) 821486
E-mail: hook_hatton@compuserve.com
Key Personnel
Chief Executive: Terence Lewis
Specialize in translation of Scientific & Technical Texts.

Indo Lingua Services Ltd
112 Leighton Rd, Kentish Town, London NW5 2RG
Tel: (0171) 4822666 *Fax:* (0171) 4852667
E-mail: indolingua@compuserve.com
Key Personnel
Man Dir: Prithvi Raj

Consultant: Pyare Shivpuri
Branch Office(s)
17B Ramesh Nagar, New Delhi 110 015
  Tel: (011) 5461055 *Fax:* (011) 5461055

Institute of Linguists
Saxon House, 48 Southwark St, London SE1 1UN
Tel: (020) 7940 3100 *Fax:* (020) 7940 3101
E-mail: info@iol.orgk.uk
Key Personnel
President: Prof J Drew
Chair: Dr J M Mitchell
Dir: E H F Ostarhild
Publication(s): *Basic Handbook for the Training of Public Service Interpreters*; *Bilingual in Britain*; *Careers Using Languages*; *Directory of Members 1996*; *Glossary of Educational Terms*; *Glossary of Social Services Terms*; *Languages & Your Career*; *Non-English Speakers & the English Legal System*; *Talk It Through*; *The Linquist* (bimonthly journal)

Institute of Translation & Interpreting
377 City Rd, London EC1V 1NDL
Tel: (020) 7713 7600 *Fax:* (020) 7713 7650
E-mail: info@iti.org.uk
Web Site: www.iti.org.uk
Key Personnel
Secretary: Jane Hibbert

Intercultural Networking Ltd (ICN)
133 John Trundle Court, London EC2Y 8DJ
Tel: (020) 7628 5876 *Fax:* (020) 7628 9147
E-mail: icn@dircon.co.uk
Web Site: www.users.dircon.co.uk/~icn/
Key Personnel
Man Dir: Atsuko Takenaka
Dir: Chieko Takanaka
Specialize in nonfiction book translation Japanese-English through to camera-ready copy.

International Languages & Translations School
365 Eugton Rd, London NW1 3AR
Tel: (020) 8882 3362 *Fax:* (020) 8882 3362
Key Personnel
Principal: Mr Li Ke-Mo
Tuition in 80 languages by correspondence, oral, telephone, fax & cassette courses. Translation, interpreting in 80 Oriental, European & African languages.

Key Language Services
Linford Forum, 32 Rockingham Drive, Linford Wood, Milton Keynes, Bucks MK14 6LY
Tel: (01908) 232101 *Fax:* (01908) 232815
E-mail: keylanguages@btinternet.com
Key Personnel
Partner: S H Clutton

Language Consultancy Services
138b Melrose Ave, London NW2 4JX
Tel: (020) 8450 5344 *Fax:* (020) 8452 9005
Key Personnel
Contact: Lucia Alvarez de Toledo

Legal & Technical Translation Services
13 Earl St, Maidstone, Kent ME14 1PL
Tel: (01622) 751537 *Fax:* (01622) 754431
E-mail: ltts@compuserve.com
Key Personnel
Dir: J M Sallares

Lexus Ltd
13 Newton Terrace, Glasgow G3 7PJ
Tel: (0141) 2215266 *Fax:* (0141) 2263139
E-mail: pt@lexus.win-uk.net

Telex: 9312134404
Key Personnel
Man Dir: Peter Terrell

Link Up Mitaka Ltd
4-12 Morton St, Leamington Spa, Warwicks CV32 5SY
Tel: (01926) 311126 *Fax:* (01926) 332990
E-mail: trans@leamington.linkup.co.uk
Web Site: www.mitaka.co.uk
Key Personnel
Administration Manager: Astird Markowski
Specialists in Far Eastern Languages.
Branch Office(s)
Mitaka BV, Herengracht 213, 1016 B9 Amsterdam

Liston Translations
169 Peckham Rye, London SE15 3HZ
Tel: (020) 7732 9431 *Fax:* (020) 7277 6862
Key Personnel
Contact: Patricia Wheeler
Legal Translation Agency.

Peak Translations
Shepherd, Kettleshulme SK23 7QU
Tel: (01663) 732074 *Fax:* (01663) 735499
E-mail: info@peak-translations.co.uk
Web Site: www.peak-translations.co.uk
Key Personnel
Contact: Ian Gordon *E-mail:* ian@peak-translations.co.uk
Founded: 1978
Also supply software translation tools for professional translators.

Marilyn Potts International Language Consultants
Member of Institute of Translation & Interpreting
St Thomas St Stables, St Thomas St, Newcastle-upon-Tyne NE1 4LE
Tel: (0191) 2324895; (0191) 2221775 *Fax:* (0191) 2616426
E-mail: 101341.533@compuserve.com
Web Site: www.marilyn-potts.co.uk
Key Personnel
Contact: Marilyn Potts
Founded: 1987
Services include translations & interpreting
Membership(s): Institute of Translation & Interpreting

Satrap Publishing & Translation
London House, Suite 21, 271 King St, London W6 9LZ
Tel: (020) 8748 9397 *Fax:* (020) 8748 9394
E-mail: satrap@btinternet.com
Key Personnel
Man Dir: Ahmad Vahdat
Founded: 1987
A single source for translation, typesetting & publishing marketing. Literary & advertising literature in major languages of the world. Specializes in Middle & Far Eastern, East & West European languages.

SEL, see Services for Export & Language (SEL)

SELTA, see Swedish-English Literary Translators' Association (SELTA)

Services for Export & Language (SEL)
Maxwell Bldg, University of Salford, Manchester M5 4WT
Tel: (0161) 7457480 *Fax:* (0161) 2955110
E-mail: sel@salford.ac.uk
Web Site: www.sel-uk.com
Key Personnel
Translations Manager: Patrick Murphy *E-mail:* p.m.murphy@salford.ac.uk

UNITED KINGDOM

Founded: 1986
Service includes translation, foreign language training & interpreting.

Swedish-English Literary Translators' Association (SELTA)
14 Grennell Close, Sutton, Surrey SM1 3LU
Tel: (020) 8641 8176 *Fax:* (020) 8641 8176
Web Site: www.swedishbookreview.com
Key Personnel
Honorary Secretary: Tom Geddes
Founded: 1982
SELTA aims to promote the publication of Swedish literature in English & to represent the interests of those involved in its translation.
Publication(s): *Swedish Book Review* (twice a year)

TransAction Translators Ltd
Redlands, Tapton House Rd, Broomhill, Sheffield, S Yorks S10 5BY
Tel: (0114) 2661103 *Fax:* (0114) 2670465
E-mail: transaction@transaction.co.uk
Key Personnel
Contact: Maryline Tergella

Translators Association
84 Drayton Gardens, London SW10 9SB
Tel: (020) 7373 6642 *Fax:* (020) 7373 5768
E-mail: info@societyofauthors.org
Web Site: www.societyofauthors.org/translators
Key Personnel
Secretary: Dorothy Sym
The Translators Association is a specialist group within The Society of Authors.
Publication(s): *In Other Words*

UPS Translations
Member of ATC, ITI, ISO9002
111 Baker St, London W1U 6RR
Tel: (020) 7837 8300 *Fax:* (020) 7486 3272
E-mail: production@upstranslations.com
Web Site: www.upstranslations.com
Key Personnel
Chairman & Man Dir: Bernard Silver
   E-mail: info@upstranslations.com
Head of Translation: Sarah Parkhurst
Founded: 1947
Translation company.
Specializes in Translation for publishing, film, video & the media.
Parent Company: United Publicity Services PLC

R Vreeland & Co
Garden Studios, 11-14 Betterton St, London WC2H 9BP
Tel: (020) 7242 8721 *Fax:* (020) 7379 0801
Key Personnel
Contact: R Vreeland

Sally Walker Language Services
43 St Nicholas St, Bristol BS1 1TP
Tel: (0117) 9291594 *Fax:* (0117) 9290633
E-mail: swls43@aol.com
Web Site: www.sallywalker.co.uk
Key Personnel
Dir: Sally Walker
Marketing Dir: David J Poole
Founded: 1969
Translation & Interpreting Service.
Specializes in 70 languages, all subjects.
Publication(s): *Sallylang* (company journal)

Branch Office(s)
244S The Exchange, Mount Stuart Square, Cardiff CF1 6ED
25 Beaufort Rd, Clifton, Bristol BS8 2JX

Wessex Translations
Member of Association of Translation Companies Institute of Translations & Interpreters
Unit A1, The Premier Centre, Abbey Park Industrial Estate, Romsey, Southampton SO51 9AQ
Tel: (01794) 512756 *Fax:* (01794) 830145
E-mail: sales@wt-languagemanagement.com
Key Personnel
Partner: Paul Stewart *E-mail:* paul@wt-languagemanagement.com
Contact: Jonathan Nater
Translations & interpreting software localisation, language training, transcription, typesetting, telemarketing, editing & proofreading, voice-overs, copywriting, web page translation.

Christine Wood Translations
7 Kings Court, Sedbergh, Cumbria LA10 5BJ
Tel: (015396) 21170 *Fax:* (015396) 21300
E-mail: cwtrans@daelnet.co.uk
Key Personnel
Dir: Christine Wood
Translations in over 30 languages; literary, commercial, technical & legal topics.

WT Language Management, see Wessex Translations

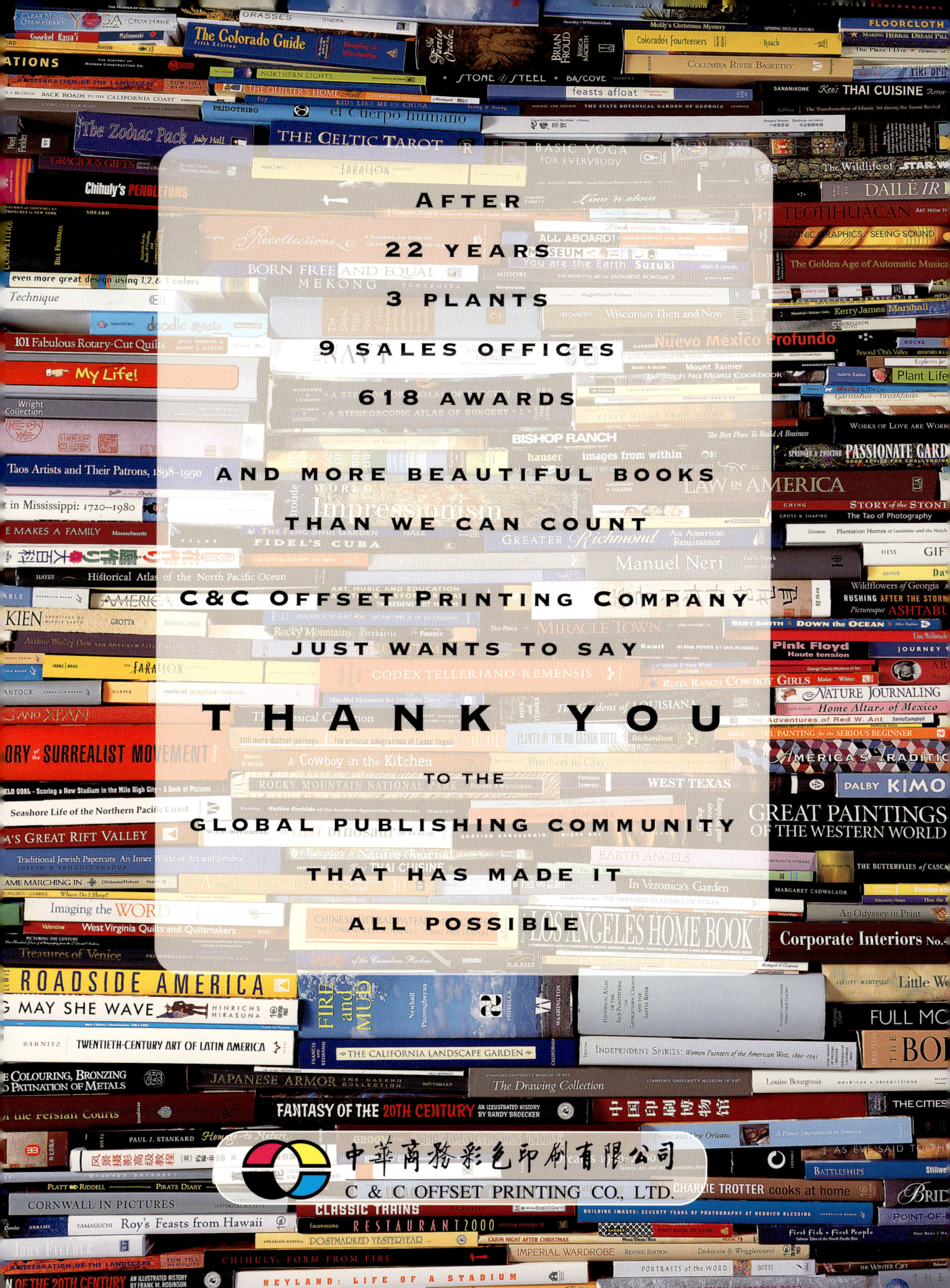

After
22 years
3 plants
9 sales offices
618 awards
and more beautiful books
than we can count
C&C Offset Printing Company
just wants to say

THANK YOU

to the
global publishing community
that has made it
all possible

中華商務彩色印刷有限公司
C & C OFFSET PRINTING CO., LTD.

中華商務彩色印刷有限公司
C & C OFFSET PRINTING CO., LTD.

MANUFACTURING PLANTS

HONG KONG
C & C Offset Printing Co., Ltd.
C & C Building, 36 Ting Lai Road
Tai Po, New Territories, Hong Kong
Tel: 852-2666-4988
Fax: 852-2666-4938
E-mail: offsetprinting@candcprinting.com

GUANGDONG
C & C Joint Printing Co. (Guangdong), Ltd.
Chunhu Industrial Estate Pinghu
Long Gang, Shenzhen, 518111, PRC
Tel: (86-755) 845-8333
Fax: (86-755) 845-9911
E-mail: guangdong@candcprinting.com

BEIJING
C & C Joint Printing Co. (Beijing), Ltd.
No.3 Donghuan North Road
Beijing Economic & Technological Development Area
Beijing 100176, PRC
Tel: (86-10) 678-72862
Fax: (86-10) 678-72861
E-mail: beijing@candcprinting.com

SALES OFFICES

PORTLAND, OR
C & C Offset Printing Co. (USA), Inc.
Post Office Box 82037
Portland, OR 97282-0037 USA
Tel: (503) 233-1834
Fax: (503) 233-7815
Email: portlandinfor@ccoffset.com

NEW YORK, NY
C & C Offset Printing Co. (NY), Inc.
401 Broadway, Suite 2015
New York, NY 10013-3005 USA
Tel: (212) 431-4210
Fax: (212) 431-3960
E-mail: newyorkinfo@ccoffset.com

UNITED KINGDOM
C & C Offset Printing Co. (U.K.), Ltd.
2 New Burlington Street, 4th Floor
W1S 2JE, London, England
Tel: 0207-287-7787
Fax: 0207-287-7187
E-mail: tracy@candcoffset.co.uk

TOKYO
C & C Printing Japan Co., Ltd.
2-6-12 Hitotsubashi, Tozaido Building 3/F
Chiyoda-Ku, Tokyo 101-0003, Japan
Tel: (81-3) 5216-4580
Fax: (81-3) 5216-4610
E-mail: mail@candcprinting.co.jp

BEIJING
C & C Joint Printing Co. (Guangdong), Ltd.
Room 706, Intercontinental Building
16 An Wai An De Road, Dongcheng District,
Beijing, 100011, PRC
Tel: (86-10) 8488-2336
Fax: (86-10) 8488-2336
E-mail: beijing@candcprinting.com

CHANGSHA
C&C Joint Printing Co.,(Guangdong), Ltd.
Rm 1218, The Building of Changsha City Commercial Bank No.1
Frong Middle Road, Changsha, Hunan 410005, PRC
tel: (86-731) 225-0288
Fax: (86-731) 225-0178
C & C Joint Printing Co., (Guangdong) Ltd.
Email: changsha@candcprinting.com

GUANGZHOU
C & C Joint Printing Co. (Guangdong), Ltd.
Room 1511, Hua Xin Building East Block, 2 Shuiyin Road
Huanshi East Guangzhou, 510010 PRC
Tel: (86-20) 3760-0979
Fax: (86-20) 3760-0977
E-mail: guangzhou@candcprinting.com

SHANGHAI
C & C Joint Printing Co. (Guangdong), Ltd.
Room 304, Fong Fa Building, No. 29 Lane 165
Dongzhu Anbin Road, Shanghai, 200050 PRC
Tel: (86-21) 6240-1305
Fax: (86-21) 6240-2090
E-mail: shanghai@candcprinting.com

XIAN
C & C Joint Printing Co., (Guangdong) Ltd.
10 Xuanfengquiao, Jian Guo Road
Xian, 71000,PRC
Tel: (86-29) 741-8407
Fax: (86-29) 743-5730
E-mail: xian@candcprinting.co

ISO 14001 :1996
Certificate No. CC1617
C&C Joint Printing Co.,(HK) Ltd.

ISO 9002: 1994
Certificate No: CC260

SUBSIDIARIES OF C&C JOINT PRINTING CO., (H.K.) LTD.

Manufacturing

Complete Book Manufacturing

This section includes companies throughout the world that offer complete book manufacturing services. Those U.S. and Canadian companies with 10% or more of their business done outside North America are also included.

Australia

ACI International Ltd
390 St Kilda Rd, 15th floor, Melbourne 3004
Tel: (03) 6058555
Key Personnel
Chairman: Brian W Scott
Man Dir, Security Printing & Computer Services Group: I D Reid

Austria

ADEVA (Akademische Druck-u Verlagsanstalt)
Auersperggasse 12, A-8010 Graz
Mailing Address: Postfach 598, A-8011 Graz
Tel: (0316) 3644 *Fax:* (0316) 364424
E-mail: info@adeva.com
Web Site: www.adeva.com *Cable:* ADEVA-GRAZ
Key Personnel
Dir: Dr Ursula Struzl
Founded: 1949
Print Runs: 300 min - 10,000 max
Business from Other Countries: 80%
Branch Office(s)
Purgleitnergasse 10, Ecke Marburgerstrabe, A-8042 Graz

Akademische Druck- u Verlagsanstalt, see ADEVA (Akademische Druck-u Verlagsanstalt)

Dr Paul Struzl GmbH, see ADEVA (Akademische Druck-u Verlagsanstalt)

Belgium

Drukkerij Lannoo NV (Lanno Printers)
Kasteelstr 97, B-8700 Tielt
Tel: (051) 424211 *Fax:* (051) 407070
E-mail: lannoo@lannooprint.be
Web Site: www.lannooprint.be
Key Personnel
General Manager & Marketing Dir: Stefaan Lannoo *E-mail:* stefaan.lannoo@lannooprint.be
Founded: 1909
Turnaround: 10 Workdays
Print Runs: 100 min - 1,000,000 max
Business from Other Countries: 30%

Canada

Aardvark Enterprises
Division of Speers Investments Ltd
204 Millbank Dr SW, Calgary, AB T2Y 2H9
Tel: 403-256-4639
Key Personnel
Pres: J Alvin Speers
Founded: 1970 (Small Press Pioneers)
Turnaround: 30 Workdays
Print Runs: 10 min - 1,000 max
Business from Other Countries: 25%

Friesens Corp
One Printers Way, Altona, MB R0G 0B0
Tel: 204-324-6401 *Fax:* 204-324-1333
E-mail: friesens@friesens.com
Key Personnel
Pres: David Friesen *E-mail:* davidf@friesens.com
Sales Mgr: Frank Friesen *E-mail:* frankf@friesens.com
Founded: 1907
Turnaround: 20-25 Workdays
Business from Other Countries: 30%
Branch Office(s)
10011 167 Court W, Lakeville, MN 55044, United States, Renee Craft *Tel:* 612-435-1997 *Fax:* 612-898-0227 *E-mail:* reneecraft@earthlink.net
Four Colour Imports, 2843 Brownboro Rd, No 102, Louisville, KY 40206, United States, George Dick *Tel:* 502-896-9644 *Fax:* 502-896-9594 *E-mail:* georged@friesens.com
Spectrum Book, 2300 Bethards Dr, Suite C, Santa Rosa, CA 95405-8568, United States, Duncan McCallum *Tel:* 707-542-6044 *Fax:* 707-542-6045 *E-mail:* specbooks@aol.com
Membership(s): BMI

Mad Dog Design Connection Inc
46 Esgore Dr, Toronto, ON M5M 3R4
Tel: 416-467-0090 *Fax:* 416-484-1140
E-mail: maddogs9@rogers.com
Key Personnel
Owner & Designer: Linda Pellowe
Designer & Digital Artist: David Szolcsanyi
Founded: 1998
Turnaround: As needed/to deadline
Business from Other Countries: 10%

Maracle Press Ltd
1156 King St E, Oshawa, ON L1H 7N4
Mailing Address: Box 606, Oshawa, ON L1H 7N4
Tel: 905-723-3438 *Fax:* 905-428-6024
E-mail: maracle@maraclepress.com
Web Site: www.maraclepress.com
Key Personnel
VP Bus Devt: Ronald G Taylor *E-mail:* rtaylor@maraclepress.com
Founded: 1920
Turnaround: 10 Workdays
Print Runs: 500 min - 500,000 max
Business from Other Countries: 20%
Membership(s): BMI; CPIA; Ontario Printing & Imaging Association; PIA

McLaren Morris & Todd Ltd
Subsidiary of Mail-Well
3270 American Dr, Mississauga, ON L4V 1B5
Tel: 905-677-3592 *Fax:* 905-677-3675
Web Site: www.mmt.ca
Key Personnel
Cont: John Mousmoules *Tel:* 905-677-3592 ext 247 *E-mail:* john@mmt.ca
Pres: Alan George
Contact: Anthony Sgro
Founded: 1956
Turnaround: 15 Workdays
Print Runs: 5,000 min - 1,000,000 max
Business from Other Countries: 10%

PrintWest
1150 Eighth Ave, Regina, SK S4R 1C9
Tel: 306-525-2304 *Fax:* 306-757-2439
E-mail: general@printwest.com
Web Site: www.printwest.com
Key Personnel
CEO: Wayne UnRuh
VP Sales & Mktg: Ken Benson
Founded: 1992
Turnaround: 15 Workdays
Print Runs: 1,000 min - 100,000 max
Business from Other Countries: 15%
Branch Office(s)
Box 2500, 2310 Millar Ave, Saskatoon, SK S7K 2C4 *Tel:* 306-665-3560 *Fax:* 306-653-1255

Productive Publications
PO Box 7200, Sta A, Toronto, ON M5W 1X8
SAN: 117-1712
Tel: 416-483-0634 *Fax:* 416-322-7434
Web Site: www.productivepublications.com
Key Personnel
Owner: Iain Williamson
Founded: 1985
Turnaround: 21 Workdays
Print Runs: 100 min - 1,000 max
Business from Other Countries: 10%

Transcontinental Printing Book Group
Division of Transcontinental Group
395 Lebeau Blvd, St-Laurent, PQ H4N 1S2
Tel: 514-337-8560 *Fax:* 514-339-2252
Web Site: www.transcontinental-gtc.com; www.transcontinental-printing.com

CANADA

Key Personnel
Sr VP, Book Group: Jacques Gregoire
US Sales Mgr: Denis Beaudin *Tel:* 514-339-2220 ext 4101 *E-mail:* beaudind@transcontinental.ca
Founded: 1976
Turnaround: 10 working days casebound; 7-10 working days softcover
Print Runs: 500 min
Business from Other Countries: 30%
Branch Office(s)
614 Yates Ave, Calumet City, IL 60409, United States, Contact: Kristopher D Levy *Tel:* 708-832-1528 *Fax:* 708-832-9510 *E-mail:* kris.levy@transcontinental.ca (Midwest)
3653 W Leland Ave, Suite One W, Chicago, IL 60625, United States, Contact: Tim Taylor *Tel:* 773-583-8155 *Fax:* 773-583-8162 *E-mail:* tim.taylor@transcontinental.com (Midwest)
19 Crown St, Milton, MA 02186-1419, United States, Contact: Mike Gazzola *Tel:* 617-696-1435 *Fax:* 617-696-1025 *E-mail:* mikebook@attbi.com (East Coast)
37 Herman Blvd, Franklin Square, NY 11010, United States, Contact: Tom Malloy *Tel:* 516-775-2980 *Fax:* 516-488-0253 *E-mail:* tmmalloy@aol.com (NY)
245 Eliot St, Ashland, MA 01721, United States, Contact: Ed Catania *Tel:* 508-881-1119 *Fax:* 508-881-7739 *E-mail:* ecatania@attbi.com (East Coast)
3175 Summit Square Dr, Suite C9, Oakton, VA 22124, United States, Contact: David Avesian *Tel:* 703-255-1332 *Fax:* 703-255-1343 *E-mail:* davesian@cox.rr.com (Southeast)
559 Lowrys Rd, Parksville, BC V9P 2R8, Contact: Mike Davies *Tel:* 250-248-9700 *Fax:* 250-248-2353 *E-mail:* bookguys@shaw.ca (West Coast)
15373 Victoria Ave, White Rock, BC V4B 1H1, Contact: Wade Davies *Tel:* 604-535-8800 *Fax:* 604-535-8802 *E-mail:* daviesw@shaw.ca (West Coast)
490 Wilfred Dr, Peterborough, ON K9K 2H1, Contact: Tom Lang *Tel:* 705-760-9594 *Fax:* 705-760-9485 *E-mail:* langt@transcontinental.ca (NY)
395 Lebeau Blvd, St-Laurent, PQ H4N 1S2, Contact: Stephane Lavoie *Tel:* 514-337-8560 *Fax:* 514-339-2252 *E-mail:* lavoies@transcontinental.ca
Membership(s): BMI; NAPL; PIA

Tri-Graphic Printing (Ottawa) Ltd
485 Industrial Ave, Ottawa, ON K1G 0Z1
Tel: 613-731-7441 *Fax:* 613-731-3741
Key Personnel
VP & Gen Mgr: Doug K Doane *E-mail:* ddoane@tri-graphic.com
VP, Prodn & Servs: Fred Malleau *Tel:* 905-665-8500 *E-mail:* fmalleau@tri-graphic.com
Founded: 1968
Turnaround: 10-15 Workdays
Print Runs: 1,000 min - 100,000 max
Business from Other Countries: 10%
Branch Office(s)
213 Byron St S, Suite 201, Whitby, ON L1N 4P7 *Tel:* 905-665-8500 *Fax:* 905-665-8501

University of Toronto Press Inc
Printing Division, 5201 Dufferin St, North York, ON M3H 5T8
Tel: 416-667-7767 *Fax:* 416-667-7803
E-mail: printing@utpress.utoronto.ca
Web Site: www.utpress.utoronto.ca
Key Personnel
Pres & Publr: George Meadows
Founded: 1901
Turnaround: 10-15 Workdays
Print Runs: 10 min - 200,000 max
Business from Other Countries: 15%
Membership(s): BMI

Webcom Ltd
3480 Pharmacy Ave, Toronto, ON M1W 2S7
Tel: 416-496-1000 *Fax:* 416-496-1537
E-mail: webcom@webcomlink.com
Web Site: www.webcomlink.com
Key Personnel
VP, Sales & Mktg: Mike Collinge
Dir, Mktg: Deborah Kupperman
Founded: 1976
Turnaround: 15 Workdays
Print Runs: 50 min - 100,000 max
Business from Other Countries: 40%

China

Hong Kong Christian Service
33 Granville Rd, Tsin Sha Tsui, Kowloon, Hong Kong SAR
Mailing Address: 33 Granville Rd, 6/F, Kowloon, Hong Kong SAR
Tel: 27316316 *Fax:* 27316333
E-mail: corpaffairs@hkcs.org
Web Site: www.hkcs.org
Key Personnel
Dir: Mr Ng Shui Lai, MBE, JP
Founded: 1952
Turnaround: 40 Workdays
Business from Other Countries: 1%
Parent Company: Hong Kong Christian Council

Jardine Wenwu Printing Co
No 21 Bei St, Xihuangchenggen, Hicheng District, Beijing

Speedflex Asia Ltd
3/F Tianjin Bldg, 167 Connaught Rd W, Hong Kong, SAR
Tel: 25422780 *Fax:* 25454026
E-mail: info@speedflex.com.hk
Web Site: www.speedflex.com.hk
Key Personnel
Sales Manager: Richard Silkstone
Founded: 1981
Turnaround: 1 Workday
Print Runs: 1 min
Business from Other Countries: 20%

Croatia

Mehanograf
Vukomerecka Cesta BB, 10040 Zagreb-Dubrava
Tel: (01) 2408567 *Fax:* (01) 2408563
Key Personnel
Dir: Zeljko Vincetic

Radin-Repro I Roto
Zagrebacka 194, 10000 Zagreb
Tel: (01) 3863111 *Fax:* (01) 3862673
E-mail: radin-repro-i-roto@zg.tel.hr
Key Personnel
Dir: Marijan Arambasin
Contact: Sanja Pusec

Vjesnik dd (Croatian Printing Plant)
Slavonska Avenija 4, 10000 Zagreb
Tel: (01) 3641 543; (01) 3641 453 *Fax:* (01) 3641 486
E-mail: hrvatska.tiskara1@zg.tel.hr
Key Personnel
General Manager: Ivan Bozicevic
Sales Manager: Irena Gnjidic
Technical Manager: Zeljko Bajs; Mijo Paradzik; Ivan Srsen
Purchasing Manager: Renata Bozickovic
Finance Manager: Koraljka Kokotovic
Founded: 1999 (In 1999 Vjesnik Publishing Company & Hrvatska tishava dd joined together to create Vjesnik dd)
Print Runs: 25,000 min - 55,000 max
Business from Other Countries: 1%

Denmark

Ingenioeren/Boger (Ingineering Books Danish Technical Press)
Skelbaekgade 4, DK-1780 Copenahagen V
Tel: 33265454 *Fax:* 33265545

Finland

Enso Oy
Kanavararta 1, 55800 Imarta
Tel: (0204) 6121 *Fax:* (02046) 24701
Key Personnel
Sales Manager: Ove Backlund; Aarno Yrjo-Koskinen

WS Bookwell Ltd
Member of Sanoma WSOY Group
Teollisuustie 4, FIN-06100 Porvoo
Tel: (019) 219 41 *Fax:* (019) 219 4800
Web Site: www.wsoy.fi/print/
Key Personnel
Man Dir: Magnus Breitenstein *E-mail:* magnus.breitenstein@bookwell.fi
Secretary: Minna Rautio *Tel:* (019) 5762402 *E-mail:* minna.rautio@wsoy.fi
Founded: 1878
Parent Company: Werner Soderstrom Corp
Ultimate Parent Company: Sonoma WSOY
Branch Office(s)
Messerdorferstr 127, 53123 Bonn, Germany, Contact: Markku Rapeli *Tel:* (0228) 986 4006 *Fax:* (0228) 986 4008
WS Bookwell AB, Borgveien 2, Ytre Enebakk N-1914, Norway, Contact: Kristen Sande *Tel:* (064) 925 840 *Fax:* (064) 925 841 *E-mail:* k.sande.wsoy@oslo.online.no
PO Box 3, Lowestoft, Suffolk NR33 8EY, United Kingdom, Contact: David Sowter *Tel:* (1502) 742 038 *Fax:* (1502) 742 039 *E-mail:* ds@wsoy.freeserve.co.uk

France

Imprimerie Bene
12 rue Pradier, F-30000 Nimes
Tel: (04) 66294897 *Fax:* (04) 66382146
Key Personnel
President: Jacques Enfer
Print Runs: 100 min - 10,000 max
Business from Other Countries: 20%

Imprimerie Descamps SA
36 place Pierre Delcourt, 59163 Conde-sur-Escaut
Tel: (03) 27400208 *Fax:* (03) 27405683
Key Personnel
Contact: Carlo Bertin
Founded: 1830
Turnaround: 2-5 Workdays
Print Runs: 800 min - 20,000 max
Business from Other Countries: 12%

Plein Chant
F-16120 Bassac
Tel: (05) 45819326 *Fax:* (05) 45819283
Key Personnel
Contact: Edmond Thomas
Founded: 1971
Print Runs: 600 min - 1,000 max
Business from Other Countries: 5%

Germany

Adobe Systems GmbH
Ohmstr, 85716 Unterschleissheim
Tel: (089) 317050 *Fax:* (089) 31705705

Ludwig Auer GmbH
Reichsstr, 17, 86609 Donauwoerth Bayern
Tel: (0906) 730 *Fax:* (0906) 73177

Bertelsmann AG
Carl-Bertelsmann Str 270, 33311 Gutersloh
Mailing Address: Postfach 111, 33311 Gutersloh
Tel: (05241) 80-0 *Fax:* (05421) 75166
E-mail: info@bestelsmann.de
Web Site: www.bertelsmann.de
Key Personnel
Division President: Frank Woessner
Founded: 1835

C L Baader Buch & Offsetdruckere GmbH & Co KG
Gutenbergstr 1, 72525 Baden-Wurttemberg
Mailing Address: Postfach 1220, 72522 Munsingen
Tel: (07381) 79192 *Fax:* (07381) 411412 *Cable:* BAADER-MUNSINGEN
Founded: 1835
Turnaround: 1 Workday
Print Runs: 1,000 min - 15,000 max

Druck & Verlagshaus Fromm GmbH & Co KG
Subsidiary of Neue Osnabruecker Zeitung, Druckzentrum Osnabrueck; Verlag A Fromm; Fromm International Publ Corp; Edition Interfrom AG
Breiter Gang 10-16, Postfach 1948, 49074 Osnabrueck
Tel: (0541) 3100 *Fax:* (0541) 310315
E-mail: druckhaus@fromm-os.de
Key Personnel
Publisher: Leo V Fromm
Chief Executive Officer: A Harms-Hunold
Founded: 1868

Media-Print Informationstechnologie GmbH
Eggertstr 28, 33100 Paderborn
Tel: (05251) 522300 *Fax:* (05251) 522480
E-mail: contact@mediaprint.de
Web Site: www.mediaprint.de
Key Personnel
Man Dir: Rainer Rings
Founded: 1993
Turnaround: 5-10 Workdays
Print Runs: 100 min - 30,000 max
Business from Other Countries: 10%

Mohndruck Graphische Betriebe GmbH
Subsidiary of Bertelsmann AG
Carl-Bertelsmann-Str 161, 33311 Guetersloh
Mailing Address: Postfach 200, 33311 Guetersloh
Tel: (05241) 802095 *Fax:* (05241) 78329
Key Personnel
Contact: Alfred Hahn
Founded: 1824
Business from Other Countries: 25%

Priese GmbH
Auerbacherstr 9, 14193 Berlin
Tel: (030) 3239089 *Fax:* (030) 3249630
Key Personnel
Contact: Elma Priese; Hans Joachim Priese

Sankt-Johannis-Druckerei
Heiligenstr 24, 77933 Lahr
Mailing Address: Postfach 5, 77922 Lahr/Schwarzw
Tel: (07821) 5810 *Fax:* (07821) 58126
Telex: 782122

Papierfabrik Scheufelen GmbH & Co KG
Adolf-Scheufelen-Str 26, 73252 Lenningen
Tel: (07026) 66-1 *Fax:* (07026) 66701

Strobel Druck & Verlag - A Strobel GmbH & Co KG
Zur Feldmuhle 9-11, 59821 Arnsberg
Mailing Address: PO Box 56 54, 59806 Arnsberg
Tel: (02931) 89000 *Fax:* (02931) 890038
E-mail: strobel-verlag.enzeigen@t-online.de
Web Site: www.ikz.de
Key Personnel
Contact: Mr Hallmann
Print Runs: 2,500 min - 90,000 max

Topic Verlag GmbH
Birkenstr 10, 85757 Karlsfeld B Munich
Tel: (08131) 97038 *Fax:* (08131) 98404
Founded: 1982
Business from Other Countries: 50%

Wissenschaftliche Verlagsgesellschaft mbH
Birkenwaldstr 44, 70191 Stuttgart
Tel: (0711) 2582-0 *Fax:* (0711) 2582-290
Key Personnel
Man Dir: Dr Christian Rotta

Hong Kong

The American Chamber of Commerce in Hong Kong
1904 Bank of America Tower, 12 Harcourt Rd, Central Hong Kong
Tel: 2526 0165 *Fax:* 2810 1289; 2596 0911
E-mail: amcham@amcham.org.hk
Key Personnel
Administration Manager: Norman Oei

Bright Future Printing Co Ltd
Sunview Industrial Building, Block D, 5/F, 3 On Yip St, Chai Wan
Tel: 25151776 *Fax:* 28972799; 25581717
Key Personnel
Chairman: Richard Ng
Turnaround: 60 Workdays (including shipping)
Print Runs: 3,000 min - 30,000 max
Business from Other Countries: 30%

C A Design, see Communication Art Design & Printing Ltd

C & C Offset Printing Co Ltd
Subsidiary of C & C Joint Printing Co (HK) Ltd under Sino United Publishing (Holdings) Ltd
C & C Bldg, 36 Ting Lai Rd, Tai Po, New Territories
Tel: (02) 666-4988 *Fax:* (02) 666-4938
E-mail: offsetprinting@candcprinting.com
Web Site: www.ccoffset.com
Key Personnel
Dir & General Manager: Xian-Qing Zhuang
Dir & Assistant General Manager: Ken Lee
Sales Manager (Overseas): Kit Wong
Sales Manager (Special Projects): Francis Ho
Dir & Executive Vice President, C & C Offset Printing Co (USA) Inc, Portland OR, USA: Charles H Clark, IV
Development Manager, C & C Offset Printing (USA) Inc, Portland, OR, USA: Jenny Whittier *Tel:* 503-233-1834 *E-mail:* jwhittier@ccoffset.com
Customer Service Manager, C & C Offset Printing Co (USA) Inc, Portland, OR, USA: Ernest Li
Dir & Executive Vice President, C & C Offset Printing Co (NY) Inc, New York, NY, USA: Simon Chan
Dir & General Manager, C & C Joint Printing Co (Guangdong) Ltd, Shenzhen, China: Jackson Leung
Deputy Sales Manager, C & C Joint Printing Co (Ghuangdong) Ltd, Shenzhen, China: Min Zhu
President, C & C Printing Japan Co Ltd, Tokyo, Japan: Masashi Otobe
Customer Service Manager, C & C Offset Printing Co (NYC), Inc, NY NY: Frances Harkness
Man Dir, C & C Joint Printing Co (Beijing), Ltd, Beijing, China: Zhang Lin Gui
Dir, C & C Offset Printing Co (UK), Ltd: Tracy Broderick
Manager, C & C Offset Printing Co (UK), Ltd: Fiona Norman
Founded: 1980
Turnaround: 42 Workdays for printing, binding & book finishing
Print Runs: 2,000 min - 200,000 max
Business from Other Countries: 60%
Branch Office(s)
C & C Joint Printing Co (Guangdong) Ltd, Chunhu Industrial Estate, Pinghu, Long Gang, Shenzhen 518111, China *Tel:* (0755) 884-1333 *Fax:* (0755) 844-2211 *E-mail:* guangdong@candcprinting.com (Plant)
C & C Printing Japan Co Ltd, Tokyodou, 6th floor, Jinbocho No 2, Bldg 127, Chiyoda-Ku, Tokyo 101, Japan *Tel:* (03) 3219-6601 *Fax:* (03) 3219-6620 *E-mail:* cctokyo@interlink.or.jp
Room 2, 9/F, 3 Chegongzhuang Main St, Xicheng District, Beijing 100044, China *Tel:* (010) 6836-5335 *Fax:* (010) 6836-5335
Room 304 Fangfa Bldg, No 29 Lane 165, Dongzhu Anbin Rd, Shanghai 200050, China *Tel:* (021) 6240-1305 *Fax:* (021) 6240-1305 *E-mail:* shanghai@candcprinting.com
Room 505 Sino Bldg, 23 Zhan Qian Rd, Guangzhou 510010, China *Tel:* (020) 8650-0602 *Fax:* (020) 8667-8882 *E-mail:* guangzhou@candcprinting.com
C & C Offset Printing Co (UK), Ltd, 2 New Burlington St, 4th fl, London W1S 2JE, United Kingdom *Tel:* (020) 7287 7787 *Fax:* (020) 7287 7187 *E-mail:* tracy@candcoffset.co.uk
U.S. Office(s): C & C Offset Printing Co (USA) Inc, 2632 SE 25 St, Suite D, Portland, OR 97202, United States *Tel:* 503-233-1834 *Fax:* 503-233-7815 *E-mail:* portlandinfo@ccoffset.com
C & C Offset Printing Co (NY) Inc, 401 Broadway, Suite 2015, New York, NY 10013-3005, United States *Tel:* 212-431-4210 *Fax:* 212-431-3960 *E-mail:* newyorkinfo@ccoffset.com

Caritas Printing Training Centre
2 Caine Rd, Caritas House, Block D, 3/F, Hong Kong
Tel: 25261148 *Fax:* 25371231
Key Personnel
General Manager: Isaac Mak
Print Runs: 1,000 min - 100,000 max
Business from Other Countries: 50%

Colorprint Offset
8 Coml Tower, Chai Wan
Tel: 28967777 *Fax:* 28896606

Key Personnel
Sales Manager: Jennifer Weston *Tel:* 9035062
Contact: Eva Lav; Ian Lee
Turnaround: Standard turnaround of 2 weeks
Print Runs: 3,000 min - 100,000 max
Business from Other Countries: 80%
Branch Office(s)
Lincoln Bldg, Suite 1149, 60 E 42 St, New York, NY 10164, United States, Lee Moncho *Tel:* 212-681-9400 *Fax:* 212-681-9362
Gainsborough House, 81 Oxford St, London W1R 1KB, United Kingdom *Tel:* (020) 7903-5060 *Fax:* (020) 7903-5063

Communication Art Design & Printing Ltd
19th Floor, China Hong Kong Tower, 8-12 Hennessy Road, Wan Chai
Tel: 28656787 *Fax:* 28663429
E-mail: cadesign@pacific.net.hk
Key Personnel
Man Dir: Rosanne Chan
Founded: 1984
Print Runs: 500 min
Business from Other Countries: 50%

Dai Nippon Printing Co (Hong Kong) Ltd
Division of Dai Nippon Printing Co Ltd
220-248 Texaco Rd, Tsuen Wan Industrial Centre, 2/F-5/F, Tsuen Wan, New Territories
Tel: 24080188 *Fax:* 24076201 *Cable:* DNPICO
Key Personnel
Administration & Finance Dir: Mr K Miya
Print Runs: 5,000 min - 200,000 max
Business from Other Countries: 85%
Branch Office(s)
Dai Nippon Printing Co Pty Ltd, 45 Clarence St, Suite 904, Level 9, KPMG Centre, Sydney NSW 2000, Australia *Tel:* (02) 9299-3155
P T Dainippon Gitakarya Printing, Jalan Ceylon 14-16, Jakarta Pusat, Indonesia
Dai Nippon Printing Co Ltd, 1-1, Ichigaya-Kagacho, 1-Chome, Shinjuku-Ku, Tokyo, Japan
Dainippon Tien Wah Printing Pte Ltd, 977 Bukit Timah Rd, Singapore 2158, Singapore *Tel:* 469-7611
Dai Nippon Printing Co Ltd, London Liaison Office, 27 Throgmorton St, 4th floor, London EC2N 2AQ, United Kingdom *Tel:* (0202) 7588-2088
U.S. Office(s): DNP America Inc, 50 California St, Suite 777, San Francisco, CA 94111, United States
DNP America Inc, 3235 Kifer Rd, Suite 100, Santa Clara, CA 95051, United States
DNP America Inc, 3858 Carson St, Suite 300, Torrance, CA 90503, United States
D N P (America) Inc, 2 Park Ave, Suite 1405, New York, NY 10016, United States

Elgin Consultants Ltd
33 Taiwan Old Tsuen, Lamma Island
Tel: 28151680
Founded: 1983
Turnaround: 21 Workdays
Business from Other Countries: 10%

Elite Printing Company Ltd
Hong Man Ind Centre, Room 1408, 2 Hong Man St, Chai Wan
Tel: 25580119 *Fax:* 28972675
E-mail: elitemkt@elite.com.hk; sales@elite.com.hk
Web Site: www.elite.com.hk
Key Personnel
Man Dir: Susan Chan
Sales & Marketing Manager: Fred Chu
Founded: 1979
Turnaround: 7-15 Workdays
Print Runs: 2,000 min - 50,000 max
Business from Other Countries: 30%

Empire Printing Ltd
3 Dai Shun St, Tai Po Ind Estate, Tai Po, New Territories
Tel: 26655193 *Fax:* 26617722
Key Personnel
Sales Manager: Lok-Tsang Li
Founded: 1978
Turnaround: 2 Workdays
Print Runs: 2,500 min - 500,000 max
Business from Other Countries: 15%

Everbest Printing Co Ltd
Block C5, 10/F, Ko Fai Industrial Bldg, 7 Ko Fai Rd, 10F, Yautong, Kowloon
Tel: (02) 7274433 *Fax:* (02) 7727687
E-mail: sales@everbest.com.hk
Key Personnel
Man Dir: Kenneth Chung
Customer Account Executive: Ronny Ng; Frankie Lee
Founded: 1954
Turnaround: 28 Workdays
Print Runs: 1,000 min - 1,000,000 max
Business from Other Countries: 90%
Branch Office(s)
Four Colour Imports Ltd, 2843 Brownsboro Rd, Louisville, KY, United States *Tel:* 502-896-9644 *E-mail:* sales@fourcolour.com
Everbest Midwest, Edina, MN, United States *Tel:* 612-944-0854
Everbest Canada, Toronto, ON, Canada *Tel:* 416-286-6688 *E-mail:* everbest@sympatico.ca

Golden Cup Printing Co Ltd
Member of Hong Kong Printers Association
6/F Seapower Industrial Centre, 177 Hoi Bun Rd, Kwun Tong, Kowloon
Tel: 23434254 *Fax:* 23415426
E-mail: sales@goldencup.com.hk
Web Site: www.goldencup.com.hk
Key Personnel
Man Dir: K K Yeung
General Manager: W K Ngan
Sales Manager: Mary Yeung *E-mail:* mary@goldencup.com.hk
Founded: 1971
Turnaround: 25 Workdays
Print Runs: 5,000 min - 200,000 max
Business from Other Countries: 80%
Branch Office(s)
Dongguan, China
Guangdong, China
Kunming, China
Yunan, China

Great Wall Graphics Ltd
2/F, 13 Wyndham St, Hong Kong
Tel: 25240014 *Fax:* 28453588
Key Personnel
Dir: Paul Zimmerman
Founded: 1982
Turnaround: 3-28 Workdays
Print Runs: 2,000 min - 500,000 max
Business from Other Countries: 50%

H & Y Printing Ltd
Blk C, 2/F Shing Tak Industrial Bldg, 44 Wong Chuk Hang Rd, Aberdeen
Tel: 28702379 *Fax:* 25550028
E-mail: hyphk@netvigator.com
Key Personnel
Contact: Jason Ma
Founded: 1996
Print Runs: 1,000 min - 100,000 max

Hill & Knowlton Asia Ltd
Subsidiary of WPP
35/F, Windsor House, 311 Gloucester Rd, Causeway Bay
Tel: 28946321
Telex: 25763551

Key Personnel
Group Dir Marketing Communications: Alistair Monteith-Hodge *E-mail:* almonte@hillanddknowlton.com.hk

Hoi Kwong Printing Co Ltd
5D Wah Ha Factory Bldg, 8 Shipyard Lane, Quarry Bay
Tel: 2562 1641 *Fax:* 2564 2142
Key Personnel
Man Dir: David Chan *Tel:* 2562 1096 *E-mail:* dchan@hoikwong.com
Founded: 1960

Hung Hing Off-set Printing Co Ltd
Subsidiary of Hung Hing Printing Group Ltd
17-19 Dai Hei St, Tai Po Industrial Estate, Tai Po, New Territories
Tel: 26648682 *Fax:* 26642070
E-mail: info@hhop.com.hk
Key Personnel
Man Dir: Matthew Yum *E-mail:* matthew@hhop.com.hk
Founded: 1950
Turnaround: 20-30 Workdays
Print Runs: 5,000 min - 1,000,000 max
Business from Other Countries: 15%

Image Printing Company Ltd
Unit 4, 4/F Cornell Centre, 50 Wing Tai Rd, Chai Wan
Tel: 28732633 *Fax:* 25583044
E-mail: imageprt@pop3.hknet.com
Key Personnel
Man Dir: Philip Chow Sung Ming
Founded: 1992
Print Runs: 1,000 min - 50,000 max
Business from Other Countries: 50%

Imago Services (HK) Ltd
653-659 Kings Rd, 6/F, Tung Chong Factory Bldg, North Point
Tel: 28113316 *Fax:* 25975253
Key Personnel
Man Dir: Kendrick Cheung

Leefung-Asco Printers Ltd
HK Worsted Mills Ind Bldg, Kwai Chung
Tel: 24216708 *Fax:* 28105530; 28105612
Key Personnel
Production Coordinator: Ms Sindy Chui
General Manager: Rebecca King

Leo Paper Products Ltd
7/F Kader Bldg, 22 Kai Cheung Rd, Kowloon Bay
Tel: 25696293 *Fax:* 25138400
E-mail: lrg@leo.com.hk
Web Site: www.leo.com.hk
Key Personnel
Man Dir: Johnny Fung *E-mail:* johnny@leo.com.hk; Michael Leung *E-mail:* michael@leo.com.hk
Marketing Dir: Kelly Fok *E-mail:* kelly@leo.com.uk
Founded: 1991
Turnaround: 15-30 Workdays
Print Runs: 5,000 min
Parent Company: Leo Paper Bags Manufacturing Ltd
Sales Office(s): Leo Paper Products (Europe) BVBA, "De Wilde Zee", Wiegstraat 19, 2000 Antwerpen, Belgium, Contact: Jan Van Gijsel *Tel:* (03) 203-0912 *Fax:* (03) 255-1303 *E-mail:* leo@leo-europe.com
Leo Paper USA, 777 108 Ave NE, Suite 1200, Bellevue, WA 98004, United States, Contact: Bijan Pakzad *Tel:* 425-646-8801 *Fax:* 425-646-8805 *E-mail:* bijan@pacificpier.com
Leo Marketing Ltd, The Malthouse, Malthouse Sq, Princes Risborough, Bucks HP27

9AB, United Kingdom *Tel:* (01844) 274-244 *Fax:* (01844) 275-105 *E-mail:* sallywood.leo@btinternet.com

Literature Ministry Department
5/F, 128 Castle Peak Rd, Shamshuipo, Kowloon
Tel: 27258558 *Fax:* 23862304
E-mail: hkccllmd@hkstar.com
Founded: 1971
Print Runs: 2,000 min - 200,000 max
Business from Other Countries: 50%

Mei Ka Printing & Publish Enterprise Ltd
Cheung Ka Industrial Bldg, Block B 8th & 9th Floor, 179-190 Connaught Rd West, Sai Ying Pin
Tel: 25401131 *Fax:* 25598718
Key Personnel
Dir: Hong Chin Huo

Midas Printing Ltd
1/F 100 Texaco Rd, Tsuen Wan, New Territories
Tel: 24076888 *Fax:* 24065800
E-mail: midas@hkstar.com
Key Personnel
Project Manager: Raymond Chan
Executive Dir: Gloria Y P Kan; John Ng
Overseas Sales Manager: Angela Lee
 Tel: 24084029 *E-mail:* bangela@midas.com.hk
Founded: 1990
Turnaround: 14-21 Workdays
Print Runs: 5,000 min - 100,000 max
Business from Other Countries: 25%

Morris Press Ltd
2802 Trend Centre, 29 Cheung Lee St, Chai Wan
Tel: 28892168 *Fax:* 28892180
Key Personnel
Dir: Raynond Shing
Turnaround: 15 Workdays
Print Runs: 5,000 min - 100,000 max
Business from Other Countries: 50%

New Island Printing Co Ltd
New Island Printing Centre, 38 Wang Lee St, Yuen Long Industrial Estate, Yuen Long, New Territories
Tel: 24428282 *Fax:* 24439882
E-mail: info@newisland.com
Web Site: www.newisland.com
Key Personnel
Dir, Business Development: John Currie
Group Dir, Sales & Marketing: Karen Fung

Palace Press International
Wah Ha Factory Bldg, 10th floor, Block C, 8 Shipyard Lane, Quarry Bay
Tel: (02) 3579019 *Fax:* (02) 5613616
E-mail: palacehk@palacepress.ocm
Web Site: www.palacepress.com
Key Personnel
Dir: Lesley Sun *E-mail:* lesley@palacepress.com
Project Manager: Maria Ramos *Tel:* 415-626-1080 ext 208 *E-mail:* maria@palacepress.com
Branch Office(s)
239-C Joo Chiat Rd, Singapore 427496, Singapore, Contact: Lesley Sun *Tel:* (0342) 3117 *Fax:* (0342) 3115 *E-mail:* ppispore@palacepress.com *Web Site:* www.palacepress.com
U.S. Office(s): 1585-A Folsom St, San Francisco, CA 94103, United States *Tel:* 415-626-1080 *Fax:* 415-626-1510 *E-mail:* ppisfo@palacepress.com *Web Site:* www.palacepress.com
180 Varick St, 10th floor, New York, NY 10014, United States *Tel:* 212-426-2622 *Fax:* 212-463-9130 *E-mail:* nyoffice@palacepress.com *Web Site:* www.palacepress.com
Palace Press Marin, 1299 Fourth St, Suite 305, San Rafael, CA 94901, United States *Tel:* 415-455-2480 *Fax:* 415-455-2490 *E-mail:* ppimarin@palacepress.com *Web Site:* www.palacepress.com

Paper Art Product Ltd
Sun Fung Ctr, Flat 819, 8/F88, Kwok Shui Rd, Kwai Chung
Tel: 24812929 *Fax:* 24892255
Turnaround: 2-4 weeks
Print Runs: 2,000 min - 100,000 max
Business from Other Countries: 80%

Paper Communication Printing Express Ltd
4A Dragon Industrial Bldg, 93 King Lam St, Cheung Sha Wan, Kowloon
Tel: 27864191 *Fax:* 27864498
E-mail: pcpe@papercom.com.hk
Key Personnel
Marketing Dir: Alam Ng
Contact: Wayne Lui
Founded: 1981
Turnaround: 28 to 56 Workdays
Print Runs: 1,000 min - 200,000 max
Business from Other Countries: 100%

Paramount Commercial Press Ltd
Subsidiary of Paramount Publishing Group Ltd
3 Chun Kwong St, Tseung Kwan O Industrial Estate, Kowloon
Tel: 28958688 *Fax:* 28978942
Key Personnel
Contact: Rosita Leung
Founded: 1968
Turnaround: 30-45 Workdays
Print Runs: 1,000 min - 1,000,000 max
Business from Other Countries: 60%

Paramount Publishing Group Limited
3 Chun Kwong St, Tseung Kwan O Industrial Estate, Kowloon
Tel: 28968688 *Fax:* 28978942
E-mail: paramountprin@navigator.com
Web Site: www.paramount.com.hk
Key Personnel
President: Victor Oh
Account Dir: Kelvin Lai
Founded: 1968
Turnaround: 30-45 Workdays
Print Runs: 1,000 min - 1,000,000 max
Business from Other Countries: 60%
U.S. Office(s): Paramount Printing Company USA Inc, 386 Park Ave S, Suite 315, New York, NY 10016, United States, President: Jason Cheng *Tel:* (212) 696-5821 *Fax:* (212) 696-5428
111 Chestnut St, Suite 508, San Francisco, CA 94111, United States, VP, Sales: Bobby Tan *Tel:* (415) 391-9111 *Fax:* (415) 398-9333

Pearl River Printing Co Ltd
Flat A, Evergreen Bldg, 13th Floor, 12 Yip Fat St, Aberdeen
Tel: 28732909 *Fax:* 28730784; 25597042
Key Personnel
Man Dir: Alan Scott Jordan
Founded: 1984
Turnaround: 5-40 Workdays
Print Runs: 500 min - 50,000 max
Business from Other Countries: 50%

Professional Publishing Co
2/F, 65, Wyndham St, Central Hong Kong
Tel: 25254623 *Fax:* 28453681
Key Personnel
Business Dir: Michael Pak
Founded: 1970
Turnaround: 20-40 Workdays
Print Runs: 5,000 min - 50,000 max
Business from Other Countries: 20%

Prontaprint Asia Ltd
1/F, Gaylord Commercial Bldg, 114 Lockhart Rd, Wanchai
Tel: 28657525 *Fax:* 28661064
E-mail: postmaster@pronta.com.hk
Key Personnel
Man Dir: Clive Howard
Founded: 1986
Business from Other Countries: 40%

Review Publishing Co Ltd
Subsidiary of Dow Jones & Co Inc
25/F Citicorp Centre, 18 Whitfield Rd, Wan Chai
Tel: 28382300 *Fax:* 25031526
Web Site: www.feer.com
Telex: 75297 *Cable:* REVIEW
Key Personnel
Editor: Nayan Chanda
Company Secretary & Finance Dir: Mr Kang Sun Tsang *E-mail:* ks.tsang@feer.com
Man Dir: Karen Mullis
Founded: 1946

Sing Cheong Printing Co Limited
Tung Chong Fty Bldg, 655 King's Rd, G/F, North Point
Tel: 25618801 *Fax:* 25659467
E-mail: info@singcheong.com.hk
Key Personnel
Dir & Manager: Karen Shen Fishel
Founded: 1965
Business from Other Countries: 96%

Sino Publishing House Ltd
Asia Harvest Commercial Center, Room 2A, Tak House, 5-11 Stanley St, Central Hong Kong
Tel: 28849963; 28973361 *Fax:* 25121154
E-mail: sunnyp@hkstar.com
Key Personnel
Dir: Stephen Stringer
Founded: 1993
Print Runs: 500 min - 500,000 max
Business from Other Countries: 75%

South China Printing Co (1988) Ltd
Subsidiary of Sing Tao Group
6/F Block B, Shatin Industrial Center, 5-7 Yuen Chun Circuit, Shatin, New Territories
Tel: 26373611 *Fax:* 26374221
Key Personnel
General Manager & Dir: Raymond Ching
Senior Division Manager: Ivan Cheung
Assistant to General Manager: Athena Yuen *E-mail:* ayuen@scpc.com.hk
Founded: 1988
Turnaround: 20 Workdays
Print Runs: 2,000 min - 150,000 max
Business from Other Countries: 98%
Branch Office(s)
Sydney, Australia, Contact: Mr Anders Hagberg *E-mail:* anders@bigpond.com
Bedfordshire, United Kingdom, Contact: Mr Alan Lynch *Tel:* (0152) 523-7455 *Fax:* (0152) 523-7756 *E-mail:* alan.lynch@LineOne.net
U.S. Office(s): Los Angeles, CA, United States, Contact: Mr Moon Chuen Lo *Tel:* (626) 291-7398 *Fax:* (626) 285-2870 *E-mail:* moonclo@earthlink.com
New York, NY, United States, Contact: Mr Peter Lawrence *Tel:* (212) 570-9010 *Fax:* (212) 628-0137 *E-mail:* scpco@aol.com

South Sea International Press Ltd
3/F, Yip Cheung Centre, 10 Fung Yip St, Chai Wan
Tel: 28971083 *Fax:* 25581473
E-mail: ssiphk@hk.super.net
Key Personnel
Man Dir: P Y Lee
Senior Manager: Franky Ho
Founded: 1984
Print Runs: 3,000 min - 500,000 max
Business from Other Countries: 80%

HONG KONG

Sunshine Press Ltd
21/F Fullager Ind Bldg, 234 Aberdeen Main Rd, Hong Kong
Tel: 25532386 *Fax:* 28732930
E-mail: spl@sunshinepress.com.hk
Key Personnel
Administrative Assistant: Trevin Tong
Contact: Joney Chan
Founded: 1976
Turnaround: 21-28 Workdays
Print Runs: 3,000 min - 500,000 max
Business from Other Countries: 25%

Unicorn International Printing Co Ltd
Blk A, 2/F, Sum Lung Ind Bldg, 11 Sun Yip St, Chai Wan
Tel: 28980238 *Fax:* 28983812
E-mail: unicorn7@netvigator.com
Key Personnel
General Manager: Paul chi-sing Choi
Founded: 1994
Turnaround: 2 weeks-1 month
Print Runs: 1,000 min - 50,000 max
Business from Other Countries: 20%

Wing King Tong Co Ltd (Printing Factory)
188 Texaco Rd, 3/F, Phase 1, Leader Industrial Centre, Tsuen Wan, New Territories
Tel: 24073287 *Fax:* 24074130
E-mail: ayan@hk.super.net
Key Personnel
Man Dir: Alex Yan *E-mail:* ayan@hk.super.net
Marketing Dir: Jeremy Kuo
Founded: 1944
Turnaround: 15 Workdays
Print Runs: 1,000 min - 100,000 max
Business from Other Countries: 95%

Ying Tat Co
Division of Quality Printing & Paper Products
Wing Wah Industrial Bldg, 8th Floor, 677 Kings Rd, Hong Kong
Tel: 25645980 *Fax:* 28111280
Key Personnel
Sales Manager: Kan Chan
Founded: 1968
Turnaround: 7-10 Workdays
Print Runs: 1,000 min - 1,000,000 max
Business from Other Countries: 30%

Hungary

Interpress Aussenhandels GmbH
Bajcsy-Zsilinszky ut 21, H-1065 Budapest
Tel: (01) 3027525; (01) 2508267 *Fax:* (01) 3027530
Key Personnel
Manager: Miklos Pollak; Sandor Kovacs; Julia Kovacs
Founded: 1991

India

Hiralal Printing Works Ltd
Subsidiary of Conway Printers Pvt Ltd
Plot No D-41/1, MIDC TTC Ind Area, Opp Turbne Tel Exch, Mumbai 400613
Tel: (022) 7672726; (022) 7683012 *Fax:* (022) 7631191
Key Personnel
Chairman: G P Agrawal
Man Dir: Mr Rakesh Kumar Agrawal
Founded: 1981

Turnaround: 40-45 Workdays
Print Runs: 5,000 min - 100,000 max
Business from Other Countries: 75%

Indonesia

Victory Offset Prima PT
Jalan Raya Pegangsaan, Dua, No 17, Jakarta 14250
Tel: (021) 460-2742; (021) 460-8968 *Fax:* (021) 460-2740; (021) 4682-0551
E-mail: info@victoryoffset.com
Web Site: www.victoryoffset.com
Key Personnel
President: Zainal F Stanley *E-mail:* zainal@victoryoffset.com
General Manager: S Wilson Pinady *E-mail:* wilson@victoryoffset.com
Founded: 1971
Turnaround: 14 days
Print Runs: 5,000 min
Business from Other Countries: 10%
Branch Office(s)
PT Victory Graficindo Printing, Jalan Raya Pegengsaan, Dua, No 17, Jakarta-Utara 14250

Ireland

Smurfit Print
33 Botanic Rd, Glasnevin, Dublin 9
Tel: (01) 303911 *Fax:* (01) 303287
Print Runs: 200 min - 5,000,000 max
Business from Other Countries: 20%
Parent Company: Jefferson Smurfit Group plc

Tower Books
13 Hawthorn Ave, Inniscarra View Estate, Ballincollig, County Cork
Tel: (021) 872294 (voice & fax)
Key Personnel
Contact: Patricia Daly
Founded: 1970
Turnaround: 7-30 Workdays
Print Runs: 300 min - 2,000 max

Israel

Chronicles Publishers Ltd
24 Haarbaah St, Tel Aviv 61200
Mailing Address: PO Box 20774, Tel Aviv 61200
Tel: (03) 5615052 *Fax:* (03) 5624104
E-mail: chronicl@inter.net.il
Key Personnel
Man Dir: Dr Yehuda Atac
Manager: Farida Yashkuner *Tel:* (03) 5613614
Founded: 1993

The Government Printer
One Miriam Ha'hashmonait St, Jerusalem 91007
Mailing Address: PO Box 765, Jerusalem 91007
Tel: (02) 5685111; (02) 5685200 *Fax:* (02) 5685226
Key Personnel
Comptroller: Shimon Hochster
Founded: 1948

Har-El Printers & Publishers
Jaffa Port, Main Gate, Jaffa 61081
Mailing Address: PO Box 8053, Jaffa 61081
Tel: (03) 6816834 *Fax:* (03) 6813563

COMPLETE BOOK

Web Site: www.interart.co.il/harel
Key Personnel
Manager: Jaacov Har-El
Export Dir: Monique L Harel *E-mail:* mharel@harelart.co.il
Founded: 1974
Turnaround: 60-90 Workdays
Print Runs: 30 min - 5,000 max
Business from Other Countries: 70%

Keterpress Enterprises Jerusalem
Industrial Zone Givat Shaul B, Jerusalem 91071
Mailing Address: PO Box 7145, Jerusalem 91071
Tel: (02) 6557822 *Fax:* (02) 6527956
E-mail: keterprs@isdn.net.il
Key Personnel
Plant Manager: Peter Tomkins *E-mail:* peter@keter-books.co.il
Sales Manager: Zvi Weller
Print Runs: 500 min - 500,000 max
Business from Other Countries: 10%
Parent Company: Keter Publishing House Ltd

Technosdar Ltd
5 Levontine St, Tel Aviv 61316
Mailing Address: PO Box 31684, Tel Aviv 65111
Tel: (03) 5607418; (03) 5605951 *Fax:* (03) 5604932
E-mail: technos@internet-zahav.net
Key Personnel
General Manager: Avraham Weiss
Founded: 1972
Turnaround: 7-16 Workdays
Business from Other Countries: 10%

Youval Tal Ltd
153 Yafo, Jerusalem 94342
Mailing Address: PO Box 2160, Jerusalem 91021
Tel: (02) 6248897 *Fax:* (02) 6245434
Key Personnel
Dir: Youval Tal

Italy

Calderini SRL
Subsidiary of Edagricole-Edizioni Agricole
Via Emilia Levante 31/2, I-40139 Bologna
Tel: (051) 62267 *Fax:* (051) 490200
E-mail: comm@calderini.agriline.it
Founded: 1960

Canale G e C SpA
Subsidiary of Istituto Grafico Bertello SpA
Via Liguria 24, 10071 Borgaro Turin
Tel: (011) 4078511 *Fax:* (011) 4078527
E-mail: info@canale.it
Web Site: www.canale.it
Key Personnel
Dir General: Canale Giacomo *E-mail:* canale@canale.it
Founded: 1915
Turnaround: 30 Workdays
Print Runs: 3,000 min
Business from Other Countries: 65%

Dedalo Litostampa SRL
Viale Luigi Jacobini 5, I-70123 Bari
Mailing Address: Casella Postale BA/19, 70123 Bari
Tel: (080) 5311400 *Fax:* (080) 5311414
Key Personnel
Man Dir: Raimondo Coga
General Manager: Sergio Coga *Tel:* (080) 5311413 *E-mail:* s.coga@edizionidedalo.it
Founded: 1965
Print Runs: 2,000 min - 10,000 max

Minerva Medica
Corso Bramante 83/85, Turin 10126
Tel: (011) 678282 *Fax:* (011) 674502
Key Personnel
President: Dr Alberto Oliaro
Founded: 1937
Print Runs: 1,000 min - 10,000 max
Business from Other Countries: 8%
Branch Office(s)
Via Spallanzani 9, Rome

Istituto Poligrafico e Zecca Dello Stato
Piazza Verdi 10, 00198 Rome
Tel: (06) 85081 *Fax:* (06) 85082517
Telex: 611008 IPZSRO
Key Personnel
Legal Representative: Giovanni Ruggeri

Valdonega SRL
via Genova 17, 37020 Arbizzano (Verona)
Tel: (045) 6020444 *Fax:* (045) 6020334
E-mail: valdoneg@valdonega.it
Key Personnel
General Manager: Martino Mardersteig
Founded: 1948
Print Runs: 1,000 min
Business from Other Countries: 70%

Republic of Korea

Daehan Printing & Publishing Co Ltd
344-12, Sangdaewon-dong, Jungwon-gu, Sungnam-City, Kyungki-do
Tel: (031) 730-3830 (i-3) *Fax:* (031) 735-8104
Web Site: www.dhpop.com
Key Personnel
President: Sungshick Kim
Manager: Jongjun Yu
Founded: 1948

Lithuania

Spindulys Printing House
Gedimino 10, 3000 Kaunas
Tel: (07) 226243; (07) 225029 *Fax:* (07) 204970
Key Personnel
Contact: Elena Kapustinskiene
Founded: 1928
Print Runs: 500 min - 100,000 max
Business from Other Countries: 6%

Madagascar

Imprimerie Catholique
127 Rue Lenine-Antanimena, Antananarivo, 101
Tel: (02) 22304

Societe Malgache d'Edition
Route des Hydrocarbures, Ankorondrano, BP 659, Antananarivo 101
Tel: (020) 2222635 *Fax:* (020) 2222254
E-mail: tribune@bow.dts.mg
Web Site: www.madagascar-tribune.com
Telex: (020) 223-40
Key Personnel
Dir of Publication: Rahaga Ramaholimihaso

Founded: 1943
Print Runs: 7,000 min - 15,000 max

Malawi

Likuni Press
Division of Odini Bookshop
PO Box 133, Lilongwe
Tel: 721135; 721388 *Fax:* 72114133
Key Personnel
Managing Editor: P I Akomenji
Bookshop Manager: D H Bvalamwendo
Chief Executive: S P Kalilombe
Founded: 1949
Print Runs: 12,000 min - 15,000 max
Business from Other Countries: 5%

Malta

Interprint Ltd - Malta
Subsidiary of Malta Government
Industrial Estate, Marsa
Tel: 240169; 222720 *Fax:* 243780; 249712
E-mail: interprintjb@camline.net.mt
Key Personnel
General Manager: Alfred Azzopardi
Sales Manager: J Bonnici
Founded: 1963
Turnaround: 15 Workdays
Print Runs: 500 min - 200,000 max
Business from Other Countries: 80%

Netherlands

Bosch en Keuning grafische bedrijven
Ericastraat 1, 3742 SG Baarn
Mailing Address: Postbus 1, 3740 AA Baarn
Tel: (035) 5412050 *Fax:* (035) 2202446
Key Personnel
Contact: P P E Rings

Collectieve Propaganda van het Nederlandse Boek (CPNB)
Keizersgracht 391, NL-1016 EJ Amsterdam
Tel: (020) 6264971 *Fax:* (020) 6231696
Key Personnel
Man Dir: Henk Kraima
Founded: 1983

CPNB, see Collectieve Propaganda van het Nederlandse Boek (CPNB)

Foundation of Marginal Printers, see Stichting Drukwerk in de Marge (Foundation of Marginal Printers)

Stichting Drukwerk in de Marge (Foundation of Marginal Printers)
Postbus 16477, 1001 RN Amsterdam
Tel: (020) 6227748 *Fax:* (020) 6227748
Key Personnel
Contact: A A Sanders
Founded: 1975

New Zealand

Bookprint Consultants Ltd
Division of Grantham House Publishing
9 Wilkinson St, Apt 6, Oriental Bay, Wellington 6001
Tel: (04) 381 3071 *Fax:* (04) 381 3067
E-mail: gstewart@iconz.co.nz
Key Personnel
Chief Executive: Graham C Stewart
Founded: 1982
Print Runs: 2,000 min - 7,500 max
Business from Other Countries: 10%

The Caxton Press
113 Victoria St, Christchurch
Mailing Address: PO Box 25088, Christchurch
Tel: (064) 3668516 *Fax:* (03) 3657840
Key Personnel
Man Dir: Bruce Bascand
Founded: 1935

John McIndoe Ltd
PO Box 694, Dunedin
Tel: (03) 4770355 *Fax:* (03) 4771982
E-mail: jmcindoe@earthlight.co.nz
Key Personnel
Man Dir: Brendan A Murphy
Founded: 1893
Print Runs: 21 min - 30 max
Business from Other Countries: 1%

PPP Printers Ltd
PO Box 22785, Christchurch
Tel: (03) 3662727 *Fax:* (03) 3654606
Key Personnel
Man Dir: D C Richardson
Founded: 1958
Turnaround: 10 Workdays
Print Runs: 100 min - 100,000 max
Business from Other Countries: 10%

Norway

ISSN Norway
National Library of Oslo, N-0203 Oslo
Mailing Address: PO Box 2674, N-0203 Oslo
Tel: 22859181 *Fax:* 22859050
E-mail: issn-norge@nb.no
Key Personnel
Dir: Mrs Kari Grethe Singsaas

Philippines

Cacho Hermanos Inc
Pines Cor, Union St, Mandaluyong City
Tel: (02) 6318362; (02) 6318363; (02) 6318364; (02) 6318365 *Fax:* (02) 6315244
E-mail: cacho@mozcom.com
Key Personnel
President: Herbert T Veloso
Founded: 1880
Turnaround: 7-120 Workdays
Print Runs: 500 min - 50,000 max
Parent Company: National Book Store

Polygraphics Trading
2665 Honduras St, Sn Isidro, 1234 Makati City
Tel: (02) 817-95-56; (02) 728-43-65; (02) 728-43-66 *Fax:* (02) 817-95-56; (02) 817-95-64

PHILIPPINES

Key Personnel
General Manager: Carlito B Bacurin
Founded: 1977
Branch Office(s)
6 Molave St, Phase II, Dona Justa Village, Angono, Rizal
Sales Office(s): 2619 Rockefeller St, Sn Isidro, 1234 Makati City

Ready Press
246 Katipunan Ave, 1109 Blueridge, Quezon City
Tel: (02) 6471163; (02) 6471227 *Fax:* (02) 6471158
E-mail: casper@pworld.net.ph
Key Personnel
General Manager: Alda Sylianteng
Turnaround: 15 Workdays
Print Runs: 5,000 min
Business from Other Countries: 10%
Parent Company: Metro Holdings Corp
Branch Office(s)
37 Balagtas St, Marikina City
Sales Office(s): 777 Burgos St, Mandaue City, Cebu

Reyes Publishing
717 Aurora Blvd, 4/F Mariwasa Bldg, 1112 Quezon City
Tel: (02) 721827 *Fax:* (02) 7218782
E-mail: reyesbub@skyinet.net
Key Personnel
Operations Manager: Roman Paolo V Reyes
Founded: 1964
Business from Other Countries: 90%

Portugal

Silabo
R Cidade de Manchester-2, 1170-100 Lisbon
Tel: (021) 8130345 *Fax:* (021) 8166719
E-mail: silabo@mail.telepac.pt
Key Personnel
Marketing Dir: Manuel Robalo
    E-mail: manuelrobalo@mail.telepac.pt
Founded: 1983
Turnaround: 5 Workdays

Romania

Editura si Atelierele Tipografice Metropol SRL
Str Stefan cel Mare, nr 2 sector 1, 7000 Bucharest
Tel: (01) 2104593; (01) 2108433 *Fax:* (01) 2106987
Key Personnel
President: Dr Bansoiu Ion
Founded: 1990
Turnaround: 3-20 Workdays
Print Runs: 500 min - 50,000 max
Business from Other Countries: 10%

Editora Paideia
Str Teleajen nr 30, Bucharest
Tel: (01) 3308006; (01) 3301678 *Fax:* (01) 3301677
E-mail: paideia@fx.ro
Key Personnel
President: Ion Bansoiu
Founded: 1990
Turnaround: 3-20 Workdays
Business from Other Countries: 10%

Singapore

Chong Moh Offset Printing Ltd
Subsidiary of Chassis Graphic Art Pte Ltd
19 Joo Koon Rd, Jurong Town 628978
Tel: 8622701 *Fax:* 8624335
E-mail: chongmoh@singnet.com.sg
Key Personnel
Chairman: James Ng
Founded: 1946
Turnaround: 10-14 Workdays
Print Runs: 1,000 min
Business from Other Countries: 35%

CS Graphics Pte Ltd
10 Tuas Avenue 20, Singapore 638822
Tel: 8610100 *Fax:* 8610190
Key Personnel
Man Dir: Mr Lee Sian Tee *E-mail:* stlee@csgraphics.com.sg
Founded: 1987
Turnaround: 80 Workdays (with pre-press); 20-60 Workdays (without pre-press)
Print Runs: 1,000 min - 200,000 max
Business from Other Countries: 100%
Sales Office(s): 7305 Sierra Dr, Granite Bay, CA 95746, United States, Contact: Rick Marment *Tel:* 916-791-9066 *Fax:* 916-791-9112
E-mail: csgraphics@csi.com

Eurasia Press Pte Ltd
10/14 Kampong Ampat-1336, Singapore 368320
Tel: 2805522 *Fax:* 2800593; 3825458
E-mail: eurasia@mbox3.singnet.com.sg
Key Personnel
Marketing Dir: Allan Fong
Founded: 1937
Turnaround: 14 Workdays
Print Runs: 500 min - 100,000 max
Business from Other Countries: 65%

HB Media Holdings Pte Ltd
Division of International Printing Division
Subsidiary of HBM Print Ltd
No 745 Toa Payoh Lorong 5, HBM Centre, Singapore 1231
Tel: 2591919 *Fax:* 3532616
Key Personnel
Senior Vice President: Paul Tan
Founded: 1980
Turnaround: 5 Workdays
Business from Other Countries: 97%
Branch Office(s)
50 Kallang Bahru No 02-14/23, Kallang Basin Industrial Estate, Singapore 339334

Ho Printing Singapore Pte Ltd
Changi South St One, Singapore 486797
Tel: 5429322 *Fax:* 2896065
Telex: RS 39685 HOFSET
Key Personnel
Sales Executive: Ho Wah Yuen
Founded: 1951
Turnaround: 35-50 Workdays
Print Runs: 5,000 min - 50,000 max
Business from Other Countries: 30%

International Press Co Pte Ltd
26 Kallang Ave, Singapore 339417
Tel: 2983800 *Fax:* 2971668
Key Personnel
Marketing Manager: Koo Kok Leong
Founded: 1972
Print Runs: 3,000 min - 50,000 max
Business from Other Countries: 60%

Khai Wah-Ferco Pte Ltd
No 61 Yishun Industrial Park A, No 02-00, Singapore 768767

COMPLETE BOOK

Tel: 7583313 *Fax:* 7582038
E-mail: kwfppi@pacific.net.sg
Key Personnel
General Manager: Sim Huat Hoe

Kim Hup Lee Printing Co Pte Ltd
22 Lim Teck Boo Rd, Singapore 1953
Tel: 2833306 *Fax:* 2889222
Key Personnel
Dir: Mr Lim Geok Khoon

Kin Keong Printing Co Pte Ltd, see Markono Print Media Pte Ltd

Magenta Lithographic Consultants
1093 Lower Delta Rd, No 04-01, Singapore 139954
Tel: 2746288
Telex: RS39478Mlcols
Key Personnel
Man Proprietor: Mr Lim Choon Kiat
Founded: 1975
Turnaround: 2-3 Workdays
Business from Other Countries: 30%

Markono Print Media Pte Ltd
Formerly Kin Keong Printing Co Pte Ltd
Subsidiary of Markono Holdings Pte Ltd
21 Neythal Rd, Singapore 628586
Tel: 62811118 *Fax:* 62866663
E-mail: sales@markono.com.sg
Key Personnel
Man Dir: Bob Lee *E-mail:* blee@markono.com.sg
Turnaround: 14 Workdays
Print Runs: 1,000 min - 100,000 max
Business from Other Countries: 20%
Branch Office(s)
Kin Keong Colour Printing (M) Sdn Bhd, Port Klang 539538

Saik Wah Press (Pte) Ltd
Blk 52 Kallang Bahru, No 07-19/20, Singapore 1233 339335
Tel: 2928759 *Fax:* 2960638
Telex: RS38564
Key Personnel
Man Dir: Mr Chin San Hwa
Founded: 1973
Turnaround: 20 Workdays
Print Runs: 1,000 min - 100,000 max
Business from Other Countries: 70%

SNP Printing Pte Ltd
97 Ubi Ave 4, Singapore 408754
Tel: 7412500 *Fax:* 2854894
E-mail: 2028095@syp.com.sg
Web Site: www.snp.com.sg
Telex: SNPRS14462
Key Personnel
President: Yeo Chee Tong
Executive Vice President: Koo Tse Chia
US Sales Manager: Patrick Chung
Turnaround: 30 Workdays
Print Runs: 2,000 min - 200,000 max
Business from Other Countries: 40%

Stamford Press Pte Ltd
209, Kallang Bahru, Singapore 339344
Tel: 2947227 *Fax:* 2944396
Telex: RS56414 STAMFO
Key Personnel
Dir: R Theyvendran
Founded: 1963
Turnaround: 3-4 Workdays for small jobs; 3-4 weeks for big jobs
Print Runs: 1,500 min - 50,000 max
Business from Other Countries: 20%

Times Printers Pte Ltd
Subsidiary of Times Publishing Group

MANUFACTURING

16 Tuas Ave 5, Singapore 639340
Tel: 8623333 *Fax:* 8621313 *Cable:* TIMESPRINT
Key Personnel
Vice President: Leong Kwok Sun
Sales Manager: Patsy Tan; Koo Kok Leong
Founded: 1968
Turnaround: 5-25 Workdays
Print Runs: 3,000 min - 300,000 max
Business from Other Countries: 75%

Toppan Company (S) Pte Ltd
Division of Toppan Printing Co Ltd
Toppan Shibaura Bldg, 3-19-26 Shibaura, Minato-ku 108-0023
Tel: 264-0654 *Fax:* 265-8298
Telex: RS 21596 *Cable:* TOPPAN
Key Personnel
Man Dir: Kohei Mochizuki
General Manager: M Sonoda
Founded: 1968
Turnaround: 3 - 4 Weeks
Print Runs: 3,000 min - 500,000 max
Business from Other Countries: 70%

Viva Lithographers Pte Ltd
Blk 3 Pasir Panjang Rd, No 06-22/23 Alexandra Distripark, Singapore 0511 118485
Tel: 2721880 *Fax:* 2735425
Key Personnel
Man Dir: Michael Oh

Slovenia

Gorenjski Tisk Printing Co
Zoisova ulica 1, 4000 Kranj
Tel: (064) 2630 *Fax:* (064) 241323
Telex: 34560 YU GOTISK
Key Personnel
Dir: Kristina Kobal
Commercial Manager: Boris Krist
Founded: 1888
Turnaround: 30 Workdays
Print Runs: 3,000 min - 15,000 max
Business from Other Countries: 50%

Spain

Offo SL
Los Mesejos 23, 28007 Madrid
Tel: (01) 5514214 *Fax:* (01) 5010699
Key Personnel
Export Manager: Jose A Martinez Minuesa

Graficas Santamaria SA
Division of Fotomecanica
Bekolarra 4, 01010 Vitoria (Alava)
Tel: (045) 229100 *Fax:* (045) 246393
Key Personnel
Contact: Jesus Alzola Aguinaco
Founded: 1963
Turnaround: 1 Workday
Print Runs: 500 min - 150,000 max
Business from Other Countries: 15%

Luis Vives (Edelvives)
Xaudaro, 25, 28034 Madrid
Tel: (076) 3344890 *Fax:* (076) 3344892
Key Personnel
Production Dir: Jesus Agudo Perez
Founded: 1890
Turnaround: 1 Workday
Business from Other Countries: 25%

Sri Lanka

Sarvodaya Vishva Lekha
No 41 Lumbini Ave, Ratmalana
Tel: (01) 714820; (01) 714829; (01) 731601
 Fax: (01) 738932
E-mail: sarvs101@sri.lanka.net
Key Personnel
Man Dir: Susiri de Silva
Founded: 1984
Print Runs: 500 min
Business from Other Countries: 5%

Sumathi Book Printing (Pvt) Ltd
Division of Sumathi Group
445/1 Prince of Wales Ave, Colombo 14
Tel: (01) 330673; (01) 330674; (01) 435225
 Fax: (01) 449593
Telex: 22104 SUMATHI CE SUMATISONS
Business from Other Countries: 75%

Switzerland

Hallwag AG
Nordring 4, 3000 Bern
Tel: (031) 423131 *Fax:* (031) 414133
Telex: 912-661 HAWA CH
Key Personnel
President: Dr Juergen Schad

IBBY, see International Board on Books for Young People (IBBY)

International Board on Books for Young People (IBBY)
Nonnenweg 12, CH-4055 Basel
Tel: (061) 2722917 *Fax:* (061) 2722757
E-mail: ibby@eye.ch
Web Site: www.ibby.org
Key Personnel
Executive Dir: Leena Maissen
President: Ms Tayo Shima
Executive Assistant: Liz Page
Founded: 1953

Ott Verlag AG (Ott Publishers, Inc)
Laenggasse 57 Postfach 22, CH-3607 Thun
Tel: (033) 221622 *Fax:* (033) 2253939

Schweizerischer Schriftstellerinnen-und Schriftsteller-Verband (Swiss Writers' Union)
Nordstr 9, 8035 Zurich
Tel: (01) 350 04 60 *Fax:* (01) 350 04 61
E-mail: letter@ch-s.ch
Web Site: www.ch-s.ch
Key Personnel
Secretary: Peter A Schmid
Founded: 1912

Swiss Writer's Union, see Schweizerischer Schriftstellerinnen-und Schriftsteller-Verband

United Republic of Tanzania

Peramiho Publications
PO Box 41, Peramiho

UNITED KINGDOM

Tel: (054) 2730 *Fax:* (054) 2917
Key Personnel
Chief Executive: Fr Gerold Rupper
Founded: 1937
Print Runs: 4,000 min - 6,000 max

Thailand

J Film Process Co Ltd
440/7 Soi Chaisamoraphum, Rangnum Rd, Phayathai, Bangkok 10400
Tel: (02) 2486888 *Fax:* (02) 2464620; (02) 2474719
Key Personnel
President: Peer Prayukvong
Vice President: Siriporn Prayukvong
Man Dir: Pira Prayookwongse
Founded: 1970
Turnaround: 6 Workdays
Print Runs: 25,000 min - 65,000 max
Business from Other Countries: 45%

Phongwarin Printing Company Ltd
299 Moo 10, Sukhumvit 107, A Muang, Samut Prakarn 10260
Tel: (02) 7498934-45; (02) 3994525-31 *Fax:* (02) 3994524; (02) 3994255
E-mail: somphong@mozart.inet.co.th
Web Site: www.phongwarin.com
Key Personnel
Man Dir: Somphong Charnsirisaksakul
Founded: 1983
Turnaround: 7 Workdays
Print Runs: 1,000 min - 500,000 max
Business from Other Countries: 5%

Thai Watana Panich Press Co Ltd
891 Rama 1 Rd, Bangkok 10330
Tel: (02) 2150060 *Fax:* (02) 2152360
E-mail: twpp@bkk.loxinfo.co.th
Telex: 72303 Thaiwat th
Key Personnel
Man Dir: Thira T Suwan
Founded: 1935
Print Runs: 5,000 min

United Kingdom

J W Arrowsmith Ltd
71 Winterstoke Rd, Bristol BS3 2NT
Tel: (0117) 9667545 *Fax:* (0117) 9637829
E-mail: jw@arrowsmith.co.uk
Web Site: www.arrowsmith.co.uk
Key Personnel
Sales Mgr: D J Hooper *E-mail:* dhooper@arrowsmith.co.uk
Founded: 1854
Turnaround: 15 Workdays
Print Runs: 500 min - 15,000 max
Business from Other Countries: 25%

BAS Printers Ltd
Over Wallop, Stockbridge, Hants SO20 8JD
Tel: (01264) 781711 *Fax:* (01264) 781116
E-mail: bas@basprint.co.uk
Web Site: www.basprint.co.uk
Key Personnel
Man Dir: David Gumn

UNITED KINGDOM

Sales Dir: Paul G Gumn *E-mail:* paul@basprint.
co.uk
Founded: 1948
Print Runs: 350 min - 40,000 max
Business from Other Countries: 10%

The Bath Press
Subsidiary of Bath Press Group PLC
Lower Bristol Rd, Bath BA2 3BL
Tel: (01225) 428101 *Fax:* (01225) 312418
Key Personnel
Man Dir: Peter Palframan
Marketing Dir: Keith Johnson
Founded: 1846
Turnaround: 10-15 Workdays
Print Runs: 3,000 min - 300,000 max
Business from Other Countries: 5%

BCS Publishing Ltd
2nd floor, Temple Court, 109 Oxford Rd, Cowley, Oxford OX4 2ER
Tel: (01865) 770099 *Fax:* (01865) 770050
Key Personnel
Man Dir: Steve McCurdy
Founded: 1993
Business from Other Countries: 40%

Bell & Bain Ltd
303 Burnfield Rd, Thornliebank, Glasgow G46 7UQ
Tel: (0141) 6495697 *Fax:* (0141) 6328733
Key Personnel
Man Dir: I Walker
Sales Dir: D Stewart
Turnaround: 7-10 Workdays
Print Runs: 100 min - 100,000 max
Business from Other Countries: 25%

Biddles Ltd
Division of W & G Baird Ltd
Woodbridge Park Estate, Woodbridge Rd, Guildford, Surrey GU1 1DA
Tel: (01483) 502224 *Fax:* (01483) 576150
Key Personnel
Man Dir: M J Read
Founded: 1885
Turnaround: 20 Workdays
Print Runs: 250 min - 50,000 max
Business from Other Countries: 8%
Branch Office(s)
Kings Lynn

Roy Bloom Ltd
Fanshaw House, 3/9 Fanshaw St, London N1 6HX
Tel: (020) 7729 5373 *Fax:* (020) 7729 2375
Key Personnel
Chairman: Roy Bloom *E-mail:* roybloom@dircon.
co.uk
Man Dir: Adam Bloom
Founded: 1969
Business from Other Countries: 40%

Book Creation Services
21 Carnaby St, London W1V 1PH
Tel: (020) 7287 0214 *Fax:* (020) 7287 8547
Key Personnel
Chairman: Hal Robinson *E-mail:* hal@zoo.co.uk
Founded: 1991
Business from Other Countries: 30%

Book Production Consultants PLC
25-27 High St, Chesterton, Cambridge CB4 1ND
Tel: (01223) 352790 *Fax:* (01223) 460718
E-mail: cw@bpccam.co.uk
Web Site: www.bpccam.co.uk
Key Personnel
Man Dir: Tony Littlechild *E-mail:* tl@bpccam.co.
uk
Founded: 1973

Print Runs: 500 min
Business from Other Countries: 25%

British Sisalkraft Ltd
Subsidiary of David S Smith (Holdings)
Commissioners Rd, Strood, Rochester, Kent ME2 4ED
Tel: (01634) 290505 *Fax:* (01634) 291029
Key Personnel
Contact: Ian O Whitty
Business from Other Countries: 27%

D Brown & Sons Ltd
14 High St, 2nd floor, Cowbridge, Vale of Glamorgan, CF71 7AG South Wales
Tel: (01446) 771475 *Fax:* (01446) 771476
Key Personnel
Dir: J M Whitaker *Tel:* (01446) 774213
Finance Dir: Jane C Brown
Founded: 1895
Business from Other Countries: 10%

Caledonian International Book Manufacturing
Westerhill Rd, Bishopbriggs, Glasgow G64 2QR
Tel: (0141) 7623000 *Fax:* (0141) 7620922
E-mail: 101622.235@compuserve.com
Key Personnel
Man Dir: Kevin McKenna
Commercial Dir: G Morrison
Group Sales Manager: Martin Platt
E-mail: martin@platt44.freeserve.co.uk
Founded: 1819

Center Print Ltd
Colwick Business Park, Private Rd 2, Colwick, Nottingham NG4 2JR
Tel: (0115) 9612277 *Fax:* (0115) 9381424
Key Personnel
Man Dir: Nicola Leslie
Print Runs: 1,000 min - 250,000 max

Chase Publishing Services
Mead, Fortescue Rd, Sidmouth, Devon EX10 9QG
Tel: (01395) 514709 *Fax:* (01395) 514709
E-mail: r.addicott@btinternet.com
Key Personnel
President: Ray Addicott *E-mail:* r.addicott@
btinternet.com
Founded: 1989

Clays Ltd
Subsidiary of St Ives Plc
Popson St, Bungay, Suffolk NR35 1ED
Tel: (01986) 893211
E-mail: clays@claysltd.co.uk
Key Personnel
Contact: Sarah Orell
Founded: 1817
Turnaround: 15 Workdays
Print Runs: 1,000 min - 1,000,000 max
Business from Other Countries: 15%

William Clowes Ltd
Goal Lane, Beccles, Suffolk NR34 9QE
Tel: (01502) 712884 *Fax:* (01502) 717003
Key Personnel
Man Dir: Alex Evans
Sales Dir: David C Browne *Tel:* (01502) 712884, Ext 240
Founded: 1803
Turnaround: 10 Workdays
Print Runs: 2,000 min
Business from Other Countries: 1%
Sales Office(s): 2 Fore St, London

Cox & Wyman Ltd
Subsidiary of Rexam Plc
Cardiff Rd, Reading RG1 8EX
Tel: (01189) 530500 *Fax:* (01189) 507222

COMPLETE BOOK

Key Personnel
General Manager: Tom Roberts
Sales Manager: Ruth Smith
Founded: 1777
Turnaround: 10 workdays
Print Runs: 2,000 min - 2,000,000 max
Business from Other Countries: 12%

Dorriston Publishers Ltd
59 Stroud Green Rd, London N4 3EG
Tel: (020) 7272 2722 *Fax:* (020) 7272 7274
Key Personnel
Man Dir: A G Dicomites

Edition
Subsidiary of Cameron Books
2 Sunny Bank Old Edinburugh Rd, Moffat Dumfriesshire DG10 9SU
Tel: (01683) 220808 *Fax:* (01683) 220012
Key Personnel
Dir: Ian Cameron; Jill Hollis
Founded: 1976

Export Booksellers Group
Division of Booksellers Association of the United Kingdom & Ireland Ltd
272 Vauxhall Bridge Rd, London SW1V 1BA
Tel: (020) 7834 5477 *Fax:* (020) 7834 8812
E-mail: mail@booksellers.org.uk
Key Personnel
Meetings Executive: John Parke *E-mail:* john.
parke@booksellers.org.uk

Robert Fletcher (Stoneclough) Ltd
Stoneclough Paper Mill, Radcliffe, Manchester M26 1EH
Tel: (01204) 571241 *Fax:* (01204) 572919
Key Personnel
Contact: John Rukin

Gardenhouse Editions
15 Grafton Sq, London SW4 0DQ
Tel: (020) 76221720 *Fax:* (020) 7720 9114
Key Personnel
Man Dir: L Johnson

Gee & Son (Denbigh) Ltd-Gwasg Gee-Gee's Press
Chapel St, Denbigh, Denbigshire LL16 3SW
Tel: (01745) 812020 *Fax:* (01745) 812825
Key Personnel
Man Dir: Emlyn Evans
Founded: 1808

Goldshield Communications Ltd
Banners Bldg, Attercliffe Rd, Sheffield S9 3QS
Tel: (0114) 2431000 *Fax:* (0114) 2433000
Key Personnel
Man Dir & Overseas-Special Projects: Sandra Potesta *E-mail:* sandra@goldcom.co.uk
Technical & Production: Stefano Potesta
Founded: 1984
Business from Other Countries: 40%

James Gowans Ltd
Subsidiary of Brown, Son & Ferguson, Ltd
4-10 Darnley St, Glasgow G41 2SD
Tel: (0141) 4293337 *Fax:* (0141) 4201694
E-mail: info@skipper.co.uk
Web Site: www.skipper.co.uk
Key Personnel
Production Dir: T Nigel Brown
Founded: 1872
Turnaround: 3-5 Workdays
Print Runs: 100 min - 10,000 max

The Guernsey Press Co Ltd
Braye Rd, Vale, Guernsey, Channel Islands GY1 3BW
Mailing Address: PO Box 57, Vale, Guernsey, Channel Islands GY1 3BW

MANUFACTURING   UNITED KINGDOM

Tel: (01481) 240240; (01481) 243657 (ISDN)
 Fax: (01481) 240290; (01481) 249147
E-mail: books@guernsey-press.com
Key Personnel
Contact: Mr T A R Duquemin
Founded: 1897
Turnaround: 10 Workdays
Print Runs: 2,000 min - 50,000 max
Business from Other Countries: 80%

Robert Hale Ltd
45-47 Clerkenwell Green, London EC1R 0HT
Tel: (020) 7251 2661 *Fax:* (020) 7490 4958
E-mail: english@halebooks.com
Web Site: www.halebooks.com
Key Personnel
Chairman: John Hare
Marketing Dir: Martin Kendall
Founded: 1936

Hammond Packaging Ltd
Division of Hammond Bindery
129 Water Lane, Holbeck, Leeds LS11 9UB
Tel: (0113) 2423548 *Fax:* (0113) 2445442
E-mail: hammpack@dial.pipex.com
Web Site: www.hammpack.co.uk
Key Personnel
Man Dir: Steve Allan
Office Manager: Susan Sheldon
Founded: 1991
Turnaround: 5-15 Workdays
Print Runs: 100 min - 500,000 max

Ikon Document Services Ltd
Subsidiary of Microgen Holdings Plc
19 The Business Centre, Molly Millars Lane, Wokingham Berks RG41 2QY
Tel: (0118) 9770510 *Fax:* (0118) 9770513
Key Personnel
Man Dir: Dave Weller
Business Development Dir: Aaron Biggs
Founded: 1972
Turnaround: 2-5 Workdays
Print Runs: 1 min - 5,000 max
Business from Other Countries: 40%
Branch Office(s)
Microgen City Park Watchmead, Welwyn Garden City, Herts AL7 1LT

Intype London Ltd
Units 3 & 4, Elm Grove Industrial Estate, Elm Grove, Wimbledon, London SW19 4HE
Tel: (020) 8947 7863 *Fax:* (020) 8947 3652
E-mail: intype@btconnect.com
Web Site: www.intype.co.uk
Key Personnel
Man Dir: Tony Chapman *E-mail:* tchap@btconnect.com
Production: Jane Rogers
Founded: 1976
Turnaround: 10-15 Workdays for proofs; 5-10 Workdays for books
Print Runs: 5 min - 2,500 max
Business from Other Countries: 5%

ITD
Faraday Rd, Rabans Lane, Aylesbury, Bucks HP19 3RY
Tel: (01296) 427211 *Fax:* (01296) 4392019
Key Personnel
Man Dir: Roy Jackson-Moore
Founded: 1976
Turnaround: 7-10 Workdays
Business from Other Countries: 10%

Gerald Judd Sales Ltd
Paper House, 104 Rochester Row, London SW1P 1JP
Tel: (020) 7828 8821 *Fax:* (020) 7828 0840
Key Personnel
Man Dir: Simon Perks

Sales Dir: Jonathan Addy
Founded: 1936

Lavenham Press Ltd
Water St, Lavenham, Sudbury, Suffolk CO10 9RN
Tel: (01787) 247436 *Fax:* (01787) 248267
E-mail: postmaster@lavenhamgroup.co.uk
Key Personnel
Man Dir: T A J Dalton
Founded: 1953
Business from Other Countries: 1%

Charles Letts & Co Ltd
Thorney Bank Industrial Estate, Dalkeith EH2 2NE
Tel: (0131) 6631971 *Fax:* (0131) 6603225
Key Personnel
Man Dir: Gordon Presly
Founded: 1796

Masons Design & Print
Viscount House, River Lane, Saltney, Chester CH4 8RH
Tel: (01244) 674433 *Fax:* (01244) 674274
E-mail: 100612.3105@compuserve.com
Key Personnel
Man Dir: Timothy Leaman
Founded: 1908
Turnaround: 5-10 Workdays
Print Runs: 500 min - 500,000 max

MPG Books Ltd
Subsidiary of Martins Printing Group
Victoria Sq, Bodmin, Cornwall PL31 1EB
Tel: (01208) 73266 *Fax:* (01208) 73603
E-mail: print@mpg-books.co.uk
Key Personnel
Sales Dir: Jeff Swift
Man Dir: Paul Dixon
Commercial Dir: Tony Chard
Founded: 1967
Turnaround: 10-15 days
Print Runs: 400 min - 10,000 max
Business from Other Countries: 5%
Parent Company: MPG Ltd

NES Arnold Ltd
Subsidiary of Group Holdings PLC
Novara House, Excelsior Rd, Ashby-de-la Zouch, Lincs LEG5 WCT
Tel: (0870) 6000 192 *Fax:* (01530) 418268
Telex: (0602) 377082
Key Personnel
Marketing Manager: Anita Ladva
 E-mail: aladva@novara.co.uk

Page Bros Ltd (Norwich)
Subsidiary of Milex Ltd
Mile Cross Lane, Norwich NR6 6SA
Tel: (01603) 429141 *Fax:* (01603) 485126
Key Personnel
Man Dir: David Armstrong
Founded: 1750
Turnaround: 10 Workdays
Print Runs: 100 min - 30,000 max
Business from Other Countries: 20%
Branch Office(s)
105-A Euston St, London NW1 2ET *Tel:* (020) 7383 2212 *Fax:* (020) 7383 4145

Paternoster Publishing
Subsidiary of STL Ltd
Kingstown Broadway, Carlisle, Cumbria CA3 0QS
Mailing Address: PO Box 300, Carlisle, Cumbria CA3 0QS
Tel: (01228) 512512 *Fax:* (01228) 514949
E-mail: info@Paternoster-Publishing.com
Web Site: www.paternoster-publishing.com

Key Personnel
Man Dir: Pieter Kwant
Founded: 1935
Print Runs: 3,000 min - 10,000 max

Pensord Press Ltd
Tram Rd Blackwood, Gwent NP2 2YA
Tel: (01495) 223721 *Fax:* (01495) 222157
Key Personnel
Dir: N G Bennays

Polestar Purnell Ltd
Subsidiary of BPC Ltd
Paulton, Bristol BS39 7LQ
Tel: (01761) 404142 *Fax:* (01761) 404198
Key Personnel
Man Dir: David Yendole
Founded: 1839

Precision Publishing Papers Ltd
Subsidiary of Ekman Cleave Group Ltd
Court Ash House, Court Ash, Yeovil, Somerset BA20 1HG
Tel: (01935) 431800 *Fax:* (01935) 431805
Key Personnel
Man Dir: Anthony J Fagan

The Q Group Plc
Remo House, 310-312 Regent St, London W1R 5AJ
Tel: (020) 7291 1600 *Fax:* (020) 7291 1699
E-mail: ppoulter@qgroupplc.com
Key Personnel
Man Dir: P F Poulter

F J Ratchford Ltd
Subsidiary of Bookcraft Supplies Ltd
Kennedy Way, Green Lane, Stockport, Cheshire SK4 2JX
Tel: (0161) 4808484 *Fax:* (0161) 4803679
Key Personnel
Dir: J P Ratchford
Founded: 1889

Redwood Books Ltd
Division of CPI (UK) Ltd
Kennet Way, Trowbridge, Wilts BA14 8RN
Tel: (01225) 769979 *Fax:* (01225) 769050
Key Personnel
Man Dir: Keith Johnson
Founded: 1993
Turnaround: 10 Workdays
Print Runs: 250 min - 20,000 max
Business from Other Countries: 8%
Branch Office(s)
London Sales Office, 22 Bloomsbury Sq, London WC1A 2NS *Tel:* (020) 7580-9328 *Fax:* (020) 7580-9337

Antony Rowe Ltd
Bumpers Farm, Chippenham SN14 6LH
Tel: (01249) 659705 *Fax:* (01249) 443103
Key Personnel
Chief Executive: Ralph Bell
Production Dir: Mike Bando
Technical Dir: Andy Burns
Secretary: Charlotte Rowe
Founded: 1983
Turnaround: 20 Workdays
Print Runs: 50 min - 2,000 max
Business from Other Countries: 2%

Scottish Braille Press
Craigmillar Park, Edinburgh EH16 5NB
Tel: (0131) 6624445 *Fax:* (0131) 6621968
E-mail: scot.braille@dial.pipex.com
Web Site: www.scottish-braille-press.org
Key Personnel
Manager: Mr J H Adams
Founded: 1891
Turnaround: 15-20 Workdays
Parent Company: Royal Blind Asylum & School

UNITED KINGDOM

Society of Authors
84 Drayton Gardens, London SW10 9SB
Tel: (020) 7373 6642 *Fax:* (020) 7373 5768
E-mail: info@societyofauthors.org
Web Site: www.societyofauthors.org
Key Personnel
General Secretary: Mark Le Fanu
Founded: 1884

M & A Thomson Litho Ltd
10/16 Colvilles Pl, Kelvin Industrial Estate, East Kilbride, Glasgow G75 0SN
Tel: (013552) 33081 *Fax:* (013552) 45439
Key Personnel
Deputy Chairman: Gary Thomson

TJ International Ltd
Subsidiary of Ulverscroft Large Print Books
Trecerus Industrial Estate, Padstow, Cornwall PL28 8RW
Tel: (01841) 532691 *Fax:* (01841) 532862
Key Personnel
Chief Executive: Angus Clark *E-mail:* Angus@tjinternational.hd.uk
Founded: 1974
Turnaround: 15 Workdays
Business from Other Countries: 5%

Toppan Printing Co (UK) Ltd
Subsidiary of Toppan Printing Co Ltd
Gillingham House, 38-44 Gillingham St, London SW1V 1HU
Tel: (020) 7828 7292 *Fax:* (020) 7828 5310
Key Personnel
President: Mr K Jo
Manager: Mr P Harty
Founded: 1983

UK Serials Group-UKSG
Hilltop, Heath End, Newbury RG20 OAP
Tel: (01635) 254292 *Fax:* (01635) 253826
E-mail: uksg.admin@dial.pipex.com
Web Site: www.uksg.org
Key Personnel
Business Manager: Alison Whitehorn
Founded: 1978

UKSG, see UK Serials Group-UKSG

United Kingdom Serials Group, see UK Serials Group-UKSG

UPM-Kymmene Ltd
Subsidiary of UPM-Kymmene Group
Norfolk House, 31 St James's Sq, London SW1Y 4JJ
Tel: (0870) 6000 876 *Fax:* (0870) 6060 876
Web Site: www.upm-kymmene.com
Key Personnel
Marketing: S P Daykin; Miss C E Burgess

Vista Computer Services Ltd
Subsidiary of Vista Computer Services Inc; Vista Computer Services; Vista Computer Services Pty
Valency House, Batchworth Lane, Northwood, Middx HA6 3HD
Tel: (01923) 820920 *Fax:* (01923) 827713
Key Personnel
Chairman: Denis Bennett
Man Dir: Colin Bottle
Marketing Manager: Marlyn Daniels
Founded: 1977
Business from Other Countries: 50%

Watkiss Automation Ltd
Subsidiary of The Watkiss Group
One Blaydon Rd, Middlefield Industrial Estate, Sandy, Beds SG19 1RZ
Tel: (01767) 682177 *Fax:* (01767) 691769

Key Personnel
Technical Dir: M Watkiss
Founded: 1959
Print Runs: 200 min - 10,000 max
Business from Other Countries: 5%

The Word Factory
Bynax House, PO Box 186, Nottingham NG11 6DU
Tel: (0115) 921-3263 *Fax:* (0115) 921-5017
E-mail: books@thewordfactory.co.uk

Zoe Books Ltd
15 Worthy Lane, Winchester SO23 7AB
Tel: (01962) 851318
E-mail: enquiries@zoebooks.co.uk
Web Site: www.zoebooks.co.uk
Key Personnel
Man Dir: Imogen Dawson *E-mail:* imogen@easynet.co.uk
Founded: 1990
Business from Other Countries: 75%

United States

A-R Editions Inc
8551 Research Way, Suite 180, Middleton, WI 53562
Tel: 608-836-9000 *Fax:* 608-831-8200
E-mail: info@areditions.com
Web Site: www.areditions.com
Key Personnel
Pres & CEO: Patrick Wall
Dir, Sales & Mktg: James L Zychowicz
  E-mail: james.zychowicz@areditions.com
Founded: 1962
Business from Other Countries: 10%

ADR/BookPrint
2012 Northern, Wichita, KS 67216
Tel: 316-522-5599 *Fax:* 316-522-5445
Web Site: www.adrbookprint.com
Key Personnel
Pres: James E Rishel
VP: Grace M Rishel *E-mail:* grace@adrbookprint.com
Prodn Mgr: Marc Seiwert
Founded: 1978
Print Runs: 50 min - 5,000 max
Business from Other Countries: 10%
Membership(s): PIA

American Pizzi Offset Corp
Subsidiary of Arti Grafiche Amilcare Pizzi (Milan)
370 Lexington Ave, Suite 1505, New York, NY 10017
Tel: 212-986-1658 *Fax:* 212-286-1887
E-mail: apocnyusa@aol.com
Key Personnel
Pres: Massimo Pizzi
Sales Mgr, US & UK: Barbara Sadick
Founded: 1914
Business from Other Countries: 50%

Asia Pacific Offset Inc
1332 Corcoran St NW, Suite 6, Washington, DC 20009
Tel: 202-462-5436 *Fax:* 202-986-4030
Web Site: www.asiapacificoffset.com
Key Personnel
Pres: Andrew Clarke *E-mail:* Andrew@asiapacificoffset.com
Dir, Sales (NY Office): Timothy Linn
  Tel: 212-941-8300 *Fax:* 212-941-9810
  E-mail: Timothy@asiapacificoffset.com
Founded: 1997

COMPLETE BOOK

Turnaround: 104 Workdays including color separation & shipping
Print Runs: 2,000 min
Business from Other Countries: 100%
Branch Office(s)
Phoenix Offset, Unit F1-2 2nd fl, Yeung Yiu Chung No 8 Industrial Bldg, 20 Wang Hoi Rd, Kowloon Bay, Hong Kong, Contact: Edmond Chan *Tel:* 2751-9962 *Fax:* 2755-8408 *E-mail:* Phoffest@netvigator.com
Sales Office(s): 225 Lafayette St, Suite 703, New York, NY 10012 *Tel:* 212-941-8300 *Fax:* 212-941-9810 *E-mail:* Timothy@asiapacificoffset.com
21 Columbus Ave, Suite 231, San Francisco, CA 94111, Dir of Sales: Rick Conant *Tel:* 415-433-3488 *Fax:* 415-433-3489 *E-mail:* Rick@asiapacificoffset.com

BookBuilders New York Ltd
353 Strawtown Rd, New City, NY 10956
Tel: 845-639-5316 *Fax:* 845-639-5318
Key Personnel
Pres: Martin Cook *E-mail:* martin@mcabooks.com
Founded: 1977
Turnaround: 30-45 Workdays
Print Runs: 2,000 min - 500,000 max
Business from Other Countries: 60%

C & C Offset Printing Co Ltd
Subsidiary of C & C Joint Printing Co (HK) Ltd under Sino United Publishing (Holdings) Ltd
2632 SE 25 Ave, Suite D, Portland, OR 97202
Mailing Address: PO Box 82037, Portland, OR 97282-0037
Tel: 503-233-1834 *Fax:* 503-233-7815
E-mail: portlandinfo@ccoffset.com
Web Site: www.ccoffset.com
Key Personnel
Dir, C & C Offset Printing Co Ltd, Portland, OR, USA: Charles H Clark, IV
  E-mail: cclark@ccoffset.com
Devt Mgr, C & C Offset Printing Co (USA) Inc, Portland, OR, USA: Jenny Whittier
  E-mail: jwhittier@ccoffset.com
Dir & Exec VP, C & C Offset Printing Co (NYC) Inc, New York, NY, USA: Simon Chan *E-mail:* schan@ccoffset.com
Cust Serv Mgr, C & C Offset Printing Co (USA) Inc, Portland, OR, USA: Ernest Li
  E-mail: ernestli@ccoffset.com
Cust Serv Mgr, C & C Offset Printing Co (NYC): Frances Harkness
  E-mail: fharkness@ccoffset.com
Dir & Gen Mgr, Hong Kong Head Office: Zhuang Xian-Qing
Dir & Asst Gen Mgr, Hong Kong Head Office: Ken Lee
Sales Mgr (Overseas), Hong Kong Head Office: Kit Wong
Sales Mgr (Special Projects), Hong Kong Head Office: Francis Ho
Dir & Gen Mgr, C & C Joint Printing Co (Guangdong) Ltd, Shenzhen, China: Jackson Leung
Deputy Sales Mgr, C & C Joint Printing Co (Guangdong) Ltd, Shenzhen, China: Simon Zhang
Pres, C & C Printing Japan Co Ltd, Tokyo, Japan: Masashi Otobe

MANUFACTURING

UNITED STATES

Man Dir, C & C Joint Printing Co (Beijing) Ltd, Beijing, China: Zhang Lin Gui
Dir, C & C Offset Printing Co (UK): Tracy Broderick
Mgr, C & C Offset Printing Co (UK): Fiona Norman
Founded: 1980
Turnaround: varies
Print Runs: 2,000 min - 200,000 max
Business from Other Countries: 60%
Branch Office(s)
C & C Printing Co (NY) Inc, 401 Broadway, Suite 2015, New York, NY 10013-3005 *Tel:* 212-431-4210 *Fax:* 212-431-3960 *E-mail:* newyorkinfo@ccoffset.com (New York City Office)
C & C Joint Printing Co (Guangdong) Ltd, Intercontinental Bldg, Rm 706, 16 An Wai An De Rd, DongCheng District, Beijing 100011, China, Contact: Mr Xiao Mungshen *Tel:* (010) 8488 2436 *Fax:* (010) 8488-2336 *E-mail:* beijing@candcprinting.com
C & C Joint Print Co (Beijing) Ltd, Beijing Economic & Technological Developent Area (BDA), No 3, Donghuan North Rd, Beijing 100176, China, Contact: Mr Zhang Lin Gui *Tel:* (010) 678 72862 *Fax:* (010) 678-72861 *E-mail:* beijing@candcprinting.com
C & C Bldg, 36 Ting Lai Rd, Tai Po, New Territories, Hong Kong *Tel:* 2666-4988 *Fax:* 2666-4938 *E-mail:* offsetprinting@candcprinting.com
C & C Joint Printing Co (Guangdong) Ltd (Changsha Office), The Building of Changsha City Commercial Bank, No 1, Frong Middle Rd, Rm 1218, Changsha, Hunan 41005, China, Contact: Ms Chen Jian *Tel:* (0731) 225 0288 *Fax:* (0731) 225 0178 *E-mail:* changsha@candcprinting.com (Regional Office)
Fang Fa Bldg, No 29, Rm 304, 165 Dongzhu Anbin Rd, Shanghai 200050, China, Contact: Ms Wu Hiaohung *Tel:* (021) 6240 1305 *Fax:* (021) 6240 2090 *E-mail:* shanghai@candcprinting.com
C & C Joint Printing Co (Guangdong) Ltd, Chunhu Industrial Estate, Pinghu, Long Gang, Shenzhen 518111, China *Tel:* (0755) 845 8333 *Fax:* (0755) 845 9111 (Plant)
C & C Printing Japan Co Ltd, Tozaido Bldg, 3F, 2-6-12 Hitotsubashi, Chiyoda-ku, Tokyo 101-0003, Japan, Contact: Mr Masashi Otobe *Tel:* (03) 5216 4580 *Fax:* (03) 5216-4610 *E-mail:* mail@candcprinting.co.jp *Web Site:* www.candcprinting.co.jp
C & C Joint Printing Co (Guangdong) Ltd (Xian Office), 10 Xuanfengquiao, Jianguo Rd, Xian 710001, China *Tel:* (029) 741 8407 *Fax:* (029) 743 5730 *E-mail:* xian@candcprinting.co
Hua Xin Bldg E Block, Rm 1511, 2 Shuiyin Rd, Huanshi East, Guangzhou 510075, China, Contact: Mr Peng Ji Shan *Tel:* (020) 3760 0979; (020) 3760 0980 *Fax:* (020) 3760 0977 *E-mail:* guangzhou@candcprinting.com
C & C Offset Printing Co (UK) Ltd, 2 New Burlington St, 4th fl, London W1S 2JE, United Kingdom *Tel:* (020) 7287-7787 *Fax:* (020) 7287-7187 *E-mail:* tracy@candcoffset.co.uk
See ad in this section and on Insert

Codra Enterprises Inc
5912 Bolsa Ave, Suite 200, Huntington Beach, CA 92649
Tel: 714-891-5652 *Fax:* 714-891-5642
E-mail: codra@codra.com
Key Personnel
Gen Mgr: Chris Kim *E-mail:* chrisk@codra.com
Founded: 1985
Turnaround: 4-6 Weeks
Print Runs: 3,000 min
Business from Other Countries: 10%
Membership(s): Pacific Northwest Booksellers Association; Publishers Association of the West

Colorprint Offset Inc
Division of Colorprint Offset (Hong Kong)
80 Park Ave, Suite 10N, New York, NY 10016
Tel: 212-681-9400 *Fax:* 212-681-9362
Key Personnel
Pres: Justin Wakefield *E-mail:* justin@colorprintoffset.com; Lee Moncho *E-mail:* lee@colorprintoffset.com
Prod Dir & Cust Serv Mgr: Kate Brady *E-mail:* kate@colorprintoffset.com
Founded: 1986
Turnaround: 15 Workdays
Print Runs: 100 min - 50,000 max
Business from Other Countries: 65%

Coneco Litho Graphics
Division of NET 2 PRESS Inc
58 Dix Ave, Glens Falls, NY 12801-7255
Mailing Address: PO Box 3255, Glen Falls, NY 12801-7255
Tel: 518-793-3823 *Fax:* 518-793-5823
Web Site: www.conecolithographics.com
Key Personnel
Pres & CEO: Garth E Grandchamp *E-mail:* garth@conecolithographics.com
Gen Mgr: Steve Webber *E-mail:* swebber@conecolithographics.com
Client Servs Mgr: Cindy Brower *E-mail:* cbrower@conecolithographics.com
Founded: 1984
Turnaround: 15 Workdays
Print Runs: 250 min - 25,000 max
Business from Other Countries: 27%

Consolidated Printers Inc
2630 Eighth St, Berkeley, CA 94710
Tel: 510-843-8524 *Fax:* 510-486-0580
E-mail: cpi@consoprinters.com
Web Site: www.consoprinters.com
Key Personnel
CEO: Lawrence A Hawkins
Founded: 1952
Turnaround: 2-20 Workdays
Print Runs: 2,000 min - 500,000 max
Business from Other Countries: 15%

Martin Cook Associates Ltd
353 Strawtown Rd, New City, NY 10956
Tel: 845-639-5316 *Fax:* 845-639-5318
Web Site: www.mcabooks.com
Key Personnel
Pres: Martin Cook *E-mail:* mcanewcity@aol.com
Founded: 1977
Turnaround: 30-45 Workdays
Print Runs: 2,000 min - 500,000 max
Business from Other Countries: 15%

CS Graphics USA Inc
Subsidiary of CS Graphics Pte Ltd Singapore
8969 Lake Ct, Granite Bay, CA 95746
Tel: 916-791-9066 *Fax:* 916-791-9112
E-mail: csgraphics@mindspring.com
Key Personnel
Mgr, Sales & Mktg: Rick Marment
Founded: 1980
Turnaround: 80 Workdays
Print Runs: 1,000 min - 75,000 max
Business from Other Countries: 30%

DNP America LLC
Subsidiary of Dai Nippon Printing Co Ltd
335 Madison Ave, 3rd fl, New York, NY 10017
Tel: 212-503-1074; 212-503-1060 *Fax:* 212-286-1505
Web Site: www.dnp.co.jp/ *Cable:* DAIPRINTS NY
Key Personnel
Pres: Yoji Yamakawa
VP & Gen Mgr, Graphic Printing: Kohei Tsumori *E-mail:* tsumori-k@mail.dnp.co.jp
Founded: 1974
Print Runs: 1,000 min - 1,000,000 max
Business from Other Countries: 54%
Branch Office(s)
577 Airport Blvd, Suite 620, Burlingame, CA 94010, Gen Mgr: Kosuke Tago *Tel:* 650-340-6061 *Fax:* 650-340-6090

Elegance Printing & Book Binding (USA)
Member of The Elegance Printing Group
708 Glen Cove Ave, Glen Head, NY 11545
Tel: 516-676-5941 *Fax:* 516-676-5973
Web Site: www.elegancebooks.com
Key Personnel
Man Dir: Frank DeLuca *E-mail:* frank@elegancebooks.com
Founded: 1977
Turnaround: Reprints ship within 14 days. New bks artwork to press within 2 wks-ship within 30 days
Print Runs: 1,000 min - 200,000 max
Business from Other Countries: 40%

Express Media Corp
1419 Donelson Pike, Nashville, TN 37217
Tel: 615-360-6400 *Fax:* 615-360-3140
E-mail: info@expressmedia.com
Web Site: www.expressmedia.com
Key Personnel
Pres: Andrew Cameron
Exec VP: Andrew S Cameron *E-mail:* ascameron@expressmedia.com
Founded: 1996
Turnaround: 3 Workdays
Print Runs: 1 min - 10,000 max
Business from Other Countries: 10%

Hamilton Printing Co
22 Hamilton Way, Castleton-on-Hudson, NY 12033
Tel: 518-732-4491 *Fax:* 518-732-7714
Key Personnel
Pres: Brian F Payne
VP, Mfg: William E Greenawalt
VP, Fin: Michael H Hart
Prod Mgr: Fred Mitchell
Sales Rep: Scott Payne; Michael C Rosenhack *E-mail:* miker@hpcbook.com; Stephen H Feuer
Founded: 1912
Turnaround: Flexible, time-sensitive scheduling
Business from Other Countries: 10%
Membership(s): BMI

Hindy's Enterprise
Division of Jinno International
3 Christine Dr, Chestnut Ridge, NY 10977-6802
Tel: 845-735-4666 *Fax:* 617-344-5905
Key Personnel
Pres: Yoh Jinno *E-mail:* jinno@hotmail.com
Founded: 1989
Turnaround: 40 Workdays
Print Runs: 500 min - 2,000,000 max
Business from Other Countries: 70%
Branch Office(s)
Melbourne Industrial Bldg, Block A, 20th fl, 16 Westlands Rd, Quarry Bay, Hong Kong *Tel:* 25166318 *Fax:* 25165161

IBT Global Ltd, see Integrated Book Technology Inc

Imago
1431 Broadway, Penthouse, New York, NY 10018
Tel: 847-358-3047 *Fax:* 212-921-8226
E-mail: imagousa@imagousa.com
Web Site: www.imagousa.com

Making great books

and

More . . .

HONG KONG
C & C Offset Printing Co., Ltd.
Kit Wong
C & C Building, 36 Ting Lai Road
Tai Po, New Territories, Hong Kong
Tel: 852-2666-4988
Fax: 852-2666-4938
E-mail: offsetprinting@candcprinting.com

UNITED KINGDOM
C & C Offset Printing Co. (UK), Ltd.
Tracy Broderick
2 New Burlington Street, 4th Floor
W1S 2JE, London, England
Tel: 0207-287-7787
Fax: 0207-287-7187
E-mail: tracy@candcoffset.co.uk

UNITED STATES

Key Personnel
Pres: Joseph E Braff *E-mail:* jbraff@imagousa.com
Sr Sales Exec: Linda Readerman
 E-mail: lreaderman@imagousa.com
Prodn Dir, USA: Howard R Musk
 E-mail: hmusk@imagousa.com
Dir, West Coast Opers: Greg Lee *Tel:* 949-661-5998 *Fax:* 949-661-8013 *E-mail:* glee@imagousa.com
Prodn Supv, West Coast: Yuhong Guo *Tel:* 949-661-5998 *Fax:* 949-661-8013 *E-mail:* yguo@imagousa.com
Dir, Midwest Opers: Bryan O'Shaughnessy *Tel:* 847-358-3047 *Fax:* 847-358-3078 *E-mail:* bo'shaughnessy@imagousa.com
Founded: 1985
Turnaround: 21 Workdays for color separations; 6 Weeks for printing & binding
Print Runs: 5,000 min
Business from Other Countries: 100%
Branch Office(s)
Imago West Coast, 31952 Camino Capistrano, Suite C-22, San Juan Capistrano, CA 92675, Prod Supv West Coast: Yuhong Guo *Tel:* 949-661-5998 *Fax:* 949-661-8013 *E-mail:* yguo@imagousa.com
Imago Midwest, 800 E Northwest Hwy, Suite 622, Palatine, IL 60067, Dir, Midwest Opers: Bryan O'Shaughnessy *Tel:* 847-358-3047 *Fax:* 847-358-3278 *E-mail:* bryano@imagousa.com
Imago (UK/Europe) Publishing Ltd, Albury Court, Albury Thame, Oxfordshire OX9 2LP, United Kingdom, Man Dir: Colin Risk *Tel:* (44) 1844 337000 *Fax:* (44) 1844 339955 *Web Site:* www.imago.co.uk
Imago Services (HKG) Ltd, 653-659 Kings Rd, 6th fl, Flat B, North Point, Hong Kong, Man Dir: Kendrick Cheung *Tel:* 2811 3316 *Fax:* 2597 5256 *Web Site:* www.imago.co.uk
Imago Productions (FE) Pte Ltd, MacPherson Industrial Complex, Suite 05-01, 5 Lorong Bakar Batu, Singapore 1334, Singapore, Man Dir: K C Ng *Tel:* 748 4433 *Fax:* 748 6082 *Web Site:* www.imago.co.uk

Integrated Book Technology Inc
Subsidiary of The IBT Group
18 Industrial Park Rd, Troy, NY 12180
Tel: 518-271-5117 *Fax:* 518-266-9422
E-mail: mail@integratedbooktechnology.com
Web Site: www.integratedbooktechnology.com
Key Personnel
CEO & Pres: John R Paeglow *E-mail:* johnp@integratedbook.com
VP & Chief Technol Officer: William Clockel *E-mail:* billc@integratedbook.com
VP, Fin: Richard Donovan *E-mail:* rickd@integratedbook.com
VP, Sales & Mktg: Robert Lindberg *E-mail:* bobl@integratedbook.com
Dir, Info Technol: Michael Whalen *E-mail:* mikew@integratedbook.com
Regl Sales: Tim Knickerbocker *E-mail:* timk@integratedbook.com
Dir, London Off: Richard Stevenson
Cust Serv Mgr: James Klein *E-mail:* jimk@integratedbook.com
Dist & Print Contact: Gary Lombardo *E-mail:* garyl@integratedbook.com
Founded: 1991
Turnaround: 1-15 Workdays
Print Runs: 10 min - 2,500 max
Business from Other Countries: 20%
Branch Office(s)
London, United Kingdom
Membership(s): BMI

Jinno International Group
3 Christine Dr, Chestnut Ridge, NY 10977
Tel: 845-735-4666 *Fax:* 617-344-5905
E-mail: jinno@hotmail.com
Key Personnel
Pres: Yoh Jinno
VP: Sharon Jinno
Founded: 1989
Turnaround: 21-30 Workdays US, 45-75 Workdays overseas
Print Runs: 500 min - 3,000,000 max
Business from Other Countries: 98%
Branch Office(s)
Hindy's Enterprise, Melbourne Industrial Bldg, 16 Westlands Rd, Block A, 20th fl, Quarry Bay, Hong Kong *Tel:* 516-6318 *Fax:* 516-5161
Wing Yiu Printing Co, Melbourne Industrial Bldg, 6th fl, Block A, 16 Westlands Rd, Quarry Bay, Hong Kong, Contact: Law Ming Wah *Tel:* 561 0283 *Fax:* 565 8233
c/o Eurasia Press Pte Ltd, 10/14 Kampong Ampat, Singapore 1336, Singapore, Contact: Allan Fong *Tel:* 280 5522 *Fax:* 280 0593
Jinno International Singapore, 710 Ang Mo Kio, Ave 8, Suite 07-2615, Singapore 2056, Singapore *Tel:* 458 0778

KNI Inc
1261 S State College Pkwy, Anaheim, CA 92806
Tel: 714-956-7300 *Fax:* 714-635-1744
E-mail: epp@kniinc.com
Web Site: www.kniinc.com
Key Personnel
Pres: Jeremy R Bernstein
VP, Admin: Judith Bernstein
VP & Sales Mgr: Peggy Bryant
VP & Cont: Dan Jacinthro
Founded: 1970
Print Runs: 50 min - 100,000 max
Business from Other Countries: 17%

Lenz & Riecker Inc
690 Union Blvd, Totowa, NJ 07512
Tel: 973-256-2456 *Fax:* 973-256-3433; 973-256-2459
E-mail: info@l-r.com
Web Site: www.l-r.com
Key Personnel
Pres: Steven Riecker
VP, Sales: G Gilrain
CFO: Barry Levinson
Founded: 1917
Turnaround: 2-20 Workdays
Print Runs: 100 min - 100,000 max
Business from Other Countries: 20%

Leo Paper USA
1180 NW Maple St, Suite 102, Issaquah, WA 98027
Tel: 425-646-8801 *Fax:* 425-646-8805
E-mail: leo@leousa.com
Web Site: www.leousa.com
Key Personnel
VP: Peter R Gillies *E-mail:* peter@leousa.com
Sales: Tom Leach *E-mail:* tom@leousa.com; Greg Witt *E-mail:* greg@leousa.com
Founded: 1983
Turnaround: 90 Workdays
Print Runs: 3,500 min - 2,000,000 max
Business from Other Countries: 20%

LK Litho
Division of The Linick Group Inc
Linick Bldg, 7 Putter Lane, Middle Island, NY 11953-0102
Tel: 631-924-8555
E-mail: linickgrp@att.net
Web Site: www.lgroup.addr.com; www.linickgroup.com
Key Personnel
VP: Roger Dextor
Founded: 1968
Turnaround: 10 Workdays
Print Runs: 2,500 min - 2,000,000 max
Business from Other Countries: 20%

Marrakech Express Inc
720 Wesley Ave, No 10, Tarpon Springs, FL 34689
Tel: 727-942-2218 *Fax:* 727-937-4758
E-mail: print@marrak.com
Web Site: www.marrak.com
Key Personnel
CEO: Peter Henzell
Prodn Mgr: Steen Sigmund
Sales/Estimator: Shirley Copperman
Founded: 1976
Turnaround: 10 days
Print Runs: 500 min - 25,000 max
Business from Other Countries: 12%

Mazer Publishing Services
Division of The Mazer Corporation
6680 Poe Ave, Dayton, OH 45414
Tel: 937-264-2600 *Fax:* 937-264-2624
E-mail: info@mazer.com
Web Site: www.mazer.com
Key Personnel
Pres: William Franklin *E-mail:* bill_franklin@mazer.com
Exec VP: Ken Fultz *E-mail:* ken_fultz@mazer.com
VP & Gen Mgr, Creative Servs: Sharon Bidwell *Fax:* 937-264-2619 *E-mail:* sharon_bidwell@mazer.com
Exec Dir, Sales: Bill Faber *Fax:* 937-264-2622 *E-mail:* bill_faber@mazer.com
Founded: 1964
Print Runs: 50 min - 25,000 max
Business from Other Countries: 10%
Branch Office(s)
2460 Sand Lake Rd, Orlando, FL 32809, Contact: Brian Blakley *Tel:* 407-859-5552 *Fax:* 407-859-0643 *E-mail:* brian_blakley@mazer.com
224 Lexington Ave, Fox River Grove, IL 60021, Contact: Dennis Bowman *Tel:* 847-639-1555 *Fax:* 847-639-1562 *E-mail:* dennis_bowman@mazer.com
22 Lehigh Rd, Wellesley, MA 02181, Contact: Ken Leahy *Tel:* 781-237-4112 *Fax:* 781-431-6184 *E-mail:* ken_leahy@mazer.com
22 Laurel Place, Upper Montclair, NJ 07043 *Tel:* 973-744-4320 *Fax:* 973-746-5608 *E-mail:* john_martel@mazer.com
3081 Glenmere Ct, Kettering, OH 45440, Contact: Mark Brewer *Tel:* 937-299-5746 *Fax:* 937-299-5761 *E-mail:* mark_brewer@mazer.com
363 Porter Rd, Bishop, TX 78602, Contact: Deborah VanLandingham *Tel:* 512-303-9758 *Fax:* 513-303-9791 *E-mail:* deborah_vanlandingham@mazer.com
Membership(s): BMI

Milanostampa/New Interlitho USA Inc
Subsidiary of Milanostampa New Interlitho Italia SpA
299 Broadway, Suite 901, New York, NY 10007
Tel: 212-964-2430 *Fax:* 212-964-2497
Web Site: www.milanostampa.com
Key Personnel
Chmn: Riccardo Sardo
Sales Rep: Rino Varrasso *E-mail:* rvarrasso@milanostampa-usa.com
Founded: 1998
Turnaround: 30 Workdays
Print Runs: 1,000 min - 3,000,000 max
Business from Other Countries: 75%
Subsidiaries: Milanostampa-New Interlitho

Palace Press International
1585-A Folsom St, San Francisco, CA 94103
Tel: 415-626-1080 *Fax:* 415-626-1510
E-mail: ppisfo@palacepress.com
Web Site: www.palacepress.com
Key Personnel
Pres: Raoul A Goff *E-mail:* raoul@palacepress.com

UNITED STATES

Dir: Gordon Goff *Tel:* 415-455-2480 ext 211 *Fax:* 415-455-2490 *E-mail:* gordon@palacepress.com
Gen Mgr: Laura Davis
Sales Mgr: Steven Goff *Tel:* 415-455-2480 *E-mail:* steven@palacepress.com
Opers Mgr: John Sopko
Founded: 1984
Turnaround: 90 Workdays
Print Runs: 3,000 min - 1,000,000 max
Business from Other Countries: 20%
Branch Office(s)
Palace Press International Los Angeles, 303 W Newby Ave, Suite C, San Gabriel, CT 91776, Contact: Sabra Chili *Tel:* 310-444-3904 *Fax:* 310-473-4799 *E-mail:* sabra@palacepress.com *Web Site:* www.palacepress.com
Palace Press International Marin, 1299 Fourth St, Suite 305, San Rafael, CA 94901, Contact: Gordon Goff *Tel:* 415-455-2480 *Fax:* 415-455-2490 *E-mail:* gordon@palacepress.com
Palace Press International New York, 180 Varick St, 10th fl, New York, NY 10014, Contact: Kelly Steis Colquitt *Tel:* 212-462-2622 *Fax:* 212-463-9130 *E-mail:* kelly@palacepress.com
Palace Press San Rafael, 1299 Fourth St, Suite 305, San Rafael, CA 94901, Contact: Lesley Sun *Tel:* 415-342-3117 *Fax:* 415-342-3115 *E-mail:* lesley@palacepress.com
Palace Press International Hong Kong, Wah Ha Factory Bldg, 10th fl, Block A, B, C & D, 8 Shipyard Lane, Quarry Bay, Hong Kong, Contact: Lesley Sun *Tel:* 357-9019 *Fax:* 561-3616 *E-mail:* palacehk@palacepress.com *Web Site:* www.palacepress.com
Palace Press, 1299 Fourth St, Suite 305, San Rafael, CA 94901, Contact: Gordon Goff *Tel:* 415-455-2480 *Fax:* 415-455-2490 *E-mail:* gordon@palacepress.com

Pioneer Graphic Scanning
Division of Jinno International
3 Christine Dr, Chestnut Ridge, NY 10977-6802
Tel: 845-735-4666 *Fax:* 617-344-5905
Key Personnel
Pres: Yoh Jinno *E-mail:* jinno@worldnet.att.net
Mktg Dir: Stewart Sum
Founded: 1989
Turnaround: 10-60 Workdays
Print Runs: 500 min - 3,000,000 max
Business from Other Countries: 95%

Printing Corp of the Americas Inc
620 SW 12 Ave, Pompano Beach, FL 33069
Tel: 954-781-8100 *Fax:* 954-781-8421
E-mail: pcaprint@bellsouth.net
Web Site: www.pcaprint.bellsouth.net
Key Personnel
Pres: Jan Tuchman
Founded: 1979
Turnaround: 5-10 Workdays
Print Runs: 500 min - 100,000 max
Business from Other Countries: 10%

Regent Publishing Services
9327 Rambler Dr, St Louis, MO 63123
Tel: 314-631-7581 *Fax:* 314-638-5113
E-mail: regentstl@aol.com
Key Personnel
Sales Dir: Carol A Davis-Tierney
Mktg Dir: James J Tierney
Founded: 1985
Turnaround: 3-4 Months
Print Runs: 2,000 min - 100,000 max
Business from Other Countries: 100%

Taylor Publishing Co
1550 W Mockingbird Lane, Dallas, TX 75235
Tel: 214-819-8100 *Fax:* 214-630-1852
E-mail: web@taylorpub.com
Web Site: www.taylorpub.com
Key Personnel
Pres: Dave Fiore
Commercial Printing/Fine Books Div: Jay Love
Dir, Mktg: Mike Taylor
Founded: 1939
Turnaround: 45 Workdays
Print Runs: 300 min - 25,000 max
Business from Other Countries: 10%

Times Publishing Group
Division of Times Publishing Ltd/Singapore
99 White Plains Rd, Tarrytown, NY 10591
Tel: 914-366-9888 *Fax:* 914-366-9898
Web Site: www.tpl.com.sg
Key Personnel
Cust Serv Exec: Bonnie Stone *E-mail:* bstone@marshallcavendish.com
Sales Mgr: Suresh Kumar *E-mail:* skumar@marshallcavendish.com
Founded: 1965
Print Runs: 2,000 min - 500,000 max
Business from Other Countries: 90%

Toppan Printing Co America Inc
Subsidiary of Toppan Printing Co Ltd
666 Fifth Ave, New York, NY 10103
Tel: 212-489-7740; 212-975-9060 *Fax:* 212-246-3067
Web Site: www.ta.toppan.com
Key Personnel
Sr VP: John Lee
Gen Sales Mgr: Shinichi Ito
Founded: 1965
Turnaround: 3-5 Months
Business from Other Countries: 10%
Branch Office(s)
4551 Glencoe Ave, Suite 230, Marina del Rey, CA 90292, Sales Mgr: Yoshihei Okamoto *Tel:* 310-823-0050 *Fax:* 310-823-0777 *Web Site:* www.ta.toppan.com

Vicks Lithograph & Printing Corp
5166 Commercial Dr, Yorkville, NY 13495
Tel: 315-736-9344 *Fax:* 315-736-1901
Key Personnel
Chmn: Dwight E "Duke" Vicks, Jr
Pres: Dwight E Vicks, III
Plant Mgr: Frank Driscoll
Sales Mgr: Pat Cotter
Founded: 1918
Turnaround: 10-20 Workdays
Print Runs: 1,000 min - 100,000 max
Business from Other Countries: 10%

Uruguay

Barreiro y Ramos SA
Juan Carlos Gomez, 1430, Montevideo 11000
Tel: (02) 986621 *Fax:* (02) 962358
Telex: 23901PB.CVJA.UY *Cable:* BAREIRAMOS
Key Personnel
President: Gaston Barreiro
Vice President: Guzman Barreiro
Founded: 1837
Print Runs: 1,000 min - 50,000 max
Business from Other Countries: 10%

Prepress Services Index

ART & DESIGN

Belgium
Drukkerij Lannoo NV, pg 1153
IMPF BV BA, pg 1153

Canada
David Berman Developments Inc, pg 1153
Celia Godkin, pg 1153
Coach House Printing, pg 1153
Leanne Franson, pg 1153
Maracle Press Ltd, pg 1153
Preney Print & Litho Inc, pg 1153
PrintWest, pg 1153
David Shaw & Associates Ltd, pg 1153
Barbara Spurll Illustration, pg 1154
University of Toronto Press Inc, pg 1154

Germany
C L Baader Buch & Offsetdruckere GmbH & Co KG, pg 1154
Priese GmbH, pg 1154
Topic Verlag GmbH, pg 1154

Hong Kong
Cristy's Atelier, pg 1155
Elegance Finance Printing Services Ltd, pg 1155
Golden Cup Printing Co Ltd, pg 1156
Mei Ka Printing & Publish Enterprise Ltd, pg 1156
Prontaprint Asia Ltd, pg 1156
Sota Graphic Arts Co Ltd, pg 1156
Ying Tat Co, pg 1157

India
Paragon Prepress Inc, pg 1157

Indonesia
Ichtiar Baru I Van Hoeve, pg 1157
Victory Offset Prima PT, pg 1157

Ireland
ICPC Ltd, pg 1157
Smurfit Print, pg 1157
Ultragraphics, pg 1157

Israel
Har-El Printers & Publishers, pg 1157

Italy
Canale G e C SpA, pg 1158

Lithuania
Spindulys Printing House, pg 1158

New Zealand
Egan-Reid Ltd, pg 1158
John McIndoe Ltd, pg 1158
PPP Printers Ltd, pg 1158

Puerto Rico
Publishing Resources Inc, pg 1158

Singapore
Craft Print Pte Ltd, pg 1159
SNP Printing Pte Ltd, pg 1159
Stamford Press Pte Ltd, pg 1159
Times Graphics, pg 1159

Slovenia
Gorenjski Tisk Printing Co, pg 1159

Spain
Graficas Santamaria SA, pg 1159

Sri Lanka
Sumathi Book Printing (Pvt) Ltd, pg 1159

United Republic of Tanzania
Peramiho Publications, pg 1160

Thailand
Phongwarin Printing Company Ltd, pg 1160

United Kingdom
BAS Printers Ltd, pg 1160
Baseline Creative Ltd, pg 1160
BCS Publishing Ltd, pg 1160
Black Bear Press Ltd, pg 1160
Book Creation Services, pg 1161
Book Production Consultants PLC, pg 1161
D Brown & Sons Ltd, pg 1161
Chase Publishing Services, pg 1161
Cooper Dale, pg 1161
Cradley Print Ltd, pg 1161
The Diagram Group, pg 1161
Edition, pg 1161
Fern House, pg 1161
Goldshield Communications Ltd, pg 1161
The Guernsey Press Co Ltd, pg 1161
Hammond Packaging Ltd, pg 1161
Holbrook Design, pg 1162
Ikon Document Services Ltd, pg 1162
Linden Artists Ltd, pg 1162
Multiplex Medway Ltd, pg 1162
Page Bros Ltd (Norwich), pg 1162
Severnside Printers Ltd, pg 1163
Watkiss Automation Ltd, pg 1163

United States
Alpina Color Graphics Inc, pg 1163
BookBuilders New York Ltd, pg 1163
Coneco Litho Graphics, pg 1164
Martin Cook Associates Ltd, pg 1164
Custom Services, pg 1164
Desktop Miracles Inc, pg 1164
DNP America LLC, pg 1164
Editoriale Bortolazzi-Stei srl, pg 1164
The Font Bureau, pg 1165
High Resolution Inc, pg 1165
Hindy's Enterprise, pg 1165
Integrated Book Technology Inc, pg 1165
ITC, pg 1165
Jinno International Group, pg 1165
Leo Paper USA, pg 1165
LK Litho, pg 1166
Mazer Publishing Services, pg 1166
Palace Press International, pg 1166
Photoengraving Inc, pg 1166
Pioneer Graphic Scanning, pg 1166
Sencor, pg 1166
SpectraComp, pg 1166
Square Two Design Inc, pg 1167
Studio 31, pg 1167
Fred Weidner & Daughter Printers, pg 1167

Uruguay
Barreiro y Ramos SA, pg 1167

COLOR SEPARATIONS

Austria
ADEVA (Akademische Druck-u Verlagsanstalt), pg 1153

Belgium
IMPF BV BA, pg 1153

Canada
Coach House Printing, pg 1153
Herzig Somerville Ltd, pg 1153
Maracle Press Ltd, pg 1153
Preney Print & Litho Inc, pg 1153
Printcrafters Inc, pg 1153
Transcontinental Printing Book Group, pg 1154

Denmark
Bianco Lunos Bogtrykkeri AS, pg 1154

Finland
Gummerus Printing, pg 1154

Germany
Media-Print Informationstechnologie GmbH, pg 1154
Mohndruck Graphische Betriebe GmbH, pg 1154
Priese GmbH, pg 1154
Topic Verlag GmbH, pg 1154
Vier-Tuerme GmbH Benedikt Press, pg 1154

Hong Kong
Best-Set Typesetter Ltd, pg 1155
Bookbuilders Ltd, pg 1155
Bright Arts Hong Kong Ltd, pg 1155
Bright Future Printing Co Ltd, pg 1155
C & C Offset Printing Co Ltd, pg 1155
Colorprint Offset, pg 1155
Dai Nippon Printing Co (Hong Kong) Ltd, pg 1155
Everbest Printing Co Ltd, pg 1156
Golden Cup Printing Co Ltd, pg 1156
The Green Pagoda Press Ltd, pg 1156
H K Scanner Arts International Ltd, pg 1156
Hindy's Enterprise Co Ltd, pg 1156
Hung Hing Off-set Printing Co Ltd, pg 1156
Image Printing Company Ltd, pg 1156
Leo Paper Products Ltd, pg 1156
Leo Reprographic Ltd, pg 1156
Midas Printing Ltd, pg 1156
New Arts Graphic Reproduction Co Ltd, pg 1156
Prontaprint Asia Ltd, pg 1156
Rainbow Graphic & Printing Co Ltd, pg 1156
Sota Graphic Arts Co Ltd, pg 1156
South Sea International Press Ltd, pg 1156
Sunshine Press Ltd, pg 1157
Toppan Printing Co (HK) Ltd, pg 1157
Wing King Tong Co Ltd (Printing Factory), pg 1157
Ying Tat Co, pg 1157

India
Hiralal Printing Works Ltd, pg 1157

Indonesia
Victory Offset Prima PT, pg 1157

Ireland
Graphic Reproductions Ltd, pg 1157
Kilkenny People/Wellbrook Press, pg 1157
Ultragraphics, pg 1157

Israel
Har-El Printers & Publishers, pg 1157
Keterpress Enterprises Jerusalem, pg 1157
Monoline Ltd, pg 1157
Technosdar Ltd, pg 1157

Italy
Canale G e C SpA, pg 1158
Dedalo Litostampa SRL, pg 1158
Nuovo Instituto Italiano d'Arti Grafiche, pg 1158
Amilcare Pizzi SpA, pg 1158

Republic of Korea
Daehan Printing & Publishing Co Ltd, pg 1158
Pyunghwa Dang Printing Co Ltd, pg 1158

Lithuania
Spindulys Printing House, pg 1158

Netherlands
Bosch en Keuning grafische bedrijven, pg 1158

New Zealand
John McIndoe Ltd, pg 1158

Portugal
Silabo, pg 1158

PREPRESS SERVICES INDEX

Singapore
Chong Moh Offset Printing Ltd, pg 1159
Chroma Graphics (Overseas) Pte Ltd, pg 1159
Craft Print Pte Ltd, pg 1159
CS Graphics Pte Ltd, pg 1159
Eurasia Press Pte Ltd, pg 1159
Ho Printing Singapore Pte Ltd, pg 1159
Markono Print Media Pte Ltd, pg 1159
Pica Overseas Color Separation Ltd, pg 1159
Sang Choy International PTE Ltd, pg 1159
SNP Printing Pte Ltd, pg 1159
Stamford Press Pte Ltd, pg 1159
Times Graphics, pg 1159
Times Printers Pte Ltd, pg 1159
Toppan Company (S) Pte Ltd, pg 1159

Slovenia
Gorenjski Tisk Printing Co, pg 1159

Spain
Graficas Santamaria SA, pg 1159

Switzerland
Photolitho AG, pg 1160

United Republic of Tanzania
Peramiho Publications, pg 1160

United Kingdom
Adroit Birmingham Ltd, pg 1160
BAS Printers Ltd, pg 1160
The Bath Press, pg 1160
Book Creation Services, pg 1161
Book Production Consultants PLC, pg 1161
D Brown & Sons Ltd, pg 1161
Butler & Tanner Ltd, pg 1161
Chase Publishing Services, pg 1161
William Clowes Ltd, pg 1161
Cradley Print Ltd, pg 1161
Essex Colour Services Ltd, pg 1161
Goldshield Communications Ltd, pg 1161
The Guernsey Press Co Ltd, pg 1161
Headley Brothers Ltd, pg 1161
Holbrook Design, pg 1162
Lowfield Printing Co Ltd, pg 1162
Martins Printing Group Ltd, pg 1162

United States
Alpina Color Graphics Inc, pg 1163
Asia Pacific Offset Inc, pg 1163
Bang Printing Co Inc, pg 1163
Best-Set Typesetter Ltd, pg 1163
Blaze International Productions Inc, pg 1163
BookBuilders New York Ltd, pg 1163
C & C Offset Printing Co Ltd, pg 1164
Colorprint Offset Inc, pg 1164
Coneco Litho Graphics, pg 1164
Martin Cook Associates Ltd, pg 1164
CS Graphics USA Inc, pg 1164
Custom Services, pg 1164
DNP America LLC, pg 1164
Editoriale Bortolazzi-Stei srl, pg 1164
Elegance Printing & Book Binding (USA), pg 1164
High Resolution Inc, pg 1165
Hindy's Enterprise, pg 1165
Jinno International Group, pg 1165
Leo Paper USA, pg 1165
Linick International Inc, pg 1166
LK Litho, pg 1166
Milanostampa/New Interlitho USA Inc, pg 1166
Palace Press International, pg 1166
Photoengraving Inc, pg 1166
Pioneer Graphic Scanning, pg 1166
Prepare Inc, pg 1166
Printing Corp of the Americas Inc, pg 1166
Quantum Colorgraphics, pg 1166
Regent Publishing Services, pg 1166
SpectraComp, pg 1166
Times Publishing Group, pg 1167
Fred Weidner & Daughter Printers, pg 1167

Uruguay
Barreiro y Ramos SA, pg 1167

COMPUTERIZED TYPESETTING

Belgium
Drukkerij Lannoo NV, pg 1153
IMPF BV BA, pg 1153

Canada
David Berman Developments Inc, pg 1153
Coach House Printing, pg 1153
Girol Books Inc, pg 1153
Maracle Press Ltd, pg 1153
Preney Print & Litho Inc, pg 1153
Transcontinental Printing Book Group, pg 1154
Tri-Graphic Printing (Ottawa) Ltd, pg 1154
University of Toronto Press Inc, pg 1154

Denmark
Bianco Lunos Bogtrykkeri AS, pg 1154

Finland
Gummerus Printing, pg 1154

France
Signes du Monde, pg 1154

Germany
C L Baader Buch & Offsetdruckere GmbH & Co KG, pg 1154
Fachhochschule Fur Druk, Studiengang Verlagswirtschaft und Verlagsherstellung, pg 1154
C Maurer Druck und Verlag, pg 1154
Media-Print Informationstechnologie GmbH, pg 1154
Mohndruck Graphische Betriebe GmbH, pg 1154
Oertel & Sporer GmbH & Co, pg 1154
Priese GmbH, pg 1154
Vier-Tuerme GmbH Benedikt Press, pg 1154

Hong Kong
Best-Set Typesetter Ltd, pg 1155
Bookbuilders Ltd, pg 1155
Caritas Printing Training Centre, pg 1155
Elegance Finance Printing Services Ltd, pg 1155
Golden Cup Printing Co Ltd, pg 1156
The Green Pagoda Press Ltd, pg 1156
Prontaprint Asia Ltd, pg 1156
Sota Graphic Arts Co Ltd, pg 1156
Sunshine Press Ltd, pg 1157
Ying Tat Co, pg 1157

India
Paragon Prepress Inc, pg 1157

Indonesia
Ichtiar Baru I Van Hoeve, pg 1157
Victory Offset Prima PT, pg 1157

Ireland
Doyle Graphics, pg 1157
ICPC Ltd, pg 1157
Smurfit Print, pg 1157

Israel
Keterpress Enterprises Jerusalem, pg 1157
Technosdar Ltd, pg 1157

Italy
Canale G e C SpA, pg 1158
Dedalo Litostampa SRL, pg 1158

Republic of Korea
Daehan Printing & Publishing Co Ltd, pg 1158

Lithuania
Spindulys Printing House, pg 1158

Madagascar
Societe Malgache d'Edition, pg 1158

New Zealand
Egan-Reid Ltd, pg 1158
John McIndoe Ltd, pg 1158

Philippines
Naldoza Printers, pg 1158
Reyes Publishing, pg 1158

Portugal
Silabo, pg 1158

Puerto Rico
Publishing Resources Inc, pg 1158

Singapore
Chong Moh Offset Printing Ltd, pg 1159
Eurasia Press Pte Ltd, pg 1159
Markono Print Media Pte Ltd, pg 1159
SNP Printing Pte Ltd, pg 1159
Stamford Press Pte Ltd, pg 1159
Times Graphics, pg 1159
Times Printers Pte Ltd, pg 1159

Slovenia
Gorenjski Tisk Printing Co, pg 1159

Switzerland
Hallwag AG, pg 1160

United Republic of Tanzania
Peramiho Publications, pg 1160

Thailand
Phongwarin Printing Company Ltd, pg 1160

United Kingdom
The Alden Group Ltd, pg 1160
AlpnetCompuType Ltd, pg 1160
J W Arrowsmith Ltd, pg 1160
Associated Translation & Typesetting, pg 1160
W & G Baird Ltd, pg 1160
BAS Printers Ltd, pg 1160
Baseline Creative Ltd, pg 1160
Black Bear Press Ltd, pg 1160
Blackmore Ltd, pg 1160
Book Creation Services, pg 1161
Book Production Consultants PLC, pg 1161
Butler & Tanner Ltd, pg 1161
Cambridge University Press - Printing Division, pg 1161
Center Print Ltd, pg 1161
The Charlesworth Group, pg 1161
Chase Publishing Services, pg 1161
William Clowes Ltd, pg 1161
Edition, pg 1161
Goldshield Communications Ltd, pg 1161
James Gowans Ltd, pg 1161
Headley Brothers Ltd, pg 1161
Heyden & Son, pg 1162
Hobbs The Printers Ltd, pg 1162
Holbrook Design, pg 1162
Ikon Document Services Ltd, pg 1162
Intype London Ltd, pg 1162
Keytec Typesetting Ltd, pg 1162
Lowfield Printing Co Ltd, pg 1162
Maney Publishing, pg 1162
MPG Colour Ltd, pg 1162
Page Bros Ltd (Norwich), pg 1162
Redwood Books Ltd, pg 1162
J R Reid Printing Group Ltd, pg 1162
Antony Rowe Ltd, pg 1162
Santype International Ltd, pg 1163
Severnside Printers Ltd, pg 1163
Thomas Technology Solutions, Inc, pg 1163
M & A Thomson Litho Ltd, pg 1163
Tradespools Ltd, pg 1163

United States
A-R Editions Inc, pg 1163
ADR/BookPrint, pg 1163
Alpina Color Graphics Inc, pg 1163
Any Photo Type, pg 1163
Bang Printing Co Inc, pg 1163
Best-Set Typesetter Ltd, pg 1163
BookBuilders New York Ltd, pg 1163
Coneco Litho Graphics, pg 1164
Martin Cook Associates Ltd, pg 1164
Custom Services, pg 1164
Datapage Technologies International Inc, pg 1164
Desktop Miracles Inc, pg 1164
Fairfield Marketing Group Inc, pg 1165
Huron Valley Graphics Inc, pg 1165
ICSI Corp, pg 1165
ITC, pg 1165
Jinno International Group, pg 1165
Lenz & Riecker Inc, pg 1165
Leo Paper USA, pg 1165
Linick International Inc, pg 1166
LK Litho, pg 1166
Mazer Publishing Services, pg 1166
Pageworks, pg 1166

MANUFACTURING

Photoengraving Inc, pg 1166
Prepare Inc, pg 1166
Sencor, pg 1166
SpectraComp, pg 1166
Studio 31, pg 1167
Taylor Publishing Co, pg 1167
Fred Weidner & Daughter Printers, pg 1167

Uruguay
Barreiro y Ramos SA, pg 1167

DATA PROCESSING SERVICES

Canada
Maracle Press Ltd, pg 1153

Hong Kong
Best-Set Typesetter Ltd, pg 1155
Sota Graphic Arts Co Ltd, pg 1156

Italy
Canale G e C SpA, pg 1158

New Zealand
Egan-Reid Ltd, pg 1158

United States
Alpina Color Graphics Inc, pg 1163
Best-Set Typesetter Ltd, pg 1163
Datapage Technologies International Inc, pg 1164
Express Media Corp, pg 1165
Fairfield Marketing Group Inc, pg 1165
Huron Valley Graphics Inc, pg 1165
Innodata Corp, pg 1165
ITC, pg 1165
Sencor, pg 1166

FOREIGN LANGUAGE COMPOSITION

Canada
David Berman Developments Inc, pg 1153
Girol Books Inc, pg 1153
Maracle Press Ltd, pg 1153
University of Toronto Press Inc, pg 1154

Denmark
Bianco Lunos Bogtrykkeri AS, pg 1154

Finland
Gummerus Printing, pg 1154

Germany
C L Baader Buch & Offsetdruckere GmbH & Co KG, pg 1154
Mohndruck Graphische Betriebe GmbH, pg 1154
Priese GmbH, pg 1154

Hong Kong
Best-Set Typesetter Ltd, pg 1155
The Green Pagoda Press Ltd, pg 1156
Prontaprint Asia Ltd, pg 1156
Sota Graphic Arts Co Ltd, pg 1156
Sunshine Press Ltd, pg 1157

Ireland
ICPC Ltd, pg 1157

Israel
Keterpress Enterprises Jerusalem, pg 1157
Technosdar Ltd, pg 1157

Italy
Canale G e C SpA, pg 1158
Dedalo Litostampa SRL, pg 1158

Republic of Korea
Daehan Printing & Publishing Co Ltd, pg 1158

Lithuania
Spindulys Printing House, pg 1158

New Zealand
Egan-Reid Ltd, pg 1158

Puerto Rico
Publishing Resources Inc, pg 1158

Singapore
Eurasia Press Pte Ltd, pg 1159
SNP Printing Pte Ltd, pg 1159
Times Graphics, pg 1159

Slovenia
Gorenjski Tisk Printing Co, pg 1159

South Africa
CTP Book Printers (Pty) Ltd, pg 1159

Spain
Graficas Santamaria SA, pg 1159

United Republic of Tanzania
Peramiho Publications, pg 1160

United Kingdom
AlpnetCompuType Ltd, pg 1160
ARADCO VSI Ltd, pg 1160
J W Arrowsmith Ltd, pg 1160
Associated Translation & Typesetting, pg 1160
Baseline Creative Ltd, pg 1160
Book Creation Services, pg 1161
Book Production Consultants PLC, pg 1161
D Brown & Sons Ltd, pg 1161
Cambridge University Press - Printing Division, pg 1161
The Charlesworth Group, pg 1161
Goldshield Communications Ltd, pg 1161
Ikon Document Services Ltd, pg 1162
Intype London Ltd, pg 1162
Maney Publishing, pg 1162
Multiplex Medway Ltd, pg 1162
Antony Rowe Ltd, pg 1162
Tradespools Ltd, pg 1163

United States
A-R Editions Inc, pg 1163
Alpina Color Graphics Inc, pg 1163
Any Photo Type, pg 1163
Best-Set Typesetter Ltd, pg 1163
BookBuilders New York Ltd, pg 1163
Custom Services, pg 1164
Datapage Technologies International Inc, pg 1164
Huron Valley Graphics Inc, pg 1165
ICSI Corp, pg 1165
Innodata Corp, pg 1165
Jinno International Group, pg 1165
Leo Paper USA, pg 1165
Palace Press International, pg 1166
Prepare Inc, pg 1166
Sencor, pg 1166
SpectraComp, pg 1166

Uruguay
Barreiro y Ramos SA, pg 1167

INDEXING

Denmark
Bianco Lunos Bogtrykkeri AS, pg 1154

Germany
C L Baader Buch & Offsetdruckere GmbH & Co KG, pg 1154
Priese GmbH, pg 1154
Topic Verlag GmbH, pg 1154

Hong Kong
Best-Set Typesetter Ltd, pg 1155
Golden Cup Printing Co Ltd, pg 1156
Midas Printing Ltd, pg 1156
South Sea International Press Ltd, pg 1156

India
Paragon Prepress Inc, pg 1157

Indonesia
Ichtiar Baru I Van Hoeve, pg 1157

Ireland
ICPC Ltd, pg 1157

Italy
Canale G e C SpA, pg 1158

Republic of Korea
Daehan Printing & Publishing Co Ltd, pg 1158

New Zealand
Egan-Reid Ltd, pg 1158
John McIndoe Ltd, pg 1158

Portugal
Silabo, pg 1158

Singapore
SNP Printing Pte Ltd, pg 1159
Toppan Company (S) Pte Ltd, pg 1159

United Republic of Tanzania
Peramiho Publications, pg 1160

United Kingdom
Book Creation Services, pg 1161
Book Production Consultants PLC, pg 1161
Chase Publishing Services, pg 1161
William Clowes Ltd, pg 1161
Fern House, pg 1161
Goldshield Communications Ltd, pg 1161
Headley Brothers Ltd, pg 1161
Hobbs The Printers Ltd, pg 1162
Ikon Document Services Ltd, pg 1162

United States
A-R Editions Inc, pg 1163
Best-Set Typesetter Ltd, pg 1163
BookBuilders New York Ltd, pg 1163
Martin Cook Associates Ltd, pg 1164
Datapage Technologies International Inc, pg 1164
Innodata Corp, pg 1165
Leo Paper USA, pg 1165
Linick International Inc, pg 1166
LK Litho, pg 1166
Sencor, pg 1166
SpectraComp, pg 1166
Fred Weidner & Daughter Printers, pg 1167

MATHEMATICS & CHEMISTRY COMPOSITION

Canada
University of Toronto Press Inc, pg 1154

Finland
Gummerus Printing, pg 1154

Hong Kong
Best-Set Typesetter Ltd, pg 1155
Golden Cup Printing Co Ltd, pg 1156

Indonesia
Ichtiar Baru I Van Hoeve, pg 1157

Ireland
ICPC Ltd, pg 1157
SciPrint Ltd, pg 1157
Smurfit Print, pg 1157

Israel
Monoline Ltd, pg 1157
Technosdar Ltd, pg 1157

Italy
Canale G e C SpA, pg 1158

Republic of Korea
Daehan Printing & Publishing Co Ltd, pg 1158

Lithuania
Spindulys Printing House, pg 1158

New Zealand
Egan-Reid Ltd, pg 1158

Portugal
Silabo, pg 1158

Singapore
Times Graphics, pg 1159

Slovenia
Gorenjski Tisk Printing Co, pg 1159

United Kingdom
J W Arrowsmith Ltd, pg 1160
Baseline Creative Ltd, pg 1160
Book Production Consultants PLC, pg 1161
Cambridge University Press - Printing Division, pg 1161

PREPRESS SERVICES INDEX

The Charlesworth Group, pg 1161
Goldshield Communications Ltd, pg 1161
Hobbs The Printers Ltd, pg 1162
Keytec Typesetting Ltd, pg 1162
Antony Rowe Ltd, pg 1162
Santype International Ltd, pg 1163
Thomas Technology Solutions, Inc, pg 1163

United States
Best-Set Typesetter Ltd, pg 1163
Datapage Technologies International Inc, pg 1164
Huron Valley Graphics Inc, pg 1165
ICSI Corp, pg 1165
ITC, pg 1165
Jinno International Group, pg 1165
Leo Paper USA, pg 1165
LK Litho, pg 1166
Prepare Inc, pg 1166
Sencor, pg 1166

MUSIC COMPOSITION

Canada
University of Toronto Press Inc, pg 1154

Germany
C L Baader Buch & Offsetdruckere GmbH & Co KG, pg 1154

Hong Kong
Golden Cup Printing Co Ltd, pg 1156
Ying Tat Co, pg 1157

Lithuania
Spindulys Printing House, pg 1158

New Zealand
Egan-Reid Ltd, pg 1158

United Republic of Tanzania
Peramiho Publications, pg 1160

United Kingdom
Holbrook Design, pg 1162

United States
A-R Editions Inc, pg 1163
Better Music Type, pg 1163
Jinno International Group, pg 1165
Leo Paper USA, pg 1165
Prepare Inc, pg 1166

NON-ROMAN ALPHABETS

Canada
University of Toronto Press Inc, pg 1154

Denmark
Bianco Lunos Bogtrykkeri AS, pg 1154

Germany
Priese GmbH, pg 1154

Hong Kong
Prontaprint Asia Ltd, pg 1156
Sunshine Press Ltd, pg 1157

Indonesia
Ichtiar Baru l Van Hoeve, pg 1157

Israel
Technosdar Ltd, pg 1157

Italy
Canale G e C SpA, pg 1158

Lithuania
Spindulys Printing House, pg 1158

New Zealand
Egan-Reid Ltd, pg 1158
John McIndoe Ltd, pg 1158

Singapore
Markono Print Media Pte Ltd, pg 1159
Times Graphics, pg 1159

Slovenia
Gorenjski Tisk Printing Co, pg 1159

United Kingdom
J W Arrowsmith Ltd, pg 1160
Book Creation Services, pg 1161
Book Production Consultants PLC, pg 1161
Goldshield Communications Ltd, pg 1161
Antony Rowe Ltd, pg 1162

United States
A-R Editions Inc, pg 1163
BookBuilders New York Ltd, pg 1163
Martin Cook Associates Ltd, pg 1164
Custom Services, pg 1164
Huron Valley Graphics Inc, pg 1165
ICSI Corp, pg 1165
Jinno International Group, pg 1165
Leo Paper USA, pg 1165
Prepare Inc, pg 1166

PRODUCTION SERVICES

Austria
ADEVA (Akademische Druck-u Verlagsanstalt), pg 1153

Canada
Aardvark Enterprises, pg 1153
David Berman Developments Inc, pg 1153
Maracle Press Ltd, pg 1153
University of Toronto Press Inc, pg 1154

Denmark
Bianco Lunos Bogtrykkeri AS, pg 1154

France
Signes du Monde, pg 1154

Germany
C L Baader Buch & Offsetdruckere GmbH & Co KG, pg 1154
Fachhochschule Fur Druk, Studiengang Verlagswirtschaft und Verlagsherstellung, pg 1154
C Maurer Druck und Verlag, pg 1154
Media-Print Informationstechnologie GmbH, pg 1154
Priese GmbH, pg 1154
Topic Verlag GmbH, pg 1154

Hong Kong
Caritas Printing Training Centre, pg 1155
Colorprint Offset, pg 1155
Cristy's Atelier, pg 1155
Dai Nippon Printing Co (Hong Kong) Ltd, pg 1155
Everbest Printing Co Ltd, pg 1156
Golden Cup Printing Co Ltd, pg 1156
The Green Pagoda Press Ltd, pg 1156
Image Printing Company Ltd, pg 1156
Mei Ka Printing & Publish Enterprise Ltd, pg 1156
New Arts Graphic Reproduction Co Ltd, pg 1156
Prontaprint Asia Ltd, pg 1156
Sota Graphic Arts Co Ltd, pg 1156
Ying Tat Co, pg 1157

Indonesia
Ichtiar Baru l Van Hoeve, pg 1157
Victory Offset Prima PT, pg 1157

Ireland
ICPC Ltd, pg 1157
Kilkenny People/Wellbrook Press, pg 1157
Ultragraphics, pg 1157

Israel
Keterpress Enterprises Jerusalem, pg 1157
Technosdar Ltd, pg 1157

Italy
Canale G e C SpA, pg 1158
Milanostampa SPA, pg 1158

Republic of Korea
Daehan Printing & Publishing Co Ltd, pg 1158

Lithuania
Spindulys Printing House, pg 1158

New Zealand
Egan-Reid Ltd, pg 1158

Puerto Rico
Publishing Resources Inc, pg 1158

Singapore
Eurasia Press Pte Ltd, pg 1159
Markono Print Media Pte Ltd, pg 1159
SNP Printing Pte Ltd, pg 1159
Stamford Press Pte Ltd, pg 1159
Times Graphics, pg 1159
Times Printers Pte Ltd, pg 1159
Toppan Company (S) Pte Ltd, pg 1159

Slovenia
Gorenjski Tisk Printing Co, pg 1159

Spain
Graficas Santamaria SA, pg 1159

Sri Lanka
Sumathi Book Printing (Pvt) Ltd, pg 1159

Switzerland
Photolitho AG, pg 1160

Thailand
Phongwarin Printing Company Ltd, pg 1160

United Kingdom
BAS Printers Ltd, pg 1160
Baseline Creative Ltd, pg 1160
Book Creation Services, pg 1161
Book Production Consultants PLC, pg 1161
D Brown & Sons Ltd, pg 1161
Caledonian International Book Manufacturing, pg 1161
Chase Publishing Services, pg 1161
William Clowes Ltd, pg 1161
Cox & Wyman Ltd, pg 1161
Fern House, pg 1161
Goldshield Communications Ltd, pg 1161
James Gowans Ltd, pg 1161
Hobbs The Printers Ltd, pg 1162
Holbrook Design, pg 1162
Ikon Document Services Ltd, pg 1162
Intype London Ltd, pg 1162
Page Bros Ltd (Norwich), pg 1162
Santype International Ltd, pg 1163
Thomas Technology Solutions, Inc, pg 1163

United States
A-R Editions Inc, pg 1163
Alpina Color Graphics Inc, pg 1163
Blaze International Productions Inc, pg 1163
BookBuilders New York Ltd, pg 1163
C & C Offset Printing Co Ltd, pg 1164
Coneco Litho Graphics, pg 1164
Martin Cook Associates Ltd, pg 1164
Custom Services, pg 1164
Datapage Technologies International Inc, pg 1164
Desktop Miracles Inc, pg 1164
DNP America LLC, pg 1164
Editoriale Bortolazzi-Stei srl, pg 1164
Elegance Printing & Book Binding (USA), pg 1164
Express Media Corp, pg 1165
High Resolution Inc, pg 1165
Hindy's Enterprise, pg 1165
Huron Valley Graphics Inc, pg 1165
Ikon Document Services, pg 1165
Innodata Corp, pg 1165
Jinno International Group, pg 1165
Leo Paper USA, pg 1165
Linick International Inc, pg 1166
LK Litho, pg 1166
Pageworks, pg 1166
Palace Press International, pg 1166
Photoengraving Inc, pg 1166
Pioneer Graphic Scanning, pg 1166
Prepare Inc, pg 1166
Printing Corp of the Americas Inc, pg 1166
Regent Publishing Services, pg 1166
Sencor, pg 1166
SpectraComp, pg 1166
Studio 31, pg 1167
Fred Weidner & Daughter Printers, pg 1167

Uruguay
Barreiro y Ramos SA, pg 1167

MANUFACTURING

PREPRESS SERVICES INDEX

PROOFING

Belgium
Drukkerij Lannoo NV, pg 1153

Canada
Coach House Printing, pg 1153
Herzig Somerville Ltd, pg 1153
Maracle Press Ltd, pg 1153
University of Toronto Press Inc, pg 1154

Denmark
Bianco Lunos Bogtrykkeri AS, pg 1154

Finland
Gummerus Printing, pg 1154

Germany
C L Baader Buch & Offsetdruckere GmbH & Co KG, pg 1154
C Maurer Druck und Verlag, pg 1154
Priese GmbH, pg 1154
Topic Verlag GmbH, pg 1154

Hong Kong
Best-Set Typesetter Ltd, pg 1155
Bright Arts Hong Kong Ltd, pg 1155
Colorprint Offset, pg 1155
Dai Nippon Printing Co (Hong Kong) Ltd, pg 1155
Golden Cup Printing Co Ltd, pg 1156
Hindy's Enterprise Co Ltd, pg 1156
Hung Hing Off-set Printing Co Ltd, pg 1156
Leo Paper Products Ltd, pg 1156
Leo Reprographic Ltd, pg 1156
Midas Printing Ltd, pg 1156
New Arts Graphic Reproduction Co Ltd, pg 1156
Prontaprint Asia Ltd, pg 1156
Sota Graphic Arts Co Ltd, pg 1156
South Sea International Press Ltd, pg 1156
Toppan Printing Co (HK) Ltd, pg 1157

India
Hiralal Printing Works Ltd, pg 1157
Paragon Prepress Inc, pg 1157

Indonesia
Victory Offset Prima PT, pg 1157

Ireland
ICPC Ltd, pg 1157
Smurfit Print, pg 1157
Ultragraphics, pg 1157

Italy
Canale G e C SpA, pg 1158

Republic of Korea
Daehan Printing & Publishing Co Ltd, pg 1158
Pyunghwa Dang Printing Co Ltd, pg 1158

Lithuania
Spindulys Printing House, pg 1158

New Zealand
Egan-Reid Ltd, pg 1158
John McIndoe Ltd, pg 1158

Portugal
Silabo, pg 1158

Singapore
CS Graphics Pte Ltd, pg 1159
Eurasia Press Pte Ltd, pg 1159
Ho Printing Singapore Pte Ltd, pg 1159
Markono Print Media Pte Ltd, pg 1159
Sang Choy International PTE Ltd, pg 1159
SNP Printing Pte Ltd, pg 1159
Stamford Press Pte Ltd, pg 1159
Times Graphics, pg 1159
Times Printers Pte Ltd, pg 1159
Toppan Company (S) Pte Ltd, pg 1159

Slovenia
Gorenjski Tisk Printing Co, pg 1159

Switzerland
Photolitho AG, pg 1160

United Republic of Tanzania
Peramiho Publications, pg 1160

United Kingdom
Book Creation Services, pg 1161
Book Production Consultants PLC, pg 1161
Chase Publishing Services, pg 1161
William Clowes Ltd, pg 1161
Essex Colour Services Ltd, pg 1161
Fern House, pg 1161
Goldshield Communications Ltd, pg 1161
The Guernsey Press Co Ltd, pg 1161
Headley Brothers Ltd, pg 1161
Hobbs The Printers Ltd, pg 1162
Holbrook Design, pg 1162
Ikon Document Services Ltd, pg 1162
Image & Print Group Ltd, pg 1162
Watkiss Automation Ltd, pg 1163

United States
Alpina Color Graphics Inc, pg 1163
Asia Pacific Offset Inc, pg 1163
Bang Printing Co Inc, pg 1163
Best-Set Typesetter Ltd, pg 1163
BookBuilders New York Ltd, pg 1163
C & C Offset Printing Co Ltd, pg 1164
Coneco Litho Graphics, pg 1164
Martin Cook Associates Ltd, pg 1164
CS Graphics USA Inc, pg 1164
Datapage Technologies International Inc, pg 1164
Desktop Miracles Inc, pg 1164
Elegance Printing & Book Binding (USA), pg 1164
High Resolution Inc, pg 1165
Huron Valley Graphics Inc, pg 1165
Ikon Document Services, pg 1165
ITC, pg 1165
Leo Paper USA, pg 1165
Linick International Inc, pg 1166
LK Litho, pg 1166
Milanostampa/New Interlitho USA Inc, pg 1166
Palace Press International, pg 1166
Photoengraving Inc, pg 1166
Regent Publishing Services, pg 1166
SpectraComp, pg 1166
Times Publishing Group, pg 1167
Fred Weidner & Daughter Printers, pg 1167

Uruguay
Barreiro y Ramos SA, pg 1167

SCIENTIFIC COMPOSITION

Canada
University of Toronto Press Inc, pg 1154

Denmark
Bianco Lunos Bogtrykkeri AS, pg 1154

Germany
C L Baader Buch & Offsetdruckere GmbH & Co KG, pg 1154
Priese GmbH, pg 1154

Hong Kong
Best-Set Typesetter Ltd, pg 1155
Golden Cup Printing Co Ltd, pg 1156

Ireland
ICPC Ltd, pg 1157
SciPrint Ltd, pg 1157
Smurfit Print, pg 1157

Israel
Monoline Ltd, pg 1157
Technosdar Ltd, pg 1157

Italy
Canale G e C SpA, pg 1158

Republic of Korea
Daehan Printing & Publishing Co Ltd, pg 1158

Lithuania
Spindulys Printing House, pg 1158

New Zealand
Egan-Reid Ltd, pg 1158

Singapore
Times Graphics, pg 1159

Slovenia
Gorenjski Tisk Printing Co, pg 1159

United Kingdom
J W Arrowsmith Ltd, pg 1160
Book Production Consultants PLC, pg 1161
Cambridge University Press - Printing Division, pg 1161
The Charlesworth Group, pg 1161
Goldshield Communications Ltd, pg 1161
Hobbs The Printers Ltd, pg 1162
Keytec Typesetting Ltd, pg 1162
Page Bros Ltd (Norwich), pg 1162
Antony Rowe Ltd, pg 1162
Santype International Ltd, pg 1163
Thomas Technology Solutions, Inc, pg 1163

United States
Datapage Technologies International Inc, pg 1164
Huron Valley Graphics Inc, pg 1165
ICSI Corp, pg 1165
Innodata Corp, pg 1165
ITC, pg 1165
Jinno International Group, pg 1165
Leo Paper USA, pg 1165
LK Litho, pg 1166
Prepare Inc, pg 1166
Sencor, pg 1166

UPC & BAR CODE SERVICES

Canada
Barcode Graphics Inc, pg 1153

United Kingdom
Axicon Auto ID Ltd, pg 1160
Holbrook Design, pg 1162

United States
C & C Offset Printing Co Ltd, pg 1164
Datapage Technologies International Inc, pg 1164
SpectraComp, pg 1166

WORD PROCESSING INTERFACE

Belgium
Drukkerij Lannoo NV, pg 1153

Canada
David Berman Developments Inc, pg 1153
Coach House Printing, pg 1153
Maracle Press Ltd, pg 1153
Tri-Graphic Printing (Ottawa) Ltd, pg 1154
University of Toronto Press Inc, pg 1154

Denmark
Bianco Lunos Bogtrykkeri AS, pg 1154

Germany
C L Baader Buch & Offsetdruckere GmbH & Co KG, pg 1154
C Maurer Druck und Verlag, pg 1154
Media-Print Informationstechnologie GmbH, pg 1154
Oertel & Sporer GmbH & Co, pg 1154
Priese GmbH, pg 1154
Topic Verlag GmbH, pg 1154
Vier-Tuerme GmbH Benedikt Press, pg 1154

Hong Kong
Golden Cup Printing Co Ltd, pg 1156
The Green Pagoda Press Ltd, pg 1156
Prontaprint Asia Ltd, pg 1156
Sota Graphic Arts Co Ltd, pg 1156

1151

PREPRESS SERVICES INDEX

Indonesia
Ichtiar Baru I Van Hoeve, pg 1157

Ireland
ICPC Ltd, pg 1157
Smurfit Print, pg 1157
Ultragraphics, pg 1157

Israel
Keterpress Enterprises Jerusalem, pg 1157
Monoline Ltd, pg 1157
Technosdar Ltd, pg 1157

Italy
Canale G e C SpA, pg 1158
Dedalo Litostampa SRL, pg 1158

Republic of Korea
Daehan Printing & Publishing Co Ltd, pg 1158

New Zealand
Egan-Reid Ltd, pg 1158
John McIndoe Ltd, pg 1158

Philippines
Naldoza Printers, pg 1158

Portugal
Silabo, pg 1158

Singapore
Eurasia Press Pte Ltd, pg 1159
Markono Print Media Pte Ltd, pg 1159
SNP Printing Pte Ltd, pg 1159
Stamford Press Pte Ltd, pg 1159
Times Graphics, pg 1159

Slovenia
Gorenjski Tisk Printing Co, pg 1159

United Republic of Tanzania
Peramiho Publications, pg 1160

United Kingdom
J W Arrowsmith Ltd, pg 1160
W & G Baird Ltd, pg 1160
BAS Printers Ltd, pg 1160
Baseline Creative Ltd, pg 1160
The Bath Press, pg 1160
Bell & Bain Ltd, pg 1160
Blackmore Ltd, pg 1160
Book Creation Services, pg 1161
D Brown & Sons Ltd, pg 1161
Chase Publishing Services, pg 1161
William Clowes Ltd, pg 1161
Goldshield Communications Ltd, pg 1161
The Guernsey Press Co Ltd, pg 1161
Hobbs The Printers Ltd, pg 1162
Holbrook Design, pg 1162
Ikon Document Services Ltd, pg 1162
Image & Print Group Ltd, pg 1162
Intype London Ltd, pg 1162
J R Reid Printing Group Ltd, pg 1162
Antony Rowe Ltd, pg 1162

Severnside Printers Ltd, pg 1163
Watkiss Automation Ltd, pg 1163

United States
A-R Editions Inc, pg 1163
Alpina Color Graphics Inc, pg 1163
American Pizzi Offset Corp, pg 1163
Bang Printing Co Inc, pg 1163
BookBuilders New York Ltd, pg 1163
Coneco Litho Graphics, pg 1164
Martin Cook Associates Ltd, pg 1164
Custom Services, pg 1164
Datapage Technologies International Inc, pg 1164
Desktop Miracles Inc, pg 1164
Huron Valley Graphics Inc, pg 1165
ICSI Corp, pg 1165
ITC, pg 1165
Lenz & Riecker Inc, pg 1165
Linick International Inc, pg 1166
LK Litho, pg 1166
Pageworks, pg 1166
Prepare Inc, pg 1166
SpectraComp, pg 1166

Prepress Services

This section includes companies throughout the world that offer a variety of prepress services. Those U.S. and Canadian companies with 10% or more of their business done outside North America are also included. Immediately preceding this section is an index classifying companies by services offered.

Austria

ADEVA (Akademische Druck-u Verlagsanstalt)
Auersperggasse 12, A-8010 Graz
Mailing Address: Postfach 598, A-8011 Graz
Tel: (0316) 3644 *Fax:* (0316) 364424
E-mail: info@adeva.com
Web Site: www.adeva.com *Cable:* ADEVA-GRAZ
Key Personnel
Dir: Dr Ursula Struzl
Contact: Doris Kellnhofer *Tel:* (0316) 3644 32
  E-mail: kellnhofer@adeva.com
Founded: 1949
Print Runs: 300 min - 10,000 max
Business from Other Countries: 80%
Branch Office(s)
Purgleitnergasse 10, Ecke Marburgerstrabe, A-8042 Graz

Akademische Druck- u Verlagsanstalt, see ADEVA (Akademische Druck-u Verlagsanstalt)

Dr Paul Struzl GmbH, see ADEVA (Akademische Druck-u Verlagsanstalt)

Belgium

Drukkerij Lannoo NV (Lanno Printers)
Kasteelstr 97, B-8700 Tielt
Tel: (051) 424211 *Fax:* (051) 407070
E-mail: lannoo@lannooprint.be
Web Site: www.lannooprint.be
Key Personnel
General Manager & Marketing Dir: Stefaan Lannoo *E-mail:* stefaan.lannoo@lannooprint.be
Founded: 1909
Turnaround: 10 Workdays
Print Runs: 100 min - 1,000,000 max
Business from Other Countries: 30%

IMPF BV BA
Sint-Amandstr 18, B-9000 Gent
Tel: (09) 2254429 *Fax:* (09) 2331338
E-mail: IMPF@xs4all.be
Key Personnel
Manager: Xavier Dewulf
Founded: 1958
Business from Other Countries: 10%

Canada

Aardvark Enterprises
Division of Speers Investments Ltd
204 Millbank Dr SW, Calgary, AB T2Y 2H9
Tel: 403-256-4639
Key Personnel
Pres: J Alvin Speers
Founded: 1970 (Small Press Pioneers)
Turnaround: 30 Workdays
Print Runs: 10 min - 1,000 max
Business from Other Countries: 25%

Barcode Graphics Inc
30 Dohme Ave, Toronto, ON M4B 3M4
Tel: 416-751-1474 *Fax:* 416-751-1575
E-mail: info@barcodegraphics.com
Web Site: www.barcodegraphics.com
Key Personnel
Pres: John Herzig *E-mail:* jherzig@barcodegraphics.com
Founded: 1981
Turnaround: 1-2 Workdays
Print Runs: 2,000,000 max
Business from Other Countries: 10%

David Berman Developments Inc
950 Gladstone Ave, Ottawa, ON K1Y 3E6
Tel: 613-728-6777 *Fax:* 613-722-5351
E-mail: info@timewise.net
Web Site: www.timewise.net
Business from Other Countries: 50%

Celia Godkin
680 Queens Quay W, Unit 411, Toronto, ON M5V 2Y9
Tel: 416-591-0491 *Fax:* 416-591-7095
E-mail: celia.godkin@utoronto.ca
Key Personnel
Illustrator: Celia Godkin
Founded: 1983
Business from Other Countries: 10%

Coach House Printing
401 Huron St, Rear, Toronto, ON M5S 2G5
Tel: 416-979-2217 *Fax:* 416-977-1158
E-mail: mail@chbooks.com
Web Site: www.chbooks.com
Key Personnel
Pres: Stan Bevington
Ed Publg: Darren Wershler-Henry
Founded: 1965
Turnaround: 14 Workdays
Print Runs: 200 min - 2,000 max
Business from Other Countries: 10%

Leanne Franson
4323 Parthenais, Montreal, PQ H2H 2G2
Tel: 514-526-4236 *Fax:* 514-526-0972
E-mail: inksports@videotron.ca
Key Personnel
Owner: Leanne Franson
Founded: 1991
Turnaround: 3-7 plus Workdays
Business from Other Countries: 50%
Membership(s): Association des Illustrateurs et d'Illustratries du Quebec

Girol Books Inc
120 Somerset St W, Ottawa, ON K2P 0H8
Mailing Address: Box 5473, Sta F, Ottawa, ON K2C 3M1
Tel: 613-233-9044 *Fax:* 613-233-9044
E-mail: info@girol.com
Web Site: www.girol.com
Key Personnel
Owner: Miguel Angel Giella; Peter Roster
Mgr: Leslie Roster *E-mail:* lroster@girol.com
Founded: 1975
Business from Other Countries: 30%

Herzig Somerville Ltd
543 Richmond St W, Suite 125, Toronto, ON M5V 1Y6
Tel: 416-681-1200 *Fax:* 416-681-1241
Web Site: www.herzig.com
Key Personnel
Pres: Mark Quesnelle
Founded: 1965
Business from Other Countries: 10%

Maracle Press Ltd
Box 606, Oshawa, ON L1H 7N4
Tel: 905-723-3438 *Fax:* 905-428-6024
E-mail: maracle@maraclepress.com
Web Site: www.maraclepress.com
Key Personnel
Pres & Gen Mgr: Bruce A Fenton
VP, Bus Devt: Ronald G Taylor *E-mail:* rtaylor@maraclepress.com
Founded: 1920
Turnaround: 10 Workdays
Print Runs: 500 min - 500,000 max
Business from Other Countries: 25%
Membership(s): BMI

Preney Print & Litho Inc
2714 Dougall Ave, Windsor, ON N9E 1R9
Tel: 519-966-3412 *Fax:* 519-966-4996
E-mail: preney@mnsi.net
Founded: 1972
Turnaround: 15 Workdays
Print Runs: 2,000 min - 1 max
Business from Other Countries: 20%

Printcrafters Inc
78 Hutchings St, Winnipeg, MB R2X 3B1
Tel: 204-633-7117 *Fax:* 204-694-1519
E-mail: printcrafters@mb.sympatico.ca
Key Personnel
Pres: Bob Payne *Tel:* 204-633-7117 ext 223
  Fax: 204-694-1594 *E-mail:* bpayne@mb.sympatico.ca
Founded: 1996 (Employee owned)
Turnaround: 5-20 Workdays
Print Runs: 200,000 min - 500,000 max
Business from Other Countries: 30%
Membership(s): CPIA

PrintWest
1150 Eighth Ave, Regina, SK S4R 1C9
Tel: 306-525-2304 *Fax:* 306-757-2439
E-mail: general@printwest.com
Web Site: www.printwest.com
Key Personnel
CEO: Wayne UnRuh
VP Sales & Mktg: Ken Benson
Founded: 1992
Turnaround: 15 Workdays
Print Runs: 1,000 min - 100,000 max
Business from Other Countries: 15%
Branch Office(s)
Box 2500, 2310 Millar Ave, Saskatoon, SK S7K 2C4 *Tel:* 306-665-3560 *Fax:* 306-653-1255

David Shaw & Associates Ltd
108 Ranleigh Ave, Toronto, ON M4N 1W9
Tel: 416-487-2019 *Fax:* 416-486-1744
E-mail: djshaw@simpatico.ca
Key Personnel
Pres: David Shaw

CANADA

Founded: 1977
Business from Other Countries: 25%

Barbara Spurll Illustration
1180 Danforth Ave, Toronto, ON M4J 1M3
Tel: 416-594-6594
E-mail: bspurll@idirect.ca
Founded: 1975
Business from Other Countries: 70%

Transcontinental Printing Book Group
Division of Transcontinental Group
395 Lebeau Blvd, St-Laurent, PQ H4N 1S2
Tel: 514-337-8560 *Fax:* 514-339-2252
Web Site: www.transcontinental-gtc.com; www.transcontinental-printing.com
Key Personnel
Sr VP, Book Group: Jacques Gregoire
US Sales Mgr: Denis Beaudin *Tel:* 514-339-2220 ext 4101 *E-mail:* beaudind@transcontinental.ca
Founded: 1976
Turnaround: 4 weeks casebound; 3 weeks softcover
Print Runs: 1,000 min
Business from Other Countries: 15%
Branch Office(s)
614 Yates Ave, Calumet City, IL 60409, United States, Contact: Kristopher D Levy *Tel:* 708-832-1528 *Fax:* 708-832-9510 *E-mail:* kris.levy@transcontinental.ca (Midwest)
3653 W Leland Ave, Suite One W, Chicago, IL 60625, United States, Contact: Tim Taylor *Tel:* 773-583-8155 *Fax:* 773-583-8162 *E-mail:* tim.taylor@transcontinental.ca (Midwest)
245 Eliot St, Ashland, MA 01721, United States, Contact: Ed Catania *Tel:* 508-881-1119 *E-mail:* ecatania@attbi.com (East Coast)
19 Crown St, Milton, MA 02186-1419, United States, Contact: Mike Gazzola *Tel:* 617-696-1435 *Fax:* 617-696-1025 *E-mail:* mikebook@attbi.com (East Coast)
37 Herman Blvd, Franklin Square, NY 11010, United States, Contact: Tom Malloy *Tel:* 516-775-2980 *Fax:* 516-488-0253 *E-mail:* tmmalloy@aol.com (NY)
3175 Summit Square Dr, Suite C9, Oakton, VA 22124, United States, Contact: David Avesian *Tel:* 703-255-1332 *Fax:* 703-255-1343 *E-mail:* davesian@cox.rr.com (Southeast)
559 Lowrys Rd, Parksville, BC V9P 2R8, Contact: Mike Davies *Tel:* 250-248-9700 *Fax:* 250-248-2353 *E-mail:* bookguys@shaw.ca (West Coast)
15373 Victoria Ave, White Rock, BC V4B 1H1, Contact: Wade Davies *Tel:* 604-535-8800 *Fax:* 604-535-8802 *E-mail:* daviesw@shaw.ca (West Coast)
490 Wilfred Dr, Peterborough, ON K9K 2H1, Contact: Tom Lang *Tel:* 705-760-9594 *Fax:* 705-760-9485 *E-mail:* langt@transcontinental.ca (NY)

Tri-Graphic Printing (Ottawa) Ltd
485 Industrial Ave, Ottawa, ON K1G 0Z1
Tel: 613-731-7441 *Fax:* 613-731-3741
Web Site: www.tri-graphic.com
Key Personnel
VP & Gen Mgr: Doug K Doane
  E-mail: ddoane@tri-graphic.com
VP, Prodn & Servs: Fred Malleau *Tel:* 905-665-8500 *E-mail:* fmalleau@tri-graphic.com
Founded: 1968
Turnaround: 10-15 Workdays
Print Runs: 1,000 min - 100,000 max
Business from Other Countries: 10%
Sales Office(s): 213 Byron St S, Suite 201, Whitby, ON L1N 4P7, VP Prod Devt: Fred Malleau *Tel:* 905-665-8500 *Fax:* 905-665-8501 *E-mail:* fmalleau@tri-graphic.com
Membership(s): BMI

University of Toronto Press Inc
Printing Division, 5201 Dufferin St, North York, ON M3H 5T8
Tel: 416-667-7767 *Fax:* 416-667-7803
E-mail: printing@utpress.utoronto.ca
Web Site: www.utpress.utoronto.ca
Key Personnel
Pres & Publr: George Meadows
Founded: 1901
Turnaround: 10-15 Workdays
Print Runs: 10 min - 200,000 max
Business from Other Countries: 15%
Membership(s): BMI

Denmark

Bianco Lunos Bogtrykkeri AS
Subsidiary of Carl Allers Etablissement AS
Otto Monsteds Gade 3, DK-1571 Copenhagen V
Tel: 33140781 *Fax:* 33913808
Key Personnel
General Manager: J Heede Sorensen
Founded: 1871

Finland

Gummerus Printing
Division of Gummerus Kirjapaino Oy
Subsidiary of Gummerus Oy
Alasinkatu 1-3, Fin-40351 Jyvaskyla
Mailing Address: PO Box 444, Fin-40351 Jyvaskyla
Tel: (014) 683525 *Fax:* (014) 676770; (014) 685166
Key Personnel
Marketing Dir: Mr Martti Aaltonen
Man Dir: Mr Jarmo Porkka
Founded: 1872
Turnaround: 20-60 Workdays
Print Runs: 1,000 min - 100,000 max
Business from Other Countries: 15%

France

Signes du Monde
1424 ch du Dupere Hubert Saint-Genez, 40380 Povartin
Tel: (06) 12 99 73 37 *Fax:* (0561) 575717
Key Personnel
Production: Hubert Saint-Genez

Germany

C L Baader Buch & Offsetdruckere GmbH & Co KG
Gutenbergstr 1, 72525 Baden-Wurttemberg
Mailing Address: Postfach 1220, 72522 Munsingen
Tel: (07381) 79192 *Fax:* (07381) 411412 *Cable:* BAADER-MUNSINGEN
Founded: 1835
Turnaround: 1 Workday
Print Runs: 1,000 min - 15,000 max

Fachhochschule Fur Druk, Studiengang Verlagswirtschaft und Verlagsherstellung
Nobelstr 10, 70569 Stuttgart
Tel: (0711) 6852807 *Fax:* (0711) 6852834
Web Site: www.fhd.stuttgart.de
Telex: 725 185 fhd d
Key Personnel
Contact: Prof Eduard H Schoenstedt

C Maurer Druck und Verlag
Schubartstr 21, 73312 Geislingen
Mailing Address: Postfach 1361, 73303 Geislingen
Tel: (07331) 9300 *Fax:* (07331) 930190
Key Personnel
Contact: Carl Otto Maurer
Founded: 1856

Media-Print Informationstechnologie GmbH
Eggertstr 28, 33100 Paderborn
Tel: (05251) 522300 *Fax:* (05251) 522480
E-mail: contact@mediaprint.de
Web Site: www.mediaprint.de
Key Personnel
Man Dir: Rainer Rings
Founded: 1993
Turnaround: 5-10 Workdays
Print Runs: 100 min - 30,000 max
Business from Other Countries: 10%

Mohndruck Graphische Betriebe GmbH
Subsidiary of Bertelsmann AG
Carl-Bertelsmann-Str 161, 33311 Guetersloh
Mailing Address: Postfach 200, 33311 Guetersloh
Tel: (05241) 802095 *Fax:* (05241) 78329
Key Personnel
Contact: Alfred Hahn
Founded: 1824
Business from Other Countries: 25%

Oertel & Sporer GmbH & Co
Burgstr 1-7, 72764 Reutlingen
Mailing Address: Postfach 1642, 72706 Reutlingen
Tel: (07121) 302555 *Fax:* (07121) 302558
Key Personnel
Publisher: Valdo Lehari
Manager & Printer: Ermo Lehari
Print Runs: 500 min - 50,000 max

Priese GmbH
Auerbacherstr 9, 14193 Berlin
Tel: (030) 3239089 *Fax:* (030) 3249630
Key Personnel
Contact: Elma Priese; Hans Joachim Priese

Topic Verlag GmbH
Birkenstr 10, 85757 Karlsfeld B Munich
Tel: (08131) 97038 *Fax:* (08131) 98404
Founded: 1982
Business from Other Countries: 50%

Vier-Tuerme GmbH Benedikt Press
Schweinfurterstr 40, 97359 Munsterschwarzach
Tel: (09324) 20214 *Fax:* (09324) 20495
Key Personnel
Contact: Josef Stoecklein
Founded: 1951
Turnaround: 8-16 Workdays
Print Runs: 300 min - 20,000 max
Business from Other Countries: 5%

SERVICES   HONG KONG

Hong Kong

Best-Set Typesetter Ltd
6 Sun Yip St, Honour Industrial Centre, Room 304, 3rd fl, Chai Wan
Tel: 2897 6033 *Fax:* 2897 5170
E-mail: bestset@bestset-typesetter.com
Web Site: www.bestset-typesetter.com
Key Personnel
Dir (Hong Kong): Johnson Yeung *Tel:* 2975 1012
  E-mail: johnson@bestset-typesetter.com
Manager: Cynthia Hui
Sales Rep: Wai Man Yeung
Founded: 1986
Turnaround: 5 workdays
Print Runs: 100 min - 200,000 max
Business from Other Countries: 98%
Branch Office(s)
3 Jiang nan Main Ave C, 3rd fl, Guangzhou, China, Contact: Patrick Au *Tel:* (020) 8441 5873 *Fax:* (020) 8441 5874
Sales Office(s): 157 Fisher Ave, Suite 6, Eastchester, NY 10709, United States, Contact: Wai Man Yeung *Tel:* 914-961-6223 *Fax:* 914-961-8212
33 Alpin Way, TW7 4RJ Isleworth, Middlesex, United Kingdom, Contact: Keith Harrocks *Tel:* (0208) 847-4947 *E-mail:* bestsetuk@bestset-typesetter.com

Bookbuilders Ltd
Unit J 13/F Yeung Yiu Chung No 8 Industrial Bldg, 20 Wang Hoi Rd, Kowloon Bay, Kowloon
Tel: 27968123 *Fax:* 27968267; 27968690
E-mail: lph@netvigator.com
Key Personnel
Man Dir: Leslie Henman
General Manager: Edward Chan

Bright Arts Hong Kong Ltd
11/F Block D Tung Chong Factory Bldg, 655-659 Kings Rd, North Point
Tel: 25620119 *Fax:* 25657031
Key Personnel
Man Dir: Sunny Shum
DTP & Systems Manager: Helen Or

Bright Future Printing Co Ltd
Sunview Industrial Building, Block D, 5/F, 3 On Yip St, Chai Wan
Tel: 25151776 *Fax:* 28972799; 25581717
Key Personnel
Chairman: Richard Ng
Turnaround: 60 Workdays (including shipping)
Print Runs: 3,000 min - 30,000 max
Business from Other Countries: 30%

C & C Offset Printing Co Ltd
Subsidiary of C & C Joint Printing Co (HK) Ltd under Sino United Publishing (Holdings) Ltd
C & C Bldg, 36 Ting Lai Rd, Tai Po, New Territories
Tel: (02) 666-4988 *Fax:* (02) 666-4938
E-mail: offsetprinting@candcprinting.com
Web Site: www.ccoffset.com
Key Personnel
Dir & General Manager: Xian-Qing Zhuang
Dir & Assistant General Manager: Ken Lee
Sales Manager (Overseas): Kit Wong
Sales Manager (Special Projects): Francis Ho
Dir & Executive Vice President, C & C Offset Printing Co (USA) Inc, Portland OR, USA: Charles H Clark, IV
Development Manager, C & C Offset Printing (USA) Inc, Portland, OR, USA: Jenny Whittier *Tel:* 503-233-1834 *E-mail:* jwhittier@ccoffset.com
Customer Service Manager, C & C Offset Printing Co (USA) Inc, Portland, OR, USA: Ernest Li
Dir & Executive Vice President, C & C Offset Printing Co (NY) Inc, New York, NY, USA: Simon Chan
Dir & General Manager, C & C Joint Printing Co (Guangdong) Ltd, Shenzhen, China: Jackson Leung
Deputy Sales Manager, C & C Joint Printing Co (Ghuangdong) Ltd, Shenzhen, China: Min Zhu
President, C & C Printing Japan Co Ltd, Tokyo, Japan: Masashi Otobe
Customer Service Manager, C & C Offset Printing Co (NYC), Inc, NY NY: Frances Harkness
Man Dir, C & C Joint Printing Co (Beijing), Ltd, Beijing, China: Zhang Lin Gui
Dir, C & C Offset Printing Co (UK), Ltd: Tracy Broderick
Manager, C & C Offset Printing Co (UK), Ltd: Fiona Norman
Founded: 1980
Turnaround: 42 Workdays for printing, binding & book finishing
Print Runs: 2,000 min - 200,000 max
Business from Other Countries: 60%
Branch Office(s)
C & C Joint Printing Co (Guangdong) Ltd, Chunhu Industrial Estate, Pinghu, Long Gang, Shenzhen 518111, China *Tel:* (0755) 844-1333 *Fax:* (0755) 844-2211 *E-mail:* guangdong@candcprinting.com (Plant)
C & C Printing Japan Co Ltd, Tokyodou, 6th floor, Jinbocho No 2, Bldg 127, Chiyoda-Ku, Tokyo 101, Japan *Tel:* (03) 3261-9650 *Fax:* (03) 3261-9655 *E-mail:* ccjtokyo@interlink.or.jp
Room 2, 9/F, 3 Chegongzhuang Main St, Xicheng District, Beijing 100044, China *Tel:* (010) 6836-5335 *Fax:* (010) 6836-5335
Room 304 Fangfa Bldg, No 29 Lane 165, Dongzhu Anbin Rd, Shanghai 200050, China *Tel:* (020) 6240-1305 *Fax:* (020) 6240-1305 *E-mail:* shanghai@candcprinting.com
Room 505 Sino Bldg, 23 Zhan Qian Rd, Guangzhou 510010, China *Tel:* (020) 8650-0602 *Fax:* (020) 8667-8882 *E-mail:* guangzhou@candcprinting.com
C & C Offset Printing Co (UK), Ltd, 2 New Burlington St, 4th fl, London W1S 2JE, United Kingdom *Tel:* (0207) 2877787 *Fax:* (0207) 2877187 *E-mail:* tracy@candcoffset.co.uk
U.S. Office(s): C & C Offset Printing Co (USA) Inc, 2632 SE 25 St, Suite D, Portland, OR 97202, United States *Tel:* 503-233-1834 *Fax:* 503-233-7814 *E-mail:* portlandinfo@ccoffset.com
C & C Offset Printing Co (NY) Inc, 401 Broadway, Suite 2015, New York, NY 10013-3005, United States *Tel:* 212-431-4210 *Fax:* 212-431-3960 *E-mail:* newyorkinfo@ccoffset.com

Caritas Printing Training Centre
2 Caine Rd, Caritas House, Block D, 3/F, Hong Kong
Tel: 25261148 *Fax:* 25371231
Key Personnel
General Manager: Isaac Mak
Print Runs: 1,000 min - 100,000 max
Business from Other Countries: 50%

Colorprint Offset
8 Coml Tower, Chai Wan
Tel: 28967777 *Fax:* 28896606
Key Personnel
Sales Manager: Jennifer Weston *Tel:* 9035062
Contact: Eva Lav; Ian Lee
Turnaround: 30-40 Workdays
Print Runs: 3,000 min - 100,000 max
Business from Other Countries: 80%

Sales Office(s): Gainsborough House, 81 Oxford St, London W1R 1KB, United Kingdom
Lincoln Bldg, Suite 1149, 60 E 42 St, New York, NY 10164, United States

Cristy's Atelier
37-39 Jervois St, Sheung Wan
Tel: 25418609 *Fax:* 28540995
E-mail: cristys@intercon.net
Founded: 1982

Dai Nippon Printing Co (Hong Kong) Ltd
Division of Dai Nippon Printing Co Ltd
220-248 Texaco Rd, Tsuen Wan Industrial Centre, 2/F-5/F, Tsuen Wan, New Territories
Tel: 24080188 *Fax:* 24076201
Web Site: www.dnp.co.jp *Cable:* DNPICO
Key Personnel
Administration & Finance Dir: Mr K Miya
Print Runs: 5,000 min - 200,000 max
Business from Other Countries: 85%
Branch Office(s)
Dai Nippon Printing Co Pty Ltd, 45 Clarence St, Suite 904, Level 9, KPMG Centre, Sydney NSW 2000, Australia
Dai Nippon Printing Co Ltd, 1-1, Ichigaya-Kagacho, 1-Chome, Shinjuku-Ku, Tokyo, Japan
Dai Nippon Printing Co (Singapore) Pte Ltd, 896 Dunearn Rd, No 04-09, Sime Darby Centre, Singapore 589472, Singapore *Tel:* 469-7611
Tien Wah Press Pte Ltd, 4 Pandan Crescent, Singapore 128475, Singapore *Tel:* 466-6222
Dai Nippon Printing Co Ltd, London Liaison Office, 27 Throgmorton St, 4th floor, London EC2N 2AQ, United Kingdom
TEP Sdn Bhd, 89, Jalan Tampoi, Kawasan Perindustrian Tampoi, 80350 Johor Bahru, Johor, Malaysia *Tel:* (07) 2369899
PT Tien Wah Press Indonesia, Janlan Tenaru, Desa Cangkir, Kec Driyorejo, Gresik 61177, Indonesia *Tel:* (031) 7507403
PT Dai Nippon Printing Indonesia, Kawasan Industri Pulogadung, Jalan Pulogadung Kaveling II, Blok H No 2-3, Jakarta Timur, Indonesia *Tel:* (021) 4610313
Dai Nippon Printing Co (Australia) PTY LTD, 45 Clarence St, Suite 904, Level 9, KPMG Centre, Sydney NSW 2000, Australia *Tel:* (02) 9299-3155
DAI Nippon IMS (America) Corp, 4524 Enterprise Dr NW, Concord, NC 28027, United States *Tel:* 704-784-8100
DAI Nippon Printing (Europe) GMBH, Berliner Allee 26, 40212 Dusseldorf, Germany *Tel:* (0211) 862018-0
DNP Denmark A/S, Skruegangen 2, DK-2690 Karlslunde, Denmark *Tel:* 4616-5100
DAI Nippon Printing (Taiwan) Co, LTD, 85 Chung Hsiao East Rd, Sec 1 Taipei, Taiwan, China *Tel:* (02) 2327-8311
Sales Office(s): DNP America Inc, 3235 Kifer Rd, Suite 100, Santa Clara, CA 95051, United States
DNP America Inc, 3858 Carson St, Suite 300, Torrance, CA 90503, United States
DNP America Inc, 7425 Mission Valley Rd, Suite 201, San Diego, CA 92108, United States *Tel:* 619-295-8111
U.S. Office(s): DNP America Inc, 50 California St, Suite 777, San Francisco, CA 94111, United States
DNP Corporation USA, 335 Madison Ave, 3rd fl, New York, NY 10017, United States *Tel:* 212-503-1060

Elegance Finance Printing Services Ltd
Subsidiary of Elegance Printing Company Limited
Suite 301, Chinachem Hollywood Centre, 1-13 Hollywood Rd, Central Hong Kong
Tel: 25212200 *Fax:* 25213616
E-mail: saledept@elegancefinptg.com

Print Runs: 500 min - 7,200 max
Business from Other Countries: 2%

Everbest Printing Co Ltd
Block C5, 10/F, Ko Fai Industrial Bldg, 7 Ko Fai Rd, 10F, Yautong, Kowloon
Tel: (02) 7274433 *Fax:* (02) 7727687
E-mail: everbest@hk.super.net; sales@everbest.com.hk
Key Personnel
Man Dir: Kenneth Chung
Customer Account Executive: Ronny Ng; Frankie Lee
Founded: 1954
Turnaround: 28 Workdays
Print Runs: 1,000 min - 1,000,000 max
Business from Other Countries: 90%
Branch Office(s)
Four Colour Imports Ltd, 2843 Brownsboro Rd, Louisville, KY, United States *Tel:* 502-896-9644 *Fax:* 502-896-9594 *E-mail:* sales@fourcolor.com *Web Site:* www.fourcolor.com
Everbest Midwest, Edina, MN, United States *Tel:* 612-944-0854 *E-mail:* sklo@juno.com
Everbest Canada, Toronto, ON, Canada *Tel:* (416) 286-6688 *E-mail:* everbestcan@sympatico.ca

Golden Cup Printing Co Ltd
6/F Seapower Industrial Centre, 177 Hoi Bun Rd, Kwun Tong, Kowloon
Tel: 23434254 *Fax:* 23415426
E-mail: sales@goldencup.com.hk
Web Site: www.goldencup.com.hk
Key Personnel
Man Dir: K K Yeung
General Manager: W K Ngan
Sales Manager: Mary Yeung *E-mail:* mary@goldencup.com.hk
Founded: 1971
Turnaround: 25 Workdays
Print Runs: 5,000 min - 200,000 max
Business from Other Countries: 80%
Branch Office(s)
Dongguan, China
Guangdong, China
Kunming, China
Yunan, China

The Green Pagoda Press Ltd
9/F, Tung Chong Factory Bldg, 653-655 Kings Rd, North Point
Tel: 25611924 *Fax:* 28110946
E-mail: gpinfo@gpp.com.hk
Key Personnel
Dir: Derek Yip
Founded: 1957
Turnaround: 1-14 days
Print Runs: 10 min - 100,000 max
Business from Other Countries: 30%

H K Scanner Arts International Ltd
Block B1, 6/F Fortune Factory Bldg, 40 Lee Chung St, Chai Wan
Tel: 29760302 *Fax:* 29760292
Key Personnel
Dir, Sales & Marketing: Wayne C Ling
Man Dir: Y C Luk

Hindy's Enterprise Co Ltd
Flat A 20/F, Melbourne Industrial Bldg, 16 Wetlands Rd, Quarry Bay
Tel: 25166318 *Fax:* 25165161
Key Personnel
General Manager: Cecilia Chung

Hung Hing Off-set Printing Co Ltd
Subsidiary of Hung Hing Printing Group Ltd
17-19 Dai Hei St, Tai Po Industrial Estate, Tai Po, New Territories
Tel: 26648682 *Fax:* 26642070
E-mail: info@hhop.com.hk
Key Personnel
Man Dir: Matthew Yum *E-mail:* matthew@hhop.com.hk
Founded: 1950
Turnaround: 20-30 Workdays
Print Runs: 5,000 min - 1,000,000 max
Business from Other Countries: 15%

Image Printing Company Ltd
Unit 4, 4/F Cornell Centre, 50 Wing Tai Rd, Chai Wan
Tel: 28732633 *Fax:* 25583044
E-mail: imageprt@pop3.hknet.com
Key Personnel
Man Dir: Philip Chow Sung Ming
Founded: 1992
Print Runs: 1,000 min - 50,000 max
Business from Other Countries: 50%

Leo Paper Products Ltd
7/F Kader Bldg, 22 Kai Cheung Rd, Kowloon Bay
Tel: 25696293 *Fax:* 25138400
E-mail: lrg@leo.com.hk
Web Site: www.leo.com.hk
Key Personnel
Deputy Man Dir: Burman Tam *E-mail:* burman@leo.com.hk
Founded: 1991
Turnaround: 15-30 Workdays
Print Runs: 5,000 min
Parent Company: Leo Paper Bags Manufacturing Ltd
Branch Office(s)
Leo Paper USA, 777 108 Ave NE, Suite 1200, Bellevue, WA 98004, United States, Contact: Bijan Pakzad *Tel:* 425-646-8801 *Fax:* 425-646-8805 *E-mail:* bijan@pacificpier.com
Sales Office(s): Leo Paper Products (Europe) BVBA, "De Wilde Zee", Wiegstraat 19, 2000 Antwerpen, Belgium, Sales Dir: Jan Van Gijsel *Tel:* (03) 203-0912 *Fax:* (03) 255-1303 *E-mail:* leo@leo-europe.com
Leo Marketing Ltd, The Malthouse, Malthouse Sq, Princes Risborough, Bucks HP27 9AB, United Kingdom, Dir: Sally Wood *Tel:* (018) 274-244 *Fax:* (018) 275-105 *E-mail:* sallywood.leo@btinternet.com

Leo Reprographic Ltd
7/F Kader Bldg, 22 Kai Cheung Rd, Kowloon Bay
Tel: (02) 569-6293 *Fax:* (02) 513-8400
E-mail: lrg@leo.com.hk
Web Site: www.leo.com.hk
Key Personnel
Managing Deputy Dir: Burman Tam *E-mail:* burman@leo.com.hk
Founded: 1991
Turnaround: 7 Workdays for 128pp A4 size
Parent Company: Leo Paper Bags Manufacturing Ltd
Sales Office(s): Leo Marketing Ltd, The Malthouse, Malthouse Sq, Princes Risborough, Bucks HP27 9AB, United Kingdom, Director: Sally Wood *Tel:* (018) 274-244 *Fax:* (018) 275-105 *E-mail:* sallywood.leo@btinternet.com
Leo Paper Products (Europe) BVBA, De Wilde Zee, Wiegstraat 19, 2000 Antwerp, Belgium, Sales Director: Jan Van Gijsel *Tel:* (03) 203-0912 *Fax:* (03) 255-1303 *E-mail:* leo@leo-europe.com
U.S. Office(s): Leo Paper USA, 777 108 Ave NE, Suite 1200, Bellevue, WA 98004, United States, Contact: Bijan Pakzad *Tel:* 425-646-8801 *Fax:* 425-646-8805 *E-mail:* bijan@pacificpier.com

Mei Ka Printing & Publish Enterprise Ltd
Cheung Ka Industrial Bldg, Block B 8th & 9th Floor, 179-190 Connaught Rd West, Sai Ying Pin
Tel: 25401131 *Fax:* 25598718
Key Personnel
Dir: Hong Chin Huo

Midas Printing Ltd
1/F 100 Texaco Rd, Tsuen Wan, New Territories
Tel: 24076888 *Fax:* 24065800; 24096875
E-mail: midas@hkstar.com
Key Personnel
Project Manager: Raymond Chan
Executive Dir: Gloria Y P Kan
Founded: 1990
Turnaround: 14-21 Workdays
Print Runs: 5,000 min - 100,000 max
Business from Other Countries: 25%

New Arts Graphic Reproduction Co Ltd
4/F Loks Industrial Bldg, 204 Tsat Tse Mui Rd, North Point
Tel: 25641323; 25618161 *Fax:* 25658262
E-mail: newarts@writeme.com
Key Personnel
Man Dir: Paul Sik-Kwong Choy
Manager: Andrew Choy *E-mail:* andchoy@netvigator.com
Founded: 1970
Business from Other Countries: 50%

Paper Communication Printing Express Ltd
4A Dragon Industrial Bldg, 93 King Lam St, Cheung Sha Wan, Kowloon
Tel: 27864191 *Fax:* 27864498
E-mail: pcpc@papercom.com.hk
Key Personnel
Marketing Dir: Alam Ng
Founded: 1981
BISAC compatible software
Turnaround: 28 to 56 Workdays
Print Runs: 1,000 min - 3,000,000 max
Business from Other Countries: 90%

Prontaprint Asia Ltd
1/F, Gaylord Commercial Bldg, 114 Lockhart Rd, Wanchai
Tel: 28657525 *Fax:* 28661064
E-mail: postmaster@pronta.com.hk
Key Personnel
Man Dir: Clive Howard
Founded: 1986
Business from Other Countries: 40%

Rainbow Graphic & Printing Co Ltd
Tseung Kwan O Industrial Estate, 8 Chun Ying St, 4/F, Kowloon
Tel: 27523423 *Fax:* 28974890
E-mail: rgarts@netvigator.com
Telex: 61310 RBART HX
Key Personnel
General Manager: Willie Lim *E-mail:* willylim@netvigator.com
Business from Other Countries: 90%

Sota Graphic Arts Co Ltd
6/F Seapower Industry Centre, 177 Hoi Bun Rd, Kwun Tong, Kowloon
Tel: 23427507 *Fax:* 23415426
E-mail: sales@goldencup.com.hk
Key Personnel
Man Dir: K K Yeung
General Manager: W K Ngan
Assistant Manager: Mary Yeung *E-mail:* mary@goldencup.com.hk
Founded: 1985
Turnaround: 10 Workdays
Print Runs: 2,000 min
Business from Other Countries: 90%

South Sea International Press Ltd
3/F, Yip Cheung Centre, 10 Fung Yip St, Chai Wan
Tel: 28971083 *Fax:* 25581473

E-mail: ssiphk@hk.super.net
Key Personnel
Man Dir: P Y Lee
Senior Manager: Franky Ho
Founded: 1984
Print Runs: 3,000 min - 500,000 max
Business from Other Countries: 80%

Sunshine Press Ltd
21/F Fullager Ind Bldg, 234 Aberdeen Main Rd, Hong Kong
Tel: 25532386 *Fax:* 28732930
E-mail: spl@sunshinepress.com.hk
Key Personnel
Administrative Assistant: Trevin Tong
Contact: Joney Chan
Founded: 1976
Turnaround: 21-28 Workdays
Print Runs: 3,000 min - 500,000 max
Business from Other Countries: 25%

Toppan Printing Co (HK) Ltd
Division of Toppan Printing Co Ltd
Yuen Long Industrial Estate, One Fuk Wang St, Yuen Long, New Territories
Tel: 24755666; 25610101 *Fax:* 24740608; 28809970
E-mail: mamada@hk.nttdata.net
Key Personnel
Man Dir: James Lee Lee
Sales Manager: Yukata Ito
Founded: 1963
Turnaround: 30 Workdays
Business from Other Countries: 25%

Wing King Tong Co Ltd (Printing Factory)
188 Texaco Rd, 3/F, Phase 1, Leader Industrial Centre, Tsuen Wan, New Territories
Tel: 24073287 *Fax:* 24074130
Key Personnel
Man Dir: Alex Yan E-mail: ayan@hk.super.net
Marketing Dir: Jeremy Kuo
Founded: 1944
Turnaround: 15 Workdays
Print Runs: 1,000 min - 100,000 max
Business from Other Countries: 95%

Ying Tat Co
Division of Quality Printing & Paper Products
Wing Wah Industrial Bldg, 8th Floor, 677 Kings Rd, Hong Kong
Tel: 25645980 *Fax:* 28111280
Key Personnel
Sales Manager: Kan Chan
Founded: 1968
Turnaround: 7-10 Workdays
Print Runs: 1,000 min - 1,000,000 max
Business from Other Countries: 30%

India

Hiralal Printing Works Ltd
Subsidiary of Conway Printers Pvt Ltd
Plot No D-41/1, MIDC TTC Ind Area, Opp Turbne Tel Exch, Mumbai 400613
Tel: (022) 7672726; (022) 7683012 *Fax:* (022) 7631191
Key Personnel
Chairman: G P Agrawal
Man Dir: Mr Rakesh Kumar Agrawal
Founded: 1981
Turnaround: 40-45 Workdays
Print Runs: 5,000 min - 100,000 max
Business from Other Countries: 75%

Paragon Prepress Inc
N-31, Kalkaji, New Delhi 110019
Tel: (011) 622 44 51 *Fax:* (011) 643 73 43
Web Site: www.paragonprepress.com
Key Personnel
CEO: S Malhotra E-mail: shailander@paragonpress.com
Production Manager: T Malhotra E-mail: tarun@paragonprepress.com
Founded: 1991

Indonesia

Ichtiar Baru l Van Hoeve
Jl Cideng Barat 62, Jakarta Barat
Tel: (021) 354533
Founded: 1972
Turnaround: 6 Workdays
Print Runs: 500 min - 18,000 max

Victory Offset Prima PT
Jalan Raya Pegangsaan, Dua, No 17, Jakarta 14250
Tel: (021) 460-2742; (021) 460-8968 *Fax:* (021) 460-2740; (021) 4682-0551
E-mail: info@victoryoffset.com
Web Site: www.victoryoffset.com
Key Personnel
President: Zainal F Stanley E-mail: zainal@victoryoffset.com
General Manager: S Wilson Pinady E-mail: wilson@victoryoffset.com
Founded: 1971
Turnaround: 14 days
Print Runs: 5,000 min
Business from Other Countries: 10%
Branch Office(s)
PT Victory Graficindo Printing, Jalan Raya Pegengsaan, Dua, No 17, Jakarta-Utara 14250

Ireland

Doyle Graphics
Esker House, Patrick St, Tullamore, Co Offaly
Tel: (0506) 21970 *Fax:* (0506) 51323
Key Personnel
Contact: Desmond Doyle
Production Manager: Tom Clarke

Graphic Reproductions Ltd
Westlink House, Old Lucan Rd, Palmerstown, Dublin 20
Tel: (01) 6230101 *Fax:* (01) 6166598; (01) 6166599
Key Personnel
Contact: David Malone; Tim Hurley
Branch Office(s)
Graphic Reproductions, 475 Park Ave S, New York, NY 10016, United States *Tel:* 212-679-4351 *Fax:* 212-679-4352

ICPC Ltd
Subsidiary of The Irish Times
Greencastle Parade, Coolock, Dublin 17
Tel: (01) 8474711 *Fax:* (01) 8474546
Key Personnel
Man Dir: Seamus McCague E-mail: seamus@icpc.ie
Production Manager: Wayne Nial E-mail: wayne@icpc.ie
Founded: 1976
Turnaround: 10 Workdays
Business from Other Countries: 95%

Kilkenny People/Wellbrook Press
34 High St, Kilkenny
Tel: (056) 21015 *Fax:* (056) 21414
Founded: 1892
Business from Other Countries: 10%

SciPrint Ltd
93-94 Industrial Estate, Shannon, Co Clare
Tel: (061) 472114; (061) 472520 *Fax:* (061) 472021
Key Personnel
Man Dir, Sales: M K Parsons
Chairman: B Lane
Founded: 1974
Turnaround: 15-20 Workdays
Print Runs: 300 min - 10,000 max
Business from Other Countries: 95%

Smurfit Print
33 Botanic Rd, Glasnevin, Dublin 9
Tel: (01) 303911 *Fax:* (01) 303287
Print Runs: 200 min - 5,000,000 max
Business from Other Countries: 20%
Parent Company: Jefferson Smurfit Group plc

Ultragraphics
Unit 78A, Cookstown Industrial Estate, Tallaght, Dublin 24
Tel: (01) 4599133 *Fax:* (01) 4512368
Key Personnel
President: Tony Lovett
Turnaround: 4-5 Workdays
Business from Other Countries: 80%

Israel

Har-El Printers & Publishers
Jaffa Port, Main Gate, Jaffa 61081
Mailing Address: PO Box 8053, Jaffa 61081
Tel: (03) 6816834 *Fax:* (03) 6813563
E-mail: mharel@harelart.co.il
Web Site: www.interart.co.il/harel
Key Personnel
Manager: Jaacov Har-El
Founded: 1974
Turnaround: 60-90 Workdays
Print Runs: 30 min - 5,000 max
Business from Other Countries: 70%

Keterpress Enterprises Jerusalem
Industrial Zone Givat Shaul B, Jerusalem 91071
Mailing Address: PO Box 7145, Jerusalem 91071
Tel: (02) 6557822 *Fax:* (02) 6527956
E-mail: keterprs@isdn.net.il
Key Personnel
Plant Manager: Peter Tomkins E-mail: peter@keter-books.co.il
Sales Manager: Zvi Weller
Print Runs: 500 min - 500,000 max
Business from Other Countries: 10%
Parent Company: Keter Publishing House Ltd

Monoline Ltd
Avnei Nezer St 3, Kiryat Sefer 71917
Tel: (08) 9741456 *Fax:* (08) 9741454
Key Personnel
Dir: S J Colthof
Founded: 1959
Business from Other Countries: 30%

Technosdar Ltd
5 Levontine St, Tel Aviv 61316
Mailing Address: PO Box 31684, Tel Aviv 65111
Tel: (03) 5607418; (03) 5605951 *Fax:* (03) 5604932
Key Personnel
General Manager: Avraham Weiss
Founded: 1972
Turnaround: 7-16 Workdays
Business from Other Countries: 10%

Italy

Canale G e C SpA
Subsidiary of Istituto Grafico Bertello SpA
Via Liguria 24, 10071 Borgaro Turin
Tel: (011) 4078511 *Fax:* (011) 4078527
E-mail: info@canale.it
Key Personnel
Dir General: Canale Giacomo *E-mail:* canale@canale.it
Founded: 1915
Turnaround: 30 Workdays
Print Runs: 3,000 min
Business from Other Countries: 65%
Parent Company: Ledi Srl; PPG Srl

Dedalo Litostampa SRL
Viale Luigi Jacobini 5, I-70123 Bari
Tel: (080) 5311400 *Fax:* (080) 5311414
Key Personnel
Man Dir: Raimondo Coga
General Manager: Sergio Coga *Tel:* (080) 5311413 *E-mail:* s.coga@edizionidedalo.it
Founded: 1965
Print Runs: 2,000 min - 10,000 max

Milanostampa SPA
Corso Ferrero 5, Farigliano 12060 Cuneo
Tel: (0173) 746111 *Fax:* (0173) 746248
E-mail: milanostamp@areacom.it
Telex: 212428
Key Personnel
Commercial Dir: Riccardo Sardo
Man Dir: Fuad Lahham
Founded: 1965
Turnaround: 15 Workdays
Print Runs: 3,000 min - 80,000 max
Business from Other Countries: 65%

Nuovo Instituto Italiano d'Arti Grafiche
Via Zanica 92, 1-24126 Bergamo
Tel: (035) 311311 *Fax:* (035) 311349
E-mail: artigraf@bertelsmann.de
Telex: (035) 300114
Founded: 1871
Turnaround: 10 Workdays
Business from Other Countries: 30%

Amilcare Pizzi SpA
Via A Pizzi, 14, 20092 Cinisello Balsamo (Milan)
Tel: (02) 618361 *Fax:* (02) 61836283
E-mail: mapizzi@tin.it
Key Personnel
Chief Executive: Massimo Pizzi
Sales Dir: Bruno Nicolis
Founded: 1914
Business from Other Countries: 45%
Branch Office(s)
Amilcare Pizzi UK, 27 Cedar Rd, Berkhamsted, Herts HP4 2LA, United Kingdom *Tel:* (02) 877692 *Fax:* (02) 875315
American Pizzi Offset Corp, 370 Lexington Ave, Suite 505, New York, NY 10017, United States *Tel:* 212-986-1658 *Fax:* 212-286-1887

Republic of Korea

Daehan Printing & Publishing Co Ltd
344-12, Sangdaewon-dong, Jungwon-gu, Sungnam-City, Kyungki-do
Tel: (031) 730-3830 (i-3) *Fax:* (031) 735-8104
E-mail: mschung@dhpop.com
Web Site: www.dhpop.com

Key Personnel
President: Sungshick Kim
Manager: Jongjun Yu
Founded: 1948

Pyunghwa Dang Printing Co Ltd
60 Kyunji-Dong, Chongro-ku, Seoul
Tel: (02) 7354001 *Fax:* (02) 7345201
E-mail: comuser@hitel.kol.co.kr *Cable:* PHDPRINTCO SEOUL
Key Personnel
President: Mr Il Soo Lee
Vice President: Mr Hae Kun Oh
Executive Dir: Mr Sang Woo Lee
Founded: 1923
Turnaround: 10 Workdays
Print Runs: 2,000 min - 500,000 max
Business from Other Countries: 7%

Lithuania

Spindulys Printing House
Gedimino 10, 3000 Kaunas
Tel: (07) 226243 *Fax:* (07) 204970
Key Personnel
Contact: Elena Kapustinskiene
Founded: 1928
Print Runs: 500 min - 100,000 max
Business from Other Countries: 6%

Madagascar

Societe Malgache d'Edition
Route des Hydrocarbures, Ankorondrano, BP 659, Antananarivo 101
Mailing Address: BP 659, Antananarivo 101
Tel: (020) 2222635 *Fax:* (020) 2222254
E-mail: tribune@bow.dts.mg
Web Site: www.madagascar-tribune.com
Telex: (020) 223-40
Key Personnel
Dir of Publication: Rahaga Ramaholimihaso
Founded: 1943
Print Runs: 7,000 min - 15,000 max

Netherlands

Bosch en Keuning grafische bedrijven
Ericastraat 1, 3742 SG Baarn
Tel: (035) 5412050 *Fax:* (035) 2202446
Key Personnel
Contact: P P E Rings

New Zealand

Egan-Reid Ltd
Level 2, 38 Ireland St, Freemans Bay, Auckland 1001
Tel: (09) 3784100 *Fax:* (09) 3784300
E-mail: books@eganreid.co.nz
Key Personnel
Man Dir: Gerard Reid *E-mail:* gerard@eganreid.co.nz
Contact: Mary Egan *E-mail:* mary@eganreid.co.nz
Founded: 1988

Turnaround: 2 Workdays
Business from Other Countries: 75%
Membership(s): Book Publishers Association of New Zealand

John McIndoe Ltd
PO Box 694, Dunedin
Tel: (03) 4770355 *Fax:* (03) 4771982
E-mail: jmcindoe@earthlight.co.nz
Key Personnel
Man Dir: Brendan A Murphy
Founded: 1893
Print Runs: 21 min - 30 max
Business from Other Countries: 1%

PPP Printers Ltd
PO Box 22785, Christchurch
Tel: (03) 3662727 *Fax:* (03) 3654606
Key Personnel
Man Dir: D C Richardson
Founded: 1958
Turnaround: 10 Workdays
Print Runs: 100 min - 100,000 max
Business from Other Countries: 10%

Philippines

Naldoza Printers
362 Tupaz St, 6000 Cebu City
Tel: (032) 261-7326 *Fax:* (032) 261-7326
E-mail: naldoza@ebu.skyinet.net
Key Personnel
Chief Executive Officer: John R Naldoza
Founded: 1989
Parent Company: Business Developers Inc
Membership(s): Philippine Printing Technical Foundation

Reyes Publishing
717 Aurora Blvd, 4/F Mariwasa Bldg, 1112 Quezon City
Tel: (02) 721827 *Fax:* (02) 7218782
E-mail: reyesbub@skyinet.net
Key Personnel
Operations Manager: Roman Paolo V Reyes
Founded: 1964
Business from Other Countries: 90%

Portugal

Silabo
R Cidade de Manchester-2, 1170-100 Lisbon
Tel: (021) 8130345 *Fax:* (021) 8166719
E-mail: silabo@mail.telepac.pt
Key Personnel
Marketing Dir: Manuel Robalo
 E-mail: manuelrobalo@mail.telepac.pt
Founded: 1983
Turnaround: 5 Workdays

Puerto Rico

Publishing Resources Inc
373 San Jorge St, 2nd Floor, Santurce 00912
Mailing Address: PO Box 41307, Minillas Station, Santurce 00940
Tel: (787) 268-8080 *Fax:* (787) 774-5781
E-mail: pri@tld.net
Key Personnel
Owner: Ronald J Chevako

Editorial Dir: Anne W Chevako
Founded: 1976
Print Runs: 500 min - 10,000 max
Business from Other Countries: 5%

Singapore

Chong Moh Offset Printing Ltd
Subsidiary of Chassis Graphic Art Pte Ltd
19 Joo Koon Rd, Jurong Town 628978
Tel: 8622701 *Fax:* 8624335
E-mail: chongmoh@singnet.com.sg
Key Personnel
Chairman: James Ng
Founded: 1946
Turnaround: 10-14 Workdays
Print Runs: 1,000 min
Business from Other Countries: 35%

Chroma Graphics (Overseas) Pte Ltd
Blk 12, Lorong Bakar Batu, No 05-08, Singapore 348745
Tel: 67423706 *Fax:* 67486712
Telex: 55962 CG SEP
Key Personnel
Man Dir: Thomas K P Chan
    E-mail: thomaschan@chromographics.com.sg
Founded: 1978
Turnaround: 7-10 Workdays
Business from Other Countries: 85%

Craft Print Pte Ltd
9 Joo Koon Circle, Jurong, Singapore 629041
Tel: 8614040 *Fax:* 8610530
E-mail: craftprt@singet.com.sq
Key Personnel
Marketing Manager: Anthony Tham

CS Graphics Pte Ltd
10 Tuas Avenue 20, Singapore 638822
Tel: 8610100 *Fax:* 8610190
E-mail: hhlee@singnet.com.sq
Key Personnel
Man Dir: Mr Lee Sian Tee *E-mail:* stlee@
    csgraphics.com.sg
Founded: 1980
Turnaround: 80 Workdays
Print Runs: 1,000 min - 100,000 max
Business from Other Countries: 100%

Eurasia Press Pte Ltd
10/14 Kampong Ampat-1336, Singapore 368320
Tel: 2805522 *Fax:* 2800593; 3825458
E-mail: eurasia@mbox3.singnet.com.sg
Key Personnel
Marketing Dir: Allan Fong
Founded: 1937
Turnaround: 14 Workdays
Print Runs: 500 min - 100,000 max
Business from Other Countries: 65%

Ho Printing Singapore Pte Ltd
Changi South St One, Singapore 486797
Tel: 5429322 *Fax:* 2896065
Telex: RS 39685 HOFSET
Key Personnel
Sales Executive: Ho Wah Yuen
Founded: 1951
Turnaround: 35-50 Workdays
Print Runs: 5,000 min - 50,000 max
Business from Other Countries: 30%

Kin Keong Printing Co Pte Ltd, see Markono Print Media Pte Ltd

Markono Print Media Pte Ltd
Formerly Kin Keong Printing Co Pte Ltd
Subsidiary of Markono Holdings Pte Ltd
21 Neythal Rd, Singapore 628586
Tel: 62811118 *Fax:* 62866663
E-mail: sales@markono.com.sg
Key Personnel
Man Dir: Bob Lee *E-mail:* blee@markono.com.sg
Turnaround: 14 Workdays
Print Runs: 1,000 min - 100,000 max
Business from Other Countries: 20%
Branch Office(s)
Kin Keong Colour Printing (M) Sdn Bhd, Port Klang 539538

Pica Overseas Color Separation Ltd
Block 55, 2nd Floor, 10-19 Ayer Rajah Crescent, Singapore 139949
Tel: 7761311 *Fax:* 7793055
Key Personnel
Dir: Thomas Ling
Founded: 1977
Turnaround: 4 Workdays
Business from Other Countries: 60%

Sang Choy International PTE Ltd
Formerly SINGAPORE SANG CHOY COLOUR SEPARATION PTE LIMITED
Harrison Ind Bldg, 05-01, 9 Harrison Rd, Singapore 369651
Tel: (065) 6289 0829 *Fax:* (065) 6282 7673
E-mail: marketing@sc-international.com.sg
Key Personnel
Dir of Operations: Almond Ko
Business from Other Countries: 50%
Branch Office(s)
806 E 14 St, Oakland, CA 94606, United States
    Tel: 510-272-9699 *Fax:* 510-272-9678

SINGAPORE SANG CHOY COLOUR SEPARATION PTE LIMITED, see Sang Choy International PTE Ltd

SNP Printing Pte Ltd
97 Ubi Ave 4, Singapore 408754
Tel: 7412500 *Fax:* 2854894
Telex: SNPRS14462
Key Personnel
President: Yeo Chee Tong
Executive Vice President: Koo Tse Chia
US Sales Manager: Patrick Chung
Turnaround: 30 Workdays
Print Runs: 2,000 min - 200,000 max
Business from Other Countries: 40%

Stamford Press Pte Ltd
209, Kallang Bahru, Singapore 339344
Tel: 2947227 *Fax:* 2944396
E-mail: stamford@singnet.com.sq
Telex: RS56414 STAMFO
Key Personnel
Dir: R Theyvendran
Founded: 1963
Turnaround: 3-4 Workdays for small jobs; 3-4 weeks for big jobs
Print Runs: 1,500 min - 50,000 max
Business from Other Countries: 20%

Times Graphics
Division of Times Printers Pte Ltd
Subsidiary of Times Publishing Ltd
Times Centre, One New Industrial Rd, Singapore 536196
Tel: 2848844 *Fax:* 2771186
Telex: RS 25713
Key Personnel
Manager: Andrew Wong Weng Fook
Founded: 1986
Turnaround: 15 Workdays
Business from Other Countries: 40%

Times Printers Pte Ltd
Subsidiary of Times Publishing Group
16 Tuas Ave 5, Singapore 639340
Tel: 8623333 *Fax:* 8621313
E-mail: timetppl@singnet.com.sq *Cable:* TIMESPRINT
Key Personnel
Vice President: Leong Kwok Sun
Sales Manager: Patsy Tan; Koo Kok Leong
Founded: 1968
Turnaround: 5-25 Workdays
Print Runs: 3,000 min - 300,000 max
Business from Other Countries: 75%

Toppan Company (S) Pte Ltd
Division of Toppan Printing Co Ltd
Toppan Shibaura Bldg, 3-19-26 Shibaura, Minato-ku 108-0023
Tel: 264-0654 *Fax:* 265-8298
Telex: RS 21596 *Cable:* TOPPAN
Key Personnel
Man Dir: Kohei Mochizuki
General Manager: M Sonoda
Founded: 1968
Turnaround: 3 - 4 Weeks
Print Runs: 3,000 min - 500,000 max
Business from Other Countries: 70%

Slovenia

Gorenjski Tisk Printing Co
Zoisova ulica 1, 4000 Kranj
Tel: (064) 2630 *Fax:* (064) 241323
Telex: 34560 YU GOTISK
Key Personnel
Dir: Kristina Kobal
Commercial Manager: Boris Krist
Founded: 1888
Turnaround: 30 Workdays
Print Runs: 3,000 min - 15,000 max
Business from Other Countries: 50%

South Africa

CTP Book Printers (Pty) Ltd
PO Box 1610, Parklands
Tel: (011) 8890600 *Fax:* (011) 8890922
E-mail: ctpjhb@iafrica.com

Spain

Graficas Santamaria SA
Division of Fotomecanica
Bekolarra 4, 01010 Vitoria (Alava)
Tel: (045) 229100 *Fax:* (045) 246393
Key Personnel
Contact: Jesus Alzola Aguinaco
Founded: 1963
Turnaround: 1 Workday
Print Runs: 500 min - 150,000 max
Business from Other Countries: 15%

Sri Lanka

Sumathi Book Printing (Pvt) Ltd
Division of Sumathi Group
445/1 Prince of Wales Ave, Colombo 14

SRI LANKA

Tel: (01) 330673; (01) 330674; (01) 435225
Fax: (01) 449593
Telex: 22104 SUMATHI CE SUMATISONS
Business from Other Countries: 75%

Switzerland

Hallwag AG
Nordring 4, 3000 Bern
Tel: (031) 423131 *Fax:* (031) 414133
E-mail: kartenverlag@hallwag.com
Telex: 912-661 HAWA CH
Key Personnel
President: Dr Juergen Schad

Photolitho AG
Industriestr 12, CH-8625 Gossau ZH
Tel: (01) 9352676 *Fax:* (01) 9353247
Key Personnel
President: Dietmar von Eicke
Administrator: Werner Holliger
Founded: 1965
Business from Other Countries: 50%

United Republic of Tanzania

Peramiho Publications
PO Box 41, Peramiho
Tel: (054) 2730 *Fax:* (054) 2917
Key Personnel
Chief Executive: Fr Gerold Rupper
Founded: 1937
Print Runs: 4,000 min - 6,000 max

Thailand

Phongwarin Printing Company Ltd
299 Moo 10, Sukhumvit 107, A Muang, Samut Prakarn 10260
Tel: (02) 7498934-45; (02) 3994525-31; (02) 7498275-79 *Fax:* (02) 3994524; (02) 3994255
Web Site: www.phongwarin.com
Key Personnel
Man Dir: Somphong Charnsirisaksakul
Founded: 1983
Turnaround: 6 Workdays
Print Runs: 1,000 min - 500,000 max
Business from Other Countries: 5%

United Kingdom

Adroit Birmingham Ltd
Cecil St, Birmingham B19 3ST
Tel: (0121) 3596831 *Fax:* (0121) 3593974
Key Personnel
Sales Manager: Jackie Robotham

The Alden Group Ltd
Osney Mead, Oxford OX2 0EF
Tel: (01865) 253200 *Fax:* (01865) 249070
E-mail: alden.press@alden.co.uk
Web Site: www.alden.co.uk
Key Personnel
Group Technical/Development Dir: Robert Hay
Sales Dir: Michael Angless
Marketing Administrator: Gemma Webb
 Tel: (01865) 253200 *E-mail:* gwebb@alden.co.uk

AlpnetCompuType Ltd
Horton Parade Horton Rd, West Drayton UB7 8EP
Tel: (01895) 440791 *Fax:* (01895) 441500
E-mail: computype@computype.co.uk
Key Personnel
Business Manager: Brian Trowse
Founded: 1976

ARADCO VSI Ltd
132 Cleveland St, London W1P 6AB
Tel: (020) 7692 7700 *Fax:* (020) 7692 7711
E-mail: aradco@compuserve.com
Key Personnel
Contact: R Dawood
Founded: 1958
Business from Other Countries: 20%

J W Arrowsmith Ltd
71 Winterstoke Rd, Bristol BS3 2NT
Tel: (0117) 9667545 *Fax:* (0117) 9637829
E-mail: jw@arrowsmith.co.uk
Key Personnel
Sales Mgr: D J Hooper *E-mail:* dhooper@arrowsmith.co.uk
Founded: 1854
Turnaround: 15 Workdays
Print Runs: 500 min - 15,000 max
Business from Other Countries: 40%

Associated Translation & Typesetting
Alexander House, 64 Robin Hood Lane, Hall Green, Birmingham B28 0JT
Tel: (0121) 603 6344 *Fax:* (0121) 603 6399
E-mail: ATTEuro@aol.com (European translation); ATTAsia@aol.com (Eastern/Asian translation)
Web Site: www.jaure.demon.co.uk
Key Personnel
Dir: Mr S Ahmed
Founded: 1971
Business from Other Countries: 50%

Axicon Auto ID Ltd
Formerly Symbol Services
Weston on the Green, Bicester, Oxon OX25 3QP
Tel: (01869) 351166 *Fax:* (01869) 351205
E-mail: sales@axicon.com
Web Site: www.axicon.com
Key Personnel
Dir: Jenny Hicks *E-mail:* jmh@axicon.com
Founded: 1981
Turnaround: 1-2 Workdays
Business from Other Countries: 30%

W & G Baird Ltd
Subsidiary of W&G Baird Holdings Ltd (parent)
Caulside Dr, Antrim BT41 2RS
Tel: (018494) 63911 *Fax:* (018494) 66250
Key Personnel
Man Dir: Dairmuid McGarry *E-mail:* diarmuid.mcgarry@wgbaird.com
Founded: 1863
Print Runs: 500 min - 100,000 max
Business from Other Countries: 45%
Branch Office(s)
Textflow, Belfast, Ireland

MSO, Belfast, Ireland
Biddles Ltd, Woodbridge Park, Woodbridge Rd, Guildford, Surrey GU1 1DA

BAS Printers Ltd
Over Wallop, Stockbridge, Hants SO20 8JD
Tel: (01264) 781711 *Fax:* (01264) 781116
E-mail: sales@basprint.co.uk
Web Site: www.basprint.co.uk
Key Personnel
Man Dir: David Gumn
Sales Dir: Paul G Gumn *E-mail:* paul@basprint.co.uk
Founded: 1948
Print Runs: 350 min - 40,000 max
Business from Other Countries: 10%

Baseline Creative Ltd
60A Northumbria Dr, Henleaze, Bristol BS9 4HW
Tel: (0117) 962 0006 *Fax:* (0117) 962 5006
E-mail: baseline@base.co.uk
Web Site: www.base.co.uk
Key Personnel
Man Dir: John Buchmueller
Business Development Manager: Nicholas J Wood
Founded: 1985
Turnaround: 30 Workdays

The Bath Press
Subsidiary of Bath Press Group PLC
Lower Bristol Rd, Bath BA2 3BL
Tel: (01225) 428101 *Fax:* (01225) 312418
Web Site: www.liberfabrica.com
Key Personnel
Man Dir: Peter Palframan
Marketing Dir: Keith Johnson
Contact: Jack McCabe *E-mail:* jmccabe@bathpress.co.uk
Founded: 1846
Turnaround: 10-15 Workdays
Print Runs: 3,000 min - 300,000 max
Business from Other Countries: 5%

BCS Publishing Ltd
Temple Court, Oxford Rd, Cowley, Oxford
Tel: (01865) 770099 *Fax:* (01865) 770050
Key Personnel
Man Dir: Steve McCurdy
Founded: 1993
Business from Other Countries: 40%

Bell & Bain Ltd
303 Burnfield Rd, Thornliebank, Glasgow G46 7UQ
Tel: (0141) 6495697 *Fax:* (0141) 6328733
E-mail: info@bell-bain.demon.co.uk
Web Site: www.bell-bain.demon.co.uk
Key Personnel
Man Dir: I Walker
Sales Dir: D Stewart
Turnaround: 7-10 Workdays
Print Runs: 100 min - 100,000 max
Business from Other Countries: 25%

Black Bear Press Ltd
King's Hedges Rd, Cambridge CB4 2PQ
Tel: (01223) 424571 *Fax:* (01223) 426877
E-mail: black_bear_pres@msn.com
Key Personnel
Man Dir: K Fentiman
Sales Dir: M W Hallam

Blackmore Ltd
Longmead, Shaftesbury, Dorset SP7 8PX
Tel: (01747) 853034 *Fax:* (01747) 854500
E-mail: sales@blackmail.blackmore.co.uk
Key Personnel
Man Dir: Chris Brickell

SERVICES
UNITED KINGDOM

Book Creation Services
21 Carnaby St, London W1V 1PH
Tel: (020) 7287 0214 *Fax:* (020) 7287 8547
E-mail: hal@zoo.co.uk
Key Personnel
Chairman: Hal Robinson *E-mail:* hal@zoo.co.uk
Founded: 1991
Business from Other Countries: 30%

Book Production Consultants PLC
25-27 High St, Chesterton, Cambridge CB4 1ND
Tel: (01223) 352790 *Fax:* (01223) 460718
Web Site: www.bpccam.co.uk
Key Personnel
Man Dir: Tony Littlechild *E-mail:* tl@bpccam.co.uk
Founded: 1973
Print Runs: 500 min
Business from Other Countries: 25%

D Brown & Sons Ltd
North Rd, Bridgend Industrial Estate, Bridgend CF31 3TP
Tel: (01656) 652447 *Fax:* (01446) 771476
E-mail: info@geminidigital.demon.co.uk
Key Personnel
Dir: J M Whitaker *Tel:* (01446) 774213
Founded: 1895
Print Runs: 1 min - 1,000,000 max
Business from Other Countries: 20%
Branch Office(s)
Eastgate Press, 62 Eastgate, Cowbridge, S Glam CF7 7AB

Butler & Tanner Ltd
The Selwood Printing Works, Frome, Somerset BA11 1NF
Tel: (01373) 451500 *Fax:* (01373) 451333
E-mail: manufacturing@butlerandtanner.com
Key Personnel
Joint Man Dir: A Huett
Sales Dir: N White

Caledonian International Book Manufacturing
Westerhill Rd, Bishopbriggs, Glasgow G64 2QR
Tel: (0141) 7623000 *Fax:* (0141) 7620922
E-mail: 101622.235@compuserve.com
Key Personnel
Man Dir: Kevin McKenna
Commercial Dir: G Morrison
Group Sales Manager: Martin Platt
  E-mail: martin@platt44.freeserve.co.uk
Founded: 1819

Cambridge University Press - Printing Division
Division of Cambridge University Press
University Printing House, Shaftesbury Rd, Cambridge CB2 2BS
Tel: (01223) 358331 *Fax:* (01223) 325672
E-mail: info@cup.cam.ac.uk
Key Personnel
Production Dir: Steve Millard *E-mail:* smillard@cup.com.ac.uk
Production Manager: Alan Dungar
Founded: 1534
Print Runs: 1 min

Center Print Ltd
Subsidiary of Beshara Press
Private Rd 2, Colwich Business Park, Colwich, Nottingham NG4 2JR
Tel: (0115) 9612277 *Fax:* (0115) 9381424
E-mail: cprint@besharapress.co.uk
Key Personnel
Man Dir: Nicola Leslie
Print Runs: 1,000 min - 250,000 max

The Charlesworth Group
254 Deighton Rd, Huddersfield, West Yorkshire HD2 1JJ
Tel: (01484) 517077 *Fax:* (01484) 517068
E-mail: sales@charlesworth.com
Key Personnel
Marketing Manager: Sarah Philp
  E-mail: s_philp@charleswater.com
Founded: 1928
Turnaround: 1 to 10 Workdays
Print Runs: 1 min - 10,000 max
Business from Other Countries: 30%

Chase Publishing Services
Mead, Fortescue Rd, Sidmouth, Devon EX10 9QG
Tel: (01395) 514709 *Fax:* (01395) 514709
E-mail: r.addicott@btinternet.com
Key Personnel
President: Ray Addicott *E-mail:* r.addicott@btinternet.com
Founded: 1989

William Clowes Ltd
Goal Lane, Beccles, Suffolk NR34 9QE
Tel: (01502) 712884 *Fax:* (01502) 717003
Key Personnel
Man Dir: Alex Evans
Sales Dir: David C Browne *Tel:* (01502) 712884, Ext 240
Founded: 1803
Turnaround: 10 Workdays
Print Runs: 2,000 min
Business from Other Countries: 1%

Cooper Dale
1a Dalling Rd, London W6 0RA
Tel: (020) 8748 6824 *Fax:* (020) 8748 5689
Key Personnel
Design Dir: Roger Pring
Founded: 1985
Print Runs: 1 min - 1,000,000 max
Business from Other Countries: 10%

Cox & Wyman Ltd
Cardiff Rd, Reading RG1 8EX
Tel: (01189) 530500 *Fax:* (01189) 507222
Key Personnel
General Manager: Tom Roberts
Sales Manager: Paul Hicks
Sales Executive: Ruth Goodman
Founded: 1777
Turnaround: 10 Workdays reprints/15 workdays new books
Print Runs: 2,000 min - 2,000,000 max
Business from Other Countries: 5%
Parent Company: Chevrillon Philippe Industrie

Cradley Print Ltd
Chester Rd, Cradley Heath, Warley, W Midlands B64 6AB
Tel: (01384) 414100 *Fax:* (01384) 414102
E-mail: sales@cradleygp.co.uk
Key Personnel
Man Dir: Chris Jordan
Turnaround: 5 Workdays
Print Runs: 1,000 min - 500,000 max
Business from Other Countries: 7%
Branch Office(s)
Quadcolor Repro

The Diagram Group
195 Kentish Town Rd, London NW5 2JU
Tel: (020) 7482 3633 *Fax:* (020) 7482 4932
E-mail: diagramuis@aol.com
Key Personnel
Contact: Bruce Robertson
Secretary: C A Dease
Founded: 1967
Business from Other Countries: 80%

Edition
Subsidiary of Cameron Books
2 Sunny Bank Old Edinburgh Rd, Moffat Dumfriesshire DG10 9SU
Tel: (01683) 220808 *Fax:* (01683) 220012
E-mail: editorial@cameronbooks.co.uk
Web Site: www.cameronbooks.co.uk
Key Personnel
Dir: Ian Cameron; Jill Hollis
Founded: 1976

Essex Colour Services Ltd
Aviation Way, Southend-on-Sea, Essex SS2 6UN
Tel: (01702) 541311 *Fax:* (01702) 540094
Web Site: www.goodspeed.co.uk
Key Personnel
Chairman: Leo Smith
Sales & Marketing Coordinator: Paula Brown
  E-mail: paula@goodspeed.co.uk
Founded: 1971
Turnaround: 5 Workdays
Print Runs: 5,000 min - 100,000 max
Business from Other Countries: 20%

Fern House
19 High St, Haddenham, Ely, Cambs CB6 3XA
Tel: (01353) 740222 *Fax:* (01353) 741987
E-mail: info@fernhouse.com
Key Personnel
Contact: Rodney Dale
Founded: 1976

Goldshield Communications Ltd
Banners Bldg, Attercliffe Rd, Sheffield S9 3QS
Tel: (0114) 2431000 *Fax:* (0114) 2433000
Key Personnel
Man Dir & Overseas-Special Projects: Sandra Potesta *E-mail:* sandra@goldcom.co.uk
Technical & Production: Stefano Potesta
Founded: 1984
Business from Other Countries: 40%

James Gowans Ltd
Subsidiary of Brown, Son & Ferguson, Ltd
4-10 Darnley St, Glasgow G41 2SD
Tel: (0141) 4293337 *Fax:* (0141) 4201694
E-mail: info@skipper.co.uk
Web Site: www.skipper.co.uk
Key Personnel
Production Dir: T Nigel Brown
Founded: 1872
Turnaround: 3-5 Workdays
Print Runs: 100 min - 10,000 max

The Guernsey Press Co Ltd
Braye Rd, Vale, Guernsey, Channel Islands GY1 3BW
Mailing Address: PO Box 57, Vale, Guernsey, Channel Islands GY1 3BW
Tel: (01481) 240240; (01481) 243657 (ISDN) *Fax:* (01481) 240290; (01481) 249147
E-mail: books@guernsey-press.com
Web Site: www.gp.guernsey-press.com
Key Personnel
Contact: Mr T A R Duquemin
Founded: 1897
Turnaround: 10 Workdays
Print Runs: 2,000 min - 50,000 max
Business from Other Countries: 80%

Hammond Packaging Ltd
Division of Hammond Bindery
129 Water Lane, Holbeck, Leeds LS11 9UB
Tel: (0113) 2423548 *Fax:* (0113) 2445442
E-mail: hammpack@dial.pipex.com
Web Site: www.hammpack.co.uk
Key Personnel
Man Dir: Steve Allan
Founded: 1991
Turnaround: 5-15 Workdays
Print Runs: 100 min - 500,000 max

Headley Brothers Ltd
Invicta Press, Queens Rd, Ashford, Kent TN24 8HH

UNITED KINGDOM   PREPRESS

Tel: (01233) 623131 *Fax:* (01233) 622704; (01233) 612345
E-mail: rpitt@headley.co.uk
Key Personnel
Sales Dir: Bruce Finn
Commercial Dir: Jon Pitt
European Sales: Ingrid Eissfeldt
Man Dir: Roger Pitt *E-mail:* rpitt@headley.co.uk
Founded: 1881
Print Runs: 1,000 min - 200,000 max
Business from Other Countries: 5%
Branch Office(s)
Headley Brothers Ltd, 3rd Floor West, High Holborn House, 52-54 High Holborn, London WC1V 6LR

Heyden & Son
Spectrum House, Hillview Gardens, London NW4 2JQ
Tel: (020) 8266 3300 *Fax:* (020) 8203 1027
E-mail: sales@heyden.com
Key Personnel
Dir: Edward Heyden

Hobbs The Printers Ltd
Brunel Rd, Totton, Hants SO40 3WX
Tel: (023) 8066 4800 *Fax:* (023) 8066 4801
E-mail: htp@tcp.co.uk
Key Personnel
Sales Manager: John Eacott *E-mail:* j.eacott@hobbs.uk.com
Commercial Dir: Terry Ozanne
Founded: 1884
Turnaround: 5-10 days litho; up to 5 days digital
Print Runs: 10 min - 50,000 max
Business from Other Countries: 4%

Holbrook Design
Holbrook House, 105 Rose Hill, Oxford OX4 4HT
Tel: (01865) 459000
E-mail: info@holbrook-design.co.uk
Key Personnel
Design Dir: Peter Tucker *E-mail:* pgt@holbrook-design.co.uk
Founded: 1974
Business from Other Countries: 20%

Ikon Document Services Ltd
Subsidiary of Microgen Holdings Plc
19 The Business Centre, Molly Millars Lane, Wokingham Berks RG41 2QY
Tel: (0118) 9770510 *Fax:* (0118) 9770513
E-mail: pamh@ikonds.co.uk
Web Site: www.ikon.com
Key Personnel
Man Dir: Dave Weller
Business Development Dir: Aaron Biggs
Founded: 1972
Turnaround: 2-5 Workdays
Print Runs: 1 min - 5,000 max
Business from Other Countries: 40%
Branch Office(s)
Microgen City Park Watchmead, Welwyn Garden City, Herts AL7 1LT

Image & Print Group Ltd
Unit 9, Oakbank Industrial Estate, Garscube Rd, Glasgow G20 7LU
Tel: (0141) 3531900 *Fax:* (0141) 3532472
E-mail: imageandprint@dial.pipex.com
Web Site: www.imageandprint.co.uk
Key Personnel
Man Dir: Ken Roberts
Production: Stephen McPhee
Founded: 1975
Turnaround: 5 Workdays
Print Runs: 1,000 min - 250,000 max

Intype London Ltd
Units 3 & 4, Elm Grove Industrial Estate, Elm Grove, Wimbledon, London SW19 4HE
Tel: (020) 8947 7863 *Fax:* (020) 8947 3652
E-mail: intype@btconnect.com
Key Personnel
Man Dir: Tony Chapman *E-mail:* tchap@btconnect.com
Production: Richard Mayne
Dir: Alan Johnson
Founded: 1976
Turnaround: 10-15 Workdays for proofs; 5-10 Workdays for books
Print Runs: 25 min - 1,000 max
Business from Other Countries: 5%

Keytec Typesetting Ltd
Unit 2-5, Hounsell Bldgs, North Mills Trading Estate, Bridport, Dorset DT6 3BE
Tel: (01308) 427580 *Fax:* (01308) 421961
E-mail: all@keytectype.co.uk
Web Site: www.keytectype.co.uk
Key Personnel
Man Dir: Mark Riddington
Founded: 1983

Linden Artists Ltd
41 Battersea Business Centre, 103 Lavender Hill, London SW11 5QL
Tel: (020) 7738 2505 *Fax:* (020) 7738 2513
Key Personnel
Dir: Dennis J Bosdet; Martin J Gibbs; Sheila Wall
Founded: 1962
Business from Other Countries: 30%

Lowfield Printing Co Ltd
9 Kennet Rd Thames Rd, Crayford, Dartford, Kent DA1 4QT
Tel: (01322) 522216 *Fax:* (01322) 555362
E-mail: lowfield@compuserve.com
Key Personnel
Dir: Ian J Starkey
Founded: 1964
Print Runs: 500 min - 20,000 max

Maney Publishing
Subsidiary of The Charlesworth Group of Companies
Hudson Rd, Leeds LS9 7DL
Tel: (0113) 249 7481 *Fax:* (0113) 248 6983
E-mail: maney@maney.co.uk
Key Personnel
Man Dir: Michael Gallico *E-mail:* m.gallico@maney.co.uk
Founded: 1900
Print Runs: 350 min - 100,000 max
Business from Other Countries: 2%

Martins Printing Group Ltd
Division of Staples Printers Ltd
The Gresham Press, Old Woking, Surrey, GU22 9LH
Tel: (01483) 757501 *Fax:* (01483) 724629
E-mail: chandler@martins-print.co.uk
Key Personnel
Group Chief Executive: M R Milton
Group Operations Dir: M R Andrew
Founded: 1930
Print Runs: 1 min - 100,000 max
Business from Other Countries: 5%
Branch Office(s)
33 Store St, London WC1E *Tel:* (020) 7436 0595 *Fax:* (020) 7436 8173 (Sales Office)

MPG Colour Ltd
Division of Martins Printing Group
Subsidiary of Staples Printers Ltd
The George Press, Trafalgar Rd, Kettering, Northamptonshire NN16 8HA
Tel: (01536) 483401 *Fax:* (01536) 481102

E-mail: print@mpg-colour.co.uk
Key Personnel
Man Dir: Simon Moore
Founded: 1945
Turnaround: 5 Workdays
Print Runs: 3,000 min - 75,000 max
Branch Office(s)
Bodmin
Peterborough
Rochester
St Albans
Wimbledon
Woking

Multiplex Medway Ltd
Gleaming Wood Dr, Lordswood Industrial Estate, Walderslade, Kent ME5 8XT
Tel: (01634) 684371 *Fax:* (01634) 683840
E-mail: enquiries@multiplex-medway.co.uk
Web Site: www.multiplex-medway.co.uk
Key Personnel
Dir: Jon Chandler
Sales Manager: Paul Adson

Page Bros Ltd (Norwich)
Subsidiary of Milex Ltd
Mile Cross Lane, Norwich NR6 6SA
Tel: (01603) 429141 *Fax:* (01603) 485126
Key Personnel
Man Dir: David Armstrong
Founded: 1750
Turnaround: 10 Workdays
Print Runs: 100 min - 30,000 max
Business from Other Countries: 20%
Branch Office(s)
105-A Euston St, London NW1 2ET *Tel:* (020) 7383 2212 *Fax:* (020) 7383 4145

Redwood Books Ltd
Division of CPI (UK) Ltd
Kennet Way, Trowbridge, Wilts BA14 8RN
Tel: (01225) 769979 *Fax:* (01225) 769050
E-mail: enquiries@redwood-books.co.uk
Web Site: www.cpi-group.net
Key Personnel
General Manager: Trevor Gee
Commercial Manager: Tony Warner *E-mail:* tony@redwood-books.co.uk
Production Manager: Peter Grant
Founded: 1993
Turnaround: 10 Workdays
Print Runs: 10 min - 20,000 max
Business from Other Countries: 8%
Parent Company: CPI France
Branch Office(s)
London Sales Office, 22 Bloomsbury Sq, London WC1A 2NS *Tel:* (020) 7580 9328 *Fax:* (020) 7580 9337

J R Reid Print & Media Group, see J R Reid Printing Group Ltd

J R Reid Printing Group Ltd
79-109 Glasgow Rd, Blantyre, Glasgow G72 0LY
Tel: (01698) 826000 *Fax:* (01698) 824944
E-mail: clindsay@reid-print-group.co.uk
Web Site: www.reid-print-group.co.uk
Key Personnel
Man Dir: John R Reid *E-mail:* johnreid@reid-print-group.co.uk

Antony Rowe Ltd
Division of Rexam Plc
14 Portman Rd, Reading, Berks RG30 1LZ
Tel: (0118) 9503911 *Fax:* (0118) 9505776
E-mail: 100546.3703@compuserve.com
Key Personnel
Chief Executive: Ralph Bell
Sales Manager: Andrew Copley
Founded: 1897
Turnaround: 10 Workdays

SERVICES

Print Runs: 50 min - 100,000 max
Business from Other Countries: 10%

Santype International Ltd
Netherhampton Rd, Salisbury SP2 8PS
Tel: (01722) 334261 *Fax:* (01722) 333171
E-mail: post@santype.com
Web Site: www.santype.com
Key Personnel
Sales Dir: John Roost *Fax:* (0870) 1372738
 E-mail: jroost@santype.co.uk
Business from Other Countries: 35%

Severnside Printers Ltd
Bridge House, Upton-on-Severn, Worcs WR8 0HG
Tel: (01684) 594521 *Fax:* (01684) 594344
Key Personnel
President & Chief Executive: Norman H Beechey
Turnaround: 14-20 Workdays
Print Runs: 500 min - 5,000 max
Business from Other Countries: 10%

Symbol Services, see Axicon Auto ID Ltd

Thomas Technology Solutions, Inc
4th Floor, Crown House, London W14 8TH
Tel: (020) 7559 9810 *Fax:* (020) 7559 9811
Web Site: www.thomastechsolutions.com
Founded: 1964

M & A Thomson Litho Ltd
10/16 Colvilles Pl, Kelvin Industrial Estate, East Kilbride, Glasgow G75 0SN
Tel: (013552) 33081 *Fax:* (013552) 45439
Web Site: www.plitho.co.uk
Key Personnel
Deputy Chairman: Gary Thomson

Tradespools Ltd
Vallis House, Robins Lane, Frome, Somerset BA11 3EG
Tel: (01373) 461475 *Fax:* (01373) 474112
E-mail: sales@tradespools.co.uk
Web Site: www.tradespools.co.uk
Key Personnel
Sales Dir: Roger Carraher
Founded: 1967
Print Runs: 1 min - 10,000 max
Business from Other Countries: 30%
Ultimate Parent Company: Antony Rowe Group

Watkiss Automation Ltd
Subsidiary of The Watkiss Group
One Blaydon Rd, Middlefield Industrial Estate, Sandy, Beds SG19 1RZ
Tel: (01767) 682177 *Fax:* (01767) 691769
E-mail: info@watkiss.com
Web Site: www.watkiss.com
Key Personnel
Technical Dir: M Watkiss
Founded: 1959
Print Runs: 200 min - 10,000 max
Business from Other Countries: 5%

United States

A-R Editions Inc
8551 Research Way, Suite 180, Middleton, WI 53562
Tel: 608-836-9000 *Fax:* 608-831-8200
E-mail: info@areditions.com
Web Site: www.areditions.com
Key Personnel
Pres & CEO: Patrick Wall

Dir, Sales & Mktg: James L Zychowicz
 E-mail: james.zychowicz@areditions.com
Founded: 1962
Business from Other Countries: 10%

ADR/BookPrint
2012 Northern, Wichita, KS 67216
Tel: 316-522-5599 *Fax:* 316-522-5445
Web Site: www.adrbookprint.com
Key Personnel
Pres: James E Rishel
VP: Grace M Rishel *E-mail:* grace@adrbookprint.com
Prodn Mgr: Marc Seiwert
Founded: 1978
Print Runs: 500 min - 5,000 max
Business from Other Countries: 10%
Membership(s): PIA

Alpina Color Graphics Inc
Subsidiary of Alpina International Inc
102 Madison Ave, New York, NY 10016
Tel: 212-683-2535 *Fax:* 212-285-2704; 212-683-2682
E-mail: graphics@alpina.net
Web Site: www.alpina.net
Key Personnel
Contact: Raj Sawhney
Founded: 1980
Turnaround: 2-3 Workdays
Print Runs: 1,000 min - 200,000 max
Business from Other Countries: 20%
Branch Office(s)
Alpina Graphics, 27 Cliff St, New York, NY 10038

American Pizzi Offset Corp
Subsidiary of Arti Grafiche Amilcare Pizzi (Milan)
370 Lexington Ave, Suite 1505, New York, NY 10017
Tel: 212-986-1658 *Fax:* 212-286-1887
E-mail: apocnyusa@aol.com
Key Personnel
Pres: Massimo Pizzi
Sales Mgr, US & UK: Barbara Sadick
Founded: 1914
Business from Other Countries: 50%

Any Photo Type
210 W 29 St, New York, NY 10001
Tel: 212-244-1130 *Fax:* 212-594-4697
Key Personnel
Pres: Harold Katzman
Founded: 1977
Turnaround: 1-2 Workdays
Business from Other Countries: 15%

Asia Pacific Offset Inc
1332 Corcoran St NW, Suite 6, Washington, DC 20009
Tel: 202-462-5436 *Fax:* 202-968-4030
Web Site: www.asiapacificoffset.com
Key Personnel
Pres: Andrew Clarke *E-mail:* Andrew@asiapacificoffset.com
Dir, Sales (NY Office): Timothy Linn
 Tel: 212-941-8300 *Fax:* 212-941-9810
 E-mail: Timothy@asiapacificoffset.com
Founded: 1997
Turnaround: 105 Workdays including color separation & shipping
Print Runs: 2,000 min
Business from Other Countries: 100%
Branch Office(s)
Phoenix Offset, Unit F1-2 2nd fl, Yeung Yiu Chung No 8 Industrial Bldg, 20 Wang Hoi Rd, Kowloon Bay, Hong Kong, Edmond Chan *Tel:* 852-2751-9962 *Fax:* 852-2755-8408
 E-mail: Phoffset@netvigator.com

Sales Office(s): 225 Lafayette St, Suite 703, New York, NY 10012 *Tel:* 212-941-8300 *Fax:* 212-941-9810 *E-mail:* Timothy@asiapacificoffset.com
21 Columbus Ave, Suite 231, San Francisco, CA 94111, Dir of Sales: Rick Conant *Tel:* 415-433-3488 *Fax:* 415-433-3489 *E-mail:* Rick@asiapacificoffset.com

Bang Printing Co Inc
3323 Oak St, Brainerd, MN 56401-0587
Mailing Address: PO Box 587, Brainerd, MN 56401-0587
Tel: 218-829-2877 *Fax:* 218-829-7145
Web Site: www.bangprinting.com
Key Personnel
VP, Sales: Todd Vanek *Tel:* 218-822-2124
 E-mail: toddv@bangprinting.com
Founded: 1899
Turnaround: 10-25 Workdays
Print Runs: 500 min - 50,000 max
Business from Other Countries: 50%

Best-Set Typesetter Ltd
Subsidiary of Excel United Co Ltd
157 Fisher Ave, Suite 6, Eastchester, NY 10709
Tel: 914-961-6223 *Fax:* 914-961-8212
E-mail: best-set-usa@msn.com
Web Site: www.bestset-typesetter.com
Key Personnel
Dir (Hong Kong): Johnson Yeung *Tel:* 2975 1012
 E-mail: johnson@bestset-typesetter.com
Sales Rep: Wai Man Yeung
Founded: 1986
Turnaround: 5 Workdays
Print Runs: 100 min - 200,000 max
Business from Other Countries: 98%
Branch Office(s)
6 Sun Yip St, Honour Industrial Centre, Room 304, 3rd fl, Chai Wan, Hong Kong
3 Jiang nan Main Ave C, 3rd fl, Guangzhou, China
33 Alpin Way, TW7 4RJ Isleworth, Middlesex, United Kingdom

Better Music Type
324 Timberdale Ct, Nashville, TN 37211
Tel: 615-833-0800
Key Personnel
Contact: Laurens A Blankers
Founded: 1977
Business from Other Countries: 30%
Membership(s): BMI

Blaze International Productions Inc
225 W 35 St, Suite 1100, New York, NY 10001
Tel: 212-967-7501 *Fax:* 212-967-7551
Key Personnel
Pres: Eugene Sanchez *Tel:* ext 222 *E-mail:* e.sanchez@blazeint.com
Founded: 1990
Turnaround: 10-15 Workdays
Print Runs: 500 min - 1,000,000 max
Business from Other Countries: 80%
Branch Office(s)
Flat 12 18/F, Kodak House, Phase 2, No 39 Healthy Street, North Point, Hong Kong
Tel: 2967 9360 *Fax:* 2967 1800

BookBuilders New York Ltd
353 Strawtown Rd, New City, NY 10956
Tel: 845-639-5316 *Fax:* 845-639-5318
Key Personnel
Pres: Martin Cook *E-mail:* martin@mcabooks.com
Founded: 1977
Turnaround: 30-45 Workdays
Print Runs: 2,000 min - 500,000 max
Business from Other Countries: 60%

UNITED STATES   PREPRESS

C & C Offset Printing Co Ltd
Subsidiary of C & C Joint Printing Co (HK) Ltd under Sino United Publishing (Holdings) Ltd
2632 SE 25 Ave, Suite D, Portland, OR 97202
Mailing Address: PO Box 82037, Portland, OR 97282-0037
Tel: 503-233-1834 Fax: 503-233-7815
E-mail: portlandinfo@ccoffset.com
Web Site: www.ccoffset.com
Key Personnel
Dir, C & C Offset Printing Co Ltd, Portland, OR, USA: Charles H Clark, IV E-mail: cclark@ccoffset.com
Devt Mgr, C & C Offset Printing Co (USA) Inc, Portland, OR, USA: Jenny Whittier E-mail: jwhittier@ccoffset.com
Dir & Exec VP, C & C Offset Printing Co (NYC) Inc, New York, NY, USA: Simon Chan E-mail: schan@ccoffset.com
Cust Serv Mgr, C & C Offset Printing Co (USA) Inc, Portland, OR, USA: Ernest Li E-mail: ernestli@ccoffset.com
Cust Serv Mgr, C & C Offset Printing Co (NYC): Frances Harkness E-mail: fharkness@ccoffset.com
Dir & Gen Mgr, Hong Kong Head Office: Zhuang Xian-Qing
Dir & Asst Gen Mgr, Hong Kong Head Office: Ken Lee
Sales Mgr (Overseas), Hong Kong Head Office: Kit Wong
Sales Mgr (Special Projects), Hong Kong Head Office: Francis Ho
Dir & Gen Mgr, C & C Joint Printing Co (Guangdong) Ltd, Shenzhen, China: Jackson Leung
Deputy Sales Mgr, C & C Joint Printing Co (Guangdong) Ltd, Shenzhen, China: Simon Zhang
Pres, C & C Printing Japan Co Ltd, Tokyo, Japan: Masashi Otobe
Man Dir, C & C Joint Printing Co (Beijing) Ltd, Beijing, China: Zhang Lin Gui
Dir, C & C Offset Printing Co (UK): Tracy Broderick
Mgr, C & C Offset Printing Co (UK): Fiona Norman
Founded: 1980
Turnaround: 42 Workdays for printing, binding & book finishing
Print Runs: 2,000 min - 200,000 max
Business from Other Countries: 60%
Branch Office(s)
C & C Printing Co (NY) Inc, 401 Broadway, Suite 2015, New York, NY 10013-3005 Tel: 212-431-4210 Fax: 212-431-3960 E-mail: newyorkinfo@ccoffset.com (New York City Office)
C & C Joint Print Co (Beijing) Ltd, Beijing Economic & Technological Developent Area (BDA), No 3, Donghuan North Rd, Beijing 100176, China, Dir & Gen Mgr: Mr Zhang Lin Gui Tel: (010) 678 72862 Fax: (010) 678-72861 E-mail: beijing@cancprinting.com
C & C Joint Printing Co (Guangdong) Ltd, Intercontinental Bldg, Rm 706, 16 An Wai An De Rd, DongCheng District, Beijing 100011, China, Contact: Mr Xiao Mungshen Tel: (010) 8488 2436 Fax: (010) 8488-2336 E-mail: beijing@cancprinting.com
Hua Xin Bldg E Block, Rm 1511, 2 Shuiyin Rd, Huanshi East, Guangzhou 510075, China, Contact: Mr Peng Ji Shan Tel: (020) 3760 0979; (020) 3760 0980 Fax: (020) 3760 0977 E-mail: guangzhou@candcprinting.com
C & C Joint Printing Co (Guangdong) Ltd, Chunhu Industrial Estate, Pinghu, Long Gang, Shenzhen 518111, China Tel: 755-845-8333 Fax: 755-885-9911 E-mail: guangdong@candcprinting.com (Plant)
C & C Bldg, 36 Ting Lai Rd, Tai Po, New Territories, Hong Kong Tel: 2666-4988 Fax: 2666-4938 E-mail: offsetprinting@candcprinting.com

C & C Joint Printing Co (Guangdong) Ltd (Changsha Office), The Building of Changsha City Commercial Bank, No 1, Frong Middle Rd, Rm 1218, Changsha, Hunan 41005, China, Contact: Ms Chen Jian Tel: (0731) 225 0288 Fax: (0731) 225 0178 E-mail: changsha@candcprinting.com (Regional Office)
Fang Fa Bldg, No 29, Rm 304, 165 Dongzhu Anbin Rd, Shanghai 200050, China Tel: (021) 6240-1305 Fax: (021) 6240-1305 E-mail: shanghai@candcprinting.com
C & C Joint Printing Co (Guangdong) Ltd (Xian Office), 10 Xuanfengquiao, Jianguo Rd, Xian 710001, China Tel: (029) 741 8407 Fax: (029) 743 5730 E-mail: xian@candcprinting.co
C & C Printing Japan Co Ltd, Tozaido Bldg, 3F, 2-6-12 Hitotsubashi, Chiyoda-ku, Tokyo 101-0003, Japan, Contact: Mr Masashi Otobe Tel: (03) 3219-6610 Fax: (03) 3219-6620 E-mail: ccjtokyo@interlink.or.jp
C & C Offset Printing Co (UK) Ltd, 2 New Burlington St, 4th fl, London W1S 2JE, United Kingdom Tel: (020) 7287 7787 Fax: (020) 7287 7187 E-mail: tracy@candcoffset.co.uk

Colorprint Offset Inc
80 Park Ave, Suite 10N, New York, NY 10016
Tel: 212-681-9400 Fax: 212-681-9362
Key Personnel
Pres: Justin Wakefield E-mail: justin@colorprintoffset.com; Lee Moncho E-mail: lee@colorprintoffset.com
Prod Dir & Cust Serv Mgr: Kate Brady E-mail: kate@colorprintoffset.com
Founded: 1986
Turnaround: 15 Workdays
Print Runs: 100 min - 50,000 max
Business from Other Countries: 65%

Coneco Litho Graphics
Division of NET 2 PRESS Inc
58 Dix Ave, Glens Falls, NY 12801-7255
Mailing Address: PO Box 3255, Glen Falls, NY 12801-7255
Tel: 518-793-3823 Fax: 518-793-5823
Web Site: www.conecolithographics.com
Key Personnel
Pres & CEO: Garth E Grandchamp E-mail: garth@conecolithographics.com
Gen Mgr: Steve Webber E-mail: swebber@conecolithographics.com
Client Servs Mgr: Cindy Brower E-mail: cbrower@conecolithographics.com
Founded: 1984
Turnaround: 15 Workdays
Print Runs: 250 min - 25,000 max
Business from Other Countries: 27%

Martin Cook Associates Ltd
353 Strawtown Rd, New City, NY 10956
Tel: 845-639-5316 Fax: 845-639-5318
E-mail: mcanewcity@aol.com
Web Site: www.mcabooks.com
Key Personnel
Pres: Martin Cook E-mail: mcanewcity@aol.com
Founded: 1977
Turnaround: 30-45 Workdays
Print Runs: 2,000 min - 300,000 max
Business from Other Countries: 15%
Membership(s): Bookbinders Guild of New York

CS Graphics USA Inc
Subsidiary of CS Graphics Pte Ltd Singapore
8969 Lake Ct, Granite Bay, CA 95746
Tel: 916-791-9066 Fax: 916-791-9112
E-mail: csgraphics@mindspring.com
Key Personnel
Mgr, Sales & Mktg: Rick Marment
Founded: 1980
Turnaround: 80 Workdays
Print Runs: 1,000 min - 75,000 max
Business from Other Countries: 30%

Custom Services
Subsidiary of Nationwide Custom Services Inc
77 Main St, Tappan, NY 10983
Mailing Address: PO Box 76, Tappan, NY 10983
Tel: 845-365-0414 Fax: 845-365-0864
Key Personnel
Owner & Pres: Norman Shaifer
VP & Mgr: Helen Newman
VP: Henry Title
Founded: 1960
Print Runs: 500 min - 10,000 max
Business from Other Countries: 30%

Datapage Technologies International Inc
222 Turner Blvd, St Peters, MO 63376-1079
Tel: 636-278-8888 Fax: 636-278-2180
Web Site: www.datapage.com
Key Personnel
Pres: Jack M Delo
VP, Sales: John E Ingerslew
VP, Publg: Linda S Blevins E-mail: lindab@datapage.com
VP, Info Systems: Ron McCafferty
Founded: 1969
Turnaround: 1-15 Workdays
Business from Other Countries: 10%

Desktop Miracles Inc
112 S Main, PMB 294, Stowe, VT 05672
Tel: 802-253-7900 Fax: 802-253-1900
Web Site: www.desktopmiracles.com
Key Personnel
Pres & CEO: Barry T Kerrigan E-mail: barry@desktopmiracles.com
Founded: 1994
Turnaround: 10-15 Workdays
Print Runs: 2,500 min
Business from Other Countries: 10%

DNP America LLC
Subsidiary of Dai Nippon Printing Co Ltd
335 Madison Ave, 3rd fl, New York, NY 10017
Tel: 212-503-1074; 212-503-1060 Fax: 212-286-1505
Web Site: www.dnp.co.jp/ Cable: DAIPRINTS NY
Key Personnel
Pres: Yoji Yamakawa
VP & Gen Mgr, Graphic Printing: Kohei Tsumori E-mail: tsumori-k@mail.dnp.co.jp
Founded: 1974
Turnaround: 30-60 Workdays
Print Runs: 1,000 min - 1,000,000 max
Business from Other Countries: 54%
Branch Office(s)
577 Airport Blvd, Suite 620, Burlingame, CA 94010, Gen Mgr: Kosuke Tago Tel: 650-340-6061 Fax: 650-340-6090

Editoriale Bortolazzi-Stei srl
39 Kane Ave, Larchmont, NY 10538
Tel: 914-834-9594 Fax: 914-833-9106
E-mail: fulvioforcellini@ebs-bortolazzi.com
Key Personnel
US Rep: Umberto Paolucci E-mail: pbert30@aol.com
Founded: 1952
Print Runs: 2,000 min - 90,000 max
Business from Other Countries: 20%
Branch Office(s)
Via Monte Comun, 40, San Giovanni Lupatoto, Verona 37057, Italy

Elegance Printing & Book Binding (USA)
Member of The Elegance Printing Group
708 Glen Cove Ave, Glen Head, NY 11545
Tel: 516-676-5941 Fax: 516-676-5973
Web Site: www.elegancebooks.com
Key Personnel
Man Dir: Frank DeLuca E-mail: frank@elegancebooks.com
Founded: 1977

SERVICES UNITED STATES

Turnaround: CTP projects, disk to proof 5 days. Reprints ship within 14 days. Proof to board books, ready to ship 3 weeks
Print Runs: 1,000 min - 200,000 max
Business from Other Countries: 40%

Equidata Philippines, see ICSl Corp

Express Media Corp
1419 Donelson Pike, Nashville, TN 37217
Tel: 615-360-6400 *Fax:* 615-360-3140
E-mail: info@expressmedia.com
Web Site: www.expressmedia.com
Key Personnel
Pres: Andrew Cameron
Founded: 1996
Turnaround: 3 Workdays
Print Runs: 1 min - 10,000 max
Business from Other Countries: 10%

Fairfield Marketing Group Inc
Subsidiary of FMG lnc
830 Sport Hill Rd, Easton, CT 06612-1250
Tel: 203-261-5585; 203-261-5568 *Fax:* 203-261-0884
E-mail: ffldmktgrp@aol.com
Key Personnel
CEO & Pres: Edward P Washchilla
VP, Fin: Pamela L Johnson
VP, Fulfillment: Jason Paul Miller *Tel:* 203-261-5585 ext 203
Founded: 1987
Turnaround: 5-10 Workdays
Print Runs: 2,500 min - 1,000,000 max
Business from Other Countries: 10%
Membership(s): BBB; DMA

The Font Bureau
326 "A" St, Boston, MA 02210
Tel: 617-423-8770 *Fax:* 617-423-8771
E-mail: typesales@fontbureau.com
Web Site: www.fontbureau.com
Key Personnel
Retail Sales Mgr: Harry Parker
Founded: 1989
Turnaround: 1 Workday
Business from Other Countries: 20%

High Resolution Inc
30 Belmont Ave, Camden, ME 04843
Tel: 207-236-3777 *Fax:* 207-236-2500
Web Site: www.highres.com
Key Personnel
Pres & Owner: Peter Koons *E-mail:* pdk@highres.com
Owner & Mktg Dir: Sandra Soards *E-mail:* sandy@high.res.com
Founded: 1986
Turnaround: 2 Workdays
Business from Other Countries: 10%

Hindy's Enterprise
Division of Jinno International
3 Christine Dr, Chestnut Ridge, NY 10977-6802
Tel: 845-735-4666 *Fax:* 617-344-5905
Key Personnel
Pres: Yoh Jinno *E-mail:* jinno@hotmail.com
Founded: 1989
Turnaround: 40 Workdays
Print Runs: 500 min - 2,000,000 max
Business from Other Countries: 70%
Branch Office(s)
Melbourne Industrial Bldg, Block A, 20th fl, 16 Westlands Rd, Quarry Bay, Hong Kong *Tel:* 2516 6318 *Fax:* 2516 5161

Huron Valley Graphics Inc
4597 Platt Rd, Ann Arbor, MI 48108
Tel: 734-477-0448 *Fax:* 734-477-0393
E-mail: custserv@hvg.com
Web Site: www.hvg.com

Key Personnel
Pres: Claudia Lybrink
Cust Serv Mgr, Sales & Mktg: Yvonne Robinson
Data Servs Mgr: Francis O'Donnell
Founded: 1971
Turnaround: 15 Workdays
Business from Other Countries: 10%

IBT Global Ltd, see lntegrated Book Technology Inc

ICSl Corp
Formerly Equidata Philippines
2274 S Arlington Rd, Akron, OH 44319
Tel: 330-645-0004; 330-786-0002 *Fax:* 330-786-0056
Web Site: www.equidataservice.com
Key Personnel
Reg Mktg Dir: Arthur Williams *E-mail:* artwilliam@worldnet.att.net
Founded: 1985
Turnaround: 1 Workday
Business from Other Countries: 30%

Ikon Document Services
399 River Rd, Hudson, MA 01749-2627
Tel: 978-562-9131 *Fax:* 978-562-4304
Key Personnel
VP: David Trombino *E-mail:* dtrombino@ikon.com
Founded: 1973
Turnaround: 3 Workdays
Print Runs: 10 min - 5,000 max
Business from Other Countries: 10%

Innodata Corp
Affiliate of Track Data Corp
3 University Plaza Dr, Suite 506, Hackensack, NJ 07601
Tel: 201-488-1200 *Fax:* 201-488-9099
E-mail: solutions@innodata.com
Web Site: www.innodata.com
Key Personnel
CEO: Jack Abahoff
Dir, Busn Devt: Joan Meyer
Founded: 1989
Turnaround: As little as 12 hours
Business from Other Countries: 25%

Integrated Book Technology Inc
Division of The IBT Group
18 Industrial Park Rd, Troy, NY 12180
Tel: 518-271-5117 *Fax:* 518-266-9422
E-mail: mail@integratedbooktechnology.com
Web Site: www.integratedbooktechnology.com
Key Personnel
CEO & Pres: John R Paeglow *E-mail:* johnp@integratedbook.com
VP & Chief Technol Officer: William Clockel *E-mail:* billc@integratedbook.com
VP, Sales & Mktg: Robert Lindberg *E-mail:* bobl@integratedbook.com
Dir, Info Technol: Michael Whalen *E-mail:* mikew@integratedbook.com
Regl Sales: Tim Knickerbocker *E-mail:* timk@integratedbook.com
Cust Serv Mgr: James Klein *E-mail:* jimk@integratedbook.com
Reg Sales: Bryan Hall
Founded: 1991
Turnaround: 1-15 Workdays
Print Runs: 10 min - 2,000 max
Business from Other Countries: 20%
Membership(s): BMI

ITC
Division of Software Services
5100 W Copans Rd, Suite 500, Margate, FL 33063
Tel: 954-623-3101 *Fax:* 954-623-3122
E-mail: team@inttype.com

Web Site: www.inttype.com
Key Personnel
Pres: Mukesh Narang
Dir, Sales & Mktg: Jane Stark *E-mail:* janes@inttype.com
Gen Mgr: Jim Thirkill
Founded: 1995
BISAC compatible software
Turnaround: 10-20 workdays - rush service available (48 hr turnaround)
Business from Other Countries: 10%

Jinno International Group
3 Christine Dr, Chestnut Ridge, NY 10977
Tel: 845-735-4666 *Fax:* 617-344-5905
E-mail: jinno@hotmail.com
Key Personnel
Pres: Yoh Jinno
VP: Sharon Jinno
Founded: 1989
Turnaround: 21-30 Workdays US, 45-75 Workdays overseas
Print Runs: 500 min - 3,000,000 max
Business from Other Countries: 98%
Branch Office(s)
Jinno International Singapore, 710 Ang Mo Kio, Ave 8, Suite 07-2615, Singapore 2056, Singapore *Tel:* 458 0778
Wing Yiu Printing Co, Melbourne Industrial Bldg, 6th fl, Block A, 16 Westlands Rd, Quarry Bay, Hong Kong, Contact: Law Ming Wah *Tel:* 561 0283 *Fax:* 565 8233
Hindy's Enterprise, Melbourne Industrial Bldg, 16 Westlands Rd, Block A, 20th fl, Quarry Bay, Hong Kong *Tel:* 516-6318 *Fax:* 516-5161
c/o Eurasia Press Pte Ltd, 10/14 Kampong Ampat, Singapore 1336, Singapore, Contact: Allan Fong *Tel:* 280 5522 *Fax:* 280 0593

Lenz & Riecker Inc
690 Union Blvd, Totowa, NJ 07512
Tel: 973-256-2456 *Fax:* 973-256-3433; 973-256-2459
E-mail: info@l-r.com
Web Site: www.l-r.com
Key Personnel
Pres: Steven Riecker
VP, Sales: G Gilrain
CFO: Barry Levinson
Founded: 1917
Turnaround: 2-20 Workdays
Print Runs: 100 min - 100,000 max
Business from Other Countries: 20%

Leo Paper USA
1180 NW Maple St, Suite 102, Issaquah, WA 98027
Tel: 425-646-8801 *Fax:* 425-646-8805
E-mail: leo@leousa.com
Web Site: www.leousa.com
Key Personnel
VP: Peter R Gillies *E-mail:* peter@leousa.com
Sales: Tom Leach *E-mail:* tom@leousa.com; Greg Witt *E-mail:* greg@leousa.com
Founded: 1983
Turnaround: 90 Workdays
Print Runs: 3,500 min - 2,000,000 max
Business from Other Countries: 20%
Branch Office(s)
Leo Paper Products Ltd, 7/F Kader Bldg, 22 Kai Cheung Rd, Kowloon Bay, Hong Kong, Man Dir: Johnny Fung *Tel:* 8841374 *Fax:* 28853520 *E-mail:* lpp@leo.com.hk *Web Site:* www.leo.com.hk
Leo Paper USA, 27 W 24 St, Suite 701, New York, NY 10010, Janine Laborne *Tel:* 917-305-0708 *Fax:* 917-305-0709
Sales Office(s): Leo Paper Products (Europe) BVBA, De Wilde Zee Wiegstraat 19, 2000 Antwerp, Belgium, Contact: Jan Van Gijsel *Tel:* (03) 203 0912 *Fax:* (03) 225-1303 *E-mail:* leo@leo-europe.com

Leo Marketing, The Malthouse, Malthouse Sq, Princes Risborough, Bucks HP27 9AB, United Kingdom, Sally Wood *Tel:* (1844) 274-244 *Fax:* (1844) 275-105 *E-mail:* sallywood.leo@btinternet.com

Linick International Inc
Division of The Linick Group Inc
Linick Bldg, 7 Putter Lane, Middle Island, NY 11953-0102
Tel: 631-924-3888
E-mail: linickgrp@att.net
Web Site: www.lgroup.addr.com; www.linickgroup.com
Key Personnel
Chmn & CEO: Dr Andrew S Linick
Treas: Marvin Glickman
Exec VP: Roger Dextor
Founded: 1972
Turnaround: 21-30 Workdays
Print Runs: 3,000 min - 50,000 max
Business from Other Countries: 30%

LK Litho
Division of The Linick Group Inc
Linick Bldg, 7 Putter Lane, Middle Island, NY 11953-0102
Tel: 631-924-3888
E-mail: linickgrp@att.net
Web Site: www.lgroup.addr.com; www.linickgroup.com
Key Personnel
VP: Roger Dextor
Founded: 1968
Turnaround: 10 Workdays
Print Runs: 5,000 min - 2,000,000 max
Business from Other Countries: 20%
Membership(s): CCA (Copywriters Council of America; DMA; LIAC

Mazer Publishing Services
Division of The Mazer Corporation
6680 Poe Ave, Dayton, OH 45414
Tel: 937-264-2600 *Fax:* 937-264-2624
E-mail: info@mazer.com
Web Site: www.mazer.com
Key Personnel
Pres: William Franklin *E-mail:* bill_franklin@mazer.com
Exec VP: Ken Fultz *E-mail:* ken_fultz@mazer.com
Exec Dir, Sales: Bill Faber *Fax:* 937-264-2622 *E-mail:* bill_faber@mazer.com
Founded: 1964
Print Runs: 50 min - 25,000 max
Business from Other Countries: 10%
Branch Office(s)
2460 Sand Lake Rd, Orlando, FL 32809, Contact: Bryan Blakley *Tel:* 407-859-5552 *Fax:* 407-859-0643 *E-mail:* bryan_blakley@mazer.com
224 Lexington Ave, Fox River Grove, IL 60021, Contact: Dennis Bowman *Tel:* 847-639-1555 *Fax:* 847-639-1562 *E-mail:* dennis_bowman@mazer.com
22 Lehigh Rd, Wellesley, MA 02181, Contact: Ken Leahy *Tel:* 781-237-4112 *Fax:* 781-431-6184 *E-mail:* ken_leahy@mazer.com
22 Laurel Place, Upper Montclair, NJ 07043, Contact: John Martel *Tel:* 973-744-4320 *Fax:* 973-746-5608 *E-mail:* john_martel@mazer.com
3081 Glenmere Ct, Kettering, OH 45440, Contact: Mark Brewer *Tel:* 937-299-5746 *Fax:* 937-299-5761 *E-mail:* mark_brewer@mazer.com
363 Porter Rd, Bishop, TX 78602, Contact: Deborah VanLandingham *Tel:* 512-303-9758 *Fax:* 512-303-9791
Membership(s): BMI

Milanostampa/New Interlitho USA Inc
Subsidiary of Milanostampa New Interlitho Italia SpA
299 Broadway, Suite 901, New York, NY 10007
Tel: 212-964-2430 *Fax:* 212-964-2497
Web Site: www.milanostampa.com
Key Personnel
Chmn: Riccardo Sardo
Sales Rep: Rino Varrasso *E-mail:* rvarrasso@milanostampa-usa.com
Founded: 1974
Turnaround: 30 Workdays
Print Runs: 1,000 min - 3,000,000 max
Business from Other Countries: 75%

Pageworks
4 Gibbons Circle, Old Saybrook, CT 06475
Tel: 860-395-2022 *Fax:* 860-388-4353
Key Personnel
Co-owner: Maggie Dana *E-mail:* maggiedana@aol.com; Jamie Temple
Founded: 1987
Business from Other Countries: 10%

Palace Press International
1585-A Folsom St, San Francisco, CA 94103
Tel: 415-626-1080 *Fax:* 415-626-1510
E-mail: ppisfo@palacepress.com
Web Site: www.palacepress.com
Key Personnel
Pres: Raoul A Goff *E-mail:* raoul@palacepress.com
Dir: Gordon Goff *Tel:* 415-455-2480 ext 211 *Fax:* 415-455-2490 *E-mail:* gordon@palacepress.com
Sales Mgr: Steven Goff *Tel:* 415-455-2480 *E-mail:* steven@palacepress.com
Proj Mgr: Maria Ramos *Tel:* 415-626-1080 ext 208 *E-mail:* maria@palacepress.ca
Founded: 1984
Turnaround: 90 Workdays
Print Runs: 3,000 min - 1,000,000 max
Business from Other Countries: 20%
Branch Office(s)
Palace Press International Los Angeles, 303 W Newby Ave, Suite C, San Gabriel, CT 91776, Contact: Sabra Chili *Tel:* 310-444-3904 *Fax:* 310-473-4799 *E-mail:* sabra@palacepress.com
Palace Press International New York, 180 Varick St, 10th fl, New York, NY 10014, Contact: Roger Ma *Tel:* 212-462-2622 *Fax:* 212-463-9130 *E-mail:* roger@palacepress.com
Palace Press San Rafael, 1299 Fourth St, Suite 305, San Rafael, CA 94901, Contact: Gordon Goff *Tel:* 415-455-2480 *Fax:* 415-455-2490 *E-mail:* gordon@palacepress.com
Palace Press International Hong Kong, Wah Ha Factory Bldg, 10th fl, Block A, B, C & D, 8 Shipyard Lane, Quarry Bay, Hong Kong, Contact: Leslie Sun *Tel:* 2357-9019 *Fax:* 2561-3616 *E-mail:* palacehk@netvigator.com *Web Site:* www.palacepress.com
Palace Press International Los Angeles, 11775 Gateway Blvd, Suite 2, Los Angeles, CA 90064, Contact: Sabra Chili *Tel:* 310-444-3904 *Fax:* 310-473-4799 *E-mail:* sabra@palacepress.com

Photoengraving Inc
502 N Willow Ave, Tampa, FL 33606
Tel: 813-253-3427 *Fax:* 813-253-5491
Key Personnel
Owner: Ed Dalton, Jr
Founded: 1953
Turnaround: 3 Workdays
Business from Other Countries: 25%

Pioneer Graphic Scanning
Division of Jinno International
3 Christine Dr, Chestnut Ridge, NY 10977-6802
Tel: 845-735-4666 *Fax:* 617-344-5905
Key Personnel
Pres: Yoh Jinno *E-mail:* jinno@worldnet.att.net
Mktg Dir: Stewart Sum
Founded: 1989
Turnaround: 10-60 Workdays
Print Runs: 500 min - 3,000,000 max
Business from Other Countries: 95%

Prepare Inc
Affiliate of Emilcomp srl
36 Woodcliff Lake Rd, Saddle River, NJ 07458
Tel: 201-934-8451 *Fax:* 201-934-2992
E-mail: csr@emilcomp.it; prepare@optonline.net
Key Personnel
Pres: Fran Daniele
VP: Rose Mello
Founded: 1987
Business from Other Countries: 50%

Printing Corp of the Americas Inc
620 SW 12 Ave, Pompano Beach, FL 33069
Tel: 954-781-8100 *Fax:* 954-781-8421
E-mail: pcaprint@bellsouth.net
Web Site: www.pcaprint.bellsouth.net
Key Personnel
Pres: Jan Tuchman
Founded: 1979
Turnaround: 5-10 Workdays
Print Runs: 500 min - 100,000 max
Business from Other Countries: 15%

Quantum Colorgraphics
166 Midland Ave, Montclair, NJ 07042
Tel: 873-783-0462 *Fax:* 973-783-0637
Web Site: www.quantumcolor.com
Key Personnel
Sr Acct Exec: Jeffrey Sestilio
Print Runs: 1,000 min - 300,000 max
Business from Other Countries: 30%

Regent Publishing Services
9327 Rambler Dr, St Louis, MO 63123
Tel: 314-631-7581 *Fax:* 314-638-5113
E-mail: regentstl@aol.com
Key Personnel
Sales Dir: Carol A Davis-Tierney
Mktg Dir: James J Tierney
Founded: 1985
Turnaround: 3-4 Months
Print Runs: 2,000 min - 100,000 max
Business from Other Countries: 100%

Sencor
240 E 56 St, 4th fl, New York, NY 10022
Tel: 212-486-0320 *Fax:* 212-486-0710
E-mail: sales@sencor.net
Web Site: www.sencor.net
Key Personnel
CEO: George Martel *E-mail:* gmartel@sencor.net
VP: Michael Martel *E-mail:* mvmartel@sencor.net
Founded: 1984
BISAC compatible software
Turnaround: 5 Workdays
Business from Other Countries: 10%
Branch Office(s)
1991 Taft Ave, Pasay City, Manila 1306, Philippines

SpectraComp
Division of Batsch Co Inc
5170 E Trindle Rd, Mechanicsburg, PA 17050
Tel: 717-697-8600 *Fax:* 717-691-0433
E-mail: info@spectracomp.com
Web Site: www.spectracomp.com
Key Personnel
Pres: Terry Fackler *E-mail:* tfackler@spectracomp.com
VP, Sales: Jeffrey Fackler
Founded: 1966
Turnaround: 1-10 Workdays
Business from Other Countries: 10%

SERVICES

Square Two Design Inc
600 Townsend St, Suite 320E, San Francisco, CA 94103
Tel: 415-437-3888 *Fax:* 415-437-3880
Web Site: www.square2.com
Key Personnel
Pres: Eddie Lee
Founded: 1992
Business from Other Countries: 10%

Studio 31
2740 SW Martha Downs Blvd, No 358, Palm City, FL 34990
Tel: 772-781-7195 *Fax:* 772-781-6044
E-mail: studio31@mindspring.com
Web Site: www.studio31.com
Key Personnel
Pres: Jim Wasserman
Founded: 1977
Business from Other Countries: 15%

Taylor Publishing Co
1550 W Mockingbird Lane, Dallas, TX 75235
Tel: 214-819-8100 *Fax:* 214-630-1852
E-mail: web@taylorpub.com
Web Site: www.taylorpub.com
Key Personnel
Pres: Dave Fiore
Dir, Fine Books & Div Sales Mgr: Jay Love
Dir, Mktg: Mike Taylor
Founded: 1939
Turnaround: 45 Workdays
Print Runs: 300 min - 25,000 max
Business from Other Countries: 10%

Times Publishing Group
Division of Times Publishing Ltd/Singapore
99 White Plains Rd, Tarrytown, NY 10591
Tel: 914-366-9888 *Fax:* 914-366-9898
Web Site: www.tpl.com.sg
Key Personnel
Cust Serv Exec: Bonnie Stone *E-mail:* bstone@marshallcavendish.com
Sales Mgr: Suresh Kumar *E-mail:* skumar@marshallcavendish.com
Founded: 1965
Print Runs: 2,000 min - 500,000 max
Business from Other Countries: 90%

Fred Weidner & Daughter Printers
15 Maiden Lane, Suite 1505, New York, NY 10038
Tel: 212-964-8676 *Fax:* 212-964-8677
E-mail: info@fwdprinters.com
Web Site: www.fwdprinters.com
Key Personnel
Contact: Frederick Weidner, III
Pres: Cynthia Weidner *E-mail:* cynthia@fwdprinters.com
Founded: 1860
Turnaround: 5-10 Workdays
Print Runs: 1,000 min - 100,000 max
Business from Other Countries: 25%

Uruguay

Barreiro y Ramos SA
Juan Carlos Gomez, 1430, Montevideo 11000
Tel: (02) 986621 *Fax:* (02) 962358
Telex: 23901PB.CVJA.UY *Cable:* BAREIRAMOS
Key Personnel
President: Gaston Barreiro
Vice President: Guzman Barreiro
Founded: 1837
Print Runs: 1,000 min - 50,000 max
Business from Other Countries: 10%

Printing, Binding & Book Finishing Index

ADHESIVE BINDING - HARD

Australia
Southwood Press Pty Ltd, pg 1193

Belgium
Drukkerij Lannoo NV, pg 1193

Canada
Appleby's Bindery Ltd, pg 1193
Printcrafters Inc, pg 1193
Transcontinental Printing Book Group, pg 1194
Tri-Graphic Printing (Ottawa) Ltd, pg 1194
University of Toronto Press Inc, pg 1194
Webcom Ltd, pg 1194

China
Speedflex Asia Ltd, pg 1194

Czech Republic
GRASPO CZ AS - Druckerei und Buchbinderei, pg 1194

Denmark
Bianco Lunos Bogtrykkeri AS, pg 1194

Finland
Gummerus Printing, pg 1194
WS Bookwell Ltd, pg 1194

Germany
C L Baader Buch & Offsetdruckerei GmbH & Co KG, pg 1194
C Maurer Druck und Verlag, pg 1195
Media-Print Informationstechnologie GmbH, pg 1195
Mohndruck Graphische Betriebe GmbH, pg 1195
Oertel & Sporer GmbH & Co, pg 1195
Priese GmbH, pg 1195
Vier-Tuerme GmbH Benedikt Press, pg 1195

Hong Kong
Best-Set Typesetter Ltd, pg 1195
C & C Offset Printing Co Ltd, pg 1195
Dai Nippon Printing Co (Hong Kong) Ltd, pg 1196
Everbest Printing Co Ltd, pg 1196
Golden Cup Printing Co Ltd, pg 1196
Hung Hing Off-set Printing Co Ltd, pg 1196
Midas Printing Ltd, pg 1197
Morris Press Ltd, pg 1197
Paramount Publishing Group Limited, pg 1197
Prontaprint Asia Ltd, pg 1197
Sing Cheong Printing Co Limited, pg 1197
Sino Publishing House Ltd, pg 1197
Unicorn International Printing Co Ltd, pg 1197
Wing King Tong Co Ltd (Printing Factory), pg 1197

Indonesia
Ichtiar Baru I Van Hoeve, pg 1198
Victory Offset Prima PT, pg 1198

Italy
Canale G e C SpA, pg 1198
Milanostampa SPA, pg 1198
Amilcare Pizzi SpA, pg 1198

Republic of Korea
Pyunghwa Dang Printing Co Ltd, pg 1199

Lithuania
Spindulys Printing House, pg 1199

New Zealand
Bookprint Consultants Ltd, pg 1199

Philippines
Cacho Hermanos Inc, pg 1199
Philippine Graphic Arts Inc, pg 1199

Singapore
CS Graphics Pte Ltd, pg 1200
Eurasia Press Pte Ltd, pg 1200
Ho Printing Singapore Pte Ltd, pg 1200
Markono Print Media Pte Ltd, pg 1200
SNP Printing Pte Ltd, pg 1200
Toppan Company (S) Pte Ltd, pg 1200
World Publications Printers Pte Ltd, pg 1201

Slovenia
Gorenjski Tisk Printing Co, pg 1201

Spain
Luis Vives (Edelvives), pg 1201

United Republic of Tanzania
Peramiho Publications, pg 1201

Thailand
J Film Process Co Ltd, pg 1201
Mavisu International Co Ltd, pg 1201

United Kingdom
Biddles Ltd, pg 1202
Caledonian International Book Manufacturing, pg 1202
Center Print Ltd, pg 1202
Clays Ltd, pg 1203
William Clowes Ltd, pg 1203
Cradley Print Ltd, pg 1203
Hammond Packaging Ltd, pg 1203
Intype London Ltd, pg 1204
Charles Letts & Co Ltd, pg 1204
Martins Printing Group Ltd, pg 1204
MPG Books Ltd, pg 1204
Redwood Books Ltd, pg 1204
Antony Rowe Ltd, pg 1204
TJ International Ltd, pg 1205
Watkiss Automation Ltd, pg 1205

United States
Bind-It Corp, pg 1205
Blaze International Productions Inc, pg 1205
BookBuilders New York Ltd, pg 1205
Colorprint Offset Inc, pg 1206
Martin Cook Associates Ltd, pg 1206
CS Graphics USA Inc, pg 1206
DNP America LLC, pg 1206
Elegance Printing & Book Binding (USA), pg 1206
Express Media Corp, pg 1206
Hamilton Printing Co, pg 1206
Hindy's Enterprise, pg 1207
Imago, pg 1207
Integrated Book Technology Inc, pg 1207
Jinno International Group, pg 1207
KNI Inc, pg 1207
Leo Paper USA, pg 1207
Linick International Inc, pg 1207
LK Litho, pg 1207
Milanostampa/New Interlitho USA Inc, pg 1208
Palace Press International, pg 1208
Regent Publishing Services, pg 1208
Spraymation Inc, pg 1208
Fred Weidner & Daughter Printers, pg 1208

Uruguay
Barreiro y Ramos SA, pg 1208

ADHESIVE BINDING - SOFT

Australia
Southwood Press Pty Ltd, pg 1193

Belgium
Drukkerij Lannoo NV, pg 1193

Canada
Appleby's Bindery Ltd, pg 1193
Coach House Printing, pg 1193
Maracle Press Ltd, pg 1193
Preney Print & Litho Inc, pg 1193
Printcrafters Inc, pg 1193
Transcontinental Printing Book Group, pg 1194
Tri-Graphic Printing (Ottawa) Ltd, pg 1194
University of Toronto Press Inc, pg 1194
Webcom Ltd, pg 1194

China
Speedflex Asia Ltd, pg 1194

Denmark
Bianco Lunos Bogtrykkeri AS, pg 1194

Finland
Gummerus Printing, pg 1194
WS Bookwell Ltd, pg 1194

Germany
C L Baader Buch & Offsetdruckerei GmbH & Co KG, pg 1194
C Maurer Druck und Verlag, pg 1195
Media-Print Informationstechnologie GmbH, pg 1195
Mohndruck Graphische Betriebe GmbH, pg 1195
Priese GmbH, pg 1195
Vier-Tuerme GmbH Benedikt Press, pg 1195

Hong Kong
Best-Set Typesetter Ltd, pg 1195
Bright Future Printing Co Ltd, pg 1195
C & C Offset Printing Co Ltd, pg 1195
Colorprint Offset, pg 1195
Dai Nippon Printing Co (Hong Kong) Ltd, pg 1196
Everbest Printing Co Ltd, pg 1196
Golden Cup Printing Co Ltd, pg 1196
Hung Hing Off-set Printing Co Ltd, pg 1196
Liang Yu Printing Factory Ltd, pg 1196
Midas Printing Ltd, pg 1197
Morris Press Ltd, pg 1197
Paramount Publishing Group Limited, pg 1197
Prontaprint Asia Ltd, pg 1197
Sheck Wah Tong Printing Press, pg 1197
Sing Cheong Printing Co Limited, pg 1197
Sino Publishing House Ltd, pg 1197
Toppan Printing Co (HK) Ltd, pg 1197
Unicorn International Printing Co Ltd, pg 1197
Wing King Tong Co Ltd (Printing Factory), pg 1197

Indonesia
Ichtiar Baru I Van Hoeve, pg 1198
Victory Offset Prima PT, pg 1198

Ireland
Kilkenny People/Wellbrook Press, pg 1198
Smurfit Print, pg 1198

Israel
Keterpress Enterprises Jerusalem, pg 1198
Technosdar Ltd, pg 1198

Italy
Canale G e C SpA, pg 1198
Milanostampa SPA, pg 1198
Minerva Medica, pg 1198
Amilcare Pizzi SpA, pg 1198

1169

PRINTING, BINDING & BOOK FINISHING INDEX

Republic of Korea
Daehan Printing & Publishing Co Ltd, pg 1199
Pyunghwa Dang Printing Co Ltd, pg 1199

Lithuania
Spindulys Printing House, pg 1199

New Zealand
Bookprint Consultants Ltd, pg 1199

Philippines
Cacho Hermanos Inc, pg 1199
Philippine Graphic Arts Inc, pg 1199

Singapore
Chong Moh Offset Printing Ltd, pg 1200
CS Graphics Pte Ltd, pg 1200
Eurasia Press Pte Ltd, pg 1200
Ho Printing Singapore Pte Ltd, pg 1200
Markono Print Media Pte Ltd, pg 1200
SNP Printing Pte Ltd, pg 1200
Times Printers Pte Ltd, pg 1200
Toppan Company (S) Pte Ltd, pg 1200
World Publications Printers Pte Ltd, pg 1201

Slovenia
Gorenjski Tisk Printing Co, pg 1201

Spain
Grafos SA Arte Sobre Papel, pg 1201
Rotedic SA, pg 1201
Luis Vives (Edelvives), pg 1201

United Republic of Tanzania
Peramiho Publications, pg 1201

Thailand
J Film Process Co Ltd, pg 1201
Mavisu International Co Ltd, pg 1201

United Kingdom
J W Arrowsmith Ltd, pg 1202
BAS Printers Ltd, pg 1202
Biddles Ltd, pg 1202
J W Braithwaite & Son Ltd, pg 1202
Caledonian International Book Manufacturing, pg 1202
Center Print Ltd, pg 1202
Clays Ltd, pg 1203
The Guernsey Press Co Ltd, pg 1203
Hammond Packaging Ltd, pg 1203
Intype London Ltd, pg 1204
Charles Letts & Co Ltd, pg 1204
Lowfield Printing Co Ltd, pg 1204
MPG Books Ltd, pg 1204
Page Bros Ltd (Norwich), pg 1204
Redwood Books Ltd, pg 1204
Antony Rowe Ltd, pg 1204
Severnside Printers Ltd, pg 1204
TJ International Ltd, pg 1205
Watkiss Automation Ltd, pg 1205
WH Trade Binders Ltd, pg 1205

United States
ADR/BookPrint, pg 1205
Bind-It Corp, pg 1205

Blaze International Productions Inc, pg 1205
BookBuilders New York Ltd, pg 1205
C & C Offset Printing Co Ltd, pg 1205
Colorprint Offset Inc, pg 1206
Coneco Litho Graphics, pg 1206
Martin Cook Associates Ltd, pg 1206
CS Graphics USA Inc, pg 1206
DNP America LLC, pg 1206
Editoriale Bortolazzi-Stei srl, pg 1206
Elegance Printing & Book Binding (USA), pg 1206
Express Media Corp, pg 1206
Hamilton Printing Co, pg 1206
Hindy's Enterprise, pg 1207
Imago, pg 1207
Integrated Book Technology Inc, pg 1207
Jinno International Group, pg 1207
Lenz & Riecker Inc, pg 1207
Leo Paper USA, pg 1207
Linick International Inc, pg 1207
LK Litho, pg 1207
Milanostampa/New Interlitho USA Inc, pg 1208
Palace Press International, pg 1208
Printing Corp of the Americas Inc, pg 1208
Regent Publishing Services, pg 1208
Spraymation Inc, pg 1208
Vicks Lithograph & Printing Corp, pg 1208
Fred Weidner & Daughter Printers, pg 1208

Uruguay
Barreiro y Ramos SA, pg 1208

BOOK PRINTING - HARDBOUND

Australia
Southwood Press Pty Ltd, pg 1193

Austria
ADEVA (Akademische Druck-u Verlagsanstalt), pg 1193

Belgium
Drukkerij Lannoo NV, pg 1193

Canada
Aardvark Enterprises, pg 1193
Coach House Printing, pg 1193
McLaren Morris & Todd Ltd, pg 1193
Printcrafters Inc, pg 1193
Transcontinental Printing Book Group, pg 1194
Tri-Graphic Printing (Ottawa) Ltd, pg 1194
University of Toronto Press Inc, pg 1194

China
Speedflex Asia Ltd, pg 1194

Denmark
Bianco Lunos Bogtrykkeri AS, pg 1194

Finland
Gummerus Printing, pg 1194
WS Bookwell Ltd, pg 1194

France
Imprimerie Gaignault, pg 1194
Signes du Monde, pg 1194

Germany
G Braun (vormals G Braun'sche Hofbuchdruckerei und Verlag), pg 1195
C Maurer Druck und Verlag, pg 1195
Media-Print Informationstechnologie GmbH, pg 1195
Mohndruck Graphische Betriebe GmbH, pg 1195
Priese GmbH, pg 1195
Vier-Tuerme GmbH Benedikt Press, pg 1195

Hong Kong
Best-Set Typesetter Ltd, pg 1195
Bookbuilders Ltd, pg 1195
Bright Future Printing Co Ltd, pg 1195
C & C Offset Printing Co Ltd, pg 1195
Caritas Printing Training Centre, pg 1195
Colorprint Offset, pg 1195
Dai Nippon Printing Co (Hong Kong) Ltd, pg 1196
Everbest Printing Co Ltd, pg 1196
Excel United Company Ltd, pg 1196
Golden Cup Printing Co Ltd, pg 1196
Hoi Kwong Printing Co Ltd, pg 1196
Hung Hing Off-set Printing Co Ltd, pg 1196
Image Printing Company Ltd, pg 1196
Kwong Fat Offset Printing Company Ltd, pg 1196
Lammar Offset Printing Co, pg 1196
Leo Paper Products Ltd, pg 1196
Liang Yu Printing Factory Ltd, pg 1196
Midas Printing Ltd, pg 1197
Morris Press Ltd, pg 1197
Paper Art Product Ltd, pg 1197
Paper Communication Printing Express Ltd, pg 1197
Paramount Publishing Group Limited, pg 1197
Prontaprint Asia Ltd, pg 1197
Sing Cheong Printing Co Limited, pg 1197
Sino Publishing House Ltd, pg 1197
South Sea International Press Ltd, pg 1197
Sun Fung Offset Binding Co Ltd, pg 1197
Sunny Printing (Hong Kong) Co Ltd, pg 1197
Sunshine Press Ltd, pg 1197
Toppan Printing Co (HK) Ltd, pg 1197
Unicorn International Printing Co Ltd, pg 1197
Wing King Tong Co Ltd (Printing Factory), pg 1197

Hungary
Interpress Aussenhandels GmbH, pg 1197
Kultura, pg 1197

Indonesia
Ichtiar Baru I Van Hoeve, pg 1198
Victory Offset Prima PT, pg 1198

Israel
Keterpress Enterprises Jerusalem, pg 1198
Monoline Ltd, pg 1198
Technosdar Ltd, pg 1198

Italy
Canale G e C SpA, pg 1198
Dedalo Litostampa SRL, pg 1198
Milanostampa SPA, pg 1198
Amilcare Pizzi SpA, pg 1198

Japan
Dai Nippon Printing Co Ltd, pg 1198

Republic of Korea
Daehan Printing & Publishing Co Ltd, pg 1199
Pyunghwa Dang Printing Co Ltd, pg 1199

Lithuania
Spindulys Printing House, pg 1199

Madagascar
Societe Malgache d'Edition, pg 1199

Malta
Interprint Ltd - Malta, pg 1199

Netherlands
Koninklijke Wohrmann Bv, pg 1199

New Zealand
Bookprint Consultants Ltd, pg 1199
John McIndoe Ltd, pg 1199
PPP Printers Ltd, pg 1199

Philippines
Cacho Hermanos Inc, pg 1199
Philippine Graphic Arts Inc, pg 1199

Portugal
Printer Portuguesa Industria Grafica Lda, pg 1199

Singapore
CS Graphics Pte Ltd, pg 1200
Eurasia Press Pte Ltd, pg 1200
Fong & Sons Printers Pte Ltd, pg 1200
Ho Printing Singapore Pte Ltd, pg 1200
International Press Co Pte Ltd, pg 1200
SNP Printing Pte Ltd, pg 1200
Tien Wah Press Pte Ltd, pg 1200
Toppan Company (S) Pte Ltd, pg 1200
World Publications Printers Pte Ltd, pg 1201

Slovenia
Gorenjski Tisk Printing Co, pg 1201

South Africa
CTP Book Printers (Pty) Ltd, pg 1201

MANUFACTURING

PRINTING, BINDING & BOOK FINISHING INDEX

Spain
Grafos SA Arte Sobre Papel, pg 1201
Printer Industria Grafica SA, pg 1201
Graficas Santamaria SA, pg 1201
Luis Vives (Edelvives), pg 1201

Sri Lanka
Sumathi Book Printing (Pvt) Ltd, pg 1201

Switzerland
Hallwag AG, pg 1201

Taiwan, Province of China
Taipei Yung Chang Printing, pg 1201

United Republic of Tanzania
Peramiho Publications, pg 1201

Thailand
J Film Process Co Ltd, pg 1201
Phongwarin Printing Company Ltd, pg 1201

United Arab Emirates
Emirates Printing Press (LLC), pg 1202

United Kingdom
The Alden Group Ltd, pg 1202
W & G Baird Ltd, pg 1202
BAS Printers Ltd, pg 1202
Ebenezer Baylis & Son Ltd, pg 1202
Biddles Ltd, pg 1202
Book Creation Services, pg 1202
Butler & Tanner Ltd, pg 1202
Caledonian International Book Manufacturing, pg 1202
Center Print Ltd, pg 1202
The Charlesworth Group, pg 1202
Clays Ltd, pg 1203
William Clowes Ltd, pg 1203
Cradley Print Ltd, pg 1203
Eagle Press, pg 1203
Goldshield Communications Ltd, pg 1203
Hammond Packaging Ltd, pg 1203
Headley Brothers Ltd, pg 1203
Intype London Ltd, pg 1204
Charles Letts & Co Ltd, pg 1204
Martins Printing Group Ltd, pg 1204
MPG Books Ltd, pg 1204
Multiplex Medway Ltd, pg 1204
George Over Ltd, pg 1204
Redwood Books Ltd, pg 1204
Antony Rowe Ltd, pg 1204
Severnside Printers Ltd, pg 1204
Stott Brothers Ltd, pg 1204
TJ International Ltd, pg 1205

United States
Asia Pacific Offset Inc, pg 1205
Blaze International Productions Inc, pg 1205
BookBuilders New York Ltd, pg 1205
Butler & Tanner Inc, pg 1205
C & C Offset Printing Co Ltd, pg 1205
Carvajal International Inc, pg 1206
Colorprint Offset Inc, pg 1206
Coneco Litho Graphics, pg 1206
Martin Cook Associates Ltd, pg 1206
CS Graphics USA Inc, pg 1206
DNP America LLC, pg 1206
Editoriale Bortolazzi-Stei srl, pg 1206
Elegance Printing & Book Binding (USA), pg 1206
Express Media Corp, pg 1206
Hamilton Printing Co, pg 1206
Hindy's Enterprise, pg 1207
Imago, pg 1207
Integrated Book Technology Inc, pg 1207
Jinno International Group, pg 1207
Leo Paper USA, pg 1207
Linick International Inc, pg 1207
LK Litho, pg 1207
Milanostampa/New Interlitho USA Inc, pg 1208
Palace Press International, pg 1208
Printing Corp of the Americas Inc, pg 1208
Regent Publishing Services, pg 1208
Taylor Publishing Co, pg 1208
Times Publishing Group, pg 1208
Fred Weidner & Daughter Printers, pg 1208

Uruguay
Barreiro y Ramos SA, pg 1208

BOOK PRINTING - MASS MARKET

Belgium
Drukkerij Lannoo NV, pg 1193

Canada
Webcom Ltd, pg 1194

Czech Republic
GRASPO CZ AS - Druckerei und Buchbinderei, pg 1194

Germany
Mohndruck Graphische Betriebe GmbH, pg 1195
Priese GmbH, pg 1195

Hong Kong
Dai Nippon Printing Co (Hong Kong) Ltd, pg 1196
Golden Cup Printing Co Ltd, pg 1196
The Green Pagoda Press Ltd, pg 1196
Hoi Kwong Printing Co Ltd, pg 1196
Midas Printing Ltd, pg 1197
Paramount Publishing Group Limited, pg 1197
Sheck Wah Tong Printing Press, pg 1197
Sing Cheong Printing Co Limited, pg 1197
Sino Publishing House Ltd, pg 1197
Unicorn International Printing Co Ltd, pg 1197

Hungary
Interpress Aussenhandels GmbH, pg 1197

India
Hiralal Printing Works Ltd, pg 1197

Indonesia
Victory Offset Prima PT, pg 1198

Ireland
Ultragraphics, pg 1198

Israel
Keterpress Enterprises Jerusalem, pg 1198

Italy
Canale G e C SpA, pg 1198
Milanostampa SPA, pg 1198
Amilcare Pizzi SpA, pg 1198

Republic of Korea
Daehan Printing & Publishing Co Ltd, pg 1199
Pyunghwa Dang Printing Co Ltd, pg 1199

Lithuania
Spindulys Printing House, pg 1199

Netherlands
Koninklijke Wohrmann Bv, pg 1199

New Zealand
Bookprint Consultants Ltd, pg 1199
John McIndoe Ltd, pg 1199

Philippines
Cacho Hermanos Inc, pg 1199

Singapore
Markono Print Media Pte Ltd, pg 1200
Times Printers Pte Ltd, pg 1200
Toppan Company (S) Pte Ltd, pg 1200

Slovenia
Gorenjski Tisk Printing Co, pg 1201

Spain
Graficas Santamaria SA, pg 1201
Luis Vives (Edelvives), pg 1201

United Republic of Tanzania
Peramiho Publications, pg 1201

Thailand
J Film Process Co Ltd, pg 1201
Mavisu International Co Ltd, pg 1201
Phongwarin Printing Company Ltd, pg 1201

United Kingdom
Caledonian International Book Manufacturing, pg 1202
Clays Ltd, pg 1203
Goldshield Communications Ltd, pg 1203
The Guernsey Press Co Ltd, pg 1203
Lavenham Press Ltd, pg 1204
Charles Letts & Co Ltd, pg 1204
Redwood Books Ltd, pg 1204

United States
Asia Pacific Offset Inc, pg 1205
Blaze International Productions Inc, pg 1205
BookBuilders New York Ltd, pg 1205
C & C Offset Printing Co Ltd, pg 1205
Carvajal International Inc, pg 1206
Colorprint Offset Inc, pg 1206
Martin Cook Associates Ltd, pg 1206
DNP America LLC, pg 1206
Express Media Corp, pg 1206
Hamilton Printing Co, pg 1206
Hindy's Enterprise, pg 1207
Jinno International Group, pg 1207
Leo Paper USA, pg 1207
Linick International Inc, pg 1207
LK Litho, pg 1207
Printing Corp of the Americas Inc, pg 1208
Times Publishing Group, pg 1208
Fred Weidner & Daughter Printers, pg 1208

BOOK PRINTING - PROFESSIONAL

Australia
Southwood Press Pty Ltd, pg 1193

Belgium
Drukkerij Lannoo NV, pg 1193

Canada
Maracle Press Ltd, pg 1193
Printcrafters Inc, pg 1193
Transcontinental Printing Book Group, pg 1194
Tri-Graphic Printing (Ottawa) Ltd, pg 1194
University of Toronto Press Inc, pg 1194
Webcom Ltd, pg 1194

China
Speedflex Asia Ltd, pg 1194

Czech Republic
GRASPO CZ AS - Druckerei und Buchbinderei, pg 1194

Denmark
Bianco Lunos Bogtrykkeri AS, pg 1194

Finland
Gummerus Printing, pg 1194

Germany
C L Baader Buch & Offsetdruckere GmbH & Co KG, pg 1194
Fachhochschule Fur Druk, Studiengang Verlagswirtschaft und Verlagsherstellung, pg 1195
G Braun (vormals G Braun'sche Hofbuchdruckerei und Verlag), pg 1195
Media-Print Informationstechnologie GmbH, pg 1195
Mohndruck Graphische Betriebe GmbH, pg 1195
Priese GmbH, pg 1195

Hong Kong
Dai Nippon Printing Co (Hong Kong) Ltd, pg 1196
Everbest Printing Co Ltd, pg 1196
Golden Cup Printing Co Ltd, pg 1196
The Green Pagoda Press Ltd, pg 1196
Hoi Kwong Printing Co Ltd, pg 1196
Image Printing Company Ltd, pg 1196

1171

PRINTING, BINDING & BOOK FINISHING INDEX

Midas Printing Ltd, pg 1197
Paper Art Product Ltd, pg 1197
Paramount Publishing Group Limited, pg 1197
Prontaprint Asia Ltd, pg 1197
Sheck Wah Tong Printing Press, pg 1197
Sing Cheong Printing Co Limited, pg 1197
Sino Publishing House Ltd, pg 1197
South Sea International Press Ltd, pg 1197
Sunshine Press Ltd, pg 1197
Unicorn International Printing Co Ltd, pg 1197
Wing King Tong Co Ltd (Printing Factory), pg 1197

Hungary
Interpress Aussenhandels GmbH, pg 1197

Indonesia
Victory Offset Prima PT, pg 1198

Ireland
Ultragraphics, pg 1198

Israel
Keterpress Enterprises Jerusalem, pg 1198
Monoline Ltd, pg 1198
Technosdar Ltd, pg 1198

Italy
Canale G e C SpA, pg 1198
Dedalo Litostampa SRL, pg 1198
Milanostampa SPA, pg 1198

Republic of Korea
Daehan Printing & Publishing Co Ltd, pg 1199
Pyunghwa Dang Printing Co Ltd, pg 1199

Madagascar
Societe Malgache d'Edition, pg 1199

New Zealand
Bookprint Consultants Ltd, pg 1199
PPP Printers Ltd, pg 1199

Philippines
Cacho Hermanos Inc, pg 1199

Portugal
Silabo, pg 1200

Singapore
Chong Moh Offset Printing Ltd, pg 1200
Eurasia Press Pte Ltd, pg 1200
Ho Printing Singapore Pte Ltd, pg 1200
PacPress Media Pte Ltd, pg 1200
SNP Printing Pte Ltd, pg 1200
Times Printers Pte Ltd, pg 1200
Toppan Company (S) Pte Ltd, pg 1200
World Publications Printers Pte Ltd, pg 1201

Slovenia
Gorenjski Tisk Printing Co, pg 1201

Spain
Grafos SA Arte Sobre Papel, pg 1201
Graficas Santamaria SA, pg 1201
Luis Vives (Edelvives), pg 1201

United Republic of Tanzania
Peramiho Publications, pg 1201

Thailand
Phongwarin Printing Company Ltd, pg 1201

United Kingdom
BAS Printers Ltd, pg 1202
Ebenezer Baylis & Son Ltd, pg 1202
Bemrose Security & Promotional Printing, pg 1202
Biddles Ltd, pg 1202
Blackmore Ltd, pg 1202
Book Creation Services, pg 1202
Butler & Tanner Ltd, pg 1202
Caledonian International Book Manufacturing, pg 1202
Cambridge University Press - Printing Division, pg 1202
The Charlesworth Group, pg 1202
Clays Ltd, pg 1203
William Clowes Ltd, pg 1203
Cradley Print Ltd, pg 1203
Goldshield Communications Ltd, pg 1203
Hammond Packaging Ltd, pg 1203
Hobbs The Printers Ltd, pg 1203
Ikon Document Services Ltd, pg 1203
Charles Letts & Co Ltd, pg 1204
MPG Books Ltd, pg 1204
Multiplex Medway Ltd, pg 1204
Redwood Books Ltd, pg 1204
Antony Rowe Ltd, pg 1204
Selwood Printing, pg 1204
Severnside Printers Ltd, pg 1204

United States
ADR/BookPrint, pg 1205
Asia Pacific Offset Inc, pg 1205
Blaze International Productions Inc, pg 1205
BookBuilders New York Ltd, pg 1205
Carvajal International Inc, pg 1206
Colorprint Offset Inc, pg 1206
Coneco Litho Graphics, pg 1206
Martin Cook Associates Ltd, pg 1206
DNP America LLC, pg 1206
Elegance Printing & Book Binding (USA), pg 1206
Express Media Corp, pg 1206
Hamilton Printing Co, pg 1206
Hindy's Enterprise, pg 1207
Imago, pg 1207
KNI Inc, pg 1207
Lenz & Riecker Inc, pg 1207
Linick International Inc, pg 1207
LK Litho, pg 1207
Marrakech Express Inc, pg 1207
Palace Press International, pg 1208
Printing Corp of the Americas Inc, pg 1208
Times Publishing Group, pg 1208
Vicks Lithograph & Printing Corp, pg 1208
Fred Weidner & Daughter Printers, pg 1208

BOOK PRINTING - SOFTBOUND

Australia
Southwood Press Pty Ltd, pg 1193

Belgium
Drukkerij Lannoo NV, pg 1193

Canada
Coach House Printing, pg 1193
Maracle Press Ltd, pg 1193
Preney Print & Litho Inc, pg 1193
Printcrafters Inc, pg 1193
Productive Publications, pg 1193
Transcontinental Printing Book Group, pg 1194
Tri-Graphic Printing (Ottawa) Ltd, pg 1194
University of Toronto Press Inc, pg 1194
Webcom Ltd, pg 1194

China
Speedflex Asia Ltd, pg 1194

Czech Republic
GRASPO CZ AS - Druckerei und Buchbinderei, pg 1194

Denmark
Bianco Lunos Bogtrykkeri AS, pg 1194

Finland
Gummerus Printing, pg 1194
WS Bookwell Ltd, pg 1194

France
Imprimerie Bene, pg 1194
Plein Chant, pg 1194
Signes du Monde, pg 1194

Germany
C Maurer Druck und Verlag, pg 1195
Mohndruck Graphische Betriebe GmbH, pg 1195
Priese GmbH, pg 1195
Vier-Tuerme GmbH Benedikt Press, pg 1195

Hong Kong
Best-Set Typesetter Ltd, pg 1195
Bookbuilders Ltd, pg 1195
Bright Future Printing Co Ltd, pg 1195
C & C Offset Printing Co Ltd, pg 1195
Caritas Printing Training Centre, pg 1195
Colorprint Offset, pg 1195
Dai Nippon Printing Co (Hong Kong) Ltd, pg 1196
Golden Cup Printing Co Ltd, pg 1196
The Green Pagoda Press Ltd, pg 1196
Hoi Kwong Printing Co Ltd, pg 1196
Hung Hing Off-set Printing Co Ltd, pg 1196
Image Printing Company Ltd, pg 1196
Leo Paper Products Ltd, pg 1196
Midas Printing Ltd, pg 1197
Morris Press Ltd, pg 1197
Paper Art Product Ltd, pg 1197

Paper Communication Printing Express Ltd, pg 1197
Paramount Publishing Group Limited, pg 1197
Prontaprint Asia Ltd, pg 1197
Sheck Wah Tong Printing Press, pg 1197
Sing Cheong Printing Co Limited, pg 1197
Sino Publishing House Ltd, pg 1197
South Sea International Press Ltd, pg 1197
Sunshine Press Ltd, pg 1197
Toppan Printing Co (HK) Ltd, pg 1197
Unicorn International Printing Co Ltd, pg 1197

Hungary
Interpress Aussenhandels GmbH, pg 1197
Kultura, pg 1197

Indonesia
Ichtiar Baru I Van Hoeve, pg 1198
Victory Offset Prima PT, pg 1198

Israel
Keterpress Enterprises Jerusalem, pg 1198
Monoline Ltd, pg 1198
Technosdar Ltd, pg 1198

Italy
Canale G e C SpA, pg 1198
Dedalo Litostampa SRL, pg 1198
Milanostampa SPA, pg 1198
Amilcare Pizzi SpA, pg 1198

Republic of Korea
Daehan Printing & Publishing Co Ltd, pg 1199
Pyunghwa Dang Printing Co Ltd, pg 1199

Lithuania
Spindulys Printing House, pg 1199

Madagascar
Societe Malgache d'Edition, pg 1199

Malaysia
Web Printers Sdn Bhd, pg 1199

Malta
Interprint Ltd - Malta, pg 1199

Netherlands
Koninklijke Wohrmann Bv, pg 1199

New Zealand
Bookprint Consultants Ltd, pg 1199
John McIndoe Ltd, pg 1199
PPP Printers Ltd, pg 1199

Philippines
Cacho Hermanos Inc, pg 1199
Philippine Graphic Arts Inc, pg 1199

Portugal
Printer Portuguesa Industria Grafica Lda, pg 1199

MANUFACTURING

PRINTING, BINDING & BOOK FINISHING INDEX

Singapore
Chong Moh Offset Printing Ltd, pg 1200
Craft Print Pte Ltd, pg 1200
CS Graphics Pte Ltd, pg 1200
Eurasia Press Pte Ltd, pg 1200
Ho Printing Singapore Pte Ltd, pg 1200
International Press Co Pte Ltd, pg 1200
Markono Print Media Pte Ltd, pg 1200
SNP Printing Pte Ltd, pg 1200
Stamford Press Pte Ltd, pg 1200
Tien Wah Press Pte Ltd, pg 1200
Times Printers Pte Ltd, pg 1200
Toppan Company (S) Pte Ltd, pg 1200
World Publications Printers Pte Ltd, pg 1201

Slovenia
Gorenjski Tisk Printing Co, pg 1201

Spain
Grafos SA Arte Sobre Papel, pg 1201
Printer Industria Grafica SA, pg 1201
Rotedic SA, pg 1201
Graficas Santamaria SA, pg 1201
Luis Vives (Edelvives), pg 1201

Sri Lanka
Sumathi Book Printing (Pvt) Ltd, pg 1201

Switzerland
Hallwag AG, pg 1201
Photolitho AG, pg 1201

United Republic of Tanzania
Peramiho Publications, pg 1201

Thailand
Mavisu International Co Ltd, pg 1201
Phongwarin Printing Company Ltd, pg 1201

United Arab Emirates
Emirates Printing Press (LLC), pg 1202

United Kingdom
J W Arrowsmith Ltd, pg 1202
BAS Printers Ltd, pg 1202
Bell & Bain Ltd, pg 1202
Biddles Ltd, pg 1202
Book Creation Services, pg 1202
Caledonian International Book Manufacturing, pg 1202
Clays Ltd, pg 1203
William Clowes Ltd, pg 1203
Cox & Wyman Ltd, pg 1203
Cradley Print Ltd, pg 1203
Goldshield Communications Ltd, pg 1203
The Guernsey Press Co Ltd, pg 1203
Headley Brothers Ltd, pg 1203
Hobbs The Printers Ltd, pg 1203
Intype London Ltd, pg 1204
Charles Letts & Co Ltd, pg 1204
Lowfield Printing Co Ltd, pg 1204
MacKays of Chatham PLC, pg 1204
MPG Books Ltd, pg 1204
George Over Ltd, pg 1204
Page Bros Ltd (Norwich), pg 1204
Redwood Books Ltd, pg 1204
Antony Rowe Ltd, pg 1204
Severnside Printers Ltd, pg 1204
TJ International Ltd, pg 1205
Watkiss Automation Ltd, pg 1205

United States
ADR/BookPrint, pg 1205
Asia Pacific Offset Inc, pg 1205
Blaze International Productions Inc, pg 1205
BookBuilders New York Ltd, pg 1205
C & C Offset Printing Co Ltd, pg 1205
Carvajal International Inc, pg 1206
Colorprint Offset Inc, pg 1206
Coneco Litho Graphics, pg 1206
Consolidated Printers Inc, pg 1206
Martin Cook Associates Ltd, pg 1206
CS Graphics USA Inc, pg 1206
DNP America LLC, pg 1206
Editoriale Bortolazzi-Stei srl, pg 1206
Elegance Printing & Book Binding (USA), pg 1206
Express Media Corp, pg 1206
Hamilton Printing Co, pg 1206
Hindy's Enterprise, pg 1207
Imago, pg 1207
Integrated Book Technology Inc, pg 1207
Jinno International Group, pg 1207
KNI Inc, pg 1207
Lenz & Riecker Inc, pg 1207
Leo Paper USA, pg 1207
LK Litho, pg 1207
Marrakech Express Inc, pg 1207
Milanostampa/New Interlitho USA Inc, pg 1208
Palace Press International, pg 1208
Printing Corp of the Americas Inc, pg 1208
Regent Publishing Services, pg 1208
Times Publishing Group, pg 1208
Vicks Lithograph & Printing Corp, pg 1208
Fred Weidner & Daughter Printers, pg 1208

Uruguay
Barreiro y Ramos SA, pg 1208

BOUND GALLEYS

Germany
Priese GmbH, pg 1195

Hong Kong
Caritas Printing Training Centre, pg 1195
Morris Press Ltd, pg 1197
Paramount Publishing Group Limited, pg 1197
Prontaprint Asia Ltd, pg 1197
Unicorn International Printing Co Ltd, pg 1197

New Zealand
Bookprint Consultants Ltd, pg 1199

Singapore
Markono Print Media Pte Ltd, pg 1200
SNP Printing Pte Ltd, pg 1200
Toppan Company (S) Pte Ltd, pg 1200
World Publications Printers Pte Ltd, pg 1201

United Republic of Tanzania
Peramiho Publications, pg 1201

United Kingdom
Redwood Books Ltd, pg 1204

United States
Asia Pacific Offset Inc, pg 1205
Coneco Litho Graphics, pg 1206
Express Media Corp, pg 1206
Integrated Book Technology Inc, pg 1207
Jinno International Group, pg 1207
Leo Paper USA, pg 1207
Linick International Inc, pg 1207
LK Litho, pg 1207
Fred Weidner & Daughter Printers, pg 1208

BURST BINDING

Australia
Southwood Press Pty Ltd, pg 1193

Canada
Tri-Graphic Printing (Ottawa) Ltd, pg 1194
Webcom Ltd, pg 1194

Germany
Priese GmbH, pg 1195

Hong Kong
Caritas Printing Training Centre, pg 1195
Everbest Printing Co Ltd, pg 1196
Golden Cup Printing Co Ltd, pg 1196
Midas Printing Ltd, pg 1197
Morris Press Ltd, pg 1197
Sheck Wah Tong Printing Press, pg 1197
Sing Cheong Printing Co Limited, pg 1197
Unicorn International Printing Co Ltd, pg 1197

Italy
Canale G e C SpA, pg 1198

New Zealand
Bookprint Consultants Ltd, pg 1199
John McIndoe Ltd, pg 1199

Singapore
Chong Moh Offset Printing Ltd, pg 1200
Toppan Company (S) Pte Ltd, pg 1200
World Publications Printers Pte Ltd, pg 1201

United Republic of Tanzania
Peramiho Publications, pg 1201

United Kingdom
Bell & Bain Ltd, pg 1202
Caledonian International Book Manufacturing, pg 1202
Center Print Ltd, pg 1202
Hammond Bindery Ltd, pg 1203
Hobbs The Printers Ltd, pg 1203
Lowfield Printing Co Ltd, pg 1204
MPG Books Ltd, pg 1204
Page Bros Ltd (Norwich), pg 1204
Redwood Books Ltd, pg 1204
TJ International Ltd, pg 1205
WH Trade Binders Ltd, pg 1205

United States
Asia Pacific Offset Inc, pg 1205
Blaze International Productions Inc, pg 1205
BookBuilders New York Ltd, pg 1205
Martin Cook Associates Ltd, pg 1206
Hamilton Printing Co, pg 1206
Integrated Book Technology Inc, pg 1207
Jinno International Group, pg 1207
Linick International Inc, pg 1207
Regent Publishing Services, pg 1208
Fred Weidner & Daughter Printers, pg 1208

CALENDAR PRINTING

Belgium
Drukkerij Lannoo NV, pg 1193

Canada
Herzig Somerville Ltd, pg 1193
McLaren Morris & Todd Ltd, pg 1193
Printcrafters Inc, pg 1193
Transcontinental Printing Book Group, pg 1194
University of Toronto Press Inc, pg 1194
Webcom Ltd, pg 1194

China
Speedflex Asia Ltd, pg 1194

Czech Republic
GRASPO CZ AS - Druckerei und Buchbinderei, pg 1194

Germany
Fachhochschule Fur Druk, Studiengang Verlagswirtschaft und Verlagsherstellung, pg 1195
C Maurer Druck und Verlag, pg 1195
Mohndruck Graphische Betriebe GmbH, pg 1195
Priese GmbH, pg 1195
Vier-Tuerme GmbH Benedikt Press, pg 1195

Hong Kong
Best-Set Typesetter Ltd, pg 1195
Bright Future Printing Co Ltd, pg 1195
C & C Offset Printing Co Ltd, pg 1195
Colorprint Offset, pg 1195
Dai Nippon Printing Co (Hong Kong) Ltd, pg 1196
Everbest Printing Co Ltd, pg 1196
Golden Cup Printing Co Ltd, pg 1196
The Green Pagoda Press Ltd, pg 1196
Hindy's Enterprise Co Ltd, pg 1196
Hoi Kwong Printing Co Ltd, pg 1196
Hung Hing Off-set Printing Co Ltd, pg 1196

PRINTING, BINDING & BOOK FINISHING INDEX

Image Printing Company Ltd, pg 1196
Midas Printing Ltd, pg 1197
Morris Press Ltd, pg 1197
Paper Art Product Ltd, pg 1197
Paper Communication Printing Express Ltd, pg 1197
Paramount Publishing Group Limited, pg 1197
Prontaprint Asia Ltd, pg 1197
Sheck Wah Tong Printing Press, pg 1197
Sing Cheong Printing Co Limited, pg 1197
Sino Publishing House Ltd, pg 1197
South Sea International Press Ltd, pg 1197
Sunshine Press Ltd, pg 1197
Toppan Printing Co (HK) Ltd, pg 1197
Unicorn International Printing Co Ltd, pg 1197
Wing King Tong Co Ltd (Printing Factory), pg 1197

Hungary
Interpress Aussenhandels GmbH, pg 1197

Indonesia
Victory Offset Prima PT, pg 1198

Ireland
Ultragraphics, pg 1198

Israel
Technosdar Ltd, pg 1198

Italy
Canale G e C SpA, pg 1198
Mariani Ritti Grafiche SRL, pg 1198
Amilcare Pizzi SpA, pg 1198

Republic of Korea
Daehan Printing & Publishing Co Ltd, pg 1199
Pyunghwa Dang Printing Co Ltd, pg 1199

Lithuania
Spindulys Printing House, pg 1199

New Zealand
Bookprint Consultants Ltd, pg 1199
John McIndoe Ltd, pg 1199
PPP Printers Ltd, pg 1199

Peru
Industrias del Envase SA, pg 1199

Philippines
Cacho Hermanos Inc, pg 1199

Singapore
Columbia Overseas Marketing Pte Ltd, pg 1200
CS Graphics Pte Ltd, pg 1200
Eurasia Press Pte Ltd, pg 1200
Ho Printing Singapore Pte Ltd, pg 1200
International Press Co Pte Ltd, pg 1200
SNP Printing Pte Ltd, pg 1200
Toppan Company (S) Pte Ltd, pg 1200
World Publications Printers Pte Ltd, pg 1201

Slovenia
Gorenjski Tisk Printing Co, pg 1201

Spain
Grafos SA Arte Sobre Papel, pg 1201
Graficas Santamaria SA, pg 1201
Luis Vives (Edelvives), pg 1201

Sri Lanka
Sumathi Book Printing (Pvt) Ltd, pg 1201

United Republic of Tanzania
Peramiho Publications, pg 1201

Thailand
J Film Process Co Ltd, pg 1201
Mavisu International Co Ltd, pg 1201
Phongwarin Printing Company Ltd, pg 1201

United Arab Emirates
Emirates Printing Press (LLC), pg 1202

United Kingdom
Center Print Ltd, pg 1202
William Clowes Ltd, pg 1203
Cradley Print Ltd, pg 1203
Essex Colour Services Ltd, pg 1203
The Guernsey Press Co Ltd, pg 1203
Headley Brothers Ltd, pg 1203
Image & Print Group Ltd, pg 1203
The Malvern Press Ltd, pg 1204
Redwood Books Ltd, pg 1204
J R Reid Printing Group Ltd, pg 1204
Severnside Printers Ltd, pg 1204

United States
Asia Pacific Offset Inc, pg 1205
Blaze International Productions Inc, pg 1205
BookBuilders New York Ltd, pg 1205
C & C Offset Printing Co Ltd, pg 1205
Carvajal International Inc, pg 1206
Colorprint Offset Inc, pg 1206
Coneco Litho Graphics, pg 1206
Martin Cook Associates Ltd, pg 1206
CS Graphics USA Inc, pg 1206
DNP America LLC, pg 1206
Editoriale Bortolazzi-Stei srl, pg 1206
Elegance Printing & Book Binding (USA), pg 1206
Hindy's Enterprise, pg 1207
Imago, pg 1207
Jinno International Group, pg 1207
KNI Inc, pg 1207
Leo Paper USA, pg 1207
Linick International Inc, pg 1207
Milanostampa/New Interlitho USA Inc, pg 1208
Palace Press International, pg 1208
Printing Corp of the Americas Inc, pg 1208
Regent Publishing Services, pg 1208
Times Publishing Group, pg 1208
Fred Weidner & Daughter Printers, pg 1208

Uruguay
Barreiro y Ramos SA, pg 1208

CASEBINDING

Belgium
Drukkerij Lannoo NV, pg 1193

Canada
Appleby's Bindery Ltd, pg 1193
Coach House Printing, pg 1193
Printcrafters Inc, pg 1193
Transcontinental Printing Book Group, pg 1194
Tri-Graphic Printing (Ottawa) Ltd, pg 1194
University of Toronto Press Inc, pg 1194

Czech Republic
GRASPO CZ AS - Druckerei und Buchbinderei, pg 1194

Denmark
Bianco Lunos Bogtrykkeri AS, pg 1194

Finland
Gummerus Printing, pg 1194

Germany
Mohndruck Graphische Betriebe GmbH, pg 1195
Priese GmbH, pg 1195

Hong Kong
Bright Future Printing Co Ltd, pg 1195
C & C Offset Printing Co Ltd, pg 1195
Caritas Printing Training Centre, pg 1195
Colorprint Offset, pg 1195
Dai Nippon Printing Co (Hong Kong) Ltd, pg 1196
Golden Cup Printing Co Ltd, pg 1196
Hung Hing Off-set Printing Co Ltd, pg 1196
Image Printing Company Ltd, pg 1196
Leo Paper Products Ltd, pg 1196
Liang Yu Printing Factory Ltd, pg 1196
Midas Printing Ltd, pg 1197
Morris Press Ltd, pg 1197
Paper Communication Printing Express Ltd, pg 1197
Paramount Publishing Group Limited, pg 1197
Prontaprint Asia Ltd, pg 1197
Sing Cheong Printing Co Limited, pg 1197
Sino Publishing House Ltd, pg 1197
Toppan Printing Co (HK) Ltd, pg 1197
Unicorn International Printing Co Ltd, pg 1197
Wing King Tong Co Ltd (Printing Factory), pg 1197

India
Hiralal Printing Works Ltd, pg 1197

Indonesia
Ichtiar Baru I Van Hoeve, pg 1198
Victory Offset Prima PT, pg 1198

Ireland
Smurfit Print, pg 1198

Israel
Keterpress Enterprises Jerusalem, pg 1198

Italy
Canale G e C SpA, pg 1198
Milanostampa SPA, pg 1198

Republic of Korea
Pyunghwa Dang Printing Co Ltd, pg 1199

Malta
Interprint Ltd - Malta, pg 1199

New Zealand
Bookprint Consultants Ltd, pg 1199
John McIndoe Ltd, pg 1199

Philippines
Cacho Hermanos Inc, pg 1199

Singapore
CS Graphics Pte Ltd, pg 1200
Eurasia Press Pte Ltd, pg 1200
Fong & Sons Printers Pte Ltd, pg 1200
Ho Printing Singapore Pte Ltd, pg 1200
International Press Co Pte Ltd, pg 1200
Kyodo Printing Co (S'pore) Pte Ltd, pg 1200
Markono Print Media Pte Ltd, pg 1200
SNP Printing Pte Ltd, pg 1200
Tien Wah Press Pte Ltd, pg 1200
Toppan Company (S) Pte Ltd, pg 1200
World Publications Printers Pte Ltd, pg 1201

Slovenia
Gorenjski Tisk Printing Co, pg 1201

Spain
Grafos SA Arte Sobre Papel, pg 1201
Graficas Santamaria SA, pg 1201

United Republic of Tanzania
Peramiho Publications, pg 1201

United Arab Emirates
Emirates Printing Press (LLC), pg 1202

United Kingdom
The Alden Group Ltd, pg 1202
BAS Printers Ltd, pg 1202
Biddles Ltd, pg 1202
Book Creation Services, pg 1202
J W Braithwaite & Son Ltd, pg 1202
Butler & Tanner Ltd, pg 1202
Caledonian International Book Manufacturing, pg 1202
Cambridge University Press - Printing Division, pg 1202
CB Print Finishers Ltd, pg 1202
Center Print Ltd, pg 1202
The Charlesworth Group, pg 1202
Cedric Chivers Ltd, pg 1203
Clays Ltd, pg 1203

MANUFACTURING

PRINTING, BINDING & BOOK FINISHING INDEX

William Clowes Ltd, pg 1203
Eagle Press, pg 1203
Goldshield Communications Ltd, pg 1203
Green Street Bindery, pg 1203
Hammond Bindery Ltd, pg 1203
Hammond Packaging Ltd, pg 1203
Headley Brothers Ltd, pg 1203
Hunter & Foulis Ltd, pg 1203
Ikon Document Services Ltd, pg 1203
Intype London Ltd, pg 1204
Charles Letts & Co Ltd, pg 1204
MacKays of Chatham PLC, pg 1204
Martins Printing Group Ltd, pg 1204
MPG Books Ltd, pg 1204
Page Bros Ltd (Norwich), pg 1204
Redwood Books Ltd, pg 1204
Antony Rowe Ltd, pg 1204
TJ International Ltd, pg 1205

United States
Asia Pacific Offset Inc, pg 1205
Blaze International Productions Inc, pg 1205
BookBuilders New York Ltd, pg 1205
Butler & Tanner Inc, pg 1205
C & C Offset Printing Co Ltd, pg 1205
Colorprint Offset Inc, pg 1206
Coneco Litho Graphics, pg 1206
Martin Cook Associates Ltd, pg 1206
CS Graphics USA Inc, pg 1206
DNP America LLC, pg 1206
Editoriale Bortolazzi-Stei srl, pg 1206
Elegance Printing & Book Binding (USA), pg 1206
Express Media Corp, pg 1206
Hamilton Printing Co, pg 1206
Imago, pg 1207
Integrated Book Technology Inc, pg 1207
Jinno International Group, pg 1207
Leo Paper USA, pg 1207
Linick International Inc, pg 1207
Milanostampa/New Interlitho USA Inc, pg 1208
Palace Press International, pg 1208
Printing Corp of the Americas Inc, pg 1208
Regent Publishing Services, pg 1208
Taylor Publishing Co, pg 1208
Times Publishing Group, pg 1208
Fred Weidner & Daughter Printers, pg 1208

Uruguay
Barreiro y Ramos SA, pg 1208

CATALOG PRiNTING

Belgium
Drukkerij Lannoo NV, pg 1193
IMPF BV BA, pg 1193

Canada
Herzig Somerville Ltd, pg 1193
Maracle Press Ltd, pg 1193
McLaren Morris & Todd Ltd, pg 1193
Preney Print & Litho Inc, pg 1193
Printcrafters Inc, pg 1193
Transcontinental Printing Book Group, pg 1194
University of Toronto Press Inc, pg 1194
Webcom Ltd, pg 1194

China
Speedflex Asia Ltd, pg 1194

Czech Republic
GRASPO CZ AS - Druckerei und Buchbinderei, pg 1194

Denmark
Bianco Lunos Bogtrykkeri AS, pg 1194

Finland
WS Bookwell Ltd, pg 1194

France
Imprimerie Gaignault, pg 1194

Germany
C L Baader Buch & Offsetdruckere GmbH & Co KG, pg 1194
Fachhochschule Fur Druk, Studiengang Verlagswirtschaft und Verlagsherstellung, pg 1195
C Maurer Druck und Verlag, pg 1195
Media-Print Informationstechnologie GmbH, pg 1195
Mohndruck Graphische Betriebe GmbH, pg 1195
Priese GmbH, pg 1195
Vier-Tuerme GmbH Benedikt Press, pg 1195

Hong Kong
Bright Future Printing Co Ltd, pg 1195
C & C Offset Printing Co Ltd, pg 1195
Colorprint Offset, pg 1195
Dai Nippon Printing Co (Hong Kong) Ltd, pg 1196
Golden Cup Printing Co Ltd, pg 1196
The Green Pagoda Press Ltd, pg 1196
Hoi Kwong Printing Co Ltd, pg 1196
Hung Hing Off-set Printing Co Ltd, pg 1196
Image Printing Company Ltd, pg 1196
Midas Printing Ltd, pg 1197
Morris Press Ltd, pg 1197
Paper Art Product Ltd, pg 1197
Paper Communication Printing Express Ltd, pg 1197
Paramount Publishing Group Limited, pg 1197
Prontaprint Asia Ltd, pg 1197
Sheck Wah Tong Printing Press, pg 1197
Sing Cheong Printing Co Limited, pg 1197
Sino Publishing House Ltd, pg 1197
South Sea International Press Ltd, pg 1197
Sunshine Press Ltd, pg 1197
Toppan Printing Co (HK) Ltd, pg 1197
Unicorn International Printing Co Ltd, pg 1197
Wing King Tong Co Ltd (Printing Factory), pg 1197

Hungary
Interpress Aussenhandels GmbH, pg 1197

India
Hiralal Printing Works Ltd, pg 1197

Indonesia
Victory Offset Prima PT, pg 1198

Ireland
Kilkenny People/Wellbrook Press, pg 1198
Smurfit Print, pg 1198
Ultragraphics, pg 1198

Israel
Keterpress Enterprises Jerusalem, pg 1198
Technosdar Ltd, pg 1198

Italy
Canale G e C SpA, pg 1198
Dedalo Litostampa SRL, pg 1198
Mariani Ritti Grafiche SRL, pg 1198
Milanostampa SPA, pg 1198
Amilcare Pizzi SpA, pg 1198

Republic of Korea
Daehan Printing & Publishing Co Ltd, pg 1199
Pyunghwa Dang Printing Co Ltd, pg 1199

Lithuania
Spindulys Printing House, pg 1199

New Zealand
Bookprint Consultants Ltd, pg 1199
John McIndoe Ltd, pg 1199
PPP Printers Ltd, pg 1199

Peru
Industrias del Envase SA, pg 1199

Singapore
Chong Moh Offset Printing Ltd, pg 1200
Columbia Overseas Marketing Pte Ltd, pg 1200
CS Graphics Pte Ltd, pg 1200
Eurasia Press Pte Ltd, pg 1200
Ho Printing Singapore Pte Ltd, pg 1200
International Press Co Pte Ltd, pg 1200
PacPress Media Pte Ltd, pg 1200
SNP Printing Pte Ltd, pg 1200
Times Printers Pte Ltd, pg 1200
Toppan Company (S) Pte Ltd, pg 1200
World Publications Printers Pte Ltd, pg 1201

Slovenia
Gorenjski Tisk Printing Co, pg 1201

Spain
Eurohueco SA, pg 1201
Grafos SA Arte Sobre Papel, pg 1201
Printer Industria Grafica SA, pg 1201
Graficas Santamaria SA, pg 1201
Luis Vives (Edelvives), pg 1201

Switzerland
Hallwag AG, pg 1201

Thailand
J Film Process Co Ltd, pg 1201
Mavisu International Co Ltd, pg 1201
Phongwarin Printing Company Ltd, pg 1201

United Kingdom
J W Arrowsmith Ltd, pg 1202
BAS Printers Ltd, pg 1202
Bemrose Security & Promotional Printing, pg 1202
Biddles Ltd, pg 1202
Black Bear Press Ltd, pg 1202
Blackmore Ltd, pg 1202
William Clowes Ltd, pg 1203
Cradley Print Ltd, pg 1203
Essex Colour Services Ltd, pg 1203
Goldshield Communications Ltd, pg 1203
The Guernsey Press Co Ltd, pg 1203
Hastings Publishing Co, pg 1203
Headley Brothers Ltd, pg 1203
Hobbs The Printers Ltd, pg 1203
Ikon Document Services Ltd, pg 1203
Image & Print Group Ltd, pg 1203
Lavenham Press Ltd, pg 1204
The Malvern Press Ltd, pg 1204
Martins Printing Group Ltd, pg 1204
Multiplex Medway Ltd, pg 1204
Redwood Books Ltd, pg 1204
J R Reid Printing Group Ltd, pg 1204
Stott Brothers Ltd, pg 1204
Watkiss Automation Ltd, pg 1205
The Wolsey Press, pg 1205

United States
ADR/BookPrint, pg 1205
Asia Pacific Offset Inc, pg 1205
BookBuilders New York Ltd, pg 1205
Butler & Tanner Inc, pg 1205
C & C Offset Printing Co Ltd, pg 1205
Carvajal International Inc, pg 1206
Colorprint Offset Inc, pg 1206
Coneco Litho Graphics, pg 1206
Consolidated Printers Inc, pg 1206
Martin Cook Associates Ltd, pg 1206
CS Graphics USA Inc, pg 1206
DNP America LLC, pg 1206
Elegance Printing & Book Binding (USA), pg 1206
Express Media Corp, pg 1206
Fairfield Marketing Group Inc, pg 1206
Hamilton Printing Co, pg 1206
Hindy's Enterprise, pg 1207
Imago, pg 1207
Jinno International Group, pg 1207
KNI Inc, pg 1207
Lenz & Riecker Inc, pg 1207
Leo Paper USA, pg 1207
Linick International Inc, pg 1207
LK Litho, pg 1207
Marrakech Express Inc, pg 1207
Palace Press International, pg 1208
Printing Corp of the Americas Inc, pg 1208
Regent Publishing Services, pg 1208
Times Publishing Group, pg 1208
Fred Weidner & Daughter Printers, pg 1208

PRINTING, BINDING & BOOK FINISHING INDEX

Uruguay
Barreiro y Ramos SA, pg 1208

COMIC BOOK PRINTING

Belgium
Drukkerij Lannoo NV, pg 1193

Canada
Preney Print & Litho Inc, pg 1193
Transcontinental Printing Book Group, pg 1194

Czech Republic
GRASPO CZ AS - Druckerei und Buchbinderei, pg 1194

Germany
Mohndruck Graphische Betriebe GmbH, pg 1195
Priese GmbH, pg 1195

Hong Kong
Dai Nippon Printing Co (Hong Kong) Ltd, pg 1196
Hoi Kwong Printing Co Ltd, pg 1196
Image Printing Company Ltd, pg 1196
Midas Printing Ltd, pg 1197
Paramount Publishing Group Limited, pg 1197
Sing Cheong Printing Co Limited, pg 1197
Sino Publishing House Ltd, pg 1197
Toppan Printing Co (HK) Ltd, pg 1197
Unicorn International Printing Co Ltd, pg 1197

Hungary
Interpress Aussenhandels GmbH, pg 1197

Italy
Canale G e C SpA, pg 1198

Republic of Korea
Daehan Printing & Publishing Co Ltd, pg 1199
Pyunghwa Dang Printing Co Ltd, pg 1199

New Zealand
Bookprint Consultants Ltd, pg 1199

Philippines
Cacho Hermanos Inc, pg 1199

Singapore
SNP Printing Pte Ltd, pg 1200
Times Printers Pte Ltd, pg 1200
Toppan Company (S) Pte Ltd, pg 1200

Slovenia
Gorenjski Tisk Printing Co, pg 1201

Spain
Graficas Santamaria SA, pg 1201
Luis Vives (Edelvives), pg 1201

United Republic of Tanzania
Peramiho Publications, pg 1201

Thailand
J Film Process Co Ltd, pg 1201
Mavisu International Co Ltd, pg 1201

United Kingdom
The Guernsey Press Co Ltd, pg 1203
Redwood Books Ltd, pg 1204
Severnside Printers Ltd, pg 1204

United States
Asia Pacific Offset Inc, pg 1205
C & C Offset Printing Co Ltd, pg 1205
DNP America LLC, pg 1206
Jinno International Group, pg 1207
Linick International Inc, pg 1207
Marrakech Express Inc, pg 1207
Palace Press International, pg 1208
Fred Weidner & Daughter Printers, pg 1208

Uruguay
Barreiro y Ramos SA, pg 1208

DIE-CUTTING

Belgium
Drukkerij Lannoo NV, pg 1193

Canada
Transcontinental Printing Book Group, pg 1194
University of Toronto Press Inc, pg 1194

China
Speedflex Asia Ltd, pg 1194

France
Signes du Monde, pg 1194

Germany
Priese GmbH, pg 1195

Hong Kong
Caritas Printing Training Centre, pg 1195
Colorprint Offset, pg 1195
Dai Nippon Printing Co (Hong Kong) Ltd, pg 1196
Everbest Printing Co Ltd, pg 1196
Golden Cup Printing Co Ltd, pg 1196
The Green Pagoda Press Ltd, pg 1196
Hung Hing Off-set Printing Co Ltd, pg 1196
Image Printing Company Ltd, pg 1196
Leo Paper Products Ltd, pg 1196
Midas Printing Ltd, pg 1197
Paper Art Product Ltd, pg 1197
Paramount Publishing Group Limited, pg 1197
Prontaprint Asia Ltd, pg 1197
Sing Cheong Printing Co Limited, pg 1197
Sino Publishing House Ltd, pg 1197
South Sea International Press Ltd, pg 1197
Unicorn International Printing Co Ltd, pg 1197
Wing King Tong Co Ltd (Printing Factory), pg 1197

Indonesia
Victory Offset Prima PT, pg 1198

Ireland
Smurfit Print, pg 1198

Israel
Technosdar Ltd, pg 1198

Italy
Canale G e C SpA, pg 1198
Dedalo Litostampa SRL, pg 1198
Amilcare Pizzi SpA, pg 1198

Republic of Korea
Daehan Printing & Publishing Co Ltd, pg 1199
Pyunghwa Dang Printing Co Ltd, pg 1199

Lithuania
Spindulys Printing House, pg 1199

New Zealand
Bookprint Consultants Ltd, pg 1199
John McIndoe Ltd, pg 1199

Singapore
Columbia Overseas Marketing Pte Ltd, pg 1200
Eurasia Press Pte Ltd, pg 1200
Ho Printing Singapore Pte Ltd, pg 1200
International Press Co Pte Ltd, pg 1200
Markono Print Media Pte Ltd, pg 1200
SNP Printing Pte Ltd, pg 1200
Stamford Press Pte Ltd, pg 1200
Toppan Company (S) Pte Ltd, pg 1200
World Publications Printers Pte Ltd, pg 1201

Spain
Grafos SA Arte Sobre Papel, pg 1201

United Republic of Tanzania
Peramiho Publications, pg 1201

Thailand
J Film Process Co Ltd, pg 1201
Mavisu International Co Ltd, pg 1201

United Arab Emirates
Emirates Printing Press (LLC), pg 1202

United Kingdom
J W Braithwaite & Son Ltd, pg 1202
Center Print Ltd, pg 1202
The Guernsey Press Co Ltd, pg 1203
Harveys Ltd, pg 1203
Image & Print Group Ltd, pg 1203
The Malvern Press Ltd, pg 1204

United States
Asia Pacific Offset Inc, pg 1205
BookBuilders New York Ltd, pg 1205
C & C Offset Printing Co Ltd, pg 1205
Colorprint Offset Inc, pg 1206
Coneco Litho Graphics, pg 1206
Martin Cook Associates Ltd, pg 1206
DNP America LLC, pg 1206
Elegance Printing & Book Binding (USA), pg 1206
Fairfield Marketing Group Inc, pg 1206
Hindy's Enterprise, pg 1207
Imago, pg 1207
Jinno International Group, pg 1207
Leo Paper USA, pg 1207
Linick International Inc, pg 1207
LK Litho, pg 1207
Milanostampa/New Interlitho USA Inc, pg 1208
Palace Press International, pg 1208
Regent Publishing Services, pg 1208
Fred Weidner & Daughter Printers, pg 1208

EDITION (HARDCOVER) BINDING

Belgium
Drukkerij Lannoo NV, pg 1193

Canada
Aardvark Enterprises, pg 1193
Appleby's Bindery Ltd, pg 1193
Transcontinental Printing Book Group, pg 1194

Czech Republic
GRASPO CZ AS - Druckerei und Buchbinderei, pg 1194

Denmark
Bianco Lunos Bogtrykkeri AS, pg 1194

France
Signes du Monde, pg 1194

Germany
Mohndruck Graphische Betriebe GmbH, pg 1195
Priese GmbH, pg 1195

Hong Kong
Best-Set Typesetter Ltd, pg 1195
Bright Future Printing Co Ltd, pg 1195
Colorprint Offset, pg 1195
Dai Nippon Printing Co (Hong Kong) Ltd, pg 1196
Everbest Printing Co Ltd, pg 1196
Golden Cup Printing Co Ltd, pg 1196
Image Printing Company Ltd, pg 1196
Midas Printing Ltd, pg 1197
Paramount Publishing Group Limited, pg 1197
Prontaprint Asia Ltd, pg 1197
Sing Cheong Printing Co Limited, pg 1197
Sino Publishing House Ltd, pg 1197

MANUFACTURING
PRINTING, BINDING & BOOK FINISHING INDEX

South Sea International Press Ltd, pg 1197
Unicorn International Printing Co Ltd, pg 1197

Indonesia
Victory Offset Prima PT, pg 1198

Israel
Har-El Printers & Publishers, pg 1198
Keterpress Enterprises Jerusalem, pg 1198
Technosdar Ltd, pg 1198

Italy
Canale G e C SpA, pg 1198
Milanostampa SPA, pg 1198
Minerva Medica, pg 1198

Republic of Korea
Pyunghwa Dang Printing Co Ltd, pg 1199

Lithuania
Spindulys Printing House, pg 1199

New Zealand
Bookprint Consultants Ltd, pg 1199
John McIndoe Ltd, pg 1199

Philippines
Cacho Hermanos Inc, pg 1199

Singapore
CS Graphics Pte Ltd, pg 1200
Eurasia Press Pte Ltd, pg 1200
Ho Printing Singapore Pte Ltd, pg 1200
International Press Co Pte Ltd, pg 1200
Markono Print Media Pte Ltd, pg 1200
SNP Printing Pte Ltd, pg 1200
Toppan Company (S) Pte Ltd, pg 1200
World Publications Printers Pte Ltd, pg 1201

Slovenia
Gorenjski Tisk Printing Co, pg 1201

Spain
Grafos SA Arte Sobre Papel, pg 1201
Luis Vives (Edelvives), pg 1201

United Republic of Tanzania
Peramiho Publications, pg 1201

Thailand
J Film Process Co Ltd, pg 1201

United Kingdom
Book Creation Services, pg 1202
Caledonian International Book Manufacturing, pg 1202
Center Print Ltd, pg 1202
Cedric Chivers Ltd, pg 1203
Clays Ltd, pg 1203
William Clowes Ltd, pg 1203
Charles Letts & Co Ltd, pg 1204
MPG Books Ltd, pg 1204
Redwood Books Ltd, pg 1204
TJ International Ltd, pg 1205

United States
Asia Pacific Offset Inc, pg 1205
Blaze International Productions Inc, pg 1205
BookBuilders New York Ltd, pg 1205
Butler & Tanner Inc, pg 1205
C & C Offset Printing Co Ltd, pg 1205
Colorprint Offset Inc, pg 1206
Martin Cook Associates Ltd, pg 1206
CS Graphics USA Inc, pg 1206
DNP America LLC, pg 1206
Editoriale Bortolazzi-Stei srl, pg 1206
Elegance Printing & Book Binding (USA), pg 1206
Express Media Corp, pg 1206
Hamilton Printing Co, pg 1206
Hindy's Enterprise, pg 1207
Imago, pg 1207
Integrated Book Technology Inc, pg 1207
Jinno International Group, pg 1207
Leo Paper USA, pg 1207
Linick International Inc, pg 1207
LK Litho, pg 1207
Milanostampa/New Interlitho USA Inc, pg 1208
Palace Press International, pg 1208
Printing Corp of the Americas Inc, pg 1208
Taylor Publishing Co, pg 1208
Times Publishing Group, pg 1208
Fred Weidner & Daughter Printers, pg 1208

Uruguay
Barreiro y Ramos SA, pg 1208

EMBOSSING

Belgium
Drukkerij Lannoo NV, pg 1193

Canada
Appleby's Bindery Ltd, pg 1193
Transcontinental Printing Book Group, pg 1194
Tri-Graphic Printing (Ottawa) Ltd, pg 1194
University of Toronto Press Inc, pg 1194

China
Speedflex Asia Ltd, pg 1194

Czech Republic
GRASPO CZ AS - Druckerei und Buchbinderei, pg 1194

Denmark
Bianco Lunos Bogtrykkeri AS, pg 1194

Finland
Gummerus Printing, pg 1194

France
Signes du Monde, pg 1194

Germany
Mohndruck Graphische Betriebe GmbH, pg 1195
Priese GmbH, pg 1195

Hong Kong
Best-Set Typesetter Ltd, pg 1195
Bright Future Printing Co Ltd, pg 1195
Caritas Printing Training Centre, pg 1195
Colorprint Offset, pg 1195
Dai Nippon Printing Co (Hong Kong) Ltd, pg 1196
Everbest Printing Co Ltd, pg 1196
Golden Cup Printing Co Ltd, pg 1196
The Green Pagoda Press Ltd, pg 1196
Hung Hing Off-set Printing Co Ltd, pg 1196
Image Printing Company Ltd, pg 1196
Leo Paper Products Ltd, pg 1196
Midas Printing Ltd, pg 1197
Morris Press Ltd, pg 1197
Paper Art Product Ltd, pg 1197
Paramount Publishing Group Limited, pg 1197
Prontaprint Asia Ltd, pg 1197
Sing Cheong Printing Co Limited, pg 1197
Sino Publishing House Ltd, pg 1197
South Sea International Press Ltd, pg 1197
Toppan Printing Co (HK) Ltd, pg 1197
Unicorn International Printing Co Ltd, pg 1197
Wing King Tong Co Ltd (Printing Factory), pg 1197

Hungary
Interpress Aussenhandels GmbH, pg 1197

Indonesia
Ichtiar Baru I Van Hoeve, pg 1198
Victory Offset Prima PT, pg 1198

Ireland
Smurfit Print, pg 1198

Israel
Keterpress Enterprises Jerusalem, pg 1198

Italy
Canale G e C SpA, pg 1198
Milanostampa SPA, pg 1198
Amilcare Pizzi SpA, pg 1198

Republic of Korea
Daehan Printing & Publishing Co Ltd, pg 1199
Pyunghwa Dang Printing Co Ltd, pg 1199

Lithuania
Spindulys Printing House, pg 1199

New Zealand
Bookprint Consultants Ltd, pg 1199
John McIndoe Ltd, pg 1199

Philippines
Cacho Hermanos Inc, pg 1199

Singapore
Columbia Overseas Marketing Pte Ltd, pg 1200
CS Graphics Pte Ltd, pg 1200
Eurasia Press Pte Ltd, pg 1200
Ho Printing Singapore Pte Ltd, pg 1200
International Press Co Pte Ltd, pg 1200
Markono Print Media Pte Ltd, pg 1200
SNP Printing Pte Ltd, pg 1200
Stamford Press Pte Ltd, pg 1200
Times Printers Pte Ltd, pg 1200
Toppan Company (S) Pte Ltd, pg 1200
World Publications Printers Pte Ltd, pg 1201

Slovenia
Gorenjski Tisk Printing Co, pg 1201

Sri Lanka
Sumathi Book Printing (Pvt) Ltd, pg 1201

Thailand
Mavisu International Co Ltd, pg 1201

United Arab Emirates
Emirates Printing Press (LLC), pg 1202

United Kingdom
Blockfoil Ltd, pg 1202
D Brown & Sons Ltd, pg 1202
Caledonian International Book Manufacturing, pg 1202
Clays Ltd, pg 1203
Cox & Wyman Ltd, pg 1203
The Guernsey Press Co Ltd, pg 1203
Hammond Packaging Ltd, pg 1203
Harveys Ltd, pg 1203
Image & Print Group Ltd, pg 1203
The Malvern Press Ltd, pg 1204
Page Bros Ltd (Norwich), pg 1204
Printafoil Ltd, pg 1204

United States
Asia Pacific Offset Inc, pg 1205
BookBuilders New York Ltd, pg 1205
C & C Offset Printing Co Ltd, pg 1205
Colorprint Offset Inc, pg 1206
Coneco Litho Graphics, pg 1206
Martin Cook Associates Ltd, pg 1206
CS Graphics USA Inc, pg 1206
D & K Group, pg 1206
DNP America LLC, pg 1206
Editoriale Bortolazzi-Stei srl, pg 1206
Elegance Printing & Book Binding (USA), pg 1206
Hindy's Enterprise, pg 1207
Imago, pg 1207
Jinno International Group, pg 1207
Leo Paper USA, pg 1207
Linick International Inc, pg 1207
LK Litho, pg 1207
Milanostampa/New Interlitho USA Inc, pg 1208
Palace Press International, pg 1208
Printing Corp of the Americas Inc, pg 1208
Regent Publishing Services, pg 1208
Taylor Publishing Co, pg 1208
Times Publishing Group, pg 1208
Fred Weidner & Daughter Printers, pg 1208

PRINTING, BINDING & BOOK FINISHING INDEX

Uruguay
Barreiro y Ramos SA, pg 1208

ENGRAVING

Belgium
Drukkerij Lannoo NV, pg 1193

Canada
Transcontinental Printing Book Group, pg 1194

China
Speedflex Asia Ltd, pg 1194

Czech Republic
GRASPO CZ AS - Druckerei und Buchbinderei, pg 1194

Denmark
Bianco Lunos Bogtrykkeri AS, pg 1194

France
Signes du Monde, pg 1194

Germany
Priese GmbH, pg 1195

Hong Kong
Midas Printing Ltd, pg 1197
Paramount Publishing Group Limited, pg 1197
Prontaprint Asia Ltd, pg 1197

Italy
Canale G e C SpA, pg 1198

Republic of Korea
Daehan Printing & Publishing Co Ltd, pg 1199

New Zealand
Bookprint Consultants Ltd, pg 1199

Philippines
Cacho Hermanos Inc, pg 1199

Singapore
SNP Printing Pte Ltd, pg 1200
Stamford Press Pte Ltd, pg 1200
Toppan Company (S) Pte Ltd, pg 1200
World Publications Printers Pte Ltd, pg 1201

Spain
Grafos SA Arte Sobre Papel, pg 1201
Graficas Santamaria SA, pg 1201

United Republic of Tanzania
Peramiho Publications, pg 1201

United Kingdom
Cox & Wyman Ltd, pg 1203
The Malvern Press Ltd, pg 1204

United States
Asia Pacific Offset Inc, pg 1205
BookBuilders New York Ltd, pg 1205
Martin Cook Associates Ltd, pg 1206

DNP America LLC, pg 1206
Elegance Printing & Book Binding (USA), pg 1206
Jinno International Group, pg 1207
Leo Paper USA, pg 1207
Linick International Inc, pg 1207
LK Litho, pg 1207
Palace Press International, pg 1208
Regent Publishing Services, pg 1208
Fred Weidner & Daughter Printers, pg 1208

FILM LAMINATING

Canada
Coach House Printing, pg 1193
Maracle Press Ltd, pg 1193
Printcrafters Inc, pg 1193
Transcontinental Printing Book Group, pg 1194
Tri-Graphic Printing (Ottawa) Ltd, pg 1194
University of Toronto Press Inc, pg 1194
Webcom Ltd, pg 1194

China
Speedflex Asia Ltd, pg 1194

Czech Republic
GRASPO CZ AS - Druckerei und Buchbinderei, pg 1194

Denmark
Bianco Lunos Bogtrykkeri AS, pg 1194

Finland
Gummerus Printing, pg 1194
WS Bookwell Ltd, pg 1194

Germany
Priese GmbH, pg 1195

Hong Kong
Best-Set Typesetter Ltd, pg 1195
Bright Future Printing Co Ltd, pg 1195
Caritas Printing Training Centre, pg 1195
Colorprint Offset, pg 1195
Dai Nippon Printing Co (Hong Kong) Ltd, pg 1196
Everbest Printing Co Ltd, pg 1196
Golden Cup Printing Co Ltd, pg 1196
Hung Hing Off-set Printing Co Ltd, pg 1196
Image Printing Company Ltd, pg 1196
Leo Paper Products Ltd, pg 1196
Midas Printing Ltd, pg 1197
Morris Press Ltd, pg 1197
Paper Communication Printing Express Ltd, pg 1197
Paramount Publishing Group Limited, pg 1197
Prontaprint Asia Ltd, pg 1197
Sing Cheong Printing Co Limited, pg 1197
Sino Publishing House Ltd, pg 1197
South Sea International Press Ltd, pg 1197
Toppan Printing Co (HK) Ltd, pg 1197
Unicorn International Printing Co Ltd, pg 1197
Wing King Tong Co Ltd (Printing Factory), pg 1197

India
Hiralal Printing Works Ltd, pg 1197

Indonesia
Ichtiar Baru I Van Hoeve, pg 1198
Victory Offset Prima PT, pg 1198

Israel
Keterpress Enterprises Jerusalem, pg 1198
Technosdar Ltd, pg 1198

Italy
Canale G e C SpA, pg 1198
Milanostampa SPA, pg 1198
Amilcare Pizzi SpA, pg 1198

Republic of Korea
Daehan Printing & Publishing Co Ltd, pg 1199
Pyunghwa Dang Printing Co Ltd, pg 1199

Lithuania
Spindulys Printing House, pg 1199

Malta
Interprint Ltd - Malta, pg 1199

New Zealand
Bookprint Consultants Ltd, pg 1199
John McIndoe Ltd, pg 1199

Philippines
Cacho Hermanos Inc, pg 1199

Singapore
Columbia Overseas Marketing Pte Ltd, pg 1200
CS Graphics Pte Ltd, pg 1200
Eurasia Press Pte Ltd, pg 1200
Ho Printing Singapore Pte Ltd, pg 1200
International Press Co Pte Ltd, pg 1200
Markono Print Media Pte Ltd, pg 1200
SNP Printing Pte Ltd, pg 1200
Stamford Press Pte Ltd, pg 1200
Tien Wah Press Pte Ltd, pg 1200
Times Printers Pte Ltd, pg 1200
Toppan Company (S) Pte Ltd, pg 1200
World Publications Printers Pte Ltd, pg 1201

Slovenia
Gorenjski Tisk Printing Co, pg 1201

Spain
Grafos SA Arte Sobre Papel, pg 1201
Rotedic SA, pg 1201
Luis Vives (Edelvives), pg 1201

Thailand
J Film Process Co Ltd, pg 1201
Mavisu International Co Ltd, pg 1201

United Arab Emirates
Emirates Printing Press (LLC), pg 1202

United Kingdom
Ebenezer Baylis & Son Ltd, pg 1202
Biddles Ltd, pg 1202
Clays Ltd, pg 1203
Cox & Wyman Ltd, pg 1203
Furnival Press, pg 1203
The Guernsey Press Co Ltd, pg 1203
Hammond Bindery Ltd, pg 1203
Hobbs The Printers Ltd, pg 1203
Hunter & Foulis Ltd, pg 1203
Intype London Ltd, pg 1204
Page Bros Ltd (Norwich), pg 1204
Peak Technologies UK Ltd, pg 1204
Redwood Books Ltd, pg 1204
Watkiss Automation Ltd, pg 1205
The Wolsey Press, pg 1205

United States
Asia Pacific Offset Inc, pg 1205
Blaze International Productions Inc, pg 1205
BookBuilders New York Ltd, pg 1205
C & C Offset Printing Co Ltd, pg 1205
Colorprint Offset Inc, pg 1206
Coneco Litho Graphics, pg 1206
Martin Cook Associates Ltd, pg 1206
CS Graphics USA Inc, pg 1206
D & K Group, pg 1206
DNP America LLC, pg 1206
Elegance Printing & Book Binding (USA), pg 1206
Express Media Corp, pg 1206
Fairfield Marketing Group Inc, pg 1206
Hindy's Enterprise, pg 1207
Imago, pg 1207
Jinno International Group, pg 1207
Lenz & Riecker Inc, pg 1207
Leo Paper USA, pg 1207
Linick International Inc, pg 1207
LK Litho, pg 1207
Milanostampa/New Interlitho USA Inc, pg 1208
Palace Press International, pg 1208
Printing Corp of the Americas Inc, pg 1208
Regent Publishing Services, pg 1208
Times Publishing Group, pg 1208
Vicks Lithograph & Printing Corp, pg 1208
Fred Weidner & Daughter Printers, pg 1208

Uruguay
Barreiro y Ramos SA, pg 1208

FOILING

Belgium
Drukkerij Lannoo NV, pg 1193

Canada
Appleby's Bindery Ltd, pg 1193
Printcrafters Inc, pg 1193
Transcontinental Printing Book Group, pg 1194
Tri-Graphic Printing (Ottawa) Ltd, pg 1194
University of Toronto Press Inc, pg 1194

China
Speedflex Asia Ltd, pg 1194

MANUFACTURING

PRINTING, BINDING & BOOK FINISHING INDEX

Czech Republic
GRASPO CZ AS - Druckerei und Buchbinderei, pg 1194

Denmark
Bianco Lunos Bogtrykkeri AS, pg 1194

Finland
Gummerus Printing, pg 1194

Germany
Priese GmbH, pg 1195

Hong Kong
Best-Set Typesetter Ltd, pg 1195
Bright Future Printing Co Ltd, pg 1195
Dai Nippon Printing Co (Hong Kong) Ltd, pg 1196
Everbest Printing Co Ltd, pg 1196
Golden Cup Printing Co Ltd, pg 1196
Hung Hing Off-set Printing Co Ltd, pg 1196
Image Printing Company Ltd, pg 1196
Leo Paper Products Ltd, pg 1196
Midas Printing Ltd, pg 1197
Morris Press Ltd, pg 1197
Paper Art Product Ltd, pg 1197
Paper Communication Printing Express Ltd, pg 1197
Paramount Publishing Group Limited, pg 1197
Prontaprint Asia Ltd, pg 1197
Sing Cheong Printing Co Limited, pg 1197
Sino Publishing House Ltd, pg 1197
South Sea International Press Ltd, pg 1197
Wing King Tong Co Ltd (Printing Factory), pg 1197

Hungary
Interpress Aussenhandels GmbH, pg 1197

Indonesia
Ichtiar Baru I Van Hoeve, pg 1198
Victory Offset Prima PT, pg 1198

Ireland
Smurfit Print, pg 1198

Israel
Keterpress Enterprises Jerusalem, pg 1198
Technosdar Ltd, pg 1198

Italy
Canale G e C SpA, pg 1198

Malta
Interprint Ltd - Malta, pg 1199

New Zealand
Bookprint Consultants Ltd, pg 1199
John McIndoe Ltd, pg 1199

Singapore
CS Graphics Pte Ltd, pg 1200
Eurasia Press Pte Ltd, pg 1200
Ho Printing Singapore Pte Ltd, pg 1200
International Press Co Pte Ltd, pg 1200
SNP Printing Pte Ltd, pg 1200
Stamford Press Pte Ltd, pg 1200
Times Printers Pte Ltd, pg 1200
Toppan Company (S) Pte Ltd, pg 1200
World Publications Printers Pte Ltd, pg 1201

Slovenia
Gorenjski Tisk Printing Co, pg 1201

Sri Lanka
Sumathi Book Printing (Pvt) Ltd, pg 1201

Thailand
J Film Process Co Ltd, pg 1201

United Arab Emirates
Emirates Printing Press (LLC), pg 1202

United Kingdom
Biddles Ltd, pg 1202
Blockfoil Ltd, pg 1202
J W Braithwaite & Son Ltd, pg 1202
Caledonian International Book Manufacturing, pg 1202
Clays Ltd, pg 1203
Cox & Wyman Ltd, pg 1203
The Guernsey Press Co Ltd, pg 1203
Hammond Packaging Ltd, pg 1203
Harveys Ltd, pg 1203
Image & Print Group Ltd, pg 1203
Charles Letts & Co Ltd, pg 1204
The Malvern Press Ltd, pg 1204
Printafoil Ltd, pg 1204

United States
Asia Pacific Offset Inc, pg 1205
BookBuilders New York Ltd, pg 1205
C & C Offset Printing Co Ltd, pg 1205
Colorprint Offset Inc, pg 1206
Coneco Litho Graphics, pg 1206
Martin Cook Associates Ltd, pg 1206
CS Graphics USA Inc, pg 1206
DNP America LLC, pg 1206
Elegance Printing & Book Binding (USA), pg 1206
Fairfield Marketing Group Inc, pg 1206
Hindy's Enterprise, pg 1207
Imago, pg 1207
Jinno International Group, pg 1207
Leo Paper USA, pg 1207
Linick International Inc, pg 1207
LK Litho, pg 1207
Palace Press International, pg 1208
Regent Publishing Services, pg 1208
Taylor Publishing Co, pg 1208
Times Publishing Group, pg 1208
Fred Weidner & Daughter Printers, pg 1208

Uruguay
Barreiro y Ramos SA, pg 1208

GILDING

Canada
Appleby's Bindery Ltd, pg 1193
University of Toronto Press Inc, pg 1194

China
Speedflex Asia Ltd, pg 1194

Czech Republic
GRASPO CZ AS - Druckerei und Buchbinderei, pg 1194

Germany
Priese GmbH, pg 1195

Hong Kong
Dai Nippon Printing Co (Hong Kong) Ltd, pg 1196
Everbest Printing Co Ltd, pg 1196
Leo Paper Products Ltd, pg 1196
Morris Press Ltd, pg 1197
Sing Cheong Printing Co Limited, pg 1197
Sino Publishing House Ltd, pg 1197
South Sea International Press Ltd, pg 1197
Unicorn International Printing Co Ltd, pg 1197
Wing King Tong Co Ltd (Printing Factory), pg 1197

Hungary
Interpress Aussenhandels GmbH, pg 1197

Indonesia
Victory Offset Prima PT, pg 1198

Israel
Technosdar Ltd, pg 1198

Italy
Milanostampa SPA, pg 1198

Republic of Korea
Pyunghwa Dang Printing Co Ltd, pg 1199

New Zealand
Bookprint Consultants Ltd, pg 1199

Singapore
Eurasia Press Pte Ltd, pg 1200
SNP Printing Pte Ltd, pg 1200

Slovenia
Gorenjski Tisk Printing Co, pg 1201

Spain
Grafos SA Arte Sobre Papel, pg 1201
Graficas Santamaria SA, pg 1201
Luis Vives (Edelvives), pg 1201

United Kingdom
Biddles Ltd, pg 1202
Caledonian International Book Manufacturing, pg 1202
Center Print Ltd, pg 1202
Clays Ltd, pg 1203
Cox & Wyman Ltd, pg 1203
Hammond Packaging Ltd, pg 1203
Charles Letts & Co Ltd, pg 1204
MPG Books Ltd, pg 1204

United States
Asia Pacific Offset Inc, pg 1205
BookBuilders New York Ltd, pg 1205
C & C Offset Printing Co Ltd, pg 1205
Martin Cook Associates Ltd, pg 1206
DNP America LLC, pg 1206
Elegance Printing & Book Binding (USA), pg 1206
Imago, pg 1207
Jinno International Group, pg 1207
Leo Paper USA, pg 1207
Linick International Inc, pg 1207
LK Litho, pg 1207
Palace Press International, pg 1208
Regent Publishing Services, pg 1208
Times Publishing Group, pg 1208
Fred Weidner & Daughter Printers, pg 1208

GLUE OR PASTE BINDING

Belgium
Drukkerij Lannoo NV, pg 1193

Canada
Appleby's Bindery Ltd, pg 1193
Printcrafters Inc, pg 1193
Transcontinental Printing Book Group, pg 1194

China
Speedflex Asia Ltd, pg 1194

Czech Republic
GRASPO CZ AS - Druckerei und Buchbinderei, pg 1194

Denmark
Bianco Lunos Bogtrykkeri AS, pg 1194

Germany
C L Baader Buch & Offsetdruckerei GmbH & Co KG, pg 1194
Priese GmbH, pg 1195
Vier-Tuerme GmbH Benedikt Press, pg 1195

Hong Kong
Dai Nippon Printing Co (Hong Kong) Ltd, pg 1196
Hung Hing Off-set Printing Co Ltd, pg 1196
Image Printing Company Ltd, pg 1196
Midas Printing Ltd, pg 1197
Morris Press Ltd, pg 1197
Paramount Publishing Group Limited, pg 1197
Prontaprint Asia Ltd, pg 1197
Sing Cheong Printing Co Limited, pg 1197
Toppan Printing Co (HK) Ltd, pg 1197
Unicorn International Printing Co Ltd, pg 1197

Indonesia
Victory Offset Prima PT, pg 1198

Ireland
Kilkenny People/Wellbrook Press, pg 1198

Italy
Canale G e C SpA, pg 1198
Milanostampa SPA, pg 1198
Minerva Medica, pg 1198

1179

PRINTING, BINDING & BOOK FINISHING INDEX — BOOK

Republic of Korea
Daehan Printing & Publishing Co Ltd, pg 1199
Pyunghwa Dang Printing Co Ltd, pg 1199

New Zealand
Bookprint Consultants Ltd, pg 1199

Singapore
Eurasia Press Pte Ltd, pg 1200
International Press Co Pte Ltd, pg 1200
Markono Print Media Pte Ltd, pg 1200
SNP Printing Pte Ltd, pg 1200
Toppan Company (S) Pte Ltd, pg 1200
World Publications Printers Pte Ltd, pg 1201

Spain
Luis Vives (Edelvives), pg 1201

United Republic of Tanzania
Peramiho Publications, pg 1201

Thailand
J Film Process Co Ltd, pg 1201
Mavisu International Co Ltd, pg 1201

United Kingdom
Clays Ltd, pg 1203
Hunter & Foulis Ltd, pg 1203
Severnside Printers Ltd, pg 1204
Watkiss Automation Ltd, pg 1205

United States
ADR/BookPrint, pg 1205
Asia Pacific Offset Inc, pg 1205
Bind-It Corp, pg 1205
BookBuilders New York Ltd, pg 1205
C & C Offset Printing Co Ltd, pg 1205
DNP America LLC, pg 1206
Elegance Printing & Book Binding (USA), pg 1206
Hindy's Enterprise, pg 1207
Imago, pg 1207
Jinno International Group, pg 1207
Leo Paper USA, pg 1207
Linick International Inc, pg 1207
Milanostampa/New Interlitho USA Inc, pg 1208
Spraymation Inc, pg 1208
Fred Weidner & Daughter Printers, pg 1208

Uruguay
Barreiro y Ramos SA, pg 1208

GRAVURE

Belgium
Drukkerij Lannoo NV, pg 1193

China
Speedflex Asia Ltd, pg 1194

Germany
Priese GmbH, pg 1195

Israel
Har-El Printers & Publishers, pg 1198
Technosdar Ltd, pg 1198

Spain
Eurohueco SA, pg 1201

United Kingdom
Cox & Wyman Ltd, pg 1203

United States
BookBuilders New York Ltd, pg 1205
DNP America LLC, pg 1206
Jinno International Group, pg 1207
Leo Paper USA, pg 1207
Linick International Inc, pg 1207
LK Litho, pg 1207
Palace Press International, pg 1208
Fred Weidner & Daughter Printers, pg 1208

HAND BOOKBINDING

Austria
ADEVA (Akademische Druck-u Verlagsanstalt), pg 1193

Canada
Aardvark Enterprises, pg 1193
Printcrafters Inc, pg 1193
University of Toronto Press Inc, pg 1194

China
Speedflex Asia Ltd, pg 1194

Finland
Gummerus Printing, pg 1194

Germany
C L Baader Buch & Offsetdruckere GmbH & Co KG, pg 1194
Fachhochschule Fur Druk, Studiengang Verlagswirtschaft und Verlagsherstellung, pg 1195
Priese GmbH, pg 1195

Hong Kong
Dai Nippon Printing Co (Hong Kong) Ltd, pg 1196
Everbest Printing Co Ltd, pg 1196
Hua Yang Printing Holding Co Ltd, pg 1196
Hung Hing Off-set Printing Co Ltd, pg 1196
Image Printing Company Ltd, pg 1196
Kwong Fat Offset Printing Company Ltd, pg 1196
Midas Printing Ltd, pg 1197
Nordica Printing Co Ltd, pg 1197
Paramount Publishing Group Limited, pg 1197
Prontaprint Asia Ltd, pg 1197
Sing Cheong Printing Co Limited, pg 1197
South Sea International Press Ltd, pg 1197
Sun Fung Offset Binding Co Ltd, pg 1197
Sunshine Press Ltd, pg 1197
Toppan Printing Co (HK) Ltd, pg 1197
Unicorn International Printing Co Ltd, pg 1197

Indonesia
Victory Offset Prima PT, pg 1198

Republic of Korea
Daehan Printing & Publishing Co Ltd, pg 1199

Lithuania
Spindulys Printing House, pg 1199

Singapore
CS Graphics Pte Ltd, pg 1200
Markono Print Media Pte Ltd, pg 1200
Toppan Company (S) Pte Ltd, pg 1200
World Publications Printers Pte Ltd, pg 1201

United Republic of Tanzania
Peramiho Publications, pg 1201

Thailand
J Film Process Co Ltd, pg 1201
Mavisu International Co Ltd, pg 1201

United Kingdom
Cedric Chivers Ltd, pg 1203
Green Street Bindery, pg 1203
Hammond Packaging Ltd, pg 1203
Ikon Document Services Ltd, pg 1203
MPG Books Ltd, pg 1204

United States
BookBuilders New York Ltd, pg 1205
C & C Offset Printing Co Ltd, pg 1205
Colorprint Offset Inc, pg 1206
CS Graphics USA Inc, pg 1206
Elegance Printing & Book Binding (USA), pg 1206
Hindy's Enterprise, pg 1207
Imago, pg 1207
Integrated Book Technology Inc, pg 1207
Leo Paper USA, pg 1207
Linick International Inc, pg 1207
Palace Press International, pg 1208
Regent Publishing Services, pg 1208
Fred Weidner & Daughter Printers, pg 1208

HOLOGRAMS

Belgium
Drukkerij Lannoo NV, pg 1193

China
Speedflex Asia Ltd, pg 1194

Germany
Mohndruck Graphische Betriebe GmbH, pg 1195
Priese GmbH, pg 1195

Hong Kong
Sing Cheong Printing Co Limited, pg 1197
Unicorn International Printing Co Ltd, pg 1197

Ireland
Smurfit Print, pg 1198

United Kingdom
Cox & Wyman Ltd, pg 1203
The Malvern Press Ltd, pg 1204
Printafoil Ltd, pg 1204

United States
BookBuilders New York Ltd, pg 1205
DNP America LLC, pg 1206
Elegance Printing & Book Binding (USA), pg 1206
Imago, pg 1207
Linick International Inc, pg 1207
LK Litho, pg 1207
Palace Press International, pg 1208
Fred Weidner & Daughter Printers, pg 1208

JOURNAL PRINTING

Austria
ADEVA (Akademische Druck-u Verlagsanstalt), pg 1193

Canada
Coach House Printing, pg 1193
Maracle Press Ltd, pg 1193
Printcrafters Inc, pg 1193
Transcontinental Printing Book Group, pg 1194
University of Toronto Press Inc, pg 1194
Webcom Ltd, pg 1194

China
Speedflex Asia Ltd, pg 1194

Czech Republic
GRASPO CZ AS - Druckerei und Buchbinderei, pg 1194

Germany
C L Baader Buch & Offsetdruckere GmbH & Co KG, pg 1194
Fachhochschule Fur Druk, Studiengang Verlagswirtschaft und Verlagsherstellung, pg 1195
G Braun (vormals G Braun'sche Hofbuchdruckerei und Verlag), pg 1195
C Maurer Druck und Verlag, pg 1195
Media-Print Informationstechnologie GmbH, pg 1195
Mohndruck Graphische Betriebe GmbH, pg 1195
Priese GmbH, pg 1195

Hong Kong
Best-Set Typesetter Ltd, pg 1195
Image Printing Company Ltd, pg 1196
Liang Yu Printing Factory Ltd, pg 1196
Midas Printing Ltd, pg 1197
Paramount Publishing Group Limited, pg 1197
Sing Cheong Printing Co Limited, pg 1197
Sino Publishing House Ltd, pg 1197
South Sea International Press Ltd, pg 1197
Toppan Printing Co (HK) Ltd, pg 1197
Unicorn International Printing Co Ltd, pg 1197

MANUFACTURING PRINTING, BINDING & BOOK FINISHING INDEX

Hungary
Interpress Aussenhandels GmbH, pg 1197

Ireland
Smurfit Print, pg 1198

Israel
Keterpress Enterprises Jerusalem, pg 1198
Monoline Ltd, pg 1198
Technosdar Ltd, pg 1198

Italy
Canale G e C SpA, pg 1198

Japan
Dai Nippon Printing Co Ltd, pg 1198

Republic of Korea
Daehan Printing & Publishing Co Ltd, pg 1199
Pyunghwa Dang Printing Co Ltd, pg 1199

Lithuania
Spindulys Printing House, pg 1199

New Zealand
Bookprint Consultants Ltd, pg 1199
PPP Printers Ltd, pg 1199

Philippines
JF Printhaus, pg 1199

Singapore
Chong Moh Offset Printing Ltd, pg 1200
Columbia Overseas Marketing Pte Ltd, pg 1200
Eurasia Press Pte Ltd, pg 1200
Markono Print Media Pte Ltd, pg 1200
PacPress Media Pte Ltd, pg 1200
SNP Printing Pte Ltd, pg 1200
Stamford Press Pte Ltd, pg 1200
Times Printers Pte Ltd, pg 1200
Toppan Company (S) Pte Ltd, pg 1200
World Publications Printers Pte Ltd, pg 1201

South Africa
CTP Book Printers (Pty) Ltd, pg 1201

Spain
Graficas Santamaria SA, pg 1201
Luis Vives (Edelvives), pg 1201

Sri Lanka
Sumathi Book Printing (Pvt) Ltd, pg 1201

Switzerland
Hallwag AG, pg 1201

United Republic of Tanzania
Peramiho Publications, pg 1201

Thailand
J Film Process Co Ltd, pg 1201

United Arab Emirates
Emirates Printing Press (LLC), pg 1202

United Kingdom
The Alden Group Ltd, pg 1202
J W Arrowsmith Ltd, pg 1202
W & G Baird Ltd, pg 1202
Bell & Bain Ltd, pg 1202
Biddles Ltd, pg 1202
Cambridge University Press - Printing Division, pg 1202
The Charlesworth Group, pg 1202
Clays Ltd, pg 1203
Cradley Print Ltd, pg 1203
R R Donnelley, pg 1203
Essex Colour Services Ltd, pg 1203
Goldshield Communications Ltd, pg 1203
Norman Hardy Printing Group, pg 1203
Hastings Publishing Co, pg 1203
Headley Brothers Ltd, pg 1203
Hobbs The Printers Ltd, pg 1203
Ikon Document Services Ltd, pg 1203
Intype London Ltd, pg 1204
Lavenham Press Ltd, pg 1204
Lowfield Printing Co Ltd, pg 1204
Multiplex Medway Ltd, pg 1204
Page Bros Ltd (Norwich), pg 1204
Redwood Books Ltd, pg 1204
J R Reid Printing Group Ltd, pg 1204
Antony Rowe Ltd, pg 1204
Severnside Printers Ltd, pg 1204
Watkiss Automation Ltd, pg 1205

United States
Asia Pacific Offset Inc, pg 1205
C & C Offset Printing Co Ltd, pg 1205
Carvajal International Inc, pg 1206
Coneco Litho Graphics, pg 1206
DNP America LLC, pg 1206
EP Graphics, pg 1206
Express Media Corp, pg 1206
Fairfield Marketing Group Inc, pg 1206
Hamilton Printing Co, pg 1206
Ikon Document Services, pg 1207
Imago, pg 1207
Integrated Book Technology Inc, pg 1207
Jinno International Group, pg 1207
KNI Inc, pg 1207
Leo Paper USA, pg 1207
Linick International Inc, pg 1207
LK Litho, pg 1207
Marrakech Express Inc, pg 1207
Palace Press International, pg 1208
Printing Corp of the Americas Inc, pg 1208
Regent Publishing Services, pg 1208
Times Publishing Group, pg 1208
Vicks Lithograph & Printing Corp, pg 1208
Fred Weidner & Daughter Printers, pg 1208

LETTERPRESS

Canada
Printcrafters Inc, pg 1193

Germany
C L Baader Buch & Offsetdruckere GmbH & Co KG, pg 1194
Fachhochschule Fur Druk, Studiengang Verlagswirtschaft und Verlagsherstellung, pg 1195
Mohndruck Graphische Betriebe GmbH, pg 1195
Priese GmbH, pg 1195

Hong Kong
The Green Pagoda Press Ltd, pg 1196
Unicorn International Printing Co Ltd, pg 1197

Hungary
Interpress Aussenhandels GmbH, pg 1197

Ireland
Ultragraphics, pg 1198

Israel
Monoline Ltd, pg 1198

Republic of Korea
Daehan Printing & Publishing Co Ltd, pg 1199

New Zealand
John McIndoe Ltd, pg 1199

Philippines
Philippine Graphic Arts Inc, pg 1199

Portugal
Silabo, pg 1200

Spain
Graficas Santamaria SA, pg 1201

Sri Lanka
Sumathi Book Printing (Pvt) Ltd, pg 1201

United Republic of Tanzania
Peramiho Publications, pg 1201

United Kingdom
Caledonian International Book Manufacturing, pg 1202
J R Reid Printing Group Ltd, pg 1204
Selwood Printing, pg 1204

United States
Fairfield Marketing Group Inc, pg 1206
Jinno International Group, pg 1207
Leo Paper USA, pg 1207
LK Litho, pg 1207
Palace Press International, pg 1208
Fred Weidner & Daughter Printers, pg 1208

Uruguay
Barreiro y Ramos SA, pg 1208

LOOSELEAF BINDING

Belgium
Drukkerij Lannoo NV, pg 1193

Canada
Maracle Press Ltd, pg 1193
Printcrafters Inc, pg 1193
Tri-Graphic Printing (Ottawa) Ltd, pg 1194
University of Toronto Press Inc, pg 1194

China
Speedflex Asia Ltd, pg 1194

Germany
Priese GmbH, pg 1195

Hong Kong
Dai Nippon Printing Co (Hong Kong) Ltd, pg 1196
Hung Hing Off-set Printing Co Ltd, pg 1196
Image Printing Company Ltd, pg 1196
Midas Printing Ltd, pg 1197
Prontaprint Asia Ltd, pg 1197
Sing Cheong Printing Co Limited, pg 1197
Sino Publishing House Ltd, pg 1197
Unicorn International Printing Co Ltd, pg 1197

Indonesia
Victory Offset Prima PT, pg 1198

Ireland
Smurfit Print, pg 1198

Israel
Technosdar Ltd, pg 1198

Italy
Canale G e C SpA, pg 1198

Netherlands
Koninklijke Wohrmann Bv, pg 1199

New Zealand
Bookprint Consultants Ltd, pg 1199

Singapore
Eurasia Press Pte Ltd, pg 1200
International Press Co Pte Ltd, pg 1200
Markono Print Media Pte Ltd, pg 1200
Stamford Press Pte Ltd, pg 1200
Toppan Company (S) Pte Ltd, pg 1200
World Publications Printers Pte Ltd, pg 1201

United Republic of Tanzania
Peramiho Publications, pg 1201

United Kingdom
J W Braithwaite & Son Ltd, pg 1202
Butler & Tanner Ltd, pg 1202
William Clowes Ltd, pg 1203
Goldshield Communications Ltd, pg 1203
Hammond Bindery Ltd, pg 1203
Harveys Ltd, pg 1203
Hobbs The Printers Ltd, pg 1203
Ikon Document Services Ltd, pg 1203
Intype London Ltd, pg 1204
Charles Letts & Co Ltd, pg 1204
Lowfield Printing Co Ltd, pg 1204

PRINTING, BINDING & BOOK FINISHING INDEX

MacKays of Chatham PLC, pg 1204
Multiplex Medway Ltd, pg 1204
Page Bros Ltd (Norwich), pg 1204
Redwood Books Ltd, pg 1204
Antony Rowe Ltd, pg 1204
M & A Thomson Litho Ltd, pg 1205
Watkiss Automation Ltd, pg 1205

United States

ADR/BookPrint, pg 1205
Asia Pacific Offset Inc, pg 1205
Bind-It Corp, pg 1205
BookBuilders New York Ltd, pg 1205
Coneco Litho Graphics, pg 1206
Martin Cook Associates Ltd, pg 1206
DNP America LLC, pg 1206
Express Media Corp, pg 1206
Hamilton Printing Co, pg 1206
Hindy's Enterprise, pg 1207
Ikon Document Services, pg 1207
Imago, pg 1207
Integrated Book Technology Inc, pg 1207
Jinno International Group, pg 1207
KNI Inc, pg 1207
Lenz & Riecker Inc, pg 1207
Leo Paper USA, pg 1207
Linick International Inc, pg 1207
LK Litho, pg 1207
Palace Press International, pg 1208
Printing Corp of the Americas Inc, pg 1208
Fred Weidner & Daughter Printers, pg 1208

MANUAL PRINTING

Belgium

Drukkerij Lannoo NV, pg 1193

Canada

Aardvark Enterprises, pg 1193
Coach House Printing, pg 1193
Maracle Press Ltd, pg 1193
Preney Print & Litho Inc, pg 1193
Printcrafters Inc, pg 1193
Transcontinental Printing Book Group, pg 1194
Tri-Graphic Printing (Ottawa) Ltd, pg 1194
University of Toronto Press Inc, pg 1194
Webcom Ltd, pg 1194

China

Speedflex Asia Ltd, pg 1194

Czech Republic

GRASPO CZ AS - Druckerei und Buchbinderei, pg 1194

Denmark

Bianco Lunos Bogtrykkeri AS, pg 1194

Finland

Gummerus Printing, pg 1194

Germany

C L Baader Buch & Offsetdruckere GmbH & Co KG, pg 1194
Mohndruck Graphische Betriebe GmbH, pg 1195
Priese GmbH, pg 1195

Hong Kong

Image Printing Company Ltd, pg 1196
Midas Printing Ltd, pg 1197
Paper Communication Printing Express Ltd, pg 1197
Paramount Publishing Group Limited, pg 1197
Prontaprint Asia Ltd, pg 1197
Sing Cheong Printing Co Limited, pg 1197
Unicorn International Printing Co Ltd, pg 1197

Hungary

Interpress Aussenhandels GmbH, pg 1197

Indonesia

Victory Offset Prima PT, pg 1198

Ireland

Smurfit Print, pg 1198

Israel

Keterpress Enterprises Jerusalem, pg 1198
Monoline Ltd, pg 1198

Italy

Canale G e C SpA, pg 1198

Republic of Korea

Daehan Printing & Publishing Co Ltd, pg 1199
Pyunghwa Dang Printing Co Ltd, pg 1199

Lithuania

Spindulys Printing House, pg 1199

New Zealand

Bookprint Consultants Ltd, pg 1199
PPP Printers Ltd, pg 1199

Portugal

Silabo, pg 1200

Singapore

Chong Moh Offset Printing Ltd, pg 1200
Ho Printing Singapore Pte Ltd, pg 1200
International Press Co Pte Ltd, pg 1200
Markono Print Media Pte Ltd, pg 1200
SNP Printing Pte Ltd, pg 1200
Times Printers Pte Ltd, pg 1200
World Publications Printers Pte Ltd, pg 1201

Slovenia

Gorenjski Tisk Printing Co, pg 1201

Spain

Graficas Santamaria SA, pg 1201
Luis Vives (Edelvives), pg 1201

Sri Lanka

Sumathi Book Printing (Pvt) Ltd, pg 1201

Thailand

J Film Process Co Ltd, pg 1201
Phongwarin Printing Company Ltd, pg 1201

United Kingdom

W & G Baird Ltd, pg 1202
Bell & Bain Ltd, pg 1202
Biddles Ltd, pg 1202
The Charlesworth Group, pg 1202
Clays Ltd, pg 1203
William Clowes Ltd, pg 1203
Goldshield Communications Ltd, pg 1203
Hobbs The Printers Ltd, pg 1203
Ikon Document Services Ltd, pg 1203
Image & Print Group Ltd, pg 1203
Intype London Ltd, pg 1204
The Malvern Press Ltd, pg 1204
Page Bros Ltd (Norwich), pg 1204
Redwood Books Ltd, pg 1204
J R Reid Printing Group Ltd, pg 1204
Antony Rowe Ltd, pg 1204
Watkiss Automation Ltd, pg 1205

United States

ADR/BookPrint, pg 1205
Asia Pacific Offset Inc, pg 1205
C & C Offset Printing Co Ltd, pg 1205
Carvajal International Inc, pg 1206
Coneco Litho Graphics, pg 1206
Consolidated Printers Inc, pg 1206
Martin Cook Associates Ltd, pg 1206
DNP America LLC, pg 1206
Elegance Printing & Book Binding (USA), pg 1206
Express Media Corp, pg 1206
Fairfield Marketing Group Inc, pg 1206
Hamilton Printing Co, pg 1206
Integrated Book Technology Inc, pg 1207
Jinno International Group, pg 1207
KNI Inc, pg 1207
Lenz & Riecker Inc, pg 1207
Linick International Inc, pg 1207
LK Litho, pg 1207
Marrakech Express Inc, pg 1207
Printing Corp of the Americas Inc, pg 1208
Regent Publishing Services, pg 1208
Times Publishing Group, pg 1208
Fred Weidner & Daughter Printers, pg 1208

Uruguay

Barreiro y Ramos SA, pg 1208

MAP PRINTING

Canada

Herzig Somerville Ltd, pg 1193
Maracle Press Ltd, pg 1193
Printcrafters Inc, pg 1193
Transcontinental Printing Book Group, pg 1194
University of Toronto Press Inc, pg 1194

Czech Republic

GRASPO CZ AS - Druckerei und Buchbinderei, pg 1194

Germany

Priese GmbH, pg 1195

Hong Kong

Dai Nippon Printing Co (Hong Kong) Ltd, pg 1196
Everbest Printing Co Ltd, pg 1196
Golden Cup Printing Co Ltd, pg 1196
Sing Cheong Printing Co Limited, pg 1197
Unicorn International Printing Co Ltd, pg 1197

Indonesia

Ichtiar Baru I Van Hoeve, pg 1198
Victory Offset Prima PT, pg 1198

Italy

Canale G e C SpA, pg 1198
Amilcare Pizzi SpA, pg 1198

Republic of Korea

Daehan Printing & Publishing Co Ltd, pg 1199
Pyunghwa Dang Printing Co Ltd, pg 1199

New Zealand

Bookprint Consultants Ltd, pg 1199
PPP Printers Ltd, pg 1199

Philippines

Cacho Hermanos Inc, pg 1199

Singapore

SNP Printing Pte Ltd, pg 1200
Toppan Company (S) Pte Ltd, pg 1200

Spain

Graficas Santamaria SA, pg 1201

Switzerland

Hallwag AG, pg 1201

Thailand

Phongwarin Printing Company Ltd, pg 1201

United Arab Emirates

Emirates Printing Press (LLC), pg 1202

United Kingdom

Goldshield Communications Ltd, pg 1203
Headley Brothers Ltd, pg 1203

United States

Asia Pacific Offset Inc, pg 1205
BookBuilders New York Ltd, pg 1205
C & C Offset Printing Co Ltd, pg 1205
Martin Cook Associates Ltd, pg 1206
DNP America LLC, pg 1206
Elegance Printing & Book Binding (USA), pg 1206
Jinno International Group, pg 1207
KNI Inc, pg 1207
Leo Paper USA, pg 1207
Printing Corp of the Americas Inc, pg 1208
Regent Publishing Services, pg 1208
Fred Weidner & Daughter Printers, pg 1208

MANUFACTURING   PRINTING, BINDING & BOOK FINISHING INDEX

Uruguay
Barreiro y Ramos SA, pg 1208

MCCAIN SEWN BINDING

China
Speedflex Asia Ltd, pg 1194

Denmark
Bianco Lunos Bogtrykkeri AS, pg 1194

Germany
Priese GmbH, pg 1195

Hong Kong
Dai Nippon Printing Co (Hong Kong) Ltd, pg 1196
Toppan Printing Co (HK) Ltd, pg 1197
Unicorn International Printing Co Ltd, pg 1197
Wing King Tong Co Ltd (Printing Factory), pg 1197

Lithuania
Spindulys Printing House, pg 1199

Philippines
Cacho Hermanos Inc, pg 1199

Singapore
Markono Print Media Pte Ltd, pg 1200
SNP Printing Pte Ltd, pg 1200
Toppan Company (S) Pte Ltd, pg 1200
World Publications Printers Pte Ltd, pg 1201

Spain
Grafos SA Arte Sobre Papel, pg 1201
Graficas Santamaria SA, pg 1201
Luis Vives (Edelvives), pg 1201

United Republic of Tanzania
Peramiho Publications, pg 1201

United Kingdom
J W Arrowsmith Ltd, pg 1202
BAS Printers Ltd, pg 1202
Goldshield Communications Ltd, pg 1203
Hobbs The Printers Ltd, pg 1203

United States
Asia Pacific Offset Inc, pg 1205
BookBuilders New York Ltd, pg 1205
Martin Cook Associates Ltd, pg 1206
DNP America LLC, pg 1206
Elegance Printing & Book Binding (USA), pg 1206
Express Media Corp, pg 1206
Hindy's Enterprise, pg 1207
Jinno International Group, pg 1207
Linick International Inc, pg 1207
Regent Publishing Services, pg 1208
Fred Weidner & Daughter Printers, pg 1208

METAL COMPOSITION

Germany
Priese GmbH, pg 1195

Hong Kong
Unicorn International Printing Co Ltd, pg 1197

Lithuania
Spindulys Printing House, pg 1199

New Zealand
John McIndoe Ltd, pg 1199

Spain
Graficas Santamaria SA, pg 1201

United Republic of Tanzania
Peramiho Publications, pg 1201

United Kingdom
J R Reid Printing Group Ltd, pg 1204
Watkiss Automation Ltd, pg 1205

United States
Fred Weidner & Daughter Printers, pg 1208

Uruguay
Barreiro y Ramos SA, pg 1208

NOTCH BINDING

Canada
Maracle Press Ltd, pg 1193
Printcrafters Inc, pg 1193
Transcontinental Printing Book Group, pg 1194
Tri-Graphic Printing (Ottawa) Ltd, pg 1194
University of Toronto Press Inc, pg 1194

Germany
Priese GmbH, pg 1195

Hong Kong
Bright Future Printing Co Ltd, pg 1195
C & C Offset Printing Co Ltd, pg 1195
Caritas Printing Training Centre, pg 1195
Dai Nippon Printing Co (Hong Kong) Ltd, pg 1196
Everbest Printing Co Ltd, pg 1196
Golden Cup Printing Co Ltd, pg 1196
Leo Paper Products Ltd, pg 1196
Midas Printing Ltd, pg 1197
Morris Press Ltd, pg 1197
Paramount Publishing Group Limited, pg 1197
South Sea International Press Ltd, pg 1197
Unicorn International Printing Co Ltd, pg 1197

Indonesia
Victory Offset Prima PT, pg 1198

Italy
Canale G e C SpA, pg 1198

New Zealand
Bookprint Consultants Ltd, pg 1199

Singapore
Chong Moh Offset Printing Ltd, pg 1200
CS Graphics Pte Ltd, pg 1200
Eurasia Press Pte Ltd, pg 1200
SNP Printing Pte Ltd, pg 1200
Toppan Company (S) Pte Ltd, pg 1200

United Republic of Tanzania
Peramiho Publications, pg 1201

United Arab Emirates
Emirates Printing Press (LLC), pg 1202

United Kingdom
Biddles Ltd, pg 1202
Caledonian International Book Manufacturing, pg 1202
Goldshield Communications Ltd, pg 1203
MPG Books Ltd, pg 1204
Page Bros Ltd (Norwich), pg 1204
Redwood Books Ltd, pg 1204
TJ International Ltd, pg 1205
Watkiss Automation Ltd, pg 1205

United States
Asia Pacific Offset Inc, pg 1205
Blaze International Productions Inc, pg 1205
BookBuilders New York Ltd, pg 1205
C & C Offset Printing Co Ltd, pg 1205
Martin Cook Associates Ltd, pg 1206
CS Graphics USA Inc, pg 1206
DNP America LLC, pg 1206
Elegance Printing & Book Binding (USA), pg 1206
Express Media Corp, pg 1206
Hamilton Printing Co, pg 1206
Hindy's Enterprise, pg 1207
Imago, pg 1207
Jinno International Group, pg 1207
Leo Paper USA, pg 1207
Linick International Inc, pg 1207
Regent Publishing Services, pg 1208
Fred Weidner & Daughter Printers, pg 1208

OFFSET PRINTING - SHEETFED

Australia
Southwood Press Pty Ltd, pg 1193

Austria
ADEVA (Akademische Druck-u Verlagsanstalt), pg 1193

Belgium
Delabie Europrint SA, pg 1193
IMPF BV BA, pg 1193

Canada
Coach House Printing, pg 1193
Herzig Somerville Ltd, pg 1193
Maracle Press Ltd, pg 1193
Preney Print & Litho Inc, pg 1193
Printcrafters Inc, pg 1193
Transcontinental Printing Book Group, pg 1194
Tri-Graphic Printing (Ottawa) Ltd, pg 1194
University of Toronto Press Inc, pg 1194
Webcom Ltd, pg 1194

Czech Republic
GRASPO CZ AS - Druckerei und Buchbinderei, pg 1194

Denmark
Bianco Lunos Bogtrykkeri AS, pg 1194

Finland
Gummerus Printing, pg 1194
WS Bookwell Ltd, pg 1194

France
Imprimerie Gaignault, pg 1194
Plein Chant, pg 1194
Signes du Monde, pg 1194

Germany
C L Baader Buch & Offsetdruckere GmbH & Co KG, pg 1194
C Maurer Druck und Verlag, pg 1195
Mohndruck Graphische Betriebe GmbH, pg 1195
Oertel & Sporer GmbH & Co, pg 1195
Priese GmbH, pg 1195
Vier-Tuerme GmbH Benedikt Press, pg 1195

Hong Kong
Best-Set Typesetter Ltd, pg 1195
Bright Future Printing Co Ltd, pg 1195
C & C Offset Printing Co Ltd, pg 1195
Caritas Printing Training Centre, pg 1195
Dai Nippon Printing Co (Hong Kong) Ltd, pg 1196
Everbest Printing Co Ltd, pg 1196
Golden Cup Printing Co Ltd, pg 1196
The Green Pagoda Press Ltd, pg 1196
Hoi Kwong Printing Co Ltd, pg 1196
Hung Hing Off-set Printing Co Ltd, pg 1196
Image Printing Company Ltd, pg 1196
Leo Paper Products Ltd, pg 1196
Liang Yu Printing Factory Ltd, pg 1196
Midas Printing Ltd, pg 1197
Morris Press Ltd, pg 1197
Paper Art Product Ltd, pg 1197
Paper Communication Printing Express Ltd, pg 1197
Paramount Publishing Group Limited, pg 1197
Prontaprint Asia Ltd, pg 1197
Sheck Wah Tong Printing Press, pg 1197
Sing Cheong Printing Co Limited, pg 1197
Sino Publishing House Ltd, pg 1197
South Sea International Press Ltd, pg 1197
Sunshine Press Ltd, pg 1197
Toppan Printing Co (HK) Ltd, pg 1197

PRINTING, BINDING & BOOK FINISHING INDEX

Unicorn International Printing Co Ltd, pg 1197
Wing King Tong Co Ltd (Printing Factory), pg 1197

Hungary
Interpress Aussenhandels GmbH, pg 1197

India
Hiralal Printing Works Ltd, pg 1197

Indonesia
Ichtiar Baru I Van Hoeve, pg 1198
Victory Offset Prima PT, pg 1198

Ireland
Kilkenny People/Wellbrook Press, pg 1198
Smurfit Print, pg 1198
Ultragraphics, pg 1198

Israel
Keterpress Enterprises Jerusalem, pg 1198
Technosdar Ltd, pg 1198

Italy
Canale G e C SpA, pg 1198
Dedalo Litostampa SRL, pg 1198
Mariani Ritti Grafiche SRL, pg 1198
Milanostampa SPA, pg 1198
Nuovo Instituto Italiano d'Arti Grafiche, pg 1198
Amilcare Pizzi SpA, pg 1198

Japan
Nissha Printing Co Ltd, pg 1198

Republic of Korea
Daehan Printing & Publishing Co Ltd, pg 1199
Pyunghwa Dang Printing Co Ltd, pg 1199

Lithuania
Spindulys Printing House, pg 1199

Malaysia
Web Printers Sdn Bhd, pg 1199

Malta
Interprint Ltd - Malta, pg 1199

Netherlands
Bosch en Keuning grafische bedrijven, pg 1199

New Zealand
Bookprint Consultants Ltd, pg 1199
John McIndoe Ltd, pg 1199
PPP Printers Ltd, pg 1199

Peru
Industrias del Envase SA, pg 1199

Philippines
Cacho Hermanos Inc, pg 1199
JF Printhaus, pg 1199
Naldoza Printers, pg 1199
Philippine Graphic Arts Inc, pg 1199

Singapore
Chong Moh Offset Printing Ltd, pg 1200
Columbia Overseas Marketing Pte Ltd, pg 1200
CS Graphics Pte Ltd, pg 1200
Eurasia Press Pte Ltd, pg 1200
Ho Printing Singapore Pte Ltd, pg 1200
International Press Co Pte Ltd, pg 1200
Markono Print Media Pte Ltd, pg 1200
PacPress Media Pte Ltd, pg 1200
SNP Printing Pte Ltd, pg 1200
Stamford Press Pte Ltd, pg 1200
Tien Wah Press Pte Ltd, pg 1200
Toppan Company (S) Pte Ltd, pg 1200
World Publications Printers Pte Ltd, pg 1201

Slovenia
Gorenjski Tisk Printing Co, pg 1201

Spain
Grafos SA Arte Sobre Papel, pg 1201
Printer Industria Grafica SA, pg 1201
Rotedic SA, pg 1201
Graficas Santamaria SA, pg 1201
Luis Vives (Edelvives), pg 1201

Sri Lanka
Sumathi Book Printing (Pvt) Ltd, pg 1201

United Republic of Tanzania
Peramiho Publications, pg 1201

Thailand
J Film Process Co Ltd, pg 1201
Mavisu International Co Ltd, pg 1201
Phongwarin Printing Company Ltd, pg 1201

United Arab Emirates
Emirates Printing Press (LLC), pg 1202

United Kingdom
The Alden Group Ltd, pg 1202
J W Arrowsmith Ltd, pg 1202
BAS Printers Ltd, pg 1202
Ebenezer Baylis & Son Ltd, pg 1202
Biddles Ltd, pg 1202
Black Bear Press Ltd, pg 1202
Blackmore Ltd, pg 1202
Butler & Tanner Ltd, pg 1202
Caledonian International Book Manufacturing, pg 1202
Cambridge University Press - Printing Division, pg 1202
The Charlesworth Group, pg 1202
Clays Ltd, pg 1203
William Clowes Ltd, pg 1203
Cox & Wyman Ltd, pg 1203
Cradley Print Ltd, pg 1203
Essex Colour Services Ltd, pg 1203
Furnival Press, pg 1203
Goldshield Communications Ltd, pg 1203
The Guernsey Press Co Ltd, pg 1203
Headley Brothers Ltd, pg 1203
Lavenham Press Ltd, pg 1204
Charles Letts & Co Ltd, pg 1204
Lowfield Printing Co Ltd, pg 1204
MacKays of Chatham PLC, pg 1204
The Malvern Press Ltd, pg 1204
MPG Books Ltd, pg 1204
Multiplex Medway Ltd, pg 1204
Redwood Books Ltd, pg 1204
J R Reid Printing Group Ltd, pg 1204
Antony Rowe Ltd, pg 1204
Selwood Printing, pg 1204
Severnside Printers Ltd, pg 1204
TJ International Ltd, pg 1205
Watkiss Automation Ltd, pg 1205

United States
ADR/BookPrint, pg 1205
Alpina Color Graphics Inc, pg 1205
Asia Pacific Offset Inc, pg 1205
Blaze International Productions Inc, pg 1205
BookBuilders New York Ltd, pg 1205
Butler & Tanner Inc, pg 1205
C & C Offset Printing Co Ltd, pg 1205
Colorprint Offset Inc, pg 1206
Coneco Litho Graphics, pg 1206
Martin Cook Associates Ltd, pg 1206
CS Graphics USA Inc, pg 1206
DNP America LLC, pg 1206
Editoriale Bortolazzi-Stei srl, pg 1206
Elegance Printing & Book Binding (USA), pg 1206
Fairfield Marketing Group Inc, pg 1206
Hamilton Printing Co, pg 1206
Hindy's Enterprise, pg 1207
Ikon Document Services, pg 1207
Imago, pg 1207
Integrated Book Technology Inc, pg 1207
Jinno International Group, pg 1207
KNI Inc, pg 1207
Lenz & Riecker Inc, pg 1207
Leo Paper USA, pg 1207
Linick International Inc, pg 1207
LK Litho, pg 1207
Marrakech Express Inc, pg 1207
Mazer Publishing Services, pg 1208
Milanostampa/New Interlitho USA Inc, pg 1208
Naturegraph Publishers Inc, pg 1208
Palace Press International, pg 1208
Printing Corp of the Americas Inc, pg 1208
Regent Publishing Services, pg 1208
Taylor Publishing Co, pg 1208
Times Publishing Group, pg 1208
Vicks Lithograph & Printing Corp, pg 1208
Fred Weidner & Daughter Printers, pg 1208

Uruguay
Barreiro y Ramos SA, pg 1208

OFFSET PRINTING - WEB

Belgium
Delabie Europrint SA, pg 1193

Canada
Arpeco Engineering, pg 1193
Maracle Press Ltd, pg 1193
Preney Print & Litho Inc, pg 1193

Transcontinental Printing Book Group, pg 1194
Tri-Graphic Printing (Ottawa) Ltd, pg 1194
Webcom Ltd, pg 1194

China
Speedflex Asia Ltd, pg 1194

Czech Republic
GRASPO CZ AS - Druckerei und Buchbinderei, pg 1194

Finland
Gummerus Printing, pg 1194
WS Bookwell Ltd, pg 1194

Germany
Mohndruck Graphische Betriebe GmbH, pg 1195
Priese GmbH, pg 1195

Hong Kong
C & C Offset Printing Co Ltd, pg 1195
Dai Nippon Printing Co (Hong Kong) Ltd, pg 1196
Paramount Publishing Group Limited, pg 1197
Toppan Printing Co (HK) Ltd, pg 1197

Hungary
Interpress Aussenhandels GmbH, pg 1197

Ireland
Kilkenny People/Wellbrook Press, pg 1198
Ultragraphics, pg 1198

Italy
Canale G e C SpA, pg 1198
Milanostampa SPA, pg 1198
Nuovo Instituto Italiano d'Arti Grafiche, pg 1198
Amilcare Pizzi SpA, pg 1198

Japan
Nissha Printing Co Ltd, pg 1198

Republic of Korea
Daehan Printing & Publishing Co Ltd, pg 1199
Pyunghwa Dang Printing Co Ltd, pg 1199

Lithuania
Spindulys Printing House, pg 1199

Malaysia
Web Printers Sdn Bhd, pg 1199

Netherlands
Bosch en Keuning grafische bedrijven, pg 1199

Philippines
Cacho Hermanos Inc, pg 1199

Singapore
Huntsmen Offset Printing Pte Ltd, pg 1200
Markono Print Media Pte Ltd, pg 1200

MANUFACTURING   PRINTING, BINDING & BOOK FINISHING INDEX

Times Printers Pte Ltd, pg 1200
Toppan Company (S) Pte Ltd, pg 1200

South Africa
CTP Book Printers (Pty) Ltd, pg 1201

Spain
Printer Industria Grafica SA, pg 1201
Rotedic SA, pg 1201

Sri Lanka
Sumathi Book Printing (Pvt) Ltd, pg 1201

United Republic of Tanzania
Peramiho Publications, pg 1201

Thailand
J Film Process Co Ltd, pg 1201

United Kingdom
Biddles Ltd, pg 1202
Blackmore Ltd, pg 1202
Caledonian International Book Manufacturing, pg 1202
Clays Ltd, pg 1203
William Clowes Ltd, pg 1203
Cox & Wyman Ltd, pg 1203
Cradley Print Ltd, pg 1203
Goldshield Communications Ltd, pg 1203
The Guernsey Press Co Ltd, pg 1203
Headley Brothers Ltd, pg 1203
Charles Letts & Co Ltd, pg 1204
MacKays of Chatham PLC, pg 1204
MPG Books Ltd, pg 1204
J R Reid Printing Group Ltd, pg 1204

United States
ADR/BookPrint, pg 1205
Asia Pacific Offset Inc, pg 1205
Blaze International Productions Inc, pg 1205
BookBuilders New York Ltd, pg 1205
Consolidated Printers Inc, pg 1206
Martin Cook Associates Ltd, pg 1206
DNP America LLC, pg 1206
Editoriale Bortolazzi-Stei srl, pg 1206
Fairfield Marketing Group Inc, pg 1206
Hamilton Printing Co, pg 1206
Imago, pg 1207
Jinno International Group, pg 1207
KNI Inc, pg 1207
Lenz & Riecker Inc, pg 1207
Linick International Inc, pg 1207
LK Litho, pg 1207
Mazer Publishing Services, pg 1208
Palace Press International, pg 1208
Printing Corp of the Americas Inc, pg 1208
Times Publishing Group, pg 1208
Vicks Lithograph & Printing Corp, pg 1208
Fred Weidner & Daughter Printers, pg 1208

ON DEMAND PRINTING

Germany
C Maurer Druck und Verlag, pg 1195

Philippines
JF Printhaus, pg 1199

United Kingdom
The Charlesworth Group, pg 1202
Redwood Books Ltd, pg 1204

United States
ADR/BookPrint, pg 1205
Asia Pacific Offset Inc, pg 1205

PERFECT (ADHESIVE) BINDING

Australia
Southwood Press Pty Ltd, pg 1193

Belgium
Drukkerij Lannoo NV, pg 1193

Canada
Appleby's Bindery Ltd, pg 1193
Coach House Printing, pg 1193
Maracle Press Ltd, pg 1193
Preney Print & Litho Inc, pg 1193
Printcrafters Inc, pg 1193
Productive Publications, pg 1193
Transcontinental Printing Book Group, pg 1194
Tri-Graphic Printing (Ottawa) Ltd, pg 1194
University of Toronto Press Inc, pg 1194
Webcom Ltd, pg 1194

China
Speedflex Asia Ltd, pg 1194

Czech Republic
GRASPO CZ AS - Druckerei und Buchbinderei, pg 1194

Denmark
Bianco Lunos Bogtrykkeri AS, pg 1194

Finland
Gummerus Printing, pg 1194

Germany
Media-Print Informationstechnologie GmbH, pg 1195
Mohndruck Graphische Betriebe GmbH, pg 1195
Priese GmbH, pg 1195
Vier-Tuerme GmbH Benedikt Press, pg 1195

Hong Kong
Bright Future Printing Co Ltd, pg 1195
C & C Offset Printing Co Ltd, pg 1195
Caritas Printing Training Centre, pg 1195
Colorprint Offset, pg 1195
Dai Nippon Printing Co (Hong Kong) Ltd, pg 1196
Everbest Printing Co Ltd, pg 1196

Golden Cup Printing Co Ltd, pg 1196
The Green Pagoda Press Ltd, pg 1196
Hung Hing Off-set Printing Co Ltd, pg 1196
Image Printing Company Ltd, pg 1196
Leo Paper Products Ltd, pg 1196
Liang Yu Printing Factory Ltd, pg 1196
Midas Printing Ltd, pg 1197
Paper Art Product Ltd, pg 1197
Paper Communication Printing Express Ltd, pg 1197
Paramount Publishing Group Limited, pg 1197
Prontaprint Asia Ltd, pg 1197
Sing Cheong Printing Co Limited, pg 1197
Sino Publishing House Ltd, pg 1197
South Sea International Press Ltd, pg 1197
Sunshine Press Ltd, pg 1197
Toppan Printing Co (HK) Ltd, pg 1197
Unicorn International Printing Co Ltd, pg 1197
Wing King Tong Co Ltd (Printing Factory), pg 1197

Hungary
Interpress Aussenhandels GmbH, pg 1197

India
Hiralal Printing Works Ltd, pg 1197

Indonesia
Victory Offset Prima PT, pg 1198

Ireland
Kilkenny People/Wellbrook Press, pg 1198
Smurfit Print, pg 1198

Israel
Keterpress Enterprises Jerusalem, pg 1198

Italy
Canale G e C SpA, pg 1198
Milanostampa SPA, pg 1198
Nuovo Instituto Italiano d'Arti Grafiche, pg 1198
Amilcare Pizzi SpA, pg 1198

Republic of Korea
Daehan Printing & Publishing Co Ltd, pg 1199
Pyunghwa Dang Printing Co Ltd, pg 1199

Lithuania
Spindulys Printing House, pg 1199

New Zealand
Bookprint Consultants Ltd, pg 1199
John McIndoe Ltd, pg 1199

Philippines
Cacho Hermanos Inc, pg 1199
Philippine Graphic Arts Inc, pg 1199

Singapore
Chong Moh Offset Printing Ltd, pg 1200
Columbia Overseas Marketing Pte Ltd, pg 1200
Craft Print Pte Ltd, pg 1200
CS Graphics Pte Ltd, pg 1200
Eurasia Press Pte Ltd, pg 1200
Ho Printing Singapore Pte Ltd, pg 1200
Huntsmen Offset Printing Pte Ltd, pg 1200
International Press Co Pte Ltd, pg 1200
Markono Print Media Pte Ltd, pg 1200
SNP Printing Pte Ltd, pg 1200
Stamford Press Pte Ltd, pg 1200
Times Printers Pte Ltd, pg 1200
Toppan Company (S) Pte Ltd, pg 1200
World Publications Printers Pte Ltd, pg 1201

Slovenia
Gorenjski Tisk Printing Co, pg 1201

Spain
Grafos SA Arte Sobre Papel, pg 1201
Printer Industria Grafica SA, pg 1201
Rotedic SA, pg 1201

Sri Lanka
Sumathi Book Printing (Pvt) Ltd, pg 1201

United Republic of Tanzania
Peramiho Publications, pg 1201

Thailand
J Film Process Co Ltd, pg 1201

United Arab Emirates
Emirates Printing Press (LLC), pg 1202

United Kingdom
J W Arrowsmith Ltd, pg 1202
BAS Printers Ltd, pg 1202
Biddles Ltd, pg 1202
Black Bear Press Ltd, pg 1202
Book Creation Services, pg 1202
J W Braithwaite & Son Ltd, pg 1202
Caledonian International Book Manufacturing, pg 1202
CB Print Finishers Ltd, pg 1202
The Charlesworth Group, pg 1202
Clays Ltd, pg 1203
William Clowes Ltd, pg 1203
Cox & Wyman Ltd, pg 1203
Cradley Print Ltd, pg 1203
Goldshield Communications Ltd, pg 1203
The Guernsey Press Co Ltd, pg 1203
Hammond Bindery Ltd, pg 1203
Headley Brothers Ltd, pg 1203
Hobbs The Printers Ltd, pg 1203
Ikon Document Services Ltd, pg 1203
Intype London Ltd, pg 1204
Lowfield Printing Co Ltd, pg 1204
MPG Books Ltd, pg 1204
Page Bros Ltd (Norwich), pg 1204
Redwood Books Ltd, pg 1204
Antony Rowe Ltd, pg 1204
Selwood Printing, pg 1204

1185

PRINTING, BINDING & BOOK FINISHING INDEX

Severnside Printers Ltd, pg 1204
TJ International Ltd, pg 1205
Watkiss Automation Ltd, pg 1205
WH Trade Binders Ltd, pg 1205

United States
ADR/BookPrint, pg 1205
Asia Pacific Offset Inc, pg 1205
Blaze International Productions Inc, pg 1205
BookBuilders New York Ltd, pg 1205
Colorprint Offset Inc, pg 1206
Coneco Litho Graphics, pg 1206
Consolidated Printers Inc, pg 1206
Martin Cook Associates Ltd, pg 1206
CS Graphics USA Inc, pg 1206
DNP America LLC, pg 1206
Elegance Printing & Book Binding (USA), pg 1206
Express Media Corp, pg 1206
Hamilton Printing Co, pg 1206
Hindy's Enterprise, pg 1207
Ikon Document Services, pg 1207
Imago, pg 1207
Integrated Book Technology Inc, pg 1207
Jinno International Group, pg 1207
KNI Inc, pg 1207
Lenz & Riecker Inc, pg 1207
Leo Paper USA, pg 1207
Linick International Inc, pg 1207
LK Litho, pg 1207
Milanostampa/New Interlitho USA Inc, pg 1208
Naturegraph Publishers Inc, pg 1208
Printing Corp of the Americas Inc, pg 1208
Regent Publishing Services, pg 1208
Times Publishing Group, pg 1208
Vicks Lithograph & Printing Corp, pg 1208
Fred Weidner & Daughter Printers, pg 1208

Uruguay
Barreiro y Ramos SA, pg 1208

PHOTOCOMPOSITION

Canada
Coach House Printing, pg 1193
Maracle Press Ltd, pg 1193
Transcontinental Printing Book Group, pg 1194
Tri-Graphic Printing (Ottawa) Ltd, pg 1194
University of Toronto Press Inc, pg 1194
Webcom Ltd, pg 1194

Czech Republic
GRASPO CZ AS - Druckerei und Buchbinderei, pg 1194

Denmark
Bianco Lunos Bogtrykkeri AS, pg 1194

France
Imprimerie Gaignault, pg 1194

Germany
C L Baader Buch & Offsetdruckere GmbH & Co KG, pg 1194
Priese GmbH, pg 1195

Hong Kong
Commercial Colorlab Ltd, pg 1195
Unicorn International Printing Co Ltd, pg 1197

Hungary
Interpress Aussenhandels GmbH, pg 1197

Ireland
Kilkenny People/Wellbrook Press, pg 1198
Smurfit Print, pg 1198

Israel
Keterpress Enterprises Jerusalem, pg 1198
Monoline Ltd, pg 1198
Technosdar Ltd, pg 1198

Italy
Canale G e C SpA, pg 1198
Dedalo Litostampa SRL, pg 1198
Minerva Medica, pg 1198
Nuovo Instituto Italiano d'Arti Grafiche, pg 1198

Republic of Korea
Daehan Printing & Publishing Co Ltd, pg 1199

Lithuania
Spindulys Printing House, pg 1199

Malta
Interprint Ltd - Malta, pg 1199

New Zealand
John McIndoe Ltd, pg 1199

Philippines
Cacho Hermanos Inc, pg 1199

Portugal
Silabo, pg 1200

Puerto Rico
Publishing Resources Inc, pg 1200

Singapore
Stamford Press Pte Ltd, pg 1200
Toppan Company (S) Pte Ltd, pg 1200

Slovenia
Gorenjski Tisk Printing Co, pg 1201

Spain
Graficas Santamaria SA, pg 1201

Switzerland
Photolitho AG, pg 1201

United Republic of Tanzania
Peramiho Publications, pg 1201

Thailand
Mavisu International Co Ltd, pg 1201

United Kingdom
J W Arrowsmith Ltd, pg 1202
Cambridge University Press - Printing Division, pg 1202
The Charlesworth Group, pg 1202
Ikon Document Services Ltd, pg 1203
Image & Print Group Ltd, pg 1203
Intype London Ltd, pg 1204
J R Reid Printing Group Ltd, pg 1204
Stott Brothers Ltd, pg 1204
Watkiss Automation Ltd, pg 1205

United States
Coneco Litho Graphics, pg 1206
Martin Cook Associates Ltd, pg 1206
Elegance Printing & Book Binding (USA), pg 1206
Ikon Document Services, pg 1207
Jinno International Group, pg 1207
Leo Paper USA, pg 1207
Linick International Inc, pg 1207
LK Litho, pg 1207
Fred Weidner & Daughter Printers, pg 1208

Uruguay
Barreiro y Ramos SA, pg 1208

PLASTIC COMB BINDING

Canada
Maracle Press Ltd, pg 1193
University of Toronto Press Inc, pg 1194

China
Speedflex Asia Ltd, pg 1194

Germany
Priese GmbH, pg 1195

Hong Kong
C & C Offset Printing Co Ltd, pg 1195
Dai Nippon Printing Co (Hong Kong) Ltd, pg 1196
The Green Pagoda Press Ltd, pg 1196
Hung Hing Off-set Printing Co Ltd, pg 1196
Image Printing Company Ltd, pg 1196
Leo Paper Products Ltd, pg 1196
Midas Printing Ltd, pg 1197
Prontaprint Asia Ltd, pg 1197
Sing Cheong Printing Co Limited, pg 1197
Sino Publishing House Ltd, pg 1197
South Sea International Press Ltd, pg 1197
Unicorn International Printing Co Ltd, pg 1197

Italy
Canale G e C SpA, pg 1198

New Zealand
Bookprint Consultants Ltd, pg 1199

Singapore
Eurasia Press Pte Ltd, pg 1200
Ho Printing Singapore Pte Ltd, pg 1200
Markono Print Media Pte Ltd, pg 1200
SNP Printing Pte Ltd, pg 1200
Toppan Company (S) Pte Ltd, pg 1200

Slovenia
Gorenjski Tisk Printing Co, pg 1201

United Republic of Tanzania
Peramiho Publications, pg 1201

United Kingdom
Biddles Ltd, pg 1202
J W Braithwaite & Son Ltd, pg 1202
Center Print Ltd, pg 1202
Ikon Document Services Ltd, pg 1203
Redwood Books Ltd, pg 1204
J R Reid Printing Group Ltd, pg 1204
Watkiss Automation Ltd, pg 1205

United States
ADR/BookPrint, pg 1205
Asia Pacific Offset Inc, pg 1205
Bind-It Corp, pg 1205
Blaze International Productions Inc, pg 1205
BookBuilders New York Ltd, pg 1205
C & C Offset Printing Co Ltd, pg 1205
Coneco Litho Graphics, pg 1206
Martin Cook Associates Ltd, pg 1206
DNP America LLC, pg 1206
Elegance Printing & Book Binding (USA), pg 1206
Express Media Corp, pg 1206
Hamilton Printing Co, pg 1206
Hindy's Enterprise, pg 1207
Ikon Document Services, pg 1207
Imago, pg 1207
Integrated Book Technology Inc, pg 1207
Jinno International Group, pg 1207
KNI Inc, pg 1207
Leo Paper USA, pg 1207
Linick International Inc, pg 1207
LK Litho, pg 1207
Printing Corp of the Americas Inc, pg 1208
Regent Publishing Services, pg 1208
Vicks Lithograph & Printing Corp, pg 1208
Fred Weidner & Daughter Printers, pg 1208

SADDLE STITCH BINDING

Belgium
Drukkerij Lannoo NV, pg 1193

Canada
Aardvark Enterprises, pg 1193
Maracle Press Ltd, pg 1193
Preney Print & Litho Inc, pg 1193
Printcrafters Inc, pg 1193
Transcontinental Printing Book Group, pg 1194
Tri-Graphic Printing (Ottawa) Ltd, pg 1194
University of Toronto Press Inc, pg 1194
Webcom Ltd, pg 1194

China
Speedflex Asia Ltd, pg 1194

MANUFACTURING

PRINTING, BINDING & BOOK FINISHING INDEX

Czech Republic
GRASPO CZ AS - Druckerei und Buchbinderei, pg 1194

Denmark
Bianco Lunos Bogtrykkeri AS, pg 1194

Germany
C Maurer Druck und Verlag, pg 1195
Priese GmbH, pg 1195

Hong Kong
Best-Set Typesetter Ltd, pg 1195
Bright Future Printing Co Ltd, pg 1195
C & C Offset Printing Co Ltd, pg 1195
Colorprint Offset, pg 1195
Dai Nippon Printing Co (Hong Kong) Ltd, pg 1196
Everbest Printing Co Ltd, pg 1196
Golden Cup Printing Co Ltd, pg 1196
The Green Pagoda Press Ltd, pg 1196
Hing Yip Printing Co Ltd, pg 1196
Hung Hing Off-set Printing Co Ltd, pg 1196
Image Printing Company Ltd, pg 1196
Leo Paper Products Ltd, pg 1196
Midas Printing Ltd, pg 1197
Morris Press Ltd, pg 1197
Paper Art Product Ltd, pg 1197
Paper Communication Printing Express Ltd, pg 1197
Paramount Publishing Group Limited, pg 1197
Prontaprint Asia Ltd, pg 1197
Sing Cheong Printing Co Limited, pg 1197
Sino Publishing House Ltd, pg 1197
South Sea International Press Ltd, pg 1197
Sunshine Press Ltd, pg 1197
Toppan Printing Co (HK) Ltd, pg 1197
Unicorn International Printing Co Ltd, pg 1197
Wing King Tong Co Ltd (Printing Factory), pg 1197

India
Hiralal Printing Works Ltd, pg 1197

Indonesia
Victory Offset Prima PT, pg 1198

Ireland
Smurfit Print, pg 1198

Israel
Keterpress Enterprises Jerusalem, pg 1198

Italy
Canale G e C SpA, pg 1198
Milanostampa SPA, pg 1198

Republic of Korea
Daehan Printing & Publishing Co Ltd, pg 1199
Pyunghwa Dang Printing Co Ltd, pg 1199

Malta
Interprint Ltd - Malta, pg 1199

New Zealand
Bookprint Consultants Ltd, pg 1199
John McIndoe Ltd, pg 1199
PPP Printers Ltd, pg 1199

Philippines
Cacho Hermanos Inc, pg 1199
Philippine Graphic Arts Inc, pg 1199

Singapore
Chong Moh Offset Printing Ltd, pg 1200
Columbia Overseas Marketing Pte Ltd, pg 1200
Eurasia Press Pte Ltd, pg 1200
Ho Printing Singapore Pte Ltd, pg 1200
Huntsmen Offset Printing Pte Ltd, pg 1200
International Press Co Pte Ltd, pg 1200
Markono Print Media Pte Ltd, pg 1200
SNP Printing Pte Ltd, pg 1200
Stamford Press Pte Ltd, pg 1200
Times Printers Pte Ltd, pg 1200
Toppan Company (S) Pte Ltd, pg 1200
World Publications Printers Pte Ltd, pg 1201

Slovenia
Gorenjski Tisk Printing Co, pg 1201

Spain
Printer Industria Grafica SA, pg 1201
Rotedic SA, pg 1201

United Republic of Tanzania
Peramiho Publications, pg 1201

Thailand
J Film Process Co Ltd, pg 1201

United Arab Emirates
Emirates Printing Press (LLC), pg 1202

United Kingdom
The Alden Group Ltd, pg 1202
J W Arrowsmith Ltd, pg 1202
BAS Printers Ltd, pg 1202
Bell & Bain Ltd, pg 1202
Biddles Ltd, pg 1202
Black Bear Press Ltd, pg 1202
Blackmore Ltd, pg 1202
Book Creation Services, pg 1202
Caledonian International Book Manufacturing, pg 1202
Cambridge University Press - Printing Division, pg 1202
Center Print Ltd, pg 1202
The Charlesworth Group, pg 1202
William Clowes Ltd, pg 1203
Cradley Print Ltd, pg 1203
Furnival Press, pg 1203
The Guernsey Press Co Ltd, pg 1203
Headley Brothers Ltd, pg 1203
Hobbs The Printers Ltd, pg 1203
Ikon Document Services Ltd, pg 1203
Intype London Ltd, pg 1204
Lowfield Printing Co Ltd, pg 1204
Redwood Books Ltd, pg 1204
J R Reid Printing Group Ltd, pg 1204
M & A Thomson Litho Ltd, pg 1205
Watkiss Automation Ltd, pg 1205

United States
ADR/BookPrint, pg 1205
Asia Pacific Offset Inc, pg 1205
Blaze International Productions Inc, pg 1205
BookBuilders New York Ltd, pg 1205
Butler & Tanner Inc, pg 1205
C & C Offset Printing Co Ltd, pg 1205
Colorprint Offset Inc, pg 1206
Coneco Litho Graphics, pg 1206
Consolidated Printers Inc, pg 1206
Martin Cook Associates Ltd, pg 1206
DNP America LLC, pg 1206
Editoriale Bortolazzi-Stei srl, pg 1206
Express Media Corp, pg 1206
Fairfield Marketing Group Inc, pg 1206
Hamilton Printing Co, pg 1206
Hindy's Enterprise, pg 1207
Ikon Document Services, pg 1207
Imago, pg 1207
Integrated Book Technology Inc, pg 1207
Jinno International Group, pg 1207
KNI Inc, pg 1207
Leo Paper USA, pg 1207
Linick International Inc, pg 1207
LK Litho, pg 1207
Milanostampa/New Interlitho USA Inc, pg 1208
Palace Press International, pg 1208
Printing Corp of the Americas Inc, pg 1208
Regent Publishing Services, pg 1208
Times Publishing Group, pg 1208
Vicks Lithograph & Printing Corp, pg 1208
Fred Weidner & Daughter Printers, pg 1208

SHORT RUN PRINTING

Austria
ADEVA (Akademische Druck-u Verlagsanstalt), pg 1193

Canada
Aardvark Enterprises, pg 1193
Coach House Printing, pg 1193
Maracle Press Ltd, pg 1193
Preney Print & Litho Inc, pg 1193
Printcrafters Inc, pg 1193
Productive Publications, pg 1193
Transcontinental Printing Book Group, pg 1194
Tri-Graphic Printing (Ottawa) Ltd, pg 1194
University of Toronto Press Inc, pg 1194
Webcom Ltd, pg 1194

China
Speedflex Asia Ltd, pg 1194

Denmark
Bianco Lunos Bogtrykkeri AS, pg 1194

Finland
Gummerus Printing, pg 1194

Germany
C L Baader Buch & Offsetdruckere GmbH & Co KG, pg 1194
C Maurer Druck und Verlag, pg 1195
Media-Print Informationstechnologie GmbH, pg 1195
Priese GmbH, pg 1195

Hong Kong
Best-Set Typesetter Ltd, pg 1195
Bright Future Printing Co Ltd, pg 1195
The Green Pagoda Press Ltd, pg 1196
Image Printing Company Ltd, pg 1196
Morris Press Ltd, pg 1197
Paper Communication Printing Express Ltd, pg 1197
Prontaprint Asia Ltd, pg 1197
Sing Cheong Printing Co Limited, pg 1197
Unicorn International Printing Co Ltd, pg 1197

Hungary
Interpress Aussenhandels GmbH, pg 1197

Ireland
Kilkenny People/Wellbrook Press, pg 1198
Smurfit Print, pg 1198
Ultragraphics, pg 1198

Israel
Har-El Printers & Publishers, pg 1198
Keterpress Enterprises Jerusalem, pg 1198
Technosdar Ltd, pg 1198

Italy
Canale G e C SpA, pg 1198

Republic of Korea
Daehan Printing & Publishing Co Ltd, pg 1199

Lithuania
Spindulys Printing House, pg 1199

Malta
Interprint Ltd - Malta, pg 1199

New Zealand
Bookprint Consultants Ltd, pg 1199
John McIndoe Ltd, pg 1199
PPP Printers Ltd, pg 1199

Philippines
Cacho Hermanos Inc, pg 1199
JF Printhaus, pg 1199

Singapore
CS Graphics Pte Ltd, pg 1200
Eurasia Press Pte Ltd, pg 1200
Fong & Sons Printers Pte Ltd, pg 1200
Ho Printing Singapore Pte Ltd, pg 1200
Kyodo Printing Co (S'pore) Pte Ltd, pg 1200

PRINTING, BINDING & BOOK FINISHING INDEX — BOOK

Markono Print Media Pte Ltd, pg 1200
SNP Printing Pte Ltd, pg 1200
Stamford Press Pte Ltd, pg 1200
Toppan Company (S) Pte Ltd, pg 1200

Slovenia
Gorenjski Tisk Printing Co, pg 1201

Spain
Graficas Santamaria SA, pg 1201

United Republic of Tanzania
Peramiho Publications, pg 1201

Thailand
Mavisu International Co Ltd, pg 1201
Phongwarin Printing Company Ltd, pg 1201

United Kingdom
J W Arrowsmith Ltd, pg 1202
BAS Printers Ltd, pg 1202
Bell & Bain Ltd, pg 1202
Biddles Ltd, pg 1202
Cambridge University Press - Printing Division, pg 1202
The Charlesworth Group, pg 1202
Cedric Chivers Ltd, pg 1203
Furnival Press, pg 1203
Goldshield Communications Ltd, pg 1203
Hammond Bindery Ltd, pg 1203
Headley Brothers Ltd, pg 1203
Hobbs The Printers Ltd, pg 1203
Ikon Document Services Ltd, pg 1203
Intype London Ltd, pg 1204
The Malvern Press Ltd, pg 1204
MPG Books Ltd, pg 1204
MPG Colour Ltd, pg 1204
Page Bros Ltd (Norwich), pg 1204
Redwood Books Ltd, pg 1204
J R Reid Printing Group Ltd, pg 1204
Antony Rowe Ltd, pg 1204
Selwood Printing, pg 1204
Severnside Printers Ltd, pg 1204
Watkiss Automation Ltd, pg 1205

United States
ADR/BookPrint, pg 1205
Asia Pacific Offset Inc, pg 1205
Blaze International Productions Inc, pg 1205
Colorprint Offset Inc, pg 1206
Coneco Litho Graphics, pg 1206
CS Graphics USA Inc, pg 1206
DNP America LLC, pg 1206
Elegance Printing & Book Binding (USA), pg 1206
Express Media Corp, pg 1206
Fairfield Marketing Group Inc, pg 1206
Hamilton Printing Co, pg 1206
Hindy's Enterprise, pg 1207
Ikon Document Services, pg 1207
Integrated Book Technology Inc, pg 1207
Jinno International Group, pg 1207
KNI Inc, pg 1207
Lenz & Riecker Inc, pg 1207
Linick International Inc, pg 1207
LK Litho, pg 1207
Marrakech Express Inc, pg 1207
Mazer Publishing Services, pg 1208
Naturegraph Publishers Inc, pg 1208
Palace Press International, pg 1208
Printing Corp of the Americas Inc, pg 1208
Taylor Publishing Co, pg 1208
Times Publishing Group, pg 1208
Fred Weidner & Daughter Printers, pg 1208

SIDE STITCH BINDING

Canada
Appleby's Bindery Ltd, pg 1193
Printcrafters Inc, pg 1193
University of Toronto Press Inc, pg 1194

China
Speedflex Asia Ltd, pg 1194

Czech Republic
GRASPO CZ AS - Druckerei und Buchbinderei, pg 1194

Germany
Media-Print Informationstechnologie GmbH, pg 1195
Priese GmbH, pg 1195

Hong Kong
Dai Nippon Printing Co (Hong Kong) Ltd, pg 1196
Everbest Printing Co Ltd, pg 1196
Golden Cup Printing Co Ltd, pg 1196
The Green Pagoda Press Ltd, pg 1196
Hung Hing Off-set Printing Co Ltd, pg 1196
Image Printing Company Ltd, pg 1196
Leo Paper Products Ltd, pg 1196
Midas Printing Ltd, pg 1197
Morris Press Ltd, pg 1197
Prontaprint Asia Ltd, pg 1197
Sing Cheong Printing Co Limited, pg 1197
Sino Publishing House Ltd, pg 1197
South Sea International Press Ltd, pg 1197
Toppan Printing Co (HK) Ltd, pg 1197
Unicorn International Printing Co Ltd, pg 1197
Wing King Tong Co Ltd (Printing Factory), pg 1197

India
Hiralal Printing Works Ltd, pg 1197

Indonesia
Victory Offset Prima PT, pg 1198

Ireland
Smurfit Print, pg 1198

Italy
Canale G e C SpA, pg 1198

Republic of Korea
Daehan Printing & Publishing Co Ltd, pg 1199

New Zealand
Bookprint Consultants Ltd, pg 1199
John McIndoe Ltd, pg 1199

Philippines
Philippine Graphic Arts Inc, pg 1199

Singapore
Eurasia Press Pte Ltd, pg 1200
Ho Printing Singapore Pte Ltd, pg 1200
Markono Print Media Pte Ltd, pg 1200

United Republic of Tanzania
Peramiho Publications, pg 1201

Thailand
J Film Process Co Ltd, pg 1201
Mavisu International Co Ltd, pg 1201

United Kingdom
J W Arrowsmith Ltd, pg 1202
J W Braithwaite & Son Ltd, pg 1202
Goldshield Communications Ltd, pg 1203
Hobbs The Printers Ltd, pg 1203
Ikon Document Services Ltd, pg 1203
Intype London Ltd, pg 1204
J R Reid Printing Group Ltd, pg 1204
Watkiss Automation Ltd, pg 1205

United States
ADR/BookPrint, pg 1205
Asia Pacific Offset Inc, pg 1205
BookBuilders New York Ltd, pg 1205
C & C Offset Printing Co Ltd, pg 1205
Coneco Litho Graphics, pg 1206
Martin Cook Associates Ltd, pg 1206
DNP America LLC, pg 1206
Elegance Printing & Book Binding (USA), pg 1206
Express Media Corp, pg 1206
Hindy's Enterprise, pg 1207
Ikon Document Services, pg 1207
Imago, pg 1207
Integrated Book Technology Inc, pg 1207
Jinno International Group, pg 1207
KNI Inc, pg 1207
Leo Paper USA, pg 1207
Linick International Inc, pg 1207
LK Litho, pg 1207
Milanostampa/New Interlitho USA Inc, pg 1208
Palace Press International, pg 1208
Printing Corp of the Americas Inc, pg 1208
Regent Publishing Services, pg 1208
Fred Weidner & Daughter Printers, pg 1208

SMYTH-TYPE SEWN BINDING

Australia
Southwood Press Pty Ltd, pg 1193

Canada
Maracle Press Ltd, pg 1193
Printcrafters Inc, pg 1193
Transcontinental Printing Book Group, pg 1194

Tri-Graphic Printing (Ottawa) Ltd, pg 1194
University of Toronto Press Inc, pg 1194

China
Speedflex Asia Ltd, pg 1194

Denmark
Bianco Lunos Bogtrykkeri AS, pg 1194

Germany
Mohndruck Graphische Betriebe GmbH, pg 1195
Priese GmbH, pg 1195

Hong Kong
Best-Set Typesetter Ltd, pg 1195
Bright Future Printing Co Ltd, pg 1195
C & C Offset Printing Co Ltd, pg 1195
Caritas Printing Training Centre, pg 1195
Colorprint Offset, pg 1195
Everbest Printing Co Ltd, pg 1196
Golden Cup Printing Co Ltd, pg 1196
Hing Yip Printing Co Ltd, pg 1196
Hung Hing Off-set Printing Co Ltd, pg 1196
Image Printing Company Ltd, pg 1196
Leo Paper Products Ltd, pg 1196
Midas Printing Ltd, pg 1197
Morris Press Ltd, pg 1197
Paper Communication Printing Express Ltd, pg 1197
Paramount Publishing Group Limited, pg 1197
Sheck Wah Tong Printing Press, pg 1197
Sing Cheong Printing Co Limited, pg 1197
Sino Publishing House Ltd, pg 1197
South Sea International Press Ltd, pg 1197
Sunshine Press Ltd, pg 1197
Toppan Printing Co (HK) Ltd, pg 1197
Unicorn International Printing Co Ltd, pg 1197
Wing King Tong Co Ltd (Printing Factory), pg 1197

Israel
Keterpress Enterprises Jerusalem, pg 1198

Italy
Canale G e C SpA, pg 1198
Dedalo Litostampa SRL, pg 1198
Milanostampa SPA, pg 1198
Amilcare Pizzi SpA, pg 1198

Republic of Korea
Pyunghwa Dang Printing Co Ltd, pg 1199

Malta
Interprint Ltd - Malta, pg 1199

Netherlands
Koninklijke Wohrmann Bv, pg 1199

MANUFACTURING PRINTING, BINDING & BOOK FINISHING INDEX

Philippines
Cacho Hermanos Inc, pg 1199
Philippine Graphic Arts Inc, pg 1199

Singapore
Chong Moh Offset Printing Ltd, pg 1200
CS Graphics Pte Ltd, pg 1200
Eurasia Press Pte Ltd, pg 1200
Ho Printing Singapore Pte Ltd, pg 1200
International Press Co Pte Ltd, pg 1200
SNP Printing Pte Ltd, pg 1200
Toppan Company (S) Pte Ltd, pg 1200

Slovenia
Gorenjski Tisk Printing Co, pg 1201

Spain
Grafos SA Arte Sobre Papel, pg 1201

United Republic of Tanzania
Peramiho Publications, pg 1201

Thailand
Mavisu International Co Ltd, pg 1201

United Arab Emirates
Emirates Printing Press (LLC), pg 1202

United Kingdom
J W Arrowsmith Ltd, pg 1202
BAS Printers Ltd, pg 1202
J W Braithwaite & Son Ltd, pg 1202
Clays Ltd, pg 1203
William Clowes Ltd, pg 1203
Goldshield Communications Ltd, pg 1203
Intype London Ltd, pg 1204
Charles Letts & Co Ltd, pg 1204
Redwood Books Ltd, pg 1204

United States
Asia Pacific Offset Inc, pg 1205
Blaze International Productions Inc, pg 1205
BookBuilders New York Ltd, pg 1205
Butler & Tanner Inc, pg 1205
C & C Offset Printing Co Ltd, pg 1205
Colorprint Offset Inc, pg 1206
Martin Cook Associates Ltd, pg 1206
CS Graphics USA Inc, pg 1206
DNP America LLC, pg 1206
Editoriale Bortolazzi-Stei srl, pg 1206
Elegance Printing & Book Binding (USA), pg 1206
Express Media Corp, pg 1206
Hamilton Printing Co, pg 1206
Hindy's Enterprise, pg 1207
Imago, pg 1207
Integrated Book Technology Inc, pg 1207
Jinno International Group, pg 1207
Leo Paper USA, pg 1207
Linick International Inc, pg 1207
Milanostampa/New Interlitho USA Inc, pg 1208
Palace Press International, pg 1208

Printing Corp of the Americas Inc, pg 1208
Regent Publishing Services, pg 1208
Times Publishing Group, pg 1208
Fred Weidner & Daughter Printers, pg 1208

SPECIALTY BINDING

Belgium
Drukkerij Lannoo NV, pg 1193

Canada
Aardvark Enterprises, pg 1193
Appleby's Bindery Ltd, pg 1193
Printcrafters Inc, pg 1193

China
Speedflex Asia Ltd, pg 1194

Germany
Priese GmbH, pg 1195

Hong Kong
Hung Hing Off-set Printing Co Ltd, pg 1196
Image Printing Company Ltd, pg 1196
Leo Paper Products Ltd, pg 1196
Morris Press Ltd, pg 1197
Prontaprint Asia Ltd, pg 1197
Sing Cheong Printing Co Limited, pg 1197

Indonesia
Victory Offset Prima PT, pg 1198

New Zealand
Bookprint Consultants Ltd, pg 1199

Singapore
SNP Printing Pte Ltd, pg 1200
Toppan Company (S) Pte Ltd, pg 1200

United Republic of Tanzania
Peramiho Publications, pg 1201

United Kingdom
Cedric Chivers Ltd, pg 1203
Hammond Packaging Ltd, pg 1203
Redwood Books Ltd, pg 1204

United States
Asia Pacific Offset Inc, pg 1205
Blaze International Productions Inc, pg 1205
BookBuilders New York Ltd, pg 1205
C & C Offset Printing Co Ltd, pg 1205
Martin Cook Associates Ltd, pg 1206
Elegance Printing & Book Binding (USA), pg 1206
Hindy's Enterprise, pg 1207
Imago, pg 1207
Jinno International Group, pg 1207
KNI Inc, pg 1207
Leo Paper USA, pg 1207
Linick International Inc, pg 1207
LK Litho, pg 1207
Palace Press International, pg 1208
Printing Corp of the Americas Inc, pg 1208

Regent Publishing Services, pg 1208
Fred Weidner & Daughter Printers, pg 1208

SPIRAL BINDING

Belgium
Drukkerij Lannoo NV, pg 1193

Canada
Maracle Press Ltd, pg 1193
Printcrafters Inc, pg 1193
Transcontinental Printing Book Group, pg 1194
University of Toronto Press Inc, pg 1194
Webcom Ltd, pg 1194

China
Speedflex Asia Ltd, pg 1194

Germany
Priese GmbH, pg 1195
Vier-Tuerme GmbH Benedikt Press, pg 1195

Hong Kong
Best-Set Typesetter Ltd, pg 1195
C & C Offset Printing Co Ltd, pg 1195
Caritas Printing Training Centre, pg 1195
Dai Nippon Printing Co (Hong Kong) Ltd, pg 1196
Everbest Printing Co Ltd, pg 1196
Hung Hing Off-set Printing Co Ltd, pg 1196
Image Printing Company Ltd, pg 1196
Leo Paper Products Ltd, pg 1196
Midas Printing Ltd, pg 1197
Morris Press Ltd, pg 1197
Paper Art Product Ltd, pg 1197
Paramount Publishing Group Limited, pg 1197
Prontaprint Asia Ltd, pg 1197
Sing Cheong Printing Co Limited, pg 1197
Sino Publishing House Ltd, pg 1197
South Sea International Press Ltd, pg 1197
Unicorn International Printing Co Ltd, pg 1197
Wing King Tong Co Ltd (Printing Factory), pg 1197

Hungary
Interpress Aussenhandels GmbH, pg 1197

India
Hiralal Printing Works Ltd, pg 1197

Indonesia
Victory Offset Prima PT, pg 1198

Israel
Technosdar Ltd, pg 1198

Italy
Canale G e C SpA, pg 1198
Amilcare Pizzi SpA, pg 1198

Lithuania
Spindulys Printing House, pg 1199

New Zealand
Bookprint Consultants Ltd, pg 1199
John McIndoe Ltd, pg 1199

Singapore
Ho Printing Singapore Pte Ltd, pg 1200
SNP Printing Pte Ltd, pg 1200
Tien Wah Press Pte Ltd, pg 1200
Toppan Company (S) Pte Ltd, pg 1200

Slovenia
Gorenjski Tisk Printing Co, pg 1201

Spain
Graficas Santamaria SA, pg 1201

United Republic of Tanzania
Peramiho Publications, pg 1201

Thailand
Mavisu International Co Ltd, pg 1201

United Kingdom
CB Print Finishers Ltd, pg 1202
Goldshield Communications Ltd, pg 1203
Ikon Document Services Ltd, pg 1203
Antony Rowe Ltd, pg 1204
Watkiss Automation Ltd, pg 1205

United States
ADR/BookPrint, pg 1205
Asia Pacific Offset Inc, pg 1205
BookBuilders New York Ltd, pg 1205
C & C Offset Printing Co Ltd, pg 1205
Colorprint Offset Inc, pg 1206
Coneco Litho Graphics, pg 1206
Martin Cook Associates Ltd, pg 1206
DNP America LLC, pg 1206
Elegance Printing & Book Binding (USA), pg 1206
Express Media Corp, pg 1206
Fairfield Marketing Group Inc, pg 1206
Hindy's Enterprise, pg 1207
Imago, pg 1207
Integrated Book Technology Inc, pg 1207
Jinno International Group, pg 1207
KNI Inc, pg 1207
Leo Paper USA, pg 1207
Linick International Inc, pg 1207
LK Litho, pg 1207
Palace Press International, pg 1208
Printing Corp of the Americas Inc, pg 1208
Regent Publishing Services, pg 1208
Vicks Lithograph & Printing Corp, pg 1208
Fred Weidner & Daughter Printers, pg 1208

Uruguay
Barreiro y Ramos SA, pg 1208

PRINTING, BINDING & BOOK FINISHING INDEX

STRUCK-IMAGE COMPOSITION

Germany
C L Baader Buch & Offsetdruckere GmbH & Co KG, pg 1194
Priese GmbH, pg 1195

Hong Kong
Commercial Colorlab Ltd, pg 1195

New Zealand
Bookprint Consultants Ltd, pg 1199
John McIndoe Ltd, pg 1199

Singapore
Toppan Company (S) Pte Ltd, pg 1200

Spain
Graficas Santamaria SA, pg 1201

United Republic of Tanzania
Peramiho Publications, pg 1201

United Kingdom
Martins Printing Group Ltd, pg 1204

United States
Fred Weidner & Daughter Printers, pg 1208

TEXTBOOK PRINTING - COLLEGE

Belgium
Drukkerij Lannoo NV, pg 1193

Canada
Maracle Press Ltd, pg 1193
McLaren Morris & Todd Ltd, pg 1193
Printcrafters Inc, pg 1193
Transcontinental Printing Book Group, pg 1194
Tri-Graphic Printing (Ottawa) Ltd, pg 1194
Webcom Ltd, pg 1194

Czech Republic
GRASPO CZ AS - Druckerei und Buchbinderei, pg 1194

Finland
Gummerus Printing, pg 1194

Germany
Priese GmbH, pg 1195

Hong Kong
Best-Set Typesetter Ltd, pg 1195
Dai Nippon Printing Co (Hong Kong) Ltd, pg 1196
Golden Cup Printing Co Ltd, pg 1196
Hoi Kwong Printing Co Ltd, pg 1196
Image Printing Company Ltd, pg 1196
Midas Printing Ltd, pg 1197
Nordica Printing Co Ltd, pg 1197
Paramount Publishing Group Limited, pg 1197
Sing Cheong Printing Co Limited, pg 1197
Sino Publishing House Ltd, pg 1197
South Sea International Press Ltd, pg 1197
Unicorn International Printing Co Ltd, pg 1197

Hungary
Interpress Aussenhandels GmbH, pg 1197

Indonesia
Victory Offset Prima PT, pg 1198

Ireland
Kilkenny People/Wellbrook Press, pg 1198
Smurfit Print, pg 1198

Israel
Monoline Ltd, pg 1198
Technosdar Ltd, pg 1198

Italy
Canale G e C SpA, pg 1198
Milanostampa SPA, pg 1198

Republic of Korea
Daehan Printing & Publishing Co Ltd, pg 1199
Pyunghwa Dang Printing Co Ltd, pg 1199

Lithuania
Spindulys Printing House, pg 1199

Malta
Interprint Ltd - Malta, pg 1199

New Zealand
Bookprint Consultants Ltd, pg 1199
PPP Printers Ltd, pg 1199

Philippines
Cacho Hermanos Inc, pg 1199

Portugal
Silabo, pg 1200

Singapore
Chong Moh Offset Printing Ltd, pg 1200
Eurasia Press Pte Ltd, pg 1200
Huntsmen Offset Printing Pte Ltd, pg 1200
Markono Print Media Pte Ltd, pg 1200
SNP Printing Pte Ltd, pg 1200
Stamford Press Pte Ltd, pg 1200
Toppan Company (S) Pte Ltd, pg 1200

Slovenia
Gorenjski Tisk Printing Co, pg 1201

Spain
Graficas Santamaria SA, pg 1201
Luis Vives (Edelvives), pg 1201

Sri Lanka
Sumathi Book Printing (Pvt) Ltd, pg 1201

United Republic of Tanzania
Peramiho Publications, pg 1201

United Kingdom
J W Arrowsmith Ltd, pg 1202
Biddles Ltd, pg 1202
Cambridge University Press - Printing Division, pg 1202
Clays Ltd, pg 1203
Goldshield Communications Ltd, pg 1203
Hobbs The Printers Ltd, pg 1203
Lavenham Press Ltd, pg 1204
Charles Letts & Co Ltd, pg 1204
MPG Books Ltd, pg 1204
Page Bros Ltd (Norwich), pg 1204
Redwood Books Ltd, pg 1204
J R Reid Printing Group Ltd, pg 1204
Antony Rowe Ltd, pg 1204
Severnside Printers Ltd, pg 1204
Watkiss Automation Ltd, pg 1205

United States
ADR/BookPrint, pg 1205
Asia Pacific Offset Inc, pg 1205
Blaze International Productions Inc, pg 1205
DNP America LLC, pg 1206
Elegance Printing & Book Binding (USA), pg 1206
Express Media Corp, pg 1206
Fairfield Marketing Group Inc, pg 1206
Hamilton Printing Co, pg 1206
Integrated Book Technology Inc, pg 1207
Jinno International Group, pg 1207
Linick International Inc, pg 1207
LK Litho, pg 1207
Marrakech Express Inc, pg 1207
Times Publishing Group, pg 1208
Fred Weidner & Daughter Printers, pg 1208

Uruguay
Barreiro y Ramos SA, pg 1208

TEXTBOOK PRINTING - EL-H1

Belgium
Drukkerij Lannoo NV, pg 1193

Canada
Maracle Press Ltd, pg 1193
Printcrafters Inc, pg 1193
Transcontinental Printing Book Group, pg 1194
Tri-Graphic Printing (Ottawa) Ltd, pg 1194
Webcom Ltd, pg 1194

Finland
Gummerus Printing, pg 1194

Germany
Mohndruck Graphische Betriebe GmbH, pg 1195
Priese GmbH, pg 1195

Hong Kong
Golden Cup Printing Co Ltd, pg 1196
Hoi Kwong Printing Co Ltd, pg 1196
Image Printing Company Ltd, pg 1196
Midas Printing Ltd, pg 1197
Nordica Printing Co Ltd, pg 1197
Paramount Publishing Group Limited, pg 1197
Sing Cheong Printing Co Limited, pg 1197
Sino Publishing House Ltd, pg 1197

Hungary
Interpress Aussenhandels GmbH, pg 1197

Ireland
Ultragraphics, pg 1198

Israel
Monoline Ltd, pg 1198
Technosdar Ltd, pg 1198

Italy
Canale G e C SpA, pg 1198
Milanostampa SPA, pg 1198

Republic of Korea
Daehan Printing & Publishing Co Ltd, pg 1199
Pyunghwa Dang Printing Co Ltd, pg 1199

New Zealand
Bookprint Consultants Ltd, pg 1199

Philippines
Cacho Hermanos Inc, pg 1199

Singapore
Chong Moh Offset Printing Ltd, pg 1200
Markono Print Media Pte Ltd, pg 1200
SNP Printing Pte Ltd, pg 1200
Toppan Company (S) Pte Ltd, pg 1200

Slovenia
Gorenjski Tisk Printing Co, pg 1201

Spain
Graficas Santamaria SA, pg 1201
Luis Vives (Edelvives), pg 1201

United Kingdom
J W Arrowsmith Ltd, pg 1202
Biddles Ltd, pg 1202
Goldshield Communications Ltd, pg 1203
Hobbs The Printers Ltd, pg 1203
Lavenham Press Ltd, pg 1204
Charles Letts & Co Ltd, pg 1204
Page Bros Ltd (Norwich), pg 1204
Antony Rowe Ltd, pg 1204
Watkiss Automation Ltd, pg 1205

United States
Asia Pacific Offset Inc, pg 1205
Blaze International Productions Inc, pg 1205
Carvajal International Inc, pg 1206
DNP America LLC, pg 1206
Elegance Printing & Book Binding (USA), pg 1206
Express Media Corp, pg 1206
Fairfield Marketing Group Inc, pg 1206
Hamilton Printing Co, pg 1206
Imago, pg 1207
Jinno International Group, pg 1207
Regent Publishing Services, pg 1208

MANUFACTURING   PRINTING, BINDING & BOOK FINISHING INDEX

Times Publishing Group, pg 1208
Fred Weidner & Daughter Printers, pg 1208

WIRE-O BINDING

Belgium
Drukkerij Lannoo NV, pg 1193

Canada
Coach House Printing, pg 1193
Maracle Press Ltd, pg 1193
Printcrafters Inc, pg 1193
Transcontinental Printing Book Group, pg 1194
University of Toronto Press Inc, pg 1194
Webcom Ltd, pg 1194

China
Speedflex Asia Ltd, pg 1194

Denmark
Bianco Lunos Bogtrykkeri AS, pg 1194

Germany
Mohndruck Graphische Betriebe GmbH, pg 1195
Oertel & Sporer GmbH & Co, pg 1195
Priese GmbH, pg 1195
Vier-Tuerme GmbH Benedikt Press, pg 1195

Hong Kong
Best-Set Typesetter Ltd, pg 1195
Bright Future Printing Co Ltd, pg 1195
C & C Offset Printing Co Ltd, pg 1195
Caritas Printing Training Centre, pg 1195
Colorprint Offset, pg 1195
Dai Nippon Printing Co (Hong Kong) Ltd, pg 1196
Golden Cup Printing Co Ltd, pg 1196
The Green Pagoda Press Ltd, pg 1196
Hing Yip Printing Co Ltd, pg 1196
Hung Hing Off-set Printing Co Ltd, pg 1196
Image Printing Company Ltd, pg 1196
Leo Paper Products Ltd, pg 1196
Liang Yu Printing Factory Ltd, pg 1196
Midas Printing Ltd, pg 1197
Morris Press Ltd, pg 1197
Paper Art Product Ltd, pg 1197
Paramount Publishing Group Limited, pg 1197
Prontaprint Asia Ltd, pg 1197
Sheck Wah Tong Printing Press, pg 1197
Sing Cheong Printing Co Limited, pg 1197
Sino Publishing House Ltd, pg 1197
South Sea International Press Ltd, pg 1197
Sunshine Press Ltd, pg 1197
Unicorn International Printing Co Ltd, pg 1197
Wing King Tong Co Ltd (Printing Factory), pg 1197

Hungary
Interpress Aussenhandels GmbH, pg 1197

Indonesia
Victory Offset Prima PT, pg 1198

Italy
Canale G e C SpA, pg 1198
Amilcare Pizzi SpA, pg 1198

New Zealand
Bookprint Consultants Ltd, pg 1199
John McIndoe Ltd, pg 1199

Singapore
Columbia Overseas Marketing Pte Ltd, pg 1200
CS Graphics Pte Ltd, pg 1200
Eurasia Press Pte Ltd, pg 1200
Ho Printing Singapore Pte Ltd, pg 1200
International Press Co Pte Ltd, pg 1200
Markono Print Media Pte Ltd, pg 1200
SNP Printing Pte Ltd, pg 1200
Stamford Press Pte Ltd, pg 1200
Toppan Company (S) Pte Ltd, pg 1200

Slovenia
Gorenjski Tisk Printing Co, pg 1201

Spain
Graficas Santamaria SA, pg 1201

United Republic of Tanzania
Peramiho Publications, pg 1201

Thailand
Mavisu International Co Ltd, pg 1201

United Arab Emirates
Emirates Printing Press (LLC), pg 1202

United Kingdom
J W Braithwaite & Son Ltd, pg 1202
CB Print Finishers Ltd, pg 1202
Center Print Ltd, pg 1202
Hammond Packaging Ltd, pg 1203
Hobbs The Printers Ltd, pg 1203
Hunter & Foulis Ltd, pg 1203
Ikon Document Services Ltd, pg 1203
Charles Letts & Co Ltd, pg 1204
Page Bros Ltd (Norwich), pg 1204
Redwood Books Ltd, pg 1204
J R Reid Printing Group Ltd, pg 1204
Antony Rowe Ltd, pg 1204
Watkiss Automation Ltd, pg 1205

United States
ADR/BookPrint, pg 1205
Asia Pacific Offset Inc, pg 1205
Blaze International Productions Inc, pg 1205
BookBuilders New York Ltd, pg 1205
C & C Offset Printing Co Ltd, pg 1205
Colorprint Offset Inc, pg 1206
Coneco Litho Graphics, pg 1206

Martin Cook Associates Ltd, pg 1206
CS Graphics USA Inc, pg 1206
DNP America LLC, pg 1206
Elegance Printing & Book Binding (USA), pg 1206
Express Media Corp, pg 1206
Hamilton Printing Co, pg 1206
Hindy's Enterprise, pg 1207
Ikon Document Services, pg 1207
Imago, pg 1207
Integrated Book Technology Inc, pg 1207
Jinno International Group, pg 1207
KNI Inc, pg 1207
Lenz & Riecker Inc, pg 1207
Leo Paper USA, pg 1207
Linick International Inc, pg 1207
LK Litho, pg 1207
Milanostampa/New Interlitho USA Inc, pg 1208
Palace Press International, pg 1208
Printing Corp of the Americas Inc, pg 1208
Regent Publishing Services, pg 1208
Fred Weidner & Daughter Printers, pg 1208

WORKBOOK PRINTING

Belgium
Drukkerij Lannoo NV, pg 1193

Canada
Maracle Press Ltd, pg 1193
Printcrafters Inc, pg 1193
Transcontinental Printing Book Group, pg 1194
Tri-Graphic Printing (Ottawa) Ltd, pg 1194
University of Toronto Press Inc, pg 1194
Webcom Ltd, pg 1194

Finland
Gummerus Printing, pg 1194

Germany
C L Baader Buch & Offsetdruckere GmbH & Co KG, pg 1194
Priese GmbH, pg 1195

Hong Kong
Best-Set Typesetter Ltd, pg 1195
Dai Nippon Printing Co (Hong Kong) Ltd, pg 1196
Golden Cup Printing Co Ltd, pg 1196
Hoi Kwong Printing Co Ltd, pg 1196
Image Printing Company Ltd, pg 1196
Midas Printing Ltd, pg 1197
Paper Communication Printing Express Ltd, pg 1197
Paramount Publishing Group Limited, pg 1197
Prontaprint Asia Ltd, pg 1197
Sing Cheong Printing Co Limited, pg 1197
Sino Publishing House Ltd, pg 1197
Unicorn International Printing Co Ltd, pg 1197

Hungary
Interpress Aussenhandels GmbH, pg 1197

India
Hiralal Printing Works Ltd, pg 1197

Ireland
Smurfit Print, pg 1198
Ultragraphics, pg 1198

Israel
Monoline Ltd, pg 1198
Technosdar Ltd, pg 1198

Italy
Canale G e C SpA, pg 1198
Milanostampa SPA, pg 1198

Republic of Korea
Daehan Printing & Publishing Co Ltd, pg 1199
Pyunghwa Dang Printing Co Ltd, pg 1199

New Zealand
Bookprint Consultants Ltd, pg 1199
PPP Printers Ltd, pg 1199

Philippines
Cacho Hermanos Inc, pg 1199
Philippine Graphic Arts Inc, pg 1199

Portugal
Silabo, pg 1200

Singapore
Chong Moh Offset Printing Ltd, pg 1200
Eurasia Press Pte Ltd, pg 1200
Markono Print Media Pte Ltd, pg 1200
SNP Printing Pte Ltd, pg 1200
Toppan Company (S) Pte Ltd, pg 1200

Slovenia
Gorenjski Tisk Printing Co, pg 1201

Spain
Graficas Santamaria SA, pg 1201
Luis Vives (Edelvives), pg 1201

Thailand
Mavisu International Co Ltd, pg 1201

United Kingdom
J W Arrowsmith Ltd, pg 1202
Biddles Ltd, pg 1202
Goldshield Communications Ltd, pg 1203
The Guernsey Press Co Ltd, pg 1203
Hobbs The Printers Ltd, pg 1203
Charles Letts & Co Ltd, pg 1204
Page Bros Ltd (Norwich), pg 1204
J R Reid Printing Group Ltd, pg 1204
Antony Rowe Ltd, pg 1204
Severnside Printers Ltd, pg 1204
Watkiss Automation Ltd, pg 1205

United States
ADR/BookPrint, pg 1205
Asia Pacific Offset Inc, pg 1205
Blaze International Productions Inc, pg 1205
Butler & Tanner Inc, pg 1205
Consolidated Printers Inc, pg 1206

PRINTING, BINDING & BOOK FINISHING INDEX

DNP America LLC, pg 1206
Express Media Corp, pg 1206
Fairfield Marketing Group Inc, pg 1206
Hamilton Printing Co, pg 1206
Ikon Document Services, pg 1207
Integrated Book Technology Inc, pg 1207
Jinno International Group, pg 1207
KNI Inc, pg 1207
Lenz & Riecker Inc, pg 1207
Linick International Inc, pg 1207
LK Litho, pg 1207
Marrakech Express Inc, pg 1207
Printing Corp of the Americas Inc, pg 1208
Vicks Lithograph & Printing Corp, pg 1208
Fred Weidner & Daughter Printers, pg 1208

Printing, Binding & Book Finishing

This section includes companies throughout the world that offer printing, binding and/or book finishing services. Those U.S. and Canadian companies with 10% or more of their business done outside North America are also included here. Immediately preceding this section is an index classifying companies by services offered.

Australia

Southwood Press Pty Ltd
76-82 Chapel St, Marrickville, NSW 2204
Tel: (02) 9560 5100 *Fax:* (02) 9550 0097
E-mail: info@southwoodpress.com.au
Web Site: www.southwoodpress.com.au
Key Personnel
Business Development Manager: Bruce Welch
Sales Manager: Elizabeth Finniecome
Founded: 1966
Turnaround: 15-20 workdays
Print Runs: 500 min - 20,000 max
Business from Other Countries: 1%

Austria

ADEVA (Akademische Druck-u Verlagsanstalt)
Auersperggasse 12, A-8010 Graz
Mailing Address: Postfach 598, A-8011 Graz
Tel: (0316) 3644 *Fax:* (0316) 364424
E-mail: info@adeva.com *Cable:* ADEVA-GRAZ
Key Personnel
Dir: Dr Ursula Struzl
Founded: 1949
Print Runs: 300 min - 10,000 max
Business from Other Countries: 80%
Branch Office(s)
Purgleitnergasse 10, Ecke Marburgerstrabe, A-8042 Graz

Akademische Druck- u Verlagsanstalt, see ADEVA (Akademische Druck-u Verlagsanstalt)

Dr Paul Struzl GmbH, see ADEVA (Akademische Druck-u Verlagsanstalt)

Belgium

Delabie Europrint SA
Avenue de l'Eurozone 8, Mouscron 7700
Tel: (056) 841306 *Fax:* (056) 840962
Key Personnel
PDG: D M Delabie
Sales Manager: Willem Mandeville
Finance: Luc Haspeslagh
Production: Debie Bertrand
Founded: 1964
Turnaround: 8 Workdays
Print Runs: 100,000 min - 1,000,000 max
Business from Other Countries: 60%

Drukkerij Lannoo NV (Lanno Printers)
Kasteelstr 97, B-8700 Tielt
Tel: (051) 424211 *Fax:* (051) 407070
E-mail: lannoo@lannooprint.be
Web Site: www.lannooprint.be
Key Personnel
General Manager & Marketing Dir: Stefaan Lannoo *E-mail:* stefaan.lannoo@lannooprint.be
Founded: 1909
Turnaround: 10 Workdays
Print Runs: 100 min - 1,000,000 max
Business from Other Countries: 30%

IMPF BV BA
Sint-Amandstr 18, B-9000 Gent
Tel: (09) 2254429 *Fax:* (09) 2331338
Key Personnel
Manager: Xavier Dewulf
Founded: 1958
Business from Other Countries: 10%

Canada

Aardvark Enterprises
Division of Speers Investments Ltd
204 Millbank Dr SW, Calgary, AB T2Y 2H9
Tel: 403-256-4639
Key Personnel
Pres: J Alvin Speers
Founded: 1970 (Small Press Pioneers)
Turnaround: 30 Workdays
Print Runs: 10 min - 1,000 max
Business from Other Countries: 25%

Appleby's Bindery Ltd
1303 Route 102, Upper Gagetown, NB E5M 1R5
Tel: 506-488-2086 *Fax:* 506-488-2086
E-mail: applbind@nbnet.nb.ca
Key Personnel
Pres & Owner: David E Appleby
Mgr: John Appleby
Founded: 1976
Turnaround: 30 Workdays
Business from Other Countries: 10%

Arpeco Engineering
7095 Ordan Dr, Mississauga, ON L5T 1K6
Tel: 905-564-5150 *Fax:* 905-564-2943
E-mail: sales@arpeco.com
Web Site: www.arpeco.com
Key Personnel
Dir, Mktg: Jim Wright
Founded: 1965
Business from Other Countries: 70%

Coach House Printing
401 Huron St, Rear, Toronto, ON M5S 2G5
Tel: 416-979-2217 *Fax:* 416-977-1158
E-mail: mail@chbooks.com
Web Site: www.chbooks.com
Key Personnel
Pres: Stan Bevington
Founded: 1965
Turnaround: 14 Workdays
Print Runs: 200 min - 2,000 max
Business from Other Countries: 10%

Herzig Somerville Ltd
543 Richmond St W, Suite 125, Toronto, ON M5V 1Y6
Tel: 416-681-1200 *Fax:* 416-681-1241
Web Site: www.herzig.com
Key Personnel
Pres: Mark Quesnelle
Founded: 1965
Business from Other Countries: 10%

Maracle Press Ltd
1156 King St E, Oshawa, ON L1H 7N4
Mailing Address: Box 606, Oshawa, ON L1H 7N4
Tel: 905-723-3438 *Fax:* 905-428-6024
E-mail: maracle@maraclepress.com
Web Site: www.maraclepress.com
Key Personnel
Pres & Gen Mgr: Bruce A Fenton
VP, Bus Devt: Ronald G Taylor *E-mail:* rtaylor@maraclepress.com
Founded: 1920
Turnaround: 10 Workdays
Print Runs: 500 min - 500,000 max
Business from Other Countries: 25%
Membership(s): BMI; CPIA; Ontario Printing & Imaging Association; PIA

McLaren Morris & Todd Ltd
3270 American Dr, Mississauga, ON L4V 1B5
Tel: 905-677-3592 *Fax:* 905-677-3675
Web Site: www.mmt.ca
Key Personnel
Pres: Alan George
Cont: John Mousmoules *Tel:* 905-677-3592 ext 247 *E-mail:* john@mmt.ca
Founded: 1956
Turnaround: 15 Workdays
Print Runs: 5,000 min - 1,000,000 max
Business from Other Countries: 10%

Preney Print & Litho Inc
2714 Dougall Ave, Windsor, ON N9E 1R9
Tel: 519-966-3412 *Fax:* 519-966-4996
E-mail: preney@mnsi.net
Founded: 1972
Turnaround: 15 Workdays
Print Runs: 2,000 min - 1 max
Business from Other Countries: 20%

Printcrafters Inc
78 Hutchings St, Winnipeg, MB R2X 3B1
Tel: 204-633-7117 *Fax:* 204-694-1519
E-mail: printcrafters@mb.sympatico.ca
Key Personnel
Pres: Bob Payne *Tel:* 204-633-7117 ext 223 *Fax:* 204-694-1594 *E-mail:* bpayne@mb.sympatico.ca
Founded: 1996 (Employee owned)
Turnaround: 5-20 Workdays
Print Runs: 500,000 min
Business from Other Countries: 30%
Membership(s): CPIA

Productive Publications
PO Box 7200, Sta A, Toronto, ON M5W 1X8
SAN: 117-1712
Tel: 416-483-0634 *Fax:* 416-322-7434
Web Site: www.productivepublications.com
Key Personnel
Owner: Iain Williamson
Founded: 1985
Turnaround: 21 Workdays
Print Runs: 100 min - 1,000 max
Business from Other Countries: 10%

CANADA

Transcontinental Printing Book Group
Division of Transcontinental Group
395 Lebeau Blvd, St-Laurent, PQ H4N 1S2
Tel: 514-337-8560 *Fax:* 514-339-2252
Web Site: www.transcontinental-gtc.com; www.transcontinental-printing.com
Key Personnel
Sr VP, Book Group: Jacques Gregoire
US Sales Mgr: Denis Beaudin *Tel:* 514-339-2220 ext 4101 *E-mail:* beaudind@transcontinental.ca
Founded: 1976
Turnaround: 15-20 workdays casebound; 10-15 workdays softcover
Print Runs: 1,000 min
Business from Other Countries: 30%
Branch Office(s)
614 Yates Ave, Calumet City, IL 60409, United States, Contact: Kristopher D Levy *Tel:* 708-832-1528 *Fax:* 708-832-9510 (Midwest)
3653 W Leland Ave, Suite One W, Chicago, IL 60625, United States, Contact: Tim Taylor *Tel:* 773-583-8155 *Fax:* 773-583-8162 *E-mail:* tim.taylor@transcontinental.ca (Midwest)
245 Eliot St, Ashland, MA 01721, United States, Contact: Ed Catania *Tel:* 508-881-1119 *Fax:* 508-881-7739 *E-mail:* ecatania@attbi.com (East Coast)
19 Crown St, Milton, MA 02186-1419, United States, Contact: Mike Gazzola *Tel:* 617-696-1435 *Fax:* 617-696-1025 *E-mail:* mikebook@attbi.com (East Coast)
37 Herman Blvd, Franklin Square, NY 11010, United States, Contact: Tom Malloy *Tel:* 516-775-2980 *Fax:* 516-488-0253 *E-mail:* tmmalloy@aol.com (NY)
3175 Summit Square Dr, Suite C9, Oakton, VA 22124, United States, Contact: David Avesian *Tel:* 703-255-1332 *Fax:* 703-255-1343 *E-mail:* davesian@cox.rr.com (Southeast)
559 Lowrys Rd, Parksville, BC V9P 2R8, Contact: Mike Davies *Tel:* 250-248-9700 *Fax:* 250-248-2353 *E-mail:* bookguys@shaw.ca (West Coast)
15373 Victoria Ave, White Rock, BC V4B 1H1, Contact: Wade Davies *Tel:* 604-535-8800 *Fax:* 604-535-8802 *E-mail:* davies@shaw.ca (West Coast)
490 Wilfred Dr, Peterborough, ON K9K 2H1, Contact: Tom Lang *Tel:* 705-760-9594 *Fax:* 705-760-9485 *E-mail:* langt@transcontinental.ca (NY)
Membership(s): BMI; NAPL; PIA

Tri-Graphic Printing (Ottawa) Ltd
485 Industrial Ave, Ottawa, ON K1G 0Z1
Tel: 613-731-7441 *Fax:* 613-731-3741
Key Personnel
VP & Gen Mgr: Doug K Doane *E-mail:* ddoane@tri-graphic.com
VP, Prodn & Servs: Fred Malleau *Tel:* 905-665-8500 *E-mail:* fmalleau@tri-graphic.com
Founded: 1968
Turnaround: 10-15 Workdays
Print Runs: 1,000 min - 100,000 max
Business from Other Countries: 10%
Branch Office(s)
213 Byron St S, Suite 201, Whitby, ON L1N 4P7 *Tel:* 905-665-8500 *Fax:* 905-665-8501

University of Toronto Press Inc
Printing Division, 5201 Dufferin St, North York, ON M3H 5T8
Tel: 416-667-7767 *Fax:* 416-667-7803
E-mail: printing@utpress.utoronto.ca
Web Site: www.utpress.utoronto.ca
Key Personnel
Pres & Publr: George Meadows
Founded: 1901
Turnaround: 10-15 Workdays
Print Runs: 10 min - 200,000 max
Business from Other Countries: 15%
Membership(s): BMI

Webcom Ltd
3480 Pharmacy Ave, Toronto, ON M1W 2S7
Tel: 416-496-1000 *Fax:* 416-496-1537
E-mail: webcom@webcomlink.com
Web Site: www.webcomlink.com
Key Personnel
VP, Sales & Mktg: Mike Collinge
Dir, Mktg: Deborah Kupperman
Founded: 1976
Turnaround: 15 Workdays
Print Runs: 50 min - 100,000 max
Business from Other Countries: 40%

China

Speedflex Asia Ltd
3/F Tianjin Bldg, 167 Connaught Rd W, Hong Kong, SAR
Tel: 25422780 *Fax:* 25454026
E-mail: info@speedflex.com.hk
Web Site: www.speedflex.com.hk
Key Personnel
Sales Manager: Richard Silkstone
Founded: 1981
Turnaround: 1 Workday
Print Runs: 1 min
Business from Other Countries: 20%

Czech Republic

GRASPO CZ AS - Druckerei und Buchbinderei
Pod Sternberkem 324, 76302 Zlin-Louky
Tel: (067) 7606111; (067) 7606246 *Fax:* (067) 7104052
E-mail: graspo@graspo.com; mp@graspo.com
Web Site: www.graspo.com
Founded: 1995
Print Runs: 1,000 min
Business from Other Countries: 50%
Branch Office(s)
Racianska 109/c, 83102 Bratislava
Sinkulova 48, 14000 Prague 4

Denmark

Bianco Lunos Bogtrykkeri AS
Subsidiary of Carl Allers Etablissement AS
Otto Monsteds Gade 3, DK-1571 Copenhagen V
Tel: 33140781 *Fax:* 33913808
Key Personnel
General Manager: J Heede Sorensen
Founded: 1871

Finland

Gummerus Printing
Subsidiary of Gummerus Oy
Alasinkatu 1-3, Fin-40351 Jyvaskyla
Mailing Address: PO Box 444, Fin-40351 Jyvaskyla
Tel: (014) 683525 *Fax:* (014) 676770; (014) 685166
Key Personnel
Marketing Dir: Mr Martti Aaltonen
Man Dir: Mr Jarmo Porkka
Founded: 1872
Turnaround: 20-60 Workdays
Print Runs: 1,000 min - 100,000 max
Business from Other Countries: 15%

WS Bookwell Ltd
Teollisuustie 4, FIN-06100 Porvoo
Tel: (019) 219 41 *Fax:* (019) 219 4800
E-mail: pekka.tykkylainen@bookwell.fi
Web Site: www.bookwell.fi
Key Personnel
Man Dir: Magnus Breitenstein *E-mail:* magnus.breitenstein@bookwell.fi
Marketing Manager: Pekka Tykkyloinen *Tel:* (019) 219 4663 *E-mail:* pekka.tykkylainen@bookwell.fi
Founded: 1878
Business from Other Countries: 50%
Parent Company: WSOY
Ultimate Parent Company: Sanoma WSOY
Branch Office(s)
Messerdorferstr 127, 53123 Bonn, Germany, Contact: Markku Rapeli *Tel:* (0228) 986 4006 *Fax:* (0228) 986 4008
PO Box 3, Lowestoft, Suffolk NR33 8EY, United Kingdom *Tel:* (502) 742 038 *Fax:* (502) 742 039

France

Imprimerie Gaignault
Route De Levroux, 36100 Issoudun
Key Personnel
Dir: Mr Marquet

Imprimerie Bene
12 rue Pradier, F-30000 Nimes
Tel: (04) 66294897 *Fax:* (04) 66382146
Key Personnel
President: Jacques Enfer
Print Runs: 100 min - 10,000 max
Business from Other Countries: 20%

Plein Chant
F-16120 Bassac
Tel: (05) 45819326 *Fax:* (05) 45819283
Key Personnel
Contact: Edmond Thomas
Founded: 1971
Print Runs: 600 min - 1,000 max
Business from Other Countries: 5%

Signes du Monde
1424 ch du Dupere Hubert Saint-Genez, 40380 Povartin
Tel: (06) 12 99 73 37 *Fax:* (0561) 575717
Key Personnel
Production: Hubert Saint-Genez

Germany

C L Baader Buch & Offsetdruckere GmbH & Co KG
Gutenbergstr 1, 72525 Baden-Wurttemberg
Mailing Address: Postfach 1220, 72522 Munsingen
Tel: (07381) 79192 *Fax:* (07381) 411412 *Cable:* BAADER-MUNSINGEN
Founded: 1835
Turnaround: 1 Workday
Print Runs: 1,000 min - 15,000 max

& BOOK FINISHING

Fachhochschule Fur Druk, Studiengang Verlagswirtschaft und Verlagsherstellung
Nobelstr 10, 70569 Stuttgart
Tel: (0711) 6852807 *Fax:* (0711) 6852834
Web Site: www.fhd-stuttgart.de
Telex: 725 185 fhd d
Key Personnel
Contact: Prof Eduard H Schoenstedt

G Braun (vormals G Braun'sche Hofbuchdruckerei und Verlag)
Karl-Friedrich-Str 14-18, 76133 Karlsruhe
Mailing Address: Postfach 1646, 76113 Karlsruhe
Tel: (0721) 165-195 *Fax:* (0721) 165-855
E-mail: volpp@gbraun-fachverlage.de
Telex: 7 826 904
Key Personnel
Marketing Dir: A Durr

C Maurer Druck und Verlag
Schubartstr 21, 73312 Geislingen
Tel: (07331) 9300 *Fax:* (07331) 930190
Web Site: www.maurer.oupiuke.de
Key Personnel
Contact: Carl Otto Maurer
Founded: 1856

Media-Print Informationstechnologie GmbH
Unit of Media-Print GmbH & Co KG
Eggertstr 28, 33100 Paderborn
Tel: (05251) 522300 *Fax:* (05251) 522480
E-mail: contact@mediaprint.de
Web Site: www.mediaprint.de
Key Personnel
Man Dir: Rainer Rings
Founded: 1993
Turnaround: 5-10 Workdays
Print Runs: 100 min - 300,000 max
Business from Other Countries: 10%

Mohndruck Graphische Betriebe GmbH
Subsidiary of Bertelsmann AG
Carl-Bertelsmann-Str 161, 33311 Guetersloh
Mailing Address: Postfach 200, 33311 Guetersloh
Tel: (05241) 802095 *Fax:* (05241) 78329
Key Personnel
Contact: Alfred Hahn
Founded: 1824
Business from Other Countries: 25%

Oertel & Sporer GmbH & Co
Burgstr 1-7, 72764 Reutlingen
Mailing Address: Postfach 1642, D-72706 Reutlingen
Tel: (07121) 302555 *Fax:* (07121) 302558
Key Personnel
Publisher: Valdo Lehari
Manager & Printer: Ermo Lehari
Print Runs: 500 min - 50,000 max

Priese GmbH
Auerbacherstr 9, 14193 Berlin
Tel: (030) 3239089 *Fax:* (030) 3249630
Key Personnel
Contact: Elma Priese; Hans Joachim Priese

Vier-Tuerme GmbH Benedikt Press
Schweinfurterstr 40, 97359 Munsterschwarzach
Tel: (09324) 20214 *Fax:* (09324) 20495
Key Personnel
Contact: Josef Stoecklein
Founded: 1951
Turnaround: 8-16 Workdays
Print Runs: 300 min - 20,000 max
Business from Other Countries: 5%

Hong Kong

Best-Set Typesetter Ltd
6 Sun Yip St, Honour Industrial Centre, 304 Third fl, Chai Wan
Tel: (02) 897 6033 *Fax:* (02) 897 5170
E-mail: bestset@bestset-typesetter.com; best-set-usa@email.msn.com
Web Site: www.bestset-typesetter.com
Key Personnel
Manager: Cynthia Hui *Tel:* 852 2975 1018
Dir: Johnson Yeung *Tel:* 852 2975 1012
Sales Representative: Wai Man Yeung *Tel:* 914 961 6223 *Fax:* 914 961 8212
Founded: 1986
Turnaround: 14 workdays
Print Runs: 500 min - 5,000,000 max
Business from Other Countries: 99%
Branch Office(s)
Best-Set Typesetter Ltd, Third Floor, No 3 Jiang Nan Main Ave C, Guangzhou, China, Johnson Yeung *Tel:* (020) 8442 5873 *Fax:* (020) 8441 5874 *E-mail:* gbestset@public.guangzhou.gd.cn
Sales Office(s): Best-Set Typesetter Ltd, 157 Fisher Ave, Suite 6, Eastchester, NY 10709, United States, Wai Man Yeung *Tel:* 914-961-6223 *Fax:* 914-961-8212 *E-mail:* best-set-usa@email.msn.com

Bookbuilders Ltd
Unit J 13/F Yeung Yiu Chung No 8 Industrial Bldg, 20 Wang Hoi Rd, Kowloon Bay, Kowloon
Tel: 27968123 *Fax:* 27968267; 27968690
E-mail: lph@netvigator.com
Key Personnel
Man Dir: Leslie Henman
General Manager: Edward Chan

Bright Future Printing Co Ltd
Subsidiary of Shiny Offset Printing Co Ltd
Sunview Industrial Building, Block D, 5/F, 3 On Yip St, Chai Wan
Tel: 25151776 *Fax:* 28972799
Key Personnel
Chairman: Richard Ng
Turnaround: 60 Workdays (including shipping)
Print Runs: 3,000 min - 30,000 max
Business from Other Countries: 30%

C & C Offset Printing Co Ltd
Subsidiary of C & C Joint Printing Co (HK) Ltd under Sino United Publishing (Holdings) Ltd
C & C Bldg, 36 Ting Lai Rd, Tai Po, New Territories
Tel: (02) 666-4988 *Fax:* (02) 666-4938
E-mail: offsetprinting@candcprinting.com
Web Site: www.ccoffset.com
Key Personnel
Dir & General Manager: Xian-Qing Zhuang
Dir & Assistant General Manager: Ken Lee
Sales Manager (Overseas): Kit Wong
Sales Manager (Special Projects): Francis Ho
Dir & Executive Vice President, C & C Offset Printing Co (USA) Inc, Portland OR, USA: Charles H Clark, IV
Development Manager, C & C Offset Printing (USA) Inc, Portland, OR, USA: Jenny Whittier *Tel:* 503-233-1834 *E-mail:* jwhittier@ccoffset.com
Customer Service Manager, C & C Offset Printing Co (USA) Inc, Portland, OR, USA: Ernest Li
Dir & Executive Vice President, C & C Offset Printing Co (NY) Inc, New York, NY, USA: Simon Chan
Dir & General Manager, C & C Joint Printing Co (Guangdong) Ltd, Shenzhen, China: Jackson Leung
Deputy Sales Manager, C & C Joint Printing Co (Ghuangdong) Ltd, Shenzhen, China: Min Zhu
President, C & C Printing Japan Co Ltd, Tokyo, Japan: Masashi Otobe
Customer Service Manager, C & C Offset Printing Co (NYC), Inc, NY NY: Frances Harkness
Man Dir, C & C Joint Printing Co (Beijing), Ltd, Beijing, China: Zhang Lin Gui
Dir, C & C Offset Printing Co (UK), Ltd: Tracy Broderick
Manager, C & C Offset Printing Co (UK), Ltd: Fiona Norman
Founded: 1980
Turnaround: 42 Workdays
Print Runs: 2,000 min - 200,000 max
Business from Other Countries: 60%
Branch Office(s)
C & C Offset Printing Co (USA) Inc, 2632 SE 25 St, Suite D, Portland, OR 97202, United States *Tel:* 503-233-1834 *Fax:* 503-233-7815 *E-mail:* portlandinfo@ccoffset.com
C & C Offset Printing Co (NY) Inc, 401 Broadway, Suite 2015, New York, NY 10013-3005, United States *Tel:* 212-431-4210 *Fax:* 212-431-3960 *E-mail:* newyorkinfo@ccoffset.com
C & C Joint Printing Co (Guangdong) Ltd, Chunhu Industrial Estate, Pinghu, Long Gang, Shenzhen 518111, China *Tel:* (0755) 884-1333 *Fax:* (0755) 884-2211 *E-mail:* guangdong@cancprinting.com (Plant)
C & C Printing Japan Co Ltd, Tokyodou, 6th floor, Jinbocho No 2, Bldg 127, Chiyoda-Ku, Tokyo 101, Japan *Tel:* (03) 3219-6610 *Fax:* (03) 3219-6620 *E-mail:* ccjtokyo@interlink.or.jp
Room 2, 9/F, 3 Chegongzhuang Main St, Xicheng District, Beijing 100044, China *Tel:* (010) 8636-5335 *Fax:* (010) 8636-5335
Room 304 Fangfa Bldg, No 29 Lane 165, Dongzhu Anbin Rd, Shanghai 200050, China *Tel:* (021) 6240-1305 *Fax:* (021) 6240-1305 *E-mail:* shanghai@candcprinting.com
Room 505 Sino Bldg, 23 Zhan Qian Rd, Guangzhou 510010, China *Tel:* (020) 8650-0602 *Fax:* (020) 8667-8882 *E-mail:* quangzhou@candcprinting.com
C & C Offset Printing Co (UK), Ltd, 2 New Burlington St, 4th fl, London W1S 2JE, United Kingdom *Tel:* (0207) 2877787 *Fax:* (0207) 2877187 *E-mail:* tracy@candcoffset.co.uk

Caritas Printing Training Centre
2 Caine Rd, Caritas House, Block D, 3/F, Hong Kong
Tel: 25261148 *Fax:* 25371231
Key Personnel
General Manager: Isaac Mak
Print Runs: 1,000 min - 100,000 max
Business from Other Countries: 50%

Colorprint Offset
8 Coml Tower, Chai Wan
Tel: 28967777 *Fax:* 28896606
Key Personnel
Sales Manager: Jennifer Weston *Tel:* 9035062
Contact: Eva Lav; Ian Lee
Turnaround: Standard 2 week turnaround
Print Runs: 3,000 min - 100,000 max
Business from Other Countries: 80%
Sales Office(s): Gainsborough House, 81 Oxford St, London W1R 1KB, United Kingdom
Lincoln Bldg, Suite 1149, 60 E 42 St, New York, NY 10164, United States

Commercial Colorlab Ltd
Aik San Factory Bldg, Quarry Bay
Tel: 25731833 *Fax:* 28934688
Key Personnel
Dir: Simon Wong; Fong Lee Yong
Turnaround: 10 Workdays
Business from Other Countries: 30%

Branch Office(s)
5/F Blk E Finance Bldg, 254-256 Des Voeux Rd, Central
Blk A 7/F Aik San Factory Bldg, 14 Westland Rd

Dai Nippon Printing Co (Hong Kong) Ltd
Division of Dai Nippon Printing Co Ltd
220-248 Texaco Rd, Tsuen Wan Industrial Centre, 2/F-5/F, Tsuen Wan, New Territories
Tel: 24080188 *Fax:* 24076201
Web Site: www.dnp.co.jp *Cable:* DNPICO
Key Personnel
Administration & Finance Dir: Mr K Miya
Print Runs: 5,000 min - 200,000 max
Business from Other Countries: 85%
Branch Office(s)
Dai Nippon Printing Co Pty Ltd, 45 Clarence St, Suite 904, Level 9, KPMG Centre, Sydney NSW 2000, Australia
Dai Nippon Printing Co Ltd, London Liaison Office, 27 Throgmorton St, 4th Floor, London EC2N 2AQ, United Kingdom
Dai Nippon Printing Co Ltd, 1-1, Ichigaya-Kagacho, 1-Chome, Shinjuku-Ku, Tokyo, Japan
DNP America Inc, 50 California St, Suite 777, San Francisco, CA 94111, United States
DNP America Inc, 3235 Kifer Rd, Suite 100, Santa Clara, CA 95051, United States
DNP America Inc, 3858 Carson St, Suite 300, Torrance, CA 90503, United States
Dai Nippon Printing Co (Singapore) Pte, Ltd, 896 Dunearn Rd, No 04-09, Sime Darby Centre, Singapore 589472, Singapore *Tel:* 469-7611
Tien Wah Press (Pte) Ltd, 4 Pandan Crescent, Singapore 128475, Singapore *Tel:* 466-6222
TWP SDN BHD, 89 Jalan Tampoi, Kawasan Perindustrian Tampoi, 80350 Johor Bahru, Johor, Malaysia *Tel:* (07) 2369899
Pt Tien Wah Press Indonesia, Jalan Tenaru, Desa Cangkir, Kec Driyorejo, Gresik 61177, Indonesia *Tel:* (031) 7507403
P T Dai Nippon Printing Indonesia, Kawasan Industri Pulogadung, Jalan Pulogadung Kaveling II, Blok H, No 2-3, Jakarta Timur, Indonesia *Tel:* (021) 4610313
DNP Corporation USA, 335 Madison Ave, 3rd Floor, New York, NY 10017, United States *Tel:* 212-503-1060
DNP (America) Inc, San Diego Sales Office, 7425 Mission Valley Rd, Suite 201, San Diego, CA 92108, United States *Tel:* 619-295-8111
DAI Nippon IMS (America) Corp, 4524 Enterprise Dr NW, Concord, NC 28027, United States *Tel:* 704-784-8100
DAI Nippon Printing (Europa) GMBH, Berliner Allee 26, 40212 Dusseldorf, Germany *Tel:* (0211) 862018-0
DNP Denmark A/S, Skruegangen 2, DK-2690 Karlslunde, Denmark *Tel:* 4616-5100
DAI Nippon Printing (Taiwan) Co, Ltd, 85 Chung Hsiao East Rd, Sec 1 Taipei, Taiwan, China *Tel:* (02) 2327-8311

Everbest Printing Co Ltd
Block C5, 10/F, Ko Fai Industrial Bldg, 7 Ko Fai Rd, 10F, Yautong, Kowloon
Tel: (02) 7274433 *Fax:* 7727687
E-mail: everbest@hk.super.net; sales@everbest.com.hk
Key Personnel
Man Dir: Kenneth Chung
Customer Account Executive: Ronny Ng; Frankie Lee
Founded: 1954
Turnaround: 28 Workdays
Print Runs: 1,000 min - 1,000,000 max
Business from Other Countries: 90%
Branch Office(s)
Four Colour Imports Ltd, 2843 Brownsboro Rd, Louisville, KY, United States *Tel:* 502-896-9644
Everbest Midwest, Edina, MN, United States *Tel:* (612) 944-0854
Everbest Canada, Toronto, ON, Canada *Tel:* 416-286-6688

Excel United Company Ltd
6/F Block A, B, E & F Sunview Industrial Bldg, 3 On Yip St, Chai Wan
Tel: 28891078 *Fax:* 28891721
Key Personnel
Dir: Samuel Chung

Golden Cup Printing Co Ltd
6/F Seapower Industrial Centre, 177 Hoi Bun Rd, Kwun Tong, Kowloon
Tel: 23434254 *Fax:* 23415426
E-mail: sales@goldencup.com.hk
Web Site: www.goldencup.com.hk
Key Personnel
Man Dir: K K Yeung
General Manager: W K Ngan
Sales Manager: Mary Yeung *E-mail:* mary@goldencup.com.hk
Founded: 1971
Turnaround: 25 Workdays
Print Runs: 5,000 min - 200,000 max
Business from Other Countries: 80%
Branch Office(s)
Dongguan, China
Guangdong, China
Kunming, China
Yunan, China

The Green Pagoda Press Ltd
9/F, Tung Chong Factory Bldg, 653-655 Kings Rd, North Point
Tel: 25611924 *Fax:* 28110946
E-mail: gpinfo@gpp.com.hk
Key Personnel
Dir: Derek Yip
Founded: 1957
Turnaround: 1-14 days
Print Runs: 10 min - 100,000 max
Business from Other Countries: 30%

Hindy's Enterprise Co Ltd
Flat A 20/F, Melbourne Industrial Bldg, 16 Wetlands Rd, Quarry Bay
Tel: 25166318 *Fax:* 25165161
Key Personnel
General Manager: Cecilia Chung

Hing Yip Printing Co Ltd
6/F Shing Tak Ind Bldg, 44 Wong Chuk Hang Rd, Aberdeen
Tel: 28147287 *Fax:* 28735317
Key Personnel
General Manager: Louis Ma
Founded: 1963
Print Runs: 1,000 min - 100,000 max
Business from Other Countries: 95%

Hoi Kwong Printing Co Ltd
5D Wah Ha Factory Bldg, 8 Shipyard Lane, Quarry Bay
Tel: 2562 1641 *Fax:* 2564 2142
E-mail: sales@hoikwong.com
Web Site: www.hoikwong.com
Key Personnel
Man Dir: David Chan *Tel:* 2562 1096
 E-mail: dchan@hoikwong.com

Hua Yang Printing Holding Co Ltd
Block A 10/F, Kong Nam Industrial Bldg, 603-9 Castle Peak Rd, Tsuen Wan, New Territories
Tel: 24167591 *Fax:* 24110235; 24166318
Key Personnel
Man Dir: Mr Chan Kok Wai
Sales & Marketing: Carl Chan

Hung Hing Off-set Printing Co Ltd
Subsidiary of Hung Hing Printing Group Ltd
17-19 Dai Hei St, Tai Po Industrial Estate, Tai Po, New Territories
Tel: 26648682 *Fax:* 26642070
E-mail: info@hhop.com.hk
Key Personnel
Man Dir: Matthew Yum *E-mail:* matthew@hhop.com.hk
Founded: 1950
Turnaround: 20-30 Workdays
Print Runs: 5,000 min - 1,000,000 max
Business from Other Countries: 15%

Image Printing Company Ltd
Unit 4, 4/F Cornell Centre, 50 Wing Tai Rd, Chai Wan
Tel: 28732633 *Fax:* 25583044
E-mail: imageprt@pop3.hknet.com
Key Personnel
Man Dir: Philip Chow Sung Ming
Founded: 1992
Print Runs: 1,000 min - 50,000 max
Business from Other Countries: 50%

Kwong Fat Offset Printing Company Ltd
10/F Block A&B, Wah Ha Factory Bldg, 8 Shipyard Lane, Quarry Bay
Tel: 25622144 *Fax:* 25657736
Key Personnel
President: Lawrence Wong
Sales Dir: Ms Stevie Wong

Lammar Offset Printing Co
Flat C, 16/F Aik Sun Factory Bldg, 14 Westlands Rd, Quarry Bay
Tel: 25631068 *Fax:* 28113375
Key Personnel
Man Dir: Mr Wu Yuk Ting

Leo Paper Products Ltd
7/F Kader Bldg, 22 Kai Cheung Rd, Kowloon Bay
Tel: (852) 28841374 *Fax:* (852) 25130698
E-mail: lpp@leo.com.hk
Web Site: www.leo.com.hk
Key Personnel
Man Dir: Johnny Fung *E-mail:* johnny@leo.com.hk; Michael Leung *E-mail:* michael@leo.com.hk
Marketing Dir: Kelly Fok *E-mail:* kelly@leo.com.uk
Founded: 1991
Turnaround: 15-30 Workdays
Print Runs: 5,000 min
Parent Company: Leo Paper Bags Manufacturing Ltd
Branch Office(s)
Leo Paper USA, 777 108 Ave NE, Suite 1200, Bellevue, WA 98004, United States, Contact: Bijan Pakzad *Tel:* 425-646-8801 *Fax:* 425-646-8805 *E-mail:* bijan@pacificpier.com
Sales Office(s): Leo Paper Products (Europe) BVBA, "De Wilde Zee", Wiegstraat 19, 2000 Antwerpen, Belgium, Contact: Jan Van Gijsel *Tel:* (03) 203-0912 *Fax:* (03) 255-1303 *E-mail:* leo@leo-europe.com
Leo Marketing Ltd, The Malthouse, Malthouse Sq, Princes Risborough, Bucks HP27 9AB, United Kingdom *Tel:* (108) 274-244 *Fax:* (018) 275-105 *E-mail:* sallywood.leo@btinternet.com

Liang Yu Printing Factory Ltd
1/F, Hip Shing Industrial Bldg, Sai Won Ho St, Shau Kei Wan
Tel: 25604453 *Fax:* 28858099
E-mail: liangyup@netvigator.com
Key Personnel
Man Dir: Eric Hui *Tel:* 25677563
Print Runs: 5,000 min - 100,000 max
Business from Other Countries: 40%

Midas Printing Ltd
1/F 100 Texaco Rd, Tsuen Wan, New Territories
Tel: 24076888 *Fax:* 24065800; 24096875
E-mail: midas@hkstar.com
Key Personnel
Project Manager: Raymond Chan
Executive Dir: Gloria Y P Kan
Founded: 1990
Turnaround: 14-21 Workdays
Print Runs: 5,000 min - 100,000 max
Business from Other Countries: 25%

Morris Press Ltd
2802 Trend Centre, 29 Cheung Lee St, Chai Wan
Tel: 28892168 *Fax:* 28892180
Key Personnel
President & Contact: Suzy P Morris
 Tel: 732-572-5185 *Fax:* 732-572-5150
 E-mail: spmorris@ix.netcom.com
Dir: Raymond Shing; Raynond Shing
Turnaround: 20 Workdays
Print Runs: 5,000 min - 100,000 max
Business from Other Countries: 50%

Nordica Printing Co Ltd
Melbourne Industrial Bldg, Block B, 3/F, 16 Westlands Rd, Quarry Bay
Tel: 25659234 *Fax:* 25656445
Key Personnel
Executive Officer, Nordica Group: Benny Kwan
Dir: Alan Wong
Manager: K P Chow

Paper Art Product Ltd
Sun Fung Ctr, Flat 819, 8/F88, Kwok Shui Rd, Kwai Chung
Tel: 24812929 *Fax:* 24892255
E-mail: paperart@netvigator.com
Turnaround: 4-8 weeks
Print Runs: 3,000 min - 1,000,000 max
Business from Other Countries: 80%

Paper Communication Printing Express Ltd
4A Dragon Industrial Bldg, 93 King Lam St, Cheung Sha Wan, Kowloon
Tel: 27864191 *Fax:* 27864498
Key Personnel
Marketing Dir: Alam Ng
Contact: Wayne Lui
Founded: 1981
Turnaround: 28 to 56 Workdays
Print Runs: 1,000 min - 100,000 max
Business from Other Countries: 10%

Paramount Publishing Group Limited
3 Chun Kwong St, Tseung Kwan O Industrial Estate, Kowloon
Tel: 28968688 *Fax:* 28978942
E-mail: paramountprin@navigator.com
Web Site: www.paramount.com.hk
Key Personnel
President: Victor Oh
Account Dir: Kelvin Lai
Founded: 1968
Turnaround: 30-45 Workdays
Print Runs: 1,000 min - 1,000,000 max
Business from Other Countries: 60%
Branch Office(s)
Paramount Printing Company USA Inc, 386 Park Ave S, Suite 315, New York, NY 10016, United States, President: Jason Cheng *Tel:* 212-696-5821 *Fax:* 212-696-5428

Prontaprint Asia Ltd
1/F, Gaylord Commercial Bldg, 114 Lockhart Rd, Wanchai
Tel: 28657525 *Fax:* 28661064
E-mail: postmaster@pronta.com.hk
Key Personnel
Man Dir: Clive Howard

Founded: 1986
Business from Other Countries: 40%

Sheck Wah Tong Printing Press
653 Kings Rd 1/F, Tung Chong Factor Bldg, North Point
Tel: 25628293 *Fax:* 25655431
Web Site: www.sheckwahtong.com
Key Personnel
Deputy Man Dir: K C Chiu *E-mail:* kcchiu@swt.com.hk
Founded: 1911
Turnaround: 20 Workdays
Print Runs: 3,000 min - 200,000 max

Sing Cheong Printing Co Limited
Tung Chong Fty Bldg, 655 King's Rd, G/F, North Point
Tel: 25618801 *Fax:* 25659467
E-mail: info@singcheong.com.hk
Key Personnel
Dir & Manager: Karen Shen Fishel
Founded: 1965
Business from Other Countries: 96%

Sino Publishing House Ltd
Asia Harvest Commercial Center, Room 2A, Tak House, 5-11 Stanley St, Central Hong Kong
Tel: 28849963; 28973361 *Fax:* 25121154
E-mail: sunnyp@hkstar.com
Key Personnel
Dir: Stephen Stringer
Founded: 1993
Print Runs: 500 min - 500,000 max
Business from Other Countries: 75%

Sota Graphic Arts Co Ltd
6/F Seapower Industry Centre, 177 Hoi Bun Rd, Kwun Tong, Kowloon
Tel: 23427507 *Fax:* 23415426
E-mail: sales@goldencup.com.hk
Key Personnel
Man Dir: K K Yeung
General Manager: W K Ngan
Assistant Manager: Mary Yeung *E-mail:* mary@goldencup.com.hk
Founded: 1985
Turnaround: 10 Workdays
Print Runs: 2,000 min
Business from Other Countries: 90%

South Sea International Press Ltd
3/F, Yip Cheung Centre, 10 Fung Yip St, Chai Wan
Tel: 28971083 *Fax:* 25581473
E-mail: ssiphk@hk.super.net
Key Personnel
Man Dir: P Y Lee
Senior Manager: Franky Ho
Founded: 1984
Print Runs: 3,000 min - 500,000 max
Business from Other Countries: 80%

Sun Fung Offset Binding Co Ltd
14B Melbourne Ind Bldg, 16 Westland Rd, Hong Kong
Tel: 25618109; 25618100 *Fax:* 28110638
E-mail: sunfung@sunfung.com.hk
Web Site: sunfung.com.hk
Key Personnel
Marketing Manager: Raymond Chau
Marketing Executive: Maria Tsang

Sunny Printing (Hong Kong) Co Ltd
Block C, Gee Tung Chang Industry Bldg, Fung Yip St, Chai Wan
Tel: 25578663 *Fax:* 28898070
E-mail: sunnyint@hkstar.com
Key Personnel
Man Dir: Albert T W Chan

Sunshine Press Ltd
21/F Fullager Ind Bldg, 234 Aberdeen Main Rd, Hong Kong
Tel: 25532386 *Fax:* 28732930
E-mail: spl@sunshinepress.com.hk
Key Personnel
Administrative Assistant: Trevin Tong
Contact: Joney Chan
Founded: 1976
Turnaround: 21-28 Workdays
Print Runs: 3,000 min - 500,000 max
Business from Other Countries: 25%

Toppan Printing Co (HK) Ltd
Division of Toppan Printing Co Ltd
Yuen Long Industrial Estate, One Fuk Wang St, Yuen Long, New Territories
Tel: 24755666; 25610101 *Fax:* 24740608; 28809970
E-mail: mamada@hk.nttdata.net
Key Personnel
Man Dir: James Lee Lee
Sales Manager: Yukata Ito
Founded: 1963
Turnaround: 30 Workdays
Business from Other Countries: 25%

Unicorn International Printing Co Ltd
Blk A, 2/F, Sum Lung Ind Bldg, 11 Sun Yip St, Chai Wan
Tel: 28980238 *Fax:* 28983812
E-mail: unicorn7@netvigator.com
Key Personnel
General Manager: Paul chi-sing Choi
Founded: 1994
Turnaround: 2 weeks-1 month
Print Runs: 1,000 min - 50,000 max
Business from Other Countries: 20%

Wing King Tong Co Ltd (Printing Factory)
188 Texaco Rd, 3/F, Phase 1, Leader Industrial Centre, Tsuen Wan, New Territories
Tel: 24073287 *Fax:* 24074130
Key Personnel
Man Dir: Alex Yan *E-mail:* ayan@hk.super.net
Marketing Dir: Jeremy Kuo
Founded: 1944
Turnaround: 15 Workdays
Print Runs: 1,000 min - 100,000 max
Business from Other Countries: 95%

Hungary

Interpress Aussenhandels GmbH
Subsidiary of ADWEST
Bajcsy-Zsilinszky ut 21, H-1065 Budapest
Tel: (01) 3027525 *Fax:* (01) 3027530
E-mail: office@interpress.hu
Web Site: www.interpress.hu
Key Personnel
Manager: Miklos Pollak; Sandor Kovacs; Julia Kovacs
Founded: 1991

Kultura
Kerek u 80, H-1035 Budapest
Tel: (01) 2501194 *Fax:* (01) 2500233
Key Personnel
Manager: Katalin Multas

India

Hiralal Printing Works Ltd
Subsidiary of Conway Printers Pvt Ltd

INDIA

Plot No D-41/1, MIDC TTC Ind Area, Opp Turbne Tel Exch, Mumbai 400613
Tel: (022) 7672726; (022) 7683012 *Fax:* (022) 7631191
Key Personnel
Chairman: G P Agrawal
Man Dir: Mr Rakesh Kumar Agrawal
Founded: 1981
Turnaround: 40-45 Workdays
Print Runs: 5,000 min - 100,000 max
Business from Other Countries: 75%

Indonesia

Ichtiar Baru I Van Hoeve
Jl Cideng Barat 62, Jakarta Barat
Tel: (021) 354533
Founded: 1972
Turnaround: 6 Workdays
Print Runs: 500 min - 18,000 max

Victory Offset Prima PT
Jalan Raya Pegangsaan, Dua, No 17, Jakarta 14250
Tel: (021) 460-8968; (021) 460-2742 *Fax:* (021) 460-2740; (021) 4682-0551
E-mail: info@victoryoffset.com
Web Site: www.victoryoffset.com
Key Personnel
President: Zainal F Stanley *E-mail:* zainal@victoryoffset.com
General Manager: S Wilson Pinady *E-mail:* wilson@victoryoffset.com
Founded: 1971
Turnaround: 14 days
Print Runs: 5,000 min
Business from Other Countries: 20%

Ireland

Kilkenny People/Wellbrook Press
34 High St, Kilkenny
Tel: (056) 21015 *Fax:* (056) 21414
Founded: 1892
Business from Other Countries: 10%

Smurfit Print
33 Botanic Rd, Glasnevin, Dublin 9
Tel: (01) 882 0500
Web Site: www.smurfit.ie
Key Personnel
Chief Executive: Niamh McGowan *Tel:* (01) 882 0501 *E-mail:* nmcgowan@smurfitprint.ie
Sales Dir: Doual Greene
Print Runs: 200 min - 5,000,000 max
Business from Other Countries: 20%
Parent Company: Jefferson Smurfit Group plc

Ultragraphics
Unit 78A, Cookstown Industrial Estate, Tallaght, Dublin 24
Tel: (01) 4599133 *Fax:* (01) 4512368
Key Personnel
President: Tony Lovett
Turnaround: 4-5 Workdays
Business from Other Countries: 80%

Israel

Har-El Printers & Publishers
Jaffa Port, Main Gate, Jaffa 61081
Mailing Address: PO Box 8053, Jaffa 61081
Tel: (03) 6816834 *Fax:* (03) 6813563
E-mail: mharel@harelart.co.il
Web Site: www.interart.co.il/harel
Key Personnel
Manager: Jaacov Har-El
Founded: 1974
Turnaround: 60-90 Workdays
Print Runs: 30 min - 5,000 max
Business from Other Countries: 70%

Keterpress Enterprises Jerusalem
Industrial Zone Givat Shaul B, Jerusalem 91071
Mailing Address: PO Box 7145, Jerusalem 91071
Tel: (02) 6557822 *Fax:* (02) 6528962
E-mail: keterprs@isdn.net.il
Key Personnel
Plant Manager: Peter Tomkins *E-mail:* peter@keter-books.co.il
Sales Manager: Zvi Weller
Print Runs: 500 min - 500,000 max
Business from Other Countries: 10%
Parent Company: Keter Publishing House Ltd

Monoline Ltd
Avnei Nezer St 3, Kiryat Sefer 71917
Tel: (08) 9741456 *Fax:* (08) 9741454
Key Personnel
Dir: S J Colthof
Founded: 1959
Business from Other Countries: 30%

Technosdar Ltd
5 Levontine St, Tel Aviv 61316
Mailing Address: PO Box 31684, Tel Aviv 65111
Tel: (03) 5607418 *Fax:* (03) 5604932
E-mail: technos@zahav.net.il
Key Personnel
General Manager: Avraham Weiss
Founded: 1972
Turnaround: 7-16 Workdays
Business from Other Countries: 10%

Italy

Canale G e C SpA
Subsidiary of Istituto Grafico Bertello SpA
Via Liguria 24, 10071 Borgaro Turin
Tel: (011) 4078511 *Fax:* (011) 4078527
E-mail: info@canale.it
Key Personnel
Dir General: Canale Giacomo *E-mail:* canale@canale.it
Founded: 1915
Turnaround: 30 Workdays
Print Runs: 3,000 min
Business from Other Countries: 65%

Dedalo Litostampa SRL
Casella Postale 362, 70123 Bari
Tel: (080) 5311400 *Fax:* (080) 5311414
Key Personnel
Man Dir: Raimondo Coga
General Manager: Sergio Coga *Tel:* (080) 5311413 *E-mail:* s.coga@edizionidedalo.it
Founded: 1965
Print Runs: 2,000 min - 10,000 max

Mariani Ritti Grafiche SRL
Via Rontgen 16, 20136 Milan
Tel: (02) 58310004 *Fax:* (02) 58310408
E-mail: ritti@tiw.it
Key Personnel
Manager: Giorgio Ritti
Founded: 1959
Business from Other Countries: 25%

Milanostampa SPA
Corso Ferrero 5, Farigliano 12060 Cuneo
Tel: (0173) 746111 *Fax:* (0173) 746248
E-mail: milanostampa@areacom.it
Telex: 212428
Key Personnel
Commercial Dir: Riccardo Sardo
Man Dir: Fuad Lahham
Founded: 1965
Turnaround: 15 Workdays
Print Runs: 3,000 min - 80,000 max
Business from Other Countries: 65%

Minerva Medica
Corso Bramante 83/85, Turin 10126
Tel: (011) 678282 *Fax:* (011) 674502
Key Personnel
President: Dr Alberto Oliaro
Founded: 1937
Print Runs: 1,000 min - 10,000 max
Business from Other Countries: 8%
Branch Office(s)
Via Spallanzani 9, Rome

Nuovo Instituto Italiano d'Arti Grafiche
Via Zanica 92, I-24126 Bergamo
Tel: (035) 311311 *Fax:* (035) 311349
Telex: (035) 300114
Founded: 1871
Turnaround: 10 Workdays
Business from Other Countries: 30%

Amilcare Pizzi SpA
Via A Pizzi, 14, 20092 Cinisello Balsamo (Milan)
Tel: (02) 618361 *Fax:* (02) 61836283
E-mail: mapizzi@tin.it
Key Personnel
Chief Executive: Massimo Pizzi
Sales Dir: Bruno Nicolis
Founded: 1914
Business from Other Countries: 45%
Branch Office(s)
Amilcare Pizzi UK, 27 Cedar Rd, Berkhamsted, Herts HP4 2LA, United Kingdom *Tel:* (01442) 877692 *Fax:* (01442) 875315
American Pizzi Offset Corp, 370 Lexington Ave, Suite 505, New York, NY 10017, United States *Tel:* 212-986-1658 *Fax:* 212-286-1887

Japan

Dai Nippon Printing Co Ltd
3-87-4 Haramachi NT Bld, Tokyo 162-01
Tel: (03) 53608602 *Fax:* (03) 53608222
Key Personnel
President: Yoshitoshi Kitajima
Dir, International Operations: Satoshi Saruwatari
Print Runs: 5,000 min - 200,000 max
Business from Other Countries: 85%
Branch Office(s)
DNP America Inc, Los Angeles, CA, United States
London, United Kingdom
Dusseldorf, Germany
Sales Office(s): New York, NY, United States
San Francisco, CA, United States
Santa Clara, CA, United States
Sydney, Australia

Nissha Printing Co Ltd
3 Mibu Hanai-cho, Nakakyo-ku, Kyoto, 604

Tel: (075) 756822000 Fax: (075) 8235322
Key Personnel
Chairman: Mr Shozo Suzuki
President: Mr Hiroshi Furukawa
International Div: Ms Yuri Miura

Republic of Korea

Daehan Printing & Publishing Co Ltd
344-12, Sangdaewon-dong, Jungwon-gu, Sungnam-City, Kyungki-do
Tel: (031) 730-3830 (i-3) *Fax:* (031) 735-8104
Web Site: www.dhpop.com
Key Personnel
President: Sungshick Kim
Manager: Jongjun Yu
Founded: 1948

Pyunghwa Dang Printing Co Ltd
60 Kyunji-Dong, Chongro-ku, Seoul
Tel: (02) 7354001 *Fax:* (02) 7345201
E-mail: phdprt@kornet.net
Key Personnel
President: Mr Il Soo Lee
Vice President: Mr Hae Kun Oh
Executive Dir: Mr Sang Woo Lee
Founded: 1923
Turnaround: 10 Workdays
Print Runs: 2,000 min - 500,000 max
Business from Other Countries: 7%

Lithuania

Spindulys Printing House
Gedimino 10, 3000 Kaunas
Tel: (07) 226243 *Fax:* (07) 204970
Key Personnel
Contact: Elena Kapustinskiene
Founded: 1928
Print Runs: 500 min - 100,000 max
Business from Other Countries: 6%

Madagascar

Societe Malgache d'Edition
Route des Hydrocarbures, Ankorondrano, BP 659, Antananarivo 101
Tel: (020) 2222635 *Fax:* (020) 2222254
E-mail: tribune@bow.dts.mg; tribune@blanbir.mg
Web Site: www.madagascar-tribune.com
Telex: (020) 223-40
Key Personnel
Dir of Publication: Rahaga Ramaholimihaso
Founded: 1943
Print Runs: 7,000 min - 15,000 max

Malaysia

Web Printers Sdn Bhd
10 Jalan Bersatu 13/4, 46700 Petaling Jaya, Selangor

Key Personnel
General Manager: Hashim Natt
Marketing Manager: Ashraf Ali

Malta

Interprint Ltd - Malta
Subsidiary of Malta Government
Industrial Estate, Marsa
Tel: 240169; 222720 *Fax:* 243780; 249712
E-mail: interprintjb@camline.net.mt
Key Personnel
General Manager: Alfred Azzopardi
Sales Manager: J Bonnici
Founded: 1963
Turnaround: 15 Workdays
Print Runs: 500 min - 20,000 max
Business from Other Countries: 80%

Netherlands

Bosch en Keuning grafische bedrijven
Ericstraat 1, 3742 SG Baarn
Mailing Address: Postbus 1, 3740 AA Baarn
Tel: (035) 5412050 *Fax:* (035) 2202446
Key Personnel
Contact: P P E Rings

Koninklijke Wohrmann Bv
Estlandsestraat 1, 7202 CP Zutphen
Tel: (0575) 582121 *Fax:* (0575) 582128

New Zealand

Bookprint Consultants Ltd
Division of Grantham House Publishing
9 Wilkinson St, Apt 6, Oriental Bay, Wellington 6001
Tel: (04) 381 3071 *Fax:* (04) 381 3067
E-mail: gstewart@iconz.co.nz
Key Personnel
Chief Executive: Graham C Stewart
Founded: 1982
Print Runs: 2,000 min - 7,500 max
Business from Other Countries: 10%

John McIndoe Ltd
PO Box 694, Dunedin
Tel: (03) 4770355 *Fax:* (03) 4771982
E-mail: jmcindoe@earthlight.co.nz
Key Personnel
Man Dir: Brendan A Murphy
Founded: 1893
Print Runs: 21 min - 30 max
Business from Other Countries: 1%

PPP Printers Ltd
PO Box 22785, Christchurch
Tel: (03) 3662727 *Fax:* (03) 3654606
Key Personnel
Man Dir: D C Richardson
Founded: 1958
Turnaround: 10 Workdays
Print Runs: 100 min - 100,000 max
Business from Other Countries: 10%

Peru

Industrias del Envase SA
Subsidiary of Cerveceria Backus & Johnson SA
Au Elmer Faucett 4766, Calla 0
Tel: (01) 5741150 *Fax:* (01) 5741787
E-mail: postmast@envase.com.pe
Web Site: www.envase.com.pe
Key Personnel
General Manager: Jose Santa Maria
Production Dir: Ing Gastavo Mansilla
Founded: 1971
Turnaround: 2 Workdays
Print Runs: 15,000 min - 1,200,000 max
Business from Other Countries: 5%

Philippines

Cacho Hermanos Inc
Pines Cor, Union St, Mandaluyong City
Tel: (02) 6330006; (02) 6318363; (02) 6318364; (02) 6318365; (02) 6318361; (02) 6318362
Fax: (02) 6315244
E-mail: cacho@mozcom.com
Key Personnel
President: Herbert T Veloso
Founded: 1880
Turnaround: 7-120 Workdays
Print Runs: 500 min - 50,000 max
Ultimate Parent Company: National Book Store

JF Printhaus
Km 83.38 Maharlika Hi-way, Brgy San Francisco, 4000 San Pablo City
Tel: (049) 562-0916
Key Personnel
Pres: Victorino F Javier, Jr
Founded: 1982
Parent Company: JF Corporation
Membership(s): Philippine Printing Technical Foundation; Printing Industries Association of the Philippines

Naldoza Printers
362 Tupaz St, 6000 Cebu City
Tel: (032) 261-7326 *Fax:* (032) 261-7326
E-mail: naldoza@ebu.skyinet.net
Key Personnel
Chief Executive Officer: John R Naldoza
Founded: 1989
Parent Company: Business Developers Inc
Membership(s): Philippine Printing Technical Foundation

Philippine Graphic Arts Inc
163 Tandang Sora St, 1400 Caloocan City
Tel: (02) 364-4591 *Fax:* (02) 631-9733
E-mail: philippinegraphicarts@yahoo.com
Key Personnel
Pres & Gen Mgr: Igmedio R Silverio

Portugal

Printer Portuguesa Industria Grafica Lda
Sao Carlos, 2725 Mem Martins
Tel: (01) 9216025 *Fax:* (01) 9218363
E-mail: lissabon.printerportuguesa@bertelsmann.de
Key Personnel
Contact: Albert Lutz

PORTUGAL

Silabo
R Cidade de Manchester-2, 1170-100 Lisbon
Tel: (021) 8130345 *Fax:* (021) 8166719
E-mail: silabo@mail.telepac.pt
Key Personnel
Marketing Dir: Manuel Robalo
    E-mail: manuelrobalo@mail.telepac.pt
Founded: 1983
Turnaround: 5 Workdays

Puerto Rico

Publishing Resources Inc
373 San Jorge St, 2nd Floor, Santurce 00912
Mailing Address: PO Box 41307, Minillas Station, Santurce 00940
Tel: (787) 268-8080 *Fax:* (787) 774-5781
E-mail: pri@tld.net
Key Personnel
Owner: Ronald J Chevako
Editorial Dir: Anne W Chevako
Founded: 1976
Print Runs: 500 min - 10,000 max
Business from Other Countries: 5%

Singapore

Chong Moh Offset Printing Ltd
Subsidiary of Chassis Graphic Art Pte Ltd
19 Joo Koon Rd, Jurong Town 628978
Tel: 8622701 *Fax:* 8624335
E-mail: chongmoh@singnet.com.sg
Key Personnel
Chairman: James Ng
Founded: 1946
Turnaround: 10-14 Workdays
Print Runs: 1,000 min
Business from Other Countries: 35%

Columbia Overseas Marketing Pte Ltd
Subsidiary of Columbia Offset Platemaking Co
77 Lorong 19 Geylang, No 02-00/05 Wing Yip Bldg, Singapore 388513
Tel: 7478607 *Fax:* 7442338
Key Personnel
Man Dir: Mr Eujin Chua
Founded: 1969
Print Runs: 1,000 min - 20,000 max
Business from Other Countries: 40%
Branch Office(s)
Columbia Binding Pte Ltd (Binding)
Columbia Laserart Pte Ltd (Printing)
Columbia Lasermould Pte Ltd (Die-cutting)

Craft Print Pte Ltd
9 Joo Koon Circle, Jurong, Singapore 629041
Tel: 8614040 *Fax:* 8610530
E-mail: craftprt@singnet.com.sg
Key Personnel
Marketing Manager: Anthony Tham

CS Graphics Pte Ltd
10 Tuas Avenue 20, Singapore 638822
Tel: 8610100 *Fax:* 8610190
E-mail: hhlee@singnet.com.sg
Key Personnel
Man Dir: Mr Lee Sian Tee *E-mail:* stlee@csgraphics.com.sg
Founded: 1980
Turnaround: 80 Workdays
Print Runs: 1,000 min - 100,000 max
Business from Other Countries: 100%

Eurasia Press Pte Ltd
10/14 Kampong Ampat-1336, Singapore 368320
Tel: 2805522 *Fax:* 2800593; 3825458
E-mail: eurasia@mbox3.singnet.com.sg
Key Personnel
Marketing Dir: Allan Fong
Founded: 1937
Turnaround: 14 Workdays
Print Runs: 500 min - 100,000 max
Business from Other Countries: 65%

Fong & Sons Printers Pte Ltd
40 Pandan Rd, Singapore 609282
Tel: 2663688 *Fax:* 2664988
Key Personnel
Man Dir: Tony Fong

Ho Printing Singapore Pte Ltd
Changi South St One, Singapore 486797
Tel: 5429322 *Fax:* 2896065
Telex: RS 39685 HOFSET
Key Personnel
Sales Executive: Ho Wah Yuen
Founded: 1951
Turnaround: 35-50 Workdays
Print Runs: 5,000 min - 50,000 max
Business from Other Countries: 30%

Huntsmen Offset Printing Pte Ltd
2 Fan Yoong Rd, Jurong Town, Singapore 629780
Tel: 2650600 *Fax:* 2658575
Key Personnel
General Manager: Heung Yam Yuen
Founded: 1970
Turnaround: 30 Workdays
Business from Other Countries: 60%

International Press Co Pte Ltd
26 Kallang Ave, Singapore 339417
Tel: 2983800 *Fax:* 2971668
Key Personnel
Marketing Manager: Koo Kok Leong
Founded: 1972
Print Runs: 3,000 min - 50,000 max
Business from Other Countries: 60%

Kin Keong Printing Co Pte Ltd, see Markono Print Media Pte Ltd

Kyodo Printing Co (S'pore) Pte Ltd
112 Neythal Rd, Jurong Town, Singapore 628599
Tel: 2652955 *Fax:* 2644939; 2610891
Telex: KSPRINT RS22144 *Cable:* SHINGPRESS
Key Personnel
Executive Secretary: Mr Ng Soo Siah

Markono Print Media Pte Ltd
Formerly Kin Keong Printing Co Pte Ltd
Subsidiary of Markono Holdings Pte Ltd
21 Neythal Rd, Singapore 628586
Tel: 62811118 *Fax:* 62866663
E-mail: sales@markono.com.sg
Key Personnel
Man Dir: Bob Lee *E-mail:* blee@markono.com.sg
Turnaround: 7 Workdays
Print Runs: 500 min - 150,000 max
Business from Other Countries: 20%
Branch Office(s)
Kin Keong Colour Printing (M) Sdn Bhd, Port Klang 539538

PacPress Media Pte Ltd
Blk 1200 Depot Close, No 01-21/27 (off Depot Rd), Telok Blangah Industrial Estate, Singapore 0410 109675
Tel: 2768090; 2730756 *Fax:* 2730060
Key Personnel
Man Dir: Mr T H Oh

PRINTING, BINDING

SNP Printing Pte Ltd
162 Bukit Merah, Central 04-3545, Singapore 150162
Tel: 2780881 *Fax:* 2766970; 2782456
E-mail: poaylim@snp.com.sg
Telex: rs56289epb
Key Personnel
President: Yeo Chee Tong
Executive Vice President: Koo Tse Chia
US Sales Manager: Patrick Chung
Turnaround: 30 Workdays
Print Runs: 2,000 min - 200,000 max
Business from Other Countries: 40%

Stamford Press Pte Ltd
209, Kallang Bahru, Singapore 339344
Tel: 2947227 *Fax:* 2944396
E-mail: stamford@singnet.com.sg
Telex: RS56414 STAMFO
Key Personnel
Dir: R Theyvendran
Founded: 1963
Turnaround: 3-4 Workdays for small jobs; 3-4 weeks for big jobs
Print Runs: 1,500 min - 50,000 max
Business from Other Countries: 20%

Tien Wah Press Pte Ltd
Subsidiary of Dai Nippon Printing Co, Ltd
4 Pandan Crescent, Singapore 128475
Tel: 64666222 *Fax:* 64693894
Key Personnel
Man Dir: Makoto Takakura
Marketing Dir: Mrs Campos-Chia Chiu Leng
Founded: 1935
Business from Other Countries: 80%
Branch Office(s)
Tien Wah Press Aust Pty Ltd, Unit 10, 130 Pacific Highway, St Leonards, 2085 Sydney, NSW, Australia *Tel:* (02) 9436-0255 *Fax:* (02) 9438-5381
Tien Wah Press France, 62 Rue Ducourdic, 75014 Paris, France *Tel:* (01) 4279-0700 *Fax:* (01) 4279-8090
Tien Wah Press, 84 Wooster St, Suite 505, New York, NY 10012, United States *Tel:* 212-274-8090 *Fax:* 212-274-0771
TWP America Inc, 2550 Ninth St, Suite 111, Berkeley, CA 94710, United States *Tel:* 510-845-9532 *Fax:* 510-845-8580
Tien Wah Press (UK) Ltd, Unit 23, The Ivories, 6-8 Northampton St, London N1 2HY, United Kingdom *Tel:* (020) 7354-3323 *Fax:* (020) 7359-8777

Times Printers Pte Ltd
Subsidiary of Times Publishing Group
16 Tuas Ave 5, Singapore 639340
Tel: 8623333 *Fax:* 8621313
E-mail: timetppl@singnet.com.sg *Cable:* TIMESPRINT
Key Personnel
Vice President: Leong Kwok Sun
Sales Manager: Patsy Tan; Koo Kok Leong
Founded: 1968
Turnaround: 5-25 Workdays
Print Runs: 3,000 min - 300,000 max
Business from Other Countries: 75%

Toppan Company (S) Pte Ltd
Division of Toppan Printing Co Ltd
Toppan Shibaura Bldg, 3-19-26 Shibaura, Minato-ku 108-0023
Tel: 264-0654 *Fax:* 265-8298
Telex: RS 21596 *Cable:* TOPPAN
Key Personnel
Man Dir: Kohei Mochizuki
General Manager: M Sonoda
Founded: 1968
Turnaround: 3 - 4 Weeks
Print Runs: 3,000 min - 500,000 max
Business from Other Countries: 70%

World Publications Printers Pte Ltd
Subsidiary of World Publications Distributors, Pte Ltd
39 Ubi Rd 1, World Publications Bldg, Singapore 408695
Tel: 7449888 *Fax:* 8406118
E-mail: wphsin@singnet.com.sg
Web Site: web.singnet.com.sg
Telex: RS 39283 WPD
Key Personnel
Chief Executive Officer & President: Mr S K Ng
Finance Dir: Mrs S K Ng
Vice President, Sales & Marketing: Ms Chan Sew Chu
Vice President, Corporate Affairs, Human Resources & Administration: Ms Dot Loh
Founded: 1982
Turnaround: 7-14 Workdays
Print Runs: 1 min - 70,000 max
Business from Other Countries: 80%

Slovenia

Gorenjski Tisk Printing Co
Zoisova ulica 1, 4000 Kranj
Tel: (064) 2630 *Fax:* (064) 241323
Telex: 34560 YU GOTISK
Key Personnel
Dir: Kristina Kobal
Commercial Manager: Boris Krist
Founded: 1888
Turnaround: 30 Workdays
Print Runs: 3,000 min - 15,000 max
Business from Other Countries: 50%

South Africa

CTP Book Printers (Pty) Ltd
PO Box 1610, Parklands
Tel: (011) 8890600 *Fax:* (011) 8890922

Spain

Eurohueco SA
Subsidiary of Arvato AG (Bertelsmann)
Apdo 30099, 08080 Barcelona
Tel: (093) 7730700 *Fax:* (093) 7730708
Key Personnel
Vice President, Sales: Clemens Brauer *Tel:* (093) 7730703 *E-mail:* c.brauer@eurohueco.es
Founded: 1985
Print Runs: 200,000 min - 15,000,000 max
Business from Other Countries: 17%
Parent Company: Arvato AG

Grafos SA Arte Sobre Papel
Sector C calle D, NO 36, E-08040 Barcelona
Tel: (093) 2618750 *Fax:* (093) 2631004
Key Personnel
Man Dir: Peter Zantop *E-mail:* peterzantop@compuserve.com
Founded: 1934
Turnaround: 30 Workdays
Print Runs: 3,000 min - 60,000 max
Business from Other Countries: 45%

Printer Industria Grafica SA
Ctra N-II, km 600, 08620 Sant Vicene dels Horts, Barcelona
Tel: (093) 6310123 *Fax:* (093) 6310205; (093) 6310206
E-mail: info@printer-spain.com
Web Site: www.printer-spain.com
Key Personnel
President: Joaquin Roca Ferrer
Business from Other Countries: 30%

Mercedes Ros Literary Agency
Castell 38, 08329 Teia, Barcelona
Tel: (093) 540 13 53 *Fax:* (093) 540 13 46
E-mail: info@mercedesros.com
Web Site: www.mercedesros.com
Key Personnel
Owner: Mercedes Ros *E-mail:* mercedes@mercedesros.com

Rotedic SA
Subsidiary of Novo Sistema
Ronda de Valdecarrizo, 13 Poligono Industrial de tres Cantos, Madrid 28760
Tel: (091) 8031676 *Fax:* (091) 8038316
Web Site: www.rotedic.com
Key Personnel
Chief Executive Officer: Alfonso de Haro C
President: Gregorio de Haro Juarez
Sales Manager & Commercial Dir: Francisco J de Haro *E-mail:* paco@rotedic.com
Founded: 1974
Print Runs: 50,000 min
Business from Other Countries: 7%

Graficas Santamaria SA
Division of Fotomecanica
Bekolarra 4, 01010 Vitoria (Alava)
Tel: (045) 229100 *Fax:* (045) 246393
Key Personnel
Contact: Jesus Alzola Aguinaco
Founded: 1963
Turnaround: 1 Workday
Print Runs: 500 min - 150,000 max
Business from Other Countries: 15%

Luis Vives (Edelvives)
Xaudaro, 25, 28034 Madrid
Tel: (076) 3344890 *Fax:* (076) 3344892
Key Personnel
Production Dir: Jesus Agudo Perez
Founded: 1890
Turnaround: 1 Workday
Business from Other Countries: 25%

Sri Lanka

Sumathi Book Printing (Pvt) Ltd
Division of Sumathi Group
445/1 Prince of Wales Ave, Colombo 14
Tel: (01) 330673; (01) 330674; (01) 435225 *Fax:* (01) 449593
E-mail: publish@slt.lk
Telex: 22104 SUMATHI CE SUMATISONS
Business from Other Countries: 75%

Switzerland

Hallwag AG
Nordring 4, 3000 Bern
Tel: (031) 423131 *Fax:* (031) 414133
E-mail: kartenverlag@hallwag.ch
Telex: 912-661 HAWA CH
Key Personnel
President: Dr Juergen Schad

Photolitho AG
Industriestr 12, CH-8625 Gossau ZH
Tel: (01) 9352676 *Fax:* (01) 9353247
Key Personnel
President: Dietmar von Eicke
Administrator: Werner Holliger
Founded: 1965
Business from Other Countries: 50%

Taiwan, Province of China

Taipei Yung Chang Printing
No 9, Lane 252, Sec 3, Chung Ching N Rd, Taipei 10318
Tel: (02) 5932392 *Fax:* (02) 5932763

United Republic of Tanzania

Peramiho Publications
PO Box 41, Peramiho
Tel: (054) 2730 *Fax:* (054) 2917
Key Personnel
Chief Executive: Fr Gerold Rupper
Founded: 1937
Print Runs: 4,000 min - 6,000 max

Thailand

J Film Process Co Ltd
440/7 Soi Chaisamoraphum, Rangnum Rd, Phayathai, Bangkok 10400
Tel: (02) 2486888 *Fax:* (02) 2464620; (02) 2474719
Key Personnel
President: Peer Prayukvong
Vice President: Siriporn Prayukvong
Man Dir: Pira Prayookwongse
Founded: 1970
Turnaround: 6 Workdays
Print Runs: 25,000 min - 65,000 max
Business from Other Countries: 45%

Mavisu International Co Ltd
11 Soi Prachanimit, Pradpatrd Phayathai, Bangkok 10400
Tel: (02) 2711148 *Fax:* (02) 2711168
Key Personnel
Man Dir: Vipavee Charoensidhi
Chairman: Marshall French
Founded: 1986
Print Runs: 15 min - 40 max
Business from Other Countries: 100%

Phongwarin Printing Company Ltd
299 Moo 10, Sukhumvit 107, A Muang, Samut Prakarn 10260
Tel: (02) 7498934-45; (02) 3994525-31; (02) 7498275-79 *Fax:* (02) 3994524; (02) 3994255
Web Site: www.phongwarin.com
Key Personnel
Man Dir: Somphong Charnsirisaksakul

Founded: 1983
Turnaround: 7 Workdays
Print Runs: 1,000 min - 500,000 max
Business from Other Countries: 5%

United Arab Emirates

Emirates Printing Press (LLC)
Member of Al Shirawi Group
PO Box 5106, Al Quoz, Dubai
Tel: (04) 347 5550; (04) 347 5544 *Fax:* (04) 347 5959
E-mail: eppdubai@emirates.net.ae
Web Site: www.eppdubai.com
Founded: 1974
Sales Office(s): Emirates Printing Press (UK) Ltd, Baylis House, Stoke Poges Lane, Slough, Berkshire SL1 3PB, United Kingdom, Sales Mgr, UK & USA: Ron Nunn *Tel:* (01753) 505612 *Fax:* (01753) 505613 *E-mail:* eppeurope@aol.com (European & USA)

United Kingdom

The Alden Group Ltd
Osney Mead, Oxford OX2 0EF
Tel: (01865) 253200 *Fax:* (01865) 249070
E-mail: alden.press@alden.co.uk
Web Site: www.alden.co.uk

J W Arrowsmith Ltd
71 Winterstoke Rd, Bristol BS3 2NT
Tel: (0117) 9667545 *Fax:* (0117) 9637829
E-mail: jw@arrowsmith.co.uk
Key Personnel
Sales Mgr: D J Hooper *E-mail:* dhooper@arrowsmith.co.uk
Founded: 1854
Turnaround: 15 Workdays
Print Runs: 500 min - 15,000 max
Business from Other Countries: 40%

W & G Baird Ltd
Subsidiary of W&G Baird Holdings Ltd (parent)
Caulside Dr, Antrim BT41 2RS
Tel: (018494) 63911 *Fax:* (018494) 66250
E-mail: wgbaird@wgbaird.com
Key Personnel
Man Dir: Dairmuid McGarry *E-mail:* diarmuid.mcgarry@wgbaird.com
Founded: 1863
Print Runs: 500 min - 100,000 max
Business from Other Countries: 45%
Branch Office(s)
MSO, Belfast, Ireland
Biddles Ltd, Woodbridge Park, Woodbridge Rd, Guildford, Surrey GU1 1DA

BAS Printers Ltd
Over Wallop, Stockbridge, Hants SO20 8JD
Tel: (01264) 781711 *Fax:* (01264) 781116
Web Site: www.basprint.co.uk
Key Personnel
Man Dir: David Gumn
Sales Dir: Paul G Gumn *E-mail:* paul@basprint.co.uk
Founded: 1948
Print Runs: 350 min - 40,000 max
Business from Other Countries: 10%

Ebenezer Baylis & Son Ltd
The Trinity Press, London Rd, Worcester WR5 2JH
Tel: (01905) 357979 *Fax:* (01905) 354919
E-mail: theworks@ebaylis.demon.co.uk
Key Personnel
Man Dir: Ian Cranston

Bell & Bain Ltd
303 Burnfield Rd, Thornliebank, Glasgow G46 7UQ
Tel: (0141) 6495697 *Fax:* (0141) 6328733
E-mail: info@bell-bain.co.uk
Key Personnel
Man Dir: I Walker
Sales Dir: D Stewart
Founded: 1831
Turnaround: 5-10 Workdays
Print Runs: 100 min - 100,000 max
Business from Other Countries: 25%

Bemrose Security & Promotional Printing
Wayzgoose Dr, Derby DE21 6XG
Mailing Address: PO Box 18, Derby DE21 6XG
Tel: (01332) 294242 *Fax:* (01332) 295848
Key Personnel
Area Sales Manager: Roger Norton
Sales Manager: Rodger Heathcote
 E-mail: rheathcote@bemrose.co.uk

Biddles Ltd
Division of W & G Baird Ltd
Woodbridge Park Estate, Woodbridge Rd, Guildford, Surrey GU1 1DA
Tel: (01483) 502224 *Fax:* (01483) 576150
E-mail: sales@biddles.co.uk
Web Site: www.biddles.co.uk
Founded: 1885
Turnaround: 20 Workdays
Print Runs: 250 min - 50,000 max
Business from Other Countries: 8%
Branch Office(s)
Kings Lynn

Black Bear Press Ltd
King's Hedges Rd, Cambridge CB4 2PQ
Tel: (01223) 424571 *Fax:* (01223) 426877
E-mail: black_bear_press@msn.com
Key Personnel
Man Dir: K Fentiman
Sales Dir: M W Hallam

Blackmore Ltd
Longmead, Shaftesbury, Dorset SP7 8PX
Tel: (01747) 853034 *Fax:* (01747) 854500
E-mail: sales@blackmail.blackmore.co.uk
Key Personnel
Man Dir: Chris Brickell

Blockfoil Ltd
Foxtail Rd, Ransomes Park Industrial Estate, Ipswich IP3 9RT
Tel: (01473) 721701 *Fax:* (01473) 270705
Key Personnel
Man Dir: Barry Corbett

Book Creation Services
21 Carnaby St, London W1V 1PH
Tel: (020) 7287 0214 *Fax:* (020) 7287 8547
Key Personnel
Chairman: Hal Robinson *E-mail:* hal@zoo.co.uk
Founded: 1991
Business from Other Countries: 30%

J W Braithwaite & Son Ltd
Pountney St, Wolverhampton WV2 4HY
Tel: (01902) 452209 *Fax:* (01902) 352918

Key Personnel
Man Dir: Bruce Kidson *E-mail:* brucekidson@jwbraithwaite.co.uk
Founded: 1901

D Brown & Sons Ltd
North Rd, Bridgend Industrial Estate, Bridgend CF31 3TP
Tel: (01446) 771475 *Fax:* (01446) 771476
E-mail: info@geminidigital.demon.co.uk
Key Personnel
Dir: J M Whitaker *Tel:* (01446) 774213
Founded: 1895
Print Runs: 1 min - 1,000,000 max
Business from Other Countries: 20%
Branch Office(s)
Eastgate Press, 62 Eastgate, Cowbridge, S Glam CF7 7AB

Butler & Tanner Ltd
The Selwood Printing Works, Frome, Somerset BA11 1NF
Tel: (01373) 451500 *Fax:* (01373) 451333
E-mail: manufacturing@butlerandtanner.com
Key Personnel
Joint Man Dir: A Huett
Sales Dir: N White

Caledonian International Book Manufacturing
Westerhill Rd, Bishopbriggs, Glasgow G64 2QR
Tel: (0141) 7623000 *Fax:* (0141) 7620922
E-mail: 101622.235@compuserve.com
Key Personnel
Man Dir: Kevin McKenna
Commercial Dir: G Morrison
Group Sales Manager: Martin Platt
 E-mail: martin@platt44.freeserve.co.uk
Founded: 1819

Cambridge University Press - Printing Division
Division of Cambridge University Press
University Printing House, Shaftesbury Rd, Cambridge CB2 2BS
Tel: (01223) 358331 *Fax:* (01223) 325672
E-mail: info@cup.cam.ac.uk
Key Personnel
Production Dir: Steve Millard *E-mail:* smillard@cup.com.ac.uk
Production Manager: Alan Dungar
Founded: 1534
Print Runs: 1 min

CB Print Finishers Ltd
Unit 4, North Tyne Industrial Estate, Newcastle Upon Tyne NE12 9TG
Tel: (0191) 2150101 *Fax:* (0191) 2701651
E-mail: sales@cbprint.co.uk
Web Site: www.cbprint.co.uk
Key Personnel
Man Dir: Paul Laidler

Center Print Ltd
Subsidiary of The Boots Co PLC
Private Rd 2, Colwich Business Park, Colwich, Nottingham NG4 2JR
Tel: (0115) 9612277 *Fax:* (0115) 9381424
E-mail: cprint@besharapress.co.uk
Key Personnel
Man Dir: Nicola Leslie
Print Runs: 1,000 min - 250,000 max

The Charlesworth Group
254 Deighton Rd, Huddersfield, West Yorkshire HD2 1JJ
Tel: (01484) 517077 *Fax:* (01484) 517068
E-mail: sales@charlesworth.com
Key Personnel
Marketing Manager: Sarah Philp
 E-mail: s_philp@charlesworth.com
Founded: 1928
Turnaround: 1-10 Workdays

& BOOK FINISHING — UNITED KINGDOM

Print Runs: 1 min - 10,000 max
Business from Other Countries: 30%

Cedric Chivers Ltd
Subsidiary of Information Preservation Ltd
One Beaufort Trade Park, Pucklechurch, Bristol BS16 9QH
Tel: (0117) 9371910 *Fax:* (0117) 9371920
E-mail: info@cedricchivers.co.uk
Web Site: www.cedricchivers.co.uk
Key Personnel
Sales & Marketing Dir: Russell Pocock
Founded: 1878
Turnaround: 15 Workdays
Print Runs: 1 min - 100 max

Clays Ltd
Subsidiary of St Ives Plc
Popson St, Bungay, Suffolk NR35 1ED
Tel: (01986) 893211
E-mail: clays@claysltd.co.uk
Key Personnel
Contact: Sarah Orell
Founded: 1817
Turnaround: 15 Workdays
Print Runs: 1,000 min - 1,000,000 max
Business from Other Countries: 15%

William Clowes Ltd
Goal Lane, Beccles, Suffolk NR34 9QE
Tel: (01502) 712884 *Fax:* (01502) 717003
Key Personnel
Man Dir: Alex Evans
Sales Dir: David C Browne *Tel:* (01502) 712884, Ext 240
Founded: 1803
Turnaround: 10 Workdays
Print Runs: 2,000 min
Business from Other Countries: 1%

Cox & Wyman Ltd
Subsidiary of Rexam Plc
Cardiff Rd, Reading RG1 8EX
Tel: (01189) 530500 *Fax:* (01189) 507222
Key Personnel
General Manager: Tom Roberts
Sales Manager: Ruth Smith
Founded: 1777
Turnaround: 10 Workdays
Print Runs: 2,000 min - 2,000,000 max
Business from Other Countries: 12%

Cradley Print Ltd
Chester Rd, Cradley Heath, Warley, W Midlands B64 6AB
Tel: (01384) 414100 *Fax:* (01384) 414102
E-mail: sales@cradleygp.co.uk
Key Personnel
Man Dir: Chris Jordan
Turnaround: 5 Workdays
Print Runs: 1,000 min - 500,000 max
Business from Other Countries: 7%
Branch Office(s)
Quadcolor Repro

R R Donnelley
Boroughbridge Rd, York YO2 5SS
Tel: (01904) 798241 *Fax:* (01904) 791017
Key Personnel
Man Dir: Roy Houston

Eagle Press
Riverside Way, Nottingham NG2 1DP
Tel: (0115) 9552335 *Fax:* (0115) 9552336
Key Personnel
Man Dir: S Keilpinski

Essex Colour Services Ltd
Aviation Way, Southend-on-Sea, Essex SS2 6UN
Tel: (01702) 541311 *Fax:* (01702) 540094
Telex: 995569
Key Personnel
Chairman: Leo Smith
Founded: 1971
Turnaround: 5 Workdays
Print Runs: 5,000 min - 100,000 max
Business from Other Countries: 20%

Furnival Press
61 Lilford Rd, London SE5 9HR
Tel: (020) 7274 2067 *Fax:* (020) 7274 6984
E-mail: furnprint@aol.com
Key Personnel
Dir: Johnny Gumb

Goldshield Communications Ltd
Banners Bldg, Attercliffe Rd, Sheffield S9 3QS
Tel: (0114) 2431000 *Fax:* (0114) 2433000
Key Personnel
Man Dir & Overseas-Special Projects: Sandra Potesta *E-mail:* sandra@goldcom.co.uk
Technical & Production: Stefano Potesta
Founded: 1984
Business from Other Countries: 40%

Green Street Bindery
9 Green St, Oxford OX4 1YB
Tel: (01865) 243540 *Fax:* (01865) 791329
Key Personnel
Contact: Garry Phipps
Turnaround: 10-15 Workdays
Print Runs: 1 min - 10,000 max
Business from Other Countries: 5%

The Guernsey Press Co Ltd
Braye Rd, Vale, Guernsey, Channel Islands GY1 3BW
Mailing Address: PO Box 57, Vale, Guernsey, Channel Islands GY1 3BW
Tel: (01481) 240240; (01481) 243657 (ISDN) *Fax:* (01481) 240290; (01481) 249147
E-mail: books@guernsey-press.com
Web Site: www.gp.guernsey-press.com
Key Personnel
Contact: Mr T A R Duquemin
Founded: 1897
Turnaround: 10 Workdays
Print Runs: 2,000 min - 50,000 max
Business from Other Countries: 80%

Hammond Bindery Ltd
Subsidiary of The Charlesworth Group
Flanshaw Way, Wakefield, West Yorks WF2 9LP
Tel: (01924) 369598 *Fax:* (01924) 364108
Key Personnel
Man Dir: Steve Allen
Sales: Brian Quarmby
Founded: 1972
Turnaround: 3-10 Workdays
Print Runs: 100 min - 250,000 max

Hammond Packaging Ltd
Division of Hammond Bindery
129 Water Lane, Holbeck, Leeds LS11 9UB
Tel: (0113) 2423548 *Fax:* (0113) 2445442
E-mail: hammpack@dial.pipex.com
Web Site: www.hammpack.co.uk
Key Personnel
Man Dir: Steve Allan
Founded: 1991
Turnaround: 5-15 Workdays
Print Runs: 100 min - 500,000 max

Norman Hardy Printing Group
Granville House, 112 Bermondsey St, London SE1 3TX
Tel: (020) 7378 1579 *Fax:* (020) 7378 6421
E-mail: info@normanwhardy.co.uk
Web Site: www.normanwhardy.com
Key Personnel
Man Dir: Stuart Hardy

Harveys Ltd
Edgefield Road Industrial Estate, Loanhead, Midlothian EH20 9SX
Tel: (0131) 4400074 *Fax:* (0131) 4403478
E-mail: sales@harveys.ltd.uk
Telex: 727985
Key Personnel
Man Dir: Tom Domke *E-mail:* tom@harvey.ltd.uk
Sales Dir: Ros Porter
Founded: 1856
Print Runs: 100 min - 250,000 max
Business from Other Countries: 10%
Branch Office(s)
Hill Head Vinyls Ltd, Old Kilpatrick, Dunbartonshire

Hastings Publishing Co
Flat 13, Whiterock House, Whiterock Rd, Hastings, East Sussex TN34 1LE
Tel: (01424) 712 765

Headley Brothers Ltd
Invicta Press, Queens Rd, Ashford, Kent TN24 8HH
Tel: (01233) 623131 *Fax:* (01233) 622704; (01233) 612345
E-mail: printing@headley.co.uk
Web Site: www.headley.co.uk
Key Personnel
Sales Dir: Bruce Finn
Commercial Dir: Jon Pitt
Man Dir: Roger Pitt *E-mail:* rpitt@headley.co.uk
Founded: 1881
Print Runs: 1,000 min - 200,000 max
Business from Other Countries: 5%

Hobbs The Printers Ltd
Brunel Rd, Totton, Hants SO40 3WX
Tel: (023) 8066 4800 *Fax:* (023) 8066 4801
E-mail: htp@tcp.co.uk
Key Personnel
Sales Manager: John Eacott *E-mail:* j.eacott@hobbs.uk.com
Commercial Dir: Terry Ozanne
Founded: 1884
Turnaround: 5-10 days litho; up to 5 days digital
Print Runs: 10 min - 50,000 max
Business from Other Countries: 4%

Hunter & Foulis Ltd
Bridgeside Works, McDonald Rd, Edinburgh EH7 4NP
Tel: (0131) 5567947 *Fax:* (0131) 5573911
E-mail: mail@hunterfoulis.co.uk
Key Personnel
Man Dir: Richard Beese
Founded: 1857

Ikon Document Services Ltd
Subsidiary of Microgen Holdings Plc
19 The Business Centre, Molly Millars Lane, Wokingham Berks RG41 2QY
Tel: (0118) 9770510 *Fax:* (0118) 9770513
E-mail: pamh@ikonds.co.uk
Web Site: www.ikon.com
Key Personnel
Man Dir: Dave Weller
Business Development Dir: Aaron Biggs
Founded: 1972
Turnaround: 2-5 Workdays
Print Runs: 1 min - 5,000 max
Business from Other Countries: 40%
Branch Office(s)
Microgen City Park Watchmead, Welwyn Garden City, Herts AL7 1LT

Image & Print Group Ltd
Unit 9, Oakbank Industrial Estate, Garscube Rd, Glasgow G20 7LU
Tel: (0141) 3531900 *Fax:* (0141) 3532472

UNITED KINGDOM   PRINTING, BINDING

E-mail: imageandprint@dial.pipex.com
Web Site: www.imageandprint.co.uk
Key Personnel
Man Dir: Ken Roberts
Production: Stephen McPhee
Founded: 1975
Turnaround: 5 Workdays
Print Runs: 1,000 min - 250,000 max

Intype London Ltd
Units 3 & 4, Elm Grove Industrial Estate, Elm Grove, Wimbledon, London SW19 4HE
Tel: (020) 8947 7863 *Fax:* (020) 8947 3652
E-mail: intype@btconnect.com
Key Personnel
Man Dir: Tony Chapman *E-mail:* tchap@btconnect.com
Production: Richard Mayne
Dir: Alan Johnson
Founded: 1976
Turnaround: 10-15 Workdays for proofs; 5-10 Workdays for books
Print Runs: 25 min - 1,000 max
Business from Other Countries: 5%

Lavenham Press Ltd
Affiliate of Terence Dalton Ltd
Water St, Lavenham, Sudbury, Suffolk CO10 9RN
Tel: (01787) 247436 *Fax:* (01787) 248267
E-mail: postmaster@lavenhamgroup.co.uk
Key Personnel
Man Dir: T A J Dalton
Founded: 1953
Business from Other Countries: 1%
Parent Company: The Lavennah Group PLC

Charles Letts & Co Ltd
Thorney Bank Industrial Estate, Dalkeith EH2 2NE
Tel: (0131) 6631971 *Fax:* (0131) 6603225
Key Personnel
Man Dir: Gordon Presly
Founded: 1796

Lowfield Printing Co Ltd
9 Kennet Rd Thames Rd, Crayford, Dartford, Kent DA1 4QT
Tel: (01322) 522216 *Fax:* (01322) 555362
E-mail: lowfield@compuserve.com
Key Personnel
Dir: Ian J Starkey
Founded: 1964
Print Runs: 500 min - 20,000 max

MacKays of Chatham PLC
Badger Rd, Lordswood, Chatham, Kent ME5 8TD
Tel: (01634) 864381 *Fax:* (01634) 867742
E-mail: mackays@mackayschatham.co.uk
Key Personnel
Dir: J A Daniels

The Malvern Press Ltd
71 Dalston Lane, London E8 2NG
Tel: (0171) 2492991 *Fax:* (0171) 2541720
Key Personnel
Man Dir: Leslie Wynn
Marketing Dir: Peter Wynn
Founded: 1953
Turnaround: 10-15 Workdays
Print Runs: 100 min
Business from Other Countries: 15%

Martins Printing Group Ltd
Division of Staples Printers Ltd
The Gresham Press, Old Woking, Surrey, GU22 9LH
Tel: (01483) 757501 *Fax:* (01483) 724629
E-mail: chandler@martins-print.co.uk

Key Personnel
Group Chief Executive: M R Milton
Group Operations Dir: M R Andrew
Founded: 1930
Print Runs: 1 min - 100,000 max
Business from Other Countries: 5%
Branch Office(s)
33 Store St, London WC1E *Tel:* (020) 7436 0595 *Fax:* (020) 7436 8173 (Sales Office)

MPG Books Ltd
Subsidiary of Martins Printing Group
Victoria Sq, Bodmin, Cornwall PL31 1EB
Tel: (01208) 73266 *Fax:* (01208) 73603
E-mail: print@mpg-books.co.uk
Key Personnel
Sales Dir: Jeff Swift
Man Dir: Paul Dixon
Commercial Dir: Tony Chard
Founded: 1967
Turnaround: 10-15 days
Print Runs: 400 min - 10,000 max
Business from Other Countries: 5%
Parent Company: MPG Ltd

MPG Colour Ltd
Division of Martins Printing Group
Subsidiary of Staples Printers Ltd
The George Press, Trafalgar Rd, Kettering, Northamptonshire NN16 8HA
Tel: (01536) 483401 *Fax:* (01536) 481102
E-mail: print@mpg-colour.co.uk
Key Personnel
Man Dir: Simon Moore
Founded: 1945
Turnaround: 5 Workdays
Print Runs: 3,000 min - 75,000 max
Branch Office(s)
Woking
Rochester
St Albans
Wimbledon
Bodmin
Peterborough

Multiplex Medway Ltd
Gleaming Wood Dr, Lordswood Industrial Estate, Walderslade, Kent ME5 8XT
Tel: (01634) 684371 *Fax:* (01634) 683840
E-mail: enquiries@multiplex-medway.co.uk
Web Site: www.multiplex-medway.co.uk
Key Personnel
Dir: Jon Chandler
Sales Manager: Paul Adson

George Over Ltd
20 Somers Rd, Rugby, Warwickshire CV22 7DH
Tel: (01788) 573621 *Fax:* (01788) 578738
E-mail: xuz23@dial.pinex.com
Key Personnel
Man Dir: A E H Gilbert
Sales Dir: Richard Gilbert

Page Bros Ltd (Norwich)
Subsidiary of Milex Ltd
Mile Cross Lane, Norwich NR6 6SA
Tel: (01603) 429141 *Fax:* (01603) 485126
Key Personnel
Man Dir: David Armstrong
Founded: 1750
Turnaround: 10 Workdays
Print Runs: 100 min - 30,000 max
Business from Other Countries: 20%
Branch Office(s)
105-A Euston St, London NW1 2ET *Tel:* (020) 7383 2212 *Fax:* (020) 7383 4145

Peak Technologies UK Ltd
Silkwood Park, Buckhurst Rd, Ascot, Berks SL56 7PW
Tel: (0) 1344-290000 *Fax:* (0) 1344 290001

E-mail: nreed@peakeurope.com
Web Site: www.peakeurope.com
Key Personnel
Man Dir: Paul O'Donnell
Parent Company: Moore Corp Ltd

Printafoil Ltd
Unit 5, Mitcham Industrial Estate, Streatham Rd, Mitcham, Surrey CR4 2AP
Tel: (0181) 6403074 *Fax:* (0181) 6402136
Key Personnel
Dir: Simon Flower

Redwood Books Ltd
Division of CPI (UK) Ltd
Kennet Way, Trowbridge, Wilts BA14 8RN
Tel: (01225) 769979 *Fax:* (01225) 769050
E-mail: enquiries@redwood-books.co.uk
Key Personnel
General Manager: Trevor Gee
Commercial Manager: Tony Warner *E-mail:* tony@redwood-books.co.uk
Production Manager: Peter Grant
Founded: 1993
Turnaround: 10 Workdays
Print Runs: 10 min - 20,000 max
Business from Other Countries: 8%
Branch Office(s)
London Sales Office, 22 Bloomsbury Sq, London WC1A 2NS *Tel:* (020) 7580-9328 *Fax:* (020) 7580-9337

J R Reid Print & Media Group, see J R Reid Printing Group Ltd

J R Reid Printing Group Ltd
79-109 Glasgow Rd, Blantyre, Glasgow G72 0LY
Tel: (01698) 826000 *Fax:* (01698) 824944
E-mail: clindsay@reid-print-group.co.uk
Web Site: www.reid-print-group.co.uk
Key Personnel
Man Dir: John R Reid *E-mail:* johnreid@reid-print-group.co.uk
Founded: 1972

Antony Rowe Ltd
Bumpers Farm, Chippenham SN14 6LH
Tel: (01249) 659705 *Fax:* (01249) 443103
E-mail: 100616.40@compuserve.com
Key Personnel
Chief Executive: Ralph Bell
Production Dir: Mike Bando
Technical Dir: Andy Burns
Founded: 1983
Turnaround: 20 Workdays
Print Runs: 50 min - 2,000 max
Business from Other Countries: 2%

Selwood Printing
Subsidiary of Lloyd's Register of Shipping
Edwood Way, Burgess Hill, West Sussex RH15 9UA
Tel: (01444) 236060 *Fax:* (01444) 245043
E-mail: systems@selwood.com
Key Personnel
Man Dir: Andrew Lowden

Severnside Printers Ltd
Bridge House, Upton-on-Severn, Worcs WR8 0HG
Tel: (01684) 594521 *Fax:* (01684) 594344
Key Personnel
President & Chief Executive: Norman H Beechey
Turnaround: 14-20 Workdays
Print Runs: 500 min - 5,000 max
Business from Other Countries: 10%

Stott Brothers Ltd
Lister Lane, Halifax, W Yorks HX1 5AJ
Tel: (01422) 362184 *Fax:* (01422) 353707

E-mail: stottbros@aol.com
Key Personnel
Man Dir: Ian Bullough

M & A Thomson Litho Ltd
10/16 Colvilles Pl, Kelvin Industrial Estate, East Kilbride, Glasgow G75 0SN
Tel: (013552) 33081 *Fax:* (013552) 45439
Web Site: www.plitho.co.uk
Key Personnel
Deputy Chairman: Gary Thomson

TJ International Ltd
Subsidiary of Ulverscroft Large Print Books
Trecerus Industrial Estate, Padstow, Cornwall PL28 8RW
Tel: (01841) 532691 *Fax:* (01841) 532862
Web Site: www.tjinterantional.com
Key Personnel
Chief Executive: Angus Clark *E-mail:* Angus@tjinternational.hd.uk
Founded: 1970
Turnaround: 15 Workdays
Business from Other Countries: 5%

Watkiss Automation Ltd
Subsidiary of The Watkiss Group
One Blaydon Rd, Middlefield Industrial Estate, Sandy, Beds SG19 1RZ
Tel: (01767) 682177 *Fax:* (01767) 691769
E-mail: info@watkiss.com
Web Site: www.watkiss.com
Key Personnel
Technical Dir: M Watkiss
Founded: 1959
Print Runs: 200 min - 10,000 max
Business from Other Countries: 5%

WH Trade Binders Ltd
Units 1-4, South March, Long March Idustrial Estate, Daventry, Northants NN11 4PH
Tel: (01327) 704911 *Fax:* (01327) 872588
E-mail: wh@whtradebinders.demon.co.uk
Key Personnel
Man Dir: Roger Westrop
Financial Manager: Adrian Johnson *E-mail:* adrian@whtradebinders.demon.co.uk
Founded: 1981
Print Runs: 10,000 min
Business from Other Countries: 1%

The Wolsey Press
The Drift, Nacton Rd, Ipswich IP3 9QR
Tel: (01473) 719377 *Fax:* (01473) 272115
E-mail: studio@wolseypress.demon.co.uk
Key Personnel
Dir: John Robinson; Colin Jennings

United States

ADR/BookPrint
2012 Northern, Wichita, KS 67216
Tel: 316-522-5599 *Fax:* 316-522-5445
Web Site: www.adrbookprint.com
Key Personnel
Pres: James E Rishel
VP: Grace M Rishel *E-mail:* grace@adrbookprint.com
Prodn Mgr: Marc Seiwert
Founded: 1978
Print Runs: 250 min - 5,000 max
Business from Other Countries: 10%
Membership(s): PIA

Alpina Color Graphics Inc
Affiliate of Alpina Copy World Inc
27 Cliff St, New York, NY 10038
Tel: 212-285-2700 *Fax:* 212-285-2704
E-mail: raj@alpinanyc.com
Web Site: www.alpina.net
Key Personnel
Contact: Raj Sawhney
CEO: Harish Sawhney *E-mail:* hs@alpina.net
Founded: 1984
Turnaround: 2-3 Workdays
Print Runs: 1,000 min - 200,000 max
Business from Other Countries: 20%

Asia Pacific Offset Inc
1332 Corcoran St NW, Suite 6, Washington, DC 20009
Tel: 202-462-5436 *Fax:* 202-968-4030
Web Site: www.asiapacificoffset.com
Key Personnel
Pres: Andrew Clarke *E-mail:* Andrew@asiapacificoffset.com
Dir, Sales (NY Office): Timothy Linn
 Tel: 212-941-8300 *Fax:* 212-941-9810
 E-mail: Timothy@asiapacificoffset.com
Founded: 1997
Turnaround: 105 Workdays including color separation & shipping
Print Runs: 2,000 min
Business from Other Countries: 100%
Branch Office(s)
Phoenix Offset, Unit F1-2 2nd fl, Yeung Yiu Chung No 8 Industrial Bldg, 20 Wang Hoi Rd, Kowloon Bay, Hong Kong, Edmond Chan *Tel:* 852-2751-9962 *Fax:* 852-2755-8408 *E-mail:* Phoffset@netvigator.com
Sales Office(s): 225 Lafayette St, Suite 703, New York, NY 10012 *Tel:* 212-941-8300 *Fax:* 212-941-9810 *E-mail:* Timothy@asiapacificoffset.com
21 Columbus Ave, Suite 231, San Francisco, CA 94111, Dir, Sales: Rick Conant *Tel:* 415-433-3488 *Fax:* 415-433-3489 *E-mail:* Rick@asiapacificoffset.com

Bind-It Corp
343 W Erie, Suite 310, Chicago, IL 60610
Tel: 312-951-1953 *Fax:* 312-951-9134
E-mail: information@bindit.com
Web Site: www.bindit.com
Key Personnel
Pres: Bill Stross
Founded: 1973
Turnaround: 14 Workdays
Business from Other Countries: 20%

Blaze International Productions Inc
225 W 35 St, Suite 1100, New York, NY 10001
Tel: 212-967-7501 *Fax:* 212-967-7551
Key Personnel
Pres: Eugene Sanchez *Tel:* ext 222 *E-mail:* e.sanchez@blazeint.com
Founded: 1990
Turnaround: 10-15 Workdays
Print Runs: 500 min - 1,000,000 max
Business from Other Countries: 80%
Branch Office(s)
Flat 12 18/F, Kodak House, Phase 2, No 39 Healthy Street, North Point, Hong Kong *Tel:* 2967 9360 *Fax:* 2967 1800

BookBuilders New York Ltd
353 Strawtown Rd, New City, NY 10956
Tel: 845-639-5316 *Fax:* 845-639-5318
Web Site: www.mcabooks.com
Key Personnel
Pres: Martin Cook *E-mail:* martin@mcabooks.com
Founded: 1977
Turnaround: 30-45 Workdays
Print Runs: 2,000 min - 500,000 max
Business from Other Countries: 60%

Butler & Tanner Inc
1776 Broadway, Suite 1710, New York, NY 10019
Tel: 212-262-4753 *Fax:* 212-262-4779
E-mail: sales@nyc.butlerandtanner.com
Web Site: www.butleratanner.com
Key Personnel
Dir, US Sales: Jeremy Snell
Founded: 1850
Turnaround: 10 days
Print Runs: 5,000 min - 100,000 max
Business from Other Countries: 10%
Parent Company: Butler & Tanner Ltd (UK)

C & C Offset Printing Co Ltd
Subsidiary of C & C Joint Printing Co (HK) Ltd under Sino United Publishing (Holdings) Ltd
2632 SE 25 Ave, Suite D, Portland, OR 97202
Mailing Address: PO Box 82037, Portland, OR 97282-0037
Tel: 503-233-1834 *Fax:* 503-233-7815
E-mail: portlandinfo@ccoffset.com
Web Site: www.ccoffset.com
Key Personnel
Dir, C & C Offset Printing Co Ltd, Portland, OR, USA: Charles H Clark, IV *E-mail:* cclark@ccoffset.com
Devt Mgr, C & C Offset Printing Co (USA) Inc, Portland, OR, USA: Jenny Whittier *E-mail:* jwhittier@ccoffset.com
Dir & Exec VP, C & C Offset Printing Co (NYC) Inc, New York, NY, USA: Simon Chan *E-mail:* schan@ccoffset.com
Cust Serv Mgr, C & C Offset Printing Co (NYC) Inc, New York, NY, USA: Frances Harkness *E-mail:* fharkness@ccoffset.com
Cust Serv Mgr, C & C Offset Printing Co (USA) Inc, Portland, OR, USA: Ernest Li *E-mail:* ernestli@ccoffset.com
Dir & Gen Mgr, Hong Kong Head Office: Zhuang Xian-Qing
Dir & Asst Gen Mgr, Hong Kong Head Office: Ken Lee
Sales Mgr (Overseas), Hong Kong Head Office: Kit Wong
Sales Mgr (Special Projects), Hong Kong Head Office: Francis Ho
Dir & Gen Mgr, C & C Joint Printing Co (Guangdong) Ltd, Shenzhen, China: Jackson Leung
Deputy Sales Mgr, C & C Joint Printing Co (Guangdong) Ltd, Shenzhen, China: Simon Zhang
Pres, C & C Printing Japan Co Ltd, Tokyo, Japan: Masashi Otobe
Man Dir, C & C Joint Printing Co (Beijing) Ltd, Beijing, China: Zhang Lin Gui
Dir, C & C Offset Printing Co (UK): Tracy Broderick
Mgr, C & C Offset Printing Co (UK): Fiona Norman
Founded: 1980
Turnaround: varies
Print Runs: 2,000 min - 200,000 max
Business from Other Countries: 60%
Branch Office(s)
C & C Joint Print Co (Beijing) Ltd, Beijing Economic & Technological Developent Area (BDA), No 3, Donghuan North Rd, Beijing 100176, China, Dir & Gen Mgr: Mr Zhang Lin Gui *Tel:* (10) 678 72862 *Fax:* (10) 678-72861 *E-mail:* beijing@candcprinting.com
C & C Joint Printing Co (Guangdong) Ltd, Intercontinental Bldg, Room 706, An Wai An De Rd, DongCheng District, Beijing 100011, China, Contact: Mr Xiao Mungshen *Tel:* (10) 8488 2436 *Fax:* (10) 8488-2336 *E-mail:* beijing@cancprinting.com
C & C Joint Printing Co (Guangdong) Ltd (Changsha Office), The Building of Changsha City Commercial Bank, No 1, Frong Middle Rd, Rm 1218, Changsha, Hunan 41005, China, Contact: Ms Chen Jian *Tel:* (731) 225

UNITED STATES — PRINTING, BINDING

0288 *Fax:* (731) 225 0178 *E-mail:* changsha@candcprinting.com (Regional Office)
Hua Xin Bldg E Block, Rm 1511, 2 Shuiyin Rd, Huanshi East, Guangzhou 510075, China, Contact: Mr Peng Ji Shan *Tel:* (20) 3760 0979; (20) 3760 0980 *Fax:* (20) 3760 0977 *E-mail:* guangzhou@candcprinting.com
Fang Fa Bldg, No 29 Land, 169 Dongzhu Anbin Rd, Shanghai 200050, China, Contact: Ms Wu Ziaohung *Tel:* (21) 6240 1305 *Fax:* (21) 6240 2090 *E-mail:* shanghai@candcprinting.com
C & C Joint Printing Co (Guangdong) Ltd, Chunhu Industrial Estate, Pinghu, Long Gang, Shenzhen 518111, China *Tel:* (755) 845 8333 *Fax:* (755) 845 9111 *E-mail:* guangzhou@candcprinting.com (Plant)
C & C Joint Printing Co (Guangdong) Ltd (Xian Office), 10 Xuanfengquiao, Jianguo Rd, Xian 710001, China *Tel:* (29) 741 8407 *Fax:* (29) 743 5730 *E-mail:* xian@candcprinting.co
C & C Offset Printing Co (UK) Ltd, 2 New Burlington St, 4th fl, London W1S 2JE, United Kingdom *Tel:* 0207-287-7787 *Fax:* 0207-287-7187 *E-mail:* tracy@candcoffset.co.uk
C & C Printing Japan Co Ltd, Tozaido Bldg, 3F, 2-6-12 Hitotsubashi, Chiyoda-ku, Tokyo 101-0003, Japan, Contact: Mr Masashi Otobe *Tel:* (3) 5216 4580 *Fax:* (3) 5216 4610 *E-mail:* mail@candcprinting.co.jp
Bookshop(s): C & C Offset Printing Co (UK) Ltd, 2 New Burlington St, 4th fl, London W1S 2JE, United Kingdom *Tel:* (207) 287 7787 *Fax:* (207) 287 7187 *E-mail:* tracy@candcoffset.co.uk

Carvajal International Inc
Division of Carvajal Inversiones
Subsidiary of Carvajal S A
901 Ponce de Leon Blvd, 9th fl, Suite 901, Coral Gables, FL 33134
Tel: 305-448-6875 *Fax:* 305-448-9942
E-mail: carinter@kanect.net
Web Site: www.dynamicgraphic.com
Key Personnel
Dir, Book Div: Guillermo Holguin
Founded: 1904
Print Runs: 3,000 min - 250,000 max
Business from Other Countries: 30%
Branch Office(s)
Carvajal S A, Calle 29 N 1, 6A-40 Cali, Colombia, Alvaro Lopez *Tel:* 572-661-8150

Colorprint Offset Inc
Division of Colorprint Offset (Hong Kong)
80 Park Ave, Suite 10N, New York, NY 10016
Tel: 212-681-9400 *Fax:* 212-681-9362
Key Personnel
Pres: Lee Moncho *E-mail:* lee@colorprintoffset.com
Prod Dir & Cust Serv Mgr: Kate Brady *E-mail:* kate@colorprintoffset.com
Founded: 1986
Turnaround: 15 Workdays
Print Runs: 100 min - 50,000 max
Business from Other Countries: 65%

Coneco Litho Graphics
Division of NET 2 PRESS Inc
58 Dix Ave, Glens Falls, NY 12801-7255
Mailing Address: PO Box 3255, Glen Falls, NY 12801-7255
Tel: 518-793-3823 *Fax:* 518-793-5823
Web Site: www.conecolithographics.com
Key Personnel
Pres & CEO: Garth E Grandchamp *E-mail:* garth@conecolithographics.com
Gen Mgr: Steve Webber *E-mail:* swebber@conecolithographics.com
Client Servs Mgr: Cindy Brower *E-mail:* cbrower@conecolithographics.com
Founded: 1984
Turnaround: 15 Workdays

Print Runs: 250 min - 25,000 max
Business from Other Countries: 27%

Consolidated Printers Inc
2630 Eighth St, Berkeley, CA 94710
Tel: 510-843-8524 *Fax:* 510-486-0580
E-mail: cpi@consoprinters.com
Web Site: www.consoprinters.com
Key Personnel
CEO: Lawrence A Hawkins
Founded: 1952
Turnaround: 2-20 Workdays
Print Runs: 2,000 min - 500,000 max
Business from Other Countries: 15%

Martin Cook Associates Ltd
353 Strawtown Rd, New City, NY 10956
Tel: 845-639-5316 *Fax:* 845-639-5318
E-mail: mcanewcity@aol.com
Web Site: www.mcabooks.com
Key Personnel
Pres: Martin Cook *E-mail:* mcanewcity@aol.com
Founded: 1977
Turnaround: 30-45 Workdays
Print Runs: 2,000 min - 500,000 max
Business from Other Countries: 15%
Membership(s): Bookbinders Guild of New York

CS Graphics USA Inc
Subsidiary of CS Graphics Pte Ltd Singapore
8969 Lake Ct, Granite Bay, CA 95746
Tel: 916-791-9066 *Fax:* 916-791-9112
E-mail: csgraphics@mindspring.com
Key Personnel
Mgr, Sales & Mktg: Rick Marment
Founded: 1980
Turnaround: 80 Workdays
Print Runs: 1,000 min - 75,000 max
Business from Other Countries: 30%

D & K Group
1795 Commerce, Elk Grove Village, IL 60007
Tel: 847-956-0160 *Fax:* 847-956-8214
E-mail: info@dkgroup.net
Web Site: www.dkgroup.com
Key Personnel
Pres: Karl Singer
VP, Sales & Mktg: Marge Hayes
Mktg Communs Coord: Holli Hagene *E-mail:* holli.hagene@dkgroup.net
Founded: 1979
Business from Other Countries: 15%

DNP America LLC
Subsidiary of Dai Nippon Printing Co Ltd
335 Madison Ave, 3rd fl, New York, NY 10017
Tel: 212-503-1074; 212-503-1060 *Fax:* 212-286-1505
Web Site: www.dnp.co.jp/ *Cable:* DAIPRINTS NY
Key Personnel
Pres: Yoji Yamakawa
VP & Gen Mgr, Graphic Printing: Kohei Tsumori *E-mail:* tsumori-k@mail.dnp.co.jp
Founded: 1974
Turnaround: 30-60 Workdays
Print Runs: 1,000,000 max
Business from Other Countries: 54%
Branch Office(s)
577 Airport Blvd, Suite 620, Burlingame, CA 94010, Kosuke Tago *Tel:* 650-340-6061 *Fax:* 650-340-6090

Editoriale Bortolazzi-Stei srl
39 Kane Ave, Larchmont, NY 10538
Tel: 914-834-9594 *Fax:* 914-833-9106
Key Personnel
US Rep: Umberto Paolucci *E-mail:* pbert30@aol.com
Founded: 1952
Print Runs: 2,000 min - 90,000 max

Business from Other Countries: 20%
Branch Office(s)
Via Monte Comun, 40, San Giovanni Lupatoto, Verona 37057, Italy

Elegance Printing & Book Binding (USA)
Member of The Elegance Printing Group
708 Glen Cove Ave, Glen Head, NY 11545
Tel: 516-676-5941 *Fax:* 516-676-5973
Web Site: www.elegancebooks.com
Key Personnel
Man Dir: Frank DeLuca *E-mail:* frank@elegancebooks.com
Founded: 1977
Turnaround: 3-4 weeks for CTP projects. Reprints ship within 14 days
Print Runs: 1,000 min - 200,000 max
Business from Other Countries: 40%

EP Graphics
169 S Jefferson St, Berne, IN 46711
Tel: 260-589-2145 *Fax:* 260-589-2810
Web Site: www.epgraphics.com
Key Personnel
Pres: Thomas Muselman
Founded: 1925
Turnaround: 15 Workdays
Print Runs: 25,000 min - 500,000 max
Business from Other Countries: 80%

Express Media Corp
1419 Donelson Pike, Nashville, TN 37217
Tel: 615-360-6400 *Fax:* 615-360-3140
E-mail: info@expressmedia.com
Web Site: www.expressmedia.com
Key Personnel
Pres: Andrew Cameron
Founded: 1996
Turnaround: 3 Workdays
Print Runs: 1 min - 10,000 max
Business from Other Countries: 10%

Fairfield Marketing Group Inc
Subsidiary of FMG Inc
830 Sport Hill Rd, Easton, CT 06612-1250
Tel: 203-261-5585; 203-261-5568 *Fax:* 203-261-0884
E-mail: ffldmktgrp@aol.com
Key Personnel
CEO & Pres: Edward P Washchilla
VP, Fin: Pamela L Johnson
VP, Fulfillment: Jason Paul Miller *Tel:* 203-261-5585 ext 203
Founded: 1987
Turnaround: 1-7 Workdays
Print Runs: 2,500 min - 10,000,000 max
Business from Other Countries: 10%
Membership(s): ABA; BBB; DMA

GAMA
Box 170, Salem, NH 03079
Tel: 603-898-2822 *Fax:* 603-898-3393
Key Personnel
Publr: Frank Romano *E-mail:* fxrppr@rit.edu
Founded: 1971
Turnaround: 80 Workdays
Print Runs: 1,000 min - 15,000 max
Business from Other Countries: 17%

Hamilton Printing Co
22 Hamilton Way, Castleton-on-Hudson, NY 12033
Tel: 518-732-4491 *Fax:* 518-732-7714
Key Personnel
Pres: Brian F Payne
VP, Mfg: William E Greenawalt
VP, Fin: Michael H Hart
Prod Mgr: Fred Mitchell
Sales Rep: Scott Payne; Michael C Rosenhack *E-mail:* miker@hpcbook.com; Stephen H Feuer
Founded: 1912
Turnaround: Flexible, time-sensitive scheduling

Business from Other Countries: 10%
Membership(s): BMI

Hindy's Enterprise
Division of Jinno International
3 Christine Dr, Chestnut Ridge, NY 10977-6802
Tel: 845-735-4666 *Fax:* 617-344-5905
Key Personnel
Pres: Yoh Jinno *E-mail:* jinno@hotmail.com
Founded: 1989
Turnaround: 40 Workdays
Print Runs: 500 min - 2,000,000 max
Business from Other Countries: 70%
Branch Office(s)
Melbourne Industrial Bldg, Block A, 20th fl, 16 Westlands Rd, Quarry Bay, Hong Kong *Tel:* 25166318 *Fax:* 25165161

IBT Global Ltd, see Integrated Book Technology Inc

Ikon Document Services
Division of Ikon Office Solutions
399 River Rd, Hudson, MA 01749-2627
Tel: 978-562-9131 *Fax:* 978-562-4304
Web Site: www.tecdoc.com
Key Personnel
VP: David Trombino *E-mail:* dtrombino@ikon.com
Founded: 1973
Turnaround: 3 Workdays
Print Runs: 5 min - 5,000 max
Business from Other Countries: 10%

Imago
1431 Broadway, Penthouse, New York, NY 10018
Tel: 847-358-3047 *Fax:* 212-921-8226
E-mail: imagousa@imagousa.com
Web Site: www.imagousa.com
Key Personnel
Pres: Joseph E Braff *E-mail:* jbraff@imagousa.com
Sr Sales Exec: Linda Readerman *E-mail:* lreaderman@imagousa.com
Prodn Dir, USA: Howard R Musk *E-mail:* hmusk@imagousa.com
Off Mgr: Susan Hirsh *E-mail:* shirsh@imagousa.com
Dir, West Coast Opers: Greg Lee *Tel:* 949-661-5998 *Fax:* 949-661-8013 *E-mail:* glee@imagousa.com
Prodn Supv, West Coast: Yuhong Guo *Tel:* 949-661-5998 *Fax:* 949-661-8013 *E-mail:* yguo@imagousa.com
Dir, Midwest Opers: Bryan O'Shaughnessy *Tel:* 847-358-3047 *Fax:* 847-358-3078 *E-mail:* bo'shaughnessy@imagousa.com
Founded: 1985
Turnaround: 21 Workdays for color separations; 6 Weeks for printing & binding
Print Runs: 5,000 min
Business from Other Countries: 100%
Branch Office(s)
Imago West Coast, 31952 Camino Capistrano, Suite C-22, San Juan Capistrano, CA 92675, Dir, West Coast Opers: Greg Lee *Tel:* 949-661-5998 *Fax:* 949-661-8013 *E-mail:* glee@imagousa.com *Web Site:* www.imagousa.com
Imago Midwest, 800 E Northwest Hwy, Suite 622, Palatine, IL 60067, Dir, Midwest Opers: Bryan O'Shaughnessy *Tel:* 847-705-3821 (ext 3854) *Fax:* 847-963-2341 *E-mail:* bryano@imagousa.com
Imago (UK/Europe) Publishing Ltd, Albury Court, Albury Thame, Oxfordshire OX9 2LP, United Kingdom, Man Dir: Richard Hayes *Tel:* 337000 *Fax:* 339935 *Web Site:* www.imago.co.uk
Imago Services (HKG) Ltd, 653-659 Kings Rd, 6th fl, Flat B, North Point, Hong Kong, Man Dir: Kendrick Cheung *Tel:* 2811 3316 *Fax:* 2597 5256

Imago Productions (FE) Pte Ltd, MacPherson Industrial Complex, Suite 05-01, 5 Lorong Bakar Batu, Singapore 1334, Singapore, Man Dir: K C Ng *Tel:* 748 4433 *Fax:* 748 6082

Integrated Book Technology Inc
Division of The IBT Group
18 Industrial Park Rd, Troy, NY 12180
Tel: 518-271-5117 *Fax:* 518-266-9422
E-mail: mail@integratedbooktechnology.com
Web Site: www.integratedbooktechnology.com
Key Personnel
CEO & Pres: John R Paeglow *E-mail:* johnp@integratedbook.com
VP & Chief Technol Officer: William Clockel *E-mail:* billc@integratedbook.com
VP, Fin: Richard Donovan *E-mail:* rickd@integratedbook.com
VP, Sales & Mktg: Robert Lindberg *E-mail:* bobl@integratedbook.com
Dir, Info Technol: Michael Whalen *E-mail:* mikew@integratedbook.com
Regl Sales: Tim Knickerbocker *E-mail:* timk@integratedbook.com
Cust Serv Mgr: James Klein *E-mail:* jimk@integratedbook.com
Contact: Beth Boniface
Founded: 1991
Turnaround: 1-15 Workdays
Print Runs: 10 min - 2,000 max
Business from Other Countries: 20%
Membership(s): BMI

Jinno International Group
3 Christine Dr, Chestnut Ridge, NY 10977
Tel: 845-735-4666 *Fax:* 617-344-5905
E-mail: jinno@hotmail.com
Key Personnel
Pres: Yoh Jinno
VP: Sharon Jinno
Founded: 1989
Turnaround: 21-30 Workdays US, 45-75 Workdays overseas
Print Runs: 500 min - 3,000,000 max
Business from Other Countries: 98%
Branch Office(s)
Hindy's Enterprise, Melbourne Industrial Bldg, 16 Westlands Rd, Block A, 20th fl, Quarry Bay, Hong Kong *Tel:* 516-6318 *Fax:* 516-5161
Wing Yiu Printing Co, Melbourne Industrial Bldg, 6th fl, Block A, 16 Westlands Rd, Quarry Bay, Hong Kong, Contact: Law Ming Wah *Tel:* 561 0283 *Fax:* 565 8233
c/o Eurasia Press Pte Ltd, 10/14 Kampong Ampat, Singapore 1336, Singapore, Contact: Allan Fong *Tel:* 280 5522 *Fax:* 280 0593
Jinno International Singapore, 710 Ang Mo Kio, Ave 8, Suite 07-2615, Singapore 2056, Singapore *Tel:* 458 0778

KNI Inc
1261 S State College Pkwy, Anaheim, CA 92806
Tel: 714-956-7300 *Fax:* 714-635-1744
E-mail: epp@kniinc.com
Web Site: www.kniinc.com
Key Personnel
Pres: Jeremy R Bernstein
VP, Admin: Judith Bernstein
VP & Sales Mgr: Peggy Bryant
VP & Controller: Dan Jacintho
Founded: 1970
Print Runs: 50 min - 100,000 max
Business from Other Countries: 17%

Lenz & Riecker Inc
690 Union Blvd, Totowa, NJ 07512
Tel: 973-256-2456 *Fax:* 973-256-3433; 973-256-2459
E-mail: info@l-r.com
Web Site: www.l-r.com
Key Personnel
Pres: Steven Riecker

CFO: Barry Levinson
VP, Sales: G Gilrain
Founded: 1917
Turnaround: 2-20 Workdays
Print Runs: 100 min - 100,000 max
Business from Other Countries: 20%
Membership(s): Association of Graphic Communications; GATF

Leo Paper USA
1180 NW Maple St, Suite 102, Issaquah, WA 98027
Tel: 425-646-8801 *Fax:* 425-646-8805
E-mail: leo@leousa.com
Web Site: www.leousa.com
Key Personnel
VP: Peter R Gillies *E-mail:* peter@leousa.com
Sales: Tom Leach *E-mail:* tom@leousa.com; Greg Witt *E-mail:* greg@leousa.com
Founded: 1983
Turnaround: 90 Workdays
Print Runs: 3,500 min - 2,000,000 max
Business from Other Countries: 20%
Branch Office(s)
Leo Paper Products Ltd, 7/F Kader Bldg, 22 Kai Cheung Rd, Kowloon Bay, Hong Kong, Man Dir: Johnny Fung *Tel:* 2884-1374 *Fax:* 2885-3520 *E-mail:* lpp@leo.com.hk *Web Site:* www.leo.com.hk
Leo Paper USA, 27 W 24 St, Suite 701, New York, NY 10010, Janine Laborne *Tel:* 917-305-0708 *Fax:* 917-305-3709 *E-mail:* leo@leousa.com
Sales Office(s): Leo Paper Products (Europe) BVBA, De Wilde Zee Wiegstraat 19, 2000 Antwerp, Belgium, Contact: Jan Van Gijsel *Tel:* (03) 203-0912 *Fax:* (03) 225-1303 *E-mail:* leo@leo-europe.com
Leo Marketing, The Malthouse, Malthouse Sq, Princes Risborough, Bucks HP27 9AB, United Kingdom, Contact: Sally Wood *Tel:* (1844) 274-244 *Fax:* (1844) 275-105 *E-mail:* sallywood.leo@btinternet.com

Linick International Inc
Division of The Linick Group Inc
Linick Bldg, 7 Putter Lane, Middle Island, NY 11953-0102
Tel: 631-924-3888 *Fax:* 631-924-3890
E-mail: linickgrp@att.net
Web Site: www.lgroup.addr.com; www.linickgroup.com
Key Personnel
Chmn & CEO: Dr Andrew S Linick
Treas: Marvin Glickman
Exec VP: Roger Dextor
Founded: 1972
Turnaround: 21-30 Workdays
Print Runs: 3,000 min - 50,000 max
Business from Other Countries: 30%

LK Litho
Division of The Linick Group Inc
Linick Bldg, 7 Putter Lane, Middle Island, NY 11953-0102
Tel: 631-924-3888
E-mail: linickgrp@att.net
Web Site: www.lgroup.addr.com/lklitho.htm
Key Personnel
VP: Roger Dextor
Founded: 1968
Turnaround: 10 Workdays
Print Runs: 2,500 min - 2,000,000 max
Business from Other Countries: 20%

Marrakech Express Inc
720 Wesley Ave, No 10, Tarpon Springs, FL 34689
Tel: 727-942-2218 *Fax:* 727-937-4758
E-mail: print@marrak.com
Web Site: www.marrak.com
Key Personnel
CEO: Peter Henzell

UNITED STATES

Prodn Mgr: Steen Sigmund
Sales/Estimator: Shirley Copperman
Founded: 1976
Turnaround: 7-10 Workdays
Print Runs: 500 min - 25,000 max
Business from Other Countries: 10%

Mazer Publishing Services
Division of The Mazer Corporation
6680 Poe Ave, Dayton, OH 45414
Tel: 937-264-2600 *Fax:* 937-264-2624
E-mail: info@mazer.com
Web Site: www.mazer.com
Key Personnel
Pres: William Franklin *E-mail:* bill_franklin@mazer.com
Exec VP: Ken Fultz *E-mail:* ken_fultz@mazer.com
Exec Dir, Sales: Bill Faber *Fax:* 937-264-2622 *E-mail:* bill_faber@mazer.com
Founded: 1964
Print Runs: 50 min - 25,000 max
Business from Other Countries: 10%
Branch Office(s)
2460 Sand Lake Rd, Orlando, FL 32809, Bryan Blakley *Tel:* 407-859-5552 *Fax:* 407-859-0643 *E-mail:* bryan_blakley@mazer.com
224 Lexington Ave, Fox River Grove, IL 60021, Dennis Bowman *Tel:* 847-639-1555 *Fax:* 847-639-1562 *E-mail:* dennis_bowman@mazer.com
22 Lehigh Rd, Wellesley, MA 02181, Ken Leahy *Tel:* 781-237-4112 *Fax:* 781-431-6184 *E-mail:* ken_leahy@mazer.com
22 Laurel Place, Upper Montclair, NJ 07043, John Martel *Tel:* 973-744-4320 *Fax:* 973-746-5608 *E-mail:* john_martel@mazer.com
3081 Glenmere Ct, Kettering, OH 45440, Mark Brewer *Tel:* 937-299-5746 *Fax:* 937-299-5761 *E-mail:* mark_brewer@mazer.com
363 Porter Rd, Bishop, TX 78602, Deborah VanLandingham *Tel:* 512-303-9758 *Fax:* 512-303-9791
Membership(s): BMI

Milanostampa/New Interlitho USA Inc
Subsidiary of Milanostampa New Interlitho Italia SpA
299 Broadway, Suite 901, New York, NY 10007
Tel: 212-964-2430 *Fax:* 212-964-2497
Web Site: www.milanostampa.com
Key Personnel
Chmn: Riccardo Sardo
Sales Rep: Rino Varrasso *E-mail:* rvarrasso@milanostampa-usa.com
Founded: 1974
Turnaround: 30 Workdays
Print Runs: 1,000 min - 3,000,000 max
Business from Other Countries: 75%

Naturegraph Publishers Inc
3543 Indian Creek Rd, Happy Camp, CA 96039
Mailing Address: PO Box 1047, Happy Camp, CA 96039
Tel: 530-493-5353 *Fax:* 530-493-5240
E-mail: nature@sisqtel.net
Web Site: www.naturegraph.com
Key Personnel
Owner & Mgr: Barbara Brown
Founded: 1946
Turnaround: 20-30 Workdays
Print Runs: 1,000 min - 10,000 max
Business from Other Countries: 10%

Palace Press International
1585-A Folsom St, San Francisco, CA 94103
Tel: 415-626-1080 *Fax:* 415-626-1510
E-mail: ppisfo@palacepress.com
Web Site: www.palacepress.com
Key Personnel
Pres: Raoul A Goff *E-mail:* raoul@palacepress.com
Dir: Gordon Goff *Tel:* 415-455-2480 ext 211 *Fax:* 415-455-2490 *E-mail:* gordon@palacepress.com
Sales Mgr: Roger Ma *Tel:* 626-282-8877 *Fax:* 626-282-6880 *E-mail:* roger@palacepress.com; Steven Goff *Tel:* 415-455-2480 *E-mail:* steven@palacepress.com
Proj Mgr: Maria Ramos *Tel:* 415-626-1080 ext 208 *E-mail:* maria@palacepress.ca
Founded: 1984
Turnaround: 90 Workdays
Print Runs: 3,000 min - 1,000,000 max
Business from Other Countries: 20%
Branch Office(s)
Palace Press International Los Angeles, 303 W Newby Ave, Suite C, San Gabriel, CT 91776, Contact: Roger Ma *Tel:* 626-282-8877 *Fax:* 626-282-6880 *E-mail:* roger@palacepress.com
Palace Press International New York, 180 Varick St, 10th fl, New York, NY 10014, Contact: Roger Ma *Tel:* 212-462-2622 *Fax:* 212-463-9130 *E-mail:* roger@palacepress.com
Palace Press San Rafael, 1299 Fourth St, Suite 305, San Rafael, CA 94901, Contact: Gordon Goff *Tel:* 415-455-2480 *Fax:* 415-455-2490 *E-mail:* gordon@palacepress.com *Web Site:* www.palacepress.com
Palace Press International Hong Kong, Wah Ha Factory Bldg, 10th fl, Block A, B, C & D, 8 Shipyard Lane, Quarry Bay, Hong Kong, Contact: Lesley Sun *Tel:* 2357-9019 *Fax:* 2561-3616 *E-mail:* lesley@palacepress.com *Web Site:* www.palacepress.com

Printing Corp of the Americas Inc
620 SW 12 Ave, Pompano Beach, FL 33069
Tel: 954-781-8100 *Fax:* 954-781-8421
E-mail: pcaprint@bellsouth.net
Web Site: www.pcaprint.bellsouth.net
Key Personnel
Pres: Jan Tuchman
Founded: 1979
Turnaround: 5-10 Workdays
Print Runs: 500 min - 100,000 max
Business from Other Countries: 15%

Regent Publishing Services
9327 Rambler Dr, St Louis, MO 63123
Tel: 314-631-7581 *Fax:* 314-638-5113
E-mail: regentstl@aol.com
Key Personnel
Sales Dir: Carol A Davis-Tierney
Mktg Dir: James J Tierney
Sales Assoc: Julia Polsen
Founded: 1985
Turnaround: 3-4 Months
Print Runs: 2,000 min - 100,000 max
Business from Other Countries: 100%

Spraymation Inc
5320 NW 35 Ave, Fort Lauderdale, FL 33309-6314
Tel: 954-484-9700 *Fax:* 954-484-9778
E-mail: sales@spraymation.com
Web Site: www.spraymation.com
Key Personnel
Natl Sales Mgr: Anthony J Diaz
Founded: 1958
Business from Other Countries: 20%

Taylor Publishing Co
1550 W Mockingbird Lane, Dallas, TX 75235
Tel: 214-819-8100 *Fax:* 214-630-1852
Web Site: www.taylorpub.com
Key Personnel
Pres: Dave Fiore
Cust Serv Rep: Jay Love
Dir, Mktg: Mike Taylor
Founded: 1939
Turnaround: 45 Workdays
Print Runs: 300 min - 25,000 max
Business from Other Countries: 10%

Times Publishing Group
Division of Times Publishing Ltd/Singapore
99 White Plains Rd, Tarrytown, NY 10591
Tel: 914-366-9888 *Fax:* 914-366-9898
Web Site: www.tpl.com.sg
Key Personnel
Cust Serv Exec: Bonnie Stone *E-mail:* bstone@marshallcavendish.com
Sales Mgr: Suresh Kumar *E-mail:* skumar@marshallcavendish.com
Founded: 1965
Print Runs: 2,000 min - 500,000 max
Business from Other Countries: 90%

Tobias Associates Inc
50 Industrial Dr, Ivyland, PA 18974-0347
Tel: 215-322-1500 *Fax:* 215-322-1504
E-mail: tobias@densitometer.com
Web Site: www.densitometer.com
Key Personnel
Adv Mgr: Robin Crowley
Founded: 1960
Business from Other Countries: 10%

Vicks Lithograph & Printing Corp
5166 Commercial Dr, Yorkville, NY 13495
Tel: 315-736-9344 *Fax:* 315-736-1901
Key Personnel
Chmn: Dwight E "Duke" Vicks, Jr
Pres: Dwight E Vicks, III
Plant Mgr: Frank Driscoll
Sales Mgr: Pat Cotter
Founded: 1918
Turnaround: 10-20 Workdays
Print Runs: 1,000 min - 100,000 max
Business from Other Countries: 10%
Membership(s): BMI; PIA

Fred Weidner & Daughter Printers
15 Maiden Lane, Suite 1505, New York, NY 10038
Tel: 212-964-8676 *Fax:* 212-964-8677
E-mail: info@fwdprinters.com
Web Site: www.fwdprinters.com
Key Personnel
Contact: Frederick Weidner, III
Pres: Cynthia Weidner *E-mail:* cynthia@fwdprinters.com
Founded: 1860
Turnaround: 5-10 Workdays
Print Runs: 1,000 min - 100,000 max
Business from Other Countries: 25%

Uruguay

Barreiro y Ramos SA
Juan Carlos Gomez, 1430, Montevideo 11000
Tel: (02) 986621 *Fax:* (02) 962358
Telex: 23901PB.CVJA.UY *Cable:* BAREIRAMOS
Key Personnel
President: Gaston Barreiro
Vice President: Guzman Barreiro
Founded: 1837
Print Runs: 1,000 min - 50,000 max
Business from Other Countries: 10%

Manufacturing Materials Index

BINDING SUPPLIES

Hong Kong
Golden Cup Printing Co Ltd, pg 1212

Singapore
CS Graphics Pte Ltd, pg 1213

Spain
Guarro Casas SA, pg 1214

United Kingdom
Harveys Ltd, pg 1214
Redwood Books Ltd, pg 1214

United States
Blaze International Productions Inc, pg 1215
Conservation Resources International Inc, pg 1215
Fibre Leather Manufacturing Corp, pg 1215
ICG/Holliston, pg 1216

BOOK COVERS

Belgium
Imprimerie Bietlot Freres SA, pg 1211

Canada
Appleby's Bindery Ltd, pg 1211
McLaren Morris & Todd Ltd, pg 1211
Printcrafters Inc, pg 1211
PrintWest, pg 1211
Transcontinental Printing Book Group, pg 1211
University of Toronto Press Inc, pg 1211

China
Speedflex Asia Ltd, pg 1211

Denmark
Bianco Lunos Bogtrykkeri AS, pg 1211

Finland
WS Bookwell Ltd, pg 1211

Germany
C L Baader Buch & Offsetdruckere GmbH & Co KG, pg 1211
Mohndruck Graphische Betriebe GmbH, pg 1211
Priese GmbH, pg 1212

Hong Kong
Dai Nippon Printing Co (Hong Kong) Ltd, pg 1212
Everbest Printing Co Ltd, pg 1212
Golden Cup Printing Co Ltd, pg 1212
The Green Pagoda Press Ltd, pg 1212
Image Printing Company Ltd, pg 1212
Mei Ka Printing & Publish Enterprise Ltd, pg 1212
Prontaprint Asia Ltd, pg 1212
Sino Publishing House Ltd, pg 1212
Wing King Tong Co Ltd (Printing Factory), pg 1212
Ying Tat Co, pg 1212

Indonesia
Ichtiar Baru 1 Van Hoeve, pg 1212
Victory Offset Prima PT, pg 1212

Ireland
SciPrint Ltd, pg 1212
Smurfit Print, pg 1213

Israel
Keterpress Enterprises Jerusalem, pg 1213

Italy
Dedalo Litostampa SRL, pg 1213
Milanostampa SPA, pg 1213

Republic of Korea
Daehan Printing & Publishing Co Ltd, pg 1213

Netherlands
BN International, pg 1213

New Zealand
Bookprint Consultants Ltd, pg 1213
John McIndoe Ltd, pg 1213

Singapore
Eurasia Press Pte Ltd, pg 1213
Ho Printing Singapore Pte Ltd, pg 1213
International Press Co Pte Ltd, pg 1213
Markono Print Media Pte Ltd, pg 1213
SNP Printing Pte Ltd, pg 1213
Times Printers Pte Ltd, pg 1213
Toppan Company (S) Pte Ltd, pg 1213

Slovenia
Gorenjski Tisk Printing Co, pg 1213

Spain
Guarro Casas SA, pg 1214

United Kingdom
Bell & Bain Ltd, pg 1214
Biddles Ltd, pg 1214
Book Creation Services, pg 1214
Caledonian International Book Manufacturing, pg 1214
Clays Ltd, pg 1214
William Clowes Ltd, pg 1214
Cox & Wyman Ltd, pg 1214
Furnival Press, pg 1214
Goldshield Communications Ltd, pg 1214
The Guernsey Press Co Ltd, pg 1214
Hammond Bindery Ltd, pg 1214
Harveys Ltd, pg 1214
Hobbs The Printers Ltd, pg 1214
Hunter & Foulis Ltd, pg 1214
Image & Print Group Ltd, pg 1214
Intype London Ltd, pg 1214
The Malvern Press Ltd, pg 1214
Page Bros Ltd (Norwich), pg 1214
Printafoil Ltd, pg 1214
Red Bridge International, pg 1214
Redwood Books Ltd, pg 1214
J R Reid Printing Group Ltd, pg 1215
Antony Rowe Ltd, pg 1215
Severnside Printers Ltd, pg 1215
Stott Brothers Ltd, pg 1215
M & A Thomson Litho Ltd, pg 1215
Watkiss Automation Ltd, pg 1215
Winter & Co UK Ltd, pg 1215
The Wolsey Press, pg 1215

United States
Bang Printing Co Inc, pg 1215
Blaze International Productions Inc, pg 1215
BookBuilders New York Ltd, pg 1215
Martin Cook Associates Ltd, pg 1215
CS Graphics USA Inc, pg 1215
D & K Group, pg 1215
Desktop Miracles Inc, pg 1215
DNP America LLC, pg 1215
Elegance Printing & Book Binding (USA), pg 1215
Fibre Leather Manufacturing Corp, pg 1215
ICG/Holliston, pg 1216
Imago, pg 1216
Integrated Book Technology Inc, pg 1216
Jinno International Group, pg 1216
Lenz & Riecker Inc, pg 1216
Linick International Inc, pg 1216
LK Litho, pg 1216
Mazer Publishing Services, pg 1216
Milanostampa/New Interlitho USA Inc, pg 1216
Printing Corp of the Americas Inc, pg 1216
Regent Publishing Services, pg 1216
Taylor Publishing Co, pg 1217
Times Publishing Group, pg 1217

Uruguay
Barreiro y Ramos SA, pg 1217

BOOK JACKETS

Belgium
Imprimerie Bietlot Freres SA, pg 1211

Canada
Appleby's Bindery Ltd, pg 1211
McLaren Morris & Todd Ltd, pg 1211
Printcrafters Inc, pg 1211
Transcontinental Printing Book Group, pg 1211
University of Toronto Press Inc, pg 1211

China
Speedflex Asia Ltd, pg 1211

Denmark
Bianco Lunos Bogtrykkeri AS, pg 1211

Finland
WS Bookwell Ltd, pg 1211

Germany
C L Baader Buch & Offsetdruckere GmbH & Co KG, pg 1211
Mohndruck Graphische Betriebe GmbH, pg 1211
Priese GmbH, pg 1212

Hong Kong
Caritas Printing Training Centre, pg 1212
Dai Nippon Printing Co (Hong Kong) Ltd, pg 1212
Everbest Printing Co Ltd, pg 1212
Golden Cup Printing Co Ltd, pg 1212
The Green Pagoda Press Ltd, pg 1212
Image Printing Company Ltd, pg 1212
Mei Ka Printing & Publish Enterprise Ltd, pg 1212
Prontaprint Asia Ltd, pg 1212
Sino Publishing House Ltd, pg 1212
Wing King Tong Co Ltd (Printing Factory), pg 1212
Ying Tat Co, pg 1212

Hungary
Interpress Aussenhandels GmbH, pg 1212

Indonesia
Ichtiar Baru 1 Van Hoeve, pg 1212

Ireland
SciPrint Ltd, pg 1212
Smurfit Print, pg 1213

Israel
Keterpress Enterprises Jerusalem, pg 1213

Italy
Dedalo Litostampa SRL, pg 1213
Milanostampa SPA, pg 1213

Republic of Korea
Daehan Printing & Publishing Co Ltd, pg 1213

New Zealand
Bookprint Consultants Ltd, pg 1213
John McIndoe Ltd, pg 1213

Singapore
Eurasia Press Pte Ltd, pg 1213
Ho Printing Singapore Pte Ltd, pg 1213
International Press Co Pte Ltd, pg 1213

MANUFACTURING MATERIALS INDEX

Markono Print Media Pte Ltd, pg 1213
SNP Printing Pte Ltd, pg 1213
Toppan Company (S) Pte Ltd, pg 1213

Slovenia
Gorenjski Tisk Printing Co, pg 1213

Spain
Guarro Casas SA, pg 1214

United Kingdom
Bell & Bain Ltd, pg 1214
Biddles Ltd, pg 1214
Book Creation Services, pg 1214
Caledonian International Book Manufacturing, pg 1214
Clays Ltd, pg 1214
William Clowes Ltd, pg 1214
Furnival Press, pg 1214
Goldshield Communications Ltd, pg 1214
The Guernsey Press Co Ltd, pg 1214
Harveys Ltd, pg 1214
Hunter & Foulis Ltd, pg 1214
Image & Print Group Ltd, pg 1214
Intype London Ltd, pg 1214
The Malvern Press Ltd, pg 1214
Page Bros Ltd (Norwich), pg 1214
Printafoil Ltd, pg 1214
Redwood Books Ltd, pg 1214
J R Reid Printing Group Ltd, pg 1215
Antony Rowe Ltd, pg 1215
Severnside Printers Ltd, pg 1215
Watkiss Automation Ltd, pg 1215
The Wolsey Press, pg 1215

United States
Bang Printing Co Inc, pg 1215
Blaze International Productions Inc, pg 1215
BookBuilders New York Ltd, pg 1215
Coneco Litho Graphics, pg 1215
Martin Cook Associates Ltd, pg 1215
CS Graphics USA Inc, pg 1215
D & K Group, pg 1215
Desktop Miracles Inc, pg 1215
DNP America LLC, pg 1215
Elegance Printing & Book Binding (USA), pg 1215
Hindy's Enterprise, pg 1216
Imago, pg 1216
Jinno International Group, pg 1216
Linick International Inc, pg 1216
LK Litho, pg 1216
Milanostampa/New Interlitho USA Inc, pg 1216
Printing Corp of the Americas Inc, pg 1216
Regent Publishing Services, pg 1216
Times Publishing Group, pg 1217

Uruguay
Barreiro y Ramos SA, pg 1217

PAPER MERCHANTS

United Kingdom
Harveys Ltd, pg 1214

United States
International Holographic Paper, pg 1216

PAPER MILLS

Spain
Guarro Casas SA, pg 1214

Manufacturing Materials

This section includes companies throughout the world involved in the production of book manufacturing materials such as paper and book cover material. Those U.S. and Canadian companies with 10% or more of their business done outside North America are also included here. Immediately preceding this section is an index classifying companies by materials manufactured.

Belgium

Imprimerie Bietlot Freres SA
rue de Rond-Point 185, B-6060 Gilly
Tel: (071) 283611 *Fax:* (071) 283620
Key Personnel
Man Dir: A Franquin
Founded: 1988
Business from Other Countries: 35%

Canada

Appleby's Bindery Ltd
1303 Route 102, Upper Gagetown, NB E5M 1R5
Tel: 506-488-2086 *Fax:* 506-488-2086
E-mail: applbind@nbnet.nb.ca
Key Personnel
Pres & Owner: David E Appleby
Mgr: John Appleby
Founded: 1976
Business from Other Countries: 10%

McLaren Morris & Todd Ltd
3270 American Dr, Mississauga, ON L4V 1B5
Tel: 905-677-3592 *Fax:* 905-677-3675
Web Site: www.mmt.ca
Key Personnel
Pres: Alan George
Cont: John Mousmoules *Tel:* 905-677-3592 ext 247 *E-mail:* john@mmt.ca
Founded: 1956
Business from Other Countries: 10%

Printcrafters Inc
78 Hutchings St, Winnipeg, MB R2X 3B1
Tel: 204-633-7117 *Fax:* 204-694-1519
E-mail: printcrafters@mb.sympatico.ca
Key Personnel
Pres: Bob Payne *Tel:* 204-633-7117 ext 223 *Fax:* 204-694-1594 *E-mail:* bpayne@mb.sympatico.ca
Founded: 1996 (Employee owned)
Business from Other Countries: 30%
Membership(s): CPIA

PrintWest
1150 Eighth Ave, Regina, SK S4R 1C9
Tel: 306-525-2304 *Fax:* 306-757-2439
E-mail: general@printwest.com
Web Site: www.printwest.com
Key Personnel
CEO: Wayne UnRuh
VP Sales & Mktg: Ken Benson
Founded: 1992
Business from Other Countries: 15%
Branch Office(s)
Box 2500, 2310 Millar Ave, Saskatoon, SK S7K 2C4 *Tel:* 306-665-3560 *Fax:* 306-653-1255

Transcontinental Printing Book Group
395 Lebeau Blvd, St-Laurent, PQ H4N 1S2
Tel: 514-337-8560 *Fax:* 514-339-2252
Web Site: www.transcontinental-gtc.com; www.transcontinental-printing.com
Key Personnel
Sr VP, Book Group: Jacques Gregoire
US Sales Mgr: Denis Beaudin *Tel:* 514-339-2220 ext 4101 *E-mail:* beaudind@transcontinental.ca
Founded: 1976
Business from Other Countries: 15%
Branch Office(s)
614 Yates Ave, Calumet City, IL 60409, United States, Contact: Kristopher D Levy *Tel:* 708-832-1528 *Fax:* 708-832-9510 *E-mail:* kris.levy@transcontinental.ca (Midwest)
3653 W Leland Ave, Suite One W, Chicago, IL 60625, United States, Contact: Tim Taylor *Tel:* 773-583-8155 *Fax:* 773-583-8162 *E-mail:* tim.taylor@transcontinental.ca (Midwest)
245 Eliot St, Ashland, MA 01721, United States, Contact: Ed Catania *Tel:* 508-881-1119 *Fax:* 508-881-7739 *E-mail:* ecantania@attbi.com (East Coast)
19 Crown St, Milton, MA 02186-1419, United States, Contact: Mike Gazzola *Tel:* 617-696-1435 *Fax:* 617-696-1025 *E-mail:* mikebook@attbi.com (East Coast)
37 Herman Blvd, Franklin Square, NY 11010, United States, Contact: Tim Malloy *Tel:* 516-775-2980 *Fax:* 516-488-0253 *E-mail:* tmmalloy@aol.com (NY)
3175 Summit Square Dr, Suite C9, Oakton, VA 22124, United States, Contact: David Avesian *Tel:* 703-255-1332 *Fax:* 703-255-1343 *E-mail:* davesian@cox.rr.com (Southeast)
559 Lowrys Rd, Parksville, BC V9P 2R8, Contact: Mike Davies *Tel:* 250-248-9700 *Fax:* 250-248-2353 *E-mail:* bookguys@shaw.ca (West Coast)
15373 Victoria Ave, White Rock, BC V4B 1H1, Contact: Wade Davies *Tel:* 604-535-8800 *Fax:* 604-535-8802 *E-mail:* davies@shaw.ca (West Coast)
490 Wilfred Dr, Peterborough, ON K9K 2H1, Contact: Tom Lang *Tel:* 705-760-9594 *Fax:* 705-760-9485 *E-mail:* langt@transcontinental.ca (NY)

University of Toronto Press Inc
Printing Division, 5201 Dufferin St, North York, ON M3H 5T8
Tel: 416-667-7767 *Fax:* 416-667-7803
E-mail: printing@utpress.utoronto.ca
Web Site: www.utpress.utoronto.ca
Key Personnel
Pres & Publr: George Meadows
Founded: 1901
Business from Other Countries: 15%
Membership(s): BMI

China

Speedflex Asia Ltd
3/F Tianjin Bldg, 167 Connaught Rd W, Hong Kong, SAR
Tel: 25422780 *Fax:* 25454026
E-mail: info@speedflex.com.hk
Key Personnel
Sales Manager: Richard Silkstone
Founded: 1981
Business from Other Countries: 20%

Denmark

Bianco Lunos Bogtrykkeri AS
Subsidiary of Carl Allers Etablissement AS
Otto Monsteds Gade 3, DK-1571 Copenhagen V
Tel: 33140781 *Fax:* 33913808
Key Personnel
General Manager: J Heede Sorensen
Founded: 1871

Finland

WS Bookwell Ltd
Subsidiary of Werner Soderstrom Corp
Teollisuustie 4, FIN-06100 Porvoo
Tel: (019) 219 41 *Fax:* (019) 219 4800
Web Site: www.wsoy.fi/print/
Key Personnel
Man Dir: Magnus Breitenstein *E-mail:* magnus.breitenstein@bookwell.fi
Secretary: Minna Rautio *Tel:* (019) 5762402 *E-mail:* minna.rautio@wsoy.fi
Founded: 1999
Business from Other Countries: 70%
Branch Office(s)
Messerdorferstr 127, 53123 Bonn, Germany, Contact: Markku Rapeli *Tel:* (0228) 986 4006 *Fax:* (0228) 986 4008
WS Bookwell AB, Borgveien 2, Ytre Enebakk N-1914, Norway, Kristen Sande *Tel:* (064) 925840 *Fax:* (064) 925841 *E-mail:* k.sande.wsoy@oslo.online.no
PO Box 3, Lowestoft, Suffolk NR33 8EY, United Kingdom, David Sowter *Tel:* (01502) 742 038 *Fax:* (01502) 742 039 *E-mail:* DS@wsoy.freeserve.co.uk

Germany

C L Baader Buch & Offsetdruckere GmbH & Co KG
Gutenbergstr 1, 72525 Baden-Wurttemberg
Mailing Address: Postfach 1220, 72522 Munsingen
Tel: (07381) 79192 *Fax:* (07381) 411412 *Cable:* BAADER-MUNSINGEN
Founded: 1835

Mohndruck Graphische Betriebe GmbH
Subsidiary of Bertelsmann AG
Carl-Bertelsmann-Str 161, 33311 Guetersloh
Mailing Address: Postfach 200, 33311 Guetersloh
Tel: (05241) 802095 *Fax:* (05241) 78329

GERMANY

Key Personnel
Contact: Alfred Hahn
Founded: 1824
Business from Other Countries: 25%

Priese GmbH
Auerbacherstr 9, 14193 Berlin
Tel: (030) 3239089 *Fax:* (030) 3249630
Key Personnel
Contact: Elma Priese; Hans Joachim Priese

Hong Kong

Caritas Printing Training Centre
2 Caine Rd, Caritas House, Block D, 3/F, Hong Kong
Tel: 25261148 *Fax:* 25371231
Key Personnel
General Manager: Isaac Mak
Business from Other Countries: 50%

Dai Nippon Printing Co (Hong Kong) Ltd
Division of Dai Nippon Printing Co Ltd
220-248 Texaco Rd, Tsuen Wan Industrial Centre, 2/F-5/F, Tsuen Wan, New Territories
Tel: 24080188 *Fax:* 24076201
Web Site: www.dnp.co.jp *Cable:* DNPICO
Key Personnel
Administration & Finance Dir: Mr K Miya
Business from Other Countries: 85%
Branch Office(s)
Dai Nippon Printing Co Pty Ltd, 45 Clarence St, Suite 904, Level 9, KPMG Centre, Sydney NSW 2000, Australia *Tel:* (02) 9299-3155
Dai Nippon Printing Co Ltd, London Liaison Office, 27 Throgmorton St, 4th floor, London EC2N 2AQ, United Kingdom *Tel:* (020) 7588-2088
Dai Nippon Printing Co Ltd, 1-1, Ichigaya-Kagacho, 1-Chome, Shinjuku-Ku, Tokyo, Japan
DNP America Inc, 50 California St, Suite 777, San Francisco, CA 94111, United States
DNP America Inc, 3235 Kifer Rd, Suite 100, Santa Clara, CA 95051, United States
DNP America Inc, 3858 Carson St, Suite 300, Torrance, CA 90503, United States
Dai Nippon Printing Co (Singapore) Pte Ltd, 896 Dunearn Rd, No 04-09, Sime Darby Centre, Singapore 589472, Singapore *Tel:* 469-7611
Tien Wah Press (Pte) Ltd, 4 Pandan Crescent, Singapore 128475, Singapore *Tel:* 466-6222
Twp Sdn Bhd, 89, Jalan Tampoi, Kawasan Perindustian Tampoi, 80350 Johor Bahru, Johor, Malaysia *Tel:* (07) 2369899
Pt Tien Wah Press Indonesia, Janlan Tenaru, Desa Cangkir, Kec Driyorejo, Gresik 61177, Indonesia *Tel:* (31) 7507403
Dnp Corporation USA, 335 Madison Ave, 3rd fl, New York, NY 10017, United States *Tel:* 212-503-1060
Dnp (America), Inc San Diego Sales Office, 7425 Mission Valley Rd, Suite 201, San Diego, CA 92108, United States *Tel:* 619-295-8111
Dai Nippon Ims (America) Corporation, 4524 Enterprise Dr NW, Concord, NC 28027, United States *Tel:* 704-784-8100
Dai Nippon Printing (Europa) Gmbh, Berliner Allee 26, 40212 Dusseldorf, Germany *Tel:* (211) 862018-0
Dnp Denmark A/S, Skruegangen 2, DK-2690 Karlslunde, Denmark *Tel:* 4616-5100
Dai Nippon Printing (Taiwan) Co, Ltd, 85 Chung Hsiao East Rd, Sec 1 Taipei, Taiwan, China *Tel:* (02) 2327-8311

Everbest Printing Co Ltd
Block C5, 10/F, Ko Fai Industrial Bldg, 7 Ko Fai Rd, 10F, Yautong, Kowloon
Tel: (02) 7274433 *Fax:* (02) 7727687
E-mail: everbest@hk.super.net; sales@everbest.com.hk
Key Personnel
Man Dir: Kenneth Chung
Customer Account Executive: Ronny Ng; Frankie Lee
Founded: 1954
Business from Other Countries: 90%
Branch Office(s)
Four Colour Imports Ltd, 2843 Brownsboro Rd, Louisville, KY, United States *Tel:* (502) 896-9644
Everbest Midwest, Edina, MN, United States *Tel:* (612) 944-0854
Everbest Canada, Toronto, ON, Canada *Tel:* (416) 286-6688

Golden Cup Printing Co Ltd
6/F Seapower Industrial Centre, 177 Hoi Bun Rd, Kwun Tong, Kowloon
Tel: 23434254 *Fax:* 23415426
E-mail: sales@goldencup.com.hk
Web Site: www.goldencup.com.hk
Key Personnel
Man Dir: K K Yeung
General Manager: W K Ngan
Sales Manager: Mary Yeung *E-mail:* mary@goldencup.com.hk
Founded: 1971
Business from Other Countries: 80%
Branch Office(s)
Dongguan, China
Guangdong, China
Kunming, China
Yunan, China

The Green Pagoda Press Ltd
9/F, Tung Chong Factory Bldg, 653-655 Kings Rd, North Point
Tel: 25611924 *Fax:* 28110946
E-mail: gpinfo@gpp.com.hk
Key Personnel
Dir: Derek Yip
Founded: 1957
Business from Other Countries: 30%

Image Printing Company Ltd
Unit 4, 4/F Cornell Centre, 50 Wing Tai Rd, Chai Wan
Tel: 28732633 *Fax:* 25583044
E-mail: imageprt@pop3.hknet.com
Key Personnel
Man Dir: Philip Chow Sung Ming
Founded: 1992
Business from Other Countries: 50%

Mei Ka Printing & Publish Enterprise Ltd
Cheung Ka Industrial Bldg, Block B 8th & 9th Floor, 179-190 Connaught Rd West, Sai Ying Pin
Tel: 25401131 *Fax:* 25598718
Key Personnel
Dir: Hong Chin Huo

Prontaprint Asia Ltd
1/F, Gaylord Commercial Bldg, 114 Lockhart Rd, Wanchai
Tel: 28657525 *Fax:* 28661064
E-mail: postmaster@pronta.com.hk
Key Personnel
Man Dir: Clive Howard
Founded: 1986
Business from Other Countries: 40%

Sino Publishing House Ltd
Asia Harvest Commercial Center, Room 2A, Tak House, 5-11 Stanley St, Central Hong Kong
Tel: 28849963 *Fax:* 25121154
E-mail: sunnyp@hkstar.com
Key Personnel
Dir: Stephen Stringer
Founded: 1993
Business from Other Countries: 75%

Wing King Tong Co Ltd (Printing Factory)
188 Texaco Rd, 3/F, Phase 1, Leader Industrial Centre, Tsuen Wan, New Territories
Tel: 24073287 *Fax:* 24074130
Key Personnel
Man Dir: Alex Yan *E-mail:* ayan@hk.super.net
Marketing Dir: Jeremy Kuo
Founded: 1944
Business from Other Countries: 95%

Ying Tat Co
Division of Quality Printing & Paper Products
Wing Wah Industrial Bldg, 8th Floor, 677 Kings Rd, Hong Kong
Tel: 25645980 *Fax:* 28111280
Key Personnel
Sales Manager: Kan Chan
Founded: 1968
Business from Other Countries: 30%

Hungary

Interpress Aussenhandels GmbH
Subsidiary of ADWEST
Bajcsy-Zsilinszky ut 21, H-1065 Budapest
Tel: (01) 3027525 *Fax:* (01) 3027530
E-mail: office@interpress.hu
Web Site: www.interpress.hu
Key Personnel
Manager: Miklos Pollak; Sandor Kovacs; Julia Kovacs
Founded: 1991

Indonesia

Ichtiar Baru I Van Hoeve
Jl Cideng Barat 62, Jakarta Barat
Tel: (021) 354533
Founded: 1972

Victory Offset Prima PT
Jalan Raya Pegangsaan, Dua, No 17, Jakarta 14250
Tel: (021) 460-2742; (021) 460-8968 *Fax:* (021) 460-2740; (021) 4682-0551
E-mail: info@victoryoffset.com
Web Site: www.victoryoffset.com
Key Personnel
President: Zainal F Stanley *E-mail:* zainal@victoryoffset.com
General Manager: S Wilson Pinady *E-mail:* wilson@victoryoffset.com
Founded: 1971
Business from Other Countries: 10%
Branch Office(s)
PT Victory Graficindo Printing, Jalan Raya Pegengsaan, Dua, No 17, Jakarta-Utara 14250

Ireland

SciPrint Ltd
93-94 Industrial Estate, Shannon, Co Clare
Tel: (061) 472114; (061) 472520 *Fax:* (061) 472021

MATERIALS

Key Personnel
Man Dir, Sales: M K Parsons
Chairman: B Lane
Founded: 1974
Business from Other Countries: 95%

Smurfit Print
33 Botanic Rd, Glasnevin, Dublin 9
Tel: (01) 303911 *Fax:* (01) 303287
Business from Other Countries: 20%
Parent Company: Jefferson Smurfit Group plc

Israel

Keterpress Enterprises Jerusalem
Industrial Zone Givat Shaul B, Jerusalem 91071
Mailing Address: PO Box 7145, Jerusalem 91071
Tel: (02) 6557822 *Fax:* (02) 6528962
Key Personnel
Plant Manager: Peter Tomkins *E-mail:* peter@keter-books.co.il
Sales Manager: Zvi Weller
Business from Other Countries: 10%
Parent Company: Keter Publishing House Ltd

Italy

Dedalo Litostampa SRL
Viale Luigi Jacobini 5, Zona Ind, 70123 Bari
Tel: (080) 5311400 *Fax:* (080) 5311414
Key Personnel
Man Dir: Raimondo Coga
General Manager: Sergio Coga *Tel:* (080) 5311413 *E-mail:* s.coga@edizionidedalo.it
Founded: 1965

Milanostampa SPA
Corso Ferrero 5, Farigliano 12060 Cuneo
Tel: (0173) 746111 *Fax:* (0173) 746248
E-mail: milanostampa@areacom.it
Telex: 212428
Key Personnel
Commercial Dir: Riccardo Sardo
Man Dir: Fuad Lahham
Founded: 1965
Business from Other Countries: 65%

Republic of Korea

Daehan Printing & Publishing Co Ltd
344-12, Sangdaewon-dong, Jungwon-gu, Sungnam-City, Kyungki-do
Tel: (031) 730-3830 (i-3) *Fax:* (031) 735-8104
Web Site: www.dhpop.com
Key Personnel
President: Sungshick Kim
Manager: Jongjun Yu
Founded: 1948

Netherlands

BN International
Rokerjweg 5, 1271 AH Huizon
Tel: (03552) 48400 *Fax:* (03552) 56004
Telex: (03552) 56004
Key Personnel
Marketing Manager: Henk Bunschoten
Founded: 1938
Business from Other Countries: 95%
Branch Office(s)
BN International UK, Unit 38, The Metro Centre, Tolpits Lane, Watford, Herts WD1 8SB, United Kingdom

New Zealand

Bookprint Consultants Ltd
Division of Grantham House Publishing
9 Wilkinson St, Apt 6, Oriental Bay, Wellington 6001
Tel: (04) 381 3071 *Fax:* (04) 381 3067
E-mail: gstewart@iconz.co.nz
Key Personnel
Chief Executive: Graham C Stewart
Founded: 1982
Business from Other Countries: 10%

John McIndoe Ltd
PO Box 694, Dunedin
Tel: (03) 4770355 *Fax:* (03) 4771982
E-mail: jmcindoe@earthlight.co.nz
Key Personnel
Man Dir: Brendan A Murphy
Founded: 1893
Business from Other Countries: 1%

Singapore

CS Graphics Pte Ltd
10 Tuas Avenue 20, Singapore 638822
Tel: 8610100 *Fax:* 8610190
E-mail: stlee@csgraphics.com.sg
Key Personnel
Man Dir: Mr Lee Sian Tee *E-mail:* stlee@csgraphics.com.sg
Founded: 1981
Business from Other Countries: 100%

Eurasia Press Pte Ltd
10/14 Kampong Ampat-1336, Singapore 368320
Tel: 2805522 *Fax:* 2800593; 3825458
E-mail: eurasia@mbox3.singnet.com.sg
Key Personnel
Marketing Dir: Allan Fong
Founded: 1937
Business from Other Countries: 65%

Ho Printing Singapore Pte Ltd
Changi South St One, Singapore 486797
Tel: 5429322 *Fax:* 2896065
Telex: RS 39685 HOFSET
Key Personnel
Sales Executive: Ho Wah Yuen
Founded: 1951
Business from Other Countries: 30%

International Press Co Pte Ltd
26 Kallang Ave, Singapore 339417
Tel: 2983800 *Fax:* 2971668
Key Personnel
Marketing Manager: Koo Kok Leong
Founded: 1972
Business from Other Countries: 60%

SPAIN

Kin Keong Printing Co Pte Ltd, see Markono Print Media Pte Ltd

Markono Print Media Pte Ltd
Formerly Kin Keong Printing Co Pte Ltd
Subsidiary of Markono Holdings Pte Ltd
21 Neythal Rd, Singapore 628586
Tel: 62811118 *Fax:* 62866663
E-mail: sales@markono.com.sg
Key Personnel
Man Dir: Bob Lee *E-mail:* blee@markono.com.sg
Business from Other Countries: 20%
Branch Office(s)
Kin Keong Colour Printing (M) Sdn Bhd, Port Klang 539538

SNP Printing Pte Ltd
97 Ubi Ave 4, Singapore 408754
Tel: 7412500 *Fax:* 2854894
E-mail: 2028095@syp.com.sg
Web Site: www.snp.com.sg
Telex: SNPRS14462
Key Personnel
President: Yeo Chee Tong
Executive Vice President: Koo Tse Chia
US Sales Manager: Patrick Chung
Business from Other Countries: 40%

Times Printers Pte Ltd
Subsidiary of Times Publishing Group
16 Tuas Ave 5, Singapore 639340
Tel: 8623333 *Fax:* 8621313
E-mail: timetppl@singnet.com.sg *Cable:* TIMESPRINT
Key Personnel
Vice President: Leong Kwok Sun
Sales Manager: Patsy Tan; Koo Kok Leong
Founded: 1968
Business from Other Countries: 75%

Toppan Company (S) Pte Ltd
Division of Toppan Printing Co Ltd
Toppan Shibaura Bldg, 3-19-26 Shibaura, Minato-ku 108-0023
Tel: 264-0654 *Fax:* 265-8298
Telex: RS 21596 *Cable:* TOPPAN
Key Personnel
Man Dir: Kohei Mochizuki
General Manager: M Sonoda
Founded: 1968
Business from Other Countries: 70%

Slovenia

Gorenjski Tisk Printing Co
Zoisova ulica 1, 4000 Kranj
Tel: (064) 2630 *Fax:* (064) 241323
Telex: 34560 YU GOTISK
Key Personnel
Dir: Kristina Kobal
Commercial Manager: Boris Krist
Founded: 1888
Business from Other Countries: 50%

Spain

Grafos SA Arte Sobre Papel
Sector C calle D, NO 36, E-08040 Barcelona
Tel: (093) 2618750 *Fax:* (093) 2631004
Key Personnel
Man Dir: Peter Zantop *E-mail:* peterzantop@compuserve.com
Founded: 1934
Business from Other Countries: 45%

SPAIN

Guarro Casas SA
Subsidiary of Arjo Wiggins Appleton
PO Box 2427, E-08080 Barcelona
Tel: (093) 7767676 *Fax:* (093) 7767630
E-mail: guarro@guarro.com
Web Site: www.guarro.com
Key Personnel
Export Executive Dir: Manuel Freijomil
  E-mail: mfreijomil@guarro.com
Founded: 1698
Business from Other Countries: 60%

United Kingdom

Bell & Bain Ltd
303 Burnfield Rd, Thornliebank, Glasgow G46 7UQ
Tel: (0141) 6495697 *Fax:* (0141) 6328733
E-mail: info@bell-bain.demon.co.uk
Key Personnel
Man Dir: I Walker
Sales Dir: D Stewart
Business from Other Countries: 25%

Biddles Ltd
Division of W & G Baird Ltd
Woodbridge Park Estate, Woodbridge Rd, Guildford, Surrey GU1 1DA
Tel: (01483) 502224 *Fax:* (01483) 576150
E-mail: sales@biddles.co.uk
Key Personnel
Man Dir: M J Read
Founded: 1885
Business from Other Countries: 8%
Branch Office(s)
Kings Lynn

Book Creation Services
21 Carnaby St, London W1V 1PH
Tel: (020) 7287 0214 *Fax:* (020) 7287 8547
Key Personnel
Chairman: Hal Robinson *E-mail:* hal@zoo.co.uk
Founded: 1991
Business from Other Countries: 30%

Caledonian International Book Manufacturing
Westerhill Rd, Bishopbriggs, Glasgow G64 2QR
Tel: (0141) 7623000 *Fax:* (0141) 7620922
E-mail: 101622.235@compuserve.com
Key Personnel
Man Dir: Kevin McKenna
Commercial Dir: G Morrison
Group Sales Manager: Martin Platt
  E-mail: martin@platt44.freeserve.co.uk
Founded: 1819

Clays Ltd
Subsidiary of St Ives Plc
Popson St, Bungay, Suffolk NR35 1ED
Tel: (01986) 893211
E-mail: clays@claysltd.co.uk
Key Personnel
Contact: Sarah Orell
Founded: 1817
Business from Other Countries: 15%

William Clowes Ltd
Goal Lane, Beccles, Suffolk NR34 9QE
Tel: (01502) 712884 *Fax:* (01502) 717003
Key Personnel
Man Dir: Alex Evans
Sales Dir: David C Browne *Tel:* (01502) 712884, Ext 240
Founded: 1803
Business from Other Countries: 1%

Cox & Wyman Ltd
Subsidiary of Rexam Plc
Cardiff Rd, Reading RG1 8EX
Tel: (01189) 530500 *Fax:* (01189) 507222
Key Personnel
General Manager: Tom Roberts
Sales Manager: Ruth Smith
Founded: 1777
Business from Other Countries: 12%

Furnival Press
61 Lilford Rd, London SE5 9HR
Tel: (020) 7274 2067 *Fax:* (020) 7274 6984
E-mail: furnprint@aol.com
Key Personnel
Dir: Johnny Gumb

Goldshield Communications Ltd
Banners Bldg, Attercliffe Rd, Sheffield S9 3QS
Tel: (0114) 2431000 *Fax:* (0114) 2433000
Key Personnel
Man Dir & Overseas-Special Projects: Sandra Potesta *E-mail:* sandra@goldcom.co.uk
Technical & Production: Stefano Potesta
Founded: 1984
Business from Other Countries: 40%

The Guernsey Press Co Ltd
Braye Rd, Vale, Guernsey, Channel Islands GY1 3BW
Mailing Address: PO Box 57, Vale, Guernsey, Channel Islands GY1 3BW
Tel: (01481) 240240; (01481) 243657 (ISDN)
  Fax: (01481) 240290; (01481) 249147
E-mail: books@guernsey-press.com
Key Personnel
Contact: Mr T A R Duquemin
Founded: 1897
Business from Other Countries: 80%

Hammond Bindery Ltd
Subsidiary of The Charlesworth Group
Flanshaw Way, Wakefield, West Yorks WF2 9LP
Tel: (01924) 369598 *Fax:* (01924) 364108
Key Personnel
Man Dir: Steve Allen
Sales: Brian Quarnby
Founded: 1972

Harveys Ltd
Edgefield Road Industrial Estate, Loanhead, Midlothian EH20 9SX
Tel: (0131) 4400074 *Fax:* (0131) 4403478
E-mail: sales@harveys.ltd.uk
Telex: 727985
Key Personnel
Man Dir: Tom Domke *E-mail:* tom@harvey.ltd.uk
Sales Dir: Ros Porter
Founded: 1856
Business from Other Countries: 10%
Branch Office(s)
Hill Head Vinyls Ltd, Old Kilpatrick, Dunbartonshire

Hobbs The Printers Ltd
Brunel Rd, Totton, Hants SO40 3WX
Tel: (023) 8066 4800 *Fax:* (023) 8066 4801
Web Site: www.hobbs.uk.com
Key Personnel
Sales Manager: John Eacott *E-mail:* j.eacott@hobbs.uk.com
Commercial Dir: Terry Ozanne
Founded: 1884
Business from Other Countries: 4%

Hunter & Foulis Ltd
Bridgeside Works, McDonald Rd, Edinburgh EH7 4NP
Tel: (0131) 5567947 *Fax:* (0131) 5573911
E-mail: mail@hunterfoulis.co.uk

Key Personnel
Man Dir: Richard Beese
Founded: 1857

Image & Print Group Ltd
Unit 9, Oakbank Industrial Estate, Garscube Rd, Glasgow G20 7LU
Tel: (0141) 3531900 *Fax:* (0141) 3532472
E-mail: imageandprint@dial.pipex.com
Web Site: www.imageandprint.co.uk
Key Personnel
Man Dir: Ken Roberts
Production: Stephen McPhee
Founded: 1975

Intype London Ltd
Units 3 & 4, Elm Grove Industrial Estate, Elm Grove, Wimbledon, London SW19 4HE
Tel: (020) 8947 7863 *Fax:* (020) 8947 3652
E-mail: intype@btconnect.com
Key Personnel
Man Dir: Tony Chapman *E-mail:* tchap@btconnect.com
Production: Moya Birchell; Richard Mayne
Founded: 1976
Business from Other Countries: 5%

The Malvern Press Ltd
71 Dalston Lane, London E8 2NG
Tel: (0171) 2492991 *Fax:* (0171) 2541720
Key Personnel
Man Dir: Leslie Wynn
Marketing Dir: Peter Wynn
Founded: 1953
Business from Other Countries: 15%

Page Bros Ltd (Norwich)
Subsidiary of Milex Ltd
Mile Cross Lane, Norwich NR6 6SA
Tel: (01603) 429141 *Fax:* (01603) 485126
Key Personnel
Man Dir: David Armstrong
Founded: 1750
Business from Other Countries: 20%
Branch Office(s)
105-A Euston St, London NW1 2ET *Tel:* (020) 7383 2212 *Fax:* (020) 1383 4145

Printafoil Ltd
Unit 5, Mitcham Industrial Estate, Streatham Rd, Mitcham, Surrey CR4 2AP
Tel: (0181) 6403074 *Fax:* (0181) 6402136
Key Personnel
Dir: Simon Flower

Red Bridge International
Subsidiary of Whitecroft PLC
Red Bridge Mill, Ainsworth, Bolton BL2 5PD
Tel: (01204) 522254 *Fax:* (01204) 384754
Web Site: www.redbridge.co.uk
Key Personnel
Sales Dir: Derek Ives *E-mail:* dives@redbridge.co.uk
Business from Other Countries: 35%

Redwood Books Ltd
Division of CPI (UK) Ltd
Kennet Way, Trowbridge, Wilts BA14 8RN
Tel: (01225) 769979 *Fax:* (01225) 769050
E-mail: enquiries@redwood-books.co.uk
Key Personnel
General Manager: Trevor Gee
Commercial Manager: Tony Warner
  E-mail: tony@redwood-books.co.uk
Production Manager: Peter Grant
Business from Other Countries: 8%
Branch Office(s)
London Sales Office, 22 Bloomsbury Sq, London WC1A 2NS *Tel:* (020) 7580-9328 *Fax:* (020) 7580-9337

MATERIALS

J R Reid Print & Media Group, see J R Reid Printing Group Ltd

J R Reid Printing Group Ltd
79-109 Glasgow Rd, Blantyre, Glasgow G72 0LY
Tel: (01698) 826000 *Fax:* (01698) 824944
E-mail: info@reid-print-group.co.uk
Web Site: www.reid-print-group.co.uk
Key Personnel
Man Dir: John R Reid *E-mail:* johnreid@reid-print-group.co.uk
Founded: 1972

Antony Rowe Ltd
Bumpers Farm, Chippenham SN14 6LH
Tel: (01249) 659705 *Fax:* (01249) 443103
E-mail: 100616.40@compuserve.com
Key Personnel
Chief Executive: Ralph Bell
Production Dir: Mike Bando
Technical Dir: Andy Burns
Founded: 1983
Business from Other Countries: 2%

Severnside Printers Ltd
Bridge House, Upton-on-Severn, Worcs WR8 0HG
Tel: (01684) 594521 *Fax:* (01684) 594344
Key Personnel
President & Chief Executive: Norman H Beechey
Business from Other Countries: 10%

Stott Brothers Ltd
Lister Lane, Halifax, W Yorks HX1 5AJ
Tel: (01422) 362184 *Fax:* (01422) 353707
E-mail: stottbros@aol.com
Key Personnel
Man Dir: Ian Bullough

M & A Thomson Litho Ltd
10/16 Colvilles Pl, Kelvin Industrial Estate, East Kilbride, Glasgow G75 0SN
Tel: (013552) 33081 *Fax:* (013552) 45439
Web Site: www.plitho.co.uk
Key Personnel
Deputy Chairman: Gary Thomson

Watkiss Automation Ltd
Subsidiary of The Watkiss Group
One Blaydon Rd, Middlefield Industrial Estate, Sandy, Beds SG19 1RZ
Tel: (01767) 682177 *Fax:* (01767) 691769
E-mail: info@watkiss.com
Web Site: www.watkiss.com
Key Personnel
Technical Dir: M Watkiss
Founded: 1959
Business from Other Countries: 5%

Winter & Co UK Ltd
Stonehill, Huntingdon, Cambs PE18 6AY
Tel: (01480) 377177 *Fax:* (01480) 377166
E-mail: sales@winteruk.com
Key Personnel
Sales Dir: Ken Armstrong
Man Dir: Richard Higgins

The Wolsey Press
The Drift, Nacton Rd, Ipswich IP3 9QR
Tel: (01473) 719377 *Fax:* (01473) 272115
E-mail: studio@wolseypress.demon.co.uk
Key Personnel
Dir: John Robinson; Colin Jennings

United States

Bang Printing Co Inc
1473 Hwy 18 E, Brainerd, MN 56401-0587
Mailing Address: PO Box 587, Brainerd, MN 56401-0587
Tel: 218-829-2877 *Fax:* 218-829-7145
Web Site: www.bangprinting.com
Key Personnel
VP, Sales: Todd Vanek *Tel:* 218-822-2124
  E-mail: toddv@bangprinting.com
Founded: 1899
Business from Other Countries: 50%

Blaze International Productions Inc
225 W 35 St, Suite 1100, New York, NY 10001
Tel: 212-967-7501 *Fax:* 212-967-7551
Key Personnel
Pres: Eugene Sanchez *Tel:* ext 222 *E-mail:* e.sanchez@blazeint.com
Founded: 1990
Business from Other Countries: 80%
Branch Office(s)
The Deepings, Hill Bottom, White Church Hill, S Oxfordshire RG8 7PT, United Kingdom
Tel: 44-1189842403
Kodak House, Phase 2, Flat 12, 18/F, No 39, Healthy St E, North Point, Hong Kong
Tel: 2967 9360 *Fax:* 2967 1800

BookBuilders New York Ltd
353 Strawtown Rd, New City, NY 10956
Tel: 845-639-5316 *Fax:* 845-639-5318
Key Personnel
Pres: Martin Cook *E-mail:* martin@mcabooks.com
Founded: 1977
Business from Other Countries: 60%

Coneco Litho Graphics
Division of NET 2 PRESS Inc
58 Dix Ave, Glens Falls, NY 12801-7255
Mailing Address: PO Box 3255, Glen Falls, NY 12801-7255
Tel: 518-793-3823 *Fax:* 518-793-5823
Founded: 1984
Business from Other Countries: 27%

Conservation Resources International Inc
8000-H Forbes Place, Springfield, VA 22151
Tel: 703-321-7730 *Fax:* 703-321-0629
E-mail: criusa@conservationresources.com
Web Site: www.conservationresources.com
Key Personnel
Pres: William K Hollinger, Jr
VP: Lavonia Hollinger
Dir, Mktg: Abby A Shaw *Tel:* 215-625-8422
  E-mail: crisales@aol.com
Business from Other Countries: 30%
Membership(s): AIC

Martin Cook Associates Ltd
353 Strawtown Rd, New City, NY 10956
Tel: 845-639-5316 *Fax:* 845-639-5318
E-mail: mcanewcity@aol.com
Web Site: www.mcabooks.com
Key Personnel
Pres: Martin Cook *E-mail:* mcanewcity@aol.com
Founded: 1977
Business from Other Countries: 15%
Membership(s): Bookbinders Guild of New York

CS Graphics USA Inc
Subsidiary of CS Graphics Pte Ltd Singapore
8969 Lake Ct, Granite Bay, CA 95746
Tel: 916-791-9066 *Fax:* 916-791-9112
E-mail: csgraphics@mindspring.com
Key Personnel
Mgr, Sales & Mktg: Rick Marment
Founded: 1980
Business from Other Countries: 30%

D & K Group
1795 Commerce, Elk Grove Village, IL 60007
Tel: 847-956-0160 *Fax:* 847-956-8214
E-mail: info@dkgroup.net
Web Site: www.dkgroup.com
Key Personnel
Pres: Karl Singer
VP, Sales & Mktg: Marge Hayes
Mktg Communs Coord: Holli Hagene
  E-mail: holli.hagene@dkgroup.net
Founded: 1979
Business from Other Countries: 15%

Desktop Miracles Inc
112 S Main, PMB 294, Stowe, VT 05672
Tel: 802-253-7900 *Fax:* 802-253-1900
Web Site: www.desktopmiracles.com
Key Personnel
Pres & CEO: Barry T Kerrigan *E-mail:* barry@desktopmiracles.com
VP: Virginia Kerrigan *E-mail:* virginia@desktopmiracles.com
Founded: 1994
Business from Other Countries: 10%

DNP America LLC
Subsidiary of Dai Nippon Printing Co Ltd
335 Madison Ave, 3rd fl, New York, NY 10017
Tel: 212-503-1074; 212-503-1060 *Fax:* 212-286-1505
Web Site: www.dnp.co.jp/ *Cable:* DAIPRINTS NY
Key Personnel
Pres: Yoji Yamakawa
VP & Gen Mgr, Graphic Printing: Kohei Tsumori
  E-mail: tsumori-k@mail.dnp.co.jp
Founded: 1974
Business from Other Countries: 54%
Branch Office(s)
577 Airport Blvd, Suite 620, Burlingame, CA 94010, Gen Mgr: Kosuke Tago *Tel:* 650-340-6061 *Fax:* 650-340-6090

Elegance Printing & Book Binding (USA)
Member of The Elegance Printing Group
708 Glen Cove Ave, Glen Head, NY 11545
Tel: 516-676-5941 *Fax:* 516-676-5973
Web Site: www.elegancebooks.com
Key Personnel
Man Dir: Frank DeLuca *E-mail:* frank@elegancebooks.com
Founded: 1977
Business from Other Countries: 40%

Fibre Leather Manufacturing Corp
686 Belleville Ave, New Bedford, MA 02745
Tel: 508-997-4557 *Fax:* 508-997-7268
E-mail: fibreleather@earthlink.net
Key Personnel
Pres: Louis Finger
VP: Daniel Finger
Sec: Carol Gutowski
Founded: 1927
Business from Other Countries: 20%

Graphic Services Corp
25 Church Hill Rd, Newtown, CT 06470
Tel: 203-270-7578 *Fax:* 203-270-1578
Web Site: www.independentcartongroup.com
Key Personnel
Pres: Andrew Willie *E-mail:* awillie633@aol.com
Off Mgr: Kathy Renzulli *E-mail:* krenzulli@independentcartongroup.com
Founded: 1990
Business from Other Countries: 10%
Membership(s): Independent Carton Group

UNITED STATES

MANUFACTURING

Hindy's Enterprise
Division of Jinno International
3 Christine Dr, Chestnut Ridge, NY 10977-6802
Tel: 845-735-4666 *Fax:* 617-344-5905
Key Personnel
Pres: Yoh Jinno *E-mail:* jinno@hotmail.com
Founded: 1989
Business from Other Countries: 70%
Branch Office(s)
Melbourne Industrial Bldg, Block A, 20th fl, 16 Westlands Rd, Quarry Bay, Hong Kong *Tel:* 25166318 *Fax:* 25165161

IBT Global Ltd, see Integrated Book Technology Inc

ICG/Holliston
Subsidiary of Industrial Coatings Group
Hwy 11-W, Holliston Mills Rd, Church Hill, TN 37642
Mailing Address: PO Box 478, Kingsport, TN 37662
Tel: 423-357-6141 *Fax:* 423-357-8840
E-mail: custserv@icg-online.com
Web Site: www.icg-online.com
Key Personnel
Pres: Robert Dwyer
Exec VP, Sales: William Waldron, III
Mktg Coord: Vicky Cardwell *E-mail:* vcardwell@holliston.com
Founded: 1897
Cover Line(s) Milled: Arrestox/Roxite B; Kennett; Pearl Linen; Sturdite
Business from Other Countries: 10%

Imago
1431 Broadway, Penthouse, New York, NY 10018
Tel: 847-358-3047 *Fax:* 212-921-8226
E-mail: imagousa@imagousa.com
Web Site: www.imagousa.com
Key Personnel
Pres: Joseph E Braff *E-mail:* jbraff@imagousa.com
Sr Sales Exec: Linda Readerman *E-mail:* lreaderman@imagousa.com
Prodn Dir, USA: Howard R Musk *E-mail:* hmusk@imagousa.com
Dir, West Coast Opers: Greg Lee *Tel:* 949-661-5998 *Fax:* 949-661-8013 *E-mail:* glee@imagousa.com
Prodn Supv, West Coast: Yuhong Guo *Tel:* 949-661-5998 *Fax:* 949-661-8013 *E-mail:* yguo@imagousa.com
Dir, Midwest Opers: Bryan O'Shaughnessy *Tel:* 847-358-3047 *Fax:* 847-358-3078 *E-mail:* bo'shaughnessy@imagousa.com
Founded: 1985
Business from Other Countries: 100%
Branch Office(s)
Imago West Coast, 31952 Camino Capistrano, Suite C-22, San Juan Capistrano, CA 92675, Dir, West Coast Opers: Greg Lee *Tel:* 949-661-5998 *Fax:* 949-661-8013 *E-mail:* glee@imagousa.com *Web Site:* www.imagousa.com
Imago Midwest, 800 E Northwest Hwy, Suite 622, Palatine, IL 60067, Dir, Midwest Opers: Bryan O'Shaughnessy *Tel:* 847-358-3047 *Fax:* 847-358-3078 *E-mail:* bryano@imagousa.com
Imago (UK/Europe) Publishing Ltd, Albury Court, Albury Thame, Oxfordshire OX9 2LP, United Kingdom, Man Dir: Colin Risk *Tel:* 337000 *Fax:* 339935 *Web Site:* www.imago.co.uk
Imago Services (HKG) Ltd, 653-659 Kings Rd, 6th fl, Flat B, North Point, Hong Kong, Man Dir: Kendrick Cheung *Tel:* 2811 3316 *Fax:* 2597 5256
Imago Productions (FE) Pte Ltd, MacPherson Industrial Complex, Suite 05-01, 5 Lorong Bakar Batu, Singapore 1334, Singapore, Man Dir: K C Ng *Tel:* 748 4433 *Fax:* 748 6082

Integrated Book Technology Inc
Division of The IBT Group
18 Industrial Park Rd, Troy, NY 12180
Tel: 518-271-5117 *Fax:* 518-266-9422
E-mail: mail@integratedbooktechnology.com
Web Site: www.integratedbooktechnology.com
Key Personnel
CEO & Pres: John R Paeglow *E-mail:* johnp@integratedbook.com
VP & Chief Technol Officer: William Clockel *E-mail:* billc@integratedbook.com
VP, Sales & Mktg: Robert Lindberg *E-mail:* bobl@integratedbook.com
Dir, Info Technol: Michael Whalen *E-mail:* mikew@integratedbook.com
Regl Sales: Tim Knickerbocker *E-mail:* timk@integratedbook.com
Cust Serv Mgr: James Klein *E-mail:* jimk@integratedbook.com
Reg Sales: Bryan Hall
Founded: 1991
Business from Other Countries: 20%
Membership(s): BMI

International Holographic Paper
Division of Pennsylvania Pulp & Paper Co
300 Highpoint Dr, Chalfont, PA 18914
Tel: 215-997-8006 *Fax:* 215-997-9005
E-mail: sales@itwholographics.com
Web Site: www.itwholographics.com
Key Personnel
VP, Sales: Phil Maniscalco
Founded: 1971
Business from Other Countries: 20%

Jinno International Group
3 Christine Dr, Chestnut Ridge, NY 10977
Tel: 845-735-4666 *Fax:* 617-344-5905
E-mail: jinno@hotmail.com
Key Personnel
Pres: Yoh Jinno
VP: Sharon Jinno
Founded: 1989
Business from Other Countries: 98%
Branch Office(s)
Hindy's Enterprise, Melbourne Industrial Bldg, 16 Westlands Rd, Block A, 20th fl, Quarry Bay, Hong Kong *Tel:* 516-6318 *Fax:* 516-5161
Wing Yiu Printing Co, Melbourne Industrial Bldg, 6th fl, Block A, 16 Westlands Rd, Quarry Bay, Hong Kong, Contact: Law Ming Wah *Tel:* 561 0283 *Fax:* 565 8233
c/o Eurasia Press Pte Ltd, 10/14 Kampong Ampat, Singapore 1336, Singapore, Contact: Allan Fong *Tel:* 280 5522 *Fax:* 280 0593
Jinno International Singapore, 710 Ang Mo Kio, Ave 8, Suite 07-2615, Singapore 2056, Singapore *Tel:* 458 0778

Lenz & Riecker Inc
690 Union Blvd, Totowa, NJ 07512
Tel: 973-256-2456 *Fax:* 973-256-3433; 973-256-2459
E-mail: info@l-r.com
Web Site: www.l-r.com
Key Personnel
Pres: Steven Riecker
CFO: Barry Levinson
VP, Sales: G Gilrain
Founded: 1917
Business from Other Countries: 20%

Linick International Inc
Division of The Linick Group Inc
Linick Bldg, 7 Putter Lane, Middle Island, NY 11953-0102
Mailing Address: PO Box 102, Middle Island, NY 11953-0102
Tel: 631-924-3888
E-mail: linickgrp@att.net
Web Site: www.lgroup.addr.com; www.linickgroup.com
Key Personnel
Chmn & CEO: Dr Andrew S Linick
Treas: Marvin Glickman
Exec VP: Roger Dextor
Founded: 1972
Business from Other Countries: 30%

LK Litho
Division of The Linick Group Inc
Linick Bldg, 7 Putter Lane, Middle Island, NY 11953-0102
Tel: 631-924-3888
E-mail: linickgrp@att.net
Web Site: www.lgroup.addr.com; www.linickgroup.com
Key Personnel
VP: Roger Dextor
Founded: 1968
Business from Other Countries: 20%

Mazer Publishing Services
Division of The Mazer Corporation
6680 Poe Ave, Dayton, OH 45414
Tel: 937-264-2600 *Fax:* 937-264-2624
E-mail: info@mazer.com
Web Site: www.mazer.com
Key Personnel
Pres: William Franklin *E-mail:* bill_franklin@mazer.com
Exec VP: Ken Fultz *E-mail:* ken_fultz@mazer.com
Exec Dir, Sales: Bill Faber *Fax:* 937-264-2622 *E-mail:* bill_faber@mazer.com
Founded: 1964
Business from Other Countries: 10%
Branch Office(s)
2460 Sand Lake Rd, Orlando, FL 32809, Bryan Blakley *Tel:* 407-859-5552 *Fax:* 407-859-0643 *E-mail:* bryan_blakley@mazer.com
224 Lexington Ave, Fox River Grove, IL 60021, Dennis Bowman *Tel:* 847-639-1555 *Fax:* 847-639-1562 *E-mail:* dennis_bowman@mazer.com
22 Lehigh Rd, Wellesley, MA 02181, Ken Leahy *Tel:* 781-237-4112 *Fax:* 781-431-6184 *E-mail:* ken_leahy@mazer.com
22 Laurel Place, Upper Montclair, NJ 07043, John Martel *Tel:* 973-744-4320 *Fax:* 973-746-5608 *E-mail:* john_martel@mazer.com
3081 Glenmere Ct, Kettering, OH 45440, Mark Brewer *Tel:* 937-299-5746 *Fax:* 937-299-5761 *E-mail:* mark_brewer@mazer.com
363 Porter Rd, Bishop, TX 78602, Steve Absher *Tel:* 512-303-9758 *Fax:* 512-303-9791 *E-mail:* steve_absher@mazer.com
Membership(s): BMI

Milanostampa/New Interlitho USA Inc
Subsidiary of Milanostampa New Interlitho Italia SpA
299 Broadway, Suite 901, New York, NY 10007
Tel: 212-964-2430 *Fax:* 212-964-2497
Web Site: www.milanostampa.com
Key Personnel
Chmn: Riccardo Sardo
Sales Rep: Rino Varrasso *E-mail:* rvarrasso@milanostampa-usa.com
Founded: 1974
Business from Other Countries: 75%

Printing Corp of the Americas Inc
620 SW 12 Ave, Pompano Beach, FL 33069
Tel: 954-781-8100 *Fax:* 954-781-8421
E-mail: pcaprint@bellsouth.net
Web Site: www.pcaprint.bellsouth.net
Key Personnel
Pres: Jan Tuchman
Founded: 1979
Business from Other Countries: 15%

Regent Publishing Services
9327 Rambler Dr, St Louis, MO 63123

Tel: 314-631-7581 *Fax:* 314-638-5113
E-mail: regentstl@aol.com
Key Personnel
Sales Dir: Carol A Davis-Tierney
Mktg Dir: James J Tierney
Founded: 1985
Business from Other Countries: 100%

Taylor Publishing Co
1550 W Mockingbird Lane, Dallas, TX 75235
Tel: 214-819-8100 *Fax:* 214-630-1852
E-mail: web@taylorpub.com
Web Site: www.taylorpub.com
Key Personnel
Pres: Dave Fiore
Dir, Fine Books & Div Sales Mgr: Jay Love
Dir, Mktg: Mike Taylor
Founded: 1939
Business from Other Countries: 10%

Times Publishing Group
Division of Times Publishing Ltd/Singapore
99 White Plains Rd, Tarrytown, NY 10591
Tel: 914-366-9888 *Fax:* 914-366-9898
Web Site: www.tpl.com.sg
Key Personnel
Cust Serv Exec: Bonnie Stone *E-mail:* bstone@marshallcavendish.com
Sales Mgr: Suresh Kumar *E-mail:* skumar@marshallcavendish.com
Founded: 1965
Business from Other Countries: 90%

Uruguay

Barreiro y Ramos SA
Juan Carlos Gomez, 1430, Montevideo 11000
Tel: (02) 986621 *Fax:* (02) 962358
Telex: 23901PB.CVJA.UY *Cable:* BAREIRAMOS
Key Personnel
President: Gaston Barreiro
Vice President: Guzman Barreiro
Founded: 1837
Business from Other Countries: 10%

Manufacturing Services & Equipment Index

BOOK MANUFACTURING EQUIPMENT

Canada
Webcom Ltd, pg 1221

United States
AWT World Trade, pg 1224
The Cleveland Vibrator Co, pg 1224
D & K Group, pg 1224

DISTRIBUTION & MAILING

Canada
Appleby's Bindery Ltd, pg 1221
Printcrafters Inc, pg 1221
PrintWest, pg 1221
Transcontinental Printing Book Group, pg 1221

China
Hong Kong Christian Service, pg 1221

Germany
C L Baader Buch & Offsetdruckere GmbH & Co KG, pg 1221
Priese GmbH, pg 1221

Hong Kong
Elegance Finance Printing Services Ltd, pg 1221
Golden Cup Printing Co Ltd, pg 1222
Prontaprint Asia Ltd, pg 1222
Sino Publishing House Ltd, pg 1222

New Zealand
Bookprint Consultants Ltd, pg 1222
John McIndoe Ltd, pg 1222

Portugal
Silabo, pg 1222

Singapore
Craft Print Pte Ltd, pg 1222
Eurasia Press Pte Ltd, pg 1222
Ho Printing Singapore Pte Ltd, pg 1222
Markono Print Media Pte Ltd, pg 1222
Times Printers Pte Ltd, pg 1222

Slovenia
Gorenjski Tisk Printing Co, pg 1222

Spain
Luis Vives (Edelvives), pg 1222

Switzerland
Schweizer Buchzentrum, pg 1223

United Republic of Tanzania
Peramiho Publications, pg 1223

Thailand
J Film Process Co Ltd, pg 1223

United Kingdom
J W Arrowsmith Ltd, pg 1223
The Bath Press, pg 1223
Book Production Consultants PLC, pg 1223
Butler & Tanner Ltd, pg 1223
Cambridge University Press - Printing Division, pg 1223
Clays Ltd, pg 1223
William Clowes Ltd, pg 1223
Cradley Print Ltd, pg 1223
Hammond Bindery Ltd, pg 1223
Headley Brothers Ltd, pg 1223
Hobbs The Printers Ltd, pg 1223
Ikon Document Services Ltd, pg 1223
Multiplex Medway Ltd, pg 1223
Page Bros Ltd (Norwich), pg 1223
Pillar Publications Ltd, pg 1223
Antony Rowe Ltd, pg 1224
TMS Development International Ltd, pg 1224
Turnaround Publisher Services, pg 1224
Watkiss Automation Ltd, pg 1224
John Wilson Booksales, pg 1224

United States
A-R Editions Inc, pg 1224
Express Media Corp, pg 1224
Fairfield Marketing Group Inc, pg 1224
Hamilton Printing Co, pg 1224
Integrated Book Technology Inc, pg 1224
InterPost North America, pg 1225
Lenz & Riecker Inc, pg 1225
LK Litho, pg 1225
Marrakech Express Inc, pg 1225
Mazer Publishing Services, pg 1225
Taylor Publishing Co, pg 1225
Times Publishing Group, pg 1225
UPS Freight Services, pg 1225
Fred Weidner & Daughter Printers, pg 1225

Uruguay
Barreiro y Ramos SA, pg 1225

MANUFACTURING BROKERS OR BROKERING

Belgium
IMPF BV BA, pg 1221

China
Hong Kong Christian Service, pg 1221

Germany
Priese GmbH, pg 1221

Hong Kong
Co-Fine Production, pg 1221
Colorcraft Ltd, pg 1221

Israel
Monoline Ltd, pg 1222

New Zealand
Bookprint Consultants Ltd, pg 1222
Egan-Reid Ltd, pg 1222

Puerto Rico
Publishing Resources Inc, pg 1222

Singapore
Imago Productions (Far East) Pte Ltd, pg 1222
SNP Printing Pte Ltd, pg 1222

United Republic of Tanzania
Peramiho Publications, pg 1223

United Kingdom
Book Production Consultants PLC, pg 1223
Chase Publishing Services, pg 1223
Goldshield Communications Ltd, pg 1223

United States
A-R Editions Inc, pg 1224
Blaze International Productions Inc, pg 1224
BookBuilders New York Ltd, pg 1224
Martin Cook Associates Ltd, pg 1224
Desktop Miracles Inc, pg 1224
Linick International Inc, pg 1225
Regent Publishing Services, pg 1225
Fred Weidner & Daughter Printers, pg 1225

Manufacturing Services & Equipment

This section includes companies throughout the world that offer manufacturing services & equipment. Those U.S. and Canadian companies with 10% or more of their business done outside North America are also included here. Immediately preceding this section is an index classifying companies by services offered.

Belgium

IMPF BV BA
Sint-Amandstr 18, B-9000 Gent
Tel: (09) 2254429 *Fax:* (09) 2331338
Key Personnel
Manager: Xavier Dewulf
Founded: 1958
Business from Other Countries: 10%

Canada

Appleby's Bindery Ltd
1303 Route 102, Upper Gagetown, NB E5M 1R5
Tel: 506-488-2086 *Fax:* 506-488-2086
E-mail: applbind@nbnet.nb.ca
Key Personnel
Pres & Owner: David E Appleby
Mgr: John Appleby
Founded: 1976
Business from Other Countries: 10%

Master Flo Technology Inc
1233 Tessier St, Hawkesbury, ON K6A 3R1
Tel: 613-636-0539 *Fax:* 613-636-0762
E-mail: info@mflo.com
Web Site: www.mflo.com
Key Personnel
VP, Opers: Tim Duffy
Founded: 1984
Business from Other Countries: 75%

Printcrafters Inc
78 Hutchings St, Winnipeg, MB R2X 3B1
Tel: 204-633-7117 *Fax:* 204-694-1519
E-mail: printcrafters@mb.sympatico.ca
Key Personnel
Pres: Bob Payne *Tel:* 204-633-7117 ext 223 *Fax:* 204-694-1594 *E-mail:* bpayne@mb.sympatico.ca
Founded: 1996 (Employee owned)
Business from Other Countries: 30%

PrintWest
1150 Eighth Ave, Regina, SK S4R 1C9
Tel: 306-525-2304 *Fax:* 306-757-2439
E-mail: general@printwest.com
Web Site: www.printwest.com
Key Personnel
CEO: Wayne UnRuh
VP Sales & Mktg: Ken Benson
Founded: 1992
Business from Other Countries: 15%
Branch Office(s)
Box 2500, 2310 Millar Ave, Saskatoon, SK S7K 2C4 *Tel:* 306-665-3560 *Fax:* 306-653-1255

Transcontinental Printing Book Group
Division of Transcontinental Group
395 Lebeau Blvd, St-Laurent, PQ H4N 1S2
Tel: 514-337-8560 *Fax:* 514-339-2252
Web Site: www.transcontinental-gtc.com; www.transcontinental-printing.com
Key Personnel
Sr VP, Book Group: Jacques Gregoire
US Sales Mgr: Denis Beaudin *Tel:* 514-339-2220 ext 4101 *E-mail:* beaudind@transcontinental.ca
Founded: 1976
Business from Other Countries: 15%
Branch Office(s)
614 Yates Ave, Calumet City, IL 60409, United States, Contact: Kristopher D Levy *Tel:* 708-832-1528 *Fax:* 708-832-9510 *E-mail:* kris.levy@transcontinantal.ca (Midwest)
3653 W Leland Ave, Suite One W, Chicago, IL 60625, United States, Contact: Tim Taylor *Tel:* 773-583-8155 *Fax:* 773-583-8162 *E-mail:* tim.taylor@transcontinental.ca (Midwest)
245 Eliot St, Ashland, MA 01721, United States, Contact: Ed Catania *Tel:* 508-881-1119 *Fax:* 508-881-7739 *E-mail:* ecatania@attnbi.com (East Coast)
19 Crown St, Milton, MA 02186-1419, United States, Contact: Michael Gazzola *Tel:* 617-696-1435 *Fax:* 617-696-1025 *E-mail:* mikebook@attbi.com (East Coast)
37 Herman Blvd, Franklin Square, NY 11010, United States, Contact: Tom Malloy *Tel:* 516-775-2980 *Fax:* 516-488-0253 *E-mail:* tmmalloy@aol.com (NY)
3175 Summit Square Dr, Suite C9, Oakton, VA 22124, United States, Contact: David Avesian *Tel:* 703-255-1332 *Fax:* 703-255-1343 *E-mail:* davesian@cox.rr.com (Southeast)
559 Lowrys Rd, Parksville, BC V9P 2R8, Contact: Mike Davies *Tel:* 250-248-9700 *Fax:* 250-248-2353 *E-mail:* bookguys@shaw.ca (West Coast)
15373 Victoria Ave, White Rock, BC V4B 1H1, Contact: Wade Davies *Tel:* 604-535-8800 *Fax:* 604-535-8802 *E-mail:* daviesw@shaw.ca (West Coast)
490 Wilfred Dr, Peterborough, ON K9K 2H1, Cont: Tom Lang *Tel:* 705-760-9594 *Fax:* 705-760-9485 *E-mail:* langt@transcontinental.ca (New York)

Webcom Ltd
3480 Pharmacy Ave, Toronto, ON M1W 2S7
Tel: 416-496-1000 *Fax:* 416-496-1537
E-mail: webcom@webcomlink.com
Web Site: www.webcomlink.com
Key Personnel
VP, Sales & Mktg: Mike Collinge
Dir, Mktg: Deborah Kupperman
Founded: 1976
Business from Other Countries: 40%
Membership(s): BMI; Canadian Book & Periodical Council; Canadian Book Manufactures Association; CPIA; PIA

China

Hong Kong Christian Service
33 Granville Rd, Tsin Sha Tsui, Kowloon, Hong Kong SAR
Tel: 27316316 *Fax:* 27316333
Founded: 1952
Business from Other Countries: 1%

France

Critiques Livres Distribution SAS
24 Rue Malmaison, BP 93, F-93172 Bagnolet Cedex
Tel: (01) 43603910 *Fax:* (01) 48973706
E-mail: critiques.livres@wanadoo.fr
Key Personnel
President: Rosalind Fay-Boehlinger
Founded: 1976
Business from Other Countries: 100%

Germany

C L Baader Buch & Offsetdruckere GmbH & Co KG
Gutenbergstr 1, 72525 Baden-Wurttemberg
Mailing Address: Postfach 1220, 72522 Munsingen
Tel: (07381) 79192 *Fax:* (07381) 411412 *Cable:* BAADER-MUNSINGEN
Founded: 1835

Priese GmbH
Auerbacherstr 9, 14193 Berlin
Tel: (030) 3239089 *Fax:* (030) 3249630
Key Personnel
Contact: Elma Priese; Hans Joachim Priese

Hong Kong

Co-Fine Production
Blk C, 10/F, Shing Teck Factory Bldg, 44 Wong Chuk Hang Rd, Hong Kong
Tel: 25180383
E-mail: cofine@netvigator.com
Key Personnel
Contact: Kenneth Derek Kan
Founded: 1988
Business from Other Countries: 30%

Colorcraft Ltd
Unit 8-9, 16/F Kodak House Phase II, 321 Java Rd, North Point
Tel: 25909033 *Fax:* 25909005; 25909271
E-mail: info.cc@colorcraft.com.hk
Web Site: www.colorcraft.com.hk
Key Personnel
Chairman & Dir: Anne Mary Walker
Business from Other Countries: 100%

Elegance Finance Printing Services Ltd
Subsidiary of Elegance Printing Company Limited
Suite 301, Chinachem Hollywood Centre, 1-13 Hollywood Rd, Central Hong Kong
Tel: 25212200 *Fax:* 25213616
E-mail: saledept@elegancefinptg.com
Business from Other Countries: 2%

HONG KONG

Golden Cup Printing Co Ltd
6/F Seapower Industrial Centre, 177 Hoi Bun Rd, Kwun Tong, Kowloon
Tel: 23434254 *Fax:* 23415426
E-mail: sales@goldencup.com.hk
Web Site: www.goldencup.com.hk
Key Personnel
Man Dir: K K Yeung
General Manager: W K Ngan
Sales Manager: Mary Yeung *E-mail:* mary@goldencup.com.hk
Founded: 1971
Business from Other Countries: 80%
Branch Office(s)
Dongguan, China
Guangdong, China
Kunming, China
Yunan, China

Prontaprint Asia Ltd
1/F, Gaylord Commercial Bldg, 114 Lockhart Rd, Wanchai
Tel: 28657525 *Fax:* 28661064
E-mail: postmaster@pronta.com.hk
Key Personnel
Man Dir: Clive Howard
Founded: 1986
Business from Other Countries: 40%

Sino Publishing House Ltd
Asia Harvest Commercial Center, Room 2A, Tak House, 5-11 Stanley St, Central Hong Kong
Tel: 28849963 *Fax:* 25121154
E-mail: sunnyp@hkstar.com
Key Personnel
Dir: Stephen Stringer
Founded: 1993
Business from Other Countries: 75%

Israel

Monoline Ltd
Avnei Nezer St 3, Kiryat Sefer 71917
Tel: (08) 9741456 *Fax:* (08) 9741454
Key Personnel
Dir: S J Colthof
Founded: 1959
Business from Other Countries: 30%

New Zealand

Bookprint Consultants Ltd
Division of Grantham House Publishing
9 Wilkinson St, Apt 6, Oriental Bay, Wellington 6001
Tel: (04) 381 3071 *Fax:* (04) 381 3067
E-mail: gstewart@iconz.co.nz
Key Personnel
Chief Executive: Graham C Stewart
Founded: 1982
Business from Other Countries: 10%

Egan-Reid Ltd
Level 2, 38 Ireland St, Freemans Bay, Auckland 1001
Tel: (09) 3784100 *Fax:* (09) 3784300
E-mail: books@eganreid.co.nz
Key Personnel
Man Dir: Gerard Reid *E-mail:* gerard@eganreid.co.nz
Contact: Mary Egan *E-mail:* mary@eganreid.co.nz
Founded: 1988

Business from Other Countries: 75%
Membership(s): Book Publishers Association of New Zealand

John McIndoe Ltd
PO Box 694, Dunedin
Tel: (03) 4770355 *Fax:* (03) 4771982
E-mail: jmcindoe@earthlight.co.nz
Key Personnel
Man Dir: Brendan A Murphy
Founded: 1893
Business from Other Countries: 1%

Portugal

Silabo
R Cidade de Manchester-2, 1170-100 Lisbon
Tel: (021) 8130345 *Fax:* (021) 8166719
E-mail: silabo@mail.telepac.pt
Key Personnel
Marketing Dir: Manuel Robalo
 E-mail: manuelrobalo@mail.telepac.pt
Founded: 1983

Puerto Rico

Publishing Resources Inc
373 San Jorge St, 2nd Floor, Santurce 00912
Mailing Address: PO Box 41307, Minillas Station, Santurce 00940
Tel: (787) 268-8080 *Fax:* (787) 774-5781
E-mail: pri@tld.net
Key Personnel
Owner: Ronald J Chevako
Editorial Dir: Anne W Chevako
Founded: 1976
Business from Other Countries: 5%

Singapore

Craft Print Pte Ltd
9 Joo Koon Circle, Jurong, Singapore 629041
Tel: 8614040 *Fax:* 8610530
E-mail: craftprt@singnet.com.sg
Key Personnel
Marketing Manager: Anthony Tham

Eurasia Press Pte Ltd
10/14 Kampong Ampat-1336, Singapore 368320
Tel: 2805522 *Fax:* 2800593; 3825458
E-mail: eurasia@mbox3.singnet.com.sg
Key Personnel
Marketing Dir: Allan Fong
Founded: 1937
Business from Other Countries: 65%

Ho Printing Singapore Pte Ltd
11-15 Harper Rd, Singapore 369676
Tel: 5429322 *Fax:* 2896065
Telex: RS 39685 HOFSET
Key Personnel
Sales Executive: Ho Wah Yuen
Founded: 1951
Business from Other Countries: 30%

Imago Productions (Far East) Pte Ltd
5 Lorong Bakar Batu, 05-01 MacPherson Industrial Complex, Singapore 348742

Tel: 7484433 *Fax:* 7486082
Key Personnel
Man Dir: K C Ng
Branch Office(s)
Imago Sales USA Inc, 310 Madison Ave, Suite 2103, New York, NY 10017, United States
Tel: 212-921-4411 *Fax:* 212-370-4542

Kin Keong Printing Co Pte Ltd, see Markono Print Media Pte Ltd

Markono Print Media Pte Ltd
Formerly Kin Keong Printing Co Pte Ltd
Subsidiary of Markono Holdings Pte Ltd
21 Neythal Rd, Singapore 628586
Tel: 62811118 *Fax:* 62866663
E-mail: sales@markono.com.sg
Key Personnel
Man Dir: Bob Lee *E-mail:* blee@markono.com.sg
Business from Other Countries: 20%
Branch Office(s)
Kin Keong Colour Printing (M) Sdn Bhd, Port Klang 539538

SNP Printing Pte Ltd
97 Ubi Ave 4, Singapore 408754
Tel: 7412500 *Fax:* 2854894
Telex: SNPRS14462
Key Personnel
President: Yeo Chee Tong
Executive Vice President: Koo Tse Chia
US Sales Manager: Patrick Chung
Business from Other Countries: 40%

Times Printers Pte Ltd
Subsidiary of Times Publishing Group
16 Tuas Ave 5, Singapore 639340
Tel: 8623333 *Fax:* 8621313
E-mail: timetppl@singnet.com.sg *Cable:* TIMESPRINT
Key Personnel
Vice President: Leong Kwok Sun
Sales Manager: Patsy Tan; Koo Kok Leong
Founded: 1968
Business from Other Countries: 75%

Slovenia

Gorenjski Tisk Printing Co
Mirka Vadnova 6, 4000 Kranj
Tel: (064) 2630 *Fax:* (064) 241323
Telex: 34560 YU GOTISK
Key Personnel
Dir: Kristina Kobal
Commercial Manager: Boris Krist
Founded: 1888
Business from Other Countries: 50%

Spain

Luis Vives (Edelvives)
Xaudaro, 25, 28034 Madrid
Tel: (091) 3344890; (091) 3344884 *Fax:* (091) 3344892; (091) 3344894
Key Personnel
Production Dir: Jesus Agudo Perez
Founded: 1890
Business from Other Countries: 25%

Switzerland

Schweizer Buchzentrum (Swiss Book Centre)
Postfach 522, CH-4601 Olten
Tel: (062) 2092525 *Fax:* (062) 2092627
Key Personnel
Dept Manager: Michael Taylor
Founded: 1882

Centre Suisse du Livre, see Schweizer Buchzentrum

Centro Svizzero del Libro, see Schweizer Buchzentrum

Swiss Book Centre, see Schweizer Buchzentrum

United Republic of Tanzania

Peramiho Publications
PO Box 41, Peramiho
Tel: (054) 2730 *Fax:* (054) 2917
Key Personnel
Chief Executive: Fr Gerold Rupper
Founded: 1937

Thailand

J Film Process Co Ltd
440/7 Soi Chaisamoraphum, Rangnum Rd, Phayathai, Bangkok 10400
Tel: (02) 2486888 *Fax:* (02) 2464620; (02) 2474719
Key Personnel
President: Peer Prayukvong
Vice President: Siriporn Prayukvong
Man Dir: Pira Prayookwongse
Founded: 1970
Business from Other Countries: 45%

United Kingdom

J W Arrowsmith Ltd
71 Winterstoke Rd, Bristol BS3 2NT
Tel: (0117) 9667545 *Fax:* (0117) 9637829
E-mail: jw@arrowsmith.co.uk
Key Personnel
Sales Mgr: D J Hooper *E-mail:* dhooper@arrowsmith.co.uk
Founded: 1854
Business from Other Countries: 40%

The Bath Press
Subsidiary of Bath Press Group PLC
Lower Bristol Rd, Bath BA2 3BL
Tel: (01225) 428101 *Fax:* (01225) 312418
Key Personnel
Man Dir: Peter Palframan
Marketing Dir: Keith Johnson
Founded: 1846
Business from Other Countries: 5%

Book Production Consultants PLC
25-27 High St, Chesterton, Cambridge CB4 1ND
Tel: (01223) 352790 *Fax:* (01223) 460718
E-mail: cw@bpccam.co.uk
Web Site: www.bpccam.co.uk
Key Personnel
Man Dir: Tony Littlechild *E-mail:* tl@bpccam.co.uk
Founded: 1973
Business from Other Countries: 25%

Butler & Tanner Ltd
The Selwood Printing Works, Frome, Somerset BA11 1NF
Tel: (01373) 451500 *Fax:* (01373) 451333
E-mail: manufacturing@butlerandtanner.com
Key Personnel
Joint Man Dir: A Huett
Sales Dir: N White

Cambridge University Press - Printing Division
Division of Cambridge University Press
University Printing House, Shaftesbury Rd, Cambridge CB2 2BS
Tel: (01223) 358331 *Fax:* (01223) 325672
Key Personnel
Production Dir: Steve Millard *E-mail:* smillard@cup.com.ac.uk
Production Manager: Peter Cunningham
Founded: 1534

Chase Publishing Services
Mead, Fortescue Rd, Sidmouth, Devon EX10 9QG
Tel: (01395) 514709 *Fax:* (01395) 514709
E-mail: r.addicott@btinternet.com
Key Personnel
President: Ray Addicott *E-mail:* r.addicott@btinternet.com
Founded: 1989

Clays Ltd
Subsidiary of St Ives Plc
Popson St, Bungay, Suffolk NR35 1ED
Tel: (01986) 893211 *Fax:* (01986) 895293
E-mail: clays@claysltd.co.uk
Key Personnel
Contact: Sarah Orell
Founded: 1817
Business from Other Countries: 15%

William Clowes Ltd
Goal Lane, Beccles, Suffolk NR34 9QE
Tel: (01502) 712884 *Fax:* (01502) 717003
Key Personnel
Man Dir: Alex Evans
Sales Dir: David C Browne *Tel:* (01502) 712884, Ext 240
Founded: 1803
Business from Other Countries: 1%

Cradley Print Ltd
Chester Rd, Cradley Heath, Warley, W Midlands B64 6AB
Tel: (01384) 414100 *Fax:* (01384) 414102
Key Personnel
Man Dir: Chris Jordan
Business from Other Countries: 7%
Branch Office(s)
Quadcolor Repro

Goldshield Communications Ltd
Banners Bldg, Attercliffe Rd, Sheffield S9 3QS
Tel: (0114) 2431000 *Fax:* (0114) 2433000
Key Personnel
Man Dir & Overseas-Special Projects: Sandra Potesta *E-mail:* sandra@goldcom.co.uk
Technical & Production: Stefano Potesta
Founded: 1984
Business from Other Countries: 40%

Hammond Bindery Ltd
Subsidiary of The Charlesworth Group
Flanshaw Way, Wakefield, West Yorks WF2 9LP
Tel: (01924) 369598 *Fax:* (01924) 364108
Key Personnel
Man Dir: Steve Allen
Sales: Brian Quarmby
Founded: 1972

Headley Brothers Ltd
Invicta Press, Queens Rd, Ashford, Kent TN24 8HH
Tel: (01233) 623131 *Fax:* (01233) 622704; (01233) 612345
Key Personnel
Man Dir: Roger Pitt *E-mail:* rpitt@headley.co.uk
Commercial Dir: Jon Pitt
Sales Dir: Bruce Finn
Founded: 1881
Business from Other Countries: 5%
Branch Office(s)
Headley Brothers Ltd, 3rd Floor West, High Holborn House, 52-54 High Holborn, London WC1V 6LR

Hobbs The Printers Ltd
Brunel Rd, Totton, Hants SO40 3WX
Tel: (023) 8066 4800 *Fax:* (023) 8066 4801
E-mail: htp@tcp.co.uk
Key Personnel
Sales Manager: John Eacott *E-mail:* j.eacott@hobbs.uk.com
Commercial Dir: Terry Ozanne
Founded: 1884
Business from Other Countries: 4%

Ikon Document Services Ltd
Subsidiary of Microgen Holdings Plc
19 The Business Centre, Molly Millars Lane, Wokingham Berks RG41 2QY
Tel: (0118) 9770510 *Fax:* (0118) 9770513
E-mail: marcb@ikonds.co.uk
Key Personnel
Man Dir: Dave Weller
Business Development Dir: Aaron Biggs
Founded: 1972
Business from Other Countries: 40%
Branch Office(s)
Microgen City Park Watchmead, Welwyn Garden City, Herts AL7 1LT

Multiplex Medway Ltd
Gleaming Wood Dr, Lordswood Industrial Estate, Walderslade, Kent ME5 8XT
Tel: (01634) 684371 *Fax:* (01634) 683840
Key Personnel
Dir: Jon Chandler
Sales Manager: Paul Adson

Page Bros Ltd (Norwich)
Subsidiary of Milex Ltd
Mile Cross Lane, Norwich NR6 6SA
Tel: (01603) 429141 *Fax:* (01603) 485126
E-mail: sco@pagesales.co.uk
Key Personnel
Man Dir: David Armstrong
Founded: 1750
Business from Other Countries: 20%
Branch Office(s)
105-A Euston St, London NW1 2ET *Tel:* (020) 7383 2212 *Fax:* (020) 7383 4145

Pillar Publications Ltd
Division of Pullar Publications Ltd
45 Woodland Grove, Weybridge, Surrey KT13 9EQ
Tel: (01932) 847629 *Fax:* (01932) 821610
E-mail: hu@bjhc.demon.co.uk

UNITED KINGDOM

Key Personnel
Owner: Dr H de Glanville
Founded: 1981
Business from Other Countries: 10%

Antony Rowe Ltd
Division of Rexam Plc
14 Portman Rd, Reading, Berks RG30 1LZ
Tel: (0118) 9503911 *Fax:* (0118) 9505776
Key Personnel
Chief Executive: Ralph Bell
Sales Manager: Andrew Copley
Founded: 1897
Business from Other Countries: 10%

TMS Development International Ltd
128 Holgate Rd, York YO24 4FL
Tel: (01904) 641640 *Fax:* (01904) 640076
E-mail: enquiry@tmsdi.com
Web Site: www.tmsdi.com
Key Personnel
Man Dir: Catherine Hick
Marketing Manager: Pat Anslow
Founded: 1989
Business from Other Countries: 30%

Turnaround Publisher Services
Unit 3, Olympia Trading Estate, Coburg Rd, London N22 6TZ
Tel: (020) 8829 3009 *Fax:* (020) 8881 5088
E-mail: turnuk@aol.com
Key Personnel
Man Dir: Bill Godber *E-mail:* bill@turnaround-uk.com
Marketing Dir: Claire Thompson *E-mail:* claire@turnaround-uk.com
Founded: 1984

Watkiss Automation Ltd
Subsidiary of The Watkiss Group
One Blaydon Rd, Middlefield Industrial Estate, Sandy, Beds SG19 1RZ
Tel: (01767) 682177 *Fax:* (01767) 691769
E-mail: info@watkiss.com
Key Personnel
Technical Dir: M Watkiss
Founded: 1959
Business from Other Countries: 5%

John Wilson Booksales
One High St, Princes Risborough, Bucks HP27 0AG
Tel: (01844) 275927 *Fax:* (01844) 274402
E-mail: jw@jwbs.co.uk
Key Personnel
Contact: John S Wilson
Founded: 1982

United States

A-R Editions Inc
8551 Research Way, Suite 180, Middleton, WI 53562
Tel: 608-836-9000 *Fax:* 608-831-8200
E-mail: info@areditions.com
Web Site: www.areditions.com
Key Personnel
Pres & CEO: Patrick Wall
Dir, Sales & Mktg: James L Zychowicz
  E-mail: james.zychowicz@areditions.com
Founded: 1962
Business from Other Countries: 10%

AWT World Trade
4321 N Knox, Chicago, IL 60641
Tel: 773-777-7100 *Fax:* 773-777-0909
E-mail: sale@awt-gpi.com
Web Site: www.awt-gpi.com
Key Personnel
Pres: Michael Green
Business from Other Countries: 25%
Sales Office(s): AWT World Trade Europe BV, Antennestr 86, 1322 AS Almere, Netherlands *Tel:* (036) 5463070 *Fax:* (036) 5463071
  E-mail: info@awt-europe.com
8984 NW 105 Way, Medley, FL *Tel:* 305-887-7500 *Fax:* 305-887-2300
Warehouse: AWT World Trade Europe BV, Antennestr 86, 1322 AS, Almere, Netherlands *Tel:* (036) 5463070 *Fax:* (036 5463071
  E-mail: info@awt-europe.com

Blaze International Productions Inc
225 W 35 St, Suite 1100, New York, NY 10001
Tel: 212-967-7501 *Fax:* 212-967-7551
Key Personnel
Pres: Eugene Sanchez *Tel:* ext 222 *E-mail:* e.sanchez@blazeint.com
Founded: 1990
Business from Other Countries: 80%
Branch Office(s)
Flat 12 18/F, Kodak House, Phase 2, No 39 Healthy Street, North Point, Hong Kong
  Tel: 2967 9360 *Fax:* 2967 1800

BookBuilders New York Ltd
353 Strawtown Rd, New City, NY 10956
Tel: 845-639-5316 *Fax:* 845-639-5318
Web Site: www.mcabooks.com
Key Personnel
Pres: Martin Cook *E-mail:* martin@mcabooks.com
Founded: 1977
Business from Other Countries: 60%

The Cleveland Vibrator Co
2828 Clinton Ave, Cleveland, OH 44113
Tel: 216-241-7157 *Fax:* 216-241-3480
E-mail: cvc@clevelandvibrators.com
Web Site: www.clevelandvibrator.com
Key Personnel
Gen Sales Mgr: Jack Steinbuch
Mktg Spec: Sue Kobylski
Founded: 1923
Business from Other Countries: 12%

Martin Cook Associates Ltd
353 Strawtown Rd, New City, NY 10956
Tel: 845-639-5316 *Fax:* 845-639-5318
E-mail: mcanewcity@aol.com
Web Site: www.mcabooks.com
Key Personnel
Pres: Martin Cook *E-mail:* mcanewcity@aol.com
Founded: 1977
Business from Other Countries: 15%
Membership(s): Bookbinders Guild of New York

Crathern Machinery Group Inc
879 Maple St, Contoocook, NH 03229-3319
Mailing Address: PO Box 187, Contoocook, NH 03229-0187
Tel: 603-746-4111 *Fax:* 603-746-4172
E-mail: info@crathern.com
Web Site: www.crathern.com
Business from Other Countries: 40%

D & K Group
1795 Commerce, Elk Grove Village, IL 60007
Tel: 847-956-0160 *Fax:* 847-956-8214
E-mail: info@dkgroup.net
Web Site: www.dkgroup.com
Key Personnel
Pres: Karl Singer
VP, Sales & Mktg: Marge Hayes
Mktg Communs Coord: Holli Hagene
  E-mail: holli.hagene@dkgroup.net
Founded: 1979
Business from Other Countries: 15%

MANUFACTURING SERVICES

Desktop Miracles Inc
112 S Main, PMB 294, Stowe, VT 05672
Tel: 802-253-7900 *Fax:* 802-253-1900
Web Site: www.desktopmiracles.com
Key Personnel
Pres & CEO: Barry T Kerrigan *E-mail:* barry@desktopmiracles.com
Founded: 1994
Business from Other Countries: 10%

Express Media Corp
1419 Donelson Pike, Nashville, TN 37217
Tel: 615-360-6400 *Fax:* 615-360-3140
E-mail: info@expressmedia.com
Web Site: www.expressmedia.com
Key Personnel
Pres: Andrew Cameron
Founded: 1996
Business from Other Countries: 10%

Fairfield Marketing Group Inc
Subsidiary of FMG Inc
830 Sport Hill Rd, Easton, CT 06612-1250
Tel: 203-261-5585; 203-261-5568 *Fax:* 203-261-0884
E-mail: ffjmktgrp@aol.com
Key Personnel
CEO & Pres: Edward P Washchilla
VP, Fin: Pamela L Johnson
VP, Fulfillment: Jason Paul Miller *Tel:* 203-261-5585 ext 203
Founded: 1987
Business from Other Countries: 10%
Membership(s): BBB; DMA

Fritz Companies Inc, see UPS Freight Services

Hamilton Printing Co
22 Hamilton Way, Castleton-on-Hudson, NY 12033
Tel: 518-732-4491 *Fax:* 518-732-7714
Key Personnel
Pres: Brian F Payne
VP, Mfg: William E Greenawalt
VP, Fin: Michael H Hart
Prod Mgr: Fred Mitchell
Sales Rep: Scott Payne; Michael C Rosenhack
  E-mail: miker@hpcbook.com; Stephen H Feuer
Founded: 1912
Business from Other Countries: 10%
Membership(s): BMI

IBT Global Ltd, see Integrated Book Technology Inc

Integrated Book Technology Inc
Division of The IBT Group
18 Industrial Park Rd, Troy, NY 12180
Tel: 518-271-5117 *Fax:* 518-266-9422
E-mail: mail@integratedbooktechnology.com
Web Site: www.integratedbooktechnology.com
Key Personnel
CEO & Pres: John R Paeglow *E-mail:* johnp@integratedbook.com
VP, Fin: Richard Donovan *E-mail:* rickd@integratedbook.com
VP & Chief Technol Officer: William Clockel
  E-mail: billc@integratedbook.com
VP, Sales & Mktg: Robert Lindberg
  E-mail: bobl@integratedbook.com
Dir, Info Technol: Michael Whalen
  E-mail: mikew@integratedbook.com
Regl Sales: Tim Knickerbocker *E-mail:* timk@integratedbook.com
Contact: Beth Boniface
Cust Serv Mgr: James Klein *E-mail:* jimk@integratedbook.com
Founded: 1991
Business from Other Countries: 20%
Membership(s): BMI

InterPost North America
Affiliate of TNT Post Group Co
200 Garden City Plaza, Suite 400, Garden City, NY 11530
E-mail: exo@tnt.com
Web Site: www.tnt.com
Key Personnel
Pres: Curtis Watson
Founded: 1958
Business from Other Countries: 100%

Lenz & Riecker Inc
690 Union Blvd, Totowa, NJ 07512
Tel: 973-256-2456 *Fax:* 973-256-3433; 973-256-2459
E-mail: info@l-r.com
Web Site: www.l-r.com
Key Personnel
Pres: Steven Riecker
CFO: Barry Levinson
VP, Sales: G Gilrain
Founded: 1917
Business from Other Countries: 20%

Linick International Inc
Division of The Linick Group Inc
Linick Bldg, 7 Putter Lane, Middle Island, NY 11953-0102
Mailing Address: PO Box 102, Middle Island, NY 11953-0102
Tel: 631-924-3888
E-mail: linickgrp@att.net
Web Site: www.lgroup.addr.com; www.linickgroup.com
Key Personnel
Chmn & CEO: Dr Andrew S Linick
Treas: Marvin Glickman
Exec VP: Roger Dextor
Founded: 1972
Business from Other Countries: 30%

LK Litho
Division of The Linick Group Inc
Linick Bldg, 7 Putter Lane, Middle Island, NY 11953-0102
Tel: 631-924-3888
E-mail: linickgrp@att.net
Web Site: www.lgroup.addr.com; www.linickgroup.com
Key Personnel
VP: Roger Dextor
Founded: 1968
Business from Other Countries: 20%

Marrakech Express Inc
720 Wesley Ave, No 10, Tarpon Springs, FL 34689
Tel: 727-942-2218 *Fax:* 727-937-4758
E-mail: print@marrak.com
Web Site: www.marrak.com
Key Personnel
CEO: Peter Henzell
Prodn Mgr: Steen Sigmund

Sales/Estimator: Shirley Copperman
Founded: 1976
Business from Other Countries: 10%

Mazer Publishing Services
Division of The Mazer Corporation
6680 Poe Ave, Dayton, OH 45414
Tel: 937-264-2600 *Fax:* 937-264-2624
E-mail: info@mazer.com
Web Site: www.mazer.com
Key Personnel
Pres: William Franklin *E-mail:* bill_franklin@mazer.com
Exec VP: Ken Fultz *E-mail:* ken_fultz@mazer.com
Founded: 1964
Business from Other Countries: 10%
Branch Office(s)
2460 Sand Lake Rd, Orlando, FL 32809, Bryan Blakley *Tel:* 407-859-5552 *Fax:* 407-859-0643 *E-mail:* bryan_blakley@mazer.com
224 Lexington Ave, Fox River Grove, IL 60021, Dennis Bowman *Tel:* 847-639-1555 *Fax:* 847-639-1562 *E-mail:* dennis_bowman@mazer.com
22 Lehigh Rd, Wellesley, MA 02181, Ken Leahy *Tel:* 781-237-4112 *Fax:* 781-431-6184 *E-mail:* ken_leahy@mazer.com
22 Laurel Place, Upper Montclair, NJ 07043, John Martel *Tel:* 973-744-4320 *Fax:* 973-745-5608 *E-mail:* john_martel@mazer.com
3081 Glenmere Ct, Kettering, OH 45440, Mark Brewer *Tel:* 937-299-5746 *Fax:* 937-299-5761 *E-mail:* mark_brewer@mazer.com
363 Porter Rd, Bishop, TX 78602, Deborah Van-Landingham *Tel:* 512-303-9758 *Fax:* 512-303-9791
Membership(s): BMI

Regent Publishing Services
9327 Rambler Dr, St Louis, MO 63123
Tel: 314-631-7581 *Fax:* 314-638-5113
E-mail: regentstl@aol.com
Key Personnel
Sales Dir: Carol A Davis-Tierney
Mktg Dir: James J Tierney
Sales Assoc: Julia Polson
Founded: 1985
Business from Other Countries: 100%

Taylor Publishing Co
1550 W Mockingbird Lane, Dallas, TX 75235
Tel: 214-819-8100 *Fax:* 214-630-1852
E-mail: web@taylorpub.com
Web Site: www.taylorpub.com
Key Personnel
Pres: Dave Fiore
Dir, Fine Books & Div Sales Mgr: Jay Love
Dir, Mktg: Mike Taylor
Founded: 1939
Business from Other Countries: 10%

Times Publishing Group
Division of Times Publishing Ltd/Singapore

99 White Plains Rd, Tarrytown, NY 10591
Tel: 914-366-9888 *Fax:* 914-366-9898
Web Site: www.tpl.com.sg
Key Personnel
Cust Serv Exec: Bonnie Stone *E-mail:* bstone@marshallcavendish.com
Sales Mgr: Suresh Kumar *E-mail:* skumar@marshallcavendish.com
Founded: 1965
Business from Other Countries: 90%

Tobias Associates Inc
50 Industrial Dr, Ivyland, PA 18974-0347
Tel: 215-322-1500 *Fax:* 215-322-1504
E-mail: tobias@densitometer.com
Web Site: www.densitometer.com
Key Personnel
Pres: Philip Tobias
Adv Mgr: Robin Crowley
VP: Charlotte Tobias
Founded: 1960
Business from Other Countries: 10%

UPS Freight Services
Formerly Fritz Companies Inc
150-20 132 Ave, Jamaica, NY 11434
Tel: 718-481-4400 *Fax:* 718-528-4191
Key Personnel
Regional Mgr: Ed Teta *E-mail:* ed.teta@fritz.com
Founded: 1933
Business from Other Countries: 50%
Warehouse: 365 Clearview Ave, Edison, NJ 08818 *Tel:* 908-225-0079 *Fax:* 908-225-1178

Fred Weidner & Daughter Printers
15 Maiden Lane, Suite 1505, New York, NY 10038
Tel: 212-964-8676 *Fax:* 212-964-8677
E-mail: info@fwdprinters.com
Web Site: www.fwdprinters.com
Key Personnel
Contact: Frederick Weidner, III
Pres: Cynthia Weidner *E-mail:* cynthia@fwdprinters.com
Founded: 1860
Business from Other Countries: 25%

Uruguay

Barreiro y Ramos SA
Juan Carlos Gomez, 1430, Montevideo 11000
Tel: (02) 986621
Telex: 23901PB.CVJA.UY *Cable:* BAREIRAMOS
Key Personnel
President: Gaston Barreiro
Vice President: Guzman Barreiro
Founded: 1837
Business from Other Countries: 10%

Book Trade Information

Book Clubs

Austria

Deutsche Buch-Gemeinschaft C A Koch's Verlag Nachfolger
Vivenotgasse 2, 1120 Vienna
Tel: (01) 8123730 *Fax:* (01) 811024
Telex: 31405
Branch Office(s)
Deutsche Buch-Gemeinschaft C A Koch's Verlag Nachfolge, Germany

Buchgemeinschaft Donauland Kremayr & Scheriau
Niederhofstr 37, 1121 Vienna
Tel: (01) 81102297 *Fax:* (01) 81102315
Telex: 131405

Buchgemeinschaft Donauland Kremayr & Scheriau, see Buchgemeinschaft Donauland Kremayr & Scheriau

Brazil

Circulo do Livro SA
Alameda Ministro Rocha de Azeredo 346, 01410 Sao Paulo
Tel: (011) 8513644 *Fax:* (011) 2827273
Telex: 31747 *Cable:* Cirlivro
Key Personnel
Man Dir: Rene Cesar Xavier dos Santos
Editorial Dir: Esnider Pizzo
Owned by: Bertelsmann AG, Germany; Abril SA Cultural e Industrial

Editora Universidade De Brasilia
SCS Rd 02 Bloco "C" No 78 Ed OK, 1, 2 & 3 Andares, 70300-500 Brasilia DF
Tel: (061) 2266874 *Fax:* (061) 2255611
E-mail: editora@unb.br *Cable:* UNIVERBRASILIA EDITORA
Established: 1961
Owned by: Fundacao Universidade de Brasilia

Chile

Clubs de Lectores Andres Bello
Ave Ricardo Lyon 946, Casilla de Correo, Providencia, Santiago
Tel: (02) 2049900; (02) 2049901 *Fax:* (02) 2253600
Telex: 240901 Edjur
Key Personnel
General Manager: Julio Serrano Lamas
Commercial Manager: Marta Mallea Araya
Established: 1947
There are two clubs: one for children (membership 20,000), the other for adults (membership 25,000).
Owned by: Editorial Andres Bello/Editorial Juridica de Chile

Colombia

Ciirculo de Lectores SA
Calle 57 No 6-35, Apdo Aereo 52111, Santafe de Bogota
Tel: 2173211; 2177720 *Fax:* 2178157
Telex: 41255 *Cable:* CIRLEC
Key Personnel
Dir: Eduardo Polo, Sr
Marketing: Rafael Vargas
Established: 1970
Number of Members: 650,000
Owned by: Casa Editorial El Tiempo

Czech Republic

ERB
Vaclavske nam 17, 11258 Prague 1
Tel: (02) 24009111 *Fax:* (02) 2320989
Telex: 121442 *Cable:* 1106
Established: 1968
Number of Members: 67,835
Owned by: Prace

Friends of Antiquity
Na Florenci 3, 11303 Prague 1
Tel: (02) 24811549; (02) 24225143 *Fax:* (02) 24226026
Key Personnel
Manager: Stefan Szerynski
Established: 1969
Number of Members: 6,000
Owned by: Nakladatelstvi Svoboda

KM C
c/o Albatros, Truhlarska 9, 11000 Prague 1
Tel: (02) 24810704; (02) 2311156; (02) 2314289 *Fax:* (02) 24810850
Young Readers' Club.
Owned by: Albatros

Odeon Buch- und Phonoclub
Narodni tr 36, 11000 Prague 1
Tel: (02) 264100 *Fax:* (02) 24225254
E-mail: odeon@comp.cz
Key Personnel
Editorial Dir: Dr Jiri Nasinec
Established: 1953
Subjects: Fiction, Art
Number of Members: 250,000
Owned by: Odeon; nakladatelstvi krasne literatury a umeni

Readers Club of Svoboda
Na Florenci 3, 11303 Prague 1
Tel: (02) 24811549; (02) 24225143 *Fax:* (02) 24226026
Key Personnel
Manager: Stefan Szerynski
Established: 1960
Provides worldwide mail order service.
Number of Members: 13,000
Owned by: Nakladatelstvi Svoboda

Denmark

Bogklubben 12 Boget A/S
Frederiksborggade 1, 1360 Copenhagen K
Tel: 33695050 *Fax:* 33695051
E-mail: b12b@bogklubben-12-boget.dk
Key Personnel
Man Dir: Jette Juliusson
Established: 1988
Subjects: General nonfiction
Owned by: Lindhardt & Ringhof I/S, Munksgaard

Egmont Wangel A/S
Gerdasgade 37, DK 250 Valby
Tel: 36156600 *Fax:* 36441162
Web Site: www.bogklubber.dk
Established: 1946
Subjects: Commercial Fiction, Children's Books, Management, True Stories
Book Club(s): Anders Ands Bogklub; Bogsamleren; Barbie Bogklubben; Management Bogklubben; Paperback Bogklubben; Virkelighedens Verden; Peter Plys Bogklubben; Anders Ands Bogklub; Bogsamleren; Barbie Bogklubben; Management Bogklubben; Paperback Bogklubben; Virkelighedens Verden; Peter Plys Bogklubben
Parent Company: Egmont

Fiction Factory International Ltd
Klareboderne 3, 1001 Copenhagen K
Tel: (043) 33 75 55 09 *Fax:* (043) 33 75 55 44
Key Personnel
Publisher: Jens Bendtsen *E-mail:* jens_bendtsen@gyldendal.dk
Established: 1987
Subjects: Children's, Adolescent, Adult (in English)
Publication(s): Fiction Factory (materials for teaching of modern languages)
Owned by: Kaleidoscope Publishers Ltd

Denmark

Gyldendals Bornebogklub
Pilestr 51, DK-1001 Copenhagen K
Tel: 33755555 *Fax:* 33755556
Web Site: www.gyldendal.dk
Telex: 15887 gyldal dk *Cable:* GYLDENDALSKE
Owned by: Gyldendal

Gyldendals Bogklub
Klareboderne 3, DK-1001 Copenhagen K
Mailing Address: PO Box 11, 1029 Copenhagen K
Tel: 33110775 *Fax:* 33110323
Web Site: www.glydendal.dk
Telex: 15887 gyldal dk *Cable:* GYLDENDALSKE
Subjects: Fiction, General Nonfiction
Owned by: Gyldendal - Nordisk Forlag A/S

Hernovs Book Club
6, Siljangade, DK-2300 Copenhagen S
Tel: 32963314 *Fax:* 32960446
E-mail: admin@hernov.dk
Owned by: Hernovs Forlag

Samlerens Bogklub
Pilestraede 51, DK-1001 Copenhagen K
Tel: 33128282 *Fax:* 33110323
Telex: 15887 gyldal dk *Cable:* GYLDENDALSKE
Subjects: Fiction, Nonfiction, Political
Owned by: Gyldendalske Boghandel - Nordisk Forlag A/S

Egypt (Arab Republic of Egypt)

Al Ahram Book Club
6, Al-Galaa' St, Cairo
Tel: (02) 748248 *Fax:* (02) 745888
Telex: 20185-92544
Owned by: Al Ahram Establishment

Finland

Aika Oy Kristilliset Kirjat (Aika Oy Christian Books)
Heikkilantie 177, 42700 Keuruu
Mailing Address: PO Box 99, Keuruu 42701
Tel: (014) 7514751 *Fax:* (014) 7514757
E-mail: aika@aikaoy.fi
Web Site: www.aikaoy.fi
Key Personnel
President & Marketing Dir: Asko Kinnunen
 Tel: (014) 7514750 *E-mail:* asko.kinnunen@aikaoy.fi
Publishing Manager: Outi Katto *Tel:* (014) 7514731 *E-mail:* outi.katto@aikaoy.fi
Established: 1995
Christian books, music & periodicals.
Number of Members: 4,000
Owned by: Ristin Voitto ry
Imprints: Hengellinen Laulukirja; Raamatun Tietosarja

Hengellinen Laulukirja, *imprint of* Aika Oy Kristilliset Kirjat

Raamatun Tietosarja, *imprint of* Aika Oy Kristilliset Kirjat

Suuri Suomalainen Kirjakerho Oy (Great Finnish Book Club Ltd)
Maistraatinportti 1, Helsinki 00240
Mailing Address: PO Box 13, FIN-00241, Helsinki
Tel: (09) 147 711 *Fax:* (09) 1496 221
E-mail: sskk.palaute@kuvalehdet.fi
Web Site: www.sskk.fi
Key Personnel
President: Pauli A Leimio *Tel:* (09) 1566 316
 E-mail: pauli.leimio@kuvalehdet.fi
Established: 1969
Book Club.
Number of Members: 280,000
Owned by: Otava Kustannusosakeyhtioe, Uudenmaankatu 10, Helsinki 00120
Parent Company: Yhtyneet Kuvalehdet Oy (United Magazines Ltd)
Ultimate Parent Company: Otava-Kuvalehdet Oy

Uudet Kirjat
Bulevardi 12, 00120 Helsinki
Mailing Address: PO Box 222, 00121 Helsinki
Tel: (09) 61681 *Fax:* (09) 6168560
Telex: 122644 Wsoy
Key Personnel
Contact: Raija Hynynen
Established: 1980
The New Books.
Number of Members: 110,000
Owned by: Werner Soederstroem Osakeyhtio (WSOY)

France

L'Amitie par le Livre
BP 1031, 25001 Besancon cedex
Tel: (03) 81820894 *Fax:* (03) 81820894
First book club founded in France in 1930, by teaching profession. It is non-profitmaking & run by voluntary effort.
Owned by: L'Amitie par le Livre

Club du Livre SA
28 rue Fortuny, M-75017 Paris
Tel: (01) 47638055 *Fax:* (01) 44404865
Key Personnel
Man Dir: Philippe Lebaud
Subjects: Art, De Luxe Editions

Jean Grassin Editeur, *imprint of* Poetes Presents

Nouveau Cercle Parisien du Livre
6 rue Bonaparte, 75006 Paris
Tel: (01) 43547195 *Fax:* (01) 40518288
Key Personnel
President: Alain de Ricou
Club is associated with publisher Galerie Lucie Weill.
Subjects: Olivier Debre Illustrations, Edmond Jabese Texts
Owned by: Au Pont des Arts; Galerie Lucie Weill

PEMF, see Publications de l'Ecole Moderne Francaise (PEMF)

Poetes Presents
Pl de Port-en-Dro, 56342 Carnac Cedex
Mailing Address: BP 75, 56342 Carnac Cedex
Tel: (02) 97529363 *Fax:* (02) 97528390
Key Personnel
President: Jean Grassin
Established: 1957

Subjects: Poetry
Book Club(s): Club de Selection des Meilleurs Livre de Poesie; Club de Selection des Meilleurs Livre de Poesie
Number of Members: 1,500
Owned by: Jean Grassin Editeur
Imprints: Jean Grassin Editeur

Publications de l'Ecole Moderne Francaise (PEMF)
Parc d'Activitites de l'Argile, Voie E, 06376 Mouans Sartoux Cedex
Tel: (016) 92921757 *Fax:* (016) 92921804 *Cable:* PEMF
This company runs five book clubs supplying series of books for children: aged 8-12 (BTJ), aged 10-15 (BT), aged over 15 (BT2); for teachers (L'Educateur), and for audiovisual supplies (BT Son).

Gerard Varin, see L'Amitie par le Livre

Germany

Bertelsmann Club
Postfach 1109, 33339 Rheda-Wiedenbrueck
Tel: (05242) 914358; (05242) 914272; (0542) 9146920 *Fax:* (05242) 916999
Telex: 931149
Key Personnel
Contact: Dr Stephan Kruemmer
Established: 1950
Number of Members: 5,600,000
Owned by: Bertelsmann AG
Branch Office(s)
290 Club-Filialen/Bertelsmann Club

Buchergilde Gutenberg
Untermainkai 66, 60329 Frankfurt am Main
Mailing Address: Postfach 160165, 60064 Frankfurt am Main
Tel: (069) 2739080 *Fax:* (069) 27390824
Owned by: Buechergilde Gutenberg Verlagsgesellschaft mbH

Deutscher Buchkreis
Am Apfelberg 18, 72076 Tuebingen
Mailing Address: Postfach 1629, 72006 Tuebingen
Tel: (07071) 96590 *Fax:* (07071) 965965
Owned by: Grabert-Verlag Wigbert Grabert

EBG Verlags GmbH
Stuttgarter Str 161, 70806 Kornwestheim
Mailing Address: PO Box 1440, 70798 Kornwestheim
Tel: (07154) 1340
Telex: 17715410 ebege d
Established: 1950
Number of Members: 1,300,000
Owned by: Bertelsmann AG

Europaeische Bildungsgemeinschaft Verlags GmbH, see EBG Verlags GmbH

Herder-Buchgemeinde
Hermann-Herder-Str 4, 79104 Freiburg
Tel: (0761) 27170 *Fax:* (0761) 2717520
Established: 1952
Subjects: Fiction & poetry, picture books
Owned by: Verlag Herder GmbH & Co KG

Wissenschaftliche Buchgesellschaft
Postfach 100110, 64201 Darmstadt
Tel: (06151) 33080 *Fax:* (06151) 3308208
E-mail: service@wbg-darmstadt.de
Established: 1949

Scientific Book Society.
Subjects: 25 Scientific Fields, 2500 titles available
Number of Members: 140,000

Greece

Sport & Hobby Book Club
19 lperidou, GR-10558 Athens
Mailing Address: PO Box 30564, GR-10033 Athens
Tel: (01) 3234217 *Fax:* (01) 3232082
E-mail: hcp@photography.gr
Key Personnel
President: Stavros Moressopoulos *E-mail:* mores.s@altavista.net
Established: 1986
Subjects: Photography, Sports, Hobbies, How-to, Music, Travel, Wine & Spirits, Animals
Number of Members: 780
Owned by: Moressopoulos SA Organizing, Publishing, Advertising, Education

Iceland

The AB Book Club (BAB)
Nybylavegur 16, 200 Kopavogur
Tel: 5643170 *Fax:* 5643190
Key Personnel
President: Fridrik Fridriksson
Editor: Bjarni Thorsfeinsson
Established: 1974
Number of Members: 8,500
Owned by: AB Almenna bokafelagid

BAB, see The AB Book Club (BAB)

Gulur Raudur Grenn og Blar Childrens Bookclub
Sidumula 7-9, 108 Reykjavik
Tel: 5102525 *Fax:* 5102525
E-mail: klubbar@mm.is
Key Personnel
Contact: Thorhildur Gardosdottir
Number of Members: 10,000
Owned by: MM Mal og menning

Heima er Bezt Book Club
Armuli 23, 108 Reykjavik
Mailing Address: Postholf 8427, 128 Reykjavik
Tel: 5531599; 5882400 *Fax:* 5888994
Key Personnel
Editor: G Baldvinsson
Owned by: Skjaldborg Ltd

The MAB Cookery Book Club
Nybylavegur 16, 200 Kopavogur
Tel: 5643170 *Fax:* 5643190
Established: 1984
Number of Members: 11,500
Owned by: AB Almenna bokafelagid

MM Mal og menning
Laugavegi 18, 101 Reykjavik
Mailing Address: Postholf 392, 121 Reykjavik
Tel: 5152500 *Fax:* 5152505
E-mail: thorai@mm.is
Web Site: www.mm.is
Key Personnel
Man Dir: Sigurdur Svavarsson
Editorial Dir: Halldor Gudmundsson
Established: 1937
Number of Members: 24,000
Publication(s): *Booksellers*

Uglan Islenski Kiljuklubburinn
Sidumula 7-9, 108 Reykjavik
Tel: 5102525
Paperback Book Club.
Number of Members: 10,000
Owned by: MM Mal og menning

Particip Verold
Njoervasundisa 15a, 104 Reykjavik
Tel: 5688433 *Fax:* 5688142
Owned by: Fjolvi; bokautgafa

India

Anand Book Club
c/o Vision Books Pvt Ltd, 24 Feroze Gandhi Rd, Lajpat Nagar-III, New Delhi 110024
Key Personnel
Dir: Sudhir Malhotra
Number of Members: 22,000
Owned by: Vision Books Pvt Ltd

Book Lovers Club
A-59 Okhla Industrial Area, Phase II, New Delhi 110020
Tel: (011) 6910050; (011) 6916209 *Fax:* (011) 6331241
E-mail: ghai@nde.vsnl.net.in *Cable:* PAPERBACKS
Established: 1986
Number of Members: 1,076
Owned by: Sterling Publishers Pvt Ltd

DC Book Club
Good Shepherd St, Kottayam, Kerala 686001
Mailing Address: PO Box 212, Kottayam, Kerala 686001
Tel: 0481 3114; 0481 3226; 0481 8214
Established: 1975
Number of Members: 2,500
Owned by: D C Books, Printers, Publishers & Booksellers

Orient Book Club
c/o Vision Books Pvt Ltd, 1590 Madarsa Rd, Kashmere Gate, Delhi 110 006
Fax: (011) 386-2935
E-mail: orientpbk@vsnl.com
Key Personnel
Dir: Sudhir Malhotra
Established: 1979
Subjects: Cookery, How-to, Fiction, Health & Fitness, Self Help, Children's Books, Investment Personal Finance
Number of Members: 40,000
Owned by: Vision Books Pvt Ltd
Parent Company: Vision Books Pvt Ltd

Star Publishers' Distributors
4/5B Asaf Ali Rd, New Delhi 110002
Tel: (011) 3274874; (011) 3268651; (011) 3261696 *Fax:* (011) 3273335; (011) 6481565
E-mail: del.starpub@axcess.net.in *Cable:* STAR PUBLIS
Key Personnel
President: Mr Amar Nath Varma
Established: 1990
Subjects: Books in English, Hindi, and other Indian Languages Linguistics, Social Sciences, Children's Books
Number of Members: 15,000

Indonesia

Himpunan Masyarakat Pencinta Buku
Jin Hasanuddin 9, Bandung, Jawa Barat
Tel: (022) 470821; (022) 470287
Established: 1979
The Association of Bibliophiles.
Number of Members: 14,300
Owned by: Eresco PT

KPI
Jln Dr Wahidin 1, Jakarta
Mailing Address: PO Box 29, Jakarta
Tel: (021) 361701; (021) 41701
Telex: 45905 Prumbp la
Established: 1982
Klub Perpustakaan Indonesia.
Number of Members: 4,500

Ireland

Doctrine & Life Book Club
42 Parnell Sq, Dublin 1
Tel: (01) 8721611 *Fax:* (01) 8731760
Key Personnel
Contact: Bernard Treaum
Number of Members: 4,000
Owned by: Dominican Publications

Religious Life Review Book Club
42 Parnell Sq, Dublin 1
Tel: (01) 8721611 *Fax:* (01) 8731760
Number of Members: 4,000
Owned by: Dominican Publications

Scripture in Church Book Club
42 Parnell Sq, Dublin 1
Tel: (01) 8721611 *Fax:* (01) 8731760
Number of Members: 6,000
Owned by: Dominican Publications

Israel

Ma'ariv Book Guild (Sifriat Ma'ariv)
3A Yoni Natanyahu St, Or-Yehuda 60376
Tel: (03) 5333333 *Fax:* (03) 5333619
Telex: 033735 *Cable:* MA'ARIV TELAVIV
Key Personnel
Dir: Yitzhak Kfir
Established: 1979
Owned by: Ma'ariv Book Guild

Italy

Isper Club
Corso Dante 122, 10126 Turin
Tel: (011) 6647803 *Fax:* (011) 6670829
Key Personnel
Contact: Grosso Marco Actis
Owned by: ISPER

Edi Thule Club
Via Gravina 95, I-90139 Palermo
Tel: (091) 323699
Owned by: Edizioni Thule
Imprints: Thule Spiritualita E Letteratura

Thule Spiritualita E Letteratura, *imprint of* Edi Thule Club

Japan

Fukuinkan Ehon Library
c/o Fukuinkan Shoten Publishers Inc, 6-3 Hon-Komagome 6 chome, Bunkyo-ku, Tokyo 113
Tel: (03) 39421226 *Fax:* (03) 39429691
Telex: J33597 Aab Forchild *Cable:* FUKUINKANSHOTEN TOKYO
Subjects: Children's Books
Owned by: Fukuinkan Shoten Publishers Inc

Kodansha Disney Children's Book Club
12-21 Otowa 2-chome, Bunkyo-ku, Tokyo 112
Tel: (03) 39446491 *Fax:* (03) 39446323
Subjects: Children's Books
Owned by: Kodan-Sha International

Bookclub Psyche
2-5 Kami-Takaido 1 chome, Suginami-ku, Tokyo 168
Tel: (03) 33290031 *Fax:* (03) 33043822
Subjects: Psychiatry
Owned by: Seiwa Shoten

Mexico

Bertelsmann de Mexico SA
Ave de la Paz No 26, Col San Angel, 01000 Mexico, DF
Tel: (05) 5501620; (05) 5489048
Telex: 1761195 Cileme
Number of Members: 200,000
Owned by: Bertelsmann AG, Germany

Club de Lectores Extemporaneos
Poniente 126-A-400, No 400, Colonia Nueva Vallejo, 07750 Mexico DF
Tel: (05) 5875424; (05) 5878785
Owned by: Editorial Extemporaneos SA

Myanmar

Sarpay Beikman Book Club
529 Merchant St, Rangoon
Tel: (01) 83611
Owned by: Sarpay Beikman Board

Netherlands

ECI voor Boeken en Grammofoonplaten BV
Laanakkerweg 14-18, 4131 PB Vianen Zh
Tel: (03473) 79214 *Fax:* (03471) 79380
Telex: 47449
Book Club(s): Nederlandse Boekenclub; Nederlandse Lezerskring Boek en Plaat BV; Nederlandse Boekenclub; Nederlandse Lezerskring Boek en Plaat BV

Nederlandse Boekenclub
Laanakkerweg 14-18, 413 1EB Vianen Zh
Mailing Address: PO Box 400, 4130 EK Vianen Zh
Tel: (03473) 79214 *Fax:* (03473) 79380
Key Personnel
Manager: A L P Bongaards
Subjects: General Fiction, Nonfiction
Book Club(s): Netherlands Book Club; Netherlands Book Club
Number of Members: 350,000
Owned by: ECI voor Boeken en Platen BV

Nederlandse Lezerskring Boek en Plaat BV
Laanakkerweg 14-18, 413 1EB Vianen Zh
Mailing Address: PO Box 400, 4130 EK Vianen Zh
Tel: (03473) 79214 *Fax:* (03473) 79380
Established: 1966
Number of Members: 500,000
Owned by: ECI voor Boeken en Platen BV

VCL
POB 5018, 8260 GA Kampen
Tel: (038) 3328912 *Fax:* (038) 3327331
Key Personnel
Contact: Mrs M Boltje *Tel:* (038) 3392524
 E-mail: mboltje@kok.nl
Owned by: Uitgeefmaatschappij J H Kok BV

New Zealand

Doubleday New Zealand Ltd, Book Club Division
One Parkway Drive, Mairangi Bay Industrial Estate, Auckland 10
Mailing Address: Private Bag, North Shore Centre, Auckland 9
Tel: (09) 4782846 *Fax:* (09) 4781609
Telex: NZ60589
Operated by Doubleday Australia Pty Ltd, Australia. Ultimate Parent Company: Bertelsmann AG, Germany.
Book Club(s): Book New Zealand; Book of the Month Club; Doubleday Book Club; Doubleday History Book Club; Doubleday Military Book Club; The Literary Guild; Doubleday Children's Book Club; Book New Zealand; Book of the Month Club; Doubleday Book Club; Doubleday History Book Club; Doubleday Military Book Club; The Literary Guild; Doubleday Children's Book Club

Nigeria

Amebo Book Club
PO Box 1970, Ibadan
Owned by: Adebara Publishing House

Onibon-Oje Book Club
Felele Layout, Molete, Ibadan
Mailing Address: PO Box 3109, Ibadan
Tel: (022) 313956
Subjects: Fiction, Drama
Owned by: Onibon-Oje Publishers

Varsity Book Club
11 Central School Rd, Onitsha
Mailing Address: PO Box 386, Onitsha
Tel: (046) 210013
Key Personnel
President: F C Ogbalu
Vice President: S U Ogbalu
Established: 1960
Subjects: Igbo, English Including Primary, Secondary and Tertiary Subjects
Owned by: Varsity Industrial Press
Branch Office(s)
14 Owerri-Orlu Rd, Owerri, Imo State

Norway

Peter Asschenfeldts Bokklubb
Postboks 1755 Vika, 0122 Oslo
Tel: 22429165 *Fax:* 22471098
Telex: 77074
Key Personnel
Manager: Willy Fordet
Established: 1978
Fiction.
Owned by: Hjemmets Bokforlag A/S

Bokklubben Bedre Ledelse
Tordenskioldsgate 6 B, 0055 Oslo
Tel: 22471000 *Fax:* 22471098
E-mail: egmont@egmont.com
Web Site: www.egmont.com
Key Personnel
Publishing Manager: Gerhard Anthun
Established: 1978
Subjects: Management, literature
Owned by: Egmont Hjemmets Bokforlag AS

De norske Bokklubbene A/S
Gullhaug Torg 1, N-0043 Oslo
Tel: 22022000 *Fax:* 22022210
Telex: 74213 Bokkl n
Key Personnel
Vice President: Jon Oestboe
Contact: Aud Norlin
Established: 1961
Subjects: Fiction & nonfiction, children & juvenile
Book Club(s): Den Norske Bokklubben; Bokklubbens Barn; Bokklubben Ekstraboker; Bokklubbens Lyrikkvaennene; Bokklubben Nye Boker; Ungdoms Bokklubben; Bokenes Verden; Dagens Boke; Villmarksklubben; Den Norske Bokklubben; Bokklubbens Barn; Bokklubben Ekstraboker; Bokklubbens Lyrikkvaennene; Bokklubben Nye Boker; Ungdoms Bokklubben; Bokenes Verden; Dagens Boke; Villmarksklubben
Number of Members: 550,000
Owned by: H Aschehoug & Co (W Nygaard) A/S; Gyldendal Norsk Forlag A/S; Tiden Norsk Forlag A/S

Damms Junior Bokklubb
Tordenskioldsgate 6 B, 0055 Oslo
Tel: 22471000 *Fax:* 22471098
E-mail: egmont@egmont.com
Web Site: www.egmont.com
Telex: 77074
Key Personnel
Manager: Willy Fordet
Subjects: Juvenile Fiction
Owned by: Egmont Hjemmets Bokforlag AS

Bokklubben Damms Leselover
Tordenskioldsgate 6 B, 0055 Oslo
Tel: 22471000 *Fax:* 22471098
E-mail: egmont@egmont.com
Web Site: www.egmont.com
Key Personnel
Manager: Willy Fordet
Established: 1978
Fiction.
Owned by: Egmont Hjemmets Bokforlag AS

Disney Junior Bokklubb
Postboks 1755 Vika, 0055 Oslo
Tel: 22471000 *Fax:* 22471098
Key Personnel
Man Dir: Cato Praner
Established: 1978
Subjects: Juvenile Fiction
Owned by: Hjemmets Bokforlag A/S

Donald Duck's Bokklubb
Tordenskioldsgate 6 B, 0055 Oslo
Tel: 22471000 *Fax:* 22471098
E-mail: egmont@egmont.com
Web Site: www.egmont.com
Key Personnel
Publishing Manager: Gerhard Anthun
Established: 1978
Subjects: Juvenile fiction
Owned by: Egmont Hjemmets Bokforlag AS

Bokklubben Feminina
Tordenskioldsgate 6 B, 0055 Oslo
Tel: 22471000 *Fax:* 22471098
Key Personnel
Man Dir: Cato Praner
Subjects: Fiction
Owned by: Egmont Hjemmets Bokforlag AS

Hjemmets Bokklubb
Tordenskioldsgate 6 B, 0055 Oslo
Tel: 22471000 *Fax:* 22471098
E-mail: egmont@egmont.com
Web Site: www.egmont.com
Key Personnel
Man Dir: Cato Praner
Established: 1978
Subjects: Fiction
Owned by: Egmont Hjemmets Bokforlag AS

Bokklubben Ny Krim
Tordenskioldsgate 6 B, 0055 Oslo
Tel: 22471000 *Fax:* 22471098
E-mail: egmont@egmont.com
Web Site: www.egmont.com
Key Personnel
Man Dir: Cato Praner
Established: 1978
Subjects: Crime fiction
Owned by: Egmont Hjemmets Bokforlag A S

Bokklubben Natur og Kultur
Drammensvn 20C, N-0255 Oslo
Mailing Address: PO Box 465 Sentrum, 0105 Oslo
Tel: 22985600 *Fax:* 22985630
Key Personnel
Editor: Hans Tarjei Skaare
Owned by: Grondahl OG Dreyers Forlag AS

De norske Bokklubbene A/S, see De norske Bokklubbene A/S

Philippines

Alemar's Best Sellers Club
Northmall Bldg, Makati Commercial Center, Makati, Metro Manila
Tel: (02) 592617
Established: 1977
Number of Members: 2,400
Owned by: Alemar's (Sibal & Son's Inc)

Portugal

Circulo de Leitores
Rua Eng Paulo de Barras, 22, Bairro de Santa Cruz, 1500 Lisbon
Tel: (021) 709221 *Fax:* (021) 707149
Telex: 18343 cilecl p
Key Personnel
Man Dir: Dr Rui Beja
Editor: Guilhermina Gomes
Established: 1971
Subjects: Fiction, Biography, Juvenile, Encyclopedias, Scientific, Historical, General Nonfiction, Special Editions, Magazines
Number of Members: 500,000
Owned by: Bertelsmann AG, Germany
Branch Office(s)
Lexicultural

Slovakia

Tatran Publishing House
Michalska 9, 81582 Bratislava
Tel: (07) 5335849 *Fax:* (07) 5335777 *Cable:* TATRAN
Key Personnel
Dir: Eva Mladekova
Established: 1947
Subjects: Classical & Modern Fiction & Nonfiction, Children's Books, Books on Art
Owned by: Tatran

Club of Young Readers
Sasinkova 5, 81519 Bratislava
Tel: (07) 5664512; (07) 5664293 *Fax:* (07) 215714
Telex: 093 421
Key Personnel
Dir: Ing Oldrich Polak
Established: 1963
Subjects: Fairy Tales, Original Slovak Literature, Prose, Poetry, Anthologies, Translations of World Literature, Scientific Literature, Critiques
Number of Members: 55,000
Owned by: Mlade leta

South Africa

Eike-Boekklub
Waltpark, 380 Bosman St, Pretoria 0002
Tel: (012) 401 0700 *Fax:* (012) 3255498
E-mail: lapa@atkv.org.za
Key Personnel
Publication & Administrative Officer: Esme Smith
E-mail: esmes@atkv.org.za
Subjects: Fiction Novels
Owned by: Lapa Publishers; Edms Bpk

Keurbiblioteek
PO Box 123, Pretoria 0001
Tel: (012) 401-0700 *Fax:* (012) 3255498
E-mail: lapa@atkv.org.za
Key Personnel
Publication & Administrative Officer: Esme Smith
E-mail: esmes@atkv.org.za
Subjects: Fiction
Owned by: Lapa Publishers (Pty) Ltd
Ultimate Parent Company: ATKV

Klub-Dagbreek
127 Mirn Rd, Newlands, Johannesburg 2092
Tel: (011) 6736725 *Fax:* (011) 6736719
Subjects: Fiction
Owned by: Perskor-uitgewery

New Day Readers Circle
PO Box 1822, Cape Town 8000
Tel: (021) 215540 *Fax:* (021) 4191865
Telex: 526922
Owned by: Lux Verbi

President Boekklub
Waltpark, 380 Bosman St, Pretoria 0002
Mailing Address: PO Box 123, Pretoria 0001
Tel: (012) 401 0700 *Fax:* (012) 3255498
E-mail: lapa@atkv.org.za
Web Site: www.lapauitgewers.org.za
Key Personnel
Publications & Administrative Officer: Esme Smith *E-mail:* esmes@atkv.org.za
Parent Company: Lapa Publishers
Ultimate Parent Company: ATKV

Klub Saffier
127 Mirn Rd, Newlands, Johannesburg 2092
Tel: (011) 6736725 *Fax:* (011) 6736719
Subjects: Fiction
Owned by: Perskor-uitgewery

Treffer-Boekklub
Posbus 123, Pretoria 0001
Tel: (012) 401 0700 *Fax:* (012) 3255498
E-mail: lapa@atkv.org.za
Subjects: Fiction
Owned by: Lapa Publishers (Pty) Ltd
Ultimate Parent Company: ATKV

Klub 707
127 Mirn Rd, Newlands, Johannesburg 2092
Tel: (011) 6736725 *Fax:* (011) 6736719
Subjects: Fiction: especially Suspense, Espionage, Detective, Thrillers (in Afrikaans)
Owned by: Perskor-uitgewery

Spain

Circulo de Lectores SA
Travessera de Gracia, 47-49, 08021 Barcelona
Tel: (093) 3660100 *Fax:* (093) 2002220
Web Site: www.circulolectores.com
Key Personnel
Dir General: Hans Meinke
Literary Dir: Jordi Nadal
Marketing Dir: Bengt Johansson
Financial Dir: Pedro Piella
Established: 1962
Number of Members: 1,540,000
Owned by: Bertelsmann AG, Germany

Sri Lanka

Book Club of the Ministry of Cultural Affairs of Sri Lanka
Transworks House, Colombo 1
Tel: (01) 437328
Owned by: Ministry of Cultural Affairs

Sweden

Allt om Hobbys Publishing Co
Oerby slottsvaeg 21, Stockholm 12021

SWEDEN

Mailing Address: PO Box 90133, Stockholm 12021
Tel: (08) 999333 *Fax:* (08) 998866
Key Personnel
President: Freddy Stenbom *E-mail:* freddy.stenbom@hobby.se
Established: 1966
Publication(s): *Allt om Hobby*
Owned by: Allt om Hobby AB

Barnens Bokklubb
PO Box 45022, 10430 Stockholm 45
Tel: (08) 4570300 *Fax:* (08) 4570331
E-mail: info@raben.se
Key Personnel
Contact: Marianne von Baumgarten-Lindberg
Established: 1977
Subjects: Children's books
Number of Members: 150,000
Publication(s): *Barn Posten; Laese Posten*
Owned by: AB Raben och Sjoegren Bokfoerlag; Bokfoerlaget Opal AB; Astrid Lindgren; Marianne von Baumgarten-Lindberg

Battre Barnomsorg
c/o Liber AB, Haelsingegatan 49, Stockholm S-11398
Mailing Address: PO Box 6471, S-11382 Stockholm
Tel: (08) 6909200 *Fax:* (08) 320851
Owned by: Liber AB

Battre Data
c/o Liber AB, Haelsingegatan 49, Stockholm S-11398
Mailing Address: PO Box 6471, S-11382 Stockholm
Tel: (08) 6909200 *Fax:* (08) 320851
Telex: 12801 S
Key Personnel
Contact: Kjell Gerdin
Established: 1983
Subjects: Computer technology
Number of Members: 1,000
Owned by: Liber AB

Battre Ledarskap
c/o Liber AB, Haelsingegatan 49, S-11398 Stockholm
Mailing Address: PO Box 6471, S-11382 Stockholm
Tel: (08) 6909200 *Fax:* (08) 6909470
Telex: 12801 S
Key Personnel
Contact: Lars Abramson
Established: 1977
Subjects: Management, Business Administration, Economics
Number of Members: 3,500
Owned by: Liber AB

Battre Marknadsforing
c/o Liber AB, Haelsingegatan 49, Stockholm S-11398
Mailing Address: PO Box 6471, S-11382 Stockholm
Tel: (08) 6909200 *Fax:* (08) 320851
Telex: 12801 S
Key Personnel
Contact: Lars Abramson
Established: 1984
Subjects: Marketing
Number of Members: 1,500
Owned by: Liber AB

Battre Skola
c/o Liber AB, Haelsingegatan 49, S-11398 Stockholm
Mailing Address: PO Box 6471, S-11382 Stockholm
Tel: (08) 6909200 *Fax:* (08) 320851
Telex: 12801 S
Key Personnel
Contact: Ingemar Ternbo
Established: 1975
Subjects: Education (book club for teachers)
Number of Members: 4,000
Owned by: Liber AB

Bokklubb Bra Bockesr
Soedra Vaegen, 263 80 Hoeganaes
Tel: (042) 339000 *Fax:* (042) 330504 *Cable:* BEBE BOOKS
Owned by: Bokfoerlaget Bra Boecker AB

Bonniers Bokklubb
PO Box 3159, 10363 Stockholm
Tel: (08) 6968000 *Fax:* (08) 6968361
Telex: 14546 Bonbook S *Cable:* BONNIERS
Key Personnel
Editor-in-Chief: Ingrid Carroll
Book Club Manager: Richard Ekstroem
Publication(s): *Bokspegeln* (The Book Mirror)
Owned by: Albert Bonniers Foerlag AB

Chef i forvaltning
c/o Liber AB, Haelsingegatan 49, S-11398 Stockholm
Mailing Address: PO Box 6471, S-11382 Stockholm
Tel: (08) 6909000 *Fax:* (08) 6909470
E-mail: export@liber.se
Web Site: www.liber.se
Owned by: Liber AB

Delta Science Fiction Bok Klubb
Box 15123, 161 15 Bromma
Tel: (08) 254781
Owned by: Delta Foerlags AB

Kalle Ankas Bokklubb
c/o Richter Egmont, Oestra Foerstadsgatan 46, S-205 75 Malmo
Tel: (040) 380600 *Fax:* (040) 933708
Telex: 33180 richt s
Owned by: Richters Foerlag AB

Kokboksklubben God Mat
c/o Richter Egmont, Oestra Foerstadsgatan 46, S-205 75 Malmo
Tel: (040) 380600 *Fax:* (040) 933708
Telex: 33180 richt s
Owned by: Richters Foerlag AB

Manadens Bok
Box 2255, 10316 Stockholm
Tel: (08) 6968520 *Fax:* (08) 6968372
E-mail: mpocket@manbok.se
Key Personnel
Dir: Magnus Nytell

Mitt foeretag
c/o Liber AB, Haelsingegatan 49, S-11398 Stockholm
Mailing Address: PO Box 6471, S-11382 Stockholm
Tel: (08) 6909000 *Fax:* (08) 320851
Telex: 12801 S
Subjects: Small businesses
Owned by: Liber AB

Reader's Digest AB
Fack 25, Kista 16493
Tel: (08) 6334800 *Fax:* (08) 7528701
E-mail: kundtjanst@readersdigest.se
Web Site: www.readersdigest.se

Richters Bokklubb
c/o Richter Egmont, Oestra Foerstadsgatan 46, S-205 75 Malmoe

Tel: (040) 380600 *Fax:* (040) 933708
Telex: 33180 richt s
Owned by: Richters Foerlag AB

Richters Ungdomsbokklubb
c/o Richter Egmont, Oestra Foerstadsgatan 46, S-20575 Malmoe
Tel: (040) 380600 *Fax:* (040) 933708
Telex: 33180 richt s
Owned by: Richters Foerlag AB

Sekreterurbokklubben
c/o Liber AB, Haelsingegatan 49, S-11398 Stockholm
Mailing Address: PO Box 6471, S-11382 Stockholm
Tel: (08) 6909200 *Fax:* (08) 6909300
Owned by: Liber AB

Serie-pocket-klubben
Landsvaegen 57, S-172 22 Sundbyberg
Mailing Address: PO Box 1074, Sundbyberg
Tel: (08) 7993110 *Fax:* (08) 7645764
Telex: 17370 semic s *Cable:* SEMICPRESS SUNDBYBERG
Owned by: Semic Press AB

Stora Familjebokklubben
c/o Bonniers foerlagen, Sveavaegen 56, S-103 63 Stockholm
Mailing Address: PO Box 3159, S-103 63 Stockholm
Tel: (08) 6968660 *Fax:* (08) 6968361
Telex: 14546 Bonbook s *Cable:* BONNIERS
Owned by: Albert Bonniers Foerlag AB

Stora Romanklubben
c/o Bonniers-foerlagen, Sveavaegen 56, S-103 63 Stockholm
Mailing Address: PO Box 3159, S-103 63 Stockholm
Tel: (08) 6968660 *Fax:* (08) 6968361
Owned by: Albert Bonniers Foerlag AB

Bokklubben Svalan
c/o Bonniers forlagen, Sveavaegen 56, S-103 63 Stockholm
Mailing Address: PO Box 3159, S-103 63 Stockholm
Tel: (08) 6968660 *Fax:* (08) 6986361
Telex: 14546 Bonbook S *Cable:* BONNIERS
Owned by: Bonnier Fakta Dokforlag AB

Underhallningsbokklubben
c/o Bonniers foerlagen, Sveavaegen 56, S-103 63 Stockholm
Mailing Address: Box 3159, S-103 63 Stockholm
Tel: (08) 6968660 *Fax:* (08) 6968361
Telex: 14546 Bonbook S *Cable:* BONNIERS
Owned by: Albert Bonniers Foerlag AB

Switzerland

Buchergilde Gutenberg AG
4601 Olten
Owned by: Edition Gutenberg

Europaring der Buch- und Schallplattenfreunde
Worblentalstr 33, 3063 Ittigen, Bern
Tel: (031) 584466
Owned by: Bertelsmann AG

NSB Buch- und Phonoclub
Schweizer Verlagshaus AG, Klausstr 10, 8008 Zurich
Tel: (01) 3833622

Key Personnel
General Manager: F Rothacher
Affiliated with Schweizer Verlagshaus AG.

Punktum AG
Klusstr 50, 8032 Zuerich
Tel: (01) 4224540 *Fax:* (01) 4224813
This club deals exclusively with children's books, intended as gifts.
Owned by: Rada Matija AG

Thailand

Science Fiction Magazine Club
105/19-2 Naret Rd, Bangkok 10500
Tel: (02) 2330302; (02) 2356931
Telex: 20657 Graphic Th
Owned by: Graphic Art Publications

United Kingdom

Adlib, *imprint of* Scholastic Publications Ltd

BCA, see Book Club Associates

Bibliophile Books
5 Thomas Rd, London E14 7BN
Tel: (020) 7515 9222 *Fax:* (020) 7538 4115
E-mail: customercare@bibliophilebooks.com
Web Site: www.bibliophilebooks.com
Key Personnel
General Manager: Anne Quigley
Established: 1979

Book Club Associates
87 Newman St, London W1P 4EN
Tel: (020) 7637 0341 *Fax:* (020) 7291 3525
Telex: 24359 B CALON *Cable:* Booklub
Key Personnel
Chief Executive: Markus Wilhelm
General Manager, Editorial: John Roberts
Established: 1966
Book Club(s): Ancient & Medieval History Book Club; Arts Guild; Children's Book of the Month Club; Classical Selection Club (Audio); EBC (Netherlands); Encounters; English Book Club (France); English Book Club (Germany); English Book Club (Norway); English Book Club (Sweden); Executive World; History Guild; Home Computer - Amiga; Home Computer - Amstrad; Home Computer - Commodore 64; Home Computer - PC; Home Computer - Spectrum Sinclair; Home Computer Atari St; Irish Book Club; Leisure Circle; Literary Guild (F); Literary Guild (M); Literary Guild Gold; Military and Aviation Book Society; Music Direct (Cass); Music Direct (R/CD); Music Direct Gold; Mystery and Thriller Guild; On the Road; Paperbacks; Plate Series; Railway Book Club; Video Direct; World Books (F); World Books (M); Ancient & Medieval History Book Club; Arts Guild; Children's Book of the Month Club; Classical Selection Club (Audio); EBC (Netherlands); Encounters; English Book Club (France); English Book Club (Germany); English Book Club (Norway); English Book Club (Sweden); Executive World; History Guild; Home Computer - Amiga; Home Computer - Amstrad; Home Computer - Commodore 64; Home Computer - PC; Home Computer - Spectrum Sinclair; Home Computer Atari St; Irish Book Club; Leisure Circle; Literary Guild (F); Literary Guild (M); Literary Guild Gold; Military and Aviation Book Society; Music Direct (Cass); Music Direct (R/CD); Music Direct Gold; Mystery and Thriller Guild; On the Road; Paperbacks; Plate Series; Railway Book Club; Video Direct; World Books (F); World Books (M)
Owned by: Reed International Books Ltd (parent company Reed Elsevier Plc); Doubleday & Company Inc, USA (parent company Bertelsmann AG, Germany)
Imprints: Guild Publishing

Book Exports, see Commonwealth Education Foundation

Bookmarks Club
265 Seven Sisters Rd, London N4 2DE
Tel: (020) 7536 9696 *Fax:* (020) 7538 0018
E-mail: 106163.77@compuserve.com
Subjects: Politics, Socialism
Owned by: IS Books Ltd

Books for Children
68 Willow Walk, London SE1 5SF
Tel: (020) 8606 3090 *Fax:* (020) 8606 3099
Established: 1977
Owned by: Time-Warner

The Bookworm Club
Rustat House, 60 Clifton Rd, Cambridge CB2 4GZ
Tel: (01223) 568650 *Fax:* (01223) 568591
E-mail: clubs@heffers.co.uk
Key Personnel
Contact: Fran Whiting
Subjects: Paperbacks for children age 8 up to the age of 13 (children's club in schools)
Owned by: W Heffer & Sons Ltd, 20 Trinity St, Cambridge CB2 3NG

Commonwealth Education Foundation
Formerly Book Exports
PO Box 367, Edgware, Middlesex HA8 7AG
Tel: (020) 8931 2359; (020) 8959 2137
Fax: (0181) 9592137
E-mail: roshanbp@aol.com
Key Personnel
Partner & Man Dir: Mr B P Lakhani
Established: 1978
Remainders at competitive prices.

Cover to Cover
Red House School Book Club, Windough Pk, Witney, Oxon OX8 5YZ
Tel: (01993) 893456 *Fax:* (01993) 6039092
Key Personnel
Man Dir: D M R Kewley
Subjects: Books for school children (11-16 years)
Owned by: Scholastic Publications Ltd

Andre Deutsch Children's Books, *imprint of* Scholastic Publications Ltd

English Book Club, see Book Club Associates

Firefly
Scholastic Ltd, Villiers House, Clarendon Ave, Leamington Spa, Warwicks CV32 5PR
Tel: (01926) 887799 *Fax:* (01926) 883331
Key Personnel
Man Dir: D M R Kewley
Office Manager: Deborah Shrives
E-mail: dshrives@scholastic.co.uk
Subjects: Books for children (3-12 years)~*Membership:* PA & PPA
Owned by: Scholastic Ltd
Ultimate Parent Company: Scholastic Inc

The Folio Society
44 Eagle St, London WC1R 4FS
Tel: (020) 7400 4242 *Fax:* (020) 7400 4242
Web Site: www.foliosoc.co.uk
Key Personnel
Editor: Sue Bradbury
Rights & Permissions: Bridget Frost
Contact: Kerry Davidson
Established: 1947
Subjects: Fiction, Poetry, Biography, History

Godfrey Cave Associates
27 Wrights Lane, London W8 5TZ
Tel: (020) 7416 3000 *Fax:* (020) 7416 3289
Key Personnel
Man Dir: Kevin Binston

Guild Publishing, *imprint of* Book Club Associates

Hippo, *imprint of* Scholastic Publications Ltd

Letterbox Library
71-73 Allen Rd, London N16 8RY
Key Personnel
Dir: Maikim Stern
Publicity & Marketing: Kerry Mason
Children's Bookclub producing quarterly catalogue & newsletter. Once-off joining fee L5.
Subjects: Non-Sexist & Multi-Cultural Children's Books

9-12 Club
Red House School Book Club, Windough Pk, Witney, Oxon OX8 5YZ
Tel: (01993) 893456 *Fax:* (0845) 6039092
Key Personnel
Managing Dir: D M R Kewley
Subjects: Books for school children (9-12 years)
Owned by: Scholastic Publications Ltd

The Poetry Book Society Ltd
Book House, 45 East Hill, London SW18 202
Tel: (020) 8870 8403 *Fax:* (020) 8877 1615
E-mail: info@poetrybooks.co.uk
Web Site: www.poetrybooks.co.uk
Key Personnel
Dir: Clare Brown *Tel:* (020) 8874 6361
 E-mail: clare@poetrybooks.co.uk
Established: 1953
Membership organization which promotes selected poetry at discounted prices.
Subjects: Poetry
Number of Members: 2,200
Publication(s): *The Bulletin* (quarterly)

Puffin Book Clubs
c/o Penguin Books Ltd, 27 Wrights Lane, London W8 5TZ
Tel: (020) 7416 3000 *Fax:* (020) 7416 3099
Key Personnel
Dir: Elaine McQuade
Incorporating Fledgling (for up to 6-year-olds), Kite (for 6 to 9-year-olds) and Post (for 9 to 13-year-olds) book clubs.
Owned by: Penguin Books Ltd

Readers Union
Berkeley Square House, Berkeley Square, London W1X 6AB
Tel: (020) 7629 8144 *Fax:* (020) 7499 9751
Telex: 264631 *Cable:* BOOKS NABBOT
Key Personnel
Marketing Dir: Lesley Godwin
Established: 1937
Book Club(s): Anglers Book Society; Belief the Religious Book Society; Birds and Natural History Book Society; Country Book Society; Country Book Society Incorporating Arena; Craft & Country Style Book Society; Craft

UNITED KINGDOM

Book Society; Craftsman Book Society; Design Book Club; Equestrian Book Society; Fieldsports Book Society; Gardeners Book Society; Golf Book Club; Maritime Book Society; Music Book Society; Nationwide & Phoenix Book Service; Needlecraft Book Society; Photographic Book Society; Ramblers & Climbers Book Society; World of Nature Book Club; World of Nature Incorporating Travel & Exploration Book Society; Anglers Book Society; Belief the Religious Book Society; Birds and Natural History Book Society; Country Book Society; Country Book Society Incorporating Arena; Craft & Country Style Book Society; Craft Book Society; Craftsman Book Society; Design Book Club; Equestrian Book Society; Fieldsports Book Society; Gardeners Book Society; Golf Book Club; Maritime Book Society; Music Book Society; Nationwide & Phoenix Book Service; Needlecraft Book Society; Photographic Book Society; Ramblers & Climbers Book Society; World of Nature Book Club; World of Nature Incorporating Travel & Exploration Book Society
Owned by: Reader's Digest Associates Ltd

The Red House Books Ltd
Windrush Park, Witney, Oxon OX8 5YF
Tel: (01993) 774171; (01993) 771144
 Fax: (01993) 776813
Key Personnel
Man Dir: David Teale
Established: 1979
Subjects: Children's
Number of Members: 350,000
Owned by: Red House Books Ltd

Scholastic Hardcover, *imprint of* Scholastic Publications Ltd

Scholastic Publications Ltd
Villiers House, Claredon Ave, Leamington Spa, Warks CV33 0JH
Tel: (01926) 887799 *Fax:* (01926) 883331
Key Personnel
Man Dir: D M R Kewley
Publishing Dir, Education Division: Ann Peel
Editorial Dir, Scholastic Children's Books: Richard Scrivener
Finance Dir: Ian Bloodworth
Trade Sales & Marketing: Gavin Lang
Operations & Distribution Dir: Philip Owen
Office Manager: Deborah Shrives
 E-mail: dshrives@scholastic.co.uk
Established: 1964
Subjects: General Education
Book Club(s): Arrow; Cover to Cover; Firefly; Arrow; Cover to Cover; Firefly
Owned by: Scholastic Inc, 730 Broadway, New York, NY, United States
Imprints: Andre Deutsch Children's Books; Hippo; Adlib; Scholastic Hardcover

6-9 Club
Red House School Book Club, Windough Pk, Witney, Oxon OX8 5YZ
Tel: (01993) 893456 *Fax:* (01993) 6039092
Key Personnel
Man Editor: D M R Kewley
Subjects: Books for school children (6-9 years)
Owned by: Scholastic Publications Ltd

Teachers Book Club
Scholastic Ltd, Villiers House, Clarendon Ave, Leamington Spa, Warwicks CV32 5PR
Tel: (01926) 887799 *Fax:* (01926) 883331
Key Personnel
Man Dir: D M R Kewley
Office Manager: Deborah Shrives
 E-mail: dshrives@scholastic.co.uk
Subjects: Books & resource materials for primary teachers
Owned by: Scholastic Ltd
Ultimate Parent Company: Scholastic Inc

The Women's Press Book Club
34 Great Sutton St, London EC1V 0LQ
Tel: (020) 7251 3007 *Fax:* (020) 7608 1938
Key Personnel
Manager: Kay Stirling *Tel:* (0207) 5539273
Established: 1980
Subjects: Books by & about women, with emphasis on fiction, women's studies, art, politics, health, biography
Number of Members: 7,000
Owned by: The Women's Press Ltd

Yugoslavia

Book Lovers' Club
Bulevar Vojvode Misica 17, 11000 Belgrade
Tel: (011) 651666; (011) 650399
Owned by: Beogradski Izdavacko-Graficki Zavod

Prosveta-Izdavako preduzece
Dobracina 30, 11000 Belgrade
Tel: (011) 642722; (011) 625766; (011) 625760
 Fax: (011) 627465

Zambia

Read-a-Book Club
Chishango Rd, Lusaka 10101
Mailing Address: PO Box 32708, Lusaka 10101
Tel: (01) 222324; (01) 236629 *Fax:* (01) 225073
Telex: 40056 *Cable:* HOUSE
Key Personnel
Man Dir: F M Chilomo
Publishing Manager: Ray Munamwimbu
Established: 1966
Publishing, printing & distribution.
Owned by: Zambia Educational Publishing House

Book Trade Organizations

The organizations listed below include publisher and bookseller associations and ISBN agencies as well as book trade and allied organizations. Listings appear under the country in which they are physically located. Some of the organizations are specific to a particular country; others are international in nature.

† indicates those organizations that are international in scope.

‡ indicates United Nations agencies with publishing activities.

◇ indicates other international organizations with publishing activities.

Additional book trade associations can be found in the sections **Literary Associations & Societies** and **Library Associations**.

Albania

◇**Lidhja e Shkrimtareve dhe e Artisteve toe Shqiperise**
National Library, Tirana
Tel: (042) 23843 *Fax:* (042) 23843
E-mail: isbn@natlib.tirana.al
Key Personnel
President: Dritero Agolli
Union of Writers & Artists of Albania.
Publication(s): *Albanaises* (quarterly, in French); *Drita* (weekly); *International Literatur* (quarterly); *Kultur Popullore* (annually, in Albanian & French); *Nentori* (monthly)

Algeria

Agence ISBN, see Bibliotheque Nationale

Bibliotheque Nationale
1 Av Frantz Fanon, Algiers
Tel: (02) 630632 *Fax:* (02) 610435

Andorra

Andorran Standard Book Numbering Agency
National Library of Andorra, Placeta Sant Esteve s/n, Andorra la Vella
Tel: 826445 *Fax:* 829445
E-mail: bncultura.gov@andorra.ad
Web Site: www.andorra.ad/bibnac
Key Personnel
Dir: Pilar Burgues

Angola

Uniao dos Escritores Angolanos (UEA)
CP 2767-C, Luanda
Tel: (02) 322155
Telex: 3056
Key Personnel
Secretary General: Luandino Vieira
Union of Angolan Writers.

Argentina

Agencia Argentina ISBN, see Camara Argentina del Libro

Camara Argentina de Publicaciones
Lavalle 437 6 D-Edif Adriatico, 6 piso, 1047 Buenos Aires
Tel: (011) 43942892 *Fax:* (011) 43942892
E-mail: publicaciones@icatel.net
Web Site: www.publicaciones.org
Key Personnel
President: Agustin dos Santos
Contact: Jorge J Serrano
Argentine Publications Association.

Camara Argentina del Libro
Ave Belgrano 1580 - 4 piso, 1093 Buenos Aires
Tel: (011) 43818383 *Fax:* (011) 43819253
E-mail: caarlibro@impsat1.com.ar
Web Site: www.editores.com *Cable:* 381-9253
Key Personnel
Dir: Noberto J Pou
Argentine Book Association.
Publication(s): *LEA*

Fundacion El Libro
Hipolito Yrigoyen 1628, Piso 5, 1344 Buenos Aires
Tel: (011) 43743288 *Fax:* (011) 43750268
E-mail: fund@libro.satlink.net
Web Site: www.el-libro.com.ar
Key Personnel
President: Jorge Naveiro
Dir: Marta V Diaz

Sociedad General de Autores de la Argentina
J A Pacheco de Melo 1820, 1126 Buenos Aires
Tel: (011) 8112582
Key Personnel
President: Isaac Aisemberg
Argentine Society of Authors.

Standard Book Numbering Agency
Camara Argentina del Libro, Ave Belgrano 1580 - 6 Piso, 1093 Buenos Aires
Tel: (011) 3819277 *Fax:* (011) 3819253
E-mail: postmaster@caarli.org.ar
Key Personnel
ISBN Administrator: Norberto Pou, Sr
Publication(s): *ISBN Directory*

Armenia

Gosudarstvenny Komitet Armjamskoj SSR po delam izdatel'stv, poligrafii, kniznoj targovli
G Kochar st 21, 375009 Yerevan 9
Tel: (02) 527595
E-mail: grapalat@arminco.com
Telex: 411871 Kniga
Key Personnel
Chairman: M F Nenashev
The USSR State Committee for Publishing, Printing and the Book Trade.

Australia

ANZAAB, see The Australian & New Zealand Association of Antiquarian Booksellers

Australia Council Literature Board
372 Elizabeth St, Surry Hills 2010
Mailing Address: PO Box 788, Strawberry Hills, Sydney, NSW 2012
Tel: (02) 9215 9000 *Fax:* (02) 9215 9111
Key Personnel
Manager: Gail Cork *Tel:* (02) 9215 9058
E-mail: g.cork@ozlo.gov.au
The Literature Board supports the writing of all forms of creative literature, including novels, short stories, poetry, publishing & promotion, plays & nonfiction (especially biography, autobiography, essays, histories, literary criticism or other expository or analytical prose). All applicants must use the Literature Board's application forms.
Publication(s): *Australia Council Support for the Arts Handbook* (1997)

The Australian & New Zealand Association of Antiquarian Booksellers
Affiliate of International League of Antiquarian Booksellers (ILAB)
69 Broadway, Nedlands, WA 6009
Tel: (0618) 9386 6103
E-mail: admin@anzaab.com
Web Site: www.anzaab.com.au
Key Personnel
President: Robert Muir
Founded: 1977

Australian Booksellers Association Inc
136 Rundle Mall, Adelaide, SA 5000
Tel: (03) 96637888 *Fax:* (03) 96637557
Key Personnel
President: Tim Peach
Executive Dir: Celia Pollock

AUSTRALIA

The ABA is a Federal Association with branches in every state & represents booksellers' interests to government bodies, publishers & other organizations.
Publication(s): *Economic Survey* (annually)

◇Australian Copyright Council
245 Chalmers St, Suite 3, Redfern, NSW 2016
Tel: (02) 9318 1788 *Fax:* (02) 9698 3536
Key Personnel
Chairman: Peter Banki
Executive Officer: Libby Baulch
Office Manager: Jennifer Bey *Tel:* (02) 9699 3247
Publication(s): *Copyright Reporter*; *Practical Guide* (Discussion paper)
ISBN Prefix(es): 0-9595513

Australian Press Council
Suite 303 149 Castlereagh St, Sydney, NSW 2000
Tel: (02) 2611930 *Fax:* (02) 2676826
Key Personnel
Executive Secretary: Jack R Herman

Australian Publishers Association Ltd
89 Jones St, Suite 60, Ultimo, NSW 2007
Tel: (02) 9281 9788 *Fax:* (02) 9281 1073
E-mail: apa@publishers.asn.au
Web Site: www.publishers.asn.au
Key Personnel
President: Greg Browne
Chief Executive: Susan Bridge
Information Officer: Sara Lovelock *E-mail:* sara.lovelock@publishers.asn.au
Founded: 1948
Trade association representing Australian book publishers.
Publication(s): *Directory of Members*; *Introduction to Book Publishing*

The Australian Society of Authors Ltd
PO Box 1566, Strawberry Hills NSW 2012
Tel: (02) 93180877 *Fax:* (02) 93180530
E-mail: asa@asauthors.org
Key Personnel
Executive Dir: Jose Borghino *E-mail:* jose@asauthors.org
Founded: 1963
Publication(s): *Australian Author* (trianually, magazine, magazine for writers, readers & people who love books); *Australian Book Contracts* (step-by-step guide to publishing contracts for authors)

Australian Society of Indexers
PO Box R598, Royal Exchange NSW 1225
Tel: (0500) 525005; (02) 94383729 *Fax:* (02) 98882229
E-mail: secretary@aussi.org
Web Site: www.aussi.org
Key Personnel
President: Alan Walker *Tel:* (02) 93680174 *E-mail:* alan.walker@s054.aone.net.au
Vice President: Michael Wyatt
Editor: Glenda Browne
Treasurer: Tricia Waters
Webmaster: Jonathan Jermey
Honorary Secretary: Lorraine Doyle
Affiliated with indexing societies in Britain, Canada, China, South Africa & USA.
Publication(s): *Australian Society of Indexers' Newsletter* (10 x/yr); *Indexers Available*
Associate Companies: American Society of Indexers; Association of Southern African Indexers & Bibliographers (ASAIB); China Society of Indexers; Indexing & Abstracting Society of Canada; Society of Indexers, United Kingdom
Branch Office(s)
ACT Region Branch, GPO Box 2069, Canberra ACT 2601
Victorian Branch, GPO Box 1251, Melbourne, Victoria 3001

South Australian Group *Tel:* (08) 8235 1535
Queensland Group *Tel:* (07) 33530120

†◇Bibliographical Society of Australia and New Zealand (BSANZ)
PO Box 1463, Wagga Wagga, NSW 2650
Tel: (02) 6931 8669 *Fax:* (02) 6931 8669
E-mail: rsalmond@pobox.com
Web Site: life.csu.edu.au/bsanz/
Key Personnel
President: D H R Spennemann
Founded: 1969
Publication(s): *Bulletin* (quarterly)
ISBN Prefix(es): 0-9598271

Christian Bookselling Association of Australia Inc
Suite 2, 7-9 President Ave, Caringbah NSW 2229
Mailing Address: PO Box 576, Caringbah NSW 1495
Tel: (02) 95243349 *Fax:* (02) 95403001
Web Site: www.christprdoz.com
Key Personnel
Executive Secretary: Jan Holt
Founded: (In existence for 28 years)
Trade organization & Member of Christian Booksellers Association (USA).
Publication(s): *CBAA News*

Copyright Agency Ltd
157 Liverpool St, Level 19, Sydney NSW 2000
Tel: (02) 93947600 *Fax:* (02) 93947601
E-mail: info@copyright.com.au
Web Site: www.copyright.com.au
Key Personnel
Chief Executive: Michael Fraser
Manager, Member Services: Jenny Longland *E-mail:* jlongland@copyright.com.au
Acts as a Copyright Collecting Society.

International Standard Book Numbering Agency, see ISBN Agency Australia

ISBN Agency Australia
18 Salmon St, Locked Bag 20, Port Melbourne, Victoria 3207
Tel: (03) 9245 7385 *Fax:* (03) 9245 7393
E-mail: isbn.agency@thorpe.com.au
Web Site: www.thorpe.com.au
Key Personnel
ISBN Coordinator: Maria Watt
Publication(s): *Australian Books In Print*
Parent Company: D W Thorpe

Mardev
Tower 2, 475 Victoria Ave, Chatswood, NSW 2067
Tel: (02) 9422 2644 *Fax:* (02) 9422 2633
E-mail: mardevlists@reedbusiness.com.au
Web Site: www.mardevlists.com
Key Personnel
Gen Manager, UK: Nick Martin
List Manager: Maureen Ryan *E-mail:* maureen.ryan@reedbusiness.com.au
Parent Company: Reed Elsevier plc
Branch Office(s)
No 1 Temasek Ave, 17-01 Millenia Tower, Singapore 039192, Singapore *Tel:* 338 3398 *Fax:* 338 1409
Quadrant House, Sutton, Surrey SM2 5AS, United Kingdom *Tel:* (020) 8643 0955 *Fax:* (020) 8652 4580 *E-mail:* mardevlists@rbo.co.uk
2 Rector St, 26th floor, New York, NY 10006, United States *Tel:* 212-584-9370 *Fax:* 212-584-9371 *E-mail:* sales@mardevlists.com

◇National Book Council Inc
71 Collins St, Melbourne, Victoria 3000
Tel: (03) 6638043 *Fax:* (03) 6638658

Key Personnel
President: Michael G Zifcak, OBE
Executive Dir: Thomas Shapcott
Publication(s): *Australian Book Review*; *Directory of Australian Authors*

Public Lending Right Scheme
MTAA House, 39 Brisbane Ave, Barton ACT 2600
Mailing Address: GPO Box 3241, Canberra, ACT 2601
Tel: (062) 711650 *Toll Free Tel:* 800 672842 (Australia only) *Fax:* (062) 711651
E-mail: plr.mail@dcita.ov.au
Web Site: www.dcita.gov.au/plr/html
Key Personnel
PLR Administrator: Paul Bootes *Tel:* (062) 711635 *E-mail:* paul.bootes@dcita.gov.au
Parent Company: Dept of Communications & the Arts
Branch Office(s)
GPO Box 3241, Canberra ACT 2601

◇Society of Women Writers
GPO Box 2621, Sydney NSW 2001
Tel: (03) 63310267
Key Personnel
Federal President: Deidre Gibson
Editor: Marilyn Arnold
Publication(s): *The Woman Writer* (bi-monthly, newsletter)
ISBN Prefix(es): 0-9587871; 0-9591144; 0-9598432
Associate Companies: Society of Women Writers & Journalists London

◇UNILINC
Level 9, 210 Clarence St, Sydney, NSW 2000
Tel: (02) 92831488 *Fax:* (02) 92679247
E-mail: rona@unilinc.edu.au
Web Site: www.unilinc.edu.au
Key Personnel
Executive Dir: Rona Wade
Founded: 1978

Austria

Bundesgremium der Buch und Medienwirtschaft, see Fachverband der Buch und Medienwirtschaft

†CIE (International Commission on Illumination Central Bureau)
Kegelgasse 27, A-1030 Vienna
Tel: (01) 71431870 *Fax:* (01) 713083818
E-mail: ciecb@ping.at
Web Site: www.cie.co.at/cie
Key Personnel
President: H A Lofberg
General Secretary: C Hermann
Founded: 1913
Subjects: Lighting

Fachverband der Buch und Medienwirtschaft
Formerly Bundesgremium der Buch und Medienwirtschaft
Wiedner-Hauptstr 63, Postfach 440, A-1045 Vienna
Tel: (01) 50105 DW 3331; (01) 50105 DW 3333 *Fax:* (01) 50105 DW 3043
E-mail: fbuchwirtschaft@wko.at
Web Site: www.buchwirtschaft.at
Key Personnel
President: Bernhard Weis
Vice President: Gustav Glockler
Man Dir: Johann Varga

†◇**Federation Internationale des Traducteurs (FIT)**
Dr Heinrich Maierstrasse 9, A-1180 Vienna
Tel: (01) 4403607; (01) 4709819 *Fax:* (01) 4403756; (01) 4708194
E-mail: info@fit.org
Web Site: www.fit.ift.org
Key Personnel
President: F Herbulot
Vice President: L Sivesind
Secretary General: Liese Katschinka
 E-mail: liese.katschinka@eunet.at
International Federation of Translators.
Publication(s): *Babel* (International journal of translation); *Translatio* (FIT Newsletter)

FIT, see Federation Internationale des Traducteurs (FIT)

◇**Hauptverband des Oesterreichischen Buchhandels** (Austrian Publishers' & Booksellers' Association)
Gruenangergasse 4, A-1010 Vienna
Tel: (01) 5121535 *Fax:* (01) 5128482
Web Site: www.buecher.at
Key Personnel
President: Dr Anton C Hilscher
Publication(s): *Adressbuch des oesterreichischen Buchhandels* (Directory of Austrian Book Trade); *Anzeiger des oesterreichischen Buchhandels* (Austrian Book Trade Gazette, 2 times/month)
Associate Companies: Verband der Antiquare Oesterreichs; Verband der oesterreichischen Buch- und Presse-Grossisten und der Werbenden Zeitschriftenhaendler; Oesterreichischer Verlegerverband; Oesterreichischer Buchhaendlerverband; Verband von selbstaendigen Verlagsvertretem Oesterreichs; Standard Book Numbering Agency

IAEA, see International Atomic Energy Agency (IAEA)

†‡**International Atomic Energy Agency (IAEA)**
Wagramer Str 5, A-1400 Vienna
Mailing Address: PO Box 100, A-1400 Vienna
Tel: (0222) 2600-0 *Fax:* (0222) 2600-7
E-mail: official.mail@iaea.org
Web Site: www.iaea.org
Key Personnel
Editorial: M F Boemeke
Public Information: M Gwozdecky
Senior Information Officer: M Fleming *Tel:* (01) 2600-21275 *E-mail:* m.fleming@iaea.org
Sales, Publicity: A Bugno; G Cazier
Founded: 1957
The International Atomic Energy Agency is an international organization within the United Nations family, having the general purpose of seeking to accelerate & enlarge the contribution of atomic energy to peace, health & prosperity throughout the world. The Agency's publications result, almost exclusively, from its own activities; published material is of intense interest only to a relatively small group of scientists & technicians
Membership: Intergovernmental Organization in Family of United Nations.
Subjects: Life Sciences, Nuclear Safety & Environmental Protection, Physics, Chemistry, Geology & Raw Materials, Reactors & Nuclear Power, Industrial Applications, Miscellaneous
Publication(s): *Meetings in Atomic Energy* (quarterly); *Nuclear Fusion* (monthly)
ISBN Prefix(es): 92-0

International Commission on Illumination Central Bureau, see CIE (International Commission on Illumination Central Bureau)

†◇**International Federation for Information Processing (IFIP)**
C/O Plamen Nedkov, Hofstrasse 3, 2361 Laxenburg
Tel: (02236) 73616 *Fax:* (02236) 736169
E-mail: ifip@ifip.or.at
Web Site: www.ifip.or.at

†‡**International Institute for Children's Literature & Reading Research (UNESCO category C)**
Mayerhofgasse 6, A-1040 Vienna
Tel: (01) 5050359; (01) 5052831 *Fax:* (01) 5050359-17; (01) 5052831-17
E-mail: office@jupendliturature.net
Web Site: www.jugendliterature.net
Key Personnel
President: Dr Hilde Hawlicek
Vice President: Alois Almer
Dir: Mag Karin Haller
Contact: Barbara Mladek *E-mail:* barbara.mladek@jugendliterature.net
Founded: 1965
Internationales Institut for Jugendliteratur und Leseforschung.
Subjects: Children & Youth Literature, Research
Publication(s): *1000 und 1 Buch* (4x annually)

Literar-Mechana, Wahrnehmungsgesellschaft fuer Urheberrechte GmbH
Linke Wienzeile 18, A-1060 Vienna VI
Tel: (01) 5872161 *Fax:* (01) 58721619
Key Personnel
Man Dir: Franz-Leo Popp
Organization for Copyright Protection.

Standard Book Numbering Agency
Gruenangergasse 4, 1010 Vienna
Tel: (01) 5121535 *Fax:* (01) 5128482
E-mail: isbn@hvb.at
Web Site: www.buecher.at
Key Personnel
Contact: Herma Papovschek
ISBN Prefix(es): 3-85103

◇**Verband der Antiquare Oesterreichs**
Gruenangergasse 4, 1010 Vienna
Tel: (01) 512 15 35 *Fax:* (01) 512 84 82
E-mail: sekretariat@hvb.at
Web Site: www.antiquare.at
Key Personnel
President: Hans-Dieter Paulusch
Austrian Antiquarian Booksellers' Association.
Publication(s): *Anzeiger des Verbandes der Antiquare Oesterreichs* (Austrian Antiquarian Booksellers' Association Gazette)

Verband der Oesterreichischen Buch-und Presse- Grossisten und der Werbenden Zeitschriftenhaendler
Gruenangergasse 4, 1010 Vienna
Tel: (01) 5121535 *Fax:* (01) 5128482
E-mail: hvb@buecher.at
Web Site: www.buecher.at
Key Personnel
President: Dr Emmerich Selch

Verband von selbstaendigen Verlagsvertreten Oesterreichs (Association of Independent Publishers Representing Austria)
Gruenangergasse 4, A-1010 Vienna
Tel: (01) 5121535 *Fax:* (01) 5128482
E-mail: hvb@buecher.at
Web Site: www.buecher.at
Key Personnel
President: Hans Jobst

Bangladesh

National Library
32, Justice Syed Mahbub Murshed Sarani, Sher-e-Bangla Nagar, Dhaka 1207
Tel: (02) 326578 *Fax:* (02) 833212
Key Personnel
Contact: Mr Shahabuddin Khan
Publication(s): *Boi* (text in Bengali)

Standard Book Numbering Agency, see National Library

Belarus

National Book Chamber of Belarus
31a Very Khoruzhey St, 220002 Minsk
Tel: (172) 2893396 *Fax:* (172) 28933963
E-mail: palata@palata.belpak.minsk.by
Key Personnel
Contact: Anatoli Voronko
Parent Company: Republic of Belarus

Standard Book Numbering Agency, see National Book Chamber of Belarus

Belgium

Association des Editeurs Belges
140 Blvd Lambermont, bte 1, B-1030 Brussels
Tel: (02) 2416580 *Fax:* (02) 2167131
Key Personnel
Dir: B Gerard
Assistant Dir: N Larock
Secretary: D Marliere
Belgian Publishers' Association.
Publication(s): *Annuaire des Editeurs belges de Langue francaise* (Belgian Publishers in French Language Annual); *Catalogue des Editeurs scientifiques*; *Donnees statistiques sur le livre belge de langue francaise*

Boek.be
Hof ter Schriecklaan 17, B-2600 Berchem, Antwerp
Tel: (03) 230 89 23 *Fax:* (03) 281 22 40
E-mail: info@boek.be
Web Site: www.boek.be
Key Personnel
President: Andre Van Halewyck
Dir: Rene Van Loon *E-mail:* rene.van.loon@boek.be
Association for the Promotion of Dutch Language Books/Books from Flanders.
Publication(s): *Adresgids voor het Boekenvan* (list of publishers & booksellers); *De Boekentrommel* (list of new children's books); *Het Boek in Vlaanderen* (list of new books); *Lijstenboek* (list of publishers & booksellers); *Tijdingen* (news)

†‡**Centre for European Policy Studies**
Place du Congres, 1, B-1000 Brussels
Tel: (02) 2293911 *Fax:* (02) 2194151; (02) 2293971
E-mail: ceps@infoboard.be
Key Personnel
President: Peter Ludlow
General Manager: Catherine Chanut
Corporate Relations Manager: Staffan Yerneck
Finances & Administration Dir: Willem Roekens
Editor: Anne Harrington

BELGIUM

Founded: 1983
Subjects: Politics, Economics, Business

EBF, see European Booksellers Federation (EBF)

†◇European Association of Directory & Database Publishers
Ave Louise 363, B-1050 Brussels
Tel: (02) 6463060 *Fax:* (02) 6463637
E-mail: mailbox@eadp.org
Web Site: www.eadp.org
Key Personnel
President: Frank-Peter Oppenborn
Secretary-General: Anne Lerat
Public Relations: Annie Komaromi
  E-mail: anniekomaromi@eadp.org
Founded: 1966
Association Europeenne des Editeurs d'Annuaires/Europaeischer Adressbuchverleger-Verband.
Publication(s): *Directories in Europe* (annually, list of members)

†◇European Booksellers Federation (EBF)
Blvd Lambermont 140/1, B-1030 Brussels
Tel: (02) 2420957 *Fax:* (02) 2420957
E-mail: eurobooks@skynet.be
Web Site: www.editeur.org/ebf.html
Key Personnel
President: John Hitchin *Tel:* (0181) 9484932
  Fax: (0181) 3320379
Vice President & Treasurer: Klaus Vorpahl
  Tel: (069) 314032-11 *Fax:* (069) 314969
General Secretary: Christiane Vuidar

†◇Federation of European Publishers (FEP)
Av de Tervueren 204, B-1150 Brussels
Tel: (02) 7701110 *Fax:* (02) 7712071
E-mail: fep.Alemann@brutele.be
Web Site: www.editeur.org/FEP.html
Key Personnel
President: Michael Gill
Dir: Mechtild Von Alemann
Contact: Mr Bergman-Tahon *E-mail:* fep.bergman@brutele.be
Founded: 1967
The Federation consists of the book associations of the European Communities & European Econo mic Area (EEA) & aims at representing jointly the interests of the European publishers for all matters arising from the Treaty of Rome, Maastricht & Amsterdam & Nice (or the Treaties).

FEP, see Federation of European Publishers (FEP)

†◇FIAF (International Federation of Film Archives)
One Rue Defacqz, 1000 Brussels
Tel: (02) 5383065 *Fax:* (02) 5344774
E-mail: fiaf@mail.interpac.be
Web Site: www.cinema.ucla.edu/fiaf
Key Personnel
Executive Secretary: Brigitte van derElst
Founded: 1938
Federation internationale des archives du film (FIAF).
Publication(s): *Bibliography of National Filmographies*; *Cataloguing Rules for Film Archives*; *Glossary of Filmographic Terms, Version II*; *Handbook for Film Archives*; *Handling, Storage & Transport of Cellulose Nitrate Film*; *International Directory of Film & TV Documentation Collections*; *International Film Archive CD-ROM*; *Journal of Film Preservation*; *Preservation & Restoration of Moving Images & Sound*; *Technical Manual of the FIAF Preservation Commission*; *The International Index to Film & Television Periodicals*

IBF, see International Booksellers Federation (IBF)

IFRRO, see International Federation of Reproduction Rights Organisations (IFRRO)

†◇International Association of Orientalist Librarians
Oost-Aziatische Bibliotheek, Kuleuven University, Mgr. Ladeuzeplein 21, 3000 Leuven
Tel: (016) 16324698 *Fax:* (016) 16324703
Web Site: www.-01.uchicago.edu/01/1aol
Key Personnel
Librarian: Mrs Benedicte Vaerman
  E-mail: benedicte.vaerman@bib.kuleuven.ac.be
Publication(s): *International Association of Orientalist Librarians Bulletin* (biannually)

†◇International Booksellers Federation (IBF)
Rue de Grand Hospice 34A, B1000 Brussels
Tel: (02) 2234940 *Fax:* (02) 2234941
E-mail: eurobooks@skynet.be
Key Personnel
President: Yvonne Steinberger
General Secretary: Christiane Vuidar
Publication(s): *Booksellers International* (different country reports); *The IBF* (IBF list of members)

†‡International Catholic Organization for Cinema & Audiovisual (OCIC)
15, Rue du Saphir, B-1030 Brussels
Tel: (02) 7344294 *Fax:* (02) 7343207
E-mail: sg@ocic.org
Web Site: www.ocic.org *Cable:* OCIC.BRUXELLES
Key Personnel
President: Henk Hoegstra
Secretary General: Robert Molhant
Founded: 1928
Subjects: African Cinema, Cinema & Religion, Video & Religion, World Cinema
Publication(s): *Cineamedia* (magazine, bimonthly)
ISBN Prefix(es): 92-9080

†◇International Federation of Reproduction Rights Organisations (IFRRO)
Rue de Prince Royal 87, B-1050 Brussels
Tel: (02) 551 08 99 *Fax:* (02) 551 08 95
E-mail: iffro@skynet.be; secretariat@ifrro.be
Web Site: www.ifrro.org
Key Personnel
President: Andre Beemsterboer
Vice President: Peter Shepherd
General Secretary: Veronica Williams
Executive Secretary: Marie-Agnes Lenoir
IFRRO links together all national Reproduction Rights Organizations (RROs) & national & international associations of rightsholders. RROs are organizations engaged in the conveyance of photocopying authorizations & royalties between rightsholders & users. IFRRO's purposes are to foster the creation of RROs worldwide; to facilitate the development of formal agreements & informal relationships between, among & on behalf of its members; & to increase public awareness of copyright & the need for effective mechanisms for conveying rights & royalties between rightsholders & users.

OCIC, see International Catholic Organization for Cinema & Audiovisual (OCIC)

†‡Tantalum-Niobium International Study Center
40 Rue Washington, B-1050 Brussels
Tel: (02) 6495158 *Fax:* (02) 6496447
E-mail: info@tanb.org
Web Site: www.tanb.org

Key Personnel
Secretary General: Judith Wickens
Subjects: Metals
ISBN Prefix(es): 92-9093

TIC, see Tantalum-Niobium International Study Center

◇Vlaamse Boekverkopersbond (VBB) (Flemish Booksellers' Association)
Hof ter Schrieckclaan 17, 2600 Berchem, Antwerp
Tel: (03) 2395740; (03) 2308835 *Fax:* (03) 2395740
E-mail: vbb@boek.be
Web Site: www.boek.be
Key Personnel
General Secretary: Luc Tessens *E-mail:* luc.tessens@vbvb.be

Vlaamse Uitgevers Vereniging (VUV) (Publishers From Flanders)
Hof ter Schrieckclaan 17, 2600 Antwerp
Tel: (03) 2308923 *Fax:* (03) 2812240
Web Site: www.vbvb.be
Key Personnel
Secretary: Jan Vanderheyden *E-mail:* jan.vanderheyden@vbvb.be
Association of Publishers of Dutch Language Books.

VUV, see Vlaamse Uitgevers Vereniging (VUV)

Bolivia

Camara Boliviana del Libro
Calle Capitan Ravelo No 2116, Casilla 682, La Paz
Tel: (02) 327039 *Fax:* (02) 327039
E-mail: cabolib@ceibo.entelnet.bo
Key Personnel
President & Dir: Rolando S Condori
Vice President: Nancy C de Montoya
Secretary: Teresa G de Alvarez
Distributions: Miguel Martinez
Sales: Jose Carlos Ciappesoni
Editorial: Nestor Castillo
Retail Sales: Walter Mercado
Bolivian Booksellers' Association.

Botswana

Standard Book Numbering Agency (Botswana)
Botswana National Library Service, Private Bag 0036, Gaborone
Tel: 352397; 352288 *Fax:* 301149
Telex: 2414 pula bd *Cable:* BONALIBS
Key Personnel
ISBN Administrator: G K Mulindwa

Brazil

ABEU, see Associacao Brasileira dar Editoras Universitarias (ABEU)

Agencia Brasileira do ISBN
c/o Biblioteca Nacional, Av Rio Branco, 219/39, 20042 Rio de Janeiro RJ
Tel: (021) 2408629; (021) 2408579 *Fax:* (021) 2204173

Telex: 2122941bnrjbr
Key Personnel
Contact: Sueli Ferreira Aleixo

Associacao Brasileira dar Editoras Universitarias (ABEU)
Universidade Federal de Santa Catarine-Campus Universitario-Trindade, Caixa Postal 476, 88040-900 Florianopolis SC
Tel: (0482) 319000 *Fax:* (0482) 344069
Telex: (0482) 240
Key Personnel
President: Alcides Buss
Brazilian Association of Academic Publishers.

Associacao Brasileira de Liverivos Antiquarios
Rua Santos Dumont 677, 25625-090 Centro Petropolis
Tel: (0242) 420376 *Fax:* (0242) 311695; (0242) 2214582
Brazilian Association of Antiquarian Booksellers.
ISBN Prefix(es): 85-7096

Brazilian National Library, see Departamento Nacional do Livro

Camara Brasileira do Livro
AlSantos 1000 - 10 andar, CEP 01418-100 Sao Paulo
Tel: (011) 3147-0870 *Fax:* (011) 3147-0870
E-mail: cbl@cbl.org.br
Web Site: www.cbl.org.br
Telex: 24788 Vrli
Key Personnel
President: Raul Wassermann
Dir: H Carlos Dias
General Manager: Aloysio T Costa
Brazilian Book Association.

Departamento Nacional do Livro (National Books Department)
Affiliate of Ministerio da Cultura Republica Federativa do Brazil
c/o Fundacao Biblioteca Nacional, Rua da Imprensa, 16, 11' and, 20030-120 Rio de Janeiro RJ
Tel: (021) 2544 85 97; (021) 2544 85 14; (021) 2544 87 03 *Fax:* (021) 2220 10 09; (021) 2240 79 29
E-mail: dnl@bn.br
Web Site: www.bn.br
Key Personnel
Dir: Elmer Correa Barbosa *E-mail:* elmer@bn.br

Sindicato Nacional dos Editores de Livros (SNEL)
SDS, Edif Venancio VI, Loja 9/17, 70000 Brasilia
Tel: (021) 2336481 *Fax:* (021) 2538502
Key Personnel
President: Sergio Abreu da Cruz Machado
Dir Secretary: Henrique Maltese
Manager: Nilson Lopes da Silva
Brazilian Publishers' Association.
Publication(s): *Informativo Bibliografico* (annually); *Jornal do SNEL* (bimonthly); *Producao Editorial Brasileira* (Brazilian Publishing Output annually)

SNEL, see Sindicato Nacional dos Editores de Livros (SNEL)

Standard Book Numbering Agency, see Agencia Brasileira do ISBN

Brunei Darussalam

Standard Book Numbering Agency
Bandar Seri Begawan 2064, Negara
Tel: (02) 382511 *Fax:* (02) 381817
Telex: bu 2774
Key Personnel
Contact: Ms Nellie Dato Paduka Haji Sunny

Bulgaria

Bulgarian National ISSN Centre
c/o St Cyril & Methodius Natl Library, Vassil Levski 88, 1504 Sophia
Tel: (02) 9461165 *Fax:* (02) 435495
Telex: 22432
Key Personnel
Dir: Antoaneta Totmanova *E-mail:* nbkm@nl.otel.net
Parent Company: St St Cyril & Methodius

◇**National ISBN Agency**
St Cyril & St Methodius National Library, Boul Vasil Leveski 88, 1037 Sofia
Tel: (02) 982811 *Fax:* (02) 435495
E-mail: nbkm@nl.otel.net
Telex: 22432 natlib
Key Personnel
ISBN Administrator: Tatjana Dermendzieva
Publication(s): *Novini ISBN i ISSN* (monthly); *Spravocnik na izdatelstva, redakcii i pecatnici v Baelgarija* (annual directory)

Standard Book Numbering Agency, see National ISBN Agency

Cameroon

†◇**Centre Regional pour la Promotion du Livre en Afrique (CREPLA)**
POB 1646, Yaounde
Tel: 224782; 2936
Key Personnel
Secretary: William Moutchia
Founded: 1962
Regional Centre for Book Promotion in Africa (co-sponsored by UNESCO).
Publication(s): *CREPLA Bulletin*

CREPLA, see Centre Regional pour la Promotion du Livre en Afrique (CREPLA)

IFORD, see Institut de Formation et de Recherche Demographiques (IFORD)

†‡**Institut de Formation et de Recherche Demographiques (IFORD)**
BP 1556, Yaounde
Tel: (023) 222471; (023) 231917 *Fax:* (023) 226793
Telex: 8304 Undevpro
Key Personnel
Man Dir: Prof Daniel M Sala-Diakanda
Founded: 1972
Subjects: Demography, Population Studies
ISBN Prefix(es): 2-905327

PAID, see Pan African Institute for Development (PAID)

†**Pan African Institute for Development (PAID)**
IPD BP 4056, Douala
Tel: 421061; 424335; 428030; 433316
Fax: 424335
E-mail: ipd.sg@cmnet.cm
Telex: 6048
Key Personnel
Pres, Governing Council: Dr Mbuki V T MWamufiya
Founded: 1964
Subjects: Rural Development
Publication(s): *An Integrated Approach to Rural Development* (IRD); *Community Health & Nutrition* (CHN); *Drought & Famine Preparedness & Response* (DFPR); *Food Self Sufficiency & Agricultural Development* (FSS); *Informal Sector & Small Scale Enterprises* (ISSE); *Popular Participation & the Promotion & Management of NGOs* (NGO); *Promoting Active Training Methods* (ATM); *Strengthening African Training & Research Institutions*; *Towards a Support Methodology* (SM); *Women & Health Programme* (W/H); *Women in Development* (WiD)

Canada

Canadian ISBN Agency, Acquisitions and Bibliographic Services Branch
National Library of Canada, 395 Wellington St, Ottawa, ON K1A 0N4
Tel: 819-994-6872 *Fax:* 819-997-7517
E-mail: isbn@nlc-bnc.ca
Web Site: www.nlc-bnc.ca/isbn/e-isbn.htm
Key Personnel
Contact: Mr David Balatti

IAML, see International Association of Music Libraries, Archives & Documentation Centres (IAML)

†◇**International Association of Music Libraries, Archives & Documentation Centres (IAML)**
c/o Cataloguing Dept, Carleton University Library, 1125 Colonel By Drive, Ottawa K1S 5B6
Tel: 613-520-2600 (ext 8150) *Fax:* 613-520-3583
Key Personnel
Sec-Gen: Alison Hall *E-mail:* alison_hall@carleton.ca
Founded: 1951
Association internationale des bibliotheques, archives et centres de documentation musicaux (AIBM)
Internationale Vereinigung der Musikbibliotheken, Musikarchive und Musikdokumentations Zentren (IVMB).
Publication(s): *Fontes artis musicae*

†◇**International Fiction Review**
University of New Brunswick, Department of Culture & Language Studies, PO Box 4400, Fredericton, NB E3B 5A3
Tel: 506-453-4636 *Fax:* 506-447-3166
E-mail: ifr@unb.ca
Web Site: www.lib.unb.ca/Texts/IFR
Key Personnel
Editor: Chris Lorey *E-mail:* lorey@unb.ca
Founded: 1974
Publication(s): *The International Fiction Review* (annually)

CANADA

ISBN/BNQ
Bibliotheque nationale du Quebec, 2275 rue Holt, Montreal, PQ H2G 3H1
Tel: 514-873-1100 (ext 319) *Fax:* 514-873-4310
E-mail: isbn@bnquebec.ca
Web Site: www.bnquebec.ca
Key Personnel
Contact: Mdme Lucie Martel
Founded: 1979
ISBN agency for Canadian francophone publishers from the private sector, for the government of Quebec & for all Quebec publishers whose principal publication language is not English.

Standard Book Numbering Agency, see Canadian ISBN Agency, Acquisitions and Bibliographic Services Branch

Standard Book Numbering Agency, see ISBN/BNQ

Chile

Camara Chilena del Libro AG
Casilla 13526, Santiago
Tel: (02) 6989519 *Fax:* (02) 6989226
E-mail: camlibro@reuna.cl
Web Site: www.camlibro.cl
Key Personnel
Manager: Carlos Franz
Chilean Association of Publishers, Distributors & Booksellers.

CELADE, see Centro Latinoamericano de Demografia (CELADE)

†‡Centro Latinoamericano de Demografia (CELADE)
Edeficio Naciones Unidas, Avda Dag Hammarskjoeld, Santiago
Mailing Address: Casilla 179-D, Santiago
Tel: (02) 2087037; (02) 2102023 *Fax:* (02) 2080196; (02) 2080252
E-mail: djaspers@eclac.cl
Web Site: www.eclac.org/Celade-Eng/index.html
Telex: 340295 UNSTGOCK *Cable:* UNATIONS
Key Personnel
Dir: Reynaldo F Bajraj
Subjects: Demography, Statistics, Sociology, Population Information & Data Processing, Periodicals
Publication(s): *Boletin Demografico* (biennially); *Notas de Poblacion* (biennially); *Revista Docpal* (annually)

PROLIBRO, see Camara Chilena del Libro AG

Standard Book Numbering Agency, see Camara Chilena del Libro AG

Standard Book Numbering Agency
c/o Camara Chilena del Libro A G, Casilla 13526, Santiago de Chile
Tel: (02) 6989519 *Fax:* (02) 6989226; (02) 6874271
E-mail: camlibro@reuna.cl
Key Personnel
President: Eduardo Castillo
Administrator: Jaime Pizarro
Publication(s): *Catalogo ISBN Libros Chilenos (Ultima Publicacion 1996)*

China

China ISBN Agency
85 Dongsi Nan Dajie, 100703 Beijing
Tel: (010) 65127806 *Fax:* (010) 65127875
Telex: 22024 cpmcp cn
Key Personnel
ISBN Contact: Yang Muzhi

Press & Publication Administration of the People's Republic of China
85 Dongsi Nandajie, Beijing 100703
Tel: (010) 5127818 *Fax:* (010) 65127875
Key Personnel
President: Song Muwen
Chief Foreign Affairs Dept: Wei Hong

Standard Book Numbering Agency, see China ISBN Agency

Colombia

Agencia Colombiana del ISBN, Camara Columbiana del Libro
Carrera 17 A No 37-27, Santafe de Bogota
Mailing Address: Apdo Aereo 8998, Santafe de Bogota
Tel: (01) 2886188 *Fax:* (01) 2873320
E-mail: camlibro@latino.net.co
Web Site: camaracolumbiandelibro.com.co
Key Personnel
Contact: Sr Jaime Bravo Navarrete

◇Camara Colombiana del Libro
Carrera 17A, No 37-27, Apdo Aereo 8998, Santafe de Bogota
Tel: (01) 2886188 *Fax:* (01) 2873320
Colombian Book Association.
Publication(s): *Correo Editorial - Boletin Bibliografico ISBN*
Associate Companies: Agencia Colombiana Del ISBN
Branch Office(s)
Camara Colombiana Del Libro Seccional Occidente

†◇Centro Regional para el Fomento del Libro en America Latina y el Caribe
Calle 70 No 9-52, Apdo Aereo 57348, Santafe de Bogota, cundinamarca
Tel: (01) 2495141; (01) 2126056 *Fax:* (01) 2554614
E-mail: cerlalc@impsat.net.co
Key Personnel
Dir: Carmen Barvo
Founded: 1971
Regional Centre for Book Promotion in Latin America and the Caribbean.
ISBN Prefix(es): 92-9057; 958-671

CERLALC, see Centro Regional para el Fomento del Libro en America Latina y el Caribe

Standard Book Numbering Agency, see Agencia Colombiana del ISBN, Camara Columbiana del Libro

Standard Book Numbering Agency
Camara Colombiana del Libro, Carrera 17A, No 37-27, Apartado Aerep 8998, Santafe de Bogota
Tel: (01) 2886188 *Fax:* (01) 2873320
E-mail: camlibro@camlibro.com.co
Web Site: www.camlibro.com.co

Key Personnel
Dir: Adriana Mejia
Contact: Gladys Torres Bazurto
Publication(s): *Libros Registrados En Colombia; Periodico Tinta Fresca*

Costa Rica

†◇AIBDA
Apdo 55, 2200 Coronado
Tel: (0506) 2290222 *Fax:* (0506) 2294741; (0506) 2292659
E-mail: aibda@iica.ac.cr
Web Site: www.iica.ac.cr
Telex: 2144 IICACR *Cable:* IICASANJOSE
Key Personnel
Executive Secretary: Michael Snarskis
Founded: 1965
Publication(s): *AIBDA Actualidades* (irregularly, free to members); *Boletin Informativo* (triannually, free to members); *Boletin Tecnico* (irregularly, available on sale); *Guia para Bibliotecas Agricolas; Quienes Quien en AIBDA*

Asociacion Interamericana de Bibliotecarios, see AIBDA

Association Interamericaine de Bibliothecaires, see AIBDA

Documentalistas y Especialistas en Informacion Agricola, see AIBDA

Documentalistes et Specialistes d'Information Agricole, see AIBDA

†‡Instituto Interamericano de Cooperacion para la Agricultura (IICA)
Apdo 55, 2200 Coronado, San Jose
Tel: (0506) 2290222 *Fax:* (0506) 2294741
Telex: 2144 lica *Cable:* IICASANJOSE
Key Personnel
Editor, General Publishing: Susana Raine
Founded: 1942
In every Latin American & Caribbean country, Canada & USA.
ISBN Prefix(es): 92-9039

Standard Book Numbering Agency
Biblioteca Nacional, San Jose 1000
Mailing Address: Apdo Postal 10008, San Jose 1000
Tel: (0506) 2331706; (0506) 212479 *Fax:* (0506) 2235510
E-mail: elenaalpizar@hotmail.com
Key Personnel
General Dir: Saborio Torres Xinia
Publication(s): *Catalogo Nacional ISBN*

Croatia

†Croatian ISBN Agency
Member of International ISBN Agency
Hrvatske bratske zajednice 4, 10000 Zagreb
Tel: (01) 6164087; (01) 6164288 *Fax:* (01) 6164371
E-mail: isbn@nsk.hr
Web Site: www.nsk.hr
Key Personnel
Contact: Daniela Zivkovic, PhD
E-mail: dzivkovic@nsk.hr
Founded: 1992
Registers publishers in Croatia in the ISBN System; maintains the Croatian Publishers

Database; holds statistics on book publishing in Croatia.
Subjects: National ISBN Agency
Publication(s): *Book & Music Publishers in Croatia: Directory*
Parent Company: National & University Library in Zagreb, Hroatske Bratske Zajednice 4, Zagreb 10000

Croatian ISMN Agency, see Croatian ISBN Agency

Cuba

Agencia Cubana del ISBN
Camara Cubana del Libro, Calle 15 No 602 esq C, Vedado, Ciudad Havana
Tel: (07) 36034 *Fax:* (07) 333441
E-mail: cclfilh@artsoft.cult.cu
Telex: 511881 feria cu
Key Personnel
Contact: Jose A Robert Gasset

◊**Ediciones Union, Union de Escritores y Artistas de Cuba**
Calle 17 No 351, Vedado, Havana
Tel: (07) 324571 *Fax:* (07) 333158
Telex: 051156364
Key Personnel
Secretary: Armando Cristobal
Union of Writers & Artists of Cuba.
Publication(s): *Union, La Gaceta de Cuba, Revista de Literatura Cubana*

Union Escritores y Artistas de Cuba, see Ediciones Union, Union de Escritores y Artistas de Cuba

Standard Book Numbering Agency, see Agencia Cubana del ISBN

Cyprus

Standard Book Numbering Agency
c/o Cyprus Centre for Registration of Books & Serials, The Cyprus Library, Eleftheria Sq, Nicosia 1011
Tel: (02) 303180; (02) 676118 *Fax:* (02) 304532
E-mail: cypruslibrary@cytanet.com.cy
Key Personnel
Dir: Dr Antonis Maratheftis
 E-mail: amaratheftis@hotmail.com
Founded: 1987
National library; Member of IFLA.
Subjects: Cyprus bibliography
ISBN Prefix(es): 9963-0

Czech Republic

◊**Ministerstvo Kultury C R, Oddeleni Tisku Oddeleni Knizi Kultury**
Maltezske, 118 11 Prague 1
Tel: (02) 24510452 *Fax:* (02) 57311376
Czech Ministry of Culture, Production Department, Publishing & Trade Book.
Publication(s): *Books in Czech Republic*

Narodni agentura ISBN v CR
Klementinum 190, 11001 Prague 1
Tel: (02) 21663306 *Fax:* (02) 21663306
E-mail: isbn@nkp.cz
Web Site: www.nkp.cz
Key Personnel
ISBN Administrator: Mr Antonin Jerabek
Publication(s): *Soupis ucastniku systemu mezinarodniho standardniho cislovani knih - ISBN - v Ceske republice* (directory of Czech publishers, annually)
Parent Company: Narodni Knihovna Ceske republiky
Associate Companies: Narodna agentura ISBN v SR

Standard Book Numbering Agency, see Narodni agentura ISBN v CR

Svaz Antikvaru CR
Karlova 2, 110 00 Prague 1
Tel: (02) 24229205 *Fax:* (02) 262186
E-mail: info@meissner.cz
Web Site: www.meissner.cz
Key Personnel
President: Petr Meissner
Contact: Vaclav Prosek
Member of ILAB (International League of Antiquarian Booksellers).

◊**Svaz ceskych knihkupcu a nakladatelu (SCKN)** (Association of Czech Booksellers & Publishers (ACBP))
Member of IPA
Jana Masaryka 56, 120 00 Prague 2
Tel: (02) 2423 90030150; (02) 90053015; (02) 22513198 *Fax:* (02) 22513198; (02) 90052991
E-mail: sckn@mbox.vol.cz
Web Site: www.sckn.cz
Key Personnel
Chairman: Jitka Undeova
Chairman of Booksellers Section, 1st Vice Chairman: Jiri Seidl
Chairman of Publishers Section, 2nd Vice Chairman: Ina Pavel Hye
Founded: 1879 (Renewed 1990)
Association of Czech Booksellers & Publishers (ACBP).
Publication(s): *Bookseller & Publisher* (Knihkupec a nakladatel, monthly); *Czech Books In Print* (Katalog kladovanych Knih) (5th edition, 2000, yearly (printed version) electronic one prepared)
ISBN Prefix(es): 80-902495
Associate Companies: Svet knihy S R O (Book World Ltd)

Denmark

Dansk ISBN - Kontor (the Danish ISBN Agency)
Dansk BiblioteksCenter, Tempovej 7-11, 2750 Ballerup
Tel: 44867777 *Fax:* 44867853
E-mail: isbn@dbc.dk
Web Site: www.isbn.kontoret.dk
Key Personnel
ISBN Administrator: Mrs Lone Olsen
 Tel: 44867741 *E-mail:* lo@dbc.dk

Den Danske Boghandlerforening (The Danish Booksellers Association)
Siljangade 6.3, DK 2200 Copenhagen S
Tel: 32542255 *Fax:* 32540041
E-mail: ddb@bogpost.dk
Web Site: www.bogguide.dk
Key Personnel
President: Jesper Moller
Dir: Olaf Winslow
Member of European Booksellers Federation (EBF) & Intranational Booksellers Federation (IBF).
Publication(s): *Bogmarkedet* (The Booktrade, The Danish Book Market with Den Danske Forlaeggerforening)

◊**Den Danske Forlaeggerforening**
18/1 Kompagnistr, 1208 Copenhagen K
Tel: 33156688 *Fax:* 33156588
E-mail: publassn@webpartner.dk
Key Personnel
Dir: JB Tune Olsen
Danish Publishers' Association.
Publication(s): *Det Danske Bogmarked* (The Danish Book Market with Den Danske Boghandlerforening); *Fortegnelse over Samhandels berettigede Boghandlere MV* (Register of Licensed Booksellers, etc)

◊**Forening for Boghaandvaerk, Nordjysk afdeling** (Association of Book Crafts, North Jutland Branch)
Hvedevaenget 5, DK-9000 Aalborg
Tel: 98127933
Web Site: www.boghaandvaerk.dle
Key Personnel
President: Bent Joergensen *E-mail:* bj@kb.dk
Treasurer & Secty: Lilli Riget
Founded: 1888
Danish Bookcraft Association.
Publication(s): *Arets bogarbejde* (Selected Books of the Year, yearbook); *Bogvennen* (The Book Lover, yearbook)
Parent Company: Forening for Boghaandvoerk, c/o Riget Consult, Thorshavnasgade 22, kl, DK-2300 Kobenhavn S

†‡**Nordic Council of Ministers Publications**
Store Strandstraede 18, DK-1255 Copenhagen K
Tel: 33960200 *Fax:* 33960202
E-mail: nmr@nmr.dk
Web Site: www.norden.org
Telex: 15544 nordmr dk
Key Personnel
Secretary General: Soren Christensen
Head, Publishing Department: Agneta Sverkel-Osterberg *Tel:* 33960410 *E-mail:* aso@nmr.dk
Founded: 1971
ISBN Prefix(es): 92-893
Number of titles published annually: 200 Print

Standard Book Numbering Agency, see Dansk ISBN - Kontor (the Danish ISBN Agency)

Ecuador

Camara Ecuatoriana del Libro
Nucleo de Pichincha, Avda Eloy Alfaro, No 355 Piso 9, Casilla 17-01-3329, Quito
Tel: (02) 553311; (02) 553314 *Fax:* (02) 222150
E-mail: celnp@hoy.net
Telex: 22096 ecuali ed
Key Personnel
Presidenta Ledo: Luis Mora Ortega

Standard Book Numbering Agency, see Camara Ecuatoriana del Libro

Egypt (Arab Republic of Egypt)

General Egyptian Book Organization
Corniche El-Nil-Boulaq, Cairo
Tel: (02) 775371; (02) 775649; (02) 5775109
 Fax: (02) 754213
Telex: 93932 Book *Cable:* GEBO
Key Personnel
Chairman: Dr Ezz El Dine Ismail
Also Publisher.
ISBN Prefix(es): 977-01

†National Information & Documentation Centre
Al-Tahrir St, Dokki, Cairo
Tel: (02) 3371696
Telex: 92111 Alsun
Key Personnel
Dir: Dr Mostago Esmat El Sarha

Standard Book Numbering Agency
National Library & Archives, Corniche El Nile, Boulac, Cairo
Tel: (02) 5750856; (02) 5751078; (02) 575886
 Fax: (02) 775385
Telex: 93932

Estonia

Estonian Publishers Association
Parnumnt 10, PO Box 3366, EE0090 Tallinn
Tel: (02) 443937 *Fax:* (02) 445720
Key Personnel
Dir: Ms A Tarvis
Affiliate member of International Publishers Association.

Standard Book Numbering Agency
Eesti Rahvusraamatukogu, National Library, Tonismagi 2, 15189 Tallinn
Tel: (02) 6307372 *Fax:* (02) 6311200
E-mail: eraamat@nlib.ee
Web Site: www.nlib.ee/textid/isbn.html
Key Personnel
Contact: Ms Mai Valtna

Ethiopia

†‡United Nations Economic Commission for Africa, ECA
PO Box 3001, Addis Ababa
Tel: (01) 517200 *Fax:* (01) 514416
Telex: 21029 *Cable:* ECA
Key Personnel
Librarian: Abdel-Rahman M Tahir

Faroe Islands

Foroya Landsbokasavn
J C Svabosgotu 16, FO-110 Torshavn
Mailing Address: PO Box 61, FO-110 Torshavn
Tel: (031) 311626 *Fax:* (031) 318895
E-mail: fonalib@flb.fo
Web Site: www.flb.fo
Key Personnel
Contact: Mr Arnbjoern O Dalsgard
 E-mail: arndal@flb.fo

Standard Book Numbering Agency, see Foroya Landsbokasavn

Fiji

Regional ISBN Centre The ISBN Officer
The University of the South Pacific Library, Suva Fiji
Mailing Address: PO Box 1168, Suva Fiji
Tel: 313900 (ext 2375) *Fax:* 300830
E-mail: mamtora_j@usp.ac.fj
Web Site: www.usp.ac.fj/~library
Telex: fj 2276

Finland

◇Finnish ISBN Agency
Helsinki University Library, Teollisuuskatu 23, FIN-00014 Helsinki
Mailing Address: PO Box 26, University of Helsinki, 00014 Helsinki
Tel: (09) 19144327; (09) 19144329 *Fax:* (09) 19144341
E-mail: marrit.hutunen@helsinki.fi
Web Site: hul.helsinki.fi/hyk/kt/kustantajat/isbn/html
Key Personnel
ISBN Administrator: Maarit Huttunen
The Finnish ISSN Center is located at the same address.

Kirjakauppaliitto Ry
Eerikinkatu 15-17 D 43-44, 00100 Helsinki
Tel: (09) 68599110 *Fax:* (09) 68599119
E-mail: toimisto@kirjakauppaliitto.fi
Key Personnel
Chief Executive: Olli Erakivi
The Booksellers' Association of Finland.
Publication(s): *Kirja-ja Paperialan kalenteri* (Book & Paperbranch register); *Kirjakauppalehti* (Bookstore Magazine)
Parent Company: Kirjakauppalehden Julkaisu Oy
Associate Companies: Suomen Kirjakaupan Saatio

Standard Book Numbering Agency, see Finnish ISBN Agency

Suomen Kirjailijaliitto
Runeberginkatu 32 C 28, SF-00100 Helsinki
Tel: (09) 445392; (09) 449752 *Fax:* (09) 492278
E-mail: suomen.kirjailijaliitto@cultnet.fi
Key Personnel
President: Jarkko Laine
Executive Secretary: Ms Paeivi Liedes
Association of Finnish Authors.
Publication(s): *Suomen Runotar*

Suomen Kustannusyhdistys
PO Box 177, FIN-00121 Helsinki
Tel: (09) 22877250 *Fax:* (09) 6121226
Web Site: www.skyry.net
Key Personnel
Dir: Veikko Sonninen
Member of the International Publishers Association & the Federation of European Publishers.
Publication(s): *Vuoden Kirjat* (List of books published in Finland)

The Finnish Book Publishers' Association, see Suomen Kustannusyhdistys

France

◇ADAGP (Societe des Auteurs dans les Arts Grarphiques et Plastiques)
11 rue Berryer, 75008 Paris
Tel: (01) 43590979 *Fax:* (01) 45634489
E-mail: adagp@adagp.fr
Web Site: www.adagp.fr
Key Personnel
Dir: Jean-Marc Gutton
Personal Assistant: Martine Bertot *Tel:* (01) 43590933 *E-mail:* bertot@adagp.fr
Founded: 1953
To administer & protect the rights of visual artists (painters, sculptors, engravers, architechts, graphists, photographers, illustrators) in matters of copyright in France.

ADELF, see Association des Ecrivains de Langue Francaise (ADELF)

ADMICAL (Association pour le Developpement du Mecenat Industriel et Commercial)
16 Rue Girardon, 75018 Paris
Tel: (01) 42552001 *Fax:* (01) 42557132
E-mail: contact@admical.org
Web Site: www.admical.org
Key Personnel
Dir: Marianne Eshet
Contact: Anne-Gaele Duriez *E-mail:* agduriez@admical.org
Association for the Development of business sponsorship.
Publication(s): *Cultural Sponsorship in Europe* (1999); *L'Actualite du Mecenat* (4 times a year); *Le Guide Juridique et Fiscal du Mecenat*; *Le Repertoire du Mecenat 2001/2002* (biennially)
ISBN Prefix(es): 2-907507

AFEM, see Association Francaise du Multimedia

AFNIL, see Agence Francophone pour la Numerotation Internationale du Livre (AFNIL)

Agence Francophone pour la Numerotation Internationale du Livre (AFNIL)
35, rue Gregoire de Tours, 75006 Paris
Tel: (01) 44412800 *Fax:* (01) 44072033
E-mail: afnil@electre.com
Key Personnel
Contact: Mrs Michele Fournier

AIEF, see Association Internationale des Etudes Francaises (AIEF)

ASFORED (Association Nationale pour la Formation et le Perfectionnement Professionnels dans les Metiers de l'Edition)
21 rue Charles-Fourier, 75013 Paris
Tel: (01) 45883981 *Fax:* (01) 45815492
Key Personnel
President: Francois (de) Waresquiel
Dir General: Pierre Tabourdeau

Association des Auteurs Autoedites
23 rue de La Sourdiere, 75001 Paris
Tel: (01) 47033664
Web Site: www.auteurs-autoedites.com

ORGANIZATIONS — FRANCE

Key Personnel
President: Robert Hentsch *E-mail:* rhentsch@club-internet.fr
Founded: 1975
Association of Author Autoedites, 500 authors members - Production: 130 books in 2000. Catalogue available on internet. Publications include poetry, art, novels, philosophy, science, teaching health.
Publication(s): *Poetry, art, novels, philosophy, science, teaching health*
Number of titles published annually: 130 Print

◇**Association Francaise du Multimedia**
8 rue Jean Gaijon, 75008 Paris
Tel: (01) 48242991 *Fax:* (01) 45231337
E-mail: info@afee.org
Web Site: www.afee.org
Key Personnel
President: Regis Poubelle
General Secretary: Pacale Ohl
French Multimedia Association.

†◇**Association Internationale de Bibliophilie**
58 rue Richelieu, c/o Bibliotheque Nationale de France, 75084 Paris Cedex 02
Tel: (01) 47037757 *Fax:* (01) 47037570
Key Personnel
Secretary-General: Jean-Marc Chatelain
Founded: 1834
International Association of Bibliophiles.
Publication(s): *Le Bulletin du Bibliophile* (biannually)

Association internationale des Critiques litteraires (NGO), see International Association of Literary Critics

†◇**Association Internationale des Etudes Francaises (AIEF)**
One rue Victor-Cousin, F-75230 Paris Cedex 05
Fax: (01) 40462588
Web Site: www.aief.eu.org
Key Personnel
Contact: Prof Antoine Compagnon
 E-mail: compagnon@aief.eu.org
Founded: 1949
International Association of French Studies.
Publication(s): *Cahiers de l'AIEF* (yearly)
ISBN Prefix(es): 2-913718
Number of titles published annually: 1 Print
Bookshop(s): Les Belles Lettres, 95 Bd Raspai, 75006 Paris

Cercle de la Librairie
35 rue Gregoire-de-Tours, Paris
Tel: (01) 44412800 *Fax:* (01) 44412865
Telex: Lifran 270838 F
Key Personnel
President: Charles Henri Flammarion
Publication(s): *Catalogue general des ouvrages parus en langue francaise* (General Catalog of Works which have appeared in the French Language); *Donnees statistiques sur l'edition du Livre en France* (French Book Production Statistics); *La Bibliographie de la France* (biblio); *Le Repertoire International des Editeurs et Diffuseurs de Langue Francaise* (International List of French Language Publishers and Distributors); *Les Livres Disponibles* (French Books in Print); *Repertoire des Livres au Format de Poche* (List of Paperback or Pocket Edition Books); *Repertoire international des Librairies de Langue francaise* (International List of French Language Bookshops)
Associate Companies: Booksellers' Circle Association of Book Trades and Industries

†◇**CISAC (Confederation Internationale des Societes d'Auteurs et de Compesiteurs)**
11 rue Kepler, 75116 Paris
Key Personnel
Secretary-General: Eric Baptiste
President: Jean Louis Tournier
Founded: 1926
Confederation internationale des Societes d'Auteurs et Compositeurs.

CITL, see College International des Traducteurs Litteraires (CITL)

College International des Traducteurs Litteraires (CITL)
Espace Van Gogh, F-13200 Arles
Tel: (04) 90497252 *Fax:* (04) 90934321
Key Personnel
Dir: Jacques Thieriot
International College of Literary Translators.
Publication(s): *Actes des Assises de la Traduction Litteraire a Arles* (1 volume per year)
Parent Company: Assises de la Traduction Litteraire A Arles

COPACEL, see Groupements Francais des Fabricants de Papiers d'Impression-Ecriture (COPACEL)

†**Council of Europe Publishing**
Palais de l'Europe, 67075 Strasbourg Cedex
Tel: (0388) 412581 *Fax:* (0388) 413910
E-mail: publishing@coe.int
Web Site: book.coe.int
Telex: 870943F
Key Personnel
Commercial Manager: Sophie Lobey
 Tel: 0388412263 *E-mail:* sophie.lobey@coe.int
Rights & Permissions Manager: Charalambos Papadopoulos *Tel:* 0388412952
 E-mail: charalambos.papadopoulos@coe.int
Editorial Manager: Francine Raveney
 Tel: 0388415114 *E-mail:* francine.raveney@coe.int
Founded: 1949
Official publisher of the Council of Europe & reflects many different aspects of the Council's work, addressing the main challenges facing European society & the world today. Our catalogue of over 1200 title in French & English includes topics ranging from international law, human rights, ethical & moral issues, society, environment, health, education & culture.
Subjects: Human Rights, Law, Criminology, Public Health, Sociology, Nature, Consumer Protection, Education, Sports, Culture, Social Security, Youth, Local Authorities
ISBN Prefix(es): 92-871

CPE (Conseil Permanent des Ecrivains)
Maison des ecrivains, 53 rue de Verneuil, 75007 Paris
Tel: (01) 49546880 *Fax:* (01) 42842087
Key Personnel
President: Maurice Cury *Tel:* (01) 40358706

◇**Dilicom**
20, rue des Grands-Augustins, 75006 Paris
Tel: (01) 43254335 *Fax:* (01) 43297688
E-mail: bf@edilectre.fr
Web Site: www.dilicom.net
Key Personnel
General Dir: Bernard de Freminville
Specialize in teleordering & teleinformation between booksellers & publishers
Electra Transmittal.

Conseil Permanent des Ecrivains, see CPE (Conseil Permanent des Ecrivains)

Association des Ecrivains de Langue Francaise (ADELF) (French Language Writers' Association)
14, rue Broussais, 75014 Paris
Tel: (01) 43219599 *Fax:* (01) 43201222
Key Personnel
President: Edmond Jouve
Secretary General: Simone Dreyfus
Founded: 1926
French Language Writers' Association.
Publication(s): *Lettres et cultures de langue francaise* (biannually)

Editions du Conseil de l'Europe, see Council of Europe Publishing

Federation de l'Imprimerie et de la Communaute Graphique-FICG
115 Blvd St-Germain, 75006 Paris
Tel: (01) 46342115 *Fax:* (01) 46337334
Key Personnel
President: Dominique Harley
Communications: Christiane Drussant
Federation of French Printers & Trade Writers.

Federation francaise des syndicats de libraries, see FFSL (Federation francaise des syndicats de libraires)

FFSL (Federation francaise des syndicats de libraires)
43 rue de Chateaudun, 75009 Paris
Tel: (01) 42820003 *Fax:* (01) 42821051
Key Personnel
President: Jean-Luc Dewas

FNPS (Federation nationale depresse d'information specialisee)
37 rue de Rome, 75008 Paris
Tel: (01) 44904360 *Fax:* (01) 44904372
Web Site: www.fnps.fr/main.asp
Key Personnel
President: Jean-Marc Detailleur
Dir: Jean-Michel Huan
French National Federation of Special Interest Press.

◇**France Edition**
115, bd Saint-Germain, 75006 Paris
Tel: (01) 44411313 *Fax:* (01) 46346383
E-mail: info@franceedition.org
Web Site: www.franceedition.org
Telex: Lifran 270838 F
Key Personnel
Chairman: Liana Levi
Man Dir, French Publishers Agency: Kathryn Nanovic-Morlet *Tel:* 212-254-4540
 E-mail: kathryn@blf.org
Specializing in promoting French books around the world, the organization of trade fairs, exhibitions, symposia, conferences & training sessions, production of catalogues devoted to specific themes, publication of a newsletter & marketing studies.
Publication(s): *La Lettre de France Edition* (marketing studies)
Branch Office(s)
French Publishers Agency/France Edition Inc, 853 Broadway, New York, NY 10003-4703, United States *Tel:* 212-254-4540 *Fax:* 212-979-6229

GFFDIE, see Groupements Francais des Fabricants de Papiers d'Impression-Ecriture (COPACEL)

Groupements Francais des Fabricants de Papiers d'Impression-Ecriture (COPACEL)
154 bd Haussmann, 75008 Paris
Tel: (01) 45628707 *Fax:* (01) 45628247

Telex: 651544
Key Personnel
President: M Claude Prince
French Manufacturer of Pocket Editions Group.

Intergovernmental Copyright Committee, see United Nations Educational, Scientific & Cultural Organization (UNESCO)

†◇International Association of Literary Critics
Affiliate of UNESCO
Hotel de Massa, 38 rue du Faubourg, St Jacques, F-75014 Paris
Tel: (01) 53101200 *Fax:* (01) 53101212
Telex: 206963
Key Personnel
President: Robert Paul Andre *Tel:* (01) 45873876
Vice President: F Malinho; Matuzewski
Founded: 1970
Association internationale des Critiques litteraires (NGO).
Publication(s): *Revue* (biannually)

†‡International Association of Universities
Maison de l, Bureau Int des Unversites, F-75732 Paris Cedex 15
Mailing Address: One Rue Miollis, F-75732 Paris Cedex 15
Tel: (01) 45 6825 45 *Fax:* (01) 47 3476 05
E-mail: iau@unesco.org
Web Site: www.unesco.org/iau
Key Personnel
Secretary General: Eva Egron-Polak
Dir, Research: Guy R Neave
Founded: 1950
International non-governmental organization.
Publication(s): *Higher Education Policy* (quarterly, journal); *International Handbook of Universities* (biannual); *Monographs: Issues in Higher Education* (biannual); *World List of Universities*

†‡International Chamber of Commerce
38 cours Albert 1er, F-75008 Paris
Tel: (01) 49532828 *Fax:* (01) 49532942
E-mail: icclib@ibnet.com; icc@iccwbo.org
Web Site: www.iccwbo.org
Telex: 650770 ICCHQ *Cable:* INCOMERC-PARIS
Key Personnel
Secretary General: Maria Livanos
ISBN Prefix(es): 92-842

†◇International Council on Archives (Conseil International des Archives)
60 rue des Francs-Bourgeois, F-75003 Paris
Tel: (01) 40276306 *Fax:* (01) 42722065
E-mail: ica@ica.org
Web Site: www.ica.org
Key Personnel
Secretary General: Mrs Joan Van Albada *Tel:* (01) 40276349 *E-mail:* vanalbada@ica.org
Publication(s): *Archivum*; *Janus*; *N'Existe Plus*

†‡International Institute for Educational Planning (IIEP)
7-9 rue Eugene-Delacroix, 75016 Paris
Tel: (01) 45037700 *Fax:* (01) 40728366
Telex: 620074 *Cable:* EDUPLAN PARIS
Key Personnel
Dir: Jacques Hallak
Publications Officer: John Hall
Founded: 1963
Established by UNESCO, IIEP is an international center for advanced training and research in educational planning. The Institute's aim is to contribute to the development of education by expanding both knowledge and the supply of competent professionals in the field of educational planning. In this endeavor the Institute cooperates with interested training and research institutions throughout the world. IIEP is financed by UNESCO and by voluntary contributions from individual member states. The program and budget of the Institute are approved by its own Governing Board. A catalogue of publications is available on request.
Subjects: Educational Planning (Administration & Management, Methologies, Manpower & Employment, School Locations, Non-formal, adult and rural Education & Literacy)
ISBN Prefix(es): 92-803

†ISSN International Centre
20 rue Bachaumont, F-75002 Paris
Tel: (01) 44882220 *Fax:* (01) 40263243
E-mail: issnic@issn.org
Web Site: www.issn.org
Key Personnel
Marketing Assistant: Zhen-Li Ha *Tel:* (01) 44 88 20 60 90 *E-mail:* ha@issn.org
Contact: P Godefroy *E-mail:* godefroy@issn.org
International Bibliographic database regarding serial publications.
Publication(s): *ISSN Register* (quarterly on CD-ROM (ISSN compact) or frequently on the web (ISSN online)); *List of Serial Title Word Abbreviations-Cumulated Edition* (1998)

Ministere des Affaires Etrangeres Division de L'Ecrit et des Mediatheques
244, boulevard Saint-Germain, 75303 Paris 07 SP
Tel: (01) 43178688 *Fax:* (01) 43178883
Key Personnel
Dir: Yves Mabin
Ministry of Foreign Affairs.
Parent Company: Association pour la diffusion de la pensee francaise (ADPF), 6 rue Ferrus, 75683 Cedex 14 Paris

†Office International des Epizooties (World Organisation for Animal Health)
12 Rue de Prony, F-75017 Paris
Tel: (01) 44151888 *Fax:* (01) 42670987
E-mail: oie@oie.int; pub.sales@oie.int
Web Site: www.oie.int
Telex: EPIZOTI 642285F
Key Personnel
Dir General: Dr Bernard Vallat
Sales & Marketing Agent: Ms Tamara Benicasa
Founded: 1924
Subjects: Veterinary science & world animal health
Publication(s): *Disease Information* (weekly, periodical); *World Animal Health in 2001* (2002, periodical)
ISBN Prefix(es): 92-9044
Total Titles: 44 Print
Distributed by SMPF Inc

†Organization for Economic Cooperation & Development (OECD)
2 rue Andre-Pascal, 75775 Paris Cedex 16
Tel: (01) 45248200 *Fax:* (01) 45248500
E-mail: news.contact@oecd.org
Web Site: www.oecd.org
Telex: 640048 *Cable:* DEVELOPECONOMIE
Key Personnel
Secretary General: Donald Johnston
Founded: 1960
Subjects: Economics, Statistics, Environment, Energy, Education, Transportation, Agriculture, Development, Finance, Urban Affairs, Labor, Science and Technology, Tourism, Consumer policy, Social problems
ISBN Prefix(es): 92-64; 92-821
Showroom(s): 33 rue Octave Feuillet, 75016 Paris
Bookshop(s): 33 rue Octave Feuillet, 75016 Paris

SACEM (Societe des Auteurs Copositeurs et Editeurs de Musique)
225 ave Charles-de-Gaulle, 92521 Neuilly-sur-Seine
Tel: (01) 47475650 *Fax:* (01) 47451294
Key Personnel
President: Gerard Calvi

SELF Syndicate of French Language Authors
Espace Lautrec, 11 rue Andre-Antoine, 75018 Paris
Tel: (01) 46711319 *Fax:* (01) 46707395
Key Personnel
President: Maguelonne Toussaint-Samat; Victoria Therame; Benjamin Lambert
Secretary General: Gerard Gaillaguet
Publication(s): *Ecrivains*

SLAM, see Syndicat National de la Librairie Ancienne et Moderne (SLAM)

SLUT, see Syndicat des Libraires Universitaires et Techniques

Societe des Auteurs Compositeurs et Editeurs de Musique, see SACEM (Societe des Auteurs Copositeurs et Editeurs de Musique)

Societe des auteurs dans les arts graphiques, plastiques et photographiques, see ADAGP (Societe des Auteurs dans les Arts Grarphiques et Plastiques)

Standard Book Numbering Agency, see Agence Francophone pour la Numerotation Internationale du Livre (AFNIL)

Standard Book Numbering Agency, see Unesco Books and Copyright Division, USBN agency

Syndicat des ecrivains de langue francaise, see SELF Syndicate of French Language Authors

Syndicat des Libraires Universitaires et Techniques
Librairie Sauramps Medical, 11 blvd Henri IV, 34000 Montpelier
Tel: (467) 413970 *Fax:* (467) 525905
Key Personnel
President: Dominique Torreilles
Secretary: Janine de Puniet

Syndicat National de la Librairie Ancienne et Moderne (SLAM)
4 rue Git-le-Coeur, F-75006 Paris
Tel: (01) 43294638; (01) 43540128 *Fax:* (01) 43254163
E-mail: slam@worldnet.fr
Web Site: www.slam-livre.fr
Key Personnel
President: Alain Marchiset
National Association of Antiquarian & Modern Booksellers.
Publication(s): *Guide du Livre Ancien et des libraires membres du Syndicat national de la Librairie Ancienne et Moderne*

◇Syndicat National de l'Edition
115 Blvd Saint-Germain, 75006 Paris
Tel: (01) 4414050 *Fax:* (01) 441 4077
Key Personnel
President: Serge Eyrolles
Deputy General: Jean Sarzana
National Union of Publishers.
Publication(s): *Abeviations des principales references en matiere juridique* (1993); *Actes du colloque sur l'edition scientifique francaise* (Fevrier, 1991); *Fiches techniques-pays (etudes du marche du livre a l'etranger)* (RFA, Espagne, Royaume-Uni); *L'edition de livres en France* (annually, statistics); *Plaquette de representation de l'edition francaise*
ISBN Prefix(es): 2-909677

ULF (Union des Libraires de France), see Union des Libraires de France (ULF)

UNESCO, see United Nations Educational, Scientific & Cultural Organization (UNESCO)

Unesco Books and Copyright Division, USBN agency
35, rue Gregoire de Tours, 75006 Paris
Tel: (01) 44412800 *Fax:* (01) 44072033
Telex: 204461; 270602
Key Personnel
Contact: Mrs Michele Fournier

Union des Libraires de France (ULF)
40 rue Gregoire-de-Tours, 75006 Paris
Tel: (01) 43298879 *Fax:* (01) 43298879
Key Personnel
President: Eric Hardin
General Delegate: Marie-Dominique Doumenc
Union of French Booksellers.
Publication(s): *La Voix des Libraires*; *Le Bullentin de l'ULF*

†◇United Nations Educational, Scientific & Cultural Organization (UNESCO)
7 Place de Fontenoy, 75352 Paris 07-SP
Tel: (01) 45 68 1000 *Fax:* 01 45 68 57 39
Web Site: www.unesco.org
Telex: 03324461 *Cable:* UNESCO PARIS
Key Personnel
Dir-General: Koichiro Matsuura
Dir, UNESCO Publishing: Milagros Del Corral
Rights: Alastair McLurg; Michiko Tanaka
Promotion: Cristina Laje; Jeanette Coulibaly
Founded: 1946
To date, UNESCO books have been translated into more than seventy languages. UNESCO acts as Standard Book Numbering Agency, administering ISBNs for UN publications. It also maintains responsibility, within its Copyright Division, for the Intergovernmental Copyright Committee. UNESCO publishes seven periodicals, including the illustrated monthly reviews, The Unesco Courier & World Heritage Review.
Subjects: Education, Science, Technology, Social Science, Culture, Communications, Human Rights, Art
ISBN Prefix(es): 92-3
Number of titles published annually: 152 Print
Total Titles: 6,000 Print

Gambia

Standard Book Numbering Agency
Gambia National Library, Reg Pye Lane, Banjul
Tel: 228312 *Fax:* 223776
E-mail: national.library@ganet.gm
Key Personnel
Chief Librarian: Abdou W Mbye *Tel:* (0220) 226491 *Fax:* (0220) 949600
Founded: 1946
National/public library service.
Branch Office(s)
Brikama Branch Library *Tel:* 484111 (Western division)

Germany

AG BDB, see Arbeitsgemeinschaft der Blindenschrift-Druckereien und Bibliotheken (AG BDB)

Arbeitsgemeinschaft der Blindenschrift-Druckereien und Bibliotheken (AG BDB)
pA Deutsche Blindenstudienanstalt e V, Am Schlag 2-A, 35037 Marburg
Mailing Address: Postfach 1160, 35001 Marburg
Tel: (06421) 606103 *Fax:* (06421) 606229; (06421) 606269
Key Personnel
President: Rainer F V Witte
Association of Braille Publishing Houses & Libraries.

Arbeitsgemeinschaft von Jugendbuchverlagen e v
avj-Geschaeftsstelle, c/o Esslinger Verlag, Postfach 100325, D-73703 Esslingen
Tel: (07153) 8262 92 *Fax:* (07153) 8262 93
E-mail: avj.ziemer@t-online.de
Key Personnel
Chairman: Mathias Berg
Manager: Susanne Ziemer
The Alliance of Publishers of Children's Books in Germany, Austria & Switzerland.
Publication(s): *Kinder und Jugendbuchverlage von A bis Z*

Arbeitskreis fur Jugendliteratur eV
Metzstrasse 14c, 81601 Munich
Mailing Address: PO Box 800124, 81601 Munich
Tel: (089) 4580806 *Fax:* (089) 45808088
E-mail: A.K.J@t-online.de
Web Site: www.ibby.org
Key Personnel
Manager: Franz Meyer
Youth Literature Committee (Section of IBBY).
Publication(s): *Auswahlliste zum Deutschen Jugendliteraturpreis* (annually); *Buch der Jugend* (annually); *Das Bilderbuch*; *Das blane Buch*; *Das Kinderbuch*; *Julet* (quarterly)

◇Borsenverein des Deutschen Buchhandels eV
Grosser Hirschgraben 17-21, 60311 Frankfurt am Main
Mailing Address: Postfach 100442, 60004 Frankfurt am Main
Tel: (069) 1306-0 *Fax:* (069) 1306-201
Key Personnel
General Manager: Dr Harald Heker
Head Information Department: Eugen Emmerling *Tel:* (69) 1306291 *Fax:* (69) 1306294 *E-mail:* emmerling@boev.de
Publication(s): *Adressbuch fuer den deutschsprachigen Buchhandel* (German-Speaking Book Trade Directory); *Archiv fuer Geschichte des Buchwesens* (Book History Archives); *Boersenblatt fuer den Deutschen Buchhandel* (German Book Journal); *Buch und Buchhandel in Zahlen* (Books & the Book Trade in Figures); *BuchJournal* (a general magazine for booksellers' customers); *Deutsche Bibliographie* (German Bibliography); *Neuerscheinungen-Sofortdienst (CIP)* (New Titles Express Service CIP); *VLB Verzeichnis lieferbarer Buecher* (German Books in Print)
Branch Office(s)
Berliner Bureau, Schiffbauerdamm 5, 10117 Berlin *Tel:* (030) 2800783-0 *Fax:* (030) 2800783-50
Leipziger Buero, Gerichtsweg 28, 04103 Leipzig *Tel:* (0341) 9954-110 *Fax:* (0341) 9954-113

Borromausverein eV
Wittelsbacherring 9, Postfach 1267, 53002 Bonn
Tel: (0228) 72580 *Fax:* (0228) 7258189
Key Personnel
President: Norbert Trippen
Publr: Rolf Pitsch

Bundesverband Deutscher Kunstverleger eV (Association of German Art Editors)
Member of Arbeitskreis Deutscher Kusthandelsverbande
Darmstaedter Landstr 3, 60594 Frankfurt Main
Mailing Address: Postfach 700 210, 60552 Frankfurt Main
Tel: (069) 629120 *Fax:* (069) 629120
Web Site: www.bdkv.de
Key Personnel
Chairman: Klaus Gerrit Friese; Ruth Leuchter
Contact: Birgit Maria Sturm *E-mail:* sturm@bdkv.de
Founded: 1989
The Federal Association of German Art Publishers is the ideal Sponsor of Kunstkoeln-International Art Fair for Art Brut, Editions & Art after 1980.

†◇Conseil international des Associations de Bibliotheques de Theologie
Postfach 250104, 50517 Cologne
Tel: (0221) 3382110 *Fax:* (0221) 3382103
Key Personnel
President: Dr A Geuns
Secretary: Dr I Dumke
International Council of Theological Library Associations.

Deutscher Komponisten-Interessenverband eV
Kadettenweg 80b, 12205 Berlin
Tel: (030) 84 31 05 80 *Fax:* (030) 84 31 05 82
Web Site: www.dkiv.allmusic.de
Key Personnel
President: Karl Heinz Wahren
Vice President: Prof Harald Banter
Manager: Manuel Neuendorf
German Composers Association.
Publication(s): *Handbuch "Komponisten der Gegnwart im Deutschen Komponisten-Interessenverband"* (1995)

†◇Gutenberg-Gesellschaft eV
Liebfrauenplatz 5, D-55116 Mainz
Tel: (06131) 22 64 20 *Fax:* (06131) 23 35 30
Key Personnel
President: Jens Beutel
Vice President: Senator Hannetraud Schultheiss
Secretary General: Gertraude Benoehr
Founded: 1901
Internationale Vereinigung fuer Geschichte und Gegenwart der Druckkunst e V
Gutenberg Gesellschaft, International Association for Past & Present History of the Art of Printing.
Subjects: Past & Present History of the Art of Printing & of the Book
Publication(s): *Gutenberg-Jahrbuch*; *Kleine Drucke*; *Sonder-Ver oeffentlichungen*
ISBN Prefix(es): 3-7755

Hessischer Verleger- und Buchhandler-Verband eV
Hessischer Verleger-und Buchhandler-Verband eV, Villa Clementine, Frankfurterstr 1, 65189 Wiesbaden
Tel: (0611) 16660-0 *Fax:* (0611) 16660-59
E-mail: buchhandelgverband.hs@t-online.de
Key Personnel
Chairman: Michael Lemling
Manager: Peter Brunner
Hessen Publishers' & Booksellers' Federation.

I A S A, see International Association of Sound & Audiovisual Archives

†International Association of Sound & Audiovisual Archives
c/o Suedwestrundfunk, Documentation & Archives Dept, 76522 Baden-Baden

GERMANY   BOOK TRADE

Mailing Address: Postfach 820, 76522 Baden-Baden
Tel: (07221) 9293487 *Fax:* (07221) 9294199
Web Site: www.llgc.org.uk/iasa/
Key Personnel
Secretary General: Albrecht Haefner
  E-mail: albrecht.haefner@swr.de
Founded: 1969
A non-governmental UNESCO-affiliated organization established to function as a medium for international co-operation between archives which preserve recorded sound & audiovisual documents.
Publication(s): *IASA Information Bulletin* (quarterly); *IASA Journal* (biannual)
ISBN Prefix(es): 0-946475

International Council of Theological Library Associations, see Conseil international des Associations de Bibliotheques de Theologie

†◇International ISBN Agency, International ISMN Agency
Staatsbibliothek zu Berlin - Preussischer Kulturbesitz, Potsdamerstr 33, 10785 Berlin
Tel: (030) 266 2498 *Fax:* (030) 2662378
E-mail: isbn@sbb.spk-berlin.de; ismn@sbb.spk.berlin.de
Web Site: isbn-international.org; ismn-international.org
Key Personnel
Dir: Dr Hartmut Walravens
Contact: Carolin Unger *E-mail:* isbn3@sbb.spk-berlin.de
Founded: 1972
This is the international ISBN office. For national offices & further details please see the ISBN System section of this book.
Publication(s): *International ISBN Users' Manual*; *International ISMN Users' Manual*; *ISBN Newsletter*; *ISMN Newsletter*; *Music Publishers' International ISMN Directory*; *Publishers' International ISBN Directory*; *The ISBN & its Uses* (video-film & sound-slide-show)

†International ISMN Agency
Potsdamer Str 33, 10785 Berlin
Tel: (030) 266 2496; (030) 266 2498; (030) 266 2338 *Fax:* (030) 266-2378
E-mail: ismn@sbb.spk-berlin.de
Web Site: ismn-international.org
Key Personnel
Dir: Dr Hartmut Walravens
Founded: 1994
Agency for the standard numbering of sheet music.
Publication(s): *ISMN Newsletter*; *ISMN Users' Manual*; *Publishers' International ISMN Directory*

International Youth Library, see Internationale Jugendbibliothek

†◇Internationale Jugendbibliothek
Schloss Blutenburg, 81247 Munich
Tel: (089) 891211-0 *Fax:* (089) 8117553
E-mail: bib@ijb.de
Web Site: www.ijb.de
Key Personnel
Chairwoman Foundations Board of Governors: Christa Spangenberg
Dir: Dr Barbara Scharioth
Publicity: Carola Gade *Tel:* (089) 891211-30
  E-mail: presse@ijb.de
Founded: 1949
International Youth Library.
Publication(s): *IJB Report* (biannually); *The White Ravens* (annual selection of international children's & youth literature)

Internationale Vereinigung fuer Geschichte und Gegenwart der Druckkunst eV, see Gutenberg-Gesellschaft eV

ISBN, see International ISBN Agency, International ISMN Agency

ISMN, see International ISMN Agency

Landesverband der Verleger und Buchhaendler Rheinland-Pfalz eV
Kaiserstr 88, 55116 Mainz
Tel: (06131) 234035 *Fax:* (06131) 230364
Rhineland-Palatinate Provincial Federation of Publishers and Booksellers.

LIBER, see Ligue des Bibliotheques Europeennes de Recherche (LIBER)

†◇Ligue des Bibliotheques Europeennes de Recherche (LIBER)
Prof Dr Hans-Albrecht Koch, Universitat Bremen, 28334 Bremen
Mailing Address: Postfach 330440, 28334 Bremen
Tel: (0421) 2183361
Key Personnel
President: Esko Haekli
League of European Research Libraries.
Publication(s): *European Research Libraries Co-operation* (The Liber Quarterly)

Norddeutscher Verleger- und Buchhaendler-Verband eV
Brahmsalle 24, 20144 Hamburg
Tel: (040) 4103161 *Fax:* (040) 2298514
North German Publishers' and Booksellers' Federation.

◇O Gracklauer Verlag und Bibliographische Agentur GmbH (O Gracklauer Publishers & Bibliographic Agency)
Wallotstr 7A, 14193 Berlin-Grunewald
Tel: (030) 8258139 *Fax:* (030) 8262039
E-mail: info@gracklauer.de
Web Site: www.gracklauer.de
Key Personnel
Owner & Man Dir: Rose M Meerwein
Suppliers of bibliographic information, title & copyright research.

Presse-Grosso, see Presse-Grosso-Bundesverband Deutscher Buch-, Zeitungs-und Zeitschriften-Grossisten eV

Presse-Grosso-Bundesverband Deutscher Buch-, Zeitungs-und Zeitschriften-Grossisten eV
Haendelstr 25-29, 50674 Cologne
Tel: (0221) 9213370 *Fax:* (0221) 92133744
E-mail: bvpg@bvpg.de
Web Site: www.pressegrosso.de
Key Personnel
Chairman: Weiner Schiessl
Manager: Gerd Kapp
Founded: 1950
Federation of German Wholesalers of Books, Newspapers and Periodicals (also known as Presse-Grosso).

International Standard Book Numbering Agency, see International Standard Buchnummer GmbH

International Standard Buchnummer GmbH
Agentur fuer die Bundesrepublik Deuschland, 60004 Frankfurt am Main
Mailing Address: Postfach 100442, 60004 Frankfurt am Main

Tel: (069) 1306387 *Fax:* (069) 1306258
E-mail: lehr@bhv.de
Web Site: www.buchandel.de
Key Personnel
Dir: Manfred Gravelius
The Booksellers' Association, Documentation & Data Processing Department (Standard Book Numbering Agency).

Stiftung Lesen
Fischtorplatz 23, 55116 Mainz
Tel: (06131) 288900 *Fax:* (06131) 230333
Key Personnel
Manager: Prof Hilmar Hoffmann

UIE, see UNESCO Institute for Education (UIE)

†◇UNESCO Institute for Education (UIE)
Feldbrunnenstr 58, 20148 Hamburg
Tel: (040) 4480410 *Fax:* (040) 4107723
E-mail: uie@unesco.org
Web Site: www.unesco.org/education/uie
Key Personnel
Dir: Dr Adama Ouane
Founded: 1951
The UIE was created in 1951 with the financial support of UNESCO & a number of member states. It is funded by Germany, UNESCO & other donors, & housed in premises provided by the City of Hamburg. It is a research, training & dissemination center which has enabled more than 2000 scholars to participate in international cooperative research projects & has developed a particular interest in lifelong education. Major areas of the current research program include the development of nonconventional approaches to primary education for out-of-school children, post-literacy & functional literacy for adults & young people, monitoring & evaluation of nonformal education programs, literacy exchange network, the legislative environment for adult education, the empowerment of women through education. Publications include over 120 titles in English, French, Spanish & Arabic & the bimonthly *International Review of Education*, for which there are concessionary subscription rates for developing countries. In the field of lifelong education & related aspects, it has published over 60 books under the series of UIE Monographs, Case Studies, Advances in Lifelong Education, UIE-Studies on Post-literacy in Industrialized Countries, other theoretical studies on Post-literacy & Continuing Education, & UIE-Studies on Functional Illiteracy in Industrialized Countries & Handbooks & Reference books, based on both theoretical & operational research.
Subjects: Literacy, Non Formal Basic Education, Continuing Education, Functional Illiteracy in Industrialized Countries, Nonformal Education, Adult Education & lifelong learning
ISBN Prefix(es): 92-820
Parent Company: UNESCO, Paris, France

Verband der Schulbuchverlage eV (Association of Text Book Publishers; Association of Test Book Publishers)
Zeppelinallee 33, 60325 Frankfurt
Mailing Address: Postfach 900540, 60445 Frankfurt am Main
Tel: (069) 703075 *Fax:* (069) 70790169
E-mail: verband-der-schulbuchverlage@t-online.de
Key Personnel
Chief Executive: Andreas Baer
Association of Publishers of Schoolbooks.

Verband der Verlage- und Buchhaendlungen Berlin-Brandenburg eV
Luetzowstr 33, 10785 Berlin
Tel: (030) 263918-0 *Fax:* (030) 263918-18

Key Personnel
President: Dietrich Simon
Manager: Detlef Bluhm
Publishers' & Booksellers' Association Berlin-Brandenburg.

Verband der Verlage und Buchhandlungen in Baden-Wuerttemberg eV (Association of Publishers & Booksellers in Baden-Wuerttemberg e V)
Paulinenstr 53, 70178 Stuttgart
Tel: (0711) 619410 *Fax:* (0711) 6194144
E-mail: buchhandelsverband@vvb-bw.de
Web Site: www.vvb-bw.de
Key Personnel
Man Dir: Johannes Scherer
Association of Publishers & Booksellers in Baden-Wuerttemberg.

Verband der Verlage und Buchhandlungen in Nordrhein-Westfalen eV (Association of Publishers & Booksellers at North Rhine Westphalia)
Marienstr 41, 40210 Duesseldorf
Tel: (0211) 864450 *Fax:* (0211) 324497
E-mail: nrw@buchhandel.de
Web Site: www.buchhandel.de/nrw
Key Personnel
Secretary: Herbert Becker
Federation of Publishers and Booksellers in North Rhine-Westphalia.

◇**Verband Deutscher Antiquare eV**
Kreuzgasse 2-4, 50667 Cologne
Mailing Address: Postfach 18 01 80, 50504 Cologne
Tel: (0221) 92548262 *Fax:* (0221) 9257932
E-mail: buch@antiquare.de
Web Site: www.antiquare.de
Key Personnel
President: Herrn Jochen Granier
Vice President: Fr Inge Utzt
German Antiquarian Booksellers' Association.
Publication(s): *Katalog zur Stuttgarter Antiquariatsmesse* (annually); *Mitgliederverzeichnis* (biannually); *zur Koelner Antiquariatsmesse empfohlen von der Internationalen Liga der Antiquariatsbuchhaendler ILAB; Katalog zu den Antiquariatstagen in Koeln* (annually)

Verband Deutscher Auskunfts und Verzichnismedien
Heerdter Sandberg 30, 40549 Duesseldorf
Tel: (0211) 577995-0 *Fax:* (0211) 577995-44
E-mail: info@vdav.org
Web Site: www.vdav.de
Key Personnel
Secretary: Petra Felkowski
Association of German Directory Publishers.

Verband katholischer Verleger und Buchhaendler eV
Adenauerallee 176, 53113 Bonn
Tel: (0228) 2421560 *Fax:* (0228) 2421561
E-mail: vkb2000@aol.com
Key Personnel
Manager: Peter J Kerp
Federation of Catholic Publishers & Booksellers.

Verlegervereinigung Rechtsinformatik eV
c/o Carl Heymanns Verlag KG, Luxemburger Str 449, 50864 Cologne
Tel: (0221) 943730 *Fax:* (0221) 94373901
Key Personnel
Chairman: Bertram Gallus
Association of Publishers of Legal Documentation.

Verwertungsgesellschaft Wort (Collecting Society Word)
Goethestr 49, 80336 Munich
Tel: (089) 514120 *Fax:* (089) 5141258
Web Site: www.vgwort.de
Key Personnel
Chairman: Lutz Franke
General Manager: Prof Ferdinand Melichar, PhD
E-mail: F.Melichar@vgwort.de
Founded: 1958
Copyright society representing authors & publishers of literary & scientific works.
Branch Office(s)
V G Wort Buero Berlin, Koethener Str 44, 10963 Berlin *Tel:* (030) 26 12 751 *Fax:* (030) 23 00 36 29

Ghana

†**Association of African Universities**
PO Box 5744, Accra-North
Tel: (021) 774495 *Fax:* (021) 774821
E-mail: secgenaau.org
Telex: 2284 Adua *Cable:* AFUNIV ACCRA
Key Personnel
President: Prof George Benneh
Secretary-General: Prof Donald Ekong
Founded: 1967
Association des Universites Africaines.
Subjects: Higher Education in Africa

Standard Book Numbering Agency
Ghana Library Board, PO Box 2970, Accra
Tel: (021) 223526; (021) 228402 *Fax:* (021) 247768
E-mail: GeorgePadmore@Africanmail.com
Web Site: www.ghanacom.gh/Padmore
Key Personnel
Contact: Omari Mensah Tenkovang
Parent Company: Ghana Library Board

†◇**Union of Writers of the African Peoples** (Union des Ecrivains Negro Africains)
c/o Ghana Association of Writers, PO Box 4414, Accra
Key Personnel
President: Atukwei Okai
General Secretary: J E Allotey-Pappoe
Objectives include the operation of a writers' publishing co-operative and the encouragement of the use of Swahili as the common language of all black African peoples.
Publication(s): *African World Alternatives*

†◇**University Bookshop**
University of Ghana, Legon
Mailing Address: PO Box LG 1, Legon
Tel: (021) 500398 *Fax:* (021) 500774
E-mail: bookshop@ug.edu.gh
Key Personnel
Manager: Emmanuel K H Tonyigah
Founded: 1948

Greece

Hellenic Federation of Publishers & Booksellers
73 Themistocleous St, 10683 Athens
Tel: (01) 3300924; (01) 3804760 *Fax:* (01) 3301617
E-mail: poev@otenet.gr
Key Personnel
President: Georgios Dardanos
Member of: International Association of Publishers; Federation of European Publishing; Federation of European Booksellers.
Publication(s): *Catalogue of the Greek Children's Books*; *General Catalogue of Greek Publishers*

Standard Book Numbering Agency
National Library of Greece, National Centre of ISBN, Panepistimiou 32, 10679 Athens
Tel: (01) 3608597; (01) 3382549 *Fax:* (01) 3611552; (01) 3608141
Telex: 216270 ypth gr
Key Personnel
ISBN Administrator: Ms Eugenia Kefallineou

Syllogos Ekdoton Bibliopolon Athinon (Publishers & Booksellers' Association of Athens)
73 Themistokleous St, 10683 Athens
Tel: (01) 3830029; (01) 3303268 *Fax:* (01) 3823222
E-mail: seva@otenet.ge
Key Personnel
President: Eleni Kanaki
Member of Hellenic Federation of Publishers & Booksellers.
Subjects: Issues concerning the book industry

Guatemala

Comite Gremial de Editores de Guatemala
Camara de Comercio de Guatemala, 10a Calle 3-80 zona 1, Guatemala City
Tel: (02) 2329053; (02) 2518381 *Fax:* (02) 2329053; (02) 2518381
Key Personnel
President: Santa Irene Piedra

Guinea

SAEC, see La Societe Africaine d'Edition et de Communication (SAEC)

La Societe Africaine d'Edition et de Communication (SAEC)
BP 555, Conakry
Tel: 461068 *Fax:* 443291
Key Personnel
PDG de la SAEC: Mr Djibril Tamsir Niane
Editorial Secretary: Mr Daouda Tamsir Niane

Guyana

CARICOM, see Regional ISBN Agency (CARICOM)

Regional ISBN Agency (CARICOM)
Caribbean Community Secretariat, Church St & Ave of the Republic, 3rd floor, Bank of Guyana Bldg, Georgetown
Mailing Address: PO Box 10827, Georgetown
Tel: (02) 69289 *Fax:* (02) 67816; (02) 66091; (02) 57341; (02) 58039
E-mail: carisec1@caricom.org; carisec2@caricom.org; carisec3@caricom.org
Web Site: www.caricom.org *Cable:* CARIBSEC GUYANA
Key Personnel
ISBN Administrator: Maureen Newton

Publication(s): *Regional Census Office, Volume of Basic Tables for Sixteen CARICOM Countries*; *Aging in the Commonwealth Caribbean*; *Caribbean development to the Year 2000: challenges, prospects and policies*; *CARICOM Model Legislation on Citzenship*; *Domestic Violence*; *Equality for Women in Employment*; *Equal Pay*; *Ingeritance*; *Maintenance & Maintenance Oredr*: *Sexual Harassment & Sexual Offences*; *CARICOM Perspective*; *CARICOM Secretary-General's report* (annually); *CARICOM'S trade: a quick reference to some summary data: 1980-1996*; *CCS Current Awareness Service: New Additions: Articles* (occasional); *Charter of Civil Society for the Caribbean Community*; *Common External Tariff of the Caribbean Common Market: based on the Harmonised Commodity Description & Coding System (HS) 2nd ed*; *Curriculum Guidelines for Family Life Education in the Caribbean: Education for Living*; *Directory of Caribbean Publishers, 3rd ed*; *Employment Problem in CARICOM Countries: the Role of Education & Training in its Existence & its Solution*; *External Public Debt & Balance of Payment of CARICOM Member States 1980-1996*; *National Accounts Digest 1980-1994*; *Regional Monograph: Intraregional & Extraregional & Extraregional Mobility: the New*; *Regional Cultural Policy of the Caribbean Community*; *Removing the Barriers: facts on the CARICOM Single Market & Economy*; *REPORT on a Comprehensive Review of the Programmes, Institutions and Organisations of the Caribbean Community*; *Socio-economic Conditions of Children & Youth in CARICOM Countries: a Situational Analysis*; *The Caribbean Community in the 1980s: report by a group of Caribbean experts*; *Towards Equity in Development: a Report on the Status of Women in Sixteen Commonwealth Caribbean Countries*; *Treaty estalighing the Caribbean Community, Chaguaramas, 4th July 1973*

Standard Book Numbering Agency, see Regional ISBN Agency (CARICOM)

Hong Kong

Books Registration Office
Leisure & Cultural Dept, Rm 805, 8/F, Lai Chi Kok Government Offices, 19 Lai Wan Rd, Lai Chi Kok, Hong Kong
Tel: 21809143 *Fax:* 21809841
E-mail: bro@lcsd.gov.hk
Key Personnel
ISBN Administrator & Librarian: Miss Chow Kam-sheung

Government Information Services
5/F, Murray Bldg, Garden Rd
Tel: (852) 2842-8728
Web Site: www.info.gov.hk/isd
Key Personnel
Dir of Information Services: Thomas Chan

Standard Book Numbering Agency, see Books Registration Office

Hungary

Magyar Iroszoevetseg
Bajza u 18 1062, Budapest H-1062
Tel: (01) 3228840 *Fax:* (01) 213419
Key Personnel
President: Bela Pomogats
Hungarian Writers' Association.
Publication(s): *Kortars*; *Magyar Naplo* (journal)

◇**Magyar Koenyvkiadok es Koenyvterjesztoek Egyesuelese**
Kertesz v.41 1/4, 1367 Budapest
Mailing Address: PO Box 130, 1367 Budapest
Tel: (01) 3432540 *Fax:* (01) 3432541
Key Personnel
President: Istvan Bart
Secretary General: Peter Zentai
Editor-in-chief: Tarjan Tamas
Association of Hungarian Publishers & Booksellers.
Publication(s): *Koenyvvilag*
ISBN Prefix(es): 963-7002; 963-7409

Orszagos Szechenyi Koenyvtar Magyar ISBN Iroda
Budavari Palota F epuelet, 1827 Budapest
Tel: (01) 224 3748 *Fax:* (01) 202-0804
Key Personnel
Head of Division: Susanne Berke *E-mail:* berk@oszk.hu
National Szechenyi Library.
ISBN Prefix(es): 963-201

Standard Book Numbering Agency, see Orszagos Szechenyi Koenyvtar Magyar ISBN Iroda

Iceland

Felag Islenskra Bokautgefenda (Icelandic Publishers' Association)
Baronsstig 5, 101 Reykjavik
Tel: 5118020 *Fax:* 5115020
E-mail: baekur@mmedia.is
Web Site: www.bokautgefa.is
Key Personnel
Chairman: Sigurdur Svavarsson
General Manager: Vilborg Hardardottir
Founded: 1889
Icelandic Publishers' Association.
Publication(s): *Bokatidindi* (annually)

Standard Book Numbering Agency of Iceland
National & University Library of Iceland, Legal Deposit Dept, Arngrimdlsgata 3, 107 Reykjavik
Tel: 5255643; 5255645 *Fax:* 5255612
E-mail: nannab@bok.hi.is
Telex: 2111 iskult
Key Personnel
Departmental Chief: Ms Nanna Bjarnadottir *E-mail:* nannab@bok.hi.is

India

AABC, see Afro-Asian Book Council (AABC)

†◇**Afro-Asian Book Council (AABC)**
4835/24 Ansari Rd, Daryaganj, New Delhi 110002
Tel: (011) 3261487 *Fax:* (011) 3267437
E-mail: sdas@ubspd.com
Key Personnel
Secretary General: Sukumar Das
Dir: Abul Hasan *E-mail:* kiran@ubspd.com
Founded: 1990
Nonprofit book promotion organization for South-South dialogue for the development of indigenous authorship & national book industries in Asia & Africa; International Book Development
Member of African Publishers Network (AP-NET), Asia-Pacific Cooperative Programme for Reading Promotion & Book Development (APPREB) & World Intellectual Property Organisation (WIPO).
Publication(s): *AABC Newsletter* (quarterly, newsletter)
Number of titles published annually: 3 Print
Total Titles: 8 Print

Assam Publishers' Association
College Hostel Rd, Panbazar, Guwahati 781 001
Tel: 543 995

Delhi State Booksellers' & Publishers' Association
Ranjit Nagar, Shiv Chowk, New Delhi 110008
Mailing Address: PO Box 1511, Delhi 11006
Tel: (011) 231867; (011) 2515726 *Fax:* (011) 2936758
Key Personnel
President: Devendra Sharma
Honorary Secretary: Bhupinder Chowdhri

Federation of Indian Publishers
Federation House 18/1-C Institutional Area, JNU Rd, Aruna Asaf Ali Marg, New Delhi 110067
Tel: (011) 6964847; (011) 6852263 *Fax:* (011) 6864054
Key Personnel
President: Shri R C Govil
Honorary General Secretary: A K Ghosh
Executive Secretary: S K Ghai
Publication(s): *Indian Book Industry Journal*

Gujarat Book Trade Federation
Navajivan Trust, PO Navajivan, Ahmedabad 380014
Tel: (079) 447 634; (079) 447 635
Key Personnel
Honorary Secretary: R N Shah
Representative body of the book trade in Gujarat.

†‡**International Crops Research Institute for the Semi-Arid Tropics (ICRISAT)**
Patancheru 502 No 324, Andhra Pradesh
Tel: 40596161 *Fax:* 40241239
E-mail: icrisat@cgnet.com
Key Personnel
Dir General: Shawki M Barghouti
Contact: R P Eaglesfield
Subjects: Agriculture
ISBN Prefix(es): 92-9066

Meerut Publishers' Association
c/o Rastogi Publications, Subhash Bazar, Shivaji Rd, Meerut 250002
Tel: (0121) 510688; (0121) 516080 *Fax:* (0121) 512545
Telex: 0549-209
Key Personnel
Partner: Mr H K Rastogi
Specializing in the field of bio-sciences, agriculture, environment & genetics for undergraduate & post graduate courses of studies in colleges & universities.
Parent Company: M/S Rastogi Publications
Associate Companies: M/S Pioneer Printers, Shiuasi Rd, Meerut

National Agency for ISBN
Ministry of Human Resource Development, Government of India, Dept of Education, New Delhi 110001
Mailing Address: B2 W 3, Curzon Rd Barracks, Kasturba Ghandi Marg, New Delhi 110001

Tel: (011) 3381739 *Fax:* (011) 3381355; (011) 3382947
Telex: 031-61336
Key Personnel
ISBN Administrator: Mr M S Sharma
Publication(s): *National Catalogue of ISBN Titles*

Standard Book Numbering Agency, see National Agency for ISBN

Indonesia

IKAPI, see Ikatan Penerbit Indonesia (IKAPI)

Ikatan Penerbit Indonesia (IKAPI)
Jl Kalipasir 32, Jakarta 10330
Tel: (021) 3141907; (021) 3146050 *Fax:* (021) 3146050
E-mail: sekretariat@ikapi.or.id
Web Site: www.ikapi.or.id
Key Personnel
President: Arselan Harahap
Secretary General: Robinson Rusdi
Association of Indonesian Book Publishers.

Indonesian ISBN Agency
Perpustakaan Nasional Indonesia, The National Library of Indonesia, Jl Salembra Raya 28, PO Box 3624, Jakarta 10002
Tel: (021) 3101411 *Fax:* (021) 3103554
E-mail: sauliah@pnri.go.id
Telex: 07345875
Key Personnel
Head, Sub Directorate of Bibliography: Sauliah Saleh

Standard Book Numbering Agency, see Indonesian ISBN Agency

Islamic Republic of Iran

Standard Book Numbering Agency
1178 Pallestine Crossroad, Enghelab Ave, Tehran 13157
Mailing Address: PO Box 13145-1483, Tehran 13157
Tel: (021) 6414991 *Fax:* (021) 6415360; (021) 6414991
E-mail: isbn@ketabnet.org
Web Site: www.ketabnet.org
Telex: 224581-IBFS-IR

Ireland

CLE: The Irish Book Publishers' Association
43/44 Temple Bar, Dublin 2
Tel: (01) 670-7393 *Fax:* (01) 670-7642
E-mail: info@publishingireland.com
Web Site: www.publishingireland.com
Key Personnel
Contact: Orla Martin

Cumann Leabharfhoilsitheoiri Eireann, see CLE: The Irish Book Publishers' Association

Irish Educational Publishers' Association
c/o Gill & Macmillan Ltd, Hume Ave, Park West, Dublin 12
Tel: (01) 500 9509 *Fax:* (01) 500 9598
Key Personnel
Secretary: Hubert Mahony *E-mail:* hmahony@gillmacmillan.ie

Israel

Book and Printing Center - Israel Export Institute
29 Hamered St, Tel Aviv 68125
Mailing Address: PO Box 50084, Tel Aviv 68125
Tel: (03) 5142916 *Fax:* (03) 5142881
E-mail: israeli@export.gov.il
Web Site: www.export.gov.il
Telex: 35613 *Cable:* MEMEX
Key Personnel
Dir: Ronit Adler *E-mail:* adler@export.gov.il
Division of the Israel Export Institute. Organizes & promotes activities relating to the export of Israeli books, publishing & printing services.
Publication(s): *Israel Book Trade Directory* (biennially)

Book Publishers' Association of Israel
29 Carlebach St, Tel-Aviv 67132
Mailing Address: PO Box 20123, Tel Aviv 67132
Tel: (03) 5614121 *Fax:* (03) 5611996
E-mail: tbpai@netvision.net.il
Key Personnel
Man Dir: Amnon Ben-Shmuel
Chairman: Shai Hausman
The Association administers two subsidiary cooperative associations & two joint publishing companies - Ma'alot & Yachdav.

Hebrew Writers Association of Israel
6 Kaplan St, Tel Aviv 64734
Mailing Address: PO Box 7111, Tel Aviv 61070
Tel: (03) 6953256 *Fax:* (03) 6919681
Key Personnel
President: Nathan Yonathan
Chairman: Dr Zahava Ben-Dov
Publication(s): *Moznayim* (monthly)

The Institute for the Translation of Hebrew Literature
23 Baruch Hirsch St, Bnei Brak
Mailing Address: PO Box 10051, Ramat Gan 52001
Tel: (03) 5796830 *Fax:* (03) 5796832
E-mail: litscene@ithl.org.il
Web Site: www.ithl.org.il
Key Personnel
Man Dir: Mrs Nilli Cohen
Office Manager: Debbie Dagan
Activities of the Institute include promotion of modern Hebrew literature in translation & co-publishing projects, literary agency services, subsidies to authors & publishers for translations of Hebrew literary works & their publication abroad; also literary agent.
Publication(s): *Bibliography of Modern Hebrew Literature in Translation* (annually); *Modern Hebrew Literature* (semi-annually)

Israel ISBN Group Agency
The Israeli Center for Public Libraries, 5 Havazelet St, Jerusalem 91002
Mailing Address: PO Box 3251, Bnei-Brak 31151
Tel: (03) 6180151 *Fax:* (03) 5798048
E-mail: id@icl.org.il
Web Site: www.icl.org.il
Key Personnel
Dir, Consulting & Publication: Ariella Z Barrett
Tel: (03) 6180151 ext 106

Parent Company: Israeli Center for Libraries
Branch Office(s)
28 Baruch Hirsh St, Bnei Brak 51131 *Tel:* (03) 6180151 ext 106 *E-mail:* ariella@icl.org.il *Web Site:* www.icl.org.il

Standard Book Numbering Agency, see Israel ISBN Group Agency

Italy

◊**Agenzia ISBN per l'Area di Lingua Italiana**
Vie Bergonzoli 5, 20127 Milan
Tel: (02) 28315996 *Fax:* (02) 28315906
Key Personnel
ISBN Administrator: Dr Michele Costa
E-mail: michele.costa@bibliografica.it
ISBN Agency for the Area of Italian Language Run by Editrice Bibliografica.
Parent Company: Associazione Italiana Editori

ALAI, see Associazione Librai Antiquari d'Italia

Associazione Italiana Editori
Via delle Erbe 2, 20121 Milan
Tel: (02) 86463091 *Fax:* (02) 89010863
E-mail: aie@aie.it
Web Site: www.aie.it
Key Personnel
Dir: Ivan Cecchini *E-mail:* ivan.cecchini@aie.it
Italian Publishers' Association.
Publication(s): *Catalogo dei Libri Italiani in Commercio*; *Giornale Della Libreria*
Branch Office(s)
via Crescenzio 19, 00193 Rome

Associazione Librai Antiquari d'Italia
Via Jacopo Nardi 6, I-50132 Florence
Tel: (055) 243253 *Fax:* (055) 243253
E-mail: alai@dada.it
Web Site: www.dada.it/alai
Key Personnel
President: Dr Giuliano Gallini
Secretary: Dr Francesco Scala
Antiquarian Booksellers' Association of Italy.

†‡**Food and Agriculture Organization of the United Nations (FAO)**
Viale delle Terme di Caracalla, I-00100 Rome
Tel: (06) 52251 *Fax:* (06) 52253152
E-mail: telex-room@fao.org
Telex: 610181 FAO I *Cable:* FOODAGRI ROME
Key Personnel
Dir-General: J Diouf
Dir Information: Karin-Lis Svarre
Chief, Sales & Marketing Group: R Sutton
Founded: 1945
The Food & Agriculture Organization (FAO), a specialized agency of the United Nations, was created in 1945. FAO Publications reflect the Organization's principal aims: to increase world agriculture production; raise levels of nutrition; and improve the conditions of rural populations. Titles include books, monographs, periodicals, technical documents, annuals, yearbooks & reports of FAO conferences & meetings. Major publications are produced in the five official UN languages (Arabic, Chinese, English, French & Spanish), & all publications & documents are available on microfiche. Unsolicited manuscripts are automatically rejected. Articles of a technical nature of no more than 2500 words on international aspects of the animal industry, food & nutrition are occasionally accepted. No payment is made.

ITALY

Subjects: Agriculture, Plant Production & Protection, Animal Production & Health, Forestry, Fisheries, Land & Water Development, Economic & Social Development, Food & Nutrition, Computerized Information Series, Educational & Training Materials
ISBN Prefix(es): 92-5; 92-851; 92-852; 92-853; 92-854; 92-855

Institute Propaganda Libraria, see IPL - Istituto Propaganda Libraria

†International Centre Study Preservation & Restoration of Cultural Property (ICCROM)
Via di San Michele 13, 00153 Rome
Tel: (06) 585531 *Fax:* (06) 58553349
E-mail: iccrom@iccrom.org
Web Site: www.iccrom.org
Key Personnel
Dir General: Nicholas Stanley-Price
Founded: 1959
Subjects: Heritage Preservation & Intergovernmental Organization
ISBN Prefix(es): 92-9077

◇IPL - Istituto Propaganda Libraria (Institute of Bookshop Advertising)
Via Mercalli 23, 20122 Milan
Tel: (02) 58301960 *Fax:* (02) 58301960
Key Personnel
Editorial Dir: Nicola Cerbino
Subjects include literature, literary criticism, fiction, history, essays, religion & philosophy.

Standard Book Numbering Agency, see Agenzia ISBN per l'Area di Lingua Italiana

Jamaica

Booksellers' Association of Jamaica
c/o Noveltry Trading Co Ltd, 53 Hanover St, Kingston
Mailing Address: PO Box 80, Kingston
Tel: (876) 922-5883; (876) 922-5661 *Fax:* (876) 922-4743
Key Personnel
President: Keith Shervington

COMLA, see The Commonwealth Library Association (COMLA)

†◇The Commonwealth Library Association (COMLA)
Mona, PO Box 144, Kingston 7
Tel: (876) 927-2123 *Fax:* (876) 927-1926
Key Personnel
President: Elizabeth Watson
Executive Secretary: Norma Amenu-Kpodo
Founded: 1972
Publication(s): *COMLA Bulletin* (Newsletter quarterly, published & distributed by Roy Sanders the Editor, PO Box 1306, Wagga Wagga, NSW 2650, Australia)

◇University of the West Indies Publishers' Association
PO Box 42, Mona, Kingston
Tel: (876) 977-2659 *Fax:* (876) 977-2660
Key Personnel
Publication Officer: Annie Paul
University of the West Indies, Mona Campus.
Publication(s): *Caribbean Geography*

Japan

ACCU, see Asia/Pacific Cultural Centre for UNESCO (ACCU)

Antiquarian Booksellers' Association of Japan
29 San-ei-cho, Shinjuku-ku, Tokyo 160-0008
Tel: (03) 33571411 *Fax:* (03) 33515855
Web Site: www.abaj.gr.jp
Key Personnel
President: Soichi Yagi

†‡Asia/Pacific Cultural Centre for UNESCO (ACCU)
6 Fukuromachi, Shinjuku-ku, Tokyo 162
Tel: (03) 32694435 *Fax:* (03) 32694510
E-mail: general@accu.or.jp *Cable:* ASCULCENTRE TOKYO
Key Personnel
Dir General: Muneharu Kusaba
Founded: 1971
Asian/Pacific Copublication Programme (ACP) is a joint program of UNESCO member states in Asia & the Pacific to produce good children's books. Regional training course on book production organized annually & Noma Concours for Picture Book Illustrations biennially.
Publication(s): *Asian/Pacific Book Development (ABD)*; *Asian/Pacific Culture (APC)*
ISBN Prefix(es): 4-946438

†The Asian Productivity Organization
1-2-10 Hirakawa-cho, Chiyoda-ku, Tokyo 102-0093
Tel: (03) 5226-3920 *Fax:* (03) 52263950
E-mail: apo@apo-tokyo.com
Web Site: www.apo-tokyo.com
Key Personnel
Secretary General: Takashi Tajima
Dir, Information & Public Relations: Kenneth Mok *Tel:* (03) 52263927 *E-mail:* ipr@apo-tokyo.com
Founded: 1961
Subjects: Productivity Improvement in APO Member Countries
ISBN Prefix(es): 92-833
Bookshop(s): Quality Resources, One Water St, White Plains, NY 10601, United States *Tel:* 212-979-8600 *Fax:* 914-791-9467

The Centre for East Asian Cultural Studies for UNESCO
The Toyo Bunko, Honkomagome 2-28-21, Bunkyo-ku, Tokyo 113
Tel: (03) 39420124 *Fax:* (03) 39420120
E-mail: nad03367@niftyserve.or.jp.
Key Personnel
Dir: Yoneo Ishii
Publications: A Tonoike
Parent Company: The Toyo Bunko Foundation

Japan Association of International Publications
Chiyoda Kaikan, 21-4 Nihonbashi 1-chome, Chuo-ku, Tokyo 103-0027
Tel: (03) 32716901 *Fax:* (03) 32716920
Web Site: www.jaip.gr.jp
Key Personnel
Chairman Board: Seishiro Murata
Secretary General: Hiroshi Takahashi
Founded: 1941
Subjects: Association of those who import & sell foreign publications, represent foreign publishers & support import of such publications
Publication(s): *JAIP Directory*
ISBN Prefix(es): 4-931516

Japan Book Publishers Association
6, Fukuro-machi, Shinjuku-ku, Tokyo 162-0828
Tel: (03) 32681303 *Fax:* (03) 32681196

BOOK TRADE

E-mail: onuki@jbpa.or.jp *Cable:* SHOSEKIKYO TOKYO
Key Personnel
President: Kunizo Asakura
Executive Dir: Tadashi Yamashita
Founded: 1957 (March)
Publication(s): *Bulletin of Japan Book Publishers Association*; *The Catalogue of Books in the Near Future*; *Japanese Books in Print CD-ROM Edition*; *Introduction to Publishing in Japan 2002-2003*

Japan Electronic Publishing Association
Tomodasanwa Bldg, 5F, 1-37, Kanda Jimbocho, Chiyoda-ku, Tokyo 101-0051
Tel: (03) 3219-2958 *Fax:* (03) 3219-2940
Web Site: www.jepa.or.jp
Key Personnel
Chairman of Board: Mr Hideki Hasegawa

Japan ISBN Agency
c/o Japan Library Publishers Bldg, 6 Fukuromachi, Shinjuku-ku, Toyko 162
Tel: (03) 32672301 *Fax:* (03) 32672304
Key Personnel
Secretary General: Naotoshi Matsudaira

Nihon Shoten Shogyo Kumiai Rengokai
2 Kanda-Surugadai 1 chome, Chiyoda-ku, Tokyo 101
Tel: (03) 32940388
Japan Federation of Commercial Co-operative of Bookstores.
Publication(s): *Kodomonohon Long-seller-list* (Children's Books: A List of Best Sellers); *Zenkoku Shoten Meibo* (Address Book of Japan Booksellers); *Zenkoku Shoten Shinbun* (Newspaper for booksellers)

◇Publishers' Association for Cultural Exchange, PACE, Japan
2-1, Sarugaku-cho 1-chome, Chiyoda-ku, Tokyo 101-0064
Tel: (03) 32915685 *Fax:* (03) 32333645
E-mail: office@pace.or.jp
Web Site: www.pace.or.jp
Key Personnel
President: Tatsuro Matsumae
Man Dir: Yasuko Korenaga
Founded: 1953
European Representation: Euro-Japanische Gesellschaft e.V. (Ohnichi Kyokai), Rossmarkt 15, 6000 Frankfurt am Main 1, Germany. Tel: (069) 285644.
Publication(s): *Directory of Japanese Publishers* (every other year); *Practical Guide to Publishing in Japan* (annually)

Standard Book Numbering Agency, see Japan ISBN Agency

Kazakstan

Book Chamber of Kazakhstan ISBN Agency
Ulica Puskina 2, Almaty 480016
Tel: (03272) 306421 *Fax:* (03272) 304265
E-mail: rntb@kaznet.kz

Standard Book Numbering Agency, see Book Chamber of Kazakhstan ISBN Agency

Kenya

†◇Eastern and Southern Africa Regional Branch of the International Council on Archives (ESARBICA)
c/o Kenya National Archives, Moi Ave, Nairobi
Mailing Address: PO Box 49210, Nairobi
Tel: (02) 228959 *Fax:* (02) 228020
E-mail: knarchives@form-net.com *Cable:* ARCHIVES NAIROBI

†International Livestock Research Institute
PO Box 30709, Nairobi
Tel: (02) 632311 *Fax:* (02) 631499
Key Personnel
Director General: Hank Fitzhugh
Sales, Production, Information, Rights & Permissions: Michael Smalley
Founded: 1974
Subjects: Livestock Research and Development in Africa
ISBN Prefix(es): 92-9053
Branch Office(s)
POB 5689, Addis Ababa, Ethiopia *Tel:* (01) 613215

Kenya Literature Bureau
Bellevue Area off Mombasa Rd, Nairobi
Mailing Address: PO Box 30022, Nairobi
Tel: (02) 722657
Key Personnel
Man Dir: S C Langat
Chief Editor: A S Githenji
ISBN Prefix(es): 9966-44

Kenya Publishers Association
c/o Phoenix Publishers Ltd, Coffee Plaza, 3rd floor, Heille Selassie Ave, Nairobi
Mailing Address: PO Box 18650, Nairobi
Tel: (02) 222309; (02) 223262 *Fax:* (02) 339875
Key Personnel
Secretary: Stanley Irura

Standard Book Numbering Agency
Kenya National Library Services, Ngong Rd, Nairobi
Mailing Address: PO Box 30573, Nairobi
Tel: (02) 718012; (02) 725859; (02) 725550 *Fax:* (02) 721749
E-mail: knls@nbnet.co.ke
Web Site: www.knls.or.ke
Telex: 23278 afrec ke
Key Personnel
Dir: S K Nganga
Publication(s): *Kenya National Bibliography*

UNEP, see United Nations Environment Programme (UNEP)

†‡United Nations Environment Programme (UNEP)
PO Box 30552, Nairobi
Tel: (02) 623331 *Fax:* (02) 520711; (02) 623692
Web Site: www.unep.org
Telex: 22068 *Cable:* UNITERRA NAIROBI
Key Personnel
Editor: Naomi Poulton *E-mail:* naomi.poulton@unep.org
Founded: 1972
Subjects: Environmental Literature
ISBN Prefix(es): 92-807
Number of titles published annually: 100 Print
U.S. Office(s): United Nations Environment Programme, Regional Office for North America, 1707 "H" St NW, Suite 300, Washington, DC 20006, United States *Tel:* 202-785-0465
E-mail: brennan.vandyke@rona.unep.org

Republic of Korea

ISBN Agency - Korea
The National Library of Korea, 60-1 Panpa-Dong, Seocho-gu, Seoul 137-702
Tel: (02) 5900627 *Fax:* (02) 5900622; (02) 5900621
E-mail: ISSNKC@sun.nl.go.kr

Korean Publishers Association
105-2 Sagan-Dong, Jongno-Gu, Seoul 110-190
Tel: (02) 735 2702 *Fax:* (02) 738 5414
E-mail: kpa@kpa21.or.kr
Web Site: www.ifrro.org/members/kpa.html
Key Personnel
President: Choon Ho Na
Secretary General: Jong Jin Jung
ISBN Prefix(es): 89-85231

Korean Publishing Research Institute
3 F Daehan Chulpan Munhwa Hoegwan, 105-2 Sagan-dong, Jongro-gu, Seoul 110-190
Tel: (02) 7399040 *Fax:* (02) 7376187
E-mail: p715@chollian.net
Key Personnel
Chief Dir: Yoon Chung-Kwang
Researcher: Park Hyun-Na

Standard Book Numbering Agency, see ISBN Agency - Korea

Kuwait

†‡Arab Centre for Medical Literature
PO Box 5225, 13053 Safat
Tel: 5338610 *Fax:* 5338618; 5338619
Key Personnel
Secretary General: Dr Abdel Rahman Al-Awadi
Subjects: Arabizing Medical Literatures
Publication(s): *Atlas of Eye Diseases in Arab Countries* (undergoing publication); *Lecture Notes on Gynaecology*; *Teeth & Health*

Latvia

†Latvian Publishers Association (Latvieas Gramatizdevefu Asociacifa)
Member of International Publishers Association
K Barona iela 36-4, 1011 Riga
Tel: (0371) 7282392 *Fax:* (0371) 7280549
E-mail: lga@gramatizdeveji.lv
Web Site: www.gramatizdeveji.lv
Key Personnel
Executive Dir: Dace Pugaca
President: Anita Rozkalne
Founded: 1993
Protection of rights & interests of publishers
Membership: International Publishers Association.

Standard Book Numbering Agency
Unit of Latvijas bibliografijas Instituts
Latvijas Bibliografijas Instituts, Anglikanu iela 5 (Bibliotekas iela), LV - 1816 Riga
Tel: (02) 7212668 *Fax:* (02) 7224587
E-mail: anitag@lbi.lnb.lv
Web Site: www.lnb.lv/eng/centrala.htm
Key Personnel
Dir, Latvian ISBN Agency: Mrs Laimdota Pruse *E-mail:* laimdotap@lbi.lnb.lv
Founded: 1993
ISBN Numbering.
Parent Company: National Library of Latvia, K.Barona 14, LV - 1235, Riga
Ultimate Parent Company: Ministry of Culture of the Republic of Latvia

Lesotho

◇Standard Book Numbering Agency
National University of Lesotho Library, Thomas Mofolo Library, Roma
Mailing Address: National University of Lesotho, PO Roma 180, Roma
Tel: 340601; 340468 *Fax:* 340000
Web Site: www.nul.ls
Telex: 4303 lo
Key Personnel
University Librarian: Dr Matseliso moshoeshoe Chadzingwa *E-mail:* m.moshoeshoe-chadzingwa@nul.ls
Founded: 1964
Education, humanities, law, science & technology, social sciences, agriculture & health sciences.

Lithuania

Lithuanian ISBN Agency
Centre of Bibliography & Book Science, Gedimino pr 51, LT-2600 Vilnius
Tel: (02) 496066 *Fax:* (02) 496055
E-mail: isbnltu@lnb.lt
Web Site: www.lnb.lt
Key Personnel
Head of Agency & Contact: Dalia Smoriginiene
ISBN Prefix(es): 9986-530

Lithuanian Publishers' Association
Z Sierakausko 15, 62600 Vilnius
Tel: (02) 332943; (02) 332943 *Fax:* (02) 330519; (02) 263157
Key Personnel
President: Aleksandras Krasnovas
Represents the interests of Lithuanian publishers.

Luxembourg

Federation Luxembourgeoise des Editeurs de Livres, ASBL
31, Blvd Konrad Adenauer, L-1115 Luxembourg
Mailing Address: BP 482, L-2014 Luxembourg
Tel: 439444 *Fax:* 439450
E-mail: promoculture@ibm.net
Key Personnel
General Secretary: Jean-Paul Schortgen
Economic Advisor: Romain Jeblick
Luxemburgish Publishers' Association.
Parent Company: Confederation Luxembourgeoise du Commerce

ISBN Agency - Luxembourg
Bibliotheque Nationale, 37 blvd F-D Roosevelt, Luxembourg
Tel: 229755-225 *Fax:* 475672
Web Site: www.bnl.lu
Key Personnel
Dir: F F Monique Kieffer
Parent Company: Bibliotheque nationale

LUXEMBOURG

†Office des Publications Officielles des Communautes Europeenes
Unit OP/3 'Publications', 2 rue Mercier, L-2985 Luxembourg
Mailing Address: BP 1003, L-2985 Luxembourg
Tel: 292942053 *Fax:* 292942025
E-mail: idea@opoce.cec.be
Web Site: www.eur-op.eu.int
Key Personnel
Dir: Lucien Emringer
Chief of Sales: Serge Brack
Chief of Marketing: N Reinert
Founded: 1969
Subjects: Economy, Law, Finance, Enterprises & Business, Energy, Foreign Relations, Agriculture, Fishing, Forestry, Tax, Employment, Labor, Environment, Scientific Research & Techniques, Information, Education, Culture, Statistics
ISBN Prefix(es): 92-77; 92-78
U.S. Office(s): Unipub, 4611-F Assembly Dr, Lanham, MD 20706-4391, United States
Tel: 800-274-4888 *Fax:* 301-459-0056

Standard Book Numbering Agency, see ISBN Agency - Luxembourg

The Former Yugoslav Republic of Macedonia

Standard Book Numbering Agency
Narodna i Univerzitetska Biblioteka, Bul Goce Delcev, br 6, 91000 Skopje
Tel: (091) 115358 *Fax:* (091) 226846
E-mail: zlata@nubsk.edu.mk
Web Site: www.nubsk.edu.mk
Key Personnel
Dir: Vera Kaljlieva

Madagascar

Office du Livre Malagasy (OLM)
Lot 111, H29 Andrefran' Ambohijanahary, Antananarivo 101
Mailing Address: BP 617, Antananarivo 101
Tel: (02) 24449
Key Personnel
Secretary General: Juliette Ratsimandrava
E-mail: ratsimandrav@initel.refer.org

Malawi

ISBN Agency (International Standard Book Number National Agency)
National Archives of Malawi, Nkuuchi St, Zomba
Mailing Address: PO Box 62, Zomba
Tel: (050) 525240; (050) 524184 *Fax:* (050) 525 362
E-mail: archives@sdnp.org.mw
Web Site: www.sdnp.org.nw/~archives/index.html
Key Personnel
Acting Director: O W Ambali
Member of ICA (International Council on Archives).
Publication(s): *National Bibliography Archives of Malawi, Zomba* (annually)
Parent Company: Ministry of Sports & Culture, Private Bag 384, Lilongwe 3

Standard Book Numbering Agency, see ISBN Agency (International Standard Book Number National Agency)

Malaysia

Malaysian Book Importers & Distributors Association
45 Jalan Tun Muhd 2, Taman Tun Dr Ismail, 60000 Kuala Lumpur
Tel: (03) 7193485 *Fax:* (03) 7181664
Key Personnel
President: Mr K Arul
Secretary: Mr Leong Fook Kwong

Malaysian Book Publishers' Association
c/o Penerbit UKM, Paras 3, University Kebangsaan Malaysia, 43600 UKM Bangi Selangor Darul Ehsan
Tel: (03) 8292840; (03) 8253485 *Fax:* (03) 8254515
Key Personnel
Honorary Secretary: Thoma Soh
Publication(s): *Malaysian Publishers Directory*

SARBICA, see Southeast Asian Regional Branch of the International Council on Archives (SARBICA)

†◇Southeast Asian Regional Branch of the International Council on Archives (SARBICA)
c/o National Archives of Malaysia, Jalan Duta, 50568 Kuala Lumpur
Tel: (03) 651 0688 *Fax:* (03) 651 5679
E-mail: query@arkib.gov.my
Web Site: arkib.gov.my/general/inter.html
Key Personnel
Chairman, Malaysia: Mrs Zakiah Hanum
Publication(s): *Southeast Asian Archives*; *Southeast Asian Microfilms Newsletter*

Standard Book Numbering Agency
c/o National Library of Malaysia, National Depository Centre, 232, Jalan Tun Razak, 50572 Kuala Lumpur
Tel: (03) 2943488; (03) 2943150; (03) 2943626 *Fax:* (03) 2927502
E-mail: isbn@www1.pnm.my
Web Site: www.pnm.my
Telex: MA 30092 *Cable:* NATLIB KUALALUMPUR

Maldive Islands

Standard Book Numbering Agency
Ministry of Education, Ghaazee Bldg, Male 20-05
Tel: 323261; 331627 *Fax:* 321201
E-mail: educator@dhivehinet.net.mv
Web Site: www.thauleem.net

Malta

◇Periodical & Book Publishers Association
Villa Yvonne 36, Ta'xbiex Terrace, Ta' Xbiex MSD 11
Mailing Address: PO Box 51, Msida MSD 11
Tel: 9882033 *Fax:* 871 2229; 169 5132
E-mail: bookpub@cwebdesign.com
Web Site: www.cwebdesign.com/pbpa.html
Key Personnel
Founder & Chairman: Joseph J Meli
E-mail: jjm@cwebdesign.com
Founded: 1989
Chairman of "Kopjamalt", The Reproduction Rights Organization for the Maltese Islands.

Standard Book Numbering Agency
Publishers Enterprises Group (PEG) Inc, PEG Bldg, UB 7 Industrial Estate, San Gwann SGN 09
Tel: 440083; 448539 *Fax:* 488908
E-mail: contact@peg.com.mt
Web Site: www.peg.com.mt
Key Personnel
Man Dir: Emanuel Debattista
Publishers & printers.

Mauritius

National ISBN Agency
Editions de l'Ocean Indien Ltee, Stanley, Rose Hill
Tel: (0230) 4646761; (0230) 4643959; (0230) 4643452 *Fax:* (0230) 4643445
E-mail: eoibooks@intnet.mu
Telex: mesynd 4739
Key Personnel
Senior Manager: Clifford Colimalay
Publishers & Distributors of books/private company.
ISBN Prefix(es): 99903-0
Parent Company: Editions de L'Ocean Indien Ltee (Publishers & Distributors)
Associate Companies: Mauritius Printing Specialists (Pte) Ltd, Stanley, Rose-Hill
Branch Office(s)
Curepipe
Flacq
Goodlands
Port Louis
Rose Hill

Standard Book Numbering Agency, see National ISBN Agency

Mexico

Camara Nacional de la Industria Editorial Mexicana
Holanda No 13, CP, 04120 Mexico 21
Tel: (05) 6045338; (05) 6882011; (05) 6882221 *Fax:* (05) 6043147; (05) 6044347
Telex: 1772969
Key Personnel
Dir: R Servin
President: A H Gayosso; J C Cramerez
Mexican Publishers' Association.
Publication(s): *Books of Mexico*; *How to obtain Mexican books and periodicals*

ORGANIZATIONS

Centro Nacional de Informacion, Agencia Nacional ISBN
Mariano Escobedo 438, 5 piso, Col Nueva Anzurez, 11590 Mexico DF
Tel: (05) 2503900 *Fax:* (05) 2031657; (05) 2307632
E-mail: jmarquez@sep.gob.mx
Telex: 1773860 psepme
Key Personnel
ISBN Administrator: Alejandra Martinez Gamboa; Ketty Garcia Agut
National Center of Information, National Agency ISBN.

†◇Consejo Interamericano de Archiveros (CITA)
c/o Archivo General de la Nacion, Apdo postal 1999, Eduardo Molina y Albaniles, Col Penitenciaria, 15350 Mexico DF
Key Personnel
Dir General: Patricia Galeana
Publication(s): *Boletin del AGN y Colecciones Graficas; Documentos de Archivonomia; Estudios Historicos; Guias y Catalogos; Informacion de Archivos Estatales y Municipales*

Standard Book Numbering Agency, see Centro Nacional de Informacion, Agencia Nacional ISBN

Republic of Moldova

Camera Nationala a Cartii din Republica Moldova, see Chambre Nationale du Livre Agence ISBN

Chambre Nationale du Livre Agence ISBN
Subsidiary of Ministry of Culture
bd Stefan cel Mare 180, of 202, 2004 Chisinau
Tel: (02) 24 65 11; (02) 24 65 42 *Fax:* (02) 24 65 11
E-mail: cameracartii@yahoo.com; cncm@moldova.cc
Web Site: www.iatp.md/cnc
Key Personnel
Dir: Valentina Chitoroaga *E-mail:* vchitoroaga@yahoo.com
Founded: 1957
ISBN Prefix(es): 9975-9532

Standard Book Numbering Agency, see Chambre Nationale du Livre Agence ISBN

Morocco

African Training and Research Centre in Administration for Development, Documentation Centre, see Centre Africain de Formation et de Recherche Administratives pour le Developpement, Centre de Documentation

Agence Marocaine de l'ISBN
Bibliotheque Generale et Archives, Service du depot legal, Av Ibn Battouta, B P 1003, Rabat
Mailing Address: BP 1003, Rabat
Tel: (07) 771890; (07) 772152 *Fax:* (07) 776062
E-mail: biblio1@onpt.net.ma
Key Personnel
ISBN Dir: Ahmed Toufiq
ISBN Agency of Morocco.

Publication(s): *Bibliographie Nationale Retrospective du Marco (1986-1995)*
Parent Company: Biliotheque Generale et Archives

†◇Centre Africain de Formation et de Recherche Administratives pour le Developpement, Centre de Documentation
Pavillon International, Blvd Mohamed V, Tangiers
Mailing Address: BP 310, Tangiers
Tel: (09) 94-26-52 *Fax:* (09) 94-14-15
Telex: 33664 *Cable:* CAFRAD TANGIER
Key Personnel
President: Mansouri Messaoud
African Training and Research Centre in Administration for Development, Documentation Centre.
Publication(s): *Directory of Administrative Information Services in Africa*

Standard Book Numbering Agency, see Agence Marocaine de l'ISBN

Namibia

ISBN Agency - Namibia
National Library of Namibia, Private Bag 13349, 9000 Windhoek
Mailing Address: Private Bag 13349, 9000 Windhoek
Tel: (061) 2935305; (061) 2935301 *Fax:* (061) 2935321
E-mail: werner@yaotto.natlib.mec.gov.na
Key Personnel
Contact: W Hillebrecht
Publication(s): *Namibia National Bibliography* (1996-)

Namibian Information Workers Association (NIWA)
PO Box 3060, Windhoek
Tel: (061) 293382 *Fax:* (061) 229808
E-mail: e.namhila@parliment.gov.na; geikhoibes@unam.na
Key Personnel
Chairperson: Ellen Ndeshi Namhila

Standard Book Numbering Agency, see ISBN Agency - Namibia

Nepal

Copyright Services Systems Centre (CSSC) Nepal, (COSESCEN)
Kamabakshee Tole, Gha 3-333, Chowk Bhitra, Kathmandu 44601-3000
Mailing Address: PO Box 3000-CSSC 15B, Kathmandu 44601-3000
Tel: (01) 212289; (01) 223036; (01) 224005
Telex: 3000 1-SB-ASS-NP
Key Personnel
President: Sugat Dass Tuladhar
Secretary General: Ganesh Lall Chhipa
Copyright Dir: Rajendra K Ranjitkar

ISBN, see National Federation of Standard Editor's Association in Nepal (NAFSEEN)

ISBN, see National Federation of Standard Periodicals Publishers Association of Nepal

NEPAL

ISBN, see National Federation of Standard Translator's Association in Nepal

ISBN, see National Standards Wholesaler's Distributor's and Subscriber's Association of Nepal (NASWDISAN)

◇National Federation of Standard Editor's Association in Nepal (NAFSEEN)
Kamabakshee Tole, Gha 3-333, Kathmandu 44601-3000
Mailing Address: PO Box 3000-NFSEA Katmandu-3-30-15B, Kathmandu 44601-3000
Tel: (01) 212289; (01) 223036; (01) 224005
Fax: (01) 223036
Telex: 3000 1-SB-ASS-NP *Cable:* NAFSEAN
Key Personnel
Secretary General: Ganesh Lall Chhipa
Editorial Dir: Ganesh Dass Chhipa
Branch Office(s)
09/63-09 Dathwee Chhen Twa Gallee, Chowk Bhitra 2nd Floor Puranco Bazaar, Arniiko-Barhabise VDC-9, Arniko Rajmarg-87 KM, Bagmati Anchal, Barhabise Mail PO Code 45303, Kathmandu Mail Centre

National Federation of Standard Periodicals Publishers Association of Nepal
Kamabakohee Tole, GHA 3-333, Kathmandu 44601-3000
Mailing Address: PO Box 3000-NFFSPP Kathmandu-3-30-15B, Kathmandu 44601-3000
Tel: 212289; 223036; 224005 *Fax:* (9771) 223036 1SB-ASS
Telex: 3000 1-SB-ASS-NP *Cable:* NAPSPEPAN
Key Personnel
Secretary General: Ganesh Lall Singh
Dir: Ganesh Dass
Branch Office(s)
Arniko-Barhabise VDC-9, Arniko Rajmarg-87 KMArniko Rajmarg-87 KM, Bagmati Anchal Barhamise Mail

◇National Federation of Standard Translator's Association in Nepal
Kamabakshee Tole, Gha 3-333, Kathmandu 44601-3000
Mailing Address: PO Box 3000-NFSTA Kathmandu-3-30-15B, Kathmandu 44601-3000
Tel: (01) 212289; (01) 223036; (01) 224005
Fax: (01) 223036 ISB-ASS
Telex: 3000 1-SB-ASS-NP *Cable:* NAFSTAN
Key Personnel
Secretary General: Ganesh Lall Chhipa
Dir: Ganesh Dass Chhipa
Branch Office(s)
09/63-16 Dathwee Chhen Twa Gallee, Chowk Bhitra 4th Floor Puranco Bazaar, Arniiko-Barhabise VDC-9, Arniko Rajmarg-87 KM, Bagmati Anchal, Barhabise Mail PO Code 45303, Kathmandu Mail Centre

◇National Standards Wholesaler's Distributor's and Subscriber's Association of Nepal (NASWDISAN)
Kamabakshee Tole, Gha 3-333, Kathmandu 44601-3000
Mailing Address: PO Box 3000-NSWDS Kathmandu-3-30-15B, Kathmandu 44601-3000
Tel: (01) 212289; (01) 223036; (01) 224005
Fax: (01) 223036
Telex: 3000 1-SB-ASS-NP
Key Personnel
Secretary General: Ganesh Lall Chhipa
Dir: Ganesh Dass Chhipa
Branch Office(s)
09/63-08 Dathwee Chhen Twa Gallee, Chowk Bhitra 5th floor Puranco Bazaar, Arniiko-Barhabise VDC-9, Arniko Rajmarg-87 KM, Bagmati anchal, Barhabise Mail PO Code 45303, Kathmandu Mail Centre

Netherlands

Centraal Boekhuis BV
Erasmusweg 10, NL-4104 AK Culemborg
Tel: (0345) 475911 *Fax:* (0345) 475343
Key Personnel
Man Dir: C J Hagenbeek
Dir, Sales & Marketing: S Berkina

Collectieve Propaganda van het Nederlandse Boek (CPNB)
Keizersgracht 391, 1016 EJ Amsterdam
Mailing Address: Postbus 10576, 1001 EN Amsterdam
Tel: (020) 6264971 *Fax:* (020) 6231696
Key Personnel
Man Dir: Henk Kraima
Foundation for the Collective Promotion of the Dutch Book.
Publication(s): *Children's Bookweek* (special publications 2); *Kinderboekenmolen, Voorleesgids* (annually); *Premium Bookweek*

†‡Cour Internationale de Justice
Palais de la Paix/Peace Palace, 2517 KJ The Hague
Tel: (070) 302 23 23 *Fax:* (070) 364 99 28
E-mail: mail@icj-cij.org
Web Site: www.icj-cij.org
Telex: 32323 *Cable:* INTERCOURT THE HAGUE
Key Personnel
Registrar & Contact: M Philippe Couvreur

CPNB, see Collectieve Propaganda van het Nederlandse Boek (CPNB)

ESOMAR, see European Society for Opinion & Marketing Research

†‡Universala Esperanto-Asocio (World Esperanto Association)
176 Nieuwe Binnenweg, NL-3015 BJ Rotterdam
Tel: (010) 4361044; (010) 4361539 *Fax:* (010) 4361751
E-mail: uea@inter.nl.net
Web Site: www.uea.org *Cable:* ESPERANTO ROTTERDAM
Key Personnel
President: Dr Renato Corsetti
Vice President: Prof Lee Chong-Yeong; Prof Humphrey Tonkin
Secretary General: Ivo Osibov
Editor: Stano Marchek
Founded: 1908
Subjects: Language problems & Esperanto as a possible solution
ISBN Prefix(es): 92-9017

†◇European Association for Health Information & Libraries
EAHIL Secretariat, Plompetorengracht 11, 3512 CA Utrecht
Tel: (030) 2619663 *Fax:* (030) 2311830
E-mail: EAHIL-secr@nic.surfnet.nl
Web Site: www.eahil.org
Key Personnel
President: Tony McSean
Secretary: Linda Lisgarten

†European Society for Opinion & Marketing Research
Vondelstraat 172, 1054 GV Amsterdam
Tel: (020) 6642141 *Fax:* (020) 6642922
E-mail: email@esomar.nl
Web Site: www.esomar.nl
Key Personnel
President: Daniel Leconte
Dir General: Juergen Schwoerer
Founded: 1948
Subjects: Marketing & opinion research

FID, see International Federation for Information & Documentation (FID)

IEA, see International Association for the Evaluation of Educational Achievement (IEA)

IFLA, see International Federation of Library Associations & Institutions (IFLA)

†◇International Association for Mass Communication Research
Postbus 67006, 1060 JA Amsterdam
Tel: (020) 6101581 *Fax:* (020) 6104821
Key Personnel
President: Prof Cees Hamelink
Administrative Secretary: Peggy Gray
Association internationale des etudes et recherches sur l'information.
Publication(s): *Communication and Democracy; Directions in Research; Mass Media and Man's View of Society; Mass Media and National Cultures; Mass Media and Socialization; New Structures of International Communication; Social Communication and Global Problems; The Role of Research*

International Association for the Evaluation of Educational Achievement (IEA)
Herengracht 487, NL-1017 BT Amsterdam
Tel: (020) 6253625 *Fax:* (020) 4207136
E-mail: department@iea.nl
Web Site: www.iea.nl
Key Personnel
Chairman: Dr Alejandro Tiana *E-mail:* atiana@edu.und.es
Executive Dir: Dr Hans Wagemaker
E-mail: hanswagemaker@compuserve.com
Manager Membership Relations: Dr Barbara Malak-Minkiewicz *E-mail:* b.malak@iea.nl
Founded: 1954
Research on educational outcomes.
Subjects: Education & various school subjects
Publication(s): *International Reports of IEA Studies*

†◇International Association of Scientific, Technical and Medical Publishers (STM)
Muurhuizen 165, 3811 EG Amersfoort
Tel: (033) 4656060 *Fax:* (033) 4656538
E-mail: lefebvre@stm.nl
Web Site: www.stm-assoc.org
Key Personnel
Secretary: Lex Lefebvre
International Trade Organization for STM, professional and scholarly publishers. Focus on copyright and legal issues, technology development & industry standards & library & users relations.

International Court of Justice, see Cour Internationale de Justice

†◇International Federation for Information & Documentation (FID)
c/o Koninklyke Bibliotheek, Prins Willem-Alexanderhof, 2509 LK The Hague
Mailing Address: General Secretariat, Postbus 90402, 2509 LK The Hague
Tel: (070) 3140671 *Fax:* (070) 3140667
E-mail: fid@fid.nl
Web Site: www.fid.nl
Key Personnel
President: Martha B Stone
Editor & Manager, PR & Publications: Theresa Stanton *E-mail:* theresa.stanton@fid.nl
Founded: 1895
Federation internationale d'Information et de documentation.
Subjects: Specialize in Business Information; Distance Learning for Librarians; Environmental Information; Infoethics; Water Information
Publication(s): *Extensions & Corrections to the UDC* (annually); *FID Directory; FID Review* (6x annually, 1999, International journal in English for information professionals)

†◇International Federation of Library Associations & Institutions (IFLA)
Postbus 95312, 2509 CH The Hague
Tel: (070) 3140884 *Fax:* (070) 3834827
E-mail: ifla@ifla.org
Web Site: www.ifla.org
Key Personnel
President: Christine Deschamps
Secretary General: Ross Shimmon
Founded: 1927
Federation internationale des associations de bibliothecaires et des bibliotheques.
Publication(s): *IFLA Annual Report* (annually); *IFLA Directory* (biennially); *IFLA Journal; IFLA Professional Reports* (series of reports published by IFLA); *IFLA Publications* (series of monographs, published by K G Saur Verlag KG, Germany); *International Cataloguing & Bibliographic Control* (quarterly)

Bureau ISBN
Centraal Boekhuis, Erasmusweg 10, 4104 AK Culemborg
Mailing Address: Postbus 360, 4100 A2 Culemborg
Tel: (0345) 475855 *Fax:* (0345) 475895
E-mail: ISBN@centraal.boekhuis.nl
Key Personnel
ISBN Administrator: Ben Klomp
Contact: Mr M G van den Heuvel
E-mail: heuvm@centraal.boekhuis.nl
Publication(s): *ISBN Manual* (2002); *ISBN Publishers List* (on diskette & computer printout)
Parent Company: Centraal Boekhuis BV

KVB Koninklijke Vereeniging van het Boekenvak (Royal Dutch Book Trade Organization)
Fredriksplein 1, 1017 XK Amsterdam
Mailing Address: Postbus 15007, 1001 MA Amsterdam
Tel: (020) 6240212 *Fax:* (020) 6208871
E-mail: info@kvb.nl
Web Site: www.kvb.nl
Key Personnel
Executive Dir: Mrs C Verberne
Founded: 1815
Association for the Promotion of the Interests of Booksellers and Publishers.
Publication(s): *Adresboek* (Address book for the Dutch Book Trade); *Boekblad* (News Magazine for the Book Trade, weekly & monthly & website www.boekblad.nl)

Nederlands Uitgeverbond (Dutch Publishers Association)
ATLAS Bldg, Block Asia, Hoogoorddreef 5, 1101 BA Amsterdam
Mailing Address: PO Box 12040, 1100 AA Amsterdam
Tel: (020) 4309150 *Fax:* (020) 4309179
E-mail: info@uitgeversverbond.nl
Web Site: www.uitgeversverbond.nl
Key Personnel
President: Prof Henk J L Vonhoff
Man Dir: J Bommer
PR Secretary: Jaap Roorda *E-mail:* j.roorda@uitgeversverbond.nl
Founded: 1880
Royal Dutch Publishers' Association.

Nederlandsche Vereeniging van Antiquaren
Postbus 364, 3500 AJ Utrecht

Tel: (030) 2319286 *Fax:* (030) 2343362
E-mail: bestbook@wxs.nl
Web Site: www.nvva.nl
Key Personnel
President: Dr F W Kuyper
Secretary: Gert Jan Bestebreurtje
Netherlands Association of Antiquarian Booksellers.

Nederlandsche Vereeniging voor Druk- en Boekkunst
van Banningstraas 2c, 2381 AV Zoeterwoude
Tel: (071) 5809634
Key Personnel
Secretary: Kees Thomassen
Netherlands Society for the Art of Printing and Book Production.
Publication(s): Mededelingen (irregularly and books)

Nederlandse Boekverkopersbond
Postbus 32, 3720 AA Bilthoven
Tel: (070) 2287956 *Fax:* (070) 2284566
Key Personnel
President: W Karssen
Executive Secretary: Mr A C Doeser
Dutch Booksellers Association.

Speurwerk Stitching betreffende het Boek
Frederiksplein 1, 1017 XK Amsterdam
Tel: (020) 6254927 *Fax:* (020) 6208871
Key Personnel
Dir: A A Herpers
Foundation for Bookmarket Research in the Netherlands.
Publication(s): Boekenvakboek 1980, 1986-88 (Publishing Industry Statistics); *Gids voor de Informatiesector 1990, 1991, 1992, 1993, 1994*; *Speurwerk Boeken Omnibus* (The Dutch Book Market - quarterly); *Structural Analysis of the Book Market in Netherlands*
Branch Office(s)
Documentation Department Speurwerk/FE, Herengracht 330, 1016 CE Amsterdam, 1016 CE Amsterdam *Tel:* (020) 6247676 *Fax:* (020) 6238869

Standard Book Numbering Agency, see Bureau ISBN

STM, see International Association of Scientific, Technical and Medical Publishers (STM)

†Technical Centre for Agricultural & Rural Co-operation
Postbus 380, NL-6700 AJ Wageningen
Tel: (0317) 467100 *Fax:* (0317) 460067
E-mail: cta@cta.nl
Web Site: www.cta.nl
Key Personnel
Head: A C Jackson *Tel:* (0317) 467127
E-mail: jackson@cta.nl
Founded: 1984
Subjects: Tropical Agriculture, Rural Development & Information & Communication Management
ISBN Prefix(es): 92-9081

Netherlands Antilles

†Bureau Intellectual Property
Berg Carmelweg 10-A, Willemstad, Curacao
Mailing Address: PO Box 3068, Curacao
Tel: (09) 465 7800; (09) 465 7802 *Fax:* (09) 465 7815; (09) 465 7692
E-mail: bipantil@curinfo.an
Key Personnel
Dir: Mr Juny J Sluis
Founded: 1893
Registration of trademarks.
Publication(s): Merkenblad (Trademark journal)
Number of titles published annually: 161 Print
Total Titles: 296 Print

New Zealand

Booksellers New Zealand
PO Box 11-377, Wellington
Tel: (04) 4728678 *Fax:* (04) 4728628
Key Personnel
Chairperson: Tony Moores
Chief Executive: Alice Heather

Booksellers NZ
North Shore Mail, PO Box 386, Auckland 9
Mailing Address: Northshore Mail Ctr, Auckland 1
Tel: (04) 4728678 *Fax:* (04) 4728628
Publication(s): NZ Publishing News (members only)
Associate Companies: Copyright Licensing Ltd

Christian Booksellers' Association (NZ Chapter)
71 Rata St, Matamata 2711
Tel: (07) 888 6010
E-mail: cba@cba.net.nz
Key Personnel
Secretary, Treasurer: Roger McRae
Currently have 54 retail members & 27 wholesale members.
Publication(s): Newsletters (bimonthly)

◇**New Zealand Council for Educational Research**
Education House, 178-182 Willis St, Wellington 6000
Mailing Address: PO Box 3237, Wellington 6000
Tel: (04) 3847939 *Fax:* (04) 3847933
Key Personnel
Dir: Dr Anne Meade *E-mail:* anne.meade@vuw.ac.nz
Publications Officer: Peter Ridder
Founded: 1934
Publication(s): New Zealand Journal of Educational Studies (set)
ISBN Prefix(es): 0-908567; 0-908916; 1-877140

New Zealand Press Council
Box 10879, The Terrace, Wellington
Tel: (04) 4735220 *Fax:* (04) 4711785
E-mail: presscouncil@asa.co.nz
Web Site: www.presscouncil.org.nz
Key Personnel
Chairman: Sir John Jeffries
Secretary: Mary Major
Founded: 1972

†◇South Pacific Association for Commonwealth Literature & Language Studies (SPACLALS)
University of Waikato, Private Bag 3105, Hamilton
Founded: 1975
Publication(s): Journal & Spaccals (biannually); *Span*

SPACLALS, see South Pacific Association for Commonwealth Literature & Language Studies (SPACLALS)

Standard Book Numbering Agency
National Library of New Zealand, Wellington 6000
Mailing Address: PO Box 1467, Wellington 6000
Tel: (04) 474 3074 *Fax:* (04) 474 3161
E-mail: isbn@natlib.govt.nz
Key Personnel
ISBN Librararian: Ms Joy Grove

Nigeria

Children's Literature Association of Nigeria
c/o Institute of African Studies, University of Ibadan, Ibadan, Oyo State
Tel: (022) 400550; (022) 400614 *Fax:* (022) 711254
Key Personnel
President: Mabel Segun

Children's Literature Documentation & Research Centre, Ibadan
UIPO Box 20744, Ibadan, Oyo State
Fax: (022) 711254
Key Personnel
Dir: Mabel Segun

Christian Booksellers Association of Nigeria
72 Yakub Gowon Way, Jos, Pleateau State
Mailing Address: Box 1322, Jos, Plateau State
Tel: 53090 *Fax:* 57684
Key Personnel
Executive Secretary: Gideon M Chimmin
Parent Company: Christian Booksellers Association USA, United States

CLIDORC, see Children's Literature Documentation & Research Centre, Ibadan

Nigerian Book Development Council
6, Obanta Rd, Apapa, Lagos
Tel: (01) 862269; (01) 862272
Key Personnel
Secretary: Alhaja M M Musa

Nigerian ISBN Agency
The Director, National Library of Nigeria, 4 Wesley St, PMB 12626 Lagos
Mailing Address: PMB 12626, Lagos
Tel: (01) 5850657 *Fax:* (01) 2631563
Telex: 21746 *Cable:* Biblios
Key Personnel
Agency Head: S E A Sonaike
Publication(s): Nigerian ISBN Manual and Directory

Nigerian Publishers Association
The Ori-Detu, Shell Close, 1st floor, Ornireke, Ibadan
Mailing Address: GPO Box 2541, Ibadan
Tel: (02) 4963007 *Fax:* (02) 4964370
Telex: 31113
Key Personnel
President: V Nwankwo
Chief: Mrs F O Orikan
Publication(s): The Publisher (biannually)

SCAUL, see Standing Conference of African University Libraries (SCAUL)

Standard Book Numbering Agency, see Nigerian ISBN Agency

NIGERIA

†◇**Standing Conference of African University Libraries (SCAUL)**
c/o E Bejide Bankole, Editor African Journal of Academic Librarianship, University of Lagos, Akoka, Yaba, Lagos
Mailing Address: Akoka, Yaba, Lagos
Tel: (01) 524968 *Fax:* (01) 822644

University Booksellers Association of Nigeria
c/o Benin University Bookshop, PMB 1154, Ugbowo Campus, Benin City
Tel: (052) 200250 (Ugbowo); (052) 200480 (Ekehuan) *Fax:* (052) 241156
Telex: 41365

Norway

Bok Og Papiransattes Forening
Ovre Vollgate 15, N-0158 Oslo
Tel: 22205197 *Fax:* 22400033
Norwegian Book Trade Employees' Association.
Publication(s): *Norsk Bokhandlermatrikkel*; *Norsk Boknokkel*

Den Norske Bokhandlerforening (The Norwegian Publishers Association)
Ovre Vollgate 15, 0158 Oslo
Tel: 22007580 *Fax:* 22333830
E-mail: dfn@forleggerforeningen.no
Web Site: www.forleggerforeningen.no
Key Personnel
Dir: K Slordahl
Norwegian Booksellers' Association.
Publication(s): *Bok og Samfunn*

†**International Union of Geological Sciences (IUGS)**
IUGS Secretariat, Geological Survey of Norway, N-7002 Trondheim
Mailing Address: PO Box 3006, Lade, N-7002 Trondheim
Tel: 73921500 *Fax:* 73502230
Key Personnel
President: Robin Brett
Secretary General: Dr R Brett
Founded: 1961
Union internationale des Sciences Geologiques.
Subjects: Earth Sciences
Publication(s): *Episodes* (quarterly)

ISBN-Kontoret Norge
National Library of Norway Oslo Division, Postbox 2674, N-0203 Oslo
Tel: 23276217 *Fax:* 23276010
E-mail: isbn-kontoret@nb.no
Web Site: www.nb.no/html/isbn_eng.html
Telex: 76078 ub n
Key Personnel
Administrator & Senior Librarian: Ms Ingebjoerg Rype
ISBN Agency.
Publication(s): *ISBN-Internasjonalt standard boknummer*
Parent Company: National Library of Norway

IUGS, see International Union of Geological Sciences (IUGS)

Norsk Musikkforleggerforening
c/o Musikk-Huset A/S, Postboks 822, Sentrum 0104 Oslo 1
Tel: 22425090 *Fax:* 22425541
Norwegian Music Publishers' Association.

Den Norske Forfatterforening
Radhusgt 7, Sentrum, Oslo
Mailing Address: Postboks 327, Sentrum, Oslo
Tel: 22424077 *Fax:* 22421107
E-mail: dnf@sn.no
Key Personnel
Secretary General: Lars Haavik
Off Manager: Tordis Fjeldstad
Norwegian Authors' Union.

Den Norske Forleggerforening
Ovre Vollgate 15, N-0158 Oslo 1
Tel: 22007580 *Fax:* 22333830
E-mail: dnf@forleggerforeningen.no
Key Personnel
Dir: Kristin Cecilie Shordahl
Secretary: Runa Systad
The Norwegian Publishers' Association. Member of IPA & FEP.

Standard Book Numbering Agency, see ISBN-Kontoret Norge

Pakistan

Standard Book Numbering Agency
Department of Librarie, National Library Bldg, Constitution Ave, Islamabad 44000
Mailing Address: PO Box 1982, Islamabad 44000
Tel: (051) 9202544-216; (051) 9202549-216
Fax: (051) 9221375
Key Personnel
ISBN Administrator: Abdul Hafeez Akhtar

Urdu Science Board
299 Upper Mall, Lahore
Tel: (042) 5758674
Branch Office(s)
Gari Khata, Manzoor Chambers, Hyderabad
Khyber Bazar, Peshawar Branch, Peshawar

Papua New Guinea

Standard Book Numbering Agency
Office of Libraries and Archives, Waigani NCD
Mailing Address: PO Box 734, Waigani NCD
Tel: 256200 *Fax:* 3251331
E-mail: ola@datec.com.pg
Telex: NE 22234
Publication(s): *ISBN Users Manual* (Second Edition, 1991)

Peru

Camara Peruana del Libro
Ave Abancay cdra 4 s/n, Lima 1
Tel: (01) 4287630 *Fax:* (01) 4277331
E-mail: jefatura@binape.gob.pe
Web Site: www.binape.gob.pe
Key Personnel
President: Julio Cesar Flores Rodriguez
Executive Dir: Dra Loyda Moran Bustamente
Administrator: Guerra Raul Guerra
Peruvian Publishers' Association.

Standard Book Numbering Agency, see Camara Peruana del Libro

Philippines

†◇**Congress of South-East Asian Librarians IV (CONSAL IV)**
National Historic Institute of the Philippines, T M Kalaw St, 100 Ermita, Manila
Mailing Address: PO Box 2926, 100 Ermita, Manila
Tel: (02) 590646 *Fax:* (02) 572644
Key Personnel
Chairman: Dr Serafin D Quiason

Philippine Educational Publishers' Association
84 P Florentino St, 3008 Quezon City
Tel: (02) 7402698 *Fax:* (02) 7115702
Key Personnel
President: D D Buhain *E-mail:* dbuhain@cnl.net
Founded: 1950

Standard Book Numbering Agency, The National Library of the Philippines
Division of Bibliographic Services Division
TM Kalaw St, 1000 Ermita, Manila
Mailing Address: PO Box 2926, Manila
Tel: (02) 5241011 *Fax:* (02) 5241011
E-mail: isbn@nlp.gov.ph
Web Site: www.nlp.gov.ph
Telex: 40726 nalib pm
Key Personnel
ISBN Administrator: Leonila DA Tominez
E-mail: leat@nlp.gov.ph
Founded: 1900
National library.
Publication(s): *Directory of Printers & Publishers*; *Philippine National Bibliography* (annually, Bibliography of works written by Filipino authors about the Philippines, cumulated quarterly)
Parent Company: The National Library of the Philippines
Ultimate Parent Company: National Commission for Culture & the Arts

Poland

AGPOL (Przedsiebiorstwo Reklamy i Wydawnictw Handlu Zagranicznego)
ul St Kierbedzia 4, skr poczt 7, 00957 Warsaw
Tel: (022) 416061 *Fax:* (022) 405607
Telex: 813364 *Cable:* Agpol Warszawa
Key Personnel
Dir: Mieczyslaw Kroker
Founded: 1956
Offers publicity services abroad for Polish foreign trade and in Poland for foreign companies.

Istytut Bibliograficzny Biblioteka Narodowa, Krajowe Biuro ISBN
Al Niepodleg losci 213, 00-973 Warsaw 22
Tel: (022) 6082410 *Fax:* (022) 6082433
E-mail: bnisbn@bn.org.pl; sadowska@bn.org.pl
Web Site: www.bn.org.pl
Telex: 816761 bn pl

Krajowe Biuro Miedzynarodowego Numeru Ksiazki ISBN
Biblioteka Narodowa, Al Niepodleglosci 213, 00-973 Warsaw
Tel: (022) 256877; (022) 6082999 *Fax:* (022) 6082433; (022) 8255251
E-mail: bnisbn@bn.org.pl
Key Personnel
Librarian: Jadwiga Sadowska

National ISBN Agency, see Krajowe Biuro Miedzynarodowego Numeru Ksiazki ISBN

Polish Chamber of Books
Krakowskie Przedmiescie 7, 00-068 Warsaw
Tel: (022) 8261201 *Fax:* (022) 8266240
E-mail: rg.pik@arspolona.com.pl
Key Personnel
President: Andrzej Chrzavnowski
Vice President: Grzegorz Majerowicz; Krzysztof Raniowski
Executive Dir: Regina Malgorzata Greda
Founded: 1990
Chamber of Commerce.

Polskie Towarzystwo Wydawcow Ksiazek
ul Mazowiecka 2/4, 00-048 Warsaw
Tel: (022) 8260735 *Fax:* (022) 8260735
Cable: PETEWUKA
Key Personnel
President: Janusz Fogler
Deputy President: Aniela Topulos
General Secretary: Donat Chruscicki
Dir: Maria Kuisz
Polish Society of Book Editors.

Przedsiebiorstwo Reklamy i Wydawnictw Handlu Zagranicznego, see AGPOL (Przedsiebiorstwo Reklamy i Wydawnictw Handlu Zagranicznego)

Standard Book Numbering Agency, see Istytut Bibliograficzny Biblioteka Narodowa, Krajowe Biuro ISBN

Stowarzyszenie Ksiegarzy Polskich
ul Mokotowska 4/6, 00641 Warsaw
Tel: (032) 2192393; (022) 256061
Web Site: www.bookweb.org/org/1322html
Key Personnel
President: Tadeusz Hussak
Association of Polish Booksellers (social organization for State book trade employees).
Publication(s): *Ksiegarz*

Zwiazek Literatow Polskich
Member of EWC (European Writers' Congress)
Krakowskie Przedmiescie 87/89, 00-079 Warsaw
Tel: (022) 826-57-85; (022) 826-08-66 *Fax:* (022) 828-39-20
Key Personnel
President: Piotr Kuncewicz
Founded: 1920
Union of Polish Writers.

Portugal

Associacao Portuguesa de Editores e Livreiros
Largo de Andaluz, 16-1 Esq, 1000 Lisbon
Tel: (021) 556241 *Fax:* (021) 3153553
Telex: 62735 Apel P *Cable:* APEL
Key Personnel
President: Dr Francisco Espadinha
Secretary General: Dr Jorge de Carvalho Sa Borges
General Manager: Jose Narciso Vieira
Portuguese Association of Publishers and Booksellers.
Publication(s): *Livros Disponiveis*; *Livros de Portugal, Boletim Bibliografico* (Portuguese Books in Print, monthly)

Standard Book Numbering Agency
Associacao Portuguesa de Editores e Livreiros, Av Estados Unidos da America, 97-6° E, 1700-167 Lisbon
Tel: (021) 8435180 *Fax:* (021) 8489377
E-mail: cdb@apel.pt
Web Site: www.apel.pt
Key Personnel
ISBN Administrator: Ms Conceicao Tome
Publication(s): *Livros Disponiveis* (Books in Print); *Portuguese Books* (CD Rom)

Puerto Rico

†◊ACURIL
PO Box 23317, San Juan 00931
Tel: (787) 764-0000 (ext 7916) *Fax:* (787) 763-5685
Key Personnel
President: Lucero Arboleda De Roa
Executive Secretary: Oneida R Ortiz *Tel:* (787) 790-8054
Association of Caribbean University, Research & Institutional Libraries.
Publication(s): *ACURIL Newsletter*; *Proceedings of Annual Conference*

Association of Caribbean University, Research & Institutional Libraries, see ACURIL

Ateneo Puertorriqueno
Apdo 9021180, San Juan 00902
Tel: (787) 721-3877 *Fax:* (787) 725-3873
Key Personnel
President: Eduardo Morales
Puerto Rican Society of Writers.

Standard Book Numbering Agency
NISC Puerto Rico, Apdo 41291, San Juan 00940-1291
Tel: (787) 724-1352 *Fax:* (787) 724-2886
E-mail: nisc@caribe.net
Key Personnel
Contact: Margaret Melcher

Qatar

Standard Book Numbering Agency
National Library, Doha
Mailing Address: PO Box 205, Doha
Tel: 429955 *Fax:* 429976
E-mail: qanaly@qatar.net.qa
Telex: 4743 qanali

Romania

†‡Centre Europeen pour l'Enseignement Superieur
39 Rue Stirbei Voda, 70732 Bucharest
Tel: (01) 3130839 *Fax:* (01) 3123567
E-mail: cepes@cepes.ro
Key Personnel
Dir: John Sadlak
Founded: 1972
Subjects: Higher Education
ISBN Prefix(es): 0-379
Number of titles published annually: 6 Print
Total Titles: 42 Print

Centrul National de Numerotare Standardizata Biblioteca Nationala (National Centre for Standard Numbering ISBN-ISSN-CIP)
Unit of Biblioteca Nationala A Romaniei
Str Ion Ghica 4, nr 4, sect 3, Bucharest 79708
Tel: (01) 3124990 *Fax:* (01) 3124990
E-mail: isbn@bibnat.ro; issn@bibnat.ro
Key Personnel
Coord & Librarian: Aurelia Persinaru
ISBN Librarian: Mihaela Leaua
CIP, Librarian: Laura Margarit
Member of ISBN International Agency & ISSN International Centre. Activities for a national ISBN & ISSN agency (record all the Romanian publishers, assign ISBN & ISSN codes, etc. In charge with the management of Romanian Cataloguing in Publication Programme & editor of CIP National Bibliography.
Publication(s): *Bibliografia Cartilor in Curs de Aparitie* (monthly, journal)
ISBN Prefix(es): 973

Societa Ziaristilor din Romania
Piata Presei Libere 1, 71341 Bucharest
Tel: (01) 6171591 *Fax:* (01) 3128266
Journalists Society of Romania.

Standard Book Numbering Agency, see Centrul National de Numerotare Standardizata Biblioteca Nationala

Uniunea Scriitorilor din Romania
Calea Victoriei 115 si 133, Bucharest
Tel: (00) 6507245 *Fax:* (00) 3129634
Telex: 11796
Romanian Writer's Union.
Publication(s): *Convorbiri Literare* (Literary Conversations); *Igaz Szo*; *Knijevni Jivot*; *Luceafarul*; *Neue Literatur*; *Orizont* (Horizon); *Romania Literara* (Literary Romania); *Secolul XX* (Twentieth Century); *Steaua* (The Star); *Utunk*; *Vatra*; *Viata Romaneasca* (Romanian Life)

Russian Federation

All-Union Book Chamber
Kremlevskaja nab 1/9, 121019 Moscow
Tel: (095) 2034653; (095) 2035608 *Fax:* (095) 2982576; (095) 2982590
E-mail: chamber@aha.ru
Web Site: www.bookchamber.ru
Key Personnel
Dir-General: Boris Lenski
Chamber also administers Russian National ISBN Agency.

†◊Association of Research Libraries & Libraries for Science & Technology in the CIS
c/o Russia National Public Library for Science & Technology, 12 Kuznetskii most, 103031 Moscow
Tel: (095) 9259288 *Fax:* (095) 9219862
E-mail: root@gpntd.msk.su
Key Personnel
President: Andrei Zemskov

International Community of Writers' Unions
Ul Povarskaja 52, 121825 Moscow
Tel: (095) 2916307 *Fax:* (095) 2919760
Key Personnel
First Secretary: T Pulator

◊The Press & Publishing Engineering Society
c/o Union of Scientific and Engineering Associations, Kursovoi per 17, 119034 Moscow
Tel: (095) 2906286 *Fax:* (095) 2918506
Key Personnel
Chairman: A Yu Ishlinskii

Scientific & production activities in book publishing.
Parent Company: Union of Scientific & Engineering Societies
Associate Companies: Ministry of Printing & Information of the Russian Federation

Publishers Association
B Nikitskaya St 44, 121069 Moscow
Tel: (095) 2021174 *Fax:* (095) 2023989
Key Personnel
Contact: M Shishigin

Publishing Council of the Academy of Sciences of the Russian Academy of Sciences
Leninsky prospekt 14, 117901 Moscow
Tel: (095) 952905 *Fax:* (095) 2379107

◇**Rossijskaja Knizhnaya Palata** (Russian Book Chamber)
Ostogenka 4, str 2, 119034 Moscow
Tel: (095) 2911278 *Fax:* (095) 2919630
E-mail: bookch@postman.tu
Web Site: www.bookchamber.ru/international
The Russian Book Chamber
All books & publications are registered & described.
Publication(s): *Knizhnava Letopis'* (Book Chronicle, weekly bulletin & 5 indexes, journal, 2002, informs about all types of books & booklets published in Russia)

Standard Book Numbering Agency
Russian ISBN Agency, Russian Book Chamber, Kremlevskaja Nab 1/9, 119019 Moscow
Tel: (095) 2034653; (095) 2035608 *Fax:* (095) 2982576; (095) 2889665
E-mail: vvc@rkp.msk.su
Key Personnel
ISBN Administrator: A Muratov
Dir General: Boris Lenski

Saudi Arabia

†◇**Arab Regional Branch of the International Council on Archives**
Institute of Public Administration Library, Riyadh 11141
Mailing Address: PO Box 205, Riyadh 11141
Tel: (01) 4761600 (ext 462)
Telex: 201160
Key Personnel
Secretary-General: Fahd Al-Askar

Standard Book Numbering Agency
King Fahad National Library, Registration & Book Numbering Department, Riyadh 11472
Mailing Address: PO Box 7572, Riyadh 11472
Tel: (01) 4645197; (01) 4624888 (ext 224)
Fax: (01) 4645341; (01) 4622707
E-mail: isbnic@kfnl.gov.sa *Cable:* 407599 KFNLR S.J.
Key Personnel
Dir: Mohammed Abdelaziz Al-Rashid

Senegal

†◇**Commission des Bibliotheques de l'AIDBA**
BP 375, Dakar
Tel: 240954
Key Personnel
Secretary: Emmanuel K W Dadzie

Association internationale pour le Developpement de la Documentation des Bibliotheques et des Archives en Afrique
International Association for the Development of Libraries and Archives in Africa.

†◇**Standing Conference of African Library Schools (SCALS)**
Universite Cheikh Anta Diop de Darkar, BP 5005, Dakar
Tel: (08) 250530 *Fax:* (08) 255219
Telex: 51-262

Singapore

SBPA, see Singapore Book Publishers' Association

Singapore Book Publishers' Association
c/o Cannon International, 86, Marine Parade Centre, No 03-213, Singapore 440086
Tel: (065) 3447801; (065) 4407409 *Fax:* (065) 4470897
E-mail: twcsbpa@singnet.com.sg
Key Personnel
President: Mr Wu Cheng Tan
Honorary Secretary: T Chandroo
Founded: 1966
Member of International Publishers Association (Geneva); Asia Pacific Publishers Association (Seoul).

Standard Book Numbering Agency
National Library Board, No 3 Changi South St 2, Tower B #03-00, Singapore 486548
Tel: 5467236 *Fax:* 5467286
E-mail: legaldep@nlb.gov.sg
Telex: Rs 26620 *Cable:* NATLIB SINGAPORE
Key Personnel
ISBN Administrators: Mrs Lim Siew Kim; Ms N Dana Lashmi
Publication(s): *Books About Singapore* (biannually); *Singapore National Bibliography* (quarterly/annually); *Singapore: National Library*; *Singapore Periodicals Index* (annually)

Slovakia

ISBN National Agency
Slovak National Library, Nam JC Hronskeho 1, 036 01 Martin
Tel: (842) 4134035 *Fax:* (842) 4734035
E-mail: isbn@snk.sk; snk@snk.sk
Web Site: www.snk.sk
Key Personnel
Contact: Mrs Jarmila Majerova
E-mail: majerova@snk.sk
Founded: 1989
Parent Company: Slovak National Library

◇**Spolok slovenskych spisovatel'ov**
Ste Fanikova 14, 81508 Bratislava
Tel: (07) 43615
Key Personnel
Honor Chairman: Ladislav Tazky
Chairman: Jaroslav Reznik
Founded: 1949
Association of Slovak Writers.
Publication(s): *Literarny Tyzdhennik* (Literary Weekly)
Associate Companies: Asociacia organizaciil Slovenska, Ste Fanikova 14, 81508 Bratislava

Slovenia

Gospodarska Zbornica Slovenije, see Zdruzenie Zaloznikov in Knjigotrzcev Slovenije Gospodarska Zbornica Slovenije

Standard Book Numbering Agency
Narodna in univerzitetna knjiznica, Turjaska 1, p p 259, 1000 Ljubljana
Tel: (01) 58 61 333 *Fax:* (01) 58 61 311
E-mail: isbn@nuk.uni-lj.si
Web Site: www.nuk.uni-lj.si/zalozniki/isbn/isbn.html

◇**Zdruzenie Zaloznikov in Knjigotrzcev Slovenije Gospodarska Zbornica Slovenije** (Association of Publishers & Booksellers of Slovenia)
Dimiceva 13, Ljubljana 1504
Tel: (01) 5898277 *Fax:* (01) 5898200; (01) 5898100
E-mail: irena.brolez@gzs.si
Web Site: www.gzs.si
Key Personnel
President, Association: Milan Matos
Member of International Publishers Association
Association of Publishers & Booksellers of Slovenia.
Publication(s): *Knjiga*

South Africa

Associated Booksellers of Southern Africa Ltd, see South African Booksellers Association

CDNL, see Conference of Directors of National Libraries (CDNL)

†◇**Conference of Directors of National Libraries (CDNL)**
State Library, c/o Corporate Communication, 0001 Pretoria
Mailing Address: PO Box 397, 0001 Pretoria
Tel: (012) 218931 *Fax:* (012) 3255984
E-mail: therese@statelib.gov.za
Key Personnel
Chairperson: P J Lor
Vice Chairperson: M A Kadir; W van Drimmelen
Founded: 1980

The Director State Library
PO Box 397, Pretoria 0001
Tel: (012) 218931 *Fax:* (012) 3255984
E-mail: rhona@statelib.pwv.gov.za

International Standard Book Numbering Agency
State Library, Attn: ISBN Agency, Pretoria 0001
Mailing Address: PO Box 397, Pretoria 0001
Tel: (012) 218931 *Fax:* (012) 3255984
E-mail: therese@statelib.pwv.gov.za

PASA, see Publishers' Association of South Africa (PASA)

Publishers' Association of South Africa (PASA)
PO Box 116, 7946 St James
Tel: (021) 7886470 *Fax:* (021) 7886469
E-mail: pasa@icon.co.za
Web Site: www.icon.co.za/~pasa
Key Personnel
Chairman: Basil Van Rooyen

Administrator: Erika Van Greunen
Publication(s): *PASA Directory* (annual list of members)

South African Booksellers Association
Formerly Associated Booksellers of Southern Africa Ltd
PO Box 870, Bellville 7530
Tel: (021) 9188616 *Fax:* (021) 9514903
E-mail: fnel@naspers.com
Web Site: sabooksellers.com
Key Personnel
President: Guru Redhi
Secretary: Peter Adams
Founded: 1998

Standard Book Numbering Agency, see The Director State Library

Spain

Agencia Espanola del ISBN
Santiago Rusinol 8, 28040 Madrid
Tel: (091) 5368830 *Fax:* (091) 5539990
Web Site: www.slt.lk/nlib
Telex: 47891 fclie
Key Personnel
Head of Service: Maria Yribarren *E-mail:* maria.yribarren@cll.mcu.es
Ministerio de Educacion y Cultura.

Asociacion de Escritores y Artistas Espanoles
Leganitos 10, 28013 Madrid
Tel: (091) 5599067 *Fax:* (091) 5599067
Key Personnel
Secretary: Jose Lopez Martinez
Spanish Writers' and Artists' Association.

Associacio d'Editors en Llengua Catalana
Valencia 279, 1r, 08009 Barcelona
Tel: (093) 155091 *Fax:* (093) 155273
E-mail: gec@gefes.es
Web Site: www.gremieditorscat.es
Association of Publishers in Catalan.

Federacion de Gremios de Editores de Espana (FGEE) (Spanish Publishers Association)
Cea Bermudez, 44-2° Dehe, Madrid 20003
Tel: (091) 5345195 *Fax:* (09) 5352625
E-mail: fgee@fge.es
Web Site: www.federacioneditores.org
Telex: 48457 Fgee E
Key Personnel
President: D Emiliano Martinez
Executive Dir: D Antonio Auila
Founded: 1978
Professional Association of Publishers.
Subjects: To represent & defend the general interests of the Spanish publishing industry

Standard Book Numbering Agency, see Agencia Espanola del ISBN

UMA, see World Blind Union (WBU) - Union Mondiale des Aveugles (UMA)

WBU, see World Blind Union (WBU) - Union Mondiale des Aveugles (UMA)

†◇World Blind Union (WBU) - Union Mondiale des Aveugles (UMA)
c/o CPB Organization Nacional de Ciegos Espanoles, La Coruna 18, E-28020 Madrid
Tel: (091) 5713685; (091) 5711236 *Fax:* (091) 5715777
E-mail: umc@once.es
Web Site: www.once.es/wbu
Key Personnel
Secretary General: Pedro Zurita
Founded: 1984
Publication(s): *The World Blind* (2x ann, Les Aveugles dans le Monde & Los Ciegos en el Mundo)

Sri Lanka

†◇The International Irrigation Management Institute
PO Box 2075, Colombo
Tel: (01) 867404 *Fax:* (01) 866854
Telex: 22318; 22907 llMIHQCE
Key Personnel
Dir General: Dr David Seckler
Head of Information: Dr James K Lenahan
Founded: 1956
An autonomous nonprofit International Organization. Member of the Consultative Group on International Agricultural Research (CGIAR).
ISBN Prefix(es): 92-9090

Sri Lanka Association of Publishers
112 S Mahinda Mawatha, Maranda, Colombo 10
Tel: (01) 695773 *Fax:* (01) 696653
E-mail: dayawansajay@hotmail.com
Key Personnel
Dir: Dayawansa Jayakody
General Secretary: Gamini Wijesuriya
Publication(s): *Hela Bima* (newspaper); *Publishing Scene* (newsletter)

†◇Standard Book Numbering Agency (ISBN Agency-Sri Lanka)
National Library & Documentation Services Board, No 14, Independence Ave, Colombo 07
Tel: (01) 674387; (01) 685197; (01) 698847 *Fax:* (01) 685201
E-mail: natlib@slt.lk
Web Site: www.slt.lk/nlib
Key Personnel
ISBN Dir: Mr M S U Amarasiri
Subjects: Social Sciences, Humanities, Science & Technology, Computer Science, Library & Information Science, Literature, Regional Interests, Mass Communication (mainly material on Sri Lanka)
Publication(s): *International Standard Book numbering in Sri Lanka* (2nd edition, brochure); *Sri Lanka (ISBN) Publishers Directory* (1991 & 1999 editions)
ISBN Prefix(es): 955-9011

Sudan

Sudanese Publishers' Association
c/o Institute of African & Asian Studies, Khartoum University, PO Box 321, Khartoum 11115
Tel: (0249) 11-77820 *Fax:* (0249) 11-77820

Suriname

Standard Book Numbering Agency
Publishers' Association Suriname, Domineestr 32, Paramaribo
Mailing Address: PO Box 1841, Paramaribo
Tel: 472545 *Fax:* 410563
E-mail: interf@sr.net
Telex: 123inco-sn
Key Personnel
ISBN Administrator: E Hogenboom

Swaziland

The Librarian, University College of Swaziland
Private Bag 4, Kwaluseni
Tel: 5184011 *Fax:* 5185276
E-mail: mmavuso@uniswac1.uniswa.sz
Web Site: library.uniswa.sz
Telex: 2087

Standard Book Numbering Agency, see The Librarian, University College of Swaziland

Sweden

Foreningen Svenska Laromedelsproducenter (The Swedish Association of Educational Publishers
Drottninggatan 97, S-11360 Stockholm
Tel: (08) 7361940 *Fax:* (08) 7361944
E-mail: fsl@forlagskansli.se
Key Personnel
Dir: Lena Westerberg *E-mail:* lena.westerberg@forlagskansli.se
Founded: 1974
Trade association for educational publishers.
ISBN Prefix(es): 91-85386
Associate Companies: The Swedish Publishers Association

Svenska Forlaggareforeningen
Drottninggatan 97, 113 60 Stockholm
Tel: (08) 7361940 *Fax:* (08) 7361944
E-mail: svf@forlagskansli.se
Key Personnel
Dir: Kristina Ahlinder
Swedish Publishers' Association.
Publication(s): *Svensk Bokhandel* (jointly with the Swedish Booksellers' Association)

The Swedish Association of Educational Publishers (Foreningen Svenska Laromedelsproducenter), see Foreningen Svenska Laromedelsproducenter (The Swedish Association of Educational Publishers

Switzerland

AIESI, see Association Internationale des Ecoles des Sciences de l'Information

ASELF, see Association Suisse des Editeurs de Langue Francaise

†◇Association Internationale des Ecoles des Sciences de l'Information
Unit of Agence Universitaire de la Francophonie
Haute Ecole de Gestion, Information et documentation, 7, route de Drize, 1227 Carouge
Tel: (022) 705 99 77 *Fax:* (022) 705 99 98
Web Site: www.aiesi.refer.org

SWITZERLAND

Key Personnel
President: Jacqueline Deschamps *Tel:* (022) 705 99 69 *E-mail:* jacqueline.deschamps@heg.ge.ch
Founded: 1977
International Association of Information Science Schools.

Association Suisse des Editeurs de Langue Francaise
Route Du Lac 2 1094 Paudex, Case Postale 1215, 1001 Lausanne
Tel: (021) 7963300 *Fax:* (021) 7963311
E-mail: aself@centrezational.cl
Telex: 455730
Key Personnel
Secretary General: Philippe Schibli
Swiss Publishers' Association (French language).
ISBN Prefix(es): 2-88303

Association Suisse des Libraires de Langue Francaise
Route Du Lac 3 1034 Paudex, Case postale 1215, 1001 Lausanne
Tel: (021) 7963300 *Fax:* (021) 7963311
E-mail: aself@centrezational.cl
Telex: 455730
Key Personnel
Secretary: Philippe Schibli
Association of Swiss French-language Bookshops.

Association Suisse Romande des Diffuseurs et Distributeurs de Livres
Route Du Lac 2 1094 Paudex, Case Postale 1215, 1001 Lausanne
Tel: (021)7963300 *Fax:* (021) 7963311
E-mail: aself@centrezational.ch
Telex: 455730
Key Personnel
Contact: Philippe Schibli
Association of Book Distributors of French-speaking Switzerland.

Buchverleger-Verband der Deutschsprachigen Schweiz (VVDS) (Swiss Publishers Association)
Alderstrasse 40 Postfach, 8034 Zurich
Tel: (01) 421 28 01 *Fax:* (01) 421 28 18
E-mail: sbvv@swissbooks.ch
Web Site: www.swissbooks.ch
Key Personnel
ISBN Administrator: Yolanda Canonica
  E-mail: yolanda.canonica@swissbooks.ch
This is the agency for German-language ISBNs.
Parent Company: Swiss Booksellers & Publishers Association

†Conference of European Churches
150 route de Ferney, 1211 Geneva 2
Mailing Address: PO Box 2100, 1211 Geneva 2
Tel: (022) 791-6111 *Fax:* (022) 791-6227
Web Site: www.cec-kek.org
Telex: 415 730 01K CH *Cable:* OIKOUMENE, GENEVA
Key Personnel
General Secretary: Keith Winston Clements
Communications Secretary: Mr Robin Gurney
  Tel: (022) 791 6485 *E-mail:* reg@cec-kek.org
Founded: 1959
Subjects: Ecumenical Theology, International Relationships
Publication(s): *God Unites; In Christ a New Creation* (English, French & German, 1992); *Springs Within the Valleys* (English, French, German, 1997); *Working Together With Him* (English, French, German, 1997)
ISBN Prefix(es): 2-88070
Branch Office(s)
Strasbourg, France
Brussels, Belgium

†◇Distripress
Beethovenstr 20, CH-8002 Zurich
Tel: (0411) 2024121 *Fax:* (0411) 2021025
E-mail: info@distripress.ch
Web Site: www.distripress.ch
Key Personnel
Man Dir: Dr Peter Emoed *E-mail:* peter.emod@distripress.ch
Founded: 1955
Association pour la Promotion de la Diffusion Internationale de la Presse
Vereinigung zur Foerderung des internationalen Pressevertriebes
Member of World Association of Newspapers, European Newspaper Publishers' Association.
Publication(s): *Distripress Gazette* (3 times a year); *Who's Who in Distripress* (annually)

IBBY, see International Board on Books for Young People (IBBY)

ILO, see International Labour Organization (ILO)

†Inter-Parliamentary Union
Union interparlementaire, pl du Petit-Saconnex, CH-1211 Geneva 19
Mailing Address: PO Box 438, CH-1211 Geneva 19
Tel: (022) 9194150 *Fax:* (022) 9194160
E-mail: postbox@mail.ipu.org
Web Site: www.ipu.org
Key Personnel
Secretary General: Anders B Johnsson
Information Officer: Luisa Ballin *Tel:* (4122) 9194116 *E-mail:* lb@mail.ipu.org
Founded: 1889
Subjects: World organization of national parliaments
Publication(s): *Codes of Conduct for Elections* (1998, CS Goodwin-Gill); *The Conference of Presiding Officers of National Parliaments* (2001); *Declaration on Criteria for Free & Fair Elections* (1994); *Democracy: Its Principles & Achievement* (1998); *Free & Fair Elections: International Law & Practice* (1994, GS Goodwin-Gill); *Handbook for Parliamentarians: Eliminating the Worst Forms of Child Labour* (2002); *Handbook for Parliamentarians: Refugee Protection, A Guide to International Refugee Law* (2001); *Handbook for Parliamentarians: Respect for International Humanitarian Law* (1999); *The Parliamentary Mandate* (2000); *Presiding Officers of National Parliamentary Assemblies* (1997, G Bergougnous); *Universal Declaration on Democracy* (1997)
ISBN Prefix(es): 92-9142

†◇International Board on Books for Young People (IBBY)
Nonnenweg 12, CH-4055 Basel
Tel: (061) 2722917 *Fax:* (061) 2722757
E-mail: ibby@eye.ch; ibby@ibby.org
Key Personnel
Executive Dir: Leena Maissen
Executive Assistant: Liz Page
Founded: 1953
Publication(s): *Bookbird: A Journal of International Children's Literature* (quarterly); *Congress Proceedings* (biennial); *IBBY Honour List* (biennial)

†‡International Commission of Jurists
81A Ave de Chatelaine, 1219 Chatelaine/Geneva
Mailing Address: PO Box 216, 1219 Chatelaine/Geneva
Tel: (022) 7884747 *Fax:* (022) 7884880
E-mail: icjch@gn.apc.org
Telex: 418 531 ICJ CH *Cable:* INTERJURISTS, GENEVA

BOOK TRADE

Key Personnel
Secretary-General: Adama Dieng
Founded: 1952
Subjects: Human Rights, International Law
Publication(s): *ICJ Newsletter; The Review*
ISBN Prefix(es): 92-9037

†‡International Institute for Labour Studies
PO Box 6, CH-1211 Geneva 22
Tel: (022) 7996128 *Fax:* (022) 7998542
E-mail: info@ils.org
Web Site: www.ils.org/inst
Telex: 415647 ilo ch
Key Personnel
Dir: Padmanabha Gopinath
Head Research Coordinator: Jean-Michel Servais

†◇International Labour Organization (ILO)
4 route des Morillons, CH-1211 Geneva 22
Tel: (022) 7996111 *Fax:* (022) 7998578
E-mail: pubvente@ilo.org
Telex: 415 647 ilo ch *Cable:* INTERLAB GENEVA
Key Personnel
Dir-General: Michel Hansenne
Chief, Publications Bureau: David Freedman
Chief, Marketing Operations: Luisito Cabrera
Rights Services: Susan Peters
Business Manager: Neal Thornton
Production Editor: May Ballerio
Editor: John Myers; Lillian Nell; Francois Crozon; Carlos Sebilla
Sales: Denis Brodier; Nicole Vallee; Gloria Manghinang
Founded: 1919
From the creation of the ILO in 1919, publishing has formed an important part of its activities. The ILO publishes books, reports & periodicals of international interest on major social, labor & economic problems & trends falling within their competence. This substantial publishing program has over 1300 titles in English, 827 in French & 650 in Spanish (editions in print) which cover studies, monographs, handbooks, training materials & periodicals.
Subjects: Reports for the *International Labor Conference*, Regional Conferences & Sectoral Meetings, Equality of Rights, International Labor Standards, Conditions of Work & Welfare Facilities, Cooperatives, Developing Countries & Technical Cooperation, Economics, Industrial Relations, Intermediate Technology, Employment & Development, Structural Adjustment, Rural Development & Employment Planning, Human Rights & Apartheid, Labor Law & Labor Administration, International Migration & Population Questions, Multinationals, Productivity & Management Development & Training, Occupational Safety & Health, Social Security, Trade Unions, Vocational Guidance & Training, Wages & Hours of Work, Vocational Rehabilitation, Workers' Education, Women's Questions, Labor Information, Statistics, Bibliographies & Periodicals, Audiovisual Material, Microfiches & CD-ROM
ISBN Prefix(es): 92-2
Branch Office(s)
Guillermo Prieto No 94, Colonia San Rafael, Ave Cordoba 950, 06470 Mexico DF, Mexico
Piso 13 y 14, 1054 Buenos Aires, Argentina
Hohenzollernstr 21, 53173 Bonn, Germany
East Court, 3rd floor, India Habitat Centre, Lodi Rd, New Delhi 110 003, India
8th floor, UNU Headquarters Bldg, 53-70 Jingumae 5-chome, Shibuya-ku, Toyko 150, Japan
Millbank Tower, 21-24 Millbank, London SW1P 4QP, United Kingdom
U.S. Office(s): ILO Publications Center, 49 Sheridan Ave, Albany, NY 12210, United States

ORGANIZATIONS   SWITZERLAND

†International Organization for Standardization (ISO)
Case Postale 56, One rue de Varembe, 1211 Geneva 20
Tel: (022) 7490111 *Fax:* (022) 7333430
E-mail: central@iso.org
Web Site: www.iso.org (online catalogue provides full listing)
Key Personnel
Acting Secretary General: Christian J Favre
Founded: 1947
Worldwide Federation of national standards bodies with some 140 members (one per country).
Subjects: Development of International Standards in all fields except electrical & electronic engineering
ISBN Prefix(es): 92-67
U.S. Office(s): American National Standards Institute (ANSI), 1819 "L" St, NW, Washington, DC 20036, United States *Tel:* 212-642-4900 *Fax:* 212-398-0023 *E-mail:* info@ansi.org *Web Site:* www.ansi.org (Postal Address: 25 W 23 St, 4th floor, New York, NY 10036)

†◇International Publishers Association
3 ave de Miremont, CH-1206 Geneva
Tel: (022) 3463018 *Fax:* (022) 3475717
E-mail: secretariat@ipa-uie.org
Web Site: www.ipa-uie.org
Key Personnel
President: Pere Vicens
Sec Gen: Benoit Muller
Assistant to Secretary General: Stephanie Tuetey
E-mail: tuetey@ipa-uie.org
Founded: 1896

†‡International Road Federation
Chemin de Blandonnet 2, CH 1214 Geneva-Vernier
Tel: (022) 3060260 *Fax:* (022) 3060270
E-mail: info@irfnet.org
Web Site: www.irfnet.org
Key Personnel
President: Alain Dupont
Dir General: M W Westerhuis
Publications: C de Jong Bozkurt
Founded: 1948
Subjects: Road Transport; Road Infrastructure
ISBN Prefix(es): 92-9106
U.S. Office(s): The Watergate Office Building, 2600 Virginia Ave NW, Suite 208, Washington, DC 20037, United States *Tel:* (202) 338-4641 *Fax:* (202) 338-8104

†‡International Telecommunication Union (ITU)
Palais des Nations, Postfach, 1211 Geneva 10
Tel: (022) 7306161 *Fax:* (022) 7306444
Telex: 421000 Uit
Key Personnel
Secretary-General: Richard E Butler
The ITU was founded in 1865 as the International Telegraphic Union. It became the International Telecommunication Union in 1934 and a specialized agency of the UN in 1947. Structure: 4 permanent organizations - General Secretariat, International Telegraph and Telephone Consultative Committee (CCITT), International Radio Consultative Committee (CCIR) and the International Frequency Registration Board (IFRB). It regulates, plans, coordinates and standardizes international telecommunications.
ISBN Prefix(es): 92-61; 92-71; 92-72; 92-73; 92-74

†‡International Union Against Cancer
Affiliate of Council for International Organizations of Medical Sciences
3 Rue du Conseil-General, 1205 Geneva
Tel: (022) 8091811 *Fax:* (022) 8091810
E-mail: info@uicc.org
Web Site: www.uicc.org
Key Personnel
Communications Manager: Steve Donnet
Tel: (022) 809 1875 *E-mail:* donnet@uicc.org
Founded: 1933
Objectives are to advance scientific & medical knowledge in research, diagnosis, treatment & prevention of cancer & promote all other aspects of the campaign against cancer throughout the world.
Publication(s): *Association of UICC Fellows Membership Directory* (2000); *International Directory of Cancer Institutes & Organizations* (on-line only)

IUCN, see World Conservation Union (IUCN)

◇Schweizerischer Buchhaendler- und Verleger-Verband SBVV
Postfach 9045, 8050 Zurich
Tel: (01) 3186430 *Fax:* (01) 3186462
E-mail: sbvv@swissbooks.ch
Web Site: www.swissbooks.ch
Key Personnel
Executive Dir: Dr Martin Dann
Secretary: Eva Heberlein
Further Education: Idda Miguel
Accountant: Ernst Kaeppeli
ISBN Agentur: Stefanie Nuebling
E-mail: stefanie.nuebling@swissbooks.ch
Swiss Booksellers' and Publishers' Association (German language).
Publication(s): *Adressbuch des Schweizer Buchhandels*; *Das Schweizer Buch*; *Der Schweizer Buchhandel* (bimonthly official organ of this association, also its French equivalent SLESR, and its Italian equivalents SESI and ALSI); *Schweizer Buecherverzeichnis*; *Verzeichnis der Auslieferungsstellen*

SLESR, see Societe des Libraires et Editeurs de la Suisse Romande (SLESR)

Societe des Libraires et Editeurs de la Suisse Romande (SLESR)
Route Du Lac 2 1094 Paudex, Case postale 1215, 1001 Lausanne
Tel: (021) 7963300 *Fax:* (021) 7963311
E-mail: aself@centrezational.cl
Key Personnel
Dir: Philippe Schibli
Booksellers' & Publishers' Association of French-speaking Switzerland.
Publication(s): *La Librairie suisse* (bimonthly official organ of this association, also its German equivalent SBVV, & its Italian equivalents SESI & ALSI)

Standard Book Numbering Agency, see Buchverleger-Verband der Deutschsprachigen Schweiz (VVDS)

UNCTAD, see United Nations Conference on Trade and Development (UNCTAD)

UNECE, see United Nations Economic Commission for Europe (UNECE)

Union Interparlementaire, see Inter-Parliamentary Union

†‡United Nations Conference on Trade and Development (UNCTAD)
Palais des Nations, CH-1211 Geneva 10
Tel: (022) 9171234; (022) 9071234 *Fax:* (022) 9070057
Telex: 412962 *Cable:* UNATIONS GENEVA
Key Personnel
Secretary-General: Rubens Ricupero
Chief Reference Service: A Von Wartensleben
E-mail: wartensleben@unctad.org
Founded: 1964
Subjects: Trade & Development

†‡United Nations Economic Commission for Europe (UNECE)
Palais des Nations, CH-1211 Geneva 10
Tel: (022) 917 44 44 *Fax:* (022) 917 05 05
E-mail: info.ece@unece.org
Web Site: www.unece.org
Telex: 41 29 62
Key Personnel
Executive Secretary: Brigita Schmoegnerova
Information Officer: Jean Michel Jakobowicz
Founded: 1947
Provides technical assistance to countries in transition & regional framework for the elaboration of conventions, norms & standards.
Subjects: Economic Analysis, Environmental, Transport, Energy, Timber, Statistics, Trade
ISBN Prefix(es): 92-1
U.S. Office(s): Regional Commissions New York Office, New York, NY 10017, United States, Director: Ms S Al-Bassam *Tel:* 212-963-8090 *Fax:* 212-963-1500 *E-mail:* rcnyo@un.org

†‡United Nations Research Institute for Social Development (UNRISD)
Palais des Nations, CH-1211 Geneva 10
Tel: (022) 917 3020 *Fax:* (022) 917 0650
E-mail: info@unrisd.org
Web Site: www.unrisd.org
Telex: 412962 UNOCH *Cable:* UNATIONS GENEVA
Key Personnel
Dir: Thandika Mkandawire
Deputy Dir: Cynthia Hewitt de Alcantara
Information Officer: Nicolas Bovay *Tel:* (022) 917 1143 *E-mail:* bovay@unrisd.org
Founded: 1963
Engages in multidisciplinary research on the social dimensions of contemporary problems affecting development.
Subjects: Technology & society; social policy & development; civil society & social movements; democracy & human rights; identities, conflict & cohesion
Publication(s): *The Accommodation of Cultural Diversity* (Case studies & public policy); *Agricultural Expansion & Tropical Deforestation: Poverty, International Trade & Land Use*; *Cambodia Reborn? The Transition to Democracy & Development*; *Derechos@Glob.net: Globalizacion y derechos humanos en America latina*; *Discours et realites des politiques participatives de gestion de l'environnement: Le cas du Senegal*; *Discours et Realites des Politiques Participatives de Geston de L'Environment*; *Ethnic Diversity & Public Policy: A Comparative Inquiry*; *Forest Policy & Politics in the Philippines: The Dynamics of Participatory Conservation*; *Gendered Poverty & Well-Being*; *Ghana's Adjustment Experience*; *La mano visible: Asumir la responsabilidad por el desarrollo social*; *Land Reform & Peasant Livelihoods: The Social Dynamics of Rural Poverty & Agrarian Reforms in Developing Countries*; *Le conflit libanais: Communautes religieuses, classes sociales et identite nationale*; *Lima megaciudad: Democracia, desarrollo y descentralizacion en sectores populares*; *Mains visibles: Assumer la responsabilite du developpement social*; *Missionaries & Mandarins: Feminist Engagement with Development Institutions*; *The Native Tourists: Mass Tourism within Developing Countries*; *Post-Conflict Eritrea: Prospects for Reconstruction & Development*; *Rebuilding Social & Economic Progress in Africa: Essays in the Memory of Philip Ndegwa*; *Renewing Social & Economic Transformation in East Central Europe*; *Rights@Glob.Net: Globalization & Human Rights in Latin America*; *Social Development & Public Policy*; *UNRISD News* (biannually,

newsletter); *Visible Hands: Taking Responsibility for Social Development*; *Whose Land? Civil Society Perspective on Land Reform & Rural Poverty Reduction, Regional Experiences from Africa, Asia & Latin America*
ISBN Prefix(es): 92-9085
Total Titles: 95 Print

†‡Universal Postal Union (UPU)
Welt post str 4, CH-3000 Berne 15
Tel: (031) 3503111 *Fax:* (031) 3503110
E-mail: info@upu.int
Web Site: www.upu.int *Cable:* UPU BERNE
Key Personnel
Dir-General: Thomas E Leavey
Head External Communications: James H Gunderson *Tel:* (031) 350 32 01 *E-mail:* james.gunderson@upu.int
Founded: 1874
Subjects: Postal matters
Publication(s): *Union Postale* (quarterly)
ISBN Prefix(es): 92-62

UNRISD, see United Nations Research Institute for Social Development (UNRISD)

UPU, see Universal Postal Union (UPU)

Vereinigung der Buchantiquare und Kupferstichhaendler in der Schweiz
Restelbergstr 82, 8044 Zurich
Tel: (01) 350-1441 *Fax:* (01) 350-1443
E-mail: mail@fluehmann.com
Web Site: www.vebuku.ch
Key Personnel
President: Alain Moisandat
Association of Antiquarians Book and Print Sellers in Switzerland.

Vereinigung des katholischen Buchandels der Schweiz
c/o Andre Hausler, Herder Verlag, Muttenzerstr 109, 4133 Pratteln 2
Tel: (061) 8210900
Association of Swiss Catholic Booksellers and Publishers.

VVDS, see Buchverleger-Verband der Deutschsprachigen Schweiz (VVDS)

WARC, see World Alliance of Reformed Churches

Weltverband der Lehrmittelfirmen, see Worlddidac

WHO, see World Health Organization (WHO)

WIPO, see World Intellectual Property Organization (WIPO)

WMO, see World Meteorological Organization

†World Alliance of Reformed Churches
150 Route de Ferney, CH-1211 Geneva 2
Mailing Address: PO Box 2100, CH-1211 Geneva 2
Tel: (022) 7916238; (022) 7916237 *Fax:* (022) 7916505
E-mail: warc@warc.ch
Web Site: www.warc.ch *Cable:* WARC GENEVA
Key Personnel
Secretary General: Rev Setri Nyomi
Administrative Assistant & Communications Office: Sally J Redondo *Tel:* (022) 791 6235 *E-mail:* sjr@warc.ch
Founded: 1875

Subjects: Biblical Studies, Regional Interests, Protestant Religion, Theology, Women's Studies, Ecological Issues, Economic & Social Justice
Publication(s): *Reformed World* (Quarterly, journal, Annual subscription); *Update* (Quarterly, newsletter, Annual subscription)
ISBN Prefix(es): 92-9075

World Association of Publishers, Manufacturers & Distributors of Educational Materials, see Worlddidac

†World Conservation Union (IUCN)
Rue Mauverney 28, CH-1196 Gland
Tel: (022) 9990001 *Fax:* (022) 9990002
E-mail: mail@hq.iucn.ch *Cable:* IUCNATURE GLAND
Key Personnel
Dir-General: David K McDowell
Founded: 1948
Subjects: Analytical reports on Eastern Europe; Biodiversity; Ecosystems; Forests; Mountains; Wetlands, Coastal & Marine Areas; Environmental Education; Environmental Law & Policy; Social Policy; Sustainable use initiatives & threatened species
ISBN Prefix(es): 2-8317; 2-88032

†‡World Health Organization (WHO)
(Organisation mondiale de la Sante)
Ave Appia, 20, CH-1211 Geneva 27
Tel: (022) 791 2111 *Fax:* (022) 791 3111
E-mail: publications@who.int
Web Site: www.who.int *Cable:* UNISANTE-GENEVE
Key Personnel
Dir General: Dr G H Brundtland
Chief, Marketing: A C Wieboldt *Tel:* (022) 791 2476 *E-mail:* wieboldta@who.int
Founded: 1948
The WHO is a specialized agency of the United Nations with primary responsibility for international health matters & public health. Through this organization the health professions of member states exchange their knowledge & experience with the aim of making possible the attainment by all citizens of the world of a level of health that will permit them to lead a socially & economically productive lives.
Subjects: Public Health, Reference, Medicine, Environmental Health
ISBN Prefix(es): 92-4
Number of titles published annually: 100 Print
Total Titles: 10,000 Print
Parent Company: Publicacoes Europa-America
U.S. Office(s): WHO Publications Center, 49 Sheridan Ave, Albany, NY 12210, United States *Tel:* 518-436-9686 *Fax:* 518-436-7433
E-mail: qcorp@compuserve.com

†◊World Intellectual Property Organization (WIPO)
34 chemin des Colombettes, Geneva 20
Tel: (022) 3389111 *Fax:* (022) 7335428
E-mail: wipo.mail@wpo.int
Key Personnel
Dir General: Dr Kamil Idris
Founded: 1967
World Intellectual Property Organization (WIPO) Responsible for the promotion of the protection of intellectual property (industrial property & copyright & neighboring rights) throughout the world. Administers, among other international conventions, the Paris Convention for the Protection of Industrial Property & the Berne Convention for the Protection of Literary & Artistic Works.
Publication(s): *Industrial Property & Copyright* (La Propriete industrielle et le Droit d'auteur, monthly in English & French, bimonthly in Spanish); *Intellectual Property in Asia & the Pacific* (quarterly in English); *International Designs Bulletin* (monthly, bilingual French & English); *PCT Gazette* (weekly in English & French); *PCT Newsletter* (monthly in English); *WIPO Gazette of International Marks-Gazette OMPI des Marques internationales* (monthly in English & French)

†◊World Meteorological Organization
Case Postale no 2300, CH-1211 Geneva 2
Tel: (022) 7308111 *Fax:* (022) 7308022
E-mail: pubsales@gateway.wmo.cch
Telex: 44 41 99 OMM CH *Cable:* METEOMOND GENEVE
Key Personnel
President: John Zillman
Secretary General: G O P Obasi
The publications of WMO include basic documents, operational publications, official records, WMO guides, technical notes, annual reports & the WMO Bulletin.
ISBN Prefix(es): 92-63
U.S. Office(s): AMS, 45 Beacon St, Boston, MA 02108, United States *Tel:* 617-227-2425 *Fax:* 617-742-8718 *E-mail:* wmopubs@9metsoc.org

World Trade Organization, see WTO (World Trade Organization)

†◊Worlddidac
Bollwerk 21, CH-3001 Bern
Mailing Address: PO Box 8866, CH-3001 Bern
Tel: (031) 311 76 82; (031) 311 76 83 *Fax:* (031) 312 17 44
E-mail: info@worlddidac.org
Web Site: www.worlddidac.org
Key Personnel
Dir: Beat Jost
World Association of Publishers, Manufacturers & Distributors of Educational Materials.

†‡WTO (World Trade Organization)
Centre William Rappard, 154 rue de Lausanne, CH-1211 Geneva 21
Tel: (022) 7395111 *Fax:* (022) 7395458
Web Site: www.wto.org
Telex: 412324 OMC; WTOCH *Cable:* OMC/WTO GENEVE
Key Personnel
Dir General: Peter Sutherland
Dir Information: Keith Rockwell
Founded: 1948
Accord general sur les Tarifs douaniers et le Commerce; Examination & negotiations of various aspects of international trade policies & practices.
Publication(s): *Basic Instruments & Selected Documents (BISD) Series* (annually); *GATT Activities* (annually); *International Trade Report* (annually); *International Trade Statistics* (annually); *The International Markets for Meat* (annually); *The World Market for Dairy Products* (annually); *Trade Policy Review series* (about 14 countries reviewed annually)
ISBN Prefix(es): 92-870

Taiwan, Province of China

Standard Book Numbering Agency
National Central Library, 20 Chungshan S Rd, Taipei 10040
Tel: (02) 23619132 (ext 705) *Fax:* (02) 23115330

E-mail: isbn@msg.ncl.edu.tw
Web Site: www.ncl.edu.tw/isbn
Key Personnel
Dir: Dr Chuang Fang-Jung
Publication(s): *ISBN Publishers' Directory* (annually)

United Republic of Tanzania

National Bibliographic Agency
Tanzania Library Service, Dar Es Salaam
Mailing Address: PO Box 9283, Dar Es Salaam
Tel: (051) 150048; (051) 110573 *Fax:* (022) 2151100
E-mail: tlsb@africaonline.co.tz
Key Personnel
Dir: E A Mwinyimvua
ISBN Administrator: Mr M S Mkenga

Standard Book Numbering Agency, see Tanzania Library Service Director

Tanzania Library Service Director
Bibi Titi Mohamed St, PO Box 9283, Dar es Salaam
Tel: (051) 2150048; (051) 2150049
E-mail: tlsb@AfricaOnline.co.tz
Key Personnel
Head, Bibliographic & Documentation Service
Dir: Ms Irene Minja
ISBN Prefix(es): 9976-65

Thailand

National Library
Tawasukree, Samsen Rd, Bangkok 10300
Tel: (02) 6285183 *Fax:* (02) 2810263
E-mail: suwksir@emisc.moe.go.th
Web Site: www.span.com.au/nlt
Telex: 84189 depfiar th
Key Personnel
Dir: Suwakhon Siriwongworawat

Publishers' and Booksellers' Association of Thailand
320 Lat Phrao 94aphat, Pracha-u-thit Rd, Bangkok 10310
Tel: (02) 5592642 *Fax:* (02) 5592643

C/O Seames, see Southeast Asian Ministers of Education Organization Regional Language Centre (SEAMEO RELC)

†◇**Southeast Asian Ministers of Education Organization Regional Language Centre (SEAMEO RELC)**
Darakarn Bldg, 920 Sukhumuit Rd, Bangkok 10110
Tel: (0662) 3910144 *Fax:* (0662) 3812587
Key Personnel
Dir: Suparak Racha-Intra
Founded: 1965
Subjects: Language Teaching & Research, Linguistics, English in multilingual, multicultural situations

Standard Book Numbering Agency, see National Library

Standard Book Numbering Agency
The National Library of Thailand, Tawasukree, Bangkok 10300
Tel: (02) 2810263; (02) 6285183 *Fax:* (02) 2815450; (02) 2810263
E-mail: suwksir@emisc.moe.go.th; suwaksir@yahoo.com
Web Site: www.span.com.au/nlt
Telex: 84189 Natlib Th
Key Personnel
Dir: Suwakhon Siriwongorawat *Tel:* (62) 2817543

†‡**United Nations Library, Bangkok**
United Nations Bldg, Rajadamnern Ave, Bangkok 10200
Tel: (02) 2881360 *Fax:* (02) 2881000
E-mail: yoo.unescap@un.org; library-escap@un.org
Telex: 82392; 82315 Escap *Cable:* ESCAP BANGKOK
Key Personnel
Librarian: Evelyn Domingo-Barker
  E-mail: domingo-barker.unescap@un.org
Subjects: Economic and Social Development in Asia and the Pacific Region
Publication(s): *Asian Bibliography* (biannually); *ESCAP Documents & Publications* (annually)

Tunisia

Agence Tunisienne de l'ISBN
Bibliotheque Nationale, 20 Souk El Attarine, BP 42, 1008 Tunis
Tel: (01) 256921 *Fax:* (01) 342700
E-mail: Bibliotheque.Nationale@Email.ati.tn

Standard Book Numbering Agency, see Agence Tunisienne de l'ISBN

Turkey

Standard Book Numbering Agency
Kultur Bakanligi, Kutuphaneler Genel Mudurlugu, Necatibey Ca No 55 Sihhiye, 06440 Ankara
Tel: (0312) 2317962 *Fax:* (0312) 2313564
E-mail: kultur@kutuphanelergm.gov.trr
Web Site: www.kutuphanelergm.gov.tr
Key Personnel
General Dir: Ms Gokcin Yalcin

Tuerk Editoerler Dernegi
No 12-3 Cagaloglu, Istanbul
Tel: (0212) 5125602 *Fax:* (0212) 5117794
Turkish Publishers' Association.

Uganda

Standard Book Numbering Agency, see Uganda Publishers and Booksellers Association

Uganda Publishers and Booksellers Association
Globe Chambers, 1st floor, Plot 2C Kampala Rd, Kampala
Mailing Address: PO Box 7732, Kampala
Tel: (041) 259163; (041) 251112 *Fax:* (041) 251160

Telex: 61272
Key Personnel
Contact: Mr Martin Okia

Ukraine

Book Chamber of Ukraine, National ISBN Agency
27, Yuri Gagarin Ave, 02094 Kiev
Tel: (44) 573-52-36 *Fax:* (44) 573-52-36
Key Personnel
Head of ISBN Agency: Iryna O Pogorelovska

Standard Book Numbering Agency, see Book Chamber of Ukraine, National ISBN Agency

United Kingdom

†**African Books Collective Ltd**
The Jam Factory, 27 Park End St, Oxford OX1 1HU
Tel: (01865) 726686 *Fax:* (01865) 793298; (01993) 709265
E-mail: abc@dial.pipex.com
Web Site: www.africanbookscollective.com
Key Personnel
Consultant: Mary Jay
Council of Management, Tanzania: Walter Bgoya
Council of Management, Kenya: Henry Chakava
Council of Management, Ghana: Woeli Dekutsey
Council of Management, Nigeria: Victor Nwankwo
Council of Management, Lesotho: Tankie Khalanyane
Founded: 1990
Donor-funded organization owned by member publishers. Has exclusive distribution rights of member publishers titles outside Africa.
Subjects: Scholarly & Academic, Literary (including Criticism), Children's Books
ISBN Prefix(es): 91-7106; 0-949229; 0-908311; 9966-831; 1-870784; 978-2601; 978-2266; 0-947479; 0-947009; 978-2264; 978-2299; 978-2321; 978-2494; 9964-970; 978-2711; 1-870716; 0-949225; 99916-31; 0-908307; 0-949932; 0-906968; 99911-31; 9964-978; 978-2492; 978-2323; 978-2276

ALPSP, see Association of Learned & Professional Society Publishers

Antiquarian Booksellers' Association
Sackville House, 40 Piccadilly, London W1V 9PA
Tel: (020) 7439 3118 *Fax:* (020) 7439 3119
E-mail: info@aba.org.uk; admin@aba.org.uk
Key Personnel
Administrators: Philippa Gibson; Deborah Stratford

Association of Authors' Agents
Drury House, 34-43 Russell St, London WC2B 5HA
Tel: (020) 7344 1000 *Fax:* (020) 7836 9541
E-mail: aaa@pfd.co.uk
Web Site: www.agentsassoc.co.uk
Key Personnel
President: Jonathan Lloyd
Treasurer: Barbara Levy
Secretary: Simon Trewin
Trade association representing the interests of UK based literary agents.

UNITED KINGDOM BOOK TRADE

Association of Learned & Professional Society Publishers
Sentosa Hill Rd, Fairlight, Hasting, East Sussex TN35 4AE
Tel: (01424) 812353 *Fax:* (0181) 6633583
E-mail: donovan@alpsp.demon.co.uk
Key Personnel
Secretary-General: B T Donovan
Publication(s): *Learned Publishing* (quarterly)

Association of Little Presses
83b London Rd, Peterborough, Cambs PE3 9BS
Tel: (020) 3851889
Key Personnel
Coordinator & Membership Secretary: Chris Jones
Chairman: Lawrence Upton
Treasurer: Peter Finch
Editor: Stan Trevor; Paul Green
Organizes book fairs.
Publication(s): *Catalogue of Little Press Books in Print* (biennially); *Getting Your Poetry Published*; *Poetry & Little Press Information (PALPI)* (biannually); *Publishing Yourself-Not Too Difficult After All*
Branch Office(s)
Consortium of London Presses, 89a Petherton Rd, London N5 2QT

Authors' Licensing & Collecting Society
Marlborough Court, 14-18 Holborn, London EC1 2LE
Tel: (020) 7395 0600 *Fax:* (020) 7395 0660
E-mail: alcs@alcs.co.uk
Key Personnel
Chairman: C Barlas
Chief Executive: Dryfdd Wyn Phillips
Communications Manager: Alex Kempner
E-mail: alex.kempner@alcs.co.uk

BACB, see British Association of Communicators in Business Ltd (BACB)

Book Development Council International (BDCI)
No 1 Kingsway, London WC2B 6XF
Tel: (020) 7565 7474 *Fax:* (020) 7836 4543
E-mail: mail@publishers.org.uk
Web Site: www.publishers.org.uk
Key Personnel
Chairman: Chris Paterson
Dir: Ian Taylor
Contact: Kate Bostock *E-mail:* kbostock@publishers.org.uk
International Division of the Publishers Association.
Parent Company: International Division of the Publishers Association UK

†◊Book Industry Communication
39-41 North Rd, London N7 9DP
Tel: (020) 7607 0021 *Fax:* (020) 7607 0415
Key Personnel
Chairman: Roger Woodham
Man Agent: Brian Green *E-mail:* brian@bic.org.uk

Book Marketing Ltd
2-4 Idol Lane, London EC3R 5DD
Tel: (020) 7398 0705 *Fax:* (020) 7626 3660
E-mail: bml@bookmarketing.co.uk
Web Site: www.bookmarketing.co.uk
Key Personnel
Man Dir: Jo Henry
Chairman: Tim Rix
Deputy Chairman: Clare Harrison
Founded: 1989
Market research agency specializing in the book industry.
ISBN Prefix(es): 1-873517

Book Tokens Ltd
Minster House, 272 Vauxhall Bridge Rd, London SW1V 1BA
Tel: (020) 7834 5488 *Fax:* (020) 7834 8781
Key Personnel
Man Dir: Stuart Mathews
Serves more than 3000 bookshops.
Parent Company: Booksellers Association of Great Britain & Ireland
Associate Companies: Booksellers Clearing House

The Book Trade Benevolent Society
Dillon Lodge, The Retreat, Abbots Rd, Kings Langley, Herts WD4 8LT
Tel: (01923) 263128 *Fax:* (01923) 270732
E-mail: btbs@booktradecharity.demon.co.uk
Web Site: www.booktradecharity.demon.co.uk
Key Personnel
President: Sally Whitaker
Chief Executive: David Hicks *Tel:* (01923) 299731
Founded: 1837
Charity-Occupational Benevolent Fund.

Books for Keeps
6 Brightfield Rd, London SE12 8QF
Tel: (020) 8852 4953 *Fax:* (020) 8318 7580
E-mail: booksforkeeps@btinternet.com
Key Personnel
Man Dir: Richard Hill
Founded: 1976
Children's Book Review Magazine.
Publication(s): *A Multicultural Guide to Children's Books: 0-16*; *Books for Keeps* (bimonthly); *Children's Books About Bullying*; *Poetry 0-13*
Parent Company: School Bookshop Association

◊Booktrust
Book House, 45 East Hill, Wandsworth, London SW18 2QZ
Tel: (020) 8516 2977 *Fax:* (020) 8516 2978
Web Site: www.booktrusted.com; www.booktrust.org.uk
Key Personnel
Prizes Administrator: Tarryn McKay *Tel:* (020) 8516 2972 *E-mail:* tarryn@booktrust.org.uk
Prizes Manager: Kate Mervyn-Jones *Tel:* (020) 8516 2973 *E-mail:* kate@booktrust.org.uk
Supported by the Arts Council of England with activities which include literary prizes such as The Man Booker Prize, The Orange Prize for Fiction & the Nestle Smarties Book Prize. Booktrust also runs the Book Information Service.
Publication(s): *Children's Books of the Year*; *Grants & Awards Annotated*; *Guide to Literary Prizes*; *The Authors & Bank Directory*
Divisions: Children's Literature Team at Booktrust (Reading-based projects & publications related to children under 16)

BPIF, see British Printing Industries Federation (BPIF)

British Association of Communicators in Business Ltd (BACB)
42 Borough High St, London SE1 1XW
Tel: (020) 7378 7139 *Fax:* (020) 7378 7140
E-mail: enquiries@bacb.org
Web Site: www.bacb.org.uk
Key Personnel
Chairman: Alison Crossley
President: Alan Peaford
Secretary General: Kathie Jones
Publication(s): *CiB News* (monthly); *Communicators in Business Magazine* (quarterly)

British Copyright Council
29-33 Berners St, Copyright House, London W1P 4AA
Tel: (020) 7359 1895 *Fax:* (020) 7359 1895
E-mail: british.copyright.council@dial.pipex.com
Key Personnel
Chairman: Maureen Duffy
Secretary: Heather Roueblatt

British Guild of Travel Writers
178 Battersea Park Rd, London SW11 4ND
Tel: (020) 7720 9009 *Fax:* (020) 7498 6153
E-mail: bgtw@garlandintl.co.uk
Key Personnel
Chairman: Martin Roberts
Contact: Ann Garland
Founded: 1960
Publication(s): *Year Book* (annually)

British Printing Industries Federation (BPIF)
11 Bedford Row, London WC1R 4DX
Tel: (020) 7242 6904 *Fax:* (020) 7405 7784
Key Personnel
Dir General: Tom Machin
Deputy Dir: David Padbury
Marketing Dir: Christine Adames
Publication(s): *Introduction to Printing Technology*; *Print Buyers Directory*; *Printing Industries* (monthly); *UK Periodical Printers*

Bryntirion Press
Bryntirion, Bridgend CF31 4DX
Tel: (01656) 655886 *Fax:* (01656) 6560095
E-mail: press@draco.co.uk
Key Personnel
Press Manager: Huw Kinsey

BSI British Standards Institution
389 Chiswick High Rd, London W4 4AL
Tel: (020) 8996 9000 *Fax:* (020) 8996 7001
E-mail: info@bsi-global.com
Web Site: www.bsi-global.com
Telex: 266933
Key Personnel
Chairman: David John
Man Dir: Stevan Breeze
Secretary: Stanley Williams
Founded: 1901
National Standards Body.
Publication(s): *Business Standards Magazine*; *13,000 British Standards*
U.S. Office(s): BSI Inc, 12110 Sunset Hills Rd, Suite 140, Reston, VA 20190-2131, United States

BTBS The Book Trade Charity, see The Book Trade Benevolent Society

†CAB International
Wallingford, Oxon OX10 8DE
Tel: (01491) 832111 *Fax:* (01491) 833508
E-mail: cabi@cabi.org
Telex: 847964 Comagg *Cable:* COMAG
Key Personnel
Distribution Manager: Roger Farnell
Journals Production Manager: Pippa Smart
Contact: Angie Barker *E-mail:* a-barker@cabi.org; Tim Hardwick
Founded: 1929
Subjects: Agriculture, Agricultural Economics, Animal Health, Animal Science, Forestry, Rural Sociology, Nutrition, Environmental Science, Human, Horticulture Health
ISBN Prefix(es): 0-85198; 0-85199

Chartered Institute of Journalists (CIJ)
2 Dock Offices, Suurrey Quays, Lower Rd, London SE16 2XU
Tel: (020) 7252 1187 *Fax:* (020) 7232 2302
E-mail: memberservices@iojco.uk
Web Site: www.ioj.co.uk

Key Personnel
President: M Moriarty
General Secretary: C J Underwood
Founded: 1884
Professional body/independent trade union.
Subjects: Journalism & Broadcasting
Publication(s): *The Journal*

Children's Book Circle
c/o Susan Barry, The Watts Publishing Group Ltd, 96 Leonard St, London EC2A 4XD
Tel: (020) 7739 2929 *Fax:* (020) 7739 2181
Key Personnel
Co-Chairperson: Susan Barry *E-mail:* susan.barry@wattspub.co.uk; Kirsten Grant

Children's Writers & Illustrators Group
Society of Authors, 84 Drayton Gardens, London SW10 9SB
Tel: (20) 7373 6642 *Fax:* (20) 7373 5768
Key Personnel
Secretary: Jo Hodder *Tel:* (20) 73736647
E-mail: johodder@societyofauthors.org
Parent Company: The Society of Authors

Christian Booksellers Association
Formerly European Christian Booksellers Association
Grampian House, 144 Deansgate, Manchester M3 3ED
Mailing Address: PO Box 30, Manchester M60 3BX
Tel: (0161) 434 7000 *Fax:* (0161) 445 2911
E-mail: info@cba-ukeurope.org
Web Site: www.cba-ukeurop.org
Key Personnel
Executive Vice Chairman: John F Macdonald
General Secretary: Barry Holmes
Founded: 1984
International trade association. Not for profit, offering a trade service to the Christian sector & some at the general sector of publishing, distribution, retailing. In UK & over 70 countries.
Publication(s): *Christian Bookstore Journal* (Monthly, Trade publications)

CICI, see Confederation of Information Communication Industries

Circle of Wine Writers
30 Wimpole St, London W1M 7AE
Tel: (020) 7486 6563 *Fax:* (020) 7486 5375
Key Personnel
President: Hugh Johnson
Chairman: Steven Spurrier
Honorary Secretary: Stephen Skeltan
Chairman: Andrew Henderson *E-mail:* andyh@mailbox.co.uk

†CODE - Europe
The Jam Factory, 27 Park End St, Oxford OX1 1HU
Tel: (01865) 202438 *Fax:* (01865) 2024390
E-mail: code_europe@compuserve.com
Publication(s): *Tailor-Made Textbooks*

Comhairle nan Leabhraichean - The Gaelic Books Council
22 Mansfield St, Glasgow G11 5QP
Tel: (0141) 337 6211 *Fax:* (0141) 341 0515
E-mail: fios@gaelicbooks.net
Web Site: www.gaelicbooks.net
Key Personnel
Chairman: Donalda MacKinnon
Dir: Ian MacDonald
Retails all Gaelic & Gaelic related titles in print.
Publication(s): *Catalog of Gaelic Books in print*; *Gaelic Poetry Posters*

Confederation of Information Communication Industries
39-41 North Rd, London N7 9DP
Tel: (020) 7607 0021 *Fax:* (020) 7607 0415
Web Site: www.cici.org.uk
Key Personnel
Manager: Brian Green *E-mail:* brian@bic.org.uk
Chairman: Peter Lalster
Dir: Clive Bradley
Operates ClClnet, containing reference databases.

◇Copyright Licensing Agency
90 Tottenham Court Rd, London W1P 9HE
Tel: (020) 7436 5931 *Fax:* (020) 7436 3986
Key Personnel
Office Manager: K Gardner
Collective administration of rights. Member of International Federation of Reproduction Rights Organizations (IFRRO).
Publication(s): *CLArion* (biannually)
Associate Companies: Authors' Licensing & Collecting Society; Publishers Licensing Society

◇Council of Academic & Professional Publishers
Division of The Publishers Association
One Kingsway, London WC2B 6XD
Tel: (020) 7565 7474 *Fax:* (020) 7836 4543
E-mail: mail@publishers.org.uk
Web Site: www.publishers.org.uk
Key Personnel
Chairman: Philip Shaw
Vice Chairman: Richard Stileman
Dir: Graham Taylor
Founded: 1977
Academic/Professional Publishing Division of the Publishers Association.
Parent Company: The Publishers Association
Associate Companies: Serial Publishers Executive

Crime Writers' Association
Meadow View, The Street, Bossingham, Canterbury, Kent CT4 6DX
Mailing Address: PO Box 63, Wakefield WF2 0WY
E-mail: info@theCWA.co.uk
Web Site: www.thecwa.co.uk
Key Personnel
Chairman: Lindsey Davis
Secretary: Judith Cutler
Founded: 1953

Cyngor Llyfrau Cymru, see Welsh Books Council

Cyngor Llyfrau Cymru Canolfan Dosbarthu, see Welsh Books Council

DACS, see Design & Artists Copyright Society (DACS)

Design & Artists Copyright Society (DACS)
Parchment House, 13 Northburgh St, London EC1 V0AH
Tel: (020) 7336 8811 *Fax:* (020) 7336 8822
E-mail: info@dacs.co.uk
Web Site: www.dacs.co.uk
Telex: 885130 FABRIX G
Key Personnel
Chief Executive: Rachel Duffield

Directory & Database Publishers Association
PO Box 23034, London W6 0RJ
Tel: (020) 8846 9707 *Fax:* (020) 0870 168 0552
Web Site: www.directory-publisher.co.uk
Key Personnel
Chairman: John Condron
Secretary: Rosemary Pettit
E-mail: RosemaryPettit@msn.com
Founded: 1970

Trade association for directory & database publishers
Membership(s): Advertising Association, Periodical Publishers Association, European Association of Directory Publishers, Advertising Standards Board of Finance, Confederation of Information Communication Industries, Digital Content Forum, Publishing National Training Organization.
Publication(s): *DPA News* (Quarterly, newsletter); *Membership Book* (Annual)
ISBN Prefix(es): 0-906247; 0-900247

Educational Publishers Council
One Kingsway, London WC2B 6XD
Tel: (020) 7565 7474 *Fax:* (020) 7836 4543
E-mail: mail@publishers.org.uk
Web Site: www.publishers.org.uk *Cable:* PUBLASOC, LONDON WC1
Key Personnel
Chairman: Philip Walters
Dir: Graham Taylor
School Books Division of The Publishers Association.
Parent Company: The Publishers Association

Educational Writers' Group
84 Drayton Gardens, London SW10 9SB
Tel: (020) 7373 6642 *Fax:* (020) 7373 5768
E-mail: info@societyofauthors.org
Web Site: www.societyofauthors.org
Key Personnel
Secretary: Elizabeth Haylett
Parent Company: The Society of Authors

Effective Publishing
58 Saint Wulszan Way, Southam, Leamington Spa, Warks CV33 0TQ
Tel: (01926) 812110
Key Personnel
Dir: Mr Chris Pratt
Associate Companies: Effective Services

European Christian Booksellers Association, see Christian Booksellers Association

†European Information Association
c/o Manchester Central Library, St Peter's Sq, Manchester M2 5PD
Tel: (0161) 2283691 *Fax:* (0161) 2366547
E-mail: eia@manchestergb.demon.co.uk
Key Personnel
Manager: Catherine Webb
Founded: 1991
Subjects: European Union Information
Publication(s): *Basic Sources of EU Information*; *EIA European Information Guides*; *EIA Quick Guides* (self-help reference cards series)
ISBN Prefix(es): 0-948272

†◇Eusidic (European Association of Information Services)
Rose Cottage, Moulsoe, Newport Pagnell, Bucks
Key Personnel
Executive Dir: Harry Collier
Administrative Secretary: Barbara Sarjeant

Federation of Children's Book Groups
c/o Janet Wild, 32 Howard Rd, Kings Heath, Birmingham B14 7PD
Tel: (0113) 4442105
Key Personnel
Secretary: Alison Dick
Books For Ever, Ripon, April 1998.

†◇The Folklore Society
University College London, Gower St, London WC1E 6BT
Tel: (020) 7387 5894
Key Personnel
President: Dr Juliette Wood
Founded: 1878

Publication(s): *Aspect of British Calendar Customs*; *Folklore (Journal of the Folklore Society)* (FLS News); *Ribbons, Bells & Squeaking Fiddlers*

The Gaelic Books Council, see Comhairle nan Leabhraichean - The Gaelic Books Council

IMO, see International Maritime Organization (IMO)

Independent Publishers Guild
Great Gransden Sandy, 4 Middle St, Bedfordshire SG19 3AD
Tel: (01767) 677753 *Fax:* (01767) 677069
Key Personnel
Secretary: Y S Messenger

Institute of Printing
The Mews, Hill House, Clanricarde Rd, Tunbridge Wells, Kent TN1 1PJ
Tel: (01892) 538118; (01892) 518028
Fax: (01892) 518028
E-mail: iop@globalprint.com
Web Site: www.globalprint.com/uk/iop
Key Personnel
Chairman: Tony White
Secretary General: David Freeland
Founded: 1980
Professional body.
Publication(s): *Professional Printer*

Institute of Scientific & Technical Communicators (ISTC)
1st fl, 17 Church Walk, St Neots, Cambs PE19 1JH
Tel: (1480) 211550 *Fax:* (1480) 211560
E-mail: istc@istc.org.uk
Web Site: www.istc.org.uk
Key Personnel
President: Iain Wright
Editor: Colin Battson
Executive Secretary: Carol Battson
Founded: 1972
Professional Association.
Subjects: Technical & Communication
Publication(s): *Communicator Journal* (4x ann)

†**International African Institute**
SOAS, Thornhaugh Str, Russell Sq, London WC1H OXG
Tel: (020) 7898 4420 *Fax:* (020) 7898 4419
E-mail: ed2@soas.ac.uk; iai@soas.ac.uk
Key Personnel
Head of Publications: Dr Elizabeth Dunstan
Tel: (020) 7898 4435
Editor, Africa: Prof Murray Last
Honorary Dir: Prof Paul Spencer
Founded: 1926
1200 institutions & individuals are subscribing & the Council includes representatives from Africa & elsewhere.
Subjects: Academic books on Africa, including History, Ethnography, Environmental Studies, Bibliography
Publication(s): *Africa* (quarterly); *African Issues* (biannually, paperback); *Classics in African Anthropology Series*; *International African Library Series* (biannually, paperback); *The Africa Bibliography* (annually)
ISBN Prefix(es): 0-85302

†◇**International Association of Agricultural Information Specialists**
c/o Margot Bellamy, CAB Int'l, 14 Queen St, Dorchester-on-Thames, Wallingford, Oxon OX10 8DE
Key Personnel
President: Jan van der Burg
Secretary-Treasurer: Margot Bellamy
Founded: 1955

Association Internationale des Specialistes de l'Information Agricoles.
Publication(s): *Quarterly IAALD Bulletin* (2/yr (one combined issue), newsletter, 2000); *World Directory of Agricultural Information Resource Centres* (1/5 yrs, 2000, Available in hard copy & on CD Rom)

†**International Association of Technological University Libraries (IATUL)**
c/o Heriot-Watt University Library, EH14 4AS Edinburgh
Tel: (0131) 451 3570 *Fax:* (0131) 451 3164
Key Personnel
President: Michael L Breaks *E-mail:* m.l.breaks@hw.ac.uk
Secretary: Judith Palmer
Founded: 1955
Publication(s): *IATUL Conference Proceedings*; *IATUL News* (quarterly)

International Book Development
6 Devonhurst Pl, Heathfield Terrace, London W4 4JD
Tel: (020) 8742 7474 *Fax:* (020) 8747 8715
Key Personnel
Man Dir: Tony Read
Dir: Amanda Buchan; Carmelle Denning; David Foster; Euan Henderson

†‡**International Maritime Organization (IMO)**
4 Albert Embankment, London SE1 7SR
Tel: (020) 7735 7611 *Fax:* (020) 7587 3210
Telex: 04423588 *Cable:* INTERMAR
Key Personnel
Information Officer: Roger Kohn *E-mail:* rkohn@imo.org
Head of Publications: Harald Grell
Founded: 1959
Subjects: Texts of International Maritime Treaties concluded under its auspices, Maritime Technical Publications, Oil Pollution Prevention, Maritime Safety
ISBN Prefix(es): 92-801

†‡**The International Molinological Society**
125 Parkside Dr, WD17 3BA Watford Herts
Mailing Address: Groothertoginnelaan 174B, 2517EV The Hague, Netherlands
Tel: (1923) 232980
Key Personnel
Chairman: M Harverson
E-mail: HarversonTims@aol.com
Publications Officer: Leo van der Drift *Tel:* (070) 3460885 *E-mail:* leo.diederik@consunet.nl
Founded: 1973
Subjects: Mills (Windmills, Watermills, Animal-Powered Mills) Technique, History, Sociology

†◇**International PEN**
9-10 Charterhouse Bldgs, Goswell Rd, London EC1M 7AT
Tel: (020) 7253 4308 *Fax:* (020) 7253 5711
E-mail: intpen@dircon.co.uk
Web Site: www.internatpen.org
Key Personnel
International President: Homero Aridjis
General-Secretary: Terry Carlbom
Founded: 1921
A World Association of Writers.
Publication(s): *PEN International* (in English & French, issued with the assistance of UNESCO)

IOJ, see Chartered Institute of Journalists (CIJ)

ISSN UK Centre
British Library, Boston Spa, Wetherby, West Yorks LS23 7BQ
Tel: (01937) 546959 *Fax:* (01937) 546562
E-mail: issn-uk@bl.uk

Telex: 557381
Key Personnel
Director: David Baron
Allocates International Standard Serial Numbers (ISSN) to serials published in UK.

ISTC, see Institute of Scientific & Technical Communicators (ISTC)

LAB, see Latin America Bureau

†◇**Latin America Bureau**
One Amwell St, London EC1R 1UL
Tel: (020) 7278 2829 *Fax:* (020) 7278 0165
E-mail: lab@gn.apc.org
Founded: 1977
Subjects: Political, Social & Economic Issues in contemporary Latin America & the Caribbean, Environmental & Women's studies

†◇**The Lewis Carroll Society**
Little Folly, 105 The Street Willesborough, Ashford, Kent TN24 ONB
E-mail: aztec@compuserve.com
Key Personnel
Honorary Secretary: Sarah Stanfield
Chairman: Dr S H Goodacre
Treasurer: Roger Allen

◇**Mardev**
Quadrant House, Sutton, Surrey SM2 5AS
Tel: (020) 8643 0955 *Fax:* (020) 8652 4580
E-mail: mardevlists@rbi.co.uk
Web Site: www.mardevlists.com
Key Personnel
General Manager: Nick Martin
Direct marketing services for publishers, academic & library mailing lists worldwide, business & professional international mailing lists, dispatch & marketing database services.
Parent Company: Reed Elsevier plc
Branch Office(s)
Tower 2, 475 Victoria Ave, Chatswood, NSW 2067, Australia *Tel:* (02) 9422 2655 *Fax:* (02) 9422 2633 *E-mail:* mardevlists@reedbusiness.com.au
No 1 Temasek Avenue, 17-01 Millenia Tower, Singapore 039192, Singapore *Tel:* 338 3398 *Fax:* 338 1409
U.S. Office(s): 2 Rector St, 26th floor, New York, NY 10006, United States *Tel:* 212-584-9370 *Fax:* 212-584-9371 *E-mail:* sales@mardevlists.com

†◇**Maritime Information Association**
c/o Marine Society, 202 Lambeth Rd, London SE1 7JW
Tel: (020) 7261 9535 *Fax:* (020) 7401 2537
Founded: 1972
Publication(s): *Marine Information* (A guide to libraries & sources of information in the UK)

◇**Music Publishers Association**
18/20 York Bldg, London WC2N 6JU
Tel: (020) 7839 7779 *Fax:* (020) 7839 7776
E-mail: mpa@mcps.co.uk
Web Site: www.mpaonline.org.uk
Key Personnel
Chairman: Andrew Potter
Deputy Chair: Jane Dyball
Chief Executive: Sarah Faulder
Trade organization for music publishers.
Publication(s): *Catalogue of Printed Music on CD-ROM*; *List of Members*; *Printed Music Distributors*

National Acquisitions Group
Lime House, poolside, Madeley, Crewe, Cheshire CW3 9HR
Tel: (01782) 750462

E-mail: nag@psilink.co.uk
Key Personnel
Administrator: Carmel Martin
Chairman: John Gill
Administrator: Diane Roberts
Publication(s): *Directory of Acquisitions Librarians in the UK & Republic of Ireland* (biannually); *NAG News* (quarterly); *Taking Stock* (biannually)

National Federation of Retail Newsagents
2 Bridgewell Pl, London EC4 0HD
Tel: (020) 7353 6816 *Fax:* (020) 7250 0927
Key Personnel
Dir: David Daniels

National Union of Journalists (Book Branch)
Acorn House, 314 Gray's Inn Rd, London WC1X 8DP
Tel: (020) 7278 7916 *Fax:* (020) 7837 8143
E-mail: book_branch@hotmail.com
Web Site: www.nujbook.org
Key Personnel
Branch Secretary: Nick Bardsley
Membership Secretary: Cath Rasbash
Founded: 1973
Trade Union.
Publication(s): *Comrade Moss* (1990, Biography)

†◇PEN Club-German Speaking Writers Abroad
Hill House, 31B Arterberry Rd, London SW20 8AG
Tel: (020) 8946 0178
Key Personnel
President: Fritz Beer
Founded: 1934
Writers association.

†◇PEN Club-Writers in Exile London Branch
46 Crouch Hall Rd, London N8 8HJ
Tel: (020) 8340 5279
Key Personnel
President: Velta Snikere
Total Titles: 8 Print

†◇The Penman Club
185 Daws Heath Rd, Benfleet, Essex SS7 2TF
Tel: (01702) 557431
Key Personnel
Secretary: Mark Sorrell
Literary advice, criticism.

Picture Research Assoc
The Studio, 5A Alvanley Gardens, London NW6 1JD
Tel: (020) 7431 9886 *Fax:* (020) 7431 9887
Key Personnel
Contact: Emma Krikler
Publication(s): *Spred* (magazine, quarterly)

†◇Private Libraries Association (PLA)
Ravelston, South View Rd, Pinner, Middlesex HA5 3YD
Web Site: www.the-old-school.demon.co.uk/pla.htm
Key Personnel
Executive Secretary: James Brown
American Membership Secretary: William A Klutts *Tel:* 901-635-2544
Canadian Membership Secretary: Alan J Horne
Editor, Private Press Books: Paul W Nash
Founded: 1956
An international society of book collectors.
Publication(s): *Private Press Books* (checklist of privately printed books); *The Private Library* (official journal)

Public Lending Right
Richard House, Sorbonne Close, Stockton-on-Tees, Cleveland TS17 6DA
Tel: (01642) 604699 *Fax:* (01642) 615641
E-mail: registrar@plr.uk.com
Web Site: www.plr.uk.com
Key Personnel
Registrar: Dr James Parker
Reports & Press Releases.
Publication(s): *Report on the Public Lending Right Scheme, 2000-01* (Annually, 2002); *Whose Loan Is It Anyway? Essays in Celebration of PLR's 20th Anniversary* (1998)

The Publishers Association
29b Montague St, London WC1B 5BH
Tel: (020) 7691 9191 *Fax:* (020) 7691 9199
E-mail: mail@publishers.org.uk
Web Site: www.publishers.org.uk
Key Personnel
President: Anthony Forbes-Watson
Chief Exec: Ronnie Williams
Dir: Graham Taylor; Ian Taylor
Annual Conference, London, April 2002. Trade association for UK publishers of books, journals & electronic publications.
Subjects: Trade association for UK publishers of books, journals & electronic publications
Publication(s): *Annual Book Trade Year Book*

Publishers Licensing Society Ltd
5 Dryden St, Covent Garden, London WC2E 9NB
Tel: (020) 7829 8486 *Fax:* (020) 7829 8488
E-mail: pls@dial.pipex.com
Web Site: www.pls.org.uk
Key Personnel
Chairman: Neil McRae
Consultant: Richard Balkwill
Chief Executive: Jens Bammel
Founded: 1981
PLS has non-exclusive licences from 1600 publishers to include their works in photocopying & digitisation licences negotiated by the Copyright Licensing Agency. PLS ensures publishers receive their share of fees collected by CLA.
Publication(s): *PLS Plus* (newsletter)
Associate Companies: Copyright Licensing Agency

SCOLMA, see Standing Conference on Library Materials on Africa (SCOLMA)

Scottish Book Marketing Group
Scottish Book Centre, 137 Dundee St, Edinburgh EH11 1BG
Tel: (0131) 2286866 *Fax:* (0131) 2283220
Publication(s): *Directory of Publishing in Scotland* (yearly); *New Scottish Books* (bi-monthly, leaflet); *Scottish Bestseller List* (fortnightly listing of bestselling books on Scotland); *Scottish Books Direct* (Home-Shopping facility for readers at home & abroad)
Associate Companies: Scottish Publishers Association *E-mail:* enquiries@scottishbooks.org *Web Site:* www.scottishbooks.org

Scottish Book Trust
The Scottish Book Centre, 137 Dundee St, Edinburgh EH11 1BG
Tel: (0131) 2293663 *Fax:* (0131) 2284293
Publication(s): *Off The Shelf: A Guide To Books & Writers for Children From Scotland*; *Shelf Life: Information, Author Information, Reviews on Books for Children in Scotland*
Parent Company: Book Trust

Scottish Newspaper Publishers' Association
48 Palmerston Pl, Edinburgh EH12 5DE
Tel: (0131) 2204353 *Fax:* (0131) 2204344
E-mail: info@snpa.org.uk
Web Site: www.snpa.org.uk
Key Personnel
Dir: Mr J B Raeburn *E-mail:* jraeburn@spef.org.uk
Trade association representing publishers of local newspapers throughout Scotland.

◇Scottish Publishers Association
Scottish Book Centre, 137 Dundee St, Edinburgh EH11 1BG
Tel: (0131) 2286866 *Fax:* (0131) 2283220
E-mail: enquiries@scottishbooks.org
Web Site: www.scottishbooks.org
Key Personnel
Dir: Lorraine Fannin
Chairman: Timothy Wright
Founded: 1973
Trade association with 80 members.
Publication(s): *Directory of Publishing in Scotland* (annually); *New Scottish Books* (6x annually)
Associate Companies: Scottish Book Marketing Group

SIBMAS, see Societe Internationale des Bibliotheques et des Musees des Arts du Spectacle (SIBMAS)

†◇Societe Internationale des Bibliotheques et des Musees des Arts du Spectacle (SIBMAS) (International Association of Libraries & Museums of the Performing Arts)
Theatre Museum, 1E Tavistock St, London WC2E 7PR
Tel: (020) 7 943 4720 *Fax:* (020) 7 943 4777
Web Site: www.theatrelibrary.org/sibmas/sibmas.html
Key Personnel
President: Dr Claudia Balk
Secretary General: Claire Hudson
Founded: 1954
International Society of Libraries & Museums for the Performing Arts.
Subjects: Performing Arts Collections, Worldwide
Publication(s): *Proceedings Bi-Annual Congresses*; *SIBMAS International Directory of Performing Arts Collections/Emmett Publishing Ltd (Haslemere 1996)*

Society of Authors
84 Drayton Gardens, London SW10 9SB
Tel: (020) 7373 6642 *Fax:* (020) 7373 5768
E-mail: info@societyofauthors.org
Web Site: www.societyofauthors.org
Key Personnel
General Secretary: Mark Le Fanu
Manager: Kate Pool *E-mail:* kpool@societyofauthors.org
Publication(s): *The Author* (quarterly)

Society of Indexers
Globe Centre, Penistone Rd, Sheffield S6 3AE
Tel: (0114) 281 3060 *Fax:* (0114) 281 3061
E-mail: admin@socind.demon.co.uk
Web Site: www.socind.demon.co.uk
Key Personnel
President: Doreen Blake
Secretary: Liza Weinkoe
Administrator: P W Burrow
Founded: 1957
Publication(s): *The Indexer*; *Training in Indexing*
Associate Companies: American Society of Indexers; Australian Society of Indexers; Indexing & Abstracting Society of Canada; Association of Southern African Indexers & Bibliographers

†◇Standing Conference on Library Materials on Africa (SCOLMA)
Commonwealth Secretariat, Marlborough House, Pall Mall, London SW14 5HX

UNITED KINGDOM   BOOK TRADE

Tel: (20) 7747 6564 *Fax:* (20) 7747 6168
E-mail: scolma@hotmail.com
Key Personnel
Chairman: Sheila Allcock
Publication(s): *African Research and Documentation*

UK International Standard Book Numbering Agency Ltd
Woolmead House W Bear Lane, Farnham GU9 7LG
Tel: (01252) 742590 *Fax:* (01252) 742526
E-mail: isbn@whitaker.co.uk
Web Site: www.whitaker.co.uk/isbn.htm
Key Personnel
Manager: Stella Griffiths
Publication(s): *International Standard Book Numbering*
Parent Company: J Whitaker & Sons Ltd

Union of Welsh Publishers & Booksellers
PO Box 103, Tregaron, Dyfed SY25 6NY
Mailing Address: c/o Gomer Press, Llandysul, Ceredigion SA44 4BQ
Tel: (1559) 362371 *Fax:* (1559) 363758
Web Site: www.wc.org.uk

†VSO Books
Voluntary Service Overseas, 317 Putney Bridge Rd, London SW15 2PN
Tel: (020) 8780 7200 *Fax:* (020) 8780 7300
E-mail: vsobooks@vso.org.uk
Web Site: www.vso.org.uk
Key Personnel
Editor: Silke Bernau *Tel:* (020) 8780 7342
Founded: 1990
Subjects: Education, Development (Health, Agriculture, Technical, Community Development)
ISBN Prefix(es): 0-9509050; 1-903697
Number of titles published annually: 3 Print
Total Titles: 22 Print

Welsh Books Council (Cyngor Llyfrau Cymru)
Castell Brychan, Aberystwyth, Aberystwyth, Wales SY23 2JB
Tel: (01970) 624455 *Fax:* (01970) 625506
E-mail: castellbrychan@cllc.org.uk
Web Site: www.cllc.org.uk; www.gwales.com
Key Personnel
Dir: Gwerfyl Pierce Jones
Deputy Dir: Pedr Ap Llwyd
Head of Marketing: D Philip Davies *E-mail:* phil.davies@cllc.org.uk
Founded: 1963
Branch Office(s)
Distribution Center, Glanyrafon Enterprise Park, Aberystwyth, Ceredigion, Wales SY23 3AQ
E-mail: distribution.centre@cllc.org.uk

Women in Publishing
Membership Officer, c/o 78 Salop Rd, London E17 7HT
E-mail: wipub@hotmail.com
Web Site: www.cyberiacafe.net/wip
Key Personnel
Membership Secretary: Natalie McCormack *Tel:* (020) 8923 2386 *E-mail:* nmccormack@waterlow.com
Founded: 1979
Promote the status of women within publishing & related fields.

†◇Writers & Scholars International
33 Islington High St, Lancaster House, London N1 9LH
Tel: (020) 7278 2313 *Fax:* (020) 7278 1878
E-mail: indexoncenso@gn.apc.org
Key Personnel
Editor: Ursula Owen
Marketing Dir: Louise Tyson
Founded: 1972

Information about censorship in the world today, covering subjects such as free speech, human rights, literature, freedom of information.
Publication(s): *Index on Censorship* (magazine)

Writers' Guild of Great Britain
430 Edgware Rd, London W2 1EH
Tel: (020) 7723 8074 *Fax:* (020) 7706 2413
E-mail: admin@writersguild.org.uk
Web Site: www.writersguild.org.uk
Key Personnel
President: John Wilsher
Chairman: Bill Morrison

United States

†American-Scandinavian Foundation
58 Park Ave, New York, NY 10016
Tel: 212-879-9779 *Fax:* 212-879-2301
E-mail: asf@amscan.org
Web Site: www.amscan.org
Key Personnel
Executive VP: Lynn Carter *E-mail:* carter@amscan.org
Publication(s): *Scan* (quarterly, newsletter); *Scandinavian Review* (triannually, cultural/literary/political magazine)

†Bernan Associates, Div of Kraus Organization, Ltd
4611-F Assembly Dr, Lanham, MD 20706-4391
Tel: 301-459-7666 *Fax:* 301-459-0056
Telex: 7108260418
Key Personnel
Sales & Publicity: Christopher Zahn
There are OAS offices/bookstores in 31 countries outside the USA.
Subjects: Development of American Nations (Regional, Social, Historical), Bibliography, Cultural Affairs, Economics, Education, Human Rights, Law, Sciences, Statistics
Publication(s): *Inter-American Review of Bibliography*
ISBN Prefix(es): 0-8270; 0-8171

IASP, see International Association of Scholarly Publishers (IASP)

†◇International Association of Law Libraries (IALL)
PO Box 5709, Washington, DC 20016-1309
Tel: 804-924-3384 *Fax:* 804-982-2232
E-mail: lbw@virginia.edu
Web Site: www.iall.org
Key Personnel
President: Larry B Wenger
Treasurer: Gloria F Chao
Secretary: Marie-Louise H Bernal
Founded: 1959
Association Internationale des Bibliotheques de Droit.
Publication(s): *International Journal of Legal Information* (Triannually, Membership); *The IALL Messenger* (Irregularly)

†◇International Association of Scholarly Publishers (IASP)
c/o Michigan State University Press, 1405 S Harrison Rd, East Lansing, MI 48823-5202
Tel: 517-355-9543 *Fax:* 517-432-2611
E-mail: bohm@pilot.msu.edu
Key Personnel
Dir: Mr F C Bohm
Founded: 1972

†◇International Association of School Librarianship
Dept 962, Box 34069, Seattle, WA 98124-1069
Tel: 604-925-0266 *Fax:* 604-925-0566
E-mail: iasl@rockland.com
Key Personnel
Executive Dir: Dr Penny Moore *E-mail:* penny.moore@xtra.co.nz
Publication(s): *Annual Conference Proceedings*; *Newsletter of the International Association of School Librarianship* (quarterly to members); *School Libraries Worldwide* (semi-annually to members, journal)

†◇International Comparative Literature Association (Association Internationale de Litterature Comparee)
Virgil Nemoianu, Catholic University, Washington, DC 20064
Tel: 416-487-6727 *Fax:* 416-487-6786
Key Personnel
President, US: Gerald Gillespie
Secretary General, Germany: Manfred Schmelling
Secretary General, US: Virgil Nemoianu
Founded: 1954

†◇International Institute of Iberoamerican Literature
University of Pittsburgh, 1312 Cathedral of Learning, Pittsburgh, PA 15260-0001
Tel: 412-624-5246 *Fax:* 412-624-0829
E-mail: iilit@pitt.edu
Web Site: www.pitt.edu/~illi
Key Personnel
Administrator: Erika Braga
Contact: Mabel Morana
Founded: 1938
Publication(s): *Memorias*; *Revista Iberoamericana* (quarterly, 1938, literary criticism journal)

†◇International League of Antiquarian Booksellers (ILAB)
400 Summit Ave, St Paul, MN 55102
Tel: 800-441-0076; 612-290-0700 *Fax:* 612-290-0646
E-mail: rulon@winternet.com
Web Site: www.ilab.org
Key Personnel
Secretary General: Rob Rulon-Miller
Founded: 1947
Publication(s): *Dictionary of the Antiquarian Book Trade* (in Danish, Dutch, English, French, German, Italian, Japanese, Spanish, Swedish); *International Directory of Antiquarian Booksellers*

†International Monetary Fund
700 19 St NW, Washington, DC
Tel: 202-623-7430 *Fax:* 202-623-7201
Key Personnel
Chief, Publication Services: Lori Michele Newsom
Editor, Rights & Permissions: Ian S McDonald
Founded: 1946
Subjects: Economics, International monetary & trade issues, Domestic fiscal & monetary topics, Activities & operations of the International Monetary Fund, Balance of payments & external adjustment problems, International finance, International statistics
Publication(s): *Annual Report on Exchange Arrangements & Exchange Restrictions*; *Direction of Trade Statistics*; *Finance & Development* (published jointly with World Bank); *World Economic Outlook*
ISBN Prefix(es): 0-939934; 1-55775

†◇International Reading Association
800 Barksdale Rd, Newark, DE 19714
Mailing Address: PO Box 8139, Newark, DE 19714-8139
Tel: 302-731-1600 *Fax:* 302-731-1057
Telex: 5106002813

Key Personnel
President: Donna Ogle
Executive Dir: Alan Farstrup
Public Information Associate: Janet Butler
Tel: 302-731-1600 ext 293 *E-mail:* jbutler@reading.org
Founded: 1956
Publication(s): *Journal of Adolescent & Adult Literary*; *Lectura y vida*; *Newspaper Reading Today*; *Reading Research Quarterly*; *The Reading Teacher*

†◇Middle East Librarians Association
University of Washington Libraries, Monographic Services, Campus Box 352900, Seattle, WA
Tel: (206) 543-8407 *Fax:* (206) 685-8049
Web Site: www.depts.washington.edu/wsx9/melahp.html
Key Personnel
Editor, Near East Division: Jonathan Rodgers
Tel: (734) 764-7555 *Fax:* (734) 763-6743
E-mail: jrodgers@umich.edu
Secretary-Treasurer: Janet Heineck *Tel:* 206-543-8405 *Fax:* 206-685-8782 *E-mail:* janeth@u.washington.edu
Publication(s): *MELA Notes* (Journal of Middle Eastern Librarianship)

SALALM, see Seminar on the Acquisition of Latin American Library Materials (SALALM)

†◇Seminar on the Acquisition of Latin American Library Materials (SALALM)
Secretariat, General Library, University of New Mexico, Albuquerque, NM 87131-1466
Tel: 505-277-5102 *Fax:* 505-277-0646
Key Personnel
Executive Secretary: Sharon A Moynahan
Publication(s): *Bibliography & Reference Series*

†◇United Nations Publications
Two UN Plaza, Room DC2-853, New York, NY 10017
Tel: 800-983-8302 *Fax:* 212-963-3489
E-mail: publications@un.org
Web Site: www.un.org/pubs/sales.htm
Telex: 62450 *Cable:* UNATIONS NYK
Key Personnel
Chief of Section: Susanna H Johnston
Marketing & Product Development: Christopher Woodthorpe
Rights & Permissions: Anne Cunningham
Rights & Permissions, Geneva: Patricia Piguet
Founded: 1945
Since 1946, United Nations has published more than 10,000 reports, studies, annual surveys, yearbooks, and monthly and quarterly periodicals in addition to the United Nations Official Records.
Reflecting the varied work of the Organization, the subjects include international trade, world and regional economic questions, international law, social questions, atomic energy, public administration, and literature concerning the role and activities of the United Nations.
Subjects: Reference, Economics, International Trade, International Law, Political Science, Social Science, Environment, Educational
ISBN Prefix(es): 92-1
Branch Office(s)
Palais des Nations, Geneva, Switzerland, Chief of Unit: Patrice Piguet

Uruguay

Camara Uruguaya del Libro
Juan D Jackson 1118, 11200 Montevideo
Tel: (02) 2414732 *Fax:* (02) 2411860
Uruguayan Publishers' Association.

Standard Book Numbering Agency
Biblioteca Nacional, Casilla de Correo 452, Montevideo
Tel: (02) 485030; (02) 496014 *Fax:* (02) 496902
Telex: 26991 biname uy
Key Personnel
Dir General: Luis Alberto Musso

Venezuela

Camara Venezolana del Libro (Venezuelan Association of Book)
Ave Andres Bello, Edificio Centro Andres Bello, Torre Oeste 11, piso 11, ofic 112-0, Caracas 1050-A
Tel: (0212) 7931347; (0212) 7931368 *Fax:* (02) 7931368
E-mail: cavelibro@cantv.net
Key Personnel
Director: M P Vargas
Venezuelan Publishers' Association.

Standard Book Numbering Agency
Venezuela National Library, Apdo 80593, Caracas 1080
Tel: (02) 938535 *Fax:* (02) 9435718
Telex: 24621 iabn vc
Key Personnel
ISBN Administrator: Bracho L Auramarina

Yugoslavia

Association of Yugoslav Publishers & Booksellers
Kneza Milosa 25/1, 11000 Belgrade
Mailing Address: PO Box 570, 11000 Belgrade
Tel: (011) 642248 *Fax:* (011) 646339
E-mail: ognjenl@eunet.yu
Key Personnel
General Dir: Mr Ognjen Lakecevic
 E-mail: ognjenl@eunet.yu
Publisher: Mrs Mirjana Popovic
Founded: 1954
Voluntary non-governmental organization. Represents members at home, abroad & by international organizations (IPA, Geneva). Organizer of the International Book Fair in Belgrade, Publishing activities.
Publication(s): *Catalog of Yugoslav Books in Print*; *Catalogue of Book Fairs in Belgrade*; *Directory of Exhibitors at the International Book Fair in Belgrade*; *Directory of Members of the Association of Yugoslav Publishers & Booksellers* (annually)
ISBN Prefix(es): 86-7115

Jugoslovenski Bibliografsko-informacijski institut, Yubin, Agencija za ISBN (Yugoslav Institute for Bibliography and Information)
Terazije 26, 11000 Belgrade
Tel: (011) 687836; (011) 688927 *Fax:* (011) 687760
E-mail: yubin@jbi.bg.ac.yu
Web Site: www.yugoslavia.com/Culture/yubin.htm
Key Personnel
Dir: Dr Radomir Glavicki
Head of International Exchange Dept: Tanja Ostojic *E-mail:* tanya@jbi.bg.ac.yu
Founded: 1950
Specializes in the production of National bibliography; organization with full responsibility.
Publication(s): *Bibliography of Yugoslavia* (Bibliografija Jugoslavije)
Number of titles published annually: 8 Print
Total Titles: 8 Print

Standard Book Numbering Agency, see Jugoslovenski Bibliografsko-informacijski institut, Yubin, Agencija za ISBN

Zambia

Booksellers' & Publishers' Association of Zambia (BPAZ)
c/o Basil Mbewe, PO Box 31838, Lusaka
Tel: (01) 225195 *Fax:* (01) 225282
Key Personnel
Executive Dir: Basil Mbewe

Standard Book Numbering Agency
c/o University of Zambia, Office of the University Librarian, Lusaka 10101
Mailing Address: PO Box 32379, Lusaka 10101
Tel: (01) 292837 (ext 1342) *Fax:* (01) 253952; (01) 250845
E-mail: library@unza.zm
Telex: ZA 40370 *Cable:* UNZA
Key Personnel
ISBN Administrator: Dr H Mwacalimba
Parent Company: Booksellers & Publishers Association of Zambia

Zimbabwe

†African Publishers' Network (APNET)
18 Van Praagh Ave, Milton Park, Harare
Tel: (04) 708418 *Fax:* (04) 708413
E-mail: apnet@mango.zw; apnet@apnet.co.zw
Web Site: www.africanpublishers.org
Key Personnel
Chairman: Mamadou Aliou Sow
Dir: Akin Fasemore
Membership/Trade Promotion Officer: Tainie Mundondo
Treasurer: Janet Njoroge
Founded: 1992
Publication(s): *African Publishing Review* (6 issues per annum); *Trade Directory 2000* (Repertoire Commercial/O Directorio Comercial, Biannual, book, 2000); *Indaba Papers*; *Thematic Catalogues*
Branch Office(s)
CP 1248, Luanda, Angola, Contact: Antonio de Brito *Tel:* (02) 331371 *Fax:* (02) 895162; (02) 332714 *E-mail:* infosec@ebonet.net
BP 1501, Yaounde, Cameroon, Contact: Freddy Ngandu *Tel:* 223554; 2223554 *Fax:* 2221761 *E-mail:* ngan_fred@yahoo.fr
PO Box 33 Panorama, Cairo, Egypt (Arab Republic of Egypt), Contact: Ashraf Hamouda *Tel:* (02) 4023399 *Fax:* (02) 4037567 *E-mail:* ahamouda@link.net
BP 542, Conakry, Guinea, Contact: Mamadou Aliou Sow *Tel:* 463507; 402849 *Fax:* 412012; 463507 *E-mail:* ganndal@mirinet.net.gn
PO Box 18033, Nairobi, Kenya, Contact: Janet Njoroge *Tel:* (02) 533665 *Fax:* (02) 540037 *E-mail:* longhorn@iconnect.co.ke
Private Bag 39, Blantyre, Malawi, Contact: Egidio Mpanga *Tel:* 670880; 670855 *Fax:* 671114 *E-mail:* dzuka@malawi.net
Ighodaro Rd, No 1, Jericho Layout, PMB 5205, Ibadan, Nigeria, Contact: Ayo Ojeniyi *Tel:* (02)

ZIMBABWE

2412268; (02) 2410943 *Fax:* (02) 2411089; (02) 2413237 *E-mail:* info@heinemannbooks.com

APNET, see African Publishers' Network (APNET)

The Literature Bureau
Ministry of Education, Sport & Culture, Causeway, Harare

Mailing Address: PO Box CY121, Causeway, Harare
Tel: (04) 333812
Key Personnel
Chief Publications Officer: B C Chitsike
ISBN Prefix(es): 0-86926

Standard Book Numbering Agency
National Archives of Zimbabwe, Causeway, Private Bag 7729, Harare

Tel: (04) 792741 *Fax:* (04) 792398
Publication(s): *Zimbabwe National Bibliography*

Zimbabwe Book Publishers Association
12 Selous Ave, Harare Causeway
Tel: (04) 750282 *Fax:* (04) 751202
Publication(s): *Directory of Zimbabwe Publishers 1995*; *Making Books*; *Zimbabwe: Books In Print 1995*

Major Book Dealers

This section contains active book dealers in one or more of the following categories: distribution, exporting, importing, major book chains, major independent booksellers, remainder dealers, and wholesalers.

Afghanistan

University of Kabul Bookstores
Jamal Mina, Kabul
Tel: 40341

Albania

Book Distribution Enterprise, see Ndermarrja Perhapjes se Librit

Ndermarrja Perhapjes se Librit
Rruga Konferenca e Pezes, Tirana
Tel: (042) 3323 *Fax:* (042) 3323
Telex: 2144 N Librit AB *Cable:* N LIBRIT TIRANA ALBANIA
Key Personnel
Dir General: Fisnik Sina
Dir Export-Import: Stefan Kume
State trading organization controlling importation of books.

Angola

Argente, Sentos & Cia Lda
CP 1314C, Luanda

Argentina

Librerias ABC SA
Ave Cordoba 685, C1054AAF Buenos Aires
Mailing Address: Casilla Correo Central 4452, C1000WBS Buenos Aires
Tel: (011) 4-314-7887 *Fax:* (011) 4-314-8106
E-mail: libabcc@datamarkets.com.ar
Web Site: www.libreriasabc.com.ar *Cable:* MOLAGENT
Key Personnel
President: Horst Stephan
Founded: 1969

American Books
Libreria Norteamericana SCA, Tucuman, 994 Buenos Aires
Tel: (011) 3963704
Key Personnel
President & Owner: Alejandro Lew
Secretary: Mrs O Matthew
Owned by: Alejandro Lew

Cosmos Libros SRL
Callaro 737, 1023 Buenos Aires
Tel: (011) 148127364; (011) 148155347
E-mail: cosmoslibros@arnet.com.ar
Key Personnel
Dir: Hugo Emilio Palacios
  E-mail: palacioshugo@arnet.com.ar
Founded: 1984
Type of Business: Distributor, Exporter, Importer, Major Independent Bookseller

Distribuidora Cuspide
Suipacha 764, 1008 Buenos Aires
Tel: (011) 3228366; (011) 3227434 *Fax:* (011) 3223456; (011) 3223465
Telex: 25477 Dicus
Key Personnel
President: Joaquin M Gil Paricio
Founded: 1960
Branch Office(s)
Suipacha 1045, 1008 Buenos Aires *Tel:* (011) 3130486
Portugal 18 Santiago, Chile *Tel:* (02) 2224978 *Fax:* (02) 2250435

Librerias Fausto
Ave Corrientes 1316, 1043 Buenos Aires
Tel: (011) 3724919
Key Personnel
Manager: Rafael Pedro Zorrilla
Owned by: Ediciones Librerias Fausto
Branch Office(s)
Ave Santa Fe 1715, 1060 Buenos Aires *Tel:* (011) 412708

Carlos Hirsch SRL
Florida 165 - 4 piso, 1333 Buenos Aires
Tel: (011) 3312391; (011) 3311787 *Fax:* (011) 3311787
Telex: 21112 Uape
Key Personnel
Manager: Leandro Moreiras; Monica Bustos
Bookshop(s): Publicitas SRL, San Marin 170, 4 Piso, of 447/448, 1004 Buenos Aires

Libreria Huemul SA
Ave Santa Fe 2237, 1123 Buenos Aires
Tel: (011) 825-2290 *Fax:* (011) 822-1666
Key Personnel
President & Manager: Antonio Rego
Also Publisher.

Libreria Kier
Ave Santa Fe 1260, 1059 Buenos Aires
Tel: (011) 8110507; (011) 8118243; (011) 8132668 *Fax:* (011) 8132668
Founded: 1907
Type of Business: Distributor, Exporter, Importer, Major Independent Bookseller
Owned by: Editorial Kier SACIFI

Ediciones Lidiun
Patagones 2463, C1282ACA Buenos Aires
Tel: (011) 4942 9002 *Fax:* (011) 942-9162
E-mail: info@ateneo.com
Web Site: www.yenny.com; www.ateneo.com
Telex: 18522 Cecba *Cable:* ATENEO
Key Personnel
President: Jorge I Letemendia
Vice Pres: Eustasio Antonio Garcia
Dir, Commercial: Jorge Gonzalez
Founded: 1912
Type of Business: Distributor, Exporter, Importer, Major Book Chain Headquarters, Major Independent Bookseller, Wholesaler
Branch Office(s)
Salguero 3172, local 2062, 1425 Buenos Aire
Obligado 2108, 1428 Buenos Aires
Bookshop(s): Florida 340, 1005 Buenos Aires
  Tel: (011) 3256801

H F Martinez de Murguia SAC y E
Av Cordoba 2270, 1120 Buenos Aires
Tel: (011) 9526173; (011) 9521088
Key Personnel
President: Agustin T Aparicio

Nueva Vision
Tucaman 3748, 1189 Buenos Aires
Tel: (011) 8631461; (011) 8635980
Key Personnel
Manager: Hector Yanover

Libreria General de Tomas Pardo SRL
Maipu 618, 1006 Buenos Aires
Tel: (011) 4322-0496 *Fax:* (011) 4393-6759

Rimecu Grupo Editorial
Av Virgen del Valle (Norte) N 634, 4700 San Fernando del Valle da Catamarca
Tel: (03833) 333136 *Fax:* (03833) 333136
Key Personnel
Contact: Luis Ricardo Mendoza Cuestas
Founded: 1991
Type of Business: Major Book Chain Headquarters, Major Independent Bookseller

Riverside Agency SAC
Mexico 3080-84 PB, 1223 Buenos Aires
Tel: (011) 957-2336 *Fax:* (011) 956-1985
Key Personnel
President: Juan Carlos Zaragoza
Founded: 1958
Type of Business: Distributor, Importer, Wholesaler

Libreria Rodriguez SA, Dto Suscripciones
Sarmiento 835, 1041 Buenos Aires
Tel: (011) 3263725; (011) 3263826; (011) 3263927
Telex: 22087 Elerre
Key Personnel
General Manager: Bautista L Tello
Also Publisher (see Ediciones L R SA).

Libreria Santa Fe
Ave Santa Fe 2386, 1123 Buenos Aires
Tel: (011) 824-5005 *Fax:* (011) 824-7932
Key Personnel
Contact: Ruben Aisenberg; Juan Pablo Aisenberg
Type of Business: Importer
Branch Office(s)
Rubaisen S & S, Avda Santa Fe 2582, Buenos Aires *Fax:* (011) 8247932
Ave Santa Fe 2928, 1425 B Buenos Aires
  Tel: (011) 8219442

Australia

Academic & General Bookshop
259 Swanston Walk, Melbourne, Victoria 3000
Tel: (03) 6633231 *Fax:* (03) 6637234
Key Personnel
Owner: Anthony Kyriacou
Founded: 1974
Branch Office(s)
Caledonia Lane, Melbourne, Victoria *Tel:* (03) 6637229 *Fax:* (03) 6637234
Bookshop(s): 196 Elgin St, Carlton 3053

Advance Book Distributors
19 Winterton Rd, Clayton 3168
Tel: (03) 95489422 *Fax:* (03) 95489411
Type of Business: Distributor

Angus & Robertson Bookshops
107 Elizabeth St, 2nd Floor, Melbourne, Victoria 3000
Tel: (03) 96708941 *Fax:* (03) 96466925
Key Personnel
General Manager: David Conners
Owned by: Brasch Pty Ltd

Australian Book Collector, *imprint of* Australian Book Collector

Australian Book Collector
PO Box 2, Uralla, NSW 2358
Tel: (02) 6778 4682 *Fax:* (02) 6778 4516
Web Site: www.ozbook.com
Key Personnel
Man Dir & Editor: Ross Burnet *E-mail:* burnet@ozbook.com
Founded: 1986
Type of Business: Distributor, Exporter, Importer, Major Independent Bookseller, Wholesaler
Imprints: Australian Book Collector; Idriess Enterprises
Bookshop(s): 100 Bridge St, Uralla 2358

Australian Government Bookshops
GPO Box 84, Canberra, ACT 2601
Tel: (062) 954031 *Fax:* (062) 954888
Web Site: www.agps.gov.au
Type of Business: Distributor, Wholesaler
Branch Office(s)
294 Adelaide St, Brisbane, Qld 4000 *Tel:* (07) 2296822 *Fax:* (07) 2291387
347 Swanston St, Melbourne, Victoria 3000 *Tel:* (03) 6633010 *Fax:* (03) 6634840
277 Flinders Mall, Townsville, Qld 4810 *Tel:* (077) 215212 *Fax:* (077) 215217
Level 3 Myer Centre, Rundle Mall, Adelaide SA 5000 *Tel:* (08) 2310144 *Fax:* (08) 2310135
512 Swift St, Albury NSW 2640 *Tel:* (060) 413788 *Fax:* (060) 412248
Commonwealth Government Bookshops, 70 Alinga St, Canberra ACT 2600 *Tel:* (062) 2477211 *Fax:* (062) 2571797
121 Liverpool St, Hobart, Tas 7000 *Tel:* (002) 237151 *Fax:* (002) 240075
Shop 24 Horwood Place, Parramatta NSW 2150 *Tel:* (02) 8938466 *Fax:* (02) 8938213
469 Wellington St, Perth WA6000 *Tel:* (09) 3224737 *Fax:* (09) 4814412
32 York St, Sydney NSW 2000 *Tel:* (02) 2996737 *Fax:* (02) 2621219

Banyan Tree Book Distributors
13 College Rd, Kent Town, SA 5067
Tel: (08) 8363-4244 *Fax:* (08) 8363-4255
E-mail: enquiries@banyantreebooks.com.au
Key Personnel
Man Dir: Susan Vanderheiden
Founded: 1990
Type of Business: Distributor

James Bennett Pty Ltd
3 Narabang Way, Belrose, NSW 2085
Mailing Address: Locked Bag 537, Frenchs Forest, NSW 2086
Tel: (02) 9986 7000 *Fax:* (02) 9986 7031
E-mail: info@bennett.com.au
Web Site: www.bennett.com.au
Key Personnel
Man Dir: Chris von Hinckeldey *E-mail:* cvh@bennett.com.au
Sales Manager: Nada Novakov
Purchasing Manager: Frank Peard
Founded: 1958
Library supplier.
Type of Business: Distributor, Exporter, Importer, Wholesaler
Owned by: B H Blackwell Ltd

Bibliotech
Division of ANUTECH
Corner Daley & Barry Drive, Acton, ACT 2601
Mailing Address: GPO Box 4, Canberra ACT 2601
Tel: (02) 62492479 *Fax:* (02) 62495677
E-mail: books@bibliotech.com.au
Key Personnel
Manager: Cathy Teager *Tel:* (02) 6249 4005 *E-mail:* cathy.teager@anutech.com.au
Book Distribution Service.
Type of Business: Distributor
Bookshop(s): Anutech Court, CNR Barry Dr & Daley Rd, Canberra ACT 2601 *Web Site:* www.anutech.com.au

Biramo Book Distributors
5 King St, Warners Bay, NSW 2282
Mailing Address: PO Box 95, Warners Bay, NSW 2282
Tel: (02) 49542626 *Fax:* (02) 49565398
E-mail: biramobooks@tpg.com.au
Key Personnel
Dir: Mr A F Rich
Founded: 1985
Type of Business: Distributor, Exporter, Importer, Wholesaler
Branch Office(s)
PO Box 14 640, Panmure, Auckland, New Zealand *Tel:* (09) 570 9089 *Fax:* (09) 570 4604

A W Birchall & Sons Pty Ltd
PO Box 170, Launceston, Tas 7250
Tel: (03) 63313011 *Toll Free Tel:* 800 806867 *Fax:* (03) 63317165
E-mail: books@birchalls.com.au
Key Personnel
Man Dir: Graeme R Tilley *E-mail:* gtilley@birchalls.com.au
Founded: 1844
Australia's oldest bookseller.
Type of Business: Importer, Major Book Chain Headquarters, Major Independent Bookseller, Wholesaler
Branch Office(s)
Students Bookshop, Burnie Tafe College, Mooreville Rd, Burnie *Tel:* (03) 64333602 *Fax:* (03) 64333716
Students Bookshop, Devonport Tafe College, 20 Valley Rd, Devonport *Tel:* (03) 64215518 *Fax:* (03) 64242581
Students Bookshop, Don College, Watkinson St, Devonport *Tel:* (03) 64244072 *Fax:* (03) 64244072
Birchalls Education Centre, 147 Bathurst St, Hobart, Tasmania *Tel:* (03) 62342122 *Fax:* (03) 62348719
Birchalls Tafe College Bookshop, 75 Campbell St, Hobart, Tasmania *Tel:* (03) 62337405 *Fax:* (03) 62311067
Bookshop(s): Students Bookshop, Alanvale Tafe College, Alanvale, Tasmania *Tel:* (03) 63364284 *Fax:* (03) 63364284

Books Australasia, see Gaston Renard Fine & Rare Books

Bookwise International
41 Pearson St, Kangaroo Point 4169
Tel: (07) 33918889
Key Personnel
Man Dir: Rod Davis
Sales Manager: Allan Barbara
Founded: 1957
Type of Business: Wholesaler
Branch Office(s)
428 George St, Sydney 2000
62 Wellington Parade, East Melbourne, Victoria 3002
4124 Hood St, Sherwood 4075

Burgewood Books
4 Diane Court, Warrandyte, Victoria 3113
Tel: (03) 98442512 (Australia); (03) 9844 2512 (International) *Fax:* (03) 98440664 (Australia); (03) 9844 0664 (International)
Key Personnel
President & Partner: Doreen Burge *E-mail:* dburge@iprimus.com.au
Vice President: Nell Charlwood
Author: Don Charlwood
Founded: 1996
Publishing.

Collins Booksellers Pty Ltd
86 Bourke St, 2nd Floor, Melbourne, Victoria 3000
Tel: (03) 96629472 *Fax:* (03) 96622527
E-mail: enquiries@collinsbooks.com.au
Web Site: www.collinsbooks.com.au
Key Personnel
Chairman & Chief Executive, OBE: Michael G Zifcak
Secretary: T J McCarthy
Founded: 1929
Type of Business: Major Book Chain Headquarters
Branch Office(s)
Canberra
New South Wales
Victoria, Queensland
Western Australia (Western Australia)

Continental Bookshop
1292 Malvern Rd, Malvern, Victoria 3144
Tel: (03) 98247711 *Fax:* (03) 98247855
Key Personnel
Owner: Harry Raynor
Owner & Mgr: Christopher Raynor *E-mail:* audio@vicnet.com.au
Founded: 1962
Foreign language books & language learning media.
Type of Business: Distributor, Exporter, Importer, Major Independent Bookseller

DA Information Services Pty Ltd
648 Whitehorse Rd, Mitcham, Victoria 3132
Mailing Address: PO Box 163, Mitcham, Victoria 3132
Tel: (03) 9210-7777 *Fax:* (03) 9210-7788
E-mail: service@dadirect.com.au
Key Personnel
Chief Executive: John Dwight
Founded: 1951
Subscription agents, Library suppliers, Electronic Information Suppliers.
Type of Business: Distributor, Importer

Daltons Books
Garema Pl, Canberra City ACT 2600
Tel: (062) 491844 *Fax:* (062) 2475753
Key Personnel
Man Dir: Teki John Dalton
Company Secretary: Margaret Ann Dalton

BOOK DEALERS — AUSTRALIA

Founded: 1968
Computer & Business, Book Specialists, Rare & Limited Edition Books.
Type of Business: Distributor, Exporter, Importer, Major Independent Bookseller
Owned by: T J Dalton Pty Ltd, PO Box 189, Claremont, WA 6010
Branch Office(s)
Dalton Books Pty Ltd

Dominie
8 Cross St, Brookvale, NSW 2100
Mailing Address: PO Box 33, Brookvale, NSW 2100
Tel: (02) 9050201 *Fax:* (02) 9055209

Dymocks Pty Ltd
424 George St, Sydney, NSW 2000
Tel: (02) 9235 0155 *Fax:* (02) 9233 7009
E-mail: service@dymocks.com.au
Web Site: www.dymocks.com.au
Key Personnel
Chairman: J P C Forsyth
Man Dir: K B Terry
General Manager, Retail: Jack McLoone
Has 60 franchise stores throughout Australia.

Foreign Language Bookshop
259 Collins St, Melbourne, Victoria 3000
Tel: (03) 96542883 *Fax:* (03) 96507664
E-mail: flb@ozonline.com.au
Web Site: www.languages.com.au
Key Personnel
Man Dir: Annette Monester
Founded: 1938
Bookstore with stock in 90 languages-books, audio learning kits software.
Type of Business: Exporter, Importer, Major Independent Bookseller

Gaanetgetal Books
21 National St, Leichhardt NSW 2040
Tel: (02) 9550-0431 *Fax:* (02) 4234-0875
E-mail: galong@ozemail.com.au
Key Personnel
President: Geoffrey Long
Vice President: Ann Long
Manager: Naomi Jacobs
Type of Business: Distributor, Importer, Major Independent Bookseller, Wholesaler
Branch Office(s)
Bolvanna, Lot 2, Foxground Rd, Foxground 2536
Bookshop(s): 22 National St, Leichhardt NWS 2040

Grahames Bookshop
Division of Horwitz Grahame Pty Ltd
506 Miller St, Cammeray, NSW 2062
Tel: (02) 9296144 *Fax:* (02) 9571814
Ten company & franchise stores nationwide.
Branch Office(s)
MLC Bldg, 105 Miller S, North Sydney, NSW 2060
Bankstown Shopping Square, Bankstown, NSW 2200
Imperial Centre, Gosford, NSW 2250
City Tatts, 200 Pitt St, Sydney, NSW 2000
Mid-City Centre, 197 Pitt St, Sydney, NSW 2000

Herron Book Distributors
39 Commercial Rd, Fortitude Valley, Qld 4006
Tel: (07) 3257 1711 *Fax:* (07) 3257 1686
E-mail: herronbooks@bigpond.com
Key Personnel
Dir: Jim Green
Founded: 1980
Promotional Book Distributor.
Type of Business: Distributor

Idriess Enterprises, *imprint of* Australian Book Collector

Internews Distribution Co
1-3 Seddon St, Bankstown, NSW 2200
Mailing Address: PO Box 36, Bankstown, NSW 2200
Tel: (02) 97074577 *Fax:* (02) 97086025
Type of Business: Distributor, Importer, Wholesaler

Kirby Book Co Pty Ltd
Suite 704, 7 Hele St, Chatswood NSW 2067
Mailing Address: Private Bag No 19, PO Alexandria, Sydney, NSW 2067
Tel: (02) 9698 2377 *Toll Free Tel:* 800 225271 *Fax:* (02) 9698 8748
Key Personnel
Chairman: John D C Reid
Co Man Dir: John A D Reid; Peter N D Reid
E-mail: preid@kirby.com.au
Founded: 1951
Australia's leading specialist wholesale distributor of oversea publications.
Type of Business: Wholesaler

Koorong Books Pty Ltd
28 West Parade, West Ryde, NSW 2114
Tel: (02) 98574477 *Fax:* (02) 98574499
E-mail: west_ryde@koorong.com.au; koorong@koorong.com.au
Web Site: www.koorong.com.au
Key Personnel
General Manager: Paul Bootes
Sr Buyer: David Dixon
Founded: 1975
Branch offices in Brisbane, Melbourne, Perth, & Sydney.
Type of Business: Importer, Major Book Chain Headquarters

Landmark Education Supplies Pty Ltd
Princes Hwy, Drouin, Victoria 3818
Tel: (056) 251701
Key Personnel
Owner: Russell Porch

Language Book Centre
Division of Abbey's Bookshops Pty Ltd
131 York St, Sydney, NSW 2000
Tel: (02) 92671397 *Fax:* (02) 92648993
E-mail: language@abbeys.com.au
Web Site: www.languagebooks.com.au
Key Personnel
Manager: Jacqueline Rychner *E-mail:* jacquir@abbeys.com.au
Man Dir: Jack Winning *Tel:* (02) 9264 3260 *E-mail:* jackw@abbeys.com.au
Founded: 1976
Type of Business: Major Independent Bookseller

Magpie Books
111 Murray St, Angaston, SA 5353
Tel: (08) 85642309
Key Personnel
Proprietor: Brian Howes *E-mail:* brhowes@dove.net.au
Founded: 1986
Publishers of directories & price guides for the antiquarian book trade.
Type of Business: Distributor
Bookshop(s): Barossa Vintage Books, 60 Murray St, Angaston 5353 *Tel:* (08) 8564 3633

Mason's Book Centre
5 Hercules St, Tullamarine, Victoria 3043
Tel: (03) 93383044 *Fax:* (03) 93382225
Key Personnel
Man Dir: W A T Mason
Dir & Secretary: D W Mason
Founded: 1967
Type of Business: Distributor, Exporter, Importer, Major Independent Bookseller
Owned by: Wenkerdea Pty Ltd

Robert Muir Old & Rare Books
69 Broadway, Nedlands 6009
Mailing Address: PO Box 364, WA 6009 Nedlands
Tel: (08) 9386 5842 *Fax:* (09) 3868211
E-mail: muir@merriweb.com.au
Web Site: www.muirbooks.com
Key Personnel
Owner: Robert Muir; Helen Muir
Founded: 1973
Member of ILAB, ABA, ANZAAB.
Type of Business: Exporter, Importer, Major Independent Bookseller

The Open Book
110 Gawler Pl, Adelaide, SA 5000
Mailing Address: GPO Box 1368, Adelaide 5001
Tel: (08) 82235468 *Toll Free Tel:* 800-888-261 *Fax:* (08) 82234552
E-mail: openbook@openbook.com.au
Web Site: www.openbook.com.au; www.lca.org.au/openbook.html
Key Personnel
National Retail Manager: Kevin Reichelt *Tel:* (08) 82239140 *E-mail:* kreichelt@openbook.com.au
Founded: 1913
Christian, religious bookstore - theological books & resources - specialty. Branch offices in Aubury, Brisbane, Hamilton, Melbourne, Sydney, Tanunda, & Toowoomba.
Type of Business: Distributor, Exporter, Importer, Major Book Chain Headquarters, Major Independent Bookseller, Wholesaler
Owned by: Openbook Publishers, 205 Halifax St, Adelaide, SA 5000

Gaston Renard Fine & Rare Books
Member of ANZAAB
PO Box 1030, Ivanhoe, Melbourne, Victoria 3079
Tel: (39) 4595040 *Fax:* (39) 4596787
E-mail: booksaus@ozemail.com.au
Key Personnel
Owner: Julien Renard
Founded: 1945
Specializes in antiquarian bookseller & publisher. Member of ANZAAB.
Type of Business: Distributor, Exporter, Importer, Major Independent Bookseller

Soundbooks
1292 Malvern Rd, Malvern, Victoria 3144
Tel: (03) 98247711 *Fax:* (03) 98247855
E-mail: audio@vicnet.com.au
Web Site: www.soundbooks.com.au
Key Personnel
Dir: Christopher Raynor *E-mail:* audio@vicnet.com.au
Founded: 1982
Specialize in audiobooks.
Type of Business: Distributor, Exporter, Importer, Major Independent Bookseller

Michael Treloar Antiqvarian Booksellers
196 North Terrace, Adelaide SA 5000
Mailing Address: GPO Box 2289, Adelaide SA 5001
Tel: (08) 82231111 *Fax:* (08) 82236599
E-mail: treloars@anzaab.com.au
Key Personnel
Owner: Michael Treloar
Founded: 1976
Type of Business: Major Independent Bookseller

La Trobe University Bookshop
La Trobe University, Kingsbury Dr, Bundoora, NT 3083
Tel: (03) 4792969 *Fax:* (03) 470-2011
Key Personnel
General Manager: I Patterson

University Co-operative Bookshop Ltd
80 Bay St, Broadway NSW 2007
Tel: (02) 93259600 *Fax:* (02) 92818390
E-mail: info@mail.coop-bookshop.com.au
Web Site: www.coop-bookshop.com.au
Key Personnel
Chief Executive Officer: Duncan Maclellan
Founded: 1958
Type of Business: Major Book Chain Headquarters, Major Independent Bookseller
Branch Office(s)
Australian Catholic University
Australian Defence Force Academy
Australian National University
Bay House
Canberra Institute of Technology
Charles Stunt University
Hornsby College of Tafe, Legal & Professional Bookshop
Macquarie University
Schools Division
Sunshine Coast University College
University of Canberra
University of England
University of Newcastle
University of New South Wales
University of Technology-Sydney
University of Sydney
University of Western Australia
University of Western Sydney-Nepean
Wagga Wagga College of Tafe
Bookshop(s): Griffith University; Southern Cross University; Sydney Institute of Technology Tertiary & Technical Books

Austria

Aichinger, Bernhard & Co GmbH
Weihburggasse 16, 1010 Vienna
Tel: (0222) 5128853 *Fax:* (0222) 5128853-13
Key Personnel
Manager: Mag Veronika Aichinger

Blackwell & Hadwiger GesmbH British Bookshop
Weihburggasse 24-26, 1010 Vienna
Tel: (01) 5121945; (01) 5132933 *Fax:* (01) 5121026
Key Personnel
Contact: Margaret Hofmaier
Founded: 1974
Type of Business: Importer, Major Independent Bookseller

British Bookshop, see Blackwell & Hadwiger GesmbH British Bookshop

Bucher-Stierle GesmbH
Kaigasse 1, Postfach 245, 5010 Salzburg
Tel: (0662) 840114 *Fax:* (0662) 8401149
E-mail: buecher-stierle@members.debis.at
Key Personnel
Owner: Vivienne Stierle
Founded: 1988
Type of Business: Exporter, Importer, Major Independent Bookseller

Der Buchfreund Universitats-Buchhandlung u Antiquariat Walter R Schaden
Sonnenfelsgasse 4, 1010 Vienna
Tel: (01) 5124856; (01) 5138289 *Fax:* (01) 5126028
E-mail: buch.schaden@vienna.at
Web Site: www.buch-schaden.at
Key Personnel
Owner: Rainer Schaden
Founded: 1955
Member of JLAB.

Type of Business: Importer, Major Independent Bookseller
Owned by: Rainer Schaden
Bookshop(s): Lugeck 7, 1010 Vienna

Dietz GmbH
Bahnstr 1, A-2351 Wr Neudorf
Tel: (0222) 5875772 *Fax:* (02236) 47127
Key Personnel
Manager: Horst Jansa; Walter Dietz
Founded: 1978
Type of Business: Importer, Wholesaler
Branch Office(s)
Airport Vienna, Vienna
Graz
Salzburg
Bookshop(s): American Discount, Rechte Wienzeile 5, 1040 Vienna

Fachbuchhandlung fur Wirtschaft und Recht Dr Karl Stropek GmbH
Waehringerstr 122, Postfach 84, A-1180 Vienna
Tel: (0222) 4795495 *Fax:* (0222) 4796230
Key Personnel
Proprietor: Eleonore Stropek
Founded: 1863
Library supplier.
Type of Business: Major Independent Bookseller

Gerold & Co
Weihburggasse 26, 1010 Vienna
Mailing Address: Postfach 597, 1011 Vienna
Tel: (01) 521 4731
Telex: 847136157 Gerol *Cable:* Geroldbuch Vienna
Key Personnel
Man Dir: Hans Neusser
Subscription agent and library jobber for European books and periodicals; also Publisher.

Hans Furstelberger
Kaufmaennisches Vereinhaus, Landstr 49, 4013 Linz
Tel: (0732) 773177 *Fax:* (0732) 784485
Type of Business: Major Independent Bookseller

A Hartleben Inhaber Dr Walter Rob
Schwarzenbergstra 6, 1015 Vienna 1
Tel: (0222) 5126236
Key Personnel
Owner: Dr Walter Rob; Dr Marion Unger-Rob
Founded: 1803
Type of Business: Distributor, Importer, Major Independent Bookseller
Branch Office(s)
Huetteldorfer Str 114, 1140 Vienna

Heidrich, Leopold, Buchhandlung u Verlagsgesellschaft
Plankengasse 7, 1010 Vienna
Tel: (0222) 5123701 *Fax:* (0222) 512370214
Key Personnel
Manager: Wolfgang Heidrich
Owned by: F Gottschalk GmbH

Verlag Johannes Heyn
Friedensgasse 23, A-9020 Klagenfurt
Tel: (0463) 33631 *Fax:* (0463) 3363133
Key Personnel
Owner: Volkmar Zechner; Gert Zechner
Type of Business: Major Independent Bookseller

Buchhandlung Karl Hofbauer KG
Hauptpl 31, Postfach 114, A-8430 Leibnitz
Tel: (03452) 82793; (03452) 82177 *Fax:* (03452) 71218
E-mail: hofbauer.buch@nextra.at
Web Site: members.nextra.at/hofbauer.buch/hofbauer.buch

Key Personnel
Manager: Jutta Hofbauer
Founded: 1963
Type of Business: Importer, Major Independent Bookseller
Branch Office(s)
A-8430 Leibnitz, Grazerg 73 *Tel:* (03452) 83166

Friedrich Hofmeister-Figaro Verlag Grossortiment und Musikalienhandlung GesmbH
Seikrgasse 12, 1015 Vienna
Tel: (01) 50576510 *Fax:* (01) 5059185
Key Personnel
Contact: Ferdinand Walcher
Type of Business: Importer, Wholesaler

Inn-Verlag, DrieBlein & Co KG
Rossaugasse 5, Postfach 29, Innsbruck 6023
Tel: (0512) 34 53 31 *Fax:* (0512) 34 12 90
E-mail: office@innverlag.at
Web Site: www.innverlag.at
Key Personnel
Production: Klaus Hagleitner
Founded: 1947
Type of Business: Distributor, Importer, Major Independent Bookseller, Wholesaler

Alexander Kerbiser KG
Wiener Str 17, Hammerpark 10, 8680 Muerzzuschlag
Tel: (03852) 4807 *Fax:* (03852) 5349
Key Personnel
Contact: E M Mueck
Founded: 1936
Type of Business: Major Independent Bookseller

Walter Klugel
Gumpendorferstr 33, 1060 Vienna
Tel: (0222) 581 84 28
Founded: 1921
Type of Business: Major Independent Bookseller

Antiquariat Walter Krieg Verlag
Karntner Str 4, 1010 Vienna
Tel: (01) 5121083
Also library supplier.
Type of Business: Exporter

Leopold Stocker Verlag
Hofgasse 5, 8011 Graz
Tel: (0316) 82 16 36 *Fax:* (0316) 83 56 12
Key Personnel
Publisher: Wolfgang Dvorak-Stocker
Founded: 1917
Type of Business: Major Independent Bookseller
Bookshop(s): Bucherquelle Buchhandlungs GmbH, Graz

Manz'sche Verlags- und Universitaetsbuchhandlung
Kohlmarkt 16, Postfach 163, A-1014 Vienna 1
Tel: (01) 531 61-0 *Fax:* (01) 531 61-181
E-mail: redaktion@manz.co.at
Telex: 75310631
Also Publisher & library supplier.
Type of Business: Exporter

Mohr-ZA Verlagsauslieferungen Ges mbH
Singerstr 12, 1010 Vienna
Mailing Address: Postfach 771, 1010 Vienna
Tel: (01) 5121676; (01) 5125711; (01) 5126994 *Fax:* (01) 111859
Key Personnel
Proprietor: Dr Gottfried Berger
Type of Business: Wholesaler

Buchhandlung Wolfgang Neugebauer
Kreuzgasse 6, 6800 Feldkirch
Tel: (05522) 74770 *Fax:* (05522) 74770
E-mail: bayer.buch@utanet.at

Founded: 1973
Also library supplier.
Type of Business: Distributor, Exporter, Importer, Major Independent Bookseller

Osterreichische Bibelgesellschaft
Breitegasse 8, 1010 Vienna
Tel: (0222) 938240
Key Personnel
Contact: Dr Jutta Henner
Founded: 1970
Type of Business: Major Independent Bookseller

Max Pock, Universitaetsbuchhandlung
Hauptplatz 1, A-8010 Graz
Tel: (0316) 825254 *Fax:* (0316) 825258; (0316) 825254-8
Telex: 031873
Key Personnel
Manager: Dr Maximilian Pock
Also library supplier.
Type of Business: Exporter

Georg Prachner KG
Kaerntner Str 30, 1010 Vienna
Tel: (0222) 5128549; (0222) 5128540 *Fax:* (0222) 5120158
Key Personnel
Man Dir: O G Prachner
Also Publisher.
Type of Business: Exporter, Importer, Major Independent Bookseller, Wholesaler

Buchhandlung Styria
Schoenaugasse 64, Postfach 435, A 8010 Graz
Tel: (0316) 80637041 *Fax:* (0316) 80637004
Key Personnel
Contact: Wolfgang Habenschuss
Owned by: Styria Druck und Verlagshaus
Branch Office(s)
Hauptpl 15, A-8720 Judenburg, Australia
Kaerntnerstr 2, A-8720 Knittelfeld
Wollzeille 2, A-1010 Vienna

J G Sydys Buchhandlung Ludwig Schubert GesmbH
Member of Hauptverband des Oesterreichischen Buchhandels
Wienerstr 19, 3100 St Poelten
Tel: (02742) 53189; (02742) 53191 *Fax:* (02742) 5318985
Web Site: members.aon.at/schubert
Key Personnel
Contact: Susanne Sandler
Founded: 1837
Type of Business: Exporter, Importer, Major Independent Bookseller

Tyrolia Verlagsanstalt GmbH
Exlgasse 20, 6020 Innsbruck
Tel: (0512) 2233-0 *Fax:* (0512) 2233-501
Telex: 053620
Key Personnel
Manager: Thaler Franz
Owned by: Verlagsanstalt Tyrolia
Branch Office(s)
Ehrwald
Fulpmes
Imst
Landeck
Lienz
Mayrhofen
Reutte
Schwaz
St Johann
Telfs
Vienna
Wattens

Urban und Schwarzenberg GmbH
Frankgasse 4, 1096 Vienna

Tel: (01) 4052731
Key Personnel
Manager: Gunter Royer
Also Publisher.
Owned by: Williams & Wilkins Ltd

Buchhandlung Veritas
Harrachstr 1-3, 4020 Linz
Tel: (0732) 776451; (0732) 776450 *Fax:* (0732) 776451239
Key Personnel
Manager: Klaus Radler
Owned by: Veritas GesmbH & Co KG

Wagner'sche Universitaetsbuchhandlung
Museumstr 4, 6021 Innsbruck
Tel: (05222) 22316
Telex: 75311457
Key Personnel
Dir: Martin Flatscher
Also library supplier.
Type of Business: Exporter

Rupertusbuchhandlung Augustin Weis und Soehne KG
Linzer Gasse 29, Postf 73, 5024 Salzburg
Tel: (0662) 71661
Key Personnel
Manager: Bernhard Weis
Also library supplier.
Type of Business: Exporter

Kunstverlag Wolfrum
Augustinerstr 10, 1010 Vienna
Tel: (0222) 5125398
Telex: 75311081 Wolb *Cable:* WITWOLF VIENNA
Key Personnel
Manager: Erich Pospisil
Man Dir: Monika Engel
Manager: Peter Engel
Founded: 1919
Also Publisher of posters, note-cards, calendars & library supplier of art books.
Type of Business: Distributor, Exporter, Importer, Major Independent Bookseller
Owned by: Monika Engel & Hubert Wolfrum

Bangladesh

Adeyle Brothers & Co
60 Patuatuly, Dhaka 1100
Tel: (02) 233508
Owned by: Genclik Kitabevi

Bangladesh Books International Ltd
73-74 Patuatuli, Dhaka 1100
Tel: (02) 232252 (ext 31); (02) 232229; (02) 256071 (ext 19)
Key Personnel
Manager: Abdul Hafiz
Also Publisher.

Dhaka Book Mart
38-2 Banglabazar, Dhaka 1100
Tel: (02) 259173

Kathakali (Bud of Spoken World)
Member of Bangladesh Book Sellers' & Publishers' Association
18 Momin Rd, Chittagong 4000
Tel: (031) 619476; (031) 619006; (031) 612625
Key Personnel
Dir, Author & Editor: Mahbubul Haque
E-mail: mhaque@abnetbd.com
Founded: 1982

Managing Authority of Chittagong University Book Center, Publisher of Chittagong Guide.
Type of Business: Distributor, Importer, Major Independent Bookseller, Wholesaler
Owned by: Mashuda Yasmin

Mullick Bros
3/1 Bangla Bazar, Dhaka 1100
Tel: (02) 280728
Also Publisher.

Puthigar Ltd
74 Farashganj, Dhaka 1100
Tel: (02) 231374; (02) 235333; (02) 259867

Barbados

The Book Source
9100407 Barbados Community College Campus, Howells Cross Rd, St Michael
Mailing Address: No 15, Tenth Ave, Belleville, Saint Michael
Tel: (246) 4310379 *Fax:* (246) 4261855
E-mail: bksource@caribsurf.com
Web Site: www.booktrace.com
Key Personnel
Dir: Beverly Smith-Hinkson *E-mail:* beverly.bksource@caribsurf.com
Founded: 1989
Book ordering service; college bookshop; online bookstore.
Type of Business: Major Independent Bookseller
Owned by: Datalore Inc
Bookshop(s): Barbados Community College

Christian Literature Crusade
St Michael Plaza, St Michael's Row, Bridgetown
Mailing Address: PO Box 1239, Bridgetown
Tel: (246) 426-9254; (246) 429-5630 *Fax:* (246) 435-6642
Key Personnel
Manager: Romain Graham
Founded: 1941
Type of Business: Distributor, Importer, Major Book Chain Headquarters
Owned by: Christian Literature Crusade

Cloister Bookstore Ltd
Hincks & Cowell Sts, Bridgetown
Tel: (246) 426-2662 *Fax:* (246) 429-7269
E-mail: cloisterbookstore@caribsurf.com
Key Personnel
Man Dir: A Musgrave
Founded: 1957
Type of Business: Distributor, Importer, Major Independent Bookseller, Wholesaler

Belgium

Acco CV
Tiensestraat 134, 3000 Leuven
Tel: (016) 291100 *Fax:* (016) 207389
Key Personnel
Manager: Rob Berrevoets
Editor: Hendrik Stubbe
Founded: 1960
Type of Business: Distributor, Exporter, Major Independent Bookseller, Wholesaler

Agence et Menageries de la Prense
Rue de la peht ile 1, 1070 Brussels
Tel: (03) 8300015 *Fax:* (03) 8254755

Key Personnel
Contact: Jean-Pierre Verbeeck; Mr Sheridan
Founded: 1850
Type of Business: Distributor, Exporter, Importer, Major Book Chain Headquarters, Wholesaler

Agora bvba
Capucienenlaan 49, 9300 Aalst
Tel: (053) 78-87-00 *Fax:* (053) 78-26-91
Key Personnel
Contact: J Van Mello
Founded: 1985
Type of Business: Distributor, Importer, Major Independent Bookseller

Altiora Averbode Uitgeverij nv
BP 51, 3271 Averbode
Tel: (013) 78-01-56 *Fax:* (013) 77-68-37

Aquila BVBA
de Beriotstraat 2, 3000 Leuven
Tel: (016) 229501 *Fax:* (016) 208419
Key Personnel
Manager: Jos Maes *E-mail:* j.maes@johannes.be
Founded: 1977
Type of Business: Distributor, Importer, Major Independent Bookseller

SA Artis-Historia
Carlistraat 1, 1140 Brussels
Tel: (02) 2409200 *Fax:* (02) 2480818
100 Bookshops throughout Belgium; Also Publisher.

Audivox
Rubenslei 23, 2018 Antwerp 1
Tel: (03) 4701784
Key Personnel
Dir: Robert Gonnissen
Founded: 1953
Specialize in the import & distribution of English & American books.

Bredero
Rozenberg 15, 2400 Mol
Tel: (014) 31-84-61 *Fax:* (014) 31-84-61
Key Personnel
Contact: E De Ridder
Type of Business: Major Independent Bookseller

De Plukvogel nv
Mechelsesteenweg 9, 1800 Vivoorde
Tel: (02) 253-06-58 *Fax:* (02) 253-06-58
Key Personnel
Contact: P Steyaert

Exhibitions International NV/SA
Kolonel Begaultlaan 17, 3012 Leuven (Wilsele)
Tel: (016) 296900 *Fax:* (016) 296129
Key Personnel
Contact: Marleen Geukens
Founded: 1989
Acts as distributor for art books, catalogues & illustrated books on gardens, travel, architecture, design, etc.
Type of Business: Distributor

Uitgeverij Het-Volk
Forelstr 22, 9000 Ghent
Tel: (09) 2656424; (09) 2656420 *Fax:* (09) 2258406
Key Personnel
Publishing Dept Manager: F Nauwelaerts
General Manager: E Korntheuer
Publishers of newspapers, magazines, books & comics.
Owned by: Drukkerij Het Volk NV
Bookshop(s): Brusselsestr 11, B-9200 Dendermonde; Kortedagsteeg 16, B-9000 Gent; Rijselstr 20, B-8900 Ieper; Markstr 24, B-8870 Izegem; Voorstr 35, B-8500 Kortrijk; Noordstr 6, B-8800 Roeselare; Maastrichtstr 65, B-3700 Tongeren; Korte Gasthuisstr 13, B-2300 Turnhout

J Story-Scientia BVBA
Van Duyseplein 8, 9000 Ghent
Tel: (09) 2255757 *Fax:* (09) 2331409
E-mail: bookshop@story.be
Web Site: www.story.be
Key Personnel
Manager: J Story
Founded: 1962
Scientific booksellers & subscription agents & publishers.
Type of Business: Distributor, Exporter, Importer, Major Independent Bookseller

Librairie des Presses Universitaires de Bruxelles
42 ave Paul Heger, 1050 Brussels
Tel: (02) 6499780 *Fax:* (02) 6477962
Scientific books.
Owned by: Presses universitaires de Bruxelles ASBL

Licap CVBA
Guimardstraat 1, 1040 Brussels 4
Tel: (02) 5099670; (02) 5099703 *Fax:* (02) 5099606
Key Personnel
Contact: Herman Deben
Founded: 1973
Type of Business: Major Independent Bookseller

Maison des Langues Vivantes-Intertaal SA
9 rue des Pierres, 1000 Brussels
Tel: (02) 5117117 *Fax:* (02) 5145820
Key Personnel
Man Dir: Pierre De Laet
Founded: 1960
Specialize in modern languages.
Type of Business: Importer, Major Independent Bookseller

Oneindige Verhaal, t bvba (The Neverending Story)
Nieuwstraat 17, 9100 Sint-Niklaas
Tel: (03) 7765225 *Fax:* (03) 7765225
E-mail: oneindigeverhaal@boekenbank.be
Key Personnel
Dir: Herwig Staes
Assistant Manager: Tim Staes *Tel:* (03) 7651730
   E-mail: timstaes@planetinternet.be
Founded: 1996
Bookstore.

Pijl Boekbedrijf nv
Bleekhofstraat 87, 2140 Antwerp
Tel: (03) 236-98-30; (03) 270-02-70 *Fax:* (03) 235-90-02
E-mail: booksell@innet.be
Key Personnel
Contact: Johan Van Hemeldonck
Type of Business: Major Book Chain Headquarters, Wholesaler

Simon Stevin NV
Zennestraat 37, 1000 Brussels 1
Tel: (02) 5121085; (02) 5138295 *Fax:* (02) 5117015
Key Personnel
Dirs: L Van Hoorick; J De Hertogh
Founded: 1930

Libris Toison d'Or SA
Espace Louise, 40-42 ave de la Toison d'Or, B-1050 Brussels
Tel: (02) 5116400 *Fax:* (02) 5140961

Key Personnel
Manager: Jacqueline Evrard
Founded: 1961
Type of Business: Major Book Chain Headquarters, Wholesaler
Owned by: Librairies du Savoir

VTB-Travel Bookshop
Division of Tui Germany
Sint-Jacobsmarkt 45, 2000 Antwerp
Tel: (03) 220-33-66 *Fax:* (03) 220-33-84
E-mail: boekhandel@vtb.be
Key Personnel
Manager: Bert van Uytsel *Tel:* (03) 220-33-68
   E-mail: bert.vanuytsel@vtb.be
Founded: 1929
Travel Bookshop; Travel Guides-Maps-Travel Necessities. Member of IMTA & VBVB.
Type of Business: Major Book Chain Headquarters, Major Independent Bookseller, Wholesaler

Wouters Import NV
Naamsestraat 48, 3000 Leuven
Tel: (016) 233481 *Fax:* (016) 398020
E-mail: info@import.wouters.be
Key Personnel
Contact: Paul Verplancke
Founded: 1989
Type of Business: Distributor, Exporter, Importer, Wholesaler
Owned by: Wouters BVBA

Benin

Libraira-Papeterie ABM
BP 889, Cotonou
Tel: 330690 (voice & fax)
Key Personnel
Vice President: Michel Goussanou
Type of Business: Distributor, Exporter, Importer, Wholesaler
Owned by: Maison d'Edition ABM
Branch Office(s)
Porto Novo
Bookshop(s): BP 889, C138 Guinkomey, Cotonou

Bolivia

Libreria los Amigos del Libro
Casilla de Correo 450, Cochabamba 15
Tel: (04) 4504150; (04) 4504151 *Fax:* (04) 4115128
E-mail: gutten@amigol.bo.net *Cable:* AMIGOL
Key Personnel
Owner: Ingrid Guttentag
Manager: Petra Guttentag; Sonia Laguna
Founded: 1945
Type of Business: Distributor, Exporter, Importer, Major Book Chain Headquarters, Wholesaler
Branch Office(s)
Airport Jorge Wilstermann, Cochabamba
Shopping Center S O F E R, Cochabamba
Av Ayacucho S-0156, Cochabamba
Bookstore San Miguel, La Paz
Bookstore en Avd 16 de Julio Edificio Alameda, La Paz
Bookstore Calle, Ingavi No 14, Santa Cruz
Calle Mercado 1315, Aerport El Alto, La Paz

Gisbert y Cia SA
Calle Comercio 1270, Plaza Murillo La Paz, La Paz
Mailing Address: Casilla Postal 195, La Paz
Tel: (02) 220 26 26 *Fax:* (02) 220 29 11
E-mail: libgis@ceibo.entelnet.bo

Key Personnel
President: Javier Gisbert
Founded: 1907
Also Publisher.
Type of Business: Distributor, Importer, Major Independent Bookseller, Wholesaler

Libreria Juventud
Plaza Murillo 519, Casilla de Correo 1489, La Paz
Tel: (02) 2406248 *Fax:* (02) 2406248
Key Personnel
Manager: Gustavo Urquizo Mendoza
Founded: 1948
Type of Business: Importer, Wholesaler
Owned by: Libreria y Editorial Juventud

Libreria la Paz
Colon 618, Casilla 539, La Paz
Tel: (02) 353323; (02) 357109 *Fax:* (02) 391513
Key Personnel
Manager: Carlos Burgos
Founded: 1900
Type of Business: Distributor, Importer, Major Independent Bookseller, Wholesaler

Bosnia and Herzegovina

Veselin Maslesa
Obala Vojvode Stepe 4, P. F 237, YU-71000 Sarajevo
Tel: (071) 214633
Telex: 41154
Also Publisher.
Type of Business: Exporter, Importer
Branch Office(s)
Maksima Gorkog 2, Pavla Goranina 2, Sarajevo
Terazije 38, Belgrade, Yugoslavia (Over 30 group bookshops)

Sarajevo Publishing, see Veselin Maslesa

Svjetlost
Muhamede Kantardzica 3, 71000 Sarajevo
Tel: (071) 443419 *Fax:* (071) 471851
Also Publisher.
Type of Business: Exporter, Importer

Botswana

Botswana Book Centre
c/o Pula Press, The Main Mall Plot 1178, Gaborone
Mailing Address: PO Box 91, Gaborone
Tel: 3952931 *Fax:* 3974315
E-mail: pulapress@botsnet.bw
Telex: 2327 Books *Cable:* Books
Key Personnel
Manager: Mae Johnson
Founded: 1826
Publisher & Member of: BOPIA.
Owned by: Botswana Book Centre Trust
Bookshop(s): Francistown Shop; Lobatse Book Shop; Maun Shop
Warehouse: Broadhurst Industrial, Gaborone *Tel:* 3912130 *Fax:* 3912029
E-mail: bookcenter@botsnet.bw

Brazil

Livraria Agir Editora
Rua dos Invalidos, 198, 20231-020 Rio de Janeiro CEP
Tel: (021) 2216424 *Fax:* (021) 2520410
Key Personnel
President: Jose de Paula Machado
Editorial Manager: Regina Lemos
Manager: Candido Guinle de Paula Machado
Founded: 1944
Type of Business: Major Book Chain Headquarters, Wholesaler
Owned by: Artes Graficas Industrias Reunidas S/A Editora

Associacao Brasiliera de Liverivos Antiquarios
Rua do Rosario 155 Centro, 20041-005 Rio de Janeiro
Tel: (021) 224-8616 *Fax:* (021) 221-4582 *Cable:* EIKOS
Founded: 1935
Type of Business: Distributor, Exporter, Importer, Major Book Chain Headquarters

Livraria Brasiliense Editora SA
Av Marques do Sao Vicente 1771, 01139-003 Sao Paulo SP
Tel: (011) 8250122 *Fax:* (011) 673024
Telex: 33271 *Cable:* DBL
Key Personnel
Contact: Claiton Celso Guerrato; Caio Graco Prado
Founded: 1943
Owned by: Editora Brasiliense SA

COLIVRO - Comercio e Distribuicao de Livros Ltda
Rua Miquel Couto 35, Loja C, Sblj. 201-7, 20070 Rio de Janeiro RJ
Tel: (021) 2243177 *Fax:* (021) 2424517
Key Personnel
Manager: Fernando Jorge da Silva
Type of Business: Distributor, Wholesaler

Columbus Cultural Editora Comercial Importacao e Exporta
Rua Alves Guimaraes, 1297 Jardim America, 05410-002 Sao Paulo SP
Tel: (011) 8648777 *Fax:* (011) 8646531
Key Personnel
Editor: Luiz Carlos Cardoso
Editor Assistant: Renata Farhat Borges
Founded: 1987
Type of Business: Exporter, Importer, Major Independent Bookseller
Owned by: Grupo Cardapio de Alimentacao

Cortez Editora e Livraria Ltda
Rua Bartira 317, Perdizes, 05009-000 Sao Paulo SP
Tel: (011) 3864 0111 *Fax:* (011) 3864 4290
E-mail: cortez@cortezeditora.com.br
Web Site: www.cortezeditora.com.br
Key Personnel
Proprietor: Jose Xavier Cortez; Potira Beserra X Cortez
Editor: Danilo A Morales
Founded: 1980
Member of Brazilian Book Association.

Livraria Cultura Editora Ltda
Ave Paulista 2073 Conj Nacional, 01311-300 Sao Paulo
Tel: (011) 2854033 *Fax:* (011) 2854457
E-mail: livros@livcultura.com.br
Telex: 1138632 *Cable:* BOOKS-S.PAULO
Key Personnel
Dir: Pedro Herz
Founded: 1969
Type of Business: Importer

Disal S/A Distribuidores Asssociados de Livros
Rua Vitoria 486/496, Centro, Sao Paulo SP 01210-000
Tel: (011) 2211011 *Fax:* (011) 2230306
E-mail: disal@disal.com.br
Web Site: www.disal.com.br
Key Personnel
President: Francisco S Canato
Founded: 1968
Type of Business: Distributor, Importer, Wholesaler
Bookshop(s): Rua Maria Antonia, 380, 01222-010 Sao Paulo/SP *Tel:* (011) 256-0264 *Fax:* (011) 256-7293; Rua Deputado Lacerda Franco, 365, 05418-000 Sao Paulo/SP *Tel:* (011) 813-5761 *Fax:* (011) 813-5761; Rua Amador Bueno, 851, 14010-070 Ribeirao Preto/SP *Tel:* (016) 610-6536

Livraria Duas Cidades Ltda
Rua Bento de Freitas 158, 01220-000 Sao Paulo SP
Tel: (011) 220-5134
Also Publisher.

Ernesto Reichmann Distribuidores de Livros LTDA
Rua Coronel Marques, 335, 03440 Sao Paulo 03440-000
Tel: (011) 2182122 *Fax:* (011) 2182122
E-mail: rrr@lb.com
Key Personnel
Dir: Reichmann Renato
Manager: Hannelore Reichmann; Antonio Francisco
Founded: 1936
Specialize in Medical & Allied Literature.
Type of Business: Distributor, Exporter, Importer, Wholesaler
Branch Office(s)
Livraria Cientifica Ernesto Reichmann LTDA, Rua Napoleao de Barros, 639, Vila Mariana, 04024-002 Sao Paulo-SP
Bookshop(s): Livraria Cientifica Ernesto Reichmann LTDA, Rua Dom Jose de Barros, 168/6o, Centro, 01038-000 Sao Paulo-SP

Global Editora e Distribuidora Ltda
Rua Pirapitingui 111, 04104-000 Sao Paulo SP
Tel: (011) 3277-7999
Key Personnel
Man Dir, Sales: Luis Alves, Jr
Founded: 1973
Type of Business: Distributor, Exporter, Importer

Livro Ibero-Americano Ltda
Rua Hermenegildo de Barros 40/42, 20241 Rio de Janeiro
Tel: (021) 221-2026; (021) 2325248; (021) 2329048 *Fax:* (065) 2528814 *Cable:* NEBRIJA
Key Personnel
Man Dir: Sir Joao Francisco J Gomes
Founded: 1946
Also Publisher.
Type of Business: Distributor, Importer, Wholesaler
Branch Office(s)
Rua Conselheiro Crispiniano 29 - 1 pav, Sao Paulo SP

ISAEC, see Editora Sinodal

Editora Letraviva Importacao Distribuidora Livros Ltd
Av Reboucas 1986, 05402-300 Sao Paulo SP
Tel: (011) 2807992 *Fax:* (011) 2807780
E-mail: letraviva@letraviva.com.br
Web Site: www.letraviva.com.br

1277

BRAZIL

Key Personnel
Contact: Bernardo J I Gurbanov
Founded: 1979
Type of Business: Distributor, Importer

LITEC (Livraria Editora Tecnica) Ltda
Rua dos Timbiras 257, 01208-010 Sao Paulo
Tel: (011) 2220477 *Fax:* (011) 2220477
E-mail: livraria@litec.net
Web Site: www.litec.com.br
Key Personnel
Manager: Antonio Clara Dos Santos; Vainer Cavalheri
Founded: 1971
Type of Business: Importer
Owned by: Livraria Editora Tecnica Ltda

Livraria Buecherstube Brooklin Ltda
Rua Bernardino de Campos, 215, 04628-001 Sao Paulo
Mailing Address: CP 21464, 04602-970 Sao Paulo
Tel: (011) 2403735; (011) 1543-38-29 *Fax:* (011) 2414315
Key Personnel
Contact: Ursula Hellner; Erica Richter

Livraria Editora Tecnica Ltd, see LITEC (Livraria Editora Tecnica) Ltda

Livraria Nobel S/A
Rua da Balsa 559, 02910 Sao Paulo SP
Tel: (011) 3933 2822; (011) 3933 2811
Fax: (011) 3931 3988
E-mail: ednobel@livrarianobel.com.br
Key Personnel
Dir, Publicity: Ary Kuflik Benclowicz
Founded: 1943
Type of Business: Distributor

Sagra-D C Luzzatto Livreiros, Editores e Distribuidores Ltda
Rua Joao Alfredo 448, Loja 1, 90050 Porto Alegre
Tel: (0512) 2275222 *Fax:* (0512) 2274438
Key Personnel
Dir: Mr Darcy Caetano Luzzatto
Founded: 1967
Type of Business: Distributor, Exporter, Importer

Papirus Editora
Rua Gabriel Penteado, 253, Campinas SP 13001-970
Tel: (0192) 313500 *Fax:* (0192) 22578
Key Personnel
Contact: Eliane Camargo
Founded: 1976
Branch Office(s)
Rua Jose Antonio Coelho, 386 Sao Paulo SP
Bookshop(s): Rua Sacramento 202, Campinas SP; Rua Sacramento 114, Campinas SP; Rua Barao de Jaguara 1331, Campinas SP

PTI, see PTI - Publicacoes Tecnicas Internacionais Ltda

PTI - Publicacoes Tecnicas Internacionais Ltda
Rua Paixoto Gomide, 209, 01409-901 Sao Paolo
Tel: (011) 2596644 *Fax:* (011) 2586990
E-mail: gerson@vortex.uol.br
Key Personnel
Contact: Pierre Grossmann
Founded: 1972
Type of Business: Distributor, Exporter, Importer
Branch Office(s)
Rua Herculano De Freitas 390, Sao Paulo, SP

Livraria Cientifica Ernesto Reichmann Ltda
Rua Dom Jose de Barros 168/6o andar, 01038 Sao Paulo
Mailing Address: PO Box 3935, 01038 Sao Paulo
Tel: (011) 2551342 *Fax:* (011) 2557501
E-mail: rrr@lb.com
Key Personnel
Manager: Renato Reichmann; Hannelore Reichmann; Antonio Francisco
Founded: 1936
Specialize in Medical & Allied Literature.
Type of Business: Distributor, Exporter, Importer, Major Book Chain Headquarters, Wholesaler
Branch Office(s)
Rua Napoleao de Barros, 639

Saraiva SA, Livreiros Editores
Ave Marques de Sao Vincente, 1697, Barra Funda, 01139-002 Sao Paulo SP
Tel: (011) 8268422 *Fax:* (011) 8260606
Telex: 1126789
Key Personnel
Man Dir: Wander Soares
Founded: 1914
Type of Business: Distributor

Editora Sinodal
Rua Amadeo Rossi 467, 93030 Sao Leopoldo RS
Tel: (051) 5926366 *Fax:* (051) 5926543
Key Personnel
Man Dir, Rights & Permissions: Eloy Teckemeier
Founded: 1948
Type of Business: Exporter, Wholesaler

Sulina Livraria Editora
Av Borges de Medeiros 1030-1036, 90000 Porto Alegre RS
Tel: (0512) 254765; (0512) 250287 *Fax:* (0512) 280734
Key Personnel
President: Vilson Nailor Noer
Founded: 1946
Type of Business: Distributor, Exporter, Importer, Major Book Chain Headquarters
Owned by: Organizacao Sulina de Representacoes SA (see Livraria Sulina Editora)
Branch Office(s)
Rua Julio de Castilbos 1657, Caxias do Sul (nine other bookshops in Porto Alegre)
AV: Nacoes Unidas, 2001 Lj 1062

Livraria Triangulo Ltda
Rua Barao de Itapetininga 255-loja 23-24, 01000 Sao Paulo SP
Tel: (011) 2550665; (011) 2310922; (011) 2310362; (011) 2310552 *Fax:* (011) 2310162
Key Personnel
Contact: Mr Carlos Roberto Gomes
Founded: 1985
Type of Business: Importer

Brunei Darussalam

The Brunel Press
PO Box 69, Kuala Belait
Tel: (03) 2344
Key Personnel
Manager: Ian MacGregor
Stockists & dealers for books handled by the Strait Times Press, Singapore.

Bulgaria

Hemus Co Inc
14 Benkovsky Str, 1000 Sofia
Tel: (02) 875902 *Fax:* (02) 870186
Telex: 22267 Hemkik
Key Personnel
Executive Dir: Anastasia Boneva
Founded: 1967
Art products, souvenirs, photo materials, records, compact discs, numismatic items, musical instruments. State owned.
Type of Business: Distributor, Exporter, Importer, Major Independent Bookseller
Bookshop(s): Hemus Books, 1b Raiko Daskalov Sq, Sofia 1000

Burundi

Imparudi (Imprimerie et Papeterie du Burundi)
BP 3010, Bujumbura
Tel: (02) 3125; (02) 7381 *Fax:* (02) 2572
Key Personnel
Contact: Mutambuka Theoneste
Type of Business: Distributor, Exporter, Importer, Wholesaler

Cameroon

Librairie Bilingue/The Bilingual Bookshop
BP 727, Yaounde
Tel: 224899 *Fax:* 232903
Telex: 8438 kn
Type of Business: Distributor, Importer, Major Independent Bookseller, Wholesaler
Owned by: Buma Kor & Co Ltd (SARL)
Branch Office(s)
Limbe
Bomenda

Presbyterian Book Depot & Printing Press Ltd (PRESBOOK)
c/o Presbookshop, BP 13, Victoria/Limbe
Tel: 332114 *Fax:* 332694
Telex: 5952 *Cable:* PRESBOOK
Key Personnel
General Manager: W Abange
Founded: 1968
Also publishers & printers.
Type of Business: Distributor, Importer
Owned by: Presbyterian Church in Cameroon
Branch Office(s)
Presbook Buea, BP 19 Buea
Presbook Douala, BP 18 Douala
Presbook Kumba, BP 87 Kumba
Presbook Kumbo, BP 4 Kumbo
Presbook Mankon, BP 39 Bamenda
Presbook Mamfe, BP 114 Mamfe
Presbook, BP 28 Tiko
Presbook Yao unde, BP 1467

Chile

Libreria Eduardo Albers
Vitacura 5648, Santiago 6670885
Mailing Address: Casilla 17, Santiago 30
Tel: (02) 2185371 *Fax:* (02) 2181458

E-mail: libreria@albers.cl
Web Site: www.albers.cl
Key Personnel
Manager: Eduardo Albers *E-mail:* ealbers@albers.cl
Founded: 1943
Type of Business: Distributor, Exporter, Importer, Major Independent Bookseller, Wholesaler

Libreria Andres Bello
Av Ricardo Lyon 946, Providencia, Santiago
Tel: (02) 2049900 *Fax:* (02) 2253600
Key Personnel
Manager: Francisco Hoyl Sotomayor
Owned by: Editorial Andres Bello/Editorial Juridica de Chile

Berenguer Editorial
Correo 9, Casilla 16598-9, Santiago

Libreria Esoterica
Huerfanos 786, Local 19, Santiago
Tel: (02) 6338430 *Fax:* (02) 6397933
E-mail: wzzdarmd@entelchile.net
Telex: 240201
Key Personnel
Owner: Walter Zuniga Zavala
Founded: 1985
Type of Business: Distributor, Exporter, Importer, Major Independent Bookseller, Wholesaler

Feria Chilena del Libro Ltda
Huerfanos 623, Casilla 10225, Santiago
Tel: (02) 6396621 *Fax:* (02) 6339374
Web Site: www.feriachilenadellibro.cl
Key Personnel
Chief Executive Officer: Juan Aldea Perez
Tel: (0562) 6323465 *E-mail:* juanaldeap@feriachilenadellibro.cl
Type of Business: Distributor, Importer, Major Book Chain Headquarters, Wholesaler

Fondo de Cultura Economica SA
Paseo Bulnes 152, Casilla 10249, Santiago
Tel: (02) 6990189 *Fax:* (02) 6962329
Founded: 1953
Type of Business: Distributor, Exporter, Importer

Editorial Francesa Espanola SA
Huelen 10, of A 3 Piso, Providencia, Santiago
Tel: (02) 235-0911; (02) 235-9734 *Fax:* (02) 236-0900
Key Personnel
General Manager: Maria Isabel Castillo
Dir, Administration & Finance: Manuel Prietu
Type of Business: Distributor, Exporter, Importer, Wholesaler
Branch Office(s)
Av Valparaiso 152, Vina del Mar

Libreria Internacional Estudio
Anibal Pinto 345, Concepcion
Tel: (041) 225533 *Fax:* (041) 244542
Key Personnel
Contact: Jorge Jimenez Arriola
Founded: 1962
Type of Business: Major Independent Bookseller

Libreria Universitaria
Maria Luisa Santander 0447, Cassilla de Correo, Providencia, Santiago 10220
Tel: (02) 2234555; (02) 2236980 *Fax:* (02) 2099455; (02) 499455
Telex: 10220
Owned by: Editorial Universitaria SA

Lila Libreria de Mujeres
Providencia 1652, Local 3, Santiago
Tel: (02) 2361725 *Fax:* (02) 2361725

Key Personnel
Manager: Jimena Pizarro
Type of Business: Major Independent Bookseller

Libreria San Pablo
Av Vicuna MacKenna, Casilla 10777, La Florida, Santiago 3746
Tel: (02) 2882026 *Fax:* (02) 6716884
Key Personnel
Manager: Antonio Taconi
Type of Business: Distributor, Exporter, Importer, Wholesaler
Owned by: Ediciones San Pablo
Branch Office(s)
Calle Pedro Montt 1772, Cienfuegos 60, Casilla Santiago
Calle Casilla 3746, Valparaiso
Calle Manuel Matta 2588, Casilla 232, Antofagasta
Hijas de San Pablo, Mackenna 6299, Santiago

China

China International Book Trading Corporation
35 Chegongzhuang Xilu, Beijing 100044
Mailing Address: PO Box 399, Beijing 100044
Tel: (010) 68412026 *Fax:* (010) 68475199
E-mail: cibtc@mail.cibtc.com.cn
Web Site: www.cibtc.com.cn *Cable:* CIBTC BEIJING
Key Personnel
President: Zhi Bin Liu
Contact: Ming Liang Yang
Founded: 1949
Type of Business: Distributor, Exporter, Importer, Major Independent Bookseller, Wholesaler
Branch Office(s)
China Book Trading GmbH, Postfach 200114, 63307 Rodermark, Germany
Tel: (06074) 95564 *Fax:* (06074) 95271
E-mail: chinabook@aol.com
Cyress Book Co Ltd, London, United Kingdom
Peace Book Co Ltd, Wingon House, 71 Desvouex Rd, Rm 901-3 & 916, Central, Hong Kong, Hong Kong *Tel:* 25222130
CIBTC Tokyo Renrakujimucho, 1-29-12 Aobadai Meguro-ky, Tokyo, Japan *Tel:* (03) 57216536 *Fax:* (03) 57216537
Cypress Book (US) Company Inc, 3450 Third St, Unit 4B, San Francisco, CA 94124, United States

China National Publications Import & Export Corp
16 Gongti East Rd, Chaoyang District, Beijing 100704
Mailing Address: PO Box 88, Beijing 100704
Tel: (010) 65066688 *Fax:* (010) 65063101
Telex: 22313 CPC CN *Cable:* PUBLIMEX
Key Personnel
President: Chen Weijiang
Type of Business: Distributor, Exporter, Importer, Wholesaler
Branch Office(s)
PO Box 4111, Shanghai
Xi Mu Tou Shi No 34, Xi'an
Siemensstr 4, Postfach 1131, 63329 Egelsbach, Germany
Unit 4, 55-57 Park Royal Rd, London NW10 7LR, United Kingdom
3F9, Shibara 2-chome Minato-ku Tokyo 108, Japan
Beijing Book Co Inc, 701 E Linden Ave, Linden, NJ 07036, United States
PO Box 525, Guangzhou

CIBTC, see China International Book Trading Corporation

Hubei Publications Import & Export Corporation
11, Zhongnan Rd, Wuchang, Wuhan 430071-027
Tel: (027) 87825561 *Fax:* (027) 87815557
E-mail: hbwwsdjkb@lbs.com
Key Personnel
Manager, Import & Export Dept: Shao-Zhang He
Founded: 1994
Books printing materials, audio-video products & other related goods both in wholesale & retail.
Type of Business: Distributor, Exporter, Importer, Major Independent Bookseller, Wholesaler
Owned by: State-owned, Manager of Import & Export Dept: Shao-zhang He

Xiamen International Book Exchange Center
No 809, East Section, South Hubin Rd, Xiamen, 361004 Fujian
Tel: (0592) 5061401 *Fax:* (0592) 5061400
E-mail: xibc@xpublic.fz.fj.cn
Key Personnel
President: Shu Yan Zhang
Type of Business: Distributor, Exporter, Importer, Major Independent Bookseller, Wholesaler

Colombia

Libreria Aguirre
Calle 53 No 49-123, Medellin Antioquia
Mailing Address: Apdo Aereo 1395, Medellin Antioquia
Tel: (04) 2394801 *Cable:* Laguirre
Key Personnel
Manager: Aura Lopez Posada
Type of Business: Importer, Major Independent Bookseller

Circulo de Lectores SA
Calle 57 No 6-35, Apdo 52111, SantaFe de Bogota Cundinamarca
Tel: (01) 2173211; (01) 2177720 *Fax:* (01) 2178157
Telex: 41255
Key Personnel
General Manager: Eduardo Polo
Dir Marketing: Rafael Vargas
Founded: 1969
Also Book Club. Branch offices in Barranquilla, Bogota, Cali, Cartagena, Manizales, Medellin, Pereira, & Tunja.
Type of Business: Distributor, Exporter, Importer, Major Book Chain Headquarters, Wholesaler
Owned by: Diario el Tiempo

Distribuidoras Unidas SA
Transversal 93 N 52-03, Santafe de Bogota, DC
Tel: 4139300 *Fax:* 4138502
Key Personnel
Legal Representative: Emiro Aristizabal

Eurolibros
Calle 40 No 20-27, Bogota
Tel: (01) 2886400 *Fax:* (01) 2450291; (01) 3401811; (01) 3401830; (01) 2886400
Key Personnel
General Dir: Carlos Roberto Jimenez
E-mail: carlosji@latino.net.co
Founded: 1983
Type of Business: Distributor, Wholesaler

Grupo Editorial Iberoamerica de Colombia SA
Carrer 2a1 No 54-78, Bogota
Mailing Address: Apdo Aereo 513, Bogota
Tel: (01) 3106553 *Fax:* (01) 3106553
E-mail: geicol@colomsat.net.co
Key Personnel
Dir General: Hernandez Rico Victor Manuel

COLOMBIA

Founded: 1991
Type of Business: Distributor, Exporter, Importer, Wholesaler

Grupo Noriega Editores de Colombia Ltda
Carrera 1a5 No 33-71, Bogota
Mailing Address: Apdo Aereo 15151, Bogota
Tel: (01) 2328336; (01) 2344929 *Fax:* (01) 2858905
E-mail: gnoriega@openway.com.co
Key Personnel
Legal Representative: Gustavo Rodriguez Garcia
Founded: 1993
Type of Business: Distributor, Importer, Wholesaler
Owned by: Editorial Limusa SA DE CV

Editorial y Libreria Herder Ltda
Carrera 11, No 73-61, SantaFe de Bogota, DC
Tel: (01) 3344853 *Fax:* (01) 2832272
Key Personnel
Legal Representative: Alvaro Gomez Robayo
Type of Business: Distributor, Exporter, Importer
Owned by: Hermann Herder e Instituto Literario

Libreria y Distribuidora Lerner Ltda
Avenida Jimenez No 4-35, Apdo Aereo 8304, SantaFe de Bogota Cundinamarca
Tel: (01) 2430567 *Fax:* (01) 2814319
Telex: 43195
Key Personnel
Manager: Luis A Burgos H
Founded: 1957
Type of Business: Importer, Major Independent Bookseller
Branch Office(s)
Calle 92 No 15-23, SantaFe de Bogota Cundinamarca *Tel:* (01) 2360580

Libreria Nacional Ltda
Unicentro-Local 1-146, Bogota
Tel: (01) 825829; (01) 833849; (01) 2139842; (01) 2139882 *Fax:* (01) 822404; (01) 2138404
Cable: LINALCO AA CALI
Key Personnel
Manager: Hernando Ordonez
Administrator General: Aura Bustamante
Gerente Bogota: Felipe Ossa
Administrador Libreria Barranquilla: Edgar Ramirez
Branch Office(s)
Carrera 53 No 75-129, Barranquilla
Unicentro Local No 1-146, Apdo Aereo 100778, Bogota *Fax:* (01) 2130484

Libreria Panamericana
Calle 12, No 34-20, Apdo Aereo 6210, Cundinamarca
Tel: (01) 2770100 *Fax:* (01) 2773599
Key Personnel
Contact: Carlos Federico Ruiz

Ediciones Paulinas (Libreria San Pablo)
Carrera 46 No 22A-90, SantaFe de Bogota Cundinamarca
Tel: (01) 2444516 *Fax:* (01) 2684288
Key Personnel
Manager: Esther Guzman
Branch offices in Barranquilla, Bogota, Cali, Cucuta, Manizales, & Medellin.
Type of Business: Distributor, Exporter, Importer, Major Book Chain Headquarters, Wholesaler
Branch Office(s)
Barranquilla
Medellin
Bogota
Cali
Cucuta
Manizales
Bookshop(s): Carrera 13 No 72-41, Bogota; Carrera 32 No 161A-04, Bogota

Libreria Temis SA
Calle 13 No 6-45, Apdo Aereo 5941, SantaFe de Bogota DDC
Tel: (01) 423035; (01) 425581; (01) 2690713; (01) 2693521 *Fax:* (01) 2925801
Founded: 1951
Type of Business: Distributor, Exporter, Importer, Wholesaler
Owned by: Editorial Temis SA, Transv 39B 17-98, SantaFe de Bogota; Nomos Impresores, SA
Branch Office(s)
Calle 52 No 42-68, Medellin
Calle 12 No 5-33, Avda Pepe Sierra No 24-25

Libreria Tercer Mundo
Transv 2-A, No 67-27, Bogota
Tel: (01) 2551539; (01) 2556691 *Fax:* (01) 2125976
E-mail: tmundoed@polcola.com.co
Key Personnel
General Manager: Santiago Pombo Vejarano
Library Dir: Juan Manuel Borda de Francisco
Founded: 1962
Owned by: Tercer Mundo Editores SA
Bookshop(s): Cra 7, No 16-91, Bogota; Cra 13, No 44-70, Bogota

Libreria Uniandes
Carrera 1 No 18A82, Bogota
Tel: (01) 2824066 (ext 2197); (01) 2824066 (ext 2198) *Fax:* (01) 2841890 *Cable:* UNIANDES
Key Personnel
General Manager: Arcesio Rodriguez P
Marketing and Sales Manager: Cesar Augusto Pena
International Trade: Luz Marina Cortes
Spanish and Latin American trade books; importers and subscription agents of academic and scientific publications.
Type of Business: Importer

Congo

Office national des Librairies Populaires (ONLP)
c/o Biblioteque Nationale Populaire, BP 1489, Brazzaville
Tel: 833485 *Fax:* 831879
Telex: 5379 *Cable:* Lipolaire Brazzaville
Key Personnel
Dir General: Ignace Taliane-Tchibamba

ONLP, see Office national des Librairies Populaires (ONLP)

The Democratic Republic of the Congo

Librairie des Presses Universitaires
Blvd du 30 Juin 4113, Kinshasa
Mailing Address: BP 1682, Kinshasa
Tel: (012) 30652
Owned by: Presses universitaires du Zaiire et l'Office du Livre (PUZ)

Librairie les Volcans
22 Ave President Mobutu, Goma
Mailing Address: BP 105, Goma
Tel: 366
Key Personnel
President: Kakule Tatsopa wa Mughalitsa
Type of Business: Distributor, Major Independent Bookseller
Owned by: Librairie Les Volcans, Publisher
Bookshop(s): Cereva

Okapi Centre de Diffusion
BP 11398, Kinshasa
Tel: (012) 31457

Librairie Saint-Paul
c/o Editions Paulines, Ave du Commerce 76, BP 335, Kinshasa
Mailing Address: BP 8505, Kinshasa
Tel: 77726
Founded: 1958
Type of Business: Distributor, Exporter, Importer, Major Independent Bookseller, Wholesaler
Owned by: Filles de Saint Paul - Congr. Internat. au service de la promotion et de l'evangelisation par les medias
Branch Office(s)
BP 505, Kisangani
BP 2447, Lubumbashi

Costa Rica

Libreria Universal Carlos Federspiel
Apdo 1532, Edificio Central, San Jose

Libreria Imprenta y Litografia Lehmann SA
Apdo 10011, San Jose
Tel: 2231212
Also Publisher.

Libreria Trejos SA
Apdo 10096, 1000 San Jose
Tel: 2242411 *Fax:* 2241528
Telex: 2858 Ltsa
Key Personnel
Manager: A Trejos

Cote d'Ivoire

CEDA, see Centre d'Edition et de Diffusion Africaines

Centre d'Edition et de Diffusion Africaines
Immeuble 60 Logements Abidjan-Plateau, BP 04, 541, Abidjan 04
Mailing Address: BP 541, Abidjan 04
Tel: 222242; 222055 *Fax:* 217262
Key Personnel
Man Dir: Venance Kacou
Also Publisher.
Type of Business: Distributor, Exporter, Importer, Wholesaler

Croatia

Tehnicka Knjiga
Jurisiceva 10, 10000 Zagreb
Tel: (041) 4810818 *Fax:* (041) 481 0821

Cuba

Ediciones Cubanas
Obispo 527 altos, Havana 1GP 10 100
Tel: (07) 631989; (07) 338942 *Fax:* (07) 338943
Telex: 0512337 *Cable:* LIBROCUBA
Key Personnel
Manager: Nancy Matos
Books, periodicals & printing material.
Type of Business: Distributor, Exporter, Importer, Major Book Chain Headquarters, Wholesaler
Owned by: Empresa de Comercio Exterior de Publicaciones
Bookshop(s): Libreria Internacional, Obispo No 528 e/ Vernaza y Villegas, Habana; Libreria La Bella Habana, Palacio del Segundo Cabo, O'Reilly No 4 Esq a Tacon, Habana Vieja

Cyprus

K P Kyriakou (Books - Stationery) Ltd
PO Box 50159, 3601 Limassol
Tel: (05) 747555 *Fax:* (05) 747047
E-mail: cybooks@logosnet.cy
Key Personnel
Man Dir: Kyriakos P Kyriakou
  E-mail: kyriakospk@webnmedia.com
Founded: 1947
Type of Business: Distributor, Exporter, Importer, Major Independent Bookseller, Wholesaler

MAM (The House of the Cyprus & Cyprological Publications)
19 Konstantinos Palaiologos Ave, Nicosia 1015
Mailing Address: PO Box 21722, Nicosia 1512
Tel: (022) 753536 *Fax:* (022) 375802
E-mail: mam@mam.cy.net
Web Site: www.mam.cy.net
Key Personnel
Manager: Fryni Michaelidou
Secretary: Mikis Michaelides
Founded: 1965
Specialize in all kinds of publications on Cyprus & in all publications by Cypriots. Authorized distributors of Cyprus Government publications & other Cypriot publishers.
Type of Business: Distributor, Exporter, Importer, Wholesaler
Bookshop(s): MAM Cyprus Publications, Stoa tou Vivliou, 5 Pesmazoglou, 10564 Athens, Greece, Manager: Matina Vossou

K Rustem & Bro
21-26 Kyrenia St, Nicosia
Mailing Address: PO Box 239, Nicosia
Tel: (02) 71041; (02) 71418; (02) 52085
Cable: RUSTEM BR 4
Bookshop(s): Tofarides Bookshop, PO Box 278, Larnaca *Tel:* (041) 54144

Czech Republic

Knihkupectvi - Antikvariat Galerie
Masarykova 15, CS-415 01 Teplice
Tel: (0417) 23966 (voice & fax)
Key Personnel
Manager: Milos Novotny
Owned by: Martina Uldrychova
Branch Office(s)
Teplice, Kapelnii 4

Denmark

Arnold Busck International Boghandel A/S
Kobmagergade 49, DK-1150 Copenhagen K
Tel: 33733500 *Fax:* 33733535
E-mail: arnold@busck.dk
Web Site: www.busck.dk
Key Personnel
Manager & Bookseller: Troels Bek *Tel:* 33733525
Founded: 1896
Export Division is at above address.
Type of Business: Exporter, Major Book Chain Headquarters, Major Independent Bookseller
Owned by: Ole Arnold Busck

Gad
Vimmelskaftet 32, 1161 Copenhagen K
Tel: (033) 150558 *Fax:* (033) 154232
Key Personnel
Manager: Erling Sievert *E-mail:* ES@gad.dk
Owned by: G E C Gads Foundation (see also G E C Gads Forlag)

Magasin du Nord A/S
Kongens Nytorv 13, 1095 Copenhagen K
Tel: 33114433 *Cable:* MAGDUNORD TELEX 15975
Key Personnel
Buyer: Alfred Jensen *Tel:* 033 182121 *Fax:* 033 182215

Nyt Nordisk Forlag Arnold Busck A/S, Publishers, see Arnold Busck International Boghandel A/S

Polyteknisk Boghandel og Forlag
Anker Engelundsvej 1, DTU, Bygn 101 A, 2800 Lyngby
Tel: 77424344 *Fax:* 77424354
E-mail: polybog@pb.dtu.dk
Key Personnel
Man Dir: Peter Langford
Founded: 1960
Type of Business: Distributor, Importer, Major Independent Bookseller, Wholesaler

C A Reitzel A/S
Postboks 1073, 1008 Copenhagen K
Tel: 33140451 *Fax:* 33140270
Key Personnel
Man Dir: Svend Olufsen
Supplies universities, scientific libraries & institutions worldwide; also Publisher.
Type of Business: Exporter, Importer

Scanvik Books Import ApS
Esplanaden 8 B, DK-1263 Copenhagen
Tel: 33127766 *Fax:* 33912882
E-mail: scanvik@bog.dk
Web Site: www.scanvik.dk
Key Personnel
Dir: John Roberts; Uwe Schultheiss
Founded: 1980
Also agent.
Type of Business: Distributor, Exporter, Importer, Wholesaler

SKT's Boghandel
Lautrupvang 15, DK-2750 Ballerup
Tel: 44686662 *Fax:* 44686660
E-mail: skt@sktbooks.dk
Key Personnel
Contact: Mark Bentley
Founded: 1968
Type of Business: Major Independent Bookseller

Studenterboghandelen ved Odense Universitet
Campusvej 55, 5230 Odense M
Tel: 66158747 *Fax:* 66158766
Key Personnel
Man Dir: Niels Lindberg
Founded: 1981
Type of Business: Importer, Major Independent Bookseller

Svensk-Norsk Bogimport A/S
Esplanaden 8, DK-1263 Copenhagen K
Tel: 33142666 *Fax:* 33143588
E-mail: snb@bog.dk
Web Site: www.snbog.dk
Key Personnel
President: Poul Brehmer
Founded: 1968
Type of Business: Distributor, Exporter, Importer, Major Independent Bookseller, Wholesaler

Tysk Bogimport ApS
Vester Voldgade 83, 1552 Copenhagen V
Tel: 33136016; 33136097 *Fax:* 33142021
Key Personnel
Contact: Eberhard Riedel
Founded: 1958
Type of Business: Distributor, Importer, Major Independent Bookseller, Wholesaler

Universitetsbogladen
Blegdamsvej 3, DK-2200 Copenhagen N
Tel: 35240444
E-mail: uniboghl@mail.teledanmark.dk.
Key Personnel
Manager: Henrik Larsen
Founded: 1968
Type of Business: Exporter, Importer, Major Independent Bookseller
Branch Office(s)
Naturfagsbogladen, Universitetsparken 13, DK-2100 Copenhagen O (natural science bookshop)
Panumbogladen, Blegdamsvej 3, DK-2200 Copenhagen N (medical bookshop)

Dominican Republic

Editorial Padilla
San Fco Macoris 14, Santo Domingo
Tel: (809) 682-0111; (809) 688-0303
Also Publisher.
Branch Office(s)
El Conde 109, Santo Domingo *Tel:* (809) 6880303

Ecuador

CD Remain Cia Ltda
Ave Repulbica 740 y Eloy Alfaro, Profesional Piso 7, Ofc 702 Casilla, 17-17-1548 Quito
Tel: (02) 224973; (02) 239328 *Fax:* (02) 505760
Type of Business: Distributor

Libreria Cientifica SA
Casilla 2905, Quito
Tel: (02) 12556

ECUADOR

Key Personnel
Manager: Alicia de Pino
Branch Office(s)
Luque 223, Guayaquil *Tel:* (04) 324650

Libreria Cima
Carlos Ibarra 200 y 10 de Agosto, Casilla 17-15-87C, Quito
Tel: (02) 571218; (02) 571318 *Cable:* CIMALE
Key Personnel
Manager: Luis A Carrera
Assistant Manager: Edgar R Freire
Type of Business: Exporter

De Cervantes Ediciones SA
Av Orellana 1811 y 10 de Agosto, Edificio El Cid, 1er piso, Quito
Tel: (02) 223062 *Fax:* (02) 523452
Key Personnel
Contact: Ismael Cervantes Quintero
Type of Business: Distributor, Exporter, Importer

Ecuazeta De Publicaciones Cia Ltda
Mariano Andrade 250 y Villalengua Urb Granda Centeno, Quito
Tel: (02) 443074 *Fax:* (02) 443074
Key Personnel
President: Jorge Zavaleta
Manager: Rocio Vacas de Alvarez
Founded: 1989
Type of Business: Distributor, Importer, Wholesaler

Edimecien Cia Ltda
Gral Aguirre 166 y Ave 10 de Agosto, Quito
Tel: (02) 502-427 *Fax:* (02) 502-429
Key Personnel
Contact: Alfredo Montoya Flores
Type of Business: Distributor, Importer, Wholesaler

Promociones Culturales Gitral SA
Ave Machala 1024 y Velez Casilla, 09-01-7278 Guayaquil
Mailing Address: PO Box 09-01-7278, Guayaquil
Tel: (02) 510510; (02) 532060; (02) 32644 *Fax:* (02) 510510; (02) 326733
Key Personnel
President: Ramon Cedeno Galarza
Type of Business: Distributor, Importer

Libreria Universitaria
Garcia Moreno 739, Apdo 2982, Quito
Tel: (02) 212521
Key Personnel
Dir: Ing Carlos E Wong Flores
Founded: 1951
Type of Business: Distributor, Exporter, Importer, Wholesaler

Ediciones Monserrat
Ave 10 de Agosto 1831 y Roca, Quito
Tel: (0222) 567 *Fax:* (0222) 541294
E-mail: edimon@uio.stnet.net
Key Personnel
Contact: Claudio C Gustavo
Type of Business: Distributor
Owned by: Monica Claudio

Egypt (Arab Republic of Egypt)

Al Arab Bookshop
23 Al-Fagalah St, Cairo 908027
Mailing Address: PO Box 29, Cairo 908027
Tel: 908025 *Cable:* ARABUKSHOP CAIRO
Key Personnel
Manager: Prof Saladin Boustany, PhD
Founded: 1900
Agent of the Library of Congress PL 480.
Type of Business: Distributor, Exporter
Owned by: Al Arab Publishing House

FHB Exporter
Ramsis Center, Cairo
Mailing Address: PO Box 159-11794, Cairo
Tel: (02) 5083898 *Fax:* (02) 5083898
E-mail: fhb@link.net
Key Personnel
Manager: Fouad H Baskharoun
Founded: 1970
Books, magazines & periodicals published in Egypt & the Arab World.
Type of Business: Distributor, Exporter, Wholesaler

Lehnert & Landrock, Bookshop and Art Publishers
44 Sherif Pasha St, 11511 Cairo
Mailing Address: PO Box 1013, 11511 Cairo
Tel: (02) 3927606; (02) 3935324 *Fax:* (02) 3934421
Key Personnel
Owner & Manager: Dr E Lambelet
Manager: Mahmud Abdel Aziz
Founded: 1924
Bookshop & art publisher.
Type of Business: Importer, Major Independent Bookseller, Wholesaler
Owned by: Edouard Lambelet & Co

Livres de France
36 Kasr el Nil St, Cairo
Tel: (02) 51512

Misr Bookshop
3 Kamel Sidkey St, Al-Fagalah, Cairo
Tel: (02) 908920
Key Personnel
Manager: Amir Saiid El-Sahhar

El Salvador

Clasicos Roxsil Editorial SA de CV
Cuarta Avenida Sur 2-3, La Libertad, Santa Tecla
Tel: 228 1832; 229 3621 *Fax:* 228 1212
Fax on Demand: 228 1212
Key Personnel
Manager: Rosa Serrano de Lopez
Chief Editorial Department: Roxana Beatriz Lopez *Tel:* 228-2646 *E-mail:* roxanabe@havegaute.com.sv
Founded: 1969
Type of Business: Distributor, Exporter, Importer, Wholesaler

Libreria Universitaria de l'Universidad de El Salvador
Ciudad Universitaria, Apdo Postal 1703, San Salvador
Tel: 259427; 256604 *Fax:* 259427
Telex: 20794

Libreria UCA
Universidad Centroamericana Jose Simeon Canas, Autopista Sur, Jardines de Guadalupe, Apdo Postal 01-575, 168 San Salvador
Tel: 240011 (ext 193); 234491 *Fax:* 2731010

Ethiopia

ECA Bookshop Co-op Society
PO Box 3001, Addis Ababa
Tel: (01) 447200

Finland

Akateeminen Kirjakauppa
Keskuskatu 1, PL 128, FIN-00101 Helsinki
Tel: (09) 12141 *Fax:* (09) 1214435
E-mail: markusanaja@stockman.mailnet.fi *Cable:* AKATEEMINEN
Key Personnel
Chief Executive: Stig-Bjorn Nyberg
Assistant: Anu Hantala
Founded: 1893
Subscriptions, CD-ROM.
Type of Business: Major Book Chain Headquarters, Major Independent Bookseller
Owned by: OY Stockmann AB
Branch Office(s)
Itakeskus
Tampere
Tapiola
Turku

Oy Satusiivet - Sagovingar AB (Lasten Parhaat Kirjat)
Simonkatu 12B-27, SF-00100 Helsinki
Tel: (09) 6933267 *Fax:* (09) 6944186
Key Personnel
President: Ritva Lemonen
Editoial Manager: Leena Jaervenpaeae
Children's Bookclub.
Owned by: Kustannus Oy Tammi

Suomalainen Kirjakauppa Oy
Koivuvaarankuja, PO Box 2, 01640 Vantaa
Tel: (00) 852751 *Fax:* (00) 8527888
Telex: 121841
Key Personnel
Man Dir: Hannu Syrjaenen
Marketing Manager: Lisbeth Kuitunen; Alto Lahdenpere
Branch offices in Espoo (3), Forssa, Hameenlinna, Hamina, Heinola, Helsinki (11), Iisalmi, Imatra, Javenpaa, Joensuu, Jyvaskyla, Kajaani, Kerava, Kotka (3), Kouvola, Kuopio, Lahti, Lappeenranta, Mikkeli (2), Pori, Raahe, Rovaniemi, Salo, Savonlinni, Seinaajoki, Tampere, Turku, Vaasa, Vantaa, Varkaus.
Type of Business: Major Book Chain Headquarters
Owned by: Rautakirja Oy

Tampereen Kirjakauppa Oy
Haemeenkatu 27, PL 21, SF-33200 Tampere
Tel: (03) 2128380 *Fax:* (03) 2122136
E-mail: trekirja@vip.fi

Web Site: www.tampereenkirjakauppa.fi
Key Personnel
Manager: Martti Helminen
Founded: 1910
Type of Business: Exporter, Importer, Major Independent Bookseller

Turun Kansallinen Kirjakauppa Oy
Linnankatu 16, 20101 Turku 10
Mailing Address: PO Box 135, 20101 Turku 10
Tel: (0921) 2502444 *Fax:* (0921) 2519348
Key Personnel
Manager: Paula Palmroth

France

Critiques Livres Distribution SAS
24 rue Malmaison, BP 93, 93172 Bagnolet Cedex
Tel: (01) 43603910 *Fax:* (01) 48973706
E-mail: critiques.livres@wanadoo.fr
Key Personnel
President: Rosalind Fay-Boehlinger
Founded: 1976
Books in the visual arts in English, French, German & Italian.
Type of Business: Distributor, Exporter, Importer, Wholesaler

Distique
5, rue du Marechal-Leclerc, 28600 Luisant
Tel: 37305700 *Fax:* 37305712
Type of Business: Distributor

Flammarion
26 rue Racine, F-75006 Paris Cedex 06
Tel: (01) 78380157; (01) 40513041 *Fax:* (01) 43292148
Telex: Flamlyo 300460 F
Key Personnel
Manager: Jean-Noel Flammarion
Also Publisher. Branches in Bordeaux, Dijon, Grenoble, Lyon, Marseilles, Montreal (Canada), & Paris.

A Van Ginneken
PO Box 1 Saint Sulpice, BP 532, 21014 Dijon Cedex
Tel: (03) 80740506 *Fax:* (03) 80740700
E-mail: hexalivre@axnet.fr
Telex: 341429
Key Personnel
Man Dir: Andries Van Ginneken
Type of Business: Distributor, Exporter, Importer, Wholesaler

Hachette Livre SA - H E D
43 quai de Grenelle, 75905 Paris Cedex
Tel: (01) 43923000 *Fax:* (01) 43923030
Key Personnel
Director: Isabelle Magnac

Lavoisier
Formerly Technique et Documentation Lavoisier
11 rue Lavoisier, 75384 Paris 08
Tel: (01) 42 65 39 95 *Fax:* (01) 42650246
E-mail: besnault@lavoisier.fr
Telex: 632020 F TDL
Key Personnel
Dir: Jacques Besnault
Founded: 1947
Type of Business: Distributor, Exporter, Importer, Major Independent Bookseller

Librairie FNAC
67 bd du General Lecherc, 92612 Clichy
Tel: 01 55215053
Key Personnel
Manager: Bertrand Picard
Assistant Dir: Garrigou Martine *E-mail:* marie-martine.garrigou@fnac.tm.fr

Librairie Generale des PUF
17 rue Soufflot, 75005 Paris Cedex
Tel: (01) 43267741 *Fax:* (01) 46332194
Owned by: Presses Universitaires de France, 12 rue Jean de Beauvais, 75006 Paris

Librairie la Hune
170 Blvd St Germain, 75006 Paris
Tel: (01) 43255406
Key Personnel
Man Dir: Georges Dupre
Owned by: Flammarion

Librairie Mollat
11 rue Vital-Carles, 33080 Bordeaux Cedex
Tel: (0556) 564040 *Fax:* (0556) 564088
Telex: 541542 F
Branch Office(s)
83-91 rue Porte-Dijeaux, 33080 Bordeaux Cedex

Office International de Documentation et Librairie (OFFILIB)
48 rue Gay-Lussac, 75240 Paris Cedex 05
Tel: (01) 43290408 *Fax:* (01) 43290612
Key Personnel
Dir: Stephanie Boudon
Type of Business: Importer, Major Independent Bookseller

OFFILIB, see Office International de Documentation et Librairie (OFFILIB)

Librairie Sauramps Medical
11 Blvd Henri-IV, 34000 Montepellier
Tel: (04) 67636880 *Fax:* (04) 67525905
E-mail: sauramps.medical@livrelmedicaux.com
Web Site: www.livrel.medicaux.com
Telex: (04) 480728
Key Personnel
Manager: Dominique Torreilles
Founded: 1977
Publisher & bookseller.
Subjects: Specialize in medicine
Type of Business: Importer, Major Independent Bookseller

Technique et Documentation Lavoisier, see Lavoisier

Librairie de l'Universite
c/o Flammarion 2, 24, rue Childebert, 69002 Lyon Cedex
Tel: (04) 78379525
Founded: 1964
Type of Business: Major Independent Bookseller
Owned by: Flammarion

Gambia

The Gambia Methodist Bookshop Ltd
16 Nelson Mandela St, Banjul
Mailing Address: PO Box 203, Banjul
Tel: 28179
Key Personnel
Manager: James Heffernan

Germany

Artibus et Literis
Friedrichstr 24-26, 40217 Duesseldorf
Mailing Address: Postfach 101053, 40001 Duesseldorf
Tel: (0211) 38810 *Fax:* (0211) 3881280
E-mail: webmaster@artibus.de
Web Site: www.artibus.de
Key Personnel
Man Partner: Horst Janssen; Klaus Janssen
Books & journals.
Type of Business: Exporter, Importer
Owned by: Horst Janssen & Klaus Janssen

Buchhandlung G D Baedeker
Kettwiger Str 33-35, 45127 Essen
Mailing Address: Postfach 100345, 45003 Essen
Tel: (0201) 20680 *Fax:* (0201) 2068-100

Bertelsmann Distribution GmbH
An der Autobahn, 33310 Gutersloh
Mailing Address: Postfach 7777, 33310 Gutersloh
Tel: (05241) 807083 *Fax:* (05241) 806006
Telex: 933827
Key Personnel
Man Dir: Dr Hans-Joachim Herzog; Hartmut Ostrowski
Also publishers' delivery service.
Type of Business: Wholesaler
Owned by: Bertelsmann AG

Blazek und Bergmann
Holzhausenstr 21, 60322 Frankfurt
Mailing Address: Postfach 200162, 60605 Frankfurt
Tel: (069) 152003-36 *Fax:* (069) 152003-44
Web Site: www.blazek.de
Versand.
Owned by: Bergmann Eike (Fr)

Bouvier GmbH & Co KG
Am Hof 28, 53113 Bonn
Mailing Address: Postfach 1268, 53113 Bonn
Tel: (0228) 729010 *Fax:* (0228) 7290179
E-mail: bouvier@books.de
Web Site: www.books.de
Key Personnel
Manager: Thomas Grundmann
Type of Business: Major Independent Bookseller
Bookshop(s): Buchhaus Gonski, Neinmarkt 18a, 50667 Cologne; Bouvier Hanim, Allee-Center, 59065 Hamm; Bouvier Koblenz, Lohrstrasse 24, 56068 Koblenz; Bouvier Siegburg, Houkt 10-19, 53721 Siegburg

Fachverlag Hans Carl GmbH
Andernacherstr 33a, 90411 Nuremberg
Mailing Address: Postfach 990153, 90268 Nuremberg
Tel: (0911) 95285-0 *Fax:* (0911) 95285-48 *Cable:* CARLVERLAG
Key Personnel
Contact: Wolfgang Illguth; Traudel Schmitt
Founded: 1861
Type of Business: Distributor, Major Independent Bookseller

Dokumente Verlag Import-Exportbuchhandlung, see Dokumente Verlag Versandbuchhandlung Librairie

Dokumente Verlag Versandbuchhandlung Librairie
Postfach 1340, 77603 Offenburg
Tel: (0781) 923699-0 *Fax:* (0781) 923699-70
E-mail: info@dokumente-verlag.de
Web Site: www.dokumente-verlag.de

Key Personnel
President: Michael Schlageter *Tel:* (0781) 92369918 *E-mail:* ms@dokumente-verlag.de
Contact: Heribert Jager
Founded: 1945
Library.
Owned by: Michael Schlageter & Heribert Jager

Erich-Weinert Universitatsbuchhandlung
Ulrichplatz 4-6, 39104 Magdeburg
Mailing Address: Postfach 1423, 39104 Magdeburg
Tel: (0391) 568590 *Fax:* (0391) 5685923
E-mail: e.angerer@weinert.de
Web Site: www.weinert.de
Founded: 1960
Type of Business: Major Independent Bookseller
Owned by: Ernst Angerer

Werner Flach Internationale Fachbuchhandlung
Schlosserstr 25, 60322 Frankfurt am Main
Tel: (069) 9591750 *Fax:* (069) 95917522
E-mail: fadibuch@flachbuch.de
Web Site: www.flachbuch.com
Key Personnel
President: Werner Flach
Founded: 1957
Type of Business: Major Independent Bookseller

R Friedlaender & Sohn GmbH Buchhaunlung & Antiquariat
Dessauer St 28-29, 10963 Berlin
Tel: (030) 2622328
Key Personnel
International Rights: Hans-Werner Kyrieleis

Graff Buchhandlung
Neuestr 23, 38100 Braunschweig
Mailing Address: Postfach 2243, 38102 Braunschweig
Tel: (0531) 480890 *Fax:* (0531) 46531
E-mail: infos@graff.de
Web Site: www.graff.de
Key Personnel
Contact: Joachim Wrensch; Thomas Wrensch
Founded: 1867
Type of Business: Major Independent Bookseller

Otto Harrassowitz Wissenschaftliche Buchhandlung & Zeitschriftenagentur
Taunusstr 5, 65183 Wiesbaden
Mailing Address: D-65174 Wiesbaden
Tel: (0611) 5300 *Fax:* (0611) 530560
E-mail: service@harrassowitz.de
Web Site: www.harrassowitz.de
Key Personnel
Dir & Managing Partner: Dr Knut Dorn
   Tel: (0611) 530200 *E-mail:* kdorn@harrassowitz.de
EDP: Friedemann Weigel
Administrative Dir: Detlef Dorn
Accounting & Finances: Ruth Becker
Founded: 1872
Service of Books & Scientific Journals to Academic & Research Libraries.
Subjects: Library Service Agency
Type of Business: Exporter, Importer, Major Independent Bookseller
Owned by: Ruth Becker, Dr Knut Dorn, Friedemann Weigel

Anton Hiersemann, Verlag
Postfach 140155, 70071 Stuttgart
Tel: (0711) 638264; (0711) 638265 *Fax:* (0711) 6369010
Key Personnel
Contact: Karl G Hiersemann
Founded: 1884
Owned by: Dr Ernst Hauswedell und Co

Heinrich Hugendubel
Verlagshaus Holzstr 28, 80469 Munich
Tel: (089) 2355860 *Fax:* (089) 23558611 *Cable:* HUGENDUBEL MUNICH

Iberoamericana Editorial Vervuert
Wielandstr 40, 60318 Frankfurt am Main
Tel: (069) 5974617 *Fax:* (069) 5978743
E-mail: info@iberoamericanalibros.com
Web Site: www.ibero-americana.net
Founded: 1975
Specialize in books & journals, Latin American & Spanish books.
Type of Business: Distributor, Exporter, Importer, Major Independent Bookseller
Parent Company: Iberoamericana de Libros y Ediciones, Amor de Dios 1, E-28014 Madrid, Spain

Koch, Neff und Oetinger & Co
Schockenriedstr 39, 70565 Stuttgart
Tel: (0711) 7860-0
Telex: 07255684 knov d stgt
Wholesaler.

Kreuz Verlag GmbH & Co KG
Breitwiesenstr 30, 70565 Stuttgart
Mailing Address: Postfach 800669, 70506 Stuttgart
Tel: (0711) 7880321 *Fax:* (0711) 7880310
E-mail: service@kreuzverlag.de
Web Site: www.kreuzverlag.de
Key Personnel
Sales: Heike Donner
Manager: Bernd Friedrich; Sabine Schubert; Olaf Carstens
Editor: Thomas Schmitz
Management Assistant: Sandra Kerschowsky
   Tel: 0711 788 03 51 *E-mail:* kerschowsky@kreuzverlag.de
Founded: 1945
Owned by: Verlagsgruppe Dornier, Dircksenstr 48, 10178 Berlin

Lange & Springer Antiquariat
Otto-Suhr-Allee 26/28, 10585 Berlin
Tel: (030) 340050; (030) 3422011 *Fax:* (030) 3405140
Web Site: www.lange-springer-antiquariat.de
Founded: 1980
Type of Business: Major Independent Bookseller

Leipziger Kommissions- und Grossbuchhandelsgesellschaft mbH, see LKG (Leipziger Kommissions- und Grossbuchhandelsgesellschaft mbH)

Georg Lingenbrink GmbH & Co, Libri
Friedensallee 273, 22763 Hamburg
Tel: (040) 853 98 0 *Fax:* (040) 853 98 300
E-mail: libri@libri.de
Web Site: www.libri.de
Key Personnel
Manager: Alfred Becht; Holger Bellmann; Dr Markus Conrad; Dr Gerhard Dust; Marga Winkler
Founded: 1928
Type of Business: Exporter, Importer, Wholesaler
Branch Office(s)
August-Schanz-Str 33, 60433 Frankfurt *Tel:* (069) 954 22 0 *Fax:* (069) 954 22 300
Europeallee, 36244 Bad Hersfeld *Tel:* (06621) 890 *Fax:* (06621) 89 13 12

LKG (Leipziger Kommissions- und Grossbuchhandelsgesellschaft mbH)
Poetzschauer Weg, 04579 Espenhain (bei Leipzig)
Tel: (034206) 650 *Fax:* (034206) 72361
E-mail: lkg.verlagsauslieferung@t-online.de
Key Personnel
Dir: Juergen Petry

Founded: 1946
Type of Business: Distributor, Exporter

J A Mayersche Buchhandlung GmbH & Co KG Abt Verlag
Matthiashofstr 28-30, 52064 Aachen
Mailing Address: Postfach 467, 52062 Aachen
Tel: (0241) 47770 *Fax:* (0241) 4777167
E-mail: info@mayersche.de
Key Personnel
Man Dir, Publicity: Helmut Falter
Founded: 1817
Branch offices in Cologne, Duisburg & Monchengladbach.
Type of Business: Distributor, Exporter, Importer, Major Independent Bookseller
Owned by: Helmut Falter

Minerva KG Internationale Fachliteratur fur Medizin und Naturwissenschaften Neue Medien
Bunsenstr 6, Postfach 101062, 64210 Darmstadt
Tel: (06151) 9880 *Fax:* (06151) 98839
Key Personnel
Contact: Stefan Gude; Christoph Gude
Founded: 1949
Type of Business: Distributor, Major Independent Bookseller
Owned by: Helmut Gude

Heinrich Petersen Hans Buchimport GmbH
Rugenbarg 256, 22549 Hamburg
Mailing Address: Postfach 530120, 22531 Hamburg
Tel: (040) 8338801 *Fax:* (040) 83388130
Key Personnel
Contact: Johann Christian Peterson

Pociao's Books
Prinz Albrechtstr 65, 53113 Bonn
Mailing Address: Postfach 190136, 53037 Bonn
Tel: (228) 229583 *Fax:* (228) 219507
E-mail: pociao@t-online.de
Web Site: pociaos-books.de
Founded: 1975
Type of Business: Distributor, Exporter, Importer, Major Independent Bookseller
Owned by: Expanded Media Editions Sans Soleil

Sachse & Heinzelmann Kunst- und Buchhandlung GmbH
Georgstr 34, 30159 Hannover
Tel: (0511) 360240 *Fax:* (0511) 324167
E-mail: info@sachse-heinselmann.de
Web Site: www.sachse-heinzelmann.de
Type of Business: Major Independent Bookseller

Sandila Import-Export Handels-GmbH
Sagestr 37, 79737 Herrischried
Tel: (07764) 93970 *Fax:* (07764) 939739
E-mail: sandila@t-online.de
Web Site: www.sandila.de
Founded: 1984
Type of Business: Distributor, Exporter, Importer, Wholesaler

Kurt Scholl
Steinhofweg 20, 69123 Heidelberg
Mailing Address: Postf 104965, 69039 Heidelberg
Tel: (06221) 707661
Founded: 1964
Type of Business: Major Independent Bookseller

SPS Verlaggsservice GmbH
Carl-Mandstr 2, 56070 Koblenz
Mailing Address: Postf 2060, 56020 Koblenz
Tel: (0261) 862662 *Fax:* (0261) 8070654
Key Personnel
Owner: Hansjochen Keilholz

Founded: 1979
Type of Business: Distributor

Stern-Verlag Janssen & Co
Friedrichstr 24-26, 40001 Dusseldorf
Mailing Address: Postfach 101053, 40217 Dusseldorf
Tel: (0211) 3881-0 *Fax:* (0211) 3881280
E-mail: buchhaus-sternverlag@t-online.de
Web Site: www.buchsv.de
Key Personnel
Man Partner: Horst Janssen; Klaus Janssen
Founded: 1900
New & antiquarian/second-hand books; journals.
Type of Business: Distributor, Exporter, Importer
Bookshop(s): Friedrichstr 24-26, 40217 Dusseldorf; Universitatsbuchhandlung, Universitatsstr 1, 40225 Dusseldorf

G Umbreit GmbH & Co KG
Mundelsheimer Strabe 3, 74321 Bietigheim-Bissingen
Mailing Address: Postfach 17 64, 74307 Bietigheim-Bissingen
Tel: (07142) 5960 *Fax:* (07142) 596199
E-mail: edv.bs@umbreit-kg.de
Key Personnel
Man Dir & Associate: Thomas Bez
Assistant Mgr, Buying Department: Martina Schlaud-Weisensee
Contact: Torben Merklinghaus *Tel:* (07142) 596 115
Founded: 1912
Type of Business: Distributor, Wholesaler

Vervuert Verlag, see Iberoamericana Editorial Vervuert

Von Kloeden KG
Wielandstr 24, 10707 Berlin
Mailing Address: Postfach 150745, 10669 Berlin
Tel: (030) 887 125 12 *Fax:* (030) 887 125 19
E-mail: v.kloeden@t-online.de
Web Site: www.vonkloeden.de; www.buchkatalog.de/vonkloeden
Key Personnel
Man Dir, Rights & Permissions: Friedrich Von Kloeden
Editorial: Uta Grabe Von Kloeden
Founded: 1967
Bookshop(s): Berlin

Berthold Winter
Postfach 128248, 10598 Berlin
Tel: (030) 3623530 *Fax:* (030) 3629693
Founded: 1920
Type of Business: Distributor, Exporter, Importer, Wholesaler

Verlags-und Sortimentsbuchhandlung Konrad Wittwer GmbH
Nordbhf Str 16, 70191 Stuttgart
Mailing Address: Postfach 105343, 70046 Stuttgart
Tel: (0711) 25070 *Fax:* (0711) 2507350
Founded: 1867
Type of Business: Major Independent Bookseller
Branch Office(s)
Koenigstr 30, 70173 Stuttgart *E-mail:* buchhans@wittwer.de *Web Site:* www.wittwer.de

Ghana

Ghana Publishing Corporation, Distribution and Sales Division
c/o Publishing Div, Private Post Bag, Tema
Tel: (022) 812921
Branches throughout Ghana.

Presbyterian Book Depot Ltd
Thorpe Rd, Accra
Mailing Address: PO Box 195, Accra
Tel: (021) 663502; (021) 663124; (021) 662415 *Fax:* (021) 665594
E-mail: pcg@africaonline.com.gh
Telex: 2525 *Cable:* BOOKS ACCRA
Key Personnel
Ag Man Dir: E Anim-Ansah
Founded: 1870
The organization comprises bookselling, stationery supply, printing (Presbyterian Press) & publishing activities (see Waterville Publishing House) Newspapers-Christian Messenger & The Presbyterian.
Type of Business: Distributor, Importer, Major Book Chain Headquarters, Major Independent Bookseller, Wholesaler
Owned by: Presbyterian Church of Ghana, PO Box 1800, Accra
Branch Office(s)
PO Box 70, Akim Oda, Mr Boakye Yiadom *Tel:* (0882) 2181
PO Box 219, Koforidua, Ms Makafui Acolatse *Tel:* (081) 22434
PO Box 1999, Kumasi, Mr G K Aboa *Tel:* (051) 28145
PO Box 16, Nkawkaw, S O Lartey *Tel:* (0842) 22010
PO Box 7, Odumase, Mr F T Lowor
PO Box 27, Tamale, K Mate *Tel:* (071) 22382
PO Box 10, Berekum, Mr Francis Yeboan *Tel:* (0642) 22029
PO Box GP 195, Accra, Twum Barima J *Tel:* (021) 663124

Queensway Bookshop and Stores Ltd
Bank Lane, Accra
Mailing Address: PO Box 4276, Accra
Tel: (021) 62707 *Cable:* Success Accra
Key Personnel
Manager: Kwaku Mensah
Suppliers of Educational, Library and HMSO Publications.
Branch Office(s)
Bank St, PO Box 20, Kumasi *Tel:* (051) 4047

University Bookshop
University of Science and Technology, University Post Office, Kumasi
Tel: (051) 60351 *Fax:* (051) 60137
E-mail: ustlib@ust.gn.apc.org *Cable:* KUMASITECH KUMASI
Key Personnel
Manager: Robert Reddick Mensah
Type of Business: Major Independent Bookseller

University Bookshop
University of Ghana, Legon, Accra
Mailing Address: PO Box 25, Legon, Accra
Tel: (021) 500398 *Fax:* (021) 500774
E-mail: addae-mensah@ug.gn.ape.org
Key Personnel
Manager: J B Teye-Adi
Founded: 1950
Type of Business: Major Independent Bookseller
Owned by: University of Ghana, Legon

Gibraltar

Gibraltar Bookshop
300 Main St, Gibraltar
Mailing Address: PO Box 816, Gibraltar
Tel: 71894 *Fax:* 75554

Key Personnel
Manager: A Benady
Type of Business: Distributor, Major Independent Bookseller

Greece

Agyra (Atkypa)
85 Kifissou Ave, 122 41 Athens
Tel: (01) 3455276; (01) 3459321; (01) 3471503 *Fax:* (01) 3474732
E-mail: agyra@agyra.gr
Bookshop(s): Pesmazoglou 5, Athens 105 64
Tel: (01) 3213507

Aithra Scientific Bookstore
One Messologiou St, 106 81 Athens
Tel: (01) 3301269 *Fax:* (01) 3302622
Key Personnel
President: Prof Vangelis Spourdagos
Founded: 1984
Specialize in books of Mathematics, Physics, Chemistry, Astronomy, Geology & Meteorology.
Type of Business: Exporter, Importer, Major Independent Bookseller, Wholesaler

Akti-Oxy Publications
27 b Mithimnis St, 112 57 Athens
Tel: 01 8676125 *Fax:* 01 8644679
E-mail: oxy@compulink.gr
Web Site: www.zoobiolon.com/oxy/
Key Personnel
President: Nikos Hatzopoulos
Vice President: Paris Coutsikos
Editor: Arhondi Korka; Tassos Nickogiannis
Secretary: Tina Anapnioti
Founded: 1995
Experimental, cultural & underground publication.
Bookshop(s): Oxy, Asklipiou 22, 10680 Athens

Alexiadou Vefa
8 Pontou, 54622 Thessaloniki
Tel: (01) 2848086 *Fax:* (01) 2849689
E-mail: vefaeditions@ath.forthnet.gr
Key Personnel
President, Author & Editor: Vefa Alexiadou
Vice President: Koszas Alexiades
Marketing Dir: Alexia Alexiadou
Founded: 1979
Type of Business: Exporter, Wholesaler
Branch Office(s)
Nevrokopiou 16, Thessaloniki

Alpha-Delta
6, Sarantaporou St, 111 44 Athens
Tel: (01) 2280027 *Fax:* (01) 2280027
Key Personnel
President: Dr Ath I Delikostopoulos
Founded: 1966
Type of Business: Wholesaler
Owned by: Alamoheilas Ltd

Anastasiadis Publications
306 Patission St, 111 41 Athens
Tel: (01) 2284013 *Fax:* (01) 2236442
Key Personnel
Contact: Pantelis Anastasiadis
Type of Business: Distributor, Wholesaler

Angeletos Sokzates
68-70 Ipirou St, 163 42 Ilioupoli, Athens
Tel: (01) 9928100 *Fax:* (01) 9940530

Aquarious
One Notara, 106 83 Athens
Tel: (01) 3842354; (01) 3617360 *Fax:* (01) 3303890

GREECE

Athina
43, Emm Benaki St, 106 81 Athens
Tel: (01) 3821308 *Fax:* (01) 3807220
Key Personnel
Contact: Mary G Mavrogianni
Type of Business: Exporter
Owned by: George Mavrogianni, 27, Emm Benaki St, 106 81 Athens

Bacharakis
13 v Konstantinou, 546 23 Thessaloniki
Mailing Address: Imeras 4, 55236 Panorama, Thessaloniki
Tel: (031) 263776 *Fax:* (031) 263776
Founded: 1967
Also Publisher.
Type of Business: Distributor, Wholesaler

Typothito G Dardanos
37 Didotou, 10680 Athens
Tel: (010) 3642003 *Fax:* (010) 3642030
E-mail: info@dardanosnet.gr
Web Site: www.dardanosnet.gr
Founded: 1993
Also acts as Publisher.
Type of Business: Distributor, Exporter, Importer, Major Book Chain Headquarters, Major Independent Bookseller

Diavlos
10 Valtetsiou St, 106 80 Athens
Tel: (01) 3631169 *Fax:* (01) 3617473
E-mail: info@diavlos-books.gr
Web Site: www.otenet.gr/diavlos
Key Personnel
President & Man Dir: Mr E Deligiannakis
Founded: 1988
Publication of scientific, computer, popular science, academic, short guides, humor books.
Type of Business: Distributor, Exporter, Major Independent Bookseller
Bookshop(s): 5 Pesmazoglov St, Athens 10564

Dion
39 Filikis Etaireias, 546 21 Thessaloniki
Tel: (031) 265042 *Fax:* (031) 265083
E-mail: dionbook@otenet.gr
Web Site: www.psarasbooks.gr
Key Personnel
Public Relations: Maria Psara
Founded: 1978
Bookshop & publications.
Type of Business: Distributor, Major Independent Bookseller, Wholesaler
Owned by: Psaras Evangelos
Parent Company: Bookshop Psaras
Showroom(s): Filiuis eterias 39
Bookshop(s): Filiuis eterias 39
Warehouse: Tzabela

Efstathiadis Group SA
3 Agiou Athanasiou St, Attikis, GR 145 65 Athens
Tel: (01) 8131593 *Fax:* (01) 8142915
Telex: 216176
Key Personnel
President: Theodore Efstathiadis
Vice President: Kyriacos Efstathiadis
Marketing Manager: Thanos Efstathiadis
Founded: 1930
Type of Business: Distributor, Exporter, Importer, Wholesaler
Branch Office(s)
14 Valtetsious St, GR-10680 Athens
4 C Cristali St, Antigonidon Sq, GR-54630 Thessaloniki
Bookshop(s): 84 Academias St, GR-10678 Athens; 14 Ethnikis Aminis St, GR- 54621 Thessaloniki

Eleftheri Skepsis
112 Ippokratous St, 114 72 Athens
Tel: (01) 3614736; (01) 3630697

G C Eleftheroudakis Co Ltd
International Bookstore, Constitution Sq, Nikis 4, GA 105 63 Athens
Tel: (01) 3222255; (01) 3229388 *Fax:* (01) 3231401; (01) 3229388
Key Personnel
Man Dir: Virginia Eleftheroudakis-Gregou
Also Publisher.

Enalios
4 El Venizelou, 143 43 Athens
Tel: (01) 2531614 *Fax:* (01) 2184854
Founded: 1996
Type of Business: Wholesaler
Owned by: Eleni Kekropoulou

Erevnites
3-5 Anaxagora St, 105 52 Athens
Mailing Address: 3-5 Gravias St, 10678 Athens
Tel: (01) 5241862; (01) 3622948
E-mail: erevnite@otenet.gr
Founded: 1991

Esoptron
107 Alexandras, 11475 Athens
Mailing Address: Armodiou 14, Athens 10552
Tel: (01) 6441169
Key Personnel
Publisher: Stamos Stinis; Pavlos Voudouris
Type of Business: Wholesaler
Bookshop(s): 49 Panepistimiou Str, 106 78 Athens (Stoa Orfeos)

Eurodiastasi
49 Kallifrona, 113 64 Athens
Tel: (01) 8610071 *Fax:* (01) 8611303
Key Personnel
Sales Manager: Yanni Mitsios
Type of Business: Exporter, Wholesaler
Owned by: Loukia Mitsa & Takis Michalopoulos

Filistor Publishing
31 Themistokleous St, 106 77 Athens
Tel: (01) 3818457
Founded: 1995
Owned by: Charalabos Grammenos

Grivas Publications
3 Irodotou St, 19300 Aspropirgos, Athens
Tel: (01) 5573470 *Fax:* (01) 5573076
E-mail: info@grivas.gr
Web Site: www.grivas.gr
Key Personnel
Man Dir: N Grivas *E-mail:* grivas@otenet.gr
Founded: 1985
Publisher of ELT Book.
Owned by: Nick & Costas Grivas

Harry Joe Patsis' European Publications' Center Ltd
62 Panepistimiou Str, 106 77 Athens
Tel: (01) 3841040; (01) 3841050 *Fax:* (01) 6232194
Key Personnel
Foreign Affairs Dir: Harry Joe Patsis
Contact: Helen Patsis; Theoharis Patsis
Founded: 1996
Type of Business: Distributor, Exporter, Importer, Major Book Chain Headquarters, Major Independent Bookseller, Wholesaler
Showroom(s): 62 Panepistiniou Str, Athens 106 77 (Same location for bookshop)

Iamvlichos
57 Marni St, 104 33 Athens
Tel: (01) 5227678 *Fax:* (01) 5226581

MAJOR

Key Personnel
General Manager: P Michalitsis
Sales Manager: K Pachidis
Founded: 1981
Owned by: P Michalitsis, K Pachidis, K Kalogeropoulos & D Doulgaridis
Bookshop(s): Sirius, Marni S, 10433 Athens

Ikaros
4 Voulis St, 105 62 Athens
Tel: (01) 3225152
Founded: 1943
Owned by: K Karydi & Ch Karydi

Kanakis Publications & Bookshop
24 Z Pigis St, 10561 Athens
Tel: (01) 3302385 *Fax:* (01) 3811902

Kapon Editions
c/o Mrs Rachel Kapon, 23-27 Makriyanni St, Athens 117 42
Tel: 92-35-098 *Fax:* (01) 92-14-089
Web Site: www.kaponeditions.gr
Key Personnel
Contact: Rachel Kapon *E-mail:* kapon_ed@otenet.gr
Founded: 1970
Also publisher.
Type of Business: Wholesaler

Kaufmann SA
9 Mavrokordatu, 106 78 Athens
Tel: (01) 3230320 *Fax:* (01) 3633967
Telex: 218187
Branch Office(s)
Academias 76, 106 78 Athens *Tel:* (01) 3627844
Siha 54 106 72 *Tel:* (01) 3643433

Kritiki
25, Koletti St, 106 77 Athens
Tel: (01) 3836460
E-mail: kritiki@hol.gr

Kyriakidis Brothers sa
11, Kon Melenikou St, 54635 Thessaloniki
Tel: (031) 210-067
E-mail: johukyr@the.forthnet.gr
Type of Business: Major Independent Bookseller, Wholesaler
Owned by: Dimitrios Kyriakidis; Tasos Kyriakidis

Lycabettus Lycabettus Press
54, Afaias St, 154 52 P Psychiko, Athens
Mailing Address: PO Box 17091, Athens 10024
Tel: (01) 6471788 *Fax:* (01) 6710666
Key Personnel
Editor: John Chapple *E-mail:* jchapple@forthnet.gr

Malliaris - Pedia
9 Aristotelous St, 546 24 Thessaloniki
Tel: (031) 278707; (031) 277113 *Fax:* (031) 264856
E-mail: info@mailiaris.gr; malliaris@classic.diavlos.gr
Web Site: www.malliaris.gr
Key Personnel
President: Antonis Malliaris
Founded: 1985
Branch Office(s)
11th Mavromihali Str, Athens *Tel:* (01) 3605874
Bookshop(s): 11th Ag Mina Str, 54624 Thessaloniki

Mavrogianni Publications
27 Emm Benaki & Solonos St, 106 81 Athens
Tel: (01) 3304628 *Fax:* (01) 3304628

Melissa Publishing House
10 Navarinou St, 106 80 Athens
Tel: (010) 3611692 *Fax:* (010) 3600865

1286

E-mail: melissa@compulink.gr
Founded: 1954

Olkos
54 Patias, 107 57 Athens
Tel: (01) 3224131 *Fax:* (01) 3253972
Key Personnel
Contact: Irene Louvzou
Founded: 1973
Type of Business: Distributor, Major Independent Bookseller, Wholesaler
Showroom(s): 5 Pezmantzoglou St, 105 64 Athens
Bookshop(s): 5 Pezmantzoglou St, 105 64 Athens

J M Pantelides Booksellers Ltd
9-11 Amerikis St, 10672 Athens
Tel: (01) 3645608 *Fax:* (01) 3636453
Telex: 224609 Paza gr
Key Personnel
Man Dir: Mrs Maro Pantelides
Founded: 1948
Type of Business: Importer, Major Book Chain Headquarters, Major Independent Bookseller, Wholesaler

Pournaras Panagiotis
12 Kastritsiou Str, 546 23 Thessaloniki
Mailing Address: PO Box 11220, 546 26 Thessaloniki
Tel: (0310) 270941 *Fax:* (0310) 228922
E-mail: pournarasbooks@the.forthnet.gr
Founded: 1962
International library suppliers & publisher.
Type of Business: Distributor, Exporter, Importer, Major Independent Bookseller

Press Photo Publications
38 Armatolon Kai Klefton, 11471 Athens
Tel: (01) 6429166 *Fax:* (01) 6443618
E-mail: photomag@photo.gr
Web Site: www.photo.gr
Founded: 1989
Type of Business: Major Independent Bookseller

Road Editions
41 Ilia Iliou St, 117 43 Athens
Tel: (01) 9296535; (01) 9296541 *Fax:* (01) 9296492
E-mail: road@enet.gr
Web Site: www.road.gr
Key Personnel
President & General Manager: Stephanos Psimenos
Editor: Ioannis Tegopoulos
Founded: 1994
Publish & retailer of maps & travel guides.
Type of Business: Exporter
Bookshop(s): 39 Ippokratous Str, Athens *Tel:* (01) 8613.242 *Fax:* (01) 3614.681; 11 Botsari Str, 16675 Glyfada *Tel:* (01) 8942.587 *Fax:* (01) 8942.582

Salto Publishers
33, Angelaki St, 546 21 Thessaloniki
Tel: (031) 262854 *Fax:* (031) 285879
E-mail: saltos@spocrk.net.gr
Key Personnel
Contact: Marina Mouratidou

Vlassi
15 Z Pigis & 2 Lontou, 10681 Athens
Tel: (01) 3812900 *Fax:* (01) 3827557
Key Personnel
President: Nikos Vlassis
Author: G R Enopoulos; K Palamas; S Melas; Oswalt Kolle
Founded: 1964

Votsis Nikos
16 Emm Benaki St, 106 78 Athens
Fax: (01) 3820646
E-mail: mvotsis@otenet.gr
Founded: 1958
Type of Business: Importer, Wholesaler

IE Zachariadou OHG (Bucherstube)
Prox Koromila 20, GR 54622 Thessaloniki
Mailing Address: PO Box 11269, GR 54110 Thessaloniki
Tel: (031) 276334 *Fax:* (031) 229936
E-mail: info@lillisbookstore.gr
Web Site: www.lillisbookstore.gr
Key Personnel
Owner: Evangelia (Lilli) Zachariadou
  E-mail: lilli@lillisbookstore.gr
Founded: 1972
German Book & Information Center, Greek General bookstore, Italian bookstore.
Type of Business: Exporter, Importer, Major Independent Bookseller

Guatemala

Piedra Santa
5 Calle 7-55, Zona 1, Tercer Nivel, Guatemala City
Tel: (02) 2329053; (02) 2201524; (02) 2201526 *Fax:* (02) 2329053
E-mail: editorialps@yahoo.com
Key Personnel
Dir: Irene Piedra Santa
  E-mail: irene_piedra_santa@hotmail.com
Founded: 1947
Also Publisher.
Type of Business: Distributor, Exporter, Importer, Major Book Chain Headquarters
Showroom(s): 11 Calle 6-50, Zona 1, Guatemala City

Libreria Tuncho Granados G
Apdo Postal 13, Guatemala City
Tel: (02) 24736; (02) 27269; (02) 21181
Branch Office(s)
La Plaza del Sol, Calle Montufar y 2 Ave, Zona 9 Guatemala City CA

Libreria Universal
13 Calle 4-16, Zona 1, Guatemala City
Tel: (02) 28484
Key Personnel
Manager: Olga A de Manrique
Owned by: Distribuidora General Universal

Guyana

Austin's Book Services
190 Church Rd, Company Pass, Cummingsburg, Georgetown
Tel: (02) 77395 *Fax:* (02) 77396
E-mail: austins@guyana.net.gy
Key Personnel
Man Dir: Lloyd F Austin
Founded: 1993
Type of Business: Distributor, Importer, Major Independent Bookseller
Bookshop(s): Austin's Book Services, 190 Church, Cummingsburg, Georgetown

Christian Book Service
242 Albert St & South Rd, Border, Georgetown
Tel: (02) 52521 *Fax:* (02) 54039

Key Personnel
Manager: Wesley Rowe
Type of Business: Major Independent Bookseller
Owned by: Full Gospel Fellowship

National Bookseller
78 Church St, Georgetown
Tel: (02) 71244 *Fax:* (02) 57309

Honduras

Libreria Universitaria Jose T Reyes
Universidad Nacional Autonoma de Honduras, PO Box 3560, Tegucigalpa DC
Tel: 228961 *Fax:* 370575
Telex: 1289

University Library, see Libreria Universitaria Jose T Reyes

Hong Kong

Enterprise International
1604 Eastern Commercial Centre 16th Floor, 393-407 Hennessy Rd, Wan Chai
Tel: 25734161 *Fax:* 28383469
E-mail: hernad@netvigator.com *Cable:* EINPRISE HONG KONG
Key Personnel
Proprietor: C P Ho *E-mail:* heruad@netvigator.com
Founded: 1978

Hong Kong Book Centre Ltd
On Lok Yuen Bldg, Basement, 25 Des Voeux Rd, Central Hong Kong
Tel: 2522 3669 *Fax:* 2868 5079
E-mail: orders@hkbookcentre.com.hk
Web Site: www.swindonbooks.com
Key Personnel
Dir: Annabella Lee
Founded: 1962

Swindon Book Co Ltd
13-15 Lock Rd, Kowloon
Tel: 2366 8555 *Fax:* 2739 4975
E-mail: swindon@netvigator.com
Web Site: www.swindonbooks.com
Telex: 50441 swin hx *Cable:* SWINDON
Key Personnel
Dir: Annabella Li
Manager: Daisy Ky Li
Book & stationery retail & distribution; filofax agency; OECD publications.
Branch Office(s)
University Book Store

Hungary

Talentum Konyves es Kereskedo Kft
Bartok B ut 106/110, Budapest 1113
Tel: (01) 2057077; (01) 2057138
Type of Business: Distributor, Importer, Wholesaler

Iceland

Boksala Studenta (The University Bookstore)
Haskola Islands, V/Hringbraut, Reykjavik IS-101
Tel: 5700777 *Fax:* 5700778
E-mail: boksala@boksala.is
Web Site: www.boksala.is
Key Personnel
Man Dir: Sigurdur Palsson
Buyer: Eysteinn Bjornsson
Founded: 1968
All subjects with a concentration on Academic & Professional Literature, Textbooks.
Type of Business: Distributor, Importer, Major Independent Bookseller
Owned by: Felagsstofnun Studenta

Bokabud Mals og menningar
Laugavegi 18, 101 Reykjavik
Mailing Address: Posthof 392, 121 Reykjavik
Tel: 5515199 *Fax:* 5623523
E-mail: mm@centrum.is
Key Personnel
Manager: Arni Einarsson
Founded: 1937
Type of Business: Distributor, Exporter, Importer, Wholesaler
Owned by: Mal og menning
Branch Office(s)
Sidumula 7-9, 108 Reykjavik

Vaka-Helgafell
Sidumuli 6, 108 Reykjavik
Tel: 5503000 *Fax:* 5503033
Key Personnel
Chairman of the Board: Olafur Ragnarsson
Man Dir: Bernhard Petersen
Dir - Publishing & Rights: Petur Mar Olafsson
Marketing Manager: Kjartan Orn Olafsson
Editor-in-Chief: Bjarni Thorsteinsson
Production Manager: Unnur Agustsdottir
Founded: 1981
Type of Business: Distributor, Importer, Wholesaler
Bookshop(s): Sidumuli 6, 108 Reykjavik

India

Affiliated East West Press Pvt Ltd
105 Nirmal Tower, 26 Barakhamba Rd, New Delhi 110001
Tel: (011) 3264180; (011) 3279113 *Fax:* (011) 3260538
E-mail: affiliat@nda.vsnl.net.in
Key Personnel
Contact: Sunny Malik
Founded: 1962
Expertise in Society Publications/Distribution; Publishers of Undergraduate/Graduate STM Books.
Type of Business: Distributor, Importer, Wholesaler
Owned by: Kamal Malik/Sunny Malik

Allied Publishers Pvt Ltd
1/13-14 Asaf Ali Rd, New Delhi
Mailing Address: PO Box 7203, New Delhi 110002
Tel: (011) 3239001; (011) 3233002; (011) 3233004; (011) 3230067; (011) 3235967
Key Personnel
Man Dir: S M Sachdev
Dir: Sunil Sachdev; Ravi Sachdev
Founded: 1934
Also Printers.
Type of Business: Distributor, Exporter, Importer, Wholesaler
Owned by: Allied Chambers (India) Ltd
Branch Office(s)
Ahmedabad
Bangalore
Calcutta
Chennai
Hyderabad
Lucknow
Mumbai
Nagpur

Atma Ram & Sons
Kashmere Gate, Delhi 110006
Mailing Address: PO Box 1429, Delhi 110006
Tel: (011) 2523082 *Cable:* BOOKS
Key Personnel
Man Dir, Publicity, Rights & Permissions: Ish Kumar Puri
Also Publisher.
Type of Business: Importer

Biblia Impex Pvt Ltd
2/18 Ansari Rd, Darya Ganj, New Delhi 110002
Tel: (011) 3278034 *Fax:* (011) 3282047
E-mail: bibimpex@giasd101.vsnl.net.in *Cable:* ELYSIUM
Key Personnel
Man Dir: P K Goel
Founded: 1980
International bookseller & subscription agent.
Type of Business: Distributor, Exporter

Books & Periodicals Agency
B-1 Inder Puri, New Delhi 110 012
Tel: (011) 5786046 *Fax:* (011) 5795554; (001) 6039477786
E-mail: bpage@de12.vsnl.net.in
Web Site: www.bpagency.com *Cable:* BACKVOLUME
Key Personnel
Proprietor: Girish Gupta
Founded: 1973
Exporter of books on South Asia & Southeast Asia. Over 100,000 titles in 356 subjects at www.bpagency.com.
Type of Business: Distributor, Exporter, Major Independent Bookseller

Books India
J-19/835 Mandir Marg, New Delhi 110 001
Tel: (011) 327 7463 *Fax:* (011) 241 2912
Key Personnel
Dir: Mr Baxi Himanshu
Founded: 1969
Type of Business: Exporter, Major Independent Bookseller

Nem Chand & Bros
Civil Lines, Roorkee 247667
Tel: (01332) 72258; (01332) 72752; (01322) 74343 *Fax:* (01332) 73258 *Cable:* ENGINJOUR
Founded: 1951
Type of Business: Distributor, Exporter, Importer, Major Independent Bookseller, Wholesaler

Current Technical Literature Co (Pvt) Ltd
Devka Mahal, Bank St, Hyderabad 500001
Tel: (033) 331333 *Cable:* Cutelico
Key Personnel
Man Dir: R K Murti
Scientific, technical & medical books.
Branch Office(s)
Calcutta
Hyderabad
Madras
New Delhi

DK Agencies (P) Ltd
A/15-17 DK Ave, Mohan Garden, Najafgarh Rd, New Delhi 110 059
Tel: (011) 535-7104; (011) 535-7105 *Fax:* (011) 535-7103
E-mail: custserv@dkagencies.com
Web Site: www.dkagencies.com
Key Personnel
Dir: Jaswant Rai Mittal; Ramesh K Mittal
E-mail: rkmittal@dkagencies.com
Senior Executive: Surya P Mittal *E-mail:* surya@dkagencies.com
Founded: 1968
Indian books & periodicals. Also multi-media (audio, video, CDs & microfilms from India). Also publisher & subscription agent.
Type of Business: Distributor, Exporter, Major Independent Bookseller, Wholesaler
Branch Office(s)
4788-90/23 Ansari Rd, Daryagarj, New Delhi 110 002 *Tel:* (011) 326-6890
Bookshop(s): 4788-90/23 Ansari Rd, Darya Ganj, New Delhi 110002 *Tel:* (011) 3266890

English Book Store
17-L Connaught Circus, New Delhi 110001
Tel: (011) 3329126 *Fax:* (011) 3321731
Key Personnel
Proprietor: Bhupinder Chowdhri
Importer - military science, aviation, nursing, foreign languages, travel, religion.

E D Galgotia & Sons
c/o Galgotia Publications Pvt Ltd, 5 Ansari Rd, Darya Ganj, New Delhi 110002
Mailing Address: PO Box 7221, New Delhi 110002
Tel: (011) 589334
Telex: 71161 Star In
Key Personnel
Dir: Suneel Galgotia; Neeraj Galgotia
Manager: P Paul
Subjects: Technical, scientific, medical & management
Type of Business: Importer, Major Independent Bookseller, Wholesaler

General Book Depot
1691 Nai Sarak, Delhi 110007
Mailing Address: PO Box 1220, Delhi 110006
Tel: (011) 3263695 *Fax:* (011) 2940861

German Book Centre
32 2nd Main Rd CIT East, Chennai 600035
Tel: (044) 4346244 *Fax:* (044) 4346529
E-mail: germanbk@vsnl.com
Web Site: germanbookcentre.com
Key Personnel
Contact: R Seshadri
Type of Business: Distributor, Importer, Wholesaler

Giri Trading Agency Pvt. Ltd
Member of Booksellers & Publishers of South India
58/2 TSV Koil St, Mylapore, Madras Chennai 600004
Tel: (044) 4943551; (044) 4940376 (Showroom); (044) 4942530 (Showroom); (044) 4953817; (044) 4953823; (044) 4611610 *Fax:* (044) 4953821
E-mail: giritrading@vsnl.com
Web Site: www.giritrading.com
Key Personnel
Dir: T S V Hari *Tel:* (044) 46116110
E-mail: tsvhari@eth.net; T S Srinivasan
Founded: 1951
Producers of audio cassettes specializing in all (A-Z) items pertaining to Hindu Religion; also acts as Publisher of English & all South Indian Language Books. Supply all items pertaining to Hindu worship.
Type of Business: Distributor, Exporter, Major Independent Bookseller, Wholesaler

Owned by: Gitaa Cassettes, T S Ranganathan; Giri Publications; Kamakoti-Tamil Monthly Magazine
Parent Company: Giri Trading Agency
Ultimate Parent Company: Giri Trading Agency Pvt. Ltd
Branch Office(s)
Modi Nivas, Bhandarkar Rd, Matunga, Mumbai 400019 *Tel:* (022) 4141344; 4122316 *Fax:* (022) 4143140 *E-mail:* giri@bom8.vsnl.net.in
Bookshop(s): 10 Kapaleeshwarar Sannadth St, Mylapore, Chennah Madras 600004 *Tel:* 4953820, 4953816

GOYL Saab, Publishers and Distributors, see General Book Depot

Higginbothams Ltd
814 Anna Salai, Madras 600002
Mailing Address: PO Box 311, Madras 600002
Tel: (044) 831-8413 *Fax:* (044) 834-590
Cable: BOOKLOVER
Key Personnel
Dir: K A Arjun
Type of Business: Importer

Hindi Book Centre
4/5-B Asaf Ali Rd, New Delhi 110002
Tel: (011) 3286757; (011) 3274874; (011) 3257220 *Fax:* (011) 3273335; (011) 6481565
E-mail: del.starpub@axcess.net.in *Cable:* STARPUBLIS
Key Personnel
Man Dir: Mr Amarnath
Executive Dir Sales: Mr Anil Varma
General books in Hindi.
Owned by: Star Publications (Pvt) Ltd

Hindustan Book Agency
P19, Green Park Extension, New Delhi 110 016
Tel: (011) 6163294; (011) 6193295; (011) 6163296 *Fax:* (011) 6193297
E-mail: hba@vsnl.com
Web Site: www.hindbook.com
Key Personnel
Partner: D K Jain; J K Jain
Founded: 1947
American Mathematical Society, Birkhauser Verlag, Cambridge University Press, IOP, Kluwer Academic Publisher, Oxford University Press, Princeton University Press, Springer Verlag, Elsevier Science.
Type of Business: Distributor

International Book House Pvt Ltd
91 Mahatma Gandhi Rd, Bangalore 560001
Tel: (0812) 2021634; (0812) 2021795 *Cable:* Interbook
Key Personnel
General Manager: C V Thambi
Manager: N Vijayaraghavan
Adult trade books.
Type of Business: Importer
Branch Office(s)
97 Residency Rd, Bangalore 560025 *Tel:* (0812) 560193
30 Homi Mody St, Bombay 400023 *Tel:* (022) 2044859

Jaicos
121-125 Mahatma Gandhi Rd, Mumbai 400023
Tel: (022) 270621 *Fax:* (022) 264-6412
E-mail: jaicopub@giasbm01.vsnl.net.in
Telex: 118-6398 JAI IN *Cable:* JAICOBOOKS
Key Personnel
Man Dir: Ashwin Shah
Editor: R H Sharma
Type of Business: Importer
Owned by: Jaico Publishing House

Branch Office(s)
Bangalore
Bombay
Calcutta
Delhi
Hyderabad
State Bank Lane, Mount Rd, Madras 600002
Bookshop(s): 127 M G Rd, Opposite Bombay University, Bombay 400023/45

B Jain Publishers Overseas
1920 Chuna Mandi St No 10, Pahar Ganj, New Delhi 110055
Mailing Address: PO Box 5775, Pahar Ganj, New Delhi
Tel: (011) 7536418; (011) 3670430; (011) 3670572 *Fax:* (011) 7536420; (011) 3610471
E-mail: bjain@vsnl.com
Web Site: www.bjainbooks.com
Key Personnel
Owner: Dr P N Jain *Tel:* (011) 2169633 *Fax:* (011) 3683400
Contact: Sh Kuldeep Jain *E-mail:* bjain@nda.vsnl.net.in
Books, handcraft items & globules.
Subjects: Medical, health & new age

Krishnamurthy K
38 Thanikachalam Rd, Madras 600017
Mailing Address: PO Box 384, Madras 600002
Tel: (044) 4344519 *Fax:* (044) 4342009
E-mail: ksm@md2.vsnl.net.in; service@kkbooks.com
Founded: 1944
Type of Business: Importer

The Modern Book Depot
15A, J L Nehru Rd, Calcutta 700013
Tel: (033) 2493102; (033) 2490933 *Fax:* (033) 2497455
E-mail: modcal@vsnl.com
Key Personnel
Owner: Dewan Chand; Prem Prakash
Founded: 1949
Type of Business: Importer, Major Independent Bookseller, Wholesaler
Owned by: Om Prakash
Branch Office(s)
Station Sq, Unit III, Bhubaneswar, 751001 Orissa

Motilal Banarsidass
41-UA Bungalow Rd, Jawahar Nagar, Delhi 110 007
Tel: (011) 391 1985; (011) 391 8335; (011) 397 4826; (011) 393 2747; (11) 393 0689; (11) 579 7221 *Fax:* (011) 393 0689; (011) 579 7221
E-mail: gloryindia@poboxes.com/mlbd@vsnl.com
Web Site: www.mlbdbooks.com *Cable:* GLORYINDIA
Key Personnel
Man Partner: N P Jain
Founded: 1903
Indological books: including Indian literature, religion, philosophy, history, culture etc; also a Publisher.
Type of Business: Distributor, Exporter, Importer, Wholesaler
Branch Office(s)
236, Sri Ranga, Ninth Main III Block, Jayanagar, Bangalore 560 0111
8 Camac St, Calcutta 700 017
120 Royapettah High Rd, Mylapore, Chennai 600004
PO Box 75, Chowk, Varanasi 221 001
Mahalaxmi Chambers, 22 Warden Rd, Mumbai 26
Ashok Raipath, opposite Patna College, Patna, Bihar 800 004
Sanas Plaza, Shop 11-13, 1302 Baji Rao Rd, Pune 411 002

Munshiram Manoharlal Publishers Pvt Ltd
54 Rani Jhansi Rd, New Delhi 110055
Mailing Address: PO Box 5715, New Delhi 110055
Tel: (011) 3671668; (011) 2673750; (011) 7538992; (011) 7536097 *Fax:* (011) 3612745
E-mail: mml@mantraonline.com *Cable:* LITERATURE NEW DELHI
Key Personnel
Man Dir: Devendra Jain
Sales Dir: Ashok Jain; Pankaj D Jain
Founded: 1952
Booksellers & Publishers.
Bookshop(s): 4416 Nai Sarak, Delhi 110006

Narosa Book Distributors Pvt Ltd
6 Community Centre, Panscheel Park, New Delhi 110017
Tel: (011) 6433992; (011) 6433818
E-mail: dlh.narosa@axcess.net.in
Telex: 3161661 *Cable:* NAROSA NEW DELHI
Key Personnel
Man Dir: N K Mehra
Production Manager: M S Sejwal
Marketing Manager: S Mehra
Branch Office(s)
2F-2G Shivan Chambers, 53 Syed Amir Ali Ave, Calcutta 700 019 *Tel:* (033) 477209
306 Shiv Centre, DBC Sector 17, PO KU Bazar, New Bombay 400 705 *Tel:* (022) 7683646
35-36 Greams Rd, Thousand Lights, Madras 600 006 *Tel:* (044) 475362

Navakarnataka Publications (P) Ltd
Embassy Centre 11 Crescent Rd, Kumara Park East, PB 5159, Bangalore, Karnataka 560001
Tel: (080) 203580; (080) 2203581; (080) 2251382
Cable: BOOKCENTRE
Key Personnel
Man Dir: R S Rajaram
Founded: 1960
Subscriptions, Publications.
Type of Business: Distributor, Exporter, Importer, Major Independent Bookseller, Wholesaler
Branch Office(s)
Kempegowda Circle SB Mutt Bldg, Bangalore, Karnataka 560009 *Tel:* (080) 2872385
Moquaddam Trade Centre, Station Road, Gulbarga, Karnataka 585102 *Tel:* (08472) 24302
K S R Road, Mangalore, Karnataka 575001 *Tel:* (0824) 441016
Ramaswamy Circle, Mysore, Karnataka 570024 *Tel:* (0821) 24094

Oxford & IBH Publishing Co Pvt Ltd
N 56 Connaught Circus, New Delhi 110001
Mailing Address: Scindia House, New Delhi 110001
Tel: (011) 3314957; (011) 3320518; (0121) 3313584 *Fax:* (011) 3322639; (011) 3713275
E-mail: oxfordpubl@axcess.net.in *Cable:* INDAMER
Key Personnel
Man Dir: Gulab Primlani
Founded: 1921
Distributing agents for FAO, ICAO, OECD, IDRC.
Type of Business: Exporter, Importer, Major Independent Bookseller, Wholesaler
Owned by: Oxford & IBH Publishing Co Pvt Ltd
Branch Office(s)
17 Park St, Calcutta 700016

Popular Book Depot
217 Raja Rammohan Roy Marg, Mumbai 400 007
Tel: (022) 382 9401; (022) 382 6762
Key Personnel
Partner: Manmohan S Bhatkal *E-mail:* bhatkal@vsnl.com
Founded: 1924

INDIA

Distribution of books, journals & educational aids.
Type of Business: Exporter, Importer
Branch Office(s)
Subscription Division, Saraswati Mandir, Jaganath Shankarshet Rd, Mumbai *Tel:* (022) 3879402
Bookshop(s): Nehru Planetarium, Worli, Mumbai 400018 *E-mail:* bhatkal@vsnl.com

Prints India
Prints House, 11 Darya Ganj, New Delhi 110 002
Tel: (011) 3268645 *Fax:* (011) 3275542
Telex: 31-61087 *Cable:* INDOLOGY
Key Personnel
Contact: V K Gupta
Founded: 1966
Also acts as Subscription Agent & Publisher.
Type of Business: Distributor, Exporter, Major Book Chain Headquarters, Major Independent Bookseller, Wholesaler
Owned by: MD Publications Pvt Ltd Co, MD House, 11 Darya Ganj, New Delhi 110002

Rupa & Co
15 Bankim Chatterjee St, College Sq, Calcutta 700073
Tel: (033) 344821; (033) 346305 *Fax:* (033) 3277294
Telex: 3166641 *Cable:* RUPANCO
Key Personnel
Man Dir: D Mehra
All subjects; also publisher.
Type of Business: Distributor, Exporter, Importer, Wholesaler
Branch Office(s)
G1 & 2 Ghaswalla Tower, P G Solanki Path, Off Lamington Rd, Near Minerva Cinema, Bombay 400 007
POB 7017, Ansari Rd, Daryaganj, New Delhi 110 002
94 South Malaka, Allahabad

Scientific Book Agency
56 D Mirza Ghalib St, Calcutta 700016
Mailing Address: PO Box 239, Calcutta 700001
Tel: (033) 292915; (033) 4642206; (033) 4638273
E-mail: psjs@cal3.usnl.net.in
Key Personnel
Editor: J Sinha; Mrs Prakriti Sinha
Founded: 1954
Also acts as publishers.
Type of Business: Distributor, Exporter, Importer, Major Independent Bookseller, Wholesaler
Bookshop(s): 79/2 Mahatma Gandhi Rd, Calcutta 700009

R R Sheth & Co
PO Box 4060, Ashram Rd, Riverside, Ahmedabad 380009
Tel: (079) 5356573
Key Personnel
Proprietor: Bhagatbhai Bhuralal Sheth *Tel:* (022) 6183182 *E-mail:* ppsheth_co@hotmail.com
Export Manager: P V Katira
Founded: 1926
Gujarati & Hindi Books, also Publisher.
Type of Business: Wholesaler
Branch Office(s)
Opp Phuvara, Gandhi Marg, Ahmedabad 380001 *Tel:* (079) 5356573

Star Publications (P) Ltd
4/5B Asaf Ali Rd, New Delhi 110002
Tel: (011) 3274874; (011) 3268651; (011) 3261696; (011) 3286757 *Fax:* (011) 3273335; (011) 6427181 *Cable:* STARPUBLIS
Key Personnel
Man Dir: Mr Amarnath Varma
All types of Indian Books, in all Indian languages & English

Also acts as publisher.
Type of Business: Distributor, Exporter

Super Book House
Sind Chambers 75 SB Singh Rd, Colaba, Bombay 400005
Tel: (022) 2830446; (022) 2830560 *Fax:* (022) 2834452
Telex: 011-83850
Key Personnel
Contact: Shoaib S Ranalui; M S Lehri
Branch Office(s)
New Delhi
Hyderabad
Bookshop(s): Ideas, 1st Floor, Doli Chambers, Next to Strand Cinema, Bombay 400005

TBI Publishers' Distributors
M-33, Donnaught Place, New Delhi 110 001
Tel: (011) 3322314; (011) 0314039 *Fax:* (011) 3325247
Key Personnel
Contact: Ravi Sabharwal
Founded: 1985
Type of Business: Distributor, Importer, Wholesaler

N M Tripathi Pvt Ltd
164 Shamaldas Gandhi Marg, Mumbai 400002
Tel: (022) 2013651; (022) 2050048
Key Personnel
Man Dir: Kartik R Tripathi
Founded: 1888
Only Gujrati Literature & Publications. Gujrati is a local Indian language.

UBS Publishers' Distributors Pvt Ltd
5 Ansari Rd, New Delhi 110002
Mailing Address: PO Box 7015, New Delhi 110002
Tel: (011) 3273601; (011) 3266645 *Fax:* (011) 3276593; (011) 3274261
E-mail: ubspd@ubspd.com
Web Site: www.gobookshopping.com *Cable:* ALLBOOKS
Key Personnel
Chairman: Mr C M Chawla
Man Dir: Mr Sukumas Das *Tel:* (011) 3276585 *E-mail:* sdas@ubspd.com
General Manager, Export Marketing: Amrit Sharma *Tel:* (011) 3271485 *E-mail:* alsharma@ubspd.com
Dir: M K Kalsi *Tel:* (011) 3245477 *E-mail:* mkkalsi@ubspd.com
Founded: 1963
Type of Business: Distributor, Exporter, Importer, Wholesaler
Branch Office(s)
10 First Main Rd, PO Box 9713, Gandhi, Nagar, Bangalore 560 009 *Tel:* (080) 2253903, 2263901, 2263902 *Fax:* (080) 2263904 *E-mail:* ubspdbng@bgl.vsnl.net.in
No 60, Nelson Manickam Rd, Aminji Karai, Chennai 600029 *Tel:* (044) 3746222, 3746351 *Fax:* (044) 3746287 *E-mail:* vijayan@che.ubspd.com
80 Noronha Rd, Cantonment, Kanpur *Tel:* (0512) 315122
8/1-B, Chowringhee Lane, Kolkata 700 016 *Tel:* (033) 2521821, 2522910, 2529473 *Fax:* (033) 2523027 *E-mail:* ubspdcal@cal.vsnl.net.in

Universal Book Shop
c/o Chugh Publications, PB No 101, 2 Starchey Rd, Civil Lines, Allahabad 21101
Tel: (0532) 603012
Key Personnel
Partner: Ramesh Chugh
Owned by: Chugh Publications

MAJOR

Universal Book Traders
80 Gokhale Market, Opp New Tishazari Courts, Delhi 110 054
Tel: (011) 221966; (011) 741101 *Fax:* (011) 2924152; (011) 7459023
Key Personnel
Partner: M G Arora; Pradeep Arora; Sanjeev Arora; Manish Arora
Founded: 1956
Type of Business: Distributor, Exporter, Importer, Major Independent Bookseller, Wholesaler
Branch Office(s)
C-27/1 Connaught Pl, Middle Circle (between Odcon & Plaza), New Delhi 110001 *Tel:* (011) 3323277

Visalaandhra Publishing House
Vignan Bhavan 4-1-435 Bank St, Hyderabad 500 001 AP
Tel: (040) 4744580 *Fax:* (040) 4735905
Founded: 1953
Publishing & marketing of general books in Telugu language.
Type of Business: Distributor, Importer, Wholesaler
Branch Office(s)
Sultan Bazar, Hyderabad 500 095 *Tel:* 4751462
Visalaandhra Book House, College Rd, Anantapur 515001 *Tel:* 20614
Visalaandhra Book House, Arundelpet, Guntur 522 002 *Tel:* 233297
Visalaandhra Book House, Main Rd, Hanmakonda 506 001 *Tel:* 577156
Visalaandhra Book House, Bank St, Hyderabad 500001 *Tel:* 4602946
Visalaandhra Book House, Kakinada 533 001 *Tel:* 378992
Visalaandhra Book House, Gandhi Rd, Tirupati 517 501 *Tel:* 22475
Visalaandhra Book House, Karl Marx Rd, Vijayawada 520002 *Tel:* 572949
Visalaandhra Book House, Main Rd, Visakhapatnam 530002 *Tel:* 502534

Indonesia

C V Toko Buku Tropen
Jl Pasar Baru 113, Jakarta 10710
Mailing Address: Tromol Pos 3604, Jakarta 10036
Tel: (021) 3811669; (021) 3813543; (021) 3805938 *Fax:* (021) 3800566
E-mail: tropen@cbn.net.id
Telex: 44122 Tropen IA *Cable:* TROPEN
Key Personnel
Manager: Mr Yohan Slamet
Man Dir: Jani Dipokusumo
Founded: 1939
University Microfilm International (UMI), Silver Platter, GALE Group, EBSCO, ProQuest.
Type of Business: Distributor, Exporter, Importer, Major Independent Bookseller, Wholesaler

Effendi Harahap Bookstore
Jl Abimanyu Raya 17-21, Semarang

Gramedia Bookshop
109 Jln Palmerah, Selatan 22, Lantai IV, Jakarta 10270
Tel: (021) 5300545 *Fax:* (021) 5486085
Key Personnel
General Manager: Indra Gunawan
Owned by: PT Gramedia
Branch Office(s)
Jl Merdeka 43, Bandung
Jl Melawai IV/13, Jakarta
Jl Pintu Air 72, Jakarta
Jl Jendral Sudirman 56, Jogjakarta
Jl Basuki Rachmat 95, Surabaya

PT BPK Gunung Mulia (Gunung Mulia Christian Publishing House Limited Company)
Member of CBA
Jln Kwitang 22-23, Jakarta Pusat 10420
Tel: (021) 3901208 *Fax on Demand:* (021) 3901633
E-mail: trade@bpkgm.com
Web Site: www.bpkgm.com
Key Personnel
President & Dir: Ichsan Gunawan
 E-mail: ichsan@bpkgm.com
Finance & Administration Dir: Viveka Nanda Leimena
Founded: 1951
Also publisher & printer.
Type of Business: Distributor, Importer, Major Book Chain Headquarters, Major Independent Bookseller
Owned by: PT BPK Gunung Mulia
Branch Office(s)
Benedict A Salindeho, Jl Cendrawasih 267 B-C-D, Makassar 90134 *Tel:* (0411) 853586 *Fax:* (0411) 855717 *E-mail:* bpkgbupg@indosat.net.id
Carolus Wirto, Jl Genteng Besar No 28, Surabaya 60275 *Tel:* (031) 5342534 *Fax:* (031) 5342534 *E-mail:* bpkgmsby@sbycentrin.net.id
Rejeki Barus, Jl Nibung Il/78, Komp Medan Plaza, Medan *Tel:* (0614) 524157 *E-mail:* bpkgmmdn@indosat.net.id
Showroom(s): Jl Kwitang 22-23, Jakarta Pusat 10420

PT Indira
Jln Borobudur 20, Jakarta
Tel: (021) 3148868; (021) 3904290 *Fax:* (021) 3929373
E-mail: indirawb@mweb.co.id
Importers of General/Trade books & Educational/Scientific/Technical books & textbooks. Library suppliers to foreign libraries of Indonesian printed books; also publisher.
Type of Business: Distributor
Branch Office(s)
Jogjakarta
Bookshop(s): JLn Borobudur 20, Jakarta

Java Books
Kelapa Gading Kirana Block A14 No 17, 14240 Jakarta 10510
Tel: (021) 4515351 (Hunting) *Fax:* (021) 4534987
E-mail: mndl@indo.net.id
Key Personnel
Contact: Mr Eric Oey; Mr Judo Suwidji; Mr Johannes Minarwan
Founded: 1985
Type of Business: Distributor, Importer
Branch Office(s)
Bali
Bandung
Jakarta
Lombok
Medan
Surabaya
Ujung Pandang
Yogyakarta

Pembimbing Masa PT
Pusat Perdagangan Senen, Blok 1, Lantai IV No 2, Jakarta Pusat
Mailing Address: PO Box 3281, Jakarta Pusat
Tel: (021) 367645
Bookshop, subscription agency.
Type of Business: Importer
Owned by: Pembimbing Masa PT
Branch Office(s)
Jl Raya Pajajaran 7, Bogor

PT Pradnya Paramita
Jln Bunga No 8 A Matraman, Jakarta 13140
Tel: (021) 8583369 *Fax:* (021) 8583369
Cable: PRADNYA JKT
Key Personnel
General Manager: Soehardjo
Administration Manager: W Moedjiono
Marketing Manager: M N Supomo
Production Manager: R E S Bujung
Also Publisher.
Branch Office(s)
Jl Kyai Maja 2A, Kebayoran Baru, Jakarta 12120, India

Islamic Republic of Iran

Nayiri Bookshop
1022 Enghelab Ave, Tehran 11339
Mailing Address: PO Box 11365-4631, Tehran 11339
Tel: (021) 677578; (021) 7536802; (021) 7537029 *Fax:* (021) 677578
Key Personnel
President: Sebouh Amirkhanian
Vice President: Mrs Seda Hartounian
Founded: 1931
Printing & Publishing of Magazines, Newspapers, in many languages, Greeting Cards, Gregorian-Armenian Art Calendars.
Type of Business: Distributor, Exporter, Importer, Major Independent Bookseller, Wholesaler

Ireland

AIS
7 Merrion Square, Dublin 2
Tel: (01) 6616522 *Fax:* (01) 6612378
Type of Business: Distributor

Book Stop
Dun Laoghaire Shopping Centre, Dun Laoghaire, Dublin
Tel: (01) 2809917; (01) 2844863
Key Personnel
Manager: John Davey
Branch Office(s)
Blackrock Shopping Centre, Blackrock, Co Dublin
Craysfort Park, Blackrock Teachers Center

The Columba Book Service
55A Spruce Ave, Stillorgan Industrial Park, Blackrock, Dublin
Tel: (01) 2942556 *Fax:* (01) 2942564
E-mail: info@columba.ie
Web Site: www.columba.ie
Key Personnel
Sales Dir: Cecilia West *E-mail:* west@columba.ie
Founded: 1986
Type of Business: Distributor

Eason & Son Ltd
80 Middle Abbey St, Dublin 1
Tel: (01) 8733811 *Fax:* (01) 8730620
Telex: 32566
Key Personnel
Chairman: Michael Ryder
Man Dir: Gordon Bolton
Founded: 1886
Type of Business: Distributor, Importer, Major Book Chain Headquarters, Major Independent Bookseller, Wholesaler

Gill & Macmillan Distribution
10 Hume Ave, Park West Dublin 12
Tel: (01) 500 9500 *Fax:* (01) 500 9599
Key Personnel
Distribution Dir: Dermot O'Brien
 E-mail: dobrien@gillmacmillan.ie
Type of Business: Distributor

Greene's Bookshop Ltd
16 Clare St, Dublin 2
Tel: (01) 6762554 *Fax:* (01) 6789091
E-mail: greenes@iol.ie
Key Personnel
Manager: P K Pembrey *Tel:* (01) 6760476
Founded: 1843
New & Secondhand Booksellers.
Type of Business: Major Independent Bookseller

Fred Hanna Ltd
27-29 Nassau St, Dublin 2
Tel: (01) 6771255; (01) 8720797 *Fax:* (01) 6714330
E-mail: hannas@indigo.ie
Founded: 1907
New & Secondhand Bookseller.
Type of Business: Major Independent Bookseller
Owned by: Fred Hanna & Family (4th Generation)
Bookshop(s): The Campus Bookshop, University College, Belfield, Dublin 4 *Tel:* (01) 2691384 *Fax:* (01) 2837002

Hodges Figgis & Co
56-58 Dawson St, Dublin 2
Tel: (01) 6774754 *Fax:* (01) 6792810; (01) 6793402
E-mail: books@hfiggis.ir
Key Personnel
Manager: Walter Pohli
Deputy Manager: Joseph Collins
Bookstall, National Institute of Higher Education, Dublin 9.
Owned by: EMI Group
Bookshop(s): Dublin City University, Dublin 9

The Library Shop
Trinity College, College St, Dublin 2
Tel: (01) 6081171 *Fax:* (01) 6081016
Web Site: www.tcd.ie/library/shop/
Telex: 93782
Key Personnel
Manager: J G Duffy *Tel:* (01) 608 1650
 E-mail: jduffy@tcd.ie
Type of Business: Major Independent Bookseller

The Mercier Bookshop Ltd
5 French Church St, Cork
Mailing Address: PO Box No 5, Cork
Tel: (021) 275040 *Fax:* (021) 274969
Key Personnel
Manager: Ms M L McNamara
Founded: 1944
Type of Business: Distributor, Exporter, Importer, Major Independent Bookseller, Wholesaler
Owned by: The Mercier Press Ltd
Branch Office(s)
Mercier Library Suppliers, 16 Humet St, Dublin 2 *Tel:* (01) 6615299 *Fax:* (01) 6618583

O'Mahony & Co Ltd
120 O'Connell St, Limerick
Tel: (061) 418155 *Fax:* (061) 414558
Web Site: www.omahonys.ie
Key Personnel
Man Dir: Frank O'Mahony *E-mail:* frank.omahony@omahonys.ie
Chairman: David O'Mahony
Founded: 1902
School & library suppliers.
Type of Business: Major Independent Bookseller

IRELAND

Branch Office(s)
Market Square, Parnell St, Ennis, Co Clare
Tel: (065) 6828355 *Fax:* (065) 6820074
E-mail: ennis.branch@omahonys.ie
University of Limerick Bookshop, National Technological Park, Limerick *Tel:* (061) 202048
E-mail: university.branch@omahonys.ie
Castle St, Tralee, Co Kerry *Tel:* (066) 7122266 *Fax:* (066) 7129442 *E-mail:* tralee.branch@omahonys.ie

Veritas Co Ltd
Veritas House, 7-8 Lower Abbey St, Dublin 1
Tel: (01) 8788177 *Fax:* (01) 8786507
Web Site: www.veritas.ie
Key Personnel
Director: Maura Nyland
Sales & Operations Manager: Maureen Sanders
Owned by: The Catholic Comunications Institute of Ireland
Branch Office(s)
Veritas, Carey's Lane, Cork
Veritas, Calgach Centre, Butcher St, Derry BT48 6PW
Veritas, 83 O'Connell St, Ennis, Co Clare
Veritas, 13 Lower Main St, Letterkenny, Co Donegal
Veritas, Adelaide St, Sligo

Israel

Academon Publishing House
Hebrew University, PO Box 24130, Jerusalem 91000
Tel: (02) 5882163 *Fax:* (02) 5815558
Web Site: www.academon.co.il
Key Personnel
Import Manager: Richard Sherman
E-mail: richard@academon.co.il
Man Dir: Itzik Lary
Founded: 1952
Academic & General Bookstore chain serving Hebrew University.
Type of Business: Importer, Major Book Chain Headquarters

Librairie Francaise Alcheh
55 Nachlat Benyamin St, Tel Aviv 65163
Mailing Address: 30 Burla St, PO Box 23758, Tel Aviv 65163
Tel: (03) 5609817; (03) 5604173 *Fax:* (03) 6994526
Key Personnel
Man Dir: Yohanan Djerassi
Founded: 1939
French & English Books.
Type of Business: Major Book Chain Headquarters
Branch Office(s)
30, Jaffa Rd, Jerusalem
55 Nachlat Benyamin St, Tel Aviv
34, Nordau St, Haifa

Books International
18 Har Pe'er St, Kiryat Gat 82221
Tel: (08) 6880939 *Fax:* (08) 6810244
E-mail: info@booksinternational.com
Web Site: www.booksinternational.com
Key Personnel
Man Dir: Shulamit Koretz
Exporter of Israeli books.
Type of Business: Distributor, Exporter

Eric Cohen Books Ltd
7 Hasadna St, Ra'anana 43650
Mailing Address: PO Box 2325, Ra'anana 43650
Tel: (09) 7478000 *Fax:* (09) 7441497
Key Personnel
Man Dir: Eric Cohen

Dyonon/Papyrus Publishing House of the Tel-Aviv
Tel Aviv University, Entin Plaza, Gate 7, Tel Aviv 61392
Mailing Address: University Student's Union, PO Box 39287, Tel Aviv 61392
Tel: (03) 6410351; (03) 6410352; (03) 6427545 (head office); (03) 6422667 (import office)
Fax: (03) 6423149
Telex: 342171 Versy ll attn Dyonon
Key Personnel
General Manager: Ittamar Herman
Import Manager: Brian Mellick
Founded: 1972
Also publisher.
Type of Business: Distributor, Exporter, Importer, Major Book Chain Headquarters, Major Independent Bookseller, Wholesaler
Branch Office(s)
Bar-Ilan University Campus

F Fischer Book Service
PO Box 7346, Haifa 31071
Tel: (04) 255830 *Fax:* (04) 244970
Key Personnel
Manager: F Fischer
Founded: 1941
Type of Business: Importer, Major Independent Bookseller

Yozmot Heiliger Ltd
3 Yohanan Hasandlar St, Tel Aviv 61560
Mailing Address: PO Box 56055, Tel Aviv 61560
Tel: (03) 528 4851 *Fax:* (03) 5285397
Key Personnel
Dir: Avi Chamo; Jacob Merynger
Founded: 1989
Subscription center, specializing in scientific & medical books.
Type of Business: Distributor, Exporter, Importer, Major Book Chain Headquarters, Major Independent Bookseller, Wholesaler

Israbook
Gefen Publishing House, 7 Ariel St, Jerusalem 91060
Mailing Address: PO Box 36004, Jerusalem 91060
Tel: (02) 5380247 *Fax:* (02) 5388423
E-mail: isragefen@netmedia.net.il
Web Site: www.israelbooks.com
Key Personnel
Publisher: Ilan Greenfield; Dror Greenfield
Founded: 1981
Type of Business: Distributor, Importer, Major Book Chain Headquarters, Major Independent Bookseller, Wholesaler
Owned by: Greenfield

Jerusalem Books Ltd
PO Box 18189, Jerusalem 91181
Tel: (02) 5321973 *Fax:* (02) 5321973
E-mail: jerbooks@netmedia.net.il
Web Site: www.jerusalembooks.co.il/index.html
Key Personnel
Contact: Helen Rivkin
Type of Business: Distributor, Exporter

Lonnie Kahn Ltd
20, Eliyaou Eitan St, Rishon Letzion 75703
Mailing Address: PO Box 49100, Tel Aviv 68105
Tel: (03) 9518418 *Fax:* (03) 9518415; (03) 9518416
Key Personnel
General Manager: Mr Itamar Karlinski

MAJOR

Founded: 1943
Type of Business: Distributor, Importer, Major Independent Bookseller, Wholesaler

Landsberger
9, Ben Yehuda St, Tel Aviv 61261
Mailing Address: PO Box 26192, Tel Aviv 61261
Tel: (03) 5176330 *Fax:* (03) 5222646
Key Personnel
Man Dir: Esther Parnes

Ludwig Mayer Jerusalem Ltd
4 Shlomzion Hamalka St, Jerusalem 91010
Mailing Address: PO Box 1174, Jerusalem 91010
Tel: (02) 6252628 *Fax:* (02) 6232640
E-mail: mayerbks@netvision.net.il
Web Site: www.mayer-books.co.il
Key Personnel
Contact: Marcel Marcus
Founded: 1908
Academic bookstore.
Type of Business: Exporter, Importer

Michlol Ltd
The Technion, Haifa 32000
Tel: (04) 8322970 *Fax:* (04) 8223854
E-mail: ws2@isdn.net.il
Key Personnel
General Dir: Samuel Weissbach
Import Manager: Daniel Ran *Tel:* (04) 8322970

Mossad Harav Kook, see Rav Kook Institute

Palphot Ltd
10 Hahagana St, Herzliya 46100
Mailing Address: PO Box 2, Herzlia 46100
Tel: (09) 9555238 *Fax:* (09) 9555238
E-mail: palphot@palphot.com
Web Site: www.palphot.com
Founded: 1934
Type of Business: Distributor, Exporter, Importer, Wholesaler

Rav Kook Institute
Maimon St, Jerusalem 910066
Mailing Address: PO Box 642, Jerusalem 910066
Tel: (02) 6526231 *Fax:* (02) 6526968
Founded: 1935
Type of Business: Exporter, Wholesaler

J Robinson & Co
31 Nachlat Benyamin St, Tel Aviv 65162
Mailing Address: PO Box 4308, Tel Aviv 65162
Tel: (03) 5605461; (03) 5601626 *Fax:* (03) 5660439
E-mail: rob_book@netvision.net.il
Key Personnel
Man Dir: Yehuda Robinson
Also antiquarian bookseller.
Type of Business: Exporter

Rubin Mass Ltd
7 Ha'Ayin Het St, Jerusalem 91009
Mailing Address: PO Box 990, Jerusalem 91009
Tel: (02) 6277863 *Fax:* (02) 6277864
E-mail: rmass@inter.net.il
Key Personnel
Man Dir: Mr Oren Mass *E-mail:* rmass@inter.net.il
Contact: Ilana Zin
Founded: 1927
Exporter of all Israeli books & periodicals.
Type of Business: Distributor, Exporter, Major Independent Bookseller, Wholesaler

Sifriat Poalim Ltd
24 Kibbutz Galuyot, Tel Aviv 68166
Mailing Address: PO Box 3768, Tel Aviv 61369
Tel: (03) 5183143 *Fax:* (03) 5183191
E-mail: akantor@inter.net.il

Web Site: www.s-poalim.co.il
Also Publisher
Membership: Israeli Book Publishers Association.

Steimatzky Group Ltd
11 Hakishon St, Bnei Brak 51114
Mailing Address: PO Box 1444, Bnei Brak 51114
Tel: (03) 5775777 *Fax:* (03) 5794567
E-mail: info@steimatzky.co.il
Web Site: www.ibooks.co.il; www.booksholyland.com
Key Personnel
Chairman: Eri M Steimatzky
Founded: 1925
Publishers' Representative & Publisher.
Type of Business: Distributor, Exporter, Importer, Major Book Chain Headquarters, Wholesaler

Yavneh Publishing House Ltd
4 Mazeh St, Tel Aviv 65213
Tel: (03) 6297856 *Fax:* (03) 6293638
Founded: 1932
Type of Business: Distributor, Exporter, Importer, Major Book Chain Headquarters, Major Independent Bookseller, Wholesaler
Owned by: Aushalom Orenstein, Nira Prieskel

Italy

Libreria All'Accademia di Randi Lorenzo & Elena snc
Via S Lucia 1, CP 1003, 35139 Padoua
Tel: (049) 8760306 *Fax:* (049) 8751825
Cable: DRAGHI PADOVA
Key Personnel
Manager: Lorenzo Randi; Eleni Randi
Type of Business: Exporter, Importer, Major Book Chain Headquarters, Major Independent Bookseller
Bookshop(s): Libreria Draghi, Via Cavour 17-19, 1, 35122 Padua *Tel:* (049) 8760306 *Fax:* (049) 8751825 (established 1850; general bookshop, foreign dept, art books); Libreria Universitaria, Via 8 Febbraio 10, I-35122 Padua *Tel:* (049) 8757244 (law, literature, university textbooks); Libreria DRAGHI-GALLEIA, Galleria S Lucia 6, I-35122 Padova *Tel:* (049) 8760306 *Fax:* (049) 8751825 (children books, guide books, dictionary, VHS films, gadgets)

Athesia Buchhandlung
Portici, 41, I-39100 Bolzano Bozen
Tel: (0471) 925203 *Fax:* (0471) 925229
Telex: 400161
Key Personnel
Head of Library: Peter Matzneller
Founded: 1907
Type of Business: Distributor, Importer, Major Book Chain Headquarters, Major Independent Bookseller, Wholesaler
Owned by: Athesiabuch GmbH
Branch Office(s)
Bressanone
Brunico
Merano
Silandro
Vipiteno

Casalini Libri
Via Benedetto da Maiano 3, Florence 50014
Tel: (055) 50181 *Fax:* (055) 5018201
E-mail: gen@casalini.it
Key Personnel
Man Dir: Barbara Casalini; Michele Casalini
Also publisher.
Type of Business: Exporter

Libreria Dante di A M Longo
Via P Costa, 39, I-48100 Ravenna
Tel: (0544) 33500 *Fax:* (0544) 217554
E-mail: longo-ra@linknet.it
Key Personnel
Manager: Alfio Longo *Tel:* (0544) 217026
E-mail: longo-ra@linknet.it
Founded: 1950
Type of Business: Exporter, Importer, Major Independent Bookseller
Owned by: Angelo Longo Editore

DEA, see DEA Diffusione Edizioni Anglo-Americane

DEA Diffusione Edizioni Anglo-Americane
Via Lima 28, I-00198 Rome
Tel: (06) 8551441 *Fax:* (06) 8543228
Key Personnel
Contact: Enrico Ligi

Libreria Feltrinelli
Via Andegari, 6, Milan 20121
Tel: (02) 86463485 *Fax:* (02) 72001064
Branch Office(s)
Piazza Porta Ravegnana 1, Bologna
Via Cavour 12-20, 50129 Florence *Tel:* (055) 292196
Via Carlo Alberto 2, Turin

Libreria S F Flaccovio
Via Ruggiero Settimo 37, 90139 Palermo
Tel: (091) 589442 *Fax:* (091) 331992
E-mail: flaccovio@lycosmail.com
Web Site: www.flaccovio.com
Key Personnel
Administrator: Sergio Flaccovio
Manager: Francesco Flaccovio
Founded: 1938
Owned by: S F Flaccovio Editore
Branch Office(s)
Libreria Dante, Quattro Canti Citta, Palermo *Tel:* 091 585927 *Fax:* 091 323103
Piazza Orlando 15, Palermo
Via E Basile 136, Palermo

FMR Ricci
Via Montecuccoli 32, 20147 Milan
Tel: (02) 414101 *Fax:* (02) 48301473
E-mail: ricci@fmrmagazine.it
Key Personnel
President: Franco Maria Ricci *E-mail:* ricci@fmrmagazine.it
Contact: Raffaella Russo
Bookshop(s): 12 rud des Beaux-Arts, Paris 75001, France *Tel:* 01 4633963; Via Farini 27, Bologna 40124 *Tel:* (05) 1231811; Via delle Belle Donne 41/R, Florence 50123 *Tel:* (05) 5283312; Via Durini 19, Milano 20122 *Tel:* (02) 798444; Via Affo 1, Parma 43100 *Tel:* (05) 1287023; Via Borgognona 4/D, Rome 00187 *Tel:* (06) 6793466; Via Carlo Alberto 12, Turin 10123 *Tel:* (01) 15629171

Gregoriana Libreria Editrice
Via Roma, 82, 35122 Padova
Tel: (049) 657493 *Fax:* (049) 662089
Founded: 1922
Type of Business: Major Independent Bookseller
Owned by: Euganea Editoriale Comunicazioni SRL, Via Roma, 82, 35122 Padova
Branch Office(s)
Via Vescovado 33, I-35100 Padua
Piazza Duomo 5, I-35100 Padua

Herder Editrice e Libreria
Piazza di Montecitorio 117/120, 00186 Rome
Tel: (06) 6795304; (06) 6794628 *Fax:* (06) 6784751
E-mail: bookcenter@herder.it; distr@herder.it
Web Site: www.herder.it

Key Personnel
Manager: Bettina Bolli
Administration: Paul Hermann Koellner
Founded: 1925
Book commerce, publishing house & distributor.
Type of Business: Distributor, Exporter, Importer, Major Independent Bookseller

Idea
Via Vigevano 41, 20144 Milan
Tel: (02) 8373949 *Fax:* (02) 8357776
Key Personnel
Publisher: Filippo Passigli

Ilisso Edizioni di Vanna Fois & CSNC
Via Guerrazzi 6, I 08100 Nuoro
Tel: (0784) 33033 *Fax:* (0784) 35413
E-mail: ilisso@ilisso.it
Web Site: www.ilisso.it
Key Personnel
Contact: Tiziana Serra
Founded: 1985
Art Books.
Owned by: Sebastiano Congiu & Vanna Fois

Libreria Editrice Minerva
Vicolodeli Archi 1, I-06081 Assisi
Tel: (075) 812381 *Fax:* (075) 816564

Opus Libri SRL
Via della Torretta 16, 50137 Florence
Tel: (055) 660833 *Fax:* (055) 670604
E-mail: opuslib@dada.it
Key Personnel
Contact: Piero Riccetti
Founded: 1980
Type of Business: Distributor, Exporter, Importer, Major Independent Bookseller, Wholesaler

Libreria Commissionaria Internazionale di Raffaele Pancaldi
Via S Petronio Vecchio 3, 40125 Bologna
Tel: (051) 229466 *Fax:* (051) 229466
Key Personnel
Manager: Raffaele Pancaldi
Founded: 1975
Type of Business: Importer, Major Independent Bookseller, Wholesaler

Libreria Internazionale Patron
Via Badini 12, 40050 Quarto Interiore Bologna
Tel: (051) 767003 *Fax:* (051) 768252
Owned by: Patron Editore SRL

Libreria Rizzoli della Rizzoli Editore SpA
Via Mecenate, 91, 20138 Milan
Tel: (02) 50951 *Fax:* (02) 5065361
Key Personnel
Manager: Aldo Allegri
Owned by: R C S Rizzoli Libri SpA
Branch Office(s)
Libreria Internazionale Rizzoli SRL, Galleria Colonna, Largo Chigi 15, Rome *Tel:* (06) 6796641

Rosenberg e Sellier SpA
Via Doria 14, 10123 Turin
Tel: (011) 8127820 *Fax:* (011) 8127808
Key Personnel
Proprietor: Ugo Gianni Rosenberg; Elvi Rosenberg
International bookseller & subscription agent.
Type of Business: Exporter, Importer

Rux Guru srl
Via Fermi, 26, 06124 Perugia
Tel: (075) 5007227 *Fax:* (075) 5051324
Key Personnel
President: Gastone Chellini
Administrator: Sara Maria Chellini

Founded: 1989
Type of Business: Distributor

Libreria Internazionale Sperling e Kupfer
Via Borgonuovo 24, Milan 20121
Tel: (02) 290341 *Fax:* (02) 6590290
Key Personnel
Manager: Francesco Bogliari

Ulrico Hoepli - Libreria Internazionale
Via Hoepli 5, I-20121 Milan
Tel: (02) 864871 *Fax:* (02) 8052886 *Cable:* HOEPLI MILAN
Key Personnel
Manager: Dr Ulrico Carlo Hoepli; Roberto Taneggi; Susanna Schwarz
Contact: Daniela Grazi
Founded: 1870
Owned by: Casa Editrice Libraria Ulrico Hoepli SpA

Jamaica

Bolivar Bookshop
1D Grove Rd, Kingston 10
Mailing Address: PO Box 413, Kingston 10
Tel: (876) 926-8799 *Fax:* (876) 968-1874
E-mail: bolivar-jamaica@colis.com
Key Personnel
Owner & Manager: Hugh Dunphy
Founded: 1965
Bookshop, Art Gallery & Antique Shop.
Parent Company: Jacaranda Holdings Ltd

Kingston Bookshop Ltd
7 Norman Rd, Lot Complex, Bldg No 10, Kingston 5
Tel: (876) 927-8899 *Cable:* FUTURITY JAMAICA
Key Personnel
Manager: S A R Fuller
Branch Office(s)
The Pavillon Shopping Center, Halfway Tree Kingston

Sangster's Book Stores Ltd
101 Water Lane, Kingston
Mailing Address: PO Box 366, Kingston
Tel: (876) 922-3640 *Fax:* (876) 922-3813
Key Personnel
Man Dir: S Kumaraswamy
Publishing & Publisher Representation.
Owned by: Gleaner Co Ltd, 7 North St, PO Box 40, Kingston
Bookshop(s): Mall, Sovereign, King St, Montego Bay

Times Store Ltd
8-12 King St, Kingston
Tel: (876) 922-4690; (876) 922-4697 *Fax:* (876) 922-4890
E-mail: chesrichards@mail.infocham.com
Telex: 3559
Key Personnel
Manager & Chief Executive Officer: George Faria
Dir: Chester Richards
Founded: 1898

Japan

Academia Scientific Book Inc
Shichi Bldg, 2-10-15 Kasuga, Bunkyo-Ku, Tokyo
Tel: (03) 3819805 *Fax:* (03) 38128509
Key Personnel
Owner: Satoshi Nakai
Branch Office(s)
Ohhomachi Hanahata 3-9-21, Tsukuba-City

Asahiya Shoten Ltd (Booksellers)
Asahi Bldg 17-9, Toyosaki 3-chome, Kita-ku, Osaka 531
Tel: (06) 3131191; (06) 3727251; (06) 3727253 *Fax:* (06) 3755650
Key Personnel
President: Takeshi Hayashima

Bookman's & Co Ltd, *imprint of* Bookman's & Co Ltd

Bookman's & Co Ltd
Member of Japan Association of International Publications
1-18 Toyosaki 3-chome, Kita-ku, Osaka 531-0072
Mailing Address: Central PO Box 1393, Osaka 530-8696
Tel: (06) 6371-4164; (06) 6371-4018 *Fax:* (06) 6371-4174
E-mail: bookman@osk3.3web.ne.jp
Web Site: www.bookmans.co.jp
Key Personnel
President: Mr Mitsunobu Nakamura
Founded: 1967
Art & architecture & graphical, industrial design photography. Textile, fashion, & interior design & human science.
Subjects: Human Science: Art & Architecture, Graphic design Industrial Design, Social Science
Type of Business: Importer, Wholesaler
Owned by: Mr M Nakamura
Imprints: Bookman's & Co Ltd

Christian Literature Society of Japan, see Kyobunkan Inc (Christian Literature Society of Japan)

France Tosho
1-12-9, Nishi-Shinjuku, PO Box 103, Shinjuku-ku, Tokyo 160-0023
Tel: (03) 3346-0396 *Fax:* (03) 3346-9154
E-mail: frtosho@blue.ocn.ne.jp
Key Personnel
Chief of the Purchase Section: Fumisate Konodo
Founded: 1967
Type of Business: Importer, Major Independent Bookseller, Wholesaler

Ikubundo Publishers Co
30-21 Hongo 5-chome, Bunkyo-ku, Tokyo 113
Tel: (03) 8145571 *Fax:* (03) 38145576

Japan Publications Trading Co Ltd (Import and Export)
1-2-1 Sarugaku-cho, Chiyoda-ku, Tokyo 101
Mailing Address: PO Box 5030 Tokyo, International, Tokyo
Tel: (03) 3292-3751 *Fax:* (03) 3290410
E-mail: jpt@po.iijnet.or.jp
Key Personnel
Export Dir: Masatoshi Sato
Import Dir: Akira Sugiyama
President: Satomi Nakabayashi
Founded: 1942
Type of Business: Distributor, Exporter, Importer, Wholesaler

Kaigai Publications Ltd (Kaigai Shuppan Boeki Kabushiki Kaisha)
21 Kanda Tsukasacho 2-chome, Chiyoda-ku, Tokyo 101
Tel: (03) 32924271 *Fax:* (03) 32924278
E-mail: admin@kaigai-pub.co.jp *Cable:* OVERSISPUB TOKYO
Key Personnel
Contact: Hajime Kuroda
Founded: 1949
Type of Business: Importer, Major Independent Bookseller
Branch Office(s)
Sendai
Tsukuba

Kaigai Shuppan Boeki Kabushiki Kaisha, see Kaigai Publications Ltd (Kaigai Shuppan Boeki Kabushiki Kaisha)

Kanda Bookshop
Tanikawa Bldg, 3-2, Kanda Surugadai, Chiyoda-ku, Tokyo 101
Tel: (03) 32553497 *Fax:* (03) 2938005; (03) 32553495
Owned by: Charles E Tuttle Co Inc
Branch Office(s)
American Club Shop, 1-2 Azabu-dai 2-chome, Minato-ku, Tokyo 106 *Tel:* (03) 5848938
Okinawa Plaza Book Shop, 242 Yamazato, Okinawa-shi, Okinawa 904 *Tel:* (0988) 333520

Kinokuniya Co Ltd
17-7, Sakuragaoka 3-chome, Shinjuku-ku, Tokyo 160
Tel: (03) 3354-0131 *Fax:* (03) 3439-3955
Also Publisher.
Type of Business: Distributor, Exporter, Importer, Major Book Chain Headquarters, Wholesaler

KPT InfoTrader Inc
New Asahi Bldg 3F, 2-3-18 Nakanoshima, Kita-ku, Osaka 530-0005
Mailing Address: CPO Box 936, Osaka 530-8694
Tel: (06) 6203 5961 *Fax:* (06) 6222 3590
E-mail: osaka@kpt-infotrader.co.jp
Key Personnel
President: Yositaka Kitao
Man Dir: Norio Komatsu
Founded: 1956
Importing books & periodicals from all over the world, for world-famous enterprises, universities, government organizations, on firm-order basis.
Type of Business: Importer
Branch Office(s)
Tokyo *Tel:* (03) 3573 3031 *Fax:* (03) 3575 4677 *E-mail:* tokyo@kpt-infotrader.co.jp
Tsukuba *Tel:* (0298) 51 8145 *Fax:* (0298) 52 9873 *E-mail:* tsukuba@kpt-infotrader.co.jp

Kyobunkan Inc (Christian Literature Society of Japan)
5-1 Ginza 4-chome, Chuo-ku, Tokyo 104
Tel: (03) 35615549 *Fax:* (03) 35355033
E-mail: kbk_fbd@msn.com
Key Personnel
Vice President: Hideo Usui
Founded: 1885
Branch offices in Fukuoka, Hiroshima, Kanazawa, Kobe, Kyoto, London (UK), Nagoya, New York (US), Okayama, Osaka, Sapporo, Sendai, Singapore, Tsukuba, & Yokohama.
Type of Business: Distributor, Importer, Major Independent Bookseller, Wholesaler

Maruzen Co Ltd
3-10 Nihonbashi 2-chome, Chuo-ku, Tokyo 103-8245
Mailing Address: PO Box 5050, Tokyo International 100-3191
Tel: (03) 3275-8582 *Fax:* (03) 3275-9072 *Cable:* MARUYA TOKYO
Key Personnel
President: Nobuo Suzuki
Executive Dir: Atsushi Suzuki
Senior General Manager: Yusaku Takahashi

BOOK DEALERS — JAPAN

General Manager, Information Resources
  Navigation Division: Tetsuro Konno
  E-mail: t_konno@maruzen.co.jp
Dir, Information Resources Navigatioin Division:
  Nobuji Ebisui
Founded: 1869
Sales of foreign & Japanese books & journals;
  scientific information retrieval services; publishing.
Type of Business: Exporter, Importer
Branch Office(s)
Kanazawa
Kobe
Kyoto

Nankodo Co Ltd
42-6 Hongo, 3 Chome, Bunkyo-ku, Tokyo 113-8410
Tel: (03) 38117239 *Fax:* (03) 38117230
Key Personnel
President: Nobuhiko Hongo
Executive Dir, Foreign Division: Masao Takahashi
Founded: 1879
Also medical publishers.
Type of Business: Distributor, Importer, Wholesaler

Nauka Ltd
30-19 Minami-Ikebukuro 2-chome, Toshima-ku,
  Tokyo 171-8551
Tel: (03) 3981-5266 *Fax:* (03) 3981-5313
E-mail: imp@nauka.co.jp
Web Site: www.nauka.co.jp
Telex: 524432 *Cable:* NAUKAINCO TOKYO
Key Personnel
President: Shuichi Sugawara
Founded: 1952
Type of Business: Distributor, Exporter, Importer,
  Major Book Chain Headquarters, Wholesaler
Bookshop(s): 1-34 Kanda-Jinbocho, Chiyoda-ku,
  Tokyo 101-0051

Nihon-Shoseki Ltd
Member of Japan Association of International
  Publications
12-6 Esakacho 2-chome, Suita City, Osaka 564-0063
Tel: (06) 6386-8601 *Fax:* (06) 6386-8620
E-mail: nihonsho@mtci.ne.jp
Key Personnel
President: Shin Tamaki
Purchasing Manager: I Tamaki
Founded: 1959
Scientific backfiles, rare & modern books, microforms & electromedias.
Type of Business: Distributor, Exporter, Wholesaler
Branch Office(s)
Toyko

Nippon Shuppan Hanbai Inc
c\o Shin-Ochanomisu Bldg, 4-3 Kandasurugadai,
  Chiyoda-ku, Tokyo 101
Tel: (03) 32331111 *Fax:* (03) 32928571
Key Personnel
Contact: Ishikawa Masakatsu
Founded: 1949
Type of Business: Distributor, Exporter, Importer

Osaka Oviss Inc
Central PO Box 292, Osaka 530-91
Tel: (06) 3527090 *Fax:* (06) 3528898
Type of Business: Importer, Major Independent
  Bookseller

Sanseido Bookstore Ltd
Member of Japan Association of International
  Publications
11-8, Kouhoku 7-chome, Adachi-ku, Tokyo 123-0872
Tel: (03) 3896 6332 *Fax:* (03) 5839 0292
E-mail: fbook_stock@mail.books-sanseido.co.jp
Web Site: www.books-sanseido.co.jp
Key Personnel
President: Tadao Kamei
Dir, Sales Dept: Ryosuke Suzuki
Manager: Osamu Suzuki
Founded: 1881
Type of Business: Importer, Major Book Chain
  Headquarters, Major Independent Bookseller
Bookshop(s): 1-1 Kanda Jimbocho, Chiyoda-ku,
  Tokyo 101

Sanyo Shuppan Boeki Co Inc
11-8 Nihonbashi-Kayabacho 1 chome, 3-11-16,
  Nihonbashi Kayabacho 1 chome, Chuo-ku,
  Tokyo 103
Mailing Address: PO Box 5037, Tokyo International 100-31
Tel: (03) 36693761
Key Personnel
President: Takeshi Katsukawa
Senior Man Dir: Koichi Ohnishi
Founded: 1956
Type of Business: Distributor, Importer, Major
  Independent Bookseller, Wholesaler
Branch Office(s)
Niihama
Osaka

Shinko Tsusho Co Ltd
7-1 Wakaba 1-chome, Shinjuku-ku, Tokyo 160
Tel: (03) 33531751 *Fax:* (03) 33532205
Key Personnel
President: Ms Keiko Nagato
Founded: 1960
Type of Business: Distributor, Importer, Wholesaler

Shiseido Booksellers Ltd
Member of Japan Association of International
  Publications
55 Koyama-Minamikazusa, Kita-ku, Kyoto 603-8149
Tel: (075) 4312345 *Fax:* (075) 4326588
E-mail: shiseido@jd5.so-net.ne.jp
Web Site: www.shiseido-book.co.jp
Key Personnel
Dir: Hiromitsu Hori
Founded: 1947
Booksellers for scholars on the field of humanities.
Type of Business: Importer, Major Independent
  Bookseller
Owned by: Mr Shuko Hori

Tohan Corporation
6-24 Higashi Goken-cho, Shinjuku-ku, Tokyo 162
Tel: (03) 32696111 *Fax:* (03)32668943
Key Personnel
President: Hirotaka Kotaki
Manager, Overseas Business Dept: Kainan Tanaka
Overseas Business Development: Takako Yuasa
  Tel: (03) 3266-9593 *Fax:* (03) 3266-8943
Overseas Sales Div: *Tel:* (03) 3266-9573 *Fax:*
  (03) 3266-8943
Also acts as literary agent.
Type of Business: Distributor, Exporter, Wholesaler

Tokyo Publications Service Ltd
Daiichi Takiguchi Bldg, 20-7 Ginza 1-chome,
  Chuo-ku, 100 Tokyo 104
Tel: (03) 35619741 *Fax:* (03) 35619743
Key Personnel
President: Kunio Kihara
Founded: 1968
Type of Business: Distributor, Exporter, Importer,
  Major Independent Bookseller, Wholesaler

Toppan Co Ltd
Toppan Shibaura Bldg, 3-19-26 Shibaura, Minato-
  ku, Tokyo 108-0023
Tel: (03) 5418-2535 *Fax:* (03) 5418-2529
Key Personnel
Chief Executive: Hiroshi Yuri *Tel:* (03) 5418-253
Man Dir: Naomi Yoshikawa
Founded: 1963
Type of Business: Distributor, Importer, Wholesaler
Branch Office(s)
Toppan Company (Singapore) Pte Ltd

Charles E Tuttle Publishing Co Inc
2-6 Suido, 1-chome Bunkyo-ku, Tokyo 112
Tel: (03) 5437 0171 *Fax:* (03) 56894927
Key Personnel
President, Singapore: Eric Oey
Man Dir: Kazuo Maekawa
Publishing Manager & Senior Editor: Erica
  Keirstead
Founded: 1948
English-language books in Japan.
Type of Business: Distributor, Exporter, Importer,
  Major Independent Bookseller, Wholesaler
Branch Office(s)
Boston, MA, United States
Osaka
Rutland, VT, United States
Bookshop(s): Kanda Shop, 1-3 Kanda-Jimbocho,
  Chiyoda-ku, Tokyo 100

United Publishers Services Ltd
Member of Times Publishing Group, Republic of
  Singapore
Kenkyu-sha Bldg, 2-9 Kanda Surugadai, Chiyoda-
  ku, Tokyo 101
Tel: (03) 3291-4541 *Fax:* (03) 3292-8610
E-mail: general@ups.co.jp
Key Personnel
President: Mark Gresham
Vice President: Junichi Takayori
The largest stock holding agent of overseas publishers in the Japanese foreign book market.
Type of Business: Distributor, Importer, Wholesaler
Owned by: Times Publishing Ltd, Singapore

**Yohan (Western Publications Distribution
Agency)**
14-9 Okubo 3-chome, Shinjuku-ku, Tokyo 169
Tel: (03) 3208-0181
Telex: 2324818 Yohan J *Cable:* BOOKYOHAN
  TOKYO
Key Personnel
Chairman: Masahiro Watanabe
President: Masanori Watanabe
Purchasing Dir: Ray Suzuki
Founded: 1953
Books & Magazines, stocklist for publishers.
  Branch offices in Fukuoka, Hiroshima, London,
  Nagoya, Osaka, Sapporo, Sendai, & Yokohama.
Type of Business: Distributor, Exporter, Importer,
  Wholesaler
Branch Office(s)
Nagoya
Osaka
Sapporo

Yushodo Co Ltd
22 Murasakino-Gonoue, Kita-ku, Kyoto 603
Tel: (075) 4619282 *Fax:* (075) 33515855
Telex: 02324136
Key Personnel
President: Mitsuo Nitta
Founded: 1932
Branch offices in Kansai, Ohtsuka, & Toyko.
Type of Business: Distributor, Exporter, Importer,
  Wholesaler

Jordan

Jordan Book Centre Co Ltd
Al-Jubeiha, Amman 11941
Mailing Address: PO Box 301, Amman 11941
Tel: (06) 676882; (06) 606882 *Fax:* (06) 602016
Telex: 21153 *Cable:* JORDAN BOOK CENTRE/ AMMAN
Key Personnel
Chief Executive: I Sharbain
Founded: 1958
Also Publisher.

Jordan Distribution Agency Co Ltd
PO Box 375, Amman 11118
Tel: (06) 4630191; (06) 4630192 *Fax:* (06) 4635152
E-mail: jda@go.com.jo
Telex: 22083 Distag Jo *Cable:* JODISTAG AMMAN
Key Personnel
Chairman: Raja Elissa
General Manager: Wadie Sayegh
Founded: 1951
Type of Business: Distributor, Exporter, Importer, Major Book Chain Headquarters, Major Independent Bookseller, Wholesaler
Owned by: Raja Elissa
Bookshop(s): Hotel Jordan Intercontinental, Amman

Sharbain's Bookshop
Jebel Amman, 1st Cir, Rainbow St, Amman
Mailing Address: PO Box 2427 Amman
Tel: (06) 638709 *Fax:* (06) 699119
Telex: 21153 sharbn jo-Bgrh-Inh *Cable:* SHARBAIN, AMMAN
Key Personnel
Owner: J I Sharbain
Founded: 1963
Type of Business: Distributor, Exporter, Importer, Major Independent Bookseller, Wholesaler

University of Jordan Bookshop
University of Jordan, Amman 11943
Mailing Address: PO Box 13307, Amman
Tel: (06) 843555 (ext 3339) *Fax:* (06) 836446
E-mail: admin@ju.edu.jo
Telex: 21153 *Cable:* UNIVERSITY OF JORDAN BOOKSHOP/AMMAN
Key Personnel
President: J J Sharbain
Founded: 1978
Owned by: JBC Co Ltd
Bookshop(s): PO Box 19903, Amman

Kenya

Book Sales (K) Ltd
PO Box 20377, Nairobi
Tel: (02) 221031; (02) 226543
Key Personnel
Chief Executive: Adrian Louis
Founded: 1976
Also Publishes.

Bookpoint Ltd
Loans House, Moi Ave, Nairobi
Mailing Address: PO Box 46449, GPO 00100 Nairobi
Tel: (02) 211156; (02) 220221; (02) 226680 *Fax:* (02) 211029
E-mail: books@africaonline.co.ke
Key Personnel
Chairman: Mohinderlal Shah
Chief Executive: Sudhir Shah
Dir: Dipak Shah
Retail-Booksellers & Stationers.
Type of Business: Exporter, Importer, Major Independent Bookseller, Wholesaler

City Bookshop Ltd
PO Box 90512, Mombasa
Tel: (011) 313149; (011) 225548 *Fax:* (011) 314815 *Cable:* CITYBOOK
Key Personnel
Man Dir: Moez T Dungerwalla
Founded: 1953
Type of Business: Distributor, Importer, Major Independent Bookseller, Wholesaler

Keswick Books & Gifts Ltd
Bruce House, Kaunda St, Nairobi
Mailing Address: PO Box 10242, Nairobi
Tel: (02) 226047; (02) 331692 *Fax:* (02) 331692
E-mail: keswick@swiftkenya.com
Key Personnel
Chief Executive: Margareta Hakanson
Founded: 1959
Type of Business: Distributor, Importer, Major Independent Bookseller
Branch Office(s)
Gospel Centre, Box 90310, Mombasa

Prestige Booksellers & Stationers
Mama Ngina St Prudential Bldg, Nairobi
Mailing Address: PO Box 45425, Nairobi
Tel: (02) 223515 *Fax:* (02) 2246796
E-mail: prest@iconnect.co.ke
Key Personnel
Chief Executive: R M Upadhyay
Contact: Dipak Upadhyay
Founded: 1972
Type of Business: Exporter, Importer, Major Independent Bookseller

Text Book Centre Ltd
Kijabe St, Nairobi
Mailing Address: PO Box 47540, Nairobi
Tel: (02) 330340 *Fax:* (02) 225779 *Cable:* TEXTBOOKS
Key Personnel
General Manager: C D Shah
Founded: 1964
Also Publisher.
Type of Business: Distributor, Exporter, Importer, Major Independent Bookseller, Wholesaler
Branch Office(s)
Sarit Centre Westlands

University of Nairobi Bookshop
PO Box 30197, Nairobi
Tel: (02) 334244 *Fax:* (02) 336885
Telex: 22095 VARSITY KE; 25561 UNIVIC KE *Cable:* VARSITY
Key Personnel
Contact: Mrs M N Muriuki
Founded: 1974
Bookseller.
Owned by: University of Nairobi

Democratic People's Republic of Korea

Korea Publications Export & Import Corporation
Yokjon-dong, Yonggwang St, Central District, Pyongyang
Tel: (02) 3818536 *Fax:* (02) 3814410
Telex: 36062 CH KP *Cable:* CHULPHANMUL, PYONGYANG
Key Personnel
Dir: Ri Yong
Head of Export Dept: Sin Hak Chol
Head of Import Dept: Jong Yong
Exporter: Mrs Kim Hye Son
Type of Business: Distributor, Exporter, Importer, Major Book Chain Headquarters, Major Independent Bookseller, Wholesaler
Bookshop(s): Changgwang Bookshop, Chollima St, Central District, Dongsong-dong

Republic of Korea

Daejon Trading Co Ltd
783-20 Pangbae-bondong, Socho-ku, Seoul
Tel: (02) 536-9555 *Fax:* (02) 536-0025
Key Personnel
Contact: Yoo Jung-Sun
Founded: 1981
Type of Business: Distributor, Importer

International Publications Service Inc (IPS)
Gongpyong Bldg, 11th Floor, 5-1 Gongpyongdong, Jongro-gu, Seoul 110-160
Mailing Address: KPO Box 496, Seoul 110-604
Tel: (02) 7342666; (02) 7342669 *Fax:* (02) 7336936
Key Personnel
President: Yong-Kook Kim
General Manager: Dong-Hyun Lee
Founded: 1983
Distributions & subscription promotions for foreign publications.
Exclusive distributor for Newsweek, Reader's Digest, National Geographic & 63 other foreign periodicals.
Branch offices in Kwangju, Kyungin, Pusan, Taejon & Taeku.
Type of Business: Distributor, Importer, Wholesaler
Branch Office(s)
Pusan
Kwangju
Kyungin
Taeku
Taejon

IPS Inc, see International Publications Service Inc (IPS)

Kyobo Book Centre Co Ltd
4F Gyobomungo 179, Naesudong Jongro-u, Seoul 110-070
Tel: (02) 333-4570 *Fax:* (02) 735-0030
Key Personnel
President: Kun-Lyu
Dir: Byung Ha-Yu; Seong Ryoung-Kim

Supervisor: Sang Sik-Ahn
Vice President: Mun Jae-Shin
Manager Information Business Team: Mr T K Kim
Type of Business: Distributor, Exporter, Importer, Major Book Chain Headquarters, Wholesaler
Owned by: Kyobo Life Insurance Co Ltd

Panmun Book Co Ltd
40 Chongno 1-ka, Changro-ku, CPO Box 1016, Seoul 110-210
Tel: (02) 720-2859; (02) 733-5300; (02) 924-0733 *Fax:* (02) 735-0376; (02) 953-2456
Telex: K27546 *Cable:* PANMUSE
Branch Office(s)
16 Kwangbok-dong, 1-ka Pusan

Science Publications Centre
201 Taegyeong Bldg 364-28, Habjeong-dong, Mapo-gu, Seoul 121-220
Tel: (02) 3254015; (02) 7336719; (02) 3254017 *Fax:* (02) 3335799

Sophia Book Service
Golden Tower 1319, 191, 2-ka Chung Jung Rd, Sodaemun Ku, Seoul 120-722
Tel: (02) 362-2036 *Fax:* (02) 362-2036
Key Personnel
Owner: Eui-Soon Chang
General Manager: Hwan Kyu Paik
Founded: 1957
Type of Business: Distributor, Exporter, Importer, Wholesaler

Universal Publications Agency Press
UPA Bldg, 54 Gyeonji-dong, Jongro-gu, Seoul 110-117
Tel: (02) 328175 *Fax:* (02) 328176
Telex: K28504 Unipub *Cable:* CHANGHOSHIN SEOUL
Key Personnel
Chairman: Chang-Ho Shin
Also Publisher.
Type of Business: Distributor

Kuwait

The Kuwait Book Shop Company Ltd
Thunayan Al-Ghanem Bldg, PO Box 2942, Safat, El-Kuwait
Tel: 2424687 *Fax:* 2420558
Telex: 30860 *Cable:* FARATOURS
Key Personnel
Owner: Bashir N Khatib

Lebanon

Librairies Antoine SAL/Librairie Antoine, A. Naufal & Freres
Sin El Fil, rue de l'Emir Bashir, BP 656 Beirut
Tel: (01) 481072; (01) 481078 *Fax:* (01) 492625

Librairie du Liban
Imm Esseily Place Riad Alsolh, BP 11-945, Beyrouth
Tel: (0357) 862957 *Fax:* (0357) 9512906
Telex: 45297 Libsay
Key Personnel
Marketing Manager: Pierre Sayegh
Founded: 1944
Also publisher.
Type of Business: Distributor, Exporter, Importer, Wholesaler

Branch Office(s)
42 Bliss St, Beirut
Rubeiz Bldg, Hamra St, Beirut *Tel:* (01) 344070

Lesotho

Mazenod Book Centre
PO Box 39, Mazenod 160
Tel: 350224 *Cable:* Mazbooks
Key Personnel
Manager: Rev Fr M Gareau

Morija Sesuto Book Depot
Church St, PO Box 4, Morija 190
Tel: 76204 *Fax:* 360009
Publishers, Books & Stationery Retailers.
Parent Company: Lesotho Evangelical Church (KEL), PO Box 260, Masery

Liberia

University Bookstore
University of Liberia, Monrovia
Mailing Address: PO Box 9020
Tel: 224671

Lithuania

Giliukas Ltd
S Lozoraicio 13, 3009 Kaunas
Tel: (07) 715950 *Fax:* (07) 709560
E-mail: giliukas@isi.kvn.lt
Key Personnel
Dir: Vyturys Jarutis
Founded: 1991
Type of Business: Distributor, Exporter, Importer, Wholesaler

Humanitas Ltd
Donelaicio 52, 3000 Kaunas
Tel: 07 423664
E-mail: info@humanitas.lt
Key Personnel
Dir: Saulius Stogevicius
Founded: 1994
Type of Business: Distributor, Importer, Major Book Chain Headquarters, Wholesaler
Bookshop(s): Tunstantis ir Viena Naktis Bookshop, Vilnius g 11, 3000 Kaunas; Vilnius Art Bookshop, Vokieciy 2, Vilnius

Luxembourg

Librairie Bourbon
11, rue du Fort Bourbon, L-1249 Luxembourg
Tel: 492206; 405070 *Fax:* 407756
Key Personnel
Manager: Charles Jourdain
Founded: 1982
Owned by: Imprimerie Saint-Paul SA, L-2988

Ernster Sarl
27 rue du Fosse, L-1536 Luxembourg
Tel: 225077-1 *Fax:* 225073
E-mail: librairie@ernster.com

Web Site: www.ernster.com
Key Personnel
Manager: Fernand Ernster *Tel:* 262740 *E-mail:* f.ernster@ernster.com
Founded: 1889
Stationary: supplies for schools, bookshop.
Bookshop(s): Ernster Belle Etoile, L-8050 Bertrange

Librairie Promoculture
14 rue Duchscher, 1424 Luxembourg
Mailing Address: BP 1142, L-1011 Luxembourg
Tel: 480691 *Fax:* 400950
E-mail: promocul@pt.lu
Key Personnel
Dir: Albert P Daming *E-mail:* daming@pt.lu
Founded: 1972
Subscription agency & technical bookshop
Also acts as Book Publisher.
Subjects: Law
Type of Business: Major Independent Bookseller
Owned by: Albert Daming, 4, Avalaon St, Luxembourg L-1159

The Former Yugoslav Republic of Macedonia

Kultura
Bul JNA 68-A, 91000 Skopje
Tel: (091) 111332 *Fax:* (091) 228608
Key Personnel
Dir: Dimitar Basevski
Commercial Dir: Arso Kokaleski
Editor: Branko Cvetkovski
Founded: 1945
Also Publisher & stationery goods supplier.
Type of Business: Distributor, Exporter, Importer, Major Independent Bookseller, Wholesaler

Makedonska kniga
ul 11 Oktomvri bb, 91000 Skopje (Macedonia)
Tel: (091) 224055 *Fax:* (091) 236951
Telex: 51637
Key Personnel
Man Dir: Branislav Mihajlovic
Thirty-one bookshops in Skopje & in all major towns in Macedonia.
Type of Business: Exporter, Importer, Wholesaler
Owned by: Makedonska kniga (Knigoizdatelstvo)

Madagascar

La Librairie de Madagascar
38 Ave de l'Independance, Antananarivo 101
Mailing Address: BP 402, Antananarivo 101
Tel: (020) 22454
Key Personnel
Manager: Yves Balanche
Founded: 1936

Librairie Mixte Sarl
37, rue 26 Jona 1960 Analakely, Antananarivo 101
Mailing Address: BP 3204, Antananrivo 101
Tel: (020) 25130
Key Personnel
Manager: Jean Razakasoa

MADAGASCAR

Librairie Universitaire
BP 566, 101 Antananarivo
Tel: (020) 24114

Societe Malgache d'Edition
route des hydrocabures Ankorondrano, BP 659, Antananarivo
Tel: (020) 2222635 *Fax:* (020) 2222254
E-mail: tribune@bow.dts.mg
Web Site: www.madagascar-tribune.com
Telex: 22340 RAMEX MG TANANARIVE
Key Personnel
Dir of Publication: Rahaga Ramaholimihaso
Founded: 1943
Also Publisher.
Type of Business: Exporter

Trano Printy Fiahyohana Loterana Malagasy
9 ave Grandidier, Antananarivo 101
Mailing Address: T.P.F.L.M., BP 533, Antananarivo
Tel: (020) 223340; (020) 24569
Also Publisher.

Malawi

Central Bookshop Ltd
PO Box 264, Blantyre
Tel: 623534 *Fax:* 633863
Key Personnel
Managing Dir: A Hamid Sacranie
Founded: 1960
School supplies, books, stationary & cards.
Type of Business: Distributor, Importer, Major Independent Bookseller
Branch Office(s)
City Centre, Lilongwe
Bookshop(s): Livingston Ave, Blantyre

CLAIM Bookshop
PO Box 503, Blantyre
Tel: 620839
Key Personnel
Manager: J T Matenje
Sales Manager: E C Mtumbati
Owned by: Christian Literature Association in Malawi

Malaysia

S Abdul Majeed & Co
No 7, Jalan 3/82B, Bangsar Utama, Off Jalan Bangsar, 59200 Kuala Lumpur
Tel: (03) 2832230 *Fax:* (03) 2825670
Key Personnel
Man Dir: A M S Alaudeen
Type of Business: Distributor, Wholesaler
Branch Office(s)
35 Jalan Sekarat, Penang

Antara Publications (M) Sdn Bhd
10th Floor Wisma Muisan, 300 Jalan Raja Laut, 50350 Kuala Lumpur
Tel: (03) 2913188 *Fax:* (03) 2913299
Key Personnel
Man Dir: Kevin Sugumaran
Type of Business: Distributor, Importer, Wholesaler
Owned by: Antara Publications (M) S/B, Singapore
Bookshop(s): BBC English Shop, Lot 2.52, 2nd Floor, Mall Complex, 100 Jalan Putra, Kuala Lumpur

Anthonian Store Sdn Bhd
Wisma Anthonian, 235 Jalan Brickfields, 50470 Kuala Lumpur
Tel: (03) 2747166
Key Personnel
Manager: K Mohanan
Also Publisher.
Branch Office(s)
Units H18/H19A, Phase 1, Level 4, Komploks Tun Abdul Razak, Julan Penang, 10000 Penang
26 Lorong Taman Ipoh Stau, Ipoh Garden South, Ipoh, Perak
26 Jalan Tekawi 5, Bangsar Baru, 59100 Kuala Lumpu *Tel:* (03) 2554596
337 Jalan Melaka Raya, Taman Melaka Raya, 75000 Melaka
68 Jalan Patu Bandar, Tunggal, 70000 Seremban
48 SS 2/67, Sungei Way, Subang, Selangor

AWL Malaysia Sdn Bhd, see Pearson Education

Badan Bookstore Sdn Bhd
28 Tingkat Bawah, Kompleks Tun Abdul Razak, 80000 Johur Bahru, Johor
Tel: (07) 2377562; (07) 2330241; (07) 330241
Key Personnel
Dir: Encik Saadon
Branch Office(s)
63, Jalan Perang, Taman Pelangi, Johor Bahru

Flo Enterprise Sdn Bhd
24 Lorong PJS 1/2A Taman Perangsans Batu 6, Jalan Kelang Lama, 46000 Petaling Jaya
Tel: (03) 7187770; (03) 7187790 *Fax:* (03) 7931066
Key Personnel
Man Dir: Johnny Leong
Type of Business: Distributor, Importer

IBS Buku Sdn Bhd
24 Jalan 20/16A, 46300 Petaling Jaya
Tel: (03) 7760514; (03) 775166; (03) 7751763 *Fax:* (03) 7765551
E-mail: ibss@ibsbuku.po.my
Key Personnel
Man Dir: Mohamed Mustafa
Founded: 1971
Type of Business: Distributor, Exporter, Importer

International Book Service, see IBS Buku Sdn Bhd

Mahir Marketing Services Sdn Bhd
7 Jl 3/82B, Bangsar Utama, Off Jalan Bangsar, 59900 Kuala Lumpur
Tel: (088) 2827372 *Fax:* (088) 718067
Telex: MA 30226 MAHIR
Key Personnel
President: Tham Ban Hing
Owned by: Mahir Holdings Sdn Bhd
Branch Office(s)
Stadrum Shah Alam, Arasi, Quadran B Seksyen 13, Shah Alam Selangor *Tel:* (03) 5501755 (03) 5501442 *Fax:* (03) 5501826

Marican Sdn Bhd
321 Jalan Tuanku Abdul Rahman, 50100 Kuala Lumpur
Tel: (03) 2981133
Telex: MA 31697 Manews *Cable:* Maricanews
Key Personnel
General Manager: C C Lo
Also Publisher.
Type of Business: Wholesaler
Branch Office(s)
171 Middle Rd, Singapore 0718, Singapore
4th Floor, Ruby Warehouse Complex, 8 Kaki Bukit Rd 2, Singapore 1441, Singapore

Mawaddah Enterprise Sdn Bhd
75 Jalan Kapitan Tam Yeong, 70000 Seremban, Negeri Sembilan
Tel: (06) 711062; (06) 722062 *Fax:* (06) 733062
E-mail: azhari@mawadah.pc.my
Key Personnel
Man Dir: Haji Azhari Hamzah
Founded: 1977
Type of Business: Distributor, Exporter, Importer, Wholesaler

MPH Distributors Sdn Bhd
1st Floor Warehouse, Bangunan Luxor, No 5 Jalan Bersatu Sect 13/4, Jalan Bersatu Sect 13/4, Jalan Semangat 46200 Petaling
Mailing Address: PO Box 1076, Jalan Semangat 46792 Petaling
Tel: (03) 7581688 *Fax:* (03) 7565995
Telex: Jcm MA 37402
Key Personnel
General Manager: Francis Heng Siang Goh
Group Financial Controller: Wong Paw
Manager: Kwai Meng Tai
Founded: 1963
Type of Business: Distributor, Importer, Major Book Chain Headquarters, Wholesaler
Owned by: MPH Group Malaysia Sdn Bhd
Bookshop(s): Bukit Bintang Plaza, Jalan Bkt Bintang, 55100 Kuala Lumpur; LG 16 Subang Parade, No 5 Jln SS 16/1, Subang Jaya; LG 30-32 Holiday Plaza, Jalan Dato Sulaiman, Century Garden, 80250 Johor Bahru; E & O Hotel, No 10 Farquhar St, 1000 Penang; 20-B 1, Jalan 20/14, Petaling Jaya; Jaya Supermarket, Section 14, 1st Floor, Petaling Jaya; F11-F13 1st Floor Alpha Angle Jalan R1, Section 1 Bandar Baru Wangsa Maju Kuala, Lumpur; No 2 Lot 22587 Jalan, Telawi Dua Bangsar Baru Kuala, Lumpur

Parry's Book Center Sdn Bhd
60 Jalan Negara Taman Melawati, 53100 Lumpur
Mailing Address: PO Box 60, 53100 Lumpur
Tel: (03) 4079179; (03) 4087235; (03) 4079176 *Fax:* (03) 4079180
Telex: Parry's MA 33243 *Cable:* PABOKCENT
Key Personnel
Dir: Abdul Wahab
Founded: 1993
University & library suppliers.

Pearson Education
3 Jalan Kilang A, Off Jalan Pencala, 46050 Selangor Darul Ehsan
Tel: (03) 7920466 *Fax:* (030) 7918005
Key Personnel
Man Dir: Wong Wee Woon
Type of Business: Distributor, Exporter

University of Malaya Co-operative Bookshop Ltd
Jalan Pantai Baru, 59700 Kuala Lumpur
Mailing Address: PO Box 1127, 59700 Kuala Lumpur
Tel: (03) 7565000; (03) 7565425 *Fax:* (03) 7563246; (03) 7554424
Telex: Unimal MA 39845
Key Personnel
Chairman: Royal Prof Ungku A Aziz
Type of Business: Distributor, Exporter, Importer, Major Independent Bookseller, Wholesaler

Mali

Librairie Deves et Chaumet
BP 64, Bamako

BOOK DEALERS   MEXICO

Malta

Audio Visual Centre Ltd
Mayflower Mansions, Bisazza St, Sliema SLM01
Tel: 330886 *Fax:* 339840
Telex: 1709 *Cable:* AUDVIS
Key Personnel
Owner: Simon Bonello
Founded: 1941
Owned by: Simon & Lydia Bonello

The Ideal Bookshop
Main Gate St, Victoria, Gozo
Mailing Address: PO Box 20, Victoria, Gozo
Tel: 553944
Key Personnel
Manager: A Vassallo
Owned by: A Vassallo and Sons Ltd
Branch Office(s)
Bxara T-Tajba, Charity St, Victoria, Gozo
 Tel: (356) 553944 (Christian Bookshop)

Merlin Library Ltd
Publications Division, Mountbatten St, Blata l-Bajda HMR 08
Tel: 221205; 234438 *Fax:* 221135
E-mail: chrigrup@keyworld.net
Key Personnel
Dir: Arthur J Gruppetta
Founded: 1964
Also Remainder Dealers.
Type of Business: Distributor, Importer, Major Independent Bookseller, Wholesaler

Giov Muscat & Co Ltd
213 St Ursola St, Valletta CMR 01
Mailing Address: PO Box 348, Valletta CMR 01
Tel: 237668; 233879; 247380 *Fax:* 240496
Key Personnel
Man Dir: J A Muscat
Founded: 1874
Type of Business: Importer, Major Independent Bookseller
Bookshop(s): 48 Merchants St, Valletta

Mauritius

Editions de l'Ocean Indien
Stanley, Rose Hill
Tel: 4642955; 4643952; 4643959; 4646761
 Fax: 4643445
Telex: 4739 *Cable:* EOI MAURITIUS
Key Personnel
Chairman: Mr Surendra Bissoondoyal
General Manager: Mr Samrat C Servansingh; Damie Ramtohul
Senior Marketing Manager: Amritlall Kundun
Founded: 1977
Also acts as publisher.
Branch offices in Curepipe, Flacq, Goodlands, Port Louis, & Rose Hill.
Type of Business: Distributor, Exporter, Importer, Major Book Chain Headquarters, Major Independent Bookseller, Wholesaler
Owned by: Government of Mauritius (60%); Longman, United Kingdom; Macmillan, United Kingdom; Nathan, France; EPB, Singapore
Bookshop(s): NPF Shopping Centre, J Koenig S Port Louis; Arcades Rond Point, Rose Hill; Arcades Salaffa, 1st Floor, Curepipe; Arcades Virginie, Flacq; Jugadambi Sharma SSS, Goodlands

Mexico

Libreria Acuario SA de CV
Tehuantepec 34, Col Roma Sur, 06760 Mexico DF
Tel: (05) 5742966; (05) 5741137 *Fax:* (05) 2642882
Founded: 1974
Type of Business: Distributor, Exporter, Importer
Bookshop(s): Ave Baja California 37-B, Col Roma Sur, Mexico 06760 DF

American Book Store SA de CV
Ave Madero No 25, Apdo 79 bis, Mexico
Tel: (05) 5127279; (05) 5127287; (05) 5120306
 Fax: (05) 5186931
Founded: 1928
Type of Business: Importer, Major Independent Bookseller
Branch Office(s)
Circuito Medicos No 2, Ciudad Satelite, 53100 Edo de Mexico *Tel:* (05) 3930682 *Fax:* (05) 5624692
Insurgentes Sur 1636, Col Credito Constructo, 03940 Mexico, DF *Tel:* (05) 6614611 *Fax:* (05) 6615109
Quintana Roo 861, Las Fuentes, Celaya, Gto *Tel:* (0461) 47301 *Fax:* (0461) 47049
Av Eugenio Garza Sada No 2404, Col Roma, Monterrey, NL *Tel:* (08) 3588028

Libreria Bellas Artes
Av Juarez 18, Col Centro, 06040 Mexico DF
Tel: (05) 5182917; (05) 5120947
Key Personnel
Manager: Miguel Noriega
Founded: 1946
Owned by: Editorial Limusa SA de CV

Central de Publicaciones SA
Ave Juarez No 4-B, 06050 Mexico DF
Tel: (05) 5104231
Owned by: Galeria de Arte Misrachi SA, Genova No 20-A, Col Jaurez 06600

Librerias de Cristal, sa de cv (Cristal Bookstores)
Tehuantepec 170, Col Roma Sur, 06760 Mexico 7 DF
Tel: (05) 5746499; (05) 5644100 *Fax:* (05) 2640983; (05) 5644100 ext 287 (fax on demand)
E-mail: biblio10@prodigy.net.mx *Cable:* EDIAPSA
Key Personnel
Dir: Benito Zychlinski
Information Bibliography Manager: Gabriel Rodriquez *Tel:* (05) 5644100 ext 210
Founded: 1939
Bookstores.
Owned by: Editorial Limusa SA de CV
Branch Office(s)
Tehuantepec 170, Col Roma Sur, 06760 Mexico City 49 MX *Tel:* (05) 6008390

Librerias Gonvill SA de CV
8 de Julio, No 825, Guadalajara, JAL 44190
Tel: (03) 6141946 *Fax:* (03) 6132282
Key Personnel
General Dir: Jorge E Gonzalez Villalobos
Administrative Dir: Tirzo F Gonzaez Letechipia
Founded: 1967
Type of Business: Distributor, Exporter, Importer, Major Book Chain Headquarters, Wholesaler

Grupo Cultural Especializado, SA
Av Popocaltepetl 510, Col Xoco, Del Benito Juarez, 03330 Mexico DF
Tel: (05) 6889831 *Fax:* (05) 6889965
Key Personnel
Dir: Mr Adrian Garcia Valades
General Manager: Ing Meliton Cross
Type of Business: Distributor, Importer, Wholesaler

Libreria Hamburgo SA
Insurgentes Sur 58, Mexico
Tel: (05) 5126796; (05) 5218265
Branch Office(s)
Insurgentes Sur 317, Mexico 11, DF *Tel:* (05) 5744015
Ribera de San Cosme 133, Mexico 4, DF *Tel:* (05) 5464736

Libreria Interacademica SA de CV
Ave Sonora 206, Mexico DF 06100
Tel: (05) 265-1165 *Fax:* (05) 265-1164
Telex: 1773596 Aldime *Cable:* LIBINTER
Key Personnel
Administrative Manager: Lourdes Reyes

Librolandia del Centro SA de CV
Matamoros 83 Retorno Gaston Madrid No 4, 83000-18 Hermosillo, Sonora 83000-18
Tel: (062) 135646; (062) 170236 *Fax:* (062) 170236
Key Personnel
Dir: Miguel A Castellanos Araujo
Type of Business: Major Independent Bookseller

MACH, see Mexican Academic Clearing House (MACH)

Mexican Academic Clearing House (MACH)
Colonia Nativitas, Apdo 13-319, 03500 Mexico
Tel: (0915) 6740779; (0915) 6740567
E-mail: hpadilla@spin.com.mx
Key Personnel
Dir General: Lic Hugo Padilla Chacon
Technical Consultant: Ario Garza Mercado
Founded: 1969
Type of Business: Exporter

Libreria Patria
Renacimiento Room 180, Col San Juan Tlihuaca, Mexico DF 02400
Tel: (05) 5613446
Key Personnel
Dir General: Rene Solis
Also Publisher.

Libreria de Porrua Hermanos y Cia, SA
Argentina 15, Apdo M-7990, Mexico DF 06020
Tel: (05) 7025467; (05) 7024574 *Fax:* (05) 7024574; (05) 7024315
E-mail: servicios@porrua.com *Cable:* PORRUAS, MEXICO
Key Personnel
President & Dir General: Jose Antonio Perez Porrua
Founded: 1900
Branch Office(s)
Av Juarez No 16
Bookshop(s): Av Rep, Argentina 15

SCRIPTA - Distribucion y Servicios Editoriales, SA de CV
Copilco 178, Edif 21/501, Col Copilco Universidad, 04340 Mexico DF
Tel: (05) 5481716 *Fax:* (05)5500564
Key Personnel
President & Dir: Bertha R Alavez Magana
Worldwide to academic libraries of scholarly books published in Latin America.
Type of Business: Distributor, Importer
Branch Office(s)
Scripta, 4011 Creek Rd, Youngstown, NY 14174, United States, Book Trade Counsellor: Lyman W Newlin *Tel:* 716-754-8145 *Fax:* 716-754-8145

1299

MEXICO

Servicio a La Iglesia Catolica AC Edicion y Distribucion de Libros Religiosos
Viaducto Tlaplan No 20, Col Ejidos de Huipulco, Mexico
Mailing Address: PO Box 22-897, Tlalpan 14370
Tel: (05) 6710269 *Fax:* (05) 5441675
Key Personnel
President: Mrs Amalia R Pino

Servicios Especializados y Representacionesen Comercio Exterior SA de CV
Norte 198 No 691 Esq, Con Av Tahel, 15510 Mexico
Tel: (05) 7609129; (05) 7605149
Key Personnel
Dir: Filiberto Vargas
Manager: Julia Gutierrez

Mongolia

State Book Trading Office
Leniny gudamch 41, Ulan-Bator
Tel: (01) 22312 *Cable:* Mongolbook

Morocco

Librairie des Colonnes
54 Blvd Pasteur, Tangier
Tel: (099) 936955 *Fax:* (099) 936955
Key Personnel
Dir: Mrs Rachel Muyal
Founded: 1947
Type of Business: Importer, Major Independent Bookseller
Owned by: Nouvelle Societe Kalila wa Dimna

Librairie des Ecoles
12 Ave Hassan II, Casablanca
Tel: (02) 266742; (02) 266743; (02) 266741 *Fax:* (02) 201003
Founded: 1947
Type of Business: Distributor, Exporter, Importer, Wholesaler

Librairie Internationale
70 rue T'ssoule, Rabat (Souissi)
Mailing Address: BP 302-10001, Rabat (Soussi)
Tel: (07) 750183 *Fax:* (07) 758661
Key Personnel
President & Owner: Mohamed Kerouach
Vice President: Brigitte Kerouach
Founded: 1960
Specialize in scientific books, CD-ROMs & multimedia.
Type of Business: Distributor, Exporter, Importer, Major Book Chain Headquarters, Major Independent Bookseller
Owned by: Kerouach Mohamed
Branch Office(s)
V Continents, 3 rue T'ssoule, Rabat (Souissi)

Librairie Livre-Service
40 Ave Allal Ben Abdellah, Rabat
Tel: (037) 724495 *Fax:* (037) 701963
Key Personnel
Executive & General Manager: Faouzi Slaoui
Type of Business: Exporter, Importer, Major Book Chain Headquarters
Bookshop(s): Librairie Livre Service, 11 Rue Tata, Casablanca *Tel:* (022) 262072 *Fax:* (022) 673089 *E-mail:* livser@iam.net.ma

SMER Diffusion
3 rue Ghazza, Rabat
Tel: (07) 723725; (07) 725960 *Fax:* (07) 701643
Telex: 3274
Key Personnel
Dir: Youssef Slaoui
Branch Office(s)
13 Ave Alaouyine, Rabat
Bookshop(s): Librarie Livre-Service, 11 rue Tata, Casablanca *Tel:* (02) 25975; Librarie de L'Agdal, angle Ave de France, Agdal, Rabat

Societe Cherifienne de Distribution et de Presse Sochepress
Angle Rues Rahal Ben Ahmed et St-Saens, Casablanca 21700
Mailing Address: BP 13683, 20300 Casablanca
Tel: (02) 22400223 *Fax:* (02) 22404032
E-mail: infolivre@sochepress.co.ma
Telex: 26660 28019 *Cable:* SOCHEPRESS CASABLANCA
Key Personnel
President, Dir General: Abdallah Lahrizi
Dir: Zhor Alaoui Belghiti; Mohamed Gounajjar; Meriem Kabbaj; Hassan Lahrizi; Maati Taimouri
Type of Business: Distributor, Exporter, Importer, Wholesaler

Myanmar

Hanthawaddy Bookshop
157 Bo Aung Gyaw St, Rangoon
Owned by: Hanthawaddy Book House

Knowledge Book House
130 Bogyoke Aung San St, Yegyaw, Rangoon
Owned by: Knowledge Printing & Publishing House

Sabe U
200 50 St, Rangoon

Sarpay Beikman Bookshop
529 Merchand St, Rangoon
Tel: (01) 83611; (01) 16611
Key Personnel
Manager: U Tin Gyi
Owned by: Sarpay Beikman Board

Sarpay Lawka
233 29 St, Rangoon

Shumawa Book House
146 Bogyoke Aung San Market, Rangoon
Owned by: Shumawa Publishing House

Thwe Thauk
185 48 St, Rangoon

Namibia

Central News Agency (CNA)
Kaiserstra Be Nord Private Bag 13176, Windhoek 9000
Tel: (061) 25625 *Fax:* (061) 227210

ELCIN Book Depot
P/Bag 2013, Ondangwa
Tel: (06756) 40211 *Fax:* (06756) 40211
Key Personnel
Contact: Anna K Kapenda
Type of Business: Major Book Chain Headquarters
Owned by: ELCIN

Swakopmunder Buchhandlung
PO Box 500, 9000 Swakopmund
Tel: (0641) 402613; (0641) 2613 *Fax:* (0641) 404183
Key Personnel
Owner: H U Delius
Founded: 1900
Type of Business: Major Independent Bookseller

Windhoeker Buchhandlung
69 Independence Ave, Windhoek 9000
Mailing Address: PO Box 1327, Windhoek
Tel: (061) 225216; (061) 33479 *Fax:* (061) 225011
Type of Business: Distributor, Importer, Major Independent Bookseller
Owned by: Bertermann

Nepal

National Standards Publisher's and Bookseller's Association Nepal (NASPUBAN)
Kamabakshee Tole, Gha 3-333, Chowk Bitra, Kathmandu 44601
Mailing Address: PO Box 3000, 15B Kathmandu 44601
Tel: (01) 212289; (01) 223036; (01) 224005 *Fax:* (01) 223036
Telex: 3000 1-SB-ASS-NP *Cable:* ANTERPRAGATISHEELSAPHOOPASA KATMANDU NEPAL
Key Personnel
Secretary General: Ganesh Lall Chhipa
Dir: Ganesh Daas Chhipa
Editorial: Aneeta Shobha Tuladhar
Sales: Padma L Tuladhar; Suneeta D Tuladhar; Parbatee S Ranjitkar
Production: Shanta S Ranjitkar
Publicity: Chandrawatee C Ranjitkar
Rights & Permissions: Renooka S Tuladhar
Man Dir: Chandra Lall Ranjitkar
Founded: 1963
Centre for Central General Selling. Order Supplies, Subscriptions & Publications.
Branch Office(s)
09-63-07, Dathwee Chhen Twa Gallee
Chowk Bhitra Purano Bazar, Arniko-Barhabise-9, Arniko Rajmarg-87K M Bagmati Anchal, Barhabise, 45303 Katmandu Mail Centre
Bookshop(s): Janapriya Pustak Bhandar, Patan Dhoka, Lalitpur; Jagriti Books Centre, Itahary Sunsary, Koshee Zone; People's Books Centre, Chenpur, Sakhuwa Sabha, Koshee Zone; People's Books & Periodicals Centre, Datraya Square, Bhaktapur; Banepa Books Depot, Banepa Nayan Bazar, Kavrepalanchok Dist; People's Friendship Books & Periodicals Shop, Dathwee Chhen Twa Gallee, Purano Bazar, Arniko Barhabise 9, Barhabise 45303; Nepal Books & Periodicals House Maisthan Tole, Birganj

Ratna Book Distributors (Pvt) Ltd
PO Box 1080, Bagbazaar, Kathmandu
Tel: (01) 223026
E-mail: rpb@wlink.com.np
Key Personnel
Manager: Govinda P Shrestha
Contact: Roshan P Shrestha
Founded: 1945
Type of Business: Distributor, Importer, Wholesaler

Branch Office(s)
Saraswati Book Centre, Near UNDP Bldg, Pulchowk, Lalitpur, Kathmandu
Ratna Pustak Bhandar, Bhotahity PO Box 98, Kathmandu *Fax:* (01) 248421 *E-mail:* rpb@wlink.com.np

Netherlands

Athenaeum Boekhandel
Spui 14-16, 1012 XA Amsterdam
Tel: (020) 6226248 *Fax:* (020) 6384901
E-mail: info@athenaeum.nl
Web Site: www.athenaeum.nl
Key Personnel
Man Dir: G Schut *Tel:* (020) 6226210 *E-mail:* g.schut@athenaeum.nl
Founded: 1966
Type of Business: Importer, Major Independent Bookseller
Branch Office(s)
Athenaeum Boekhandel Haarlem, Gedempte Oude Gracht 70, 2011 GT Haarlem
Tel: (023) 5318755 *Fax:* (023) 5322603
E-mail: haarlem@athenaeum.nl
Athenaeum Boekhandel Hogeschoolboekhandel, Kohnstammhuis DO.31, Wibautstraat 2-4, 1091 GM Amsterdam *Tel:* (020) 5995553 *Fax:* (020) 4686186 *E-mail:* wibaut@athenaeum.nl

John Benjamins Publishing Co
Klaprozenweg 105, 1033 NN Amsterdam
Mailing Address: Postbus 36224, 1020 ME Amsterdam
Tel: (020) 6304747 *Fax:* (020) 6739773
E-mail: customer.services@benjamins.nl
Web Site: www.benjamins.com
Key Personnel
Dir: John Benjamins
General Manager: Paul Peranteau *Tel:* 215-836-1200 *E-mail:* paul@benjamins.com
Also Publisher & Antiquarian.
Branch Office(s)
Benjamins North America Inc, 821 Bethlehem Pike, Erdenheim, PA 19038, United States
Tel: 215-836-1200 *Fax:* 215-836-1204

Broese BV
Stadhuisbrug 5, 3511 Utrecht
Mailing Address: Postbus 38, 3500 AA Utrecht
Tel: (030) 2335200 *Fax:* (030) 2314071
E-mail: info@broese.net
Web Site: www.broese.net
Telex: 40411 Boek
Key Personnel
Man Dir: H Wijnants
Zandweg 69C, Postbus 783454 ZH de' Meern. Tel: (03406) 64224 Telex: 40411 Boek Fax: (03406) 67670.
Type of Business: Distributor, Exporter, Importer
Owned by: Wolters Kluwer NV
Bookshop(s): Stadhuisbrug 5, 3511 pk Utrecht; Heidelberglaan 2, 3584 cs Utrecht (Uithof)

Bruna BV
Meidoornkade 12, 3990 AE Houten
Mailing Address: Postbus 800, 3990 DV Houten
Tel: (0800) 0230535
E-mail: klantenservice@bruna.com
Web Site: www.bruna.nl
Telex: 47518
Key Personnel
President: J V Hanegem
Owned by: Buehrmann-Tetterode NV
Bookshop(s): A P Standaard Boekhandel (Delft, Zaandam); Boekhandel Bergmans (Maastricht); Boekhandel H Coebergh Haarlem; Boekhandel Hugo Jonkers (Eindhoven); Moderne Boekhandel (Amsterdam); Boekhandel Mosmans ('s Hertogenbosch); Boekhandel Revers en van Brummen (Dordrecht); Boekhandel F Schoth (Boxmeer); Ten Have en Hoofdstadboekhandel (Amsterdam); Boekhandel Van Broek (Zeist); Boekhandel Van Leeuwen (Roosendaal)

Dekker v d Vegt
Marikemstraat 29, 6511 PX Nijmegen
Mailing Address: Postbus 9016, 6500 GT Nijmegen
Tel: (024) 3221010 *Fax:* (024) 3242111
E-mail: mariken@dekker.nl
Key Personnel
Manager: P H M Hooghof
Founded: 1856
Type of Business: Major Independent Bookseller
Owned by: Boehhandels Groep Nederland
Branch Office(s)
Koningstr 31, 6811 DG Arnhem *Tel:* (026) 4452345 *Fax:* (026) 3511018 *E-mail:* arnhem@dekker.nl
Th van Aquinostr 1A, Nijmegen *Tel:* (024) 355127 *Fax:* (024) 3560720 *E-mail:* campus@dekker.nl
Brandstr 23, Sittard *Tel:* (046) 4528100 *Fax:* (046) 4581606 *E-mail:* sittard@dekker.nl

European Book Service
3454 ZJ De Maern, 3454 PK De Meern
Mailing Address: Postbus 130, 3454 PK De Meern
Tel: (030) 6660211 *Fax:* (030) 6662674
Key Personnel
Man Dir: S Valk
Export Manager: R Puyk

Boekhandel Gianotten BV
Postbus 90117, 5000 LA Tilburg
Tel: (013) 4651111 *Fax:* (013) 4635390
Key Personnel
Manager: A J H Gunsing
Owned by: Boekhandels Groep Nederland
Branch Office(s)
Breda
Beneluxlaan 59, 5042 WK T Tilburg *Tel:* (013) 682991
Tilburg

Ginsberg Univ Boekhandel
Breestraat 127-129, 2300 PA Leiden
Mailing Address: Postbus 9003, 2300 PA Leiden
Tel: (071) 124642; (071) 141773 *Fax:* (071) 127505
E-mail: ginsberg@euronet.nl
Key Personnel
Manager: R Egan
Type of Business: Major Independent Bookseller

ICOB/Atrium
Ondernemingsweg 60, 2404 HN Alphen aan den Rijn
Mailing Address: Postbus 392, 2400 AJ Alphen aan den Rijn
Tel: (0172) 437231 *Fax:* (01720) 39379
Key Personnel
Man Dir: Hans Meijer
Publisher: Dennis Friedhoff
Founded: 1965
Also publisher.
Type of Business: Remainder Dealer

Martinus Nijhoff International BV
Koraalrood 50, 2718 SC Zoetermeer
Mailing Address: Postbus 58, 9700 MB Groningen
Tel: (050) 5226286 *Fax:* (079) 615698
E-mail: 100137.3636@compuserve.com
Key Personnel
Managers: Bas Guijt; Peter Van Hout
Promotion Manager: Steven Beij
Founded: 1853
Type of Business: Distributor, Major Independent Bookseller

Nilsson & Lamm BV, Algemene Import Boekhandel
Pampuslaan 212, Postbus 195, 1380 AD Weesp
Tel: (0294) 465044 *Fax:* (0294) 415054
E-mail: nilam@euronet.nl
Key Personnel
Man Dir: P Bleekrode
Sales & Distribution Dir: W J van Loon
Marketing Dir: J Kuijzer
Founded: 1880
Type of Business: Distributor, Wholesaler

Pegasus Publishers & Booksellers
Singel 367, NL-1012 WL Amsterdam
Mailing Address: PO Box 11470, 1001 GL Amsterdam
Tel: (020) 6231138 *Fax:* (020) 6203478
E-mail: pegasus@pegasusboek.nl
Web Site: www.pegasusboek.nl
Key Personnel
Dir: Joop F Yisberg
Founded: 1945
Type of Business: Exporter, Importer, Major Independent Bookseller

Scheltema
Koningsplein 20, 1017 BB Amsterdam
Mailing Address: Postbus 271, 1000 AG Amsterdam
Tel: (020) 5231411 *Fax:* (020) 6227684
E-mail: shv@dds.nl
Web Site: www.scheltema.nl
Key Personnel
General Manager: H Wijnants
Sales Managers: A Luinstra; C Noordhoek; Mrs T Scholtens
Founded: 1853
Type of Business: Major Independent Bookseller
Owned by: Boekhandels Groep Nederland

Schuyt & Co Uitgevers en Importeurs BV
Gedempte Oude Gracht 35, 2011 GL Haarlem
Mailing Address: Postbus 563, 2011 mGL Haarlem
Tel: (023) 5325440 *Fax:* (023) 5327017
Key Personnel
President: Karl C Schuyt
Owned by: Schuyt & Co Beheer BV

Valeton b v
Nes 39, 1012 KC Amsterdam
Tel: (020) 6201454 *Fax:* (020) 6279209
Key Personnel
President: Alexander Valeton
Vice President: Heleen Van Ketwich-Verschuur
Founded: 1990
Type of Business: Distributor, Exporter, Importer, Major Book Chain Headquarters, Wholesaler
Owned by: Alexander Valeton
Bookshop(s): Dam 8, 1012 CG Amsterdam; Westzeeoyk 20, Rotterdam

Van Piere Boeken
Heuvel Galerie 190 & 232, 5600 CE Eindhoven
Mailing Address: PO Box 2200, 5600 CE Eindhoven
Tel: (040) 2444045 *Fax:* (040) 2463945
E-mail: pierboek@euronet.nl
Key Personnel
Manager: Chris de Plot
Founded: 1848
Type of Business: Major Independent Bookseller
Owned by: Van Piere Wristers Booksellers

H de Vries Boeken
Jacoijnestaat 3-7, 2000 AG Haarlem
Mailing Address: Postbus 274, 2000 AG Haarlem
Tel: (023) 5319458 *Fax:* (023) 5311680

NETHERLANDS

Key Personnel
Man Dir: R H C de Vries; K de Vries Kuijper
Manager, General Bookshop: G Braaksma
Manager, School Textbooks: A Kroenburg
Founded: 1905
Type of Business: Major Independent Bookseller

Netherlands Antilles

De WitAruba Boekhandel
L G Smith Blvd 110, Oranjestad, Aruba
Tel: (0297) 823500 *Fax:* (0297) 821575
    Cable: DEWITSTORES
Key Personnel
Man Dir: R de Zwart
Stationery, souvenirs, gifts, clothing.
Type of Business: Distributor, Importer, Major Independent Bookseller
Owned by: De Wit Stores NV

New Zealand

Arts Centre Bookshop
28 Worcester St, Christchurch
Mailing Address: PO Box 845, Christchurch
Tel: (03) 3655277 *Fax:* (03) 3653293
Type of Business: Major Independent Bookseller

Bennetts Bookshop Ltd
38-42 Broadway, Palmerston North
Mailing Address: PO Box 138, Palmerston North
Tel: (06) 3283009 *Fax:* (06) 3282836 *Cable:* Bennibooks
Key Personnel
Group General Manager: Trevor Day
7 Stores nationwide.
Owned by: The Rank Group Ltd
Branch Office(s)
Bennetts University Book Centre Ltd, Private Bag, Massey University, Palmerston North *Tel:* (063) 66020 *Fax:* (063) 66716
Bennetts University Book Centre Waikato Ltd, PO Box 13066, Hillcrest, Hamilton *Tel:* (071) 62255

Blackmore's Booksellers BLA
284 Trafalgar St, Nelson
Tel: (03) 5489992 *Fax:* (03) 5466779
Key Personnel
Partner: Tim Blackmore; Jennifer Blackmore
Type of Business: Major Independent Bookseller

Hedley's Bookshop Ltd
150 Queen St, Masterton
Mailing Address: PO Box 746, Masterton
Tel: (06) 3782875 *Fax:* (06) 3782570
Key Personnel
Manager: David Hedley
Founded: 1907
Also publisher.
Type of Business: Distributor, Major Independent Bookseller
Branch Office(s)
Hedley Australia, 4 Farm Rd, Alphington, Melbourne, Victoria 3078, Australia *Tel:* (02) 4992645 *Fax:* (03) 4994060
Bookshop(s): Hedley's Bookshop (BAM), Mezzanine level, Central Library Bldg, 65 Victoria St, Wellington *Tel:* (04) 4731730 *Fax:* (04) 4711635

Janeff Books (JM & MJ Books Ltd)
16 Te Mata Rd, Havelock North 4230
Tel: (070) 777783
Key Personnel
Owner: Max Dempsey; Margaret Dempsey
Type of Business: Major Independent Bookseller

JM & MJ Books Ltd, see Janeff Books (JM & MJ Books Ltd)

Kydds Paper Plus
66 Hakiaha St, Taumarunui
Tel: (07) 8957430 *Fax:* (07) 8957977
Key Personnel
Owner: Mrs J J Kydd
Type of Business: Major Independent Bookseller

Lincoln University Bookshop
Lincoln Univ, Springs Rd, Canterbury
Mailing Address: PO Box 94, Canterbury
Tel: (03) 3253892 *Fax:* (03) 3253615
Key Personnel
Supervisor: Bronwyn Mclean *E-mail:* mcleanb@lincoln.ac.nz
Type of Business: Major Independent Bookseller
Owned by: Lincoln University

Living Word Distribution
52 Collingwood St, Hamilton 2001
Tel: (07) 839 5607 *Fax:* (07) 834 3916
E-mail: livingword.ltd@xtra.co.nz
Key Personnel
Executive Dir: G T Hooper
Founded: 1977
Subjects: Books, gifts, music & video, retailer
Type of Business: Distributor, Exporter, Importer, Major Independent Bookseller, Wholesaler
Parent Company: Living Word Distributors Ltd

McLeods Booksellers
Hinemoa Centre Hinemoa St, Rotorua
Mailing Address: PO Box 623, Rotorua
Tel: (07) 3485388 *Fax:* (07) 3490288
E-mail: mcleods@clear.net.nz
Web Site: www.mcleodsbooks.co.nz
Key Personnel
Manager: D C Thorp
Founded: 1944
Traditional, stock-holding combining selection & service with latest bibliographic technology. Specialise in: Maori books & floral art books.
Type of Business: Major Independent Bookseller

Omega Distributors Ltd
10 Andrew Baxter Dr, Mangere, 1701 Auckland
Mailing Address: PO Box 107025, Airport Oaks Mangere, 1730 Auckland
Tel: (09) 2570081 *Fax:* (09) 2570082
E-mail: books@omegavision.co.nz
Key Personnel
Executive Dir: Graham Walker
General Manager: M J Frith
Founded: 1958
Christian Book/Bible/Gift Distributors
Memberships: Booksellers Association of New Zealand; Christian Booksellers Association of New Zealand.
Type of Business: Distributor, Importer
Owned by: Vision Resources Ltd

One Way Book Centre
122 Manchester St, Christchurch 1
Tel: (03) 3663657 *Fax:* (03) 3664445
Key Personnel
Manager: Bruce McFarlane
Type of Business: Distributor, Importer, Major Independent Bookseller, Wholesaler

Pathfinder Bookshop
38 Lorne St, Auckland

MAJOR

Mailing Address: PO Box 1050000, Auckland
Tel: (09) 3790147 *Fax:* (09) 3098167
Founded: 1981
Type of Business: Major Independent Bookseller

Peaceful Living Publications
Unit 7B 42 Courtney Rd, Tauranga, BOP
Mailing Address: PO Box 300, Tauranga, BOP
Tel: (071) 5718105 *Fax:* (071) 5718513
E-mail: books@peaceful-living.co.nz
Key Personnel
Manager: Wayne Morgan
Office Manager: Maria Rawson
Metaphysics, mysticism, health, tarot cards, audio cassettes & CDs, self awareness & New Age literature.
Type of Business: Distributor

School Supplies Limited
Symonds St, Auckland
Tel: (09) 3023215 *Fax:* (09) 3023209
Telex: NZ 63426
Key Personnel
General Manager: Graham Wadams
Curriculum Resource Manager: Michaela Davis
Type of Business: Distributor, Importer, Wholesaler
Owned by: Whitcoulls Group Ltd, 186 Queen St, Private Bag, Auckland 92028

South Pacific Books Imports Ltd
PO Box 68-097, Newton, Auckland 2
Tel: (09) 3762142 *Fax:* (09) 3762141
E-mail: sales@soupacbooks.co.nz
Web Site: www.soupacbooks.co.nz
Key Personnel
Man Dir: Alan McEldowney
Founded: 1984
Book wholesaler.
Warehouse: 6 King St, Grey Lynn, Auckland

South Sea Books
37 Holliss Ave, Christchurch
Tel: (03) 3317630
E-mail: southsea@ihug.co.nz
Web Site: www.abebooks.com/home/southsea
Key Personnel
Owner: Glenn Haszard
Founded: 1984
Type of Business: Exporter, Importer, Major Independent Bookseller, Wholesaler
Owned by: Glenn Charles Haszard

Techbooks
Private Bag 99939, Newmarket, Auckland
Tel: (09) 5240132 *Fax:* (09) 5233769
Key Personnel
Man Dir: Colin Greenwood
Founded: 1983
Type of Business: Major Independent Bookseller
Branch Office(s)
82 Waring Taylor St, Welington
Bookshop(s): 378-380 Broadway, Newmarket

Unity Books Lt
57 Willis St, Wellington
Tel: (04) 499 4245 *Fax:* (04) 499 4246
E-mail: unity.books@clear.net.n2
Key Personnel
Dir: A H Preston
Manager: Tilly Lloyd
Type of Business: Major Independent Bookseller
Bookshop(s): Unity Books, 19 High St, Auckland *Tel:* (09) 3070731 *Fax:* (09) 3734883

University Book Shop (Auckland) Ltd
Student Union Bldg, 34 Princes St, Auckland 1
Mailing Address: PO Box 90944, Auckland Mail Centre, Auckland 1001
Tel: (09) 3771869 *Fax:* (09) 3094278
E-mail: ubsauck@ubsbooks.co.nz

Web Site: www.ubsbooks.co.nz *Cable:* UNIBOOKS
Key Personnel
Manager: John Pringle
Founded: 1966
Type of Business: Importer, Major Independent Bookseller
Owned by: Whitcoulls Ltd/Auckland University Students Association
Bookshop(s): 2 Lorne St, Auckland 1; Tamaki Campus, Merton Rd, Auckland 5

University Book Shop (Canterbury) Ltd
University of Canterbury, University Dr Christchurch
Mailing Address: Private Bag 4748, Christchurch
Tel: (03) 488579 *Fax:* (03) 3488851
Web Site: www.canterbury.ac.nz
Key Personnel
Manager: David Ault *E-mail:* david@ubscan.co.nz
Founded: 1971
Type of Business: Exporter, Importer, Major Independent Bookseller

University Book Shop (Otago) Ltd
378 Great King St, Dunedin
Mailing Address: PO Box 6060, Dunedin
Tel: (03) 4776976 *Fax:* (03) 4776571
E-mail: ubs@xtra.co.nz
Web Site: www.unibooks.co.nz
Key Personnel
Manager: Bill Noble
Founded: 1945
Type of Business: Major Independent Bookseller

Whitcoulls Ltd
Private Bag 92098, 186 Queen St, Auckland
Tel: (09) 3092233 *Fax:* (09) 3095503
Telex: NZ 60402
Key Personnel
Chief Executive: David Brown
General Manager: David Worley
55 Stores nationwide.
Owned by: The Rank Group

Nicaragua

Libreria Tecnologica Universitaria
Universidad Centroamericana, Pista de la Resistencia, Managua
Mailing Address: Apdo 69, Managua
Tel: (02) 773026 *Fax:* (02) 670106

Libreria Universitaria
Universidad Nacional Autonoma de Nicaragua, Recinto Universitario-Ruben, Dario, Managua
Tel: (0311) 2612; (0311) 2613

Nigeria

Ahmadu Bello University Bookshop Ltd
Kaduna State, PMB 1094, Zaria
Tel: (069) 550054
Key Personnel
General Manager: K A Momoh; Mrs Amnim

Benin University Bookshop
University of Benin, PMB 1154, Ugbowo Campus, Benin City
Tel: (052) 240115 ext 217 *Fax:* (052) 241156

Telex: 41365
Key Personnel
Manager: S O Ehiede

Challenge Bookshops
c/o ECWA Productions Ltd, 10, Kano Rd, Jos
Mailing Address: PMB 2010, Jos
Tel: (073) 53897; (073) 52230
Key Personnel
General Manager: E C Nwobilo
Type of Business: Wholesaler
Owned by: ECWA Productions Ltd

CSS Bookshops, Agency & Publishing Division
19 Broad St, Lagos, Lagos State
Mailing Address: PO Box 174, Lagos
Tel: (01) 2633081; (01) 2637009; (01) 2637023; (01) 2633010 *Fax:* (01) 2637089
Key Personnel
Chief Executive: Dayo Alabi
Chief Accountant: Kola Olaitan
Founded: 1869
Also Publisher.
Type of Business: Distributor, Importer, Major Book Chain Headquarters, Wholesaler
Owned by: The Church of Nigeria

Fola Abbey Educational Book Services, Fola Abbey Bookshops Ltd
One Odulami Lane, off Kakawa St, Lagos, Lagos State
Tel: (01) 2636679 *Fax:* (01) 825268
Key Personnel
Chief Executive: Hakeem A Sanni
Suppliers of all Nigerian publications to Universities, Libraries & individuals.
Type of Business: Exporter

Mabrochi International Co Ltd
143 Moshood Abiola Way, Ebute Metta (West), Lagos State
Mailing Address: PO Box 1509, Surulere PO, Lagos State
Tel: (01) 2662275 *Fax on Demand:* (01) 2662275
E-mail: mabrochiadol@yahoo.com
Key Personnel
Sales Executive: Adol C Ofoegbu
Founded: 1976
Specialize in mail order services worldwide. Academic jobber for overseas universities & libraries. Subscription agent for Nigerian publications.
Type of Business: Distributor, Exporter, Importer, Major Independent Bookseller, Wholesaler
Branch Office(s)
7 Oyabiyi St, Yaba, Lagos (Tertiary textbooks)

Nigerian Book Suppliers Ltd
54-56 Bankhole St, Lagos, Lagos State
Mailing Address: PO Box 3870, Lagos, Lagos State
Tel: (01) 22407
Telex: 20202 Tds Box 052 Ikeja
Key Personnel
Man Dir: B Fatayi-Williams
Bookseller and library supplier specializing in professional books (especially legal, management, banking and accountancy), Africana, mass market paperback fiction, and library titles for tertiary level libraries.

Odusote Bookstores Ltd
68, Lagos Bye-Pass, Oke Ado, Ibadan
Mailing Address: PO Box 244, Ibadan
Tel: (02) 316451 *Fax:* (02) 315654
Telex: 31215 (Odbook NG) *Cable:* ODBOOK, IBADAN
Key Personnel
Man Dir: Ola Odusote
Manager: Olufemi Odusote
Founded: 1964

Type of Business: Distributor, Wholesaler
Branch Office(s)
177 Herbert Macaulay St, Yaba, Lagos State
Tel: (01) 861248

University Bookshop Ltd
Obafemi Awolowo University, Ile-Ife, Osun State
Tel: (036) 230290 *Cable:* BOOKSHOP IFEVARSITY
Key Personnel
Man Dir: Oyeniyi Osundina
Founded: 1964
Type of Business: Major Independent Bookseller
Owned by: Obafemi Awolowo University
Branch Office(s)
Ado-Ekiti
Osogbo

University Bookshop (Nigeria) Ltd
University of Ibadan, Ibadan, Oyo State
Tel: (02) 400550 (ext 1208); (02) 400550 (ext 1047); (02) 400614 (ext 1244); (02) 400614 (ext 1042)
Key Personnel
General Manager: Akin Aqbebi
Branch Office(s)
University College Hospital

University of Lagos Bookshop
PMB 1013, University of Lagos, Idiaraba, Lagos
Tel: (01) 820279 *Fax:* (01) 822644
Telex: 26983 Unilag.NG *Cable:* UNIVERSITY OF LAGOS
Key Personnel
Manager: Mrs Oluronke Orimalade
Founded: 1966
Type of Business: Importer
Branch Office(s)
College of Medicine, University of Lagos, Idi-Araba, Surulere, Lagos

University of Nigeria Bookshop Ltd
Nsukka
Tel: (042) 332077; (042) 771911
Key Personnel
Manager: B U Ezugwu

John West Publications Co Ltd
208-212, Broad Street, Lagos
Mailing Address: PO Box 2416, Lagos
Tel: (01) 932011
Telex: John West Ikeja
Key Personnel
Man Dir: Alhaji Lateef Kayode Jakande

Norway

A/L Biblioteksentralen (The Norwegian Library Bureau)
Postboks 6142, Etterstad, 0602 Oslo 6
Tel: 22673480 *Fax:* 22196443
Key Personnel
Administrative Dir: Arnt Seljeseth
Head of Book/Media Dept: Toril Anderson
Founded: 1952
Bibliographic products & service; Materials, furnishings & interior architects for libraries.

Forlagsentralen ANS
Furuset, Postboks 1, 1001 Oslo
Tel: 22329600 *Fax:* 22329601
E-mail: forlagsentralen@forlagsentralen.no
Key Personnel
President: Eivind T Skogseide
Founded: 1964
Type of Business: Distributor

F Beyer Bok-Og Papirhandel A/S
Strandgt 4, 5013 Bergen
Tel: 055321180 *Fax:* 055326465 *Cable:*
BOKBEYER BERGEN
Key Personnel
Manager: Hans Erik Hansen

Gardum A/S
Soregaten 22, Soluberggaten 11A, N-4001 Stavanger
Mailing Address: Postboks 242, N-4001 Stavinger
Tel: 04520200; 04520400 *Fax:* 04520680
Key Personnel
Manager: Rein Fridtjot Gardum Gardum

Libris Emo AS
Boks 40, 2013 Skjetten
Tel: 63849200 *Fax:* 63849345
Key Personnel
President: Torgeir Daal
Chain Dir: Morten Aas
Founded: 1972
Type of Business: Major Book Chain Headquarters
Owned by: Aker RG1

Lyngs Bokhandel A/S
Postboks 327, 7001 Trondheim
Tel: 73512544 *Fax:* 73512544
Key Personnel
Manager: Ragnvald C Knudsen
Founded: 1927
Type of Business: Major Independent Bookseller

Olaf Norlis Bokhandel A/S
Universitetsgaten 24, N-0162 Oslo
Tel: 22004300 *Fax:* 22422651
Key Personnel
Manager: Tom Vister
Marketing Manager: Hans Petter Yssen
Founded: 1890
Specialize in medicine, education, business, computers, travel, Scandinavian literature, books in minority & immigrant languages & library supplier.
Type of Business: Distributor, Exporter, Importer, Major Independent Bookseller, Wholesaler
Owned by: H Aschehoug & Co W Nygaard A/S

Norsk Bokdistribusjon
Vakaasveien 7, N-1360 Nesbru
Mailing Address: PO Box 203, N-1379 Nesbru
Tel: 66983980 *Fax:* 66845590
E-mail: vv@vettviten.no
Web Site: www.vettviten.no
Key Personnel
Sales & Marketing Manager: Jo Lien
Publisher: Jan Lien
Founded: 1987
Specialize in computer science, technology & medicine.
Type of Business: Distributor, Importer, Wholesaler
Owned by: Vett & Viten as

Erik Qvist Bokhandel A/S
Drammensveien 16, N-0558 Oslo
Tel: 22440326 *Fax:* 22558889
E-mail: qvist.libris@qvist.no
Key Personnel
Chairman: Erik Chr Qvist
Man Dir: Harald Qvist
Founded: 1905
Type of Business: Major Book Chain Headquarters, Major Independent Bookseller
Bookshop(s): F Beyers Bokhandel A/S, Strand Gt 4, 5013 Bergen; F Beyer, Lodin Leppsg+7, 500 Bergen *Tel:* 55318180

Sentraldistribusjon ANS
c/o Cappelens, Postboks 350, 0101 Sentrum, Oslo
Tel: 22365000 *Fax:* 22365040
Key Personnel
President: Roland Hellberg
Vice President: Jan Erik Stokke
Type of Business: Distributor
Owned by: Cappelens Publishing

Tanum Karl Johan A/S
Karl Johansgate 43, Postboks 1177, 0107 Sentrum, Oslo 1
Tel: 22411100 *Fax:* 22333275
Telex: 72427 Tanum N *Cable:* TANUMBOK
Key Personnel
Dir: Petter A Knudsen
Manager: Bjorg Andreassen
Type of Business: Exporter, Importer, Wholesaler

Tapir
N-7005 Trondheim
Tel: 73593226; 73598422 *Fax:* 73598494; 73598494
Key Personnel
Manager: Hans G Auganaes
Manager, Book Division: Johan Kristengard
Founded: 1921
Type of Business: Distributor, Exporter, Importer, Major Independent Bookseller, Wholesaler

Unipa A/S
Postboks 2607 Mohlenpris, N-5836 Bergen
Tel: 55318405 *Fax:* 55324270
E-mail: unipa@online.no
Key Personnel
Man Dir: Terje Bergesen
Type of Business: Major Book Chain Headquarters

Wennergren-Cappelen A/S
Ovre Vollgt 15, Sentrum, NO-0105 Oslo
Mailing Address: Postboks 738 Sentrum, NO-0105 Oslo
Tel: 23357250 *Fax:* 22337104
E-mail: wenca@wenca.no
Key Personnel
President: Glenn Andersen
Founded: 1829
Also Publishers, Stamp Dealers & Antiquariat.
Type of Business: Distributor, Importer, Wholesaler
Parent Company: Cap AS
Ultimate Parent Company: J W Cappelen (Also owner)

Pakistan

Comprehensive Book Service
56-New Urdu Bazar, Mohan Rd, Karachi 74200
Tel: (021) 214682 *Fax:* (021) 2632131
E-mail: shahzad@cbs.khi.sdnpk.undp.org
Telex: 23035 Pcokr *Cable:* GOODBOOKS
Key Personnel
Proprietor: Shahzad Najmee
Publishers, booksellers and library suppliers.
Type of Business: Distributor, Exporter, Importer, Major Independent Bookseller, Wholesaler

Ferozsons (Private) Ltd
60 Shahrah-e-Quaid-e-Azam, Lahore
Tel: (042) 111626262 *Fax:* (042) 6369204
E-mail: support@ferozsons.com.pk *Cable:* FEROZSONS
Key Personnel
Man Dir, Publicity: A Salam
Dir: Mr Zaheer Salam
Dir, Business Development: Muqeet Salam
Manager, Rawalpindi: Aftab A Tariq
Manager, Karachi: Ms Gul Afshan
Founded: 1894
Also Publisher & Printer.
Type of Business: Distributor, Exporter, Importer, Major Independent Bookseller, Wholesaler
Branch Office(s)
1st floor, Mehran Heights, Main Clifton Rd, Karachi
277 Peshawar Rd, Rawalpindi

Liberty Books (Pvt) Ltd
3 Rafig Plaza, M R Kayani Rd, Saddar Karachi 74400
Mailing Address: PO Box 7427, Saddar Karachi 74400
Tel: (021) 111311113 *Fax:* (021) 5684319
E-mail: libertybooks@libertybooks.com
Web Site: www.libertybooks.com
Key Personnel
Managing Dir: A Hussein
Sales Dir: Saleem Hussein
Founded: 1948
Type of Business: Distributor, Importer, Wholesaler
Branch Office(s)
Pearl Continental Hotel, Karachi
Hotel Marriott, Karachi
Hotel Sheraton & Clifton, Karachi
Distribution Division, 3 Rafiq Plaza, Inverarity Rd, Saddar, Karachi *Tel:* (021) 5683026

NGM Communication
Gulberg Colony, Lahore 54660
Mailing Address: PO Box 3041, Lahore 54660 Punjab
Tel: (042) 5713849
E-mail: ngm@shoa.net; anjeeam@anjeeam.com
Web Site: www.ngm.web-page.net
Key Personnel
Editor: Andy Nizami
Founded: 1980
Member of The Pakistan Publishers & Booksellers Association (Karachi Zone). Commercial & Government Booksellers. Dealers in Back issues. International subscription Agents for Pakistani Journals, Periodicals, Serials & Newspapers. Library Suppliers. Publishers' Representatives. Bankers; Habib Bank Limited.
Type of Business: Distributor, Exporter, Major Book Chain Headquarters, Major Independent Bookseller, Wholesaler
Owned by: Fatima Nizami

Pak American Commercial (Pvt) Ltd
53/2 Kashmir Rd, Rawalpindi, Cantt 3
Tel: (021) 563709 *Fax:* (021) 565190 *Cable:* PAKACINC KARACHI
Key Personnel
Dir: Ahsan Jaffri
Retail bookseller & subscription agent; also publisher.
Type of Business: Importer, Major Independent Bookseller, Wholesaler
Branch Office(s)
Pak American Commercial (Pvt) Ltd, 1st Floor, Pak Chambers, 5 Temple Rd, Lahore
53/2 Kashmir Rd, PO Box 294, Rawalpindi *Tel:* (051) 63709

Pak Book Corporation
Aziz Chambers, 21 Queen's Rd, 54000 Lahore
Tel: (042) 111 636 636 *Fax:* (042) 6362328
E-mail: pbc@brain.net.pk
Key Personnel
Man Dir: M A Khan Akter
Dir: M Iqbal Cheema
Founded: 1975
Deal with scientific books, journals & films & CD-ROM databases.
Type of Business: Distributor, Exporter, Importer, Wholesaler
Branch Office(s)
G-6/1/1, Khayaban-E-Suhawardy, Islamabad
Star Centre, Main Tariq Rd, PECHS, Karachi

Paramount Books (Pvt) Ltd
PECH Society, 152/0 Block 2, Karachi 75400
Tel: (021) 4550661; (021) 4551630
Telex: 25856 PBL PAK *Cable:* PARABOOKS KARACHI
Key Personnel
Dir: Iqbal S Mohammad
Manager: Saleem A Latif
Founded: 1947
Type of Business: Distributor, Wholesaler
Branch Office(s)
Lahore
Rawalpindi

Royal Book Co
232 Saddar Cooperative Market, Abdullah Haroon Rd, Karachi 74400
Tel: (021) 5684244; (021) 5670628; (021) 5653418 *Fax:* (021) 5653419
E-mail: royalbook@hotmail.com
Leading Publisher.
Type of Business: Distributor, Exporter, Importer, Major Independent Bookseller, Wholesaler
Branch Office(s)
402 Rehman Centre, Zaibunnisa St, Karachi 74400 *Tel:* (021) 5670628
Showroom(s): BE 5 Rex Centre, Zaibunnisa St, Karachi 74400

West-Pakistan Publishing Co (Pvt) Ltd
17 Urdu Bazar, Lahore
Mailing Address: GPO Box No 374, Lahore
Tel: (042) 52427 *Cable:* WESPUBLISH LAHORE
Key Personnel
Chief Executive: Syed Ahsan Shah
Founded: 1932
Also Publisher.
Type of Business: Exporter, Importer, Wholesaler

Panama

Libreria Cultural Panamena SA
Via Espana 16, Apdo 2018, Panama
Tel: 2235628; 2236267 *Fax:* 2237280 *Cable:* CULPASA
Key Personnel
Manager: Amador j Fraguela
Founded: 1955
Type of Business: Distributor, Exporter, Importer, Major Book Chain Headquarters, Wholesaler
Owned by: Libreria Cultural Panamena SA, Distribudoira Cultural y Manfer SA

Libreria Menendez
Galerias Obarrio, Via Brasil, Panama
Tel: 2258996
Branch Office(s)
Libreria Menendez Paitilla
Libreria Santa Ana, Plaza Santa Ana
Ave Justo Arosemena y Calle 36

Papua New Guinea

University Book Shop Inc
University Papua New Guinea, Boroko National Capitol District
Mailing Address: PO Box 4819
Tel: 267375 *Fax:* 260961
Telex: NE 22366
Key Personnel
Manager: E Guy

Paraguay

Libreria Comuneros
Cerro Cora 289, Casella Correo 930, Asuncion
Tel: (021) 446176; (021) 444667 *Fax:* (021) 444667
Key Personnel
Proprietor: Oscar R Rolon
Type of Business: Distributor, Exporter, Importer, Major Independent Bookseller, Wholesaler

Libreria Internacional SA
Estrella 723, Asuncion
Mailing Address: Casilla de Correi 991, Asuncion
Tel: (021) 491423 *Fax:* (021) 449730
Key Personnel
Manager: Victor Buzo
Founded: 1953
Type of Business: Distributor, Importer, Wholesaler
Bookshop(s): Casa Central, Estrella 723, Asuncion

Agencia de Librerias Nizza SA
Eligio Ayala 1073, Casilla de Correo 2596, Asuncion
Tel: (021) 47160
Owned by: Ediciones Nizza

Peru

Librerias ABC SA
Sta Catalina 217, Apdo 53, Arequipa
Tel: (054) 422900; (054) 422902 *Fax:* (054) 422901 *Cable:* MOLAGENT LIMA
Key Personnel
Man Dir: Herbert H Moll
Branch Office(s)
Edificio El Pacifico, Miraflores
Centro Comercial Todos, San Isidro

Adriatica
Jr Junin no 555, Trujillo
Tel: (044) 251145 *Fax:* (044) 256712
E-mail: adriatica@pc-vertas.com
Key Personnel
Manager: Adriana Doig Mannucci
Founded: 1994
Type of Business: Distributor, Importer, Major Independent Bookseller

Distribuidora Importadora Durand SA
Jr San Pedro 311-313, Lima 34
Tel: (014) 4452113 *Fax:* (014) 4463190
Key Personnel
General Dir: Arturo Durand Gamero
Type of Business: Distributor, Importer, Wholesaler

Ediciones Euroamericanas SA
Av Emancipacion 234, Lima 1
Tel: (014) 4274686 *Fax:* (014) 4280545
Key Personnel
Manager: Juan Moncayo Larrea
Founded: 1985
Type of Business: Distributor, Importer, Wholesaler

Ediciones Zeta SCR Ltda
Pachacutec No 1414, Jesus Maria, Casilla 4050 Lima
Tel: (014) 4729890; (014) 4720781 *Fax:* (014) 4725942; (014) 4750094 *Cable:* EDIZETA LIMA
Key Personnel
Manager: Jorge Zavaleta
Founded: 1978
Type of Business: Distributor, Importer, Wholesaler
Bookshop(s): Zeta Bookstore SRL, Cmdte Espinar 219, Miraflores, Lima

Liberia Editorial Minerva-Miraflores
Av Larco No 299, Miraflores, Lima 18
Tel: (014) 4475499 *Fax:* (014) 4458583
E-mail: minerva@chavin-rcp-net-pe
Key Personnel
General Dir: Sandro Mariategui Chiappe
Type of Business: Distributor, Importer, Major Book Chain Headquarters, Major Independent Bookseller, Wholesaler
Branch Office(s)
Miraflores, Surquillo San Borja
Bookshop(s): Av La Paz Nro 210, Miraflores; Av Primavera 2593, San Borja

Libreria l'Universidad, Nicolas Ojeda Fierro e Hijos SRL Ltda
Ave Nicolas de Pierola 639, Lima
Tel: (014) 282461; (014) 282036
Branch Office(s)
Ave Nicolas de Pierola 681, Lima *Tel:* 282036

Sociedad Biblica Peruana Asociacion Cultural
Av Petit Thouars No 991, Lima 1
Tel: (014) 4330232 *Fax:* (014) 4336389
E-mail: sbpac01@telemail.telematic.edu.pe
Key Personnel
General Secretary: Ing P A Quiroz
Founded: 1947
Type of Business: Distributor, Exporter, Importer
Owned by: SBP

Libreria Studium SA
Pl Francia 1164, Lima 1
Tel: (01) 275960; (01) 326278; (01) 325528 *Fax:* (01) 4325354
Key Personnel
Purchasing & Exporting Manager: Sergio Costa B
Also Publisher.
Branch Office(s)
Calle Moral 107A-107B, Arequipa
Calle Arequipa 110, Ayacucho
Saenz Pena 625, Callao
Elias Aguirre 251, Chiclayo
Meson de la Estrella 144, Cuzco
Calle Real 377, Huancayo
Tacna 145, Ica
Prospero 268-270, Iquitos
Colmena 626, Lima
Jiron de la Union 560, Lima
Ave Larco 720, Miraflores
Tacna 216, Piura
Francisco Pizarro 533, Trujillo

Libreria y Distribuidora de la Universidad Nacional Mayor de San Marcos
Av Venezuela Cuadra 34 s/n Ciudad Universitaria, 1 Apdo 454 Lima
Tel: (014) 640560 *Fax:* (014) 640560
Key Personnel
Administrator: Edilberto Chuchon Huamani
Type of Business: Distributor, Importer

Philippines

Alemar's
Northmall Bldg, Makati Commercial Center, Metro Manila
Tel: (02) 592617
Telex: 23312 Rhp ph bx 1102
Owned by: Phoenix Publishing House Inc
Branch Office(s)
Pl del Rosario, cnr Junquera St, Cebu City
Fiesta Carnival, Cubao, Quezon City
CM Recto St, Davao Cit
1428 Taft Ave, Manila
526 United Nations Ave, Manila
769 Rizal Ave, Manila
Holiday Plaza Libertad Cnr, F B Harrison St, Pasay City
927 Quezon Ave, Quezon City

Bookmark Inc
264-A Pablo Ocampo Sr Ave, Makati City
Mailing Address: PO Box 1171, Metro Manila
Tel: (0632) 8958061; (02) 868061; (02) 868062; (02) 868063; (02) 868064; (02) 868065
Fax: (02) 8160745 *Cable:* BOOKMARK MANILA
Key Personnel
General Manager: Jose Maria Lorenzo Tan
Also Bookselling, Publishing & Retailing.
Type of Business: Exporter
Owned by: Filipino Corporation
Bookshop(s): 357 T Pinpin, Escolta, Manila
Tel: (02) 481804; Greenbelt, Makati *Tel:* (02) 8151088; Paseo, Makati *Tel:* (02) 877169; Buendia Ave, Makati *Tel:* (02) 871126; Twin Cinema Arcade, Alabang *Tel:* (02) 8423187; Quezon Ave, Quezon City *Tel:* (02) 976349; Taft Ave, Manila *Tel:* (02) 593359; Session Rd, Baguio *Tel:* 4424912; Maharlika Livelihood Center, Baguio; Mayflower Plaza, Mandaluyong *Tel:* (02) 6321081; Shaw Blvd, Mandaluyong *Tel:* (02) 790584; International School, Makati *Tel:* (02) 886327; Aurora Blvd, Quezon City *Tel:* (02) 989114; San Fernando, La Union

Felta Book Sales Inc
Fortune Bldg, Ground Floor, 160 Legaspi St, Legaspi Village, Makati Metro Manila
Tel: (02) 8178155; (02) 8177773 *Fax:* (02) 8181188; (02) 9114103
Key Personnel
President: Felicito Abiva
Founded: 1969
US & UK Publisher's Representative (Educational, Children's Books, Mass Paperback); Licensee of Educational Materials (Elem - High School); Journal Subscription Agent (Medical & Professional).
Type of Business: Distributor, Wholesaler
Branch Office(s)
110 Nathan St, White Plains, Quezon City

Goodwill Trading Co Inc
711 Rizal Av, Sta Cruz, Manila
Tel: (02) 403610
Telex: 27302 Gtc Ph *Cable:* Gotrade Manila
Key Personnel
President & General Manager: Manuel Cancio

G Miranda & Sons
1242-1246 Asturias St, Sampalac, Manila
Tel: (02) 7121620 *Fax:* (02) 7120502 *Cable:* MIRANDASONS
Key Personnel
Manager: Eloisa D Miranda
Branch Office(s)
Miranda Davao, C M Recto Ave, Davao City
Miranda UP, UP Shopping Centre, Diliman, Quezon City
Miranda Espana, 1404 Espana St, Manila
Miranda Recto, 1887 C M Recto Ave, Manila
Miranda Morayta, 844 N Reyes St, Morayta, Manila
Miranda Cubao, Aurora Blvd, Cubao, Quezon City

National Book Store Inc
Quad Alpha Centrum, 125 Pioneer St, Mandaluyong City 1550
Tel: (02) 6318061; (02) 6318062; (02) 6318063; (02) 6318064; (02) 6318065; (02) 6318066
Telex: 27890 NBS-PH; 41144 NBS-PM
Cable: Nabost Manila
Key Personnel
General Manager: Mrs Socorro C Ramos
Also Publisher.

Philippine Education Co Inc
Esguerra Bldg 1, 140 Amorsolo St, 7th floor, Legaspi Village, 1229 Makati
Tel: (02) 487215; (02) 487317
Telex: 7222321 *Cable:* Pecoi Manila
Key Personnel
General Manager: Antero L Soriano
Also Publisher.
Branch Office(s)
Makati Commercial Center, West Drive Arcade, Makati
Cubao
Araneta Center
Broadway Centrum, Dona Juana Rodriguez & Aurora Blvd, Quezon City

Popular Book Store
305 Tomas Morato St, Quezon City
Tel: (02) 372-2162 *Fax:* (02) 372-2050
E-mail: popular@pworld.net.ph *Cable:* POBOST
Key Personnel
Pres & Gen Mgr: Katherine Ann Po
Type of Business: Distributor, Importer, Major Independent Bookseller, Wholesaler
Owned by: Popular Trading Corporation

Rex Book Store Inc
84 P Florentino Ave, 1008 Quezon City
Tel: (02) 7414956
Key Personnel
President: Dominador D Buhain
Vice President & General Manager: Mario Buhain
Editorial Manager: Mrs Flor Cabangis
Branch Office(s)
Rex Miscellaneous & Book Store, Greenhills, San Juan
Rex Book Store Cebu
Rex Book Store Davao
Rex Book Store Makati
Rex Book Store Mandaluyong
Bookshop(s): Rex Book Store, Recto, 1977 C M Recto Ave, Manila

Reyes Publishing, Inc
4th Floor, Mariwasa Bldg, 717 Aurora Blvd, 1112 Quezon City
Tel: (02) 721-7492; (02) 722-1827; (02) 726-4274; (02) 721-8792 *Fax:* (02) 721-8782
E-mail: reyespub@skyinet.net
Telex: 63740 Vri pn *Cable:* VERAREYES MANILA
Key Personnel
President: Luis Reyes
Manager: Paolo Reyes
Founded: 1986

Poland

ABE Marketing
ul Grzybowska 37A, 00-855 Warsaw
SAN: 128-0031
Tel: (022) 6540675 *Fax:* (022) 6520767
E-mail: info@abe.com.pl
Web Site: www.abe.com.pl/
Key Personnel
President: Marek Nowakowski *E-mail:* marek.nowakowski@abe.com.pl
Subscription Manager: Irena Ksiezopolska *E-mail:* irena.ksiezopolska@abe.com.pl
Founded: 1991
Polish sole agent for K G Saur Verlag Munich; subscription services.
Type of Business: Importer, Major Independent Bookseller
Branch Office(s)
Rynek Podgorski 9, Cracow *Tel:* (012) 6562102 *Fax:* (012) 6562102 *E-mail:* krakow@abe.com.pl
ul Wincentego Pola 16, 44-100 Gliwice *Tel:* (032) 3393150 *Fax:* (032) 3393150 *E-mail:* gliwice@abe.com.pl
Bookshop(s): Academic Bookstore Gliwice, ul Wincentego Pola 16, 44-100 Gliwice *Tel:* (032) 339 3150 *Fax:* (032) 339 3150 *E-mail:* gliwice@abe.com.pl; Academic Bookstore Warsaw

Centrala Handlu Zagranicznego ARS Polona SA (Foreign Trade Enterprise ARS Polona Joint Stock Company)
Krakowskie Przedmiescie 7, 00-068 Warsaw
Mailing Address: PO Box 1001, 00-950 Warsaw
Tel: (022) 8261201; (022) 8266248 *Fax:* (022) 8265334; (022) 8264763
E-mail: arspolona@arspolona.com.pl
Web Site: www.arspolona.com.pl *Cable:* ARS POLONA WARSZAWA
Key Personnel
Commercial Dir: Aleksandra Stepien
Manager, Book Dept: Jacek Salwa
Founded: 1953
Export & import of books & periodicals as well as publish books. Export & import of musical instruments & philately Organizer of Warsaw International & National Book Fairs.
Type of Business: Distributor, Exporter, Importer, Wholesaler

Chamber of Books
c/o PWN Polish Scientific Publishers, ul Hoza 62, 00-682 Warsaw
Tel: (022) 6215571; (022) 6254170
Key Personnel
President: Grzegorz Boguta
Vice President: Grzegorz Majerowicz

Dom Ksiazki, Panstwowe Przedesiebiorstwo
ul Smolensk 33, 31-112 Krakow
Tel: (012) 4225472; (012) 4228202 *Fax:* (012) 4228202
Key Personnel
Dir Gen: Kazimierz Mrowczyk
Vice Manager: Stanislaw Zahorodny
Founded: 1950
Type of Business: Major Book Chain Headquarters, Wholesaler

Portugal

Centro Antiquar do Alecrim A Trindade
Rua do Alecrim, 79-81, 1200 Lisbon
Tel: (021) 3424660 *Fax:* (021) 3470180
E-mail: np75ae@mail.telepac.pt
Key Personnel
Contact: Antonio Trindade
Type of Business: Major Independent Bookseller

BOOK DEALERS — PORTUGAL

Sociedades Livreiras Bertrand
Rua Anchieta 29-1, 1200 Lisbon
Tel: (021) 320084 *Fax:* (021) 3468286
Telex: 42748
Key Personnel
Man Dir: Antero Braga
Assistant Dir: Carlos Vilar
Founded: 1727
Branch offices in Aveiro, Coimbra, Faro, Lisbon, Porto & Vianna do Castelo.
Owned by: Bertrand Editora Lda

A Tavares de Carvalho
Av da Republica, 46-3, 1050 Lisbon
Tel: (021) 7970377 *Fax:* (021) 7958880
Key Personnel
Owner: A Tavares de Carvalho
Founded: 1959
Medium stock of old rare books in all fields, but mainly in Portuguese & Spanish 16th Century books.

CDL (Central Distribuidora Livreira) Sarl
Bairro Bela Vista Arm 2 P-30, 2735 Cacem Agualua-Cacem
Tel: (01) 4264422; (01) 769744; (01) 779825
Key Personnel
Dir: Mario Lino

Central Distribuidora Livreira, see CDL (Central Distribuidora Livreira) Sarl

Destarte, Lda
Rua Sto Antonio da Gloria, 90, 1250-218 Lisbon
Tel: (021) 3465155 *Fax:* (021) 3475811
E-mail: destarte@esoterica.pt
Key Personnel
Man Dir: Jorge Linhares *Tel:* (021) 3479164
Founded: 1980
Type of Business: Distributor, Importer
Imprints: Edicoes Destarte
Branch Office(s)
Livraria Linhares

Dinapress
Largo Dr Antonio de Sousa Macedo, 2, 1200 Lisbon
Tel: (021) 608992 *Fax:* (021) 608992
E-mail: dinalivro@ip.pt
Key Personnel
Marketing: Joel Antero D'Aguiar S Amaro
Founded: 1989
Type of Business: Exporter, Wholesaler
Owned by: Sr Silverio Pedroso Amaro
Bookshop(s): Centro Cultural Brasi Leiro, Largo Dr Antonio de Sousa Macedo, 2, 1200 Lisbon

Distri Cultural Lda
Rua Vasco da Gamma, 4-4A, 2685 Sacavem
Tel: (01) 9425394 *Fax:* (01) 9425214
Telex: 16588 Eliber
Key Personnel
Man Dir: Karl-Heinz Petzler
Sales Dir: Carlos Alberto
Marketing & Promotion: Martin E Wragg
Founded: 1980
Main Agencies: Oxford University Press, Hachette, Lanenscheidt, Max Hueber, Kuemmerly & Frey, Berlitz, Pan MacMillan, Harper Collins, RandomHouse, Bantom Doubleday Dell.
Type of Business: Distributor

Distri Lojas-Sociedade Livreira Lda
c/o Distri Cultural, LDA Rue Vasco de Gama 4-4A, P-2685 Sacavem
Tel: (01) 9425394 *Fax:* (01) 9425214
Telex: 62483
Key Personnel
Man Dir: Luis Santos
Sales Manager: Luis Alves
Commercial Contact: Jorge Mourao
Founded: 1977
Bookshops in Cascais, Coimbra, Estoril, & Sintra Porto (1); Braga, & Algarve (6); Lisbon (11).
Owned by: Grupo Distri

Distribuidora Editora Vral, Lda
Apdo 119, Queluz Codex
Tel: (01) 4393978 *Fax:* (01) 4373558
Key Personnel
Contact: Victor Martins
Type of Business: Distributor, Exporter, Importer, Major Independent Bookseller

Domingos Castro
Travessa dos Frois, 3-2, 2000 Santarem
Tel: (043) 332920 *Fax:* (043) 27406
Founded: 1984
Type of Business: Distributor, Wholesaler
Branch Office(s)
Rua da Costa, 14-1 Fre, Lisbon
Rua Nartiags Lizgadade, 190-3, 4000 Porto

ECL
Rua D Manuel 11, 33-5, 4050 Porto
Tel: (02) 600-40-01 *Fax:* (02) 609-96-15
E-mail: ecl@mail.telepac.pt
Founded: 1990
Type of Business: Distributor

EDC -Empresa De Divulgacao Cultural, SA
c\o Editorial Verbo, Rua Carlos Testa 1-2, 1000 Lisbon
Tel: (021) 562131 *Fax:* (021) 562139
Telex: 15177
Owned by: Editorial Verbo SA

Edicoei Tecnicas & Culturais, Lda, see Domingos Castro

Edicoes Destarte, *imprint of* Destarte, Lda

Electroliber Lda
Rua Vasco da Gama, n 4-4 Apartado 164, 2686 Sacavem
Tel: (01) 9425394 *Fax:* (01) 9425214
Telex: 16588 *Cable:* TELEGRAMAS ELECTROLIBER
Key Personnel
Contact: Pedro R de Vasconcelos; Antonio J Faria
Type of Business: Distributor
Branch Office(s)
Porto-Albufeira-Funchal

Esquina-Livraria e Papelaria Lda
Rua Afonso Lopes Vieira, 126 (AO FOCO), 4100-020 Porto
Tel: (022) 6065234 *Fax:* (022) 6053878
E-mail: livrariaesquina@mail.telepac.pt
Key Personnel
Manager: Luis Barroso *Tel:* (022) 6065314
Also deals in secondhand books.
Type of Business: Wholesaler

Livraria Ferin, Ltda
R Nova do Almada 70-74, 1249-098 Lisbon
Tel: (01) 213424422; (01) 213469033 *Fax:* (01) 213471101
E-mail: livraria.ferin@mail.telepac.pt
Key Personnel
President & General Manager: Margarida Dias Pinheiro
Founded: 1840
Type of Business: Exporter, Importer, Wholesaler

Julio de Figueiredo, Lda
Rua Antonio Pereira Carrilho, 5-10, 1000 Lisbon
Tel: (021) 8460784 *Fax:* (021) 8464164
E-mail: jlfig@individual.eunet.pt
Key Personnel
Contact: Julio Figueiredo
Type of Business: Distributor, Importer

Figueirinhas, Lda
Rua da Prata, 208-20, 1100 Lisbon
Tel: (021) 8879268 *Fax:* (021) 8879639
E-mail: correio@liv_figueirinhas.pt
Key Personnel
Contact: Francisco Pimenta
Type of Business: Distributor

Livraria Guimaraes
Rua da Misericordia, 68-70, 1200 Lisbon
Tel: (021) 3462436 *Fax:* (021) 3462620
Key Personnel
Man Dir: Isabel Leao
Founded: 1899
Also Publishes under Guimaraes Editores Lda (at above address).

Hipocrates - Livros Tecnicos, Lda
Av Praia da Vitoria, 45, 1000 Lisbon
Tel: (021) 3571247 *Fax:* (021) 3571247
Key Personnel
Contact: Norberto Boletas
Founded: 1976
Type of Business: Importer

International Book Centre
c/o Distri Cultural, Rua Vasco de Gama, 4-4a, 2685 Sacavem
Key Personnel
Man Dir: Karl-Heinz Petzler
Assistant Dir: Beatriz Mestrinho
Owned by: Distri Cultural (Grupo Distri)

Jayantilal Jamnadas, Lda
Rua Elias Garcia Lt 30-lj E-Amadora, 2700 Amadora
Tel: (01) 4960951
Founded: 1987
Type of Business: Major Independent Bookseller

Livraria Barata, Antonio D M Barata
Ave de Roma 11-A, 1000 Lisbon
Tel: (021) 8481631 *Fax:* (021) 8403344
Key Personnel
Contact: Graca Didier

Livraria Buchholz, Lda
Rua Duque de Palmela, 4, 1250-098 Lisbon
Tel: (021) 3170580 *Fax:* (021) 3522634
E-mail: buchholz@mail.telepac.pt
Web Site: www.buchholz.pt
Key Personnel
Man Dir: Karin Sousa Ferreira *Tel:* (021) 3170589
Founded: 1943
General & academic titles in Portuguese, English/American, French, German & Spanish language.
Type of Business: Exporter, Importer

Livraria Caravana
Rua Jose da Costa Guerreiro, 8100 Loule
Tel: (089) 462879 *Fax:* (089) 462871
Founded: 1996
Also Tobacco & Stationer's Shop.
Type of Business: Major Independent Bookseller

Livraria Latina
Rua de Sta Catarina, 2-10, 4000-441 Porto
Tel: (022) 2001294 *Fax:* (022) 2086053
Key Personnel
Contact: Henrique Perdigao
Founded: 1941
Also book publisher.
Type of Business: Importer, Major Independent Bookseller, Wholesaler

PORTUGAL

Livraria Ler, Lda
Rua Almeida e Sousa, 24-C, 1300 Lisbon
Tel: (021) 3888371
Key Personnel
Dir: Luis Alves Dias
Founded: 1970
Type of Business: Distributor

Livraria Manuel Ferreira
Rua Formosa, 21, 4000 Porto
Tel: (02) 563237
E-mail: manuelferreira@ip.pt
Key Personnel
Contact: Paulo Ferreira

Livraria Teorema 1-Cogitum Livrarias Lda
Shopping Center Massama, Loja 41, 2745 Queluz
Mailing Address: Largo Padre Anerico, Lote 249, Loja B, 2745 Queluz
Tel: 4304430 *Fax:* 4394909; 4394431
E-mail: cogitum@ip.pt
Key Personnel
Contact: Joao Nuno Cruz
Founded: 1991
Owned by: Cogitum Uvrarias Lda

Lojas Europa-America
Apdo 8, Mem Martins Codex
Tel: (01) 9211461 *Fax:* (01) 9217940
Owned by: Publicacoes Europa-America Lda
Branch Office(s)
Ave 25 de Abril 48, Almada
Centro Comercial Pao de Acucar, Lojas 6,7 - Estrade a Nacional 6, Cascais
Ave 28 de Maio 61, Castelo Branco
Arcadas do Parque, Estoril
Pr Ferreira de Almeida 21-22, Faro
Rua Jose Relvas 15 B-C, Parede
Ave Antonio Enes 14-B, Queluz
Ave Elias Garcia 104-B, Queluz

Editorial Noticias
Rua Padre Luis Aparicio, n 10, 1150-248 Lisbon
Tel: (021) 3552130 *Fax:* (021) 3552168

Editorial O Livro Lda
Rua Claudio Nunes 121, 1500 Lisbon
Tel: (021) 704709 *Fax:* (021) 7783536
Key Personnel
Man Dir: Carlos de Moura
Editorial: Carlos Perdigao
Also publisher.
Branch Office(s)
Rua da Boa Hora, 36 & 68, Porto *Tel:* (021) 2005739 *Fax:* (021) 2005736

Patio-Livraria Inglesa
Rua da Carreira, 43, 9000 Funchal
Tel: (0291) 224490 *Fax:* (0291) 232077
E-mail: patiolivros@mail.pt
Founded: 1981
Specialize in exporting books worldwide & in the supply of Portuguese/Brazilian publications. Carry in stock all available books on Madeira.
Type of Business: Distributor, Exporter, Importer, Major Book Chain Headquarters

Livraria Portugal (Dias e Andrade Lda)
Rua do Carmo 70, Apdo 2681, 1200 Lisbon
Tel: (021) 3474982
Key Personnel
Manager: Henrique Arronches; Jose Simocs; Jose Reis; Manuel Dias
Founded: 1941
Type of Business: Distributor, Exporter, Importer

Livraria Sa da Costa
Praca Luis de Camoes 22-4, 1200 Lisbon
Tel: (021) 3460721

Key Personnel
Manager: Manuel F da Costa
Owned by: Sa da Costa Editora

Sodilivros
Tv Estevao Pinto, 6-A, 1000 Lisbon
Tel: (021) 658902 *Fax:* (021) 3876281
Key Personnel
Contact: Jorge De Azevedo
Founded: 1985
Type of Business: Distributor

Livraria Sousa e Almeida Lda
Rau da Fabrica 40-42, 4050-245 Porto
Tel: (02) 22 050 073 *Fax:* (02) 22 050 073
E-mail: sousaealmeida@net.sapo.pt

Puerto Rico

Bookstore, Institute of Puerto Rican Culture
PO Box 4184, San Juan 00905
Tel: (787) 724-0910 *Fax:* (787) 723-8393
Key Personnel
Owner & Manager, Institute de Cultura Puertoriquena: Rene Grullon Nunez
Stock includes subjects on music, Puerto Rico, history, humanities, short stories, poetry & literature. Also carry maps & sheet music.

Universidad de Puerto Rico-Recinto de Rio Piedras
Universidad de Puerto Rico, Recinto de Rio Pideras, 00932 Rio Piedras 00931
Mailing Address: PO Box 23345 UPR Station, 00931 San Juan
Tel: (787) 764-0000; (787) 763-3930 *Fax:* (787) 764-2250
Key Personnel
Acting Dir Administrator: Mrs Lily A Garcia Ricard
State University Bookstore.

Qatar

Arabian Bookshop
PO Box 7884, Doha
Tel: 448292 *Fax:* 449653
Telex: 5078 Majed DH

Reunion

Cazal SA
42 Rue Alexis de Villeneuve, Saint-Denis
Tel: 213264 *Fax:* 410977
Telex: 916453
Key Personnel
President: Philippe Baloukjy
Imprints, Printing, Advertising.

Librairie Universsitaire de la Reunion
29, Av de la Victoire, Saint Denis 97489
Tel: 210758
Key Personnel
Manager: Apavou

Romania

Artexim - Foreign Trade Co
Piata Scinteii sect 1, 7000 Bucharest
Tel: (01) 157672
Telex: 011191
Carries out all the commercial operations connected with book import and export.

Libraria Universitatii
Str Universitatii 1, R-3400 Cluj-Napoca
Tel: (064) 18107; (064) 14267
Libraria Universitatii belongs to the state and is under the rule of the Bookshops' Center, Dostoievski Street No 71.

Russian Federation

Mezhdunarodnaya Kniga
ul Dimitrova 39, 117044 Moscow
Tel: (095) 2384600
Telex: 411160 MKN SU
Key Personnel
Dir: Yuri V Kurenkov
Export organization for books, periodicals, printing equipment, audio and video recordings, and other cultural goods. Other services include co-editions, copyright, and arranging of fairs and exhibitions abroad and in Russia.

Rwanda

Librairie Universitaire
BP 117, Butare
Tel: 30272; 30273
Owned by: Universite Nationale du Rwanda, faculte du Droit

Saudi Arabia

Dar Al-Ulum Publishers, Booksellers & Distributors
Sixteen Street, Riyadh 11431
Mailing Address: PO Box 1050, Riyadh 11431
Tel: (01) 4777121 *Fax:* (01) 4793446
Telex: 203094 *Cable:* OHALI RIYADH
Key Personnel
Proprietor: Abdulla N Al-Ohali; Mohammad S Al-Kadi
Manager, Foreign Books: Gaafar I At-Tai
Also Publishers.
Type of Business: Distributor
Bookshop(s): Sitteen St, Sitteen St

International Bookshops
PO Box 22348, Riyadh 11495
Tel: (03) 4641851 *Fax:* (03) 4641851
Key Personnel
Owner: Said H AlSalah
General Manager: Basim S AlSalah
Also publisher.
Type of Business: Distributor, Importer, Major Independent Bookseller
Branch Office(s)
Dana Shopping Center, Damman
4 Seasons Center, Rakah
King Fahd St & 28 St

Tihama Bookshops
PO Box 8963, Jeddah 21492
Tel: (02) 6444444 *Fax:* (02) 6519277
Key Personnel
Manager: Hassan Assad; Mansour Linjawi
Manager, English Language Books: Ahmed Shafi
Owned by: Tihama Advertising Co

Senegal

Librairie Clairafrique
2, rue El Hadj Mbaye Gueye, BP 2005, Dakar
Tel: 222169 *Fax:* 218409
Telex: 21403 Clairaf
Key Personnel
Manager: Pauline Kemayi
Founded: 1951
Type of Business: Distributor, Major Independent Bookseller
Owned by: Archdiocese de Dahar

Sierra Leone

Njala University College Bookshop
Njala University, Freetown
Cable: Njalunbooks
Key Personnel
Manager: J D Kappia

Singapore

Info Access & Distribution
Blk 113 Eunos Av 3, No 07-03 Gordon Industrial Bldg, Singapore 409839
Tel: 7418422 *Fax:* 7418821
E-mail: andrew@accesshost.com.sg
Key Personnel
Contact: Mr Lee Pit Teong
Founded: 1990
Type of Business: Remainder Dealer
Branch Office(s)
Hong Kong
Taiwan
Thailand

Marketasia Distributors (S) Pte Ltd
Pan-I Complex, 601 Sims Dr, No 04-05, Singapore 387382
Tel: 67448483; 67448486 *Fax:* 67448497
E-mail: marketasia@pacific.net.sg
Web Site: www.marketasia.com.sg
Key Personnel
Dir: Johnson Lee *E-mail:* jl@marketasia.com.sg
Founded: 1987
Specialize in the publishing & distributing of books & magazines.
Type of Business: Distributor, Importer
Owned by: Johnson Lee & Quek Chin Hu

Masagung Books Pte Ltd
41 Sixth Ave, Off Bukit Timah Rd, Singapore 276483
Tel: 4683276
Telex: rs 34500 A; B Gasing
Also Publisher.

MPH Bookstores (S) Pte Ltd
601 Sims Drive, No 03-21, Pan-I Complex, Singapore 387382
Tel: 7485050; 7471088 *Fax:* 7440620; 7472630
Telex: RS 35853 Mphmag *Cable:* EMPRESS SINGAPORE
Key Personnel
Marketing Manager: Lawrence Geoffrey
Bookshop(s): 71-77 Stamford Rd, Singapore 178895; Cold Storage Jelita, 293 Holland Rd, Jalan Jelita 278628 *Tel:* 4689405; Isetan Dhoby Ghavt, B1-01-20-11, Orchard Rd, Singapore 238824 *Tel:* 3381888

Pacific Book Centre (S) Pte Ltd
c/o Pan Pacific Distributors Ltd, 597 Havelock Rd, Singapore 0316
Tel: 2616288 *Fax:* 2616088
Telex: 36496
Key Personnel
Man Dir: Low Tai Ee
Manager: Lawrence Tan
Owned by: Pan Pacific Publications Pte Ltd, 16 Fan Yoong Rd, Singapore 629793
Branch Office(s)
Queenstown Branch, Apt Blk 6C, 01-48 Margaret Drive, Singapore 142006 *Tel:* 4745701
Alexandra Branch, Apt Blk 136, 01-155 Alexandra Rd, Singapore 150136 *Tel:* 4740577
Havelock Branch, Apt Blk 22, 01-675 Havelock Rd, Singapore 160022 *Tel:* 2724326
Pasir Panjang Branch, 02-02 PSA Bldg, 460 Alexandra Rd, Singapore 119963 *Tel:* 2781090
Bras Basah Branch, Bain St, 02-69 Block 231, Bras Basah Complex, Singapore 180231 *Tel:* 3381024
Jurong East Branch, Block 130 01-221, Jurong East St 13, Singapore 600130 *Tel:* 5666153
Bukit Batok Branch, Blk 283, Bukit Batok East Ave 3 01-275, Singapore 650283 *Tel:* 5674649

Publishers Marketing Services Pte Ltd
10-C Jalan Ampas, Suite 07-01, Ho Seng Lee Flatted Warehouse, Singapore 329513
Tel: 2565166 *Fax:* 2530008
Key Personnel
Office Manager: Nicklaus Tan
Deputy Man Dir: Raymond Lim
Founded: 1980
Type of Business: Distributor, Exporter, Importer, Wholesaler
Owned by: Brian Lim

Select Books Pte Ltd
19 Tanglin Rd No 03-15, Tanglin Shopping Centre, Singapore 247909
Tel: 7321515 *Fax:* 7360855
E-mail: info@selectbooks.com.sg *Cable:* SELBOOKS
Key Personnel
Man Dir: Lena U Wen Lim
Admin Manager: Mrs Ng San May
Founded: 1976
Publisher & Retailer of books about SE Asia.
Type of Business: Distributor, Exporter, Importer, Major Independent Bookseller

STM Publishers Services Pte Ltd
352 Larong Chuan, No 01-05 Laurel Park, Singapore 556783
Tel: 62864998 *Fax:* 62882116
E-mail: tonypoh@pacific.net.sg
Key Personnel
Dir: Tony Poh *E-mail:* tonypoh@pacific.net.sg
Founded: 1993
Subjects: STM, Social Science, Arts, Education, Agriculture & Humanities-Publishers representing agent for SE & NE Asia Laws.
Type of Business: Distributor
Branch Office(s)
Chin Shan Information Service Ltd, 10F-1 No 166 Jiang Yi Rd, Chong Ho 235, Taipei Hsien, Taiwan, Province of China *E-mail:* csis@csis.com.tw

STP Distributors Pte Ltd
Times Centre, One New Industrial Rd, Singapore 536196
Tel: 2848844 *Fax:* 2610164; 2854871
Telex: rs 28068 STP *Cable:* STPSALES SINGAPORE
Key Personnel
Senior Vice President: Michael Kok Pun Liew
Owned by: Times Publishing Group

Times The Bookshop
Times Centre, One New Industrial Rd, Singapore 536196
Tel: 2848844 *Fax:* 2771186
Telex: RS 25713 *Cable:* Times Singapore
Key Personnel
Manager: Arthur Lee
Owned by: Times Publishing Ltd

The World Book Co (Pte) Ltd
Bras Basah Complex, Block 231, Bain St No 04-57, Singapore 180231
Tel: 3382323 *Fax:* 3371186
Telex: rs 36020 Wbksin
Key Personnel
General Manager: H P Foo

Slovakia

Slovart Co Ltd
Nam Slobody 6, 817 64 Bratislava
Tel: (07) 230229 *Fax:* (07) 46256
Telex: 93394 Slov
Type of Business: Exporter, Importer

Slovenia

Cankarjeva Zalozba
Kopitarjeva Ulica 2, SLO-1000 Ljubljana
Tel: (061) 219419 *Fax:* (061) 13 23 144; (061) 318 782
E-mail: cankar.zalozba@cankarjeva-z.si
Also publisher & antiquarian bookseller.
Type of Business: Exporter, Importer
Branch Office(s)
Kopitarjeva 2, Ljubljana
Miklosiceva 16, Ljubljana
Slovenska 37, Ljubljana
Trg osvoboditve 7, Ljubljana
Trzaska 59, Ljubljana
1 junija 27, Trbovlje
Usnjarska stolpic S 15, Vrhnika
Zaloska 35, Ljubljana

Co Libri
Presernova 5, 1000 Ljubljana
Tel: (061) 1255111 *Fax:* (061) 224454
Key Personnel
Man Dir: Mrs Majda Sikosek
Editor: Mr Vasja Krasevec
Founded: 1946
Also publisher.
Type of Business: Distributor, Exporter, Importer, Wholesaler

Sraka International
Valanticevo 17, 8000 Novo Mesto
Tel: (068) 23174 *Fax:* (068) 24094
Key Personnel
Dir & Editor: Drago Vovk
Founded: 1990
Type of Business: Distributor, Exporter, Importer
Owned by: Drago & Bozica Vovk

SLOVENIA

Tehniska Zalozba Slovenije
Lepi pot 6, 1111 Ljubljana
Mailing Address: Postfach 541, 1000 Ljubljana
Tel: (061) 213733 *Fax:* (061) 218246
Type of Business: Distributor, Major Independent Bookseller, Wholesaler

South Africa

Aloe Educational
PO Box 4349, Johannesburg 2000
Tel: (011) 8393719 *Fax:* (011) 8393720
Key Personnel
Chief Executive: Lionel N Schroder
Founded: 1968
Library suppliers & booksellers.
Owned by: Aloe Book Agency (Pty) Ltd

Book Promotions
PO Box 5, Plumstead 7800
Tel: (021) 7060949 *Fax:* (021) 7060940
E-mail: enquiries@bookpro.co.za
Key Personnel
Man Dir: Roy G Mansell *Tel:* (021) 7060949 ext 231 *E-mail:* roy@bookpro.co.za
Distributor, Importer.
Type of Business: Distributor, Importer

Central News Agency Ltd
PO Box 10799, Johannesburg 2000
Tel: (011) 4917500
Branch Office(s)
PO Box 9, Cape Town 8000 *Tel:* (021) 541261
PO Box 938, Durban 4000 *Tel:* (031) 451875
(also 250 branches throughout the country)

CNA, see Central News Agency Ltd

Faradawn cc
PO Box 1903, Saxonwold 2132
Tel: (011) 8851787; (011) 8851847 *Fax:* (011) 8851829
Key Personnel
Members: Lorraine Shalekoff; Lesley Thomas
Founded: 1983
Publishers Representatives, Book & Map Distributors.
Type of Business: Distributor, Importer, Wholesaler

Fogarty's Bookshop
Shop 20, Walmer Park Shopping Centre, Main St, Walmer-Port Elizabeth 6070
Mailing Address: PO Box 1881, Port Elizabeth 6000
Tel: (041) 3681425; (041) 3681454 *Fax:* (041) 3681279
Key Personnel
Manager: Teresa Fogarty *E-mail:* fogartys@global.co.za
Type of Business: Major Independent Bookseller

HAUM Booksellers
PO Box 460, Pretoria 0001
Tel: (012) 3228474
Telex: 320962 SA
Key Personnel
Manager: T Botha
Owned by: HAUM

Juta & Co Ltd
Mercury Crescent, Hillstar Industrial Township, Wetton 7780
Mailing Address: PO Box 14373, Kenwyn 7790
Tel: (021) 7975101 *Fax:* (021) 7970121
Type of Business: Major Independent Bookseller

Owned by: Juta Holdings (Pty) Ltd
Bookshop(s): Cape Town Bookshop, One Bree St, PO Box 30, Cape Town *Tel:* (021) 418-3260 *Fax:* (021) 418-1282 *E-mail:* ctbooks@juta.co.za; Bellville, Louvville Place, Church Square, PO Box 1605, Bellville 7535 *Tel:* (021) 948-7700 *Fax:* (021) 946-1657 *E-mail:* bbbooks@juta.co.za; Parow, Shoprite Park, Shop 19/20, 262 Voortrekker Rd, Parow 7500 *Tel:* (021) 418-3260 *Fax:* (021) 930-7962 *E-mail:* pabooks@juta.co.za; Johannesburg, Mezzanine fl, 111 Commissioner St, PO Box 1010, Johannesburg 2000 *Tel:* (011) 333-5521 *Fax:* (011) 333-4810 *E-mail:* jhbbooks@juta.co.za; Randburg, 3 Garden St, Bordeaux 2194 *Tel:* (011) 886-8595 *E-mail:* rbgbooks@juta.co.za; Pretoria, Hatfield Plaza, 1st Floor, 1122 Burnett St, Private Bag 12, Brooklyn 0011 *Tel:* (012) 362-5800 *Fax:* (012) 362-5744 *E-mail:* ptabooks@juta.co.za; Durban, 216 Stranger St, PO Box 50197, Musgrave Rd, Durban 4062 *Tel:* (031) 37-3970 *Fax:* (031) 37-1819 *E-mail:* dbnbooks@juta.co.za

Leo Books
PO Box 6836, Roggebaai, Cape Town 8012
Tel: (021) 406-3315 *Fax:* (021) 406-2926
E-mail: leobooks@nbh.nasper.co.za
Key Personnel
Contact: Peter Martin
Type of Business: Distributor

Logans University Bookshop (Pty) Ltd
39 Gale St, Durban 4001
Tel: (031) 3076530 *Fax:* (031) 3073230
Owned by: The Literary Group (Pty) Ltd
Branch Office(s)
100 Mansfield Rd, Durban *Tel:* 218223 (Technikon)
660 Umbilo Rd, Durban (Medical Books)
Nedbank Plaza, Durban Rd, PMB 301 Pietermaritzburg *Tel:* (0331) 941588

Maskew Miller Longman
PO Box 396, Cape Town 8000
Tel: (021) 531 7750 *Fax:* (021) 5314049
E-mail: firstname@mml.co.za
Telex: 526053 SA *Cable:* MASKEWMILLER
Key Personnel
Chief Executive: Fatima Dada
Publishing Dir: J Pienaar
Founded: 1893
Also publisher.
Type of Business: Importer, Wholesaler

MBEU Christian Bookshop
PO Box 74, Sibasa Venda
Tel: (015) 58147 *Fax:* (015) 932258
Key Personnel
Chief Executive: B Cronje
Branch Office(s)
Makhado
Siloam
Thohoyandou
Louis Trichardt

Media House Publications Pty Ltd
PO Box 782395, Sandton 2146
Tel: (011) 8826237 *Fax:* (011) 8829652
Key Personnel
Contact: Kate Everingham
Founded: 1983
Type of Business: Distributor, Exporter, Importer, Wholesaler
Owned by: Book Services International SA Pty Ltd

Nasou Via Afrika
PO Box 5197, 8000 Cape Town
Tel: (021) 4063001 *Fax:* (021) 4062922
E-mail: nasouhk@nbh.naspers.co.za

MAJOR

Key Personnel
Manager Administration & Retail: Mr G Naude
Type of Business: Distributor, Importer, Major Book Chain Headquarters
Owned by: National Educational Group
Branch Office(s)
Bloemfontein
East London
George
Newcastle
Port Elizabeth
PO Box 11945 Hatfield 0028, Pretoria *Tel:* (012) 3429971 *Fax:* (012) 3429972
Randburg
Upington
Bellville
Pinetown

Shuter & Shooter (Pty) Ltd
PO Box 618, Ferndale 2160
Tel: (0331) 427419 *Fax:* (0331) 943096
Key Personnel
Man Dir: D Ryder
Also Publisher.
Branch Office(s)
PO Box 618, Ferndale 2160 *Tel:* (011) 7928363 *Fax:* (011) 7927024
Bookshop(s): 230 Church St, Pietermaritzburg 3201

The Struik Publishing Group
80 McKenzie St, 8000 Cape Town
Mailing Address: PO Box 1144, 8000 Cape Town
Tel: (021) 4624360 *Fax:* (021) 4624379
Cable: DEKENA
Key Personnel
Executive: Gerrit Struik

Technical Books Ltd
PO Box 2866, Cape Town 8000
Tel: (021) 4216540 *Fax:* (021) 4216593
E-mail: techbkct@mweb.co.za
Key Personnel
Chief Executive: Anthony Shapiro *E-mail:* tony@techbooks.co.za
Founded: 1929
STM book specialist.
Type of Business: Distributor, Importer, Major Independent Bookseller, Wholesaler
Bookshop(s): 10th floor Anreith Centre, Hans Strijdom Ave, Cape Town 8001

United Book Distributors (Pty) Ltd
1st Floor, Permad House, 28 Betty St, Jeppestown, Hillbrow 2001
Mailing Address: PO Box 17294, Hillbrow 2001
Tel: 614431
Telex: 482991 SA *Cable:* Unibooks
Key Personnel
Manager: J Gordin
Type of Business: Distributor, Wholesaler

Van Schaik Bookstore University Bookshop
PO Box 2355, 7550 Bellville
Tel: (021) 9188500 *Fax:* (021) 9511670
E-mail: vsblv@vanschaik.com
Web Site: www.vsonline.co.za *Cable:* BOOKSCHAIK
Key Personnel
Gen Mgr: Chris Wolf *E-mail:* cwolf@vanschaik.com
Founded: 1917
Owned by: Nasionale Boekhandel Ltd

Spain

Agencia General de Libreria Internacional SL (AGLI)
Islas Marshall 1, 28035 Madrid
Tel: (091) 3736640 *Fax:* (091) 3732740
Key Personnel
Contact: President
Bookshop(s): Libreria Jose Ma Padrino Barquillo, 21, 28004 Madrid *Tel:* (091) 5325361 *Fax:* (091) 5328569

AGLI - Agencia General de Libreria Internacional SL, see Agencia General de Libreria Internacional SL (AGLI)

Alibri Libreria, SL
Balmes 26, 08007 Barcelona
Tel: (093) 317 0578 *Fax:* (093) 412 2702
E-mail: books-world@books-world.com
Cable: HERDER
Key Personnel
General Manager: Gerardo Nahm
Founded: 1925
Academic bookshop.
Type of Business: Exporter, Importer, Major Independent Bookseller
Owned by: Andreas Valtl

Libreria Ancora y Delfin
Av Diagonal 564, 08021 Barcelona
Tel: (093) 2000746 *Fax:* (093) 2000757
E-mail: ancorayclefin@cambraben.es
Key Personnel
Contact: Eulalia Teixidor de Ventos
Founded: 1956
Bookshop.
Owned by: Ancora y Delfin SL

Libreria Bosch
Ronda Universidad 11, 08007 Barcelona
Tel: (093) 3175308; (093) 3175358; (093) 3175558 *Fax:* (093) 4122764
E-mail: info@libreriabosch.es
Web Site: www.libreriabosch.es *Cable:* BOSLIBRI
Key Personnel
Manager: Javier Bosch
Founded: 1889
General Bookstore.
Type of Business: Distributor, Exporter, Importer, Major Independent Bookseller
Owned by: Libreria Bosch, SL

Celesa (Spanish Books Export Center)
Laurel N° 21, 28005 Madrid
Tel: (091) 5170170 *Fax:* (091) 5173481
E-mail: celesa@infornet.es
Web Site: www.celesa.es
Key Personnel
Dir: D Jose Maria Redondo Suarez
Founded: 1986
Specialize in the export of any book published in Spain.
Type of Business: Exporter
Owned by: 100 Editoriales Espanolas y Ministerio Cultura

Libreria DELSA
Serrano, No 80, 28006 Madrid
Tel: (091) 5751541 *Fax:* (091) 5758414
Key Personnel
Contact: Silvela Sonsoles
21 Branches throughout Spain DELSA de Publicaciones SA is also at the above address.

Diaz de Santos SA - Libreria Cientifico-Tecnica
Juan Bravo 3-A, 28006 Madrid
Tel: (091) 4312482 *Fax:* (091) 5755563
Telex: 45141 Dsan E
Owned by: Diaz de Santos SA
Branch Office(s)
Diaz de Santos SA - Libreria Cientifico-Tecnica, Calle Balmes 417/419, 08022 Barcelona *Tel:* (093) 2128647
Diaz de Santos SA - Agropecuaria, Calle Lagasca 38, 28001 Madrid *Tel:* (091) 4312482
Diaz de Santos SA - Libreria Medica, Calle Maldonado 6, 28006 Madrid *Tel:* (091) 4312482
Bookshop(s): Libreria Agropecuaria, Lagasca 38

EDHASA (Editora y Distribuidora Hispano-Americana SA)
Av Diagonal, 519-521, 2, 08029 Barcelona
Tel: (093) 4949720 *Fax:* (093) 4194584
E-mail: info@edhasa.es
Web Site: www.edhasa.es
Key Personnel
Editorial Dir: Daniel Fernandez *E-mail:* d.fdez@edhasa.es
Publisher's Assistant: Virginia Elizondo *E-mail:* v.elizondo@edhasa.es
Founded: 1946
Subjects: Fine Editions, Illustrated Books, General Trade Books-Hardcover, Juvenile & Young Adult Books, Translations, Economics, Fiction, History, How-To, Literature, Literary, Literary Criticism, Essays, Management, Maritime, Philosophy, Romance, Science Fiction, Fantasy, Travel
Type of Business: Distributor, Exporter

Editora y Distribuidora Hispano Americana SA (EDHASA), see EDHASA (Editora y Distribuidora Hispano-Americana SA)

Enrique Libreria
Libreros 8, E-28004 Madrid
Tel: (091) 5228088
Key Personnel
Contact: Enrique Bataller Ferrandiz
Founded: 1971
Type of Business: Exporter, Importer, Major Independent Bookseller

Casa del Libro Espasa-Calpe SA
Carretera de Irun KM 12, 200, 28049 Madrid
Mailing Address: Apdo de Correos 547, 28049 Madrid
Tel: (091) 3589689 *Fax:* (091) 3589505
Telex: 48850 ESPACE *Cable:* ESPACALPE
Owned by: Editorial Espasa-Calpe SA
Branch Office(s)
Colon de Larreategui 41, 48009 Bilbao *Tel:* (04) 4232005

Libreria Hispano Americana
Gran Via de Les Corts Catalanes 594, 08007 Barcelona
Tel: (093) 3175337; (093) 3180079 *Fax:* (093) 3189339
Key Personnel
Manager: Josep M Boixareu Vilaplana
Commercial Manager: Jose Romero Gonzalez
Founded: 1941
Specialize in Scientific & Technical Books.
Type of Business: Importer, Major Independent Bookseller

Hogar del Libro, SA
Ramelleres, 17, 08001 Barcelona
Tel: (093) 3182700 *Fax:* (093) 3010399
Key Personnel
Dir: Sebastia Fabregues
Branch Office(s)
Pg Placa Major 12, 08202 Sabadell
Pg Placa Major 34, 08202 Sabadell *Tel:* (03) 7255959
Hogar del Libro-Baricentro, Carretera Barcelona a Sabadell, Local No 135 *Tel:* (03) 7186310
Bookshop(s): Elisabets 6, 08001 Barcelona

Marcial Pons Librero
Calle San Sotero 6, 28037 Madrid
Tel: (091) 3043303 *Fax:* (091) 7541218
E-mail: ediciones@marcialpons.es
Founded: 1948
Type of Business: Distributor, Exporter, Importer, Major Independent Bookseller, Wholesaler
Bookshop(s): Law, Barbara de Braganza, 8, 28004 Madrid; Economics, Plaza de las Salesas, 10, 28004 Madrid; Humanities, Plaza Conde del Valle de Suchill, 8, 28015 Madrid

H F Martinez de Murguia SA
Valverde 30, 28004 Madrid
Tel: (091) 5227053 *Fax:* (091) 5313786
Key Personnel
Manager: Francisco Gugel
Supplier of books published in Spain.
Type of Business: Distributor, Exporter, Importer, Wholesaler

Mundi-Prensa Libros, SA
Castello 37, 28001 Madrid
Tel: (091) 4363700 *Fax:* (091) 5753998
E-mail: libreria@mundiprensa.es
Web Site: www.mundiprensa.com
Key Personnel
Gneral Manager: Jose Maria Hernandez *E-mail:* hernandez@mundiprensa.es
Founded: 1948
Publisher, bookseller & subscription agency.
Type of Business: Distributor, Exporter, Importer, Major Book Chain Headquarters, Major Independent Bookseller, Wholesaler
Branch Office(s)
Barcelona
Mexico City
Bookshop(s): Libreria Mundi-Prensa

Libreria Passim SA
Floridablanca, 54-58 Ent 4 B, 08015 Barcelona, Cataluna
Tel: (093) 4574757 *Fax:* (093) 4574757
E-mail: passim@intercom.es
Key Personnel
Manager: Alex Pujol
Publishes catalogs of new & out-of-print books about Spain & Latin America published in Spain. Specialize in sales to universities & libraries.
Type of Business: Exporter, Major Independent Bookseller

Libreria Pons SL
Felix Latassa, 33, 50006 Zaragoza
Mailing Address: Felix Latassa, 33, 50006 Zaragoza
Tel: (0976) 359037 *Fax:* (0976) 356072
E-mail: promedit@libreriapons-zaragoza.com
Web Site: www.libreriapons-zaragoza.com
Key Personnel
Dir: Juan F Pons
Founded: 1951
Library supplier.
Type of Business: Distributor, Importer, Major Independent Bookseller

PPC Editorial y Distribuidora, SA
Enrique Jardiel Poncela 4, 28016 Madrid
Tel: (091) 359-2300 *Fax:* (091) 345-0282
Telex: 45051 *Cable:* PEPECE
Key Personnel
President: Antonio Montero Moreno
Vice President: Juan Luis Acebal Lujan
Dir: Angel Alos Cortes
Type of Business: Distributor, Exporter, Major Book Chain Headquarters
Owned by: PPC

SPAIN

Branch Office(s)
Libreria Pastoral, Velazquez 2, 04002 Almeria
Libreria P P C, Canuda 9, 08002 Barcelona
Libreria Piedelatorre, 29015 Malaga
Libreria Selecta, San Felipe Neri 10, 07002 Palma de Mallorca
Libreria Concilio, Teniente Coronel Segui 1, 41001 Sevilla
Libreria Promocion, c/o Conde de Cardenas 5, 14002 Cordoba

Promocion Popular Cristiana, see PPC Editorial y Distribuidora, SA

Libreria Rubinos - 1860 SA
Alcala 98, 28009 Madrid
Tel: (091) 4352239 *Fax:* (091) 5753272
Key Personnel
Administrator: Antonio Rubinos Casanueva
Type of Business: Distributor, Exporter, Importer, Major Book Chain Headquarters, Major Independent Bookseller, Wholesaler

Sri Lanka

Bright Book Centre (Pvt) Ltd
S-27 1st Floor, Colombo Central Super Market Complex, Colombo 11
Mailing Address: PO Box 162, Colombo 0011
Tel: (01) 434770 *Fax:* (01) 333279
Key Personnel
President: Pon Sakthivel
Founded: 1990
Specialize in book publishing & distributing.
Type of Business: Distributor, Exporter, Importer, Major Independent Bookseller, Wholesaler
Branch Office(s)
77/24 Jampeetta Lane, Colombo 13

KVG de Silva & Sons
415 Galle Rd, Colombo 4
Tel: (01) 84146 *Fax:* (01) 588875
Telex: 22658 GLAXY CE
Key Personnel
President: K V J De Silva
Founded: 1898
Dealers in Rare Books & Maps of Sri Lanka & Sri Lankan Islands & old views of Sri Lanka.
Type of Business: Distributor, Importer, Major Independent Bookseller
Branch Office(s)
Serendib Gallery, 100 Galle Rd, Colombo 4
Bookshop(s): K V G's Bookstore, Liberty Plaza, Colombo 3

Lake House Bookshop
100 Sir Chittampalam Gardiner Mawatha, Colombo 2
Tel: (01) 32104; (01) 432105
Telex: 21266 Lakexpo Ce *Cable:* BOOKSALES
Key Personnel
Dir & General Manager: Victor Walatara
Founded: 1941
Also publisher.
Type of Business: Distributor, Exporter, Importer, Major Independent Bookseller, Wholesaler
Owned by: Lake House Investments Ltd, 40, WAD Ramanayake Mawatha, Colombo 2
Branch Office(s)
Liberty Plaza, Dehiwela, Hyde Park Corner

Sadeepa Bookshop
No 1060, Maradana Rd, Borella Colombo 8
Tel: (01) 686114; (01) 694289; (01) 678043 *Fax:* (01) 683813
E-mail: sadeepabk@itmin.com
Web Site: www.neatron-com/sadeepabk

Key Personnel
General Manager: Nimal Sarathchandra
Founded: 1987
Also printer & publisher.
Type of Business: Distributor, Importer, Major Book Chain Headquarters, Major Independent Bookseller, Wholesaler
Owned by: Sarath Chandra Wanniatchi
Branch Office(s)
Sadeepa Print Shop, 1121 B, Maradana Rd, Colombo 8
YMBA Bldg, Colombo 8

Sarasavi Book Shop Pvt Ltd
Subsidiary of Sarasavi Group of Companies
30, Stanley Thilakaratne Mawatha, Nugegoda 10250
Mailing Address: PO Box 89, Nugegoda 10250
Tel: (01) 852519; (01) 820983; (01) 820230; (074) 304546 *Fax:* (01) 821454; (01) 509503
E-mail: sarasavi@slt.lk
Web Site: www.sarasavibooks.com
Key Personnel
Chairman & Man Dir: Mr H D Premasiri
Founded: 1948
Membership(s): Sri Lanka Book Publishers' Association, Book Sellers Association of Ceylon, British Book Sellers Association, Sri Lanka Book Sellers Association.
Type of Business: Importer, Major Independent Bookseller
Imprints: Sarasavi Publishers
Branch Office(s)
Colombo Fort-44/9 YMBA Bldg *Tel:* (01) 326831
Colombo 8-1/50 YMBA Bldg, Borella *Tel:* (01) 698886
Kandy-86 D S Senanayake Veediya *Tel:* (08) 234036
Matara-74 Kumarathunga Mawatha *Tel:* (041) 28406
Warehouse: 3/1 Saint John's Church Rd, Nugegoda

Sarasavi Publishers, *imprint of* Sarasavi Book Shop Pvt Ltd

Sudan

Bashir Bookshop
PO Box 1118, Khartoum

The Khartoum Bookshop, see The New Bookshop

The New Bookshop
Zubeir Pasha St, Khartoum
Mailing Address: PO Box 968, Khartoum
Tel: (011) 774425
Telex: 22159 sd *Cable:* Newstand Khartoum
Key Personnel
Owner: P N Flanginis
Founded: 1957
Subjects: Member of the Sudan Chamber of Commerce-Khartoum
Type of Business: Distributor, Importer, Wholesaler

The Nile Bookshop
41 New Extension St, Khartoum
Mailing Address: PO Box 8036, Khartoum
Tel: (011) 43737; (011) 44189 *Cable:* NILE
Type of Business: Distributor, Importer, Major Independent Bookseller

The Sudan Bookshop Ltd
PO Box 156, Khartoum
Tel: (011) 74123; (011) 76781

Telex: 22480 sisco km *Cable:* Bookshop Khartoum
Key Personnel
Man Dir: Joseph A Tadros

University of Khartoum Bookshop
PO Box 321, Khartoum
Tel: (011) 80558
Key Personnel
Manager: Dr Khalid El-Mubarak
Owned by: Khartoum University Press

Sweden

Akerbloms Universitetsbokhandel
Affiliate of Bokia
Oestra Radhusgatan 6, Umea
Mailing Address: Box 83, S-90103 Umea
Tel: (090) 711250 *Fax:* (090) 711260
E-mail: swedish.books@akerbloms.se
Key Personnel
Manager: Mats Gyllengahm *E-mail:* mats.gyllengahm@bokia.se
Founded: 1843
Type of Business: Importer, Major Independent Bookseller

Akademibokhandeln/Almqvist & Wiksell
Maester Samuelsgatan 32, 113 98 Stockholm
Mailing Address: Box 7634, Stockholm
Tel: (08) 6909200 *Fax:* (08) 6909300
Founded: 1953
Group Members: Akademibokhandeln/Ecksersteins, Lundequistska.
Type of Business: Exporter, Importer, Major Book Chain Headquarters

Almqvist och Wiksell Bokhandel AB
Master Samuelsgatan 32, 10394 Stockholm
Mailing Address: Box 7634, 113 98 Stockholm
Tel: (08) 6136100 *Fax:* (08) 242543; (08) 208036
Telex: 12430
Member of Esselte Bokhandel Group.

Fritzes Booksellers
Regeringsgatan 12, 106 47 Stockholm
Mailing Address: PO Box 16356, 106 47 Stockholm
Tel: (08) 6909090 *Fax:* (08) 8205021
Telex: 12387 Fritzes S
Key Personnel
Man Dir: Hans Davidson
Owned by: Wennergven-Williams AB

AB Gleerups Universitetsbokhandeln
Box 172, 22100 Lund
Tel: (046) 196000 *Fax:* (046) 184247; (046) 196027
Key Personnel
Manager: Peter Dahl
President: Kjell Dyster-Aas
Type of Business: Distributor, Importer, Major Independent Bookseller, Wholesaler

Soederbokhandeln Hansson och Bruce AB
Goetgatan 37, 102 66 Stockholm
Mailing Address: PO Box 4086, 102 61 Stockholm
Tel: (08) 405432; (08) 6405433 *Fax:* (08) 6441315
Key Personnel
Manager: Stig Sunnerholm
Founded: 1874

Konst-Bibliofilen
Bangata 17, 11629 Stockholm

Mailing Address: PO Box 2042, Stockholm 10311
Tel: (08) 6407868
Key Personnel
Contact: Stefan Schueler
Founded: 1972
Monographs on living Swedish artists.
Type of Business: Major Independent Bookseller

Esselte Bokhandel Lundequistska
Oestra Agatan 31, 751 25 Uppsala
Mailing Address: PO Box 610, 751 25 Uppsala
Tel: (018) 139830 *Fax:* (018) 695837
Telex: 76255 Lundeg S
Key Personnel
Manager: Hans Molander
Member of Esselte Bokhandel Group.

AB Nordiska Bokhandeln
c/o Molander Brotvagen 32, 161 39 Bromma
Mailing Address: PO Box 161, 101 39 Bromma
Tel: (08) 269809 *Fax:* (08) 254246
Telex: 12430
Member of Esselte Bokhandel Group.
Owned by: AB Nordiska Bokhandelns Foerlag

Samdistribution AB
c/o Bonnier Forlagen, 103 63 Stockholm
Mailing Address: PO Box 3159, 103 63 Stockholm
Tel: (08) 6968000 *Fax:* (08) 6968361
Key Personnel
President: Soren Wahlund
Founded: 1975
Warehousing of books (Book Trade, Book Services & Book Club Members).
Type of Business: Distributor
Owned by: Bonnierfoerlagen AB

Wettergrens Bokhandel AB
Vaestra Hamngatan 22, 411 17 Goeteborg
Tel: (031) 894500 *Fax:* (031) 7062520
Key Personnel
Contact: Carl Wettergren
Founded: 1882
Type of Business: Major Independent Bookseller

Switzerland

H R Balmer AG Buchhandlung Verlag Verlagsauslieferung
Neugasse 12, Postfach 960, CH-6301 Zug
Tel: (041) 711 47 37 *Fax:* (041) 711 09 17
Key Personnel
Contact: Christoph Balmer
Type of Business: Distributor, Importer, Major Independent Bookseller, Wholesaler
Bookshop(s): Buches Balmer, Metalli-Allee, Baarerstr 22, 6304 Zug

Brunner Buecher AG, see Buchhandlung zum Elsasser AG

Buchhandlung zum Elsasser AG
Limmatquai 18, Postfach 8022, 8001 Zurich
Tel: (01) 2610847; (01) 2511612 *Fax:* (01) 2610897
Telex: 57268
Key Personnel
Manager: Mr Hansruedi Brunner

Fehr'sche Buchhandlung AG
Schmiedgasse 16, 9001 St Gallen
Tel: (075) 221152; (075) 231381
Key Personnel
Manager: B Brun

Hans Huber
Langgassstrasse 76, CH-3000 Berne 9
Tel: (031) 3004500 *Fax:* (031) 3004590
E-mail: admin@hanshuber.com
Web Site: verlag.hanshuber.com
Founded: 1927
Also publisher.
Type of Business: Distributor, Exporter, Importer, Major Independent Bookseller
Branch Office(s)
Zeltweg 6, CH-8032 Zurich *Tel:* (01) 2523360 (Medicine, Psychology, Science)

Buchhandlung Meili & Co
Fronwagplatz 13, Postfach 409, CH-8200 Schaffhausen
Tel: (053) 254144 *Fax:* (053) 254746
Telex: 76777 Meibuch
Owned by: Peter Meili & Co

No Name Photo Gallery, see PEP Buchhandlung & No Name Photo Gallery

Orell Fuessli Verlag
Nuschelerstr 22, Postf 8022, Zurich 3
Tel: (01) 2113630 *Fax:* (01) 4667412
Telex: (01) 813021 orla ch
Key Personnel
Manager: Dr Manfred Hiefner-Hug
Also Publisher.

PEP Buchhandlung & No Name Photo Gallery
Unterer Heuberg 2, CH-4051 Basel
Mailing Address: Postfach 9, 4142 Muchenstein 2
Tel: (061) 352065
Key Personnel
Vice President: Victor Zwimpfer
Founded: 1980
Bookstore specializing in photo, film, art, tattoo, Indian literature & photo gallery.
Type of Business: Distributor, Exporter, Importer, Major Book Chain Headquarters, Major Independent Bookseller
Owned by: Tobias Toggweiler

Pilgermission Buch & Brunnen-Verlag Basel
Wallstr 6, CH-4002 Basel
Tel: (061) 234406 *Fax:* (061) 2646010
Key Personnel
Contact: Hans-Peter Zueblin

Quellen-Verlag
Gallusstr 20, 9001 St Gallen
Tel: (071) 227 47 77 *Fax:* (071) 227 47 58

Hans R Rohr
Moehrlistr 130, CH-8006 Zurich
Tel: (01) 3614846
Founded: 1921
Branch Office(s)
Filmbuchhandlung Rohr, Oberdorfstr 3, CH-8024 Zurich (Film/Cinema)

Buchhandlung Scherz AG
Markgasse 25, Postfach 66, CH-3000 Berne
Tel: (031) 227337 *Fax:* (031) 210375
Owned by: Scherz Verlag AG

Schweizer Buchzentrum (Swiss Book Centre)
Postfach 522, CH-4600 Olten
Tel: (062) 476161 *Fax:* (062) 465676
Type of Business: Distributor

Buchhandlung Staeheli AG
Bederstr 77, CH-8021 Zurich
Tel: (01) 2099111 *Fax:* (01) 2099112
E-mail: info@staehelibooks.ch
Web Site: www.staehelibooks.ch *Cable:* STAEHELIBOOKS
Key Personnel
Chief Executive Officer: Claus Gretener
E-mail: claus.gretener@staehelibooks.ch
Founded: 1934
Booksellers & Subscription Agents
Online Bookshop.
Type of Business: Importer, Major Independent Bookseller
Bookshop(s): 4/5 Am Weinplatz, 8021 Zurich

Staeheli's Bookshops Ltd, see Buchhandlung Staeheli AG

Centre Suisse du Livre, see Schweizer Buchzentrum

Centro Svizzero del Libro, see Schweizer Buchzentrum

Swiss Book Centre, see Schweizer Buchzentrum

Wepf & Co AG
Eisengasse 5, Postfach, CH-4001 Basel
Tel: (061) 269 85 15 (Germany) *Fax:* (061) 261 35 97 (Germany)
E-mail: wepf@dial.eunet.ch
Web Site: www.wepf.ch *Cable:* WEPFCO BASEL
Key Personnel
Dir: H U Herrmann
Also Publisher & Antiquarian Bookshop.
Branch Office(s)
PO Box 1948, Hauptstr 400, 79576 Weil am Rhein, Germany *Tel:* (07621) 75028 *Fax:* (07621) 75992
5, quai des Bateliers, F-67000 Strasbourg, France *Tel:* (0388) 371327 *Fax:* (0388) 240096

Syrian Arab Republic

Avicenne Librairie Internationale
Rue Tajhiz St, Damascus Boite Postale 2456
Mailing Address: Box 2456, Damascus
Tel: (011) 2212911; (011) 2244477 *Fax:* (011) 2219833
E-mail: avicenne@net.sy
Telex: Ortexo 419120 SY
Key Personnel
Manager: Jean-Pierre Dummar
Founded: 1963
Entertainment Articles.
Type of Business: Distributor, Importer, Major Book Chain Headquarters
Owned by: Meridien Bookshop, Kuwatly St, Jean Pierre Dummar
Branch Office(s)
Sheraton Bookshop, Amawiia Sq, Damascus *Tel:* (011) 2229300
Amir Poloee Bookshop, Aleppo *Tel:* (021) 2246510
Safir Bookshop, Homs *Tel:* (031) 412400

Taiwan, Province of China

The Children's Book Store Company Ltd
10, Lane 992 Section 5 Min Sheng East Rd, Taipei

TAIWAN, PROVINCE OF CHINA

Tel: (02) 7628222 *Fax:* (02) 7604322
Key Personnel
Chief Exec: Chang Yao-Hwa
Founded: 1955
Type of Business: Wholesaler

Mei Ya Publications Inc (Sueling Inc)
10F 82 Fuhsing S Rd, Sec 2, Taipei 106
Tel: (02) 7037481 *Fax:* (02) 7033847
Telex: 11240 Sueling
Key Personnel
Manager: Julia Lee
Specialize in College and University textbook reprints (all copyrighted).

United Republic of Tanzania

The Dar Es Salaam Bookshop
Makunganya St, Dar Es Salaam
Mailing Address: PO Box 9030, Dar Es Salaam
Tel: (051) 23416
Key Personnel
Manager: C Salu

International Bookshop
PO Box 21341, Dar Es Salaam
Tel: (051) 21930; (051) 27458
Telex: 41334 Intpub Tz
Key Personnel
Dir: Murtaza Alidina
Retail Outlets: Les Nouvelles, Kilimanjaro Hotel, Dar Es Salaam.

Readit Books
PO Box 20986, Dar es Salaam
Tel: (022) 2184077 *Fax:* (022) 2181077
E-mail: readitbooks@yahoo.com

University of Dar Es Salaam Bookshop
Unit of Dar es Salaam University Press Ltd
PO Box 35182, Dar Es Salaam
Tel: (022) 2410093; (022) 2410500 (ext 2568) *Fax:* (022) 2410137
Key Personnel
Ag Marketing Manager: Mr A Kanuya *Tel:* (022) 2410300
Type of Business: Importer, Major Independent Bookseller
Owned by: University of Dar Es Salaam

Thailand

Asia Books Co Ltd
No 5 Sukhumvit Rd, SOI 61, Bangkok 10110
Mailing Address: PO Box 40, 10110 Bangkok
Tel: (02) 7159000 *Fax:* (02) 3811621; (02) 3912277
E-mail: information@asiabooks.com
Web Site: www.asiabooks.com
Key Personnel
Owner: Vinai Suttharoj
Dir: Anakepeerasak Rachanee *Tel:* (02) 7159166 *E-mail:* rachanee@asiabooks.com
Founded: 1969
Publisher, Distributor & chain of English language bookshops in Thailand.
Type of Business: Distributor, Importer, Major Book Chain Headquarters, Wholesaler
Showroom(s): Central City Bangna, 3rd floor, Central City Plaza, Room 309, Bangna-Trat Rd, KM 3 Bangkok *Tel:* (02) 3610743; (02) 3610744 *Fax:* (02) 3610745; Emporium Shopping Complex, 3rd floor next to the main entrance to Emporium Dept Store, Sukhumvit Rd, Bangkok *Tel:* (02) 6648565-7 *Fax:* (02) 6648548; Landmark A, Branch 1st floor, Landmark Plaza, Sukjumvit Rd, Bangkok *Tel:* (02) 2525839; (02) 2525456 *Fax:* (02) 2515993; Landmark Z: Art & Architecture Book Center, 3rd floor, Landmark Plaza, Sukhumvit Rd, Bangkok *Tel:* (02) 2525655; (02) 2529901 *Fax:* (02) 2515993; Peninsula: Asia Books Professional Bookshop, 2nd floor, Peninsula Plaza, Rajdamri Rd, Bangkok *Tel:* (02) 2539786; (02) 2539788 *Fax:* (02) 2540737; Seacon Square, 2nd floor, Srinakarin Rd, Bangkok *Tel:* (02) 7218867-8 *Fax:* (02) 7218869; Siam Discovery Center, 4th floor near the connecting walk to Siam Center, Bangkok *Tel:* (02) 6580418-20 *Fax:* (02) 6580421; Sukhumvit: Asia Books General Books Shop, 221 Sukhumvit Rd (Between Soi 15 & 17), Bangkok *Tel:* (02) 2527277; (02) 6510428 *Fax:* (02) 2516042; Thaniya: Professional Book Center, 3rd floor, Thaniya Plaza, Silom Rd, Bangkok *Tel:* (02) 2312106; (02) 2312107 *Fax:* (02) 2312108; Times Square, 2nd floor, Time Square Shopping & Plaza, Sukhumvit Rd (between Soi 12 & 14), Bangkok *Tel:* (02) 2500162; (02) 2500163 *Fax:* (02) 2500164; World Trade Centre, 3rd floor, Zone C, Phase II Rajdamri Rd, Bangkok *Tel:* (02) 2556209; (02) 2556210 *Fax:* (02) 2556211

Central Book Distribution Co, Ltd
306 Silom Rd, Bangkok 10500
Tel: (02) 367-5565 (direct); (02) 367-5030-41 (ext 181 & 178) *Fax:* (02) 367-5049
Telex: 82768 Cetrac Th *Cable:* CETRAC BANGKOK
Key Personnel
Owner: Tieng Chirathivat
Man Dir: Ratana Norabhanlobh *E-mail:* ratanan@cmg.co.th
Founded: 1948
Type of Business: Distributor, Exporter, Importer, Wholesaler

Christian Bookstore
14 Pramuan Rd, Bangkok 10500
Tel: (02) 234-7991
Key Personnel
Manager: Urai Kithpraditkul
Type of Business: Distributor, Importer, Major Book Chain Headquarters, Wholesaler

Nibhondh Co Ltd
40-42 Charoen Krung Rd Siyaeg Phaya Sri, Bangkok 10100
Tel: (02) 2212611; (02) 2211553
Key Personnel
Manager: Sumetra Kongsiri
English books at the above address; English, Thai books and magazines at Nibhondh (sikak), 40-42 New Rd, Bangkok.

Odeon Book Store Lp
Opp Odeon Theatre, Wang Burapha, Bangkok 10500
Tel: (02) 2210742; (02) 2216567 *Fax:* (02) 2253300; (02) 2548806
Key Personnel
Manager: Prasarn Santiwathana
Branch Office(s)
218/10-2 soil Siam Sq, Rama 1 Rd, Bangkok 10500

Suksit Siam Co Ltd
1715 Rama IV Rd, Bangkok 10500

MAJOR

Fax: (02) 2511630
Key Personnel
Manager, Publicity: Mrs Nilchawee Sivaraksa
Also library suppliers.
Type of Business: Importer

Suriwong Book Centre, Ltd
54 Sridonchai Rd, Chiang Mai 50100
Mailing Address: PO Box 44, Chiang Mai 50000
Tel: (053) 281052 *Fax:* (053) 271902
E-mail: suriwong@loxinfo.co.th
Key Personnel
Man Dir: Joy Jittidecharaks
Book Retailer in Thai & English, medical journals agent.
Bookshop(s): 54 Sridonchai Rd, Chiang Mai 50100 *E-mail:* suriwong@loxinfo.co.th

Suriyaban Bookstore
c/o Suriyaban Publishers, 14 Pramuan Rd, Bangkok 10500
Tel: (02) 2347991; (02) 2347992
Key Personnel
Manager: Surapon Byboribankul
Owned by: Suriyaban Publishers

White Lotus Co Ltd
16 Soi 47 Sukhumwit Rd, Bangkok 10110
Mailing Address: PO Box 1141, Bangkok 10110
Tel: (02) 3324915
Key Personnel
Chief Executive: D Ande
Founded: 1972
Also Publisher.
Type of Business: Distributor, Exporter, Importer, Wholesaler

Togo

Librairie/Editions Nouvelles Editions Africaines du TOGO
F239 du 13 Janvier, BP 4862, Lome
Mailing Address: 00228 Lome
Tel: 216761 *Fax:* 221003
Key Personnel
Contact: Fatai Joseph Aguiar
Sales Administrator: Takougnadi
Owned by: Les Nouvelles Editions Africaines du TOGO (NEA-TOGO)
Bookshop(s): 239 Blvd du 13 Janvier, Lome; Tokoin Doumassesse VB, Lome

Librairie Walter
25 rue du Grand Marche, BP 397, Lome

Trinidad & Tobago

Campus Corner Ltd
72 Pembroke St, Port of Spain
Tel: (868) 623-1678 *Fax:* (868) 623-1678
Key Personnel
Manager: Hilton S Young
Founded: 1973
Type of Business: Distributor, Importer, Major Independent Bookseller, Wholesaler

Charran's Bookshop (1978) Ltd
c/o Charran's Educational Publishers, 58 Western Main Rd, St James
Tel: (868) 6223832

BOOK DEALERS UNITED KINGDOM

Key Personnel
Manager: Betty Charran
Owned by: Charran Educational Publishers
Bookshop(s): Muir Marshall Ltd, 64a Independence Sq, Port of Spain

Tunisia

Librairie Art et Culture
24 Ave Taieb M'hiri, 7000 Bizerte
Tel: (02) 31072 *Fax:* (02) 431372
Key Personnel
Contact: Mr Limam Nouredine
Type of Business: Distributor

Editions Bouslama
15 Av de France, 1000 Tunis
Tel: (01) 245612
Also publisher.
Branch Office(s)
53 rue Nahas Pacha, Tunis
7 rue Amilcar, Tunis

Societe Nationale d'Edition et de Diffusion
5 ave de Carthage, 1000 Tunis
Tel: (01) 255000
Also publisher.

Turkey

ABC Kitabevi Sanayi Tic AS
Tunel Maydan 1, 80030 Beyoglu, Istanbul
Tel: (0212) 2762404 *Fax:* (0212) 2851860
Telex: 46963 Abca Tr
Key Personnel
Manager: Hamit Calcskan
Owned by: Genclik Kitabevi

Arkadas Ltd
Mithatpasa cad 28/C, Yenisehir, Ankara 06441
Tel: (0312) 4344624; (0312) 3548300 *Fax:* (0312) 4356057
Key Personnel
Chairman & Owner: Cumhur Ozdemir
  E-mail: cumhuro@arkadas.com.tr
Editor: Meltem Ozdemir *E-mail:* meltemo@arkadas.com.tr
Retail Trade of Book Stationery, Music Cassettes, Compact Discs, Import Diskettes, Poster & Print, Publishing.
Type of Business: Distributor, Importer, Major Independent Bookseller, Wholesaler

Fen Kitabevi
Milli Muedafaa Cad 14/7, Ankara
Tel: (0312) 4253111 *Fax:* (0312) 4185109; (0312) 4171733
Founded: 1975
Type of Business: Importer, Major Independent Bookseller, Wholesaler
Owned by: Guellueoglu/Mehmet S

Redhouse Bookstore
Rizapasa Yokusu 50, 34450 Eminonu/Istanbul
Tel: (01) 5221498 *Fax:* (01) 5190883
Telex: 23554 Peet Tr *Cable:* PEET ISTANBUL TR
Key Personnel
Manager: Charles H Brown
Owned by: Redhouse Press

Uganda

Uganda Bookshop
Ebenezer Bldg, Plot 4, Colville St, Kampala
Mailing Address: PO Box 7145
Tel: (041) 243756 *Fax:* (041) 245597 *Cable:* BOOKSHOP
Key Personnel
General Manager: Stephen Rostron
Founded: 1927
Type of Business: Distributor, Importer, Major Book Chain Headquarters, Major Independent Bookseller, Wholesaler
Owned by: Church of Uganda, PO Box 6246, Kampala

United Kingdom

Abbeydale, *imprint of* Bookmart Ltd

Africa Book Centre Ltd
38 King St, Covent Garden, London WC2E 8JT
Tel: (020) 7240 6649 *Fax:* (020) 7497 0309
  Toll Free Fax: (0845) 458 1579 (UK only)
E-mail: orders@africabookcentre.com
Web Site: www.africabookcentre.com
Key Personnel
Man Dir: Anthony W Zurbrugg *Tel:* (020) 7836 3020 *E-mail:* tz@africabookcentre.com
Founded: 1989
Member of Booksellers' Association (UK)
Also Publishers' Agent.
Type of Business: Distributor, Exporter, Importer, Major Independent Bookseller, Wholesaler
Warehouse: Central Books Ltd, 99 Wallis Rd, London E9 5LN *Tel:* (020) 8986 4854 *E-mail:* orders@centralbooks.com (Also distribution)

African Books Collective Ltd
The Jam Factory, 27 Park End St, Oxford OX1 1HU
Tel: (01865) 726686 *Fax:* (01865) 793298; (01993) 709265
E-mail: abc@dial.pipex.com
Web Site: www.africanbookscollective.com
Key Personnel
Consultant: Mary Jay
Marketing: Justin Cox
Customer Services Manager: Krisia Cook
Founded: 1989
Marketing & distribution of books published in Africa by 51 publishers from 12 countries. Scholarly, literature & children's, English language titles & Swahiti children's books.
Type of Business: Distributor
Owned by: African Publishers Collective
Warehouse: Unit 3, Off Pytts Lane, Burford Oxon OX18 4SJ

Afterhurst Ltd
27 Palmeira Mansions, Church Rd, Hove, East Sussex BN3 2FA
Tel: (01273) 748427 *Fax:* (01273) 722180
E-mail: dirdist@erlbaum.co.uk
Key Personnel
Sales Manager: Linda Jarrett
Type of Business: Distributor
Owned by: Taylor & Francis Ltd, 1 Gunpowder Sq, London EC4A 3DE

Airlift Book Co
8 The Arena, Mollison Ave, Enfield, Middlesex EN3 7NJ
Tel: (0181) 8040400 *Fax:* (0181) 8040044
Key Personnel
Man Dir: J Bailey
Founded: 1981
Type of Business: Distributor

Albany Book Co Ltd
30 Clydeholm Rd, Clydeside Industrial Estate, Glasgow G14 0BJ
Tel: (0141) 9542271
Telex: 777253
Key Personnel
Man Dir: Andrew T Haigh
Dir: Jonathan Ridge; Mike Jones; Joseph Halpin
Bookshop(s): Book Services (Scotland) Ltd, 32 Finlas St, Glasgow G22 5DU (School Textbook Supply); College Bookshop, Jordanhill College, Southbrae Dr, Glasgow G13 1PP (Educational Book Supply)

Aldington Books Ltd
Unit 3B, Frith Business Centre, Frith Rd, Aldington, Kent TN25 7HJ
Tel: (01233) 720123 *Fax:* (01233) 721272
E-mail: sales@aldingtonbooks.co.uk
Web Site: www.aldingtonbooks.com.uk

The Anglo American Book Company Ltd
Crown Buildings, Bancyfelin, Carmarthen SA33 5ND
Tel: (01267) 211880 *Fax:* (01267) 211882
E-mail: books@anglo-american.co.uk
Key Personnel
Man Dir: Dr Martin Roberts
Marketing Dir: David Bowman
Founded: 1992
Mail order book seller & distributor.
Type of Business: Distributor, Exporter, Importer

Apex Books Concern
Darus Salaam, 89 Norfolk Rd, Littlehampton, West Sussex BN17 5HE
Tel: (01903) 739042; (01903) 734432
  Fax: (01903) 734432; (0870) 056 7860
E-mail: enquiries@apexbooks.co.uk
Web Site: www.apexbooks.co.uk
Key Personnel
Man Dir: S Dean *Tel:* (01903) 734682
Dir: A Dean; Ms M Hughes
Founded: 1950
Specialist in religious & cultural studies. Books, journals, videos, slides, microforms in all subjects.
Type of Business: Distributor, Exporter, Importer

Art Books International Ltd
One Stewarts Court, 220 Stewarts Rd, London SW8 4UD
Tel: (020) 7720 1503 *Fax:* (020) 7720 3158
Key Personnel
Man Dir: Stanley Kekwick
Sales Manager: Fiona Smith
Head of Accounts: Stephen Coke
Founded: 1991
Type of Business: Distributor

Art Data
12 Bell Industrial Estate, 50 Cunningham St, London W4 5HB
Tel: (020) 8747 1061 *Fax:* (020) 8742 2319
Key Personnel
Contact: Mr T G Borton

Ashgrove Press
Imprint of Hollydata Publishers Ltd
3 Town Barton, Norton St Philip, Bath BA2 7LN
Tel: (01373) 834900 *Fax:* (01373) 834900
Web Site: www.ashgrovepublishing.com
Founded: 1980

1315

UNITED KINGDOM

Austicks Headrow Bookshop
91 The Headrow, Leeds LS1 6LJ
Tel: (0113) 2433099
Key Personnel
Manager: John Prime

Bailey Distribution Ltd
Subsidiary of Bailey Brothers & Swinfen Ltd
Montifield Industrial Estate, Learoyd Rd, Units 1A & 1B, New Romney, Kent TN28 8XU
Tel: (01797) 366905 *Fax:* (01797) 366638
Key Personnel
Dir: R P Mortimore
Founded: 1978
Type of Business: Distributor

B McCall Barbour
28 George IV Bridge, Edinburgh EH1 1ES
Tel: (0131) 2254816 *Fax:* (0131) 2254816
Key Personnel
Partner: Dr T C Danson-Smith
Founded: 1900
Christian Publishers.
Type of Business: Distributor, Exporter, Importer, Major Independent Bookseller, Wholesaler

Bargain Book Sales
2b Moore Park Rd, London SW6 2JT
Tel: (020) 7385 7007 *Fax:* (020) 7385 7007
Key Personnel
Owner & Dir: Graham Snell
Founded: 1975
Specializes in high-quality remainders, especially illustrated books on the Fine & Applied Arts, Graphics, Architecture, Photography, the Cinema & Music.
Type of Business: Remainder Dealer

Bay Foreign Language Books
Member of Bookseller's Association
Unit 3B Frith Business Centre, Frith Rd Aldington, Ashford Kent TN25 7HJ
Tel: (01233) 720020 *Fax:* (01233) 721272
E-mail: sales@baylanguagebooks.co.uk
Web Site: www.baylanguagebooks.co.uk
Key Personnel
Partner & Dir: Jan Barker
Dir: A R P Lennox-Kay
Founded: 1990
Publishers, University Library supply; over 480 languages in 2000-2001 catalogue.
Member of Bookseller's Association.
Type of Business: Distributor, Exporter, Importer, Major Independent Bookseller, Wholesaler

George Bayntun Booksellers
Manvers St, Bath BA1 1JW
Tel: (01225) 466000 *Fax:* (01225) 482122
Key Personnel
Proprietor & Owner: Edward Bayntun Coward
Founded: 1894
Rare Books, First Editions & Fine Bindings.

BEBC Distribution
Unit 15 Albion Close, Newtown Business Park, Parkstone Poole, Dorset BH12 3LL
Mailing Address: PO Box 1496, Parkstone Poole Dorset BH12 3LL
Tel: (01202) 715555 *Fax:* (01202) 715556
E-mail: bebc@bebc.co.uk
Web Site: www.bebc.co.uk
Key Personnel
Distribution Manager: Charles Kipping
  E-mail: charlesk@bebc.co.uk
Founded: 1974
Owned by: Bournemouth English Book Centre

Bertrams
The Nest, Rosary Rd, Norwich, Norfolk NR1 1TF
Tel: (01603) 216666 *Fax:* (01603) 611201
E-mail: books@bertrams.com
Key Personnel
Chairman: Kip Bertram
Chief Executive: Julian Rivers
Dir: Nigel Bertram
Co-Secretary: Mrs E Bertram
Buying Dept Manager: Mike Butler
Trade Manager: Barry Robinson
Founded: 1966
Type of Business: Exporter, Wholesaler

Bibliophile Books
5 Thomas Rd, London E14 7BN
Tel: (020) 7515 9222 *Fax:* (020) 7538 4115
E-mail: customercare@bibliophilebooks.com
Web Site: www.bibliophilebooks.com
Key Personnel
Chief Executive: Anne Quigley
Type of Business: Remainder Dealer

Biblios Publishers Distribution Services Ltd
Old London Rd, Washington RH20 3BN
Tel: (01903) 892346 *Fax:* (01903) 893383
E-mail: biblios@biblios.co.uk
Key Personnel
Administration Manager: Helen Negus
  E-mail: helenn@biblios.co.uk
Founded: 1976
Type of Business: Distributor

Birmingham Museums & Art Gallery
Division of Birmingham City Council
Chamberlain Sq, Birmingham B3 3DH
Tel: (0121) 3032834
E-mail: bmag_enq@birmingham.gov.uk
Web Site: www.bmag.org.uk
Key Personnel
Senior Assistant Dir: Mr G Allen
Administrator: J Swancutt *Tel:* (0121) 3033964
  E-mail: jackie_swancutt@birmingham.gov.uk
Museum & art gallery.

Blackwell Retail
48-51 Broad St, Oxford, Oxon OX1 3AJ
Tel: (01865) 792792 *Fax:* (01865) 794143
E-mail: sales@blackwell.co.uk
Telex: 83118 *Cable:* BOOKS OXFORD
Key Personnel
Man Dir: Alan Leitch
Type of Business: Exporter, Major Independent Bookseller
Bookshop(s): Blackwell's University Bookshop, 99 High St, Old Aberdeen AB25 3EN *Tel:* (01224) 486102 *Fax:* (01224) 276162; Blackwell's, 12-14 Upperkirkgate, Aberdeen AB10 1BG *Tel:* (01224) 644528 *Fax:* (01224) 630032; Blackwell's College Shop, Northern College, Hilton Place, Aberdeen AB10 1FA *Tel:* (01224) 488640; Blackwell's Medical Bookshop, University Medical School, Polwarth Bldg, Foresterhill, Aberdeen AB25 2ZD *Tel:* (01224) 683431; Blackwell's Business & Law Bookshop, 3 Windsor Arcade, Birmingham B2 5LG *Tel:* (0121) 2334969 *Fax:* (0121) 2363652; Blackwell's College Bookshop, Sandwell College, Wednesbury Campus, Woden Road South, Wednesbury WS10 0PE *Tel:* (0121) 5057711; Blackwell's Academic Bookshop, Bolton Institute, Deane Rd, Bolton BL3 5AB *Tel:* (01204) 521580; Blackwell's, 11 Bond St, Brighton BN1 1JL *Tel:* (01273) 329012; (01273) 329396 *Fax:* 01273) 329277; Blackwell's University Bookshop, University of Brighton, Mezzanine Floor, Cockroft Bldg, Moulsecoomb, Brighton *Tel:* (01273) 571974; (01273) 642020 *Fax:* (01273) 620556; Blackwell's Academic Bookshop, University of Brighton, Friston House, Village Way, Falmer, Brighton BN1 9PH *Tel:* (01273) 692624/643464; Blackwell's, 89 Park St, Bristol BS1 5PW *Tel:* (0117) 9276602 *Fax:* (0117) 9251854; Blackwell's University Bookshop, The University of the West of England, Coldharbour Lane, Bristol BS16 1Qy *Tel:* (0117) 9652573 *Fax:* (0117) 9750437; Blackwell's University Bookshop, University of Wales, College of Cardiff, University of Cardiff, Senghennydd, Cardiff CF2 4AG *Tel:* (01222) 340673; Blackwell's Medical Bookshop, The Concourse, University Hospital of Wales, Cardiff CF4 4XW *Tel:* (01222) 762878; Blackwell's, 13-17 Royal Arcade, Cardiff CF1 2PR *Tel:* (01222) 395036 *Fax:* (01222) 345680; Blackwell's at UWIC, Colchester Ave, Cardiff CF3 7XR *Tel:* (01222) 506307; Blackwell's, 4 Cornhill, Dorchester DT1 1BB *Tel:* (01305) 264081 *Fax:* (01305) 260551; Blackwell's University Bookshop, University of Dundee, 95 Nethergate, Dundee DD1 4DH *Tel:* (01382) 322184 *Fax:* (01382) 227048; Blackwell's Medical Bookshop, Ninewells Hospital, Dundee DD1 9SY *Tel:* (01382) 566551; Blackwell's College Bookshop, Northern College of Education, Gardyne Rd, Broughty Ferry, Dundee DD5 1NY *Tel:* (01753) 464277; Alden & Blackwell, Eton College, Windsor, Berkshire SL4 6DF *Tel:* (01753) 863849 *Fax:* (01753) 832453; Blackwell's University Bookshop, University of Exeter, Stocker Rd, Exeter EX4 4QA *Tel:* (01392) 59456 *Fax:* (01392) 411207; Blackwell's University Bookshop, School of Education, University of Exeter, Exeter EX1 2LU *Tel:* (01392) 264956; Blackwell's University Bookshop, Exmouth Campus, University of Plymouth, Douglas Ave, Exmouth EX8 2AT *Tel:* (01395) 225215; Blackwell's Business & Law Bookshop, 83 St Vincent St, Glasgow G2 5TF *Tel:* (0141) 2211369 *Fax:* (0141) 2211440; Blackwell's University Bookshop, University of Liverpool, Alsop Bldg, Brownlow Hill, Liverpool L3 5TX *Tel:* (0151) 7098146 *Fax:* 0151 7096653; Blackwell's University Bookshop, Aldham Robarts Learning Resource Centre, Liverpool Hohn Moores University, Maryland St, Liverpool L1 9DE *Tel:* (0151) 2313175; Blackwell's, 100 Charing Cross Rd, London WC2H 0JG *Tel:* (0207) 2925100 *Fax:* (0207) 2409665; Blackwell's University Bookshop, University of North London, 158 Holloway Rd, London *Tel:* (0207) 7004786 *Fax:* (0207) 7007687; Blackwell's University Bookshop, University of North London, Ladbroke House, 62-66 Highbury Grove, London N5 2AD *Tel:* (0207) 7535087 ext 5193; Blackwell's University Bookshop, 119-122 London Rd, London SE1 6LF *Tel:* (0207) 9285378 *Fax:* (0207) 2619536; Blackwell's University Bookshop, Faculty of the Built Environment, South Bank University, Wandsworth Rd, London SW8 2JZ *Tel:* (0207) 8158302 *Fax:* (0207) 8158302; Blackwell's Business & Law Bookshop, 243-244 High Holborn, London WC1V 7DZ *Tel:* (0207) 8319501 *Fax:* (0207) 4059412; Blackwell's College Bookshop, Holborn College of Law, 200 Greyhound Rd, London W14 9RY *Tel:* (0207) 3813731; Blackwell's City Bookshop, 11 Copthall Ave, London EC2R 7DJ *Tel:* (0207) 6381991 *Fax:* (0207) 6381594; Blackwell's Medical Bookshop, Royal Free Hospital, School of Medicine, University of London, Rowland Hill St, London NW3 2PF *Tel:* (0207) 8302180 *Fax:* (0207) 8302180; Blackwell's Medical Bookshop, King's College School of Medicine & Dentistry, Bessemer Rd, London SE5 9PJ *Tel:* (0207) 3464074 *Fax:* (0207) 3464074; Blackwell's Academic Bookshop, Union Bldg, Loughborough University, Ashby Rd, Loughborough LE11 3TT *Tel:* (01509) 219788 *Fax:* (01509) 219754; Blackwell's University Bookshop, Faculty of Agriculture & Food Sciences, Sutton Bonington, Loughborough LE12 5RD *Tel:* (0115) 9516017; Blackwell's University Bookshop, The Precinct Centre, Oxford Rd, Manchester M13 9RN *Tel:* (0161) 8344019 *Fax:* (0161)

BOOK DEALERS — UNITED KINGDOM

8329240; Blackwell's, University Library, UMIST, Sackville St, Manchester M60 1QD *Tel:* (0161) 2004936; Blackwell's, Manchester Business School, Booth St, West Manchester M15 6PB *Tel:* 0161) 2756320; Blackwell's Academic Bookshop, The Elizabeth Gaskell Site, Manchester Metropolitan University, Hathersage Rd, Manchester M13 0JA; Blackwell's, 141 Percy St, Newcastle Upon Tyne NE1 7RS *Tel:* (0191) 232 6421 *Fax:* (0191) 260 2536; Blackwell's University Bookshop, University of Nottingham, Portland Bldg, University Park, Nottingham NG7 2RD *Tel:* (0115) 9587063 *Fax:* (0115) 9505935; Blackwell's Medical Bookshop, Queen's Medical Centre, Clifton Blvd, Nottingham NG7 2UH *Tel:* (0115) 9780938 *Fax:* (0115) 9709980; Blackwell's Arts Centre Bookshop, Arts Centre, University Park, Nottingham NG7 2UH *Tel:* (0115) 9515057; Blackwell's University Bookshop, Nottingham Trent University, Chaucer Bldg, Goldsmith St, Nottingham NG1 5LT *Tel:* (0115) 9417307 *Fax:* (0115) 9417311; Blackwell's University Bookshop, Nottingham Trent University, Clifton Campus, Clifton Lane, Clifton, Nottingham NG11 8NS *Tel:* (0115) 9844474 *Fax:* (0115) 9211410; Blackwell's University Bookshop, Oxford Brookes University, Gipsy Lane, Headington, Oxford OX3 0BP *Tel:* (01865) 483063; (01865) 792792; Blackwell's Medical Bookshop, John Radcliffe Hospital, Headington, Oxford OX3 9DU *Tel:* (01865) 741663 *Fax:* (01865) 741663; Blackwell's Art Bookshop, 27 Broad St, Oxford OX1 2AS *Tel:* (01865) 792792 *Fax:* (01865) 794143; Blackwell's Map & Travel Shop, 53 Broad St, Oxford OX1 3BQ *Tel:* (01865) 792792 *Fax:* (01865) 794143; Blackwell's Music Shop, 38 Holywell St, Oxford OX1 3SW *Tel:* (01865) 792792 *Fax:* (01865) 248833; Blackwell's Children's Bookshop, 8 Broad St, Oxford OX1 3AJ *Tel:* (01865) 792792 *Fax:* (01865) 790937; Blackwell's Rare Books, 38 Holywell s, Oxford OX1 3SW *Tel:* (01865) 792792 *Fax:* (01865) 248833; Blackwell's Paperback Bookshop, 23-25 Broad St, Oxford OX1 3AX *Tel:* (01865) 248870; (01865) 792792 *Fax:* (01865) 794143; Blackwell's University Bookshop, University of Glamorgan, LLantwit, Treforest, Pontypridd, Mid-Glamorgan CF37 1DL *Tel:* (01443) 401502 *Fax:* (01443) 400791; Blackwell's Academic Bookshop, University of Portsmouth, 6-7 Charterhouse, Lord Montgomery Way, Portsmouth PO1 1SB *Tel:* (01705) 832813 *Fax:* (01705) 832813; Blackwell's Academic Bookshop, University of Portsmouth, Milton Site, Locksway Rd, Milton, Portsmouth PO4 8JF *Tel:* (01705) 844181; Blackwell's, 12-16 Arundel Way, Portsmouth PO1 1NZ *Tel:* (01705) 825552 *Fax:* (01705) 851032; Blackwell's University Bookshop, University Library Bldg, University of Central Lancashire, 52 St Peter's Square, Preston PR1 2HZ *Tel:* (01772) 254462; (01772) 893990 *Fax:* (01772) 202313; Blackwell's, 6-12 Kings Rd, Reading RG1 3AA *Tel:* (0118) 9595555 *Fax:* (0118) 9509638; The Friar Street Bookshop, 142-143 Friar St, Reading RG1 1EX *Tel:* (0118) 9573082; Blackwell's College Bookshop, University College of Ripon & York St John, College Road, Ripon, North Yorkshire HG4 2QX *Tel:* (01765) 602961 ext 242; Blackwell's University Bookshop, University of Salford, Horlock Court, University Rd, Salford M5 4WT *Tel:* (0161) 7374565 *Fax:* (0161) 7430566; Blackwell's University Bookshop, Sheffield Hallam University, City Campus, Pond St, Sheffield S1 1WB *Tel:* (0114) 2752152 *Fax:* (0114) 2798950; Blackwell's, 156-160 West St, Sheffield S1 3ST *Tel:* (0114) 2738906 *Fax:* (0114) 2700935; Blackwell's, Broomhill, 220 Fulwood Rd, Sheffield S10 3BB *Tel:* (0114) 2660820; Blackwell's, Broomhill, 220 Fulwood Rd, Sheffield S10 3BB *Tel:* (0114) 2660820; Blackwell's Academic bookshop, Southampton Institute, Sir James Matthews Bldg, 157-187 Above Bar St, Southampton SO14 7JT *Tel:* (01703) 631806 *Fax:* (01703) 631787; Blackwell's University Bookshop, University of Sunderland, Edinburgh Bldg, Chester Rd, Sunderland SR1 3SD *Tel:* (0191) 5152908 *Fax:* (0191) 5140462; Blackwell's University Bookshop, University of Sunderland, St Peter's Campus, St Peter's Way, Monkwearmouth, Sunderland SR6 0DD *Tel:* (0191) 5153985; Blackwell's at South Devon College, McKay Bldg, Newton Rd, Torquay TQ2 5BY *Tel:* (01803) 386407 *Fax:* (01803) 291992; Blackwell's University Bookshop, University of York, Heslington, York YO1 5DD *Tel:* (01904) 432715 *Fax:* (01904) 413420; Blackwell's, 32 Stonegate, Yoek YO1 2AP *Tel:* (01904) 624531 *Fax:* (01904) 623294; Blackwell's Academic Bookshop, York College of Further & Higher Education, Tadcaster Rd, Dringhouses, York YO2 1UA *Tel:* (01904) 770438

Roy Bloom Ltd
Fanshaw House, 3-9 Fanshaw St, London N1 6HX
Tel: (020) 7729 5373 *Fax:* (020) 7729 2375
Key Personnel
Chairman: Roy Bloom *E-mail:* roybloom@dircon.co.uk
Man Dir: Adam Bloom
Sales: Paul White
Founded: 1969
Specialize in publishers' overstocks & remainders.
Type of Business: Remainder Dealer

Book Exports, see Commonwealth Education Foundation

Book Representation & Distribution Ltd
Hadleigh Hall, London Rd, Hadleigh, Essex SS7 2DE
Tel: (01702) 552912 *Fax:* (01702) 556095
E-mail: mail@bookreps.com
Web Site: www.bookreps.com
Key Personnel
Man Dir: Dan Levey
Secretary: Doreen Mann
Accountant: Richard Foster
Sales Manager: Celia Stocks
Marketing Manager: Don Brown
Founded: 1988
Type of Business: Distributor, Exporter, Importer

Bookmark Remainders
Riverdell Illand, Launceston, Cornwall PL15 7LS
Tel: (01566) 782728 *Fax:* (01566) 776061
Key Personnel
Man Dir: Andrew Rattray
Founded: 1954
Remainder specialists.
Type of Business: Remainder Dealer

Bookmart Ltd
Desford Rd, Enderby, Leicester LE9 5AD
Tel: (0116) 2751800 *Fax:* (0116) 2750507
E-mail: books@bookmart.co.uk
Key Personnel
Man Dir: Philip E Parkin
Finance Dir: Andrew Painter
Co-Edition Sales Manager: Linda Williams
Founded: 1989
Publisher & distributor, promotional books.
Imprints: Abbeydale; Silverdale
Branch Office(s)
Regent St, London

Bookpoint Ltd
39 Milton Park, Abingdon, Oxfordshire OX14 4TD
Tel: (01235) 400400 *Fax:* (01235) 861038; (01235) orders 821511
E-mail: firstname.lastname@bookpoint.co.uk
Telex: 837091 bookpt g
Key Personnel
Man Dir: Tony Bryars
Founded: 1973
Type of Business: Distributor
Owned by: Hodder Headline PLC

Books for Europe Ltd
3 Sutton Court, 92 Grange Rd, London W5 3PG
Tel: (020) 8840 6672
Key Personnel
Man Dir: Juliusz Komarnicki *Tel:* (091) 9671539 *Fax:* (091) 9667865
Type of Business: Exporter

Books from India (UK) Ltd
45 Museum St, London WC1A 1LR
Tel: (020) 7405-3784 *Fax:* (020) 7831-4517
Key Personnel
Contact: Shreeram Vidyarthi
Founded: 1978
Also publisher.
Type of Business: Distributor, Exporter, Importer, Major Independent Bookseller, Wholesaler
Branch Office(s)
Asia Publishing House Ltd, Borden Villa, Borden Lane, Sittingbourne, Kent ME10 1BY
Tel: (01795) 473149 *Fax:* (01795) 473149

Bookworld Wholesale
Unit 10, Hodfar Rd, Sandy Lane Industrial Estate, Stourpont-on-Severn, Worcs DY13 9QB
Tel: (01299) 823330 *Fax:* (01299) 829970
Key Personnel
Partner: Lian Clark; Janet Gainham; Justin Gainham; Leslie Gainham
Founded: 1988
Specialize in transport, military & modelling books.
Type of Business: Distributor, Exporter, Importer, Wholesaler

Booth-Clibborn Editions, see Internos Books

Botes Librair
Parkhurst Mews, Parkhurst Rd, Bexhill, East Sussex TN40 1DW
Mailing Address: PO Box 22, Bexhill, East Sussex TN40 1DW
Tel: (01424) 210871 *Fax:* (01424) 734506; (01424) 731262
E-mail: 100450.3641@compuserve.com
Key Personnel
President: David L Gould
Founded: 1964
Library suppliers, educational supplies & specialists in medical & scientific publications.
Type of Business: Exporter, Wholesaler
Branch Office(s)
Botes Unifoyle Ltd, International School Book Distributors
Bookshop(s): Books Unlimited, PO Box 22, Bexhill, East Sussex TN40 1DW

BPL Remainders
Princess House, 50 Eastcastle St, Suite 275, London W1N 7AP
Tel: (020) 7636 5070; (020) 7631 5070 *Fax:* (020) 7580 3001
Telex: 22303
Key Personnel
General Manager: K Fox
Export Sales Administrator: Francesca Ferguson
Founded: 1982
Type of Business: Remainder Dealer

Bradt Travel Guides Ltd
19 High St, Chalfont St Peter, Saint Peter Bucks SL9 9QE
Tel: (01753) 893444 *Fax:* (01753) 892333
E-mail: info@bradt-travelguides.com
Web Site: www.bradt-travelguides.com
Key Personnel
President: Hilary Bradt
Office Manager: Debbie Hunter
Founded: 1972
US Distributor: Globe Pequot Press.
Type of Business: Exporter

The Bridge Book Co Ltd
Winton House, Wintonlea, Monument Way West, Woking, Surrey GU21 5EN
Tel: (01483) 720505 *Fax:* (01483) 756143
E-mail: bridgepem@aol.com
Key Personnel
Man Dir: M J Pemberton
Founded: 1962
Type of Business: Distributor, Exporter, Importer, Remainder Dealer
Parent Company: Chrysalis Books Ltd

Bridge Bookshop Ltd
Shore Rd, Isle of Man, Port Erin IM9 6HL
Tel: (01624) 833376 *Fax:* (01624) 835381
Key Personnel
Manager: Joan Hook
Dir: Rosemary Pickard
Founded: 1953
Type of Business: Exporter, Major Independent Bookseller
Owned by: Rosemary & Alan Pickard

Browne's Bookstore
56 Mill Rd, Cambridge CB1 2AS
Tel: (01223) 350968 *Fax:* (01223) 353456
E-mail: brownes_books@msn.com
Key Personnel
Contact: Mrs G H Browne
Founded: 1976
Specialize in mail order, library supplies.
Type of Business: Exporter, Major Independent Bookseller

Bushwood Books
6 Marksbury Ave, Kew Gardens, Surrey TW9 4JF
Tel: (0208) 3928585 *Fax:* (0208) 3929876
E-mail: bushwd@aol.com
Key Personnel
Contact: Richard Hansen; Victoria Hansen
Founded: 1984
Type of Business: Distributor
Owned by: Ultraco Ltd

Cedar Media
7-9 Church Hill, Loughton, Essex IG10 1QP
Tel: (020) 8508 8856 *Fax:* (020) 8508 8856
E-mail: cedarmedia@btinternet.com
Key Personnel
Dir: Marie L Barnett; Roger Barnett
Founded: 1987
Marketing, distribution of reference publication concerning EU & Europe as a whole.
Type of Business: Distributor, Exporter, Importer

Central Books
99 Wallis Rd, London E9 5LN
Tel: (020) 8986 4854 *Fax:* (020) 8533 5821
E-mail: orders@centralbooks.com
Key Personnel
Man Dir: William Norris
Sales Manager: Mark Chilver
Accounts: Dave Cope
Founded: 1939
Type of Business: Distributor, Exporter, Importer, Major Independent Bookseller

Clarke Associates Ltd
2-3 Denmark St, Bristol BS1 5DQ
Tel: (0117) 968864 *Fax:* (0117) 9226437
Key Personnel
Chairman, Man Dir: Malcolm Clarke
Dir: Susan C Phillips
Founded: 1982
Publishing Consultants.
Type of Business: Distributor, Exporter, Importer
Owned by: Clarke Associates Ltd

Clipper Distribution Services
Windmill Grove, Portchester, Hants PO16 9HT
Tel: (01705) 200080 *Fax:* (01705) 200090
Key Personnel
Contact: John Delieu
Founded: 1988
Type of Business: Distributor

Colt Associates
The Old School, Brewhouse Hill, Wheathampstead, St Albans, Herts AL4 8AN
Tel: (0158) 2834292 *Fax:* (0158) 825778
Key Personnel
President: Roger Lloyd-Taylor
Founded: 1977
Other branch offices located in China, Hong Kong & Manila.
Branch Office(s)
Toyko, Japan

Combined Book Services
Units I-K, Paddock Wood Distribution Center, Paddock Wood, Tonbridge, Kent TN12 6UU
Tel: (01892) 837171 *Fax:* (01892) 837272
E-mail: orders@combook.co.uk
Key Personnel
Man Dir: Charles Turner
Mail order book distribution.
Type of Business: Distributor, Exporter, Importer, Wholesaler

Commonwealth Education Foundation
Formerly Book Exports
PO Box 367, Edgware, Middlesex HA8 7AG
Tel: (0208) 9312359 *Fax:* (0208) 9592137
E-mail: rushanbp@aol.com
Founded: 1989
Suppliers of any book to any country, single volume to complete libraries. Free of charge.

Computer Bookshops Ltd
205 Formans Rd, Sparkhill, Birmingham B11 3AXL
Tel: (0121) 7783333 *Fax:* (0121) 6060469
E-mail: info@compbook.co.uk
Web Site: www.compbook.co.uk
Key Personnel
Chairman: I K Maclean
Man Dir: Donna Jones
Head of Marketing: Paul Savill *E-mail:* pauls@compbook.co.uk
Founded: 1978
Type of Business: Distributor, Wholesaler

Coningsby International Bookshop Services
22 School Lane, Coningsby, Lincoln LN4 4WX
Tel: (01526) 342231 *Fax:* (01526) 344367
E-mail: service@coningsby.com
Web Site: www.coningsby.com
Key Personnel
Owner: Clive Sharples; Ruth Sharples
Founded: 1976
Type of Business: Exporter, Major Independent Bookseller

Cordee Ltd
3a De Montfort St, Leicester LE1 7HD
Tel: (0116) 254 3579 *Fax:* (0116) 247 1176
Founded: 1973
Specialize in recreation & travel.
Type of Business: Distributor, Wholesaler

The Crafts Council
44A Pentonville Rd, London N1 9BY
Tel: (020) 7806 2559 *Fax:* (020) 7837 6891
Key Personnel
Manager: Jo Swait *Tel:* (020) 7806 2557
 E-mail: j-swait@craftscouncil.org.uk
Contact: Lisa Daniel
Founded: 1971
Government-financed body promoting Britain's artist craftsman, craft books & catalogs.
Bookshop(s): The Gallery Shop, 44A Pentonville Rd, London N1 9BY

Crofthouse Books Ltd
39 Alexandra Rd, Addlestone, Weybridge, Surrey KT15 2PQ
Tel: (01932) 845559 *Fax:* (01932) 849528; (01932) 830006
E-mail: croft@croftbook.co.uk
Web Site: www.crofthouse.co.uk
Key Personnel
Dir: David H Smith
Type of Business: Distributor, Exporter, Importer, Major Independent Bookseller

Cyngor Llyfrau Cymru Canolfan Dosbarthu, see Welsh Books Council: Distribution Centre

D Services
6 Euston St, Freemen's Common, Leicester LE2 7SS
Tel: (0116) 2547671 *Fax:* (0116) 2544670
Key Personnel
General Manager: Trevor Martin
Sales Manager: John Timmis
Founded: 1973
Type of Business: Distributor
Owned by: W H Smith

Dawson UK Ltd, Books Division
Crane Close, Denington Industrial Estate, Wellingborough, Northants NN8 2QG
Tel: (01933) 274444 *Fax:* (01933) 225993
E-mail: bksales@dawson.co.uk
Key Personnel
Chief Executive: B C Ingleby
European Book Division Manager: Diane Kerr
European Publisher Relations Manager: Eric Le Strat
Marketing Manager, UK: M Johnson
Founded: 1809
Subscription Agent.
Type of Business: Distributor, Exporter, Importer
Owned by: Dawson Holdings Plc
Associate Companies: Dawson UK Subscription & Technology Divisions, Cannon House, Folkestone, Kent CT19 5EE

Delta Books Worldwide
39 Alexandra Rd, Addlestone Weybridge, Surrey KT15 2PQ
Tel: (01932) 854776 *Fax:* (01932) 849528
Key Personnel
Contact: Eileen Fryer
Type of Business: Distributor, Exporter, Wholesaler

Dillons, The Bookstore
Royal House, Princes Gate, Homer Rd, Solihull B11 3QQ
Tel: (0121) 6314333
Branch offices in Aberdeen, Birmingham, Bromley, Cambridge, Canterbury, Charing Cross, Chichester, Coventry, Crawrey, Croydon, Derby, Ealing, Egham, Harrogate, Leicester, Liverpool, London, Manchester, Nottingham, Oxford, & Wolverhampton.
Owned by: THORN EMI Home Electronics (UK) Ltd

BOOK DEALERS UNITED KINGDOM

Branch Office(s)
Charing Cross
Chichester
Coventry

Dillons City Business Book Store
72 Park Rd, London WC2N 5EJ
Tel: (020) 7628 7479 *Fax:* (020) 7628 7871
E-mail: loncbus@dillons.eunet.co.uk
Key Personnel
Manager: Amanda Panedli

The Economists' Bookshop
Clare Market, Portugal St, London WC2A 2AB
Tel: (020) 7405 5531 *Fax:* (020) 7430 1584
E-mail: economists@waterstones.co.uk
Key Personnel
General Manager: Sue Tarratt
Owned by: The EMI Group -Dillons Group, Royal House, Prince's Gate House Rd, Solihull, W Ruplands BG1 3QQ
Branch Office(s)
The Barbican Business Book Centre, 9 Moorfields, London *Tel:* (020) 7628 7479
Bookshop(s): City Poly Bookshop, Moorgate, London EC2; City University Bookshop, Northampton Square, London EC1V 0HB; Queen Mary and Westfield College Bookshop, Mile End Rd, London E1 4NS; Brunel University Bookshop, Cleveland Rd, Uxbridge, Middlesex

Electronica Books & Media Ltd
Sunbury International Business Center, Brookland Close, Sunbury-on-Thames, Middlesex TW16 7DX
Tel: (01932) 765119 *Fax:* (01932) 765429
Key Personnel
Dir: Michael Geelan
Founded: 1988
Type of Business: Distributor, Exporter, Importer, Wholesaler

Elstead Maps
Badgery Hookley Lane, Elstead Godalming, Surrey GU8 6JE
Tel: (01252) 703472 *Fax:* (01252) 703971
E-mail: maps@elstead.co.uk
Web Site: www.elstead.co.uk
Key Personnel
Proprietor: Stephen Colebrooke *E-mail:* stephen@elstead.co.uk
Founded: 1981
Mail order retailers.

European Schoolbooks Ltd
The Runnings, Cheltenham GL51 9PQ
Tel: (01242) 245252 *Fax:* (01242) 224137
Key Personnel
Man Dir: Frank A Preiss *E-mail:* fap@esb.co.uk
Founded: 1964
Specialists in major European languages other than English.
Type of Business: Distributor, Importer, Wholesaler
Bookshop(s): The European Bookshop, 5 Warwick St, London W1R 5RA

Eurospan Distribution Center Ltd
Bolholt Walshaw Rd, Bury, Lancs BL8 1RP
Tel: (0161) 7642296 *Fax:* (0161) 7648213
E-mail: chris@e_d_c.co.uk
Key Personnel
Man Dir: Peter Kershaw Taylor
Founded: 1969
Type of Business: Distributor

Clive Farahar & Sophie Dupre Booksellers
Horsebrook House, XV The Green, Calne, Wilts SN11 8DQ
Tel: (01249) 821121 *Fax:* (01249) 821202
E-mail: post@faraharupre.co.uk
Web Site: www.faraharupre.co.uk
Key Personnel
Contact: Sophie Dupre *E-mail:* sophie@faraharadupre.co.uk
Founded: 1981
Antiquarian books on voyages & travels. Autograph letters, signed photos, signed books, photography in all fields especially royalty & literature.
Type of Business: Major Independent Bookseller

T C Farries & Co Ltd
Irongray Rd, Lochside, Dumfries DG2 0LH
Tel: (01387) 720755 *Fax:* (01387) 721105
Key Personnel
Chairman: D W N Landale
Sales Dir: Mrs L Bennett
Man Dir: P D R Landale
Finance Dir: J McGrillis
Founded: 1982
Type of Business: Distributor, Exporter, Major Independent Bookseller, Wholesaler

W & G Foyle Ltd
113-119 Charing Cross Rd, London WC2H 0EB
Tel: (020) 7437 5660
Key Personnel
Manager: John Cruickshanks

Freelance Market News Ltd
Sevendale House, 7 Dale St, Manchester M1 1JB
Tel: (0161) 2282362 *Fax:* (0161) 2283533
E-mail: fmn@writersbureau.com
Web Site: www.writersbureau.com
Key Personnel
Editor: Angela Cox
Founded: 1968
Type of Business: Distributor, Exporter, Importer, Major Independent Bookseller, Wholesaler
Owned by: The Writers Bureau

Walter H Gardner & Co
16 Chalton Dr, London N2 0QW
Tel: (20) 8458 3202 *Fax:* (20) 8458 8499
Key Personnel
Man Partner: Walter H Gardner
Sales & Marketing: Mrs D Gardner
Type of Business: Remainder Dealer

Gardners Books
One Whittle Dr, Eastbourne, East Sussex BN23 6HQ
Tel: (01323) 521555 *Fax:* (01323) 521666
E-mail: export@gardners.com
Web Site: www.gardners.com
Key Personnel
Dir, Export Sales: Warwick Bailey *E-mail:* wbailey@gardners.com
Contact: Mike Burge
International Book Wholesalers.
Type of Business: Exporter, Wholesaler

Gazelle Book Services Ltd
Falcon House, Queen Sq, Lancaster LA1 1RN
Tel: (01524) 68765 *Fax:* (01524) 63232
E-mail: gazellebooks@talk21.com
Web Site: www.gazellebook.co.uk
Key Personnel
Man Dir: Trevor Witcher *E-mail:* trevor.gazelle@talk21.com
Dir: Brian Haywood; Mark Trotter
Founded: 1988
Type of Business: Distributor

George Gregory Bookseller
Manvers St, Bath BA1 1JW
Tel: (01225) 466000 *Fax:* (01225) 482122
Key Personnel
President: Mrs C A W Bayntun-Coward
Founded: 1846
Old Books, Maps & Prints.

William George's Sons Ltd
89 Park St, Bristol BS1 5PW
Tel: (0117) 9276602
Key Personnel
Manager: Duncan Dewfall

John Gifford Ltd, see W & G Foyle Ltd

Godfrey Cave Associates Ltd
27 Wrights Lane, London W8 5TZ
Tel: (020) 7416 3000 *Fax:* (020) 7416 3289
Key Personnel
Man Dir: Kevin Binston
Sales Dir: Deborah Wright
Sales Manager: Patrick Duffin
Publishing, Liason Manager: Roz Scott
Founded: 1972
Type of Business: Remainder Dealer

Godfrey Cave Holdings Ltd
27 Wrights Lane, London W8 5TZ
Tel: (020) 7416 3000 *Fax:* (020) 7416 3099
Comprised of Godfrey Cave Associates, Bloomsbury Editions, Omega Books, Benson Books.
Type of Business: Remainder Dealer

Gracewing/Fowler Wright Books
Gracewing House, 2 Southern Ave, Leominster Herefordshire HR6 0QF
Tel: (0568) 616835 *Fax:* (0568) 613289
Key Personnel
Man Dir: Tom Longford
Founded: 1958
Type of Business: Distributor, Exporter, Importer, Major Independent Bookseller, Wholesaler

Grange Books PLC
The Grange, Units 1-6, Kingsnorth Industrial Estate, Hoo, Nr Rochester, Kent ME3 9ND
Tel: (01634) 256 000 *Fax:* (01634) 255 500
E-mail: grangebooks@aol.com
Web Site: www.grangebooks.co.uk
Key Personnel
Man Dir: Michael Ash
Founded: 1972
Specialize in Illustrated Adult Nonfiction, Children's, Promotional, Reprint & Remainder Books; Publisher of promotional books co-editions.
Type of Business: Remainder Dealer

Grantham Book Services Ltd
Isaac Newton Way, Alma Park Industrial Estate, Grantham, Lincs NG31 9SD
Tel: (01476) 541000; (01476) 541 080 (orders) *Fax:* (01476) 541061
E-mail: orders@gbs.tbs-ltd.co.uk
Key Personnel
Chairman: David Pemberton
Man Dir: Graham Miller
Founded: 1975
Contract Distribution (Publishing).
Type of Business: Distributor
Owned by: Random House Group

Green Street Bookshop (Mail Order)
Yardleys, 12 Newbiggen St, Thaxted, Essex CM6 2QR
Tel: (01371) 831449 *Fax:* (01371) 831599
E-mail: info@gsb.org.uk
Web Site: www.gsb.org.uk
Key Personnel
Manager: Tahira Whiteman *E-mail:* sales@gsb.org.uk
Founded: 1983
Specialize in books on Islam/Muslim World. International mail-order catalogs & library supplies issued, Islamic Library Consultancy.

Type of Business: Distributor, Exporter, Importer, Major Independent Bookseller
Parent Company: Muslim Academic Trust

Haigh & Hochland Ltd
Harniman House, 391-401 Oxford Rd, Manchester M13 9QA
Tel: (061) 2734156 *Fax:* (061) 2734340
Key Personnel
Man Dir: Michael Beattie
Founded: 1951
Type of Business: Distributor, Exporter, Importer, Major Independent Bookseller

Hammicks Bookshops Ltd
Hammicks House, Browells Lane, Feltham, Middlesex TW13 7EE
Tel: (0181) 8995060 (head office & general inquiries) *Fax:* (0181) 8995075
Key Personnel
Man Dir: Trevor Goul-Wheeker
Finance Dir: Mike Dobbie
Book & Product Manager: Sue Baker
Founded: 1968
There are Hammick's Bookshops at Andover, Barnset, Basingstoke, Bracknell, Bristol, Cheltenham, Chichester, Epsom, Farnham, Hammersmith, Harrogate, Harrow, Hemel Hempstead, Horsham, Leamington Spa, London, Luton, Maidenhead, Manchester, Oldham, Peterborough, Redhill, Southend, Southport, Stockport, Windsor, Woking.
Type of Business: Major Book Chain Headquarters

Hatchards Ltd
187 Piccadilly, London W1J 9LE
Tel: (020) 7439 9921 *Fax:* (020) 7494 1313
E-mail: books@hatchards.co.uk
Web Site: www.hatchards.co.uk
Key Personnel
General Manager: Roger Katz
Marketing Assistant: Mark Hammett
Founded: 1797
Booksellers.
Owned by: EMI
Ultimate Parent Company: HMV Media Group

Health Sciences Associates International
15 Roehampton Lane, London SW15 5LS
Tel: (020) 8876 2340 *Fax:* (020) 8392 9845
Key Personnel
Contact: Neville Mendelson
Founded: 1982
Specialize in marketing, promote & sell by direct mail & displays medical veterinary & nursing journals, books & electronic publications direct to doctors & allied professions throughout Europe. Also offers US professional medical societies & publishers an office address in Europe, London, for receipt of orders & inquiries.
Type of Business: Distributor

Heffers Booksellers & Library Suppliers
20 Trinity St, Cambridge Cambs CB2 3NG
Tel: (01223) 568568 *Fax:* (01223) 568591
E-mail: heffers@heffers.co.uk
Web Site: www.heffers.co.uk
Telex: 81298
Key Personnel
Man Dir: Mark Wait
Founded: 1876
Type of Business: Exporter, Major Independent Bookseller
Owned by: W Heffer & Sons Ltd
Branch Office(s)
Heffers-Sound, 19 Trinity St, Cambridge (recorded music on cassette & compact disc, spoken word cassettes)
13 Trinity St, Cambridge

Cambridge (art & architecture plus Deighton, Bell- antiquarian and secondhand books)
Grafton Centre, Cambridge (general books)
30 Trinity S, Cambridge (children's books)
31 St Andrews St, Cambridge (paperbacks & videos)

Hellenic Bookservice
91 Fortess Rd, Kentish Town, London NW5 1AG
Tel: (020) 72679499 *Fax:* (020) 72679498
E-mail: hellenicbooks@btinternet.com
Web Site: www.hellenicbookservice.com
Key Personnel
Partner: Monica Williams
Founded: 1966
Independent Bookseller.

Thomas Heneage Art Books
42 Duke St, St James's, London SW1Y 6DJ
Tel: (020) 7930 9223 *Fax:* (020) 7839 9223
E-mail: artbooks@heneage.com
Key Personnel
Man Dir: Thomas Heneage
Type of Business: Major Independent Bookseller
Owned by: Thomas Heneage

The Holt Jackson Book Co Ltd
Preston Rd, Lytham, Lancs FY8 5AX
Tel: (01253) 737464 *Fax:* (01253) 733361
E-mail: info@holtjackson.co.uk
Web Site: www.holtjackson.co.uk
Key Personnel
Chairman: J K Holden *E-mail:* kholden@holtjackson.co.uk
Deputy Chairman: J M Pewtress
Acquisitions Manager: Tom Lee
Sales & Customer Care Dir: Anne Ollie
Finance Dir: Carole Perk
Founded: 1932
Type of Business: Exporter, Major Independent Bookseller, Wholesaler

Brian Inns Booksales & Services
9 Ashley Crescent, Warwick CV34 6QH
Tel: (01926) 498428 *Fax:* (01926) 498428
Key Personnel
Man Dir: Brian Inns
Founded: 1989
Sales consultant & sales agency.

International Thomson Publishing Services Ltd, see Thomson Publishing Services

Internos Books
12 Percy St, London W1P 9FB
Tel: (020) 7637 4255 *Fax:* (020) 7637 4251
Key Personnel
President: E Booth-Clibborn
Editor: M Sutcliffe
Sales Dir: J Booth-Clibborn
Founded: 1987
Type of Business: Distributor, Exporter, Importer, Wholesaler
Owned by: Booth-Clibborn Editions

Richard Joseph Publishers Ltd
PO Box 6123, Basingstoke, Hants RG25 2WE
Tel: (01256) 811314 *Fax:* (01256) 336362
E-mail: rjoe01@aol.com
Web Site: www.sheppardsdirectories.co.uk
Key Personnel
Man Dir: Richard Joseph
Founded: 1990
Also acts as print consultant
Joint owner of Sheppard's Book Search with Book Data Ltd.

Kuperard, *imprint of* Kuperard

Kuperard
Division of Bravo Ltd
311 Ballards Lane, London N12 8LY
Tel: (020) 8446 2440 *Fax:* (020) 8446 2441
E-mail: kuperard@bravo.clara.net
Web Site: www.kuperard.co.uk
Key Personnel
Man Dir: Joshua Kuperard *E-mail:* joshua@bravo.clara.net
Sales & Marketing Manager: Martin Kaye
Founded: 1986
Publisher.
Type of Business: Distributor, Exporter, Importer
Imprints: Kuperard

Lavis Marketing
73 Lime Walk, Headington, Oxford OX3 7AD
Tel: (01865) 767575 *Fax:* (01865) 750079
E-mail: orders@lavismarketing.co.uk
Key Personnel
Contact: James H Lavis *E-mail:* jim@lavismarketing.co.uk
Founded: 1982
Type of Business: Distributor

The Lexicon Bookshop
63 Strand St, Douglas IM1 2RL
Tel: (01624) 673004 *Fax:* (01624) 661959
Key Personnel
Proprietor: D W Ashworth
Founded: 1936
Type of Business: Major Independent Bookseller

Lister Art Books of Southport
PO Box 31, Southport PR9 8BF
Tel: (01704) 232033 *Fax:* (01704) 505926
E-mail: sales@laboox.demon.co.uk
Key Personnel
Contact: Graham Lister
Books on Antiques & Collecting; USA Co represented.
Type of Business: Distributor, Importer

Littlehampton Book Services Ltd
Faraday Close, Durrington, West Sussex BN13 3RB
Tel: (01903) 828500 *Fax:* (01903) 828625
E-mail: rcm@lbsltd.co.uk
Key Personnel
Man Dir: Martin Evans
Distribution Dir: Alan Joy
Finance Dir: Basil May
Type of Business: Distributor
Owned by: Orion Publishing Group, 5 Upper St Martin's Lane, London WC2H 9EA

Chris Lloyd Sales & Marketing Services
Stanley House, 3 Fleets Lane, Poole Dorset BH15 3AJ
Tel: (01202) 649930 *Fax:* (01202) 649950
E-mail: chrlloyd@globalnet.co.uk
Founded: 1986
Type of Business: Distributor, Importer

Lomond, *imprint of* Lomond Books

Lomond Books
No 36, West Shore Rd, Granton, Edinburgh EH5 1QD
Tel: (0131) 5512261 *Toll Free Tel:* 800 0286943 (orders only) *Fax:* (0131) 5521703
E-mail: sales@lomand-books.co.uk
Key Personnel
Man Dir: David Flatman
Sales & Marketing Dir: Trevor Maher
Sales Manager: Duncan Baxter
Also retailer & publisher.
Type of Business: Remainder Dealer, Wholesaler
Imprints: Lomond

BOOK DEALERS — UNITED KINGDOM

Mallory International Ltd
Potter's Market, West Hill, Ottery St Mary, Devon EX11 1TY
Tel: (01404) 815310 *Fax:* (01404) 812245
E-mail: sales@malloryint.co.uk
Web Site: www.malloryint.co.uk
Key Personnel
Executive Dir: Norman Guthrie
Dir: Mrs Clare Guthrie *E-mail:* clare@malloryint.co.uk; Julian Hardinge; Mrs Ulrike Hardinge
Founded: 1989
International booksellers.
Type of Business: Distributor, Exporter, Importer, Major Independent Bookseller

Marston Book Services Ltd
PO Box 269, Abingdon, Oxford OX14 4YN
Tel: (01235) 46550 *Fax:* (01235) 46555
Telex: 837515
Key Personnel
Man Dir: Charles Ashford
Type of Business: Distributor

Menoshire Ltd
Unit 13, 21 Wadsworth Rd, Perivale, Greenford, Middlesex UB6 7LQ
Tel: (0181) 5667344 *Fax:* (0181) 9912439
Key Personnel
Man Dir: J M Treacy
Type of Business: Exporter, Importer, Wholesaler

Meresborough Books
17 Station Rd, Rainham, Gillingham, Kent ME8 7RS
Tel: (01634) 371591 *Fax:* (01634) 262114
E-mail: shop@rainhambookshop.co.uk
Web Site: www.rainhambookshop.co.uk
Key Personnel
Manager: Hamish Mackay-Miller
Type of Business: Major Independent Bookseller, Wholesaler

Millbank Books Ltd
The Court Yard, The Old Monastery, Windhill, Bishop's Stortford, Herts CM23 2PE
Tel: (01279) 655233 *Fax:* (01279) 655244
E-mail: caw@millbank.demon.co.uk
Key Personnel
Dir: Diana Walsh; Christine Walsh
Founded: 1987
Distributors of General Nonfiction in the UK, Europe & Middle East; Import Specialist Titles from USA, Singapore, Malaysia, Australia & South Africa; Also act as UK agents for overseas publishers to sell the rights of their titles to UK publishers.
Type of Business: Distributor, Exporter, Importer

Morley Books
Elmfield Rd, Morley, Leeds LS27 0NN
Tel: (0113) 2012900 *Fax:* (0113) 2012929
E-mail: frank_schubert@cyphergroup.com
Web Site: www.cyphergroup.com
Key Personnel
Buyer: Steve Ream
Founded: 1947
Owned by: Johnstown Press

Motilal (UK) Books of India
PO Box 324, Borehamwood, Herts WD6 1NB
Tel: (0208) 9051244 *Fax:* (0208) 9051108
E-mail: info@mlbduk.com
Web Site: www.mlbduk.com
Key Personnel
Owner & Distribution Dir: Ray McLennan
Founded: 1982
Import, Export & Distribution Agency for books published in India.
Type of Business: Distributor, Exporter, Importer
Parent Company: Money Savers (London) Ltd

Music Book Distributors Ltd
44 Station Way, Buckhurst Hill, Essex IG9 6LN
Tel: (0181) 5591522 *Fax:* (0181) 5591522
Key Personnel
Dir: Neil Taylor
Founded: 1988
Type of Business: Wholesaler

Northern Map Distributors
101 Broadfield Rd, Sheffield S8 0XH
Tel: (01142) 582660 *Toll Free Tel:* 800 834920
Key Personnel
Partner: David N Smith
Founded: 1975
Map & Guide Wholesaler.
Subjects: LAM-FORD Maps
Type of Business: Wholesaler

Orbis Books (London) Ltd
206 Blythe Rd, London W14 0HH
Tel: (020) 7602 5541 *Fax:* (020) 8742 7686
E-mail: bookshop@orbis-books.co.uk
Key Personnel
Dir: Jerzy Kulczycki
Specialize in books in English on Central & Eastern Europe. Stockholders of books in Polish, Czech, Slovak & Bulgarian.
Type of Business: Exporter, Importer, Major Independent Bookseller

Parfitts Book Services
50 Imber Rd, Warminster, Wilts BA12 0BN
Tel: (01985) 216371 *Fax:* (01985) 212982
E-mail: parfitts@cix.compulink.co.uk
Key Personnel
Dir: J E Parfitt
Type of Business: Distributor, Exporter, Importer, Major Independent Bookseller, Wholesaler

Plymbridge Distributors Ltd
Plymbridge House, Estover Rd, Plymouth PL6 7PZ
Tel: (01752) 202300 *Fax:* (01752) 202330
E-mail: orders@plymbridge.com
Web Site: www.plymbridge.com
Key Personnel
Man Dir: Michael W Beevers
Type of Business: Distributor

H Pordes Ltd
58-60 Charing Cross Rd, London WC2H 0BB
Tel: (020) 8445 1273 *Fax:* (020) 8445 5510
Key Personnel
Dir: Henry Pordes; N Pordes
Manager: Gino Della Ragione
Founded: 1975
Wholesale only-buying & selling of remainders. Also publisher.
Type of Business: Remainder Dealer

Promotional Reprint Co Ltd
Kiln House, 210 New Kings Rd, London SW6 4NZ
Tel: (020) 7736 5666 *Fax:* (020) 7736 5777
Type of Business: Remainder Dealer

Rainham Bookshop, see Meresborough Books

Ramboro Books Plc
Bibliophile House, 10 Blenheim Court, Brewery Rd, 202-208 New North Rd, London N7 9NT
Tel: (020) 7700 7444 *Fax:* (020) 7700 4552
E-mail: enquiries@ramboro.co.uk
Key Personnel
International Sales Dir: Tim Finch
 E-mail: tfinch@chrysalisbooks.co.uk
Type of Business: Remainder Dealer

Randall & Swift Ltd
44 Station Way, Buckhurst Hill, Essex IG9 6LN
Tel: (0181) 5591522 *Fax:* (0181) 5591522
Key Personnel
Dir: Neil Taylor
Founded: 1979
Supplier of printed music & music books to libraries.

The Richmond Publishing Co Ltd
PO Box 96, Slough SL2 3RS
Tel: (01753) 643104 *Fax:* (01753) 646553
E-mail: rpc@richmond.co.uk
Key Personnel
Man Dir: Mrs S J Davie
Founded: 1970
Type of Business: Distributor, Exporter, Importer, Major Independent Bookseller, Wholesaler

RICS Books
Surveyor Court, Westwood Business Park, Coventry CV4 8JE
Tel: (020) 7222 7000 *Fax:* (0171) 2229430
E-mail: rbsbooks@rics.co.uk
Key Personnel
Man Dir: Angela Martland
Founded: 1981
Distributor for 11 US publishers.
Type of Business: Distributor, Major Independent Bookseller
Owned by: Royal Institution of Chartered Surveyors (RICS)
Branch Office(s)
RICS Books Mail Order, Surveyor Court, Westwood Way, Coventry CV4 8JE

Louise Ross & Co, Ltd
Mulberry House, 8 Mount Rd, Lansdown, Bath, Avon BA1 5PW
Tel: (01225) 448786 *Fax:* (01225) 448789
Key Personnel
Man Dir: Louise Ross *E-mail:* lross@britishlibrary.net
Founded: 1977
Antiquarian & literary books, first editions only; also acts as publisher.
Type of Business: Major Independent Bookseller
Owned by: Ross Press

Roundhouse Publishing Ltd
Millstone, Limers Lane, Northam EX39 2RG
Tel: (01237) 474474 *Fax:* (01237) 474774
E-mail: roundhouse.group@ukgateway.net
Web Site: www.roundhouse.net
Key Personnel
President & Chief Executive: Alan T Goodworth
Founded: 1991
Distributor of small/medium publisher lists from USA, Canada & Australia.
Type of Business: Distributor, Exporter, Importer, Wholesaler
Warehouse: Orca Book Services, Poole

Royal Institution of Chartered Surveyors, see RICS Books

Sandpiper Books Ltd
24 Langroyd Rd, London SW17 7PL
Tel: (020) 8767 7421 *Fax:* (020) 8682 0280
E-mail: sandpiper@sandpiper.co.uk
Key Personnel
Sales Manager: Chris Harley *E-mail:* charley@sandpiper.co.uk
Contact: Robert Collie
Founded: 1984
Specializing in scholarly & literary remainders, good quality arts, reprints of academic monographs with Oxford University Press.
Type of Business: Remainder Dealer
Showroom(s): 4/S Academy Buildings, Lower Ground Floor, Fanshaw St, London N1 6LQ

UNITED KINGDOM

Saqi Books
26 Westbourne Grove, London W2 5RH
Tel: (020) 7229 8543; (020) 7221 9347
 Fax: (020) 7229 7492
E-mail: saqibooks@dial.pipex.com
Web Site: www.saqibooks.com
Key Personnel
Contact: Mai Ghoussoub
Editorial Manager: Sarah Al-Hamad
 E-mail: sarah@saqibooks.com
Founded: 1979
Type of Business: Exporter, Importer, Major Independent Bookseller
Owned by: A & S Gaspard; M Ghoussoub; K & H Makija

Derek Searle Associates
Cippenham Lodge, Cippenham Lane, Slough, Berks SL1 5AN
Tel: (01753) 539295 *Fax:* (02753) 551863
E-mail: dsapublish@aol.com
Key Personnel
Contact: Mrs Maureen Corrington
Founded: 1991
Act as Independent Sales & Marketing Agents on behalf of client Publishers.

Send the Light Ltd
PO Box 300, Carlisle, Cumbria CA3 0QS
Tel: (01228) 512512 *Fax:* (01228) 514949
E-mail: nancy.ursh@stl.org
Key Personnel
Chief Executive: Keith Danby
Man Dir, Publishing: Mark Finnie
Founded: 1965
Publish & distribute books to advance the Christian faith.
Type of Business: Distributor, Wholesaler
Subsidiaries: Paternoster Publishing

Shelwing Ltd
4 Pleydell Gardens, Folkestone, Kent CT20 2DN
Tel: (01303) 850501 *Fax:* (01303) 850162
E-mail: info@shelwing.com
Web Site: www.shelwing.com
Key Personnel
Chairman: John Bailey
Publicity: Eileen Marshall
Founded: 1983
Warehousing, Jacket mailing & Mailing List compilation; UK agents for Scarecrow Press, Inc & McFarland & Company, Inc.

Sherratt & Hughes
c/o WHSmith Retail Ltd, Freepost (sce 4410), Swindon, Wilts SN3 3XS
Tel: (01793) 695195
Key Personnel
Manager: J D Siverns
Incorporating Bowes & Bowes Books.
Owned by: WHSmith & Son Ltd

Shogun International Ltd
87 Gayford Rd, London W12 9BY
Tel: (020) 8749 2022 *Fax:* (020) 8740 1086
Key Personnel
Manager: P Tai
Founded: 1974
Manufactured supply of martial arts equipment, clothing & books (on martial arts only).
Type of Business: Distributor, Exporter, Importer, Wholesaler

Silverdale, *imprint of* Bookmart Ltd

John Smith & Son (Glasgow) Ltd
57-61 St Vincent St, Glasgow G2 5TB
Tel: (0141) 2217472 *Fax:* (0141) 2484412
Telex: 778881 Jssglw G *Cable:* BOOKS: GLASGOW
Founded: 1751

WH Smith PLC
Nations House PLC, 103 Wigmore St, London W1U 1WH
Tel: (020) 7409 3222 *Fax:* (020) 7514 9633
Web Site: www.whsmith.co.uk/awards
Key Personnel
Chairman: Jeremy Hardie
Corporate Affairs Dir: Tim Blythe
Founded: 1792
There are 400 High Street Stores & 100 airport & station bookstores throughout the UK & 100 specialist bookshops, operating under the name of Waterstones.
Type of Business: Distributor, Major Independent Bookseller

Springfield Books Ltd
Norman Rd, Denby Dale, Huddersfield, West Yorkshire HD8 8TH
Tel: (01484) 864955 *Fax:* (01484) 865443
Key Personnel
Sales Manager, Publicity: Paula Brennan
Founded: 1984
Type of Business: Distributor

The Stationery Office
Publications Centre, 51 Nine Elms Lane, London SW8 5DR
Mailing Address: PO Box 29, Norwich NR3 1GN
Tel: (020) 7600 5522 *Fax:* (020) 7873 8200 (orders)
Web Site: www.theso.co.uk
Key Personnel
Export Manager: Brian Tierney *Tel:* (020) 7873 8211 *Fax:* (020) 7873 8203 *E-mail:* brian.tierney@theso.co.uk
Sales Manager: Rebecca Barley
Publicity Manager: Michelle Brown
Bibliographics Manager: Peter Gutteridge
Editorial: Philip Brooks *Tel:* (1603) 605532
 E-mail: phil.brooks@theso.co.uk
Contact: Jamie Precious
Founded: 1786
Publishes for UK government departments & a wide variety of public bodies on subjects covering academic & general interests. Also, the UK distributor for international organizations including UN, UNESCO, FAO, WHO, OECD, EU & IMF.
Type of Business: Distributor, Exporter

STL, see Send the Light Ltd

THE, see Total Home Entertainment

James Thin, Bookseller
53-59 South Bridge, Edinburgh EH1 1YS
Tel: (0131) 622 8222 *Fax:* (0131) 557 8149
E-mail: enquiries@jthin.co.uk
Web Site: www.jamesthin.co.uk
Key Personnel
Non-Exec Chmn: D Ainslie Thin
Man Dir: Jackie Thin
Dirs: Malcolm Gibson; Ken Lemond; Andrew Thin; James Thin; Graham White
Assistant to Man Dir: Dayle Coltman *Tel:* (0131) 622 8281 *E-mail:* dayle.coltman@jthin.co.uk
Founded: 1848
Specialize in the publication of Scottish interest & outdoor books under the Mercat Press imprint.
Type of Business: Major Independent Bookseller
Bookshop(s): James Thin Ltd, Unit 21-23, Sovereign S/Ctr, Weston-Super-Mare, Avon BS23 1HL; James Thin Ltd, 15 Sandgate, Ayr KA7 1BG; The Lanes, 77 Lowther St, Carlisle CA3 8EF; James Thin Ltd, 18/26 Church Crescent, Dumfries DG1 1DQ; James Thin Ltd, 7/8 High St, Dundee DD1 1SS; James Thin Ltd, 53/59 South Bridge, Edinburgh EH1 1YS; James Thin Ltd, 59 George St, Edinburgh EH2 2JQ; James Thin Ltd, 29 Buccleuch St, Edinburgh E48 9JR; James Thin Ltd, Hugh Nisbet Bldg, Heriot-Watt University, Riccarton Campus, Edinburgh EH14 2AS; James Thin Ltd, Kings Bldg Bookshop, W Mains Rd, Edinburgh EH9 3 JR; Gyle, 35 Gyle Ave, South Gyle Broadway, Edinburgh EH12 9JT; James Thin Ltd, 22/24 Thackery Mall, Fareham Shopping Centre, Fareham, Hants PO16 OPQ; James Thin Ltd, Unit SU45, The Lakeside Centre, West Thurrock, Grays, Essex RM16 1ZF; James Thin Ltd, Mid Level, Unit 55-56, The Exchange, Ilford, Essex IG1 IAA; James Thin Ltd, 29 Union St, Inverness IV1 1QA; James Thin Ltd, 87 Grampian Rd, Aviemore, Inverness-shire PH22 1RH; James Thin Ltd, Unit LSU 2, Centre Court Shopping Centre, Wimbledon, London SW19 8YE; James Thin Ltd, Unit 26, Treaty Centre, Hounslow, Middlesex TW3 IES; James Thin Ltd, 2A Mercer Walk, The Pavilions, Uxbridge, Middlsex 1LU 1LY; James Thin Ltd, 20/21 Castle Mall, Norwich, Norfolk NR1 3XJ; James Thin Ltd, Unit SU44, The Peacocks Centre, Woking, Surrey GU21 1GD; James Thin Ltd, University Bookshop, Student's Union, St Mary's Pl, St Andrews, Fife KY16 9UZ; James Thin, 176 High St, Perth PH1 5UN; James Thin, 5 New St, Huddersfield, Yorkshire HD1 2AX

Thomson Publishing Services
Formerly International Thomson Publishing Services Ltd
Cheriton House, North Way, Andover SP10 5BE
Tel: (01264) 332424 *Fax:* (01264) 364418
Key Personnel
General Manager: Barry Hinchmore
Customer Service Dir: Carrie Willicome
Chief Accountant: Jo Jewell
Founded: 1988
Type of Business: Distributor
Owned by: The Thomson Corp

Thornton's of Oxford Ltd
11 Broad St, Oxford OX1 3AR
Tel: (01865) 242939 *Fax:* (01865) 204021
E-mail: thorntons@booknews.demon.co.uk
Web Site: www.demon.co.uk/thorntons
Key Personnel
Man Dir: Willem A Meeuws
Founded: 1835
Also Publisher.
Type of Business: Distributor, Exporter, Importer, Major Independent Bookseller

Tiger Books International PLC
26A York St, Twickenham, Middlesex TW1 3LJ
Tel: (0181) 8925577 *Fax:* (0181) 8916550
Key Personnel
Man Dir: Grahame Parish
Founded: 1985
Type of Business: Remainder Dealer

Titles Old and Rare Books of Oxford
15 Turl St, Oxford OX1 3DQ
Tel: (01865) 727928 *Fax:* (01865) 727928
Key Personnel
Contact: G Stone; R Stone
Founded: 1972
Specialize in History of Science, Travel, Agriculture, Literature, General Antiquarian & Secondhand Books.
Type of Business: Major Independent Bookseller

Total Home Entertainment
Unit One, Rosevale Business Park, Newcastle-under-Lyme, Staffs ST5 7QT
Tel: (01782) 566566 *Fax:* (01782) 565400
E-mail: thenews@the.co.uk
Key Personnel
Man Dir: Alasdair Ogilvie

BOOK DEALERS — UNITED KINGDOM

Sales & Marketing Dir, Books: Phil Scarlet
Wholesaler for Home Entertainment software including books, videos, music, multimedia products, electronic games & accessories. Multi-lingual export service & advice centre based in London.
Type of Business: Distributor, Exporter, Wholesaler
Owned by: John Menzies (UK) Ltd
Branch Office(s)
The International Export Office, Unit 4, Elsinore House, 77 Fulham Palace Rd, London W6 8JA

Troika
North Rd, London N7 9DP
Tel: (020) 7619 0800 *Fax:* (020) 7619 0801
Key Personnel
Man Dir: Aidan Lunn
Founded: 1983
Independent Representatives.

John Trotter Books
80 East End Rd, London N32SY
Tel: (020) 8349 9484 *Fax:* (020) 8346 7430
Founded: 1973
Also Publishers & Remainder Dealers.
Type of Business: Major Independent Bookseller

Turnaround Publisher Services
Unit 3, Olympia Trading Estate, Coburg Rd, London N22 6TZ
Tel: (020) 8829 3009 *Fax:* (020) 8881 5088
E-mail: info@turnaround-uk.com
Web Site: www.turnaround-uk.com
Key Personnel
Man Dir: Bill Godber *E-mail:* bill@turnaround-uk.com
Marketing Dir: Claire Thompson *E-mail:* claire@turnaround-uk.com
Founded: 1984
Book distributor of a wide range of US, UK & Irish based publishers to the UK & continental Europe.
Member of Publishers' Association (UK) & Bookseller's Association (UK).
Type of Business: Distributor, Exporter, Importer, Wholesaler

Turpin Distribution Services Ltd
Division of Swets Publisher Services
Blackhorse Rd, Letchworth, Herts SG6 1HN
Tel: (01462) 672555 *Fax:* (01462) 480947
Web Site: www.turpin-distribution.com; www.turpinbooks.com (online bookshop)
Key Personnel
Man Dir: Lorna M Summers
Sales Manager: Kathy Law *E-mail:* lawk@turpinltd.com
Founded: 1968
Provide worldwide distribution of books & fulfillment of journals for academic & learned publishers from US & UK locations. Customized service includes invoicing in the publisher's name & using the publisher's own trading terms. Management reports are available 24/7 via internet. Mulilingual customer care & customer relationship. Multiple currencies.
Type of Business: Distributor
Owned by: Swets & Zeitlinger BV, Heereweg 347 B, 2161 SZ Lisse, Netherlands; Swets & Zeitlinger BV, PO Box 800, 2160 SZ Lisse, Netherlands (Mailing address)
Branch Office(s)
Turpin North America
Warehouse: 440 Creamery Way, Suite A, Exton, PA 19341, United States

UBS Publishers' Distributors Ltd
475 N Circular Rd, Neasden, London NW2 7QG
Tel: (020) 84508667 *Fax:* (020) 8452 6612 (attn: UBSPD)
E-mail: ubspd@gobookshopping.com
Web Site: www.gobookshopping.com
Key Personnel
Dir: M K Kalsi
Founded: 1937
Represent over 400 Indian publishers, stocks 2 million books in India & has constant liaisons with over 2000 commercial publishers, research institutions & government depts & disseminate information about their new publications through their weekly bulletins as well as their subject-wise catalogs.
Type of Business: Distributor, Exporter, Importer, Wholesaler
Branch Office(s)
Banglore, India
Bombay, India
Calcutta, India
Kanpur, India
Madras, India
New Delhi, India
Patna, India

United Book Suppliers
689 Antrim Rd, Newtownabbey, Co Antrim BT36 8RN
Tel: (01232) 832362 *Fax:* (01232) 848780
Key Personnel
Man Dir: John Lindsay
Founded: 1981
Type of Business: Distributor, Exporter, Wholesaler

University of London
External Publications Rm 265, Senate House, Malet St, London WC1E 7HU
Tel: (020) 7636 8000 ext 3268 *Fax:* (020) 7636 5874
Key Personnel
Publications Officer: S M Masters
Type of Business: Major Independent Bookseller

Robert Vaughan Antiquarian Booksellers
20 Chapel St, Stratford-Upon-Avon, Warwicks CV37 6EP
Tel: (01789) 205312
Key Personnel
Contact: Mlle C M Vaughan
Founded: 1953
Type of Business: Major Independent Bookseller

Vine House Distribution Ltd
Affiliate of Vine House Book Promotion
Waldenbury, North Common, Chailey, East Sussex BN8 4DR
Tel: (0182) 5723398 *Fax:* (0182) 5724188
E-mail: sales@vinehouseuk.co.uk
Web Site: www.vinehouseuk.co.uk
Key Personnel
Man Dir: Richard Squibb
Founded: 1987
International book distributors, including representation & public relations.
Type of Business: Distributor, Exporter, Importer
Warehouse: Mullany Business Park, Deanland Rd, Golden Cross, East Sussex BN27 3RP

Peter Ward Book Exports
Unit 3, Taylors Yard, 67 Alderbrook Rd, London SW12 8AD
Tel: (020) 8772 3300 *Fax:* (020) 8772 3309
E-mail: pwbookex@dircon.co.uk
Key Personnel
Partner & President: Peter Ward
Vice President: Richard Ward
Founded: 1974
Publishers' representatives.
Type of Business: Exporter, Major Independent Bookseller, Wholesaler

Waterstone & Co Ltd
Capital Court, Capital Interchange Way, Brentford, Middlesex TW8 0EX
Tel: (0181) 7423800 *Fax:* (0181) 7420215
Numerous branches throughout the UK.

Welsh Books Council: Distribution Centre
(Cyngor Llyfrau Cymru Canolfan Dosbarthu)
Glanyrafon Enterprise Park, Llanbadarn, Aberystwyth, Ceredigion, Wales SY23 3AQ
Tel: (01970) 624455 *Fax:* (01970) 625506
E-mail: distribution.centre@cllc.org.uk
Web Site: www.gwales.com; www.cllc.org.uk
Key Personnel
Dir: Miss Gwerfyl Pierce Jones
Manager: Dafydd Charles Jones
Head of Marketing: Dr David Philip Davies
 E-mail: phil.davies@cllc.org.uk
Deputy Dir: Pedr Ap Llwyd
Founded: 1963
Type of Business: Distributor, Wholesaler
Owned by: Welsh Books Council

Whitaker TeleOrdering
Woolmead House West, Bear Lane, Farnham, Surrey GU9 7LG
Tel: (01252) 742542 *Fax:* (01252) 742543
E-mail: help@teleord.co.uk
Web Site: www.whitaker.co.uk
Key Personnel
Dir: Paul Pounsford
Order Routing & EDI Communication Network.
Owned by: J Whitaker & Sons Ltd

WJ Williams & Son (Books) Ltd
Ashcroft, Small Meadow, Barton under Needwood, Staffordshire DE13 8BA
Tel: (01283) 712948 *Fax:* (01283) 716807
E-mail: mail@williams-books.co.uk
Web Site: www.williams-books.co.uk
Key Personnel
Owner, Dir & Chief Executive: Anthony B Williams
Founded: 1972
Wholesale remainder bookseller & reprint publisher.
Type of Business: Remainder Dealer
Imprints: Wrens Park Publishing

Wisdom Books
25 Stanley Rd, Ilford, Essex LG1 1RW
Tel: (0208) 553 5020 *Fax:* (0208) 553 5122
E-mail: enquiries@wisdombooks.org
Web Site: www.wisdombooks.org
Key Personnel
Man Dir: Dennis Heslop
Sales Manager: Mike Gilmore
Title Research: Leigh Wyman
Office Manager: Philip Bradley
Orders: Jonathon Steyn
Founded: 1989
Specialize in all traditions of Buddhism.
Type of Business: Distributor, Importer, Wholesaler

Witherby & Co Ltd
Book Dept, 2nd floor, 32-36 Aylesbury St, London EC1R 0ET
Tel: (020) 7251 5341 *Fax:* (020) 7251 1296
E-mail: books@witherbys.co.uk
Web Site: www.witherbys.com
Key Personnel
Man Dir & Publisher: Alan Witherby
 E-mail: alanw@witherby.co.uk
Founded: 1740
Specializes in insurance & shipping publications.
Subjects: Risk management
Type of Business: Exporter, Major Independent Bookseller
Bookshop(s): 20 Aldermanbury, London EC2V 7HY *Tel:* (0207) 972 0152 *Fax:* (0207) 417 4431

Woodfield & Stanley Ltd
Broad Lane, Moldgreen, Huddersfield HD5 9BX
Tel: (01484) 421467; (01484) 532401
 Fax: (01484) 510237
Web Site: www.woodfield-stanley.co.uk
Key Personnel
Man Dir: P G Chadwick
Founded: 1946
Type of Business: Distributor, Major Independent Bookseller, Wholesaler

World Leisure Marketing
11 Newmarket Court, Derby DE24 8NW
Tel: (01332) 573737 *Fax:* (01332) 573399
E-mail: office@wlmsales.co.uk
Web Site: www.maps-guides.com
Key Personnel
Man Dir: John Whitby
Sales Dir: John Grundy
Founded: 1991
Type of Business: Distributor, Exporter, Importer

Wrens Park Publishing, *imprint of* WJ Williams & Son (Books) Ltd

Roy Yates Books
Smallfields Cottage, Cox Green, Rudgwick, Horsham, West Sussex RH12 3DE
Tel: (01403) 822299 *Fax:* (01403) 823012
Key Personnel
Proprietor: Roy Yates
Founded: 1987
Type of Business: Distributor, Exporter, Importer, Major Independent Bookseller, Wholesaler

Uruguay

Albe Libros Tecnicos SRL
Cerrito 566, Casilla de Correos 1603, 11000 Montevideo
Tel: (02) 957528; (02) 957485 *Fax:* (02) 957528
Key Personnel
Bookstore & Editorial: Daniel Aljanati
Distributor: Jaime Daniel Aljanati
Founded: 1950
Type of Business: Distributor, Exporter, Importer, Major Independent Bookseller, Wholesaler
Owned by: Nuestra Tierra (publishing) & Distribuidora Albe SRL (distribution), Cerrito 566, Montevideo 1100

America Latina
18 de Julio 2089, Montevideo
Tel: (02) 415127 *Fax:* (02) 495568
Key Personnel
Manager: Ismael Munoz
Founded: 1962
Type of Business: Distributor, Importer, Major Independent Bookseller, Wholesaler

Barreiro y Ramos SA
JC Gomez 1430, 1100 Montevideo
Tel: (02) 986621 *Fax:* (02) 962358
Key Personnel
Pres: Dr Gaston Barreiro Zorrilla
Also Publisher.
Branch Office(s)
Ave General Artigas 714, Las Piedras
Arocena 1599, Montevideo
Ave 18 de Julio 1852, Montevideo
Ave 18 de Julio 941, Montevideo
Ave 8 de Octubre 3728, Montevideo
Ave Agraciada 3945, Montevideo
Ave Rivera 2684, Montevideo
Calle 21 de Setiembre 2753, Montevideo
Minas 1491, Montevideo

Feria del Libro
Ave 18 de Julio 1308, Montevideo
Tel: (02) 902070 *Fax:* (02) 902070
Key Personnel
Manager: Domingo A Maestro
Type of Business: Distributor, Importer, Major Book Chain Headquarters, Wholesaler

Libreria Amalio M Fernandez SRL
25 de Mayo 477, planta baja ofic 11, 11000 Montevideo
Tel: (02) 852684 *Fax:* (02) 852684
Founded: 1951
Type of Business: Distributor, Exporter, Importer, Major Independent Bookseller, Wholesaler

El Galeon
Juan Carlos Gomez 1327, 11000 Montevideo
Mailing Address: Casilla de Correos Suite 458, 11000 Montevideo
Tel: (02) 9156139; (02) 9157909 *Fax:* (02) 9157909
E-mail: elgaleon@netgate.com.uy
Web Site: www.elgaleonlibros.com *Cable:* GALLEONBOOK MONTEVIDEO
Key Personnel
Proprietor: Roberto Cataldo
Founded: 1973
Antiquarian bookseller specializing in history, literature, art, politics; also chart engraving.
Type of Business: Distributor, Exporter, Importer, Major Independent Bookseller, Wholesaler

Libreria Linardi y Risso
Juan Carlos Gomez 1435, 11000 Montevideo
Tel: (02) 915 7129 *Fax:* (02) 915 7328
E-mail: lyrbooks@linardiyrisso.com
Key Personnel
Manager: Andres Linardi; Alvaro J Risso
Founded: 1944
Antiquarian bookseller; Uruguayan Current Books.
Type of Business: Distributor, Exporter, Major Independent Bookseller

Palacio del Libro
25 de Mayo 577, Casilla de Correo 371, Montevideo
Tel: (02) 959019 *Fax:* (02) 957543
Key Personnel
Man Dir: Daniel Mussini
Vice President: Liliana Mussini
Editorial Graphic Bindery workshop.
Type of Business: Distributor, Exporter, Importer, Major Independent Bookseller, Wholesaler

Venezuela

Libreria del Este
52 Avda Francisco de Miranda Edificio Galipan, Apdo 60-337, Caracas 1060-A 106
Tel: (02) 9511297; (02) 9512307; (02) 9511705
Key Personnel
Manager: Tomas Pericas
Exclusive distributors of World Bank, United Nations, UNESCO, OIT publications.
Type of Business: Distributor

Fundacion Kuai-Mare
c/o Instituto Autonomo Biblioteca Nacional y de Servicios de Bibliotecas, Calla Soledad, Edif Rogi 1, Piso 3, Zona Industrial la Trinidad, Apdo 80593, Caracas 1080
Tel: (02) 938535 ext 213; (02) 9418011 (ext 227)
 Fax: (02) 9415219
Telex: 24621
This is the distribution side of the Instituto Autonomo Biblioteca Nacional y de Servicios de Bibliotecas, specializing in publications by Venezuelan official, cultural and university organizations. There are five other branches.

Medica Paris Libreria
Gran Av, Calle Real de Sabana Grande, Apdo 60681, Edif Medica Paris, Caracas 106
Tel: (02) 7816044; (02) 7821464; (02) 78190452709; (02) 727425 *Fax:* (02) 7931753
Telex: 21420 DISME VC
Key Personnel
Manager: Pierre Paneyko
Founded: 1975

Organizacion de Bienestar Estudiantil (OBE)
Universidad Central de Venezuela, Aptdo 47004, Caracas 1041
Tel: (02) 6054050 (ext 4200, 4201 & 4202)
 Fax: (02) 6930638

Libreria Tecnica Vega
Plaza Las Tres Gracias, Edificio Odeon, Los Chagauramos, Caracas 1010-A
Mailing Address: Apdo 51662, Caracas, Los Chaguaramos 1010-A
Tel: (02) 6221397 *Fax:* (02) 6622092 *Cable:* EDIVEGA
Key Personnel
Manager: Lucia Ribas
Owned by: Fernando Vega, Ediciones Vega SRL

Yugoslavia

Forum
Vojvode Misica 1, 21000 Novi Sad
Mailing Address: PO Box 200, 21000 Novi Sad
Tel: (021) 57216 *Fax:* (021) 57216
Also Publisher.
Type of Business: Exporter, Importer

Jugoslovenska Knjiga (Yugoslav Book; Yugoslav Book)
Tera 21OE 2+/2 PF 36, 11000 Belgrade
Mailing Address: PO Box 36, 11000 Belgrade
Tel: (011) 3340025 *Fax:* (011) 3231079
Key Personnel
Deputy General Dir: Stanika Buser
 E-mail: juknjiga@eumet.yu
Publish books, periodicals & newspapers
Member of Association of Yugoslav Publishers & Booksellers.
Type of Business: Exporter, Importer
Bookshop(s): Knez Mimailova 2, 11000 Belgrade
Warehouse: Gunouuceu Venac 10, 11000 Belgrade

Nolit Publishing House
Terazije 27/II, YU-11000 Belgrade
Mailing Address: PO Box 369, YU-11000 Belgrade
Tel: (011) 3245017; (011) 3228872 *Fax:* (011) 627285
Telex: 11-603 *Cable:* NOLIT BGD
Key Personnel
General Manager: Radivoje Nesic
Editor-in-Chief: Milos Stambolic
Thirty bookshops throughout Yugoslavia.
Type of Business: Distributor, Exporter, Importer, Major Book Chain Headquarters, Major Independent Bookseller, Wholesaler
Owned by: Nolit Publishing House

Prosveta
Dobracina 30, YU-11000 Belgrade
Tel: (011) 642772 (import); (011) 625766
 Fax: (011) 627-465

Also Publisher. Over fifty bookshops throughout Yugoslavia.
Type of Business: Exporter, Importer

Vuk Karadzic
Kraljevica Marka 9, Postanski fah 762, 11000 Belgrade
Tel: (011) 628066; (011) 628043 *Fax:* (011) 623150
Key Personnel
Man Dir: Ancic Vojin
Also Publisher.
Type of Business: Exporter, Importer

Zambia

Primrose Books and Periodicals
PO Box 23382, Kitwe
Tel: (02) 210817

University Bookshop
University of Zambia, Lusaka
Mailing Address: PO Box 32379, Lusaka
Tel: (01) 294690; (01) 290319 *Fax:* (01) 253952; (01) 294690
Telex: ZA 44370
Key Personnel
Bookshop Manager: Hudson Unene
  E-mail: hunene@admin.unza.zm
Accountant: E E Sinyolo
Bookshop Supervisor: M Soko
Founded: 1967
Membership: Booksellers & Publishers Association of Zambia (BPAZ), Pan African Booksellers Association (PABA).
Type of Business: Distributor, Exporter, Importer, Major Independent Bookseller

Owned by: The University of Zambia
Branch Office(s)
Pakati Arcade-Lusaka Hotel Outlet, Box 32379, Lusaka

Zambia Catholic Bookshop (Mission Press)
Franciscan Centre, Chifubu Rd, Ndola
Mailing Address: PO Box 71581, Ndola
Tel: (02) 680456; (02) 680466 *Fax:* (02) 680484
E-mail: mpress@zamnet.zm
Type of Business: Distributor, Exporter, Importer, Wholesaler

Zimbabwe

Book Centre, Textbook Sales (Pvt) Ltd
Affiliate of Tutorial Press
4 Conald Rd, Harare
Mailing Address: PO Box 37799, Harare
Tel: (04) 790691 *Fax:* (04) 751690 *Cable:* TEXTBOOK
Key Personnel
Man Dir: A Wallace
Publisher: Mr G McCullough
Founded: 1956
Branch offices in Bulawayo, Gweru, Masvingo, Mutare, & Rusape.
Type of Business: Distributor, Importer, Major Book Chain Headquarters, Wholesaler
Bookshop(s): 16 George Silundika Ave, Harare

Kingstons Ltd
105 Victoria St, Harare
Mailing Address: PO Box 2374, Harare
Tel: (04) 750547; (04) 750548; (04) 750549; (04) 750550 *Fax:* (04) 723697
Telex: (04) 723697
Key Personnel
Man Dir: Elliot Mugamu

Also retailer with 19 branches in Zimbabwe & one in Bobwana.
Type of Business: Wholesaler

The Literature Bureau
Ministry of Education, Sport & Culture, Causeway, Harare
Mailing Address: PO Box CY121, Causeway, Harare
Tel: (04) 726929 *Cable:* LITBURO
Key Personnel
Chief Publications Officer: B C Chitsike
Also Publisher.
Type of Business: Distributor, Wholesaler

Mambo Bookshop
Senga Rd, PO Box 779, Gweru
Tel: (0154) 4016; (0154) 4017 *Fax:* (0154) 51991
E-mail: mambo@icon.co.zw
Key Personnel
General Manager: Fr Ron Gentile
Type of Business: Distributor, Exporter, Importer, Major Independent Bookseller, Wholesaler
Owned by: Mambo Press
Bookshop(s): Speke Ave/First St, Harare
  Tel: (0154) 705899; Gweru Bookshop, PO Box 779, Gweru *Tel:* (0154) 705899; Mambo Masvingo Bookshop, PO Box 1010, Masvingo *Tel:* (0139) 64566; Bulawago, PO Box 799, Gweru (19) 61162

National Books of Zimbabwe
c/o Apex Corp, Plot 332 Birmingham Rd, Southerton, Harare
Mailing Address: PO Box 647, Harare
Tel: (04) 703257; (04) 703258
Key Personnel
Chief Executive: A J Henderson
(Apex Holdings (Pvt) Ltd trade under the above name).
Owned by: Apex Corporation of Zimbabwe
Branch Office(s)
PO Box 2020, Bulawayo

Book Trade Reference Books & Journals

Featuring publications for and about the book trade and book publishing industries, titles listed may be relative to one specific country or may be of international relevance. Titles are arranged alphabetically by the country where the publisher is located or the country to which the title relates.

ϕ indicates those publications of international scope.

The type of publication appears in parentheses after the title:

        (B) - Book   (J) - Journal   (P) - Periodical

For library-related publications see **Library Reference Books & Journals**.

Albania

Bibliografia kombetare e Librit Shqip
(Albanian National Bibliography of Books) (J)
Published by National Library
Tirana
Tel: (042) 23843 *Fax:* (042) 23843
Quarterly.

Drita (P)
Published by Union of Writers and Artists of Albania
Baboci 37z, Tirana
Published weekly.

Kultura Popullore (P)
Published by Academie des Sciences de la RPSA, Institut de Culture Populaire
Rruga Kont Urani 3, Tirana
Tel: (042) 22323 *Fax:* (042) 23818
Published in Albanian, biannually; in French, annually.

Les Lettres Albanaises (P)
Published by Union of Writers and Artists of Albania
Baboci 37z, Tirana
Tel: (042) 27989
Published in French, quarterly.

Libri (The Book) (J)
Published by National Library
Tirana
Tel: (042) 23843 *Fax:* (042) 23843

Nentori (P)
Published by Union of Writers and Artists of Albania
Baboci 37z, Tirana
Tel: (042) 27989
Monthly.

Algeria

Bibliographie de l'Algerie (J)
Published by Bibliotheque Nationale
BP 127, Hamma El Annassers, 16000 Algiers
Tel: (021) 67 18 67; (021) 67 19 67 *Fax:* (021) 68 23 00
Published in Arabic & French (Selon lalangue du document).
Biannually.
100 DA; $22 US
ISSN: 1111-4835

Argentina

Boletin (Bulletin) (P)
Published by Sociedad Argentina de Escritores (SADE)
Uruguay 1371, 1016 Buenos Aires
Tel: (011) 811-3520 *Fax:* (011) 813-0773
Bimonthly.

Boletin de la Academia Argentina de Letras
(Bulletin of the Argentine Academy of Literature) (P)
Published by Academia Argentina de Letras (Bulletin of the Argentine Academy of Literature)
Sanchez de Bustamante 2663, C1425DVA Buenos Aires
Tel: (011) 4-8023814; (011) 4-8027509; (011) 4-8025161 *Fax:* (011) 4-8028340
E-mail: aaldespa@fibertel.com.ar; aaladmin@fibertel.com.ar; aalbibl@fibertel.com.ar
Key Personnel
Librarian: Alejandro E Parada
Quarterly.
ISSN: 0001-3757

Criterio (P)
Published by Kriterion SA
Junin 627, 1026 Buenos Aires
Tel: (011) 8160920; (011) 8144400 *Fax:* (011) 8144400

Davar (P)
Published by Fundacion Sociedad Hebraica Argentina
Sarmiento 2233, 1044 Buenos Aires
Tel: (011) 952-2170

Australia

APA Directory of Members (B)
Published by Australian Publishers Association Ltd
89 Jones St, Suite 60, Ultimo, NSW 2007
Tel: (02) 9281 9788 *Fax:* (02) 9281 1073
E-mail: apa@publishers.asn.au
Web Site: www.publishers.asn.au
Key Personnel
Chief Executive: Susan Bridge
Annually.
128 pp, $27.50 (AUS)

AUMLA (P)
Published by Australasian Universities Language & Literature Association
EMSAH School, University of Queensland, Private Bag 4800, Brisbane 4072
Tel: (07) 3365 2552 *Fax:* (07) 3365 2799
Key Personnel
Editor: Lloyd Davis *E-mail:* lloyd.davis@mailbox.ug.edu.au
Journal of literary criticism, language & cultural studies; published in English with occasional articles in French, German or Spanish.
First published 1953.
bi-annually.
170 pp
ISSN: 0001-2793

The Australian Author (P)
Published by The Australian Society of Authors Ltd
PO Box 1566, Strawberry Hills, NSW 2012
Tel: (02) 93180877 *Fax:* (02) 93180530
E-mail: asauthors@peg.pegasus.o2.au
Web Site: www.asaauthors.org
Key Personnel
Editor: Helen Stanwix
Quarterly.

Australian Book Review (J)
Published by National Book Council Inc
PO Box 2320, Richmond, South Victoria 3121
Tel: (03) 9429 6700 *Fax:* (03) 9429 2288
E-mail: abr@vicnet.net.au
Web Site: avoca.vicnet.net.au/~abr/
Key Personnel
Editor: Helen Daniel
Published 10 times a year. Publishes reviews & articles on Australian books & writing.

Australian Books in Print (B)
Published by D W Thorpe
18 Salmon St, Locked Bag 20, Port Melbourne, Victoria 3207
Tel: (03) 9245 7370; (03) 9245 7389 (customer service) *Fax:* (03) 9245 7395
E-mail: yoursay@thorpe.com.au; customer.service@thorpe.com.au
Web Site: www.thorpe.com.au
Key Personnel
Editor: Karen Hewitt
Information on over 100,000 Australian titles in print as well as publisher & distributor information. Other useful book trade related information included. Also available on microfiche & CD-ROM.
First published 1956.
Annual.
2500 pp
ISBN(s): 1-86452-041-8 (2 vol set)
ISSN: 0067-172X

Australian Bookseller & Publisher (P)
Published by D W Thorpe

AUSTRALIA

18 Salmon St, Locked Bag 20, Port Melbourne, Victoria 3207
Tel: (03) 9245 7370; (03) 9245 7389 (customer service) *Fax:* (03) 9245 7395
E-mail: bookseller.publisher@thorpe.com.au; yoursay@thorpe.com.au; customer.service@thorpe.com.au
Web Site: www.thorpe.com.au
Key Personnel
Publisher: Paulene Morey
First published 1921.
11x/yr.
ISSN: 0004-8763

Australian Literary Studies (P)
Published by University of Queensland Press
PO Box 6042, Saint Lucia, Qld 4067
Tel: (07) 33652452 *Fax:* (07) 33651988
Key Personnel
Editor: Dr Leigh Dale
Journals Administrator: Rosemary Chay
  E-mail: rosiec@uqp.uq.edu.au
Academic/scholarly publication.
Biennially.
Vol 20, Nos 3 & 4, 2002, AUD $82-00 (45.72 US dollars)
ISSN: 0004-9697

Australian Society of Indexers Newsletter (J)
Published by Australian Society of Indexers
PO Box R598, Royal Exchange NSW 1225
Tel: (0500) 525005; (02) 94383729
E-mail: mindexer@interconnect.com.au
Web Site: www.zeta.org.au/~aussi
Key Personnel
Editor: Glenda Browne
Available by E-mail, some discounts available.
Monthly; excluding January & December.

Biblionews & Australian Notes & Queries (J)
Published by Book Collectors' Society of Australia
16 Edwin St (South), Croydon, NSW 2132
Tel: (02) 9798 8984 *Fax:* (02) 9798 8984
E-mail: jeff@bcspl.com.au
Key Personnel
Ed: Brian Taylor
Secretary: Jeff Bidgood
Quarterly, to members.

Brouhaha (P)
Published by Corporate Image
Grosvenor St, Sydney, NSW 2000
Mailing Address: PO Box N110, Sydney, NSW 2000
Tel: (02) 423861
Published quarterly.

ƒBSANZ Bulletin (J)
Published by Bibliographical Society of Australia and New Zealand (BSANZ)
Baillieu Library, University of Melbourne, Parkville, Vic 3053
Tel: (03) 8344 5366
Key Personnel
Editor: Brian Hubber *E-mail:* morrison@unimelb.edu.au
Quarterly.

Guide to New Australian Books (P)
Published by D W Thorpe
18 Salmon St, Locked Bag 20, Port Melbourne, Victoria 3207
Tel: (03) 9245 7370; (03) 9245 7389 (customer service) *Fax:* (03) 9245 7395
E-mail: yoursay@thorpe.com.au; customer.service@thorpe.com.au
Web Site: www.thorpe.com.au
Listings & descriptions for newly published Australian books, along with information about forthcoming titles. Additional information includes author & editor.
First published 1990.
6x/yr.
ISSN: 1035-5391

Introduction to Book Publishing (B)
Published by Australian Publishers Association Ltd
89 Jones St, Suite 60, Ultimo, NSW 2007
Tel: (02) 9281 9788 *Fax:* (02) 9281 1073
E-mail: apa@publishers.asn.au
Web Site: www.publishers.asn.au
55 pp, $16.50 AUS

Island (P)
Published by Island Magazine Inc
PO Box 210, Sandy Bay, Tas 7005
Tel: (03) 62262325 *Fax:* (03) 62262172
E-mail: island@tassie.net.au
Web Site: www.islandmag.com
Key Personnel
Editor: David Owen
Literary Magazine.
Quarterly.

New Ceylon Writing (P)
Published by Macquarie University
School of English and Linguistics, North Ryde, NSW 2109
Tel: (02) 8058776 *Fax:* (02) 8057849
Creative and critical writing.

New Zealand Books in Print (B)
Published by D W Thorpe
18 Salmon St, Locked Bag 20, Port Melbourne, Victoria 3207
Tel: (03) 9245 7370; (03) 9245 7389 (customer service) *Fax:* (03) 9245 7395
E-mail: yoursay@thorpe.com.au; customer.service@thorpe.com.au
Web Site: www.thorpe.com.au
Bibliographic data on over 14,000 books in print from New Zealand & the Pacific Island states. Includes information on publishers, distributors, trade associations, as well as information about booksellers, literary awards & other book trade related information.
First published 1964.
Annual.
29: 850 pp, L55
ISBN(s): 1-86452-036-1
ISSN: 0157-7662

Overland (P)
Published by The O L Society Ltd
Melbourne, Victoria 8001
Mailing Address: PO Box 14146 MCMC, Melbourne, Victoria 8001
Tel: (03) 96884163 *Fax:* (03) 96884883
E-mail: overland@vu.edu.au
Key Personnel
Editor: Ian Syson *E-mail:* ian.syson@vu.edu.au
Quarterly.

Periodicals in Print and Online: Australia, New Zealand & Asia Pacific (B)
Published by Bookman Press Pty Ltd
607 Saint Kilda Rd, Level 8, Melbourne, Victoria 3004
Tel: (03) 9521 3250 *Fax:* (03) 9521 3270
E-mail: fayg@bookman.com.au
Web Site: www.bookman.com.au
First published 1981.
ISSN: 1322-3895

Quadrant (P)
Published by Quadrant Magazine Co Inc
47 George St, Fitzroy, Victoria 3065
Mailing Address: PO Box 1495, Collingwood, Victoria 3066
Tel: (03) 94176855 *Fax:* (03) 94162980
E-mail: quadrnt@ozemail.com.au
Key Personnel
Ed: P P McGuiness
Ten times per year.

Reading Time (P)
Published by Children's Book Council of Australia
Box 62, Ashmont, NSW 2650
Tel: (02) 69254907 *Fax:* (02) 69254907
Key Personnel
Editor & Publisher: Dr John Cohen
  E-mail: jcohen@ozemail.com.au
Yearly index to reviews & articles.
Quarterly.
44 pp
ISSN: 0155-218X

Southerly (P)
Published by English Association, Sydney Branch
PO Box 555, Leichhardt, NSW 2040
Tel: (02) 8182591; (02) 5643322 *Fax:* (02) 8185332
Southerly publishes short stories, poetry & literary criticism about Australian writers.
First published 1939.
Quarterly.

Victorian Government Publications (VGP) (J)
Published by State Library of Victoria
328 Swanston St, Melbourne, Vic 3000
Tel: (03) 96699920 *Fax:* (03) 96699888
Web Site: dargo.vicnet.net.au/vgb
Telex: AA38104
Key Personnel
Government Publications Librarian: Dianne Beaumont *E-mail:* dianneb@slv.vic.gov.au
Monthly.

Weekly Book Newsletter (P)
Published by D W Thorpe
18 Salmon St, Locked Bag 20, Port Melbourne, Victoria 3207
Mailing Address: Locked Bag 20, Port Melbourne, Victoria 3207
Tel: (03) 9245 7370; (03) 9245 7389 (customer service) *Fax:* (03) 9245 7395
E-mail: blue.newsletter@thorpe.com.au; yoursay@thorpe.com.au; customer.service@thorpe.com.au
Web Site: www.thorpe.com.au
Key Personnel
Editor: Andrew Wilkins *Tel:* (03) 9245 7392 *Fax:* (03) 9245 7395 *E-mail:* andrew.wilkins@thorpe.com.au
First published 1972.
Weekly (49 issues/yr).
ISSN: 0812-7042
Parent Company: R R Bowker
Ultimate Parent Company: Cambridge Information Group

Westerly (P)
Published by The Center for Studies in Australian Literature
English Communication & Cultural Studies, University of Western Australia, Crawley, WA 6009
Tel: (08) 93802101 *Fax:* (08) 93801030
E-mail: westerly@cyllene.uwa.edu.au
Web Site: www.arts.uwa.edu.au/westerly
Annually.

Writers and Photographers Marketing Guide: Directory of Australian and New Zealand Literary and Photo Markets (B)
Published by Australian Writers' Professional Service

c/o G R Pittaway, PO Box 28, Collins St, Melbourne, Victoria 3001
Tel: (03) 6546211; (054) 468275 *Fax:* (03) 6509648

Austria

Adressbuch des oesterreichischen Buchhandels (Directory of Austrian Book Trade) (B)
Published by Hauptverband des Oesterreichischen Buchhandels (Austrian Publishers' & Booksellers' Association)
Gruenangergasse 4, 1010 Vienna
Tel: (01) 5121535 *Fax:* (01) 5128482
E-mail: hbv@buecher.at
Web Site: www.buecher.at

Anzeiger des oesterreichischen Buchhandels (Austrian Book Trade Gazette) (J)
Published by Hauptverband des Oesterreichischen Buchhandels (Austrian Publishers' & Booksellers' Association)
Gruenangergasse 4, 1010 Vienna
Tel: (01) 5121535; (0222) 5121535 *Fax:* (01) 512153521; (01) 5128482
Semi-monthly.

Anzeiger des Verbandes der Antiquare Oesterreichs (J)
Published by Verband der Antiquare Oesterreichs
Gruenangergasse 4, 1010 Vienna
Tel: (01) 512 15 35 *Fax:* (01) 512153521
Austrian Antiquarian Booksellers' Association Gazette.

Autorensolidaritaet (Solidarity of Authors) (P)
Published by Interessengemeinschaft oesterreichischer Autorinnen und Autoren
Literaturhaus, Seidengasse 13, A-1070 Vienna
Tel: (01) 526204413 *Fax:* (01) 526204450
E-mail: ig@literaturhaus.at
quarterly.

Die Rampe (P)
Amt der Ooe Landesregierung, Institut fuer Kulturfoerderung, Spittelwiese 4, 4010 Linz
Tel: (0732) 772015491 *Fax:* (0732) 772011786
E-mail: k.post@ooe.gv.at
Web Site: www.ooe.gv.at
First published 1975.
5.20 euros

Die Literatur der oesterreichischen Kunst-, Kultur- und Autorenverlage (Austrian Publishing in Arts, Culture & Literature) (B)
Published by Interessengemeinschaft oesterreichischer Autorinnen und Autoren
Literaturhaus, Seidengasse 13, A-1070 Vienna
Tel: (01) 526204413 *Fax:* (01) 526204450
E-mail: ig@literaturhaus.at
Web Site: www.literaturhaus.at/lh/ig

Literatur und Kritik (Literature & Criticism) (P)
Published by Otto Mueller Verlag GesmbH & Co KG
Ernst-Thun-Str 11, A-5020 Salzburg
Tel: (0662) 881974 *Fax:* (0662) 872387
E-mail: otto.muellerverlag@salzburg.co.at
Key Personnel
Editor: Kourl-Markus Gauss
First published 1966.
5 times a year.
OS 93; DM 1350
ISSN: 0024-466X

Manuskripte (Manuscripts) (P)
Published by Dr Alfred Kolleritsch
Sackstrasse 17, A-8010 Graz
Tel: (0316) 825608 *Fax:* (0316) 825608
Journal for literature, art, & criticism.

Modern Austrian Literature (P)
Published by Arthur Schnitzler International Research Association
Dept of Literatures and Languages, University of California, Riverside, CA 92521
Tel: (0909) 787-4314 *Fax:* (0909) 779-2160
E-mail: austrian@citrus.ucr.edu
Text & summaries in English & German.

Sprachkunst, Beitraege zur Literaturwissenschaft (Art of Language, Contributions to the Study of Literature) (P)
Published by Oesterreichischen Akademie der Wissenschaften Kommission fuer Literaturwissenschaft
Dr Ignaz-Seipel-Platz 2, A-1010 Vienna
Mailing Address: PO Box 471, A-1011 Vienna
Tel: (01) 51581481 *Fax:* (01) 5139541
E-mail: verlag@oeaw.ac.at
Web Site: www.oeaw.ac.at/einheiten/verlag
Publication of articles particularly on poetical works, on literary history & poetics, reviews in addition. The language is German, English, French & Russian.

Stueckeboerse Katalog (J)
Published by Gerhard Ruiss
im Literaturhaus, Seidengasse 13, 1070 Vienna
Tel: (01) 526204418 *Fax:* (01) 526204430
E-mail: ig@literaturhaus.at
Web Site: www.literaturhaus.at/lh/ig
Catalogue of unpublished & published Austrian dramatic works.

Bangladesh

Bangladesh National Bibliography (J)
Published by National Library of Bangladesh
32, Justice Syed Mahabub Morshed Sarani, Sher-e-Bangla Nagar (Agargaon), Dhaka 1207
Annual.

Barbados

National Bibliography of Barbados (B)
Published by Naional Library Service
Coleridge St, Bridgetown
Tel: (246) 436-6081 *Fax:* (246) 436-1501
E-mail: natil@caribsurf.com

Belarus

Letopis Pechati Belarusi (Byelorussian National Bibliography) (J)
Published by Nationalnaya Knizhnaya Palata Belarus (National Book Chamber of Belarus)
ul v Karuzhai, 31a, 220002 Minsk
Tel: (0172) 289-33-96 *Fax:* (0172) 289-33-96
E-mail: palata@palata.beipak.mihsk.BY
ISSN: 0130-9218

Neman (P)
Published by Belorussian Writers' Union
Pro Skaryny 39, 220005 Minsk
Tel: (095) 2384967
Literary, artistic, socio-political magazine
The Nemen.
Monthly.

Belgium

Adresgids Voor Het Boekenvak (B)
Published by Boek.be
Hof ter Schrieklaan 17, B-2600 Berchem, Antwerp
Tel: (03) 230 89 23 *Fax:* (03) 281 22 40
E-mail: info@boek.be
Web Site: www.boek.be
A list of Dutch booksellers & publishers.
First published 1929.
Annually.

Annuaire (B)
Published by Commission Belge de Bibliographie et de Bibliologie
4 blvd de l'Empereur, B-1000 Brussels
Tel: (02) 80510464 *Fax:* (080) 80510465; (02) 5131503
Annually.

Belgische Bibliografie (J)
Published by Koninklijke Bibliotheek Alber I
4 blvd de l'Empereur, 1000 Brussels
Tel: (02) 5195701 *Fax:* (02) 5195716
Web Site: www.kbr.be/bb/brbb001.html
Key Personnel
Contact: Willy Vanderpijpen *E-mail:* vdpijpen@kbr.be
Monthly.

Dietsche Warande en Belfort (P)
Published by Uitgeverij Peeters Leuven (Belgie)
Bondgenotenlaan 153, B-3000 Leuven
Tel: (016) 235170 *Fax:* (016) 228500
Web Site: www.peeters-leuven.be
Journal for literature, art & spiritual life.

De Gulden Passer (P)
Published by Vereeniging der Antwerpsche Bibliophielene
c/o Museum Plantin-Moretus, Vrijdagmarkt 22, B-2000 Antwerp
Tel: (03) 2330294; (03) 2322455 *Fax:* (03) 2262516
Antwerp Association of Bibliophiles.

Le Livre et l'Estampe (The Book & The Print) (P)
Published by Societe Royale des Bibliophiles et Iconophiles de Belgique
4 blvd de l'Empereur, B-1000 Brussels
Biannually.

Neerlandia (P)
Published by Algemeen-Nederlands Verbond
Gallaitstraat 86, B-1030 Brussels
Tel: (020) 241 31 64 *Fax:* (020) 241 31 64
E-mail: info.anv@edpnet.be
Web Site: www.algemeennederlandsverbond.org
5 times/yr.

Revue generale (General Review) (P)
Published by De Boeck et Larcier SA
Fond Jean Paques, 4, B-1348 Louvain-la-Neuve
Tel: (010) 866629; (010) 482511 *Fax:* (010) 866691; (010) 482650
E-mail: revue.generale@euronet.be
Web Site: www.deboeck.be

Key Personnel
Contact: Agnes Duquenne *Tel:* (010) 482610
 E-mail: agnes.duquenne@deboeck.be
Publication includes general information on Belgian politics, economics, literature, etc.
First published 1865.
6 times/yr.
ISSN: 0777-2287

Streven (P)
Prinsstraat 15, B-2000 Antwerp
Tel: (03) 212 10 20 *Fax:* (03) 212 10 22
E-mail: streven@skynet.be
Web Site: www.come.to/streven
Magazine on Culture & Society, published monthly.
First published 1933.
Monthly (except August).
96 pp
ISSN: 0039-2324

Bolivia

Bio-Bibliografia Boliviana (Bolivian Bibliography) (J)
Published by Werner Guttentag y Rita Arze Editorial los Amigos del Libro
Casilla de Correo 450, Cochabamba 15
Tel: (04) 4504150 *Fax:* (04) 4115128
Key Personnel
Owner: Werner T Guttentag *E-mail:* gutten@amigol.bo.net
Annually.
Parent Company: Los Amigos del Libro

Bolivian Booknews (B)
Published by Editorial los Amigos del Libro
Casilla de Correo 450, Cochabamba 15
Tel: (04) 4504150 *Fax:* (04) 4115128
Key Personnel
Owner: Werner Guttentag *E-mail:* gutten@amigol.bo.net
Monthly.

Bosnia and Herzegovina

Izraz (P)
Published by Sour Svjetlost
Petra Preradovica 3, 71000 Sarajevo
Mailing Address: PO Box 129, 71000 Sarajevo
Journal of literary & artistic criticism.

Botswana

The National Bibliography of Botswana (P)
Published by Botswana National Library Service
Private Bag 0036, Gaborone
Tel: (031) 352397
Three per year.

Brazil

Bibliografia Brasileira (Brazilian Bibliography) (J)
Published by Biblioteca Nacional
Ave Rio Branco 219-39, 20040-008 Rio de Janeiro
Tel: (021) 2628255 *Fax:* (021) 2204173
E-mail: aromano@ars.bn.br

Jornal do SNEL/Producao Editorial Brasileria (SNEL Newspaper/Brazilian Editorial Production) (B)
Published by Sindicato Nacional dos Editores de Livros (SNEL)
SDS Edif Venancio VI, Loja 9/17, 7000 Brasilia
Tel: (021) 2336481 *Fax:* (021) 2538502
Telex: (021) 37063

Veritas (P)
Published by Pontificia Universidade Catolica do Rio Grande do Sul
c/o Antoninho M Naime Caixa Posta 12001, 90620 Porto Alegre RS
Tel: (051) 3391511 *Fax:* (051) 3391564
Telex: (051) 3349

Bulgaria

Balgarski disertacii (Bulgarian Dissertations) (P)
Published by Cyril & Methodius National Library
88 V Levski Blvd, 1504 Sofia
Tel: (02) 9882811 *Fax:* (02) 435495
Key Personnel
Contact: Stefka Penceva
First published 1973.
Annual.
ISSN: 0323-9411

Balgarski knigopis, Seria 1 (B)
Published by Cyril & Methodius National Library
88 V Levski Blvd, 1504 Sofia
Tel: (02) 9882811 *Fax:* (02) 435495
Key Personnel
Contact: Efrosina Angelova *E-mail:* angelova@nl.oltel.net
First published 1969.
Annual.
ISSN: 0323-9713

Balgarski periodichen Pechat, Seria 4 (Bulgarian Periodicals, Series 4) (P)
Published by Cyril & Methodius National Library (Narodna Biblioteka Kirili i Metodi)
88 Vassil Levski Blvd, 1504 Sofia
Tel: (02) 9882811 *Fax:* (02) 435495
E-mail: issn@nl.otel.net
Key Personnel
Contact: Ilona Kalojanova *Tel:* (02) 9882811 ext 273, 281
(Bulgarian Periodicals), part of *Bulgarska Nacionalna Bibliografija*.
First published 1967.
Annually.
ISSN: 0032-9764

Bibliographia na Balgarskata Bibliographia (Bibliography of Bulgarian Bibliographies) (B)
Published by Cyril & Methodius National Library
88 V Levski Blvd, 1504 Sofia
Tel: (02) 9882811 *Fax:* (02) 435495
Key Personnel
Contact: Tzvetanka Pancheva
First published 1965.
Annual.
ISSN: 0204-7373

Bulgarski knigopis, Seria 1 (The National Bibliography) (P)
Published by Cyril & Methodius National Library
88 V Levski Blvd, 1504 Sofia
Tel: (02) 9882811 *Fax:* (02) 435495
Key Personnel
Contact: Efrosina Angelova *E-mail:* angelova@nl.oltel.net
First published 1897.
Monthly.
ISSN: 0323-9616

Diskographia (B)
Published by Cyril & Methodius National Library
88 V Levski Blvd, 1504 Sofia
Tel: (02) 9882811 *Fax:* (02) 435495
Key Personnel
Contact: Alexander Kasabov
annual.
ISSN: 1310-9154

Letopis na Statiite ot Balgarskite Spisania i Sbornici (Articles from Bulgarian Journals & Collections) (P)
Published by Cyril & Methodius National Library
88 V Levski Blvd, 1504 Sofia
Tel: (02) 9882811 *Fax:* (02) 435495
Key Personnel
Contact: Liulia Kostova
First published 1952.
Monthly.
ISSN: 0324-0398

Letopis na statiite ot balgarskite vestnici (Articles from Bulgarian Newspapers) (P)
Published by Cyril & Methodius National Library
88 V Levski Blvd, 1504 Sofia
Tel: (02) 9882811 *Fax:* (02) 435495
Key Personnel
Contact: Maria Gavrilova
First published 1952.
Monthly.
ISSN: 0324-0347

Literaturen Forum (P)
Published by Literaturen Forum OOD
Prince Alexandre Batenberg, 4, 1040 Sofia
Tel: (02) 392215; (02) 390215; (02) 881069
 Fax: (02) 881069
Published weekly.

Literaturna Misal (Literary Thought) (P)
Published by Bulgarian Academy of Sciences, Institute of Literature
Shipchenski prohod 52 bl 17, 1113 Sofia
Tel: (02) 701830
Key Personnel
Associate Dir: Prof Stefan Kozhuharov
Text in Bulgarian. Contents page in English & French.

Chile

Bibliografia chilena (Chilean Bibliographies) (J)
Published by Biblioteca Nacional de Chile
Alameda L. Bernardo O'Higgins 651, Correo Central, Clasificador 1.105 Santiago
Tel: (02) 6338957; (02) 6381151 *Fax:* (02) 6380461; (02) 6381975
E-mail: bnescrit@oris.renib.cl
Key Personnel
Contact: Pedro Pablo Zegers

Efimeros (Ephemerals) (P)
Published by Biblioteca del Congreso Nacional
Huerfanos 1117-2 piso, Santiago
Mailing Address: CP 1199, Edificio del Congreso Nacional, Santiago
Tel: (02) 2701700 *Fax:* (02) 6961143
E-mail: direcbcn@congreso.cl

Mapocho (P)
Published by Biblioteca Nacional de Chile
Avda Bernardo O'Higgins 651, Clasificador 1400, Santiago
Tel: (02) 3605200; (02) 6381151 *Fax:* (02) 6380461
Distributor Editorial University.

Revista Chilena de Literatura (Chilean Review of Literature) (P)
Published by Universidad de Chile Facultad de Filosofia y Humanidades, Deparmento de Literatura
Casilla 10136-Correo Central, Santiago
Tel: (02) 6787022 *Fax:* (02) 2716823
E-mail: crosenfe@abello.dic.uchile.cl

China

China Today (P)
Published by China Welfare Institute
24 Baiwanzhuang Rd, Beijing 100037
Tel: (010) 8326037 *Fax:* (010) 8328338
Web Site: www.chinatoday.com
Published in English, French, Arabic, German, English braille & Chinese.
Monthly.

Chinese Literature (P)
Published by Chinese Literature Press
24 Baiwanzhuang Rd, Beijing 100037
Tel: (010) 8326678 *Fax:* (010) 8326678
Subscriptions to: China International Book Trading Corporation (CIBTC) (Guoji Shudian), PO Box 399, Beijing 100044
English & French editions; also publishes paperback novels & collections of short stories & poems under the logo Panda Books.

Directory of Publishers in China (B)
Published by Foreign Languages Press of China
24 Baiwanzhuanglu Rd, Beijing 100037
Tel: (010) 68327750; (010) 8320579 *Fax:* (010) 68326642; (010) 8317390
E-mail: flpcn@public3.bta.net.cn

Zhongguo jia shu mu (Chinese National Bibliography) (B)
Published by Bibliography & Document Press
National Library of China, 7 Wenjinjie St, 100802 Beijing 00802
Tel: (010) 6016633 ext 295 *Fax:* (010) 8419291
Telex: 222211 NLC CN *Cable:* 0848

Colombia

Anuario Bibliografico Colombiano (Colombian Bibliographical Annual) (J)
Published by Instituto Caro y Cuervo
Carrera 11 No 64-37 Apdo Aereo 51502, Santafe de Bogota, Cundinamarca
Tel: (01) 255-82-89; (01) 558289 *Fax:* (01) 217-02-43
Annually.

ϕ**Boletin Informativo CERLALC** (J)
Published by Centro Regional para el Fomento del Libro en America Latina y el Caribe (CERLALC)
Calle 70 No 9-52, Apdo Aereo, 57348 Bogota
Tel: (01) 3217501 *Fax:* (01) 3217503
E-mail: cerlalc@impsat.net.co
Key Personnel
Editor: Margarita Mendieta
Regional Center for the Promotion of Books in Latin America & the Caribbean.

Directorio Latinoamericano de Editoriales, Distribuidoras y Librerias (B)
Published by Centro Regional para el Fomento del Libro en America Latina y el Caribe
Calle 70 No 9-52, Apdo Aereo 57348, Santafe de Bogota Cundinamarca
Tel: (01) 2126056; (01) 2495141; (01) 3125690 *Fax:* (01) 2554614
E-mail: cerlalc@ipmsat.net.co
Key Personnel
Dir: Carmen Barvo
Dos nuevos publicaciones en Dd-Rom, anexo folletos. Para titulos no en inges, favor de proveer traduccion en Asimismo, el libro Manual de edicio.

Tinta Fresca (ISBN Bibliographical Bulletin/Editorial Mail) (J)
Published by Camara Colombiana del Libro
Carrera 17A No 37-27, Bogota
Tel: (01) 2886188 *Fax:* (01) 2873320
Quarterly.

The Democratic Republic of the Congo

Bibliographie Nationale (B)
Published by Bibliotheque Nacionale
BP 410, Kinshasa-Gombe
Telex: 21216 CAU ZR
Zaire Bibliography.

Costa Rica

Anuario bibliografico costarricense (Annual Costa Rican Bibliography) (J)
Published by Asociacion Costarricense de Bibliotecarios
Apdo 3308, San Jose

Catalogo Nacional ISBN (National ISBN Catalog) (J)
Published by Direccion General de Bibliotecas y Biblioteca Nacional
Apdo 10008-1000, Calle 15-17, Acdas 3Y3b, San Jose
Tel: 2331706; 2212436; 2212479 *Fax:* 2235510
Key Personnel
Contact: Marco A Chacon Monge

Indice de Revistas Nacionales (Catalog of National Periodicals) (J)
Published by Direccion General de Bibliotecas y Biblioteca Nacional
Apdo 10008-1000, San Jose
Tel: 2212436; 2212479 *Fax:* 2235510

Cote d'Ivoire

Bibliographie de la Cote-d'Ivoire (Ivory Coast Bibliography) (J)
Published by Bibliotheque Nationale
BP V180, Abidjan
First published 1969.
Annually in two volumes.

Revue de Litterature de l'esthetique negre-africaines & edition de livres Scolaires, de litterature Jenerale et d'encyclopedie (P)
Published by Les Nouvelles Editions Africaines
One blvd de Marseille, 01 Abidjan
Mailing Address: BP 3525, 01 Abidjan
Tel: 32-12-51; 32-16-22; 32-60-09
Telex: Cote d Ivoire 22564

Croatia

Forum (J)
Published by Hrvatska Akademija Zhanosti i Umjethosti, Razred Za Suvremenu knjizevnost
Zrinski trg 11, 10000 Zagreb
Tel: (041) 433661 *Fax:* (041) 433383
Key Personnel
Editor: Slavko Mihalic
Journal of the Section for Contemporary Literature of the Croatian Academy of Sciences and Arts; text in Croatian.

Cuba

Taller Literario (P)
Published by Biblioteca Central de la Universidad de Oriente
Avda Patricio Lumumba S-N, Santiago de Cuba
Tel: (0226) 3-1973 *Fax:* (0226) 3-2689
Key Personnel
Librarian: Caridad Velaquez Alazar
Literary Workshop.

Union (P)
Published by Ediciones Union, Union de Escritores y Artistas de Cuba
Calle 17 No 351, Vedado, Havana
Tel: (07) 324551; (07) 324571 *Fax:* (07) 333158
Key Personnel
Dir: Jorge Lois Arcos

Czech Republic

Casopis Narodniho muzea Rada historicka (The Bulletin of the National Museum Series: History) (P)
Published by Narodni Muzeum
Vaclavske nam 68, 115 79 Prague 1
Tel: (02) 24497350 *Fax:* (02) 22246047
Summaries in English, French, German & Russian.
Quarterly.

CZECH REPUBLIC

Casopis Narodniho muzea Rada prirodovedna
(The Bulletin of the National Museum Series: Natural Science) (P)
Published by Narodni Muzeum
Vaclavske nam 68, 115 79 Prague 1
Tel: (02) 24497350 *Fax:* (02) 22246047
Summaries in English, French, German & Russian.
Quarterly.

Czech Books For You (J)
Published by Artia Pegass Press Co Ltd
Palac Metro, Nardoni tr 25, 11121 Prague 1
Tel: (02) 266568; (02) 262081 *Fax:* (02) 24227872
Telex: 161065 ARTA C *Cable:* ARTIASPOL PRAHA
Quarterly bulletin with annotations and prices of approximately 200 of the most interesting books published in the Czech Republic during the previous quarter.

Muzejni a vlastivedna prace (Museum & Local History) (P)
Published by Narodni Muzeum
Vaclavske nam 68, 115 79 Prague 1
Tel: (02) 24497350 *Fax:* (02) 22246047
Summaries in English, French, German & Russian.
Quarterly.

Numismaticke listy (Numismatics Journal) (P)
Published by Narodni Muzeum
Vaclavske nam 68, 115 79 Prague 1
Tel: (02) 24497350 *Fax:* (02) 22246047
Summaries in English, French, German & Russian.
Six times a year.

Sbornik Narodniho muzea Rada A: Historie
(Collection of the National Museum Series A: History) (P)
Published by Narodni Muzeum
Vaclavske nam 68, 115 79 Prague 1
Tel: (02) 24497350 *Fax:* (02) 22246047
Summaries in English, French, German & Russian.
Quarterly.

Sbornik Narodniho muzea Rada B: Prirodni vedy (Collection of the National Museum Series B: Natural Science) (P)
Published by Narodni Muzeum
Vaclavske nam 68, 115 79 Prague 1
Tel: (02) 24497350 *Fax:* (02) 22246047
Key Personnel
Ed: Jiri Kvacek
Manager: Lukas Viktora
In English or German, also in Czechoslovakian with English & German summaries.
Quarterly.

Sbornik Narodniho muzea Rada C: Literarni historie (Magazine of the National Museum of Prague, Series C: Literary History) (P)
Published by Narodni Muzeum
Vaclavske nam 68, 115 79 Prague 1
Tel: (02) 24497350 *Fax:* (02) 22246047
Key Personnel
Ed: Helga Turkova
Manager: Lukas Viktora *Tel:* (02) 24497450 *Fax:* (02) 264919 *E-mail:* lukas.viktora@nm.cz
Summaries in English, French, German & Russian.
Quarterly.

Svetova Literatura (P)
Published by Odeon, nakladatelstvi krasne literatury a umeni
Ma Sarykovo nabr 26, 110 00 Prague 1
Tel: (02) 422912999 (voice & fax)
Review of Foreign Literature.

Denmark

Bogormen (J)
Published by Danske Boghandler Medhjaelperforening (The Bookworm, Journal for Book Trade Employees)
Siljangade 6, 2300 Copenhagen S
Tel: 31542255 *Fax:* 31572422
4 times per year.

Born og Boger (Children & Books) (P)
Published by Danmarks Skolebiblioteksforening
Vesterbrogade 20, DK-1620 Copenhagen V
Tel: 33253222 *Fax:* 33253223
E-mail: komskolbib@internet.dk
Key Personnel
Editor: Niels Jacobsen
English Summary. Periodical concerning books & other cultural values for children & young adults.

Danish Literary Magazine (P)
Published by The Danish Literature Information Centre
Christians Brugge 1, DK-1219 Copenhagen
Tel: 33320725 *Fax:* 33911545
E-mail: danlit@inet.uni.c.dk
Key Personnel
Dir: Tim Smedegaard

Dansk Bogfortegnelse (Danish National Bibliography, Books) (J)
Published by Danish Bibliographic Centre
Tempovej 7-11, 2750 Ballerup
Tel: 44867777 *Fax:* 44867891
E-mail: dbc@dbc.dk

Fortegnelse over Samhandelsberettigede Boghandlere MV (B)
Published by Den Danske Forlaeggerforening
Kompagmislraede 18, 1208 Copenhagen K
Tel: 33156688 *Fax:* 33156588
Register of Booksellers etc.

Hvedekorn (P)
Published by Borgens Forlag A/S
Valbygardsvej 33, 2500 Valby
Tel: 36153615 *Fax:* 36153616
Magazine for poetry & graphics.

Nordisk Exlibris Tidsskrift (Scandinavian Bookplate Periodical) (P)
Published by Dansk Exlibris Selskab
PO Box 1519, 2770 Copenhagen
Tel: 46769166 *Fax:* 46769167
E-mail: 113071.3716@compuserve.com
Key Personnel
Editor: Christian Sorensen
ISSN: 0029-1323

Orbis Litterarum (P)
Published by Blackwell Munksgaaard
Norre Sogade 35, DK-1370 Copenhagen K
Mailing Address: PO Box 2148, 1016 Copenhagen K
Tel: 77333333 *Fax:* 77333377
E-mail: headoffice@munksgaard.dk
Web Site: www.blackwellmunksgaard.com
Key Personnel
Editor: Prof Morton Nojgard
International Review of literary studies; text mainly in English, occasionally in French & German.

Produktionshaandbogen (Production Handbook) (B)
Published by Forlaget de Grafiske Haandboeger
Finsensvej 80, 2000 Frederiksberg
Tel: 38883222 *Fax:* 38883038
Key Personnel
Contact: Ilse Rosenback
Directory of prepress, printing & print-finishing companies in Denmark.

Egypt (Arab Republic of Egypt)

Lotus; Afro-Asian Writings (P)
Published by Permanent Bureau of Afro-Asian Writers
104 Sharia Kasr El-Aini, Cairo
Important quarterly review published for the Permanent Bureau of Afro-Asian Writers.

Ethiopia

Ethiopian Publications: Books, Pamphlets, Annuals & Periodical Articles (P)
Published by Addis Ababa University, Institute of Ethiopian Studies
PO Box 1176, Addis Ababa
Tel: (01) 119469 *Fax:* (01) 552688
E-mail: ics@padis.gn.apc.org
Ethiopian National Bibliography.
Annually.

List of Ethiopian Authors (B)
Published by Addis Ababa University Press
PO Box 1176, Addis Ababa
Tel: (01) 115673 *Fax:* (01) 550655

Fiji

Publications Bulletin (J)
Published by Fiji Government Printing Department
Box 2225, Government Buildings, Suva
Tel: 385999 *Fax:* 370203
E-mail: webmaster@fiji.gov.fj
Web Site: www.fiji.gov.fj
Semi-annually.

ǂ**South Pacific Bibliography** (J)
Published by University of the South Pacific Library
PO Box 1168, Suva
Tel: 3313900 (ext 2375) *Fax:* 3300830
E-mail: library@usp.ac.fj
Web Site: www.usp.ac.fjl~library
Published biennially.

ǂ**South Pacific Periodicals Index** (B)
Published by University of the South Pacific Library
PO Box 1168, Suva
Tel: 3313900 (ext 2375) *Fax:* 3300830
E-mail: library@usp.ac.fj
Web Site: www.usp.ac.fjl~library

Finland

Bokvaennen (The Bibliophile) (J)
Published by Boknoje, Barnens
Box 1253, 251-12 Helsinki
Tel: (042) 136415 *Fax:* (042) 147132
Key Personnel
Editor: Lars Forsberg

Books from Finland (J)
Published by Helsinki University Library
University of Helsinki, Unioninkatu 36, FIN-00014 Helsinki
Mailing Address: University of Helsinki, PO Box 15, FIN-00014 Helsinki
Tel: (09) 1357942 *Fax:* (09) 1357942
E-mail: bff@helsinki.fi
Web Site: www.lib.helsinki.fi/bff
Key Personnel
Editor-in-Chief: Kristina Carlson
Editor: Soila Lehtonen
Editor (London): Hildi Hawkins
A literary journal published in English of books from & about Finland.
First published 1967.
Quarterly.
80 pp, Annual subscription 27 euros, 20 euros in Finland & Scandinavia
ISSN: 0006-7490

The Finnish National Bibliography (P)
Published by Helsinki University Library
Slavonic Library, PB 15, Helsingin Yliopisto, 00014 Unioninkatu 36
Fax: (00) 7084441
Also on microfiche; monthly with annual cumulation.

Horisont (P)
Published by Svenska Oesterbottens Litteraturfoerening
c/o Sandin, Radhusgatan 50 c 53, FIN-65100 Vasa
Tel: (061) 3128426 *Fax:* (061) 3242210
E-mail: horisont50@hotmail.com
Literary magazine.
First published 1954.
4 issues/ yr.
30 euros/4 issues
ISSN: 0439-5530

Kirjakauppalehti (Book Trade Journal) (J)
Published by Kirjamedia Oy
Eerikinkatu 15-17 D43-44, 00100 Helsinki
Tel: (09) 68599114 *Fax:* (09) 68599119
Key Personnel
Editor-in-Chief: Annika Asvik

Parnasso (P)
Published by Yhtyneet Kuvalehdet Oy
Maistraatinportti 1, SF-00240 Helsinki
Tel: (00) 1566531 *Fax:* (00) 1566505

Skrifter utgivna av Svenska Litteratursaellskapet i Finland (P)
Published by Svenska Litteratursaellskapet i Finland (Society of Swedish Literature in Finland)
Riddareg 5, FIN 00170 Helsinki 17
Tel: (09) 618777 *Fax:* (09) 6187 7377
Key Personnel
Editor: Nina Edgren-Henrichson *E-mail:* nina.edgren-henrichson@sls.fi
Scholarly publications in history, literature, ethnology, Scandinavian languages, social & political sciences.
ISSN: 0039-6842

Virittaejae (P)
Published by Society for the Study of Finnish Castrenianum, PL3, 00014 University of Helsinki
Tel: (09) 191 24342 *Fax:* (09) 1913321
Web Site: www.helsinki.fi/jarj/kks/virittaja
Key Personnel
Editor: Marja-Liisa Helasvuo; Susanna Shore
Summaries in English, French & German
The Kinder.
First published 1897.
Quarterly (4 numbers per vol).
54 euros (47 euros if paid through a Finnish bank)
ISSN: 0042-6806

France

ƒ**Bibliotheques et Musees des Arts du Spectacle dans le Monde** (Performing Arts Libraries and Museums of the World) (B)
Published by Societe Internationale des Bibliotheques-Musees des Arts du Spectacle
Centre National de la Recherche Scientifique (CNRS), 3-5 rue Michel-Ange, 75794 Paris Cedex 16
Tel: (01) 44964000 *Fax:* (01) 44965000

ƒ**Bulletin du Bibliophile** (J)
Published by Association Internationale Bibliophile
Electre-Editions du Cercle de la Librarie, 35 rue Gregoire-de-Tours, 75006 Paris
Tel: (01) 44412800 *Fax:* (01) 43296895
Published in English, French, German, Italian & Spanish
Biannually, June & December.

Choisir (P)
Published by Centre National de Documentation Pedagogique (CNDP)
29 rue d'Ulm, 75230 Paris Cedex 05
Tel: (01) 46349000 *Fax:* (01) 46345544
Key Personnel
Editor: J Lanfranchi

ƒ**Copyright Bulletin** (J)
Published by UNESCO
Division of Art & Cultural Enterprise
Unit of Creativity & Copyright
7, Place de Fontenoy, 75352 Paris 07-SP
Tel: (01) 45684702; (01) 45684705 *Fax:* (01) 45685589
E-mail: m.e.guerassimos@unesco.org
Web Site: www.upo.unesco.org/publications; www.unesco.org/culture/copyright
Published in English, French, Spanish, Chinese & Russian.
Quarterly.
80 pp

ƒ**Copyright Laws & Treaties of the World** (B)
Published by UNESCO Publishing
7 Place de Fontenoy, 75352 Paris 07-SP
Tel: (01) 45684930 *Fax:* (01) 45685737
E-mail: publishing.promotion@unesco.org
Web Site: www.unesco.org/publications
Telex: 204461
Key Personnel
Dir, General: Koichiro Matsuura
Dir, UNESCO Publishing: Chandran Nair
Editorial Dir: Michiko Tanaka
Rights & Permissions: Georgina Almeida
Promotion & Sales: Cristina Laje
UNESCO acts as Standard Book Numbering Agency, administering ISBNs for UN publications. It also maintains responsibility, within its Copyright Division, for the Intergovernmental Copyright Committee. UNESCO publishes monographs, CD-ROMs, scientific maps & journals on education, culture, sciences & communication.
Annually.

Critique (P)
Published by Les Editions de Minuit SA
7 rue Bernard-Palissy, F-75006 Paris
Tel: (01) 45442316
Key Personnel
Contact: Isabelle Chave
General review of publications in France & abroad.

ƒ**Directory of Documentation, Libraries and Archives Services in Africa** (B)
Published by UNESCO Publishing
Office of Public Information, 7 Place de Fontenoy, F-75352 Paris 07-SP
Tel: (01) 45681682 *Fax:* (01) 4565823
Web Site: www.unesco.org/publications
Telex: 204461

Documentation, technique scientifique et commerciale (J)
Published by Librairie Lavoisier
11 rue Lavoisier, 75384 Paris Cedex 08
Tel: (01) 42657167 *Fax:* (01) 42650246
E-mail: group@lavoisier.fr
Web Site: www.lavoisier.fr
Documentation - Technical, Scientific & Commercial. Text & summaries in English, French & German.

Donnees statistiques sur l'edition du Livre en France (French Book Production Statistics) (B)
Published by Syndicat National de l'Edition
115 Blvd Saint Germain, 75006 Paris
Tel: (01) 4441 4050 *Fax:* (01) 4441 4077

ƒ**Index Translationum, International Bibliography of Translations** (B)
Published by UNESCO
7, Place de Fontenoy, 75352 Paris 07-SP
Tel: (01) 45684310; (01) 45684311 *Fax:* (01) 45685591
E-mail: index@unesco.org
Web Site: www.unesco.org/culture/xtrans
Bibliography available on CD-ROM & Internet only.
Annual cummulative edition.
8, $45 (US)
ISBN(s): 92-3-003809-1
ISSN: 1020-1386

Information Litteraire (P)
Published by Presses Universitaires 'de Besancon
95 blvd Raspail, F-75006 Paris
Tel: (01) 45485826 *Fax:* (01) 45485860
Editions J-B Bailliere, 10 rue Thenard, F-75005 Paris.

ƒ**International Association of Literary Critics Review** (J)
Published by International Association of Literary Critics
Hotel de Massa, 38 rue du Faubourg, St Jacques, 75014 Paris
Tel: (01) 40513300 *Fax:* (01) 45873876

ƒ**Lettre Internationale (Revue)** (International Letter Review) (J)
41, rue Bobillot, 75013 Paris
Mailing Address: 27, rue St Ambroise, 75011 Paris
Tel: (01) 42470200; (01) 42470734 *Fax:* (01) 42338324
Published in 9 languages.

Litterature (P)
Published by Larousse et Universite Paris-8
21 rue du Montparnasse, F-75283 Paris Cedex 6

FRANCE

Tel: (01) 44394400 *Fax:* (01) 44394343
Key Personnel
Editor: Francois Tremolieres

Livres au Format de Poche (Paperback Books) (B)
Published by Electre
35 rue Gregoire de Tours, 75279 Paris Cedex 06
Tel: (01) 44412800 *Fax:* (01) 44412865; (01) 44412855; (01) 44412800
E-mail: commercial@electre.com
Annually.
2001, $43.61 F
ISBN(s): 2-7654-0812-2

Livres de France (Books of France) (J)
Published by Pierre Louis Rozynes
35 rue Gregoire de Tours, 75006 Paris
Tel: (01) 44412800 *Fax:* (01) 43297785
E-mail: livrebdo@electre.com
Guide to published books & trade information.
Monthly.
Parent Company: Livres Hebdo/ Electre

Livres Disponibles (B)
Published by Editions du Cercle de la Librairie
35 rue Gregoire de Tours, 75006 Paris Cedex
Tel: (01) 44412800 *Fax:* (01) 43296895
French Books in Print. Also available on microfiche, from database (Electre), & CD-ROM.
Annually.

Livres Hebdo (Weekly Books) (J)
Published by Pierre Louis Rozynes
35 rue Gregoire de Tours, 75279 Paris Cedex 06
Tel: (01) 44412800 *Fax:* (01) 43297785
E-mail: livrebdo@electre.com
Book market weekly trade journal.
Parent Company: Electre

Magazine litteraire (P)
Published by Magazine-Expansion
40 rue des Saints-Peres, 75007 Paris
Tel: (01) 45441451 *Fax:* (01) 45488636
E-mail: magazine@magazine-litteraire.com
Web Site: www.magazine-litteraire.com
Literary magazine.
Monthly.
108 pp
ISSN: 0024-9807

La Nouvelle Revue francaise (P)
Published by Editions Gallimard
5 rue Sebastien-Bottin, 75328 Paris Cedex 07
Tel: (01) 49544200
Key Personnel
Editor: Michel Braudeau
First published 1909.
Quarterly.
352 pp
ISSN: 0029-4802

Quinzaine litteraire (Literary Fortnightly) (P)
Published by Selis la Quinzaine Litteraire
135 rue Saint-Martin, F-75194 Paris 4
Tel: (01) 48874857 *Fax:* (01) 48871301

Repertoire international des Editeurs et Diffuseurs de Langue francaise (International List of French Language Publishers and Distributors) (B)
Published by Editions du Cercle de la Librairie
35 rue Gregoire de Tours, 75006 Paris
Tel: (01) 44412861 *Fax:* (01) 44412865
Telex: lifran 270838
Annually.

Revue de Litterature comparee (Review of Comparative Literature) (P)
Published by Didier Erudition

6 rue de la Sorbonne, 75005 Paris
Tel: (01) 43544757 *Fax:* (01) 40517385
Text in English & French.

Revue des Etudes Italiennes (Review of Italian Studies) (P)
Published by Societe des Etudes Italiennes (Paris)
Centre Malesherbes, 108, Boulevard Malesherbes, 75850 Paris Cedex 17
Tel: (01) 43 18 41 66; (01) 43 18 41 69 *Fax:* (01) 43 18 41 71
Key Personnel
Dir: Francois Livi *E-mail:* francois.livi@paris4.sorbonne.fr
Biannually.
160 pp, 40 Euros
ISSN: 0035-2047

La Revue des Livres pour Enfants (Children's Books Review Magazine) (P)
Published by La Joie par les Livres
8 rue St-Bon, F-75004 Paris
Tel: (01) 48876195 *Fax:* (01) 48870852

Gambia

National Bibliography of the Gambia (B)
Published by Gambia National Library
Reg Pye Lane, PMB 552, Banjul
Tel: 228312 *Fax:* 223776

Georgia

Sakmatsvilo Literaturis Moambe (Bulletin of Children's Literature) (J)
Published by Nakaduli
Ketskhoveli 5, 380007 Tbilisi

Germany

ƒ**Adressbuch fuer den deutschsprachigen Buchhandel** (B)
Published by Buchhaendler-Vereinigung Verlag GmbH
Grosser Hirschgraben 17-21, 60311 Frankfurt
Mailing Address: Postfach 100442, 60004 Frankfurt
Tel: (069) 1306243 *Fax:* (069) 1306382
E-mail: weber@bhv.de
Telex: 413573 buchvd
Directory of the German-language Book Trade.

The African Book Publishing Record (ABPR) (P)
Published by K G Saur Verlag GmbH, A Gale/ Thomson Learning Company
Unit of Thomson Learning
Ortlerstr 8, 81373 Munich
Mailing Address: Postfach 70 16 20, 81316 Munich
Tel: (089) 76902-0 *Fax:* (089) 76902-150
E-mail: info@saur.de
Web Site: www.saur.de
Telex: 5212067
Bibliographical tool which offers systematic & comprehensive coverage of new & forthcoming African publications in a single source, providing full bibliographic & acquisitions data. Also

BOOK TRADE REFERENCE

includes an extensive book review section & features news, reports & articles about African book trade activities & developments.
Quarterly.
Parent Company: Gale
Ultimate Parent Company: The Thomson Corporation

African Books in Print/Livres Africains Desponibles (5th ed) (B)
Published by K G Saur Verlag GmbH, A Gale/ Thomson Learning Company
Unit of Thomson Learning
Ortlerstr 8, 81373 Munich
Mailing Address: Postfach 70 16 20, 81316 Munich
Tel: (089) 76902-0 *Fax:* (089) 76902-150
E-mail: info@saur.de
Web Site: www.saur.de
Telex: 5212067
Major reference work containing full bibliographic details on 24,000 books, published in 45 African countries by more than 700 publishers & research institutions with publishing programs.
5th edition
ISBN(s): 3-598-07684-3
Parent Company: Gale
Ultimate Parent Company: The Thomson Corporation

African Studies Abstracts (J)
Published by K G Saur Verlag GmbH, A Gale/ Thomson Learning Company
Unit of Thomson Learning
Ortlerstr 8, 81373 Munich
Mailing Address: Postfach 70 16 20, 81316 Munich
Tel: (089) 76902-0 *Fax:* (089) 76902-150
E-mail: info@saur.de
Web Site: www.saur.de
Abstracting journal providing coverage of all the leading journals in the field of African Studies, Third World countries & development issues. Each issue contains approximately 450 abstracts Published on behalf of the African Studies Centre, Leiden, Netherlands.
Parent Company: Gale
Ultimate Parent Company: The Thomson Corporation

Akzente (P)
Published by Carl Hanser Verlag
Kolberger Str 22, 81679 Munich
Tel: (089) 998300 *Fax:* (089) 984809
E-mail: info@hanser.de
Web Site: www.hanser.de/verlag/

Archiv fuer Geschichte des Buchwesens (Archive for History Books) (J)
Published by Buchhaendler-Vereinigung Verlag GmbH
Grosser Hirschgraben 17-21, 60004 Frankfurt
Mailing Address: Postfach 100442, 60004 Frankfurt
Tel: (069) 1306287 *Fax:* (069) 1306382
E-mail: agb@buchhaendler-vereinigung.de
Telex: 413573 buchvd
First published 1958.
2 times/yr.
ISBN(s): 3-7657-2187-5
ISSN: 0066-6327

Besprechungen Annotationen (P)
Published by Einkaufszentrale fur offentliche Bibliotheken BmbH
Bismarckstr 3, 72705 Reutlingen
Mailing Address: Postfach 1542, 72705 Reutlingen
Tel: (07121) 144-0 *Fax:* (07121) 144-280

BOOKS & JOURNALS GERMANY

Boersenblatt fuer den Deutschen Buchhandel/Frankfurt am Main und Leipzig (Official Journal of the German Book Trade) (J)
Published by Borsenverein des Deutschen Buchhandels eV
Grosser Hirschgraben 17-21, 60311 Frankfurt am Main
Mailing Address: Postfach 100442, 60004 Frankfurt am Main
Tel: (069) 1306 363 *Fax:* (069) 2899 86
E-mail: boersenblatt@buchhandles-veseinigung.de
Telex: 413573 buchvd
First published 1834.
ISSN: 0940-0044

Buch Aktuell (Topical Book) (P)
Published by Harenberg Kommunikation Verlags- und Medien GmbH & Co KG
Koenigswall 21, 44137 Dortmund
Tel: (0231) 90560 *Fax:* (0231) 9056110
E-mail: 100126.3422@compuserve.com

Buch und Buchhandel in Zahlen (Books & the Book Trade in Figures) (B)
Published by Borsenverein des Deutschen Buchhandels eV
Grosser Hirschgraben 17-21, 60311 Frankfurt am Main
Mailing Address: Postfach 100442, 60004 Frankfurt am Main
Tel: (069) 1306335 *Fax:* (069) 1306396
Telex: 413573 buchvd
Key Personnel
Contact: Eva Martin

Buchhaendler heute (The Bookseller Today) (J)
Published by Triltsch Druck und Verlag GmbH & Co KG
Herzogstr 53, 40215 Duesseldorf
Tel: (0211) 38636-0 *Fax:* (0211) 38636-13
E-mail: wehling@triltschverlag.de
Web Site: www.triltschverlag.de
Book Trade.
Monthly.

BuchJournal (J)
Published by Borsenverein des Deutschen Buchhandels eV
Grosser Hirschgraben 17-21, 60311 Frankfurt am Main
Mailing Address: Postfach 100442, 60004 Frankfurt am Main
Tel: (069) 1306248 *Fax:* (069) 1306201
E-mail: kammann@bhr.de
Key Personnel
Contact: Petra Kammann
General magazine for booksellers' customers.
Quarterly.

BuchMarkt (Book Market) (J)
Published by Verlag K. Werner GmbH
Sperberweg 4A, 40668 Meerbusch
Mailing Address: 32
Tel: (02150) 919100 *Fax:* (02150) 919191
Key Personnel
Editor-in Chief: Christian von Zittwitz
Journal for the book trade in German-speaking areas.

Buchreport (Book Report) (J)
Published by Harenberg Kommunikation Verlags- und Medien GmbH & Co KG
Koenigswall 21, 44137 Dortmund
Mailing Address: Postfach 101852, 44018 Dortmund
Tel: (0231) 90560 *Fax:* (0231) 9056111
E-mail: post@harenberg.de
Web Site: www.buchreport.de
Largest independent magazine for booksellers in German-speaking areas.

First published 1970.
Weekly.
ISSN: 1615-0732

Buecherkarren (Book Cart) (J)
Published by Verlag Volk & Welt GmbH
Oranienstr 164/165, 10969 Berlin
Tel: (030) 61689530 *Fax:* (030) 61689540 *Cable:* VOLKWELT BERLIN
List of company publications to the general reader.
Two to three times a year.

Buecherkommentare (Book Commentaries) (P)
Published by Rombach GmbH Druck und Verlagshaus & Co
Unterwerkstr 5, 79115 Freiburg
Mailing Address: Postfach 5109, 79013 Freiburg
Tel: (0761) 4500294; (0761) 4500 0 *Fax:* (0761) 4500 2125
Telex: uber 772728

Bulletin Jugend und Literatur (Youth & Literature Bulletin) (P)
Published by Neuland-Verlagsgesellschaft mbH
PO Box 1422, 21496 Geesthacht
Tel: (04152) 81342 *Fax:* (04152) 81343
E-mail: vertrieb@neuland.com
Web Site: www.neuland.com
Key Personnel
Editor: Brigitte Briese
First published 1969.
monthly.
36 pp
ISSN: 0045-351X

Deutsche Nationalbibliographie (German National Bibliography) (J)
Published by Deutsche Bibliothek Frankfurt am Main
Buchhaendler-Vereinigung GmbH, 60004 Frankfurt am Main
Mailing Address: Postfach 100442, 60004 Frankfurt am Main
Tel: (069) 1306243 *Fax:* (069) 1306201
E-mail: vertrieb@buchhaendler-vereingung.de
Web Site: www.buchhaendler-vereingung.de
Key Personnel
Contact: Marlies Ney
Publisher located at Grosser Hirschgraben 17-21, Frankfurt am Main.

⌀**Dictionnaire pratique de l'Edition en 20 Langues (Woerterbuch des Verlagswesens in 20 Sprachen)** (Publishers Practical Dictionary in Twenty Languages) (B)
Published by K G Saur Verlag GmbH, A Gale/Thomson Learning Company
Unit of Thomson Learning
Ortlerstr 8, 81373 Munich
Mailing Address: Postfach 70 16 20, 81316 Munich
Tel: (089) 76902-0 *Fax:* (089) 76902-150
E-mail: info@saur.de
Web Site: www.saur.de
Telex: 5212067
Parent Company: Gale
Ultimate Parent Company: The Thomson Corporation

Directory of Special Collections in Western Europe (B)
Published by K G Saur Verlag GmbH, A Gale/Thomson Learning Company
Unit of Thomson Learning
Ortlerstr 8, 81373 Munich
Mailing Address: Postfach 70 16 20, 81316 Munich
Tel: (089) 76902-0 *Fax:* (089) 76902-150
E-mail: info@saur.de
Web Site: www.saur.de

Parent Company: Gale
Ultimate Parent Company: The Thomson Corporation

Flugpost - Informationsdienst Luftfahrt (Airmail-Aviation Information Service) (P)
Published by Flugpost Verlag Peter Pletschacher
Kolpingring 16, 82041 Oberhaching
Tel: (089) 6138900 *Fax:* (089) 613890-10
Key Personnel
Manager: Peter Pletschacher
Weekly.

⌀**Frankfurt Book Fair** (B)
Published by Ausstellungs-und Messe-GmbH des Borsenvereins des Deutschen Buchhandels
Reineckstr 3, 60313 Frankfurt am Main
Mailing Address: Postfach 100116, 60001 Frankfurt am Main
Tel: (069) 21020 *Fax:* (069) 2102 227; (069) 2102 277
E-mail: exhibition@book-fair.com
Web Site: www.frankfurt-book-fair.com
Key Personnel
Dir: Helga Jansohn
Deputy Dir: Galoi Rauch-Kneer

⌀**Gesamtverzeichnis des deutschsprachigen Schrifttums** (Bibliography of German Language Publications) (B)
Published by K G Saur Verlag GmbH, A Gale/Thomson Learning Company
Unit of Thomson Learning
Ortlerstr 8, 81373 Munich
Mailing Address: Postfach 70 16 20, 81316 Munich
Tel: (089) 76902-0 *Fax:* (089) 76902-150
E-mail: info@saur.de
Web Site: www.saur.de
Telex: 5212067
Covers 1700-1965.
Parent Company: Gale
Ultimate Parent Company: The Thomson Corporation

⌀**Gesamtverzeichnis des deutschsprachigen Schrifttums ausserhalb des Buchhandels** (Bibliography of German Language Publications Outside the Booktrade) (B)
Published by K G Saur Verlag GmbH, A Gale/Thomson Learning Company
Unit of Thomson Learning
Ortlerstr 8, 81373 Munich
Mailing Address: Postfach 70 16 20, 81316 Munich
Tel: (089) 76902-0 *Fax:* (089) 76902-150
E-mail: info@saur.de
Web Site: www.saur.de
Telex: 5212067
Covers 1966-1980.
Parent Company: Gale
Ultimate Parent Company: The Thomson Corporation

⌀**Gesamtverzeichnis Deutschsprachiger Hochschulschriften 1966-1980** (Bibliography of German Language Academic Publications 1966-1980) (B)
Published by K G Saur Verlag GmbH, A Gale/Thomson Learning Company
Unit of Thomson Learning
Ortlerstr 8, 81373 Munich
Mailing Address: Postfach 70 16 20, 81316 Munich
Tel: (089) 76902-0 *Fax:* (089) 76902-150
E-mail: info@saur.de
Web Site: www.saur.de
Telex: 5212067
Parent Company: Gale
Ultimate Parent Company: The Thomson Corporation

ƒ**Guide to Microforms in Print** (B)
Published by K G Saur Verlag GmbH, A Gale/
 Thomson Learning Company
Unit of Thomson Learning
Ortlerstr 8, 81373 Munich
Mailing Address: Postfach 70 16 20, 81316 Munich
Tel: (089) 76902-0 *Fax:* (089) 76902-150
E-mail: info@saur.de
Web Site: www.saur.de
Telex: 5212067
Parent Company: Gale
Ultimate Parent Company: The Thomson Corporation

Guide to Microforms in Print: Author/Title (P)
Published by K G Saur Verlag GmbH, A Gale/
 Thomson Learning Company
Unit of Thomson Learning
Ortlerstr 8, 81373 Munich
Mailing Address: Postfach 70 16 20, 81316 Munich
Tel: (089) 76902-0 *Fax:* (089) 76902-150
E-mail: info@saur.de
Web Site: www.saur.de
Telex: 5212067
Cumulative alphabetical list of books, journals & other materials available form US & foreign publishers in microform.
Annual.
1999: 2100 pp, $430
ISBN(s): 3-598-11392-7
Parent Company: Gale
Ultimate Parent Company: The Thomson Corporation

Hebbeljahrbuch (Hebbel Year Book) (P)
Published by Westholsteinische Verlagsanstalt und Verlagsdruckerei Boyens & Co
Am Wulf-Isebrand Platz, 25746 Heide Holstein
Mailing Address: Postfach 1880, 25738 Heide Holstein
Tel: (0481) 68862 *Fax:* (0481) 6886467
E-mail: buchverlagch@nordsee.de

Die Horen (P)
Published by Wirtschaftsverlag NW, Verlag Fuer neue Wissenschaft GmbH
Buergermeister-Smidtstr 74-76, 27568 Bremerhaven
Mailing Address: Postfach 101110, 27511 Bremerhaven
Tel: (0471) 945440 *Fax:* (0471) 9454477
E-mail: vertrieb@nw-verlag.de
Web Site: www.nw-verlag.de
First published 1955.
Quarterly.
31 euros & postage (1 year subscription)
ISSN: 0018-4942

Imprimatur (J)
Published by Gesellschaft der Bibliophilen
Harrasowitz Verlag, 65174 Wiesbaden
Tel: (0611) 530570
E-mail: verlag@harrassowitz.de
Web Site: www.harrassowtiz.de
Among other things history of books, printers, bookmindedness.
ISSN: 0073-5620

International African Bibliography (J)
Published by K G Saur Verlag GmbH, A Gale/
 Thomson Learning Company
Unit of Thomson Learning
Ortlerstr 8, 81373 Munich
Mailing Address: Postfach 70 16 20, 81316 Munich
Tel: (089) 76902-0 *Fax:* (089) 76902-150
E-mail: info@saur.de
Web Site: www.saur.de
Telex: 5212067
Indexes the latest books, articles & papers published internationally on Africa.
Quarterly.
Parent Company: Gale
Ultimate Parent Company: The Thomson Corporation

ƒ**International Book Trade Directory** (B)
Published by K G Saur Verlag GmbH, A Gale/
 Thomson Learning Company
Unit of Thomson Learning
Ortlerstr 8, 81373 Munich
Mailing Address: Postfach 70 16 20, 81316 Munich
Tel: (089) 76902-0 *Fax:* (089) 76902-150
E-mail: info@saur.de
Web Site: www.saur.de
Telex: 5212067
Listing details of booksellers in 134 countries outside the US and Canada.
Parent Company: Gale
Ultimate Parent Company: The Thomson Corporation

ƒ**International Cataloguing and Bibliographic Control** (J)
Published by IFLA UBCIM Programme
c/o die Deutsche Bibliothek, Adickesallee 1, 60322 Frankfurt am Main
Tel: (069) 1525 1140; (069) 1525 1441
 Fax: (069) 1525 1142
E-mail: iflaubcim@dbf.ddb.de
Web Site: www.ifla.org/vi/3/ubcim.htm
Key Personnel
Editor: Ms Marie-France Plassard
Quarterly.

ƒ**Jahrbuch der Auktionspreise fuer Buecher, Handschriften und Autographen** (German Book Prices Current) (B)
Published by Dr Ernst Hauswedell & Co Verlag
Haldenstr 30, 70376 Stuttgart
Mailing Address: Postfach 140155, 70071 Stuttgart
Tel: (0711) 54 99 71-11 *Fax:* (0711) 54 99 71-21
E-mail: hiersemann.hauswedell.verlage@t-online.de
Web Site: www.hauswedell.de
Key Personnel
Contact: Reinhold Busch
Publication contains Book auction prices in Germany, Austria, Switzerland & the Netherlands.

LIBER Quarterly: The Journal of European Research Libraries (J)
Published by K G Saur Verlag GmbH, A Gale/
 Thomson Learning Company
Unit of Thomson Learning
Ortlerstr 8, 81373 Munich
Mailing Address: Postfach 70 16 20, 81316 Munich
Tel: (089) 76902-0 *Fax:* (089) 76902-150
Web Site: www.lib.dk/liber/liberq
Key Personnel
Editor: Dr Peter te Boekhorst *Tel:* (0251) 83 2 40 64 *Fax:* (0251) 83 2 83 98 *E-mail:* boekho@uni-muenster.de; llrike Scholle *Tel:* (0251) 83 2 40 64 *Fax:* (0251) 83 2 83 98 *E-mail:* scholul@uni-muenster.de
Published in English, French & German.
First published 1972.
Quarterly.
Free to member of LIBER, can be purchased separately
ISSN: 1435-5205

LiteraturNachrichten (Literary News) (P)
Published by Society for the Promotion of African, Asian & Latin American Literature
Reineckstr 3, 60313 Frankfurt
Mailing Address: Postfach 10 01 16, 60001 Frankfurt
Tel: (069) 2102247 *Fax:* (069) 2102227
E-mail: litprom@book-fair.com
Web Site: www.litprom.de
The only quarterly in Germany to report about literary developments in the Southern hemisphere.
First published 1983.
quarterly.
36 pp, Euro 15.00 aq
ISSN: 0935-7807

ƒ**Microform & Imaging Review** (J)
Published by K G Saur Verlag GmbH, A Gale/
 Thomson Learning Company
Unit of Thomson Learning
Ortlerstr 8, 81373 Munich
Mailing Address: Postfach 70 16 20, 81316 Munich
Tel: (089) 76902-0 *Fax:* (089) 76902-150
E-mail: info@saur.de
Web Site: www.saur.de
Telex: 5212067
Parent Company: Gale
Ultimate Parent Company: The Thomson Corporation

Neue deutsche Literatur (New German Literature) (P)
Published by Aufbau-Verlag GmbH
Neue Promenade 6, 10178 Berlin
Tel: (030) 28394238 *Fax:* (030) 28394100
E-mail: ndl@aufbau-verlag.de
Web Site: www.aufbau-verlag.de
Key Personnel
Editor: Juergen Engler
Periodical for German Literature & Reviews.
First published 1953.
Bimonthly.
192 pp, L10 (15.37 US dollars)
ISSN: 0028-3150

Neue Rundschau (New Review) (P)
Published by Martin Bauer
Neue Gruenstr 17, 10179 Berlin
Tel: (030) 308639 12 *Fax:* (030) 308639 10
E-mail: bauersfv@aol.com
Web Site: www.s-fischer.de
First published 1890.
Quarterly.
ISBN(s): 3-10-809045-3
ISSN: 0028-3347
Parent Company: S Fischer Verlag, Berlin

ƒ**Publishers' International ISBN Directory** (B)
Published by K G Saur Verlag GmbH, A Gale/
 Thomson Learning Company
Unit of Thomson Learning
Ortlerstr 8, 81373 Munich
Mailing Address: Postfach 70 16 20, 81316 Munich
Tel: (089) 76902-0 *Fax:* (089) 76902-150
E-mail: info@saur.de
Web Site: www.saur.de
Telex: 5212067
Parent Company: Gale
Ultimate Parent Company: The Thomson Corporation

Quickborn (P)
Published by Quickborn, Vereinigung fuer Niederdeutsche Sprache und Literatur eV
Alexanderstr, 16, 20099 Hamburg
Tel: (040) 240809 *Fax:* (040) 240809
Key Personnel
Editor: Dirk Roemmer
Magazine for literature & poetry in the low German dialects.

Schriften und Zeugnisse zur Buchgeschichte Veroeffentlichungen des Leipziger Arbeitskreises zur Geschichte des Buchwesens; Leipziger Jahrbuch zur Buchgeschichte (B)
Published by Leipziger Arbeitskreis zur Geschichte des Buchwesens, Harassowitz Verlag
65174 Wiesbaden
Tel: (0611) 5300 *Fax:* (0611) 530570
E-mail: poethe@dbl.ddb.de
History of books, the booktrade, publishers & printers.
ISSN: 0942-4709

Sinn und Form (Contents & Form) (P)
Published by Akademie der Kunste, Aufbau-Verlag Berlin-Brandenburg
Tucholskystr 2, 10117 Berlin
Tel: (030) 28884880 *Fax:* (030) 28884884
E-mail: sinnform@adk.de
Web Site: www.sinn-und-form.de
Key Personnel
Chief Editor: Sebastian Kleinschmidt
Contributions to literature. Articles on literature & humanities.
First published 1949.
Bimonthly.
144 pp, 9 euros
ISSN: 0037-5756

ƒ**Subject Guide to Microforms in Print** (B)
Published by K G Saur Verlag GmbH, A Gale/Thomson Learning Company
Unit of Thomson Learning
Ortlerstr 8, 81373 Munich
Mailing Address: Postfach 70 16 20, 81316 Munich
Tel: (089) 76902-0 *Fax:* (089) 76902-150
E-mail: info@saur.de
Web Site: www.saur.de
Telex: 5212067
Parent Company: Gale
Ultimate Parent Company: The Thomson Corporation

Der Ubersetzer (The Translator) (J)
Published by Verband deutschsprachiger Uebersetzer literarischer und wissenschaftlicher Werke eV (VDU)
Fuerststr 17, 7400 Tuebingen
Tel: (089) 2710994 *Fax:* (089) 2718272

Verlage 2002/2003, Deutschland, Oesterreich, Schweiz und auslaendischer Verlage mit deutschen Auslieferungen (Publishers 2002/2003 Germany, Austria, Switzerland & Foreign Publishers with German Distributions) (B)
Published by Verlag der Schillerbuchhandlung Hans Banger OHG
Guldenbachstr 1, 50935 Cologne
Tel: (0221) 46014-0 *Fax:* (0221) 46014-25
E-mail: banger@banger.de
Web Site: www.banger.de
Key Personnel
Editor: Ruth Jepsen
Available on CD-ROM.
Annual.
1008 pp
ISBN(s): 3-87856-096-6
ISSN: 1439-0736

Verlagsventretungen 2002/2003, Deutschland, Oesterreich, Schweiz (B)
Published by Verlag der Schillerbuchhandlung Hans Banger OHG
Guldenbachstr 1, 50935 Cologne
Tel: (0221) 46014-0 *Fax:* (0221) 46014-25
E-mail: banger@banger.de
Web Site: www.banger.de
Key Personnel
Editor: Ruth Jepsen
Annual.
448 pp
ISBN(s): 3-87856-098-2
ISSN: 0944-3754

Verzeichnis Lieferbarer Buecher (German Books in Print) (B)
Published by K G Saur Verlag GmbH, A Gale/Thomson Learning Company
Unit of Thomson Learning
Ortlerstr 8, 81373 Munich
Mailing Address: Postfach 70 16 20, 81316 Munich
Tel: (089) 76902-0 *Fax:* (089) 76902-150
E-mail: info@saur.de
Web Site: www.saur.de
Telex: 5212067
Editor, Buchhaendler-Veriningung, Frankfurt.
Parent Company: Gale
Ultimate Parent Company: The Thomson Corporation

ƒ**Who's Who at the Frankfurt Book Fair** (B)
Published by K G Saur Verlag GmbH, A Gale/Thomson Learning Company
Unit of Thomson Learning
Ortlerstr 8, 81373 Munich
Mailing Address: Postfach 70 16 20, 81316 Munich
Tel: (089) 76902-0 *Fax:* (089) 76902-150
E-mail: info@saur.de
Web Site: www.saur.de
Telex: 5212067
An International Publishers' Guide
A listing of publishers at the Frankfurt Book Fair, their addresses and the representatives chosen to attend the fair and their functions.
Parent Company: Gale
Ultimate Parent Company: The Thomson Corporation

Wolfenbuetteler Notizen zur Buchgeschichte (Wolfenbuetteler Notes on the History of Books) (J)
Published by Harrassowitz Verlag
Taunusstr 14, 65183 Wiesbaden
Tel: (0611) 530-0 *Fax:* (0611) 530-570; (0611) 530-560 (orders)
E-mail: verlag@harrassowitz.de; service@harrassowitz.de
Web Site: www.harrassowitz.de
Biannually.
ISSN: 0341-2253

Zeitschriften 2002 Deutserland-Oesterreich-Schweiz (German Language Periodical) (B)
Published by Verlag der Schillerbuchhandlung Hans Banger OHG
Guldenbachstr 1, 50935 Cologne
Tel: (0221) 46014-0 *Fax:* (0221) 46014-25
E-mail: banger@banger.de
Web Site: www.banger.de
Key Personnel
Editor: Ruth Jepsen
Available on CD-ROM.
Annual.
1427 pp
ISBN(s): 3-87856-094-X
ISSN: 1439-0728

Ghana

Asemka (P)
Published by University of Cape Coast
c/o French Department, University of Cape Coast, Cape Coast
Tel: 32483; 32480 (ext 220) *Fax:* 32485
Telex: 2552
Key Personnel
General Editor: Prof Y S Boafo

Ghana National Bibliography (J)
Published by George Padmore Research Library on African Affairs
PO Box 2970, Accra
Tel: (021) 228402; (021) 223526 *Fax:* (021) 247768
First published 1965.
Biannual with annual cummulation.
$20 for biannual, $60 for annual
ISSN: 0855-0255

Greece

Nea Hestia (P)
Published by G C Eleftheroudakis SA
Nikis 4, 10563 Athens
Tel: (01) 3229388 *Fax:* (01) 3239821
Text in Greek.

Guatemala

Alero (Eaves) (P)
Published by Universidad de San Carlos de Guatemala
Ciudad Universitaria, Zona 12, 01012 Guatemala
Tel: (02) 760790 *Fax:* (02) 767221

Guyana

Guyanese National Bibliography (B)
Published by National Library
76-77 Main & Church Sts, Georgetown
Mailing Address: PO Box 10240, Georgetown
Tel: (02) 62699; (02) 62690; (02) 74052; (02) 74053
Quarterly.

Hong Kong

PEN News (P)
Published by Hong Kong Chinese PEN Centre
Mongkok Post Office, Kowloon
Mailing Address: PO Box 78521, Mongkok Post Office, Kowloon
Text in Chinese.

Hungary

ƒ**Helikon Irodalomtudomanyi Szemle** (Helikon Review of General & Comparative Literature) (J)
Published by Magyar Tudomanyos Akademia Irodalomtudomanyi Intezete (HAS Institute of Literary Studies)

Menesi ut 11-13, 1118 Budapest
Tel: (01) 1665938
Summaries published in French, Russian & German.

The Hungarian Quarterly (P)
Published by The Hungarian Quarterly Society
Naphegy Tier 8, Budapest H-1016
Mailing Address: PO Box 3, Budapest H-1426
Tel: (01) 3756722 *Fax:* (01) 3188297
E-mail: hungq@hungary.com; quarterly@mail.datanet.hu
Telex: 224371; 225859
Key Personnel
Editor: Miklos Vajda
Text in English.
ISBN(s): 963-7262; 963-7560

Literatura (P)
Published by Akademiai Kiado
PO Box 245, H-1519 Budapest
Tel: (01) 1811991 *Fax:* (01) 1811991
Telex: 226228 aknyoh

Iceland

Arsskyrsla (B)
Published by Borgarbokasafn
Thingholtsstr 27, 101 Reykjavik
Tel: 5257155 *Fax:* 114643
ISBN(s): 9979-9326

Skirnir (J)
Published by Hid Islenzka Bokmenntafelag
Sidumula 21, 128 Reykjavik
Mailing Address: Postholf 8935, 128 Reykjavik
Tel: 5889060 *Fax:* 5889095
E-mail: hib@islandia.is
Web Site: www.arctic.is/hib
Key Personnel
Editor: Sveinn Yngvi Egilsson; Svavar H Svavarsson
Journal of the Icelandic Literary Society involving Icelandic Cultural Studies.
Biannually.

India

ɸ**Marg** (B)
Published by Marg Publications
Army & Navy Bldg, 3rd Floor, 148 Mahatma Gandhi Rd, Fort Mumbai 400001
Tel: (022) 2842520; (022) 2821151; (022) 2049131 (ext 7828) *Fax:* (022) 2047102
E-mail: margpub@tata.com; margpub@vsnl.com
Web Site: www.marg-art.org
Key Personnel
Contact: Radhika Sabavala
Publication on Indian art, culture & related civilizations.
First published 1946.
Quarterly.
140 pp

ɸ**African Books Newsletter** (J)
Published by Intertrade Publications
55 Gariahat Rd, Calcutta 700019
Mailing Address: PO Box 10210, Calcutta 700019
Tel: (033) 475-4872; (033) 475-5069
Check list of recent books published in English, arranged according to subject.

ɸ**Akavita** (Blank Verse) (P)
Published by Samkaleen Prakashan
2762, Rajguru Marg, Paharganj, New Delhi 110055
Tel: (011) 3523520; (011) 3518197
Text in Hindi.
First published 1976.
Quarterly.
Annual subscription - Inland: Rs 80; Overseas: $24 US (seamail); $32 (airmail)
ISSN: 0970-096X

ɸ**Art & Poetry Today** (P)
Published by Samkaleen Prakashan
2762, Rajguru Marg, Paharganj, New Delhi 110055
Tel: (011) 3523520; (011) 3518197
Text in English.
First published 1976.
Quarterly.
Annual subscription - Inland: Rs 80; Overseas: $24 US (seamail); $32 (airmail)
ISSN: 0970-1001

ɸ**Asian Books Newsletter** (J)
Published by Intertrade Publications
55 Gariahat Rd, Calcutta 700019
Mailing Address: PO Box 10210, Calcutta 700019
Tel: (033) 475-4872; (033) 475-5069
Checklist of recent books published in English, arranged according to subject.

Creative Forum (P)
Published by Bahri Publications
997A/9 Gobindpuri, Kalkaji, New Delhi 110019
Mailing Address: PO Box 4453, New Delhi 110019
Tel: (011) 6448606; (011) 6445710 *Fax:* (011) 6448606
E-mail: bahrius@vsnl.com
Web Site: bahripublications.org
Key Personnel
Publisher& Editor: Ujjal Singh Bahri
A journal of current literary practices.
Quarterly.
Rs 400 (US 90) per annum

D K Fortnight (J)
Published by D K Publishers' Distributors (P) Ltd
One Ansari Rd, Daryaganj, New Delhi 110002
Tel: (011) 3278368 *Fax:* (011) 3264368
Web Site: dkpdindia.com
Telex: 31-66778
Key Personnel
Editor: Praveen Mittal
Lists the new books released during each fortnight in the market by various publishers to reach the information to the target audience as early as possible; also contains an editorial on book industry.

ɸ**D K Yearbook** (B)
Published by D K Publishers' Distributors (P) Ltd
One Ansari Rd, Daryaganj, New Delhi 110002
Tel: (011) 3278368 *Fax:* (011) 3264368
Web Site: dkpdindia.com
Telex: 31-66778
Key Personnel
Chief Editor: Parmil Mittal
Published in English; covers social sciences, humanities & sciences.
Annually.

Directory of Indian Publishers & Distributors 1994 (B)
Published by Indian Bibliographic Centre
76, Chandrika Colony, Sigra, 221010 Varanasi
Tel: (0542) 221337 *Fax:* (0542) 222337

E-mail: rishipub@satyam.net.in
Reference book for librarians, publishers, distributors & booksellers.

Indian Author (P)
Published by Authors Guild of India
F-12 Jangpura Ext, New Delhi 110014
Tel: (011) 4315063; (011) 6847950 *Fax:* (011) 3321189

Indian Book Industry (J)
Published by Federation of Indian Publishers
18/6 Institutional Area, near JNU, New Delhi 110067
Tel: (011) 6964847; (011) 6852263 *Fax:* (011) 6864054
The journal is a publication devoted to production, promotion, & distribution of books. There are six issues in a year & every issue has a focus on a particular subject. For example, the issue of April 1995 was a special issue on the National Convention of Indian Language Publishers held from 7-9 April 1995.
Bimonthly.

Indian Books & Foreign Books (B)
Published by Researchco Reprints
25-B/2, New Rohtak Rd, New Delhi 110005
Tel: (011) 6781565 *Fax:* (011) 7276256
Telex: 31-79055 *Cable:* SEARCHBOOK
Annual bibliography of books in English.

Indian Books in Print (J)
Published by Indian Bibliographies Bureau
219 Kadambari, 19-IX Rohini, Delhi 110085
Tel: (011) 7564112; (011) 7553211 *Fax:* (011) 7564112
E-mail: ibb_indian_bibliographies@hotmail.com
Key Personnel
Assistant Manager: Ms Bimla Rawat
First published 1969.
Annually.
21st: 3400 pp, $250 US
ISSN: 0971-1589

Indian Horizons (J)
Published by Indian Council for Cultural Relations
Indraprastha Estate, New Delhi 110002
Tel: (011) 3379309 *Fax:* (011) 3778639
E-mail: iccr@vsnl.com
A journal in English on Indian Culture and the arts, and of cultural relations past and present between India and the world. Contents include articles, fiction and review.
$40.00
ISBN(s): 0019-7203

Indian Journal of Applied Linguistics (P)
Published by Bahri Publications
997A/9 Gobindpuri, Kalkaji, New Delhi 110019
Mailing Address: PO Box 4453, New Delhi
Tel: (011) 6448606; (011) 6445710 *Fax:* (011) 6448606
E-mail: bahrius@vsnl.com
Web Site: bahripublications.org
Key Personnel
Editor: Mr Ujjal Singh Bahri
Publishers of scholarly books & journals in linguistics, literature, translation, communication & creative literature.
1-2x annually.
160 pp, $90 (US)
ISSN: 0379-0037

Indian Literary Review (P)
Published by Chetna Publications
Shastri Gali No 3, Maujpur, New Delhi 110053

Indian Literature (P)
Published by National Academy of Letters: Sahitya Akademi

BOOKS & JOURNALS

INDIA

Sahitya Akademi, Rabindra Bhavan, 35 Ferozeshah Rd, New Delhi 110001
Tel: (011) 3387064 *Fax:* (011) 3382428
Telex: 31; 65445 SAND IN
Bimonthly, text in English.

Indian National Bibliography (J)
Published by Central Reference Library
Belvedere, Calcutta 700027
Tel: (033) 479172122; (033) 4481529 *Fax:* (033) 4791722
E-mail: crlinb@cal3.vsnl.net.in
Web Site: www.crlindia.org
Key Personnel
Contact: K K Kochukoshy
Index Indiana: Journal for Indian language periodicals, published quarterly in Roman Script.
Monthly with annual cumulation.

The Indian PEN (P)
Published by The PEN All-India Centre
40 New Marine Lines, Mumbai 400020
Tel: (022) 2032175
Key Personnel
Editor: Mr Nissim Ezekiel
Text in English.
Quarterly.

Indian Publishers' Directory (B)
Published by Mukherjee & Co Pvt Ltd
P-27B, CIT Rd, Scheme 52, Calcutta WB 700014
Tel: (033) 341606

International Journal of Communication (P)
Published by Bahri Publications
997A/9 Gobindpuri, Kalkaji, New Delhi 110019
Mailing Address: PO Box 4453, New Delhi 110019
Tel: (011) 6448606; (011) 6445710 *Fax:* (011) 6448606
E-mail: bahrius@vsnl.com
Web Site: bahripublications.org
Key Personnel
Publisher& Editor: Ujjal Singh Bahri
First published 1990.
1-2x annually.
240 pp, $90 (US)

International Journal of Translation (P)
Published by Bahri Publications
997A/9 Gobindpuri, Kalkaji, New Delhi 110019
Mailing Address: PO Box 4453, New Delhi 110019
Tel: (011) 6448606; (011) 6445710 *Fax:* (011) 6448606
E-mail: bahrius@vsnl.com
Web Site: bahripublications.org
Key Personnel
Publisher& Editor: Ujjal Singh Bahri
A review of translation studies.
1-2x annually.
160 pp, $90 (US)
ISSN: 0970-9819

Katha-Sahitya (J)
Published by Mitra & Ghosh Publishers Pvt Ltd
10 Shyama Charan Dey St, Calcutta 700073
Tel: (033) 316420
Key Personnel
Contact: Roy Sabitendranath *Tel:* (033) 415 5889; 415 4597
Monthly literary journal. Regular Features: editorial, book review, magazine review, news about authors. Special issues: Puja Issue, published on the eve of Durga Puja & Book Fair Issue published on the eve of Calcutta Book Fair.
First published 1949.
Monthly.
128 pp, IRS $6.00 per copy. Annual Subscriptions IRS $145.00 for India
ISSN: 0971-7137

Lalit Kala (P)
Published by Lalit Kala Akademi
c/o National Academy of Art, Rabindra Bhavan, New Delhi 110001
Tel: (011) 387241

Language Forum (P)
Published by Bahri Publications
997A/9 Gobindpuri, Kalkaji, New Delhi 110019
Mailing Address: PO Box 4453, New Delhi 110019
Tel: (011) 6448606; (011) 6445710 *Fax:* (011) 6448606
E-mail: bahrius@vsnl.com
Web Site: bahripublications.org
Key Personnel
Editor: Mr Ujjal Singh Bahri
Biannual journal of language & literature.
First published 1975.
1-2x annually.
200 pp, $90 (US)
ISSN: 0253-5071

⌽**Latin American Books Newsletter** (J)
Published by Intertrade Publications
55 Gariahat Rd, Calcutta 700019
Mailing Address: PO Box 10210, Calcutta 700019
Tel: (033) 475-4872; (033) 475-5069
Key Personnel
Editor: John A Gillard

The Literary Criterion (P)
Published by Dhvanyaloka, Mysore
Bangalore University English Department, Jnana Bharathi, Bangalore 560 056
Tel: (080) 3355299
Key Personnel
Editor: C D Narasimhaiah; C N Srinath

Literary Half-Yearly (P)
Published by Literary Press
Anjali 96, 7 Main, Jayalakshmipurum, Mysore 570012
Tel: 513030
First published 1960.
Semi-annually.

⌽**Marg** (P)
Published by Marg Publications
Army & Navy Bldg, 3rd Floor, 148 Mahatma Gandhi Rd, Fort Mumbai 400001
Tel: (022) 2842520; (022) 2821151; (022) 2049131 (ext 7828) *Fax:* (022) 2047102
E-mail: margpub@tata.com; margpub@vsnl.com
Web Site: www.marg-art.org
Key Personnel
Contact: Radhika Sabavala
Publication on Indian art, culture & related civilizations.
First published 1946.
Quarterly.
100 pp
ISSN: 0972-1444

Miscellany (P)
Published by Writers Workshop
162/92 Lake Gardens, Calcutta 700045

MIWA: Major Indian Works Annual (J)
Published by D K Agencies (P) Ltd
A/15-17 DK Ave, Mohan Garden, Off Najafgarh Rd, New Delhi 110059
Tel: (011) 535-7104; (011) 535-7105 *Fax:* (011) 535-7103
E-mail: custserv@dkagencies.com
Web Site: www.dkagencies.com
A bibliography of significant English language works from India.
Annually.
ISSN: 0971-4669

⌽**Pacific Islands Books News Letters** (J)
Published by Intertrade Publications
55 Gariahat Rd, Calcutta 700019
Mailing Address: PO Box 10210, Calcutta 700019
Tel: (033) 475-4872; (033) 475-5069

Pustak Parichaya (J)
Published by Indian Publishing House
93 A Lenin Sarani, Calcutta 700013
Tel: (033) 3275267
Text in Hindi.

Recent Indian Books (J)
Published by Federation of Publishers & Booksellers Associations in India
4833/24 Govind Lane, Ansari Rd, 1st Floor, New Delhi 110002
Tel: (011) 3272845

⌽**Samkaleen Kala Aur Kavita** (Contemporary Art & Poetry) (P)
Published by Samkaleen Prakashan
2762, Rajguru Marg, Paharganj, New Delhi 110055
Tel: (011) 3523520; (011) 3518197
Key Personnel
Editor: Krishan Khullar
Text in Hindi.
First published 1976.
Quarterly.
32 pp
ISBN(s): 81-7083
ISSN: 0970-0986

Samkalin Bharatiya Sahitya (Contemporary Indian Literature) (P)
Published by National Academy of Letters: Sahitya Akademi
Sahitya Akademi, Rabindra Bhavan, 35 Ferozeshah Rd, New Delhi 110001
Tel: (011) 3387064; (011) 3386626 *Fax:* (011) 3382428
E-mail: secy@ndb.vsnl.net.in
Web Site: www.sahitya-akademi.org
Telex: SAHITYAKAR
Key Personnel
Editor: Girdhar Rathi *Tel:* (011) 2225714
  E-mail: girdharrathi@yahoo.co.in
Creative & critical writings in Hindi & translation into Hindi from all the Indian languages.
First published 1980.
Bi-monthly.
200 pp, $10 (USA), L 6; $50 (USA), L 30 (Airmail)
ISSN: 0970-8367
Branch Office(s)
YA-4 Sahvikas, 68 Patparganj, I P Extension, Delhi 10092

Samskrita Pratibha (P)
Published by National Academy of Letters: Sahitya Akademi
Sahitya Akademi, Rabindra Bhavan, 35 Ferozeshah Rd, New Delhi 110001
Tel: (011) 3387064 *Fax:* (011) 3382428
Telex: 31; 65445 SAND IN *Cable:* SAHITYAKAR
Twice yearly journal of creative writing in Sanskrit.

⌽**Yuva Kavi** (Young Poets) (P)
Published by Samkaleen Prakashan
2762, Rajguru Marg, Paharganj, New Delhi 110055
Tel: (011) 3523520 *Fax:* (011) 3518197
Text in Hindi.
First published 1976.
Quarterly.

32 pp
ISBN(s): 81-7083
ISSN: 0970-0978

Islamic Republic of Iran

A Bibliography of Mathematics (B)
Published by The National Library of Iran
Anahita Alley, Africa St, Tehran 19176
Mailing Address: Shahid Bahonar St, Tehran 19548
Tel: (021) 2280937 *Fax:* (021) 2288680
E-mail: nli@nli.ir
Key Personnel
Senior Research Librarian: Mrs Poori Soltani
   E-mail: poorisoltani@yahoo.com
Compiler: M Rahbari
$30

A Bibliography of the Folklores, Manners and Customs of Isfahan (B)
Published by The National Library of Iran
Anahita Alley, Africa St, Tehran 19176
Mailing Address: Shahid Bahonar St, Tehran 19548
Tel: (021) 2288680 *Fax:* (021) 2288680
E-mail: nli@nli.ir
Key Personnel
Senior Research Librarian: Mrs Poori Soltani
   E-mail: poorisoltani@yahoo.com
Author: Ms Nahid Habibi Azad
First, $20

Bibliography of the Medical Manuscripts in Iran (B)
Published by The National Library of Iran
Anahita Alley, Africa St, Tehran 19176
Mailing Address: Shahid Bahonar St, Tehran 19548
Tel: (021) 280 86 80 *Fax:* (021) 280 86 80
E-mail: nli@nli.ir
Key Personnel
Senior Research Librarian: Mrs Poori Soltani
   E-mail: poorisoltani@yahoo.com
First published 1992.
1st: 325 pp, 36001 (Rls)

Catalogue de Precieux Ouvrages Scientifiques Francais de la Bibliotheque National de la Republique Islamique d'Iran (Catalog of Valuable French Works in the National Library of Iran) (B)
Published by The National Library of Iran
Anahita Alley, Africa St, Tehran 19176
Mailing Address: Shahid Bahonar St, Tehran 19548
Tel: (021) 2280937 *Fax:* (021) 2288680
E-mail: nli@nli.ir
Key Personnel
Senior Research Librarian: Mrs Poori Soltani
   E-mail: poorisoltani@yahoo.com
Compiler: Ms Shohreh Taravatil
First published 1993.
$25

Catalogue of Newspapers in the National Library of Iran (B)
Published by The National Library of Iran
Anahita Alley, Africa St, Tehran 19176
Mailing Address: Shahid Bahonar St, Tehran 19548
Tel: (021) 2288680 *Fax:* (021) 2288680
E-mail: nli@nli.ir
First published 1977.
1st: 3341 pp

Class PQ: French Literature, Individual Authors 18, 19, 20th Centuries: Based on the Library of Congress Classification (B)
Published by The National Library of Iran
Anahita Alley, Africa St, Tehran 19176
Mailing Address: Sh Bahonar Str, 19548 Tehran
Tel: (021) 22 886 80 *Fax:* (021) 22 886 80
E-mail: nli@nli.ir
Key Personnel
Senior Research Librarian: Mrs Poori Soltani
   E-mail: poorisaltani@yahoo.com
First published 1994.
1st: 185 pp, $25

Directory of Documentation Centres, Special Libraries & University Libraries of Iran, 2nd Edition (B)
Published by The National Library of Iran
Anahita Alley, Africa St, Tehran 19176
Mailing Address: Sh Bahonar Str, 19548 Tehran
Tel: (021) 280 86 80 *Fax:* (021) 280 86 80
E-mail: nli@nli.ir

A Directory of Iranian Periodicals & Newspapers (B)
Published by The National Library of Iran
Anahita Alley, Africa St, Tehran 19176
Mailing Address: Shahid Bahonar St, Tehran 19548
Tel: (021) 2280937 *Fax:* (021) 2288680
E-mail: nli@nli.ir
Key Personnel
Senior Research Librarian: Mrs Poori Soltani
   E-mail: poorisoltani@yahoo.com
First published 1994.
Annually.
$50
ISBN(s): 964-446-040-5
ISSN: 1028-7035

The Iranian National Bibliography (P)
Published by The National Library of Iran
Anahita Alley, Africa St, Tehran 19176
Mailing Address: Shahid Bahonar St, Tehran 19548
E-mail: nli@nli.ir
Key Personnel
Senior Research Librarian: Mrs Poori Soltani
   E-mail: poorisoltani@yahoo.com
First published 1963.
Semiannually.
ISSN: 0075-0522

Pahlavi Text: Transcript, Translation (B)
Published by The National Library of Iran
Anahita Alley, Africa St, Tehran 19176
Mailing Address: Sh Bahonar Str, 19548 Tehran
Tel: (021) 8088971 *Fax:* (021) 8088950
E-mail: nli@nli.ir
Key Personnel
Senior Research Librarian: Mrs Poori Soltani
   E-mail: poorisoltani@yahoo.com
First published 1992.
1st edition: 563 pp

Political Life of Imam Khomeini (B)
Published by The National Library of Iran
Anahita Alley, Africa St, Tehran 19176
Mailing Address: Shahid Bahonar St, Tehran 19548
Tel: (021) 280 86 80 *Fax:* (021) 280 86 80
E-mail: nli@nli.ir

Rules & Standards for Publishing Books (B)
Published by The National Library of Iran
Anahita Alley, Africa St, Tehran 19176
Mailing Address: Shahid Bahonar St, Tehran 19548

Tel: (021) 2280937 *Fax:* (021) 2288680
E-mail: nli@nli.ir
Key Personnel
Senior Research Librarian: Mrs Poori Soltani
   E-mail: poorisaltani@yahoo.com
2nd (1988): 42 pp, $10

Ruznameye Dowlat-e Alliyah Iran (B)
Published by The National Library of Iran
Anahita Alley, Africa St, Tehran 19176
Mailing Address: Shahid Bahonar St, Tehran 19548
Tel: (021) 2280932 *Fax:* (021) 2288680
E-mail: nli@nli.ir
This is a reprint of an old newspaper.
1st, $50

Iraq

Iraqi National Bibliography (J)
Published by National Library
Bab-el-Muaddum, Baghdad
Tel: (01) 4164190
Triannually.

Ireland

Books Ireland (J)
Published by Jeremy Addis
11 Newgrove Ave, Dublin 4
Tel: (01) 2692185 *Fax:* (01) 2604927
E-mail: booksi@eircom.net
The trade journal & review medium of the Irish publishing industry, published nine times a year.
First published 1976.
3 Euros
ISSN: 0376-6039

Comhar (Cooperation) (P)
5 Rae Mhuirfean, Ath Cliath 2
Tel: (01) 6785443 *Fax:* (01) 6785443
Text in Irish.

Journal of the Irish Colleges of Physicians & Surgeons (J)
Published by Irish Colleges of Physicians & Surgeons
The Mercer Library, Mercer St Lower, Dublin 2
Tel: (01) 402 2196 *Fax:* (01) 402 2457
E-mail: jicps@rcsi.ie
Web Site: www.rcsi.ie
Quarterly.

Israel

Ariel: The Israel Review of Arts & Letters (P)
Published by The Israel Foreign Ministry
Department, Cultural Affairs, Ministry of Foreign Affairs, Hakirya 94383
Tel: (02) 6432147 *Fax:* (02) 6437502
E-mail: debasher@netvision.net.il
Web Site: www.israel-mfa.gov.il
Key Personnel
Editor: Asher Weill
First published 1962.
Quarterly.
96 pp
ISSN: 0004-1343

Israel Book Trade Directory (B)
Published by Weill Publishers
PO Box 7705, Jerusalem 91076
Tel: (02) 6432147 *Fax:* (02) 6437502
E-mail: debasher@netvision.net.il
Biennially.

Jerusalem Report (P)
22 Yosef Rivlin St, Jerusalem 91017
Mailing Address: PO Box 1805, Jerusalem 91017
Tel: (02) 6291011 *Fax:* (02) 6291037
E-mail: jrep@attmail.com
Web Site: www.jreport.virtual.co.il
Key Personnel
Editor: Hirsh Goodman

Kiryat Sefer (kiryat sefer) (P)
Published by Hebrew University of Jerusalem
Edmond J Safra Campus, Jerusalem 91341
Mailing Address: PO Box 34165, Jerusalem 91341
Tel: (02) 6585019 *Fax:* (02) 6511771
E-mail: jnl@savion.huji.ac.il
Web Site: jnul.huji.ac.il/rambi
Telex: 25307
Biographical quarterly.

Modern Hebrew Literature (P)
Published by The Institute for the Translation of Hebrew Literature
PO Box 1005 1, Ramat Gan 5200 1
Tel: (03) 579 6830 *Fax:* (03) 579 6832
E-mail: hamachon@inter.net.il
Telex: 341118 BXTV IL ext 1272 *Cable:* TARGUM TELAVIV
Key Personnel
Man Dir: Mrs Nilli Cohen
Published semiannually.

Italy

Andersen-Il Mondo dell'Infanzia (J)
Published by Feguagiskia' Studios
Via Crosa di Vergagni 3R, 16124 Genova
Tel: (010) 2757544 *Fax:* (010) 2510838
Text in Italian. Contains articles on CYL, teaching, theatre & film as well as literary competitions. Includes reviews & news.

Belfagor (P)
Published by Casa Editrice Leo S Olschki
Casella Postale 66, I-50100 Florence
Tel: (055) 6530684 *Fax:* (055) 6530214
E-mail: celso@olschki.it
Web Site: www.olschki.it
Key Personnel
Publisher: Leo S Olschki
Review of literature & information.
First published 1946.
6 times/yr.
128 pp
ISSN: 0005-8351

La Bibliofilia (P)
Published by Casa Editrice Leo S Olschki
Casella Postale 66, I-50100 Florence
Tel: (055) 6530684 *Fax:* (055) 6530214
E-mail: celso@olschki.it
Web Site: www.olschki.it
Key Personnel
Publisher: Leo S Olschki
Text in English, French, German & Italian. Bibliophily, History of Printing.
First published 1899.
3 times/yr.
110 pp
ISSN: 0006-0941

Bibliografia Nazionale Italiana (Italian National Bibliography) (J)
Published by Central Institute of the Union Catalog of Italian Libraries & Bibliographical Information
Viale del Castro Pretorio 105, I-00185 Rome
Tel: (06) 4454701 *Fax:* (06) 4959302
E-mail: depinedo@itcaspur.caspur.it

Catalogo dei Libri in Commercio (Catalog of Books in Print) (B)
Published by Editrice Bibliografica SpA
Via Bergonzoli 1/5, 20127 Milan
Tel: (02) 28315996 *Fax:* (02) 28315906
Sponsored by Associazone Italiana Editori, listing 325,000 Italian titles.

Catalogo del Periodici Italiani (Catalogue of Italian Periodicals) (B)
Published by Editrice Bibliografica SpA
Via Bergonzoli 1/5, 20127 Milan
Tel: (02) 28315996 *Fax:* (02) 28315906

Giornale della Libreria (Book Trade Journal) (J)
Published by Editrice Bibliografica SpA
Member of Organ of Italian Publishers Association
Via Bergonzoli 1/5, 20127 Milan
Tel: (02) 28315996 *Fax:* (02) 28315906
Monthly.
102.30 Euro

giornale storico della letteratura italiana (Historical Journal of Italian Literature) (P)
Published by Loescher Editore SRL
Via Vittorio Amedeo Il 18, 10121 Turin
Tel: (011) 5654111 *Fax:* (011) 5625822

Gli Editori Italiani (The Italian Publishers) (B)
Published by Editrice Bibliografica SpA
Viale Vittorio Veneto 24, 20124 Milan
Tel: (02) 28315996 *Fax:* (02) 28315906
3,200 Italian publisher listings.

Lettere Italiane (P)
Published by Casa Editrice Leo S Olschki
Casella Postale 66, I-50100 Florence
Tel: (055) 6530684 *Fax:* (055) 6530214
E-mail: celso@olschki.it
Web Site: www.olschki.it
History of Italian Literature.
First published 1949.
Quarterly.
170 pp
ISSN: 0024-1334

Libri e Riviste d'Italia (Italian Books & Periodicals) (J)
Published by Instituto Poligrafico Dello Stato
Piazza Verdi 10, Rome
Tel: (06) 85082175 *Fax:* (06) 85082517
Available in Italian editions & international editions in English, French, German & Spanish.

Nuova Corrente (New Current) (P)
Published by Tilgher-Genova sas
Via Assarotti 31/15, 16122 Genova
Tel: (010) 8391140 *Fax:* (010) 87 06 53
E-mail: tilgher@tilgher.it
Web Site: www.tilgher.it
Text in several languages.
First published 1954.
2 times/yr.
71.000 (Italy); 102.000 (foreign)

Paideia (P)
Published by Carlo Cordie-Giuseppe Scarpat
Via Corsica 130, I-25125 Brescia
Tel: (030) 222094 *Fax:* (030) 223269
Literary review with bibliographical information; text in English, French, German & Italian.

La Rassegna della Letteratura Italiana (Italian Literature Review) (P)
Published by Casa Editrice le Lettere
Costa San Giorgio 28, 50125 Florence
Tel: (055) 2342710 *Fax:* (055) 2346010

Rivista di Letteratura Moderne e Comparate (Review of Modern and Comparative Literature) (P)
Published by Pacini Editore Srl
Via Gherardesca, 56121 Ospedaletto, Pisa
Tel: (050) 313011 *Fax:* (050) 3130300
E-mail: pacini.editore@pacinieditore.it
Web Site: www.pacinieditore.it
Text in English, French and Italian.

Uomini e Libri (Men and Books) (P)
Published by Edizioni Effe Emme
Viale E Caldara 8, 20122 Milan

Jamaica

Book Production in Jamaica: A Select List of Jamaican Publications (B)
Published by Jamaica Library Service
2 Tom Redcam Dr, Kingston 5
Mailing Address: PO Box 58, Kingston 5
Tel: (876) 926-3310 *Fax:* (876) 926-2188
E-mail: jamlibs@cwjamaica.com

ϕ**Caribbean Quarterly** (J)
Published by Cultural Studies Initiative, Vice Chancellery
University of the West Indies, Mona, Kingston 7
Mailing Address: PO Box 1, Mona, Kingston 7
Tel: (876) 977 1689 *Fax:* (876) 977 6105
E-mail: carbqtly@uwimom.edu.jm
Key Personnel
Editor: Rex Nettleford
Contact: Dr V Salter *E-mail:* vsalter@uwimona.edu.jm
First published 1949.
Quarterly.
120 pp
ISSN: 0008-6495

Jamaican National Bibliography (J)
Published by National Library of Jamaica
12 East St, Kingston
Mailing Address: PO Box 823, Kingston
Tel: (876) 967-1526 *Fax:* (876) 922-5567
E-mail: nlj@infochan.com
Web Site: www.nlj.org.jm *Cable:* NALIBJAM
Key Personnel
Editor: Byron Palmer *Tel:* (876) 967-2494
The Jamaican National Bibliography lists all material published in Jamaica, works by Jamaicans published outside of the country, as well as works about Jamaica.

Japan

Asian/Pacific Book Development (ABD) (J)
Published by Asia/Pacific Cultural Centre for UNESCO (ACCU)
6 Fukuro-machi, Shinjuku-ku, Tokyo 162
Tel: (03) 32694435 *Fax:* (03) 32694510
E-mail: general@accu.or.jp *Cable:* ASCULCENTRE

JAPAN

Key Personnel
Editor-in-Chief: Shigeo Miyamoto
Provides information, news items relating to books, publishing & promotional activities in Asia & the Pacific contributed by more than twenty national correspondents.
Quarterly.

Biblia (J)
Published by Tenri University Press
Tenri Central Library, Tenri-SHI Nara 632-8577
Tel: (0743) 631515 *Fax:* (0743) 637728
Text in Japanese.

Bulletin of Japan Book Publishers Association (J)
Published by Japan Book Publishers Association
6, Fukuro-machi, Shinjuku-ku, Tokyo 162-0828
Tel: (03) 32681303 *Fax:* (03) 32681196
Web Site: www.jbpa.or.jp

The Catalog of Books in the Near Future (Korekara deru Hon) (P)
Published by Japan Book Publishers Association
6, Fukuro-machi, Shinjuku-ku, Tokyo 162-0828
Tel: (03) 32681303 *Fax:* (03) 32681196
Web Site: www.jbpa.or.jp

A Comprehensive Bibliography of Japanese Periodicals (P)
Published by The Shuppan News Co Ltd
3-2-4 Misaki-cho 3 chome, Chiyoda-ku, Tokyo 101
Tel: (03) 32622076

A Comprehensive Catalog of Collected Works, Publishers in Japan (J)
Published by The Shuppan News Co Ltd
3-2-4 Misaki-cho 3 chome, Chiyoda-ku, Tokyo 101
Tel: (03) 32622076

Directory of Japanese Publishing Industry (J)
Published by Publishers' Association for Cultural Exchange, PACE, Japan
2-1, Sarugaku-cho 1-chome, Chiyoda-ku, Tokyo 101
Tel: (03) 32915685 *Fax:* (03) 32333645
Statistics of the Japanese publishing world.

Doitsu Bungaku (P)
Published by Nippon Dokubungakkai
c/o Ikubundo, Hongo 5-30-21, Bunkyo-ku, Tokyo 113-0033
Key Personnel
President: Prof Takao Tsunekawa
German Literature.
First published 1947.

Doshisha Literature (J)
Published by Doshisha University, English Literary Society
Karasuma Imadegawa, Kamikyo-ku, Kyoto 602
Tel: (075) 2513371 *Fax:* (075) 2513059
E-mail: kkitao@mail.doshisha.ac.jp
Web Site: english.doshisha.ac.jp/gakkai/
Journal of English literature and philology; text in English.

An Introduction to Publishing in Japan (B)
Published by Japan Book Publishers Association
6, Fukuro-machi, Shinjuku-ku, Tokyo 162-0828
Tel: (03) 32681303 *Fax:* (03) 32681196
Web Site: www.jbpa.or.jp *Cable:* SHOSEKIKYO TOKOYO 1

Japan Directory of Professional Associations (B)
Published by Intercontinental Marketing Corp
Wako 5 Bldg 5th Floor, 1-19-8 Kakigaracho Nihombashi, Chuo-ku, Tokyo 103-0014
Mailing Address: IPO Box 5056, Tokyo 100-3191
Tel: (03) 36617458 *Fax:* (03) 36679646
E-mail: imcbook@ibm.net
Web Site: www.twics.com/~imcbooks
Key Personnel
Editor: Warren E Ball
Lists important associations, societies & many institutions, many of which are significant publishers or otherwise valuable information sources.

Japan English Publications in Print (B)
Published by Intercontinental Marketing Corp
Wako 5 Bldg 5th Floor, 1-19-8 Kakigaracho Nihombashi, Chuo-ku, Tokyo 103-0014
Mailing Address: IPO Box 5056, Tokyo 100-3191
Tel: (03) 36617458 *Fax:* (03) 36679646
E-mail: imcbook@ibm.net
Web Site: www.twics.com/~imcbooks/JEPP3A.htm
Key Personnel
Editor: Warren E Ball
English journals, books, directories & other publications, published in Japan.

Japanese Books in Print (B)
Published by Japan Book Publishers Association
6, Fukuro-machi, Shinjuku-ku, Tokyo 162-0828
Tel: (03) 32681303 *Fax:* (03) 32681196
Web Site: www.jbpa.or.jp

Japanese Literature Today (P)
Published by Japan PEN Club
Room 265, Syuwa Residential Hotel, 9-1-7 Akaska, Minato-ku, Tokyo 107
Tel: (03) 34021171 *Fax:* (03) 34025951
Published annually (1976-1985).

Japanese Publications News and Reviews (J)
Published by Shuppan News Co Ltd
3-2-4 Masaki-cho 3 Chome, Chiyoda-ku, Tokyo 101
Tel: (03) 32622076

JPG Letter (J)
Published by Intercontinental Marketing Corp
Wako 5 Bldg 5th Floor, 1-19-8 Kakigaracho Nihombashi, Chuo-ku, Tokyo 103-0014
Mailing Address: IPO Box 5056, Tokyo 100-3191
Tel: (03) 36617458 *Fax:* (03) 36679646
E-mail: imcbook@ibm.net
Web Site: www.twics.com/~imcbooks/JEPP3A.htm
Key Personnel
Editor: Warren E Ball
Newsletter containing information on new English publications (periodicals & books) that are published in Japan & other southeast & east Asian countries.
Monthly.

Practical Guide to Publishing in Japan (B)
Published by Publishers' Association for Cultural Exchange, PACE, Japan
2-1, Sarugaku-cho 1-chome, Chiyoda-ku, Tokyo 101
Tel: (03) 32915685 *Fax:* (03) 32333645

Sheppard's Book Dealers in Japan (B)
Published by Richard Joseph Publishers Ltd
Unit 2, Monks Walk, Farnham, Surrey GU9 8HT, UK
Tel: (01256) 811314 *Fax:* (01256) 336362
E-mail: rjoe01@aol.com
Web Site: www.sheppardsdirectories.co.uk
Antiquarian & second hand book dealers.
L24; US $48

Shinkan News (J)
Published by Tohan Corporation
6-24 Higashigoken-cho, Shinjuku-ku, Tokyo 162-8710
Fax: (03) 3269-6111

Shuppan Nenkan (J)
Published by Shuppan News Co Ltd
3-2-4 Masaki-cho 3 Chome, Chiyoda-ku, Tokyo 101
Tel: (03) 32622076
Information on publishing for the previous year.
Annually.

Shuppan Nyusu (J)
Published by Shuppan News Co Ltd
3-2-4 Masaki-cho 3 Chome, Chiyoda-ku, Tokyo 101
Tel: (03) 32622076
Publishers' News.
Three times a month.

Studies in English Literature (P)
Published by Nihon Eibungakkai
501 Kenkyusha Bldg, 9 Surugadai 2-chome, Kanda, Chiyoda-ku, Tokyo 101-0062
Tel: (03) 32937528 *Fax:* (03) 323937539
Published annually in Japanese & English.

Umi (P)
Published by Chuo-Koron-Sha Inc
2-8-7 Kyobashi, Chuo-ku, Tokyo 104
Tel: (03) 3563-3666 *Fax:* (03) 3561 5920

Jordan

Jordanian National Bibliography (B)
Published by Jordan Library Association
PO Box 6289, Amman
Tel: (06) 629412
Annually.

Palestinian Bibliography: A List of Books Published by the Arabs in Palestine 1948-1980 (B)
Published by Jordan Library Association
PO Box 6289, Amman
Tel: (06) 629412

Palestinian-Jordanian Bibliography (B)
Published by Jordan Library Association
PO Box 6289, Amman
Tel: (06) 629412

Kazakstan

Prostor (The Expose) (P)
Published by Kazakh Writers' Union
Dr Albai Khana, 105, 480091 Almaty
Tel: (3272) 696319 *Fax:* (3272) 691058
Literary, artistic, socio-political magazine.
Monthly.

Kenya

African Journal of Health Sciences (J)
Published by African Forum for Health Sciences
PO Box 54840, Nairobi
Tel: (02) 722541 *Fax:* (02) 720030

E-mail: kemrilib@healthnet.or.ke
Web Site: www.kemri.org
Key Personnel
Ed: Dr Davy Koech
First published 1994.
ISSN: 1022-9272

African Urban Quarterly (J)
Published by African Urban Quarterly Limited, Centre for Urban Research
University of Nairobi, Chiromo Campus, ICIPE Bldg, Riverside Dr, Nairobi
Mailing Address: PO Box 51336, 00200 City Square, Nairobi
Tel: (02) 449231; (02) 448218; (02) 449186
 Fax: (02) 336885; (02) 444110; (02) 718548
International & interdisciplinary journal that covers all aspects of urbanization & regional planning from the most theoretical to the most imperical. AUQ serves as a central clearing house for research with analytical, descriptive, evaluative, & prescriptive problems concerned with comparative urbanization & regional planning in Africa with the rest of the world. Topics covered include agriculture, demography, transportation, medicine, politics, geography, history, sociology, economics, mathematics, urbanization, anthropology, archeology, education, law & environmental studies as they affect the quality of human life in both rural as well as in urban areas.
1 pp, $130 USD
ISSN: 0747-6108

Kenya National Bibliography (B)
Published by Kenya National Library Service
PO Box 30573, Nairobi
Tel: (02) 725550; (02) 725551; (02) 725569; (02) 725983 *Fax:* (02) 721749
E-mail: knls@nbnet.co.ke
Web Site: www.knls.or.ke
Key Personnel
Dir: S K Ng'anga

Republic of Korea

Books from Korea (B)
Published by Korean Publishers Association
105-2 Sagan-Dong, Jongno-Gu, Seoul 110-190
Tel: (02) 735 2702 *Fax:* (02) 738 5414
E-mail: kpa@kpa21.or.kr
Web Site: www.kpa21.or.kr
Key Personnel
Secretary General: Jong Jin Jung
Published annually; text in English.

Catalog of Government Publications (B)
Published by National Assembly Library
One Yoido-dong, Seoul
Tel: (02) 7843565 *Fax:* (02) 7884193
Telex: 25849
Includes University Publications.

Korean National Bibliography (J)
Published by The National Library of Korea
60-1 Panpo-dong, Seocho-gu, Seoul 137-702
Tel: (02) 5355458 *Fax:* (02) 3534167
E-mail: nlkpc@sun.nl.or.kr

Korean Publication Yearbook (B)
Published by Korean Publishers Association
105-2 Sagan-Dong, Jongno-Gu, Seoul 110-190
Tel: (02) 735 2702 *Fax:* (02) 738 5414
E-mail: kpa@kpa21.or.kr
Web Site: www.kpa21.or.kr

Key Personnel
Secretary General: Jong Jin Jung
Text in Korean.
Annual.

Korean Publishers Directory (B)
Published by Korean Publishers Association
105-2 Sagan-Dong, Jongno-Gu, Seoul 110-190
Tel: (02) 735 2702 *Fax:* (02) 738 5414
E-mail: kpa@kpa21.or.kr
Web Site: www.kpa21.or.kr
Key Personnel
Secretary General: Jong Jin Jung
Published annually; text in English.

KPA Journal (J)
Published by Korean Publishers Association
105-2 Sagan-Dong, Jongno-Gu, Seoul 110-190
Tel: (02) 735 2702 *Fax:* (02) 738 5414
E-mail: kpa@kpa21.or.kr
Web Site: www.kpa21.or.kr
Key Personnel
Secretary General: Jong Jin Jung
Published monthly, in Korean.

Latvia

Daugava (P)
Published by Daugava Ltd
Balasta Dambis, 3, Riga LV-1081
Tel: (02) 465996
Literary magazine.
Bimonthly.

Luxembourg

Bibliographie Luxembourgeoise (Luxembourg Bibliography) (J)
Published by Bibliotheque Nationale du Grand-Duche de Luxembourg
37 blvd F D Roosevelt, 2450 Luxembourg
Tel: 226255 *Fax:* 475672
Web Site: www.bibnatlux.etat.lu

Kritikon Litterarum (P)
Published by Thesen Verlag Vowinckel
3 pl de la Gare, 6674 Mertert
Tel: 748715 *Fax:* 26740429
First published 1972.
Biannually.
173 euros/vol
ISSN: 0340-9767

The Former Yugoslav Republic of Macedonia

Macedonian Review (P)
Published by Cultural Life-Kulturen Zivot
Ruzveltova 6, 91001 Skopje
Mailing Address: PO Box 85, 91001 Skopje
Tel: (091) 239134; (091) 226105
Cultural Life.

Razgledi (P)
Published by Marsala Tita Iv Baraka, Skopje
Ul Ivo Ribar-Lola 66, 91000 Skopje
Mailing Address: Box 37, 91000 Skopje
Review of literature, art and culture; text in Macedonian.

Stremez (P)
Published by Interesna Zaednica na Kulturata Pri Lep
Centar za kultura M Cepenkov, 97500 Prilep
Tel: 27308; 21703 *Fax:* 21703
Journal for literature and culture; text in Macedonian.

Madagascar

Bibliographie annuelle de Madagascar (Madagascar Annual Bibliography) (B)
Published by Bibliotheque Universitarie, Campus Universitaire
Campus Universitaire d'Ankatso, BP 908, Antananarivo 101
Tel: (02) 23228
E-mail: buunivtanamg@minitel.refer.org
Annual.

Bibliographie Nationale de Madagascar (Madagascar National Bibliography) (B)
Published by Bibliotheque Nationale (Sous la Direction de Ralaisaholimanana Louis)
Bibliotheque Nationale, ANOSY, BP 257, Antananarivo
Tel: (022) 25872 *Fax:* (022) 29448

Malaysia

Bibliografi Negara Malaysia (Malaysian National Bibliography) (J)
Published by Perpustakaan Negara Malaysia, Technical Services Div
232, Jalan Tun Razak, 50572 Kuala Lumpur
Tel: (03) 2943488; (03) 2943150 *Fax:* (03) 2929767
Telex: 30092
Key Personnel
Editor: Nafisah Ahmad

Malay Literature (P)
Published by Dewan Bahasa dan Pustaka
Jl Dewan Bahasa, 50460 Kuala Lumpur
Tel: (03) 21481011; (03) 21447269 *Fax:* (03) 21443875
Web Site: www.dbp.gov.my
Key Personnel
Head, Comparative Literature Dept: Mrs Zalila Shariff *E-mail:* zalila@dbp.gov.my
National Language & Literary Agency of Malaysia.
June & Dec.
RM 10.00
ISSN: 0128-1186

ƒ**Southeast Asian Archives** (J)
Published by Southeast Asian Regional Branch of the International Council on Archives (SARBICA)
c/o National Archives of Malaysia, Jalan Duta, 50568 Kuala Lumpur
Tel: (03) 6510688 *Fax:* (03) 6515679
E-mail: query@arkib.gov.my
Web Site: arkib.gov.my/general/inter.html

Malta

Malta National Bibliography (B)
Published by Malta National Library
36 Old Treasury St, Valletta CMR 02
Tel: 224338 *Fax:* 235992
Key Personnel
Contact: M Mallia
Published annually.

Mauritius

Quarterly Memorandum of Books Printed in Mauritius and Registered in the Archives (J)
Published by Mauritius Archives
Development Bank of Mauritius Complex, Petite Riviere, Beau-Bassin

Mexico

Bibliografia Mexicana (Mexican Bibliography) (B)
Published by Biblioteca Nacional de Mexico
Centro Cultural, Cuidad Universitaria, Deleg Coyoacan, 04510 Mexico DF
Tel: (05) 6226807 *Fax:* (05) 6650951
E-mail: libros@biblional.bibliog.unam.mx
Key Personnel
Contact: Roxana L Mejia Murillo

Boletin Bibliografico Mexicano (Mexican Bibliographical Bulletin) (J)
Published by Libreria de Porrua Hermanos y Cia, SA
A Rep de Argentina 15, 06020 Mexico, DF
Tel: (05) 7025467 *Fax:* (05) 7024574
Web Site: www.luit.com/porrua/home.html *Cable:* PORRAUS MEXICO
Key Personnel
Ed: Jose Antonio Perez Porrua

Boletin del Instituto de Investigaciones Bibliograficas (Bulletin of the Institute of Bibliographic Research) (J)
Published by Instituto de Investigaciones Bibliograficas
Centro Cultural, Cuidad Universitaria, Deleg Coyoacan, 04510 Mexico, DF
Tel: (05) 6226807; (05) 6226811 *Fax:* (05) 6650951
E-mail: libros@biblional.bibliog.unam.mx
Book Review & Historic Articles on Mexico & Latin America.

Cuadernos Americanos (American Notebooks) (P)
Published by Universidad Nacional Autonoma de Mexico (National University of Mexico)
Torre 1 de Humanidades PB 20 piso, Ciudad Universitaria, 04510 Mexico, DF
Tel: (05) 6221902 *Fax:* (05) 6162515
E-mail: cuadamer@servidor.unam.mx
Our America, Monograph; Our America, Permanent collection; 500 Years After, Commemorative collection of the 500 years of the arrival of Columbus to America; Annual Latin America, permanent collection.
Triannually.

How to Obtain Mexican Books and Periodicals (B)
Published by Camara Nacional de la Industria Editorial Mexicana
Holanda 13, Col San Diego Churubusco, 04120 Coyoacan Mexico, DF
Tel: (05) 6887122; (05) 6882011; (05) 6882221 *Fax:* (05) 6043147
Information on the Mexican publishing industry, including a list of principal exporters of Mexican books.

Libros de Mexico (Books of Mexico) (J)
Published by Camara Nacional de la Industria Editorial Mexicana
Holanda 13, Col San Diego Churubusco, 04120 Coyoacan Mexico, DF
Tel: (05) 6887122 *Fax:* (05) 6043147
E-mail: ciecprom@inetcorp.net.mx
Web Site: www.libromex.com.mx
Quarterly review of book trade.

Morocco

Bibliographie Nationale Marocaine (Moroccan National Bibliography) (B)
Published by Bibliotheque Generale et Archives du Maroc
Av Ibn Battouta, Rabat
Mailing Address: BP 1003, Rabat
Tel: (07) 771890 *Fax:* (07) 776062
Semi-annually.

Nepal

Nepalese National Bibliography (J)
Published by Tribhuvan University Central Library
Kirtipur, Kathmandu
Tel: (01) 331317 *Fax:* (01) 331964
Key Personnel
Llibrarian: Krishna Mani Bhandary
E-mail: kmani@npl.healthnet.org

Netherlands

Amsterdamer Publikationen zur Sprache und Literatur (P)
Published by Rodopi
Tijnmuiden 7, 1046 AK Amsterdam
Tel: (020) 6114821 *Fax:* (020) 4472979
E-mail: f.van.der.zee@rodopi.nl
Web Site: www.rodopi.nl
Germanic Languages & Literatures.

ƒ**Babel (International Journal of Translation)** (J)
Published by Federation Internationale des Traducteurs (FIT)
John Benjamins Publishing Co, Amsteldijk 44, 1070 AN Amsterdam
Mailing Address: PO Box 75577, 1070 AN Amsterdam
Tel: (020) 6738156 *Fax:* (020) 6792956
Web Site: www.benjamins.nl

ƒ**Bibliotheca Orientalis** (J)
Published by Nederlands Instituut voor Het Nabije Oosten
Postbus 9515, 2300 RA Leiden
Tel: (071) 5272036 *Fax:* (071) 5272020
International bibliograghical & reviewing journal for Near Eastern & Mediterranean studies, published in English, French & German.
Bimonthly.

Boekblad (J)
Published by Koninklijke Vereeniging ter bevordering van de belangen des Boekhandels/Boekblad bv
Frederiksplein 1, 1001 MA Amsterdam
Mailing Address: Postbus 15007, 1001 MA Amsterdam
Tel: (020) 6253131 *Fax:* (020) 6220908
E-mail: redactie@boekblad.kvb.nl
Web Site: www.boekblad.nl
News-sheet for the book trade.
Daily, weekly, monthly.

Brinkman's Cumulatieve Catalogus (Brinkman's Cumulative Book Catalog) (J)
Published by Bohn Stafleu Van Loghum BV
De Molen 77, 3990 GA Houten
Mailing Address: Postbus 246, 3990 GA Houten
Tel: (0172) 466321 *Fax:* (0172) 435527

Castrum Peregrini (P)
Published by Castrum Peregrini Presse
PO Box 645, 1000 AP Amsterdam
Tel: (020) 6235287 *Fax:* (020) 6247096
Journal for literature & art; text in German.

Deutsche Buecher (The German Books) (J)
Published by Rodopi
Tijnmuiden 7, 1046 AK Amsterdam
Tel: (020) 6114821 *Fax:* (020) 4472979
E-mail: f.van.der.zee@rodopi.nl
Web Site: www.rodopi.com
Text in German.
Branch Office(s)
Weidler Buchverlag, Postfach 210315, D-10503 Berlin

Forum der Letteren (P)
Published by Smits BV
Postbus 276, 2501 CG The Hague
Tel: (070) 3895390 *Fax:* (070) 3802135

Gids voor de Informatiesector 1994 (B)
Published by NBLC
Postbus 43300, 2504 AH The Hague
Tel: (070) 3090380 *Fax:* (070) 3090200
(Boekenvakboek, 1991) Publishing Industry Statistics.

Het Nederlandse Boek (The Dutch Book) (J)
Published by Nederlandse Boek
De Lairessestraat 108, 1071 PK Amsterdam
Tel: (020) 6233187
New Pocket-Books & Paperbacks included.
6 times/yr.
24 pp, 10 euros
ISSN: 0166-0586

Hollands Maandblad (Holland Monthly) (P)
Published by Stichting Hollands Maandblad
Herengracht 481, 1017 BT Amsterdam
Tel: (020) 5249800 *Fax:* (020) 6276851
E-mail: hollandsmaandblad@contact-bv.nl

ƒ**IFLA Directory** (J)
Published by International Federation of Library Associations & Institutions
c/o Koninklijke Bibliothek, Prins Willem-Alexanderhof 5, The Hague
Mailing Address: PO Box 95312, 2509 The Hague
Tel: (070) 3140884 *Fax:* (070) 3834827
E-mail: ifla@ifla.org

Web Site: www.ifla.org
Biennially.
ISSN: 0074-6002

De negentiende EEUW (The Nineteenth Century) (P)
Published by Maatschappij der Nederlandse Letterkunde, Werkgroep Negentiende Eeuw
Groothertoginnelaan 260, 2517 EZ The Hague
Tel: (70) 3106455
Web Site: www.leidenuniv.nl/host/mnl/wkgrp19/
Key Personnel
Contact: Dr A van Kalmthout *E-mail:* a.b.g.m. van.kalmthout@let.rug.nl
First published 1977.
240 pp
ISSN: 1381-8546

Quaerendo (P)
Published by Brill Academic Publishers
PO Box 9000, 2300 PA Leiden
Tel: (071) 5353500 *Fax:* (071) 317532
E-mail: cs@brill.nl
A quarterly journal from the Low Countries devoted to manuscripts and printed books; text mainly in English, occasionally in French and German.

De Revisor (P)
Published by Em Querido's Uitgeverij BV
Singel 262, NL-1016 AC Amsterdam
Tel: (020) 5511262 *Fax:* (020) 6203509
Key Personnel
Editorial Secretary: Fleur Speet

Speurwerk Boeken Omnibus (The Dutch Book Market) (J)
Published by Stichting Speurwerk betreffende het Boek
Frederiksplein 1, 1017 XK Amsterdam
Tel: (020) 6254927 *Fax:* (020) 6208871
Quarterly.

New Zealand

Te Rarangi Pukapuka Matua o Aotearoa (New Zealand National Bibliography) (J)
Published by National Library of New Zealand (Te Puna Matauranga o Aotearoa)
PO Box 1467, Wellington 6004
Tel: (04) 4743000 *Fax:* (04) 4743042
E-mail: tepuna@natlib.govt.nz
Web Site: www.natlib.govt.nz
First published 1961.
Monthly online version; cumulative on CD-ROM. 830 NZ dollars (405.29 US dollars) for 1 CD-ROM annually; 1200 NZ dollars (585.96 US dollars) 2 CD-ROMs annually; monthly website version free & free on CD-ROM for International clients
ISSN: 0028-8497

Nigeria

ƒAfrican Journal of Academic Librarianship (P)
Published by Standing Conference of African University Libraries (SCAUL)
Akoka, Yaba, Lagos
Mailing Address: PO Box 46, Akoka, Yaba, Lagos
Tel: (01) 524968

The Benin Review (J)
Published by Ethiope Publishing Corporation
34 Murtala Mohammed St, Benin City
Mailing Address: PMB 1332, Benin City, Bendel State
Tel: (052) 243036
Telex: 41110
Key Personnel
Editor: Abio la Irele
The journal covers all the arts in Africa, both traditionally and modern, and is also concerned with cultural life in the Black World generally.

ƒHeritage (J)
Published by Heritage Books
2-8 Calcutta Crescent Gate 4, Apapa, Lagos
Mailing Address: PO Box 610, 101251 Apapa, Lagos
Tel: (01) 871333; (01) 875389
Key Personnel
Editor: Naiwu Osahon
African arts & letters.
Quarterly.

The Muse (P)
Published by English Association at Nsukka
University of Nigena, Dept of English, Nsukka
Tel: 771911
Telex: 51496
Key Personnel
Editor: Onyedika L Okwuonu
Irregularly.

National Bibliography of Nigeria (J)
Published by National Library of Nigeria-Reserch & Development Dept
Dantata House, Central Business District, PMB 1, Abuja
Mailing Address: PMB 12626, Lagos
Tel: (01) 2600220 *Fax:* (09) 2347517
Cumulations before 1971 published by the Ibadan University Press.
First published 1950.
Annually, also available as a weekly service.

Northern Nigerian Publications (J)
Published by Ahmadu Bello University Press Ltd
PMB 1094, Zaria, Kaduna State
Tel: (069) 50054
Telex: 75241
Annually.

Publishing in Nigeria (B)
Published by Ethiope Publishing Corporation
34 Murtala Mohammed St, Benin City, Bendel State
Mailing Address: PMB 1332, Benin City, Bendel State
Tel: (052) 243036
Telex: 41110

Serials in Print in Nigeria (B)
Published by National Library of Nigeria-Reserch & Development Dept
Dantata House, Central Business District, PMB 1, Abuja
Mailing Address: PMB 12626, Lagos
Tel: (01) 2600220

Norway

Bok Og Samfunn (J)
Published by Norwegian Booksellers Association
Ovre Vollgate 15, N-0158 Oslo 1
Tel: 22411290 *Fax:* 22411289
E-mail: bokogsamfunn@boknett.no

Web Site: www.boknett.no/bos.html
Trade journal for the Norwegian book trade.

Edda (P)
Published by Scandinavian University Press
Universitetsforlaget, N-0608 Oslo 1
Mailing Address: PO Box 2959-Toeyen, N-0608 Oslo 1
Tel: 22575400 *Fax:* 22857353
E-mail: subscription@scupino.
Web Site: www.scupino
Literary research
Scandinavian.

The Norseman (P)
Published by Nordmanns-Forbundet (The Norse Federation)
Raadhusgate 23B, N-0158 Oslo
Tel: (022) 3357170 *Fax:* (022) 3357175
E-mail: norseman@norseman.no
Key Personnel
Editor-in-Chief: Kjetil A Flatin
Editor: Gunnar Gran
5 times/yr.
64 pp
ISSN: 0029-1846

Norsk Bokhandlermatrikkel (Norwegian Booksellers Membership List) (B)
Published by Bok Og Papiransattes Forening
Ovre Vollgate 15, N-0158 Oslo
Tel: 22205197 *Fax:* 22420033

Samtiden (J)
Published by H Aschehoug & Co (W Nygaard)
Sehesteds gate 3, Postboks 363 Sentrum, 0102 Oslo
Tel: 22400400 *Fax:* 22206395
E-mail: epost@aschehoug.no
Web Site: www.aschehoug.no
Key Personnel
Asst Editor: Erik V Jacobson *E-mail:* erik.jacobsen@aschehoug.no
Journal for politics, literature & other social questions.

ƒScandinavian Public Library Quarterly (SPLQ) (J)
Published by Statens Bibliotektilsyn
PO Box 8145 Dep, 0033 Oslo
Tel: 22523051 *Fax:* 22525198; 22523051
E-mail: mboedtke@online.no
Key Personnel
Editor: Marit Lund Bodtker
Editor, Norway: Ellen Hjortsaeter
Editor, Denmark: Elisabeth Lylloff
Editor, Finland: Sirpa Schueler
Editor, Sweden: Elisabeth Nilsson

Syn og Segn (Vision & Tradition) (P)
Published by Det Norske Samlaget
Postboks 4672 Sofienberg, 0506 Oslo
Tel: 22687600 *Fax:* 22687502
E-mail: syn.og.segn@samlaget.no
Web Site: www.samlaget.no
Major Norwegian review on political & cultural affairs.
Quarterly.

Vinduet (The Window) (P)
Published by Gyldenal Norsk Forlag
Sehesteds gt 4, 0164 Oslo 1
Mailing Address: PO Box 6860, St Olavs plass, 0130 Oslo
Tel: 22034244 *Fax:* 22034105
E-mail: @gyldenal.no
Web Site: www.vinduet.no
Telex: 72 880 gyldn n
Quarterly.

Pakistan

Ham Qalam (P)
Published by Pakistan Writers' Guild
11 Abbok Rd Anarkali/ One Mentgomrey Rd, Lahore
Tel: (042) 6367124
Monthly.

Pakistan Book Trade Directory (B)
Published by Library Promotion Bureau
Karachi University Campus, Dastagir Society, Federal B Area, Karachi 75270
Mailing Address: PO Box 8421, Karachi 75270
Tel: (021) 479001 *Fax:* (021) 473226
Key Personnel
Chief Editor: Mr Adil Usmani

Pakistan National Bibliography (Qaumi Kitabiaat-E-Pakistan) (J)
Published by Department of Libraries, National Library of Pakistan
Constitution Ave, Islamabad
Tel: (051) 9202544; (051) 9202549; (051) 9206436; (051) 9206440 *Fax:* (051) 221375
E-mail: nlpba@isb.paknet.com.pk
Web Site: www.nlp.gov.pk
Key Personnel
Editor, PNB: M Irshad Sherwani
First published 1962.
Annually.
1996: 300 pp, $60 USD

Papua New Guinea

Bikmaus (P)
Published by National Research Institute of Papua New Guinea
Cultural Studies Division, PO Box 1432, Boroko, National Capital District
Mailing Address: PO Box 5854, Boroko
Tel: 253200; 25-4644 *Fax:* 253042
Published quarterly.

Office of Libraries and Archives, Papua, New Guinea (J)
Published by National Library Service of Papua New Guinea
PO Box 734, Waigani NCD
Tel: 3256200 *Fax:* 3251331
Telex: NE 22234
Key Personnel
Dir General: Daniel Paraide *Tel:* 3258013
E-mail: paraide@daltron.com.ps
Annually.

Peru

Bibliografia Peruana (Peruvian National Bibliography) (J)
Published by Biblioteca Nacional del Peru
Ave Abancay 4, Cdra s/n, Apdo 2335, Lima 1
Tel: (01) 287690 ext 147; (01) 428-7690
Fax: (01) 4277331
Key Personnel
Director: Sinesio Lopez
First published 1943.
annual.
2000, $45

Revista Peruana de Cultura (Peruvian Review of Culture) (P)
Published by Instituto Nacional de Cultura
Casilla 5247, Ancash 390, Lima
Tel: (014) 287990

Textual (P)
Published by Instituto Nacional de Cultura
Casilla 5247, Ancash 390, Lima
Tel: (014) 287990
Key Personnel
Dir: Dr Fernando Silva Santisteban

Philippines

Diliman Review (P)
Published by University of the Philippines, Sciences, Arts, & Letters, & Social Sciences & Philosophy
Palma Hall Annex, 2nd Floor, 1101 Diliman, Quezon City
Tel: (02) 982471; (02) 995071
Web Site: www.upd.edu.ph
Key Personnel
Editor: Eddie E Eswetura

Philippine Studies (P)
Published by Ateneo de Manila University Press
PO Box 154, 1099 Manila
Tel: (632) 4265984; (632) 4266001 *Fax:* (632) 4265909
E-mail: unipress@admn.edu.ph
Publishes articles, notes & reviews in the humanities, literature, history, social sciences, philosophy & Philippine arts.
Quarterly.
ISSN: 0031-7837

Poland

Ksiegarz (The Bookseller) (J)
Published by Stowarzyszenie Ksiegarzy Polskich
ul Batorego 24, 43-100 Tychy
Tel: (032) 2192393
E-mail: sklep@ksiegarz.com
Web Site: www.ksiegarz.com.pl

Pamietnik Teatralny (P)
Published by Polish Academy of Sciences, Institute of Art
ul Dluga 28, 00-950 Warsaw
Tel: (022) 8313271 *Fax:* (022) 8313149
History of Polish Theatre, published quarterly.

Polish Publishers and Booksellers (B)
Published by Panstwowy Instytut Wydawniczy (PIW) (National Publishing Institute)
ul Foksal 17, Skrytka pocztowa 377, 00-372 Warsaw
Tel: (022) 8260201; (022) 8260205 *Fax:* (022) 8261536
Telex: 814306
Text in English.

Ruch Wydawniczy w Liczbach (Polish Publishing in Figures) (B)
Published by Biblioteka Narodowa
Al Niepodleglosci 213, 02 086 Warsaw 22
Tel: (022) 6082639 *Fax:* (022) 6082408
E-mail: statystyka@bn.org.pl
Key Personnel
Editor: Krystyna Bankowska-Bober

First published 1955.
Yearly.
102 pp
ISSN: 0511-1196

Soon to Appear (J)
Published by AGPOL (Przedsiebiorstwo Reklamy i Wydawnictw Handlu Zagranicznego)
ul Kerbedzia 4, 00-957 Warsaw
Tel: (022) 416061 *Fax:* (022) 405607
Telex: 813364
French, German & Russian editions.

Portugal

Livros de Portugal (Portuguese Books) (J)
Published by Associacao Portuguesa de Editores e Livreiros
Av Estados Unidos da America, 97 6 Esq, 1700 Lisbon
Tel: (021) 8435180 *Fax:* (021) 8489377
Telex: 62735

Livros Disponiveis (B)
Published by Associacao Portuguesa de Editores e Livreiros
Av Estados Unidos da America, 97 6 Esq, 1700-004 Lisbon
Tel: (021) 8435180 *Fax:* (021) 8489377
E-mail: adm@apel.pt
Web Site: www.apel.pt
Portuguese Books in Print (CD-ROM).
Annual.
36.41 euros

O Mundo do Edicao Luso-Brasileira (B)
Published by Publicacoes Europa-America Lda
Apdo 8, Mem Martins Cedex
Tel: (01) 9211461 *Fax:* (01) 9217940
Telex: 42255 peap
The World of Publishing, Portugal & Brazil.

Puerto Rico

Atenea (P)
Published by University of Puerto Rico at Mayaguez, College of Arts and Sciences
Mayaguez Campus, Mayaguez 00681
Tel: (787) 834-3031
Text in Spanish, English, French and Italian.

⨍**Guide to Review of Books From And About Hispanic America** (B)
Published by AMM Editions
c/o Pontifical Catholic University of Puerto Rico, Ponce 00732
Mailing Address: Box 151, Sta 6, Ponce 00732
Tel: (787) 841-2000 *Fax:* (787) 840-4295
Annually.

Romania

Bibliografia Romaniei (J)
Published by National Library
Str Ion Ghica 4, Sec 3, Bucharest R-79708
Tel: (01) 3157063; (01) 3142434 (ext 232)
Fax: (01) 3123381
E-mail: go@bibnat.ro
Romanian National Bibliography.
First published 1952.

Bimonthly.
156 pp
ISSN: 1221-9126

Cahiers Roumains d'Etudes Litteraires
(Periodical of Romanian Literary Studies) (P)
Published by Euresis - Cahiers Roumains d'Etudes Litteraires
Editura Univers, Piata Presei Libere NR 1, 79739 Bucharest
Tel: (01) 2226629 *Fax:* (01) 2225652
Text in French & English, occasionally in German, Russian, Spanish & Italian.

Convorbiri Literare (Literary Conversations) (P)
Published by Writers' Union of the Socialist Republic of Romania
Calea Victoriei 115, Bucharest
Tel: (01) 6507245 *Fax:* (01) 3129634
Telex: 11796
Key Personnel
Editor: Corneliu Sturzu

Manuscriptum (P)
Published by The Ministery of Culture
B-dul Dacia, nr 12, sector 1, 71116 Bucharest
Tel: (01) 6502096 *Fax:* (01) 6424169
Manuscripts, Literary documents in Romanian, or bilingual, if necessary; Summaries in French, English, German & Russian.

Revista de Istorie si Teorie Literara (Review of Literary History and Theory) (P)
Published by Academia Romana
Calea 13 Septembrie 13, R-76117 Bucharest
Summaries in French and Russian.

Romania Literara (Literary Romania) (P)
Published by Writers' Union of the Socialist Republic of Romania
Calea Victoriei 115, Bucharest
Tel: (01) 6507245 *Fax:* (01) 3129634
Telex: 11796
Key Personnel
Dir: Nicolae Manolescu

Romanian Review (P)
Published by Foreign Languages Press Romania
PO Box 33-28, Bucharest 71341
Tel: (01) 2228481 *Fax:* (01) 2230528
Text in English, French & German (monthly), Russian (quarterly).

Secolul XX (Twentieth Century) (P)
Published by Writers' Union of the Socialist Republic of Romania
Calea Victoriei 115, Bucharest
Tel: (01) 6507245 *Fax:* (01) 3129634
Telex: 11796
Key Personnel
Editor: Don Haulica

Steaua (P)
Published by Writers' Union of the Socialist Republic of Romania
Calea Victoriei 115, Bucharest
Tel: (01) 6507245 *Fax:* (01) 3129634
Telex: 11796
Key Personnel
Editor-in-Chief: Aurel Rau

Russian Federation

Avrora (Aurora) (J)
Published by Russian Federation Union of Writers
Novy Arbat, 18, Moscow
Tel: (095) 202 5959 *Fax:* (095) 956 9215
E-mail: sekretar@avrora.ru
Key Personnel
Editor: E Shevelyov
Literary, artistic and socio-political journal.
Monthly.

Bibliografiya (Bibliography) (J)
Published by Izdatel'stvo Kniznaya palata
Sushchevskii val 64, 129272 Moscow
Tel: (095) 2888643; (095) 2889238
Telex: 411167 GBLSU
Bimonthly.

Druzhba Narodov (People's Friendship) (P)
Published by Soyuz Pisatelei Rossii
Povarskaya ul, 52, 121827 Moscow
Tel: (095) 2916227; (095) 2916354
Web Site: www.russia.agama.com/r_club/journals/drushba.nar/contence.htm
Literary, artistic, socio-political magazine.
Monthly.

Knizhnaya Letopis' (Book Chronicle) (J)
Published by Rossijskaja Knizhnaya Palata (Russian Book Chamber)
Vl Ostogenka, 4, 119034 Moscow
Tel: (095) 2916843 *Fax:* (095) 2919630
E-mail: bookch@postman.ru
Web Site: www.bookchamber.ru/international
Book Annals; published by Book Chamber International.
First published 1807.
Weekly bulletin.
160 pp, 520 US
ISSN: 0869-5962

Knizhnaya Moskva: Putevoditel'-Spravochnik (Books in Moscow A Guide and Handbook) (B)
Published by Reklama
ul Cajkouskogo 7, 121099 Moscow
Tel: (095) 2052101

Knizhnoe Obozrenie (J)
Published by Ministerstvo Pechati i Informatsii Rossi
Sushchevskiival, 64, 129272 Moscow
Tel: (095) 2384967 *Fax:* (095) 2384967
Telex: 411167 GBLSU
Book Reviews.

Letopis' Periodicheskikh i Prodolzhaiushchikhsya Izdanii (J)
Published by Letopis' Chronicle
Durasovskij per 9, 102001 Moscow
Tel: (095) 2972557
Periodicals and Continuations.

Literaturnaya Rossiya (Literary Russia) (P)
Published by Izdatelsroe objedinenie pisatelei
Tsvetnoi bul 30, Moscow 103662
Tel: (095) 2004005; (095) 2002324 *Fax:* (095) 2002755
Weekly.

Literaturnoe Obozrenie/Literary Review (Magazine) (Literary Review) (P)
Published by Vitaly/Benkin
ul Dobroljubova, 9/11, Moscow 127254
Tel: (095) 2199263 *Fax:* (095) 2180398
Journal of critics and bibliography.
Bimonthly.

Molodaya Gvardiya (The Young Guards) (P)
Published by ZAO, Journal Molodaya gvadiya
Novodmitrovakaya ul 5-A, Moscow 125015
Tel: (095) 2858829 *Fax:* (095) 2855690
Literary, artistic, socio-political magazine.
Monthly.

Moskva (Moscow) (P)
Published by Soyuz Pisatelei Rossii
Ul Arbat, 20, Moscow 121918
Tel: (095) 9219626 *Fax:* (095) 2910732
E-mail: moskva@jurmos.msk.ru
Key Personnel
Editor: L L Borodin
Literary, artistic, socio-political illustrated magazine.
Monthly.

Nash Sovremennik (Our Contemporary) (P)
Published by RSFSR Writers' Union
Tsvetnoi bul, 32, Moscow 103750
Tel: (095) 2002424 *Fax:* (095) 2002305
Literary, artistic, socio-political magazine.
Monthly.

Neva (P)
Published by NEVA Monthly Ltd
Nevskii prospect, 3, St Petersburg 191186
Tel: (0812) 3126478; (0812) 3158472 *Fax:* (0812) 3126478
Literary, artistic, socio-political illustrated magazine, black & white photos.
Monthly.

Novye Knigi (New Books) (J)
Published by Mezdunarodnaja Kniga
B Yakimanka, 39, 117049 Moscow
Tel: (095) 2384600; (095) 2330066 *Fax:* (095) 2302117
E-mail: postmaster@mkniga.msk.su
Telex: 411160
18 Issues a year.

Novyi Mir (P)
Published by Sergei/Yakovlev
Maly Putinkovsky per, 1-2, Moscow 103806
Tel: (095) 2095702 *Fax:* (095) 2000829
Literary, artistic and socio-political illustrated journal.
First published 1925.
Monthly.

Russkaya Literatura (Russian Literature) (P)
Published by Academy of Sciences, Institute of Russian Literature, Pushkin's House
Naberejnaya Makarova, 4, 199034 St Petersburg
Tel: (0812) 2181601
Historical and literary journal.

Slovo (P)
Published by Izdatel'st vol Kzinzhnaya Palata
Sushchevskii val 64, Moscow 129272
Tel: (095) 2384967 *Fax:* (095) 2384634
Telex: 411 169 GBLSU
Now Word.

Voprosy Literatury (Questions of Literature) (P)
Published by Institute of World Literature
B Gnezdnikovskii per, 10, 103009 Moscow
Tel: (095) 2294977 *Fax:* (095) 2296471
Telex: 411950POEMA SU *Cable:* 103009
Key Personnel
Editor in Chief: L Lazarev

RUSSIAN FEDERATION

Znamya (The Banner) (P)
ul Nikoskaja 8/1, Moscow 103863
Tel: (095) 9241346 *Fax:* (095) 9213272
Literary, artistic, socio-political magazine.

Zvezda (The Star) (P)
ul Mokhovaya 20, St Petersburg D-28
Tel: (0812) 2728948
Literary, artistic, socio-political magazine.
Monthly.

Senegal

Bibliographie du Senegal (Bibliographies of Senegal) (J)
Published by Archives du Senegal, Immeuble administratif
Ave Leopold Sedar Senghor, Dakar
Tel: 217021 *Fax:* 225126
E-mail: bdas@primature.sn
ISBN(s): 0378-9942

⫻**Bibliographie nationale courante de l' Annee...des pays d' Afrique d' expression francaise** (National Bibliography for the Year...of Francophone African Countries) (B)
Published by Ecole de Bibliothecaires, Archivistes, et Documentalistes de Dakar
Universite Cheikh Anta Diop De Dakar, Faculty of Arts & Sciences, BP 3252, Dakar
Tel: 257660 *Fax:* 255219
Key Personnel
Dir: Ousmane Sane
Bibliography covering books & other materials published in Francophone Africa.
First published 1967.
Annual.

Sierra Leone

Sierra Leone Publications (J)
Published by Sierra Leone Library Board
PO Box 326, Freetown
Tel: (022) 23848; (022) 223848
The national bibliography, published annually since 1962.

Singapore

Books about Singapore (B)
Published by National Reference Library
Library Supply Centre, 3 Changi South St 2 Tower B, #03-00, Singapore 486548
Tel: 6546 7265 *Fax:* 6546 7209
E-mail: ref@nlb.gov.sg
Web Site: www.lib.gov.sg
Biennially.
ISSN: 0068-0176
Parent Company: National Library Board

NBDCS News (J)
Published by National Book Development Council of Singapore
One Temasek Ave, 17-01 Millenia Tower, Singapore 039192
Tel: 4343651 *Fax:* 8832393
Quarterly.
Free

Singapore Book World (J)
Published by National Book Development Council of Singapore
One Temasek Ave, 17-01 Millenia Tower, Singapore 039192
Tel: 4343651 *Fax:* 8832393
Reviews of Singapore published books & articles on the book trade & reading trends.

Singapore National Bibliography (SNB) (J)
Published by National Library Board Singapore, Library Support Services
3 Changi South St 2 Tower B, No 03-00, Singapore 486548
Tel: 65467225; 65467262
E-mail: nazimahsyed@nlb.gov.sg
Web Site: www.nlb.gov.sg
Telex: RS 26620 NATLIB
Annual accumulation.
Every 6 months.
ISSN: 0218-6454

Singapore Periodicals Index (B)
Published by National Reference Library
Library Supply Centre, 3 Changi South St 2 Tower B, #03-00, Singapore 486548
Tel: 65467225; 65467262 *Fax:* 3309611; 3371470
Telex: RS 26620 NATLIB
Published annually.

Slovakia

Kniha (The Book) (P)
Published by Vydavatel' Sky odbor
Ul L Novomeskeho 32, 03652 Martin
Tel: (0842) 31861 *Fax:* (0842) 32454

Literatura (Slovak Literature) (P)
Published by Veda Publishing House of the Slovak Academy of Sciences
Bradacova 7, 852 86 Bratislava
Tel: (07) 57312; (07) 831172; (07) 832254 *Fax:* (07) 835391; (07) 832254
Contents page and summaries in German and Russian.

Slovak Books in Print (J)
Published by Slovart Co Ltd
nam Slobody 6, 81764 Bratislava
Tel: (07) 230229
Telex: 93394 slov c

Slovenske pohlady na literaturu a umenie (Slovak View on Literature & Art) (P)
Published by Vydavatel'stvo Spolku slovensky ch spisovatel'ov sro
Lavrinska 2, 813 08 Bratislava
Tel: (07) 334316; (07) 334374; (07) 332334; (07) 5332671 *Fax:* (07) 335411

Slowakei (Slovakia) (P)
Published by Matus-Cernak-Institut, Kulturelles Zentrum der Slowaken in Deutschland
Postfach 100924, 50449 Cologne, Germany
Literary, scientific and political review.

Slovenia

Slovenska Bibliografija (J)
Published by Narodna in Univerzitetna Knjiznica, Ljubljana (National and University Library)

Narodna in Univerzitetna Knjiznica, Turjaska 1, 1001 Ljubljana
Tel: (01) 2001-100; (61) 2001 115 *Fax:* (01) 4257-293
Slovene Bibliography.
Quarterly.
ISSN: 0353-1716

South Africa

Acta Classica (P)
Published by Classical Association of South Africa
c/o Academia Latina, University of Pretoria, Pretoria 0002
Tel: (012) 4202368 *Fax:* (012) 4204008
E-mail: bothmh@alpha.unisa.ac.za
Key Personnel
Editor: Danig B Lombard
Annually.

Akroterion (P)
Published by University of Stellenbosch Dept of Classics
Private Bag X1, Matieland, Stellenbosch 7602
Tel: (021) 808-3136 *Fax:* (021) 808-4336
E-mail: classics@maties.sun.ac.za

Catalog of Books (English) Published in Southern Africa, Still in Print (1970) (B)
Published by Struik Publishers (Pty) Ltd
PO Box 1144, 8000 Cape Town
Tel: (021) 216740; (021) 517128; (021) 462-4360 *Fax:* (021) 216744; (021) 462-4379

English in Africa (P)
Published by Institute for the Study of English in Africa, Rhodes University
St Peter's Bldg (off Somerset St), Grahamstown 6140
Mailing Address: PO Box 94, Grahamstown 6140
Tel: (046) 6038565 *Fax:* (046) 6038566
E-mail: j.king@ru.ac.za
Web Site: www.ru.ac.za/institutes/isea/eia/index.htm
Key Personnel
Editor: Craig Mackenzie
Managing Editor: Prof Laurence Wright
Editorial Assistant: Marion Baxter
Published biennially in May & December. Primary source material: critical articles & book reviews on all aspects of African literature written in English.
Biennially.
$22 US; L16 (2 issues)
ISSN: 0376-8902

Journal of Literary Studies (P)
Published by Journal of Literary Studies, Unisa Printers
Theory of Literature, UNISA, POB 392, Pretoria 0001
Tel: (012) 4296614; (012) 4296700; (012) 4296058 *Fax:* (012) 4293221
E-mail: graberc@alpha.unisa.ac.za
Journal to provide a forum for the discussion of literary theory, methodology, research & related matters, features articles, commentary, book reviews & general announcements.

New Coin Poetry (P)
Published by Institute for the Study of English in Africa, Rhodes University
St Peter's Bldg (off Somerset St), Grahamstown 6140
Mailing Address: PO Box 94, Grahamstown 6140
Tel: (046) 6038565 *Fax:* (046) 6038566

E-mail: j.king@ru.ac.za
Web Site: www.ru.ac.za/institutes/isea/newcoin/
Key Personnel
Editor: Joan Metelerkamp
Managing Editor: Prof Laurence Wright
Editorial Assistant: Marion Baxter
New South African poetry, interviews with poets & poetry reviews.
Biennially in July & Dec.
90 pp, $15 US; L8.50 (2 issues)
ISSN: 0028-4459

New Contrast (P)
Published by South African Literary Journal Ltd
PO Box 3841, Cape Town 8000
Publishes South African poetry, short fiction, essays, criticisms, book reviews, graphic art & general cultural commentary. Does not discriminate on the basis of race, gender, political persuasion or religious creed.

scrutiny2: issues in English studies in Southern Africa (P)
Published by University of South Africa Library
PO Box 392, Pretoria 0003
Tel: (012) 4296602; (012) 4296342 Fax: (012) 4293221
E-mail: unisa-press@unisa.ac.za
Web Site: www.unisa.ac.za/dept/press/onjourn.html
Telex: 3777 Cable: UNISA
Literary articles & reviews.
Biennially in May & Sept.

ɟShakespeare in Southern Africa (P)
Published by Shakespeare Society of Southern Africa
c/o ISEA, Rhodes University, Grahamstown 6140
Mailing Address: PO Box 94, Grahamstown 6140
Tel: (0461) 6038565 Fax: (0461) 6038566
E-mail: mbaxter@ru.ac.za
Web Site: www.ru.ac.za/affiliates/isea/shakespeare
Key Personnel
Editor: Prof Brian Pearce E-mail: brianp@dit.ac.za
Contact: Prof Laurence Wright E-mail: l.wright@ru.ac.za
Articles, commentary & reviews on all aspects of Shakespearean studies & performance, with a particular emphasis on the response to Shakespeare in Southern Africa.
First published 1987.
Annual.
100 pp, $120 per annum
ISSN: 1011-582X

South African Journal of African Languages (P)
Published by African Language Association of Southern Africa
South African Bureau for Scientific Publications, PO Box 1758, Pretoria 0001
Tel: (012) 3226404 Fax: (012) 3207803
E-mail: bspman@icon.co.za
Web Site: www.safest.org.za/bsp
Quarterly.

Staffrider (P)
Published by Congress of South African Writers
PO Box 421007, Fordsburg 2033
Tel: 8332530 Fax: 8332532

Spain

Bibliografia Espanola Monografias (Spanish Bibliography) (J)
Published by Biblioteca Nacional de Espana
Plaza del Rey 1, 28004 Madrid
Mailing Address: Paseo De Recoletos, 20-22, Madrid 28001
Tel: (091) 5447443; (091) 5807856 Fax: (091) 5807873
E-mail: webmaster@bne.es; p.dominguez@bne.es
Web Site: www.bne.es

Bibliografia Espanola: Suplemento de Publicaciones Periodicas (Periodical Publications Supplement to Spanish Bibliography) (J)
Published by Biblioteca Nacional de Espana
Plaza del Rey 1, 28004 Madrid
Tel: (091) 5447443; (091) 5807856 Fax: (091) 5807873
E-mail: webmaster@bne.es
Web Site: www.bne.es

Catalan Review (P)
Published by North American Catalan Society, Publicacions de L'Abadia de Monserriat
Ausias March 92-98, 08013 Barcelona
Tel: (093) 8940720 Fax: (093) 3175992
E-mail: pamsa@pamsa.com
Web Site: www.indiana.edu/~nacs/CReview.htm; www.pamsa.com
Current and past issues of Catalan Review can be purchased from: Merce Vidal Tibbits, Dept of Modern Langauges & Literatures, Howard Univ, Washington, DC 20059.

Delibros (J)
Published by Delibros SA
Orense, 4-10a plauta, 28020 Madrid
Tel: (091) 5981789 Fax: (091) 5563685

Libros Espanoles en Venta: Repertorio Anual (B)
Published by Agencia Espanola del ISBN
Agencia Espanol ISBN, Calle Santiago Rusinol 8, 28040 Madrid
Tel: (091) 5368830 Fax: (091) 5539990
Spanish Books in Print. Annual five volume compilation of monthly periodicals.

Litoral (P)
Published by Visor Libros
Isaac Peral, 18, 28015 Madrid
Tel: (091) 5436134; (091) 5492655 Fax: (091) 5448695
Monthly poetry review.

Nuestro Tiempo (Our Time) (P)
Published by Servicio de Publicaciones de la Universidad de Navarra, SA
Edif. Bibliotecas, Campus Universitario, 31080 Pamplona
Tel: (048) 252700

Razon y Fe (Reason & Faith) (P)
Published by Centro Loyola de Estudios y Communicacion Social
Pablo Aranda 3, 28006 Madrid
Tel: (091) 5624930 Fax: (091) 5634073
Spanish-American review.

Revista de Occidente (Review of the West) (P)
Published by Instituto Universitario Ortega y Gasset
Fortuny 53, 28010 Madrid
Tel: (091) 3104412 Fax: (091) 3084007

Serra d'Or (P)
Published by Publicacions de l'Abadia de Montserrat
Ausias March 92-98, Apdo 244, 08013 Barcelona
Tel: (093) 2430302; (093) 2450303; (093) 2657923 Fax: (093) 2473594
Key Personnel
Editor: Maur M Boix

Sri Lanka

Sri Lanka (ISBN) Publishers Directory (1994 edition) (B)
Published by National Library & Documentation Services Board
No 14, Independence Ave, Colombo 07
Mailing Address: PO Box 1764, Colombo 07
Tel: (01) 685198; (01) 685203; (01) 698847
Fax: (01) 685201
E-mail: nldsb@mail.natlib.lk
Key Personnel
Dir General: Mr M S U Amarasiri Tel: (01) 687581 E-mail: dgnl@sltnet.lk
This directory includes 1080 Sri Lankan Publishers. It is divided into two parts: namely, Alphabetical Section & Numerical Section. In each section, the publishers are categorized into three groups: Commercial, Governmental & Non-Governmental Institutions & Author/Private Publishers. The ISBN Publishers Directory is computerized & the database is updated monthly.

Sri Lanka National Bibliography (J)
Published by Sri Lanka National Library Services Board
No 14 Independence Ave, Colombo 7
Mailing Address: PO Box 1764, Colombo 7
Tel: (01) 698847 Fax: (01) 685201
E-mail: natlib@slt.lk
Web Site: www.slt.lk/nlib
Text in English, Sinhalese & Tamil.
Quarterly.
US $50 (postage included)

Vidoyaya Journal of Social Science (J)
Published by University of Sri Jayewardenepura
Gangodawila, Nugegoda
Tel: 553194 Fax: 852604
Key Personnel
Editor-in-Chief: Winston E Ratnayake
ISBN(s): 955-9054

Swaziland

Swaziland National Bibliography (J)
Published by University of Swaziland Library
Private Bag 4, Kwaluseni
Tel: 85108 Fax: 85276
Published irregularly.

Sweden

Bonniers Litteraera Magasin (Bonniers Literary Magazine) (P)
Published by Albert Bonniers Forlag
Box 3159, 103 63 Stockholm 3
Tel: (08) 7996308 Fax: (08) 6968359
E-mail: blm@bok.bonnier.se

Svensk Bokfoerteckning (J)
Published by Kungliga Biblioteket, Tidnings AB Svensk Bokhandel
PO Box 5039, S-102-41 Stockholm

SWEDEN

Tel: (08) 4634000 *Fax:* (08) 4634004
E-mail: kungl.biblioteket@kb.se
Swedish National Bibliography.

Svensk Bokhandel (J)
Published by Tidnings AB Svensk Bokhandel
Birkagatan 16 C, 11386 Stockholm
Mailing Address: PO Box 6888, S-11386 Stockholm
Tel: (08) 54541770 *Fax:* (08) 54541775
Swedish Book Trade. Jointly with Swedish Booksellers' Association.

Svenska Bokfoerlaeggarefoereningen (B)
Published by Swedish Publishers' Association
Drottninggatan 97, 2 tr, 11360 Stockholm
Tel: (08) 7361940 *Fax:* (08) 7361944
E-mail: svf@forlagskansli.se
Web Site: www.forlagskansli.se
Swedish Publishers' Association list of members & agents, together with book trade associates & organizations.

Text (J)
Published by Dahlia Books, International Publishers & Booksellers
Box 1025, 751 40 Uppsala
Tel: (018) 101098 *Fax:* (018) 100525
Bibliographical journal, in English & Swedish.

Switzerland

Adressbuch des Schweizer Buchhandels (B)
Published by Schweizerischer Buchhaendler- und Verleger-Verband SBVV
Postfach 9045, 8050 Zurich
Tel: (01) 3186444 *Fax:* (01) 3186462
Directory of the Swiss book trade, containing lists of publishers, booksellers, distributors, trade organizations & cross-reference indexes.

Bookbird: A Journal of International Children's Literature (J)
Published by International Board on Books for Young People (IBBY)
Nonnenweg 12, CH-4055 Basel
Tel: (061) 2722917 *Fax:* (061) 2722757
E-mail: ibby@eye.ch
Web Site: www.ibby.org
Key Personnel
Executive Dir: Leena Maissen
Covers many facets of international children's literature & includes news from IBBY & the IBBY National Sections.
Quarterly.
ISSN: 0006-7377

Cenobio (P)
Published by Ignazio Bonoli, Flavio Catenazzi, Franco Lanza, Carlo Monti, Marcello Ostinelli
PO Box 174, CH-6903 Lugano 3
Tel: (091) 9668508; (091) 9681048 *Fax:* (091) 9665156 *Cable:* CH-6943 VEZIA
Text in French & Italian.

Drehpunkt (Pivot) (P)
Published by Lenos Verlag
Spalentorweg 12, CH-4051 Basel
Mailing Address: Postfach 164, CH-4016 Basel
Tel: (061) 253414 *Fax:* (061) 2613518

Edition (J)
Published by Stauffacher Verlag AG
Limmatquai 36, 8001 Zurich
Tel: (01) 474175
Book advertiser.

Etudes de Lettres (Literary Studies) (P)
Published by Universite de Lausanne
Faculte des Lettres, CH-1015 Lausanne
Tel: (021) 692-2907; (021) 692-2909 *Fax:* (021) 692-3045
E-mail: anne.joho@dlett.unil.ch
Web Site: www.unil.ch
Key Personnel
Editor: Johannes Bronkhorst
First published 1960.
4 times/yr.
170 pp, 18 francs for single volume; 26 francs for double volumes
ISSN: 0014-2026

ƒ**International Publishers Association Proceedings of Congress** (B)
Published by International Publishers Association
3 ave de Miremont, CH-1206 Geneva
Tel: (022) 3463018 *Fax:* (022) 3475717
E-mail: info@ipa-uie.org
Web Site: www.ipa-uie.org
Telex: 3421883 *Cable:* INPUBLASS
Key Personnel
Secretary-General: J Alexis Koutchoumow

Jugendliteratur (J)
Published by Schweizerischer Bund fuer Jugendliteratur
Zentralsekretariat, Gewerbstr 8, 6330 Cham
Tel: (042) 413140 *Fax:* (041) 420159
E-mail: sbj@bluewin.ch
Key Personnel
Chief Editor: Jutta Radel
Quarterly.

Librarium (J)
Published by Schweizerische Bibliophilen - Gesellschaft
c/o Prof Dr Werner G Zimmerman, Hadlaubstr 42, 8044 Zurich
Text in German, French, Italian & English.

orte (P)
Published by Orte-Verlag
Wirtschaft Kreuz, CH-9427 Zelg-Wolfhaden
Tel: (071) 8881456

ƒ**La Propriete industrielle et le droit d'auteur** (Industrial Property & Copyright) (P)
Published by World Intellectual Property Organization (WIPO)
34 chemin des Colombettes, Geneva 20
Mailing Address: PO Box 18, CH-1211 Geneva 20
Tel: (022) 7309111 *Fax:* (022) 7335428
Web Site: www.wipo.org
Telex: 412912 ompi ch
Key Personnel
Head Information Section: Laurent Manderieux
Monthly, English & French; Bimonthly, Spanish.

Das Schweizer Buch (J)
Published by Schweizerischer Buchhaendler- und Verleger-Verband SBVV
PO Box 9050, 8050 Zurich
Tel: (01) 3186400 *Fax:* (01) 3186462
The Swiss Book. Bibliographical bulletin. Cosponsored by Schweizerische Landesbibliothek.

Schweizer Buchhandel (The Swiss Book Trade) (J)
Published by Schweizerischer Buchhaendler- und Verleger-Verband SBVV
Postfach 9045, 8050 Zurich
Mailing Address: Postfach 9045, 8050 Zurich
Tel: (01) 3186444 *Fax:* (01) 3186462
E-mail: sbw@dw.krinfo.ch

Schweizer Monatshefte (Swiss Monthly Magazine) (P)
Published by Gesellschaft Schweizer Monatshefte
Vogelsangstr 52, 8006 Zurich
Tel: (01) 3612621 *Fax:* (01) 3637005
Monthly.

Swiss National Bibliography (J)
Published by Schweizerische Landesbibliothek (Bibliotheque nationale suisse)
Hallwylstr 15, 3003 Berne
Tel: (031) 3228911 (Secretary) *Fax:* (031) 3228463
E-mail: IZ-Helvetica@slb.admin.ch

Verlag Prufen & Handeln (P)
Published by Prufen & Handeln/Examiner et Agir
CH-8215 Hallau
Tel: (052) 6813144 *Fax:* (052) 6814014
Web Site: www.klettgau.ch.pruefen&handeln
Cable: MEMOPRESS; Prufen & Handeln; Aktion Volk & Parlament
Journalism & literature; text in German. Short information on politics, economics & religion with commentary. Summary in French.
Parent Company: Aktion Vold und Parlament
Ultimate Parent Company: Action Peuple et Parlement

Taiwan, Province of China

Chinese National Bibliography (J)
Published by National Central Library
20 Chungshan S Rd, 10040 Taipei
Tel: (02) 23619132 *Fax:* (02) 23110155
E-mail: chengkk@msg.ncl.edu.tw
Text in Chinese.

The Chinese PEN (P)
Published by International PEN, Taipei Chinese Center
5th Floor, 33-4 Lane 180 Kwang Fu South Rd, Taipei 10553
Tel: (02) 7219101 *Fax:* (02) 7219101
Published quarterly in English.

Counter Attack (P)
Published by National Institute for Compilation and Translation
247 Chou-Shan Rd, Taipei
Fax: (02) 23629256
Key Personnel
Dir: Chi-chun Tseng
First published 1932.

Shu mo chi kan (J)
Published by Student Book Co Ltd
198, Hop'ing East Road, Sec 1, Taipei
Tel: (02) 3634156 *Fax:* (02) 3636334
Quarterly bibliography, text in Chinese.

Tamkang Review (P)
Published by Tamkang University, Graduate Institute of Western Languages & Literature
Tamsui, Taipei Hsien, Taiwan 25137
Tel: (02) 6215656 (ext 329) *Fax:* (02) 6209912
E-mail: lindsay@hpap.tku.edu.tw
Journal mainly devoted to comparative studies between Chinese & foreign literatures; text in English.

United Republic of Tanzania

Government and Tanu Publications List (J)
Published by Government Printer
PO Box 9124, Dar es Salaam

Tanzania National Bibliography (J)
Published by Tanzania Library Services Board
Bibi Titi Mohamed St, PO Box 9283, Dar es Salaam
Tel: (022) 2150048; (022) 2150049 *Fax:* (022) 2151100
E-mail: tlsb@africaonline.co.tz
The National bibliography was published annually from 1969-1982; monthly from 1983-1988. It is now published annually.
First published 1974.
ISSN: 0856-003X

Umma (P)
Published by University of Dar Es Salaam
Department of Literature, Dar Es Salaam
Mailing Address: PO Box 35041, Dar Es Salaam
Tel: (051) 43500 (ext 2311) *Fax:* (051) 43395
Biannual literary magazine published under the auspices of the Department of Literature, University of Dar Es Salaam.

Trinidad & Tobago

Directory of Publishers, Printers and Booksellers in Trinidad and Tobago (B)
Published by University of the West Indies (Trinidad & Tobago)
The Main Library, St Augustine
Tel: (868) 662-2002 (ext 2132) *Fax:* (868) 662-9238
E-mail: mainlib@library.uwi.tt
Telex: 24520 VWI-Wg
Key Personnel
Author: Maureen Henry
Revised edition 1990.

Tunisia

Repertoire des Unites de Documentation en Tunisia (B)
Published by Bibliotheque Nationale
20, Souk-el-'Attariine, BP 42, 1000 Tunis RP
Tel: (01) 256921; (01) 249902; (01) 245338
Fax: (01) 342700
Telex: 14032

Turkey

Turkiye Bibliyografyasi (Turkish National Bibliography) (J)
Published by National Library of Turkey
Bahcelievler, 06490 Ankara
Tel: (0312) 2224768 *Fax:* (0312) 2230451
E-mail: katalog@mkutup.gov.tr
Web Site: www.mkutup.gov.tr
Key Personnel
Librarian: Nurhan Naneci
First published 1928.
Monthly.
Annual subscription $48 foreign countries
ISSN: 0041-4328

Varlik (Existence) (P)
Published by Varlik Yayinlari AS
Piyerloti Cad 7-9, Gemberlitas, Istanbul 34400
Tel: (0212) 518-0048 (Direct); (0212) 516-2004
Fax: (0212) 516-2005
E-mail: varlik@isbank.net.tr; varlik@varlik.com.tr
Web Site: www.varlik.com.tr
Key Personnel
Editor: Filiz Nayir Deniztekin
Business Manager: Osman Deniztekin
First published 1933.
Monthly.
2,000,000 TL; USD 1.80
ISSN: 1300-1728

United Kingdom

IRWI, see Information Research Watch International (IRWI)

ƒ**AAB's British Bibliography of Rare & Out-of-Print Publications** (P)
Published by Magna Graecia's Publishers (UK)
PO Box 342, Oxford OX2 7YF
Tel: (01865) 792610 *Fax:* (01865) 792611
E-mail: magnagraecias@aol.com
Web Site: www.magnagraeciaspublishers.co.uk
Key Personnel
Editor: Luigi Gigliotti
General Editor: Louis de Sybaris
Weekly.
ISBN(s): 0-86340-002-7
ISSN: 1362-8534

ƒ**AAB's Guide to Private English Language Schools in the United Kingdom for Overseas Students** (B)
Published by Magna Graecia's Publishers (UK)
PO Box 342, Oxford OX2 7YF
Tel: (01865) 792610 *Fax:* (01865) 792611
E-mail: magnagraecias@aol.com
Web Site: www.magnagraeciaspublishers.co.uk
Key Personnel
Editor: Luigi Gigliotti
General Editor: Louis de Sybaris
Annually.
ISBN(s): 0-95077-280-1
ISSN: 1363-1993

ƒ**AAB's Register of Wanted Publications** (B)
Published by Magna Graecia's Publishers (UK)
PO Box 342, Oxford OX2 7YF
Tel: (01865) 792610; (01865) 790686
Fax: (01865) 792611
E-mail: magnagraecias@aol.com
Web Site: www.magnagraeciaspublishers.co.uk
Key Personnel
Editor: Luigi Gigliotti
General Editor: L de Sybaris
First published 1976.
Weekly.
ISBN(s): 0-86340-020-5
ISSN: 0966-2413

ƒ**Abstracts in New Technologies & Engineering** (J)
Formerly Current Technology Index
Published by CSA (Cambridge Scientific Abstracts)
Windsor Court, East Grinstead House, East Grinstead, West Sussex RH19 1XA
Tel: (01342) 326972 *Fax:* (01342) 336197
E-mail: service@csa.com
Web Site: www.csa.com
An index, with abstracts, to scientific & technical periodicals, published in the UK & US.
Bimonthly (journal); Quarterly (CD-ROM); Monthly (web).
$1145 euros, $1750 US, $1170 euros (rest of world)
ISSN: 1367-9899
Parent Company: Cambridge Information Group

ƒ**Advertiser's Annual 2001-2002** (B)
Published by Hollis Publishing Ltd
Harlequin House, 7 High St, Teddington, Middlesex TW11 8EL
Tel: (020) 8977 7711 *Fax:* (020) 8977 1133
E-mail: orders@hollis-pr.co.uk; hollis@hollis-pr.co.uk
Web Site: www.hollis-pr.co.uk
Annual.
77, L260 (400 US dollars) (including p&p)
ISBN(s): 0-900967-889

ƒ**African Publishers Networking Directory 1997/98** (B)
Published by African Books Collective Ltd
The Jam Factory, 27 Park End St, Oxford OX1 1HU
Tel: (01865) 726686 *Fax:* (01865) 793298; (01993) 709265
E-mail: abc@dial.pipex.com
Key Personnel
Consultant: Mary Jay
Resource directory of major African publishers.

The African Publishing Companion: A Resource Guide (B)
Published by Hans Zell Publishing Consultants
Glais Bheinn, Locharron, Ross-shire IV54 8YB
Tel: (01520) 722951 *Fax:* (01520) 722953
Web Site: www.hanszell.co.uk; www.africanpublishingcompanion.com
Key Personnel
Publisher & Editor: Hans M Zell *E-mail:* hzell@dial.pipex.com
Concise yet detailed information about many aspects of African publishing & book trade. Over 1,600 entries, extensively cross referenced. Purchase of book includes 24 month access to the online version.
First published 2002.
Biannually.
256 pp, L80 (130 US dollars)
ISBN(s): 0-9541029-0-8

ƒ**African Research & Documentation** (J)
Published by Standing Conference on Library Materials on Africa (SCOLMA)
c/o Exeter University Library, Srocker Rd, Exeter EX4 4PT
Tel: (01392) 263865 *Fax:* (01392) 263871
Web Site: www.soas.ac.uk/scolna
Key Personnel
Subscription Manager: Helen Muirden *E-mail:* h.j.muirden@exeter.ac.uk

Agenda (P)
Published by The Agenda & Editions Charitable Trust
5 Cranbourne Court, Albert Bridge Rd, London SW11 4PE
Tel: (020) 7228 0700 *Fax:* (020) 7228 0700
Quarterly.

UNITED KINGDOM   BOOK TRADE REFERENCE

ɸAlexandria: Journal of National &
   International Library & Information Issues
   (J)
Published by Ashgate Publishing Ltd
Gower House, Croft Rd, Aldershot, Hants GU11
   3HR
Tel: (01252) 331551 Fax: (01252) 317446
E-mail: info@ashgatepub.demon.co.uk

Ambit (P)
Published by Dr Martin Bax
17 Priory Gardens, London N6 5QY
Tel: (020) 8340 3566
Web Site: www.ambit.co.uk; ambitmagazine.co.uk
Poetry, Prose, Short Fiction, Illustration & Re-
   views.
First published 1959.
Quarterly.
96 pp, L24 UK; L26/$52 US
ISSN: 0002-6972

The Author (P)
Published by Society of Authors
84 Drayton Gardens, London SW10 9SB
Tel: (020) 7373 6642 Fax: (020) 7373 5768
E-mail: TheAuthor@societyofauthors.org
Web Site: www.societyofauthors.org
Key Personnel
Editor: Derek Parker
Manager: Kate Pool E-mail: kpool@
   societyofauthors.org
Quarterly.
ISSN: 0005-0628

ɸBeishon Publications Ltd (J)
15 Micawber St, London N1 7TB
Tel: (020) 7336 6650 Fax: (020) 7336 6640
E-mail: beishon@ibm.net
ISSN: 0958-3866

Bibliography of Books in Polish or Relating to
   Poland Published Outside Poland (P)
Published by The Polish Library
238-246 King St, London W6 0RF
Tel: (020) 8741 0474 Fax: (020) 8741 7724
E-mail: bibliotekapolska@posklibrary.fsnet.co.uk
First published 1953.

Book & Magazine Collector (J)
Published by Diamond Publishing Group Ltd
43-45 St Mary's Rd, Ealing, London W5 5RQ
Tel: (020) 8579 1082 Fax: (020) 8566 2024

ɸBook-Auction Records (B)
Published by Dawson Book Division
Crane Close, Wellingborough NN8 2QG
Tel: (01933) 274444 Fax: (01933) 225933
E-mail: coles@dawson.co.uk
Web Site: www.dawson.co.uk
Priced & annotated report of international book
   auctions.
Annually.

The Book Collector (P)
Published by The Collector Ltd
PO Box 12426, London W11 3GW
Tel: (020) 7792 3492 Fax: (020) 7792 3492
E-mail: info@thebookcollector.co.uk
Web Site: www.thebookcollector.co.uk
Key Personnel
Editor: Nicolas J Barker
Antiquarian books & bibliography.
First published 1952.
Quarterly.
152 pp

BookBank (J)
Published by J Whitaker & Sons Ltd
Endeavour House, 189 Shaftesbury Ave, London
   WC2H 8TJ

Tel: (020) 7420 6006 Fax: (020) 7836 6781
E-mail: sales@whitaker.co.uk
Web Site: www.whitaker.co.uk
Service combining the BookBank database with
   the Southern African Books in Print listing of
   over 30,000 titles from 800 publishers.
Monthly.

BookBank OP (J)
Published by J Whitaker & Sons Ltd
Endeavour House, 189 Shaftesbury Ave, London
   WC2H 8TJ
Tel: (020) 7420 6006 Fax: (020) 7836 6781
E-mail: sales@whitaker.co.uk
Web Site: www.whitaker.co.uk
Key Personnel
Marketing Dir: Marie Lester
CD-ROM containing details of over 800,000 out
   of print titles & is updated quarterly.

BookBank with THORPE-ROM (J)
Published by J Whitaker & Sons Ltd
Endeavour House, 189 Shaftesbury Ave, London
   WC2H 8TJ
Tel: (020) 7420 6006 Fax: (020) 7836 6781
Web Site: www.whitaker.co.uk
Key Personnel
Marketing Dir: Marie Lester
CD-ROM containing all the information listed
   on BookBank with the addition of full biblio-
   graphic details for English language books pub-
   lished in Australia, New Zealand & the Pacific
   Islands.

Bookdealers in India & the Orient (B)
Published by Richard Joseph Publishers Ltd
PO Box 6123, Basingstoke, Hants RG25 2WE
Tel: (01256) 811314 Fax: (01256) 336362
E-mail: rjoe01@aol.com
Web Site: www.sheppardsdirectories.co.uk
A directory of antiquarian booksellers in India &
   oriental countries.
Occasionally.
2nd, L24; US $48

Books for Keeps (J)
Published by School Bookshop Association
6 Brightfield Rd, London SE12 8QF
Tel: (020) 8852 4953 Fax: (020) 8318 7580
E-mail: booksforkeeps@btinternet.com
Reviews of Children's Books.

Books in Polish or Relating to Poland (P)
Published by The Polish Library
238-246 King St, London W6 0RF
Tel: (020) 8741 0474 Fax: (020) 8741 7724
E-mail: bibliotekapolska@posklibrary.fsnet.co.uk
Web Site: www.posk.org
First published 1950.

Books in Scotland (J)
Published by Ramsay Head Press
9 Glenisla Gardens, Edinburgh EH9 2HR
Tel: (0131) 662 1915
Key Personnel
Editorial Dir & International Rights: Conrad K
   Wilson
Quarterly magazine.

Books In The Media (J)
Published by Bookwatch Ltd
15-Up, East St, Lewin's Yard, Chesham, Bucks
   HP5 1HQ
Tel: (01494) 792269 Fax: (01494) 784850
E-mail: 100615.1643@compuserve.com
Weekly listings of all National Daily & Sunday
   Press Reviews, TV & Radio Program Tie-ins,
   Serializations, Best Seller Lists & some Trade
   News & Comment, Inc Sales Index. Founded
   1979.
Saturdays.

Books Magazine (P)
Published by Publishing News Ltd
39 Store St, London WC1E 7DB
Tel: (020) 7404 0304 Fax: (020) 7242 1865;
   (020) 7242 0762
Published bimonthly.

ɸBooks: The International Market (B)
Published by Euromonitor PLC
60-61 Britton St, London EC1M 5UX
Tel: (020) 7251 8024 Fax: (020) 7608 3149
E-mail: info@euromonitor.com
Web Site: www.euromonitor.com
Telex: 21120 MONREF G
Appraisal of the international book market cover-
   ing UK, USA, Spain, Japan, Germany, France
   & Italy.
Annually.

The Bookseller (P)
Published by VNU Entertainment Media UK Ltd
Endeavour House, 189 Shaftesbury Ave, London
   WC2H 8TJ
Tel: (020) 7420 6006 Fax: (020) 7836 6781;
   (020) 7420 6102 (advertising); (020) 7420
   6103 (editorial)
E-mail: information@bookseller.co.uk
Web Site: www.thebookseller.com
Book trade newspaper.
First published 1858.
Weekly.
ISSN: 0006-7539
Parent Company: VNU Business Media Inc
Ultimate Parent Company: VNU NV

Bookselling (J)
Published by Booksellers Association of the
   United Kingdom & Ireland
Minister House, 272 Vauxhall Bridge Rd, London
   SW1V 1BA
Tel: (020) 7834 5477 Fax: (020) 7834 8812
E-mail: mail@booksellers.org.uk
Web Site: www.booksellers.org.uk
ISSN: 0969-4862

BPIF List of Members (B)
Published by British Printing Industries Federation (BPIF)
11 Bedford Row, London WC1R 4DX
Tel: (020) 7915 8300 Fax: (020) 7405 7784
Directory of information on the BPIF & the Printing Industry.

ɸBritish Humanities Index (BHI) (J)
Published by CSA (Cambridge Scientific Ab-
   stracts)
Windsor Court, East Grinstead House, East Grin-
   stead, West Sussex RH19 1XA
Tel: (01342) 326972 Fax: (01342) 336197
E-mail: service@csa.com
Web Site: www.csa.com
Indexes humanities-related articles published by
   British newspapers & journals.
Quarterly (journal & CD-ROM), Monthly (web).
Print subscription: $750 euros, $1160 US, $775
   euros (rest of world); CD-ROM $1250 euros;
   Web $1425 euros
ISSN: 0007-0815
Parent Company: Cambridge Information Group

British National Bibliography (J)
Published by The British Library National Biblio-
   graphic Service
Boston Spa, Wetherby, W Yorks LS23 7BQ
Tel: (01937) 546613 Fax: (01937) 546586
E-mail: nbs-info@bl.uk
Web Site: www.bl.uk
British National Bibliography is available in-print,
   on-line & on CD-ROM.
First published 1950.

1352

BOOKS & JOURNALS

UNITED KINGDOM

Weekly with 2 interim cumulations for Jan-April & May-August; annual volume.
ISSN: 0007-1544

Carousel - The Guide to Children's Books (B)
Published by David & Jenny Blanch
7 Carrs Lane, Birmingham B4 7TG
Tel: (0121) 643 6411 *Fax:* (0121) 643 3152
E-mail: carousel.guide@virgin.net
Published triannually.

Cencrastus (P)
One Abbeymount Techbase, 2 Easter Rd, Edinburgh EH8 8EJ
Tel: (0131) 6615687 *Fax:* (0131) 6615687
E-mail: 106536.755@compuserve.com
Scottish & International literature, arts and affairs.
Quarterly.

Chapman (P)
Published by Chapman Magazine
4 Broughton Pl, Edinburgh, Scotland EH1 3RX
Tel: (0131) 5572207 *Fax:* (0131) 5569565
E-mail: edition@chapman-pub.co.uk
Web Site: www.chapman-pub.co.uk
Key Personnel
Editor: Joy Hendry
Assistant Editor: Gerry Stewart
Literary/magazine publisher.
First published 1970.
Triannually.
97: 144 pp, 4 pound 95p
ISBN(s): 0906772
ISSN: 0308-2695

China: A Survey of the Book Market (B)
Published by British Council, Publishing Promotion Unit
Bridgewater House, 58 Whitworth St, Manchester M1 6BB
Tel: (0161) 9577182 *Fax:* (0161) 9577168
E-mail: publishing.promotion@britcoun.org
Web Site: www.britcoun.org

ƒ**The Clio Montessori Series** (B)
Published by ABC-CLIO
35A Great Clarendon St, Oxford OX2 6AT
Tel: (01865) 311350 *Fax:* (01865) 311358
E-mail: oxford@abc-clio.ltd.uk
Web Site: www.abc-clio.com
Covers education.

Critical Quarterly (P)
Published by Blackwell Publishers
108 Cowley Rd, Oxford OX4 1JF
Tel: (01865) 791100 *Fax:* (01865) 791347
E-mail: jnlinfo@blackwellpublishers.co.uk
Web Site: www.blackwellpublishers.co.uk
Telex: 837022 OXBOOK G

Current British Directories (B)
Published by CBD Research Ltd
15 Wickham Rd, Beckenham, Kent BR3 5JS
Tel: (020) 8650 7745 *Fax:* (020) 8650 0768
E-mail: cbd@cbdresearch.freeserve.co.uk
Web Site: www.cbdresearch.com
A guide to the directories published in the UK & Ireland.
First published 1952.
irregular.
14
ISBN(s): 0-900-246-936

Current Research in Library & Information Science (CRLIS), see Information Research Watch International (IRWI)

Current Technology Index, see Abstracts in New Technologies & Engineering

ƒ**Dictionary of International Biography** (B)
Published by Melrose Press Ltd
St Thomas Pl, Ely, Cambs CB7 4GG
Tel: (01353) 646600 *Fax:* (01353) 646601
General reference publication listing leading individuals from all fields of interest.

Directory of Members (B)
Published by Booksellers Association of the United Kingdom & Ireland
Minister House, 272 Vauxhall Bridge Rd, London SW1V 1BA
Tel: (020) 7834 5477 *Fax:* (020) 7834 8812
E-mail: mail@booksellers.org.uk
Web Site: www.booksellers.org.uk
L31 plus L5 overseas delivery (47.65 US dollars plus 7.69 overseas delivery)
ISBN(s): 0-907972-837

Directory of Publishing in Scotland (B)
Published by Scottish Publishers Association
Scottish Book Centre, 137 Dundee St, Edinburgh EH11 1BG
Tel: (0131) 2286866 *Fax:* (0131) 2283220
E-mail: info@scottishbooks.co
Web Site: www.scottishbooks.co
Key Personnel
Administrator: Carol Lothian *E-mail:* carol.lothian@scottishbooks.org
Handbook for the Scottish book world, listing Scottish publishers, details of related organizations, the addresses of major Scottish bookshops, & information on support services.
Annually.

Directory of Publishing: United Kingdom, Commonwealth & Overseas (B)
Published by The Continuum International Publishing Group Ltd
The Tower Bldg, 11 York Rd, London SE1 7NX
Tel: (020) 7922 0880 *Fax:* (020) 7922 0881
Web Site: www.continuum-books.com

Directory of UK & Irish Book Publishers including distributors, sales agents & wholesalers (B)
Published by Booksellers Association of the United Kingdom & Ireland
Minister House, 272 Vauxhall Bridge Rd, London SW1V 1BA
Tel: (020) 7834 5477 *Fax:* (020) 7834 8812
E-mail: mail@booksellers.org.uk
Web Site: www.booksellers.org.uk
Full details on over 3000 UK & Irish publishers & their UK distributors, including imprints.
First published 1954.
Annual.
2001: 900 pp, L60 (90.23 US dollars)
ISBN(s): 0-907-972-780

Envoi (P)
44 Rudyard Rd, Biddulph Moor, Staffs ST8 7JN
Tel: (01782) 517892
Published triannually.

ƒ**The Europa World Yearbook** (B)
Published by Europa Publications
11 New Fetter Lane, London EC4P 4EE
Tel: (020) 7822 4300 *Fax:* (020) 7822 4329
E-mail: sales.europa@tandf.co.uk
Web Site: www.europapublications.com
Over 4000 pages of up-to-date statistics & directory information surveying over 250 countries & territories & outlines over 1650 international organizations.
First published 1926.
Annually in two volumes.
43, $895
ISBN(s): 185743-130-8
Parent Company: Taylor & Francis Group

ƒ**European Book World** (B)
Published by Anderson Rand Ltd
Russell Court, Cambridge CB2 1HL
Tel: (01223) 566640 *Fax:* (01223) 566643
E-mail: ar.info@dial.pipex.com
Detailed information on Publishers, Libraries & Booksellers throughout West & Eastern Europe, including former USSR. Details on over 150,000 organizations. Printed & CD-ROM.

Global BookBank (J)
Published by J Whitaker & Sons Ltd
Endeavour House, 189 Shaftesbury Ave, London WC2H 8TJ
Tel: (020) 7420 6006 *Fax:* (020) 7836 6781
CD-ROM containing the combined Whitaker, Bowker & DW Thorpe in-print & forthcoming databases form the most comprehensive listing available of English language books, maps & associated products. There are 2 services: Premium-2 discs for comprehensive searching, Finder-1 disc for fast searching & ordering.

ƒ**Global Publishing** (B)
Published by Euromonitor PLC
60-61 Britton St, London EC1M 5UX
Tel: (020) 7251 8024 *Fax:* (020) 7608 3149
E-mail: info@euromonitor.com
Web Site: www.euromonitor.com
Market research report covering consumer & business books, electronics & print, distributed by retail, institutional, direct mail & mail order in 51 countries.

The Good Book Guide (P)
24 Seward St, London EC1V 3GB
Tel: (020) 7490 9900 *Fax:* (020) 7490 9909
E-mail: enquiries@good-book-guide.co.uk
Monthly book review magazine, subscription only.

Granta (P)
Published by Granta Publications Ltd
2-3 Hanover Yard, Noel Rd, Islington, London N1 8BE
Tel: (020) 7704 9776 *Fax:* (020) 7704 0474

Guide to Literary Prizes (B)
Published by Booktrust
Book House, 45 E Hill, Wandsworth, London SW18 2QZ
Tel: (020) 8516 2977 *Fax:* (020) 8516 2978
E-mail: booktrust@dial.pipex.com

ƒ**The Indexer** (J)
Published by Society of Indexers
Globe Centre, Penistone Rd, Sheffield S6 3AE
Tel: (0171) 4034947
Journal of Australian, American, Canadian & Southern African & British Societies of Indexers.

ƒ**Information Europe** (J)
Published by Beishon Publications Ltd
15 Micawber St, London N1 7TB
Tel: (020) 7336 6650 *Fax:* (020) 7336 6640
E-mail: beishon@ibm.net

ƒ**Information Research Watch International (IRWI)** (J)
Formerly Current Research in Library & Information Science (CRLIS)
Published by CSA (Cambridge Scientific Abstracts)
Windsor Court, East Grinstead House, East Grinstead, West Sussex RH19 1XA
Tel: (01342) 336159 *Fax:* (01342) 336197
E-mail: service@csa.com; tjones@csa.com (sales); support@csa.com (technical support); eurosupport@csa.com (support in Europe)

UNITED KINGDOM

Web Site: www.csa.com
Key Personnel
Editor: Mrs Pirkko Elliott *E-mail:* pirkko@dial.piper.com
Newsletter providing brief reports of research in library & information science, electronic publishing & use of the internet, & related fields such as publishing, museums, archives, records management, & information industry. Also includes an editorial & two articles per issue on aspects of research in library & information science..
First published 1980.
Bimonthly.
24 pp, Annual subscription includes access to a web database. Europe L350, $1535, other nations L360
ISSN: 1470-1391
Parent Company: Cambridge Information Group

⌀International Information & Library Review (J)
Published by Academic Press Ltd
24-28 Oval Rd, London NW1 7DX
Tel: (020) 7267 4466 *Fax:* (020) 7482 2293
Published quarterly.

⌀International Organizations Series (B)
Published by ABC-CLIO
35A Great Clarendon St, Oxford OX2 6AT
Tel: (01865) 311350 *Fax:* (01865) 311358
E-mail: oxford@abc-clio.ltd.uk
Web Site: www.abc-clio.com
Available in North America from Transaction Books.

⌀International Printing Sourcebook (B)
Published by Pira International
Randalls Rd, Leatherhead, Surrey KT22 7RU
Tel: (01372) 802080 *Fax:* (01372) 802079
E-mail: publications@pira.co.uk
Web Site: www.piranet.com
Covers pulp & paper, packaging, publishing & printing.

ISBN Listing - On Microfiche (J)
Published by J Whitaker & Sons Ltd
Endeavour House, 189 Shaftesbury Ave, London WC2H 8TJ
Tel: (020) 7420 6006 *Fax:* (020) 7836 6781
Web Site: www.whitaker.co.uk
Listing in ISBN sequence of over 1,500,000 titles on the Whitaker database. Includes 850,000 out-of-print titles.

⌀The Journal of Commonwealth Literature (J)
Published by CSA (Cambridge Scientific Abstracts)
Windsor Court, East Grinstead House, East Grinstead, West Sussex RH19 1XA
Tel: (01342) 326972 *Fax:* (01342) 336198
E-mail: service@csa.com
Web Site: www.csa.com
Key Personnel
Editor: John Thieme; Geraldine Stoneham
Critical & bibliographical forum in the field of Commonwealth writing. Published triannually, the first two issues contain critical comment on all aspects of Commonwealth & related literatures. The third issue contains a comprehensive bibliography of publications in the field.
3x/yr.
L115
ISSN: 0021-9894
Parent Company: Cambridge Information Group

Learned Publishing (J)
Published by Association of Learned & Professional Society Publishers
South House, The Street, Clapham, Worthing, West Sussex BN13 3UU
Tel: (01903) 871686 *Fax:* (01903) 871457
Web Site: www.alpsp.org.uk
Key Personnel
Editor: Michele Beujaunin
Secretary General: Sally Morris
Quarterly.
80 pp
ISSN: 0953-1513

⌀Library Association Record (J)
Published by Facet Publishing
7 Ridgmount St, London WC1E 7AE
Tel: (020) 7255 0594 *Fax:* (020) 7255 0591
E-mail: record@la-hq.org.uk
Web Site: www.fdgroup.co.uk
The news magazine of *The Library Association*, sent to all members & available on subscription to non-members. Also accompanied, 5 times per year, by Library Technology.
Monthly.

Literary Review (P)
Published by Namara Group
44 Lexington St, London W1R 3LW
Tel: (020) 7437 9392 *Fax:* (020) 7734 1844
E-mail: litrev@dircon.co.uk
Web Site: www.litreview.com
Monthly reviews of the best newly published fiction & non-fiction.
First published 1979.
Monthly.
64 pp, L3 (Sterling); $7 USD per issue
ISSN: 0144-4360

⌀LOGOS (J)
Published by Whurr Publishers Ltd
19b Compton Terrace, London N1 2UN
Tel: (020) 7359 5979 *Fax:* (020) 7226 5290
E-mail: info@whurr.co.uk
Web Site: www.whurr.co.uk

London Review of Books (P)
Published by LRB Ltd
28 Little Russell St, London WC1A 2HN
Tel: (020) 7209 1141 *Toll Free Tel:* (800) 258-2066 *Fax:* (020) 7209 1151
E-mail: edit@lrb.co.uk
Web Site: www.lrb.co.uk
Key Personnel
Editor: Mary-Kay Wilmers
Bimonthly.
L2.95 (3.95 US dollar)
ISSN: 0260-9592

New Books in German (J)
Published by Society of Authors
c/o Goethe Institut, 50 Princes Gate, Exhibition Rd, London SW7 2PH
Tel: (020) 7596 4023 *Fax:* (020) 7594 0245
E-mail: nbg@london.goethe.org
Web Site: www.new-books-in-german.com
Key Personnel
Editor: Astrid Kurth *E-mail:* aekurth@web.de
Reviews German language literature (Swiss, Austrian & German) in English to promote sales into the British & US markets.
Semi-annual.

⌀New Review of Academic Librarianship (J)
Published by Taylor Graham Publishing
48 Regent St, Cambridge CB2 1FD
Web Site: www.taylorgraham.com
First published 1995.
Annual.
ISSN: 1361-4533
Branch Office(s)
PMB 187, 12021 Wilshire Blvd, Los Angeles, CA 90025, United States

⌀New Review of Children's Literature & Librarianship (J)
Published by Taylor Graham Publishing
48 Regent St, Cambridge CB2 1FD
Web Site: www.taylorgraham.com
First published 1995.
Annual.
ISSN: 1361-4541
Branch Office(s)
PMB 187, 12021 Wilshire Blvd, Los Angeles, CA 90025, United States

⌀New Review of Hypermedia & Multimedia (J)
Published by Taylor Graham Publishing
48 Regent St, Cambridge CB2 1FD
Web Site: www.taylorgraham.com
First published 1995.
Annual.
ISSN: 1361-4568
Branch Office(s)
PMB 187, 12021 Wilshire Blvd, Los Angeles, CA 90025, United States

⌀New Review of Information & Library Research (J)
Published by Taylor Graham Publishing
48 Regent St, Cambridge CB2 1FD
Web Site: www.taylorgraham.com
First published 1995.
Annual.
ISSN: 1361-455X

⌀New Review of Information Networking (J)
Published by Taylor Graham Publishing
48 Regent St, Cambridge CB2 1FD
Web Site: www.taylorgraham.com
First published 1995.
Annual.
ISSN: 1361-4576
Branch Office(s)
PMB 187, 12021 Wilshire Blvd, Los Angeles, CA 90025, United States

100 Best Books 1999 (B)
Published by BookTrust
Book House, 45 East Hill, Wandsworth, London SW18 2QZ
Tel: (020) 8516 2984 *Fax:* (020) 8516 2978
Key Personnel
Contact: Ann Newton
Young Book Trust selection of paperbacks for children 12 & under.

OP Title Listing - On Microfiche (B)
Published by J Whitaker & Sons Ltd
Endeavour House, 189 Shaftesbury Ave, London WC2H 8TJ
Tel: (020) 7420 6006 *Fax:* (020) 7836 6781
Listing of 900,000 out of print titles.

Orbis (P)
27 Valley View, Primrose, Jarrow Tyne & Wear, Warwicks NE32 5QT
Tel: (0191) 4897055 *Fax:* (0191) 4897055; (0191) 4301297
Independent British literary quarterly with international connections; publishes mainly poetry, but uses some prose & letters; also features news, educational & review columns.

Outlets for Specialist New Books in the UK: A Subject Classified, Descriptive Directory (B)
Published by Peter Marcan Publications
PO Box 3158, London SE1 4RA
Tel: (020) 7357 0368
Entries on some 800 businesses of many kinds (including museum/art gallery shops, periodicals & associations, as well as related directories).

Outposts Poetry Quarterly (P)
Published by Hippopotamus Press

22, Whitewell Rd, Frome, Frome, Somerset BA11 4EL
Tel: (01373) 466653 *Fax:* (01373) 466653
Key Personnel
Editor: Roland John
New poetry, translations, essays & reviews.

ɸPartners in African Publishing (J)
Published by CODE - Europe
The Jam Factory, 27 Park End St, Oxford OX1 1HU
Tel: (01865) 202438 *Fax:* (01865) 2024390

ɸPEN International (J)
Published by International PEN
9-10 Charterhouse Bldgs, Goswell Rd, London EC1M 7AT
Tel: (020) 7253 4308 *Fax:* (020) 7253 5711
E-mail: intpen@dircon.co.uk
Web Site: www.internatpen.org
Published in English & French & issued with the assistance of UNESCO.
First published 1981.
Semiannual.
100 pp
ISSN: 1010-4534

Phillip's International Paper Directory (B)
Published by CMP Data & Information Services
Division of CMP Information Ltd
Riverbank House, Angel Lane, Tonbridge, Kent TN9 1SE
Tel: (01732) 377591 *Fax:* (01732) 377479
E-mail: orders@cmpinformation.com
Web Site: www.cmpdata.co.uk
Key Personnel
Commerical Dir: Duncan Clark
First published 1904.
Annual.
752 pp, L150
ISBN(s): 0-86382-488-9
ISSN: 0954-8521

Planet - The Welsh Internationalist (P)
Published by Berw Cyf
PO Box 44, Aberystwyth, Ceredigion SY23 3ZZ
Tel: (01970) 611255 *Fax:* (01970) 611197
E-mail: planet.enquiries@planetmagazine.org.uk
Web Site: www.planetmagazine.org.uk
Key Personnel
Editor: John Barnie
Associate Editor: Helle Michelsen; Owain Wilkins
First published 1970.
6 times/yr.
128 pp
ISSN: 0048-4288

PN Review (P)
Published by Carcanet Press Ltd
Fourth Floor, Conavon Court, 12-16 Blackfriars St, Manchester M3 5BQ
Tel: (0161) 834 8730 *Fax:* (0161) 832 0084
E-mail: pnr@carcanet.u-net.com
Key Personnel
Editorial & Man Dir: Michael Schmidt
Features poetry & literary criticism.
Bimonthly.

Poetry Now (P)
Published by Forward Press Ltd
Remus House, Coltsfoot Drive, Woodston, Peterborough PE2 7BU
Tel: (01733) 890099 *Fax:* (01733) 230751
Quarterly.
$15/year
Parent Company: Forward Press Ltd

Poetry Review (P)
Published by The Poetry Society Inc
22 Betterton St, London WC2H 9BX
Tel: (020) 7420 9883 *Fax:* (020) 7240 4818
E-mail: poetryreview@poetrysociety.org.uk
Poetry & reviews.
Quarterly.

PR Planner Europe (J)
Published by Media Information Ltd
Chess House, 34 German St, Chesham, Bucks HP5 1SJ
Tel: (0870) 7360016 (UK); (1494) 797260 (Int) *Fax:* (0870) 7360011 (UK); (1494) 797224
E-mail: prplanner@mediainfo.co.uk
Key Personnel
Marketing Manager: Wendy Thompson
Press Directory.
Quarterly.
Parent Company: The Observer Group

Printing Trades Directory (B)
Published by CMP Data & Information Services
Riverbank House, Angel Lane, Tonbridge, Kent TN9 1SE
Tel: (01732) 377591 *Fax:* (01732) 377479
E-mail: orders@cmpinformation.com
Web Site: www.cmpdata.co.uk
Key Personnel
Commercial Dir: Duncan Clark *Tel:* (01732) 377423 *Fax:* (01732) 368324
Editor: Philip Dury *Tel:* (01732) 377542 *Fax:* (01732) 377483
Marketing Manager: Alison Prangnell *Tel:* (01732) 377627 *Fax:* (01732) 368324 *E-mail:* aprangnell@cmpinformation.com
Comprehensive directory on the UK print industry. Used by manufacturers, printers & print buyers.
First published 1960.
42nd, L115
ISBN(s): 0-86382-512-5
ISSN: 0079-5372

Printing World (J)
Published by United Business Media International plc
Sovereign House, Sovereign Way, Tonbridge, Kent TN9 1RW
Tel: (01732) 377507 *Fax:* (01732) 377316
E-mail: nwhichelow@ubminteratiara.com
Web Site: www.dotprint.com
Key Personnel
Editor: Tony Brown *E-mail:* abrown@ubminternational.com
Publisher: Andy Jordan *E-mail:* ajordan@ubminternatinal.com
Marketing Manager: Nicky Whichelow *E-mail:* nwhichelow@ubminternational.com
Weekly.
$2.75, Annual Subscription $142 US

ɸPrivate Press Books (B)
Published by Private Libraries Association (PLA)
Ravelston, South View Rd, Pinner, Middlesex HA5 3YD
Key Personnel
Executive Secretary: James Brown
Editor, Private Press Books: Paul W Nash
Annual bibliography of the work of private presses throughout the world.

ɸThe Rialto (P)
PO Box 309, Aylsham, Norwich, Norfolk NR11 6LN
Web Site: www.therialto.co.uk
Key Personnel
Editor: Michael Mackmin
Poety magazine.
First published 1984.
3 times per year.
56 pp, L18 sterling only, annual subscription
ISSN: 0268-5981

The School Librarian (P)
Published by School Library Association
Liden Library, Barrington Close, Liden, Swindon, Wilts SN3 6HF
Tel: (01793) 791787 *Fax:* (01793) 537374
E-mail: info@sla.org.uk
Web Site: www.eduweb.co.uk
Key Personnel
Editor: Raymond Astbury

ɸSerials In The British Library (J)
Published by The British Library National Bibliographic Service
Boston Spa, Wetherby, W Yorks LS23 7BQ
Tel: (01937) 546585 *Fax:* (01937) 546586
E-mail: nbs-info@bl.uk
Web Site: www.bl.uk
List all new serial titles acquired by the British Library reference departments & all UK serials received through legal deport. Coverage is worldwide & all subject areas.
Three printed issues, annual cumulation.

ɸSheppard's Book Dealers in Europe (B)
Published by Richard Joseph Publishers Ltd
PO Box 6123, Basingstoke, Hants RG25 2WE
Tel: (01256) 811314 *Fax:* (01256) 336362
E-mail: rjoe01@aol.com
Web Site: www.sheppardsdirectories.co.uk
Antiquarian & second hand book dealers.
First published 1967.
L27; US $54

Sheppard's Book Dealers in The British Isles (B)
Published by Richard Joseph Publishers Ltd
PO Box 6123, Basingstoke, Hants RG25 2WE
Tel: (01256) 811314 *Fax:* (01256) 336362
E-mail: rjoe01@aol.com
Web Site: www.sheppardsdirectories.co.uk
Antiquarian & second hand book dealers.
Annual.
L30; US $60

ɸSheppard's Dealers in Collectables (B)
Published by Richard Joseph Publishers Ltd
Unit 2, Monk Walk, Room 10, Farnham, Surrey GU9 8HT
Tel: (01256) 811314 *Fax:* (01256) 336362
E-mail: rjoe01@aol.com
Web Site: www.sheppardsdirectories.co.uk
Key Personnel
Editor: Miss A Lake
Dealers of new & old collectables.
L18; US $36

ɸSheppard's International Directory of Ephemera Dealers (B)
Published by Richard Joseph Publishers Ltd
PO Box 6123, Basingstoke, Hants RG25 2WE
Tel: (01256) 811314 *Fax:* (01256) 336362
E-mail: rjoe01@aol.com
Web Site: www.sheppardsdirectories.co.uk
Dealers of Ephemera.
First published 1994.
Every 6 years.
300 pp, L27; US $56

ɸSheppard's International Directory of Print & Map Sellers (B)
Published by Richard Joseph Publishers Ltd
PO Box 6123, Basingstoke, Hants RG25 2WE
Tel: (01256) 811314 *Fax:* (01256) 336362
E-mail: rjoe01@aol.com
Web Site: www.sheppardsdirectories.co.uk
Antiquarian & second hand print & map sellers.
4th, L27; US $54

Signal (P)
Published by Thimble Press

Lockwood, Station Rd, South Woodchester, Stroud, Glos GL5 5EQ
Tel: (01453) 755566 *Fax:* (01453) 878599
Approaches to children's books.
Triannually.

ƒ**Slavonica** (J)
Published by University of Manchester/Sheffield Academic Press
Department of Russian Studies, University of Manchester, Arts Bldg, Oxford Rd, Manchester M13 9PL
Tel: (0161) 2753138 *Fax:* (0161) 2753031
Web Site: www.art.man.ac.uk/russian/slavonic.htm
Key Personnel
Editor: Jakaterina Young *E-mail:* katya.young@man.ac.uk
Academic Publication.
First published 1983.
Biennially.
120 pp
ISSN: 1361-7427
Ultimate Parent Company: Continuum

Stand Magazine (P)
179 Wingrove Rd, Newcastle-upon-Tyne NE4 9DA
Tel: (0191) 2733280 *Fax:* (0191) 2733280
Literary magazine published quarterly.

Swedish Book Review (P)
Published by Swedish-English Literary Translators Association
Bronygaer, Llanybydder SA40 95A
Tel: (01570) 480373; (01570) 424751 (Subscriptions) *Fax:* (01570) 481281; (01570) 421091 (Subscriptions)
E-mail: sbr@lillsverige.demon.co.uk
Web Site: www.swedishbookreview.com
Key Personnel
Editor: Mr L Thompson
Half yearly translators review, in English, of works written in Swedish, originating from Sweden or Swedish writers in Finland, with translations into English.
First published 1983.
Biennially.
L15; US $25; SEK 200
ISSN: 0265-8119

The Times Literary Supplement (P)
Published by The Times Supplements Ltd
Admiral House, 66-68 East Smithfield, London E1 9XY
Tel: (020) 7782 3000 *Fax:* (020) 7782 3100
Web Site: www.nytimes.com
Weekly.

UK Book Printers (B)
Published by Book Production Section BPIF
British Printing Industries Federation, 11 Bedford Row, London WC1R 4DX
Tel: (020) 7915 8300 *Fax:* (020) 7405 7784
E-mail: info@bpif.org.uk
Web Site: www.bpif.org.uk
Key Personnel
Editor: Leigh Martins
Biannually.

UK Periodical Printers (B)
Published by Periodical Printers Section BPIF
British Printing Industries Federation, 11 Bedford Row, London WC1R 4DX
Tel: (020) 7915 8300 *Fax:* (020) 7405 7784
E-mail: info@bpif.org.uk
Web Site: www.bpif.org.uk
Key Personnel
Editor: Leigh Martins
Yearbook.

ƒ**UKBookWorld 2002 CD-ROM** (B)
Published by Clique Ltd
7 Pulleyn Dr, York Y024 1DY
Tel: (01904) 631752 *Fax:* (01904) 651325
E-mail: cole@clique.co.uk
Web Site: www.clique.co.uk
Price guide/reference 850,000+ books (second-hand/rare/out of print) on CD. Published annually in April.

Vigil (P)
Published by Vigil Publications
12 Priory Mead, Bruton, Somerset BA10 0DZ
Tel: (01749) 813349
Poetry & Prose with the accent on developments in form & structure applied to contemporary themes.

Walford's Guide to Reference Material (B)
Published by Facet Publishing
7 Ridgmount St, London WC1E 7AE
Tel: (020) 7255 0590 *Fax:* (020) 7255 0591
E-mail: info@facetpublishing.co.uk
Web Site: www.facetpublishing.co.uk
Key Personnel
Production Manager: Kathryn Beecroft *Tel:* (020) 7255 0595 *E-mail:* k.beecroft@facetpublishing.co.uk
First published 1959.
Annually.
8th edition, 3 volumes

Whitaker ROM (J)
Published by J Whitaker & Sons Ltd
Endeavour House, 189 Shaftesbury Ave, London WC2H 8TJ
Tel: (020) 7420 6006 *Fax:* (020) 7836 6781
TFPL Internation CD-ROM Directory containing information on over 10,000 CD-ROMs & multimedia titles. Updated semi-annually.

Whitaker's Almanack (B)
Published by The Stationery Office
The Publications Centre, 51 Nine Elms Lane, London SW8 5DR
Mailing Address: PO Box 276, London SW8 4DT
Tel: (020) 7600 5522 *Fax:* (020) 7873 8200 (orders)
E-mail: whitakers.almanack@theso.co.uk
Web Site: www.tsonline.co.uk
General reference book including information on British government.
First published 1868.
Annual.
1200 pp, $40
ISBN(s): 0117022799

ƒ**Whitaker's Books In Print: The Reference Catalog of Current Literature** (B)
Published by J Whitaker & Sons Ltd
Endeavour House, 189 Shaftesbury Ave, London WC2H 8TJ
Tel: (020) 7420 6006 *Fax:* (020) 7379 5469
E-mail: sales@whitaker.co.uk
Web Site: www.whitaker.co.uk
Listing (in English) of books published or on sale in the UK & Western Europe plus a directory of 30,000 publishers in five volumes.
Annually.

Whitaker's Directory of Publishers (B)
Published by J Whitaker & Sons Ltd
Endeavour House, 189 Shaftesbury Ave, London WC2H 8TJ
Tel: (020) 7420 6006 *Fax:* (020) 7836 6781
Lists over 8000 most active publishers in the UK.

ƒ**Who's Who in Asia & The Pacific Nations** (B)
Published by Melrose Press Ltd
St Thomas Pl, Ely, Cambs CB7 4GG
Tel: (01353) 646600 *Fax:* (01353) 646601
E-mail: info@melrosepress.co.uk
Web Site: www.melrosepress.co.uk
Career profiles of leading achievers from this increasingly influential region.
First published 1989.
4th: 523 pp, L95.00 GBP
ISBN(s): 0-948875-631

ƒ**Willing's Press Guide** (J)
Published by Media Information Ltd
Affiliate of Romeike Media Intelligence
Chess House, 34 Germain St, Chesham, Bucks HP5 1SJ
Tel: (0870) 7360015 (UK); (014) 94 797300 (Int) *Fax:* (0870) 7360011 (UK); (014) 94 797224 (Int)
E-mail: willings@mediainfo.co.uk
Web Site: www.willingspressguide.com
Key Personnel
Sales Consultant: Michelle Frick
Award winning Willings Press Guide is firmly established as the most accurate, comprehensive & up to date media guide currently available.
Annually.
L170-Vol 1 (UK); L170-Vol 2 (International); L225-Vol 1&2; L275-CD-ROM; L275-Online

ƒ**World Bibliographical Series** (B)
Published by ABC-CLIO
35A Great Clarendon St, Oxford OX2 6AT
Tel: (01865) 311350 *Fax:* (01865) 311358
E-mail: oxford@abc-clio.ltd.uk
Web Site: www.abc-clio.com

ƒ**The World Book Report 1999** (J)
Published by Euromonitor
60-61 Britton St, London EC1M 5NA
Tel: (020) 7251 1105 *Fax:* (020) 7608 3149
Analysis of the book market worldwide.

ƒ**The World of Learning** (B)
Published by Europa Publications
11 New Fetter Lane, London EC4P 4EE
Tel: (020) 7822 4300 *Fax:* (020) 7822 4329
E-mail: info.europa@tandf.co.uk
Web Site: www.europapublications.co.uk; www.europapublications.com
Directory lists over 26,000 academic institutions world-wide together with more than 150,000 staff & officials.
Annually.
Parent Company: Taylor & Francis

ƒ**World Photographers Reference Series** (B)
Published by ABC-CLIO
35A Great Clarendon St, Oxford OX2 6AT
Tel: (01865) 311350 *Fax:* (01865) 311358
E-mail: oxford@abc-clio.ltd.uk
Web Site: www.abc-clio.com
Available in North America from: G K Hall.

ƒ**Writers' & Artists' Yearbook** (B)
Published by A & C Black Publishers Ltd
37 Soho Sq, London W1D 3QZ
Tel: (020) 7287 5338 *Fax:* (020) 7734 6856
E-mail: wayb@acblack.com
Key Personnel
Editorial: Christine Robinson
Annually in September.
Parent Company: Bloomsbury Publishing PLC

Writers' Circles Handbook (B)
Published by Jill Dick
Oldacre, Horderns Park Rd, Chapel-en-le Frith, High Peak SK23 9SY
Tel: (01298) 812305
Web Site: www.cix.co.uk/~oldacre/index.htm; www.btinternet.com

Key Personnel
Editor: Jill Dick *E-mail:* jillie@cix.co.uk
L5 post free

Writers News (P)
PO Box 4, Nairn IV12 4HU
Tel: (01667) 454441 *Fax:* (01667) 454401
Information on Markets, Competitions, Short Story Competitions, How-To Articles, for both the established & aspiring writer.

United States

ƒ**American Libraries Magazine** (J)
Published by American Library Association (ALA)
50 E Huron St, Chicago, IL 60611
Tel: 312-440-0901 *Fax:* 312-280-3256
E-mail: americanlibraries@ala.org
Web Site: www.ala.org/alonline

ƒ**Book Review Index** (B)
Published by The Gale Group
27500 Drake Rd, Farmington Hills, MI 48331-3535
Tel: 248-699-4253 *Fax:* (248) 699-8061
E-mail: galeord@gale.com
Web Site: www.gale.com
Telex: (313) 961-6637
Includes listings from outside the US and Canada.

ƒ**Booklist & Reference Books Bulletin** (J)
Published by American Library Association (ALA)
50 E Huron St, Chicago, IL 60611
Tel: 312-944-6780 *Fax:* 312-944-7841
E-mail: bsegedin@ala.org
Web Site: www.ala.org/booklist

ƒ**Bookman's Price Index** (B)
Published by The Gale Group
27500 Drake Rd, Farmington Hills, MI 48331-3535
Tel: 248-699-4253 *Toll Free Tel:* 800- 877-4253
Fax: (248) 699-8061
E-mail: galeord@gale.com
Web Site: www.gale.com

ƒ**Choice Magazine** (J)
Published by American Library Association (ALA)
50 E Huron St, Chicago, IL 60611
Tel: 312-944-6780 *Fax:* 312-944-7841
Web Site: www.ala.org/acrl/choice/home.html

ƒ**Contemporary Authors** (B)
Published by The Gale Group
27500 Drake Rd, Farmington Hills, MI 48331-3535
Tel: 248-699-4253 *Toll Free Tel:* 800- 877-4253
Fax: (248) 699-8061
E-mail: galeord@gale.com
Web Site: www.gale.com
Includes listings also from outside the US & Canada. There are three separate publications under this title: Regular Series, New Revisions & Autobiographies.

ƒ**Directory of Special Libraries and Information Centers** (B)
Published by The Gale Group
27500 Drake Rd, Farmington Hills, MI 48331-3535
Tel: 248-699-4253 *Toll Free Tel:* 800- 877-4253
Fax: 248-699-8061
E-mail: galeord@gale.com

Web Site: www.gale.com
US, Canada & International.

ƒ**Guide to Reference Books** (B)
Published by American Library Association (ALA)
50 E Huron St, Chicago, IL 60611
Tel: 312-944-6780 *Toll Free Tel:* 800-545-2433
Fax: 312-440-9374

The Historical Novels Review (J)
Published by Historical Novel Society
824 Heritage Dr, Addison, IL 60101
Mailing Address: Booth Library, Eastern Illinois University, 600 Lincoln Ave, Charleston, IL 61920
Tel: 217-581-7538 *Fax:* 217-581-7534
E-mail: cfsinc@eiu.edu (editorial); hns@lensman.org (subscription)
Web Site: www.historicalnovelsociety.org
Key Personnel
Coordinating Ed (US): Sarah Nesbeitt
  E-mail: cfsln@eiu.edu
Coordinating Ed (UK): Sally Zigmond
  E-mail: sallyzigmond@hotmail.com
US Membership Sec: Tracey Callison
  E-mail: hns@lensman.org
Reviews of currently published historical fiction from the US and Great Britain.
First published 1997.
Quarterly.
54 pp, $38 airmail, $30 surface, available with membership only
ISSN: 1471-7492

ƒ**Inter-American Review of Bibliography (Revista Interamericana de Bibliografia)** (J)
Published by Organization of American States, Department of Publications
1889 F St NW, Washington, DC 20006-4499
Tel: 202-458-3000 *Fax:* 202-458-3534

ƒ**International Directory of Children's Literature** (B)
Published by George Kurian Reference Books
PO Box 519, Baldwin Place, NY, NY 10505
Tel: 914-962-3287 *Fax:* 914-962-3287
Key Personnel
Editor: George Kurian
Reference Book Publisher.
First published 1974.
Quarterly.
5th: 128 pp
ISBN(s): 0-8160-1411-6

International Literary Market Place (B)
Published by Information Today, Inc
630 Central Ave, New Providence, NJ 07974
Tel: 908-286-1090 *Fax:* 908-219-0192
E-mail: custserv@infotoday.com
Web Site: www.literarymarketplace.com
Directory of companies & individuals in the book publishing trade, covering 180 countries outside the US & Canada. Entries included for more than 10,000 publishers & 4300 book organizations, including agents, booksellers & library associations. The US & Canada are covered by Literary Market Place.
Annually.
36th: 1730 pp, $219.00 US dollars
ISBN(s): 1-57387-144-3
ISSN: 0074-6827

Literary Market Place (B)
Published by Information Today, Inc
630 Central Ave, New Providence, NJ 07974
Tel: 908-286-1090 *Fax:* 908-219-0192
E-mail: custserv@infotoday.com
Web Site: www.literarymarketplace.com
Directory of over 40,000 companies & individuals US & Canadian publishing. A two volume set, each containing two alphabetical names & numbers indexes, one for key companies listed & one for individuals. The rest of the world is covered by International Literary Market Place.
Annually.
62nd: 2149 pp, $299.00 US dollars
ISBN(s): 1-57387-132-X
ISSN: 0000-1155

ƒ**Review - Latin American Literature & Arts** (J)
Published by Americas Society
680 Park Ave, 4th Floor, New York, NY 10021
Tel: 212-249-8950 *Fax:* 212-249-5868
E-mail: dshapiro@as-coa.org
Web Site: www.americas-society.org
Contemporary Latin American literature in English translation.
Bienially; May & November.

ƒ**Scandinavian Review** (J)
Published by American-Scandinavian Foundation
58 Park Ave, New York, NY 10016
Tel: 212-879-9779 *Fax:* 212-879-2301; 212-249-3444
E-mail: asf@amscan.org
Web Site: www.amscan.org
Key Personnel
Editor: Adrienne Gyongy *E-mail:* agyongy@amscan.org
Cultural/literary/political magazine.
Triannually.

Solander
Published by Historical Novel Society
824 Heritage Dr, Addison, IL 60101
Mailing Address: 7 Ticehurst Close, Worth, Crawley, West Sussex RH10 7GN, United Kingdom
Tel: 217-581-7538 *Fax:* 217-581-7534
Web Site: www.historicalnovelsociety.org
Key Personnel
Editor: Sarah Cuthbertson
  E-mail: sarah76cuthbert@aol.com
Fiction Editor: Richard Lee *E-mail:* histnovel@aol.com
US Membership Sec: Tracey Callison
  E-mail: hns@lensman.org
Literary magazine for historical fiction, with articles, interviews & short fiction.
First published 1997.
Semi-annually.
38 pp, $38 airmail; $30 surface, available with membership only
ISSN: 1471-7484

Ulrich's International Periodicals Directory,
see Ulrich's Periodicals Directory

ƒ**Ulrich's Periodicals Directory** (B)
Published by R R Bowker LLC
Subsidiary of Cambridge Information Group Inc
630 Central Ave, New Providence, NJ 07974
Tel: 908-219-0199 *Toll Free Tel:* 800-521-8110
Fax: 908-219-0812
E-mail: ulrichs@bowker.com
Web Site: www.bowker.com; www.ulrichsweb.com
Key Personnel
Dir, Serials: Edgar Adcock
Dir, Sales: Serge Sarkis
Five volume set, arranged by subject classification, includes periodicals, newsletters, newspapers, annuals & irregular serials published worldwide. Also available on the Internet, CD-ROM, online & magnetic tape.
First published 1932.
Annual.
41st, 2003: 12000 pp, $699.00
ISBN(s): 0-8352-4503-9
ISSN: 0000-2100

ZIMBABWE

ɟUnited Nations Publications (B)
United Nations Plaza, Sales Section, Rm DC2-853, New York, NY 10017
Tel: 212-963-8302 *Toll Free Tel:* 800-253-9646
Fax: 212-963-3489
E-mail: publications@un.org
Web Site: www.un.org/publications

ɟThe Writers Directory (B)
Published by St James Press
27500 Drake Rd, Farmington Hills, MI 48331-3535
Tel: 248-699-4253 *Toll Free Tel:* 800-877-4253
Fax: 248-699-8061
E-mail: galeord@gale.com
Web Site: www.gale.com
Key Personnel
Editor: Miranda Serrara
Published biennially.

Uruguay

Anuario bibliografico Uruguayo 1968-
(Uruguayan Bibliographical Annual 1968-) (B)
Published by Biblioteca Nacional del Uruguay
Av 18 de Julio 1790, Casilla de Correo 452, Montevideo
Tel: (02) 485030; (02) 402-08-12 *Fax:* (02) 496902; (02) 401-67-16
Supplement published annually.
400 pp

Venezuela

Bibliografia Venezolana (Venezuelan Bibliography) (B)
Published by Instituto Autonomo, Biblioteca Nacional y de Servicios de Bibliotecas
Apdo 80593, Prados del Este, Caracas 1080A
Tel: (02) 938535; (02) 9418011 (ext 213-227)
Fax: (02) 9415219
Telex: 24621 VC

Viet Nam

Thu' muc quoc gia Vietnam (J)
Published by National Library of Vietnam
31 Trang Thi, 10000 Hanoi
Tel: (04) 8252643
National Bibliography. Monthly, with annual cumulation.

Van Hoc (P)
Published by Van Hoc Publishing House
49 Tran Hung Dao St, Hanoi
Tel: (04) 4252570

Yugoslavia

Bagdala (P)
Published by Izdavacko preduzece
Zakiceva 5-7, 37000 Krusevac
Tel: (037) 39209
Literature, art and culture; text in Serbo-Croation.

Bibliografija Domacih i stranih knjiga (Review of Domestic & Foreign Books & Articles) (P)
Published by Centar za Vojnonaucnu Dokumentaciju i Informacije
Baolkanska 53/a, 11000 Belgrade
Tel: (011) 656122; (011) 22575; (011) 2358710

Bibliografija Jugoslavije (Bibliography of Yugoslavia) (J)
Published by Jugoslovenski Bibliografsko-Informacijski Institut (Yubin)
Terazije 26, 11000 Belgrade
Tel: (011) 687836 *Fax:* (011) 687760
E-mail: yubin@jbi.bg.ac.yu
Web Site: www.jbi.bg.ac.yu
Key Personnel
Dir General: Radomir Glavicki, PhD
The National Bibliography of Yugoslavia/Production.
First published 1950.
Bi-monthly.
100 pp
ISSN: 0523-2201

Catalogue of Books Published by Yugoslav Publishers (B)
Published by Association of Yugoslav Publishers & Booksellers
Kneza Milosa 25/1, 11000 Belgrade
Tel: (011) 642248; (011) 642533 *Fax:* (011) 646339
Key Personnel
General Dir: Mr Ognjen Lakecevic
E-mail: ognjenl@eunet.yu

Directory of Members (B)
Published by Association of Yugoslav Publishers & Booksellers
Kneza Milosa 25/1, 11000 Belgrade
Mailing Address: PO Box 570, 11000 Belgrade
Tel: (011) 642248; (011) 642533 *Fax:* (011) 646339
Key Personnel
General Dir: Mr Ognjen Lakecevic
E-mail: ognjenl@eunet.yu
Directory of Yugoslav Publishers & Booksellers.

Katalog Medunarodnog Sajma Knjiga u Beogradu (Catalogue of the International Book Fair in Belgrade) (B)
Published by Association of Yugoslav Publishers & Booksellers
Kneza Milosa 25/1, 11000 Belgrade
Tel: (011) 642248; (011) 642533 *Fax:* (011) 646339
Key Personnel
General Dir: Mr Ognjen Lakecevic
E-mail: ognjenl@eunet.yu

Knjizevne Novine (Literary News) (P)
pf 23, Gospodar Jovanova 5, 11000 Belgrade
Tel: (011) 637-518; (011) 638-159; (011) 639-631
Fax: (011) 637-518; (011) 638-168
Key Personnel
Editor: Dragan M Jeremic

Lumina (P)
Published by Libertatea
Zarka Zrenjanina 7, 26000 Pancevo
Tel: (013) 33-51; (013) 46-447 *Fax:* (013) 46-447
Key Personnel
Editor: Ion Balan
Literary and cultural review.

Savremenik (P)
Published by Knjizevne Novine
pf 23, Gospodar Jovanova 5, 11000 Belgrade
Tel: (011) 637-518; (011) 638-159; (011) 639-631
Fax: (011) 637-518; (011) 638-168
Text in Serbo-Croation.
Monthly.

Zambia

National Bibliography of Zambia (B)
Published by National Archives of Zambia
PO Box RW 50010, Lusaka
Tel: (01) 254080; (01) 254081

Zimbabwe

ɟAfrican Publishing Review (J)
Published by African Publishers' Network (AP-NET)
18 Van Praagh Ave, Milton Park, Harare
Mailing Address: PO Box 3773, Harare
Tel: (04) 708413; (04) 708418; (04) 708405
Fax: (04) 708413
E-mail: apnet@mango.zw; apnet@apnet.co.zw
Web Site: www.africanpublishers.org
Newsletter.
Bimonthly.

Zimbabwe National Bibliography (B)
Published by National Archives of Zimbabwe
PB 7729, Causeway, Harare
Tel: (04) 792741 *Fax:* (04) 792398

Literary Associations & Prizes

Literary Associations & Societies

Listed in this section are literary associations and societies. Listings appear alphabetically under the country in which they are located. Other book trade associations and organizations can be found in the sections **Book Trade Organizations** and **Library Associations**.

Argentina

Academia Argentina de Letras (Bulletin of the Argentine Academy of Literature)
Sanchez de Bustamante 2663, C1425DVA Buenos Aires
Tel: (011) 4-8023814; (011) 4-8025161; (011) 4-8027509 *Fax:* (011) 4-8028340
E-mail: aaldespa@fibertel.com.ar; aaladmin@fibertel.com.ar; aalbibl@fibertel.com.ar
Key Personnel
President: Pedro Luis Barcia
General Secretary: Rodolfo Modern
Treasurer: Federico Peltzer
Founded: 1931
Specialize in philosophy, literature & linguistics.
Publication(s): *Boletin de la Academia Argentina de Letras* (quarterly); *Serie de acuerdos acerca del Idioma*; *Serie de Clasicos Angentinos*; *Serie Estudios academicos y otras publicaciones*; *Serie Estudios Linguisticos y Filologicos*; *Serie Homenajes*

PEN Club Argentino-Centro Internacional de la Asociacion PEN
Rivadavia 4060, 1205 Buenos Aires
Key Personnel
President: Miguel A Olivera
Secretary: Luis Ricardo Furlan; Alicia Bermolen
Publication(s): *Boletin* (and books)

Australia

Association for the Study of Australian Literature Ltd
School of Humanities, Griffith University, Nathan, Brisbane, Qld 4111
Tel: (07) 38757165 *Fax:* (07) 38757730
E-mail: p.buckridge@hum.gu.edu.au
Key Personnel
President: Prof Robert Dixon
Secretary: Dr Patrick Buckridge
Publication(s): *Notes & Furphies*

Australasian Association for Lexicography
Bond University, Gold Coast, Qld 4229
Tel: (07) 5595-2502 *Fax:* (07) 5595-2545
E-mail: bill_krebs@bond.edu.au
Web Site: www.anu.edu.au/linguistics/alex/
Key Personnel
Secretary: Bill Krebs
Publication(s): *Australex* (newsletter)

Australian Library Publishers' Society
Barr Smith Library, University of Adelaide, Adelaide, SA 5005
Tel: (08) 8303 5370 *Fax:* (08) 8303 4369
Web Site: www.library.adelaide.edu.au/ual/publ/alps/
Key Personnel
Convener & University Librarian: Ray Choate
Tel: (08) 8303 4064 *E-mail:* ray.choate@adelaide.edu.au
Represents 33 library publishers & markets approximately 300 publications.
Publication(s): *Catalogue of Members Publications* (5th edition)

Australian Literature Society, see Association for the Study of Australian Literature Ltd

The Australian Society of Authors Ltd
PO Box 1566, Strawberry Hills, NSW 2012
Tel: (02) 93180877 *Fax:* (02) 93180530
E-mail: asa@asauthors.org
Key Personnel
Executive Dir: Jose Borghino *E-mail:* jose@asauthors.org
Founded: 1963
Publication(s): *Australian Book Contracts*; *The Australian Author* (3 times a year, magazine)

Australian Writers' Guild Ltd
60 Kellett St, Kings Cross, NSW 2011
Tel: (02) 93577888 *Fax:* (02) 93577776
E-mail: awgsyd@ozemail.com.au
Web Site: www.ozemail.com.au/~awgsyd/index.htm/
Key Personnel
Executive Officer: Chris Sharp
President: Geoffrey Atherden
Publication(s): *A Matter of Cultural Sovereignty* (a symposium); *The Writers' Directory: writers for screen, stage, radio & television in Australia*

Bibliographical Society of Australia and New Zealand (BSANZ)
National Library of Australia, Canberra, ACT 2600
Tel: (03) 9052689 *Fax:* (03) 9052610
Key Personnel
Secretary: Richard Overell
Publication(s): *Broadsheet* (triannually); *Bulletin* (quarterly)

Children's Book Council of Australia
PO Box 470, Mount Lawley, WA 6929
Tel: (08) 9371 5018
Web Site: www.cbc.org.au
Key Personnel
President: Margot Hillel
Secretary: Anne Hanzl
Branches in New South Wales, Queensland, South Australia, Tasmania, Victoria, Western Australia, Australian Capital Territory, Northern Territory.
Publication(s): *Reading Time* (quarterly New South Wales Branch)

Fellowship of Australian Writers
PO Box 448, Rozelle, NSW 2039
Key Personnel
President: Beverley Earnsham
Secretary: Alan Russell
Twenty-one regional branches in suburbs of Sydney & country towns; 1,000 members.
Publication(s): *Bulletin* (Bimonthly)

Fellowship of Australian Writers (Vic) Inc
PO Box 528, Camberwell, Victoria, ACT 3124
Tel: (03) 93493722 *Fax:* (02) 93493722
Key Personnel
President: Adrian Peniston-Bird
All awards open the second week of September & close the third week of November each year.
Membership 2,500.

NSW Writers' Centre
PO Box 1056, Rozelle, NSW 2039
Tel: (02) 95559757 *Fax:* (02) 98181327
E-mail: nswwc@ozemail.com.au
Web Site: www.nswwriterscentre.org.au
Key Personnel
Chairman: Prof Michael Wilding
Executive Dir: Irina Dunn
Founded: 1991
Resource & information centre for emerging & professional writers.
Publication(s): *Newswrite* (monthly)

International PEN (Melbourne Centre)
PO Box 2273, Caulfield Junction, Victoria 3161
Tel: (03) 95097257 *Fax:* (03) 95097257
Key Personnel
President: Judith Buckrich *E-mail:* buckrich@netspace.net.au
Secretary: Danik Bancilhon

International PEN Sydney Centre
POB 1384, Rozelle, NSW 2039
Tel: (02) 95559931 *Fax:* (02) 96928836
Key Personnel
President: Yvonne Preston
E-mail: yvonnepreston@one.net.au
Publication(s): *Newsletter* (quarterly)

Poetry Society of Australia
Grosvenor St, Sydney, NSW 2000
Mailing Address: PO Box N110, Sydney, NSW 2000

AUSTRALIA

Tel: (02) 423861
Key Personnel
Joint Secretary: Robert Adamson; Debra Adamson
Publication(s): *New Poetry* (quarterly; also poems, articles, reviews, notes and comments, interviews)

Austria

Oesterreichische Gesellschaft fuer Literatur (Austrian Literary Society)
Herrengasse 5, A-1010 Vienna
Tel: (01) 5338159; (01) 5338159 *Fax:* (01) 5334067
E-mail: office@ogl.at
Web Site: www.ogl.at
Key Personnel
President: Marianne Gruber
Vice President: Helmuth A Niederle
Founded: 1961
Austrian Literary Society.

Institut fur Oesterreichkunde (Institute for the Knowledge of Austria)
Hanuschgasse 3/3, A-1010 Vienna
Tel: (01) 512-79-32 *Fax:* (01) 512-79-32
E-mail: loek.wirtschaftsgeschichte@univie.ac.at
Key Personnel
President: Prof Ernst Bruckmueller, PhD *Tel:* (01) 4277 41312 *E-mail:* ernst.bruckmueller@univie.ac.at
Secretary General: Bernhard Zimmermann
Founded: 1957
Publication(s): *Oesterreich Archiv* (yearly, book); *Oesterreich in Geschichte und Literatur (mit Geographie)* (bimonthly, journal); *Schriften des Institutes fuer Oesterreichkunde* (yearly, book); *Schriftenreihe Literatur des Institutes fuer Oesterreichkunde*

Oesterreichischer PEN-Club
Concordia Haus Bankgasse 8, A-1010 Vienna 1
Tel: (01) 5334459 *Fax:* (01) 5328749
Key Personnel
President: Dr Wolfgang Georg Fischer
Secretary: Dr Peter Marginter
Publication(s): *Pen-Nachrichten* (biannually)

Bahrain

Bahrain Writers & Literators Association
PO Box 1010, Manama
Key Personnel
President: Ali al-Shargawi
Secretary: Fareed Ramadan

Bangladesh

Society of Arts, Literature and Welfare
Society Park, K C Dey Rd, Chittagong
Key Personnel
General Secretary: Nesar Ahmed Chowdhury

Belgium

Academie Royale de Langue et de Litterature Francaise
Palais des Academies, One rue Ducale, 1000 Brussels
Tel: (02) 5115687; (02) 5116757
Key Personnel
Dir: Raymond Trousson
Vice Dir: Georges-Henri Dumont
Secretary: Andre Goosse
Royal Academy of French Language and Literature.
Publication(s): *Bulletin, Annuaire, Memoires*

Academie Royale des Sciences, des Lettres et des Beaux-Arts de Belgique
des Academis, rue Ducale 1, 1000 Brussels
Tel: (02) 5502211 *Fax:* (02) 5502205
Key Personnel
Secretary: Baron Philippe Roberts-Jones
Belgian Royal Academy of Sciences, Letters and Fine Arts.
Publication(s): *Biannual Bulletins, Memoirs, Year Book*

Antwerp Bibliophile Society
Museum Plantin-Moretus, Vrijdagmarkt 22, 2000 Antwerp
Tel: (03) 2330294 *Fax:* (03) 2262516
E-mail: francine.demav@amtwerpa.be
Key Personnel
President: Prof L Voet, PhD
Secretarys: Prof G Persoons, PhD; Prof L De Pavw-De Veen, PhD
Vereeniging der Antwerpsche Bibliophielen.
Publication(s): *De Gulden Passer*

Association des Ecrivains Belges de Langue Francaise
Maison Camille Lemonnier - Maison des Ecrivains, 150 chaussee de Wavre, 1050 Brussels
Tel: (02) 512 2968 *Fax:* (02) 502 4373
Key Personnel
President: France Bastia
Vice President: Prof Emile Kesteman; Marie Nicolai
Secretary General: Jean Lacroix
Association of Belgian Writers in the French Language.
Publication(s): *Nos Lettres* (ten times a year)

Commission Belge de Bibliographie et de Bibliologie
4 blvd de l'Empereur, 1000 Brussels
Mailing Address: Rue du Centre 10, B-6670 Gouvy
Tel: (080) 510464 *Fax:* (080) 80510465
Key Personnel
Treasurer: Mireille Verbeke-Vanlaecken
E-mail: chriverb@skynet.be
Belgian Commission of Bibliography & Bibliology.
Publication(s): *Annuaire* (yearbook); *Coll: Bibliographia Belgica*

KANTL, see Koninklijke Academie voor Nederlandse Taal- en Letterkunde

Koninklijke Academie voor Nederlandse Taal-en Letterkunde (Royal Academy of Dutch Language & Literature (Belgium))
Koningstraat 18, B-9000 Gent
Tel: (09) 265 93 40 *Fax:* (09) 265 93 49
E-mail: secretariaat@kantl.be
Web Site: www.kantl.be

LITERARY ASSOCIATIONS

Key Personnel
Permanent Secretary: Prof Dr Georges de Schutter
Librarian: Marijke De Wit *Tel:* (09) 265 93 43
E-mail: mdewit@kantl.be
Founded: 1886
Royal Academy of Dutch Language & Literature.
Publication(s): *Jaarboek van de Koninklijke Academie voor Nederlandse Taal-en Letterkunde* (annual); *Verslagen en Mededelingen van de Koninklijke Academie voor Nederlandse Taal-en Letterkunde* (3x/yr)

Koninklijke Academie voor Wetenschappen Letteren en Schone Kunsten Van Belgie
Paleis der Academien, Hertogsstr 1, B-1000 Brussels
Tel: (02) 550 23 23 *Fax:* (02) 550 23 25; (02) 5502325
Key Personnel
Publications Officer: Gilbert Reynderg *Tel:* (02) 550 23 32 *E-mail:* gilbert.reynders@kvab.be
Permanent Secretary: Niceas Schamp
Dutch-speaking Royal Belgian Academy of Sciences, Letters & Fine Arts.
Publication(s): *Collectanea Biblica et Religiosa Antiqua*; *Collectanea Hellenistica*; *Collectanea Maritima*; *Corpus Catalogorum Belgii*; *Fontes Historiae Artis Neerlandicae*; *Iuris Scripta Historica*; *Iusti Lipsi Epistolae (The Correspondence of J Lipsius)*; *(Memoirs) & Fine Arts*; *National Biography*; *Proceedings Department of Letters*; *Studia Europea*; *Studies in Belgian economic history*; *Year Book*

International PEN Club, Belgian French-Speaking Centre
10 Ave des Cerfs, 1950 Kraainem
Tel: (02) 7314847 *Fax:* (02) 7314847
Key Personnel
President: Huguette de Broqueville
Secretary: Titanne Simons
Founded: 1922
A voice of literature worldwide, bringing together poets, novelists, essayists, historians, critics, translators, editors, journalists & screenwriters. Members are united in a common concern for the craft & art of writing & a commitment to freedom of expression through the written word.

PEN Club-Belgian
Wiesbeek 41, 9255 Buggenhout
Tel: (052) 351118 *Fax:* (052) 351119
Key Personnel
President: Monika Van Paemel
Secretary: M Fernand Auwera

SABAM, see Societe Belge des Auteurs, Compositeurs et Editeurs (SABAM)

SL(L)W, see Societe de Langue et de Litterature Wallonnes ASBL

Societe Belge des Auteurs, Compositeurs et Editeurs (SABAM)
75-77 rue d'Arlon, 1040 Brussels
Tel: (02) 2868211 *Fax:* (02) 2311800
E-mail: 101641.2761@compuserve.com
Key Personnel
President: Jacques Leduc
Man Dir: Paul Louka; Roger Van Ransbeek
General Manager: Peter Van Rompaey
Contact: Joseph Dethier; Jean Darlier
Belgian Society of Authors, Composers & Publishers.
Publication(s): *Bulletin* (quarterly)

Societe de Langue et de Litterature Wallonnes ASBL (Society for Walloon Language & Literature)
Universite de Liege, 7 place du XX Aout, 4000 Liege
Tel: (086) 344432
E-mail: sllw.be@skynet.be
Web Site: users.skynet.be/sllw
Key Personnel
President: Guy Belleflamme
Vice President & Editor: Marie-Buy Boutier
Secretary: Victor George
Publication(s): *Chronique de la Societe de Langue et de Litterature wallonnes* (periodically); *Dialectes de Wallonie* (periodically)

Bolivia

PEN Club de Bolivia (Centro Internacional de Escritores)
Calle Goitia 17, Casilla 149, La Paz
Key Personnel
Secretary: Yolanda Bedregal de Conitzer

Brazil

Academia Amazonense de Letras
Rua Ramos Ferreira 1009, Manaus, AM
Key Personnel
President: Djalma Batista
Secretary: Genesino Braga
Librarian: Mario Ypiranga Monteiro
Amazonas Academy of Letters.
Publication(s): *Revista*

Academia Brasileira de Letras
Ave Presidente Wilson 203, 20030 Rio de Janeiro, RJ
Key Personnel
Secretary General: Abgar Renault
Librarian: Barbosa Lima Sobrinho
Publication(s): *Revista*

Academia Catarinense de Letras
Edif Jose Daux, Rua Vidal Ramos, 88000 Florianopolis, SC
Mailing Address: Av Irineu Bornahusen 5000, Caixa Postal 912, Florianopolis SC 88010-970
Tel: 2342166
Key Personnel
President: Paschoal Apostolo Pitsica
Secretary General: Jali Meirinho
Librarian: Pedro Bertolino
Santa Catarina Academy of Letters.
Publication(s): *Revista* (annual)

Academia Cearense de Letras
Palacio Senador Alencar, Rua Sao Paulo 51, 60030 Fortaleza, CE
Key Personnel
President: Claudio Martins
Secretary General: Itamar de Santiago Espindola
Ceara Academy of Letters.
Publication(s): *Colecao Antonio Sales*; *Colecao Dolor Barreira*; *Revista da Academia Cearense de Letras*

Academia de Letras da Bahia
Av Joana Angelica 198 Nazare, 40050 Salvador BA
Tel: (071) 243-7614 *Fax:* (071) 243-7614
Key Personnel
President: Claudio Veiga
Vice President: Wilson Lins
Secretary: Edivaldo M Boaventura
Bahia Academy of Letters.
Publication(s): *Revista* (Annually)

Academia de Letras de Piaui
64000-490 Teresina, Pl
Key Personnel
President: Jose de Arimathea Tito Filho
Piaui Academy of Letters.
Publication(s): *Revista*

Academia Mineira de Letras
Rua da Bahia 1466, 30160 Belo Horizonte MG
Key Personnel
President: Vivaldi Moreira
Minas Gerais Academy of Letters.

Academia Paraibana de Letras
Rua Duque de Caxias 25, CP 334, 58000 Joao Pessoa, PB
Key Personnel
President: Afonso Pereira da Silva
General Secretary: Aurelio Moreno de Albuquerque
Paraiba Academy of Letters.
Publication(s): *Revista*

Academia Paulista de Letras
Largo do Arouche 312, 01219 Sao Paulo, SP
Key Personnel
President: Antonio A S Amora
Sao Paulo Academy of Letters.
Publication(s): *Biblioteca Academia Paulista de Letras*; *Revista da Academia Paulista de Letras*

Academia Pernambucana de Letras
Ave Rui Barbosa 1596, Gracas, 52050-000 Recife PE
Tel: (081) 2682211
Key Personnel
President: Luiz de Magalhaes Melo
Secretary: Dr Lucilo Varejao Filho
Pernambuco Academy of Letters.
Publication(s): *Revista*

PEN Clube do Brasil (Associacao Universal de Escritores)
Praia do Flamengo 172-11, Rio de Janeiro 2000
Key Personnel
President: Prof Marcos Almir Madeira
Secretary: Maria Cecilia Ribas Carneiro
Publication(s): *Boletim* (novels, poetry)

Bulgaria

Bulgarian Academy of Sciences, Institute of Literature
15 Noemvri 1, 1040 Sofia
Tel: (02) 84141 *Fax:* (02) 880448
Key Personnel
Associate Dir: Prof Stefan Kozhuharov
Publication(s): *Literatourna Missul* (Literary Thought)

Bulgarian Writers' Union
A Kanchev 5, 1000 Sofia
Tel: (02) 898346 *Fax:* (02) 880685
Key Personnel
President: N Haitov
Publication(s): *Literaturen Front* (weekly); *Obzor* (Survey, quarterly; text in English, Spanish & French); *Plamak* (The Flame, monthly); *Savremennik* (quarterly); *Septemvri* (monthly); *Slaveiche* (monthly, for children)

China

China PEN Centre
Chinese Writers Activity Center, 25 Dongtuchenglu, Beijing 10013
Fax: 8610 64221704
Key Personnel
President: Mr Ba Jin
Secretary: Mr Bi Shuowang

Colombia

Instituto Colombiano de Cultura Hispanica
Calle 12, No 2-41, Apdo 5454, Bogota
Tel: (01) 3413857 *Fax:* (01) 2811051
Key Personnel
Dir: William Jaramillo Meja
General Secretary: Clemencia Vallejo de Meja
Publication(s): *Flora de la Real Expedicion Botanica del Nuevo*

Instituto Caro y Cuervo
Carrera 11, No 64-37, Apdo Aereo 51502, Bogota
Tel: (01) 2557753 *Fax:* (01) 217-02-43
E-mail: carocuer@interred.gov.co
Key Personnel
Dir: Ignacio Chaves Cuevas
Secretary General: Carlos Julio Luque Cagua
Founded: 1942
Linguistics, Philology & Literature.

PEN Internacional de Colombia
Apdo Aereo 101830, Bogota 10
Tel: (01) 2846761; (01) 2561540 *Fax:* (01) 2184236
Key Personnel
President: Cecilia Balcazar de Bucher, PhD
Secretary: Gloria Guardia
PEN International of Colombian Writers.

Congo

Congolese Pen Club
BP 2181, Brazzaville
Tel: 813601 *Fax:* 813601
Key Personnel
President: Emmanuel B Dongala

Czech Republic

Matice moravska
Gorkeho 14, 60200 Brno
Tel: (05) 750050 *Fax:* (05) 753050
Key Personnel
President: Prof Jan Janak, Jr
Secretary: Dr Jiri Malir
Publication(s): *Casopis Matice moravske* (biannually)

Czech PEN Centre
Member of International PEN Centre
Hermanova 33, 17000 Praha 7, 9, 28th Octoberstr, 110 00 Prague 1
Tel: (02) 24235546 *Fax:* (02) 24221926

E-mail: centrum@pen.cz
Web Site: www.pen.cz
Key Personnel
President: Jiri Stransky *E-mail:* jiri@pen.cz
Secretary: Libuse Ludvikova *Tel:* (02) 24234343
    E-mail: libuse@pen.cz
Founded: 1925

Denmark

Dansk Forfatterforening
Tordenskjolds Gard, Strandgade 6, DK-1401 Copenhagen K
Tel: 32955100 *Fax:* 32540115
E-mail: danskforfatterforening@
    danskforfatterforening.dk
Web Site: www.danskforfatterforening.dk
Key Personnel
President: Mr Knud Vilby
Founded: 1894
Danish Writers' Association.
Publication(s): *Forfatteren* (8 yearly)

Det Danske Sprog - og Litterurselskab
    (Society for Danish Language & Literature)
Christians Brygge 1, 1219 Copenhagen K
Tel: 33130660 *Fax:* 33140608
E-mail: sekretariat@dsl.dk
Web Site: www.dsl.dk
Key Personnel
President: Iver Kjaer
Contact: Nicholai Reinseth *E-mail:* nr@dsl.dk
Founded: 1911
Society for Danish Language & Literature.

Det Kongelige Danske Videnskabernes Selskab
    (The Royal Danish Academy of Sciences & Letters)
H C Andersens Blvd 35, DK-1553 Copenhagen V
Tel: 33435300 *Fax:* 33435301
E-mail: kvds@royalacademy.dk
Web Site: www.royalacademy.dk
Key Personnel
President: Birger Munk Olsen
Secretary: Ole Hansen
Editor: Flemming Lundgreen-Nielsen
Founded: 1742
Royal Danish Academy of Sciences & Letters.
Publication(s): *Biologiske Skrifter*; *Historisk-filosofiske Meddelelser*; *Historisk-filosofiske Skrifter*; *Oversigt* (annual report; four-monograph series)

Nyt Dansk Litterurselskab
Hotelvej 9, 2640 Hedehusene
Tel: 4659 5520 *Fax:* 4659 5520
E-mail: ndl@ndl.dk
Key Personnel
President: Morten Bagger
Manager: Anne Warming
New Danish Society for Literature.
Aims, Publication/Republication of books in short supply in libraries. Special activity, Magnaprint (large print books for partially sighted).

Ecuador

Casa de la Cultura Ecuatoriana Benjamin Carrion
Av 6 de Dicimbre 794, Apdo 67, Quito
Key Personnel
President: Ledo Camilo Restrepo
Secretary General: Ledo Sergiovelez

Academia Ecuatoriana de la Lengua
Apdo 3460, Quito
Tel: (02) 226-870
Key Personnel
President: Galo Rene Perez
Secretary: Piedad Larrea Borja
Publication(s): *Memorias de la Academia de la hengua*

Egypt (Arab Republic of Egypt)

Atelier, L
6 Victor Bassili St, 6 Pharaana St, Azarita, Alexandria
Tel: (03) 4820526 *Fax:* (03) 4837662
Key Personnel
Honorary President: Prof Naima El-Shishiny
Honorary Secretary: D Farouk Wahba
Society of Artists & Writers.

High Council of Arts & Literature
9 Sharia Hassan Sabri, Zamalek, Cairo

Finland

Finlands svenska forfattareforening (Society of Swedish Authors in Finland)
URHO Kekkonens gata 8B 14, FIN-00100 Helsingfors
Tel: (09) 446266 *Fax:* (09) 446871
Key Personnel
President: Thomas Wulff
Secretary: Merete Jensen
Society of Swedish Authors in Finland; Member of The Three Seas Writer's & Translator's Council, European Writer's Congress, Baltic Writer's Council, Nordic Writer's Council.

Finnish Academy of Science & Letters, see Suomalainen Tiedeakatemia

Kirjallisuudentutkijain Seura (Finnish Literary Research Society)
Department of Finnish Literature, University of Helsinki, PL 3, Fabianink 33, 00014 Helsinki
Tel: (09) 19122658 *Fax:* (09) 19123008
Web Site: www.helsinki.fi/jarj/skts
Telex: 124690
Key Personnel
President: Prof Kaimikkoven *Tel:* (09) 40 8289924
Secretary: Mirjam Ilvas
The Literary Research Society.
Publication(s): *Kirjallisuudentutkijain Seuran Vuosikirja* (The Yearbook of the Literary Research Society)

Finnish PEN Center
Kauppakartanonkatu 26 G 86, 00930 Helsinki 93
Tel: (09) 1996448 *Fax:* (09) 1996540
Key Personnel
President: Elisabeth Nordgren
Secretary: Sanna Jaatinen

Suomalainen Tiedeakatemia
Mariankatu 5, 00170 Helsinki
Tel: (09) 636800 *Fax:* (09) 660117

Key Personnel
President: Heikki Solin
Secretary General: Pentti Kauranen
Finnish Academy of Science & Letters.
Publication(s): *Annales Academiae Scientiarum Fennicae, Mathematica*; *Folklore Fellows' Communications*; *Vuosikirja* (Yearbook)

Suomalaisen Kirjallisuuden Seura (Finnish Literature Society)
Hallituskatu 1, 00170 Helsinki
Mailing Address: PO Box 259, 00170 Helsinki
Tel: (09) 131231 *Fax:* (09) 13123220
E-mail: sks-kirjasto@helsinki.fi
Key Personnel
Secretary-General: Urpo Vento
Publisher: Matti Suurpaeae
Librarian: Henni Ilomaeki
Dir, Folklore Archive: Pekka Laaksonen
Dir, Literature Archive: Kaarina Sala
Dir, Finnish Literature Information Centre: Marja-Leena Rautalin
Specialize in folklore, ethnology, literary research, Finnish language, cultural history.
Publication(s): *Studia Fennica*; *Suomi*; *Tietolipas*; *Toimituksia* (irregular)

Svenska Litteratursaellskapet i Finland
    (Society of Swedish Literature in Finland)
Riddaregatan 5, FIN-00170 Helsinki
Tel: (09) 618777 *Fax:* (09) 6187 7377
E-mail: sls@mail.sls.fi
Web Site: www.sls.fi
Key Personnel
President: Prof Hakan Andersson
Editor: Nina Edgren-Henrichson *E-mail:* nina.edgren-henrichson@sls.fi
Founded: 1885
Swedish Literary Society in Finland.
Publication(s): *Skrifter utgivna av Svenska Litteratursaellskapet i Finland* (Writings)

Svenska Oesterbottens Litteraturfoerening
Handelsesplanden 23A, SF-65100 Vasa
Tel: (06) 3128426 *Fax:* (06) 3242210
Key Personnel
Contact: Gun Anderssen
Swedish Oesterbottens Literary Association.
Publication(s): *Horisont*

France

Academie Goncourte, Socieete de gens de Lettres
c/o Drouant, Place Gaillon, 75002 Paris
Key Personnel
Presidents: Herve Bazin; Francis Nourissier
Responsible for annual prizes-poetry scholarships, best romance novels, biographies.

Centre National du Livre
53 rue de Verneuil, 75343 Paris Cedex 07
Tel: (01) 49546868 *Fax:* (01) 45491021
Web Site: www.centrenationaldulivre.fr
Key Personnel
President: Jean-Sebastien Dupuit
Secretary General: Michel Marian
National Literary Centre.

Association d'Information et de Defense des Auteurs - Calcre
BP 17, 94404 Vitry-sur-Seine
E-mail: secr@calcre.com
Web Site: www.calcre.com
Key Personnel
President: Roger Gaillard
Secretary: Claude Aubert
Founded: 1979

Publication(s): *Arlit - Annuaire des Revues Litteraires & Cie* (3 times/yr); *Audace - Annuaire a l'Usage des Auteurs Cherchant un Editeur* (3 times/yr); *Ecrire & Editer* (bimonthly, magazine); *Savelivre - Guide des Salons et des Fetes du Livre* (4 times/yr)

Maison des Ecrivains (Writers' House)
53 rue de Verneuil, 75007 Paris
Tel: (01) 49546880 *Fax:* (01) 42842087
E-mail: courrier@maison-des-ecrivains.asso.fr
Web Site: www.maison-des-ecrivains.asso.fr
Key Personnel
President: Claude Esteban
Dir: Alain Lance

PEN Club Francais
6 rue Francois-Miron, 75004 Paris
Tel: (01) 42773787 *Fax:* (01) 42786487
Key Personnel
President: Jean Orizet

PEN Club de Suisse romande
c/o Mme Mantilleri, 217 route de Vovray, 74160 Collonges s/s Saleve
Tel: (022) 50-43-69-35
Key Personnel
President: Jean-Pierre Moulin
Secretary: Bridgitte Mantilleri
PEN Club for French-speaking Switzerland.
Publication(s): *PEN Club romand Newsletter* (biannually)

SNAC, see Syndicat National des Auteurs et Compositeurs

Societe des Auteurs et Compositeurs Dramatiques (SACD)
11 bis rue Ballu, 75442 Paris Cedex 09
Tel: (01) 40234444 *Fax:* (01) 45267428
E-mail: infosacd@sacd.fr
Key Personnel
Dir Communications: Beatrice Clerc
Publication(s): *SACD*

Societe des Gens de Lettres de France
Hotel de Massa, 38, rue du Faubourg-Saint-Jacques, 75014 Paris
Tel: (01) 53 10 12 00 *Fax:* (01) 53 10 12 12
E-mail: sgdlf@wanadoo.fr
Web Site: www.sgdl.org
Telex: 206 963 F
Key Personnel
President: Alain Absire
First Vice President: Marie-France Briselance
Secretary-General: Jean Claude Bologne
Treasurer: Francois Taillandier
Publication(s): *Journal des Lettres et de l'Audiovisuel*; *Revue des Lettres et de l'Audiovisuel*

la Societe des Poetes Francais
Siege social 16, rue Monsieur le Prince, 75006 Paris
Fax: (01) 40469982
E-mail: poetesfrancais@aol.com
Web Site: www.societedespoetesfrancais.asso.fr
Key Personnel
President: Vital Heurtebize
Secretary General: Linda Bastide
Publication(s): *Bulletin* (triannually)

Societe d'Etudes Dantesques
Centre Universitaire Mediterraneen, 65 Promenade-des- Anglais, 06000 Nice
Key Personnel
Secretary General: Simon Lorenzi

Societe d'Histoire Litteraire de la France
112 rue Monge, 75005 Paris
Mailing Address: BP 173, 75005 Paris
Tel: (01) 45872330 *Fax:* (01) 45872330
Key Personnel
President: R Pomeau
French Literary History Association.
Publication(s): *Revue d'Histoire litteraire de la France* (alternate months)

Syndicat National des Auteurs et Compositeurs
80 rue Taitbout, 75009 Paris Cedex 09
Tel: (01) 42805282
E-mail: snac@calva.net
Web Site: www.snac.fr
Key Personnel
President: Jacques Vigoureux
Honorary President: Jean Drejac; Antoine Duhamel

Germany

Adalbert Stifter Verein eV (Adalbert Stifter Association)
Hochstr 8, 81669 Munich
Tel: (089) 4489807 *Fax:* (089) 4891148
E-mail: asv.kulturinstitul@t-online.de
Key Personnel
Chairman: Prof Otto Herbert Hajek
Manager: Dr Peter Becher
Contact: Dr Sigrid Canz
Founded: 1947
Information brochure in German, Czech & English; literature, art, cultural history of Bohemia & Moravia.
Publication(s): *Stifter-Jahrbuch/Neue Folge* (since 1987)

Bundesverband junger Autoren und Autorinnen eV
Kannenbaeckerstr 9, 53340 Meckenheim
Mailing Address: Postfach 200303, 53133 Bonn
Tel: (22258) 7889 *Fax:* (2225) 7889
E-mail: bvjaa@t-online.de
Web Site: www.bvja-online.de
Key Personnel
Chairman: Heike Prassel
Manager: Thomas Stichtenoth
Founded: 1987
Publication(s): *Konzepte*; *LiteraturMagazin*

Deutsche Akademie fuer Sprache und Dichtung (German Academy of Language & Poetry)
Alexandraweg 23, 64287 Darmstadt
Tel: (06151) 40920 *Fax:* (06151) 409299
E-mail: Deutsche.Akademie@T-Online.de
Web Site: www.deutscheakademie.de
Key Personnel
President: Prof Dr Christian Meier
Secretary-General: Dr Gerhard Dette
Press Officer: Corinna Blattmann *Tel:* (06151) 409216
German Academy of Language & Poetry.
Publication(s): *Dichtung & Sprache* (irregularly); *Jahrbuch der Deutschen Akademie fuer Sprache & Dichtung* (annually); *Preisschriften* (annually); *Veroeffentlichungen der Deutschen Akademie fuer Sprache & Dichtung* (irregularly)

Deutscher Literaturfonds eV
Alexandraweg 23, 64287 Darmstadt
Tel: (06151) 40930 *Fax:* (06151) 409333
Web Site: stadt.darmstadt.gmd.de/kultur/literatur/lit-fond.html
Key Personnel
Contact: Dr Gerhard Dette

Deutsches PEN-Zentrum (Ost) (East German PEN Center)
Kulturbrauerei Schoenhauser Allee 36-39, 10435 Berlin
Tel: (030) 304413904 *Fax:* (030) 304413904
Key Personnel
President: Prof Dieter Schlenstedt
Secretary: Joochen Laabs

Gesellschaft fur Interkulturelle Germanistik eV (GIG)
c/o Institut fur Literaturwissenschaft der Universitat, Universitat Friderciana-Karlsruhe, Kaiserstr 12, 76128 Karlsruhe
Tel: (0721) 6080 *Fax:* (0721) 6084290
Key Personnel
President, University Bayreuth: Prof A Wierlacher, PhD
Vice President, University Karlsruhe: Prof B Thum, PhD

Gesellschaft zur Foerderung der Literatur aus Afrika Asien und Lateinamerika eV
Reineckstr 3, 60313 Frankfurt am Main
Mailing Address: Postfach 100116, 60001 Frankfurt am Main
Tel: (069) 2102247 *Fax:* (069) 2102227
E-mail: litprom@book-fair.com
Web Site: www.litprom.de
Key Personnel
Dir: Peter Ripken
President: Peter Weidhaas
The Society seeks to promote German translations of creative writing from Africa, Asia & Latin America. It works as a non-profit agency & as a consultant for German language publishers & Third World publishers who have translation rights to offer. It is organizing reading tours & special promotion campaigns & is also in charge of a special programme for translations grants into German.
Publication(s): *Literaturnachrichten* (quarterly in German)

Goethe-Gesellschaft in Weimar eV
Burgplatz 4, 99403 Weimar
Mailing Address: Postfach 2251, 99403 Weimar
Tel: (3643) 202050 *Fax:* (3643) 202061
E-mail: goetheges@aol.com
Web Site: www.goethe-gessellschaft.de
Key Personnel
President (Weimar): Dr Jochen Golz
Vice President (Dusseldorf): Dr Volkmar Hansen
Contact: Dr Petra Oberhauser
Founded: 1885
Publication(s): *Goethe-Jahrbuch* (yearbook)

Gutenberg-Gesellschaft-Internationale Vereinigung fur Geschichte und Gegenwart der Druckkunst eV
Liebfrauenplatz 5, D-55116 Mainz
Tel: (06131) 22 64 20 *Fax:* (06131) 23 35 30
Key Personnel
President: Jens Beutel
Vice President: Senator Hannetraud Schultheiss
Publishing Manager: Dr Stephan Fuessel
Secretary General: Gertraude Benoehr
June 1998, Guntenberg-Museum, Mainz.
Publication(s): *Gutenberg-Jahrbuch: Kleine Drucke der Gutenberg-Gesellschaft*

Literarischer Verein in Stuttgart eV
Haldenstr 30, 70376 Stuttgart
Mailing Address: Postfach 140155, 70071 Stuttgart
Tel: (0711) 5499710 *Fax:* (0711) 54997121
Key Personnel
President: Gerd Hiersemann *E-mail:* hiersemann.hauswedell.verlage@t-online.de
The Society's goal (founded in 1839) is to publish the texts of valuable unpublished manuscripts & old printed texts in a new form

GERMANY

- especially with regard to old German literature.
Publication(s): *Bibliothek des Literarischen Vereins in Stuttgart* (Vol 1 1842 - Vol 318 1996)

Literarisches Colloquium Berlin
Am Sandwerder 5, 14109 Berlin
Tel: (030) 8169960 *Fax:* (030) 81699619
Web Site: www.lcb.de
Key Personnel
Contact: Thomas Geiger *Tel:* (030) 181699613
  E-mail: geiger@lcb.de
Founded: 1963
Publication(s): *Sprache im technischen Zeitalter* (quarterly)

Maximilian-Gesellschaft eV
Haldenstr 30, 70376 Stuttgart
Mailing Address: Postfach 140155, 70071 Stuttgart
Tel: (0711) 5499711 *Fax:* (0711) 54997121
E-mail: hiersemann.hauswedell.verlage@t-online.de
Web Site: www.maximilian-gesellschaft.de
Key Personnel
Chairman: Prof Horst Gronemeyer, PhD
Producer: Reinhold Busch
Book Collectors Society.

PEN Zentrum Bundesrepublik Deutschland
Sandstrasse 10, 64283 Darmstadt
Tel: (06151) 23120 *Fax:* (06151) 293414
Key Personnel
President: Carl Amery
Secretary: Hans Werner Schwarze

Society for the Promotion of African, Asian and Latin American Literature, see Gesellschaft zur Foerderung der Literatur aus Afrika Asien und Lateinamerika eV

Greece

Kentron Ekdoseos Ellinon Syngrafeon
Akadimia Athinon, Odos Anagnostopoulou 14, 10673 Athens
Tel: (01) 3612541 *Fax:* (01) 3602691
Centre for the Publication of Ancient Greek Authors.

Haiti

Le Bibliophile (The Book Lover)
Caphaitien
Key Personnel
President: Silvio Faschi
Secretary: Louis Toussaint
Publication(s): *La Citadelle* (weekly); *Stella* (monthly)

Hong Kong

Chinese Language Society of Hong Kong
18/F Kam Chung Bldg, 19-21 Hennessy Rd, Hong Kong
Tel: (02) 5284853
Key Personnel
Secretary: Leung Nga Mei

Hong Kong Chinese PEN Centre
Victoria Park Mansion, 15th Floor, Flat A, Paterson St, Hong Kong
Mailing Address: PO Box 78521, Mongkok Post Office, Kowloon
Key Personnel
President: Chu Chih-Tai
Secretary: William Hsu
Publication(s): *PEN News* (weekly in Chinese)

Hong Kong English PEN Centre
21 Wun Sha St, Flat 20D, Tai Hang, Hong Kong
Tel: 25774168 *Fax:* 25774168
Key Personnel
President: Fred S Armentrout
Vice President: Peter Stambler
Secretary: Ruth Barzel
Publication(s): *Vietnamese Writers in Hong Kong's Camps, A Caselist*

Hungary

Hungarian PEN Centre, see Magyar PEN Club

Magyar Irodalomtoerteneti Tarsasag (Society of Hungarian Literary History)
Piarista Koez 1, 1052 Budapest
Tel: (01) 377819 *Fax:* (01) 3377819
Key Personnel
President: Sandor Ivan Kovacs
General Secretary: Praznovszky Mihaly
Founded: 1912
Society of Hungarian Literary History.
Publication(s): *Irodalomtoertenet*

Magyar Tudomanyos Akademia Irodalomtudomanyi Intezete (HAS Institute of Literary Studies)
Menesi u 11-13, 1118 Budapest
Tel: (01) 3858790 *Fax:* (01) 3853876
Key Personnel
Dir Prof: Laszlo Szorenyi
Institute of Literary Studies of the Hungarian Academy of Sciences.
Publication(s): *Helikon* (bimonthly); *Irodalomtoerteneti Fuezetek* (papers); *Irodalomtoerteneti Koenyvtar* (monographs); *Irodalomtoerteneti Koezlemenyek* (quarterly); *Literatura* (quarterly); *Neohelicon* (quarterly)
Ultimate Parent Company: Hungarian Academy of Science (HAS)

Magyar PEN Club
Karolyi Mihalyut 16, 1056 Budapest
Tel: (01) 3184143 *Fax:* (01) 1171722
Key Personnel
President: Mr Gabor Goergey
Secretary: Fanos Benyhe
Publication(s): *The Hungarian PEN, Le PEN hongrois* (yearly bulletin)

Iceland

Hid Islenzka Bokmenntafelag
Sidumula 21, 128 Reykjavik
Mailing Address: Postholf 8935, 128 Reykjavik
E-mail: hib@islandia.is
Key Personnel
President: Sigurdur Lindal
Secretary: Reynir Axelsson
Icelandic Literary Society.
Publication(s): *Annual Journal, Skirnir* (biannually)

International PEN Centre
PO Box 33, Reykjavik
Key Personnel
President: Thor Vilhjalmsson
Secretary: Einar Karason

Rithofundasamband Islands (The Icelandic Writers' Union)
Dyngjuvegi 8, 104 Reykjavik
Tel: 5683190 *Fax:* 5683192
E-mail: rsi@rsi.is
Web Site: www.rsi.is
Key Personnel
Chairman: Adalsteinn Asberg Sigurdsson
Man Dir: Ragnheidur Tryggvadottir
Founded: 1974
Writers' Union of Iceland.
Publication(s): *Frettabref* (Newsletter)

India

National Academy of Letters, India, see Sahitya Akademi

The PEN All-India Centre
Affiliate of PEN International
40 New Marine Lines, Mumbai 400020
Tel: (022) 2032175
E-mail: ambika.sirkar@gems.vsnl.net.in
  Cable: CARE ARYAHATA BOMBAY
Key Personnel
President: Annada Sankar
Acting Secretary & Treasurer: Ranjit Hoskote
Honorary Secretary-Treasurer: Prof Nissim Ezekiel
Member, Executive Committee: Rameshchandra Sirkar
Publication(s): *Asian Liturature: Poetry, Short Stories & Essays*; *Assamese Literature*; *Bengali Liturature*; *Drama in Modern india & Writer's Responsibility in a Rapidly Changing World*; *India Writers Meet*; *Indian Lituature of Today*; *Indian Writers at Chidambaram*; *Indian Writers in Conference*; *Indian Writers in Council*; *Indo-Anglian Liturature*; *The Novel in Modern India*; *Telugu Literature*; *The Indian PEN* (quarterly); *Writers in Free India*; *Writing in India*

Sahitya Akademi
Rabindra Bhawan, 35 Ferozshah Rd, New Delhi 110001
Tel: (011) 3387064 *Fax:* (011) 3382428
  Cable: SAHITYAKAR
Key Personnel
President: Prof Anantha Murphy
Vice President: Mr Ramakanta Rath
Secretary: Prof K Satchidanandan *Tel:* (011) 3386626
Editor: Prof H S Shivaprakash; Mr Girdhar Rathi
National Academy of Letters; regional offices in Bombay, Calcutta, Madras and Bangalone.
Publication(s): *Indian Literature* (English, bimonthly); *Samkaleen Bharateeya Sahitya* (Hindi, bimonthly); *Samskrita Pratibha* (Sanskrit, biannually)

Indonesia

PEN Centre
c/o Jalan Cemara 6, Jakarta, Pusat

Tel: (093) 3905837 *Fax:* (093) 325890
Key Personnel
Secretary: Dr Toeti Heraty Noerhadi

Ireland

Irish Academy of Letters
School of Irish Studies, Thomas Prior House, Merrion Rd, Dublin 4
Key Personnel
Secretary: Sean J White

Irish PEN
Rosslyn, Killarney Rd, Bray, Co Wicklow
Key Personnel
President: Mr O Z Whitehead
Secretary: Arthur Flynn

Israel

ACUM Ltd (Society of Authors, Composers & Music Publishers in Israel)
ACUM House 9, Tuval St, Ramat-Gan 52117
Mailing Address: PO Box 1704, Ramat-Gan 52117
Tel: (03) 6113400 *Fax:* (03) 6122629
E-mail: acum@acum.org.il
Web Site: www.acum.org.il
Key Personnel
Dir General: Yorik Ben-David
Secretary: Nilli Werker
Reprint Rights Department: Hany Moshe
Executive Secretary: Efrat Fishbein
International Affairs Manager: Evelyne Sahar
Tel: (03) 6113420 *E-mail:* eves@acum.org.il
Founded: 1936
Administration of authors & composers' rights
Member of BIEM, CISAC.

ELEAS, see English Language Editors' Association (ELEAS)

English Language Editors' Association (ELEAS)
PO Box 6925, Jerusalem
Tel: (02) 586-5772 *Fax:* (02) 586-6411
Web Site: www.geocities.com/jewishgroups/8Eleas.html
Key Personnel
Contact: David Grossman *E-mail:* davidg@macam.ac.il

Mekise Nirdamim Society
PO Box 4344, Jerusalem
Tel: (02) 636072
Key Personnel
President: Prof S Abramson
Secretary: Prof I Tashma
Publishes Hebrew works of the older classical Jewish literature.

Palestinian PEN Centre
Al Khaldi St 4, Wadi Al Juz, Jerusalem
Tel: (02) 6262970 *Fax:* (02) 6264620
Key Personnel
President: Hanan Awwad

Israeli PEN Centre
6 Kaplan St, Tel Aviv 61070
Mailing Address: PO Box 7203, Tel Aviv 61070
Tel: (03) 6964937 *Fax:* (03) 6964937

Key Personnel
President: Mr Sandu David
Secretary: Ms Shulamit Kuriansky

Italy

Accademia Nazionale di Scienze, Lettere ed Arti (National Academy of Sciences, Literatures & Arts)
Palazzo Coccapani, Corso Vittorio Emanuelle II 59, 41100 Modena
Tel: (059) 225566 *Fax:* (059) 225566
E-mail: biblio.asla@cedoc.mo.it
Key Personnel
Contact: Prof Ferdinando Taddei
Publication(s): *Atti e Memorie* (annual)

Accademia Nazionale Virgiliana di Scienze, Lettere e Arti
Via Accademia 47, 46100 Mantua 46100
Tel: (0376) 320314 *Fax:* (0376) 222774
Key Personnel
President: Prof Claudio Gallico
Publication(s): *Atti di Convegni tenuti presso l'Accademia Virgiliana; Atti e Memorie NS* (annually)

Accademia Petrarca di Lettere, Arti e Scienze
Via dell'Orto, 52100 Arezzo
Tel: (0575) 24700
Key Personnel
President: Prof Alberto Fatucchi
Secretary: Dr Tullio Bensi
Contact: Rag Luciano Nocenti
Petrarch Academy of Letters, Arts & Science.
Publication(s): *Atti e Memorie della Accademia, Studi Petrarcheschi*

Istituto Lombardo Accademia di Scienze e Lettere
Via Brera 28, 20121 Milan
Tel: (02) 864087 *Fax:* (02) 86461388
E-mail: istituto.lombardo@unimi.it
Key Personnel
President: Prof Antonio Padoa Schioppa
Vice President: Prof Emilio Gatti

Keats-Shelley Memorial Association
Piazza di Spagna 26, 00187 Rome
Tel: (06) 6784235 *Fax:* (06) 6784167
E-mail: info@keats-shelley-house.org
Web Site: www.keats-shelley-house.org
Key Personnel
Dir: Catherine Payling
Founded: 1903
Publication(s): *Review*

PEN International Centre
Via Daverio 7, 20122 Milan
Key Personnel
President: Mario Luzi
Secretary General: Marie Brunelli

Societa Dante Alighieri
Palazzo di Firenze, Piazza Firenze 27, 00186 Rome
Tel: (06) 6873694
Key Personnel
Secretary General: Giuseppe Cota
For the teaching & diffusion of Italian language & culture throughout the World.
Publication(s): *Pagine della Dante* (quarterly)

Societa Dantesca Italiana
Via dell'Arte della Lana 1, 50123 Florence
Tel: (055) 287134 *Fax:* (055) 211316
E-mail: sdi@leonet.it; sdi.biblio@leonet.it; sdi.biblio2@leonet.it
Web Site: www.danteonline.it
Key Personnel
President: Prof Francesco Mazzoni, PhD
Founded: 1888
Italian Dante Society.
Publication(s): *Edizione Nazionale delle Opere di Dante Alighieri; Quaderni degli Studi Danteschi; Quaderni del Centro Studi e Documentazione Dantesca e Medievale; Studi Danteschi* (Annual)

Japan

Japan PEN Club
Rm 265 Syuwa Residential Hotel, 9-1-7 Akasaka, Minato-ku, Tokyo
Tel: (03) 34021171; (03) 34021172 *Fax:* (03) 34025951
Key Personnel
Secretary: Hotsuki Ozaki
Publication(s): *Japanese Literature Today* (annually since 1976)

Nihon Dokubungakkai
c/o Ikubundo, Hongo 5-30-21, Bunkyo-ku, Tokyo 113-0033
Key Personnel
Contact: Prof Takao Tsunekawa
Japanese Society of German Literature.
Publication(s): *Doitsu Bungaku* (German Literature biannually)

Nihon Eibungakkai
501 Kenkyusha Bldg, 9 Surugadai 2-Chome, Kanda, Chiyoda-ku, Tokyo 101-0062
Tel: (03) 32937528 *Fax:* (03) 323937539
Key Personnel
President: Kazuhisa Takahashi
English Literary Society of Japan.
Publication(s): *Studies in English Literature* (tri-annually)

Nippon Hikaku Bungakukai
Aoyamagakuih University, Shibuya-ku, Tokyo
Key Personnel
President: K Nakajam
Secretary General: Saburo Ota
Comparative Literature Society of Japan.

Nippon Rosiya Bungakkai
c/o Baba-ken, Tokyo Institute of Technology, 2-12-1 O- okayama, Meguro-ku, Tokyo 152
Key Personnel
President: Togo Masanobu
Secretary General: T Egawa
Russian Literary Society in Japan.

Republic of Korea

Korean PEN Centre
Rm 1105, Oseong B/D, 13-5 Youido-dong, Yongdungpo-ku, Seoul 150010
Tel: (02) 782 1337; (02) 782 1338 *Fax:* (02) 786 1090
E-mail: penkon2001@yahoo.co.kr
Key Personnel
Executive Dir: Prof Yearn Hong Choi *Tel:* (02) 785 4429

REPUBLIC OF KOREA

President: Prof Ki Jo Song
Publication(s): *Korean Literature Today* (quarterly)

Liechtenstein

PEN Club Liechtenstein
Postfach 416, FL-9490 Vaduz
Tel: (0423) 2327271 *Fax:* (0423) 2328071
E-mail: pen@schlapp.li *Cable:* PEN CLUB
Key Personnel
Secretary: Dr Manfred Schlapp
  E-mail: manfred@schlapp.li
Publication(s): *Zifferblatt* (annually)

The Former Yugoslav Republic of Macedonia

Dru-stvo na Pisatelite na Makedonija
Maksim Gorki 18, 91000 Skopje
Tel: (091) 117668 *Fax:* (091) 228345
Key Personnel
President: Jovan Pavlovski
Secretaries: Paskal Gilovski; Svetlana Hristova-Jocic
Society of Writers of Macedonia.

Macedonian PEN - Skopje
Str Maksim Gorki 18, 91000 Skopje
Tel: (091) 130054 *Fax:* (091) 117668
Key Personnel
President: Mme Kata Kulavkova
Secretary: M Eftim Kletnikov

Sojuz na drustvata za makedonski jazik i literatura
Filolski fakultet, 91000 Skopje
Key Personnel
President: Elena Bendevska
Secretary: Ljupco Mitrevski
Union of Associations for Macedonian Language & Literature.
Publication(s): *Literaturen zbor* (Literary Word)

Malaysia

Dewan Bahasa dan Pustaka
Jl Dewan Bahasa, 50460 Kuala Lumpur
Tel: (03) 21481011; (03) 2481820 *Fax:* (03) 21443875
Telex: MA 32683
Key Personnel
Dir General: Haji Jumaat Moho Noor
National Language & Literary Agency.
Publication(s): *Dewan Bahasa*; *Dewan Budaya*; *Dewan Masyarakat*; *Dewan Pelajar*; *Dewan Sastera* (monthly); *Dewan Siswa* (monthly); *Tenggara* (half-yearly)

Mexico

Mexican PEN Centre
Amsterdam 266-int.6, Col. Hipodramo/Gndesa, Mexico, DF 06170 EC1M 7AT
Tel: (05) 574-4882 *Fax:* (05) 264-0813
Key Personnel
President: Victor Manuel Mendiola
  E-mail: victorma@mail.internet.com.mx
Secretary: Jose Maria Espinosa
Publication(s): *Directorio de Escritores* (annually)

Nepal

Nepal PEN Centre
PO Box 8975 EPC 533, Kathmandu
Fax: (01) 522346
E-mail: archana@icimod.org.np; grana@saligram.mos.com.np
Key Personnel
President: Dr D C Gautam
Vice President: Nagendra Raj Sharma
Secretary General: Greta Rana
Working Secretary: Archana Singh Karki
Publication(s): *Jane Eyre (in Nepali)* (With help from the Bronte Society, Translator-S Rai)

Netherlands

Maatschappij der Nederlandse Letterkunde
  (Society of Netherlands Literature)
Universiteitsbibliotheek, 2300 RA Leiden
Mailing Address: Postbus 9501, 2300 RA Leiden
Tel: (071) 5144962 *Fax:* (071) 5272836
E-mail: mnl@library.leidenuniv.nl
Key Personnel
Secretary: Dr Leo L van Maris
Publication(s): *Indische Letteren* (quarterly); *Jaarboek der Maatschappij* (annually); *De negentiende eeuw* (quarterly); *Tijdschrift voor Nederlandse Taal- en Letterkunde* (quarterly)

Netherlands Centre of the International PEN
Rogneurdonk 17, 1218 Maastricht
Tel: (043) 433498 *Fax:* (043) 433498
Key Personnel
President: Hans Van de Waarsenburg

Edgar Wallace Society
Kohlbergsgracht 40, NL-6462 CD Kerkrade HP6 5JG
Tel: (045) 5670050 *Fax:* (045) 5670070
Key Personnel
President: Penelope Wallace
Organizer: Kai J Hinz
Publication(s): *Crimson Circle* (quarterly magazine)

New Zealand

New Zealand Book Council
Old Wool House, 1st Floor, 139-141 Reclherston St, Wellington
Tel: (04) 4991569 *Fax:* (04) 4991424
Web Site: www.vuw.ac.n3/n3bookcouncil
Key Personnel
President: Sir Ken Keilk

Dir: Karen Ross *E-mail:* director@bookcouncil.org.nz
Publication(s): *Book Buyers in New Zealand*; *Books You Couldn't Buy* (censorship in New Zealand); *Landmarks of New Zealand Writing to 1945*; *Writers in Schools*

New Zealand Council for Educational Research
Education House, 178-182 Willis St, Wellington 1
Mailing Address: PO Box 3237, Wellington 1
Tel: (04) 3847939 *Fax:* (04) 3847933
Key Personnel
Dir: Dr Anne Meade *E-mail:* anne.meade@vuw.ac.nz

New Zealand Society of Authors
Mount Eden, Auckland 10
Mailing Address: PO Box 67013, Mount Eden, Auckland
E-mail: nzsa@clear.net.nz
Web Site: www.authors.org.nz
Key Personnel
Executive Secretary: Jenny Jones *Tel:* (09) 6308077
Publication(s): *New Zealand Author* (bimonthly)

New Zealand Writers Guild
PO Box 47 886, Ponsonby, Auckland 1034
Tel: (09) 360 1408 *Fax:* (09) 360-1409
E-mail: info@nzwritersguild.org.nz
Web Site: www.nzwritersguild.org.nz
Key Personnel
Executive Dir: Dominic Sheehan

PEN NZ Inc, see New Zealand Society of Authors

Norway

Information Office for Norwegian Literature Abroad, see NORLA (Information Office for Norwegian Literature Abroad)

NORLA (Information Office for Norwegian Literature Abroad)
Bygdoy Alle 21, N-0262 Oslo
Tel: 22122540 *Fax:* 22122544
E-mail: firmapost@norla.no
Web Site: www.norla.no
Key Personnel
Dir: Kristin Brudevoll
Literary Advisor: Andrine Pollen
Founded: 1978
State supported foundation offering grants to translations of Norwegian literature.
Publication(s): *Selected Norwegian Fiction*

Norske Akademi for Sprog og Litteratur
Inkognitogt 24, 0256, Oslo 2
Key Personnel
President: Helge Nordahl
Secretary: Prof Sissel Lange-Nielsen
Norwegian Academy for Language & Literature.

Det Norske Videnskaps-Akademi
Drammensveien 78, 0271 Oslo
Mailing Address: Drammensueien 78, 0271 Oslo
Tel: 22121090 *Fax:* 22121099
E-mail: dnva@online.no
Web Site: www.dnva.no
Key Personnel
Honorary President: HM The King
President: Prof Inger Moen
Vice President: Lars Wallaoe
Secretary General: Reidun Sirevag

Norwegian PEN Centre
Etterstadgat 25, N-0658 Oslo 3
Tel: 22194551 *Fax:* 22194551
Key Personnel
President: Kjell Olaf Jensen

Pakistan

Anjuman Taraqqi-e-Urdu Pakistan
Baba-e-Urdu Rd, 159 Block 7, Gulshane-e Igbal, Karachi 75300
Tel: (021) 461406; (021) 4973296; (021) 7724023
Key Personnel
President: N H Jafarey
Secretary: Jamiluddin A'Ali
For the promotion of the Urdu language and literature.
Publication(s): *Qaumi Zaban* (monthly); *Urdu* (quarterly)

Pakistan Writers' Guild
11 Abbok Rd, Anarkali, Lahore
Key Personnel
Research Officer: Inamul Haq Javeid
Secretary General: Mohamed Tufail
Publication(s): *Ham Qalam* (monthly)

Sindhi Adabi Board
PO Box 12, Hyderabad, Sind
Tel: (0221) 771276
Key Personnel
Chairman: Muhammad Ibrahim Joyo
Secretary: Ghulam Rabbani Agro
To promote the language, literature & culture of the Sind region.

Panama

PEN Club-Panamanian
PO Box 1824, Panama 1
Tel: 263-8822 *Fax:* 263-9918
Key Personnel
President: Jose Franco
Secretary: Dr Juan David Morgan

Paraguay

PEN Club del Paraguay
Casilla de Correo 487, Asuncion
Key Personnel
President: Jose-Luis Appleyard
Secretary: Guido Rodriguez Alcala

Philippines

International PEN Centre, Philippine Chapter
531 Padre Faura, 1099 Ermita, Manila
Mailing Address: PO Box 3959, 1099 Manila
Tel: (02) 5230870 *Fax:* (02) 5255038 *Cable:* SOLDAD MANILA
Key Personnel
President: Alejandro Roces
National Secretary: F Sionil Jose

Poland

Instytut Badan Literackich PAN
Nowy Swiat 72, Palac Staszica, 00-330 Warsaw
Tel: (022) 8269945
Key Personnel
Dir: Prof Alina Witkowska; Prof Elizbicta Sarnawska-Temeriusz
Institute of Literary Research of the Polish Academy of Sciences.
Publication(s): *Kwartalnik Historii Prasy Polskiej* (Quarterly of the History of the Polish Press); *Literary Studies in Poland* (semi-annually); *Pamietnik Literacki* (Literary Journal, quarterly)

Polish PEN Club
ul Krakowskie Przedmiescie 87/89, 00-079 Warsaw
Tel: (022) 8265784 *Fax:* (022) 8260589
Key Personnel
President: Jacek Bochenski
Secretary: Ewa Krasinska

Towarzystwo Literackie im Adama Mickiewicza
Nowy Swiat 72, 00-330 Warsaw
Tel: (022) 265231 (ext 279)
Key Personnel
President: Prof Zdzislaw Libera, PhD
Mickiewicz Literary Society.
Publication(s): *Rocznik* (Yearbook)

Portugal

Instituto Portugues da Sociedade Cientifica de Goerres
c/o Universidade Catolica Portuguesa, Palma de Cima, 1600 Lisbon
Tel: (021) 7265554 *Fax:* (021) 7260546
E-mail: mrato@reitoria.ucp.pt
Key Personnel
Contact: Maria Eugenia Rato
Portuguese Institute of the Goerres Research Society.
Publication(s): *Portugiesische Forschungen der Goerres Gesellschaft* (Researches in Portuguese)

PEN Clube Portugues
Subsidiary of PEN International
Rua Emb Martins Janeira, 15-6-ESQ, 1750-097 Lisbon
Mailing Address: Rua Emb Martins Janeira 15-6-E, 1750-097 Lisbon
Tel: (021) 7573452 *Fax:* (021) 7573452
E-mail: penclube@mail.telepac.pt
Key Personnel
President: Casimiro de Brito
Secretary: Manuel Frias Martins
Founded: 1978
Writers' Association.

Sociedade Portuguesa de Autores
Ave Duque de Loule 31, 1069 Lisbon Codex
Tel: (021) 578320 *Fax:* (021) 3530257 *Cable:* AUTORES
Key Personnel
President: Dr Luiz Francisco Rebello
Vice President: Dr Alvaro Salazar
Publication(s): *Autores*

Puerto Rico

Puerto Rican PEN Centre (PEN Club of Puerto Rico)
Hernandez 721, No 11N, San Juan 00907
Tel: (787) 724-0869 *Fax:* (787) 724-2060
Key Personnel
President: Dr Carlos Varo
Secretary: Maria E Ramos

Romania

Romanian PEN Centre
56 Transilvaniei St, 70778 Bucharest
Tel: (01) 3111112 *Fax:* (01) 3125854
Key Personnel
President: Ana Blandiana
Secretary: Mircea Martin

Societatea de Stiinte Filologice din Romania (SSF)
Bd Schitul Magureanu, nr 1, sector 5, 79664 Bucharest 1
Tel: (01) 6151792 *Fax:* (01) 6151792
Key Personnel
Pres: Paul Cornea
Secretary General: Mircea Franculescu
Contact: Florentina Samihaian
Publication(s): *Buletinul SSF*; *Limba si literatura* (journal); *Limba si Literatura Romania* (journal)

SSF, see Societatea de Stiinte Filologice din Romania (SSF)

Russian Federation

PEN Club-Russian
Russian PEN Centre Neglinnaya St 18/1 Bldg 2, 103031 Moscow
Tel: (095) 2094589; (095) 2093171 *Fax:* (095) 2000293
E-mail: 7416.g23@g23.relcom.ru
Key Personnel
Dir General: Alexandr Tkachenko
Editor: Mikhail Kaminsky
Contact: Y Tutchaninova

Senegal

PEN Club du Senegal
Rue 1 Prolongee Pointe, Dakar
Tel: 210471; 258009 *Fax:* 211632
Key Personnel
President: Ousmane Sembene
Secretary: Alioune Badara Beye

Slovenia

Slovene PEN Centre
Tomsiceva 12, 61000 Ljubljana
Tel: (01) 4254847
Key Personnel
President: Marko Kravos
Secretary: Iztok Ososnik
Publication(s): *Litterae Slovenicae*

Spain

Ateneo Cientifico, Literario y Artistico
Calle del Prado 21, Madrid
Tel: (01) 4296251
Key Personnel
President: Jose Prat Garcia
General Secretary: David M Rivas Infante
Scientific, Literary & Artistic Athenaeum.

Ateneo Cientifico, Literario y Artistico
Calle Cifuentes 25, Mahon, Minorca, Balearic Islands
Tel: (071) 360553
Key Personnel
President: Francesc Tutzo Bennasar
Secretary: Miguel Angel Limon Pons
Scientific, Literary & Artistic Athenaeum.
Publication(s): *Revista de Menorca* (quarterly)

Galician Pen Club
Carretas 21, 15705 Santiago De Compostela
Tel: (081) 587750
E-mail: rabade@ctv.esp
Key Personnel
President: Luis G Tusar
Secretary: Helena Villa Maneiro

Real Academia Sevillana de Buenas Letras
Abades 14, 41004 Seville
Tel: (05) 4225200
Key Personnel
Dir: Eduardo Ybarra Hidalgo
Secretary: Dr Rogelio Reyes Cano
Librarian: Alfredo Jimenez Nunez
Seville Royal Academy of Belles Lettres.
Publication(s): *Boletin de Buenas Letras* (quarterly)

Reial Academia de Bones Lletres
Bisbe Cacador, 3, 08002 Barcelona
Tel: (093) 310-2349 *Fax:* (093) 3102349
Key Personnel
President: Eduard Ripoll
Secretary: Frederic Udina
Librarian: Francisco Marsa
Royal Academy of Belles Lettres.
Publication(s): *Boletin, Memorias*

Sociedad de Ciencias, Letras y Artes El Museo Canario
Dr Chil 25, Las Palmas, Canary Islands 35001
Tel: (028) 33 68 00 *Fax:* (028) 33 68 01
E-mail: emuseo@ext.step.es
Key Personnel
President: Victor Montelongo Parada
Dir: Diego Lopez Diaz
Scientific, Literary & Art Society.
Publication(s): *El Museo Canario* (quarterly)

Sweden

Kungl Vitterhets Historie och Antikvitets Akademien (The Royal Academy of Letters, History & Antiquities)
Villagatan 3, S-114 86 Stockholm
Mailing Address: Box 5622, S-114 86 Stockholm
Tel: (08) 4404280 *Fax:* (08) 4404290
E-mail: kansli@vitterhetsakad.se
Web Site: www.vitterhetsakad.se
Key Personnel
President: Prof Anders Jeffner
Secretary-General: Prof Ulf Sporrong
Founded: 1753
Royal Academy of Letters, History & Antiquities.
Publication(s): *Arkiv (Archives)* (irregularly); *Arsbok (Yearbook)* (annually); *Fornvaennen (Journal of Swedish Antiquarian Research)* (4 times/yr); *Handlingar (Proceedings)* (irregularly); *Monografier (Monographs)* (irregularly)

Svenska Penklubben (Swedish Centre of International PEN)
c/o Natur och Kultur, PO Box 27323, 10254 Stockholm
Tel: (08) 4538677 *Fax:* (08) 4538794
Key Personnel
President: Ljiljana Dufgran
Publisher: Christian Reimers *E-mail:* christian.reimers@nok.se

Centro Uruguayo PEN
c/o Ana J Valdes, 104 20 Stockholm
Mailing Address: Box 8190, 104 20 Stockholm
Fax: (08) 155320
Key Personnel
President: Enrique Estrazulas
Secretary: Augus Poet

Samfundet De Nio (The Academy of the Nine)
c/o Anders R Oehman, Villagatan 14, SE-114 32 Stockholm
Tel: (08) 411 15 42 *Fax:* (08) 21 19 15
Key Personnel
Secretary: Anders R Oehman
President: Inge Jonsson
Founded: 1913

Svenska Penklubben, see Svenska Penklubben (Swedish Centre of International PEN)

Switzerland

Ecrivains Suisses du Groupe d'Olten, see Schweizer Autorinnen und Autoren Gruppe Olten

Gesellschaft fur deutsche Sprache und Literatur in Zurich
Deutsches Seminar der Universitaet Zuerich, Schonberggasseg, CH-8001 Zurich
Tel: (01) 6342571 *Fax:* (01) 6344905
E-mail: uguenthe@ds.unizh.ch
Key Personnel
President: Dr Ulla Gunther
Society for German Language & Literature in Zurich.

Schweizer Autorinnen und Autoren Gruppe Olten
Industriestr 23, CH-8500 Frauenfeld
Tel: (052) 7288933 *Fax:* (052) 7288932
E-mail: sekretariate@gruppe.olten
Key Personnel
President: Peter Honer
Secretary: Jochen Kelter
Contact: Rita Knecht

PEN Internazionale - Centro della Svizzera Italiana e Romancia
Postfach 314, CH-6932 Lugano-Breganzona 1
Tel: (091) 8039325 *Fax:* (091) 8039300
Key Personnel
President: Johannes Avv Clemente
Secretary: Attilia F Venturini
Publication(s): *Viceversa PEN International Centro Della Svizzera Italiana e Retoromancia, 1997*

Swiss-German PEN Club Centre
Industriestr 21, CH-8500 Frauenfeld
Tel: (031) 3724085 *Fax:* (031) 3723032
Key Personnel
President: Brechbuehl Beat
General Secretary: Barbara Traber
Publication(s): *PEN-Brief* (in German)

Schweizerische Bibliophilen -Gesellschaft
Voltastr 43, 8044 Zuerich
Key Personnel
President: Dr Conrad Ulrich *Tel:* (01) 252 6349
Swiss Society of Bibliophiles.
Publication(s): *Librarium* (published triannually since 1958)

Schweizerischer Bund fuer Jugendliteratur
Gewerbestr 8, CH-6330 Cham
Tel: 7413140 *Fax:* 7400159
E-mail: sbj@bluewin.ch
Name: Swiss Federation for Youth Literature.
Publication(s): *Autoren ud Referenten der Deutschschweiz*; *Das Buch-Dein Freund* (yearbook for lower and middle grades); *Das Buch fuer Dich* (list of recommended books; yearly); *Information Buch Oberstufe* (yearbook for upper grades); *Jugendliteratur* (quarterly journal)

Schweizerischer Schriftstellerinnen-und Schriftsteller-Verband (Swiss Writers' Union)
Nordstr 9, CH-8035 Zurich
Tel: (01) 3500460 *Fax:* (01) 3500461
E-mail: letter@ch-s.ch
Web Site: www.ch-s.ch
Key Personnel
Secretary: Peter A Schmid
Founded: 1912
Publication(s): *Neuer Judische Literatur in der Switzerland*; *Zweifache Eigenheit*

Swiss Writer's Union, see Schweizerischer Schriftstellerinnen-und Schriftsteller-Verband

Taiwan, Province of China

China National Association of Literature and the Arts
No 4, Lane 22, Nuigpo St West, Taipei

The Taipei Chinese PEN Centre
4th Floor, 4 Lane 68, When Chou St, Taipei 106, ROC
Tel: (02) 23693609 *Fax:* (02) 23699948
Cable: TAIPENCLUB
Key Personnel
President: Prof Yu Kwang-chung
Secretary: Mrs Sarah Jen-Hui Hsiang
Publication(s): *The Chinese PEN* (quarterly, text in English)

Thailand

Thailand PEN Centre
2/49 Ranong 1 Rd, Khet Dusit, Bangkok 10300
Tel: (02) 6685147; (02) 2792621
Key Personnel
President: Srisurang Poolthupya
Secretary: Wannee Phudhchareonthong
Founded: 1958
Non-profit literary society.
Publication(s): *Thailand PEN Journal* (journal)

The Siam Society
131 Soi Asoke, Sukhumvit 21, Bangkok 10110
Tel: (02) 6616470 *Fax:* (02) 2583491
Key Personnel
President: Bangkok Chowkwanyun
Coordinator: Kanitha Kasina-ubol
Publication(s): *Journal of the Siam Society* (annually); *Natural History Bulletin of the Siam Society* (annually)

Tunisia

Institut des Belles Lettres Arabes
12 rue Jamaa el Haoua, 1008 Tunis Bab Menara
Tel: (01) 560133 *Fax:* (01) 572683
E-mail: ibla@gnet.tn
Key Personnel
Dir: Jean Fontaine
Institute of Arab Belles Lettres.
Publication(s): *Revue IBLA* (biannual study of cultural problems in the Arab-Moslem world)

Union des Ecrivains Tunisiens
20 ave de Paris, Tunis 1000
Tel: (01) 257591
Key Personnel
President: Mohamed Laroussi Metoui
Secretary General: Souf Abiol
Tunisian Writers' Union.

Turkey

PEN Yazarlar Dernegi
General Yazgan, Sok 10/10, 80050, Tunel, Istanbul
Tel: (0212) 2920026 *Fax:* (0212) 2526314; (0212) 2920026
Key Personnel
President: Sukran Kurdakul
PEN - Turkish Centre.

United Kingdom

Yr Academi Gymreig (The Welsh Academy)
Mount Stuart House, 3rd floor, Mount Stuart Sq, Cardiff CF10 5FQ
Tel: (029) 20472266 *Fax:* (029) 20492930
E-mail: post@academi.org
Web Site: www.academi.org
Key Personnel
Chief Executive Officer: Peter Finch
Founded: 1959
The Welsh National Literature Promotion Agency & Society of Writers.
Publication(s): *Auto*; *Taliesin*

Alliance of Literary Societies
22 Belmont Grove, Havant, Hants P09 3PU
Tel: (023) 92475855 *Fax:* (0870) 0560330
Web Site: www.sndc.demon.co.uk/als.htm
Key Personnel
President: Susan Hill
Honorary Secretary: Rosemary Culley
  E-mail: rosemary@sndc.demon.co.uk
Publication(s): *Open Book* (Annually)

Arts Council of Wales
9 Museum Pl, Cardiff CF1 3NX
Tel: (02920) 376500 *Fax:* (01222) 221447
E-mail: information@ccc-acw.org.uk
Web Site: www.ccc-acw.org.uk
Key Personnel
Chief Executive: Frances Medley
Senior Literature Officer: Tony Bianchi

Aslib, The Association for Information Management
Stone House Ct, London EC3A 7PB
Tel: (01274) 777 700 *Fax:* (020) 7903 0011
E-mail: pubs@aslib.com
Web Site: www.aslib.co.uk
Key Personnel
Chief Executive: Roger Bowes
Head of Publications: Sarah Blair
Publication(s): *Directory of Information Sources in the UK* (biennially)

The Association for Information Management, see Aslib, The Association for Information Management

Association for Scottish Literary Studies
Dept of Scottish History, University of Glasgow, 9 University Gardens, Glasgow G12 8QH
Tel: (0141) 330 5309 *Fax:* (0141) 330 5309
Web Site: www.asls.org.uk
Key Personnel
General Manager: Duncan Jones *E-mail:* djones@scothist.arts.gla.ac.uk
Secretary: Jim Alison
Honorary Treasurer: Tom Ralph
Membership Secretary: Isobel McCallum
Founded: 1970
See also under Publishers.
Publication(s): *New Writing Scotland* (annually); *Scot Lit* (biannually); *Scottish Language* (annually); *Scottish Studies Review* (biannually)

Association of Art Historians
70 Cowcross St, London EC1M 6EJ
Tel: (020) 7490 3211 *Fax:* (020) 7490 3277
E-mail: admin@aah.org.uk
Web Site: www.aah.org.uk
Key Personnel
Chair: Prof Toshio Watanabe
Honorary Secy: Dr Penny McCracken
Administrator: Andrew Falconer
Founded: 1974
Professional arts organization which promotes the study of art history.
Publication(s): *The Art Book* (quarterly); *Art History* (5x/yr); *Bulletin* (triannually, bulletin)

Association of British Science Writers
23 Savile Row, London W1X 2NB
Tel: (020) 7439 1205 *Fax:* (020) 7973 3051
Key Personnel
President: Sir Francis Graham-Smith
Secretary: Dr Peter Briggs
Publication(s): *Science Reporter* (monthly)

Jane Austen Memorial Trust
Jane Austen's House, Chawton Alton, Hants GU34 1SD
Tel: (01420) 83262 *Fax:* (01420) 83262
Key Personnel
Administration: Thomas Carpenter
Assistant Administrator: Ann Channon
Publication(s): *Jane Austen's House* (guidebook)

Authors' Club
40 Dover St, London W1S 4NP
Tel: (020) 7499 8581 *Fax:* (020) 7409 0913
Key Personnel
Secretary: Ann De Le Grange

Francis Bacon Society Inc
C/O G N Salway, Lee House, Flat 1, 75A Effra Rd London SW19 8PS
Key Personnel
Honorary Vice President: Mary Brameld
Chairman: T D Bokenham, Esq
Designated Chairman: P A Welsford
Librarian: Prof John Spiers
Founded: 1886
Old Established Society; Custodians of the Francis Bacon Tradition.
Publication(s): *Baconiana* (periodically)

The Beatrix Potter Society
Resources for Business, South Park Rd, Macclesfield SK11 6SH
Tel: (01625) 267880 *Fax:* (01625) 267879
E-mail: bps@resources.demon.co.uk
Key Personnel
Chair: Judy Taylor
Founded: 1980
The Society promotes study & appreciation of Potter's life & works, holds regular talks & biennial Study Conference in Lake District.
Publication(s): *Books about Beatrix Potter's Life & Work* (quarterly, newsletter)

E F Benson, see The Tilling Society

E F Benson Society
The Old Coach House, High St, Rye, Sussex TN31 7JF
Tel: (01797) 223114
Key Personnel
Chair: Keith Cavers
Secretary: Allan Downend
Founded: 1984
Literary society.
Publication(s): *Bensoniana Onwards Now 3*; *The Benson's*; *The Dodo* (annual, journal)

BookPower
Formerly Educational Low-Priced Sponsored Text
305-307 Chiswick High Rd, London W4 4HH
Tel: (020) 8742 8232 *Fax:* (020) 8747 8715
E-mail: bookpower@ibd.uk.net
Web Site: www.bookpower.org
Key Personnel
Head Administration: Eileen Gillow
Founded: 1996
Charity.

Books Across the Sea
The English-Speaking Union, Dartmouth House, 37 Charles St, London W1X 8AB
Tel: (020) 7993 3338 *Fax:* (020) 7495 6108
E-mail: esu@mailbox.ulcc.ac.uk
Web Site: es.libfl.ru/eng/esu/esu-books.html
Key Personnel
Librarian: Andrea K Wathern
President: HRH The Duke of Edinburgh, KG, KT, OM
Dir General: Valerie Mitchell
Chairman: The Baroness Brigstocke
Publication(s): *Ambassador Booklist*

UNITED KINGDOM LITERARY ASSOCIATIONS

British Fantasy Society
2 Harwood St, Stockport, Cheshire SK4 1JJ
Tel: (0161) 6004125
Web Site: www.geocities.com/solto/6859
Key Personnel
President: Ramsey Campbell
Vice President: Mike Chinn
Secretary: Robert Parkinson
Publication(s): *Chills*; *Dark Horizons Newsletter*; *Mystique*

The British Science Fiction Association Ltd
44 White Way, Kidlington, Oxon OX5 2XA
Tel: (01865) 371734
E-mail: bsfa@acnestis.demon.co.uk
Key Personnel
Membership Secretary: Paul Billinger
Administrator: Vikki Lee France
Founded: 1948
Publication(s): *Focus* (biannual SF writers' magazine); *Matrix* (bimonthly newsletter); *Vector* (bimonthly critical journal)

The Bronte Society
The Bronte Parsonage Museum, Haworth, Keighley, W Yorks BD22 8DR
Tel: (01535) 642323 *Fax:* (01535) 647131
E-mail: bronte@bronte.prestel.co.uk
Web Site: www.bronte.org.uk
Key Personnel
Membership Development Officer: Rebecca Bishop *Tel:* (01535) 640195 *E-mail:* rebecca.bishop@bronte.org.uk
Founded: 1893
Publication(s): *Bronte Studies* (three times a year); *Gazette* (biannually)

Byron Society (International)
Byron House, 6 Gertrude St, London SW10 0JN
Tel: (020) 7352 5112
Key Personnel
Honorary Dir: Mrs Elma Dangerfield, OBE
Publication(s): *The Byron Journal* (annual)

Randolph Caldecott Society
Clatterwick House, Little Leigh, Northwich, Cheshire CW8 4RJ
Tel: (01606) 891303
Key Personnel
Secy: Kenn Oultram
Founded: 1970
Publication(s): *Caldecott Sketch*

Cambridge Bibliographical Society
University Library, West Rd, Cambridge CB3 9DR
Tel: (01223) 333123 *Fax:* (01223) 333160
E-mail: cbs@ula.cam.ac.uk
Key Personnel
Honorary Secretary: N A Smith
 E-mail: nas1000@cam.ac.uk
Founded: 1949
Publication(s): *Monographs* (irregularly); *Transactions* (annually)

The Centre for Creative Communities
118 Commercial St, London E1 6NF
Tel: (020) 7247 5385 *Fax:* (020) 7247 5256
E-mail: baaa@easynet.co.uk
Key Personnel
Executive Dir: Jennifer Williams

Children's Books History Society
25 Field Way, Hoddesdon, Herts EN11 0QN
Tel: (01992) 464885 *Fax:* (01992) 464885
E-mail: cbhs@abcgarrelt.demon.co.uk
Key Personnel
Chairman: Morna Daniels
Secretary: Mrs Pat Garrett
Treasurer: Sarah Jardine-Willoughby
Founded: 1969
In 1990 a biennial Harvey Darton Award was established for a book published in English, which extends our knowledge of some aspect of British children's literature of the past.
Publication(s): *CBHS Newsletter* (3x/ann, newsletter)

The John Clare Society
The Stables, 1a West St, Helpston, Peterborough PE6 7DU
Tel: (01733) 252678 *Fax:* (01733) 252678
Web Site: www.thezone.virgin.net/linda.curry/jclaresoceity.htm
Key Personnel
President: Ronald Blythe
Vice President: Prof Eric Robinson; Edward Storey; Prof Kelsey Thornton
Editor: Dr John Goodridge
Member Secretary: Linda Curry
Honorary Secretary: Peter Moyse *E-mail:* moyse.helpston@talk21.com
Founded: 1981
To promote a wider & deeper knowledge of the poet, John Clare (1793-1864).
Publication(s): *The John Clare Society Journal* (annual July)

The Joseph Conrad Society (UK)
c/o POSK, 238-46 King St, London W6 0RF
E-mail: k.carabine@ukc.ac.uk; allansimmons@compuserve.com
Web Site: www.bathspa.ac.uk/conrad/
Key Personnel
President: Philip Conrad
Secretary: Hugh Epstein *E-mail:* hepstein@freecall-uk.co.uk
Founded: 1973
Literary society devoted to all aspects of the study of the works & life of Joseph Conrad (1857-1924).
Publication(s): *The Conradian* (2x ann)

Critics' Circle
c/o The Stage Newspaper, 47 Bermondsey St, London SE1 3XT
Tel: (020) 7403 1818 (ext 148) *Fax:* (020) 7357 9287
Key Personnel
Contact: Catherine Cooper

Daresbury Lewis Carroll Society
Clatterwick House, Little Leigh, Northwich, Cheshire CW8 4RJ
Tel: (01606) 891303
Key Personnel
Secretary: Kenn Oultram
Founded: 1970
Publication(s): *Stuff & Nonsense*

The Dickens Fellowship
Dickens House, 48 Doughty St, London WC1N 2LF
Tel: (020) 7405 2127 *Fax:* (020) 7831 5175
Key Personnel
Honorary General Secretary: Dr Tony R Williams *E-mail:* arwilliams33@compuserve.com; Mrs Thelma Grove
Editor: Prof Malcolm Andrews
Affiliated to the Alliance of Literary Societies, The Birmingham & Midland Institute, 9 Margaret St, Birmingham, B 3BS.
Publication(s): *The Dickensian* (triannually); *Mr Dick's Kite* (Newsletter triannually)

The Dorothy L Sayers Society
Rose Cottage, Malthouse Lane, Hurstpierpoint, West Sussex BN6 9JY
Tel: (01273) 833444 *Fax:* (01273) 835988
E-mail: jasmine@bredon.demon.co.uk
Key Personnel
Chairman: Christopher J Dean
Honorary Secretaries: Lenelle Davis; Jasmine Simeone
Founded: 1976
Publication(s): *Poetry of Dorothy L Sayers*; *Sidelights on Sayers* (annual proceedings)

Early English Text Society
Christ Church, Oxford OX1 1DP
Web Site: eets.org.uk
Key Personnel
Honorary Dir: Prof John Burrow
Executive Secretary: R F S Hamer
Founded: 1864

Edinburgh Bibliographical Society
Dept of Special Collections, Edinburgh University Library, George Sq, Edinburgh EH8 9LJ
Tel: (0131) 6503412 *Fax:* (0131) 6506863
E-mail: exkb33@srv1.lib.ed.ac.uk
Telex: 727442
Key Personnel
Honorary Secretary: M Simpson
Publication(s): *Transactions* (biennial - for members only)

Educational Low-Priced Sponsored Text, see BookPower

The Eighteen Nineties Society
97d Brixton Rd, London SW9 6EE
Tel: (020) 7582 4690
Key Personnel
President: Elizabeth The Countess of Longford
Patron: HRH Princess Michael of Kent
Chair: Martyn Goff
Treasurer: Martin Paisher
Honorary Secretary: G Krishnamurti
Publication(s): *The Journal of the Eighteen Nineties Societies* (annually); *The Keynote* (quarterly newsletter)

The George Eliot Fellowship
71 Stepping Stones Rd, Coventry CV5 8JT
Tel: (024) 7659 2231
Key Personnel
President: Jonathan G Ouvry
Vice President: Rosemary Ashton, PhD; A S Byatt; Tenniel Evans; Beryl Gray, PhD; Graham Handley, PhD; Ruth Harris; John Rignall, PhD; Harriet Williams; Michael Wolff; Margaret Wolfit; Gabriel Woolf
Secretary: Hr Kathleen Adams
Founded: 1930
Publication(s): *George Eliot Review* (annually); *Pitkin Guide to George Eliot (illustrated)*; *Those Of Us Who Loved Her: The Men In George Eliot's Life*

Thomas Ellis Memorial Fund
University Registry, Univ of Wales, Cathays Park, Cardiff CF10 3NS
Tel: (029) 2038 2656 *Fax:* (029) 2078 6259
E-mail: awards@wales.ac.uk
Key Personnel
Secretary General: Dr Lynn Williams

English Association
University Leicester, University Rd, Leicester LE1 7RH
Tel: (0116) 2523982 *Fax:* (0116) 2522301
E-mail: engassoc@le.ac.uk
Web Site: www.le.ac.uk/engassoc/
Key Personnel
Chair: Elaine Treharne
Chief Executive: Helen Lucas *Tel:* (0116) 252 2300 *E-mail:* hl11@le.ac.uk
Founded: 1906
Publication(s): *EA Newsletter* (3 times annually); *English* (3 times annually); *English 4-11* (3 times annually); *Essays and Studies* (annually); *The Use of English* (3 times annually); *The*

The English-Speaking Union of the Commonwealth
37 Charles St, London W1J 5ED
Tel: (020) 7529 1550 *Fax:* (020) 7495 6108
E-mail: esu@esu.org
Web Site: www.esu.org
Key Personnel
Dir General: Valerie Mitchell
Librarian: Andrea Wathern *Tel:* (020) 7529 1587
  E-mail: library@esu.org
Founded: 1918
Branches worldwide in 52 countries.
Publication(s): *Concord*

Hakluyt Society
c/o Map Library, The British Library, Great Russell St, 96 Euston Rd, London NW1 2DB
Tel: (01428) 641850 *Fax:* (01428) 641933
E-mail: office@hakluyt.com
Web Site: www.hakluyt.com
Key Personnel
President: Sarah Tyacke
Administrator: Richard Bateman
Publications of scholarly editions of records of voyages, travels & other geographical material of the past.
Publication(s): *The Hakluyt Society* (third series)

Thomas Hardy Society
PO Box 1438, Dorchester, Dorset DT1 1YH
Tel: (01305) 251501 *Fax:* (01305) 251501
E-mail: info@hardysociety.org
Web Site: hardysociety.org
Key Personnel
Chair: Dr Simon Curtis
Secretary: Olive Blackburn
List of publications available.
Publication(s): *The Thomas Hardy Journal* (3 times/yr)

The Richard Jefferies Society
Eidsvoll, Bedwells Heath, Boars Hill, Oxford OX1 5JE
Tel: 01865 735678
Web Site: web.sirius.com/~treitel/jefferies.html
Key Personnel
President: Prof Jeremy Hooker
Secretary: Phyllis Treitel
Founded: 1950
Publication(s): *The Richard Jefferies Society Journal*

Keats-Shelley Memorial Association
10 Lansdowne Rd, Tunbridge Wells TN1 2NJ
Tel: (01892) 533452 *Fax:* (01892) 519142
Key Personnel
Honorary Treasurer: R Cavaliero
Publication(s): *Keats-Shelley Review* (annual)

Kipling Society
6 Clifton Rd, Maida Vale, London W9 1S5
Tel: (020) 7286 0194 *Fax:* (020) 7286 0194
Web Site: www.kipling.org.uk
Key Personnel
Honorary Secretary: Jane Keskar *E-mail:* jane@keskar.fsworld.co.uk
Founded: 1927
Publication(s): *The Kipling Journal* (quarterly)

Charles Lamb Society
BM Elia, London WC1N 3XX
Key Personnel
Chairman: N R D Powell
Publication(s): *The Charles Lamb Bulletin* (quarterly)

Lancashire Authors' Association
Heatherslade, 5 Quakerfields, Westhoughton, Bolton, Lancs BL5 2BJ
Tel: (01942) 791390
Key Personnel
Chairman: George W White
General Secretary: Eric Holt
Publication(s): *Lancashire Miscellany* (1987/8/90 cassette tapes); *The Record* (quarterly)

Friends of Arthur Machen
5 Birch Terrace, Hanging Birch Lane, Horam, East Sussex TN21 0PA
Tel: (01633) 422520 *Fax:* (0633) 421055
Web Site: www.machensoc.demon.co.uk
Key Personnel
President: Barry Humphries
Secretary: Adrian Eckersley *E-mail:* adrian@machensoc.demon.co.uk
Patron: Julian Lloyd Webber
Publication(s): *Avallaunius* (Journal); *The Silurist* (News Letter)

Medical Writers Group
Society of Authors, 84 Drayton Gardens, London SW10 9SB
Tel: (020) 7373 6642 *Fax:* (020) 7373 5768
E-mail: info@societyofauthors.org
Web Site: www.societyofauthors.org
Key Personnel
Contact: Dorothy Sym
Divisions: The Society of Authors

The Mervyn Peake Society
Rupera, Trinity Rd, Mistley, Manningtree, Essex CO11 2HL
Tel: (01206) 396 130
Key Personnel
Contact: Yvonne McLean

William Morris Society
Kelmscott House, 26 Upper Mall, London W6 9TA
Tel: (020) 8741 3735 *Fax:* (020) 8748 5207
Key Personnel
President: Linda Parry
Editor: Dr Rosie Miles
Publication(s): *Biannual Journal*

Oxford Bibliographical Society
c/o Bodleian Library, Oxford OX1 3BG
Tel: (01865) 277102 *Fax:* (01865) 277182
Telex: 83656
Key Personnel
Secretary: Mrs M Szurko
Publication(s): *First Series* (Vols 1-VII, 1923-46); *New Series* (Vol I, 1948-, Vol 23, 1992); *Occasional Publications* (No 1, 1967-); *Third Series* (Vol 1, 1996)

English Centre of International PEN
152-156 Kentish Town Rd, London NW1 9QB
Tel: (020) 7267 9444 *Fax:* (020) 7267 9304
E-mail: enquiries@pen.org.uk
Web Site: www.pen.org.uk
Key Personnel
President: Victoria Glendinning
Executive Dir: Diana Reich
Programme Dir, Writers in Prison Committee: Lucy Popescu
Membership Secretary: Simon Burt
Publication(s): *PEN News* (biannual, newsletter)

PEN Scottish Centre
26 E Clyde St, Helensburgh G80 7PG
Tel: (01436) 672010
Key Personnel
President: Mr Robin Lloyd-James
Secretary: Simon Berry

The Poetry Society Inc
22 Betterton St, London WC2H 9BX
Tel: (020) 7420 9880 *Fax:* (020) 7240 4818
E-mail: poetryreview@poetrysociety.org.uk
Web Site: www.poetrysociety.org.uk
Key Personnel
Dir: Christina Patterson
Membership Manager: Vera Di Campli San Vito
  Tel: (020) 7420 9881
Publication(s): *Jumpstart: Poetry in the Secondary School*; *Poems on the the Underground Posters*; *The Poetry Book for Primary Schools*; *Poetry News*; *Poetry Review*

The Arthur Ransome Society Ltd (TARS)
Abbot Hall, Art Gallery & Museum, Kirkland, Kendal, Cumbria LA9 5AL
Tel: (01539) 722464
E-mail: tarsinfo@arthur-ransome.org
Web Site: www.arthur-ransome.org/ar
Key Personnel
President: Norman Willis
Company Secretary: Dr Bill Janes
Branch offices located in Australia, Japan, New Zealand & United States.
Publication(s): *Literary Conference Papers* (biannual); *Mixed Moss* (biannual); *Outlaw* (biannual); *Signals* (biannual)

Romantic Novelists' Association
One Beechwood Ct, The Street, Synderstone, Norfolk PE31 8SD
Tel: (01827) 714776 (voice & fax)
Web Site: freespace.virgin.net/marina.oliver/apfrm.htm
Key Personnel
Chairman: Jean Saunders
Honorary Secretary: Joyce Bell

Royal Literary Fund
3 Johnson's Court, off Fleet St, London EC4A 3EA
Tel: (020) 7353 7150 *Fax:* (020) 7353 7150
Key Personnel
President: Sir Stephen Tumim
General Secretary: Eileen Gunn
Publication(s): *Archives of the Royal Literary Fund 1790-1918* (printed guide & microfilm)

The Royal Society for the Encouragement of Arts, Manufactures & Commerce-RSA
8 John Adam St, London WC2N 6EZ
Tel: (020) 7930 5115 *Fax:* (020) 7839 5805
Key Personnel
Acting Dir: James Sandison

Royal Society of Literature of the United Kingdom
Somerset House, Strand, London WC2R 1LA
Tel: (020) 7845 4676 *Fax:* (020) 7845 4679
E-mail: info@rslit.org
Web Site: www.rslit.org
Key Personnel
Secretary: Mrs M Fergusson
Assistant Secretary: Julia Abel Smith *Tel:* (020) 7845 4677 *E-mail:* julia@rslit.org
Founded: 1820
Registered charity.
Publication(s): *News From the Royal Society of Literature*

The Ruskin Society of London
Subsidiary of The Royal Society of Literature
351 Woodstock Rd, Oxford OX2 7NX
Tel: (01865) 310987; (01865) 515962
  Fax: (01865) 240448
Key Personnel
Secretary: A Hardy
Founded: 1980

Articles & news of Ruskinian interest & nineteenth century literary history.
Publication(s): *The Ruskin Gazette* (Annually, journal)

Shakespearean Authorship Trust
11 Old Sq, Lincoln's Inn, London WC2A 3TS
Tel: (020) 7242 6995 *Fax:* (020) 7242 6995
Key Personnel
Chairman: Dr L L Ware
Honorary Secretary: Dr D W Vessey
Publication(s): *The Bard* (last published May 1984)

The Shaw Society
51 Farmfield Rd, Bromley, Kent BR1 4NF
Tel: (020) 86973619 *Fax:* (020) 86973619
Key Personnel
Editor: T F Evans
General Secretary: Barbara Smoker
Treasurer: R Abrahams
Publication(s): *The Shavian* (every nine months)

Society for the Study of Medieval Languages and Literature
Dept of English, De Montfort University, Leicester LF1 9BH
Mailing Address: St Hugh's College, St Margaret's Rd, Oxford OX2 6LE
Tel: (01865) 270665 *Fax:* (01865) 270600
Key Personnel
President: Mr AVC Schmidt
Secretary: Dr Roger Dalrymple *E-mail:* roger.dalrymple@st-hughs.ox.ac.uk
Treasurer: Dr D G Pattison
Publication(s): *Medium Aevum/Medium Aevum Monographs* (new series)

Society of Freelance Editors & Proofreaders
Mermaid House, One Mermaid Court, London SE1 1HR
Tel: (020) 7403 5141 *Fax:* (020) 7407 1193
E-mail: admin@sfep.org.uk
Web Site: www.sfep.org.uk
Key Personnel
Chair: Naomi Laredo
Founded: 1988
Professional body providing training, information, support, electronic resources & newsletters.
Publication(s): *CopyRight* (magazine)

The Society of Women Writers & Journalists
Calvers Farm, Thelveton, Diss, Norfolk IP23 4NG
Tel: (01379) 740550 *Fax:* (01379) 741716
Web Site: www.author.co.uk/swwj.html
Key Personnel
Secretary/Vice Chairman: Jean Hawkes
Membership Secretary: Joyce Elsden *Tel:* (1903) 774688 *Fax:* (1903) 230266
Publication(s): *The Woman Writer*

TARS, see The Arthur Ransome Society Ltd (TARS)

The Tilling Society
5 Friars Bank, Guestling, Hastings TN35 4EJ
Fax: (01424) 813237
Key Personnel
Joint-Secretary: Cynthia Reavell; Tony Reavell
Founded: 1982
Publication(s): *E F Benson as Mayor of Rye* (book); *Tilling Society Newsletter* (biannually, newsletter)

The Tolkien Society
201 Prestbury Rd, Cheltehnam, Glocs GL521 3ER
Tel: (01242) 529757
Key Personnel
Secretary: Sally Kennett
Publication(s): *Amon Hen* (bulletin, 6 issues a year); *Mallorn* (journal, annually)

Translators Association
c/o Society of Authors, 84 Drayton Gradens, London SW10 9SB
Tel: (020) 7373 6642 *Fax:* (020) 7373 5768
E-mail: info@societyofauthors.org
Web Site: www.societyofauthors.org
Key Personnel
Secretary: Dorothy Sym
The Association is a specialist group representing published literary translators within the Society of Authors.
Publication(s): *In Other Words* (journal); *Quick Guide to Literary Translation*

H G Wells Society
49 Beckingthorpe Dr, Bottesford, Nottingham NG13 0DN
Web Site: hgwellsusa.50megs.com
Key Personnel
Secretary: Dr J R Hammond
Founded: 1960
Publication(s): *The Wellsian* (annually); *H G Wells: A Comprehensive Bibliography*

The Welsh Academy, see Yr Academi Gymreig

West Country Writers' Association
High Wotton, Wotton Lane, Lympstone, Exmouth, Devon EX8 5AY
Tel: (01395) 222749
Key Personnel
Secretary: Mrs Judy Joss
Founded: 1951

Uruguay

Academia Nacional de Letras
Ituzaingo 1255, 11000 Montevideo
Tel: (02) 9152374 *Fax:* (02) 0167460
Telex: 23133 Mec Ug
Key Personnel
President of Academy: Antonio Cravotto
Secretary of Academy: Carlos Jones
Publication(s): *Boletin de la Academia Nacional de Letras*; *Revista Nacional*

Venezuela

Centro Venezolano del PEN Internacional
Apdo de Correos 14413, Caracas 1010-A
Tel: (02) 5616691; (02) 5617589; (02) 5617287 *Fax:* (02) 5718064
Telex: 26217 Biaya *Cable:* BIAYACUCH
Key Personnel
President: Dr Jose Ramon Medina
Secretary: Oswaldo Trejo
Publication(s): *Con Textos; Coleccion Plural*

Yugoslavia

Serbian PEN Centre
Francuska br 7, 11000 Belgrade
Tel: (011) 626081 *Fax:* (011) 635979
Key Personnel
President: Miodrag Perisic
Secretary: Dr Kosta Cavoski
Publication(s): *Pismo* (quarterly, published jointly with "Jovan Popovic" Library, Zemun)

Zimbabwe

The Literature Bureau
Ministry of Education, Sport & Culture, Causeway, Harare
Mailing Address: PO Box CY121, Causeway, Harare
Tel: (04) 333812
Key Personnel
Chief Publications Officer: B C Chitsike

The Zimbabwe Writers Union
Gloag High School, PO Box 61, Bulawayo
Tel: (09) 531305
Key Personnel
President: D Mungoshi
Secretary General: Pathisa Nyathi

Literary Prizes

Prizes and awards are listed alphabetically under the country where the sponsor is located. In some instances, recipients are restricted to the country in which the prize or award is presented.

☆ indicates those prizes with no geographical restriction placed upon recipients.

Argentina

Concurso Literario Premio Emece
Emece Editores SA
Av Independencia 1668, C 1100 ABQ Buenos Aires
Tel: (011) 4382-4043; (011) 4382-4045
Web Site: www.emece.com.ar
Key Personnel
Editorial Department: Ms Mirta Mallo
E-mail: mmallo@eplaneta.com.ar
Established: 1954
For the best unpublished novel or book of short stories in the Spanish language.

National Prize for Literature
Argentina Ministry of Education & Justice
Subsecretary of Culture, Eizzurno 935, 1020 Buenos Aires
For best works of prose & poetry. Awarded every three years.

Premio Academia Nacional de la Historia
Academia Nacional de la Historia
Balcarce 139, 1064 Buenos Aires
Tel: (021) 3315147 *Fax:* (011) 3314633
E-mail: postmaster@anh.edu.ar
National Academy of History Award.

Australia

Greater Dandenong Short Story Competition, see Greater Dandenong Writing Awards

The Age Book of the Year Awards
The Age
250 Spencer St, Melbourne, Victoria 3000
Tel: (03) 6004211 *Fax:* (03) 6707514
Two prizes will be awarded by 'The Age' to the two Australian books of outstanding literary merit which best express Australia's identity or character: one prize for a work of imaginative writing, the other for a nonfiction work. One will be named 'The Age' Book of the Year and will receive a $4000 prize. The other the best work in its category, and will receive a $3000 prize.

Alexander Henderson Award
Australian Institute of Genealogical Studies Inc
1/41 Railway Rd, Blackburn, Melbourne, Victoria 3130
Mailing Address: PO Box 339, Blackburn, Melbourne, Victoria 3130
Tel: (03) 98773789 *Fax:* (03) 98779066
E-mail: aigs@alphalink.com.au
Web Site: www.alphalink.com.au/~aigs/index.htm
Established: 1973
Best Australian family history book, written & entered for the award.
Closing Date: Nov 30 each year
Presented: Last Friday of May

The Alice Literary Award
Society of Women Writers (Australia)
c/o The President, GPO Box 121A, Melbourne, Victoria 3001
Tel: (03) 2986117
Presented by the Society of Women Writers (Australia) biennially for a distinguished & long-term contribution to literature by an Australian woman. First presented in 1978.

APA Book Design Awards
Australian Publishers Association Ltd
89 Jones St, Suite 60, Ultimo, NSW 2007
Tel: (02) 9281 9788 *Fax:* (02) 9281 1073
E-mail: apa@publishers.asn.au
Web Site: www.publishers.asn.au
Key Personnel
Contact: Susan Bridge
Recognizes creativity, excellence & innovation in contemporary Australian book design. Books entered must have been designed in Australia & published for the first time during the preceding calendar year. There are 20 award categories which feature prizes to the value of $1000. Entries open in October & close in January. Winners are announced at the Book Design Awards, held in conjunction with the Australian Book Fair at Darling Harbour in June.

APA Campus Bookstore of the Year Award
Formerly Tertiary Bookseller of the Year Award
Australian Publishers Association Ltd
89 Jones St, Suite 60, Ultimo, NSW 2007
Tel: (02) 9281 9788 *Fax:* (02) 9281 1073
E-mail: apa@publishers.asn.au
Web Site: www.publishers.asn.au

APA Publisher of the Year Award
Australian Publishers Association Ltd
89 Jones St, Suite 60, Ultimo, NSW 2007
Tel: (02) 9281 9788 *Fax:* (02) 9281 1073
E-mail: apa@publishers.asn.au
Web Site: www.publishers.asn.au
Peer-assessment award, acknowledging professional performance by organizations during the previous calendar year.
Presented: Australian Book Industry Awards Dinner at the Australian Book Fair in June, Annually in June

The Kitty Archer-Burton Award
Society of Women Writers (Australia)
c/o The President, GPO Box 121A, Melbourne, Victoria 3001
Tel: (03) 2986117
Presented by the Society of Women Writers (Australia) biennially for verse by a youth of under 19 years of age. First presented in 1979.

Arts Queensland Judith Wright Calanthe Award for Poetry
Brisbane Writers Festival Association Inc
PO Box 3567, South Brisbane, Qld 4101
Tel: (07) 3255 0254 *Fax:* (07) 3255 0362
E-mail: writers@qpac.com.au
Established: 1997
Award for poetry by an Australian author.
Other Sponsor(s): Arts Queensland
Closing Date: July 2003
Presented: Oct 2003

Arts Queensland Steele Rudd Short Story Award
Brisbane Writers Festival Association Inc
PO Box 3567, South Brisbane, Qld 4101
Tel: (07) 3255 0254 *Fax:* (07) 3255 0362
E-mail: writers@qpac.com.au
Established: 1997
Award for a collection of short stories by an Australian author.
Other Sponsor(s): Arts Queensland
Closing Date: July 2003
Presented: Oct 2003

Australian Literature Society Gold Medal
Association for the Study of Australian Literature
School of Humanities & General Studies, Univ of W Sidney, MacArthur Campus, Campbelltown, ACT 2560
Tel: (046) 203151 *Fax:* (046) 281298
Award originated by Colonel, the Honourable R A Crouch in 1899 & continued by the Australian Literature Society until 1983 when the ALS incorporated with the Association for the Study of Australian Literature. It is awarded annually for the most outstanding Australian literary work, or for outstanding services to Australian literature.

Australian Vogel Literary Award
Allen & Unwin Pty Ltd, The Australian Newspaper, Vogel Breads
PO Box 8500, Saint Leonards, NSW 2065
Tel: (02) 8425 0100 *Fax:* (02) 99062218
Web Site: www.allenandunwin.com
Key Personnel
Contact: Emma Sorensen *E-mail:* emmas@allenandunwin.com
Established: 1980
Literary Award for an unpublished manuscript by Australian authors under 35 years of age.
Other Sponsor(s): The Australian Newspaper
Closing Date: May annually
Presented: Sept/Oct

The Marten Bequest Travelling Scholarships
Permanent Ltd
35 Clarence St, Sydney, NSW 2000
Tel: (02) 8295 8191 *Fax:* (02) 8295 8693
Key Personnel
Awards Administrator: Linda Ingaldo
E-mail: linda.ingaldo@permanentgroup.com.au
Six scholarships awarded annually. $18,000 awarded for study in the following area(s): singing, instrumental music, painting, ballet, sculpture, architecture, prose, poetry & acting. Entrants must be born in Australia & between the ages of 21-35 (except in the field of ballet: ages 17-35).
Award: Scholarship
Closing Date: Oct/Nov of year previous

Bronze Swagman Award
Winton Tourist Promotion Association
PO Box 44, Winton, Qld 4735

AUSTRALIA

Tel: (07) 46571466 *Fax:* (07) 46571886
Key Personnel
Secretary: I Jempson
Awarded for Bush Verse. Book verse available in December of each year.
Award: Annually; Bronze statuette of The Swagman, sculpted by Daphne Mayo, valued at $2500 & a Winton opal, valued at $150
Closing Date: Jan 31
Presented: Easter Annually

R Carson-Gold Memorial Short Story Competition
Fellowship of Australian Writers Queensland
PO Box 1871, Brisbane, Qld 4001
Awarded annually. Closes 23 April. Short story by Australian with Australian setting. 1st Prize $600, 2nd Prize $300, 3rd Prize $100. Administered by the Union Fidelity Trust Company of Australia.

Children's Book of the Year Awards
Children's Book Council of Australia
PO Box 275, Carlton S, Victoria 3053
Tel: (03) 9349 3111
Awarded annually by the Children's Book Council of Australia.
(1) Book of the Year, established 1946.
(2) Junior Book of the Year, established 1982.
(3) Picture Book of the Year established 1952. $30,000 to be distributed amongst the winners & honor books (possibility of two) in each category.
(4) The Eve Pownall Information Book Award (nonfiction) established 1993. $10,000 to be distributed between winner & up to two honor books.

The City of Brisbane Prize for Asia-Pacific Travel Writing
Brisbane Writers Festival Association Inc
PO Box 3567, South Brisbane, Qld 4101
Tel: (07) 3255 0254 *Fax:* (07) 3255 0362
E-mail: writers@qpac.com.au
Key Personnel
Production Coordinator: Catherine Sheedy
Established: 1997
Other Sponsor(s): Brisbane City Council
Closing Date: July 2003
Presented: Brisbane Writers Festival, Oct 2003

Tom Collins Poetry Prize
Western Australia Fellowship of Australian Writers
Tom Collins House, 88 Wood St, Swanbourne, WA 6010
Mailing Address: FAWWA, PO Box 312, Cottesloe, WA 6011
Tel: (09) 3844771 *Fax:* (09) 3844854
E-mail: fawwa@iinet.net.au
Key Personnel
President: Gwenda Steff
First awarded in 1977. Administered by Western Australia FAW, and sponsored by J Furphy & Sons, Shepparton, Victoria, since 1984, for a poem of up to 60 lines. Three prizes: $500 open, $200 for the highest commended entry, & $100 (x3) commended. Closing date 31 December.

C H Currey Memorial Fellowship
State Library of NSW Press
Macquarie St, Sydney, NSW 2000
Tel: (02) 92731414 *Fax:* (02) 92731248
E-mail: library@ilanet.slnsw.gov.au
Web Site: www.s/nsw.gov.au

Emeritus Awards
Australia Council Literature Board
PO Box 788, Strawberry Hills, NSW 2012

Tel: (02) 9215 9000; (02) 9215 9056 *Fax:* (02) 9215 9111
Web Site: www.ozco.gov.au
Key Personnel
Administrator: Maggie Joel *E-mail:* m.joel@ozco.gov.au
Open to Australian writers over the age of 65 who must be nominated by other people. They must have produced a critically acclaimed body of work over a long creative life. Nominators must give evidence that the maximum annual income of the nominated writer is less than $40,000.
Closing Date: Nomination May 15

FAW Anne Elder Poetry Award
Fellowship of Australian Writers (Vic) Inc
33 Windsor Crescent, Camberwell, Victoria 3127
Tel: (03) 98973977
First prize $1000 & second prize $500 awarded to writers whose first book of poetry has been published during 1994. An award is possible where up to four poets contribute to a book, providing it is the first published book-length collection of poetry by the authors concerned. Book must be at least 20 pages. Self-published works are eligible. Publishers & authors can also submit entries. Three copies of each book required & will not be returned. Open to Australia residents only. The award opens the second week of September & closes the third week of November each year.

FAW Australian Unity Literature Award
Fellowship of Australian Writers (Vic) Inc
33 Windsor Crescent, Camberwell, Victoria 3127
Tel: (03) 98973977
Award for work of sustained quality & distinction with an Australian theme, first published during 1995. Three copies of the book are required & will not be returned. A prize of $1500 will be offered. Open to Australia residents only. The award opens the second week of September & closes the third week of November each year.

FAW C J Dennis Poetry Award
Fellowship of Australian Writers (Vic) Inc
33 Windsor Crescent, Camberwell, Victoria 3127
Tel: (03) 98973977
Award to a young writer (10-14 years). Only one copy of poem required. Prizes of $100 & $50 will be awarded. Open to Australia residents only. The award opens the second week of September & closes the third week of November each year.

FAW Christopher Brennan Award
Fellowship of Australian Writers (Vic) Inc
33 Windsor Crescent, Camberwell, Victoria 3127
Tel: (03) 98973977
A plaque designed by sculptor Michael Meszaros is awarded to a poet in Australia whose work is of sustained distinction. Entries not required. Open to Australia residents only. The award opens the second week of September & closes the third week of November each year.

FAW Fedora Anderson Poetry Award
Fellowship of Australian Writers (Vic) Inc
33 Windsor Crescent, Camberwell, Victoria 3127
Tel: (03) 98973977
Award to a young writer (15-20 years). One copy of the poem is required. Prizes of $150 and $75 will be awarded. Open to Australia residents only. The award opens the second week of September & closes the third week of November each year.

FAW Mary Grant Bruce Story Award for Children's Literature
Fellowship of Australian Writers (Vic) Inc

33 Windsor Crescent, Camberwell, Victoria 3127
Tel: (03) 98973977
Award to recognize and honor the contribution by Mary Grant Bruce to children's literature, to promote Sale & district as her birthplace, and to encourage the writing of higher quality children's short stories. The trust is administered by the City of Sale. The story should be aimed at young readers aged between 10-15 years. Entries may be no longer than 5000 words. Two copies of the story are required. More than one entry may be submitted. $600 award to winner of open section. Second prize $300. Others may be commended. Writers living in the Gippsland area, as described by Municipal boundaries, are also eligible for separate $200 award. Open to Australia residents only.
The award opens the second week of September & closes the third week of November each year.

FAW Mavis Thorpe Clark Award
Fellowship of Australian Writers (Vic) Inc
33 Windsor Crescent, Camberwell, Victoria 3127
Tel: (03) 98973977
Awarded to postprimary students. One prize is for an individual submission & the other for a group entry. With the exception of school newspapers, all other kinds of creative writing are eligible. At least 10 items required, but volume is not of great importance. Individual submissions are restricted to one per student, but schools may submit more than one group entry. All entrants must be attending the same postprimary school in Australia & the work original & written in the current calendar year. Presentation, layout & design are not key criteria, but entries should be securely bound in some way. Only one copy of each entry required. Open to Australia residents only.
Award: Two prizes of $150
Closing Date: Opens the 2nd week of Sept; closes the 3rd week of Nov

The Festival Awards for Literature
Arts South Australia
GPO Box 2308, Adelaide, SA 5001
Tel: (08) 82077100 *Fax:* (08) 82077159
Web Site: www.arts.sa.gov.au
Key Personnel
Project Manager: Penelope Curtin
The awards are offered biennially by the South Australian Government & announced during Writers' Week of the Adelaide Festival of Arts. The seven awards offered are: (1) The National Fiction Award for a published novel or a collection of short stories ($16,000); (2) The John Bray Award for Poetry for a published collection of poetry ($16,000); (3) The National Children's Literature Award for a published children's book, fiction or nonfiction ($16,000); (4) The National Nonfiction Award for a published work of nonfiction ($16,000); (5) The Jill Blewett Playwright's Award for a play script performed by a professional theatre company or a professional production unit ($16,000); (6) Carclew Fellowship, a fellowship of up to 6 months at Carclew, open to writers resident in South Australia ($16,000); (7) South Australian Premier's Literary Award for the most outstanding published work submitted to the Festival for Literature (extra $5000 added to winner's $15,000 category prize). Authors of published works must be citizens or residents of Australia.

The Miles Franklin Literary Award
Permanent Ltd
35 Clarence St, Sydney, NSW 2000
Tel: (02) 8295 8191 *Fax:* (02) 8295 8693

Key Personnel
Awards Administrator: Linda Ingaldo
 E-mail: linda.ingaldo@permanentgroup.com.au
Established: 1957
Australia's most prestigious literary award. Award to the novel or play which is the best for its year & which represents Australia's life in any of its phases. Annual award.
Award: $28000 AUD
Closing Date: Dec 15
Presented: State Library of NSW, May/June

The Mary Gilmore Award
Association for the Study of Australian Literature
School of Humanities & General Studies, Univ of W Sydney, Macarthur Campus, Campbelltown ACT 2560
Tel: (046) 203151 *Fax:* (046) 281298
Awarded annually for the best first book of poetry published in Australia during the previous calendar year. Originated in 1985.

Grants for Writers (New Work & Fellowships)
Australia Council Literature Board
PO Box 788, Strawberry Hills, NSW 2012
Tel: (02) 9215 9000 *Fax:* (02) 9215 9111
E-mail: v.fay@ozco.gov.au
Web Site: www.ozco.gov.au
Key Personnel
Administrator: Maggie Joel *E-mail:* m.joel@ozco.gov.au
New Work & Fellowship categories offer grants ranging from $5000 to $80,000 to Australian writers. Projects are accepted in the following areas: fiction, literary non-fiction, poetry, children's literature, writing for stage or radio. Minimum publication/performance requirements apply. One closing date per year.
Closing Date: May 15

Greater Dandenong Writing Awards
Formerly Greater Dandenong Short Story Competition
City of Greater Dandenong
397-405 Springvale Rd, Springvale, Victoria 3171
Mailing Address: PO Box 200, Springvale, Victoria 3171
Tel: (03) 9239-5100 *Fax:* (03) 9329-5916
E-mail: cultural.development@rgd.vic.gov.au
Web Site: www.greaterdandenong.com
Key Personnel
Project Officer: Sarah Portanier *Tel:* (03) 9239 5141
Established: 1979
Multicultural literary event with categories for stories & poems.
Closing Date: June 30 annually

Grenfell Henry Lawson Festival of Arts Awards
Henry Lawson Festival of Arts
PO Box 77, Grenfell, NSW 2810
Tel: (063) 431779 *Fax:* (063) 431548
Telex: 437156
Awarded annually in June with engraved bronze statuettes created by Sydney sculptor Alan Ingham, and cash. Awards are made for short story up to 5000 words, verse, art and the words and music of an Australian popular song; also a bush ballad.

Lyndall Hadow/Donald Stuart Short Story Award
Western Australia Fellowship of Australian Writers
Tom Collins House, 88 Wood St, Swanbourne, WA 6010
Mailing Address: FAWWA, PO Box 312, Cottesloe, WA 6011
Tel: (09) 3844771 *Fax:* (09) 3844854
E-mail: fawwa@iinet.net.au

Key Personnel
President: Gwenda Steff
Executive Officer: Sally Green
Administered by Western Australia FAW for a short story not exceeding 3,000 words. Two prizes: $400 open, the other $100 for the highest commended entry. Alternates (even years) with Donald Stuart Short Story Award (odd years). Closing date 30 June.

The Grace Leven Prize for Poetry
Perpetual Trustee Co Ltd
39 Hunter St, Sydney, NSW 2000
Mailing Address: PO Box 4172, Sydney, NSW 2001
Tel: (02) 92293951 *Toll Free Tel:* 800 501227 *Fax:* (02) 92293957
E-mail: foundations@perpetual.com.au
Instituted under the will of William Baylebridge, the Australian poet, who died in 1942. This prize of $400 is offered annually for the best volume of poetry published during the twelve months immediately preceding the year in which the award is made. Competitors must be either Australian born, & writing as Australians, or they must be naturalized in Australia & have lived in that country for at least ten years. The volume chosen may have been published in any country, but copies of it must be freely obtainable in Australia.

The Walter McRae Russell Award
Association for the Study of Australian Literature
School of Humanities & General Studies, University of W Sidney, McArthur Campus, Campbelltown ACT 2560
Tel: (046) 203151 *Fax:* (046) 281298
Awarded annually for the best first work of literary scholarship on an Australian subject published during the previous calendar year. Originated in 1983.

The Charles Meeking Award
Society of Women Writers (Australia)
c/o The President, GPO Box 121A, Melbourne, Victoria 3001
Tel: (03) 2986117
Presented by the Society of Women Writers (Australia) biennially for verse by an Australian woman. First presented in 1979.

Metcalfe Medallion
Australian Library & Information Association (ALIA)
Queen Victoria Terrace, Canberra ACT 2600
Mailing Address: PO Box E441, Kingston, ACT 2604
Tel: (02) 62851877 *Fax:* (02) 62822249
Web Site: www.vicnet.net.au/vicnet/libraries/alla.html

The Kathleen Mitchell Award
Permanent Ltd
35 Clarence St, Sydney, NSW 2000
Tel: (02) 8295 8191 *Fax:* (02) 8295 8693
Key Personnel
Awards Administrator: Linda Ingaldo
 E-mail: linda.ingaldo@permanentgroup.com.au
Established: 1996
Biannual award for published authors under the age of 30 in the two calendar years preceding the award.
Award: $5000 AUD

National Book Council Awards for Australian Literature
National Book Council Inc
PO Box 2320, Richmond, South Victoria 3121
Tel: (03) 9663 8655 *Fax:* (03) 9963 8658
Key Personnel
Executive Dir: Tom Shapcott

There are four awards. The NBC Banjo Awards for Australian Literature consist of two equal prizes of $15,000 (one for fiction, the other nonfiction). There is also an NBC Turnbull Fox Phillips Poetry Award, to the value of $7500. They are awarded for books which in the opinion of the judges, are of the highest literary merit & which make outstanding contributions to Australian literature. The Order of Australia Book Prize is awarded triennially & will next be held in January 2003. A prize of $15,000 will be awarded to a book which promotes a sense of national unity & pride.

NBC Medal
National Book Council Inc
PO Box 2320, Richmond, South Victoria 3121
Tel: (03) 96638655 *Fax:* (03) 9429 2288
First established as Bookman of the Year Award in 1975; became NBC Medal 1986. The medal is awarded to someone who has made a sustained contribution over many years to the Australian book world.

New South Wales Ministry for the Arts
New South Wales Premier's Literary Awards
St James Centre, Level 9, 111 Elizabeth St, Sydney 2000
Mailing Address: PO Box A-226, Sydney South NSW 1235
Tel: (02) 92285533 *Fax:* (02) 922847722
E-mail: ministry@arts.nsw.gov.au
Web Site: www.arts.nsw.gov.au
Established: 1979
Presented by the New South Wales Government to honor distinguished achievement by Australian writers. The Ethnic Affairs Commission Award of $10,000 is offered for a work which reflects an aspect of Australia's multicultural society. In addition, the committee judging the book awards may propose that a special award, (usually $5,000), with or without prize money, be made for a work not readily covered by the existing categories, or in recognition of a writer's achievements generally. Winners in all categories also receive commemorative medallions.
Award: Fiction $20,000; Non-fiction $20,000; Poetry $15,000; A Children's Book $15,000; Play, film, television or radio script $15,000; Literary Critism $15,000; Book of the year an additional $2,000; Ethnic Affairs Commission Award about Australia's multiculture $10,000

New South Wales Writer's Fellowship
New South Wales Premier's Literary Awards
St James Centre, Level 9, 111 Elizabeth St, Sydney 2000
Tel: (02) 92285533 *Fax:* (02) 922847722
Web Site: www.arts.nsw.gov.au
Awarded by the New South Wales Government in conjunction with the New South Wales Premier's Literary Awards, the Fellowship, valued at $10,000 in 1995, is normally awarded to supplement a writer's income during work on an approved project likely to result in literary work of significant quality, or be of lasting benefit to the applicant's experience & development as a writer or the advancement of Australian literature in general. Applicants are required to have been resident three years prior to & at the time of application.

Colin Roderick Award
Foundation for Australian Literary Studies
School of Humanities, James Cook University, Townsville, Qld 4811
Tel: (0747) 814451; (0747) 814426 *Fax:* (0747) 815655
Established: 1965
$5000 & the H T Priestley Medal from the Townsville Foundation for Australian Literary Studies at the James Cook University. The

AUSTRALIA

award is made to the author of the best book in any field of writing dealing with any aspect of Australian life.
Closing Date: February 28
Presented: Townsville, Australia, September 13

Walter Stone Memorial Award
Fellowship of Australian Writers (NSW)
GPO Box 488, Rozelle, NSW 2039
Tel: (02) 5461814
For a monograph, biography or bibliography on some aspect of Australian literature. Biennial prize of $500 plus certificate.

Storywriting & Art Project Prize
Australia Department of Veterans' Affairs Public Relations Dept
Heidelberg Repatriation Hospital, Banksia St, Heidelberg West, Victoria 3081
Mailing Address: PO Box 21, Wooden, ACT 2606
Tel: (03) 4902646 *Fax:* (03) 4997427
Web Site: www.dva.gov.au/index

TDK Australian Audio Book Awards
National Library of Australia
Parkes Pl, Canberra, ACT 2600
Tel: (06) 6262-1111 *Fax:* (06) 6257-1703
E-mail: mdickens@nla.gov.au
Web Site: www.nla.gov.au

Tertiary Bookseller of the Year Award, see APA Campus Bookstore of the Year Award

Victorian Premier's Literary Awards
State Library of Victoria
328 Swanston St, Melbourne, Vic 3000
Tel: (03) 8664 7277 *Fax:* (03) 9639 4189
E-mail: pla@slv.vic.gov.au
Web Site: www.statelibrary.vic.gov.au/pla
Founded in 1985 on the occasion of the centenary of the births of Vance & Nettie Palmer. Open to Australian writers with works first published or performed between May 1, 2001 & April 30, 2002. The annual awards are (1) Vance Palmer Prize for a work of fiction ($20,000), (2) Nettie Palmer Prize for a work of nonfiction ($20,000), (3) Louis Esson Prize for Drama ($12,000), (4) C J Dennis Prize for Poetry ($12,000), (5) Kraft Foods Prize for Young Adult Fiction ($12,000), (6) Dinny O'Hearn/SBS Book Prize for Literary Translation ($12,000) & (7) Alfred Deakin Prize for an Essay Advancing Public Debate ($12,000). The applications are to be given to the Project Officer.
Closing Date: Early May each year
Presented: Mid-October

Patrick White Literary Award
Perpetual Trustee Co Ltd
39 Hunter St, Sydney, NSW 2000
Mailing Address: PO Box 4172, Sydney, NSW 2001
Tel: (02) 92293951 Toll Free *Tel:* 800 501227 *Fax:* (02) 92293957
E-mail: foundations@perpetual.com.au
Key Personnel
Charitable Trusts Manager: Susan Ahmelman
Patrick White applied his Nobel Prize money to establish a trust to make an annual award to an Australian writer who has not been adequately recognized. Submissions are not required.

Young Australians Best Book Award
Young Australians Best Book Award Council
PO Box 238, Kew, Victoria 3101
Tel: (03) 98897749
E-mail: yabbabooks@yahoo.com
Web Site: www.vicnet.net.au/~yabba

Key Personnel
President: Graham Davey *E-mail:* daveyg@netspace.net.au
Treasurer: Richard Bennett
Established: 1986
Citation from Children.
Awarded annually.
Closing Date: Student nominations are sought in Term 1 (Feb-April)
Presented: Awards Ceremony, November

Austria

Austrian Award of Merit for Children's Literature
Bundeskanzleramt, Kunstsektion
Abteilung Il 15, Schottengasse 1, A-1014 Vienna
Tel: (01) 5315-7560 *Fax:* (01) 5315-7561
Key Personnel
Contact: Dr Peter Schneck *E-mail:* peter.schneck@bka.gv.at
Established: 1980
Conferred on an author, illustrator & translator in appreciation of his life's work.
Award: 150,000 Schillings awarded in a two year cycle

Austrian Children's & Juvenile Book Awards
Bundeskanzleramt, Kunstsektion
Abteilung Il 15, Schottengasse 1, A-1014 Vienna
Tel: (01) 5315-7560 *Fax:* (01) 5315-7561
Key Personnel
Contact: Dr Peter Schneck *E-mail:* peter.schneck@bka.gv.at
Established: 1955
There are seven categories: four for books for children & young people, an "Austrian Children's & Young People's Nonfiction Book Prize", "Austrian Children's & Young People's Translation Prize" & an "Austrian Children's & Young People's Prize" for book illustration.
Award: 250,000 Schillings to be shared by the prize winners. Prizewinning books are purchased by the Ministry of Education Arts in the amount of 140,000 Schillings

Austrian National Award for Poetry for Children
Bundeskanzleramt, Kunstsektion
Schottengasse 1, A-1014 Vienna
Tel: (01) 53157560 *Fax:* (01) 53157561
Key Personnel
Contact: Peter Schneck *E-mail:* peter.schneck@bmwf.gv.at
Established: 1993
For the complete works of an author of poetry for children in German language.
Award: 75,000 Schillings awarded every two years

Austrian Promotional Award for Children's Literature
Bundeskanzlermt, Kunstsektion
Schottengasse 1, A-1014 Vienna
Tel: (01) 53157560 *Fax:* (01) 53157561
Key Personnel
Contact: Peter Schneck *E-mail:* peter.schneck@bke.gv.at
Established: 1996
Conferred on an author, illustrator or translator in appreciation of his outstanding contributions to children's literature.
Award: 75,000 Schillings every two years

☆**Austrian State Prize for European Literature**
Bundeskanzleramt-Kunstsektion
BKA Kunstsektion, Abt Il/5, Schottengasse 1, A-1014 Vienna

LITERARY

Tel: (01) 53157550 *Fax:* (01) 53157557
Key Personnel
Contact: Dr Robert Stocker
Established: 1965
Presented by the Austrian Minister of Education to a European author (with the exception of an Austrian national) whose work has also been acclaimed outside his own country; this must be demonstrated by translation. No applications; The prize is awarded on the recommendation of an independent jury.
Award: 300,000 Australian Schillings & testimonial awarded annually

Ehrenpreis des oesterreichischen Buchhandels
The Austrian Booksellers & Publishers Association
Gruenangergasse 4, A-1010 Vienna
Tel: (01) 512 15 35 *Fax:* (01) 512 84 82
E-mail: hvb@buecher.at
Web Site: www.buecher.at

FIT Astrid Lindgren Translation Prize
International Federation of Translators
Dr Heinrich Maierstr 9, A-1180 Vienna
Tel: (01) 4403607 *Fax:* (01) 4403756
Web Site: www.fit.ift.org

☆**FIT Best Periodical Award**
Federation internationale des Traducteurs (FIT)
Dr Heinrich Maierstr 9, A-1180 Vienna
Tel: (01) 4403607 *Fax:* (01) 4403756
Web Site: www.fit.ift.org
Key Personnel
President: Adolfo Gentile
(1) Established in 1970 and sponsored by Carl-Bertil Nathhorst-Stiftelser (Stockholm, Sweden). Awarded every three or four years, for (a) a literary and (b) a nonliterary translation which make an outstanding contribution to the improvement of the quality of translation.

Great Austrian State Prize
Bundeskanzleramt-Kunstsektion
BKA Kunstsektion, Abt Il/5, Schottengasse 1, A-1014 Vienna
Tel: (01) 53157550 *Fax:* (01) 53157557
This prize alternates between literature, music & the fine arts. Awarded by Oesterreichischer Kunstsenat. No applications.
Award: 300,000 Schillings for life's work

Grosse Literaturstipendien des Landes Tirol
Amt der Tiroler Landesregierung
Sillgasse 8, A-6020 Innsbruck
Tel: (0512) 576377202 *Fax:* (0512) 576377200

Michael Haberlandt Medal
Verein fur Volkskunde
Laudongasse 19, A-1080 Vienna
Tel: (01) 4068905 *Fax:* (01) 4085342
E-mail: volkskundemuseum.wien@netway.at

Oesterreichischer Staatspreis fur literarische Ubersetzer (Austrian State Prize for Literary Translators)
Bundeskanzleramt-Kunstsektion
BKA Kunstsektion, Abt Il/5, Schottengasse 1, A-1014 Vienna
Tel: (01) 53157550 *Fax:* (01) 53157557
Key Personnel
Contact: Dr Robert Stocker
Award: 100,000 Schillings

Rauriser Encouragement Award
Salzburger Landesregierung
Kulturabteilung, Postfach 527, 5010 Salzburg
Tel: (0662) 80422729 *Fax:* (0662) 80422119
E-mail: kultur@salzburg.gv.at
Web Site: www.salzburg.gv.at/kultur

Key Personnel
Contact: Dr Herbert Mayrhofer *E-mail:* herbert.mayrhofer@salzburg.gv.at
Annual literary award sponsored by the Salzburg provincial government & the village of Rauris. 3,634 euros awarded for a specific topic, as decided by jury.

Rauriser Literature Prize
Salzburger Landesregierung
Kulturabteilung, Postfach 527, 5010 Salzburg
Tel: (0662) 80422729 *Fax:* (0662) 80422119
E-mail: kultur@salzburg.gv.at
Web Site: www.salzburg.gv.at/kultur
Key Personnel
Contact: Dr Herbert Mayrhofer *E-mail:* herbert.mayrhofer@salzburg.gv.at
For an outstanding first publication in prose, as decided by jury.
Other Sponsor(s): Salzburg provincial government
Award: 7,270 euros annually

Recognition Prize/Foerderungspreis fuer Literatur
Bundeskanzleramt-Kunstsektion
Abt II/5, Schottengasse 1, 1014 Vienna
Tel: (01) 53157550 *Fax:* (01) 53157620
Awarded by jury. No applications.
Award: 100,000 Schillings

State Scholarship for Literature
Bundeskanzleramt-Kunstsektion
BKA Kunstsektion, Abt II/5, Schottengasse 1, A-1014 Vienna
Tel: (01) 53157550 *Fax:* (01) 53157557
Awarded by jury. Submissions accepted.
Award: Twenty given each year; 15,000 Schillings each month for twelve months

Otto Stoessl-Preis
Otto Stoessl-Stiftung
Semmelweisgasse 9, A-8010 Graz
Tel: (0316) 8016-4611 *Fax:* (0316) 8016-4633
Key Personnel
Contact: Dr Christoph Binder *E-mail:* christoph.binder@stmk.gv.at
Established: 1981
Unpublished German stories.
Award: Literature prize 4000 EURO
Closing Date: End of every 2nd year (2001, 2003...)
Presented: Vienna, End of every second year (2002, 2004...)

Georg Trakl Prize
Salzburger Landesregierung
Kulturabteilung, Postfach 527, 5010 Salzburg
Tel: (0662) 80422729 *Fax:* (0662) 80422119
E-mail: kultur@salzburg.gv.at
Web Site: www.salzburg.gv.at/kultur
Key Personnel
Contact: Dr Herbert Mayrhofer *E-mail:* herbert.mayrhofer@salzburg.gv.at
An irregular award to a writer of lyric poetry for his/her complete poetical works.
Award: 7270 euros

Upper Austria Culture Prize for Literature
Upper Austria State Government
Institut fuer Kulturfoerderung, Spittelwiese 4, A-4010 Linz
Tel: (0732) 27205486 *Fax:* (0732) 27207786

City of Vienna Encouragement Prize
City of Vienna Magistrate
Magistratsabteilung 7-Kultur, 8, Friedrich-Schmidt-Platz 5, A-1082 Vienna
Tel: (01) 400084767 *Fax:* (01) 40007104
Established: 1951
Awarded to talented young writers (under 40 years of age) whose previous work is worthy of recognition & whose development shows promise. Candidates must be Austrian citizens who have either lived for three years in Vienna or who work in the city.
Award: 40,000 schillings annually

City of Vienna Prize
City of Vienna Magistrate
Magistratsabteilung 7-Kultur, 8, Friedrich-Schmidt-Platz 5, A-1082 Vienna
Tel: (01) 400084767 *Fax:* (01) 40007104
Originally founded in 1947. An annual award of 100,000 Schillings is made to an author for total literary output.

City of Vienna Prize for Books for Children & Young People
City of Vienna Magistrate
Magistratsabteilung 7-Kultur, 8, Friedrich-Schmidt-Platz 5, A-1082 Vienna
Tel: (01) 400084716; (01) 400084717 *Fax:* (01) 40007216
Web Site: www.magwien.gv.at/ma07/index.htm
Key Personnel
Contact: Ernestine Pecksteiner *E-mail:* pec@m07.magwien.gv.at
Awarded annually by the City of Vienna for distinguished books for children & young people, including illustration.

Anton Wildgans Prize of Austrian Industry
Vereinigung der Oesterreichischen Industrie
Schwarzenbergplatz 4, 1031 Vienna
Tel: (01) 0222 71135 *Fax:* (01) 713 6899
Key Personnel
Contact: Ilse Steiner *E-mail:* i.steiner@iv-net.at
Awarded annually, at the beginning of the autumn, to an Austrian lyric poet, dramatist, novelist or essayist, young or middle aged. The author must be an Austrian citizen, writing in German, who lives either in Austria or abroad. Awarded by a committee. No applications.
Award: Maximum prize 7500 euros

Writers Scholarship for Literature
Bundeskanzleramt-Kunstsektion
BKA Kunstsektion, Abt II/5, Schottengasse 1, A-1014 Vienna
Mailing Address: Postfach 65, A-1014 Vienna
Tel: (01) 53157550 *Fax:* (01) 53157557
Ten given each year. 4000 Schillings each month for twelve months, awarded by jury. Submissions accepted.

Wuerdigungspreis (Lower Austria Prize of Honor)
AMT der Niederosterreichischen Landesregierung-Kulturabteilung
Landhausplatz 1, A-3109 St Polten
Tel: (02742) 200 *Fax:* (02742) 200 3279

Bangladesh

Bangla Academy Literary Awards
Bangla Academy
Language & Literary Section, Burdwan House, Dhaka 1000
Tel: (02) 5001314 *Cable:* ACADEMY, DHAKA
Two awards annually for an overall outstanding contribution to Bangla literature. 25,000 taka each.

Belgium

Goblet d'Alviella Prize
Academie Royale de Belgique
Palais des Academies, One rue Ducale, 1000 Brussels
Tel: (02) 5144064; (02) 5144256 *Fax:* (02) 5502205
For the best work of a strictly scientific & objective character relating to the history of religions, published by a Belgian author. 50,000 francs. Awarded every five years.

Lode Baekelmans Prize
Koninklijke Academie voor Nederlandse Taal- en Letterkunde (Royal Academy of Dutch Language & Literature (Belgium))
Koningstraat 18, B-9000 Gent
Tel: (09) 265 93 40 *Fax:* (09) 265 93 49
E-mail: info@kantl.be
Key Personnel
Librarian: Marijke De Wit *Tel:* (09) 265 93 43
E-mail: mdewit@kantl.be
Established: 1940
For the best literary work in Dutch - novel, poetry, play, radio play, essay, etc - dealing with the sea, sailors, navigation, the harbor, inland navigation or related topics. Recipients must be Belgian nationals.
Award: 1860 EUR awarded triennially
Closing Date: February 1, 2003

Internationale Eugene Baie Prijs (International Eugene Baie Prize)
Province of Antwerp/Eugene Baie Foundation
Koningin Elisabethlei 22, B-2018 Antwerp
Tel: (03) 2405011 *Fax:* (03) 2406470
Eugene Baie International Prize.

Karel Barbier Prize
Koninklijke Academie voor Nederlandse Taal- en Letterkunde (Royal Academy of Dutch Language & Literature (Belgium))
Koningstraat 18, B-9000 Gent
Tel: (09) 265 93 40 *Fax:* (09) 265 93 49
E-mail: info@kantl.be
Key Personnel
Librarian: Marijke De Wit *Tel:* (09) 265 93 43
E-mail: mdewit@kantl.be
Established: 1927
For the best historical novel in Dutch, with a national-historical theme. Short stories & romanticized biographies also taken into consideration. Recipients must be Belgian nationals.
Award: 500 EUR awarded biannually
Closing Date: February 1, 2003

August Beernaert Prize
Koninklijke Academie voor Nederlandse Taal- en Letterkunde (Royal Academy of Dutch Language & Literature (Belgium))
Koningstraat 18, B-9000 Gent
Tel: (09) 265 93 40 *Fax:* (09) 265 93 49
E-mail: info@kantl.be
Key Personnel
Librarian: Marijke De Wit *Tel:* (09) 265 93 43
E-mail: mdewit@kantl.be
Established: 1912
For the best literary work in Dutch, irrespective of the genre, published or unpublished. Recipients must be Belgian nationals.
Award: 1240 EUR awarded biennially
Closing Date: February 1, 2002

Beernaert Prize
Academie Royale de Langue et de Litterature Francaises
rue Ducale, 1, B-1000 Brussels

For the most outstanding work of a Belgian author written in French language.
Award: awarded annually

Belgian Government Prizes for Literature
Counseil de la Communaute francaise de Belgique
Rue de la Loi 6, B-1000 Brussels
Tel: (02) 5063811 *Fax:* (02) 5063980
An annual State Prize for Literature, in turn awarded for prose, drama, poetry & essay.
Award: 150,000 francs

☆Anton Bergmann Prize
Academie Royale de Belgique
Palais des Academies, One rue Ducale, 1000 Brussels
Tel: (02) 5502211; (02) 5144256 *Fax:* (02) 5502205
For the author of a historical account or monograph, written in Dutch & relating to a Flemish town or community in Belgium. 50,000 Belgian francs. Awarded every five years for a work appearing in print or (provisionally) in manuscript form, during the period. Foreign authors may also compete, provided work is in Dutch & is published in Belgium or the Netherlands.

Ernest Bouvier-Parviliez Prize
Academie Royale de Langue et de Litterature Francaise
Palais des Academies, One rue Ducale, B-1000 Brussels
For the entire work of a Belgian author written in French. Awarded every four years.

Constant de Horion Prize
Association des Ecrivains Belges de Langue Francaise
Maison Camille Lemonnier, Maison des Ecrivains, 15, 150 Chaussee de Wavre, 1050 Brussels
Tel: (02) 512 2968 *Fax:* (02) 502 4373
Key Personnel
President: France Bastia
Vice President: Prof Emile Kesteman
Established: 1977
Founded by Baron Jean Constant (the writer Constant de Horion), for recognition of the best essay on literary history or literary criticism by an established Belgian writer, or a literary aspect of French expressionism. Belgian writers over forty years of age are eligible. 50,000 francs awarded biennially.
Award: 50,000 FB
Closing Date: 11/30/2001

Arthur H Cornette Prize
Koninklijke Academie voor Nederlandse Taal- en Letterkunde (Royal Academy of Dutch Language & Literature (Belgium))
Koningstraat 18, B-9000 Gent
Tel: (09) 265 93 40 *Fax:* (09) 265 93 49
E-mail: info@kantl.be
Key Personnel
Librarian: Marijke De Wit *Tel:* (09) 265 93 43
E-mail: mdewit@kantl.be
Established: 1950
For the best literary essay, written in Dutch, published or unpublished. Recipients must be Belgian nationals.
Award: 1500 EUR awarded every five years
Closing Date: February 1, 2006

☆Albert Counson Prize
Academie Royale de Langue et de Litterature Francaise
Palais des Academies, One rue Ducale, B-1000 Brussels

Tel: (02) 5115687
For a scholarly work on romance languages, in relation to or connected with Belgium. Monetary prize. Awarded every five years.

☆Franz Cumont Prize
Academie Royale de Belgique
Palais de Academies, One rue Ducale, B-1000 Brussels
Tel: (02) 5502211; (02) 5144256 *Fax:* (02) 5502205
For a work by a Belgian or foreign author dealing with the history of religion or science in antiquity, ie in the Mediterranean area prior to the time of Mohammed. No application necessary. The prize cannot be divided, except where one or more authors have acted in collaboration. 100,000 Belgian francs. Awarded triennially.

Nestor de Tiere Prize
Koninklijke Academie voor Nederlandse Taal- en Letterkunde (Royal Academy of Dutch Language & Literature (Belgium))
Koningstraat 18, B-9000 Ghent
Tel: (09) 265 93 40 *Fax:* (09) 265 93 49
E-mail: info@kantl.be
Key Personnel
Librarian: Marijke De Wit *Tel:* (09) 265 93 43
E-mail: mdewit@kantl.be
Established: 1930
For the best play written in Dutch. Recipients must be Belgian nationals.
Award: 500 EUR awarded biennially
Closing Date: December 10, 2001

Felix Denayer Prize
Academie Royale de Langue et de Litterature Francaise
Palais de Academies, One rue Ducale, B-1000 Brussels
For a single work or the entire literary work of a Belgian written in French. Awarded annually.

Prix Ernest Discailles
Academie Royale de Langue et de Litterature Francaise
Palais de Academies, One rue Ducale, B-1000 Brussels
Tel: (02) 5502211; (02) 5144256 *Fax:* (02) 5502205
For a distinguished literary work written in French, preferably by a poet.
Award: Biennially

☆Ernest Discailles Prize
Academie Royale de Belgique
Palais des Academies, One rue Ducale, 1000 Brussels
Tel: (02) 5502211; (02) 5144256 *Fax:* (02) 5502205
Alternates between the best work on the history of French literature & on contemporary history. Open to (1) Belgians, (2) foreigners who are studying or have studied at the University of Ghent. Awarded every five years.
Award: 60,000 Belgian francs

Jules Duculot Prize
Academie Royale de Belgique
Palais des Academies, One rue Ducale, 1000 Brussels
Tel: (02) 5144256; (02) 5502211 *Fax:* (02) 5502205
For a work in print or manuscript form, written in French, dealing with the history of philosophy. Awarded only to Belgians, or to foreigners holding an academic grade granted by a Belgian university. Printed work must have been published in the five years prior to the end of the relevant period. The prize is awarded for what appears the most deserving work, irrespective of whether it has been submitted for entry or not.
Award: 180,000 francs every five years

Charles Duvivier Prize
Academie Royale de Belgique
Palais des Academies, One rue Ducale, 1000 Brussels
Tel: (02) 5502211; (02) 5144256 *Fax:* (02) 5502205
For the Belgian author of the best work on the history of Belgian or foreign law, or on the history of Belgian political, judicial or administrative institutions. 50,000 francs.

Joris Eeckhout Prize
Koninklijke Academie voor Nederlandse Taal- en Letterkunde (Royal Academy of Dutch Language & Literature (Belgium))
Koningstraat 18, B-9000 Gent
Tel: (09) 265 93 40 *Fax:* (09) 265 93 49
E-mail: info@kantl.be
Key Personnel
Librarian: Marijke De Wit *Tel:* (09) 265 93 43
E-mail: mdewit@kantl.be
Established: 1937
For the best literary essay about an author, written in Dutch, at least 100 pages, published or unpublished. Recipients must be Belgian nationals.
Award: 500 EUR awarded biennially
Closing Date: February 1, 2002

Professor Doctor Leon Elaut Prize
Koninklijke Academie voor Nederlandse Taal- en Letterkunde (Royal Academy of Dutch Language & Literature (Belgium))
Koningstr 18, B-9000 Ghent
Tel: (09) 265 93 40 *Fax:* (09) 265 93 49
E-mail: info@kantl.be
Key Personnel
Librarian: Marijke De Wit *Tel:* (09) 265 93 43
E-mail: mdewit@kantl.be
Established: 1981
For the best monograph, written in Dutch, about cultural history of Flanders, 1815-1940 in connection with the Flemish movement.
Award: 2480 EUR biennially
Closing Date: February 1, 2002

☆Camille Engelman Prize
Academie Royale de Langue et de Litterature Francaise
Palais des Academies, One rue Ducale, B-1000 Brussels
Tel: (02) 5115687
For the outstanding literary work of the year (published or unpublished) written in French. Monetary prize. Awarded annually.

Joseph Gantrelle Prize
Academie Royale de Belgique
Palais des Academies, One rue Ducale, 1000 Brussels
Tel: (02) 5502211; (02) 5144256 *Fax:* (02) 5502205
For a work in classical philology. 60,000 francs. Awarded biennially to Belgian authors.

Guido Gezelle Prize
Koninklijke Academie voor Nederlandse Taal- en Letterkunde (Royal Academy of Dutch Language & Literature (Belgium))
Koningstraat 18, B-9000 Gent
Tel: (09) 265 93 40 *Fax:* (09) 265 93 49
E-mail: info@kantl.be
Key Personnel
Librarian: Marijke De Wit *Tel:* (09) 265 93 43
E-mail: mdewit@kantl.be
Established: 1941

For the best volume of Dutch poetry, published or unpublished. Recipients must be Belgian nationals.
Award: 1240 EUR awarded every 5 years
Closing Date: February 1, 2002

Maurice Gilliams Prize
Koninklijke Academie voor Nederlandse Taal- en Letterkunde (Royal Academy of Dutch Language & Literature (Belgium))
Koningstraat 18, B-9000 Gent
Tel: (09) 265 93 40 *Fax:* (09) 265 93 49
E-mail: info@kantl.be
Key Personnel
Librarian: Marijke De Wit *Tel:* (09) 265 93 43
E-mail: mdewit@kantl.be
Established: 1985
For the best volume of poetry, the best essay about poetry or for a complete poetical work, written in Dutch. Nationality of the recipient is not taken into account.
Award: 2480 EUR awarded every four years
Closing Date: February 1, 2002

Tobie Jonckheere Prize
Academie Royale de Belgique
Palais des Academies, One rue Ducale, 1000 Brussels
Tel: (02) 5502211; (02) 5144256 *Fax:* (02) 5502205
For a work, in published or manuscript form, devoted to the educational sciences. 60,000 francs. Awarded every three years.

Hubert Krains Prize
Association des Ecrivains Belges de Langue Francaise
Maison Camille Lemonnier-Maison des Ecrivains, 150 Chaussee de Wavre, 1050 Brussels
Tel: (02) 512 2968 *Fax:* (02) 502 4373
Key Personnel
Secretary General: Jean Lacroix
Vice President: Prof Emile Kesteman
Established: 1950
For the unpublished work of a writer below the age of 40. Founded in 1950 by the Association of Belgian Writers in the French Language in memory of one of its presidents.
Award: 500 euros awarded biennially (alternately prose & poetry)
Closing Date: September 15, 2001

Rene Lyr Prize for Poetry
Association des Ecrivains Belges de Langue Francaise
Maison Camille Lemonnier - Maison des Ecrivains, 150 Chaussee de Wavre, 1050 Brussels
Tel: (02) 512 2968 *Fax:* (02) 502 4373
Key Personnel
President: France Bastia
Vice President: Prof Emile Kesteman
Established: 1959
Founded under Friends of Rene Lyr patronage & awarded every three years to a French-language poet for published or unpublished, non-prize-winning work. All poets of French expressionism are eligible. 25,000 francs.
Other Sponsor(s): The Family of Rene Lyr
Award: 875 euros
Closing Date: April 30, 2002

Malpertuis Prize
Academie Royale de Langue et de Litterature Francaise
Palais des Academies, One rue Ducale, B-1000 Brussels
For an outstanding contribution to Belgian literature in the field of drama, poetry, short story or essay written in French. Awarded biennially.

Joseph-Edmond Marchal Prize
Academie Royale de Belgique
Palais des Academies, One rue Ducale, 1000 Brussels
Tel: (02) 5502211; (02) 5502212 *Fax:* (02) 5502205
For the Belgian author of the best work, in print or in manuscript form, on national antiques or archaeology.
Award: 60,000 francs every 5 years

Arthur Merghelynck Prize
Koninklijke Academie voor Nederlandse Taal- en Letterkunde (Royal Academy of Dutch Language & Literature (Belgium))
Koningstraat 18, B-9000 Gent
Tel: (09) 265 93 40 *Fax:* (09) 265 93 49
E-mail: info@kantl.be
Key Personnel
Librarian: Marijke De Wit *Tel:* (09) 265 93 43
E-mail: mdewit@kantl.be
Established: 1946
For the two best literary works, one prose the other poetry, including essays about prose or poetry, written in Dutch, published or unpublished. Recipients must be Belgian nationals.
Award: 1240 EUR for each prize, awarded triennially
Closing Date: February 1, 2003

Albert Mockel Grand Prize for Poetry
Academie Royale de Langue et de Litterature Francaise
Palais des Academies, One rue Ducale, B-1000 Brussels
For the best Belgian poet writing in French. Awarded every five years.

Gilles Nelod Prize
Association des Ecrivains Belges de Langue Francaise
Maison Camille Lemonnier - Maison des Ecivains, 150 Chaussee de Wavre, 1050 Brussels
Tel: (02) 512 2968 *Fax:* (02) 502 4373
Key Personnel
President: France Bastia
Vice President: Prof Emile Kesteman
Established: 1984
Founded by Gilles Nelod & administered by the Association of Belgian Writers in the French Language. Awarded biennially for a previously unpublished work of fiction.
Award: 250 euros
Closing Date: 5/10/2001

Order of the Crown Prize
Belgium Ministry of Foreign Affairs
Service des Ordres, Rue Belliard 65, B-1040 Brussels
Tel: (02) 5013511 *Fax:* (02) 5013669

Alex Pasquier Prize
Association des Ecrivains Belges de Langue Francaise
Maison Camille Lemonnier - Maison de Ecrivains, 15, 150 Chaussee de Wavre, 1050 Brussels
Tel: (02) 512 2968 *Fax:* (02) 502 4373
Key Personnel
President: France Bastia
Vice President: Prof Emile Kesteman
Established: 1972
Established in memory of Association president Alex Pasquier, by his widow, for recognition of the best historical novel, published or unpublished, during the preceding five years by a Belgian writer in the French language.
Award: 625 euros
Closing Date: 9/15/2002

Prix de Stassart
Academie Royale de Belgique Classe des Lettres et des Sciences Morales et Politiques
Palais des Academies, Rue Ducale 1, B-1000 Brussels
Tel: (02) 5502211; (02) 5144256 *Fax:* (02) 5502205

Prix Henri Lavachery
Academie Royale de Belgique Classe des Lettres et des Sciences Morales et Politiques
Palais des Academies, Rue Ducale 1, B-1000 Brussels
Tel: (02) 5502211; (02) 5144256 *Fax:* (02) 5502205

Prize for Literature of the Parliament of the French Community of Belgium
Parliament of the French Community of Belgium (Prix litteraire de Parlement de la Communaute francais de Belgique)
Rue de la Loi 6, B-1012 Brussels
Tel: (02) 5063929 *Fax:* (02) 5063853
Key Personnel
Contact: N Ryelandt *E-mail:* ryelandtn@pcf.be
Award: 150,000 FB
Closing Date: February 1

Victor Rossel Prize
Le Soir
21 Place de Louvain, B-1000 Brussels
Tel: (02) 2255555 *Fax:* (02) 2255910
E-mail: journal@lesior.be
For the best novel, or collection of short stories published during the year, written in French by a Belgian author.
Award: 200,000 francs awarded annually

de Saint-Genois Prize
Academie Royale de Belgique
Palais des Academies, One rue Ducale, 1000 Brussels
Tel: (02) 5502211; (02) 5144256 *Fax:* (02) 5502205
For the author of the best historical or literary work written in Dutch. 50,000 francs. Awarded every five years.

Ary Sleeks Prize
Koninklijke Academie voor Nederlandse Taal- en Letterkunde (Royal Academy of Dutch Language & Literature (Belgium))
Koningstraat 18, B-9000 Gent
Tel: (09) 265 93 40 *Fax:* (09) 265 93 49
E-mail: info@kantl.be
Key Personnel
Librarian: Marijke De Wit *Tel:* (09) 265 93 43
E-mail: mdewit@kantl.be
Established: 1974
The Ary Sleeke Prize recognizes the best novel, volume of short stories or an essay, published or unpublished. Recipients must be Belgian nationals.
Award: 620 EUR triennially
Closing Date: February 1, 2002

Suzanne Tassier Prize
Academie Royale de Belgique
Palais des Adademies, One rue Ducale, B-1000 Brussels
Tel: (02) 5502211; (02) 5144256 *Fax:* (02) 5502205
For a Belgian woman who, following study at a Belgian university, has obtained at least a Doctorate. The prize is awarded for a major scientific work, dealing with a subject from history, law, philology or the social sciences: failing a meritorious work from one of these branches, then for a subject from the natural sciences, medicine or mathematics. Preference will be

BELGIUM

given to a work of an historical nature, in its widest sense.
Award: 70,000 francs every two years

Auguste Teirlinck Prize
Academie Royale de Belgique
Palais de Academies, One rue Ducale, B-1000 Brussels
Tel: (02) 5502211; (02) 5144256 *Fax:* (02) 5502205
For a contribution to Flemish literature. 50,000 francs. Awarded every five years.

Troubadour de la SABAM
Belgische Vereniging van Auteurs, Componisten en Uitgevers (Socete Belge des Auteurs, Compositeurs et Editeurs
c/o Awards Committee, Rue d'Arlon 75-77, B-1040 Brussels
Tel: (02) 2868211 *Fax:* (02) 2311800
E-mail: 101641.2761@compuserve.com
Web Site: www.sabam.be
Established: 1951
Recognizes living poets of any nationality whose works have significantly influenced world poetry..
Award: 100,000 Belgian francs biennially

Bolivia

Premios Nacionales de Cultura
Ministerio de Educacion
Avda Arce 2408, La Paz
Tel: (02) 373260
For recognition of achievements in literature, the arts or science. Monetary prizes & a medal are given biannually.

Concurso Nacional de Novela Erich Guttentag
(Erich Guttentag National Novel Competition)
Editorial Los Amigos del Libro
Av Ayacucho S-0156, Casilla 450, Cochabamba Casilla 450
Tel: (042) 4-504150; (042) 4-504151 *Fax:* (591) 411 5128
E-mail: gutten@amigol.bo.net
Key Personnel
President: Werner Guttentag

Franz Tamayo Prize
La Paz Municipal Mayor's Office
Oficial Mayor de Cultura, La Paz
For outstanding literary work. Prizes of 15,000 and 5000 Bolivian pesos. Awarded annually.

Brazil

Graca Aranha Prize
PEN Clube do Brasil (Associacao Universal de Escritores)
Praia do Flamengo 172 - 10 andar, 2000 Rio de Janeiro RJ
Tel: (021) 2850491
For the best Brazilian novel.

Afonso Arinos Prize
Academia Brasileira de Letras
Ave Presidente Wilson 203, 20030 Rio de Janeiro RJ
Tel: (021) 2205441
For the best work of fiction published or written during the two years preceding the year of award. Awarded annually.

Olavo Bilac Prize
Academia Brasileira de Letras
Av Presidente Wilson 203, 20030 Rio de Janeiro RJ
Tel: (021) 2205441
For the best book of poetry. Awarded annually.

Jabuti Prize
Instituto Brasil-Estados Unidos
Ave N S de Copacabana 690, 11 andar, 22050-000 Rio de Janeiro RJ
Tel: (021) 2558332 *Fax:* (021) 2558332
Web Site: www.lbeuce.com.br/eng/
Awarded annually for best literary composition published in previous year.

Monteiro Lobato Prize
Academia Brasileira de Letras
Av Presidente Wilson 203, 20030 Rio de Janeiro RJ
Tel: (021) 2205441
For children's literature. Awarded annually.

Julia Lopes de Ameida Prize
Academia Brasileira de Letras
Av Presidente Wilson 203, 20030 Rio de Janeiro RJ
Tel: (021) 2205441
For the best unpublished or published literary work written by a woman, preferably for a novel or collection of short stories. Awarded annually.

Machado de Assis Prize
Academia Brasileira de Letras
Av Presidente Wilson 203, 20030 Rio de Janeiro RJ
Tel: (021) 2205441
Founded in 1943, this award is to an outstanding Brazilian writer for the sum of his work. Awarded annually. One of Brazil's highest literary honors.

Odorico Mendes Prize
Funarte Fudacao Nacional De Arte
Rua da Imprensa, 16, 5 Andar-Centro, 20030 Rio de Janeiro RJ
Tel: (021) 2976116; (021) 2624895 *Fax:* (021) 2624895
For the best translation from foreign literature into the Portuguese language. Awarded annually.

National Book Institute Prizes
Instituto Nacional do Livro
SCRN, 704/705, B1 C, No 40, 2 andaer, 70730 Brasilia DF
Tel: (061) 2742315
For outstanding unpublished literary works of fiction, poetry, history and essays. In addition, one prize is awarded for the best unpublished work of children's literature & another for illustrations of books for children. Awarded annually.

Luisa Claudio de Sousa Prize
PEN Clube do Brasil (Associacao Universal de Escritores)
Praia do Flamengo 172 - 10 andar, 2000 Rio de Janeiro RJ
Tel: (021) 2850491
For the best book published in the previous year. Novels, plays, literary history & criticism works are considered.

Jose Verissimo Prize
Funarte Fudacao Nacional De Arte
Rua da Imprensa, 16, 5 Andar-Centro, 20030 Rio de Janeiro RJ

Tel: (021) 2976116 *Fax:* (021) 2624895
For the best essay & a work of scholarship. Awarded annually.

Bulgaria

International Vaptsarov Prize
Union of Bulgarian Writers
Angel Kanchev 5, BG-1040 Sofia
Tel: (02) 874711 *Fax:* (02) 874757

Canada

☆**The Acorn-Rukeyser Chapbook Contest**
Mekler & Deahl
237 Prospect St S, Hamilton, ON L8M 2Z6
Tel: 905-312-1779 *Fax:* 905-312-8285
Web Site: www.meklerdeahl.com
Key Personnel
Managing Partner: James Deahl *E-mail:* james@meklerdeahl.com
Poems may be published or unpublished & must be within the People's Poetry tradition as exemplified by the work of Milton Acorn & Muriel Rukeyser. An entry will be a poetry mss of up to 30 typed pages with simultaneous submissions being accepted. All entries will be returned after the winning chapbook is published & all entrants will receive a copy of the winning chapbook.
Address entries to Acorn-Rukeyser Chapbook Contest, Mekler & Deahl, Publishers, 237 Prospect St South, Hamilton, ON, Canada L8M 2Z6.
Award: Fifty copies of chapbook & cash prize of $100
Closing Date: Last day of September 2000

☆**The Herb Barrett Award**
Hamilton Haiku Press
237 Prospect St South, Hamilton, ON L8M 2Z6
Tel: 905-312-1779
Web Site: www.meklerdeahl.com
Key Personnel
Managing Partner: James Deahl *E-mail:* james@meklerdeahl.com
For short poetry in the haiku tradition. Poems must be no more than 4 lines long. They may or may not follow the traditional 17-syllable form, but should be in the haiku tradition. Poems may be published or unpublished. Up to 10 poems may be submitted per entry. Manuscripts must be typed or word-processed, one poem per page, on letter-sized paper, with no identifying marks. Name, address & phone number, with titles or first lines, should be on a separate sheet of paper. All entrants will receive one copy of the anthology. Entrants with poetry in the anthology will receive one additional copy. Copyright remains with the author.
Award: 1st prize $200 US, 2nd prize $150 US, 3rd prize $100 US, other prizes: anthology publication
Closing Date: Postmarked by November 30, 2002

☆**Lorne Pierce Medal**
Royal Society of Canada
283 Sparks St, Ottawa, ON K1R 7X9
Tel: 613-991-6990 *Fax:* 613-991-6996
E-mail: adminrsc@rsc.ca
Key Personnel
Contact: Sophie Buoro

Established 1926. For achievement & conspicuous merit in the field of imaginative or critical literature, in English or French. Medal awarded biennially.

☆**The Sandburg-Livesay**
Mekler & Deahl
237 Prospect St S, Hamilton, ON L8M 2Z6
Tel: 905-312-1779 *Fax:* 905-312-8285
Web Site: www.meklerdeahl.com
Key Personnel
Managing Partner: James Deahl *E-mail:* james@meklerdeahl.com
Poems may be published or unpublished.
Award: Fifty copies of chapbook & cash prize of $250; first runner-up $150; second runner-up $100
Closing Date: Oct 31, 2002

Chile

National Prize for Literature (Premio Nacional de Literatura)
Ministerio de Educacion de Chile
Ave Libertador Bernardo O'Higgins, 1371 Santiago
Established: 1942
To recognize an author's sum of work.
Award: A monetary prize awarded annually

Colombia

☆**Felix Restrepo Prize**
Academia Colombiana
Carrera 3A, Numero 17-34, Piso 3, Apdo Aereo 44763, Bogota, DC
Tel: (01) 3414805 *Fax:* (01) 2838552
E-mail: accefyn@colciencias.gov.co
Web Site: www.accefyn.org.co
For distinguished contributions to philology.
Award: 100,000 Colombian pesos & publication of work, awarded annually

Jose Maria Vergara y Vergara Prize
Ministerio de Educacion Nacional
Centro Administrativo Nacional (CAN), 501 Avda Eldorado, Bogota DE
Tel: (01) 2224597 *Fax:* (01) 2224530
For Colombian authors, to promote literary development. Diploma plus 10,000 Colombian pesos. Awarded annually.

Costa Rica

Editorial Costa Rica Literary Prize
Editorial Costa Rica
Apdo 10010, San Jose 1000
Tel: 253-5354 *Fax:* 253-5091
E-mail: editocr@racsa.co.cr
Key Personnel
General Manager: Ana Patricia Cartin
Founded in 1973, this annual award is to encourage creative writing generally. The prize is rotated in order to be open to all genres - fiction, stories, theatre, essays, short stories, poetry, biography, history. The most recent winner was Eduardo Oconitrillo.

Aquileo J Echeverria Prize
Costa Rican Ministry of Culture, Youth and Sport
Apdo 10227, San Jose 1000
Tel: 33 14 71 *Fax:* 33 7066
For Costa Rican citizens who have excelled in the fields of literature (novel, short story, poetry, essay, scientific literature), history, theatre, music, fine arts. 40,000 colones divided between the selected works. Total sum of awards cannot exceed 8,000,000 colones. Awarded annually.

Joven Creacion Literary Prize
Editorial Costa Rica
Apdo 10010, San Jose 1000
Tel: 253-5354 *Fax:* 253-5091
E-mail: editocr@racsa.co.cr
Key Personnel
General Manager: Ana Patricia Cartin
Formed in 1976 in collaboration with the Associacion de Autores, with the aim of stimulating young writing in the fields of poetry & narrative/stories.

Carmen Lyra Literary Prize
Editorial Costa Rica
Apdo 10010, San Jose 1000
Tel: 253-5354 *Fax:* 253-5091
E-mail: editocr@racsa.co.cr
Founded in 1974 in honour of the writer Maria Isabel Carvajal (pseudonym Carmen Lyra), this annual award is to encourage the writing of literature intended for children & young people.

Premio Poesia y Narrativa
Editorial Universitaria Centroamericana (EDUCA)
Ciudad Universitatar Rodrigo Facio, Apdo 64, San Jose 2060
Tel: 2243727 *Fax:* 2539141
E-mail: educacr@sol.racsa.co.cr
Key Personnel
Dir: Sebastian Vaquerano

Cuba

☆**Casa de las Americas Literary Award**
Casa de las Americas
Calle 3ra y G, El Vedado, Havana 10400
Tel: (07) 55 27 15; (07) 55 27 06; (07) 55 27 09 *Fax:* (07) 327272; (07) 334554
E-mail: cil@casa.cult.cu
Web Site: www.casa.cult.cu
An annual prize of US $3,000 (or equivalent in national currency) is awarded to an author for unpublished work in one or other of the following genres: novels, plays, 'testimonial' books, essays on artistic & literary themes - Brazilian & French Caribbean (or national language) works; short stories, poetry, essays on historical & social themes, books for children & young people & Anglo-Caribbean (or national language) works. The winning work will be published.

Czech Republic

Mlada Fronta Publishing House Prize
Radlicka 61, 15000 Prague 5
Tel: (02) 2527 6120 *Fax:* (02) 2527 6176
Key Personnel
Dir: Martina Hartova *E-mail:* hartova@mf.cz
Awarded annually by the publishing house Mlada fronta (Young Front) for literary works of prose, poetry, journalism, popular science, also translations, published by them during the preceding year.

Jaroslav Seifert Prize
Charta 77 Foundation
Melantrichova 5, CZ-11000 Prague 1
Tel: (02) 24225092 *Fax:* (02) 24213647
E-mail: charta77@mbox.vol.cz
Web Site: www.bariery.cz
Key Personnel
Program Dir: Indira Bornova *Tel:* (02) 24230216
Established: 1986
For recognition of the best work in Czech & Slovak literature.
Other Sponsor(s): Zivnostenska Banka, Prague
Award: 250,000 Czech crowns & a diploma made by one of the well known Czechoslovak artists
Closing Date: Spring every year
Presented: Zivnostenska Banka, Prague, Autumn

Denmark

Emil Aarestrup Prize
Dansk Forfatterforening
Strandgade 6, DK-1401 Copenhagen K
Tel: 32955100 *Fax:* 32540115
For outstanding poetry. DKr 7000 & a medal. Awarded annually.

The H C Andersen Prize
Dansk Forfatterforening
Strandgade 6, DK-1401 Copenhagen K
Tel: 32955100 *Fax:* 32540115
For scientists & writers connected with H C Andersen, for outstanding contributions to Danish literature. DKr 45,000. Awarded annually.

Martin Andersen Nex Prize
Dansk Forfatterforening
Strandgade 6, DK-1401 Copenhagen K
Tel: 32955100 *Fax:* 32540115
DKr 5000. Awarded annually.

Herman Bang Memorial Prize
Dansk Forfatterforening
Strandgade 6, DK-1401 Copenhagen K
Tel: 32955100 *Fax:* 32540115
For works of prose. DKr 5000. Awarded annually.

Danish Academy Prize for Literature
Danish Academy
Vognmagergade 7, DK-1120 Copenhagen K
Tel: 33131112 *Fax:* 33328045 *Cable:* LAWOFF
For an outstanding work of literature. DKr 300,000. Awarded biannually.

Danish Prize for Children's Literature
Danish Ministry of Cultural Affairs
The Media & Grants Secretariat, Nybrogade 10, 1203 Copenhagen K
Tel: 33923040 *Fax:* 33146428
E-mail: tips@kulturtilskud.dk
Web Site: www.kulturtilskud.min.dk
Key Personnel
Consultant: Eva Jensen *Tel:* 33923583 *E-mail:* ej@kulturtilskud.dk
Established: 1954
For the best Danish books for children & teenagers.
Award: DKr 30,000 awarded annually

Danish Writers' Association Non-Fiction Prize
Dansk Forfatterforening
Strandgade 6, DK-1401 Copenhagen K
Tel: 32955100 *Fax:* 32540115
DKr 30,000. Awarded annually.

Denmark

Danmarks Skolebibliotekarforenings Bornebogspris
Danish School Librarian Association
Gogevej 2, DK-4130 Viby
Tel: 46193440 *Fax:* 46194349

Dansk Oversaetterforbunds Aerespris
Dansk Forfatterforening
Strandgade 6, DK-1401 Copenhagen K
Tel: 32955100 *Fax:* 32540115
For the outstanding translation into Danish of one or more significant works. Awarded annually.
Award: Dkr 5000

Johannes Ewald Prize
Dansk Forfatterforening
DK-1401, Strandgade 6, Copenhagen K
Tel: 32955100 *Fax:* 32540115
For prose, poetry & dramatic works. DKr 6000. Awarded annually.

Soren Gyldendal Prize
Gyldendalske Boghandel - Nordisk Forlag A/S
Klareboderne 3, 1001 Copenhagen K
Tel: 33755555 *Fax:* 33755556
E-mail: gyldendal@gyldendal.dk
Web Site: www.gyldendal.dk
Telex: 15887 Gyldal Dk
Key Personnel
Man Dir: Stig Andersen
Secretary: Annie Auhagen *Tel:* (33) 755523
E-mail: annie_auhagen@gyldendal.dk
For Danish authors from any field whose work is of great literary value.
Award: DKr 150,000 awarded annually
Closing Date: Cannot be applied for

Holberg Medal
Dansk Forfatterforening
Strandgade 6, DK-1401 Copenhagen K
Tel: 32955100 *Fax:* 32540115
For outstanding contributions to Danish literature. DKr 35,000 & a medal. Awarded annually.

Adam Gottlob Oehlenschlaeger Prize
Dansk Forfatterforening
Strandgade 6, DK-1401 Copenhagen K
Tel: 32955100 *Fax:* 32540115
For prose works & poetry. DKr 6000. Awarded annually.

Edvard Pedersens Biblioteksfonds Forfatterpris
Danish Library Association
c/o Flemming Ettrup, Secretary, Telegrafvej 5, DK-2750 Ballerup
Tel: 33250935 *Fax:* 33257900
E-mail: dkf@dlf.dk
Web Site: www.litteraturpriser.dk/pris/epfond.htm; www.edvardp.dk; www.dbf.dk
Key Personnel
President: Mogens Damm

Henrik Pontoppidan Memorial Prize
Dansk Forfatterforening
Strandgade 6, DK-1401 Copenhagen
Tel: 32955100 *Fax:* 32540115
For outstanding contributions to Danish literature. Awarded annually.
Award: DKr 20,000

Finland

Finlandia Junior Prize
Suomen Kirjasaatio (Finnish Book Foundation)
Lonnrotinkatu 11 A, 00120 Helsinki
Mailing Address: PO Box 177, FIN-00121 Helsinki
Tel: (09) 228 77 250 *Fax:* (09) 612 1226
Web Site: www.skyry.net
Key Personnel
Contact: Veikko Sonninen *E-mail:* veikko.sonninen@skyry.net
For the outstanding Finnish children's book of the year. Awarded annually.
Award: 26,000 euros

Rudolf Koivu Prize
Grafia Ry
Uudenmaankatu 11B9, SF-00120 Helsinki
Tel: (09) 601941 *Fax:* (09) 601140
Key Personnel
Chairman: Mr Kari Kakko
For the illustrator of the year's best Finnish picture-book for children. Organized by Grafia Ry & awarded every other year.

Arvid Lydecken Prize
Suomen Nuorisokirjailijat ry
Palomaeentie 13 B, c/o Tuija Lehtinen, SF-02730 Espoo
Tel: (09) 852 2176
Web Site: www.nuorisokirjailijat.fi
Key Personnel
Chairman: Mrs Tuija Lehtinen *E-mail:* tuileh@netti.fi
For the writer of the year's best Finnish book for children.
Award: Awarded annually

State Prizes for Literature
Ministry of Education, Finland
Meritullinkatu 10, SF-00171 Helsinki
Mailing Address: PO Box 293, SF-0071 Helsinki
Tel: (00) 134171 *Fax:* (00) 1359335
Web Site: www.minedu.fi
Prizes for the best literary works. Awarded annually.

France

Prix de l'Academie des Sciences Arts et Belles Lettres de Dijon (Dijon Academy of Sciences, Art & Literature Prize)
Academie des Sciences Arts et Belles Lettres de Dijon
Bibliotheque Municipale de Dijon, 5 Rue de l'Ecole de Droit, F-21000 Dijon
Tel: (80) 303639 *Fax:* (80) 499968

Prix de l'Academie Mallarme
Academie Mallarme
Espace Culturel, 16 rue Monsieur Le Prince, 75006 Paris
Tel: (01) 46227125
Key Personnel
Secretary General: Charles Dobzynski
Mallarme Academic Prize.

Prix ALPHA de la Nouvelle
Aspects Artistiques Litteraires et Photographiques de la region Hazebrouckoise
9 Ave Pierre-Curie, F-59190 Hazebrouck
Tel: 28410744

Prix Guillaume Apollinaire
22 rue des Felibres, F-91600 Savigny-S/Orge
Tel: (01) 6996 3524

Prix Antonin Artaud
Association des Ecrivains du Rouergue
BP 307, F-12003 Rodez Cedex
Tel: (05) 65781307; (05) 65778849 (Secretary)

Francois-Joseph Audiffred Prize
Academie des Sciences Morales et Politiques, Institut de France
23 quai de Conti, F-75270 Paris Cedex 06
Tel: (01) 43263135 *Fax:* (01) 43295510
For a published work best qualified to inspire love of ethics & virtue & to discourage egoism and envy; or to stimulate knowledge & appreciation of the Country of France. Awarded annually.

Joseph Autran Prize
la Societe des Poetes Francais
Siege social 16, rue Monsieur le Prince, 75006 Paris
Tel: (01) 40469982 *Fax:* (01) 40469982
E-mail: poetesfrancais@aol.com
Web Site: www.societedespoetesfrancais.asso.fr
Key Personnel
President: Vital Heurtebize
Secretary General: Linda Bastide
Created by the Countess of Miramon-Fitz-James. Awarded annually to a poet for the whole of his work.

Prix Baudelaire
Societe des Gens de Lettres de France
Hotel de Massa, 38 rue du Faubourg Saint-Jacques, F-75014 Paris
Tel: (01) 531012 00 *Fax:* (01) 531012 12
Key Personnel
President: Alain Absire
First Vice President: Marie-France Briselance
Secretary General: Jean Claude Bologne
Treasurer: Francois Taillandier
Awards the best French translation of an English work to which the author is native of the United Kingdom or one of the Commonwealth Countries. Awarded each spring.
Award: 2250 euros
Presented: British Council, Paris

Pascal Bonetti Grand Prize
la Societe des Poetes Francais
Siege social 16, rue Monsieur le Prince, 75006 Paris
Tel: (01) 40469982 *Fax:* (01) 40469982
E-mail: poetesfrancais@aol.com
Web Site: www.societedespoetesfrancais.asso.fr
Key Personnel
President: Vital Heurtebize
Secretary General: Linda Bastide
Annual award of 1000 francs for the entire work of a poet.

Prix Bordin
Institut de France Academie des Beaux Arts
Institut de France, 23 Quai de Conti, F-75006 Paris Cedex 06
Tel: (01) 44414320

Louis Castex Prize
Academie Francaise, Institut de France
23 quai de Conti, F-75006 Paris
Tel: (01) 43295510
For a literary work celebrating a major voyage of exploration or archaeological or ethnological discovery. Fictional romance excluded. Awarded annually.

Chateauneuf-du-Pape Grand Prize
la Societe des Poetes Francais
Siege social 16, rue Monsieur le Prince, 75006 Paris
Tel: (01) 40469982 *Fax:* (01) 40469982
E-mail: poetesfrancais@aol.com
Web Site: www.societedespoetesfrancais.asso.fr

Key Personnel
President: Vital Heurtebize
Secretary General: Linda Bastide
Instituted by the town of Chateauneuf-du-Pape and other cities in the same area. Awarded every two years for a poetic work (unpublished, or published in previous five years) which, irrespective of subject, appears most deserving for its formal purity and lofty sentiments. 1,000 francs. Awarded preferably to a young poet.

Honore Chavee Prize
Academie des Inscriptions et Belles Lettres, Institut de France
23 quai de Conti, F-75270 Paris Cedex 06
Tel: (01) 44414310 *Fax:* (01) 44414311
To encourage work in linguistics & in particular, research on romance languages. Awarded biennially.

Prix Maurice-Edgar Coindreau
Societe des Gens de Lettres de France
Hotel de Massa, 38 rue du Faubourg-Saint-Jacques, F-75014 Paris
Tel: (01) 53 10 12 00 *Fax:* (01) 53 10 12 12
Key Personnel
President: Alain Absire
First Vice President: Marie-France Briselance
Secretary General: Jean Claude Bologne
Treasurer: Francois Taillandier
Rewards a literary translation for American work.
Award: 2250 euros

Concours de Nouvelles
Mairie de Palaiseau
Service culturel de la mairie, F-91120 Palaiseau
Tel: (01) 60143960 *Fax:* (01) 60143960

Albert Dauzat Prize
la Societe des Poetes Francais
Siege social 16, rue Monsieur le Prince, 75006 Paris
Tel: (01) 40469982 *Fax:* (01) 40469982
E-mail: poetesfrancais@aol.com
Web Site: www.societedespoetesfrancais.asso.fr
Key Personnel
President: Vital Heurtebize
Secretary General: Linda Bastide
Awarded annually for a poetic work in praise of animals.

Eve Delacroix Prize
Academie Francaise, Institut de France
23 quai de Conti, F-75006 Paris
Tel: (01) 43295510
For a literary work, essay or novel combining literary quality, a sense of human dignity & the responsibilities of authorship. 5,000 francs. Awarded annually.

Deldebat de Gonzalya Foundation Prize
la Societe des Poetes Francais
Siege social 16, rue Monsieur le Prince, 75006 Paris
Tel: (01) 40469982 *Fax:* (01) 40469982
E-mail: poetesfrancais@aol.com
Web Site: www.societedespoetesfrancais.asso.fr
Key Personnel
President: Vital Heurtebize
Secretary General: Linda Bastide
Founded in 1941, a medal is awarded every two years for a small body of poems classical in form and noble in inspiration.

Marceline Desbordes-Valmore Prize
la Societe des Poetes Francais
Siege social 16, rue Monsieur le Prince, 75006 Paris
Tel: (01) 40469982 *Fax:* (01) 40469982
E-mail: poetesfrancais@aol.com
Web Site: www.societedespoetesfrancais.asso.fr

Key Personnel
President: Vital Heurtebize
Secretary General: Linda Bastide
Created by President Andre Foulon de Vaulx. Founded 1937. Awarded annually to a female member of the Poetry Society, with a recognized talent at the height of its development.

Deux Magots Prize (Prix des Deux Magots)
Cafe des Deux Magots
6 Pl Saint Germain des Pres, 75006 Paris
Tel: (01) 45485525; (01) 45487357 *Fax:* (01) 45493129
E-mail: cafe.lesdeuxmagots@free.fr
Web Site: www.lesdeuxmagots.com
Key Personnel
Dir: M J Mathivat
Established: 1933
The prize originated in Paris.
Award: 7700 euros

Alfred Dutens Prize
Academie des Inscriptions et Belles Lettres, Institut de France
23 quai de Conti, F-75270 Paris Cedex 06
Tel: (01) 44414310 *Fax:* (01) 44414311
For the most useful work on linguistics. Awarded every ten years.

Erlanger Foundation Prize
la Societe des Poetes Francais
Siege social 16, rue Monsieur le Prince, 75006 Paris
Tel: (01) 40469982 *Fax:* (01) 40469982
E-mail: poetesfrancais@aol.com
Web Site: www.societedespoetesfrancais.asso.fr
Key Personnel
President: Vital Heurtebize
Secretary General: Linda Bastide
Founded in 1921, a medal awarded every five years for a poem, 150 lines maximum, written by someone who has served in front line of combat.

Prix Paul Feval de Litterature Populaire
Societe des Gens de Lettres de France
Hotel de Massa, 38 rue du Faubourg Saint-Jacques, F-75014 Paris
Tel: (01) 531012 00 *Fax:* (01) 531012 12
E-mail: sgdlf@wanadoo.fr
Web Site: www.sgdl.org
Key Personnel
President: Alain Absire
First Vice President: Marie-France Briselance
Secretary General: Jean Claude Bologne
Treasurer: Francois Taillandier
Award: 3000 euros

Jean Finot Prize
Academie des Sciences Morales et Politiques, Institut de France
23 quai de Conti, F-75270 Paris Cedex 06
Tel: (01) 43263135 *Fax:* (01) 43295510
For a work of a humanitarian social trend. Awarded every two years.

Ernest Fleury Prize
la Societe des Poetes Francais
Siege social 16, rue Monsieur le Prince, 75006 Paris
Tel: (01) 40469982 *Fax:* (01) 40469982
E-mail: poetesfrancais@aol.com
Web Site: www.societedespoetesfrancais.asso.fr
Key Personnel
President: Vital Heurtebize
Secretary General: Linda Bastide
Instituted by Marthe-Claire Fleury in memory of her father, the poet Ernest Fleury. It is awarded annually for the whole of a poet's work (classical poetry, published or not).

Marshal Foch Prize
Academie Francaise, Institut de France
23 quai de Conti, F-75006 Paris
Tel: (01) 43295510
For a book on the future of the nation's defence by a French officer, engineer, scholar or philosopher. Awarded every two years.

Fouraignan Foundation Prize
la Societe des Poetes Francais
Siege social 16, rue Monsieur le Prince, 75006 Paris
Tel: (01) 40469982 *Fax:* (01) 40469982
E-mail: poetesfrancais@aol.com
Web Site: www.societedespoetesfrancais.asso.fr
Key Personnel
President: Vital Heurtebize
Secretary General: Linda Bastide
Founded in 1914, a medal awarded every five years for a collection of poems in 18th century French style, inspired by current events.

Gegner Prize
Academie des Sciences Morales et Politiques, Institut de France
23 quai de Conti, F-75270 Paris Cedex 06
Tel: (01) 43263135 *Fax:* (01) 43295510
To a philosopher-writer whose works contribute to the progress of philosophic science. Awarded annually.

Giles Prize
Academie des Inscriptions et Belles Lettres, Institut de France
23 quai de Conti, F-75270 Paris Cedex 06
Tel: (01) 44414310 *Fax:* (01) 44414311
For a work on China, Japan or the Far East. Awarded every two years to a French national only.

Goncourt Prize
Academie Goncourte, Socieete de gens de Lettres
Place Gaillon, 75002 Paris
Tel: (01) 42651516 *Fax:* (01) 4703498
Founded by E de Goncourt, 1914, the annual prize honors a prose work by a younger writer with originality of spirit and form. The novel is the preferred medium. The award is the same as when the prize was originated, 50 francs. The Academy also awards each year, in various French towns, prizes for short story, biography, historical novel & poetry. These awards range from 10,000 to 50,000 francs.

☆**Grand Prix de la Francophonie**
Academie Francaise, Institut de France
23 quai de Conti, F-75006 Paris
Tel: (01) 43295510
Established in 1986 by the Government of Canada in collaboration with the Academie Francaise. The Government of Canada donated C$400,000 as a founding sum with the expectation that other countries, organizations & groups would make further contributions. The prize is to reward the work of a French-speaking writer who has contributed in an outstanding manner to the upholding & exemplification of the French language. The prize can also be for literary or philosophical work which individually or collectively has assured the regeneration of the French language in the fields of science, technology or information. Annual award of 400,000 French francs.

Grand Prix de la Nouvelle
Societe des Gens de Lettres de France
Hotel de Massa, 38 rue du Faubourg-Saint-Jacques, F-75014 Paris
Tel: (01) 531012 00 *Fax:* (01) 531012 12
Key Personnel
President: Alain Absire

First Vice President: Marie-France Briselance
Secretary General: Jean Claude Bologne
Treasurer: Francois Taillandier
Award: 3000 euros

Grand Prix de Litterature de la Societe des Gens de Lettres pour l'ensemble de l'oeuvre
Societe des Gens de Lettres de France
Hotel de Massa, 38 rue du Faubourg Saint-Jacques, F-75014 Paris
Tel: (01) 53 10 12 00 *Fax:* (01) 53 10 12 12
E-mail: sgdlf@wanadoo.fr
Web Site: www.sgdl.org
Key Personnel
President: Alain Absire
First Vice President: Marie-France Briselance
Secretary General: Jean Claude Bologne
Treasurer: Francois Taillandier
Award: 7000 euros

Grand Prix de Poesie de la Societe des Gens de Lettres pour l'ensemble de l'oeuvre
Societe des Gens de Lettres de France
Hotel de Massa, 38 rue du Faubourg Saint-Jacques, F-75014 Paris
Tel: (01) 531012 00 *Fax:* (01) 531012 12
Key Personnel
President: Alain Absire
First Vice President: Marie-France Briselance
Secretary General: Jean Claude Bologne
Treasurer: Francois Taillandier
Award: 7000 euros

Grand Prix International de Poesie de la Ville de Grenoble
Societe des Poetes et Artistes de France
30 CRS-J-Jaures, F-38000 Grenoble
Tel: (01) 76475483

Grand Prix Litteraire de l'Afrique Noire
(Black Africa Literary Prize)
Association des Ecrivains de Langue Francaise (ADELF) (French Language Writers' Association)
14 rue Broussais, F-75014 Paris
Tel: (01) 43219599 *Fax:* (01) 43201222

Grand Prix SDGL du Livre des Arts
Societe des Gens de Lettres de France
Hotel de Massa, 38 rue du Faubourg Saint-Jacques, F-75014 Paris
Tel: (01) 531012 00 *Fax:* (01) 531012 12
Key Personnel
President: Alain Absire
First Vice President: Marie-France Briselance
Secretary General: Jean Claude Bologne
Treasurer: Francois Taillandier
For recognition of outstanding works completed in the past year.
Award: 3000 euros

Grand Prix SGDL de l'oeuvre Multimedia
Societe des Gens de Lettres de France
Hotel de Massa, 38 rue du Faubourg Saint Jacques, F-75014 Paris
Tel: (01) 531012 00 *Fax:* (01) 531012 12
Key Personnel
President: Alain Absire
First Vice President: Marie-France Briselance
Secretary General: Jean Claude Bologne
Treasurer: Francois Taillandier
Award: 3000 euros

Grand Prix SGDL du Livre d'Histoire
Societe des Gens de Lettres de France
Hotel de Massa, 38 rue du Faubourg St Jacques, F-75014 Paris
Tel: (01) 531012 00 *Fax:* (01) 531012 12
Key Personnel
President: Alain Absire
First Vice President: Marie-France Briselance
Secretary General: Jean Claude Bologne
Treasurer: Francois Taillandier
To recognize the author of an historical work.
Award: 3000 euros

Grand Prix SGDL du Livre Jeunesse
Societe des Gens de Lettres de France
Hotel de Massa, 38 rue du Faubourg Saint-Jacques, F-75014 Paris
Tel: (01) 531012 00 *Fax:* (01) 531012 12
Key Personnel
President: Alain Absire
First Vice President: Marie-France Briselance
Secretary General: Jean Claude Bologne
Treasurer: Francois Taillandier
Established: 1982
For recognition of a book intended for young people by its qualities of invention, writing and presentation. Works written in French and published before March of the preceding year may be submitted by the author or editor. Awarded annually.
Award: 3000 euros

Grand Prix SGDL du Roman
Societe des Gens de Lettres de France
Hotel de Massa, 38 rue du Faubourg Saint-Jacques, F-75014 Paris
Tel: (01) 53 10 12 00 *Fax:* (01) 53 10 12 12
E-mail: sgdlf@wanadoo.fr
Web Site: www.sgdl.org
Key Personnel
President: Alain Absire
First Vice President: Marie-France Briselance
Secretary General: Jean Claude Bologne
Treasurer: Francois Taillandier
For recognition of an outstanding novel. Works published within the preceding year may be submitted.
Award: 3000 euros

Grand Prix SGDL du site Internet litteraire
Societe des Gens de Lettres de France
Hotel de Massa, 38 rue du Faubourg Saint Jacques, F-75014 Paris
Tel: (01) 531012 00 *Fax:* (01) 531012 12
Key Personnel
President: Alain Absire
First Vice President: Marie-France Briselance
Secretary General: Jean Claude Bologne
Treasurer: Francois Taillandier
Award: 3000 euros

Grand Prize for French Poets
la Societe des Poetes Francais
Siege social 16, rue Monsieur le Prince, 75006 Paris
Tel: (01) 40469982 *Fax:* (01) 40469982
E-mail: poetesfrancais@aol.com
Web Site: www.societedespoetesfrancais.asso.fr
Key Personnel
President: Vital Heurtebize
Secretary General: Linda Bastide
Awarded annually since 1936, for the whole body of a poet's work, as decided by the Committee of the Societe des Poetes (no applications allowed).

Grand Prize for Literature
Academie Francaise, Institut de France
23 quai de Conti, F-75006 Paris
Tel: (01) 43295510
To a prose-writer for one or more works noteworthy in form & inspiration. Awarded every two years.

Grand Prize for Poetry
Academie Francaise, Institut de France
23 quai de Conti, F-75006 Paris
Tel: (01) 43295510
100,000 francs. Awarded annually.

☆**Grand Prize for the Influence of the French Language**
Academie Francaise, Institut de France
23 quai de Conti, F-75006 Paris
Tel: (01) 43295510
For work contributing to the influence of the French language. Monetary prize awarded annually.

Grands Prix d'Histoire Chateaubriand - la Vallee-aux-Loups
Maison de Chateaubriand
87 rue Chateaubriand, F-92290 Chatenay-Malabry
Tel: (01) 47025861 *Fax:* (01) 47020557

Cardinal Grente Prize
Academie Francaise, Institut de France
23 quai de Conti, F-75006 Paris
Tel: (01) 43295510
Awarded biennially for the entire works of a regular or secular member of the Roman Catholic clergy.

Edmond Haraucourt Prize
la Societe des Poetes Francais
Siege social 16, rue Monsieur le Prince, 75006 Paris
Tel: (01) 40469982 *Fax:* (01) 40469982
E-mail: poetesfrancais@aol.com
Web Site: www.societedespoetesfrancais.asso.fr
Key Personnel
President: Vital Heurtebize
Secretary General: Linda Bastide
Replaces the J-M Renaitour Prize. Awarded annually to a member of the Societe des Poetes (no applications allowed).

☆**Heredia Prize**
Academie Francaise, Institut de France
23 quai de Conti, F-75006 Paris
Tel: (01) 43295510
Monetary award given in alternate years to (1) a Latin American writer for a piece of prose or poetry written in French, (2) the author of a collection of printed sonnets.

Clovis Hugues Award
la Societe des Poetes Francais
Siege social 16, rue Monsieur le Prince, 75006 Paris
Tel: (01) 40469982 *Fax:* (01) 40469982
E-mail: poetesfrancais@aol.com
Web Site: www.societedespoetesfrancais.asso.fr
Key Personnel
President: Vital Heurtebize
Secretary General: Linda Bastide
Awarded annually to a poet whose work is inspired by the same sentiments of social brotherhood as moved Clovis Hugues.

Interallie Prize
Cercle Interallie
33 rue du Fg St Honore, F-75008 Paris
Tel: (01) 42659600
Awarded since 1930 for a high quality novel, preferably written by a journalist. Awarded annually.

☆**International French Friendship Prize**
la Societe des Poetes Francais
Siege social 16, rue Monsieur le Prince, 75006 Paris
Tel: (01) 40469982 *Fax:* (01) 40469982
E-mail: poetesfrancais@aol.com
Web Site: www.societedespoetesfrancais.asso.fr
Key Personnel
President: Vital Heurtebize
Secretary General: Linda Bastide
For poetry written in French by a foreigner. Awarded biennially.

PRIZES — FRANCE

Jean-Christophe Prizes
la Societe des Poetes Francais
Siege social 16, rue Monsieur le Prince, 75006 Paris
Tel: (01) 40469982 *Fax:* (01) 40469982
E-mail: poetesfrancais@aol.com
Web Site: www.societedespoetesfrancais.asso.fr
Key Personnel
President: Vital Heurtebize
Secretary General: Linda Bastide
Offered by Mrs Alice Cluchier in memory of the young tragedian, her son. Awarded every two years to young poets for a manuscript of minimum ten poems in classical form or in free verse.

☆Stanislas Julien Prize
Academie des Inscriptions et Belles Lettres, Institut de France
23 quai de Conti, F-75270 Paris Cedex 06
Tel: (01) 44414310 *Fax:* (01) 44414311
For the best work related to China. Monetary prize. Awarded annually.

☆Kalinga Prize for the Popularization of Science
UNESCO Publishing
One, rue Miollis, F-75352 Paris
Tel: (01) 45684143 *Fax:* (01) 4565823
Web Site: www.unesco.org/general/eng/about/prizes/prsc.html; www.unesco.org/science/unesco_intern_sc_prizes.htm
Key Personnel
Assistant Editor for Science: Susan Schneegans
E-mail: s.schneegans@unesco.org
Established: 1951
This prize, awarded annually by UNESCO, was established by the Kalinga Foundation Trust in 1951. The recipient must have distinguished him or herself in the course of a brilliant career as science writer, editor, lecturer, film producer, radio/TV program director or presenter. The National Commission for UNESCO within each country forwards a single nomination to UNESCO on the basis of recommendations from national bodies, including science journals, national associations for the advancement of science.
Other Sponsor(s): Kalinga Foundation Trust (India)
Award: L 2000
Closing Date: June
Presented: India in even years; Paris (UNESCO Hq) in odd years, November

Prix Halperine Kaminsky
Societe des Gens de Lettres de France
Hotel de Massa, 38 rue du Faubourg Saint-Jacques, F-75014 Paris
Tel: (01) 531012 00 *Fax:* (01) 531012 12
Key Personnel
President: Alain Absire
First Vice President: Marie-France Briselance
Secretary General: Jean Claude Bologne
Treasurer: Francois Taillandier
Comprised of two prizes: Le Prix Halperine-Kaminsky Consecration, 7000 euros & Le Prix Halperine-Kaminsky Decouverte, 1500 euros.

Prix Roger Kowalski/Prix de Poesie de la Ville de Lyon
Ville de Lyon
c/o Division des Affaires Culturelles, BP 1065, F-69205 Lyon Cedex 01
Annual prize awarded to a living poet for a French language manuscript.

Georges Lafenestre Foundation Prize
la Societe des Poetes Francais
Siege social 16, rue Monsieur le Prince, 75006 Paris
Tel: (01) 40469982 *Fax:* (01) 40469982
E-mail: poetesfrancais@aol.com
Web Site: www.societedespoetesfrancais.asso.fr
Key Personnel
President: Vital Heurtebize
Secretary General: Linda Bastide
Founded in 1938 by the family of Georges Lafenestre on the occasion of the poet's centenary, a medal is given for an unpublished poem of high inspiration & classical form, 150 lines maximum.

Prix Valery Larbaud
Association International des Amis de Valery Larbaud
Les Eygalades B, 116 rue Edmond-Carrieu, 30900 Nimes
Tel: (01) 04 6664 9402

Sebastien-Charles Leconte Foundation Prize
la Societe des Poetes Francais
Siege social 16, rue Monsieur le Prince, 75006 Paris
Tel: (01) 40469982 *Fax:* (01) 40469982
E-mail: poetesfrancais@aol.com
Web Site: www.societedespoetesfrancais.asso.fr
Key Personnel
President: Vital Heurtebize
Secretary General: Linda Bastide
Founded in 1935 by Jean-Michel Renaitour, and awarded biennially in honor of a volume of classical poetry published in the preceding two years.

☆Literary Critics' Grand Prize
la Societe des Poetes Francais
Siege social 16, rue Monsieur le Prince, 75006 Paris
Tel: (01) 40469982 *Fax:* (01) 40469982
E-mail: poetesfrancais@aol.com
Web Site: www.societedespoetesfrancais.asso.fr
Telex: 206 963 F
Key Personnel
President: Vital Heurtebize
Secretary General: Linda Bastide
For the best work of literary criticism or literary history. Established in 1959. 10,000 French francs, awarded annually.

Paul Lofler Foundation Prize
la Societe des Poetes Francais
Siege social 16, rue Monsieur le Prince, 75006 Paris
Tel: (01) 40469982 *Fax:* (01) 40469982
E-mail: poetesfrancais@aol.com
Web Site: www.societedespoetesfrancais.asso.fr
Key Personnel
President: Vital Heurtebize
Secretary General: Linda Bastide
Awarded every two years for the best sonnet submitted for competition to the Societe des Poetes.

Jean Mace Prize
Ligue Francaise de l'Enseignement et de l'Education Permanente
3 rue Recamier, F-75341 Paris Cedex 07
Tel: (01) 43589748
E-mail: ligue-sri@ligue.cie.fv
Web Site: www.lalique.cie.fv
For works on any field of activity in which the French League for Teaching & Continuing Education is involved. Awarded annually.

Maison de Poesie
Fondation Emile Blemont
11 bis, rue Ballu, F-75009 Paris
Tel: (01) 40234599

☆Mandat des Poetes Prize
Pierre Bearn
60 rue Monsieur-le-Prince, F-75006 Paris
Tel: (01) 43262273
Founded in 1950 by Pierre Bearn, to aid a French-language poet of talent, young or old, in time of need. Awarded annually.

Prix Medicis de l'Essai
Prix Medicis
25 rue Dombasle, 75015 Paris
Tel: (01) 48287690 *Fax:* (01) 48287690
Key Personnel
Secretary General: Francine Mallet
E-mail: dominique.larre@wanadoo.fr
Established: 1985
For the best essay in French, including translated writing, appearing during the preceding year. Monetary prize. Awarded annually.
Presented: Paris, France, Annually in early November

Prix Medicis Etranger
Prix Medicis
25 rue Dombasle, 75015 Paris
Tel: (01) 48287690 *Fax:* (01) 48287690
Key Personnel
Secretary General: Francine Mallet
E-mail: dominique.larre@wanadoo.fr
Established: 1970
For the best foreign novel appearing in French during the preceding year. Awarded annually.
Presented: Paris, France, November

Medicis Prize
Prix Medicis
25 rue Dombasle, 75015 Paris
Tel: (01) 48287690 *Fax:* (01) 48287690
Key Personnel
Secretary General: Francine Mallet
E-mail: dominique.larre@wanadoo.fr
Established: 1958
Awarded to an avant-garde novel, story or collection whose publication has not been accompanied by the celebrity or fame the author's talent deserves.
Presented: Paris, France, Annually in November

Prix du Meilleur Livre Etranger
24, rue de Oudinot, F-75007 Paris
Tel: (01) 45671898 *Fax:* (01) 45447924
Prize for the Best Foreign Book.

Grand Prix Thyde Monnier de la SGDL
Societe des Gens de Lettres de France
Hotel de Massa, 38 rue du Faubourg Saint-Jacques, F-75014 Paris
Tel: (01) 531012 00 *Fax:* (01) 531012 12
Key Personnel
President: Alain Absire
First Vice President: Marie-France Briselance
Secretary General: Jean Claude Bologne
Treasurer: Francois Taillandier
Established: 1975
For recognition of a cycle of novels or for a separate work (novel, essay or collection of poems) published during the preceding two years. Writers whose talents have not brought them material success are eligible. Awarded annually.
Award: 3000 euros

Prix de Poesie Louis Montalte
Societe des Gens de Lettres de France
Hotel de Massa, 38 rue du Faubourg Saint-Jacques, F-75014 Paris
Tel: (01) 531012 00 *Fax:* (01) 531012 12
Key Personnel
President: Alain Absire
First Vice President: Marie-France Briselance
Secretary General: Jean Claude Bologne
Treasurer: Francois Taillandier
For recognition of the complete works of a known poet.
Award: 3000 euros

FRANCE   LITERARY

Montyon Prize
Académie Francaise, Institut de France
23 quai de Conti, F-75006 Paris
Tel: (01) 43295510
For any work published by a French author showing qualities of practical idealism. Awarded annually.

Eugene Le Mouel Foundation Prize
la Societe des Poetes Francais
Siege social 16, rue Monsieur le Prince, 75006 Paris
Tel: (01) 40469982 *Fax:* (01) 40469982
E-mail: poetesfrancais@aol.com
Web Site: www.societedespoetesfrancais.asso.fr
Key Personnel
President: Vital Heurtebize
Secretary General: Linda Bastide
Founded in 1936, this is a medal awarded every five years for a poem in any genre, but preferably inspired by Eugene Le Mouel.

National Grand Prize for Literature
Ministere de la Culture et de la Communication, Direction du livre et de la Lecture
DIC, 3 rue de Valois, F-75042 Paris Cedex 01
Tel: (01) 40158778 *Fax:* (01) 42869736
Established in 1950. To the writer who has contributed most to French literature. 50,000 francs. Awarded annually.

National Grand Prize for Translation
Ministere de la Culture et de la Communication, Direction du livre et de la Lecture
DIC, 3 rue de Valois, F-75042 Paris Cedex 01
Tel: (01) 40158778 *Fax:* (01) 42869736
Established: 1985
To the translator who has contributed most to the standard of literary translation into the French language. Awarded annually.
Award: 30,000 francs

Prix Gerard de Nerval
Societe des Gens de Lettres de France
Hotel de Massa, 38 rue du Faubourg Saint-Jacques, F-75014 Paris
Tel: (01) 53 10 12 00 *Fax:* (01) 53 10 12 12
E-mail: sgdlf@wanadoo.fr
Web Site: www.sgdl.org
Key Personnel
President: Alain Absire
First Vice President: Marie-France Briselance
Secretary General: Jean Claude Bologne
Treasurer: Francois Taillandier
Established: 1989
For recognition of an outstanding translation of a German work.
Award: 3000 euros

Grand Prix d'Histoire Nationale Maurice Payard (Maurice Payard National History Grand Prize)
Academie Nationale de Reims
7 rue des Ecoles, 51100 Reims
Mailing Address: 38 rue Gambetta, 51100 Reims
Tel: (0326) 910449 *Fax:* (0326) 910449
Key Personnel
Secretary General: Patrick Demouy *Tel:* (0326) 479819 *E-mail:* patrick.demouy@laposte.net
Administrative Secretary: Philippe Petit-Stervinou
Established: 1978
Champagne History.
Award: 1500 euros
Presented: July

De Pimodan Foundation Prize
la Societe des Poetes Francais
Siege social 16, rue Monsieur le Prince, 75006 Paris
Tel: (01) 40469982 *Fax:* (01) 40469982
E-mail: poetesfrancais@aol.com
Web Site: www.societedespoetesfrancais.asso.fr
Key Personnel
President: Vital Heurtebize
Secretary General: Linda Bastide
Founded in 1926, a medal is awarded every five years to a regional poet celebrating his land.

Charles Pitou Foundation Prize
la Societe des Poetes Francais
Siege social 16, rue Monsieur le Prince, 75006 Paris
Tel: (01) 40469982 *Fax:* (01) 40469982
E-mail: poetesfrancais@aol.com
Web Site: www.societedespoetesfrancais.asso.fr
Key Personnel
President: Vital Heurtebize
Secretary General: Linda Bastide
Founded 1928, a medal is awarded every five years for a poem in strictly classical form celebrating a French province, preferably Normandy.

Grand Prix Poncetton de la SGDL
Societe des Gens de Lettres de France
Hotel de Massa, 38 rue du Faubourg Saint Jacques, F-75014 Paris
Tel: (01) 531012 00 *Fax:* (01) 531012 12
Key Personnel
President: Alain Absire
First Vice President: Marie-France Briselance
Secretary General: Jean Claude Bologne
Treasurer: Francois Taillandier
Established: 1970
For recognition of the total works of a writer whose value has not been recognized and whose situation has been seriously affected.
Award: 3000 euros

Prix de la Critique Peotique
la Societe des Poetes Francais
Siege social 16, rue Monsieur le Prince, 75006 Paris
Tel: (01) 40469982 *Fax:* (01) 40469982
E-mail: poetesfrancais@aol.com
Web Site: www.societedespoetesfrancais.asso.fr
Key Personnel
President: Vital Heurtebize
Secretary General: Linda Bastide
Awarded every two years for a work or body of work of poetic criticism or exegesis.

Prix de la reedition
Societe des Gens de Lettres de France
Hotel de Massa, 38 rue du Faubourg Saint Jacques, F-75014 Paris
Tel: (01) 531012 00 *Fax:* (01) 531012 12
Key Personnel
President: Alain Absire
First Vice President: Marie-France Briselance
Secretary General: Jean Claude Bologne
Treasurer: Francois Taillandier
Award: 1500 euros

Prix Universalis
Encylopaedia Universalis
18, rue de Tilsitt, F-75017 Paris
Tel: (01) 45727272 *Fax:* (01) 45720343
Web Site: www.universalis.fr

Concours Promethee (Promethee Competition)
L'Atelier Imaginaire
BP 2, F-65290 Juillan
Tel: (062) 32 03 70 *Fax:* (062) 32 03 70

Prose Poetique Prize
la Societe des Poetes Francais
Siege social 16, rue Monsieur le Prince, 75006 Paris
Tel: (01) 40469982 *Fax:* (01) 40469982
E-mail: poetesfrancais@aol.com
Web Site: www.societedespoetesfrancais.asso.fr
Key Personnel
President: Vital Heurtebize
Secretary General: Linda Bastide
Awarded every five years at discretion of Committee of Societe des Poetes for a work of poetry which ignores classical prosody but is essentially poetic in spirit.

☆**Lucien de Reinach Prize**
Academie des Sciences Morales et Politiques, Institut de France
23 quai de Conti, F-75270 Paris Cedex 06
Tel: (01) 43263135 *Fax:* (01) 43295510
Awarded every other year for the best original work written in French in the most recent two years on an overseas subject.

Duchess of Rohan Foundation Prize
la Societe des Poetes Francais
Siege social 16, rue Monsieur le Prince, 75006 Paris
Tel: (01) 40469982 *Fax:* (01) 40469982
E-mail: poetesfrancais@aol.com
Web Site: www.societedespoetesfrancais.asso.fr
Key Personnel
President: Vital Heurtebize
Secretary General: Linda Bastide
Medal awarded every five years to a poet, preferably young, who submits work of maximum 200 lines in competition.

☆**Rose of French Poets Award**
la Societe des Poetes Francais
Siege social 16, rue Monsieur le Prince, 75006 Paris
Tel: (01) 40469982 *Fax:* (01) 40469982
E-mail: poetesfrancais@aol.com
Web Site: www.societedespoetesfrancais.asso.fr
Key Personnel
President: Vital Heurtebize
Secretary General: Linda Bastide
Established 1949. For a foreign poet who has celebrated France in his verse. Medal awarded every two years.

Grand Prix SGDL de l'Essai
Societe des Gens de Lettres de France
Hotel de Massa, 38 rue du Faubourg Saint-Jacques, F-75014 Paris
Tel: (01) 531012 00 *Fax:* (01) 531012 12
Key Personnel
President: Alain Absire
First Vice President: Marie-France Briselance
Secretary General: Jean Claude Bologne
Treasurer: Francois Taillandier
Established: 1984
For recognition of an outstanding essay.
Award: 3000 euros

Prix Tristan Tzara de Traduction (Franco-Hongrois)
Societe des Gens de Lettres de France
Hotel de Massa, 38 rue du Faubourg Saint-Jacques, F-75014 Paris
Tel: (01) 531012 00 *Fax:* (01) 531012 12
Key Personnel
President: Alain Absire
First Vice President: Marie-France Briselance
Secretary General: Jean Claude Bologne
Treasurer: Francois Taillandier
Established: 1986
For recognition of the Hungarian translation of a French work.
Award: 1500 euros

Prix de Poesie Charles Vildrac
Societe des Gens de Lettres de France
Hotel de Massa, 38 rue du Faubourg Saint-Jacques, F-75014 Paris
Tel: (01) 531012 00 *Fax:* (01) 531012 12
Key Personnel
President: Alain Absire

First Vice President: Marie-France Briselance
Secretary General: Jean Claude Bologne
Treasurer: Francois Taillandier
Established: 1973
To recognize a writer of a collection of poems published during the year preceding the award. Writers under 40 years of age are eligible. Awarded annually.
Award: 1500 euros

Volney Prize
Institut de France
23 quai de Conti, F-75006 Paris
Tel: (01) 43295510
For a work in comparative philology.

Germany

Adelbert-von-Chamisso-Preis der Robert Bosch Stiftung
Bavarian Academy of Fine Arts
Max-Joseph-Platz 3, D-80539 Munich
Tel: (089) 2900770 *Fax:* (089) 29007723
E-mail: info@badsk.de
Web Site: www.badsk.de
Key Personnel
Contact: Dr Oswald Georg Bauer
Annual.
Other Sponsor(s): Robert Bosch Stiftung

Andreas-Gryphius-Preis
Art Society
Hafenmarkt 2, W-73728 Esslingen/Neckar
Tel: (0711) 43969010 *Fax:* (0711) 39690123

Grosser Literaturpreis der Bayerischen Akademie der Schonen Kunste
Bavarian Academy of Fine Arts
Max-Joseph-Platz 3, D-80539 Munich
Tel: (089) 2900770 *Fax:* (089) 29007723
E-mail: info@badsk.de
Web Site: www.badsk.de
Key Personnel
Contact: Dr Oswald Georg Bauer
Annual.

Berlin Art Prizes
Akademie der Kunste, Berlin
Hanseatenweg 10, D-10557 Berlin 21
Tel: (030) 390 76-0 *Fax:* (030) 390 76-175
E-mail: info@adk.de
Web Site: www.adk.de
Established: 1948
Major literary award given for a body of work by the Akademie der Kuenste (Academy of Arts). The award, Fontane-Preis, is made once every six years (a similar award being made in other disciplines in the intervening five years). In addition, 'encouragement' prizes of 10,000 DM are given annually by the Akademie in each of the six disciplines - this includes one for literature & one for film/TV/radio work (which may be for writing).
Award: 30,000 DM
Presented: March 18 annually

Horst Bienek Award for Poetry
Bavarian Academy of Fine Arts
Max-Joseph-Platz 3, D-80539 Munich
Tel: (089) 2900770 *Fax:* (089) 29007723
E-mail: info@badsk.de
Web Site: www.badsk.de
Key Personnel
Contact: Dr Oswald Georg Bauer
Annual.
Other Sponsor(s): Robert Bosch Stiftung

☆**Bremen Literatur Prize**
Bremen City Council
Herdentorsteinweg 7, D-28195 Bremen
Tel: (0421) 3612718 *Fax:* (0421) 3614091
E-mail: CHinrichs@kultur.bremen.de
Established by Senat der Frein Hansestadt Foundation to encourage German-speaking poets & writers. Awarded annually for a single work.
Award: 30,000 DM

☆**Bremen Literature Encouragement Prize**
Bremen City Council
Herdentorsteinweg 7, 28195 Bremen
Tel: (0421) 3612718 *Fax:* (0421) 3614091
E-mail: chinrichs@kultur.bremen.de
Established: 1977
Established by Rudolf-Alexander-Schroeder Foundation to encourage young German-speaking poets & writers.
Award: 10,000 DM awarded annually for a single work

Georg-Buechner Preis
Deutsche Akademie fuer Sprache und Dichtung (German Academy of Language & Poetry)
Alexandraweg 23, D-64287 Darmstadt
Tel: (06151) 40920 *Fax:* (06151) 409299
E-mail: deutsche.akademie@t-online.de
Web Site: www.deutscheakademie.de
Key Personnel
General-Secretary: Dr Gerhard Dette
Press Officer: Corinna Blattmann *Tel:* (06151) 409216
Established: 1951
Award: 40,000 euros
Presented: Autumn annually

Buxtehuder Bulle
Stadt Buxtehude
Kulturbuero, Stavenert 5, 21614 Buxtehude
Mailing Address: Postfach 15 55, 21605 Buxtehude
Tel: (04161) 501 441 *Fax:* (04161) 501 423
E-mail: stadtverwaltung@buxtehude.de
Established: 1971
A literary prize given to the best book (young readers aged 14-18) published in Germany during the preceding year. By internal nomination only.
Award: 5,000 Eur & a plaque awarded annually

Christoph-Martin-Wieland-Preis
Freundeskreis zur Internationalen Forderung Literarischer und Wissenschaftlicher Uebersetzungen
Runtstr 56, 79102 Freiburg

City of Munich Prizes
Landeshauptstadt Muenchen Kulturreferat
Burgstr 4, 80313 Munich
Tel: (089) 233 26991 *Fax:* (089) 233 21262
Web Site: www.muenchen.de
Established: 1977
For recognition of lifetime achievement in the arts by authors and artists of Munich. Prizes awarded for each of the following categories: Literature - to honor an outstanding literary collection, established in 1991; Film - to honor special achievements in film, established in 1992; Journalism - to honor an outstanding journalistic work in print, radio, or television, established in 1992; Art - for special achievements in the field of fine arts, established in 1991; Architecture - for an outstanding exceptional project designed & constructed in Munich, established in 1977; Design - for an outstanding design achievement, established in 1992; Music - for deserving musicians & musical groups in all fields and all genres of music, established in 1992; Theatre, established in 1992; and Dance (triennial), established in 1993: Discontinued.
Award: Prizes of 7,500 euros awarded for categories biennially

Deutscher Jugendliteratur Preis
Arbeitskreis fur Jugendliteratur eV
Schloerstr 10, W-80634 Munich
Tel: (089) 1684052 *Fax:* (089) 1684066
German Section of the International Board on Books for Young People.

Alfred-Doeblin Preis
Akademie der Kunste, Berlin
Hanseatenweg 10, D-10557 Berlin 21
Tel: (030) 390 76-0 *Fax:* (030) 39000771
Inaugurated in 1983, this award will generally be made every one or two years for unpublished work of an epic nature. The amount awarded will be up to 20,000 DM.

Annette von Droste Huelshoff Preis
Landschaftsverband Westfalen - Lippe Abteilung Kulturpflege
Warendorfer Str 24, W-48147 Muenster
Tel: (0251) 5913856 *Fax:* (0251) 591268
E-mail: abt.kulturpflege@lwl.org
Key Personnel
Contact: Prof Dr Manfred Balzer
Established: 1946
For recognition of special achievement in poetry written in either high or low German. Every third time it can be awarded for creative musical achievement. Recipients must be natives or residents of the Westfalian - Lippe region of Germany. Established by Provinzialverband Westfalen in memory of the German & Westfalian poetess, Annette von Droste-Hulshoff (1797-1848). Formerly: Westfaelischer Literaturpreis.
Award: 25,000 DM & a certificate awarded biennially

Konrad Duden Prize
Stadt Mannheim, Amt fuer Rats und Oeffentlichkeitsarbeit
Postfach 103051, 68030 Mannheim
Tel: (0621) 9645 *Fax:* (0621) 105882
E-mail: masta@mannheim.de
Web Site: www.mannheim.de
Key Personnel
Contact: Kirsten Batzler *E-mail:* kirsten.batzler@mannheim.de
Awarded biennially to personalities who have particularly contributed to the German language. The award is connected with a monetary prize of 12,500 euros & is noncompetitive.

Sigmund Freud Preis Fluer Wissenschaftliche Prosa
Deutsche Akademie fuer Sprache und Dichtung (German Academy of Language & Poetry)
Alexandraweg 23, D-64287 Darmstadt
Tel: (06151) 40920 *Fax:* (06151) 409299
E-mail: deutsche.akademie@t-online.de
Web Site: www.deutscheakademie.de
Key Personnel
Secretary-General: Dr Gerhard Dette
Press Officer: Corinna Blattmann *Tel:* (06151) 409216
Established: 1964
Award: 12,500 euros
Presented: Autumn annually

Friedenspreis des Deutschen Buchhandels
(Peace Prize of the German Book Trade)
Borsenverein des Deutschen Buchhandels eV
Grosser Hirschgraben 17-21, 60311 Frankfurt am Main
Mailing Address: Postfach 100442, 60004 Frankfurt am Main

GERMANY

Tel: (069) 1306228 *Fax:* (069) 1306382
E-mail: presse@boev.de
Web Site: www.boersenverein.de
Established: 1950
The prize is an amount made up exclusively of donations from publishers & booksellers. The Peace Prize is an impressive indication of the book trade's commitment to serve international understanding by its activities. According to tradition, the prize has been awarded annually. The prize is awarded during the Frankfurt Book Fair which is held each autumn.
Award: 15,000 Euros
Presented: The Frankfurt Book Fair, Autumn

Friedrich-Gerstaecker Preis-der Stadt Braunschweig
Stadt Braunschweig-Kulturinstitut
Steintorwall 3, 38100 Braunschweig
Tel: (0531) 470 4840 *Fax:* (0531) 470 4809
E-mail: kulturinstitut@braunschweig.de
Award: 6000 EUR awarded biennially

☆The German Youth Literature Award
Arbeitskreis fur Jugendliteratur eV
Metzstr 14C, 81667 Munich
Tel: (089) 1684052 *Fax:* (089) 1684066
The German Youth Literature Award is given by the Federal Ministry for Women & Youth. The selection of the books & the arrangements for granting the award are in the hands of the Arbeitskreis fuer Jugendliteratur eV, a body in which the organizations concerned with promoting good books for the young in Germany are represented. The selection is restricted to books published in the German language, primarily books from Germany, Austria & Switzerland (translations included). The rules for the award have been altered periodically. The award consists of a total of four prizes, each 15,000 DM, which can be awarded for picture-books, fiction, nonfiction & for appreciation of outstanding achievement.

Grosser Literature Preis
Bayerische Akademie der schonen Kunste
Max Joseph Platz 3, W-80539 Munich
Tel: (089) 2900770 *Fax:* (089) 29007723
To a poet or writer for his whole work. A monetary prize awarded annually.

Friedrich Gundolf Preis fuer die Vermittlung Deutscher Kultur im Ausland (Friedrich Gundolf Prize for German Culture in Foreign Countries)
Deutsche Akademie fuer Sprache und Dichtung
(German Academy of Language & Poetry)
Alexandraweg 23, D-64287 Darmstadt
Tel: (06151) 40920 *Fax:* (06151) 409299
E-mail: deutsche.akademie@t-online.de
Web Site: www.deutscheakademie.de
Key Personnel
Secretary-General: Dr Gerhard Dette
Press Officer: Corinna Blattmann *Tel:* (06151) 409216
Established: 1964
Award: 12,500 euros
Presented: Spring annually

Johann-Peter-Hebel-Preis
Ministerium fur Wisserschaft, Forschung und Kunst Baden-Wurttemberg
Hauptstatterstrasse 67, W-70029 Stuttgart 10
Mailing Address: Postfach 10 34 38, W-70029 Stuttgart
Tel: (0711) 6442660 *Fax:* (0711) 6442659
E-mail: presse@mwk-bw.de

☆Wilhelm Heinse Medal for Literature in Essay Form
Akademie der Wissenschaften und der Literatur, Klasse der Literatur
Geschwister-Scholl-Strasse 2, W-55131 Mainz
Tel: (06131) 577102 *Fax:* (06131) 577111
Founded in 1978 & awarded annually. Henceforth awarded biennially.

Ricarda-Huch-Preis
City of Darmstadt
c/o Hauptamt, Magistrat, Luisenplatz 5, Postfach 11 07 80, W-64283 Darmstadt 11
Tel: (06151) 132023 *Fax:* (06151) 133398

☆Inter Nationes Culture Prize
Inter Nationes eV
Kennedyalle 91-103, D-53175 Bonn
Tel: (0228) 8800 *Fax:* (0228) 880457
E-mail: planuug@internations.de
Web Site: www.inter-nationes.de
Established: 1968
To recognize publishers, historians, writers, translators, etc., who have made a valuable contribution to international understanding in cultural fields. Awarded to foreign nationals only. Formerly:(1988) Inter Nationes - Preis fur Werke der Literatur und bildenden Kunst.
Award: 10,000 DM and a personally dedicated booklet awarded every two years

International Youth Library, see White Ravens

Thomas Mann Prize
Hansestadt Lubeck-Bereich Kunst und Kultur
Schildstr 12, D-23539 Luebeck 1
Tel: (0451) 122-4100 *Fax:* (0451) 122-4106
Established: 1975
Founded in honor of Thomas Mann, to celebrate the 100th anniversary of his birth. The prize will be awarded to personalities who have, through their literary work, shown the humanitarian spirit set out in the work of Thomas Mann. 15,000 DM. Awarded triennially. No application fee.

Johann-Heinrich-Merck-Preis fuer literarische Kritik und Essay (J H Merck Prize for Literary Criticism & Essay)
Deutsche Akademie fuer Sprache und Dichtung
(German Academy of Language & Poetry)
Alexandraweg 23, D-64287 Darmstadt
Tel: (06151) 40920 *Fax:* (06151) 409299
E-mail: deutsche.akademie@t-online.de
Web Site: www.deutscheakademie.de
Key Personnel
General-Secretary: Dr Gerhard Dette
Press Officer: Corinna Blattmann *Tel:* (06151) 409216
Established: 1964
The German Academy of Language & Poetry prize for literary criticism.
Award: 12,500 euros
Presented: Autumn annually

Rolandpreis fur Kunst im offentlichen Raum
Senator for Bildung, Wissenschaft, Kunst und Sport
Rembertiring 8-12, D-28195 Bremen
Tel: (0421) 3612717; (0421) 3612718 *Fax:* (0421) 3614091
Bremen City Council.

Literaturpreis der Stadt-Dortmund-Nelly-Sachs-Preis (The Literary Prize of Dortmund City-Nelly Sachs Prize)
Kulturbuero der Stadt Dortmund
Kleppingstr 21-23, W-44122 Dortmund
Tel: (0231) 50 25442 *Fax:* (0231) 50 22497

LITERARY

Key Personnel
Contact: Hans-Georg Schuk *E-mail:* hg.schuk@t-online.de
Established: 1961
Instituted by the Dortmund City Council. Awarded every two years to personalities who have produced outstanding creative work in the art or cultural field.
Award: 15,000 euros

Schiller Prize
Stadt Mannheim, Amt fuer Rats und Oeffentlichkeitsarbeit
Postfach 103051, 68030 Mannheim
Tel: (0621) 9627 *Fax:* (0621) 105882
E-mail: masta@mannheim.de
Key Personnel
Contact: Rainer Gluth *E-mail:* rainer.gluth@mannheim.de
Prize awarded to persons who have contributed significantly to cultural development by their total works or an individual work of outstanding quality, or whose previous work shows promise in the cultural field. This award is connected with a monetary prize totaling 25,000 DM & is to be awarded every four years.

Literaturpreis der Landeshauptstadt Stuttgart
(Stuttgart Literary Prize)
Landeshauptstadt Stuttgart
Kulturamt, Postfach 106034, Eichstrasse 9, 70173 Stuttgart
Tel: (0711) 2163062 *Fax:* (0711) 2167628
Telex: 722854 Kult d

Thaddaeus-Troll-Preis
Foerderkreis Deutscher Schriftsteller in Baden-Wurttemberg eV
Rosenbergstr 96, 70176 Stuttgart
Fax: (0711) 6365364
E-mail: info@schriftsteller-in-bawue.de
Web Site: www.schriftsteller-in-bawue.de
Established: 1981
Foerderpreis.
Closing Date: application not possible

Johann-Heinrich-Voss-Preis fuer Uebersetzung
Deutsche Akademie fuer Sprache und Dichtung
(German Academy of Language & Poetry)
Alexandraweg 23, D-64287 Darmstadt
Tel: (06151) 40920 *Fax:* (06151) 409299
E-mail: deutsche.akademie@t-online.de
Web Site: www.deutscheakademie.de
Key Personnel
Press Officer: Corinna Blattmann *Tel:* (06151) 409216
Established: 1958
Germany Academy of Language & Poetry.
Award: 15,000 euros
Presented: Spring annually

Walter Tiemann Award
Leipzig College of Graphic Arts & Book Design
Wachterstr 11, 04107 Leipzig
Tel: (0341) 21350 *Fax:* (0341) 2135166
E-mail: hgb@hbg-leipzig.de
Web Site: www.hgb-leipzig.de
Key Personnel
Public Administration & Public Relations: Sibylle Schulz Shibru
To recognize independent publishers, small publishers & printing-presses. One to three different titles published within the preceding two years may be submitted. Established in honor of Walter Tiemann, a teacher & the rector from 1920 to 1945 at the former Leipzig Academie for Graphic Arts and Book Production, now the College of Graphic Arts and Book Design, Leipzig.
Award: A small sculpture & 10,000 DM for first prize; 3,000 DM for second prize; 2,000 DM for third prize

White Ravens
Internationale Jugendbibliothek
Schloss Blutenburg, D-81247 Munich
Tel: (089) 8912110 *Fax:* (089) 8117553
E-mail: bib@ijb.de
Web Site: www.ijb.de
Established: 1983
To promote high quality children's books of international interest. About 250 children's books, by authors & illustrators from all over the world, are given recognition. Children's books submitted by publishers during the year prior to the award are considered. White Ravens books are listed in the annual international selected bibliography & exhibited during the Children's Book Fair in Bologna, Italy & thereafter upon request in libraries & other institutions. Titles in over 30 languages from 50 countries.
Award: Annually
Closing Date: December
Presented: Bologna Children's Book Fair, Italy, April

Greece

Book Prizes of the Circle of the Greek Children's Book
Circle of the Greek Children's Book IBBY (Greek Section)
28, Bouboulinas Str, GR-106 82 Athens
Tel: (01) 8222296 *Fax:* (01) 8222296
Key Personnel
President: Loty Petrovits *Tel:* (01) 8223008
   E-mail: loty@eexi.gz
Established: 1970
Awarded annually for various types of children's literature.
Award: Prizes range from 1,000 to 1,500 Euro

Parnassos Foundation Prize
Parnassos Society
8 St Georges Kazytsis Sq, GR-105 61 Athens
Tel: (01) 3221917 *Fax:* (01) 3249398
Established: 1980
To provide recognition for the best play of the year.
Award: A monetary prize & honorary recognition awarded annually

Haiti

Prix litteraire Henri Deschamps (Henri Deschamps Literary Prize)
Maison Henri Deschamps, Grand Rue
Les Enterprises Deschamps-Frisch SA, No 318 Blvd JJ Dessalines, Port-au-Prince
Mailing Address: PO Box 164, Port-au-Prince
Tel: (509) 2232215; (509) 2232216 *Fax:* (509) 2214976
E-mail: entdeschamps@gdfhaiti.com
Key Personnel
Secretary General: Paulette Poujol Oriol
Established: 1975
Open to unpublished Haitian writers, on any subject. Awarded annually.
Award: 10,000 Gdes & free publishing copies 1000

Hong Kong

Awards for Creative Writing in Chinese
Hong Kong Public Libraries
66 Causeway Rd, Causeway Bay, Hong Kong
Tel: 2921 0208 *Fax:* 2415 8211
E-mail: enquiries@lcsd.gov.hk
Web Site: www.hkpl.gov.hk
Key Personnel
Assistant Dir: Michael Mak *E-mail:* mklmak@lcsd.gov.hk
Senior Librarian (Extension Activities): Sun Tinny YM *Tel:* 2921 2687 *E-mail:* tymsun@lcsd.gov.hk
Established: 1979
Awarded to residents of Hong Kong aged 16 & over, under six categories (prose, poetry, fiction, literary criticism, children's storybook & children's picture book) to cultivate interest in creative writing in Chinese.
Award: Awarded biennially; First prize is HK$12,000 for each category

Hong Kong Biennial Award for Chinese Literature
Hong Kong Public Libraries
66 Causeway Rd, Causeway Bay, Hong Kong
Tel: (02) 2921 0208 *Fax:* (02) 2415 8211
E-mail: enquiries@lcsd.gov.hk
Web Site: www.hkpl.gov.hk
Key Personnel
Senior Librarian (Extension Activities): Sun Tinny YM *Tel:* 2921 2687 *E-mail:* tymsun@lcsd.gov.hk
Established: 1991
By open nomination. To give recognition to the outstanding achievements of established Hong Kong writers & to encourage them to write quality literary work. Awards presented for fiction, prose, poetry, children's literature & literary criticism, published in Hong Kong in the previous two years & written in Chinese.
Award: Biennially; In 1997 each award was HK$50,000

Hungary

Jozsef Attila Prize
Ministry of Culture & Education
Szalay-utca 10/14, H-1055 Budapest
Tel: (01) 1530600 *Fax:* (01) 1533553
For highly significant work in prose or poetry. Given to writers, poets & critics. Since 1950 awarded to 8-10 people a year.

Robert Graves Prize
Hungarian Writers' Union
Magyar Iroszovetseg, Bajza utca 18, H-1062 Budapest
Tel: (01) 429568 *Fax:* (01) 213419

Kossuth Prize
Mueveloedesi Miniszterium
Kossuth Lajos-Ter 1-3, H-1055 Budapest, V
Tel: (01) 1120600 *Fax:* (01) 530124
Founded 1948. An irregular award to outstanding artists, including writers.

☆**Hungarian PEN Club Medal**
Hungarian PEN Centre
V Karolyi Mihaly U 16, H-1051 Budapest H-1053
Tel: (01) 184143
For translation of Hungarian literary work into foreign languages. Awarded when merited.

State Prize
Office of the Prime Minister
Kossuth Lajos-Ter 1-3, H-1055 Budapest, V
Tel: (01) 1120600 *Fax:* (01) 530124
Annual national prize for most exceptional & outstanding creative works. Of over a hundred recipients each year, one or more writers receive this award.

Szakszervezete Muveszeti Kulturalis Dij
National Confederation of Hungarian Trade Unions (Magyar Szakszervezetek Orszagos Szovetsege)
Dozsa Gyoergy ut 84/B, H-1415 Budapest
Tel: (01) 3225033 *Fax:* (01) 3421924
Awarded annually. Established in 1958 by the Central Council of Hungarian Trade Unions, prizes are awarded to artists, scientists, educators, as well as for literary works. Nominees are people who excel in improving worker-artist contacts and in disseminating knowledge. Selection is by public opinion poll.
Trade Union's Art & Cultural Prize.

India

Bhai Santokh Singh Award
Haryana Sahitya Akademi
Kothi No 897, Sector-2, Panchkula 134112
Tel: (0172) 565521; (0172) 563340
Key Personnel
Dir: A S Shergill
Awarded annually to an Indian national domiciled in Haryana State for contributions to the development of Panjabi literature. Presented for the life long contribution to the Panjabi writer once in a lifetime.

I C Chacko Award
Kerala Sahitya Akademi
Town Hall Rd, Thrissur 680020 Kerala
Tel: (011) 331069
Key Personnel
Secretary: Payipra Radhakrishnan
For the best book published in Malayalam during the preceding three years in the fields of science and linguistics. 2000 Indian rupees awarded annually. Enquiries to Kerala Sahitya Akademi, PO Box 501, Town Hall Rd, Trichur 680020, Kerala State.

Escorts Book Award
Dehli Management Association
India Habitat Centre, Core 6A, 1st Floor, Lodhi Rd, New Delhi 110003
Tel: (011) 4649552 *Fax:* (011) 4649553
E-mail: dmadelhi@ndb.vsnl.net.in
Key Personnel
Program Manager: S Kumar
Instituted by Escorts Ltd in 1965 and administered by Delhi Management Association. For original books on management principles & practices by Indian writers. 5000 & 3000 Indian rupees each. Awarded annually.

Indian Books Centre Oriental Studies Award
Sri Satguru Publications
40/5 Shakti Nagar, New Delhi 110007
Tel: (011) 7126497 *Fax:* (011) 7227336
For the best work in Oriental Studies, published in Sanskrit, English, Tibetan or Hindi. 1100 Indian rupees, a shawl & a citation are awarded on a regular basis.

Jnanpith Award
Bharatiya Jnanpith
18 Institutional Area, Lodi Rd, New Delhi 110 003
Tel: (011) 4626467; (011) 698417

INDIA

Kerala Sahitya Akademi Awards
Kerala Sahitya Akademi
Town Hall Rd, Thrissur 680020 Kerala
Tel: (0487) 331069
Key Personnel
Secretary: Payipra Radhakrishnan
For literary works in Malayalam published during the preceding three years, in the following categories: fiction; drama; poetry; short stories; novels; literary criticism; (biography; autobiography; travelogs & humor); scientific & scholarly works (including philosophy; education; sociology). 5000 Indian rupees for each award.

Kesari Award
DC Books
Good Shepard St, Kottayam, Kerala 686001
Mailing Address: PO Box 212, Kottayam, Kerala 686001
Tel: 3114; 8214
Best unpublished novel in Malayalam, 3,000 Indian rupees. Awarded annually.

C B Kumar Award
Kerala Sahitya Akademi
Town Hall Rd, Thrissur 680020 Kerala
Tel: (011) 331069
Key Personnel
Secretary: Payipra Radhakrishnan
For best collection of essays in Malayalam. 1500 Indian rupees awarded annually.

Kuttippuzha Award
Kerala Sahitya Akademi
Town Hall Rd, Thrissur 680020 Kerala
Tel: (011) 331069
Key Personnel
Secretary: Payipra Radhakrishnan
For the best book of criticism published in Malayalam during the preceding three years. 2000 Indian rupees awarded once every two years.

Law Books in Hindu Prize
Indian Law Institute
Opposite Supreme Court, Bhagwandas Rd, New Delhi 110 001
Tel: (011) 389429 *Fax:* (011) 3782140
Awarded annually for law books/manuscripts in Hindi. The first prize is 10,000 Indian rupees & prizes up to 100,000 Indian rupees may be awarded.

Mahrishi Vedvyasa Prize
Haryana Sahitya Akademi
Kothi No 897, Sector-2, Panchkula 134112
Tel: (0172) 565521
Awarded annually to an Indian national domiciled in Haryana State for contribution towards the development of Sanskrit literature. 11000 Indian rupees.

Meera Award
Rajasthan Sahitya Akademi
Palace, Udaipur, Rajasthan
Tel: 83717; 83629
Founded 1959. For best literary work in Hindi. 11,000 Indian rupees awarded annually.

K R Namboodiri Award
Kerala Sahitya Akademi
Town Hall Rd, Thrissur 680020 Kerala
Tel: (011) 331069
Key Personnel
Secretary: Payipra Radhakrishnan
For best work on Vedic literature in Malayalam. 2000 Indian rupees awarded annually.

Pandit Lakhmi Chand Prize
Haryana Sahitya Akademi
Kothi No 897, Sector-2, Panchkula 134112
Tel: (0172) 565521
Awarded annually to an Indian national for outstanding work on literature, art, history & culture of Haryana, 11000 Indian rupees.

M P Paul Award
D C Books
Good Shepard St, Kottayam, Kerala 686001
Mailing Address: PO Box 214, Kottayam, Kerala 686001
Tel: 3114; 8214
For best unpublished fiction in Malayalam. Awarded annually.
Award: 3000 Indian rupees

M P Paul Prize
Sahitya Pravarthaka Co-operative Society Ltd
PO Box 94, Kottayam, Kerala 686001
Tel: 4111; 4112
For best published fiction in Malayalam. 1000 Indian rupees awarded annually.

Sahitya Akademi Award
Sahitya Akademi
Rabindra Bhavan, 35 Ferozshah Rd, New Delhi 110 001
Tel: (011) 3387064 *Fax:* (011) 3382428
E-mail: secy@ndb.vsnl.net.in
Web Site: www.sahitya-akademi.org.
Key Personnel
Secretary: Prof K Satchidanandan *Tel:* (011) 3386626
Established: 1955
For outstanding literary works written in each of the 22 languages of India recognized by the Indian National Academy of Letters (Sahitya Akademi). 25,000 Indian rupees each. Awarded annually to Indian nationals only.
Award: National Award
Closing Date: December annually
Presented: New Delhi, February annually

Sahitya Pravarthaka Benefit Fund Awards
Sahitya Pravarthaka Co-operative Society Ltd
PO Box 94, Kottayam, Kerala 686001
Tel: 4111; 4112
For best works in Malayalam. Five prizes of 2000 Indian rupees each awarded annually.

Sur Award
Haryana Sahitya Akademi
Kothi No 897, Sector-2, Panchkula 134112
Tel: (0172) 565521
Awarded annually to an Indian national domiciled in Haryana State for outstanding contribution to development of Hindi, Sanskrit & Haryanvi.
Award: 25,000 Indian rupees

Sree Padmanabha Swami Prize
Kerala Sahitya Akademi
Town Hall Rd, Thrissur 680020 Kerala
Tel: (011) 331069
Key Personnel
Secretary: Payipra Radhakrishnan
For the best children's literature published in Malayalam during the preceding three years. 2500 Indian rupees awarded annually.

Tagore Literacy Award
Indian Adult Education Association
17-B Indraprastha Estate, New Dehli 110 002
Tel: (011) 3722206 *Fax:* (011) 3355306
Recognition of outstanding contribution to promotion of women's literacy & adult education in India.

Urdu Akademy Awards
Urdu Academy Delhi
Ghata Masjid Rd, Daryaganj, New Delhi 1100021
Awarded annually to Indian nationals for Urdu literature.

Islamic Republic of Iran

Children's Book Council Award (Jayezeh Showraye Ketabe Koodak)
Children's Book Council of Iran
PO Box 13145-133, Enghelab Vahid Nazari 69, Tehran 13158
Tel: (021) 6408074; (021) 6405878 *Fax:* (021) 8002369
Web Site: www.schoolnet.or.ir/~cbc
Key Personnel
General Secretary: Noushine Ansari
E-mail: anmo@kanoon.net
Established: 1963
For recognition of a contribution in the field of children's literature. Iranian writers, illustrators & translations are eligible. Established by A Yamini Sharif.
Award: A plaque or diploma is awarded annually
Presented: CBCI Annual Meeting, January each year

Ireland

Aosdana Membership
The Arts Council/An Chomhairle Ealaion
70 Merrion Sq, Dublin 2
Tel: (01) 6180200 *Fax:* (01) 6761302
E-mail: info@artscouncil.ie
Web Site: www.artscouncil.ie
Key Personnel
Registrar: Patricia Quinn
Special honorary affiliation of creative artists, which also provides annuities up to 11,072 euro. To be eligible for membership, the artist must have been born in Ireland or been a resident of Ireland for five years, must not be less than 35 years of age & must have produced a body of works. Membership is by election.

The Clo lar-Chonnacta Literary Award
Clo Iar-Chonnachta Teo
Indreabhan, Conamara, Co Galway
Tel: (091) 593307 *Fax:* (091) 593362
E-mail: cic@iol.ie
Key Personnel
General Manager: Deirdre O'Toole
The Clo Iar-Chonnacta Literary Award & 5000 pounds will be presented annually for a newly written & unpublished work in the Irish language. 2001 Short Story or Long Play.
Closing Date: December

Denis Devlin Memorial Award for Poetry
The Arts Council/An Chomhairle Ealaion
70 Merrion Sq, Dublin 2
Tel: (01) 6180200 *Fax:* (01) 6761302
E-mail: info@artscouncil.ie
Web Site: www.artscouncil.ie
Given for the finest collection of poetry in the English language by an Irish citizen published in the previous three years. Value IR L1500.

Gregory Medal
Irish Academy of Letters, School of Irish Studies

4 Ailesbury Grove, Dundum, Dublin 14
For distinction in letters or outstanding literary work in Irish. Awarded periodically.

☆**International Fiction Prize**
Irish Times Ltd
10-16 D'Olier St, Dublin 2
Tel: (01) 6792022 *Fax:* (01) 6773282
Awarded biannually for a work of fiction written in English & published in Ireland, the United Kingdom or the United States within a two year period from August 1 of the previous year to July 31 of the year of the prize. Four titles are shortlisted for this prize.

☆**The Irish Literature Prize: Fiction**
Irish Times Ltd
10-16 D'Olier St, Dublin 2
Tel: (01) 6792022 *Fax:* (01) 6773282
Awarded biannually along with the Poetry Prize. Books can be in either English or Irish & published in Ireland, the United Kingdom or the United States within a two-year time period from August 1 & July 31 of the year of the prize. Three books are shortlisted for this prize.

☆**The Irish Literature Prize: Nonfiction**
Irish Times Ltd
10-16 D'Olier St, Dublin 2
Tel: (01) 6792022 *Fax:* (01) 6773282
Awarded biannually along with the First Book Prize. Books can be in either English or Irish & published in Ireland, the United Kingdom or the United States within a two-year period from August 1 & July 31 of the year of the prize. Three books are shortlisted for this prize.

☆**The Irish Literature Prize: Poetry**
Irish Times Ltd
10-16 D'Olier St, Dublin 2
Tel: (01) 6792022 *Fax:* (01) 6773282
Awarded biannually along with the Fiction Prize. Books can be in either English or Irish & published in Ireland, the United Kingdom or the United States withing a two-year period from August 1 & July 31 of the year of the prize. Three books are shortlisted for this prize.

Macaulay Fellowship
The Arts Council/An Chomhairle Ealaion
70 Merrion Sq, Dublin 2
Tel: (01) 6180200 *Fax:* (01) 6761302
E-mail: info@artscouncil.ie
Web Site: www.artscouncil.ie
Awarded in literature every triennially to young Irish writers who are usually under 30 years of age; this fellowship is valued at IRL 3500.

Novel Prize
Irish Academy of Letters, School of Irish Studies
4 Ailesbury Grove, Dundum, Dublin 14
For the best novel written in Irish. Awarded annually.

☆**The Prize for Poetry in Irish/An Duais don bhFiliiocht in Gaeilge**
The Arts Council/An Chomhairle Ealaion
70 Merrion Sq, Dublin 2
Tel: (01) 6180200 *Fax:* (01) 6761302
E-mail: info@artscouncil.ie
This prize, established 1962 is awarded to the author of the best book of poetry in the Irish language (Gaelic) published in the previous three years. Its value is Irish L1500.

Rooney Prize for Irish Literature
Rooney Prize Committee
Strathin, Templecarrig, Delgany Co, Wicklow
Tel: (01) 2874769 *Fax:* (01) 2872595

Key Personnel
Chairman: Jim Sherwin *E-mail:* jsherwin@rol.ue
Annual award for Irish Literature of IRL5,000. A noncompetitive Prize to encourage young Irish creative talent. Enquiries to Jim Sherwin at above address.

Marten Toonder Award
The Arts Council/An Chomhairle Ealaion
70 Merrion Sq, Dublin 2
Tel: (01) 6180200 *Fax:* (01) 6761302
E-mail: info@artscouncil.ie
Web Site: www.artscouncil.ie
Awarded in literature every three years. Value IR L7875/10000.

Israel

ACUM Prize for Literature and Music
Society of Authors, Composers and Music Publishers in Israel
PO Box 14220, 61140 Tel Aviv
Tel: (03) 6850115 *Fax:* (03) 5620119
Established: 1957
To encourage creative work in the fields of literature & music. Israeli citizens are eligible.
Award: Monetary prizes annually

Award for Original Hebrew Novel
Mordechai Bernstein Literary Prizes Association
c/o The Book Publishers Association of Israel, 29 Carlebach St, 67132 Tel Aviv
Tel: (03) 5614121 *Fax:* (03) 5611996
E-mail: info@tbpai.co.il
Established: 1981
To encourage authors under the age of 50 who write Hebrew novels. Established to honor Mordechal Bernstein, an Israeli author.
Award: Monetary award, biennially

Award for Original Hebrew Poetry
Mordechai Bernstein Literary Prizes Association
c/o The Book Publishers Association of Israel, 29 Carlebach St, 67132 Tel Aviv
Tel: (03) 5614121 *Fax:* (03) 5611996
E-mail: info@tbpai.co.il
Established: 1981
To encourage Hebrew poets under the age of 50. Established in honor of Mordechai Bernstein, an Israeli author.
Award: A monetary prize is awarded biennially

Bialik Prize for Literature
Tel-Aviv-Yafo Municipality
Dept of Municipal Prizes, Tel Aviv
The highest literary award of the Tel-Aviv-Yafo Municipality, awarded in two categories: belles-lettres & Jewish studies. 80,000 shekels. Awarded annually.

Brenner Prize
Hebrew Writers' Association in Israel
PO Box 7111, Tel Aviv
Tel: (03) 253-256
In recognition of outstanding literary works. 12,000 shekels. Awarded annually.

Israeli Prize in Humanities and Social Sciences
Israeli Ministry of Education and Culture
Rechov Shivtei Yisrael 34, 91911 Jerusalem
Tel: (02) 278211
For the most original, outstanding contribution to the humanities & social sciences. 110,000 shekels. Awarded annually in each one of the following areas: (1) Judaica, Modern Hebrew Literature & Education; (2) the Humanities & the Social Sciences; (3) the Arts; (4) Science & Technology; (5) outstanding life-long service to the welfare of Israeli society.

☆**The Jerusalem Prize For Freedom of the Individual in Society**
Jerusalem International Book Fair
PO Box 775, Jerusalem 91007
Tel: (02) 6297922; (02) 6297868 *Fax:* (02) 6243144
E-mail: jer_fair@netvision.net.il
Web Site: www.jerusalembookfair.com
Key Personnel
Man Dir: Zev Birger
Contact: Annette Aaronson
Established in 1963 & is awarded during the Jerusalem International Book Fair which is held every two years. The award is made to a world-renowned author whose works express the idea of the freedom of the individual in society.
Award: $5,000 cash
Presented: Jerusalem International Book Fair, March 21, 2001

Shazar Prize
Israel Ministry of Education & Culture
Rechov Shivtei Yisrael 34, 91911 Jerusalem
Tel: (02) 278-211
Awarded to immigrant writers, young authors & writers dealing with the Holocaust. 5000-12,000 shekels to each author. Awarded annually.

Tchernichowsky Prize
Tel-Aviv-Yafo Municipality
Dept of Municipal Prizes, Tel Aviv
For outstanding translations into Hebrew. 60,000 shekels divided between two translators: one of belles-lettres and one of scientific material. Awarded biennially.

Italy

Andersen Prize
Sestri Levante Municipality
Piazza Matteotti 3, Sestri Levante, GE
Tel: (0185) 4781 *Fax:* (0185) 41064
Web Site: www.premioandersen.it
To recognize the year's best fairy tale for children. Professional or amateur writers are eligible.

Bagutta Prize
Bagutta Restaurant
Via Bagutta 14, I-20121 Milan
Tel: (02) 702767 *Fax:* (02) 799613
Founded in 1927 for the best book of the year, given for several literary forms including the novel & poetry. 50,000,000 lire, awarded annually.

Bologna Ragazzi Prize for Children and Youth, see BolognaRagazzi Award

☆**BolognaRagazzi Award**
Formerly Bologna Ragazzi Prize for Children and Youth
Bologna Children's Book Fair
Piazza della Costituzione 6, I-40128 Bologna
Tel: (051) 282111 *Fax:* (051) 6374011
E-mail: bookfair@bolognafiere.it
Web Site: www.bookfair.bolognafiere.it
Key Personnel
Man Dir: Giuseppe Fini
Established: 1966

To reward the best publishing projects selected among the works presented by the exhibitors of the Book Fair.
Presented: Annually

Isle of Elba - Rafaello Brignetti Literary Award
Premio Letterario Isola d'Elba - Raffaello Brignetti
c/o Azienda di Promozione Turistica, Calata Italia 26, I-57037 Portoferraio
Tel: (0565) 914671 *Fax:* (0565) 916350
For recognition of outstanding works of prose, poetry, or literary essays. Works by European authors published in Italy or translated into Italian during the previous year are eligible. Formerly: (1984) Premio Letterario Isola d'Elba. Renamed in 1984 in honor of Raffaello Brignetti.
Award: 10,000,000 Italian lire annually

Campieillo Prize
Campiello Foundation
Calle Due Portoni no 6, I-30172 Mestre (Venice)
Tel: (041) 983463 *Fax:* (041) 985395
Telex: 420380
Instituted in 1963 and promoted by the seven industrial association founder members of Fondazione Campiello. For a previously unpublished work of fiction. Annual award of 16,000,000 lire.

☆Giosue Carduccie Prize
Bologna University
via Zamboni 33, I-40100 Bologna
Tel: (51) 228621
Established 1950. For poetry, monographs & essays on poetry & poets. 1,500,000 lire. Awarded annually.

Castello-Sanguinetto Prize
Comune di Sanquinetto
Interno Castello 2, I-37058 Sanguinetto, VR
Tel: (0442) 81066 *Fax:* (0442) 365150
Web Site: www.verno.net/servizi/spettaen.htm
Established: 1951
To encourage the development of novels for young readers between 11 and 14 years of age. The novel must be published in Italy before July 15 of the current year. Established by Professor Giulletto Accordi.
Other Sponsor(s): Cassa di Risparmio di Verona - Vicenza e Belluno
Award: 4,000,000 lire for first prize; second prize 2000 lire; both awarded annually

Certamen Capitolinum
Istituto Nazionale di Studi Romani
Piazza dei Cavalieri di Malta 2, I-00153 Rome
Tel: (06) 5743442; (06) 5743445 *Fax:* (06) 5743447
E-mail: studiromani@studizomani.it
Web Site: www.studiromani.it
Key Personnel
President: Prof Mario Petrucciani
Dir: Dr Fernanda Roscetti
Established: 1950
To provide recognition for the best works on the Latin language & literature. Teachers, scholars & students are eligible.
Award: (1) First prize - 600,000 lire & a silver sculpture of a she-wolf, (2) second prize - 300,000 lire & a silver medallion, (3) third prize - 100,000 lire & a diploma (to students), and (4) honorable mentions awarded annually

☆Antonio Feltrinelli Prize
Accademia Nazionale dei Lincei
Palazzo Corsini, via della Lungara 10, I-00165 Rome
Tel: (06) 650831

Each year the Lincei Academy (the National Italian Academy of Sciences) awards Antonio Feltrinelli prizes for accomplishment in the various branches of sciences, humanities, and literature. These prizes were instituted by an Italian businessman who died in 1942 & bequeathed his fortune to the Academy for the purpose of "rewarding toil, study, intelligence . . . those men who with greater success distinguished themselves with high achievements in art & science, since they are the true benefactors of their own country as well as of all humanity". The literature award is granted every five years & the amount varies.

Grinzane Cavour Prize
Grinzane Cavour Prize Association
Via Montebello 21, I-10124 Turin
Tel: (011) 8126847 *Fax:* (011) 8125456
E-mail: grinzane@attin.it
Established: 1982
To encourage the diffusion of reading in the Italian school, especially of books of contemporary fiction. Literary critics, scholars, writers, journalists & people in the world of Italian culture judge the books. Established by Prof. Giuliano Soria. Awarded annually in five categories: contemporary Italian fiction; contemporary foreign fiction translated into Italian; an international prize for the complete works of a foreign writer; young beginning author, aged less than forty; essay writing.
Other Sponsor(s): Fondazione Cassa di Risparmio di Torino; Provincia di Torino; Regione Piemonte; SEAT
Award: International prize for the complete works of a foreign writer - 10,000,000 lire; all others 7,000,000 lire

☆Naples Prize for Literature
Fondazione Premio Napoli
Palazzo Reale-Piazza Plebiscito, I-80132 Naples
Tel: (081) 403187; (081) 422362 *Fax:* (081) 402023
Key Personnel
Contact: Carmen Petillo
Established: 1954
For recognition of an outstanding work of literature in Italian. Italian & non-Italian authors are eligible.
Award: 10,000,000 Italian lire and a plaque awarded annually

Laura Orvieto Prize
Fondazione Premio Laura Orvieto
Archivo Contemporaneo del Gabinetto, GP Vieusseux, Via Maggio 42, I-50125 Florence
Tel: (055) 213295 *Fax:* (055) 213188
Established: 1954
To provide recognition for the manuscript of a book of fiction for children from 8 to 11 years of age. Italian authors are eligible. Established by Adriana Guasconi Orvieto in memory of Laura Orvieto.
Award: Monetary prizes awarded biennially

Premio Langhe Ceretto
Biblioteca Civica G Ferrero
via Vittorio Emanuele, 19, Alba
Tel: (0173) 290092 *Fax:* (0173) 362075
E-mail: cn0002@biblioteche.regione.piemonte.it
Key Personnel
Secretary: Dr Gianfranco Maggi

Strega Prize
Strega Alberti Benevento
Corso Rinascimento 41, I-00186 Rome
Tel: (06) 540346 *Fax:* (06) 892919
Web Site: www.cnet.it/fair/alberti
Founded in 1947 by Maria Bellonci and Guido Alberti for a work of fiction.

Viareggio Prizes
Premio Viareggio
Via Francesco Borgatti 25, I-00191 Rome
Tel: (06) 3283736
Web Site: www.circle.intesc.it/eder/crofil/narita/97/italia/viaregg.htm
Founded in 1929, since 1967 the annual award has been divided into three sections: fiction, nonfiction & poetry. Annually given to foreign writers & poets 25,000,000 lire.

Japan

Female Writers Literary Award (Joryu Bungaku Award)
Chuo-Koron-Sha Inc
2-8-7 Kyobashi, Chou-ku, Tokyo 104
Tel: (03) 35631261 *Fax:* (03) 35615920
For the best novel. 1,000,000 yen. Awarded annually.

Gunzo for Fiction du Critique Prize
Kodansha
Otowa Daini Bldg, 2-12-21 Otowa 2-chome, Bunkyo-ku, Tokyo 112
Tel: (03) 9446491 *Fax:* (03) 9449915
Established: 1967
To provide recognition for an outstanding work of fiction by a new writer. Formerly known as the Gunzo Fiction Prize.
Award: 500,000 yen

Japan Translation Prize for Publisher
Japan Society of Translators
c/o Orion Press, 1-55 Kanda-Jimbocho, Chiyoda-ku, Tokyo
Tel: (03) 32943936 *Fax:* (03) 33061251
For outstanding translations. Awarded annually.

Kodansha Cultural Prize in Publishing for Book Design
Kodansha
Otowa Daini Bldg, 2-12-21 Otowa, Bunkyo-ku, Tokyo 112
Tel: (03) 9446491 *Fax:* (03) 9449915
The most recent winners were Eiji Sakagawa & Yoko Yamamoto for L no Okurikmono (Shueisha).
Award: 1,000,000 yen

Kodansha Cultural Prize in Publishing for Illustrations
Kodansha
Otowa Daini Bldg, 2-12-21 Otowa 2-chome, Bunkyo-ku, Tokyo 112
Tel: (03) 9446491 *Fax:* (03) 9449915
Key Personnel
Contact: Tetsu Shirai
Established 1970 for the best work of illustration, awarded annually. The most recent winner was Yasuhiro Yomogida for Kakashinagaya (Yomiuri Shimbun).
Award: 1,000,000 yen

Kodansha Cultural Prize in Publishing for Photographs
Kodansha
Otowa Daini Bldg, 2-12-21 Otowa, Bunkyo-ku, Tokyo 112
Tel: (03) 9446491 *Fax:* (03) 9449915
The most recent winner was Koichi Imaeda for Aozameta Soviet (Bungeishunju) & Russian Roulette (Shinchosha).
Award: 1,000,000 yen

PRIZES   JAPAN

Kodansha Cultural Prize in Publishing for Picture Books
Kodansha
Otowa Daini Bldg, 2-12-21 Otowa, Bunkyo-ku, Tokyo 112
Tel: (03) 9446491 *Fax:* (03) 9449915
Key Personnel
Contact: Tetsu Shirai
Established 1970 for the most outstanding picture book, awarded annually. The most recent winner was Miho Takeda for Tonari no Seki no Masuda-kun (Popurasha).
Award: 1,000,000 yen

Kodansha Essay Prize
Kodansha
2-12-21 Otowa 2-chome, Otowa Daini Bldg, Bunkyo-ku, Tokyo 112
Tel: (03) 9446491 *Fax:* (03) 9449915
Key Personnel
Contact: Tetsu Shirai
Established 1985 for the best essay. 1,000,000 yen awarded annually.

Kodansha Nonfiction Prize
Kodansha
2-12-21 Otowa 2-chome, Otowa Daini Bldg, Bunkyo-ku, Tokyo 112
Tel: (03) 9446491 *Fax:* (03) 9449915
Key Personnel
Contact: Tetsu Shirai
Established 1979 for the best nonfiction work. 1,000,000 yen, awarded annually. The most recent winners were Miyoko Kudo for Kudo Shasinkan no Showa (Asahi Shimbunsha) & Yukiharu Takahashi for Soubou no Daichi (Kodansha).

Kodansha Prize for Comics
Kodansha
Otowa Daini Bldg, 2-12-21 Otowa, Bunkyo-ku, Tokyo 112
Tel: (03) 9446491 *Fax:* (03) 9449915
1,000,000 yen. The most recent winners were Joji Morikawa for Hajime no Ippo (Kodansha), Mieko Ohsaka for Eien no Nohara (Shueisha), Kenshi Hirokane for Kacho Shima Kosaku (Kodansha) & Jun Fukami for Wari (Kodansha).

Yukio Mishima Award
Shincho-Sha Co Ltd
71 Yarai-cho, Shinjuku-ku, Tokyo 162-8711
Tel: (03) 32665543 *Fax:* (03) 32665234
Established 1987. For a literary work (novel, criticism, poetry, drama) written by a new or moderately well-known writer and published during the preceding year. Annual award of commemorative plaque & 1,000,000 yen.

Noma Award for Publishing in Africa
Kodansha
Otowa Daini Bldg, 2-12-21 Otowa, Bunkyo-ku, Tokyo 112
Tel: (03) 9446491 *Fax:* (03) 9449915
Established: 1980
To encourage the development of the African publishing industry. The most recent winner was NIYI Osunddre for Waiting Laughters (Malthouse Press Ltd).
Award: $5000

Noma Award for the Translation of Japanese Literature
Kodansha
Otowa Daini Bldg, 2-12-21 Otowa 2-chome, Bunkyo-ku, Tokyo 112
Tel: (03) 9446491 *Fax:* (03) 9449915
Established in 1990 for the best translation of a post-1926 Japanese novel or essay. $10,000.

Noma Concours for Picture Book Illustrations
Kodansha
Otowa Daini Bldg, 2-12-21 Otowa 2-chome, Bunkyo-ku, Tokyo 112
Tel: (03) 9446491 *Fax:* (03) 9449915
Established to promote high standards in children's book illustration. $2000.

Noma Juvenile Literature Prize for New Writers
Kodansha
Otowa Daini Bldg, 2-12-21 Otowa 2-chome, Bunkyo-ku, Tokyo 112-01
Tel: (03) 9446491 *Fax:* (03) 9449915
Key Personnel
Contact: Tetsu Shirai
Established 1963 for the best juvenile novel by a new writer. 1,000,000 yen, awarded annually.

Noma Literacy Prize
Kodansha
Otowa Daini Bldg, 2-12-21 Otowa 2-chome, Bunkyo-ku, Tokyo 112
Tel: (03) 9446491 *Fax:* (03) 9449915
Established to honor an individual or group working to improve literacy levels in the Third World. $10,000.

Noma Literature Prize for New Writers
Kodansha
Otowa Daini Bldg, 2-12-21 Otowa, Bunkyo-ku, Tokyo 112
Tel: (03) 9446491 *Fax:* (03) 9449915
Key Personnel
Contact: Tetsu Shirai
Established 1979 for the best novel by a new writer. 1,000,000 yen, awarded annually. The most recent winner was Yoriko Shono for Nanimo shitenai (Kodansha Ltd).

Noma Prize for Juvenile Literature
Kodansha
Otowa Daini Bldg, 2-12-21 Otowa 2-chome, Bunkyo-ku, Tokyo 112
Tel: (03) 9446491 *Fax:* (03) 9449915
Key Personnel
Contact: Tetsu Shirai
Established 1963 for the best juvenile novel. 2,000,000 yen. Awarded annually. The most recent winners were Ashiko Imamura for Kagarichan (Kodansha) & Tadaaki Mori for Ho Misake Made (Kumon Shuppan).

Noma Prize for Literature
Kodansha
Otowa Daini Bldg, 2-12-21 Otowa 2-chrome, Bunkyo-ku, Tokyo 112
Tel: (03) 9446491 *Fax:* (03) 9449915
Key Personnel
Contact: Tetsu Shirai
Established 1941 for the best Japanese novel of the year. 3,000,000 yen. Awarded annually.

Osaragi Jiro Prize
Asahi Shimbun Publishing Co
Osaragi Jiro Prize Office, 5-3-2 Tsukiji, Chou-Ku, Tokyo 104-11
Tel: (03) 35450131
Web Site: www.mmip.or.jp/asahishimbun/index-e.html
Established: 1974
For recognition of outstanding work in the field of literature. Established in memory of Jiro Osaragi, one of the most popular novelists in Japan.
Award: 2,000,000 yen awarded annually

Oya Soichi Nonfiction Prize
The Society for the Promotion of Japanese Literature
Bungei Shunju Publishing Co 3-23 Kioi-cho, Chiyoda-ku, Tokyo 102-8008
Tel: (03) 32651211 *Fax:* (03) 32652624
Key Personnel
Contact: Kazukiyo Takahashi
To encourage new nonfiction writers. 1,000,000 yen, plus around-the-world air ticket, contributed by JAL Co Ltd. Awarded annually.

Printing Culture Prize
Japan Federation of Printing Industries
1-16-8 Shintomi, Chuo-ku, Tokyo
Tel: (03) 35536051; (03) 35536079 *Fax:* (03) 35536079
Established: 1987
To provide recognition in the field of printing for a work that is artistically, historically & academically valuable. Formerly, Insatsu Bunka Sho.
Award: Monetary award & plaque awarded every four years

Shincho Gakugei-Sho
Shincho-Sha Co Ltd
71 Yarai-cho, Shinjuku-ku, Tokyo 162-8711
Tel: (03) 32665543 *Fax:* (03) 32665234
Established 1987. For a creative work of nonfiction contributing to Japanese art, literature or culture & published during the preceding year. Annual award of commemorative plaque & 1,000,000 yen.

Tanizaki Junichiro Prize
Chuo-Koron-Sha Inc
2-8-7 Kyobashi, Chuo-ku, Tokyo 104
Tel: (03) 35631261 *Fax:* (03) 3561 5920
To recall the works by Tanizaki & to celebrate the publisher's birthday. 1,000,000 yen. Awarded annually.

Shugoro Yamamoto Award
Shincho-Sha Co Ltd
71 Yarai-cho, Shinjuku-ku, Tokyo 162
Tel: (03) 32665543 *Fax:* (03) 32665234
Established 1987. For an outstanding novel written by a new or moderately well-known writer & published during the preceding year. Annual award of commemorative plaque & 1,000,000 yen.

Yomiuri Literature Prize
Yomiuri Newspapers Publishing Co
c/o Office of International Affairs, 1-7-1 Ohtemachi, Chiyoda-ku, Tokyo 100-55
Tel: (03) 32421111 *Fax:* (03) 32460888
Established in 1950 for the best work in six categories: novel, essay & travels, drama, literary study & translation, poetry & haiku, critique & biography. 1,000,000 yen each, awarded annually. The latest prize winners in each category were: Takako Takahashi for Ikari no Ko (Kodansha Ltd) & Hideo Takubo for Kaizu (Kodansha Ltd) (joint award, novel); Inako Sata for Tsuki no En (Kodansha Ltd) (essay & travels); Fumi Saito for Hakadorikayukamu (Fushiki Shoin Publishing Co) (poetry & haiku); Masaaki Kanno for Stephane Mallarme (Chuokoron-Sha Inc) & Chiaki Matsudaira for Anabasis (Chikuma Shobo Publishing Co Ltd) (joint award, literary study & translation). There were no awards in the categories of drama & critique & biography.

Yoshikawa Eiji Cultural Prize
Kodansha
Otowa Daini Bldg, 2-12-21 Otowa 2-chome, Bunkyo-ku, Tokyo 112
Tel: (03) 9446491 *Fax:* (03) 9449915
1,000,000 yen.

Yoshikawa Eiji Literature Prize
Kodansha

JAPAN

Otowa Daini Bldg, 2-12-21 Otowa 2-chome, Bunkyo-ku, Tokyo 112
Tel: (03) 9446491 *Fax:* (03) 9449915
Key Personnel
Contact: Tetsu Shirai
Established 1967 for a popular novel. 3,000,000 yen, awarded annually.

Yoshikawa Eiji Literature Prize for New Writers
Kodansha
Otowa Daini Bldg, 2-12-21 Otowa, Bunkyo-ku, Tokyo 112
Tel: (03) 9446491 *Fax:* (03) 9449915
Key Personnel
Contact: Tetsu Shirai
Established 1980 for a popular novel for a new writer. 1,000,000 yen, awarded annually. The most recent winners were Ramo Nakajima for Konya Subete no Barde (Kodansha) & Miyuki Miyabe for Honjo Fukagawa Fushigizoshi (Shinjimbutsu Ohraisha).

Kenya

Jomo Kenyatta Prize for Literature
Kenya Publishers Association
Oxford Univ Press, East and Central Africa, Nairobi
Mailing Address: PO Box 72532, Nairobi
Tel: (02) 336377
Awarded annually to provide recognition for an outstanding literary work written in the English or Swahili languages. Authors from Kenya, Uganda, or Tanzania were eligible.
Award: 10,000 Kenya shillings, divided between a work in English & a work in Swahili

Republic of Korea

Korean Literature Translation Award
Korean Culture & Fine Arts Foundation
1-130 Dong Soong-Dong Chongro-ku, Seoul 110
Mailing Address: PO Box Kwang Hwa Moon 947, Seoul 110-510
Tel: (02) 7604563 *Fax:* (02) 7604694
E-mail: paca@caibs.kcaf.or.kr
Web Site: www.kcaf.or.kr
Key Personnel
Contact: Park Eun Young
Awarded biennially to encourage people engaged in the translation & publication abroad of Korean literature; If there is no work of sufficient merit for the grand prize, the finest entry will be awarded $30,000.
Award: Grand prize - $50,000; each of two work-of-merit prize winners - $10,000

Liechtenstein

Liechtenstein-Preis zur Foerderung Zeitgenoessischer Literatur
PEN Club Liechtenstein
PO Box 416, FL-9490 Vaduz
Tel: (0423) 2327271 *Fax:* (0423) 2328071
Liechtenstein Prize for the Advancement of Literature.

Luxembourg

Trophee International de la Reliure d'Art (Art of Bookbinding International Trophy)
ARA International
58, Domaine Mehlstrachen, 6942 Niederanven
Tel: 34 85 91 *Fax:* 34 85 91

Madagascar

Literature Prize
Malagasy Ministry of Culture, Communication & Leisure
Antsahovola, BP 305, 101 Antananarivo
Tel: (02) 27092
For an outstanding novel. 130,000 Malagasy francs. Awarded every two years.

Malaysia

Anugerah Sastera Negara Prize
Dewan Bahasa dan Pustaka
Jl Dewan Bahasa, 50460 Kuala Lumpur
Tel: (03) 21481011 *Fax:* (03) 21443875
Telex: 32683 DBP MA
National Literary Award. Founded 1980, the highest governmental award to an author writing in the national language, who has made a major contribution to the development of the country's literature. Award consists of M$30,000, publication facilities and other benefits.

Dewan Bahasa Dan Pustaka Prize
Dewan Bahasa Dan Pustaka
Government of Malaysia, Language & Literary Agency, Rohanl Rustam, Chief Librarian, 50926 Kuala Lumpur
Mailing Address: PO Box 10803, Kuala Lumpur 50926
Tel: (03) 2481011 *Fax:* (03) 2482726
Malaysian Literary Prize. Founded 1982, & awarded by the Malaysian Government biennially for creative writing in the national language, covering short story, novel, poetry & drama, & with the aim of encouraging new talent & enhancing the quality of the national literature.

Mexico

Concurso de Cuento de Ciencia Ficcion (Science Fiction Story Competition)
National Autonomous University of Mexico, Ciudad Universitaria
Delegacion - Coyoacan, 04510 Mexico City, DF
Tel: (05) 5505215

Jorge Cuesta National Poetry Prize
Gobierno del Estado de Veracruz-Llave
Instituto Veracruzano de Cultura Francisco Canal s/n esq, 91700 Veracruz
Tel: (029) 316994; (029) 316967 *Fax:* (029) 316962

☆**Rafael Heliodoro Valle Prize**
National Library of Mexico
Insurgentes Sur 3000, Centro Cultural Universitario, 04510 Mexico City DF
Tel: (05) 6226801 *Fax:* (05) 650951
Founded in 1976 to reward an especially notable writer (in odd-numbered years; in even numbered years to an historian for research work & synthesis). The candidate must have been born in Latin America, over age 50, and the work written in Spanish or Portuguese. 20,000,000 Mexican pesos prize, plus diploma & gold medal.

National Prize for Linguistics & Literature
Senate of the Republic
Mexico Camara de Senadores, c/o Comision Medalla Belisario Dominquez, Xicotencatl, 06018 Mexico City
Tel: (05) 5844662
For the best literary works in the fields of the novel, poetry, essay, biography, drama & motion picture scriptwriting. 100,000 Mexican pesos. Awarded annually.

Premio Internacional de Novela Nuevo Leon (Nuevo Leon International Novel Prize)
Ediciones Castillo SA de CV
Calle Morelos Ote 451, Monterrey
Tel: (083) 445200; (083) 450918; (083) 332498 *Fax:* (083) 431619; (083) 332804

☆**Alfonso Reyes Prize**
Senate of the Republic
Consejo del Premio Nacional de Ciencias y Artes, Argentina 28, Oficina 124, 06029 Mexico DF
Tel: (05) 5844662
Founded 1973. Awarded by the Federal Government of Mexico to an author of any nationality for his or her literary output on the study of the works of Alfonso Reyes or on Mexico. The amount of this prize is 20,000,000 pesos.

Jose Ruben Romero (Premio de Novela Jose Ruben Romero)
Instituto Nacional de Bellas Artes
Auditorio Nacional, Bosque de Chapultepec, Miguel Hidalgo, 11580 Mexico City DF
Tel: (05) 5207241 *Fax:* (05) 5202724
Established: 1978
To recognize unpublished novels of outstanding literary quality by authors in the Spanish language who are residents of Mexico. Works to be considered should be 120-300 pages in length. Established in memory of the Mexican author.
Other Sponsor(s): State of Michoacan
Award: 20,000,000 Mexican pesos & a certificate awarded annually

Juan Rulfo First Novel Prize (Premio Juan Rulfo Para Primera Novela)
Instituto Nacional de Bellas Artes
Auditorio Nacional, Bosque de Chapultepec, Miguel Hidalgo, 11580 Mexico City DF
Tel: (05) 5207241 *Fax:* (05) 5202724
Established: 1980
To recognize the best first novel by an author in the Spanish language residing in Mexico. Works to be considered should be 120-300 pages in length. Established in memory of the Mexican author.
Other Sponsor(s): State of Guerrero
Award: 10,000,000 Mexican pesos & a certificate awarded annually

Premio Xavier Villaurrutia de Escritores para Escritores
Sociedad Alfonsina Internacional AC
Ave Transmisiones 42, 01790 Mexico City DF

Tel: (05) 6831217
For poetry, prose, novel, short story, drama or essays by new or young authors. Prizes totalling 30,000,000 pesos are awarded annually.

Monaco

☆Prix Litteraire Prince Pierre-de-Monaco
Foundation Prince Pierre de Monaco
Le Winter Palace, 4, boulevard des Moulins, MC-98000 Monte Carlo
Tel: (093) 158303 *Fax:* (093) 506694
Key Personnel
Administrator: Beatrice Dunoyer *Tel:* (093) 158776
Secretary General: Rainier Rocchi
Restricted to French-speaking writers. For the entire literary work of one author. 100,000 French francs awarded annually. No applications accepted.

Myanmar

National Literary Awards
Sarpay Beikman Board
529 Merchant St, Yangon
When the Burma Translation Society (now renamed Sarpay Beikman Board) was founded in 1947 it established the Best-Published-Novel-of-the-Year Prize with prize money of K1000. The awards were gradually increased & in 1962 Sarpay Beikman was offering nine awards.
When Sarpay Beikman was taken over by the Revolutionary Government in August 1963 the Awards were transformed into National Literary Awards. More literary awards were gradually added & there are now 13 awards for the best published novel of the year, the best collection of short stories, the best belles letters, the best book of knowledge (arts), the best book of knowledge (science), the best book of poems, the best translation of a world classic, the best translation in the general knowledge field, the best published play, the best book for children, the best book for youth, the best book on Burmese culture & the best book on political affairs.
Each national literary award now draws prize money of K6000.

Netherlands

Henriette de Beaufort-prijs (Henriette de Beaufort Prize)
Maatschappij der Nederlandse Letterkunde (Society of Netherlands Literature)
Witte Singel 27, Universiteitsbibliotheek Leiden, NL-2300 RA Leiden
Mailing Address: Universiteitsbibliotheek, PO Box 9501, 2300 RA Leiden
Tel: (071) 5144962 *Fax:* (071) 5272836
E-mail: mnl@library.leidenuniv.nl
Web Site: www.leidenuniv.nl/host/mnl
Key Personnel
Secretary: Dr Leo L van Maris
Established: 1985
Awarded triennially to recognize the author of a biographical work. Awarded alternately to a Dutch & a Flemish author.
Award: 2500 euros

F Bordewijk Prize
Jan Campert Foundation
PO Box 12654, NL-2500 DP The Hague
Tel: (070) 3533637 *Fax:* (070) 3533058
Key Personnel
Secretary: A P Spijkers
For the best Dutch novel.
Award: 10,000 Dutch florins awarded annually

Jan Campert Prize
Jan Campert Foundation
PO Box 12654, NL-2500 DP The Hague
Tel: (070) 3533637 *Fax:* (070) 3533058
Key Personnel
Secretary: A P Spijkers
For outstanding Dutch poetry.
Award: 10,000 Dutch florins awarded annually

Charlotte Kohlerprijs
Stichting Charlotte Kohler
Huddestraat 7, NL-1018 HB Amsterdam
Tel: (020) 6240803 *Fax:* (020) 5963413
E-mail: bureau@VSenV.nl
Key Personnel
Contact: Mrs A de Boer

Hendrik de Vries Award
City Council of Groningen
Trompsingel 27, NL-9724 DA Groningen
Tel: (050) 3676254 *Fax:* (050) 3676249
Established: 2001
To recognize achievement in or contribution to literature & the visual arts. The entry must, in some way, be related to Groningen or to the work of Hendrik de Vries. Established in honor of Hendrik de Vries (1896-1989), a poet & painter.
Award: 5.672 euros awarded to young artists. The award has to be used to create some kind of art project

Frans Erensprijs
Stichting Frans Erensprijs
Europalaan 49, NL-6226 CN Maastricht
Tel: (043) 3635340
Established: 1986
To recognize a Dutch author for memoirs, essays, or creative literary works in prose or poetry. Named for Frans Erens, a Dutch author (1857-1935). Prize winners: Kees Fens (1986), Anton Koolhaas (1989), Gerric Komrij (1992), Jacq Vogelaar (1995).
Award: 10,000 Dutch guilders awarded every three years

Dr Wijnaendts Francken Prijs
Maatschappij der Nederlandse Letterkunde (Society of Netherlands Literature)
Universiteitsbibliotheek Leiden, Witte Singel 27, NL-2300 RA Leiden
Mailing Address: Universiteitsbibliotheek, PO Box 9501, 2300 RA Leiden
Tel: (071) 5144962 *Fax:* (071) 5272836
E-mail: mnl@library.leidenuniv.nl
Web Site: www.leidenuniv.nl/host/mnl
Key Personnel
Secretary: Dr Leo L van Maris
Established: 1934
Awarded triennially for a work written in Dutch alternately in one of following categories: (1) essays & literary criticism, (2) cultural history.
Award: 2500 euros

Gold Pencil, Gouden Griffel
Collective Promotion of the Netherlands Book
Postbus 10576, NL-1001 EN Amsterdam
Tel: (020) 6264971 *Fax:* (020) 6231696
Established 1971. For the best Dutch children's books - A Golden Slate & 3000 Dutch florins. For Dutch or foreign, translated books - Silver Slate Pencils (maximum 8). Also a Golden Brush & 3000 Dutch florins for the best Dutch illustrated children's book & two silver Brushes for Dutch or foreign, translated illustrated work. Awarded annually. Occasionally a Golden Key for children's/young persons' book with new developments (technically or in subject matter) is awarded.

☆Herman Gorter Prize (Poetry)
Amsterdam City Government, Stichting Amsterdams Fonds voor de Kunst
Herengracht 609, 1017 CE Amsterdam
Tel: (020) 5200520 *Fax:* (020) 6238389
E-mail: afk@afk.nl
Web Site: www.afk.nl
Established: 1972
Subsidies, grants & prizes for the arts. Annual art awards of the city of Amsterdam, no application.

The G H's-Gravesande Prize
Jan Campert Foundation
PO Box 12654, NL-2500 DP The Hague
Tel: (070) 3533637 *Fax:* (070) 3533058
Key Personnel
Secretary: A P Spijkers
For special services to literature.
Award: 10,000 Dutch florins awarded triennially

J Greshoff Prize
Jan Campert Foundation
PO Box 12654, NL-2500 DP The Hague
Tel: (070) 3533637 *Fax:* (070) 3533058
Key Personnel
Secretary: A P Spijkers
For the best Dutch essay.
Award: 10,000 Dutch florins awarded biennially

Nienke van Hichtum Prize
Jan Campert Foundation
PO Box 12654, NL-2500 DP The Hague
Tel: (070) 3533637 *Fax:* (070) 3533058
Key Personnel
Secretary: A P Spijkers
For the best Dutch children's book.
Award: 10,000 Dutch florins awarded every two years

P C Hooft Prize for Literature
Stichting P C Hooft-prijs voor Letterkunde
Postbus 90515, Prins Willem, Alexanderhof 5, NL-2595 LM The Hague
Tel: (070) 3339666 *Fax:* (070) 3477941
For important & original literary works in Dutch. 75,000 Dutch florins. Awarded annually where possible: one year for poetry, the next year for prose, the next year for literary essay.

Lucy B & C W van der Hoogt Prize
Maatschappij der Nederlandse Letterkunde (Society of Netherlands Literature)
Universiteitsbibliotheek, Leiden Witte Singel 27, NL-2300 RA Leiden
Mailing Address: Universiteitsbibliotheek, PO Box 9501, 2300 RA Leiden
Tel: (071) 5144962 *Fax:* (071) 5272836
E-mail: mnl@library.leidenuniv.nl
Web Site: www.leidenuniv.nl/host/mnl
Key Personnel
Secretary: Dr Leo L van Maris
Established: 1921
Awarded to a promising Dutch or Flemish writer.
Award: 6000 euros & a medal awarded annually

Busken Huet Prize (Biography/Essay)
Amsterdam City Government, Stichting Amsterdams Fonds voor de Kunst
Herengracht 609, 1017 CE Amsterdam
Tel: (020) 5200520 *Fax:* (020) 6238389
E-mail: afk@afk.nl

NETHERLANDS

Web Site: www.afk.nl
Established: 1973
Subsidies, grants & prizes for the Arts. Annual art awards of the city of Amsterdam, no application.

Constantijn Huygens Prize
Jan Campert Foundation
PO Box 12654, NL-2500 DP The Hague
Tel: (070) 3533637 *Fax:* (070) 3533058
Key Personnel
Secretary: A P Spijkers
To a distinguished Dutch author for all his works.
Award: 20,000 Dutch florins awarded annually

Multatuli Prize
Amsterdam City Government, Stichting Amsterdams Fonds voor de Kunst
Herengracht 609, 1017 CE Amsterdam
Tel: (020) 5200520 *Fax:* (020) 623-8389
E-mail: afk@afk.nl
Web Site: www.afk.nl
Key Personnel
Contact: Desmond Spruyt
Established: 1972
Subsidies, grants & prizes for the arts.
Closing Date: No application

Prijs der Nederlandse Letteren
Nederlandse Taalunie (Dutch Language Union)
Postbus 10595, 2501-HN The Hague
Tel: (070) 3469548 *Fax:* (070) 3659818
Key Personnel
General Secretary: Koen Jaspaert
Established 1956. To the most outstanding prose writer, essay writer, drama writer or poet in the Netherlands or in Belgium writing in Dutch. 16,000 Euro. Awarded triennially.

☆**Martinus Nijhoff Prijs voor Vertalingen**
Prince Bernhard Cultural Foundation
Herengracht 476, NL-1017 CB Amsterdam
Mailing Address: Postbus 19750, NL-1000 GT Amsterdam
Tel: (020) 5206130 *Fax:* (020) 6238499
E-mail: info@cultuurfonds.nl
Web Site: www.prinsbernhardfonds.nl/groen/grbbot.html
Established 1953. For translation of literary work into & from Dutch. 100,000 Dutch florins. Awarded annually.
Martinus Nijhoff Prize for Translators.

Henriette Roland Holst Prijs
Maatschappij der Nederlandse Letterkunde (Society of Netherlands Literature)
Universiteitsbibliotheek Leiden, Witte Singel 27, NL-2300 RA Leiden
Mailing Address: Universiteitsbibliotheek, PO Box 9501, 2300 RA Leiden
Tel: (071) 5144962 *Fax:* (071) 5272836
E-mail: mnl@library.leidenuniv.nl
Web Site: www.leidenuniv.nl/host/mnl
Key Personnel
Secretary: Dr Leo L van Maris
Established: 1957
Awarded triennially for a work written in Dutch & reflecting social concerns.
Award: 2500 euros

☆**Jenny Smelik IBBY Prize**
Dutch Section of the International Board on Books for Young People
PO Box 17162, NL-1001 JD Amsterdam
Tel: (020) 6363708 *Fax:* (020) 6363708
Established: 1983
To recognize alternately an author & an illustrator of children's books who contribute to a better understanding of minorities. Selection is by nomination & application. Established by Klasina Smelik in honor of the children's book author, Jenny Smelik-Kiggen. Formerly: Jenny Smilik-Kiggenprijs.
Award: 2000 euro biennial by the Dutch section of IBBY

Theo Thijssen Prize for Children's & Youth Literature
Stichting P C Hooft-prijs voor Letterkunde
Postbus 90515, Prins Willem, Alexanderhof 5, NL-2595 LM The Hague
Tel: (070) 3339666 *Fax:* (070) 3477941
Key Personnel
Secretary: Aad Meinderts *E-mail:* aad.meinderts@nlmd.nl
For the best author's work for children & young people. 75,000 Dutch florins. Awarded triennially.

New Zealand

Bank of New Zealand Essay Award
Bank of New Zealand
BNZ Tower, Level 5, 125 Queen St, Auckland
Tel: (03) 353-2004 *Toll Free Tel:* 800 502900
Fax: (03) 353-2600
Web Site: www.bnz.co.nz
Key Personnel
Sponsorship & Events Consultant: Lyndal McMeeking *E-mail:* lyndal_mcmeeking@bnz.co.nz
Open to essays on a topic of the writers choice. Entries must not have been published or broadcast. Entrants have to be either born in New Zealand or New Zealand citizens or residents for 3 years. Awarded biennially.

Bank of New Zealand Katherine Mansfield Award
Bank of New Zealand
BNZ Tower, Level 5, 125 Queen St, Auckland
Tel: (03) 353-2004 *Toll Free Tel:* 800 502900
Fax: (03) 353-2600
Web Site: www.bnz.co.nz
Key Personnel
Sponsorship & Event Consultant: Lyndal McMeeking *E-mail:* lyndal_mcmeeking@bnz.co.nz
For an unpublished short story. Sponsored by the Bank of New Zealand. Entrants to be either born in New Zealand or New Zealand citizens or residents for 3 years. Awarded biennially.

Bank of New Zealand Novice Writer's Award
Bank of New Zealand
BNZ Tower, Level 5, 125 Queen St, Auckland
Tel: (03) 353-2004 *Toll Free Tel:* 800 502900
Fax: (03) 353-2600
Web Site: www.bnz.co.nz
Key Personnel
Sponsorship & Events Consultant: Lyndal McMeeking *E-mail:* lyndal_mcmeeking@bnz.co.nz
Open to writers whose works have not previously been published or broadcast for payment. Entrants must be either born in New Zealand, or New Zealand citizens or resident for 3 years. Awarded biennially.

Bank of New Zealand Young Writers' Award
Bank of New Zealand
BNZ Tower, Level 5, 125 Queen St, Auckland
Tel: (03) 353-2004 *Toll Free Tel:* 800 502900
Fax: (03) 353-2600
Web Site: www.bnz.co.nz
Key Personnel
Sponsorship & Event Consultant: Lyndal McMeeking *E-mail:* lyndal_mcmeeking@bnz.co.nz
For an unpublished short story written by a secondary-school pupil (over 13 years). The entrant must be either born in New Zealand or a New Zealand citizen or resident for 3 years. Awarded biennially.

Best First Book of Fiction Award
New Zealand Society of Authors
Mount Eden, Auckland
Mailing Address: PO Box 67013, Mount Eden, Auckland
Tel: (09) 6308077
E-mail: nzsa@clear.net.nz
Web Site: www.authors.org.nz
Key Personnel
Executive Secretary: Jenny Jones *Tel:* (09) 6308077
Established 1944. This prize incorporates the Hubert Church Award & is for the best first book of fiction 48 pages or more (24 pages if a work of drama), written by a New Zealand citizen or a person resident in New Zealand throughout the previous five years. NZ $1000. Awarded annually.

PEN Best First Book of Nonfiction Award
New Zealand Society of Authors
PO Box 67013, Mount Eden, Auckland
Tel: (09) 6308077 *Fax:* (09) 6308077
E-mail: nzsa@clear.net.nz
Web Site: www.authors.org.nz
Key Personnel
Executive Secretary: Jenny Jones *Tel:* (09) 6308077
For the best first book of published nonfiction of 48 pages or more, written by a New Zealand citizen or a person resident in New Zealand throughout the previous five years. Awarded annually. Prize of NZ $1000.

Best First Book of Poetry Award
New Zealand Society of Authors
Mount Eden, Auckland
Mailing Address: PO Box 67013, Mount Eden, Auckland
Tel: (09) 6308077
E-mail: nzsa@clear.net.nz
Web Site: www.authors.org.nz
Key Personnel
Executive Secretary: Jenny Jones *Tel:* (09) 6308077
Established 1940. This prize incorporates the Jessie Mackay Award & is for the best first book of published poetry, of 24 pages or more, written by a New Zealand citizen or a person resident in New Zealand throughout the previous five years. NZ $1000. Awarded annually.

Buckland Literary Award
Trustees Executors & Agency Company of New Zealand Ltd
24 Water St, Dunedin 9001
Tel: (03) 779 466 *Fax:* (03) 799 466
Founded in 1966 by the late Freda M Buckland for the work of the highest literary merit by a New Zealand writer. Awarded annually.

Russell Clark Award
Library & Information Association of New Zealand Aotearoa (LIANZA)
Old Wool House, Level 5, 139-141 Featherston St, Wellington 6001
Mailing Address: PO Box 12-212, Wellington 6038
Tel: (04) 4735834 *Fax:* (04) 4991480
E-mail: office@lianza.org.nz
Web Site: www.lianza.org.nz
Key Personnel
Office Manager: Steve Williams *E-mail:* steve@lianza.org.nz

Established 1975 for the most distinguished illustrations for a children's book. Illustrator must be a citizen or resident of New Zealand. Bronze medal & NZ $1000. Awarded annually.

Elsie Locke Award
Formerly Young People's Nonfiction Award
Library & Information Association of New Zealand Aotearoa (LIANZA)
Old Wool House, Level 5, 139-141 Featherston St, Wellington 6001
Mailing Address: PO Box 12-212, Wellington 6038
Tel: (04) 4735834 *Fax:* (04) 4991480
E-mail: office@lianza.org.nz
Web Site: www.lianza.org.nz
Key Personnel
Office Manager: Steve Williams *E-mail:* steve@lianza.org.nz
Established: 1986
Awarded annually for the most distinguished contribution to nonfiction writing for young people. Author(s) must be a citizen or resident of New Zealand.
Award: Medal & NZ $1000

Esther Glen Award
Library & Information Association of New Zealand Aotearoa (LIANZA)
Old Wool House, Level 5, 139-141 Featherston St, Wellington 6001
Mailing Address: PO Box 12-212, Wellington 6038
Tel: (04) 4735834 *Fax:* (04) 4991480
E-mail: office@lianza.org.nz
Web Site: www.lianza.org.nz
Key Personnel
Office Manager: Steve Williams *E-mail:* steve@lianza.org.nz
Established: 1944
For the best children's book of fiction by an author who is a citizen of, or resident in, New Zealand. Bronze medal & NZ $1000. Awarded annually.
Presented: Annual Conference

Montana New Zealand Book Awards
Booksellers NZ
Book House, 86 Boulcott St, Wellington
Mailing Address: PO Box 11-377, Wellington
Tel: (04) 4728678 *Fax:* (04) 4728628
Key Personnel
Contact: John Barr *E-mail:* johnbarr@booksellerz.cc.mail.compuserve.com
Established: 1967
For the book of the year based on: (1) quality of writing & illustrations; (2) quality of editing, design & production; (3) impact on the community. Open only to books by New Zealand authors produced by New Zealand book publishers.
Other Sponsor(s): Creative New Zealand
Award: First prize NZ $20,000, second NZ $10,000, third NZ $5000
Presented: July

New Zealand Post Children's Book Awards
Booksellers New Zealand
PO Box 11-377, Wellington
Tel: (04) 728678 *Fax:* (04) 728628
Key Personnel
Contact: John Schiff
Sponsored by Aim Toothpaste Division of Lever Rexona Ltd & awarded annually. The Awards aim to provide recognition & reward to New Zealand authors & illustrators of high-quality children's literature & are awarded in four categories: (1) NZ $5000 to the author of the best Junior Fiction book; (2) NZ $2500 each to the author & illustrator of the best children's picture book (one award of NZ $5000 where the author & illustrator are the same person); (3) NZ $5000 to the author of the best Senior Fiction book; (4) NZ $5000 to the author of the best nonfiction book; (5) one award of NZ $1000 to a promising first children's book.
Other Sponsor(s): Creative New Zealand

Young People's Nonfiction Award, see Elsie Locke Award

Nigeria

Concord Press Award for Academic Publishing
Concord Press Board of Trustees
Enuwa Sq, Ile-Ife
Mailing Address: PO Box 845, Ile-Ife
Tel: (036) 230190
Established 1984. Sponsored by M K O Abiola (founder & Chairman of the Concord Press of Nigeria Ltd). The principal aim of the Award is to encourage publication of works by Nigerian authors & scholars which are suitable as textbooks at University level. 25,000 naira awarded annually.

Delta Fiction Award
Delta Publications (Nigeria) Ltd
PO Box 1172, 172 Ogui Rd, Enugu
Tel: (042) 253215
For an unpublished novel on any subject, although theme should have an international flavor.
Award: 10,000 naira

Distinguished Authors Award
c/o University Bookshop Ltd
Obafemi Awolowo University, Ile-Ife, Osun State
Tel: (036) 230290

Federal Radio Corporation of Nigeria
Federal Radio Corporation of Nigeria, Broadcasting House
Ikoyi, PMB 12504, Lagos
Tel: (01) 2690301; (01) 681954 *Fax:* (01) 2690073
Telex: 21484
Various literary & drama competitions are sponsored by the Federal Radio Corporation of Nigeria, Lagos, from time to time.
Branch Office(s)
FRCN, PMB 5003, Ibadan
PMB 71, Abuja
Broadcasting House, Onitsha Rd, Enugu, Enugu
PO Box 250, Kaduna

Nigerian Book Development Council Book Prize
Nigerian Book Development Council
6 Obanta Rd, Apapa, Lagos
Tel: (01) 862269; (01) 862272
For the best book of social significance by a Nigerian author. 200 naira awarded annually.

Nigerian Book Development Council Literary Prize
Nigerian Book Development Council
6 Obanta Rd, Apapa, Lagos
Tel: (01) 862269; (01) 962272
For the best book written by a Nigerian & published in Nigeria (excluding children's books). 300 naira awarded annually.

Norway

Bastian Prize
The Norwegian Association of Literary Translators
Raasdhusgaten 7, N-0150 Oslo X
Mailing Address: Postboks 579, Sentrum, 0105 Oslo
Tel: 22478090 *Fax:* 22420356
Web Site: www.boknett.no/no
Key Personnel
Contact: Hilde Sveinsson *E-mail:* hilde@translators.no
Awarded annually for an outstanding translation to Norwegian.
Closing Date: Annually Jan 15

N W Damm Children's Book Prize
N W Damm og Son A/S
PO Box 1755, Kristian August gt 3, N-0122 Oslo
Tel: 02941500 *Fax:* 02360874
Established: 1952
Award: 60,000 Norwegian kroner biennially

Literature Awards for Children and Young People
Ministry of Cultural Affairs Norwegian Directorate for Public Libraries
Kronprinsensgate 9, N-0033 Oslo 1
Mailing Address: PO Box 8145 DEP, N-0033 Oslo 1
Tel: 21021700 *Fax:* 21021701
E-mail: sb@bibtils.no
Web Site: www.samson.bibtils.no
Key Personnel
Librarian: Elin Thomsen *Tel:* 21021725
E-mail: elin.thomsen@bibtils.no
Established: 1949
For the best books for children in the following categories: novel (ca 40,000 Norwegian kroner), picture book (ca 40,000 Norwegian kroner), illustrations, new-comer, translations (new Norwegian), translations (literary Norwegian), facts & comics. Awarded annually.
Presented: Annually

Norske Akademis Pris Til Minne om Thorleif Dahl
Norwegian Academy for Language and Literature
Inkognitogt 24, N-0256 Oslo
Tel: 22562950 *Fax:* 22553743

Tarjei Vesaas Debutant Prize
Den Norske Forfatterforening
Radhusgata 7, Oslo 1
To a writer under 30 for the best first book of prose or poetry. 14,000 Norwegian kroner. Awarded annually.

Pakistan

Adamjee Prize
Pakistan Writers' Guild
11 Abbok Rd, Anarkali, Lahore
Founded in 1960 for the best book of creative and progressive poetry, novel, short story, drama, travelogue or biography. 20,000 rupees. Awarded annually. Administered by the Pakistan Writers' Guild in Karachi.

Dawood Prize for Literature
Pakistan Writers' Guild
11 Abbok Rd, Anarkali, Lahore

PAKISTAN

Founded in 1963 for the best books on literary research, literary history, literary criticism; for research works on the Pakistan movement; and for the best translation. 25,000 rupees. Sponsored by the Dawood Foundation. Awarded annually.

Habib Bank Prize for Literature
Pakistan Writers' Guild
11 Abbok Rd, Anarkali, Lahore
Founded in 1968 for the best translation or adaptation of the year (into English or a Pakistani language) of a modern or classical work in any Pakistani language, 25,000 rupees. Awarded annually.

National Bank of Pakistan Prize for Literature
Pakistan Writers' Guild
11 Abbok Rd, Anarkali, Lahore
Founded in 1964 for the best books on economics & scientific, technical & professional subjects. 25,000 rupees. Awarded annually.

President's Award for Pride of Performance
Pakistan Ministry of Education
Block D Pakistan Secretariat, Islamabad
Tel: (051) 825001
For notable achievements in literature. Awarded annually.

Prizes for Manuscripts of Juveniles
Pakistan Writers' Guild
11 Abbok Rd, Anarkali, Lahore
Six prizes for creative writing in the field of children's literature in the Urdu language. Awarded annually.

Regional Literature Awards
Pakistan Writers' Guild
11 Abbok Rd, Anarkali, Lahore
For the best literary works, including the novel, short story, drama, poetry, biography, travel, literary criticism or research work, in each of the four regional languages of Punjabi, Pushto, Sindhi & Gujrati. Awarded annually.

United Bank Prize for Literature
Pakistan Writers' Guild
11 Abbok Rd, Anarkali, Lahore
Founded in 1967 for books in Urdu and Bengali in the following categories: for children up to 15 years of age; and poetry or prose, fiction or nonfiction, for young children. 20,000 rupees. Awarded annually.

Panama

Literary Prize
Revista Nacional de Cultura, Instito Nacional de Cultura
Apdo 662, Panama 1
Tel: 228-4952 Fax: 228-0101
Key Personnel
Dir: A Ortega
Founded in 1946 by Ricardo Miro to pay tribute to those who furthered the cause of learning, arts & sciences. Awarded annually. A prize of $2000 is given in each of five sections: poetry, short story, fiction, theatre, essay.

Philippines

Cultural Centre of the Philippines Literary Awards/Literature Grants
Cultural Centre of the Philippines
CCP Complex, Roxas Blvd, 1004 Metro Manila
Mailing Address: PO Box 310, 1004 Metro Manila
Tel: (02) 8321125
Telex: 40518 CULTURE PM Cable: CULTURE PM
Key Personnel
Division Chief, Literature Division: Herminio S Beltran, Jr Tel: (02) 834-0347 Fax: (02) 832 5120 E-mail: ccp@ccp.admin.edu.ph
Awarded annually for the best volume of verse, essay, fiction & best play written in Filipino & other Philippine languages. Open to resident Filipino citizens. Prizes 10,000 Philippine pesos in each category. Prizes also for second & third places. Winning works are published in the series of CCP literary quarterly journal, 'Ani'. CCP Literature Grants award 25,000 Philippine pesos for a novel & 15,000 each for poetry, short fiction, essay, play & children's literature.

Don Carlos Palanca Memorial Awards for Literature Contest
Carlos Palanca Foundation Inc
Ground Floor, CPJ Bldg, 105 Carlos Palanca, Jr St, Legaspi Village, Makati, Metro Manila
Tel: (02) 8183681 Fax: (02) 8174045
Established: 1950
Cash, certificate & medals.

Poland

Cracow City Literary Prize
Zwiazek Literatow Polskich
Kolberga 10-4, PL-31-160 Krakow
Tel: (022) 268421 Fax: (022) 228855 Cable: ZLP KRAKOW KRUPNICZA 22 - PL
Key Personnel
Vice President Writer & Journalist: Leszek Maruta Tel: 012 423 43 55
For the entire work of an author whose life & writings were connected with Cracow. Awarded annually.

Nagroda Literacka SBP (Literary Prize of PLA)
Stowarzyszenie Bibliotekarzy Polskich
ul Konopczynskiego 5-7, PL 00-953 Warsaw
Tel: (022) 8230270
Established: 1983
For recognition of work that has had an impact on publishing activity; Outstanding works of fiction & nonfiction are considered; Opinions of the local branches of PLA are sought in the selection process..
Award: A plaque, diploma & registration awarded annually

Jan Parandowski Prize
Polish PEN Club
Krakowskie Przedmiescie 87/89, PL-00-079 Warsaw
Tel: (022) 265784 Fax: (022) 260589
E-mail: penclub@ikp.atm.com.pl
Purpose is to commemorate Jan Parandowski's personality and works. Every Polish author of literary merit is eligible.
Award: Annually

PEN Club Prizes for Editors
Polish PEN Club
Krakowskie Przedmiescie 87/89, PL 00-079 Warsaw
Tel: (022) 265784 Fax: (022) 260589
E-mail: penclub@ikp.atm.com.pl
Purpose is to award the best editorial work. Every Polish editor of editorial merit is eligible.
Award: Annually

PEN Club Prizes for Essay, Prose & Poetry
Polish PEN Club
Krakowskie Przedmiescie 87/89, PL 00-079 Warsaw
Tel: (022) 265784 Fax: (022) 260589
E-mail: penclub@ikp.atm.com.pl
Purpose is to award the best literary works in the year. Polish essayists, prose writers & poets are eligible.
Award: Annually

PEN Club Prizes for Translators of Foreign Literature into Polish
Polish PEN Club
Krakowskie Przedmiescie 87/89, PL-00-079 Warsaw
Tel: (022) 265784 Fax: (022) 260589
E-mail: penclub@ikp.atm.com.pl
Purpose is to promote foreign literature in Poland. Open to all Polish translators of foreign literature into Polish.
Award: Annually

PEN Club Prizes for Translators of Polish Literature into Foreign Languages
Polish PEN Club
Krakowskie Przedmiescie 87/89, PL-00-079 Warsaw
Tel: (022) 265784 Fax: (022) 260589
E-mail: penclub@ikp.atm.com.pl
Purpose is to promote Polish literature abroad. All foreign translators of Polish literature & poetry are eligible.
Award: Annually

Polish Prime Minister Award for Literature for Children and Youth
Polish Prime Minister's Office
Al Ujazdowskie 1/3, PL 00-583 Warsaw
For the entire work of an author of books for children & young people. Awards biennially.

☆**Polish Society of Authors (Zaiks) Prizes**
Stowarzyszenie Authorow Zaiks (Nagrody i Wyrozniania Stowarzyszenia Autorow ZAIKS)
ul Hipoteczna 2, PL-00-092 Warsaw
Tel: (022) 827 65 15 Fax: (022) 828 92 04
E-mail: zaike@zaiks.org.pl
Web Site: www.zaiks.org.pl
Literary award for translators, est 1966, awarded annually; Award for the promotion of Polish creativity, est 1990, awarded annually; Varasviane Award: for workds devoted to Warsaw, est 1988, awarded bi-annually; Award for creative achievements in choreography, est 2001, awarded bi-annually; Medal of ZAIKS.

Ksawery Pruszynski Prize
Polish PEN Club
Krakowskie Przedmiescie 87/89, PL 00-079 Warsaw
Tel: (022) 265784 Fax: (022) 260589
E-mail: penclub@ikp.atm.com.pl
Purpose is to commemorate the personality & output of Ksawery Pruxynski. Polish prose writers & essayists of editorial merit are eligible.
Award: Annually

Jan Strzelecki Prize
Polish PEN Club

Krakowskie Przedmiescie 87/89, PL-00-079 Warsaw
Tel: (022) 265784 *Fax:* (022) 260589
E-mail: penclub@ikp.atm.com.pl
Purpose is to commemorate Jan Strzelecki's personality & works. Polish authors, essayists & sociologists are eligible.
Award: Annually

Commander Kazimierz Szczesny Prize
Polish PEN Club
Krakowskie Przedmiescie 87/89, PL 00-079 Warsaw
Tel: (022) 265784 *Fax:* (022) 260589
E-mail: penclub@ikp.atm.com.pl
Purpose is to commemorate Commander Kazimierz Szczesny. Polish marine writers & authors whose works are connected with the sea are eligible.
Award: Every third year

Portugal

Calouste Gulbenkian Translation Prize
Lisbon Academy of Sciences
Rua da Academie das Ciencias 19, P-1200 Lisbon
Tel: (021) 3463866 *Fax:* (021) 3420395
Recognizes the best translator of a work of fiction, a play, or a work of poetry from a foreign language into Portuguese. Aesthetic & vernacular qualities of the translation are considered by the jury. Portuguese translators whose works are published during the year of the award are eligible..
Award: Two prizes of 20,000 escudos each, one for prose & one for poetry, annually
Closing Date: 1975

Ricardo Malheiros Prize
Acedemia Das Ciencias De Lisboa
rua Academia das Ciencieas 19, P-1200 Lisbon
Tel: (021) 3463866 *Fax:* (021) 3420395
6,000 escudos awarded annually to an author for a work of imaginative literature.

National Award for Poetry and the Novel
Associacao Portuguesa de Escritores (Portuguese Association of Writers)
Rua de S Domingos a Lapa 17, P-1200 Lisbon
Tel: (021) 320467
Two prizes, one for the best book of poetry & the other for the best novel or book of short stories. 50,000 escudos each. Awarded annually.

National Essay Award
Associacao Portuguesa de Escritores (Portuguese Association of Writers)
Rua de S Domingos a Lapa 17, P-1200 Lisbon
Tel: (021) 320467
For the best essay written by a Portuguese author & printed in Portuguese. 50,000 escudos. Awarded biennially.

Revelation Awards (Poetry and Prose)
Associacao Portuguesa de Escritores (Portuguese Association of Writers)
Rua de S Domingos a Lapa 17, P-1200 Lisbon
Tel: (021) 320467
Four prizes, two given for the best unpublished manuscript of poetry & two for prose. 5,000 escudos. Awarded annually.

Revelation Prize for Children's Literature
Associacao Portuguesa de Escritores (Portuguese Association of Writers)
Rua de S Domingos a Lapa 17, P-1200 Lisbon
Tel: (021) 320467
For the best book written for readers between four & sixteen. 15,000 escudos. Awarded annually.
Award: 100,000 escudos

Aquilino Ribeiro Literary Prize
Lisbon Academy of Sciences
Rua da Academia das Ciencias 19, P-1200 Lisbon
Tel: (021) 3463866 *Fax:* (021) 3420395

Romania

Romanian Writers' Union Prizes
Uniunea Scriitorilor din Romania
Calea Victoriei 133, 71102 Bucharest
Tel: (01) 507245 *Fax:* (01) 505594
For an outstanding contribution to Romanian literature in poetry, prose, drama, literary criticism, history of literature, literary reportage, literature for children and youth, translations from world literature, and for a promising new literary work by a young writer. Awarded annually (separate prizes are awarded by Bucharest, Cluj, Jassy, Timisoara, Craiova, Sibiu, Brasov and Tiirgu-Mures Writers' Associations. Awarded annually. For further information contact the appropriate Associations of the Writers' Union of the Socialist Republic of Romania).

Singapore

National Book Development Council of Singapore Book Awards
National Book Development Council of Singapore
One Temasek Ave, 17-01 Millenia Tower, Singapore 039192
Tel: 4343651 *Fax:* 8832393
First awarded in 1976 for outstanding works of creative and non creative writing by local authors in any of the four official languages (Malay, English, Chinese, and Tamil). The awards are for fiction, poetry, drama, nonfiction, and children's and young people's books. Up to 15 prizes of 500 to 2000 Singapore dollars. Awarded biennially.

Slovakia

Mlade leta Prize
Young Years Publishing House
Peter Cacko, Nam SNP 12, CS-815 19 Bratislava
Tel: (07) 364475 *Fax:* (07) 364563
For existing works or for outstanding achievements in the field of juvenile literature. The executive body of the Frano Kral Prize is the Slovak Literary Fund, the Circle of Friends of Childrens Books in Slovakia and publishing house Mlade leta. The prize is awarded annually.

☆**Pavol Orszagh-Hviezdoslav Prize**
Association of Slovak Writers (Spolak Slovenskych Spisovatelov)
Stefanikova 14, 815 08 Bratislava
Tel: (07) 43615
Awarded annually by the Union of Slovak Writers to outstanding translators of Slovak literature abroad during the preceding year. 10,000 crowns, plus a fortnight in Slovakia.

Slovenia

International Literary Award Vilenica
Slovene Writers' Association
Tomsiceva 12, 1001 Ljubljana
Tel: (061) 42 52 340 *Fax:* (061) 25 14 144; (061) 42 16 430
E-mail: barbara.subert@yuest.arnes.si

South Africa

Academy Prize for Translated Work
Formerly Translation Prize
South African Academy for Science & Arts, Engelenburghuis
Pretoria 0001
Tel: (012) 3281082 *Fax:* (012) 3285091
Key Personnel
Contact: Dr D J C Geldenhuys
Established: 1948
For translations into Afrikaans of belletristic work from any other language. Awarded every three years.
Award: 2500 rand

Alba Bouwer Prize
South African Academy for Science & Arts, Engelenburghuis
Pretoria 0001
Tel: (012) 3281082 *Fax:* (012) 3285091
Key Personnel
Contact: Dr D J C Geldenhuys
For recognition of Afrikaans literature for children 7-12 years old. A monetary prize donated by the Akademie is awarded triennially.

CNA Literary Award
CNA (Central News Agency)
c/o Public Relations, Johannesburg 2000
Mailing Address: PO Box 10799, Johannesburg 2000
Tel: (011) 4917902 *Fax:* (011) 4930777
E-mail: angelaa@cna.co.za
Established in 1961 for the best original works, one in English & one in Afrikaans, published for the first time during the calendar year of the competition. R15,500 rand each for the winner & 3500 rand for the runners-up in both the English & Afrikaans categories, with an additional prize of 3000 rand for the best debut work published in each category. Awarded annually. Books must be in one of following categories: novel, short story, poetry, biography, drama, history, travel. Authors must be South African citizens or registered permanent residents of South Africa.

English Association (South African Branch) Literary Competition
English Association
B204 Devonshire Hill, Grotto Rd, Rondebosch, Cape Town 7700
Tel: (021) 6854242
For original unpublished manuscripts by residents of Southern Africa. Subject, literary form & amount of award vary from year to year. Three prizes are usually awarded annually according to the standard reached.

SOUTH AFRICA

Percy FitzPatrick Prize
English Academy of Southern Africa
PO Box 124, Wits 2050
Tel: (011) 717-9339 *Fax:* (011) 717-9339
E-mail: engac@cosmos.wits.ac.za
Key Personnel
Administrative Officer: Mrs C James
Awarded biennially. Recognizes achievement by Southern African writers publishing in South Africa in the field of children's books.
Award: 2000 rand

Katrine Harries Award
Library & Information Association of South Africa (LIASA)
PO Box 1598, Pretoria 0001
Tel: (012) 481 2870 *Fax:* (012) 481 2873
E-mail: liasa@liasa.org.za
Web Site: www.liasa.org.za
Key Personnel
Executive Dir: Mrs Gwenda Thomas
For outstanding illustrations in South African children's books, regardless of language. Awarded annually.

Hertzog Prize
South African Academy for Science & Arts, Engelenburghuis
574 Ziervogel St, Arcadia, Pretoria 0083
Mailing Address: Private Bag X11, Arcadia, Pretoria 0007
Tel: (012) 3285082 *Fax:* (012) 3285091
E-mail: akademie@mweb.co.za
Web Site: www.akademie.co.za
Key Personnel
Contact: Mrs L E Brink
Established: 1914
A prestige prize for Afrikaans literature. Prizes are awarded in rotation for poetry, drama and prose. Awarded annually.
Award: 17,000 rand & 18 ct gold medal

W A Hofmeyr Prize
Tafelberg Publishers Ltd
PO Box 879, 28 Wale St, Cape Town 8000
Tel: (021) 4241320 *Fax:* (021) 4241320
Awarded for the best literary work published by Tafelberg, Human & Rousseau, Nasou, Via Afrika, JL van Schaik & Jonathan Ball.
Award: R5000 & gold medallion (1 ounce pure gold) annually

Tienie Holloway Medal
South African Academy for Science & Arts, Engelenburghuis
Pretoria 0001
Tel: (012) 3281082 *Fax:* (012) 3285091
Key Personnel
Contact: Dr D J C Geldenhuys
Established in 1969 by Dr J E Holloway. A gold medal is awarded every triennially to a writer who has produced the best work in Afrikaans literature for infants.

C P Hoogenhout Award
Library & Information Association of South Africa (LIASA)
Menlo Park, Pretoria 0102
Mailing Address: PO Box 124, Wits 2050
Tel: (012) 464967 *Fax:* (012) 464967
To encourage the production of outstanding Afrikaans children's books. Awarded biannually.

C J Langenhoven Prize
South African Academy for Science & Arts, Engelenburghuis
Pretoria 0001
Tel: (012) 3281082 *Fax:* (012) 3285091

Key Personnel
Contact: Dr D J C Geldenhuys
For outstanding work in field of Afrikaans linguistics. Awarded triennially.

Louis Hiemstra Prize for Non-fiction
South African Academy for Science & Arts, Engelenburghuis
574 Ziervogel St, Arcadia, Pretoria 0083
Mailing Address: Private Bag X11, Arcadia, Pretoria 0007
Tel: (012) 3285082 *Fax:* (012) 3285091
E-mail: akademie@mweb.co.za
Web Site: www.akademie.co.za
Established: 2001
Awarded for non-fiction work in Afrikaans. Awarded every three years.
Award: 20,000 rand

H Recht Malan Prize
Tafelberg Publishers Ltd
PO Box 879, 28 Wale St, Cape Town 8000
Mailing Address: PO Box 879, Cape Town 8000
Tel: (021) 4241320 *Fax:* (021) 4241320
Awarded annually for the best nonfiction book published by Tafelberg, Human & Rousseau, Nasou, Via Afrika, JL van Schaik & Jonathan Ball, R5000.00 & gold medallion (1 ounce pure gold).

Eugene Marais Prize
South African Academy for Science & Arts, Engelenburghuis
Pretoria 0001
Tel: (012) 3281082 *Fax:* (012) 3285091
Key Personnel
Contact: Dr D J C Geldenhuys
Established: 1961
For a first or early work of belletristic publication in Afrikaans. The prize can be awarded only once to any particular writer. Awarded annually.
Award: 11,000 rand

MER Prize
Tafelberg Publishers Ltd
PO Box 879, 28 Wale St, Cape Town 8000
Tel: (021) 4241320 *Fax:* (021) 4241320
Key Personnel
Contact: Riellela de Jage *E-mail:* rdejage@tafelberg.com
Awarded for the best children's book published by Tafelberg, Human & Rousseau, Nasou, Via Afrika, J L van Schaik & Jonathan Ball.
Award: R5000 & gold medallion (1 ounce pure gold) annually

Perskor Prize for Light Reading
Perskor Publishers
PO Box 845, Johannesburg 2000
Tel: (011) 776-9111
5000 rand awarded every triennially.

Perskor Prize for Literature
Perskor Publishers
PO Box 845, Johannesburg 2000
Tel: (011) 776-9111
For the best literary work published in Afrikaans by Perskor. 5000 rand awarded biannually.

Perskor Prize for Youth Literature
Perskor Publishers
PO Box 845, Johannesburg 2000
Tel: (011) 776-9111
For the best youth work published in Afrikaans by Perskor. 5000 rand awarded biannually.

Gustav Preller Prize
South African Academy for Science & Arts, Engelenburghuis

Pretoria 0001
Tel: (012) 3281082 *Fax:* (012) 3285091
Key Personnel
Contact: Dr D J C Geldenhuys
For literary science & literary criticism in Afrikaans. Awarded triennially.

Thomas Pringle Awards
English Academy of Southern Africa
PO Box 124, Wits 2050
Tel: (011) 717-9339 *Fax:* (011) 717-9339
E-mail: engac@cosmos.wits.ac.za
Key Personnel
Administrative Officer: Mrs C James
Awarded every year in three of five categories, including play, book, film & television reviews in newspapers & periodicals; literary articles or substantial book reviews in academic & other journals & in newspapers; articles on language & the teaching of English in academic, teachers' & other journals & in newspapers; short stories & one-act plays in periodicals; & poetry in periodicals.
Other Sponsor(s): FNB Vita
Award: 2000 rand prize in each category

Scheepers Prize
South African Academy for Science & Arts, Engelenburghuis
Pretoria 0001
Tel: (012) 3281082 *Fax:* (012) 3285091
Key Personnel
Contact: Dr D J C Geldenhuys
For the best book written for children. Awarded triennially.

Olive Schreiner Prize for English Literature
English Academy of Southern Africa
PO Box 124, Wits 2050
Tel: (011) 717-9339 *Fax:* (011) 717-9339
E-mail: engac@cosmos.wits.ac.za
Key Personnel
Administrative Officer: Mrs C James
For original literary work in English by a promising South African writer & published in South Africa. Awarded annually in one of the following categories: prose, poetry, drama.
Other Sponsor(s): FNB Vita
Award: 5000 rand

South African Academy for Science & Arts Prizes
South African Academy for Science & Arts, Engelenburghuis
Pretoria 0001
Tel: (012) 3281082 *Fax:* (012) 3285091
Key Personnel
Contact: Dr D J C Geldenhuys
The Academy awards a number of prizes for works in Afrikaans; the following are noted in this section: Alba Bouwer Prize; Hertzog Prize; Tienie Holloway Medal; C J Langenhoven Prize; Eugene Marais Prize; Gustav Preller Prize; Scheepers Prize; Translation Prize. See individual entries for details.

Translation Prize, see Academy Prize for Translated Work

Spain

Premio Apel les Mestres, see Premio Destino Infantil-Apel.les Mestres

Miguel de Cervantes Prize
Direccion General del Libro y Bibliotecas, Ministerio de Cultura
Plaza del Rey 1, E-28004 Madrid

Tel: (091) 5325089 *Fax:* (091) 5321222
For the work of a writer who has made an outstanding contribution to Spanish Literature. 15,000,000 pesetas. Awarded annually.

☆Premio Destino Infantil-Apel.les Mestres
(Destino Children's Book Prize)
Formerly Premio Apel les Mestres
Ediciones Destino
Provenza 260 5a Planta, E-08008 Barcelona
Tel: (093) 496 70 01 *Fax:* (093) 496 70 02
E-mail: edicionesdestino@stl.logiccontrol.es
Web Site: www.edestino.es
Key Personnel
Editor: Patrizia Campana *E-mail:* pcampana@edestino.es
Established: 1980
Open to all illustrated literary works which have not been published in any form & are intended for children. Works can be in Spanish, Catalan, Basque, Galician, English, French or Italian. Exists to acknowledge creative effort in the world of illustrated books.
Award: 4500 euros
Closing Date: September 2002
Presented: October annually

Espejo de Espana Prize
Editorial Planeta SA
Corcega 273-279, E-08008 Barcelona
Tel: (093) 228 58 00 *Fax:* (093) 217 71 40
Telex: 93458 EDTPE
Established: 1975
Awarded for an essay.
Award: 4,000,000 pesetas annually

Fastenrath Prize
Real Academia Espanola
Felilpe IV 4, Madrid
Tel: (091) 4203613 *Fax:* (091) 4200079
Established 1909 for works of excellence written in the Spanish language. 500,000 pesetas. Awarded annually in rotation for the following categories of writing: poetry; essays, criticism; novel or story; history, biography; drama.

Hucha de Oro Prize
Confederacion Espanola de Cajas de Ahorros (CECA)
Departmento de Comunicacion y Relacioues Externes, Calle de Alcala 27, E-28014 Madrid
Tel: (091) 5965628 *Fax:* (091) 5965737
Telex: 27304
For an unpublished short story in Castilian. Annual awards are made in which the two main prizewinners are selected from the previously-chosen to the limit of 20 winners of the Hucha de Plata prizes (25,000 pesetas & a chest of silver each). The winner of the Hucha de Oro first prize receives 1,000,000 pesetas & a chest of gold (hucha de oro); the winner of the second prize receives 500,000 pesetas & a miniature chest of gold.

Lazarillo Prize
Organizacion Espanola para Libro Infantilly Juvenil
Santiago Rusinol 8, E-28040 Madrid
Tel: (091) 5530821 *Fax:* (091) 5539990

Ramon Llull Prize
Editorial Planeta SA
Corcega 273-279, E-08008 Barcelona
Tel: (093) 228 58 00 *Fax:* (093) 217 71 40
Web Site: www.editorial.planeta.es
Telex: 93458 EDTPE
Key Personnel
Chairman: Jose Manuel Lara Hernandez
Established: 1968
Founded for the purpose of contributing to the increase & promotion of narrative in Catalan.

Since 1995 it has accepted both fictional works (novels, narratives, etc.) & nonfictional works (essays, memoirs, biographies, etc).
Award: 10,000,000 pesetas
Presented: Jan annually

Premio Nadal (Nadal Prize)
Ediciones Destino
Provenza 260 5a Planta, E-08008 Barcelona
Tel: (093) 496 70 01 *Fax:* (093) 496 70 02
E-mail: edicionesdestino@stl.logiccontrol.es
Web Site: www.edestino.es
Key Personnel
Editor: Joaquim Palau Fau
Secretary: Yolanda Bolsa *E-mail:* ybolsa@edestino.es
Established: 1944
The Nadal Prize is the oldest literary prize to be awarded to novels written in Spanish. Starting with the 2001 prize, novels presented for this award will also be competing for the Premio Destino-Guion script award, which will be awarded to the best novel according to its potential for adaptation to a film or audio-visual script.
Award: 3,000,000 pesetas (winner); 1,000,000 pesetas (runner-up)
Presented: Jan annually

National Prize for Illustration of Children's Literature
Direccion General del Libro y Bibliotecas, Ministerio de Cultura
Plaza del Rey 1, E-28004 Madrid
Tel: (091) 5325089 *Fax:* (091) 5321222
An annual award of 1,000,000 pesetas for the best illustrations in a book for children or young people. Awarded in alternate years in each category.

National Prize for Literature
Direccion General del Libro y Bibliotecas, Ministerio de Cultura
Plaza del Rey 1, E-28004 Madrid
Tel: (091) 5325089 *Fax:* (091) 5321222
Founded 1984. Three annual awards of 2,500,000 pesetas each for the best books of poetry, fiction and essays published in the previous year in one of the official languages of Spain. The most recent winners were Antonio Gamoneda (poetry), Antonio Munoz-Molina (fiction) and Gabriel Albiac (essays).

National Prize of Spanish Letters
Direccion General del Libro y Bibliotecas, Ministerio de Cultura
Plaza del Rey 1, E-28004 Madrid
Tel: (091) 5325089 *Fax:* (091) 5321222
Founded 1986. An award of 5,000,000 pesetas in recognition of an author, writing in one of the official Spanish languages, for the whole of his work.

National Prizes for Children's Literature
Direccion General del Libro y Bibliotecas, Ministerio de Cultura
Plaza del Rey 1, E-28004 Madrid
Tel: (091) 5325089 *Fax:* (091) 5321222
Founded 1978. Two annual awards of 1,500,000 pesetas (for an original work) and 1,000,000 pestas (for a translation) are made for the best literary works intended for children or young people, written in any of the official languages of Spain. Awarded in alternate years in each category.

☆Leopoldo Panero Prize
Instituto de Cooperacion Iberoamericana
Avda de los Reyes Catolicos 4, Ciudad Universitaria, 28040 Madrid

Tel: (091) 5838100 *Fax:* (091) 5838310
For poetry in Spanish, 150,000 pesetas. Awarded annually.

☆Planeta Prize
Editorial Planeta SA
Corcega 273-279, E-08008 Barcelona
Tel: (093) 228 58 00 *Fax:* (093) 217 71 40
Web Site: www.editorial.planeta.es
Key Personnel
Chairman: Jose Manuel Lara Hernandez
Established: 1952
Promotes Spanish authors. The award is 50,000,000 pesos for the winner & 12,000,000 for the runner-up. Presented annually in Oct
Argentina: presented for the ninth year. Given for previously unpublished works in Spanish, continuing in its objective of promoting the production of novels. The award is 50,000 pesos for the winner & 10,000 for the runner-up. Presented annually in Oct
Chile: Awarded for the first time in 2000 for journalistic research. May be entered by journalists or writers with works referring to Chilean subject matter in any written journalistic genre: information, report, chronicle, biography, analysis or interview. Pieces may be the work of a single author or of several. An award of 5,000,000 pesos is presented annually in Oct
Columbia: prize awarded in recognition of the life & works of, alternately, a journalist & historian. An award of 7,000,000 pesos is presented annually in Dec.

Premi Josep Pla (Josep Pla Prize)
Ediciones Destino
Provenza 260 5a Planta, E-08008 Barcelona
Tel: (093) 496 70 01 *Fax:* (093) 496 70 02
E-mail: edicionesdestino@stl.logiccontrol.es
Web Site: www.edestino.es
Key Personnel
Editor: Joaquim Palau Fau
Secretary: Yolanda Bolsa *E-mail:* ybolsa@edestino.es
Established: 1969
Awarded for prose in Catalan without limits in terms of genre (novels, short stories, accounts, travel books, memoirs or biographies).
Award: 1,000,000 pesetas
Presented: Jan annually

Prince of Austrias Prizes
Fundacion Principado de Asturias
General Yague 2, E-33004 Oviedo
Tel: (08) 5258755 *Fax:* (08) 5242104
E-mail: info@fpa.es
Web Site: www.fpa.es

Alvarez Quintero Prize
Real Academia Espanola
Felilpe IV 4, Madrid
Tel: (091) 4203613 *Fax:* (091) 4200079
Established 1949 for the best work in two categories alternately: novel or story collection & theatrical works. 100,000 pesetas. Awarded biennially.

Reading and Writing National Competition
Direccion General del Libro y Bibliotecas, Ministerio de Cultura
Plaza del Rey 1, E-28004 Madrid
Tel: (091) 5325089 *Fax:* (091) 5321222
Founded 1978. An annual competition for students at COU, BUP or equivalent levels of 'Formacion Profesional'. Prizes are given for literary works, in any of the official languages of Spain, related to an important figure in Spanish literature. Prize winners are selected from 150 qualifying works. First, second and third prizes are of 55,000, 50,000 and 45,000 pesetas respectively, and further prizes of 25,000 pesetas each may be awarded. A second group of awards is made for students at

EGB level for illustrations related to an important figure in Spanish literature. Prizes are of 55,000 pesetas, 50,000 pesetas and 45,000 pesetas and further prizes of 25,000 pesetas each may be awarded. Winners must use the prize money exclusively for the purchase of books.

Rivadeneyra Prizes
Real Academia Espanola
Felilpe IV 4, Madrid
Tel: (091) 4203613 *Fax:* (091) 4200079
Established 1940 for the best work on Spanish literature & linguistics. Two prizes, of 300,000 pesetas & 200,000 pesetas. Awarded annually.

☆La Sonrisa Vertical Prize
La Sonrisa Vertical, Tusquets Editores
Cesare Cantu, 8, E-08023 Barcelona
Tel: (093) 2530400 *Fax:* (093) 4176703
Telex: 99061 TUSQ E
Founded in 1978 in homage to Lopez Barbadillo. Awarded annually for the best erotic novel written in Spanish or another language of the Spanish State. The prize is 1,000,000 pesetas advance on the work prior to publication, together with an artistic object.

Sri Lanka

Literary Prizes for Sinhala Literature
Ministry of Cultural Affairs
255, Bauddhaloka Mawatha, Colombo 7
Tel: (01) 545777
For the best books published in the previous year in the Sinhala language in the following categories: novels, short stories, poetry, translations, children's literature, scientific literature, drama; also three awards in miscellaneous literary areas and awards for original works in Pali, Sanskrit and Arabic. 5000 Sri Lanka rupees each, excepting children's literature for which the prize is 2000 rupees. Awarded annually.

D R Wijewardene Memorial Award
Lake House Bookshop
100, Sir Chittampalam Gardiner Mawatha, PO Box 244, Colombo 2
Tel: (01) 430581; (01) 430582; (01) 432105
Fax: (01) 432104
E-mail: bookshop@sri.lanka.net
Telex: 21266 LAKEXPO CE BOOKSALES
Key Personnel
Chairman: Mr R S Wijewardena
General Manager: Mr Sarath De Silva
Established: 1984
Established by the Lake House Bookshop, Colombo, for the best unpublished manuscript of a novel or short story collection in Sinhala. The most recent winner was Mrs Shanthi Disanayake. Awarded annually.
Award: 40,000 Sir Lanka rupees
Closing Date: November
Presented: Sri Lanka Foundation, Colombo 7, June

Sweden

Carl Akermarks Stipendium
Swedish Academy
PO Box 2118, 103 13 Stockholm
Tel: (08) 106524 *Fax:* (08) 244225
E-mail: sekretariat@svenskaakademien.se
Web Site: www.svenskaakademien.se

Reward for theatre. This award cannot be applied for.
Award: Five prizes of 20,000 Swedish kronor annually

Aniara Priset
Sveriges Allmaenna Biblioteksfoerening
PO Box 3127, S-103 62 Stockholm
Tel: (08) 54513230 *Fax:* (08) 54513231
E-mail: christina.stenberg@sab.se
Swedish Library Association.

Bellman Prize
Swedish Academy
PO Box 2118, 103 13 Stockholm
Tel: (08) 106524 *Fax:* (08) 244225
E-mail: sekretariat@svenskaakademien.se
Web Site: www.svenskaakademien.se
For poetry. This prize cannot be applied for.
Award: 200,000 Swedish crowns annually

Blekinge County Council Culture Prize
Blekinge County Council
Kansliet, S-37181 Karlskrona
Tel: (0455) 734023 *Fax:* (0455) 80250
E-mail: landstinget.blekinge@ltblekinge.se
Established: 1964
Recognizes a person or organization for a valuable contribution to science, arts, poetry, literature, music, dance, theatre, journalism or free education.
Award: 50,000 Swedish kronor annually

Gerard Bonnier's Prize
Swedish Academy
PO Box 2118, 103 13 Stockholm
Tel: (08) 106524 *Fax:* (08) 244225
E-mail: sekretariat@svenskaakademien.se
Web Site: www.svenskaakademien.se
One prize to a writer active in the fields within the Academy's mandate. This award cannot be applied for.
Award: 125,000 Swedish crowns annually

Dobloug Prize
Swedish Academy
PO Box 2118, 103 13 Stockholm
Tel: (08) 106524 *Fax:* (08) 244225
E-mail: sekretariat@svenskaakademien.se
Web Site: www.svenskaakademien.se
For outstanding literary work by two Norwegian & two Swedish writers. This award cannot be applied for.
Award: Two prizes of 80,000 Swedish crowns in each category awarded annually

Signe Ekblad-Eldh Prize
Swedish Academy
PO Box 2118, 103 13 Stockholm
Tel: (08) 106524 *Fax:* (08) 244225
E-mail: sekretariat@svenskaakademien.se
Web Site: www.svenskaakademien.se
To famous Swedish writers. This award cannot be applied for.
Award: 70,000 Swedish crowns annually

Gun & Olof Engqvist Prize
Swedish Academy
PO Box 2118, 103 13 Stockholm
Tel: (08) 106524 *Fax:* (08) 244225
E-mail: sekretariat@svenskaakademien.se
Web Site: www.svenskaakademien.se
For Swedish Literature & Cultural Journalism. This award cannot be applied for.
Award: 100,000 Swedish crowns awarded annually

Lydia & Herman Eriksson Prize
Swedish Academy
PO Box 2118, 103 13 Stockholm
Tel: (08) 106524 *Fax:* (08) 244225
E-mail: sekretariat@svenskaakademien.se
Web Site: www.svenskaakademien.se
Awarded to a Swedish writer for a work of prose or poetry. This prize cannot be applied for.
Award: 70,000 Swedish crowns every second year

Nils Holgersson Plaque
Sveriges Allmaenna Biblioteksfoerening
PO Box 3127, S-103 62 Stockholm
Tel: (08) 54513230 *Fax:* (08) 54513231
E-mail: info@biblioteksforeningen.org
Web Site: www.biblioteksforeningen.org
Established: 1950
Swedish Library Association.

Nils Holgersson Plaque
Svensk Biblioteksforening
PO Box 3127, S-103 62 Stockholm
Tel: (08) 54513230 *Fax:* (08) 54513231
E-mail: info@biblioteksforeningen.org
Web Site: www.biblioteksforeningen.org
Established: 1950

Kalleberger Prize
Swedish Academy
PO Box 2118, 103 13 Stockholm
Tel: (08) 106524 *Fax:* (08) 244225
E-mail: sekretariat@svenskaakademien.se
Web Site: www.svenskaakademien.se
An award in memory of Tekla Hansson to a Swedish writer for a work of prose or poetry. This prize cannot be applied for.
Award: 30,000 Swedish crowns annually

Kellgren Prize
Swedish Academy
PO Box 2118, 10313 Stockholm
Tel: (08) 106524 *Fax:* (08) 244225
E-mail: sekretariat@svenskaakademien.se
Web Site: www.svenskaakademien.se
For important achievements in any of the fields of the Academy. This prize cannot be applied for.
Award: 125,000 Swedish crowns annually

Literary Award
Svenska Dagbladet
Ralambsvagen 7, S-105 17 Stockholm
Tel: (08) 135000 *Fax:* (08) 523497
Established: 1944
To encourage Swedish theatre design, and to recognize contributions during the preceding theatre season. Awarded annually.
Award: 25,000 Swedish kronor

☆Nobel Prize for Literature
Swedish Academy
PO Box 2118, 103 13 Stockholm
Tel: (08) 106524 *Fax:* (08) 244225
E-mail: sekretariat@svenskaakademien.se
Web Site: www.svenskaakademien.se
Of all the literary prizes, the Nobel Prize for literature is the biggest in value & in honor bestowed. It is one of the five prizes founded by Alfred Nobel (1833-1896); the other four awards are for physics, chemistry, physiology or medicine, & peace. By the terms of Nobel's will, the prize for literature is to be given to the person "who shall have produced in the field of literature the most distinguished work of an idealistic tendency." The award is administered by the Swedish Academy in Stockholm & official presentation is made on December 10, the anniversary of Nobel's death. No one may apply for the Nobel Prize, there is no competition. It is awarded to an author usually for their total literary output & not for any single work.
Award: A gold medal, a diploma & a sum of money; the amount in 2001 was 10,000,000 Swedish crowns

☆**Nordic Council Literature Prize**
Nordic Council, Swedish Delegation
Riksdagen, S-100 12 Stockholm
Tel: (08) 7865049 *Fax:* (08) 7866129
Key Personnel
Secretary General: Eva Smekal *E-mail:* eva.smekal@riksdagen.se
Established: 1962
Nordic Council's Literature Prize is awarded annually for a Literary work in the fiction, genre, written in one of the languages of the Nordic countries. It can be a novel, a play, a collection - of poems, short stories or essays - or another work which meets high literary & artistic standards. The aim is to increase interest in Nordic literature & establish a Nordic book marker.
Presented: Nordic Council Conference or a session in Feb or March

Margit Pahlson Prize
Swedish Academy
PO Box 2118, 103 13 Stockholm
Tel: (08) 106524 *Fax:* (08) 244225
E-mail: sekretariat@svenskaakademien.se
Web Site: www.svenskaakademien.se
For achievements of particular significance for the Swedish language. This award cannot be applied for.
Award: 100,000 Swedish crowns annually

Swedish Academy Nordic Prize
Swedish Academy
PO Box 2118, 103 13 Stockholm
Tel: (08) 106524 *Fax:* (08) 244225
E-mail: sekretariat@svenskaakademien.se
Web Site: www.svenskaakademien.se
For important achievements in any of the fields of interest of the Academy. Citizens of any of the Scandinavian countries are eligible. This award cannot be applied for.
Award: 250,000 Swedish crowns annually

Swedish Academy Prizes
Swedish Academy
PO Box 2118, 103 13 Stockholm
Tel: (08) 106524 *Fax:* (08) 244225
E-mail: sekretariat@svenskaakademien.se
Web Site: www.svenskaakademien.se
In addition to those fully listed individually, the Swedish Academy awards the following prizes: Ida Baeckman Prize (Literature/Journalism: biennial); Beskow Prize (Literary: biennial); Blom Prize (Swedish Language: annual); Karin Gierow Prizes (for (1) Cultural Information: annual; (2) Promotion of Knowledge: annual; Axel Hirsch Prize (Biographic/Historic: annual); Ilona Kohrtz Prize (Prose/Poetry: annual); Royal Prize (Cultural/Literary: annual); Birger Schoeldstroem Prize (Literary History/Biography: every 4 years); Schueck Prize (Literary History: annual); Swedish Language & Literature Teachers' Prize (annual); Swedish Linguistics Prize (annual); Swedish into Foreign Language Translation Prize (annual); Translation into Swedish Prize (annual); Zibet Prize (Literary/Historic referring to reign of Gustav III: biennial); miscellaneous prizes for work in literary or linguistic fields.
These prizes cannot be applied for.

Swedish Authors' Fund Awards
Swedish Authors' Fund
Klara Norra Kyrkogata 29, Box 1106, S-11181 Stockholm
Tel: (08) 4404550 *Fax:* (08) 4404565
E-mail: svff@svff.se
Web Site: www.svff.se
Key Personnel
Secretariat: Jesper Soderstrom *E-mail:* jesper.soderstrom@svff.se
To recognize authors, translators & illustrators who have made special contributions within their own fields; Main purpose of the fund is to administer the Swedish system of library loan compensation to authors, translators & book illustrators.
Award: 20,000 Swedish kronor each, annually

Lena Vendelfelt Prize
Swedish Academy
PO Box 2118, 103 13 Stockholm
Tel: (08) 106524 *Fax:* (08) 244225
E-mail: sekretariat@svenskaakademien.se
Web Site: www.svenskaakademein.se
For a literary work, mainly poetry. This prize cannot be applied for.
Award: 30,000 Swedish crowns annually

Switzerland

☆**Hans Christian Andersen Awards**
International Board on Books for Young People (IBBY)
Nonnenweg 12, CH-4055 Basel
Tel: (061) 2722917 *Fax:* (061) 2722757
E-mail: ibby@eye.ch
Web Site: www.ibby.org
Key Personnel
Executive Dir: Leena Maissen
Executive Assistant: Liz Page
The International Board on Books for Young People (IBBY) gives these awards every two years to a living author & a living illustrator who, through their works, have made distinguished contributions to international children's & young adult literature. (Until 1966 a prize was awarded for a specific book & to an author only.) A jury of ten members, appointed by the Executive Committee of IBBY, makes the decision from nominations submitted from member countries all over the world.
Other Sponsor(s): Nissan Motor Corp
Award: Biennial

Anne Frank Literary Award
Anne Frank-Fonds
Steinengrahen 18, CH-4051 Basel
Tel: (061) 2741174 *Fax:* (061) 2741175

Grand Prix Ramuz
Foundation C F Ramuz
Case Postale 181, CH-1009 Pully
Tel: (021) 721 3643
Key Personnel
Contact: Rebetez Maurice
Established: 1955
To recognize a writer for his entire work. Swiss authors writing in the French language are eligible.
Award: 15,000 Swiss francs every five years

Grosser Schillerpreis
Schweizerische Schillerstiftung, Fondation Schiller Suisse
Mattenway 4, CH-8126-3270 Aarberg
Tel: 032 393 72 64
Key Personnel
Secretary: Agnes Aeschlimann
Prizes for Swiss citizens only.

☆**IBBY-Asahi Reading Promotion Award**
International Board on Books for Young People (IBBY)
Nonnenweg 12, CH-4055 Basel
Tel: (061) 2722917 *Fax:* (061) 2722757
E-mail: ibby@eye.ch
Web Site: www.ibby.org
Key Personnel
Executive Dir: Leena Maissen
Co-sponsored by the Japanese newspaper company Asahi Shimbun since 1987 & presented by IBBY every year to a group or institution that is making a significant contribution to book promotion programs for children & young adults.
Award: 1,000,000 yen

☆**IBBY Honour List**
International Board on Books for Young People (IBBY)
Nonnenweg 12, CH-4055 Basel
Tel: (061) 2722917 *Fax:* (061) 2722757
E-mail: ibby@eye.ch
Web Site: www.ibby.org
Key Personnel
Executive Dir: Leena Maissen
Executive Assistant: Liz Page
Biennial selection of outstanding, recently published books, honoring writers, illustrators & translators from IBBY member countries. Titles are selected by the National Sections. The Honor List Diplomas are presented to the recipients at the IBBY Congresses.
Award: Biennially

Inner Swiss Literature Award
Inner Swiss Cultural Foundation
Justiz, Gemeinde und Kultur Departement des Kantous Luzern, Kultur und Jugendforderung, Bahnhofstr 18, 6002 Lucerne
Tel: (041) 2285206 *Fax:* (041) 2100573
Key Personnel
Contact: Daniel Huber *E-mail:* daniel.huber@lu.ch
Established: 1951
For recognition of outstanding literary work; Authors living in the central part of Switzerland (Innerschweiz, cantons: Lucerne, Uri, Schwyz, Obwalden, Nidwalden, & Zug) or who originate from those areas are eligible.
Award: 20,000 Swiss francs & a certificate awarded annually

International Award for the Furtherance of Human Understanding
The International Organization for the Elimination of All Forms of Racial Discrimination (EAFORD)
5 Rte des Morillions, bureau No 475, 1211 Geneva 2
Mailing Address: Case Postale 2100, 1211 Geneva 2
Tel: (022) 7886233 *Fax:* (022) 7886233
Annual International Award for outstanding published work in English, French, Arabic, Spanish or Portuguese dealing with questions of racism & racial discrimination.

☆**Gottfried Keller Prize**
Martin Bodmer-Stiftung fur einen Gottfried Keller-Preis
c/o Thomas Bodner, PO Box 1425, CH-8032 Zurich
Established: 1921
Founded by Martin Bodmer for Swiss & other writers who have honored the Swiss spirit.
Award: 25,000 Swiss francs biennially

Prix Liberte Litteraire
Foundation Armleder
Hotel Richemond, CH-1206 Geneva
Tel: (022) 7311400 *Fax:* (022) 7312414
Freedom Literary Prize.

Prix Litteraire de la Ville de La Chaux-de-Fonds et de la Revue (Literary Review Prize of La Chaux de Fronds)
Editions
19-21 Rue du Manege, CH-2301 La Chaux de Fonds
Tel: (032) 9682418 *Fax:* (032) 9682750

SWITZERLAND

Preis der Schweizerische Schillerstiftung
Schweizerische Schillerstiftung, Fondation Schiller Suisse
Mattenway 4, CH-8126-3270 Aarberg
Tel: 032 393 72 64
Key Personnel
Secretary: Agnes Aeschlimann
Prize for Swiss citizens, or foreigners living in Switzerland for a minimum of five years.

City of Zurich Literary Prize
Praesidialdepartement der Stadt Zurich
Postfach, 8022 Zurich
Tel: (01) 2163125 *Fax:* (01) 2121404
E-mail: musik.literatur@prd.stzh.ch
Key Personnel
Contact: Roman Hess
Established: 1930
Founded by the City of Zurich to reward an author for his or her whole literary work. No applications or nominations accepted.
Award: 50,000 Swiss francs awarded at irregular intervals

Thailand

Bangkok Bank Foundation Prize
Bangkok Bank Foundation
333 Silom Rd, Bangkok 10500
Tel: (02) 2343333 *Fax:* (02) 2365913
For prose or poetry in Thai concerning history, art, culture, religion, social affairs, philosophy or new creative ideas. 50,000 baht each for prose and poetry. Awarded annually.

Turkey

Award for Literature and Scientific Publications
Turkish Language Institution (Turk Dil Kurumu)
Ataturk Bulvari, 217, Kavaklidere, TR-06680 Ankara
Tel: (0312) 4286100 *Fax:* (0312) 4285288
E-mail: bim@tdk.gov.tr
Web Site: www.tdk.gov.tr
Key Personnel
President: Dr Hasan Eren
To encourage and sponsor Research and studies in Turkish Language Literature and Linguistics.

United Kingdom

BP Natural World Book Prize, see Natural World Book Prize

The Booker Prize, see The Man Booker Prize

☆**Academi Cardiff International Poetry Competition**
Academi
Mount Stuart House, Mount Stuart Sq, Cardiff, Wales CF10 5FQ
Tel: (029) 472266 *Fax:* (029) 492930
E-mail: post@academi.org
Web Site: www.academi.org
Established: 1986
Awarded annually. Poems in the English language of no more than 50 lines on any subject. Open to all nationalities. First prize L5000; second prize L750; third prize L500; ten prizes L250.
Closing Date: 6/1/2003

J R Ackerley Prize for Autobiography
English Centre of International PEN
152-156 Kentish Town Rd, London NW1 9QB
Tel: (020) 7267 9444 *Fax:* (020) 7267 9304
E-mail: enquiries@pen.org.uk
Web Site: www.pen.org.uk
Key Personnel
President: Victoria Glendinning
Executive Dir: Diana Reich
Established: 1982
Annual award for a literary autobiography written in English by an author of British nationality & published in the UK in the previous year.
Award: L1000 & a silver Dupont pen
Presented: PEN International Writers' Day

Airey Neave Research Award
The Airey Neave Trust
House of Commons, London SW1A 0AA
Tel: (020) 7495 0554 *Fax:* (020) 7491 1118

☆**Alexander Prize**
Royal Historical Society
University College London, Gower St, London WC1E 6BT
Tel: (020) 7387 7532 *Fax:* (020) 7387 7532
E-mail: royalhistsoc@ucl.ac.uk
Web Site: www.rhs.ac.uk
Key Personnel
Executive Secretary: Joy McCarthy
For an essay in English on a historical subject: must be a genuine work of original research. Candidates must either be under the age of 35 or be registered for a higher degree or have been registered for such a degree within the last three years. Must not exceed 8,000 words including foot-notes & can relate to any historical subject. Candidates are required to state the total number of words of their entry. It may be derived from a doctoral thesis (either in progress or completed) but it should be self-contained & suitable for reading as a lecture. No more than one essay submitted per year.
To apply: send one typescript copy of the essay, without identification of the author, with a cover letter (stating name, address, date of birth, institution, details of degree registration where relevant & essay title).
Award: L250 or a silver medal

Apple Tree Award
Reach: National Resource Centre for Children with Reading Difficulties
Wellington House, Wellington Rd, Wokingham, Berks RG40 2AG
Tel: (0118) 9891101 *Fax:* (0118) 9790989
E-mail: reach-reading.demon.co.uk
Creative writing prize for children with language difficulties.

The Rosemary Arthur Award
The National Poetry Foundation
27 Mill Rd, Fareham, Hants PO16 0TH
Tel: (01329) 822218 *Fax:* (01329) 822218
The award consists of the complete funding for a book of the poet's work, a suitably inscribed brass & glass carriage clock & L100 in cash. Rosemary Arthur is sponsor.

☆**Arts Council Awards & Bursaries**
Arts Council of England
14 Great Peter St, London SW1P 3NQ
Tel: (020) 7973 6431 *Fax:* (020) 7973 6590
Web Site: www.artscouncil.org.uk
Intended to provide experienced playwrights with an opportunity to research & develop work for theater independent of financial pressures & free from the need to write for a particular market. Full details of the help given to playwrights is available on request.

The Arts Council of Wales Book of the Year Awards
Arts Council of Wales
Holst House, 9 Museum Pl, Cardiff CF1 3NX
Tel: (02920) 376500 *Fax:* (02920) 221447
Key Personnel
Contact: Ms Lleucu Siencyn
Since 1968, The Arts Council of Wales has given awards to Welsh authors (by birth of residence) whose books are of exceptional literary merit. The books may be written in English or Welsh. The prizes are awarded to recognize achievement, to draw attention to writers of promise & to encourage the writing of creative literature in English & Welsh. Two prizes of L3,000 are awarded annually to winners & L1,000 to four other short-listed authors.
Other Sponsor(s): Hay-on-Wye Festival of Literature
Presented: Hay-on-Wye Festival of Literature

☆**Arvon Foundation International Poetry Competition**
Arvon Foundation Ltd
42A Buckingham Palace Rd, 2nd floor, London SW1W 0RE
Tel: (020) 7931 7611 *Fax:* (020) 7963 0961
E-mail: comps@arvonfoundation.org
First organized in 1980. Entries for the competition must be previously unpublished poems of any length written in English. An anthology of winning poems, and those selected by the judges for special commendation, are published by the Arvon Foundation.

Authors' Club Best First Novel Award
Authors' Club
40 Dover St, London W1S 4NP
Tel: (020) 7499 8581 *Fax:* (020) 7409 0913
Key Personnel
Secretary: Ann de La Grange
For the most promising first novel published in English in the United Kingdom in the preceding year.
Award: L1000 awarded annually
Closing Date: Nov 2002

Authors' Club Sir Banister Fletcher Award
Authors' Club
40 Dover St, London W1S 4NP
Tel: (020) 7499 8581 *Fax:* (020) 7409 0913
Key Personnel
Secretary: Ann de La Grange
For the most deserving book on architecture or the arts.
Award: L1000 awarded annually

Aventis Prizes for Science Books
Formerly Rhone-Poulenc Prizes for Science Books
Aventis Pharma Ltd
c/o Copus, 6-9 Carlton House Terrace, London SW1Y 5AG
Tel: (020) 7451 2579 ext 2579 *Fax:* (020) 7451 2693
E-mail: bookprize@copus.org.uk
Web Site: www.aventissciencebookprizes.com
Key Personnel
Copus Manager: Natasha Martineau
    E-mail: natasha.martineau@copus.org.uk
Spirit Publicity: Reeta Bhatiani *E-mail:* reeta@spiritpublicity.com
Established: 1988

PRIZES — UNITED KINGDOM

Prizes were established to celebrate the best in popular science writing & are awarded annually to books that make science more accessible to readers of all ages & backgrounds. The Prizes are organized by Copus-The Science Communication Partnership.
Award: Up to L30,000 awarded annually in two categories: General (L10,000) for a book with a general readership; Junior (L10,000) for a book for under-14's. Up to 5 shortlisted authors in each category receive L1,000 each

☆BBC WILDLIFE Magazine Awards for Nature Writing
BBC WILDLIFE Magazine
Broadcasting House, Whiteladies Rd, Bristol BS8 2LR
Tel: (0117) 9738402 *Fax:* (0117) 9467075
E-mail: wildlife.magazine@bbc.co.uk
Key Personnel
Editor: Rosamund Kidman Cox
Competition Organizer & Editorial Assistant: Nina Epton
Annual awards for essays of not more than 800 words based on personal observations or reflections on nature. The main award is L1,000; should this be won by a professional writer, a second award of L200 is made to the best essay by an amateur. There are also two awards for younger writers & a number of runner-up prizes.

☆Benson Medal
Royal Society of Literature of the United Kingdom
Somerset House, Strand, London WC2R 1LA
Tel: (20) 7845 4676 *Fax:* (20) 7845 4679
E-mail: info@rslit.org
Web Site: www.rslit.org
Key Personnel
Chairman: Ronald Harwood
Assistant Secretary: Julia Abel Smith *Tel:* (020) 7845 4677 *E-mail:* julia@rslit.org
Established: 1961
Founded 1961 by Dr. A C Benson. For a body of meritorious work in poetry, fiction, history, biography or belles lettres. A silver medal given periodically at the discretion of the Council of the Royal Society of Literature. Applications are not invited.
Award: Occasional Award

☆David Berry Prize
Royal Historical Society
University College London, Gower St, London WC1E 6BT
Tel: (020) 7387 7532 *Fax:* (020) 7387 7532
E-mail: royalhistsoc@ucl.ac.uk
Web Site: www.rhs.ac.uk
Key Personnel
Executive Secretary: Joy McCarthy
For an essay in English on a subject, to be selected by the candidates, dealing with Scottish history. The essay submitted must be a genuine work of research based on original (manuscript or printed) materials. The essay should be between 6,000 & 10,000 words in length (excluding foot-notes & appendices). It must be submitted in typescript. The author's name should not appear on the typescript & should be submitted separately. No person to whom the prize has been awarded may enter for any subsequent competition for the prize.
Award: Monetary prize awarded annually

Besterman/McColvin Medal
Chartered Institute of Library & Information Professionals
7 Ridgmount St, London WC1E 7AE
Tel: (020) 7255 0650 *Fax:* (020) 7255 0501
E-mail: marketing@cilip.org.uk
Web Site: www.cilip.org.uk
For outstanding works of reference published in the UK. One for print & one for electronic formats. Eligible works are those published from Jan 1, 2001 until July 5, 2002. The judges will assess the authority, scope & coverage, arrangement & currency of the information, quality of indexing, adequacy of references, physical presentation, originality & value for money.
Award: 500 UK Pounds & certificate
Presented: Sept

James Tait Black Memorial Prizes
University of Edinburgh
David Hume Tower, George Sq, Edinburgh EH8 9JX
Tel: (0131) 650 3619 *Fax:* (0131) 650 6898
Web Site: www.ed.ac.uk/~englitw3/jtbinf.htm
Key Personnel
Contact: Sheila Strathdee *E-mail:* s.strathdee@ed.ac.uk
Established: 1919
These literary prizes were founded by the late Mrs Janet Coats Black in memory of her husband, a partner in the publishing house of A&C Black Ltd, London. Mrs Black set aside L11,000 to be used for two prizes of whatever income the fund would produce after paying expenses. The prizes, supplemented by the Scottish Arts Council, now amount annually to approximately L3000 each. Literary Prizes are awarded to the best biography & to the best work of fiction published during the calendar year Oct 1st to Sept 30th.

The K Blundell Trust
Society of Authors
84 Drayton Gardens, London SW10 9SB
Tel: (020) 7373 6642 *Fax:* (020) 7373 5768
E-mail: info@societyofauthors.org
Web Site: www.societyofauthors.org
Concerns grants to published British authors under 40 years of age & to published authors who need additional funding to write their next book.
Closing Date: April 30 & October 31

☆Boardman Tasker Prize for Mountain Literature
Boardman Tasker Charitable Trust
Pound House, Llangennith, Swansea, Wales SA3 1JQ
Tel: (01792) 386 215 *Fax:* (01792) 386 215
Web Site: www.boardmantasker.com
Key Personnel
Contact: Margaret Body *E-mail:* margaretbody@lineone.net
Established: 1983
Established to commemorate the lives of distinguished mountaineers Peter Boardman & Joe Tasker who died in 1982 on Mount Everest. An annual prize of L2000 will go to an author of a published work of nonfiction or fiction, written in the English language, initially or in translation, which makes an outstanding contribution to mountain literature; published between November 1st of previous year & October 31st of year of the prize.
Award: L2000 awarded annually
Closing Date: August 1 of year in which the prize is offered
Presented: Alpine Club, London, UK, November

☆The Man Booker Prize
Formerly The Booker Prize
Booktrust
Book House, 45 E Hill, Wandsworth, London SW18 2QZ
Tel: (020) 8516 2977 *Fax:* (020) 8516 2978
Web Site: www.booktrusted.com; www.themanbookerprize.com
Key Personnel
Prize Administrator: Tarryn McKay *Tel:* (020) 8516 2972 *E-mail:* tarryn@booktrust.org.uk
Contact: Kate Mervyn-Jones *E-mail:* kate@booktrust.org.uk
Established: 1969
Prize of L50,000 donated by the Man Group plc & administered by Booktrust, for any full-length novel, written in English by a citizen of The Commonwealth, or the Republic of Ireland. Any United Kingdom publisher who publishes works of fiction may enter up to two novels, with scheduled publication dates between 1st October & 30 September. In addition, publishers may enter any current novel by an author who has previously been shortlisted or won the Booker Prize.
Other Sponsor(s): The Man Group plc
Award: L50,000
Presented: Annually

The Bridport Prize Poetry & Short Stories
Bridport Arts Centre
South St, Bridport, Dorset DT6 3NR
Tel: (01308) 459444 *Fax:* (01308) 459166
E-mail: info@bridport-arts.com
Web Site: www.bridportprize.org.uk
Award: 1st Prize in each category: L3,000; 2nd Prize L1,000; 3rd Prize L500
Closing Date: June 30th each year
Presented: Bridport Arts Centre, 10-26-02 (last Saturday of October, each year)

British Book Awards
Publishing News Ltd
39 Store St, London WC1E 7DB
Tel: (020) 7692 2900 *Fax:* (020) 7419 2111
E-mail: mailbox@publishingnews.co.uk
Web Site: www.publishingnews.co.uk
Key Personnel
Organizer: Merric Davidson *Tel:* (01580) 212041 *E-mail:* nibbies@mdla.co.uk
Established: 1989
The UK Book Trade 'OSCARS'.
Other Sponsor(s): 15 Corporate sponsors including Reader's Digest, Virgin, KPMG
Closing Date: mid-November
Presented: Grosvenor House on Park Lane, February Annually

British Comparative Literature Association/British Centre for Literary Translation Prize
British Comparative Literature Association/British Centre for Literary Translation
UEA, Norwich NR4 7TJ
Tel: (01603) 592143 *Fax:* (01603) 250599
E-mail: transcomp@uea.ac.uk
Key Personnel
Contact: Dr Jean Boase-Beier *Tel:* (01603) 593360 *E-mail:* J.Boase-Beier@uea.ac.uk
Literary translation includes poetry, fiction or literary prose, from any period; maximum 25 typed pages. First Prize: L350; Second Prize: L200; Third Prize: L100; other entries may receive commendations.
Award: Monetary Prize
Closing Date: January 31 annually
Presented: BCLA Prize Giving, July

British Science Fiction Awards
The British Science Fiction Association Ltd
44 White Way, Kidlington, Oxon 0X5 2XA
Key Personnel
Awards Administrator: Chris Hill
Awarded annually for the best science fiction book published in Britain for the first time in the previous year. Also BSFA awards for the best short story & artwork.

The Calouste Gulbenkian Foundation Prize
Society of Authors - Translators Association
84 Drayton Gardens, London SW10 9SB

Tel: (020) 7373 6642 *Fax:* (020) 7373 5768
E-mail: info@societyofauthors.org
Web Site: www.societyofauthors.org
The triennial prize is for translations of works from any period by a Portuguese national. The translation must have been first published in the UK.
Award: L1000
Closing Date: December 20

The Carey Award
Society of Indexers
Globe Centre, Penistone Rd, Sheffield S6 3AE
Tel: (0114) 281 3060 *Fax:* (0114) 281 3061
E-mail: admin@socind.demon.co.uk
Web Site: www.socind.demon.co.uk
Key Personnel
Administrator: P W Burrow
The award is made by Council for services to indexing.

Carnegie Medal
Chartered Institute of Library & Information Professionals
7 Ridgmount St, London WC1E 7AE
Tel: (020) 7255 0650 *Fax:* (020) 7255 0501
E-mail: info@cilip.org.uk
Web Site: www.cilip.org.uk
Key Personnel
Marketing Manager: Louisa Myatt
Established: 1936
To commemorate the centenary of Andrew Carnegie's birth in 1835. Annual award for an outstanding book for children written in English & first published during the preceding year in the UK. Recommendations for the award are made by members of The Library Association. Winner selected by Youth Libraries Group.

Children's Award
Arts Council of England
14 Great Peter St, London SW1P 3NQ
Tel: (020) 7973 6431 *Fax:* (020) 7973 6983
Web Site: www.artscouncil.org.uk
Celebrates the accomplishments & raises the profile of theatre for children & most especially, playwrights who work in this field.

Children's Book Award
Federation of Children's Book Groups
The Old Malt House, Wilts SN8 2DW
Tel: (01672) 540629 *Fax:* (01672) 41280
Key Personnel
Coordinator: Marianne Adey
E-mail: marianneadey@aol.com
Founded 1980. Awarded annually by the Federation of Children's Book Groups for the best work of fiction (published in the United Kingdom). Chosen by children for children.

☆**Cholmondeley Award for Poets**
Society of Authors
84 Drayton Gardens, London SW10 9SB
Tel: (020) 7373 6642 *Fax:* (020) 7373 5768
E-mail: info@societyofauthors.org
Web Site: www.societyofauthors.org
Established by the late Dowager Marchioness of Cholmondeley in 1966 for 'the benefit & encouragement of poets of any age, sex or nationality'. The noncompetitive award is for work generally, not for a specific book & submissions are not required. Approximately L8000 awarded annually.

Arthur C Clarke Award
Science Fiction Foundation, British Science Fiction Association, Science Museum
60 Bournemouth Rd, Folkestone, Kent CT19 5AZ
Tel: (01303) 232939 *Fax:* (01303) 252939
E-mail: clarke@appomattox.demon.co.uk
Web Site: www.clarkeaward.com
Key Personnel
Administrator: Paul Kincaid
Established: 1986
For the best science fiction novel published in the United Kingdom. The winner is chosen by a panel of six judges representing the Science Fiction Foundation, the British Science Fiction Association & the International Science Policy Foundation.
Award: Annual award of an engraved bookend & L2003
Presented: The Science Museum, London, Mid-May

David Cohen British Literature Prize
Arts Council of England
14 Great Peter St, London SW1P 3NQ
Tel: (020) 7973 6431 *Fax:* (020) 7973 6983
Administered by the Arts Council in association with Coutts & Co, this prize will be awarded biennially in recognition of the entire body of a writer's work.

Commonwealth Writers Prize
Commonwealth Foundation
Marlborough House, Pall Mall, London SW1Y 5HY
Tel: (020) 516 2972 *Fax:* (020) 516 2978
E-mail: geninfo@commonwealth.int
Web Site: www.commonwealthfoundation/programmes/programme.cfm
Established in 1987. Awarded Annually.

☆**Duff Cooper Prize**
Duff Cooper
54 St Maur Rd, London SW6 4DP
Tel: (020) 7736 3729 *Fax:* (020) 7731 7638
Key Personnel
Prize Administrator: Ms Artemis Cooper
First awarded 1956. For a literary work of history, biography, poetry or politics supported by a recognized publisher in English or French. The prize is the interest from a Trust Fund. Awarded annually.

☆**The Rose Mary Crawshay Prize**
British Academy
20-21 Cornwall Terrace, London NW1 4QP
Tel: (020) 7487 5966 *Fax:* (020) 7224 3807
E-mail: basec@britac.ac.uk
Web Site: www.brita3.britac.ac.uk
Founded 1888. Awarded by the Council of the British Academy to women writers of any nationality for an historical or critical work of value on any subject concerning English literature. Preference is given to works on Byron, Shelley or Keats. One or more prizes awarded annually. Applications are not sought.

CWA Cartier Diamond Dagger Award
Crime Writers' Association
Meadow View, The Street, Bossingham, Canterbury, Kent CT4 6DX
Mailing Address: PO Box 63, Wakefield WF2 0WY
E-mail: info@theCWA.co.uk
Web Site: www.thecwa.co.uk
Key Personnel
Chairman: Lindsey Davis
Secretary: Judith Cutler
Inaugurated 1986 & sponsored by Cartier in conjunction with the Crime Writers' Association. For outstanding contribution to the genre. Silver book with diamond dagger plunged into it. Personal memento of diamond brooch or tiepin.

CWA John Creasey Memorial Award
Crime Writers' Association
Meadow View, The Street, Bossingham, Canterbury, Kent CT4 6DX
Mailing Address: PO Box 63, Wakefield WF2 0WY
E-mail: info@theCWA.co.uk
Web Site: www.thecwa.co.uk
Key Personnel
Chairman: Lindsey Davis
Secretary: Judith Cutler
Founded 1973 & sponsored by Chivers Press. Annual award of magnifying glass with onyx handle & inscribed plate & check for best crime novel by author who has not previously published a full-length work of fiction. Submission by publishers only.

CWA Gold Dagger Award for Fiction
Crime Writers' Association
Meadow View, The Street, Bossingham, Canterbury, Kent CT4 6DX
Mailing Address: PO Box 63, Wakefield WF2 0WY
E-mail: info@theCWA.co.uk
Web Site: www.thecwa.co.uk
Key Personnel
Chairman: Lindsey Davis
Secretary: Judith Cutler
Inaugurated 1955, revised 1960. A gilded dagger & check for the best crime-fiction novel of the year awarded annually by a panel of reviewers. Submission by publishers only.

CWA Macallan Gold Dagger Award for Nonfiction
Crime Writers' Association
Meadow View, The Street, Bossingham, Canterbury, Kent CT4 6DX
Mailing Address: PO Box 63, Wakefield WF2 0WY
Web Site: www.thecwa.co.uk
Key Personnel
Chairman: Lindsey Davis
Secretary: Judith Cutler
Inaugurated 1978. Winner is selected by an independent panel. The winner receives a Gilded Dagger in inscribed case & a check. Submission by publishers only.

CWA Macallen Short Story Dagger Award
Crime Writers' Association
Meadow View, The Street, Bossingham, Canterbury, Kent CT4 6DX
Mailing Address: PO Box 63, Wakefield WF2 0WY
E-mail: info@theCWA.co.uk
Web Site: www.thecwa.co.uk
Key Personnel
Chairman: Lindsey Davis
Secretary: Judith Cutler
Awarded for a short story published in a crime anthology in 1997. Submission by publishers only. Prize - L5000.

CWA Silver Dagger Award
Crime Writers' Association
Meadow View, The Street, Bossingham, Canterbury, Kent CT4 6DX
Mailing Address: PO Box 63, Wakefield WF2 0WY
E-mail: info@theCWA.co.uk
Web Site: www.thecwa.co.uk
Key Personnel
Chairman: Lindsey Davis
Secretary: Judith Cutler
Inaugurated 1955, revised 1969. A silvered dagger & check for the runner-up.

☆**Isaac Deutscher Memorial Prize**
Lloyds Bank Ltd
71 Lombard St, London EC3 P3BS

Instituted 1968. For a work published or in typescript in any of the main European languages which contributes to the development of Marxist thought. L100 awarded annually.

Encore Award
Society of Authors
84 Drayton Gardens, London SW10 9SB
Tel: (020) 7373 6642 *Fax:* (020) 7373 5768
E-mail: info@societyofauthors.org
Web Site: www.societyofauthors.org
Awarded to a second novel (or novels) judged to be the best first published in the UK during the year preceding the year in which the award is presented; publisher entry only.
Award: L10,000 (14,159 US dollars) shared between the winners
Closing Date: Nov 30
Presented: Spring

☆**Christopher Ewart-Biggs Memorial Prize**
Hugo Arnold
33a Brondesbury Rd, London NW6
Established in 1977 to commemorate Christopher Ewart-Biggs, the British Ambassador to Ireland, who was assassinated in Dublin in 1976. This award is made biennially to writings from any nationality where the published work contributes most to peace and understanding in Ireland, closer ties between the peoples of Britain & Ireland, or to cooperation between the partners of the European Community. Entries should be in English or French & the prize is L4000.

☆**The Geoffrey Faber Memorial Prize**
Faber & Faber Ltd
3 Queen's Sq, London WC1N 3AU
Tel: (020) 7465 0045 *Fax:* (020) 7465 0034
Established in 1963 by Faber & Faber Ltd as a memorial to the founder & first Chairman of the firm, this prize of L1000 is awarded annually. It is given in alternate years, for a volume of verse & for a volume of prose fiction. It is given to that volume of verse or prose fiction first published originally in the United Kingdom during the two years preceding the year in which the Award is given which is, in the opinion of the judges, of the greatest literary merit. To be eligible for the prize the volume of verse or prose fiction in question must be by a writer who is: (a) not more than forty years old at the date of publication, (b) a citizen of the United Kingdom & Colonies, of any other Commonwealth state, of Ireland or of the Republic of South Africa. There are three judges, who are reviewers of poetry or fiction as the case may be, & they are nominated each year by the editors or literary editors of newspapers & magazines which regularly publish such reviews. Faber & Faber invite nominations from such editors & literary editors. No submissions for the prize are to be made.

Eleanor Farjeon Award
Scholastic UK Group
Watts Publishing Group, 96 Leonard St, London EC2A 4XD
Tel: (020) 7739 2929 *Fax:* (020) 7739 2318
Key Personnel
Promotions & Marketing: Susan Barry
 E-mail: susan.barry@waltspub.co.uk
The Eleanor Farjeon Award was established in 1965 to commemorate the work of the late children's author. The Children's Book Circle makes an annual award of L500 (minimum) which may be given to a librarian, teacher, author, artist, publisher, reviewer, bookseller or television producer who, in the judgment of the Awards Committee, is considered to have done outstanding work for children's books. Sponsored by Books for Children.
Presented: Year 2000

FCI Competition Essay
Fan Circle International
Cronk-Y-Voddy, 21 Rectory Rd, Coltishall NR12 7HF

The Fidler Award
Scottish Book Trust
Scottish Book Centre, 137 Dundee St, Edinburgh EH11 1BG
Tel: (0131) 2293663 *Fax:* (0131) 2284293
E-mail: Scottish.book.trust@dial.pipex.com
Web Site: www.scottishbooktrust.com
Key Personnel
Chief Executive, Scotland: Lindsay Fraser
First Awarded in 1983. Annual award of L1000 and a trophy for an unpublished novel written for 8-12 year olds. The author may have had previous books published, but this must be the first for this age range. The award is sponsored by Hodde Childrens Books will publish the winning entry.

John Florio Prize
Society of Authors - Translators Association
84 Drayton Gardens, London SW10 9SB
Tel: (020) 7373 6642 *Fax:* (020) 7373 5768
E-mail: info@societyofauthors.org
Web Site: www.societyofauthors.org
Established in 1963 under the auspices of the Italian Institute & the British-Italian Society & named after John Florio. For the best translation into English of a twentieth-century Italian work of literary merit & general interest, published by a British publisher during the preceding two years. L1000.
Closing Date: December 20

Fraenkel Prize in Contemporary History
Institute of Contemporary History & Wiener Library
4 Devonshire St, London W1W 5BH
Tel: (020) 7636 7247 *Fax:* (020) 7436 6428
E-mail: info@wienerlibrary.co.uk
Web Site: www.wienerlibrary.co.uk
Key Personnel
Administrative Co-ordinator: Rod Digges
Inaugurated in 1989 by Mr Ernst Fraenkel. Two awards: one of US $6000 for any entrant & one of US $4000 for entrants who have yet to publish a major work.
Closing Date: May 10

David Gemmell Cup
Hastings Writer's Group
1 Page Lane, Bexhill TN39 3RD
Tel: 212647

Gibb Memorial Trust
E J W Gibb Memorial Trust
2 Penarth Pl, Cambridge CB3 9LU
Tel: (01223) 566630 *Fax:* (01223) 511182
Web Site: www.arisandphillips.com
Key Personnel
Secretary to the Trustees: P R Bligh
 E-mail: prbligh@btinternet.com
Publishers of works about Persian, Turkish & Arabic history & religions.

Gladstone History Book Prize
University College London
Royal Historical Society, Grower St, London WC1E 6BT
Tel: (020) 7387 7532 *Fax:* (020) 7387 7532
E-mail: royalhistsoc@ucl.ac.uk
Web Site: www.rhs.ac.uk
Key Personnel
Executive Secretary: Joy McCarthy
Established: 1998
Based on any historical subject which is not primarily related to British history. Must be its author's first solely written history book & published in English during the calendar year 2003 by a scholar normally resident in the UK. Must be an original & scholarly work of historical research. Author or Publisher should submit three copies (non-returnable) of an eligible book by the end of the year.
Award: Annual award
Closing Date: Dec 31, 2002
Presented: Royal Historical Society's annual reception, July 2003

Glenfiddich Food & Drink Awards
William Grant & Sons
Independence House, 84 Lower Mortlake Rd, Richmond, Surrey TW9 2HS
Tel: (020) 8322 1188 *Fax:* (020) 8322 1695
Web Site: www.glenfiddisch.com
Key Personnel
Chairman, Glenfiddich Food & Drink Awards: Heather Graham
Public Relations Officer: K Fiennes-Price
Established: 1969
Food & Drink.
Closing Date: January
Presented: January

Edgar Graham Book Prize
School of Oriental & African Studies
Geography Department, Thornhaugh St, Russell Sq, London WC1H 0XG
Tel: (020) 7898 4570 *Fax:* (020) 7898 4599
Key Personnel
Secretary: C Darfour *E-mail:* cd16@soas.ac.uk
Award of L1500 is given biennially to a work of original scholarship published in English on agricultural &/or industrial development in Asia &/or Africa.

Kate Greenaway Medal
Chartered Institute of Library & Information Professionals
7 Ridgmount St, London WC1E 7AE
Tel: (020) 7255 0650 *Fax:* www.cilip.org.uk
E-mail: info@cilip.org.uk
Web Site: www.cilip.org.uk
Key Personnel
Marketing Manager: Louisa Myatt
First awarded 1955. Offered annually by CILIP for the most distinguished work in the illustration of children's books first published in the United Kingdom during the preceding year. Winners selected by Youth Libraries Group.

Eric Gregory Trust Fund Awards
Society of Authors
84 Drayton Gardens, London SW10 9SB
Tel: (020) 7373 6642 *Fax:* (020) 7373 5768
E-mail: info@societyofauthors.org
Web Site: www.societyofauthors.org
A number of awards are made each year to encourage young British poets. Candidates for awards must be British subjects by birth, ordinarily resident in the United Kingdom & under the age of 30 on 31 March in the year of the award. Candidates must submit a published or unpublished volume of belles lettres, poetry or drama-poems by 31 October each year.
Closing Date: October 31

☆**The Guardian Award for Children's Fiction**
The Guardian
119 Farringdon Rd, London EC1R 3ER
Tel: (020) 7278 2332 *Fax:* (020) 7713 4366
Instituted in 1967 and awarded annually. The prize of L500 (subject to revision) is given for an outstanding work of fiction for children by a citizen of The Commonwealth.

UNITED KINGDOM LITERARY

☆**The Guardian Fiction Prize**
The Guardian
119 Farringdon Rd, London EC1R 3ER
Tel: (020) 7278 2332 *Fax:* (020) 7713 4366
Telex: 8811746
Instituted in 1965 & awarded annually. The prize of L3000 to the winner is given for a novel published by a citizen of Britain or The Commonwealth & is intended to encourage work, originality & promise.

Hawthornden Prize
Hawthornden Literary Institute
Hawthornden Castle, Lasswade, Midlothian EH18 1EG
Tel: (0131) 4402180
Key Personnel
Administrator: Dr Kusnetz
Established: 1919
Founded in 1919 by Miss Alice Warrender, it is awarded annually to a British subject under age 41 for the best work of imaginative literature. It is especially designed to encourage young authors, and the word 'imaginative' is given a broad interpretation. Biographies are not excluded. Books do not have to be submitted for the prize; it is awarded without competition. A panel of judges chooses the winner.
Award: Annually

Francis Head Bequest
Society of Authors
84 Drayton Gardens, London SW10 9SB
Tel: (020) 7373 6642 *Fax:* (020) 7373 5768
E-mail: info@societyofauthors.org
Web Site: www.societyofauthors.org
Concerns grants to British authors over 35 years of age, who are suffering from illness, financial difficulty or temporary setbacks.

Heinemann Award for Literature
Royal Society of Literature of the United Kingdom
Somerset House, Strand, London WC2R 1LA
Tel: (020) 7845 4676 *Fax:* (020) 7845 4679
E-mail: info@rslit.org
Key Personnel
Assistant Secretary: Julia Abel Smith *Tel:* (020) 7845 4677 *E-mail:* julia@rslit.org
Established: 1944
A foundation was established in 1944 through a bequest in the will of the late William Heinemann, eminent British publisher. The Royal Society of Literature administers the annual foundation award which is 'primarily to reward those classes of literature which are less remunerative, namely, poetry, criticism, biography, history, etc' & 'to encourage the production of works of real merit'. The amount of the award is L5000 specified. Submitted works must have been written originally in English & published during the calendar year previous to the year in which the prize is presented.
Closing Date: Dec 15 annually
Presented: June annually

Felicia Hemans Prize for Lyrical Poetry
University of Liverpool
12 Abercromby Sq, Liverpool L69 3BX
Mailing Address: PO Box 147, Liverpool
Tel: (0151) 7942458 *Fax:* (0151) 7086502
E-mail: p.blythe@liv.ac.uk
Telex: 627095
For a poem by past or present members and students of the University of Liverpool.
Award: Books or cash awarded annually

William Hill Sports Book of the Year
William Hill Organizaton
Greenside House, 50 Station Rd, Wood Green, London N22 4TP
Tel: (020) 8365 7211 *Fax:* (020) 8889 0472

Lakeland Book of the Year Awards
Cumbria Tourist Board
Ashleigh, Holly Rd, Windermere, Cumbria LA23 2AQ
Tel: (015394) 44444 *Fax:* (015394) 44041
These annual awards were established in 1984 by Hunter Davies & Cumbria Tourist Board. The Hunter Davies Award is for a book which best helps visitors or residents to enjoy a greater love or understanding of life in Cumbria - the Lake District. The Tullie House Prize is for a book which best helps develop a greater appreciation of the built and/or natural environment of Cumbria. The Barclays Bank Award is for the best small book on any aspect of Cumbria life, people or culture. The Border Television Prize is for a book which best illustrates the beauty & character of Cumbria.

Ian Saint James Literary Award
Collins Publishers
8 Grafton St, London W1X 3LA
Tel: (020) 7493 7070
Founded 1989 to encourage writers of short stories who have not previously had work published in book form. L1000 will go to each of the twelve best stories, and from these the L11,000 winner and two runners-up (L4000 and L1000) will be chosen. To be awarded annually.

The Independent Foreign Fiction Award
The Independent
40 City Rd, London EC1Y 2DB
Tel: (020) 7253 1222 *Fax:* (020) 7962 0016

International Short Story Competition/International Poetry Competition 2000
Stand Magazine
Haltwhistle House, George St, Newcastle Tyne, Tyne & Wear NE4 75L
Tel: (0191) 2733280
E-mail: dlatane@vcu.edu; standsubscription@cablenet.co.uk
Key Personnel
Admin: Linda Goldsmith
Sample copies available for $13 (US) from David Latane, Dept of English, VCU, Richmond, VA 23284, USA.

Natural World Book Prize
Formerly BP Natural World Book Prize
Booktrust
Book House, 45 E Hill, Wandsworth, London SW18 2QZ
Tel: (020) 8516 2977 *Fax:* (020) 8516 2978
Web Site: www.booktrusted.com
Key Personnel
Prizes Administrator: Tarryn McKay *Tel:* (020) 8516 2972 *E-mail:* tarryn@booktrust.org.uk
Contact: Kate Mervyn-Jones *E-mail:* kate@booktrust.org.uk
Established: 1987
A L5000 prize will be awarded to the author(s) of the book which most imaginatively promotes the conservation of the natural environment & all its animals & plants. The judges reserve the right to award a prize of L1000 for a runner-up. All entries must be published in the UK, by a UK publisher between June 1 & the following May 31. This award is open to any nationality. The author(s) must be alive at the time of submission.
Other Sponsor(s): BP, The Wildlife Trusts & Subbuteo Books
Award: L5000 annually awarded to adults

☆**Kraszna-Krausz Book Awards**
Kraszna-Krausz Foundation
Park House London Rd, High Wycombe, Bucks HP11 1B2
Tel: (1494) 450171 *Fax:* (1494) 441815
Sponsored by the Kraszna-Krausz Foundation, these international Awards are made to encourage & recognize outstanding achievements in the publishing & writing of books on the art, history, practice & technology of photography & of the moving image.
The Awards are made annually, with prizes for books on still photography alternating with those for books on the moving image (film, television, video). There will be prizes of L10,000 for the winner in each of two categories, with L1000 awards for the runners-up.

Lancashire County Library Children's Book of the Year Award
Lancashire County Library
County Library Manager, County Library Headquarters, County Hall, PO Box 61, Preston PR1 8RJ
Tel: (01772) 264018 *Fax:* (01772) 264880
E-mail: library@lcl.lancscc.gov.uk
Web Site: www.lancashire.gov.uk/libraries/
Key Personnel
Contact: David G Lightfoot *E-mail:* david.lightfoot@lcl.lancscc.gov.uk
Established: 1986
Annual award, sponsored by The University of Central Lancashire, given for a work of fiction or a collection of short stories by a single author. The book should be suitable for 11-14 year olds.
Award: L500 & an engraved decanter

Ralph Lewis Award
University of Sussex Library
Brighton BN1 9QL
Tel: (01273) 678158 *Fax:* (01273) 678441
E-mail: library@sussex.ac.uk
Key Personnel
Contact: Deborah Shorley

London Writers' Competition
Arts Office: Wandsworth Borough Council
Town Hall, Wandsworth High St, London SW18 2PU
Tel: (020) 8871 8711 *Fax:* (020) 8871 7630
The competition is open to London writers only & has both short story, poetry & play sections.

The Agnes Mure Mackenzie Award
The Saltire Society
Saltire Court, 20 Castle Terrace, Edinburgh EH1 2EG
Tel: (0131) 5561836 *Fax:* (0131) 5571675
This award is given biennially for a published work of Scottish Historical Research.

☆**Enid McLeod Prize**
Franco-British Society
Room 623 Linen Hall, 162-168 Regent St, London W1R 5TB
Tel: (020) 7734 0815 *Fax:* (020) 7734 0815
Founded 1981. An annual prize for the book (published in the UK) judged to have contributed the most to Franco-British understanding.

The Macmillan Prize for Children's Picture Book Illustration
Macmillan Children's Books
25 Eccleston Place, London SW1F 9NF
Tel: (020) 7014 6000 *Fax:* (020) 7014 6001
Key Personnel
Contact: Bonnie Saunders
Established: 1986
This annual award was established in 1986 in order to stimulate new work from young illustrators in British art schools. Open to all art

students in higher education establishments in the UK.
Award: L1000, L500 & L250, plus the possibility of publication

Macmillan Silver Pen Award for Short Stories
English Centre of International PEN
152-156 Kentish Town Rd, London NW1 9QB
Tel: (020) 7267 9444 *Fax:* (020) 7267 9304
E-mail: enquiries@pen.org.uk
Web Site: www.pen.org.uk
Key Personnel
President: Victoria Glendinning
Executive Dir: Diana Reich
Presented annually for a collection of short stories written in English by an author of British nationality & published in the UK in the previous year.
Other Sponsor(s): Macmillan Publishers; ST Dupont; Stern Family (nonfiction award in-memory of James Stern)
Award: L500 & a silver Dupont pen
Presented: PEN International Writers' Day

Marsh Award for Children's Literature in Translation
Authors' Club
40 Dover St, London W1X 3RB
Tel: (020) 7499 8581 *Fax:* (020) 7409 0913
Established: 1995
Sponsored by the Marsh Christian Trust, the award aims to encourage translation of foreign children's books into English. It is a biennial award (first year: 1996), open to British translations of books for 4-16 year-olds, published in the UK by a British publisher. Any category will be considered with the exception of encyclopedias & reference. No electronic books.
Award: L750

Marsh Biography Award
Authors' Club
40 Dover St, London W1S 4NP
Tel: (020) 7499 8581 *Fax:* (020) 7409 0913
Established in 1986, this national biography biennial award is sponsored by B P Marsh & Co Ltd. Publishers are invited to submit one biography by a British author. The prize was first awarded by the Authors' Club in 1987 & consisted of a trophy & a check for L3500.

Kurt Maschler Award
Booktrust
Book House, 45 E Hill, Wandsworth, London SW18 2QZ
Tel: (020) 8516 2977 *Fax:* (020) 8516 2978
Web Site: www.booktrusted.com
Key Personnel
Prizes Manager: Kate Mervyn-Jones *Tel:* (020) 8516 2973 *E-mail:* kate@booktrust.org.uk
Prize Administrator: Tarryn McKay *Tel:* (020) 8516 2972 *E-mail:* tarryn@booktrust.org.uk
Established: 1982
The Kurt Maschler Award is awarded annually for a work of imagination for children in which text & illustration are integrated so that each enhances & balances the other. The winning author & illustrator will receive an 'Emil' - a bronze statue of Erich Kaestner's famous character as visualized by Walter Trier. All entries must be published in the UK by a UK publisher & authors/illustrators must be of British nationality, or other nationals who have been resident in the British Isles for at least 10 years. Publication must be in the calendar year of the prize (ie books published during 2001 will be eligible for the 2001 prize).
Other Sponsor(s): Tom Maschler
Award: L1,000 annually

☆**MCA Book Prize**
Management Consultancies Association (MCA)
11 W Halkin St, London SW1X 8JL
Tel: (020) 7235 3897 *Fax:* (020) 7235 0825
E-mail: MCA@MCA.org.uk
Web Site: www.mca.org.uk
Key Personnel
Awards Administrator: Andrea Livingstone
Deputy Dir: Will White
It is aimed to recognize & reward British writers of management books & to offer encouragement to writers whose books contribute stimulating, original & progressive ideas on management issues.
Award: L5000 annually

The Michael Powell Book Award
British Film Institute
21 Stephen St, London W1P 1PL
Tel: (020) 7255 1444 *Fax:* (020) 7436 7950
This annual award, first made in 1983, is given to a book published in Britain dealing with film or television by a UK author. The award takes the form of a specially commissioned plaque.

MIND Book of the Year
MIND Publications
Granta House, 15-17 Broadway, London E15 4BQ
Tel: (020) 8519 2122 *Fax:* (020) 8522 1725
E-mail: a.mccarthy@mind.org.uk
Web Site: www.mind.org.uk
Key Personnel
Information Dir: Anny Brackx *Tel:* (020) 8221 9660 *Fax:* (020) 7221 9681 *E-mail:* a.brackx@mind.org.uk
Established: 1981
Inaugurated in 1981 by MIND & the National Book League in memory of Allen Lane. Awarded annually to the author of the book (fiction or nonfiction) which outstandingly furthers public awareness of mental health problems.
Award: L1500

Scott Moncrieff Prize
Society of Authors - Translators Association
84 Drayton Gardens, London SW10 9SB
Tel: (020) 7373 6642 *Fax:* (020) 7373 5768
E-mail: info@societyofauthors.org
Web Site: www.societyofauthors.org
Established in 1964 under the auspices of the Translators Association of the Society of Authors to be awarded annually for the best translation published by a British publisher during the previous year. Only translations of French twentieth-century works of literary merit & general interest will be considered. The work should be entered by the publisher & not the individual translator.
Closing Date: December 20

Mother Goose Award
Books for Children
c/o Brettenham House, Lancaster Place, London WC2E 7TL
Tel: (020) 7322 1451 *Fax:* (020) 7322 1488
E-mail: liz_flanagan@time-inc.com
Established 1979 as an annual award for the most exciting newcomer to children's book illustration in the United Kingdom, the competition is open to all illustrators who have published a first major book for children between March 1st and February 28th/29th of the preceding year. The award takes the form of a bronzed goose egg, a scroll and L1000 for the winner.

☆**The Shiva Naipaul Memorial Prize**
Spectator
56 Doughty St, London WC1N 2LL
Tel: (020) 7405 1706 *Fax:* (020) 7242 0603
Founded 1985 & awarded annually. A prize of L3000 is given to an English-language writer of any nationality under 35 years of age best able to describe a visit to a foreign place or people. The award will not be for travel writing in the conventional sense, but for the most acute & profound observation of cultures &/or scenes (which could be within the writer's native country) evidently alien to the writer. The winning entry will be published in 'The Spectator'. Submissions should not previously have been published & should not be more than 4000 words.

National Poetry Competition
The Poetry Society Inc
22 Betterton St, London WC2H 9BX
Tel: (020) 7420 9880 *Fax:* (020) 7240 4818
E-mail: poetryreview@poetrysociety.org.uk
Web Site: www.poetrysociety.org.uk
Founded 1978. Awarded annually for a poem written in English. L5000 first prize, L1000 second, L500 third & ten of L50. Closing date October 31st. Send SAE for entry form or visit website.

The Nestle Smarties Book Prize
Booktrust
Book House, 45 E Hill, Wandsworth, London SW18 2QZ
Tel: (020) 8516 2977 *Fax:* (020) 8516 2978
Web Site: www.booktrusted.com
Key Personnel
Prize Administrator: Tarryn McKay *Tel:* (020) 8516 2972 *E-mail:* tarryn@booktrust.org.uk
Contact: Elizabeth Bananuka
Established: 1985
To encourage high standards & stimulate interest in children's books. The prize is only open to works of fiction or poetry for children, written in English by a citizen of the UK, or an author resident in the UK. The author of the book must be living at the time of publication. The adult panel read over 260 books from which they must choose three from each category. The age categories are 5 & under, 6-8 & 9-11. The shortlisted books are then given to the Young Judges, who have to read the books & decide which book gets Gold, Silver & Bronze. The Young Judges are chosen from classes of school children, who have to complete tasks set for their age category. A new Young Judge category was added a couple of years ago, chosen from Kids' Club Networks. They read & judge the 6-8 books.
Other Sponsor(s): Nestle

New Writers Award
Romantic Novelists' Association
16 St Briacway, Exmouth EX8 5RN
Tel: (01395) 279659
Key Personnel
New Writers' Organizer & Contact: Margaret James *E-mail:* margaret@jamesk.freeserve.co.uk
Established: 1960
For an unpublished romantic novel.
Other Sponsor(s): RNA
Award: Trophy & cash prize
Closing Date: Sept annually
Presented: Party in London, May annually

☆**The Noma Award for Publishing in Africa**
PO Box 128, Witney, Oxon OX8 5XU
Tel: (01993) 775235 *Fax:* (01993) 709265
Key Personnel
Secretary to the NOMA Award Managing Committee: Mary Jay *E-mail:* maryljay@aol.com
Established: 1979
Established by the late Shoichi Noma, formerly President of the Japanese publishing company Kodansha Ltd, for African writers & scholars whose work is published in Africa. The annual award is given for an outstanding work in any of the following categories (1) scholarly or academic, (2) children's books, (3) literature

& creative writing (including fiction, drama or poetry).
Award: $10,000 (US)
Closing Date: March 28
Presented: Various places, mainly within Africa

Observer National Children's Poetry Competition
The Observer
119 Farrington Rd, London EUR 3ER
Tel: (020) 7278 2332 *Fax:* (020) 7278 1449
First awarded in 1986 and sponsored then and in 1987 and 1988 by the Water Authorities Association, the competition is open to three age groups: 10 years and under, 11-14 years and 15-18 years. There is an additional prize for the best group of poems from any school.

Outposts Poetry Competition
Hippopotamus Press
22 Whitewell Rd, Frome, Somerset BA11 4EL
Tel: (0373) 466653 *Fax:* (0373) 466653
Key Personnel
Competition Organizer: M Pargitter
Established: 1991
Awarded annually in the Autumn for new poetry adjudicated by a great poet. First prize approximately L500.

Parker Romantic Novel of the Year
Romantic Novelists' Association
2 Broad Oak Lane, Wigginton, York Y032 2SB
Tel: 01904 765035
Key Personnel
Award Organizer: Joan Emery
Established: 1960
Established as the RNA Major Award. For the best romantic novel (modern or historical) published during the year. Open to non-members.
Other Sponsor(s): Parker Pen Co
Award: L5000 cash prize awarded annually
Closing Date: November of each year
Presented: Awards luncheon, London, April each year

Premio Valle Inclan
Society of Authors - Translators Association
84 Drayton Gardens, London SW10 9SB
Tel: (020) 7373 6642 *Fax:* (020) 7373 5768
E-mail: info@societyofauthors.org
Web Site: www.societyofauthors.org
This annual prize is for published translations of full length Spanish works of literary merit & general interest (the original must have been written in Spanish but can be from any period & from anywhere in the world). The translation must have been first published in the UK. L1000.
Closing Date: December 20

☆**Quadrennial Prize for Bibliography**
International League of Antiquarian Booksellers
Wynches Barn, Herts SG10 6BA
Fax: (01279) 842 830
To the author of the best work, published or unpublished, of learned bibliography, of research into the history of the book or typography, or a book of general interest on the subject. The competition is open, without restriction, but entries must be submitted in a language which is universally read. An already published work is eligible only if it has an imprint bearing a date within the four years preceding the closing date for submission. Entries in the form of a specialized catalogue of one or more books destined for sale are not eligible, nor periodicals or public library catalogues. Any further information relating to the prize for Bibliography awarded by ILAB can be obtained from the National Associations of Antiquarian Booksellers.

Award: US $10,000 every four years
Presented: Summer 2002

☆**Trevor Reese Memorial Prize**
Institute of Commonwealth Studies
University of London, 28 Russell Sq, London WC1B 5DS
Tel: (020) 7862 8844 *Fax:* (020) 7862 8820
E-mail: ics@sas.ac.uk
Web Site: www.sas.ac.uk/commonwealthstudies/
Key Personnel
Events & Publicity Officer: Stephanie Kearins
 Tel: (020) 7862 8825 *E-mail:* skearins@sas.ac.uk
Established: 1976
The prize was established from a memorial fund to Dr Trevor Reese, Reader in Imperial Studies at the Institute of Commonwealth Studies, who died in 1976. The adjudicators are interested in wide-ranging publications, but the terms of the Prize specifically apply to scholarly works usually by a single author, in the field of Imperial & Commonwealth history.
Award: L1000 biennually

Rhone-Poulenc Prizes for Science Books, see Aventis Prizes for Science Books

☆**John Llewellyn Rhys Prize**
Booktrust
Book House, 45 E Hill, Wandsworth, London SW18 2QZ
Tel: (020) 8516 2977 *Fax:* (020) 8516 2978
Web Site: www.booktrusted.com
Key Personnel
Prize Administrator: Tarryn McKay *Tel:* (020) 8516 2972 *E-mail:* tarryn@booktrust.org.uk
Prizes Manager: Susy Behr *Tel:* (20) 8516 2993 *E-mail:* susy@booktrust.org.uk
Established: 1942
Founded by Jane Oliver, the widow of John Llewellyn Rhys, a young writer killed in action in World War II. To be eligible, entries may be any work of literature written by a British or Commonwealth writer under the age of 35 at the time of publication. Books must be written in English & published in the UK during the year of the Prize. Previous winners of the prize may not enter. This prize is open to published works only, entries submitted by UK publisher only.
Other Sponsor(s): The Mail on Sunday
Award: L500 awarded annually

The Rio Tinto David Watt Memorial Prize
Rio Tint PLC
6 Saint James's Sq, London SW1Y 4LD
Tel: (020) 7930 2399 *Fax:* (020) 7930 3249
Closing Date: March 31, 2001

The Robinson Medal
Chartered Institute of Library & Information Professionals
7 Ridgmount St, London WC1E 7AE
Tel: (020) 7255 0650 *Fax:* (020) 7255 0501
E-mail: info@cilip.org.uk
Web Site: www.cilip.org.uk
Key Personnel
Marketing Manager: Louisa Myatt
Awarded biennially to recognize innovation & excellence in library administration and administrative procedures. It is aimed specifically at attracting submissions from people working at paraprofessional levels in the library and information field.

The Royal Society of Medicine Prizes for Medical Writing & Illustration
The Society of Authors, Medical Writers Group
84 Drayton Gardens, London SW10 9SB
Tel: (020) 7373 6642 *Fax:* (020) 7373 5768

E-mail: info@societyofauthors.org
Web Site: www.societyofauthors.org
Key Personnel
Contact: Dorothy Sym

Sasakawa Prize
Society of Authors - Translators Association
84 Drayton Gardens, London SW10 9SB
Tel: (020) 7373 6642 *Fax:* (020) 7373 5768
E-mail: info@societyofauthors.org
Web Site: www.societyofauthors.org
This prize is for translations of full length Japanese works of literary merit & general interest, from any period. The translation must have been first published in the UK. Award: L2000.

Schlegel-Tieck Prize
Society of Authors - Translators Association
84 Drayton Gardens, London SW10 9SB
Tel: (020) 7373 6642 *Fax:* (020) 7373 5768
E-mail: info@societyofauthors.org
Web Site: www.societyofauthors.org
Established in 1964 under the auspices of the Translators Association, a subsidiary organization of the Society of Authors, to be awarded annually for the best translation published by a British publisher during the previous year. Only translations of German twentieth-century works of literary merit & general interest will be considered. The work should be entered by the publisher & not the individual translator.
Closing Date: December 20

Scottish Arts Council Book Awards
The Scottish Arts Council
Literature Dept, 12 Manor Pl, Edinburgh EH3 7DD
Tel: (0131) 2266051 *Fax:* (0131) 2259833
E-mail: administrator@scottisharts.org.uk
Web Site: www.sac.org.uk
Key Personnel
Secretary to Literary Director: Catherine Allan
 E-mail: catherine.allan@scottisharts.org.uk
A limited number of Awards (usually 10 per year), value L1000 each, are made twice yearly by the Scottish Arts Council to the authors of published books of literary merit written by Scots, by writers resident in Scotland, or on topics of Scottish interest. Most categories of books are eligible for consideration, but specialist, technical & academic books are outside the remit one award of $3000 is made annually to the author of a book for children. Books are submitted by the authors' publishers. Children's Book Awards (3 per year) value L1000 each, are made.

The Scottish Book of the Year Award & Scottish First Book of the Year by a New Author
The Saltire Society
Saltire Court, 20 Castle Terrace, Edinburgh EH1 2EG
Tel: (0131) 5561836 *Fax:* (0131) 5571675
Key Personnel
Contact: Kathleen Munro
Award established in 1982 by The Saltire Society & now funded by The Scotsman. Awarded for a book of a literary nature written by an author of Scottish descent or living in Scotland, or a book which deals with the work or life of a Scot or with a Scottish problem, event or situation. The Scotsman contributes substantial monetary sums to be awarded annually.

Scottish International Open Poetry Competition
Ayshire Writers & Artists Society
Irvine, Ayrshire KA11 3BW
Mailing Address: 42 Tollerton Dr, Irvine, Ayrshire KA11 3BW

Tel: (01294) 276381
Longest running poetry competition in UK. Free entry. Open to established & aspiring poets but two IRC's required.

Andre Simon Fund Book Awards
Andre Simon Memorial Fund
5 Sion Hill Pl, Bath BA1 5SJ
Tel: (01225) 336305 *Fax:* (01225) 421862

W H Smith Young Writers' Competition
WH Smith PLC
Nations House PLC, 103 Wigmore St, London W1U 1WH
Tel: (020) 7409 3222 *Fax:* (020) 7514 9633
Web Site: www.whsmith.co.uk/awards
Established in 1959 as the Children's Literary Competition, & previously run by the 'Daily Mirror', the competition aims to encourage creativity in written English. Open to all children in the United Kingdom & of British nationality abroad, up to the age of 16 years. Ninety-three awards including cash prizes to schools & children totalling more than L7000 are made & the award-winning work is published in book form.

☆WHSmith Literary Award
WH Smith PLC
Nations House, 103 Wigmore Street, London W1H 0WH
Tel: (020) 7514 9623 *Fax:* (020) 7514 9635
Web Site: www.whsmith.co.uk/awards
Established: 1959
The prize is awarded to a work of fiction or non-fiction that makes an outstanding contribution to English literature & written by an author from The UK, The Commonwealth or The Republic of Ireland. The winner is chosen by nomination, entries are not required. Prize L10,000.

Somerset Maugham Award
Society of Authors
84 Drayton Gardens, London SW10 9SB
Tel: (020) 7373 6642 *Fax:* (020) 7373 5768
E-mail: info@societyofauthors.org
Web Site: www.societyofauthors.org
Founded 1946 by Somerset Maugham to encourage young British writers to travel abroad. Given to a promising author of a published work of poetry, fiction, criticism, biography, history, philosophy, belles lettres or travel. Candidates must be British subjects by birth & ordinarily resident in the United Kingdom & under age 35. Awards must be used for foreign travel.
Closing Date: December 20

☆Stand Magazine International Short Story Competition
Stand Magazine
Haltwhistle House, George St, Newcastle Tyne, Tyne & Wear NE4 75L
Tel: (0191) 2733280
E-mail: standsubscription@cablenet.co.uk
Key Personnel
Admin: Linda Goldsmith
Founded in 1983, & hosted by the Cheltenham Festival of Literature to encourage & promote the work of new or unknown short-story writers. Awarded biennially. First prize of L1250, further prizes totalling L1000 & runners-up prizes of one-year subscriptions to the magazine. Please send UK stamped-addressed envelope or two international reply coupons.

☆Stand Magazine Poetry Competition
Stand Magazine
Haltwhistle House, George St, Newcastle Tyne, Tyne & Wear NE4 75L
Tel: (0191) 2733280
Founded in 1996. Awarded biennially. L2500 in prizes. Offers publication to the first ten poems & have allotted a limit of 500 lines. Send a stamped addressed envelope (UK) or two international reply coupons (abroad).

James Stern Silver Pen Award for Nonfiction
English Centre of International PEN
152-156 Kentish Town Rd, London NW1 9QB
Tel: (020) 7267 9444 *Fax:* (020) 7267 9304
E-mail: enquiries@pen.org.uk
Web Site: www.pen.org.uk
Key Personnel
President: Victoria Glendinning
Executive Dir: Diana Reich
Awarded annually for a work of nonfiction written in English by an author of British nationality & published in the UK in the previous year.
Award: L1000 & a silver Dupont pen
Presented: PEN International Writers' Day

Sunday Times Small Publishers Award
The Sunday Times
One Pennington St, London E1 9XW
Tel: (020) 7782 5718 *Fax:* (020) 7782 5658
Annual award for the best independent publisher in the UK which produces between 5 & 40 titles in a calendar year.

☆Thomas Cook Daily Telegraph Travel Book Award
The Thomas Cook Group & The Daily Telegraph
Carpenter Lodge, Thorpe Wood, Peterborough PE3 6PU
Tel: (01733) 503560 *Fax:* (01733) 503596
Web Site: www.thetravelbookaward.com
Key Personnel
Contact: Joan Lee *Tel:* (01733) 503566
E-mail: joan.lee@thomascook.com
One Award: L10,000 for the travel narrative which most inspires in the reader the desire to travel. Books published Jan 1 - Dec 31 in the preceding year.
Other Sponsor(s): The Daily Telegraph

☆The Times Educational Supplement Information Book Award
Times Educational Supplement
Admiral House, 66-68 East Smithfield, London E1W 1BX
Mailing Address: PO Box 495, London E1W 2XY
Tel: (020) 7782 3000 *Fax:* (020) 7782 3200
Web Site: www.tes.co.uk

☆The Times Educational Supplement Schoolbook Award
Times Educational Supplement
Admiral House, 66-68 East Smithfield, London E1W 1BX
Mailing Address: PO Box 495, London E1W 2XY
Tel: (020) 7782 3000 *Fax:* (020) 7782 3200
Web Site: www.tes.co.uk
The Award is administered jointly by the TES & the Educational Publishers Council. There are two categories, Primary, for children ages 5-11 & Secondary, for young people ages 11-16. Prizes are to be awarded to the authors of the most outstanding schoolbooks in the subject of National Curriculum Books (subject decided each year). The category changes annually. To be eligible, books must have originated in Great Britain, final entry date usually Dec 31. No proof copies can be considered. There is no limit to the number of entries but the publishers are asked to be selective in their entries & no books may be entered simultaneously for the Schoolbook Award & the TES Information Book Awards. One copy of each entry should be sent directly to TES & to each of the judges.

Tom-Gallon Trust Award
Society of Authors
84 Drayton Gardens, London SW10 9SB
Tel: (020) 7373 6642 *Fax:* (020) 7373 5768
E-mail: info@societyofauthors.org
Web Site: www.societyofauthors.org
Founded 1943. This prize of not more than L1000 is awarded biennially to short story writers of limited means. Entrants must submit a list of already published fiction, one published or unpublished short story, & a brief statement of their financial position & willingness to devote substantial time to writing fiction as soon as they are financially able.
Closing Date: September 30

☆The Betty Trask Awards
Society of Authors
84 Drayton Gardens, London SW10 9SB
Tel: (020) 7373 6642 *Fax:* (020) 7373 5768
E-mail: info@societyofauthors.org
Web Site: www.societyofauthors.org
Established in 1983, the Awards are for the benefit of authors under 35 years of age who are Commonwealth citizens & are given for a first novel (published or unpublished) of a romantic or traditional nature. First awarded in 1984 the total value of prizes is L25,000. All winners are required to use the money for a period or periods of foreign travel with a view to increasing their experience & knowledge for future literary benefit.
Closing Date: January 31

Travelling Scholarships
Society of Authors
84 Drayton Gardens, London SW10 9SB
Tel: (020) 7373 6642 *Fax:* (020) 7373 5768
E-mail: info@societyofauthors.org
Web Site: www.societyofauthors.org
Established in 1944 to enable British Writers to keep in touch with their colleagues abroad. Honorary Scholarships are awarded for a body of work & submissions are not accepted.

VER Poets Open Competition
VER Poets
Haycroft, 61-63 Chiswell Green Lane, St Albans, Herts AL2 3AL
Tel: (01727) 867005
Key Personnel
President: John Cotton
Vice President: John Mole
Chairman: Ray Badman
Editor & Organiser: May Badman
Established: 1966
Award: Total Prizes L1,000 (as L500, L300, 2x L100) & winner & selected included in Anthology
Closing Date: April 30
Presented: St Albans, June 21, 2003

Vondel Translation Prize
Society of Authors - Translators Association
84 Drayton Gardens, London SW10 9SB
Tel: (020) 7373 6642 *Fax:* (020) 7373 5768
E-mail: info@societyofauthors.org
Web Site: www.societyofauthors.org
The biennial prize is for translations of works into English of Dutch & Flemish works of literary merit & general interest. The translation must have been first published in the UK or the USA. The prize is worth L2000 & (subject to confirmation).
Closing Date: December 20

Walford Award
Chartered Institute of Library & Information Professionals
7 Ridgmount St, London WC1E 7AE

UNITED KINGDOM

Tel: (020) 7255 0650 *Fax:* (020) 7255 0501
E-mail: marketing@cilip.org.uk
Web Site: www.cilip.org.uk
Presented to an individual who has made a sustained & continual contribution to the science & art of bibliography in the UK. The nominee need not be a resident in the UK.
Award: 500 UK pounds & certificate

Wheatley Medal
Chartered Institute of Library & Information Professionals
7 Ridgmount St, London WC1E 7AE
Tel: (020) 7255 0650 *Fax:* (020) 7255 0501
E-mail: marketing@cilip.org.uk
Web Site: www.cilip.org.uk
Established: 1961
Presented in association with The Society of Indexers, for an outstanding printed index published in the UK between Jan 1, 2000 & April 27, 2001. Indexes will be judged on clarity, comprehensiveness, choice of terms & headings, use of cross reference, avoidance of strings of undifferentiated page references, layout, presentation, overall impact of the index & relevance to text.
Award: 500 UK Pounds, certificate, gold medal
Presented: Awards ceremony, Sept

Whitbread Book Awards
Booksellers Association of the United Kingdom & Ireland
Minister House, 272 Vauxhall Bridge Rd, London SW1V 1BA
Tel: (020) 7834 5477 *Fax:* (020) 7834 8812
E-mail: mail@booksellers.org.uk
Web Site: www.whitbread-bookawards.co.uk
Key Personnel
Contact: Denise Bayat
Established: 1971
The awards celebrate & promote the best contemporary British writing. Judged in two stages & offering a total of L50,000 prize money. The awards are open to five categories: Novel, Biography, Poetry & Children's Book of the Year. The Novel, First Novel, Biography & Poetry Awards are judged by a panel of three judges & the winner of each category receives an award of L5,000. Three adult judges & two young judges select a shortlist of four books for the Whitbread Children's Book of the Year. The final judges then select the Whitbread Children's Book of the Year, worth L5,000 & then go on to choose the Whitbread Book of the Year from the winners of the Novel, First Novel, Biography & Poetry Awards & the winner of the Whitbread Children's Book of the Year. The winner receives a check for L25,000. Writers must have lived in Great Britain & Ireland for three or more years. Submissions must be received from publishers. Closing date is early July.

Whitfield Prize
Royal Historical Society
University College London, Gower St, London WC1E 6BT
Tel: (020) 7387 7532 *Fax:* (020) 7387 7532
E-mail: royalhistsoc@ucl.ac.uk
Web Site: www.rhs.ac.uk
Key Personnel
Executive Secretary: Joy McCarthy
For a new book on British history.
Award: L1000 awarded annually

John Whiting Award
Arts Council of England
14 Great Peter St, London SW1P 3NQ
Tel: (020) 7973 6431 *Fax:* (020) 7973 6983
Web Site: www.artscouncil.org.uk

Key Personnel
Assistant Drama Officer: Jemima Lee
E-mail: jemima.lee@artscouncil.org.uk
Award is intended to help future careers & enhance reputations of British playwrights & to draw to public attention the importance of writers in contemporary theatre.

Meyer Whitworth Award
Arts Council of England
14 Great Peter St, London SW1P 3NQ
Tel: (020) 7973 6431 *Fax:* (020) 7973 6983
Web Site: www.artscouncil.org.uk
Intended to help further the careers of UK playwrights who are not yet established.

Wilkins International Memorial Poetry Prize
Birmingham & Midland Institute
9 Margaret St, Birmingham B3 3BS
Tel: (0121) 236 3591 *Fax:* (0121) 212 4577
Web Site: www.bmi.org.uk
Key Personnel
Administrator & General Secretary: Philip Fisher
Established in 1983. The poems submitted must be in English, not more than 40 lines in length, unpublished & should not have been accepted for publication elsewhere or entered in any other poetry competition. There is a lower age limit of 16 years.
Award: Total Prizes L1000, 1st Prize L500
Closing Date: August 31
Presented: Year 2000

Winifred Holtby Memorial Prize
Royal Society of Literature of the United Kingdom
Somerset House, Strand, London WC2R 1LA
Tel: (020) 7845 4676 *Fax:* (020) 7845 4679
E-mail: info@rslit.org
Key Personnel
Assistant Secretary: Julia Abel Smith *Tel:* (020) 7845 4677 *E-mail:* julia@rslit.org
Established: 1966
Founded in 1966 by Vera Brittain in memory of Winifred Holtby. An annual award for the best regional novel of its year; if no suitable work of fiction can be found the jury may consider works of nonfiction. Submissions by publishers, not by individual authors. Award Type is for regional fiction.
Closing Date: Dec 15, 2002 (entries are not accepted until mid-October)
Presented: St Bride Institute, London, June 2003

Wolfson History Prize
The Wolfson Foundation
8 Queen Anne St, London W1G 9LD
Tel: (020) 7323 5730 *Fax:* (020) 7323 3241
Key Personnel
Prize Administrator: Yee-Lin Tan *Tel:* (020) 7323 5730 ext 213 *E-mail:* yee-lin.tan@wolfson.org.uk
Established: 1972
One or two awards totaling up to L30,000 are made annually to British authors of historical writing which is considered both scholarly & accessible to the general reader.

Writers' Bursaries
Arts Council of England
14 Great Peter St, London SW1P 3NQ
Tel: (020) 7973 6431 *Fax:* (020) 7973 6983
Web Site: www.artscouncil.org.uk
Fifteen awards of L7000: open to published writers resident in England who need funds to complete a work in progress.

☆Yorkshire Post Book of the Year Award
Yorkshire Post Newspapers Ltd
Wellington St, Leeds LS1 1RF
Mailing Address: PO Box 168, Leeds LS1 1RF

Tel: (0532) 432701 *Fax:* (0532) 2388909
Key Personnel
Organizer: Margaret Brown
Instituted 1964 for the best book published each year in the United Kingdom called 'Book of the Year' Award. Translations, reissues & works of a strictly scientific or technical nature are excluded. In addition, there is a Best First Work Award for a new author. There are also special annual awards for books selected to advance the popular appreciation of art & music.

United States

☆American-Scandinavian Foundation Translation Prize
American-Scandinavian Foundation
58 Park Ave, New York, NY 10016
Tel: 212-879-9779 *Fax:* 212-879-2301; 212-249-3444
E-mail: asf@amscan.org
Web Site: www.amscan.org
Key Personnel
Editor: Adrienne Gyongy *E-mail:* agyongy@amscan.org
Initiated in 1980 by 'Scandinavian Review' (three per year) to bring best of contemporary Scandinavian literature to American readers. There is a prize of US $2,000, either for poetry or fiction, in addition to publication. Awarded annually for the best translation of work by a Danish, Finnish, Icelandic, Norwegian or Swedish author born after 1800; for more details request rules.
Closing Date: Postmark deadline of June 1

☆The Bologna New Media Prize
Children's Software Revue & The Bologna Children's Book Fair
44 Main St, Flemington, NJ 08822
Tel: 908-284-0404 *Fax:* 908-284-0405
Web Site: www.bolognanewmediaprize.com
Key Personnel
Editor: Warren Buckleitner *E-mail:* buckleit@aol.com
Established: 1997
Children's interactive media.
Closing Date: Annually December 15
Presented: Bologna, Italy, Annually in April

☆Children's Book Award
International Reading Association
800 Barksdale Rd, Newark, DE 19714
Mailing Address: PO Box 8139, Newark, DE 19714-8139
Tel: 302-731-1600 *Fax:* 302-731-1057
Key Personnel
Public Information Associate: Janet Butler *Tel:* 302-731-1600 ext 293 *E-mail:* jbutler@reading.org
Established 1974. Awarded annually for a first or second book (any language) to authors who show unusual promise in the children's/young adult book field. There are three categories: Primary (ages preschool - 8), Intermediate (Ages 9-13) & Young Adult (Ages 14-17). Entries in languages other than English must include a one-page abstract in English & a translation into English of one chapter or similar selection.
Award: Four awards of US $500 for fist or second published book
Presented: San Francisco, 2002

☆Clarence L Holte Literary Prize
Phelps-Stokes Fund

74 Trinity Place, Suite 1303, New York, NY 10006
Tel: 212-619-8100 Fax: 212-619-5108
Key Personnel
Contact: Dr Wilbert LeMelle
Founded in 1977. Awarded for published writings of excellence in literature & the humanities making important contributions to the cultural heritage of Africa & the African Diaspora. The prize is awarded biennially.
Presented: Year 2000

☆Hugo Awards
World Science Fiction Society
PO Box 426159, Kendall Square Station, Cambridge, MA 02142
Web Site: www.wsfa.org
Established 1953 as Science Fiction Achievement Awards for the best science fiction writing in several categories. Chrome-plated rocket ship model awarded annually.

☆IBC International Book Award
International Book Committee (IBC)
800 Barksdale Rd, Newark, DE 19714
Mailing Address: PO Box 8139, Newark, DE 19714
Tel: 302-731-1600 Fax: 302-731-1057
Key Personnel
Chairman: Alan Farstrup
Vice Chairman: Leena Maissen
Established: 1972
Founded by book professionals as an outgrowth of the Support Committee for the Unesco International Book Year, the award is granted annually to outstanding persons or groups for their contribution to the promotion of books & reading internationally.

☆The Irish American Cultural Institute Literary Awards
The Irish American Cultural Institute
One Lackawanna Pl, Morristown, NJ
Tel: 973-605-1991 Fax: 973-605-8875
E-mail: irishway@aol.com
Established: 1966
For writers in the Irish or English language. Butler awards total US $10,000 for each language in alternate years & there is a US $5000 O'Shaughnessy award for poetry. There is also funding to primary research on Irish-American themes. No application procedure.
Closing Date: Fall
Presented: Fall of the following year

☆The Kiriyama Pacific Rim Book Prize
The Kiriyama Pacific Rim Institute
650 Delancey St, Suite 101, San Francisco, CA 94107
Tel: 415-777-1763 Fax: 415-422-5933
E-mail: admin@pacificrimvoices.org
Web Site: www.pacificrimvoices.org
Key Personnel
Project Coordinator: Jeannine Cuevas
Established: 1996
Annual prize for the book judged to have contributed most to understanding among Pacific Rim countries. Books must be published in English, either originating in English or translated into English. Books published between October 31, 2000 & October 31, 2001 are eligible for the 2001 prize. Open to nonfiction or fiction of any genre.
Award: $30,000 US ($15,000 to winning authors, fiction & nonfiction)
Closing Date: July 3
Presented: Annually in late October/early November

☆Neustadt International Prize for Literature
World Literature Today
University of Oklahoma, 110 Monnet Hall, Norman, OK 73019-4033
Tel: 405-325-4531 Fax: 405-325-7495
Key Personnel
Executive Dir: Robert Con Davis-Undiano
'World Literature Today', an international literary quarterly, established in 1969 a biennial award for distinguished & continuing artistic achievement in the fields of poetry, drama or fiction. A new international jury of twelve is appointed for each successive award by the editor in consultation with the editorial board. Each juror presents one candidate for the prize. A majority (seven) of the jury must be present for the deliberations & the final voting. Representative selections of a candidate's work must be available to the jury in either French or English translation. Announcement of the winner is made in February or March, & the award is officially presented at The University of Oklahoma, Norman, Oklahoma, every other year. The prize is an award certificate, a replica of an eagle's feather in silver, & US $50,000. 'World Literature Today' dedicates one issue to the recipient. The University of Oklahoma Press will seriously consider the publication of a book by or on the winner. Prize not open to application.

☆Pegasus Prize for Literature
Mobil Corporation
3225 Gallows Rd, Fairfax, VA 22037
Tel: 703-846-3000 Fax: 703-846-4669
Established in 1977 & sponsored by Mobil Oil Corporation affiliates to encourage the recognition of distinguished works from countries whose literature is rarely translated into English. Usually awarded every two years. Prize of approximately US $3000, a medal, translation into English & publication by the Louisiana State University Press (USA).

Venezuela

☆Romulo Gallegos Novel Prize
National Council For Culture
Torre Norte piso 16 - Centro Simon Bolivar, Apdo 50995, Caracas
The prize was established in 1965 by the National Institute of Culture & Fine Arts of the Republic of Venezuela. Originally instituted to mark the 80th anniversary of the birth of the illustrious author Romulo Gallegos, which was celebrated in August 1964, the first award was made in 1967, the 400th anniversary of the founding of Caracas - brthplace of the novelist. Competition is open to any writer from Latin America, Spain or the Philippines whose novel is written in Spanish & has been published originally in one of the countries of the above designated areas. The amount of the prize is approximately $22,223 & will be granted every five years. Enquiries to Centro de Estudios Latinoamericanos 'Romulo Gallegos', Apdo 75667, Caracas 1070A, Venezuela.

National Prize for Literature
Concejo Nacional de la Cultura (CONAC)
Torre Norte, piso 16, Centro Simon Bolivar, Apdo 50995, Caracas
Tel: (02) 914611
Awarded annually to the best Venezuelan author. 30,000 bolivares. Also includes contestants in narrative prose and essays.

Zimbabwe

The Literature Bureau Annual Literary Award
The Literature Bureau
Ministry of Education, Sport & Culture, Causeway, Harare
Mailing Address: PO Box CY121, Causeway, Harare
Tel: (04) 333812
500 Zimbabwe dollars for the best works in Shona & Ndebele. Most genres, including translations, qualify for entry.

Book Trade Calendar

Calendar of Book Trade & Promotional Events—Alphabetical Index of Sponsors

Adelaide Festival
Adelaide Writers' Week
  February 2004, pg 1441

Advanstar Communications
AIIM 2003 Show & Conference
  April 2003, pg 1433

Advanstar Expositions
ON DEMAND
  April 2003, pg 1434

Advertising Research Foundation
Advertising Research Foundation Annual Convention Research Infoplex
  April 2003, pg 1432

ALA, see American Library Association (ALA)

American Association of Advertising Agencies
American Association of Advertising Agencies Management Conference & Annual Meeting
  April 2003, pg 1433
Creative Conference
  November 2002, pg 1428
  November 2004, pg 1444
Media Conference & Trade Show
  March 2003, pg 1432

American Booksellers Association
ABA Convention & Trade Exhibit
  May 2003, pg 1434

American Forest & Paper Association
Paper Week
  March 2003, pg 1432

American Institute of Graphic Arts (AIGA)
Business & Design Conference
  October 2002, pg 1427
  Autumn 2004, pg 1443
National Design Conference
  October 2003, pg 1440

American Library Association (ALA)
American Library Association Annual Conference
  June 2003, pg 1436
  June 2004, pg 1443
  June 2005, pg 1445
  June 2006, pg 1446
American Library Association Mid-Winter Meeting
  January 2003, pg 1429
  January 2004, pg 1441
National Library Week
  April 2003, pg 1434
  April 2004, pg 1442
  April 2005, pg 1445
  April 2006, pg 1446
  April 2007, pg 1447

American Medical Writers Association
American Medical Writers Association Annual Conference
  October 2002, pg 1427
  September 2003, pg 1438
  October 2004, pg 1444

American Schools of Oriental Research
American Academy of Religion
  November 2002, pg 1428
  November 2003, pg 1440
  November 2004, pg 1444
  November 2005, pg 1446
  November 2006, pg 1446
  November 2007, pg 1447

American Society for Quality
Annual Quality Congress
  May 2003, pg 1434
Quest for Excellence
  March 2003, pg 1432

American Translators Association (ATA)
American Translators Association Annual Conference
  November 2002, pg 1428
  November 2003, pg 1440

Amsterdam RAI
Amsterdam International Printing Allied Industries Trade Fair (Grafivak)
  May 2003, pg 1434

Antiquarian Booksellers' Association of America
International Book Fair/Los Angeles Book Fair
  February 2004, pg 1441
International Book Fair/San Francisco Book Fair
  February 2003, pg 1430

ANZAAB, see The Australian & New Zealand Association of Antiquarian Booksellers

Arbeitsgemeinschaft des Blindenschrift-Druckereien und Bibliotheken (AG BDB)
Association of Braille Publishing Houses & Libraries Annual Conference
  Autumn 2002, pg 1427
  Autumn 2003, pg 1438

ARLIS/UK & Ireland, The Art Libraries Society
ARLIS/UK & Ireland Annual Conference
  July 2003, pg 1437

Ars Polona - Warsaw International Book Fair Office
Warsaw International Book Fair
  May 2003, pg 1436

Associated Collegiate Press (ACP)
National College Media Convention
  October 2002, pg 1427
  November 2003, pg 1441
  November 2004, pg 1444

Associated Writing Programs (AWP)
Associated Writing Programs Annual Conference
  March 2003, pg 1431
  March 2004, pg 1442

Association Expositions & Services
BookExpo America (BEA)
  May 2003, pg 1434

Association of American Publishers Inc (AAP)
Association of American Publishers Annual Meeting
  February 2003, pg 1430
Association of American Publishers Annual Meeting for Small & Independent Publishers
  February 2003, pg 1430
Association of American Publishers Professional & Scholarly Publishing Divison Annual Meeting
  February 2003, pg 1430
Association of American Publishers School Division Annual Meeting
  February 2003, pg 1430

Association of American University Presses (AAUP)
Association of American University Presses Annual Meeting
  June 2003, pg 1436

Association of Directory Publishers
Association of Directory Publishers Annual Meeting
  Spring 2003, pg 1431

Association of Yugoslav Publishers & Booksellers
Belgrade International Book Fair
  October 2002, pg 1427
  October 2003, pg 1439

Ausstellungs-und Messe-GmbH des Borsenvereins des Deutschen Buchhandels
Frankfurt Book Fair
  October 2002, pg 1427
  October 2003, pg 1440
  October 2004, pg 1444
  October 2005, pg 1445
  October 2006, pg 1446

The Australian & New Zealand Association of Antiquarian Booksellers
ANZAAB Book Fair
  November 2002, pg 1428

1415

ALPHABETICAL INDEX OF SPONSORS

BASH, see Booksellers Association of the United Kingdom & Ireland

BIBF Management Office, CNPIEC
Beijing International Book Fair
May 2003, pg 1434

Bibliographical Society of Canada/La Societe bibliographique du Canada
Bibliographical Society of Canada/La Societe bibliographique du Canada Annual Meeting
June 2003, pg 1436

Binding Industries Association International
Binding Industries Association International Conference
April 2003, pg 1433

Bock.be
De Boekenbeurs
October 2002, pg 1427
October 2003, pg 1439

Bok & Bibliotek
Goteborg International Book Fair
September 2003, pg 1438
September 2004, pg 1444

BolognaFiere
Bologna Children's Book Fair
April 2003, pg 1433

Book Manufacturers' Institute Inc (BMI)
BMI Annual Conference
November 2002, pg 1428
October 2003, pg 1439
BMI Management Conference
April 2003, pg 1433

Bookbuilders West
Annual Bookbuilders West Book Show
December 2002, pg 1429
BookTech East 2003
March 2003, pg 1431

Booksellers Association of the United Kingdom & Ireland
Booksellers Association of Great Britain & Ireland Annual Conference
April 2003, pg 1433

British & Irish Association of Law Librarians
British & Irish Association of Law Librarians Annual Conference
June 2003, pg 1436

The Bronte Society
The Bronte Society Annual General Meeting
June 2003, pg 1436

Bulgarian Book Publishers Association
Sofia International Book Fair
December 2003, pg 1441

Business & Industrial Trade Fairs Ltd
Graphic Arts
August 2003, pg 1438
Print & Pack Expo
August 2003, pg 1438

Canadian Library Association (CLA)
Canadian Library Association Annual Convention & Tradeshow
June 2003, pg 1436

Canon Communications
Eastpack: The Power of Packaging
June 2003, pg 1436
SouthPack
April 2003, pg 1434
Westpack
February 2003, pg 1431

Catholic Press Association of the US & Canada
Catholic Press Association of the US and Canada Annual Convention
May 2003, pg 1434

CBA
CBA Expo 2003
January 2003, pg 1429
CBA International Convention
July 2003, pg 1437

Chartered Institute of Library & Information Professionals
Umbrella 2003
July 2003, pg 1437

The Children's Book Council Inc (CBC)
Children's Book Week
November 2003, pg 1440
November 2004, pg 1444
November 2005, pg 1446
Young People's Poetry Week
April 2003, pg 1434

Christian Booksellers Convention Ltd
Christian Booksellers Convention
March 2003, pg 1432

Church & Synagogue Library Association
Church & Synagogue Library Association Conference
July 2003, pg 1437
July 2004, pg 1443

Ciana Ltd
London Remainder & Promotional Book Fair
January 2003, pg 1430

CILIP, see Chartered Institute of Library & Information Professionals

Colorado Center for the Book
Rocky Mountain Book Festival
Spring 2003, pg 1431
Spring 2004, pg 1442

Consejo Nacional para la Cultura y las Artes
FILIJ/International Book Fair for Children & Youth
November 2002, pg 1428

Deutsche Gesellschaft fur Informationswissenschaft und informationspraxis eV
DGI Annual Meeting & Online Conference
Spring 2003, pg 1431

The Direct Marketing Association Inc (The DMA)
DMA Annual Conference & Exhibition
October 2003, pg 1439

Distripress
Distripress Annual Congress
September 2003, pg 1438
September 2004, pg 1444

CALENDAR OF BOOK TRADE

Dog Writers' Association of America Inc (DWAA)
Dog Writers' Association of America Annual Meeting
February 2003, pg 1430

The Dorothy L Sayers Society
The Dorothy L Sayers Society Annual Convention
August 2003, pg 1438

Edinburgh International Book Festival
Edinburgh International Book Festival
August 2003, pg 1438

Educational Computer Conferences Inc
Technology, Reading & Learning Difficulties
January 2003, pg 1430

English Association
English Association Semiannual Teachers' Conference
October 2003, pg 1439

European Association of Directory Publishers
European Association of Directory Publishers Annual Conference
September 2003, pg 1438

Evangelical Christian Publishers Association
Building Governmental Relationships
November 2003, pg 1440
General Trade Publishing & Retailing
May 2004, pg 1442
Introducing ECPA Publishing University
November 2004, pg 1444
Truth and Consequences
April 2003, pg 1434
Working Together Building the Business Ministering Effectively
November 2002, pg 1429

Evangelical Press Association (EPA)
Evangelical Press Association Annual Conference
May 2003, pg 1435

Expo Source
Internet Expo Printing & Graphics Arts Expo
May 2003, pg 1435

Federacion de Gremios de Editores de Espana (FGEE) (Spanish Publishers Association)
LIBER Feria Internacional del Libro
October 2002, pg 1427
October 2003, pg 1440
September 2004, pg 1444
October 2005, pg 1445
September 2006, pg 1446

Federation of Children's Book Groups
Federation of Children's Book Groups Annual Conference
April 2003, pg 1433

Feria Internacional del Libro
Feria Internacional del Libro
November 2002, pg 1428
November 2003, pg 1441
November 2004, pg 1444

Football Writers Association of America
Football Writers Association of America Annual Meeting
January 2003, pg 1429

Fundacion El Libro
Buenos Aires International Book Fair
April 2003, pg 1433
Fundacion El Libro Professionals' Meeting
April 2003, pg 1433

ALPHABETICAL INDEX OF SPONSORS

Garden Writers Association of America
Garden Writers Association of America Meeting & Symposium
August 2003, pg 1438

General Directorate of International Book Exhibitions & Fairs
Moscow International Book Fair
September 2003, pg 1439
September 2004, pg 1444

General Egyptian Book Organization
Cairo International Book Fair
November 2002, pg 1428

Ghana Trade Fair Co Ltd
Ghana International Book Fair
November 2002, pg 1428
Autumn 2004, pg 1443

Graphic Arts Show Company
Graphic Arts/The Charlotte Show
March 2003, pg 1432
Gutenberg Festival
May 2003, pg 1435
June 2004, pg 1443

Gravure Association of America Inc
Gravure Association of America Convention
May 2003, pg 1435

Guadalajara International Book Fair
Guadalajara International Book Fair
November 2002, pg 1428
November 2003, pg 1441

Gutenberg-Gesellschaft eV
Gutenberg Gesellschaft Annual General Meeting
June 2003, pg 1436
June 2004, pg 1443

Hong Kong Trade Development Council
Hong Kong Book Fair
July 2003, pg 1437
July 2004, pg 1443
July 2005, pg 1445

IAML, see International Association of Music Libraries, Archives & Documentation Centres

IBBY, see International Board on Books for Young People (IBBY)

IDE Alliance
PRIMEX 2003, Print Media Executive Conference
February 2003, pg 1431
Spectrum 2003
September 2003, pg 1439

IDG World Expo
Macworld Conference & Expo
January 2003, pg 1430
July 2003, pg 1437

IFLA, see International Federation of Library Associations & Institutions (IFLA)

INCHEBA as
Biblioteka International Book Fair
November 2002, pg 1428

Information Today, Inc
InfoToday
May 2003, pg 1435

Institute of Printing
Institute of Printing National Annual General Meeting
May 2003, pg 1435

Instituto Tecnologico y de Estudios Superiores de Monterrey
Monterrey International Book Fair
October 2002, pg 1427
October 2003, pg 1440

Inter American Press Association (IAPA)
Inter American Press Association General Assembly
October 2002, pg 1427
October 2003, pg 1440
Inter American Press Association Mid-Year Meeting
March 2003, pg 1432

International Association of Business Communicators (IABC)
International Association of Business Communicators Conference
June 2003, pg 1436

International Association of Music Libraries, Archives & Documentation Centres
International Association of Music Libraries, Archives & Documentation Centres Conference
July 2003, pg 1437
August 2004, pg 1443

International Board on Books for Young People (IBBY)
International Board on Books for Young People Biennial Congress
September 2004, pg 1444
September 2006, pg 1446
International Children's Book Day
April 2003, pg 1433
April 2004, pg 1442

International Council on Archives (Conseil International des Archives)
International Congress on Archives
August 2004, pg 1443

International Electronic Publishing Research Centre Ltd (IEPRC)
Electronic Publishing International
June 2003, pg 1436

International Federation of Film Archives (Federation Internationale des Archives du Film)
FIAF Congress
June 2003, pg 1436
April 2004, pg 1442
April 2005, pg 1445
April 2006, pg 1446

International Federation of Library Associations & Institutions (IFLA)
IFLA General Conference & Council
August 2003, pg 1438
August 2004, pg 1443
August 2005, pg 1445
August 2006, pg 1446

International Newspaper Financial Executives
International Newspaper Financial Executives Annual Conference
June 2003, pg 1436
June 2004, pg 1443
June 2005, pg 1445

International PEN
World Congress of International PEN
November 2003, pg 1441

International Plate Printers', Die Stampers' & Engravers' Union of North America
International Plate Printers', Die Stampers' & Engravers' Union of North America Mini Meeting
June 2003, pg 1437

International Prepress Association
International Prepress Association Marketing & Sales Conference
February 2003, pg 1431

International Publishers Association
IPA Congress
June 2004, pg 1443

International Reading Association
International Reading Association Annual Convention
May 2003, pg 1435

Internationale Vereinigung fuer Geschichte und Gegenwart der Druckkunst eV, see Gutenberg-Gesellschaft eV

Jerusalem International Book Fair
Jerusalem International Book Fair
March 2003, pg 1432

Jewish Book Council
Jewish Book Month
November 2002, pg 1429

Key3Media Events
COMDEX/Fall
November 2002, pg 1428
November 2003, pg 1441
Seybold Seminars
September 2003, pg 1439

Learned Information (Europe) Ltd
Online Information
December 2002, pg 1429
December 2003, pg 1441

Leipziger Messe GmbH, Projektteam Buchmesse
Leipzig Book Fair
March 2003, pg 1432
March 2004, pg 1442

Library Association of Alberta
Alberta Library Conference
April 2003, pg 1433
April 2004, pg 1442

Luckwaldt Messen
Quod Libet/International Antiquarian Book Fair & Artists Books
May 2003, pg 1435
May 2004, pg 1442

Media Central
Folio:Midwest
March 2003, pg 1432
The Folio:Show
October 2002, pg 1427
Folio:West
April 2003, pg 1433

Miami Book Fair International
Miami Book Fair International
November 2002, pg 1429
November 2003, pg 1441

Modern Language Association of America (MLA)
Modern Language Association of America Annual Convention
December 2002, pg 1429

NASW, see National Association of Science Writers (NASW)

ALPHABETICAL INDEX OF SPONSORS

National Association of College Stores (NACS)
CAMEX
   March 2003, pg 1432
   February 2004, pg 1441

National Association of Printing Ink Manufacturers
National Association of Printing Ink Manufacturers Annual Convention
   April 2003, pg 1433
   March 2004, pg 1442

National Association of Science Writers (NASW)
National Association of Science Writers Annual Meeting
   February 2003, pg 1431
   February 2004, pg 1441

National Federation of Press Women Inc (NFPW)
National Federation of Press Women National Conference
   September 2003, pg 1439

National Newspaper Association
National Newspaper Association Annual Convention & Trade Show
   October 2003, pg 1440
   October 2004, pg 1444
National Newspaper Association Annual Government Affairs Conference
   March 2003, pg 1432

The National Press Foundation
National Press Foundation Annual Awards Dinner
   February 2003, pg 1431

New Atlantic Independent Booksellers Association (NAIBA)
New Atlantic Independent Booksellers Association Annual Trade Show
   Autumn 2003, pg 1438

New York Is Book Country
New York is Book Country
   September 2003, pg 1439

Newsletter & Electronic Publishers Association
International Newsletter & Specialized - Information Conference
   June 2003, pg 1436
Newsletter Marketing Conference
   December 2002, pg 1429

Newspaper Association of America (NAA)
Newspaper Association of America Annual Convention
   April 2003, pg 1434
   April 2004, pg 1442
   April 2005, pg 1445
NEXPO®
   June 2003, pg 1437
   June 2004, pg 1443

North American Agricultural Journalists
North American Agricultural Journalists Spring Meeting
   April 2003, pg 1434

NPES The Association for Suppliers of Printing, Publishing and Converting Technologies
NPES The Association for Suppliers of Printing, Publishing and Converting Technologies Annual Conference
   October 2002, pg 1428
   October 2003, pg 1440

Outdoor Writers Association of America
Outdoor Writers Association of America Annual Conference
   June 2003, pg 1437

Pacific Printing & Imaging Association
Pacific Printing & Imaging Association Northwest Regional Industry Event
   Spring 2003, pg 1431

Packaging Machinery Manufacturers Institute
PACK EXPO
   November 2002, pg 1429
   October 2003, pg 1440

Penton Media
Internet World UK
   June 2003, pg 1437

Periodical Writers' Association of Canada
Periodical Writers' Association of Canada Annual General Meeting
   May 2003, pg 1435

Photographic Society of America Inc (PSA)
PSA International Conference of Photography
   September 2003, pg 1439

Post Newsweek Tech Media Group
FOSE
   April 2003, pg 1433

Poznan International Fair Ltd
Infosystem Fairs
   April 2003, pg 1433
Poligrafia
   April 2003, pg 1434

Premedia Business
The National Center for Database Marketing
   December 2002, pg 1429

PrintImage International
The Quick Print Show
   March 2003, pg 1432

Printing Association of Florida Inc
Graphics of the Americas
   January 2003, pg 1430

Printing Industries of America Inc
Print Sales & Marketing Conference
   June 2003, pg 1437

Publishers Association of the South (PAS)
Publishers Association of the South Fall Conference & Annual Meeting
   September 2003, pg 1439
Publishers Winter Conclave
   January 2003, pg 1430

Reed Exhibition Companies
Asia International Book Fair/International Library Expo
   April 2004, pg 1442
Book Expo Canada
   June 2003, pg 1436
EM: Electronic Book & Multimedia Fair
   April 2003, pg 1433
Pacprint
   May 2005, pg 1445
Printex 03
   May 2003, pg 1435
TIBF: Tokyo International Book Fair
   April 2003, pg 1434

CALENDAR OF BOOK TRADE

Reed Exhibition Companies (UK)
London Book Fair
   March 2003, pg 1432
Northprint
   May 2003, pg 1435

Reed Messe Salzburg
Dataprint
   April 2003, pg 1433

Reed Midem
MILIA: The World's Interactive Content Marketplace
   February 2003, pg 1431
WEM: The World Education Market
   May 2003, pg 1436

Reed-OIP
Salon du Livre de Jeunesse Childrens Book Fair
   November 2002, pg 1429
Salon du Livre: Paris Book Fair
   March 2003, pg 1432

Reed Tradex Co Ltd
Thai Print: The International Trade Exhibition for Printing Machinery, Graphic Art Equipment, Pre-Press Solutions, Materials & Supplies
   September 2003, pg 1439

Research & Engineering Council of the Graphic Arts Industry Inc
Binding, Finishing & Distribution Seminar
   April 2003, pg 1433

Romance Writers of America
RWA Annual National Conference
   July 2003, pg 1437
   July 2004, pg 1443
   July 2005, pg 1445
   July 2006, pg 1446

SABEW, see Society of American Business Editors & Writers Inc

Salon du Livre de Montreal
Salon du Livre de Montreal
   November 2002, pg 1429
   November 2003, pg 1441

School Library Association
School Library Association Annual Conference
   June 2003, pg 1437
   June 2004, pg 1443

Science Fiction Research Association Inc
Science Fiction Research Association Annual Conference
   June 2003, pg 1437

Small Press Center
Small Press Book Fair
   March 2003, pg 1432
   March 2004, pg 1442

Small Publishers Association of North America (SPAN)
SPAN Conference
   October 2002, pg 1428
   October 2003, pg 1440

Societe de Foires Internationales de Luxembourg, Societe Anonyme
Antiques & Fine Arts Exhibition/Luxembourg Book Festival
   March 2003, pg 1431
   March 2004, pg 1442
   March 2005, pg 1445

& PROMOTIONAL EVENTS

Society for Imaging Science & Technology (IS&T)
Color Imaging Conference - Color Science Systems & Applications
November 2002, pg 1428
November 2003, pg 1440
DPP 2003 - International Conference on Digital Production Printing
May 2003, pg 1435
NIP 19: The 19th International Congress on Digital Printing Technologies
September 2003, pg 1439
The PICS Conference
May 2003, pg 1435

Society for Scholarly Publishing
Society for Scholarly Publishing Annual Meeting
May 2003, pg 1435

Society of American Business Editors & Writers Inc
Society of American Business Editors & Writers Annual Convention and Exhibition
April 2003, pg 1434

Society of Children's Book Writers & Illustrators (SCBWI)
International Conference on Writing & Illustrating for Children
February 2003, pg 1430
August 2003, pg 1438

The Society of Professional Journalists
Society of Professional Journalists National Convention
September 2003, pg 1439

South African Booksellers Association
South African Booksellers Association Annual Conference
August 2003, pg 1438

Southeast Booksellers Association (SEBA)
Southeast Booksellers Association Annual Meeting & Trade Show
September 2003, pg 1439

Southern California Writers' Conference San Diego
Southern California Writers' Conference San Diego
February 2003, pg 1431

Spanish Evangelical Publishers Association (SEPA)/Associacion de Editores Evangelicos and Editorial Unilit
Exposicion de Literatura Cristiana (EXPOLIT) Book Fair
February 2003, pg 1430
May 2003, pg 1435
May 2004, pg 1442

Special Libraries Association (SLA)
Special Libraries Association Annual Conference
June 2003, pg 1437
June 2004, pg 1443
Special Libraries Association Winter Meeting & Education Conference
January 2003, pg 1430
January 2004, pg 1441

SPIE - The International Society for Optical Engineering
IS&T/SPIE Electronic Imaging Science & Technology
January 2003, pg 1430

Technical Association of the Pulp & Paper Industry (TAPPI)
AICC/TAPPI SuperCorrExpo® 2004
November 2004, pg 1444
China Paper
November 2002, pg 1428
Corrugated Containers Conference & CorrExpo
October 2002, pg 1427
October 2003, pg 1439
Fall Technical Conference & Trade Fair
October 2003, pg 1440
October 2004, pg 1444
Spring Technical Conference & Trade Fair
May 2003, pg 1435
TAPPI 8th Advanced Coating Fundamentals Symposium
May 2003, pg 1435

Texas Graphic Arts Educational Foundation
Southwestern Graphics
June 2003, pg 1437

Texas Outdoor Writers Association
Texas Outdoor Writers Association Annual Conference
February 2003, pg 1431

Trade Promotion Services Ltd
Spring Fair Birmingham
February 2003, pg 1431

Tueyap Tuem Fuarcilik Yapim AS
Istanbul Book Fair
November 2003, pg 1441

UK Serials Group
UKSG Annual Conference & Exhibition
April 2003, pg 1434
March 2004, pg 1442
April 2005, pg 1445
April 2006, pg 1446

ALPHABETICAL INDEX OF SPONSORS

Verband der Verlage und Buchhandlungen in Baden-Wuerttemberg eV (Association of Publishers & Booksellers in Baden-Wuerttemberg e V)
Buch-IBO
March 2003, pg 1431
Karlsruher Buecherschau (Karlsruhe Book Exhibition)
November 2002, pg 1429
Stuttgarter Buchwochen (Stuttgart Bookweeks)
November 2002, pg 1429
November 2003, pg 1441
November 2004, pg 1444
November 2005, pg 1446
November 2006, pg 1446
November 2007, pg 1447

Virginia Festival of the Book
Virginia Festival of the Book
March 2003, pg 1432

Vystavisti Flora Olomoucas
Fair of Books & Literary Festival
Autumn 2002, pg 1427

Web Offset Association
Annual Web Offset Association Conference
May 2003, pg 1436
April 2004, pg 1442
May 2005, pg 1445

Weltverband der Lehrmittelfirmen, see Worlddidac

World Association of Publishers, Manufacturers & Distributors of Educational Materials, see Worlddidac

Worlddidac
China Didac/WORLDDIDAC Chengdu
October 2002, pg 1427
WORLDDIDAC 2003 Mexico
February 2003, pg 1431

Writer's Summer School
Writer's Summer School
August 2003, pg 1438

Xplor International
Xplor Global Conference
October 2002, pg 1428
October 2003, pg 1440
November 2004, pg 1445
October 2005, pg 1446

Zagrebacki Velesajam
INTERLIBER-EDUCA International Fair of Books & Teaching Appliances
November 2002, pg 1429

Zimbabwe International Book Fair
Zimbabwe International Book Fair
August 2003, pg 1438

Calendar of Book Trade & Promotional Events—Alphabetical Index of Events

ABA Convention & Trade Exhibit
May 2003, pg 1434

Adelaide Writers' Week
February 2004, pg 1441

Advertising Research Foundation Annual Convention Research Infoplex
April 2003, pg 1432

AICC/TAPPI SuperCorrExpo® 2004
November 2004, pg 1444

AIIM 2003 Show & Conference
April 2003, pg 1433

Alberta Library Conference
April 2003, pg 1433
April 2004, pg 1442

American Academy of Religion
November 2002, pg 1428
November 2003, pg 1440
November 2004, pg 1444
November 2005, pg 1446
November 2006, pg 1446
November 2007, pg 1447

American Association of Advertising Agencies Management Conference & Annual Meeting
April 2003, pg 1433

American Library Association Annual Conference
June 2003, pg 1436
June 2004, pg 1443
June 2005, pg 1445
June 2006, pg 1446

American Library Association Mid-Winter Meeting
January 2003, pg 1429
January 2004, pg 1441

American Medical Writers Association Annual Conference
October 2002, pg 1427
September 2003, pg 1438
October 2004, pg 1444

American Translators Association Annual Conference
November 2002, pg 1428
November 2003, pg 1440

Amsterdam International Printing Allied Industries Trade Fair (Grafivak)
May 2003, pg 1434

Annual Quality Congress
Formerly Quality Press Annual Quality Congress
May 2003, pg 1434

Antiques & Fine Arts Exhibition/Luxembourg Book Festival
March 2003, pg 1431
March 2004, pg 1442
March 2005, pg 1445

ANZAAB Book Fair
November 2002, pg 1428

ARLIS/UK & Ireland Annual Conference
July 2003, pg 1437

Asia International Book Fair/International Library Expo
April 2004, pg 1442

Associated Writing Programs Annual Conference
March 2003, pg 1431
March 2004, pg 1442

Association of American Publishers Annual Meeting
February 2003, pg 1430

Association of American Publishers Annual Meeting for Small & Independent Publishers
February 2003, pg 1430

Association of American Publishers Professional & Scholarly Publishing Divison Annual Meeting
February 2003, pg 1430

Association of American Publishers School Division Annual Meeting
February 2003, pg 1430

Association of American University Presses Annual Meeting
June 2003, pg 1436

Association of Braille Publishing Houses & Libraries Annual Conference
Autumn 2002, pg 1427
Autumn 2003, pg 1438

Association of Directory Publishers Annual Meeting
Spring 2003, pg 1431

Beijing International Book Fair
May 2003, pg 1434

Belgrade International Book Fair
October 2002, pg 1427
October 2003, pg 1439

Bibliographical Society of Canada/La Societe bibliographique du Canada Annual Meeting
June 2003, pg 1436

Biblioteka International Book Fair
November 2002, pg 1428

Binding, Finishing & Distribution Seminar
April 2003, pg 1433

Binding Industries Association International Conference
April 2003, pg 1433

BMI Annual Conference
November 2002, pg 1428
October 2003, pg 1439

BMI Management Conference
April 2003, pg 1433

Bologna Children's Book Fair
April 2003, pg 1433

Book Expo Canada
Formerly Canadian Booksellers Association Annual Convention & Tradeshow
June 2003, pg 1436

Annual Bookbuilders West Book Show
December 2002, pg 1429

BookExpo America (BEA)
May 2003, pg 1434

Booksellers Association of Great Britain & Ireland Annual Conference
April 2003, pg 1433

BookTech East 2003
March 2003, pg 1431

British & Irish Association of Law Librarians Annual Conference
June 2003, pg 1436

The Bronte Society Annual General Meeting
June 2003, pg 1436

Buch-IBO
March 2003, pg 1431

Buenos Aires International Book Fair
April 2003, pg 1433

Building Governmental Relationships
Formerly Exploring General Trade Publishing in the Big Apple
November 2003, pg 1440

Business & Design Conference
October 2002, pg 1427
Autumn 2004, pg 1443

Cairo International Book Fair
November 2002, pg 1428

CAMEX
March 2003, pg 1432
February 2004, pg 1441

Canadian Booksellers Association Annual Convention & Tradeshow, see Book Expo Canada

Canadian Library Association Annual Convention & Tradeshow
June 2003, pg 1436

Catholic Press Association of the US and Canada Annual Convention
May 2003, pg 1434

ALPHABETICAL INDEX OF EVENTS

CBA Expo 2003
January 2003, pg 1429

CBA International Convention
July 2003, pg 1437

Children's Book Week
November 2003, pg 1440
November 2004, pg 1444
November 2005, pg 1446

China Didac/WORLDDIDAC Chengdu
Formerly China Didac/WORLDDIDAC Shanghai
October 2002, pg 1427

China Didac/WORLDDIDAC Shanghai, see China Didac/WORLDDIDAC Chengdu

China Paper
November 2002, pg 1428

Christian Booksellers Convention
March 2003, pg 1432

Church & Synagogue Library Association Conference
July 2003, pg 1437
July 2004, pg 1443

Color Imaging Conference - Color Science Systems & Applications
November 2002, pg 1428
November 2003, pg 1440

COMDEX/Fall
November 2002, pg 1428
November 2003, pg 1441

Corrugated Containers Conference & CorrExpo
Formerly International Corrugated Containers Conference & Trade Fair
October 2002, pg 1427
October 2003, pg 1439

Creative Conference
November 2002, pg 1428
November 2004, pg 1444

Dataprint
April 2003, pg 1433

De Boekenbeurs
October 2002, pg 1427
October 2003, pg 1439

DG1 Annual Meeting & Online Conference
Spring 2003, pg 1431

Distripress Annual Congress
September 2003, pg 1438
September 2004, pg 1444

DMA Annual Conference & Exhibition
October 2003, pg 1439

Dog Writers' Association of America Annual Meeting
February 2003, pg 1430

The Dorothy L Sayers Society Annual Convention
August 2003, pg 1438

DPP 2003 - International Conference on Digital Production Printing
May 2003, pg 1435

Eastpack: The Power of Packaging
June 2003, pg 1436

Edinburgh International Book Festival
August 2003, pg 1438

Electronic Publishing International
June 2003, pg 1436

EM: Electronic Book & Multimedia Fair
April 2003, pg 1433

English Association Semiannual Teachers' Conference
October 2003, pg 1439

European Association of Directory Publishers Annual Conference
September 2003, pg 1438

Evangelical Press Association Annual Conference
May 2003, pg 1435

Exploring General Trade Publishing in the Big Apple, see Building Governmental Relationships

Exposicion de Literatura Cristiana (EXPOLIT) Book Fair
February 2003, pg 1430
May 2003, pg 1435
May 2004, pg 1442

Fair of Books & Literary Festival
Autumn 2002, pg 1427

Fall Technical Conference & Trade Fair
October 2003, pg 1440
October 2004, pg 1444

Federation of Children's Book Groups Annual Conference
April 2003, pg 1433

Feria Internacional del Libro
November 2002, pg 1428
November 2003, pg 1441
November 2004, pg 1444

FIAF Congress
June 2003, pg 1436
April 2004, pg 1442
April 2005, pg 1445
April 2006, pg 1446

FILIJ/International Book Fair for Children & Youth
November 2002, pg 1428

Flanders Book Fair, see De Boekenbeurs

Folio:Midwest
March 2003, pg 1432

The Folio:Show
October 2002, pg 1427

Folio:West
April 2003, pg 1433

Football Writers Association of America Annual Meeting
January 2003, pg 1429

FOSE
April 2003, pg 1433

CALENDAR OF BOOK TRADE

Frankfurt Book Fair
October 2002, pg 1427
October 2003, pg 1440
October 2004, pg 1444
October 2005, pg 1445
October 2006, pg 1446

Fundacion El Libro Professionals' Meeting
April 2003, pg 1433

The Future Role of Sales Reps, see Working Together Building the Business Ministering Effectively

Garden Writers Association of America Meeting & Symposium
August 2003, pg 1438

General Trade Publishing & Retailing
May 2004, pg 1442

Ghana International Book Fair
November 2002, pg 1428
Autumn 2004, pg 1443

Goteborg International Book Fair
September 2003, pg 1438
September 2004, pg 1444

Graphic Arts
Formerly International Graphic Arts Technology Exhibition for Asia
August 2003, pg 1438

Graphic Arts/The Charlotte Show
March 2003, pg 1432

Graphics of the Americas
January 2003, pg 1430

Gravure Association of America Convention
May 2003, pg 1435

Guadalajara International Book Fair
November 2002, pg 1428
November 2003, pg 1441

Gutenberg Festival
May 2003, pg 1435
June 2004, pg 1443

Gutenberg Gesellschaft Annual General Meeting
June 2003, pg 1436
June 2004, pg 1443

Hong Kong Book Fair
July 2003, pg 1437
July 2004, pg 1443
July 2005, pg 1445

IEPRC Annual Conference, see Electronic Publishing International

IFLA General Conference & Council
August 2003, pg 1438
August 2004, pg 1443
August 2005, pg 1445
August 2006, pg 1446

Infosystem Fairs
April 2003, pg 1433

InfoToday
May 2003, pg 1435

Institute of Printing National Annual General Meeting
May 2003, pg 1435

& PROMOTIONAL EVENTS

Inter American Press Association General Assembly
October 2002, pg 1427
October 2003, pg 1440

Inter American Press Association Mid-Year Meeting
March 2003, pg 1432

INTERLIBER-EDUCA International Fair of Books & Teaching Appliances
November 2002, pg 1429

International Association of Business Communicators Conference
June 2003, pg 1436

International Association of Music Libraries, Archives & Documentation Centres Conference
July 2003, pg 1437
August 2004, pg 1443

International Board on Books for Young People Biennial Congress
September 2004, pg 1444
September 2006, pg 1446

International Book Fair/Los Angeles Book Fair
February 2004, pg 1441

International Book Fair/San Francisco Book Fair
February 2003, pg 1430

International Children's Book Day
April 2003, pg 1433
April 2004, pg 1442

International Conference on Writing & Illustrating for Children
Formerly National Conference on Writing & Illustrating for Children
February 2003, pg 1430
August 2003, pg 1438

International Congress on Archives
August 2004, pg 1443

International Corrugated Containers Conference & Trade Fair, see Corrugated Containers Conference & CorrExpo

International Graphic Arts Technology Exhibition for Asia, see Graphic Arts

International Newsletter & Specialized - Information Conference
June 2003, pg 1436

International Newspaper Financial Executives Annual Conference
June 2003, pg 1436
June 2004, pg 1443
June 2005, pg 1445

International Plate Printers', Die Stampers' & Engravers' Union of North America Mini Meeting
June 2003, pg 1437

International Prepress Association Marketing & Sales Conference
February 2003, pg 1431

International Printing & Packaging Machinery and Materials Exhibition for Asia, see Print & Pack Expo

International Reading Association Annual Convention
May 2003, pg 1435

Internet Expo Printing & Graphics Arts Expo
May 2003, pg 1435

Internet World UK
June 2003, pg 1437

Introducing ECPA Publishing University
November 2004, pg 1444

IPA Congress
June 2004, pg 1443

IS&T/SPIE Electronic Imaging Science & Technology
January 2003, pg 1430

Istanbul Book Fair
November 2003, pg 1441

Jerusalem International Book Fair
March 2003, pg 1432

Jewish Book Month
November 2002, pg 1429

Karlsruher Buecherschau (Karlsruhe Book Exhibition)
November 2002, pg 1429

Leipzig Book Fair
March 2003, pg 1432
March 2004, pg 1442

LIBER Feria Internacional del Libro
October 2002, pg 1427
October 2003, pg 1440
September 2004, pg 1444
October 2005, pg 1445
September 2006, pg 1446

London Book Fair
March 2003, pg 1432

London Remainder & Promotional Book Fair
January 2003, pg 1430

Macworld Conference & Expo
January 2003, pg 1430
July 2003, pg 1437

Media Conference & Trade Show
March 2003, pg 1432

Miami Book Fair International
November 2002, pg 1429
November 2003, pg 1441

MILIA: The World's Interactive Content Marketplace
February 2003, pg 1431

Modern Language Association of America Annual Convention
December 2002, pg 1429

Monterrey International Book Fair
October 2002, pg 1427
October 2003, pg 1440

Montreal Book Show, see Salon du Livre de Montreal

Moscow International Book Fair
September 2003, pg 1439
September 2004, pg 1444

ALPHABETICAL INDEX OF EVENTS

National Association of Printing Ink Manufacturers Annual Convention
April 2003, pg 1433
March 2004, pg 1442

National Association of Science Writers Annual Meeting
February 2003, pg 1431
February 2004, pg 1441

The National Center for Database Marketing
December 2002, pg 1429

National College Media Convention
October 2002, pg 1427
November 2003, pg 1441
November 2004, pg 1444

National Conference on Writing & Illustrating for Children, see International Conference on Writing & Illustrating for Children

National Design Conference
October 2003, pg 1440

National Federation of Press Women National Conference
September 2003, pg 1439

National Library Week
April 2003, pg 1434
April 2004, pg 1442
April 2005, pg 1445
April 2006, pg 1446
April 2007, pg 1447

National Newspaper Association Annual Convention & Trade Show
October 2003, pg 1440
October 2004, pg 1444

National Newspaper Association Annual Government Affairs Conference
March 2003, pg 1432

National Press Foundation Annual Awards Dinner
February 2003, pg 1431

New Atlantic Independent Booksellers Association Annual Trade Show
Autumn 2003, pg 1438

New York is Book Country
September 2003, pg 1439

Newsletter Marketing Conference
December 2002, pg 1429

Newspaper Association of America Annual Convention
April 2003, pg 1434
April 2004, pg 1442
April 2005, pg 1445

NEXPO®
June 2003, pg 1437
June 2004, pg 1443

NIP 19: The 19th International Congress on Digital Printing Technologies
September 2003, pg 1439

North American Agricultural Journalists Spring Meeting
April 2003, pg 1434

Northprint
May 2003, pg 1435

1423

ALPHABETICAL INDEX OF EVENTS

NPES The Association for Suppliers of Printing, Publishing and Converting Technologies Annual Conference
October 2002, pg 1428
October 2003, pg 1440

ON DEMAND
April 2003, pg 1434

Online Information
December 2002, pg 1429
December 2003, pg 1441

Outdoor Writers Association of America Annual Conference
June 2003, pg 1437

Pacific Printing & Imaging Association Northwest Regional Industry Event
Formerly TechGraphics New Media
Spring 2003, pg 1431

PACK EXPO
November 2002, pg 1429
October 2003, pg 1440

Pacprint
May 2005, pg 1445

Paper Week
March 2003, pg 1432

Periodical Writers' Association of Canada Annual General Meeting
May 2003, pg 1435

The PICS Conference
May 2003, pg 1435

Poligrafia
April 2003, pg 1434

PRIMEX 2003, Print Media Executive Conference
February 2003, pg 1431

Print & Pack Expo
Formerly International Printing & Packaging Machinery and Materials Exhibition for Asia
August 2003, pg 1438

Print Sales & Marketing Conference
June 2003, pg 1437

Printex 03
May 2003, pg 1435

PSA International Conference of Photography
September 2003, pg 1439

Publishers Association of the South Fall Conference & Annual Meeting
September 2003, pg 1439

Publishers Winter Conclave
January 2003, pg 1430

Quality Press Annual Quality Congress, see Annual Quality Congress

Quest for Excellence
March 2003, pg 1432

The Quick Print Show
March 2003, pg 1432

Quod Libet/International Antiquarian Book Fair & Artists Books
May 2003, pg 1435
May 2004, pg 1442

Rocky Mountain Book Festival
Spring 2003, pg 1431
Spring 2004, pg 1442

RWA Annual National Conference
July 2003, pg 1437
July 2004, pg 1443
July 2005, pg 1445
July 2006, pg 1446

Salon du Livre de Jeunesse Childrens Book Fair
November 2002, pg 1429

Salon du Livre de Montreal
November 2002, pg 1429
November 2003, pg 1441

Salon du Livre: Paris Book Fair
March 2003, pg 1432

School Library Association Annual Conference
June 2003, pg 1437
June 2004, pg 1443

Science Fiction Research Association Annual Conference
June 2003, pg 1437

Seybold Seminars
September 2003, pg 1439

Small Press Book Fair
March 2003, pg 1432
March 2004, pg 1442

Society for Scholarly Publishing Annual Meeting
May 2003, pg 1435

Society of American Business Editors & Writers Annual Convention and Exhibition
April 2003, pg 1434

Society of Professional Journalists National Convention
September 2003, pg 1439

Sofia International Book Fair
December 2003, pg 1441

South African Booksellers Association Annual Conference
August 2003, pg 1438

Southeast Booksellers Association Annual Meeting & Trade Show
September 2003, pg 1439

Southern California Writers' Conference San Diego
February 2003, pg 1431

SouthPack
April 2003, pg 1434

Southwestern Graphics
June 2003, pg 1437

SPAN Conference
October 2002, pg 1428
October 2003, pg 1440

Special Libraries Association Annual Conference
June 2003, pg 1437
June 2004, pg 1443

Special Libraries Association Winter Meeting & Education Conference
January 2003, pg 1430
January 2004, pg 1441

Spectrum 2003
September 2003, pg 1439

Spring Fair Birmingham
February 2003, pg 1431

Spring Technical Conference & Trade Fair
May 2003, pg 1435

Stuttgarter Buchwochen (Stuttgart Bookweeks)
November 2002, pg 1429
November 2003, pg 1441
November 2004, pg 1444
November 2005, pg 1446
November 2006, pg 1446
November 2007, pg 1447

TAPPI 8th Advanced Coating Fundamentals Symposium
May 2003, pg 1435

TechGraphics New Media, see Pacific Printing & Imaging Association Northwest Regional Industry Event

Technology, Reading & Learning Difficulties
January 2003, pg 1430

Texas Outdoor Writers Association Annual Conference
February 2003, pg 1431

Thai Print: The International Trade Exhibition for Printing Machinery, Graphic Art Equipment, Pre-Press Solutions, Materials & Supplies
September 2003, pg 1439

TIBF: Tokyo International Book Fair
April 2003, pg 1434

Truth and Consequences
Formerly Who Are We Publishing For
April 2003, pg 1434

UKSG Annual Conference & Exhibition
April 2003, pg 1434
March 2004, pg 1442
April 2005, pg 1445
April 2006, pg 1446

Umbrella 2003
July 2003, pg 1437

VABook, see Virginia Festival of the Book

Virginia Festival of the Book
March 2003, pg 1432

Warsaw International Book Fair
May 2003, pg 1436

Annual Web Offset Association Conference
May 2003, pg 1436
April 2004, pg 1442
May 2005, pg 1445

WEM: The World Education Market
May 2003, pg 1436

& PROMOTIONAL EVENTS

Westpack
February 2003, pg 1431

Who Are We Publishing For, see Truth and Consequences

Working Together Building the Business Ministering Effectively
Formerly The Future Role of Sales Reps
November 2002, pg 1429

World Congress of International PEN
November 2003, pg 1441

WORLDDIDAC 2003 Mexico
February 2003, pg 1431

Writer's Summer School
August 2003, pg 1438

Xplor Global Conference
October 2002, pg 1428

ALPHABETICAL INDEX OF EVENTS

October 2003, pg 1440
November 2004, pg 1445
October 2005, pg 1446

Young People's Poetry Week
April 2003, pg 1434

Zimbabwe International Book Fair
August 2003, pg 1438

Calendar of Book Trade & Promotional Events

Arranged chronologically by year and month, this section lists book trade events worldwide. Preceding this section are two indexes: the Sponsor Index is an alphabetical list of event sponsors followed by the names and dates of those events they sponsor; the Event Index is an alphabetical list of events along with the dates on which the events are held.

2002

AUTUMN

Association of Braille Publishing Houses & Libraries Annual Conference
Sponsored by Arbeitsgemeinschaft des Blindenschrift-Druckereien und Bibliotheken (AG BDB)
pA Deutsche Blinden-Bibliother, AM Schlag 8-10, 35037 Marburg an der Lahn, Germany
Mailing Address: Postfach 1160, 35001 Marburg an der Lahn, Germany
Tel: (06421) 6060 *Fax:* (06421) 606269
E-mail: info@blista.de
Web Site: www.blista.de
Key Personnel
Pres & Libr Dir: Rainer F V Witte *E-mail:* witt@blista.de
Location: German Institute for the Blind, Marburg/Lahn, Germany
Autumn 2002

Fair of Books & Literary Festival
Sponsored by Vystavisti Flora Olomoucas
Wolkerova 17, 771 11 Olomouc, Czech Republic
Mailing Address: PO Box 46, Olomouc 77111, Czech Republic
Tel: (068) 414021 *Fax:* (068) 5413370
E-mail: expo@flora-ol.cz
Web Site: www.flora-ol.cz
Autumn 2002

OCTOBER

American Medical Writers Association Annual Conference
Sponsored by American Medical Writers Association
40 W Gude Dr, Suite 101, Rockville, MD 20850-1192, United States
Tel: 301-294-5303 *Fax:* 301-294-9006
E-mail: amwa@amwa.org
Web Site: www.amwa.org
Location: Town & Country Hotel, San Diego, CA, USA
Oct 30-Nov 2, 2002

Belgrade International Book Fair
Sponsored by Association of Yugoslav Publishers & Booksellers
Kneza Milosa 25/1, 11000 Belgrade, Yugoslavia
Tel: (011) 642248; (011) 642533 *Fax:* (011) 646339
Web Site: www.beobookfair.co.yu
Key Personnel
General Dir: Mr Ognjen Lakecevic
 E-mail: ognjenl@eunet.yu
Location: Belgrade, Yugoslavia
Oct 22-28, 2002

Business & Design Conference
Sponsored by American Institute of Graphic Arts (AIGA)
164 Fifth Ave, New York, NY 10010, United States
Tel: 212-807-1990 (ext 223) *Fax:* 212-807-1799
E-mail: aiganswers@aiga.org; programs@aiga.org
Web Site: www.aiga.org
Key Personnel
Exec Dir: Richard Grefe
Biennial event.
Location: Hyatt Regency, Minneapolis, MN, USA
Oct 25-27, 2002

China Didac/WORLDDIDAC Chengdu
Formerly China Didac/WORLDDIDAC Shanghai
Sponsored by Worlddidac
Bollwerk 21, CH-3001 Bern, Switzerland
Mailing Address: PO Box 8866, CH-3001 Bern, Switzerland
Tel: (031) 311 76 82 *Fax:* (031) 312 17 44
E-mail: info@worlddidac.org
Web Site: www.worlddidac.org
Key Personnel
Proj Mgr: Madeleine Kihm *E-mail:* kihm@worlddidac.org
International exhibition for educational materials, professional training & e-learning.
Location: Chengdu, China
Oct 21-23, 2002

Corrugated Containers Conference & CorrExpo
Formerly International Corrugated Containers Conference & Trade Fair
Sponsored by Technical Association of the Pulp & Paper Industry (TAPPI)
15 Technology Pkwy S, Norcross, GA 30092, United States
Mailing Address: PO Box 105113, Atlanta, GA 30348-5113, United States
Tel: 770-446-1400 *Fax:* 770-446-6947
Web Site: www.tappi.org
Key Personnel
Publg Dir: Mary Beth Bennett
Adv Asst: Keith Hudson *E-mail:* khudson@tappi.org
Dir, Admin: Jeff Petro
Corp Rel Dir: Clare Reagan *E-mail:* creagan@tappi.org
Admin: Julie Anne Wiley
Location: Indianapolis Convention Center & RCA Dome, Indianapolis, IN, USA
Oct 27-30, 2002

De Boekenbeurs (Flanders Book Fair)
Sponsored by Bock.be
Hof ter Shrieklaan 17, 2600 Berchem/Antwerp, Belgium
Tel: (03) 2308923 *Fax:* (03) 2812240
E-mail: info@boek.be
Web Site: www.boek.be
Location: Bouwcentrum, Jan van Rijswijcklaan 191, Antwerp, Belgium
Oct 31- Nov 10, 2002

The Folio:Show
Sponsored by Media Central
470 Park Ave, 8th fl, New York, NY 10016, United States
Tel: 212-545-3630 *Fax:* 917-981-2924
E-mail: folioshow@mediacentral.com
Web Site: www.folioshow.com; www.mediacentral.com
Location: New York Hilton, New York, NY, USA
Oct 28-30, 2002

Frankfurt Book Fair
Sponsored by Ausstellungs-und Messe-GmbH des Borsenvereins des Deutschen Buchhandels
Reinecksstr 3, 60313 Frankfurt am Main, Germany
Mailing Address: Postfach 100116, 60001 Frankfurt am Main, Germany
Tel: (069) 21020 *Fax:* (069) 2102 227
E-mail: info@book-fair.com
Web Site: www.frankfurt-book-fair.com *Cable:* BUCHMESSE
Key Personnel
CEO: Lorenzo Rudolf
Location: Frankfurt Fairgrounds, Frankfurt, Germany
Oct 9-14, 2002

Inter American Press Association General Assembly
Sponsored by Inter American Press Association (IAPA)
1801 SW Third Ave, Miami, FL 33129, United States
Tel: 305-634-2465 *Fax:* 305-635-2272
E-mail: info@sipia.org
Web Site: www.sipiapa.org
Location: Lima, Peru
Oct 25-29, 2002

LIBER Feria Internacional del Libro
Sponsored by Federacion de Gremios de Editores de Espana (FGEE) (Spanish Publishers Association)
Cea Bermudez, 44-2º Dehe, Madrid 20003, Spain
Tel: (091) 5345195 *Fax:* (091) 5352625
E-mail: fgee@fge.es
Web Site: www.federacioneditores.org
Location: Barcelona, Spain
Oct 2-5, 2002

Monterrey International Book Fair
Sponsored by Instituto Tecnologico y de Estudios Superiores de Monterrey
Av Eugenio Garza Sada 2501, Col Tecnologico, 648497 Monterrey, Nuevo Leon, Mexico
Tel: (08) 328 43 28 *Fax:* (08) 359 96 23
E-mail: filmty@fil.mty.itesm.mx
Web Site: fil.mty.itesm.mx
Key Personnel
Opers Dir: Armando Ruiz
Location: Cintemex, Monterrey, Mexico
Oct 12-20, 2002

National College Media Convention
Sponsored by Associated Collegiate Press (ACP)
Subsidiary of National Scholastic Press Assn
2221 University Ave SE, Suite 121, Minneapolis, MN 55414, United States
Tel: 612-625-8335 *Fax:* 612-626-0720
E-mail: info@studentpress.org
Web Site: www.studentpress.journ.umn.edu/acp
Location: Hyatt Hotel, Orlando, FL, USA
Oct 31-Nov 3, 2002

NPES The Association for Suppliers of Printing, Publishing and Converting Technologies Annual Conference
Sponsored by NPES The Association for Suppliers of Printing, Publishing and Converting Technologies
1899 Preston White Dr, Reston, VA 20191-4367, United States
Tel: 703-264-7200 *Fax:* 703-620-0994
E-mail: npes@npes.org
Web Site: www.npes.org
Key Personnel
Pres: Regis J Delmontagne
Dir, Communs & Mktg: Carol J Hurlburt
 E-mail: churlbur@npes.org
Trade Association representing companies which manufacture equipment, systems, software & supplies used in printing, publishing & converting.
Location: Napa, CA, USA
Oct 26-28, 2002

SPAN Conference
Sponsored by Small Publishers Association of North America (SPAN)
425 Cedar St, Buena Vista, CO 81211, United States
Mailing Address: PO Box 1306, Buena Vista, CO 81211-1306, United States
Tel: 719-395-4790 *Fax:* 719-395-8374
E-mail: span@spannet.org
Web Site: www.spannet.org
Key Personnel
Exec Dir: Marilyn Ross
Busn Dir: Tom Ross
A meaty, in-depth college for independent presses, authors & self-publishers. Emphasis is on "can-do" marketing/PR strategies.
Location: Denver, CO, USA
Oct 18-20, 2002

Xplor Global Conference
Sponsored by Xplor International
24238 Hawthorne Blvd, Torrance, CA 90505-6505, United States
Tel: 310-791-9521 *Fax:* 310-375-4240
E-mail: info@xplor.org
Web Site: www.xplor.org
Key Personnel
Communs Asst: Steven Barry
Location: Anaheim, CA, USA
Oct 27-30, 2002

NOVEMBER

American Academy of Religion
Sponsored by American Schools of Oriental Research
825 Houston Mill Rd, Atlanta, GA 30329, United States
Tel: 404-727-3049; 404-727-7920 *Fax:* 404-727-7959
Web Site: www.aarweb.org
Key Personnel
Meeting Coord: Shannon Planck
Location: Toronto, ON, Canada
Nov 23-26, 2002

American Translators Association Annual Conference
Sponsored by American Translators Association (ATA)
225 Reinekers Lane, Suite 590, Alexandria, VA 22314, United States
Tel: 703-683-6100 *Fax:* 703-683-6122
E-mail: ata@atanet.org
Web Site: www.atanet.org

Key Personnel
Exec Dir: Walter Bacak *Tel:* 703-683-6100 ext 3006 *E-mail:* walter@atanet.org
Location: Hyatt Regency Hotel, Atlanta, GA, USA
Nov 6-9, 2002

ANZAAB Book Fair
Sponsored by The Australian & New Zealand Association of Antiquarian Booksellers
Affiliate of International League of Antipoarian Booksellers
69 Broadway, Nedlands, WA 6009, Australia
Tel: (0618) 9386 6103 *Fax:* (0618) 9386 8211
E-mail: admin@anzaab.com
Web Site: www.anzaab.com
Key Personnel
Pres: Robert Muir
Location: Malvern Town Hall, Melbourne, Victoria, Australia
Nov 8-10, 2002

Biblioteka International Book Fair
Sponsored by INCHEBA as
Viedenska cesta 7, 852 51 Bratislava, Slovakia
Tel: (02) 6727 2135 *Fax:* (02) 6727 2143
E-mail: info@incheba.sk
Web Site: www.incheba.sk
Location: INCHEBA Exhibition & Convention Centre, Bratislava, Slovakia
Nov 7-10, 2002

BMI Annual Conference
Sponsored by Book Manufacturers' Institute Inc (BMI)
65 William St, Suite 300, Wellesley, MA 02481-3800, United States
Tel: 781-239-0103 *Fax:* 781-239-0106
E-mail: bmibook@aol.com
Web Site: www.bmibook.org
Key Personnel
Exec VP: Stephen P Snyder
Location: Arizona Biltmore, Phoenix, AZ, USA
Nov 3-6, 2002

Cairo International Book Fair
Sponsored by General Egyptian Book Organization
Corniche El-Nil, Boulaq, Cairo, Egypt (Arab Republic of Egypt)
Tel: (02) 5775371; (02) 5775109; (02) 4500342; (02) 5775545 *Fax:* (02) 5754213; (02) 5764276; (02) 4529677 *Cable:* GEBO
Key Personnel
Commercial Sector & Fairs: Mr Samir Saad Khalil *E-mail:* s.s.khalil@usa.net
Location: International Fairground, Cairo, Egypt
Nov 20-Dec 5, 2002

China Paper
Sponsored by Technical Association of the Pulp & Paper Industry (TAPPI)
15 Technology Pkwy S, Norcross, GA 30092, United States
Mailing Address: PO Box 105113, Atlanta, GA 30348-5113, United States
Tel: 770-446-1400 *Fax:* 770-446-6947
Web Site: www.tappi.org
Key Personnel
Publg Dir: Mary Beth Bennett
Adv Asst: Keith Hudson *E-mail:* khudson@tappi.org
Dir, Admin: Jeff Petro
Corp Rel Dir: Clare Reagan *E-mail:* creagan@tappi.org
Location: Shanghai, China
Nov 12-15, 2002

Color Imaging Conference - Color Science Systems & Applications
Sponsored by Society for Imaging Science & Technology (IS&T)
7003 Kilworth Lane, Springfield, VA 22151, United States
Tel: 703-642-9090 *Fax:* 703-642-9094
E-mail: info@imaging.org
Web Site: www.imaging.org
Key Personnel
Gen Co-chair: Ricardo Motta; Lindsay MacDonald
Location: SunBurst Resort, Scottsdale, AZ, USA
Nov 12-15, 2002

COMDEX/Fall
Sponsored by Key3Media Events
117 Kendrick St, Suite 600, Needham, MA 02494, United States
Tel: 781-433-1500 *Fax:* 781-433-1800
E-mail: sell@comdex.com
Web Site: www.comdex.com
Telex: 174273
Location: Las Vegas, NV, USA
Nov 18-22, 2002

Creative Conference
Sponsored by American Association of Advertising Agencies
405 Lexington Ave, 18th fl, New York, NY 10174-1801, United States
Tel: 212-682-2500 *Fax:* 212-682-8391
Web Site: www.aaaa.org
Key Personnel
Pres & CEO: O Burtch Drake
Sr VP & Dir, Pub Aff: John Wolfe
Nov 13-15, 2002

Feria Internacional del Libro
Alemania 1370, 39-130 CP, Postal Jal, De, Guadalajara 44170, Mexico
Tel: (03) 8125560; (03) 3810 0331 *Fax:* (03) 8122841; (033) 3810 0379
E-mail: fil@fil.com.mx; filny@aol.com
Web Site: fil.com.mx
Location: Guadalajara Convention Center, Guadalajara, Mexico
Nov 30-Dec 8, 2002

FILIJ/International Book Fair for Children & Youth
Sponsored by Consejo Nacional para la Cultura y las Artes
Calz Mexico Coyoacan 371, Col Xoco, Mexico, DF, Mexico
Fax: (05) 6058731
E-mail: dgp.cnca@concaulta.gob.mx
Location: Centro Nacional de las Artes, Mexico City, Mexico
Nov 9-17, 2002

Ghana International Book Fair
Sponsored by Ghana Trade Fair Co Ltd
Trade Fair Centre, Accra, Ghana
Mailing Address: PO Box TF 111, Accra, Ghana
Tel: (021) 776611; (021) 772376; (021) 776614; (024) 622891 *Fax:* (021) 772012
E-mail: gtfc@ghana.com; tfa@ighmail.com
Location: Ghana International Trade Fair Centre, Accra, Ghana
Nov 6-12, 2002

Guadalajara International Book Fair
Div of Humanities NAC 5225, City College of New York, New York, NY 10031, United States
Tel: 212-650-7925 *Fax:* 212-650-7912
E-mail: filny@aol.com
Web Site: www.fil.com.mx
Key Personnel
US Rep: David Unger

& PROMOTIONAL EVENTS

Held annually in Guadalajara, Mexico, the Guadalajara International Book Fair is the most important event for Spanish book professionals.
Location: Guadalajara. Mexico
Nov 30-Dec 8, 2002

INTERLIBER-EDUCA International Fair of Books & Teaching Appliances
Sponsored by Zagrebacki Velesajam
Avenija Dubrovnik 15, 10020 Zagreb, Croatia
Tel: (01) 6503111 *Fax:* (01) 6520643
E-mail: zagvel@zv.hr
Web Site: www.zv.hr
Key Personnel
Project Manager: Berislav Cizmek *Tel:* (01) 6903-395 *Fax:* (01) 6503-112 *E-mail:* bcizmek@zv.hr
Location: Zagreb Fair Ground, Zagreb, Croatia
Nov 12-16, 2002

Jewish Book Month
Sponsored by Jewish Book Council
15 E 26 St, New York, NY 10010-1579, United States
Tel: 212-532-4949 (ext 297) *Fax:* 212-481-4174
E-mail: jbc@jewishbooks.org
Web Site: www.jewishbookcouncil.org
Key Personnel
Exec Dir: Carolyn Starman Hessel
  E-mail: carolynhessel@jewishbooks.org
Nov-Dec, 2002

Karlsruher Buecherschau (Karlsruhe Book Exhibition)
Sponsored by Verband der Verlage und Buchhandlungen in Baden-Wuerttemberg eV (Association of Publishers & Booksellers in Baden-Wuerttemberg e V)
Paulinenstr 53, 70178 Stuttgart, Germany
Tel: (0711) 619410 *Fax:* (0711) 6194144
E-mail: buchhandelsverband@vvb-bw.de
Web Site: www.vvb-bw.de
Key Personnel
Exhibition Mgr: Ursula Kettenmann *Tel:* (0711) 61941 26 *E-mail:* kettenmann@vvb-bw.de
Location: Karlsruhe, Germany
Nov 15-Dec 8, 2002

Miami Book Fair International
300 NE Second Ave, Suite 1501, Miami, FL 33132, United States
Tel: 305-237-3258 *Fax:* 305-237-3645
E-mail: bookfair@mdcc.edu
Web Site: www.miamibookfair.com
Location: Miami-Dade Community College, Wolfson Campus, Miami, FL, USA
Nov 17-24, 2002

PACK EXPO
Sponsored by Packaging Machinery Manufacturers Institute
4350 N Fairfax Dr, Suite 600, Arlington, VA 22203, United States
Tel: 703-243-8555 *Fax:* 703-243-3038
E-mail: expo@pmmi.org
Web Site: www.packexpo.com
Key Personnel
Exhibitor Servs Coord: Kim Beaulieu
  E-mail: kbeaulieu@packexpo.com
Location: McCormick Place, Chicago, IL, USA
Nov 3-7, 2002

Salon du Livre de Jeunesse Childrens Book Fair
Sponsored by Reed-OIP
Subsidiary of Reed Exhibition Companies
11 rue du Colonel Pierre Avia, 75015 Paris, France
Tel: (01) 41 90 47 47 *Fax:* (01) 41 90 47 00
E-mail: livre@reed-oip.fr; info@reed-oip.fr
Web Site: www.reed-oip.fr; www.ldj.tm.fr

Key Personnel
Contact: Denis-Luc Panthin *E-mail:* panthin@ldj.tm.fr
France's leading publishing event dedicated to children's books.
Location: Montreal, PQ, Canada
Nov 27-Dec 2, 2002

Salon du Livre de Montreal (Montreal Book Show)
480 Boul St-Laurent, Suite 403, Montreal, PQ H2Y 3Y7, Canada
Tel: (514) 845-2365 *Fax:* (514) 845-7119
E-mail: slm.info@videotron.ca
Web Site: www.salondulivredemontreal.com
Key Personnel
Dir-Gen: Francine Bois
Exhibition Servs: Sebastien Barange
Location: Place Bonaventure Exhibition Hall, Montreal, PQ, Canada
Nov 14-18, 2002

Stuttgarter Buchwochen (Stuttgart Bookweeks)
Sponsored by Verband der Verlage und Buchhandlungen in Baden-Wuerttemberg eV (Association of Publishers & Booksellers in Baden-Wuerttemberg e V)
Paulinenstr 53, 70178 Stuttgart, Germany
Tel: (0711) 619410 *Fax:* (0711) 6194144
E-mail: buchhandelsverband@vvb-bw.de
Key Personnel
Contact: Maike Dreyer *Tel:* (0711) 61941 28 *E-mail:* dreyer@vvb-bw.de
Location: Stuttgart, Germany
Nov 14-Dec 8, 2002

Working Together Building the Business Ministering Effectively
Formerly The Future Role of Sales Reps
Sponsored by Evangelical Christian Publishers Association
1969 E Broadway Rd, Suite 2, Tempe, AZ 85282, United States
Tel: 480-966-3998 *Fax:* 480-966-1944
Web Site: www.ecpa.org
Key Personnel
Pres: Doug Ross *E-mail:* dross@ecpa.org
Location: Tucson, AZ, USA
Nov 2-6, 2002

DECEMBER

Annual Bookbuilders West Book Show
Sponsored by Bookbuilders West
PO Box 7046, San Francisco, CA 94120-9727, United States
Tel: 415-273-5790
E-mail: bookshow@bookbuilders.org
Web Site: www.bookbuilders.org
Key Personnel
Pres: Michelle Bisson Savoy
Treas: Mike O'Brien
Location: San Francisco, CA, USA
Dec 3, 2002

Modern Language Association of America Annual Convention
Sponsored by Modern Language Association of America (MLA)
26 Broadway, 3rd fl, New York, NY 10004, United States
Tel: 646-576-5000 *Fax:* 646-576-5160
E-mail: afrankel@mla.org
Web Site: www.mla.org
Key Personnel
Dir, Conventions: Maribeth T Kraus
Assoc Dir, Conventions: Karin Bagnall

Location: New York, NY, USA
Dec 27-30, 2002

The National Center for Database Marketing
Sponsored by Premedia Business
11 River Bend Dr S, Stamford, CT 06907, United States
Mailing Address: PO Box 4949, Stamford, CT 06907-0949, United States
Tel: 203-358-9900 *Fax:* 203-358-5831
Web Site: www.primedia.com
Dec 9-11, 2002

Newsletter Marketing Conference
Sponsored by Newsletter & Electronic Publishers Association
1501 Wilson Blvd, Suite 509, Arlington, VA 22209, United States
Tel: 703-527-2333 *Fax:* 703-841-0629
E-mail: nepa@newsletters.org
Web Site: www.newsletters.org
Key Personnel
Exec Dir: Patti Wysocki
Location: Caesars Palace, Las Vegas, NV, USA
Dec 4-6, 2002

Online Information
Sponsored by Learned Information (Europe) Ltd
Subsidiary of VNU Business Information Europe
Woodside, Hinksey Hill, Oxford OX1 5BE, United Kingdom
Tel: (01865) 388000 *Fax:* (01865) 736354
E-mail: marketing@learned.co.uk
Web Site: www.learned.co.uk
Key Personnel
Mktg Mgr: Rebekah Hart
Location: Olympia Grand Hall, London, UK
Dec 3-5, 2002

2003

JANUARY

American Library Association Mid-Winter Meeting
Sponsored by American Library Association (ALA)
50 E Huron St, Chicago, IL 60611, United States
Tel: 312-280-3200 *Fax:* 312-944-7841
E-mail: ala@ala.org
Web Site: www.ala.org/events
Key Personnel
Public Info Dir: Deborah Davis
Press Officer: Belia Ortega
Dir, Intl Rel: Michael Dowling
Location: Philadelphia, PA, USA
Jan 24-29, 2003

CBA Expo 2003
Sponsored by CBA
9240 Explorer Dr, Colorado Springs, CO 80920, United States
Mailing Address: PO Box 62000, Colorado Springs, CO 80962-2000, United States
Tel: 719-265-9895 *Fax:* 719-272-3510
Web Site: www.cbaonline.org
Key Personnel
Pres: William Anderson
VP & COO: Dorothy Gore
Convention & Expositions Mgr: Scott Graham
Location: Indianapolis, IN, USA
Jan 27-31, 2003

Football Writers Association of America Annual Meeting
Sponsored by Football Writers Association of America

18652 Vista Del Sol, Dallas, TX 75287, United States
Tel: 972-713-6198 Fax: 972-713-6198
E-mail: tigerfwaa@aol.com
Web Site: www.fwaa.com; www.footballwriters.com
Key Personnel
Pres, USA Today: Kelly Whiteside
1st VP, Arkansas - Democrat - Gazette: Wally Hall
2nd VP, New York Daily News: Dick Weiss
Location: Tempe, AZ, USA
Jan 2-4, 2003

Graphics of the Americas
Sponsored by Printing Association of Florida Inc
6095 NW 167 St, Suite D7, Hialeah, FL 33015, United States
Mailing Address: PO Box 170010, Hialeah, FL 33017-0010, United States
Tel: 305-558-4855 Fax: 305-823-8965
E-mail: goa@pafgraf.org
Web Site: www.graphicsoftheamericas.com
Key Personnel
VP, Trade Shows: Chris Price
 E-mail: chrisp4goa@aol.com
Location: Miami Beach Convention Center, Miami Beach, FL, USA
Jan 24-26, 2003

IS&T/SPIE Electronic Imaging Science & Technology
Sponsored by SPIE - The International Society for Optical Engineering
1000 20 St, Bellingham, WA 98225, United States
Mailing Address: PO Box 10, Bellingham, WA 98225, United States
Tel: 360-676-3290 Fax: 360-647-1445
E-mail: exhibition@spie.org
Web Site: www.spie.org
Key Personnel
Gen Co-chair: Martin Freeman; Sethuraman Panchanathan
Location: Santa Clara, CA, USA
Jan 20-24, 2003

London Remainder & Promotional Book Fair
Sponsored by Ciana Ltd
4/5 Academy Bldgs, Fanshaw St, London N1 6LQ, United Kingdom
Tel: (020) 7729 6044 Fax: (020) 7729 3365
E-mail: enquiries@ciana.co.uk
Web Site: www.ciana.co.uk
Location: Hilton Brighton Metropole Hotel, King's Rd, Brighton, UK
Jan 12-13, 2003

Macworld Conference & Expo
Sponsored by IDG World Expo
Unit of IDG
3 Speen St, Framingham, MA 01701, United States
Tel: 508-424-4800 Fax: 508-620-6668
Web Site: www.macworldexpo.com
Key Personnel
VP: Rob Scheschareg
Location: Moscone Convention Center, San Francisco, CA, USA
Jan 6-10, 2003

Publishers Winter Conclave
Sponsored by Publishers Association of the South (PAS)
4412 Fletcher St, Panama City, FL 32405-1017, United States
Tel: 850-914-0766 Fax: 850-769-4348
E-mail: executive@pubsouth.org
Web Site: www.pubsouth.org
Key Personnel
Pres: Joseph Billingsley

Assn Exec: Pat Sabiston
Location: The Maison Dupuy, New Orleans, LA, USA
Jan 17-19, 2003

Special Libraries Association Winter Meeting & Education Conference
Sponsored by Special Libraries Association (SLA)
1700 18 St NW, Washington, DC 20009-2514, United States
Tel: 202-234-4700 Fax: 202-265-9317
E-mail: sla@sla.org
Web Site: www.sla.org
Key Personnel
Interim Dir: Lynn Smith
Location: Hyatt Regency, New Orleans, LA, USA
Jan 23-25, 2003

Technology, Reading & Learning Difficulties
Sponsored by Educational Computer Conferences Inc
19 Calvert Ct, Piedmont, CA 94611-3435, United States
Tel: 510-594-1249 Fax: 510-594-1838
E-mail: exhibits@trld.com
Web Site: www.trld.com
Key Personnel
Contact: Diane Frost
Location: San Francisco, CA, USA
Jan 16-18, 2003

FEBRUARY

Association of American Publishers Annual Meeting
Sponsored by Association of American Publishers Inc (AAP)
71 Fifth Ave, 2nd fl, New York, NY 10003-3004, United States
Tel: 212-255-0200 Fax: 212-255-7007
Web Site: www.publishers.org
Key Personnel
Pres & CEO: Patricia S Schroeder Tel: 202-347-3375 Fax: 202-347-3690
Location: Renaissance Mayflower Hotel, Washington, DC, USA
Feb 26-27, 2003

Association of American Publishers Annual Meeting for Small & Independent Publishers
Sponsored by Association of American Publishers Inc (AAP)
71 Fifth Ave, 2nd fl, New York, NY 10003-3004, United States
Tel: 212-255-0200 Fax: 212-255-7007
Web Site: www.publishers.org
Key Personnel
Pres & CEO: Patricia S Schroeder Tel: 202-347-3375 Fax: 202-347-3690
Location: Renaissance Mayflower Hotel, Washington, DC, USA
Feb 26, 2003

Association of American Publishers Professional & Scholarly Publishing Divison Annual Meeting
Sponsored by Association of American Publishers Inc (AAP)
71 Fifth Ave, 2nd fl, New York, NY 10003-3004, United States
Tel: 212-255-0200 Fax: 212-255-7007
Web Site: www.publishers.org
Key Personnel
Pres & CEO: Patricia S Schroeder Tel: 202-347-3375 Fax: 202-347-3690

Location: Mayflower Hotel, Washington, DC, USA
Feb 3-5, 2003

Association of American Publishers School Division Annual Meeting
Sponsored by Association of American Publishers Inc (AAP)
71 Fifth Ave, 2nd fl, New York, NY 10003-3004, United States
Tel: 212-255-0200 Fax: 212-255-7007
Web Site: www.publishers.org
Key Personnel
Pres & CEO: Patricia S Schroeder Tel: 202-347-3375 Fax: 202-347-3690
Location: The Registry Resort, Naples, FL, USA
Feb 6-7, 2003

Dog Writers' Association of America Annual Meeting
Sponsored by Dog Writers' Association of America Inc (DWAA)
173 Union Rd, Coatesville, PA 19320, United States
Tel: 610-384-2436 Fax: 610-384-2471
E-mail: rhydowen@aol.com
Web Site: www.dwaa.org
Key Personnel
Pres: Chris Walkowicz
Sec: Pat Santi
Location: South Gate Tower Hotel, New York, NY, USA
Feb 9, 2003

Exposicion de Literatura Cristiana (EXPOLIT) Book Fair
Sponsored by Spanish Evangelical Publishers Association (SEPA)/Associacion de Editores Evangelicos and Editorial Unilit
1360 NW 88 Ave, Miami, FL 33172, United States
Tel: 305-592-6136 (ext 105) Fax: 305-592-0087
E-mail: expolit@editorialunilit.com
Web Site: www.expolit.com
Key Personnel
Pres, SEPA: Esteban Fernandez
Pres, EXPOLIT: David Ecklebarger
Spanish Christian Literature Convention.
Location: El Salvador, South America
Feb 25-March 1, 2003

International Book Fair/San Francisco Book Fair
Sponsored by Antiquarian Booksellers' Association of America
20 W 44 St, 4th fl, New York, NY 10036, United States
Tel: 212-944-8291 Fax: 212-944-8293
E-mail: abaa@panix.com
Web Site: www.abaa.org
Key Personnel
Dir: Liane Wade
Location: San Francisco, CA, USA
Feb 2003

International Conference on Writing & Illustrating for Children
Formerly National Conference on Writing & Illustrating for Children
Sponsored by Society of Children's Book Writers & Illustrators (SCBWI)
8271 Beverly Blvd, Los Angeles, CA 90048, United States
Tel: 323-782-1010 Fax: 323-782-1892
E-mail: scbwi@scbwi.org
Web Site: www.scbwi.org
Key Personnel
Pres: Steve Mooser
Location: New York, NY, USA
Feb 2003

International Prepress Association Marketing & Sales Conference
Sponsored by International Prepress Association
7200 France Ave S, Suite 223, Edina, MN 55435, United States
Tel: 952-896-1908 *Fax:* 952-896-0181
E-mail: info@ipa.org
Web Site: www.ipa.org
Key Personnel
Pres: Steven Bonoff *E-mail:* steve@ipa.org
Location: Florida, USA
Feb 6-9, 2003

MILIA: The World's Interactive Content Marketplace
Sponsored by Reed Midem
Subsidiary of Reed Exhibition Companies
11 rue du Colonel Pierre-Avia, 75726 Paris Cedex 15, France
Tel: (01) 41 90 44 00 *Fax:* (01) 41 90 44 09
E-mail: info@milia.com
Web Site: www.milia.com
Key Personnel
Contact: Maud Chevalier *E-mail:* maud.chevalier@reedmidem.com
Location: Palais des Festivals, Cannes, France
Feb 2-4, 2003

National Association of Science Writers Annual Meeting
Sponsored by National Association of Science Writers (NASW)
PO Box 890, Hedgesville, WV 25427, United States
Tel: 304-754-5077 *Fax:* 304-754-5076
Web Site: www.nasw.org
Key Personnel
Exec Dir: Diane McGurgan *E-mail:* diane@nasw.org
Location: Denver, CO, USA
Feb 13-18, 2003

National Press Foundation Annual Awards Dinner
Sponsored by The National Press Foundation
1211 Connecticut Ave NW, Suite 310, Washington, DC 20036, United States
Tel: 202-663-7280 *Fax:* 202-530-2855
E-mail: npf@nationalpress.org
Web Site: www.nationalpress.org
Location: Washington, DC, USA
Feb 27, 2003

PRIMEX 2003, Print Media Executive Conference
Sponsored by IDE Alliance
100 Daingerfield Rd, Alexandria, VA 22314-2888, United States
Tel: 703-837-1070 *Fax:* 703-837-1072
Web Site: www.idealliance.org
Location: The Registry Resort, Naples, FL, USA
Feb 12-15, 2003

Southern California Writers' Conference San Diego
Division of Random Cove, IE
4406 Park Blvd, Suite E, San Diego, CA 92116, United States
Tel: 619-233-4651 *Fax:* 253-390-8577
E-mail: wewrite@writersconference.com
Web Site: www.writersconference.com
Key Personnel
Exec Dir: Michael Gregory *E-mail:* msg@writersconference.com
Location: San Diego, CA, USA
Feb 14-17, 2003

Spring Fair Birmingham
Sponsored by Trade Promotion Services Ltd
Leon House, 19th fl, 233 High St, Croydon CR0 9XT, United Kingdom
Tel: (020) 8277 5863; (020) 8277 5830 (sales)
E-mail: info@emap.com
Web Site: www.springfair.com
Location: National Exhibition Centre, Birmingham, UK
Feb 2-6, 2003

Texas Outdoor Writers Association Annual Conference
Sponsored by Texas Outdoor Writers Association
7503 Bayswater, Amarillo, TX 79119, United States
Tel: 806-345-3280 *Fax:* 806-372-3717
E-mail: l.leschper@worldnet.att.net
Web Site: www.towa.org
Key Personnel
Exec Dir: Lee Leschper
Pres: Mark McDonald
Feb 2003

Westpack
Sponsored by Canon Communications
11444 W Olympic Blvd, Suite 900, Los Angeles, CA 90064, United States
Tel: 310-445-4200 *Fax:* 310-445-4299
Web Site: www.cancom.com
Biennial event.
Location: Anaheim Convention Center, Anaheim, CA, USA
Feb 19-21, 2003

WORLDDIDAC 2003 Mexico
Sponsored by Worlddidac
Bollwerk 21, CH-3001 Bern, Switzerland
Mailing Address: PO Box 8866, CH-3001 Bern, Switzerland
Tel: (031) 311 76 82 *Fax:* (031) 312 17 44
E-mail: info@worlddidac.org
Web Site: www.worlddidac.org
Key Personnel
Project Mgr: Esther Schindles *E-mail:* schindles@worlddidac.org
International exhibition for educational materials, professional training & e-learning.
Location: Mexico
Feb 12-14, 2003

SPRING

Association of Directory Publishers Annual Meeting
Sponsored by Association of Directory Publishers
116 Cass St, Traverse City, MI 49685, United States
Mailing Address: PO Box 1929, Traverse City, MI 49685, United States
Fax: 231-486-2182
E-mail: hq@adp.org
Web Site: www.adp.org
Key Personnel
Pres & CEO: R Lawrence Angove
Spring 2003

DGI Annual Meeting & Online Conference
Sponsored by Deutsche Gesellschaft fur Informationswissenschaft und informationspraxis eV
Ostbahnhofstr 13, 60314 Frankfurt am Main, Germany
Tel: (069) 430313 *Fax:* (069) 4909096
E-mail: dgd@darmstadt.gmd.de
Location: Frankfurt Fairgrounds, Frankfurt, Germany
Spring 2003

Pacific Printing & Imaging Association Northwest Regional Industry Event
Formerly TechGraphics New Media
Sponsored by Pacific Printing & Imaging Association
5319 SW Westgate Dr, Suite 117, Portland, OR 97221-2430, United States
Tel: 503-297-3328 *Fax:* 503-297-3320
E-mail: events@pacprinting.com
Web Site: www.ppi-assoc.org
Key Personnel
Exec Dir: Marcus Sassaman *E-mail:* marcus@pacprinting.com
Spring 2003

Rocky Mountain Book Festival
Sponsored by Colorado Center for the Book
2123 Downing St, Denver, CO 80205, United States
Tel: 303-839-8320 *Fax:* 303-839-8319
E-mail: ccftb@compuserve.com
Web Site: www.coloradobook.org
Key Personnel
Exec Dir: Christiane H Citron
Non profit organization promoting love of books.
Location: Denver, CO, USA
Spring 2003

MARCH

Antiques & Fine Arts Exhibition/Luxembourg Book Festival
Sponsored by Societe de Foires Internationales de Luxembourg, Societe Anonyme
2088 Luxembourg, Luxembourg
Tel: 43991 *Fax:* 4399315
E-mail: fil@fil.lu
Location: Luxembourg Conference & Exhibition Center, Luxembourg, Luxembourg
March 13-16, 2003

Associated Writing Programs Annual Conference
Sponsored by Associated Writing Programs (AWP)
George Mason University, MS-1E3, Fairfax, VA 22030, United States
Tel: 703-993-4301 *Fax:* 703-993-4302
E-mail: awp@gmu.edu
Web Site: www.awpwriter.org
Key Personnel
Exec Dir: D W Fenza
Dir of Conferences: Un J Lee
Association of writers & writing programs.
Location: Baltimore, MD, USA
Feb 2-March 1, 2003

BookTech East 2003
Sponsored by Bookbuilders West
PO Box 7046, San Francisco, CA 94120-9727, United States
Tel: 415-273-5790
E-mail: bookshow@bookbuilders.org
Web Site: www.booktechexpo.com
Key Personnel
Pres: Michelle Bisson Savoy
Location: Hilton, New York, NY, USA
March 3-5, 2003

Buch-IBO
Sponsored by Verband der Verlage und Buchhandlungen in Baden-Wuerttemberg eV (Association of Publishers & Booksellers in Baden-Wuerttemberg e V)
Division of Internationale Bodensee-Messe, Friedrichshafen
Paulinenstr 53, 70178 Stuttgart, Germany
Tel: (0711) 619410 *Fax:* (0711) 6194144
E-mail: buchhandelsverband@vvb-bw.de
Web Site: www.vvb-bw.de

Location: International Bodensee-Messe, Friedrichshafen, Germany
March 22-30, 2003

CAMEX
Sponsored by National Association of College Stores (NACS)
500 E Lorain St, Oberlin, OH 44074-1294, United States
Tel: 440-775-7777 *Fax:* 440-775-4769
E-mail: info@nacs.org
Web Site: www.nacs.org
Key Personnel
CEO: Brian Cartier
PR Dir: Laura Nakoneczny *Tel:* 440-775-7777, ext 2351 *E-mail:* lnakoneczny@nacs.org
Conference & tradeshow dedicated exclusively to the more than $10 billion collegiate retailing industry.
Location: St Louis, MO, USA
March 7-11, 2003

Christian Booksellers Convention
Sponsored by Christian Booksellers Convention Ltd
Victoria House, Victoria Rd, Buckhurst Hill, Essex 1G9 5EX, United Kingdom
Tel: (020) 5592975; (020) 8559 1180 *Fax:* (020) 5029062
E-mail: 100067.1226@compuserve.com
Location: Doncaster Exhibition & Conference Center, Doncaster, UK
March 2003

Folio:Midwest
Sponsored by Media Central
470 Park Ave, 8th fl, New York, NY 10016, United States
Tel: 212-545-3630 *Fax:* 917-981-2924
E-mail: folioshow@mediacentral.com
Web Site: www.folioshow.com; www.mediacentral.com
Location: Sheraton Chicago Hotel & Towers, Chicago, IL, USA
March 10-11, 2003

Graphic Arts/The Charlotte Show
Sponsored by Graphic Arts Show Company
1899 Preston White Dr, Reston, VA 20191-4367, United States
Tel: 703-264-7200 *Fax:* 703-620-9187
E-mail: info@gasc.org
Web Site: www.gasc.org
Telex: NPES MCLN
Key Personnel
Pres: Regis J Delmontagne
Biennial event featuring equipment, products & services for graphic communications industry.
Location: Charlotte Convention Center, Charlotte, NC, USA
March 13-15, 2003

Inter American Press Association Mid-Year Meeting
Sponsored by Inter American Press Association (IAPA)
1801 SW Third Ave, Miami, FL 33129, United States
Tel: 305-634-2465 *Fax:* 305-635-2272
Web Site: www.sipiapa.org
Key Personnel
Exec Dir: Julio E Munoz
Location: El Salvador
March 21-25, 2003

Jerusalem International Book Fair
PO Box 775, Jerusalem 91007, Israel
Tel: (02) 6297922; (02) 6297868 *Fax:* (02) 6243144
E-mail: jer_fair@netvision.net.il
Web Site: www.jerusalembookfair.com

Key Personnel
Man Dir: Zev Birger
Location: Jerusalem Convention (Interna) Center, Jerusalem, Israel
March 30-April 4, 2003

Leipzig Book Fair
Sponsored by Leipziger Messe GmbH, Projektteam Buchmesse
Messe-Allee 1, 04356 Leipzig, Germany
Mailing Address: Postfach 100 720, 04007 Leipzig, Germany
Tel: (0341) 6788240 *Fax:* (0341) 6788242
E-mail: info@leipziger-buchmesse.de
Web Site: www.leipziger-buchmesse.de
Key Personnel
Exhibition Dir: Oliver Zille *Tel:* (0341) 678 8241 *Fax:* (0341) 678 8242
Location: Neues Messegelande, Leipzig, Germany
March 20-23, 2003

London Book Fair
Sponsored by Reed Exhibition Companies (UK)
Oriel House, 26 The Quadrant, Richmond, Surrey TW9 1DL, United Kingdom
Tel: (020) 8910 7815 *Fax:* (020) 8910 7930
Web Site: www.lbf-virtual.com
Telex: 8951389 ITFLONG
Key Personnel
Key Acct Mgr: Catriana Stemp *E-mail:* catriana.stemp@reedexpo.co.uk
Sales Exec: Ruth Moses *E-mail:* ruth.moses@reedexpo.co.uk
Spring publishing event attended by publishers, booksellers, literary agents, librarians, authors, production & content managers & international rights agents.
Location: Olympia Exhibition Centre, Hammersmith Rd, London, UK
March 16-18, 2003

Media Conference & Trade Show
Sponsored by American Association of Advertising Agencies
405 Lexington Ave, 18th fl, New York, NY 10174-1801, United States
Tel: 212-682-2500 *Fax:* 212-682-8391
Web Site: www.aaaa.org
Key Personnel
Pres & CEO: O Burtch Drake
Sr VP & Dir, Pub Aff: John Wolfe
Location: Hilton, New Orleans, LA, USA
March 5-6, 2003

National Newspaper Association Annual Government Affairs Conference
Sponsored by National Newspaper Association
500 N Washington St, 2nd fl, Falls Church, VA 22046-3514, United States
Mailing Address: PO Box 5737, Arlington, VA 22205, United States
Tel: 703-534-1278 *Fax:* 703-534-5751
E-mail: info@nna.org
Web Site: www.nna.org
Location: Hyatt Regency Capitol Hill, Washington, DC, USA
March 19-22, 2003

Paper Week
Sponsored by American Forest & Paper Association
1111 19 St NW, Suite 800, Washington, DC 20036, United States
Tel: 202-463-2700 *Fax:* 202-463-2785
E-mail: info@afandpa.org
Web Site: www.afandpa.org; www.paperweek.org
Key Personnel
Pres & CEO: W Henson Moore
Location: Waldorf-Astoria Hotel, New York, NY, USA
March 9-11, 2003

Quest for Excellence
Sponsored by American Society for Quality
600 N Plankinton Ave, Milwaukee, WI 53203, United States
Tel: 414-272-8575 *Fax:* 414-272-1734
E-mail: cs@asq.org
Web Site: www.asq.org
Telex: 31-6567
Key Personnel
Exec Dir: Paul Borawski
Education Mgr: Shirley Krentz
Dir, Progs & Opers: Brian LeHouillier
Location: Marriott Wardham Park Hotel, Washington, DC, USA
March 30-April 2, 2003

The Quick Print Show
Sponsored by PrintImage International
70 E Lake St, Suite 333, Chicago, IL 60601, United States
Tel: 312-726-8015 *Fax:* 312-726-8113
Web Site: www.printimage.org
Key Personnel
Pres & CEO: Steve Johnson
Location: Las Vegas, NV, USA
March 2-5, 2003

Salon du Livre: Paris Book Fair
Sponsored by Reed-OIP
Subsidiary of Reed Exhibition Companies
11 rue du Colonel Pierre Avia, 75015 Paris, France
Tel: (01) 41 90 47 47 *Fax:* (01) 41 90 47 49
E-mail: livre@reed-oip.fr
Web Site: www.reed-oip.fr
Annual international publishing event for publishers, booksellers, teachers & librarians. Open to the trade & the public.
Location: Paris Expo-Porte de Versailles, Paris, France
March 22-27, 2003

Small Press Book Fair
Sponsored by Small Press Center
20 W 44 St, New York, NY 10036, United States
Tel: 212-764-7021 *Fax:* 212-354-5365
E-mail: info@smallpress.org
Web Site: www.smallpress.org
Key Personnel
Dir: Karin Taylor
Location: Small Press Center, New York, NY, USA
March 29-30, 2003

Virginia Festival of the Book
Division of Virginia Foundation for the Humanities
145 Ednam Dr, Charlottesville, VA 22903, United States
Tel: 434-924-6890 *Fax:* 434-296-4714
E-mail: vabook@virginia.edu
Web Site: www.vabook.org
Key Personnel
Program Dir: Nancy Damon *Tel:* 434-924-7548
Program Assoc: Kevin McFadden
 E-mail: kjm7a@virginia.edu
Location: Charlottesville, VA, USA
March 19-23, 2003

APRIL

Advertising Research Foundation Annual Convention Research Infoplex
Sponsored by Advertising Research Foundation
641 Lexington Ave, New York, NY 10022, United States
Tel: 212-751-5656 *Fax:* 212-319-5265
Web Site: www.thearf.org

Key Personnel
Pres: James Spaeth
Sr VP, Communs: Carol White
Man Ed: Kathryn Kucharski Grubb *Tel:* 212-751-5656 ext 226 *E-mail:* kathy@thearf.org
Location: New York Hilton, New York, NY, USA
April 7-9, 2003

AIIM 2003 Show & Conference
Sponsored by Advanstar Communications
1100 Wayne Ave, Suite 1120, Silver Spring, MD 20910, United States
Tel: 301-587-8202 *Fax:* 301-587-2711
E-mail: aiim@aiim.org
Web Site: www.aiim.org
Key Personnel
Natl Acct Coord: Daniel Espinosa
Gen Mgr: Brian Randall
Location: Jacob K Javits Convention Center, New York, NY, USA
April 7-9, 2003

Alberta Library Conference
Sponsored by Library Association of Alberta
80 Baker Crescent NW, Calgary, AB T2L 1R4, Canada
Tel: 403-284-5818 *Fax:* 403-282-6646
Web Site: www.laa.ab.ca
Key Personnel
Pres: Pat Cavill
Exec Dir: Christine Sheppard *E-mail:* shepparc@cadvision.com
Location: Jasper Park Lodge, Jasper, AB, Canada
April 24-27, 2003

American Association of Advertising Agencies Management Conference & Annual Meeting
Sponsored by American Association of Advertising Agencies
405 Lexington Ave, 18th fl, New York, NY 10174-1801, United States
Tel: 212-682-2500 *Fax:* 212-682-8391
Web Site: www.aaaa.org
Key Personnel
Pres & CEO: O Burtch Drake
Sr VP & Dir, Pub Aff: John Wolfe
Location: Ritz-Carlton, New Orleans, LA, USA
April 9-11, 2003

Binding, Finishing & Distribution Seminar
Sponsored by Research & Engineering Council of the Graphic Arts Industry Inc
PO Box 1086, White Stone, VA 22578-1086, United States
Tel: 804-436-9922 *Fax:* 804-436-9511
E-mail: recouncil@rivnet.net
Web Site: www.recouncil.org
Key Personnel
Man Dir: Ronald L Mihills
Location: Marriott O'Hare, Chicago, IL, USA
April 9-10, 2003

Binding Industries Association International Conference
Sponsored by Binding Industries Association International
Affiliate of Special Industry Group of Printing Industries of America Inc
70 E Lake St, Suite 300, Chicago, IL 60601, United States
Tel: 312-372-7606 *Fax:* 312-704-5025
E-mail: bia1@ix.netcom.com
Web Site: www.bindingindustries.org
Key Personnel
Exec Dir: Joanne Rock
Location: Saddlebrook Resort, Tampa, FL, USA
April 4-6, 2003

BMI Management Conference
Sponsored by Book Manufacturers' Institute Inc (BMI)
65 William St, Suite 300, Wellesley, MA 02481-3800, United States
Tel: 781-239-0103 *Fax:* 781-239-0106
E-mail: bmibook@aol.com
Web Site: www.bmibook.org
Key Personnel
Exec VP: Stephen P Snyder
Location: The Villas at Grand Cypress, Orlando, FL, USA
April 27-29, 2003

Bologna Children's Book Fair
Sponsored by BolognaFiere
Piazza Costituzione 6, 40128 Bologna, Italy
Tel: (051) 282 361; (051) 282 242 *Fax:* (051) 6 374 011
E-mail: dir.com@bolognafiere.it; dir.gen@bolognafiere.it; bookfair@bolognafiere.it
Web Site: www.bolognafiere.it/bookfair
Telex: 511248 *Cable:* BOLOGNAFIERE BOLOGNA
Location: Bologna Fairground, Piazza Costituzione 6, Bologna, Italy
April 2-5, 2003

Booksellers Association of Great Britain & Ireland Annual Conference
Sponsored by Booksellers Association of the United Kingdom & Ireland
Minster House, 272-274 Vauxhall Bridge Rd, London SW1V 1BA, United Kingdom
Tel: (020) 7802 0802 *Fax:* (020) 7802 0803
E-mail: mail@booksellers.org.uk
Web Site: www.booksellers.org.uk
Location: Dublin, Ireland
April 27-29, 2003

Buenos Aires International Book Fair
Sponsored by Fundacion El Libro
Hipolito Yrigoyen 1628 - 5 piso, C1089AAF Buenos Aires, Argentina
Tel: (011) 4374 3288 *Fax:* (011) 4375 0268
E-mail: fundacion@el-libro.com.ar
Web Site: www.el-libro.com.ar
Key Personnel
Proj Mgr: Marta Diaz
Location: Buenos Aires, Argentina
April 2003

Dataprint
Sponsored by Reed Messe Salzburg
Am Messezentrum 6, 5021 Salzburg, Austria
Mailing Address: Postfach 285, 5021 Salzburg, Austria
Tel: (0662) 44770 *Fax:* (0662) 4477161
E-mail: info@reedexpo.at
Web Site: www.reedexpo.at
Key Personnel
Dir: Johann Jungreithmair
Trade fair for print media & digital production.
Location: Design Center, Linz, Austria
April 1-4, 2003

EM: Electronic Book & Multimedia Fair
Sponsored by Reed Exhibition Companies
18F Shinjuku Nomura Bldg, 1-26-2 Nishishinjuku, Shinjuku-ku, Toyko 163-0570, Japan
Tel: (03) 3349 8501 *Fax:* (03) 3344 2400
E-mail: rej@reedexpo.co.jp
Key Personnel
Show Mgr: Keifuke Amano
Location: Tokyo Big Sight, Tokyo, Japan
April 2003

Federation of Children's Book Groups Annual Conference
Sponsored by Federation of Children's Book Groups
2 Bridge Wood View, Horsforth, Leeds, West Yorkshire LS18 5PE, United Kingdom
Tel: (0113) 2588910 *Fax:* (0113) 2575409; (0113) 2588920
E-mail: info@fcbg.org.uk
Web Site: www.fcbg.org.uk
Location: St Felix School, Southwold, Suffolk, East Anglia, UK
April 11-13, 2003

Folio:West
Sponsored by Media Central
470 Park Ave, 8th fl, New York, NY 10016, United States
Tel: 212-545-3630 *Fax:* 917-981-2924
E-mail: folioshow@mediacentral.com
Web Site: www.mediacentral.com; www.folioshow.com
April 23-25, 2003

FOSE
Sponsored by Post Newsweek Tech Media Group
8500 Leesburg Pike, Suite 7500, Vienna, VA 22182-2412, United States
Tel: 703-848-2800 *Fax:* 703-226-1279
Web Site: www.fose.com; www.postnewsweektech.com
Location: Washington Convention Center, Washington, DC, USA
April 8-10, 2003

Fundacion El Libro Professionals' Meeting
Sponsored by Fundacion El Libro
Hipolito Yrigoyen 1628 - 5 piso, C1089AAF Buenos Aires, Argentina
Tel: (011) 4374 3288 *Fax:* (011) 4375 0268
E-mail: fundacion@el-libro.com.ar
Web Site: www.el-libro.com.ar
Key Personnel
Proj Mgr: Marta Diaz
Location: La Rural, Buenos Aires, Argentina
April 14-16, 2003

Infosystem Fairs
Sponsored by Poznan International Fair Ltd
ul Glogowska 14, 60-734 Poznan, Poland
Tel: (061) 8692 599; (061) 8692 295; (061) 866 4314 *Fax:* (061) 8660 707
E-mail: infosystem@mtp.com.pl
Web Site: infosystem.mtp.com.pl
Telex: 413251
Location: Poznan, Poland
April 8-11, 2003

International Children's Book Day
Sponsored by International Board on Books for Young People (IBBY)
Nonnenweg 12, CH-4055 Basel, Switzerland
Mailing Address: Nonnenweg 12, Postfach, Basel Ch-4003, Switzerland
Tel: (061) 2722917 *Fax:* (061) 2722757
E-mail: ibby@ibby.org
Web Site: www.ibby.org
Theme: International Children's Book Day.
Location: Worldwide
April 2, 2003

National Association of Printing Ink Manufacturers Annual Convention
Sponsored by National Association of Printing Ink Manufacturers
581 Main St, Woodbridge, NJ 07095, United States
Tel: 732-855-1525 *Fax:* 732-855-1838
E-mail: napim@napim.org
Web Site: www.napim.org
Key Personnel
Exec Dir: James Coleman
Trade association.
Location: Registry Resort, Naples, FL, USA
April 6-9, 2003

National Library Week
Sponsored by American Library Association (ALA)
50 E Huron St, Chicago, IL 60611, United States
Tel: 312-944-6780 *Fax:* 312-944-8520
E-mail: pio@ala.org
Web Site: www.ala.org/events
Key Personnel
Dir: Marc Gould *E-mail:* mgould@ala.org
Press Officer: Larra Clark *E-mail:* lclark@ala.org
Location: Nationwide throughout the USA
April 6-12, 2003

Newspaper Association of America Annual Convention
Sponsored by Newspaper Association of America (NAA)
1921 Gallows Rd, Suite 600, Vienna, VA 22182, United States
Tel: 703-902-1600 *Fax:* 703-902-1843
E-mail: laths@naa.org
Web Site: www.naa.org
Key Personnel
Pres & CEO: John Sturm
Location: Sheraton, Seattle, WA, USA
April 27-30, 2003

North American Agricultural Journalists Spring Meeting
Sponsored by North American Agricultural Journalists
Texas A & M University, 2112 TAMU, College Station, TX 77843-2112, United States
Mailing Address: 2604 Cumberland Ct, College Station, TX 77845, United States
Tel: 979-845-2872 *Fax:* 979-845-2414
Web Site: naaj.tamu.edu
Key Personnel
Exec Sec, Treas: Kathleen Phillips *E-mail:* kaphillips@tamu.edu
Location: Washington, DC, USA
April 6-8, 2003

ON DEMAND
Sponsored by Advanstar Expositions
440 Wheelers Farm Rd, Suite 101, Milford, CT 06460, United States
Tel: 203-701-0144 *Fax:* 203-882-1800
E-mail: ondemand@advanstar.com
Web Site: www.ondemandexpo.com
Key Personnel
Group Show Dir: Brian Randell
Digital printing & publishing.
Location: Jacob K Javitz Convention Center, New York, NY, USA
April 7-9, 2003

Poligrafia
Sponsored by Poznan International Fair Ltd
ul Glogowska 14, 60-734 Poznan, Poland
Tel: (061) 8692 599; (061) 8692 295; (061) 866 4314 *Fax:* (061) 8660 707
E-mail: info@mtp.com.pl
Web Site: www.mtp.com.pl
Key Personnel
Proj Team Mgr: Jerzy Kaczmarek *Tel:* (061) 869 21 38
International fair of printing machines, materials & services.
April 8-11, 2003

Society of American Business Editors & Writers Annual Convention and Exhibition
Sponsored by Society of American Business Editors & Writers Inc
University of Missouri, School of Journalism, 134 Neff Anne X, Columbia, MO 65211-1200, United States
Tel: 573-882-7862 *Fax:* 573-884-1372
E-mail: sabew@missouri.edu
Web Site: www.sabew.org

Key Personnel
Exec Dir: Carolyn Guniss
Exec Asst: Helen Pattrin
Location: Royal Sonesta Hotel, Boston, MA, USA
April 27-29, 2003

SouthPack
Sponsored by Canon Communications
11444 W Olympic Blvd, Suite 900, Los Angeles, CA 90064, United States
Tel: 310-445-4200 *Fax:* 310-445-4299
Web Site: www.cancom.com
Biennial.
Location: Georgia World Congress Center, Atlanta, GA, USA
April 30-May 1, 2003

TIBF: Tokyo International Book Fair
Sponsored by Reed Exhibition Companies
18F Shinjuku Nomura Bldg, 1-26-2 Nishishinjuku, Shinjuku-ku, Toyko 163-0570, Japan
Tel: (03) 3349 8507 *Fax:* (03) 3344 2400
E-mail: tibf-eng@reedexpo.co.jp
Web Site: www.reedexpo.co.jp/tibf
Key Personnel
Show Mgr: Keifuke Amano
Organized by the executive committee of TIBF.
Location: Tokyo Big Sight, Tokyo, Japan
April 24-27, 2003

Truth and Consequences
Formerly Who Are We Publishing For
Sponsored by Evangelical Christian Publishers Association
1969 E Broadway Rd, Suite 2, Tempe, AZ 85282, United States
Tel: 480-966-3998 *Fax:* 480-966-1944
Web Site: www.ecpa.org
Key Personnel
Pres: Doug Ross *E-mail:* dross@ecpa.org
Location: Riverside, CA, USA
April 26-30, 2003

UKSG Annual Conference & Exhibition
Sponsored by UK Serials Group
Hilltop, Heath End, Newbury RG20 0AP, United Kingdom
Tel: (01635) 254292 *Fax:* (01635) 253826
E-mail: uksg.admin@dial.pipex.com
Location: Heriot-Watt University, Edinburgh, UK
April 7-9, 2003

Young People's Poetry Week
Sponsored by The Children's Book Council Inc (CBC)
12 W 37 St, 2nd fl, New York, NY 10118-7480, United States
Tel: 212-966-1990 *Fax:* 212-966-2073
Web Site: www.cbcbooks.org/html/poetry_week.html
Key Personnel
VP, Dir of Mktg: JoAnn Sabatino-Falkenstein *Tel:* 212-966-1990 ext 305 *E-mail:* joann.sabatino_falkenstein@cbcbooks.org
Location: USA
April 14-20, 2003

MAY

ABA Convention & Trade Exhibit
Sponsored by American Booksellers Association
828 S Broadway, Tarrytown, NY 10591, United States
Tel: 914-591-2665 *Fax:* 914-591-2720
E-mail: info@bookweb.org
Web Site: www.bookweb.org
Held in conjunction with BookExpo America.

Location: Los Angeles Convention Center, Los Angeles, CA, USA
May 28-June 1, 2003

Amsterdam International Printing Allied Industries Trade Fair (Grafivak)
Sponsored by Amsterdam RAI
RAI, Europaplein, Amsterdam 1078-GZ, Netherlands
Mailing Address: PO Box 77777, Amsterdam 1070-MS, Netherlands
Tel: (020) 5491212 *Fax:* (020) 5491843
E-mail: grafivak@rai.nl
Web Site: www.grafivak.nl
Key Personnel
Proj Mgr: Esther Zeilstra *E-mail:* ezeilstra@rai.nl
Location: Amsterdam IRAI Exhibition Center, Amsterdam, Netherlands
May 13-17, 2003

Annual Quality Congress
Formerly Quality Press Annual Quality Congress
Sponsored by American Society for Quality
600 N Plankinton Ave, Milwaukee, WI 53203, United States
Tel: 414-272-8575 *Fax:* 414-272-1734
E-mail: cs@asq.org
Web Site: www.asq.org
Telex: 31-6567
Key Personnel
Exec Dir: Paul Borawski
Education Mgr: Shirley Krentz
Dir, Progs & Opers: Brian LeHouillier
Location: Kansas City Convention Center, Kansas City, MO, USA
May 19-21, 2003

Beijing International Book Fair
Sponsored by BIBF Management Office, CNPIEC
16 Gongti E Rd, Chaoyang District, Beijing 100020, China
Tel: (010) 65063080 *Fax:* (010) 65063101; (010) 65089188
E-mail: bibffo@bibf.net
Web Site: www.bibf.net
Location: Beijing Exhibition Center, Beijing, China
May 19-23, 2003

BookExpo America (BEA)
Sponsored by Association Expositions & Services
Affiliate of Reed Exhibition Companies
383 Main Ave, Norwalk, CT 06851, United States
Tel: 203-840-5614 *Fax:* 203-840-5580
E-mail: inquiry@bookexpo.america.com
Web Site: bookexpoamerica.com
Key Personnel
Sr VP: Tony Calanca
Industry VP & Show Mgr: Greg Topalian
Mktg Dir: Tom Kobak
Sales Dir: Steven Rosato
Location: Los Angeles Convention Center, Los Angeles, CA, USA
May 28-June 1, 2003

Catholic Press Association of the US and Canada Annual Convention
Sponsored by Catholic Press Association of the US & Canada
3555 Veterans Memorial Hwy, Unit O, Ronkonkoma, NY 11779, United States
Tel: 631-471-4730 *Fax:* 631-471-4804
E-mail: cathjourn@aol.com
Web Site: www.catholicpress.org
Key Personnel
Exec Dir: Owen P McGovern
Location: Atlanta, GA, USA
May 26-28, 2003

& PROMOTIONAL EVENTS

DPP 2003 - International Conference on Digital Production Printing
Sponsored by Society for Imaging Science & Technology (IS&T)
7003 Kilworth Lane, Springfield, VA 22151, United States
Tel: 703-642-9090 *Fax:* 703-642-9094
E-mail: info@imaging.org
Web Site: www.imaging.org
Key Personnel
Gen Chair: Ignacio Fons
Location: Hilton Barcelona Hotel, Barcelona, Spain
May 18-21, 2003

Evangelical Press Association Annual Conference
Sponsored by Evangelical Press Association (EPA)
PO Box 28129, Crystal, MN 55428, United States
Tel: 763-535-4793 *Fax:* 763-535-4794
E-mail: director@epassoc.org
Web Site: www.epassoc.org
Key Personnel
Exec Dir: Doug Trouton
Location: Atlanta, GA, USA
May 4-11, 2003

Exposicion de Literatura Cristiana (EXPOLIT) Book Fair
Sponsored by Spanish Evangelical Publishers Association (SEPA)/Asociacion de Editores Evangelicos and Editorial Unilit
1360 NW 88 Ave, Miami, FL 33172, United States
Tel: 305-592-6136 (ext 105) *Fax:* 305-592-0087
E-mail: expolit@editorialunilit.com
Web Site: www.expolit.com
Key Personnel
Pres, SEPA: Esteban Fernandez
Pres, EXPOLIT: David Ecklebarger
Spanish Christian Literature Convention.
Location: Miami, FL, USA
May 15-20, 2003

Gravure Association of America Convention
Sponsored by Gravure Association of America Inc
1200-A Scottsville Rd, Rochester, NY 14624, United States
Tel: 585-436-2150 *Fax:* 585-436-7689
E-mail: gaa@gaa.org
Web Site: www.gaa.org
Key Personnel
Meeting Planner: Pamela Schenk
Location: Westin Resort, Hilton Head, SC, USA
May 18-21, 2003

Gutenberg Festival
Sponsored by Graphic Arts Show Company
1899 Preston White Dr, Reston, VA 20191-4367, United States
Tel: 703-264-7200 *Fax:* 703-620-9187
E-mail: info@gasc.org
Web Site: www.gasc.org
Key Personnel
Dir, Communs: David Paulos
Annual trade show for graphic design, digital prepress, printing, publishing & converting.
Location: Long Beach Convention Center, Long Beach, CA, USA
May 1-3, 2003

InfoToday
Sponsored by Information Today, Inc
143 Old Marlton Pike, Medford, NJ 08055-8750, United States
Tel: 609-654-6266 *Fax:* 609-654-4309
E-mail: custserv@infotoday.com
Web Site: www.infotoday.com
Key Personnel
Conference Dir: Kathy Hogan-Bayer
Global conference & exhibition on electronic information & knowledge management.
Location: New York Hilton & Towers, New York, NY, USA
May 6-8, 2003

Institute of Printing National Annual General Meeting
Sponsored by Institute of Printing
The Mews, Hill House, Clanricarde Rd, Tunbridge Wells, Kent TN1 1PJ, United Kingdom
Tel: (01892) 538118 *Fax:* (01892) 518028
E-mail: admin@instituteofpainting.org
Web Site: www.instituteofprinting.org
Location: Norwich, Norfolk, UK
May 16-18, 2003

International Reading Association Annual Convention
Sponsored by International Reading Association
800 Barksdale Rd, Newark, DE 19711, United States
Mailing Address: PO Box 8139, Newark, DE 19714-8139, United States
Tel: 302-731-1600 *Fax:* 302-731-1057
E-mail: conferences@reading.org
Web Site: www.reading.org
Key Personnel
Pres: Jerry L Johns
Exec Dir: Alan E Farstrup
Location: Orlando, FL, USA
May 4-9, 2003

Internet Expo Printing & Graphics Arts Expo
Sponsored by Expo Source
8041 Hosbrook, Suite 201, Cincinnati, OH 45236, United States
Tel: 513-936-0054 *Fax:* 513-936-0451
E-mail: exposource@fuse.net
Web Site: exposupersite.com
Key Personnel
Show Mgr: Jim Klaserner
Location: Cincinnati Convention Center, Cincinnati, OH, USA
May 19-20, 2003

Northprint
Sponsored by Reed Exhibition Companies (UK)
Oriel House, 26 The Quadrant, Richmond, Surrey TW9 1DL, United Kingdom
Tel: (020) 8910 7910 *Fax:* (020) 8910 7813
E-mail: northprint.helpline@reedexpo.co.uk
Web Site: www.northprintexpo.co.uk
Telex: 8951389 ITFLONG
Key Personnel
Exhibition Dir: Andrew Furness *E-mail:* andrew.furness@reedexpo.co.uk
Sales Mgr: Steve Powell *E-mail:* steve.powell@reedexpo.co.uk
Mktg Mgr: Helen Beckett *E-mail:* helen.beckett@reedexpo.co.uk
Location: Harrogate Exhibition Centre, Harrogate, UK
May 13-15, 2003

Periodical Writers' Association of Canada Annual General Meeting
Sponsored by Periodical Writers' Association of Canada
54 Wolseley St, Suite 203, Toronto, ON M5T 1A5, Canada
Tel: 416-504-1645 *Fax:* 416-504-9079
E-mail: info@pwac.ca
Web Site: www.pwac.ca; www.writers.ca
Key Personnel
Exec Dir: Susan Stevenson
Location: Edmonton, AB, Canada
May 23-June 1, 2003

The PICS Conference
Sponsored by Society for Imaging Science & Technology (IS&T)
7003 Kilworth Lane, Springfield, VA 22151, United States
Tel: 703-642-9090 *Fax:* 703-642-9094
E-mail: info@imaging.org
Web Site: www.imaging.org
Key Personnel
Gen Co-chair: Johnan McCann; Mary McCann
Location: Hyatt Regency Hotel, Rochester, NY, USA
May 13-16, 2003

Printex 03
Sponsored by Reed Exhibition Companies
PO Box 764, Rozelle NSW 2039, Australia
Tel: (02) 9422 2500 *Fax:* (02) 9422 2555
E-mail: stf_management@msn.com.au
Web Site: www.printex.net.au
PrintEx brings the latest printing & graphic communications technologies to the industry. Presented by Graphic Arts Merchants Association of Australia Inc. (GAMAA) & The Printing Industries Association of Australia (PIAA).
Location: Sydney Convention & Exhibition Centre, Darling Harbour, Sydney, NSW, Australia
May 29-31, 2003

Quod Libet/International Antiquarian Book Fair & Artists Books
Sponsored by Luckwaldt Messen
Brueckhorst strasse 34, 24641 Sievershuetten, Germany
Tel: (040) 194 8101 *Fax:* (040) 194 636
E-mail: frauke@luckwaldt.de
Web Site: www.quod-libet.com
Location: Hamburger Boerse, Adolphsplatz 1, Hamburg, Germany
May 9-11, 2003

Society for Scholarly Publishing Annual Meeting
Sponsored by Society for Scholarly Publishing
10200 W 44 Ave, Suite 304, Wheat Ridge, CO 80033-2840, United States
Tel: 303-422-3914 *Fax:* 303-422-8894
E-mail: ssp@resourcenter.com
Web Site: www.sspnet.org
Location: Hyatt Regency Baltimore, Baltimore, MD, USA
May 28-30, 2003

Spring Technical Conference & Trade Fair
Sponsored by Technical Association of the Pulp & Paper Industry (TAPPI)
15 Technology Pkwy S, Norcross, GA 30092, United States
Tel: 770-446-1400 *Fax:* 770-446-6947
Web Site: www.tappi.org
Location: Chicago, IL, USA
May 11-14, 2003

TAPPI 8th Advanced Coating Fundamentals Symposium
Sponsored by Technical Association of the Pulp & Paper Industry (TAPPI)
15 Technology Pkwy S, Norcross, GA 30092, United States
Mailing Address: PO Box 105113, Atlanta, GA 30348-5113, United States
Tel: 770-446-1400 *Fax:* 770-446-6947
Web Site: www.tappi.org
Key Personnel
Publg Dir: Mary Beth Bennett
Adv Asst: Keith Hudson *E-mail:* khudson@tappi.org
Dir, Admin: Jeff Petro
Corp Rel Dir: Clare Reagan *E-mail:* creagan@tappi.org
Admin: Julie Anne Wiley

Location: Sheridan Chicago Hotel & Towers, Chicago, IL, USA
May 8-10, 2003

Warsaw International Book Fair
Sponsored by Ars Polona - Warsaw International Book Fair Office
Krakowskie Przedmiescie 7, 00-068 Warsaw, Poland
Tel: (022) 826-12-01; (022) 826-92-56 *Fax:* (022) 826-92-56
E-mail: mtk@arspolona.com.pl
Web Site: www.bookfair.pl
Key Personnel
Sec Gen: Ms Joanna Aleksandrowicz
  E-mail: joannaa@arspolona.com.pl
Location: Palace of Culture & Science, Warsaw, Poland
May 14-18, 2003

Annual Web Offset Association Conference
Sponsored by Web Offset Association Division of Printing Industries of America Inc
100 Daingerfield Rd, Alexandria, VA 22314, United States
Tel: 703-519-8100; 703-519-8142 *Fax:* 703-519-7109
Web Site: www.gain.net
Key Personnel
Meetings Mgr: Jonna Swan
Location: Opryland, Nashville, TN, USA
May 4-7, 2003

WEM: The World Education Market
Sponsored by Reed Midem
11 rue du Colonel Pierre-Avia, 75726 Paris Cedex 15, France
Tel: (01) 41 90 44 00 *Fax:* (01) 41 90 44 09
Web Site: www.reedmidemorg.com
Key Personnel
Contact: Dominique Wasquel *E-mail:* dominique.wasquel@reedmidem.com
Provides a one-stop international shopping forum, showcasing educational resources for all levels & ages of learners, for use in the classroom, the workplace or the home.
Location: Lisbon, Portugal
May 21-23, 2003

JUNE

American Library Association Annual Conference
Sponsored by American Library Association (ALA)
50 E Huron St, Chicago, IL 60611, United States
Tel: 312-280-3200 *Fax:* 312-944-7841
E-mail: ala@ala.org
Web Site: www.ala.org
Key Personnel
Public Info Dir: Deborah Davis
Press Officer: Belia Ortega
Dir, Intl Rel: Michael Dowling
Location: Toronto, ON, Canada
June 19-25, 2003

Association of American University Presses Annual Meeting
Sponsored by Association of American University Presses (AAUP)
71 W 23 St, Suite 901, New York, NY 10010, United States
Tel: 212-989-1010 *Fax:* 212-989-0176
E-mail: info@ aaupnet.org
Web Site: www.aaupnet.org
Key Personnel
Exec Dir: Peter J Givler
Asst Dir: Timothy Muench

Admin Mgr: Linda McCall *Tel:* 212-989-1010 Ext 30 *E-mail:* lmccall@aaupnet.org
Membership Mgr: Susan Patton *Tel:* 212-989-1010, ext 25 *E-mail:* spatton@aaupnet.org
Location: Hyatt Regency, St Louis, MO, USA
June 22-25, 2003

Bibliographical Society of Canada/La Societe bibliographique du Canada Annual Meeting
Sponsored by Bibliographical Society of Canada/ La Societe bibliographique du Canada
PO Box 575, Sta P, Toronto, ON M5S 2T1, Canada
Tel: 416-946-3173
E-mail: mcgaughe@yorku.ca
Web Site: www.library.utoronto.ca
Key Personnel
Pres: Peter McNally
Location: Toronto, ON, Canada
June 16, 2003

Book Expo Canada
Formerly Canadian Booksellers Association Annual Convention & Tradeshow
Sponsored by Reed Exhibition Companies
3761 Victoria Park Ave, Unit One, Toronto, ON M1W 3S2, Canada
Tel: 416-491-7565 *Toll Free Tel:* 888-322-7333 *Fax:* 416-491-7096
E-mail: jsickinger@reedexpo.com
Web Site: www.cbabook.org; www.cbabook.com; www.bookexpo.ca
Key Personnel
Show Mgr: Jennifer Sickinger
Location: Metro Toronto Convention Centre, Toronto, ON, Canada
June 4-7, 2003

British & Irish Association of Law Librarians Annual Conference
Sponsored by British & Irish Association of Law Librarians
26 Myton Crescent, Warwick CV34 6QA, United Kingdom
Tel: (01926) 491717 *Fax:* (01926) 491717
Key Personnel
BIALL Administer: Susan Frost
Location: Cardiff, UK
June 2003

The Bronte Society Annual General Meeting
Sponsored by The Bronte Society
The Bronte Parsonage Museum, Haworth, Keighley, W Yorks BD22 8DR, United Kingdom
Tel: (01535) 642323 *Fax:* (01535) 647131
E-mail: bronte@bronte.prestel.co.uk
Web Site: www.bronte.org.uk
Location: Haworth, UK
June 4, 2003

Canadian Library Association Annual Convention & Tradeshow
Sponsored by Canadian Library Association (CLA)
328 Frank St, Ottawa, ON K2P 0X8, Canada
Tel: 613-232-9625 *Fax:* 613-563-9895
E-mail: info@cla.ca
Web Site: www.cla.ca
Key Personnel
Exec Dir: Vicki Whitmell *E-mail:* vwhitmel@cla.ca
Location: Metro Toronto Convention Centre, Toronto, ON, Canada
June 19-25, 2003

Eastpack: The Power of Packaging
Sponsored by Canon Communications
11444 W Olympic Blvd, Suite 900, Los Angeles, CA 90064, United States
Tel: 310-445-4200 *Fax:* 310-445-4299
Web Site: www.cancom.com

Location: Jacob K Javits Convention Center, New York, NY, USA
June 2-4, 2003

Electronic Publishing International
Sponsored by International Electronic Publishing Research Centre Ltd (IEPRC)
PO Box 83, Leatherhead, Surrey KT22 7AZ, United Kingdom
Tel: (011) 1372-373646; (011) 1372-278335 *Fax:* (011) 1372-379732
E-mail: admin@ieprc.org
Web Site: www.ieprc.org
Telex: 929810
Location: Darmstadt, Germany
June 2003

FIAF Congress
Sponsored by International Federation of Film Archives (Federation Internationale des Archives du Film)
Rue Defacqz 1, 1000 Brussels, Belgium
Tel: (02) 5383065 *Fax:* (02) 5344774
E-mail: info@fiafnet.org
Web Site: www.fiafnet.org
Key Personnel
Sr Adminstr: Christian Dimitriu
Location: Stockholm, Sweden & Helsinki, Finland
June 2-10, 2003

Gutenberg Gesellschaft Annual General Meeting
Sponsored by Gutenberg-Gesellschaft eV
Liebfrauenplatz 5, D-55116 Mainz, Germany
Tel: (06131) 22 64 20 *Fax:* (06131) 23 35 30
E-mail: gutenberg-gesellschaft@freenet.de
Web Site: www.gutenberg-gesellschaft.uni-mainz. de
Key Personnel
Sec Gen: Gertraude Benoehr
Location: Museum Mainz, City Hall, Mainz, Germany
June 21, 2003

International Association of Business Communicators Conference
Sponsored by International Association of Business Communicators (IABC)
One Hallidie Plaza, Suite 600, San Francisco, CA 94102, United States
Tel: 415-544-4700 *Fax:* 415-544-4747
E-mail: service_center@iabc.com
Web Site: www.iabc.com
Key Personnel
Pres: Julie Freeman
Location: Toronto, ON, Canada
June 8-11, 2003

International Newsletter & Specialized - Information Conference
Sponsored by Newsletter & Electronic Publishers Association
1501 Wilson Blvd, Suite 509, Arlington, VA 22209, United States
Tel: 703-527-2333 *Fax:* 703-841-0629
E-mail: nepa@newsletters.org
Web Site: www.newsletters.org
Key Personnel
Exec Dir: Patti Wysocki
Location: Renaissance Mayflower Hotel, Washington, DC, USA
June 1-3, 2003

International Newspaper Financial Executives Annual Conference
Sponsored by International Newspaper Financial Executives
21525 Ridgetop Circle, Suite 200, Sterling, VA 20166, United States
Tel: 703-421-4060 *Fax:* 703-421-4068
E-mail: infehq@infe.org

Web Site: www.infe.org
Key Personnel
VP & Exec Dir: Robert J Kasabian
E-mail: bkasabian@infe.org
June 21-25, 2003

International Plate Printers', Die Stampers' & Engravers' Union of North America Mini Meeting
Sponsored by International Plate Printers', Die Stampers' & Engravers' Union of North America
3957 Smoke Rd, Doylestown, PA 18901, United States
Tel: 215-340-2843
Key Personnel
Sec & Treas: James Kopernick
Location: Philadelphia, PA, USA
June 2003

Internet World UK
Sponsored by Penton Media
16 Thordal Circle, Darien, CT 06880, United States
Tel: 203-559-2800 Fax: 203-559-2840
E-mail: information@penton.com
Web Site: www.internetworld.co.uk
Location: Earls Court One, London, UK
June 3-5, 2003

NEXPO®
Sponsored by Newspaper Association of America (NAA)
1921 Gallows Rd, Suite 600, Vienna, VA 22182, United States
Tel: 703-902-1600 Fax: 703-902-1843
E-mail: laths@naa.org
Web Site: www.nexpo.com
Key Personnel
Dir of Exhibition Sales: Brad Smith
Annual technical exposition & conference for newspapers.
Location: Las Vegas Convention Center, Las Vegas, NV, USA
June 16-19, 2003

Outdoor Writers Association of America Annual Conference
Sponsored by Outdoor Writers Association of America
158 Lower Georges Valley Rd, Spring Mills, PA 16875, United States
Tel: 814-364-9557 Fax: 814-364-9558
E-mail: eking4owaa@cs.com
Web Site: www.owaa.org
Location: Columbia, MO, USA
June 14-18, 2003

Print Sales & Marketing Conference
Sponsored by Printing Industries of America Inc
100 Daingerfield Rd, Alexandria, VA 22314, United States
Tel: 703-519-8143 Fax: 703-519-7109
Web Site: www.gain.net
Location: Bernalillo, New Mexico
June 22-25, 2003

School Library Association Annual Conference
Sponsored by School Library Association
Unit 2, Lotmead Business Village, Lotmead Farm, Wanborough, Swindon, Wilts SN4 0UY, United Kingdom
Tel: (01793) 791787 Fax: (01793) 791786
E-mail: info@sla.org.uk
Web Site: www.sla.org.uk
Key Personnel
Chief Executive: Kathy Lemaire E-mail: kathy@sla.org.uk
Location: University of Leicester, Leicester, UK
June 27-29, 2003

Science Fiction Research Association Annual Conference
Sponsored by Science Fiction Research Association Inc
University of California, Psychology, One Shields Ave, Mentor, CA 95616-8686, United States
Tel: 530-752-1699
Web Site: www.sfra.org
Key Personnel
Pres: Prof Alan C Elms
Location: University of Guelph, Guelph, ON, Canada
June 26-29, 2003

Southwestern Graphics
Sponsored by Texas Graphic Arts Educational Foundation
13410 Preston Rd, No 1-100, Dallas, TX 75240-5299, United States
E-mail: info@swgraphics.com
Web Site: www.swgraphics.com
Key Personnel
Asst Show Mgr: Laura Bates
Location: Alamodome, San Antonio, TX, USA
June 5-7, 2003

Special Libraries Association Annual Conference
Sponsored by Special Libraries Association (SLA)
1700 18 St NW, Washington, DC 20009-2514, United States
Tel: 202-234-4700 Fax: 202-265-9317
E-mail: sla@sla.org
Web Site: www.sla.org
Key Personnel
Interim Dir: Lynn Smith
Location: Hilton New York; Marriott Marquis & Sheraton New York, New York, NY, USA
June 7-12, 2003

JULY

ARLIS/UK & Ireland Annual Conference
Sponsored by ARLIS/UK & Ireland, The Art Libraries Society
18 College Rd, B60 2NE Bromsgrove, United Kingdom
Tel: (01527) 579298 Fax: (01527) 579298
E-mail: sfrench@arlis.demon.co.uk
Web Site: www.arlis.org.uk
Key Personnel
Administrator: Sonia French E-mail: sfrench@arlis.demon.co.uk
Chair: Margaret Young
Theme "New Ways of Seeing Art Information".
Location: University of Sussex, Brighton, UK
July 3-6, 2003

CBA International Convention
Sponsored by CBA
9240 Explorer Dr, Colorado Springs, CO 80920, United States
Mailing Address: PO Box 62000, Colorado Springs, CO 80962-2000, United States
Tel: 719-265-9895 Fax: 719-272-3510
Web Site: www.cbaonline.org
Key Personnel
Pres: William Anderson
VP & COO: Dorothy Gore
Convention & Expositions Mgr: Scott Graham
For almost 50 years, the annual CBA International Convention has been our industry's single-most impacting week. During this week, people of the industry form all over the world meet face-to-face for buying & selling, education, inspiration, fellowship & future planning. Here individuals unite to further the mission of seeing Christian product impact lives for God's kingdom the world over. And at this unique gathering, our industry's strength is most evident & our goals are most clearly in focus. It is, in short, the most important week in the ministry of your business & of the industry as a whole.
Location: Orange County Convention Center, Orlando, FL, USA
July 12-17, 2003

Church & Synagogue Library Association Conference
Sponsored by Church & Synagogue Library Association
PO Box 19357, Portland, OR 97280-0357, United States
Tel: 503-244-6919 Fax: 503-977-3734
E-mail: csla@worldaccessnet.com
Web Site: www.worldaccessnet.com/~csla
Location: Brookfield, WI, USA
July 28-30, 2003

Hong Kong Book Fair
Sponsored by Hong Kong Trade Development Council
Unit 13, Expo Galleria, One Expo Dr, Wanchai, Hong Kong
Tel: (02) 5844333 Fax: (02) 8240026
E-mail: exhibitions@tdc.org.hk
Web Site: hkbookfair.tdc.org.hk
Key Personnel
Sales Adminstrator: Joyce P F Laing
Location: Hong Kong Convention & Exhibition Center, One Harbour Rd, Wanchai, Hong Kong
July 22-28, 2003

International Association of Music Libraries, Archives & Documentation Centres Conference
Sponsored by International Association of Music Libraries, Archives & Documentation Centres
c/o Carleton University Library, 1125 Colonel By Drive, Ottawa, ON K1S 5B6, Canada
Tel: 613-520-2600 (ext 8150) Fax: 613-520-3583
Web Site: www.cilea.it/music/iaml/iamlhome.htm
Key Personnel
Sec-Gen: Alison Hall E-mail: alison_hall@carleton.ca
Location: Tallinn, Estonia
July 7-12, 2003

Macworld Conference & Expo
Sponsored by IDG World Expo
Unit of IDG
3 Speen St, Framingham, MA 01701, United States
Tel: 508-424-4800 Fax: 508-620-6668
Web Site: www.macworldexpo.com
Key Personnel
VP: Rob Scheschareg
Location: Jacob K Javits Convention Center, New York, NY, USA
July 14-18, 2003

RWA Annual National Conference
Sponsored by Romance Writers of America
3707 FM 1960 West, Suite 555, Houston, TX 77068, United States
Tel: 281-440-6885 Fax: 281-440-7510
E-mail: info@rwanational.org
Web Site: www.rwanational.org
Key Personnel
Exec Dir: Allison Kelley E-mail: akelley@rwanational.org
Location: New York, NY, USA
July 16-19, 2003

Umbrella 2003
Sponsored by Chartered Institute of Library & Information Professionals

7 Ridgmount St, London WC1E 7AE, United Kingdom
Tel: (020) 7255 0543 *Fax:* (020) 7255 0541
E-mail: info@la-hq.org.uk; info@cilip.org.uk
Web Site: www.cilip.org.uk; www.cilip.org.uk
Location: UMIST, Manchester, UK
July 3-5, 2003

AUGUST

The Dorothy L Sayers Society Annual Convention
Sponsored by The Dorothy L Sayers Society
Rose Cottage, Malthouse Lane, Hurstpierpoint, West Sussex BN6 9JY, United Kingdom
Tel: (01273) 833444 *Fax:* (01273) 835988
E-mail: seona@sayers.org.uk
Web Site: www.sayers.org.uk
Location: Royal Holloway College, UK
Aug 2003

Edinburgh International Book Festival
Scottish Book Centre, 137 Dundee St, Edinburgh EH11 1BG, United Kingdom
Tel: (0131) 2285444 *Fax:* (0131) 2284333
E-mail: admin@edbookfest.co.uk
Web Site: www.edbookfest.co.uk
Key Personnel
Dir: Catherine Lockerbie
Location: Charlotte Square Gardens, Edinburgh, UK
Aug 9-25, 2003

Garden Writers Association of America Meeting & Symposium
Sponsored by Garden Writers Association of America
10210 Leatherleaf Ct, Manassas, VA 20111, United States
Tel: 703-257-1032 *Fax:* 703-257-0213
E-mail: info@gwaa.org
Web Site: www.gwaa.org
Key Personnel
Pres: Bill Aldrich
Exec Dir: Nona Wolfran-Koivula
Location: Indian Lakes Resort, Chicago, IL, USA
Aug 14-19, 2003

Graphic Arts
Formerly International Graphic Arts Technology Exhibition for Asia
Sponsored by Business & Industrial Trade Fairs Ltd
Unit 103-105, New East Ocean Centre, 9 Science Museum Rd, Tsimshatsui East, Kowloon, Hong Kong
Tel: 28652633 *Fax:* 28661770; 28662076
E-mail: enquiry@bitf.com.hk
Web Site: www.bitf.com.hk
Key Personnel
Senior Manager: Louis Leung
Location: Hong Kong Convention & Exhibition Centre, Hong Kong
Aug 2003

IFLA General Conference & Council
Sponsored by International Federation of Library Associations & Institutions (IFLA)
Postbus 95312, 2509 CH The Hague, Netherlands
Tel: (070) 3140884 *Fax:* (070) 3834827
E-mail: ifla@ifla.org
Web Site: www.ifla.org
Location: Berlin, Germany
Aug 2003

International Conference on Writing & Illustrating for Children
Formerly National Conference on Writing & Illustrating for Children
Sponsored by Society of Children's Book Writers & Illustrators (SCBWI)
8271 Beverly Blvd, Los Angeles, CA 90048, United States
Tel: 323-782-1010 *Fax:* 323-782-1892
E-mail: scbwi@scbwi.org
Web Site: www.scbwi.org
Key Personnel
Pres: Steve Mooser
Location: Century Plaza Hotel & Spa, Los Angeles, CA, USA
Aug 15-18, 2003

Print & Pack Expo
Formerly International Printing & Packaging Machinery and Materials Exhibition for Asia
Sponsored by Business & Industrial Trade Fairs Ltd
Unit 103-105, New East Ocean Centre, 9 Science Museum Rd, Tsimshatsui East, Kowloon, Hong Kong
Tel: 28652633 *Fax:* 28661770; 28662076
E-mail: enquiry@bitf.com.hk
Web Site: www.bitf.com.hk
Key Personnel
Senior Manager: Louis Leung
Location: Hong Kong Convention & Exhibition Centre, Hong Kong
Aug 2003

South African Booksellers Association Annual Conference
Sponsored by South African Booksellers Association
PO Box 870, Bellville 7535, South Africa
Tel: (021) 918-8616 *Fax:* (021) 951-4903
Location: Durban, South Africa
Aug 19-20, 2003

Writer's Summer School
PO Box 5532, Heanor, Derbyshire DE75 7YF, United Kingdom
Tel: (07050) 630949 *Fax:* (07050) 630949
E-mail: gxk@cs.nott.ac.uk
Web Site: www.wss.org.uk; www.swanwickwss.freeserve.co.uk/home.html
A week-long summer school of informal talks & discussion groups, forums, panels, quizzes, competition & a lot of fun. Open to everyone, from absolute beginners to published authors. Held annually in August.
Location: The Hayes Conference Centre, Swanwick, Derbyshire, UK
Aug 2003

Zimbabwe International Book Fair
PO Box 21303, London WC2E 8PH, United Kingdom
Tel: (020) 7836 8501 *Fax:* (020) 7836 8501
E-mail: international@zibf.org
Web Site: www.zibf.org
Location: Harare Gardens, Harare, Zimbabwe
Aug 6-10, 2003

AUTUMN

Association of Braille Publishing Houses & Libraries Annual Conference
Sponsored by Arbeitsgemeinschaft des Blindenschrift-Druckereien und Bibliotheken (AG BDB)
pA Deutsche Blinden-Bibliother, AM Schlag 8-10, 35037 Marburg an der Lahn, Germany
Mailing Address: Postfach 1160, 35001 Marburg an der Lahn, Germany
Tel: (06421) 6060 *Fax:* (06421) 606269
E-mail: info@blista.de
Web Site: www.blista.de
Key Personnel
Pres & Libr Dir: Rainer F V Witte *E-mail:* witt@blista.de
Location: German Institute for the Blind, Marburg/Lahn, Germany
Autumn 2003

New Atlantic Independent Booksellers Association Annual Trade Show
Sponsored by New Atlantic Independent Booksellers Association (NAIBA)
2667 Hyacinth St, Westbury, NY 11590, United States
Tel: 516-333-0681 *Fax:* 516-333-0689
E-mail: info@naiba.com; readingent@aol.com
Web Site: www.naiba.com
Key Personnel
Exec Dir: Eileen Dengler
Autumn 2003

SEPTEMBER

American Medical Writers Association Annual Conference
Sponsored by American Medical Writers Association
40 W Gude Dr, Suite 101, Rockville, MD 20850-1192, United States
Tel: 301-294-5303 *Fax:* 301-294-9006
E-mail: amwa@amwa.org
Web Site: www.amwa.org
Location: Inter-Continental, Miami, FL, USA
Sept 18-20, 2003

Distripress Annual Congress
Sponsored by Distripress
Beethovenstr 20, CH-8002 Zurich, Switzerland
Tel: (01) 2024121 *Fax:* (01) 2021025
E-mail: info@distripress.ch
Web Site: www.distripress.ch
Key Personnel
Dir: Dr Peter Emod *E-mail:* peter.emod@distripress.ch
Non-profit association promoting the free international circulation of the press.
Location: Dublin, Ireland
Sept 14-18, 2003

European Association of Directory Publishers Annual Conference
Sponsored by European Association of Directory Publishers
Ave Franklin Roosevelt, 127, 1050 Brussels, Belgium
Tel: (02) 6463060 *Fax:* (02) 6463637
E-mail: mailbox@eadp.org
Web Site: www.eadp.org
Location: Budapest, Hungary
Sept 17-19, 2003

Goteborg International Book Fair
Sponsored by Bok & Bibliotek
412 94 Goteborg, Sweden
Tel: (031) 7088400 *Fax:* (031) 209103
Web Site: www.bok-bibliotek.com
Key Personnel
Man Dir: Anna Falck *E-mail:* anna.falck@bok-bibliotek.se
Exhibition Mgr: Lisa Oden *E-mail:* lo@bok-bibliotek.se
Location: Swedish Exhibition & Congress Centre, Goteborg, Sweden
Sept 25-28, 2003

& PROMOTIONAL EVENTS

Moscow International Book Fair
Sponsored by General Directorate of International Book Exhibitions & Fairs
16 Malaya Dmitrovka St, Moscow 127006, Russian Federation
Tel: (095) 2994034; (095) 2999790; (095) 2993466 *Fax:* (095) 9732132; (095) 2992539
E-mail: exhibitions@elnet.msk.ru
Web Site: www.bookfair.ru; www.mibf.ru
Key Personnel
Gen Dir: Mr Nikolay Ph Ovsyannikov
Location: All Russian Exhibition Centre, Moscow, Russia
Sept 3-8, 2003

National Federation of Press Women National Conference
Sponsored by National Federation of Press Women Inc (NFPW)
PO Box 5556, Arlington, VA 22205-0056, United States
Tel: 703-534-2500 *Fax:* 703-534-5751
E-mail: presswomen@aol.com
Web Site: www.nfpw.org
Key Personnel
Exec Dir: Carol Pierce
Location: Wyndham Hotel, Wilmington, DE, USA
Sept 4-6, 2003

New York is Book Country
Sponsored by New York Is Book Country
c/o C2 Media, 423 W 55 St, New York, NY 10019, United States
Tel: 646-557-6625 *Fax:* 646-557-6400
E-mail: nyibc@c2media.com
Key Personnel
Exec Dir: Courtney Muller
Annual five-day literary festival throughout the city, culminating in the Sunday, books-only street fair on Fifth Ave between 48th & 57th Streets, New York, NY, USA.
Location: New York, NY, USA
Sept 17-21, 2003

NIP 19: The 19th International Congress on Digital Printing Technologies
Sponsored by Society for Imaging Science & Technology (IS&T)
7003 Kilworth Lane, Springfield, VA 22151, United States
Tel: 703-642-9090 *Fax:* 703-642-9094
E-mail: info@imaging.org
Web Site: www.imaging.org
Location: Hyatt Regency Hotel, New Orleans, LA, USA
Sept 28-Oct 3, 2003

PSA International Conference of Photography
Sponsored by Photographic Society of America Inc (PSA)
3000 United Founders Blvd, Suite 103, Oklahoma City, OK 73112-3940, United States
Tel: 405-843-1437 *Fax:* 405-843-1438
Web Site: www.psa-photo.org
Key Personnel
VP, Conventions: Ms Icy Sowards
Location: Houston, TX, USA
Sept 1-6, 2003

Publishers Association of the South Fall Conference & Annual Meeting
Sponsored by Publishers Association of the South (PAS)
4412 Fletcher St, Panama City, FL 32405-1017, United States
Tel: 850-914-0766 *Fax:* 850-769-4348
E-mail: executive@pubsouth.org
Web Site: www.pubsouth.org
Key Personnel
Pres: Joseph Billingsley

Assn Exec: Pat Sabiston
Location: Jekyll Island, GA, USA
Sept 18-19, 2003

Seybold Seminars
Sponsored by Key3Media Events
303 Vintage Park Dr, Foster City, CA 94404, United States
Tel: 650-578-6900 *Fax:* 650-525-0194
Web Site: www.key3media.com/seyboldseminars/
Key Personnel
VP & Gen Mgr: Gene Gable
Location: Moscone Convention Center, San Francisco, CA, USA
Sept 29-Oct 2, 2003

Society of Professional Journalists National Convention
Sponsored by The Society of Professional Journalists
Eugene S Pulliam National Journalism Center, 3909 N Meridian St, Indianapolis, IN 46208, United States
Tel: 317-927-8000 *Fax:* 317-920-4789
E-mail: spj@spj.org
Web Site: www.spj.org
Key Personnel
Exec Dir: Terrance G Harper
Deputy Dir: Julie Grimes
Programs Coord: Carrie Copeland
Location: Tampa, FL, USA
Sept 10-12, 2003

Southeast Booksellers Association Annual Meeting & Trade Show
Sponsored by Southeast Booksellers Association (SEBA)
2730 Devine St, Columbia, SC 29205, United States
Tel: 803-252-7755 *Fax:* 803-252-8589
E-mail: sebajewell@aol.com; info@sebaweb.org
Web Site: www.sebaweb.org
Location: Jekyl Island, GA, USA
Sept 19-21, 2003

Spectrum 2003
Sponsored by IDE Alliance
100 Daingerfield Rd, Alexandria, VA 22314-2888, United States
Tel: 703-837-1070 *Fax:* 703-837-1072
Web Site: www.idealliance.org
Location: Sheraton El Conquistador, Tuscon, AZ, USA
Sept 14-18, 2003

Thai Print: The International Trade Exhibition for Printing Machinery, Graphic Art Equipment, Pre-Press Solutions, Materials & Supplies
Sponsored by Reed Tradex Co Ltd
100/68-69, 32nd fl, Sathorn Nakorn Tower, North Sathorn Rd, Silom Bangrak, Bangkok 10500, Thailand
Tel: (02) 636 7272 *Fax:* (02) 636 7282
E-mail: rtdx@reedtradex.co.th; ask@reedtradex.co.th
Web Site: www.reedtradex.co.th
Co-organized by the Thai Printing Association.
Location: Bangkok International Trade & Exhibition Centre, Bangkok, Thailand
Sept 2003

OCTOBER

Belgrade International Book Fair
Sponsored by Association of Yugoslav Publishers & Booksellers

Kneza Milosa 25/1, 11000 Belgrade, Yugoslavia
Tel: (011) 642248; (011) 642533 *Fax:* (011) 646339
Web Site: www.beobookfair.co.yu
Key Personnel
General Dir: Mr Ognjen Lakecevic
E-mail: ognjenl@eunet.yu
Location: Belgrade, Yugoslavia
Oct 23-29, 2003

BMI Annual Conference
Sponsored by Book Manufacturers' Institute Inc (BMI)
65 William St, Suite 300, Wellesley, MA 02481-3800, United States
Tel: 781-239-0103 *Fax:* 781-239-0106
E-mail: bmibook@aol.com
Web Site: www.bmibook.org
Key Personnel
Exec VP: Stephen P Snyder
Location: The Breakers, Palm Beach, FL, USA
Oct 26-29, 2003

Corrugated Containers Conference & CorrExpo
Formerly International Corrugated Containers Conference & Trade Fair
Sponsored by Technical Association of the Pulp & Paper Industry (TAPPI)
15 Technology Pkwy S, Norcross, GA 30092, United States
Mailing Address: PO Box 105113, Atlanta, GA 30348-5113, United States
Tel: 770-446-1400 *Fax:* 770-446-6947
Web Site: www.tappi.org
Key Personnel
Publg Dir: Mary Beth Bennett
Adv Asst: Keith Hudson *E-mail:* khudson@tappi.org
Dir, Admin: Jeff Petro
Corp Rel Dir: Clare Reagan *E-mail:* creagan@tappi.org
Admin: Julie Anne Wiley
Location: Hyatt Regency Dallas, Dallas, TX, USA
Oct 12-15, 2003

De Boekenbeurs (Flanders Book Fair)
Sponsored by Bock.be
Hof ter Shrieklaan 17, 2600 Berchem/Antwerp, Belgium
Tel: (03) 2308923 *Fax:* (03) 2812240
E-mail: info@boek.be
Web Site: www.boek.be
Location: Bouwcentrum, Jan van Rijswijcklaan 191, Antwerp, Belgium
Oct 2003

DMA Annual Conference & Exhibition
Sponsored by The Direct Marketing Association Inc (The DMA)
1120 Avenue of the Americas, New York, NY 10036, United States
Tel: 212-768-7277 *Fax:* 212-302-6714
E-mail: conference@the-dma.org
Web Site: www.dmaannual.com
Location: Orange County Convention Center, Orlando, Fl, USA
Oct 12-15, 2003

English Association Semiannual Teachers' Conference
Sponsored by English Association
University of Leicester, University Rd, Leicester LE1 7RH, United Kingdom
Tel: (0116) 2523982 *Fax:* (0116) 2522301
E-mail: engassoc@le.ac.uk
Key Personnel
Chief Exec: Helen Lucas
Conference Org: Louise Callen
Membership Coord: Jeremy Wiltshire
Oct 2003

Fall Technical Conference & Trade Fair
Sponsored by Technical Association of the Pulp & Paper Industry (TAPPI)
15 Technology Pkwy S, Norcross, GA 30092, United States
Mailing Address: PO Box 105113, Atlanta, GA 30348-5113, United States
Tel: 770-446-1400 *Fax:* 770-446-6947
Web Site: www.tappi.org
Key Personnel
Publg Dir: Mary Beth Bennett
Adv Asst: Keith Hudson *E-mail:* khudson@tappi.org
Dir, Admin: Jeff Petro
Corp Rel Dir: Clare Reagan *E-mail:* creagan@tappi.org
Admin: Julie Anne Wiley
Location: Hyatt Chicago, Chicago, IL, USA
Oct 24-31, 2003

Frankfurt Book Fair
Sponsored by Ausstellungs-und Messe-GmbH des Borsenvereins des Deutschen Buchhandels
Reineckssstr 3, 60313 Frankfurt am Main, Germany
Mailing Address: Postfach 100116, 60001 Frankfurt am Main, Germany
Tel: (069) 21020 *Fax:* (069) 2102 227
E-mail: info@book-fair.com
Web Site: www.frankfurt-book-fair.com *Cable:* BUCHMESSE
Key Personnel
CEO: Lorenzo Rudolf
Location: Frankfurt Fairgrounds, Frankfurt, Germany
Oct 8-13, 2003

Inter American Press Association General Assembly
Sponsored by Inter American Press Association (IAPA)
1801 SW Third Ave, Miami, FL 33129, United States
Tel: 305-634-2465 *Fax:* 305-635-3272
E-mail: info@sipia.org
Web Site: www.sipiapa.org
Location: Westin Hotel, Chicago, IL, USA
Oct 10-14. 2003

LIBER Feria Internacional del Libro
Sponsored by Federacion de Gremios de Editores de Espana (FGEE) (Spanish Publishers Association)
Cea Bermudez, 44-2° Dehe, Madrid 20003, Spain
Tel: (091) 5345195 *Fax:* (091) 5352625
E-mail: fgee@fge.es
Web Site: www.federacioneditores.org
Location: Madrid, Spain
Oct 1-4, 2003

Monterrey International Book Fair
Sponsored by Instituto Tecnologico y de Estudios Superiores de Monterrey
Av Eugenio Garza Sada 2501, Col Tecnologico, 648497 Monterrey, Nuevo Leon, Mexico
Tel: (08) 328 43 28 *Fax:* (08) 359 96 23
E-mail: filmty@fil.mty.itesm.mx
Web Site: fil.mty.itesm.mx
Key Personnel
Opers Dir: Armando Ruiz
Location: Cintemex, Monterrey, Mexico
Oct 11-19, 2003

National Design Conference
Sponsored by American Institute of Graphic Arts (AIGA)
164 Fifth Ave, New York, NY 10010, United States
Tel: 212-807-1990 (ext 323) *Fax:* 212-807-1799
E-mail: aiganswers@aiga.org; programs@aiga.org
Web Site: www.aiga.org

Key Personnel
Exec Dir: Richard Grefe
Biennial event.
Location: Vancouver, BC, Canada
Oct 23-26, 2003

National Newspaper Association Annual Convention & Trade Show
Sponsored by National Newspaper Association
PO Box 7540, Columbia, MO 65205-7450, United States
Tel: 573-882-4021 *Fax:* 573-884-5490
E-mail: info@nna.org
Web Site: www.nna.org
Key Personnel
Exec VP & CEO: Brian Steffens
Location: Hyatt Regency, Crown Center, Kansas City, MO, USA
Oct 1-4, 2003

NPES The Association for Suppliers of Printing, Publishing and Converting Technologies Annual Conference
Sponsored by NPES The Association for Suppliers of Printing, Publishing and Converting Technologies
1899 Preston White Dr, Reston, VA 20191-4367, United States
Tel: 703-264-7200 *Fax:* 703-620-0994
E-mail: npes@npes.org
Web Site: www.npes.org
Key Personnel
Pres: Regis J Delmontagne
Dir, Communs & Mktg: Carol J Hurlburt *E-mail:* churlbur@npes.org
Trade Association representing companies which manufacture equipment, systems, software & supplies used in printing, publishing & converting.
Location: Sea Island, GA, USA
Oct 25-28, 2003

PACK EXPO
Sponsored by Packaging Machinery Manufacturers Institute
4350 N Fairfax Dr, Suite 600, Arlington, VA 22203, United States
Tel: 703-243-8555 *Fax:* 703-243-3038
E-mail: expo@pmmi.org
Web Site: www.packexpo.com
Key Personnel
Exhibitor Servs Coord: Kim Beaulieu *E-mail:* kbeaulieu@packexpo.com
Location: Las Vegas Convention Center, Las Vegas, NV, USA
Oct 13-15, 2003

SPAN Conference
Sponsored by Small Publishers Association of North America (SPAN)
425 Cedar St, Buena Vista, CO 81211, United States
Mailing Address: PO Box 1306, Buena Vista, CO 81211-1306, United States
Tel: 719-395-4790 *Fax:* 719-395-8374
E-mail: span@spannet.org
Web Site: www.spannet.org
Key Personnel
Exec Dir: Marilyn Ross
Busn Dir: Tom Ross
A meaty, in-depth college for independent presses, authors & self-publishers. Emphasis is on "can-do" marketing/PR strategies.
Location: Los Angeles, CA
Oct 24-26, 2003

Xplor Global Conference
Sponsored by Xplor International
24238 Hawthorne Blvd, Torrance, CA 90505-6505, United States
Tel: 310-791-9521 *Fax:* 310-375-4240

E-mail: info@xplor.org
Web Site: www.xplor.org
Key Personnel
Communs Asst: Steven Barry
Location: Atlanta, GA, USA
Oct 25-31, 2003

NOVEMBER

American Academy of Religion
Sponsored by American Schools of Oriental Research
825 Houston Mill Rd, Atlanta, GA 30329, United States
Tel: 404-727-3049; 404-727-7920 *Fax:* 404-727-7959
Web Site: www.aarweb.org
Key Personnel
Meeting Coord: Shannon Planck
Location: Atlanta, GA, USA
Nov 22-25, 2003

American Translators Association Annual Conference
Sponsored by American Translators Association (ATA)
225 Reinekers Lane, Suite 590, Alexandria, VA 22314, United States
Tel: 703-683-6100 *Fax:* 703-683-6122
E-mail: ata@atanet.org
Web Site: www.atanet.org
Key Personnel
Exec Dir: Walter Bacak *Tel:* 703-683-6100 ext 3006 *E-mail:* walter@atanet.org
Location: Pointe South Mountain Resort, Phoenix, AZ, USA
Nov 5-8, 2003

Building Governmental Relationships
Formerly Exploring General Trade Publishing in the Big Apple
Sponsored by Evangelical Christian Publishers Association
1969 E Broadway Rd, Suite 2, Tempe, AZ 85282, United States
Tel: 480-966-3998 *Fax:* 480-966-1944
Web Site: www.ecpa.org
Key Personnel
Pres: Doug Ross *E-mail:* dross@ecpa.org
Location: Washington, DC, USA
Nov 2-4, 2003

Children's Book Week
Sponsored by The Children's Book Council Inc (CBC)
12 W 37 St, 2nd fl, New York, NY 10118-7480, United States
Tel: 212-966-1990 *Fax:* 212-966-2073
Web Site: www.cbcbooks.org/html/book_week.html
Key Personnel
VP, Dir of Mktg: JoAnn Sabatino-Falkenstein *Tel:* 212-966-1990 ext 305 *E-mail:* joann.sabatino_falkenstein@cbcbooks.org
Location: Nationwide across the USA, Theme: "Book Time"
Nov 17-23, 2003

Color Imaging Conference - Color Science Systems & Applications
Sponsored by Society for Imaging Science & Technology (IS&T)
7003 Kilworth Lane, Springfield, VA 22151, United States
Tel: 703-642-9090 *Fax:* 703-642-9094
E-mail: info@imaging.org
Web Site: www.imaging.org

& PROMOTIONAL EVENTS

Key Personnel
Gen Co-chair: Ricardo Motta; Lindsay MacDonald
Location: SunBurst Resort, Scottsdale, AZ, USA
Nov 4-7, 2003

COMDEX/Fall
Sponsored by Key3Media Events
117 Kendrick St, Suite 600, Needham, MA 02494, United States
Tel: 781-433-1500 *Fax:* 781-433-1800
E-mail: sell@comdex.com
Web Site: www.comdex.com
Telex: 174273
Location: Las Vegas, NV, USA
Nov 2003

Feria Internacional del Libro
Alemania 1370, 39-130 CP, Postal Jal, De, Guadalajara 44170, Mexico
Tel: (03) 8125560; (033) 3810 0331 *Fax:* (03) 8122841; (033) 3810 0379
E-mail: fil@fil.com.mx; filny@aol.com
Web Site: fil.com.mx
Location: Guadalajara, Mexico
Nov 29-Dec 7, 2003

Guadalajara International Book Fair
Div of Humanities NAC 5225, City College of New York, New York, NY 10031, United States
Tel: 212-650-7925 *Fax:* 212-650-7912
E-mail: filny@aol.com
Web Site: www.fil.com.mx
Key Personnel
US Rep: David Unger
Held annually in Guadalajara, Mexico, the Guadalajara International Book Fair is the most important event for Spanish book professionals.
Location: Guadalajara. Mexico
Nov 29-Dec 7, 2003

Istanbul Book Fair
Sponsored by Tueyap Tuem Fuarcilik Yapim AS
Gazeteciler Mahellesi, Saglam Fikir Sokak No 19, 80300 Esentepe-Istanbul, Turkey
Tel: (0212) 2123100 *Fax:* (0212) 2123098
E-mail: artlink@tuyap.com.tr
Web Site: www.tuyap.com
Location: Tueyap Istanbul Exhibition Palace, Istanbul, Turkey
Nov 1-9, 2003

Miami Book Fair International
300 NE Second Ave, Suite 1501, Miami, FL 33132, United States
Tel: 305-237-3258 *Fax:* 305-237-3645
E-mail: bookfair@mdcc.edu
Web Site: www.miamibookfair.com
Location: Miami-Dade Community College, Wolfson Campus, Miami, FL, USA
Nov 17-23, 2003

National College Media Convention
Sponsored by Associated Collegiate Press (ACP)
Subsidiary of National Scholastic Press Assn
2221 University Ave SE, Suite 121, Minneapolis, MN 55414, United States
Tel: 612-625-8335 *Fax:* 612-626-0720
E-mail: info@studentpress.org
Web Site: www.studentpress.journ.umn.edu/acp
Location: Hyatt Dallas Reunion, Dallas, TX, USA
Nov 6-9, 2003

Salon du Livre de Montreal (Montreal Book Show)
480 Boul St-Laurent, Suite 403, Montreal, PQ H2Y 3Y7, Canada
Tel: (514) 845-2365 *Fax:* (514) 845-7119
E-mail: slm.info@videotron.ca
Web Site: www.salondulivredemontreal.com

Key Personnel
Dir-Gen: Francine Bois
Exhibition Servs: Sebastien Barange
Location: Place Bonaventure Exhibition Hall, Montreal, PQ, Canada
Nov 13-17, 2003

Stuttgarter Buchwochen (Stuttgart Bookweeks)
Sponsored by Verband der Verlage und Buchhandlungen in Baden-Wuerttemberg eV (Association of Publishers & Booksellers in Baden-Wuerttemberg e V)
Paulinenstr 53, 70178 Stuttgart, Germany
Tel: (0711) 619410 *Fax:* (0711) 6194144
E-mail: buchhandelsverband@vvb-bw.de
Key Personnel
Contact: Maike Dreyer *Tel:* (0711) 61941 28 *E-mail:* dreyer@vvb-bw.de
Location: Haus der Wirtschaft, Stuttgart, Germany
Nov 13-Dec 6, 2003

World Congress of International PEN
Sponsored by International PEN
9-10 Charterhouse Bldgs, Goswell Rd, London EC1M 7AT, United Kingdom
Tel: (020) 7253 4308 *Fax:* (020) 7253 5711
E-mail: intpen@dircon.co.uk
Web Site: www.internatpen.org
Location: Mexico City, Mexico
Nov 24-Dec 1, 2003

DECEMBER

Online Information
Sponsored by Learned Information (Europe) Ltd
Subsidiary of VNU Business Information Europe
Woodside, Hinksey Hill, Oxford OX1 5BE, United Kingdom
Tel: (01865) 388000 *Fax:* (01865) 736354
E-mail: marketing@learned.co.uk
Web Site: www.learned.co.uk
Key Personnel
Mktg Mgr: Rebekah Hart
Location: Olympia Grand Hall, London, UK
Dec 2-4, 2003

Sofia International Book Fair
Sponsored by Bulgarian Book Publishers Association
11 Slaveikov Sq, 1000 Sofia, Bulgaria
Mailing Address: PO Box 1046, 1000 Sofia, Bulgaria
Tel: (02) 986 79 93; (02) 986 79 70 *Fax:* (02) 986 79 93
E-mail: bba@otel.net
Web Site: www.bba-bg.org
Key Personnel
Dir: Raymond Wagenstein
Location: National Palace of Culture, Sofia, Bulgaria
Dec 2003

2004

JANUARY

American Library Association Mid-Winter Meeting
Sponsored by American Library Association (ALA)
50 E Huron St, Chicago, IL 60611, United States
Tel: 312-280-3200 *Fax:* 312-944-7841
E-mail: ala@ala.org
Web Site: www.ala.org/events

Key Personnel
Public Info Dir: Deborah Davis
Press Officer: Belia Ortega
Dir, Intl Rel: Michael Dowling
Location: San Diego, CA, USA
Jan 9-14, 2004

Special Libraries Association Winter Meeting & Education Conference
Sponsored by Special Libraries Association (SLA)
1700 18 St NW, Washington, DC 20009-2514, United States
Tel: 202-234-4700 *Fax:* 202-265-9317
E-mail: sla@sla.org
Web Site: www.sla.org
Key Personnel
Interim Dir: Lynn Smith
Location: Albuquerque, NM, USA
Jan 22-24, 2004

FEBRUARY

Adelaide Writers' Week
Sponsored by Adelaide Festival
105 Hindley St, Adelaide, SA 5000, Australia
Mailing Address: Adelaide Festival Corporation, PO Box 8116, Station Arcade, Adelaide, SA 5000, Australia
Tel: (08) 8216 4444 *Fax:* (08) 8216 4455
E-mail: rwight@adelaidefestival.net.au
Web Site: www.adelaidefestival.org.au; www.adelaidefestivalofideas.com.au
Location: Pioneer Women's Memorial Gardens, King William St, Adelaide, Australia
Feb 29-March 5, 2004

CAMEX
Sponsored by National Association of College Stores (NACS)
500 E Lorain St, Oberlin, OH 44074-1294, United States
Tel: 440-775-7777 *Fax:* 440-775-4769
E-mail: info@nacs.org
Web Site: www.nacs.org
Key Personnel
CEO: Brian Cartier
PR Dir: Laura Nakoneczny *Tel:* 440-775-7777, ext 2351 *E-mail:* lnakoneczny@nacs.org
Conference & tradeshow dedicated exclusively to the more than $10 billion collegiate retailing industry.
Location: San Antonio, TX, USA
Feb 27-March 2, 2004

International Book Fair/Los Angeles Book Fair
Sponsored by Antiquarian Booksellers' Association of America
20 W 44 St, 4th fl, New York, NY 10036, United States
Tel: 212-944-8291 *Fax:* 212-944-8293
E-mail: abaa@panix.com
Web Site: www.abaa.org
Key Personnel
Dir: Liane Wade
Location: Los Angeles, CA, USA
Feb 2004

National Association of Science Writers Annual Meeting
Sponsored by National Association of Science Writers (NASW)
PO Box 890, Hedgesville, WV 25427, United States
Tel: 304-754-5077 *Fax:* 304-754-5076
Web Site: www.nasw.org

Key Personnel
Exec Dir: Diane McGurgan *E-mail:* diane@nasw.org
Location: Seattle, WA, USA
Feb 2004

SPRING

Rocky Mountain Book Festival
Sponsored by Colorado Center for the Book
2123 Downing St, Denver, CO 80205, United States
Tel: 303-839-8320 *Fax:* 303-839-8319
E-mail: ccftb@compuserve.com
Web Site: www.coloradobook.org
Key Personnel
Exec Dir: Christiane H Citron
Non profit organization promoting love of books.
Location: Denver, CO, USA
Spring 2004

MARCH

Antiques & Fine Arts Exhibition/Luxembourg Book Festival
Sponsored by Societe de Foires Internationales de Luxembourg, Societe Anonyme
2088 Luxembourg, Luxembourg
Tel: 43991 *Fax:* 4399315
E-mail: fil@fil.lu
Location: Luxembourg Conference & Exhibition Center, Luxembourg, Luxembourg
March 11-14, 2004

Associated Writing Programs Annual Conference
Sponsored by Associated Writing Programs (AWP)
George Mason University, MS-1E3, Fairfax, VA 22030, United States
Tel: 703-993-4301 *Fax:* 703-993-4302
E-mail: awp@gmu.edu
Web Site: www.awpwriter.org
Key Personnel
Exec Dir: D W Fenza
Dir of Conferences: Un J Lee
Association of writers & writing programs.
Location: Chicago, IL, USA
March 24-27, 2004

Leipzig Book Fair
Sponsored by Leipziger Messe GmbH, Projekt-team Buchmesse
Messe-Allee 1, 04356 Leipzig, Germany
Mailing Address: Postfach 100 720, 04007 Leipzig, Germany
Tel: (0341) 6788240 *Fax:* (0341) 6788242
E-mail: info@leipziger-buchmesse.de
Web Site: www.leipziger-buchmesse.de
Key Personnel
Exhibition Dir: Oliver Zille *Tel:* (0341) 678 8241 *Fax:* (0341) 678 8242
Location: Neues Messegelande, Leipzig, Germany
March 25-28, 2004

National Association of Printing Ink Manufacturers Annual Convention
Sponsored by National Association of Printing Ink Manufacturers
581 Main St, Woodbridge, NJ 07095, United States
Tel: 732-855-1525 *Fax:* 732-855-1838
E-mail: napim@napim.org
Web Site: www.napim.org

Key Personnel
Exec Dir: James Coleman
Trade association.
Location: LaQuinta Resort, LaQuinta, CA, USA
March 28-31, 2004

Small Press Book Fair
Sponsored by Small Press Center
20 W 44 St, New York, NY 10036, United States
Tel: 212-764-7021 *Fax:* 212-354-5365
E-mail: info@smallpress.org
Web Site: www.smallpress.org
Key Personnel
Dir: Karin Taylor
Location: Small Press Center, New York, NY, USA
March 2004

UKSG Annual Conference & Exhibition
Sponsored by UK Serials Group
Hilltop, Heath End, Newbury RG20 0AP, United Kingdom
Tel: (01635) 254292 *Fax:* (01635) 253826
E-mail: uksg.admin@dial.pipex.com
Location: UMIST, Manchester, UK
March 29-31, 2004

APRIL

Alberta Library Conference
Sponsored by Library Association of Alberta
80 Baker Crescent NW, Calgary, AB T2L 1R4, Canada
Tel: 403-284-5818 *Fax:* 403-282-6646
Web Site: www.laa.ab.ca
Key Personnel
Pres: Pat Cavill
Exec Dir: Christine Sheppard *E-mail:* shepparc@cadvision.com
Location: Jasper Park Lodge, Jasper, AB, Canada
April 29-May 2, 2004

Asia International Book Fair/International Library Expo
Sponsored by Reed Exhibition Companies
One Temasek Ave, Suite 17-01, Millenia Tower, Singapore, Singapore
Tel: 0338 2002 *Fax:* 0338 2112
E-mail: ask@reedexpo.com.sg; sp@reedexpo.com.sg
Location: Singapore International Convention & Exhibition Centre, Singapore, Singapore
April 2004

FIAF Congress
Sponsored by International Federation of Film Archives (Federation Internationale des Archives du Film)
Rue Defacqz 1, 1000 Brussels, Belgium
Tel: (02) 5383065 *Fax:* (02) 5344774
E-mail: info@fiafnet.org
Web Site: www.fiafnet.org
Key Personnel
Sr Adminstr: Christian Dimitriu
Location: Hanoi, Vietnam
April 18-24, 2004

International Children's Book Day
Sponsored by International Board on Books for Young People (IBBY)
Nonnenweg 12, CH-4055 Basel, Switzerland
Mailing Address: Nonnenweg 12, Postfach, Basel Ch-4003, Switzerland
Tel: (061) 2722917 *Fax:* (061) 2722757
E-mail: ibby@ibby.org
Web Site: www.ibby.org
Theme: International Children's Book Day.

Location: Worldwide
April 2, 2004

National Library Week
Sponsored by American Library Association (ALA)
50 E Huron St, Chicago, IL 60611, United States
Tel: 312-944-6780 *Fax:* 312-944-8520
E-mail: pio@ala.org
Web Site: www.ala.org/events
Key Personnel
Dir: Marc Gould *E-mail:* mgould@ala.org
Press Officer: Larra Clark *E-mail:* lclark@ala.org
Location: Nationwide throughout the USA
April 18-24, 2004

Newspaper Association of America Annual Convention
Sponsored by Newspaper Association of America (NAA)
1921 Gallows Rd, Suite 600, Vienna, VA 22182, United States
Tel: 703-902-1600 *Fax:* 703-902-1843
E-mail: laths@naa.org
Web Site: www.naa.org
Key Personnel
Pres & CEO: John Sturm
Location: Omni Shoreham Hotel, Washington, DC, USA
April 20-23, 2004

Annual Web Offset Association Conference
Sponsored by Web Offset Association
Division of Printing Industries of America Inc
100 Daingerfield Rd, Alexandria, VA 22314, United States
Tel: 703-519-8100; 703-519-8142 *Fax:* 703-519-7109
Web Site: www.gain.net
Key Personnel
Meetings Mgr: Jonna Swan
Location: Chicago, IL, USA
April 18-21, 2004

MAY

Exposicion de Literatura Cristiana (EXPOLIT) Book Fair
Sponsored by Spanish Evangelical Publishers Association (SEPA)/Associacion de Editores Evangelicos and Editorial Unilit
1360 NW 88 Ave, Miami, FL 33172, United States
Tel: 305-592-6136 (ext 105) *Fax:* 305-592-0087
E-mail: expolit@editorialunilit.com
Web Site: www.expolit.com
Key Personnel
Pres, SEPA: Esteban Fernandez
Pres, EXPOLIT: David Ecklebarger
Spanish Christian Literature Convention.
Location: Miami, FL, USA
May 14-19, 2004

General Trade Publishing & Retailing
Sponsored by Evangelical Christian Publishers Association
1969 E Broadway Rd, Suite 2, Tempe, AZ 85282, United States
Tel: 480-966-3998 *Fax:* 480-966-1944
Web Site: www.ecpa.org
Key Personnel
Pres: Doug Ross *E-mail:* dross@ecpa.org
May 1-5, 2004

Quod Libet/International Antiquarian Book Fair & Artists Books
Sponsored by Luckwaldt Messen
Bruechhorst strasse 34, 24641 Sievershuetten, Germany

Tel: (040) 194 8101 *Fax:* (040) 194 636
E-mail: frauke@luckwaldt.de
Web Site: www.quod-libet.com
May 7-9

JUNE

American Library Association Annual Conference
Sponsored by American Library Association (ALA)
50 E Huron St, Chicago, IL 60611, United States
Tel: 312-280-3200 *Fax:* 312-944-7841
E-mail: ala@ala.org
Web Site: www.ala.org
Key Personnel
Public Info Dir: Deborah Davis
Press Officer: Belia Ortega
Dir, Intl Rel: Michael Dowling
Location: Orlando, FL, USA
June 24-30, 2004

Gutenberg Festival
Sponsored by Graphic Arts Show Company
1899 Preston White Dr, Reston, VA 20191-4367, United States
Tel: 703-264-7200 *Fax:* 703-620-9187
E-mail: info@gasc.org
Web Site: www.gasc.org
Key Personnel
Dir, Commus: David Paulos
Annual trade show for graphic design, digital pre-press, printing, publishing & converting.
Location: Long Beach Convention Center, Long Beach, CA, USA
June 17-19, 2004

Gutenberg Gesellschaft Annual General Meeting
Sponsored by Gutenberg-Gesellschaft eV
Liebfrauenplatz 5, D-55116 Mainz, Germany
Tel: (06131) 22 64 20 *Fax:* (06131) 23 35 30
E-mail: gutenberg-gesellschaft@freenet.de
Web Site: www.gutenberg-gesellschaft.uni-mainz.de
Key Personnel
Sec Gen: Gertraude Benoehr
Location: Museum Mainz, City Hall, Mainz, Germany
June 26, 2004

International Newspaper Financial Executives Annual Conference
Sponsored by International Newspaper Financial Executives
21525 Ridgetop Circle, Suite 200, Sterling, VA 20166, United States
Tel: 703-421-4060 *Fax:* 703-421-4068
E-mail: infehq@infe.org
Web Site: www.infe.org
Key Personnel
VP & Exec Dir: Robert J Kasabian
 E-mail: bkasabian@infe.org
Location: Washington, DC
June 26-30, 2004

IPA Congress
Sponsored by International Publishers Association
3 ave de Miremont, CH-1206 Geneva, Switzerland
Tel: (022) 3463018 *Fax:* (022) 3475717
E-mail: info@ipa-uie.org
Web Site: www.ipa-uie.org
Key Personnel
Sec Gen: Benoit Muller
Location: Berlin, Germany
June 21-24, 2004

NEXPO®
Sponsored by Newspaper Association of America (NAA)
1921 Gallows Rd, Suite 600, Vienna, VA 22182, United States
Tel: 703-902-1600 *Fax:* 703-902-1843
E-mail: laths@naa.org
Web Site: www.nexpo.com
Key Personnel
Dir of Exhibition Sales: Brad Smith
Annual technical exposition & conference for newspapers.
Location: Washington, DC
June 26-29, 2004

School Library Association Annual Conference
Sponsored by School Library Association
Unit 2, Lotmead Business Village, Lotmead Farm, Wanborough, Swindon, Wilts SN4 0UY, United Kingdom
Tel: (01793) 791787 *Fax:* (01793) 791786
E-mail: info@sla.org.uk
Web Site: www.sla.org.uk
Key Personnel
Chief Executive: Kathy Lemaire *E-mail:* kathy@sla.org.uk
Location: Dublin, Ireland
June 2004

Special Libraries Association Annual Conference
Sponsored by Special Libraries Association (SLA)
1700 18 St NW, Washington, DC 20009-2514, United States
Tel: 202-234-4700 *Fax:* 202-265-9317
E-mail: sla@sla.org
Web Site: www.sla.org
Key Personnel
Interim Dir: Lynn Smith
Location: Nashville, TN, USA
June 5-10, 2004

JULY

Church & Synagogue Library Association Conference
Sponsored by Church & Synagogue Library Association
PO Box 19357, Portland, OR 97280-0357, United States
Tel: 503-244-6919 *Fax:* 503-977-3734
E-mail: csla@worldaccessnet.com
Web Site: www.worldaccessnet.com/~csla
Location: Indianapolis, IN, USA
July 2004

Hong Kong Book Fair
Sponsored by Hong Kong Trade Development Council
Unit 13, Expo Galleria, One Expo Dr, Wanchai, Hong Kong
Tel: (02) 5844333 *Fax:* (02) 8240026
E-mail: exhibitions@tdc.org.hk
Web Site: hkbookfair.tdc.org.hk
Key Personnel
Sales Adminstrator: Joyce P F Laing
Location: Hong Kong Convention & Exhibition Center, One Harbour Rd, Wanchai, Hong Kong
July 2004

RWA Annual National Conference
Sponsored by Romance Writers of America
3707 FM 1960 West, Suite 555, Houston, TX 77068, United States
Tel: 281-440-6885 *Fax:* 281-440-7510
E-mail: info@rwanational.org
Web Site: www.rwanational.org

Key Personnel
Exec Dir: Allison Kelley *E-mail:* akelley@rwanational.org
Location: Dallas, TX, USA
July 28-31, 2004

AUGUST

IFLA General Conference & Council
Sponsored by International Federation of Library Associations & Institutions (IFLA)
Postbus 95312, 2509 CH The Hague, Netherlands
Tel: (070) 3140884 *Fax:* (070) 3834827
E-mail: ifla@ifla.org
Web Site: www.ifla.org
Location: Buenos Aires, Argentina
Aug 2004

International Association of Music Libraries, Archives & Documentation Centres Conference
Sponsored by International Association of Music Libraries, Archives & Documentation Centres
c/o Carleton University Library, 1125 Colonel By Drive, Ottawa, ON K1S 5B6, Canada
Tel: 613-520-2600 (ext 8150) *Fax:* 613-520-3583
Web Site: www.cilea.it/music/iaml/iamlhome.htm
Key Personnel
Sec-Gen: Alison Hall *E-mail:* alison_hall@carleton.ca
Location: Oslo, Norway
Aug 8-14, 2004

International Congress on Archives
Sponsored by International Council on Archives (Conseil International des Archives)
60 rue des Francs-Bourgeois, 75003 Paris, France
Tel: (01) 40276306; (01) 40276349; (01) 40276134 *Fax:* (01) 42722065
E-mail: ica@ica.org
Web Site: www.ica.org
Key Personnel
Sec Gen: Mr Joan Van Albada
Location: Wein, Austria
Aug 23-28, 2004

AUTUMN

Business & Design Conference
Sponsored by American Institute of Graphic Arts (AIGA)
164 Fifth Ave, New York, NY 10010, United States
Tel: 212-807-1990 (ext 223) *Fax:* 212-807-1799
E-mail: aiganswers@aiga.org; programs@aiga.org
Web Site: www.aiga.org
Key Personnel
Exec Dir: Richard Grefe
Biennial event.
Autumn 2004

Ghana International Book Fair
Sponsored by Ghana Trade Fair Co Ltd
Trade Fair Centre, Accra, Ghana
Mailing Address: PO Box TF 111, Accra, Ghana
Tel: (021) 776611; (021) 772376; (021) 776614; (024) 622891 *Fax:* (021) 772012
E-mail: gtfc@ghana.com; tfa@ighmail.com
Location: Ghana International Trade Fair Centre, Accra, Ghana
Autumn 2004

SEPTEMBER

Distripress Annual Congress
Sponsored by Distripress
Beethovenstr 20, CH-8002 Zurich, Switzerland
Tel: (01) 2024121 *Fax:* (01) 2021025
E-mail: info@distripress.ch
Web Site: www.distripress.ch
Key Personnel
Dir: Dr Peter Emod *E-mail:* peter.emod@distripress.ch
Non-profit association promoting the free international circulation of the press.
Location: Vancouver, BC, Canada
Sept 12-16, 2004

Goteborg International Book Fair
Sponsored by Bok & Bibliotek
412 94 Goteborg, Sweden
Tel: (031) 7088400 *Fax:* (031) 209103
Web Site: www.bok-bibliotek.com
Key Personnel
Man Dir: Anna Falck *E-mail:* anna.falck@bok-bibliotek.se
Exhibition Mgr: Lisa Oden *E-mail:* lo@bok-bibliotek.se
Sept 2004

International Board on Books for Young People Biennial Congress
Sponsored by International Board on Books for Young People (IBBY)
Nonnenweg 12, CH-4055 Basel, Switzerland
Mailing Address: Nonnenweg 12, Postfach, Basel Ch-4003, Switzerland
Tel: (061) 2722917 *Fax:* (061) 2722757
E-mail: ibby@eye.ch
Web Site: www.ibby.org
Location: Cape Town, South Africa
Sept 5-9, 2004

LIBER Feria Internacional del Libro
Sponsored by Federacion de Gremios de Editores de Espana (FGEE) (Spanish Publishers Association)
Cea Bermudez, 44-2° Dehe, Madrid 20003, Spain
Tel: (091) 5345195 *Fax:* (091) 5352625
E-mail: fgee@fge.es
Web Site: www.federacioneditores.org
Location: Barcelona, Spain
Sept 29-Oct 1, 2004

Moscow International Book Fair
Sponsored by General Directorate of International Book Exhibitions & Fairs
16 Malaya Dmitrovka St, Moscow 127006, Russian Federation
Tel: (095) 2994034; (095) 2999790; (095) 2993466 *Fax:* (095) 9732132; (095) 2992539
E-mail: exhibitions@elnet.msk.ru
Web Site: www.bookfair.ru; www.mibf.ru
Key Personnel
Gen Dir: Mr Nikolay Ph Ovsyannikov
Location: All Russian Exhibition Centre, Moscow, Russia
Sept 1-6, 2004

OCTOBER

American Medical Writers Association Annual Conference
Sponsored by American Medical Writers Association
40 W Gude Dr, Suite 101, Rockville, MD 20850-1192, United States
Tel: 301-294-5303 *Fax:* 301-294-9006
E-mail: amwa@amwa.org
Web Site: www.amwa.org
Location: Adam's Mark Hotel, St Louis, MO, USA
Oct 21-23, 2004

Fall Technical Conference & Trade Fair
Sponsored by Technical Association of the Pulp & Paper Industry (TAPPI)
15 Technology Pkwy S, Norcross, GA 30092, United States
Mailing Address: PO Box 105113, Atlanta, GA 30348-5113, United States
Tel: 770-446-1400 *Fax:* 770-446-6947
Web Site: www.tappi.org
Key Personnel
Publg Dir: Mary Beth Bennett
Adv Asst: Keith Hudson *E-mail:* khudson@tappi.org
Dir, Admin: Jeff Petro
Corp Rel Dir: Clare Reagan *E-mail:* creagan@tappi.org
Admin: Julie Anne Wiley
Location: Atlanta Marriott Marquis, Atlanta, GA, USA
Oct 17-21, 2004

Frankfurt Book Fair
Sponsored by Ausstellungs-und Messe-GmbH des Borsenvereins des Deutschen Buchhandels
Reinecksstr 3, 60313 Frankfurt am Main, Germany
Mailing Address: Postfach 100116, 60001 Frankfurt am Main, Germany
Tel: (069) 21020 *Fax:* (069) 2102 227
E-mail: info@book-fair.com
Web Site: www.frankfurt-book-fair.com *Cable:* BUCHMESSE
Key Personnel
CEO: Lorenzo Rudolf
Location: Frankfurt Fairgrounds, Frankfurt, Germany
Oct 6-10, 2004

National Newspaper Association Annual Convention & Trade Show
Sponsored by National Newspaper Association
PO Box 7540, Columbia, MO 65205-7450, United States
Tel: 573-882-4021 *Fax:* 573-884-5490
E-mail: info@nna.org
Web Site: www.nna.org
Key Personnel
Exec VP & CEO: Brian Steffens
Location: Adam's Mark, Denver, CO, USA
Oct 13-16, 2004

NOVEMBER

AICC/TAPPI SuperCorrExpo® 2004
Sponsored by Technical Association of the Pulp & Paper Industry (TAPPI)
15 Technology Pkwy S, Norcross, GA 30092, United States
Mailing Address: PO Box 105113, Atlanta, GA 30348-5113, United States
Tel: 770-446-1400 *Fax:* 770-446-6947
Web Site: www.tappi.org
Key Personnel
Publg Dir: Mary Beth Bennett
Adv Asst: Keith Hudson *E-mail:* khudson@tappi.org
Dir, Admin: Jeff Petro
Corp Rel Dir: Clare Reagan *E-mail:* creagan@tappi.org
Location: Georgia World Congress Center, Atlanta, GA, USA
Nov 8-12, 2004

American Academy of Religion
Sponsored by American Schools of Oriental Research
825 Houston Mill Rd, Atlanta, GA 30329, United States
Tel: 404-727-3049; 404-727-7920 *Fax:* 404-727-7959
Web Site: www.aarweb.org
Key Personnel
Meeting Coord: Shannon Planck
Location: San Antonio, TX, USA
Nov 20-23, 2004

Children's Book Week
Sponsored by The Children's Book Council Inc (CBC)
12 W 37 St, 2nd fl, New York, NY 10118-7480, United States
Tel: 212-966-1990 *Fax:* 212-966-2073
Web Site: www.cbcbooks.org/html/book_week.html
Key Personnel
VP, Dir of Mktg: JoAnn Sabatino-Falkenstein
Tel: 212-966-1990 ext 305 *E-mail:* joann.sabatino_falkenstein@cbcbooks.org
Nov 15-21, 2004

Creative Conference
Sponsored by American Association of Advertising Agencies
405 Lexington Ave, 18th fl, New York, NY 10174-1801, United States
Tel: 212-682-2500 *Fax:* 212-682-8391
Web Site: www.aaaa.org
Key Personnel
Pres & CEO: O Burtch Drake
Sr VP & Dir, Pub Aff: John Wolfe
Nov 2004

Feria Internacional del Libro
Alemania 1370, 39-130 CP, Postal Jal, De, Guadalajara 44170, Mexico
Tel: (03) 8125560; (033) 3810 0331 *Fax:* (03) 8122841; (033) 3810 0379
E-mail: fil@fil.com.mx; filny@aol.com
Web Site: fil.com.mx
Location: Guadalajara, Mexico
Nov 27-Dec 5, 2004

Introducing ECPA Publishing University
Sponsored by Evangelical Christian Publishers Association
1969 E Broadway Rd, Suite 2, Tempe, AZ 85282, United States
Tel: 480-966-3998 *Fax:* 480-966-1944
Web Site: www.ecpa.org
Key Personnel
Pres: Doug Ross *E-mail:* dross@ecpa.org
Nov 7-9, 2004

National College Media Convention
Sponsored by Associated Collegiate Press (ACP)
Subsidiary of National Scholastic Press Assn
2221 University Ave SE, Suite 121, Minneapolis, MN 55414, United States
Tel: 612-625-8335 *Fax:* 612-626-0720
E-mail: info@studentpress.org
Web Site: www.studentpress.journ.umn.edu/acp
Location: Nashville Convention Center, Nashville, TN, USA
Nov 4-7, 2004

Stuttgarter Buchwochen (Stuttgart Bookweeks)
Sponsored by Verband der Verlage und Buchhandlungen in Baden-Wuerttemberg eV (Association of Publishers & Booksellers in Baden-Wuerttemberg e V)
Paulinenstr 53, 70178 Stuttgart, Germany
Tel: (0711) 619410 *Fax:* (0711) 6194144
E-mail: buchhandelsverband@vvb-bw.de

& PROMOTIONAL EVENTS

Key Personnel
Contact: Maike Dreyer *Tel:* (0711) 61941 28
 E-mail: dreyer@vvb-bw.de
Location: Haus der Wirtschaft, Stuttgart, Germany
Nov 12-Dec 5, 2004

Xplor Global Conference
Sponsored by Xplor International
24238 Hawthorne Blvd, Torrance, CA 90505-6505, United States
Tel: 310-791-9521 *Fax:* 310-375-4240
E-mail: info@xplor.org
Web Site: www.xplor.org
Key Personnel
Communs Asst: Steven Barry
Location: San Diego, CA, USA
Nov 7-12, 2004

2005
MARCH

Antiques & Fine Arts Exhibition/Luxembourg Book Festival
Sponsored by Societe de Foires Internationales de Luxembourg, Societe Anonyme
2088 Luxembourg, Luxembourg
Tel: 43991 *Fax:* 4399315
E-mail: fil@fil.lu
Location: Luxembourg Conference & Exhibition Center, Luxembourg, Luxembourg
March 10-13, 2005

APRIL

FIAF Congress
Sponsored by International Federation of Film Archives (Federation Internationale des Archives du Film)
Rue Defacqz 1, 1000 Brussels, Belgium
Tel: (02) 5383065 *Fax:* (02) 5344774
E-mail: info@fiafnet.org
Web Site: www.fiafnet.org
Key Personnel
Sr Adminstr: Christian Dimitriu
Location: Ljubljana, Slovenia
April 2005

National Library Week
Sponsored by American Library Association (ALA)
50 E Huron St, Chicago, IL 60611, United States
Tel: 312-944-6780 *Fax:* 312-944-8520
E-mail: pio@ala.org
Web Site: www.ala.org/events
Key Personnel
Dir: Marc Gould *E-mail:* mgould@ala.org
Press Officer: Larra Clark *E-mail:* lclark@ala.org
Location: Nationwide throughout the USA
April 10-16, 2005

Newspaper Association of America Annual Convention
Sponsored by Newspaper Association of America (NAA)
1921 Gallows Rd, Suite 600, Vienna, VA 22182, United States
Tel: 703-902-1600 *Fax:* 703-902-1843
E-mail: laths@naa.org
Web Site: www.naa.org
Key Personnel
Pres & CEO: John Sturm
Location: Fairmont, San Francisco, CA, USA
April 17-20, 2005

UKSG Annual Conference & Exhibition
Sponsored by UK Serials Group
Hilltop, Heath End, Newbury RG20 0AP, United Kingdom
Tel: (01635) 254292 *Fax:* (01635) 253826
E-mail: uksg.admin@dial.pipex.com
Location: Heriot-Watt University, Edinburgh, UK
April 11-13, 2005

MAY

Pacprint
Sponsored by Reed Exhibition Companies
475 Victoria Ave, Chatswood, NSW 2067, Australia
Mailing Address: Locked Bag 2555, Chatswood, NSW 2067, Australia
Tel: (02) 9422 2500 *Fax:* (02) 9422 2555
E-mail: ask@reedexpo.com.au
Key Personnel
Contact: Norm Lembke *E-mail:* norm.lembke@reedexpo.com.au
Location: Melbourne Convention & Exhibition Centre, Melbourne, Australia
May 1, 2005

Annual Web Offset Association Conference
Sponsored by Web Offset Association
Division of Printing Industries of America Inc
100 Daingerfield Rd, Alexandria, VA 22314, United States
Tel: 703-519-8100; 703-519-8142 *Fax:* 703-519-7109
Web Site: www.gain.net
Key Personnel
Meetings Mgr: Jonna Swan
Location: Opryland Texas, Grapenne, TX, USA
May 1-4, 2005

JUNE

American Library Association Annual Conference
Sponsored by American Library Association (ALA)
50 E Huron St, Chicago, IL 60611, United States
Tel: 312-280-3200 *Fax:* 312-944-7841
E-mail: ala@ala.org
Web Site: www.ala.org
Key Personnel
Public Info Dir: Deborah Davis
Press Officer: Belia Ortega
Dir, Intl Rel: Michael Dowling
Location: Chicago, IL, USA
June 23-29, 2005

International Newspaper Financial Executives Annual Conference
Sponsored by International Newspaper Financial Executives
21525 Ridgetop Circle, Suite 200, Sterling, VA 20166, United States
Tel: 703-421-4060 *Fax:* 703-421-4068
E-mail: infehq@infe.org
Web Site: www.infe.org
Key Personnel
VP & Exec Dir: Robert J Kasabian
 E-mail: bkasabian@infe.org
Location: Hilton at Walt Disney World Village, Orlando, FL, USA
June 25-29, 2005

JULY

Hong Kong Book Fair
Sponsored by Hong Kong Trade Development Council
Unit 13, Expo Galleria, One Expo Dr, Wanchai, Hong Kong
Tel: (02) 5844333 *Fax:* (02) 8240026
E-mail: exhibitions@tdc.org.hk
Web Site: hkbookfair.tdc.org.hk
Key Personnel
Sales Adminstrator: Joyce P F Laing
Location: Hong Kong Convention & Exhibition Center, One Harbour Rd, Wanchai, Hong Kong
July 2005

RWA Annual National Conference
Sponsored by Romance Writers of America
3707 FM 1960 West, Suite 555, Houston, TX 77068, United States
Tel: 281-440-6885 *Fax:* 281-440-7510
E-mail: info@rwanational.org
Web Site: www.rwanational.org
Key Personnel
Exec Dir: Allison Kelley *E-mail:* akelley@rwanational.org
Location: Reno, NV, USA
July 27-30, 2005

AUGUST

IFLA General Conference & Council
Sponsored by International Federation of Library Associations & Institutions (IFLA)
Postbus 95312, 2509 CH The Hague, Netherlands
Tel: (070) 3140884 *Fax:* (070) 3834827
E-mail: ifla@ifla.org
Web Site: www.ifla.org
Location: Oslo, Norway
Aug 2005

OCTOBER

Frankfurt Book Fair
Sponsored by Ausstellungs-und Messe-GmbH des Borsenvereins des Deutschen Buchhandels
Reinecksstr 3, 60313 Frankfurt am Main, Germany
Mailing Address: Postfach 100116, 60001 Frankfurt am Main, Germany
Tel: (069) 21020 *Fax:* (069) 2102 227
E-mail: info@book-fair.com
Web Site: www.frankfurt-book-fair.com *Cable:* BUCHMESSE
Key Personnel
CEO: Lorenzo Rudolf
Location: Frankfurt Fairgrounds, Frankfurt, Germany
Oct 15-24, 2005

LIBER Feria Internacional del Libro
Sponsored by Federacion de Gremios de Editores de Espana (FGEE) (Spanish Publishers Association)
Cea Bermudez, 44-2° Dehe, Madrid 20003, Spain
Tel: (091) 5345195 *Fax:* (091) 5352625
E-mail: fgee@fge.es
Web Site: www.federacioneditores.org
Location: Madrid, Spain
Oct 12-15, 2005

Xplor Global Conference
Sponsored by Xplor International
24238 Hawthorne Blvd, Torrance, CA 90505-6505, United States
Tel: 310-791-9521 *Fax:* 310-375-4240
E-mail: info@xplor.org
Web Site: www.xplor.org
Key Personnel
Communs Asst: Steven Barry
Location: San Diego, CA, USA
Oct 30-Nov 4, 2005

NOVEMBER

American Academy of Religion
Sponsored by American Schools of Oriental Research
825 Houston Mill Rd, Atlanta, GA 30329, United States
Tel: 404-727-3049; 404-727-7920 *Fax:* 404-727-7959
Web Site: www.aarweb.org
Key Personnel
Meeting Coord: Shannon Planck
Location: Philadelphia, PA, USA
Nov 19-22, 2005

Children's Book Week
Sponsored by The Children's Book Council Inc (CBC)
12 W 37 St, 2nd fl, New York, NY 10118-7480, United States
Tel: 212-966-1990 *Fax:* 212-966-2073
Web Site: www.cbcbooks.org/html/book_week.html
Key Personnel
VP, Dir of Mktg: JoAnn Sabatino-Falkenstein *Tel:* 212-966-1990 ext 305 *E-mail:* joann.sabatino_falkenstein@cbcbooks.org
Nov 14-20, 2005

Stuttgarter Buchwochen (Stuttgart Bookweeks)
Sponsored by Verband der Verlage und Buchhandlungen in Baden-Wuerttemberg eV (Association of Publishers & Booksellers in Baden-Wuerttemberg e V)
Paulinenstr 53, 70178 Stuttgart, Germany
Tel: (0711) 619410 *Fax:* (0711) 6194144
E-mail: buchhandelsverband@vvb-bw.de
Key Personnel
Contact: Maike Dreyer *Tel:* (0711) 61941 28 *E-mail:* dreyer@vvb-bw.de
Location: Haus der Wirtschaft, Stuttgart, Germany
Nov 11-Dec 4, 2005

2006
APRIL

FIAF Congress
Sponsored by International Federation of Film Archives (Federation Internationale des Archives du Film)
Rue Defacqz 1, 1000 Brussels, Belgium
Tel: (02) 5383065 *Fax:* (02) 5344774
E-mail: info@fiafnet.org
Web Site: www.fiafnet.org
Key Personnel
Sr Adminstr: Christian Dimitriu
Location: Sao Paulo & Rio de Janeiro, Brazil
April 2006

National Library Week
Sponsored by American Library Association (ALA)
50 E Huron St, Chicago, IL 60611, United States
Tel: 312-944-6780 *Fax:* 312-944-8520
E-mail: pio@ala.org
Web Site: www.ala.org/events
Key Personnel
Dir: Marc Gould *E-mail:* mgould@ala.org
Press Officer: Larra Clark *E-mail:* lclark@ala.org
Location: Nationwide throughout the USA
April 2-8, 2006

UKSG Annual Conference & Exhibition
Sponsored by UK Serials Group
Hilltop, Heath End, Newbury RG20 0AP, United Kingdom
Tel: (01635) 254292 *Fax:* (01635) 253826
E-mail: uksg.admin@dial.pipex.com
Location: University of Warwick, Coventry, UK
April 3-5, 2006

JUNE

American Library Association Annual Conference
Sponsored by American Library Association (ALA)
50 E Huron St, Chicago, IL 60611, United States
Tel: 312-280-3200 *Fax:* 312-944-7841
E-mail: ala@ala.org
Web Site: www.ala.org
Key Personnel
Public Info Dir: Deborah Davis
Press Officer: Belia Ortega
Dir, Intl Rel: Michael Dowling
Location: New Orleans, LA, USA
June 22-28, 2006

JULY

RWA Annual National Conference
Sponsored by Romance Writers of America
3707 FM 1960 West, Suite 555, Houston, TX 77068, United States
Tel: 281-440-6885 *Fax:* 281-440-7510
E-mail: info@rwanational.org
Web Site: www.rwanational.org
Key Personnel
Exec Dir: Allison Kelley *E-mail:* akelley@rwanational.org
Location: Atlanta, GA, USA
July 26-29, 2006

AUGUST

IFLA General Conference & Council
Sponsored by International Federation of Library Associations & Institutions (IFLA)
Postbus 95312, 2509 CH The Hague, Netherlands
Tel: (070) 3140884 *Fax:* (070) 3834827
E-mail: ifla@ifla.org
Web Site: www.ifla.org
Location: Seoul, Korea
Aug 2006

SEPTEMBER

International Board on Books for Young People Biennial Congress
Sponsored by International Board on Books for Young People (IBBY)
Nonnenweg 12, CH-4055 Basel, Switzerland
Mailing Address: Nonnenweg 12, Postfach, Basel Ch-4003, Switzerland
Tel: (061) 2722917 *Fax:* (061) 2722757
E-mail: ibby@eye.ch
Web Site: www.ibby.org
Location: Beijing, China
Sept 20-24, 2006

LIBER Feria Internacional del Libro
Sponsored by Federacion de Gremios de Editores de Espana (FGEE) (Spanish Publishers Association)
Cea Bermudez, 44-2° Dehe, Madrid 20003, Spain
Tel: (091) 5345195 *Fax:* (091) 5352625
E-mail: fgee@fge.es
Web Site: www.federacioneditores.org
Location: Barcelona, Spain
Sept 27-30, 2006

OCTOBER

Frankfurt Book Fair
Sponsored by Ausstellungs-und Messe-GmbH des Borsenvereins des Deutschen Buchhandels
Reinecksstr 3, 60313 Frankfurt am Main, Germany
Mailing Address: Postfach 100116, 60001 Frankfurt am Main, Germany
Tel: (069) 21020 *Fax:* (069) 2102 227
E-mail: info@book-fair.com
Web Site: www.frankfurt-book-fair.com *Cable:* BUCHMESSE
Key Personnel
CEO: Lorenzo Rudolf
Location: Frankfurt Fairgrounds, Frankfurt, Germany
Oct 4-9, 2006

NOVEMBER

American Academy of Religion
Sponsored by American Schools of Oriental Research
825 Houston Mill Rd, Atlanta, GA 30329, United States
Tel: 404-727-3049; 404-727-7920 *Fax:* 404-727-7959
Web Site: www.aarweb.org
Key Personnel
Meeting Coord: Shannon Planck
Location: Washington, DC, USA
Nov 18-21, 2006

Stuttgarter Buchwochen (Stuttgart Bookweeks)
Sponsored by Verband der Verlage und Buchhandlungen in Baden-Wuerttemberg eV (Association of Publishers & Booksellers in Baden-Wuerttemberg e V)
Paulinenstr 53, 70178 Stuttgart, Germany
Tel: (0711) 619410 *Fax:* (0711) 6194144
E-mail: buchhandelsverband@vvb-bw.de
Key Personnel
Contact: Maike Dreyer *Tel:* (0711) 61941 28 *E-mail:* dreyer@vvb-bw.de
Location: Haus der Wirtschaft, Stuttgart, Germany
Nov-Dec

2007
APRIL

National Library Week
Sponsored by American Library Association (ALA)
50 E Huron St, Chicago, IL 60611, United States
Tel: 312-944-6780 *Fax:* 312-944-8520
E-mail: pio@ala.org
Web Site: www.ala.org/events
Key Personnel
Dir: Marc Gould *E-mail:* mgould@ala.org
Press Officer: Larra Clark *E-mail:* lclark@ala.org
Location: Nationwide throughout the USA
April 15-21, 2007

NOVEMBER

American Academy of Religion
Sponsored by American Schools of Oriental Research
825 Houston Mill Rd, Atlanta, GA 30329, United States
Tel: 404-727-3049; 404-727-7920 *Fax:* 404-727-7959
Web Site: www.aarweb.org
Key Personnel
Meeting Coord: Shannon Planck
Location: San Diego, CA, USA
Nov 17-20, 2007

Stuttgarter Buchwochen (Stuttgart Bookweeks)
Sponsored by Verband der Verlage und Buchhandlungen in Baden-Wuerttemberg eV (Association of Publishers & Booksellers in Baden-Wuerttemberg e V)
Paulinenstr 53, 70178 Stuttgart, Germany
Tel: (0711) 619410 *Fax:* (0711) 6194144
E-mail: buchhandelsverband@vvb-bw.de
Key Personnel
Contact: Maike Dreyer *Tel:* (0711) 61941 28
E-mail: dreyer@vvb-bw.de
Location: Haus der Wirtschaft, Stuttgart, Germany
Nov-Dec

Library Resources

Major Libraries

The majority of the libraries and archives listed are those associated with government or educational institutions. Many are also involved in publishing activities.

Afghanistan

Institute of Education Library, Kabul University
Jamal Mina, Kabul
Tel: 42594

Library of the Press & Information Department
Sanaii Wat, Kabul
Key Personnel
Dir: Mohammed Sarwar Rona

Ministry of Education Library
Kabul
Key Personnel
Chief Officer: Mohamad Quasem Hilaman

Library of the National Bank
Ibn Sina Wat, Kabul
Key Personnel
Dir: A Aziz

Public Library
Charaii-i-Malik Asghar, Kabul
Key Personnel
Dir: Mohamad Omar Seddiqui

University Library
Kabul
Tel: 42594

Albania

Botim i Bibliotekes Kombetare
Sheshi Skenderbe, Tirana
Tel: (042) 23843 *Fax:* (04) 23843
E-mail: plasari@san.com.al
Key Personnel
Dir: Mr Aurel Plasari
National Library.
Publication(s): *Bibliografia kombeetare e Republikees see Shipeerisee, Periodiku* (Albanian National Bibliography of Periodicals); *Bibliografia kombeetare e Republikees see Shqipeerise Libri* (Albanian National Bibliography of Books)

Shkoder Public Library
Shkoder

Algeria

Agence ISBN, see Bibliotheque Nationale

Bibliotheque Municipale de Constantine
Hotel de Ville, Constantine

Bibliotheque Nationale
One Ave du Docteur Frantz Fanon, Algiers 1600
Tel: (063) 0632
Key Personnel
Dir: Mohamed Aissa-Oumoussa
Publication(s): *Bibliographie de l'Algerie* (biannually, in Arabic and French)

Ecole nationale polytechnique, Bibliotheque
10 ave Pasteur, El-Harrach, BP 182, Algiers
Tel: (052) 1027 *Fax:* (052) 2973
E-mail: enp@ist.cerist.dz
Telex: 64147 Enp
Key Personnel
Librarian: K Amara

Institut National Agronomique, Bibliotheque
One av Pasteur, Hacen-Badi, El-Harrach, Algiers
Tel: (052) 1987 *Fax:* (052) 3547
Telex: 64143 Dz
Key Personnel
Chief Librarian: Rosa Issolah
Publication(s): *Annals de l'INA*

Institut Pasteur d'Algerie, Bibliotheque
rue du Dr Laveran, Alger
Tel: (065) 8860 *Fax:* (067) 2503
Telex: 65-337; 65-627
Key Personnel
Dir: Prof F Boulahbal

Archives nationales
BP 61, Algiers - Gare
Tel: (054) 2160 *Fax:* (054) 1616
Telex: 62524
Key Personnel
Dir: Abdelkrim Badjada

Bibliotheque Centrale, Universite d'Alger
2 rue Didouche Mourad, Algiers
Tel: (064) 6970
Telex: 5385
Key Personnel
Librarian: Zoulikha Bekaddour

Bibliotheque de l'Universite de Constantine
Route de Ain el Bey, BP 325, Constantine
Tel: (069) 7385
Telex: 92436

Key Personnel
Chief Librarian: Noureddine Talhour
Publication(s): *Des Catalogues Thematiques*

Universite d'Oran, Bibliotheque
Es-Senia, BP 1524, Oran
Tel: (036) 2788 *Fax:* (038) 8672
Telex: 22993 UNIRX DZ

Angola

Direccao Provincial Servicos de Geologia e Minas de Angola Biblioteca
CP 1260C, Luanda
Tel: (02) 322766
Telex: 3324

Biblioteca Municipal de Luanda
CP 1227, Luanda
Tel: (02) 392297 *Fax:* (02) 33902
Key Personnel
Librarian: Antonio Jose Emidio De Brito

Biblioteca Nacional de Angola
Av Comandante Jika CP 2915, Luanda
Tel: (02) 326299 *Fax:* (02) 326299
E-mail: biblioteca@netangola.com
Telex: 4129 Mincult
Key Personnel
Dir: Maria Jose Faria Ramos
Founded: 1969
Publication(s): *Novas* (News)

Universidade de Luanda Biblioteca
Av 4 de Fevereiro 7 CP 815, Luanda
Tel: (02) 30517 *Fax:* (02) 330520
Telex: 3076
Key Personnel
Librarian: Jeronimo Octavio Xavier Belo

Argentina

Biblioteca Argentina Dr Juan Alvarez
Pte Roca 731, 2000 Rosario, C Postal 2000
Tel: (041) 802538; (041) 802539 *Fax:* (041) 802561
E-mail: biblarg@rosario.gov.ar
Key Personnel
Contact: Maria del Carmen D'Angelo

ARGENTINA

Biblioteca del Banco Central de la Republica Argentina (Central Bank of the Argentine Republic)
San Martin 216-1piso, 1004 Buenos Aires
Tel: (011) 4348 3772; (011) 4348 3500 (ext 2571 & 2801) *Fax:* (011) 4348 3771
E-mail: biblio@bcra.gov.ar
Web Site: www.bcra.gov.ar
Telex: 24031 BCFEXAR
Key Personnel
Chief Librarian: Marta S Gutierrez
 E-mail: mgutierrez@bcra.gov.ar
Library of the Central Bank.
Publication(s): *Boletin Estadistico* (monthly); *Boletin Monetario y Financiero* (quarterly); *Central de Deudores* (monthly); *Informacion de Entidades Financieras* (monthly); *Informe Anual del Presidente al Congreso de la Nac* (annual); *Resumen de las Regulaciones del Sistema Financiero Argentino* (biannual)

Biblioteca Nacional
Aguero 2502, Buenos Aires 1425
Tel: (011) 4806-6155; (011) 4806-6157 *Fax:* (011) 4806-6157
E-mail: postmaster@siscor.bibnal.edu.ar
Key Personnel
Dir: Oscar Sbarra Mitre

Biblioteca Nacional de Maestros
Pizzurno 953, 1020 Buenos Aires
Tel: (011) 8110275 *Fax:* (011) 8110275
Key Personnel
Dir: Lic Graciela Perrone
National Teachers' Library.
Publication(s): *Historia de la Biblioteca Nacional de Maestros*; *La Biblioteca* (monthly)

Biblioteca del Congreso de la Nacion (National Library of Congress)
Rivadavia 1850, 1033 Buenos Aires
Tel: (011) 4761641 *Fax:* (011) 954-1067
Key Personnel
Dir of Technical Processes: Lic Liliana Casteran Racedo
National Library of Congress.

Sistema de Bibliotecas y de Informacion
Universidad de Buenos Aires, Azcuenaga 280, 1029 Buenos Aires
Tel: (011) 9511366 *Fax:* (011) 49526557
E-mail: postmaster@sisbi.uba.ar
Telex: 18694-IBUBA-AR
Key Personnel
General Coordinator: Dr Susana Soto
Jefe de Procesos Tecnicos: Elsa Elena Elizalde

Universidad de Buenos Aires, Sistema de Bibliotecas y de Informacion
Azcuenaga 280, 1029 Buenos Aires
Tel: (011) 9511366 *Fax:* (011) 9526557
E-mail: postmaster@sisbi.uba.ar
Telex: 18694

Biblioteca Central, Universidad del Salvador
Presidente Peron 1818, 1040 Buenos Aires
Tel: (011) 400422; (011) 3710422
E-mail: uds-bibl@salvador.edu.ar

Biblioteca Mayor de la Universidad Nacional de Cordoba (Major Library, University of Cordoleo, Argentine)
Calle Obispo Trejo 242, Casilla de Correo 63 Cordoba X50001YF
Tel: (351) 4331072 *Fax:* (351) 4331079
E-mail: cendoc@sri.hejo.unc.edu.ar
Web Site: www.bmayor.unc.edu.ar
Key Personnel
Deputy Dir: Lic Rosa M Bestani
Founded: 1613

Principal Library of the National University of Cordoba
The Library also possesses collections from the 16th, 17th & 18th centuries.
Publication(s): *Informativo* (irregular)

Biblioteca de la Universidad Nacional de La Plata
Plaza Rocha 137, 1900 La Plata
Tel: (021) 25-5004 *Fax:* (021) 255004
E-mail: bulap@cespivm2.bitnet
Telex: 31151 Bulap
Key Personnel
Dir: Carlos Jose Tejo

Universidad Nacional del Litoral
Blvd Pellegrin, 2750 Santa Fe
Tel: (042) 571110
E-mail: deopint@unl.edu.ar
Key Personnel
Dir: Beatriz S Perez Risso de Costa

Aruba

Biblioteca Nacional Aruba (Aruba National Library)
George Maduro St 13, Oranjestad
Tel: (0297) 821580 *Fax:* (0297) 821580
E-mail: bna@setarnet.aw
Telex: bc 5060
Key Personnel
Acting Dir: Astrid J T Britten
System Librarian & Acting Dir: Lilian A Semeleer
Founded: 1949
National & Public Library; Member of *Acuril-IFLA*.
Branch Office(s)
Filiaal San Nicolaas, Peter Stuyvesant Straat Z/N, San Nicolas *E-mail:* sn@setarnet.aw

Australia

Archives Office of New South Wales
2 Globe St, The Rocks, Sydney, NSW 2000
Tel: (02) 2370200 *Fax:* (02) 2370142
Key Personnel
Principal Archivist: D J Cross
Branch Office(s)
76 Miller Red, Villawood

Australian National University Library
Cor Fellows & Garran Rd, Canberra, ACT 0200
Mailing Address: GPO Box 4, Canberra, ACT 0200
Tel: (02) 6125 2003 *Fax:* (02) 6125 0058
Key Personnel
University Librarian: C R Steele *Tel:* (02) 6249 0083 *E-mail:* colin.steele@anu.edu.au
Publication(s): *User response to URICA: a catalogue on line*

Barr Smith Press, University of Adelaide Library
The University of Adelaide Library, The University of Adelaide, Adelaide, SA 5005
Tel: (08) 8303 5370 *Fax:* (08) 8303 4369
Web Site: www.library.adelaide.edu.au
Key Personnel
University Librarian: Ray Choate *Tel:* (08) 8303 4064 *E-mail:* ray.choate@adelaide.edu.au
Publication(s): *Joanna & Robert, the Barr Smith's Life in Letters, 1853-1919* (1996); *Poems & Recollections of the Past* (1996)

CSIRO (Commonwealth Scientific & Industrial Research Organization)
Limestone Ave, Campbell, ACT 2612
Mailing Address: PO Box 225, Dickson, ACT 2602
Tel: (03) 4187333 *Fax:* (03) 4190459
Web Site: www.csiro.au
Telex: 30236
Key Personnel
Chief Executive: Malcolm McIntosh
Chairman: Prof A Clarke
Library Network Services provides cost effective, specialized library services to CSIRO's Network of 45 libraries throughout Australia & delivery of a complete range of library services to staff of the Information Services Branch.

Library & Information Service of Western Australia, see State Library of Western Australia

Monash University Library
Box 4, Monash University, Victoria 3800
Tel: (03) 99052662 *Fax:* (03) 99052610
E-mail: equery@lib.monash.edu.au
Key Personnel
University Librarian: Cathrine Harboe-Ree

The State Library of New South Wales
Macquarie St, Sydney, NSW 2000
Tel: (02) 92731414 *Fax:* (02) 92731255
E-mail: library@sl.nsw.gov.au
Web Site: www.sl.nsw.gov.au
Key Personnel
State Librarian: D Schmidmaier
Founded: 1826
Publication(s): *Public Library News* (newsletter); *Public Library Statistics* (annually)

State Library of Queensland
Queensland Cultural Centre, Southbank, South Brisbane, Qld 4101
Tel: (07) 38407666 *Fax:* (07) 38462421
Key Personnel
Librarian: Des Stephens
Manager, Public Affairs: Yvonne Kennedy *Tel:* (07) 38407776 *E-mail:* y.kennedy@slq.qld.gov.au
Includes the John Oxley Library of Queensland History.
Publication(s): *Annual Report of the Library Board of Queensland*; *Directory of State and Public Library Service in Queensland* (annually); *North Queensland Towns and Districts Bibliography* (1975); *Public Libraries in Queensland: Statistical Bulletin* (annually); *Queensland Government Publications,* (1977-quarterly); *The Development of State Libraries and their effect on the Public Library Movement in Australia* (1809-1964)

State Library of South Australia
North Terrace, Adelaide, SA 5000
Mailing Address: GPO Box 419, Adelaide SA 5001
Tel: (08) 82077200 *Fax:* (08) 82077247
Web Site: www.slsa.sa.gov.au
Key Personnel
Dir: Bronwyn Halliday
Chairman: Peter Wylie
Publication(s): *Collection Development Policy* (orig 1995); *Extra Extra* (3 issues per year); *Strategic Plan* (1993-2020)

State Library of Tasmania
91 Murray St, Hobart, Tas 7000
Tel: (03) 6233 7511 *Fax:* (03) 6231 0927
E-mail: state.library@education.tas.gov.au
Web Site: www.statelibrary.education.tas.gov.au

Key Personnel
Dir: Siobhan Gaskell *E-mail:* siobhan.gaskell@education.tas.gov.au
Senior Librarian (Policy Planning): Bridget Hutton *Tel:* (03) 6233 6815 *E-mail:* bridget.hutton@education.tas.gov.au
Founded: 1850
State library & public library service.

State Library of Victoria
328 Swanston St, Melbourne, Vic 3000
Tel: (03) 8664 7000 *Fax:* (03) 96699888; (03) 96699958
Key Personnel
Chief Executive & State Librarian: Frances Awcock
Publication(s): *La Trobe Library Journal* (biannually); *Victorian Government Publications* (monthly)

State Library of Western Australia
Formerly Library & Information Service of Western Australia
Alexander Library Bldg, Perth Cultural Centre, Perth, WA 6000
Tel: (08) 9427 3111 *Fax:* (08) 9427 3256
E-mail: info@liswa.wa.gov.au
Web Site: www.liswa.wa.gov.au
Key Personnel
Chief Executive Officer & State Librarian: Claire Forte
Publication(s): *Guide to the Genealogical Collection of the State Reference Library*

University of Melbourne Library
Baillieu Library, Parkville, Victoria 3052
Tel: (03) 83445382 *Fax:* (03) 83449879
Telex: 30815
Key Personnel
Vice Principal: H M Hayes *E-mail:* h.hayes@unimelb.edu.au

University of New South Wales Library
Sydney, NSW 2052
Tel: (02) 93852615 *Fax:* (02) 93858002
E-mail: information@unsw.edu.au
Web Site: www.library.edu.au
Key Personnel
Librarian: M E Bate
Founded: 1948

University of Queensland Library
Saint Lucia, Qld 4072
Tel: (07) 33656209 *Fax:* (07) 33657317
Key Personnel
Librarian: Janine Schmidt

University of South Australia Library
Holbrooks Rd, Underdale, SA 5032
Tel: (08) 83026611 *Fax:* (08) 83026756
Web Site: www.library.unisa.edu.au
Key Personnel
Librarian: Dr Alan Bundy *E-mail:* alan.bundy@unisa.edu.au
Publisher of library science texts & conference proceedings.

University of Sydney Library
Parramatta Rd, Sydney, NSW 2006
Tel: (02) 93512990 *Fax:* (02) 93512890
Key Personnel
Librarian: John Shipp

University of Technology, Sydney Library
PO Box 123, Broadway, NSW 2007
Tel: (02) 95142000 *Fax:* (02) 95141551
Key Personnel
Librarian: Stephen V O'Connor
Publication(s): *Library Link* (newsletter, quarterly)

University of Western Australia Library
Stirling Highway, Nedlands, WA 6009
Tel: (09) 3802344 *Fax:* (09) 3801012
E-mail: liboff@uniwa.uwa.edu.av
Telex: 92992 Uniwa *Cable:* Uniwest
Key Personnel
Librarian: John Arfield

Austria

Amtsbibliothek des Bundesministeriums fur Unterricht, und Kulturelle Angelegenheiten und des Bundesministeriums fur Wissenschaft und Verkehr
Minoritenplaz 5, Postfach 65, A-1014 Vienna
Tel: (01) 531200 *Fax:* (01) 53120-5172
Telex: 115532
Key Personnel
Manager: Dr Norbert Neumann
Publication(s): *Euro-Dok: Bildung, Forschung, Kultur, Kunst, Unterricht, Wissenschaft*; *Forschungspolitische Dokumentation* (Political Research Documentation); *Veroeffentlichungen: Zuwachsverzeichnis*

Bibliothek der Osterreichischen Akademie der Wissenschaften
Dr-Ignaz-Seipel-Platz 2, A-1010 Vienna
Tel: (01) 51581262
E-mail: bibliothe@oeaw.ac.at
Web Site: www.oeaw.ac.at
Telex: (01) 12628
Key Personnel
Assistant Professor: Dr Christine Harrauer
E-mail: christine.harrauer@oeaw.ac.at
Library of the Austrian Academy of Science.
Publication(s): *Kosmos und Mythos*; *Meliouchos*

Bibliothek des Benediktinerklosters Melk in Niederoesterreich
A-3390 Stift, Melk
Tel: (02752) 52312342 *Fax:* (02752) 5231252
Key Personnel
Librarian: P Gottfried Glassner
E-mail: gglassner@magnet.at
Library of the Melk Benedictine Monastery in Lower Austria.
Publication(s): *Die Anfaenge der Melker Bibliothek* (1996)

Bibliothek des Osterreichischen Patentamtes
Kohlmarkt 8-10, A-1014 Vienna
Tel: (01) 53424; (01) 53140 *Fax:* (01) 53424; (01) 53110
E-mail: weiding@at-patent.co.at
Telex: 136847 OEPA
Key Personnel
President: Dr Otmar Rafeiner
Librarian: Dr Ingrid Weidinger
Library of the Austrian Patent Office.
Publication(s): *Oestereichischer Musteronzeiger*; *Ostereichisches Gebroiuchsmusterblett*; *Oesterreichischer Markenanzeiger*; *Oesterreichisches Patentblatt*; *Patentschriften*

Universitaetsbibliothek Graz (University Library Graz)
Universitaetspl 3a, A-8010 Graz
Tel: (0316) 380 3101; (0316) 380 3102; (0316) 380 3100 *Fax:* (0316) 384 987
Web Site: www.ub.kfunigtaz.ac.at
Key Personnel
Librarian: Dr Sigrid Reinitzer *E-mail:* sigrid.reinitzer@kfunigraz.ac.at
Founded: 1573

Publication(s): *Jahresbericht* (annually, 1973); *News (Informationsschrift der Universitaetsbibliothek Graz)* (Heft 1 1987)
Parent Company: Karl-Franzens Universitat Graz, Universitaetsplatz 3, A-8010 Graz

Universitaetsbibliothek Innsbruck
Innrain 50, A-6010 Innsbruck
Tel: (0512) 5072401 *Fax:* (0512) 5072864
Telex: 553708
Key Personnel
Dir: Dr Walter Neuhauser
Publication(s): *Vom Codex zum Computer*

Oberoesterreichische Landesbibliothek (Regional Library Upper Austria)
Schillerpl 2, Postfach 129, 4021 Linz 2
Tel: (0732) 6640710 *Fax:* (0732) 664071-44
E-mail: landesbibliothek@ooe.gv.at
Web Site: www.landesbibliothek.at
Key Personnel
Dir: Dr Christian Enichlmayr *Tel:* (0732) 66407722 *E-mail:* christian.enichlmayr@ooe.gv.at
Founded: 1774
Reference Library.
Parent Company: Land Oberoesterreich

Oesterreichisches Staatsarchiv (Austrian State Archives)
Nottendorfer, Gasse 2, A-1030 Vienna
Tel: (01) 79540-0 *Fax:* (01) 79540 (ext 109)
E-mail: gdpost@oesta.gv.at
Web Site: www.oesta.gv.at
Key Personnel
General Dir: Prof Dr Lorenz Mikoletzky *Tel:* (01) 79540-100 *E-mail:* lorenz.mikoletzky@oesta.gv.at
Personnel & Administrative Dir: Luzia Owajko
Dir, Archives of the Republic: Hr Dr Manfred Fink
Dir, Library of Austrian State Archives: Hr Dr Adolf Gaisbauer
Dir, Finance Archives: Hr Dr Christian Sapper
Dir, War Archive: Hr Dr Christoph Tepperberg
Dir, Courthouse & State Archives: Hr Prof Dr Leopold Auer
Provisional Dir, General Adminstrative Archive: Dr Gerald Theimer
Founded: 1945
Publication(s): *Mitteilungen des Oesterreichischen Staatsarchivs* (Annually)

Osterreichische Nationalbibliothek (Austrian National Library)
Josefspl 1, 1015 Vienna
Tel: (01) 534100 *Fax:* (01) 533704983
Telex: 112624 AOenb
Key Personnel
Dir General: Dr Hans Marthe
Publication(s): *Informationsfuehrer Bibliotheken und Dokumentations- stellen in Oesterreich* (Information Guide to Libraries and Documentation Centres in Austria)

Steiermaerkische Landesbibliothek
Kalchberggasse 2, A-8011 Graz
Mailing Address: Postfach 861, A-8011 Graz
Tel: (0316) 80164600 *Fax:* (0316) 80164633
E-mail: post@stlbib.stmk.gv.at
Web Site: www.stmk.gv.at/verwaltung/stlbib/start.stm
Key Personnel
Dir: Dr Joseph F Desput
Librarian: Dr Hannes Lambauer *Tel:* (0316) 80164609
Founded: 1811
Public Scientific Library.
Publication(s): *Veroeffentlichungen der Steiermaerkischen Landesbibliothek 24: Joerg-Martin Willnauer: Die Steiermark in Wort und Schild*

(2000, Scientific series concerning Styrian literature history & history of culture); *Geschichte und Gegenwart* (History & the Present, quarterly, 2000, Scientific journal)

Universitaetsbibliothek der Technischen Universitaet Wien (Vienna University of Technology Library)
Resselgasse 4, A-1040 Vienna
Tel: (01) 58801 44051 *Fax:* (01) 5880144099
E-mail: info@mail.ub.tuwien.ac.at
Web Site: www.ub.tuwien.ac.at
Key Personnel
Librarian: Dr Peter Kubalek
Founded: 1815
Focuses on the Natural & Technical Sciences but also covers related subjects such as Environmental Technology.

Universitaetsbibliothek Salzburg
Universitatsbibliothek Hauptbibliothek Hofstallgasse 2-4, A-5020 Salzburg
Tel: (0662) 842576 *Fax:* (0662) 842576680
Key Personnel
Librarian: Dr Christine Unterrainer
E-mail: christine.unterrainer@sbg.ac.at

Vienna International Centre Library
Wagramestr 5, Postfach 100, A-1400 Vienna
Tel: (01) 2600 *Fax:* (01) 2600 29584
E-mail: vicl@iaea.org
Telex: 112645 *Cable:* Inatom Vienna

Universitaetsbibliothek Wien (Vienna University Library)
Dr-Karl-Lueger-Ring 1, A-1010 Vienna
Tel: (01) 427715001 *Fax:* (01) 42779150
E-mail: info.ub@univie.ac.at
Web Site: www.ub.unvie.ac.at
Key Personnel
Librarian: Dr Ilse Dosoudil *E-mail:* ilse.dosoudil@univie.ac.at
Founded: 1365

Wiener Stadt- und Landesarchiv
One Rathaus, A-1082 Vienna
Tel: (01) 4000; (01) 84808 *Fax:* (01) 4000; (01) 9984819; (01) 1-4000-7238 (international)
E-mail: post@m08.magwien.gv.at
Key Personnel
Dir: Dr Ferdinand Opll
Vienna Municipal Archives.
Publication(s): *Veroeffentlichungen des Wiener Stadt-und Landesarchivs*

Wiener Stadt- und Landesbibliothek
Rathaus, A-1082 Vienna
Tel: (01) 400084915 *Fax:* (01) 40007219
E-mail: post@m09.magwien.gv.et
Web Site: www.stadtbibliothek.wien.at
Key Personnel
Man Dir: Walter Obermaier
Vienna Municipal & County Library.

Azerbaijan

Azerbaidzhanskaya gosudarstvennaya biblioteka im M F Akhundova (M F Akhundov State Library of Azerbaijan Republic)
Khagani 29, 370601 Baku
Tel: (012) 934003
Key Personnel
Dir: L Yu Gafurova
Publication(s): *Azerbaijan in Foreign Press* (Bibliographic Indexes); *Scientific Transactions of M F Akhundov State Library*

Bahamas

The College of the Bahamas Library
Poinciana Dr & Thompson Blvd, PO Box N4912, Nassau
Tel: (242) 323-7930 *Fax:* (242) 326-7834
E-mail: library@cob.edu.bs
Web Site: www.cob.edu.bs
Key Personnel
Dir: Ms Willamae Johnson *Tel:* (242) 302-4552
E-mail: coblibwj@cob.edu.bs
Founded: 1975
Has branches in Freeport, Grand Bahama & New Providence.
Publication(s): *Bahamas Reference Collection: a Bibliography* (1980, with irregular supplements); *The Chickcharney Express* (Irregular); *The Library Informer* (per semester, newsletter)
Parent Company: The College of the Bahamas

Nassau Public Library
PO Box N3210, Nassau
Tel: (242) 322-4907

Sir Charles Hayword Lending Library
PO Box F40040, Freeport
Key Personnel
Contact: Elaine B Talma

Bahrain

Bahrain Centre for Studies, Research Library & Information Dept
PO Box 496, Manama
Tel: 754757 *Fax:* 754678
Telex: 9764 BCSR BN
Key Personnel
Library Dir: Najim Rashid

College of Medicine Library, Arabian Gulf University
Arabian Gulf University, Manama
Mailing Address: PO Box 26671, Manama
Tel: 440044 *Fax:* 440002
E-mail: suad@mail.agu.edu.bh
Telex: 7319
Key Personnel
Librarian: Suad Al-Khalifa

Manama Central Library
PO Box 43, Manama
Tel: 231105 *Fax:* 274036
Key Personnel
Dir of Public Libraries: Mansoor Mohamed Sarhan

University of Bahrain
PO Box 32038, Isa Town
Tel: 682748 *Fax:* 681465
Telex: 9258
Key Personnel
Dir & Librarian: Hedi Talbi *E-mail:* talbi@admin.uob.bh
Assistant Dir (Isa Town): Mrs Al-Khalifa Tahani
Assistant Dir (Sakhir): Mr Nadim Joseph Hammond

Bangladesh

Bangladesh Central Public Library
Ministry Cult Affairs, 10, Kazi Nazrul Islam Ave, Shahbagh, Dhaka 1000
Tel: (02) 500819
Key Personnel
Dir: Dr A F M Badive-Rahman

Bangladesh Institute of Development Studies Library
E-17 Agargaon, Sher-e Bangle Nagar, Motiheel Commercial Area, Dhaka 7 2
Mailing Address: PO Box 3854, Dhaka 7 2
Tel: (02) 9118999; (02) 813023 *Cable:* BIDECON DHAKA
Key Personnel
Chief Librarian: Nilufar Akhter

National Library of Bangladesh
Sher-e-Bangla Nagar Agargaon, Dhaka 1207
Tel: (02) 326572; (02) 312733; (02) 318704
Key Personnel
Dir: Dr Sharif Uddin Ahmed *Tel:* (02) 9112733

British Council Library
GPO Box 161, Dhaka 1000
Tel: (02) 868905; (02) 868907; (02) 868867 *Fax:* (02) 863375; (02) 870483
Web Site: www.britishcouncil.org/bangladesh/
Telex: 642470 Bric
Key Personnel
Dir: Tom Cowin *E-mail:* tcowin@thebritishcouncil.net

Dhaka University Library
Dhaka 1000
Tel: (02) 505789 *Fax:* (02) 865583
Key Personnel
Librarian: Dr Serajul Islam

University of Rajshahi Library
Rajshahi 6205
Tel: (0721) 750666 *Fax:* (0721) 750064
E-mail: rajuce@citechco.net
Key Personnel
Administrator: Prof Abaydur Rahman Pramanik
Founded: 1955

Barbados

National Library Service
Coleridge St, Bridgetown
Tel: (0246) 436-6081 *Fax:* (0246) 436-1501
Key Personnel
Dir: Dr J Y Blackman
Publication(s): *National Bibliography of Barbados*; *West Indian Collection*
Branch Office(s)
Main Lending Library, Coleridge St, Bridgetown
Tel: (0246) 4366081

University of the West Indies Library (Barbados)
Main Library, Bridgetown
Mailing Address: PO Box 1334, Bridgetown
Tel: (246) 417-4444 *Fax:* (246) 417-4460
Telex: 2257 Univados *Cable:* UNIVADOS BARBADOS
Key Personnel
Librarian: Michael Gill *E-mail:* gillme@caribsurg.com

Belarus

National Library of Belarus
9 Chyrvonaarmejskaja St, 220636 Minsk
Tel: (0172) 275463 *Fax:* (0172) 292494
E-mail: sol@nacbibl.minsk.by
Key Personnel
Librarian & Dir: Galina N Alejnik
Publication(s): *Chernobyl* (bibliographic index 3 times a year); *Cultural Life of Belarus* (monthly); *Current literature on the history of Belarus and its historical science* (bibliographic index 3 times a year); *Signal Information on Culture & Arts* (weekly); *Social Sciences* (monthly)

Belgium

AMVC-Letterenhuis (Archives & Museum of Flemish Culture - Literature Centre)
Minderbroedersstraat 22, B-2000 Antwerp
Tel: (03) 222 9320 *Fax:* (03) 222 9321
E-mail: amvc@cs.antwerpen.be
Web Site: www.antwerpen.be/cultuur/amvc
Key Personnel
Curator: Leen Van Dijck *Tel:* (03) 222 9329
 E-mail: helena.vandijck@cs.antwerpen.be
Founded: 1933
Archives & Museum of Flemish Culture.

Archives generales du Royaume
2-4 rue de Ruysbroeck, B-1000 Brussels
Tel: (02) 5137680 *Fax:* (02) 5137681
National Archives.

Bibliotheque Central du Minstere de l'Education Nationale
43 rue de Stassart, 1050 Brussels
Tel: (02) 5110830 *Fax:* (02) 5134333
Key Personnel
Dir: J M Andrin

Bibliotheque du Musee Royal de Mariemont
100 chaussee de Mariemont, B-7140 Morlanwelz-Mariemont
Tel: (064) 212193 *Fax:* (064) 262924
Key Personnel
Librarian: M B Delattre
Publication(s): *Bulletin d'Information* (quarterly); *Cahiers de Mariemont* (annually); *Catalogues d'Expositions, Monographies, Dossiers Pedagogiques*

Bibliotheque Fonds Quetelet
6 rue de l'Industrie, 1000 Brussels
Tel: (02) 5066054 *Fax:* (02) 5028425
Key Personnel
Librarian: E Van Wesemael
Library of the Ministry of Economic Affairs.
Publication(s): *Accroissements de la Bibliotheque Centrale Fonds Quetelet* (monthly)

Bibliotheque Royale Albert Ier
4 blvd de l'Empereur, 1000 Brussels
Tel: (02) 5195311 *Fax:* (02) 5195454
Telex: 21157
Key Personnel
Dir: Pierre Cockshaw
Koninklijke Bibliotheek Albert I.
Publication(s): *Bibliograhie de Belgique (Belgisch Bibliographie)* (monthly); *Bulletin de la BR (KB Bulletin)* (quarterly)

Bibliotheques de l'Universite Libre de Bruxelles
50 ave Franklin D Roosevelt, 1050 Brussels
Tel: (02) 6502378 *Fax:* (02) 6502370
E-mail: bibulb@vlb.ac.be
Key Personnel
Librarian: Jean-Pierre Devroey

Centre d'Information et de Conservation de l'Universite de Liege
One pl Cockerill, 4000 Liege
Tel: (04) 3665206 *Fax:* (04) 3665702
Key Personnel
Head Librarian: Nicole Haesenne
Chief Librarian: Dr J Denooz *E-mail:* joseph.denooz@ulg.ac.be
Publication(s): *Bibliotheca Universitatis Leodiensis*

Goethe-Institut
58 rue Belliard, 1040 Brussels
Tel: (02) 2303970 *Fax:* (02) 2307725
E-mail: goethe.library@infoboard.be
Key Personnel
Librarian: Dr Bernhard Beutler

Institut Royal des Sciences Naturelles de Belgique, Bibliotheque (Royal Belgian Institute of Natural Sciences)
KBIN-Library/Documentation Service, Vautierstraat 29, B-1000 Brussels
Tel: (02) 627 41 89 *Fax:* (02) 627 41 13
E-mail: bib@naturalsciences.be
Web Site: www.naturalsciences.be
Telex: INSNAT
Key Personnel
Librarian: Laurent Meese *Tel:* (02) 627 42 49
 E-mail: laurent.meese@naturalsciences.be
Head Department Vertebrates: J Govaere
Founded: 1846
Publication(s): *Biology* (annually, bulletin, 2001); *Earth Sciences* (annually, bulletin, 2002); *Entomology* (annually, bulletin, 2001); *Documents de Travail de L'IR Sc N B*

Katholieke Universiteit Leuven
Universiteitsbibliotheek, Mgr Ladeuzeplein 21, B-3000 Leuven
Tel: (016) 324660; (016) 324601 *Fax:* (016) 324616
Web Site: www.bib.kuleuven.ac.be
Key Personnel
Librarian: Raf Dekeyser *E-mail:* raf.dekeyser@bib.kuleuven.ac.be
University Library of Louvain.
Publication(s): *Ex officina* (Bulletin of the Friends of Louvain University Library)

Bibliotheque Universitaire Moretus Plantin (University Library Moretus Plantin)
Unit of The University of Namur
19 rue Grandgagnage, B-5000 Namur
Tel: (081) 724630 *Fax:* (081) 724645
E-mail: bump@fundp.ac.be
Web Site: www.fundp.ac.be/bump
Key Personnel
Chief Librarian: Prof R Noel
Secretary: Yvette Wilquet *E-mail:* yvettewilquet@fundp.ac.be
Academic library.

Bibliotheque du Parlement
Rue de la Loi 13, 1000 Brussels
Tel: (02) 5499200 *Fax:* (02) 5499497
Key Personnel
Librarian: Roland Van Nieuwenborgh

Museum Plantin-Moretus
Vrijdagmarkt 22, 2000 Antwerp
Tel: (03) 221 14 50; (03) 221 14 51 *Fax:* (03) 221 14 71
E-mail: museum.plantin.moretus@antwerpen.be
Web Site: www.antwerpen.be/cultuur/museum_plantinmoretus/
Key Personnel
Dir: Dr Francine de Nave
Publication(s): *About types, books & prints. Didactic brochure for the Plantin-Moretus Museum & City Prints Gallery* (1989, monograph); *Plantin-Moretus Museum Antwerp (Musea Nostra)* (1995, monograph); *The Illustration of Books Published by the Moretuses* (1996, monograph)

Stadsbibliotheek (Library of the City of Antwerp)
Hendrik Conscienceplein 4, B-2000 Antwerp
Tel: (03) 2068711 *Fax:* (03) 2068775
E-mail: sba@antwerpes.be
Key Personnel
Dir: R Rennenberg
Founded: 1481
Reference library concentrating on humanities.

Bibliotheek Universitair Centrum
Middelheimlaan 1, B-2020 Antwerp
Tel: (03) 2180788; (03) 2180794 *Fax:* (03) 2180652
E-mail: benoni@mare.ruca.ua.ac.be
Key Personnel
Contact: Dr B van Styvendaele

Universite Catholique de Louvain
Place de l'Universite 1, B-1348 Louvain-la-Neuve
Tel: (010) 478187 *Fax:* (010) 478298
E-mail: sceb@sceb.ucl.ac.be
Web Site: www.bib.ucl.ac.be
Key Personnel
Chief Librarian: Charles-Henri Nyns
 E-mail: nyns@sceb.ucl.ac.be

Universiteit Antwerpen Bibliotheek UFSIA (University of Antwerp UFSIA Library)
Prinsstr 9, B-2000 Antwerp
Tel: (03) 2204996 *Fax:* (03) 2204437
E-mail: ludo.simons@ufsia.ac.be
Web Site: lib.ua.ac.be
Telex: 33599 Ufsia
Key Personnel
Chief Librarian: L Simons
Dir: Theo Boeckx *Tel:* (03) 2204448
 E-mail: theo.boeckx@ufsia.ac.be
Founded: 1852
Universiteit Antwerpen consists of Universitaire Faculteiten Sint-Ignatius (UFSIA), Universitaire Instelling Antwerpen (UIA), Rijksuniversitair Centrum Antwerpen (RUCA), each with its own library. The above entry details refer to UFSIA.

University Library of Louvain (Leuven), see Katholieke Universiteit Leuven

University Library of Louvain (Louvain-la-Neuve) Les Bibliotheques de l'Universite Catholique de Louvain, see Universite Catholique de Louvain

Vrije Universiteit Brussel Universiteitsbibliotheek
Campus Oefenplein, Pleinlaan 2, B-1050 Brussels
Tel: (02) 6292111 *Fax:* (02) 6292282
E-mail: snamenwi@vnet3.uub.ac.be
Telex: 61051

Belize

National Library Service of Belize
Princess Margaret Drive, Belize City

BELIZE

Mailing Address: PO Box 287, Belize City
Tel: (02) 2234248; (02) 2234249 *Fax:* (02) 2234246
E-mail: nls@btl.net
Web Site: www.nlsbze.bz
Key Personnel
Chief Librarian: Mrs Joy L Ysaguirre
Committed to the promotion of a more informed, aware & literate society & seeks to provide universal access to information through the maintenance of a National Library & Public Library service.
Memberships: Comla; ACURIL; ABINIA-AC; IFLA; INFOLAC.
Parent Company: Ministry of Education, Government of Belize

Benin

Bibliotheque Nationale du Benin
BP 401, Porto Novo
Tel: 212585
Key Personnel
Dir: H N Amoussou
Publication(s): *Les Numeras de la Bibliographie Nationale*

Bibliotheque Universitaire Centrale
Abomey-Calavy, Cotonou
Mailing Address: BP 526, Cotonou
Tel: 360074
Telex: 5010 *Cable:* Biblionationale
Key Personnel
Chief Librarian: Pascal A I Gandaho

Direction des Archives Nationales du Benin
Direction des Archives Nationales, BP 629, Porto Novo
Tel: 213079 *Fax:* 213079
Telex: 5347
Key Personnel
Dir: Elise R Paraiso *Tel:* 050266; 223497
Founded: 1913
Memberships: CIA; AIAF; WARBICA.
Publication(s): *Bulletin des Archives*; *Guide de l'usager*; *Memoire du Benin*; *Repertoire Serie E: Affaires politiques*; *Repertoire Serie N: Affaires Militaires*; *Repertoire Serie Q: Affaires Economiques*

Bermuda

Bermuda Archives
Government Administration Bldg, 30 Parliament St, Hamilton HM12
Tel: (0441) 2929847
Key Personnel
Archivist: Karla M Haywood
Publication(s): *A Guide to the Records of Bermuda* (1980)

Bermuda College Library
21 College Rise, Paget
Mailing Address: PG BX, Paget PG 04
Tel: (441) 236-9000 *Fax:* (441) 236-8888
Key Personnel
Librarian: Daurene V Aubrey

Bermuda National Library
Par-la-Ville, Hamilton HM11
Tel: (0441) 295-2905 *Fax:* (0441) 292-8443
E-mail: bdanatlib@gov.bm
Telex: 3775 Modus

Key Personnel
Head Librarian: C Joanne Brangman
 E-mail: jbrangman@gov.bm
Technical Services Librarian: Patrice A Carvell
 E-mail: pcarvell@gov.bm
Adult Services Librarian: Julie Bean
 E-mail: jbean@gov.bm
Youth Services Librarian: Marla Smith
 E-mail: msmith@gov.bm
Publication(s): *Bermuda National Bibliography* (quarterly)
Branch Office(s)
Bermuda Youth Library *E-mail:* youthlib@gov.bm
Mobile Library

Bolivia

Biblioteca del Congreso Nacional
Ed ex-Banco Central de Bolivia, P1, Calle Ayacucho, Esq, Mercado, La Paz
Tel: (02) 314731 *Fax:* (02) 392402
Telex: 3204

Biblioteca y Archivo Nacional de Bolivia
Calle Bolivar, Casilla 338, Sucre
Tel: (064) 1481
Key Personnel
Dir: Gunnar Mendoza

Biblioteca de la Direccion de Cultura
Alacaldia Municipal, Casilla 1856, La Paz 1832
Library of Cultural Affairs Administration.

Universidad Boliviana Tomas Frias, Departmento de Bibliotecas
Biblioteca Central, Av del Maestro, Casilla 54, Potosi
Tel: (062) 27313
Key Personnel
Dir: Julia B De Lopez
Publication(s): *Boletin del Departamento de Bibliotecas* (and occasional papers)

Biblioteca Central de la Universidad Mayor de San Andres
Ave Villazon 1995, Casilla 6548, La Paz
Tel: (02) 25568
Key Personnel
Dir, Lic: Alberto Crespo Rodas

Biblioteca Central de la Universidad Mayor de San Francisco Xavier
Plaza 25 de Mayo, Casilla 212, Sucre
Key Personnel
Dir: Agar Penaranda

Biblioteca Central Universitaria 'Jose Antonio Arze'
Casilla 992, Cochabamba
Tel: (042) 31733 *Fax:* (042) 31691
Telex: 6363
Key Personnel
Dir: Dr Luis Alberto Ponce
Publication(s): *Boletin Bibliografico*; *Notas Bibliotecologicas*

Bosnia and Herzegovina

Narodna i univerzitetska biblioteka Bosne i Hercegovine
ul Obala 42, 71000 Sarajevo

Tel: (071) 533204
Key Personnel
Head: Dr Enes Kujundzjc
National & University Library of Bosnia & Herzegovina.

Botswana

Botswana National Library Service
Private Bag X2044, Mmabatho 8681
Tel: (019231) 352397 *Fax:* (019231) 22063
 Cable: Bonalibs
Key Personnel
Acting Dir of Library Service: S Khutsoane
Publication(s): *The National Bibliography of Botswana*

Botswana National Archives & Records Services
PO Box 239, Gaborone
Tel: 311820 *Fax:* 308545
E-mail: archives@gov.bw
Telex: 2994BD *Cable:* HOMES
Key Personnel
Dir: Ms K P Kgabi
Principal Archivist: C T Nengomasha; A S B Akhaabi
Librarian: A R Adekanmbi
Founded: 1967
Provides a national archives services to preserve for posterity historically important records & data for research, education & reference.
Publication(s): *Botswana National Archives & Records Services Library Accessions List* (Yearly)

Geological Survey Department Library
PO Box 14, Lobatse
Tel: (0330) 330327 *Fax:* (0330) 332013
Telex: 2293 Geo *Cable:* Rocks Lobatse
Key Personnel
Dir: T P MacLacha

The National Institute of Development Research & Documentation
University of Botswana, Private Bag UB 0022, Gaborone
Tel: 351151 *Fax:* 356591
E-mail: nir@wn.apc.org
Key Personnel
Senior Documentalist: Stella B Monageng

University of Botswana Library
Plot 4775 Nyerere Dr, Gaborone
Mailing Address: Private Bag 00390, Gaborone, Botswana
Tel: 3552295 *Fax:* 356291; 356591
Telex: 2429
Key Personnel
Dir: H K Raseroka *E-mail:* raseroka@mopipi.ub.bw
Founded: 1971

Brazil

Arquivo Nacional
Rua Azeredo Coutinho, 77 3 Andar, 7th floor, 20230-170 Rio de Janeiro
Tel: (021) 252-2617 *Fax:* (021) 252 9821
Telex: 2134103
Key Personnel
General Dir: Jaime Antones Da Silva

Publication(s): *ACERVO-Revista do Arquivo Nacional*; *Serie de Publicacoes Historicas*; *Serie de Publicacoes Tecnicas*; *Serie Instrumentos de Trabalho*; *Serie Publicacoes Avulsas*

Biblioteca do Ministerio das Relacoes Exteriores
Esplanada dos Ministerios, Anexo 2, Terreo, 70170-900 Brasilia DF
Tel: (061) 2116359 *Fax:* (061) 2237362
Cable: 1319
Key Personnel
Dir, Librarian: Maria Salete Carvalho Reis
Publication(s): *Referencia de Periodicos* (monthly)

Biblioteca Municipal Mario de Andrade
Rua da Consolacao 94, Sao Paulo 01302
Tel: (011) 2394384 *Fax:* (011) 2393459
Key Personnel
Dir: Lucia Neiza Pereira DaSilva
Contact: Marli Monteiro
Publication(s): *Boletim Bibliografico Biblioteca Mario de Andrade* (quarterly)

Biblioteca Publica do Estado do Rio de Janeiro
Ave Presidente Vargas 1261, Rio de Janeiro, RJ 20071-004
Tel: (021) 2246184 *Fax:* (021) 2526810
E-mail: bperj@callnet.com.br
Key Personnel
Dir General: Ana Ligia Silva Medeiros

Centro de Documentacao e Informacao da Camara dos Deputados
Palacio do Congresso Nacional, Praca dos Tres Poderes, 70160-900 Brasilia DF
Tel: (061) 3186785 *Fax:* (061) 3182171
Telex: 0611164
Key Personnel
Dir: Suelena Pinto Bandeira
House of Representatives' Centre of Documentation & Information.

Fundacao Biblioteca Nacional
Ave Rio Branco 219-39, 20040-008 Rio de Janeiro RJ
Tel: (021) 22408079 *Fax:* (021) 2204173
E-mail: portella@bn.br
Web Site: www.bn.br
Key Personnel
President: Eduardo Mattos Portella
Publication(s): *Anais da Biblioteca Nacional*; *Bibliografia Brasileira*; *Brazilian Book Magazine*; *revista "Poesia Sempre"*

SIBi/USP, see Sistema Integrado de Bibliotecas da Universidade de Sao Paulo (SIBi)

Sociedade Brasileira de Cultura Inglesa - Biblioteca
Rua Raul Pompeia 231, 3 andar, CP5215, Rio de Janeiro RJ
Tel: (021) 2870990 ext 303 *Fax:* (021) 2676474
Key Personnel
Contact: Ma de Fatima B Goncalves
Publication(s): *Library News*

Universidade de Brasilia, Biblioteca Central
Campus Universitario, Asa Norte, CP 152951, 70910 Brasilia DF
Tel: (061) 2742412
Telex: 1083
Key Personnel
Dir: Pereira O'Dilon

Sistema Integrado de Bibliotecas da Universidade de Sao Paulo (SIBi) (University of Sao Paulo Integrated Library System)
Av Prof Luciano Gualberto, Trav J, 374-1 andar, Predio da Antiga Reitoria, Cid Universitaria, 05508-900 Sao Paulo SP
Mailing Address: CP 3751, 05508-900 Sao Paulo SP
Tel: (011) 3031-7448 *Fax:* (011) 3815-2142
E-mail: dtsibi@org.usp.br
Web Site: www.usp.br/sibi
Telex: 81465
Key Personnel
Dir: Teresinha Das Gracas Coletta
Publication(s): *SIBI Informa, Catalogos de Teses e Producao Docente, Intenacao* (available online)

Biblioteca Central da Universidade Federal do Parana
CP 441, Rua Gen Carneiro 370/80, 80060-150 Curitiba, Parana PR
Tel: (041) 2645545 *Fax:* (041) 2627784
Telex: 5100
Key Personnel
Dir: Elayne Margareth Schloegel

Centro de Ciencias da Saude da Universidade Federal do Rio de Janeiro
Biblioteca Central - bloco L Cidade Universitaria Ilha do Fundao, ZC-32, POB 68032, Rio de Janeiro RJ 22306
Tel: (021) 2951397 *Fax:* (021) 2952346 *Cable:* C P 68032
Key Personnel
Librarian: Maria R A A Uriarte
Medical School Library of the University of Rio de Janeiro.

Universidade Federal do Rio Grande do Sul (UFRGS), Biblioteca Central
Paulo Gama, Terreo de Reitoria, CP 2303 90001 Porto Alegre RS RS
Tel: (051) 3163065 *Fax:* (051) 3163984
E-mail: biblioteca@bc.ufrgs.br
Telex: 0511055
Key Personnel
Librarians: Ana Maria Galvao; Veleida Blank

Brunei Darussalam

Perpustakaan Dewan Bahasa dan Pustaka Brunei, Kementerian Kebudayaan, Belia dan Sukan
Jalan Elizabeth II, Bandar Seri Begawan 2064
Tel: (02) 235501 *Fax:* (02) 224763
Key Personnel
Librarian: Hj Abu Bakar Hj Zainal
National Language & Literature Bureau Library.
Publication(s): *Acquis List*; *Ind Exes*

Bulgaria

Bulgarian Academy of Sciences, Central Library
15 Noemvri 1, 1040 Sofia
Tel: (02) 878966 *Fax:* (02) 803127
E-mail: banlib@bgcict.acad.bg
Telex: 22424
Key Personnel
Associate Prof: Dincho Krastev

Publication(s): *Bulgarian Academic Books* (catalog is published only by the Publishing House of Bulgarian Academy of Sciences); *Problemi na specialnite biblioteki* (Problems of special libraries irregular); *Problems Of Special Libraries; Collected Papers*

Central Agricultural Library, National Agro-industrial Union
bul Tzarigradsko Shosse 125, Sofia
Tel: (02) 709168

Central Medical Library
ul G Sofiiski 1, 1431 Sofia
Tel: (02) 523171 *Fax:* (02) 523171
E-mail: medlib@bgcict.bitnet
Key Personnel
Dir: Petar Dabschev, MD

Central State Archives
Division of General Department of Archives of the Republic of Bulgaris
Moskovska 5, 1000 Sofia
Tel: (02) 940 0104 *Fax:* (02) 9801443
Key Personnel
Dir: G Chernev
Founded: 1993
Collecting, registering, handling, preserving, using & making accessible to the public the archival holdings of the state agencies, public & private bodies.
Parent Company: General Department of Archives of the Republic of Bulgaria
Ultimate Parent Company: Council of Ministers

Central State Archives of the People's Republic of Bulgaria, see General Department of Archives of the Republic of Bulgaria

Central Technical Library
50, Dr GM Dimitrov Blvd, Sofia 1125
Tel: (02) 702935 *Fax:* (02) 710157
E-mail: ctb@nacid.nat.bg
Web Site: www.nacid.nat.bg
Key Personnel
Dir: Valentina Slavcheva *E-mail:* vs@nacid.nat.bg
Founded: 1962
Parent Company: National Centre for Information & Documentation (NACID)

General Department of Archives of the Republic of Bulgaria
Formerly Central State Archives of the People's Republic of Bulgaria
Moskovska 5, 1000 Sofia
Tel: (02) 9400101 *Fax:* (02) 980 14 43
E-mail: gua@mail.orbitel.bg
Key Personnel
Chairman: Atanas Atanassov *Tel:* (02) 9400105
Founded: 1977
Administration, coordination, control, publishing of archival records.
Publication(s): *Archival Review*; *Bulletin of the State Archives*; *The Archives are Speaking* (series of archives editions)

Central Library of the Higher Technical Institutes
Blvd Dragan Cankov 2, 1421 Sofia
Tel: (02) 665274 *Fax:* (02) 656863
E-mail: lib@vaeg.acad.bg
Telex: 23574
Key Personnel
Dir: A Todorova

National Library 'Ivan Vazov'
17 ul Vaptsarov, 4000 Plovdiv
Tel: (032) 62 29 15
E-mail: nbiv@plovdiv.techno-link.com
Web Site: fobos.primasoft.bg/libplovdiv

BULGARIA

Key Personnel
Dir: Radka Koleva
Publication(s): *Plovdivski kraj* (annually)
Branch Office(s)
15, Avksentii Veleshki S, 4000 Plovdiv
49, Dimitar Talev St, 4004 Plovdiv

S S Saint Cyril & Saint Methodius National Library
88 V Levski Blvd, 1504 Sofia
Tel: (02) 882811 *Fax:* (02) 435495
E-mail: nbkm@bgcict.acad.bg
Key Personnel
Librarian: Dr Vera L Gancheva
Publication(s): *Bibliotekar* (The Librarian); *Bibliotekite v Bulgariya* (Bulgarian Libraries); *Bibliotekoznanie, Bibliografiya, Knigoznanie, Nauchna Informatsiya* (Library Science, Bibliography, Scientific Information); *Bulgarska Nacionalna Bibliografija, Ser 1-8* (The National Bibliography); *Bulgarski Knigopis* (Bulgarian Books); *Bulgarski periodicen Pecat* (Bulgarian Periodicals - each part of The National Bibliography)

Sofia City & District State Archives
Moskovska 5, 1000 Sofia
Tel: (02) 9400106 *Fax:* (02) 980 1443
Key Personnel
Dir: Kr Milcheva
Founded: 1952
Collecting, registering, handling, use & making available to the public the archives about Sofia & Sofia district.
Parent Company: General Department of Archives of the Republic of Bulgaria
Ultimate Parent Company: Council of Ministers

Sofiiski Universitet Kliment Ohridsky Biblioteka
Tzar Osvoboditel 15 Blvd, Sofia
Tel: (02) 467584; (02) 9443719 *Fax:* (02) 467170
E-mail: lsu@libsu.uni-sofia.bg
Web Site: www.libsu.uni-sofia.bg
Telex: 23296 Suko RBG
Key Personnel
Dir: Ivanka Yankova *E-mail:* yankova@libsu.uni-sofia.bg
Founded: 1888

University of Sofia Library, see Sofiiski Universitet Kliment Ohridsky Biblioteka

Burkina Faso

Centre National des Archives
Presidence du Faso, BP 7030, Ouagadougou
Tel: 336196 *Fax:* 314926
Telex: 5221
Key Personnel
Dir: Didier E Ouedraogo

Universite de Ouagadougou
BP 7021, Ouagadougou
Tel: 307064
Telex: 5270 UV

Burundi

Bibliotheque Publique
BP 960, Bujumbura

National Library of Burundi
BP 1095, Bujumbura
Tel: 021 62 73 *Fax:* 021 92 95
E-mail: biefbdi@cbinf.com

Office National du Tourisme (ONT)
BP 902, 2, Avenue des Euphorbes, Bujumbura
Tel: (02) 2202; (02) 2023; (02) 4208 *Fax:* (02) 9390
Telex: Cab Pub BDI 5081, 5082
Key Personnel
Dir: Hermenegilde Nimbona
Branch Office(s)
7, Boulevard de l'Uprona, Bujumbura
Aeroport International de Bujumbura

Bibliotheque de l'Universite du Burundi
29, av de l'Uprona, Bujumbura
Mailing Address: BP 1320, Bujumbura
Tel: (022) 5196; (022) 5446; (022) 2857
Cable: UNIVARWA
Key Personnel
Chief Librarian: Tharlisse Nsabimana

Cameroon

Archives Bibliotheque nationales du Cameroon
BP 1053, Yaounde
Tel: 220078
Key Personnel
Dir: Emerant Mbon Mekompomb

Universite de Yaounde, Bibliotheque
BP 337, Yaounde
Tel: 220744
Telex: 8384
Key Personnel
Librarian: Peter Nkangafaok Chateh
Publication(s): *Etudes et Recherches en Bibliotheconomie*

Universite de Yaounde Ecole Normale Superieure, Bibliotheque
BP 337, Yaounde
Tel: 220744
Telex: 8384

University of Dschang Central Library
PO Box 96, Dschang
Tel: 45-13-81 *Fax:* 45-23-81
Telex: 7013KN
Key Personnel
Librarian: Martin Tehinde

Central African Republic

Bibliotheque Universitaire de Bangui
BP 1450, Bangui
Tel: 612000
Telex: 5283
Key Personnel
Dir: Thomas Poussoumandji

Chad

Centre De Documentation Universitaire (CDU)
(University Documentation Center)
Av Mobutu, N'Djamena
Mailing Address: BP 1117, N'Djamena
Tel: (0235) 51 44 44; (0235) 51 62 68
Fax: (0235) 51 40 33
E-mail: rectorat@intnet.td
Key Personnel
Chief Librarian: Mr Koulassim Doumtangar
Founded: 1972
Parent Company: Universite De N'Djamena

Centre de Recherche des Archives et de Documentation (CRAD)
BP 731, N'Djamena
Tel: (051) 2327
Telex: 524 SKD UNESCO *Cable:* VNESCO NDJAMENA
Key Personnel
Dir: Dr Khalil Alio
Chief of Center, Librarian: Ngaryaka Neldjita
Publication(s): *COMNAT*

CRAD, see Centre de Recherche des Archives et de Documentation (CRAD)

Chile

Biblioteca del Congreso Nacional
Huerfanos 1117, Piso 2, Santiago
Tel: (02) 2701700 *Fax:* (02) 2701766
E-mail: xfeliu@biblioteca.congreso.cl
Key Personnel
Dir: Ximena Feliu Silva
Library of Congress.
Publication(s): *Boletin Informativo*; *Estudios*; *Serie Estudios*; *Temas de Actualidad* (triannually)
Branch Office(s)
Edificio del Congreso Nacional, Victoria S/N, Valparaiso

Biblioteca Nacional de Chile
Avda B O'Higgins 651, 1400 Santiago
Tel: (02) 3605239 *Fax:* (02) 6380461
Key Personnel
Dir: Clara Budnik S *E-mail:* cl.budnik@oris.renib.cl
Subject Dir: Gonzalo Catalan Bertoni
National Library of the Office of Libraries, Archives & Museums.
Publication(s): *Bibliografia chilena* (formerly 'Anuario de la Prensa', 1982); *Referencias Criticas sobre Autores Chilenos* (Annually, 1988)

Ediciones Universidad Technologica Metropolitana
Casilla 9845 Correo Central, Santiago
Tel: (02) 7877962 *Fax:* (02) 7877925
Key Personnel
Dir Comite Editorial: Hector Gomez-Fuentes *E-mail:* hector.gomez@utem.cl
Founded: 1989
Academic text in Humanities, Social Sciences, Pure & Applied Sciences.

Pontificia Universidad Catolica de Chile Sistema de Bibliotecas
Vicuna Mackenna 4860, Casilla 306-Correo 22, Santiago
Tel: (02) 6864615 *Fax:* (02) 6865852
Key Personnel
Dir: Maria Luisa Arenas Franco

Biblioteca de la Universidad Catolica de Valparaiso
Ave Brasil 2950, Casilla 4059, Valparaiso
Tel: (032) 273261 *Fax:* (032) 273183
Telex: 230389 Ucv
Key Personnel
Dir: Yolanda Soto Vergara

Biblioteca Central de la Universidad de Chile
Arturo Prat 23, Casilla 10-D, Santiago
Tel: (02) 717997
Key Personnel
Dir: Alamiro de Avila Martel

Universidad de Concepcion Direccion de Bibliotecas
Barrio Universitario, Casilla 1807, Concepcion
Tel: (041) 234985 *Fax:* (041) 244796
Key Personnel
Dir: Maria Nieves Alsonso Martinez

China

Chongqing Library
One Changjiang Rd A, Chongqing, Sichuan Province
Tel: 54832
Key Personnel
Dir: Li Pujie

Dalian University of Technology
2 Linggong Rd, Ganjingzi District, Dalian, Liaoning 116024
Tel: (0411) 4708620 *Fax:* (0411) 4671872
E-mail: lib@dlut.edu.cn
Web Site: www.dlut.edu.cn
Telex: 86231 DUTCN *Cable:* 7108
Key Personnel
Professor: Xie Maozhao *E-mail:* xmz@dlut.edu.cn
Publication(s): *Computational Structural Mechanics & Applications*; *Journal of Dalian University of Technology*; *Journal of Mathematical Research & Exposition*

The Documentation and Information Centre of the Chinese Academy of Sciences, see Library of Chinese Academy of Sciences

Fudan University Library
220 Handan Lu, Shanghai 200433
Tel: (021) 65492222 (ext 3162) *Fax:* (021) 65649814
E-mail: zfqin@fudan.edu.cn.f
Key Personnel
Professor: Xu Peng; Qin Zeng-Fu
Publication(s): *Mathematical Analysis* (Lectures on Higher Mathematics)

Liaoning Library
5 Wenxingli, Shenyang Lu (Section 2), Shenyang, Liaoning Province

Library of Chinese Academy of Sciences
Formerly The Documentation and Information Centre of the Chinese Academy of Sciences
8 Kexueyuan, Nanlu, Zhongguancun, Beijing 100080
Tel: (010) 62566847 *Fax:* (010) 62566846
E-mail: office@mail.las.ac.cn
Telex: 83020
Key Personnel
Dir: Xu Yinchi
Membership(s): IFLA.

Nanjing tushuguan
66 Chengxian St, Nanjing, 210018 Jiangsu Province
Tel: 7717619
Key Personnel
Vice President: Yuan da-zhi; Lu zi-bo; Gong ai-dong
Nanking Library.
Publication(s): *Journal of Jiangsu Library Science*

The National Library of China
39 Baishiqiao Rd, Haidian, Beijing 100081
Tel: (010) 68415566 *Fax:* (010) 68419271
E-mail: cjsun@sun.ihep.ac.cn
Telex: 222211 NLC CN *Cable:* 0848
Key Personnel
Dir: Liu Jiping; Ren Joyu
Zhongguo guojia tushuguan; formerly National Library of Beijing, Beijing Library, Peking Library, National Library of Peking, etc.
Publication(s): *Chinese Classification - A System Used in Chinese Libraries*; *Documentation* (series); *Journal of The National Library of China*; *The National Catalogue of Foreign Periodicals*

Peking University Library
Haidian District, Beijing 100871
Tel: (010) 62751051 *Fax:* (010) 62761008
E-mail: office@lib.pku.edu.cn
Key Personnel
Librarian: Dai Longji *Tel:* (010) 62753503
E-mail: dailj@lib.pku.edu.cn
Founded: 1902

Qinghua daxue tushuguan
Qinghuayuan, West Suburb, Beijing
Tel: (010) 62594591 *Fax:* (010) 6256278
Telex: 22617
Key Personnel
Dir: Shu Wen Hao
Qinghua University Library.

Library of the Renmin University of China
175 Haidian Rd, Beijing 100872
Tel: (010) 62511371; (010) 62511014 *Fax:* (010) 62515332; (010) 62566374
Key Personnel
Contact: Yang Dongliag *E-mail:* yangpj@sun.ihep.ac.cn

Shanghai Academy of Social Sciences Library
1575 Wanhang du Lu, Shanghai
Tel: (021) 2522657 *Cable:* 7306
Key Personnel
Dir: Xie-Jun Chen

Shanghai tushuguan (Shanghai Library)
Hiaihai Rd, Shanghai
Tel: (021) 3273176 *Fax:* (021) 3278493
Key Personnel
Dir: Shu Qing Zho
Hon Dir: Gu Ting-long
Shanghai Library.

Xiamen University Library
Division of Xiamen University
422, Siming Nan Rd, Xiamen, Fujian 361005
Tel: (0592) 2186127 *Fax:* (0592) 2182360
E-mail: xiaodh@xmu.edu.cn
Web Site: library.xmu.edu.cn (Chinese BG)
Key Personnel
Chief Librarian: Dr Mingguang Chen
Founded: 1921
Specialize in book borrowing & reading, document, information services.

Xie Maozhao, see Dalian University of Technology

Yunnan Provincial Library
2 Chihu Nanlu, Kunming, Yunnan Province
Tel: (0871) 5298
Key Personnel
Dir: Wu Rui

ZheJiang Provincial Library
102 Daxue Rd, Hangzhou, Zhejiang
Tel: (0571) 773414; (0571) 7046414 *Fax:* (0571) 7046263
Key Personnel
Chief Officer: Wang Xiaoliang
Chekiang Library, Hangchow.

Zhongguo guojia tushuguan, see The National Library of China

Zhongshan Library of Guangdong Province
211 Wenming Rd, Guangzhou (Canton), Guangdong Province
Tel: (020) 330676
Key Personnel
Chief Librarian: Huang Jungui
Also 81 Wende Rd, Guangdong (Canton) Tel: (020) 330349.

Colombia

Biblioteca Luis-Angel Arango Banco de la Republica (Luis Angel Arango Library-Central Bank of Colombia)
Carrera 5a, No 11-68, Apdo Aereo 3531, Santafe de Bogota DC
Tel: (01) 2827840 *Fax:* (01) 2863881
E-mail: wbiblio@banrep.gov.co
Web Site: www.banrep.gov.co *Cable:* REDESBANCO BIBLIOTECA
Key Personnel
Dir: Jorge Orlando Melo *E-mail:* jmelogo@banrep.gov.co
Publication(s): *Boletin Cultural y Bibliografico* (quarterly); *Estudios sobre Politica Economica* (biannually)

Archivo General de la Nacion de Colombia
Calle 24, 5-60 Piso 4, Santafe de Bogota
Tel: (01) 416015 *Fax:* (01) 3372019
Key Personnel
Dir: Jorge Palacios Preciado
National Archives.

BAC, see Biblioteca Agropecuaria de Colombia (BAC)

Biblioteca Agropecuaria de Colombia (BAC)
Apdo Aereo 240142, Eldorado, Santafe de Bogota
Mailing Address: Apdo. Aereo 240142, Las Palmas
Tel: (01) 2861507 (ext 3428); (01) 2813088
Fax: (01) 2813088
E-mail: fsalazar@caldas.colciencias.gov.co
Key Personnel
Dir: Francisco Salazar Alonso
Farming and Livestock Library of Colombia.

Biblioteca Nacional de Colombia
Calle 24 No 5-60, Apdo 27600, Bogota
Tel: (01) 2414029 *Fax:* (01) 2414030
Key Personnel
Dir: Carlos Jose Reyes
Publication(s): *Revista Senderos*

British Council Library
Calle 87 No 12-79, Apdo Aereo 089231, Bogota 1
Tel: (01) 2579632 *Fax:* (01) 2187754
E-mail: brit.council@bc-bogota.bcouncil.org

COLOMBIA

Web Site: www.britishcouncil.org/colombia/
Telex: 45715 Bcoun
Key Personnel
Librarian: Maria Clemencia de Bohorquez

Centro de Estudios sobre Desarrollo Economico CEDE
Carrera IE 18A-10, Apdo Aereo 4976, Bogota
Tel: (01) 3520466 *Fax:* (01) 2841890
E-mail: cede@uniandes.edu.co
Telex: 42343 Unand
Key Personnel
Dir: Jose Leibovich Goldenberg
Librarian: Angela Marie Mesia De Restrepo
Centre for Studies on Economic Development.

Fundacion Universidad Externado de Colombia
Apdo Aereo 034141, Calle 12, No 1-17 Este, Bogota
Tel: (01) 2826066 *Fax:* (01) 2847769
E-mail: uextpub3@impsat.net.co
Key Personnel
Dir: Lina Espitaleta DeVillegris

Pontificia Universidad Javeriana, Facultad de Comunicacion y Lenguaje
Departamento de Ciencia de la Informacion, Carrera 7 No 41-00, Bogota
Tel: (01) 2858177 *Fax:* (01) 2887896; (01) 2850973
E-mail: incabarc@javercol.javeriana.edu.co
Key Personnel
Dir: Luz Maria Carbarcas Santoya

Universidad de los Andes, Biblioteca General, Ramon de Zubiria
Carrera 1 E No 18A-10, Apdo Aereo 4976, Bogota
Tel: (01) 2866309; (01) 3520466 *Fax:* (01) 2860489; (01) 2841890
E-mail: secgral@uniandes.edu.ca
Telex: 42343
Key Personnel
Librarian: Angela Maria Mejia de Restrepo

Universidad de Antioquia, Escuela Interamericana de Bibliotecologia, Biblioteca
Calle 67X Carrera 53, 1226 Medellin
Tel: (04) 2105140 *Fax:* (04) 2116939
Key Personnel
Dir: Carlos A Cadavid
Memberships: FID; ALA; AIBDA; IFLA; SALALM; Asociacion Latinoamericana de Archivos; The Library Association; ACURIL.
Publication(s): *Bibliografia Bibliotecologica*; *Bibliografica y de Obras de Referencia Colombianas* (Bibliography of Library Science, Bibliography and Colombian Works of Reference)

Universidad de los Andes, Centro de Estudios sobre Desarrollo Economico (CEDE), see Centro de Estudios sobre Desarrollo Economico CEDE

Universidad Nacional de Colombia, Biblioteca Central
Ciudad Universitaria, Apdo Aereo 14490, Bogota
Tel: (01) 2691743
E-mail: refer@biblioteca.campus.unal.edu.co
Key Personnel
Dir: Victor Albis
Contact: A Takahashi

Congo

Bibliotheque Universitaire, Universite Marien Ngouabi
BP 2025, Brazzaville
Tel: 811430; 831430
Key Personnel
Dir: F Wellot Samba
Librarian: Innocent Mabiala
Publication(s): *Annales*; *Dimi*; *Repertoire d'auteurs congolais*; *Revue d'histoire anthropologie* (Also other lists & catalogs)

Centre Culturel Francais, Bibliotheque
BP 2141, Brazzaville
Tel: 832566 *Fax:* 83-25-66

Bibliotheque Nationale Populaire
BP 1489, Brazzaville
Tel: 833485
Key Personnel
Dir: Pierre Mayola
Publication(s): *Repertorie bibliographique nationale*

The Democratic Republic of the Congo

Archives nationales du Zaiire
42a ave de la Justice, BP 3428, Kinshasa-Gombe
Tel: (012) 31083
Key Personnel
Librarian: Kiobe Lumenga-Neso
Publication(s): *Kinshasa. Genese et Sites Historiques* (Arnaza-Bief 1995)

Bibliotheque Centrale de l'Universite de Kisangani
Campus de Kisangani, BP 2012, Kisangani
Tel: 2948
Key Personnel
Chief Librarian: Muzila Label Kakes

Bibliotheque Centrale, Universite de Kinshasa
BP 125, Kinshasa XI
Tel: 77920 ext 161
Publication(s): *Annales de la Bibliotheque Centrile de Kinshasa*

Bibliotheque Publique de Kinshasa
10 bd Tshatshi, BP 410, Kinshasa
Tel: (012) 3070
Key Personnel
Librarian: B Mongu

Institut Pedagogique National
BP 8815, Kinshasa 1
Tel: (012) 80573

Institut pour la Recherche Scientifique en Afrique Centrale (IRSAC)
Bibliotheque Centra, Lwiro, Bukavu
Key Personnel
Chief Librarian: Mburunge Murhagane

IRSAC, see Institut pour la Recherche Scientifique en Afrique Centrale (IRSAC)

Bibliotheque Centrale de l'Universite de Lubumbashi
BP 2896, Lubumbashi
Key Personnel
Librarian: Mubadi Sule Mwanansuka

Costa Rica

Biblioteca Nacional
Calle 15-17, Acdas 3y3b, Apdo 10008-1000, San Jose
Tel: 2331706 *Fax:* 2235510
Telex: 3334 Dider
Key Personnel
Dir: Guadalupe Rodriguez
Contact: Marco A Chacon Monge
Publication(s): *Catalogo Nacional ISBN*; *Indice de Diarios y Semanarios de Costa Rica* (Catalog of Costa Rican Daily & Weekly Newspapers); *Indice de Revistas Nacionales* (Catalog of National Periodicals)

Biblioteca Mark Twain, Centro Cultural Costarricense-Norteamericano
Apdo 1489, San Jose 1000
Tel: 2259433 *Fax:* 2241480
E-mail: bncsjcr@sol.racsa.co.cr
Key Personnel
Librarian: Guisella Ruiz

Universidad de Costa Rica Sistema de Bibliotecas, Documentacion e Informacion
Ciudad Universitaria Rodrigo Facio, Apdo 2060, 2060 San Jose
Tel: 2536152; 2535323 *Fax:* 234809; 2074163; 230452
E-mail: mazamora@sibdi.bldt.ucr.ac.cr
Telex: UNICORI 2544
Key Personnel
Dir: Dr Adrian Araya Marin; Maria Julia Vargas; Aurora Zamora
Publication(s): *Agronomia Costarricense* (semiannually); *Annario del Cooperativismo en Costa Rica* (08030480xx); *Anuario de Estudios Centroamericanos* (annually); *Ciencia Y Tecnologia* (semiannually); *Ciencias Economicas* (semiannually); *Ciencias Matematicas* (semiannually); *Educacion* (semiannually); *Escena: Revista Teatral* (semiannually); *Herencia* (semiannually); *Ingenieria* (semiannually); *Kanina: Revista de Artes Y Letras* (semiannually); *Revista de Biologia Tropical* (semiannually); *Revista de Filologia Y Linguistica* (semiannually); *Revista de Filosofia* (semiannually); *Revista de Historia* (semiannually); *Revista Geologica de America Central* (semiannually); *Revistas de Ciencias Sociales* (quarterly)

Cote d'Ivoire

Archives de Cote d'Ivoire
BP V126, Abidjan
Tel: 324158
Telex: 22296
Key Personnel
Dir: Dominique Tchriffo

Bibliotheque Centrale de la Cote d'Ivoire
BPV 6243, Abidjan-Treichville

Tel: 323872
Key Personnel
Librarian: P Zelli Any-Grah

Bibliotheque de l'Universite Nationale de Cote d'Ivoire
22 BP 384, Abidjan
Tel: 440847
Telex: 3469
Key Personnel
Dir: Francoise N'Goran
Publication(s): *Annales de l'Universite d'Abidjan*

Bibliotheque Municipale
BP 24, Plateau, Abidjan

Bibliotheque Nationale
BP V180, Abidjan
Tel: 213872
Key Personnel
Librarian: Ambroise Agnero
Publication(s): *Bibliographie de la Cote-d'Ivoire*

Centre Culturel Francais, Bibliotheque
Av Franchet dEsperey, Angle rue Botreau Roussel, Abidjan
Mailing Address: 01 BP 3995, Abidjan
Tel: 211599; 225628 *Fax:* 227132
E-mail: cef@ci.refer.org
Telex: 22465 Miscop Ci
Key Personnel
Dir: Michel Janis
Librarian: Gerard Audovin

INADES (Institut Africain pour le Developpment Economique et Social)
15 av Jean Jaures, Abidjan 08
Mailing Address: BP 2088, Abidjan 08
Tel: 224404720 *Fax:* 22448438
E-mail: inades@ci.refer.org; inades@africaonline.co.ci
Web Site: www.inades.ci.refer.org
Key Personnel
Librarian: Maria Vial
Publication(s): *COURRIER* (trimonthly); *Manuels de Bibliotheconomic* (quarterly)

Croatia

Nacionalna i Sveucilisna Biblioteka
PO Box 550, 10000 Zagreb
Tel: (041) 6164009 *Fax:* (041) 6164186
Key Personnel
Dir: Dr Ivan Mihel
Chief Librarian: Dr Josip Stipanov
National & University Library.
Publication(s): *Bibliografija knjiga tiskanih u SR Hrvatskoj*; *Bibliografija rasprava, clanaka i knjizevnih radova u casopisima SR Hrvatske*; *Grada za hrvatsku retrospektivnu bibliografiju*

Cuba

Archivo Historico de la Provincia Ciudad de la Habana
Compostela No 906 esq San Isidro, Havana
Tel: (07) 629436 *Fax:* (07) 338089
E-mail: arnac@ceniai.cus
Key Personnel
Dir Dra: Berarda Salabarra Abraham

Biblioteca Central de la Universidad de Oriente
Ave Patricio Lumumba, Santiago
Tel: (0226) 31973 *Fax:* (0226) 32989
E-mail: jrcobo@ict.uo.edu.cu
Key Personnel
Librarian: Maura Gonzalez

Biblioteca del Instituto Pre-Universitario de la Habana
Zulueta y San Jose, Havana
Key Personnel
Dir: Jose Manuel
Library of the Pre-University Institute of Education.

Biblioteca Historica Cubana y Americana
Municipio de la Habana, Oficina del Historiador de la Ciudad, Havana
Cuban & American Historical Library.

Biblioteca Nacional Jose Marti
Plaza de la Revolucion, Apdo Oficial 3, Havana
Tel: (07) 708277
Telex: 511963 Bnjm
Key Personnel
Editor: Maria Terry Gonzales
National Library.
Publication(s): *Bibliografia Cubana*; *Bibliografias Especializadas*; *Boletines Bibliograficas e Informacion Senal*; *Documentos Extranjeros Adquiridos*; *Ediciones Especializadas sobre la Cultura y el Arte*; *Indice General de Publicaciones Periodicas Cubanas*; *Revista de la Biblioteca Nacional Jose Marti*
Branch Office(s)
Ninguna

Biblioteca Jose Antonio Echeverria
calle 3ra, esquina a G, El Vedado, Havana 10400
Tel: (07) 552705 *Fax:* (07) 334554
E-mail: casa@tinored cu
Telex: 511019
Key Personnel
Dir: Ernest Sierra
Specialize in Latin-American Literature, History & Sociology.

IDICT, see Instituto de Informacion Cientifica y Tecnologica (IDICT) Ministerio de Ciencia, Technolia y Medio Ambiente (CITMA)

Instituto de Informacion Cientifica y Tecnologica (IDICT) Ministerio de Ciencia, Technolia y Medio Ambiente (CITMA)
Capitolio Nacional, Apdo 2019, Havana
Tel: (07) 62-6501; 60-3411 *Fax:* (07) 33-8237
E-mail: garriga@ceniai.inf.cu
Telex: 511203 *Cable:* 62-6501 IDICT CU
Key Personnel
Gen Dir: Nicolas Garriga
Dir: Jesus Martinez; Luis A Mourelos; Eduardo Orozco; Gloria Ponjuan
Publication(s): *Cubaciencia*; *Directorio Biomundi*
Branch Office(s)
Biblioteca Nacional de Ciencia y Tecnica (BNCT)
Centro de Estudios y Desarollo Profesional en Ciencias de la Informacion (PROINFO)
Centro de Intercambio Automatizado (CENIAI)
Consultoria en Biotecnologia e Industria Medico-Farmaceutica (BIOMUNDI)

Instituto de Literatura y Lingueistica
Salvador Allende 710, Havana
Tel: (07) 785405 *Fax:* (07) 338054; (07) 331325
Telex: 511290 acdcp cu
Key Personnel
Dir: Yolanda Ricardo Garcell
Vice Dir: Nuria Gregori Torada
Librarian: Pedro Luis Suarez Sola

Biblioteca Manuel Sanguily
Ministerio de Relaciones Exteriores, Calzada y G, Vedado, Havana
Key Personnel
Dir Dra: Madelaine Teran

Biblioteca General de la Universidad Central de las Villas (Central Library of Central University of Las Villas)
Carretera Camajvani Km 5, 5, Santa Clara
Tel: 81178 *Fax:* 81682; 81608
E-mail: ucludri@ucentral.quantum.inf.cu
Key Personnel
Lib Inquiries: Jose Rivero Diaz
Founded: 1959
Subdivided into small branches for technical & social matters regarding careers studied in the University. Specific reference (eg cybernetics, economics, etc).

Universidad de la Habana, Direccion de Informacion Cientifica y Tecnica
Ruben Martinez Villena Cl 302 esq A15 Vedado, Havana
Tel: (07) 333768 *Fax:* (07) 325774
Telex: 0512210 Dict Uh
Key Personnel
Dir: Dr Maria Christina Santos *E-mail:* cristina@dist.uh.cu

Cyprus

The Library of the Archbishop Macarios III Foundation
PO Box 21269, 1505 Nicosia
Tel: (02) 430008 *Fax:* (02) 430667
Key Personnel
Dir: Dr M Stavrou

British Council Library
3 Museum St, Nicosia
Mailing Address: PO Box 5654, Nicosia
Tel: (02) 442152 *Fax:* (02) 477257
E-mail: stamatis.dracos@britcoun.org.cy
Web Site: www.britcoun.org/cyprus
Telex: 3911 Briconic
Key Personnel
Deputy Librarian: Joan Georghallides

Cyprus Library
Eleftheria Sq, 1011 Nicosia
Tel: (022) 303180; (022) 676118 *Fax:* (022) 304532
E-mail: cypruslibrary@cytanet.com.cy
Key Personnel
Librarian: Antonis Maratheftis
  E-mail: amaratheftis@hotmail.com
Founded: 1987
Publication(s): *Cyprus Bibliography*
Parent Company: Ministry of Education and Culture

Library of the Cyprus Museum - Dept of Antiquities
Museum St 1, Nicosia
Mailing Address: PO Box 22024, Nicosia
Tel: (022) 865848 *Fax:* (022) 303148
Key Personnel
Librarian: Maria Economidou

Municipal Library
PO Box 41, Famagusta
Key Personnel
Chief Librarian: Ch Christofides

CYPRUS

Library of the Paedagogiki Institute Academia (College of Education)
c/o Ministry of Education, PO Box 512, Nicosia
Tel: (02) 305933
Key Personnel
Librarian: Maria Demetriou; Soula Agdpiou

Library of Phaneromeni, see The Library of the Archbishop Macarios III Foundation

Sultan's Library
Evcaf, Nicosia

Cyprus Turkish Public Library
Kizilay Ave, Nicosia
Tel: (02) 83257
Key Personnel
Chief Librarian: Fatma Oenen

Czech Republic

Knihovna Narodniho muzea (The National Museum Library)
Vaclavske nam 68, 115 79 Prague 1
Tel: (02) 24497111 *Fax:* (02) 24226488
E-mail: nm@nm.cz
Key Personnel
Dir: Helga Turkova, PhD *E-mail:* helga.turkova@nm.cz
National Museum Library.
Publication(s): *Sbornik Narodniho muzea, Rada C: literarni historie* (Journal/Magazine of the National Museum Prague, series C: Literary History, quarterly, 1996, summaries in English, French, German, Russian)

Mestska knihovna v Praze
Marianske Nam 1, 11572 Prague 1
Tel: (02) 22113300 *Fax:* (02) 22113305
E-mail: bimkovaa@mlp.czi
Key Personnel
Dir: Anna Bimkova
The City Library in Prague.

Moravska Zemska Knihovna (Moravian Library)
Kounicova 65a, Brno 601 87
Tel: (05) 41646111 *Fax:* (05) 41646101
E-mail: mzk@mzk.cz
Web Site: www.mzk.cz
Key Personnel
Dir: Dr Jaromir Kubicek *Tel:* (05) 41646110
 E-mail: kubicek@mzk.cz
Founded: 1808

Moravska Zemska Knihovna-Technicka Knihovna
Veveri 95, 658 42 Brno
Tel: (05) 42162150 *Fax:* (05) 747758
E-mail: pokorna@mzk.cz
Key Personnel
Chief Librarian: Milada Pokorna
Dir: J Kubicek
Moravian Library, Technical Library.

Narodni knihovna Ceske republiky (The National Library of the Czech Republic)
Klementinum 190, Prague 11001
Tel: (02) 21663277 *Fax:* (02) 21663277
Web Site: www.nkp.cz
Key Personnel
Dir: Dr Vojtech Balik
Public Relations: Libuse Piherova, PhD
 E-mail: libuse.piherova@nkp.cz
Founded: 1777

Publication(s): *Ceska narodni bibliografie Knihy* (The Czech National Bibliography-Books, annually, Czech Books); *Narodni Knihovna* (National Library, quarterly); *Narodni bibliografie Ceske republiky, Hudebniny* (The National Bibliography of the Czech Republic-Music, quarterly, Czech Music)
Parent Company: The Ministry of the Culture of the Czech Republic

Pamatnik narodniho pisemnictvi (Museum of Czech Literature)
Division of Ministry of Culture, Czech Rep
Strahov, Strahovske nadvori 1, 11838 Prague
Tel: (02) 20516695 *Fax:* (02) 20517277
Key Personnel
Dir: Dr Eva Wolfova *E-mail:* wolfova@pamatniknarodnihopisemnictvi.cz
Museum of Czech Literature.
Membership(s): ICOM.
Publication(s): *Literarni Archiv-Almanac* (annually)

Parlamentni Knihovna (Parliamentary Library)
Division of Office of the Chamber of Deputies
Snemovni 4, 11826 Prague 1
Tel: (02) 57534409 *Fax:* (02) 57534408
Web Site: www.psp.ez/kps/knih/
Key Personnel
Director: Dr Karel Sosna *E-mail:* sosna@psp.cz
Founded: 1857
Member of IFLA & ECPRD.
Parent Company: Chamber of Deputies of the Czech Parliament

Statni technicka knihovna (State Technical Library)
Marianske nam 5, 11001 Prague 1
Mailing Address: PO Box 206, 11001 Prague 1
Tel: (02) 2166 3480 *Fax:* (02) 2222 1340
E-mail: techlib@stk.cz
Web Site: www.stk.cz
Key Personnel
Dir: Martin Svoboda
Contact: Dr Jan Bayer *E-mail:* j.bayer@stk.cz
State Technical Library.

Vedecka knihovna V olomouci (Research Library in Olomouc)
Ostruznicka 3, 779 11 Olomouc
Mailing Address: PO Box 9, 779 11 Olomouc
Tel: (068) 522 23 75 *Fax:* (068) 522 57 74
E-mail: info@vkol.cz
Web Site: www.vkoe.cz
Key Personnel
Contact: Dr Marie Nadvornikova, PhD *Tel:* (068) 522 23 28
Founded: 1573
Research Library.

Vysoka skola banska - Technicka Univerzita Ostrava (VSB - Technical University of Ostrava)
17 listopadu 15, 708 33 Ostrava, Poruba
Tel: (069) 6991278 *Fax:* (069) 6917301
Key Personnel
University Librarian: Daniela Tkacikova
 E-mail: Daniela.Tkacikova@vsb.cz

Denmark

Aalborg Universitetsbibliotek (Aalborg University Library)
Langagervej 2, DK-9220 Aalborg
Mailing Address: Postboks 8200, DK-9220 Aalborg
Tel: 96359400 *Fax:* 98156859

E-mail: aub@aub.auc.dk
Web Site: www.aub.auc.dk
Key Personnel
Chief Librarian: Niels-Henrik Gylstorff
Information Coordinator: Karen Dissing
 Tel: 96359343 *E-mail:* karen@aub.auc.dk

Arhus Kommunes Biblioteker
Mollegade 1, DK-8000 Aarhus C
Tel: 87304500 *Fax:* 87304639
Key Personnel
Chief Librarian: Rolf Hapel
Arhus Public Library.

Biblioteksstyrelsen (Danish National Library Authority)
Nyhavn 31 E, 1051 Copenhagen K
Tel: 33733373 *Fax:* 33733372
E-mail: bs@bs.dk
Web Site: www.bs.dk
Key Personnel
Dir: Jens Thorhauge
Contact: Vibeke Cranfield *E-mail:* vhc@bs.dk
Government agency under the Danish Ministry of Culture.
Publication(s): *Nyt fra Nyhavn* (Quarterly, Info on library related matters)

Danmarks BlindeBibliotek (The Danish National Library for the Blind)
Teglvaerksgade 37, 2100 Copenhagen 0
Tel: 39274444 *Fax:* 39274454
E-mail: dbb@dbb.dk
Web Site: www.dbb.dk
Key Personnel
Dir: Elsebeth Tank
Contact: Lisbeth Trinskjer
The Danish National Library for the Blind (DBB).

Danmarks Natur-og Laegevidenskabelige Bibliotek, Universitet sbiblioteket (The Danish National Library of Science & Medicine)
Norre Alle 49, DK-2200 Copenhagen N
Tel: 35396523 *Fax:* 35398533
E-mail: dnlb@dnlb.dk
Web Site: www.dnlb.dk
Key Personnel
Advisory Librarian: Torsten Schlichtkrall
 Tel: 35396523 ext 245 *E-mail:* ts@dnlb.dk
Chief Librarian: Mette Stockmarr
Founded: 1482
The Danish National Library of Science & Medicine, Copenhagen University Library.
Publication(s): *Acta Historica Scientiarum Naturalium et Medicinalium*; *Skrifter Udgivet of Danmarks Natur-og Laegevedenskabelige Bibliotek, Kobenhavns Universitets Bibiotek*

Danmarks Paedagogiske Bibliotek (National Library of Education)
Emdrupvej 101, DK-2400 Copenhagen NV
Mailing Address: PO Box 840, DK-2400 Copenhagen NV
Tel: 39696633 *Fax:* 39551000
E-mail: dpb@dpb.dpu.dk
Web Site: www.dpb.dpu.dk/
Key Personnel
Dir: Soren Carlsen
Deputy Dir: Jakob Andersen *E-mail:* jak@dpb.dpu.dk

Danmarks Statistik Biblioteket
Skt Kields Plads 11, DK-2100 Copenhagen O
Mailing Address: Sejrogade 11, DK-2100 Copenhagen O
Tel: 39173030 *Fax:* 39173003
E-mail: bib@dst.dk
Key Personnel
Librarian: Soren Carlsen
National Statistical Library.

Danmarks Tekniske Videncenter (DTV)
Anker Engelunds Vej 1, DK-2800 Lyngby
Mailing Address: PO Box 777, DK-2800 Lyngby
Tel: 45257200 *Fax:* 45883040
E-mail: dtv@dtv.dk
Web Site: www.dtv.dk
Key Personnel
Dir: Annette Winkel Schwarz
Technical Knowledge Center & Library of Denmark.

Frederiksberg Kommunes Biblioteker
(Frederiksberg Library)
Solbjergvej 21-25, DK-2000 Frederiksberg
Tel: (045) 38211800 *Fax:* (045) 38211799
E-mail: bib@fkb.dk
Web Site: www.fkb.dk
Telex: 16548 fkbib
Key Personnel
Chief Librarian: Anne Moeller-Rasmussen
  E-mail: amr@fkb.dk
Founded: 1887
Public library.

Gentofte Bibliotekerne
Ahlmanns Alle 6, DK-2900 Hellerup
Tel: 39627500 *Fax:* 39627507
Key Personnel
Chief Librarian: Laone Gladbo
Gentofte Municipal Library.

Kobenhavns Kommunes Biblioteker
Islands Brygge 37, 2300 Copenhagen S
Tel: 33664650 *Fax:* 33667061
E-mail: ibertelsen.kff@ipost.kk.dk
Telex: 16648
Key Personnel
City Librarian: Jan Ostergaard
Copenhagen Municipal Libraries.
Publication(s): *Arsberetning* (annual report)

Kobenhavns Stadsarkiv (City Archives of Copenhagen)
Radhuset, DK-1599 Copenhagen V
Tel: 33662370 *Fax:* 33667039
E-mail: stadsarkiv@kff.kk.dk
Web Site: www.ksa.kk.dk
Key Personnel
Head Archivist: Henrik Gautier
Copenhagen City Archives.
Publication(s): *Historiske Meddelelser om Kobenhavn* (Historical Yearbook)

Det Kongelige Bibliotek
Sgren Kierkegaards Plads, PO Box 2149, DK-1016 Copenhagen K
Tel: 33474747 *Fax:* 3332 9846
E-mail: kb@kb.dk
Web Site: www.kb.dk
Key Personnel
Dir-General: Erland Kolding Nielsen
Sectional Librarian: Birgitte Hvidt *Tel:* 33474323
  E-mail: bhv@kb.dk
Founded: 1648
Publication(s): *Catalogue of Oriental Manuscript; Xylographs, etc in Danish Collections* (irregular, 1966); *Fund og Forskning i Det Kongelige Biblioteks Samlinger* (annually, 1961, Discovery & Research in the Collections in the Royal Library)
Branch Office(s)
The Royal Library Amager, Njalsgade 80
  Tel: 3347 4747 *Fax:* 3393 2218
The Royal Library Fiolstraede, Fiolstraede 1
  Tel: 3347 4747 *Fax:* 3393 2218

Det nordjyske Landsbibliotek
Nytorv 26, DK-9100 Aalborg
Mailing Address: PO Box 839, DK-9100 Aalborg
Tel: 99314400 *Fax:* 99314433
E-mail: njl@njl.dk
Key Personnel
Librarian: Kirsten Boel
Central Library for the County of North Jutland.

Odense Centralbibliotek
Ostre Stationsuej 15, 5000 Odense C
Tel: 66131372 *Fax:* 66137337
Key Personnel
Chief Librarian: Soeren Egelund
Odense County Library.

Odense Universitetsbibliotek
Campusvej 55, DK-5230 Odense M
Tel: 65501000 *Fax:* 66158162
E-mail: sdub@bib.sdu.dk
Key Personnel
Dir & Librarian: Aase Lindahl *Tel:* 65502683
University Library of Southern Denmark.

Rigsarkivet (Danish National Archives)
Rigsdagsgarden 9, DK-1218 Copenhagen K
Tel: 33923310 *Fax:* 33153239
E-mail: mailbox@ra.sa.dk
Web Site: www.sa.dk
Key Personnel
National Archivist: Johan Peter Noack
Secretary: Helle Gjellerup *Tel:* 33922336
  E-mail: hg@ra.sa.dk
Danish National Archives.
Publication(s): *Siden Saxo*

Roskilde University Library
Universitetsvej 1, DK-4000 Roskilde
Mailing Address: PO Box 258, DK-4000 Roskilde
Tel: 46742000 *Fax:* 46743090
E-mail: rub@ruc.dk
Key Personnel
Dir: Niels Senius Clausen *Tel:* 46742215
  E-mail: nsc@rub.ruc.dk
Founded: 1971

Statsbiblioteket (State & University Library, Aarhus)
Universitetsparken, DK-8000 Arhus C
Tel: 89462022 *Fax:* 89462220
E-mail: sb@statsbiblioteket.dk
Telex: 64515
Key Personnel
Library Dir: Niels Mark
State & University Library.
Publication(s): *Avismikrofilm i Statsbiblioteket; Journalism, Media & Communication; Ongoing Research in Denmark, Finland, Norway & Sweden; Nordicom; Bibliography of Nordic Mass Communication Literature* (ISSN 0105-1385)

Dominican Republic

Biblioteca Dominicana
Chapel of the Dominican Order, Santo Domingo
Key Personnel
Dir: Jose Rijo

Biblioteca Nacional
Cesar Nicolas Penson 91, Plaza de la Cultura, Santo Domingo
Key Personnel
Dir: Roberto DeSoto
National Library.

Biblioteca de la Camara Oficial de Comercio, Agricultura e Industria del Distrito Nacional
Arzobispo Nouel 206, Altos, Apdo 815, Santo Domingo
Tel: (809) 682-2688 *Fax:* (809) 685-2228
Library of the Chamber of Commerce, Agriculture and Industry.

Universidad Nacional Pedro Henriquez Urena
Biblioteca Carretera Duarte km 6 1/2 y 5 1/2, Apdo 1423, Santo Domingo
Tel: (0809) 542-6888 (ext 2301-2315)
  Fax: (0809) 566-2206; (0809) 540-3803
E-mail: biblioteca@unphu.edu.do
Web Site: www.unphu.edu.do/biblioteca.html
Key Personnel
Librarian: Carmen Iris Olivo
Publication(s): *Revista Aula 2da Epoca y Campus; Revista de Ciencias Juridicas y Politicas*

Biblioteca Municipal de Santo Domingo
Padre Billini 18, Santo Domingo
Key Personnel
Librarian: Luz Del Carmen Rijo

Biblioteca de la Secretaria de Estado de Relaciones Exteriores
Estancia Ramfis, Santo Domingo
Key Personnel
Dir: Dr Prospero J Mella Chavier
Library of the Secretariat of Foreign Affairs.

Biblioteca de la Universidad Autonoma de Santo Domingo
Ciudad Universitaria, Apdo 1355, Santo Domingo
Key Personnel
Dir: Martha Maria DeCastro Cotes

Ecuador

Archivo Nacional de Historia
Avda 6 de Diciembre 332, Apdo 67, Quito
Key Personnel
Dir: Jorge A Garces
National Historical Archives.

Biblioteca Ecuatoriana 'Aurelio Espinosa Polit'
Apdo 17-01-160, Quito
Tel: (02) 596420
Key Personnel
Dir: Rev Julian G Bravo *E-mail:* beap@uio.satnet.net
Publication(s): *Diccionaris Bibliografico Ecuatoriano* (Vols I, II, III & IV)

Biblioteca Nacional del Ecuador
12 de Octobre 555, Apdo 67, Quito
Tel: (02) 528840
Key Personnel
Dir: Dr Eugenio Espejo
National Library.

Biblioteca de la Casa de la Cultura Ecuatoriana, see Biblioteca Nacional Eugenio Espejo de la Casa de la Cultura Ecuatoriana

Biblioteca Nacional Eugenio Espejo de la Casa de la Cultura Ecuatoriana
Nucleo de Guayas, a de Octubre y, Pedro Moncayo, Apdo 3542, Guayaquil
Tel: (02) 528840
Key Personnel
Dir Lic: Ruth Garaicoa Soria
Library of Ecuadorian Culture.

Museo y Biblioteca Municipal
Ave 10 de Agosto entre Chile y Calle Pedro Carbo Palacio, Municipal Apdo 6069, Guayaquil
Tel: (04) 515738
Key Personnel
Dir: Patricia De Quevedo

Biblioteca de la Universidad Central de Ecuador
Ciudad Universitaria, Apdo 166, Quito
Tel: (02) 524714

Biblioteca General, Universidad de Guayaquil
C Chile 900, Apdo 3834, Guayaquil
Tel: (04) 282440 *Fax:* (04) 329905
Telex: 3179
Key Personnel
Dir: Leonor Villao de Santander

Egypt (Arab Republic of Egypt)

Alexandria Municipal Library
18 Sharia Menasha Moharrem Bey, Alexandria
Key Personnel
Chief Librarian: Sheikh Beshir Beshir El Shindi

American University in Cairo Library
113 Sharia Kasr El Aini, Cairo
Mailing Address: PO Box 2511, 11511 Cairo
Tel: (02) 3576904 *Fax:* (02) 5943824
Telex: 92224 AUCAI UN EGYPT
Key Personnel
Dean, Libraries & Learning Technologies: Shahira El Sawy *E-mail:* selsawy@aucegypt.edu
Head, ILL/Doc Del & Electronic Resource Services: Hoda El Ridi *Tel:* (02) 3576365 *E-mail:* elridi@aucegypt.edu

Al- Azhar University Library
Nasr City, Cairo
Tel: (02) 904051; (02) 706097
Key Personnel
Librarian: M E A Hady

Egyptian National Library (Dar-ul-Kutub)
Sharia Corniche El-Nil, Bulaq, Cairo
Tel: (02) 900232
Key Personnel
General Dir: Ali Abdul Mohsen

Ein Shams University Library
Abbasiyah Kasr-El-Zaafran, Cairo
Tel: (02) 2847827 *Fax:* (02) 2847824
Key Personnel
Librarian: Nasr El Din Abdel Rahman

Institute of Arab Research & Studies Library
One Tolombat St, Garden City, Cairo
Mailing Address: PO Box 229, Garden City, Cairo
Tel: (02) 3551648 *Fax:* (02) 3562543
Telex: 928642 Alcso *Cable:* IREALEA CAIRO
Key Personnel
President: Prof M S Abulezz, PhD
Dir: Prof Ahmed Youssef

Ministry of Education Library
16 Sharia El-Falaki, Cairo
Tel: (02) 8544805
Key Personnel
Dir: Hassen Abdel Shafi

Ministry of Justice Library
Midan, Lazoghli, Saida, Cairo
Tel: (02) 20806
Key Personnel
Librarian: Fekry Abou-El-Kheir

National Archives
Al-Qalcah, Cairo

National Assembly Library
Palace of the National Assembly, Majlisal-Shab St, Cairo
Mailing Address: PO Box 1183, Cairo
Tel: (02) 3540279 *Fax:* (02) 3548977
Telex: 20054

National Information & Documentation Centre
Al-Tahrir St, Dokki, Cairo
Tel: (02) 3371696
Key Personnel
Dir: Dr Mostaga Esmat El-Sarha
Publication(s): *Directory of Scientific & Technical Libraries*

University of Ain Shams Library, see Ein Shams University Library

University of Alexandria Library
22 Sharia al-Gueish, Shatby, Alexandria
Tel: (03) 5971675 *Fax:* (03) 5960720
Telex: 54467
Key Personnel
Chief Librarian: Khalid El Ramady

University of Cairo Library
Gameet el Qahira Street, Giza, Cairo
Tel: (02) 5729584 *Fax:* (02) 628884
Key Personnel
General Dir: Fatina Ibrahim

El Salvador

Biblioteca Nacional
8a Ave Norte y Calle Delgado, San Salvador
Tel: 216312
Key Personnel
Dir: Jose Astul Yanes

Biblioteca de la Universidad Centroamericana 'Jose Simeon Canas' (Biblioteca "Florentino Idoate" de la Univrsidad Centroamericana "Jose Simeon Canas")
Jardines de Guadalupe, Autopista Sur, Apdo 168, San Salvador
Tel: 2734400 *Fax:* 2731010
E-mail: ucabib.director@bib.uca.edu.sv
Key Personnel
Dir: Katherine Miller *E-mail:* kmiller@uca.bib.edu.sv
Publication(s): *Estudios Centro Americanas (ECA)*

Biblioteca Central de la Universidad de El Salvador
Ciudad Universitaria, Final 25 Av Norte, Apdo 143, San Salvador
Tel: 2250278 *Fax:* 2250278
E-mail: sb@biblio.ues.edu.sv
Key Personnel
Dir: Ana Aurora de Kapsalis
Publication(s): *Boletin* (monthly); *Lista de Acquisiciones Recientes* (monthly)

Eritrea

University of Asmara Library
PO Box 1220, Asmara
Tel: (01) 161926; (01) 162553 *Fax:* (01) 162236
Telex: 42091 *Cable:* ASMUNIV
Key Personnel
Dir & Librarian: Assefaw Abraha *E-mail:* assefawa@lib.usa.edu.er
Parent Company: University of Asmara
Ultimate Parent Company: Ministry of Education

Estonia

National Library of Estonia
Tonismaegi 2, EE0100 Tallinn
Tel: (02) 6307500 *Fax:* (02) 6311410
E-mail: nlib@venus.nlib.ee
Key Personnel
General Dir: Dr Ivi Eenmaa
The National Library of Estonia is also the Parliamentary Library of Estonia; it is the central library in the field of humanities & art.
Publication(s): *Eesti Rahvusbibliograafia: Artiklid* (The Estonian National Bibliography: Articles from Serials); *Eesti Rahvusraamatukogu: Raamatud* (The Estonian National Bibliography: Books)

Tartu University Library (Tartu Ulikooli Raamatukogu)
One W Struve Str, 50091 Tartu
Tel: (07) 375 700 (Director); (07) 375 703 (Secretary) *Fax:* (07) 375 701
E-mail: library@utlib.ee
Web Site: www.utlib.ee
Key Personnel
Library Dir: Toomas Liivamagi *Tel:* (07) 375 700 *E-mail:* toomas@utlib.ee
Founded: 1802
Member of Association of European Research Libraries (LIBER); Association of Libraries of the Baltic Area *Bibliotheca Baltica* ; European Association of Health Information Libraries (EAHIL); International Association of Music Libraries (IAML); European Information Association (EIA) and its branch for Baltic & Nordic Countries.
Publication(s): *Eksliibrised Tartu Ulikooli Raamatukogus* (Bookplates in Tartu University Library, irregular, 1975, Four publications to introduce the collection); *Publicationes Bibliothecae Universitatis Litterarum Tartuensis* (irregular, 1973, Introduces Tartu University Library collections of manuscripts); *Raamat-aegrestaureerimine* (Book-Time-Restoration, irregular, 1969); *Raamatukogu toeid* (Publications of Tartu University Libary. 1-XI, papers on the library, 1968); *Tartu (Riiklik) Uelikool* (Tartu State University, The Bibliography of Works Published, irregular, Records all the works published by university faculty & students); *Tartu Uelikooli Raamatukogu vanagraafika kogu kataloogid* (Tartu University Library collections of graphic art sicne 15th centruy, irregular, 1974, Nine publications about English, German, Flemish, Dutch, Italian and French works of graphic art); *Tartu Ulikooli Raamatukogu aastaraamat* (Tartu University Library Yearbook, regular, 1996, Contains annual report, list of donations and research articles)

Ethiopia

Addis Ababa University Library
PO Box 1176, Addis Ababa
Tel: (01) 115673; (01) 550844 *Fax:* (01) 550655
Telex: 21205 *Cable:* AAUNIV
Key Personnel
Librarian: Dr Taye Tadesse
Publication(s): *List of Ethiopian Authors* (monograph)

Agricultural Institute Library
PO Box 307, Jimma
Tel: (07) 110102
Key Personnel
Librarian: Goitom Ghebru

Alemaya University of Agriculture Library
PO Box 138, Dire Dawa
Tel: (05) 111399 *Fax:* (05) 114008
Key Personnel
Assistant Librarian: Tesfaye Salilew

British Council Library
Artistic Bldg, Adoua Ave, Addis Ababa
Mailing Address: PO Box 1043, Addis Ababa
Tel: (01) 550022 *Fax:* (01) 552544
Telex: 21561
Key Personnel
Librarian: Seyoum Gebre-Hiwot
Specialize in provision of library & information services.

Institute of Ethiopian Studies Library
PO Box 1176, Addis Ababa
Tel: (01) 550844; (01) 119469 *Fax:* (01) 552688
E-mail: ies.aau@telecom.net.et
Telex: 21205 *Cable:* AA N IV
Key Personnel
Librarian: Girma Jemaneh
Founded: 1963
Publication(s): *Ethiopian Publications* (annually); *List of Current Periodical Publications* (biannually)
Parent Company: Addis Ababa University

National Library and Archives of Ethiopia
PO Box 717, Addis Ababa
Tel: (01) 512241
Key Personnel
Librarian: Almaz Mengistu

Organization for African Unity Library
PO Box 3243, Addis Ababa
Tel: (01) 517700 (ext 211) *Fax:* (01) 513036
Telex: 21046 *Cable:* OAU
Key Personnel
Chief Librarian: Mrs J C Ranaivoravelo

United Nations Economic Commission for Africa Library
Africa Hall, Addis Ababa
Mailing Address: PO Box 3001, Addis Ababa
Tel: (01) 517200 *Fax:* (01) 514416; (01) 512233
E-mail: eca.info@un.org
Web Site: www.un.org.depts/eca
Telex: 21029 *Cable:* Eca Addis Ababa
Key Personnel
Librarian: Fathi S Daif
Founded: 1958
Publication(s): *Africa Index: Selected articles on socio-economic development* (quarterly)

Faroe Islands

Foroya Landsbokasavn
J C Svabosgotu 16, FO-110 Torshavn
Mailing Address: PO Box 61, FO-110 Torshavn
Tel: 29811626 *Fax:* 29818895
E-mail: fonalib@flb.fo
Key Personnel
Librarian: Martin Naes
Publication(s): *The Faroese* (book list)

Standard Book Numbering Agency, see Foroya Landsbokasavn

Fiji

Library Service of Fiji
Government Buildings, Suva
Mailing Address: PO Box 2526, Suva
Tel: 315303 *Fax:* 314994
Key Personnel
Chief Librarian: Humesh Prasad *Tel:* 315303
Senior Librarian: Shafig Gafoor
Publication(s): *Fiji National Bibliography* (annually)
Parent Company: Ministry of Education
Branch Office(s)
Northern Regional Library, Labasa
Western Regional Library, PO Box 150, Lautoka

National Archives of Fiji
25 Carnarvon St, Suva
Mailing Address: PO Box 2125, Suva
Tel: 304144 *Cable:* ARCHIVIST
Key Personnel
Archivist: Setareki Turnaceva

Suva City Library
Victoria Parade, Suva
Mailing Address: GPO Box 176, Suva
Tel: 313433 *Fax:* 302158 *Cable:* TOWN CLERK SUVA
Key Personnel
Chief Librarian: Ms Lalita Sudhakar Lal
Publication(s): *Suva City Council* (annual report)

University of the South Pacific Library
PO Box 1168, Suva
Tel: 313900 (ext 2282) *Fax:* 3300830
Telex: 2276
Key Personnel
Librarian: Esther Williams *E-mail:* williams_e@usp.ac.fj
Coordination Unit for Pacific Islands Marine Resources Information System (PIMRIS), Regional Center for Population Information Network (POPIN).
Publication(s): *PIC Newsletter* (quarterly); *PIMRIS Newsletter* (quarterly); *South Pacific Bibliography* (biennially); *South Pacific Periodicals Index*; *South Pacific Research Register* (biennially)

Finland

Abo Akademis bibliotek (Abo Akademi University Library)
Domkyrkogt 2-4, 20500 Abo
Tel: (02) 2154180 *Fax:* (02) 2154795
E-mail: ill@abo.fi
Key Personnel
Librarian: Tore Ahlback
Contact: Anders Ekberg *E-mail:* anders.ekberg@abo.fi
Publication(s): *Skrifter utgivna av Abo Akademis bibliotek*

Eduskunnan Kirjasto (Library of Parliament, Finland)
Aurorankatu 6, FIN-00102 Helsinki
Tel: (00) 4321 *Fax:* (00) 4323495
E-mail: library@eduskunta.fi
Web Site: www.eduskunta.fi/kirjasto/
Key Personnel
Library Dir: Tuula H Laaksovirta
Secretary: Satu Saarikivi *E-mail:* satu.saarikivi@eduskunta.fi
Library of Parliament.
Publication(s): *Bibliographia iuridica Fennica*

Helsingin Kaupunginkirjasto - yleisten kirjastojen keskuskirjasto (Helsinki City Library - Central Library for Public Libraries)
Rautatielaisenkatu 8, FIN-00520 Helsinki
Mailing Address: PO Box 4100, FIN-00099 City of Helsinki
Tel: (09) 3108511 *Fax:* (09) 31085517
E-mail: city.library@hel.fi
Key Personnel
Library Dir: Ms Maija Berndtson
Executive Assistant: Reita Hamalainen *Tel:* (09) 31085520 *E-mail:* reita.hamalainen@hel.fi

Helsinki University Library
Helsingin Yliopisto, FIN-00014 Unioninkatu 36
Mailing Address: Box 15, Helsingin Yliopisto, FIN-00014 Unioninkatu 36
Tel: (09) 19122709 *Fax:* (09) 19122719
E-mail: hyk.palvelu@helsinki.fi
Telex: 121538 Hyk
Key Personnel
Librarian: Prof Esko Haekli
Founded: 1640
Publication(s): *Books from Finland* (quarterly, mostly in English, but also in French & German); *Publications of the University Library at Helsinki*; *The Finnish National Bibliography* (CD-ROM)
Parent Company: University of Helsinki
Branch Office(s)
Slavonic Library, PB 15, Helsingin Yliopisto, 00014 Unioninkatu 36 *Tel:* (09) 19123196
American Resource Center, Box 15, Helsingin Yliopisto, 00014 Unioninkatu 36 *Tel:* (09) 19124048 *Fax:* (09) 652940 *E-mail:* ARC@usembassy.fi

Joensuun Yliopisto
Kirjasto Yliopistokatu 2 PL 107, 80101 Joensuu
Tel: (013) 2511 *Fax:* (0251) 2050
E-mail: joyle@joyl.joensuun.ti
Telex: 46223
Key Personnel
Librarian: Tuulikki Nurminen
Joensuu University.

Jyvaskylan Yliopiston Kirjasto (Jyvaskyla University Library)
Seminaarinkatu 15, FIN-40014 Jyvaskylan Yliopisto
Mailing Address: PO Box 35 (B), FIN-40014 Jyvaskyla
Tel: (014) 2603373 *Fax:* (014) 2603371
E-mail: jyk@Library.jyu.fi
Key Personnel
Dir: Pirjo Vatanen
Librarian: Kaija Nygard *Tel:* (014) 260 3374
E-mail: kaija.nygord@library.jyu.fi
Founded: 1863
Jyvaskyla University Library.
Parent Company: Jyvaskylan Yliopiston (Jyvaskyla University)

FINLAND

Kansallisarkisto Kirjasto (National Archives of Finland/Library)
Rauhankatu 17, FIN-00170 Helsinki
Mailing Address: PO Box 258, FIN-00171 Helsinki
Tel: (09) 228521 *Fax:* (09) 176302
E-mail: national_archives@narc.fi
Web Site: www.narc.fi
Key Personnel
Head of Library: Elisa Orrman *E-mail:* elisa.orrman@narc.fi
Library Assistant: Marjut Nuikka *E-mail:* marjut.nuikka@narc.fi
Founded: 1869
National Archives of Finland.

Library of Statistics, see Statistics Finland Library

Oulun Yliopiston Kirjasto
Linnanmaa, SF-90571 Oulu
Mailing Address: PL 450, SF-90571 Oulu
Tel: (081) 5531011 *Fax:* (081) 5569135
Telex: 32256 Oyk
Key Personnel
Acting Chief Librarian: Paeivi Kytoemaeki
Oulu University Library.
Publication(s): *Acta Universitatis Ouluensis* (Publications of Oulu University Library)

Sibelius-Akatemian Kirjasto
Toeoeloenkatu 28, SF-00260 Helsinki
Tel: (09) 4054539 *Fax:* (09) 4054542
E-mail: ikoskimi@siba.fi
Key Personnel
Librarian: Irmeli Koskimies
Sibelius Academy Library.

Statistics Finland Library
Tyoepajakatu 13B, FIN-00022 Helsinki
Mailing Address: PO Box 2B, FIN-00022 Helsinki
Tel: (09) 17342220 *Fax:* (09) 17342279
E-mail: kirjasto.tilastokeskus@stat.fi
Web Site: www.stat/fi/tk/kk/index_en.html
Key Personnel
Chief Librarian: Hellevi Yrjoelae

Tampereen Yliopiston Kirjasto (Tampere University Library)
Yliopistonkatu 38, SF-33101 Tampere
Mailing Address: PO Box 617, SF-33101 Tampere
Tel: (03) 2156111 *Fax:* (03) 2157493
Web Site: www.uta.fi/~kimiii
Telex: 22263 Tayk
Key Personnel
Chief Librarian: Dr Mirja Iivonen *E-mail:* mirja.t.iivonen@uta.fi
Founded: 1925
Library of the University of Tampere.
Publication(s): *University Publications*

Teknillisen Korkeakoulun Kirjasto
Otaniementie 9, SF-02150 Espoo
Tel: (00) 4514112 *Fax:* (00) 4514132
E-mail: infolib@hut.fi
Key Personnel
Dir of Libraries: Ari Muhonen
Head of Information Services: Irma Pasanen
Helsinki University of Technology Library (National Resource Library for Technology in Finland).
Publication(s): *Annual Bibliography of the Helsinki University of Technology* (online only); *Research at HUT* (annual, online only); *Tenttu* (online only)

TERKKO, see Terveystieteiden keskuskirjasto (TERKKO)

Terveystieteiden keskuskirjasto (TERKKO)
Haartmanink 4, SF-00290 Helsinki
Tel: (00) 19126644 *Fax:* (00) 2410385
E-mail: terkko-info@helinski.fi
National Library of Health Sciences.
Publication(s): *FINMED/MEDIC* (bibliography & database)

Turun Yliopiston Kirjasto (Turku University Library)
FIN-20500 Turku
Tel: (02) 3336163 *Fax:* (02) 3335050
E-mail: annales@utu.fi
Telex: 62123 Tyk
Key Personnel
Librarian: Tuulikki Nurminen
Turku University Library.
Publication(s): *Annales Universitatis Turkuensis*

France

American Library in Paris
10, rue du General-Camou, 75007 Paris
Tel: (01) 53591260 *Fax:* (01) 45502583
E-mail: alparis@cybercable.fr
Web Site: www.ourworld.compuserve.com/homepages/alp/
Key Personnel
Dir: Kay G Rader
Assistant Dir: Adele Witt
Reference Librarian: A Delumeau *Tel:* (01) 53591262 *E-mail:* delumeau@cybercable.fr
Founded: 1920
Special Collections: Gregory Usher Cookbook Collection; Marlene Dietrich Collection. Specialize in social sciences, humanities, US history & civilization, literary criticism.

Bibliotheque Universitaire Antilles-Guyane (BUAG)
BP 7210, Campus de Schoelcher, 97275 Schoelcher Cedex
Tel: (05) 96727530 *Fax:* (05) 96727527
Key Personnel
Dir: M F Bernabe
Librarian In-Charge, Section Martinique: Jacques Dalquier *E-mail:* j.dalquier@martinique.univ-ag.fr
In-Charge, Section Guyane: N Clement-Martin
In-Charge, Section Guadeloupe: C Vassilieff

Archives Nationales
60 rue des Francs-Bourgeois, F-75141 Paris Cedex 03
Tel: (01) 40276131 *Fax:* (01) 40276601
Key Personnel
Dir: H Lerch
Branch Office(s)
09/63-02 Dathwee Chhen Twa Gallee, Chowk Bhitra 2nd Floor Purano Bazaar, Arniko-Barhabise VDC-9, Arniko Rajmarg-87 K M, Bagmati Anchal, Barhabise Mail PO Code 45303, Kathmandu Mail Centre, Nepal

Bibliotheque de l' Arsenal
Division of Bibliotheque Nationale de France
One rue de Sully, F-75004 Paris
Tel: (01) 53012525 *Fax:* (01) 42770163
E-mail: arsenal@bnf.fr
Key Personnel
Dir & Chief Librarian: Bruno Blasselle *E-mail:* bruno.blasselle@bnf.fr

Bibliotheque Centrale du Museum National d'Histoire Naturelle
38 rue Geoffry-Saint Hilaire, Paris
Tel: (01) 40793627 *Fax:* (01) 40793656

Key Personnel
Dir: Michele Mauries
Chief Librarian: Monique Duereux

Bibliotheque d'Art et d'Archeologie Jacques Doucet
Division of Universites de Paris IV et Paris I
2/4 rue Vivienne, 75083 Paris Cedex 02
Tel: (01) 47037620 *Fax:* (01) 47038925
E-mail: baa@paris4.sorbonne.fr
Key Personnel
Chief Librarian: Francoise Lemelle
This is a Paris University library.

Bibliotheque Historique de la Ville de Paris
24 rue Pavee, 75004 Paris
Tel: (01) 44592940 *Fax:* (01) 42740316
Key Personnel
Curator: Jean Derens

Bibliotheque Interuniversitaire de Montpellier
Bibliotheque Inter Universitaire, 60, rue des Etats Generaux, 34965 Montpellier Cedex 2
Tel: (04) 67 13 43 50 *Fax:* (04) 67 13 43 51
Key Personnel
Chief Librarian: Pierre Gaillard
Publication(s): *Le Musee Atger (The Atger Museum)*; *Relais*

Bibliotheque Municipale
One rue de La Borderie, 35042 Rennes Cedex
Tel: (02) 99630909; (02) 99879898 *Fax:* (02) 99360596; (02) 99879899
E-mail: bm-rennes@univ-rennes1.fr
Key Personnel
Contact: Marie-Therese Pouillias
Publication(s): *Cinq cents ans d'imprimerie en Bretagne, 1484-1985* (catalog); *Jean Larcher* (catalog); *Le Femme 1900 dans les collections Henri Polles* (catalog); *Le Pelletier* (dictionary); *Le Romantisme breton: collection Henri Polles*, *L'itinerarie de Kenneth White* (catalog); *Paul Feval, 1816-1887*

Bibliotheque Municipale de Besancon
One rue de la Bibliotheque, BP09, F-25012 Besancon Cedex
Tel: (01) 81812089 *Fax:* (01) 81619877
Key Personnel
Librarian: Helene Richard *E-mail:* helene.richard@besancon.com

Bibliotheque Municipale de Grenoble
12 blvd Marechal Lyautey, 38021 Grenoble Cedex 1
Mailing Address: BP 1095, 38000 Grenoble Cedex 1
Tel: (076) 0476862100 *Fax:* (076) 0476862119
E-mail: bmei@upmf-grenoble.fr
Key Personnel
Librarians: Sylvie Crouzet; Catherine Pouyet
Publication(s): *Bibliotheque municipale de Grenoble, Catalogue general auteurs des livres imprimes jusqu'a 1900* (1980, 12 vols available from K G Saur, Germany)

Bibliotheque Municipale de Lyon
30 blvd Vivier-Merle, F-69431 Lyon cedex 03
Tel: (07) 78621800 *Fax:* (07) 78621949
E-mail: bm@bm-lyon.fr
Web Site: www.bm-lyon.fr
Key Personnel
Librarian: Patrick Bazin *Tel:* (04) 7862 1924
E-mail: pbazin@bm-lyon.fr

Bibliotheque Nationale de France
11 quai Francois Mauriac, 75013 Paris
Tel: (01) 53795379 *Fax:* (01) 47037734
Key Personnel
President: Jean Pierre Angremy

Dir General: Philippe Belaval
National Library.

Bibliotheque Nationale et Universitaire de Strasbourg
5 rue du Marechal Joffre, BP 1029/F, F-67070 Strasbourg cedex
Tel: (03) 88252800 *Fax:* (03) 88252803
Key Personnel
Administrator: Gerard Littler
(main address & Management & Legal Section); 6 place de la Republique, BP 1029/F, F-67070 Strasbourg cedex Tel: 88252800 (Alsace Region Affairs Section); 3 bis rue du Marechal Joffre, BP 1029/F, F-67070 Strasbourg cedex Tel: 88252846.
Publication(s): *Bibliographie alsacienne*; *Catalogue critique des manuscrits persans*; *Papyrus grecs de la BNUS*

Bibliotheque Universitaire d'Avignon et des Pays du Vaucluse
74 Rue Louis Pasteur, 84029 Avignon Cedex 1
Tel: (04) 90162500 *Fax:* (04) 90162510
Key Personnel
Dir: Francoise Febvre

Bibliotheque Municipale de Bordeaux
85 cours du Marechal Juin, 33075 Bordeaux cedex
Tel: (05) 56243251 *Fax:* (05) 56249408
Key Personnel
Dir: Pierre Botineau

BUAG, see Bibliotheque Universitaire Antilles-Guyane (BUAG)

La Documentation Francaise
29 Quai Voltaire, 75340 Paris Cedex 07
Mailing Address: 124, rue Henri-Barbusse, 93308 Aubervilliers
Tel: (01) 40157000 *Fax:* (01) 40 15 68 00
Key Personnel
Man Dir: Sophie Moati
Commercial Dir: Alain-Marie Bassy
Editorial Dir: M Meusy
Chief Sales: Bernard Meunier

Bibliotheque de Documentation Internationale Contemporaine
Centre Universitaire, 6 allee de l'Universite, F-92001 Nanterre cedex
Tel: (01) 40977900 *Fax:* (01) 40977940
E-mail: courrier.bdic@u-paris10.fr
Key Personnel
Dir: Genevieve Dreyfus-Armand
This is a Paris University library.
Publication(s): *Collection des Publications de la BDIC*

Ecole Nationale Superieure des Sciences de l'information et des bibliotheques (ENSSIB)
17-21 Blvd du 11 Novembre 1918, 69623 Villeurbanne cedex
Tel: (04) 72444343; (04) 72444307 *Fax:* (04) 72442788
E-mail: com@enssib.fr; dupuigre@enssib.fr
Key Personnel
Dir: Francois Dupuigrenet-Desroussilles
Dir, Publications: Anne Meyer
Publication(s): *Bulletin des bibliotheques de France*; *Editions de l'Enssib*; *Monographies en sciences de l'information et des bibliotheques* (travaux d'etude et de recherche)

Bibliotheque de Geographie
191 rue St-Jacques, F-75005 Paris
Tel: (01) 44324461; (01) 44321463 *Fax:* (01) 44321467
Key Personnel
Librarian: Joseph Maie
This is a Paris University library.

INIST (Institut de p Information Scientifique et Technique), see Institut de l'Information Scientifique et Technique (INIST)

Bibliotheque de l'Institut de France
23 quai de Conti, F-75006 Paris
Tel: (01) 44414410 *Fax:* (01) 44414411
Key Personnel
Dir & Librarian: Mireille Pastoureau
Founded: 1795

Institut de l'Information Scientifique et Technique (INIST)
Affiliate of CNRS (French National Centre for Scientific Research)
2 Allee du Parc de Brabois, 54514 Vandoeuvre-les-Nancy Cedex
Tel: (03) 83504600 *Fax:* (03) 83504650
E-mail: infoclient@inist.fr
Web Site: www.inist.fr
Key Personnel
Dir: A Pain Chanudet
Founded: 1988
INIST-CNRS, the leading French scientific & technical information center, is a service unit of the French National Centre for Scientific Research (CNRS). It uses its unique pool of expertise in Europe, to collect basic & applied research publications in cooperation with some hundred French & international organizations. INIST-CNRS produces multidisciplinary & multilingual bibliographical databases - PASCAL, FRANCIS & ARTICLE@INIST - listing documents published in most areas of Science & Technology, Medicine, the Humanities, Social Sciences & Economics. INIST-CNRS is also the leading scientific & technical document delivery service in France (700,000) document copies supplied each year).
Publication(s): *Articlesciences* (3000 each day, 1990); *Francis* (monthly updates, 1972); *Pascal* (weekly updates, 1973)

Bibliotheque Interuniversitaire des Langues Orientales
4 rue de Lille, F-75007 Paris
Tel: (01) 44778720 *Fax:* (01) 44778730
E-mail: biulo@idf.ext.jussieu.fr
Key Personnel
Dir: Nelly Guillaume *E-mail:* guillaum@idf.ext.jussieu.fr
Founded: 1868
Paris University Library.

Bibliotheque Mazarine
23 quai de Conti, F-75006 Paris
Tel: (01) 44414406 *Fax:* (01) 44414407
Key Personnel
Chief Curator & Dir: Christian Peligry
E-mail: christian.peligry@mazarine.univ-paris5.fr

Bibliotheque Interuniversitaire de Medecine
12 rue de l'Ecole de Medecine, F-75270 Paris Cedex 06
Tel: (01) 40461616 *Fax:* (01) 44411020
Key Personnel
Dir & Chief Curator: P Casseyre
This is a Paris University library.
Publication(s): *Catalogue des Periodiques de la Bibliotheque (1976-1981)*; *Bibliotheque de l'ancienne Faculte de Medecine de Paris: Catalogue des Livres du XVIe siecle extrait du catalogue general du fonds ancien*

Bibliotheque Municipale de Nancy
43 rue Stanislas, 54042 Nancy Cedex
Tel: (03) 83373883 *Fax:* (03) 83379182
E-mail: bmnancy@mairie-nancy.fr
Key Personnel
Chief Librarian: Andre Markiewicz
Founded: 1750

Bibliotheque du Musee de l'Homme
Palais de Chaillot, Pl du Trocadero, F-75116 Paris
Tel: (01) 44057203; (01) 44057272 *Fax:* (01) 44057212
Key Personnel
Dir: Jacqueline Dubois

Bibliotheque Interuniversitaire de Pharmacie
4 ave de l'Observatoire, F-75270 Paris Cedex 6
Tel: (01) 53739517 (ext 9523) *Fax:* (01) 53739520
E-mail: piketty@pharmacie.univ_paris5.fr
Key Personnel
Librarian: Francoise Malet
This is a Paris University library seat of CADIST for culture (Beauty culture: perfumes & cosmetics).

Bibliotheque Sainte-Genevieve
10 pl du Pantheon, F-75005 Paris
Tel: (01) 44419797 *Fax:* (01) 44419796
E-mail: bsg@univ.paris1.fr
Key Personnel
Librarian: Nathalie Jullian
This is a Paris University library & public library.

Service commun de la documentation de l'Universite de Lille III
DULJVA, Pont de Bois, BP 99, 59652 Villeneuve d'Ascq Cedex
Tel: (03) 20417000 *Fax:* (065) 20914650
E-mail: scd@univ.lille3.fr
Key Personnel
Dir: Jean-Paul Chadourne

Bibliotheque de la Sorbonne
13 rue de la Sorbonne, F-75257 Paris Cedex 5
Tel: (01) 40463027 *Fax:* (01) 40463044
E-mail: adminst@biu.sorbonne.fr
Web Site: www.sorbonne.fr
Key Personnel
Chief Librarian: Marie-Bernadette Jullien
E-mail: bjullien@biu.sorbonne.fr
Founded: 1762
This is a Paris Interuniversity library.
Branch Office(s)
Lettres et Sciences humaines

Universite de Toulouse-Mirail
Bibliotheque Universitaire 5, allees Machado, F 31106 Toulouse Cedex 01
Mailing Address: BU Lettres, BP 1350, F 31106 Toulouse Cedex 01
Tel: 50 40 44; 50 40 64 *Fax:* 50 40 50
Key Personnel
Librarian: Francoise Leroi *E-mail:* francoise.leroi@univ.tlse2.fr
Chief Librarian: J Claude Annezer
Publication(s): *Anglophonia*; *Caravelle*; *Champs du Signe*; *Criticon*; *Litteratures*; *Pallas*

Universites de Nancy
Bibliotheque Interuniversitaire 11 pl Carnot, 54042 Nancy Cedex
Tel: (08) 83370213 *Fax:* (08) 83355790
Key Personnel
Librarian: Claude Gerard

French Guiana

Institut Francais de Recherche Scientifique pour le Developpement en Cooperation
Centre ORSTOM de Cayenne, Bibliotheque, BP 165, 97323 Cayenne cedex
Tel: 302785 *Fax:* 319855
Key Personnel
Dir: Guy Rocheteau
Office of Scientific & Technical Research Overseas.
Publication(s): *La Nature et l'Homme* (irregular publication)

Gabon

Bibliotheque de l'Universite Omar Bongo
Blvd Leon M'Ba, Libreville
Mailing Address: BP 13131, Libreville
Tel: 732956; 732033
Telex: 5336
Key Personnel
Dir: Mrs Anicette Odimbossoukou
Publication(s): *Inventaire du fonds documentaire, par discipline* (annually); *Liste des nouvelles acquisitions* (quarterly); *Liste des periodiques en cours* (annually)

Centre Bibliotheque d'Information
BP 750, Libreville
Tel: 21115

Direction Generale des Archives Nationales, de la Bibliotheque Nationale et de la Documentation Gabonaise (DGABD)
BP 1188, Libreville
Tel: 736310 *Fax:* 730972
Key Personnel
Archives Dir: Rene G Sonnet-Azize
Dir: Jean Paul Mifouna

Gambia

Gambia College Library
Western Division, Brikama
Tel: 84812
Key Personnel
Librarian: Rosanna A Jallon Ndaw-Jallow
President: N S Z Njie

The Gambia National Library
Reg Pye Lane, PMB 552, Banjul
Tel: 28312 *Fax:* 223776
Key Personnel
Chief Librarian: Mary E Fye

Georgia

Gosudarstvennaya Respublikanskaya biblioteka Gruzinskoi SSR im K Marksai
Kecchoveli ul 5, Tblisi 380007
Tel: (08832) 999286 (Director's Office)
Fax: (08832) 998095
Key Personnel
Dir: Alexander Kartozia
State Republican Karl Marx Library of the Georgian SSR.

Germany

Badische Landesbibliothek
Erbprinzenstr 15, 76133 Karlsruhe
Tel: (0721) 1752001 *Fax:* (0721) 1752333
E-mail: sekretariat@blb-karlsruhe.de; infozentrum@blb-karlsruhe.de
Web Site: www.blb-karlsruhe.de
Key Personnel
Librarian: Dr Peter Michael Ehrle
Man Assistant: Dr Martina Rebmann *Tel:* (0721) 1752262 *E-mail:* rebmann@blb-karlsruhe.de
Founded: 1500

Staatsbibliothek Bamberg
Neue Residenz, Domplatz 8, 96049 Bamberg
Tel: (0951) 54014 *Fax:* (0951) 54615
Key Personnel
Chief Librarian: Dr Bernhard Schemmel
Publication(s): *Auserlesene Schrift-Bilder*; *Bambergische Bildhauerzeichnungen des Rokoko und Klassizismus*; *Das Allgemeine Krankenhaus Fuerstbischof Franz Ludwig von Erthals in Bamberg von 1789*; *Der Bamberger Psalter*; *Der Bamberger Siddur*; *Deutsche Grammatiken vom Humanismus bis zur Aufklaerung*; *Die Entdeckung der Fraenkischen Schweiz im Spiegel der Graphik*; *Die Ingenieur- und Zeichenakademie des Leopold Westen und ihre Entwicklung*; *Die Neuen Welten in alten Buechern*; *Friedrich Karl Rupprecht*; *Fuers Schoene Geschlecht*; *Handschriften aus dem Augustiner-Chorherrenstift Neunkirchen am Brand*; *Johann Lukas Schoenlein*; *Karl Theodor von Buseck 1803-1860*; *Staatsbibliothek Bamberg*; *Vergil 2000 Jahre*

Bayerische Staatsbibliothek
Ludwigstr 16, 80328 Munich, Bavaria
Tel: (089) 286380 *Fax:* (089) 286382200
E-mail: direktion@bsb-muenchen.de
Web Site: www.bsb.muenchen.de
Key Personnel
Librarian: Dr H Leskien; Peter Schnitzlein *Tel:* (089) 286382429 *E-mail:* schnitzlein@bsb.muenchen.de
Founded: 1558
Bavarian State Library.
Publication(s): *Bayerische Staatsbibliothek:* (ein Selbstportrait); *Jahresbericht* (annually)

Technische Universitat Bergakademie Freiberg
c/o Universitatsbibliothek Georgius Agricola, Argricolastrasse 10, 09599 Frieberg
Tel: (03731) 392959 *Fax:* (03731) 393289
E-mail: unibib@ub.tu-freiberg.de
Key Personnel
Librarian: Karin Mittenzwei
Publication(s): *Veroffentlichungen der Wissenschaftler der TU Bergakademie Freiberg*

Bibliothek des Instituts fuer Weltwirtschaft, see Deutsche Zentralbibliothek fuer Wirtschaftswissenschaften (ZBW)/Bibliothek des Instituts fuer Weltwirtschaft

Bibliothek fur Zeitgeschichte/Library of Contemporary History
Konrad Adenauerstr 8, 70173 Stuttgart
Mailing Address: Postfach 105441, 70047 Stuttgart
Tel: (0711) 2124516 *Fax:* (0711) 2124517
E-mail: bfz@mailserver.wlb-stuggart.de
Web Site: www.wlb-stuggart.de/~bfz/bfz.htm
Key Personnel
Dir: Dr Gerhard Hirschfeld
This library is housed in same building as the Wuerttembergische Landesbibliothek, covering library (approx 310,000 books & approx 650 current periodicals), archives, documentation center for grey literature, research facilities, etc.
Publication(s): *Schriften der Bibliothek fuer Zeitgeschichte NF*; *Stuttgarter Vortraege zur Zeitgeschichte*
Parent Company: Wuerttembergische Landse Bibliothek
Ultimate Parent Company: Land Baden-Wuerttemberg

Bibliotheks und Informationssystem der Universitaet Oldenburg
Uhlhornsweg 49-55, Oldenburg 26129
Mailing Address: Postfach 2541, Oldenburg 26015
Tel: (0441) 7984001 *Fax:* (0441) 798-4040
E-mail: zi@bis.uni-oldenburg.de
Web Site: www.bis.uni-oldenburg.de/
Telex: 25655 unoldd
Key Personnel
Librarian: Hans-Joahim Waetjen
E-mail: waetjen@bis.uni-oldenburg.de
Founded: 1974
Research library, scientific publishing house, media centre.

Universitaet Bonn
Universitaets -und Landesbibliothek, Adenauerralle 39-41, 53113 Bonn
Mailing Address: Postfach 2460, 53014 Bonn
Tel: (0228) 737350 *Fax:* (0228) 737546
E-mail: ulb@ulb.uni-bonn.de
Key Personnel
Librarian: Dr Renate Vogt *E-mail:* vogt@ulb.uni-bonn.de
Publication(s): *Universitaets -und Landesbibliothek Bonn*

Technische Universitaet Braunschweig
Universitaetsbibliothek Pockelsstr 14, 38106 Braunschweig
Mailing Address: Postfach 3329, 38023 Braunschweig
Tel: (0531) 3915011 *Fax:* (0531) 3915836
E-mail: ub@tu-bs.de
Key Personnel
Librarian: Prof Dietmar Brandes, PhD
Publication(s): *Veroeffentlichungen der Universitaetsbibliothek Braunschweig*

Die Deutsche Bibliothek
Adickesallee 1, 60322 Frankfurt am Main
Tel: (069) 15250 *Fax:* (069) 15251010
E-mail: info@dma.ddb.de
Web Site: www.ddb.de
Key Personnel
President: Dr Elisabeth Niggemann
Acting Representative: Ute Schwens
Contact: Kathrin Ansorge *Tel:* (069) 15251004 *E-mail:* ansorge@dbf.ddb.de
Founded: 1947
National Library & National Bibliographic Agency.
Publication(s): *Bibliographie der im Ausland erschienenen deutschsprachigen Veroeffentlichungen*; *Deutsche Nationalbibliographie*
Branch Office(s)
Deutsches Musikarchiv Berlin, Gaertner St 25-32, 12207 Berlin, Acting Representative: Ingo Kolasa *Tel:* 030 770020 *Fax:* 030 77002299 *E-mail:* info@dma.ddb.de *Web Site:* www.ddb.de
Deutsche Buecherei Leipzig, Deutscher Platz 1, Leipzig, Acting Representative: Inmgard Spencker *Tel:* (0341) 22710 *Fax:* (0341) 2271444 *E-mail:* info@dbl.ddb.de *Web Site:* www.ddb.de

LIBRARIES — GERMANY

Deutsche Buecherei Leipzig, see Die Deutsche Bibliothek

Deutsche Zentralbibliothek fuer Wirtschaftswissenschaften (ZBW)/Bibliothek des Instituts fuer Weltwirtschaft
Duesternbrooker Weg 120, 24105 Kiel
Tel: (0431) 8814-383 *Fax:* (0431) 8814520
E-mail: info@zbw.ifw-kiel.de *Cable:* WELTWIRTSCHAFT KIEL
Key Personnel
Dir: H Thomsen *E-mail:* h.thomsen@zbw.ijw-kiel.de
Contact: Iris Reimers *E-mail:* zbw@zbw.ijw-kiel.de
German National Library for Economics; Deutsche Zentralbibliothele fuer Wirtschaftswissenschaften.
Publication(s): *Bibliography on Economic Transition in Eastern Europe*; *Bibliography on German Unification*; *Im Dienste der Wirtschaftswissenschaften*; *Kieler Bibliographien zu aktuellen oekonomischen Themen*; *Kieler Schriftumskunden zu Wirtschaft und Gesellschaft*; *Statistiche Uebersichten fuer das Jahr 2001*; *Thesaurus der ZBW*; *Wirtschaftswissenschafte Literatur*: (Bibliothek, Dokumentation, Information. 2001, Kiel)

Deutscher Bundestag Bibliothek
Bibliothek, Platz der Republik, 11011 Berlin
Tel: (030) 22732372 *Fax:* (030) 22736087
Web Site: www.bundestag.de
Telex: 0886808

Deutsches Bucharchiv Munchen, Institut fur Buchwissenschaften
Von-der-Tann-Str 5, 80539 Munich
Tel: (089) 7901220 *Fax:* (089) 7901419
E-mail: kontakt@bucharchiv.de
Web Site: www.bucharchiv.de
Key Personnel
Doctor of Law: Prof Ludwig Delp *Tel:* (089) 7901190
Institute for Book Research.
Publication(s): *Buchwissenschafiliche Beitraege aus dem Deutschen Bucharchiv Muenchen*
Branch Office(s)
Bibliothek, Salvatorplatz 1, 80333 Munich *Tel:* 089 2919510 *Fax:* 089 29195195

Deutsches Musikarchiv Berlin, see Die Deutsche Bibliothek

Die Deutsche Bibliothek/Deutsche Bucherei Leipzig
Deutscher Platz, 04103 Leipzig
Tel: (0341) 22710 *Fax:* (0341) 2271444
E-mail: info@dbl.ddb.de
Web Site: www.ddb.de
Key Personnel
Dir: Dr Elisabeth Niggemann
Contact: Joerg Raeuber; Birgit Schneider
National Library & National Bibliography Agency.
Publication(s): *Deutsche Nationalbibliographie* (German National Bibliography, weekly)

Universitaet Dortmund
Universitaetsbibliothek Vogelpothsweg 76, 44227 Dortmund
Tel: (0231) 7554029; (0231) 7554001; (0231) 4554030 *Fax:* (0231) 7554032
Telex: 822445 Unido d
Key Personnel
Librarian: Marlene Nagelsmeier-Linke

Universitaetsbibliothek Eichstaett
Universitaetsallee 1, 85072 Eichstaett
Tel: (08421) 931330 *Fax:* (08421) 931791
E-mail: ub-direktion@ku-eichstaett.de
Key Personnel
Librarian: Hermann Holzbauer

Ernst-Moritz-Arndt Universitat Greifswald, Universitatsbibliothek
Rubenowstr 4, 17487 Greifswald
Tel: (03834) 861502 *Fax:* (03834) 861501
E-mail: ub@rz.uni-greifswald.de
Key Personnel
Dir: Dr Hans-Armin Knoeppel
Founded: 1604
Publication(s): *Buchmalerei aus Handschriften und Drucken der Universitaetsbibliothek Greifswald*; *Die Vitae Pomeranorum*

Fachhochschule Dortmund (University of Applied Sciences)
Vogelpoths Weg 76, 44227 Dortmund
Mailing Address: Postfach 105018, 44047 Dortmund
Tel: (0231) 7554047 *Fax:* (0231) 7554604
E-mail: bibliothek@fhb.fh-dortmund.de
Web Site: www.fhb.fh.dortmund.de
Key Personnel
Librarian: Dr Robert Klitzke *E-mail:* klitzke@fhb.fh-dortmund.de
Founded: 1972

Fachhochschule Stuttgart Hochschule der Medien (University of Applied Sciences School of Media)
Wolframstr 32, 70191 Stuttgart
Tel: (0711) 257060 *Fax:* (0711) 25706300
E-mail: info@hdm-stuttgart.de; friedling@hdm-stuttgart.de
Web Site: www.hdm-stuttgart.de
Key Personnel
Contact: Prof Agnes Juelkenbeck; Prof Alexander Roos; Prof Peter Vodosek *E-mail:* vodosek@hdm-stuggart.de
Founded: 1942
Information material on demand.
Publication(s): *HDM aktuell* (biannually)

Freie Universitaet Berlin (Free University of Berlin)
Universitaetsbibliothek Garystr 39, 14195 Berlin
Tel: (030) 83854224; (030) 83854093 *Fax:* (030) 83853738
E-mail: leitung@ub.fu-berlin.de
Web Site: www.ub.fu-berlin.de
Key Personnel
Librarian: Ulrich Naumann *E-mail:* naumann@ub.fu-berlin.de
Founded: 1952

Hamburgisches Welt-Wirtschafts-Archiv (HWWA) Bibliothek (Hamburg Institute of International Economics)
Neuer Jungfernstieg 21, 20347 Hamburg
Tel: (040) 42834 242 *Fax:* (040) 42834 550
E-mail: biblio@hwwa.de
Web Site: www.hwwa.de
Key Personnel
Head, Library: Wolfgang Scherwath *E-mail:* scherwath@hwwa.de
Founded: 1908
Special library for economy.

Universitaetsbibliothek Hannover und Technische Informationsbibliothek (University Library of Hannover & Technical Information Library)
Universitatsbibliothek und TIB Welfengarten 1B, 30167 Hannover
Mailing Address: Postfach 6080, 30167 Hannover
Tel: (0511) 7622268 *Fax:* (0511) 715936
E-mail: ubtib@tib.uni-hannover.de
Web Site: www.tib.uni-hannover.de
Key Personnel
Head Librarian: Uwe Rosemann
Deputy Librarians: Dr Irina Sens; Petra Duren
Founded: 1831 ((University Library of Hannover; Technical Information Library founded in 1959))
Document Delivery.
Publication(s): *TIBORDER-Document Delivery System* (online catalog on STN International)

Herzog August Bibliothek
Lessingplatz 1, 38299 Wolfenbuettel
Mailing Address: Postfach 1364, 38299 Wolfenbuettel
Tel: (05331) 8080 *Fax:* (05331) 808173; (05331) 808134
E-mail: direktor@hab.de
Key Personnel
Dir: Prof Paul Raabe, PhD; Prof Helwig Schmidt-Olintzer

Herzogin Anna Amalia Bibliothek
Platz der Demokratie 1, 99423 Weimar
Mailing Address: Postfach 2012, 99401 Weimar
Tel: (03643) 545200 *Fax:* (03643) 545220
E-mail: haab@weimar-klassik.de
Key Personnel
Dir: Dr Michael Knoche
Library is part of the Stiftung Weimarer Klassik.
Publication(s): *Internationale Bibliographie zur Deutschen Klassik, 1750-1850*
Parent Company: Stiftung Weimarer Klassik

Hessische Landes und Hochschulbibliothek Darmstadt
Division of Technische Universitat Darmstadt
Schloss, 64283 Darmstadt
Tel: (06151) 165800 *Fax:* (06151) 165897
E-mail: auskunft@lhb.tu-darmstadt.de
Web Site: elib.tu-darmstadt.de/lhb
Key Personnel
Librarian: Dr Hans Georg Nolte-Fischer
Executive Secretary: Doris Michel *Tel:* (06151) 165801 *E-mail:* michel@lhb.tu-darmstadt.de
Founded: 1568
The Hesse State & University Library.
Branch Office(s)
Zweigbibliothek Lichtwiese, El Lissitzkystr 1, 64287 Darmstadt *Tel:* (06151) 165867 *E-mail:* monikah@lhb.tu-darmstadt.de
Patentinformationszentrum, Schoefferstr 8, 64295 Darmstadt *E-mail:* info@main-piz.de *Web Site:* www.patent.fh-darmstadt.de

Technische Hochschule Aachen (Aachen University of Technology)
Hochschulbibliothek Templergraben 61, 52062 Aachen
Mailing Address: RWTH Aachen, 52056 Aachen
Tel: (0241) 804445 *Fax:* (0241) 8888273
Telex: 0832704
Key Personnel
Librarian: Ulrike Eich
Founded: 1870

Humboldt Universitaet zu Berlin
Universitaetsbibliothek, Dorotheenstr 27, 10117 Berlin 70099
Tel: (030) 20933212 *Fax:* (030) 20933207
E-mail: info@ub.hu-berlin.de
Web Site: www.ub.hu-berlin.de

Ibero-Amerikanisches Institut Preussischer Kulturbesitz (Ibero American Institute)
Potsdamerstr 37, 10785 Berlin
Mailing Address: Postfach 1247, 10722 Berlin
Tel: (030) 2662520 *Fax:* (030) 2662503
E-mail: iai@iai.spk-berlin.de
Web Site: www.iai.spk-berlin.de
Telex: 183160 staab d

Key Personnel
Dir: Dr Gunther Maihold
Library Dir: Peter Altekrueger *Tel:* (030) 2662533
 E-mail: altekrueger@iai.spk-berlin.de
Founded: 1930
Research institute & special library for Latin America, Spain & Portugal
Membership: Lasa, Salalm, Redial, Adlaf, Liber.
Publication(s): Biblioteca Luso-Brasileira (book); *Bibliotheca Iberoamericana* (book); *Ibero-Analysen* (book); *Ibero-Bibliographien* (book); *Iberoamericana, Indiana* (journal)

International Youth Library, see Internationale Jugendbibliothek

Internationale Jugendbibliothek
Schloss Blutenburg, 81247 Munich
Tel: (089) 8912110 *Fax:* (089) 8117553
E-mail: bib@ijb.de
Key Personnel
Contact: Carola Gade *Tel:* (089) 89121130
International children & youth literature, posters, original illustrations, manuscripts & handwriting. 520,000 volumes in over 730 languages & 250 current magazines.
Publication(s): IJB Report (biannual report)

Universitat Konstanz
Universitatsbibliothek Universitatsstr 10, 78464 Konstanz
Mailing Address: Postfach 5560, 78461 Konstanz
Tel: (07531) 882800 *Fax:* (07531) 883082
Telex: 073359
Key Personnel
Librarian: Klaus Franken

Leipziger Staedtische Bibliotheken
Wilhelm-Leuschner-Platz 10/11, 04107 Leipzig
Mailing Address: Postfach 100927, 04009 Leipzig
Tel: (0341) 123 53 43 *Fax:* (0341) 123 53 05
E-mail: stadtbib@leipzig.de
Web Site: www.leipzig.de/stadtbib.htm
Key Personnel
Dir: Reinhard Stridde

Library of Contemporary History, see Bibliothek fur Zeitgeschichte/Library of Contemporary History

Landesbibliothek Mecklenburg-Vorpommern
Am Dom 2, 19055 Schwerin
Mailing Address: Postfach 011013, 19010 Schwerin
Tel: (0385) 558440 *Fax:* (0385) 5584424
E-mail: lb@lbmv.de
Web Site: www.lbmv.de
Key Personnel
Dir: Dr R Juergen Wegener *E-mail:* wegener@lbmv.de
Publication(s): CD-ROM Geschichtliche Bibliographie von Mecklenburg von den Anfangen bis 1945 (1998, bibiography); *Mecklenburg-Vorpommersche Bibliographie* (annually, bibliographical yearbook); *Periodica aus Mecklenburg-Vorpommern* (1996, bibliography of in Meckl-Vorp published newspapers, journals, yearbooks)
Branch Office(s)
Musikaliensammlung, Molkereistr 3, 19053 Schwerin, Herr Jedeck *Tel:* (0385) 5584431 *Fax:* (0385) 5584439 *E-mail:* jedeck@lbmv.de

Niedersaechsische Landesbibliothek
Waterloostr 8, 30169 Hannover
Tel: (0511) 12670 *Fax:* (0511) 12 67202
E-mail: nlb@zb.nlb-hannover.de
Web Site: www.nlb-hannover.de
Key Personnel
Librarian: Dr Wolfgang Dittrich *Tel:* (0511) 126301 *E-mail:* wolfgang.dittrich@zb.nlb-hannover.de
Founded: 1665

Niedersaechsische Staats- und Universitaetsbibliothek Goettingen (Lower Saxony State & University Library Goettingen)
Division of University of Goettingen
Platz der Goettinger Sieben 1, 37073 Goettingen
Mailing Address: 37070 Goettingen
Tel: (0551) 395212 (Secretariat); (0551) 393079 (Chemie); (0551) 392360 (Physik) *Fax:* (0551) 395222; (0551) 395220 (Bereichsbibliothek Medizin)
E-mail: sub@mail.sub.uni-goettingen.de
Web Site: www.sub.uni-goettingen.de
Key Personnel
Dir: Prof Elmar Mittler, PhD *Tel:* (0551) 395210 *E-mail:* mittler@mail.sub.uni-goettingen.de
Founded: 1734

Universitatsbibliothek Regensburg
Universitatsstr 31, 93053 Regensburg
Tel: (0941) 943390003 *Fax:* (0941) 9433285
Telex: 65658 unire d
Key Personnel
Contact: Dr Friedrich Geisselmann
 E-mail: friedrichgeisselmann@bibliothek.uni-regensburg.de

Rheinische Landesbibliothek Koblenz (Rhenish Regional Library of the German 'Land' Rhineland Palatinate)
Bahnofplatz 14, 56068 Koblenz
Mailing Address: PO Box 201352, 56013 Koblenz
Tel: (0261) 9150040 *Fax:* (0261) 9150091
E-mail: info@rlb.de
Web Site: www.rlb.de
Key Personnel
Dir: Dr Ernst-Ludwig Berz *Tel:* (0261) 9150014 *Fax:* (0261) 9150090 *E-mail:* berz@rlb.de
General Research Library.

Universitaet Rostock Universitaetsbibliothek
Altbettelmoenschtrasse 4, 18051 Rostock
Tel: (0381) 4982283 *Fax:* (0381) 4982270
E-mail: ub-sekretariat@ub.uni-rostock.de00.de
Key Personnel
Dir: Dr Ing Peter Hoffmann *E-mail:* peter.hoffmann@ub.uni-rostock.de

Saarlaendische Universitaets und Landesbibliothek (University & State Library of the Saarland)
Im Stadtisald, Geb 3, 66123 Saarbruecken
Mailing Address: Postfach 151141, 66041 Saarbruecken
Tel: (0681) 3022070 *Fax:* (0681) 3022796
E-mail: sulb@sulb.uni-saarland.de
Web Site: www.sulb.uni-saarland.de
Key Personnel
Dir: Prof Bernd Hagenau
Acquisitions: Gabriele Mohrbach *Tel:* (0681) 302 2087 *E-mail:* g.mohrbach@sulb.uni-saarland.de
Founded: 1950
Specialize in academic library.
Parent Company: Univsersitaet des Saarlandes
Branch Office(s)
Medizinische Bibliothek, 66421 Homburg, Contact: Reinhard Kraemer *Tel:* (0684) 162 6059 *Fax:* (0684) 162 6033 *E-mail:* m.kraemer@sulb.uni-saarland.de

Saechsische Landesbibliothek- Staats- und Universitaetsbibliothek Dresden
01054 Dresden
Tel: (0351) 4634308 *Fax:* (0351) 4637173
E-mail: direktion@slub-dresden.de
Key Personnel
Dir General: Prof Juergen Hering
Publication(s): Aurich, Frank; Die Anfange des Buchdrucks in Dresden; Bibliographie Geschichte der Technik; Hagemeyer, Kerstin: Ober Naumann, den guten Menschen und groBen Kuunstler; Loesch, Perk: L'art de la fortification; Saechsische Bibliographie; Schwarze Kopfe; SLUB-Kurier; Tradition und Herausforderung

Walther-Schuecking-Institut fuer Internationales Recht an der Universitaet Kiel
Christian-Albrechts-Platz 4, 24118 Kiel
Tel: (0431) 8802367 *Fax:* (0431) 8801619
E-mail: fb.internat-recht@ub.uni-kiel.de
Telex: 292656 Cauki
Publication(s): German Yearbook Of International Law; Veroeffentlichungen des Walther-Schuecking-Instituts fuer Internationales Recht (series)

Staats- und Universitaetsbibliothek Hamburg Carl von Ossietzky
Von-Melle Park 3, 20146 Hamburg
Tel: (040) 42838 2233 *Fax:* (040) 42838-3352
E-mail: auskunft@sub.uni-hamburg.de
Web Site: www.sub.uni-hamburg.de
Key Personnel
Dir: Prof Peter Rau, PhD
Founded: 1479
State & University Library. All areas of science; Special collections: Policies & Peace Research, Science of Administration, Spain & Portugal. Coastal & sea fishing, language & culture of North American Indians & Eskimos.

Staats- und Universitatsbibliothek Bremen
PF 330160, 28331 Bremen
Mailing Address: Bibliothekstrasse, 28359 Bremen
Tel: (0421) 2182601 *Fax:* (0421) 2182614
E-mail: suub@zfn.uni-bremen.de
Telex: 0245811 unibr d
Key Personnel
Library Dir: Annette Rath-Beckmann

Staatsbibliothek zu Berlin - Preussischer Kulturbesitz (Berlin State Library - Prussian Cultural Foundation)
Unter den Linden 8, Haus 1, 10117 Berlin-Mitte
Mailing Address: Potsdamer Str 33, 10785 Berlin
Tel: (030) 266-0 *Fax:* (030) 266-1721; (030) 266-2319
E-mail: generaldiv@sbb.spk-berlin.de
Web Site: staatsbibliothek-berlin.de
Key Personnel
General Dir: Graham Jefcoate
Contact: Jeanette Lamble *E-mail:* jeanette.lamble@sbb.spk-berlin.de
Founded: 1661
International Research Library.
Publication(s): Beitraege aus der Staatsbibliothek zu Berlin - PK (irregularly); *International ISBN Publishers' Directory* (annually); *ISBN Newsletter* (irregularly); *ISBN Review* (annually); *ISMN Newsletter* (irregularly); *Jahresbericht* (annually); *Kartographische Bestandsverzeichnisse* (irregularly); *Kataloge der Handschriftenabteilung, Reihe 1: Handschriften & Reihe 2: Nachlaesse* (irregularly); *Kataloge der Musikabteilung* (irregularly); *Ausstellungskataloge USW* (irregularly, exhibition catalogues); *Veroeffentlichungen der Osteuropa-Abteilung* (irregularly)
Parent Company: Stiftung Preussischer Kulturbesitz (Prussian Cultural Foundation)

Stadt Frankfurt a Main Stadt-und Universitaetsbibliothek
Bockenheimer Landstr 134-138, 60325 Frankfurt am Main
Tel: (069) 21239-381 *Fax:* (069) 21239-062

E-mail: ditektion@stub.uni-frankfurt.de
Key Personnel
Librarian: B Dugall

Stadt- und Universitaetsbibliothek
Bockenheimer Landstr 134-138, 60325 Frankfurt am Main
Tel: (069) 21239381 *Fax:* (069) 21239062
E-mail: direktion@uni-frankfurt.com
Key Personnel
Dir: Mr Dugall

Thueringer Universitaets- und Landesbibliothek Jena
Bibliotheksplalt 2, 07743 Jena
Tel: (03641) 940 000 *Fax:* (03641) 940 002
E-mail: thulb@thulb.uni-jena.de
Key Personnel
Librarian: Dr Sabine Wefers
Publication(s): *Keine Aenderungen*; *Thueringen - Bibliographic (Online)*

Universitat Ulm
Universitatsbibliothek Schlossbau 38, 89079 Ulm
Tel: (0731) 502-01 *Fax:* (0731) 5022038
Telex: 0712567
Key Personnel
Dir: S Franke

Universitaet Kaiserslautern
Paul-Ehrlich-Str, Geb 32, 67633 Kaiserslautern
Mailing Address: Postfach 2040, 67608 Kaiserslautern
Tel: (0631) 2052241 *Fax:* (0631) 2052355
E-mail: unibib@ub.uni-kl.de
Web Site: www.uni-kl.de/bibliothek

Universitaets - und Landesbibliothek Sachsen-Anhalt
August-Bebel-Str 13 u 50, 06098 Halle/Saale
Tel: (0345) 5522001 *Fax:* (0345) 5527140
E-mail: direktion@bibliothek.uni-halle.de
Key Personnel
Dir: Dr Heiner Schnelling *Tel:* (0345) 5522000 *E-mail:* schnelling@bibliothek.uni-halle.de
Founded: 1696

Universitaets und Landesbiblothek Muenster
Krummer Timpen 3-5, 48143 Muenster
Mailing Address: Postfach 8029, 48043 Muenster
Tel: (0251) 8324022 *Fax:* (0251) 8328398
E-mail: ulbmail@uni-muenster.de
Key Personnel
Contact: Dr Roswitha Poll

Universitaets- und Stadtbibliothek (Cologne University & City Library)
Universitatsbibliothek 33, 50931 Cologne
Tel: (0221) 4702260; (0221) 4702214 *Fax:* (0221) 4705166
E-mail: usbsekr@ub.uni-koeln.de; sekretariat@ub.uni-koeln.de
Web Site: www.nb.nui-koeln.de
Key Personnel
Dir & Professor: Dr Wolfgang Schmitz
Contact: Anne Fuentes *Tel:* (0221) 4703307 *E-mail:* fuentes@ub.uni-koeln.de
Founded: 1920

Universitaetsbibliothek
Werthmannplatz 2, 79098 Freiburg im Breisgau
Mailing Address: Postfach 1629, 79016 Freiburg im Breisgau
Tel: (0761) 2033900 (management); (0761) 2033918 (inquiries) *Fax:* (0761) 2033987
E-mail: info@ub.uni-freiburg.de
Web Site: www.ub.uni-freiburg.de
Key Personnel
Dir: Baerbel Schubel

Contact: Dr Suehl-Strohmenger *Tel:* (0761) 203 3924 *E-mail:* suehl@ub.uni-freiburg.de
Publication(s): *Festschrift: Tradition-Organisation-Innovation*; *Reihe: Schriften der Universitaets Bibliothek Freiburg*

Universitaetsbibliothek Bamberg
Feldkirchenstr 21, Zufahrt: Am Heidelsteig, 96052 Bamberg
Mailing Address: Postfach 2705, 96018 Bamberg
Tel: (0951) 8631503 *Fax:* (0951) 8631565
E-mail: unibibliothek.bamberg@unibib.uni-bamberg.de
Key Personnel
Chief Librarian: Dr Dieter Karasek *E-mail:* dieter.karasek@unibib.uni-bamberg.de

Universitaetsbibliothek Bochum
Universitaetsstr 150, 44780 Bochum
Tel: (49234) 3222350; (49234) 3222351 *Fax:* (49234) 3214736
Web Site: www.ub.ruhr-uni-bochum.de
Key Personnel
Dir: Dr Erdmute Lapp *E-mail:* erda.lapp@ruhr-uni-bochum.de
Publication(s): *Bibliotheksfuehrer* (2002); *Ruhr-Universitaet Bochum* (1978)

Universitaetsbibliothek Erlangen-Nuernberg
Universitaetsstr 4, 91054 Erlangen
Tel: (09131) 85-22151 *Fax:* (09131) 85-29309
E-mail: direktion@bib.uni-erlangen.de
Web Site: www.ub.uni-erlangen.de
Key Personnel
Dir: Dr Hans-Otto Keunecke

Universitaetsbibliothek Heidelberg
Ploeck 107-109, 69117 Heidelberg
Mailing Address: Postfach 105749, 69047 Heidelberg
Tel: (06221) 542380 *Fax:* (06221) 542623
E-mail: ub@ub.uni-heidelberg.de
Key Personnel
Dir: Dr Hermann Josef Dorpinghaus
Publication(s): *Bibliothek-Forschung und Praxis*; *Bibliothek und Wissenschaft*; *Heidelberger Bibliothehsschriften*; *Neuerwerbungslisten der Sondersammelgebiete Aegyptologie, Klassische Archaeologie, Mittlere und Neuere Kunstgeschichte*; *Zeitschriftenverzeichnis Aegyptologie, Klassische Archaeologie und Mittlere und Neuere Kunstgeschichte*; *Heidelberger Zeitschriftenverzeichnis*

Universitaetsbibliothek Leipzig
Universitaetsbibliothek, Beethovenstr 6, 04107 Leipzig
Tel: (0341) 9730500 *Fax:* (0341) 9730599
E-mail: ba@ub.uni-leipzig.de
Key Personnel
Dir: Dr Phil Ekkehard Henschke
Publication(s): *Geschriebenes aber bleibt*

Universitaetsbibliothek Mannheim
Schloss Ostfluegel, 68131 Mannheim
Tel: (0621) 181 2941 *Fax:* (0621) 181 2939
E-mail: biblubma@bib.uni-mannheim.de
Web Site: www.bib.uni-mannheim.de
Key Personnel
Dir Dipl Phys: Benz Christian

Universitaetsbibliothek Tuebingen
Wilhelmstr 32, 72016 Tuebingen
Mailing Address: Postfach 2620, 72016 Tuebingen
Tel: (07071) 2972577 *Fax:* (07071) 293123
E-mail: sekretariat@ub.uni-tuebingen.de
Key Personnel
Contact: Dr Berndt von Egidy

Universitaetsbibliothek Wuppertal
Gauss-Str 20, 42119 Wuppertal
Mailing Address: Postfach 100127, 42001 Wuppertal
Tel: (0202) 439-2690 *Fax:* (0202) 439-2695
E-mail: ubwupper@bib.uni-wuppertal.de
Web Site: www.bib.uni-wuppertal.de
Key Personnel
Librarian: Dr Dieter Staeglich

Universitat Wuerzburg
Universitaetsbibliothek Am Hubland, 97074 Wuerzburg
Tel: (931) 8885943 *Fax:* (931) 8885970
E-mail: direktion@bibliothek.uni-wuerzburg.de
Web Site: www.bibliothek.uni-wuerzburg.de
Key Personnel
Librarian: K Suedekum
Publication(s): *Verzeichnis auf Anfrage*

Universitatbibliothek (University Library)
Alte Munze 16, 49076 Osnabruck
Mailing Address: Postfach 4469, 49034 Osnabruck
Tel: (0541) 9694320 *Fax:* (0541) 9694482
E-mail: aaa@uni-osnabrueck.de
Web Site: www.uni-osnabrueck.de
Key Personnel
Librarian: Eilhard Cordes
Founded: 1974
Publication(s): *Ausstellungs Kataloge*
Parent Company: University of Osnabruck

Universitatsbibliothek Augsburg
Universitatsstr 22, 86159 Augsburg
Mailing Address: Universitaetsbibliothek Augsburg, 86135 Augsburg
Tel: (0821) 5985300 *Fax:* (0821) 5985354
E-mail: dir@bibliothek.uni-augsburg.de
Web Site: www.bibliothek.uni-augsburg.de
Telex: 53830
Key Personnel
Contact: Eva Schoeppl *Tel:* (0821) 5985304 *E-mail:* eva.schoeppl@bibliothek.uni-augsburg.de
Founded: 1970

Wissenschaftliche Allgemeinbibliothek der Stadt Erfurt
Dompl 1, 99084 Erfurt
Mailing Address: Postfach 243, 99084 Erfurt
Tel: (0361) 5624876; (0361) 6551590 *Fax:* (0361) 6462071; (0361) 6551599
Key Personnel
Contact: Heidemarie Trenkmann

Wuerttembergische Landesbibliothek
Konrad-Adenauerstr 8, 70173 Stuttgart
Mailing Address: Postfach 105441, 70047 Stuttgart
Tel: (0711) 2124424 *Fax:* (0711) 2124422
E-mail: direktion@wlb-stuttgart.de
Web Site: www.wlb-stuttgart.de
Key Personnel
Dir: Dr H Kowark
Contact: Horst Hilger *Tel:* (0711) 2124390; (0711) 2124504 *E-mail:* hilger@wlb-stuttgart.de
Founded: 1765
Regional library for the state of Baden-Wurttemberg, currently comprised of 4.65 million media items.
Publication(s): *Ausstellungs- und Bestandskataloge*

Zentral- und Landesbibliothek Berlin (ZLB) (Central & Regional Library of Berlin)
Blucherplatz 1, 10922 Berlin
Tel: (030) 902260; (030) 90226-401 *Fax:* (030) 90226-494
E-mail: info@zlb.de
Web Site: www.zlb.de

Key Personnel
General Dir: Dr Claudia Lux *Tel:* (030) 90226-450 *E-mail:* lux@zlb.de
Founded: 1901
Full library & information services.

ZLB, see Zentral- und Landesbibliothek Berlin (ZLB)

Ghana

Balme Library, see University of Ghana Library

British Council Library
Liberia Rd, Accra
Mailing Address: PO Box 771, Accra
Tel: (021) 244744; (021) 663979 *Fax:* (021) 240330
Telex: 2369 brico gh
Key Personnel
Education Information Officer: Benjamin Addo *E-mail:* benjaminaddo@bcgha.africainline.com.gh
Head Libraries & Information Services: Ruth Osci

Council for Scientific & Industrial Research-Institute for Scientific & Technological Information
PO Box M 32, Accra
Tel: (021) 778808; (021) 764822
E-mail: csir@ghana.com; cemensah@hotmail.com
Web Site: www.csir.org.gh
Telex: SCIENCES
Key Personnel
Dir: C Entsuah-Mensah
Council for Scientific & Industrial Research Library.
Publication(s): *CSIR Newsletter* (quarterly); *Directory of high level manpower* (every 5 years); *Directory of Research Projects (Science & Technology) in Ghana (1990)* (every 5 years); *Directory of Special and Research Libraries in Ghana*; *Ghana Journal of Agricultural Science* (semi-annual); *Ghana Journal of Science* (semi-annual); *Ghana Science Abstracts* (annually); *Union List of Scientific Serials in Ghanaian Libraries (1976)*

CSIR-INSTI, see Council for Scientific & Industrial Research-Institute for Scientific & Technological Information

Geological Survey Department Reference Library
Ministry of Lands & Mineral Resources, Accra
Mailing Address: PO Box M80, Accra
Tel: (021) 228093 *Fax:* (021) 228063
Key Personnel
Librarian: E Hammond

George Padmore Research Library on African Affairs
PO Box 2970, Accra
Tel: (021) 228402
Key Personnel
Librarian: Sarah Kanda; Christina D T Kwei
Publication(s): *Current Ghana Bibliography* (every two months); *Ghana National Bibliography* (annually)

Ghana Library Board
Thorpe Rd, Accra
Mailing Address: PO Box 663, Accra
Tel: (021) 662795 *Cable:* GHANLIB ACCRA
Key Personnel
Dir & Librarian: David Cornelius
The Research Library on African Affairs, a division of the Ghana Library Board performs some functions of a National Library for Ghana.
Publication(s): *Ghana National Bibliography, A Guide to Creative Writing by Africans in English* (Annual Report)

Ghana Institute of Management & Public Administration, Library & Documentation Centre
Greenhill, Achimota, Accra
Mailing Address: PO Box 50, Achimota
Tel: 4016813 ext 224 1 *Fax:* 667681
Telex: 2551 Gimpa Gh *Cable:* GIMPA ACHIMOTA
Key Personnel
Librarian: Moses Osei Bonsu

Institute of African Studies Library
University of Ghana, Legon, Accra
Mailing Address: PO Box 73, Legon, Accra
Tel: (021) 500512 *Fax:* (021) 667701; (021) 500512; (021) 502397
E-mail: africans@africanline.com.gh
Key Personnel
Assistant Librarian: Mrs Olive Adoah
Founded: 1901
Publication(s): *Research Review* (magazine)

Kwame Nkrumah University of Science & Technology Library
Private Post Bag, Kumasi
Tel: (051) 60199; (051) 60133 *Fax:* (051) 60358
E-mail: ustlib@libr.ug.edu.gh
Key Personnel
University Librarian: Mrs H R Asamoah-Hassan
Founded: 1951

School of Administration Library
University of Ghana, Legon, Accra
Mailing Address: PO Box 78, Legin, Accra
Tel: (021) 765915 *Fax:* (021) 777024
E-mail: soa@ug.gn.apc.org
Key Personnel
Librarian: Mr G Odartey-Cofie
Publication(s): *Journal of Management Studies* (Ghana)

Statistical Service
Economic Library, Accra
Mailing Address: PO Box 1098, Accra
Tel: (021) 666512 *Fax:* (021) 667069
Telex: 2205 MIFAEP GH
Key Personnel
Government Statistician: Dr Oti Boateng Daasebre
Deputy Government Statisticians: Dr K A Twum-Baah; Mr K Addomah-Gyabaah
Information Officer: Mr J Y Amankrah
Collection, compilation, analysis, publication & dissemination of statistical information.

University of Cape Coast Library
PMB, University Post Office, Cape Coast
Tel: (042) 24409; (042) 32480 *Fax:* (042) 32485
Telex: 2552 UCC GH
Key Personnel
Librarian: Richard Arkaifie

University of Ghana Library
Balme Library, Legon, Accra
Mailing Address: PO Box 24, Legon, Accra
Tel: (021) 775309; (021) 500014; (021) 302347 *Fax:* (021) 667701
E-mail: balme@ug.gn.apc.org *Cable:* UNIVERSITY LEGON
Key Personnel
Librarian: Mrs C O Kisiedu

Gibraltar

Gibraltar Garrison Library
2 Library Gardens, Gibraltar
Mailing Address: PO Box 374, Gibraltar
Tel: 77418 *Fax:* 79927
Key Personnel
Secretary: J M Searle
Gibraltor & Western Mediterranean Research by arrangement with secretary.

Gibraltar Library Service, see John Mackintosh Hall Library

John Mackintosh Hall Library
John Mackintosh Hall, 308 Main St, Gibraltar
Tel: 78000 *Fax:* 40843
Key Personnel
Dir: Geraldine Finlayson *E-mail:* gfjmh@gibnet.gi
Free lending library set up under will of late John Mackintosh, mainly adult fiction & nonfiction. Now incorporating the Gibraltar Library Service.

Greece

Athens Academy Library
28 Odos Venizelou, 106 79 Athens
Tel: (01) 3600209

British Council Library
Kolonaki Sq, 106 73 Athens
Mailing Address: PO Box 3488, 10210 Athens
Tel: (01) 3692333 *Fax:* (01) 3634769
E-mail: british.council@britcoun.gr
Telex: 218799 Bric Gr
Key Personnel
Library Services Officer: Vana Dadakaridov *E-mail:* vana.dadakaridov@britcoun.gr

Ethnikon Idryma Erevnon
48 Vassileos Constantinou Ave, GR-11635 Athens
Tel: (01) 722981115 *Fax:* (01) 7246618
Telex: 224064 EIE GR
Key Personnel
Man Dir: Prof B Maglaris
President: Prof Nikos Athanassiades
National Hellenic Research Foundation.

Eugenides Foundation Technical Library
Leophoros Syngrou Ave 387, 17564 Athens
Tel: (01) 9411181 *Fax:* (01) 9417372
E-mail: library@eugenides_found.edu.gr
Cable: FONDATIONEVGE
Key Personnel
Librarian: Hara Brindesi

Gennadius Library
American School of Classical Studies at Athens, Odos Souidias 61, GR-10676 Athens
Tel: (01) 7210536 *Fax:* (01) 7237767
E-mail: djord@leon.nrcps.ariadne-t.gr
Key Personnel
Librarian: David Jordan
Dir: Dr Haris Kalligas
Publication(s): *The New Griffon, No 1, 1991* (In Greek)

National Library of Greece
Odos el Benizelu 32, 10679 Athens
Tel: (01) 3614413 *Fax:* (01) 3608495

E-mail: nikolopoulos@sysa.nlg.ariaolne-t.gr
Key Personnel
Dir: Dr Panayotis G Nicolopoulos

Library of the National Technological University of Athens
Odos 28, Octovriou 42, 106 82 Athens

Library of the Technical Chamber of Greece
Odos Lekka 23-25, 105 62 Athens
Tel: (01) 3254590 *Fax:* (01) 3237525

Library of the University of Crete
Rethimnon
Tel: (0831) 77900 *Fax:* (0831) 77909
Telex: 291145
Key Personnel
Librarian: Michael Tzekakis

Library of the University of Thessaloniki
c/o Aristotelian University of Thessaloniki, Panepistimiou, 540 06 Thessaloniki
Tel: (031) 996703 *Fax:* (031) 206138
Telex: 0412181 auth
Key Personnel
Librarian: D Dimitriou

Guatemala

Archivo General de Centro
America, 4a Ave 7-16, Zona 1, Guatemala City
Key Personnel
Dir: Arturo Valdes

Biblioteca Nacional de Guatemala
5 Avda 7-26, Zona 1, Guatemala City
Tel: (02) 2322443 *Fax:* (02) 2539071
E-mail: vicast@biblionet.edu.gt
Key Personnel
Librarian: Victor Castillo Lopez
National Library of Guatemala.

Biblioteca Central de la Universidad de San Carlos
Ciudad Universitaria, Zona 12, Guatemala City
Tel: (02) 767117
Key Personnel
Acting Dir: Lieda Ofelia Aguilar
Publication(s): *Boletin Bibliografico*; *Boletin Contenidos*

Guinea

Bibliotheque Nationale
BP 561, Conakry
Tel: (04) 61010
Key Personnel
Librarian: Lansana Sylla

Guyana

Guyana Medical Science Library
Georgetown Hospital Compound, Georgetown
Key Personnel
Librarian: Mrs Jennifer Wilson

National Library
PO Box 10240, Georgetown
Tel: (02) 62699
Key Personnel
Chief Librarian: Gwyneth E Browman
Publication(s): *Guyanese National Bibliography*

Haiti

Bibliotheque du Petit Seminaire
Port-au-Prince

Bibliotheque Haitienne des Freres de l'I.C., Saint Louis de Gonzague
180 Rue du Centre, BP 1758, Port-au-Prince HT 6110
Tel: 2232148; 2237508
Key Personnel
Dir: Br Ernest Even
Founded: 1920
Secteurs les plus importants du fonds documentaire; a) collections de journaux des XIXe et XXe siecles b) histoire de Saint-Domingue et de l'Haiti contemporaine c) litterature haitienne.

Bibliotheque Nationale d'Haiti (National Library)
193 rue du Centre, Port-au-Prince
Tel: 20236 *Fax:* 38773
Key Personnel
Dir: Francoise Beaulieu Thybulle

Holy See (Vatican City State)

Biblioteca Apostolica Vaticana
Cortile del Belvedere, 00120 Vatican City
Tel: (06) 69883302 *Fax:* (06) 69884795
E-mail: bav@librs6k.vatlib.it
Telex: 2024 Dirgental VA
Key Personnel
Prefect: Prof Don Raffaele Farina
Vatican Apostolic Library.

Honduras

Biblioteca Nacional de Honduras
Ave Salvador Mendieta No 411, Tegucigalpa
Tel: 228577 *Fax:* 228577
E-mail: binah%bn@sdnhon.org; binah@ns.hondunet.net
Key Personnel
Dir: Hector Roberto Luna

Sistema Bibliotecario
c/o Universidad Nacional Autonoma de Honduras, Ciudad Univeritaria, Tegucigalpa
Tel: 322204 *Fax:* 310675
Telex: 1289 Unah Ho
Key Personnel
Dir: Orfylia S Pinel
Publication(s): *Boletin del Sistema Bibliotecario*

Hong Kong

British Council Library
3 Supreme Court Rd, Admirality, Hong Kong
Tel: 2913 5125 *Fax:* 2913 5121
Telex: 74141 bcoun hx
Key Personnel
Assistant Dir, Information: L J Nairn

Chinese University of Hong Kong Library System
Shatin, New Territories
Tel: 2609-7301; 2609-7302 *Fax:* 2603-6952
E-mail: library@cuhk.edu.hk
Web Site: www.lib.cuhk.edu.hk/
Telex: 50301 Cuhk Hx *Cable:* SINOVERSITY
Key Personnel
University Librarian: Dr Colin Storey *Tel:* 2609-7318 *E-mail:* storey@cuhk.edu.hk
Publication(s): *Catalogue of the Chinese Rare Books in the Libraries of The Chinese University of Hong Kong*; *History of Medicine:* (an Annotated Bibliography of Titles at The Chinese University of Hong Kong No 7); *Newspapers of Hong Kong, 1841-1979* (No 6); *Serials of Hong Kong, 1845* (No 5); *Union Catalogue of Asian Fine Arts Collection* (No 8)
Branch Office(s)
Architecture Library *Tel:* 2609 6599 *Fax:* 2603 6584
Chung Chi College Library *Tel:* 2609 6969 *Fax:* 2603 5793
Li Ping Medical Library *Tel:* 2632 2459 *Fax:* 2637 7817
New Asia College Library *Tel:* 2609 7657 *Fax:* 2603 5796
United College Library *Tel:* 2609 7565 *Fax:* 2603 5729

The Hong Kong Polytechnic University Library
Hung Hom, Kowloon
Tel: 2766 6857 *Fax:* 2765 8274
Key Personnel
University Librarian: Barry Burton
   E-mail: lbbarry@polyu.edu.hk
Publication(s): *Hongkongiana:* (an index to selected Hong Kong periodicals electronic database)

Hong Kong Public Libraries
11/F Hong Kong Central Library, 66 Causeway Rd, Hong Kong
Tel: 2921 0208 *Fax:* 2415 8211
E-mail: enquiries@lcsd.gov.hk
Web Site: www.hkpl.gov.hk
Key Personnel
Assistant Dir: Michael Mak *E-mail:* mklmak@lcsd.gov.hk
Provide free public library services through a network of 69 libraries.

Sun Yat-Sen Library
172-174 Boundary St, Kowloon
Tel: 23365291
Key Personnel
Librarian: Mrs Megie M L Tong

University of Hong Kong Libraries
University of Hong Kong, Pokfulam Rd
Tel: 2859 7000; 2859 2203 *Fax:* 2858 9420
E-mail: libadmin@hkucc.hku.hk
Web Site: www.hku.hk/lib/
Key Personnel
Librarian: Dr Anthony W Ferguson
Deputy Librarian: Peter Sidorko; Lawrence Wai Hong Tam
Sub-Librarian (Administration): Shirley Sin
   Tel: 2859 2217 *E-mail:* syysin@hkucc.hku.hk

Founded: 1912
Publication(s): *The University of Hong Kong Libraries Publications Series*

Hungary

BME KTK, see Budapesti Muszaki es Guzdasagtudomanyi Egyetem Orszagos Muszaki Informacios Kozpont es Konyvtar

Budapesti Kozgazdasagtudomanyi es Allamigazoatasi Luyutemi Egyetem Kozponti Konyvtar (Budapest University of Economic Science & Public Administration-Central Library)
Zsil u 2, 1093 Budapest
Mailing Address: Postfach 489, 1093 Budapest 5
Tel: (01) 2175827 *Fax:* (01) 2174910
E-mail: huszar@mail.lib
Web Site: www.lib.bke.hu
Key Personnel
Librarian: Dr Hedvig Huszar
Central Library of Budapest University of Economic Sciences.

Budapesti Muszaki es Guzdasagtudomanyi Egyetem Orszagos Muszaki Informacios Kozpont es Konyvtar (Budapest University of Technology & Economics, National Technical Information Centre & Library)
Budafoki u 4-6, H-1111 Budapest
Tel: (01) 463-2441 *Fax:* (01) 463-2440
Key Personnel
Dir: Ilona Fonyo *E-mail:* ifonyo@omikk.bme.hu

Foszekesegyhazi Konyvtar (Cathedral Library)
Pazmany P U 2, H-2500 Esztergom
Tel: 33411891
E-mail: bibliotheca@ehf.hu *Cable:* BIBLIOTHECA ESZTERGOM
Key Personnel
Dir: Bela Czekli
Cathedral Library.

Fovarosi Szabo Ervin Konyvtar
Vlll Szabo Ervin ter 1, 1088 Budapest
Mailing Address: PO Box 487, 1371 Budapest
Tel: (01) 1185815 *Fax:* (01) 1185914
E-mail: h7448kis@huelia.bitnet
Key Personnel
Dir: Jenoe Kiss
Ervin Szabo Metropolitan Library.

Jozsef Attila Tudomanyegyetem Egyetemi Koenyvtar
Dugonics ter 13, 6701 Szeged
Mailing Address: Postfach 393, 6701 Szeged
Tel: (062) 454036 *Fax:* (062) 312718
E-mail: mader@bibl.u-szeged.hu
Key Personnel
Chief Librarian: Dr Bela Mader
University Library of the Attila Jozsef University.
Publication(s): *Acta Bibliothecaria* (all irregular); *Acta Universitatis Szegediensis de Attila Jozsef Nominatae*; *Dissertationes ex Bibliotheca Universitatis de Attila Jozsef nominatae*; *Koenyvtartoerteneti Fuezetek* (History of Libraries series, with German summaries, five vols published out of projected ten)

Koezponti Statisztikai Hivatal Koenyvtar es Dokumentacios Szolgalat
Keleti Karoly u 5, Budapest 1525
Mailing Address: Postfach 10, H-1525 Budapest
Tel: (01) 3456105 *Fax:* (01) 3456112

Key Personnel
Dir General: Dr Istvan Csahok *E-mail:* istvan.csahok@ksh.gov.hu
Library & Documentation Service of the Central Statistical Office.
Publication(s): *Magyarorszag toerteneti helysegnevtara 1773-1808* (Historical Gazetteer of Hungary, 2000); *Statisztikai modszerek-Temadokumentacio* (Statistical Methods-Surveys of Literature on Various Subjects, 2000); *Szakbibliografiak-Statisztikai adatforrasok bibliografia* (Special Bibliographies-Sources of Statistical Data Bibliography, 2002); *Toerteneti statisztikai fuezetek* (Papers on Historical Statistics, 2000); *Toerteneti statisztikai tanulmanyok* (Studies on Historical Statistics, 2000)

Kossuth Lajos Tudomanyegyetem Egyetemi Koenyvtar
Egyetem Ter 1, Pf 39, 4010 Debrecen
Tel: (052) 410443 *Fax:* (052) 316835
E-mail: ilevay@giant.lib.klte.hu
Telex: 72200
Key Personnel
Chief Librarian: Dr Olga Gomba
Dir General: Dr Iren Levay
Lajos Kossuth University Library.

Magyar Orszagos Leveltar (MOL) (National Archives of Hungary)
Becsi kapu ter 4, 1014 Budapest 1
Mailing Address: Postafiok 3, Budapest 1250
Tel: (01) 3565811 *Fax:* (01) 2121619
E-mail: mail@natarch.hu
Web Site: www.natarch.hu
Key Personnel
Dir: Lajos Gecsenyi, PhD *Tel:* (01) 3560975 *E-mail:* gecsenyi@natarch.hu
Founded: 1756
National Archives of Hungary.
Publication(s): *Leveltari Kozlemenyek* (Archival Publications, biannually, 1923, academical & scholar); *Magyar Orszagos Leveltar Kiadvanyai* (Publications of National Archives of Hungary, biannually)

Magyar Tudomanyos Akademia Koenyvtara (Library of the Hungarian Academy of Sciences)
Arany J u 1, Budapest 1051
Mailing Address: PF 1002, H-1245 Budapest
Tel: (01) 411 6100 *Fax:* (01) 311 6954
E-mail: mtak@vax.mtak.hu
Web Site: w3.mtak.hu
Key Personnel
Deputy Dir General: Dr Alojzia Domsa *E-mail:* domsa@vax.mtak.hu
Founded: 1826
Library of the Hungarian Academy of Sciences/Library of the HAS.
Publication(s): *Budapest Oriental Reprints Ser A & Ser B* (irregular, scientific monographs); *Catalogi Collectionis Manuscriptorum Bibliothecae Academiae Scientiarum Hungaricae* (irregular, catalogues of the holdings); *Oriental Studies* (irregular, scientific monographs); *Publicationes Bibliothecae Academiae Scientiarum Hungaricae* (irregular, scientific monographs)

MOL, see Magyar Orszagos Leveltar (MOL)

Orszagos Muoszaki, Informacios Koozpont es Koonyvtar (OMIKK) (National Technical Information Centre & Library)
1428 Budapest, Muzeum u 17, Budapest H-1428
Mailing Address: Postafiok 12, Budapest H-1428
Tel: (01) 3384074; (01) 3382300 *Fax:* (01) 3382414
E-mail: fotik@omk.omikk.hu

Key Personnel
Dir General: Akos Robert Herman, PhD *E-mail:* har@omk.omikk.hu
Librarian: Peter Szanto
Translation Department, offers translation from Hungarian & other languages
National Technical Information Centre & Library.
Publication(s): *Tudomanyos es Muoszaki Tajekoztatas* (Scientific & Technical Information)

Orszagos Szechenyi Koenyvtar
Budavari Palota F epuelet, 1827 Budapest
Tel: (01) 2243700 *Fax:* (01) 202-0804
E-mail: viki@oszk.hu
Key Personnel
Dir General: Geza Poprady
National Center for Library Science & Methodology, Hungarian national ISBN & ISDS Center.
Publication(s): *A magyar irodalom es irodalomtudomany bibliografaja* (Bibliography of Hungarian Literature & Literary Studies); *Az Orszagos Szechenyi Koenyvtar evkoenyve* (National Szechenyi Library Year Book); *Hungariaka informacio* (Hungarica information); *Kurrens Kuelfoeldi idoeszaki Kiadvanyok a Magyar Koenyvtarakban* (Current Foreign Periodical Publications in Hungarian Libraries); *Magyar Koenyveszet* (Cumulation of Hungarian national bibliography. Bibliography of books, annually); *Magyar nemzeti bibliografia Idoszaki kiadvanyok bibliografiaja* (Hungarian national bibliography of serials); *Magyar nemzeti bibliografia. Idoszaki kiadvanyok repertoriuma* (Hungarian national bibliography. Repertory of periodicals); *Magyar nemzeti bibliografia Koenyvek bibliografiaja* (Hungarian National Bibliography Bibliography of Books); *Magyar nemzeti bibliografia. Zenemuvek bibliografiaja* (Hungarian national bibliography of music scores & records); *Mikrofilmek cimjegyzeke. Idoszaki kiadvanyok* (List of Microfilm Titles. Periodical Publications); *Mikrofilmek cimjegyzeke. Modern nyomtatvanyok* (List of Microfilm Titles. Modern Printed Matter); *Mikrofilmek cimjegyzeke. Szines grafikai plakatok* (List of Microfilm Titles. Colored Graphic Posters); *Mikrofilmek cimjegyzeke. Zenei gyujtemeny. Zenemukeziratok* (List of Microfilm Titles. Music Collection. Music Manuscripts); *Uj periodikumok* (New periodicals)

Sarospataki Reformatus- Kollegium Tudomanyos Gyuejtemenyei Nagykoenyvtar
Rakoczy ut 1, 3950 Sarospatak
Tel: 4111057
Key Personnel
Dir: Michael Szentimrel
The Library of Scientific Collections of the Reformed College of Saroapatak.

Iceland

Kennarahaskoli Islands (Iceland University of Education)
v/Stakkahlid, 105 Reykjavik
Tel: 5633800; 5633863 *Fax:* 5633914
Web Site: www.khi.is/bok
Key Personnel
Learning Center Dir: Kristin Indridadottir *E-mail:* kindr@khi.is

Landsbokasafn Islands-Haskolabokasafn
Arngrimsgafa 3, 107 Reykjavik 107
Tel: 5255600 *Fax:* 5255615
E-mail: lbs@bok.hi.is
Web Site: www.bok.hi.is

Key Personnel
National Librarian: Einar Sigurdsson
E-mail: einsig@bok.hi.is
National Library & University Library of Iceland.
Publication(s): *Handritasafn Landsbokasafns* (catalog of Manuscripts); *Islensk bokaskra* (Icelandic National Bibliography); *Islensk Hljodritaskra* (Bibliography of Icelandic Sound Recordings, supplement to Islensk bokaskra); *Ritmennf (annual journal))*

Borgarbokasafn Reykjavikur (Reykjavik City Library)
Tryggvagata 15, 101 Reykjavik
Tel: 5631717 *Fax:* 5631705
E-mail: borgarbokasafn@skyrr.is
Web Site: www.borgarbokasafn.is
Key Personnel
City Librarian: Anna Torfadottir
Office Manager: Kolbrun Hanksdottir
 E-mail: kolbrun@borgarbokasafn.is
Founded: 1923
Publication(s): *Arsskyrsla*
Branch Office(s)
Foldasafn, Grafarvogskirkju, 112 Reykjavik
 Tel: 5675320
Gerduberg, Gerduberg 3-5, 109 Reykjavik
 Tel: 5579122
Kringlusafn, Listabraut 3, 103 *Tel:* 5806200
Seljasafn, Holmascli 4-6, 109 Reykjavik
 Tel: 5873320
Solheimasafn, Solheimum 27, 104 Reykjavik
 Tel: 5536814

India

American Information Resource Center
Division of Public Affairs Section, American Embassy
The American Center, 24 Kasturba Gandhi Marg, New Delhi 110001
Tel: (011) 3316841; (011) 3314251; (011) 3316841 *Fax:* (011) 3329499
E-mail: newdelhi@usia.gov; libel@pd.state.gov
Web Site: americanlibrary.in.library.net
Key Personnel
AIRC Dir: Veena Chawla
Public library.

Bombay University Library
University Rd Fort, Bombay 400032
Tel: (022) 2652819 *Fax:* (022) 2652832
Key Personnel
Librarian: Dr S R Ganpule

British Council Libraries
17, Kasturba Gandhi Marg, New Delhi 110001
Tel: (011) 3711401 *Fax:* (011) 3710717
Web Site: www.britishcouncil.org/india/
Key Personnel
Head, Library & Info Services: P Jayarajan
 E-mail: jayarajan@in.britishcouncil.org
Branch Office(s)
39 St Mark's Rd, Bangalore 560001
GTB Complex, Roshanpura Naka, Bhopal 462003
5, Shakesphere sarani, Calcutta 700071 *Tel:* (033) 2825944 *Fax:* (033) 2824804 *E-mail:* calcutta.library@in.britishcouncil.org
SCO 36-38, Sector 8C, Madhya Marg, Chandigarh 160008 *Tel:* (0172) 546540 *Fax:* (0172) 547540 *E-mail:* chandigarh.library@in.britishcouncil.org
737 Anna Salai, Chennai 600002 *Tel:* (044) 8525002 *Fax:* (044) 8523234 *E-mail:* channai.library@in.britishcouncil.org
5-9-22 Sarovar Centre, Secretariat Rd, Hyderabad 560004
Mayfair Bldg, Hazratganj, Lucknow 226001
Mittal Towers "A" Wing, 1st fl, Nariman Point, Mumbai 400021 *Tel:* (022) 2823530 *Fax:* (022) 2852024 *E-mail:* mumbai.library@in.britishcouncil.org
B P Koirala Marg, Patna 800001
917/1 Ferugusson College Rd, Shivaji Nagar, Pune 411004
YMCA Bldg, Thiruvananthapuram 695001
Bhaikaka Bhawan, Law Garden, Ellisbridge, Ahmedabad, 380 006 Gujarat *Tel:* (079) 656-0693 *Fax:* (079) 449493

Central Library
Vadodara, Gujaat, Baroda 390006
Tel: (0265) 540133
Key Personnel
State Librarian: Bakulesh Bhuta
Publication(s): *Granth Deep* (quarterly)

Central Secretariat Library
Govt of India, G Wing, Shastri Bhavan, New Delhi 110001
Tel: (011) 3389684 *Fax:* (011) 3384846
E-mail: rootofcsl@delnet.ren.nic.in
Key Personnel
Dir: Kalpana Dasgupta

Delhi Public Library
S P Mukherjee Marg, New Delhi 110006
Tel: (011) 2916881
Key Personnel
Dir: Dr Banwari Lal

Delhi University Library System
University Enclave, Delhi 110007
Tel: (011) 7667848 *Fax:* (011) 7666404
E-mail: crl@delnet.ven.nic.in
Key Personnel
University Librarian: M L Saini

Gujarat Vidyapith Granthalaya
Ashram Rd, Gandhi Bhavan, Ahmedabad 380014
Tel: (079) 7541148 *Fax:* (079) 7542547
E-mail: gujvi@adinet.emet.in
Telex: 121-6254 GUVI IN
Key Personnel
Librarian: K K Bhausar
Combined university, state central & public library.
Publication(s): *Gujarati Samayik Lekh Suchi* (Gujarati Indexing of Articles from Selected Gujarati Journals); *Tapas Nibandh Suchi* (Gujarati Bibliography of Dissertations)

Indian Council of World Affairs Library
Sapru House, Barakhamba Rd, New Delhi 110001
Tel: (011) 3317246 *Fax:* (011) 3317248
Cable: INTERASIA
Key Personnel
Acting Librarian: Man Singh Deora
 E-mail: dgicwa@hotmail.com
Publication(s): *Documentation on Asia* (annually)

Indian Institute of Management
Vikram Sarabhai Library, Vastrapur, Ahmedabad 380 015
Tel: (079) 6307241; (079) 6324980 *Fax:* (079) 6306896
Key Personnel
Dir: Jahar Saha
Librarian: Ashok Jambhekar *E-mail:* ashokj@iimahd.ernet.in
Founded: 1962

Indian Institute of Technology Central Library
Central Library IITPO, Chennai 600036
Tel: (044) 2351365 *Fax:* (044) 2350509
E-mail: lib@iitm.ernet.in
Telex: 418926 *Cable:* TECHNOLOGY
Key Personnel
Librarian: Dr Harish Chandra

Institute for Social & Economic Change Library
Nagarbhavi PO, Bangalore 560 072
Tel: (080) 3355468; (080) 3387010 *Fax:* (080) 3387008
E-mail: ssisec@ren.nic.in
Key Personnel
Librarian: V K Jain
Dir: P V Shenol

The Asiatic Society of Bombay
Town Hall, Bombay 400023
Tel: (022) 2860956
E-mail: asbl@giasbom2.vsnl.net.in
Key Personnel
President: Dr D R SarDesai
Vice President: Smt N M Pandit; Dr M D Paradkar; Mr Mirza Boman; Dr Mani Kamerkar
Honorary Secretary: Mrs Vimal N Shah
Editor: Dr V M Kulkarni; Dr Devangana Desai
Publication(s): *Journal of the Asiatic Society of Bombay & Monographs*

Madras Literary Society Library
College Rd, Chennai 600006
Key Personnel
Manager: P N Balasundaram

National Archives of India
Janpath, New Delhi 110001
Tel: (011) 383436
Key Personnel
Librarian: R C Puri
Dir General: S Sarkar

The National Library, Government of India
Belvedere, Calcutta 700027
Tel: (033) 4791381 *Fax:* (033) 4791462
Telex: 8117 *Cable:* LIBRARIAN
Key Personnel
Dir: Hariit Singh
Publication(s): *India's National Library*; *India's National Library: Systematization and Modernization*; *The National Library and Public Libraries in India*

Nehru Memorial Museum and Library (NMML)
Teen Murti House, New Delhi 110011
Tel: (011) 3015333; (011) 3017089 *Fax:* (011) 37923296
Key Personnel
Dir: Dr O P Kejariwal
Librarian: Mrs Kanwal Verma
Research Center on Modern Indian History, with emphasis on Indian Nationalism; 2, 09, 904 vols; large collections of newspapers, microfilms, private papers, institutional records, photographs & oral history recordings.

Pt Ravishankar Shukla University Library
Raipur 492002
Tel: 23970
Key Personnel
Librarian: Rameshwar Singh

Sahitya Akademi Library
Rabindra Bhavan, 35 Ferozeshah Rd, New Delhi 110001
Tel: (011) 3387064 *Fax:* (011) 3382428
Cable: SAHITYAKAR
Key Personnel
President: Prof Anantha Murphy
Librarian: K C Dutt
National Academy of Letters Library.
Publication(s): *Indian Literary Index* (biannually)

INDIA

State Central Library
Afzalgunj, Hyderabad 12
Tel: (040) 43107
Key Personnel
Librarian: T V Vedamrutham

Indonesia

Arsip Nasional Republik Indonesia
Jl Ampera Raya, Cilandak, Timar, Jakarta 12560
Tel: (021) 7805851 *Fax:* (021) 7805812
E-mail: anrinet@indosat.net.id
Key Personnel
Reference & Information Service: Dr Noerhadi Magetsari
National Archives.

British Council Library
S Widjojo Centre, Jl Jenderal Sudirman 71, Jakarta 12190
Tel: (021) 2524115; (021) 2524122; (021) 2524126 *Fax:* (021) 2524129
Telex: 45246 BRICOUN JKT
Key Personnel
Librarian: Toosye Damayanti

CALTD, see Center for Agricultural Library & Technology Dissemination (CALTD)

Center for Agricultural Library & Technology Dissemination (CALTD) (Pusat Perpustakaan dan Penyebaran Teknalogi Pertanian)
Formerly National Library for Agricultural Sciences
Jl Ir Haji Juanda 20, Bogor 16122
Tel: (0251) 321746 *Fax:* (0251) 326561
E-mail: pustaka@booor.net
Web Site: pustaka.bogor.net *Cable:* Pustaka
Key Personnel
Dir: Dr Tjeppy D Soedjana
Founded: 1842
Publication(s): *Indonesian Journal of Agricultural Science (IJAS)*
Parent Company: Agency for Agricultural Research & Development

Perpustakaan Dewan Perwakilan Rakjat - RI
Jl Jenderal Gatot Subroto, Jakarta, Pusat 10270
Tel: (021) 5715220 *Fax:* (021) 5715884
Telex: 65396 RHM OPR
Key Personnel
Chief Librarian: Mrs Roemningsih
Parliamentary Library of Indonesia.
Publication(s): *Aquisition List*

Pusat Dokumentasi dan Informasi Ilmiah
Gatot Subroto 10, Jakarta 4298
Mailing Address: PO Box 4298, Jakarta 4298
Tel: (021) 5733465 *Fax:* (021) 5733467
Telex: 62875 IA *Cable:* PDII
Key Personnel
Contact: Mr B Sudarsono
Indonesian Centre for Scientific Documentation & Information.
Publication(s): *Baca* (Read bimonthly); *Bibliografi Khusus* (Special Bibliographies irregular); *Direktori Perpustakaan Khusus dan Sumber Informasi di Indonesia* (Directory of Special Libraries and Information Sources in Indonesia irregular); *Indeks Laporan Penelitian dan Survei* (Index of Research and Survey Report annual; and lists of acquisitions books and microfiches); *Indeks Majalah Ilmiah Indonesia* (Index of Indonesian Learned Periodicals semi-annual)

Library of Hasanuddin University
Perpustakaan Pusat, Universitas Hasanuddin, Kampus Tamalanrea, Ujung Pandang 90245
Tel: (0411) 512026 *Fax:* (0411) 510088
Telex: 7179 UNHAS
Key Personnel
Head Librarian: Rosdiani Rachim

Hatta Foundation Library
Perpustakaan, Jl Solo 155, Yogyakarta 55281
Tel: (0274) 87747 *Fax:* (0274) 87747
Key Personnel
Librarian: R Soedjatmiko
Contact: Fauzie Ridjal
Hatta Foundation Library.
Branch Office(s)
Perpustakaan Yayasan Hatta, Jl Adisutjipto 155, Yogyakarta 55281

Perpustakaan Pusat Institut Teknologi Bandung
Jl Ganesya, No 10, Bandung 40132
Tel: (022) 2500089 *Fax:* (022) 2500089
Telex: ITB BD 28324
Key Personnel
Chief Librarian: Dr Adjat Sakri
Librarian: Dr I Nyoman Susila
Central Library, Bandung Institute of Technology.
Publication(s): *Proceedings Institut Teknologi Bandung*

Perpustakaan Islam
Jl P Mangkubumi 38, Yogyakarta
Tel: (0274) 2078
Key Personnel
Dir: Dr H Asyhuri Dahlan
Librarian: Moh Amien Mansoer
Islamic Library.

Perpustakaan Nasional
Salemba Raya 28, Jakarta 10002
Mailing Address: PO Box 3624, Jakarta 10002
Tel: (021) 3101411 *Fax:* (021) 3103551
Key Personnel
Dir: Ms Mastini Hardjo Prakoso
National Library of Indonesia.

National Library for Agricultural Sciences, see Center for Agricultural Library & Technology Dissemination (CALTD)

National Library of Indonesia, see Perpustakaan Nasional

Library of Political and Social History
Medan Merdeka Selatan 11, Jakarta
Tel: (021) 360136
Key Personnel
Librarian: Dr Soekarman
Publication(s): *Index Pemilu* (Index of General Elections); *Press index; Index Artikel Tentang Negara* (Index of Official Publications)

Universitas Udayana Library
Jl PB Sudirman, Bukit Jimbaran, Denpasar, Bali
Tel: (0361) 71854 ext 151; (0361) 701139 *Fax:* (0361) 71607; (0361) 701907
Key Personnel
Librarian: Dr I Gusti Nyeman Tirtayasa
Publication(s): *Bibliografi*

Islamic Republic of Iran

Ferdowsi University of Mashhad Central Library & Documentation Centre
PO Box 1163-91375, Mashhad
Tel: (051) 818113-14 *Fax:* (051) 818113
Telex: 512271
Key Personnel
General Dir: Dr M T Eclalati

Institution of Libraries, Museums & Documentation Centre of Astan Quds Razavi, see Organizations of Libraries, Museums & Documentation Centre of Astan Quds

IRANDOC, see Iranian Information Documentation Centre

Iranian Information Documentation Centre
Affiliate of Ministry of Culture & Higher Education
1188 Englab St, Tehran
Mailing Address: PO Box 13185-1371, Tehran
Tel: (021) 6494954; (021) 6462548 *Fax:* (021) 6462254
E-mail: info@irandoc.ac.ir
Web Site: www.irandoc.ac.ir
Telex: 6415330 *Cable:* ASNDIRAN
Key Personnel
Dir: Hussein Gharibi
International Relations Manager: Mr Parviz Shahriari
Contact: Mr Dariush Saberi
Founded: 1968
Engaged in Information Sciences Fields. Main activities include production & dissemination of Iranian scientific information (Persian); Research on Information Science; Iranian Dissertion Abstracts (students graduated in Iran & abroad); Research Projects Abstracts; Iranian Scientific Meetings And Proceedings; Iranian Government Reports & many other topics which are all online free. Researchers can access to the materials via visiting our web page, periodicals & connecting to SABA intranet which is our local network, otherwise they can apply for searching the documents by letter or coming to the Search Unit of our library.
Publication(s): *Current Research in Iranian Universities and Research Centers*; *Directory of Scientific Meeting Held In Iran*; *Dissertion Abstracts of Iranian Graduates Abroad*; *Index to Latin periodicals available in Iranian special libraries*; *Iranian Dissertion Abstracts*; *Iranian Government Report*; *Iranian Scholars and Experts Database*; *The Abstract of Scientific and Technical reports*

The Islamic Republic of Iran Parliament Library, No 2 (Ketab-Khane-ye Majles-e Shora-ye Eslami, no 2) (Library, Museum & Documentation Center of the Islamic Consultative Assembly, No 2)
Baharestan Sq, PO Box 11365-866, Tehran
Tel: (021) 6135429; (021) 6135335 *Fax:* (021) 3130919; (021) 3129385
Fax on Demand: (021) 3124339
E-mail: webmaster@majlislib.com
Web Site: www.majlislib.org
Key Personnel
Dir: Seyyed Mohammad Ali Ahmadi Abhari
Tel: (021) 3130920 *Fax:* (021) 3124339
E-mail: Abhari@majlislib.com

Founded: 1950
Library & information Services.
Ultimate Parent Company: Majles-e Shora-ye Eslami (The Islamic Consultative Assembly)

The Islamic Republic of Iran Parliament Library, No 1 (Ketabkhane-ye Majles-e Shora-ye Elsami, No 1) (Library, Museum & Documentation Center of the Islamic Consultative Assembly Number 1)
Baharestan Sq, PO Box 11365-866, Tehran
Tel: (021) 3130919; (021) 3126092 *Fax:* (021) 3130919; (021) 3129385; (021) 3124339
Fax on Demand: (021) 3124339
E-mail: frelations@majlislib.com; irparlib@majlislib.com; info@majlislib.com
Web Site: www.majlislib.org
Key Personnel
Dir: Seyyed Mohammad Ali Ahmadi Abhari
Tel: (021) 3130920 *Fax:* (021) 3124339
E-mail: abhari@majlislib.com
Founded: 1923
Library & information services; manuscripts collection; indexing of the manuscripts; publishing; renovation, maintenance, disinfection & antiacidification of old books & manuscripts; making microfilms.
Ultimate Parent Company: Majles-e Shora-ye Eslami (The Islamic Consultative Assembly)

The National Library of the Islamic Republic of Iran
Anahita Alley, Africa St, Tehran 19176
Tel: (021) 2288680 (voice & fax) *Fax:* (021) 8088950
E-mail: natlibir@neda.net
Key Personnel
Dir: Dr Mohammed Khatami
Publication(s): *A Bibliography of the Folklore of Isfahan*; *A Catalogue of the manuscripts in the National Library of Iran*; *A Directory of Iranian Periodicals & Newspapers*; *Catalog of Valuable French Works in the National Library of Iran*; *Glossary of Library Terms*; *List of Persian Subject Headings*; *Persian Author Marks*; *Political Life of Imain Khomevni*; *Rules & Standards for Publishing Books*; *Technical Services* (8th edition); *The Iranian National Bibliography*; *The Name Authority List of Authors & Famous People*

Organizations of Libraries, Museums & Documentation Centre of Astan Quds
Formerly Institution of Libraries, Museums & Documentation Centre of Astan Quds Razavi
PO Box 91735-177, Mashhad
Tel: (098511) 2216009 *Fax:* (098511) 2220845
E-mail: radad@imamreza.or.ir; astanlib@imamreza.or.ir
Web Site: www.aqlibrary.org
Key Personnel
Dir General: Dr A M Baradaran Rafiei
Publication(s): *Library & Information Science Quarterly* (quarterly)
Parent Company: Astan Quds Razavi

Shiraz University
Zand Ave, Shiraz 71944
Tel: (071) 6260011; (071) 59220 *Fax:* (071) 669225
Telex: 65912; 332169
Key Personnel
President: Dr Z Hayati *E-mail:* zhayati@rose.shirazu.ac.ir; Dr M Ershad Langroodi
Acquisition Librarian: N Amitaimoor

University of Isfahan Library
Hezar Jerib Ave, Isfahan
Tel: (031) 71071; (031) 685141 *Fax:* (031) 275145

Telex: 312295 IREU IR
Key Personnel
Dir of Libraries: M Jamshidian Ph D

Central Library, University of Tabriz
Central Library & Documentation Center, University of Tabriz, Tabriz
Tel: (041) 344705 *Fax:* (041) 344705
Telex: 412045 TBUN-IR
Key Personnel
Dir: A Adine Ghahramani; Dr G H Tasbihi

Central Library & Documentation Centre of University of Teheran
Enghelab Ave, Teheran
Tel: (021) 6112503 *Fax:* (021) 6409348
Telex: 13944; 222966

Iraq

Al-Awqaf
Bab Al-Muadham, Baghdad
Mailing Address: PO Box 14146, Baghdad
Tel: (01) 4169362 *Fax:* (01) 4167790
Telex: 2785
Key Personnel
Librarian: Jassim Al-Juboori
Dir: Afaf Abidul Latif
Library of Waqfs.
Branch Office(s)
Adhamiya, Mosul
Main Mosque, Anbar
Al-Qazzaza Library, Baghdad
Munier Al-Qadhi Library, Baghdad
Amarah
Diala
Kerkuk
Nasiriyah
Sulaymaniyah

The Diwan Library, Ministry of Education
Educational Campus, Baghdad
Tel: (01) 8860000-2178
Telex: 2259
Key Personnel
Librarian: Dr Kadhim G Al-Khazraji

Library of the Iraq Museum
Salhiya Quarter, Baghdad West
Tel: (01) 8879687
Key Personnel
Dir: Dr Muyad Said Damerji; Zounab Sadiq

Library of the Mosul Museum
Dawassa, Mosul
Key Personnel
Dir: Hazmin A Hameed

Mosul Public Library
1930 Abdul-Halim Al-Lawand, Mosul
Tel: (060) 810162 *Fax:* (060) 814765
Telex: 8011
Key Personnel
Gen Dir: Adran S Natheev

National Centre of Archives
Nat Library Bldg, 2nd Floor, Bab-el-Muaddam, Baghdad
Tel: (01) 4164190 *Cable:* CENTARCHIV
Key Personnel
Dir General: Salim Al-Alousi
Located at The Building of the National Library, 2nd floor, Baghdad.

National Library
Bab-el-Muaddum, Baghdad
Tel: (01) 4164190
Key Personnel
Dir: Abdul Hameed Alwaehi
Publication(s): *al-Maktaba al-Arabia Journal*; *Iraqi National Bibliography* (triannually)

Scientific Documentation Centre
Central Science Library, Abu Nuas Rd, Baghdad
Mailing Address: PO Box 2441, Baghdad
Tel: (01) 7760023
Telex: 2187 Bathilmi IK
Key Personnel
Dir: Dr Faik Abdul S Razzaq

Central Library of the University of Baghdad
Jadiriya, Baghdad
Mailing Address: PO Box 47303, Baghdad
Tel: (01) 7763091 *Fax:* (01) 7763592
Telex: 2197
Key Personnel
Librarian: Dr Zeki Al-Werdi

Central Library of the University of Basrah
Basrah
Tel: (040) 417914
Telex: 207025
Key Personnel
Librarian: Dr Tarik Al-Manassir

Central Library of the University of Mosul
Mosul
Tel: (060) 810162 *Fax:* (060) 814765
Telex: 8011
Key Personnel
Dir General: Dr Adnan S Natheev

Central Library of the University of Salahaddin
Arbil
Tel: 23102
Telex: 218510
Key Personnel
Dir: Dr Abdull S Abbas

Ireland

The Chester Beatty Library
Dublin Castle, Dublin 2
Tel: (01) 4070750 *Fax:* (01) 4070760
E-mail: info@cbl.ie
Web Site: www.cbl.ie
Key Personnel
Dir & Librarian: Dr Michael Ryan
Reference Librarian: Celine Ward *Tel:* (01) 4070757 *E-mail:* cward@cbl.ie
Among items on display at the Library is material showing the development of the written word from 2700 BC (the date of the Library's earliest clay tablet) down to modern times.

Boole Library, see University College Cork, Boole Library

Central Catholic Library
74 Merrion Sq South, Dublin 2
Tel: (01) 6761264
Key Personnel
Librarian: Teresa Whitington

Dublin Public Libraries
Cumberland House, Fenian St, Dublin 2
Tel: (01) 6644800 *Fax:* (01) 6761628
E-mail: dublin.city.libs@iol.ie
Telex: 33287

Key Personnel
Dublin City Librarian & Dir: Deirdre Ellis-King
Headquarters of the International IMPAC Dublin Literary Awards.

James Hardiman Library, see National University of Ireland Galway (NUI, Galway)

Leabharlann Boole, see University College Cork, Boole Library

National Archives
Bishop St, Dublin 8
Tel: (01) 4072 300 *Fax:* (01) 4072 333
E-mail: mail@nationalarchives.ie
Web Site: www.nationalarchives.ie
Key Personnel
Dir: Dr David Craig

National Library of Ireland
Kildare St, Dublin 2
Tel: (01) 6618811 *Fax:* (01) 6766690
Key Personnel
Editor: Dr Noel Kissane
Dir: Brendan O'Donoghue
The National Library of Ireland publishes material from its collection in the medium of folders, facsimile documents, illustrated booklets & books.
Publication(s): *Ex Camera, 1860-1960* (1990); *James Joyce* (1982); *Parnell - A Documentary History* (1991); *The Irish Face* (1987); *The Irish Famine: A Documentary History* (1995); *The Irish Publishing Record* (annually from 1989-); *The James Joyce/Paul Leon Papers* (1992); *Treasures from the National Library of Ireland* (1994); *W B Yeats & His Circle* (1989); *Writers, Racouteurs & Notable History* (1993)

National University of Ireland Galway (NUI, Galway)
Galway
Tel: (091) 524809 *Fax:* (091) 522394
Web Site: www.library.nuigalway.ie
Key Personnel
Chief Librarian: Marie Reddan *E-mail:* marie.reddan@nuigalway.ie
Founded: 1845
University library.

Oireachtas Library
Leinster House, Kildare St, Dublin 2
Tel: (01) 6183412 *Fax:* (01) 6184376
Key Personnel
Librarian: Maura Corcoran
Selective works of parliamentary interest.

Representative Church Body Library
Braemor Park, Churchtown, Dublin 14
Tel: (01) 4923979 *Fax:* (01) 4924770
E-mail: library@ireland.anglican.org
Web Site: www.ireland.anglican.org/library/library.html
Key Personnel
Librarian & Archivist: Raymond Refaussé
Founded: 1932
Publication(s): *A Handlist of Church of Ireland Parish Registers in the Representative Church Body Library*; *A Handlist of Church of Ireland Vestry Minute Books in the Representative Church Body Library*; *A Library on the Move. Twenty Five Years of the Representative Church Body Library in Churchtown*; *Register of Holy Trinity Church, Cork, 1643-1668* (1998); *Register of the Cathedral Church of St Columb, Derry, 1703-1732*; *Register of the Cathedral Church of St Columb, Derry, 1732-1775*; *Register of the Church of St Thomas, Lisnagarvey, Co Antrim, 1637-1646*; *Register of the Parish of Leixlip, Co Kildare, 1665-1778*; *Register of the Parish of St Thomas, Dublin, 1750-1791*; *Registers of the Parish of St John the Evangelist, Dublin* (book)

Royal College of Surgeons in Ireland Library
Mercer Library, Mercer Street Lower, Dublin 2
Tel: (01) 4022411 *Fax:* (01) 4022457
E-mail: library@rcsi.ie
Web Site: www.rcsi.ie
Key Personnel
Librarian: Miss B M Doran
Deputy Librarian: Hugh Brazier *Tel:* (01) 4022406 *E-mail:* hbrazier@rcsi.ie
Publication(s): *Journal of the Irish Colleges of Physicians and Surgeons*
Branch Office(s)
Beaumont Hospital Library, Beaumont Rd, Dublin 9 *Tel:* (01) 836 7396 *E-mail:* bhlibrary@rcsi.ie

Royal Dublin Society Library
Ballsbridge, Dublin 4
Tel: (01) 6680866; (01) 2407288 *Fax:* (01) 6604014 *Cable:* SOCIETY, DUBLIN
Key Personnel
Librarian: Mary Kelleher *E-mail:* mary.kelleher@rds.ie
Founded: 1731
Private Society.

Trinity College Library Dublin
College St, Dublin 2
Tel: (01) 608 1665 *Fax:* (01) 608 3774
Web Site: www.tcd.ie/library
Telex: 93782
Key Personnel
Librarian & College Archivist: William G Simpson *Tel:* (01) 608 1661 *E-mail:* wsimpson@tcd.ie
Founded: 1592
Academic & legal deposit library.
Publication(s): *Long Room*
Parent Company: Trinity College Dublin

University College Cork, Boole Library
Cork
Tel: (021) 276871 *Fax:* (021) 903119
E-mail: library@ucc.ie
Telex: 7605 Unicei
Key Personnel
President: Dr Michael Mortell
Librarian: John Fitzgerald
Deputy Librarian: Edward Fahy

University College Dublin Library
Belfield, Dublin 4
Tel: (01) 716 7694 *Fax:* (01) 283 7667
E-mail: library@ucd.ie
Web Site: www.ucd.ie/library
Key Personnel
Librarian: S Phillips

Israel

Central Library of Agricultural Science
ARO PO Box 12, Rehovot 76100
Tel: (08) 481270 *Fax:* (03) 993998
Telex: 381331
Key Personnel
Dir: N Barzely

Bar Ilan University Central Library
c/o Wurzweiler Central Library, PO Box 90,000, Ramat Gan 52900
Tel: (03) 5318486; (03) 5318357 *Fax:* (03) 5349233

Key Personnel
University Librarian: Ya'akov Aronson *E-mail:* aronson@mail.biu.ac.il
Founded: 1955
Publication(s): *Hebrew Subject Headings for use in Cataloging* (updated semi-annually); *Index to literary supplements of the Daily Hebrew Press* (annual)

Ben-Gurion University of the Negev Library
PO Box 653, Beer Sheva 84105
Tel: (07) 6461401 *Fax:* (07) 6472940
Key Personnel
Dir: Avner Shmuelevitz

Central Library for the Blind, Visually Impaired & Handicapped
4 Hahistadrut St, Netanaya 42441
Tel: (09) 8620166 *Fax:* (09) 8626346
E-mail: office@clfb.org.il
Web Site: www.clfb.org.il
Key Personnel
Dir: Uri Cohen *Tel:* (03) 6315555 *Fax:* (03) 6315577
Branch Office(s)
Elinore & Athol Burns, 66 Moshe Dayan St, Yad-Eliyahu, Tel Aviv

The Central Archives for the History of the Jewish People
PO Box 1149, Jerusalem 91010
Tel: (02) 635716 *Fax:* (02) 635716
E-mail: archives@vms.huji.ac.il
Web Site: www.sites.huji.ac.il/archives
Key Personnel
Dir: Assouline Hadassah
Formerly Jewish Historical General Archives.

Development Study Center
Herzl St, Rehovot 76122
Mailing Address: PO Box 2355, Rehovot 76122
Tel: (08) 474111 *Fax:* (08) 475884
E-mail: dsc@netvision.net.il
Key Personnel
Dir: Dr Dafna Schwartz

Dvir Bialik Municipal Central Public Library
14 Hibat-Zion St, Ramat Gan
Tel: (03) 786375
Key Personnel
Librarian: Hadassah Pelach

Hebrew University of Jerusalem
Formerly Jewish National & University Library
Edmond J Safra Campus, Jerusalem 91341
Mailing Address: PO Box 34165, Jerusalem 91341
Tel: (02) 6585017 *Fax:* (02) 6511771
Web Site: jnul.huji.ac.il/rambi
Key Personnel
Dir: Prof Yoram Tsafrir
Publication(s): *Index of Articles on Jewish Studies* (online); *Kiryat Sefer* (quarterly, bibliographical)

Israel State Archives
Prime Minister's Office, Kiryat Ben-Gurion, Bldg 3, Jerusalem 91919
Tel: (02) 5680680 *Fax:* (02) 6793375
Key Personnel
Dir: M Mossek
Publication(s): *Documents on the Foreign Policy of Israel* (series); *Israel Government Publications* (annually)

Jerusalem City (Public) Library
11 Bezalel St, Jerusalem 94591
Mailing Address: PO Box 1409, Jerusalem 94591
Tel: (02) 226785 *Fax:* (02) 255785
Key Personnel
Dir: A Vilner

LIBRARIES

Jewish National & University Library, see Hebrew University of Jerusalem

Knesset Library
Kiryat Ben Gurion, The Knesset Bldg, 91 950 Jerusalem
Tel: (02) 753333 *Fax:* (02) 5662733
E-mail: sifriaz@netvision.net.il
Key Personnel
Librarian: Sandra Fine

Pevsner Public Library
54 Pevsner St, Haifa 31053
Mailing Address: PO Box 5345, Haifa 31053
Tel: (04) 667766
Key Personnel
Librarian: Dr S Back

Shaar Zion Library
Division of Culture
25 King Saul Blvd, Tel Aviv
Mailing Address: PO Box 33235, Tel Aviv
Tel: 03 6910141
Key Personnel
Library Dir: Ora Nebenzahl
Ultimate Parent Company: Tel Aviv Municipality

Technion - Israel Institute of Technology Libraries
Technion City, Elyachar Library, Haifa 32000
Tel: (04) 292507 (Elyachar Central Library) *Fax:* (04) 8233501
Telex: 46650
Key Personnel
Dir: Nurit Roitberg

Tel Aviv University Library
PO Box 39040, Tel Aviv 69978
Tel: (03) 640-8111 *Fax:* (03) 6409598
E-mail: tauinfo@post.tau.ac.il
Web Site: www.tau.ac.il
Telex: 342227 versy1L
Key Personnel
Dir: Dr Dan Simon

University of Haifa Library
Abba Khoushy Rd, Mt Carmel Central, Haifa 31905
Tel: (04) 257753; (04) 8240289 *Fax:* (04) 342104; (04) 8257753
E-mail: sever@lib.haifa.ac.il
Key Personnel
Dir: Prof Shmuel Sever
Publication(s): *Index to Hebrew Periodicals* (semi-annually, CD-ROM)

Weizmann Institute of Science Libraries
Herzl St, PO Box 26, Rehovot 76100
Tel: (08) 9343583 (W1X Central Library); (08) 9343211 (Weizmann Institute) *Fax:* (08) 9344176
E-mail: rapinsk@wisemail.weizmann.ac.il
Web Site: www.weizmann.acie/wis-library/home.htn
Key Personnel
Chief Librarian: Ilana Pollack *E-mail:* ilana.pollack@weizmann.ac.il

Italy

Biblioteca Ambrosiana
Piazza Pio XI 2, 20123 Milan
Tel: (02) 806921 *Fax:* (02) 80692210
Key Personnel
Librarian: Gianfranco Ravasi
Publication(s): *Fontes Ambrosiani*

Biblioteca Angelica
Piazza S Agostino 8, 00186 Rome
Tel: (06) 6868041; (06) 6875874 *Fax:* (06) 6832312; (06) 6832312
Key Personnel
Dir: Armida Batori
Paola Munafo e Nicoletta Muratore: La Biblioteca Angelica, Roma, Instituto Poligrafico dello Stato (1989).

Biblioteca Comunale dell' Archiginnasio
Piazza Galvani 1, 40124 Bologna
Tel: (051) 276811 *Fax:* (051) 261160
E-mail: archiginnasio@comune.bologna.it
Web Site: www.archiginnasio.it
Key Personnel
Dir: Dr Pierangelo Bellettini
Founded: 1801
Publication(s): *L'Archiginnasio: Bollettino della Biblioteca Comunale di Bologna* (annually)

Archivio Centrale dello Stato
Piazzale degli Archivi, EUR, 00144 Rome
Tel: (06) 5920371 *Fax:* (06) 5413620
Key Personnel
Dir: Prof Paolo Carucci
Librarian: Eugenia Nieddu
National Archives.
Publication(s): *Bollettino Delle Nuove Accessioni*

Biblioteca dell'Archivio Storico Civico e Biblioteca Trivulziana
Castello Sforzesco, 20121 Milan
Tel: (02) 62083946 *Fax:* (02) 875926
Key Personnel
Librarian: Dr Giovanni M Piazza
Library publications are sent free by request or in exchange for other publications.

Biblioteca Centrale della Regione Siciliana gia Biblioteca Nazionale di Palermo
Corso Vittorio Emanuele 431, 90134 Palermo
Tel: (091) 6967644; (091) 6967642 *Fax:* (091) 6967644
Key Personnel
Dir DSSA: Carmela Perretta

Biblioteca Medicea Laurenziana
Member of Associazione Italiana Biblioteche (AIB)
Affiliate of Ministero per i Beni e le Attivita Culturali
Piazza San Lorenzo 9, 50123 Florence
Tel: (055) 210760 *Fax:* (055) 2302992
E-mail: medicea@unifi.it
Web Site: www.bml.firenze.sbn.it
Key Personnel
Chief Librarian: Franca Arduini

Biblioteca Nazionale Braidense
Via Brera 28, 20121 Milan
Tel: (02) 86460907 *Fax:* (02) 72023910
Key Personnel
Dir: Dr Goffredo Dotti
Contact: Dr Arminda Batori

Biblioteca Nazionale Centrale
Piazza dei Cavalleggeri 1B, 50122 Florence
Tel: (055) 249191 *Fax:* (055) 2342482
Key Personnel
Dir: Dr Antonia Ida Fontana

Biblioteca Nazionale Centrale Vittorio Emanuele II
Viale Castro Pretorio 105, 00185 Rome
Tel: (06) 49891 *Fax:* (06) 4457635
Key Personnel
Dir: Dott Livia Borghetti
Publication(s): *Bollettino delle opere moderne straniere acquiste dalle Biblioteche Pubbliche statali Italiane; Quaderni della Biblioteca nazionale centrale di Roma; Studi guide, cataloghi*

Biblioteca Nazionale Vittorio Emanuele III
Piazza del Plebiscito, Palazzo Reale, 80132 Naples
Tel: (081) 407921; (081) 7819111 *Fax:* (081) 403820
E-mail: Emanuele@librari.beniculturali.it
Key Personnel
Dir: Mauro Giancaspro
Librarian: Anna Giaccio *Tel:* (081) 7819215
Publication(s): *I Quaderni della Biblioteca Nazionale de Napoli*

Biblioteca Nazionale Universitaria
Piazza Carlo Alberto 3, Turin 10123
Tel: (011) 889737 *Fax:* (011) 817778
E-mail: bntsbnol@itocsivm.csi.it
Key Personnel
Dir: Dr Lenardo Seluaggi

Biblioteca Nazionale Marciana
San Marco 7, 30124 Venice
Tel: (041) 5208788 *Fax:* (041) 5238803
E-mail: biblioteca@marciana.venezia.sbn.it
Web Site: www.marciana.venezia.sbn.it/
Key Personnel
Dir: Dr Marino Zorzi
Publication(s): *Miscellanea Marciana*

Biblioteca Universitaria
Subsidiary of Biblioteca Estense
Biblioteca Estense Universitaria, Piazza S Agostino 337, 41100 Modena
Tel: (059) 222248 *Fax:* (059) 230195
E-mail: biblio.estense@cedoc.mo.it
Key Personnel
Chief Librarian: Dr Ernesto Milano
Economics, medicine, engineering, mathematics.

Biblioteca Musicale S Cecilia
Via dei Greci 18, Rome 00187
Tel: (06) 6784552 ext 235 *Fax:* (06) 6784555
Key Personnel
Librarian: Dr Domenico Carboni

Biblioteca Estense Universitaria
Largo Porta S Agostino 337, 41100 Modena
Tel: (059) 222248 *Fax:* (059) 230195
E-mail: estense@kril.cedoc.unimo.it; biblio.estense@cedoc.mo.it
Web Site: www.cedoc.mo.it/estense
Key Personnel
Dir: Dr Ernesto Milano

European University Institute Library
Badia Fiesolana, Via dei Roccettini 9, 50016 San Domino
Tel: (055) 4685379 *Fax:* (055) 468544
E-mail: biblio@iue.it
Telex: 571528 Iue *Cable:* UNIVEUR
Key Personnel
Librarian: Peter Hertner

Biblioteca Comunale Malatestiana
Piazza Bufalini 1, 47023 Cesena (Forli)
Tel: (0547) 610892 *Fax:* (0547) 21237
Key Personnel
Librarian: Dr Lorenzo Baldacchini

Biblioteca Universitaria di Padua
Via S Biagio 7, 35121 Padua
Tel: (049) 8240211; (049) 8240241 *Fax:* (049) 8762711
E-mail: bupd@librari.beniculturali.it
Web Site: www.unipd.it/bibliotecauniversitaria

ITALY

Key Personnel
Librarian: Rosalba Suriano
Founded: 1629

Biblioteca Riccardiana
Via dei Ginori 10, 50129 Florence
Tel: (055) 212586 *Fax:* (055) 211379
Key Personnel
Dir: Dott Giovanna Lazzi

Biblioteca Nazionale Sagarriga Visconti Volpi
Palazzo Ateneo, Piazza Umberto 1, 70122 Bari
Tel: (080) 5212534 *Fax:* (080) 5212667
Key Personnel
Dir: Marie Theresa Tafuri DiMeligano

Universita degli Studi di Firenze, Biblioteca di Lettre e Filosofia
Piazza Brunelleschi, 4, 50121 Florence
Tel: (055) 27571 *Fax:* (055) 243471; (055) 264194
Key Personnel
Dir: Dr Angelo Marino *E-mail:* marino@cesitl.unifi.it
Librarian: A M Tammaro

Universita di Roma 'La Sapienza'
Division of Uffieio Centrale Per I Beni Librari E Istituti Culturali
Piazzale Aldo Moro 5, 00185 Rome
Tel: (06) 4456820; (06) 4474021 *Fax:* (06) 4474024
E-mail: alessandrina@librari.beniculturali.it
Web Site: www.alessandrina.librari.beniculturali.it
Key Personnel
Dir: Maria Concetta Petrollo *E-mail:* petrollo@uniromal.it
Publication(s): *Catalogo Del Fondo Leopardiano*; *Inchiostri Per L'Infanzia*; *Voci Di Roma*
Parent Company: Ministero Per I Beni E Le Attivita Culturali

Jamaica

Jamaica Archives
King & Manchester Sts, Spanish Town
Tel: (876) 984-2581 *Fax:* (876) 984-8254
Key Personnel
Government Archivist: Elizabeth Williams

Jamaica Library Service
2 Tom Redcam Dr, Kingston 5
Mailing Address: PO Box 58, Kingston 5
Tel: (876) 926-3310; (876) 926-3312 *Fax:* (876) 926-2188
Key Personnel
Dir: Gloria E Salmon
Publication(s): *Book Production in Jamaica: A Select List of Jamaican Publications*; *Jamaica: A Select Bibliography 1900-1963*; *Jamaica Library Service 21 Years of Progress in Pictures 1948-1969*; *Jamaica Poetry: A Checklist, Slavery to the Present*; *Reflections on Black River*; *What's New in Librarianship*

National Library of Jamaica
12-16 East St, Kingston
Mailing Address: PO Box 823, Kingston
Tel: (876) 967-1526 *Fax:* (876) 922-5567
E-mail: nlj@infochan.com
Web Site: www.nlj.org.jm *Cable:* NALIBJAM
Key Personnel
Dir: John Aarons
The Library is the National Reference Library of Jamaica. Its main functions are to collect and preserve the national imprint, to serve as the bibliographic center for Jamaica and the focal point of the national information system.
Publication(s): *Gleaner* (of Jamaica); *Jamaican National Bibliography* (Occasional bibliography series); *The Gleaner* (Index monthly index to the)

Northern Carribean University
Hiram S Walters Resource Center, Mandeville
Tel: (876) 962-2204 *Fax:* (876) 962-0075
E-mail: hswalters@netscape.net
Web Site: www.w.college.edu
Key Personnel
Library Dir: Heather Rodriguez Richards
Branch Office(s)
Andrews School of Nursing, Kingston

United Theological College of the West Indies
Golding Ave, Kingston 7
Mailing Address: PO Box 136, Kingston 7
Tel: (876) 927-2868 *Fax:* (876) 977-0812
E-mail: unitheol@cwjamaica.com
Web Site: www.utcwi.edu.jm
Key Personnel
Acting President: Rev Lewin Williams, PhD
Librarian: Miss Adenike Soyibo *Tel:* (876) 927-1724 *E-mail:* asoyibo@hotmail.com
Founded: 1966
Theological Seminary.
Publication(s): *Caribbean Journal of Religious Studies* (biennially)

University of Technology, Jamaica
Calvin McKain Library, 237 Old Hope Rd, Kingston 6
Tel: (876) 927-1680; (876) 927-1688 *Fax:* (876) 927-1614
E-mail: library@utech.edu.jm
Web Site: www.utechjamaica.edu.jm
Key Personnel
University Librarian: Hermine C Salmon
Founded: 1958

University of the West Indies Library (Jamaica)
Main Library, Mona, Kingston 7
Tel: (876) 927-2123 *Fax:* (876) 927-1926
E-mail: manlibry@uwimona.edu.jm
Web Site: www.library.uwimona.edu.jm:1104
Telex: 2123 *Cable:* UNIVERS
Key Personnel
University/Campus Librarian: Ms Stephney Ferguson *Tel:* (876) 970-2945 *E-mail:* sfergusn@uwimona.edu.jm
Founded: 1948
Educational Institution.
Publication(s): *Medical Caribbeana: An Index to Caribbean Health Sciences Literature* (Library Annual Report); *Research for Development, Vol 1* (1998, Bibliography of staff publications 1993-1998); *Research for Development: Strengthening Our Tourism Product* (Bibliography)
Branch Office(s)
Medical Library
Science Library

Japan

Gifu Diagaku Fuzoku Toshokan
1-1 Yanagido, Gifu 501-11
Tel: (0582) 801111

Hokkaido University Library
Kita-8, Nishi-5, Kitakyu-shu, Sapporo, Hokkaido 060
Tel: (011) 7162111 *Fax:* (011) 7464595
Key Personnel
Lib Prof: T Sanbong
Librarian: Hiroshi Yoshida
Publication(s): *Yuin* (The Hokkaido University Library Bulletin, in Japanese, quarterly)

International Documentation Center, The University of Tokyo
General Library, Univ of Tokyo, 7-3-1, Bunkyo-Ku, Tokyo 113-0033
Tel: (03) 38122111 ext 2645 *Fax:* (03) 58002426
E-mail: kokusai@lib.u-tokyo.ac.jp
Key Personnel
Head Librarian: Akira Ohno
Librarian: Ms Kayu Sakata
Publication(s): *Watakushitachi no Kokuren* (The Japanese brochure about the United Nations published in 1995)

Kokuritsu Kobunshokan
3-2 Kitanomarukoen, Chiyoda-ku, Tokyo 102
Tel: (03) 32140621 *Fax:* (03) 32128806
Key Personnel
Dir Gen: Kazumasa Iwahashi
National Archives of Japan.

Kyoto Sangyo University Library
Kamigamo Motoyama, Kita-ku, Kyoto 603
Tel: (075) 7012151 *Fax:* (075) 7051447
Key Personnel
Dir: Satora Yabunaka

Kyushu University Library
6-10-1 Hakozaki, Higashi-ku, Fukuoka 812
Tel: (092) 6411101; (092) 6422111
Key Personnel
Librarian: S Arikana

School of Library & Information Science
Keio University, 2-15-45 Mita Minato-ku, Tokyo 108
Tel: (03) 34534511
Key Personnel
Librarian: Motoko Sekiguchi

National Diet Library
1-10-1 Nagata-cho, Chiyoda-ku, Tokyo 100-8924
Tel: (03) 35812331 *Fax:* (03) 35082934
E-mail: kokusai@ndl.go.jp
Web Site: www.ndl.go.jp
Key Personnel
Librarian: Masao Tobari
Dir Planning & Cooperation Division: Yukiko Saito
Founded: 1948
As The only national library in Japan, provides services for the Diet, for the government & for the general public. All publications in Japan are deposited with the Library, which produces the database of domestic publications.
Publication(s): *Biburosu* (Biblos, quarterly, on-line); *Nihon kagakugijutsu kankei chikuji kankobutsu soran* (Directory of Japanese Scientific Periodicals, 1997, on-line); *Nihon zenkoku shoshi* (Japanese National Bibliography, weekly, on-line); *NDL Newsletter* (bimonthly, on-line); *Refarensu* (Reference, monthly)

Osaka University Library
1-4 Machikaneyama-cho, Toyonaka, Osaka 560
Tel: (06) 8505045 *Fax:* (06) 8505052
Key Personnel
Dir, Library Services: Takeshi Hayashi

Osaka Prefectural Nakanoshima Library
1-2-10 Nakanoshima, Kita-ku, Osaka 530
Tel: (06) 2030474 *Fax:* (06) 2034914
Key Personnel
Head Librarian: Shigemitsu Nakayama

Tenri Central Library
Tenri University, 1050 Somanouchi-machi, Tenrishi, Nara 632-8577
Tel: (0743) 631515 *Fax:* (0743) 637728
E-mail: info@tcl.gr.jp
Web Site: www.tcl.gr.jp
Key Personnel
Chief Librarian: Keiichiro Moroi

Tohoku University Library
Kawauchi, Sendai, Miyagi 980
Tel: (0222) 2175933; (0221) 2174844 *Fax:* (0222) 2175949; (0222) 217846
E-mail: desk@library.tohoku.ac.jp

Tokyo Metropolitan Central Library
5-7-13 Minami-Azabu, Minato-ku, Tokyo 106 8577
Tel: (03) 34428451 *Fax:* (03) 34478924
Web Site: www.library.metro.tokyo.jp/
Key Personnel
Dir: Okabe Kazukuni

The Toyo Bunko
Honkomagome 2-28-21, Bunkyo-ku, Tokyo 113 0021
Tel: (03) 39420121 *Fax:* (03) 39420258
E-mail: webmaster@toyo-bunko.or.jp
Web Site: www.toyo-bunko.or.jp/toyobunko-e
Key Personnel
Dir: Yoshinobu Shiba
Founded: 1924
Also Centre for East Asian Cultural Studies for UNESCO, for which publications include various directories, bibliographies & monographs.
Publication(s): *Asian Research Trends: A Humanities & Social Science Review* (journal, annually); *Memoirs of the Research Department of the Toyo Bunko* (journal, annually)

University of Tokyo Library
7-3-1, Hongo, Bunkyo-ku, Tokyo 113
Tel: (03) 38122111 *Fax:* (03) 38164208
E-mail: kikaku@lib.u-tokyo.ac.jp
Key Personnel
Dir: K Rodumoto

Waseda University Library
1-6-1 Nishiwaseda, Shinjuku-ku, Tokyo 160
Tel: (03) 32034141
E-mail: intl-ac@mn.naseda.ac.jp
Telex: 2323280
Key Personnel
Librarian: T Hamada
Publication(s): *Bulletin of Waseda University Library*

Jordan

Amman Public Library
PO Box 182181, Amman
Tel: (06) 637111; (06) 627718 *Fax:* (06) 649420
Telex: 21969 Amcity Jo
Key Personnel
City Librarian: Abdul-Fattah Al-Homran

British Council Library
Rainbow St, Amman Centre, Amman 11118
Mailing Address: PO Box 634, Amman 11118
Tel: (06) 4636147; (06) 4636148 *Fax:* (06) 4656413
Web Site: www.britishcouncil.org.jo
Key Personnel
Information Officer: Sonia Kawas *E-mail:* sonia.kawas@britishcouncil.org.jo
Founded: 1950

The Department of the National Library
AL-Sharif Hussein Ben Ali St, Amman
Mailing Address: PO Box 6070, Amman
Tel: (06) 610311 *Fax:* (06) 616832
Key Personnel
Dir General: Ousama Mikadi

Jordan University of Science and Technology Library
c/o University of Jordan Central Library, Amman
Mailing Address: PO Box 20670, Amman
Tel: (06) 843555 *Fax:* (06) 832318
Telex: 21629
Key Personnel
Dir: Dr Salah Jarrar

Mu'tah University Library
PO Box 7, Mu'tah, Al Karak
Tel: (06) 617860 *Fax:* (03) 654061
Telex: 63003 Mu'tah JO
Key Personnel
Dir: Amin Al-Najdawi

Public Library
PO Box 348, Irbid 1957
Key Personnel
Librarian: Anwar Ishaq Al-Nshiwat

Royal Scientific Society Library
PO Box 925819, Amman
Tel: (06) 844700 *Fax:* (06) 844806
Telex: 21276 RAMAH
Key Personnel
President: Dr Youssef Mussier

University of Jordan Library
Amman
Mailing Address: PO Box 20670, Amman
Tel: (06) 843555 *Fax:* (06) 832318
Telex: 21629 Unvj jo
Key Personnel
Acting Dir: Dr Salah Jarrar
Publication(s): *Al-Maktaba* (monthly newsletter); *Arab References till 1980* (in Arabic); *Jordanian Publications in 1982*; *Periodical Holdings* (in English and Arabic); *The Library Guide* (in English and Arabic)

Yarmouk University Library
PO Box 566, Irbid 21163
Tel: (02) 271100 ext 2870 *Fax:* (02) 7271273
Web Site: www.yu.edu.jo
Telex: 51566 Yarmuk Jo *Cable:* Yarmouk Jordan
Key Personnel
Dir: M Savaveh
Founded: 1976
Specialize in education/library.

Kazakstan

Kazakhstan Academy of Sciences
Central Library of the Kazakh Academy of Science, ul Shevchenko 28, 480021 Almaty
Tel: (03272) 628341 (voice & fax)
Key Personnel
Dir: K K Abugalieva

Kenya

Egerton University Library
PO Box 536, Njoro
Tel: (037) 61620 *Fax:* (037) 61527
E-mail: eu-vc@net2000kc.com
Telex: 33075
Key Personnel
Librarian: S C Otenya
Publication(s): *Egerton University Journal*

Kabete Library
c/o University of Nairobi, Main (Ghandi) Library, Nairobi
Mailing Address: PO Box 30197, Nairobi
Tel: (02) 334244 *Fax:* (02) 336885
Key Personnel
Acting Librarian: S Mathangani

Kenya Agricultural Research Institute
PO Box 57811, Nairobi
Tel: (02) 32880 *Fax:* (0154) 583384
Key Personnel
Librarian: Daniel NJoroge Kanijane

Kenya National Archives & Documentation Service
Library, Kenya National Archives Bldg, Moi Ave, Nairobi
Mailing Address: PO Box 49210, Nairobi
Tel: (02) 228959 *Fax:* (02) 228020
E-mail: knarchives@kenyaweb.com
Telex: 228020 *Cable:* ARCHIVES
Key Personnel
Dir: Musila Musembi
Librarian: Wekalao Namande
Founded: 1946
Publication(s): *Acquisitions guides* (various)

Kenya National Library Service
Ngong Rd, Nairobi
Mailing Address: PO Box 30573, Nairobi
Tel: (02) 725550 *Fax:* (02) 721749
E-mail: knls@nbnet.co.ke
Web Site: www.knls.or.ke *Cable:* KENLIB
Key Personnel
Dir: S K Ng'Anga
Publication(s): *Kenya National Bibliography*; *Kenyan Periodicals Directory*

Kenya Polytechnic Library
Haile Selassie Ave, Nairobi
Mailing Address: PO Box 52428, Nairobi
Tel: (02) 338231
Key Personnel
Librarian: S K Ng'Anga

Kenya School of Law
PO Box 30369, Nairobi
Key Personnel
Chief Librarian: Peter Okoth

Kenya Technical Teachers' College Library
PO Box 44600, Nairobi
Tel: (02) 520211 *Fax:* (02) 520037
Telex: 22981 kttcol
Key Personnel
Librarian: G M King'ori
Publication(s): *Mwalimu Kenya Education Supplement* (monthly); *Secondary School Library Facilities in Central Province, Kenya*; *Serials Literature, Exploitation and Use in Libraries*; *The Problems of Providing Library Services to School Children in Developing Countries*

Kenyatta University Library
PO Box 43844, Nairobi
Tel: (02) 810901 *Fax:* (02) 810759
Telex: 25483
Key Personnel
Librarian: James Mwangi Nganga
Publication(s): *Directory of Research in the University*; *Education in Kenya: an Index* (1984); *Education in Kenya since Independence: a bibliography* (1963-1983)

KENYA

McMillan Memorial Library
Banda St, Nairobi
Mailing Address: PO Box 40791, Nairobi
Tel: (02) 21844
Key Personnel
Chief Librarian: A O Esilaba

Mines & Geological Department Library
Kencom House, City Hall Way, Moi Ave, Nairobi
Mailing Address: PO Box 30009, Nairobi
Tel: (02) 29621 *Cable:* Mineralogy
Key Personnel
Commissioner: C Y O Owayo

Ministry of Agriculture & Livestock Development Library
Kilimo House, Nairobi
Mailing Address: PO Box 30028, Nairobi
Tel: (02) 718870 *Fax:* (02) 725774
Telex: 22766 minag ke
Under the charge of The Library Services Co-ordinator.
Publication(s): *Economic Review of Agriculture*

Mombasa Polytechnic Library
Tom Myoba Ave, Mombasa
Mailing Address: PO Box 90420, Mombasa
Tel: (011) 492222
Key Personnel
Librarian: R Kasina

National Public Health Laboratory Services (Medical Department)
Kenyatta National Hospital, NPHLS Bldg, Nairobi
Mailing Address: PO Box 20750, Nairobi
Tel: (02) 725601 *Fax:* (02) 729504
Key Personnel
Dir: Dr Jack Nyamongo

University of Nairobi Libraries
University Way, GPO 00100 Nairobi
Mailing Address: PO Box 30197, GPO 00100 Nairobi
Tel: (02) 334244 *Fax:* (02) 336885
E-mail: jkml@uonbi.ac.ke
Web Site: www.uonbi.ac.ke
Telex: 22095-Varsity KE *Cable:* VARSITY NAIROBI
Key Personnel
University Librarian: Salome W Mathangani
 E-mail: salma@uonbi.ac.ke
Specialize in supporting study, teaching and research needs of the University of Nairobi.
Branch Office(s)
Chiromo Library, College of Biological and Physical Sciences, Chiromo, Nairobi *Tel:* (02) 43181-90
Kabete Library, PO Box 30197, College of Agriculture and Veterinary Sciences, Kabete, Nairobi *Tel:* (02) 632143; (02) 631277
Kikuyu Library, College of Education and External Studies, PO Box 92, Kikuyu *Tel:* (02) 32021; (02) 32016; (02) 31117-8
Lower Kabete Library, Lower Kabete, Nairobi *Tel:* (02) 732160/5
Parklands Law Library, Parklands Campus, Parklands, Nairobi *Tel:* (02) 742261-4
ADD, State House Road, Nairobi *Tel:* (02) 724520/5 (Architecture Design & Development)
Medical, Ngong Road, Nairobi *Tel:* 02 726300

Democratic People's Republic of Korea

State Central Library
c/o Grand People's Study House, Pyongyang
Mailing Address: PO Box 200, Pyongyang
Tel: (02) 34066

Republic of Korea

Dongguk University Central Library
26, 3-ga Pil-dong, Jung-gu, Seoul
Tel: (02) 2603114 *Fax:* (02) 2771274

Ewha Womans University Central Library
11-1 Daehyun-dong, Sudaemun-gu, Seoul 120-750
Tel: (02) 3602114 *Fax:* (02) 3935903
E-mail: libacq@mm.ewha.ac.kr
Key Personnel
Librarian: Bong Hee Kim

Korea University Library
5-1-2 Anamdong, Sungbuk-ku, Sungbuk-ku, Seoul
Tel: (02) 942641; (02) 942649; (02) 944381; (02) 944389 *Fax:* (02) 9225820

Korea Development Institute Library
207-41, Chongnyangri-dong, Dongdaemun-ku, Seoul 130-012
Mailing Address: PO Box 113, Chong Nyang, Seoul 130-012
Tel: (02) 958 4262 *Fax:* (02) 958 4261
E-mail: libyhj@kdiux.kdi.re.kr
Web Site: www.kdi.re.kr
Key Personnel
Chief Librarian: Hwajin Yoon
Founded: 1971
Economics Research Institution.

Kyungpook National University Central Library
1370 Sankyuk-dong Puk-ku, Taegu 702-701
Tel: (053) 9555516 *Fax:* (053) 9506533

National Assembly Library
One Youido-dong, Yeongdeungpo-gu, Seoul
Tel: (02) 7884101; (02) 7843565 *Fax:* (02) 7884301; (02) 7884193
E-mail: cdcol@nanet.go.jp
Telex: 25849
Key Personnel
Librarian: Chong-Il Park
Publication(s): *Acquisition List (in Korean)* (bimonthly & annually); *Index to Korean-Language Periodicals (in Korean)* (bimonthly & annually); *Index to Korean Laws and Statutes (in Korean)* (biennially); *Index to National Assembly Debates (in Korean)* (irregularly); *Index to Recent Periodical Articles of Major Interests (in Korean)* (monthly); *Issue Briefs (in Korean)* (irregularly); *Legislative Information Analysis (in Korean)* (quarterly); *List of Theses for Doctors' and Masters' Degrees Awarded in Korea (in Korean)* (annually); *National Assembly Library Review (in Korean)* (bimonthly)

National Central Library, see The National Library of Korea

The National Library of Korea
Formerly National Central Library
San 60-1 Banpo-Dong, Seocho-Gu, Seoul 137-702
Tel: (02) 5354142; (02) 5900548 *Fax:* (02) 5965749
E-mail: nlkpc@sun.nl.or.kr
Key Personnel
Librarian: Hyun-Taek Shin
Publication(s): *Bibliographie Index of Korea*; *Korean National Bibliography*
Branch Office(s)
635 Yeoksam-dong, Kangnam-gu, Seoul

Seoul National University Library
SAN 56-1, Shillim-Dong, Kwanak-Gu, Seoul 151-742
Tel: (02) 880-5284 *Fax:* (02) 8712972
E-mail: joongyo@plaza.snu.ac.kr

United Nations Depository Library
1 Anam-dong, Sungbuk-gu, Seoul
Tel: (02) 3290-1492 *Fax:* (02) 922-4633
E-mail: mgc@kulib.korea.ac.kr
Key Personnel
Chief Librarian: Kim Deoug Hoon

Yonsei University Library
134 Shinchon-dong, Seodaemoon-ku, Seoul 120-749
Tel: (02) 3613308 *Fax:* (02) 3936803
E-mail: sbchang@bubble.yonsei.ac.kr

Kuwait

Kuwait University Library
PO Box 17140, Kuwait
Tel: 4813182 *Fax:* 4816095
Telex: 22616
Key Personnel
Dir: Dr Husain A Al-Ansari
Publication(s): *The Library Bulletin*

Kuwait National Library, see National Library of Kuwait

National Library of Kuwait
Formerly Kuwait National Library
Mubarakiya St, (Opposite) Al-Muzaini Exchange, Kuwait City
Mailing Address: PO Box 26182, 13122 Safat
Tel: 2415192; 2415190 *Fax:* 2415195
E-mail: nccalknl@ncc.moc.kw *Cable:* Thaquf
Key Personnel
Dir General: Wafa'a H Al-Sane
Founded: 1994
National Depository, ISBN, UN Depository.
Parent Company: National Council for Culture, Arts & Letters

National Scientific and Technical Information Center (NSTIC)
Kuwait Institute for Scientific Research, 13109 Safat
Mailing Address: PO Box 24885, 13109 Safat
Tel: 4818713 *Fax:* 4836097
Telex: Kisr Kt 22299 *Cable:* SCIENCE KUWAIT
Key Personnel
Dir: Mrs Ferial Al-Freih

Laos People's Democratic Republic

Bibliotheque Nationale
BP 122, Vientiane
Tel: (021) 212452; (021) 222485 *Fax:* (021) 213029
E-mail: pfd-mill@pan.laos.net.la

Latvia

LNB, see National Library of Latvia

National Library of Latvia (Latvijas Nacionala Biblioteka)
14 K Barona Str, LV-1423 Riga
Tel: (02) 7289874 *Fax:* (02) 7280851
E-mail: lnb@lbi.lnb.lv
Web Site: www.latnet.lv/lnb
Key Personnel
Dir: Mr Andris Vilks *E-mail:* andrisv@lbi.lnb.lv
Founded: 1919
The National Library of Latvia is the keeper of all printed matter of the Republic of Latvia, the developer of national bibliographic resources & the center for development of a system of state libraries. NLL, coordinating with other libraries, forms a depository of national literature & performs the functions of an interlibrary loan center in Latvia.
Publication(s): *Latviesu zinatne un literatura*; *Latvijas preses hronika* (ISSN 1017-7604)

Lebanon

American University of Beirut Libraries
Bliss St, Riad El Solh, Beirut 1107 2020
Mailing Address: PO Box 11-0236, Riad El Solh, Beirut 1107 2020
Tel: (01) 340460 *Fax:* (01) 744703
E-mail: library@aub.edu.lb
Web Site: www.aub.edu.lb/
Telex: 20801 *Cable:* AMUNOB
Key Personnel
University Librarian: Helen Bikhazi
Constituent Libraries: Jafet Memorial Library (Central Library), Farm Library; Science and Agriculture Library; Engineering and Architecture Library.

Library of Beirut Arab University
PO Box 11-5020, Beirut
Tel: (01) 300110 *Fax:* (01) 818402
E-mail: bau@inco.com.lb

Bibliotheque de l'Ecole Superieure des Lettres
rue de Damas, BP 1931, Beirut

Faculte des Sciences Medicales, Bibliotheque
Damascus St, BP 115076 Riyad El-Solh, Beirut
Tel: (01) 614001-2-3 *Fax:* (01) 614054
E-mail: msamaha@usj.edu.lb
Web Site: www.usj.edu.lb
Parent Company: Universite Saint Joseph

Library of the Faculty of Engineering
Universite St Joseph, PO Box 1514, Beirut
Tel: (01) 395606
Key Personnel
Librarian: Henri Ketterer

Library of the Faculty of Law
Universite St Joseph, Rue de Damas, Beirut
Mailing Address: BP 175208, Beirut
Tel: (01) 426 456 *Fax:* (01) 423 369
Publication(s): *Proche-Orient, Etudes Juridiques*

Bibliotheque de l'Institut Francais d'Archeologie du Proche Orient
Rue de Damas, Beirut
Mailing Address: PO Box 11-1424, Beirut
Tel: (01) 615 844 *Fax:* (01) 615 866
E-mail: ifapo@lb.refer.org
Key Personnel
Dir: Jean-Marie Dentzer
Publication(s): *Bibliotheque Archeologique et Historique* (147 titles); *Syria, Revue d'art oriental et d'archeologie* (annually, 2 vols)

Nami C Jafet Memorial Library, see American University of Beirut Libraries

Bibliotheque Nationale du Liban
BP 11-945, Beirut
Tel: (01) 862957 *Fax:* (01) 374079

Library of the Near East School of Theology
PO Box 13-5780, Chouran, Beirut
Tel: (01) 354194 *Fax:* (01) 347129
E-mail: nest.lib@inco.com.lb
Telex: 44246 NEST LE
Key Personnel
Librarian: David A Kerry
Founded: 1932
Publication(s): *Theological Review*

Library of the Monastery of St-Saviour (Basilian Missionary Order of St-Saviour)
Saida

Bibliotheque Orientale
rue de l'Universite St Joseph 755, Beirut
Mailing Address: PO Box 166, Beirut
Tel: (01) 200297
E-mail: bibor@cyberia.net.lb
Key Personnel
Dir: Martin J McDermott

Lesotho

British Council Library
Hobson's Sq, Maseru 100
Mailing Address: PO Box 429, 100 Maseru
Tel: 312609 *Fax:* 310363
E-mail: libsupbc@adelfang.co.za
Key Personnel
Library Supervisor: Zanedde Nsibirwa

Lesotho National Library Service
Kingsway Rd, Griffith Hill Junction, Maseru 100
Mailing Address: PO Box 985, Maseru 100
Tel: 323100 *Fax:* 327890
Telex: 4228
Key Personnel
Librarian: Ms Dikeledi J Setlogelo

National University of Lesotho Library
Thomas Mofolo Library, Via Maseru, Roma 180
Tel: 340601 *Fax:* 340000
Telex: 4303 10 *Cable:* UNITER
Key Personnel
University Librarian: Dr Matseliso moshoeshoe Chadzingwa *E-mail:* m.moshoeshoe-chadzingwa@nul.ls

Liberia

Cuttington University College Library
Episcopal Church Off Bldg, Monrovia
Mailing Address: PO Box 10-277, 1000 Monrovia 10
Tel: 227413

Government Public Library
Ashmun St, Monrovia

University of Liberia Libraries
PO Box 9020, Monrovia
Tel: 224671
Key Personnel
Dir: Dr C Wesley Armstrong

Libyan Arab Jamahiriya

Benghazi Public Library
Shar a Umar al-Mukhtar, Benghazi
Tel: (061) 96379

Al- Fateh University, The Central Library
PO Box 13482, Tripoli
Tel: (022) 605441 *Fax:* (022) 605460
Telex: 20629

Government Library
14 Shar'a al-Jazair, Tripoli

National Archives
Castello, Tripoli
Tel: (02133) 40166

National Library
PO Box 9127, Benghazi
Tel: (061) 90509 *Fax:* (061) 96379
Telex: 40107

University of Garyounis Library
SPLA Jamahiriya, Benghazi
Mailing Address: PO Box 1308, Benghazi
Tel: (022) 29021
Telex: 40175 unigarly
Key Personnel
Librarian: Ahmed M Gallal

Liechtenstein

Liechtensteinische Landesbibliothek
Oeffentliche Stiftung, Gerberweg 5, 9490 Vaduz
Mailing Address: Postfach 385, 9490 Vaduz
Tel: 2366362 *Fax:* 2331419
E-mail: labibl@firstlink.li
Web Site: www.lbfl.li
Key Personnel
Dir: Dr Ospelt Alois
Founded: 1961
National Library.
Publication(s): *Liechtensteinische Bibliographie*

Lithuania

Martynas Mazvydas National Library of Lithuania (Lietuvos Nacionaline Martyno Mazvydo Biblioteka)
Gedimino pr 51, LT-2600 Vilnius
Tel: (02) 497023 *Fax:* (02) 496129
E-mail: biblio@lnb.lt
Web Site: www.lnb.lt
Key Personnel
Deputy Dir & Dir, Bibliography & Book Science Center: Dr Regina Varniene
Deputy Dir & Dir, Library Research Center: Vytautas Gudaitis
Deputy Dir: Algirdas Plioplys
Librarian: Dr Vladas Bulavas
Founded: 1919
Library & information services.
Publication(s): *Bibliografijos Zinios* (Bibliography News, monthly); *Lietuvos Spaudos Statistika* (Lithuanian Press Statistics, annually); *Tarp Knygu* (In the World of Books, monthly); *Mokslo darbai* (Works of Sciences:, annually)

Vilnius University Library (Vilniaus Universiteto Biblioteka)
Universiteto 3, 2633-LT Vilnius
Tel: (02) 687101 *Fax:* (02) 687104
E-mail: mb@mb.vu.lt
Web Site: www.mb.vu.lt
Key Personnel
Dir & Librarian: B Butkeviciene *E-mail:* birute.butkeviciene@mb.vu.lt
Founded: 1570
Member of Lithuanian Academic Libraries Association.

Luxembourg

Bibliotheque de la Ville
26 rue Emile Mayrisch, Esch-sur-Alzette 4002
Tel: 547383
Key Personnel
Librarian: Fernand Roeltgen

Bibliotheque Nationale (National Library)
37, blvd F-D Roosevelt, L-2450 Luxembourg
Tel: 229755-1 *Fax:* 475672
Key Personnel
Dir: Dr Monique Kieffer *E-mail:* monique.kieffer@bi.etat.lu
Publication(s): *Bibliographie d'histoire luxembourgeoise*; *Bibliographie luxembourgeoise*

Archives Nationales (National Archives)
Plateau du St-Esprit, BP 6, 2010 Luxembourg
Tel: 4786660 *Fax:* 474692
Key Personnel
Dir: Dr Cornel Meder
Publication(s): *Publications des Anlux, Plusieurs Series* (catalogs, repertories, reprints)

Macau

Biblioteca Central de Macau
Av Conselheiro Ferreira de Almeida No 89A-B, Macao
Tel: 371623 *Fax:* 318756
Key Personnel
Chief Librarian: Ophelia Tang
Publication(s): *Boletim Bibliografico de Macau*

The Former Yugoslav Republic of Macedonia

Arhiv na Makedonija
Biblioteka, Kej Dimitar Vlahov bb, Skopje
Mailing Address: P0 Box 496, 91001 Skopje
Tel: (091) 116571 *Fax:* (091) 115827
Key Personnel
Dir: Kiro Dojcinovski
Archives of Macedonia.

Narodna i univerzitetska biblioteka Kliment Ohridski ('Kliment Ohridski' National and University Library)
bulevar 'Goce Delcev' br 6, 91000 Skopje
Mailing Address: PP 566, 91000 Skopje
Tel: (091) 115177 *Fax:* (091) 226846
E-mail: kliment@nubski.edu.mk
Publication(s): *Bibliografija KPJ-SKM 1919-1979*; *Bilten na izdanija od oblasta na samoupravuvanjeto vo Jugoslavija*; *Katalog na staropecateni i retki knigi vo Narodnata i Univerzitetskata Biblioteka 'Kliment Ohridski' - Skopje*; *Makedonska Bibliografija*

Madagascar

Bibliotheque Universitaire
Campus Universitaire d'Ankatso, PO Box 908, Antananarivo
Tel: (02) 23228
E-mail: buunivtanamg@minitel.refer.org
Key Personnel
Dir: Jean-Noel Randriantsara
Publication(s): *Bibliographie annuelle de Madagascar*

Bibliotheque du Centre Culturel Albert Camus
14 Ave de l'Independance, BP 488, Antananarivo
Tel: (02) 23647 *Fax:* (02) 21338
E-mail: medccac@dts.ng
Telex: 22507
Key Personnel
Contact: Singare Reinhard Veionique

Bibliotheque Nationale Malagasy
Anosy, BP 257, Antananarivo
Tel: (02) 25872 *Fax:* (02) 29448

Bibliotheque Municipale
Av du 18 juin, BP 729, Antananarivo
Tel: (04) 21176
Key Personnel
President: Julien Razafimandimbilaza
Librarian: Albert Denis Rakoto

Archives Nationales de Madagascar
BP 3384, Antananarivo
Key Personnel
Dir: Mdme Sahondra Andriamihamina

Malawi

British Council Library
PO Box 30222, Lilongwe 3
Tel: 783244 *Fax:* 782945
Web Site: www.britishcouncil.org/malawi/
Telex: 44476 Bricoun Ml

Bunda College of Agriculture Library
PO Box 219, Lilongwe
Tel: 277222 *Fax:* 277364; 277251
E-mail: bundalibrary@bunda.sdup.org.mw
Web Site: www.bunda.sdnp.org.mw
Telex: 43622 Bunda Ml *Cable:* BUNDAGRIC
Key Personnel
Librarian: Margaret E Ngwira
Parent Company: Bunda College of Agriculture, University of Malawi

Malawi National Library Service
Area 13, Capital City, Lilongwe 3
Mailing Address: PO Box 30314, Lilongwe 3
Tel: 783700
Key Personnel
National Librarian: R S Mabomba

National Archives of Malawi
Mkulichi Rd, Zomba
Mailing Address: PO Box 62, Zomba
Tel: 522922 *Fax:* 522148
Key Personnel
Librarian: D D Najira
Publication(s): *Malawi National Bibliography*

University of Malawi Libraries
PO Box 280, Zomba
Tel: 524222; 525935 *Fax:* 525225
Telex: 44742
Key Personnel
Librarian: Steve S Mwiyeriwa *E-mail:* smwiyeriwa@unima.wn.apc.org; smwiyeriwa@chirunga.sdnp.org.mw
Founded: 1965
Publication(s): *An Annotated Bibliography of Education in Malawi*; *Directory of Malawi Libraries*; *Library Bulletin*; *Report on University Libraries*
Parent Company: University of Malawi
Branch Office(s)
Bunda College of Agriculture Library
Chancellor College Library
College of Medicine Library
Kamuzu College of Nursing Library
Polytechnic Library

University of Malawi, Polytechnic Library
PB 303, Chichiri, Blantyre 3
Tel: 670411 *Fax:* 670578
Telex: 44613 Polytec
Key Personnel
Librarian: Paul Kanthambi

Malaysia

British Council Library
Jl Bukit Aman, 50480 Kuala Lumpur
Mailing Address: PO Box 10539, 50480 Kuala Lumpur
Tel: (03) 2987555 *Fax:* (03) 2937214
E-mail: brcokl@britcoun.org.my
Web Site: www.britcoun.org.my
Telex: MA 31052
Key Personnel
Librarian & Information Services Manager: Ms Gaik Sim Khoo

Branch Office(s)
3 World Quay, 10300 Penang
PO Box 10746, Sabah
PO Box 615, Sarawak

Ministry of Agriculture Library
Wisma Tani, Jl Sultan Salahuddin, 50624 Kuala Lumpur
Tel: (03) 2982011 *Fax:* (03) 2913758
Telex: TANIAN MA 33045 *Cable:* TANI KUALA LUMPUR
Key Personnel
Librarian: Mrs Pathmavathy Satyahoorthy
Publication(s): *Bulletin of the Ministry of Agriculture* (irregular); *Malaysian Agricultural Journal* (biannual)

Ministry of Environment & Public Health, Library Division
Jl P Ramlee, 93572 Kuching Sarawak
Tel: (082) 242911 *Fax:* (082) 246552
Key Personnel
Chief Librarian: Johnny Kueh

National Archives of Malaysia
Jalan Duta, 50568 Kuala Lumpur
Tel: (03) 2543244 *Fax:* (03) 2555679 *Cable:* ARKIB KUALALUMPUR
Key Personnel
Dir-Gen: Mrs Zakiah Hanum Nor
Other publications include Acquisitions List, List of Record & Archives Groups available for researchs bibliographies & others.
Publication(s): *Annual Report of the National Archives* (Bulletins)

National Library of Malaysia (Gift & Exchange Unit)
232, Jalan Tun Razak, 50572 Kuala Lumpur
Tel: (03) 2943488 *Fax:* (03) 2927899
E-mail: pnmweb@www.pnm.my
Telex: MA NATLIB 30092
Key Personnel
Dir-General: Mariam Abdul Kadir
Publication(s): *Bibliography of books in Bahasa Malaysia*; *Directory of Librarians in Malaysia*; *Directory of Libraries in Malaysia*; *Index to Malaysian Conferences* (annually); *Malaysian National Bibliography* (quarterly, annually); *Malaysian Newspaper Index* (quarterly); *Malaysian Periodicals Index* (biannually)

National University of Malaysia Library
Perpustakaan, 43600 Bangi, Selangor
Tel: (03) 8250001 *Fax:* (03) 8256484
Telex: MA 31496
Key Personnel
Chief Librarian: Muslim Norsham
  E-mail: norsham@pkrisc.cc.ukm.my
Holds Malay Library Collection (approx 30,000 titles).
Publication(s): *Katalog Koleksi Melayu, Penerbit Ukm 1990*

Perpustakaan Negeri Sabah, see Sabah State Library

Rubber Research Institute of Malaysia Library
Jl Ampang, Peti Surat 10150, 50908 Kuala Lumpur
Tel: (03) 4567033 *Fax:* (03) 4573512
Telex: Rrim MA 30369 *Cable:* SEARCHING
Key Personnel
Librarian: H S Kaw
Publication(s): *Journal Natural Rubber Research* (Planters' Bulletin)

Sabah State Library
Lot A, Tingkat 1, Bangunan Kedai Baru Keningau, 8900 Keningau, Sabah
Tel: (088) 54333 *Fax:* (088) 233167
E-mail: pns@sbh.lib.edu.my
Key Personnel
Dir: Datuk Adeline Leong

SEACEN, see South East Asian Central Banks (SEACEN) Research & Training Centre

Selangor Public Library
c/o Perpustakaan Raja Tun Uda, Persiaran, Perdagangan, 40572 Shah Alam, Selangor
Tel: (03) 5597667 *Fax:* (03) 5596045
E-mail: ppas@sel.lib.edu.my
Key Personnel
Dir: Mrs Shahaneem Mustafa

South East Asian Central Banks (SEACEN) Research & Training Centre
Lorong Universiti A, Petaling Jaya
Tel: (03) 7568622 *Fax:* (03) 7574616
E-mail: info@seacen.po.my
Web Site: www.bnm.gov.my/seacen/index.htm
Key Personnel
Chief Librarian: Zainon Zubir *E-mail:* zzainon@seacen.po.my

Tun Razak Library
Jl Panglima Bukit Gantang Wahat, 3000 Ipoh, Perak
Tel: (05) 508073
Publication(s): *Accession Lists* (in English, Malay, Chinese and Tamil); *Malaysiana Collection* (plus supplement)

Library Tun Seri Lanang, Universiti Kebangsaan Malaysia
43600 Bangi, Selangor
Tel: (03) 8250001 *Fax:* (03) 8256484
E-mail: norsham@pkrisc.cc.ukm.my
Telex: 34196

Universiti Putra Malaysia Library (UPM)
43400UPM, Serdang, Selangor
Tel: (03) 9486101 *Fax:* (03) 9483244
E-mail: cans@admin.upm.edu.my
Telex: Uniper MA 37454 *Cable:* UNIPERTAMA SUNGAI BESI
Key Personnel
Chief Librarian: Ms Abdul Hamid Kamariah
Publication(s): *INFORMAN* (Library Newletter); *TUNAS* (Malaysian Agriculture Information Bulletin)

University Library, Universiti Sains Malaysia
Minden, 11800 Penang
Tel: (04) 6577888; (04) 6585518 *Fax:* (04) 6571526
E-mail: chieflib@notes.usm.my
Web Site: www.lib.usm.my
Telex: USMLIB MA40254 *Cable:* UNISAINS
Key Personnel
Chief Librarian: Noor Ida Yang Rashdi *Tel:* (04) 6577888, Ext 3700
Founded: 1969
Academic Library - student population 23,000.
Publication(s): *Bibliography series* (irregular); *Midas Bulletin* (6/yr)

Universiti Teknologi Malaysia
University Teknologi M'sia, Skudai, 81310 Johor
Tel: (07) 5576160 *Fax:* (07) 5579376
E-mail: psz@utm.my
Telex: MA 60205 *Cable:* UNITEK MA
Key Personnel
Vice Chancellor: Dr Ahmad Zaharudin bin Idrus
Assistant Registrar: Ahmad Musthafa B Jamil
  Tel: (07) 5502465 *E-mail:* musthafa@pendaftar.utm.my
Publication(s): *Berita Unitek, Berita Satelit*; *Jurnal Teknologi*

University of Malaysia Library
Lembah Pantai, 50603 Kuala Lumpur
Tel: (03) 7560022 *Fax:* (03) 7564004
Key Personnel
Librarian: Dr Zaiton Osman *E-mail:* zaiton@cc.um.edu.my
Publication(s): *Kekal Abadi* (quarterly newsletter); *Maklumat Semasa* (monthly)

University of Technology Malaysia, see Universiti Teknologi Malaysia

UPM, see Universiti Putra Malaysia Library (UPM)

Mali

Bibliotheque du Centre Culturel Francais de Bamako
Ambassade de France, BP 1547, Bamako
Tel: 224019
Telex: 2569
Key Personnel
Librarian: Veronique Reinhard-Singare

Bibliotheque Nationale
av Kasse Keita, BP 159, Bamako
Tel: 224963

Centre francais de Documentation, see Bibliotheque du Centre Culturel Francais de Bamako

Ecole normale superieure
Bibliotheque, BP 241, Bamako
Tel: 222189

Faculte de Medecine de Pharmuacie et d'Odonto-Stomatologie
Bibliotheque, BP 1805, Bamako
Tel: 225277 *Fax:* 228109; 229658
E-mail: diawara@mrtcbko.malinet.ml
Key Personnel
Librarian: Diawara Cheick Oumar

Malta

Gozo Public Library
Vajringa St, Victoria, Gozo
Tel: 556200 *Fax:* 555944
Key Personnel
Librarian: George V Borg *Tel:* 561510
  E-mail: georgev.borg@magnet.mt
Founded: 1853

National Library of Malta
36 Old Treasury St, CMR 02 Valletta CMR 02
Tel: 224338 *Fax:* 235992
E-mail: joseph.boffa@magnet.mt
Key Personnel
Librarian: John B Sultana
Contact: M Vella
Publication(s): *Malta National Bibliography*

University of Malta Library
Tal-Qrow, Msida
Tel: 333903 *Fax:* 336450
Telex: 407 Hieduc *Cable:* UNIVERSITY MALTA

Key Personnel
Librarian: Dr Paul Xuereb
Publication(s): *Il-Poezija Bil-Malti, 1964-74* (A Bibliography of Maltese Bibliographies 1978)

Martinique

Archives departementales de la Martinique
19 Rue Saint John-Perse, Fort-de-France-FWI F-97263
Mailing Address: BP 649, 97262 Fort-de-France
Tel: 638846 *Fax:* 700450
Key Personnel
Dir: Dominique Taffin
Publication(s): *Guide des Archives de la Martinique* (Voir Liste complete ci-jointe, 1978); *Conscil Souverain de la Martinique Inventaire analytique* (1985-1999); *Tome I*; *Tome II*

Bibliotheque Victor Schoelcher
rue de la Liberte, BP 640, 97200 Fort-de-France
Tel: 04702667 *Fax:* 04724555
Key Personnel
Librarian: Jacqueline Leger

Mauritania

Arab Library
Chinguetti

Bibliotheque Nationale
BP 20, Nouakchott
Tel: 022435

Direction des Archives Nationales, Bibliotheque Publique et Centre du Documentation
av de l'Independence, BP 77, Nouakchott
Tel: 52317 (ext 32)
Telex: Prim 580 Mtn
Key Personnel
Dir: Moktar Ould Hemeina

Mauritius

British Council Library
Royal Rd, Rose Hill
Mailing Address: PO Box 111, Rose Hill
Tel: 4549550 *Fax:* 4549553
E-mail: britcouncil@intnet.mu
Web Site: www.britishcouncil.org/mauritius
Key Personnel
Dir: Mrs Shoba Pannappa

Carnegie Library
Queen Elizabeth II Ave, Curepipe
Tel: 6742287 *Fax:* 6765054
Key Personnel
Senior Librarian: T K Hurrynag-Ramnauth
Tel: 675 4041
Large collection of material on historical background of Mauritius & original manuscripts, papers on colonization by French & British.
Parent Company: Municipal Council of Curepipe
Ultimate Parent Company: Ministry of Local Government & Environment

City Library
City Hall Municipality of Port Louis, Port Louis

Mailing Address: PO Box 422, Port Louis
Tel: 212083 ext 161-163 *Fax:* 2124258 *Cable:* CERNE/PORT LOUIS
Key Personnel
Librarian: Gaetan Benoit
Publication(s): *Bibliography: Mauritiana in City Library*; *Literary Publishing & Bibliographical Control in Mauritius*; *Newspapers Index: Mauritius*

Mauritius Archives
Bank of Mauritius Complex, Petite Riviere
Tel: 088469
Key Personnel
Dir: Dr P H Sooprayen
Publication(s): *Annual Report of the Archives Department* (including a bibliographical supplement); *Quarterly Memorandum of Books Printed in Mauritius and Registered in the Archives*

Mauritius Institute Public Library
PO Box 54, Port Louis
Tel: 2120639 *Fax:* 2125717
Key Personnel
Head Librarian: Sewannah Ankiah

University of Mauritius Library
Library, Reduit
Tel: 4541041 *Fax:* 4549642
Telex: 4621
Key Personnel
Chief Librarian: B R Goordyal
E-mail: goordyal@dovc.uom.ac.mu
Publication(s): *Journal of the University of Mauritius* (irregular); *University of Mauritius Calendar*; *University of Mauritius Report* (annually)

Mexico

Biblioteca Nacional de Antropologia E Historia
Paseo de la Reforma y Calzada Gandhi s/n, Col Polanco, CP 11560, Mexico, DF
Tel: (05) 5536342 *Toll Free Fax:* 52-86-17-43
E-mail: colecciones.bnah@inah.gob.mx
Web Site: www.inah.gob.mx
Key Personnel
Contact: Dr Cesar Moheno; Miguel Najera Perez
Founded: 1888
Parent Company: Instituto Nacional de Antropologia e Historia
Branch Office(s)
Subireccion de Documentacion

Archivo General de la Nacion
Tacuba 8, Apdo 1999, Eduardo Molina y Albaniles, Col Penitenciaria, 15350 Mexico 1
Tel: (05) 5851833
Key Personnel
Dir: Leonor Ortiz M Prieto
Publication(s): *Boletin*

Biblioteca Benjamin Franklin (USIS)
Londres 16, Col Juarez, Mexico, DF
Tel: (05) 2099100 *Fax:* (05) 5910075
E-mail: refbbf@usia.gov
Publication(s): *Boletin de Seleccion de Adquisiciones Recientes* (quarterly)

Biblioteca Central
Universidad Autonoma Chapingo, 56230 Chapingo
Tel: (0595) 50877 *Fax:* (0595) 50877
E-mail: rsuarez@taurusl.chapings.mx

Key Personnel
Librarian: Rosa Maria Ojeda-Trejo
Previously named Escuela Nacional de Agricultura Periodicals. Chapingo, Revista de Geografia Agricola, Textual.

Direccion General de Bibliotecas de la Universidad Nacional Autonoma de Mexico
Ciudad Universitaria, Circuito Interior, 04510 Mexico
Tel: (05) 6221603 *Fax:* (05) 6160664
E-mail: jadolfo@servidor.unam.mx
Key Personnel
Librarian: Adolfo Rodriguez
Publication(s): *Directorio de Bibliotecas UNAM*; *Librunam*; *Seriunam* (Catalogo de Publicaciones); *Tesiunam*

Biblioteca de Mexico
Plaza de la Ciudadela 6, 06040 Mexico
Tel: (05) 7091113; (05) 7091469 *Fax:* (05) 7091173
E-mail: bibmex@servidor.ynam.mx
Key Personnel
Librarian: Carmen E de Moreno

Biblioteca Nacional de Mexico
Centro Cultural, Ciudad Universitaria, Delegacion Coyoacan, Apdo 29-124, 04510 Mexico
Tel: (05) 6226808 *Fax:* (05) 6650951
E-mail: liceaj@biblional.bibliog.unam.mx
Key Personnel
Dir: Jose Guadalupe Moreno De Alba
Publication(s): *Bibliografia Mexicana*; *Boletin del Instituto de Investigaciones Bibliograficas* (annually)

Centro de Informacion Cientifica y Humanistica
Universidad Nacional Autonoma de Mexico, Ciudad Universitaria, Villa Obregon, 04510 Mexico, DF
Tel: (05) 6223966 *Fax:* (05) 6162557
Telex: 01774523
Key Personnel
Dir: Mtro Juan Voutssas Marquez
Unidad de Bibliotecas de Investigacion Cientifica de la UNAM.

Biblioteca del Congreso de la Union
Tacuba 29, Centro Historico, Del Cuauhtemoc, Mexico
Tel: (05) 5103866 *Fax:* (05) 5121085

Hemeroteca Nacional de Mexico
Centro Cultural, Ciudad Universitaria, Del Coyoacan, 04510 Mexico DF
Tel: (05) 6226808 *Fax:* (065) 665-0951
Key Personnel
Dir: Jose Moreno de Alba
National Periodicals Library.

Biblioteca del Instituto Anglo-Mexicano de Cultura
Antonio Caso 127, Col San Rafael, DF CP 06470 Mexico
Tel: (05) 5664500 *Fax:* (05) 5666739
Telex: 01772938 Brcome
Key Personnel
Head Librarian: Aurora P Vela
Anglo-Mexican Cultural Institute.

Instituto de Investigaciones Electricas
Apdo 1-475, 62001 Cuernavaca, Mor
Tel: (073) 183811 *Fax:* (073) 182521
E-mail: postmaster@iie.org.mx
Telex: 17-76352 IIEMME
Key Personnel
Executive Dir: Pablo Mulas

Biblioteca del Instituto Panamericano de Geografia e Historia
Ex-Arzobispado 29, Col Observatorio, Deleg Miguel Hidalgo, 11860 Mexico, DF
Tel: (05) 2775888 *Fax:* (05) 2716172
Key Personnel
Secretary General: Dr Chester J Zelaya-Goodman
Publications Coordinator: Jaime Curenom
Pan American Institute of Geography & History.
Publication(s): *Ver Informacion Adjunta*

Instituto Tecnologico y de Estdios Superiores de Monterrey Biblioteca
Ave Eugenio Garza Sada 2501 Sur, 64849 Monterrey, NL
Tel: (081) 8328-4096 *Fax:* (081) 8328-4067
Web Site: cib.mty.itesm.mx
Key Personnel
Librarian: Miguel A Arreola
 E-mail: miguel_arreola@itesm.mx
Publication(s): *Transferencia* (Strategic Studies Center monthly)

ITESM Biblioteca, see Instituto Tecnologico y de Estdios Superiores de Monterrey Biblioteca

Biblioteca de la Universidad Iberoamericana
Centro de Informacion Academica, Prolongacion Paseo de la Reforma No 880, Col Lomas se Santa Fe, Delegacion Alvaro Obregon, 01210 Mexico, DF
Tel: (05) 2923508; (05) 2674249 *Fax:* (05) 2923008; (05) 2922838; (05) 2674249; (05) 2674000 (ext 47-05)
Key Personnel
Dir: Ing Pilar Verdejo Paris
Contact: Sonia Bacha Baz *E-mail:* sonia.bacha@uia.mx

Biblioteca Daniel Cosio Villegas El Colegio de Mexico AC
Camino al Ajusco 20, Col Pedregal Sta Teresa, CP 10740, Mexico, DF
Mailing Address: Apdo Postal 20-671, CP 01000 Mexico, DF
Tel: (055) 5449 3000; (055) 5449 2909; (055) 5449 2936 *Fax:* (055) 5645 0464; (055) 5645 4584
E-mail: biblio@colmex.mx
Web Site: biblio.colmex.mx
Telex: 1777585 COLME *Cable:* COLME
Key Personnel
Library Dir: Alvaro Quijano Solis
 E-mail: quijano@colmex.mx
Interim Dir: Micaela Chavez Villa *E-mail:* mch@colmex.mx
Founded: 1940
Graduate institution for research & education in the social sciences & the humanities.
Publication(s): *Boletin de la BDCV*
Parent Company: El Colegio de Mexico

Monaco

Bibliotheque Louis Notari (Library Louis Notari)
8 rue Louis Notari, MC 98000 Monaco
Tel: 93152940 *Fax:* 93152941
Key Personnel
Dir: Herve Barral
Administrative Sectretary: Catherine Notari

Mongolia

State Archives
Ulan-Bator State Public Library of Mongolia, Chinggis Av 3, Ulan-Bator 11
Tel: (01) 323100
Key Personnel
Dir: M Bayaizul

Morocco

Bibliotheque Ben Youssef
Dar Glaoui, Rue Rmila, Marrakesh Medina
Tel: (04) 25465
Key Personnel
Dir: Seddik Bellarbi

Bibliotheque Generale et Archives du Maroc
Ave Ibn Battouta, Rabat
Mailing Address: BP 1003, Rabat
Tel: (07) 771890 *Fax:* (07) 776062
E-mail: bgarabat@iam.net.ma
Key Personnel
Librarian: Ahmed Toufiq
Publication(s): *Bibliographie nationale marocaine*

British Council Library
39 Rue de Tanger, Rabat
Mailing Address: BP 427, Rabat
Tel: (07) 760836 *Fax:* (07) 760850
E-mail: britcoun.morocco@britishcouncil.org.ma
Web Site: www.britishcouncil.org/morocco
Telex: 36293
Key Personnel
Dir: Graham McCulloch
Librarian: Abdellatif Mazouz
British Cultural Centre.

Centre National de Documentation
BP 826, Rabat 10004
Tel: (07) 774944 *Fax:* (07) 773134
E-mail: magridoc@wizarat-sukkan.sukkan.gov.ma
Key Personnel
Dir: Ahmed Fassi Fihri
Publication(s): *voir liste jointe*

Bibliotheque de la Communaute Urbaine de Casablanca
142, Av des Forces Armees Royales, Casablanca
Tel: (02) 314170
Key Personnel
Dir: Haj Mohamed Bouzid

Bibliotheque Generale et Archives
BP 692, Tetouan
Tel: (096) 3258
Key Personnel
Librarian: M M Dellero

Institut Scientifique
Ave Ibn Battouta, BP 703, Rabat
Tel: (07) 774548 *Fax:* (07) 774540
Telex: MADILM 36361M
Key Personnel
Chief de Service: Abdellatif Bayed
Publication(s): *Bulletin de l'Institut Scientifique*; *Documents de l'Institut Scientifique*; *Travaux de l'Institut Scientifique*

Bibliotheque de l'Universite Quaraouyine
Place des Seffarines, BP 790, Fes

Mozambique

Biblioteca Municipal
Pacos de Concelho, Maputo

Biblioteca Nacional de Mocambique
CP 141, Maputo
Tel: (01) 425676
Key Personnel
Librarian: Joaquim Chigogoro Mussassa

Direccao Nacional de Geologia (Centro de Documentacao)
Praca 25 de Junho, No 380, CP 217 Maputo
Tel: (01) 424031-4; (01) 420797 *Fax:* (01) 429216
E-mail: geologia@zebra.uem.mz
Telex: 6-584 GEOMI MO
Key Personnel
National Dir: Joao Marques
National Deputy Dir: Elias Daudi
Publication(s): *Boletim Geologico*

Arquivo Historico de Mocambique
 (Mozambique Historical Archives)
Division of Eduardo Mondlane University
Ave Filipe Samuel Magaia, 717, CP 2033 Maputo
Mailing Address: PO Box 2033, 715 Maputo
Tel: (01) 421177; (01) 421178 *Fax:* (01) 423428
E-mail: ahm@ahm.mz
Web Site: www.ahm.mz
Key Personnel
Dir: Maria Ines Nogueira da Costa
Editor: J P Borges Coelho
Librarian: Antonio Sopa
Specialize in administrative and colonial archives 19th & 20th centuries. Bibliographic, cartographic, photographic and poster collectives.
Publication(s): *Arquivo* (Archive, every six weeks, bulletin, 1987); *Documentos* (annually, series); *Estudos* (Studies, 7x/yr, series)

Bibliotecas da Universidade Eduardo Mondlane
Direccao dos Servicos de Documentacao, CP 257 Maputo
Tel: (01) 425972 *Fax:* (01) 428128
Telex: 6-718 UEM MO
Key Personnel
Head of Services: Wanda do Amaral
 E-mail: wanda@nambu.uem.mz
The University Eduardo Mondlane does not have a Central Library, but controls 15 departmental libraries; Direccao id responsible for all library & documentation services throughout the University.

Myanmar

Institute of Economics Library
University Estate, Yangon
Mailing Address: PO Box 473, Yangon
Tel: (01) 532433

Institute of Education Library
University Estate, Yangon
Tel: (01) 31345

Magwe Degree College Library
University Campus, Magwe
Tel: (63) 21030
Key Personnel
Dir: Khin Myint Myint

MYANMAR

Mandalay University Library
University of Mandalay, University Estate, Mandalay
Tel: (02) 21211
Key Personnel
Librarian: U Myint Thein

National Library
Town Hall, Strand Rd, Yangon
Tel: (01) 272058

Universities' Central Library
Main University Estate, Yangon
Tel: (01) 31144

Namibia

National Archives of Namibia
4 Luederitz St, Private Bag 13250, Windhoek 9000
Tel: (061) 2934308 *Fax:* (061) 239042
E-mail: natarch@witbooi.natarch.mec.gov.na
Key Personnel
Acting Chief: J Kutzner

National Library
Private Bag 13349, Windhoek 9000
Tel: (061) 2934490 *Fax:* (061) 229808
E-mail: johan@natlib.mec.gov.na
Key Personnel
Chief, National Library: Mr J Loubser
Librarian: M K Hoffmann

Windhoek Public Library
Luederitz St, Private Bag 13183, Windhoek 9000
Tel: (061) 224899 *Fax:* (061) 212169
Key Personnel
Librarian: Mrs L Hansmann

Nepal

British Council Library
Kanti Path, Kathmandu
Mailing Address: PO Box 640, Kathmandu
Tel: (01) 221305; (01) 223796 *Fax:* (01) 224076
E-mail: bcnepal@bc-nepal.wlink.com.np
Web Site: www.britcoun.org/nepal/neplis.htm
Telex: 2382 Bricon NP
Key Personnel
Dir: Barbara Wickham

Madan Puraskar Library
Lalitpur
Tel: (01) 521014 *Fax:* (01) 536390
E-mail: kmldxt@wlink.com.np
Key Personnel
Librarian: Kamalmani Dixit
   E-mail: kamalmanidixit@hotmail.com
Founded: 1956

National Library, see Nepal National Library

Nepal National Library
Formerly National Library
Harihar Bhawan, PO Box 182, Lalitpur
Tel: (01) 521132
E-mail: nnl@nnl.wlink.com.np
Key Personnel
Chief Librarian: Dasharath Thapa

Tribhuvan University Central Library
Kirtipur, Katmandu
Tel: (01) 331317 *Fax:* (01) 226964
Publication(s): *Bibliography of non-alignment, 1982; Bibliography of Population and Family Planning, 1981; Nepalese National Bibliography; Nepal's Foreign Affaires* (bibliographical guide to resources in the Tucl, 1974)

Netherlands

Bibliotheek van het Centraal Bureau voor de Statistiek (Statistics Netherlands Library)
Prinses Beatrixlaan 428, 2273 XZ Voorburg
Mailing Address: Postbus 4000, 2270 JM Voorburg
Tel: (070) 3375151 *Fax:* (070) 3375984
E-mail: bibliotheek@cbs.nl
Web Site: www.cbs.nl
Telex: 32692 cbs nl
Key Personnel
Librarian: Ms M F Wijngaarden *Tel:* (070) 3375149 *E-mail:* mwei@cbs.nl

Bibliotheek Wageningen UR (Wageningen University & Research Centre Library)
Jan Kopshuis, Generaal Foulkesweg 19, Wageningen
Mailing Address: PO Box 9100, 6700 HA Wageningen
Tel: (07) 484440 *Fax:* (07) 484761
E-mail: bluwpudoc@secr.bib.wau.nl
Web Site: www.agralin.nl
Key Personnel
Chief Librarian: Dr L J M Waaijers
Public Relations Officer: Macel van Berkum
   Tel: (0317) 484537 *E-mail:* marcel.vanberkum@id.bib.wau.nl
Wageningen UR Library.

DBA, see Dienst Bibliotheek en Archief

Dienst Bibliotheek en Archief
Spui 68, 2511 BT The Hague
Mailing Address: Postbox 12653, 2500 DP The Hague
Tel: (070) 3534455 *Fax:* (070) 3534504
E-mail: sear@dbadenhaag.nl
Key Personnel
Librarian: W M Renes
Public Library.

Bibliotheek Technische Universiteit Eindhoven (Eindhoven University of Technology Library)
Den Dolech 2, 5612 AZ Eindhoven
Mailing Address: Postbus 90159, 5600 RM Eindhoven
Tel: (040) 2472381 *Fax:* (040) 2447015
E-mail: helpdesk.bib@tue.nl

EVD eenheid Bibliotheek
Ministerie van Economische Zaken, Diviesie Informatie Eenheid, Bibliotheek, Bezuidenhoutseweg 181, 2594 AH The Hague
Tel: (070) 3797210 *Fax:* (070) 3797878
Telex: 31099 Ecza nl *Cable:* ECONINF
Key Personnel
Librarian: G P van der Sluys

Internationaal Instituut voor Sociale Geschiedenis
Cruquiusweg 31, 1019 AT Amsterdam
Tel: (020) 6685866 *Fax:* (020) 6654181
E-mail: inf.gen@iisg.nl
Web Site: www.iisg.nl
Key Personnel
General Dir: J Kloosterman

International Institute of Social History.
Publication(s): *Catalogs & Monograph Series; International Review of Social History*

Koninklijke Bibliotheek
Prins Willem Alexanderhof 5, 2509 LK The Hague
Mailing Address: Postbus 90407, 2509 LK The Hague
Tel: (070) 3140911 *Fax:* (070) 3140651
E-mail: secretariaat@konbib.nl
Telex: 31500
Royal (National) Library.
Publication(s): *Bibliography of Translations* (from the Dutch); *Dutch Bibliography - Brinkman's Cumulatieve Catalogues*

Museum Van Het Boek/Museum Meermanno-Westree-nianum
Prinsessegracht 30, 2514 AP The Hague
Tel: (070) 3462700 *Fax:* (070) 3630350
Key Personnel
Dir: Dr J A Brandenbarg
National Book Museum.

Nederlands Instituut voor Wetenschappelijke Informatiediensten
Postbus 95110, 1090 HC Amsterdam
Tel: (020) 4628628 *Fax:* (020) 6685079
E-mail: info@niwi.knaw.nl
Web Site: www.niwi.knaw.nl
Library of Royal Netherlands Academy of Arts & Sciences.

NIWI, see Nederlands Instituut voor Wetenschappelijke Informatiediensten

Openbare Bibliotheek/Gemeentearchief, see Dienst Bibliotheek en Archief

Rijksmuseum Library
Yan Luykenstraat 1A, 1071 XY Amsterdam
Mailing Address: PO Box 74888, 1070 DN Amsterdam
Tel: (020) 6747267 *Fax:* (020) 6747001
E-mail: bibliotheek@rijksmuseum.nl
Web Site: www.rijksmuseum.nl
Key Personnel
Contact: G J Koot *Tel:* (020) 6747250 *E-mail:* g.koot@rijksmuseum.nl
Founded: 1885
Art history.

Bibliotheek der Rijksuniversiteit te Groningen
Broerstr 4, 9712 CP Groningen
Mailing Address: Postbus 559, 9700 AN Groningen
Tel: (050) 3635002 *Fax:* (050) 3634996
E-mail: secretarial@ub.rug.nl
Key Personnel
Dir: Dr A C Klugkist *E-mail:* a.c.klugkist@ub.rug.nl

Gemeentebibliotheek Rotterdam
Hoogstr 110, 3011 PV Rotterdam
Mailing Address: Postbus 22140, 3003 DC Rotterdam
Tel: (010) 2816100 *Fax:* (010) 2816181
Telex: 25221 gbr nl
Key Personnel
Librarian: F H Meijer
Rotterdam Municipal Library.

Stichting Arnhemse Openbare en Gelderse Wetenschappelijke Bibliotheek
Koningstr 26, 6811 DG Arnhem
Mailing Address: Postbus 1168, 6801 ML Arnhem
Tel: (026) 3543111 *Fax:* (026) 4458616
Web Site: www.biblioarnhem.nl

Key Personnel
Head: Dr P G Aalbers
Librarian: A J Hovy *E-mail:* j.hovy@
 biblioarnhem.nl
Founded: 1853
Public Library.

Universiteitsbibliotheek
Universiteit van Amsterdam, Singel 425, 1012 WP Amsterdam
Mailing Address: Postbus 19185, 1000 GD Amsterdam
Tel: (020) 5252301 *Fax:* (020) 5252311
E-mail: secr@uba.uva.nl
Key Personnel
Librarian: Dr N Verhagen

Universiteitsbibliotheek Leiden (University Library)
Witte Singel 27, 2311 BG Leiden
Mailing Address: Postbus 9501, 2300 RA Leiden
Tel: (071) 5272801 *Fax:* (071) 5272836
E-mail: secretariaat@library.leidenuniv.nl
Key Personnel
Librarian: P W J L Gerretsen

Universiteitsbibliotheek Nijmegen
Erasmuslaan 36, 6525 GG Nijmegen
Mailing Address: Postbus 9100, 6500 HA Hijmegen
Tel: (024) 3612440 *Fax:* (080) 3615944
E-mail: secretariaat@ubn.kun.nl

Universiteitsbibliotheek Utrecht
Wittevrouwenstr 7-11, 3512 CS Utrecht
Mailing Address: Postbus 16007, 3500 DA Utrecht
Tel: (030) 2538002 *Fax:* (030) 2538398
Telex: 47103
Key Personnel
Librarian: J S M Savenije
Contact: L C Kuiper-Brussen *Tel:* (030) 253-6643
 E-mail: l.kuiper@library.uu.nl
University Library, Utrecht.
Publication(s): *Handschriften en Oude Drukken van de Utrechtse Universiteits bibliothek* (MSS and Old Books of University Library, Utrecht: Exhibition Catalogue 1984); *Illuminated and Decorated Medieval Manuscripts in the University Library Utrecht* (illustrated catalogue); *The Utrecht Psalter, Picturing the Psalms of David* (CD-ROM); *Vier eeuwen Universiteitsbibliotheek Utrecht (Four Centuries University Library, Utrecht: Part 1 1584-1878)* (summary in English)

Universiteit Wageningen, see Bibliotheek Wageningen UR

Netherlands Antilles

Openbare Bibliotheek
Abr M Chumaceiro Blvd 17, Willemstad, Curacao
Tel: (09) 4617055 *Fax:* (09) 4656247
Key Personnel
Librarian: Rose Marie de Paula

Universiteits-Bibliotheek, Universiteit van de Nederlandse Antillen
Jan Noorduynweg 111, Willemstad, Curacao
Mailing Address: PO Box 3059, Willemstad, Curacao
Tel: (09) 84422 *Fax:* (09) 85465

Telex: 110111
Key Personnel
Librarian: Stanley R Criens

New Caledonia

Bibliotheque Bernheim, Bibliotheque territoriale de la Nouvelle-Caledonie
BP G1, Route Territoriale 13, Noumea Cedex
Tel: 272343 *Fax:* 276588
Key Personnel
Librarian: Jean-Francois Carrez-Corral

Secretariat of the Pacific Community Library
95 Promenade Roger Laroque, Noumea 98868
Mailing Address: PO Box D5, Noumea
Tel: 262000 *Fax:* 263818
E-mail: library@spc.int
Web Site: www.spc.int/library
Telex: 3139NM Sopacom *Cable:* SOUTH PACOM
Key Personnel
Librarian: Mark Perkins *E-mail:* markp@spc.int
Founded: 1947
To support development in the Pacific via SPC programs.
Ultimate Parent Company: Pacific Community
Branch Office(s)
Suva, Fiji

New Zealand

Archives New Zealand (Te Whare Tohu Tohituhinga O Aotearoa)
10 Mulgrave St, Wellington
Mailing Address: PO Box 12050, Wellington
Tel: (04) 4995595 *Fax:* (04) 4956210
E-mail: enquiries@archives.govt.nz
Web Site: www.archives.govt.nz
Key Personnel
Chief Archivist: Dianne Macaskill
Specialize in the preservation of Government records.
Parent Company: NZ Government

Auckland City Libraries
Wellesley St, Auckland 1
Mailing Address: PO Box 4138, Auckland 1
Tel: (09) 3770209 *Fax:* (09) 3077741
Telex: 2750
Key Personnel
City Librarian: Barbara Birkbeck

Canterbury University Library
Private Bag 4800, Christchurch
Tel: (03) 3667001 *Fax:* (03) 3642055
Telex: 4144 unicant
Key Personnel
Librarian: R W Hlavac *E-mail:* r.hlavac@libr.canterbury.ac.nz

Christchurch City Libraries
Cr Oxford Terrace, Gloucester St, Christchurch 1
Mailing Address: PO Box 1466, Christchurch 1
Tel: (03) 3796914 *Fax:* (03) 3651751
Key Personnel
Library Manager: Sue Sutherland
Promotions & Publications Coordinator: Sasha Bowers *E-mail:* sasha.bowers@govt.nz

Marketing & Development Manager: Glenda Fulten *Tel:* (03) 3727840 *E-mail:* glenda.fulten@ccc.govt.nz
Publication(s): *Bookmark* (monthly); *Connect* (monthly)

Dunedin Public Libraries
Moray Place, Dunedin
Mailing Address: PO Box 5542, Dunedin
Tel: (03) 4743690 *Fax:* (03) 4743660
E-mail: library@dcc.govt.nz
Key Personnel
Library Services Manager: Bernie Hawke
Collection Dev Libn: Barbara Frame *Tel:* (03) 4743620 *E-mail:* bframe@dcc.govt.wz
Founded: 1908
Public Library.
Parent Company: Dunedin City Council

Napier Public Library
Station St, Napier
Mailing Address: PO Box 940, Napier
Tel: (06) 8344180
E-mail: library@napier.govt.nz
Key Personnel
Manager: Leslie Clague
Customer Services Manager: Wendy Gosling *Tel:* (06) 8344139
Branch Office(s)
Taradale Library, White St, Taradale, Napier

National Library of New Zealand (Te Puna Matauranga o Aotearoa)
70 Molesworth St, Wellington 1
Mailing Address: PO Box 1467, Wellington 6004
Tel: (04) 4743000 *Fax:* (04) 4743035; (04) 858077
Telex: NZ (04) 4730-080
Key Personnel
National Librarian: Christopher Blake

North Shore City Libraries
Private Bag 93508, Takapuna, North Shore City
Tel: (09) 4868460 *Fax:* (09) 4868519
Web Site: www.shorelibraries.govt.nz
Key Personnel
Library Services Manager: Geoff Chamberlain *Tel:* (09) 4868461 *E-mail:* geoffc@shorelibraries.govt.nz

Palmerston North Public Library
The Square & Main St, Palmerston North
Mailing Address: PO Box 1948, Palmerston North
Tel: (06) 3583076 *Fax:* (06) 3568869
E-mail: library@pnlibrary.manawatan.planet.co.nz

Parliamentary Library
Parliament Bldg, Wellington 6001
Tel: (04) 4719623 *Fax:* (04) 4711250
E-mail: moira.fraser@parliament.govt.nz
Key Personnel
Parliamentary Librarian: Moira Fraser

Alexander Turnbull Library
Division of National Library of New Zealand/Te Puna Matauranga o Aotearoa
National Library of New Zealand, National Library Bldg, Molesworth St, Wellington, North, Wellington 1
Mailing Address: PO Box 12349, Wellington North, Wellington
Tel: (04) 4743000 *Fax:* (04) 4743063
E-mail: atl@natlib.govt.nz
Key Personnel
Chief Librarian: Margaret Calder
Reader Education Librarian: Janet Horncy *Tel:* (04) 474 3048 *E-mail:* janet.horncy@natlib.govt.nz
Research library within the National Library of New Zealand. Listing of publications avail-

NEW ZEALAND

able on the National Library of New Zealand website-www.natlib.govt.nz/ under the heading "Using our collections", select 'What's available', 'Alexander Turnbull Library'.
Publication(s): *Turnbull Library Record* (1 issue per annum)

University of Auckland Library
5 Alfred St, Auckland
Mailing Address: PO Box 92019, Auckland
Tel: (09) 3737999 *Fax:* (09) 3737565
E-mail: library@auckland.ac.nz
Web Site: www2.auckland.ac.nz/lbr/libhome.htm
Key Personnel
University Librarian: Janet Copsey *Tel:* (09) 3737599 ext 7352 *E-mail:* jl.copsey@auckland.ac.nz

University of Otago Library
Cumberland St, Dunedin
Mailing Address: PO Box 56, Dunedin
Tel: (03) 4791100 *Fax:* (03) 4798947
E-mail: office.central@library.otago.ac.nz
Key Personnel
Librarian: M J Wooliscroft

Wellington City Libraries
65 Victoria St, Wellington 1
Mailing Address: PO Box 1992, Wellington 1
Tel: (04) 8014040 *Fax:* (04) 8014047
Key Personnel
Manager: Jane Hill *E-mail:* hill_j@wcc.govt.nz
Contact: Robin Dinnan

Nicaragua

Archivo Nacional de Nicaragua
Biblioteca Especializada, 6a C 402, Apdo 2087, Managua
Tel: (02) 226290 *Fax:* (02) 22722
E-mail: binanic@tmx.com.nic
Key Personnel
Dir: Alfredo Gonzalez Vilchez
Publication(s): *Boletin*

Biblioteca Nacional
C del Triunfo 302, Managua
Mailing Address: Apdo 101, Managua
Tel: (02) 97517 *Fax:* (02) 94387

INCAE, see Instituto Centroamericano de Administracion de Empresas (INCAE) Library

Instituto Centroamericano de Administracion de Empresas (INCAE) Library
Apdo 2485, Managua
Tel: (02) 58446-8
Telex: 2360
Key Personnel
Associate Dir: Antonio Acevedo E
Publication(s): *Revista INCAE*

Ruben Dario, see Biblioteca Nacional

Universidad Centroamericana
Apdo 69, Managua
Tel: (02) 773026 *Fax:* (02) 670106
E-mail: ucanic@nicarao.apc.org
Telex: 2296
Key Personnel
Librarian: Conny Mendez R

Niger

Centre d'Enseignement Superieur de Niamey
Bibliotheque, BP 237, Niamey
Tel: 732713 *Fax:* 733862
Telex: uninim 5258 hi
University Education Centre.

Bibliotheqe l'Ecole nationale d'administration du Niger
BP 542, Niamey
Tel: 723183
Key Personnel
Librarian: Mme Yacouba Halimatou

Institut de Recherche en Sciences Humaines
BP 318, Niamey
Tel: 735141
Telex: 5258
Key Personnel
Librarian: Sai'dou Harouna
Publication(s): *Etudes Nigeriennes*

Bibliotheque de l'Universite de Niamey
BP 237, 10896 Niamey
Tel: 732713 *Fax:* 733862
Telex: 5258

Nigeria

Ahmadu Bello University Library
PMB 1041, Zaria, Kaduna
Tel: (069) 32081; (069) 32082
Telex: 75241 Zarabu Ng
Publication(s): *Northern Nigerian Publications* (annually)

Anambra State Library Board
Market Rd, PMB 01026, Enugu
Tel: (042) 334103 *Cable:* LIBRARIES ENUGU
Key Personnel
Librarian: C N Ekweozoh

Bendel State Library
17 James Watt Rd, Benin City, Bendel State
Mailing Address: PMB 1127, Benin City, Bendel State
Tel: (052) 200810 *Cable:* LIBRARY BENIN
Key Personnel
Dir: D O Oboro
Publication(s): *Bendel Library Journal*

Benin University Library
PMB 1154, Benin City
Tel: (052) 600553 *Fax:* (052) 241156
Telex: 41365
Key Personnel
University Librarian: S A Tamah
Publication(s): *List of Serials*

IAR, see Institute for Agricultural Research (IAR)

Institute for Agricultural Research (IAR)
PMB 1044, Samaru-Zaria
Tel: (069) 50681 *Fax:* (069) 50563
Key Personnel
Dir: Prof J P Voh
Publication(s): *KWIC Index to the Abstracting & Indexing*; *Library Accession List* (monthly); *List of Current Serials in the Library* (annually); *Subject Bibliographies on Nigeria Agriculture*

International Institute of Tropical Agriculture Library
Oyo Rd, Ibadan, Oyo State
Mailing Address: PMB 5320, Ibadan, Oyo State
Tel: (02) 2412626 *Fax:* (02) 8741772276 via INMARSAT
E-mail: iita@cgnet.com
Telex: 31417; 31159 Tropib Ng *Cable:* TROPFOUND IKEJA
Key Personnel
Head, Information Services: Dr C Brelet
Publication(s): *IITA Annual Report*; *IITA Research*

University of Jos Library
Bauchi Rd, Plateau State
Mailing Address: PMB 2084, Plateau State
Tel: (073) 610514 *Fax:* (073) 610514
E-mail: library@unijos.edu.ng
Telex: 81136 Unijos NG *Cable:* LIBRARIAN UNIJOS
Key Personnel
University Librarian: Mrs A B Ojoade
Publication(s): *Nigerian Periodicals Index* (1986)

Library Board of Kaduna State
PMB 2061, Kaduna
Tel: (062) 242590
Key Personnel
Dir: J A Maigari
Publication(s): *Biographies of Governors of Former Northern Nigeria & Kaduna State, 1960-1990*; *Meet Our Friends*; *Proceedings of the First Kaduna State Book Fair*; *Proceedings of the First Northern States Book Fair*; *Proceedings of the Second Kaduna State Book Fair*

Kano State Library Board
PMB 3094, Kano
Tel: (064) 645614
Key Personnel
Dir: Alhaji Shehu Mukhtar
Publication(s): *Library Guide*

Kenneth Dike Library
Ibadan
Tel: (02) 8103118 *Fax:* (02) 8103118
E-mail: library@kdl.ui.edu.ng
Key Personnel
Librarian: Joseph Ezenwani Ikem
Publication(s): *Library Record* (monthly)

Lagos City Council Libraries
48 Broad St, Lagos
Mailing Address: PMB 2025, Lagos
Tel: (01) 50246

National Archives of Nigeria Library
University of Ibadan Post Office, PMB 4, Ibadan
Tel: (022) 415000 *Cable:* DARCHNES
Key Personnel
Dir: Comfort Aina Ukwu

National Library of Nigeria-Reserch & Development Dept
Dantata House, Central Business District, PMB 1, Abuja
Mailing Address: PMB 12626, Lagos
Tel: (01) 2600220 *Fax:* (09) 2347517
Telex: 21746 Nat Lib Ng *Cable:* BIBLIOS
Key Personnel
Dir: Muazu H Wali
Secretary: B O Ifediba
Publication(s): *Afribiblios* (biannually); *Libraries in Nigeria, a Directory*; *National Bibliography of Nigeria*; *Nigerbiblios* (quarterly); *Nigerian Books in Print*; *Nominal List of Practicing Librarians in Nigeria*; *Serials in Print in Nigeria*

Nnamdi Azikiwe Library
University of Nigeria, Enugu State, Nsukka 0042
Tel: (042) 771444 *Fax:* (042) 770644; (042) 771500
E-mail: misunn@aol.com
Telex: Ulions 51496 *Cable:* NIGERSITY LIBRARY
Key Personnel
Acting Librarian: C C Uwechie
Collection includes 9000 items in microform; CD-ROM facilities available.
Publication(s): *Nsukka Library Notes*; *Readers' Guide* (Annual Report); *UNLAN* (University of Nigeria Library Accessions and News)

Obafemi Awolowo University Library
c/o Hezekiah Oluwasanmi Library, Ile-Ife
Tel: (036) 230291 ext 2287; (036) 230290
Fax: (036) 230291 (ext 2287)
E-mail: ul@libraryoauife.edu.ng
Key Personnel
Librarian: Adedeji Adelabu

University of Lagos Library
Akoka, Yaba, Lagos
Tel: (01) 821273 *Fax:* (01) 822644
Telex: 26983
Key Personnel
Librarian: S A Orimoloye

University of Nigeria
Nnamdi Azikiwe Library, Nsukka, Enugu State
Tel: (042) 771444 *Fax:* (042) 770644; (042) 771500
E-mail: misunn@aol.com
Telex: 51496 ULIONS NG
Key Personnel
University Librarian: Emenike Ikeqbune
Founded: 1960

Norway

Bergen offentlige Bibliotek (Bergen Public Library)
Stromgaten 6, 5015 Bergen
Tel: 55568500 *Fax:* 55568555
Web Site: www.bergen.folkebibl.no
Key Personnel
Dir: Trine Kolderup Flaten *E-mail:* trine@bergen.folkebib.no
Founded: 1872
Bergen Public Library.

Deichmanske Bibliotek
Henrik Ibsens gate 1, 0179 Oslo 1
Tel: 22032900 *Fax:* 22113389
Telex: 18337 deich n
Key Personnel
Chief Librarian: Liv Saeteren
City Library of Oslo.

Drammen Folkebibliotek
Gamle Kirkeplass 7, 3001 Drammen
Mailing Address: Postboks 1136, 3001 Drammen
Tel: 32806300 *Fax:* 32806453
E-mail: magne@drmbib.bibsyst.no
Key Personnel
Chief Librarian: Magne Hauge
Public Library of Drammen; County Library of Buskerud.

Styret for det Industrielle Rettsvern Information Department
Kobehavngaten 10, Oslo
Mailing Address: Postboks 8160 Dep, 0033 Oslo 1
Tel: 22387300 *Fax:* 22387301
Telex: 19152 nopat n
Key Personnel
Assistant Dir General: Per Olaf Ranger
Library of the Norwegian Patent Office.

Kristiansand Folkebibliotek
Postboks 476, 4664, Raedhusgt 11, Kristiansand 4611
Tel: 38124910 *Fax:* 38124949
Key Personnel
Chief Librarian: Anne Kristin Undlien
Municipal Library.

Nobelinstituttet (Nobel Institute)
Biblioteket, Drammensveien 19, 0255 Oslo
Tel: 22129320 *Fax:* 22129310
Web Site: www.nobel.no
Key Personnel
Head Librarian: Anne C Kjelling *Tel:* 22129321
E-mail: ack@nobel.no
Founded: 1904
Library covers following fields: international relations, international law, peace, & international economics.

Norges Landbrukshogskoles Bibliotek
Postboks 5012, 1432 As NLH
Tel: 64947500 *Fax:* 64947670
E-mail: biblutl@bibl.nlh.no
Library of the Agricultural University of Norway
The University Library/Information Technology Department of the Agricultural University of Norway.

Riksarkivet
Folke Bernadottes vei 21, Oslo
Mailing Address: Postboks 4013, Ulleval Stadion, 0806 Oslo
Tel: 22022600 *Fax:* 22237489
E-mail: riksarkivet@riksarkivaren.dep.no
Web Site: www.riksarkivet.no; www.arkivverket.no
National Archives of Norway.

Statistisk sentralbyras bibliotek og informasjonssenter (Statistics Norway-Library & Information Centre)
Kongens gate 6, 0033 Oslo
Mailing Address: Postboks 8131 Dep, 0033 Oslo 1
Tel: 21090000; 21094642; 21094643
Fax: 21094973; 21094504
E-mail: biblioteket@ssb.no
Web Site: www.ssb.no *Cable:* STATISTIKK
Key Personnel
Head Librarian: Hilde Rodland *Tel:* 21094633
E-mail: hilde.rodland@ssb.no
Library of Statistics Norway.

Universitetsbiblioteket i Bergen
Haakon Sheteligspl 7, 5007 Bergen
Tel: 55582500 *Fax:* 55589703
E-mail: adm@ub.uib.no
Telex: 42690 ubb n
Key Personnel
Librarian: Kari Garnes

Universitetsbiblioteket i Oslo
Drammensveien 42, 0242 Oslo
Tel: 22855050 *Fax:* 22859050
E-mail: ubofjernlaan@ub.uio.no
Key Personnel
Librarian: Jan Erik Roeed
Publication(s): *Bibliografi over Norges offentlige publikasjoner 1956-1990*; *Helse-NOTA 1992-*; *Kataloger pa mikrofilm kort*; *Maskinlesbare data*; *Mikrofilmer* (35mm Norske aviser, Norske tidsskrifter, Norske og utenlandske boker); *Nansen bilde data base pa CD-ROM*; *Nasjonalbibliografiske data NBDATA 1962-* (CD-ROM); *Nordisk samkatalog for periodika CDNOSP*; *Norsk bokfortegnelse*; *Norsk bokfortegnelse: Musikktrykk*; *Norsk lokalhistorisk litteratur 1946-1979*; *Norsk lokalhistorisk litteratur 1971-1990*; *Norsk musikkfortegnelse: lydfestinger*; *Norsk musikkfortegnelse: notetrykk*; *Norsk periodikafortegnelse 1993-*; *Norsk samkatalog for boker CDSAM 1981-*; *Norsk samkatalog for boker CDSAM 1983-*; *Norske tidsskriftartikler 1980-*; *Norske tidsskrifter 1971-1983*; *NOSP adresseliste*; *UBO: Brosjyrer*; *UBO: Diverse publikasjonerk*; *UBO: Skrifter*; *UBO: Veiledninger*

Universitetsbiblioteket i Trondheim
Hogskoleringen 1, 7034 Trondheim
Tel: 73595110 *Fax:* 73595103
E-mail: ubit@ub.ntnu.no
Telex: 55384 Bibl n
Key Personnel
Chief Librarian: Kari Christensen
University Library of Trondheim. Incorporating libraries of the College of Arts and Sciences and of the Museum (formerly Library of the Royal Norwegian Society of Sciences & Letters, DKNVS).

University of Oslo Library, see Universitetsbiblioteket i Oslo

Pakistan

British Council Library
Block 14, Civic Centre G6, Islamabad
Mailing Address: PO Box 1135, Islamabad
Tel: (051) 111424424 *Fax:* (051) 111425425
E-mail: peterellwood@britishcouncil.bg
Web Site: www.britishcouncil.pk
Telex: 54644
Key Personnel
Dir: Peter Ellwood
Deputy Dir: John Payne
Asst Dir, Library & Information Services: Jonathan Smith

Ewing Memorial Library
Forman Christian College, Lahore 16
Key Personnel
Librarian: Jacob Lal Din

Dr Mahmud Husain Library
University Campus, Karachi 75270
Tel: (021) 474953 *Fax:* (021) 4969277
Key Personnel
Librarian: M K Alam
Publication(s): *Guide to Bibliographical Sources* (Catalog of rare books)

Islamic Research Institute Library
PO Box 1035, Islamabad 44000
Tel: (051) 9261761-5; (051) 2252816
Telex: 54068 IIU Pak *Cable:* ISLAMSERCH
Key Personnel
Dir General: Zafar Ishaq Ansari
Ultimate Parent Company: International Islamic University, Islamabad

National Archives of Pakistan
Administrative Block Area, N Block, Pak Secretariat, Islamabad
Tel: (051) 9202044; (051) 9214569 *Fax:* (051) 817323; (051) 9203545
Web Site: www.unesco.org/web.world/mdm/1999/eng/pakistan
Telex: ARCHIVES
Key Personnel
Dir General: Mr Ijaz Mohiuddin
Dir: Mr Mond Ramzan

PAKISTAN

Founded: 1951
Storage & presentation of historical & public records
Member of International Council on Archives (ICA).
Publication(s): *Pakistan Archives* (biannual journal, journal)
Branch Office(s)
Karachi, Frere Market Rd *Tel:* (021) 7765232

National Library of Pakistan
Constitution Av, Islamabad 44000
Mailing Address: PO Box 1982, Islamabad 44000
Tel: (051) 9214523 *Fax:* (051) 92213754
E-mail: nlpiba@isb.paknet.com.pk
Key Personnel
Dir: M A Zaheer *Tel:* (051) 9206584
Contact: A H Akhtar

Pakistan Institute of Development Economics
PO Box 1091, Islamabad 44000
Tel: (051) 9206616 *Fax:* (051) 9210886
E-mail: pide@isb.paknet.com.pk
Web Site: www.pide.org.pk
Key Personnel
Editor: Dr A R Kemal
Deputy Chief, Library & Documentation: Zafar J Naqvi *Tel:* (051) 9214041 *E-mail:* naqvizj@hotmail.com
Founded: 1957
Research.
Publication(s): *Pakistan Development Review* (quarterly)

Pakistan Institute of Nuclear Science & Technology Library, Science Information Division
Nilore, Islamabad
Tel: (051) 452350 *Fax:* (051) 429533
E-mail: ctc@shell.portal.com
Telex: 5725 Atcom Pk
Key Personnel
Head, Scientific Information Division: Dr Abdullah Sadiq
Principal Librarian: Mohammad Shafique

Pakistan Scientific and Technological Information Centre (PASTIC)
Quaid-i-Azam University Campus, Islamabad
Tel: (051) 824161 *Fax:* (051) 9201341
E-mail: pnc%pastic@sdnpk.undp.org.pk
Key Personnel
Dir General, Pastic: Dr Muhammad Afzal *Tel:* (051) 9201340 *E-mail:* pstic@paknet2.ptc.pk
Dir: Sheikh M Hanif
Publication(s): *Directory of Scientific Periodicals of Pakistan* (annually); *Pakistan Science Abstracts* (quarterly)

Punjab University Library
Shahrah-e-al-Beruni, Lahore 2
Mailing Address: Quaid-e-Azam Campus, Lahore 54590
Tel: (042) 868853
Key Personnel
Chief Librarian: Ahmad Naseer

Punjab Public Library
Library Rd, Lahore 54000
Tel: (042) 9211649 *Fax:* (042) 9211651
E-mail: pplinfo@brain.net.pk
Web Site: www.brain.net.pk/pplinfo
Key Personnel
Secretary/Chief Librarian: Hafiz Khudea Bekhsh

Sind University Central Library
University of Sind, Allama ll Kazi Campus, Jamshoro, Sind
Tel: (0221) 671292 ext 58
Key Personnel
Librarian: Mohammad Ishaquel Laghari

University of Baluchistan Library
Sariab Rd, Quetta
Tel: (081) 41770
Key Personnel
Librarian: Murtaza Ghulam Brohi

University of Engineering & Technology Central Library
Grand Trunk Rd, Lahore 54890
Tel: (042) 6829243 *Fax:* (042) 6822566
E-mail: central_library@yahoo.com
Web Site: www.uet.edu.pk *Cable:* UNIVENGTECH
Key Personnel
Librarian: Abdul Hameed
Assistant Librarian: Muhammad Saeed *Tel:* 6822667
Founded: 1961
Publication(s): *Central Library Bulletin* (bimonthly)

Panama

Biblioteca Nacional
Ernesto J Castillero R, Apdo 2444, Panama
Key Personnel
Dir: Prof Algis Borrero
Publication(s): *Bibliografías nacionales*

Biblioteca Bio-Medica del Laboratorio Conmemorativo Gorgas
Av Justo Arosemena 35-30, Apdo 6991, Panama 5
Tel: (02) 274111 *Fax:* (02) 254366
E-mail: igorgas@sin.fonet
Telex: 3433 *Cable:* GOMELA
Key Personnel
Dir: Dr Rolando E Saenz
Librarian: Nora E Osses; Gloria O de Cano
Branch Office(s)
PO Box 935, APO, Miami, FL, United States
Gorgas Memorial Laboratory
Bio-medical Research Library

Universidad de Panama, Biblioteca Interamericana Simon Bolivar
Estafeta Universitaria, Apdo 3277, Panama
Tel: 2636133
Key Personnel
Librarian: Nuria F de Gonzalez
Publication(s): *Boletin Bibliografico*

Papua New Guinea

Office of Libraries and Archives, Papua, New Guinea
PO Box 734, Waigani
Tel: 3256200 *Fax:* 3251331
E-mail: ola@datec.com.pg *Cable:* PNG LIB BOROKO
Key Personnel
Dir General: Daniel Paraide
Publication(s): *Ola Nius (formerly National Library Nius)*; *Papua New Guinea National Bibliography*; *Selective Index to the Times of Papua New Guinea*

Papua New Guinea Institute of Public Administration Library (PNGIPA)
PO Box 1216, Port Moresby, Boroko
Tel: 3260433 *Fax:* 3261654
Telex: 23011 *Cable:* PNGIPA
Key Personnel
Contact: Lewis Kusso-Alles
Publication(s): *Administration for Development* (college journal)
Branch Office(s)
Papua New Guinea Institute of Public Administration, Boroko

PNGIPA Library, see Papua New Guinea Institute of Public Administration Library (PNGIPA)

Michael Somare Library
University, National Capital District 134, Waigani 134
Mailing Address: PO Box 319, Waigani 134
Tel: (0675) 3267280 *Fax:* (0675) 3267187
E-mail: 100352.216@compuserve.com
Telex: ne 22366
Key Personnel
Contact: Florence J Griffin
Publication(s): *Guide to Manuscripts in the New Guinea Collection* (by Nancy Lutton 1980); *New Guinea Periodical Index* (quarterly)

Paraguay

Biblioteca y Archivo Nacionales
Mariscal Estigarriba, 95 Asuncion
National Library and Archives.

Biblioteca de la Sociedad Científica del Paraguay
Avda Espana 505, Asuncion
Tel: (021) 24832
Library of the Paraguayan Scientific Society.

Peru

ALIDE, see Asociacion Latinoamericana de Instituciones Financieras Para El Desarrollo (ALIDE)

Archivo General de la Nacion del Peru
Calle Manuel Cuadros s/n, Palacio de Justicia, Apdo 3124, Lima
Tel: (014) 275930 *Fax:* (014) 282829
E-mail: emendoza@agn.minjus.gos.pe
Key Personnel
Chief Librarian & Dir: Aida Mendoza Navarro

Asociacion Latinoamericana de Instituciones Financieras Para El Desarrollo (ALIDE)
(Latin American Association of Development Financing Institutions)
Paseo de la Republica, 3211 Lima, San Isidro
Mailing Address: Apartado Postal 3988, Lima 100
Tel: (01) 4422400 *Fax:* (01) 4428105
E-mail: sg@alide.org.pe
Web Site: www.alide.org.pe
Key Personnel
Secretary General: Rommel Acevedo
Head, Institutional Relations Division: Eduardo Vasquez *E-mail:* dri@alide.org.pe
Founded: 1968

Represents institutions that finance development in Latin America & the Caribbean. Provides information & documentation related to development banking fields of interest, as well as having information on materials relative to specific economic sectors & technological aspects. Collects specialized documentation concerned with banking & financing development
Membership: World Federation of Development Financing Institutions (WFDFI).
Publication(s): *Boletin Alide* (Alide Bulletin, 6 times annually, dedicated to the provision of articles & analytical information, in depth studies & documents of a technical & legal nature related to banking & financing development); *Memoria Annual* (annually, report)

Biblioteca Central de la Universidad Nacional de San Agustin
Cuidad Universitaria s/n, Apdo 23, Arequipa
Tel: (054) 229719

Biblioteca Central de la Universidad Nacional Mayor de San Marcos
Simon Rodriquez 681, Apdo 454, Lima 1
Tel: (01) 4285210 *Fax:* (01) 4285210
E-mail: ogeibl@sanfer.edu.pe

Biblioteca Nacional
Av Abancay, 4a Cuadra S/N, Lima 1
Tel: (014) 287690 *Fax:* (01) 4277331
E-mail: jefatura@binape.gob.pe
Key Personnel
Dir: Sinesio Lopez Jimenez
Publication(s): *Anuario Bibliografico Peruano* (Bibliographical Annual of Peru, Annual); *Bibliografia Nacional* (Peruvian monthly Bibliographical Information, Annual, 2000); *Boletin de la Biblioteca Nacional* (Bulletin of the National Library); *Gaceta Bibliotecaria* (Library Gazette, Irregular); *Revista Fenix* (Phoeniz Magazine, magazine)

ESAN - Escuela de Administracion de Negocios para Graduados, Direccion de Investigacion
Alonso de Molina, Monterrico Chico, Surco, Lima 33
Mailing Address: Apdo 1846, Lima 100
Tel: (01) 3451565 *Fax:* (01) 3451328
E-mail: cendoc@esan.edu.pe
Key Personnel
Dir: Carlos Tejada Oshiro

Biblioteca Central de la Pontificia Universidad Catolica del Peru
Av Universitaria Cdra 18, San Miguel, Apdos 1761, Lima 32
Tel: (01) 4602870 (ext 176) *Fax:* (01) 4633773
E-mail: biblio@pucp.edu.pe
Key Personnel
Rector: Hugo Sarabia
Books & journals sold by Fondo Editorial de la Pontificia Universidad Catokuca del Peru.
Publication(s): *Books* (13 academic journals)

Universidad del Pacifico Libreria
Av Salaverry 2020, Jesus Maria, Apdo 4683, Lima 11
Tel: (014) 712277 *Fax:* (01) 2650958
E-mail: dri@up.edu.pe
Telex: 25650
Key Personnel
Dir: P Visconti
Publication(s): *Apuntes*; *Counterbalance Points* (monthly); *Intercampus*

Universidad Nacional San Antonio Abad del Cusco
Av de la Cultura, Apdo 921, Cuzco
Tel: (084) 222271; (084) 224303

Philippines

Ateneo de Manila University Libraries, see Rizal Library

Far Eastern University Library
Quezon Bd, 2806 Manila
Mailing Address: PO Box 609, 2806 Manila
Tel: (02) 7413421
Key Personnel
Dir: Celedonio O Resurreccion
Publication(s): *Far Eastern University Journal*

Manila City Library
Alvarez St, Santa Cruz, Manila
Mailing Address: City Hall, 3rd fl, Manila
Key Personnel
City Librarian: Filemon L Gecolew

National Library
Ermita, TM Kalaw St, 1000 Manila
Mailing Address: PO Box 2926, 1000 Manila
Tel: (02) 5253196 (Filipiniana); (02) 582271 (Reference); (02) 582660 (Public Documents) *Fax:* (02) 5242329
E-mail: amb@max.ph.net
Telex: (02) 505143 (Filipiniana); 582271 (Reference); 582660; 582511 (Public Documents)
Cable: NALIBPHILS
Key Personnel
Contact: Dr Serafin Quiason

Philippine Normal College Library & Library Science Departments
Taft Ave, Manila
Tel: (02) 5270372 *Fax:* (02) 5270372
Key Personnel
Contact: Calixta Aquirre

Rizal Library
Formerly Ateneo de Manila University Libraries
Katipunan Ave, Loyola Heights, 1108 Quezon City, Metro Manila
Mailing Address: PO Box 154, 1099 Manila
Tel: (02) 426-6001; 5800-5816 (Local) *Fax:* (02) 426-5961
Web Site: rizal.lib.admn.edu.ph
Key Personnel
Dir: Mrs Lourdes T David *E-mail:* latdavid@admu.edu.ph
Founded: 1969
Educational institution.
Parent Company: Ateneo de Manila University

Science & Technology Information Institute Department of Science & Technology
Bicutan, Taguig, Manila
Mailing Address: PO Box 3596, Manila
Tel: (02) 8220954
Key Personnel
Chief: Dr Irene D Amores
Publication(s): *Philippine Science & Technology Abstracts*; *R & D Philippines*; *SEA Abstracts*; *Series of Philippine Scientific Bibliographies*; *Union Catalogue of NISST*; *Union List of Serials of NSTA and its Agencies*

Silliman University Library
Silliman University Library, 6200 Dumaguete City, 1101 Negros Oriental
Mailing Address: 6200 Dumaguete City, Negros Oriental
Tel: (035) 4227208; (035) 4226002 *Fax:* (035) 4227208
E-mail: sulib@su.edu.ph
Web Site: su.edu.ph
Key Personnel
President: Agustin A Pulido
University Librarian: Lorna T Yso *E-mail:* lty@su.edu.ph
Founded: 1901
Educational institution.
Publication(s): *Convergence* (annual, journal, 1994, multidisciplinary journal of the arts & sciences); *Sands & Coral* (annual, journal, 1948, student literary journal); *Silliman Journal* (semi-annual, journal, 1954, humanities & sciences); *Silliman University Library Bulletin* (bi-monthly, newsletter, 1971, contains news about the library personnel, resources, services & facilities)

Ramona S Tirona Memorial Library
The Philippine Women's University, Taft Ave, 1004 Manila
Tel: (02) 5268421 (loc 176) *Fax:* (02) 5266935
Key Personnel
Librarian: Dionisia M Angeles
Publication(s): *Administrative Bulletin*; *Philippine Educational Forum*; *PWU Bulletin/FTB Bulletin*; *The Alumni Link and Philippine Women's University Forum*; *The Link*

University of Manila Central Library
546 Dr M V de los Santos St, Sampaloc, 1008 Manila
Tel: (02) 7413637 *Fax:* (02) 7413640

University of San Carlos Library System
P del Rosario St, 6401 Cebu City
Mailing Address: PO Box 182, 6401 Cebu City
Tel: (032) 220432; (032) 2540432 *Fax:* (032) 54341; (032) 2540432
E-mail: direklib@pinya.usc.edu.ph
Web Site: www.use.edu.ph/administration/library
Cable: STEYL CEBU
Key Personnel
Dir, Libraries: Marilou P Tadlip

University of Santo Tomas Library
Espana St, Manila
Tel: (02) 210081 *Fax:* (02) 7409709
E-mail: clib1@ustcc.ust.edu.ph
Web Site: www.library.ust.edu.ph
Key Personnel
Chief Librarian: Erlinda F Flores
Contact: Fr Angel A Aparicio *Tel:* (02) 7313034
Founded: 1611

University of the East Library
Claro M Recto Ave, 2806 Manila
Tel: (02) 7358544 *Fax:* (02) 7356976
E-mail: uel@mozcom.com
Key Personnel
Chief Librarian: Narcisa F Tioco

University of the Philippines Diliman University Library
Gonzalez Hall, Diliman, 3004 Quezon City
Tel: (02) 926 1877 *Fax:* (02) 92 1876
E-mail: salvacion.arlante@up.edu.ph
Web Site: www.mainlib.upd.edu.ph
Key Personnel
University Librarian: Salvacion M Arlante
Founded: 1922
Publication(s): *Index to Philippine Periodicals (IPP)* (Quarterly)

Poland

Naczelna Dyrekcja Archiwow Panstwowych
Ul Dluga 6, Skr poczt 1005, 00950 Warsaw

Tel: (022) 8313206; (022) 8313208 *Fax:* (022) 8317563
Key Personnel
Contact: Doc dr hab Daria Nalecz
Main Directorate of the Polish State Archives.
Publication(s): *Archeion, Teki archiwalne*

Archiwum Glowne Akt Dawnych
Ul Dluga 7, 00-263 Warsaw
Tel: (022) 8311525 (ext 28) *Fax:* (022) 8311608
Key Personnel
Dir: Dr Wladyslaw Stepniak
Central Archives for Historical Documents.
Publication(s): *Miscellanea Historico-archivistica*

Biblioteka Jagiellonska (Jagiellonian Library; Jagiellonian Library)
Aleja Mickiewicza 22, 30-059 Krakow
Tel: (012) 6331971 (Director); (012) 6336377 (Operator); (012) 6330903 (Secretariat) *Fax:* (012) 6330903
Key Personnel
Dir: Dr Krzysztof Zamorski *E-mail:* zamorski@if.uj.edu.pl
Deputy Dir: Ryszard Juchniewicz; Teresa Malik *Tel:* (012) 6339882 *E-mail:* malikter@if.uj.edu.pl; Zdislaw Pietrzyk, PhD
Founded: 1364
Publication(s): *Biuletyn Biblioteki Jagiellonskiej* (The Jagiellonian Library Bulletin, annually)
Parent Company: Uniwersytet Jagiellonski (Jagiellonian University)

Biblioteka Narodowa
ul Niepodleglosci 213, 00-973 Warsaw
Mailing Address: Al Niepodleglosci 213, PO Box 36, 00-973 Warsaw 22
Tel: (022) 8255733 *Fax:* (022) 8255251
E-mail: biblnar@bn.org.pl; bndyrekt@bn.org.pl
Key Personnel
Dir: Prof Adam Manikowski
The National Library. See also Instytut Bibliograficzny, a division of the National Library.
Publication(s): *Biuletyn Informacyjny Biblioteki Narodowej* (The National Library Information Bulletin); *Rocznik Biblioteki Narodowej* (The National Library Yearbook)

Biblioteka Publiczna m st Warszawy - Biblioteka Glowna Wojewodztwa Mazowieckiego (The Warsaw Public Library-The Central Library of Masovia Province)
Ul Koszykowa 26/28, 00-553 Warsaw
Mailing Address: PO Box 365, 00-950 Warsaw
Tel: (022) 6217852 *Fax:* (022) 6211968
E-mail: Biblioteka@biblpubl.haw.pl
Web Site: www.biblpubl.waw.pl
Key Personnel
Manager: Janina Jagielska
Head, Planning Dept: Joanna Kacprzak *Tel:* (022) 628 2001 ext 161 *E-mail:* dzial.fachowo.organizacyjny@biblpubl.waw.pl
Founded: 1907
Public Library of Warsaw.
Publication(s): *Prace Biblioteki Publicznej m st Warszawy* (The Works of Warsaw Public Library, irregularly); *Sesje varsavianistyczne* (Varsaviana Sessions, irregularly)

Biblioteka Uniwersytecka w Warszawie (Warsaw University Library)
Ul Dobra 56/60, 00-312 Warsaw
Tel: (022) 5525660; (022) 5525181 *Fax:* (022) 5525181
E-mail: buw@mail.uw.edu.pl
Web Site: www.buw.uw.edu.pl
Key Personnel
Librarian: Dr Henryk Hollender
Founded: 1817
Publication(s): *Prace Biblioteki Uniwersyteckiej w Warszawie - Acta Bibliothecae* (irregularly)

Biblioteka Uniwersytecka w Poznaniu (Poznan University Library)
Ul Ratajczaka 38-40, 61-816 Poznan
Tel: (061) 852-29-55; (061) 829-38-00 *Fax:* (061) 829-38-24
E-mail: library@amu.edu.pl
Web Site: lib.amu.edu.pl
Telex: 412714 Bup
Key Personnel
Dir: Dr Artur Jazdon *E-mail:* jazar@amu.edu.pl
Founded: 1919
Publication(s): *Biblioteka* (annually); *Zeszyty Naukowe Biblioteki Uniwersyteckiej w Poznaniv* (irregular)
Parent Company: Uniwersytek im Adama Mickiewicza w Poznaniu (UAM)

Politechnika Gdanska
ul Narutowicza 11/12, 80952 Gdansk Wrzeszcz
Tel: (058) 3415791 *Fax:* (058) 3415821
E-mail: mainlibr@sunrise.pg.gda.pl; jligman@sunrise.pg.gda.pl
Web Site: www.pg.gda.pl
Telex: 415821
Key Personnel
Manager: Miroslaw Komendecki
Publication(s): *Bibliografia publikacji pracownikow Politechniki Gdanskiej* (Bibliographic Publication of the Employees of the Technical University of Gdansk); *Raporty Wydzialow PG* (Annual, Berichte der Fakultaten der TU Gdansk); *Wykaz nabytkow BG PG* (Monthly, Directory of New Recruting of the Central Library of Gdansk); *Zhistorii Politechniki Gdanskiej* (Quarterly, The History of the Technical University of Gdansk)

Biblioteka Gdanska PAN
Ul Walowa 15, 80858 Gdansk
Tel: (058) 312251-54 *Fax:* (058) 312970
E-mail: bgpan@task.gda.pl
Key Personnel
Librarian: Zbigniew Nowak
Publication(s): *Libri Gedanenses* (annually)

Glowna Biblioteka Lekarska
Ul Chocimska 22, 00791 Warsaw
Tel: (022) 497851 *Fax:* (022) 497802
E-mail: gbl@atos.warman.com.pl
Telex: 814820
Key Personnel
Dir: Prof Janusz Kapuscik
Central Medical Library.
Publication(s): *Biuletyn GBL*; *Polska Bibliografia Lekanska*

Biblioteka Glowna Politechniki Warszawskiej
Pl Politechniki 1, 00-661 Warsaw
Tel: (022) 6211370 *Fax:* (022) 6287184
E-mail: bgpw@bg.pw.edu.pl
Library of the Technical University of Warsaw.

Instytut Bibliograficzny
Division of National Library - Biblioteka Narodowa
Biblioteka Narodowa, Al Niepodleglosci 213, 00-973 Warsaw 22
Mailing Address: PO Box 36, Warsaw 22
Tel: (022) 6082946 *Fax:* (022) 8255251
E-mail: sadowska@bn.org.pl
Telex: 816761 Bn Pl
Key Personnel
Librarian: Jadwiga Sadowska, PhD
Bibliographical Institute (a Division of the National Library - see Biblioteka Narodowa).
Publication(s): *Bibliografia Bibliografii Polskich* (Bibliography of Polish Bibliographies, Annual); *Bibliografia Wydawnictw Ciagych* (Bibliography of Serials, Annual); *Bibliografia Zawartosci Czasopism* (Index to Periodicals, Monthly); *Polonica Zagraniczne* (Foreign Polonica, Annual); *Polska Bibliografia Bibliologiczna* (Polish Bibliography of Library Science, Annual); *Przewodnik Bibliograficzny* (Bibliographical Guide, Weekly); *Ruch Wydawniczy w Liczbach* (Polish Publishing in Figures, Annual)

Politechnika Krakowska im Tadeusza Kosciuszki (Cracow University of Technology)
Member of IATUL
Ul Warszawska 24, 31155 Krakow
Tel: (12) 6282014 *Fax:* (12) 6332909; (12) 6282014
E-mail: listy@biblos.pk.edu.pl
Web Site: www.biblios.pk.edu.pl
Key Personnel
Librarian: Marek M Gorski *E-mail:* gorski@biblos.pk.edu.pl

Politechnika Slaska (The Silesian Technical University)
Biblioteka Glowna, ul Kaszubska 23, Gliwice 44-100
Tel: (032) 23412 69 *Fax:* (032) 23715 51
E-mail: info@bibgl.polsl.gliwice.pl
Key Personnel
Manager: Halina Baluka
Founded: 1945

Politechnika Wroclawska/Biblioteka Glowna i OINT (Wroclaw University of Technology/Main Library & Scientific Information Centre)
Wybrzeze Wyspianskiego 27, 50370 Wroclaw
Tel: (071) 3202305 *Fax:* (071) 3282960
E-mail: bg@bg.pwr.wroc.pl
Key Personnel
Dir: Henryk Szarski
Librarian: Lucja Talarczyk-Malcher
Publication(s): *Acta of Bioengineering and Biomechanics*; *Architectus*; *Badania Operacyjne i Decyzje*; *Environment Protection Engineering*; *Fizykochemiczne Problemy Mineralurgii*; *Inzynieria Chemiczna i Procesowa*; *Optica Applicata*; *Studia Geotechnica and Mechanica*; *Systems Science*

Polska Fundacja Spraw Miedzynarodowych (Polish Foundation of International Affairs)
Ul Warecka 1a, PL 00-950 Warsaw
Mailing Address: PO Box 1000, PL00-950 Warsaw
Tel: (022) 8278888; (022) 5239086 *Fax:* (022) 5239027
E-mail: warecka@qdnet.pl
Key Personnel
Head of Publications: Aleksandra Zieleniec *E-mail:* warecka@qdnet.pl
Publication(s): *The Polish Quarterly of International Affairs* (quarterly); *Yearbook of Polish Foreign Policy* (Annually)

Biblioteka Slaska (Silesian Library)
Plac Rady Europy 1, 40-021 Katowice
Tel: (032) 208 38 75 *Fax:* (032) 208 37 20
E-mail: bsl@libra.bs.katowice.pl; bsl@bs.katowice.pl
Web Site: www.bs.katowice.pl
Key Personnel
Dir: Prof Jan Malicki *Tel:* (032) 206 06 875
Research library. Main special collections covering: literature, history, law, religion, social science & economy, special Silesian collection.
Publication(s): *Bibliografia Slaska* (Yearly); *Ksiaznica Slaska* (irregular, bulletin, Provides information on the Silesian Library activites & articles on the history of Silesian books)

Uniwersytet Szczecinski
Ul A Mickiewicza 16, 70384 Szczecin
Tel: (091) 845338 *Fax:* (09) 845338

E-mail: livre.bibl@univ.szczecin.pl Cable: 422719
Key Personnel
Rector of University: Prof Tadeusz Wierzabicki
Dir: Jolanta Goc
Publication(s): *Przeglad Zachodniopomorski* (quarterly)

Biblioteka Uniwersytecka we Wroclawiu
(Library of the University of Wroclaw)
Ul Karola Szajnochy 10, 50-076 Wroclaw
Tel: (071) 3463129 *Fax:* (071) 3463166
E-mail: infnauk@bu.uni.wroc.pl
Web Site: www.bu.uni.wroc.pl
Key Personnel
Director: Dr Andrzej Ladomirski
Founded: 1945
University Library Wroclaw.
Publication(s): *Bibliothecalia Wratislaviensia* (irregular, newspaper, 1995)

Uniwersytet Gdanski
Biblioteka Glowna UG, ul Armii Krajowej 110, 81824 Sopot
Tel: (058) 5509005; (058) 5511117 *Fax:* (058) 5515221
E-mail: bib@bg.univ.gda.pl; info@bg.univ.gda.pl
Web Site: www.bg.univ.gda.pl/library/
Key Personnel
Librarian: Urszula Sawicka
Founded: 1970

Biblioteka Uniwersytecka w Torruniu (Nicholas Copernicus University Library)
Ul Gagarina 13, 87-100 Torun
Tel: (056) 654 29 52; (056) 61 14 408 *Fax:* (056) 652 04 19
E-mail: umklibr@bu.uni.torun.pl; sekrretariat@bu.uni.torrum.pl
Web Site: www.bu.uni.torrum.pl/en
Key Personnel
Librarian: Stefan Czaja
Founded: 1945
Library of the Mikolaj Kopernik University in Torun.
Parent Company: Uniwersytet Mikolaja Kopernika w Torruniu

Portugal

Biblioteca da Academia das Ciencias de Lisboa
Rua da Academia das Ciencias 19, P-1200 Lisbon
Tel: (021) 3463866
Library of the Academy of Sciences.

Biblioteca da Ajuda
Palacio da Ajuda, 1300 Lisbon
Tel: (021) 3638592 *Fax:* (021) 3638592
Key Personnel
Dir: Francisco Delfim Cunha Leao

Biblioteca Geral da Universidade de Coimbra
Largo Porta Ferrea, 3000-447 Coimbra Codex
Tel: (0239) 859800 *Fax:* (0239) 827135
E-mail: bguc@ci.uc.pt
Telex: (039) 52275
Key Personnel
Dir: Prof Anibal Pinto De Castro
  E-mail: acastro@ci.uc.pt
Publication(s): *Acta Universitatis Conimbrigensis*; *Biblioteca da Universidade de Coimbra*; *Biblioteca Geralda Universidade de Coimbra*; *Divulgacao Bibliografica*; *Revista da Universidade de Coimbra*; *Sumarios das Publicacoes Periodicas Portuguesas*

Biblioteca Nacional
Campo Grande 83, 1749-081 Lisbon
Tel: (021) 217982000 *Fax:* (021) 217982140
E-mail: bn@bn.pt
Web Site: www.bn.pt
Key Personnel
Deputy Dir: Fernanda Maria Campos *Tel:* (021) 217982022 *E-mail:* fcampos@bn.pt
Founded: 1796
National Library.
Publication(s): *Bibliografia Nacional Portuguesa* (2x/yr, Portuguese National Bibliography in CD-ROM); *Leituras: Revista da Biblioteca Nacional* (2x/yr)

Biblioteca Popular de Lisboa
Rua Academia das Ciencias, 19 Rua Ivens, 35, 1294 Lisbon codex
Tel: (021) 369883
Key Personnel
Contact: Belkiss Pousao Lopes

Biblioteca Publica de Evora
Largo Conde de Vila Flor, 7000 Evora
Tel: (066) 22369 *Fax:* (066) 742081
Public Library.
Publication(s): *Evora, BPADE, 1988*; *Isabel Cid-Incunabulos da Biblioteca Publica e Arquivo Distrital de Evora-Catalogo Abreviado*; *Isabel Cid-Incunabulos E Seus Possuidores, Estudo das marcas de posse dos incunabulos da Biblioteca Publica e Arquivo Distrital de Evora, Lisboa INIC, 1988*; *Isabel Cid-Lil Vicente e asua Epoca, Evora, 1992*

Biblioteca Publica Municipal do Porto
Jardim de Sao Lazaro, 4099 Porto Codex
Tel: (02) 572147 *Fax:* (02) 5106139
Key Personnel
Dir: L Cabral
Municipal Library of Porto.

Fundacao para a Ciencia e a Tecnologia/Servico de Informacao e Documentacao(SID)
Av D Carlos 1, 126,2, 1200 Lisbon
Tel: (01) 3924440 *Fax:* (01) 3957284
Telex: 12290 junic
Key Personnel
Dir: Dr Gabriela Lopes da Silva *E-mail:* G.L.Silva@fct.mct.pt
Centre of Scientific & Technical Information, a branch of the Junta Nacional de Investigacao Cientifica e Technologia (National Council for Scientific & Technological Research).
Publication(s): *Guia de servicos di Documentacao e di Bibliotecas em Portugal*

Instituto dos Arquivos Nacionais/Torre do Tombo
Alameda da Universidade, 1600 Lisbon
Tel: (01) 7811500 *Fax:* (01) 7937230
E-mail: dc@iantt.pt
Telex: 65729 ANTTP
Key Personnel
Head of Division: Dr Maria de Lurdes Henriques

Biblioteca do Palacio Nacional de Mafra
Terreiro de D Joao V, 2640 Mafra
Tel: (0261) 817550 *Fax:* (0261) 811947
Key Personnel
Dir: Maria Margarida Montenegro

Universidade do Minho (Minho University)
Largo do Paco, 4709 Braga Codex
Tel: (0253) 604150 *Fax:* (0253) 678590
Web Site: www.sdum.uminho.pt
Telex: 132135
Key Personnel
Dir Documentation Services: Armindo R Cardoso
  E-mail: acardoso@sdum.uminho.pt

Librarian: Eloy Rodrigues *Tel:* (253) 510119
  E-mail: eloy@sdum.uminho.pt
Founded: 1973

Puerto Rico

Archivo General de Puerto Rico
Instituto de Cultura Puertorriquena, Apto 4184, San Juan 00902
Tel: (787) 722-2113 *Fax:* (787) 722-9097
Key Personnel
Dir: Nelly V Cruz Rodriquez
National Archives of Puerto Rico.

Biblioteca General de Puerto Rico (General Library of Puerto Rico)
Instituto de Cultura Puertorriquena, Ponce de Leon 500, San Juan 00908
Mailing Address: PO Box 9024184, San Juan 00902-4184
Tel: (787) 722-2113 *Fax:* (787) 724-0330
Key Personnel
Dir: Ines Flores-Forastieri
Founded: 1967
Library.

Caribbean & Latin American Studies Library
University Station, Apdo 21927, Rio Piedras 00931-1927
Tel: (787) 764-0000 (ext 3319) *Fax:* (787) 763-5685
E-mail: utorres@upracd.upr.clu.edu
Key Personnel
Librarian: Victor F Torres-Ortiz
Research collection open to the general public.

Inter American University of Puerto Rico Library
Bo Canelas, Carr 2 K.8, Arecibo 00614-4050
Mailing Address: PO Box 4050, Arecibo 00614-4050
Tel: (787) 878-5475 (ext 320) *Fax:* (787) 880-1624
E-mail: sabreu@uiprl.inter.edu

University of Puerto Rico, General Library, Mayaguez Campus
College Station, Mayaguez 00709-5000
Mailing Address: PO Box 5000, Mayaguez 00709-5000
Tel: (787) 832-4040 (ext 2255) *Fax:* (787) 834-3031
Key Personnel
Contact: Grace Quinones-Seda

University of Puerto Rico, Medical Sciences Campus Library
Medical Center Area Rio Piedras, San Juan 00936-5067
Mailing Address: PO Box 365067, San Juan 00936-5067
Tel: (787) 758-2525 *Fax:* (787) 282-6438
Telex: 3859173
Key Personnel
Dir: Francisca Corrada

University of Puerto Rico, Library System, Rio Piedras Campus
PO Box 23302, San Juan 00931-3302
Tel: (787) 764-0000 (ext 3296) *Fax:* (787) 764-0270
Key Personnel
Dir: Ramon A Budet *Tel:* (787) 764-0000 ext 5085 *E-mail:* RBudet@rrpac.upr.clu.edu

Acting Associate Dir: Myra Torres Alamo
 E-mail: mytorres@rrpac.upr.clu.edu
Publication(s): *Al Dia, Entorno; Biblionotas; Boletines de Divulgacion; Lumbre; Perspectiva; Servicio de Alerta*

Qatar

Qatar National Library
PO Box 205, Doha
Tel: 429955 *Fax:* 429976
Telex: 4743 Qanali DH
Key Personnel
Dir: Mohammed Hamad Al-Nassr
Branch Office(s)
Al Khansa
Al- Shekh Ali
Al-Khore
Al-Rayyan
Al-Shamal
Al-Wakra

Qatar University Library
PO Box 2713, Doha
Tel: 832222; 892406 *Fax:* 83511
Telex: 4630 Unvsty DH

Reunion

Archives departementales
Le Chaudron, 97490 Sainte-Clotilde
Tel: 212829
Key Personnel
Librarian: Jullien Benoit

Bibliotheque Departemental de Pret
One pl Joffre, 97400 St-Denis
Tel: 210324 *Fax:* 214130
Key Personnel
Librarian: Marie-Colette Maujean

Mediatheque de Saint Pierre
BP 396, rue du College Arthur, 97458 St-Pierre Cedex
Tel: 96 71 91 *Fax:* 25 74 10
Web Site: www.mediatheque-saintpierre.fr
Key Personnel
Librarian: Linda Koo Seen Lin *E-mail:* ksl@mediatheque-saintpierre.fr

SCD, see Universite de la Reunion, Service Commun de la Documentation

Universite de la Reunion, Service Commun de la Documentation
15 Ave Rene Cassin, BP 7152, 97715 St-Denis Cedex
Tel: 938379 *Fax:* 938364
Key Personnel
Dir: Lefe Bure
Conservateur General: Anne-Marie Blanc

Romania

Academia de Studii Economice, Biblioteca Centrala
Piata Romana 6, 70167 Bucharest
Tel: (01) 115960
Telex: Asero 11863

Arhivele Nationale ale Romaniei (National Archives of Romania)
B-dul Elisabeta 49, Bucharest 70602
Tel: (01) 3152503 *Fax:* (01) 3125841
Key Personnel
General Dir: Dr Costin Fenesan
Member of the International Association of Francopone Archives; International Council of Archives.
Publication(s): *Historical Abstract & America-History & Life* (article abstracts & index)

Biblioteca Centrala Universitara
Str transilvaniei nr 6, sector 1, 70778 Bucharest
Tel: (01) 6154240; (01) 6156584 *Fax:* (01) 6132842
E-mail: stoica@bcub.ro
Key Personnel
Dir: Dr Ion Stoica
Deputy Dirs: Ivona Dumitrescu; Dr Mircea Regneala
Publication(s): *Literatura romana; Ghid bibliografic Partea I: Surse. Partea a II-a: Scriitori. Vol.I: A-L. Vol.II: M-Z. 1979, 1982, 1983*

Biblioteca Nationala a Romaniei (National Library of Romania)
Str Ion Ghica 4, 79708 Bucharest
Tel: (01) 3157063 *Fax:* (01) 3123381
E-mail: go@bibnat.ro
Key Personnel
Dir: Ion Dan Erceanu
Founded: 1955
National Library of Romania.

Biblioteca Centrala Universitara Mihail Eminescu (Central University Library)
Str Pacurari, nr 4, 6600 Iasi
Tel: (032) 316281 *Fax:* (032) 261796
Web Site: www.bcu-iasi.ro
Key Personnel
Dir: Prof Al Calinescu
Parent Company: Ministry of Education & Research

INID, see Institutul National de Informare si Documentare (INID)

Institutul National de Informare si Documentare (INID) (National Institute for Information & Documentation)
Str George Enescu 27-29, Sector 1, 70074 Bucharest
Tel: (01) 6134010 *Fax:* (01) 3126734
E-mail: inid@iniduw.inid.ro
Telex: 11247
Key Personnel
General Dir: Ana-Eugenia Negulescu, MA
Publication(s): *Abstracts of Romanian Scientific & Technical Literature* (in English, French & Romanian); *Buletin de referate din literatura stiintifica si tehnica romana; Information & Documentation Problems/Probleme de informare si documentare* (in English & Romanian)

Biblioteca Municipala Mihail Sadoveanu
Str Take Ionescu nr 4, 79711 Bucharest
Tel: (01) 2113625 *Fax:* (01) 2113625
Key Personnel
Assistant Dir: Rodica Cosmaciuc
Founded: 1935
Memberships: EBLIDA; IFLA; IMTAMEL.
Publication(s): *The Bibliography of Bucharest City* (1996); *Biblioteca Bucurestilor* (Bucharest's Library Review, monthly, 1998); *Foaia Cartierului* (Neighborhood's Review, monthly)

Universitatea Transilvania Din Brasov Biblioteca Centrala (Transylvania University of Brasov Central Library)
B-dul Eroilor nr 9, 2200 Brasov
Tel: (068) 475348 *Fax:* (068) 475348
E-mail: libr@vega.unitbv.ro
Web Site: www.unitbu.ro/biblio/bib_home.htm
Key Personnel
Dir: Aurel Negrutiu
Head, Library Service: Andrea Deaconescu
 E-mail: deacon@vega.unitbv.ro
Founded: 1948
Specialize in academic library, engineering, forestry, wood industry, humanities, sciences, medicine, music & economy.
Parent Company: Transilvania University of Brasov

Universitatea de Medicina si Farmacie Biblioteca Centrala (Central Library of the University of Medicine & Pharmacy; Central Library of the Univeristy of Medicine and Pharmacy)
Division of Government of Romania
Avram Iancu 31, 3400 Cluj-napoca
Tel: (064) 192629 *Fax:* (064) 190832
Web Site: www.bib.umfcluj.ro
Key Personnel
Dir: Iona Robu *E-mail:* irobu@umfcluj.ro
Founded: 1948
Central Library of the University of Medicine and Pharmacy.
Parent Company: University of Medicine & Pharmacy Ministry of Education

Biblioteca Universitatii Politehnica Bucuresti
Splaiul Independentei 313, Cod 77206, Bucharest 16
Tel: (01) 3127044 *Fax:* (01) 3125365
Telex: 10252 ipolb
Key Personnel
Librarian: Dan-Radu Popescu
 E-mail: dr_popescu@chim.upb.ro
Contact: Lucia Verbinski

Russian Federation

Fundamental Library of the Academy of Medical Sciences
Baltiiskaya Ul 8, 125874 Moscow
Tel: (095) 155-17-93
Key Personnel
Contact: G I Bakhereva

Biblioteka Akademii Nauk Rossii (Russian Academy of Sciences Library)
Birzevaja linija 1, 199034 St Petersburg
Tel: (0812) 3283592 *Fax:* (0812) 3287436
E-mail: ban@info.rasl.spb.ru
Web Site: www.ban.tu
Key Personnel
Contact: Dr Valerij Leonov
Founded: 1714

All-Russian Patent Technical Library
Berezhkovskaya naberezhnaya 24, 121857 Moscow
Tel: (095) 2406425 *Fax:* (095) 2404437
E-mail: vptb@aha.ru
Telex: 411774 bipat SU
Key Personnel
Library Dir: V I Amelkina
Deputy Dir: O I Kosolapov

Central State Archives
Vyborgskaya 3, 125212 Moscow

Tel: (095) 1597383
Key Personnel
Dir: A Prokopenko

Gosudarstvennaya publichnaya istoricheskaya biblioteka Rossii
Starosadskij per 9, 101000 Moscow
Tel: (095) 9256514 *Fax:* (095) 9284332; (095) 9256514
E-mail: maf@shpl.ru
Key Personnel
Dir: Dr Mikhail Dmitrievich Afanasiev
State Public Historical Library of Russia.

Gosudarstvennaya publichnaya nauchno-tekhnicheskaya biblioteka SSSR
Kuznetskii most 12, 103031 Moscow
Tel: (095) 9259288 *Fax:* (095) 9219862
E-mail: root@gpntb.msk.su
Telex: 411180
Key Personnel
Dir: A I Zemskov
State Public Scientific and Technical Library of the USSR.

Institut Nauchnoy Informatsii po Obschestvennym Naukam, Rossijskoj Akademii Nauk RF
Krasikova ul 28/21, 117418 Moscow V-418
Tel: (095) 1288881; (095) 1288930 *Fax:* (095) 4202261
Institute of Scientific Information in the Social Sciences of the Russian Academie of Sciences, Russian Federation.

Nauchnaya biblioteka im M Gor'kogo Sankt-Petersburgskogo (Scientific Library of St Petersburg University)
Universitetskaya naberezhnaya 7/9, 199034 St Petersburg
Tel: (0812) 328 27 41; (0812) 218955 (Reference & Information) *Fax:* (0812) 328 27 41
E-mail: info@mail.lib.pu.ru
Web Site: www.lib.pu.ru
Key Personnel
Dir: N A Sheshina
Vice Dir: Marina Karpova
M Gor'kii Scientific Library of the State University of St Petersburg.

Petrozavodskij Gosudarstvennyj Universitet
prospekt Lenina 33, 185640 Petrozavodsk
Tel: (08142) 775148 *Fax:* (08142) 71021
E-mail: postmaster@mainpgn.kardia.su
Key Personnel
Dir: M P Otlivanchick

Rossiiskaya Nacionalnaya biblioteka
Sadovaya ul 18, 191069 St Petersburg D-69
Tel: (0812) 3109850 *Fax:* (0812) 3106148
E-mail: mb@glas.apc.org
Key Personnel
Economic Relations Coordinator: D B Guschin
National Library of Russia.

Gosudarstvennaya publichnaya nauchno-tekhnicheskaya biblioteka Sibirskogo otdeleniya Rossiiskoi Akademii Nauk
Voskhod 15, 630200 Novosibirsk 200
Tel: (0382) 661860 (Director); (0382) 661991
  Fax: (0382) 663365
E-mail: root@libr.nsk.su
Telex: 133220 *Cable:* 1023 LIBRO
Key Personnel
Dir: Prof Boris Stepanovich Yelepov
Deputy Dir: Yelena Borisovna Soboleva
Secretary, International Ties: Vera Nicolaevna Cabanova
State Public Scientific Technological Library of the Siberian Branch Academy of Sciences of Russia.

Russian State Historical Archives
Angliiskaya nab 4, 190000 St Petersburg
Tel: (0812) 311-09-26 *Fax:* (0812) 311-22-52
Key Personnel
Dir: V G Gerasimov

Sankt-Peterburgskogo Gosudarstvennogo Universiteta
Universiteskaya nab, 7-9, 199034 St Petersburg
Tel: (0812) 2182741 *Fax:* (0812) 2182741
Key Personnel
Vice Dir: M Karpova

Scientific Library of St Petersburg University, see Nauchnaya biblioteka im M Gor'kogo Sankt-Petersburgskogo

Scientific Library Voronezh State University
Ul Pushkinskaya, 148, 344049 Rostov-na-Donu
Tel: (08632) 654363 *Fax:* (08632) 645335
E-mail: root@lib.vsu.ru
Key Personnel
Librarian: Svetlana Yants

Scientific Library Voronezh State University
prospekt Revoljucii 24, 394000 Voronezh
Tel: (0732) 55-35-59 *Fax:* (0732) 78-97-55
E-mail: root@lib.vsu.ru
Web Site: www.lib.vsu.ru
Key Personnel
Librarian: Svetlana Yants
Founded: 1918

State Archives of the Russian Federation
Bolshaya Pirogovskaya ul 17, 119817 Moscow
Tel: (095) 2458184 *Fax:* (095) 2451287

Vserossijskaja gosudarstvennaja biblioteka inostrannoj literatury im M I Rudomino (M I Rudomino All-Russia State Library for Foreign Literature)
Nikolojamskaya ul, 1, Moscow 109189
Tel: (095) 9153621 *Fax:* (095) 9153637
E-mail: vgbil@libfl.ru
Web Site: www.libfl.ru
Key Personnel
Dir General: Ekaterina Genieva
Founded: 1922
General research & public library, an international cultural center
Member of International Federation of Library Associations & Institutions (IFLA), Russian Library Association.

Rwanda

Bibliotheque de l'Institut National de la Recherche Scientifique
BP 192, Butare
Tel: 30395 *Fax:* 30939
Telex: 22605

Service de l'Information et des Archives Nationales
Presidence de la Republique, BP 15, Kigali
Tel: 75432
Telex: 22517
Key Personnel
Dir: Charles Uyisenga

Bibliotheque de l'Universite Nationale du Rwanda
BP 117, Butare
Tel: 30372
Telex: 22605
Key Personnel
Dir: Claudien Ntarwanda

Samoa

Nelson Memorial Public Library
PO Box 598, Apia
Tel: (0685) 21028 *Fax:* (0685) 21028
Web Site: www.samoa.com
Key Personnel
Chief Librarian: Ms Jacinta P Godinet
  E-mail: jpgodinet@lesamoa.net
Founded: 1960

Saudi Arabia

Imam Mohamed Bin Saud University Library
PO Box 5701, Riyadh 11432
Tel: (01) 2580812 *Fax:* (01) 4020886
Telex: 401166 Univer SJ
Key Personnel
Acting Dean of Library Affairs: Dr Mohamed Al Zeer

Institute of Public Administration Library
PO Box 205, Riyadh 11141
Tel: (01) 4768888 *Fax:* (01) 4792136
E-mail: library@ipa.edu.sa
Telex: 404360 SJ *Cable:* IPADMIN
Key Personnel
Dir of Libraries: Mostafa M Sadhan
Publication(s): *Maktabat Al Idarah* (Library Administration, quarterly)

Islamic University Central Library
PO Box 170, Al-Madinah Al-Munawarah, Medina
Tel: (04) 8474080 *Fax:* (04) 8474560
Telex: 570022 Islami SJ
Key Personnel
University Rector: Dr Abdullah Saleh Alobeid
Dean & Library Affairs & Man Dir: Dr Mohammad Yakub Turkustani
Editor in Chief: Dr Ali Sultan Alhakamy

King Abdulasiz University Library
PO Box 1026, Jeddah 21441
Tel: (02) 6879033 *Fax:* (02) 6405974
Telex: 401141 Kauni SJ
Key Personnel
Librarian: Dr Mofakhar H Khan
A Central Library with 10 branches in various faculties.
Publication(s): *Annual Index of Umm Al-Qura* (Arabic); *Catalogue of MSS in the Central Library* (Arabic); *Dissertations on Saudi Arabia* (English)

King Abdulaziz Public Library
PO Box 86486, Riyadh 11622
Tel: (01) 4911300; (01) 4911304 *Fax:* (01) 4911949
E-mail: kapl@anet.net.sa
Telex: 406444 KAPL
Key Personnel
Dir General: Faisal A Al-Muammar

King Faisal University Library
PO Box 1982, Dammam 31441

SAUDI ARABIA

Tel: (03) 8574456 *Fax:* (03) 8576748
Telex: 870020 FAISAL SJ
Key Personnel
Vice Dean of Libraries: Dr Mohammed
  M Al-Abdullah *Tel:* (03) 8574456
  E-mail: alabdullah1963@yahoo.com
Librarian, College of Medicine: Mr Abdulhamid
  Abualsoud *Tel:* (03) 8577000 (ext 353)

King Saud University Library
PO Box 22480, Riyadh 11495
Tel: (01) 4676148 *Fax:* (01) 4676162
Web Site: www.ksu.edu.sa
Telex: 201019 Ksu SJ *Cable:* University
Key Personnel
Dean: Dr Sulaiman S Al-Ogla *E-mail:* sfalogla@.
  ksu.edu.sa
Founded: 1979
Publication(s): *Directory of Libraries in Saudi
  Arabia* (1979)

National Library
King Faisal St, Riyadh

Umm al Qura University Library
PO Box 407/715, Mecca
Tel: (02) 5564770 *Fax:* (02) 556562
Telex: 540026 Jammka SJ
Key Personnel
Dean of Library Affairs: Dr Hammad M Ae-
  Thomaly

Senegal

L'Alliance francaise, Bibliotheque
2 Rue Assane N Doye, Dakar
Tel: 8210822

Archives du Senegal
Immeuble administratif, ave Leopold Sedar Sen-
  ghor, Dakar
Tel: 8235072 *Fax:* 8225126
E-mail: pmardi@primature.sn
Key Personnel
Dir: Saliou Mbaye
National Archives of Senegal.
Publication(s): *Bibliographie du Senegal* (annual
  report); *Dictionnaire de sigles et acronymes en
  usage au Senegal* (1990, monographic); *Guide
  de Archives de l'AOF* (monographic); *Histoire
  des institutions coloniales Francaise en Afrique
  de l'ouest (1816-1960)* (1991, monographic)

**Ecole des Bibliothecaires, Archivistes et
  Documentalistes de l'Universite Cheikh Anta
  Diop de Dakar**
BP 3252, Dakar
Tel: 8240542; 8257660 *Fax:* 252883; 8240542
Telex: 51-262 UNIVDAK SG
Key Personnel
Dir: Sane Ousmane

IDEP, see Institut Africain de Developpement
  Economique et de Planification (IDEP),
  Bibliotheque

**Institut Africain de Developpement
  Economique et de Planification (IDEP),
  Bibliotheque**
BP 3186, Dakar
Tel: 8231020 *Fax:* 8222964
E-mail: idep@sonatel.senet.net
Telex: 51579 Idep *Cable:* IDEP

**Institut Fondamental d'Afrique Noire,
  Bibliotheque**
BP 206, Dakar
Tel: (0221) 250090
E-mail: bibifan@ifan.refer.sn
Telex: 51262
Key Personnel
Librarian: Gora Dia

**Universite Cheikh Anta Diop de Dakar,
  Bibliotheque Universitaire**
BP 2006, Dakar
Tel: 825 02 79 *Fax:* 824 23 79
Telex: 5126256 UNIVDAK
Key Personnel
Dir: Ms Henri Sene *Tel:* 824 69 81
  E-mail: hsene@ucad.sn
Founded: 1957
University Library.
Publication(s): *Collective Catalogue of Memoires*;
  Collective Catalogue of Periodicals; *Collective
  National Catalogue of Periodical Publications*
Parent Company: Universite Cheikh Anta Diop
  de Dakar

Sierra Leone

Public Archives of Sierra Leone
Fourah Bay College, PB87, Freetown
Tel: (022) 27337
Key Personnel
Hon Govt Archivist Prof: Akintola J G Wyse

British Council Library
Tower Hill, Freetown
Mailing Address: PO Box 124, Freetown
Tel: 222223 *Fax:* 224123
E-mail: bcouncil@sierratel.sl
Web Site: www.britishcouncil.org/sierraleone/
Telex: 3453 Bricon SL
Key Personnel
Contact: Abator Thomas

Fourah Bay College Library
University of Sierra Leone, Freetown
Mailing Address: PO Box 87, Freetown
Tel: (022) 229471 *Cable:* FOURAH BAY
Key Personnel
Librarian: Deanna Thomas

Milton Margai Teachers' College Library
Goderich hr, Freetown
Tel: (022) 024305

**Njala University College Library (University of
  Sierra Leone)**
PB, Freetown
Key Personnel
Librarian: A N T Deen

Sierra Leone Library Board
Rokel St, Freetown
Mailing Address: PO Box 326, Freetown
Tel: (022) 23848
Key Personnel
Chief Librarian: Mrs I O'Brien-Coker
Publication(s): *Sierra Leone Publications* (annu-
  ally)

United States Information Service Library
c/o American Embassy, 8 Walpole, Freetown
Tel: 226481 *Fax:* 225471
Telex: 3509
Key Personnel
Librarian: Florence Nylander

University of Sierra Leone, see Njala University
  College Library (University of Sierra Leone)

Singapore

National Archives of Singapore
140 Hill St Bldg, Singapore 0617 179868
Tel: 3380000 *Fax:* 3393583

National Reference Library
One Temasek Ave 06-00, Singapore 039192
Tel: 3377355 *Fax:* 3309611
Telex: rs 26620 *Cable:* NATLIB SINGAPORE
Key Personnel
Dir: Mrs Hedwig Anuar
Publication(s): *Accessions List* (monthly); *Check-
  list of Current Serials*; *Government Services
  Directory* (second edition); *Masterlist of South-
  east Asian Microforms Supplement* (Bibliogra-
  phies, booklists, library guides periodically);
  Singapore National Bibliography (quarterly,
  with annual supplement); *Singapore Periodicals
  Index* (annually); *The Memoranda of Books
  Registered in the 'Catalogue of Books Printed
  or Published in Singapore' under the Provisions of the Printers and Publishers Act*; *Union
  Catalogue of Scientific and Technical Serials*

National University of Singapore Library
10 Kent Ridge Crescent, Singapore 119260
Tel: 7722069 *Fax:* 7771272
E-mail: clbsec@nus.edu.sg
Telex: RS 33943 UNISPO
Key Personnel
Librarian: Jill Quah
Publication(s): *LINUS Newsletter of the NUS
  Library*; *NUS Library Guide* (folder); *Singa-
  pore Conference Index*; *SMC Ondisc CD-ROM*
  (contains PERIND database: Index to Period-
  ical Articles relating to Singapore, Malaysia,
  Brunei & ASEAN; Singapore/Malaysia Collec-
  tion database; NUS Theses Collection database)
Branch Office(s)
Central Library
Chinese Library
Hon Sui Sen Memorial Library
Law Library
Medical Library
Science Library

Slovakia

Centrum Vedecko-Technickych Informaci SR
Slovak Centre of Scientific & Technical Informa-
  tion, Namestie slobody 19, 81223 Bratislava
Tel: (07) 362419 *Fax:* (07) 323527
E-mail: cvti@tbb1.sltk.stuba.sk
Key Personnel
Dir: Dipl Ing Jan Kurak
Deputy Dir: Vlasta Cikatricisova
Slovak Centre of Scientific & Technical Informa-
  tion.
Publication(s): *Bulletin Centra VTI SR* (Signale
  informacie); *EURO-info*; *Infotrend*

Univerzitna Kniznica
Michalska 1, 814 17 Bratislava
Tel: (07) 5333247 *Fax:* (07) 5334246
Key Personnel
Librarian: PhDr Emil Vontorcik
Manager: Peter Tausche
Diplomat: Julius Balogh

Univerzita Pavla Jozefa Safarika
Srobarova 2, 04180 Kosice
Tel: (095) 6222608 *Fax:* (095) 766959
E-mail: zahrodd@kosice.upjs.sk
Key Personnel
Dir: Darina Kozuchova

Univerzitna kniznica
Michalska 1, 81417 Bratislava
Tel: (07) 5333247 *Fax:* (07) 5334246
Telex: 93255 Uknz
Key Personnel
Dir: Dr Emil Vontorcik
University Library.

Ustredna kniznica Slovenskej akademie vied
(The Central Library of the Slovak Academy of Sciences)
Klemensova 19, 81467 Bratislava
Tel: (07) 5292 1733 *Fax:* (07) 52921733
E-mail: knizhorv@klemens.savba.sk
Web Site: www.savba.sk/sav/inst/uk/uksav.html
Key Personnel
Dir: Dr Marcela Horvathova
Central Library of the Slovak Academy of Sciences.
Publication(s): *Informacny Bulletin UK SAV* (Bulletin)
Parent Company: Slovak Academy of Sciences

Vydavatel' Sky odbor
ul Ladisalva Novomeskeho 32, 03652 Martin
Tel: (0842) 31861 *Fax:* (0842) 33188
E-mail: snk@matica.sk
Telex: 075331
Key Personnel
General Dir: Daniela Slizova
Slovak National Library.
Publication(s): *Hudobny archiv* (Music Archive); *Kniha* (The Book); *Kniznice a informacie* (libraries and scientific information every two months); *Literarnomuzejny letopis* (Literary Museum Annals); *Literarny archiv* (Literary Archive); *Slovaci v zahranici* (The Slovaks abroad annually); *Slovenska narodna bibliografia* (Slovak National Bibliography monthly); *Slovensko* (Slovakia monthly)

Slovenia

Arhiv Republike Slovenije (Archives of the Republic of Slovenia)
Zvezdarska 1, pp 21, 1127 Ljubljana
Tel: (01) 2414200 *Fax:* (01) 2414269
E-mail: ars@gov.si
Key Personnel
Dir: Vladimir Zumer *E-mail:* vladimir.zumer@gov.si
Librarian: Alenka Hren *Tel:* (01) 2412218
E-mail: alenka.hren@gov.si
Publication(s): *Arhivi* (Sources); *Inventarji* (Inventories); *Katalogi* (Catalogs); *Viri* (Sources); *Vodniki* (Guides)

Univerza Ljubljana
Kongresni trg 12, 1000 Ljubljana
Tel: (061) 1254055 *Fax:* (061) 1254053
Telex: 32285 NUK-LJB-YU *Cable:* NUK LJUBLJANA
Key Personnel
Librarian: Lenart Setinc

Narodna in Univerzitetna Knjiznica, Ljubljana
(National and University Library)
Turjaska 1, 1000 Ljubljana
Mailing Address: PO Box 259, 1001 Ljubljana
Tel: (01) 2001-100 *Fax:* (01) 4257-293
Telex: 32285 *Cable:* NUK LJUBLJANA
Key Personnel
Man Dir: Lenart Setinc
Dir General of Library Programs: Jakac-Bizjak Vilenka
National & University Library.
Publication(s): *Knjiznicarske novice*; *Signalne informacije*; *Slovenska bibliografija*

Somalia

Biblioteca dell'Universita Nazionale della Somalia
PO Box 15, Mogadishu

National Library of Somalia
PO Box 1754, Mogadishu
Tel: 22758

South Africa

Bloemfontein Public Library
Municipality of Bloemfontein, 43 West Burger St, Bloemfontein 9300
Mailing Address: PO Box 20606, Bloemfontein 9300
Tel: (051) 71993 *Fax:* (051) 4058604
E-mail: pat@dux.bfncouncil.co.za
Key Personnel
City Librarian: P J van der Walt

Cape Provincial Library Service
PO Box 2108, Cape Town 8000
Tel: (021) 4109111 *Fax:* (021) 4197541

Cape Town City Libraries
Old Drill Hall, Parade St, Cape Town 8000
Mailing Address: PO Box 4728, Cape Town 8000
Tel: (021) 4624400 *Fax:* (021) 4615981
Key Personnel
City Librarian: Mr H C F Heymann
E-mail: hheymann@ctcc.gov.za

Council for Scientific & Industrial Research, see CSIR Information Services

CSIR Information Services
Meiring Naude Rd Scientia, PO Box 395, Pretoria 0001
Mailing Address: PO Box 217, Pretoria 0001
Tel: (012) 8412911 *Fax:* (012) 3491154
Telex: 32043
Key Personnel
Head: Dr Ben Fouche
Marketing Manager: M Whitfield
Scientific, technological & business information, decision support value-added services, electronic real-time access to local & international databases.

Department of Arts, Culture, Science and Technology
Oranje-Nassau Bldg, Schoeman St, PB X894, Pretoria 0001
Tel: (012) 3146033; (012) 3146032; (012) 3146031 *Fax:* (012) 3232720
E-mail: ab02@acts1.pwv.gov.2a
Key Personnel
Librarian: D E Mohlakwana
Publication(s): *Library News*

Durban Metropolitan Library
PO Box 917, Durban 4000
Tel: (031) 300-6911 *Fax:* (031) 300-6301
E-mail: michelej@durban.gov.2a
Key Personnel
Dir Libraries: R Jayaram
Publication(s): *Bookworm* (staff quarterly magazine)

East London Municipal Library
Gladstone & Buxton Sts 2, East London 5201
Mailing Address: PO Box 652, East London 5200
Tel: (0431) 24991 *Fax:* (431) 431729
Key Personnel
Manager: Mrs M M Davidson

Education Library & Information Services, see EDULIS (Education Library & Information Services)

EDULIS (Education Library & Information Services)
P/B X9099, 9 Dorp St, Cape Town 8000
Tel: (021) 4835265; (021) 4835266; (021) 4835267 *Fax:* (021) 4835747
Key Personnel
Head: Mrs Lyne Metcalfe *E-mail:* lmetcalf@pawc.wcape.gov.za
Publication(s): *RESENSIONES: RECOMMENDED CURRICULUM RESOURCE MATERIAL FOR SECONDARY PRIMARY PREPRIMA* (Annually)
Parent Company: Western Cape Education Department
Ultimate Parent Company: Provincial Administration of the Western Cape

Free State Provincial Library & Information Services
Provincial Government Bldg, 12th floor, Elizabeth St, Bloemfontein 9301
Mailing Address: Private Bag 20606, Bloemfontein 9300
Tel: (051) 4054680 *Fax:* (051) 4033567
E-mail: jacomien@majuba.ofs.gov.za
Web Site: mangaung.ofs.gov.za/library/index/htm
Cable: ORANVRY
Key Personnel
Dir: J J Schimper *Tel:* (051) 4054681
Founded: 1948
Publication(s): *Free State Libraries* (quarterly, journal)

Harold Holmes Library, see Johannesburg College of Education, Harold Holmes Library

Johannesburg College of Education, Harold Holmes Library
27 St Andrews Rd, Parktown, Johannesburg 2193
Tel: (011) 6421417 *Fax:* (011) 6436312
Key Personnel
Chief Librarian: J B Crow

Johannesburg Public Library
Library Gardens, Corner of Market & Fraser Streets, Johannesburg 2001
Tel: (011) 8363787 *Fax:* (011) 8366607
E-mail: library@mj.org.za
Key Personnel
Librarian: E J Bevan *E-mail:* jbevan@mj.org.za
Founded: 1890
Publication(s): *Local Government Library Bulletin* (irregular)

Kempton Park Public Library
Civic Centre, Kempton Park 1620
Mailing Address: PO Box 13, Kempton Park 1620
Tel: (011) 9212150 *Fax:* (011) 9750921
Key Personnel
Chief Librarian: J H van der Walt

SOUTH AFRICA

Kimberley Public Library
Chapel St, Kimberley 8300
Mailing Address: PO Box 627, Kimberley 8300
Tel: (053) 8306241 *Fax:* (053) 8331954
E-mail: fritz@kbymun.org.za
Key Personnel
City Librarian: Mr F H van Dyke
Founded: 1878
City Public Libraries including 6 branches & 18 depots.
Parent Company: Sol Plaatje Municipality
Branch Office(s)
Africana Library *E-mail:* afrilib@global.co.za
Judy Scott Library

Kwa-Zulu Natal Provincial Library Service
230 Prince Alfred St, 3201 Pietermaritzburg 3201
Mailing Address: PB X9016, Pietermaritzburg 3200
Tel: (0331) 3940241 *Fax:* (0331) 3942237
E-mail: bawar@kzntl.gov.za
Telex: 643030
Key Personnel
Deputy Dir: Dr Rookaya Bawa
Contact: Janet Hart *E-mail:* hartj@natalia.kzntl.gov.za
Publication(s): *KZN Librarian* (Journal of Kwa-Zulu Natal Provincial Library Service)

Library of Parliament
PO Box 18, Cape Town 8000
Tel: (021) 4032140 *Fax:* (021) 4614331
Key Personnel
Chief Librarian: G Swanepoel

Natal Archives Depot, see State Archives Service: Natal Archives Depot

Natal Society Library
Churchill Sq, Church St, Pietermaritzburg 3200
Mailing Address: PO Box 415, Pietermaritzburg 3200
Tel: (033) 3452383 *Fax:* (033) 3940095
E-mail: nsl@alphafuturenet.co.za
Key Personnel
Dir: Mr J C Morrison
Founded: 1851
Publication(s): *Aids Bibliography* (5 vols); *Natalia* (historical journal)

National Archives, Cape Town Archives Repository, Library
Formerly State Archives, Cape Town Archives Repository, Library
72 Roeland St, Cape Town 8001
Mailing Address: PB X9025, Cape Town 8000
Tel: (021) 4624050 *Fax:* (021) 4652960
E-mail: capearch01@hotmail.com
Web Site: www.national.archives.gov.za
Key Personnel
Archivist: Miss L Du Plessis

National Archives of South Africa, Orange Free State Archives Repository, Library/Free State Provincial Archives
29 Badenhorst St, Bloemfontein
Mailing Address: PB X20504, Bloemfontein 9300
Tel: (051) 5226762 *Fax:* (051) 5226765
Fax on Demand: (051) 5226765
E-mail: fsarch01@hotmail.com
Web Site: www.national.archives.gov.za
Key Personnel
Contact: Mr P F Wheeler

National Archives Repository, Library
24 Hamilton St, Pretoria 0001
Mailing Address: Private Bag X236, 0001 Pretoria
Tel: (012) 3235300 *Fax:* (012) 3235287
E-mail: arg50@acts4.pwv.gov.za
Web Site: www.national.archives.gov.za

Key Personnel
National Archivist: Dr G A Dominy
Founded: 1909
Parent Company: National Archives & Record Services

Pretoria Public Library
Sammy Marks Place, Pretoria 0002
Mailing Address: PO Box 2673, Pretoria 0001
Tel: (012) 3088837 *Fax:* (012) 3088873
Key Personnel
City Librarian: Elke Hansen

Rhodes University Library
PO Box 184, Grahamstown 6140
Tel: (046) 603-8436 *Fax:* (046) 622-3487
E-mail: library@ru.ac.za
Web Site: www.rhodes.ac.za/library/
Key Personnel
Chief Librarian: M A E Kenyon *Tel:* (046) 6038079 *E-mail:* m.kenyon@ru.ac.za

Royal Society of South Africa Library
PO Box 594, c/o University Capetown, Rondebosch 7700, Cape Town 8000
Tel: (021) 6502543 *Fax:* (021) 6502726
E-mail: roysoc@psipsy.uct.ac.za
Telex: 5-214-39 SA
Key Personnel
President: O W Prozesky
Editor: J R E Lutjeharms
Honorary Librarian: D E Rawlings
Publication(s): *Transactions of the Royal Society of South Africa* (irregular)

South African Library
PO Box 496, Queen Victoria St, Cape Town 8000
Tel: (021) 246320 *Fax:* (021) 244848
E-mail: macmahon@salib.ac.za
Key Personnel
Dir: P E Westra

South African Library for the Blind
PO Box 115, Grahamstown 6140
Tel: (0461) 27226 *Fax:* (0461) 27650
E-mail: blindlib@iafrica.com
Key Personnel
Dir: Mr N J Snyman

State Library
239 Vermeulen St, Pretoria 0001
Mailing Address: PO Box 397, Pretoria 0001
Tel: (012) 218931 *Fax:* (012) 3255984
E-mail: hvdwalt@statelib.pwv.gov.za
Key Personnel
Dir: Dr Peter J Lor
Publication(s): *Contributions to Library Science*; *Directory of South African Publishers*; *Index to South African Periodicals (ISAP)*; *Micrographic Series Indexes*; *Periodicals in Southern African Libraries (PISAL)*; *SANB (South African National Bibliography)*

State Archives, Cape Town Archives Repository, Library, see National Archives, Cape Town Archives Repository, Library

State Archives Service: Natal Archives Depot
231 Pietermaritz St, PB X9012, Pietermaritzburg 3200
Tel: (0331) 424712 *Fax:* (0331) 944353
Key Personnel
Chief Archivist: J N Hawley

Transvaal Provincial Library and Museum Service
Paul Krueger St, Pretoria 0001
Mailing Address: PO Box 413, Pretoria 0001
Tel: (012) 3227632 *Fax:* (012) 3227939
Telex: 30302 *Cable:* TRANSATOR

Key Personnel
Contact: Dinah van Driel
Publication(s): *Overvaal Musea, Book parade*

University of Cape Town Libraries
Private Bag, Rondebosch, Cape 7700
Tel: (021) 650-3097 *Fax:* (021) 689-7568
Telex: 5720327
Key Personnel
Librarian: A S C Hooper
Publication(s): *Bibliographical series* (irregularly); *Jagger Journal* (annually); *Varia series* (irregularly)

University of Port Elizabeth Library
Summerstrand, PB X6058, Port Elizabeth 6000
Tel: (041) 5042281 *Fax:* (041) 5042280
E-mail: libref@upe.ac.za *Cable:* UNIPE
Key Personnel
Scientific Editor: Mr S J Gerber
Publication(s): *UPE Publication Series*

University of Pretoria Academic Information Services
Hillcrest, Pretoria 0002
Tel: (012) 420-2235 *Fax:* (012) 362-5100 *Cable:* PUNIV
Key Personnel
Dir: Prof E D Gerryts *E-mail:* gerryts@acinfo.up.ac.za

University of South Africa Library
PO Box 392, Pretoria 0003
Tel: (012) 4293131 *Fax:* (012) 4292925
E-mail: willej@alpha.unisa.ac.za *Cable:* UNISA PRETORIA
Key Personnel
Executive Dir: Prof J Willemse
Publication(s): *Mousaion* (in collaboration with the University of South Africa's Dept of Information Science)

University of Stellenbosch Library
PB 5036, Stellenbosch 7535
Tel: (021) 959-2911 *Fax:* (021) 959-3627
E-mail: jhvi@maties.sun.ac.za
Telex: 526661
Key Personnel
Senior Dir, Library Services: Prof J H Viljoen

University of the Western Cape Library
Modderdam Rd, PB X17, Bellville 7530
Tel: (021) 976161 *Fax:* (021) 576661
Telex: 576661
Key Personnel
Acting University Librarian: R W Pfeiffer

University of the Witwatersrand Library
One Jan Smuts Av, Johannesburg 2001
Mailing Address: PO Box X1, PO Wits, Johannesburg 2050
Tel: (011) 716-2330 *Fax:* (011) 403-1421
E-mail: 056heath@libris.wwl.wits.ac.za
Telex: 422460 *Cable:* UNIWITS
Key Personnel
Librarian: H M Edwards

Spain

Archivo General de Indias
Avda de la Constitucion, 41004 Seville
Tel: (05) 4500532 *Fax:* (05) 4219485
Key Personnel
Contact: Rosario Parra Cala
Archives of the Indies.

LIBRARIES

Archivo Historico Nacional
Serrano 115, 28006 Madrid
Tel: (091) 5618003
Key Personnel
Dir: Dra Ma Concepcion Contel Barea
National Historical Archives.

Archivo y Biblioteca Capitulares
Cathedral of Toledo, Toledo 45001
Tel: (025) 212423 *Fax:* (025) 212423
E-mail: archicapto@terra.es
Web Site: architoledo.org
Key Personnel
Dir: Dr Ramon Gonzalvez Ruiz; Dr Angel Fernandez Collado
Archives and Library of the Cathedral Chapter.

Biblioteca Bergnes de las Casas . Bibioteca de Catalunya
Gran Via de les Corts Catalanes, 657 bis, 08010 Barcelona
Tel: (093) 2659003 *Fax:* (093) 2656635
Key Personnel
Librarian: Maria Artal
Library attached to Biblioteca de Catalunya.

Biblioteca de Catalunya
Carrer of l'Hospital, 56, 08001 Barcelona
Tel: (093) 2702300 *Fax:* (093) 270-23-02
E-mail: bcpublic@bnc.es
Web Site: www.gencat.es/bc/
Key Personnel
Dir: Mrs Vinyet Panyella
Chief of Difussion Area: Montserrat Fonoll
  E-mail: mfonoll@bnc.es
National Library of Catalonia.
Publication(s): *Nota Bene* (bimonthly, Information bulletin of the biblioteca de Catalunya)

Biblioteca General de Humanidades, CSIC
Duque de Medinaceli, 6, 28014 Madrid
Tel: (091) 4292017 *Fax:* (091) 4296823
E-mail: medina@bib.csic.es

Biblioteca Nacional
Paseo de Recoletos 20, 28071 Madrid
Tel: (091) 5807800 *Fax:* (091) 5775634
Key Personnel
Dir: Alicia Giron Garcia

The British Council Library
P General Martinez Campos, 31, 28010 Madrid
Tel: (091) 3373500 *Fax:* (091) 3373573
E-mail: information@bc-madrid.sprint.com
Web Site: www.britishcouncil.org/spain/
Key Personnel
Contact: Antonia Dominguez

Biblioteca General de Humanidades Consejo Superior de Investigaciones Cientificas
Duque de Medincceli 6, 28014 Madrid
Tel: (091) 4292017; (091) 5854883 *Fax:* (091) 4296823; (091) 5854883
E-mail: medina@bib.csic.es
Web Site: www.csic.es/cbic/BGH/bgh.htm
Key Personnel
Library Dir: Carmen Perez-Montes
  E-mail: carmela@bib.csic.es
Library of the Council for Scientific Research.

Biblioteca de la Agencia Espanola de Cooperacion Internacional
Avda Reyes Catolicos 4, 28040 Madrid
Tel: (091) 5838524 *Fax:* (091) 5838525
Library of the Institute of Spanish-American Fellowship.

Archivo de la Corona de Aragon
Almogavars 77, 08018 Barcelona
Tel: (093) 4854285 *Fax:* (093) 3001252
Key Personnel
Dir: Rafael Conde y Delgado de Molina
Royal Archives of Aragon.
Publication(s): *Coleccion de Documentos Ineditos del Archivo de la Corona de Aragon (from 1847)*

Fundacion Esade
Marques de Mulhacen, 40-42, 08034 Barcelona
Tel: (093) 2806162 *Fax:* (093) 2048105
Web Site: www.esade.es/biblio
Telex: 98286
Key Personnel
Head Librarian: Francisca Buxo *E-mail:* buxo@esade.edu

Hemeroteca Municipal de Madrid
Calle Conde Duque 9-11, 28015 Madrid
Tel: (091) 5885771
Key Personnel
Director: Carlos Dorado Fernandez
Madrid Periodical Library.

Biblioteca de Menendez Pelayo
Rubio 6, 39007 Santander
Tel: (042) 234534
Key Personnel
Librarian: Manuel Revuelta Sanudo
Publication(s): *Boletin de la Biblioteca de Menendez Pelayo* (annually); *Estudios de literatura y pensamiento hispanicos* (series); *La Biblioteca de Menendez Pelayo*

Patrimonio Nacional, Real Biblioteca
Palacio Real, Calle Bailen s/n, 28071 Madrid
Tel: (091) 4548733; (091) 4548732; (091) 4548732 *Fax:* (091) 4548867
Key Personnel
Dir: Maria Luisa Lopez-Vidriero
  E-mail: lvidriero@patrimonionacional.es
Library of the Royal Palace.

Servicio de Biblioteca
Aptdo 69, 48080 Bilbao
Tel: (04) 6006125 *Fax:* (04) 6006049
E-mail: biblioteca.cruces@hcru.osakidetza.net
Service in information & scientific documentation in health sciences.
Publication(s): *Catalogo Publicaciones y Series Periodicas Medicina*

Universidad Autonoma - Biblioteca Universitaria
Carretera de Colmenar Viejo, Km 15, E-28049 Madrid
Tel: (091) 3974399 *Fax:* (091) 3975058
Web Site: www.uam.es
Key Personnel
Contact: Maria Sintes *E-mail:* msintes@olmo.bibcen.uam.es

Biblioteca de la Universidad Complutense
Pabellon de Gobierno, Ciudad Universitaria, s/n, 28040 Madrid
Tel: (091) 5490256 *Fax:* (091) 3943437
Key Personnel
Librarian: Marta Torres Santo Domingo

Universidad de Cantabria Biblioteca
Av de Los Castros, s/n, 39005 Santander
Tel: (042) 201180 *Fax:* (042) 201183
Key Personnel
Dir: Javier Martinez *E-mail:* pvier.martinez@gastion.unican.es

Universidad Pontificia de Salamanca, Biblioteca
Compania 5, 37002 Salamanca
Tel: (0923) 277118 *Fax:* (0923) 277118

E-mail: bibliotecaio.general@upsa.es
Web Site: www.upsa.es/biblioteca.html

Universitat Autonoma de Barcelona Servei de Biblioteques
Campus Universitari-Edifici N, Primera Planta, 08193 Bellaterra, Barcelona
Tel: (093) 581 1015 *Fax:* (093) 581 3219
Telex: 52040 EDVCIE
Key Personnel
Dir: Joan Gomez Escofet *E-mail:* joan.gomez.escofet@uab.es
Deputy Librarian: Nuria Balague *E-mail:* nuria.balague@uab.es
Publication(s): *Biblioteca Informacions*

Biblioteca de la Universitat de Barcelona
Gran Via 585, 08007 Barcelona
Tel: (093) 3184266 *Fax:* (093) 3025947
E-mail: sbib@org.ub.es
Key Personnel
Librarian: Dolors Lamarca Morell
Publication(s): *Memoria*; *Red de Bibliothecas Universitarias*

Sri Lanka

British Council Information Resource Centre
49 Alfred House Gardens, Colombo 3
Mailing Address: PO Box 753, Colombo 3
Tel: (01) 581171; (01) 581172; (01) 587078
  Fax: (01) 587079
E-mail: inquiries@britishcouncil.lk
Web Site: www.britishcouncil.lk
Key Personnel
Dir: Susan Maingay
Manager, Information & Customer Service: Srimani Colonne *E-mail:* srimani.colonne@britishcouncil.lk
Founded: 1949
Branch Office(s)
178, DS Sennanayake Veediya, Kanoy

Colombo Public Library
15 Marcus Fernando Mawatha, Colombo 7
Tel: (01) 691968; (01) 696530; (01) 695156
  Fax: (01) 691968
Key Personnel
Chief Librarian: M D H Jayawardhana
Founded: 1925
Publication(s): *Libraries and People*; *A Manual for Public Libraries in Sri Lanka*; *Road to Wisdom*; *Glimpses of Colombo*
Parent Company: Colombo Municipal Council

Industrial Technology Institute Information Services Centre
363 Bauddhaloka Mawatha, Colombo 7
Mailing Address: PO Box 787
Tel: (01) 698624 *Fax:* (01) 697994; (01) 686567; (01) 698624
Telex: 21248 MININD CE Attention CISIR
  Cable: CISIR
Key Personnel
Manager, Information Services: Dilmani Warnasuriya *E-mail:* dilmani@iti.lk
Founded: 1955

Department of National Archives
7 Reid Ave, Colombo 7
Mailing Address: PO Box 1414, Colombo 7
Tel: (01) 694523 *Cable:* ARCHIVES
Key Personnel
Dir: Dr Winalaratwe

National Library & Documentation Services Board
No 14, Independence Ave, Colombo 07

SRI LANKA

Mailing Address: PO Box 1764, Colombo 07
Tel: (01) 6852003; (01) 685199; (01) 698847
Fax: (01) 685201
E-mail: nldsb@mail.natlib.lk
Key Personnel
Dir, General: M S U Amarasiri *Tel:* (01) 687581
E-mail: dgnl@sltnet.lk
Publication(s): *Directory of Social Science Libraries, Information Centres & Data Bases in Sri Lanka*; *International Standard Book Numbering in Sri Lanka* (brochure); *Library News* (quarterly); *Sri Lanka Conference Index, 1976-1986, 1987-1990, 1991-1992* (Sri Lanka Newspaper article Index-1993); *Sri Lanka (ISBN) Publishers Directory, 1991 edition*; *Sri Lanka National Bibliography* (monthly)

National Museum Library of Sri Lanka (NMLSL)
PO Box 854, Colombo 7
Tel: (01) 693314 *Fax:* (01) 693314
Key Personnel
Contact: Lionel R Amarakoon
See also Department of National Museums (Publisher).
Publication(s): *Spolia Zeylanica: Bulletin of the National Museums of Sri Lanka*; *Sri Lanka Periodicals Index*; *Ceylon Periodicals Directory (Annual Supplements)*

NMLSL, see National Museum Library of Sri Lanka (NMLSL)

University of Peradeniya Library
University Park, Peradeniya
Mailing Address: PO Box 35, Peradeniya
Tel: (08) 388678; (08) 388301 (ext 2040); (08) 388301 (ext 2042); 386003-04 *Fax:* (08) 388678
E-mail: lib@mail.pdn.ac.lk
Web Site: www.pdn.ac.lk
Key Personnel
Librarian: N T S A Senadeera *E-mail:* sena@lib.pdn.ac.uk
Founded: 1921
Publication(s): *Ceylon Journal of Science: Biological Sciences* (irregular, academic journal); *Ceylon Journal of Science: Physical Sciences* (irregular, academic journal); *Modern Sri Lanka Studies* (irregular, academic journal); *Sri Lanka Journals of the Humanities* (irregular, academic journal)

Sudan

ACADI, see Arab Organization for Agricultural Development

AOAD, see Arab Organization for Agricultural Development

Arab Center for Agricultural Documentation, see Arab Organization for Agricultural Development

Arab Organization for Agricultural Development
St No 7, Al Alamarat, Khartoum 11111
Mailing Address: PO Box 474, Khartoum 11111
Tel: (011) 472176; (011) 472183 *Fax:* (011) 471402
E-mail: aoad@sudanmail.net
Web Site: www.aoad.org
Telex: 22554 AOAD SD *Cable:* AOAD KHARTOUM

Key Personnel
Dir General: Dr Salem AL-Lozi
Deputy Dir General: Dr El-Tag Fadlallah

British Council Library
14 Abu Sinn St, Khartoum
Mailing Address: PO Box 1253, Khartoum
Tel: (011) 780817 *Fax:* (011) 774935
E-mail: don.sloan@bc-khartoum.bcouncil.org
Web Site: www.britishcouncil.org/sudan/
Telex: 23114 Bckht Sd
Key Personnel
Librarian: Ali Hassan Salih

Khartoum Polytechnic Library
PO Box 407, Khartoum
Tel: 78922
Key Personnel
Librarian: Mohammad Bakheit

National Records Office Library
Jumhuria Av, Khartoum
Mailing Address: PO Box 1914, Khartoum
Tel: 76082
Key Personnel
Librarian: Abdel Aziz Gabir Mohamed

Neelain University
Affiliate of Ministry of Higher Education & Scientific Research
Deanary of Libraries, Khartoum
Mailing Address: PO Box 12702, Khartoum
Tel: (011) 776433
E-mail: alageedseed Ahmed@hotmail.com
Founded: 1992
Academic Teaching & lecturing.

Omdurman Islamic University
PO Box 382, Omdurman
Tel: 51489

University of Khartoum Library
PO Box 321, Khartoum 11115

Suriname

Bibliotheek Cultureel Centrum Suriname
Gravenstr 112-114, Paramaribo
Mailing Address: PO Box 1241, Paramaribo
Tel: 472369; 473309 *Fax:* 476516
E-mail: sccs@sr.net; stgccs1947@hotmail.com
Key Personnel
Dir: J M L Roozer
Founded: 1947
Library of the Cultural Centre Suriname.

Swaziland

Swaziland National Library Service
Headquarters and Mbabane Library, Mbabane
Mailing Address: PO Box 1461, Mbabane
Tel: 42633 *Fax:* 43863
Telex: 2270 Wd
Key Personnel
Dir: B J K Kingsley

Swaziland College of Technology Library
PO Box 69, Mbabane
Tel: 42681 *Fax:* 44521

University of Swaziland Library
PO Box 4, Kwaluseni

Tel: 84011; 2264 (Manzini) *Fax:* 85276
Telex: 2087 WD
Key Personnel
Librarian: Mrs M R Mavuso
Publication(s): *Serials in Swaziland University Libraries* (irregularly); *Swaziland National Bibliography* (irregularly)

Sweden

Goteborgs Stadsbibliotek
Gaetaplatsen, S-402 29 Gothenburg
Mailing Address: PO Box 5404, S-402 29 Gothenburg
Tel: (031) 61-65-00 *Fax:* (031) 61-66-93
City Library and County Library.

Goteborgs Universitetsbibliotek
Centralbiblioteket, Renstroemsgatan 4, S-405 30 Goteburg
Mailing Address: PO Box 222, S-40530 Goteburg
Tel: (031) 7731000 *Fax:* (031) 163797
E-mail: library@ub.gu.se
Key Personnel
Librarian: John Erik Nordstrand
Publication(s): *Acta Bibliothecae Universitatis Gothoburgensis* (irregularly); *New Literature on Women. A Bibliography* (quarterly)

Kungl Tekniska Hoegskolan (Royal Institute of Technology Library)
Valhallavaegen 81, 100 44 Stockholm
Tel: (08) 7906000 *Fax:* (08) 109199
Telex: 10389

Kungliga Biblioteket
Box 5039, S-102 41 Stockholm 5
Tel: (08) 4634000 *Fax:* (08) 4634004
E-mail: kungl.biblioteket@kb.se
Web Site: www.kb.se
Key Personnel
National Librarian: Tomas Lidman *E-mail:* tomas.lidman@kb.se
The Royal Library - National Library of Sweden.
Publication(s): *Acta Bibliothecae Regiae Stockholmiensis*; *Bibliography of Swedish Sheet Music* (On Line only); *Kungl Bibliotekets Utstaellningskatalog*; *Rapport*; *Suecana Extranea* (On Line only); *Svensk Bokfoertecknking* (Swedish National Bibliography); *Svensk Musikfoerteckning* (Swedish Periodicals); *Svensk Periodicafoerteckning* (Swedish Periodicals)

Lunds Universitets Bibliotek
Lend University Libraries, PO Box 134, S-221 00 Lund
Tel: (046) 222 00 00 *Fax:* (046) 222 36 82
E-mail: lub@lub.lu.se
Web Site: www.lub.lu.se
Telex: 32208 lub Lund
Key Personnel
Dir: Lars Bjornshauge *E-mail:* lars.bjornshauge@lub.lu.se
Senior Administrative Officer: Berit Nilsson
Tel: (046) 222 9204 *E-mail:* berit.nilsson@lub.lu.se
Publication(s): *Scripta Academica*

Malmoe Stadsbibliotek
Kung Oscars v, 211 33 Malmoe
Tel: (040) 6608500 *Fax:* (040) 6608681
Web Site: www2.malmo.stadsbibliotek.org
Key Personnel
Librarian: Gunilla Konradsson Mortin; Ulla Brohed *Tel:* (040) 6608680 *E-mail:* ulla.brohed@mail.stadsbibliotek.org
City Library, Lending Centre for Southern & Western Sweden.

LIBRARIES

Riksarkivet
Fyrverkarbacken 13-17, 102 29 Stockholm
Mailing Address: Box 12541, 102 29 Stockholm
Tel: (08) 7376350 *Fax:* (08) 7376474
National Record Office, National Archives of Sweden.

Statistics Sweden Library
Box 24300, S-10451 Stockholm
Tel: (08) 7835066 *Fax:* (08) 7834045
E-mail: library@scb.se
Key Personnel
Chief Librarian: Rolf-Allan Norrmosse
Library of Statistics Sweden.
Publication(s): *Statistics from Individual Countries: National Statistics from Sweden and other Countries; Statistics from International Organizations and other (issuing) Bodies*

Stockholms Stadsbibliotek
Sveavaegen 73, 113-83 Stockholm
Mailing Address: Box 6502, 113 83 Stockholm
Tel: (08) 50831100 *Fax:* (08) 50831210
Telex: 19478
Key Personnel
City Librarian: Ian Boman
City Library of Stockholm.

Stockholms Universitetsbibliotek
Universitetsvaegen 10, S-106 91 Stockholm
Tel: (08) 162000 *Fax:* (08) 152800
Web Site: www.sub.su.se
Key Personnel
Head of Information & IT Department: Gunilla Lilie Bauer *Tel:* (08) 162747 *E-mail:* gunilla.lilie.bauer@sub.swe
Librarian: Gunnar Sahlin
This Library which incorporates the Library of the Royal Swedish Academy of Sciences (Kungliga Svenska Vetenskapsakadamiens Bibliotek) covering Humanities, Law, Social Sciences, Mathematics & Natural Sciences, psychology & education.
Publication(s): *Stockholms universitetsbibliotek Rapport*

Svenska Barnboksinstitutet
Odengatan 61, SE-113 22 Stockholm
Tel: (08) 54542050 *Fax:* (08) 54542054
E-mail: info@sbi.kb.se; biblioteket@sbi.kb.se
Web Site: www.sbi.kb.se
Key Personnel
Dir: Sonja Svensson
Head Librarian: Cecilia Ostlund *E-mail:* cecilia.ostlund@sbi.kb.se
Founded: 1965
Swedish Institute for Children's Books.
Publication(s): *Barnboken: Svenska Barnboksinstitutets Tidskrift* (ISSN 0347-772X) (biennually, 1978, English Summary)

Sveriges Lantbruksuniversitets Bibliotek
Central Library, Ultunabiblioteket, 750 07 Uppsala
Mailing Address: Box 7071, 750 07 Uppsala
Tel: (018) 671000 *Fax:* (018) 672853
E-mail: ultunabiblioteket@bibul.slu.se
Telex: 76062
Key Personnel
Dir: Sten F Vedi
Libraries of the Swedish University of Agricultural Sciences.

Umea University Library
Universitetsomradet, hus C, SE-901 74 Umea
Tel: (090) 7865000 *Fax:* (090) 7869626
E-mail: www.bibliotekschefen@ub.umu.se
Web Site: www.ub.umu.se
Key Personnel
Librarian: Lars-Ake Idahl *Tel:* (090) 7869680
E-mail: lars-ake.idahl@ub.umu.se
Parent Company: Umea University

Uppsala Universitetsbibliotek
Dag Hammarskjoelds vaeg 1, 751 20 Uppsala
Mailing Address: Box 510, 751 20 Uppsala
Tel: (018) 4713900 *Fax:* (018) 4713913
Key Personnel
Librarian: Thomas Tottie
Publication(s): *Acta Bibliothecae R Universitatis Upsaliensis; Scripta Minora Bibliothecae R Universitatis Upsaliensis; Uppsala Universitetsbiblioteks Utstaellningskataloger*

Switzerland

Bibliotheca Bodmeriana (Fondation Martin Bodmer)
19-21 route du Guignard, CP 7, 1223 Cologny
Tel: (022) 7074433 *Fax:* (022) 7074430
Key Personnel
Dir: Dr Martin Bircher
Founded: 1971

Bibliotheque Cantonale et Universitaire de Lausanne
Palais de Ramine, 1005 Lausanne
Tel: (021) 3167880 *Fax:* (021) 3167870
Key Personnel
Dir: Hubert Villard
Vice Dir: Silvia Kimmeier

Bibliotheque Cantonale et Universitaire (Kantons- und Universitatsbibliothek)
Rue Joseph-Pillere 2, 1701 Fribourg
Tel: (026) 3051313 *Fax:* (026) 3051377
E-mail: bcu@etatfr.ch

Bibliotheque de la Ville, see Bibliotheque Publique et Universitaire de Neuchatel

Bibliotheque nationale suisse, see Schweizerische Landesbibliothek (Bibliotheque nationale suisse)

Bibliotheque Publique et Universitaire de Geneve
Promenade des Bastions, CH-1211 Geneva 4
Tel: (022) 4182800 *Fax:* (022) 4182801
E-mail: info.bpu@ville-ge.ch
Key Personnel
Dir: Alain L Jacquesson *Tel:* (022) 41882828
E-mail: alain.jacquesson@bpu.ville-ge.ch
Founded: 1562
Publication(s): *Compte rendu* (annually)

Bibliotheque Publique et Universitaire de Neuchatel
3 pl Numa-Droz, 2000 Neuchatel
Tel: (032) 717-73-00 *Fax:* (032) 717-73-09
Key Personnel
Librarian: Michel Schlup
Publication(s): *Ville de Neuchatel: Bibliotheques et Musees* (annually)

Bureau International du Travail, see International Labour Office, Bureau of Library & Information Services

ETH- Bibliothek (Eidgenossische Technische Hochschule Bibliothek)
Raemistr 101, CH-8092 Zurich
Tel: (01) 6322549 *Fax:* (01) 6321357
Telex: 817178 Bibl Ch
Key Personnel
Head, Acquisitions: Maria Strauss *Tel:* (01) 6322124 *E-mail:* strauss@library.ethz.ch
Contact: Dr Wolfram Neubauer
Library of the Swiss Federal Institute of Technology.

ILO, see International Labour Office, Bureau of Library & Information Services

International Labour Office, Bureau of Library & Information Services
4, rte des Morillons, CH-1211 Geneva 22
Tel: (022) 7998675 *Fax:* (022) 7996516
E-mail: bibl@ilo.org
Key Personnel
Manager: L Stoddart
Publication(s): *Helecon CD-ROM International 1980; ILO Manual for Labour Information Centers (1992)* (available in English, French or Spanish); *ILO Thesaurus 1998: Labour, Employment & Training Terminology* (in English, French & Spanish); *Labordoc* (data base in English, French & Spanish)

Schweizerische Landesbibliothek (Bibliotheque nationale suisse)
Division of Federal Office of Culture
Hallwylstr 15, CH-3003 Berne
Tel: (031) 3228911 (Secretary); (031) 3228979 (Lending Dept); 3228935 (Information)
Fax: (031) 3228463
E-mail: 1Z-Helvetica@slb.admin.ch
Key Personnel
Dir: Dr Jean-Frederic Jauslin
Swiss National Library.
Publication(s): *Das Schweizer Buch* (national bibliography); *The Swiss National Library*

Schweizerisches Wirtschaftsarchiv (Archives Economiques Suisses)
Petersgraben 51, 4003 Basel
Mailing Address: Postfach 664, 4003 Basel
Tel: (061) 2673219 *Fax:* (061) 2673208
Key Personnel
Dir: Johanna Gisler *E-mail:* gisler@ubaclu.unibas.ch
Founded: 1910
Swiss Economic Archives.

Schweizerisches Bundesarchiv (Swiss Federal Archives)
Archivstr 24, CH-3003 Bern
Tel: (031) 322 89 89 *Fax:* (031) 322 78 23
E-mail: bundesarchiv@bar.admin.ch
Web Site: www.bundesarchiv.ch
Key Personnel
Contact: Hans von Ruette *E-mail:* hans.vonruette@bar.admin.ch
Founded: 1798
Swiss Federal Archives.

Stadt- und Universitaetsbibliothek
Muenstergasse 61, Bern 7
Mailing Address: Postfach 3000, Bern 7
Tel: (031) 3203211 *Fax:* (031) 3203299
E-mail: info@stub.unibe.ch
Web Site: www.stub.unibe.ch
Key Personnel
Librarian: Prof Robert Barth
Contact: Michael Haldemann *Tel:* (031) 3203236
E-mail: haldemann@stub.unibe.ch

Stiftsbibliothek (Abbey Library of St Gall)
Klosterhof 6d, 9004 St Gallen
Tel: (071) 2273416 *Fax:* (071) 2273418
E-mail: stibi@stibi.ch
Web Site: www.stibi.ch
Key Personnel
Librarian: Prof Ernst Tremp

Contact & Lic Phil: Theres Flury *Tel:* (071)
2273417 *E-mail:* theres.flury@kk-stibi.sg.ch
Historical library with a unique collection of early medieval manuscripts.

United Nations Library
Palais des Nations, 8-14 Av de la Paix, 1211 Geneva 10
Tel: (022) 9174181 *Fax:* (022) 9170028
Telex: 412962

Oeffentliche Bibliothek der Universitaet Basel
Schoenbeinstr 20, 4056 Basel
Tel: (061) 2673130 *Fax:* (061) 2673103
Key Personnel
Dir: H Hug
Public Library of Basel University.
Publication(s): *Jahresbericht* (Occasional Papers & Indexes in the Series Publikationen der Universitaetsbibliothek)
Branch Office(s)
Medizinbibliothek, Hebelstr 20, CH-4031 Basel
WWZ-Bibliothek, Petersgraben 51, CH-4051 Basel

Universitat Zentralbibliothek Zuerich
Zaehringerpl 6, CH-8025 Zurich
Tel: (01) 2683100 *Fax:* (01) 2683290
Key Personnel
Librarian: Dr Hermann Koestler

Syrian Arab Republic

Al Maktabah Al Wataniah
Bab El-Faradj, Aleppo
Key Personnel
Librarian: Younis Roshdi
National Library.

Assad National Library
Malki St, Damascus
Mailing Address: PO Box 3639, Damascus
Tel: (011) 338255 *Fax:* (011) 3320804
Telex: 419134
Key Personnel
Librarian: Ghassan Lahham
Publication(s): *Analytical Index to Syrian Periodicals; List of Syrian Dissertations; Syrian National Bibliography*

Damascus University Library
Damascus
Mailing Address: PO Box 3003, Damascus
Tel: (011) 2119840
Telex: 411971
Key Personnel
Contact: Nizar Oyoun El-Soud
Publication(s): *Bibliography of the Middle East*

Public Library of Latakia
Latakia, Syria
Key Personnel
Dir: Mohamad Ali Nitayfi

Al Zahiriah
Bab el Barid, Damascus
Tel: (011) 112813
National Library.

Taiwan, Province of China

Bureau of International Exchange of Publications
National Central Library, 20 Chung Shan South St, Taipei 10040
Tel: (02) 23169132 *Fax:* (02) 23110155
Key Personnel
Bureau Chief: Teresa Wang Chang
E-mail: teresa@msg.ncl.edu.tu
Publication(s): *Chinese Cultural Organizations Directory; National Central Library Newsletter*

Dr Sun Yat-sen Library
2F, 505 Jen Ai Rd, Sect 4, Taipei 116
Tel: (02) 27297030 *Fax:* (02) 27582460

Fu Ssu-Nien Library, Institute of History & Philology, Academia Sinica
130 Yen Chiu Yuan Rd, Sec 2 Nankang, Taipei 11521
Tel: (02) 27829555 (ext 136) *Fax:* (02) 27868834
Key Personnel
Dir: Juei-hsiu Wu

National Central Library
20 Chung Shan S Rd, Taipei 10001
Tel: (02) 23619132 *Fax:* (02) 23110155
Key Personnel
Dir: Dr Juang Fang-Rung
Publication(s): *Index to Chinese Periodical Literature; National Bibliography of the Republic of China; National Union List of Chinese Periodicals of the Republic of China; Union Catalog of Books in the Republic of China; Yearbook of Libraries in the Republic of China*

National Taiwan University Library
Library, One Roosevelt Rd, Sec 4, Taipei 106
Tel: (02) 2363-6810 *Fax:* (02) 23634344
E-mail: ntulib@ms.cc.ntu.edu.tw
Web Site: www.lib.ntu.edu.tw
Key Personnel
Dir: Ming-der Wu
Founded: 1928
Publication(s): *An Atlas Plants from the Tanaka Collection at National Taiwan Univeristy Library; Bibliography of the Works of Dr Tyozaburo Tanaka; Catalog of Chinese Stitched Binding Books in the National Taiwan University; Catalog of National Taiwan University Publications (1946-1985); Catalog of the Tanaka Collection at National Taiwan University Library; Ino kanori and Taiwan Studies; a special exhibition of Ino Collections; List of Publications of the Faculty & Staff of the National Taiwan University Theses & Dissertations (1959-1985); National Taiwan University Catalog of Old Japanese Materials on Taiwan Studies; National Taiwan University Catalog of Rare Books Title Index; National Taiwan University Catalog of Rare Rooks; National Taiwan University College of Law Catalog of Old Japanese Materials on Taiwan Studies; National Taiwan University Library Newsletter* (bimonthly, newsletter); *National Taiwan University List of Serials in Chinese, Japanese & Korean Languages; National Taiwan University Union List of Collected Mainland Periodicals; Supplement & Index Report on the Present Status of Documents on Taiwanese History at the National Taiwan University; University Library Quarterly*

National War College Library
Yangmingshan, Taipei
Tel: (02) 3619132 *Fax:* (02) 3110155
Key Personnel
Contact: Lo Mou-pin

Taiwan Branch Library, National Central Library
One Hsinshen S Rd, Section 1, Taipei 106
Mailing Address: PO Box 106, Taipei 106
Tel: (02) 7718528
Key Personnel
Library Dir: Wei-jei Lin
Librarian: Hui-Hsien Jill Yu
List of Nonchinese serials of National Central Library Taiwan Branch.
Publication(s): *Catalog on China in Western Languages; N C L Taiwan Branch Bulletin; Southeast Asia Catalog*

Tajikistan

Gousudarstvennaja Biblioteka Respublika Tadzkistan im Firdousi
prosp Rudaki, 734025 Dusanbe
Tel: (03772) 27-47-26
Key Personnel
Librarian: S Goibnazarov

United Republic of Tanzania

British Council Library
Samora Ave, Ohio St, Dar Es Salaam
Mailing Address: PO Box 9100, Dar Es Salaam
Tel: (051) 116574 *Fax:* (051) 112669
E-mail: oreste.makafu@tz.britcoun.org
Web Site: www.britishcouncil.org/tanzania/
Telex: 41719 *Cable:* BRICO
Key Personnel
Librarian: Oreste Makafu

Eastern & Southern African Management Institute (ESAMI)
PO Box 3030, Arusha
Tel: 8383; 8388 *Fax:* 8285
E-mail: esamihg@yako.habar.co.tz
Telex: 42076
Key Personnel
Assistant Serials Librarian: Grace Lema
Publication(s): *African Management Development Forum* (biannual); *ESAMI Newsletter* (quarterly)
Branch Office(s)
Harare
Kampala
Lilongwe
Lusaka
Maputo
Mbabawe
Nairobi

Institute of Development Management Library
Mzumbe
Mailing Address: PO Box 1, Mzumbe
Tel: (023) 260-4380-4 *Fax:* (023) 260-4382
E-mail: idm@raha.com

Telex: idm morogoro
Key Personnel
Chief Librarian: Matilda Kuzilwa
    E-mail: matildakuz@yahoo.com.uk

Kivukoni College Library
PO Box 9193, Dar Es Salaam
Tel: (051) 820047
Telex: 41390
Key Personnel
Librarian: George M Gwahemba

Makumira Lutheran Theological College Library
PO Box 55, Usa River
Telex: 42054
Key Personnel
Chief Librarian: Ndelilio Mbise *Tel:* 255 057 8599
Founded: 1947
Theology, East Africana.
Publication(s): *Africa Theological Journal & Larida la Uchungagi*

Sokoine University of Agriculture Library
Chuo Kikuu, Morogoro
Mailing Address: PO Box 3000, Morogoro
Tel: (056) 3511 *Fax:* (056) 4088
E-mail: sua@hnettan.gn.apc.org
Telex: 55308 Univmo Tz *Cable:* Uniagric Morogoro
Key Personnel
Librarian: Ms E V Chiduo
Publication(s): *Annual Record of Research; Bibliography of Higher Degree Theseses & Dissertations held by the Library of the Sokoine University of Agriculture; Library Accessions List* (quarterly); *The Green Revolution: A Bibliography*
Branch Office(s)
Mazimbu Library

Tanzania Library Service
Bibi Titi Mohamed St, PO Box 9283, Dar es Salaam
Tel: (051) 2150048; (051) 150923
Telex: Tanlis
Key Personnel
Dir: E A Mwinyimvua
Publication(s): *Tanzania National Bibliography; Directory of Libraries in Tanzania* (1984)

University of Dar es Salaam Library
PO Box 35092, Dar Es Salaam
Tel: (051) 43241 *Fax:* (051) 43241
E-mail: libdirec@udsm.ac.tz
Telex: 41561
Key Personnel
Dir: Dr John M Newa
Publication(s): *East Africana Accessions Bulletin; Tanzania Regional Bib Series; University of Dar Es Salaam Library Journal*

Thailand

British Council Library
254 Chulalongkorn 64, Siam Sq 2, Phyathai Rd, Pathumwan, Bangkok 10330
Tel: (02) 6525480; (02) 2526136 *Fax:* (02) 2535312
E-mail: bc.bangkok@britcoun.or.th
Web Site: www.britcoun.org/thailand/
Telex: 72058
Key Personnel
Dir: Dr John Richards
British Education Information provider.

Centers of Academic Resources Chulalongkorn University
Phya Thai Rd, Bangkok 10330
Tel: (02) 218-2905 *Fax:* (02) 215-3617
E-mail: prachak@chulkn.cav.chula.ac.th
Key Personnel
Dir: Dr Prachak Poomvises
Includes Central Library, Thailand Information Center and Audiovisual Center.
Publication(s): *Academic Resources Journal; Union Catalog of Chulalongkorn University Libraries; Union List of Serials in Thailand* (automated)

Main Library, Kasetsart University
50 Phaholyothin Rd, Bangkok 10903
Tel: (02) 5611369
Key Personnel
Librarian: Mrs Piboonsin Watanapongse

National Archives Division
Fine Arts Department, Samsen Rd, Bangkok 10300
Tel: (02) 2811599 *Fax:* (02) 28115341

The National Library of Thailand
Samsen Rd, Bangkok 10300
Tel: (02) 2815212 *Fax:* (02) 2810263
E-mail: suwaksir@emisc.moc
Telex: 84189 Natlib Th
Key Personnel
Dir: Mrs Kullasap Gesmankit

Siriraj Medical Library
Mahidol University, Siriraj Hospital, Prannok Rd, Bangkok 10700
Tel: (02) 4113112 ext 325 *Fax:* (02) 4128418
Key Personnel
Librarian: Mrs Kannigar Chollampe

Srinakharinwirot University, Central Library
Sukhumwit Rd 23, Bangkok 10110
Tel: (02) 2584002; (02) 2584003 *Fax:* (02) 2604514
E-mail: pimol@psm.swu.ac.tt
Telex: 72270 Unisirin Th
Key Personnel
Dir: Mr Chaleo Pansida

Thai National Documentation Centre (TNDC)
196 Phahonyothin Rd, Bang Khen, Bangkok 10900
Tel: (02) 579112130 *Fax:* (02) 5798594
Telex: 21392 TISTR TH *Cable:* TISTR/BANGKOK
Key Personnel
Dir: Mrs Nongphanga Chitrakorn
Publication(s): *Abstracts of TISTR Technical Reports; List of Scientific and Technical Literature Relating to Thailand; Scientific Serials in Thai Libraries; Thai Abstracts; TISTR Bibliographical Series*

Thammasat University Libraries
2 Prachand Rd, Bangkok 10200
Tel: (02) 6235176 *Fax:* (02) 6235173
E-mail: tulib@alpha.tu.ac.th
Web Site: 192.150.249.123/
Telex: 72432 Tamsat TH
Key Personnel
Dir: Nuanchawee Suthamwong
Librarian: Mrs Chooman Thirakit *Tel:* (02) 613 3518 *E-mail:* chuman@alpha.tu.ac.th
Founded: 1934
Academic libraries.
Publication(s): *Biography Index; Dom Thad* (biennial, journal); *International Symposium on Information: Standards for Bibliographic Control; Thai Royal Gazette Index; The Advancement of Librarianship* (a workshop to identify & assess needs in Southeast Asia & to formulate project proposals)

Togo

Bibliotheque Nationale
Ave Sarawaka, BP1002, Lome
Tel: 216367; 210410 *Fax:* 221967
Telex: 5322 Minedue
Key Personnel
Dir: Mamah Zakari
Publication(s): *Bibliographie Nationale*

Bibliotheque de l'Universite du Benin
BP 1515, Lome
Tel: 213027 *Fax:* 218595
Telex: 52 - 58

Trinidad & Tobago

Central Library of Trinidad & Tobago, see National Library & Information System Authority (NALIS)

National Archives
Unit of Minister of Communications - Information Services
The Government Archivist, 105 St Vincent St, Port of Spain
Mailing Address: PO Box 763, Port of Spain
Tel: (868) 6252689 *Fax:* (868) 6252629
E-mail: natt@tstt.neth
Key Personnel
Government Archivist: Helena Leonce
Founded: 1960
Preserves the documentary heritage of Trinidad & Tobago.

National Library & Information System Authority (NALIS)
109 Abercromby St, Port of Spain
Tel: (0868) 624-5835; (0868) 623-6137; (0868) 623-4844; (0868) 627-2319 *Fax:* (0868) 625-5369 *Fax on Demand:* 624-3120
E-mail: nalis@nalis.gov.tt
Web Site: www.nalis.gov.tt *Cable:* Centralib Trinidad
Key Personnel
Executive Dir: Pamella Benson
Founded: 1998
National Library System.
Publication(s): *Trinadad & Tabago National Bibliography* (Annual)

Trinidad Public Library, see National Library & Information System Authority (NALIS)

University of the West Indies Library (Trinidad & Tobago)
St Augustine
Tel: (0868) 662-2002 (ext 2132) *Fax:* (0868) 662-9238
E-mail: mainlib@library.uwi.tt
Telex: 24520 Uwi-Wg *Cable:* STOMATA, PORT OF SPAIN
Key Personnel
Contact: Dr Margaret D Rouse-Jones
Publication(s): *CARINDEX: Science & Technology; CARINDEX: Social Sciences & Humani-*

ties; *Directory of Publishers, Printers & Booksellers in Trinidad & Tobago*; *OPreP Newsletter*

Tunisia

Archives nationales
Le Premier Ministere, La Casbash, 1020 Tunis
Tel: (01) 560556 *Fax:* (01) 569175
Key Personnel
Dir: Moncef Fakhfakh

Bibliotheque Nationale
20 Souk-el-Attarine, 1008, BP 42 Tunis
Tel: (01) 245338 *Fax:* (01) 342700
Key Personnel
Librarian: Ibrahim M Chabbouh
Publication(s): *Bibliographie Nationale: Publications en serie*; *Bibliographie nationale: Publications officielles et non officielles*; *Bibliographies Specialisees (Themes tunisiens notamment)*; *Fahras al-Makhtuetat (catalogue des manuscrits)*; *Informations bibliographiques*; *Repertoire des Unites de Documentation en Tunisie*

British Council Library
c/o British Embassy, 5 pl de la Victoire, Tunis 1015 RP
Tel: (01) 259053 *Fax:* (01) 353411
E-mail: general.enquiries@bc.tunis.bcouncil.org
Web Site: www.britishcouncil.org/tunisia

Centre de Recherches et d'Etudes Administratives
24 ave du Docteur Calmette, Mutuelleville, 1002 Tunis
Tel: (01) 846167 *Fax:* (01) 787205
Telex: Ena 13198
Key Personnel
Dir: Mohamed Hedi Touati
Publication(s): *Revue tunisienne d'Administration Publique* (semiannually)

CREA, see Centre de Recherches et d'Etudes Administratives

Bibliotheque de la Faculte des Sciences de Tunis
Campus Universitaire Manar II, 2092 Tunis
Tel: (01) 873366

Institut de Presse & des Sciences de l'Information Universite La Manouba
Campus Universitaire-La Manouba, Tunis 2010
Tel: (01) 600 831; (01) 600 981 *Fax:* (01) 600 465
Telex: 15254 IPSI.TN
Key Personnel
Director: Hassen Mustapha *E-mail:* mustapha.hassen@ipsi.rau.tn
Publication(s): *Revue Tunisienne de Communication*

Turkey

Ankara University Library
Tandogan Meydani, Ankara Diskapi
Tel: (0312) 472100723
Key Personnel
Librarian: Dr Sekine Karakas

The Beyazit State Library
Imaret Sok 18, Istanbul, Beyazit
Tel: (0212) 5222488 *Fax:* (0212) 5261133
Key Personnel
Librarian: Yusuf Tavacl

Bilkent University Library
Bilkent, 06533 Ankara
Tel: (0312) 266-4472 *Fax:* (0312) 266-4391
Web Site: www.library.bilkent.edu.tr
Key Personnel
University Librarian: Phyllis L Erdogan
E-mail: librdirector@bilkent.edu.tr
Founded: 1986
Membership: IFLA, LIBER, ALA, LA (UK), IATUL, MELA, IAML.
Branch Office(s)
Bilkent University East Campus Library, 06533 Ankara *Tel:* (312) 266-5117
E-mail: eastlibrary@bilkent.edu.tr

Bogazici University Library
Bebek, 80815, Istanbul
Tel: (0212) 2631500 *Fax:* (0212) 2656357
Telex: 26411
Key Personnel
Dir: Ender Altug

The Grand National Assembly of Turkey Library & Documentation TBMM (TBMM Kutuephane Dokuemantasyon ve Tercueme Mueduerluegue)
Bakanliklar, Ankara 06543
Tel: (0312) 4206835 *Fax:* (0312) 4207548
E-mail: library@tbmm.gov.tr
Web Site: www.tbmm.gov.tr
Key Personnel
Dir: Ali Riza Cihan *E-mail:* acihan@tbmm.gov.tr
Memberships: APLAP; ECPRD; IFLA; LIBER.

Istanbul Universitesi Merkez Kuetuephanesi
Beyazit, Istanbul
Tel: (0212) 5140380 *Fax:* (0212) 5111219
E-mail: acpay-ed@mam.net.tr
Key Personnel
Librarian: Guelguen Sayari
Istanbul University Central Library.

Middle East Technical University Library
Member of IATUL
Ismet Inonu Bulvari, 06531 Ankara
Tel: (0312) 2102780; (0312) 2102782 *Fax:* (0312) 2101119
E-mail: lib-hot-line@metu.edu.tr
Telex: 42761
Key Personnel
Library Acting Dir: Prof Buelent Karasoezen, PhD *E-mail:* bulent@metu.edu.tr

Milliii Kuetuephane
Bahcelievler, 06490 Ankara
Tel: (0312) 2223812 (ext 4148) *Fax:* (0312) 2230451
Key Personnel
Librarian: Sahika Unal
National Library.
Publication(s): *Turkiye Bibliyografyasi*

Library of the Mineral Research and Exploration General Directorate
Ismet Inoenue Bulvari, Ankara 06520
Tel: (0312) 2873430 *Fax:* (0310) 2879188
Web Site: www.mta.gov.tr
Telex: 42741 42060mta tr *Cable:* METEA/ANKARA
Key Personnel
Librarian: Gonul Kocer
Founded: 1935
Specialize in books on mining exploration, geological investigation, earth investigations.

Publication(s): *Bulletin of the Mineral Reserch & Exploration* (bulletin)
Parent Company: Bureau of Mines, USA
Ultimate Parent Company: BROM, France

National Library of Izmir
Milli Kuetuphane Caddesi No 39, Izmir
Tel: (0232) 4842002 *Fax:* (0232) 4821703
Key Personnel
Dir: Ali Riza Atay
Publication(s): *Izmir Milli Kuetuphanesi, Yazma Eserler Katalogu, Vol 1 ve 2* (Manuscript Catalogue of Izmir National Library Vol 1 & Vol II)

Sueleymaniye Kuetuephanesi
Istanbul
Tel: (0212) 5206460
Key Personnel
Librarian: Muammer Ulker
Dir: Nuammer Uelker
Library of the Sueleymaniye.
Publication(s): *Nail Bayraktar* (1984, catalog of the important Arabic manuscripts in Bagdatli Vehbi Efendi Library, Istanbul); *The Union Catalogue Islamic Medical Manuscripts in Turkish Library* (1984); *Turkiye Yazmalari Toplu Katalogiu (TUYATOK)* (The union catalogue of manuscripts in Turkey)

Technical University Library
Ayazaga, Maslak 86026, Istanbul
Tel: (0212) 2763596 *Fax:* (0212) 2761734
Key Personnel
Contact: Nurten Atalik

Tuerdok (Turkish Scientific and Technical Documentation Centre)
Ataturk Bulvari 221, Kavaklidere 06100 Ankara
Tel: (0312) 468-53-00; (0312) 4673657
Fax: (0312) 4277489
Telex: 43186 Btak Tr *Cable:* TUBITAK, ANKARA

Turkmenistan

National Library of Turkmenistan
Pl K Marksa, 744000 Ashkhabad
Tel: (03632) 253254
Key Personnel
Dir: Nazar Atabaevich Kurbanov

Uganda

Central Reference Library
c/o Public Libraries Board Headquarters, 11-13 Buganda Rd, Kampala
Mailing Address: PO Box 4262, Kampala
Tel: (041) 233633 *Fax:* (041) 348625
E-mail: library@imul.com
Key Personnel
Dir: P Birungi
Founded: 1972

Albert Cook Medical Library
Makerere Medical School, Kampala
Mailing Address: PO Box 7072, Kampala
Tel: (041) 534149 *Fax:* (041) 530024
E-mail: acook@uga.healthnet.org *Cable:* MAKUNIKA KAMPALA

LIBRARIES

Key Personnel
Deputy University Librarian: Maria Goretti Musoke
Publication(s): *East African Medical Bibliography* (bimonthly); *The Uganda Health Information Digest* (three times)

Makerere University Library
PO Box 16002, Kampala
Tel: (041) 31041; (041) 31042 *Cable:* MAKUNIKA
Key Personnel
Librarian: James Mugasha

Makerere Institute of Social Research Library
PO Box 16022, Kampala
Tel: (041) 554582 *Fax:* (041) 532821
E-mail: misrlib@imul.com

Public Libraries Board
11-13 Buganda Rd, 11 Bombo Rd, Kampala
Mailing Address: PO Box 4262, Kampala
Tel: (041) 233633 *Fax:* (041) 348625
E-mail: library@imul.com *Cable:* LIBRARY, KAMPALA
Key Personnel
Dir: P K Birungi
Founded: 1964
Nation-wide public library service.

Uganda Polytechnic Library at Uganda Technical College
PO Box 7181, Kampala
Tel: (041) 285211 *Fax:* (041) 222643 *Cable:* TECHNICAL
Key Personnel
Chief Librarian: R Nganwa

Ukraine

Vernadsky Central Scientific Library of the National Academy of Sciences of Ukraine
pr 40-richya Zhovtnya 3, 252650 Kiev 34
Tel: (044) 2658104 *Fax:* (044) 2643398
Key Personnel
Dir: M I Senchenko

United Arab Emirates

Centre for Documentation & Research
Abu Dhabi
Mailing Address: PO Box 5884, Abu Dhabi
Tel: (02) 4445400 *Fax:* (02) 4445811
Founded: 1988
Archival Collections.
Publication(s): *Documents of UAE* (annually)
Ultimate Parent Company: Abu Dhabi Government

National Library
Cultural Foundation, Old Palace, Abu Dhabi
Mailing Address: PO Box 2380, Abu Dhabi
Tel: (02) 215300 *Fax:* (02) 217472
Telex: 22414 Culcen Em
Key Personnel
Dir: Jumaa Alqubaisi

United Kingdom

Belfast Public Library
Central Library, Royal Ave, Belfast BT1 1EA
Tel: (01232) 243233 *Fax:* (01232) 332819
Telex: 747359
Key Personnel
Chief Librarian: J N Montgomery

Birmingham Library Information Services
Central Library, Chamberlain Sq, Birmingham B3 3HQ
Tel: (0121) 303 4511 *Fax:* ((0121) 303 2861
Telex: 337655
Key Personnel
Contact: Mrs Marjorie Westley *Tel:* (0121) 303 2868 *E-mail:* marje.westley@birmingham.gov.uk
Assistant Dir: V M Griffiths
Publication(s): *A Royal Town & Its Park OOP*; *An Account of Harborne OOP*; *Birmingham Street Names OOP*; *Briefing* (bimonthly); *Bygone Bartley Green*; *Guide to Religious Periodical Literature OOP* (quarterly); *Kingstanding Past & Present OOP*; *National Socialist Literature in Birmingham Reference Library*; *News Review* (5 issues a week); *Statistics & Market Research* (monthly); *The Nine Days in Birmingham*; *The Shakespeare Library OOP*; *The Story of Rednal OOP*; *Birmingham Between the Wars*; *In the Midst of Life*; *Lost Railways of BirminghamWords*; *Directory of the Irish in Birmingham*; *Struggling Manor*

Bodleian Library
Broad St, Oxford OX1 3BG
Tel: (01865) 277000 *Fax:* (01865) 277182
E-mail: vaisey@vax.ox.ac.uk
Telex: 83656
Key Personnel
Librarian: R P Carr

British Library Document Supply Centre
Boston Spa, Wetherby, W Yorks LS23 7BQ
Tel: (01937) 546060 *Fax:* (01937) 546333
Key Personnel
Publishing Officer: Dr Dorothy Dryden
Publications Officer: Andrea Seed
See also entry under Publishers.
Publication(s): *Alphanumeric Reports Publications Index*; *Books at Boston Spa* (on microfiche); *Boston Spa Books* (on CD-ROM); *Boston Spa Conferences* (on CD-ROM); *Boston Spa Serials* (on CD-ROM); *British Reports, Translations & Theses*; *Current Serials Received*; *Directory of Acronyms*; *Focus on British Biological & Medical Research*; *Focus on British Business & Management Science Research*; *Focus on British Engineering & Computer Sciences Research*; *East-West Links*; *Index of Conference Proceedings* (monthly with annual cumulations); *Index of Conference Proceedings 1964-1988*; *Inside Conferences* (on CD-ROM); *Inside Information* (on CD-ROM); *Keyword Index to Serial Titles* (on microfiche); *POPSI-The Popular Song Index*

The British Library
96 Euston Road, London NW1 2DB
Tel: (020) 7412 7000 *Fax:* (020) 7412 7268
Key Personnel
Dir General, Collections and Services: D Bradbury
See individual entries for details of divisions
See also entry under Publishers.
Publication(s): *British Library Journal* (biannually); *British National Bibliography*; *Catalogue of Additions to the Manuscripts in the British Library*; *Guide to the Department of Oriental Manuscripts & Printed Books* (General Books & Monographs on Science & Humanities Subjects)
Branch Office(s)
The British Library Document Supply Centre, Boston Spa Wetherby, West Yorks

The British Library National Bibliographic Service
Boston Spa, Wetherby, W Yorkshire LS23 7BQ
Tel: (01937) 546585 *Fax:* (01937) 546586
E-mail: nbs-info@bl.uk
Web Site: www.bl.uk
See also entry under Publishers; also publishes a wide range of books of interest to the general reader & collector, including facsimiles of items in our renowned collection & works of general bibliography.
Publication(s): *Fiction on Fiche* (quarterly); *Books in English* (Bi-monthly); *British National Bibliography* (weekly); *British National Film & Video Guide* (quarterly & annually); *Name Authority List* (monthly); *Serials in the British Library* (quarterly); *British National Bibliography for Report Literature* (monthly); *The UKMARC & Anglo-American Authority Formats: A Cataloguer's Guide* (1998); *The UKMARC Exchange Record Format* (1997); *UK Marc Manual: A cataloguer's Guide to the Bibliographic Format* (1996)

British Library, Newspaper Library
Colindale Ave, London NW9 5HE
Tel: (020) 7412 7353 *Fax:* (020) 7412 7379
E-mail: newspaper@bl.uk
Web Site: www.bl.uk
Telex: 21462
Key Personnel
Newspaper Librarian: Edmund King *Tel:* (020) 7412 7362 *E-mail:* ed.king@bl.uk
Editor of the Newsletter: Christopher Skelton-Foord
The National Collection of British & Overseas newspapers.

British Library of Political & Economic Science
London School of Economics, 10 Portugal St, London WC2A 2HD
Tel: (020) 7955 7219 *Fax:* (020) 7955 7454
E-mail: library@lse.ac.uk
Key Personnel
Librarian & Dir Information Services: Lynne J Brindley
Not a British Library division.
Publication(s): *The International Bibliography of the Social Sciences*

British Library Oriental & India Office Collections
96 Euston Rd, London NW1 2DB
Tel: (020) 7412 7873 *Fax:* (020) 7412 7641
E-mail: oioc-enquiries@bl.uk
Web Site: www.bl.uk
Key Personnel
Dir: G W Shaw
Publication(s): *Calcutta: City of Palaces* (1990); *Catalogue of the Nevill Collection of Sinhalese Mss* (4 vols, 1987-1990); *Catalogue of the Urdu, Panjabi, Pashto and Kashmiri Documents in the India Office Library and Records* (1990); *Descriptive Catalogue of the Batala Collection of Mughal Documents 1527-1757* (1990); *General Guide to the India Officer Records* (1988); *Oriental Gardens* (1991); *The Life of the Buddha* (1992)
Orders to: Turpin Distribution Services Ltd, Blackhorse Rd, Letchworth, Herts SG6 1HN
Tel: (01462) 672555 *Fax:* (01462) 480947

UNITED KINGDOM

The British Library, Science Technology & Innovation Information Services
Science Technology & Innovation Information Services, 96 Euston Rd, London NW1 2DB
Tel: (020) 7412 7288; (020) 7412 7494; (020) 7412 7496
E-mail: scitech@bl.uk; social-policy@bl.uk; patents-information@bl.uk
Web Site: www.bl.uk
Key Personnel
Head of Library: Julia Stocken
List of seminars & publications available upon request. The national library for science, technology, business, patents & the social sciences, is the most comprehensive reference collection in Western Europe of such literature from the whole world. Inquiries are also handled by telephone, fax & e-mail. The library has inquiry & referral services (especially in business information, the environment, industrial property, health care & the social sciences); online database search, photocopy & linguistic aid services; runs courses & seminars, & provides a wide range of publications from newsletters to definitive bibliographies.

Cambridge University Library
West Rd, Cambridge CB3 9DR
Tel: (01223) 333000 *Fax:* (01223) 333160
E-mail: library@ula.cam.ac.uk
Web Site: www.lib.cam.ac.uk/publications
Key Personnel
Librarian: Mr P K Fox
Deputy Librarian: Mr D J Hall; Ms A Murray
Founded: 1400
List of publications available on request from the library offices.
Branch Office(s)
Betty & Gordon Moore Library, Wilberforce Rd, Cambridge CB3 0WD *Tel:* (01223) 365670 *Fax:* (01223) 365678 *E-mail:* science@ula.cam.ac.uk
Medical Library, Addenbrooke's Hospital, Hills Rd, Cambridge CB2 2SP *Tel:* (01223) 336750 *Fax:* (01223) 331918
Scientific Periodicals Library, Arts School, Bene't St, Cambridge CB2 3PY *Tel:* (01223) 334742 *Fax:* (01223) 334748 *E-mail:* mlw1003@cam.ac.uk
Squire Law Library, 10 West Rd, Cambridge CB3 9DZ *Tel:* (01223) 330077 *Fax:* (01223) 330048

Durham Chapter Library
The College, Durham DH1 3EH
Tel: (0191) 386-2489 *Fax:* (0191) 386-4267
Web Site: www.durhamcathedral.co.uk/
Key Personnel
Deputy Chapter Librarian: Roger C Norris
E-mail: r.c.norris@durham.ac.uk

Durham University Library
Stockton Rd, Durham DH1 3LY
Tel: (0191) 3743018 *Fax:* (0191) 3747481
Key Personnel
Librarian: Dr J T D Hall

Edinburgh University Library
30-38 George Sq, Edinburgh EH8 9LJ
Tel: (0131) 650 3384; (0131) 650 3374 (reference & information services) *Fax:* (0131) 667 9780; (0131) 650 3380 (administration); (0131) 650 6863 (special collections)
E-mail: library@ed.ac.uk
Web Site: www.lib.ed.ac.uk
Key Personnel
Librarian: Ian R M Mowat
Dept Librarian: Sheila E Cannell
Founded: 1580
Publication(s): *Catalogue of Printed Books* (1988 microfiche); *Catalogue of the Library of The Rev James Nairn* (Guides, Leaflets, Exhibition Catalogs); *Collection of Historical Essays* (1982); *Edinburgh University Library, 1580-1980*; *Manuscript Treasures of Edinburgh University Library* (1980)

Edinburgh City Libraries, see Edinburgh City Library & Information Services

Edinburgh City Library & Information Services
Formerly Edinburgh City Libraries
Central Library, George IV Bridge, Edinburgh EH1 1EG
Tel: (0131) 242 8000 *Fax:* (0131) 242 8007
E-mail: eclis@edinburgh.gov.uk
Web Site: www.edinburgh.gov.uk/libraries
Key Personnel
Head, Lib & Info Servs: W Wallace
Founded: 1890
Public library service.
Parent Company: Culture & Leisure Dept
Ultimate Parent Company: City of Edinburgh Council

University of Exeter
University Library, Stocker Rd, Exeter EX4 4PT
Tel: (01392) 263869 *Fax:* (01392) 263871
E-mail: library@exeter.ac.uk
Web Site: www.ex.ac.uk/library/
Key Personnel
Librarian: A T Paterson

Glasgow City Libraries and Archives, the Mitchell Library
North St, Glasgow G3 7DN
Tel: (0141) 287-2999 *Fax:* (0141) 287-2815
Key Personnel
Commercial Manager: Verina Litster
Publication(s): *West of Scotland Census Returns & Old Parochial Registers* (a directory of public library holdings in the West of Scotland)

University of Glasgow
University Library, Hillhead St, Glasgow G12 8QE
Tel: (0141) 3306704 *Fax:* (0141) 3304952
E-mail: library@lib.gla.ac.uk
Web Site: www.lib.gla.ac.uk
Key Personnel
Dir, Library Services: Christine Bailey
Founded: 1451
Specialize in university higher education.

Guildhall Library
Aldermanbury, London EC2P 2EJ
Tel: (020) 7332 1868 (ext 1870) *Fax:* (020) 7600 3384
Key Personnel
Librarian: Melvyn Barnes

Institute of Development Studies
University of Sussex, Falmer, Brighton BN1 9RE
Tel: (01273) 606261 *Fax:* (01273) 621202; (01273) 691647
Telex: 877997 IDSBTN G
Key Personnel
Head, Communications: Geoff Barnard

Leeds University Library
Leeds LS2 9JT
Tel: (0113) 2336388; (0113) 2335501 *Fax:* (0113) 2335561
E-mail: library@library.novell.leeds.ac.uk
Key Personnel
Dir, Library Services: J Wilkinson
Founded: 1874
Publication(s): *A Catalogue of the Icelandic Collection*; *Catalogue of German Literature Printed in the 17th & 18th Centuries*; *Catalogue of the Romany Collection*; *The Brotherton Collection* (its contents described with illustrations of fifty books and manuscripts)

University of Leicester
University Library, University Rd, Leicester LE1 9QD
Mailing Address: PO Box 248, Leicester LE1 9QD
Tel: (0116) 2522042 *Fax:* (0116) 2522066
E-mail: library@lx.ac.uk
Key Personnel
Librarian: Dr Timothy Hobbs

Liverpool Libraries & Information Services
William Brown St, Liverpool L3 8EW
Tel: (0151) 2255429 *Fax:* (0151) 2335886
Key Personnel
Head of Library & Information Services: Joyce Little
Publication(s): *Liverpool-Capital of the Slave Trade*; *Liverpool Women at War*; *The Battle of the Atlantic* (personal memories)

The Mitchell Library, see Glasgow City Libraries and Archives, the Mitchell Library

National Library for the Blind
Cromwell Rd, Bredbury, Stockport, Cheshire SK6 2SG
Tel: (0161) 355 2000 *Fax:* (0161) 355 2098
E-mail: enquiries@nlbuk.org
Web Site: www.nlbuk.org
Key Personnel
Chief Executive: Helen Brazier
Communications Manager: Carol Youlton
Tel: (0161) 355 2079 *E-mail:* carol-youlton@ulbuk.org
Head, Marketing: Mark Drury
Founded: 1882
A leading national agency in the provision of library services for visually impaired people & Europe's largest lending library for people who cannot read print.

National Library of Scotland
George IV Bridge, Edinburgh EH1 1EW
Tel: (0131) 2264531 *Fax:* (0131) 6224803
E-mail: enquiries@nls.uk
Web Site: www.nls.uk
Key Personnel
Librarian: Martyn Wade
Deputy Head of Public Programmes: J Cromarty
Tel: (0131) 622 4810 *E-mail:* j.cromarty@nls.uk
Head of Public Programmes: K J S Gibson
Publication(s): *Catalogue of Manuscripts* (eight volumes); *Directory of Scottish Newspapers* (1984); *Scottish Family Histories* (1986); *Scottish Gaelic Union Catalogue* (1984); *Special & Named Printed Collections in the National Library of Scotland*, Ed G Hogg (1999)

National Library of Wales
Penglais Aberystwyth, Ceredigion SY23 3BU
Tel: (01970) 632800 *Fax:* (01970) 615709
E-mail: holi@llgc.org.uk
Web Site: www.llgc.org.uk
Key Personnel
Librarian: Mr Andrew M W Green
National Library.
Publication(s): *Llyfryddiaeth Cymru - A Bibliography of Wales* (no longer published on paper, available only as an online service on the web catalog); *The National Library of Wales Journal* (semiannually, academic, based on the library's holdings)

The Natural History Museum Library
Cromwell Rd, South Kensington, London SW7 5BD
Tel: (020) 7942 5460 *Fax:* (020) 7942 5559

Key Personnel
Head of Library & Information Services: Ray Lester
Founded: 1881

Oxford University, Taylor Institution Library
St Giles', Oxford OX1 3NA
Tel: (01865) 278158 (issue desk); (01865) 278161; (01865) 278154 (office) *Fax:* (01865) 278165
E-mail: enquiries@taylib.ox.ac.uk
Web Site: www.taylib.ox.ac.uk
Key Personnel
Librarian: Ms E A Chapman
Deputy Librarian: Ms A J Peters
Contact: Mrs E A C Baird *Tel:* (01865) 278162
Founded: 1845
Graduate research library for modern languages.

PRONI (Public Record Office of Northern Ireland)
66 Balmoral Ave, Belfast BT9 6NY
Tel: (02890) 251318 *Fax:* (02890) 255999
E-mail: proni@nics.gov.uk
Web Site: www.proni.nics.gov.uk/index.htm
Key Personnel
Deputy Keeper & Chief Executive: Dr Gerry Slater *E-mail:* slaterg.proni@doeni.gov.uk

Public Record Office
Kew, Richmond, Surrey TW9 4DU
Tel: (0208) 3925265 *Fax:* (0208) 3925266
E-mail: enquiries@pro.gov.uk
Web Site: www.pro.gov.uk
Key Personnel
Head of Enterprises: Anne Kilminster *Tel:* (0208) 3925206 *E-mail:* anne.kilminster@pro.gov.uk
Founded: 1838
National archive for the records of the British courts of law & central departments of state.

John Rylands University Library of Manchester
Oxford Rd, Manchester M13 9PP
Tel: (0161) 2753738 (Main Library Bldg); (0161) 8345343 (Deansgate Bldg) *Fax:* (0161) 2737488 (Main Library Bldg); (0161) 8345574 (Deansgate Bldg)
Key Personnel
Librarian: Mr W G Simpson
Administation officer: Peter Wadsworth *Tel:* (0161) 275 3760 *E-mail:* peter.wadsworth@man.ac.uk
Publication(s): *The Bulletin of the John Rylands University Library of Manchester*

School of Oriental & African Studies Library
University of London, Thornhough St, Russell Sq, London WC1H 0XG
Tel: (020) 7323 6109 *Fax:* (020) 7636 2834
E-mail: kw@soas.ac.uk
Key Personnel
Librarian: Mr Keith Webster
Publication(s): *Library Catalogue* (1978-84 supplement on microfiche); *Library Guide*

Scottish Poetry Library
5 Crichton's Close, Edinburgh EH8 8DT
Tel: (031) 557-2876 *Fax:* (031) 557-8393
E-mail: inquiries@spl.org.uk
Web Site: www.spl.org.uk
Key Personnel
Dir: Robyn Marsack
Librarian: Iain Young *E-mail:* librarian1@spl.org.uk
Founded: 1984
Free lending & reference library specializing in Scottish & international poetry of mainly 20th century. Computer index to poetry now available online. Travelling van service provided. Stock includes books, audio & video tapes, periodicals, news cuttings. Workshops for children organized in term-time & holidays.
Publication(s): *Index to Scottish Poetry Magazines* (forthcoming, Vols 1-9 published)

Trinity College Library
Cambridge CB2 1TQ
Tel: (01223) 338488 *Fax:* (01223) 338532
Key Personnel
Librarian: D J McKitterick

ULL, see University of London Library

University of Aberdeen
Queen Mother Library, Meston Walk, Aberdeen AB24 2UE
Tel: (01224) 272579 *Fax:* (01224) 487048
E-mail: library@abdn.ac.uk
Web Site: www.abdn.ac.uk/diss/library
Key Personnel
Manager, Library Division: Ms Carole Munro *Tel:* (01224) 273321 *E-mail:* c.munro@abdn.ac.uk
Contact: Christine A Miller *Tel:* (01224) 272572 *E-mail:* c.a.miller@abdn.ac.uk
Founded: 1495
University library.
Publication(s): *George Washington Wilson Photographic Series* (irregular, Based on the Library's archive of Victorian glass plate negatives)
Branch Office(s)
Education Library (Agriculture & forestry)
Medical Library
Taylor Library (Law & European documentation centre)

University of London Library
Senate House, Malet St, London WC1E 7HU
Tel: (020) 7862 8500 *Fax:* (020) 7862 8480
E-mail: ull@ull.ac.uk
Web Site: www.ull.ac.uk
Key Personnel
University Librarian: Mrs E Robinson
Founded: 1837
Academic Research Library.
Publication(s): *Catalogue of Goldsmiths' Library of Economic Literature, Vol I-V* (Guides; Brochures)

The University of Reading
Reading University Library, Whiteknights, PO Box 223, Reading, Berks RG6 6AE
Tel: (0118) 9318770 *Fax:* (0118) 9316636
E-mail: library@reading.ac.uk
Web Site: www.library.rdg.ac.uk
Key Personnel
Librarian: Julia Munro
Founded: 1892
University Library.
Publication(s): *Beckett at Reading: catalogue of the Beckett manuscript collection at the University of Reading* (catalog, 1998); *Beckett's Dream Notebook* (1999); *Catalogue of the collection of children's books 1617-1939 in the Library of the University of Reading* (catalog, 1988); *The Cole Library of early medicine & zoology, Part 2, 1800 to present day & supplement* (catalog, 1975); *The Cole Library of early medicine & zoology, Part 1: 1472-1800* (catalog, 1969); *The Finzi book room at the University of Reading* (catalog, 1981); *Historical farm records: a summary guide to manuscripts and other material collected by the Institute of Agricultural History and Museum of English Rural Life* (1973); *The Ideal Core of the Onion: Reading Beckett Archives* (1992); *The Kingsley Read alphabet collection* (catalog, 1983); *Records management in British universities: a survey with some suggestions* (1978); *Robert Gibbings 1889-1958* (1989); *The Samuel Beckett collection* (catalog, 1978); *W M Childs: an account of his life and work* (1976)

University of Southampton
University Library, University Rd, Highfield, Southampton SO17 1BJ
Tel: (01703) 592180 *Fax:* (01703) 593007
Telex: 47661
Key Personnel
Librarian: B Naylor

Wellcome Library for the History & Understanding of Medicine
Affiliate of Welcome Trust Centre for the History of Medicine at UCL
183 Euston Rd, London NW1 2BE
Tel: (020) 7611 8582 *Fax:* (020) 7611 8369
E-mail: library@wellcome.ac.uk
Web Site: library.wellcome.ac.uk
Key Personnel
Librarian: David Pearson
Contact: Ms Sue Gold *Tel:* (20) 7611 8386 *E-mail:* s.gold@wellcome.ac.uk
Exists to promote understanding of the history & wider social & ethical aspects of medicine. It builds upon the major international collections formed by Sir Henry Wellcome & still actively developed, to provide research & enquiry facilities which are available to the public & academic communities free of charge.
Parent Company: Wellcome Trust

Westminster Abbey Library
Westminster Abbey, London SW1P 3PA
Tel: (020) 7222 5152 *Fax:* (020) 7654 4827
E-mail: library@westminster-abbey.org
Key Personnel
Librarian: Dr Tony A Trowles *E-mail:* tony.trowles@westminster-abbey.org

Uruguay

Biblioteca Nacional del Uruguay
18 de Julio 1790, Casilla 452, Montevideo
Tel: (02) 485030 *Fax:* (02) 496902
Key Personnel
Dir: Prof Rafael Gomensoro
Publication(s): *Anuario Bibliografico Uruguayo 1968-*; *Directorio de Servicios de Informacion y Documentacion en el Uruguay, 1988-*; *Revista Archivo, 1987-*; *Revista Biblioteca Nacional 1966-*; *Uruguay: Indice de publicaciones periodicas en ciencia y tecnologia 1981-1983, 1986-*
Branch Office(s)
Oficina de Ventas, Instituto Nacional del Libro, San Jose, 1116 Montevideo *Tel:* (02) 986740

Centro Nacional de Documentacion Cientifica, Tecnica y Economics (CNDCTE)
18 de Julio 1790, Casilla 452, Montevideo
Tel: (02) 485030 *Fax:* (02) 496902
Part of the National Library (Biblioteca National del Uruguay).
Publication(s): *Directorio de Servicios de Informacion y Documentacion en el Uruguay*; *Indice de publicaciones periodicas en ciencia y tecnologia 1981-1983*

Biblioteca Central y Publicaciones del Consejo de Educacion Secundaria
Eduardo Acevedo 1427, Piso 1, Montevideo
Tel: (02) 484273; (02) 483051 *Fax:* (02) 481252
Key Personnel
Dir: David Yudchak

URUGUAY

Biblioteca Facultad de Humanidades y Ciencias de la Educacion
Magallanes 1577, Montevideo
Tel: (02) 488185 *Fax:* (02) 484303
E-mail: biblio@fhudec.edu.uy
Key Personnel
Librarian: Margarita Llado

Biblioteca Municipal Dr Joaquin de Salterain
Ciudadela 1225, Montevideo
Key Personnel
Contact: Rolando Brianes

Biblioteca del Museo Historico Nacional
Casa Rivera, C Rincon 437, CP 11000 Montevideo
Tel: (02) 951051
Key Personnel
Contact: Elisa Silva Cazet

Biblioteca del Palacio Legislativo, see Biblioteca del Poder Legislativo

Biblioteca del Poder Legislativo
Av Libertador Brigadier Gral Lavelleja y Av de las Layes, s/n, Avda Libertador Brigadier Gral Lavelleja y Avda Gral Flores, Montevideo
Tel: (02) 409111 *Fax:* (02) 235538
Telex: 23203
Key Personnel
Librarian: Mazzeo Condenanza; Luis H Boions Pombo
Library of the Legislative Power.
Publication(s): *Anales Parlamentarios* (semestrial); *Bibliografia Uruguaya* (irregularly); *Boletin Bibliografico* (monthly); *Fichas Analiticas de Articulos de Publicaciones Periodicas* (monthly)

Uzbekistan

Alisher Navoi National Library of Uzbekistan
5 Mustakillik St, 700078 Tashkent
Tel: (099871) 1391658 *Fax:* (099871) 1391658; (099871) 1330908
E-mail: navoi@physic.uzsci.net
Key Personnel
Dir: Z Isomiddinov
Founded: 1870

Venezuela

Archivo General de la Nacion (AG)
Santa Capilla a Carmelitas 5, Caracas 1010
Key Personnel
Dir: Dr Mario Briceno Perozo

Biblioteca de la Universidad Catolica 'Andres Bello'
Montalban, La Vega Apdo 29068, Caracas 1021
Tel: (02) 475110 *Fax:* (02) 4223897
Key Personnel
Librarian: Emilio Piriz Perez

Biblioteca del Congreso
Esq de Pajaritos, 3er piso, Monjas a Padre Sierre, Edif Jose Maria Vargas, Caracas 1010
Tel: (02) 4832344 *Fax:* (02) 4832904
Telex: 21252 CCASSVC
Key Personnel
Contact: Dr Gabriela Nino de Desarollo

Biblioteca Nacional
Final Av Panteon Esq Fe a Remedios, Caracas
Mailing Address: Apdo 6525, Caracas
Tel: (02) 5059141 *Fax:* (02) 5059159
E-mail: vbetanc@reaccium.ve
Telex: 24621 IASBN
Key Personnel
Dir: Lic Virginia Betancourt
See also Instituto Autonomo Biblioteca Nacional y de Servicios de Bibliotecas.

Instituto Autonomo, Biblioteca Nacional y de Servicios de Bibliotecas
Final Av Panteon Esq Fe a Remedios, Apdo 6525, Caracas 1010-A
Tel: (02) 5059141 *Fax:* (02) 5059159
Telex: 24621 Iabn Vc
Key Personnel
Dir Lic: Virginia Betancourt
National Library, Public Library Services, Audio-visual Archive of Venezuela.
Publication(s): *Anuarios Bibliograficos* (to 1977); *Bibliografia Venezolana* (from 1978); *Catalogo de Publicaciones Oficiales; Informe Anual*

Biblioteca Marcel Roche del Instituto Venezolano de Investigaciones Cientificas (Marcel Roche Library of the Venezuelan Institute for Scientific Research)
Altos de Pipe, Km 11 Carretera Panamericana, Apdo 21827, Caracas 1020-A
Tel: (02) 5041512 *Fax:* (02) 5041423
E-mail: xjayaro@ivic.ivic.ve
Telex: 21657 *Cable:* IVICSAS
Key Personnel
Librarian: Xiomara Jayaro

Biblioteca Central de la Universidad Central de Venezuela
Ciudad Universitaria Los Chaguaramos, Apdo 104, Caracas 105
Tel: (02) 6628427 *Fax:* (02) 6622486
Telex: 28479
Key Personnel
Librarian: Dr Eudis Borra

Servicios Bibliotecarios Universidad de los Andes (Serbiula)
Edif Administrativo piso 5, Merida 5101
Tel: (0274) 2402731; (0274) 2402729 *Fax:* (0274) 2402507; (0274) 2402748
E-mail: adquisi@serbi.ula.ve
Web Site: www.serbi.ula.ve
Telex: 74206 BMULA-VC
Key Personnel
Coordinator: Jesus Rivero M
Contact: Arnold B Conquet Alcala *Tel:* (0274) 2401227 *E-mail:* canjedon@serbi.ula.ve
Founded: 1980
University library services.

Biblioteca Central de la Universidad de Zulia
Apdo de Correos 526, Maracaibo 4011
Tel: (061) 515390
Key Personnel
Librarian: Elga Ortega
Publication(s): *Boletin* (biennially)

Viet Nam

General Scientific Library of Ho Chi Minh City
69 Ly tu Trong, Ho Chi Minh City
Tel: (08) 225055 *Fax:* (08) 299318
Key Personnel
Dir: Mrs Trinh-Ngoc-Hanh

National Library of Vietnam
31 Trang Thi, Hanoi
Tel: (04) 8252643 *Fax:* (04) 253357
E-mail: tdung@nlv01.gov.vn
Key Personnel
Librarian: Nguyen The Duc
Publication(s): *Cong tac Thu' vien-Thu' muc* (Journal of Library and Bibliography); *Thu' muc quoc gia Viet nam* (National Bibliography)

Social Sciences Library
34 Ly tu Trong, Ho Chi Minh City
Tel: (08) 8296744 *Fax:* (08) 223735
Key Personnel
Dir: Tran Minh Duc

Yemen

British Council Library
Beit Al Mottahar, Harat Handhal, Sana'a
Mailing Address: PO Box 2157, Sana'a
Tel: (01) 275584 *Fax:* (01) 274128
Telex: 2748 Brcoun Ye

Library of the Great Mosque of Sana'a
Al Jamia al Kabir, Sana'a

Miswat Library
Aden
(Previously called Lake Library. Administration by Aden Municipality).

Yugoslavia

Centralna Narodna Biblioteka SR Crne Gore (Central National Library of Montenegro)
X Bulevar Lenjina 163 Pf 57, 81250 Cetinje
Tel: (086) 31143 *Fax:* (086) 31726
E-mail: cnb@cg.yu
Web Site: www.heritage.cg.yu
Key Personnel
Dir: Dr Cedomir Draskovic
Founded: 1946
Central National Library of Montenegro, national depository, general scientific library; special collection of Montenegrina, old & rare books.
Publication(s): *Bibliografski vjesnik* (3x/yr)

Biblioteka Matice Srpske (Matica Srpska Library)
Ul Matice srpska 1, 21000 Novi Sad
Tel: (021) 420199 *Fax:* (021) 28574
E-mail: bms@bms.nsac.yu
Key Personnel
Dir: Miro Vuksanovic *Tel:* (021) 28910
E-mail: miro@bms.ns.ac.yu
Founded: 1826
Library & information work.
Member of the International Federation of Library Associations & Institutions (IFLA).
Publication(s): *Matica Srpska Library Guide*

Narodna Biblioteka Srbije (National Library of Serbia)
Skerliceva 1, Belgrade 11000
Tel: (011) 451242 *Fax:* (011) 451289
Web Site: www.nbs.bg.ac.yu
Telex: 12 208 NB SRB YU
Key Personnel
Dir: Milomar Petrovic; Mr Sreten Ugricic
Dir for International Relations: Vesna Injac
E-mail: injac@nbs.bg.ac.yu
Head, Publishing & Editor: Djurdjic Ljiljana

LIBRARIES

Founded: 1832
Publishing Department of the National Library of Serbia.

Arhiv Srbije (Archives of Serbia)
Karnegijeva 2, YU-11000 Belgrade
Tel: (011) 3370781 *Fax:* (011) 3370246
E-mail: arhvserb@eunet.yu
Key Personnel
Dir: Milorad M Radevic
Librarian: Tatjana Jovanovic; Mrs L Mirkovic

Biblioteka Srpske Akademije Nauka i Umetnosti (Library of the Serbian Academy of Sciences & Arts)
Knez Milhailova 35, 11001 Belgrade
Mailing Address: PO Box 366, 11001 Belgrade
Tel: (011) 3342400 *Fax:* (011) 182825; (011) 639120
E-mail: admin@bib.sanu.ac.yu
Web Site: www.sanu.ac.yu
Key Personnel
Exchange Librarian (Englishing speaking Countries): Prof Spomenka Ninic *Tel:* (011) 3342400 ext 233 *E-mail:* ninic@bib.sanu.ac.yu
Dir, Library of SASA & Librarian: Prof Mr Niksa Stipcevic
Founded: 1842
Publication(s): *Izdanja Biblioteke Srske Akademije Nauka i Umetnosti*

Univerzitet u Beogradu biblioteka 'Svetozar Markovic'
Bul revolucije 71, PP 349, 11000 Belgrade
Tel: (011) 3370509 *Fax:* (011) 3370354
Key Personnel
Librarian: Ivan Gadjanski
University Library 'Svetozar Markovic'.

Zambia

C B U Library, see The Copperbelt University Library

The Copperbelt University Library
Division of Ministry of Education
Member of Association of African Universities
Jambo Dr, Kitwe
Mailing Address: PO Box 21692, Kitwe
Tel: (02) 222066; (02) 223972 *Fax:* (02) 222469; (02) 223972
E-mail: library@cbu.ac.zm
Telex: ZA 53270
Key Personnel
Librarian: Maurice C Lundu *E-mail:* lundum@cbu.ac.zm
Founded: 1987
Academic institution.
Parent Company: Copperbelt University
Ultimate Parent Company: Government of the Republic of Zambia

Hammarskjold Memorial Library
Division of Mindolo Ecumenical Foundation
PO Box 21493, Kitwe
Tel: (02) 214572; (02) 219012; (02) 211488 *Fax:* (02) 211001
Telex: 52050 Za *Cable:* MINCEN KITWE
Key Personnel
Librarian: Dunstan Chikonka
Founded: 1963
Information provision to the foundation's participant's & many other copperbelt residents interested in various research programs.
Publication(s): *Mindolo* (weekly); *Mindolo World* (biannually, various reports of conferences & research programs)

Evelyn Hone College Library
Church Rd, Lusaka
Mailing Address: PO Box 30029, Lusaka
Tel: 211557
Key Personnel
Librarian: Regina Shula

Kitwe Public Library
Kaunda Sq, Kitwe
Mailing Address: PO Box 20070, Kitwe
Tel: 213685

Lusaka City Library
Katondo Rd, Lusaka
Mailing Address: PO Box 31304, Lusaka
Tel: (01) 227282
Telex: 40157 Za
Key Personnel
City Librarian: J C Nkole

National Archives of Zambia
PO Box 50010, Lusaka
Tel: (01) 254081 *Fax:* (01) 254080
E-mail: naz@zamnet.zm
Key Personnel
Dir: N M Mutiti
Publication(s): *List of Periodicals in the National Archives of Zambia*; *National Archives of Zambia Annual Reports*; *National Bibliography of Zambia*

National Institute of Public Administration Library
PO Box 31990, 10101 Lusaka
Tel: (01) 228802
Telex: 40523
Key Personnel
Librarian: A G Kasonso

Natural Resources Development College Library
PO Box 310099, Lusaka
Tel: (01) 281328 *Fax:* (01) 224639 *Cable:* NATIVE LUSAKA
Key Personnel
Librarian: M M Misengo

Ndola Public Library
218 Independence Way, Ndola
Mailing Address: PO Box 70388, Ndola
Tel: 617173
Telex: 30270
Key Personnel
Librarian: K Mumba Chisaka

Northern Technical College Library
Chela Rd, Ndola
Mailing Address: PO Box 250093, Ndola
Tel: (02) 680142 *Fax:* (02) 680423
E-mail: nortec@zamtel.zm
Key Personnel
Librarian: P Nabombe

University of Zambia Press (UNZA Press)
PO Box 32379, Lusaka
Tel: (01) 290740; (01) 290409 *Fax:* (01) 253952
Telex: 44370 Za *Cable:* UNZA-Press
Key Personnel
Publisher: Samuel Kasankha
Membership: Book Sellers & Publishers Association of Zambia.
Publication(s): *Six Scholarly & Academic Journals* (biannual)
Parent Company: University of Zambia

Zambia Library Service
Division of Ministry of Education
Unit of Zambia Library Association
Haile Salassie Ave, Longacres, Lusaka
Mailing Address: PO Box 30802, Lusaka
Tel: (01) 254993 *Fax:* (01) 254993 *Cable:* ZAMLIBS
Key Personnel
Deputy Chief Librarian: E M Msadabwe
Publication(s): *Annual Report* (annually); *Teacher/Librarians* (biannually, newsletter)

Zimbabwe

Bulawayo Public Library
100 Fort St, Bulawayo
Tel: (09) 60965 *Fax on Demand:* (09) 60965
E-mail: bpl@netconnect.co.zw
Web Site: www.angelfire.com/kg/bpl
Key Personnel
Librarian & Secretary: Robin W Doust
Founded: 1896
Public library & legal deposit (archive) collection.

National Free Library of Zimbabwe
Dugald Niven Library, 12th Ave South Park, Bulawayo
Mailing Address: PO Box 1773, Bulawayo
Tel: (09) 62359 *Fax:* (09) 77662
Telex: 33128
Key Personnel
Chief Librarian: D E Barron

Geological Survey of Zimbabwe
PO Box CY 210, Causeway, Harare
Tel: (04) 726342 *Fax:* (04) 739601
Telex: 22416 MINESZW *Cable:* MINES
Key Personnel
Dir: S M N Ncube

Harare City Library
PO Box 1087, Harare
Tel: (04) 751834; 751835
Key Personnel
Librarian: Mrs M Ross-Smith

Harare Polytechnic Library
Herbert Chitepo Ave, Harare
Mailing Address: PO Box CY-407, Causeway, Harare
Tel: (04) 752311
Key Personnel
Head: Miss A M Powell
Founded: 1924
Ultimate Parent Company: Ministry of Higher Education

National Archives of Zimbabwe
Private Bag 7729, Causeway, Harare
Tel: (04) 792741 *Fax:* (04) 792398
Key Personnel
Editor: O Wytete
Publication(s): *Guides to the National Archives collections* (series); *Zimbabwe National Bibliography*; *Directory of Libraries in Zimbabwe* (1986)

Library of Parliament
PO Box CY 298, Causeway, Harare
Tel: (04) 700181 ext 2131; (04) 700181 ext 132 *Fax:* (04) 795548
Telex: 24064
Key Personnel
Librarian: N Masawi

Turner Memorial Library
Queensway Civic Complex, Kingsway, POB 48, Mutare
Tel: (0120) 63412 *Fax:* (0120) 61002
Key Personnel
Head, Library Services: Mr Darlington Mandowo

ZIMBABWE

Founded: 1936
Membership: Zimbabwe Library Association; United Nations Associated Libraries (UNAL).
Parent Company: City of Mutare (Municipality)
Branch Office(s)
Dangamvura Public Library & Sakubva Public Library, PO Box 448, Mutare

University of Zimbabwe Library
PO Box MP167, Mount Pleasant, Harare
Tel: (04) 303211 *Fax:* (04) 333407
E-mail: mainlib@uzlib.uz.zw
Telex: 26580 Univ Z Zw *Cable:* UNIVERSITY
Key Personnel
Librarian: S M Made

Library Associations

Listed below are library or library-related associations. Other book trade associations and organizations can be found in **Literary Associations & Societies** and **Book Trade Organizations**.

Albania

Council of Libraries
Ruga Abdi Toptani, No 3, Tirana
Tel: (042) 7984; (042) 7823
Key Personnel
President: M Domi

Algeria

Institut de Bibliotheconomie et des Sciences Documentaires
Universite d'Alger, 2 rue Didouche Mourad, Algiers
Tel: 647971
Key Personnel
Librarian: Abdellah Abdi
Institute of Library Economics and Documentation.

Argentina

ABGRA (Asociacion de Bibliotecarios Graduados de la Republica Argentina)
Tucuman 1424, 8piso D, 1050 Buenos Aires
Tel: (011) 3730571; (011) 3848095 *Fax:* (011) 3730571; (011) 3715269
E-mail: postmaster@abgra.org.ar
Key Personnel
President: Ana Maria Peruchena Zimmermann
Vice President: Alberto Ataulfo Lucero
Executive Secretary: Rosa Emma Monfasani
Association of Graduate Librarians of Argentina.
Publication(s): *Referencias Revista*

Asociacion Argentina de Bibliotecas y Centros de Informacion Cientificos y Tecnicos
Ave Santa Fe 1145, 1059 Buenos Aires
Tel: (011) 3938406
Key Personnel
President: Abilio Bassets
Technical Secretary: Ernesto G Gietz
Argentian Association of Scientific & Technical Libraries & Information Centres.

Asociacion de Bibliotecarios Graduados de la Republica Argentina, see ABGRA (Asociacion de Bibliotecarios Graduados de la Republica Argentina)

Centro de Documentacion Bibliotecologica
Universidad Nacional del Sur, Avda Alem 1253, 8000 Bahia Blanca
Tel: (091) 28035 *Fax:* (091) 551447
Telex: 81712 ARDUIOR
Key Personnel
Dir: Atilio Peralta
Centre for Library Science Documentation.
Publication(s): *Bibliografia Bibliotecologica Argentina* (Argentine Library Science Bibliography); *Documentacion Bibliotecologica*; *Guia de las Bibliotecas Universitarias Argentinas* (Guide to Argentine University Libraries); *Junta de Bibliotecas Universitarias Nacionales Argentinas* (National Joint of Argentine University Libraries); *Quien es Quien en la Bibliotecologia Argentina* (Who's Who in Argentine Library Science)

Instituto de Bibliografia del Ministerio de Educacion de la Provincia de Buenos Aires
Calle 47 No 510 - 6 piso, 1900 La Plata
Tel: (021) 35915
Key Personnel
Dir: Maria del Carmen Crespi de Bustos
Publication(s): *Bibliografia Argentina de Historia*; *Boletin de Informacion Bibliografica*

Australia

Australian Law Librarians' Group, Inc
Butterworths Library, Level 12, 475-495 Victoria Ave, Chatswood NSW 2067
Mailing Address: PO Box 821, Sydney, NSW 1043
Tel: (02) 9422 2335 *Fax:* (02) 9422 2417
Web Site: www.allg.asn.au
Key Personnel
National Convenor: Jennie Speirs
E-mail: jspeirs@piper-alderman.com.au
Founded: 1969
Publication(s): *Australian Law Librarian*

Australian Library and Information Association
PO Box E441, Kingston, ACT 2604
Tel: (02) 62851877 *Fax:* (02) 62822249
E-mail: enquiry@alia.org.au
Key Personnel
President: Joyce Kirk
Executive Dir: Jennifer Nicholson
Founded: 1937
Publication(s): *Australian Academic and Research Libraries* (quarterly); *Australian Library Journal* (quarterly); *Australian Special Libraries News*; *Cataloguing Australia*; *Conference Proceedings* (biennially); *Directory of Special Libraries in Australia*; *Incite* (Newsletter); *Library Services in Distance Education*; *Orana* (Children's Libraries Newsletter); *Periodicals for School Libraries*; *Teacher Librarians: the mid 80s and beyond*

Australian Society of Archivists
c/o Queensland State Archives, PO Box 1397, Sunnybank Hills, Qld 4109
Tel: (07) 38758742 *Fax:* (07) 38758764
E-mail: shicks@gil.com.au; asa@asap.unimelb.edu.au
Web Site: www.archives.qld.gov.au; www.archivenet.gov.au/asa/asa
Key Personnel
President: Kathryn Dan
Secretary: Fiona Burn
Man Editor: Shauna Hicks
Publication(s): *Archives and Manuscripts* (biannually); *ASA Bulletin* (six times a year); *Debates & Discourses: Selected Australian Writings in Archival Theory, 1951-1990*; *Directory of Archives in Australia*

CAVAL, see Cooperative Action by Victorian Academic Libraries (CAVAL)

Cooperative Action by Victorian Academic Libraries (CAVAL)
4 Park Dr, Bundoora, Victoria 3083
Tel: (03) 94592722 *Fax:* (03) 94592733
E-mail: caval@caval.edu.au; richardj@caval.edu.au
Key Personnel
Executive Dir: Geoff Payne
Publication(s): *CAVAL* (newsletter)

Council of Australian State Libraries
c/o State Library of New South Wales, Macguarie St, Sydney NSW
Tel: (02) 92731414 *Fax:* (07) 38462421
Telex: 92231
Key Personnel
Chairperson: D H Stephens

National Library of Australia
Parkes Pl, Canberra, ACT 2600
Tel: (06) 2621111 *Fax:* (06) 62571703
Web Site: www.nla.gov.au
Telex: 62100
Key Personnel
Publication Dir: Dr Paul Hetherington
Editorial & Production Coordinator: Heather Clark *Tel:* (02) 62621593 *E-mail:* hclark@nla.gov.au

Austria

Dokumentationsstelle fur neuere Osterreichische Literatur
Seidengasse 13, 1070 Vienna
Tel: (01) 5262044 *Fax:* (01) 526204430
E-mail: hl@literaturhans.at
Web Site: www.literaturhans.at
Key Personnel
Dir: Dr Heinz Lunzer
Founded: 1965
Documentation Centre for Modern Austrian Literature.
Publication(s): *Zirkular* (quarterly)

Oesterreichische Gesellschaft fuer Dokumentation und Information (Austrian Documentation Society)
Member of FID
c/o TermNet, Simmeringer Hauptstr 24, A-1110 Vienna
Tel: (01) 74040280 *Fax:* (01) 74040281
E-mail: oegdi@oegdi.at
Web Site: www.oegdi.at
Key Personnel
Pres: Gerhard Richter
Contact: Edit Kifer
Austrian Society for Documentation & Information.
Publication(s): *Oegdi Aktuell*

Austria

Oesterreichisches Institut fuer Bibliotheksforschung, Dokumentations- und Informationswesen
Resselgasse 4, 1040 Vienna
Key Personnel
Chairman: J Wawrosch
Austrian Institute for Library Research, Documentation and Information.

Vereinigung Oesterreichischer Bibliothekarinnen und Bibliothekare (VOeB)
Theodor-Koruustr 38, 1082 Graz
Tel: (01) 400084915 *Fax:* (01) 40007219
Key Personnel
President: Dr Sigrid Reinitzer *Tel:* (0316) 380-3101; 380-3102; 380-3103 *Fax:* (0316) 38 49 87 *E-mail:* sigrid.reinitzer@kfunigraz.ac.at
Secretary: Dr Brigitte Schaffer *Tel:* (0316) 68 58 77-43 *Fax:* (0316) 68 58 77-39 *E-mail:* brigitte.schaffer@pa.asn-graz.ac.at
Association of Austrian Librarians.
Publication(s): *Biblos* (quarterly, bulletin); *Mitteilungen* (quarterly, bulletin); *Verleger-Publisher: Gesellschaft der Freunde der Oesterreichischen National-bibliothek* (published in German)

VOeB, see Vereinigung Oesterreichischer Bibliothekarinnen und Bibliothekare (VOeB)

Bangladesh

National Library of Bangladesh
Member of IFLA (International Federation of Library Association)
32, Justice Syed Mahabub Morshed Sarani, Sher-e-Bangla Nagar (Agargaon), Dhaka 1207
Tel: (02) 326572; (02) 9118704 *Fax:* (02) 9118704
Key Personnel
Dir: Dr Sharif Uddin Ahmed *Tel:* (02) 9112733
Founded: 1972
Collection, preservation & reproduction of books & other documents; reference & readers service. ISBN Agency of all publications. Hold seminars, exhibitions & workshops to create awareness of Library services.
Publication(s): *Artical Index* (annually); *Bangladesh National Bibliography* (annually); *Public Library Directory* (annually)
Parent Company: Ministry of Cultural Affairs

The Library Association of Bangladesh
c/o Safia Kanal National Public, Library Bldg, Shahbagh, Ramna, Dhaka 1000
Tel: (02) 504269; (02) 8619408
E-mail: msik@icddrb.org
Key Personnel
President: M Shamsul Islam Khan
Vice President: Kazi Abdul Mazed; Dr Md Abdul Matir; Md Harun-ar-Rashid
General Secretary: Kh Fazlur Rahman
Treasurer: Md Abdul Latif
Founded: 1956
Work for the professional development in Bangladesh & offers training courses.
Publication(s): *The Eastern Librarian* (twice a year); *Upatta* (newsletter, quarterly, text in Bengali)

Barbados

Library Association of Barbados
PO Box 827E, Bridgetown
Key Personnel
President: Shirley Yearwood
Secretary: Hazelyn Devonish
Publication(s): *Bulletin* (irregular); *Update* (irregular, newsletter)

Belgium

APBD, see Association Professionnelle des Bibliothecaires et Documentalistes (APBD)

Archief- en Bibliotheekwezen in Belgie
4 blvd de l'Empereur, 1000 Brussels
Tel: (02) 5195351 *Fax:* (02) 5195533
Telex: 21157
Key Personnel
General Secretary: Wim De Vos *E-mail:* wim.devos@kbr.be
Belgian Association of Archivists and Librarians (Archives et Bibliotheques de Belgique).
Publication(s): *Archives et Bibliotheques de Belgique* (Text in Dutch, English, French, German, Italian, Latin and Spanish)

Association Belge de Documentation (Belgian Association for Documentation)
Chaussee de Wavre 1683, Waversesteenweg, B-1160 Brussels
Tel: (02) 6755862 *Fax:* (02) 6727446
E-mail: abdbvd@abd-bvd.be
Web Site: www.abd-bvd.be
Key Personnel
President: Philippe Laurent
Treasurer: Miguel Lambotte
Founded: 1947
Memberships: EBLIDA; ECIA.
Publication(s): *ABD-BVD Info* (newsletter); *Cahiers de la Documentation - Bladen voor Documentatie* (quarterly, text in Dutch, English & French)

Association des Archivistes et Bibliotheques, see Archief- en Bibliotheekwezen in Belgie

Association des Bibliothecaires Belges d'Expression Francaise
c/o rue Vandevandel 39, B-1470 Genappe
Tel: (067) 771477 *Fax:* (067) 771477
E-mail: abbef@freeworld.be; abbef.be@gate71.be
Key Personnel
President: Michel Dagneau *E-mail:* michel.dagneau@freeworld.be
Association of French-speaking Librarians from Belgium.
Publication(s): *Le Bibliothecaire: Revue d'Information culturelle et bibliographique*

Association Professionnelle des Bibliothecaires et Documentalistes (APBD)
7 rue des Marronniers, 5651 Thy-Le Chateau
Tel: (071) 614335 *Fax:* (071) 611634
E-mail: biblio.hainaut@skynet.be
Key Personnel
President: Jean-Claude Trefois
Secretary: Laurence Hennaux
Publication(s): *Bloc-notes*; *Un cadeau, un livre* (annual selection of children's books)

Scientific & Technical Information Service
Bd de l'Empereur 4 Keizerslaan, B-1000 Brussels
Tel: (02) 5195640 *Fax:* (02) 5195645
E-mail: info@stis.fgov.be
Web Site: www.stis.fgov.be
Key Personnel
Dir: Dr Jean Moulin *Tel:* (02) 5195656
E-mail: jean.moulin@stis.fgov.be
Publication(s): *The Electronic Information Services Industry in Belgium 1997-1999*
Parent Company: Federal Office for Scientific, Technical & Cultural Affairs

SIST-DWTI, see Scientific & Technical Information Service

Vereniging van Religieus-Wetenschappelijke Bibliothecarissen (Association of Religious Academic Librarians)
Sint Michielsstraat 6, 3000 Leuven
Tel: (016) 323807 *Fax:* (016) 323862
E-mail: etiennedhondt@theo.kuleuven.ac.be
Web Site: www.theo.kuleuven.ac.be/beth
Key Personnel
President: E D'Hondt
Secretary: K van de Casteele
Founded: 1965
Member: Bibliotheques Europeennes de Theologie (BETH).
Publication(s): *VRB-Informatie* (quarterly)

Vlaamse Vereniging voor Bibliotheek-Archief-en Documentatiewezen (VVBAD) (Flemish Association for Libraries, Archives & Documentation Centres)
Statiestraat 179, B-2600 Berchem Antwerp
Tel: (03) 2814457 *Fax:* (03) 2188077
E-mail: vvbad@vvbad.be
Web Site: www.vvbad.be
Key Personnel
President: Geert Puype
Executive Dir: Marc Storms *E-mail:* marc.storms@vvbad.be
Secretary: Myriam Lemmens
Founded: 1921
Flemish Association of Librarians, Archivists, Documentalists & Information Professionals.
Publication(s): *Archiefkunde* (monographs); *Bibliotheek- en Archiefgids* (Library & Archive Guide 6 times a year); *Bibliotheekkunde* (monographs); *INFO* (monthly membership journal); *Vlaamse Archief-, Bibliotheek- en Documentatiegids* (every 2 years, an address guide to archives, libraries & documentation centers in Dutch-speaking part of Belgium)

VRB, see Vereniging van Religieus-Wetenschappelijke Bibliothecarissen

Belize

Belize Library Association
c/o Central Library, Bliss Institute, Belize City
Mailing Address: PO Box 287, Belize City
Tel: (02) 7267
Key Personnel
Secretary: Robert Hulse
President: H W Young
Publication(s): *Belize Library Association Bulletin*

Bolivia

Asociacion Boliviana de Bibliotecarios (ABB)
c/o Biblioteca y Archivo Nacional, Calle Bolivar, Sucre
Key Personnel
Dir: Gunnar Mendoza
Bolivian Library Association.

Centro Nacional de Documentacion Cientifica y Tecnologica - Universidad Mayor De S an Andres
Calle Ayacucho No 205, Casilla 9357, La Paz
Tel: (02) 359586; (02) 359587 *Fax:* (02) 359491
Telex: 3438 UMSA-BV
Key Personnel
Contact: Ruben Valle Vera
National Scientific & Technological Documentation Centre.
Publication(s): *Bibliography Series* (3-5 a year); *Boletin Accesos* (quarterly); *Current Events* (annually)

Bosnia and Herzegovina

Drustvo Bibliotekara Bosne i Hercegovine
Zmaja od Bosne 8B, 71000 Sarajevo
Tel: (071) 212-435 *Fax:* (071) 212-435
Key Personnel
President: Nevenka Hajdarovic *E-mail:* nevenka@utic.net.ba
Publisher: Emina Memija
Librarians' Society of Bosnia & Herzegovina.
Publication(s): *Bibliotekarstvo* (yearly)

Botswana

Botswana Library Association
PO Box 1310, Gaborone
Tel: (031) 3552295 *Fax:* (031) 357291
Telex: 2429BD
Key Personnel
Chairman: F M Lamusse
Secretary: A M Mbangiwa *E-mail:* mbrngiwa@noka.ub.bw
Publication(s): *Botswana Library Association Journal*

Brazil

Associacao dos Arquivistas Brasileiros
(Association of Brazilian Archivists)
Rua da Candelaria, 9-Sala 1004, Centro, Rio de Janeiro RJ
Tel: (021) 2337142 *Fax:* (021) 2337142
Key Personnel
President: Lia Temporal Malcher
Secretary: Laura Regina Xavier
Publication(s): *Arquivo & Administracao* (biannually); *Associacao dos Arquivistas Brasileiros* (Association of Brazilian Archivists, bulletin)

Instituto Brasileiro de Informacao em Ciencia e Tecnologia
SAS Quadra 05 Lote 06 Bloco H, 70070-000 Brasilia DF
Tel: (061) 2176111 *Fax:* (061) 2262677
Telex: (061) 2481
Key Personnel
Dir: Jose Rincon Ferreira
Publication(s): *Bibliografia Brasileira de Ciencia da Informacao* (Brazilian Bibliography of Information Science, annually); *Bibliografic Brasileira de Politica Cientifica e Tecnologica* (Brazilian Bibliography of Political Science & Technology); *Boletim Qualidade & Produtividade* (Quality & Productivity Bulletin, quarterly); *Calendario de Eventos em C&T* (Calendar of Events in C&I, quarterly); *Ciencia da Informacao* (Information Science, biannually); *Informativo IBICT* (Informative IBICT, biannually)

Federacao Brasileira de Associacoes de Bibliotecarios - Comissao Brasileira de Documentacao Juridica (FEBAB/CBDJ)
Rua Avonhandava 40, Cj 110, 01306 Sao Paulo
Tel: (011) 2579979 *Fax:* (011) 2830747
Key Personnel
President: Joao Carlos Gomes Ribeiro
Executive Secretary: Tania Cordeiro Alvarez; Wilma Rosa
Brazilian Federation of Library Associations - Brazilian Committee of Legal Documentation.
Publication(s): *Noticias* (News; many publications dealing with legal and related matters)

IBICT, see Instituto Brasileiro de Informacao em Ciencia e Tecnologia

Brunei Darussalam

Persatuan Perpustakaan Kebangsaan Negara Brunei
c/o Language & Literature Bureau Library, Jalan Elizabeth II, Bandar Seri Begawan
Tel: (02) 235501
Key Personnel
Contact: Abu Bakar Bin
National Library Association of Brunei.

Cameroon

Association des Bibliothecaires, Archivistes, Documentalistes et Museographes du Cameroon (ABADCAM)
Universite de Yaounde, Bibliotheque Universitaire, BP 337, Yaounde
Tel: 220744 *Fax:* 221320
Telex: 8384
Key Personnel
Librarian: P N Chateh
Association of Librarians, Archivists, Documentalists and Museum Curators of Cameroon.
Publication(s): *Newsletter*

Canada

IAML, see International Association of Music Libraries, Archives & Documentation Centres

International Association of Music Libraries, Archives & Documentation Centres
Alison Hall, Cataloguing Dept, Careton University Library, 1125 Colonel By Dr, Ottawa, ON, ON K1S 5B6
Tel: 613-520-2600 (ext 8150) *Fax:* 613-520-3583
Publication(s): *Fontes Artis Musicae*

Chile

Colegio de Bibliotecarios de Chile AG
Diagonal Paraguay 383, Dept 122, Santiago 6510017
Tel: (02) 222 56 52 *Fax:* (02) 635 50 23
E-mail: cdb@transtar.cl
Web Site: www.bibliotecarios.cl
Key Personnel
President: Esmerelda Ramos Ramos
Secretary: Monica Nunez
Chilean Library Association.
Publication(s): *Indices de Publicaciones Periodicas en Bibliotecologia* (Catalogue of Periodical Publications on Librarianship); *Micronoticias*

CONICYT (National Commission for Science & Technology)
Departamento de Informacion, Casilla 297-V, Canada 308, Correo 21, Santiago
Tel: (02) 3654450 *Fax:* (02) 6551395
E-mail: info@conicyt.cl
Web Site: www.conicyt.cl
Key Personnel
Head of Dept: Ana Maria Prat *Tel:* (02) 3654455
Publication(s): *Serie Directorios*; *Serie Informacion y Documentacion*

China

China Society for Library Science
39 Bai Shi Qiao Rd, Beijing 100081
Tel: (010) 68415566 ext 5563; (010) 68417815 *Fax:* (010) 68419271
Telex: 222211
Key Personnel
President: Liu Deyou
Secretary General: Liu Xiangsheng
Publication(s): *Bulletin of the China Library Science*

Colombia

Asociacion Colombiana de Bibliotecarios
Calle 10 No 3-16, Apdo Aereo 30883, Bogota
Tel: (01) 2694219
Key Personnel
Pres: Saul Sanchez Toro
Colombian Library Association.
Publication(s): *Boletin*

Congo

Direction Generale des Services de Bibliotheques, Archives et Documentation
Bibliotheque Nationale Populaire, BP 114, BP 1489 Brazzaville
Tel: 833485
Key Personnel
Dir: Pierre Mayola
General Management of Library, Archives and Documentation Services.

The Democratic Republic of the Congo

Association Zairoise des Archivistes, Bibliothecaires et Documentalistes
BP 805, Kinshasa X1
Tel: (012) 30123; (012) 30124
Key Personnel
Executive Secretary: E Kabeba-Bangasa
Zaire Association of Archivists, Librarians and Documentalists.
Publication(s): *Mukanda*

Costa Rica

Asociacion Costarricense de Bibliotecarios
Apdo 3308, San Jose
Key Personnel
Secretary-General: Nelly Kopper
Costa Rican Association of Librarians.
Publication(s): *Anuario bibliografico costarricense* (Boletin)

Cote d'Ivoire

Association pour le Developpement de la Documentation, des Bibliotheques et Archives de la Cote d'Ivoire (ADBACI)
c/o Bibliotheque Nationale, BP V 180, Abidjan
Tel: 213872
Key Personnel
Dir: Ambroise Agnero
Secretary General: Cangah Guy

Croatia

HKD, see Hrvatsko knjiznicarsko drustvo

Hrvatsko knjiznicarsko drustvo (Croation Library Association)
Ulica Hrvatske bratske zajednice 4, 10000 Zagreb
Tel: (41) 6164 037; (41) 6164 210; (41) 6159 320
Fax: (41) 6164 186
E-mail: hbd@nsk.hr
Web Site: pubwww.srce.hr/hkd
Key Personnel
President: Dubravka Stancin-Rosic *Tel:* (01) 616 4037
Secretary: Dunja-Marija Gabriel
Founded: 1940
Croatian Library Association
Membership: IFLA (International Federation of Library Associations), EBLIDA (European Bureau of Library, Information & Documentation Associations).
Publication(s): *Vjesnik bibliotekara Hrvatske* (semiannually, 1950, scientific magazine)

Cuba

Library Association of Cuba
Biblioteca Nacional Jose Marti, Apdo 6881, Ave de Independencia e/20 de Mayo y Aranguren, Plaza de la Revolucion Josee Martii, Havana
Tel: (07) 708277
Telex: 0571963
Key Personnel
Dir: Marta Terry Gonzalez
Vice President: Blanca Mercedes Mesa; Elisa Masiques

Cyprus

Library Association of Cyprus
PO Box 1039, Nicosia
Key Personnel
Secretary: Paris G Rossos
President: Costas D Stephanov
Publication(s): *Deltion Vivliothikarion* (Library Bulletin)

Czech Republic

Svaz knihovniku informacnich pracovniku Ceske republiky (SKIP) (Association of Library & Information Professionals of the Czech Republic)
C/O Narodni Knihovna, Klementinum 190, 110 01 Prague 1
Mailing Address: National Library, Klementinum 190, 11000 Praha
Tel: (02) 21663338 *Fax:* (02) 21663175
Web Site: www.nkp.cz
Key Personnel
President: Vit Richter *E-mail:* vit.richter@nkp.cz
Honorary Pres: Dr Jarmila Burgetova *Tel:* (02) 3115030 *E-mail:* jarmila.burgetova@seznam.cz
Founded: 1968
Association of Library & Information Professionals of Czech Republic
Membership(s): IFLA.
Publication(s): *SKIP* (4x ann, bulletin)

Denmark

Arkivarforeningen
c/o Landsarkivet for Sjaelland, jagtvej 10, 2200 Copenhagen K K
Tel: 31393520 *Fax:* 33153239
Key Personnel
President: Tyge Krogh
Secretary: Charlotte Steinmark
Archives Society.
Publication(s): *Kommunal opgavelosning 1842-1970* (Odense University Press, 1990)

Danmarks Biblioteksforening (Danish Library Association)
Vesterbrogade 20/5, 1620 Copenhagen V
Tel: 33250935 *Fax:* 33257900
Key Personnel
Dir: Winnie Vitzansky
Publication(s): *Biblioteksvejviser* (Library Guide); *Bogens Verden* (Library Journal); *Danmarks Biblioteker* (Members Magazine)

Danmarks Forskningsbiblioteksforening
Postboks 2149, 1016 Kobenhavn K
Tel: 33936222 *Fax:* 33919596
E-mail: df@kb.dk
Key Personnel
President: Erland Kolding
Secretary: D Skovgaard
Danish Research Library Association: Section 1 Research Libraries; Section 2 Staff members of Danish Research Libraries.
Publication(s): *DF-Revy*

Dansk Musikbiblioteksforening (Danish Music Library Organization)
Member of Association of Danish Music Libraries (Danish section of AIBM/IAML)
c/o Det Kgl Bibliotek, Postbox 2149, DK-1016 Copenhagen K
Tel: 33474316 *Fax:* 33474710
E-mail: dmbf@kb.dk
Web Site: www.dmbf.sb.aau.dk
Key Personnel
President: Kirsten Voss-Eliasson
Publication(s): *Musik BIB* (quarterly, 2000)

Kommunernes Skolebiblioteksforening
Vesterbrogade 20, DK-1620 Copenhagen V
Tel: 33253222 *Fax:* 33253223
E-mail: komskolbib@internet.dk
Web Site: www.ksbk.dk
Key Personnel
Chief Executive: Paul Erik Sorensen
Editor: Niels Jacobsen
Association of Danish School Libraries.
Publication(s): *Born og Boger* (Children & Books); *Skolebiblioteksarbogen* (School Libraries Annual; also books dealing with youth culture, English summary)

Dominican Republic

Asociacion Dominicana de Bibliotecarios (ASODOBI)
c/o Biblioteca Nacional, Plaza de la Cultura, Cesar Nicolas Penson 91, Santo Domingo
Tel: (809) 688-4086
Key Personnel
President: Prospero J Mella-Chavier
Secretary-General: Ms V Regus
Dominican Association of Librarians.
Publication(s): *El Papiro*

ASODOBI, see Asociacion Dominicana de Bibliotecarios (ASODOBI)

Departamento de Documentacion y Bibliotecas
Galeria Nacional de Bellas Artes y Cultos, Santo Domingo
Key Personnel
Dir: Dr Jose de J Alvarez Valverde
Library and Documentation Service.

Grupo Bibliografico Nacional de la Republica Dominicana
Archivo General de la Nacion, Calle ME Diaz, Santo Domingo

Ecuador

Asociacion Ecuatoriana de Bibliotecarios (AEB)
c/o Casa de la Cultura Ecuatoriana 'Benjamin Carrion', Apdo 67, Ave 6 de Diciembre 794, Quito
Tel: (02) 528840; Headquarters: (02 263474)
Key Personnel
President: Eulalia Galarza
Ecuadorian Library Association.
Publication(s): *Unidad Bibliotecaria*

Egypt (Arab Republic of Egypt)

Egyptian Association for Library & Information Science
c/o Dept Archives, Librarianship & Information Science, Faculty of Arts, University of Cairo, Cairo
Tel: (02) 5676365 *Fax:* (02) 5729659
Key Personnel
President: Dr S Khalifa
Secretary: M Hosam El-Din
Publication(s): *Alam al-Maktabat* (Library World)

El Salvador

Asociacion de Bibliotecarios de El Salvador
Biblioteca Nacional, 8A Ave Norte y Calle Delgado, San Salvador
Tel: 216312
El Salvador Library Association.
Publication(s): *Informa* (Newsletter monthly)

Asociacion General de Archivistas de El Salvador
Archivo General de la Nacion, Palacio Nacional, San Salvador
Tel: 229418
Association of Archivists of El Salvador.

Ethiopia

Ethiopian Library & Information Association
PO Box 30530, Addis Ababa
Tel: (01) 518020 *Fax:* (01) 552544
Key Personnel
President: Mulugeta Hunde
Secretary: Girma Makonnen
Publication(s): *Bulletin*; *Directory of Ethiopian Libraries*

Finland

Finnish Library Association, see Suomen Kirjastoseura

Bibliothecarii Medicinae Fenniae
c/o National Library of Health Sciences, Haartmaninkatu 4, FIN-00290 Helsinki
Tel: (09) 19126645 *Fax:* (09) 19126652
Key Personnel
President: Merja Jauhiainen *Tel:* (09) 47 47 2384
E-mail: merja.jauhiainen@occuphealth.fi
Founded: 1980
Memberships: IFLA (International Federation of Library Associations & Institutions); EAHIL (European Association for Health Information & Libraries Association); NAMHI (Nordic Association for Medical & Health Information).

Suomen Kirjastoseura
Vuorikatu 22 A18, FIN-00100 Helsinki
Tel: (09) 622 1399; (09) 694 1854 (education); (09) 694 1878 (information); (09) 694 1856 (Kirjastolehi); (09) 694 1858 (Secretary General) *Fax:* (09) 622 1466
E-mail: fla@fla.fi
Key Personnel
Secretary-General: Sinikka Sipila
President: Kaarina Dromberg
Finnish Library Association.
Publication(s): *Kirjastolehti* (Library Journal)

Suomen Tieteellinen Kirjastoseura
PO Box 39, 00014 University of Helsinki
Tel: (09) 3653148 *Fax:* (09) 3652907
E-mail: meri.kuula@arcada.fi
Key Personnel
President: Tuula Ruhanen *E-mail:* tuula.ruhanen@helsinki.fi
Secretary: Meri Kuula
Finnish Research Library Association.
Publication(s): *Guide to Research Libraries & Information Services in Finland*; *Signum* (eight times a year text in Finnish)

Tietohuollon Neuvottelukunta
c/o Ministry of Education, Meritullinkatu, 00171 Helsinki
Mailing Address: PO Box 293, 00171 Helsinki
Tel: (09) 134171 *Fax:* (09) 1359335
Telex: 122109 Mined
Key Personnel
Chairman: Veikko Litzen
Secretary General: Annu Jylhae-Pyykoenen
Finnish Council for Information Provision.

France

ABEF, see Association des Bibliotheques Chretiennes France (ABEF)

ADBS, see L'Association des Professionnels de l'Information et de la Documentation (ADBS)

Association des Archivistes Francais
60 rue des Francs-Bourgeois, 75141 Paris cedex 3
Tel: (01) 40276000
Key Personnel
President: Jean-Luc Eichenlaub
Secretary: Jean LePottier
Association of French Archivists.
Publication(s): *La Gazette des Archives*
Branch Office(s)
Centre de Formation, 9 rue Rodier, 75009 Paris

Association des Bibliothecaires Francais
31 rue de Chabrol, 75010 Paris
Tel: (01) 55331030 *Fax:* (01) 55301031
E-mail: abf@abf.asso.fr
Web Site: www.abf.asso.fr
Key Personnel
President: Gerard Briand
General Secretary: Jan-Francois Jacques
Founded: 1906
Association of French Librarians.
Publication(s): *Bulletin d'informations de l'ABF*

Association des Bibliotheques Chretiennes France (ABEF)
9 Bd Voltaire, 21000 Dijon
Tel: (03) 80631478
Key Personnel
Executive Secretary: Bernard Stelly
Association of Ecclesiastical Libraries in France.
Publication(s): *Bulletin de liaison de l'ABEF* (ISSN 0066-8958)

Association des Diplomes de l'Ecole de Bibliothecaires-Documentalistes
c/o Bibliotheque du Saulchoir, 43 bis rue de la Glaciere, 75013 Paris
Tel: (01) 45870533 *Fax:* (01) 43310756
E-mail: pofier@citiz.fr
Key Personnel
Secretary: M Potier
Association of Graduates of the School of Librarians and Documentalists.
Publication(s): *Bulletin d'Information* (annual)

F A D B E N, see Federation des Enseignants Documentalistes de l'Education nationale

Federation des Enseignants Documentalistes de l'Education nationale
25 rue Claude Tiller, 75012 Paris 12
Tel: (01) 43724560; (03) 8588898 *Fax:* (03) 8588898
E-mail: fadben@insat.com
Key Personnel
President: Mrs France Vernotte
General Secretary: Mrs Claude Morizio
Federation of Associations of National Educational Record Clerks and Librarians.
Publication(s): *La Lettre* (quarterly); *Mediadoc* (triannually)

L'Association des Professionnels de l'Information et de la Documentation (ADBS)
25 rue Claude Tillier, 75012 Paris
Tel: (01) 43722525 *Fax:* (01) 43723041
E-mail: adbs@adbs.fr
Web Site: www.adbs.fr
Key Personnel
President: Florence Wilhelm
French Association of Information and documentation Professionals.
Publication(s): *Documentaliste - Sciences de l'Information et ouvrages Specialises*

Germany

A Sp B, see Arbeitsgemeinschaft der Spezialbibliotheken eV (ASpB)

Arbeitsgemeinschaft der Archive und Bibliotheken in der evangelischen Kirche
Veilhofstr 28, 90489 Nuremberg
Mailing Address: Postfach 250429, 90129 Nuremburg
Tel: (0911) 588690 *Fax:* (0911) 5886969
E-mail: LKANuernberg@t-online.de
Web Site: home.t-online.de/home/LKANuernberg/lkantit.htm
Key Personnel
President: Dr Helmut Baier
Joint Association of Archives & Libraries in the Evangelical Church.

Publication(s): *Aus Evangelischen Archiven, Neue Folge der Allgemeinen Mitteilungen der AABevk; Veroeffentlichungen der AABevK* (Publications of the AABevK)

Arbeitsgemeinschaft der Regionalbibliotheken
Konrad-Adenauer Str 8, 70173 Stuttgart
Mailing Address: Postfach 105441, 70047 Stuttgart
Tel: (0711) 212 4424 *Fax:* (0711) 212 4422
E-mail: direktion@wlb-stuttgart.de
Key Personnel
President: Dr Hannsjorg Kouarte
Joint Association of Regional Libraries.

Arbeitsgemeinschaft der Spezialbibliotheken eV (ASpB) (Association of Special Libraries, Germany)
c/o Forschungszentrum, Julich GmbH, Zentralbibliothek, 52425 Julich
Tel: (02461) 61-2907; (02461) 61-5368
Fax: (02461) 61-6103
Web Site: www.aspb.de
Key Personnel
Chairman: Dr Rafael Ball, PhD *E-mail:* r.ball@ft-juelich.de
Project Manager & Secretary Dir: Edith Salz *E-mail:* e.salz@fz-juelich.de
Founded: 1946
Membership: International Federation of Library Associations & Institutions (IFLA).
Publication(s): *Bericht ueber elie Tagungi elekrouischer* (every 2 years, newsletter, conference report)

Arbeitsgemeinschaft fur juristisches Bibliotheks- und Dokumentationswesen
Teilbibliothek Recht der, Universitatsbibliothek, 93042 Regensburg
Tel: (0941) 9432497 *Fax:* (0941) 9433285
Key Personnel
Chairwoman: Dr Cornelie Butz
Editor: Heinz-Guenther Black
Joint Association for Law Libraries and Legal Documentation.
Publication(s): *Arbeitshefte* (irregularly); *Mitteilungen der Arbeitsgemeinschaft fuer juristisches Bibliotheks- und Dokumentationswesen* (triannually)

Arbeitsgemeinschaft fur medizinisches Bibliothekswesen
c/o Boehringer Mannheim GmbH Zentralbibliothek, Sandhoferstr 116, 68305 Mannheim
Mailing Address: Postfach 310120, 68261 Mannheim
Tel: (0621) 7592376 *Fax:* (0621) 7594419
Key Personnel
Chairman: Peter Stadler

BDB, see Bundesvereinigung Deutscher Bibliotheksverbande (BDB)

Berufsverband Information Bibliothek (BIB)
Formerly Verein der Bibliothekare und Assistenten
Postfach 1324, 72703 Reutlingen
Tel: (07121) 34910 *Fax:* (07121) 300433
E-mail: mail@bib-info.de
Web Site: www.bib-info.de
Key Personnel
President: Klaus Peter Bottger *Tel:* (208) 4554141 *E-mail:* klaus.peter.boettger@sdadt-mh.de
Secretary: Katharina Boulanger
Association of Librarians.
Publication(s): *BuB-Forum for Bibliothek und Information* (from: Postfach 1324, 72703 Reutlingen)

Bundesvereinigung Deutscher Bibliotheksverbande (BDB)
Strasse des 17, Juni 114, 10623 Berlin
Tel: (030) 39001480 *Fax:* (030) 39001484
E-mail: dbv@bdbibl.de
Web Site: www.bdbibl.deldbv
Key Personnel
Forewoman: Prof Birgit Dankert
Contact: Elke Daempfert *E-mail:* daempfert@bdbibl.de
Association of German Library & Librarian Associations.
Publication(s): *Ausbildung im Europaeischen Rahmen-Abschlussbericht; BDB-Jahresbericht 1989/90; Bibkliotheken '93; Bibliotheken in der Informationsgesellschaft; Bibliotheksdienst; Drehscheibe der Information; Menschen, Buecher und Computer; Umsetzung der EG-Richtlinien zum Vermiet-und Verleihrecht*
Branch Office(s)
Fadbodsdule Hamburg, Griudellof 30, 20146 Hamburg

DBV, see Deutscher Bibliotheksverband eV (DBV)

Deutsche Exlibris Gesellschaft ev (German Bookplate Society)
Member of F I S A E
Am Loewentor 46, Koblenz, Rheinland-Pfalz 56075
Tel: (0261) 57885 *Fax:* (0261) 9523494
Web Site: www.exlibris-gesellschaft.de
Key Personnel
President: Dr Gernot Blum *E-mail:* info@exlibris-blum.de
Secretary: Birgit M A Goebel *E-mail:* birgit.goebel@t-online.de
Publication(s): *Jahrbuch Exlibriskunst und Graphik* (annually)

Deutsche Gesellschaft fur Informationswissenschaft und informationspraxis eV
Ostbahnhofstr 13, 60314 Frankfurt, AM 1
Tel: (069) 430313 *Fax:* (069) 4909096
E-mail: dgd@darmstadt.gmd.de
Web Site: www.dgd.de
Key Personnel
President: Dr Horst Neiber
Contact: Hans Nerlich
German Society for Information Science & Information Practice.
Publication(s): *nfd-Information Wissenschaft und Praxis* (Documentation)

Deutscher Bibliotheksverband eV (DBV)
Strasse des 17, Juni 114, 10623 Berlin
Tel: (030) 39001480 *Fax:* (030) 39001484
E-mail: dbv@bdbibl.de
Web Site: www.bdbibl.de/bv
Key Personnel
President: Dr Christof Eichert
Chairman: Dr Georg Ruppelt
Contact: Elke Daempfert *E-mail:* daempfert@bdbibl.de
Association of German Libraries.
Publication(s): *D B V-Info* (annually)

Deutscher Verband Evangelischer Buchereien eV
Buergerstr 2a, 37073 Goettingen
Tel: (0551) 5007590 *Fax:* (0551) 704415
E-mail: dveb@evlka.de
Key Personnel
Chairman: Dr Eckart V Vietinghoff
Manager: Gabriele Kassenbrock
German Association of Protestant Libraries.
Publication(s): *Der Evangelische Buchberater* (quarterly); *Handwoerterbuch der evangelischen Buechereiarbeit 1980*

Deutsches Bibliotheksinstitut
Kurt-Schumacher-Damm 12-16, 13405 Berlin
Tel: (030) 41034-0 *Fax:* (030) 403410-0
E-mail: www@dbi-berlin.de
Key Personnel
Dir: Prof Gunter Beyersdorff
German Library Institute.
Publication(s): *also several reference books, monographs, bibliographical & statistical services; Bibliotheks Info* (monthly); *Bibliotheksdienst* (monthly); *Forum Musikbibliothek* (quarterly); *Schulbibliothek aktuell* (quarterly)
Branch Office(s)
Luisenstr 57, 10117 Berlin

GBDL, see Gesellschaft fur Bibliothekswesen und Dokumentation des Landbaues (GBDL)

Gesellschaft fur Bibliothekswesen und Dokumentation des Landbaues (GBDL)
Affiliate of Arbcitsgemeinschaft der Specialbibliotheken e v (ASpB)
TU Muenchen, 85350 Freising
Tel: (08161) 714029 *Fax:* (08161) 715093
Key Personnel
President: Prof W Laux, PhD
Secretary: Dr Birgid Schlindwein *E-mail:* schlind@weihenstephan.de
Society for Librarianship & Documentation in Agriculture.
Publication(s): *Mitteilungen der Gesellschaft fuer Bibliothekswesen und Dokumentation des Landbaues*

Informationszentrum fuer Informationswissenschaft und -praxis (IZ)
Fachhochschule Potsdam, Friedrich-Ebert-Str 4, 14467 Potsdam
Mailing Address: Postfach 600608, 14406 Potsdam
Tel: (0331) 5802210 *Fax:* (0331) 5802229
E-mail: iz@fh-potsdam.de
Documentation & Information Society.

NABD, see Normenausschuss Bibliotheks- und Dokumentationswesen (NABD) im DIN Deutsches Institut fuer Normung eV

Normenausschuss Bibliotheks- und Dokumentationswesen (NABD) im DIN Deutsches Institut fuer Normung eV
Burggrafenstr 6, 10787 Berlin
Mailing Address: 10772 Berlin
Tel: (030) 26012791 *Fax:* (030) 26011231
Web Site: www.din.de/set/gremien/nas/ *Cable:* DEUTSCHNORMEN BERLIN
Key Personnel
Manager: Edith Lechner *E-mail:* lechner@nabd.din.de

VdA - Verband deutscher Archivarinnen und Archivare e V (Association of German Archivists)
Formerly Verein deutscher Archivare (VdA)
Marstallstr 2, 99423 Weimar 99423
Mailing Address: Postfach 2119, 99402 Weimar
Tel: (03643) 870-235 *Fax:* (03643) 870-164
E-mail: info@vda.archiv.net
Web Site: www.vda.archiv.net
Key Personnel
Chairman: Dr Volker Wahl *E-mail:* wahl@vda.archiv.net
Contact: Thilo Bauer *E-mail:* bauer@vda.archiv.net
Founded: 1946
Association of German Archivists.
Publication(s): *Archive in der Bundesrepublik Deutschland, Oesterreich & der Schweiz* (Register of Archives in Germany, Austria & Switzerland-at irregular intervals of several years)

Verein der Bibliothekare und Assistenten, see Berufsverband Information Bibliothek (BIB)

Verein der Diplom-Bibliothekare an wissenschaftlichen Bibliotheken eV
c/o Universitaetsbibliothek, Am Hubland, 97074 Wuerzburg
Tel: (0221) 5747161 *Fax:* (0221) 5747110
Key Personnel
Chairman: Marianne Saule
Association of Certified Librarians at Academic Libraries.
Publication(s): *Rundschreiben*

Verein deutscher Archivare (VdA), see VdA - Verband deutscher Archivarinnen und Archivare e V

Verein Deutscher Bibliothekar eV
Krummer Timpen 3-5, 48143 Munsten
Tel: (0251) 8324032 *Fax:* (0251) 8328398
Key Personnel
President: Dr Klaus Hilgemann
E-mail: hilgema@ui-muenster.de
Secretary: Dr Lydiia Jungnickel
Association of German Librarians.
Publication(s): *Jahrbuch der deutschen Bibliotheken* (Yearbook of German Libraries); *Zeitschrift fuer Bibliothekswesen und Bibliographie* (Journal of Library Science and Bibliography)

Wuerttembergische Bibliotheksgesellschaft
Konrad-Adenauerstr 8, 70047 Stuttgart
Mailing Address: Posttach 10 54 41, 70047 Stuttgart
Tel: (0711) 2124428 *Fax:* (0711) 2124422
E-mail: wbg@mailserver.wlb-stutthart.de
Web Site: www.wlb-stuttgart.de
Key Personnel
Secretary: Elisabeth Tosta
Society of Friends of the Wuerttemberg State Library.

Ghana

Ghana Library Association
PO Box 4105, Accra
Tel: (02) 668 731
Key Personnel
Secretary: A W K Insaidoo
President: E S Asiedo
Publication(s): *Ghana Library Journal* (irregular)

Greece

Enosis Hellinon Bibliothekarion
Themistocleus 73, 10683 Athens
Tel: (01) 3226625
Key Personnel
President: K Xatzopoulou
General Secretary: E Kalogeraky
Greek Library Association.

Guinea

Direction de la Recherche Scientifique et Techniques
Bibliothelique nationale, BP 561, Conakry
Tel: (04) 461010
Key Personnel
Dir: Lansana Sylla
National Research & Documentation Institute.

Guyana

Guyana Library Association
c/o National Library, Church St & Ave of the Republic, Georgetown
Tel: (02) 62690; (02) 62699
Key Personnel
President: Hetty London
Secretary: Jean Harripersaud

Holy See (Vatican City State)

Biblioteca Apostolica Vaticana
Cortile del Belvedere, 00120 Vatican City
Tel: (06) 69883302 *Fax:* (06) 69884795
E-mail: bav@librsbk.vatlib.it
Telex: 2024 Dirgental VA
Key Personnel
Prefect: Prof Don Raffaele Farina

Honduras

Asociacion de Bibliotecarios y Archivistas de Honduras
11a Calle, 1a y 2a Avdas No 105, Comayagueela DC, Tegucigalpa
Key Personnel
President: Francisca de Escoto Espinoza
Secretary General: Juan Angel R Ayes
Association of Librarians & Archivists of Honduras.
Publication(s): *Catalogo de Prestamo*

Hong Kong

Hong Kong Library Association
GPO 10095
E-mail: hklib@hklib.org.hk
Web Site: www.hklib.org.hk
Key Personnel
President: Tommy Yeung
Honorary Secretary: Venia Mak *Tel:* 26168562
E-mail: hklib@hklib.org.hk
Journal Price $150 (local) US $30 (overseas), plus postage.
Publication(s): *Journal of the Hong Kong Library Association* (irregular)

Hungary

Magyar Koenyvtarosok Egyesuelete
(Association of Hungarian Librarians)
Hold u 6, H-1054 Budapest
Tel: (01) 311 8634 *Fax:* (01) 311 8634
E-mail: mke@oszk.hu
Web Site: www.mke.oszk.hu
Key Personnel
President: Dr Zoltan Ambrus *Tel:* (06) 454 354 ext 108 *E-mail:* ambrus@athos.bmk.hu
General Secretary: Mrs Katalin Haraszti *Tel:* (01) 441 4854 *E-mail:* haraszti@ogyk.hu
Founded: 1935
Association of Hungarian Librarians.

Iceland

Bokavardafelag Islands
PO Box 1497, 121 Reykjavik
Tel: 564-2050 *Fax:* 564-3877
Key Personnel
President: H A Hardarson
Secretary: A Agnarsdottir
Icelandic Library Association.
Publication(s): *Bokasafnid* (The Library); *Fregnir* (Newsletter)

India

Documentation Research and Training Centre
Eighth Mile, Mysore Rd, R V College Post, Bangalore 560059
Tel: (080) 604648 *Fax:* (080) 8430265
E-mail: drtc@isibang.ernet.in
Telex: 8458376 Isib In *Cable:* STATISTICA
Key Personnel
Head Prof: M A Gopinath
Contact: I K Ravichandra
Indian Statistical Institute.
Publication(s): *Annual Seminar, DRTC* (annually); *Refresher Seminar, DRTC* (annually)

IASLIC, see Indian Association of Special Libraries & Information Centres (IASLIC)

Indian Association of Academic Librarians
c/o Dr Zakir Husein Library, Jamia Milia Islamia University, Jamia Nagar, New Delhi 110025
Tel: (011) 6831717
Key Personnel
Secretary: M M Kashyap

Indian Association of Special Libraries & Information Centres (IASLIC)
P 291, CIT Scheme No 6M, Kankurgachi, Calcutta 700054
Tel: (033) 334-9651
Key Personnel
Publisher: J M Das
Publication(s): *Directory of Special & Research Libraries in India* (Newsletter 12 a year); *Indian Library Science Abstracts* (4 a year)

Indian Library Association
A/40-41, Flat 201, Ansal Bldg, Dr Mukerjee Nagar, Delhi 110009
Tel: (011) 7117743
Key Personnel
President: P S G Kumar
Editor, ILA Newsletter: P S G Kumar

Indonesia

Ikatan Pustakawan Indonesia
Jalan Merdeka Selatan No 21, Jakarta, Pusat
Mailing Address: PO Box 3624, 10002 Jakarta, Pusat
Tel: (021) 342529 *Fax:* (021) 3103554
Key Personnel
President: S Kartosdono
Indonesian Library Association.
Publication(s): *Majalah Ikatan Pustakawan Indonesia*

Iraq

Arab Archivists Institute
c/o National Centre of Archives, National Library Bldg, 2nd Floor, Bab-el-Muaddum, Baghdad
Mailing Address: PO Box 594, Baghdad
Key Personnel
Dir: Salim Al-Alousi

Iraq Library Association
c/o National Library, Bab-el-Muaddum, Baghdad
Tel: (01) 4164190
Key Personnel
Dir: Abdul Hameed Al-Alawchi

Ireland

Central Catholic Library Association Inc
74 Merrion Sq South, Dublin 2
Tel: (01) 6761264
Key Personnel
Librarian: Teresa Whitington

An Chomhairle Leabharlanna (Library Council)
53 & 54 Upper Mount St, Dublin 2
Tel: (01) 6761167 *Fax:* (01) 6766721
E-mail: info@librarycouncil.ie
Web Site: www.librarycouncil.ie
Key Personnel
Dir: Mrs N McDermott
Research & Information Officer: Alun Bevan *Tel:* (01) 6789905 *E-mail:* abevan@librarycouncil.ie
Library Council. This is the development agency for public libraries in Ireland.
Publication(s): *Annual Report* (annual); *Irish Library News* (monthly)

Cumann Leabharlann na h-Eireann (Library Association of Ireland)
53 Upper Mount St, Dublin
Tel: (01) 6619000 *Fax:* (01) 6761628
Web Site: www.libraryassociation.ie
Key Personnel
President: Marjory Sliney *Tel:* (01) 845-2026 *E-mail:* msliney@circon.net
Honorary Secretary: Geraldine McHugh
Founded: 1928
Member of IFLA & EBLIDA.
Publication(s): *An Leabharlann* (Published jointly with CILIP-Northern Ireland); *The Library Association of Ireland* (4 per year, Published jointly with CILIP-Northern Ireland)

National Library of Ireland Society
Kildare St, Dublin 2
Tel: (01) 6030200 *Fax:* (01) 6766690
Key Personnel
Dir: Brendan O'Donoghue
Secretary: G Lyne

Israel

Israel Librarians & Information Specialists Association
17 Strauss St, 91001 Jerusalem
Mailing Address: PO Box 238, 91001 Jerusalem
Tel: (02) 62072868 *Fax:* (02) 625628
Key Personnel
President: Benjamin Schachter
Publication(s): *The Reader's Aid (Yad Lakore)-Israel Journal for Libraries and Archives*

Israel Society of Libraries & Information Centers (ASMI)
Member of IFLA
97 Yaffo St, Klal House, Room 707, 91281 Jerusalem
Mailing Address: POB 28273, 91281 Jerusalem
Tel: (02) 6249421 *Fax:* (02) 6249421
E-mail: asmi@asmi.org.il
Web Site: www.asmi.org.il
Key Personnel
Chairperson: Shoshana Langerman *Tel:* (02) 5632756 *Fax:* (02) 5630640 *E-mail:* shala@barak-online.net
Publication(s): *Information & Librarianship* (irregular, 2 issues per volume, 2002)

The Israeli Center for Libraries
PO Box 3251, 31155 Bnei-Brak
Tel: (03) 6180151 *Fax:* (03) 5798048
E-mail: icl@icl.org.il
Web Site: www.icl.org.il
Key Personnel
Chairman: Jacob Agmon
Dir: Orly Onn
Publication(s): *Basifriot* (newspaper); *Yad-la-Kore* (The Reader's Aid library quarterly, & library monographs)

Italy

Associazione Italiana Biblioteche
CP 2461, 00100 Rome, A-D
Tel: (06) 4463532 *Fax:* (06) 4441139
E-mail: aib@aib.it
Web Site: www.aib.it
Key Personnel
President: I Poggiali
Secretary: A Paoli
Editorial Office: Maria Teresa Natale *E-mail:* natale@aib.it
Italian Library Association.
Publication(s): *AIB Notizie* (monthly); *Bollettino AIB* (quarterly); *Rapporti AIB* (irregularly)

Istituto Centrale per il Catalogo Unico delle Biblioteche Italiane e per le Informazioni Bibliografiche
Viale del Castro Pretorio, 00185 Rome
Tel: (06) 4454701 *Fax:* (06) 4959302
Key Personnel
Dir: Dr Giovanna Mazzola Merola
Central Institute of the Union Catalogue of Italian Libraries & Bibliographical Information.
Publication(s): *Bibliografia di Inventari e Cataloghi a Stampa dei Manoscritti*; *Bibliografia Nazionale Italiana*; *Catalogo Collettivo di Periodici - Archivio ISRDS/CNR*; *I Emilia Romagna - Il Friuli Venezia Giulia*; *Le Edizioni Italiane del XVI sec, Guida alla Catalogazione per Autori delle Stampe, Inventari Non a Stampa di Manoscritti*; *Periodici Italiani 1886-1981*; *Quaderno RICA*; *Regole Italiane di Catalogazione per Autori*; *Soggettario per i Cataloghi delle Biblioteche Italiane*

Jamaica

Jamaica Library Association
PO Box 58, Kingston 5
Tel: (876) 63310 *Fax:* (876) 62188
Key Personnel
President: P Kerr
Secretary: F Salmon
Honorary Secretary: Valda Adeyiga
Publication(s): *JLA News* (quarterly)

Japan

Gakujutsu Bunken Fukyu-Kai
c/o Tokyo Institute of Technology, 2-12-1 O-okayama, Meguro-ku, Tokyo 152
Key Personnel
President: Shu Kanbara
Association for Science Documents Information.

Information Processing Society of Japan
7th floor, Shibaura-Maekawa Bldg, 3-16-20, Shibaura, Minato-ku, Tokyo 108
Tel: (03) 54843535 *Fax:* (03) 54843534
E-mail: lizuka@ipsj.or.jp; tsuchi@ipsj.or.jp; somo@ipsj.or.jp
Key Personnel
President: Dr Iwao Tada
Service Division Manager: Yoshio Tsuchikawa
Publication(s): *Joho-shori* (Journal of IPSJ, Japanese, monthly); *Transactions of IPSJ* (Japanese, monthly)

Joho Kagaku Gijutsu Kyokai
Sasaki Bldg, 5-7 Koisikawa 2, Bunkyo-ku, Tokyo
Key Personnel
President: T Gondoh
General Manager: Yukio Ichikawa
Information Science & Technology Association (INFOSTA).
Publication(s): *(microfiche, biannually)* (Journal of Information Science & Technology Association)

Mita Society for Library & Information Science
School of Library & Information Science, Keio University, 2-15-45 Mita, Minato-ku, Tokyo 108-8345
Tel: (03) 34533920
Key Personnel
President: Kimio Hosono
Secretary: Satoko Suzuki *E-mail:* mslis@slis.keio.ac.jp
Publication(s): *Library & Information Science* (biannually)

Nihon Toshokan Kyokai
1-11-14 Shinkawa, Chuo-ku, Tokyo 104 0033
Tel: (03) 35230841 *Fax:* (03) 34217588
E-mail: info@jla.or.jp
Key Personnel
Secretary-General: Reiko Sakagawa
Japan Library Association.

Publication(s): *Gendai no Toshokan* (quarterly); *Nippon no Sankotosho Shikiban* (quarterly); *Nippon no Toshokan* (annually); *Sentei Tosho Somokuroku* (annually, Standard Catalog of Selected Books); *Toshokan Nenkan* (annually, Library Year Book); *Toshokan Zasshi* (monthly)

Nihon Toshokan Joho Gakka: Nihon Toshok Johogakkai (Japan Society of Library & Information Science)
c/o Faculty of Letters, Aichi Shukutoku University, 9 Katahira, Nagakute, Nagakute-cho, Aichi-gun, Aichi 480-1197
Tel: (03) 561624111
Key Personnel
President: Maso Nagasawa
Executive Secretary: Tomohide Muranushi
Contact: Shinichi Toda *Tel:* (03) 3945 7444
  E-mail: toda@hakusrv.toyo.ac.jp
Founded: 1953
Promotion of library & information science.
Publication(s): *Nihon Toshokan Joho Gakkaishi* (Journal of Japan Society of Library & Information Science, quarterly)

Nippon Igaku Toshokan Kyokai
Gakkai Center Bldg, 5F, 2-4-16 Yayoi, Bunkyo-ku, Tokyo 113
Tel: (03) 38151942 *Fax:* (03) 38151608
E-mail: jmlahq@nisiq.net
Key Personnel
Secretary: Junzo Tsuno
The Japan Medical Library Association.
Publication(s): *Igakutoshokan*; *List of current periodicals acquired by the Japanese Medical, Dental and Pharmaceutical Libraries*; *Union Catalogue of Foreign Books in the Libraries of Japan Medical Schools*

Nippon Yakugaku Toshokan Kyogikai
c/o Library, Faculty of Pharmaceutical Sciences, University of Tokyo, Hongo 7-3-1, Bunkyo-ku, Tokyo 113
Tel: (03) 38122111
Japan Pharmaceutical Library Association.
Publication(s): *Yakugaku Toshokan* (Pharmaceutical Library Bulletin)

Senmon Toshokan Kyogikai (SENTOKYO)
c/o Japan Library Association, Bldg F6, 1-11-14 Shinkawa, Chuo-ku, Tokyo 104-0033
Tel: (03) 3537-8335 *Fax:* (03) 3537-8336
E-mail: jsla@jsla.or.jp
Web Site: www.jsla.or.jp
Key Personnel
President: Kousaku Inaba
Executive Dir: Fumihisa Nakagawa
Japan Special Libraries Association.
Publication(s): *Bulletins* (six times a year); *Directory of Special Libraries* (in Japanese)

SENTOKYO, see Senmon Toshokan Kyogikai (SENTOKYO)

Jordan

Jordan Library Association
PO Box 6289, Amman
Tel: (06) 629412
Key Personnel
President: Anwar Akroush
Secretary: Yousra Abu Ajamieh
Publication(s): *Anglo-American Cataloguing Rules* (2nd Edition; in Arabic, 1983); *Directory of Jordanian Periodicals* (1982); *Directory of Libraries and Librarians in Jordan* (bilingual, 1984); *Directory of Libraries in Jordan 1976*; *Introduction to Librarianship and Information Science* (in Arabic, 1982); *Jordanian National Bibliography* (annually); *Palestinian-Jordanian Bibliography 1900-1970 and 1971-1975*; *Rissalat al-Maktaba* (The Message of the Library quarterly); *Technical Processing of Information* (in Arabic); *The Palestinian Bibliography: a List of Books Published by the Arabs in Palestine 1948-1980*

Kenya

Kenya Library Association
PO Box 46031, Nairobi
Tel: (02) 214917 *Fax:* (02) 336885
Key Personnel
Chairman: Jacinta Were *E-mail:* jwere@ken.healthnet.org
Secretary: Alice Bulogosi
Publication(s): *Kelias News* (bimonthly); *Maktaba Journal* (biannually)

Republic of Korea

Hanguk Seoji Hakhoe
c/o National Assembly Library, 1 Yeodong, Yeogdungpo-gu, Seoul
Tel: (02) 784-3561 *Fax:* (02) 788-3385
Korean Bibliographical Society.

Hanguk Tosogwan Hakhoe
c/o Dept of Library Science, Sung Kyun Kwan University, 53, 3-ga, Myungryun-dong, Chongro-ku, Seoul 110-745
Tel: (02) 7600114 *Fax:* (02) 7442453
Korean Library Science Society.
Publication(s): *Tosogwan Hak* (Journal of the Korean Library Science Society, Korean with English abstracts)

Korean Library Association
60-1 Panpo Dong, Seocho-ku, Seoul
Tel: (02) 5354868 *Fax:* (02) 5355616
E-mail: klanet@hitel.net
Key Personnel
President: Ki Nam Shin
Executive Dir: Won Ho Jo
Publication(s): *KLA Bulletin* (bi-monthly); *Korean Cataloguing Rules*; *Korean Decimal Classification*; *Statistics on Libraries in Korea* (Annual); *The Patterns of Book Cover Design in Korea (1392-1945)*

Korean Research & Development Library Association (KORDELA)
Room 0411 KIST Library, Cheongryang, Seoul
Mailing Address: POB 131, Cheongryang, Seoul
Tel: (02) 9673692 *Fax:* (02) 29634013
Telex: 27380 Kistrok K
Key Personnel
President: Ke Hong Park
Secretary: Keon Tak Oh

Kuwait

Kuwait University Library
PO Box 17140, Kuwait City
Key Personnel
Dir: Dr Husain A Al-Ansari
Publication(s): *The University Library*

Laos People's Democratic Republic

Association des Bibliothecaires Laotiens
c/o Direction de la Bibliotheque Nationale, Ministry of Information & Culture, BP 122, Vientiane
Tel: (021) 212452 *Fax:* (021) 213029
E-mail: pfd-mill@pan.laos.net.la
Key Personnel
Dir: Somthong
Association of Laos Librarians.

Latvia

Library Association of Latvia
Latvian National Library, Kr Barona iela 14, 1423 Riga
Tel: (0132) 728-98-74 *Fax:* (0132) 728-08-51
E-mail: lnb@com.latnet.lv
Telex: TEMA SU
Key Personnel
President: Aldis Abele
Dir: Andris Vilks
Vice President: Silvia Linina
Editor: Antra Purina
Publication(s): *Nota Bene* (quarterly journal)

Lebanon

The Lebanese Library Association
c/o American University of Beirut, University Library/Serials Dept, Beirut
Mailing Address: PO Box 113/5367, Beirut
Tel: (01) 374374 ext 2606 *Fax:* (01) 351 706
Telex: 20801
Key Personnel
President: Mr Fawz Abdalleh
Executive Secretary: Rudaynah Shoujah
Publication(s): *Al-Nashrah* (3 times yr, bulletin)

Lesotho

Lesotho Library Association
Private Bag A26, Maseru
Cable: Lelia Maseru
Key Personnel
Chairman: S M Mohai
Secretary: N Taole
Publication(s): *Lesotho Library Association Newsletter* (annually)

Lithuania

Lithuanian Librarians Association
Sv Ignoto 6-108, LT-2600 Vilnius
Tel: (02) 750340 *Fax:* (02) 750340
E-mail: lbd@vpu.lt
Web Site: www.lbd.lt
Key Personnel
Vice President: Emilija Banionyte *E-mail:* emilija.banionyte@vpu.lt
Founded: 1935

The Former Yugoslav Republic of Macedonia

Bibliotekarsko Drustvo na Makedonija
(Macedonian Library Association)
Bul Goce Delcev 6, 91000 Skopje
Mailing Address: PO Box 566, 91000 Skopje
Tel: (091) 212 736; (091) 115 177 (ext 39)
Fax: (091) 232649
E-mail: mile@nubsk.edu.mk; bmile47@yahoo.com
Key Personnel
President: Mile Boseski
Secretary: Poliksena Matkovska
Union of Librarians' Associations of Macedonia Official titles: Savez drustava bibliotečkih radnika Jugoslavije (Serbo-Croatian), Sojuz na drustvata na bibliotecnite rabotnici na Yugoslavija (Macedonian), Zveza durstev bibliotecnih delavcev Jugoslavije (Slovene). The headquarters of the League is situated in each of the six republics & two provinces of Yugoslavia in turn & changes every two years.
Publication(s): *Bibliotekarska iskra*

Malawi

The Malawi Library Association
PO Box 429, Zomba
Tel: (050) 522222 *Fax:* (050) 523225
Key Personnel
Chairman: Joseph J Uta
Secretary: Vote D Somba
Publication(s): *Libraries in Malawi: Textbook for Library Assistants*; *MALA Bulletin*; *Manual for Small Libraries*

Malaysia

Persatuan Perpustakaan Malaysia
PO Box 12545, 50782 Kuala Lumpur
Tel: (03) 273114 *Fax:* (03) 2731167
Key Personnel
President: Chew Wing Foong
Secretary: Leni Abdul Latif
Honorary Secretary: Ahmad Ridzuan Wan Chik
Library Association of Malaysia.
Publication(s): *Berita PPM* (bimonthly); *Majallah Perpustakaan Malaysia* (annually); *Sumber Pustaka* (official newsletter)

Mali

Association Malienne des Bibliothecaires, Archivistes et Documentalistes
c/o Bibliotheque Nationale du Mali, BP 159, Ave Kasse Keiita, Bamako
Tel: 224963
Key Personnel
Dir: Mamadou Konoba Keiita

Malta

Malta Library & Information Association (MaLIA)
c/o University Library, Msida MSD 06
Tel: (0356) 21322054
Web Site: www.malia-malta.org
Key Personnel
Secretary: Robert Mizzi *E-mail:* robmiz@mail.global.net.mt
Chairperson: Joseph R Grima
Founded: 1969
Publication(s): *Directory of Libraries & Information Units in Malta* (1996); *Directory of Publishers, Printers, Book Designers & Book Dealers in Malta*; *MaLIA Newletter* (quarterly)

Mauritania

Association Mauritanienne des Bibliothecaires, Archivistes et Documentalistes
c/o Bibliotheque Nationale BP 20, Nouakchott
Key Personnel
President: O Diouwara
Secretary: Sid'Ahmed Fall dit Dah

Mauritius

Mauritius Library Association
c/o The British Council, Royal Rd, Rose Hill
Mailing Address: POB 111, Rose Hill
Tel: 4549550; 4549551; 4549552 *Fax:* 4549553
E-mail: bcouncil@intnet.mu
Web Site: www.britishcouncil.org/mauritius/
Key Personnel
President: K Appadoo
Secretary: S Rughoo
Publication(s): *Mauritius Library Association Newsletter* (quarterly)

Mexico

AMBAC, see Asociacion Mexicana de Bibliotecarios AC (AMBAC)

Asociacion Mexicana de Bibliotecarios AC (AMBAC)
Apdo 27-651, Administracion de Correos 27, Mexico, DF 06760
Tel: (05) 5751135
E-mail: ambac@solar.sar.net
Key Personnel
President: Elsa M Ramirez Leyva
Secretary: Jose L Almanza Morales
Publication(s): *Memorias de Jornadas*; *Noticiero* (Bulletin)

Escuela Nacional de Biblioteconomia y Archivonomia
Viaducto Miguel Aleman 155, Mexico City, DF 13
Key Personnel
Dir: Prof Eduardo Salas Estrada
National School of Librarianship and Archives.
Publication(s): *Bibliotecas y Archivos*

Instituto de Investigaciones Bibliograficas
Biblioteca Nacional de Mexico & Hemeroteca Nacional de Mexico, Insurgentes Sur S/N Centro Cultural, Ciudad Universitaria, 04510 Mexico, DF
Tel: (05) 6226808 *Fax:* (05) 6650951
Key Personnel
Dir: Jose Guadalupe Moreno De Alba
Coordinators: Judith Licea De Arenas; Aurora Cano Andaluz
Institute of Bibliographic Research.
Publication(s): *Bibliografia Mexicana*

Myanmar

Myanmar Library Association
c/o National Library, Strand Rd, Yangon
Key Personnel
Chief Librarian: U Khin Maung Tin

Nepal

Nepal Library Association
c/o National Library, Harihar Bhawan, Pulchowk Library, PO Box 2773 Kathmandu
Tel: (01) 521132
Key Personnel
Librarian: Shusila Dwivedi

Netherlands

Koninklijke Vereniging van Archivarissen in Nederland
Cruquisweg 31, 1019 AT Amsterdam
Tel: (070) 3478656 *Fax:* (070) 3825790
Key Personnel
Off Dir: Mrs Marjoke de Roos
Royal Association of Archivists in the Netherlands.
Publication(s): *Almanak van het Nederlands archiefwezen*; *Archievenblad*

FOBID, see Stichting Federatie van Organisaties van Bibliotheek-, Informatie-, Dokumentatiewezen (FOBID)

IFLA, see International Federation of Library Associations & Institutions (IFLA)

International Federation of Library Associations & Institutions (IFLA)
PO Box 95312, 2509 CH The Hague
Tel: (070) 3140884 *Fax:* (070) 3834827
E-mail: ifla@ifla.org

Web Site: www.ifla.org
Key Personnel
Secretary General: Ross Shimmon
See also under International Organizations section.

NBBI, see Nederlands Bureau voor Bibliotheekwezen en Informatieverzorging (NBBI)

NBLC Vereniging van Openbare Bibliotheken (NBLC, Netherlands Public Library Association)
Platina weg 10, 2544 EZ The Hague
Mailing Address: PO Box 43300, 2504 AH The Hague
Tel: (070) 3090100 *Fax:* (070) 3090200
Telex: nblc nl
Key Personnel
Executive Dir: J E van der Putten
Contact: Marian Koren *Tel:* (070) 3090115
E-mail: koren@nblc.nl
Founded: 1972
National Association of Public Libraries, IFLA & EBLIDA.
Publication(s): *Bibliotheek Blad* (2 times weekly, Library Journal)

Nederlands Bureau voor Bibliotheekwezen en Informatieverzorging (NBBI)
Burg Van Karnebeeclaan 19, 2585 The Hague
Tel: (070) 3607833 *Fax:* (070) 3615011
Key Personnel
Dir: Dr J DeVuyst
Contact: W Leys
Library & information science.

Nederlandse Vereniging voor beroepsbeoefenaren in de bibliotheeck-informatie-en kennissector (The Netherland Association of Librarians, Documentalists & Information Specialists)
NVB-Verenigingsbureau Plompetorengracht 11, 3512 CA Utrecht
Tel: (030) 2311263 *Fax:* (030) 2311830
E-mail: nvbinfo@wxs.nl
Web Site: www.kb.b.nl/nvb
Key Personnel
President: Dr J S M Savenye
Netherlands Librarians' Society.

Stichting Federatie van Organisaties van Bibliotheek-, Informatie-, Dokumentatiewezen (FOBID)
Postbus 43300, 2504 AH Den Haag
Tel: (070) 3090107 *Fax:* (070) 3090200
E-mail: fobid@nblc.nl
Key Personnel
Chairman: Dr J H de Swart
Secretary: George Koers
Federation of Library Information & Documentation Organizations.
Publication(s): *Cataloguing Rules* (parts 1-8); *Library & Documentation Centres in the Netherlands*; *Library & Documentation Guide*

Netherlands Antilles

Antillion Library Association
c/o Openbare Bibliotheek Curacao, Abr M Chumaceiro Blvd, Willemstad, Curacao
Tel: (09) 4617055 *Fax:* (09) 4656247
Key Personnel
Secretary: Ms Marvis Amerikaan
Publication(s): *APLA Newsletter*

New Zealand

International Association of Music Libraries, New Zealand Branch, Inc
Wellington Public Library, Wellington
Mailing Address: PO Box 1992, Wellington
Tel: (04) 8014040 *Fax:* (04) 8014047
Key Personnel
Secretary: Joanne Horner
Publication(s): *Bibliography of Writings about New Zealand Music Published to end of 1983*; *Crescendo*; *Directory of New Zealand Musical Organizations*; *Orchestral Scores* (Performing Editions list); *Sing!* (Choral Scores Catalogue)

Library & Information Association of New Zealand Aotearoa (LIANZA)
Old Wool House, Level 5, 139-141 Featherston St, Wellington 6001
Mailing Address: PO Box 12-212, Wellington 6038
Tel: (04) 4735834 *Fax:* (04) 4991480
Key Personnel
President: Lisa Tocker
Office Manager: Steve Williams *E-mail:* steve@lianza.org.nz
Founded: 1910
Professional Association.
Publication(s): *DILSINZ* (Directory of information & library services in New Zealand); *Library Life* (magazine, 11 per year); *New Zealand Libraries* (biannual); *Public Libraries of New Zealand* (1995); *Public Library Statistics* (1999); *Valuing the Economic Costs and Benefits of Libraries* (1996); *Who's Who in New Zealand Libraries* (1990)

Nicaragua

Asociacion Nicaraguense de Bibliotecarios y Profesionales a Fines
Apdo Postal 3257, Managua
Key Personnel
Executive Secretary: Susana Morales Hernandez
Nicaraguan Association of Librarians.

Nigeria

Anambra State School Libraries Association
c/o University of Nigeria, Enugu Campus Library, Enugu
Tel: (042) 252080; (042) 332091 *Cable:* Nigersity Enugu
Key Personnel
Honorary Secretary: Virginia W Dike
Publication(s): *Manual for School Libraries on Small Budgets*; *School Libraries Bulletin* (triannually)

Nigerian Library Association
c/o National Library of Nigeria, Gidan Isa, Festival Rd, Garki District, Area 10, Abuja
Tel: (01) 2600220 *Fax:* (01) 631563
Telex: 21746
Key Personnel
President: A O Banjo
Secretary: D D Bwayili
(There are also regional associations in the various states under the umbrella of the Nigerian Library Association).
Publication(s): *Nigerian Libraries* (three a year); *NLA Newsletter*

Norway

Arkivarforeningen
c/o Riksarkivet, Folke Bernadottes Vei 21, 0806 Oslo
Mailing Address: Postboks 10, 0807 Oslo
Tel: 22022600 *Fax:* 22237489
The Association of Archivists.
Publication(s): *Norsk arkivforum*

Norsk Bibliotekforening
Malerhaugveien 20, N-0661 Oslo
Tel: 22688550 *Fax:* 22672368
Key Personnel
Dir: Berit Aaker
Norwegian Library Association.
Publication(s): *Internkontakt*

Riksbibliotektjenesten
Kronprinsensgt 9, Vika, Oslo
Mailing Address: Postboks 8046 Dep, N-0030 Oslo
Tel: 23 11 89 00 *Fax:* 23 11 89 01
E-mail: rbt@rbt.no
Key Personnel
Acting Dir General: Kirsten Engelstad
National Office for Research & Documentation, Academic & Professional Libraries.
Publication(s): *Handbook of Research & Special Libraries* (irregularly); *Skrifter fra Riksbibliotektjenesten* (irregularly); *Synopsis* (6 per year)

Pakistan

Government of Pakistan Department of Libraries
National Library of Pakistan, Constitution Ave, Islamabad
Mailing Address: POB 1982, Islamabad
Tel: (051) 9214523 *Fax:* (051) 9221375
E-mail: nlpiba@paknet2.ptc.pk
Key Personnel
Dir General: Abdul Hafeez Akhtar
Editor: Amjad Majeed
Publication(s): *Accessions List Pakistan* (monthly); *Pakistan National Bibliography* (annually)

Karachi University Library Science Alumni Association
c/o University of Karachi, Dept of Library Science, Karachi 75270
Tel: (021) 479001
Key Personnel
Secretary: S Zia Haider

Library Promotion Bureau
Karachi University Campus, Karachi 75270
Mailing Address: PO Box 8421, Karachi 75270
Key Personnel
President: M Adil Usmani
Secretary General: Nasim Fatima
Publication(s): *Bibliographical Services Throughout Pakistan* (2nd Edition); *Documents Procurement Service*; *Libraries of Pakistan*; *Pakistan Book Trade Directory*; *Pakistan Library Bulletin* (quarterly); *Secondary School Library*

Resources & Services in Pakistan; University Librarianship in Pakistan; Who's Who in Library & Information Science

Pakistan Library Association (PLA)
c/o Pakistan Inst Development Economics, Univ Campus, Islamabad
Mailing Address: PO Box 1091, Islamabad
Tel: (051) 9214041 *Fax:* (051) 9210886
Key Personnel
President: Sain Malik
Secretary General: Atta Ullah
Vice President, Federal Branch: Zafar Javed Naqvi *E-mail:* pide@ish.paknet.com.pk
Founded: 1957
Publication(s): *Code of Ethics for Librarians; PLA Newsletter; Public Libraries Facilities in Pakistan; Standards of College Libraries; Standards of Special Libraries; Standards of University Libraries*

Panama

Asociacion de Bibliotecarios Graduados del Istmo de Panama
c/o Director de la Biblioteca Bio-Medica de Laboratorio Conmemorativo Gorgas, Avda Justo Arosemena No 35-30, Apdo 6991, Panama 5
Tel: 2227411 *Fax:* 2254366
Key Personnel
President: Prof Manuel Victor De Las Casas
Secretary: Iris de Espinosa
Association of Graduate Librarians of the Isthmus of Panama (AGLIP).

Asociacion Panamena de Bibliotecarios
c/o Biblioteca Interamericana Simon Bolivar, Estafeta Universitaria, Panama City
Key Personnel
President: Bexie Rodriguez de Leon
Panama Library Association.
Publication(s): *Boletin*

Paraguay

Asociacion de Bibliotecarios Universitarios del Paraguay
c/o Prof Yoshiko M de Freundorfer, Head, Escuela de Bibliotecologia, Universidad Nacional de Asuncion, Asuncion Casilla 910, 2064 Asuncion
Tel: (021) 507080 *Fax:* (021) 213734
Key Personnel
President: Prof Gloria Ondina Ortiz C
Secretary: Celia Villamayor de Diaz
Paraguayan Association of University Librarians.

Peru

Asociacion de Archiveros del Peru (ADAP)
Archivo Central Salaverry 2020 Jesus Mario, Universidad del Pacifico, 11 Lima 11
Tel: (01) 4712277 *Fax:* (01) 2650958
E-mail: dri@u8p.edu.pe
Key Personnel
President: Jose Luis Abanto Arrelucea
1a Vocal: Yolanda Auqui Chayez
2a Vocal: Denise Ballivian Seminario
Peruvian Association of Archivists.

Asociacion Peruana de Bibliotecarios (APB)
Bellavista 561 Miraflores Apdo 995, Lima 18
Tel: (01) 474869
Key Personnel
President: Martha Fernandez de Lopez
Secretary: Luzmila Tello de Medina
Peruvian Association of Librarians.

Biblioteca Agricola Nacional/Universidad Nacional Agraria La Molina
Av La Universidad, s/n La Molina, Apdo 456, Lima 12
Tel: (01) 4352035 *Fax:* (01) 4352473
E-mail: ban@unaln.edu.pe
Key Personnel
Contact: Alejandro Fukusaki Yoshizawd
Association of Agricultural Librarians.

Philippines

Association of Special Libraries of the Philippines (ASLP)
National Library Bldg, Room 301, T M Kalaw St, 2801 Manila
Tel: (02) 590177 *Fax:* (02) 590177
Key Personnel
President: Zenaida F Lucas
Secretary: Socorro G Elevera
Publication(s): *ASLP Bulletin* (annually); *Directory of Special Library Resources and Research Facilities in the Philippines*

Bibliographical Society of the Philippines
National Library of the Philippines, T M Kalaw, 1000 Ermita, Manila
Mailing Address: PO Box 2926, 1000 Ermita, Manila
Tel: (02) 583252; (02) 5253196 *Fax:* (02) 502329; (02) 5242329
E-mail: amb@max.ph.net
Key Personnel
Secretary-Treasurer: Leticia R Maloles

Philippine Librarians Association Inc
c/o National Library, T M Kalaw St, Room 301, 1000 Manila, Ermita
Mailing Address: PO Box 2926, 1000 Manila, Erimta
Tel: (02) 590177
Key Personnel
President: Atty Antonio M Sontos
Secretary: Rosemarie Rosali
Publication(s): *PLAI Bulletin* (annually); *PLAI Newsletter* (biannaully)

Poland

Stowarzyszenie Bibliotekarzy Polskich
8-10 Czerwca, 2001 Warsaw-Miedzeszyn
Tel: (022) 8230270 *Fax:* (022) 8225133
Key Personnel
Chairman: Stanislaw Czajka
Secretary General: Janina Jagielska
Polish Librarians' Association.
Publication(s): *Bibliotekarz* (The Librarian); *Poradnik Bibliotekarza* (The Librarian's Adviser); *Przeglad Biblioteczny* (Library Review)

Portugal

Associacao Portuguesa de Bibliotecarios, Arquivistas e Documentalistas (The Portuguese Association of Librarians Archivists & Documentalists)
R Morais Soares, 43C-1 DTD, 1900-341 Lisbon Codex
Tel: (021) 8154479; (021) 8134697 *Fax:* (021) 8154508
E-mail: badbn@mail.telepac.pt
Key Personnel
President: Ernestina de Castro
Contact: Sandrine Jercaeret
Portuguese Association of Librarians, Archivists & Documentalists.
Publication(s): *Cadernos de Biblioteconomia, Arquivistica e Documentacao* (biannually)

Puerto Rico

Sociedad de Bibliotecarios de Puerto Rico
Apdo 22898, Universidad de Puerto Rico Station, San Juan 00931
Tel: (787) 764-0000 (ext 5204) *Fax:* (787) 763-5685
E-mail: vtorres@upracd.upr.clu.edu
Key Personnel
President: Aura Jimenez de Panepinto
Secretary: Olga L Hernandez
Society of Librarians of Puerto Rico.
Publication(s): *Boletin, Informa* (Newsletter); *Cuadernos Bibliotecologicos, Cuadernos Bibliograficos*

Senegal

ASBAD, see Association Senegalaise de Bibliothecaires, Archivistes et Documentalistes, (ASBAD)

Association Senegalaise de Bibliothecaires, Archivistes et Documentalistes, (ASBAD)
BP 3252, Dakar
Tel: 246981 *Fax:* 242379
Key Personnel
President: Marietou Diongue Diop
Secretary: Emmanuel Kabou
Publication(s): *Canal-ist*

Sierra Leone

Sierra Leone Association of Archivists, Librarians and Information Scientists (SLAALIS)
c/o Sierra Leone Library Board, Freetown
Mailing Address: PO Box 326, Freetown
Tel: 223848
Key Personnel
President: Deanna Thomas
Publication(s): *SLAALIS Bulletin* (quarterly)

Singapore

Library Association of Singapore
c/o Bukit Merah Central, Singapore 911537
Mailing Address: PO Box 0693, Singapore 911537
Key Personnel
Honorary Secretary: Siti Hanifah Mustapha
Congress of South East Asian Libraries, Singapore, 2000.
Publication(s): *Directory of Information Databases in Singapore*; *Directory of Libraries in Singapore*; *Singapore Libraries* (annually); *Singapore Libraries Bulletin* (quarterly)

Slovenia

ZBDS, see Zveza bibliotekarskih drustev Slovenije (ZBDS) Slovenian Library Association

Zveza bibliotekarskih drustev Slovenije (ZBDS) Slovenian Library Association
(Union of Associations of Slovene Librarians)
Turjaska 1, 1000 Ljubljana
Tel: (01) 200 1193 *Fax:* (01) 251 3052
Web Site: www.zbds-zveza.si
Key Personnel
President: Irena Sesek *Tel:* (01) 586 1309 *E-mail:* irena.sesek@nuk.uni-lj.si
Secretary: Liljana Hubej
Founded: 1947
Library Association of Slovenia.
Publication(s): *Knjiznica* (Library, quarterly, 1957)

South Africa

African Library Association of South Africa (ALASA), see Library & Information Association of South Africa (LIASA)

LIASA, see Library & Information Association of South Africa (LIASA)

Library & Information Association of South Africa (LIASA)
Formerly African Library Association of South Africa (ALASA); South African Institute for Librarianship & Information Science (SAILIS)
PO Box 1598, Pretoria 0001
Tel: (012) 481 2870; (012) 481 2871; (012) 481 2872; (012) 481 2875 *Fax:* (012) 481 2873
E-mail: liasa@liasa.org.za
Web Site: www.liasa.org.za
Key Personnel
Executive Dir: Mrs Gwenda Thomas
Publication(s): *LIASA-IN-Touch* (quarterly, magazine); *LIASA News* (quarterly, newsletter); *South African Journal of Library and Information Science* (biannually, journal)

South African Institute for Librarianship & Information Science (SAILIS), see Library & Information Association of South Africa (LIASA)

Spain

Asociacion Espanola de Archiveros, Bibliotecarios, Museologos y Documentalistas
Recoletos 5, 28001 Madrid
Tel: (091) 5751727 *Fax:* (091) 5751727
Key Personnel
President: Julia M Rodriguez Barrero
Spanish Association of Archivists, Librarians, Curators and Documentalists.
Publication(s): *Boletin* (with bibliography section)

Sri Lanka

National Library of Sri Lanka Library Services Board
No 14, Independence Ave, Colombo 07
Mailing Address: PO Box 1764, Colombo 07
Tel: (01) 685203; (01) 685199; (01) 698847 *Fax:* (01) 685201
E-mail: nldsb@mail.natlib.lk
Key Personnel
Dir, General: M S U Amarasiri *Tel:* (01) 687581 *E-mail:* dgnl@sltnet.lk
Publication(s): *Sri Lanka News paper article Index-1993* (conference index); *Directory of Social Science Libraries, Information Centres & Data Bases in Sri Lanka*; *International Standard Book Numbering in Sri Lanka* (brochure); *Library News* (quarterly); *Pustakala Dave Bhanda*; *Sri Lanka (ISBN) Publishers Directory*; *Sri Lanka National Bibliography* (monthly)

Sri Lanka Library Association
Professional Center, 275/75 Bauddhaloka Mawatha, Colombo 7
Tel: (01) 589103
E-mail: postmast@slla.ac.lk
Key Personnel
President: Mr Harrison Perera
Vice President: Mrs Sumana Jayasuriya; Mrs Daya Ratnayake
Secretary: Mr Wilfred Ranasinghe
Publication Officer: Mrs Swarna Jayatillake
Assistant Secretary: Mrs Deepali Talagala
Education Officer: Mr H M Guneratna Banda
Assistant Education Officer: Mr J Ratnayake
Treasurer: Mr Anton D Nallathamby
Librarian: Mr M B M Fairooz
Publication(s): *SLLA News Letter* (quarterly); *Sri Lanka Library Review* (biannually)

Swaziland

Swaziland Library Association
PO Box 2309, Mbabane
Tel: 43101 *Fax:* 42641
Telex: 2270 wd (c; o British Council)
Key Personnel
Chairman: L Dlamini
Secretary: P Muswazi

Sweden

Svenska Arkivsamfundet (Swedish Society of Archivists)
Malmtorgsg 3, S-10339 Stockholm
Tel: (08) 405100 *Fax:* (08) 6579564
Web Site: www.arkivsamfundet.org
Key Personnel
President: Berndt Fredriksson *E-mail:* berndt.fredriksson@foreign.office.se
Swedish Association of Archivists.
Publication(s): *Arkiv, Samhaelle, Forskning* (Archives, Society, Research, biannually)

Sveriges Allmaenna Biblioteksfoerening
Saltmaetargatan 3A, S-103 62 Stockholm
Mailing Address: PO Box 3127, S-103 62 Stockholm
Tel: (08) 54513230; (08) 54513230 (SAB office) *Fax:* (08) 54513231
Web Site: www.sab.se/
Key Personnel
Secretary General: Christina Stenberg *Tel:* (08) 54513233 *E-mail:* christina.stenberg@sab.se
Editor & Chief: Marianne Steinsaphir *E-mail:* m.steinsaphir@bbl.sab.se
Swedish Library Association.
Publication(s): *Biblioteksbladet* (The Library Journal, 10x/yr)

Tekniska Litteratursaellskapet
Box 55580, S-102 04 Stockholm
Tel: (08) 6782320 *Fax:* (08) 6782301
E-mail: kansliet@tls.se
Key Personnel
President: L Lindskog
Secretary: K Wahl
Swedish Society for Technical Documentation.
Publication(s): *Tidskrift foer Dokumentation* (quarterly)

Switzerland

Association des Bibliotheques et Bibliothecaires Suisses
Effingerstr 35, CH-3008 Bern
Tel: (031) 3824240 *Fax:* (031) 3824648
E-mail: bbs@bbs.ch
Web Site: www.bbs.ch
Key Personnel
General Secretary: Marianne Tschaeppat *E-mail:* tschaeppaet@bbs.ch
Association of Swiss Librarians & Libraries.
Publication(s): *Arbido* (jointly with Swiss Association for Documentation & Swiss Association of Archivists monthly)

Schweizerische Vereinigung fur Dokumentation
Schmidgasse 4, Postfach 601, CH-6301 Zug
Tel: (041) 7264505 *Fax:* (041) 7264509
Key Personnel
President: St Hollaander
Secretary: H Schweuk

Verband der Bibliotheken und der Bibliothekarinnen/Bibliothekare der Schweiz (BBS), see Association des Bibliotheques et Bibliothecaires Suisses

Verein Schweizerischer Archivarinnen und Archivare (Association des archivistes suisses/Associazione degli archivista svizzeri/Uniun da las asrchivarias e dals archivaris svizzers)
Member of ICA
Schweizerisches Bundesarchiv, Aarchivsor 24, 3003 Bern
Tel: (031) 322 89 89; (031) 322 92 85
Web Site: www.staluzern.ch/vsa
Key Personnel
Pres: Andreas Lellerhals *E-mail:* andreas.lellerhals@bar.admin.ch
Founded: 1922

SWITZERLAND

Association of Swiss Archivists.
Publication(s): *Arbido*

Taiwan, Province of China

Library Association of China
National Central Library, 20 Chungshan S Rd, Taipei 100-01
Tel: (02) 23312475 *Fax:* (02) 23700899
E-mail: lac@msg.ncl.edu.tw
Web Site: www.lac.ncl.edu.tw
Key Personnel
President: Huang Shih-wson
Secretary General: Teresa Wang Chang
Publication(s): *Library Association of China Bulletin* (semi-annually); *Library Association of China Newsletter* (quarterly)

United Republic of Tanzania

Tanzania Library Association
POB 2645, Dar Es Salaam
Tel: (051) 4026121
Key Personnel
Chairman: T E Mlaki
Secretary: Ms A Ngaiza
Publication(s): *Matukio* (TLA newsletter); *Someni* (journal)

Thailand

Thai Library Association
273 Vibhavadee Rangsit Rd Phayathai, Bangkok 10400
Tel: (02) 2712084
Key Personnel
President: K Chavallt
Secretary: Miss Karnmanee Suckcharoen

Togo

Association Togolaise pour le Developpement de la Documentation des Bibliotheques, Archives et Musees
c/o Bibliotheque de l'Universite du Benin, BP 1515, Lome
Tel: 213027 *Fax:* 218784
Key Personnel
Secretary: E E Amah

ATODBAM, see Association Togolaise pour le Developpement de la Documentation des Bibliotheques, Archives et Musees

Trinidad & Tobago

Library Association of Trinidad & Tobago
PO Box 1275, Port of Spain
Tel: (0868) 687 0194
Key Personnel
President: Gemma Crichton
Secretary: Ernesta Greenidge *E-mail:* secretary@latt.org.tt
Founded: 1960
Publication(s): *Blatt* (Bulletin of the Library Association of Trinidad and Tobago annually)

Tunisia

Association Tunisienne des Documentalistes, Bibliothecaires et Archivistes
BP 380, 1015 Tunis
Key Personnel
President: Ahmed Ksibi
Tunisian Association of Record-Keepers, Librarians and Archivists.
Publication(s): *L'Enfant et la Lecture*; *RASSID*

Turkey

Tuerk Kueuephaneciler Dernegi
Elguen Sok-8/8, 06440 Yenisehir, Ankara
Tel: (0312) 2301325 *Fax:* (0312) 2320453
Key Personnel
President: A Berberoglu
Secretary: A Kaygusuz
Turkish Librarians' Association.
Publication(s): *Tuerk Kuetuiphaneciligi* (4 a year)

Uganda

Uganda Library Association
PO Box 5894, Kampala
Tel: (0141) 285001 ext 4
Key Personnel
Chairman: Elisam Naghra
Secretary: Charles Batembyze
Founded: 1972
Discussing the usage of libraries & their information resources in Uganda.
Publication(s): *Uganda Information Bulletin* (quarterly, newsletter); *Ugandan Libraries* (biannual)

United Kingdom

ARLIS/UK & Ireland, The Art Libraries Society
18 College Rd, Bromsgrove, Worcs B60 2NE
Tel: (01527) 579298 *Fax:* (01527) 579298
Key Personnel
Administrator: Sonia French *E-mail:* sfrench@arlis.demon.co.uk
Founded: 1969
Professional body for librarians & all concerned with the documentation of virtual art.
Publication(s): *ARLIS News-sheet* (6 times a year); *Art Libraries Journal* (quarterly); *Annual Directory* (annually)

Aslib, The Association for Information Management
60/62 Toller Lane, Bradford BD8 9BY
Tel: (01274) 777 700 *Fax:* (01274) 785 200
E-mail: pubs@aslib.com
Web Site: www.aslib.co.uk
Key Personnel
Dir: R B Bowes
Head of Publications: Sarah Blair
Publication(s): *Aslib Book Guide* (monthly); *Aslib Proceedings* (monthly); *Current Awareness Abstracts* (monthly); *Forthcoming International Scientific & Technical References* (quarterly); *International Journal of Electronic Library Reseach* (quarterly); *IT Link* (monthly); *Journal of Documentation* (annually); *Managing Information* (monthly); *Program* (quarterly)

Association of London Chief Librarians
c/o Central Library, St Nicholas Way, Sutton Surrey SM1 1EA
Tel: (0181) 7704760 *Fax:* (0181) 7704777
Key Personnel
Head Libraries & Heritage: Trevor Knight

The Association for Information Management, see Aslib, The Association for Information Management

Association of British Theological & Philosophical Libraries
Dr Williams's Library, 14 Gordon Sq, London WC1H 0AG
Tel: (020) 7387 3727
Key Personnel
Secretary: Colin Clarke *E-mail:* colin.clarke@dwlib.co.uk
Publication(s): *Bulletin of ABTAPL* (triannually); *Guide to Theological & Religious Studies Collections & Great Britain & Ireland*

Bibliographical Society
c/o The Wellcome Library, 183 Easton Rd, London NW1 2BE
Tel: (020) 7611 7244 *Fax:* (020) 7611 8703
Key Personnel
Honorary Secretary: David Pearson *E-mail:* d.pearson@wellcome.ac.uk
Founded: 1892
Publication(s): *The Library* (quarterly, various books on bibliographical subjects)

Book Aid International
39-41 Coldharbour Lane, Camberwell, London SE5 9NR
Tel: (020) 7733 3577 *Fax:* (020) 7978 8006
E-mail: info@bookaid.org
Web Site: www.bookaid.org
Key Personnel
Chairman: Tim Rix
Dir: Sara Harrity
Deputy Dir: David Membrey *E-mail:* david.membrey@bookaid.org
Book aid charity sending about 750,000 new & used books a year to partners in developing world countries & supporting development of local publishing.

British & Irish Association of Law Librarians
Lincoln's Inn Library, London W2CA 3TN
Tel: (020) 7242 4371 *Fax:* (020) 7404 1864
E-mail: holborn@linclib.sonnet.co.uk

ASSOCIATIONS

Key Personnel
Honorary Secretary: Guy Holborn
Publication(s): *The Law Librarian*

Chartered Institute of Library & Information Professionals
Formerly The Library Association; Institute of Information Scientists
7 Ridgmount St, London WC1E 7AE
Tel: (020) 7255 0500; (020) 7255 0505 (textphone) *Fax:* (020) 7255 0501
E-mail: info@cilip.org.uk
Web Site: www.cilip.org.uk
Key Personnel
Chief Executive: Bob McKee
Member Services: Sue Brown
Founded: 2002
Professional body for librarians & information managers.
Publication(s): *Update* (monthly, magazine)
Imprints: Facet Publishing

CILIP, see Chartered Institute of Library & Information Professionals

Circle of State Librarians
Home Office Library, ISU Resources, Queen Anne's Gate, London SW1H 9AT
Tel: (020) 7273 4463
Key Personnel
Honorary Secy: Miss L A Cooper
Publication(s): *State Librarian* (triannually)

CSL, see Circle of State Librarians

Facet Publishing, *imprint of* Chartered Institute of Library & Information Professionals

Facet Publishing
Imprint of Chartered Institute of Library & Information Professionals (CILIP)
7 Ridgmount St, London WC1E 7AE
Tel: (020) 7255 0594 *Fax:* (020) 7255 0591
E-mail: info@facetpublishing.co.uk
Web Site: www.facetpublishing.co.uk
Key Personnel
Man Dir: Janet Liebster
Publisher: Helen Carley
Marketing Executive: Mark O'Loughlin *Tel:* (020) 7255 0597 *E-mail:* mark.o'loughlin@facetpublishing.co.uk
Professional body for librarians & information managers.
Publication(s): *A Directory of Libraries in the UK & Ireland*; *A Directory of Rare Books & Special Collections in the UK & Ireland*; *A Guide to World Language Dictionaries*; *The Successful LIS Professional Series*; *Walfords Guide to Reference Material* (3 vols)

Friends of the National Libraries
The British Library, Great Russell St, London WC1B 3DG
Tel: (020) 7412 7559
Key Personnel
Chairman: Lord Egremont
Honorary Secretary: Michael Borrie

Impact
c/o The Library Association, 7 Ridgmount St, London WC1E 7AE
Mailing Address: Engineering Employer's Federation, Broadway House, Tothill St, London SW1H 9NQ
Tel: (020) 7222 7777; (020) 7636 7543 *Fax:* (020) 7222 2782; (020) 7436 7218
Key Personnel
President: Peter Loewenstein
The National Conference, Reading, May 1998.

Publication(s): *Adult Sequels*; *Children's Sequels*; *EU Information Sources*; *Counter Point Series*; *Cumulated Fiction Index*; *Fiction Index*; *Junior Fiction Index*; *Picture Book Index*

Institute of Information Scientists, see Chartered Institute of Library & Information Professionals

International Association of Music Libraries, Archives & Documentation Centres (UK & Irl Branch)
Edinburgh City Libraries, 9 George IV Bridge, Edinburgh EH1 1EG
Tel: (0131) 242 8053 *Fax:* (0131) 242 8009
Key Personnel
General Secretary: Peter Baxter
E-mail: pbbaxter@hotmail.com
Founded: 1953
Publication(s): *Brio* (biannually)

The Library Association, see Chartered Institute of Library & Information Professionals

School Library Association
Unit 2, Lotmead Business Village, Lotmead Farm, Wanborough, Swindon, Wilts SN4 0UY
Tel: (01793) 791787 *Fax:* (01793) 791786
E-mail: info@sla.org.uk
Web Site: www.sla.org.uk
Key Personnel
President: Prof Frank N Hogg
Chief Executive: Kathy Lemaire *E-mail:* kathy@sla.org.uk
Founded: 1937
Promote the development of effective school libraries through advocacy, publishing & training.
Publication(s): *The School Librarian* (quarterly; also practical guidelines on school library management & annotated book lists)

Scottish Library Association
One John St, Hamilton ML3 7EU
Tel: (01698) 458888 *Fax:* (01698) 458899; (01698) 628159
E-mail: sla@slainte.org.uk
Web Site: www.slainte.org.uk
Key Personnel
Dir: Robert Craig, Obe
Publication(s): *Scottish Libraries* (every two months)

SHINE-Scottish Health Information Network
c/o Maureen Thom, Management Development Group, Scottish Health Center Library, Crewe Rd South, Edinburgh EH4 2LF
Tel: (0131) 6232535 *Fax:* (0131) 3152369
E-mail: mdg@ednet.co.uk
Key Personnel
Contact: Maureen Thom
Publication(s): *Directory of Health Information Resources in Scotland*
Branch Office(s)
Erskine Medical Library, Hugh Robson Bldg, George Square, Edinburgh EH8 9XE *Tel:* (031) 650-3692

Society of Archivists
40 Northampton Rd, London EC1R OHB
Tel: (020) 7278 8630 *Fax:* (020) 7278 2107
E-mail: societyofarchivists@archives.org.uk
Web Site: www.archives.org.uk
Key Personnel
Executive Secretary: Mr P S Cleary
Publication(s): *Careers Opportunities* (monthly); *Journal of the Society of Archivists* (biannually, newsletter)

Society of College, National & University Libraries (SCONUL)
102 Euston St, London NW1 2HA
Tel: (020) 7387 0317 *Fax:* (020) 7383 3197
Key Personnel
Executive Secretary: A J C Bainton

The Society of County Librarians
Leeds Library & Information Service, The Town Hall, The Headrow, Leeds LS1 8NZ
Tel: (0113) 2478330 *Fax:* (0113) 2478331
Key Personnel
Assistant Dir: Catherine Blanshard
E-mail: catherine.blanshard@leeds.gov.uk
Aim is to further the position of public libraries across England, Northern Ireland & Wales to influence decision makers.

Welsh Library Association
c/o Publications Office, Dept of Information & Library Studies, Llanbadarn Fawr, Aberystwyth Dyfed SY23 3AS
Tel: (01970) 622174 *Fax:* (01970) 622190
E-mail: hle@aber.ac.uk
Key Personnel
Executive Officer: Huw Evans *E-mail:* hle@aber.ac.uk
Subjects: Professional Association
Publication(s): *Index to Poetry Wales, Wales, O M Edwards, Welsh Outlook*; *Who's Who In Welsh Librarianship 1999*; *Mynegai i Cymru, Yr Efrydydd, Llenor, Lleufer, Taliesin, Y Traethodydd*; *Teifi Library Project*; *The Festiniog Railway 1954-1994: A Bibliography, Andrew R Johnson*

Uruguay

Agrupacion Bibliotecologica del Uruguay
(Group Librarian of Uruguay)
Cerro Largo 1666, Montevideo 11200
Tel: (02) 400 57 40
Key Personnel
President: Luis Alberto Musso
Founded: 1964
Uruguayan Library & Archive Science Association.
Publication(s): *Anales del Senado del Uruguay* (Annals of the Senate of Uruguay, 1971); *Aportes para la historia de la bibliotecologia en el Uruguay* (Library Proffesion story, 1969); *Archivos del Uruguay* (Uruguay archives, 1974); *Bibliografia bibliografica y bibliotecologica* (Bibliography, 1964); *Bibliografia de Historia del Uruguay* (Bibliography History, 1977); *Bibliografia uruguaya sobre Brasil* (Brasil Bibliography, 1973); *La Estrella del sur-Indice* (The Southern Star, 1968); *Colonizacion Canaria en la Banda Oriental del Uruguay* (Canary of Uruguay Colonization, 1997); *El Dia - Indice General Alfabetico* (The Day - Indice General Alfabetico); *Fernandez Saldana, relacion de su obra bibliografica* (Fernandez Saldana Bibliography, 1989); *El Rio de la Plata en el Archivo General de Indias* (The River Plate in Archive General of Indias, 1997); *De Libros y lectores* (Books and Readers, 2000); *Uruguay-Brasil y sus medallas* (Uruguay Brasil Medals, 1976)

Asociacion de Bibliotecologos del Uruguay
(Uruguayan Library Association)
Eduardo V Haedo 2255, 11200 Montevideo
Mailing Address: PO Box 1315, 11000 Montevideo
Tel: (02) 4099989 *Fax:* (02) 4099989
E-mail: ABU@adinet.com.uy
Key Personnel
President: Eduardo Correa

Venezuela

Colegio de Bibliotecologos y Archivologos de Venezuela, see Venezuelan Library & Archives Association

Venezuelan Library & Archives Association
Apdo 6283, Caracas
Tel: (02) 5721858
Key Personnel
President: Elsi Jimenez de Diaz

Viet Nam

Hoi Thu-Vien Viet Nam
National Library of Viet Nam, 31 Trang Thi, 10000 Hanoi
Tel: (04) 8252643
Vietnamese Library Association.
Publication(s): *Thu'-Vien Tap-san* (Library Bulletin)

Yugoslavia

Jugoslovenski Bibliografsko-Informacijski Institut (Yugoslav Institute for Bibliography & Information)
Terazije 26, 11000 Belgrade
Tel: (011) 687836; (011) 688927 *Fax:* (011) 687760; (011) 38111
Key Personnel
Dir: Dr Radomir Glavicki
Yugoslav Institute for Bibliography information publishes Bibliografija Jugoslavije (Yugoslavia Bibliography) which includes books, pamphlets, music scores & articles of literary, scientific interest, philology, art & sport.
Publication(s): *Belgrade*; *Universal Decimal Classification, International* (Serbacroatian version)

Zambia

Zambia Library Association
PO Box 32839, Lusaka
Key Personnel
Chairman: C Zulu
Honorary Secretary: W C Mulalami
Publication(s): *Zambia Library Association Journal*; *Zambia Library Association Newsletter*

Zimbabwe

Library & Information Science Society
c/o Harare Polytechnic, Causeway, Harare
Mailing Address: PO Box CY 8074, Causeway, Harare
Tel: (04) 752311
Key Personnel
Contact: Dakarai Mashava

Zimbabwe Library Association
PO Box 3133, Harare
Key Personnel
Chairman: Driden Kunaka
Honorary Secretary: Albert Masheka
Publication(s): *The Zimbabwean Librarian*

Founded: 1978
Professional Association.
Publication(s): *Panel de Noticias* (News Board, monthly; free to members only)

Library Reference Books & Journals

The publications in this section are library related and are listed alphabetically under the country of the publisher.

The type of publication appears in parentheses after the title:

    (B) - Book   (J) - Journal   (P) - Periodical

For information on reference books, journals and periodicals relating to the book publishing industry see **Book Trade Reference Books & Journals**.

Argentina

Guia de las Bibliotecas Universitarias Argentinas (Guide to Argentine University Libraries) (B)
Published by Centro de Documentacion Bibliotecologica, Universidad Nacional del Sur
Avda Alem 1253, 8000 Bahia Blanca
Tel: (091) 28035 ext 255 *Fax:* (091) 551447
Key Personnel
Chief Librarian: Marta Ibarlucca

Referencias (References) (J)
Published by AGBRA (Asociacion de Bibliotecarios Graduados de la Republica Argentina)
Tucuman 1424, 8 piso D, 1050 Buenos Aires
Tel: (011) 4373-0571 *Fax:* (011) 4371-5269
E-mail: abgra@ciudad.com.ar
Web Site: abgra.sisbi-uba.ar
Key Personnel
President: Ana Maria Peruchena Zimmermann

Australia

ABN Catalogue (J)
Published by Australian Bibliographic Network, National Library of Australia
Parkes Pl, Canberra, ACT 2600
Tel: (02) 6262-1111 *Fax:* (02) 6257-1703
E-mail: www@nla.gov.au
Web Site: www.nla.gov.au
Bimonthly.

Access (J)
Published by Australian School Library Association Inc
PO Box 450, Belconnen, ACT 2616
Tel: (02) 62311870 *Fax:* (02) 62312092
E-mail: asladaw@atrax.net.au
Web Site: www.asla.org.au
Quarterly.

Australian Academic & Research Libraries (J)
Published by Australian Library & Information Association
PO Box E441, Kingston, ACT 2604
Tel: (02) 6285-1877 *Fax:* (02) 6282-2249
E-mail: pre@comserver.canberra.edu.au
Key Personnel
Editor: Dr Peter Clayton
Quarterly.
$106 AUD (overseas Air)

Australian Librarian's Manual (Vols I, II & III) (B)
Published by Australian Library & Information Association (ALIA)
Kingston, ACT 2604
Mailing Address: PO Box E441, Kingston, ACT 2604
Tel: (02) 62851877 *Fax:* (02) 62822249
E-mail: enquiry@alia.org.au
Web Site: www.alia.org.au
Key Personnel
Editor: David J Jones

Australian Libraries: the Essential Directory (B)
Published by Auslib Press Pty Ltd
PO Box 622, Blackwood, SA 5051
Tel: (08) 8278 4363 *Fax:* (08) 8278 4000
E-mail: auslib@mail.camtech.met.au
Biennially.

Australian Library Journal (J)
Published by Australian Library & Information Association
9-11 Napier Close, Deakin 2600
Mailing Address: PO Box E441, Kingston, ACT 2604
Tel: (02) 6285-1877 *Fax:* (02) 6282-2249
E-mail: alj@alia.org.au
Web Site: www.alia.org.au/alj
Key Personnel
Editor: John Levett
Academic/scholarly publication.
First published 1951.
Quarterly.
$106 AUD (Overseas air)

Cataloguing Australia (J)
Published by Australian Library & Information Association
9-11 Napier Close, Deakin 2600
Mailing Address: PO Box E441, Kingston, ACT 2604
Tel: (02) 6285-1877 *Fax:* (02) 6282-2249
E-mail: enquiry@alia.org.au
Quarterly.

Directory of Special Libraries in Australia (B)
Published by Australian Library & Information Association
9-11 Napier Close, Deakin 2600
Mailing Address: PO Box E441, Kingston, ACT 2604
Tel: (02) 6285-1877 *Fax:* (02) 6282-2249
Key Personnel
Editor: David J Jones

inCite (J)
Published by Australian Library & Information Association
9-11 Napier Close, Deakin 2600
Mailing Address: PO Box E441, Kingston, ACT 2604
Tel: (02) 6285-1877 *Fax:* (02) 6282-2249
E-mail: incite@alia.org.au
Web Site: www.alia.org.au
Key Personnel
Editor: Emma Davis *E-mail:* emma.davis@alia.org.au
Managing Editor: Ivan Trundle
Newsletter.
First published 1980.
Monthly.
$AUD 129.00 (Overseas air)
ISSN: 0158-0876

Orana (J)
Published by Australian Library & Information Association
9-11 Napier Close, Deakin ACT 2600
Tel: (02) 6285 1877 *Fax:* (02) 6282 2249
E-mail: enquiry@alia.org.au
Web Site: www.alia.org.au
Key Personnel
Editor: Margaret Steinberger
Production Editor: Shirley Campbell
 E-mail: shirley.campbell@alianet.alia.org.au
Children's, youth services & school libraries journal.
3 times per year.
ISSN: 0045-6705

Our Heritage: A Directory to Archives and Manuscript Repositories in Australia (B)
Published by Australian Society of Archivists
PO Box 34, Dickson, Act 2602
Tel: (06) 2093633 *Fax:* (06) 2093931
Key Personnel
Dir General: G E Nichols

La Trobe Journal (P)
Published by Friends of the State Library of Victoria
328 Swanston St, Melbourne, Victoria 3000
Tel: (03) 9669-9888 *Fax:* (03) 9663-1480
E-mail: webinfo@slv.vic.gov.au
Web Site: www.slv.vic.gov.au
Key Personnel
Editor: Prof John Barnes *E-mail:* rjbarnes@latrobe.edu.au
Biannually.
ISSN: 1441-3760

Austria

Biblos (J)
Published by Gesellschaft der Freunde der Osterreichischen Nationalbibliothek
Boenlau Verlag GmbH & Co, Sachsenplatz 4-6, A-1201 Vienna
Tel: (01) 3302427; (01) 3302420 *Fax:* (01) 3302432
Telex: 12624
Austrian journal for book & library personnel, documentation, bibliography & bibliophily; published in English & German.
First published 1952.
Semiannually.

Austria

INFODOC 1994 Bibliotheken, Informations- und Dokumentationseinrichtungen in Oesterreich (Information Guide to Libraries and Documentation Centres in Austria) (B)
Published by Bundesministerium fur Wissenschaft, Forschung, und Kunst
Minoritenplatz 5, 111/1, 1010 Vienna
Tel: (01) 53120 *Fax:* (01) 6530; (01) 53120

Mitteilungen der Vereinigung oesterreichischer Bibliothekarinnen und Bibliothekare (Bulletin of the Association of Austrian Librarians) (J)
Published by Vereinigung Oesterreichischer Bibliothekarinnen und Bibliothekare (VOeB)
Innrain 50, A-6010 Innsbruck
Tel: (0512) 4000-84936 *Fax:* (0512) 5072893
Key Personnel
Manager & Editor: Maria Seissel *E-mail:* maria.sei551@uibk.ac.at
First published 1948.
Quarterly.
ISSN: 1022-2588

Scrinium (J)
Published by Verband Oesterreichischer Archivare
Postfach 164, A-1014 Vienna
Tel: (01) 79540450 *Fax:* (01) 79540109
Key Personnel
Ed: Rainer Egger
Journal of the Association of Austrian Archivists.
First published 1969.
Biannually.
ISSN: 1012-0327

Bangladesh

Eastern Librarian (P)
Published by The Library Association of Bangladesh
c/o Bangladesh Central Public Library Bldg, Institute of Library & Information Science Bldg, Shahbagh Ramna, Shahbagh, Dhaka 1000
Tel: (02) 504269
E-mail: msik@icddrb.org
Key Personnel
Ed: M Shamsol Islam Khan
Published biannually, text in English.
First published 1966.
ISSN: 1021-3651

Barbados

Bulletin of the Library Association of Barbados (J)
Published by Library Association of Barbados
PO Box 827E, Bridgetown
Key Personnel
President: Shirley Yearwood
Irregularly.
First published 1968.

Belgium

Archives et Bibliotheques de Belgique (Library Archives of Belgium) (J)
Boulevard de l'Empereur 4, B-1000 Brussels
Tel: (02) 519 5393 *Fax:* (02) 519 5679
Key Personnel
Chairman & Rights & Permissions: Frank Daelemans *E-mail:* frank.daelemans@klr.be
Text in Dutch, English, French, German, Italian, Latin & Spanish.
First published 1923.
Irregular, 1-2 a year.
ISSN: 0003-9748

Bibliotheek- & archiefgids (Library & Archive Guide) (J)
Published by Vlaamse Vereniging voor Bibliotheek- Archief-en Documentatiewezen (VVBAD) (Flemish Association for Libraries, Archives & Documentation Centres)
Statiestraat 179, 2600 Antwerp
Tel: (03) 2814457 *Fax:* (03) 2188077
Web Site: www.vvbad.be
Key Personnel
Editor: Peter Van den Broeck
Editorial Secretary: Marijke Hoflack *E-mail:* marijke.hoflack@vvbad.be
First published 1922.
Bi-monthly.
48 pp
ISSN: 0772-7003

Cahiers de la Documentation (J)
Published by Association Belge de Documentation (Belgian Association for Documentation)
Chaussee de Wavre 1683, Waversesteenweg, Brussels 1160
Tel: (02) 6755862 *Fax:* (02) 6727446
E-mail: abdbvd@abd-bvd.be
Web Site: www.abd-bvd.be
Text in Dutch, English & French.
First published 1947.
Quarterly.
49.58 Euro/year
ISSN: 0007-9804

Bosnia and Herzegovina

Bibliotekarstvo (Librarianship) (J)
Published by Drustvo Bibliotekara Bosne i Hercegovine
Zmaja od Bosne 8B, 71000 Sarajevo
Tel: (071) 212-435; (071) 275301 *Fax:* (071) 212-435; (071) 533204
Key Personnel
President: Nevenka Hajdarovic *E-mail:* nevenka@utic.net.ba
First published 1956.
ISSN: 0006-1832

Brazil

Ciencia da Informacao (J)
Published by Instituto Brasileiro de Informacao em Ciencia e Tecnologia
SAS Qd 5, Lote 6, Bloco H, CEP 70070-000 Brasilia DF
Tel: (061) 2176369 *Fax:* (061) 2262677
Key Personnel
Dir: Jose Rincon Ferreira
Information Science (triannually).

Noticias (J)
Published by Federacao Brasileira de Associacoes de Bibliotecarios - Comissao Brasileira de Documentacao Juridica (FEBAB/CBDJ)
Rua Avanhandava 40, Conj 110, 01306 Sao Paulo
Tel: (011) 2579979
Key Personnel
President: Joao Carlos Gomes Ribeiro
News.

Bulgaria

Biblioteka (J)
Published by St Cyril & St Methodius National Library
Vassil Levski 88, 1504 Sofia
Tel: (02) 882811 *Fax:* (02) 435495
E-mail: nbkm@bgcict.acad.bg
Key Personnel
Dir Prof: Dr Kiril Topalov
The Library.

China

Library & Information Service (P)
Published by Library of Chinese Academy of Sciences
8 Kexueyuan, Nanlu, Zhongguancun, Beijing 100080
Tel: (010) 62566847 *Fax:* (010) 62566846
Key Personnel
Dir: Xu Yinchi
Every 2 months.

Colombia

Boletin (Bulletin) (J)
Published by Asociacion Colombiana de Bibliotecarios
Calle 10 No 3-16, Apdo Aereo 30883, Bogota
Tel: (01) 2694219
Key Personnel
President: Saul Sanchez Toro
Quarterly.

Boletin Cultural y Bibliografico (Cultural & Bibliographical Bulletin) (J)
Published by Biblioteca Luis-Angel Arango Banco de la Republica (Luis Angel Arango Library-Central Bank of Colombia)
Calle 11 No 4-14, Apdo Aeero 3531, Bogota
Tel: (01) 2827840 *Fax:* (01) 2863881
E-mail: wbiblio@banrep.gov.co
Web Site: www.banrep.gov.co
Quarterly.

Croatia

Vjesnik bibliotekara Hrvatske (Croatian Librarians' Report) (J)
Published by Hrvatsko knjiznicarsko drustvo (Croation Library Association)
Ulica Hrvatske bratske zajednice 4, 10000 Zagreb
Tel: (01) 616 4130 *Fax:* (01) 616 4786
E-mail: hkd@nsk.hr
Web Site: pubwww.srce.hr/hkd
Key Personnel
President: Dubravka Stancin-Rosic *Tel:* (01) 616 4037
Editor-in-Chief: Tinka Katic *E-mail:* tkatic@nsk.hr

Text in Croatian, English, German; summaries in Croatian & English. Back issues available.
Quarterly.
ISSN: 0507-1925

Cuba

Revista de la Biblioteca Nacional Jose Marti (Jose Marti National Library Review) (J)
Published by Biblioteca Nacional Jose Marti
Apdo 6881, Avda de Independencia e/20 de Mayo y Aranquern, Plaza de la Revolucion Jose Marti, Havana
Tel: (07) 96091
Telex: 511963
Key Personnel
Editor: Julio Le Riverend
Triannually.
$15
ISSN: 0006-1727

Denmark

Biblioteksarbog (Library Yearbook) (B)
Published by Danish National Library Authority
Tempovej 7-11, 2750 Ballerup
Tel: 44867777 *Fax:* 44867891
E-mail: dbc@dbc.dk
Web Site: www.dbc.dk
Key Personnel
Man Dir: Mogens Brabrand Jensen
Dir: Kirsten Waneck

Bibliotekspressen (The Library Press) (J)
Published by Bibliotekarforbundet
Lindevangs Alle 2, DK-2000 Frederiksberg
Tel: 38881770 *Fax:* 38883101
E-mail: bpr@bf.dk
Web Site: www.bf.dk/bpr.htm
Key Personnel
Editor: Per Nyeng *E-mail:* pr@bf.dk; Hanne Folmer Schade *E-mail:* hfs@bf.dk
ISSN: 1395-0401

Biblioteksvejviser (Library Guide) (B)
Published by Danmarks Biblioteksforening (Danish Library Association)
Vesterbrogade 205, 1620 Copenhagen
Tel: 33250935 *Fax:* 33257900
E-mail: dbf@dbf.dk
Web Site: www.dbf.dk
Key Personnel
Dir: Winnie Vitzansky
Editor: Hanne Klemmed *E-mail:* hk@dbf.dk
First published 1970.
Annually.
$345
ISBN(s): 87-90849-13-2

Bogens Verden (Book Magazine) (J)
Published by Danmarks Biblioteksforening (Danish Library Association)
Vesterbrogade 205, 1620 Copenhagen
Tel: 33250935 *Fax:* 33257900
E-mail: dbf@dbf.dk
Web Site: www.dbf.dk
Key Personnel
Dir: Winnie Vitzansky
Editor: Bruno Svindborg
Magazine for Danish & foreign literature & culture.
First published 1918.
6 times a year.
ISSN: 0006-5692

Danmarks Biblioteker (J)
Published by Danmarks Biblioteksforening (Danish Library Association)
Vesterbrogade 205, 1620 Copenhagen
Tel: 33250935 *Fax:* 33257900
E-mail: dbf@dbf.dk
Web Site: www.dbf.dk
Key Personnel
Dir: Winnie Vitzansky
Newsletter from the Danish Library Association.
First published 1987.
10 times a year.
ISSN: 0902-7270

DF-Revy (J)
Published by Danmarks Forskningsbiblioteksforening
Aarhus School of Business Library, Fuglesangs Alle 4, 8210 Aarhus V
Tel: 89486542 *Fax:* 86159627
E-mail: kin@asb.dk
Key Personnel
President: Erland Kolding Nielsen
Editor: Kirsten Krogh Kruuse

Over Broen - Library Student's Journal (J)
Published by Danmarks Biblioteksskole/Royal School of Librarianship
Birketinget 6, DK-2300 Copenhagen S
Tel: 31586066 Lok 522 *Fax:* 32840201
E-mail: K943CWL@db.dk
Key Personnel
Librarian: Ivar A. L. Hoel

Skolebiblioteksarbogen (School Libraries Annual) (B)
Published by Danmarks Skolebiblioteksforening
Vesterbrogade 20, DK-1620 Copenhagen V
Tel: 33253222 *Fax:* 33253223
E-mail: komskolbib@internet.dk

Egypt (Arab Republic of Egypt)

Directory of Scientific and Technical Libraries (B)
Published by National Information & Documentation Centre
Al-Tahrir St, Dokki, Cairo
Tel: (02) 3371696 *Fax:* (02) 3371696
Key Personnel
Dir: Dr Mostago Esmat El Sarha

Ethiopia

Bulletin (J)
Published by Ethiopian Library & Information Association
PO Box 30530, Addis Ababa
Tel: (01) 518020
Key Personnel
President: Mulugeta Hunde
Published biannually.

Bulletin (J)
Published by Ethiopian Manuscript Microfilm Library
PO Box 30530, Addis Ababa
Tel: (01) 110844
Published quarterly.

Directory of Ethiopian Libraries (B)
Published by Ethiopian Library & Information Association
PO Box 30530, Addis Ababa
Tel: (01) 518020
Key Personnel
President: Tamirat Mota

Fiji

Handbook for Teacher Librarians (B)
Published by Library Service of Fiji
Ministry of Education, Government Buildings, Suva
Mailing Address: PO Box 2526, Suva
Tel: 315303 *Fax:* 314994
Key Personnel
Principal Librarian: Humesh Prasad

Journal (P)
Published by Fiji Library Association (FLA)
c/o Editor, Government Buildings, Suva
Mailing Address: PO Box 2125, Suva
Tel: 304144 *Fax:* 304144
Telex: FJ2276 *Cable:* UNIVERSITY SUVA
Newsletter also.

Finland

Guide to Research Libraries & Information Services in Finland (B)
Published by Suomen Tieteellinen Kirjastoseura
PO Box 217, 00171 Helsinki
Tel: (09) 3653148 *Fax:* (09) 3652907
E-mail: meri.kuula@arcada.fi
Key Personnel
President: Arja-Riitta Haarala

Kirjastolehti (Bulletin) (J)
Published by Suomen Kirjastoseura
Vuorikatu 22 A18, 00100 Helsinki
Tel: (09) 6221340 *Fax:* (09) 6221466
E-mail: verho@fla.fi
Web Site: www.fla.fi/kirjastolehti
Key Personnel
President: Kaarina Dromberg
First published 1908.
8 times a year.
40 pp
ISSN: 0023-1843

Signum (J)
Published by Suomen Tieteellinen Kirjastoseura
Library of Parliament, Aurorankatu 6, 00-102 Fi-Helsinki
Tel: (09) 432 3485 *Fax:* (09) 432 3495
Web Site: www.pro.tsv.fi/stks
Key Personnel
Editor: Paivikki Karhula *E-mail:* paivikki.karhula@eduskunta.fi
First published 1968.
Eight times yearly.

France

Documentaliste - Sciences de l'Information
(Documentalist - Information Sciences) (J)
Published by L'Association des Professionnels de l'Information et de la Documentation (ADBS)
25 rue Claude Tillier, F-75012 Paris
Tel: (01) 43722525 *Fax:* (01) 43723041
E-mail: adbs@adbs.fr
Web Site: www.adbs.fr
Key Personnel
President: Florence Wilhelm
Director of the Review: Serge Cacaly
Editor: Jean Michel Rauzier
General Manager: David Cayre
French review devoted to techniques, professions, services & policies in the information & library fields & to research in information sciences, with particular focus on European & French-speaking countries. Abstracts in English.
First published 1964.
5 yearly.
80 pp
ISSN: 0395-3858

INTER BCD (J)
Published by Centre d'Etude de la Documentation et de l'Information Scolaires
16, rue des Belles-Croix, 91150 Etampes
Tel: (01) 64943951 *Fax:* (01) 64945499
E-mail: cedis@calvanet.calvacom.fr
Key Personnel
Publr: Michel Mouillet
Editor: Marie Noelle Michaut
Journal for specialist librarians.
Biannually.
ISSN: 1270-1467

INTER CDI (J)
Published by Centre d'Etude de la Documentation et de l'Information Scolaires
16, rue des Belles Croix, 91150 Etampes
Tel: (01) 64943951 *Fax:* (01) 64945499
E-mail: cedis@calvanet.calvacom.fr
Key Personnel
Publr: Michel Mouillet
Journal for Specialist Librarians (second level).
Bimonthly.
ISSN: 0242-2999

Scribeco (J)
Published by Institut National de la Statistique et des Etudes Economiques (INSEE)
One rue Vincent Avriol, 80027 Amiens Cedex
Tel: (03) 22927322 *Fax:* (03) 22979295
E-mail: inseeactualites@insee.fr
Bibliographic bulletin.
First published 1986.
6 times/yr.
ISSN: 0769-0509

Germany

Beitraege zum Buch-und Bibliothekswesen (B)
Published by Harrassowitz Verlag
Taunusstr 14, 65183 Wiesbaden
Tel: (0611) 530-0 *Fax:* (0611) 530-570; (0611) 530-560 (orders)
E-mail: verlag@harrassowitz.de; service@harrassowitz.de
Web Site: www.harrassowitz.de
Key Personnel
Editor: Michael Knoche
Rights & Permissions: Robert Gietz
This book series deals with, among other things, library science, bibliographies & the history of books, libraries & publishing houses.
6 times yearly.
ISBN(s): 3-447 3-8086
ISSN: 0408-8107

Bibliothek und Wissenschaft (Libraries & Science) (J)
Published by Harrassowitz Verlag
Taunusstr 14, 65183 Wiesbaden
Tel: (0611) 530-0 *Fax:* (0611) 530-570; (0611) 530-560 (orders)
E-mail: verlag@harrassowitz.de; service@harrassowitz.de
Web Site: www.harrassowitz.de
Key Personnel
Publicity Dir: Robert Gietz *Tel:* (0611) 530-551
E-mail: rgietz@harrassowitz.de
History of books, libraries & science.
Annually.

Buchprofile (J)
Published by Borromausverein eV
Wittelsbacherring 9, 53115 Bonn
Mailing Address: Postfach 1267, 53115 Bonn
Tel: (0228) 72580 *Fax:* (0228) 7258189
Key Personnel
Publr: Rolf Pitsch
Editor: Herbert Stangl
Book profile for Catholic library work.

Buchwissenschaftliche Beitraege aus dem Deutschen Bucharchiv Muenchen (Articles of the German Archives in Munich) (B)
Published by Harrassowitz Verlag
Taunusstr 14, 65183 Wiesbaden
Tel: (0611) 530-0 *Fax:* (0611) 530-570; (0611) 530-560 (orders)
E-mail: verlag@harrassowitz.de; service@harrassowitz.de
Web Site: www.harrassowitz.de
Key Personnel
Rights & Permissions: Robert Gietz
Editor: Ludwig Delp; Ursula Neumann
This book series deals, among other things, with the history of books, libraries, literature & publishing houses.
Irregularly.
ISSN: 0724-7001

Busse/Ernestus/Plassmann - Libraries in the Federal Republic of Germany (1983) (B)
Published by Harrassowitz Verlag
Taunusstr 14, 65183 Wiesbaden
Tel: (0611) 530-0 *Fax:* (0611) 530-570; (0611) 530-570
E-mail: verlag@harrassowitz.de; service@harrassowitz.de
Web Site: www.harrassowitz.de
Key Personnel
Rights & Permissions: Robert Gietz
The work outlines the organization of the libraries of Western Germany.
ISBN(s): 3-447 3-8086

Die Deutsche Bibliothek (The German Library) (B)
Published by Die Deutsche Bibliothek/Deutsche Buecherei Leipzig
Adickeallee 1, 60322 Frankfurt
Tel: (069) 15250 *Fax:* (069) 15251010
E-mail: info@dbf.ddb.de
Key Personnel
Contact: Dr Elisabeth Niggemann
Annual/weekly/monthly/semi-annual.

Erwerbung in Deutschen Bibliotheken (Acquisitions Departments of German Libraries) (B)
Published by Harrassowitz Verlag
Taunusstr 14, 65183 Wiesbaden
Tel: (0611) 530-0 *Fax:* (0611) 530-570; (0611) 530-560 (orders)
E-mail: verlag@harrassowitz.de; service@harrassowitz.de
Web Site: www.harrassowitz.de
Key Personnel
Rights & Permissions: Robert Gietz
Biennially.
ISBN(s): 3-447-3-8086

Geschichte des Buchhandels (History of the Book Trade) (B)
Published by Harrassowitz Verlag
Taunusstr 14, 65183 Wiesbaden
Tel: (0611) 530-0 *Fax:* (0611) 530-570; (0611) 530-570
E-mail: verlag@harrassowitz.de; service@harrassowitz.de
Web Site: www.harrassowitz.de
Key Personnel
Rights & Permissions: Robert Gietz
The series deals with the history of the international booktrade. Presently the following volumes are available Germany, Netherlands, Hungary, Norway, Russia & Soviet Union.
Irregularly.
ISSN: 0941-7877

Gesellschaft fuer das Buch (Society for the Book) (J)
Published by Harrassowitz Verlag
Taunusstr 14, 65183 Wiesbaden
Tel: (0611) 530-0 *Fax:* (0611) 530-570; (0611) 530-560 (orders)
E-mail: verlag@harrassowitz.de; service@harrassowitz.de
Web Site: www.harrassowitz.de
Key Personnel
Rights & Permissions: Robert Gietz
First published 1995.
Irregularly.
ISSN: 0948-5007

Handbuch der Bibliotheken (Directory of Libraries) (B)
Published by K G Saur Verlag GmbH, A Gale/Thomson Learning Company
Unit of Thomson Learning
Ortlerstr 8, 81373 Munich
Mailing Address: Postfach 70 16 20, 81316 Munich
Tel: (089) 76902-0 *Fax:* (089) 76902-150
E-mail: info@saur.de
Web Site: www.saur.de
Telex: 5212067
Bundesrepublik Deutschland, Oesterreich, Schweiz, Germany, Austria, Switzerland.
Parent Company: Gale
Ultimate Parent Company: The Thomson Corporation

IFLA Journal (J)
Published by K G Saur Verlag GmbH, A Gale/Thomson Learning Company
Unit of Thomson Learning
Ortlerstr 8, 81373 Munich
Mailing Address: Postfach 70 16 20, 81316 Munich
Tel: (089) 76902-0 *Fax:* (089) 76902-150
E-mail: info@saur.de
Web Site: www.saur.de
Telex: 5212067
Parent Company: Gale
Ultimate Parent Company: The Thomson Corporation

IFLA Publications (B)
Published by K G Saur Verlag GmbH, A Gale/Thomson Learning Company
Unit of Thomson Learning

Ortlerstr 8, 81373 Munich
Mailing Address: Postfach 70 16 20, 81316 Munich
Tel: (089) 76902-0 *Fax:* (089) 76902-150
E-mail: info@saur.de
Web Site: www.saur.de
Telex: 5212067
A series of publications related to the International Federation of Library Associations and Institutions.
Parent Company: Gale
Ultimate Parent Company: The Thomson Corporation

Jahrbuch der Deutschen Bibliotheken
(Yearbook of German Libraries) (B)
Published by Harrassowitz Verlag
Taunusstr 14, 65183 Wiesbaden
Tel: (0611) 530-0 *Fax:* (0611) 530-570; (0611) 530-570
E-mail: verlag@harrassowitz.de; service@harrassowitz.de
Web Site: www.harrassowitz.de
Information about German Scientific Libraries.
First published 1902.
Biennially.
ISSN: 0075-2223

Leipziger Jahrbuch zur Buchgeschichte (J)
Published by Harrassowitz Verlag
Taunusstr 14, 65183 Wiesbaden
Tel: (0611) 530-0 *Fax:* (0611) 530-570; (0611) 530-560 (orders)
E-mail: verlag@harrassowitz.de; service@harrassowitz.de
Web Site: www.harrassowitz.de
Key Personnel
Editor: Thomas Keiderling; Lothar Poethe; Volker Titel
History of books, of the booktrade, of publishers & of printers.
ISSN: 0940-1954

Librarianship and Information Work Worldwide (B)
Published by K G Saur Verlag GmbH, A Gale/Thomson Learning Company
Unit of Thomson Learning
Ortlerstr 8, 81373 Munich
Mailing Address: Postfach 70 16 20, 81316 Munich
Tel: (089) 76902-0 *Fax:* (089) 76902-150
E-mail: info@saur.de
Web Site: www.saur.de
Parent Company: Gale
Ultimate Parent Company: The Thomson Corporation

Marginalien Zeitschrift fuer Buchkunst und Bibliophilie (Marginal Notes - Journal for Book Art & Bibliophilic) (J)
Published by Harrassowitz Verlag
Taunusstr 14, 65183 Wiesbaden
Tel: (0611) 530-0 *Fax:* (0611) 530-570; (0611) 530-560 (orders)
E-mail: verlag@harrassowitz.de; service@harrassowitz.de
Web Site: www.harrassowitz.de
Quarterly.
ISSN: 0025-2948

John Roger Paas, The German Political Broadsheet 1600-1700 (B)
Published by Harrassowitz Verlag
Taunusstr 14, 65183 Wiesbaden
Tel: (0611) 530-0 *Fax:* (0611) 530-570; (0611) 530-560 (orders)
E-mail: verlag@harrassowitz.de; service@harrassowitz.de
Web Site: www.harrassowitz.de

Key Personnel
Rights & Permissions: Robert Gietz
The edition will comprise approximately 10 volumes & 4-index volume. Over 3000 broadsheets are reproduced in full site. Approximately 7000 individual copies are cited. Available volumes: 1 (1600-1615), 2 (1616-1619), 3 (1620-1621), 4 (1622-1629), 5 (1630-1631), 6 (1632).
ISBN(s): 3-447; 3-8086

Schulbibliothek aktuell (School Library Today) (J)
Published by Deutsches Bibliotheksinstitut
Kurt-Schumacher-Damm 12-16, 13405 Berlin
Tel: (030) 41034-0 *Fax:* (030) 403410-0
E-mail: www@dbi-berlin.de
Web Site: www.dbi-berlin.de
Key Personnel
Dir: Prof Gunter Beyersdorff
First published 1975.
Quarterly.
ISSN: 0341-471X

Wolfenbuetteler Schriften zur Geschichte des Buchwesens (J)
Published by Harrassowitz Verlag
Taunusstr 14, 65183 Wiesbaden
Tel: (0611) 530-0 *Fax:* (0611) 530-570; (0611) 530-560 (orders)
E-mail: verlag@harrassowitz.de; service@harrassowitz.de
Web Site: www.harrassowitz.de
Key Personnel
Rights & Permissions: Robert Gietz
This journal series deals with the history of books, libraries & publishing houses. Published in cooperation with Herzog August Bibliothek.
First published 1977.
Irregular.
ISSN: 0724-9586

World Guide to Libraries (B)
Published by K G Saur Verlag GmbH, A Gale/Thomson Learning Company
Ortlerstr 8, 81373 Munich
Mailing Address: Postfach 70 16 20, 81316 Munich
Tel: (089) 76902-0 *Fax:* (089) 76902-150
E-mail: info@saur.de
Web Site: www.saur.de
Telex: 5212067
Furnishes details on 47,000 libraries in 167 countries. Covers national, general research, university, school, government, corporate, ecclesiastical, special & public libraries with over 30,000 volumes. Alphabetical index.
1200 pp
ISBN(s): 3-598-20725-5
Parent Company: Gale
Ultimate Parent Company: The Thomson Corporation
U.S. Office(s): Thomson Learning

World Guide to Special Libraries (B)
Published by K G Saur Verlag GmbH, A Gale/Thomson Learning Company
Unit of Thomson Learning
Ortlerstr 8, 81373 Munich
Mailing Address: Postfach 70 16 20, 81316 Munich
Tel: (089) 76902-0 *Fax:* (089) 76902-150
E-mail: info@saur.de
Web Site: www.saur.de
Telex: 5212067
Parent Company: Gale
Ultimate Parent Company: The Thomson Corporation

Zeitschrift fuer Bibliothekswesen und Bibliographie (Journal of Library Science & Bibliography) (J)
Published by Vittorio Klostermann GmbH
Frauenlobstr 22, 60487 Frankfurt am Main
Mailing Address: Postfach 900601, 60446 Frankfurt am Main
Tel: (069) 97 08 16-0 *Fax:* (069) 70 80 38
E-mail: verlag@klostermann.de
Web Site: www.klostermann.de
Key Personnel
Editor: Dr Elisabeth Niggemann
6x annually.
ISSN: 0044-2380

Ghana

Directory of Libraries in Ghana, (B)
Published by Department of Library and Archival Sciences
c/o University of Ghana, POB 25, Legon, Nr Accra
Tel: (021) 302347 *Fax:* (021) 667701
E-mail: balme@ug.gn.apc.org.
Telex: 2556
Key Personnel
Librarian: C O Kisiedu

Directory of Research and Special Libraries in Ghana (B)
Published by Council for Scientific and Industrial Research
PO Box M 32, Accra
Tel: (021) 777651 *Fax:* (021) 777655
E-mail: ghastnet@ncs.ccm.gh
Key Personnel
Dir Prof: W. S. Al-Hassan

Ghana Library Journal (J)
Published by Ghana Library Association
PO Box 5015, Accra
Tel: 668731
Key Personnel
President: E S Asiedo
Annually.
ISSN: 0016-9552

Guyana

Bulletin (J)
Published by Guyana Library Association
c/o National Library, 176-177 Church St & Ave of the Republic, Georgetown
Tel: (02) 62690
Key Personnel
Editor: Wenda Stevenson
First published 1970.
Semiannually.
ISSN: 1023-3385

Honduras

Catalogo de Prestamo (Loan Catalog) (J)
Published by Asociacion de Bibliotecarios y Archivistas de Honduras
lla Calle, 1a y 2A Avdas No 105, Comayagueela, DC Tegucigalpa
Key Personnel
President: Francisca de Escoto Espinoza
Monthly.

Hong Kong

Journal of the Hong Kong Library Association (J)
Published by Hong Kong Library Association
PO Box 10095, Hong Kong
Tel: (02) 859-8902 *Fax:* (02) 915-2458
E-mail: hkla@hk.super.net
Web Site: www.hk.super.net/~hkla
Key Personnel
President: Alima Tuet
Rights & Permissions: Esther Woo
 E-mail: emwwoo@hkucc.hku.hk
Text in English and Chinese.
ISSN: 0073-3237

Hungary

Hungarian Library & Information Science Abstracts (J)
Published by Orszagos Szechenyi Koenyvtar Magyar ISBN Iroda
Budavari Palota F epuelet, 1827 Budapest
Tel: (01) 224-3795 *Fax:* (01) 202-0804
E-mail: lnagypal@oszk.hu
Telex: 224226 bibln h
Key Personnel
Dir General: Geza Poprady
Text in English.
Semiannually.
ISSN: 0046-8304

Koenyvtari Figyeloe Uj folyam (Library Review) (J)
Published by Orszagos Szechenyi Koenyvtar Magyar ISBN Iroda
Budavari Palota F epuelet, 1827 Budapest
Tel: (01) 224-3795 *Fax:* (01) 202-0804
E-mail: kovacs@oszk.hu
Telex: 224226 bibln h
Key Personnel
Dir General: Geza Poprady
Text in Hungarian; summaries in English & German.
Quarterly.
ISSN: 0865-0276

Koenyvtartoerteneti Fuezetek (History of Libraries series) (J)
Published by Jozsef Attila Tudomanyegyetem Egyetemi Koenyvtar
Dugonics-ter 13, 6701 Szeged
Tel: (062) 324022 *Fax:* (062) 312718
E-mail: mader@bibl.u-szeged.hu

Magyar koenyvtari szakirodalom bibliografiaja (Bibliography on Hungarian Library Literature) (J)
Published by Orszagos Szechenyi Koenyvtar Magyar ISBN Iroda
Budavari Palota F epuelet, 1827 Budapest
Tel: (01) 224-3795 *Fax:* (01) 202-0804
Telex: 224226 bibln h
Key Personnel
Dir General: Geza Poprady
Text in Hungarian.
Quarterly.
ISSN: 0133-736X

Iceland

Fregnir & Bokasafnid (J)
Published by Icelandic Library Association
Box 1497, 121 Reykjavik
Tel: 564-2050 *Fax:* 564-3877
Key Personnel
President: H A Hardarson
Newsletter.

India

Annals of Library & Information Studies (J)
Formerly Annals of Library Science & Documentation
Published by Indian National Scientific Documentation Centre (INSDOC)
14 Satsang Vihar Marg, Off SJS Sansanwal Marg, New Delhi 110067
Tel: (011) 6863609 *Fax:* (011) 6862228
E-mail: mcs@ndf.vsnl.net.in
Web Site: www.insdoc.org
Telex: 031-73099
Key Personnel
Dir: Mr V K Gupta
Text in English.
First published 1954.
Quarterly.
ISSN: 0972-5423

Annals of Library Science & Documentation, see Annals of Library & Information Studies

Books of the Week Bulletin (J)
Published by D K Agencies (P) Ltd
A/15-17 DK Ave, Mohan Garden, Off Najafgarh Rd, New Delhi 110059
Tel: (011) 535-7104; (011) 535-7105 *Fax:* (011) 535-7103
E-mail: custserv@dkagencies.com
Web Site: www.dkagencies.com
Source for bibliographical details of English language publications published from India.
Weekly.

Bulletin (J)
Published by Indian Library Association
A/40-41, Flat 201, Ansal Bldgs, Dr Mukherjee Nagar, Delhi 110009
Tel: (07) 117743
Key Personnel
President: P S G Kumar
Editor: S Ansari
Text in English.
First published 1965.
Quarterly.

D K Newsletter (J)
Published by D K Agencies (P) Ltd
A/15-17 DK Ave, Mohan Garden, Off Najafgarh Rd, New Delhi 110059
Tel: (011) 535-7104; (011) 535-7105 *Fax:* (011) 535-7103
E-mail: custserv@dkagencies.com
Web Site: www.dkagencies.com
News & Reviews of Indian Publications in English.
First published 1975.
Quarterly.
ISSN: 0971-4448

Directory of Special & Research Libraries in India (B)
Published by Indian Association of Special Libraries & Information Centres
P 291, CIT Scheme No 6M, Kankurgachi, Calcutta 700054
Tel: (033) 334-9651
Key Personnel
Pres: Dr M G Som

GILA Bulletin (J)
Published by Government of India Librarians Association
A/40-41, Flat 201, Ansal Bldgs, Dr Mukhevjee Nagar, Delhi 110009
Tel: 711-7743
Published quarterly.

IASLIC Bulletin (J)
Published by Indian Association of Special Libraries & Information Centres
P 291, CIT Scheme No 6M, Kankurgachi, Calcutta 700054
Tel: (033) 334-9651
Key Personnel
Pres: Dr M G Som
Text in English.
First published 1956.
Quarterly.

Indian Library Science Abstracts (J)
Published by Indian Association of Special Libraries & Information Centres
P 291, CIT Scheme No 6M, Kankurgachi, Calcutta 700054
Tel: (033) 334-9651
Key Personnel
Pres: Dr M G Som
Annual.
ISSN: 0019-5790

Indian Publications Catalog (B)
Published by D K Agencies (P) Ltd
A/15-17 DK Ave, Mohan Garden, Off Najafgarh Rd, New Delhi 110059
Tel: (011) 535-7104; (011) 535-7105 *Fax:* (011) 535-7103
E-mail: custserv@dkagencies.com
Web Site: www.dkagencies.com
Bibliographic information for public libraries.

Journal of Library & Information Science (J)
Published by Department of Library and Information Science
Department of Library & Information Science, University of Delhi, Delhi 110007
Tel: (011) 7666656
First published 1976.
Biannually.
ISSN: 0970-714X

Journal of Library Science (J)
Published by Nagpur University
Rabindranath Tagore Marg, Nagpur, Maharashtra 440001
Tel: 525417

Karnatak Granthalaya (J)
Published by Granthalaya Vijnana Prakashana Gulbarga University, Gulbarga 585106 Karnataka
Tel: (08472) 21446 *Fax:* (08472) 21632
Text in Kannada, contents page in English and Kannada.
First published 1969.
Quarterly.
ISSN: 0022-9083

The National Library and Public Libraries in India (B)
Published by The National Library
Belvedere, Calcutta 700027
Tel: (033) 479-1381 *Fax:* (033) 479-1462
Key Personnel
Dir: Dr A N Banerjee

Special Listings (J)
Published by D K Agencies (P) Ltd
A/15-17 DK Ave, Mohan Garden, Off Najafgarh Rd, New Delhi 110059
Tel: (011) 535-7104; (011) 535-7105 *Fax:* (011) 535-7103
E-mail: custserv@dkagencies.com
Web Site: www.dkagencies.com
Information by subject on books & back numbers of Indian periodicals.

Subscribers' Guide to Indian Periodicals/Serials (J)
Published by D K Agencies (P) Ltd
A/15-17 DK Ave, Mohan Garden, Off Najafgarh Rd, New Delhi 110059
Tel: (011) 535-7104; (011) 535-7105 *Fax:* (011) 535-7103
E-mail: custserv@dkagencies.com
Web Site: www.dkagencies.com

Indonesia

Baca (Read) (J)
Published by Indonesian Institute of Sciences, Centre for Scientific Documentation & Information
Lembaga Ilmu Pengetahuan Indonesia, Pusat Dokumentasi dan Informasi Irmiah, Jakarta
Mailing Address: POB 4298, Jakarta 12042
Tel: (021) 5733465 *Fax:* (021) 5733467
E-mail: admin@pdii.lipi.go.id
Key Personnel
Editor: Antari Wahyuning Mawarti
  E-mail: Antari_s@hotmail.com
First published 1974.
Quarterly.
ISSN: 0125-9008

Berita Bulanan (Monthly Bulletin) (J)
Published by National Bibliographic Centre
c/o Library of Political & Social History, Medan Merdeka Selatan 11, Jakarta

Majalah Ikatan Pustakawan Indonesia (J)
Published by Indonesian Library Association
Jl Imamj Bonjol 1, POB 3624, Jakarta 10002
Tel: 342529
Key Personnel
President: M H Prakoso
Indonesian Library Association Journal.

Islamic Republic of Iran

The Authority File of the Iranian Governmental Corporate Bodies (B)
Published by The National Library of Iran
Sh Bahonar Str, 19548 Tehran
Tel: (021) 280 86 80 *Fax:* (021) 280 86 80

A Catalog of the Manuscripts in the National Library of Iran (B)
Published by The National Library of Iran
Sh Bahonar Str, 19548 Tehran
Tel: (021) 280 86 80 *Fax:* (021) 280 86 80
E-mail: nli@nli.ir
Key Personnel
Manuscript Dept: H Aximi

A Catalog of the Persian Maps in the National Library of the Islamic Republic of Iran (B)
Published by The National Library of Iran
Anahita Alley, Africa St, PO Box 11365/9597, Tehran 19176
Tel: (021) 280 86 80 *Fax:* (021) 280 86 80

Class DSR: History of Iran (B)
Published by The National Library of Iran
Sh Bahonar Str, 19548 Tehran
Tel: (021) 2280937 *Fax:* (021) 2288680
E-mail: nli@nli.ir
Key Personnel
Author & Research Librarian: Kamran Fani
An adaptation of Library of Congress Classification.
First published 1980.
3rd (2000): 198 pp, $50
ISBN(s): 964-446-056-1

Class PIR: Iranian Languages & Literature (B)
Published by The National Library of Iran
Sh Bahonar Str, 19548 Tehran
Tel: (021) 280 86 80 *Fax:* (021) 280 86 80
Based on the Library of Congress Classification.

Dewey Decimal Classification: Geography of Iran, 3rd Edition (B)
Published by The National Library of Iran
Sh Bahonar Str, 19548 Tehran
Tel: (021) 280 86 80 *Fax:* (021) 280 86 80
E-mail: nli@nli.ir

Dewey Decimal Classification: History of Iran (B)
Published by The National Library of Iran
Sh Bahonar Str, 19548 Tehran
Mailing Address: Shahid Bahonar St, Tehran 19548
Tel: (021) 2280937 *Fax:* (021) 2288680
E-mail: nli@nli.ir
Key Personnel
Author & Research Librarian: Kamran Fani
Senior Research Librarian: Mrs Poori Soltani
  E-mail: poorisaltani@yahoo.com
First published 1982.
3rd (1999), $20
ISBN(s): 964-446-037-5

Dewey Decimal Classification: Iranian Languages (B)
Published by The National Library of Iran
Sh Bahonar Str, 19548 Tehran
Mailing Address: Shahid Bahonar St, Tehran 19548
Tel: (021) 2280937 *Fax:* (021) 2288680
E-mail: nli@nli.ir
Key Personnel
Senior Research Librarian: Mrs Poori Soltani
  E-mail: poorisoltani@yahoo.com
First published 1988.
3rd (1998), $15
ISBN(s): 964-446-031-6

Dewey Decimal Classification: Iranian Literature (B)
Published by The National Library of Iran
Sh Bahonar Str, 19548 Tehran
Mailing Address: Shahid Bahonar St, Tehran 19548
Tel: (021) 2280937 *Fax:* (021) 2288680
E-mail: nli@nli.ir
Key Personnel
Senior Research Librarian: Mrs Poori Soltani
  E-mail: poorisoltani@yahoo.com
Text in Persian.
First published 1972.
2nd (1998), $50
ISBN(s): 964-446-032-4

Dewey Decimal Classification: Islam, 3rd Edition (B)
Published by The National Library of Iran
Sh Bahonar Str, 19548 Tehran
Tel: (021) 280 86 80 *Fax:* (021) 280 86 80
E-mail: nli@nli.ir
Key Personnel
Senior Research Librarian: Mrs Poori Soltani
  E-mail: poorisaltani@yahoo.com
3rd

A Directory of Iranian Newspapers (B)
Published by The National Library of Iran
Sh Bahonar Str, 19548 Tehran
Tel: (021) 280 86 80 *Fax:* (021) 2288680
Annually.

Farsi Author Mark, to be used with the Library of Congress Classification Schedules (B)
Published by The National Library of Iran
Sh Bahonar Str, 19548 Tehran
Tel: (021) 2288680 *Fax:* (021) 2288680
E-mail: nli@nli.ir
Key Personnel
Senior Research Librarian: Poori Soltani
  Tel: (021) 2280937 *E-mail:* poorisoltani@yahoo.com
First published 1997.
3: 34 pp

Faslname-yi Ketab (J)
Published by The National Library of Iran
Shahid Bahonar St, Tehran 19548
Tel: (021) 280 86 80 *Fax:* (021) 280 86 80
E-mail: nli@nli.ir
Key Personnel
Editor: Abbas Horri
Journal of The National Library of Iran.
First published 1990.
Quarterly.
ISSN: 1022-6451

List of Persian Subject Headings (B)
Published by The National Library of Iran
Sh Bahonar Str, 19548 Tehran
Mailing Address: Shahid Bahonar St, Tehran 19548
Tel: (021) 2280937 *Fax:* (021) 2288680
E-mail: nli@nli.ir
Key Personnel
Senior Research Librarian: Mrs Poori Soltani
  E-mail: poorisaltani@yahoo.com
3 vols.
First published 1993.
3rd (2002), $50
ISBN(s): 964-446-070-7

Persian Author Mark (B)
Published by The National Library of Iran
Sh Bahonar Str, 19548 Tehran
Mailing Address: Shahid Bahonar St, Tehran 19548
Tel: (021) 280 86 80 *Fax:* (021) 280 86 80
E-mail: nli@nli.ir
Three-Figure Table, Based on Cutter-Sanborn.
2nd

Rules for Filing Persian Catalog Card, 2nd Edition (B)
Published by The National Library of Iran
Sh Bahonar Str, 19548 Tehran
Tel: (021) 280 86 80 *Fax:* (021) 280 86 80
E-mail: nli@nli.ir

Technical Services, 8th Edition (B)
Published by The National Library of Iran
Sh Bahonar Str, 19548 Tehran
Mailing Address: Shahid Bahonar St, Tehran 19548

ISLAMIC REPUBLIC OF IRAN

Tel: (021) 280 86 80 *Fax:* (021) 280 86 80
E-mail: nli@nli.ir
8th, $501
ISBN(s): 964-446-029-4

Iraq

Arab Archives Journal (J)
Published by National Centre of Archives
National Library Bldg, 2nd Floor, Bab-el-Muaddum, POB 594, Baghdad
Key Personnel
Dir General: Salim Al-Alousi

Ireland

Directory of Libraries & Information Services in Ireland (B)
Published by Library Association of Ireland & CILIP (Northern Ireland)
53 Upper Mount St, Dublin 2
Tel: (01) 6619000 *Fax:* (01) 6761628
E-mail: laisec@iol.ie
Web Site: www.libraryassociation.ie
Key Personnel
President: Marjory Sliney *Tel:* (01) 8452026
  E-mail: msliney@eircom.net;marjory.sliney@fingalcoco.ie
Available online only.

Irish Library News (J)
Published by An Chomhairle Leabharlanna (Library Council)
53 & 54 Upper Mount St, Dublin 2
Tel: (01) 6761167 *Fax:* (01) 6766721
E-mail: info@librarycouncil.ie
Web Site: www.librarycouncil.ie
Key Personnel
Dir: Norma McDermott
Newssheet issued free to libraries.
First published 1977.
Monthly.
ISSN: 0332-0049

An Leabharlann (Irish Library) (J)
Published by Library Association of Ireland & CILIP-Northern Ireland
53 Upper Mount St, Dublin 2
Tel: (01) 6619000 *Fax:* (01) 6761628
Web Site: www.libraryassociation.ie
Key Personnel
President: Marjory Sliney *Tel:* (01) 8452026
  E-mail: msliney@eircom.net

Long Room (J)
Published by Friends of the Library
Trinity College, College St, Dublin 2
Tel: (01) 6082087 *Fax:* (01) 6719003
E-mail: vkinane@lib1.tcd.ie
Telex: 93782
Key Personnel
Editor: Vincent Kinane
Ireland's Journal for the History of the Book.
Annually.

Israel

Bibliography of Modern Hebrew Literature in Translation (B)
Published by The Institute for the Translation of Hebrew Literature
23 Baruch Hirsch St, Bnei Brak
Mailing Address: PO Box 1005 1, Ramat Gan 5200 1
Tel: (03) 579 6830 *Fax:* (03) 579 6832
E-mail: hamachon@inter.net.il; litscene@ithl.org.il
Web Site: www.ithl.org.il
Key Personnel
Man Dir: Mrs Nilli Cohen
First published 1979.
Annually.
ISSN: 0334-309X

Index to Hebrew Periodicals (J)
Published by Centre for Public Libraries
PO Box 242, 91002 Jerusalem
Tel: (02) 6252949 *Fax:* (02) 6250620
Key Personnel
Chairman: Jacob Agmon
Available on CD-ROM only.
Annually.

Information & Librarianship (J)
Published by Israel Society of Libraries and Information Centers
97 Yaffo St, Klal House, Room 707, Jerusalem 94340
Mailing Address: PO Box 28273, Jerusalem 91281
Tel: (02) 6249421 *Fax:* (02) 6249421
E-mail: asmi@asmi.org.il
Key Personnel
Chairperson: Shoshana Langerman
  E-mail: shola@barak-online.net
Biannually.

Yad-La-kore (P)
Published by The Israeli Center for Libraries
PO Box 242, 91002 Jerusalem
Tel: (02) 6252949 *Fax:* (02) 3250620
E-mail: rochelle@actcom.co.il
Key Personnel
Dir: Dr Martin Weyl
The Reader's Aid - Israel Journal for Libraries and Archives.
First published 1946.
Quarterly.
ISSN: 0334-200X

Italy

Accademie e Biblioteche d'Italia (Academies and Libraries of Italy) (J)
Published by Ministero per Beni Culturali e Ambientali
Casa Editrice Fratelli Palombi, Via del Gracchi 181-185, I-00192 Rome
Tel: (06) 3214150 *Fax:* (06) 3214752
E-mail: flli.palombi@mail.stm.it
Frequency.
96 pp
ISSN: 0393-4451

Bollettino AIB (AIB Bulletin) (J)
Published by Italian Library Association (Associazione Italiana Biblioteche)
CP 24 61, 00100 Rome
Tel: (06) 4463532 *Fax:* (06) 4441139
E-mail: bollettino@aib.it
Web Site: www.aib.it/aib/boll/boll.htm
Key Personnel
Editor: Giovanni Solimine
Contact: Maria Teresa Natale
Quarterly.
ISSN: 1121-1490

Catalogo Collettivo di Periodici - Archivio ISRDS/CNR (Catalog of Collective Periodicals) (B)
Published by Istituto Centrale per il Catalogo Unico delle Biblioteche Italiane e per le Informazioni; Bibliografiche
Viale del Castro Pretorio, I-00185 Rome
Tel: (06) 4454701 *Fax:* (06) 4959292
Key Personnel
Dir: Dr Giovanna Mazzola Merola
Contains listings of over 46,000 periodicals in 1500 libraries.

Periodici Italiani 1886-1981 (Italian Periodicals) (B)
Published by Istituto Centrale Catalogo Unico delle Biblioteche Italiane e per le Informazione Bibliografiche
Viale del Castro Pretorio, I-00185 Rome
Tel: (06) 4454701 *Fax:* (06) 4959292
Key Personnel
Dir: Dr Giovanna Mazzola Merola

Regole Italiane di Catalogazione per Autori (Italian Rules of Cataloging by Author) (B)
Published by Istituto Centrale per il Catalogo Unico delle Biblioteche Italiane e per le Informazioni Bibliografiche
Viale del Castro Pretorio, I-00185 Rome
Tel: (06) 4454701 *Fax:* (06) 4959292
Key Personnel
Dir: Dr Giovanna Mazzola Merola

Soggettario per i Cataloghi delle Biblioteche Italiane (Subject Collections in Italian Libraries) (J)
Published by Istituto Centrale per il Catalogo Unico delle Biblioteche Italiane e per le Informazioni Bibliografiche
Viale del Castro Pretorio, 00185 Rome
Tel: (06) 4454701 *Fax:* (06) 4959302
Key Personnel
Dir: Dr Giovanna Mazzola Merola

Jamaica

JLA Bulletin (J)
Published by Jamaica Library Association
PO Box 58, Kingston 5
Fax: (876) 927-2944
Key Personnel
President: P Kerr
First published 1950.
Annually.

JLA News (B)
Published by Jamaica Library Association
PO Box 58, Kingston 5
Tel: (876) 927-2944
Key Personnel
President: P Kerr
News of current events in the libraries of Jamaica.
Quarterly.

Japan

A Survey of Special Collections in Japan (B)
Published by The Shuppan News Co Ltd
40-7 Kanda-Jimbo-cho 2 Chome, Chyoda-Ku,
  Chiyoda-ku, Tokyo 101
Tel: (03) 32622076
ISBN(s): 4-7852

Biblos (J)
Published by National Diet Library
1-10-1 Nagata-cho, Chiyoda-ku, Tokyo 100-8924
Tel: (03) 35812331 *Fax:* (03) 35082934
E-mail: kokusai@ndl.go.jp
Web Site: www.ndl.go.jp
Key Personnel
Dir, Planning & Cooperation Dept: Yukiko Saito
Online magazine for branch, executive, judicial & other special libraries.
ISSN: 1344-8412

Bulletin of the Japan Special Libraries Association (J)
Published by Japan Special Libraries Association
c/o National Diet Library, 10-1, Nagatacho 1-chome, Chiyoda-ku, Tokyo 100
Tel: (03) 35812331 *Fax:* (03) 35979104
Abstracts in English.

Directory of Special Libraries (B)
Published by Japan Special Libraries Association
c/o National Diet Library, 10-1, Nagotacho 1-chome, Chiyoda-ku, Tokyo 100
Tel: (03) 35812331 *Fax:* (03) 35979104
Entry names also in English.

Gendai no Toshokan (J)
Published by Japan Library Association
1-10 Taishido 1-chome, Setagaya-ku, Tokyo 154
Tel: (03) 34106411 *Fax:* (03) 34217588
Libraries Today.

Handbook (B)
Published by Japan Special Libraries Association
c/o National Diet Library, 10-1, Nagatacho 1-chome, Chiyoda-ku, Tokyo 100
Tel: (03) 35812331 *Fax:* (03) 35979104
Text in Japanese.

Journal of Information Science and Technology Association (J)
Published by Information Science and Technology Association
Sasaki Bldg, 5-7 Koisikawa-2, Bunkyo-ku, Tokyo 112
Tel: (03) 38133791 *Fax:* (03) 38133793

Nippon no Sankotosho Shikiban (J)
Published by Japan Library Association
1-10 Taishido 1-chome, Setagaya-ku, Tokyo 154
Tel: (03) 34106411 *Fax:* (03) 34217588
Guide to Japanese Reference Books.

Nippon no Toshokan (B)
Published by Japan Library Association
1-10 Taishido 1-chome, Setagaya-ku, Tokyo 154
Tel: (03) 34106411 *Fax:* (03) 34217588
Statistics on Libraries in Japan: annual statistics & directory of public & university libraries.

Reference (J)
Published by National Diet Library
1-10-1 Nagata-cho, Chiyoda-ku, Tokyo 100-8924
Tel: (03) 35812331 *Fax:* (03) 35082934
E-mail: kokusai@ndl.go.jp
Web Site: www.ndl.go.jp
Key Personnel
Dir, Planning & Cooperation Dept: Yukiko Saito
First published 1951.
Monthly.
ISSN: 0034-2912

Toshokan Zasshi (J)
Published by Japan Library Association
1-10 Taishido 1-chome, Setagaya-ku, Tokyo 154
Tel: (03) 34106411 *Fax:* (03) 34217588
Library Journal.

Jordan

Directory of Libraries in Jordan (B)
Published by Jordan Library Association
PO Box 6289, Amman
Tel: (06) 629412
Key Personnel
President: Anwar Akroush
Bilingual, 1984.

Directory of Periodicals in Jordan (B)
Published by Jordan Library Association
PO Box 6289, Amman
Tel: (06) 629412
Key Personnel
President: Anwar Akroush

Rissalat al-Maktaba (J)
Published by Jordan Library Association
PO Box 6289, Amman
Tel: (06) 629412
Key Personnel
President: Anwar Akroush
The Message of the Library, text in Arabic, summaries in English.

Kenya

Accessions List of the Library of Congress Office, Nairobi, Kenya (P)
Published by US Library of Congress Office
PO Box 30598, Nairobi
Tel: (02) 442321; (02) 446348 *Fax:* (02) 445580
E-mail: nairobi@libeon-kenya.org
Web Site: www.icipe.org/locnairobi
Key Personnel
Field Director: Paul J Steere
Bimonthly.
ISSN: 1527-5396

Maktaba (J)
Published by Kenya Library Association
PO Box 46031, Nairobi
Tel: (02) 334244 *Fax:* (02) 336885
Key Personnel
Chairman: Jacinta Were *E-mail:* jwere@ken.healthnet.org
Official journal of the Kenya Library Association.
Biannually.

Republic of Korea

Bibliographic Index of Korea (B)
Published by The National Library of Korea
60-1 Panpo-dong, Seocho-gu, Seoul 137-702
Tel: (02) 5354142 *Fax:* (02) 5965749
E-mail: nlkpc@sun.nl.or.kr
Key Personnel
Dir: Gi-Young Jeong

Chonggi Kanhaengmul Kisa Saegin (Index to Korean Language Periodicals) (J)
Published by National Assembly Library
One Yoido-dong, Seoul
Tel: (02) 7843565 *Fax:* (02) 7884193
Telex: 25849
Key Personnel
Librarian: Chong-Il Park
Bimonthly.

Journal of the Korean Society for Library & Information Science (J)
Published by Korean Society for Library & Information Science
SungKyunKwan University, 53, 3-ga, Myungnyun-dong, Chongno-gu, Seoul 110-745
Tel: (02) 760-0330 *Fax:* (02) 760-0326
Key Personnel
President: Eun-Chul Lee *E-mail:* eclee@skku.ac.kr
Text in Korean with English abstracts.
First published 1970.
Quarterly.
300 pp
ISSN: 1225-598X

KLA Bulletin (J)
Published by Korean Library Association
60-1, Panpo-dong, Seocho-ku, Seoul
Tel: (02) 5354868 *Fax:* (02) 5355616
E-mail: klanet@hitel.net
Key Personnel
President: Shin Ki Nam
Bimonthly.

Korean Cataloguing Rules (B)
Published by Korean Library Association
60-1, Panpo-dong, Seocho-ku, Seoul
Tel: (02) 5354868 *Fax:* (02) 5355616
Key Personnel
President: Shin Ki Nam

Korean Library Association Bulletin (J)
Published by Korean Library Association
60-1, Panpo-dong, Seocho-ku, Seoul
Tel: (02) 5354868 *Fax:* (02) 5355616
E-mail: klanet@hitel.net
Key Personnel
President: Shin Ki Nam
Bimonthly.

Kukhoe Tosogwanbo (National Assembly Library Review) (J)
Published by National Assembly Library
One Yoido-dong, Seoul
Tel: (02) 7843565 *Fax:* (02) 7884193
Telex: 25849
Key Personnel
Librarian: Chong-Il Park
Bimonthly.

Statistics on Libraries in Korea (J)
Published by Korean Library Association
60-1, Panpo-dong, Seocho-ku, Seoul
Tel: (02) 5354868 *Fax:* (02) 5355616
E-mail: klanet@hitel.net
Key Personnel
President: Shin Ki Nam
Annually.
ISSN: 1225-5521

Kuwait

The Library Bulletin (P)
Published by Kuwait University Library
PO Box 17140, Kuwait City
Key Personnel
Dir: Dr Husain A Al-Ansari

The University Library (P)
Published by Kuwait University Library
PO Box 17140, Kuwait City
Key Personnel
Dir: Dr Husain A Al-Ansari

Lebanon

Newsletter (J)
Published by The Lebanese Library Association
c/o American University of Beirut, University Library/Gifts & Exchange, Beirut
Mailing Address: PO Box 113/5367
Tel: (01) 340740 ext 2603 *Fax:* (0212) 478-1995 (USA)
Telex: 2080
Key Personnel
President: Marouf Rafi

The Former Yugoslav Republic of Macedonia

Bibliotekarska iskra (J)
Published by Bibliotekarsko Drustvo na Makedonija
Narodna i univerziteska biblioteka "Kliment Ohridski", Bul Goce Delcev-6, Skopje 91000
Tel: (091) 115-177 *Fax:* (091) 230-874
Librarian Association of Macedonia.

Madagascar

Newsletter (J)
Published by Association de Bibliothecaires, Documentalistes, Archivistes et Museographes de Madagascar
Bibliotheque Nationale, Anosy, BP 257, 101 Antananarivo
Tel: (02) 25872
Key Personnel
Dir: L Ralaisholimanana

Malawi

Directory of Malawi Libraries (B)
Published by University of Malawi Libraries
PO Box 280, Zomba
Tel: 522222 *Fax:* 523225
E-mail: smwiyeriwa@unima.wn.apc.org

Mala Bulletin (J)
Published by Malawi Library Association
PO Box 429, Zomba
Tel: (050) 522222 *Fax:* (050) 523225
Key Personnel
President: Ralph Masanjika

Malaysia

Directory of Libraries in Malaysia (B)
Published by National Library of Malaysia (Gift & Exchange Unit)
232 Jalan Tun Razak, 50572 Kuala Lumpur
Tel: (03) 2943488 *Fax:* (03) 2927899
Telex: 30092
Key Personnel
Dir-General: Mariam Abdul Kadir

Majallah Perpustakaan Malaysia (J)
Published by Persatuan Perpustakaan Malaysia
PO Box 12545, Kuala Lumpur
Official journal, text in English and Malay.

Sumber Pustaka (J)
Published by Persatuan Perpustakaan Malaysia
PO Box 12545, 50782 Kuala Lumpur
Tel: (03) 273114 *Fax:* (03) 2731167
Malaysian Library Association official newsletter, text in English and Malay.

Malta

A Bibliography of Maltese Bibliographies (B)
Published by University of Malta Library
Msida
Tel: 333903 *Fax:* 336450
Key Personnel
Chancellor: Prof J Rizzo Naudi
Librarian: Dr Paul Xuereb
First published 1993.

Malia Newsletter (J)
Published by Malta Library & Information Association
c/o University Library, Msida MSD 06
Web Site: www.malia-malta.org
Key Personnel
Chairman: Joseph R Grima
Honorary Secretary: Robert Mizzi
    E-mail: robmiz@global.net.mt

Mauritius

Mauritius Library Association Newsletter (J)
Published by Mauritius Library Association
c/o British Council, Royal Rd, Rose Hill
Mailing Address: POB 111, Rose Hill
Tel: 4549550
Web Site: www.britishcouncil.org/mauritius/
Quarterly.

Memorandum of Books printed in Mauritius and registered in the Archives Office (B)
Published by Mauritius Archives
Development Bank of Mauritius Complex, Petite Riviere
Tel: 2334299

Mexico

Boletin (J)
Published by Instituto de Investigaciones Bibliograficas
c/o Biblioteca Nacional de Mexico & Hemeroteca Nacional de Mexico, Insurgentes Sur s/n, Centro Cultural, Ciudad Universitaria, 04510 Mexico, DF
Tel: (05) 6226805 *Fax:* (05) 6650951
Key Personnel
Dir: Jose Moreno De Alba
Bulletin of the Institute of Bibliographic Research.

Centro de Bibliotecologia, Archivologia e Informacion Anuario (B)
Published by Universidad Nacional Autonoma de Mexico (National University of Mexico)
Torre 1 de Humanidades PB 20 piso, Ciudad Universitaria, 04510 Mexico, DF
Tel: (05) 6221603 *Fax:* (05) 6160664
Key Personnel
Dir: Adolfo Rodriquez Gallardo
Annual of Library Science, Archives, and Information Science.

Noticiero de la AMBAC (News of the Mexican Association of Librarians) (J)
Published by Asociacion Mexicana de Bibliotecarios AC (AMBAC)
Apdo 27-651, 06760, Mexico DF
Tel: (05) 5751135 *Fax:* (05) 5751135
E-mail: ambac@solar.sar.net
Key Personnel
Contact: Elsa M Martinez

Netherlands

Bibliotheck Blad (Library Journal) (J)
Published by Vereniging NBLC
Platinaweg 10, 2504 AH The Hague 2544 EZ
Mailing Address: PO Box 43300, 2504 AH The Hague 5
Tel: (070) 3090100 *Fax:* (070) 3090200
E-mail: bibliotheckblad@nblc.nl

Brinkman's Cumulative Catalog (B)
Published by Bohn Stafleu Van Loghum BV
Postbus 246, 3990 GA Houten
Tel: (0172) 466321 *Fax:* (0172) 435527
E-mail: klantenservice@bsl.nl
Dutch National Bibliography.

Informatie Professional (J)
Published by Nederlandse Vereniging voor beroepsbeoefenaren in de bibliotheeck-informatie-en kennissector (The Netherland Association of Librarians, Documentalists & Information Specialists)
c/o NVB-Verenigingsbureau Plompetorengracht 11, 3512 CA Utrecht
Tel: (030) 2311263 *Fax:* (030) 2311830
Key Personnel
President: Dr J S M Savenye
Professional journal for librarians, researchers & documentalists (joint publication).

Nederlands Archievenblad (Netherlands) (J)
Published by Vereniging van Archivaissen in Nederland
Postbus 11645, 2502 AP The Hague

Tel: (070) 3478656 *Fax:* (070) 3825790
Key Personnel
Contact: P Brood

New Zealand

Library Life (J)
Published by Library & Information Association of New Zealand Aotearoa (LIANZA)
Old Wool House, Level 5, 139-141 Featherston St, Wellington 6001
Mailing Address: PO Box 12-212, Wellington 6038
Tel: (04) 4735834 *Fax:* (04) 4991480
E-mail: office@lianza.org.nz
Web Site: www.lianza.org.nz
Key Personnel
President: Lisa Tocker
Office Manager: Steve Williams *E-mail:* steve@lianza.org.nz
11 times a year (not January).

New Zealand Libraries (J)
Published by Library & Information Association of New Zealand Aotearoa (LIANZA)
Old Wool House, Level 5, 139-141 Featherston St, Wellington 6001
Mailing Address: PO Box 12-212, Wellington 6038
Tel: (04) 4735834 *Fax:* (04) 4991480
E-mail: office@lianza.org.nz
Key Personnel
Editor: Barbara Frame
Semi-annually.
ISSN: 0028-8381

Public Libraries of New Zealand 1995 (B)
Published by Library & Information Association of New Zealand Aotearoa (LIANZA)
Old Wool House, Level 5, 139-141 Featherston St, Wellington 6001
Mailing Address: PO Box 12-212, Wellington 6038
Tel: (04) 4735834 *Fax:* (04) 4991480
E-mail: office@lianza.org.nz
Web Site: www.lianza.org.nz
Key Personnel
President: Lisa Tocker
Office Manager: Steve Williams *E-mail:* steve@lianza.org.nz
Directory with contact details & indexes.

Nigeria

Afribiblios (J)
Published by National Library of Nigeria-Reserch & Development Dept
Dantata House, Central Business District, PMB 1, Abuja
Mailing Address: PMB 12626, Lagos
Tel: (09) 2346772 *Fax:* (09) 2347517
Key Personnel
Chairman: Francis Z Gana
Biannually.

Bendel Library Journal (J)
Published by Edo State Library Board
17 James Watt Rd, Benin City
Mailing Address: PMB 1127, Benin City
Tel: (052) 200810
Key Personnel
Dir: J O U oDiase

Libraries in Nigeria: A Directory (B)
Published by National Library of Nigeria-Reserch & Development Dept
Dantata House, Central Business District, PMB 1, Abuja
Tel: (09) 2346772; (09) 2346773 *Fax:* (09) 2347517
E-mail: nln.rusd@nlbn.org
Telex: 21746
Key Personnel
National Librarian: Mrs O O Omolayole

Library Forum (J)
Published by Nigerian Library Association
c/o National Library Association, 4 Wesley St, PMB 12626, Lagos
Tel: (01) 2600220 *Fax:* (01) 631563
Telex: 21746
Key Personnel
Chairman: Francis Z Gana
Quarterly.

Library Record (J)
Published by Kenneth Dike Library
University of Ibadan, Ibadan
Tel: (02) 8103118 *Fax:* (02) 8103118
E-mail: library@ibadan.ac.ng.; library@kdl.ui.edu.ng
Key Personnel
Librarian: Joseph Ezenwani Ikem
Monthly.

Nigerian Libraries (J)
Published by Nigerian Library Association
c/o National Library of Nigeria, PMB 12626 4 Wesley St, Lagos
Tel: (01) 2600220 *Fax:* (01) 631563
Telex: 21746
Key Personnel
Chairman: Francis Z Gana
Three issues a year, the official publication of the Nigerian Library Association; the Association also publishes a mimeographed newsletter.

Nigerian Periodicals Review (J)
Published by ABIC Books & Equipment Ltd
18 Kenyatta St, Enugu
Mailing Address: PO Box 13740
Tel: (042) 331827 *Fax:* (042) 334811

NLA Newsletter (J)
Published by Nigerian Library Association
c/o National Library of Nigera, 4 Wesley St, PMB 12626, Lagos
Tel: (01) 2600220 *Fax:* (01) 631563
Telex: 21746
Key Personnel
Chairman: Francis Z Gana

Nominal List of Practicing Librarians in Nigeria (B)
Published by National Library of Nigeria-Reserch & Development Dept
Dantata House, Central Business District, PMB 1, Abuja
Mailing Address: PMB 12626, Lagos
Tel: (01) 2600220 *Fax:* (09) 2347517
Telex: 21746
Key Personnel
Chairman: Francis Z Gana
Annually
Names and addresses of practicing librarians at 59 libraries in Nigeria.

Nsukka Library Notes (J)
Published by Nnamdi Azikiwe Library
University of Nigeria, Nsukka, Enugu State
Tel: (042) 771444 *Fax:* (042) 770644
Telex: ULIONS NG 51496
Key Personnel
Librarian: C C Uwechie

School Libraries Bulletin (J)
Published by Anambra State School Libraries Association
c/o Dept of Library Science, University of Nigeria, Enugu Campus, Enugu
Tel: (42) 334103

Norway

Bok og Bibliotek (Books & Libraries) (J)
Published by Statens bibliotektilsyn
Munkedamsveien 62A, 0033 Oslo 8
Mailing Address: PO Box 8145 DEP, M-0033 Oslo
Tel: 22832585 *Fax:* 22831552
Key Personnel
Dir: Asbjorn Langeland
Editor: M Boedtker

Pakistan

Libraries of Pakistan (B)
Published by Library Promotion Bureau
Karachi University Campus, Dastagir Society, Federal B Area, Karachi 75270
Mailing Address: PO Box 8421, Karachi 75270
Tel: (021) 453560
Key Personnel
Dir: Dr Manzoor Ahmed

Pakistan Library Bulletin (P)
Published by Library Promotion Bureau
Karachi University Campus, Dastagir Society, Federal B Area, Karachi 75270
Mailing Address: PO Box 8421, Karachi 75270
Tel: (021) 6335605
Key Personnel
Dir: Dr Manzoor Ahmed
Quarterly.

Plan for Development of Libraries in Pakistan (B)
Published by Library Promotion Bureau
Karachi University Campus, Dastagir Society, Federal B Area, Karachi 75270
Mailing Address: PO Box 8421, Karachi 75270
Tel: (021) 453560

Public Libraries Facilities in Pakistan (B)
Published by Pakistan Library Association (PLA)
c/o International Islamic University, Islamabad
Mailing Address: PO Box 1243, Islamabad
Tel: (051) 855127 *Fax:* (051) 853360
Telex: 54068
Key Personnel
Chief Librarian: Munhammad Riaz

Papua New Guinea

Directory of Libraries in Papua New Guinea (B)
Published by Papua New Guinea Library Association
PO Box 5560, Boroko
Tel: 252405 *Fax:* 259447

PAPUA NEW GUINEA

Telex: 23472
Key Personnel
Dir: Soroi Marepo Eoe

Guide to Manuscripts in the New Guinea Collection (B)
Published by University of Papua New Guinea Library
University Post Office, Waigani
Mailing Address: PO Box 319, Waigani
Tel: 267280 *Fax:* 267187
Telex: 22366
Key Personnel
Librarian: Florence Griffin
By Nancy Lutton (1980).

Peru

Boletin Bibliografico (J)
Published by Biblioteca Central de la Universidad Nacional Mayor de San Marcos
Pasaje Simon Rodriquez 697, Lima
Tel: (014) 4285210 *Fax:* (014) 4285210
Key Personnel
Dir: Dr Oswaldo Salaverry Garcia
Bibliographical Bulletin.

Boletin de la Biblioteca Nacional del Peru (National Library of Peru Bulletin) (J)
Published by Biblioteca Nacional del Peru
Avda Abancay 4ta cuadra, Lima 1
Tel: (01) 428-7690 *Fax:* (01) 427-7331
E-mail: jefatura@binape.gob.pe
Key Personnel
Director: Sinesio Lopez
First published 1943.
irregular.

FENIX Revista de la Biblioteca Nacional del Peru (FENIX National Library of Peru Review) (J)
Published by Biblioteca Nacional del Peru
Avda Abancay 4ta cuadra, Lima 1
Tel: (01) 428-7690; (01) 428-7696 *Fax:* (01) 427-7331
E-mail: jefatura@binape.gob.pe
Web Site: www.binape.gob.pe
Key Personnel
Director: Sinesio Lopez
First published 1944.
irregular.
42 (2001), $30
ISSN: 0015-0002

Gaceta Bibliotecaria Del Peru (Library Gazette) (J)
Published by Biblioteca Nacional del Peru
Apdo 2335, Avda Abancay 4ta cuadra s/n, Lima
Tel: (01) 4287690 *Fax:* (01) 4277331
E-mail: jefatura@binape.gob.pe
Key Personnel
Director: Sinesio Lopez
First published 1963.
irregular.
37 (1987)

Philippines

Bulletin (J)
Published by Association of Special Libraries of the Philippines (ASLP)
National Library Bldg, Room 301, T M Kalaw St, 2801 Manila
Tel: (02) 590177 *Fax:* (02) 590177
Key Personnel
President: Zenaida F Lucas
Quarterly.

Bulletin (J)
Published by Philippine Librarians Association Inc
c/o National Library, T M Kalaw St, Room 301, 1000 Manila, Ermita
Tel: (02) 5253196 *Fax:* (02) 5242329
E-mail: amb@max.ph.net

Directory of Special Library Resources and Research Facilities in the Philippines (B)
Published by Association of Special Libraries of the Philippines (ASLP)
National Library Bldg, Room 301, T M Kalaw St, 2801 Manila
Tel: (02) 590177 *Fax:* (02) 590177
Key Personnel
President: Zenaida F Lucas

Index to Philippine Periodicals (IPP) (B)
Published by University of the Philippines Library, Indexing Section
Gonzalez Hall, Diliman, 1101 Quezon City
Tel: (02) 926 1877 *Fax:* (02) 926 1876
E-mail: salvacion.arlante@up.edu.ph
Web Site: www.mainlib.upd.edu.ph
First published 1946.
Quarterly.

Journal of Philippine Librarianship (J)
Published by University of the Philippines, Institute of Library Science
3/F Gonzalez Hall, Main Library Bldg, UP Diliman, Quezon City 1101
Tel: (02) 920 5367 *Fax:* (02) 920 5367
Key Personnel
Business Manager: Nathalie N de la Torre
E-mail: nathalie8_4@yahoo.com
Text in English.
Annually.
$15
ISSN: 0022-359X

Newsletter (J)
Published by Bibliographical Society of the Philippines
c/o National Library of the Philippines, T M Kalaw St, 1000 Ermita, Manila
Mailing Address: PO Box 2926, 1000 Ermita, Manila
Tel: (02) 5253196 *Fax:* 5242329
E-mail: amb@max.ph.net

Newsletter (J)
Published by University of the Philippines, Institute of Library Science
Diliman, Gonzalez Hall, 1101 Quezon City
Tel: (02) 920 5367 *Fax:* (02) 920 5367
Key Personnel
Business Manager: Nathalie N de la Torre
E-mail: nathalie8_4@yahoo.com
Text in English.
Annually.
ISSN: 0300-3612

Philippine National Bibliography (J)
Published by National Library of the Philippines
PO Box 2926, T M Kalaw, 1000 Ermita, Manila
Tel: (02) 525-31-96 *Fax:* (02) 524-23-29
E-mail: nanie@nlp.gov.ph
Web Site: www.nlp.gov.ph
Key Personnel
Dir: Prudenciana C Cruz
Published quarterly with annual cumulation.
Parent Company: National Commission for Culture & the Arts

Poland

Bibliografia Wydawnictw CIAGLYCH (Bibliography of Polish Serials) (J)
Published by Biblioteka Narodowa
Al Niepodleglosci 213, 00-973 Warsaw 22
Tel: (022) 608 2409
Web Site: www.bn.org.pl
Telex: 813702 BNPL; 816761 *Cable:* AL NIEPODLEGLOSCI
Key Personnel
Librarian: Grazyna Federowicz
Annually.

Bibliotekarz (The Librarian) (J)
Published by Polish Librarians' Association
ul Konopczynskiego 5-7, 00-953 Warsaw
Tel: (022) 275296
Key Personnel
President: Stanislaw Czaja
Text in Polish. Summaries in English and Russian.

Biblioteki Publiczne w Liczbach (Public Libraries in Figures) (B)
Published by Biblioteka Narodowa
Al Niepodleglosci 213, 02 086 Warsaw 22
Mailing Address: PO Box 36, 00-973 Warsaw
Tel: (022) 8255733 *Fax:* (022) 6082999
Telex: 816761
Key Personnel
Dir: Prof Adam Manikowski

Informator Adresowy Podstawowych Placowek Informacji Naukowej i Technicznej (B)
Published by Centralne Laboratorium Przemys Zlemniacanego (Starch and Potato Products Research Laboratory)
Zwierzyniecka 18, 60-814 Poznan
Tel: (061) 8668045 *Fax:* (061) 8417610
E-mail: clpz@man.poznan.pl
Web Site: www.clpz.posnan.pl

Informator Biblioteczny (Library Guide) (B)
Published by Polish Librarians' Association
ul Konopczynskiego 5-7, 00-953 Warsaw
Tel: (022) 275296
E-mail: ekrysiak@plearn.edu.pl
Web Site: ciuw.warman.net.pl/alf/sbp/index.html
Key Personnel
President: Stanislaw Czajka

Informator Nauki Polskiej (Polish Research Directory) (B)
Published by Osrodek Przetwarzania Informacji
al Niepodleglosci 188b, 00-950 Warsaw
Mailing Address: PO Box 355, 00-950 Warsaw
Tel: (022) 256178 *Fax:* (022) 253319
E-mail: wasiak@atos.warman.com.pl
Key Personnel
Dir: Waclaw Wasiak *E-mail:* wasiak@atos.warman.com.pl
Available in Polish & English language versions, five volumes.

Informator o Bibliotekach Wspolpracujacych w Ramach Specjalizacji Zbiorow (Information About Modern Libraries Working on Group Specializations) (B)
Published by Biblioteka Glowna Politechniki Warszawskiej
Plac Politechniki 1, 00-661 Warsaw
Tel: (022) 6211370 *Fax:* (022) 6211370
Key Personnel
Dir: E Dudzinska

Komputerowe Bazy Danych o Nauce i Technice
(Computerized Databases on Science & Technology) (B)
Published by Osrodek Przetwarzania Informacji
al Niepodleglosci 188b, 00-950 Warsaw
Mailing Address: PO Box 355, 00-950 Warsaw
Tel: (022) 256178 *Fax:* (022) 253319
E-mail: wasiak@atos.warman.com.pl
Key Personnel
Dir: Waclaw Wasiak *E-mail:* wasiak@atos.warman.com.pl

Nauka, Informacja, Biznes (Science, Information, Business) (P)
Published by Osrodek Przetwarzania Informacji
al Niepodleglosci 188b, 00-950 Warsaw
Mailing Address: PO Box 355, 00-950 Warsaw
Tel: (022) 256178 *Fax:* (022) 253319
E-mail: wasiak@atos.warman.com.pl
Key Personnel
Dir: Waclaw Wasiak *E-mail:* wasiak@atos.warman.com.pl
Seven mathematical series.
Quarterly.

Nuka, Informacja, Biznes-Katalog Rozpraw Doktorskich i Habilitacyjnych (Science, Information, Business-Catalogue of Doctoral & Habilitational Dissertations) (P)
Published by Osrodek Przetwarzania Informacji
al Niepodleglosci 188b, 00-950 Warsaw
Mailing Address: PO Box 355, 00-950 Warsaw
Tel: (022) 256178 *Fax:* (022) 253319
Key Personnel
Dir: Waclaw Wasiak *E-mail:* wasiak@atos.warman.com.pl
Annually.

Placowki Informacji Naukowej i Technicznej w Polsce (Scientific & Technical Information Centres in Poland) (B)
Published by Osrodek Przetwarzania Informacji
al Niepodleglosci 188b, 00-950 Warsaw
Mailing Address: PO Box 355, 00-950 Warsaw
Tel: (022) 256178 *Fax:* (022) 253319
Key Personnel
Dir: Waclaw Wasiak *E-mail:* wasiak@atos.warman.com.pl

Polska Bibliografia Bibliologiczna (Polish Bibliography of Library Science) (B)
Published by Biblioteka Narodowa
Al Niepodlegtosci 213, 00-973 Warsaw 22
Mailing Address: PO Box 36, 00-973 Warsaw 22
Tel: (022) 259271 *Fax:* (022) 6082999
Telex: 816761
Key Personnel
Dir: Prof Adam Manikowski

Poradnik Bibliotekarza (The Librarian's Adviser) (J)
Published by Polish Librarians' Association
ul Konopczynskiego 5-7, 00-953 Warsaw
Tel: (022) 275296 *Fax:* (022) 223541
Key Personnel
President: Stanislaw Czaja

Research & Development Units & Scientific Institutions-R&D Tender '95 (B)
Published by Osrodek Przetwarzania Informacji
al Niepodleglosci 188b, 00-950 Warsaw
Mailing Address: PO Box 355, 00-950 Warsaw
Tel: (022) 256178 *Fax:* (022) 253319
Key Personnel
Dir: Waclaw Wasiak *E-mail:* wasiak@atos.warman.com.pl

Rocznik Biblioteki Narodowej (National Library Yearbook) (B)
Published by Biblioteka Narodowa
Al Niepodleglosci 213, PO Box 36, 00-973 Warsaw 22
Tel: (022) 259271 *Fax:* (022) 6082999
Telex: 816761
Covers scientific library science with text in Polish with English summaries.

Portugal

Boletim de Bibliografia Portuguesa (J)
Published by Instituto da Biblioteca Nacional e do Livro
Campo Grande 83, 1751 Lisbon codex
Tel: (021) 7950130 *Fax:* (021) 7933607
Portuguese Bibliographic Bulletin.

Cadernos de Biblioteconomia, Arquivistica e Documentacao (Library Management, Archives & Documentation) (J)
Published by Associacao Portuguesa de Bibliotecarios, Arquivistas e Documentalistas (The Portuguese Association of Librarians Archivists & Documentalists)
R Morais Soares, 43C-1 DTD, 1900 Lisbon Codex
Tel: (021) 8154479; (021) 8134697 *Fax:* (021) 8154508
E-mail: badbn@mail.telepac.pt
Key Personnel
Dir: Antonio Pina Falcao
Triannually.

Guia de Servicios de Documentacao e de Bibliotecas em Portugal (List of Portuguese Libraries & Documentation Services) (B)
Published by Fundacao para a Ciencia e a Tecnologia/Servico de Informacao e Documentacao(SID)
Av D Carlos 1 126, 1249-074 Lisbon
Tel: (021) 3924440 *Fax:* (021) 3957284
E-mail: sid@fct.mct.pt
Web Site: www.fct.mct.pt
Key Personnel
President: Prof Fernando Ramoa Ribeiro
Dir: Dr Gabriela Lopes da Silva *E-mail:* G.L.Silva@fct.mct.pt
Internet database only at www.fct.mct.pt, option: Bibliotecas com Revistas de C&T.

Sumarios das Publicacoes Periodicas Portuguesas (Current Contents of Portuguese Periodicals) (J)
Published by Biblioteca Geral da Universidade de Coimbra
Largo da Porta Ferrea, 3000-447 Coimbra
Tel: (0239) 859800 *Fax:* (0239) 827135
E-mail: bguc@ci.uc.pt
Key Personnel
Dir: Prof Anibal Pinto De Castro
E-mail: acastro@ci.uc.pt

Romania

ABSI - Abstracte in bibliologie si stiinta informarii (ABSI - Abstracts in Library & Information Science) (J)
Published by National Library
Str Ion Ghica 4, 79708 Bucharest
Tel: (01) 3142434 (ext 111); (01) 3142434 (ext 131) *Fax:* (01) 3123381
E-mail: go@bibnat.ro
Key Personnel
Chief Editor: Ioana Varlan
ABSI- Abstracts in Library & Information Science.
First published 1960.
Monthly.
51 pp
ISSN: 1220-3092

Biblioteconomie Culegere de Traduceri Prelucrate (Librarianship: Collected Adapted Translations) (J)
Published by National Library
Str Ion Ghica 4, 79708 Bucharest
Tel: (01)3142434 (ext 111); (01) 3142434 (ext 126); (01) 3142434 (ext 131) *Fax:* (01) 3123381
E-mail: go@bibnat.ro
Key Personnel
Chief Editor: Anca Moraru
Librarianship: Collected adapted translations.
First published 1964.
Quarterly.
95 pp
ISSN: 1220-3076

Information & Documentation Problems (J)
Published by National Institute for Information & Documentation
Str George Enescu 27-29, Sector 1, R-70141 Bucharest
Tel: (01) 6134010 *Fax:* (01) 3126734
E-mail: inid@iniduw.inid.ro
Telex: 11247
Key Personnel
Contact: Gheorghe Anghel
About 500 different publications in Romanian, periodicals (science, know-hows, machines, products, works, etc).

Russian Federation

Bibliotechnoe delo i Bibliografiya Bibliografieheskaya informatsiya (Library Science and Theory of Bibliography, Bibliographic Information) (B)
Published by Russian State Library
3/5 Vozdvizhenka, 101000 Moscow
Tel: (095) 202-79-47 *Fax:* (095) 2002255
E-mail: bvpress@rsl.ru
Telex: 411167 GBL SU
Key Personnel
Dir: Vladimir K Egorov

Biblioteka (The Librarian) (J)
Published by Ministry of Culture
Prospekt Marksa ll-1, 121019 Moscow
Tel: (095) 2026308
Telex: 411167 GBLSU

Biblioteka v epohu peremen. Informatsionnyj sbornik (J)
Published by Russian State Library
3/5 Vozdvizhenka, 101000 Moscow
Tel: (095) 202 83 12 *Fax:* (095) 202 83 12
E-mail: aisnikl@rsl.ru
Web Site: www.rsl.ru
Key Personnel
Dir: Dr Vladimir V Fedorov *Tel:* (095) 203 84 12
E-mail: gek@rsl.ru
First published 1999.
quarterly.
160 pp, $50

Bibliotekovedenie (Library Science) (J)
Published by Russian State Library
3/5 Vozdvizhenka, 101000 Moscow

RUSSIAN FEDERATION

Tel: (095) 202-79-47 *Fax:* (095) 203-93-90; (095) 90-60-62
E-mail: bvpress@rsl.ru
Key Personnel
Gen Dir: Victor Fedorov

Bibliotekovedenie i Bibliografiya za Rubezhom-Librarianship & Bibliography Abroad (Librarianship & Bibliography Abroad) (B)
Published by Russian State Library
3/5 Vozdvizhenka, 101000 Moscow
Tel: (095) 202-79-47 *Fax:* (095) 2002255
E-mail: bvpress@rsl.ru
Telex: 411167 GBL SU
Key Personnel
Dir: Vladimir K Egorov

Esteticheskoe vospitanie Referativno-Bibliograficheskaya informatsiya (Aesthetic Education Bibliographic Information) (B)
Published by Russian State Library
3/5 Vozdvizhenka, 101000 Moscow
Tel: (095) 202-79-47 *Fax:* (095) 2002255
E-mail: irgb@glas.apc.org
Telex: 411167 GBL SU

Izobrazitelnoye Iskustvo, Bibliograficheskaya Informatsiya (Fine Art, Bibliographic Information) (B)
Published by Russian State Library
3/5 Vozdvizhenka, 101000 Moscow
Tel: (095) 202-79-47 *Fax:* (095) 2002255
E-mail: bvpress@rsl.ru
Telex: 411167 GBL SU
Key Personnel
Dir: Vladimir K Egorov
Theory & practice of fine art in Russia & abroad.

Kultura v Sovremennom Mire, Informatsionni Sbornik (Culture in the Modern World, Serial Information) (B)
Published by Russian State Library
3/5 Vozdvizhenka, 101000 Moscow
Tel: (095) 202-79-47 *Fax:* (095) 2002255
E-mail: bvpress@rsl.ru
Telex: 411167 GBL SU
Key Personnel
Dir: Vladimir K Egorov
The world cultural process, cultural policy, views & analyses, innovation in culture & art.

Kultura, Kulturologiya, Referativno-bibliograficheskaya informatsiya (Culture, Culturology, Bibliographic Information) (J)
Published by Russian State Library
3/5 Vozdvizhenka, 101000 Moscow
Tel: (095) 202 83 12 *Fax:* (095) 202 83 12
E-mail: aisnikl@rsl.ru
Key Personnel
Dir: Dr Vladimir V Fedorov *Tel:* (095) 203 84 12
E-mail: gek@rsl.ru

Massovaya Biblioteca. Teoriya i Practica (Public Library. Theory & Practice) (B)
Published by Russian State Library
3/5 Vozdvizhenka, 101000 Moscow
Tel: (095) 202-79-47 *Fax:* (095) 203-93-90
E-mail: bvpress@rsl.ru
Key Personnel
Dir: Vladimir K Egorov
Serial information publication.

Materialnaya Baza Sfery Kulturi, Informatsionni Sbornik (Material Base of the Cultural Sphere, Serial Information) (B)
Published by Russian State Library
3/5 Vozdvizhenka, 101000 Moscow
Tel: (095) 202-79-47 *Fax:* (095) 2002255

E-mail: bvpress@rsl.ru
Telex: 411167 GBL SU
Key Personnel
Dir: Vladimir K Egorov
Material & technical facilities, economy, management in culture.

Mir Bibliotek Segodnya (Library World Today) (J)
Published by Russian State Library
3/5 Vozdvizhenka, 101000 Moscow
Tel: (095) 202-79-47 *Fax:* (095) 203-93-90
E-mail: bvpress@rsl.ru
Key Personnel
Editor-in-Chief: L Majzewa
Original & abstract information on Russian & world libraries. Serial information publication.

Muzeynoe delo i ohrana pamyatnikov. Referativno-bibliograficheskaya informatsiya (Museums & Protection of monuments. Bibliographic Information) (J)
Published by Russian State Library
3/5 Vozdvizhenka, 101000 Moscow
Tel: (095) 202 83 12 *Fax:* (095) 202 83 12
E-mail: aisnikl@rsl.ru
Key Personnel
Dir: Dr Vladimir V Fedorov *Tel:* (095) 203 84 12
E-mail: gek@rsl.ru

Muzika, Bibliograficheskaya Informatsiya (Music, Bibliographic Information) (B)
Published by Russian State Library
3/5 Vozdvizhenka, 101000 Moscow
Tel: (095) 202-79-47 *Fax:* (095) 2002255
E-mail: bvpress@rsl.ru
Telex: 411167 GBL SU
Key Personnel
Dir: Vladimir K Egorov
Theory, history & genres of music.

Narodnoie Tvorchestvo: Sociokulturnaya Deyatelnost v Sfere Dosuga, Informatsionni Sbornik (Sociocultural Activity in the Sphere of Leisure, Serial Information) (B)
Published by Russian State Library
3/5 Vozdvizhenka, 101000 Moscow
Tel: (095) 202-79-47 *Fax:* (095) 2002255
E-mail: bvpress@rsl.ru
Key Personnel
Dir: Vladimir K Egorov
Folk art, amateur activity & national traditional art.

Nauchnye i tekhnicheskie biblioteki (Scientific and Technical Libraries) (J)
Published by Russia National Public Library for Science and Technology
Kusnetsky most 12, Moscow 103031
Tel: (095) 9259288 *Fax:* (095) 9219862
E-mail: root@gpntb.msk.ru
Telex: 411167 GBLSU
Key Personnel
Dir: Dr A I Zemskov

Nauka o Kulture. Itogi i perspektivy. Informatsionnyj sbornik (Culture Science. Results & Perspectives. Serial Information) (J)
Published by Russian State Library
3/5 Vozdvizhenka, 101000 Moscow
Tel: (095) 202 83 12 *Fax:* (095) 202 83 12
E-mail: aisnikl@rsl.ru
Key Personnel
Dir: Dr Vladimir V Fedorov *Tel:* (095) 203 84 12
E-mail: gek@rsl.ru

Panorama kulturnoi zhizni Rossiyskoi Federatsii. Informatsionnyj sbornik (Panorama of Cultural Life in Russian Federation. Serial Information) (J)
Published by Russian State Library

3/5 Vozdvizhenka, 101000 Moscow
Tel: (095) 202 83 12 *Fax:* (095) 202 83 12
E-mail: aisnikl@rsl.ru
Key Personnel
Dir: Dr Vladimir V Fedorov *Tel:* (095) 203 84 12
E-mail: gek@rsl.ru

Panorama kulturnoi zhizni stran SNG i Baltii. Informatsionnyj sbornik (Panorama of Cultural Life in the States of the CIS & in the Baltic States. Serial Information) (J)
Published by Russian State Library
3/5 Vozdvizhenka, 101000 Moscow
Tel: (095) 202 83 12 *Fax:* (095) 202 83 12
E-mail: aisnikl@rsl.ru
Key Personnel
Dir: Dr Vladimir V Fedorov *Tel:* (095) 203 84 12
E-mail: gek@rsl.ru

Panorama kulturnoi zhizni zarubezhnyh stran. Informatsionnyj sbornik (Panorama of Cultural Life Abroad. Serial Information) (J)
Published by Russian State Library
3/5 Vozdvizhenka, 101000 Moscow
Tel: (095) 202 83 12 *Fax:* (095) 202 83 12
Key Personnel
Dir: Dr Vladimir V Fedorov *Tel:* (095) 203 84 12
E-mail: gek@rsl.ru

Russkaya Kultura Vne Granits (Russian Culture Beyond Frontiers) (B)
Published by Russian State Library
3/5 Vozdvizhenka, 101000 Moscow
Tel: (095) 202-79-47 *Fax:* (095) 2002255
E-mail: bvpress@rsl.ru
Key Personnel
Dir: Vladimir K Egorov
Serial Information Culture, History, & Policy.

Sociokulturnaya Deyatelnost v Sfere Dosuga, Referativno-Bibliograficheskaya Informatsiya (Sociocultural Activities in the Sphere of Leisure, Bibliographic Information) (B)
Published by Russian State Library
3/5 Vozdvizhenka, 101000 Moscow
Tel: (095) 202-79-47 *Fax:* (095) 2002255
E-mail: bvpress@rsl.ru
Telex: 411167 GBL SU
Key Personnel
Dir: Vladimir K Egorov
Problems of outdoor recreation.

Zrelischnie Iskustva Referativno-Bibliograficheskaya Informatsiya (Performing Arts, Bibliographic Information) (B)
Published by Russian State Library
3/5 Vozdvizhenka, 101000 Moscow
Tel: (095) 202-79-47 *Fax:* (095) 2002255
E-mail: bvpress@rsl.ru
Telex: 411167 GBL SU
Key Personnel
Dir: Vladimir K Egorov
Theatre, circus, dance & music hall art.

Saudi Arabia

Bulletin (J)
Published by National Library
King Faisal St, Riyadh
Key Personnel
Dir: Abdur Rahman Al Sarra

Directory of Libraries in Saudi Arabia (B)
Published by King Saud University Library
PO Box 22480, Riyadh 11495

Tel: (01) 4676148 *Fax:* (01) 4676162
E-mail: fl01001@ksu.edu.sa
Key Personnel
Dean: Dr Sulaiman Al-Ogla
First published 1979.
215 pp

Senegal

Repertoire des Bibliotheques et Organismes de Documentation au Senegal (Catalogue of the Libraries and Documentation Centres of Senegal) (B)
Published by Ecole des Bibliothecaires, Archivistes et Documentalistes de l'Universite Cheikh Anta Diop de Dakar
Faculty of Arts & Social Sciences, BP 3252 Dakar
Tel: 8257660
Key Personnel
Dir: Ousmane Sane
Archives and documentation centres throughout Senegal. Information on 124 libraries.

Sierra Leone

SLAALIS Bulletin (J)
Published by Sierra Leone Association of Archivists, Librarians and Information Scientists
PO Box 326, Freetown
Tel: (022) 23848
Key Personnel
Chief Librarian: Irene O'Brien-Coker
Published quarterly.

Singapore

Directory of Libraries in Singapore (B)
Published by Library Association of Singapore
Bukit Merah Central, c/o Branch Library, Singapore 159835
Mailing Address: PO Box 0693, Singapore 911537
Key Personnel
President: Choy Fatt Cheong

Singapore Libraries (B)
Published by Library Association of Singapore
Bukit Merah Central, c/o Branch Library, Singapore 159835
Mailing Address: PO Box 0693, Singapore 911537
Key Personnel
President: Choy Fatt Cheong
Published annually.

Singapore Libraries Bulletin (P)
Published by Library Association of Singapore
Bukit Merah Central, c/o Branch Library, Singapore 159835
Mailing Address: PO Box 0693, Singapore 911537
Key Personnel
President: Choy Fatt Cheong
Published quarterly.

Singapore Periodicals Index (P)
Published by National Library Board Singapore, Library Supply Services
Tower B, 3rd Story, No 3, Changi South St 2, Singapore 486548
Tel: 65467265 *Fax:* 65467209
E-mail: spi@nlb.gov.sg *Cable:* RS 26620 NATLIB
Key Personnel
Librarian: Hamidah Abdullah *Tel:* 65467296
E-mail: hamidah.abdullah@nlb.gov.sg
Serial (CD-ROM).
First published 1996.
Annually.
ISSN: 0218-902X

Slovenia

Knjiznica: Revija za Podrocje Bibliotekarstva in Informacijske Znanosti (Library: Journal for Library & Information Science) (J)
Published by Zveza bibliotekarskih drustev Slovenije (ZBDS) Slovenian Library Association (Union of Associations of Slovene Librarians)
Turjaska 1, 1000 Ljubljana
Tel: (061) 2001 207 *Fax:* (061) 2001 192
Web Site: www.zbds-zveza.si
Key Personnel
Editor: Melita Ambrozic *E-mail:* melita.ambrozic@nuk.uni-lj.si
Text in Slovenian; Summaries in English. Library & information sciences.
First published 1957.
Quarterly.
150 pp, $30 Vol
ISSN: 0023-2424

South Africa

The Cape Librarian (P)
Published by Cape Provincial Library Service
PO Box 2108, Cape Town 8000
Tel: (021) 4109111 *Fax:* (021) 4197541
Key Personnel
Dir: N. F. Van Der Merwe
Text in Afrikaans & English.

Free State Libraries (J)
Published by Free State Information Services Directorate
Private Bag X20606, Bloemfontein 9300
Tel: (051) 4054680 *Fax:* (051) 4054036
E-mail: loader@majuba.ofs.gov.za; jacomien@majuba.ofs.gov.za
Telex: 267056t

Index to South African Periodicals (ISAP) (J)
Published by State Library
PO Box 397, Pretoria 0001
Tel: (012) 218931 *Fax:* (012) 3255984
E-mail: askotze@statelib.pwv.gov.za
Key Personnel
Dir: Dr Peter J Lor

Kwaznaplis (J)
Published by Kwazulu Natal Provincial Library Services
PB X9016, Pietermaritzburg 3200
Tel: (0331) 940241 *Fax:* (0331) 942237
E-mail: hartj@natalia.kzntl.gov.za
Key Personnel
Deputy Dir: Dr Rookaya Bawa

LIASA News (J)
Published by Library & Information Association of South Africa (LIASA)
PO Box 1598, Pretoria 0001
Tel: (012) 481 2870 *Fax:* (012) 481 2873
E-mail: liasa@liasa.org.za
Web Site: www.liasa.org.za
Key Personnel
Executive Dir: Mrs Gwenda Thomas
Quarterly.

Local Government Library Bulletin (J)
Published by Johannesburg Public Library
Market Sq, Johannesburg 2001
Tel: (011) 8363787 *Fax:* (011) 8366607
Key Personnel
Librarian: E J Bevan *E-mail:* jbevan@mj.org.za
Monthly.
free

Mousaion (P)
Published by Unisa Press
University of South Africa, Pretoria 0003
Mailing Address: PO Box 392, Pretoria 0001
Tel: (012) 4293111 *Fax:* (012) 4293221
E-mail: unisa-press@unisa.ac.za
Web Site: www.unisa.ac.za
Telex: 350068 *Cable:* UNISA
Key Personnel
Editor: Prof J A Kruger

Periodicals in Southern African Libraries (PISAL) (J)
Published by State Library
PO Box 397, Pretoria 0001
Tel: (012) 218931 *Fax:* (012) 3255984
Key Personnel
Dir: Dr Peter J Lor

Quarterly Bulletin of the South African Library (J)
Published by South African Library
PO Box 496, Cape Town 8000
Tel: (021) 246320 *Fax:* (021) 244848

South African Journal of Library & Information Science (J)
Published by Library & Information Association of South Africa (LIASA)
PO Box 1598, Pretoria 0001
Tel: (012) 481 2870 *Fax:* (012) 481 2873
E-mail: liasa@liasa.org.za
Web Site: www.liasa.org.za
Key Personnel
Executive Dir: Mrs Gwenda Thomas
Bianually.

South African Journal of Library & Information Science (J)
Published by Bureau for Scientific Publications
PO Box 1758, Pretoria 0001
Tel: (012) 3226404 *Fax:* (012) 3207803
E-mail: bspman@icon.co.za
Web Site: www.safest.org.za/bsp
Telex: 350068

South African National Bibliography (SANB) (J)
Published by State Library
PO Box 397, Pretoria 0001
Tel: (012) 218931 *Fax:* (012) 3255984
Quarterly issues, annual cumulation.

Spain

Biblioteca Hispana (Spanish Library) (B)
Published by Consejo Superior de Investigaciones Cientificas
Vitruvio, 8, 28006 Madrid
SAN: 001-1347
Tel: (091) 2619800 *Fax:* (091) 4113077
Key Personnel
Pres: Cesar Nombela Cano

Sri Lanka

Directory of Social Science Libraries, Information Centres and Data Bases in Sri Lanka 1990 (B)
Published by National Library & Documentation Services Board
No 14, Independence Ave, Colombo 07
Tel: (01) 698847 *Fax:* (01) 685201
E-mail: natlib@slt.lk
Web Site: www.slt.lk/nlib
Key Personnel
Dir: MS Upali Amarzsiri
Other publications relevent to Social Sciences, Conference Index; Selected Bibliography on SAARC; Sri Lanka Pustakala Namawaliya; Sri Lanka Rajaye Prakashana Namawaliya; Directory of Libraries in Sri Lanka; Directory of Social Scientists in Sri Lanka Part 1; Bibliography on Kataragama; Bibliography on Mahindagamanaya; Lama Grantha Namawaliaya; Pustakala Dave Bhanda; Sri Lanka Newspaper article index.

Library News (J)
Published by National Library & Documentation Services Board
No 14, Independence Ave, Colombo 07
Tel: (01) 698847; (01) 674387 *Fax:* (01) 685201
E-mail: natlib@slt.lk
Web Site: www.slt.lk/nlib
Key Personnel
Dir General: Mr M S U Amarasiri *Tel:* (01) 687581 *E-mail:* dgnl@sltnet.lk
Quarterly.
ISSN: 1391-0000

Sri Lanka Library Review (J)
Published by Sri Lanka Library Association
275/75 Bauddhaloka Mawatha, Colombo 7
Tel: (01) 589103
E-mail: postmast@slla.ac.lk
Key Personnel
Contact: Mrs Swarna Jayatilleke

Sri Lanka Periodicals Directory (J)
Published by National Museum Library of Sri Lanka (NMLSL)
PO Box 854, Colombo 7
Tel: (01) 595366
Annual supplements.

Sri Lanka Periodicals Index (P)
Published by National Museum Library of Sri Lanka (NMLSL)
Sir Marcus Fernando Mawatha, Colombo 7
Mailing Address: PO Box 854, Colombo 7
Tel: (01) 595366

Swaziland

Directory of Swaziland Libraries (B)
Published by University of Swaziland Library
Private Bag 4, Kwaluseni
Tel: 84011 *Fax:* 85276
Key Personnel
Chancellor: HM King Mswati, lll
Published irregularly.

Serials in Swaziland University Libraries (B)
Published by University of Swaziland Library
Private Bag 4, Kwaluseni
Tel: 84011 *Fax:* 85276
E-mail: mmavuso@uniswacl.uniswa.sz
Telex: 2087
Published irregularly.

Sweden

Biblioteksbladet (Library Journal) (J)
Published by Sveriges Allmaenna Biblioteksfoerening
PO Box 3127, S-103 62 Stockholm
Tel: (08) 54513230 *Fax:* (08) 54513231
Text in Scandinavian languages with summaries in English.

Svensk periodicafoerteckning (Current Swedish Periodicals) (B)
Published by Kungliga Biblioteket, Bibliografiska avdelningen
Box 5039, 10241 Stockholm
Tel: (08) 4634000 *Fax:* (08) 4634004
Telex: 19640 KBS S

Tidskrift foer Dokumentation (Documentation Periodical) (J)
Published by Tekniska Litteratursaellskapet
Box 55580, S-102 04 Stockholm
Tel: (08) 6782320 *Fax:* (08) 6782301
E-mail: kansliet@tls.se
Web Site: www.tls.se
Text in Swedish, with summaries & occasional articles in English Nordic Journal of Documentation.

Switzerland

Arbido (J)
Published by Association des Bibliotheques et Bibliothecaires Suisses
Sekretariat BBS, Effingstr 35, CH-3008 Bern
Tel: (031) 382 42 40 *Fax:* (031) 382 46 48
E-mail: bbs@bbs.ch
Key Personnel
President: Dr Peter Wille

Syrian Arab Republic

Damascus University Library Review (J)
Published by Damascus University Press
Damascus
Tel: (011) 215100
Telex: 411971

Taiwan, Province of China

Chung-hua min-kuo t'u-shu-kuan nien-chien (B)
Published by National Central Library
20 Chungshan S Rd, Taipei 10040
Tel: (02) 23619132 *Fax:* (02) 23110155
Key Personnel
Dir: Dr Tseng Chi-Chun
Yearbook of Libraries in the Republic of China.

Chung-kuo t'u-shu-kuan hsueh-hui hui-pao (J)
Published by Library Association of China
c/o National Central Library, 20 Chungshan S Rd, Taipei 10040
Tel: (02) 23312475 *Fax:* (02) 23700899
Key Personnel
Pres: James HC Hu
Bulletin of the Library Association of China.

Journal of Library and Information Science (J)
Published by Department of Adult & Continuing Education, National Taiwan Normal University
162, Section 1, Hoping East Rd, Taipei 10610
Tel: (02) 3625101; (02) 3625102 *Fax:* (02) 3946506; (02) 3626341
Key Personnel
Pres: Hsi-Muh Leu

Tseng-pu hsiu-ting Chung-hua min-kuo Chung-wen ch'i-k'an lien-ho mu-lu (B)
Published by National Central Library
20 Chungshan S Rd, Taipei 10040
Tel: (02) 23619132 *Fax:* (02) 23110155
Key Personnel
Dir: Tseng Chi-Chun
National Union List of Chinese Periodicals of the Republic of China.

United Republic of Tanzania

Directory of Libraries, Museums and Archives in Tanzania (B)
Published by Tanzania Library Services Board
Bibi Titi Mohamed St, PO Box 9283, Dar es Salaam
Tel: (051) 110572; (051) 110573
Key Personnel
Dir General: Ellezer A Mwinyimvua
1979.

Matukio (J)
Published by Tanzania Library Association
PO Box 33433, Dar es Salaam
Key Personnel
Chairman: Dr Alli Mcharzao

Thailand

An Annotated Bibliography of Librarianship in Thailand (B)
Published by Department of Library Science, Chulalongkorn University, Faculty of Arts
Phaya Thai Rd, Bangkok 10330
Tel: (02) 215-0871 *Fax:* (02) 215-4804
Telex: 20217
Key Personnel
Prof: Dr Boonrod Binson

Bulletin (J)
Published by Thai Library Association
273 Vibhavadee Rangsit Rd, Phyathai, Bangkok 10400
Tel: (02) 2712084
Key Personnel
Pres: M Chavalit

List of Scientific Libraries in Thailand (B)
Published by Thai National Documentation Centre (TNDC)
196 Phahon Yothin Rd, Bangkok 10900
Tel: (02) 579112130 *Fax:* (02) 5798594
Telex: 21392
Key Personnel
Dir: Mrs Nongphanga Chitrakorn

Trinidad & Tobago

Bulletin (J)
Published by Library Association of Trinidad & Tobago
PO Box 1275, Port of Spain
Tel: (868) 687-0194
Web Site: www.latt.org.tt
Key Personnel
President: Gemma Crichton
Secretary: Ernesta Greenidge *E-mail:* secretary@latt.org.tt
Bulletin of the Library Association of Trinidad and Tobago.

Tunisia

Rassid (J)
Published by Association Tunisienne des Documentalistes, Bibliothecaires et Archivistes
BP 380, 1015 Tunis
Tel: (01) 245338
Key Personnel
Pres: Daly Abdelbaki
Chief Redactor: Mohamed Abdelsaoued
First published 1970.
quarterly.
60 pp, $25/yr
ISSN: 0330-8782

United Kingdom

Archives (J)
Published by British Records Association
c/o London Metropolitan Archives, 40 Northampton Rd, London EC1R OHB
Tel: (020) 7833 0428 *Fax:* (020) 7833 0416
Archives-Journal of the British Records Association Internet Home Page: http://ihr.sas.ac.uk/ihr/associnstits/bra.html.
ISBN(s): 0-900222

Art Libraries Journal (J)
Published by ARLIS/UK & Ireland, The Art Libraries Society
18 College Rd, Bromsgrove, Wores B60 2NE
Tel: (01527) 579298 *Fax:* (01527) 579298
Key Personnel
Editor: Gillian Varley
L52
ISSN: 0307-4722

Aslib Book Guide (J)
Published by Aslib, The Association for Information Management
60/62 Toller Lane, Bradford BD8 9BY
Tel: (01274) 777 700 *Fax:* (01274) 785 200
E-mail: pubs@aslib.com
Web Site: www.aslib.co.uk
Telex: 23667
Monthly.

Bibliography of Printed Works on London History to 1939 (B)
Published by Facet Publishing
7 Ridgmount St, London WC1 7AE
Tel: (020) 7255 0594 *Fax:* (020) 7255 0591
E-mail: info@facetpublishing.co.uk
Web Site: www.facetpublishing.co.uk
First bibliography on London History.
First published 1994.
895 pp
ISBN(s): 1-85604-074-7

The Bibliotheck (P)
Published by Library Association, Scottish Group, University College & Research Section
Goerge IV Bridge, Edinburgh, EH1 1EW Scotland G12 8QE
Tel: (0131) 226-4531 *Fax:* (0131) 220-6662
E-mail: enquiries@nls.uk
A Scottish journal of bibliography and allied topics.

Brio (J)
Published by International Association of Music Libraries (UK & Ireland Branch)
Royal Northern College of Music, 124 Oxford Rd, Manchester M13 9RD
Tel: (0161) 907 5245 *Fax:* (0161) 9273 7611
Web Site: www.rncm.ac.uk
Key Personnel
Editor: Geoff Thomason *E-mail:* geoff.thomason@rncm.ac.uk
Brio contains articles relevant to the music library profession, reviews of books & scores, & a listing of current work in music librarianship.
First published 1964.
2 issues per yr, May & November.
ISSN: 0007-0173

Chartered Institute of Library & Information Professionals Yearbook, see CILIP Yearbook

CILIP Yearbook (B)
Formerly Library Association Yearbook
Published by Facet Publishing
7 Ridgmount St, London WC1E 7AE
Tel: (020) 7255 0594 *Fax:* (020) 7255 0591
E-mail: info@facetpublishing.co.uk
Web Site: www.facetpublishing.co.uk
Key Personnel
Editor: K A Beecroft
Listing of officers, members, Royal Charter & bylaws.
Annual.

Directory of Acquisitions Librarians in the UK & Republic of Ireland (B)
Published by National Acquisitions Group
Lime House, Poolside, Madeley, Crewe CW3 9DX
Tel: (01782) 750462 *Fax:* (01782) 750462
E-mail: nag@psilink.co.uk
Key Personnel
Administrator: Carmel Martin; Diane Roberts
8th

Directory of Information Sources in the UK (B)
Published by Aslib, The Association for Information Management
60/62 Toller Lane, Bradford BD8 9BY
Tel: (01274) 777 700 *Fax:* (01274) 785 200
E-mail: pubs@aslib.com
Web Site: www.aslib.co.uk
Telex: 23667
Listing of over 9,000 organizations in the UK.

Directory of Rare Book & Special Collections in the UK & Republic of Ireland (B)
Published by Facet Publishing
7 Ridgmount St, London WC1E 7AE
Tel: (020) 7255 0594 *Fax:* (020) 7255 0591
E-mail: info@facetpublishing.co.uk
Web Site: www.facetpublishing.co.uk
Key Personnel
Editor: Barry Bloomfield
Details of the rare & special collections of over 1200 libraries.

Impact: Journal of the Career Development Group (J)
Published by Chartered Institute of Library & Information Professionals
Music Library, University of Reading, 35 Upper Redlands Rd, Reading RG1 5JE
Tel: (0118) 931 8413
Web Site: www.careerdevelopmentgroup.org.uk
Bimonthly.
20 pp
ISSN: 1468-1625

Interlending & Document Supply (J)
Published by MCB University Press Ltd
60/62 Toller Lane, Bradford, W Yorks BD8 9BY
Tel: (01274) 777700 *Fax:* (01274) 785200
E-mail: editorial@mcb.co.uk
Web Site: www.mcb.co.uk

ɟJournal of Documentation (J)
Published by Emerald
60/62 Toller Lane, Bradford BD8 9BY
Tel: (01274) 777 700 *Fax:* (01274) 785 200
E-mail: jdoc@emeraldinsight.com
Web Site: www.emeraldinsight.com
Key Personnel
Man Editor: Diane Heath
First published 1944.
6 times/yr.
Vol 58 (2002): 720 pp
ISSN: 0022-0418
Parent Company: MCB UP Ltd

Journal of Information Science (JIS) (J)
Published by CSA (Cambridge Scientific Abstracts)
Windsor Court, East Grinstead House, East Grinstead, West Sussex RH19 1XA
Tel: (01342) 326972 *Fax:* (01342) 336198
E-mail: service@csa.com
Web Site: www.csa.com
Key Personnel
Editor: Alan Gilchrist

UNITED KINGDOM

Bimonthly.
L205
ISSN: 0165-5515
Parent Company: Cambridge Information Group

Journal of the Society of Archivists (J)
Published by Carfax Publishing Co
PO Box 25, Abingdon, Oxon OX14 3UE
Tel: (01235) 555335
The JSA is a journal for archivists, record managers & conservators worldwide. Published biannually.
ISBN(s): 0-902879

The Law Librarian (P)
Published by British & Irish Association of Law Librarians/Sweet & Maxwell Ltd
100 Avenue Road, London NW3 3PF
Tel: (020) 7393 7000 *Fax:* (020) 7393 7020
Telex: 335101 PINCO G

The Libraries Directory (B)
Published by James Clarke & Co Ltd
PO Box 60, Cambridge CB1 2NT
Tel: (01223) 350865 *Fax:* (01223) 366951
E-mail: publishing@jamesclarke.co.uk
Web Site: www.jamesclarke.co.uk
Key Personnel
Man Dir: Adrian Brink
Editor: Iain Walker
Directory of Public Libraries, Special Libraries, Record Offices, Archives & Library Organizations in the UK & Ireland.
First published 1890.
Biennially.
2000-2002: 510 pp, L99
ISBN(s): 0-227-67956-3 (Hardcover); 0-227-67957-1 (CD-ROM Reference Edition (Stand Alone) L150+VAT); 0-227-67958-X (CD-ROM Marketing Edition (Stand Alone) L225+VAT); 0-227-67959-8 (CD-ROM Reference Edition (Network) L275+VAT); 0-227-67960-1 (CD-ROM Marketing Edition (Network) L350+VAT)
ISSN: 0961-4575

Libraries in The United Kingdom & The Republic of Ireland (B)
Published by Facet Publishing
7 Ridgmount St, London WC1E 7AE
Tel: (020) 7255 0594 *Fax:* (020) 7255 0591
E-mail: info@facetpublishing.co.uk
Web Site: www.facetpublishing.co.uk
Listing of public library services & a select list of academic & other library addresses.
Annually.
29th: 464 pp, L37.50
ISBN(s): 1-85604-450-5

The Library (P)
Published by Bibliographical Society
c/o Wellcome Institute, 183 Euston Rd, London NW1 2BE
Tel: (020) 7412 7579 *Fax:* (020) 7412 7577
E-mail: martin.davies@bl.uk
Key Personnel
President: R Myers
Bibliography.
Quarterly.

Library and Information Science Abstracts (LISA) (J)
Published by CSA (Cambridge Scientific Abstracts)
Windsor Court, East Grinstead House, East Grinstead, West Sussex RH19 1XA
Tel: (01342) 336163 *Fax:* (01342) 336197
E-mail: service@csa.com; tjones@csa.com (sales); support@csa.com (technical support)
Web Site: www.csa.com
Key Personnel
Editor: Lilian Lincoln *E-mail:* llincoln@csa.com

Monthly publication. Indexes & abstracts 500 periodicals from over 65 countries in over 20 languages. Current awareness & search service for information about library & information science & related areas including the internet & information industry. Also available as a CD-ROM searchable database & as a web database.
First published 1969.
Monthly.
100 pp, Annual subscription for 11 issues plus cumulated annual index: Europe L650, $1010,
ISSN: 0024-2179
Parent Company: Cambridge Information Group

Library Association Record (J)
Published by Facet Publishing
7 Ridgmount St, London WC1E 7AE
Tel: (020) 7255 0594 *Fax:* (020) 7255 0591
E-mail: info@facetpublishing.co.uk
Web Site: www.facetpublishing.co.uk
Key Personnel
Chief Executive: Bob McKee
Editor: Elspeth Hyams
Monthly.

Library Association Yearbook, see CILIP Yearbook

Library Review (J)
Published by MCB University Press Ltd
60-62 Toller Lane, Bradford, W York BD8 9BY
Tel: (01274) 777700 *Fax:* (01274) 785200
E-mail: editorial@mcb.co.uk
Web Site: www.mcb.co.uk

LISA, see Library and Information Science Abstracts (LISA)

Managing Information (J)
Published by Aslib, The Association for Information Management
Stone House Ct, London EC3A 7PB
Tel: (01274) 777 700 *Fax:* (020) 7903 0011
E-mail: pubs@aslib.com
Web Site: www.aslib.co.uk
Biennial.

New Library World (J)
Published by MCB University Press Ltd
60-62 Toller Lane, Bradford, W York BD8 9BY
Tel: (01274) 777700 *Fax:* (01274) 785200
E-mail: editorial@mcb.co.uk
Web Site: www.mcb.co.uk
Incorporates Information & Library Manager.

The Private Library (P)
Published by Private Libraries Association (PLA)
Ravelston, South View Rd, Pinner, Middlesex HA5 3YD
E-mail: dchambers@aol.com
Web Site: www.the-old-school.demon.uk/pla.htm
Key Personnel
Executive Secretary: James Brown
Editor, Private Press Books: Paul W Nash
Concerned with book collecting.
First published 1957.
Quarterly.
48 pp
ISSN: 0032-8898

Reference Reviews (J)
Published by MCB University Press Ltd
60/62 Toller Lane, Bradford, W Yorks BD8 9BY
Tel: (01274) 777700 *Fax:* (01274) 785200
E-mail: editorial@mcb.co.uk
Web Site: www.mcb.co.uk
Reviews of current reference materials, electronic version only.

LIBRARY REFERENCE

Scottish Libraries (J)
Published by Scottish Library Association
One John St, Hamilton ML3 7EU
Tel: (01698) 458888 *Fax:* (01698) 458899; (01698) 428159
E-mail: sla@slainte.org.uk
Key Personnel
President: Stuart James

The SLG Directory to Children's and School Library Services in the British Isles (B)
Published by Library Association, School Libraries Group
c/o Mrs Mary Day, 10 Newlyn Close, Stevenage, Herts SG1 2JD
Tel: (01438) 353264
2nd edition
ISBN(s): 0-85365; 0-948933

State Librarian (J)
Published by Circle of State Librarians
Stationary Office, 51 Nine Elms Lane, London SW8 5DR
Tel: (020) 7787 3011 *Fax:* (020) 7873 8463
E-mail: book.orders@theso.co.uk
Web Site: www.national-publishing.co.uk

Uruguay

Bibliografia y documentacion en el Uruguay (Bibliography and Documentation in Uruguay) (B)
Published by Agrupacion Bibliotecologica del Uruguay (Group Librarian of Uruguay)
Cerro Largo 1666, Montevideo 11200
Tel: (02) 400 57 40
Key Personnel
Pres: Luis Alberto Musso

Revista de la Biblioteca Nacional (National Library Review) (J)
Published by Biblioteca Nacional del Uruguay
18 de Julio 1790, Casilla de Correo 452, Montevideo
Tel: (02) 485030 *Fax:* (02) 496902

Viet Nam

Cong tac Thu' vien-Thu' muc (Journal of Library & Bibliography) (J)
Published by National Library of Vietnam
31 Trang Thi, 10000 Hanoi
Tel: (04) 52643
Key Personnel
Dir: Nguyen The Duc

Yugoslavia

Biblioteke u Jugoslaviji (Libraries in Yugoslavia) (B)
Published by Jugoslovenski Bibliografsko-informacijski institut, Yubin, Agencija za ISBN (Yugoslav Institute for Bibliography and Information)
Terazije 26, 1000 Belgrade
Tel: (011) 687836 *Fax:* (011) 687760

Biblioteke u SR Srbiji (Libraries in Serbia) (B)
Published by Narodna Biblioteka Srbije (National Library of Serbia)
Skerliceva 1, Belgrade 11000
Tel: (011) 451242
Key Personnel
Dir: Milomir Petrovic

Zambia

Directory of Libraries in Zambia (B)
Published by Zambia Library Association
PO Box 32839, Lusaka
Provides details on all the major libraries in the country.

Zambia Library Association Journal (J)
Published by Zambia Library Association
PO Box 32839, Lusaka
Key Personnel
Chair: Mrs C Zulu

Zimbabwe

Directory of Libraries (B)
Published by National Archives of Zimbabwe
PB 7729, Causeway, Harare
Tel: (04) 792741 *Fax:* (04) 792398
Key Personnel
Dir: S Njovana

The Zimbabwe Librarian (P)
Published by Zimbabwe Library Association
PO Box 3133, Harare
Tel: (04) 792641 *Fax:* (04) 703050
Key Personnel
Editor: Hikawa Mkuleko

Industry Yellow Pages

Arranged alphabetically by company/organization name, the industry yellow pages include the page number(s) where the listing can be found as well as the organization's country, telephone, fax, e-mail address and web address. Companies/organizations listed in the following sections are excluded from the yellow pages: **Book Trade Reference Books and Journals; Literary Prizes; Calendar of Book Trade & Promotional Events** and **Library Reference Books & Journals**.

A A Publishing (United Kingdom) *Tel:* (01256) 491522 *Fax:* (01256) 322575 *E-mail:* helen.taylor@theaa.com *Web Site:* 195.89.185.89/aapub/home.asp, pg 644

A & A (Italy) *Tel:* (02) 876999 *Fax:* (02) 877928, pg 374

A & A & A Edicoes e Promocoes Internacionais Ltda (Brazil) *Tel:* (024) 221-1467 *Fax:* (024) 221-3669, pg 77

A & A Farmar (Ireland) *Tel:* (01) 4963625 *Fax:* (01) 4970107 *E-mail:* afarmar@iol.ie *Web Site:* farmarbooks.com, pg 358

A & B Personal Management Ltd (United Kingdom) *Tel:* (020) 7839 4433 *Fax:* (020) 7930 5738, pg 1117

A Francke Verlag (Tubingen und Basel) (Germany) *Tel:* (07071) 97970 *Fax:* (07071) 75288 *E-mail:* foolfrancke@tonline.de *Web Site:* www.geist.de/francke/info-D.html, pg 191

Editions A M Metailie (France) *Tel:* (01) 55 42 83 00 *Fax:* (01) 55428304 *E-mail:* presse@metailie.info *Web Site:* www.metailie.info, pg 145

A-Mail Academic (United Kingdom) *Tel:* (020) 7871 9139 *Fax:* (020) 7871 9140 *E-mail:* a-mail@djlb.co.uk *Web Site:* www.a-mail.co.uk, pg 644

A-R Editions Inc (United States) *Tel:* 608-836-9000 *Fax:* 608-831-8200 *E-mail:* info@areditions.com *Web Site:* www.areditions.com, pg 1142, 1163, 1224

A-Z Ediciones y Publications (Spain) *Tel:* (091) 4427793 *Fax:* (091) 4425940, pg 561

A/L Biblioteksentralen (The Norwegian Library Bureau) (Norway) *Tel:* 22673480 *Fax:* 22196443, pg 1303

Aache Ediciones (Spain) *Tel:* (0949) 220 438 *E-mail:* ediciones@aache.com *Web Site:* www.aache.com, pg 561

Aafzam Ltd (Zambia) *Tel:* (01) 223261, pg 766

Aalborg Universitetsbibliotek (Denmark) *Tel:* 96359400 *Fax:* 98156859 *E-mail:* aub@aub.auc.dk *Web Site:* www.aub.auc.dk, pg 1460

Aarachne Verlag (Austria) *Tel:* (01) 2855353 *Fax:* (01) 2855353 *Web Site:* www.aarachne.at, pg 49

Aardvark Enterprises (Canada) *Tel:* 403-256-4639, pg 1131, 1153, 1193

Aare-Verlag (Switzerland) *Tel:* (062) 8368626 *Fax:* (062) 8245780, pg 607

Aarhus Universitetsforlag (Denmark) *Tel:* 89425370 *Fax:* 89425380 *E-mail:* unipress@au.dk *Web Site:* www.unipress.dk, pg 129

The AB Book Club (BAB) (Iceland) *Tel:* 5643170 *Fax:* 5643190, pg 1229

AB Svenska Laromedel-Editum (Finland) *Tel:* (09) 8043188 *Fax:* (09) 8043257, pg 141

ABA Books (New Zealand) *Tel:* (07) 8549360 *Fax:* (07) 8549361 *Web Site:* www.ababooks.co.nz, pg 488

Editorial Abaco de Rodolfo Depalma SRL (Argentina) *Tel:* (011) 4371-1675 *Fax:* (011) 43711675 *E-mail:* info@abacoeditorial.com.ar *Web Site:* www.abacoeditorial.com.ar, pg 2

Mandira Jaya Abadi (Indonesia) *Tel:* (024) 519547; (024) 316150 *Fax:* (024) 542189, pg 353

Publicacions de l'Abadia de Montserrat (Spain) *Tel:* (093) 2450303; (093) 2657923; (093) 2430302 *Fax:* (093) 2473594 *E-mail:* pamsa@pamsa.com *Web Site:* www.pamsa.com, pg 561

Abagar Pablioing (Bulgaria) *Tel:* (02) 702826 *Fax:* (02) 702926, pg 94

Abagar, Veliko Tarnovo (Bulgaria) *Tel:* (062) 43936; (062) 47814 *Fax:* (062) 46993, pg 94

Abakus Musik Barbara Fietz (Germany) *Tel:* (06478) 2250 *Fax:* (06478) 1355 *E-mail:* hotline@abakus-musik.de *Web Site:* www.abakus-musik.de, pg 191

Abakus Verlag GmbH (Austria) *Tel:* (0662) 662 24 65 84, pg 49

Abbotsford Publishing (United Kingdom) *Tel:* (01543) 255749, pg 644

ABC Books (Australian Broadcasting Corporation) (Australia) *Tel:* (02) 9950 3999 *Fax:* (02) 9950 3888 *E-mail:* abcbooks@your.abc.net.au *Web Site:* abcshop.com.au, pg 10

ABC der Deutschen Wirtschaft, Verlagsgesellschaft mbH (Germany) *Tel:* (06151) 38920 *Fax:* (06151) 33164; (06151) 389280 *E-mail:* info@abconline.de *Web Site:* www.abconline.de, pg 191

ABC Editions (France) *Tel:* (01) 48122222 *Fax:* (01) 48122239, pg 145

ABC Kitabevi AS (Turkey) *Tel:* (0212) 2762404 *Fax:* (0212) 2851860, pg 638

ABC Kitabevi Sanayi Tic AS (Turkey) *Tel:* (0212) 2762404 *Fax:* (0212) 2851860, pg 1315

Librerias ABC SA (Argentina) *Tel:* (011) 4-314-7887 *Fax:* (011) 4-314-8106 *E-mail:* libabcc@datamarkets.com.ar *Web Site:* www.libreriasabc.com.ar, pg 1271

Librerias ABC SA (Peru) *Tel:* (054) 422900; (054) 422902 *Fax:* (054) 422901, pg 511, 1305

ABC-CLIO (United Kingdom) *Tel:* (01865) 311350 *Fax:* (01865) 311358 *E-mail:* oxford@abc-clio.ltd.uk *Web Site:* www.abc-clio.com, pg 644

Ben Abdallah Editions (Tunisia) *Tel:* (01) 237011 *Fax:* (01) 786290, pg 637

S Abdul Majeed & Co (Malaysia) *Tel:* (03) 2832230 *Fax:* (03) 2825670, pg 451, 1298

ABE Marketing (Poland) *Tel:* (022) 6540675 *Fax:* (022) 6520767 *E-mail:* info@abe.com.pl *Web Site:* www.abe.com.pl/, pg 1306

Gruppo Abele (Italy) *Tel:* (011) 54,54,89; (011) 814,42,715 *Fax:* (011) 54.52.41 *E-mail:* egamedia@mbox.vol.it, pg 374

Abeledo-Perrot SAE e I (Argentina) *Tel:* (011) 4124-9750 *Fax:* (011) 4371-5156 *E-mail:* editorial@abeledo-perrot.com, pg 2

Abercastle Publications (United Kingdom) *Tel:* (01239) 811267, pg 644

Edizioni Abete (Italy) *Tel:* (06) 225821 *Fax:* (06) 2282960, pg 374

ABG Professional Information (United Kingdom) *Tel:* (020) 7920 8991 *Fax:* (020) 7920 8992 *E-mail:* info@abgpublications.co.uk *Web Site:* www.abgpublications.co.uk, pg 644

ABGRA (Asociacion de Bibliotecarios Graduados de la Republica Argentina) (Argentina) *Tel:* (011) 3730571; (011) 3848095 *Fax:* (011) 3730571; (011) 3715269 *E-mail:* postmaster@abgra.org.ar, pg 1511

Abhinav Publications (India) *Tel:* (011) 666387; (011) 660932; (011) 6524658; (011) 6566387; (011) 6562784 *Fax:* (011) 6857009 *Web Site:* www.abhinavexports.com, pg 329

Abhishek Publications (India) *Tel:* (0172) 707562 *Fax:* (0172) 704668, pg 329

ABIC Books & Equipment Ltd (Nigeria) *Tel:* (042) 331827 *Fax:* (042) 334811, pg 497

Abimo (Belgium) *Tel:* (052) 462407 *Fax:* (052) 461962 *E-mail:* info@abimo-uitgeverij.com *Web Site:* www.abimo-uitgeverij.com, pg 63

Abisega Publishers (Nigeria) Ltd (Nigeria) *Tel:* (022) 415802, pg 497

Editrice Abitare Segesta (Italy) *Tel:* (02) 76.09.02.11 *Fax:* (02) 76.02.31.40 *Web Site:* www.abitare.it, pg 374

Abiva Publishing House Inc (Philippines) *Tel:* (02) 7120245 *Fax:* (02) 7320308 *E-mail:* abiva@asiagate.net, pg 512

Libraira-Papeterie ABM (Benin) *Tel:* 330690 (voice & fax), pg 1276

Abo Akademis forlag - Abo Akademi University Press (Finland) *Tel:* (02) 2153292 *Fax:* (02) 2154490 *E-mail:* forlaget@abo.fi *Web Site:* www.abo.fi/instut/forlag, pg 141

Abo Akademis bibliotek (Finland) *Tel:* (02) 2154180 *Fax:* (02) 2154795 *E-mail:* ill@abo.fi, pg 1463

Aboriginal Studies Press (Australia) *Tel:* (02) 6246 1111 *Fax:* (02) 6261 4285 *E-mail:* sales@aiatsis.gov.au *Web Site:* www.aiatsis.gov.au, pg 10

Editorial Abril SA (Argentina) *Tel:* (011) 3752450; (011) 3752451, pg 2

Abril SA (Brazil) *Tel:* (011) 3990-1322 *Fax:* (011) 3990-2100 *Web Site:* pp.uol.com/br, pg 77

Absolute Press (United Kingdom) *Tel:* (01225) 316 013 *Fax:* (01225) 445 836 *E-mail:* info@absolutepress.demon.co.uk, pg 644

Ediciones Abya-Yala (Ecuador) *Tel:* (02) 562633; (02) 506247 *Fax:* (02) 506255 *E-mail:* admin-info@abyayala.org; editorial@abyayala.org; enlace@abyayala.org *Web Site:* www.abyayala.org, pg 137

Yr Academi Gymreig (United Kingdom) *Tel:* (029) 20472266 *Fax:* (029) 20492930 *E-mail:* post@academi.org *Web Site:* www.academi.org, pg 1369

Academia (Czech Republic) *Tel:* (02) 2494 1976 *Fax:* (02) 24212582 *Web Site:* www.academia.cz, pg 122

Academia (Lithuania) *Tel:* (02) 626851 *Fax:* (02) 226351, pg 445

Academia Amazonense de Letras (Brazil), pg 1361

Academia Argentina de Letras (Argentina) *Tel:* (011) 4-8023814; (011) 4-8027509; (011) 4-8025161 *Fax:* (011) 4-8028340 *E-mail:* aaldespa@fibertel.com.ar; aaladmin@fibertel.com.ar; aalbibl@fibertel.com.ar, pg 2

Academia Argentina de Letras (Argentina) *Tel:* (011) 4-8023814; (011) 4-8025161; (011) 4-8027509 *Fax:* (011) 4-8028340 *E-mail:* aaldespa@fibertel.com.ar; aaladmin@fibertel.com.ar; aalbibl@fibertel.com.ar, pg 1359

Academia Brasileira de Letras (Brazil), pg 1361

Academia-Bruylant (Belgium) *Tel:* (010) 45 23 95 *Fax:* (010) 45 44 80 *E-mail:* academia-bruylant@skynet.be *Web Site:* www.academia-bruylant.be, pg 63

Academia Catarinense de Letras (Brazil) *Tel:* 2342166, pg 1361

Academia Cearense de Letras (Brazil), pg 1361

Academia das Ciencias de Lisboa (Portugal) *Tel:* (021) 3463866, pg 522

Biblioteca da Academia das Ciencias de Lisboa (Portugal) *Tel:* (021) 3463866, pg 1493

Academia de Centro America (Costa Rica) *Tel:* 224-6644; 227520 *Fax:* 2246642 *E-mail:* academia@sol.racsa.co.cr, pg 115

Academia de la Llingua Asturiana (Spain) *Tel:* (098) 5211837 *Fax:* (098) 5226816 *E-mail:* alla@asturnet.es *Web Site:* www.asturnet.es/alla, pg 561

Academia de Letras da Bahia (Brazil) *Tel:* (071) 243-7614 *Fax:* (071) 243-7614, pg 1361

Academia de Letras de Piaui (Brazil), pg 1361

Academia de Studii Economice, Biblioteca Centrala (Romania) *Tel:* (01) 115960, pg 1494

Academia Mineira de Letras (Brazil), pg 1361

Academia Nacional de Letras (Uruguay) *Tel:* (02) 9152374 *Fax:* (02) 0167460, pg 1372

Academia Nacional de la Historia (Venezuela) *Tel:* (02) 4817547; (02) 4839435; (02) 486720 *Fax:* (02) 4817547, pg 761

Academia Nicaraguense de la Lengua (Nicaragua), pg 497

Academia Paraibana de Letras (Brazil), pg 1361

Academia Paulista de Letras (Brazil), pg 1361

Academia Pernambucana de Letras (Brazil) *Tel:* (081) 2682211, pg 1361

Academia Press (Belgium) *Tel:* (09) 233.80.88 *Fax:* (09) 233.14.09 *E-mail:* info@academiapress.be *Web Site:* www.academiapress.be, pg 64

Academia Publications P Ltd (Malaysia) *Tel:* (03) 572455, pg 451

Academia Scientific Book Inc (Japan) *Tel:* (03) 3819805 *Fax:* (03) 38128509, pg 1294

Academic & General Bookshop (Australia) *Tel:* (03) 6633231 *Fax:* (03) 6637234, pg 1272

Academic Book Corporation (India) *Tel:* (0522) 418421; (0522) 416584 *Fax:* (0522) 22061; (0522) 210376, pg 329

Academic Books Pvt Ltd (Zimbabwe) *Tel:* (04) 706729; (04) 704910 *Fax:* (04) 702071, pg 767

The Academic Press (India) *Tel:* (124) 6322779; (124) 6322005 *Fax:* (124) 6324782 *E-mail:* indoc@indiatimes.com, pg 329

Academic Press Ltd (United Kingdom) *Tel:* (020) 7482-2893 *Fax:* (020) 7267-4752 *E-mail:* 25775ACPRESG,ap@acad.com, pg 644

Academic Publishers (Bangladesh) *Tel:* (02) 507355; (02) 507366 *Fax:* (02) 863060, pg 62

Academic Publishers (India) *Tel:* (033) 241-4857 *Fax:* (033) 241-3702 *E-mail:* acabooks@cal.vsnl.net.in, pg 329

Academie Goncourte, Socieete de gens de Lettres (France), pg 1362

Academie Nationale de Reims (France) *Tel:* (0326) 910449 *Fax:* (0326) 910449, pg 145

Academie Royale de Langue et de Litterature Francaise (Belgium) *Tel:* (02) 5115687; (02) 5116757, pg 1360

Academie Royale des Sciences, des Lettres et des Beaux-Arts de Belgique (Belgium) *Tel:* (02) 5502211 *Fax:* (02) 5502205, pg 1360

Editura Academiei Romane (Romania) *Tel:* (01) 6317400; (01) 6314460, pg 531

Academon Publishing House (Israel) *Tel:* (02) 5811326; (02) 5811327 *Fax:* (02) 5815558, pg 365

Academon Publishing House (Israel) *Tel:* (02) 5882163 *Fax:* (02) 5815558 *Web Site:* www.academon.co.il, pg 1292

Academy of Education Planning & Management (AEPAM) (Pakistan) *Tel:* (051) 250731 *Fax:* (051) 856495, pg 506

Academy of the Hebrew Language (Israel) *Tel:* (02) 6493555 *Fax:* (02) 5617065 *E-mail:* acad2u@vms.huji.ac.il *Web Site:* hebrew-academy.huji.ac.il, pg 365

Fundamental Library of the Academy of Medical Sciences (Russian Federation) *Tel:* (095) 155-17-93, pg 1494

Academy Science Publishers (Kenya) *Tel:* (02) 884402-5 *Fax:* (02) 884406 *E-mail:* asp@arcc.or.ke, pg 430

Academy of Sciences Publishing House (Democratic People's Republic of Korea) *Tel:* (02) 51956, pg 434

Acair Ltd (United Kingdom) *Tel:* (01851) 703 020 *Fax:* (01851) 703 294 *E-mail:* enquiries@acairbooks.com *Web Site:* www.acairbooks.com, pg 645

Acantilado (Spain) *Tel:* (093) 2123808 *Fax:* (093) 4182317 *E-mail:* qcrema@mito.ibernet.com, pg 561

Acantilado (Spain) *Tel:* (093) 4144906 *Fax:* (093) 4147107 *E-mail:* correo@elacantilado.com *Web Site:* www.elacantilado.com, pg 561

Editorial Acanto SA (Spain) *Tel:* (093) 4189093 *Fax:* (093) 4189088 *E-mail:* acanto@globalcom.es, pg 561

Acbrecht Kraus Verlag GmbH (Germany) *Tel:* (089) 99 84 01-0 *Fax:* (089) 4372-2440 *E-mail:* vertrieb.verlagsgruppe@bertelsmann.de, pg 191

Accademia (Milano) (Italy) *Tel:* (02) 2552593, pg 374

Libreria All'Accademia di Randi Lorenzo & Elena snc (Italy) *Tel:* (049) 8760306 *Fax:* (049) 8751825, pg 1293

Accademia Nazionale di Scienze, Lettere ed Arti (Italy) *Tel:* (059) 225566 *Fax:* (059) 225566 *E-mail:* biblio.asla@cedoc.mo.it, pg 1365

Accademia Nazionale Virgiliana di Scienze, Lettere e Arti (Italy) *Tel:* (0376) 320314 *Fax:* (0376) 222774, pg 1365

Accademia Petrarca di Lettere, Arti e Scienze (Italy) *Tel:* (0575) 24700, pg 1365

Accedo Verlagsgesellschaft mbH (Germany) *Tel:* (089) 935714 *Fax:* (089) 9294109 *E-mail:* accedoverlag@web.de *Web Site:* www.accedoverlag.de, pg 191

Access International Services (Morocco) *Tel:* (02) 316068 *Fax:* (02) 304685, pg 469

Access Press (Australia) *Tel:* (08) 93793188 *Fax:* (08) 93793199, pg 10

Acco CV (Belgium) *Tel:* (016) 29 11 00 *Fax:* (016) 20 73 89, pg 64

Acco CV (Belgium) *Tel:* (016) 291100 *Fax:* (016) 207389, pg 1275

Acento Editorial (Spain) *Tel:* (091) 5088996; (091) 5085145; (091) 4228800 *Fax:* (091) 5089927; (091) 5084974 *E-mail:* sm@hispanica.net, pg 561

ACER Agencia Literaria (Spain) *Tel:* (091) 3692061 *Fax:* (091) 3692052, pg 1116

ACER Press (Australia) *Tel:* (03) 9277 5555 *Fax:* (03) 9277 5500 *E-mail:* sales@acer.edu.au *Web Site:* www.acer.edu.au, pg 10

Editorial Acervo SL (Spain) *Tel:* (093) 2122664 *Fax:* (093) 2122706 *E-mail:* editorial_acervo@hotmail.com, pg 561

Ach Publishing House (Israel) *Tel:* (04) 727227; (04) 7222096 *Fax:* (04) 417839, pg 365

Achiasaf Publishing House Ltd (Israel) *Tel:* (09) 8851390 *Fax:* (09) 8851391 *E-mail:* info@achiasaf.co.il *Web Site:* www.achiasaf.co.il, pg 365

Achiever (Israel) *Tel:* (02) 6253627 *Fax:* (02) 6255740, pg 365

ACHPER Inc (Australian Council for Health, Physical Education & Recreation) (Australia) *Tel:* (08) 8340 3388 *Fax:* (08) 8340 3399 *E-mail:* achper@achper.org.au *Web Site:* www.achper.org.au, pg 10

Achterbahn AG Buch (Germany) *Tel:* (0431) 702-800 *Fax:* (0431) 7028-228 *E-mail:* 100424.1232@compuserve.com, pg 191

ACI International Ltd (Australia) *Tel:* (03) 6058555, pg 1131

Joh van Acken GmbH & Co KG (Germany) *Tel:* (02151) 44 00-0 *Fax:* (02151) 44 00-11 *E-mail:* verlag@vanacken.de *Web Site:* www.spendengrusskarten.de/willkommen.html, pg 191

R van Acken GmbH Druckerei und Verlag (Germany) *Tel:* (0591) 97312-0 *Fax:* (0591) 74631, pg 191

F A Ackermanns Kunstverlag GmbH (Germany) *Tel:* (089) 78580826 *Fax:* (089) 7858028 *E-mail:* info@ackermannkalender.de *Web Site:* www.ackermannkalender.de, pg 191

Editorial Acme SA (Argentina) *Tel:* (011) 4328-1508; (011) 4328-1662 *Fax:* (011) 4328-9345 *E-mail:* acme@redynet.com.ar, pg 3

Aconcagua Ediciones y Publicaciones SA (Mexico) *Tel:* (05) 5361292, pg 457

Acorn Books (South Africa) *Tel:* (011) 8805768 *Fax:* (011) 8805768 *E-mail:* acorbook@iafrica.com, pg 552

ACP Publishing Pty Ltd (Australia) *Tel:* (02) 9282 8000 *Fax:* (02) 9267 4361 *Web Site:* www.acp.com.au, pg 10

ACR Edition Internationale (Art Creation Realisation) (France) *Tel:* (01) 47 88 14 92 *Fax:* (01) 43 33 38 81 *E-mail:* acredition@acr-edition.com *Web Site:* www.acr-edition.com, pg 145

Editorial Acribia SA (Spain) *Tel:* (0976) 232089 *Fax:* (0976) 219212 *E-mail:* acribia@red3i.es, pg 561

Act 3 Publishing (United Kingdom) *Tel:* (020) 7402 2231, pg 645

Acta Universitatis Gothoburgensis (Sweden) *Tel:* (031) 7731000 *Fax:* (031) 7734064 *E-mail:* library@ub.gu.se *Web Site:* www.gu.se, pg 599

Actes Graphiques (France) *Tel:* (04) 77 59 28 95; (06) 09 42 21 13 *Fax:* (04) 77592903 *Web Site:* www.actes-graphiques.com, pg 145

Editions Actes Sud (France) *Tel:* (04) 90 49 86 91 *Fax:* (04) 90 96 95 25 *E-mail:* contact@actes-sud.fr *Web Site:* www.actes-sud.fr, pg 146

Actinic Press Ltd (United Kingdom) *Tel:* (01684) 540154 *Fax:* (01684) 540154, pg 645

Action Artistique de la Ville de Paris (France) *Tel:* (01) 43 25 30 30 *Fax:* (01) 43 25 17 69 *E-mail:* aavp@club-internet.fr, pg 146

Action Editora Ltda (Brazil) *Tel:* (021) 3325-7229 *Fax:* (021) 3325-7229 *Web Site:* editora.com.br, pg 77

Action Magazine (Zimbabwe) *Tel:* (04) 747213-7-274 *Fax:* (04) 747409 *E-mail:* actionmg@cst.co.zw *Web Site:* www.cst.co.zw/action, pg 767

Action Publications (Cyprus) *Tel:* (02) 444104 *Fax:* (02) 450048, pg 121

Action Publishers (Kenya) *Tel:* (02) 506700, pg 430

YELLOW PAGES

Actualquarto (Belgium) *Tel:* (071) 21.61.53 *Fax:* (071) 21.77.13, pg 64

Libreria Acuario SA de CV (Mexico) *Tel:* (05) 5742966; (05) 5741137 *Fax:* (05) 2642882, pg 1299

ACUM Ltd (Society of Authors, Composers & Music Publishers in Israel) (Israel) *Tel:* (03) 6113400 *Fax:* (03) 6122629 *E-mail:* acum@acum.org.il *Web Site:* www.acum.org.il, pg 1365

ACURIL (Puerto Rico) *Tel:* (787) 764-0000 (ext 7916) *Fax:* (787) 763-5685, pg 1257

Ad-Ex Translations Ltd (United Kingdom) *Tel:* (020) 8542 7809 *Fax:* (020) 8543 1253 *E-mail:* adx@cable.inet.co.uk, pg 1128

ADA Edita Tokyo Co Ltd (Japan) *Tel:* (03) 34031581 *Fax:* (03) 34031582, pg 414

Ada Korn Editora SA (Argentina) *Tel:* (011) 4374-6199 *Fax:* (011) 4374-9699 *E-mail:* adakorn@datamarket.com.ar, pg 3

Ada Press Publishers (Turkey) *Tel:* (0212) 243 1778; (0212) 243 1779 *Fax:* (0212) 249 3545, pg 638

ADAC Verlag GmBH (Germany) *Tel:* (06196) 6096-0 *Fax:* (06196) 27450 *E-mail:* info@cartotravel.de *Web Site:* www.cartotravel.de, pg 191

Adaex Educational Publications Ltd (Ghana) *Tel:* (024) 367145 *E-mail:* epublication@yahoo.com, pg 306

ADAGP (Societe des Auteurs dans les Arts Grarphiques et Plastiques) (France) *Tel:* (01) 43590979 *Fax:* (01) 45634489 *E-mail:* adagp@adagp.fr *Web Site:* www.adagp.fr, pg 1242

Adalbert Stifter Verein eV (Germany) *Tel:* (089) 4489807 *Fax:* (089) 4891148 *E-mail:* asv.kulturinstitul@t-online.de, pg 1363

Adamantine Press Ltd (United Kingdom), pg 645

Centro de Estudios Adams-Ediciones Valbuena SA (Spain) *Tel:* (091) 4459335 *Fax:* (091) 5933973 *E-mail:* adams@adams.es *Web Site:* www.adams.es, pg 561

Mario Adda Editore SNC (Italy) *Tel:* (080) 5539502 *Fax:* (080) 5539502, pg 374

Addis Ababa University Library (Ethiopia) *Tel:* (01) 115673; (01) 550844 *Fax:* (01) 550655, pg 1463

Addis Ababa University Press (Ethiopia) *Tel:* (01) 119418; (01) 550844 (ext 227) *Fax:* (01) 550655, pg 141

Addison-Wesley (Singapore) Pte Ltd (India) *Tel:* (011) 214 6067 *Fax:* (011) 214 6071 *E-mail:* info@pearsoned.co.in *Web Site:* www.pearsonedindia.com, pg 329

Adea Edizioni (Italy) *Tel:* (02) 69006933 *Fax:* (02) 69007135, pg 374

Adebara Publishers Ltd (Nigeria), pg 497

Adelphi Edizioni SpA (Italy) *Tel:* (02) 725731 *Fax:* (02) 89010337 *E-mail:* rightsdept@adelphi.it *Web Site:* www.adelphi.it; www.adelphiaua.it, pg 374

ADEVA (Akademische Druck-u Verlagsanstalt) (Austria) *Tel:* (0316) 3644 *Fax:* (0316) 364424 *E-mail:* info@adeva.com *Web Site:* www.adeva.com, pg 1131, 1153

ADEVA (Akademische Druck-u Verlagsanstalt) (Austria) *Tel:* (0316) 3644 *Fax:* (0316) 364424 *E-mail:* info@adeva.com, pg 1193

Adeyle Brothers & Co (Bangladesh) *Tel:* (02) 233508, pg 62, 1275

ADIRA (Switzerland) *Tel:* (022) 312 25 43 *Fax:* (022) 312 26 13 *E-mail:* adira@adira.net *Web Site:* www.adira.net, pg 607

Adivinar y Multiplicar, SA de CV (Mexico) *Tel:* (05) 604-4511 *Fax:* (05) 604-1583 *E-mail:* multipli@compuserve.com.mx, pg 457

Deborah Adlam (United Kingdom) *Tel:* (0131) 6676048, pg 1128

Adlard Coles Nautical (United Kingdom) *Tel:* (020) 7758 0200 *Fax:* (020) 7831 8478 *E-mail:* adlardcoles@acblack.co.uk *Web Site:* www.adlardcoles.co.uk, pg 645

ADMICAL (Association pour le Developpement du Mecenat Industriel et Commercial) (France) *Tel:* (01) 42552001 *Fax:* (01) 42557132 *E-mail:* contact@admical.org *Web Site:* www.admical.org, pg 1242

Adobe Systems GmbH (Germany) *Tel:* (089) 317050 *Fax:* (089) 31705705, pg 1133

Adonia-Verlag (Switzerland) *Tel:* (01) 9801930 *Fax:* (01) 9800622 *E-mail:* advonia.verlag@bluewin.ch *Web Site:* www.libroplus.ch/adonia, pg 608

ADPF Publications (France) *Tel:* (01) 43 13 11 00 *Fax:* (01) 43 13 11 25 *Web Site:* www.france.diplomatie.fr; www.adpf.asso.fr, pg 146

ADR/BookPrint (United States) *Tel:* 316-522-5599 *Fax:* 316-522-5445 *Web Site:* www.adrbookprint.com, pg 1142, 1163, 1205

Adrian (France) *Tel:* (01) 42364429 *Fax:* (01) 42364429, pg 146

Adriatica (Peru) *Tel:* (044) 251145 *Fax:* (044) 256712 *E-mail:* adriatica@pc-vertas.com, pg 1305

Adriatica Editrice (Italy) *Tel:* (080) 5211341 *Fax:* (080) 5235640 *E-mail:* edit_adriatica@teseo.it *Web Site:* www.teseo.it/edit_adriatica, pg 374

Adroit Birmingham Ltd (United Kingdom) *Tel:* (0121) 3596831 *Fax:* (0121) 3593974, pg 1160

Adsale Publishing Co Ltd (Hong Kong) *Tel:* (02) 8118897 *Fax:* (02) 5165119 *E-mail:* publishing@adsalepub.com.hk *Web Site:* www.adsalepub.com.hk, pg 318

Advaita Ashrama (India) *Tel:* (033) 2440898; (033) 2452383; (033) 2164000 *Fax:* (033) 2450050 *E-mail:* advaita@vsnl.com *Web Site:* education.vsnl.com/advaita/advtoc.html, pg 329

Advance Book Distributors (Australia) *Tel:* (03) 95489422 *Fax:* (03) 95489411, pg 1272

The Advancement Centre (Australia) *Tel:* (02) 9896-2311, pg 11

Advent Indonesia Publishing (Indonesia) *Tel:* (022) 630392; (022) 642006 *Fax:* (022) 630588, pg 353

Advent Kiado (Hungary) *Tel:* (01) 2565205 *Fax:* (01) 2565205, pg 323

The Advent Press (Ghana) *Tel:* (021) 777861; (021) 775327 *Fax:* (021) 774338; (021) 2119, pg 306

Adverbum SARL (France) *Tel:* (04) 92812881 *Fax:* (04) 92813711 *E-mail:* info@adverbum.fr *Web Site:* www.adverbum.fr, pg 146

Advisory Unit: Computers in Education (United Kingdom) *Tel:* (01707) 266714 *Fax:* (01707) 273684 *E-mail:* sales@advisory-unit.org.uk *Web Site:* www.advisory-unit.org.uk, pg 645

Adwinsa Publications (Ghana) Ltd (Ghana) *Tel:* (021) 221654; (021) 21577, pg 306

Adyar-Verlag (Germany) *Tel:* (07950) 925010 *Fax:* (07950) 925029, pg 191

AE Technical Translation Services (United Kingdom) *Tel:* (01286) 650667 *Fax:* (01286) 650500, pg 1128

Editorial AEDOS SA (Spain) *Tel:* (093) 4883492 *Fax:* (093) 4877659, pg 561

Aeneas Verlagsgesellschaft GmbH (Austria) *Tel:* (02236) 25422, pg 49

AENOR (Asociacion Espanola de Normalizacion y Certificacion) (Spain) *Tel:* (091) 914 32 60 00 *Fax:* (091) 913 10 40 32 *E-mail:* info@aenor.es *Web Site:* www.aenor.es, pg 561

Aeolian Press (Australia) *Tel:* (08) 9761 2772 *Fax:* (08) 9761 4151, pg 11

Aeolus Press BV (Netherlands) *Tel:* (0344) 572055 *Fax:* (0344) 572562 *E-mail:* aeolus@swets.hl, pg 472

THE AFRICAN LITERATURE CLUB

Centre Aequatoria (Belgium) *Tel:* (016) 46 44 84 *Fax:* (016) 46 44 84 *Web Site:* www.aequatoria.be; www.abbol.com, pg 64

Aerogie-Verlag (Germany) *Tel:* (030) 6 76 32 00 *Fax:* (030) 6 76 32 00, pg 191

Aerospace Publications (Australia) *Tel:* (02) 6280 0111 *Fax:* (02) 6280 0007 *Web Site:* www.ausaviation.com, pg 11

AEskan (Iceland) *Tel:* 551-0248, pg 327

Aesthetica (Italy) *Tel:* (091) 308290 *Fax:* (091) 308290 *E-mail:* aesthetica@unipa.it, pg 374

Afa Yayincilik Sanayi Tic AS (Turkey) *Tel:* (0212) 2453967 *Fax:* (0212) 2444362, pg 638

Editorial Afers, SL (Spain) *Tel:* (096) 1268654 *Fax:* (096) 1272582 *E-mail:* afers@provicom.com *Web Site:* www.provicom.com/afers, pg 561

Affiliated East West Press Pvt Ltd (India) *Tel:* (011) 3315398; (011) 3279113 *Fax:* (011) 3260538 *E-mail:* aewp.newdel@axcess.net.in, pg 329

Affiliated East West Press Pvt Ltd (India) *Tel:* (011) 3264180; (011) 3279113 *Fax:* (011) 3260538 *E-mail:* affiliat@nda.vsnl.net.in, pg 1288

Affonso & Reichmann Editores Associados (Brazil) *Tel:* (021) 507-1270 *Fax:* (021) 507-1270, pg 78

A4 Publications Ltd (United Kingdom) *Tel:* (01384) 440591 *Fax:* (01384) 440582, pg 645

Afram Publications (Ghana) Ltd (Ghana) *Tel:* (021) 412561; (021) 024 278844; (021) 024 278855 *E-mail:* aframpub@punchgh.com, pg 306

Africa Book Centre Ltd (United Kingdom) *Tel:* (020) 7240 6649 *Fax:* (020) 7497 0309 *Toll Free Fax:* (0845) 458 1579 (UK only) *E-mail:* orders@africabookcentre.com *Web Site:* www.africabookcentre.com, pg 1315

Africa Book Services (EA) Ltd (Kenya) *Tel:* (02) 223641 *Fax:* (02) 330272 *E-mail:* abs@mref.co.ke, pg 430

Africa Christian Press (Ghana) *Tel:* (021) 244147; (021) 244148 *Fax:* (021) 220271; (021) 668115 *E-mail:* acpbooks@ghana.com, pg 306

Africa Film & TV t/a Z Promotions (Zimbabwe) *Tel:* (04) 726972; (04) 726795 *Fax:* (04) 726796 *E-mail:* info@africfilmtv.com *Web Site:* www.africafilmtv.com, pg 767

Africa Literatura Arte Cultura - ALAC (Portugal) *Tel:* (01) 4192274, pg 522

Books for Africa Publishing House (Zimbabwe) *Tel:* (04) 794329 *Fax:* (04) 61881, pg 767

Nouvelles Editions Africaines du Senegal (NEAS) (Senegal) *Tel:* (0221) 8211381; (0221) 8221580 *Fax:* (0221) 8223604 *E-mail:* neas@telecomplus.sn, pg 544

African Association for Literacy & Adult Education (AALAE) (Kenya) *Tel:* (02) 222391; (02) 331512, pg 431

African Books Collective Ltd (United Kingdom) *Tel:* (01865) 726686 *Fax:* (01865) 793298; (01993) 709265 *E-mail:* abc@dial.pipex.com *Web Site:* www.africanbookscollective.com, pg 1263, 1315

African Centre for Technology Studies (ACTS) (Kenya) *Tel:* (02) 524700; (02) 524000 *Fax:* (02) 524701; (02) 524001 *E-mail:* acts@cgiar.org *Web Site:* www.acts.or.ke, pg 431

African Council for Communication Education (Kenya) *Tel:* (02) 541440; (02) 540820 ext 289, pg 431

African Cultural Centre (Mauritius) *Tel:* 2124131 *Fax:* 2088620, pg 457

The African Literature Club (Germany) *Tel:* (06221) 411861 *Fax:* (06221) 411861, pg 191

AFRICAN PUBLISHERS' NETWORK (APNET)   INDUSTRY

African Publishers' Network (APNET) (Zimbabwe) *Tel:* (04) 708418 *Fax:* (04) 708413 *E-mail:* apnet@mango.zw; apnet@apnet.co.zw *Web Site:* www.africanpublishers.org, pg 1269

African Universities Press (Nigeria) *Tel:* (022) 317218, pg 497

Africana-FEP Publishers Ltd (Nigeria) *Tel:* (046) 210669, pg 498

Afro-Asian Book Council (AABC) (India) *Tel:* (011) 3261487 *Fax:* (011) 3267437 *E-mail:* sdas@ubspd.com, pg 1248

Edicoes Afrontamento (Portugal) *Tel:* (02) 489271 *Fax:* (02) 491777 *E-mail:* afrontamento@mail.telepac.pt, pg 522

Afterhurst Ltd (United Kingdom) *Tel:* (01273) 748427 *Fax:* (01273) 722180 *E-mail:* dirdist@erlbaum.co.uk, pg 1315

Agalma Psicanalise Editora Ltda (Brazil) *Tel:* (071) 332-8776 *Fax:* (071) 245-7883 *E-mail:* agalma@agalma.com.br *Web Site:* www.agalma.com.br, pg 78

Agam Kala Prakashan (India) *Tel:* (011) 7212195; (011) 7401485; (011) 7401486 *Fax:* (011) 7401485, pg 330

AGAPE (Yugoslavia) *Tel:* (021) 469-474 *Fax:* (021) 469-382 *E-mail:* agape@eunet.yu *Web Site:* www.agape.hu, pg 764

Agape Ferences Nyomda es Konyvkiado Kft (Hungary) *Tel:* (062) 444-002 *Fax:* (062) 442-592 *E-mail:* agape@tiszanet.hu, pg 323

Editorial AGATA SA de CV (Mexico) *Tel:* (03) 6584392 *Fax:* (03) 6138429, pg 457

Age Concern Books (United Kingdom) *Tel:* (020) 8765 7200 *E-mail:* infodep@ace.org.uk *Web Site:* www.ageconcern.org.uk, pg 645

Editions L'Age d'Homme - La Cite (Switzerland) *Tel:* (021) 3120095 *Fax:* (021) 3208440, pg 608

Agence Bibliographique de L'Enseignement Superieur (France) *Tel:* (04) 67 54 84 10 *Fax:* (04) 67 54 84 14 *E-mail:* nom@abes.fr *Web Site:* www.abes.fr, pg 146

Agence de Distribution de Presse (Senegal) *Tel:* (08) 320278 *Fax:* (08) 324915 *E-mail:* adpresse@telecomplus.sn, pg 544

Agence de l'Est (Czech Republic) *Tel:* (02) 602 978 281 *Fax:* (02) 2278 1937 *E-mail:* agencedelest@mbox.vol.cz, pg 1110

Agence et Menageries de la Prense (Belgium) *Tel:* (03) 8300015 *Fax:* (03) 8254755, pg 1275

Agence Francophone pour la Numerotation Internationale du Livre (AFNIL) (France) *Tel:* (01) 44412800 *Fax:* (01) 44072033 *E-mail:* afnil@electre.com, pg 1242

Agence Hoffman (Germany) *Tel:* (089) 3084807 *Fax:* (089) 3082108, pg 1111

Agence Marocaine de l'ISBN (Morocco) *Tel:* (07) 771890; (07) 772152 *Fax:* (07) 776062 *E-mail:* biblio1@onpt.net.ma, pg 1253

Agence Tunisienne de l'ISBN (Tunisia) *Tel:* (01) 256921 *Fax:* (01) 342700 *E-mail:* Bibliotheque.Nationale@Email.ati.tn, pg 1263

Agencia Brasileira do ISBN (Brazil) *Tel:* (021) 2408629; (021) 2408579 *Fax:* (021) 2204173, pg 1238

Agencia Colombiana del ISBN, Camara Columbiana del Libro (Colombia) *Tel:* (01) 2886188 *Fax:* (01) 2873320 *E-mail:* camlibro@latino.net.co *Web Site:* camaracolumbiandelibro.com.co, pg 1240

Agencia Espanola de Cooperacion (Spain) *Tel:* (091) 5838100; (091) 5838254; (091) 5838101; (091) 5838102 *Fax:* (091) 5838310; (091) 5838311; (091) 5838313, pg 562

Agencia Espanola del ISBN (Spain) *Tel:* (091) 5368830 *Fax:* (091) 5539990 *Web Site:* www.slt.lk/nlib, pg 1259

Agencia General de Libreria Internacional SL (AGLI) (Spain) *Tel:* (091) 3736640 *Fax:* (091) 3732740, pg 1311

Agencia Literaria Balcells Mello e Souza Riff S/C Ltda (Brazil) *Tel:* (021) 22876299 *Fax:* (021) 22676393, pg 1109

Agencija Za Ikonomicesko Programirane i Razvitie (Bulgaria) *Tel:* (02) 9816597 *Fax:* (02) 466110 *E-mail:* aecd@sf.cit.bg, pg 94

The Agency (London) Ltd (United Kingdom) *Tel:* (020) 7727 1346 *Fax:* (020) 7727 9037 *E-mail:* info@theagency.co.uk *Web Site:* www.agentsassoc.co.uk, pg 1117

Agens-Werk, Geyer & Reisser, Druck und Verlagsgesellschaft mbH (Austria) *Tel:* (01) 545641 *Fax:* (01) 544564166, pg 49

Agentur des Rauhen Hauses Hamburg GmbH (Germany) *Tel:* (040) 53 53 88-0 *Fax:* (040) 53 53 88-43 *E-mail:* kundenservice@agentur-rauhes-haus.de *Web Site:* www.agentur-rauhes-haus.de, pg 192

Agenzia ISBN per l'Area di Lingua Italiana (Italy) *Tel:* (02) 28315996 *Fax:* (02) 28315906, pg 1249

Agenzia Letteraria Internazionale (Italy) *Tel:* (02) 86463418; (02) 865445; (02) 861572 *Fax:* (02) 876222, pg 1113

Agertofts Forlag A/S (Denmark) *Tel:* 046151248 *Fax:* 046151248, pg 129

Livraria Agir Editora (Brazil) *Tel:* (021) 2216424 *Fax:* (021) 2520410, pg 1277

AGIR S/A Editora (Brazil) *Tel:* (021) 509-6424; (021) 252-8261 *Fax:* (021) 509-0410 *E-mail:* info@agireditora.com.br *Web Site:* www.visualnet.com.br/cmaya/cm-ft-01.htm, pg 78

Agis Verlag GmbH (Germany) *Tel:* (07221) 95 75-0 *Fax:* (07221) 6 68 10 *E-mail:* info@agis-verlag.de, pg 192

AGM doo (Croatia) *Tel:* (01) 4856309; (01) 4856307 *Fax:* (01) 4856316 *E-mail:* agm@agm.hr *Web Site:* www.agm.hr, pg 118

Edizioni della Fondazione Giovanni Agnelli (Italy) *Tel:* (011) 6500500 *Fax:* (011) 6502777 *E-mail:* staff@fga.it *Web Site:* www.fondazione-agnelli.it, pg 375

Agni Publishing House (Russian Federation) *Tel:* (08462) 70-32-87; (08462) 70-23-87 (ext 445 - Orders) *Fax:* (08462) 70-23-85 *E-mail:* cdk@transit.samara.ru; support@agniart.ru (distribution & ordering) *Web Site:* www.agni.samara.ru, pg 537

Uitgeversmaatschappij Agon (Netherlands) *Tel:* (020) 5247500 *Fax:* (020) 6224937, pg 472

Agora bvba (Belgium) *Tel:* (053) 78-87-00 *Fax:* (053) 78-26-91, pg 1276

Agora Editorial (Spain) *Tel:* (095) 2228699; (095) 2221847 *Fax:* (095) 2226411, pg 562

Editora Agora Ltda (Brazil) *Tel:* (011) 38723322 *Fax:* (011) 38727476 *E-mail:* agora@editoraagora.com.br *Web Site:* www.editoraagora.com.br, pg 78

De Agostini Scolastica (Italy) *Tel:* (02) 380861 *Fax:* (02) 38086448 *Web Site:* www.scuola.com/inviarisposta.html, pg 375

AGPOL (Przedsiebiorstwo Reklamy i Wydawnictw Handlu Zagranicznego) (Poland) *Tel:* (022) 416061 *Fax:* (022) 405607, pg 1256

Agrargazdasagi Kutato es Informatikai Intezet (Hungary) *Tel:* (01) 1171011 *Fax:* (01) 1377037, pg 323

Agricole Publishing Academy (India) *Tel:* (011) 69 48 25, pg 330

Agricultural Institute Library (Ethiopia) *Tel:* (07) 110102, pg 1463

Central Library of Agricultural Science (Israel) *Tel:* (08) 481270 *Fax:* (03) 993998, pg 1476

Agrivet Publishers (Namibia) *Tel:* (061) 228909 *Fax:* (061) 230619 *E-mail:* agriveti@iafrica.com.ma, pg 471

Ediciones Agrotecnicas, SL (Spain) *Tel:* (091) 5175248; (091) 5473515 *Fax:* (091) 5474506 *E-mail:* agrotecnicas@agrotecnica.com *Web Site:* www.agrotecnica.com, pg 562

Agrupacion Bibliotecologica del Uruguay (Uruguay) *Tel:* (02) 400 57 40, pg 1525

AGT Editor SA (Mexico) *Tel:* (05) 5164261 *Fax:* (05) 2771696, pg 457

Editorial Aguaclara (Spain) *Tel:* (096) 5240064 *Fax:* (096) 5259302 *E-mail:* edit.aguaclara@natural.es, pg 562

Agudat Sabah (Israel) *Tel:* (09) 8620544 *Fax:* (09) 8620546, pg 365

Aguilar Altea Taurus Alfaguara SA de Ediciones (Argentina) *Tel:* (011) 4912-7220 *Fax:* (011) 4912-7440 *Web Site:* www.alfaguara.com.ar, pg 3

Aguilar Altea Taurus Alfaguara SA de CV (Mexico) *Tel:* (05) 6888277 *Fax:* (05) 6011067, pg 457

Aguilar SA de Ediciones (Spain) *Tel:* (091) 7449060 *Fax:* (091) 7449093 *E-mail:* limarquezes@santillana.es *Web Site:* www.gruposantillana.com, pg 562

Libreria Aguirre (Colombia) *Tel:* (04) 2394801, pg 1279

Agyra (Greece) *Tel:* (01) 3455276; (01) 3459321; (01) 3471503 *Fax:* (01) 3474732 *E-mail:* agyra@agyra.gr, pg 1285

AHB Publications (Australia), pg 11

Ahmadu Bello University Bookshop Ltd (Nigeria) *Tel:* (069) 550054, pg 1303

Ahmadu Bello University Library (Nigeria) *Tel:* (069) 32081; (069) 32082, pg 1488

Ahmadu Bello University Press Ltd (Nigeria) *Tel:* (069) 550054 *E-mail:* abupl@abu.edu.ng, pg 498

Ahn Graphics (Republic of Korea) *Tel:* (02) 7632320; (02) 7438066 *Fax:* (02) 7433352 *E-mail:* 100050.1023@compuserve.com; ahnO1dh@chollian.dacom.co.kr *Web Site:* www.ag.co.kr, pg 434

Al Ahram Book Club (Egypt (Arab Republic of Egypt)) *Tel:* (02) 748248 *Fax:* (02) 745888, pg 1228

Al Ahram Establishment (Egypt (Arab Republic of Egypt)) *Tel:* (02) 748248 *Fax:* (02) 745888, pg 138, 1125

Ahriman-Verlag GmbH (Germany) *Tel:* (0761) 502303 *Fax:* (0761) 502247 *E-mail:* ahriman@t-online.de *Web Site:* www.ahriman.com, pg 192

Ai Chih Book Co Ltd (Taiwan, Province of China) *Tel:* (07) 8121571 *Fax:* (07) 8121534, pg 629

Ai Interactive Ltd (United Kingdom) *Tel:* (01235) 529595 *Fax:* (01235) 520205 *E-mail:* medical@andromeda-interactive.co.uk *Web Site:* www.andromeda-interactive.co.uk, pg 645

AIB Associazione Italiana Biblioteche (Italy) *Tel:* (06) 4463532 *Fax:* (06) 4441139 *E-mail:* aib@aib.it *Web Site:* www.aib.it, pg 375

AIBDA (Costa Rica) *Tel:* (0506) 2290222 *Fax:* (0506) 2294741; (0506) 2292659 *E-mail:* aibda@iica.ac.cr *Web Site:* www.iica.ac.cr, pg 1240

Aichinger, Bernhard & Co GmbH (Austria) *Tel:* (0222) 5128853 *Fax:* (0222) 5128853-13, pg 1274

aid infodienst - Verbraucherdienst, Ernaehrung, Landwirtschaft eV (Germany) *Tel:* (0228) 8499-0 *Fax:* (0228) 9526952; (0228) 8499-177 *E-mail:* aid@aid.de *Web Site:* www.aid.de, pg 192

Aide Editora e Comercio de Livros Ltda (Brazil) *Tel:* (021) 2589-9926 *Fax:* (021) 2589-9926 *E-mail:* aideeditora@radnet.com.br *Web Site:* www.radnet.com.br/aideditora, pg 78

Aika Oy Kristilliset Kirjat (Finland) *Tel:* (014) 7514751 *Fax:* (014) 7514757 *E-mail:* aika@aikaoy.fi *Web Site:* www.aikaoy.fi, pg 141, 1228

Aiki News (Japan) *Tel:* (03) 33596265, pg 414

Aina-e-Adab (Pakistan) *Tel:* (042) 54069, pg 506

Aion Verlag (Romania) *Tel:* (059) 14795, pg 531

Air Gallery Edition, Helmut Kreuzer (Germany) *Tel:* (08122) 84487 *Fax:* (08122) 84487, pg 192

Air Larko Panorama, ALP (Cyprus) *Tel:* (06) 236181 *Fax:* (06) 245046, pg 121

Airis Press (Russian Federation) *Tel:* (095) 9561684; (095) 7852925 *Fax:* (095) 9561684; (095) 7852925 *E-mail:* rolf@airis.ru *Web Site:* www.airis.ru, pg 537

Airlife Publishing Ltd (United Kingdom) *Tel:* (01743) 235651 *Fax:* (01743) 232944 *E-mail:* info@airlifebooks.com *Web Site:* www.airlifebooks.com, pg 645

Airlift Book Co (United Kingdom) *Tel:* (0181) 8040400 *Fax:* (0181) 8040044, pg 1315

AIS (Ireland) *Tel:* (01) 6616522 *Fax:* (01) 6612378, pg 358, 1291

Aisthesis Verlag Dr Detlev Kopp und Dr Michael Vogt (Germany) *Tel:* (0521) 172604; (0521) 172812 *Fax:* (0521) 172812 *E-mail:* aisthesis@bitel.net *Web Site:* www.fechenbach.de, pg 192

Aithra Scientific Bookstore (Greece) *Tel:* (01) 3301269 *Fax:* (01) 3302622, pg 1285

AITI (Associazione Italiana Traduttoried Interpreti) (Italy) *Tel:* (06) 88327535 *Fax:* (06) 88327535 *E-mail:* aiti@maix.it *Web Site:* www.mix.it/AITI, pg 1127

AITIM (Asociacion de Investigacion Tecnica de las industrias de la Madera y Corcho) (Spain) *Tel:* (091) 5425864 *Fax:* (091) 5590512 *E-mail:* informame@aitim.es *Web Site:* www.aitim.es, pg 562

Gillon Aitken Associates Ltd (United Kingdom) *Tel:* (020) 7351 7561 *Fax:* (020) 7352 9105 *E-mail:* 100303.1765@compuserve.com, pg 1118

Editura Aius (Romania) *Tel:* (051) 112786 *Fax:* (051) 113965 *E-mail:* aius@oltenia.ro, pg 531

Ajanta Books International (India) *Tel:* (011) 3926182 *Fax:* (011) 7415016 *E-mail:* ajantabi@ndf.vsnl.net.in; ajantabi@id.erh.net, pg 1112

Ajanta Publications (India) (India) *Tel:* (011) 7415106; (011) 2926182; (011) 725 8630 *Fax:* (011) 7415016; (011) 7132908; (011) 7213076, pg 330

Ajstan Publishers (Armenia) *Tel:* (02) 528520, pg 10

Biblioteca da Ajuda (Portugal) *Tel:* (021) 3638592 *Fax:* (021) 3638592, pg 1493

AK Press & Distribution (United Kingdom) *Tel:* (0131) 5555165 *Fax:* (0131) 5555215 *E-mail:* ak@akedin.demon.co.uk *Web Site:* www.akuk.com, pg 645

Akademiai Kiado (Hungary) *Tel:* (01) 4668282 *Fax:* (01) 4668251, pg 323

Akademie Verlag GmbH (Germany) *Tel:* (030) 422006-05 *Fax:* (030) 422006-57 *E-mail:* mktg@akademie-verlag.de *Web Site:* www.akademie-verlag.de, pg 192

Akademiforlaget Corona AB (Sweden) *Tel:* (040) 189480 *Fax:* (040) 184570 *E-mail:* kundservice@cor.se *Web Site:* www.cor.se, pg 599

Akademiforlaget Goteborgslitteratur (Sweden) *Tel:* (031) 813410 *Fax:* (031) 811492 *E-mail:* sales@akg.se, pg 600

Biblioteka Akademii Nauk Rossii (Russian Federation) *Tel:* (0812) 3283592 *Fax:* (0812) 3287436 *E-mail:* ban@info.rasl.spb.ru *Web Site:* www.ban.tu, pg 1494

Akademische Druck-u Verlagsanstalt Dr Paul Struzl GmbH (Austria) *Tel:* (0316) 3644 *Fax:* (0316) 36 44-24 *E-mail:* info@adeva.com *Web Site:* www.adeva.com, pg 49

Akademisk Forlag (Denmark) *Tel:* 33 43 40 80 *Fax:* 33 43 40 99 *E-mail:* info@akademisk.dk *Web Site:* www.akademisk.dk, pg 129

Libreria Akadia Editorial (Argentina) *Tel:* (011) 4961-8614; (011) 4961-8595 *Fax:* (011) 4961-8614 *E-mail:* akadia@syb.com.ar, pg 3

Akadoma CV (Indonesia) *Tel:* (021) 3904323, pg 353

Akajase Enterprises (United Republic of Tanzania) *Tel:* (051) 26121, pg 633

Ediciones Akal SA (Spain) *Tel:* (091) 6565611; (091) 6565157; (091) 8061996 *Fax:* (091) 6564911; (091) 8044028 *E-mail:* admon@akal.com, pg 562

Akateeminen Kirjakauppa (Finland) *Tel:* (09) 12141 *Fax:* (09) 1214435 *E-mail:* markusanaja@stockman.mailnet.fi, pg 1282

Akateeminen Kustannusliike Oy (Finland) *Tel:* (09) 434 2320, pg 141

Akcali Copyright Agency (Turkey) *Tel:* (0216) 3388771; (0216) 3485160 *Fax:* (0216) 3490778 *E-mail:* akcali@attglobal.net, pg 1117

Akdeniz Yayincilik (Turkey) *Tel:* (0212) 5268012; (0212) 5224045 *Fax:* (0212) 5268011; (0212) 6290027, pg 638

Akerbloms Universitetsbokhandel (Sweden) *Tel:* (090) 711250 *Fax:* (090) 711260 *E-mail:* swedish.books@akerbloms.se, pg 1312

Azerbaidzhanskaya gosudarstvennaya biblioteka im M F Akhundova (Azerbaijan) *Tel:* (012) 934003, pg 1452

Akita Shoten Publishing Co Ltd (Japan) *Tel:* (03) 32647249 *Fax:* (03) 32659076, pg 414

Akohi Editions (Cote d'Ivoire) *Tel:* 24 39 54 79 *Fax:* 24 39 75 58, pg 117

Editions Akpagnon (Togo) *Tel:* 220244 *Fax:* 220244, pg 636

Akritas (Greece) *Tel:* (01) 9334685 *Fax:* (01) 9311436, pg 308

M Akselrad (Germany) *Tel:* (06221) 183030 *Fax:* (06221) 181223 *E-mail:* m_akselrad@compuserve.com, pg 192

Akshat Publications (India) *Tel:* (011) 7247234; (011) 7114425; (011) 7240483 *Fax:* (011) 7254734; (011) 7218836, pg 330

Akson Charemtat (S/B Akson) (Thailand) *Tel:* (02) 2214587 *Fax:* (02) 2255356, pg 635

Akti-Oxy Publications (Greece) *Tel:* 01 8676125 *Fax:* 01 8644679 *E-mail:* oxy@compulink.gr *Web Site:* www.zoobiolon.com/oxy/, pg 1285

Al-Fatah University, General Administration of Libraries, Printing & Publications (Libyan Arab Jamahiriya) *Tel:* (02133) 621988, pg 444

Editions Al-Fourkane (Morocco) *Tel:* (02) 983351 *Fax:* (02) 983351, pg 469

Editions Al Liamm (France) *Tel:* 0298021084, pg 146

Al Maktabah Al Wataniah (Syrian Arab Republic), pg 1502

AL Publishers (India) *Tel:* (040) 7611600, pg 330

Al-Tanwir Al Ilmi (Scientific Enlightenment Publishing House) (Jordan) *Tel:* (026) 4899619 *Fax:* (026) 4899619, pg 430

Aladdin Books Ltd (United Kingdom) *Tel:* (020) 7323 3319 *Fax:* (020) 7323 4829 *E-mail:* sales@aladdin1.dircon.co.uk, pg 645

Alamire vzw, Music Publishers (Belgium) *Tel:* (011) 610 510 *Fax:* (011) 610 511 *E-mail:* info@alamire.com *Web Site:* www.alamire.com, pg 64

Alamo Hellas (Greece) *Tel:* (01) 2280027 *Fax:* (01) 2280027, pg 308

Editorial 'Alas' (Spain) *Tel:* (093) 4537506; (093) 3233445 *Fax:* (093) 4537506 *E-mail:* sala@editorial-alas.com *Web Site:* www.editorial-alas.com, pg 562

Alba (Italy) *Tel:* (0532) 249854 *Fax:* (0532) 249854 *E-mail:* alba_editrice@virgilio.it *Web Site:* digilander.libero.it/albaeditrice, pg 375

Alba Fachverlag GmbH und Co KG (Germany) *Tel:* (0211) 52013-51 *Fax:* (0211) 52013-18 *Web Site:* www.alba-verlag.de, pg 192

Albah Publishers (Nigeria), pg 498

J H Goehre Albanus Verlag (Switzerland) *Tel:* (052) 293503, pg 608

Albany Book Co Ltd (United Kingdom) *Tel:* (0141) 9542271, pg 1315

Albarello Verlag GmbH (Germany) *Tel:* (0202) 2058 8279 *Fax:* (0202) 2058 80534, pg 192

Albatros (Poland) *Tel:* (022) 842-9867 *Fax:* (022) 842-9867, pg 516

Editura Albatros (Romania) *Tel:* (01) 2228493 *Fax:* (01) 2228493, pg 531

Albatros Publishing House, Co Ltd (Czech Republic) *Tel:* (02) 24810704; (02) 2311156; (02) 24314289 *Fax:* (02) 24810850 *E-mail:* albatros@bonton.cz *Web Site:* www.albatros.cz, pg 122

Editorial Albatros SACI (Argentina) *Tel:* (011) 4807-2030 *Fax:* (011) 4807-2010 *E-mail:* info@edalbatros.com.ar *Web Site:* www.edalbatros.com.ar, pg 3

Albe Libros Technicos (Uruguay) *Tel:* (02) 957485 *Fax:* (02) 957528, pg 759

Albe Libros Tecnicos SRL (Uruguay) *Tel:* (02) 957528; (02) 957485 *Fax:* (02) 957528, pg 1324

Verlag Karl Alber GmbH (Germany) *Tel:* (0761) 27 17-365 *Fax:* (0761) 27 17-212 *E-mail:* alber-buch@alber.freinet.de *Web Site:* www.alber.freinet.de, pg 192

Alberdania SL (Spain) *Tel:* (0943) 632814 *Fax:* (0943) 638055 *E-mail:* alberdania@ctv.es *Web Site:* www.alberdania.com, pg 562

Libreria Eduardo Albers (Chile) *Tel:* (02) 2185371 *Fax:* (02) 2181458 *E-mail:* libreria@albers.cl *Web Site:* www.albers.cl, pg 1278

Albert Bonniers Forlag (Sweden) *Tel:* (08) 696 8620 *Fax:* (08) 696 8369; (08) 696 8347 *E-mail:* info@abforlag.bonnier.se *Web Site:* www.albertbonniersforlag.com, pg 600

Albert Nauck & Co (Germany) *Tel:* (0221) 94373-0 *Fax:* (0221) 94373-901, pg 192

Albert Propster Verlag und Buchhandlung (Germany) *Tel:* (0831) 22797 *Fax:* (0831) 201732, pg 192

Ermanno Albertelli Editore (Italy) *Tel:* (0521) 290387 *Fax:* (0521) 290387, pg 375

Alberti Libraio Editore (Italy) *Tel:* (0323) 402534 *Fax:* (0323) 401074 *E-mail:* alberti_libraio_editore@hotmail.com *Web Site:* www.albertilibraioeditore.it, pg 375

Alberts XII (Latvia) *Tel:* (02) 7285183 *Fax:* (02) 7332427, pg 441

Editions Albin Michel (France) *Tel:* (01) 42 79 10 00 *Fax:* (01) 43 27 21 58 *Web Site:* www.albin-michel.fr, pg 146

E Albrecht Verlags-Kommanditgesellschaft (Germany) *Tel:* (089) 85 85 31 00 *Fax:* (089) 85 85 31 99 *E-mail:* av@albrecht.de, pg 192

Verlag und Antiquariat Frank Albrecht (Germany) *Tel:* (06203) 65713 *Fax:* (06203) 65311 *E-mail:* albrecht@antiquariat.com *Web Site:* www.antiquariat.com, pg 192

Librairie Francaise Alcheh (Israel) *Tel:* (03) 5609817; (03) 5604173 *Fax:* (03) 6994526, pg 1292

Alcor-Edimpex (Verlag) Ltd (Romania) *Tel:* (01) 665-34-40 *Fax:* (01) 665 34 40 *E-mail:* ed_alcor@yahoo.com *Web Site:* www.rotravel.com/alcor, pg 531

The Alden Group Ltd (United Kingdom) Tel: (01865) 253200 Fax: (01865) 249070 E-mail: alden.press@alden.co.uk Web Site: www.alden.co.uk, pg 1160, 1202

Aldington Books Ltd (United Kingdom) Tel: (01233) 720123 Fax: (01233) 721272 E-mail: sales@aldingtonbooks.co.uk Web Site: www.aldingtonbooks.com.uk, pg 1315

Aldwych Press Ltd (United Kingdom) Tel: (020) 7240 0856 Fax: (020) 7379 0609 E-mail: info@eurospan.co.uk Web Site: www.eurospan.co.uk, pg 645

Centro Antiquar do Alecrim A Trindade (Portugal) Tel: (021) 3424660 Fax: (021) 3470180 E-mail: np75ae@mail.telepac.pt, pg 1306

Aleko, Nakladatelska Divize (Czech Republic) Tel: (02) 6921024; (02) 6921025 Fax: (02) 6921025, pg 122

Aleks Print Publishing House (Bulgaria) Tel: (052) 823147 Fax: (052) 823147, pg 94

Aleks Soft (Bulgaria) Tel: (078) 46136 Fax: (078) 46136, pg 94

Alekto Verlag GmbH (Austria) Tel: (0463) 515 230; (0463) 593 217 Fax: (0463) 503 351 E-mail: bali@bali.co.at Web Site: bali.co.at, pg 49

Livraria Alema (Brazil) Tel: (0473) 3264558 Fax: (0473) 3263062, pg 78

Alemar's (Philippines) Tel: (02) 592617, pg 1306

Alemar's Best Sellers Club (Philippines) Tel: (02) 592617, pg 1231

Alemaya University of Agriculture Library (Ethiopia) Tel: (05) 111399 Fax: (05) 114008, pg 1463

Aleph (Italy) Tel: (0935) 500368 Fax: (0935) 500568, pg 375

El Aleph Editores (Spain) Tel: (093) 443 71 00 Fax: (093) 443 71 30 E-mail: correu@grup62.com Web Site: www.grup62.com, pg 562

Aletheia Publishing (Australia) Tel: (07) 38552056 E-mail: aletheia@powerup.com.au, pg 11

Alexander Verlag Berlin (Germany) Tel: (030) 3021826 Fax: (030) 3029408 E-mail: info@alexander-verlag.com Web Site: www.alexander-verlag.com, pg 192

Alexandria Municipal Library (Egypt (Arab Republic of Egypt)), pg 1462

Alexiadou Vefa Editions (Greece) Tel: (01) 2848086; (031) 245151 Fax: (01) 2849689; (01) 2846984 E-mail: vefaeditions@ath.forthnet.gr Web Site: www.addgr.com/comp/vefa, pg 309

Alexiadou Vefa (Greece) Tel: (01) 2848086 Fax: (01) 2849689 E-mail: vefaeditions@ath.forthnet.gr, pg 1285

ALFA dd za izdavacke, graficke i trgovacke poslove (Croatia) Tel: (01) 4666 066; (01) 4666 077 Fax: (01) 4666 258 E-mail: alfa-zg@zg.tel.hr, pg 118

Alfa-Narodna Knjiga (Yugoslavia) Tel: (011) 3221-484; (011) 3227-426; (011) 3223-910 Fax: (011) 3227-946 E-mail: alfankkl@eunet.yu Web Site: www.narodnaknjiga.co.yu, pg 764

Editora Alfa Omega Ltda (Brazil) Tel: (011) 3062-6400; (011) 3062-6690 Fax: (011) 3083-0746 E-mail: alfaomega@alfaomega.com.br Web Site: www.alfaomega.com.br, pg 78

ALFA OMEGA Grupo Editor (Mexico) Tel: (05) 5119203 Fax: (052) 2077158 E-mail: 74054.1612@compuserve.com, pg 458

Publicacoes Alfa SA (Portugal) Tel: (021) 917 2807 Fax: (021) 917 0130, pg 522

Wydawnictwa Normalizacyjne Alfa-Wero (Poland) Tel: (02) 6218750; (02) 6216751 Fax: (02) 6218750, pg 516

Alfabeta Bokforlag AB (Sweden) Tel: (08) 7149353; (08) 7149336 Fax: (08) 6432431 E-mail: info@alfabeta.se Web Site: www.alfamedia.se, pg 600

Alfabeta Impresores Ltda (Chile) Tel: (02) 6397765 Fax: (02) 6391752, pg 99

Alfadil Ediciones (Venezuela) Tel: (02) 762-3036; (02) 761-3576; (02) 715-676 Fax: (02) 7620210 E-mail: alfagrupo@compuserve.com, pg 761

Alfagrama SRL ediciones (Argentina) Tel: (011) 4342-2452; (011) 4345-2299 Fax: (011) 4345-5411 E-mail: libros@alfagram.com.ar Web Site: www.alfagrama.com.ar, pg 3

Alfaguara Ediciones SA - Grupo Santillana (Spain) Tel: (091) 744 90 60 Fax: (091) 744 92 24 Web Site: www.alfaguara.santillana.es, pg 562

Libreria Alfani Editrice SRL (Italy) Tel: (055) 2398800 Fax: (055) 284397 E-mail: info@librerialfani.it, pg 375

Ediciones Alfar SA (Spain) Tel: (05) 4406100; (05) 4406366; (05) 4406614 Fax: (05) 4402580, pg 562

Edicions Alfons el Magnanim, Institucio Valenciana d'Estudis i Investigacio (Spain) Tel: (06) 3883544; (06) 3883555 Fax: (06) 3883568 Web Site: www.alfonselmagnanim.com, pg 562

Algarve (Lithuania) Tel: (02) 725910; (02) 721635 Fax: (02) 721462, pg 445

Editorial Algazara (Spain) Tel: (095) 2358284 Fax: (095) 2333175, pg 562

Les Editions Algeriennes En-Nahdha (Algeria) Tel: (021) 737627 Fax: (021) 737627, pg 2

Sheikh Shaukat Ali & Sons (Pakistan) Tel: (021) 214585 Fax: (021) 212289, pg 506

Alianza Editorial de Argentina SA (Argentina) Tel: (011) 4342-4426; (011) 4342-9029 Fax: (011) 4342-4426; (011) 4342-9025, pg 3

Alianza Editorial Mexicana (Mexico) Tel: (05) 6704887; (05) 6704712, pg 458

Alianza Editorial SA (Spain) Tel: (091) 3938888 Fax: (091) 3207480 E-mail: alianza@anaya.es Web Site: www.alianzaeditorial.es, pg 562

Alibaba Verlag GmbH (Germany) Tel: (069) 590097 Fax: (069) 559855 Web Site: www.alibaba-verlag.de, pg 193

Alibri Libreria, SL (Spain) Tel: (093) 317 0578 Fax: (093) 412 2702 E-mail: books-world@books-world.com, pg 1311

Edizioni Alice (Italy) Tel: (091) 9729393 Fax: (091) 9718779, pg 375

Alice-Kan (Japan) Tel: (03) 59767013 Fax: (03) 39438396, pg 414

Alinari Fratelli SpA Istituto di Edizioni Artistiche (Italy) Tel: (055) 23951 Fax: (055) 262857 E-mail: infomore@alinari.it Web Site: www.alinari.com, pg 375

Alinco SA - Aura Comunicacio (Spain) Tel: (093) 2172054 Fax: (093) 2373469, pg 563

Alinea (Italy) Tel: (055) 333428 Fax: (055) 331013 E-mail: info@alinea.it, pg 375

Alinea A/S (Denmark) Tel: 33694666 Fax: 33694660 E-mail: alinea@alinea.dk; skoleservice@alinea.dk Web Site: www.alinea.dk, pg 129

Alisher Navoi National Library of Uzbekistan (Uzbekistan) Tel: (099871) 1391658 Fax: (099871) 1391658; (099871) 1330908 E-mail: navoi@physic.uzsci.net, pg 1508

ALITHIA Publishing Co (Cyprus) Tel: (02) 463040 Fax: (02) 463945, pg 121

Alkim Kitapcilik-Yayimcilik (Turkey), pg 638

Alkor-Edition Kassel GmbH (Germany) Tel: (0561) 3105-280 Fax: (0561) 37755 E-mail: alkor-edition@baerenreiter.com Web Site: www.alkor-edition.com, pg 193

Editora All (Romania) Tel: (01) 402 26 00 Fax: (01) 402 26 10 E-mail: info@all.ro Web Site: www.all.ro, pg 531

All-Russian Patent Technical Library (Russian Federation) Tel: (095) 2406425 Fax: (095) 2404437 E-mail: vptb@aha.ru, pg 1494

All-Union Book Chamber (Russian Federation) Tel: (095) 2034653; (095) 2035608 Fax: (095) 2982576; (095) 2982590 E-mail: chamber@aha.ru Web Site: www.bookchamber.ru, pg 1257

Ian Allan Publishing Ltd (United Kingdom) Tel: (01932) 266600 Fax: (01932) 266601 E-mail: info@ianallanpub.co.uk Web Site: www.ianallan.com, pg 646

Umberto Allemandi & Co Publishing (United Kingdom) Tel: (020) 7735 3331 Fax: (020) 7735 3332 E-mail: feedback@theartnewspaper.com Web Site: www.theartnewspaper.com, pg 646

Umberto Allemandi & C SRL (Italy) Tel: (011) 8199111 Fax: (011) 8193090 E-mail: allemandi@aztel.it, pg 375

Allen & Unwin Pty Ltd, The Australian Newspaper, Vogel Breads (Australia) Tel: (02) 8425 0100 Fax: (02) 9906 2218 E-mail: frontdesk@allenandunwin.com Web Site: www.allenandunwin.com, pg 11

Allert de Lange BV (Netherlands) Tel: (02) 6246744 Fax: (020) 6384975, pg 472

L'Alliance francaise, Bibliotheque (Senegal) Tel: 8210822, pg 1496

Alliance of Literary Societies (United Kingdom) Tel: (023) 92475855 Fax: (0870) 0560330 Web Site: www.sndc.demon.co.uk/als.htm, pg 1369

Alliance West African Publishers & Co (Nigeria) Tel: (085) 230798, pg 498

Allied Book Centre (India) Tel: (0135) 656526; (0135) 650949; (0135) 9837066875 Fax: (0135) 656554, pg 330

Allied Mouse Ltd (United Kingdom) Tel: (01349) 865400 Fax: (01349) 866066 E-mail: info@heartstone.co.uk Web Site: www.heartstone.co.uk, pg 646

Allied Publishers Pvt Ltd (India) Tel: (011) 3239001; (011) 3233002 Web Site: www.alliedpublishers.com, pg 330

Allied Publishers Pvt Ltd (India) Tel: (011) 3239001; (011) 3233002; (011) 3233004; (011) 3230067; (011) 3235967, pg 1288

All'Insegna del Giglio (Italy) Tel: (055) 451.593 Fax: (055) 450,030, pg 375

Allison & Busby (United Kingdom) Tel: (020) 7738 7888 Fax: (020) 7733 4244 E-mail: all@allisonbusby.co.uk Web Site: www.allisonandbusby.com, pg 646

Allt om Hobby AB (Sweden) Tel: (08) 999333 Fax: (08) 998866, pg 600

Allt om Hobbys Publishing Co (Sweden) Tel: (08) 999333 Fax: (08) 998866, pg 1231

Alma (Denmark) Tel: 48 25 54 41 Fax: 48 25 20 41, pg 129

Alma Littera (Lithuania) Tel: (02) 617927; (02) 624695 Fax: (02) 617927 E-mail: post@almali.lt Web Site: www.almali.lt, pg 445

Alma'Arif PT (Indonesia) Tel: (022) 4207177 Fax: (022) 439194, pg 353

Livraria Almedina (Portugal) Tel: (039) 26199 Fax: (039) 851901 E-mail: livrarialmedina@mail.telepac.pt, pg 522

Almenna Bokafelagid (Iceland) Tel: 5643170 Fax: 5643190, pg 327

Akademibokhandeln/Almqvist & Wiksell (Sweden) Tel: (08) 6909200 Fax: (08) 6909300, pg 1312

Almqvist och Wiksell Bokhandel AB (Sweden) Tel: (08) 6136100 Fax: (08) 242543; (08) 208036, pg 1312

Almqvist och Wiksell International (Sweden) Tel: (08) 7282500 Fax: (08) 338707 E-mail: scand.mongr@awi.se, pg 600

Aloe Educational (South Africa) *Tel:* (011) 8393719 *Fax:* (011) 8393720, pg 1310

Forlaget alokke AS (Denmark) *Tel:* 75671119 *Fax:* 75671074 *E-mail:* alokke@get2net.dk, pg 129

Alouette Verlag (Germany) *Tel:* (040) 712 23 53 *Fax:* (040) 713 41 88 *E-mail:* webmaster@alouette-verlag.de *Web Site:* www.alouette-verlag.de, pg 193

Ediciones Alpe (Mexico) *Tel:* (05) 5365749; (05) 2033157 *Fax:* (05) 2033157, pg 458

Alpha-Delta (Greece) *Tel:* (01) 2280027 *Fax:* (01) 2280027, pg 1285

Alpha Literatur Verlag/Alpha Presse (Germany) *Tel:* (069) 555325 *Fax:* (069) 558361, pg 193

Editions Alphee (Monaco) *Tel:* (093) 30-40-06 *Fax:* (099) 99-67-18, pg 468

Alpina Color Graphics Inc (United States) *Tel:* 212-683-2535 *Fax:* 212-683-2704; 212-683-2682 *E-mail:* graphics@alpina.net *Web Site:* www.alpina.net, pg 1163

Alpina Color Graphics Inc (United States) *Tel:* 212-285-2700 *Fax:* 212-285-2704 *E-mail:* raj@alpinanyc.com *Web Site:* www.alpina.net, pg 1205

Alpine Fine Arts Books Ltd (United Kingdom) *Tel:* (020) 7935 0797 *Fax:* (020) 7935 0656, pg 646

Alpnet UK (United Kingdom) *Tel:* (0181) 6883852 *Fax:* (0181) 6888888 *E-mail:* croydon@alpnet.com, pg 1128

AlpnetCompuType Ltd (United Kingdom) *Tel:* (01895) 440791 *Fax:* (01895) 441500 *E-mail:* computype@computype.co.uk, pg 1160

ALS-Verlag GmbH (Germany) *Tel:* (06074) 82160 *Fax:* (06074) 27322 *E-mail:* info@als-verlag.de *Web Site:* www.als-verlag.de, pg 193

Alsatia SA (France) *Tel:* (03) 89 45 21 53 *Fax:* (03) 89 45 18 98, pg 146

Alta Fulla Editorial (Spain) *Tel:* (093) 4590708; (093) 4591363 *Fax:* (093) 2075203 *E-mail:* altafulla@altafulla.com *Web Site:* www.altafulla.com, pg 563

Altamira BV (Netherlands) *Tel:* (023) 5286882 *Fax:* (023) 5288097, pg 472

Altberliner Verlag GmbH (Germany) *Tel:* (030) 284 992-0 *Fax:* (030) 284 992-20 *E-mail:* presse@altberliner.de *Web Site:* www.altberliner.de, pg 193

Altea, Taurus, Alfaguara SA (Spain) *Tel:* (091) 7449060 *Fax:* (091) 7449224 *E-mail:* clientes@santillana.es *Web Site:* www.alfaguara.santillana.es, pg 563

Ediciones Altera SL (Spain) *Tel:* (093) 4519537 *Fax:* (093) 4517441 *E-mail:* editorial@altera.net, pg 563

Altera Forlag A/S (Norway) *Tel:* 22569590 *Fax:* 22565088, pg 502

Alternative Editura (Romania) *Tel:* (01) 2234966; (01) 2229468 *Fax:* (01) 6756074; (01) 2234971, pg 532

Editions Alternatives (France) *Tel:* (01) 43 26 26 82 *Fax:* (01) 43290270 *E-mail:* ealterna@club-internet.fr, pg 146

ALTESS Editions Argel (France) *Tel:* (01) 64403589 *Fax:* (01) 64402757 *E-mail:* eliaur@club-internet.fr *Web Site:* www.ifrance.com/3eMillenaire/altess/index.htm, pg 146

Altin Kitaplar Yayinevi (Turkey) *Tel:* (0212) 5224045; (0212) 3394359 *Fax:* (0212) 5268011, pg 638

Altina (Belgium) *Tel:* (059) 80-16-51 *Fax:* (059) 51-27-17, pg 64

Altiora Averbode Uitgeverij nv (Belgium) *Tel:* (013) 78-01-56 *Fax:* (013) 77-68-37, pg 1276

Aluminium-Verlag Marketing & Kommunikation GmbH (Germany) *Tel:* (0211) 4796227 *Fax:* (0211) 4796412 *Web Site:* www.alu-verlag.com, pg 193

Alumni PT (Indonesia) *Tel:* (022) 2501251; (022) 2503039; (022) 2503038 *Fax:* (022) 2503044, pg 353

Alun Books (United Kingdom) *Tel:* (01639) 886186 *E-mail:* enquiries@alunbooks.co.uk *Web Site:* www.alunbooks.co.uk, pg 646

Biblioteca Argentina Dr Juan Alvarez (Argentina) *Tel:* (041) 802538; (041) 802539 *Fax:* (041) 802561 *E-mail:* biblarg@rosario.gov.ar, pg 1449

Livraria Francisco Alves Editora SA (Brazil) *Tel:* (021) 221-3198 *Fax:* (021) 242-8215, pg 78

Alyssa Editions (Tunisia) *Tel:* 740989 *Fax:* 733659, pg 637

Alzieu Editions (France) *Tel:* (04) 76 51 09 51 *Fax:* (04) 76 51 09 51 *E-mail:* editions-alzieu@wanadoo.fr, pg 146

Am Oved Publishers Ltd (Israel) *Tel:* (03) 6291526 *Fax:* (03) 6298911, pg 365

AMA nakladatelstvi (Czech Republic) *Tel:* (0618) 265 84 *Fax:* (0618) 228 31 *E-mail:* rstudio@login.cz, pg 123

Armenio Amado Editora de Simoes, Beirao & Ca Lda (Portugal) *Tel:* (039) 92150 *Fax:* (039) 851901, pg 522

Amalthea srl (Italy) *Tel:* (081) 7334785 *Fax:* (081) 7334785 *Web Site:* www.amalthea.it, pg 375

Amalthea-Verlag (Austria) *Tel:* (01) 712 35 60 *Fax:* (01) 713 89 95 *Web Site:* www.amalthea.at, pg 49

Pustaka Aman Press Sdn Bhd (Malaysia) *Tel:* (09) 781849 *Fax:* (09) 784058, pg 451

Amanda (Denmark) *Tel:* 33790110 *Fax:* 33790011 *E-mail:* forlag@dansklf.dk, pg 130

Amar Prakashan (India) *Tel:* (011) 713182, pg 330

Editions de l'Amateur (France) *Tel:* (01) 45 77 08 05 *Fax:* (01) 45799715, pg 147

Amazonas Editores Ltda (Colombia) *Tel:* (091) 8621443; (091) 6762596; (091) 6760616; (091) 6760656; (091) 6180256; (091) 2182760 *Fax:* (091) 8620081; (091) 2762596; (091) 6180326, pg 111

Ambar Prakashan (India) *Tel:* (011) 7770067; (011) 522997; (011) 7525528 *Fax:* (011) 7776058 *E-mail:* bitambar@bol.net.in, pg 330

Amber Books Ltd (United Kingdom) *Tel:* (020) 75207600 *Fax:* (020) 75207606 *E-mail:* amber-books@dial.pipex.com, pg 646

Amber Lane Press Ltd (United Kingdom) *Tel:* (01608) 810024 *Fax:* (01608) 810024 *E-mail:* jamberlane@aol.com, pg 646

Amberwood Publishing Ltd (United Kingdom) *Tel:* (01634) 290115 *Fax:* (01634) 290761 *E-mail:* books@amberwoodpublishing.com *Web Site:* www.amberwoodpublishing.com, pg 646

Ambit Serveis Editorials, SA (Spain) *Tel:* (093) 4881342 *Fax:* (093) 4874772, pg 563

Uitgeverij Ambo BV (Netherlands) *Tel:* (020) 5245411 *Fax:* (020) 4200422, pg 472

Amboss-Verlag E Widmer (Switzerland) *Tel:* (071) 711236; (071) 714590 *Fax:* (071) 714590, pg 608

Editions Ambozontany (Madagascar) *Tel:* (07) 50027; (07) 51441, pg 450

Librairie Ambozontany (Madagascar) *Tel:* (07) 50027; (07) 51441, pg 450

Biblioteca Ambrosiana (Italy) *Tel:* (02) 806921 *Fax:* (02) 80692210, pg 1477

Amebo Book Club (Nigeria), pg 1230

America Latina (Uruguay) *Tel:* (02) 415127 *Fax:* (02) 495568, pg 1324

American Books (Argentina) *Tel:* (011) 3963704, pg 1271

American Book Store SA de CV (Mexico) *Tel:* (05) 5127279; (05) 5127284; (05) 5120306 *Fax:* (05) 5186931, pg 1299

The American Chamber of Commerce in Hong Kong (Hong Kong) *Tel:* 2526 0165 *Fax:* 2810 1289; 2596 0911 *E-mail:* amcham@amcham.org.hk, pg 1133

American Chamber of Commerce of Jamaica (Jamaica) *Tel:* (876) 929-7866 *Fax:* (876) 929-8597, pg 412

The American Chamber of Commerce in Japan (Japan) *Tel:* (03) 34335381 *Fax:* (03) 34361446, pg 414

American Information Resource Center (India) *Tel:* (011) 3316841; (011) 3314251; (011) 3316841 *Fax:* (011) 3329499 *E-mail:* newdelhi@usia.gov; libel@pd.state.gov *Web Site:* americanlibrary.in.library.net, pg 1473

American Library in Paris (France) *Tel:* (01) 53591260 *Fax:* (01) 45502583 *E-mail:* alparis@cybercable.fr *Web Site:* www.ourworld.compuserve.com/homepages/alp/, pg 1464

American Pizzi Offset Corp (United States) *Tel:* 212-986-1658 *Fax:* 212-286-1887 *E-mail:* apocnyusa@aol.com, pg 1142, 1163

American-Scandinavian Foundation (United States) *Tel:* 212-879-9779 *Fax:* 212-879-2301 *E-mail:* asf@amscan.org *Web Site:* www.amscan.org, pg 1268

American Technical Publishers (United Kingdom) *Tel:* (01462) 437933 *Fax:* (01462) 433678 *E-mail:* atp@ameritech.co.uk *Web Site:* www.ameritech.co.uk, pg 646

American University in Cairo Library (Egypt (Arab Republic of Egypt)) *Tel:* (02) 3576904 *Fax:* (02) 5943824, pg 1462

American University in Cairo Press (Egypt (Arab Republic of Egypt)) *Tel:* (02) 3542964 *Fax:* (02) 3557565, pg 138

American University of Beirut Libraries (Lebanon) *Tel:* (01) 340460 *Fax:* (01) 744703 *E-mail:* library@aub.edu.lb *Web Site:* www.aub.edu.lb/, pg 1481

Amerind Publishing Co (P) Ltd (India) *Tel:* (011) 3324578; (011) 3320518, pg 1124

Amerindian Research Unit (Guyana) *Tel:* (02) 4930 *Fax:* (02) 54885 *Web Site:* gold.sdnp.org.gy/uog/, pg 316

Editions d'Amerique et d'Orient, Adrien Maisonneuve (France) *Tel:* (01) 43 26 86 35 *Fax:* (01) 43 54 59 54 *E-mail:* maisonneuve@maisonneuve-adrien.com, pg 147

Editions Amez (France) *Tel:* (03) 88845656 *Fax:* (03) 88845684, pg 147

Amichai Publishing House Ltd (Israel) *Tel:* (09) 8859099 *Fax:* (09) 8853464, pg 365

Amigo Translations Ltd (United Kingdom) *Tel:* (0121) 7426905 *Fax:* (0121) 7420583, pg 1128

Libreria los Amigos del Libro (Bolivia) *Tel:* (04) 4504150; (04) 4504151 *Fax:* (04) 4115128 *E-mail:* gutten@amigol.bo.net, pg 1276

Los Amigos del Libro Ediciones (Bolivia) *Tel:* (04) 4504150; (04) 4504151 *Fax:* (04) 4115128 *Web Site:* www.librosbolivia.com, pg 76

Amir Kabir Book Publishing & Distribution Co (Islamic Republic of Iran) *Tel:* (021) 6463487; (021) 390752 *Fax:* (021) 6461931, pg 357

L'Amitie par le Livre (France) *Tel:* (03) 81820894 *Fax:* (03) 81820894, pg 147, 1228

Amiza Associate Malaysia Sdn Bhd (Malaysia) *Tel:* (03) 7036100 *Fax:* (03) 7034268, pg 451

AMK Interaksi Sdn Bhd (Malaysia) *Tel:* (03) 215306 *Fax:* (03) 718067, pg 451

Amman Public Library (Jordan) *Tel:* (06) 637111; (06) 627718 *Fax:* (06) 649420, pg 1479

Ammann Verlag & Co (Switzerland) *Tel:* (01) 268 10 40 *Fax:* (01) 268 10 50 *E-mail:* info@ammann.ch *Web Site:* www.ammann.ch, pg 608

Amnesty International VZW (Belgium) *Tel:* (03) 271.16.16 *Fax:* (03) 235.78.12 *E-mail:* amnesty@aivl.be *Web Site:* www.aivl.be, pg 64

Amnesty International Publications (United Kingdom) *Tel:* (020) 7814 6200 *Fax:* (020) 7833 1510 *E-mail:* information@amnesty.org.uk *Web Site:* www.amnesty.org.uk, pg 647

Amnistia Internacional Editorial SL (Spain) *Tel:* (091) 310 12 77 *Fax:* (091) 319 53 34 *E-mail:* amnistia.internacional@a-i.es *Web Site:* www.a-i.es, pg 563

Amorrortu Editores SA (Argentina) *Tel:* (011) 4816-5812; (011) 4816-5869 *Fax:* (011) 4816-3321 *E-mail:* amorrortueditores@vianetworks.net.ar, pg 3

The Ampersand Press (CI) Ltd (United Kingdom) *Tel:* (01481) 823462, pg 647

Editions Amphora SA (France) *Tel:* (01) 43 29 03 04; (01) 43 26 10 87 *Fax:* (01) 43 29 49 49; (01) 40 46 85 76 *Web Site:* www.ed-amphora.fr, pg 147

Editions Amrita SA (France) *Tel:* (05) 53507954 *Fax:* (05) 53508020 *E-mail:* amrita.editions@perigord.com, pg 147

Amtsbibliothek des Bundesministeriums fur Unterricht, und Kulturelle Angelegenheiten und des Bundesministeriums fur Wissenschaft und Verkehr (Austria) *Tel:* (01) 531200 *Fax:* (01) 53120-5172, pg 1451

AMV Ediciones (Spain) *Tel:* (091) 5336926; (091) 5349368 *Fax:* (091) 5530286 *Web Site:* www.amvediciones.com, pg 563

AMVC-Letterenhuis (Belgium) *Tel:* (03) 222 9320 *Fax:* (03) 222 9321 *E-mail:* amvc@cs.antwerpen.be *Web Site:* www.antwerpen.be/cultuur/amvc, pg 1453

An Gum (Ireland) *Tel:* (01) 8734700 *Fax:* (01) 8731140 *E-mail:* gum@educ.irlgov.ie, pg 358

Anabas-Verlag Guenter Kaempf GmbH & Co KG (Germany) *Tel:* (069) 94 21 98 71 *Fax:* (069) 94 21 98 72 *E-mail:* info@anabas-verlag.com, pg 193

L'Anabase (France) *Tel:* (01) 30410747 *Fax:* (01) 34858073, pg 147

Edizioni Anabasi SpA (Italy) *Tel:* (02) 76.02.12.72 *Fax:* (02) 76.02.13.32, pg 375

Editorial Anagrama (Spain) *Tel:* (093) 2037652 *Fax:* (093) 2037738 *E-mail:* anagrama@anagrama-ed.es *Web Site:* www.anagrama-ed.es, pg 563

Anako Editions (France) *Tel:* (01) 43 94 92 88 *Fax:* (01) 43 94 02 45 *E-mail:* anako.editions@anako.com *Web Site:* www.anako.com, pg 147

Anam Publishing Co (Republic of Korea) *Tel:* (02) 22380491 *Fax:* (02) 22524334, pg 434

Anambra State Library Board (Nigeria) *Tel:* (042) 334103, pg 1488

Anambra State School Libraries Association (Nigeria) *Tel:* (042) 252080; (042) 332091, pg 1521

Anand Book Club (India), pg 1229

Ananda Publishers Pvt Ltd (India) *Tel:* (033) 2414352; (033) 2413417; (033) 344362 *Fax:* (033) 2253240; (033) 2253241 *E-mail:* ananda@cal3.vsnl.net.in *Web Site:* www.anandapub.com, pg 330

Anansi Uitgewers (South Africa) *Tel:* (021) 968511 *Fax:* (021) 969698, pg 552

Anastasiadis Publications (Greece) *Tel:* (01) 2284013 *Fax:* (01) 2236442, pg 1285

Ediciones Anaya SA (Spain) *Tel:* (091) 393 86 00 *Fax:* (091) 320 91 29; (091) 742 66 31 *E-mail:* cga@anaya.es *Web Site:* www.anaya.es, pg 563

Anaya Educacion (Spain) *Tel:* (091) 393 86 00 *Fax:* (091) 742 66 31; (091) 320 91 29 *E-mail:* cga@anaya.es *Web Site:* www.anaya.es, pg 563

Anaya-Touring Club (Spain) *Tel:* (091) 393 86 00 *Fax:* (091) 742 66 31; (091) 320 91 29 *E-mail:* cga@anaya.es *Web Site:* www.anaya.es, pg 563

Libraire Ancienne Noel Anselot (Belgium) *Tel:* (060) 6165 6091 *Fax:* (060) 6165 6091, pg 64

El Ancora Editores (Colombia) *Tel:* (01) 283 9040; (01) 342 6224; (01) 283 9235 *Fax:* (01) 283 9235 *E-mail:* ancoraed@interred.net.co, pg 111

Editrice Ancora (Italy) *Tel:* (02) 3456081 *Fax:* (02) 34560866 *E-mail:* editrice@ancora-libri.it *Web Site:* www.ancora-libri.it, pg 375

Libreria Ancora y Delfin (Spain) *Tel:* (093) 2000746 *Fax:* (093) 2000757 *E-mail:* ancorayclefin@cambraben.es, pg 1311

Editions l'Ancre de Marine (France) *Tel:* 99 56 78 43 *Fax:* 99 40 00 77, pg 147

Andernach Atelier Verlag (AVA) (Germany) *Tel:* (02241) 31640 *Fax:* (02241) 316436, pg 193

Andersen Press Ltd (United Kingdom) *Tel:* (020) 7840 8701 *Fax:* (020) 7233 6263 *E-mail:* andersenpress@randomhouse.co.uk *Web Site:* www.andersenpress.co.uk, pg 647

Robert Andersen & Associates Pty Ltd (Australia) *Tel:* (03) 4893968 *Fax:* (03) 4822416 *E-mail:* 100357.354@compuserve.com *Web Site:* www.educationprofile.com.au, pg 11

Darley Anderson Literary TV & Film Agency (United Kingdom) *Tel:* (020) 7385 6652 *Fax:* (020) 7386 5571 *E-mail:* dander6652@aol.comm, pg 1118

Michelle Anderson Publishing Pty Ltd (Australia) *Tel:* (03) 9662 2282 *Fax:* (03) 9662 2527 *E-mail:* hocpub@collinsbooks.com.au; hillofcontent@bizland.com, pg 11

Anderson Rand Ltd (United Kingdom) *Tel:* (01223) 467313 *Fax:* (01223) 316144 *E-mail:* ar.info@dial.pipex.com *Web Site:* turboguide.com/data2/cdprod1/doc/cd-rom.publisher/A/Anderson.Rand.Ltd.html, pg 647

Andi Offset (Indonesia) *Tel:* (0274) 561881 *Fax:* (0274) 588282 *E-mail:* andi_pub@indo.net.id, pg 354

Andina Publishing House (Bulgaria) *Tel:* (052) 257002, pg 94

Andorran Standard Book Numbering Agency (Andorra) *Tel:* 826445 *Fax:* 829445 *E-mail:* bncultura.gov@andorra.ad *Web Site:* www.andorra.ad/bibnac, pg 1235

Andreas und Andreas Verlagsbuchhandel (Austria) *Tel:* (0662) 64350008 *Fax:* (0662) 6435002, pg 49

Andrena Publishers (Lithuania) *Tel:* (02) 703834; (02) 627015 *E-mail:* andrena@takas.lt, pg 445

AndreouChr- Publishers (Cyprus) *Tel:* (02) 666877 *Fax:* (02) 666878 *E-mail:* andzeou2@cytanet.com.cy, pg 122

Chris Andrews Publications (United Kingdom) *Tel:* (01865) 723404 *Fax:* (01865) 725294 *E-mail:* enquiries@cap-ox.com *Web Site:* www.cap-ox.com, pg 647

Andromeda Oxford Ltd (United Kingdom) *Tel:* (01235) 550 296 *Fax:* (01235) 550 330 *E-mail:* mail@andromeda.co.uk *Web Site:* www.andromeda.co.uk, pg 647

Angel Publications (Australia) *Tel:* (02) 48211463, pg 11

Angeletos Sokzates (Greece) *Tel:* (01) 9928100 *Fax:* (01) 9940530, pg 1285

Franco Angeli SRL (Italy) *Tel:* (02) 28 37 141 *Fax:* (02) 26 14 47 93 *E-mail:* fran@francoangeli.it, pg 375

Biblioteca Angelica (Italy) *Tel:* (06) 6868041; (06) 6875874 *Fax:* (06) 6832312; (06) 6832312, pg 1477

Angelika und Lothar Binding (Germany) *Tel:* (06221) 20955 *Fax:* (06221) 181846 *Web Site:* www.binding-singles.de, pg 193

CV Angkasa CV (Publishers) (Indonesia) *Tel:* (022) 4208955; (022) 4204795 *Fax:* (022) 439183, pg 354

The Anglo American Book Company Ltd (United Kingdom) *Tel:* (01267) 211880 *Fax:* (01267) 211882 *E-mail:* books@anglo-american.co.uk, pg 1315

Anglo-Didactica, SL Editorial (Spain) *Tel:* (091) 3780188 *Fax:* (091) 3780188 *E-mail:* anglodidac@aregen.net, pg 563

Anglo-German Foundation for the Study of Industrial Society (United Kingdom) *Tel:* (020) 7823 1123 *Fax:* (020) 7823 2324 *E-mail:* info@agf.org.uk *Web Site:* www.agf.org.uk, pg 647

Angus & Robertson Bookshops (Australia) *Tel:* (03) 96708941 *Fax:* (03) 96466925, pg 1272

Anhui People's Publishing House (China) *Tel:* (0551) 257134; (0551) 253673, pg 102

Anixis Publications (Greece) *Tel:* (01) 6205436 *Fax:* (01) 8079357, pg 309

Anjuman Taraqqi-e-Urdu Pakistan (Pakistan) *Tel:* (021) 461406; (021) 4973296; (021) 7724023, pg 1367

Ankara University Library (Turkey) *Tel:* (0312) 472100723, pg 1504

Ankh-Hermes BV (Netherlands) *Tel:* (0570) 678900 *Fax:* (0570) 624632 *E-mail:* ankh-hermes.nl@pi.net, pg 472

Ankur Prakashani (Bangladesh) *Tel:* (02) 9569121; (02) 9553635 *Fax:* (02) 9567730 *E-mail:* ankur@bangla.net *Web Site:* www.nutra.org/html/ankur.html, pg 62

Ankur Publishing House (India) *Tel:* (022) 543 2817; (022) 536 9907 *Fax:* (022) 543 2817 *E-mail:* ankur@bom3.vsnl.net.in *Web Site:* www.satyamplastics.com/ankurpublishing/, pg 330

Anmol Publications Pvt Ltd (India) *Tel:* (011) 3255577; (011) 3261597; (011) 3278000 *Fax:* (011) 3280289 *E-mail:* anmol@nde.vsnl.net.in *Web Site:* www.anmolbooks.com, pg 331

Editions d'Annabelle (France) *Tel:* (01) 47420161 *Fax:* (01) 47424214, pg 147

Annales de la Recherche Urbaine (France) *Tel:* (01) 40816371 *Fax:* (01) 40816378 *Web Site:* www.equipement.gouv.fr, pg 147

Anowuo Educational Publications (Ghana) *Tel:* (021) 669961, pg 306

Anrich Verlag GmbH (Germany) *Tel:* (06201) 6007-0; (06201) 6007-358 *Fax:* (06201) 6007-92 *E-mail:* g.anrich@beltz.de, pg 193

Forlagsentralen ANS (Norway) *Tel:* 22329600 *Fax:* 22329601 *E-mail:* forlagsentralen@forlagsentralen.no, pg 1303

Ansay Pty Ltd (Australia) *Tel:* (02) 5602044 *Fax:* (02) 5694585, pg 11

Antara Publications (M) Sdn Bhd (Malaysia) *Tel:* (03) 2913188 *Fax:* (03) 2913299, pg 1298

Pustaka Antara (Malaysia) *Tel:* (03) 2925823 *Fax:* (03) 2917997, pg 451

PT Pustaka Antara Publishing & Printing (Indonesia) *Tel:* (021) 3156994; (021) 3156995 *Fax:* (021) 322745 *E-mail:* nacelod@indo.net.id, pg 354

Antenna Edicoes Tecnicas Ltda (Brazil) *Tel:* (021) 223-2442 *Fax:* (021) 263-8840 *E-mail:* antenna@unisys.com.br, pg 78

Antex Verlag-Hans Joachin Schuhmacher (Germany) *Tel:* (033603) 40410 *Fax:* (033603) 40400, pg 193

Edition Anthese (France) *Tel:* (01) 46 56 06 67 *Fax:* (01) 49 85 09 92, pg 147

Anthonian Store Sdn Bhd (Malaysia) *Tel:* (03) 2747166, pg 1298

Uitgeverij Anthos (Netherlands) *Tel:* (020) 5245411 *Fax:* (020) 4200422 *E-mail:* info@amboanthos.nl, pg 472

Editorial Anthropos del Hombre (Spain) *Tel:* (093) 6972296 *Fax:* (093) 6972296, pg 563

Editions Anthropos Sarl (France) *Tel:* (01) 45781292 *Fax:* (01) 45750567, pg 147

Edicoes Antigona (Portugal) *Tel:* (021) 749483 *Fax:* (021) 749483, pg 522

Bibliotheque Universitaire Antilles-Guyane (BUAG) (France) *Tel:* (05) 96727530 *Fax:* (05) 96727527, pg 1464

Antillion Library Association (Netherlands Antilles) *Tel:* (09) 4617055 *Fax:* (09) 4656247, pg 1521

Antiqua-Verlag GmbH (Germany) *Tel:* (07746) 2273 *Fax:* (07746) 2260, pg 194

Antiquarian Booksellers' Association (United Kingdom) *Tel:* (020) 7439 3118 *Fax:* (020) 7439 3119 *E-mail:* info@aba.org.uk; admin@aba.org.uk, pg 1263

Antiquarian Booksellers' Association of Japan (Japan) *Tel:* (03) 33571411 *Fax:* (03) 33515855 *Web Site:* www.abaj.gr.jp, pg 1250

Antiquariat und Verlag Auvermann Keip GmbH (Germany) *Tel:* (06021) 59 05 0 *Fax:* (06021) 59 05 42 *E-mail:* info@keip.net *Web Site:* www.keip.net, pg 194

Antiquariats-Union Vertriebs GmbH & Co KG (Germany) *Tel:* (04131) 983504 *Web Site:* www.restauflagen.de, pg 194

Antique Collectors' Club Ltd (United Kingdom) *Tel:* (01394) 385501 *Fax:* (01394) 384434 *E-mail:* sales@antique-acc.com *Web Site:* www.antique-acc.com, pg 647

Antiques & Collectors Guides Ltd (United Kingdom) *Tel:* (0141) 8480880 *Fax:* (0141) 8892063, pg 647

Librairies Antoine SAL/Librairie Antoine, A. Naufal & Freres (Lebanon) *Tel:* (01) 481072; (01) 481078 *Fax:* (01) 492625, pg 1297

Antonius-Verlag (Switzerland) *Tel:* (032) 625 37 42, pg 608

Biblioteca Nacional de Antropologia E Historia (Mexico) *Tel:* (05) 5536342 *Toll Free Fax:* 52-86-17-43 *E-mail:* colecciones.bnah@inah.gob.mx *Web Site:* www.inah.gob.mx, pg 1484

Editora Antroposofica Ltda (Brazil) *Tel:* (011) 2464550 *Fax:* (011) 2479714 *E-mail:* editora@antroposofica.com.br *Web Site:* www.sab.org.br/edit; www.antroposofica.com.br, pg 78

Editrice Antroposofica SRL (Italy) *Tel:* (02) 7491197, pg 375

Antroposofsko Izdatelstvo Dimo R Daskalov OOD (Bulgaria) *Tel:* (042) 54481, pg 94

Maison d'Edition Protestante ANTSO (Madagascar) *Tel:* (022) 20886 *Fax:* (022) 26372 *E-mail:* fjkm@dts.mg, pg 450

Antwerp Bibliophile Society (Belgium) *Tel:* (03) 2330294 *Fax:* (03) 2262516 *E-mail:* francine.demav@amtwerpa.be, pg 1360

Anvil Books Ltd (Ireland) *Tel:* (01) 4973628 *Fax:* (01) 4968263, pg 358

Anvil Press (Zimbabwe) *Tel:* (04) 792551; (04) 739681, pg 767

Anvil Press Poetry Ltd (United Kingdom) *Tel:* (020) 8469 3033 *Fax:* (020) 8469 3363 *E-mail:* info@anvilpresspoetry.com *Web Site:* www.anvilpresspoetry.com, pg 648

Anvil Publishing Inc (Philippines) *Tel:* (02) 9140155; (02) 6711899 *Fax:* (02) 6719235 *E-mail:* anvil@fc.emc.com.ph; pubdept@anvil.com.ph, pg 512

Any Photo Type (United States) *Tel:* 212-244-1130 *Fax:* 212-594-4697, pg 1163

Anzea Publishers Ltd (Australia) *Tel:* (02) 7631211 *Fax:* (02) 7643201, pg 11

Ao Livro Tecnico Industria e Comercio Ltda (Brazil) *Tel:* (021) 580-6230; (021) 580-1168 *Fax:* (021) 580-9955 *Web Site:* www.editoraaolivrotecnico.com.br, pg 78

Aoki Shoten Co Ltd (Japan) *Tel:* (03) 32192341 *Fax:* (03) 32192585, pg 414

AOL-Verlag Frohmut Menze (Germany) *Tel:* (07227) 95 88-0 *Fax:* (07227) 95 88-95 *E-mail:* info@aol-verlag.de; bestellung@aol-verlag.de *Web Site:* www.aol-verlag.de, pg 194

Aoraki Press Ltd (New Zealand) *Tel:* (04) 3858528 *Fax:* (03) 3858528 *E-mail:* aorakipr@actrix.gen.nz, pg 488

AP Information Services (United Kingdom) *Tel:* (020) 8349 9988 *Fax:* (020) 8349 9797 *E-mail:* info@ap-info.co.uk *Web Site:* www.ap-info.co.uk, pg 648

APA (Academic Publishers Associated) (Netherlands) *Tel:* (020) 6265544 *E-mail:* info@apa-publishers.com, pg 472

APA Production Pte Ltd (Singapore) *Tel:* 8651600 *Fax:* 8616438, pg 545

APAC Publishers Services (Singapore) *Tel:* 7478662 *Fax:* 7478916, pg 545

Apaginastantas - Cooperativa de Servicos Culturais (Portugal) *Tel:* (021) 668987, pg 522

Editions APESS ASBL (Luxembourg) *Tel:* (045) 808358 *Fax:* (045) 802813 *E-mail:* apess@education.lu *Web Site:* www.restena.lu/apess, pg 447

Apex Books Concern (United Kingdom) *Tel:* (01903) 739042; (01903) 734432 *Fax:* (01903) 734432; (0870) 056 7860 *E-mail:* enquiries@apexbooks.co.uk *Web Site:* www.apexbooks.co.uk, pg 1315

Apex Publishing (Oman) *Tel:* 799388 *Fax:* 793316 *E-mail:* apexoman@gto.net.om, pg 506

Apex Publishing Ltd (United Kingdom) *E-mail:* enquiry@apexpublishing.co.uk *Web Site:* www.apexpublishing.co.uk, pg 648

Verlag der Apfel (Austria) *Tel:* (01) 52 661 52 *Fax:* (01) 5228718, pg 49

APH Publishing Corp (India) *Tel:* (011) 5100581; (011) 5410924; (011) 3285807 *Fax:* (011) 3274050 *E-mail:* aph@mantrasonline.com, pg 331

Verlag APHAIA Svea Haske, Sonja Schumann GbR (Germany) *Tel:* (030) 813 39 98 *Fax:* (030) 813 39 98 *E-mail:* info@aphaia-verlag.de *Web Site:* www.aphaia-verlag.de, pg 194

Apimondia (Italy) *Tel:* (06) 6852286 *Fax:* (06) 6852286 *E-mail:* apimondia@mclink.it *Web Site:* www.apimondia.org, pg 375

Apocalipsis Digital (Cuba) *Tel:* (07) 816625 *E-mail:* adigital@tinored.cu; adigital@colombus.cu, pg 120

Apogeo srl - Editrice di Informatica (Italy) *Tel:* (02) 461920 *Fax:* (02) 4815382 *E-mail:* apogeo@apgeoline.com, pg 375

Apollo-Verlag Paul Lincke GmbH (Germany) *Tel:* (06131) 246300 *Fax:* (06131) 246861 *E-mail:* apollo@schott-musik.de, pg 194

Apollo's Reklame en Uitgeversburo (Suriname), pg 599

Apostolado da Oracao Secretariado Nacional (Portugal) *Tel:* (053) 22485 *Fax:* (053) 615631, pg 522

Apostolato della Preghiera (Italy) *Tel:* (06) 697.607.1 *Fax:* (06) 67.81.063 *E-mail:* adp@adp.it *Web Site:* www.adp.it, pg 376

Biblioteca Apostolica Vaticana (Holy See (Vatican City State)) *Tel:* (06) 69879402 *Fax:* (06) 69884795 *E-mail:* bav@librs6k.vatlib.it, pg 317

Biblioteca Apostolica Vaticana (Holy See (Vatican City State)) *Tel:* (06) 69883302 *Fax:* (06) 69884795 *E-mail:* bav@librs6k.vatlib.it, pg 1471

Biblioteca Apostolica Vaticana (Holy See (Vatican City State)) *Tel:* (06) 69883302 *Fax:* (06) 69884795 *E-mail:* bav@librsbk.vatlib.it, pg 1517

Apostoliki Diakonia tis Ekklisias tis Helladas (Greece) *Tel:* (010) 7272331 *Fax:* (010) 7238149 *E-mail:* apostoliki-diakonia@ath.forthnet.gr *Web Site:* www.apostoliki-diakonia.gr, pg 309

Forlaget Apostrof ApS (Denmark) *Tel:* 3920 8420 *Fax:* 3920 8453 *E-mail:* info@apostrof.dk *Web Site:* www.apostrof.dk, pg 130

Apotekarsocietetens Forlag (Sweden) *Tel:* (08) 7235000 *Fax:* (08) 205511, pg 600

Apple Books (Zambia) *Tel:* (01) 211216 *Fax:* (01) 224855, pg 766

Apple Press (United Kingdom) *Tel:* (01273) 727268 *Fax:* (01273) 727269 *E-mail:* gailN@RotoVision.com *Web Site:* www.quarto.com, pg 648

Appleby's Bindery Ltd (Canada) *Tel:* 506-488-2086 *Fax:* 506-488-2086 *E-mail:* applbind@nbnet.nb.ca, pg 1193, 1211, 1221

Appletree Press Ltd (United Kingdom) *Tel:* (028) 9024 3074 *Fax:* (028) 9024 6756 *E-mail:* reception@appletree.ie *Web Site:* www.appletree.ie, pg 648

Appropriate Technology Development Group (Inc) WA (Australia) *Tel:* (08) 9336 1262 *Fax:* (08) 9430 5729 *E-mail:* apace@argo.net.au *Web Site:* www.argo.net.au/apace, pg 11

APRD - Association pour la Recherche et l'Information demographiques (France) *Tel:* (01) 44321400 *Fax:* (01) 40462588, pg 147

Aquamarin Verlag (Germany) *Tel:* (08092) 9444 *Fax:* (08092) 1614 *E-mail:* aquamarin-verlag@t-online.de, pg 194

Aquanut Agencies Pte Ltd (Singapore) *Tel:* 7753614 *Fax:* 7753614 *E-mail:* aquanut@singnet.com.sg *Web Site:* www.aquanut.com.sg, pg 545

Aquarela Galleries (Trinidad & Tobago) *Tel:* 6255982 *Fax:* 6245217, pg 636

Editora Aquariana Ltda (Brazil) *Tel:* (11) 5031 1500 *Fax:* (11) 5031 3462 *E-mail:* aquariana@ground.com.br, pg 78

Aquarious (Greece) *Tel:* (01) 3842354; (01) 3617360 *Fax:* (01) 3303890, pg 1285

Aquarius (Greece) *Tel:* (361) 7360, pg 309

Aquarius Library (United Kingdom) *Tel:* (01424) 721196 *Fax:* (01424) 717704 *E-mail:* aquarius.lib@clara.net *Web Site:* www.aquariuscollection.com, pg 1118

Aquila BVBA (Belgium) *Tel:* (016) 229501 *Fax:* (016) 208419, pg 1276

Aquila Press (Australia) *Tel:* (02) 8268 3344 *Fax:* (02) 9283 3987 *E-mail:* sales@youthworks.asn.au, pg 11

ARA International (Luxembourg) *Tel:* (352) 34 85 91 *Fax:* (352) 34 85 91 *E-mail:* amisrelart@pt.lu, pg 447

Arab Archivists Institute (Iraq), pg 1518

Arab Library (Mauritania), pg 1484

Al Arab Bookshop (Egypt (Arab Republic of Egypt)) *Tel:* 908025, pg 1282

Arab Centre for Medical Literature (Kuwait) *Tel:* 5338610 *Fax:* 5338618; 5338619, pg 1251

Arab Communicators (Bahrain) *Tel:* (0973) 254 258 *Fax:* (0973) 531 837, pg 61

Arab Institute for Research and Publishing (Lebanon) *Tel:* (01) 807900 *Fax:* (01) 96266; (01) 685501, pg 442

Arab Organization for Agricultural Development (Sudan) *Tel:* (011) 78760; (011) 78761; (011) 78762; (011) 78763 *Fax:* (011) 471402 *E-mail:* aoad@sudanmail.net, pg 598

Arab Organization for Agricultural Development (Sudan) *Tel:* (011) 472176; (011) 472183 *Fax:* (011) 471402 *E-mail:* aoad@sudanmail.net *Web Site:* www.aoad.org, pg 1500

Al Arab Publishing House (Egypt (Arab Republic of Egypt)) *Tel:* (02) 908027, pg 138

ARAB REGIONAL BRANCH OF THE INTERNATIONAL COUNCIL ON ARCHIVES INDUSTRY

Arab Regional Branch of the International Council on Archives (Saudi Arabia) *Tel:* (01) 4761600 (ext 462), pg 1258

Arab Scientific Publishers BP (Lebanon) *Tel:* (01) 811385 *Fax:* (01) 860138; (01) 861311 *Web Site:* www.asp.com.lb, pg 442

Arabian Bookshop (Qatar) *Tel:* 448292 *Fax:* 449653, pg 1308

Arabian Focus Pty Ltd (Australia) *Tel:* (07) 3425-1766; (07) 851180; (07) 34251180 *Fax:* (07) 34251857, pg 11

ARADCO VSI Ltd (United Kingdom) *Tel:* (020) 7692 7700 *Fax:* (020) 7692 7711, pg 1128

ARADCO VSI Ltd (United Kingdom) *Tel:* (020) 7692 7700 *Fax:* (020) 7692 7711 *E-mail:* aradco@compuserve.com, pg 1160

Arambol, SL (Spain) *Tel:* (091) 3194057 *Fax:* (091) 3194057 *E-mail:* arambolsl@hotmail.com, pg 563

Biblioteca Luis-Angel Arango Banco de la Republica (Colombia) *Tel:* (01) 2827840 *Fax:* (01) 2863881 *E-mail:* wbiblio@banrep.gov.co *Web Site:* www.banrep.gov.co, pg 1457

arani-Verlag GmbH (Germany) *Tel:* (030) 691-7073 *Fax:* (030) 691-4067, pg 194

Aranyhal Konyvkiado Goldfish Publishing (Hungary) *Tel:* (01) 2396721; (01) 2391851 *Fax:* (01) 2396721 *E-mail:* sprinter@com.kibernet.hu, pg 323

Editorial Aranzadi SA (Spain) *Tel:* (0948) 297 297 *Fax:* (0948) 197 200 *E-mail:* clientes@aranzadi.es *Web Site:* www.aranzadi.es, pg 564

Editorial Franciscana Aranzazu (Spain) *Tel:* (043) 780797; (043) 780951 *Fax:* (043) 783370, pg 564

Ararat Verlag und Druckerei (Romania) *Tel:* (01) 3111425; (01) 6134050 *Fax:* (01) 3111420, pg 532

Aratron, IK (Bulgaria) *Tel:* (02) 980-74-55 *Fax:* (02) 958-19-31 *E-mail:* aratron@techno-link.com, pg 94

M J Bezerra de Araujo Editora Ltda (Brazil) *Tel:* (021) 5024435 *Fax:* (021) 5024435, pg 78

L'Arbalete (France) *Tel:* (04) 72933434 *Fax:* (04) 72933400, pg 147

BV Uitgeverij de Arbeiderspers (Netherlands) *Tel:* (020) 5247500 *Fax:* (020) 6224937 *E-mail:* info@arbeiderspers.nl, pg 473

Arbeiterpresse Verlag GmbH (Germany) *Tel:* (0201) 6462106 *Fax:* (0201) 6462108 *E-mail:* vertrieb@arbeiterpresse.de *Web Site:* www.arbeiterpresse.de, pg 194

Arbeitsgemeinschaft der Archive und Bibliotheken in der evangelischen Kirche (Germany) *Tel:* (0911) 588690 *Fax:* (0911) 5886969 *E-mail:* LKANuernberg@t-online.de *Web Site:* home.t-online.de/home/LKANuernberg/Ikantit.htm, pg 1515

Arbeitsgemeinschaft der Blindenschrift-Druckereien und Bibliotheken (AG BDB) (Germany) *Tel:* (06421) 606103 *Fax:* (06421) 606229; (06421) 606269, pg 1245

Arbeitsgemeinschaft der Regionalbibliotheken (Germany) *Tel:* (0711) 212 4424 *Fax:* (0711) 212 4422 *E-mail:* direktion@wlb-stuttgart.de, pg 1516

Arbeitsgemeinschaft der Spezialbibliotheken eV (ASpB) (Germany) *Tel:* (02461) 61-2907; (02461) 61-5368 *Fax:* (02461) 61-6103 *Web Site:* www.aspb.de, pg 1516

Arbeitsgemeinschaft fur juristisches Bibliotheks- und Dokumentationswesen (Germany) *Tel:* (0941) 9432497 *Fax:* (0941) 9433285, pg 1516

Arbeitsgemeinschaft fur medizinisches Bibliothekswesen (Germany) *Tel:* (0621) 7592376 *Fax:* (0621) 7594419, pg 1516

Arbeitsgemeinschaft von Jugendbuchverlagen e v (Germany) *Tel:* (07153) 8262 92 *Fax:* (07153) 8262 93 *E-mail:* avj.ziemer@t-online.de, pg 1245

Arbeitsgruppe LOK Report eV (Germany) *Tel:* (030) 86 40 92 62 *Fax:* (030) 86 40 92 64 *E-mail:* redaktion@lok-report.de *Web Site:* www.lok-report.de, pg 194

Arbeitskreis fur Jugendliteratur eV (Germany) *Tel:* (089) 4580806 *Fax:* (089) 45808088 *E-mail:* A.K.J@t-online.de *Web Site:* www.ibby.org, pg 1245

Arbol Editorial SA de CV (Mexico) *Tel:* (05) 6884828; (05) 6886458, pg 458

Uitgeverij Arbor (Netherlands) *Tel:* (035) 5422141 *Fax:* (035) 15433, pg 473

Editorial Arca SRL (Uruguay) *Tel:* (02) 900318 *Fax:* (02) 901887; (02) 930188, pg 760

Arcadia Edizioni Srl (Italy) *Tel:* (059) 76.60.34 *Fax:* (059) 77.92.79 *E-mail:* edizioni@arcadiabooks.com *Web Site:* www.arcadiabooks.com, pg 376

Arcadia Verlag GmbH (Germany) *Tel:* (040) 4141000 *Fax:* (040) 41410041 *E-mail:* contact@sikorski.de *Web Site:* www.sikorski.de, pg 194

Editions Arcam (France) *Tel:* (01) 42729312 *E-mail:* phreatiq@multimania.com, pg 147

Arcanta Aries Gruppo Editoriale (Italy) *Tel:* (049) 8712477 *Fax:* (049) 8713851, pg 376

AB Arcanum (Sweden) *Tel:* (031) 871516 *Fax:* (031) 270925, pg 600

ARCHA sro Vydavatel 'stro (Slovakia) *Tel:* (07) 5315586; (07) 54415609 *Fax:* (07) 5441586 *E-mail:* archa@internet.sk, pg 549

Archaeological Publications (Australia) *Tel:* (03) 95230549 *Fax:* (03) 95230549 *E-mail:* auraweb@hotmail.com, pg 12

The Library of the Archbishop Macarios III Foundation (Cyprus) *Tel:* (02) 430008 *Fax:* (02) 430667, pg 1459

L'Arche Editeur (France) *Tel:* (01) 46334645 *Fax:* (01) 46335640 *E-mail:* contact@arche-editeur.com *Web Site:* www.arche-editeur.com, pg 147

Arche Verlag AG, Raabe und Vitali (Switzerland) *Tel:* (01) 2522410 *Fax:* (01) 2611115, pg 608

Archief- en Bibliotheekwezen in Belgie (Belgium) *Tel:* (02) 5195351 *Fax:* (02) 5195533, pg 1512

Biblioteca Comunale dell' Archiginnasio (Italy) *Tel:* (051) 276811 *Fax:* (051) 261160 *E-mail:* archiginnasio@comune.bologna.it *Web Site:* www.archiginnasio.it, pg 1477

Archimede Edizioni (Italy) *Tel:* (02) 76 00 98 81 *Fax:* (02) 76 01 42 94, pg 376

Archinto snc (Italy) *Tel:* (02) 86460237 *Fax:* (02) 86451955 *E-mail:* lettere@mcm.it; info@archinto.it *Web Site:* www.archinto.it, pg 376

L'Archipel (France) *Tel:* (01) 55807740 *Fax:* (01) 55807741 *E-mail:* ecricom@wanadoo.fr, pg 148

Archipelago Press (Singapore) *Tel:* 2248044 *Fax:* 2247400 *E-mail:* edm@pacific.net.sg, pg 545

Architectura & Natura (Netherlands) *Tel:* (020) 6236186 *Fax:* (020) 6382303 *E-mail:* kemme@architectrua.nl, pg 473

Architectural Association Publications (United Kingdom) *Tel:* (020) 7887 4021; (020) 7887 4000 *Fax:* (020) 7414 0783 *E-mail:* publications@aaschool.ac.uk *Web Site:* www.aaschool.ac.uk/publications, pg 648

Koninklijke Vereniging van Archivarissen in Nederland (Netherlands) *Tel:* (070) 3478656 *Fax:* (070) 3825790, pg 1520

Archives de Cote d'Ivoire (Cote d'Ivoire) *Tel:* 324158, pg 1458

Archives departementales (Reunion) *Tel:* 212829, pg 1494

Public Archives of Sierra Leone (Sierra Leone) *Tel:* (022) 27337, pg 1496

Archives Bibliotheque nationales du Cameroon (Cameroon) *Tel:* 220078, pg 1456

Archives departementales de la Martinique (Martinique) *Tel:* 638846 *Fax:* 700450, pg 1484

Archives du Senegal (Senegal) *Tel:* 8235072 *Fax:* 8225126 *E-mail:* pmardi@primature.sn, pg 1496

Archives generales du Royaume (Belgium) *Tel:* (02) 5137680 *Fax:* (02) 5137681, pg 1453

Archives Nationales (France) *Tel:* (01) 40276131 *Fax:* (01) 40276601, pg 1464

Archives nationales (Tunisia) *Tel:* (01) 560556 *Fax:* (01) 569175, pg 1504

Archives nationales du Zaiire (The Democratic Republic of the Congo) *Tel:* (012) 31083, pg 1458

Archives New Zealand (New Zealand) *Tel:* (04) 4995595 *Fax:* (04) 4956210 *E-mail:* enquiries@archives.govt.nz *Web Site:* www.archives.govt.nz, pg 1487

Archives Office of New South Wales (Australia) *Tel:* (02) 2370200 *Fax:* (02) 2370142, pg 1450

Archivio Centrale dello Stato (Italy) *Tel:* (06) 5920371 *Fax:* (06) 5413620, pg 1477

Archivio Guido Izzi Edizioni (Italy) *Tel:* (06) 383193 *Fax:* (06) 39734433, pg 376

Archivio Segreto Vaticano (Holy See (Vatican City State)) *Tel:* (06) 69883314 *Fax:* (06) 69885574, pg 317

Biblioteca dell'Archivio Storico Civico e Biblioteca Trivulziana (Italy) *Tel:* (02) 62083946 *Fax:* (02) 875926, pg 1477

Archivio Storico Ticinese (Switzerland) *Tel:* (092) 8256622 *Fax:* (092) 8251874, pg 608

Archivo General de la Nacion de Colombia (Colombia) *Tel:* (01) 416015 *Fax:* (01) 3372019, pg 1457

Archivo General de Centro (Guatemala), pg 1471

Archivo General de la Nacion (Mexico) *Tel:* (05) 5851833, pg 1484

Archivo General de la Nacion del Peru (Peru) *Tel:* (014) 275930 *Fax:* (014) 282829 *E-mail:* emendoza@agn.minjus.gos.pe, pg 1490

Archivo General de Puerto Rico (Puerto Rico) *Tel:* (787) 722-2113 *Fax:* (787) 722-9097, pg 1493

Archivo General de Indias (Spain) *Tel:* (05) 4500532 *Fax:* (05) 4219485, pg 1498

Archivo General de la Nacion (AG) (Venezuela), pg 1508

Archivo Historico de la Provincia Ciudad de la Habana (Cuba) *Tel:* (07) 629436 *Fax:* (07) 338089 *E-mail:* arnac@ceniai.cus, pg 1459

Archivo Historico Nacional (Spain) *Tel:* (091) 5618003, pg 1499

Archivo Nacional de Historia (Ecuador), pg 1461

Archivo Nacional de Nicaragua (Nicaragua) *Tel:* (02) 226290 *Fax:* (02) 22722 *E-mail:* binanic@tmx.com.nic, pg 1488

Archivo y Biblioteca Capitulares (Spain) *Tel:* (025) 212423 *Fax:* (025) 212423 *E-mail:* archicapto@terra.es *Web Site:* architoledo.org, pg 1499

L'Archivolto (Italy) *Tel:* (02) 29010444; (02) 29010424 *Fax:* (02) 29001942 *E-mail:* info@archivolto.com *Web Site:* www.archivolto.com, pg 376

Naczelna Dyrekcja Archiwow Panstwowych (Poland) *Tel:* (022) 8313206; (022) 8313208 *Fax:* (022) 8317563, pg 1491

Archiwum Glowne Akt Dawnych (Poland) *Tel:* (022) 8311525 (ext 28) *Fax:* (022) 8311608, pg 1492

Arco Editorial SA (Spain) *Tel:* (093) 4184910 *Fax:* (093) 2118139 *E-mail:* arcoedit@idgrup.ibernet.com, pg 564

Arco Libros SL (Spain) *Tel:* (091) 4153687; (091) 4161371; (091) 5196651 *Fax:* (091) 4135907 *E-mail:* arcolibros@arcomuralla.com *Web Site:* www.arcomuralla.com, pg 564

Arcs Editions (Tunisia) *Tel:* (01) 351617, pg 637

ARCult Media (Germany) *Tel:* (0228) 211059 *Fax:* (0228) 217493 *E-mail:* info@arcultmedia.de *Web Site:* www.arcultmedia.de, pg 194

Arcus-Medien Wolfgang Steinhardt (Germany) *Tel:* (030) 8 32 50 41 *Fax:* (030) 8 32 73 23, pg 194

Ardey-Verlag GmbH (Germany) *Tel:* (0251) 4132-0 *Fax:* (0251) 4132-20 *Web Site:* www.ardey-verlag.de, pg 194

Publications Aredit (France) *Tel:* 20267981, pg 148

Uitgeverij Arena BV (Netherlands) *Tel:* (020) 5540500 *Fax:* (020) 4216868 *E-mail:* arenaasd@wxs.nl, pg 473

Arena Verlag GmbH (Germany) *Tel:* (0931) 79 644-0 *Fax:* (0931) 79 644-13, pg 194

Edizioni ARES (Italy) *Tel:* (02) 29514202 *Fax:* (02) 29520163 *E-mail:* aresed@tin.it *Web Site:* www.ares.mi.it, pg 376

Arevik (Armenia) *Tel:* (02) 524561, pg 10

Argalia Editore delle Arti Grafiche Editoriali SRL (Italy) *Tel:* (0722) 328733 *Fax:* (0722) 328756, pg 376

Argente, Sentos & Cia Lda (Angola), pg 1271

Editorial Argentina Plaza y Janes SA (Argentina) *Tel:* (011) 4862-6769; (011) 4862-6785 *Fax:* (011) 4864-4970, pg 3

Argentine Bible Society (Argentina) *Tel:* (011) 4312-3533 *Fax:* (011) 4312-3400 *E-mail:* socbiblicaarg@biblica.org *Web Site:* www.biblesociety.org, pg 3

ARGO-RISK Publisher (Russian Federation) *Tel:* (095) 4768538 *Fax:* (095) 2926511 *E-mail:* zayats@glas.apc.org, pg 537

Argo Spoken Word (United Kingdom) *Tel:* (020) 8910 5000 *Fax:* (020) 8910 5400, pg 648

Argon Verlag GmbH (Germany) *Tel:* (030) 25 37 38-0; (030) 25 37 38-301 (ISDN) *Fax:* (030) 25 37 38-99 *E-mail:* info@argon-verlag.de *Web Site:* www.argon-verlag.de, pg 195

Editorial Argos Vergara SA (Spain) *Tel:* (093) 5808124 *Fax:* (093) 6921851, pg 564

Argosy Press (Zimbabwe) *Tel:* (04) 704766; (04) 704715 *Fax:* (04) 752162, pg 768

Argument-Verlag (Germany) *Tel:* (040) 401800-0 *Fax:* (040) 401800-20 *E-mail:* verlag@argument.de *Web Site:* www.argument.de, pg 195

Arguval Editorial SA (Spain) *Tel:* (095) 2318784; (095) 2360213 *Fax:* (095) 2323715, pg 564

Argyll Publishing (United Kingdom) *Tel:* (01369) 820229 *Fax:* (01369) 820372 *E-mail:* argyll.publishing@virgin.net *Web Site:* freespace.virgin.net/bruntsfield.com/dt2001/argyll, pg 648

Arhiv na Makedonija (The Former Yugoslav Republic of Macedonia) *Tel:* (091) 116571 *Fax:* (091) 115827, pg 1482

Arhiv Republike Slovenije (Slovenia) *Tel:* (01) 2414200 *Fax:* (01) 2414269 *E-mail:* ars@gov.si, pg 1497

Arhivele Nationale ale Romaniei (Romania) *Tel:* (01) 3152503 *Fax:* (01) 3125841, pg 1494

Arhus Kommunes Biblioteker (Denmark) *Tel:* 87304500 *Fax:* 87304639, pg 1460

Editorial Ariel SA (Spain) *Tel:* (093) 496 70 30 *Fax:* (093) 496 70 32 *E-mail:* editorial@ariel.es *Web Site:* www.ariel.es, pg 564

Ariel Lydbokforlag (Norway) *Tel:* 64943510 *Fax:* 64943510, pg 502

Ariel Publishing House (Israel) *Tel:* (02) 6434540 *Fax:* (02) 6436164, pg 365

Aries-Verlag Paul Johannes Muller (Germany) *Tel:* (08661) 8209 *Fax:* (08661) 985 980 *E-mail:* pjm@aries-verlag.de, pg 195

Arihant Publishers (India) *Tel:* (0141) 515192, pg 331

Ario Company Ltd (Republic of Korea) *Tel:* (02) 7122001; (02) 712203 *Fax:* (02) 7023156, pg 434

Aris & Phillips Ltd (United Kingdom) *Tel:* (01985) 213409 *Fax:* (01985) 212910 *E-mail:* aris.phillips@btinternet.com *Web Site:* www.arisandphillips.com, pg 648

Ariston Editions (Switzerland) *Tel:* (071) 6727218 *Fax:* (071) 6727219 *E-mail:* 106420.3235@compuserve.com, pg 608

Uitgeverij Aristos (Netherlands) *Tel:* 073 6136416 *E-mail:* aristos@xs4all.nl *Web Site:* www.xs4all.nl/~aristos, pg 473

Aritbus et Historiae, Rivista Internationale di arti visive ecinema, Institut IRSA - Verlagsanstatt (Austria) *Tel:* (01) 7130136 *Fax:* (01) 7130130 *E-mail:* irsa@irsa.com.pl *Web Site:* www.irsa.com.pl, pg 49

Ark Boeken Publishing House (Netherlands) *Tel:* (020) 6114847 *Fax:* (020) 6114864 *E-mail:* arkboeken@wxs.nl, pg 473

Edizioni Arka SRL (Italy) *Tel:* (02) 4818230 *Fax:* (02) 4816752 *E-mail:* arka.edizioni@tin.it, pg 376

Arkadas Ltd (Turkey) *Tel:* (0312) 4344624 *Fax:* (0312) 4356057, pg 639

Arkadas Ltd (Turkey) *Tel:* (0312) 4344624; (0312) 3548300 *Fax:* (0312) 4356057, pg 1315

Wydawnictwo Arkady (Poland) *Tel:* (022) 8268980; (022) 8267079; (022) 8269316; (022) 6358344 *Fax:* (022) 8274194 *E-mail:* arkady@arkady.com.pl *Web Site:* arkady.com.pl, pg 516

Arkana Verlag Tete Bottger Rainer Wunderlich GmbH (Germany) *Tel:* (0551) 41709 *Fax:* (0551) 43868, pg 195

Uitgeverij Jan van Arkel (Netherlands) *Tel:* (030) 2731840 *Fax:* (030) 2733614 *E-mail:* i-books@antenna.nl *Web Site:* www.antenna.bl/i-books, pg 473

Arkeoloji Ve Sanat Yayinlari (Turkey) *Tel:* (212) 293 0378 *Fax:* (212) 245 6877 *E-mail:* arkeolojisanat@superonline.com *Web Site:* www.arkeolojisanat.com, pg 639

Arkin Kitabevi (Turkey) *Tel:* (0212) 5229224; (0212) 5132384; (0212) 5413620 *Fax:* (0212) 5121901, pg 639

Arkitektens Forlag (Denmark) *Tel:* 32836900 *Fax:* 32836940 *E-mail:* eksp@arkfo.dk *Web Site:* www.arkitektens-forlag.dk, pg 130

Arkitektur Forlag AB (Sweden) *Tel:* (08) 6796105 *Fax:* (08) 6115270 *E-mail:* redaktionen@arkitektur.se *Web Site:* www.arkitektur.se, pg 600

Arkivarforeningen (Denmark) *Tel:* 31393520 *Fax:* 33153239, pg 1514

Arkivarforeningen (Norway) *Tel:* 22022600 *Fax:* 22237489, pg 1521

Arktos (Italy) *Tel:* (011) 9773941 *Fax:* (011) 9773941, pg 376

Arlekin-Wydawnictwo Harlequin Enterprises sp zoo (Poland) *Tel:* (022) 499498 *Fax:* (022) 499557, pg 516

ARLIS/UK & Ireland, The Art Libraries Society (United Kingdom) *Tel:* (01527) 579298 *Fax:* (01527) 579298, pg 1524

Armada Publishing House (Russian Federation) *Tel:* (095) 4544301; (095) 45431526 *Fax:* (095) 4542481 *E-mail:* riv@armada.msk.su, pg 537

Armadillo Publishers (Australia) *Tel:* (03) 9844-4558 *Fax:* (03) 9489-5576, pg 12

Editions de l'Armancon (France) *Tel:* (03) 80 64 41 87 *Fax:* (03) 80 64 46 96 *Web Site:* www.editions-armancon.fr/presentation.htm, pg 148

Editore Armando Armando SRL (Italy) *Tel:* (06) 5894525 *Fax:* (06) 5818564 *E-mail:* amministrazione@armando.it *Web Site:* www.armando.it, pg 376

Armenia Editions (Switzerland) *Tel:* (079) 447 4593 *Fax:* (079) 447 4593, pg 608

Gruppo Editoriale Armenia SpA (Italy) *Tel:* (02) 683911 *Fax:* (02) 6684884 *E-mail:* armenia@armenia.it; armenia@mr-net.it *Web Site:* www.armenia.it, pg 376

Armitano Editores CA (Venezuela) *Tel:* (02) 2342565; (02) 2342568; (02) 2340865 *Fax:* (02) 2341647 *E-mail:* armiedit@telcel.net.ve *Web Site:* www.armitano.com, pg 761

Editorial Armonia SA (Mexico) *Tel:* (05) 687266, pg 458

Arms & Armour Press (United Kingdom) *Tel:* (020) 7420 5555 *Fax:* (020) 7420 5555, pg 648

Livraria Arnado Lda (Portugal) *Tel:* (039) 27573 *Fax:* (039) 22598, pg 522

Arnaud Editore SRL (Italy) *Tel:* (055) 216485 *Fax:* (055) 260466, pg 376

Arnette-Blackwell (France) *Tel:* (01) 45496500 *Fax:* (01) 45491288, pg 148

Arnkrone Forlaget A/S (Denmark) *Tel:* 32507000 *Fax:* 32522652, pg 130

Arnold (United Kingdom) *Tel:* (020) 7873 6000 *Fax:* (020) 7873 6325 *E-mail:* feedback.arnold@hodder.co.uk *Web Site:* www.arnoldpublishers.com, pg 648

Edward Arnold (Australia) Pty Ltd (Australia) *Tel:* (03) 98599011 *Fax:* (03) 98599141, pg 12

Arnoldsche Verlagsanstalt GmbH (Germany) *Tel:* (0711) 645618-0 *Fax:* (0711) 645618-79 *E-mail:* art@arnoldsche.com *Web Site:* www.arnoldsche.com, pg 195

Aromolaran Publishing Co Ltd (Nigeria) *Tel:* (02) 24392, pg 498

Arpeco Engineering (Canada) *Tel:* 905-564-5150 *Fax:* 905-564-2943 *E-mail:* sales@arpeco.com *Web Site:* www.arpeco.com, pg 1193

Arpoador (Uruguay) *Tel:* (02) 707826 *Fax:* (02) 717278, pg 760

Arquivo Nacional (Brazil) *Tel:* (021) 252 2617 *Fax:* (021) 252 9821 *E-mail:* arqnacdg@rio.com.br, pg 79

Arquivo Nacional (Brazil) *Tel:* (021) 252-2617 *Fax:* (021) 252 9821, pg 1454

Arquivo Universidade de Coimbra (Portugal) *Tel:* (039) 25422 *Fax:* (039) 25841, pg 522

Arrayan Editores (Chile) *Tel:* (02) 4314200 *Fax:* (02) 2741041 *E-mail:* web@arrayan.cl *Web Site:* www.arrayan.cl, pg 99

J W Arrowsmith Ltd (United Kingdom) *Tel:* (0117) 9667545 *Fax:* (0117) 9637829 *E-mail:* jw@arrowsmith.co.uk *Web Site:* www.arrowsmith.co.uk, pg 1139

J W Arrowsmith Ltd (United Kingdom) *Tel:* (0117) 9667545 *Fax:* (0117) 9637829 *E-mail:* jw@arrowsmith.co.uk, pg 1160, 1202, 1223

Ars Edition GmbH (Germany) *Tel:* (089) 381006-77 *Fax:* (089) 381006-58, pg 195

Ars Longa Publishing House (Romania) *Tel:* (0232) 215078 *Fax:* (0232) 215078 *E-mail:* arslonga@mail.dntis.ro, pg 532

Ars Poetica Editora Ltda (Brazil) *Tel:* (011) 2405598 *Fax:* (011) 5312648, pg 79

Ars Scribendi bv Uitgeverij (Netherlands) *Tel:* (0348) 443998 *Fax:* (0348) 444076 *E-mail:* info@arsscribendi.com *Web Site:* www.arsscribendi.com, pg 473

ARS VIVENDI VERLAG   INDUSTRY

Ars Vivendi Verlag (Germany) *Tel:* (091) 03-719 29 0 *Fax:* (091) 03 719 59 19 *E-mail:* ars@arsvivendi.com *Web Site:* www.arsvivendi.com, pg 195

Bibliotheque de l' Arsenal (France) *Tel:* (01) 53012525 *Fax:* (01) 42770163 *E-mail:* arsenal@bnf.fr, pg 1464

Arsenale Editrice SRL (Italy) *Tel:* (041) 5240610 *Fax:* (041) 5221579; (041) 5240865, pg 376

D I Arsenidis Publications (Greece) *Tel:* (01) 36-29-538; (01) 36-33923 *Fax:* (01) 36-18-707 *Web Site:* www.arsenidis.gr/NavFrame_en.htm, pg 309

Arsip Nasional Republik Indonesia (Indonesia) *Tel:* (021) 7805851 *Fax:* (021) 7805812 *E-mail:* anrinet@indosat.net.id, pg 1474

Arsorigo Co Ltd (Taiwan, Province of China) *Tel:* (02) 7252387 *Fax:* (02) 7252387, pg 629

Art & Metiers Du Livre/Editions (France) *Tel:* (01) 42 27 32 36 *Fax:* (01) 47 63 25 52 *E-mail:* infos@faton.fr *Web Site:* www.art-metiers-du-livre.com/revue.html, pg 148

Art Book Co Ltd (Taiwan, Province of China) *Tel:* (02) 23620578 *Fax:* (02) 23623594 *E-mail:* artbook@ms43.hinet.net, pg 629

Art Books International Ltd (United Kingdom) *Tel:* (020) 7720 1503; (020) 7578 1222 *Fax:* (020) 7720 3158 *E-mail:* artbooks@a-b-i.demon.co.uk, pg 649

Art Books International Ltd (United Kingdom) *Tel:* (020) 7720 1503 *Fax:* (020) 7720 3158, pg 1315

Art Data (United Kingdom) *Tel:* (020) 8747 1061 *Fax:* (020) 8742 2319, pg 1315

Art Directors Club Verlag GmbH (Germany) *Tel:* (030) 59 00 31 0 *Fax:* (030) 59 00 31 0 *E-mail:* adc@adc.de *Web Site:* www.adc.de, pg 195

Librairie Art et Culture (Tunisia) *Tel:* (02) 31072 *Fax:* (02) 431372, pg 1315

Art Gallery of South Australia Bookshop (Australia) *Tel:* (08) 8207 7029 *Fax:* (08) 8207 7069 *E-mail:* agsa.bookshop@saugov.sa.gov.au *Web Site:* www.artgallery.sa.gov.au, pg 12

Art Gallery of Western Australia (Australia) *Tel:* (08) 9492 6600 *Fax:* (08) 9492 6655 *E-mail:* admin@artgallery.wa.gov.au *Web Site:* www.artgallery.wa.gov.au, pg 12

Art House Group (Finland) *Tel:* (09) 6933725 *Fax:* (09) 6933762, pg 142

Art on the Move (Australia) *Tel:* (08) 9227 7505 *Fax:* (08) 9227 5304 *E-mail:* artmoves@highwayl.com.an *Web Site:* www.imago.com.au/artmoves, pg 12

Art Price Annual ADEC (France) *Tel:* (01) 478 220 000 *Fax:* (01) 478 220 606, pg 148

Art Sales Index Ltd (United Kingdom) *Tel:* (01784) 451145 *Fax:* (01784) 451144 *E-mail:* asi@art-sales-index.com, pg 649

The Art Trade Press Ltd (United Kingdom) *Tel:* (023) 9248 4943, pg 649

Artava Ltd (Latvia) *Tel:* (02) 7830254 *Fax:* (02) 7830254 *E-mail:* arta@latnet.lv, pg 441

ARTC/OLOR (Germany) *Tel:* (02381) 980190 *Fax:* (02381) 9801999, pg 195

Artech House (United Kingdom) *Tel:* (020) 7596 8750 *Fax:* (020) 7630 0166 *E-mail:* artech-uk@artechhouse.com *Web Site:* www.artechhouse.com, pg 649

Artel SC (Belgium) *Tel:* (081) 21 37 00 *Fax:* (081) 21 23 72 *E-mail:* erasme@skynet.be, pg 64

Artema (Italy) *Tel:* (011) 386500 *Fax:* (011) 3853244 *E-mail:* cse@estorinese.inet.it, pg 377

Artemis Publishing Pty Ltd (Australia) *Tel:* (03) 6143920 *Fax:* (03) 6701252 *E-mail:* jasart@magnafield.com.au *Web Site:* www.magnafield.com.au/~jasart, pg 12

Artemis Verlag (Romania) *Tel:* (01) 2226661, pg 532

Edizioni Artes (Italy) *Tel:* (02) 70209917 *Fax:* (02) 70209919, pg 377

Artes de Mexico y del Mundo, SA de CV (Mexico) *Tel:* (05) 208 3217 *Fax:* (05) 525 5925 *E-mail:* artesmex@internet.com.mx; artesdemexico@artesdemexico.com *Web Site:* www.artesdemexico.com, pg 458

Artes e Oficios Editora Ltda (Brazil) *Tel:* (051) 311 0832; (051) 311 5442 *Fax:* (051) 311 0832 *E-mail:* artesofi@pro.via-rs.com.br, pg 79

Artetech Publishing Co (United Kingdom) *Tel:* (01225) 862482 *Fax:* (01225) 865601, pg 649

Artexim - Foreign Trade Co (Romania) *Tel:* (01) 157672, pg 1308

Arthur James Ltd (United Kingdom) *Tel:* (01962) 736880 *Fax:* (01962) 736881 *E-mail:* office@johnhunt-publishing.com *Web Site:* www.johnhunt-publishing.com, pg 649

Artibus et Literis (Germany) *Tel:* (0211) 38810 *Fax:* (0211) 3881280 *E-mail:* webmaster@artibus.de *Web Site:* www.artibus.de, pg 1283

Artioli Editore in Modena (Italy) *Tel:* (059) 827181 *Fax:* (059) 826819 *E-mail:* artiolip@pianeta.it, pg 377

SA Artis-Historia (Belgium) *Tel:* (078) 150.150 *Fax:* (078) 150.150 *E-mail:* info@artis-historia.be *Web Site:* www.artis-historia.bc, pg 64

SA Artis-Historia (Belgium) *Tel:* (02) 2409200 *Fax:* (02) 2480818, pg 1276

Artisjus (Hungary) *Tel:* (01) 2121553 *Fax:* (01) 2121552, pg 1112

The Artist Publishing Co (Taiwan, Province of China) *Tel:* (02) 3932780; (02) 23932780 *Fax:* (02) 3932012; (02) 23932012, pg 629

ARTMED (Brazil) *Tel:* (051) 3303444; (051) 3318244 *Fax:* (051) 3302378 *E-mail:* artmed@artmed.com.br *Web Site:* www.artmed.com.br, pg 79

Artmoves (Australia) *Tel:* (03) 96500744; (03) 98828116 *Fax:* (03) 98828162; (03) 96506916 *E-mail:* rastawoman@msn.com, pg 12

ArTresor naklada (Croatia) *Tel:* (01) 4846 791 *Fax:* (01) 4846 916 *E-mail:* artresor@zg.tel.hr, pg 118

Arts & Antiques Edition Munich Verlag, Buch & Kunsthandel GmbH (Germany) *Tel:* (089) 349830 *Fax:* (089) 349834 *E-mail:* wine-price@wine-auction-world.com, pg 195

Arts Centre Bookshop (New Zealand) *Tel:* (03) 3655277 *Fax:* (03) 3653293, pg 1302

Arts Council of England (United Kingdom) *Tel:* (020) 7333 0100 *Fax:* (020) 7973 6590 *E-mail:* enquiries@artscouncil.org.uk *Web Site:* www.artscouncil.org.uk, pg 649

Arts Council of Wales (United Kingdom) *Tel:* (02920) 376500 *Fax:* (01222) 221447 *E-mail:* information@ccc-acw.org.uk *Web Site:* www.ccc-acw.org.uk, pg 1369

Compagnie Francaise des Arts Graphiques SA (France) *Tel:* (01) 46243925, pg 148

Wydawnictwa Artystyczne i Filmowe (Poland) *Tel:* (022) 8455301; (022) 8455584; (022) 8455465; (022) 8453936 *Fax:* (022) 8455584; (022) 8455465; (022) 8453936, pg 516

Arun-Verlag (Germany) *Tel:* (036743) 233-0 *Fax:* (036743) 233-17 *E-mail:* info@arun-verlag.de *Web Site:* www.arun-verlag.de, pg 195

Arvore Coop de Actividades Artisticas, CRL (Portugal) *Tel:* (02) 383867 *Fax:* (02) 2002684, pg 522

Arya Medi Publishing House (India) *Tel:* (011) 5717012 *Fax:* (011) 5715850, pg 331

AS Narbuto Leidykla (AS Narbutas' Publishers) (Lithuania) *Tel:* (075) 420868 *Fax:* (075) 429335, pg 445

AS Publishing (United Kingdom) *Tel:* (020) 8458 3552 *Fax:* (020) 8458 0618 *E-mail:* asp@dircon.co.uk, pg 649

Asa Editions (France) *Tel:* (01) 47704290 *Fax:* (01) 47704298 *Web Site:* www.asaeditions.com, pg 148

Asahiya Shoten Ltd (Booksellers) (Japan) *Tel:* (06) 3131191; (06) 3727251; (06) 3727253 *Fax:* (06) 3755650, pg 1294

Asahiya Shuppan (Japan) *Tel:* (03) 32670865 *Fax:* (03) 32680928, pg 414

Asakura Publishing Co Ltd (Japan) *Tel:* (03) 32600141 *Fax:* (03) 32600180, pg 414

Asam Establishment for Publishing & Distribution (Saudi Arabia) *Tel:* (01) 4453732 *Fax:* (01) 4412583, pg 543

Asamblea Legislativa, Biblioteca Monsenor Sanabria (Costa Rica) *Tel:* 223-2396; 243-2397 *Fax:* 243-2400 *E-mail:* jvolio@congreso.aleg.go.cr; vvargas@congreso.aleg.go.cr; epaniagu@congreso.aleg.go.cr, pg 115

Roland Asanger Verlag GmbH (Germany) *Tel:* (08744) 7262 *Fax:* (08744) 967755 *E-mail:* verlag@asanger.de *Web Site:* www.asanger.de, pg 195

The Asano Agency, Inc (Japan) *Tel:* (03) 39434171 *Fax:* (03) 39437637, pg 1113

Aschehoug Dansk Forlag A/S (Denmark) *Tel:* 33305522 *Fax:* 33305822 *E-mail:* info@ash.egmont.com *Web Site:* www.aschehoug.dk, pg 130

Aschehoug Forlag (Norway) *Tel:* 22400400 *Fax:* 22429467, pg 502

H Aschehoug & Co (W Nygaard) A/S (Norway) *Tel:* 22400400 *Fax:* 22206395 *E-mail:* epost@aschehoug.no *Web Site:* www.aschehoug.no, pg 502

Aschendorffsche Verlagsbuchhandlung GmbH & Co KG (Germany) *Tel:* (0251) 690133 *Fax:* (0251) 690143 *E-mail:* buchverlag@aschendorff.de *Web Site:* www.aschendorff.de/buch, pg 195

Asclepios Edition Lothar Baus (Germany) *Tel:* (06841) 71863 *E-mail:* lotharbaus@web.de *Web Site:* www.asclepiosedition.de, pg 196

Ascona Presse (Switzerland) *Tel:* (091) 7911334 *Fax:* (091) 7911334, pg 608

Asempa Publishers (Ghana) *Tel:* (021) 221706; (021) 233084 *Fax:* (021) 776725; (021) 233130; (021) 235140 *E-mail:* asempa@ghana.com, pg 306

ASFORED (Association Nationale pour la Formation et le Perfectionnement Professionnels dans les Metiers de l'Edition) (France) *Tel:* (01) 45883981 *Fax:* (01) 45815492, pg 1242

Asgard Publishing Services (United Kingdom) *Tel:* (0113) 2741037 *Fax:* (0113) 2741037 *E-mail:* info@asgardpublishing.co.uk *Web Site:* www.asgardpublishing.co.uk, pg 1128

Ashanti Publishing (South Africa) *Tel:* (011) 8032506 *Fax:* (011) 8035094, pg 552

Ashgate Publishing Ltd (United Kingdom) *Tel:* (01252) 331551 *Fax:* (01252) 317446 *E-mail:* info@ashgatepub.co.uk *Web Site:* www.ashgate.com, pg 649

Ashgrove Press (United Kingdom) *Tel:* (020) 7713-7540 *Fax:* (020) 7713-7541 *E-mail:* gmo73@dial.pipex.com *Web Site:* www.ashgrovepublishing.com, pg 650

Ashgrove Press (United Kingdom) *Tel:* (01373) 834900 *Fax:* (01373) 834900 *Web Site:* www.ashgrovepublishing.com, pg 1315

Ashling Books (Australia) *Tel:* (02) 62591027, pg 12

Ashmolean Museum Publications (United Kingdom) *Tel:* (01865) 278010 *Fax:* (01865) 278018 *E-mail:* publications@ashmus.ox.ac.uk *Web Site:* www.ashmol.ox.ac.uk/ash/publications, pg 650

Sheikh Muhammad Ashraf Publishers (Pakistan) *Tel:* (042) 353171; (042) 353489 *Fax:* (042) 353489, pg 506

Ashton & Denton Publishing Co (CI) Ltd (United Kingdom) *Tel:* (01534) 735461; (01534) 727976 *Fax:* (01534) 875805, pg 650

Asia Books Co Ltd (Thailand) *Tel:* (02) 7159000 *Fax:* (02) 3811621; (02) 3912277 *E-mail:* information@asiabooks.com *Web Site:* www.asiabooks.com, pg 1314

Asia Pacific Business Press Inc (India) *Tel:* (011) 3923955; (011) 3935654 *Fax:* (011) 3941561 *E-mail:* niir@vsnl.com *Web Site:* www.niir.org, pg 331

Asia Pacific Communications Ltd (Hong Kong) *Tel:* (02) 8610102 *Fax:* (02) 5296816 *E-mail:* asiapac@attglobal.net, pg 318

Asia/Pacific Cultural Centre for UNESCO (ACCU) (Japan) *Tel:* (03) 32694435 *Fax:* (03) 32694510 *E-mail:* general@accu.or.jp, pg 1250

Asia Pacific Offset Inc (United States) *Tel:* 202-462-5436 *Fax:* 202-986-4030 *Web Site:* www.asiapacificoffset.com, pg 1142

Asia Pacific Offset Inc (United States) *Tel:* 202-462-5436 *Fax:* 202-968-4030 *Web Site:* www.asiapacificoffset.com, pg 1163, 1205

Asia 2000 Ltd (China) *Tel:* (02) 530 1409 *Fax:* (02) 526 1107 *E-mail:* info@asia2000.com.hk, pg 102

Asian Culture Co (Taiwan, Province of China) *Tel:* (02) 5072606 *Fax:* (02) 5074260, pg 629

Asian Educational Services (India) *Tel:* (011) 668594; (011) 660187; (011) 6851586 *Fax:* (011) 6852805; (011) 6855499 *E-mail:* asianeds@nda.vsnl.net.in, pg 331

The Asian Productivity Organization (Japan) *Tel:* (03) 5226-3920 *Fax:* (03) 52263950 *E-mail:* apo@apo-tokyo.com *Web Site:* www.apo-tokyo.com, pg 1250

Asian Trading Corporation (India) *Tel:* (080) 51807; (080) 579410; (080) 5587807 *Fax:* (080) 5596363 *E-mail:* atc@mcdecom.net, pg 331

Asiapac Books Pte Ltd (Singapore) *Tel:* 3928455 *Fax:* 3926455 *E-mail:* apacbks@singnet.com.sg *Web Site:* www.asiapacbooks.com, pg 545

ASK Ltd (Ukraine) *Tel:* (044) 241-94-96; (044) 456-72-51 *Fax:* (044) 455-58-89 *E-mail:* ask.sale@i.com.ua, pg 643

Aslib, The Association for Information Management (United Kingdom) *Tel:* (01274) 777 700 *Fax:* (020) 7903 0011 *E-mail:* aslib@aslib.com; pubs@aslib.com *Web Site:* www.aslib.co.uk, pg 650

Aslib, The Association for Information Management (United Kingdom) *Tel:* (01274) 777 700 *Fax:* (020) 7903 0011 *E-mail:* pubs@aslib.com *Web Site:* www.aslib.co.uk, pg 1369

Aslib, The Association for Information Management (United Kingdom) *Tel:* (01274) 777 700 *Fax:* (01274) 785 200 *E-mail:* pubs@aslib.com *Web Site:* www.aslib.co.uk, pg 1524

Asociacion de Bibliotecarios de El Salvador (El Salvador) *Tel:* 216312, pg 1515

Asociacion de Bibliotecarios Graduados del Istmo de Panama (Panama) *Tel:* 2227411 *Fax:* 2254366, pg 1522

Asociacion de Bibliotecarios Universitarios del Paraguay (Paraguay) *Tel:* (021) 507080 *Fax:* (021) 213734, pg 1522

Asociacion Argentina de Bibliotecas y Centros de Informacion Cientificos y Tecnicos (Argentina) *Tel:* (011) 3938406, pg 1511

Asociacion Bautista Argentina de Publicaciones (Argentina) *Tel:* (011) 863-6745 *Fax:* (011) 863-6745, pg 3

Asociacion Boliviana de Bibliotecarios (ABB) (Bolivia), pg 1512

Asociacion Colombiana de Bibliotecarios (Colombia) *Tel:* (01) 2694219, pg 1513

Asociacion Costarricense de Bibliotecarios (Costa Rica), pg 1514

Asociacion de Archiveros del Peru (ADAP) (Peru) *Tel:* (01) 4712277 *Fax:* (01) 2650958 *E-mail:* dri@u8p.edu.pe, pg 1522

Asociacion de Bibliotecarios y Archivistas de Honduras (Honduras), pg 1517

Asociacion de Bibliotecologos del Uruguay (Uruguay) *Tel:* (02) 4099989 *Fax:* (02) 4099989 *E-mail:* ABU@adinet.com.uy, pg 1525

Asociacion de Escritores y Artistas Espanoles (Spain) *Tel:* (091) 5599067 *Fax:* (091) 5599067, pg 1259

Asociacion Dominicana de Bibliotecarios (ASODOBI) (Dominican Republic) *Tel:* (809) 688-4086, pg 1514

Asociacion Ecuatoriana de Bibliotecarios (AEB) (Ecuador) *Tel:* (02) 528840; Headquarters: (02 263474), pg 1515

Asociacion Espanola de Archiveros, Bibliotecarios, Museologos y Documentalistas (Spain) *Tel:* (091) 5751727 *Fax:* (091) 5751727, pg 1523

Asociacion General de Archivistas de El Salvador (El Salvador) *Tel:* 229418, pg 1515

Asociacion Latinoamericana de Instituciones Financieras Para El Desarrollo (ALIDE) (Peru) *Tel:* (01) 4422400 *Fax:* (01) 4428105 *E-mail:* sg@alide.org.pe *Web Site:* www.alide.org.pe, pg 1490

Asociacion Instituto Linguistico de Verano (Colombia) *Tel:* 2829886; 2821047; 3416185 *Fax:* 2860358 *E-mail:* langaffairs_cob@sil.org, pg 111

Asociacion Mexicana de Bibliotecarios AC (AMBAC) (Mexico) *Tel:* (05) 5751135 *E-mail:* ambac@solar.sar.net, pg 1520

Asociacion Nicaraguense de Bibliotecarios y Profesionales a Fines (Nicaragua), pg 1521

Asociacion Panamena de Bibliotecarios (Panama), pg 1522

Asociacion para el Progreso de la Direccion (APD) (Spain) *Tel:* (094) 423 22 50 *Fax:* (094) 423 62 49 *E-mail:* apd@bil.apd.es *Web Site:* www.apd.es, pg 564

Asociacion Peruana de Bibliotecarios (APB) (Peru) *Tel:* (01) 474869, pg 1522

Editores Asociados Mexicanos SA de CV (EDAMEX) (Mexico) *Tel:* (05) 5598588 *Fax:* (05) 5757035, pg 458

Aspect Press (New Zealand) *Tel:* (06) 368-2887, pg 488

Aspect Press Ltd (Russian Federation) *Tel:* (095) 3094062 *Fax:* (095) 3091166 *E-mail:* info@aspectpress.ru *Web Site:* www.aspectpress.ru, pg 537

ASR Publications (Pakistan) *Tel:* (042) 5882617; (042) 5882618; (042) 877613; (42) 877496 *Fax:* (042) 5882617; (042) 5711575 *E-mail:* iwsl@asr.edunet.sdnpk.undp.org or iwsl@asr.brain.net.pk, pg 506

Assad National Library (Syrian Arab Republic) *Tel:* (011) 338255 *Fax:* (011) 3320804, pg 1502

Assam Publishers' Association (India) *Tel:* 543 995, pg 1248

Peter Asschenfeldts Bokklubb (Norway) *Tel:* 22429165 *Fax:* 22471098, pg 1230

Assemblies of God Mission (Papua New Guinea) *Tel:* 881256, pg 510

Assert Publishing (Australia) *Tel:* (09) 398-8279 *Fax:* (09) 398-8279, pg 12

Assimil NV (Belgium) *Tel:* (02) 5114502 *Fax:* (02) 5129138 *E-mail:* assimilbenelux@wanadoo.be *Web Site:* www.assimil.be, pg 64

Editions Assimil SA (France) *Tel:* (01) 45768737 *Fax:* (01) 45940655 *E-mail:* contact@assimil.com *Web Site:* www.assimil.com, pg 148

Assimil GmbH (Germany) *Tel:* (02426) 9400 *Fax:* (02426) 4862 *E-mail:* kontakt@assimil.com *Web Site:* www.assimil.com, pg 196

Assirio & Alvim (Portugal) *Tel:* (021) 555580 *Fax:* (021) 3152935, pg 522

Asso Verlag (Germany) *Tel:* (0208) 802356 *Fax:* (0208) 809882, pg 196

Associacao Arvore da Vida (Brazil) *Tel:* (011) 2185399 *Fax:* (011) 2181401 *E-mail:* editora@eavida.com.br, pg 79

Associacao Brasileira dar Editoras Universitarias (ABEU) (Brazil) *Tel:* (0482) 319000 *Fax:* (0482) 344069, pg 1239

Associacao Brasileira de Liverivos Antiquarios (Brazil) *Tel:* (021) 224-8616 *Fax:* (021) 221-4582, pg 79

Associacao Brasileira de Liverivos Antiquarios (Brazil) *Tel:* (0242) 420376 *Fax:* (0242) 311695; (0242) 2214582, pg 1239

Associacao Brasileira de Liverivos Antiquarios (Brazil) *Tel:* (021) 224-8616 *Fax:* (021) 221-4582, pg 1277

Associacao dos Arquivistas Brasileiros (Brazil) *Tel:* (021) 2337142 *Fax:* (021) 2337142, pg 1513

Associacao dos Escritores Mocambicanos (AEMO) (Mozambique) *Tel:* (01) 420727, pg 470

Associacao Palas Athena do Brasil (Brazil) *Tel:* (011) 3209-6288 *Fax:* (011) 3277-8137 *E-mail:* grafica@palasathena.org; editora@palasathena.org *Web Site:* www.palasathena.org, pg 79

Associacao Portuguesa de Bibliotecarios, Arquivistas e Documentalistas (Portugal) *Tel:* (021) 8154479; (021) 8134697 *Fax:* (021) 8154508 *E-mail:* badbn@mail.telepac.pt, pg 1522

Associacao Portuguesa de Editores e Livreiros (Portugal) *Tel:* (021) 556241 *Fax:* (021) 3153553, pg 1257

Associacio d'Editors en Llengua Catalana (Spain) *Tel:* (093) 155091 *Fax:* (093) 155273 *E-mail:* gec@gefes.es *Web Site:* www.gremieditorscat.es, pg 1259

Associated Educational Distributors (M) Sdn Bhd (Malaysia) *Tel:* (06) 2844786 *Fax:* (06) 2844697, pg 451

Associated Publishing House (India) *Tel:* (011) 2429392, pg 331

Associated Translation & Typesetting (United Kingdom) *Tel:* (0121) 603 6344 *Fax:* (0121) 603 6399 *E-mail:* ATTEuro@aol.com (European translation); ATTAsia@aol.com (Eastern/Asian translation); ATTgraphic@jaure.demon.com (web design/graphics), pg 1128

Associated Translation & Typesetting (United Kingdom) *Tel:* (0121) 603 6344 *Fax:* (0121) 603 6399 *E-mail:* ATTEuro@aol.com (European translation); ATTAsia@aol.com (Eastern/Asian translation) *Web Site:* www.jaure.demon.co.uk, pg 1160

Association des Bibliothecaires, Archivistes, Documentalistes et Museographes du Cameroon (ABADCAM) (Cameroon) *Tel:* 220744 *Fax:* 221320, pg 1513

Association pour le Developpement de la Documentation, des Bibliotheques et Archives de la Cote d'Ivoire (ADBACI) (Cote d'Ivoire) *Tel:* 213872, pg 1514

L'Association (France) *Tel:* (01) 43558587 *Fax:* (01) 43558621 *E-mail:* lassocia@club-internet.fr, pg 148

Association des Archivistes Francais (France) *Tel:* (01) 40276000, pg 1515

Association des Bibliotheques et Bibliothecaires Suisses (Switzerland) *Tel:* (031) 3824240 *Fax:* (031) 3824648 *E-mail:* bbs@bbs.ch *Web Site:* www.bbs.ch, pg 1523

Association of London Chief Librarians (United Kingdom) *Tel:* (0181) 7704760 *Fax:* (0181) 7704777, pg 1524

Association Belge de Documentation (Belgium) *Tel:* (02) 6755862 *Fax:* (02) 6727446 *E-mail:* abdbvd@abd-bvd.be *Web Site:* www.abd-bvd.be, pg 1512

Association de la Recherche Historique et Sociale (Morocco) *Tel:* 918239, pg 469

Association des Auteurs Autoedites (France) *Tel:* (01) 47033664 *Web Site:* www.auteurs-autoedites.com, pg 1242

Association des Bibliothecaires Laotiens (Laos People's Democratic Republic) *Tel:* (021) 212452 *Fax:* (021) 213029 *E-mail:* pfd-mill@pan.laos.net.la, pg 1519

Association des Bibliothecaires Belges d'Expression Francaise (Belgium) *Tel:* (067) 771477 *Fax:* (067) 771477 *E-mail:* abbef@freeworld.be; abbef.be@gate71.be, pg 1512

Association des Bibliothecaires Francais (France) *Tel:* (01) 55331030 *Fax:* (01) 55301031 *E-mail:* abf@abf.asso.fr *Web Site:* www.abf.asso.fr, pg 1515

Association des Bibliotheques Chretiennes France (ABEF) (France) *Tel:* (03) 80631478, pg 1515

Association des Diplomes de l'Ecole de Bibliothecaires-Documentalistes (France) *Tel:* (01) 45870533 *Fax:* (01) 43310756 *E-mail:* pofier@citiz.fr, pg 1515

Association des Ecrivains Belges de Langue Francaise (Belgium) *Tel:* (02) 512 2968 *Fax:* (02) 502 4373, pg 1360

Association des Ecrivains Reunionnais/ocean Indien (ADER) (Reunion) *Tel:* 437607 *Fax:* 437607, pg 531

Association des Editeurs Belges (Belgium) *Tel:* (02) 2416580 *Fax:* (02) 2167131, pg 1237

Association for Scottish Literary Studies (United Kingdom) *Tel:* (0141) 330 5309 *Fax:* (0141) 330 5309 *Web Site:* www.asls.org.uk, pg 650, 1369

Association for the Study of Australian Literature Ltd (Australia) *Tel:* (07) 38757165 *Fax:* (07) 38757730 *E-mail:* p.buckridge@hum.gu.edu.au., pg 1359

Association Francaise de Normalisation (France) *Tel:* (01) 41 62 80 00 *Fax:* (01) 49 17 90 00 *Web Site:* www.afnor.fr, pg 148

Association Francaise du Multimedia (France) *Tel:* (01) 48242991 *Fax:* (01) 45231337 *E-mail:* info@afee.org *Web Site:* www.afee.org, pg 1243

Association Internationale de Bibliophilie (France) *Tel:* (01) 47037757 *Fax:* (01) 47037570, pg 1243

Association Internationale des Ecoles des Sciences de l'Information (Switzerland) *Tel:* (022) 705 99 77 *Fax:* (022) 705 99 98 *Web Site:* www.aiesi.refer.org, pg 1259

Association Internationale des Etudes Francaises (AIEF) (France) *Fax:* (01) 40462588 *Web Site:* www.aief.eu.org, pg 1243

Association Malienne des Bibliothecaires, Archivistes et Documentalistes (Mali) *Tel:* 224963, pg 1520

Association Mauritanienne des Bibliothecaires, Archivistes et Documentalistes (Mauritania), pg 1520

Association of African Universities (Ghana) *Tel:* (021) 774495 *Fax:* (021) 774821 *E-mail:* secgenaau.org, pg 1247

Association of Art Historians (United Kingdom) *Tel:* (020) 7490 3211 *Fax:* (020) 7490 3277 *E-mail:* admin@aah.org.uk *Web Site:* www.aah.org.uk, pg 1369

Association of Authors' Agents (United Kingdom) *Tel:* (020) 7344 1000 *Fax:* (020) 7836 9541 *E-mail:* aaa@pfd.co.uk *Web Site:* www.agentsassoc.co.uk, pg 1263

Association of British Science Writers (United Kingdom) *Tel:* (020) 7439 1205 *Fax:* (020) 7973 3051, pg 1369

Association of British Theological & Philosophical Libraries (United Kingdom) *Tel:* (020) 7387 3727, pg 1524

Association of Commonwealth Universities (ACU) (United Kingdom) *Tel:* (020) 7380 6700 *Fax:* (020) 7387 2655 *E-mail:* info@acu.ac.uk *Web Site:* www.acu.ac.uk, pg 650

Association of Development Agencies (Jamaica) *Tel:* (876) 9602319; (876) 9683605 *Fax:* (876) 9298773, pg 412

Association of Learned & Professional Society Publishers (United Kingdom) *Tel:* (01424) 812353 *Fax:* (0181) 6633583 *E-mail:* donovan@alpsp.demon.co.uk, pg 1264

Association of Little Presses (United Kingdom) *Tel:* (020) 3851889, pg 1264

Association of Research Libraries & Libraries for Science & Technology in the CIS (Russian Federation) *Tel:* (095) 9259288 *Fax:* (095) 9219862 *E-mail:* root@gpntd.msk.su, pg 1257

Association of Special Libraries of the Philippines (ASLP) (Philippines) *Tel:* (02) 590177 *Fax:* (02) 590177, pg 1522

Association of Yugoslav Publishers & Booksellers (Yugoslavia) *Tel:* (011) 642533; (011) 646841 *Fax:* (011) 646339, pg 764

Association of Yugoslav Publishers & Booksellers (Yugoslavia) *Tel:* (011) 642248 *Fax:* (011) 646339 *E-mail:* ognjenl@eunet.yu, pg 1269

Association Professionnelle des Bibliothecaires et Documentalistes (APBD) (Belgium) *Tel:* (071) 614335 *Fax:* (071) 611634 *E-mail:* biblio.hainaut@skynet.be, pg 1512

Association for Science Education (United Kingdom) *Tel:* (01707) 283001 *Fax:* (01707) 266532 *E-mail:* ase@asehq.telme.com *Web Site:* www.ase.org.uk, pg 650

Association Senegalaise de Bibliothecaires, Archivistes et Documentalistes, (ASBAD) (Senegal) *Tel:* 246981 *Fax:* 242379, pg 1522

Association Suisse des Editeurs de Langue Francaise (Switzerland) *Tel:* (021) 7963300 *Fax:* (021) 7963311 *E-mail:* aself@centrezational.cl, pg 608, 1260

Association Suisse des Libraires de Langue Francaise (Switzerland) *Tel:* (021) 7963300 *Fax:* (021) 7963311 *E-mail:* aself@centrezational.cl, pg 1260

Association Suisse des Traducteurs Terminologues et Interpretes (ASTTI) (Switzerland) *Tel:* (031) 3123303 *Fax:* (031) 3121250, pg 1127

Association Suisse Romande des Diffuseurs et Distributeurs de Livres (Switzerland) *Tel:* (021)7963300 *Fax:* (021) 7963311 *E-mail:* aself@centrezational.ch, pg 1260

Association Togolaise pour le Developpement de la Documentation des Bibliotheques, Archives et Musees (Togo) *Tel:* 213027 *Fax:* 218784, pg 1524

Association Tunisienne des Documentalistes, Bibliothecaires et Archivistes (Tunisia), pg 1524

Association Zairoise des Archivistes, Bibliothecaires et Documentalistes (The Democratic Republic of the Congo) *Tel:* (012) 30123; (012) 30124, pg 1514

Associazione Italiana Biblioteche (Italy) *Tel:* (06) 4463532 *Fax:* (06) 4441139 *E-mail:* aib@aib.it *Web Site:* www.aib.it, pg 1518

Associazione Italiana Editori (Italy) *Tel:* (02) 86463091 *Fax:* (02) 89010863 *E-mail:* aie@aie.it *Web Site:* www.aie.it, pg 1249

Associazione Librai Antiquari d'Italia (Italy) *Tel:* (055) 243253 *Fax:* (055) 243253 *E-mail:* alai@dada.it *Web Site:* www.dada.it/alai, pg 1249

Astor-Verlag, Willibald Schlager (Austria) *Tel:* (01) 9144281 *Fax:* (01) 9144281, pg 49

Editorial Astrea de Alfredo y Ricardo Depalma SRL (Argentina) *Tel:* (011) 4382-1880 *Fax:* (011) 4382-4203 *E-mail:* info@astrea.com.ar *Web Site:* www.astrea.com.ar, pg 3

Editorial Astri SA (Spain) *Tel:* (093) 6801207 *Fax:* (093) 6803194 *E-mail:* astri@astri.es; astri@mundivia.es *Web Site:* www.astri.es, pg 564

Astrodata AG (Switzerland) *Tel:* (01) 7001012 *Fax:* (01) 7001610 *E-mail:* wettswil@astrodata.ch *Web Site:* www.astrodata.ch, pg 608

Casa Editrice Astrolabio-Ubaldini Editore (Italy) *Tel:* (06) 854 22 45; (06) 855 21 31 *Fax:* (06) 855 27 56 *E-mail:* astrolabio.gana@alphacomm.it, pg 377

Astrolog Publishing House (Israel) *Tel:* (09) 7412044 *Fax:* (09) 7442714, pg 365

AT Verlag (Switzerland) *Tel:* (062) 836 6666 *Fax:* (062) 836 6667 *E-mail:* info.buchverlag@azag.ch *Web Site:* www.at-verlag.ch, pg 608

Editrice Atanor SRL (Italy) *Tel:* (06) 7024595 *Fax:* (06) 7014422, pg 377

Ataturk Kultur, Dil ve Tarih, Yusek Kurumu Baskanligi (Turkey) *Tel:* (0312) 4286100, pg 639

Ataturk Universitesi (Turkey) *Tel:* (0442) 2343677; (0442) 2184172 *Fax:* (0442) 17140, pg 639

Les Editions de l'Atelier SA (France) *Tel:* (01) 44089515 *Fax:* (01) 44089500, pg 148

Verlag Atelier im Bauernhaus (Germany) *Tel:* (04293) 491; (04293) 493 *Fax:* (04293) 1238, pg 196

Atelier Books (United Kingdom) *Tel:* (0131) 5574050 *Fax:* (0131) 5578382 *E-mail:* mail@bournefineart.co.uk *Web Site:* www.bournefineart.co.uk/books.html, pg 650

Atelier, L (Egypt (Arab Republic of Egypt)) *Tel:* (03) 4820526 *Fax:* (03) 4837662, pg 1362

Atelier National de Reproduction des Theses (France) *Tel:* (03) 20 30 86 73 *Fax:* (03) 20 54 21 95 *E-mail:* anrt@univ-lille3.fr, pg 148

Atelier Publishing Co Ltd (Japan) *Tel:* (03) 33572741 *Fax:* (03) 33572194, pg 414

Atelier Verlag Andernach (AVA) (Germany) *Tel:* (02632) 44432 *Fax:* (02632) 31383, pg 196

Editura si Atelierele Tipografice Metropol SRL (Romania) *Tel:* (01) 2104593; (01) 2108433 *Fax:* (01) 2106987, pg 1138

Les Ateliers d'Orion (France) *Tel:* (04) 66 21 87 02 *Fax:* (04) 66 21 85 39, pg 148

Ateliers et Presses de Taize (France) *Tel:* 3 85 50 30 30 *Fax:* 3 85 50 30 15 *E-mail:* rencontres@taize.fr *Web Site:* www.taize.fr, pg 148

Atena (Poland) *Tel:* (061) 228685 *Fax:* (061) 524082 *E-mail:* atena@poz1.commet.pl, pg 516

Atena Kustannus Oy (Finland) *Tel:* (014) 620192 *Fax:* (014) 620190, pg 142

Sociedad de Educacion Atenas SA (Spain) *Tel:* (091) 5480127 *Fax:* (091) 5591771, pg 564

Ateneo Cientifico, Literario y Artistico (Spain) *Tel:* (01) 4296251, pg 1368

Ateneo Cientifico, Literario y Artistico (Spain) *Tel:* (071) 360553, pg 1368

Editorial Ateneo de Caracas (Venezuela) *Tel:* (02) 5734622 (ext 33); (02) 5754475 (orders); (02) 5734400; (02) 5734600 *Fax:* (02) 5754475, pg 762

Ateneo de Manila University Press (Philippines) *Tel:* (02) 4265984; (02) 4261238 *Fax:* (02) 4265909 *E-mail:* unipress@pusit.admu.edu.ph (business/operations), pg 512

Ateneo Puertorriqueno (Puerto Rico) *Tel:* (787) 721-3877 *Fax:* (787) 725-3873, pg 1257

Athena Press (Australia) *Tel:* (02) 9357-3720 *Fax:* (02) 9357-3720, pg 12

Athenaeum Boekhandel (Netherlands) *Tel:* (020) 6226248 *Fax:* (020) 6384901 *E-mail:* info@athenaeum.nl *Web Site:* www.athenaeum.nl, pg 1301

Athenaeum Verlag AG (Switzerland) *Tel:* (091) 571536, pg 608

Editora Atheneu Ltda (Brazil) *Tel:* (011) 220-9186 *Fax:* (011) 221-3389 *E-mail:* atheneau@nutecnet.com.br *Web Site:* www.atheneu.com.br, pg 79

Atheneum Forlag A/S (Norway) *Tel:* 64978000 *Fax:* 64978001, pg 502

Athens Academy Library (Greece) *Tel:* (01) 3600209, pg 1470

Athesia Buchhandlung (Italy) *Tel:* (0471) 925203 *Fax:* (0471) 925229, pg 1293

Verlagsanstalt Athesia (Italy) *Tel:* (0471) 925203 *Fax:* (0471) 925207, pg 377

Athina (Greece) *Tel:* (01) 3821308 *Fax:* (01) 3807220, pg 1286

Athina, Mary Mavrogiannis (Greece) *Tel:* (01) 3821308; (01) 3807220 *Fax:* (01) 3838228, pg 309

The Athlone Press Ltd (United Kingdom) *Tel:* (020) 8458 0888 *Fax:* (020) 8201 8115 *E-mail:* athlonepress@btinternet.com *Web Site:* www.transcomm.ox.ac.uk/wwwroot/athlone_press.htm, pg 650

Editora Atica SA (Brazil) *Tel:* (011) 278 93 22 *Fax:* (011) 277 41 46, pg 79

Atica, SA Editores e Livreiros (Portugal) *Tel:* (021) 8153220 *Fax:* (021) 8153219, pg 522

Atlantic Transport Publishers (United Kingdom) *Tel:* (01326) 373656 *Fax:* (01326) 378309; (01326) 373656, pg 650

Atlantica Editrice SARL (Italy), pg 377

Editorial Atlantida SA (Argentina) *Tel:* (011) 4331-4591; (011) 4331-4599 *Fax:* (011) 3313341 *Web Site:* www.atlantida.com.ar, pg 3

Atlantis M Pechlivanides & Co SA (Greece) *Tel:* (01) 9220071 *Fax:* (01) 9247341, pg 309

Atlantis Musikbuch (Germany) *Tel:* (06131) 246-0 *Fax:* (06131) 246-211, pg 196

Atlantis sro (Czech Republic) *Tel:* (05) 42213552 *Fax:* (05) 42214425, pg 123

Atlantis-Verlag AG (Switzerland) *Tel:* (010) 2622717 *Fax:* (01) 2512615, pg 608

Atlantisz Kiado (Hungary) *Tel:* (01) 2663870 *Fax:* (01) 2663870 *E-mail:* atlantis@budapest.hu, pg 323

Atlas (Greece) *Tel:* (01) 3627342 *Fax:* (01) 3300257, pg 309

Editions Atlas (France) *Tel:* (01) 40 74 38 38 *Fax:* (01) 49 53 07 25 *E-mail:* contact@editionsatlas.fr *Web Site:* www.editionsatlas.fr, pg 148

Editora Atlas SA (Brazil) *Tel:* (011) 221 9144 *Fax:* (011) 220 7830 *E-mail:* edatlas@editora-atlas.com.br *Web Site:* www.edatlas.com.br, pg 79

Atlas Press (United Kingdom) *Tel:* (020) 7490 8742 *Fax:* (021) 7490 8742 *E-mail:* atlaspress@compuserve.com *Web Site:* www.atlaspress.co.uk, pg 651

Atma Ram & Sons (India) *Tel:* (011) 2523082; (011) 2946466 *E-mail:* yogesh2@ndf.vsnl.net.in, pg 331

Atma Ram & Sons (India) *Tel:* (011) 2523082, pg 1288

ATP - Packager (France) *Tel:* (0473) 19 58 80 *Fax:* (0473) 195899 *E-mail:* atp.chamalieres@wanadoo.fr, pg 149

Ediciones Atril (Spain) *Tel:* (091) 6911000 *Fax:* (091) 6916380, pg 564

Atrium Verlag AG (Switzerland) *Tel:* (01) 2613035; (01) 473035 *Fax:* (01) 2615436, pg 609

Attic Press Ltd (Ireland) *Tel:* (021) 4321 725 *Fax:* (021) 315 329 *E-mail:* atticirl@iol.ie *Web Site:* www.iol.ie/~atticirl/, pg 358

Atuakkiorfik A/S Det Greenland Publishers (Denmark) *Tel:* 322122 *Fax:* 322500 *E-mail:* henri@atuakkiorfik.gl *Web Site:* www.atuakkiorfik.gl, pg 130

Scoop/Au Vent des Iles (French Polynesia) *Tel:* (689) 43 54 56 *Fax:* (689) 42 61 74 *E-mail:* contact@tahiti-books.com *Web Site:* www.tahiti-books.com, pg 190

Aubanel SA (France) *Tel:* (01) 40515200; (01) 40515205, pg 149

Editions de l'Aube (France) *Tel:* (04) 90 07 46 60 *Fax:* (04) 90 07 53 02, pg 149

Editions Aubier-Montaigne SA (France) *Tel:* (01) 40 51 31 00 *Fax:* (01) 43 29 21 48, pg 149

Auckland City Libraries (New Zealand) *Tel:* (09) 3770209 *Fax:* (09) 3077741, pg 1487

Auckland University Press (New Zealand) *Tel:* (09) 373 7528 *Fax:* (09) 373 7465 *E-mail:* aup@auckland.ac.nz *Web Site:* www.auckland.ac.nz/aup/, pg 488

Audio Visual Centre Ltd (Malta) *Tel:* 330886 *Fax:* 339840, pg 1299

Audivox (Belgium) *Tel:* (03) 4701784, pg 1276

AUE-Verlag GmbH (Germany) *Tel:* (06298) 1328 *Fax:* (06298) 4298 *E-mail:* aue-verlag@web.de *Web Site:* www.aue-verlag.com, pg 196

Ludwig Auer GmbH (Germany) *Tel:* (0906) 730 *Fax:* (0906) 73177, pg 1133

Auer Verlag GmbH (Germany) *Tel:* (0906) 730 *Fax:* (0906) 73177; (0906) 73178 *E-mail:* info@auer-verlag.de *Web Site:* www.auer-verlag.de, pg 196

Aufbau Taschenbuch Verlag GmbH (Germany) *Tel:* (030) 283 94-0 *Fax:* (030) 283 94 100 *E-mail:* info@aufbau-verlag.de *Web Site:* www.aufbau-verlag.de, pg 196

Aufbau-Verlag GmbH (Germany) *Tel:* (030) 28 394-0 *Fax:* (030) 28 394-100 *E-mail:* info@aufbau-verlag.de *Web Site:* www2.aufbauverlag.de, pg 196

Aufstieg-Verlag GmbH (Germany) *Tel:* (0871) 54112 *Fax:* (0871) 54112 *Web Site:* www.aufstieg-verlag.de, pg 196

August Guse Verlag GmbH (Germany) *Tel:* (06039) 480110 *Fax:* (06039) 480148 *E-mail:* info@guese.de *Web Site:* www.guese.de, pg 196

J J Augustin GmbH Verlag (Germany) *Tel:* (04124) 20442046 *Fax:* (04124) 4709, pg 196

Augustin-Verlag (Switzerland) *Tel:* (052) 649 31 31 *Fax:* (052) 649 31 94 *E-mail:* augustin@augustin.ch, pg 609

Augustinus-Verlag Wurzburg Inh Augustinerprovinz (Germany) *Tel:* (0931) 3097400 *Fax:* (0931) 3097401 *Web Site:* www.augustiner.de, pg 196

Augustus Verlag (Germany) *Tel:* (0821) 7004-700 *Fax:* (0821) 7004-179 *Web Site:* www.droemer-weltbild.de, pg 196

Editions d'Aujourd'hui (Les Introuvables) (France) *Tel:* (01) 43547910 *Fax:* (01) 43298620, pg 149

Aulis Publishers (United Kingdom) *Tel:* (01373) 451 777 *Fax:* (01373) 452 888 *E-mail:* info@aulis.com *Web Site:* www.aulis.com, pg 651

Aulis Verlag Deubner & Co KG (Germany) *Tel:* (0221) 9514540 *Fax:* (0221) 518443, pg 197

AULOS sro (Czech Republic) *Tel:* (02) 536863 *Fax:* (02) 90004536 *E-mail:* aulos@volny.cz, pg 123

Aurelia Books PVBA (Belgium) *Tel:* (091) 82 55 82 *Fax:* (091) 82 72 47, pg 64

Auroa (Indonesia) *Tel:* (021) 5810413, pg 354

Aurora (Czech Republic) *Tel:* (02) 24 21 43 26 *Fax:* (02) 24 21 43 26 *E-mail:* aurora@aurora-books.cz *Web Site:* www.aurora-books.cz, pg 123

Aurora Art Publishers (Russian Federation) *Tel:* (0812) 3123753 *Fax:* (0812) 3125460, pg 537

Aurora Semanario Israeli de Actualidad (Israel) *Tel:* (03) 5462785; (03) 5463297 *Fax:* (03) 5625082 *E-mail:* aurorail@netvision.net.il, pg 365

Aurum Press Ltd (United Kingdom) *Tel:* (020) 7637 3225 *Fax:* (020) 7580 2469 *Web Site:* www.aurumpress.co.uk/top2.htm, pg 651

Aurum Verlag GmbH (Germany) *Tel:* (0531) 708790 *Fax:* (0531) 708706 *E-mail:* westermann_wsv@bs.magicvillage.de, pg 197

Auslib Press Pty Ltd (Australia) *Tel:* (08) 8278 4363 *Fax:* (08) 8278 4000 *E-mail:* info@auslib.com.au *Web Site:* www.auslib.com.au, pg 12

Ausmed Publications Pty Ltd (Australia) *Tel:* (03) 9375-7311 *Fax:* (03) 9375-7299 *E-mail:* ausmed@ausmed.com.au *Web Site:* www.ausmed.com.au, pg 12

Aussaat Verlag (Germany) *Tel:* (02845) 392234 *Fax:* (02845) 392250 *E-mail:* info@neukirchener-verlag.de *Web Site:* www.aussaat-verlag.de, pg 197

Aussie Books (Australia) *Tel:* (07) 3345 4253 *Fax:* (07) 3344 1582 *E-mail:* sildale@yahoo.com *Web Site:* www.treasureenterprises.com, pg 12

Aussies Afire Publishing (Australia) *Tel:* (02) 6581 0654 *Fax:* (02) 6581 0745 *Web Site:* www.gracechurchpm.org.au, pg 13

Austed Publishing Co (Australia) *Tel:* (08) 9388 8099 *Fax:* (08) 9245 8247 *E-mail:* netquery@austed.com.au, pg 13

Jane Austen Memorial Trust (United Kingdom) *Tel:* (01420) 83262 *Fax:* (01420) 83262, pg 1369

Austicks Headrow Bookshop (United Kingdom) *Tel:* (0113) 2433099, pg 1316

Austin's Book Services (Guyana) *Tel:* (02) 77395 *Fax:* (02) 77396 *E-mail:* austins@guyana.net.gy, pg 1287

Australasian Association for Lexicography (Australia) *Tel:* (07) 5595-2502 *Fax:* (07) 5595-2545 *E-mail:* bill_krebs@bond.edu.au *Web Site:* www.anu.edu.au/linguistics/alex/, pg 1359

Australasian Medical Publishing Company Ltd (AMPCO) (Australia) *Tel:* (02) 9562 6666 *Fax:* (02) 9562 6600 *E-mail:* ampco@ampco.com.au *Web Site:* www.ampco.com.au, pg 13

Australasian Textiles Publishers (Australia) *Tel:* (03) 5255 5500 *Fax:* (03) 5256 1668 *Web Site:* www.atfmag.com, pg 13

Australia Council Literature Board (Australia) *Tel:* (02) 9215 9000 *Fax:* (02) 9215 9111, pg 1235

Australian Academic Press Pty Ltd (Australia) *Tel:* (07) 3257 1176 *Fax:* (07) 3252 5908 *E-mail:* info@australianacademicpress.com.au *Web Site:* www.australianacademicpress.com.au, pg 13

Australian Academy of Science (Australia) *Tel:* (02) 6247 5777 *Fax:* (02) 6257 4620 *E-mail:* aas@science.org.au *Web Site:* www.science.org.au, pg 13

The Australian & New Zealand Association of Antiquarian Booksellers (Australia) *Tel:* (0618) 9386 6103 *E-mail:* admin@anzaab.com *Web Site:* www.anzaab.com.au, pg 1235

Australian Book Collector (Australia) *Tel:* (02) 6778 4682 *Fax:* (02) 6778 4516 *Web Site:* www.ozbook.com, pg 1272

Australian Booksellers Association Inc (Australia) *Tel:* (03) 96637888 *Fax:* (03) 96637557, pg 1235

Australian Broadcasting Authority (Australia) *Tel:* (02) 9344 7700 *Toll Free Tel:* 800 22 6667 *Fax:* (02) 9334 7799; (02) 93447700 *E-mail:* info@aba.gov.au *Web Site:* www.aba.gov.au, pg 13

Australian Chart Book Pty Ltd (Australia) *Tel:* (02) 9489 4786 *Fax:* (02) 9487 2089 *E-mail:* davidkent@austchartbook.com.au *Web Site:* www.austchartbook.com.au, pg 13

Australian Copyright Council (Australia) *Tel:* (02) 9318 1788 *Fax:* (02) 9698 3536, pg 1236

The Australian Council for Educational Research Ltd (Australia) *Tel:* (03) 9277 5555 *Fax:* (03) 9277 5500, pg 13

Australian Film Television & Radio School (Australia) *Tel:* (02) 9805-6611 *Fax:* (02) 9887-1030 *E-mail:* info_nsw@aftrs.edu.au *Web Site:* www.aftrs.edu.au, pg 13

Australian Government Bookshops (Australia) *Tel:* (062) 954031 *Fax:* (062) 954888 *Web Site:* www.agps.gov.au, pg 1272

Australian Government Publishing Service (Australia) *Tel:* (062) 62954031 *Fax:* (062) 62954888 *Web Site:* www.agps.gov.au, pg 13

Australian Institute of Criminology (Australia) *Tel:* (02) 6260 9200 *Fax:* (02) 6260 9201 *E-mail:* aicpress@aic.gov.au *Web Site:* www.aic.gov.au, pg 13

Australian Institute of Family Studies (AIFS) (Australia) *Tel:* (03) 9214 7888 *Fax:* (03) 9214 7839 *Web Site:* www.aifs.org.au, pg 13

Australian Large Print Pty Ltd (Australia) *Tel:* (03) 3380666 *Fax:* (03) 3380975 *E-mail:* alpav@tpgl.com.au, pg 14

Australian Law Librarians' Group, Inc (Australia) *Tel:* (02) 9422 2335 *Fax:* (02) 9422 2417 *Web Site:* www.allg.asn.au, pg 1511

Australian Library and Information Association (Australia) *Tel:* (02) 62851877 *Fax:* (02) 62822249 *E-mail:* enquiry@alia.org.au, pg 1511

Australian Library Publishers' Society (Australia) *Tel:* (08) 8303 5370 *Fax:* (08) 8303 4369 *Web Site:* www.library.adelaide.edu.au/ual/publ/alps/, pg 1359

Australian Marine Conservation Society Inc (AMCS) (Australia) *Tel:* (07) 3848 5235 *Toll Free Tel:* 800 066 299 *Fax:* (07) 3892 5814 *E-mail:* amcs@amcs.org.au *Web Site:* www.amcs.org.au, pg 14

Australian National University Library (Australia) *Tel:* (02) 6125 2003 *Fax:* (02) 6125 0058, pg 1450

Australian Press Council (Australia) *Tel:* (02) 2611930 *Fax:* (02) 2676826, pg 1236

Australian Publishers Association Ltd (Australia) *Tel:* (02) 9281 9788 *Fax:* (02) 9281 1073 *E-mail:* apa@publishers.asn.au *Web Site:* www.publishers.asn.au, pg 1236

Australian Scholarly Publishing (Australia) *Tel:* (03) 8175208 *Fax:* (03) 8176431 *E-mail:* aspic@ozemail.com.au, pg 14

Australian Society of Archivists (Australia) *Tel:* (07) 38758742 *Fax:* (07) 38758764 *E-mail:* shicks@gil.com.au; asa@asap.unimelb.edu.au *Web Site:* www.archives.qld.gov.au; www.archivenet.gov.au/asa/asa, pg 1511

The Australian Society of Authors Ltd (Australia) *Tel:* (02) 93180877 *Fax:* (02) 93180530 *E-mail:* asa@asauthors.org, pg 1236, 1359

Australian Society of Indexers (Australia) *Tel:* (0500) 525005; (02) 94383729 *Fax:* (02) 98882229 *E-mail:* secretary@aussi.org *Web Site:* www.aussi.org, pg 1236

Australian Writers' Guild Ltd (Australia) *Tel:* (02) 93577888 *Fax:* (02) 93577776 *E-mail:* awgsyd@ozemail.com.au *Web Site:* www.ozemail.com.au/~awgsyd/index.htm/, pg 1359

Authors' Club (United Kingdom) *Tel:* (020) 7499 8581 *Fax:* (020) 7409 0913, pg 1369

Authors' Licensing & Collecting Society (United Kingdom) *Tel:* (020) 7395 0600 *Fax:* (020) 7395 0660 *E-mail:* alcs@alcs.co.uk, pg 1264

Authors Press (India) *Tel:* (011) 2436299; (011) 2460145 *Fax:* (011) 2460145 *E-mail:* authorspress@yahoo.com, pg 331

Automobilia srl (Italy) *Tel:* (02) 48021671 *Fax:* (02) 48194968, pg 377

Bundesverband junger Autoren und Autorinnen eV (Germany) *Tel:* (22258) 7889 *Fax:* (2225) 7889 *E-mail:* bvjaa@t-online.de *Web Site:* www.bvja-online.de, pg 1363

Verlag der Autoren GmbH & Co KG (Germany) *Tel:* (069) 2385740 *Fax:* (069) 24277644 *E-mail:* buch@verlag-der-autoren.de *Web Site:* www.verlag-der-autoren.de, pg 197

Autorensolidaritat - Verlag der Interessengemeinschaft osterreichischer Autorinnen und Autoren (Austria) *Tel:* (01) 526 20 44-13 *Fax:* (01) 526 20 44-55 *E-mail:* ig@literaturhaus.at, pg 49

Biblioteca de Autores Cristianos (Spain) *Tel:* (091) 3090862; (091) 3090973 *Fax:* (091) 3091980 *E-mail:* bacventas@planalfa.es, pg 564

Autovision Verlag Guther Co (Germany) *Tel:* (040) 810327 *Fax:* (040) 87932995, pg 197

Autrement Editions (France) *Tel:* (01) 40260606 *Fax:* (01) 40260026 *E-mail:* contact@autrement.com *Web Site:* www.autrement.com, pg 149

Autres Temps (France) *Tel:* (0491) 26 80 33 *Fax:* (0491) 41 11 01, pg 149

Autumn Publishing Ltd (United Kingdom) *Tel:* (01243) 531660 *Fax:* (01243) 774433 *Web Site:* www.autumnpublishing.co.uk, pg 651

Editions Philippe Auzou (France) *Tel:* (01) 40338400 *Fax:* (01) 47972008, pg 149

AV Studio Reklamno-vydavatel 'ska agentura (Slovakia) *Tel:* (07) 726297 *Fax:* (07) 726297, pg 549

AVA-Autoren- und Verlags-Agentur GmbH (Germany) *Tel:* (08152) 925883 *Fax:* (08152) 3076 *E-mail:* avagmbh@aol.com, pg 1111

AVACO - Christian Mass Communications Center (Japan) *Tel:* (03) 32034121 *Fax:* (03) 32034186 *E-mail:* avaco@ppp.fastnet.or.jp, pg 414

Editions l'Avant-Scene de Prette Technique (France) *Tel:* (01) 46342820 *Fax:* (01) 43545014, pg 149

Editorial Avante SA de Cv (Mexico) *Tel:* (05) 5855400 *Fax:* (05) 5855298, pg 458

Editorial 'Avante!' (Portugal) *Tel:* (021) 8429836 *Fax:* (021) 8429849, pg 522

Aventinum Nakladatelstvi (Czech Republic) *Tel:* (02) 4021907; (02) 4019069; (02) 40193056 *Fax:* (02) 4018534 *Web Site:* www.piscia.comp.cz/knihy/kni-aq09_cz.htm, pg 123

NV Uitgeverij Altiora Averbode (Belgium) *Tel:* (013) 780141 *Fax:* (013) 773311 *E-mail:* averbode.publ@verbode.be, pg 64

Averbode Publishers (Belgium) *Tel:* (013) 780111 *Fax:* (013) 780183; (013) 780179 *E-mail:* averbode.publ@verbode.be *Web Site:* www.averbode.com, pg 64

Avero Publications Ltd (United Kingdom) *Tel:* (0191) 2615790 *Fax:* (0191) 2611209 *E-mail:* nstc@newcastle.ac.uk, pg 651

Avgvstinvs (Spain) *Tel:* (091) 5342070 *Fax:* (091) 5544801 *E-mail:* revista@avgvstinvs.org *Web Site:* www.avgvstinvs.org, pg 564

Aviani Editore (Italy) *Tel:* (0432) 46478 *Fax:* (0432) 43420, pg 377

Aviatic Verlag GmbH (Germany) *Tel:* (089) 613890-0 *Fax:* (089) 613890-10 *E-mail:* aviatic@t-online.de *Web Site:* www.aviatic.de, pg 197

Aviation Industry Press (China) *Tel:* (010) 4221690 *Fax:* (010) 4221696, pg 102

Avicenne Librairie Internationale (Syrian Arab Republic) *Tel:* (011) 2212911; (011) 2244477 *Fax:* (011) 2219833 *E-mail:* avicenne@net.sy, pg 1313

Monte Avila Editores Latinoamericana CA (Venezuela) *Tel:* (02) 2659871 *Fax:* (02) 2667226; (02) 2659871 *E-mail:* alemar@telcel.net.ve, pg 762

Avinash Reference Publications (India) *Tel:* (0231) 21024 *Fax:* (0231) 27262, pg 331

AvivA Britta Jurgs GmbH (Germany) *Tel:* (030) 39731372 *Fax:* (030) 39731371 *E-mail:* aviva@txt.de *Web Site:* www.aviva-verlag.de, pg 197

Avoca Publications (Ireland) *Tel:* (01) 889218, pg 358

Avots (Latvia) *Tel:* (02) 7225824; (02) 7211394 *Fax:* (02) 7225824, pg 441

Award Publications Ltd (United Kingdom) *Tel:* (020) 7388 7800 *Fax:* (020) 7388 7887 *E-mail:* info@award.abel.co.uk, pg 651

Al-Awqaf (Iraq) *Tel:* (01) 4169362 *Fax:* (01) 4167790, pg 1475

AWT World Trade (United States) *Tel:* 773-777-7100 *Fax:* 773-777-0909 *E-mail:* sale@awt-gpi.com *Web Site:* www.awt-gpi.com, pg 1224

Axel Juncker Verlag Jacobi KG (Germany) *Tel:* (089) 360960 *Fax:* (089) 36096222, pg 197

Axicon Auto ID Ltd (United Kingdom) *Tel:* (01869) 351166 *Fax:* (01869) 351205 *E-mail:* sales@axicon.com *Web Site:* www.axicon.com, pg 1160

Axiom Publishers & Distributors (Australia) *Tel:* (08) 83627052 *E-mail:* axiompub@camtech.net.au, pg 14

Axiotelis G (Greece) *Tel:* (01) 3610091; (01) 3618247 *Fax:* (01) 3610887, pg 309

Biblioteca Ayacucho (Venezuela) *Tel:* (02) 5644402; (02) 5643583 *Fax:* (02) 5634223, pg 762

Ayalga Ediciones SA (Spain) *Tel:* (085) 5500599; (085) 501299 *Fax:* (085) 5500869, pg 564

Al-Ayam Press Co Ltd (Sudan), pg 598

Aydin Yayincilik (Turkey) *Tel:* (0427) 2506; (0427) 3850042 *Fax:* (0385) 3923; (0385) 2853925, pg 639

Editorial Ayuso (Spain) *Tel:* (091) 2228080, pg 564

AZ Bertelsmann Direct GmbH (Germany) *Tel:* (05241) 805046 *Fax:* (05241) 809336 *E-mail:* az@bertelsmann.de *Web Site:* www.az.bertelsmann.de, pg 197

AZ Editora SA (Argentina) *Tel:* (011) 4961-4036; (011) 4961-4037; (011) 4961-4038; (011) 4961-0088 *Fax:* (011) 4961-0089 *E-mail:* promocion@azeditora.com.ar, pg 3

AZernesr (Azerbaijan) *Tel:* (012) 925015, pg 61

Al- Azhar University Library (Egypt (Arab Republic of Egypt)) *Tel:* (02) 904051; (02) 706097, pg 1462

La Azotea Editorial Fotografica SRL (Argentina) *Tel:* (011) 4811-0931 *Fax:* (011) 4811-0931 *E-mail:* azotea@laazotea.com.ar *Web Site:* www.laazotea.com, pg 4

Editorial Azteca SA (Mexico) *Tel:* (05) 5261157, pg 458

B & B (Republic of Korea) *Tel:* (02) 540-4425 *Fax:* (02) 517-8793, pg 434

B & B Verlag Anita und Klaus Buscher (Germany) *Tel:* (06321) 968485 *Fax:* (06321) 968486, pg 197

Ediciones B, SA (Spain) *Tel:* (093) 484 66 00 *Fax:* (093) 232 46 60 *Web Site:* www.edicionesb.es; www.edicionesb.com, pg 565

B I Publications Pvt Ltd (India) *Tel:* (011) 3274443; (011) 3259352; (011) 3255118 *Fax:* (011) 3261290 *E-mail:* bigroup@del3.vsnl.net.in, pg 331

B M Israel BV (Netherlands) *Tel:* (020) 6247040 *Fax:* (020) 6382355 *E-mail:* bmisrael@xs4all.nl *Web Site:* www.nvva/israelbm, pg 473

b small publishing (United Kingdom) *Tel:* (020) 8974 6851 *Fax:* (020) 8974 6845 *E-mail:* info@bsmall.co.uk *Web Site:* homepage.ntlworld.com/codework/welcome.htm, pg 651

Ba-reunsa Publishing Co (Republic of Korea) *Tel:* (02) 5123217 *Fax:* (02) 5463217, pg 434

Auteursbureau Greta Baars-Jelgersma (Netherlands) *Tel:* (024) 6963336 *Fax:* (024) 6963293 *Web Site:* home.hetnet.nl/~jelgersma696, pg 1114

Bernard Babani (Publishing) Ltd (United Kingdom) *Tel:* (020) 7603 2581; (020) 7603 7296 *Fax:* (020) 7603 8203 *E-mail:* enquiries@babanibooks.com *Web Site:* www.babanibooks.com, pg 651

Babel Verlag Kevin Perryman (Germany) *Tel:* (08243) 961691 *Fax:* (08243) 961614 *E-mail:* info@babel-verlag.de *Web Site:* www.babel-verlag.de, pg 197

Baberu Inc (Japan) *Tel:* (03) 32952306 *Fax:* (03) 32957128, pg 414

Babtext Nakladatelska Spolecnost (Czech Republic) *Tel:* (02) 435 992 *Fax:* (02) 768992; (02) 61221868, pg 123

Joan Bacchus-Xavier (Trinidad & Tobago) *Tel:* 6225588 *Fax:* 6251330, pg 636

Bacharakis (Greece) *Tel:* (031) 263776 *Fax:* (031) 263776, pg 1286

J P Bachem Verlag GmbH (Germany) *Tel:* (0221) 1619-0 *Fax:* (0221) 1619159; (0221) 1619231 (Vertrieb) *E-mail:* info@bachem-verlag.de *Web Site:* www.bachem-verlag.de, pg 197

Dr Bachmaier Verlag GmbH (Germany) *Tel:* (089) 685120; (089) 68008255 *Fax:* (089) 685120; (089) 68008255 *E-mail:* contact@verlag-drbachmaier.de *Web Site:* www.verlag-drbachmaier.de, pg 197

Backhuys Publishers BV (Netherlands) *Tel:* (071) 5170208 *Fax:* (071) 5171856 *E-mail:* backhuys@backhuys.com *Web Site:* www.backhuys.com, pg 473

Francis Bacon Society Inc (United Kingdom), pg 1369

Editions de la Baconniere SA (Switzerland) *Tel:* (022) 8690017 *Fax:* (022) 8690015 *E-mail:* DEB@medecinehygiene.ch, pg 609

Badan Bookstore Sdn Bhd (Malaysia) *Tel:* (07) 2377562; (07) 2330241; (07) 330241, pg 1298

Badan Penerbit Kristen Gunung Mulia (Indonesia) *Tel:* (021) 3901208 *Fax:* (021) 3901633 *E-mail:* trade@bpkgm.com *Web Site:* www.bpkgm.com, pg 354

Badenia Verlag und Druckerei GmbH (Germany) *Tel:* (0721) 95450 *Fax:* (0721) 9545125 *E-mail:* verlag@badeniaverlag.de *Web Site:* www.badeniaverlag.badeniaonline.de, pg 197

Badische Landesbibliothek (Germany) *Tel:* (0721) 1752001 *Fax:* (0721) 1752333 *E-mail:* sekretariat@blb-karlsruhe.de; infozentrum@blb-karlsruhe.de *Web Site:* www.blb-karlsruhe.de, pg 1466

Badischer Landwirtschafts-Verlag GmbH (Germany) *Tel:* (0761) 2713342 *Fax:* (0761) 2021887 *E-mail:* redaktion@blv-freiburg.de, pg 197

Buchhandlung G D Baedeker (Germany) *Tel:* (0201) 20680 *Fax:* (0201) 2068-100, pg 1283

U Baer Verlag (Switzerland) *Tel:* (01) 3835500 *Fax:* (01) 3836883, pg 609

Barenreiter Verlag Basel AG (Switzerland) *Tel:* (061) 395898; (061) 395899 *Fax:* (061) 3079660 *E-mail:* baerenreiter_ch@compuserve.com *Web Site:* www.baerenreiter.com, pg 609

Buchhandlung Baeschlin (Switzerland) *Tel:* (058) 611126, pg 609

K P Bagchi & Co (India) *Tel:* (033) 267474; (033) 269496 *Fax:* (033) 2482973, pg 332

Baha'i (Italy) *Tel:* (06) 9334334 *Fax:* (06) 9334335, pg 377

Baha'i Publishing Trust (United Kingdom) *Tel:* (01572) 722780 *Fax:* (01572) 724280 *E-mail:* sales@bahaibooks.co.uk *Web Site:* www.bahai-publishing-trust.co.uk, pg 651

Baha'i Publishing Trust of India (India) *Tel:* (011) 6818990; (011) 6819391 *Fax:* (011) 6812703 *E-mail:* bptindia@del3.vsnl.net.in; publisher@bahaindia.org *Web Site:* www.bahaindia.org, pg 332

Baha'i Verlag GmbH (Germany) *Tel:* (06192) 22921 *Fax:* (06192) 22936 *E-mail:* info@bahai-verlag.de *Web Site:* www.bahaipublishers.org, pg 198

Maison d'Editions Baha'ies ASBL (Belgium) *Tel:* (02) 647 07 49 *Fax:* (02) 646 21 77 *Web Site:* www.adeb.irisnet.be, pg 64

R G Bahnsen (Australia) *Tel:* (08) 2630670, pg 14

Bahnsport Aktuell Verlag GmbH (Germany) *Tel:* (06184) 923330; (06184) 923350, pg 198

Bahrain Centre for Studies, Research Library & Information Dept (Bahrain) *Tel:* 754757 *Fax:* 754678, pg 1452

Bahrain Writers & Literators Association (Bahrain), pg 1360

Baifukan Co Ltd (Japan) *Tel:* (03) 32625270 *Fax:* (03) 32625276, pg 414

Baile del Sol, Colectivo Cultural (Spain) *Tel:* (0922) 54-53-45 *E-mail:* bailesol@idecnet.com; bailesol@club.idecnet.com; bailesol@teleline.es, pg 565

Bailey Distribution Ltd (United Kingdom) *Tel:* (01797) 366905 *Fax:* (01797) 366638, pg 1316

Bill Bailey Publishers' Representatives (United Kingdom) *Tel:* (01626) 331079 *Fax:* (01626) 331080 *E-mail:* billbailey.pubrep@eclipse.co.uk *Web Site:* www.healthpress.co.uk, pg 651

Bailey Brothers & Swinfen Ltd (United Kingdom) *Tel:* (01797) 366905 *Fax:* (01797) 366638, pg 651

Editions J B Bailliere (France) *Tel:* (01) 55 33 69 00 *Fax:* (01) 55 33 68 07, pg 149

Bailliere Tindall Limited (United Kingdom) *Tel:* (020) 7424 4200 *Fax:* (020) 7482 4752, pg 652

W & G Baird Ltd (United Kingdom) *Tel:* (018494) 63911 *Fax:* (018494) 66250, pg 1160

W & G Baird Ltd (United Kingdom) *Tel:* (018494) 63911 *Fax:* (018494) 66250 *E-mail:* wgbaird@wgbaird.com, pg 1202

Bakalar spol sro (Czech Republic) *Tel:* (019) 523197, pg 123

Baken-Verlag Walter Schnoor (Germany) *Tel:* (04822) 1671; (04192) 1784, pg 198

Bakermat NV (Belgium) *Tel:* (015) 42 05 08 *Fax:* (015) 42 05 73 *E-mail:* info@bakermat.com *Web Site:* www.bakermat.com, pg 65

Bakyoung Publishing Co (Republic of Korea) *Tel:* (02) 7336771; (02) 7336773 *Fax:* (02) 7364818, pg 434

Bal-eon (Republic of Korea) *Tel:* (02) 9293546; (02) 9293547 *Fax:* (02) 9293548, pg 434

Balai Pustaka (Indonesia) *Tel:* (021) 3447003; (021) 3447006; (021) 7650228; (021) 7650229 *Fax:* (021) 3446555; (021) 7650704 *E-mail:* mail@balaiperaga.com; pustakaperaga@lycos.com *Web Site:* www.balaiperaga.com, pg 354

Edition Balance Marion Gunther Bonsack (Germany) *Tel:* (03621) 750061 *Fax:* (0721) 151315156 *E-mail:* info@edition-balance.de, pg 198

Uitgeverij Balans (Netherlands) *Tel:* (020) 6268982 *Fax:* (020) 6223481 *E-mail:* balans@uitgeverijbalans.nl *Web Site:* www.uitgeverijbalans.nl, pg 473

Balassi Kiado Kft (Hungary) *Tel:* (01) 1755064; (01) 1162885 *E-mail:* balassi@mail.datanet.hu, pg 323

Carmen Balcells Agencia Literaria SA (Spain) *Tel:* (093) 2008933 *Fax:* (093) 2007041 *E-mail:* ag-balcells@ag-balcells.com, pg 1116

Editions Baleine (France) *Tel:* (01) 43724960 *Fax:* (01) 43728760, pg 149

Izdatelstvo na Balgarskata Akademija na Naukite (Bulgaria) *Tel:* (02) 720922; (02) 722466 *Fax:* (02) 700204, pg 94

A A Balkema (Netherlands) *Tel:* (010) 4145822 *Fax:* (010) 4135947 *E-mail:* orders@swets.nl *Web Site:* www.balkema.nl, pg 473

Jonathan Ball Publishers (South Africa) *Tel:* (011) 622-2900 *Fax:* (011) 622-7610, pg 552

Editions Balland (France) *Tel:* (01) 43 25 74 40 *Fax:* (01) 46 33 56 21, pg 149

Ballinakella Press (Ireland) *Tel:* (061) 927030 *Fax:* (061) 927418 *E-mail:* info@ballinakella.com, pg 358

H R Balmer AG Verlag (Switzerland) *Tel:* (042) 2144141; (042) 214735 *Fax:* (042) 210917, pg 609

H R Balmer AG Buchhandlung Verlag Verlagsauslieferung (Switzerland) *Tel:* (041) 711 47 37 *Fax:* (041) 711 09 17, pg 1313

Baltos Lankos (Lithuania) *Tel:* (02) 220126 *Fax:* (02) 220152 *E-mail:* baltos.lankos@post.omnitel.net, pg 445

Baltzer Science Publishers (Netherlands) *Tel:* (020) 471051 *Fax:* (020) 4710152 *E-mail:* publish@baltzer.nl *Web Site:* www.baltzer.nl, pg 474

Staatsbibliothek Bamberg (Germany) *Tel:* (0951) 54014 *Fax:* (0951) 54615, pg 1466

Editorial Banca y Comercio SA de CV (Mexico) *Tel:* (05) 5353587, pg 458

Bancaria Editrice SpA (Italy) *Tel:* (06) 6767391; (06) 6767392; (06) 6767393 *Fax:* (06) 6767397, pg 377

Bandansan (Thailand) *Tel:* (02) 825511, pg 635

Bandicoot Books (Australia) *Tel:* (03) 6267 1223 *Web Site:* www.bandicootbooks.com, pg 14

Bang Printing Co Inc (United States) *Tel:* 218-829-2877 *Fax:* 218-829-7145 *Web Site:* www.bangprinting.com, pg 1163, 1215

The Bangalore Printing & Publishing Co Ltd (India) *Tel:* (0812) 601638; (0812) 6601027 *Fax:* (0812) 6679279 *Web Site:* www.bangalorepress.com, pg 332

C Bange GmbH & Co KG (Germany) *Tel:* (09274) 94130 *Fax:* (09274) 94132 *E-mail:* service@bange-verlag.de *Web Site:* www.bange-verlag.de, pg 198

Bangladesh Publishers (Bangladesh) *Tel:* (02) 233135, pg 62

Bangladesh Books International Ltd (Bangladesh) *Tel:* (02) 232252 (ext 31); (02) 232229; (02) 256071 (ext 19), pg 1275

Bangladesh Central Public Library (Bangladesh) *Tel:* (02) 500819, pg 1452

Bangladesh Government Press, Ministry of Establishment, Government of the Peoples Republic of Bangladesh (Bangladesh) *Tel:* (02) 8122845 *Fax:* (02) 8113095 *E-mail:* adab@bdonline.com, pg 62

Bangladesh Institute of Development Studies Library (Bangladesh) *Tel:* (02) 9118999; (02) 813023, pg 1452

National Library of Bangladesh (Bangladesh) *Tel:* (02) 326572; (02) 312733; (02) 318704, pg 1452

National Library of Bangladesh (Bangladesh) *Tel:* (02) 326572; (02) 9118704 *Fax:* (02) 9118704, pg 1512

Bani Mandir, Book-Sellers, Publishers & Educational Suppliers (India) *Tel:* (0361) 540465; (0361) 520241; (0361) 30485, pg 332

Bank-Verlag GmbH (Germany) *Tel:* (0221) 54900 *Fax:* (0221) 5490120 *E-mail:* bank-verlag@bank-verlag.de *Web Site:* www.bank-verlag.de, pg 198

Bannakhan (Thailand) *Tel:* (02) 227796, pg 635

Bannakit Trading (Thailand) *Tel:* (02) 2825520; (02) 2827537; (02) 2814213 *Fax:* (02) 2820076, pg 635

The Banner of Truth Trust (United Kingdom) *Tel:* (0131) 337 7310 *Fax:* (0131) 346 7484 *E-mail:* info@bannetoftruth.co.uk *Web Site:* www.banneroftruth.co.uk, pg 652

Banson (United Kingdom) *Tel:* (020) 7729 7315; (020) 7613 1388 *Fax:* (020) 7729 7870 *E-mail:* banson@ourplanet.com, pg 652

BANYAN TREE BOOK DISTRIBUTORS   INDUSTRY

Banyan Tree Book Distributors (Australia) *Tel:* (08) 8363-4244 *Fax:* (08) 8363-4255 *E-mail:* enquiries@banyantreebooks.com.au, pg 1272

Bar Ilan University Central Library (Israel) *Tel:* (03) 5318486; (03) 5318357 *Fax:* (03) 5349233, pg 1476

Bar Ilan University Press (Israel) *Tel:* (03) 5318401; (03) 5318575 *Fax:* (03) 5353446 *E-mail:* press@mail.biu.ac.il *Web Site:* www.biu.ac.il/Press, pg 365

Editorial Barath SA (Spain) *Tel:* (091) 4496049, pg 565

Baraza la Kiswahili la Taifa (United Republic of Tanzania) *Tel:* (051) 23452; (051) 24139, pg 1128

Barbados National Trust (Barbados) *Tel:* 426-2421 *Fax:* 429-9055 *E-mail:* natrust@sunbeach.net, pg 1109

B McCall Barbour (United Kingdom) *Tel:* (0131) 2254816 *Fax:* (0131) 2254816, pg 1316

McCall Barbour (United Kingdom) *Tel:* (0131) 225-4816 *Fax:* (0131) 225-4816 *E-mail:* ashbethany43@hotmail.com, pg 652

Editorial Barcanova SA (Spain) *Tel:* (093) 2172054 *Fax:* (093) 2373469 *E-mail:* barcanova@barcanova.es *Web Site:* www.barcanova.es, pg 565

Editorial Barcino SA (Spain) *Tel:* (093) 2186888 *Fax:* (093) 2186888 *E-mail:* ebarcino@editorialbarcino.com *Web Site:* www.editorialbarcino.com, pg 565

Barcode Graphics Inc (Canada) *Tel:* 416-751-1474 *Fax:* 416-751-1575 *E-mail:* info@barcodegraphics.com *Web Site:* www.barcodegraphics.com, pg 1153

Hjalmar R Bardarson (Iceland) *Tel:* 5550729, pg 327

Bardi Editore srl (Italy) *Tel:* (06) 4817656 *Fax:* (06) 48912514 *E-mail:* bardied@tin.it *Web Site:* www.bardieditore.com, pg 377

Bardon-Chinese Media Agency (Taiwan, Province of China) *Tel:* (02) 23655753 *Fax:* (02) 23658148; (02) 23652615 *Web Site:* www.bardonchinese.com, pg 1117

Barenreiter-Verlag Karl-Votterle GmbH & Co KG (Germany) *Tel:* (0561) 31050 *Fax:* (0561) 3105176 *E-mail:* info@baerenreiter.com *Web Site:* www.baerenreiter.com, pg 198

Bargain Book Sales (United Kingdom) *Tel:* (020) 7385 7007 *Fax:* (020) 7385 7007, pg 1316

Bargezzi-Verlag AG (Switzerland) *Tel:* (031) 221380; (031) 211434 *Fax:* (031) 3113071, pg 609

Barkfire Press (New Zealand) *Tel:* (09) 3031039 *Fax:* (09) 3031059 *E-mail:* info@barkfire.com, pg 488

Barmarick Publications (United Kingdom) *Tel:* (01964) 630033 *Fax:* (01964) 631716 *E-mail:* hr24@dial.pipex.com, pg 652

Barn Dance Publications Ltd (United Kingdom) *Tel:* (020) 8657 2813 *Fax:* (020) 8651 6080 *E-mail:* barndance@pubs.co.uk *Web Site:* www.barndancepublications.co.uk, pg 652

Barnens Bokklubb (Sweden) *Tel:* (08) 4570300 *Fax:* (08) 4570331 *E-mail:* info@raben.se, pg 1232

Baronet (Czech Republic) *Tel:* (02) 74 77 18 06 (ext 31) *Fax:* (02) 74 77 38 70 *E-mail:* baronet.odbyt@volny.cz *Web Site:* www.baronet-knihy.cz; www.baronet.cz; www.knihy.de, pg 123

Barr Smith Press, University of Adelaide Library (Australia) *Tel:* (08) 8303 5370 *Fax:* (08) 8303 4369 *Web Site:* www.library.adelaide.edu.au, pg 1450

Barreiro y Ramos SA (Uruguay) *Tel:* (02) 986621 *Fax:* (02) 962358, (02 958283), pg 760

Barreiro y Ramos SA (Uruguay) *Tel:* (02) 986621 *Fax:* (02) 962358, pg 1146, 1167, 1208, 1217

Barreiro y Ramos SA (Uruguay) *Tel:* (02) 986621, pg 1225

Barreiro y Ramos SA (Uruguay) *Tel:* (02) 986621 *Fax:* (02) 962358, pg 1324

Barrister & Principal (Czech Republic) *Tel:* (05) 45211015 *Fax:* (05) 45210607 *E-mail:* barrister@barrister.cz, pg 123

La Bartavelle (France) *Tel:* 37821450 *Fax:* 37821463, pg 149

Verlag Dr Albert Bartens KG (Germany) *Tel:* (030) 8035678 *Fax:* (030) 8032049, pg 198

Johann Ambrosius Barth GmbH (Germany) *Tel:* (0341) 9929200 *Fax:* (0341) 9929209, pg 198

Otto Wilhelm Barth-Verlag KG (Germany) *Tel:* (089) 92170 *Fax:* (089) 9217168, pg 198

Editions A Barthelemy (France) *Tel:* (04) 90036000 *Fax:* (04) 90036009 *E-mail:* infos@editions-barthelemy.com *Web Site:* www.editions-barthelemy.com, pg 149

Bartkowiaks Forum Book Art (Germany) *Tel:* (040) 2793674 *Fax:* (040) 2704397 *E-mail:* 0402793674-1@t-online.de *Web Site:* www.forumbookart.com, pg 198

Bartleby & Co (Belgium) *Tel:* (02) 538 10 51 *E-mail:* bartleby@skynet.be, pg 65

Bartschi Publishing (Switzerland) *Tel:* 01 7373528, pg 609

BAS Printers Ltd (United Kingdom) *Tel:* (01264) 781711 *Fax:* (01264) 781116 *E-mail:* bas@basprint.co.uk *Web Site:* www.basprint.co.uk, pg 1139

BAS Printers Ltd (United Kingdom) *Tel:* (01264) 781711 *Fax:* (01264) 781116 *E-mail:* sales@basprint.co.uk *Web Site:* www.basprint.co.uk, pg 1160

BAS Printers Ltd (United Kingdom) *Tel:* (01264) 781711 *Fax:* (01264) 781116 *Web Site:* www.basprint.co.uk, pg 1202

Basam Books Oy (Finland) *Tel:* (09) 605391 *Fax:* (09) 4521261, pg 142

Baseball Magazine-Sha Co Ltd (Japan) *Tel:* (03) 32380285 *Fax:* (03) 32380084, pg 415

Baseline Creative Ltd (United Kingdom) *Tel:* (0117) 962 0006 *Fax:* (0117) 962 5006 *E-mail:* baseline@base.co.uk *Web Site:* www.base.co.uk, pg 1160

Bashir Bookshop (Sudan), pg 1312

Basica Editora (Portugal) *Tel:* (021) 779273, pg 522

Basileia Verlag (Switzerland) *Tel:* (061) 251766 *Fax:* (061) 2688321; (061) 232523, pg 609

Basilisken-Presse (Germany) *Tel:* 06421 15188, pg 198

Basilius Presse AG (Switzerland) *Tel:* (061) 228004; (061) 228005 *Fax:* (061) 232523, pg 609

BasisDruck Verlag GmbH (Germany) *Tel:* (030) 4457680 *Fax:* (030) 4459599 *E-mail:* basisdruck@planet-interkom.de *Web Site:* www.basisdruck.de, pg 198

Bassermann Verlag (Germany) *Tel:* (089) 43 72-0 *E-mail:* vertrieb.verlagsgruppe@bertelsmann.de *Web Site:* www.randomhouse.de/bassermann, pg 198

Bastei Luebbe Taschenbuecher (Germany) *Tel:* (02202) 121-0 *Fax:* (02202) 121-933 *E-mail:* info@luebbe.de *Web Site:* www.luebbe.de, pg 199

Bastei Verlag (Germany) *Tel:* (02202) 121-0 *Fax:* (02202) 121-936 *E-mail:* info@bastei.de *Web Site:* www.bastei.de, pg 199

Bastogi (Italy) *Tel:* (0881) 725070 *Fax:* (0881) 677513, pg 377

Ediciones Bat (Chile) *Tel:* (02) 2743171 *Fax:* (02) 2250261, pg 99

David Bateman Ltd (New Zealand) *Tel:* (09) 4444680 *Fax:* (09) 4440389, pg 488

The Bath Press (United Kingdom) *Tel:* (01225) 428101 *Fax:* (01225) 312418, pg 1140

The Bath Press (United Kingdom) *Tel:* (01225) 428101 *Fax:* (01225) 312418 *Web Site:* www.liberfabrica.com, pg 1160

The Bath Press (United Kingdom) *Tel:* (01225) 428101 *Fax:* (01225) 312418, pg 1223

Batsford Ltd (United Kingdom) *Tel:* (020) 7471 1100 *Fax:* (020) 7471 1101 *E-mail:* info@batsford.com, pg 652

Casa Editrice Luigi Battei (Italy) *Tel:* (0521) 233733 *Fax:* (0521) 231291, pg 377

Battenberg Verlag (Germany) *Tel:* (089) 9271280 *Fax:* (089) 9271236, pg 199

Battre Barnomsorg (Sweden) *Tel:* (08) 6909200 *Fax:* (08) 320851, pg 1232

Battre Data (Sweden) *Tel:* (08) 6909200 *Fax:* (08) 320851, pg 1232

Battre Ledarskap (Sweden) *Tel:* (08) 6909200 *Fax:* (08) 6909470, pg 1232

Battre Marknadsforing (Sweden) *Tel:* (08) 6909200 *Fax:* (08) 320851, pg 1232

Battre Skola (Sweden) *Tel:* (08) 6909200 *Fax:* (08) 320851, pg 1232

Societe Nouvelle Rene Baudouin (France) *Tel:* (01) 43290050 *Fax:* (01) 43257241, pg 149

Verlag Hermann Bauer KG (Germany) *Tel:* (0761) 70820 *Fax:* (0761) 701811 *E-mail:* info@hermann-bauer.de *Web Site:* www.hermann-bauer.de, pg 199

N E Bauman Moscow State Technical University Publishers (Russian Federation) *Tel:* (095) 2614597 *Fax:* (095) 2636707; (095) 2654298, pg 537

Baumann GmbH & Co KG (Germany) *Tel:* (09221) 949401; (09221) 949382; (09221) 949360 *Fax:* (09221) 84434 *E-mail:* service@baumann-online.de, pg 199

Dr Wolfgang Baur Verlag Kunst & Alltag (Germany) *Tel:* (089) 217514 *Fax:* (089) 217515 *E-mail:* mail@kunstalltag.de *Web Site:* www.kunstalltag.de, pg 199

Institut fuer Baustoffe, Massivbau und Brandschutz/Bibliothek (Germany) *Tel:* (0531) 391 5454 *Fax:* (0531) 391 5900 *E-mail:* ibmb@tu-bs.de *Web Site:* www.ibmb.tu-bs.de, pg 199

Bautz Traugott (Germany) *Tel:* (05521) 5700; (05521) 5588 *Fax:* (05521) 5780 *Web Site:* www.bautz.de, pg 199

Bauverlag GmbH (Germany) *Tel:* (06123) 7000 *Fax:* (06123) 700122, pg 199

Colin Baxter Photography Ltd (United Kingdom) *Tel:* (01479) 873999 *Fax:* (01479) 873888 *E-mail:* sales@colinbaxter.co.uk *Web Site:* www.colinbaxter.co.uk; www.worldlifelibrary.co.uk, pg 652

Bay Foreign Language Books (United Kingdom) *Tel:* (01233) 720020 *Fax:* (01233) 721272 *E-mail:* sales@baylanguagebooks.co.uk *Web Site:* www.baylanguagebooks.co.uk, pg 1316

Bay View Books Ltd (United Kingdom) *Tel:* (01237) 479225; (01237) 421285 *Fax:* (01237) 421286, pg 652

Bayard Presse - Department Livre (France) *Tel:* (01) 44 35 60 60 *Fax:* (01) 44 35 61 61 *Web Site:* www.bayardpresse.com, pg 149

Bayda Books (Australia) *Tel:* (0613) 9380-2988 *Fax:* (0613) 9380-2988 *E-mail:* bayda@ozemail.com.au *Web Site:* www.ozemail.com.au/~bayda/, pg 14

Bayerische Akademie der Wissenschaften (Germany) *Tel:* (089) 230310 *Fax:* (089) 23031100 *Web Site:* www.badw.de, pg 199

Bayerische Staatsbibliothek (Germany) *Tel:* (089) 286380 *Fax:* (089) 286382200 *E-mail:* direktion@bsb-muenchen.de *Web Site:* www.bsb.muenchen.de, pg 1466

Bayerische Verlagsanstalt GmbH (Germany) *Tel:* (0951) 967120 *Fax:* (0951) 96712235, pg 199

Bayerischer Schulbuch-Verlag GmbH (Germany) *Tel:* (089) 450510 *Fax:* (089) 45051200, pg 199

Ebenezer Baylis & Son Ltd (United Kingdom) *Tel:* (01905) 357979 *Fax:* (01905) 354919 *E-mail:* theworks@ebaylis.demon.co.uk, pg 1202

Joycelyn Bayne (Australia) *Tel:* (08) 3561748, pg 14

George Bayntun Booksellers (United Kingdom) *Tel:* (01225) 466000 *Fax:* (01225) 482122, pg 1316

BBC Audiobooks (United Kingdom) *Tel:* (01225) 335 336 *Fax:* (01225) 310 771; (01225) 448 005; (01225) 422 585 *E-mail:* sales@chivers.co.uk; info@chivers.co.uk *Web Site:* www.chivers.co.uk, pg 652

BBC English (United Kingdom) *Tel:* (020) 8576 2221 *Fax:* (020) 8576 3040, pg 652

BBC Television Training (United Kingdom) *Tel:* (01923) 855632 *Fax:* (01923) 855632, pg 653

BBC Worldwide Publishers (United Kingdom) *Tel:* (020) 8576 2570 *Fax:* (020) 8749 8766 *E-mail:* bbcsales@bbc.co.uk *Web Site:* www.bbcworldwide.com, pg 653

BCA (United Kingdom) *Tel:* (020) 7637 0341 *Fax:* (020) 7291 3525, pg 653

BCM Media Inc (Republic of Korea) *Tel:* (02) 567-0644; (02) 533-0089 *Fax:* (02) 552-9169 *E-mail:* bcmpub@nuri.net *Web Site:* www.bcm.co.kr, pg 434

BCS Publishing Ltd (United Kingdom) *Tel:* (01865) 770099 *Fax:* (01865) 770050, pg 1140, 1160

be.bra verlag GmbH (Germany) *Tel:* (030) 44023810 *Fax:* (030) 44023819 *E-mail:* info@bebraverlag.de *Web Site:* www.bebraverlag.de, pg 199

Beacon Verlag Koerber OHG (Germany) *Tel:* (06322) 2056 *Fax:* (06322) 2056, pg 199

Beaconsfield Publishers Ltd (United Kingdom) *Tel:* (01494) 672118 *Fax:* (01494) 672118 *E-mail:* books@beaconsfield-publishers.co.uk *Web Site:* www.beaconsfield-publishers.co.uk, pg 653

Ruth Bean Publishers (United Kingdom) *Tel:* (01234) 720356 *Fax:* (01234) 720590 *E-mail:* ruthbean@onetel.net.uk, pg 653

Beas Ediciones SRL (Argentina) *Tel:* (011) 4923-4030; (011) 4924-5337 *Fax:* (011) 4924-0217, pg 4

Beascoa SA Ediciones (Spain) *Tel:* (093) 3196517; (093) 3934380 *Fax:* (093) 3107694; (093) 3934389 *E-mail:* info@beascoa.com, pg 565

Editions des Beatitudes, Pneumatheque (France) *Tel:* (02) 54 88 21 18 *Fax:* (02) 54 88 97 73 *E-mail:* edd.etrangers@wandadoo.com *Web Site:* www.editions-beatitudes.fr, pg 150

The Beatrix Potter Society (United Kingdom) *Tel:* (01625) 267880 *Fax:* (01625) 267879 *E-mail:* bps@resources.demon.co.uk, pg 1369

Beatriz Viterbo Editora (Argentina) *Tel:* (041) 4827560 *Fax:* (041) 4261919 *E-mail:* beatrizviterbo@arnet.com.ar, pg 4

The Chester Beatty Library (Ireland) *Tel:* (01) 4070750 *Fax:* (01) 4070760 *E-mail:* info@cbl.ie *Web Site:* www.cbl.ie, pg 1475

Beauchesne Editeur (France) *Tel:* (01) 53 10 08 18 *Fax:* (01) 53 10 85 19, pg 150

Beaver Publishing Ltd (United Kingdom) *Tel:* (01625) 586670 *Fax:* (01625) 586782, pg 653

Beazer Publishing Company Pty Ltd (Australia) *Tel:* (03) 5156 0556 *Fax:* (03) 5156 0556 *E-mail:* beazer@s140.aone.net.au *Web Site:* www.beazerpublishing.com, pg 14

Mitchell Beazley (United Kingdom) *Tel:* (020) 7531 8400; (020) 7531 8480 (UK sales); (020) 7531 8481 (special sales); (020) 7531 8479 (marketing); (020) 7531 8488 (publicity); (020) 7531 8482 (export sales); (020) 7531 8484 (foreign rights); (020) 7531 8476 (US sales) *Fax:* (020) 7531 8650 *E-mail:* enquiries@mitchell-beazley.co.uk *Web Site:* www.mitchell-beazley.com, pg 653

BEBC Distribution (United Kingdom) *Tel:* (01202) 715555 *Fax:* (01202) 715556 *E-mail:* bebc@bebc.co.uk *Web Site:* www.bebc.co.uk, pg 1316

Ludwig Bechauf Verlag (Germany) *Tel:* (0521) 130648 *Fax:* (0521) 139347, pg 200

Bechtermunz Verlag (Germany) *Tel:* (0821) 70040 *Fax:* (0821) 7004-179, pg 200

Bechtle Graphische Betriebe und Verlagsgesellschaft mbH und Co KG (Germany) *Tel:* (0711) 29088-0 *Fax:* (0711) 29088-154, pg 200

Beck & Gluckler Verlag GmbH & Co KG (Germany) *Tel:* (0761) 701530 *Fax:* (0761) 701580, pg 200

Verlag C H Beck (OHG) (Germany) *Tel:* (089) 381890 *Fax:* (089) 38189402 (Sales); (089) 38189398 (Editorial) *E-mail:* bestellung@beck.de *Web Site:* www.beck.de, pg 200

Barbara Beckett Publishing Pty Ltd (Australia) *Tel:* (02) 3312871 *Fax:* (02) 3603106 *Web Site:* bbeckett-peg.apc.org, pg 14

Bedout Editores SA (Colombia) *Tel:* (04) 5112900 *Fax:* (04) 2517946, pg 111

Bokklubben Bedre Ledelse (Norway) *Tel:* 22471000 *Fax:* 22471098 *E-mail:* egmont@egmont.com *Web Site:* www.egmont.com, pg 1230

Bedriftsokonomens Forlag A/S (Norway) *Tel:* 22985800 *Fax:* 22985841, pg 502

Beerenverlag (Germany) *Tel:* (0611) 376316 *Fax:* (0611) 376316, pg 200

Beginners Publishers (Ghana) *Tel:* (021) 503040 *Fax:* (051) 772642 Attn: Beginners Publishers, pg 306

Beijing Ancient Books Publishing House (China) *Tel:* (010) 2016699 313; (010) 2013122 *Fax:* (010) 2012339 *E-mail:* geo@bph.com.cn, pg 102

Beijing Arts & Crafts Publishing House (China) *Tel:* (010) 4035477; (010) 4031811, pg 102

Beijing Education Publishing House (China) *Tel:* (010) 2016699-268; (010) 62013122 *Fax:* (010) 2012339 *E-mail:* geo@bph.com.cn, pg 102

Beijing Fine Arts & Photography Publishing House (China) *Tel:* (010) 2016699; (010) 62016699-315 *Fax:* (010) 2012339 *E-mail:* geo@bph.com.cn, pg 102

Beijing Juvenile & Children's Books Publishing House (China) *Tel:* (010) 2016699-350; (010) 62013122 *Fax:* (010) 2012339 *E-mail:* geo@bph.com.cn, pg 102

Beijing Medical Univ Press (China) *Tel:* (010) 62092249 *Fax:* (010) 62029848 *E-mail:* bmupress@public.fhnet.cn.net *Web Site:* www.bjmu.edu.cn, pg 102

Beijing Publishing House (China) *Tel:* (010) 62012335 *Fax:* (010) 62012339 *E-mail:* geo@bph.com.cn *Web Site:* www.bph.com.cn, pg 102

Beijing University Press (China) *Tel:* (010) 2561166-3672 *Fax:* (010) 2564095 *E-mail:* psj@pup.pku.edu.cn, pg 102

Dr Ivana Beil, Internationale Handelsvermitlung im Medien- und Verlagswesen (Germany) *Tel:* (06201) 14611 *Fax:* (06201) 17280, pg 1111

Library of Beirut Arab University (Lebanon) *Tel:* (01) 300110 *Fax:* (01) 818402 *E-mail:* bau@inco.com.lb, pg 1481

Academie Tunisienne des Sciences, des Lettres et des Arts Beit El Hekma (Tunisia) *Tel:* (01) 277275; (01) 731696 *Fax:* (01) 731204, pg 637

Belarus (The Belorussia) (Belarus) *Tel:* (0172) 238742 *Fax:* (0172) 238731, pg 63

Beleke KG Verlag (Germany) *Tel:* (0201) 81300 *Fax:* (0201) 8130108 *E-mail:* info@beleke.de *Web Site:* www.beleke.edu, pg 200

Belfast Public Library (United Kingdom) *Tel:* (01232) 243233 *Fax:* (01232) 332819, pg 1505

Editions Belfond (France) *Tel:* (01) 45-44-38-23 *Fax:* (01) 45 44 98 04, pg 150

Belforte Editore Libraio srl (Italy) *Tel:* (0586) 887379 *Fax:* (0586) 889668 *E-mail:* belforte@librinformatica.it, pg 377

Fundacion Editorial de Belgrano (Argentina) *Tel:* (011) 4772-4014 *Fax:* (011) 4775-8788, pg 4

Editions Belin (France) *Tel:* (01) 55 42 84 00 *Fax:* (01) 43 25 18 29 *E-mail:* contact@edition-belin.fr *Web Site:* www.editions-belin.com, pg 150

Belitha Press Ltd (United Kingdom) *Tel:* (020) 7978 6330 *Fax:* (020) 7223 4936 *E-mail:* info@belithapress.co.uk *Web Site:* www.belithapress.co.uk, pg 653

Belize Library Association (Belize) *Tel:* (02) 7267, pg 1512

Bell & Bain Ltd (United Kingdom) *Tel:* (0141) 6495697 *Fax:* (0141) 6328733, pg 1140

Bell & Bain Ltd (United Kingdom) *Tel:* (0141) 6495697 *Fax:* (0141) 6328733 *E-mail:* info@bell-bain.demon.co.uk *Web Site:* www.bell-bain.demon.co.uk, pg 1160

Bell & Bain Ltd (United Kingdom) *Tel:* (0141) 6495697 *Fax:* (0141) 6328733 *E-mail:* info@bell-bain.co.uk, pg 1202

Bell & Bain Ltd (United Kingdom) *Tel:* (0141) 6495697 *Fax:* (0141) 6328733 *E-mail:* info@bell-bain.demon.co.uk, pg 1214

Libreria Bellas Artes (Mexico) *Tel:* (05) 5182917; (05) 5120947, pg 1299

Ediciones Bellaterra SA (Spain) *Tel:* (093) 3390511; (093) 3499786 *Fax:* (093) 3520851, pg 565

Bellcourt Books (Australia) *Tel:* 055 72 1310 *Fax:* 055 72 1310, pg 14

Editions Belle Riviere (Switzerland) *Tel:* (024) 498 40 49 *Fax:* (024) 498 40 46, pg 609

Societe d'Edition Les Belles Lettres (France) *Tel:* (01) 44398420 *Fax:* (01) 45449288 *Web Site:* www.lesbelleslettres.com, pg 150

Bellew Publishing Co Ltd (United Kingdom) *Tel:* (020) 8673 5611 *Fax:* (020) 8675 2142, pg 653

Biblioteca de la Universidad Catolica 'Andres Bello' (Venezuela) *Tel:* (02) 475110 *Fax:* (02) 4223897, pg 1508

Editorial Andres Bello/Editorial Juridica de Chile (Chile) *Tel:* (02) 2049900; (02) 4619500 *Fax:* (02) 2253600 *Web Site:* www.editorialandresbello.com, pg 100

Clubs de Lectores Andres Bello (Chile) *Tel:* (02) 2049900; (02) 2049901 *Fax:* (02) 2253600, pg 1227

Libreria Andres Bello (Chile) *Tel:* (02) 2049900 *Fax:* (02) 2253600, pg 1279

Belaruskaya Encyklapedyya (Belarus) *Tel:* (0172) 284 1767; (0172) 284 0600; (0172) 284 0983, pg 63

Belser Wissenschaftlicher Dienst (Germany) *Tel:* (07054) 2475 *Fax:* (07054) 2639 *E-mail:* 101553.3467@compuserve.com *Web Site:* www.belser.com, pg 200

Julius Beltz GmbH & Co KG (Germany) *Tel:* (06201) 60070 *Fax:* (06201) 6007-310 *E-mail:* info@beltz.de *Web Site:* www.beltz.de, pg 200

BeMa (Italy) *Tel:* (02) 2552451 *Fax:* (02) 27000692, pg 377

Bemrose Security & Promotional Printing (United Kingdom) *Tel:* (01332) 294242 *Fax:* (01332) 295848, pg 1202

Bemust doo Novinsko-Izdavacko stamparsko i trgovacko preduzece (Bosnia and Herzegovina) *Tel:* (033) 414-050; (033) 414-051 *Fax:* (033) 414-050; (033) 414-051 *E-mail:* bemust@bih.net.ba, pg 77

Ben and Company Ltd (United Republic of Tanzania) *Tel:* (051) 67407 *Fax:* (051) 112440, pg 633

Ben-Gurion University of the Negev Library (Israel) *Tel:* (07) 6461401 *Fax:* (07) 6472940, pg 1476

Bibliotheque Ben Youssef (Morocco) *Tel:* (04) 25465, pg 1485

Ben-Zvi Institute (Israel) *Tel:* (02) 5398844 *Fax:* (02) 5612329 *E-mail:* mahonzvi@h2.hum.huji.ac.il *Web Site:* www.ybz.org.il, pg 365

Bendel State Library (Nigeria) *Tel:* (052) 200810, pg 1488

James Bendon Ltd (Cyprus) *Tel:* (05) 323047 *Fax:* (05) 2563 2352 *E-mail:* books@jamesbendon.com *Web Site:* www.jamesbendon.com, pg 122

Benefit Publishing Co (Hong Kong), pg 318

Benghazi Public Library (Libyan Arab Jamahiriya) *Tel:* (061) 96379, pg 1481

Benin University Bookshop (Nigeria) *Tel:* (052) 240115 ext 217 *Fax:* (052) 241156, pg 1303

Benin University Library (Nigeria) *Tel:* (052) 600553 *Fax:* (052) 241156, pg 1488

Eliane Benisti Literary Agency (France) *Tel:* (01) 42228533 *Fax:* (01) 45441817 *E-mail:* benisti@compuserve.com, pg 1110

Biblioteca Benjamin Franklin (USIS) (Mexico) *Tel:* (05) 2099100 *Fax:* (05) 5910075 *E-mail:* refbbf@usia.gov, pg 1484

John Benjamins BV (Netherlands) *Tel:* (020) 6304747 *Fax:* (020) 6739773 *E-mail:* customer.services@benjamins.nl *Web Site:* www.benjamins.com, pg 474

John Benjamins Publishing Co (Netherlands) *Tel:* (020) 6304747 *Fax:* (020) 6739773 *E-mail:* customer.services@benjamins.nl *Web Site:* www.benjamins.com, pg 1301

Petra Bornhauber Benleo Verlag (Germany) *Tel:* (02271) 4782-0 *Fax:* (02271) 4782-20 *Web Site:* www.benleo.de, pg 200

James Bennett Pty Ltd (Australia) *Tel:* (02) 9986 7000 *Fax:* (02) 9986 7031 *E-mail:* info@bennett.com.au *Web Site:* www.bennett.com.au, pg 1272

Bennetts Bookshop Ltd (New Zealand) *Tel:* (06) 3283009 *Fax:* (06) 3282836, pg 1302

E F Benson Society (United Kingdom) *Tel:* (01797) 223114, pg 1369

Benteli Verlag (Switzerland) *Tel:* (031) 9608484 *Fax:* (031) 9617414 *E-mail:* info@benteliverlag.ch *Web Site:* www.benteliverlag.ch, pg 609

John Bentley Book Agencies (New Zealand) *Tel:* (09) 4736920 *Fax:* (09) 4736920 *E-mail:* sjsb@connected.net.nzed, pg 1115

Benziger Verlag AG (Switzerland) *Tel:* (01) 2527050 *Fax:* (01) 2624792, pg 609

Beobachter Buchverlag (Switzerland) *Tel:* (01) 8296111 *Fax:* (01) 8103791 *Web Site:* www.beobachter.ch, pg 609

Beogradski Izdavacko-Graficki Zavod (Yugoslavia) *Tel:* (011) 650-399; (011) 651-666 *Fax:* (011) 651-841, pg 764

Berchtold Haller Verlag (Switzerland) *Tel:* (031) 334 03 03 *Fax:* (031) 334 03 06, pg 609

Berenguer Editorial (Chile), pg 1279

Berg International Editeurs (France) *Tel:* (01) 43267273 *Fax:* (01) 46339499, pg 150

Berg Publishers (United Kingdom) *Tel:* (01865) 245104 *Fax:* (01865) 791165 *E-mail:* enquiry@bergpublishers.com *Web Site:* www.bergpublishers.com, pg 654

Bergadis (Greece) *Tel:* (01) 3614263, pg 309

Technische Universitat Bergakademie Freiberg (Germany) *Tel:* (03731) 392959 *Fax:* (03731) 393289 *E-mail:* unibib@ub.tu-freiberg.de, pg 1466

Bergen offentlige Bibliotek (Norway) *Tel:* 55568500 *Fax:* 55568555 *Web Site:* www.bergen.folkebibl.no, pg 1489

Berger-Levrault SA (France) *Tel:* (03) 83 38 83 83 *Fax:* (03) 83 38 86 10; (03) 83 38 37 12 *E-mail:* blc@berger-levrault.fr *Web Site:* www.berger-levrault.fr, pg 150

Berghahn Books Ltd (United Kingdom) *Tel:* (01865) 250011 *Fax:* (01865) 250056 *E-mail:* info@berghahnbooks.com *Web Site:* www.berghahnbooks.com, pg 654

Berghs (Sweden) *Tel:* (08) 316559 *Fax:* (08) 327745, pg 600

Bergli Books AG (Switzerland) *Tel:* (061) 373 27 77 *Fax:* (061) 373 27 28 *E-mail:* info@bergli.ch *Web Site:* www.bergli.ch, pg 609

Bergmoser & Holler Verlag GmbH (Germany) *Tel:* (0241) 93888123 *Fax:* (0241) 93888188 *E-mail:* kontakt@buhv.de *Web Site:* www.buhv.de, pg 200

Biblioteca Bergnes de las Casas . Bibioteca de Catalunya (Spain) *Tel:* (093) 2659003 *Fax:* (093) 2656635, pg 1499

Bergstadtverlag Wilhelm Gottlieb Korn GmbH Wuerzburg (Germany) *Tel:* (07571) 728170 *Fax:* (07571) 728280, pg 200

Bergverlag Rudolf Rother GmbH (Germany) *Tel:* (089) 6086690 *Fax:* (089) 60866969 *E-mail:* bergverlag@rother.de *Web Site:* www.rother.de, pg 200

Beri Publishing (Australia) *Tel:* (03) 98091434 *Fax:* (03) 98091434 *E-mail:* beripub@ozemail.com.au, pg 14

Berichthaus Verlag, Dr Conrad Ulrich (Switzerland) *Tel:* (01) 2526349 *Fax:* (01) 2526426, pg 609

Berita Publishing Sdn Bhd (Malaysia) *Tel:* (03) 2824322 *Fax:* (03) 2821605, pg 451

Berkeley Brasil Editora Ltda (Brazil) *Tel:* (011) 3649-4663 *Fax:* (011) 261-1342 *E-mail:* berkeley@siciliano.com.br *Web Site:* berkeley.com.br, pg 79

The Berlin Agency (Germany) *Tel:* (030) 88677000 *Fax:* (030) 88677011 *E-mail:* junglindemann@berlinagency.de, pg 1111

Berlin Verlag Arno Spitz GmbH (Germany) *Tel:* (030) 8417700 *Fax:* (030) 84177021 *E-mail:* berlin-verlag.spitz@t-online.de *Web Site:* www.berlin-verlag.de, pg 200

Berliner Debatte Wissenschafts Verlag, GSFP-Gesellschaft fur Sozialwissen-schaftliche Forschung und Publizistik mbH &Co KG (Germany) *Tel:* (030) 44651355 *Fax:* (030) 44651358 *E-mail:* web@berlinerdebatte.de *Web Site:* www.berlinerdebatte.de, pg 201

Berliner Handpresse Wolfgang Joerg und Erich Schonig (Germany) *Tel:* (030) 6148728; (030) 6142605, pg 201

Berliner Zeitung (Germany) *Tel:* (030) 2327-9 *Fax:* (030) 2327-5681 *E-mail:* berlinerzeitung@berlinonline.de *Web Site:* www.berlinzeitung.de, pg 201

Berlitz (UK) Ltd (United Kingdom) *Tel:* (020) 7611 9640 *Fax:* (020) 7611 9656 *E-mail:* publishing@berlitz.co.uk *Web Site:* www.berlitz.com, pg 654

David Berman Developments Inc (Canada) *Tel:* 613-728-6777 *Fax:* 613-722-5351 *E-mail:* info@timewise.net *Web Site:* www.timewise.net, pg 1153

Bermuda Archives (Bermuda) *Tel:* (0441) 2929847, pg 1454

Bermuda College Library (Bermuda) *Tel:* (441) 236-9000 *Fax:* (441) 236-8888, pg 1454

Bermuda National Library (Bermuda) *Tel:* (0441) 295-2905 *Fax:* (0441) 292-8443 *E-mail:* bdanatlib@gov.bm, pg 1454

Bermudian Publishing Co (Bermuda) *Tel:* (441) 295-0695 *Fax:* (441) 295-8616 *E-mail:* berpub@ibl.bm *Web Site:* www.bermuda.bm, pg 76

Luigi Bernabo Associates SRL (Italy) *Tel:* (02) 58306332; (02) 58306378 *Fax:* (02) 58306312, pg 1113

Bernal Publishing (Australia) *Tel:* (0613) 9808-3775 *Fax:* (0613) 9888-7572 *E-mail:* sales@bernalpublishing.com *Web Site:* www.bernalpublishing.com, pg 14

Bernan Associates, Div of Kraus Organization, Ltd (United States) *Tel:* 301-459-7666 *Fax:* 301-459-0056, pg 1268

Bernard und Graefe Verlag (Germany) *Tel:* (0228) 64830 *Fax:* (0228) 6483106 *E-mail:* 101336.245@compuserve.com, pg 201

Berndtson & Berndtson GmbH Verlag-Publishing (Germany) *Tel:* (08141) 32410 *Fax:* (08141) 324120 *E-mail:* redaktion@berndtson.de *Web Site:* www.mapmyway.com, pg 201

A Bernecker Verlag GmbH (Germany) *Tel:* (05661) 731-0 *Fax:* (05661) 731111 *Web Site:* www.bernecker.de, pg 201

Verlag Alexander Bernhardt (Austria) *Tel:* (05242) 6213149 *Fax:* (05242) 72801 *E-mail:* bernhardt@grafswerk.org; c.bernhardt@tirol.com, pg 49

Bibliotheque Bernheim, Bibliotheque territoriale de la Nouvelle-Caledonie (New Caledonia) *Tel:* 272343 *Fax:* 276588, pg 1487

Beroa-Verlag (Switzerland) *Tel:* (01) 4801313 *Fax:* (01) 4801312, pg 609

Bertello Edizioni (Italy) *Tel:* (0171) 266861; (0171) 699002 *Fax:* (0171) 697729; (0171) 266861, pg 377

Bertelsmann AG (Germany) *Tel:* (05241) 80-0 *Fax:* (05421) 75166 *E-mail:* info@bestelsmann.de *Web Site:* www.bertelsmann.de, pg 1133

C Bertelsmann Verlag GmbH (Germany) *Tel:* (089) 4372-0 *Fax:* (089) 4372-2812 *E-mail:* vertrieb.verlagsgruppe@bertelsmann.de *Web Site:* www.randomhouse.de, pg 201

Bertelsmann Club (Germany) *Tel:* (05242) 914358; (05242) 914272; (0542) 9146920 *Fax:* (05242) 916999, pg 1228

Bertelsmann de Mexico SA (Mexico) *Tel:* (05) 5501620; (05) 5489048, pg 1230

Bertelsmann Distribution GmbH (Germany) *Tel:* (05241) 807083 *Fax:* (05241) 806006, pg 1283

Bertelsmann Lexikon Verlag GmbH (Germany) *Tel:* (05241) 800 *Fax:* (05241) 73075 *E-mail:* vertrieb.verlagsgruppe@bertelsmann.de *Web Site:* www.lexiconverlag.de/lexiconverlag.html, pg 201

Verlag Bertelsmann Stiftung (Germany) *Tel:* (05241) 8181197 *Fax:* (05241) 8181931 *E-mail:* sabine.klemm@bertelsmann.de *Web Site:* www.bertelsmann-stiftung.de/verlag, pg 201

W Bertelsmann Verlag GmbH & Co KG (Germany) *Tel:* (0521) 911-01-0 *Fax:* (0521) 911 01-79 *E-mail:* wbv@wbv.de *Web Site:* www.wbv.de; www.berufsbildung.de; www.berufe.net, pg 201

BertelsmannSpringer Science & Business Media GmbH (Germany) *Tel:* (030) 82787-0 *Fax:* (030) 8274091 *Web Site:* www.bertelsmannspringer.de, pg 202

Robert Berthold Photography (Australia) *Tel:* (02) 9887-3986 *Fax:* (02) 9887-3986, pg 14

Editions Bertout (France) *Tel:* (02) 35 04 69 68 *Fax:* (02) 35846327, pg 150

Bertrams (United Kingdom) *Tel:* (01603) 216666 *Fax:* (01603) 611201 *E-mail:* books@bertrams.com, pg 1316

Editora Bertrand Brasil Ltda (Brazil) *Tel:* (021) 2585 2070 *Fax:* (021) 2585 2087 *E-mail:* professor@bertrandbrasil.com.br *Web Site:* www.bertrandbrasil.com.br, pg 79

Bertrand Editora Lda (Portugal) *Tel:* (021) 3468286 *Fax:* (021) 3479728, pg 522

Sociedades Livreiras Bertrand (Portugal) *Tel:* (021) 320084 *Fax:* (021) 3468286, pg 1307

Editions Bertrandl-Lacoste (France) *Tel:* (01) 53 40 53 53 *Fax:* (01) 42 33 82 47 *E-mail:* contact@bertrand-lacoste.fr *Web Site:* www.bertrand-lacoste.fr, pg 150

Verlag Beruf + Schule Belz KG (Germany) *Tel:* (04821) 40140 *Fax:* (04821) 4941 *E-mail:* info@verlag-beruf-schule.de *Web Site:* www.verlag-beruf-schule.de, pg 202

Berufsverband Information Bibliothek (BIB) (Germany) *Tel:* (07121) 34910 *Fax:* (07121) 300433 *E-mail:* mail@bib-info.de *Web Site:* www.bib-info.de, pg 1516

Best-Set Typesetter Ltd (Hong Kong) *Tel:* 2897 6033 *Fax:* 2897 5170 *E-mail:* bestset@bestset-typesetter.com *Web Site:* www.bestset-typesetter.com, pg 1155

Best-Set Typesetter Ltd (Hong Kong) *Tel:* (02) 897 6033 *Fax:* (02) 897 5170 *E-mail:* bestset@bestset-typesetter.com; best-set-usa@email.msn.com *Web Site:* www.bestset-typesetter.com, pg 1195

Best-Set Typesetter Ltd (United States) *Tel:* 914-961-6223 *Fax:* 914-961-8212 *E-mail:* best-set-usa@msn.com *Web Site:* www.bestset-typesetter.com, pg 1163

Verlag Das Beste GmbH (Germany) *Tel:* (0711) 66020 *Fax:* (0711) 6602858 *E-mail:* verlag@readersdigest.de *Web Site:* www.dasbeste.de; www.readersdigest.de, pg 202

Bet-El Publishers (South Africa) *Tel:* (012) 3294508, pg 553

Beta Editorial SA (Spain) *Tel:* (093) 2804640 *Fax:* (093) 2806320, pg 565

Beta Medical Publishers (Greece) *Tel:* (010) 6714340; (010) 6714371 *Fax:* (010) 6715015 *E-mail:* betamedarts@hol.gr *Web Site:* www.betamedarts.gr, pg 309

Editora Betania S/C (Brazil) *Tel:* (031) 4511122 *Fax:* (031) 4476088 *E-mail:* betania@prover.com.br, pg 79

Bethania Verlag (Austria) *Tel:* (01) 6672216, pg 49

Bettendorf'sche Verlagsanstalt GmbH (Germany) *Tel:* (089) 29088-0 *Fax:* (089) 356384-20, pg 202

Better Music Type (United States) *Tel:* 615-833-0800, pg 1163

Bettex, Editions Medicales Roland (Switzerland) *Tel:* (022) 7029311 *Fax:* (022) 7029355, pg 609

Annette Betz Verlag im Verlag Carl Ueberreuter (Austria) *Tel:* (01) 404440 *Fax:* (01) 404445 *Web Site:* www.annettebetz.com; www.ueberreuter.at, pg 49

Betzel Verlag GmbH (Germany) *Tel:* (050) 21914869 *Fax:* (050) 21914868 *E-mail:* betzelverlag@proximedia.de *Web Site:* www.proximedia.com/local/20000099001, pg 202

Beust Verlag GmbH (Germany) *Tel:* (089) 230895-0 *Fax:* (089) 266471 *E-mail:* mail@beustverlag.de, pg 202

Beuth Verlag GmbH (Germany) *Tel:* (030) 26010 *Fax:* (030) 26011260 *E-mail:* info@beuth.de *Web Site:* www.beuth.de; www.mybeuth.de, pg 202

Bewitched Books (Australia) *Tel:* (03) 9751-1931, pg 15

The Beyazit State Library (Turkey) *Tel:* (0212) 5222488 *Fax:* (0212) 5261133, pg 1504

Editions Beyeler (Switzerland) *Tel:* (061) 206 97 00 *Fax:* (061) 206 97 19, pg 610

F Beyer Bok-Og Papirhandel A/S (Norway) *Tel:* 055321180 *Fax:* 055326465, pg 1304

Joachim Beyer Verlag (Germany) *Tel:* (09274) 95051 *Fax:* (09274) 95053 *E-mail:* Beyer.Verlag@t-online.de *Web Site:* www.derschachladen.de, pg 202

Bezalel Academy of Arts & Design (Israel) *Tel:* (02) 589 3313 *Fax:* (02) 582 3094 *E-mail:* ouriel@bezalel.ac.il *Web Site:* www.bezalel.ac.il, pg 365

Bezerr-Editorae e Distribuidora de Abel Antonio Bezerra (Portugal) *Tel:* (053) 22604 *Fax:* (053) 617105, pg 522

De Bezige Bij (Netherlands) *Tel:* (020) 3059810 *Fax:* (020) 3059824 *E-mail:* info@debezigebij.nl *Web Site:* www.debezigebij.nl, pg 474

BFI Publishing (United Kingdom) *Tel:* (020) 7957 4789 *Fax:* (020) 74367950; (020) 76362516 *E-mail:* publishing@bfi.org.uk *Web Site:* www.bfi.org.uk, pg 654

BBT Bhaktivedanta Book Trust (Germany) *Tel:* (06782) 2214 *E-mail:* p.huy@t-online.de, pg 202

Bharat Law House Pvt Ltd (India) *Tel:* (011) 791 0001; (011) 791 0002; (011) 791 0003 *Fax:* (011) 791 0004 *E-mail:* blh@nda.vsnl.net.in *Web Site:* www.bharatlawhouse.com, pg 332

Bharat Publishing House (India) *Tel:* (011) 575 7081 *Fax:* (011) 367 6058 *E-mail:* bitambar@bol.net.in, pg 332

Bharatiya Samijik Vigyan Auusandhan Parishad (India) *Tel:* (011) 6179834; (011) 6179838; (011) 6179679 *Fax:* (011) 6179836 *E-mail:* info@icssr.org *Web Site:* www.ecssr.org, pg 332

Bharatiya Vidya Bhavan (India) *Tel:* (022) 3631261; (022) 8118261; (022) 8118262 *Fax:* (022) 3630058, pg 333

Bhawan Book Service, Publishers & Distributors (India) *Tel:* 2258836; 271559 *Fax:* 265315, pg 333

Mauritus Bhojpuri Institute (Mauritius) *Tel:* 2082956 *Fax:* 4643445, pg 457

Bhratara Karya Aksara (Indonesia) *Tel:* 021 81858, pg 354

Bi-bong Publishing Co (Republic of Korea) *Tel:* (02) 3142-6555 *Fax:* (02) 3142-6556, pg 435

The Bialik Institute (Israel) *Tel:* (02) 6783554 *Fax:* (02) 6783706 *E-mail:* bialik@actcom.co.il, pg 365

Bianco (Italy) *Tel:* (06) 8554962 *Fax:* (06) 8844703, pg 377

Bianco Lunos Bogtrykkeri AS (Denmark) *Tel:* 33140781 *Fax:* 33913808, pg 1154, 1194, 1211

Bibellesbund Verlag (Switzerland) *Tel:* (052) 2451445 *Fax:* (052) 2451446 *E-mail:* info@bibellesebund.ch *Web Site:* www.bibellesebund.ch, pg 610

Bibelselskabets Forlag og Vajsenhusets Forlag (Denmark) *Tel:* 33127835 *Fax:* 33932150 *E-mail:* bibelselskabet@bibelselskabet.dk *Web Site:* www.bibelselskabet.dk, pg 130

Bible Reading Fellowship (United Kingdom) *Tel:* (01865) 319700 *Fax:* (01865) 319701 *E-mail:* enquiries@brf.org.uk *Web Site:* www.brf.org.uk, pg 654

Bible Society (United Kingdom) *Tel:* (01793) 418100 *Fax:* (01793) 418118 *E-mail:* info@bfbs.org.uk *Web Site:* www.biblesociety.org.uk, pg 654

Bible Society in Australia National Headquarters (Australia) *Tel:* (02) 9829 9000 *Fax:* (02) 98294685 *E-mail:* customer.service@bible.org.au *Web Site:* www.biblesociety.com.au, pg 15

Bible Society of Namibia (Namibia) *Tel:* (061) 235090 *Fax:* (061) 228663, pg 471

Bible Society of South Africa (South Africa) *Tel:* (021) 212040 *Fax:* (021) 4194846, pg 553

Biblia Impex Pvt Ltd (India) *Tel:* (011) 3278034; (011) 3262515 *Fax:* (011) 3282047 *E-mail:* bibimpex@giasd101.vsnl.net.in, pg 333

Biblia Impex Pvt Ltd (India) *Tel:* (011) 3278034 *Fax:* (011) 3282047 *E-mail:* bibimpex@giasd101.vsnl.net.in, pg 1288

Biblio-Zeller Verlag (Germany) *Tel:* (0541) 404590 *Fax:* (0541) 41255 *E-mail:* zeller@zeller.os.emnet.de *Web Site:* www.militaria-biblio.de, pg 202

Bibliografica Internacional SA (Chile) *Tel:* (02) 6394057 *Fax:* (02) 6397693, pg 100

Bibliographical Society of Australia and New Zealand (BSANZ) (Australia) *Tel:* (03) 9052689 *Fax:* (03) 9052610, pg 1359

Bibliographical Society of the Philippines (Philippines) *Tel:* (02) 583252; (02) 5253196 *Fax:* (02) 502329; (02) 5242329 *E-mail:* amb@max.ph.net, pg 1522

Bibliographical Society (United Kingdom) *Tel:* (020) 7611 7244 *Fax:* (020) 7611 8703, pg 1524

Bibliographical Society of Australia and New Zealand (BSANZ) (Australia) *Tel:* (02) 6931 8669 *Fax:* (02) 6931 8669 *E-mail:* rsalmond@pobox.com *Web Site:* life.csu.edu.au/bsanz/, pg 1236

Bibliographisches Institut & F A Brockhaus AG (Germany) *Tel:* (0621) 3901-01 *Fax:* (0621) 3901-3 91 *Web Site:* www.brockhaus.de, pg 203

Bibliographisches Institut und F A Brockhaus AG (Switzerland) *Tel:* (01) 2120800 *Fax:* (01) 7108325, pg 610

Bibliographisches Institut GmbH (Germany) *Tel:* (0341) 97 86-30 *Fax:* (0341) 97 86-5 60, pg 203

Bibliography Institute of the National Library of Latvia (Latvia) *Tel:* (02) 7225135 *Fax:* (02) 7224587 *E-mail:* anitag@lnb.lv *Web Site:* www.lnb.lv, pg 441

Bibliomed - Medizinische Verlagsgesellschaft mbH (Germany) *Tel:* (05661) 73440 *Fax:* (05661) 8360 *E-mail:* info@bibliomed.de *Web Site:* www.bibliomed.de, pg 203

Le Bibliophile (The Book Lover) (Haiti), pg 1364

Bibliophile Books (United Kingdom) *Tel:* (020) 7515 9222 *Fax:* (020) 7538 4115 *E-mail:* customercare@bibliophilebooks.com *Web Site:* www.bibliophilebooks.com, pg 1233, 1316

Verlag Bibliophile Drucke von Josef Stocker AG (Switzerland) *Tel:* (01) 7404444, pg 610

Bibliopolis - Edizioni di Filosofia e Scienze Srl (Italy) *Tel:* (081) 664606 *Fax:* (081) 7616273 *E-mail:* info@bibliopolis.it *Web Site:* www.bibliopolis.it, pg 377

Biblios Publishers Distribution Services Ltd (United Kingdom) *Tel:* (01903) 892346 *Fax:* (01903) 893383 *E-mail:* biblios@biblios.co.uk, pg 1316

Biblioteca Agricola Nacional/Universidad Nacional Agraria La Molina (Peru) *Tel:* (01) 4352035 *Fax:* (01) 4352473 *E-mail:* ban@unaln.edu.pe, pg 1522

Biblioteca Agropecuaria de Colombia (BAC) (Colombia) *Tel:* (01) 2861507 (ext 3428); (01) 2813088 *Fax:* (01) 2813088 *E-mail:* fsalazar@caldas.colciencias.gov.co, pg 1457

Biblioteca Central (Mexico) *Tel:* (0595) 50877 *Fax:* (0595) 50877 *E-mail:* rsuarez@taurusl.chapings.mx, pg 1484

Biblioteca Central de la Universidad de Oriente (Cuba) *Tel:* (0226) 31973 *Fax:* (0226) 32989 *E-mail:* jrcobo@ict.uo.edu.cu, pg 1459

Biblioteca Central de la Universidad Nacional de San Agustin (Peru) *Tel:* (054) 229719, pg 1491

Biblioteca Central de la Universidad Nacional Mayor de San Marcos (Peru) *Tel:* (01) 4285210 *Fax:* (01) 4285210 *E-mail:* ogeibl@sanfer.edu.pe, pg 1491

Biblioteca Central de Macau (Macau) *Tel:* 371623 *Fax:* 318756, pg 1482

Direccion General de Bibliotecas de la Universidad Nacional Autonoma de Mexico (Mexico) *Tel:* (05) 6221603 *Fax:* (05) 6160664 *E-mail:* jadolfo@servidor.unam.mx, pg 1484

Biblioteca Centrala Universitara (Romania) *Tel:* (01) 6154240; (01) 6156584 *Fax:* (01) 6132842 *E-mail:* stoica@bcub.ro, pg 1494

Biblioteca Centrale della Regione Siciliana gia Biblioteca Nazionale di Palermo (Italy) *Tel:* (091) 6967644; (091) 6967642 *Fax:* (091) 6967644, pg 1477

Biblioteca de Catalunya (Spain) *Tel:* (093) 2702300 *Fax:* (093) 2702304 *E-mail:* bcpublic@bnc.es *Web Site:* www.gencat.es/bc/, pg 565

Biblioteca de Catalunya (Spain) *Tel:* (093) 2702300 *Fax:* (093) 270-23-02 *E-mail:* bcpublic@bnc.es *Web Site:* www.gencat.es/bc/, pg 1499

Biblioteca de Mexico (Mexico) *Tel:* (05) 7091113; (05) 7091469 *Fax:* (05) 7091173 *E-mail:* bibmex@servidor.ynam.mx, pg 1484

Biblioteca del Banco Central de la Republica Argentina (Argentina) *Tel:* (011) 4348 3772; (011) 4348 3500 (ext 2571 & 2801) *Fax:* (011) 4348 3771 *E-mail:* biblio@bcra.gov.ar *Web Site:* www.bcra.gov.ar, pg 1450

Biblioteca del Congreso (Venezuela) *Tel:* (02) 4832344 *Fax:* (02) 4832904, pg 1508

Biblioteca del Congreso Nacional (Bolivia) *Tel:* (02) 314731 *Fax:* (02) 392402, pg 1454

Biblioteca del Congreso Nacional (Chile) *Tel:* (02) 2701700 *Fax:* (02) 2701766 *E-mail:* xfeliu@biblioteca.congreso.cl, pg 1456

Biblioteca del Instituto Pre-Universitario de la Habana (Cuba), pg 1459

Biblioteca dell'Universita Nazionale della Somalia (Somalia), pg 1497

Biblioteca do Ministerio das Relacoes Exteriores (Brazil) *Tel:* (061) 2116359 *Fax:* (061) 2237362, pg 1455

Biblioteca Dominicana (Dominican Republic), pg 1461

Biblioteca Ecuatoriana 'Aurelio Espinosa Polit' (Ecuador) *Tel:* (02) 492190 *Fax:* (02) 493928 *E-mail:* beaep@isio.satnet.net *Web Site:* www.cultura.com.ec, pg 137

Biblioteca Ecuatoriana 'Aurelio Espinosa Polit' (Ecuador) *Tel:* (02) 596420, pg 1461

Biblioteca General de Puerto Rico (Puerto Rico) *Tel:* (787) 722-2113 *Fax:* (787) 724-0330, pg 1493

Biblioteca General de Humanidades, CSIC (Spain) *Tel:* (091) 4292017 *Fax:* (091) 4296823 *E-mail:* medina@bib.csic.es, pg 1499

Biblioteca Geral da Universidade de Coimbra (Portugal) *Tel:* (0239) 859800; (0239) 859800 *Fax:* (0239) 827135 *E-mail:* bguc@ci.uc.pt, pg 523

Biblioteca Geral da Universidade de Coimbra (Portugal) *Tel:* (0239) 859800 *Fax:* (0239) 827135 *E-mail:* bguc@ci.uc.pt, pg 1493

Biblioteca Historica Cubana y Americana (Cuba), pg 1459

Biblioteca Medicea Laurenziana (Italy) *Tel:* (055) 210760 *Fax:* (055) 2302992 *E-mail:* medicea@unifi.it *Web Site:* www.bml.firenze.sbn.it, pg 1477

Biblioteca Municipal Mario de Andrade (Brazil) *Tel:* (011) 2394384 *Fax:* (011) 2393459, pg 1455

Biblioteca Municipal (Mozambique), pg 1485

Biblioteca Nacional (Angola) *Tel:* (02) 322070 *Fax:* (02) 323979, pg 2

Biblioteca Nacional (Argentina) *Tel:* (011) 4806-6155; (011) 4806-6157 *Fax:* (011) 4806-6157 *E-mail:* postmaster@siscor.bibnal.edu.ar, pg 1450

Biblioteca Nacional Aruba (Aruba) *Tel:* (0297) 821580 *Fax:* (0297) 821580 *E-mail:* bna@setarnet.aw, pg 1450

Biblioteca Nacional de Colombia (Colombia) *Tel:* (01) 2414029 *Fax:* (01) 2414030, pg 1457

Biblioteca Nacional (Costa Rica) *Tel:* 2331706 *Fax:* 2235510, pg 1458

Biblioteca Nacional Jose Marti (Cuba) *Tel:* (07) 708277, pg 1459

Biblioteca Nacional (Dominican Republic), pg 1461

Biblioteca Nacional del Ecuador (Ecuador) *Tel:* (02) 528840, pg 1461

Biblioteca Nacional (El Salvador) *Tel:* 216312, pg 1462

Biblioteca Nacional de Guatemala (Guatemala) *Tel:* (02) 2322443 *Fax:* (02) 2539071 *E-mail:* vicast@biblionet.edu.gt, pg 1471

Biblioteca Nacional de Honduras (Honduras) *Tel:* 228577 *Fax:* 228577 *E-mail:* binah%bn@sdnhon.org; binah@ns.hondunet.net, pg 1471

Biblioteca Nacional de Mexico (Mexico) *Tel:* (05) 6226808 *Fax:* (05) 6650951 *E-mail:* liceaj@biblional.bibliog.unam.mx, pg 1484

Biblioteca Nacional de Mocambique (Mozambique) *Tel:* (01) 425676, pg 1485

Biblioteca Nacional (Nicaragua) *Tel:* (02) 97517 *Fax:* (02) 94387, pg 1488

Biblioteca Nacional (Panama), pg 1490

Biblioteca Nacional (Peru) *Tel:* (01) 4287690 *Fax:* (01) 4277331, pg 511

Biblioteca Nacional (Peru) *Tel:* (014) 287690 *Fax:* (01) 4277331 *E-mail:* jefatura@binape.gob.pe, pg 1491

Biblioteca Nacional (Portugal) *Tel:* (021) 217982000 *Fax:* (021) 217982140 *E-mail:* bn@bn.pt *Web Site:* www.bn.pt, pg 1493

Biblioteca Nacional (Spain) *Tel:* (091) 5807800 *Fax:* (091) 5775634, pg 1499

Biblioteca Nacional (Venezuela) *Tel:* (02) 5059141 *Fax:* (02) 5059159 *E-mail:* vbetanc@reaccium.ve, pg 1508

Biblioteca Nacional de Chile (Chile) *Tel:* (02) 3605239 *Fax:* (02) 6380461, pg 1456

Biblioteca Nacional de Maestros (Argentina) *Tel:* (011) 8110275 *Fax:* (011) 8110275, pg 1450

Biblioteca Nacional del Uruguay (Uruguay) *Tel:* (02) 485030 *Fax:* (02) 496902, pg 1507

Biblioteca Nationala a Romaniei (Romania) *Tel:* (01) 3157063 *Fax:* (01) 3123381 *E-mail:* go@bibnat.ro, pg 1494

Biblioteca Nazionale Braidense (Italy) *Tel:* (02) 86460907 *Fax:* (02) 72023910, pg 1477

Biblioteca Nazionale Centrale Vittorio Emanuele II (Italy) *Tel:* (06) 49891 *Fax:* (06) 4457635, pg 1477

Biblioteca Nazionale Centrale (Italy) *Tel:* (055) 249191 *Fax:* (055) 2342482, pg 1477

Biblioteca Nazionale Universitaria (Italy) *Tel:* (011) 889737 *Fax:* (011) 817778 *E-mail:* bntsbnol@itocsivm.csi.it, pg 1477

Biblioteca Nazionale Vittorio Emanuele III (Italy) *Tel:* (081) 407921; (081) 7819111 *Fax:* (081) 403820 *E-mail:* Emanuele@librari.beniculturali.it, pg 1477

Biblioteca Nazionale Marciana (Italy) *Tel:* (041) 5208788 *Fax:* (041) 5238803 *E-mail:* biblioteca@marciana.venezia.sbn.it *Web Site:* www.marciana.venezia.sbn.it/, pg 1477

Editorial Biblioteca Nueva SL (Spain) *Tel:* (091) 3100436; (091) 3081592; (091) 411-2020 *Fax:* (091) 3198235; (091) 745-2630 *E-mail:* editorial@bibliotecanueva.com; imago@teleline.es, pg 565

Biblioteca Popular de Lisboa (Portugal) *Tel:* (021) 369883, pg 1493

Biblioteca Publica do Estado do Rio de Janeiro (Brazil) *Tel:* (021) 2246184 *Fax:* (021) 2526810 *E-mail:* bperj@callnet.com.br, pg 1455

Biblioteca Publica de Evora (Portugal) *Tel:* (066) 22369 *Fax:* (066) 742081, pg 1493

Biblioteca Publica Municipal do Porto (Portugal) *Tel:* (02) 565361; (02) 572147 *Fax:* (02) 5106139, pg 523

Biblioteca Publica Municipal do Porto (Portugal) *Tel:* (02) 572147 *Fax:* (02) 5106139, pg 1493

Biblioteca Universitaria (Italy) *Tel:* (059) 222248 *Fax:* (059) 230195 *E-mail:* biblio.estense@cedoc.mo.it, pg 1477

Biblioteca y Archivo Nacional de Bolivia (Bolivia) *Tel:* (064) 1481, pg 1454

Biblioteca y Archivo Nacionales (Paraguay), pg 1490

Bibliotech (Australia) *Tel:* (02) 62492479 *Fax:* (02) 62495677 *E-mail:* books@bibliotech.com.au, pg 1272

Biblioteka Jagiellonska (Poland) *Tel:* (012) 6331971 (Director); (012) 6336377 (Operator); (012) 6330903 (Secretariat) *Fax:* (012) 6330903, pg 1492

Biblioteka Narodowa (Poland) *Tel:* (022) 8255733; (022) 8259271 *Fax:* (022) 8255251 *E-mail:* biblnar@bn.org.pl; bndyrekt@bn.org.pl, pg 516

Biblioteka Narodowa (Poland) *Tel:* (022) 8255733 *Fax:* (022) 8255251 *E-mail:* biblnar@bn.org.pl; bndyrekt@bn.org.pl, pg 1492

Biblioteka Publiczna m st Warszawy - Biblioteka Glowna Wojewodztwa Mazowieckiego (Poland) *Tel:* (022) 6217852 *Fax:* (022) 6211968 *E-mail:* Biblioteka@biblpubl.haw.pl *Web Site:* www.biblpubl.waw.pl, pg 1492

Biblioteka Uniwersytecka w Warszawie (Poland) *Tel:* (022) 5525660; (022) 5525181 *Fax:* (022) 5525181 *E-mail:* buw@mail.uw.edu.pl *Web Site:* www.buw.uw.edu.pl, pg 1492

Biblioteka Uniwersytecka w Poznaniu (Poland) *Tel:* (061) 852-29-55; (061) 829-38-00 *Fax:* (061) 829-38-24 *E-mail:* library@amu.edu.pl *Web Site:* lib.amu.edu.pl, pg 1492

Bibliotekarsko Drustvo na Makedonija (The Former Yugoslav Republic of Macedonia) *Tel:* (091) 212 736; (091) 115 177 (ext 39) *Fax:* (091) 232649 *E-mail:* mile@nubsk.edu.mk; bmile47@yahoo.com, pg 1520

Biblioteksstyrelsen (Denmark) *Tel:* 33733373 *Fax:* 33733372 *E-mail:* bs@bs.dk *Web Site:* www.bs.dk, pg 1460

Bibliotekstjaenst AB (Sweden) *Tel:* (046) 180000 *Fax:* (046) 180125, pg 600

Bibliotheca Bodmeriana (Switzerland) *Tel:* (022) 7074433 *Fax:* (022) 7074430, pg 1501

Bibliotheca di Gabriele Chiusano (Italy) *Tel:* (0771) 744350, pg 378

Bibliotheek van het Centraal Bureau voor de Statistiek (Netherlands) *Tel:* (070) 3375151 *Fax:* (070) 3375984 *E-mail:* bibliotheek@cbs.nl *Web Site:* www.cbs.nl, pg 1486

Bibliotheek Wageningen UR (Netherlands) *Tel:* (07) 484440 *Fax:* (07) 484761 *E-mail:* bluwpudoc@secr.bib.wau.nl *Web Site:* www.agralin.nl, pg 1486

Bibliothek der Osterreichischen Akademie der Wissenschaften (Austria) *Tel:* (01) 51581262 *E-mail:* bibliothe@oeaw.ac.at *Web Site:* www.oeaw.ac.at, pg 1451

Bibliothek des Benediktinerklosters Melk in Niederoesterreich (Austria) *Tel:* (02752) 52312342 *Fax:* (02752) 5231252, pg 1451

Bibliothek des Osterreichischen Patentamtes (Austria) *Tel:* (01) 53424; (01) 53140 *Fax:* (01) 53424; (01) 53110 *E-mail:* weiding@at-patent.co.at, pg 1451

Bibliothek fur Zeitgeschichte/Library of Contemporary History (Germany) *Tel:* (0711) 2124516 *Fax:* (0711) 2124517 *E-mail:* bfz@mailserver.wlb-stuggart.de *Web Site:* www.wlb-stuggart.de/~bfz/bfz.htm, pg 1466

Bibliotheks und Informationssystem der Universitaet Oldenburg (Germany) *Tel:* (0441) 7984001 *Fax:* (0441) 798-4040 *E-mail:* zi@bis.uni-oldenburg.de *Web Site:* www.bis.uni-oldenburg.de/, pg 1466

Bibliotheque Cantonale et Universitaire de Lausanne (Switzerland) *Tel:* (021) 3167880 *Fax:* (021) 3167870, pg 1501

Bibliotheque Cantonale et Universitaire (Kantons- und Universitatsbibliothek) (Switzerland) *Tel:* (026) 3051313 *Fax:* (026) 3051377 *E-mail:* bcu@etatfr.ch, pg 1501

YELLOW PAGES

Bibliotheque Central du Minstere de l'Education Nationale (Belgium) *Tel:* (02) 5110830 *Fax:* (02) 5134333, pg 1453

Bibliotheque Centrale de la Cote d'Ivoire (Cote d'Ivoire) *Tel:* 323872, pg 1458

Bibliotheque Centrale de l'Universite de Kisangani (The Democratic Republic of the Congo) *Tel:* 2948, pg 1458

Bibliotheque Centrale du Museum National d'Histoire Naturelle (France) *Tel:* (01) 40793627 *Fax:* (01) 40793656, pg 1464

Bibliotheque Centrale, Universite de Kinshasa (The Democratic Republic of the Congo) *Tel:* 77920 ext 161, pg 1458

Bibliotheque d'Art et d'Archeologie Jacques Doucet (France) *Tel:* (01) 47037620 *Fax:* (01) 47038925 *E-mail:* baa@paris4.sorbonne.fr, pg 1464

Bibliotheque de l'Institut National de la Recherche Scientifique (Rwanda) *Tel:* 30395 *Fax:* 30939, pg 1495

Bibliotheque de l'Universite Omar Bongo (Gabon) *Tel:* 732956; 732033, pg 1466

Bibliotheque de la Ville (Luxembourg) *Tel:* 547383, pg 1482

Bibliotheque de l'Ecole Superieure des Lettres (Lebanon), pg 1481

Bibliotheque de l'Universite Nationale de Cote d'Ivoire (Cote d'Ivoire) *Tel:* 440847, pg 1459

Bibliotheque Departemental de Pret (Reunion) *Tel:* 210324 *Fax:* 214130, pg 1494

Bibliotheque des Arts (France) *Tel:* (01) 40467590, pg 150

La Bibliotheque des Arts (Switzerland) *Tel:* (021) 3123667; (021) 239334 *Fax:* (021) 3213615, pg 610

Bibliotheque du Centre Culturel Francais de Bamako (Mali) *Tel:* 224019, pg 1483

Bibliotheque du Musee Royal de Mariemont (Belgium) *Tel:* (064) 212193 *Fax:* (064) 262924, pg 1453

Bibliotheque du Petit Seminaire (Haiti), pg 1471

Bibliotheque Fonds Quetelet (Belgium) *Tel:* (02) 5066054 *Fax:* (02) 5028425, pg 1453

Bibliotheque Generale et Archives du Maroc (Morocco) *Tel:* (07) 771890 *Fax:* (07) 776062 *E-mail:* bgarabat@iam.net.ma, pg 1485

Bibliotheque Haitienne des Freres de l'I.C., Saint Louis de Gonzague (Haiti) *Tel:* 2232148; 2237508, pg 1471

Bibliotheque Historique de la Ville de Paris (France) *Tel:* (01) 44592940 *Fax:* (01) 42740316, pg 1464

Bibliotheque Interuniversitaire de Montpellier (France) *Tel:* (04) 67 13 43 50 *Fax:* (04) 67 13 43 51, pg 1464

Bibliotheque Louis Notari (Monaco) *Tel:* 93152940 *Fax:* 93152941, pg 1485

Bibliotheque Municipale (Cote d'Ivoire), pg 1459

Bibliotheque Municipale (France) *Tel:* (02) 99630909; (02) 99879898 *Fax:* (02) 99360596; (02) 99879899 *E-mail:* bm-rennes@univ-rennes1.fr, pg 1464

Bibliotheque Municipale de Besancon (France) *Tel:* (01) 81812089 *Fax:* (01) 81619877, pg 1464

Bibliotheque Municipale de Constantine (Algeria), pg 1449

Bibliotheque Municipale de Grenoble (France) *Tel:* (076) 0476862100 *Fax:* (076) 0476862119 *E-mail:* bmei@upmf-grenoble.fr, pg 1464

Bibliotheque Municipale de Lyon (France) *Tel:* (07) 78621800 *Fax:* (07) 78621949 *E-mail:* bm@bm-lyon.fr *Web Site:* www.bm-lyon.fr, pg 1464

Bibliotheque Nationale (Algeria) *Tel:* (02) 630632 *Fax:* (02) 610435, pg 1235

Bibliotheque Nationale (Algeria) *Tel:* (063) 0632, pg 1449

Bibliotheque Nationale (Cote d'Ivoire) *Tel:* 213872, pg 1459

Bibliotheque Nationale (Guinea) *Tel:* (04) 61010, pg 1471

Bibliotheque Nationale (Mali) *Tel:* 224963, pg 1483

Bibliotheque Nationale (Mauritania) *Tel:* 022435, pg 1484

Bibliotheque Nationale (Togo) *Tel:* 216367; 210410 *Fax:* 221967, pg 1503

Bibliotheque Nationale (Tunisia) *Tel:* (01) 245338 *Fax:* (01) 342700, pg 1504

Bibliotheque Nationale de France (France) *Tel:* (01) 53 79 88 98; (01) 53 79 81 75 *Fax:* (01) 53 79 81 72 *E-mail:* commercial@bnf.fr *Web Site:* editionsl.bnf.fr, pg 150

Bibliotheque Nationale de France (France) *Tel:* (01) 53795379 *Fax:* (01) 47037734, pg 1464

Bibliotheque Nationale d'Haiti (National Library) (Haiti) *Tel:* 20236 *Fax:* 38773, pg 1471

Bibliotheque Nationale du Benin (Benin) *Tel:* 212585, pg 1454

Bibliotheque Nationale et Universitaire de Strasbourg (France) *Tel:* (03) 88252800 *Fax:* (03) 88252803, pg 1465

Bibliotheque Publique (Burundi), pg 1456

Bibliotheque Publique de Kinshasa (The Democratic Republic of the Congo) *Tel:* (012) 3070, pg 1458

Bibliotheque Publique et Universitaire de Geneve (Switzerland) *Tel:* (022) 4182800 *Fax:* (022) 4182801 *E-mail:* info.bpu@ville-ge.ch, pg 1501

Bibliotheque Publique et Universitaire de Neuchatel (Switzerland) *Tel:* (032) 717-73-00 *Fax:* (032) 717-73-09, pg 1501

Bibliotheque Royale Albert Ier (Belgium) *Tel:* (02) 5195311 *Fax:* (02) 5195454, pg 1453

Bibliotheque Universitaire (Madagascar) *Tel:* (02) 23228 *E-mail:* buunivtanamg@minitel.refer.org, pg 1482

Bibliotheque Universitaire Centrale (Benin) *Tel:* 360074, pg 1454

Bibliotheque Universitaire d'Avignon et des Pays du Vaucluse (France) *Tel:* (04) 90162500 *Fax:* (04) 90162510, pg 1465

Bibliotheque Universitaire, Universite Marien Ngouabi (Congo) *Tel:* 811430; 831430, pg 1458

Bibliotheques de l'Universite Libre de Bruxelles (Belgium) *Tel:* (02) 6502378 *Fax:* (02) 6502370 *E-mail:* bibulb@vlb.ac.be, pg 1453

Societe Biblique Francaise (France) *Tel:* (01) 39945051 *Fax:* (01) 39905351 *E-mail:* contacts@alliance-biblique-fr.org *Web Site:* www.la-bible.net, pg 150

Biblos srl (Italy) *Tel:* (049) 5975236 *Fax:* (049) 5972841, pg 378

Biddles Ltd (United Kingdom) *Tel:* (01483) 502224 *Fax:* (01483) 576150, pg 1140

Biddles Ltd (United Kingdom) *Tel:* (01483) 502224 *Fax:* (01483) 576150 *E-mail:* sales@biddles.co.uk *Web Site:* www.biddles.co.uk, pg 1202

Biddles Ltd (United Kingdom) *Tel:* (01483) 502224 *Fax:* (01483) 576150 *E-mail:* sales@biddles.co.uk, pg 1214

Der Baum Wolfgang Biedermann Verlag (Austria) *Tel:* (01) 9319053, pg 49

Bielefelder Verlagsanstalt GmbH & Co KG Richard Kaselowsky (Germany) *Tel:* (0521) 595 0 *Fax:* (0521) 595 518 *E-mail:* kontakt@bva-bielefeld.de *Web Site:* www.bva-bielefeld.de, pg 203

EDITORIAL BIOSFERA CA

Bierman og Bierman I/S (Denmark) *Tel:* 75320288 *Fax:* 75321548 *E-mail:* mail@bierman.dk *Web Site:* www.bierman.dk, pg 130

Biermann Verlag GmbH (Germany) *Tel:* (02236) 376-0 *Fax:* (02236) 376-999 *E-mail:* info@biermann.net *Web Site:* www.biermann-online.de, pg 203

Big Apple Tuttle-Mori Agency Inc (China) *Tel:* (010) 64020119; (02) 25067828 *Fax:* (010) 64020119 *E-mail:* 76540.101@compuserve.com, pg 1109

Big Balloon BV (Netherlands) *Tel:* (023) 5176620; (023) 5176642 *Fax:* (023) 5176630; (023) 5176640 *Web Site:* www.bigballoon.nl, pg 474

BIG Database Publishing Pvt Ltd (India), pg 333

Big Tree Publishing (Republic of Korea) *Tel:* (02) 7369653 *Fax:* (02) 7328694 *E-mail:* kennamu@unitel.co.kr, pg 435

Bihar Hindi Granth Akademi (India) *Tel:* (0612) 671432, pg 333

Erven J Bijleveld (Netherlands) *Tel:* (030) 2317688 *Fax:* (030) 2368675, pg 474

Bijutsu Shuppan-Sha, Ltd (Japan) *Tel:* (03) 32342151 *Fax:* (03) 32349451 *Web Site:* www.bijutsu.co.jp, pg 415

Bilal Muslim Mission of Tanzania (United Republic of Tanzania) *Tel:* (051) 30345; (051) 50924 *Fax:* (051) 116550 *E-mail:* bilal@raha.com, pg 633

Bilblioteka Nov den - Sajuz na Svobodnite Demokrati (Union of Free Democrats) (Bulgaria) *Tel:* (02) 773-982 *Fax:* (02) 327972, pg 94

BILD Publications (United Kingdom) *Tel:* (01562) 723010 *Fax:* (01562) 723029 *E-mail:* enquiries@bild.org.uk *Web Site:* www.bild.org.uk, pg 654

Bild und Heimat Verlagsgesellschaft GmbH (Germany) *Tel:* (03765) 78 15-0 *Fax:* (03765) 1 22 45, pg 203

Bildarchiv Preussischer Kulturbesitz bpk (Germany) *Tel:* (030) 278 792 0 *E-mail:* bildarchiv@bpk.spk-berlin.de *Web Site:* www.bildarchiv-bpk.de, pg 203

Bilden Bilgisayar (Turkey) *Tel:* (0216) 449 52 50 *Fax:* (0216) 449 52 51 *E-mail:* bilden@bilden.com.tr *Web Site:* www.bilden.com.tr, pg 639

BW Bildung und Wissen Verlag und Software GmbH (Germany) *Tel:* (0911) 96 76-179 *Fax:* (0911) 96 76-189 *E-mail:* info@bwverlag.de *Web Site:* www.bwverlag.de, pg 203

Bilkent University Library (Turkey) *Tel:* (0312) 266-4472 *Fax:* (0312) 266-4391 *Web Site:* www.library.bilkent.edu.tr, pg 1504

Bina Aksara Parta (Indonesia) *Tel:* (361) 95240, pg 354

Bina Cipta PT (Indonesia) *Tel:* (022) 2504319 *Fax:* (022) 2504319, pg 354

Bina Ilmu (Indonesia) *Tel:* (031) 5323214; (031) 5340076 *Fax:* (031) 5315421, pg 354

Bina Rena Pariwara (Indonesia) *Tel:* (021) 7901938; (021) 7901939 *Fax:* (021) 7901939, pg 354

Bind-It Corp (United States) *Tel:* 312-951-1953 *Fax:* 312-951-9134 *E-mail:* information@bindit.com *Web Site:* www.bindit.com, pg 1205

Bindernagelsche Buchhandlung (Germany) *Tel:* (06031) 55 64 *Fax:* (06031) 6 48 40, pg 203

Guy Binsfeld & Co Sarl (Luxembourg) *Tel:* 496868 *Fax:* 488770, pg 447

Bio Concepts Publishing (Australia) *Tel:* (07) 33525088 *Fax:* (07) 33566081 *E-mail:* orthplet@ozemail.com.au *Web Site:* www.bioconcepts.com.au, pg 15

Editoriale Bios (Italy) *Tel:* (0984) 398300 *Fax:* (0984) 398300, pg 378

BIOS Scientific Publishers Ltd (United Kingdom) *Tel:* (01865) 726286 *Fax:* (01865) 246823 *Web Site:* www.bios.co.uk, pg 654

Editorial Biosfera CA (Venezuela) *Tel:* (02) 7528892; (02) 7519119 *Fax:* (02) 7519320, pg 762

BIR Publishing (Republic of Korea) *Tel:* (02) 515 2000 *Fax:* (02) 515 2007 *Web Site:* www.bir.co.kr, pg 435

Biramo Book Distributors (Australia) *Tel:* (02) 49542626 *Fax:* (02) 49565398 *E-mail:* biramobooks@tpg.com.au, pg 1272

A W Birchall & Sons Pty Ltd (Australia) *Tel:* (03) 63313011 *Toll Free Tel:* 800 806867 *Fax:* (03) 63317165 *E-mail:* books@birchalls.com.au, pg 1272

Birchgrove Books (Australia) *Tel:* (02) 98105040 *Fax:* (02) 98106053 *E-mail:* 100406.343@compuserve.com, pg 15

Birkhauser Verlag AG (Switzerland) *Tel:* (061) 2050707 *Fax:* (061) 2050799 *E-mail:* info@birkhauser.ch; sales@birkhauser.ch *Web Site:* www.birkhauser.ch, pg 610

Birkner & Co Zweigniederlassung Mecklenburg-Vorpommern (Germany) *Tel:* (040) 85308502 *Fax:* (040) 85308381, pg 203

Birlinn Ltd (United Kingdom) *Tel:* (0131) 668 4371 *Fax:* (0131) 668 4466 *E-mail:* info@birlinn.co.uk *Web Site:* www.birlinn.co.uk, pg 655

Birmingham Books (United Kingdom) *Tel:* (0121) 235 2868; (0121) 235 4511 *Fax:* (0121) 233 9702; (0121) 233 4458, pg 655

Birmingham Library Information Services (United Kingdom) *Tel:* (0121) 303 4511; (0121) 233 9702; (0121) 235 2868 *Fax:* (0121) 233 4458 *E-mail:* central.library@birmingham.gov.uk *Web Site:* www.birmingham.gov.uk, pg 655

Birmingham Library Information Services (United Kingdom) *Tel:* (0121) 303 4511 *Fax:* ((0121) 303 2861, pg 1505

Birmingham Museums & Art Gallery (United Kingdom) *Tel:* (0121) 3032834 *E-mail:* bmag_enq@birmingham.gov.uk *Web Site:* www.bmag.org.uk, pg 1316

Societe Nouvelle Adam Biro (France) *Tel:* (01) 44 59 84 59 *Fax:* (01) 44 59 87 17, pg 150

Biro Penyediaan Teks Itm (Biroteks) (Malaysia) *Tel:* (03) 59271 ext 495 *Fax:* (03) 500226; (03) 55692733, pg 451

Biro Pusat Statistik (Indonesia) *Tel:* (021) 3810291; (021) 3841195; (021) 3842508 *Fax:* (021) 3857046, pg 354

Birsen Yayinevi (Turkey) *Tel:* (0212) 5278578; (0212) 5137588 *Fax:* (0212) 5270895, pg 639

BIS Publishers (Netherlands) *Tel:* (020) 6205171 *Fax:* (020) 6279251 *E-mail:* bispub@XS4all-nl, pg 474

Bishopsgate Press Ltd (United Kingdom) *Tel:* (01732) 833778 *Fax:* (01732) 833090, pg 655

Bitan Publishers Ltd (Israel) *Tel:* (03) 6040089 *Fax:* (03) 5404792, pg 365

BKV-Brasilienkunde Verlag GmbH (Germany) *Tel:* (05452) 4598 *Fax:* (05452) 4357 *E-mail:* brasilien@T-Online.de *Web Site:* www.brasilienkunde.de; home.t-online.de/home/Brasilien, pg 203

BLA Publishing Ltd (United Kingdom) *Tel:* (01342) 318980 *Fax:* (01342) 410980, pg 655

A & C Black Publishers Ltd (United Kingdom) *Tel:* (020) 7758 0200 *Fax:* (020) 7758 0222 *E-mail:* enquiries@acblack.co.uk *Web Site:* www.acblack.co.uk, pg 655

Black Academy Press (Nigeria) *Tel:* (083) 230606; (083) 232606, pg 498

Black Ace Books (United Kingdom) *Tel:* (01307) 465096 *Fax:* (01307) 465494 *Web Site:* www.blackacebooks.com, pg 655

Black Bear Press Ltd (United Kingdom) *Tel:* (01223) 424571 *Fax:* (01223) 426877 *E-mail:* black_bear_pres@msn.com, pg 1160

Black Bear Press Ltd (United Kingdom) *Tel:* (01223) 424571 *Fax:* (01223) 426877 *E-mail:* black_bear_press@msn.com, pg 1202

Black Dog Books (Australia) *Tel:* (03) 9419 9406 *Fax:* (03) 9419 1214 *E-mail:* dog@bdb.com.au *Web Site:* www.bdb.com.au, pg 15

Black Mask Ltd (Ghana) *Tel:* (021) 234577 *Fax:* (021) 231431, pg 306

Black Spring Press Ltd (United Kingdom) *Tel:* (020) 7639 2492 *Fax:* (020) 7639 2508 *E-mail:* bsp@blackspring.demon.co.uk, pg 655

Blackbooks Co-operative for Aborigines Ltd (Australia) *Tel:* (0612) 9660 3444 *Fax:* (0612) 9660 1924 *E-mail:* Tranby@tranby.com.au *Web Site:* www.midcoast.com.au, pg 15

Blackhead Ink Publishing (Australia) *Tel:* (065) 592981 *Fax:* (065) 510518, pg 15

Blackie Children's Books (United Kingdom) *Tel:* (020) 7416 3000 *Fax:* (020) 7416 3086, pg 655

Blackmore Ltd (United Kingdom) *Tel:* (01747) 853034 *Fax:* (01747) 854500 *E-mail:* sales@blackmail.blackmore.co.uk, pg 1160, 1202

Blackmore's Booksellers BLA (New Zealand) *Tel:* (03) 5489992 *Fax:* (03) 5466779, pg 1302

Blackstaff Press (United Kingdom) *Tel:* (028) 9066 8074 *Fax:* (028) 9066 8207 *E-mail:* info@blackstaffpress.com *Web Site:* www.blackstaffpress.com, pg 655

Blackstone Press Pty Ltd (Australia) *Tel:* (02) 9389 7677 *E-mail:* c.l.e.@laams.com.au, pg 15

Blackwell & Hadwiger GesmbH British Bookshop (Austria) *Tel:* (01) 5121945; (01) 5132933 *Fax:* (01) 5121026, pg 1274

Blackwell Munksgaaard (Denmark) *Tel:* 77333333 *Fax:* 77333377 *E-mail:* headoffice@munksgaard.dk *Web Site:* www.blackwellmunksgaard.com, pg 130

Blackwell Publishers (United Kingdom) *Tel:* (01865) 791100 *Fax:* (01865) 791347 *Web Site:* www.blackwellpublishers.co.uk, pg 655

Blackwell Retail (United Kingdom) *Tel:* (01865) 792792 *Fax:* (01865) 794143 *E-mail:* sales@blackwell.co.uk, pg 1316

Blackwell Science Ltd (United Kingdom) *Tel:* (01865) 206206 *Fax:* (01865) 721205 *E-mail:* shona.macdonald@blacksci.co.uk, pg 656

Blackwell Science Pty Ltd (Australia) *Tel:* (03) 93470300 *Fax:* (03) 9347 5001 *E-mail:* dimi.katsiens@blacksci-asia.com.au *Web Site:* www.blacksci.co.uk, pg 15

Blackwell Wissenschafts-Verlag GmbH (Germany) *Tel:* (030) 32 79 06-0 *Fax:* (030) 32 79 06-10 *E-mail:* verlag@blackwis.de; rights@blackwis.de *Web Site:* www.blackwis.de, pg 203

Bladkompaniet A/S (Norway) *Tel:* 22902400 *Fax:* 22902401, pg 503

Horst Blaich Pty Ltd (Australia) *Tel:* (03) 7202658 *Fax:* (03) 7624225, pg 15

Joan Blair (Australia) *Tel:* (02) 42321642, pg 15

William Blake & Co (France) *Tel:* (05) 56 31 42 20 *Fax:* (05) 56 31 45 47 *Web Site:* www.editions-william-blake-and-co.com, pg 150

Blaketon Hall Ltd (United Kingdom) *Tel:* (01392) 210 602 *Fax:* (01392) 421 165 *E-mail:* sales@blaketonhall.co.uk *Web Site:* www.blaketonhall.co.uk, pg 656

Editions Gerard Blanchart & Cie SA (Belgium) *Tel:* (02) 4783706 *Fax:* (02) 4786429, pg 65

Editions Blanco SA (Belgium) *Tel:* (02) 7720320 *Fax:* (02) 7706429, pg 65

Blandford Publishing Ltd (United Kingdom) *Tel:* (01202) 665432 *Fax:* (01202) 666219, pg 656

Blanvalet VerlagGmbH (Germany) *Tel:* (089) 4372-0 *Fax:* (089) 4372-2812 *E-mail:* vertrieb.verlagsgruppe@bertelsmann.de, pg 204

Verlag Die Blaue Eule (Germany) *Tel:* (0201) 8 77 69 63 *Fax:* (0201) 8 7769 64 *E-mail:* info@die-blaue-eule.de *Web Site:* www.die-blaue-eule.de, pg 204

Blaukreuz-Verlag Bern (Switzerland) *Tel:* (031) 3015866; (031) 3015243 *Fax:* (031) 3005869, pg 610

Blaukreuz-Verlag Wuppertal (Germany) *Tel:* (0202) 6200361 *Fax:* (0202) 6200381 *E-mail:* bkv@blaukreuz.de *Web Site:* www.blaukreuz.de, pg 204

Blay-Foldex (France) *Tel:* (01) 49889210 *Fax:* (01) 49889209 *Web Site:* 195.11.148.32:8055, pg 151

Blaze International Productions Inc (United States) *Tel:* 212-967-7501 *Fax:* 212-967-7551, pg 1163, 1205, 1215, 1224

Blazek und Bergmann (Germany) *Tel:* (069) 152003-36 *Fax:* (069) 152003-44 *Web Site:* www.blazek.de, pg 1283

Bleicher Verlag GmbH (Germany) *Tel:* (07156) 43 08-20 *Fax:* (07156) 43 08-40 *E-mail:* info@bleicher_verlag.de *Web Site:* www.bleicher-verlag.de, pg 204

Verlag Wolfgang Bleiweis (Germany) *Tel:* (09721) 26721 *Fax:* (09721) 26751, pg 204

BLIC, russko-Baltijskij informaciionnyj centr, AO (Russian Federation) *Tel:* (0812) 3112252 *Fax:* (0812) 3112252; (0812) 1135896 *E-mail:* blitz@blitz.spb.ru, pg 537

Central Library for the Blind, Visually Impaired & Handicapped (Israel) *Tel:* (09) 8620166 *Fax:* (09) 8626346 *E-mail:* office@clfb.org.il *Web Site:* www.clfb.org.il, pg 1476

Bloch Editores SA (Brazil) *Tel:* (021) 205-8682 *Fax:* (021) 205-8682 *E-mail:* blocheditores@ieq.com.br *Web Site:* www.blocheditores.hpg.ig.com.br, pg 79

Blockfoil Ltd (United Kingdom) *Tel:* (01473) 721701 *Fax:* (01473) 270705, pg 1202

Bloemfontein Public Library (South Africa) *Tel:* (051) 71993 *Fax:* (051) 4058604 *E-mail:* pat@dux.bfncouncil.co.za, pg 1497

H W Blok Uitgeverij BV (Netherlands) *Tel:* (036) 5485480 *Fax:* (036) 5485499, pg 474

Nakladatelstvi Blok (Czech Republic) *Tel:* (05) 42321245 *Fax:* (05) 42321245, pg 123

Blondel La Rougery SARL (France) *Tel:* (01) 48949452 *Fax:* (01) 48949438, pg 151

Bloodaxe Books Ltd (United Kingdom) *Tel:* (01434) 240 500 *Fax:* (01434) 240 505 *E-mail:* editor@bloodaxebooks.demon.co.uk *Web Site:* www.bloodaxebooks.com, pg 656

Roy Bloom Ltd (United Kingdom) *Tel:* (020) 7729 5373 *Fax:* (020) 7729 2375, pg 1140, 1317

Bloomings Books (Australia) *Tel:* (03) 9427 1234; (03) 9427 1490 *Fax:* (03) 9427 9066, pg 15

Bloomsbury Publishing PLC (United Kingdom) *Tel:* (020) 7494 2111 *Fax:* (020) 7434 0151 *E-mail:* csm@bloomsbury.com *Web Site:* www.bloomsburymagazine.com, pg 656

Blorenge Books (United Kingdom) *Tel:* (01873) 856114, pg 656

Eberhargd Blottner Verlag (Germany) *Tel:* (06128) 2 36 00 *Fax:* (06128) 21180 *E-mail:* blottner@blottner.de *Web Site:* www.blottner.de, pg 204

Blubber Head Press (Australia) *Tel:* (03) 6223 8644 *Fax:* (03) 6223 8644 *E-mail:* books@astrolabebooks.com.au, pg 15

Editora Edgard Blucher Ltda (Brazil) *Tel:* (011) 3078-5366 *Fax:* (011) 3079-2707 *E-mail:* eblucher@uol.com.br, pg 80

Blueprint (United Kingdom) *Tel:* (01372) 802080 *Fax:* (01372) 802079 *E-mail:* publications@pira.co.uk, pg 656

Brigitte Blume (Germany) *Tel:* (089) 1418639 *Fax:* (089) 1418639, pg 204

BLV Verlagsgesellschaft mbH (Germany) *Tel:* (089) 127050 *Fax:* (089) 12705354 *E-mail:* blv.verlag@blu.de *Web Site:* www.blv.de, pg 204

BMJ Publishing Group (United Kingdom) *Tel:* (020) 7387 4499; (020) 7383 6245 *Fax:* (020) 7383 6661; (020) 7383 6662 *E-mail:* customerservices@bmjbooks.com *Web Site:* www.bmjpg.com, pg 656

BN International (Netherlands) *Tel:* (03552) 48400 *Fax:* (03552) 56004, pg 1213

Bo-jinjae Printing Co Ltd (Republic of Korea) *Tel:* (02) 6792351; (02) 6792355 *Fax:* (02) 6762821, pg 435

Bo Moon Dang (Republic of Korea) *Tel:* (02) 7047025 *Fax:* (02) 7042324, pg 435

Bo Ri (Republic of Korea) *Tel:* (02) 3233676 *Fax:* (02) 3240285, pg 435

Board of Studies (Australia) *Tel:* (02) 9367 8111 *Fax:* (02) 9367 8484 *Web Site:* www.boardofstudies.nsw.edu.au, pg 15

Boat Books Group (Australia) *Tel:* (02) 94391133 *Fax:* (02) 94398517 *E-mail:* boatbook@boatbooks-aus.com.au, pg 15

De Boccard Edition-Diffusion (France) *Tel:* (01) 43 26 00 37 *Fax:* (01) 43 54 85 83, pg 151

Verlag Erwin Bochinsky GmbH & Co KG (Germany) *Tel:* (069) 2 71 37 89-0 *Fax:* (069) 2 71 37 89-94 *Web Site:* www.das-musikinstrument.de, pg 204

Bock und Herchen Verlag (Germany) *Tel:* (02224) 57 75 *Fax:* (02224) 7 83 10 *E-mail:* buh@bock-net.de *Web Site:* www.b-u-b.de, pg 204

Bodleian Library (United Kingdom) *Tel:* (01865) 277000 *Fax:* (01865) 277182 *E-mail:* vaisey@vax.ox.ac.uk, pg 1505

Les Editions de la Fondation Martin Bodmer (Switzerland) *Tel:* (022) 7362370 *Fax:* (022) 7001540, pg 610

De Boeck et Larcier SA (Belgium) *Tel:* (010) 48 25 11 *Fax:* (010) 48 26 50 *Web Site:* www.larcier.be/larcier.html, pg 65

Boehlau-Verlag GmbH & Cie (Germany) *Tel:* (0221) 91 39 0-0 *Fax:* (0221) 91 39 0-11 *E-mail:* vertrieb@boehlau.de *Web Site:* www.boehlau.de, pg 204

Boehlau Verlag GmbH & Co KG (Austria) *Tel:* (01) 330 24 27 *Fax:* (01) 330 24 32 *Web Site:* www.boehlau.at, pg 50

Verlag Hermann Boehlaus Nachfolger Weimar GmbH & Co (Germany) *Tel:* (03643) 8508-90 *Fax:* (03643) 8508-92, pg 205

Boek Promotions BV (Netherlands) *Tel:* (035) 5310154, pg 474

Boek.be (Belgium) *Tel:* (03) 230 89 23 *Fax:* (03) 281 22 40 *E-mail:* info@boek.be *Web Site:* www.boek.be, pg 1237

Boekencentrum BV (Netherlands) *Tel:* (079) 3615481 *Fax:* (079) 3615489 *E-mail:* info@boekencentrum.nl *Web Site:* www.boeckencentrum.nl, pg 474

De Boekerij BV (Netherlands) *Tel:* (020) 5353135 *Fax:* (020) 5353130 *E-mail:* info@boekery.nl, pg 474

BoekWerk (Netherlands) *Tel:* (050) 5265559 *Fax:* (050) 5268198, pg 474

Klaus Boer Verlag (Germany) *Tel:* (089) 13938099 *Fax:* (089) 13989098 *E-mail:* boerv@online.de *Web Site:* www.boerverlag.de, pg 205

Borsenverein des Deutschen Buchhandels eV (Germany) *Tel:* (069) 1306-0 *Fax:* (069) 1306-201, pg 1245

Bogan's Forlag (Denmark) *Tel:* 48188055 *Fax:* 48188769, pg 130

Bogazici University Library (Turkey) *Tel:* (0212) 2631500 *Fax:* (0212) 2656357, pg 1504

Bogfabrikken Fakta ApS (Denmark) *Tel:* 35373533 *Fax:* 35373299, pg 130

Bogklubben 12 Boget A/S (Denmark) *Tel:* 33695050 *Fax:* 33695051 *E-mail:* b12b@bogklubben-12-boget.dk, pg 1227

Bohem Press Kinderbuchverlag (Switzerland) *Tel:* (01) 4407000 *Fax:* (01) 4407001 *E-mail:* bohem@dial.eunet.ch, pg 610

Bohmann Druck und Verlag GmbH & Co KG (Austria) *Tel:* (01) 740950 *Fax:* (01) 74095 183 *Web Site:* www.bohmann.co.at, pg 50

Bohn Stafleu Van Loghum BV (Netherlands) *Tel:* (0172) 466321 *Fax:* (0172) 435527, pg 474

Boighar (Bangladesh) *Tel:* (031) 252745, pg 62

Boinkie Publishers (Australia) *Tel:* (02) 588-7010 *Fax:* (02) 9311-3428, pg 15

Edition Boiselle (Germany) *Tel:* (06232) 629662 *Fax:* (06232) 629664 *E-mail:* info@edition-boiselle.de *Web Site:* www.edition-boiselle.de, pg 205

Bojko Kacarmazov (Bulgaria) *Tel:* (02) 654969 *Fax:* (02) 654969 *E-mail:* eto@einet.bg, pg 94

Bok Og Papiransattes Forening (Norway) *Tel:* 22205197 *Fax:* 22400033, pg 1256

Bokaforlag Birtingur (Iceland) *Tel:* 5627700 *Fax:* 5627710, pg 327

Bokautgafan Orn og Orlygur ehf (Iceland) *Tel:* 5671777 *Fax:* 5671240; 5684866, pg 327

Bokavardafelag Islands (Iceland) *Tel:* 564-2050 *Fax:* 564-3877, pg 1517

Bokaverslun Sigfusar Eymundssonar (Iceland) *Tel:* 13135 *Fax:* 15078, pg 327

Bokforlaget Atlantis AB (Sweden) *Tel:* (08) 7830440 *Fax:* (08) 6617285 *E-mail:* mail@atlantis-publishers.se, pg 600

Bokforlaget Bra Bocker AB (Sweden) *Tel:* (040) 665 46 00 *Fax:* (040) 665 46 22 *E-mail:* kundservice@bbb.se *Web Site:* www.bbb.se, pg 600

Bokforlaget Cordia AB (Sweden) *Tel:* (08) 702 79 90 *Fax:* (08) 641 45 85, pg 600

Bokforlaget Fabel AB (Sweden) *Tel:* (08) 869080 *Fax:* (08) 7495021, pg 600

Bokforlaget Opal AB (Sweden) *Tel:* (08) 282179 *Fax:* (08) 296623, pg 600

Bokforlaget Plus AB (Sweden) *Tel:* (08) 6547408, pg 600

Bokforlaget Rediviva, Facsimileforlaget (Sweden) *Tel:* (08) 257007, pg 600

Bokforlaget Settern AB (Sweden) *Tel:* (0435) 80070; (0435) 80400 *Fax:* (0435) 80400 *E-mail:* info@settern.se *Web Site:* www.settern.se, pg 601

Bokforlaget Spektra AB (Sweden) *Tel:* (035) 36030 *Fax:* (035) 36177, pg 601

Bokklubb Bra Bockesr (Sweden) *Tel:* (042) 339000 *Fax:* (042) 330504, pg 1232

De norske Bokklubbene A/S (Norway) *Tel:* 22022000 *Fax:* 22022210, pg 1230

Boksala Studenta (The University Bookstore) (Iceland) *Tel:* 5700777 *Fax:* 5700778 *E-mail:* boksala@boksala.is *Web Site:* www.boksala.is, pg 1288

Bolanz Verlag fur Alle (Germany) *Tel:* (07541) 33 6 99 *Fax:* (07541) 32467, pg 205

Bold ADS (Zimbabwe) *Tel:* (04) 621321; (04) 621327 *Fax:* (04) 621328, pg 768

CB-Verlag Carl Boldt (Germany) *Tel:* (030) 833 70 87 *Fax:* (030) 833 91 25 *E-mail:* cb-verlag@t-online.de, pg 205

Boletin Oficial del Estado (Spain) *Tel:* (091) 3841700; (091) 3841701; (091) 2365303 *Fax:* (091) 5382349 *Web Site:* www.boe.es, pg 565

Bolivar Bookshop (Jamaica) *Tel:* (876) 926-8799 *Fax:* (876) 968-1874 *E-mail:* bolivar-jamaica@colis.com, pg 1294

Bollati Boringhieri Editore Srl (Italy) *Tel:* (011) 5591711 *Fax:* (011) 543024 *E-mail:* info@bollatiboringhieri.it; rightsdept@bollatiboringhieri.it, pg 378

Herbert Bolles (Australia) *Tel:* (02) 45 67 7350, pg 15

Bollmann-Bildkarten-Verlag GmbH & Co KG (Germany) *Tel:* (0531) 332069 *Fax:* (0531) 353064 *E-mail:* info@bollmann-bildkarten.de *Web Site:* www.bollmann-bildkarten.de, pg 205

David Bolt Associates (United Kingdom) *Tel:* (01483) 721118 *Fax:* (01483) 721118, pg 1118

Bombay University Library (India) *Tel:* (022) 2652819 *Fax:* (022) 2652832, pg 1473

Bompiani-RCS Libri (Italy) *Tel:* (02) 50951 *Fax:* (02) 5065361 *Web Site:* www.reslibri.it, pg 378

Bonacci editore (Italy) *Tel:* (06) 68300004 *Fax:* (06) 68806382 *E-mail:* info@bonacci.it *Web Site:* www.bonacci.it, pg 378

Bonafides Verlags-Anstalt (Liechtenstein) *Tel:* (075) 82510, pg 444

Giuseppe Bonanno Editore (Italy) *Tel:* (095) 601984 *Fax:* (095) 604380, pg 378

Frances Bond Literary Services (South Africa) *Tel:* (031) 2624532 *Fax:* (031) 2622620 *E-mail:* fbond@mweb.com.za, pg 1116

Casa Editrice Bonechi (Italy) *Tel:* (055) 576841 *Fax:* (055) 5000766 *E-mail:* bonechi@bonechi.it *Web Site:* www.bonechi.it., pg 378

Bonechi-Edizioni Il Turismo Srl (Italy) *Tel:* (055) 2398224 *Fax:* (055) 216366, pg 378

Verlag Aurel Bongers (Germany) *Tel:* (02361) 27000 *Fax:* (02361) 27007, pg 205

Ditta F Bongiovanni SAS (Italy) *Tel:* (051) 225722 *Fax:* (051) 226128, pg 378

Bonifatius GmbH Druck-Buch-Verlag (Germany) *Tel:* (05251) 153 171 *Fax:* (05251) 153 104 *Web Site:* www.bonifatius.de, pg 205

Universitaet Bonn (Germany) *Tel:* (0228) 737350 *Fax:* (0228) 737546 *E-mail:* ulb@ulb.uni-bonn.de, pg 1466

Editions Andre Bonne (France) *Tel:* (01) 45150061 *Fax:* (01) 45218175, pg 151

Bonnier Audio (Sweden) *Tel:* (08) 6968760 *Fax:* (08) 6968757, pg 601

Bonnier Audio (Sweden) *Tel:* 08 6968760; 08 6968757, pg 601

Bonnier Carlsen Bokforlag AB (Sweden) *Tel:* (08) 59895500 *Fax:* (08) 4538945, pg 601

Bonnier Publications AS (Denmark) *Tel:* 32833100 *Fax:* 32833123 *Web Site:* www.bonnierpublications.com, pg 130

Bonnier Utbildning AB (Sweden) *Tel:* (08) 6968590 *Fax:* (08) 6968610, pg 601

Albert Bonniers Forlag (Sweden) *Tel:* (08) 6968000 *Fax:* (08) 6968361, pg 601

Bonniers Bokklubb (Sweden) *Tel:* (08) 6968000 *Fax:* (08) 6968361, pg 1232

Bonniers Specialmagasiner A/S Bogdivisionen (Denmark) *Tel:* 39 17 20 00 *Fax:* 39 17 23 00, pg 130

Bonsai-Centrum (Germany) *Tel:* (06221) 8491-0 *Fax:* (06221) 849130 *E-mail:* info@bonsai-centrum.de *Web Site:* www.bonsai-centrum.de, pg 205

Bonsignori Editore SRL (Italy) *Tel:* (06) 5881496 *Fax:* (06) 5882839 *E-mail:* redazione@bonsignori.it, pg 378

Bonum Editorial SACI (Argentina) *Tel:* (011) 4554-1414 *Fax:* (011) 4554-1414, pg 4

Adolf Bonz Verlag GmbH (Germany) *Tel:* (05300) 901053 *Fax:* (0503) 901053, pg 205

BOOBOOK PUBLICATIONS

Boobook Publications (Australia) *Tel:* (049) 97 0811 *Fax:* (049) 97 1089, pg 15

Book Agencies of Tasmania (Australia) *Tel:* (03) 62 477 405 *Fax:* (03) 62 471 116 *E-mail:* bookagencies@trump.net.au *Web Site:* www.ontas.com.au/book_agencies/contact.htm, pg 16

Book Aid International (United Kingdom) *Tel:* (020) 7733 3577 *Fax:* (020) 7978 8006 *E-mail:* info@bookaid.org *Web Site:* www.bookaid.org, pg 1524

Book and Printing Center - Israel Export Institute (Israel) *Tel:* (03) 5142916 *Fax:* (03) 5142881 *E-mail:* israeli@export.gov.il *Web Site:* www.export.gov.il, pg 1249

Book Centre, Textbook Sales (Pvt) Ltd (Zimbabwe) *Tel:* (04) 790691 *Fax:* (04) 751690, pg 1325

Book Chamber of Kazakhstan ISBN Agency (Kazakstan) *Tel:* (03272) 306421 *Fax:* (03272) 304265 *E-mail:* rntb@kaznet.kz, pg 1250

Book Chamber of Ukraine, National ISBN Agency (Ukraine) *Tel:* (44) 573-52-36 *Fax:* (44) 573-52-36, pg 1263

Book Circle (India) *Tel:* (011) 3266258; (011) 3288283; (011) 3241513 *Fax:* (011) 3263050 *E-mail:* thebookcircle@yahoo.com *Web Site:* www.meditechbooks.com, pg 333

Book Club Associates (United Kingdom) *Tel:* (020) 7637 0341 *Fax:* (020) 7291 3525, pg 1233

Book Collectors' Society of Australia (Australia) *Tel:* (02) 9798 8984 *Fax:* (02) 9798 8984 *E-mail:* jeff@bcspl.com.au, pg 16

The Book Company Publishing Pty Ltd (Australia) *Tel:* (02) 94863711 *Fax:* (02) 94863722 *E-mail:* sales@thebookcompany.com.au *Web Site:* www.thebookcompany.com.au, pg 16

Book Creation Services (United Kingdom) *Tel:* (020) 7287 0214 *Fax:* (020) 7287 8547, pg 1140

Book Creation Services (United Kingdom) *Tel:* (020) 7287 0214 *Fax:* (020) 7287 8547 *E-mail:* hal@zoo.co.uk, pg 1161

Book Creation Services (United Kingdom) *Tel:* (020) 7287 0214 *Fax:* (020) 7287 8547, pg 1202, 1214

Book Data (United Kingdom) *Tel:* (020) 8843 8600 *Fax:* (020) 8843 8744 *E-mail:* info@bookdata.co.uk; sales@bookdata.co.uk *Web Site:* www.bookdata.co.uk; www.ehaus.co.uk, pg 657

Book Data Asia Pacific (New Zealand) *Tel:* (09) 360 3294 *Fax:* (09) 360 8853 *E-mail:* info@bookdata.co.nz *Web Site:* www.bookdata.com, pg 488

Book Development Council International (BDCI) (United Kingdom) *Tel:* (020) 7565 7474 *Fax:* (020) 7836 4543 *E-mail:* mail@publishers.org.uk *Web Site:* www.publishers.org.uk, pg 1264

Book Editore (Italy) *Tel:* (051) 714720 *Fax:* (051) 711216, pg 378

Book Faith India (India) *Tel:* (011) 7132459 *Fax:* (011) 7249674 *E-mail:* pilgrim@del2.vsnl.net.in, pg 333

The Book Guild Ltd (United Kingdom) *Tel:* (01273) 472534 *Fax:* (01273) 476472 *E-mail:* info@bookguild.co.uk *Web Site:* www.bookguild.co.uk, pg 657

The Book House (Pakistan) *Tel:* (042) 61212; (042) 232415 *Fax:* (042) 6360955, pg 506

Book Industry Communication (United Kingdom) *Tel:* (020) 7607 0021 *Fax:* (020) 7607 0415, pg 1264

Book Lovers Club (India) *Tel:* (011) 6910050; (011) 6916209 *Fax:* (011) 6331241 *E-mail:* ghai@nde.vsnl.net.in, pg 1229

Book Lovers' Club (Yugoslavia) *Tel:* (011) 651666; (011) 650399, pg 1234

Book Marketing Ltd (China) *Tel:* (02) 5620121 *Fax:* (02) 5650187, pg 102

Book Marketing Ltd (United Kingdom) *Tel:* (020) 7398 0705 *Fax:* (020) 7626 3660 *E-mail:* bml@bookmarketing.co.uk, pg 657

Book Marketing Ltd (United Kingdom) *Tel:* (020) 7398 0705 *Fax:* (020) 7626 3660 *E-mail:* bml@bookmarketing.co.uk *Web Site:* www.bookmarketing.co.uk, pg 1264

Book Packaging & Marketing (United Kingdom) *Tel:* (01327) 858380 *Fax:* (01327) 858380, pg 657

Book Production Consultants PLC (United Kingdom) *Tel:* (01223) 352790 *Fax:* (01223) 460718 *E-mail:* cw@bpccam.co.uk *Web Site:* www.bpccam.co.uk, pg 1118, 1140

Book Production Consultants PLC (United Kingdom) *Tel:* (01223) 352790 *Fax:* (01223) 460718 *Web Site:* www.bpccam.co.uk, pg 1161

Book Production Consultants PLC (United Kingdom) *Tel:* (01223) 352790 *Fax:* (01223) 460718 *E-mail:* cw@bpccam.co.uk *Web Site:* www.bpccam.co.uk, pg 1223

Book Promotions (South Africa) *Tel:* (021) 7060949 *Fax:* (021) 7060940 *E-mail:* enquiries@bookpro.co.za, pg 1310

The Book Publishers Association of Israel (Israel) *Tel:* (03) 5614121 *Fax:* (03) 5611996 *E-mail:* info@tbpai.co.il, pg 366

Book Publishers' Association of Israel (Israel) *Tel:* (03) 5614121 *Fax:* (03) 5611996 *E-mail:* tbpai@netvision.net.il, pg 1249

The Book Publishers' Association of Israel, International Promotion and Literary Rights Department (Israel) *Tel:* (03) 5614121 *Fax:* (03) 5611996 *E-mail:* rights@tbpai.co.il *Web Site:* www.tbpai.co.il, pg 1112

Book Publishing Institute (Afghanistan), pg 1

Book Representation & Distribution Ltd (United Kingdom) *Tel:* (01702) 552912 *Fax:* (01702) 556095 *E-mail:* mail@bookreps.com *Web Site:* www.bookreps.com, pg 1317

Book Representation & Publishing Co Ltd (Nigeria) *Tel:* (022) 710242, pg 498

Book Sales (K) Ltd (Kenya), pg 431

Book Sales (K) Ltd (Kenya) *Tel:* (02) 221031; (02) 226543, pg 1296

The Book Source (Barbados) *Tel:* (246) 4310379 *Fax:* (246) 4261855 *E-mail:* bksource@caribsurf.com *Web Site:* www.booktrace.com, pg 1275

Book Stop (Ireland) *Tel:* (01) 2809917; (01) 2844863, pg 1291

Book Studio (Finland) *Tel:* (0914) 451441 *Fax:* (0914) 419142 *E-mail:* books@bookstudio.fi *Web Site:* www.bookstudio.fi, pg 142

Book Tokens Ltd (United Kingdom) *Tel:* (020) 7834 5488 *Fax:* (020) 7834 8781, pg 1264

The Book Trade Benevolent Society (United Kingdom) *Tel:* (01923) 263128 *Fax:* (01923) 270732 *E-mail:* btbs@booktradecharity.demon.co.uk *Web Site:* www.booktradecharity.demon.co.uk, pg 1264

Bookbank SL (Spain) *Tel:* (091) 3733539 *Fax:* (091) 3165591, pg 1116

Bookbank SL Agencia Literaria (Spain) *Tel:* (091) 3733539 *Fax:* (091) 3165591 *E-mail:* bookbank@nexo.es, pg 565

Bookbuilders Ltd (Hong Kong) *Tel:* 27968123 *Fax:* 27968267; 27968690 *E-mail:* lph@netvigator.com, pg 1155, 1195

BookBuilders New York Ltd (United States) *Tel:* 845-639-5316 *Fax:* 845-639-5318, pg 1142, 1163

BookBuilders New York Ltd (United States) *Tel:* 845-639-5316 *Fax:* 845-639-5318 *Web Site:* www.mcabooks.com, pg 1205

BookBuilders New York Ltd (United States) *Tel:* 845-639-5316 *Fax:* 845-639-5318, pg 1215

BookBuilders New York Ltd (United States) *Tel:* 845-639-5316 *Fax:* 845-639-5318 *Web Site:* www.mcabooks.com, pg 1224

Bookionics (India) *Tel:* (040) 593654 *Fax:* (040) 595678 *E-mail:* bookionics@yahoo.com *Web Site:* www.bookionics.com, pg 333

Booklink (United Kingdom) *Tel:* (01923) 828612 *Fax:* (01923) 828455 *E-mail:* booklink@aol.com, pg 1118

Booklinks Corporation (India) *Tel:* (0842) 558561, pg 334

Bookmaker (France) *Tel:* (01) 43548434 *Fax:* (01) 43547102 *E-mail:* bookmake@club-internet.fr, pg 151

Bookmakers Design & Production Ltd (New Zealand) *Tel:* (09) 784572 *Fax:* (09) 784572, pg 489

Bookman Books, Ltd (Taiwan, Province of China) *Tel:* (02) 3658617 *Fax:* (02) 3653548, pg 629

Bookman Consultants Ltd (Kenya) *Tel:* (02) 336771 *Fax:* (02) 217267, pg 431

Bookman Literary Agency (Denmark) *Tel:* 45892520 *Fax:* 45892501 *E-mail:* IHL@bookman.dk, pg 1110

Bookman Press Pty Ltd (Australia) *Tel:* (03) 9521 3250 *Fax:* (03) 9521 3270 *E-mail:* fayg@bookman.com.au *Web Site:* www.bookman.com.au, pg 16

Bookman Printing & Publishing House Inc (Philippines) *Tel:* (02) 7124813; (02) 7123587; (02) 7408108 *Fax:* (02) 7124843 *E-mail:* bookman@info.com.ph, pg 512

Bookman's & Co Ltd (Japan) *Tel:* (06) 6371-4164; (06) 6371-4018 *Fax:* (06) 6371-4174 *E-mail:* bookman@osk3.3web.ne.jp *Web Site:* www.bookmans.co.jp, pg 1294

Bookmark Remainders (United Kingdom) *Tel:* (01566) 782728 *Fax:* (01566) 776061, pg 1317

Bookmark Inc (Philippines) *Tel:* (0632) 8958061 *Fax:* (0632) 8970824 *E-mail:* bookmark@info.com.ph *Web Site:* www.bookmark.com, pg 512

Bookmark Inc (Philippines) *Tel:* (0632) 8958061; (02) 868061; (02) 868062; (02) 868063; (02) 868064; (02) 868065 *Fax:* (02) 8160745, pg 1306

Bookmarks Club (United Kingdom) *Tel:* (020) 7536 9696 *Fax:* (020) 7538 0018 *E-mail:* 106163.77@compuserve.com, pg 1233

Bookmarks Publications (United Kingdom) *Tel:* (020) 7637 1848 *Fax:* (020) 7637 3416 *Web Site:* www.bookmarks.uk.com, pg 657

Bookmart Ltd (United Kingdom) *Tel:* (0116) 2751800 *Fax:* (0116) 2750507 *E-mail:* books@bookmart.co.uk, pg 1317

Bookpoint Ltd (Kenya) *Tel:* (02) 211156; (02) 220221; (02) 226680 *Fax:* (02) 211029 *E-mail:* books@africaonline.co.ke, pg 1296

Bookpoint Ltd (United Kingdom) *Tel:* (01235) 400400 *Fax:* (01235) 861038; (01235) orders 821511 *E-mail:* firstname.lastname@bookpoint.co.uk, pg 1317

BookPower (United Kingdom) *Tel:* (020) 8742 8232 *Fax:* (020) 8747 8715 *E-mail:* bookpower@ibd.uk.net *Web Site:* www.bookpower.org, pg 1369

Bookprint Consultants Ltd (New Zealand) *Tel:* (04) 381 3071 *Fax:* (04) 381 3067 *E-mail:* gstewart@iconz.co.nz, pg 1137, 1199, 1213, 1222

Books Across the Sea (United Kingdom) *Tel:* (020) 7993 3338 *Fax:* (020) 7495 6108 *E-mail:* esu@mailbox.ulcc.ac.uk *Web Site:* es.libfl.ru/eng/esu/esu-books.html, pg 1369

Books & Books (India) *Tel:* (011) 551252, pg 334

Books & Periodicals Agency (India) *Tel:* (011) 5786046 *Fax:* (011) 5795554; (001) 6039477786 *E-mail:* bpage@del2.vsnl.net.in *Web Site:* www.bpagency.com, pg 1288

Books for Children (United Kingdom) *Tel:* (020) 8606 3090 *Fax:* (020) 8606 3099, pg 1233

Books for Europe Ltd (United Kingdom) *Tel:* (020) 8840 6672 *Fax:* (020) 8840 6672 *E-mail:* bfekoma@dial.eunet.ch, pg 657

Books for Europe Ltd (United Kingdom) *Tel:* (020) 8840 6672, pg 1317

Books for Keeps (United Kingdom) *Tel:* (020) 8852 4953 *Fax:* (020) 8318 7580 *E-mail:* booksforkeeps@btinternet.com, pg 1264

Books for Our Times (Australia) *Tel:* (08) 3709990 *Fax:* (08) 3709995 *E-mail:* creativefax@cobweb.com.au, pg 16

Books for Pleasure Inc (Philippines) *Tel:* (02) 771807 *Fax:* (02) 7275240, pg 512

Books from India (UK) Ltd (United Kingdom) *Tel:* (020) 7405-3784 *Fax:* (020) 7831-4517, pg 1317

Books in the Attic Publishers Ltd (Israel) *Tel:* (03) 248324 *Fax:* (03) 623630, pg 366

Books India (India) *Tel:* (011) 327 7463 *Fax:* (011) 241 2912, pg 1288

Books International (Israel) *Tel:* (08) 6880939 *Fax:* (08) 6810244 *E-mail:* info@booksinternational.com *Web Site:* www.booksinternational.com, pg 1292

Books International (United Kingdom) *Tel:* (01252) 376564 *Fax:* (01252) 370181 *E-mail:* booksinter@aol.com *Web Site:* www.books-international.co.uk/, pg 657

Books of Zimbabwe Publishing Co (Pvt) Ltd (United Kingdom) *Tel:* (079) 41959026 *E-mail:* info@booksofzimbabwe.co.za *Web Site:* www.booksofzimbabwe.co.za, pg 657

Books Registration Office (Hong Kong) *Tel:* 21809143 *Fax:* 21809841 *E-mail:* bro@lcsd.gov.hk, pg 1248

Booksellers' & Publishers' Association of Zambia (BPAZ) (Zambia) *Tel:* (01) 225195 *Fax:* (01) 225282, pg 1269

Booksellers' Association of Jamaica (Jamaica) *Tel:* (876) 922-5883; (876) 922-5661 *Fax:* (876) 922-4743, pg 1250

Booksellers New Zealand (New Zealand) *Tel:* (04) 4728678 *Fax:* (04) 4728628, pg 1255

Booksellers NZ (New Zealand) *Tel:* (04) 4728678 *Fax:* (04) 4728628, pg 1255

Bookstore, Institute of Puerto Rican Culture (Puerto Rico) *Tel:* (787) 724-0910 *Fax:* (787) 723-8393, pg 1308

Booktrust (United Kingdom) *Tel:* (020) 8516 2977 *Fax:* (020) 8516 2978 *Web Site:* www.booktrusted.com; www.booktrust.org.uk, pg 1264

Bookwise International (Australia) *Tel:* (07) 33918889, pg 1272

Bookworld (Zambia) *Tel:* (01) 225195 *Fax:* (01) 225282, pg 766

Bookworld Wholesale (United Kingdom) *Tel:* (01299) 823330 *Fax:* (01299) 829970, pg 1317

The Bookworm Club (United Kingdom) *Tel:* (01223) 568650 *Fax:* (01223) 568591 *E-mail:* clubs@heffers.co.uk, pg 1233

Boolarong Press (Australia) *Tel:* (07) 8541920 *Fax:* (07) 8541705, pg 16

Boom Uitgeverij (Netherlands) *Tel:* (0522) 257012 *Fax:* (0522) 266198, pg 474

Boombana Publications (Australia) *Tel:* (07) 3289 8106 *Fax:* (07) 3289 8107 *E-mail:* J.Lacherez@uq.net.au *Web Site:* www.boombanapublications.com, pg 16

Richard Boorberg Verlag GmbH & Co (Germany) *Tel:* (0711) 73 85-0 *Fax:* (0711) 73 85-100 *Web Site:* www.boorberg.de, pg 205

Boosey & Hawkes Music Publishers Ltd (United Kingdom) *Tel:* (020) 7580 2060 *Fax:* (020) 7291 7109 *Web Site:* www.boosey.com/publishing, pg 657

Boosey & Hawkes Music Publishers LTD, London (Germany) *Tel:* (030) 25001300 *Fax:* (030) 25001399 *E-mail:* musikverlag@boosey.com *Web Site:* www.boosey.com/publishing, pg 205

Boostan Publishing House (Israel) *Tel:* (03) 9221821 *Fax:* (03) 9221299, pg 366

BOOX (Sweden) *Tel:* (08) 4113700 *Fax:* (08) 4115330 *E-mail:* info@boox.se, pg 601

Edizioni Bora SNC di E Brandani & C (Italy) *Tel:* (051) 356133 *Fax:* (051) 374394 *E-mail:* daniele.brandani@mailbox.dsnet.it, pg 378

Borba (Yugoslavia) *Tel:* (011) 3243-437; (011) 3234-531; (011) 3239-038 *Fax:* (011) 3244-913, pg 764

Editions Bordas (France) *Tel:* (01) 44395445 *Fax:* (01) 44394350, pg 151

Pierre Bordas et Fils (France) *Tel:* (01) 43 25 04 51 *Fax:* (01) 43 25 47 84 *E-mail:* pierre.bordas.filsd@wanadoo.fr, pg 151

Bibliotheque Municipale de Bordeaux (France) *Tel:* (05) 56243251 *Fax:* (05) 56249408, pg 1465

Presses Universitaires de Bordeaux (PUB) (France) *Tel:* (05) 57 12 44 22 *Fax:* (05) 57 12 45 34 *E-mail:* pub@montaigne.u-bordeaux.fr *Web Site:* www.montaigne.u-bordeaux.fr, pg 151

Borgens Forlag A/S (Denmark) *Tel:* 36 15 36 15 *Fax:* 36 15 36 16 *E-mail:* post@borgen.dk *Web Site:* www.borgen.dk, pg 130

Borim Publishing Co (Republic of Korea) *Tel:* (02) 31412221 *Fax:* (02) 31418474, pg 435

Edizioni Borla SRL (Italy) *Tel:* (06) 39376728 *Fax:* (06) 39376620, pg 378

Born-Verlag (Germany) *Tel:* (0561) 40950 *Fax:* (0561) 4095112 *E-mail:* info.born@ec-jugend.de *Web Site:* www.born-buch.de, pg 205

Bornegudstjeneste-Forlaget (Denmark) *Tel:* 75934455 *Fax:* 75924275 *E-mail:* lohse@imh.dk, pg 130

Editions Bornemann (France) *Tel:* (01) 42 82 74 44 *Fax:* (01) 48 74 14 88, pg 151

Borromausverein eV (Germany) *Tel:* (0228) 72580 *Fax:* (0228) 7258189, pg 1245

Editions Emile Borschette (Luxembourg) *Tel:* 87177 *Fax:* 879599, pg 447

Borsens Forlag (Denmark) *Tel:* 33320102 *Fax:* 33935422 *E-mail:* borsens.forlag@borsen.dk, pg 130

Bosch & Keuning (Netherlands) *Tel:* (035) 12050 *Fax:* (035) 2202446, pg 474

Antoni Bosch Editor SA (Spain) *Tel:* (093) 206 07 30 *Fax:* (093) 206 07 31 *E-mail:* info@antonibosch.com *Web Site:* www.antonibosch.com, pg 565

Bosch Casa Editorial SA (Spain) *Tel:* (093) 4548437; (093) 4544629; (093) 4521050 *Fax:* (093) 3236736 *E-mail:* bosch@boschce.es *Web Site:* www.boschce.es, pg 565

Bosch en Keuning grafische bedrijven (Netherlands) *Tel:* (035) 5412050 *Fax:* (035) 2202446, pg 1137, 1158, 1199

J M Bosch Editor (Spain) *Tel:* (093) 3175308 *Fax:* (093) 4122764 *E-mail:* jmbos@libreriabosch.es *Web Site:* www.libreriabosch.es/jmb, pg 565

Libreria Bosch (Spain) *Tel:* (093) 3175308; (093) 3175358; (093) 3175558 *Fax:* (093) 4122764 *E-mail:* info@libreriabosch.es *Web Site:* www.libreriabosch.es, pg 1311

Editorial M J Bosch, SL (Spain) *Tel:* (093) 4512335 *E-mail:* mjbosch@colon.net, pg 565

C Bosendahl (Germany) *Tel:* (05751) 40000 *Fax:* (05751) 400077, pg 205

Gustav Bosse GmbH & Co KG (Germany) *Tel:* (0561) 31 05-0 *Fax:* (0561) 31 05-2 40 *E-mail:* info@bosse-verlag.de *Web Site:* www.bosse-verlag.de, pg 205

BOSZ scp (Poland) *Tel:* (013) 469 90 00 *Fax:* (013) 469 61 88 *E-mail:* boszsc@ks.onet.pl *Web Site:* www.bosz.com.pl, pg 516

Botanisch-Zoologische Gesellschaft (Liechtenstein) *Tel:* (00423) 2324819 *Fax:* (00423) 2332819 *E-mail:* renat@pingnet.li, pg 444

Libreria y Ediciones Botas SA (Mexico) *Tel:* (05) 5223896 *Fax:* (02) 702 54 03 *E-mail:* botas@mail.nextgeninter.net.mx, pg 458

Bote & Bock Musikalienhandelsgesellschaft mbH (Germany) *Tel:* (030) 2500-1300 *Fax:* (030) 2500-1399 *E-mail:* musikverlag@boosey.com, pg 206

Ediciones Botella al Mar (Argentina) *Tel:* (011) 4803-8246, pg 4

Botes Librair (United Kingdom) *Tel:* (01424) 210871 *Fax:* (01424) 734506; (01424) 731262 *E-mail:* 100450.3641@compuserve.com, pg 1317

Botim i Bibliotekes Kombetare (Albania) *Tel:* (042) 23843 *Fax:* (04) 23843 *E-mail:* plasari@san.com.al, pg 1449

Botimpex Publications Import-Export Agency (Albania) *Tel:* (042) 34023 *Fax:* (042) 26886 *E-mail:* botimpex@albaniaonline.org; botimpex@iccal.org *Web Site:* pages.albaniaonline.net/botimpex/, pg 1

Botswana National Library Service (Botswana) *Tel:* (019231) 352397 *Fax:* (019231) 22063, pg 1454

Botswana Library Association (Botswana) *Tel:* (031) 3552295 *Fax:* (031) 357291, pg 1513

Botswana Book Centre (Botswana) *Tel:* 3952931 *Fax:* 3974315 *E-mail:* pulapress@botsnet.bw, pg 1277

Botswana National Archives & Records Services (Botswana) *Tel:* 311820 *Fax:* 308545 *E-mail:* archives@gov.bw, pg 1454

The Botswana Society (Botswana) *Tel:* 351500 *Fax:* 359321 *E-mail:* botsoc@info.bw *Web Site:* ubh.tripod.com/bsoc/botsoc.htm, pg 77

Bottin SA (France) *Tel:* (01) 49 81 56 56 *Fax:* (01) 49 81 56 76, pg 151

Boukoumanis' Editions (Greece) *Tel:* (01) 3618502; (01) 3637436 *Fax:* (01) 3630669 *E-mail:* info@boukoumanis.gr *Web Site:* www.boukoumanis.gr, pg 309

Boulevard Books UK/The Babel Guides (United Kingdom) *Tel:* (01865) 712931 *Fax:* (01865) 712931 *E-mail:* raybabel@dircon.co.uk *Web Site:* www.raybabel.dircon.co.uk, pg 657

Bounty Books (United Kingdom) *Tel:* (020) 7531 8600 *Fax:* (020) 7531 8607 *Web Site:* www.bountybooks.co.uk, pg 657

Librairie Bourbon (Luxembourg) *Tel:* 492206; 405070 *Fax:* 407756, pg 1297

Bourdeaux-Capelle SA (Belgium) *Tel:* (082) 222283; (082) 222277 *Fax:* (082) 226378, pg 65

Editions Bouslama (Tunisia) *Tel:* (01) 245612 *Fax:* (01) 381100, pg 637

Editions Bouslama (Tunisia) *Tel:* (01) 245612, pg 1315

Bouvier GmbH & Co KG (Germany) *Tel:* (0228) 729010 *Fax:* (0228) 7290179 *E-mail:* bouvier@books.de *Web Site:* www.books.de, pg 1283

Bouvier Verlag (Germany) *Tel:* (0228) 729010 *Fax:* (0228) 637909 *E-mail:* verlag@books.de, pg 206

Bovolenta (Italy) *Tel:* (0532) 750737, pg 378

M J Bowen & Pty Ltd (Australia) *Tel:* (03) 95613425 *Fax:* (03) 98829405, pg 16

Bowerdean Publishing Co Ltd (United Kingdom) *Tel:* (020) 8788 0938 *Fax:* (020) 8788 0938 *Web Site:* www.bowerdean.co.uk/, pg 658

Boxtree Ltd (United Kingdom) *Tel:* (020) 7881 8000 *Fax:* (020) 7881 8001, pg 658

Marion Boyars Publishers Ltd (United Kingdom) *Tel:* (020) 8788 9522 *Fax:* (020) 8789 8122 *E-mail:* marion.boyars@talk21.com *Web Site:* www.marionboyars.co.uk, pg 658

David Boyce Publishing (Australia) *Tel:* (02) 6997484, pg 16

Boydell & Brewer Ltd (United Kingdom) *Tel:* (01394) 411320 *Fax:* (01394) 411477 *E-mail:* boydell@boydell.co.uk *Web Site:* www.boydell.co.uk, pg 658

BPB Publications (India) *Tel:* (011) 3281723; (011) 3272329 *Fax:* (011) 3266427 *E-mail:* bokks@bpbpub.com, pg 334

BPL Remainders (United Kingdom) *Tel:* (020) 7636 5070; (020) 7631 5070 *Fax:* (020) 7580 3001, pg 1317

BPP Publishing Ltd (United Kingdom) *Tel:* (020) 8740 2222 *Fax:* (020) 8740 1111 *E-mail:* info@bpp.com *Web Site:* www.bpp.com, pg 658

BPS Books (British Psychological Society) (United Kingdom) *Tel:* (0116) 254 9568 *Fax:* (0116) 247 0787 *E-mail:* enquiry@bps.org.uk *Web Site:* www.bps.org.uk, pg 658

BR Publishing Corporation (India) *Tel:* (011) 7430113; (011) 7143353, pg 334

Dr Barry Bracewell-Milnes (United Kingdom) *Tel:* (01737) 350736, pg 658

Bradt Travel Guides Ltd (United Kingdom) *Tel:* (01753) 893444 *Fax:* (01753) 892333 *E-mail:* info@bradt-travelguides.com *Web Site:* www.bradt-travelguides.com, pg 658, 1318

Bragelonne (France) *Tel:* (01) 4818 1970 *Fax:* (01) 4818 0247 *E-mail:* info@bragelonne.fr *Web Site:* www.bragelonne.fr, pg 151

Louis Braille Audio (Australia) *Tel:* (03) 9864 9645 *Fax:* (03) 9864 9646 *E-mail:* lba.sales@visionaustralia.org.au *Web Site:* www.louisbrailleaudio.com, pg 16

Braintrust Marketing Services Ges mbH Verlag (Austria) *Tel:* (01) 40416-0 *Fax:* (01) 40416-33 *E-mail:* braintrust@magnet.at *Web Site:* www.braintrust.at, pg 50

J W Braithwaite & Son Ltd (United Kingdom) *Tel:* (01902) 452209 *Fax:* (01902) 352918, pg 1202

Verlag Brandenburger Tor GmbH (Germany) *Tel:* (030) 2834171 *Fax:* (030) 2834916, pg 206

Brandenburgisches Verlagshaus in der Dornier Medienholding GmbH (Germany) *Tel:* (030) 28447-112; (030) 28447-113 *Fax:* (030) 28447-123 *E-mail:* info@dornier-verlage.de *Web Site:* www.dornier-verlage.de, pg 206

Brandes & Apsel Verlag GmbH (Germany) *Tel:* (069) 957 301 86 *Fax:* (069) 957 301 87 *E-mail:* brandes-apsel@t-online.de *Web Site:* www.brandes-apsel-verlag.de, pg 206

Brandon Book Publishers Ltd (Ireland) *Tel:* (066) 51463 *Fax:* (066) 51234, pg 359

Christian Brandstatter Verlagsgesellschaft GmbH (Austria) *Tel:* (01) 4083814; (01) 4083815 *Fax:* (01) 4087200 *E-mail:* books@oebv.co.et, pg 50

Oscar Brandstetter Verlag GmbH & Co KG (Germany) *Tel:* (0611) 9 91 20-0 *Fax:* (0611) 3 08 37 85 *E-mail:* brandstetter-verlag@t-online.de *Web Site:* www.brandstetter-verlag.de, pg 206

Editora do Brasil SA (Brazil) *Tel:* (011) 222 0211 *Fax:* (011) 222 5583, pg 80

Instituto Brasileiro de Edicoes Pedagogicas (IBEP) (Brazil) *Tel:* (011) 6099-7799 *Fax:* (011) 6694-5338 *Web Site:* www.ibep-nacional.com.br, pg 80

Instituto Brasileiro de Informacao em Ciencia e Tecnologia (Brazil) *Tel:* (061) 217-6360; (061) 217-6350 *Fax:* (061) 226-2677 *E-mail:* webmaster@ibick.br *Web Site:* www.ibict.br, pg 80

Instituto Brasileiro de Informacao em Ciencia e Tecnologia (Brazil) *Tel:* (061) 2176111 *Fax:* (061) 2262677, pg 1513

Brasilia Editora (J Carvalho Branco) (Portugal) *Tel:* (02) 2055854 *Fax:* (02) 2055854, pg 523

Editora Brasiliense SA (Brazil) *Tel:* (011) 6671-2016 *Fax:* (011) 6671-5946 *E-mail:* brasilienseedit@uol.com.br *Web Site:* www.editorabrasiliense.com.br, pg 80

Livraria Brasiliense Editora SA (Brazil) *Tel:* (011) 8250122 *Fax:* (011) 673024, pg 1277

Brasilivros Editora e Distribuidora Ltda (Brazil) *Tel:* (011) 3284-8155 *Fax:* (011) 2850305; (011) 2856406, pg 80

Brassey's UK Ltd (United Kingdom) *Tel:* (020) 7471 1100 *Fax:* (020) 7471 1101 *E-mail:* info@batsford.com *Web Site:* www.batsford.com, pg 658

Technische Universitaet Braunschweig (Germany) *Tel:* (0531) 3915011 *Fax:* (0531) 3915836 *E-mail:* ub@tu-bs.de, pg 1466

Breakthrough Ltd - Breakthrough Publishers (Hong Kong) *Tel:* 2735 8848 *Fax:* 2690 2603 *E-mail:* admin@el2100.com *Web Site:* www.teachlikethis.com, pg 318

Breal (France) *Tel:* (01) 48122222 *Fax:* (01) 48122239 *Web Site:* www.editions-breal.fr/contacts/default_main.asp, pg 151

Nicholas Brealey Publishing (United Kingdom) *Tel:* (020) 7239 0360 *Fax:* (020) 7239 0370 *E-mail:* sales@nbrealey-books.com *Web Site:* www.nbrealey-books.com, pg 659

Bredero (Belgium) *Tel:* (014) 31-84-61 *Fax:* (014) 31-84-61, pg 1276

Bredero (Netherlands Antilles) *Tel:* (09) 7376751, pg 488

Breedon Books Publishing Company Ltd (United Kingdom) *Tel:* (01332) 384235 *Fax:* (01332) 292755 *E-mail:* sales@breedonpublishing.co.uk *Web Site:* www.breedonbooks.co.uk, pg 659

Breese Books Ltd (United Kingdom) *Tel:* (020) 7727 9426 *Fax:* (020) 7229 3395 *Web Site:* www.sherlockholmes.co.uk; www.abracadabra.co.uk, pg 659

Breitkopf & Hartel (Germany) *Tel:* (0611) 450080 *Fax:* (0611) 4500859; (0611) 4500860; (0611) 4500861 *E-mail:* info@breitkopf.com *Web Site:* www.breitkopf.com; www.breitkopf.de, pg 206

Emgleo Breiz (France) *Tel:* (02) 98026817 *Fax:* (02) 98026817 *E-mail:* emgleobreiz@hotmail.com *Web Site:* emgleo-breiz.online.fr/, pg 151

Breklumer Buchhandlung und Verlag (Germany) *Tel:* (04671) 910020 *Fax:* (04671) 910030 *E-mail:* verlag@breklumer.de *Web Site:* www.breklumer.de, pg 206

Editions Jacques Bremond (France) *Tel:* (04) 66 37 27 40 *Fax:* (04) 66 37 27 40, pg 151

Joh & Sohn Brendow Verlag GmbH (Germany) *Tel:* (02841) 97761-21 *Fax:* (02841) 97761-30 *E-mail:* brendow.verlag@brendow.de *Web Site:* www.brendow.de, pg 206

Edizioni Brenner (Italy) *Tel:* (0984) 74537 *Fax:* (0984) 74537, pg 378

BrennGlas Verlag Assenheim Juergen Seuss (Germany) *Tel:* (06034) 3663 *Fax:* (06034) 3663 *Web Site:* www.minipresse.de, pg 206

The Brenthurst Press (Pty) Ltd (South Africa) *Tel:* (011) 6466024 *Fax:* (011) 4861651 *E-mail:* orders@brenthurst.co.az, pg 553

Brepols Publishers NV (Belgium) *Tel:* (014) 448020 *Fax:* (014) 428919 *E-mail:* info.publishers@brepols.com *Web Site:* www.brepols.net, pg 65

Edizioni Bresciane (Italy) *Tel:* (030) 393589 *Fax:* (030) 393589, pg 378

Breslich & Foss (United Kingdom) *Tel:* (020) 7580 8774 *Fax:* (020) 7580 8784 *E-mail:* sales@breslichfoss.com, pg 659

Breslov Research Institute (Israel) *Tel:* (02) 5824641 *Fax:* (02) 5825542 *E-mail:* info@breslov.org *Web Site:* www.breslov.org/catalog.html, pg 366

Alain Brethe Editions (France) *Tel:* (01) 30609862; (01) 42039570, pg 152

Editore Giorgio Bretschneider (Italy) *Tel:* (06) 6879361 *Fax:* (06) 6864543 *E-mail:* info@bretschneider.it *Web Site:* www.bretschneider.it, pg 378

Brewin Books Ltd (United Kingdom) *Tel:* (01527) 854228 *Fax:* (01527) 852746 *E-mail:* enquiries@brewinbooks.com *Web Site:* www.brewinbooks.com, pg 659

Editions BRGM (France) *Tel:* (02) 38643028 *Fax:* (02) 38643682 *E-mail:* infoterreve@brgm.fr *Web Site:* www.infoterre.brgm.fr, pg 152

Brick Row Publishing Co Ltd (New Zealand) *Tel:* (09) 4106993 *Fax:* (09) 4106993, pg 489

The Bridge Book Co Ltd (United Kingdom) *Tel:* (01483) 720505 *Fax:* (01483) 756143 *E-mail:* bridgepem@aol.com, pg 1318

Bridge Books (United Kingdom) *Tel:* (01978) 262377 *Fax:* (01978) 358661, pg 659

Bridge Bookshop Ltd (United Kingdom) *Tel:* (01624) 833376 *Fax:* (01624) 835381, pg 1318

Bridge To Peace Publications (Australia) *Tel:* (02) 9875 1912 *Fax:* books@bridgetopeace.com.au; adesso@bridgetopeace.com.au *Web Site:* www.bridgetopeace.com.au, pg 16

Bridgeway Publications (Australia) *Tel:* (07) 3390 4323 *Fax:* (07) 3390 4323 *E-mail:* info@bridgeway.org.au *Web Site:* www.bridgeway.org.au, pg 16

Brigg Verlag Franz-Josef Buchler KG (Germany) *Tel:* (0821) 711347 *Fax:* (0821) 711347, pg 206

Bright Arts Hong Kong Ltd (Hong Kong) *Tel:* 25620119 *Fax:* 25657031, pg 1155

Bright Book Centre (Pvt) Ltd (Sri Lanka) *Tel:* (01) 434770 *Fax:* (01) 333279, pg 1312

Bright Concepts Printing House (Philippines) *Tel:* (0917) 6473803 *E-mail:* dawnphilatelics@yahoo.com, pg 512

Bright Future Printing Co Ltd (Hong Kong) *Tel:* 25151776 *Fax:* 28972799; 25581717, pg 1133, 1155

Bright Future Printing Co Ltd (Hong Kong) *Tel:* 25151776 *Fax:* 28972799, pg 1195

Brijbasi Printers Pvt Ltd (India) *Tel:* (011) 6914115; (011) 6841897 *Fax:* (011) 6837835, pg 334

Brill Academic Publishers (Netherlands) *Tel:* (071) 53 53 566 *Fax:* (071) 53 17 532 *E-mail:* cs@brill.nl *Web Site:* www.brill.nl, pg 475

Brilliant Publications (United Kingdom) *Tel:* (01525) 229720 *Fax:* (01525) 229725 *E-mail:* sales@brilliantpublications.co.uk *Web Site:* www.brilliantpublications.co.uk, pg 659

Brimax Books (United Kingdom) *Tel:* (020) 7531 8400 *Fax:* (020) 7531 8607 *Web Site:* www.brimax.co.uk, pg 659

Brinque Book Editora de Livros Ltda (Brazil) *Tel:* (011) 37428142 *Fax:* (011) 37432235 *E-mail:* brinquebook@infantil.net, pg 80

The British Academy (United Kingdom) *Tel:* (020) 7969 5200 *Fax:* (020) 7969 5300 *E-mail:* secretary@britac.ac.uk *Web Site:* www.britac.ac.uk, pg 659

British & Irish Association of Law Librarians (United Kingdom) *Tel:* (020) 7242 4371 *Fax:* (020) 7404 1864 *E-mail:* holborn@linclib.sonnet.co.uk, pg 1524

BAAF: Adoption & Fostering (United Kingdom) *Tel:* (020) 7593 2000 *Fax:* (020) 7593 2001 *E-mail:* mail@baaf.org.uk *Web Site:* www.baaf.org.uk, pg 659

British Association of Communicators in Business Ltd (BACB) (United Kingdom) *Tel:* (020) 7378 7139 *Fax:* (020) 7378 7140 *E-mail:* enquiries@bacb.org *Web Site:* www.bacb.org.uk, pg 1264

British Cement Association (United Kingdom) *Tel:* (01344) 762676 *Fax:* (01344) 761214 *E-mail:* library@bca.org.uk *Web Site:* www.bca.org.uk, pg 660

British Copyright Council (United Kingdom) *Tel:* (020) 7359 1895 *Fax:* (020) 7359 1895 *E-mail:* british.copyright.council@dial.pipex.com, pg 1264

British Council Library (Cyprus) *Tel:* (02) 442152 *Fax:* (02) 477257 *E-mail:* stamatis.dracos@britcoun.org.cy *Web Site:* www.britcoun.org/cyprus, pg 1459

British Council Library (Ethiopia) *Tel:* (01) 550022 *Fax:* (01) 552544, pg 1463

British Council Library (Ghana) *Tel:* (021) 244744; (021) 663979 *Fax:* (021) 240330, pg 1470

British Council Library (Hong Kong) *Tel:* 2913 5125 *Fax:* 2913 5121, pg 1471

British Council Library (Indonesia) *Tel:* (021) 2524115; (021) 2524122; (021) 2524126 *Fax:* (021) 2524129, pg 1474

British Council Library (Jordan) *Tel:* (06) 4636147; (06) 4636148 *Fax:* (06) 4656413 *Web Site:* www.britishcouncil.org.jo, pg 1479

British Council Library (Malawi) *Tel:* 783244 *Fax:* 782945 *Web Site:* www.britishcouncil.org/malawi/, pg 1482

British Council Library (Malaysia) *Tel:* (03) 2987555 *Fax:* (03) 2937214 *E-mail:* brcokl@britcoun.org.my *Web Site:* www.britcoun.org.my, pg 1482

British Council Library (Pakistan) *Tel:* (051) 111424424 *Fax:* (051) 111425425 *E-mail:* peterellwood@britishcouncil.bg *Web Site:* www.britishcouncil.pk, pg 1489

British Council Library (Sierra Leone) *Tel:* 222223 *Fax:* 224123 *E-mail:* bcouncil@sierratel.sl *Web Site:* www.britishcouncil.org/sierraleone/, pg 1496

The British Council Library (Spain) *Tel:* (091) 3373500 *Fax:* (091) 3373573 *E-mail:* information@bc-madrid.sprint.com *Web Site:* www.britishcouncil.org/spain/, pg 1499

British Council Library (Sudan) *Tel:* (011) 780817 *Fax:* (011) 774935 *E-mail:* don.sloan@bc-khartoum.bcouncil.org *Web Site:* www.britishcouncil.org/sudan/, pg 1500

British Council Library (United Republic of Tanzania) *Tel:* (051) 116574 *Fax:* (051) 112669 *E-mail:* oreste.makafu@tz.britcoun.org *Web Site:* www.britishcouncil.org/tanzania/, pg 1502

British Council Library (Thailand) *Tel:* (02) 6525480; (02) 2526136 *Fax:* (02) 2535312 *E-mail:* bc.bangkok@britcoun.or.th *Web Site:* www.britcoun.org/thailand/, pg 1503

British Council Library (Tunisia) *Tel:* (01) 259053 *Fax:* (01) 353411 *E-mail:* general.enquiries@bc.tunis.bcouncil.org *Web Site:* www.britishcouncil.org/tunisia, pg 1504

British Council Library (Yemen) *Tel:* (01) 275584 *Fax:* (01) 274128, pg 1508

The British Council, Design, Publishing & Print Department (United Kingdom) *Tel:* (020) 7930 8466 *Fax:* (020) 7389 6347 *Web Site:* www.britishcouncil.org, pg 660

British Council Information Resource Centre (Sri Lanka) *Tel:* (01) 581171; (01) 581172; (01) 587078 *Fax:* (01) 587079 *E-mail:* inquiries@britishcouncil.lk *Web Site:* www.britishcouncil.lk, pg 1499

British Council Libraries (India) *Tel:* (011) 3711401 *Fax:* (011) 3710717 *E-mail:* www.britishcouncil.org/india/, pg 1473

British Council Library (Bangladesh) *Tel:* (02) 868905; (02) 868907; (02) 868867 *Fax:* (02) 863375; (02) 870483 *Web Site:* www.britishcouncil.org/bangladesh/, pg 1452

British Council Library (Colombia) *Tel:* (01) 2579632 *Fax:* (01) 2187754 *E-mail:* brit.council@bc-bogota.bcouncil.org *Web Site:* www.britishcouncil.org/colombia/, pg 1457

British Council Library (Greece) *Tel:* (01) 3692333 *Fax:* (01) 3634769 *E-mail:* british.council@britcoun.gr, pg 1470

British Council Library (Lesotho) *Tel:* 312609 *Fax:* 310363 *E-mail:* libsupbc@adelfang.co.za, pg 1481

British Council Library (Mauritius) *Tel:* 4549550 *Fax:* 4549553 *E-mail:* britcouncil@intnet.mu *Web Site:* www.britishcouncil.org/mauritius, pg 1484

British Council Library (Morocco) *Tel:* (07) 760836 *Fax:* (07) 760850 *E-mail:* britcoun.morocco@britishcouncil.org.ma *Web Site:* www.britishcouncil.org/morocco, pg 1485

British Council Library (Nepal) *Tel:* (01) 221305; (01) 223796 *Fax:* (01) 224076 *E-mail:* bcnepal@bc-nepal.wlink.com.np *Web Site:* www.britcoun.org/nepal/neplis.htm, pg 1486

British Educational Communication & Technology Agency (BECTA) (United Kingdom) *Tel:* (024) 7641 6994 *Fax:* (024) 7641 1418 *E-mail:* becta@becta.org.uk *Web Site:* www.becta.org.uk, pg 660

British Fantasy Society (United Kingdom) *Tel:* (0161) 6004125 *Web Site:* www.geocities.com/solto/6859, pg 1370

British Guild of Travel Writers (United Kingdom) *Tel:* (020) 7720 9009 *Fax:* (020) 7498 6153 *E-mail:* bgtw@garlandintl.co.uk, pg 1264

British Horse Society (United Kingdom) *Tel:* (08701) 202 244 *Fax:* (01926) 707 800 *E-mail:* enquiry@bhs.org.uk *Web Site:* www.bhs.org.uk, pg 660

British Institute in Eastern Africa (Kenya) *Tel:* (02) 43330; (02) 43721 *Fax:* (02) 43365 *E-mail:* britinst@insightkenya.com, pg 431

British Library Document Supply Centre (United Kingdom) *Tel:* (01937) 546060 *Fax:* (01937) 546333, pg 1505

The British Library (United Kingdom) *Tel:* (020) 7412 7000 *Fax:* (020) 7412 7268, pg 1505

The British Library National Bibliographic Service (United Kingdom) *Tel:* (01937) 546585 *Fax:* (01937) 546586 *E-mail:* nbs-info@bl.uk *Web Site:* www.bl.uk, pg 660, 1505

British Library, Newspaper Library (United Kingdom) *Tel:* (020) 7412 7353 *Fax:* (020) 7412 7379 *E-mail:* newspaper@bl.uk *Web Site:* www.bl.uk, pg 1505

British Library of Political & Economic Science (United Kingdom) *Tel:* (020) 7955 7219 *Fax:* (020) 7955 7454 *E-mail:* library@lse.ac.uk, pg 1505

British Library Oriental & India Office Collections (United Kingdom) *Tel:* (020) 7412 7873 *Fax:* (020) 7412 7641 *E-mail:* oioc-enquiries@bl.uk *Web Site:* www.bl.uk, pg 1505

British Library Publications (United Kingdom) *Tel:* (020) 7412 7704 *Fax:* (020) 7412 7768 *E-mail:* blpublications@bl.uk *Web Site:* www.bl.uk, pg 660

British Library Document Supply Centre, Publications Marketing (United Kingdom) *Tel:* (01937) 546060 *Fax:* (01937) 546333 *Web Site:* www.bl.uk, pg 660

The British Library, Science Technology & Innovation Information Services (United Kingdom) *Tel:* (020) 7412 7288; (020) 7412 7494; (020) 7412 7496 *E-mail:* scitech@bl.uk; social-policy@bl.uk; patents-information@bl.uk *Web Site:* www.bl.uk, pg 1506

British Museum Press (United Kingdom) *Tel:* (020) 7323 1234 *Fax:* (020) 7436 7315 *Web Site:* www.britishmuseum.co.uk, pg 660

British Printing Industries Federation (BPIF) (United Kingdom) *Tel:* (020) 7242 6904 *Fax:* (020) 7405 7784, pg 1264

The British Science Fiction Association Ltd (United Kingdom) *Tel:* (01865) 371734 *E-mail:* bsfa@acnestis.demon.co.uk, pg 1370

British Sisalkraft Ltd (United Kingdom) *Tel:* (01634) 290505 *Fax:* (01634) 291029, pg 1140

British Tourist Authority (United Kingdom) *Tel:* (020) 8846 9000 *Fax:* (020) 8846 0302 *Web Site:* www.visitbritain.com, pg 660

Verlag Ekkehard & Ulrich Brockhaus GmbH & Co KG (Germany) *Tel:* (0212) 65 87-29; (0172) 2 55 59 61 *Fax:* (0202) 42 82 82; (0212) 65 87-99 *E-mail:* mail@verlag-brockhaus.de *Web Site:* www.verlag-brockhaus.de, pg 206

Brockhaus/Kommission GmbH (Germany) *Tel:* (07154) 1327-0 *Fax:* (07154) 1327-13, pg 206

R Brockhaus Verlag (Germany) *Tel:* (02104) 968600; (02104) 968620 (sales) *Fax:* (02104) 968601 *E-mail:* edit@brockhaus-verlag.de *Web Site:* www.brockhaus-verlag.de, pg 206

Brody (Czech Republic) *Tel:* (02) 22252077; (02) 376630 *E-mail:* brody@draha.czcom.cz *Web Site:* www.brody.cz, pg 123

Vanden Broele NV (Belgium) *Tel:* (050) 456 177 *Fax:* (050) 456 199 *E-mail:* graphic.group@vandenbroele.be *Web Site:* www.vandenbroele.be, pg 65

Broese BV (Netherlands) *Tel:* (030) 2335200 *Fax:* (030) 2314071 *E-mail:* info@broese.net *Web Site:* www.broese.net, pg 1301

Brombergs Bokforlag AB (Sweden) *Tel:* (08) 56262080 *Fax:* (08) 56262085 *E-mail:* info@brombergs.se *Web Site:* www.brombergs.se, pg 601

Edicions Bromera SL (Spain) *Tel:* (096) 2402254 *Fax:* (096) 2403191 *E-mail:* illa@bromera.com; bromera@bromera.com *Web Site:* www.bromera.com, pg 566

The Bronte Society (United Kingdom) *Tel:* (01535) 642323 *Fax:* (01535) 647131 *E-mail:* bronte@bronte.prestel.co.uk *Web Site:* www.bronte.org.uk, pg 1370

Brooker's Ltd (New Zealand) *Tel:* (04) 4998178 *Fax:* (04) 4998173 *E-mail:* service@brookers.co.nz, pg 489

Brookfield Press (Australia) *Tel:* (07) 3374-1053 *Fax:* (07) 3374-2059, pg 16

Brookfield Press (New Zealand) *Tel:* (09) 5765438 *Fax:* (09) 5736222, pg 489

Brooklands Books Ltd (United Kingdom) *Tel:* (01932) 865051 *Fax:* (01932) 868803 *E-mail:* info@brooklands-books.com *Web Site:* www.brooklands-books.com, pg 660

Broteria Associacao Cultural e Cientifica (Portugal) *Tel:* (021) 3961660 *Fax:* (021) 3956629, pg 523

Michele Broutta Oeuvres Graphiques Contemporaines (France) *Tel:* (01) 45779379 *Fax:* (01) 40590432, pg 152

Curtis Brown (Australia) Pty Ltd (Australia) *Tel:* (02) 93315301; (02) 93616161 *Fax:* (02) 93603935 *E-mail:* info@curtisbrown.com.au, pg 1109

Curtis Brown (United Kingdom) *Tel:* (020) 7396 6600 *Fax:* (020) 7396 0110 *E-mail:* cb@curtisbrown.co.uk, pg 1118

D Brown & Sons Ltd (United Kingdom) *Tel:* (01446) 771475 *Fax:* (01446) 771476, pg 1140

D Brown & Sons Ltd (United Kingdom) *Tel:* (01656) 652447 *Fax:* (01446) 771476 *E-mail:* info@geminidigital.demon.co.uk, pg 1161

D Brown & Sons Ltd (United Kingdom) *Tel:* (01446) 771475 *Fax:* (01446) 771476 *E-mail:* info@geminidigital.demon.co.uk, pg 1202

Ediciones Brown SA (Peru) *Tel:* (01) 4462753 *Fax:* (01) 4462753, pg 511

The Brown Reference Group PLC (United Kingdom) *Tel:* (020) 7920 7500 *Fax:* (020) 7920 7501 *E-mail:* info@brownpartworks.co.uk *Web Site:* www.brownpartworks.co.uk, pg 660

Robert Brown & Associates Australia Pty Ltd (Australia) *Tel:* (063) 318577 *Fax:* (063) 321273, pg 16

Brown, Son & Ferguson, Ltd (United Kingdom) *Tel:* (0141) 4291234 *Fax:* (0141) 4201694 *E-mail:* enquiry@skipper.co.uk *Web Site:* www.skipper.co.uk, pg 661

Brown Wells & Jacobs Ltd (United Kingdom) *Tel:* (020) 8771 5115 *Fax:* (020) 8771 9994 *E-mail:* postmaster@popking.demon.co.uk *Web Site:* www.bwj.org, pg 661

Browne's Bookstore (United Kingdom) *Tel:* (01223) 350968 *Fax:* (01223) 353456 *E-mail:* brownes_books@msn.com, pg 1318

Brud Nevez (France) *Tel:* (02) 98449842 *Fax:* (02) 98804970, pg 152

Bruecke-Verlag Kurt Schmersow (Germany) *Tel:* (05121) 91 92 0 *Fax:* (05121) 91 92 20 *Web Site:* www.bruecke-verlag.de, pg 207

Bruehlsche Uni-Druckerei Verlag, der Giessener Anzeiger GmbH & Co KG (Germany) *Tel:* (0641) 95040 *Fax:* (0641) 9504100, pg 207

BRUEN-Verlag, Gorenflo (Germany) *Tel:* (06142) 61434 *Fax:* (06142) 61259 *E-mail:* 0614261434-1@t-online.de, pg 207

Bruna BV (Netherlands) *Tel:* (0800) 0230535 *E-mail:* klantenservice@bruna.com *Web Site:* www.bruna.nl, pg 1301

Uitgeverij A W Bruna en Zoon NV (Netherlands) *Tel:* (030) 2470411 *Fax:* (030) 2410018 *E-mail:* a.w.bruna@awbruna.nl; multimedia@awbruna.nl *Web Site:* www.awbruna.nl, pg 475

A W Bruna Uitgevers BV (Netherlands) *Tel:* (030) 2470411 *Fax:* (030) 2410018 *E-mail:* a.w.bruna@awbruna.nl, pg 475

The Brunel Press (Brunei Darussalam) *Tel:* (03) 2344, pg 1278

Brunnen-Verlag Basel (Switzerland) *Tel:* (061) 234406 *Fax:* (061) 2956069, pg 610

Brunnen-Verlag GmbH (Germany) *Tel:* (0641) 6059-0 *Fax:* (0641) 6059-100 *E-mail:* brunnen.gi@t-online.de *Web Site:* www.brunnen-verlag.de, pg 207

Editorial Bruno (Spain) *Tel:* (091) 3610448 *Fax:* (091) 3613133 *E-mail:* info@editorial-bruno.es *Web Site:* www.editorial-bruno.es, pg 566

Asociacion Editorial Bruno (Peru) *Tel:* (01) 4237890; (01) 4251248, pg 511

F Bruns Bokhandel og Forlag A/S (Norway) *Tel:* 73510022 *Fax:* 73509320 *E-mail:* brunslb@online.no, pg 503

Eteblissements Emile Bruylant SA (Belgium) *Tel:* (02) 512.98.45 *Fax:* (02) 511.72.02 *E-mail:* info@bruylant.be *Web Site:* www.bruylant.be, pg 65

Felicity Bryan (United Kingdom) *Tel:* (01865) 513816 *Fax:* (01865) 310055, pg 1118

Bryntirion Press (United Kingdom) *Tel:* (01656) 656095 *Fax:* (01656) 656095 *E-mail:* press@draco.co.uk, pg 661

Bryntirion Press (United Kingdom) *Tel:* (01656) 655886 *Fax:* (01656) 6560095 *E-mail:* press@draco.co.uk, pg 1264

Bryson Agency Australia Pty Ltd Fran Bryson (Australia), pg 1109

BS Publications (India) *Tel:* (040) 4758216 *Fax:* (040) 4756271 *E-mail:* booksynd@hd2.dot.net.in, pg 334

BSE Verlag Dr Bernhard Schuttengruber (Austria) *Tel:* (0316) 839600; 283170, pg 50

BSI British Standards Institution (United Kingdom) *Tel:* (020) 8996 9000 *Fax:* (020) 8996 7001 *E-mail:* info@bsi-global.com *Web Site:* www.bsi-global.com, pg 1264

BSI - ELOR Editions Jeunesse (France) *Tel:* (02) 99912280 *Fax:* (02) 99913445, pg 152

BSMPS - M/s Bishen Singh Mahendra Pal Singh (India) *Tel:* (0135) 655748 *Fax:* (0135) 650107 *E-mail:* info@bishensinghbooks.com *Web Site:* www.bishensinghbooks.com, pg 334

Edizioni Bucalo SNC (Italy) *Tel:* (0773) 410036 *Fax:* (0773) 410036 *Web Site:* www.bucalo.it, pg 379

C L Baader Buch & Offsetdruckere GmbH & Co KG (Germany) *Tel:* (07381) 79192 *Fax:* (07381) 411412, pg 1133, 1154, 1194, 1211, 1221

Buch- und Kunstverlag Kleinheinrich (Germany) *Tel:* (06071) 55572 *Fax:* (06071) 55572, pg 207

Buch und Verlagsdruckerei AG (Liechtenstein), pg 444

Verlag Bucheli (Switzerland) *Tel:* (042) 221736 *Fax:* (042) 417115, pg 610

Verlag C J Bucher GmbH (Germany) *Tel:* (089) 51480-20 *Fax:* (089) 5148-2233, pg 207

Bucher-Stierle GesmbH (Austria) *Tel:* (0662) 840114 *Fax:* (0662) 8401149 *E-mail:* buecher-stierle@members.debis.at, pg 1274

Editions Buchet/Chastel (France) *Tel:* (01) 44320560; (01) 44320563 (sales) *Fax:* (01) 44320561 *E-mail:* buchet.chastel@wanadoo.fr *Web Site:* www.theatre-contemporain.net/editions/buchet/buchet.htm, pg 152

Der Buchfreund Universitats-Buchhandlung u Antiquariat Walter R Schaden (Austria) *Tel:* (01) 5124856; (01) 5138289 *Fax:* (01) 5126028 *E-mail:* buch.schaden@vienna.at *Web Site:* www.buch-schaden.at, pg 1274

Buchhaendler-Vereinigung GmbH (Germany) *Tel:* (069) 1306-0; (069) 1306-339 (Boersenblatt); (069) 1306-340 (Boersenblatt) *Fax:* (069) 1306-201 *E-mail:* info@buchhaendler-vereinigung.de *Web Site:* www.buchhaendler-vereinigung.de, pg 207

Buchhandlung WUV Dolmetsch (Austria) *Tel:* (01) 3685704 *Fax:* (01) 3109023 *E-mail:* fachverlag@servicebetriebe.at, pg 50

Buchheim-Verlag (Germany) *Tel:* (08157) 1221 *Fax:* (08157) 3143, pg 207

Buchkultur Verlags GmbH Zeitschrift fuer Literatur & Kunst (Austria) *Tel:* (01) 7863380 *Fax:* (01) 7863380-10 *E-mail:* office@buchkultur.net *Web Site:* www.buchkultur.net, pg 50

BuchMarkt Verlag K Werner GmbH (Germany) *Tel:* (02150) 9191-0 *Fax:* (02150) 919191 *E-mail:* redaktion@buchmarkt.de *Web Site:* buchmarkt.de, pg 207

C C Buchners Verlag (Germany) *Tel:* (0951) 96 501-0 *Fax:* (0951) 61-774 *E-mail:* service@ccbuchner.de *Web Site:* www.ccbuchner.de, pg 207

Buchverlag Basler Zeitung (Switzerland) *Tel:* (061) 661111 *Fax:* (061) 6391343 *E-mail:* order@baz.ch, pg 610

Buchverlag Junge Welt GmbH (Germany) *Tel:* (030) 231079 0 *Fax:* (030) 2826989 *E-mail:* bvjw.berlin@t-online.de *Web Site:* www.buchverlagjw.com, pg 207

Buchverlage Langen-Mueller/Herbig (Germany) *Tel:* (089) 2 90 88-0 *Fax:* (089) 29088-144; (089) 29088-155; (089) 29088-178 *Web Site:* www.herbig.net, pg 207

Buchverleger-Verband der Deutschsprachigen Schweiz (VVDS) (Switzerland) *Tel:* (01) 421 28 01 *Fax:* (01) 421 28 18 *E-mail:* sbvv@swissbooks.ch *Web Site:* www.swissbooks.ch, pg 1260

The Buckman Agency (United Kingdom) *Tel:* (01608) 683677 *Fax:* (01608) 683449, pg 1118

Budapesti Kozgazdasagtudomanyi es Allamigazoatasi Luyutemi Egyetem Kozponti Konyvtar (Hungary) *Tel:* (01) 2175827 *Fax:* (01) 2174910 *E-mail:* huszar@mail.lib *Web Site:* www.lib.bke.hu, pg 1472

Budapesti Muszaki es Guzdasagtudomanyi Egyetem Orszagos Muszaki Informacios Kozpont es Konyvtar (Hungary) *Tel:* (01) 463-2441 *Fax:* (01) 463-2440, pg 1472

Buddhist Publication Society Inc (Sri Lanka) *Tel:* (08) 223679; (08) 237283 *Fax:* (08) 223679 *E-mail:* bps@ids.lk; bps@metta.lk, pg 596

Budget Books Pty Ltd (Australia) *Tel:* (03) 5516111 *Fax:* (03) 6466925, pg 16

Buchergilde Gutenberg (Germany) *Tel:* (069) 2739080 *Fax:* (069) 27390824, pg 1228

Buchergilde Gutenberg AG (Switzerland), pg 1232

Buchergilde Gutenberg Verlagsgesellschaft mbH (Germany) *Tel:* (069) 27 39 08-0 *Fax:* (069) 27 39 08-26; (069) 27 39 08-25 *Web Site:* www.buechergilde.de, pg 207

Buechse der Pandora Verlags-GmbH (Germany) *Tel:* (06441) 911312 *Fax:* (06441) 911314, pg 207

Buffetti (Italy) *Tel:* (06) 231951 *Fax:* (06) 23195490, pg 379

Bugra Suisse Burchler Grafino AG (Switzerland) *Tel:* (031) 548111 *Fax:* (031) 544562, pg 610

Buijten en Schipperheijn BV Drukkerij en Uitg Mij v/h (Netherlands) *Tel:* (20) 5241010 *Fax:* (20) 5241011 *E-mail:* info@bijten.nl, pg 475

Building & Road Research Institute (BRRI) (Ghana) *Tel:* (051) 60064; (051) 60065 *Fax:* (051) 60080 *E-mail:* brri@ghana.com *Web Site:* www.csir.org.gh/brri.html, pg 306

De l'edition Bukie Banane (Mauritius) *Tel:* 4542327, pg 457

P T Bulan Bintang (Indonesia) *Tel:* (021) 3901651; (021) 3901652 *Fax:* (021) 3107027, pg 354

Bulawayo Public Library (Zimbabwe) *Tel:* (09) 60965 *E-mail:* bpl@netconnect.co.zw *Web Site:* www.angelfire.com/kg/bpl, pg 1509

Bulgarian Academy of Sciences, Institute of Literature (Bulgaria) *Tel:* (02) 84141 *Fax:* (02) 880448, pg 1361

Bulgarian Academy of Sciences, Central Library (Bulgaria) *Tel:* (02) 878966 *Fax:* (02) 803127 *E-mail:* banlib@bgcict.acad.bg, pg 1455

Bulgarian National ISSN Centre (Bulgaria) *Tel:* (02) 9461165 *Fax:* (02) 435495, pg 1239

Bulgarian Writers' Union (Bulgaria) *Tel:* (02) 898346 *Fax:* (02) 880685, pg 1361

Bulgarski Houdozhnik Publishers (Bulgaria) *Tel:* (02) 467285 *Fax:* (02) 946 0212, pg 94

Bulgarski Pissatel (Bulgaria) *Tel:* (02) 875873; (02) 873454; (02) 874527 *Fax:* (02) 872495, pg 94

The Bulletin Newspaper (Zimbabwe) *Tel:* (9) 78831; (9) 880591 *Fax:* (9) 78835 *E-mail:* dirpub@mweb.co.zw, pg 768

Bulvest 2000 Ltd (Bulgaria) *Tel:* (02) 9833286; (02) 9833169 *Fax:* (02) 9815464 *E-mail:* bulvest@internet-bg.net, pg 94

Bulzoni Editore SRL (Le Edizioni Universitarie d'Italia) (Italy) *Tel:* (06) 4455207 *Fax:* (06) 4450355, pg 379

Bum-Woo Publishing Co (Republic of Korea) *Tel:* (02) 7172121; (02) 7172122 *Fax:* (02) 7170429, pg 435

Editions Buma Kor (Cameroon) *Tel:* (023) 7 23 07 68 *Fax:* (023) 23 29 03, pg 99

Bumi Aksara PT (Indonesia) *Tel:* (021) 4717049; (021) 4700988 *Fax:* (021) 4700989, pg 354

Bun-ichi Sogo Shuppan (Japan) *Tel:* (03) 32357341 *Fax:* (03) 32691402 *E-mail:* bunichi@vinet.or.jp, pg 415

Bund demokratischer Wissenschaftlerinnen und Wissenschafler eV (BdWi) (Germany) *Tel:* (06421) 2 13 95 *Fax:* (06421) 2 46 54 *E-mail:* verlag@bdwi.de *Web Site:* www.bdwi.de, pg 207

Bund Deutscher Schriftsteller (Germany) *Tel:* (06074) 47566 *Fax:* (06074) 47540 *Web Site:* www.bund-deutscher-schriftsteller.de, pg 208

Bund fuer deutsche Schrift und Sprache (Germany) *Tel:* (04435) 1313 *Fax:* (04435) 3623 *Web Site:* www.bfds.de, pg 208

Bund-Verlag GmbH (Germany) *Tel:* (069) 79 50 10 0 *Fax:* (069) 79 50 10 10 *E-mail:* kontakt@bund-verlag.de *Web Site:* www.bund-verlag.de, pg 208

Bunda College of Agriculture Library (Malawi) *Tel:* 277222 *Fax:* 277364; 277251 *E-mail:* bundalibrary@bunda.sdup.org.mw *Web Site:* www.bunda.sdnp.org.mw, pg 1482

Bundes-Verlag GmbH (Germany) *Tel:* (02302) 930 93-0 *Fax:* (02302) 930 93-10 *E-mail:* info@bundesverlag.de *Web Site:* www.bundes-verlag.de, pg 208

Bundesanzeiger Verlagsgesellschaft (Germany) *Tel:* (0221) 9 76 68-0 *Fax:* (0221) 9 76 68-278 *E-mail:* vcotiicb@bundesanzeiger.de *Web Site:* www.bundesanzeiger.de, pg 208

Bundesverband der Dolmetscher und Ubersetzer eV (BDU) (Germany) *Tel:* (030) 88712830 *Fax:* (030) 88712840 *E-mail:* bdue-bgs@t-online.de *Web Site:* www.bdue.de, pg 1125

Bundesverband Deutscher Kunstverleger eV (Germany) *Tel:* (069) 629120 *Fax:* (069) 629120 *Web Site:* www.bdkv.de, pg 1245

Bundesvereinigung Deutscher Bibliotheksverbande (BDB) (Germany) *Tel:* (030) 39001480 *Fax:* (030) 39001484 *E-mail:* dbv@bdbibl.de *Web Site:* www.bdbibl.deldbv, pg 1516

Bunkasha Publishing Co, Ltd (Japan) *Tel:* (03) 32225111 *Fax:* (03) 32223666 *E-mail:* fukai@bunkasha.co.jp, pg 415

Bunkashobo-Hakubun-Sha (Japan) *Tel:* (03) 39472034 *Fax:* (03) 39474976, pg 415

Editions du Buot (France) *Tel:* (01) 53388110 *Fax:* (01) 53388119, pg 152

Burckhardthaus-Laetare Verlag GmbH (Germany) *Tel:* (069) 8400030 *Fax:* (069) 84000333, pg 208

Aenne Burda Verlag (Germany) *Tel:* (0781) 8402 *Fax:* (0781) 3386, pg 208

Bureau of International Exchange of Publications (Taiwan, Province of China) *Tel:* (02) 23169132 *Fax:* (02) 23110155, pg 1502

Bureau des Longitudes de France (France) *Tel:* (01) 43265902 *Fax:* (01) 43268090 *E-mail:* contact@bureau-des-longitudes.fr *Web Site:* www.bureau-des-longitudes.fr/, pg 152

Bureau for Indigenous Languages (Namibia) *Tel:* (061) 24601, pg 471

Bureau Intellectual Property (Netherlands Antilles) *Tel:* (09) 465 7800; (09) 465 7802 *Fax:* (09) 465 7815; (09) 465 7692 *E-mail:* bipantil@curinfo.an, pg 1255

Bureau of Ghana Languages (Ghana) *Tel:* (021) 64130; (021) 65194, pg 306

Bureau of Ghana Languages (Ghana) *Tel:* (021) 64130; (021) 65194; (021) 65461 ext 514, pg 1126

Bureau of Resource Sciences (Australia) *Tel:* (02) 6272 4282 *Fax:* (02) 6272 4747 *Web Site:* www.infomine.com/index/suppliers/Bureau_of_Resource_Sciences, Australia.html, pg 16

Bureau of Statistics (United Republic of Tanzania) *Tel:* (051) 111634; (051) 111635 *Fax:* (051) 112352 *E-mail:* kento@raha.com, pg 633

Ulrich Burgdorf/Homeopathic Publishing House (Germany) *Tel:* (0551) 796050 *Fax:* (0551) 796955 *E-mail:* Burgdorf-Verlag@t-online.de *Web Site:* www.burgdorf-verlag.de, pg 208

Fachverlag fur Burgerinformation, Eigenvelag (Austria) *Tel:* (0316) 686727 *Fax:* (0316) 673078, pg 50

Burgewood Books (Australia) *Tel:* (03) 98442512 (Australia); (03) 9844 2512 (International) *Fax:* (03) 98440664 (Australia); (03) 9844 0664 (International), pg 1272

Edmund Burke Publisher (Ireland) *Tel:* (01) 2882159 *Fax:* (01) 2834080 *E-mail:* deburca@indigo.ie, pg 359

Kartographischer Verlag Busche GmbH (Germany) *Tel:* (0231) 4 44 77-0 *Fax:* (0231) 4 44 77-77 *E-mail:* info@kvbusche.de *Web Site:* www.kvbusche.de, pg 208

Arnold Busck International Boghandel A/S (Denmark) *Tel:* 33733500 *Fax:* 33733535 *E-mail:* arnold@busck.dk *Web Site:* www.busck.dk, pg 1281

Bush Press Communications Ltd (New Zealand) *Tel:* (09) 486 2667 *Fax:* (09) 486 2667 *E-mail:* bush.press@clear.net.nz, pg 489

Bushwood Books (United Kingdom) *Tel:* (0208) 3928585 *Fax:* (0208) 3929876 *E-mail:* bushwd@aol.com, pg 1318

Business & Industrial Publication Co Ltd (Hong Kong) *Tel:* (02) 25273377 *Fax:* (02) 28667732, pg 318

Business Bureau Christchurch (New Zealand) *Tel:* (03) 3585287, pg 489

Business Center for Academic Societies Japan (Japan) *Tel:* (03) 58145811 *Fax:* (03) 58145822 *E-mail:* gen@bcasj.or.jp, pg 415

Business Contact BV (Netherlands) *Tel:* (020) 5249800 *Fax:* (020) 6276851 *E-mail:* businesscontact@contact-bv.nl *Web Site:* www.boekenwereld.com, pg 475

Business Directory of Lanka Limited (Sri Lanka) *Tel:* (01) 577563; (01) 577793 *Fax:* (01) 586135 *E-mail:* info@lanka.com *Web Site:* www.lanka.com, pg 596

Business Monitor International (United Kingdom) *Tel:* (020) 7248 0468 *Fax:* (020) 7248 0467 *E-mail:* subs@businessmonitor.com *Web Site:* www.businessmonitor.com, pg 661

Business Traveller Asia Pacific (Hong Kong) *Tel:* (02) 25119317 *Fax:* (02) 25196846 *E-mail:* biztrvlr@netvigator.com, pg 318

Business Tutors (Barbados) *Tel:* (246) 428-5664 *Fax:* (246) 429-4854 *E-mail:* pchad@caribsurf.com, pg 63

Helmut Buske Verlag GmbH (Germany) *Tel:* (040) 2999580 *Fax:* (040) 29995820 *E-mail:* info@buske.de *Web Site:* buske.de, pg 208

Verlag Busse und Seewald GmbH (Germany) *Tel:* (05221) 77 5-0 *Fax:* (05221) 77 52 04 *E-mail:* info@busse-seewald.de *Web Site:* www.busse-seewald.de, pg 208

Butler & Tanner Inc (United States) *Tel:* 212-262-4753 *Fax:* 212-262-4779 *E-mail:* sales@nyc.butlerandtanner.com *Web Site:* www.butleratanner.com, pg 1205

Butler & Tanner Ltd (United Kingdom) *Tel:* (01373) 451500 *Fax:* (01373) 451333 *E-mail:* manufacturing@butlerandtanner.com, pg 1161, 1202, 1223

Butterworth-Heinemann Ltd (United Kingdom) *Tel:* (01865) 310366; 781-904-2500 (editorial & marketing) *Toll Free Tel:* 800-366-2665 (Customer Service & Sales) *Fax:* (01865) 310898; 781-904-2620 (sales); 781-904-2640 (editorial & marketing) *Toll Free Fax:* 800-446-6520 (customer service) *E-mail:* collegerep@bhusa.com (academic sales); buseditors@bhusa.com (business); bhmarketing@repp.co.uk (business marketing); conventions@bhusa.com (conventions); dpeditors@bhusa.com (digital press); engeditors@bhusa.com (engineering); editors@focalpress.com (focal press); gen@bhusa.com (general sales); internetrep@bhusa.com (internet reseller sales); mededitors@bhusa.com (medical); newsneseditors@bhusa.com (newnes press); bhukorders@repp.co.uk (orders); securityeditors@bhusa.com (security); specialsales@bhusa.com (special & bulk sales); techsupport@bhusa.com (techeditors@bhusa.com (technoloby); tradesales@bhusa.com (trade (book store) sales) *Web Site:* www.butterworth.heinemann.co.uk, pg 661

Butterworths Australia Ltd (Australia) *Tel:* (02) 9422 2222 *Fax:* (02) 9422 2444 *E-mail:* orders@butterworths.com.au *Web Site:* www.butterworths.com.au, pg 16

Butterworths Hong Kong (Hong Kong) *Tel:* 2965 1400 *Fax:* 2976 0840 *E-mail:* customer.care@butterworths-hk.com *Web Site:* www.butterworths-hk.com, pg 318

Butterworths New Zealand Ltd (New Zealand) *Tel:* (04) 385 1479 *Fax:* (04) 385 1598 *E-mail:* Customer.Relations@butterworths.co.nz *Web Site:* www.butterworths.co.nz, pg 489

Butterworths South Africa (South Africa) *Tel:* (031) 268 3111; (031) 268 3007 (customer service) *Fax:* (031) 268 3100; (021) 268 3109 (customer service) *Web Site:* www.butterworths.co.za, pg 553

Butterworths Tolley (United Kingdom) *Tel:* (020) 7400 2500; (020) 8662 2000 (customer service) *Fax:* (020) 7400 2842; (020) 8662 2012 (customer service) *E-mail:* customer-services@butterworths.com *Web Site:* www.butterworths.co.uk, pg 661

Butzon & Bercker GmbH (Germany) *Tel:* (02832) 929-0 *Fax:* (02832) 929-211 *E-mail:* service@butzonbercker.de *Web Site:* www.butzonbercker.de, pg 208

BV Uitgevery NZV (Nederlandse Zondagsschool Vereniging) (Netherlands) *Tel:* (035) 6285285 *Fax:* (035) 6241319, pg 475

Bycornute Books (United Kingdom) *Tel:* (01323) 649053, pg 1118

Byggforlaget (Sweden) *Tel:* (08) 6653650 *Fax:* (08) 6616901 *Web Site:* www.byggforlaget.se, pg 601

Byron Society (International) (United Kingdom) *Tel:* (020) 7352 5112, pg 1370

BZZTOH Publishers (Netherlands) *Tel:* (070) 3632934 *Fax:* (070) 3631932 *E-mail:* info@bzztoh.nl *Web Site:* www.bzztoh.nl, pg 475

C & C Offset Printing Co Ltd (Hong Kong) *Tel:* (02) 666-4988 *Fax:* (02) 666-4938 *E-mail:* offsetprinting@candcprinting.com *Web Site:* www.ccoffset.com, pg 1133, 1155, 1195

C & C Offset Printing Co Ltd (United States) *Tel:* 503-233-1834 *Fax:* 503-233-7815 *E-mail:* portlandinfo@ccoffset.com *Web Site:* www.ccoffset.com, pg 1142, 1164, 1205

C&S Publications (New Zealand) *Tel:* (0812) 56807 *Fax:* (0812) 8966583, pg 489

C V Toko Buku Tropen (Indonesia) *Tel:* (021) 3811669; (021) 3813543; (021) 3805938 *Fax:* (021) 3800566 *E-mail:* tropen@cbn.net.id, pg 1290

Ca Luna Forlaget (Denmark) *Tel:* 86828688 *Fax:* 86828664 *E-mail:* caluna@caluna.dk *Web Site:* www.caluna.dk, pg 131

Caann Verlag, Klaus Wagner (Germany) *Tel:* (08121) 9 32 71 *Fax:* (08121) 9 32 78 *E-mail:* webmaster@caann-verlag.de *Web Site:* www.caann-verlag.de, pg 208

CAB International (United Kingdom) *Tel:* (01491) 832111 *Fax:* (01491) 833508 *E-mail:* cabi@cabi.org, pg 1264

Ediciones el Caballito SA (Mexico) *Tel:* (05) 5903653; (05) 5963400, pg 458

CABI Publishing (United Kingdom) *Tel:* (01491) 832111 *Fax:* (01491) 833508 *E-mail:* publishing@cabi.org *Web Site:* www.cabi-publishing.org, pg 662

Cabildo Insular de Gran Canaria Departamento de Ediciones (Spain) *Tel:* (0928) 381020 *Fax:* (0928) 381627 *Web Site:* www.grancanaria.com, pg 566

Cabinet Conseil CCMLA (Morocco) *Tel:* (07) 770229; (07) 770264 *Fax:* (07) 770264, pg 469

Cacho Hermanos Inc (Philippines) *Tel:* (02) 6318362; (02) 6318363; (02) 6318364; (02) 6318365 *Fax:* (02) 6315244 *E-mail:* cacho@mozcom.com, pg 1137

Cacho Hermanos Inc (Philippines) *Tel:* (02) 6330006; (02) 6318363; (02) 6318364; (02) 6318365; (02) 6318361; (02) 6318362 *Fax:* (02) 6315244 *E-mail:* cacho@mozcom.com, pg 1199

Cacho Publishing House, Inc (Philippines) *Tel:* (02) 6318361 *Fax:* (02) 6315244 *E-mail:* cacho@s.com.ph, pg 512

Cacucci Editore (Italy) *Tel:* (080) 5214220 *Fax:* (080) 5234777, pg 379

Cadans (Netherlands) *Tel:* (020) 6206263 *Fax:* (020) 6209253, pg 475

Cadence Publicacoes Internacionais Ltda (Brazil) *Tel:* (021) 2637885 *Fax:* (021) 2830812 *E-mail:* cadence@mtecnet.com.br, pg 80

Edizioni Cadmo SRL (Italy) *Tel:* (055) 50181 *Fax:* (055) 50181201, pg 379

Cadmos Verlag GmbH (Germany) *Tel:* (04131) 981 666 *Fax:* (04131) 981 668 *E-mail:* info@cadmos.de *Web Site:* www.cadmos.de, pg 208

Cadogan Guides (United Kingdom) *Tel:* (020) 8600 3550 *Fax:* (020) 8600 3599 *E-mail:* info@cadoganguides.com; editorial@codoganguides.com; advertising@cadoganguides.com; publicity@cadoganguides.com; marketing@cadoganguides.com *Web Site:* www.cadoganguides.com, pg 662

Le Cadratin (France) *Tel:* (01) 42821701 *Fax:* (01) 42821701, pg 152

Caglayan Kitabevi (Turkey) *Tel:* (0212) 2491794 *Fax:* (0212) 1491794, pg 639

Editions des Cahiers Bourbonnais (France) *Tel:* (04) 70568061 *Fax:* (04) 70568080 *E-mail:* ecb@cahiers-bourbonnais.com *Web Site:* www.cahiers-bourbonnais.com/barre_liens.htm, pg 152

Editions Cahiers d'Art (France) *Tel:* (01) 45487673 *Fax:* (01) 45449850 *E-mail:* cahiersart@aol.com, pg 152

Cahiers de la Renaissance Vaudoise (Switzerland) *Tel:* (021) 3121914 *Fax:* (021) 3126714, pg 610

Les Cahiers Fiscaux Europeens Sarl (France) *Tel:* (04) 93538939 *Fax:* (04) 93536628 *E-mail:* auteurs@fontaneau.com *Web Site:* www.fontaneau.com/cfe99.htm, pg 152

Cahiers Luxembourgeois (Luxembourg) *Tel:* 338885 *Fax:* 336513, pg 447

Cairns Art Society Inc (Australia) *Tel:* (07) 4039 1122 *E-mail:* cas@internetnorth.com.au, pg 17

Cairo University Press (Egypt (Arab Republic of Egypt)) *Tel:* (02) 846144, pg 138

Caja de Ahorros del Mediterraneo-Obras Sociales (Spain) *Tel:* (06) 5906363; (06) 5905785 *Fax:* (06) 5905828 *Web Site:* www.cam.es, pg 566

Calambur Editorial, SL (Spain) *Tel:* (091) 913553033 *Fax:* (091) 913553033 *E-mail:* calambur@calambureditorial.com *Web Site:* www.calambureditorial.com, pg 566

Calamo Editorial (Spain) *Tel:* (096) 5130581 *Fax:* (096) 5115345 *E-mail:* calamo@lobocom.es, pg 566

Randolph Caldecott Society (United Kingdom) *Tel:* (01606) 891303, pg 1370

Calder Publications Ltd (United Kingdom) *Tel:* (020) 7633 0599 *E-mail:* info@calderpublications.com *Web Site:* www.calderpublications.com, pg 662

Calderini SRL (Italy) *Tel:* (051) 62267 *Fax:* (051) 490200 *E-mail:* comm@calderini.agriline.it, pg 1136

Caledonian International Book Manufacturing (United Kingdom) *Tel:* (0141) 7623000 *Fax:* (0141) 7620922 *E-mail:* 101622.235@compuserve.com, pg 1140, 1161, 1202, 1214

Calesa SA Editorial La (Spain) *Tel:* (083) 351215; (083) 353575; (0983) 348102 *Fax:* (0983) 358550 *E-mail:* editorial@la-calesa.com, pg 566

Uitgeverij G F Callenbach BV (Netherlands) *Tel:* (038) 3392555 *Fax:* (038) 3328912, pg 475

Callis Editora Ltda (Brazil) *Tel:* (011) 3842-2066 *Fax:* (011) 3849-5882 *E-mail:* callis@sanet.com.br *Web Site:* www.callis.com.br, pg 80

Verlag Georg D W Callwey GmbH & Co (Germany) *Tel:* (089) 4360050 *Fax:* (089) 436005113 *Web Site:* www.callwey.de, pg 208

Editions Calmann-Levy SA (France) *Tel:* (01) 47 42 38 33 *Fax:* (01) 47 42 77 81, pg 152

Calosci (Italy) *Tel:* (0575) 678282 *Fax:* (0575) 678282 *E-mail:* info@calosci.com *Web Site:* www.calosci.com, pg 379

Calvary Press (Sri Lanka) *Tel:* (01) 553110, pg 596

Calwer Verlag Stuttgart eV (Germany) *Tel:* (0711) 167 22-0 *Fax:* (0711) 167 22 77 *E-mail:* info@calwer.com *Web Site:* www.calwer.com, pg 209

Camara Argentina de Publicaciones (Argentina) *Tel:* (011) 43942892 *Fax:* (011) 43942892 *E-mail:* publicaciones@icatel.net *Web Site:* www.publicaciones.org, pg 1235

Camara Argentina del Libro (Argentina) *Tel:* (011) 43818383 *Fax:* (011) 43819253 *E-mail:* caarlibro@impsat1.com.ar *Web Site:* www.editores.com, pg 1235

Camara Boliviana del Libro (Bolivia) *Tel:* (02) 327039 *Fax:* (02) 327039 *E-mail:* cabolib@ceibo.entelnet.bo, pg 1238

Camara Brasileira do Livro (Brazil) *Tel:* (011) 3147-0870 *Fax:* (011) 3147-0870 *E-mail:* cbl@cbl.org.br *Web Site:* www.cbl.org.br, pg 1239

Camara Chilena del Libro AG (Chile) *Tel:* (02) 6989519 *Fax:* (02) 6989226 *E-mail:* camlibro@reuna.cl *Web Site:* www.camlibro.cl, pg 1240

Camara Colombiana del Libro (Colombia) *Tel:* (01) 2886188 *Fax:* (01) 2873320, pg 1240

Camara Dos Deputados Coordenacao De Publicacoes (Brazil) *Tel:* (061) 318-5151 *Fax:* (061) 318-2190 *E-mail:* publicacoes.cedi@camara.gov.br *Web Site:* www.camara.gov.br, pg 80

Camara Ecuatoriana del Libro (Ecuador) *Tel:* (02) 553311; (02) 553314 *Fax:* (02) 222150 *E-mail:* celnp@hoy.net, pg 1241

Camara Municipal de Castelo (Portugal) *Tel:* (058) 828580 *Fax:* (058) 829811, pg 523

Camara Nacional de la Industria Editorial Mexicana (Mexico) *Tel:* (05) 6045338; (05) 6882011; (05) 6882221 *Fax:* (05) 6043147; (05) 6044347, pg 1252

Biblioteca de la Camara Oficial de Comercio, Agricultura e Industria del Distrito Nacional (Dominican Republic) *Tel:* (809) 682-2688 *Fax:* (809) 685-2228, pg 1461

Camara Peruana del Libro (Peru) *Tel:* (01) 4287630 *Fax:* (01) 4277331 *E-mail:* jefatura@binape.gob.pe *Web Site:* www.binape.gob.pe, pg 1256

Camara Uruguaya del Libro (Uruguay) *Tel:* (02) 2414732 *Fax:* (02) 2411860, pg 1269

Camara Venezolana del Libro (Venezuela) *Tel:* (0212) 7931347; (0212) 7931368 *Fax:* (02) 7931368 *E-mail:* cavelibro@cantv.net, pg 1269

Cambridge Bibliographical Society (United Kingdom) *Tel:* (01223) 333123 *Fax:* (01223) 333160 *E-mail:* cbs@ula.cam.ac.uk, pg 1370

Cambridge University Press (Australia) *Tel:* (03) 95680322 *Fax:* (03) 95631517 *E-mail:* info@cambridge.edu.au *Web Site:* www.cambridge.edu.au, pg 17

Cambridge University Library (United Kingdom) *Tel:* (01223) 333000 *Fax:* (01223) 333160 *E-mail:* library@ula.cam.ac.uk *Web Site:* www.lib.cam.ac.uk/publications, pg 1506

Cambridge University Press (United Kingdom) *Tel:* (01223) 312393 *Fax:* (01223) 315052 *E-mail:* information@cup.cam.ac.uk; uksales@cambridge.org (sales); editorial@cambridge.org (editorial enquiries); rights@cambridge.org (rights & permission); www@cambridge.org (web services) *Web Site:* www.uk.cambridge.org, pg 662

Cambridge University Press - Printing Division (United Kingdom) *Tel:* (01223) 358331 *Fax:* (01223) 325672 *E-mail:* info@cup.cam.ac.uk, pg 1161, 1202

Cambridge University Press - Printing Division (United Kingdom) *Tel:* (01223) 358331 *Fax:* (01223) 325672, pg 1223

Camden Press Ltd (United Kingdom) *Tel:* (020) 7226 2061 *Fax:* (020) 7226 2418, pg 662

Camera Austria (Austria) *Tel:* (0316) 81 55 50-0 *Fax:* (0316) 81 55 50-9 *E-mail:* camera.austria@styria.com *Web Site:* www.camera-austria.at, pg 50

Camera dei Deputati Ufficio Pubblicazioni Informazione Parlamentare (Italy) *Tel:* (06) 67609328 *Fax:* (06) 6781326 *Web Site:* www.camera.it, pg 379

Camerapix Publishers International Ltd (Kenya) *Tel:* (02) 448923; (02) 448924; (02) 448925 *Fax:* (02) 448926; (02) 448927 *E-mail:* info@camerapix.com *Web Site:* www.camerapix.com, pg 431

Camerapix Publishers Intl Ltd (United Kingdom) *Tel:* (020) 8449 5503 *Fax:* (020) 8449 8120 *E-mail:* camerapixuk@btinternet.com, pg 662

Cameron & Hollis (United Kingdom) *Tel:* (01683) 220808 *Fax:* (01683) 220012 *E-mail:* editorial@cameronbooks.co.uk; sales@cameronbooks.co.uk (orders) *Web Site:* www.cameronbooks.co.uk, pg 663

Editorial Caminho SARL (Portugal) *Tel:* (021) 3152683 *Fax:* (021) 534346 *E-mail:* caminho@mail.telepac.pt, pg 523

Editora Caminho Suave Ltda (Brazil) *Tel:* (011) 2783377 *Fax:* (011) 2783537, pg 80

Campanotto (Italy) *Tel:* (0432) 699390; (0432) 690155 *Fax:* (0432) 644728, pg 379

Campbell Thomson & McLaughlin Ltd (United Kingdom) *Tel:* (020) 7242 0958 *Fax:* (020) 7242 2408, pg 1118

Les Editions Camphill (Switzerland) *Tel:* (021) 8062269 *Fax:* (021) 8061897, pg 610

Instituto Campineiro de Ensino Agricola Ltda (Brazil) *Tel:* (019) 3272-2280; (019) 3272-2677 *Fax:* (019) 3272-6004 *E-mail:* icea@icea.com.br *Web Site:* www.icea.com.br, pg 80

Campinia Media VZW (Belgium) *Tel:* (014) 59 09 59 *Fax:* (014) 59 03 44 *E-mail:* info@campiniamedia.be *Web Site:* www.campiniamedia.be, pg 65

Campus Corner Ltd (Trinidad & Tobago) *Tel:* (868) 623-1678 *Fax:* (868) 623-1678, pg 1314

Editora Campus Ltda (Brazil) *Tel:* (021) 509 5340 *Fax:* (021) 507 1991 *E-mail:* info@campus.com.br *Web Site:* www.campus.com.br, pg 80

Campus Evangelical Fellowship, Literature Department (Taiwan, Province of China) *Tel:* (02) 23653665-331 *Fax:* (02) 3680303 *E-mail:* publish@campus.org.tw, pg 629

Campus Publishing Ltd (Ireland) *Tel:* (091) 524662; (091) 767408 *Fax:* (091) 527505, pg 359

Campus Verlag GmbH (Germany) *Tel:* (069) 976 516-0 *Fax:* (069) 976 516-78 *E-mail:* info@campus.de *Web Site:* www.campus.de, pg 209 campusbooks Medien AG (Germany) *Tel:* (089) 18921730 *Fax:* (089) 18921731 *E-mail:* partner@campusbooks.de *Web Site:* www.campusbooks.de, pg 209

Bibliotheque du Centre Culturel Albert Camus (Madagascar) *Tel:* (02) 23647 *Fax:* (02) 21338 *E-mail:* medccac@dts.ng, pg 1482

Canadian ISBN Agency, Acquisitions and Bibliographic Services Branch (Canada) *Tel:* 819-994-6872 *Fax:* 819-997-7517 *E-mail:* isbn@nlc-bnc.ca *Web Site:* www.nlc-bnc.ca/isbn/e-isbn.htm, pg 1239

Editions Canal (France) *Tel:* (01) 42222730 *Fax:* (01) 42223025, pg 152

Canale G e C SpA (Italy) *Tel:* (011) 4078511 *Fax:* (011) 4078527 *E-mail:* info@canale.it *Web Site:* www.canale.it, pg 1136

Canale G e C SpA (Italy) *Tel:* (011) 4078511 *Fax:* (011) 4078527 *E-mail:* info@canale.it, pg 1158, 1198

Candlelight Trust T/A Candlelight Farm (Australia) *Tel:* (08) 92520456 *Fax:* (08) 92520456 *Web Site:* www.cfpermaculture.com, pg 17

Editorial Cangallo SACI (Argentina) *Tel:* (011) 4331-0204; (011) 4331-8848, pg 4

Canis Vydavatelstvi a Nakladatelstvi (Czech Republic) *Tel:* (02) 251096, pg 123

Cankarjeva Zalozba (Slovenia) *Tel:* (061) 21-419 *Fax:* (061) 214250, pg 551

Cankarjeva Zalozba (Slovenia) *Tel:* (061) 219419 *Fax:* (061) 13 23 144; (061) 318 782 *E-mail:* cankar.zalozba@cankarjeva-z.si, pg 1309

Cannon International (Singapore) *Tel:* 3323639; 3447801 *Fax:* 3323273 *E-mail:* legaldep@nlb.gov.sq.hdtsdnl@technet.sq, pg 545

Canoe Press (Jamaica) *Tel:* (876) 977-2659 *Fax:* (876) 977-2660 *E-mail:* salex@uwimona.edu.jm, pg 412

Canongate Books Ltd (United Kingdom) *Tel:* (0131) 557 5111 *Fax:* (0131) 557 5211 *E-mail:* salesandmark@canongate.co.uk; customerservices@canongate.co.uk *Web Site:* www.canongate.net, pg 663

Editions Canope (France) *Tel:* (04) 73-93-82-90 *Fax:* (04) 73-39-33-00 *E-mail:* editions.canope@wanadoo.fr *Web Site:* editionscanope.com, pg 152

Canova SRL (Italy) *Tel:* (0422) 382383 *Fax:* (0422) 382383, pg 379

Editorial Cantabrica SA (Spain) *Tel:* (04) 4245307 *Fax:* (04) 4231984, pg 566

Edizioni Cantagalli (Italy) *Tel:* (0577) 42102 *Fax:* (0577) 45363 *E-mail:* cantagalli@edizionicantagalli.com *Web Site:* www.edizionicantagalli.com, pg 379

Uitgeverij Cantecleer BV (Netherlands) *Tel:* (035) 5486601 *Fax:* (035) 5486615, pg 475

Canterbury University Library (New Zealand) *Tel:* (03) 3667001 *Fax:* (03) 3642055, pg 1487

Canterbury University Press (New Zealand) *Tel:* (03) 364-2914 *Fax:* (03) 364-2044 *E-mail:* mail@cup.canterbury.ac.nz, pg 489

Dr Cantz'sche, Druckerei GmbH & Co, Cantz Verlag (Germany) *Tel:* (0711) 4405-0 *Fax:* (0711) 4405-220 *E-mail:* bklein@jfink.de, pg 209

Capall Bann Publishing (United Kingdom) *Tel:* (01635) 247050 (sales); (1635) 248711 (editorial) *Fax:* (01635) 247050 (sales); (01635) 248711 (editorial) *E-mail:* enquiries@capallbann.co.uk *Web Site:* www.capallbann.co.uk, pg 663

Cape Catley (New Zealand) *Tel:* (09) 445-9668 *Fax:* (09) 445-9668 *E-mail:* cape.catley@xtra.co.nz *Web Site:* www.capecatleybooks.co.nz, pg 489

Cape Provincial Library Service (South Africa) *Tel:* (021) 4109111 *Fax:* (021) 4197541, pg 1497

Cape Provincial Library Service (South Africa) *Tel:* (021) 5910095 *Fax:* (021) 4102261, pg 553

Cape Town City Libraries (South Africa) *Tel:* (021) 4624400 *Fax:* (021) 4615981, pg 1497

Editorial Capitan San Luis (Cuba) *Tel:* (07) 234475; (07) 307397 *Fax:* (07) 332070, pg 120

Capitol Publishing House Inc (Philippines) *Tel:* (02) 997061; (02) 997062; (02) 997063; (02) 997064; (02) 997065 *Fax:* (02) 990535, pg 513

Capone Editore SRL (Italy) *Tel:* (0832) 612618 *Fax:* (0832) 611877, pg 379

J W Cappelens Forlag A/S (Norway) *Tel:* 22365000 *Fax:* 22365040, pg 503

Nuova Casa Editrice Licinio Cappelli GEM srl (Italy) *Tel:* (051) 239060 *Fax:* (051) 239286 *E-mail:* info@cappellieditore.com *Web Site:* www.cappellieditore.com, pg 379

Capstone Publishing Ltd (United Kingdom) *Tel:* (01865) 798623 *Fax:* (01865) 240941 *E-mail:* capstone_publishing@msn.com *Web Site:* www.capstone.co.uk, pg 663

Captain Jonas Publications (Australia) *Tel:* (07) 9555230 *Fax:* (07) 4956-2633, pg 17

Capu (Portugal) *Tel:* (021) 8492869 *Fax:* (021) 8409361, pg 523

Editions Capucines (Mauritius) *Tel:* 4641563 *Fax:* 4641563 *E-mail:* edcapsee@intnet.mu, pg 457

Editions Caracteres (France) *Tel:* (01) 43379698 *Fax:* (01) 43372610 *E-mail:* caracteres2000@aol.com *Web Site:* www.editions-caracteres.fr/contact.htm, pg 152

Editions Caraiibes SA (Haiti) *Tel:* 23179, pg 317

Caramel SA (Belgium) *Tel:* (02) 2632051 *Fax:* (02) 2632050 *E-mail:* caramel@skynet.be, pg 65

Editora Caravela (Portugal) *Tel:* (021) 155848 *Fax:* (021) 155848, pg 523

Carcanet Press Ltd (United Kingdom) *Tel:* (0161) 834 8730 *Fax:* (0161) 832 0084 *E-mail:* pnr@carcanet.u-net.com *Web Site:* www.carcanet.co.uk, pg 663

Cardiff Academic Press (United Kingdom) *Tel:* (029) 2056 03 *Fax:* (029) 2055 4909 *E-mail:* drakegroup@btinternet.com, pg 663

Cardinal Publishing Ltd (United Kingdom) *Tel:* (020) 8444 4666 *Fax:* (020) 8444 5637, pg 663

Careers & Educational Publishers Ltd (Ireland) *Tel:* (094) 71093, pg 359

Careers & Occupational Information Centre (COIC) (United Kingdom) *Tel:* (0114) 259 4564 *Fax:* (0114) 259 3439, pg 663

Carfax Publishing Ltd (United Kingdom) *Tel:* (01235) 401000 *Fax:* (01235) 401550 *E-mail:* sales@carfax.co.uk, pg 663

Carib Research & Publications Inc (Barbados) *Tel:* (246) 438-0580, pg 63

Caribbean & Latin American Studies Library (Puerto Rico) *Tel:* (787) 764-0000 (ext 3319) *Fax:* (787) 763-5685 *E-mail:* utorres@upracd.upr.clu.edu, pg 1493

Caribbean Authors Publishing (Jamaica) *Tel:* (876) 929-1226 *Fax:* (876) 929-3721, pg 412

Caribbean Community Secretariat (Guyana) *Tel:* (02) 692809 *Fax:* (02) 267816; (02) 257341; (02) 258031 *E-mail:* carisec1@caricom.org; carisec2@caricom.org; carisec3@caricom.org *Web Site:* www.caricom.org, pg 317

Caribbean Epidemiology Centre (Trinidad & Tobago) *Tel:* 6224261; 6224262 *Fax:* 622-2792 *E-mail:* cec_email@carec.paho.org, pg 636

Caribbean Food & Nutrition Institute (Jamaica) *Tel:* (876) 927-3829, pg 412

The Caribbean Law Publishing Co Ltd (Jamaica) *Tel:* (876) 927-2085 *Fax:* (876) 977-0243, pg 412

Caribbean Telecommunications Union (Trinidad & Tobago) *Tel:* 6283185 *Fax:* 6286037 *E-mail:* ctunion@tstt.net.tt, pg 636

Carinthia Verlag (Austria) *Tel:* (0463) 50 12 20-212 *Fax:* (0463) 50 12 20-214 *Web Site:* www.verlag.carinthia.com, pg 50

Carit Andersens Forlag A/S (Denmark) *Tel:* 436222 *Fax:* 435151 *E-mail:* info@caritandersens.dk *Web Site:* www.caritandersen.dk, pg 131

Caritas Printing Training Centre (Hong Kong) *Tel:* 25261148 *Fax:* 25371231, pg 1133, 1155, 1195, 1212

Carl-Auer-Systeme Verlag (Germany) *Tel:* (06221) 64 38 0 *Fax:* (06221) 64 38 22 *E-mail:* info@carl-auer.de *Web Site:* www.carl-auer.de, pg 209

Fachverlag Hans Carl GmbH (Germany) *Tel:* (0911) 95285-0 *Fax:* (0911) 95285-48; (0911) 9528571; (0911) 9528561 *E-mail:* info@hanscarl.com *Web Site:* www.hanscarl.com, pg 209

Fachverlag Hans Carl GmbH (Germany) *Tel:* (0911) 95285-0 *Fax:* (0911) 95285-48, pg 1283

Carl Link Verlag-Gesellschaft mbH Fachverlag fur Verwaltungsrecht (Germany) *Tel:* (09261) 969-0 *Fax:* (09261) 969-699 *E-mail:* info@carllink.de *Web Site:* www.carllink.de, pg 209

Carlong Publishers (Caribbean) Ltd (Jamaica) *Tel:* (876) 923-6505 *Fax:* (876) 923-7003 *E-mail:* sales@carlpub.com, pg 412

Forlaget Carlsen A/S (Denmark) *Tel:* 44443233 *Fax:* 44443633 *E-mail:* carlsen@carlsen.dk *Web Site:* www.carlsen.dk, pg 131

Carlsen Verlag GmbH (Germany) *Tel:* (040) 39 804 0 *Fax:* (040) 39 804 390, pg 209

Carlsson Bokfoerlag AB (Sweden) *Tel:* (08) 4112349 *Fax:* (08) 7968457, pg 601

Carlton Publishing Group (United Kingdom) *Tel:* (020) 7612 0400 *Fax:* (020) 7612 0401 *E-mail:* enquires@carltonbooks.co.uk *Web Site:* www.carltonbooks.co.uk, pg 664

Carmelitana VZW (Belgium) *Tel:* (09) 225.48.36 *Fax:* (09) 224.06.01 *E-mail:* boekhandel@carmelitana.be *Web Site:* www.carmelitana.be, pg 65

Edizioni Carmelitane (Italy) *Tel:* (06) 79847482 *Fax:* (06) 79845387, pg 379

Carnegie Library (Mauritius) *Tel:* 6742287 *Fax:* 6765054, pg 1484

Carnell Literary Agency (United Kingdom) *Tel:* (01279) 723626 *Fax:* (01279) 600308, pg 1118

Caroline van Gelderen Literary Agency (Netherlands) *Tel:* (035) 6241336 *Fax:* (035) 6232740 *E-mail:* mail@carvang.nl, pg 1114

Jon Carpenter Publishing (United Kingdom) *Tel:* (01608) 811969 *Fax:* (016808) 811969, pg 664

Editions Didier Carpentier (France) *Tel:* (01) 48780072 *Fax:* (01) 42829199, pg 152

Alzira Chagas Carpigiani (Brazil) *Tel:* (011) 849-0189 *Fax:* (011) 227-3384 *E-mail:* kerredit@uol.com.br, pg 80

Casa Musicale Edizioni Carrara SRL (Italy) *Tel:* (035) 243618 *Fax:* (035) 270298, pg 379

Carre d'Art Edition Archigraphie (Switzerland) *Tel:* (022) 3115750 *Fax:* (022) 3122121, pg 610

Carrick Media (United Kingdom) *Tel:* (01294) 311322 *Fax:* (01294) 311322 *E-mail:* enquiries@carrickmedia.demon.co.uk, pg 664

Edizioni Carroccio (Italy) *Tel:* (049) 700568 *Fax:* (049) 700568, pg 379

Carroggio SA de Ediciones (Spain) *Tel:* (093) 4949922 *Fax:* (093) 4949923 *E-mail:* editorial@carroggio.es *Web Site:* www.carroggio.com, pg 566

CARTA, THE ISRAEL MAP & PUBLISHING CO LTD   INDUSTRY

Carta, The Israel Map & Publishing Co Ltd (Israel) *Tel:* (02) 6783355 *Fax:* (02) 6782373 *E-mail:* cartaben@netvision.net.il *Web Site:* www.holyland-jerusalem.com, pg 366

Editura Cartea Romaneasca (Romania) *Tel:* (01) 3123733; (01) 6148802 *Fax:* (01) 3110025, pg 532

Edizioni Cartedit SRL (Italy) *Tel:* (0373) 277410 *Fax:* (0373) 277405, pg 379

Carter's Publications (Australia) *Tel:* (02) 9450 0011 *Fax:* (02) 9450 2532 *E-mail:* info@carters.com.au *Web Site:* www.carters.com.au, pg 17

Carto BVBA (Belgium) *Tel:* (02) 26803455 *Fax:* (02) 2680345, pg 65

Cartoeristiek (Federatie van Belgische Autobus- en Autocarondernemers) (BAAV) (Belgium) *Tel:* (051) 226060 *Fax:* (051) 229273, pg 66

Edizioni Cartografiche Milanesi (Italy) *Tel:* (02) 6193747 *Fax:* (02) 66402281 *E-mail:* info@ortelio-ecm.it, pg 379

Cartographia Ltd (Hungary) *Tel:* (01) 363 3639 *Fax:* (01) 363 4639 *Web Site:* www.cartographia.hu, pg 323

Cartoon-Caricature-Contor Arno Koch-CCC (Germany) *Tel:* (089) 3233669 *Fax:* (089) 3226859 *E-mail:* ccc@c5.net *Web Site:* www.c5.net, pg 1111

The Cartoon Cave (United Kingdom) *Tel:* (01780) 460689; (01780) 460757 *Fax:* (01780) 460689 *Web Site:* www.cartooncave.co.uk, pg 664

Cartoon Creation (Belgium) *Tel:* (02) 6520220 *Fax:* (02) 6520160, pg 66

Carvajal SA (Peru) *Tel:* (01) 440-9685 *Fax:* (01) 440-4871, pg 511

Carvajal International Inc (United States) *Tel:* 305-448-6875 *Fax:* 305-448-9942 *E-mail:* carinter@kanect.net *Web Site:* www.dynamicgraphic.com, pg 1206

A Tavares de Carvalho (Portugal) *Tel:* (021) 7970377 *Fax:* (021) 7958880, pg 1307

Casa de las Americas (Cuba) *Tel:* (07) 327271; (07) 323588 *Fax:* (07) 327272, pg 120

Casa de Velazquez (Spain) *Tel:* (091) 4551580 *Fax:* (091) 5446870 *E-mail:* bcv@bibli.cvz.es *Web Site:* www.casadevelazquez.org, pg 566

Casa Editora Abril (Cuba) *Tel:* (07) 624330 *E-mail:* eabril@jcce.org.cu *Web Site:* www.almamater.cu, pg 120

Casa Editoriala Independenta Europa (Romania) *Tel:* (051) 153487; (051) 425801 *Fax:* (051) 425801, pg 532

Casa Editrice Felice Le Monnier (Italy) *Tel:* (055) 64910 *Fax:* (055) 643983 *E-mail:* monnier@tin.it, pg 380

Casa Editrice Giuseppe Principato Spa (Italy) *Tel:* (02) 312025 *Fax:* (02) 33104295 *E-mail:* info@principato.it, pg 380

Casa Editrice Libraria Ulrico Hoepli SpA (Italy) *Tel:* (02) 864871 *Fax:* (02) 8052886 *E-mail:* hoepli@hoepli.it, pg 380

Casa Editrice Lint Srl (Italy) *Tel:* (040) 360396 *Fax:* (040) 361354, pg 380

Edizioni Casagrande SA (Switzerland) *Tel:* (091) 8256622 *Fax:* (091) 8251874 *E-mail:* casagrande@casagrande-online.ch *Web Site:* www.casagrande-online.ch, pg 611

Casalini Libri (Italy) *Tel:* (055) 50181 *Fax:* (055) 5018201, pg 380

Casalini Libri (Italy) *Tel:* (055) 50181 *Fax:* (055) 5018201 *E-mail:* gen@casalini.it, pg 1293

Editorial Casals SA (Spain) *Tel:* (093) 2449550 *Fax:* (093) 2656895 *E-mail:* casals@editorialcasals.com *Web Site:* www.editorialcasals.com, pg 566

Editorial Casariego (Spain) *Tel:* (091) 4424339; (091) 4425178; (091) 4411330; (091) 4416829 *Fax:* (091) 4426224 *E-mail:* casariego@btlink.net *Web Site:* www.casariego.com, pg 566

Casarotto Ramsay & Associates Ltd (United Kingdom) *Tel:* (020) 7287 4450 *Fax:* (020) 7287 9128 *E-mail:* agents@casarotto.uk.com *Web Site:* www.casarotto.uk.com, pg 1118

Edistudio di Brunetto Casini (Italy) *Tel:* (050) 48670 *Fax:* (050) 500585 *E-mail:* edistudio@sirius.pisa.it, pg 380

Casket Publications (Australia) *Tel:* (02) 98058878; (02) 94819145; (02) 98755382 *Fax:* (02) 98506593; (02) 98755382, pg 17

Casopisni zavod Uradni list Republike Slovenije (Slovenia) *Tel:* (061) 1251419; (061) 1252357 *Fax:* (061) 224337 *E-mail:* url@uradni-list.si, pg 551

Frank Cass Publishers (United Kingdom) *Tel:* (020) 8920 2100 *Fax:* (020) 8447 8548 *E-mail:* info@frankcass.com *Web Site:* www.frankcass.com, pg 664

Cassell & Co (United Kingdom) *Tel:* (020) 7420 5555 *Fax:* (020) 7240 7261; (020) 7240 8531, pg 664

Casset Ediciones SL (Spain) *Tel:* (091) 5043584 *Fax:* (091) 2508841, pg 566

Editorial Castalia (Spain) *Tel:* (091) 3198940; (091) 3195857 *Fax:* (091) 3102442 *E-mail:* castalia@infornet.es *Web Site:* www.castalia.es, pg 566

Casa Editrice Castalia (Italy) *Tel:* (011) 4374176 *Fax:* (011) 4374176, pg 380

Editions Casteilla (France) *Tel:* (01) 30141930 *Fax:* (01) 34603132 *E-mail:* info@casteilla.fr *Web Site:* www.casteilla.fr/contact/princ_contact.htm, pg 153

Edizioni Castello di Antonio Careddu (Italy) *Tel:* (070) 562296 *Fax:* (070) 562296, pg 380

Il Castello srl (Italy) *Tel:* (02) 48401629 *Fax:* (02) 4453617 *E-mail:* il_castello@tin.it, pg 380

Editions Casterman (France) *Tel:* (01) 55 28 12 00 *Fax:* (01) 55 28 12 60 *Web Site:* www.casterman.com, pg 153

Editions Casterman SA (Belgium) *Tel:* (02) 209 83 00 *Fax:* (02) 209 83 01 *Web Site:* www.casterman.com, pg 66

Editions Casterman SA (Belgium) *Tel:* (032) 22098300 *Fax:* (032) 22098301 *Web Site:* www.casterman.com, pg 66

Casterman NV (Netherlands) *Tel:* (0321) 313553 *Fax:* (0321) 318205, pg 475

Castle House Publications Ltd (United Kingdom) *Tel:* (01892) 539606 *Fax:* (01892) 517773; (01892) 517005 *E-mail:* enquiries@castlehouse.co.uk *Web Site:* www.castlehouse.co.uk, pg 664

Castle Publications SA (Switzerland) *Tel:* (022) 511036; (022) 7884222 *Fax:* (022) 7511111; (022) 7884240, pg 611

Castle Translations (United Kingdom) *Tel:* (01524) 841169 *Fax:* (01524) 381721 *E-mail:* info@castletranslations.co.uk *Web Site:* www.castletranslations.co.uk, pg 1128

Castlemead Publications (United Kingdom) *Tel:* (01920) 465525 *Fax:* (01920) 465545 *E-mail:* sales@castlemeadpublications.fsnet.co.uk *Web Site:* www.castlemeadpublications.fsnet.co.uk, pg 665

Le Castor Astral (France) *Tel:* (01) 48401490 *Fax:* (01) 48401973 *E-mail:* swproduction@magic.fr *Web Site:* perso.magic.fr/swproduction/castocau.html, pg 153

Il Castoro (Italy) *Tel:* (02) 29513529 *Fax:* (02) 29529896 *E-mail:* castoro@riavarea.com, pg 380

Edicios do Castro (Spain) *Tel:* (0981) 621494; (0981) 620937; (0981) 620200 *Fax:* (0981) 623804 *E-mail:* edicios.ocastro@sargadelos.com *Web Site:* www.sargadelos.com, pg 566

Castrum Peregrini Presse (Netherlands) *Tel:* (020) 235287 *Fax:* (020) 6247096 *E-mail:* mail@castrumperegrini.nl *Web Site:* castrumperegrini.nl, pg 475

Catchfire Press Inc (Australia) *Tel:* (02) 49264029 *E-mail:* catchfire@idl.com.au *Web Site:* cust.idl.com/au/catchfire/hmpage04.html, pg 17

Ediciones Catedra SA (Spain) *Tel:* (091) 3200119; (091) 3938800; (091) 3938787 *Fax:* (091) 7426631; (091) 7412118 *E-mail:* catedra@catedra.com *Web Site:* www.catedra.com, pg 566

Cathedral Books Ltd (Ireland) *Tel:* (01) 8787372 *Fax:* (01) 8787704 *E-mail:* cathedra@indigo.ie, pg 359

Kyle Cathie Ltd (United Kingdom) *Tel:* (020) 7692 7215 *Fax:* (020) 7692 7260 *E-mail:* general.enquiries@kyle-cathie.com *Web Site:* www.kylecathie.co.uk, pg 665

Central Catholic Library (Ireland) *Tel:* (01) 6761264, pg 1475

Catholic Institute for International Relations (United Kingdom) *Tel:* (020) 7354 0883 *Fax:* (020) 7359 0017 *E-mail:* ciir@ciir.org *Web Site:* www.ciir.org, pg 665

Catholic Institute of Sydney (Australia) *Tel:* (02) 9752 9530 *Fax:* (02) 9746 6022 *E-mail:* cisinfo@cis.catholic.edu.au *Web Site:* www.cis.catholic.edu.au, pg 17

Central Catholic Library Association Inc (Ireland) *Tel:* (01) 6761264, pg 1518

Catholic Supplies (NZ) LTD (New Zealand) *Tel:* (04) 3843665 *Fax:* (04) 3843663 *E-mail:* sales@catholicsupplies.co.nz *Web Site:* www.catholicsupplies.co.nz, pg 489

Imprimerie Catholique (Madagascar) *Tel:* (02) 22304, pg 1137

Catia Monser Eggcup-Verlag (Germany) *Tel:* (0211) 215122 *Fax:* (0211) 215122 *E-mail:* cmonserev@aol.com *Web Site:* members.aol.com/CMonserEV, pg 209

Causeway Press Ltd (United Kingdom) *Tel:* (01695) 576048; (01695) 577360 *Fax:* (01695) 570714 *E-mail:* davidalcorn.causewaypress@btinternet.com, pg 665

Caux Books (Switzerland) *Tel:* (041) 422213 *Fax:* (021) 9629465 *E-mail:* bookch@caux.ch, pg 611

Caux Edition SA (Switzerland) *Tel:* (021) 9629469 *Fax:* (021) 9629465, pg 611

Paul Cave Publications Ltd (United Kingdom) *Tel:* (01703) 223591; (01703) 333457 *Fax:* (01703) 227190 *E-mail:* lanksmag@zone.co.uk, pg 665

Verlag Bo Cavefors (Switzerland) *Tel:* (01) 2017200, pg 611

Marshall Cavendish Books (Singapore) *Tel:* (065) 2848844 *Fax:* (065) 2854871 *E-mail:* te@corp.tpl.com.sg *Web Site:* www.timesone.com.sg/te, pg 545

Marshall Cavendish Partworks Ltd (United Kingdom) *Tel:* (01424) 756 565 *Fax:* (01424) 755 519 *E-mail:* enquiries@woodgt.co.uk *Web Site:* www.marshallcavendish.co.uk, pg 665

Cavendish Publishing Pty Ltd (Australia) *Tel:* (02) 99182199 *Web Site:* www.cavendishpublishing.com, pg 17

Cavendish Publishing Ltd (United Kingdom) *Tel:* (020) 7278 8000 *Fax:* (020) 7278 8080 *E-mail:* info@cavendishpublishing.com *Web Site:* www.cavendishpublishing.com, pg 665

Caversham Broshures (South Africa) *Tel:* (031) 7017021 *Fax:* (031) 7017036, pg 553

The Caxton Press (New Zealand) *Tel:* (03) 3668516 *Fax:* (03) 3657840, pg 490

The Caxton Press (New Zealand) *Tel:* (064) 3668516 *Fax:* (03) 3657840, pg 1137

Editorial Caymi SACI (Argentina) *Tel:* (011) 4305-0784 *Fax:* (011) 4304-2474, pg 4

Cazal SA (Reunion) *Tel:* 213264 *Fax:* 410977, pg 1308

CB Print Finishers Ltd (United Kingdom) *Tel:* (0191) 2150101 *Fax:* (0191) 2701651 *E-mail:* sales@cbprint.co.uk *Web Site:* www.cbprint.co.uk, pg 1202

CBA Translations (United Kingdom) *Tel:* (01) 1404822284 *Fax:* (01) 1404823136 *E-mail:* enquires@cbatranslations.freeserve.co.uk *Web Site:* www.cbatranslations.freeserve.co.uk, pg 1128

CBD Research Ltd (United Kingdom) *Tel:* (020) 8650 7745 *Fax:* (020) 8650 0768 *E-mail:* cbd@cbdresearch.com *Web Site:* www.cbdresearch.com, pg 665

CCH Editions Ltd (United Kingdom) *Tel:* (01869) 253300 *Fax:* (01869) 874700 *E-mail:* customer.services@cch.co.uk, pg 665

CCH New Zealand Ltd (New Zealand) *Tel:* (09) 488 2760 *Fax:* (09) 489 3312 *E-mail:* nzsales@cch.co.nz *Web Site:* www.cch.co.nz, pg 490

CD Remain Cia Ltda (Ecuador) *Tel:* (02) 224973; (02) 239328 *Fax:* (02) 505760, pg 1281

CDL (Central Distribuidora Livreira) Sarl (Portugal) *Tel:* (01) 4264422; (01) 769744; (01) 779825, pg 1307

CEAC, Grupo Editorial SA (Spain) *Tel:* (093) 3073004 *Fax:* (093) 2660067 *E-mail:* atencioncliente@ceacedit.com; info@ceacedit.com *Web Site:* www.ceacedit.com; www.editorialceac.com, pg 567

Editorial la Cebra SA de CV (Mexico) *Tel:* (05) 2779529 *Fax:* (05) 2737866 *E-mail:* 74173.1014@compuserve.com, pg 458

CEC-Cosmic Energy Connections (Germany) *Tel:* (0761) 7059 632 *Fax:* (0761) 7059 633, pg 209

Biblioteca Musicale S Cecilia (Italy) *Tel:* (06) 6784552 ext 235 *Fax:* (06) 6784555, pg 1477

CED (Italy) *Tel:* (089) 254252 *Fax:* (089) 254262 *E-mail:* ced@pamdoraezimet.it, pg 380

CED-Samsom (Belgium) *Tel:* (02) 7231111 *Fax:* (02) 7231050 *E-mail:* customer.cedsamson@wkb.be *Web Site:* www.cedsamson.be, pg 66

CEDAM (Casa Editrice Dr A Milani) (Italy) *Tel:* (049) 8239111 *Fax:* (049) 8752900 *E-mail:* info@cedam.com *Web Site:* www.cedam.com, pg 380

Cedar Media (United Kingdom) *Tel:* (020) 8508 8856 *Fax:* (020) 8508 8856 *E-mail:* cedarmedia@btinternet.com, pg 1318

Cedel, Ediciones Jose O Avila Monteso ES (Spain) *Tel:* (093) 2156039 *Fax:* (093) 2156088 *E-mail:* cedel@wbsite.es, pg 567

CEEBA Publications Antenne d'Autriche (Austria) *Tel:* (02236) 803115 *Fax:* (02236) 8033 *E-mail:* ceeba@steyler.at *Web Site:* www.steyler.at/, pg 50

Editions du CEFAL (Belgium) *Tel:* (04) 254 25 20 *Fax:* (04) 254 24 40 *E-mail:* cefal.celes@skynet.be *Web Site:* www.cefal.com, pg 66

CEIC Alfons El Vell (Spain) *Tel:* (06) 2876551 *Fax:* (06) 2875286, pg 567

Cekit SA (Colombia) *Tel:* (01) 333535; (01) 345075; (01) 352575 *Fax:* (01) 342615 *Web Site:* www.cekit.com.co, pg 111

Celebrity Educational Publishers (Singapore) *Tel:* 7857274 *Fax:* 7489108, pg 545

Celeluck Co Ltd (Hong Kong) *Tel:* (02) 8939197; (02) 8939147 *Fax:* (02) 8915591 *E-mail:* open@open.com.hk *Web Site:* www.open.com.hk, pg 318

Celesa (Spain) *Tel:* (091) 5170170 *Fax:* (091) 5173481 *E-mail:* celesa@infornet.es *Web Site:* www.celesa.es, pg 1311

Celeste Ediciones (Spain) *Tel:* (01) 3100599; (002) 118298 *Fax:* (01) 3100459 *E-mail:* info@celesteediciones.com *Web Site:* www.celesteediciones.com, pg 567

Celia Godkin (Canada) *Tel:* 416-591-0491 *Fax:* 416-591-7095 *E-mail:* celia.godkin@utoronto.ca, pg 1153

CELID (Italy) *Tel:* (011) 2489326 *Fax:* (011) 2489329, pg 380

CELSE (Compagnie d'Editions Libres, Sociales et Economiques SA) (France) *Tel:* (01) 42674123 *Fax:* (01) 42274020 *E-mail:* celse@celsedit.com *Web Site:* www.celsedit.com, pg 153

Celta Editora, Lda (Portugal) *Tel:* (01) 4417433 *Fax:* (01) 4417733, pg 523

Celuc Libri (Italy) *Tel:* (02) 86450776 *Fax:* (02) 86451424, pg 380

CEM Publishers Ltd (Nigeria), pg 498

Cemagref Editions (France) *Tel:* (01) 4096 62 85 *Fax:* (01) 4096 61 64 *E-mail:* info@cemagref.fr *Web Site:* www.cemagref.fr, pg 153

Sociedad Fondo Editorial Cenamec (Venezuela) *Tel:* (02) 229133; (02) 229511 *Fax:* (02) 225077, pg 762

Editions Cenomane (France) *Tel:* (02) 43242157 *Fax:* (02) 43771916, pg 153

Cent Pages (France) *Tel:* (02) 38121620 *Fax:* (04) 38121629 *E-mail:* editions@editions-centpages.fr *Web Site:* www.editions-centpages.fr/contact/contact.htm, pg 153

Centaur Press (1954) (United Kingdom) *Tel:* (020) 7431 4391 *Fax:* (020) 7431 5129 *E-mail:* books@opengatepress.co.uk *Web Site:* www.opengatepress.co.uk, pg 665

Centaurus-Verlagsgesellschaft GmbH (Germany) *Tel:* (07643) 93 39-0 *Fax:* (07643) 93 39-11 *E-mail:* info@centaurus-verlag.de *Web Site:* www.centaurus-verlag.de, pg 209

Centenary Publishing House Ltd (Uganda) *Tel:* (041) 241599 *Fax:* (041) 250427, pg 642

Centenary of Technical Education in Bairnsdale Group (Australia) *Tel:* (03) 5152-4556, pg 17

Center for Advanced Welsh & Celtic Studies (United Kingdom) *Tel:* (01970) 626717 *Fax:* (01970) 627066 *E-mail:* cawcs@wales.ac.uk *Web Site:* www.aber.ac.uk/~awcwww/s/cyflwyniad.html, pg 665

Center for Agricultural Library & Technology Dissemination (CALTD) (Indonesia) *Tel:* (0251) 321746 *Fax:* (0251) 326561 *E-mail:* pustaka@booor.net *Web Site:* pustaka.bogor.net, pg 1474

The Center for Romanian Studies (Romania) *Tel:* (032) 219000 *Fax:* (032) 219010 *E-mail:* csr@romanianstudies.ro *Web Site:* www.romanianstudies.ro, pg 532

Center Print Ltd (United Kingdom) *Tel:* (0115) 9612277 *Fax:* (0115) 9381424, pg 1140

Center Print Ltd (United Kingdom) *Tel:* (0115) 9612277 *Fax:* (0115) 9381424 *E-mail:* cprint@besharapress.co.uk, pg 1161, 1202

Centers of Academic Resources Chulalongkorn University (Thailand) *Tel:* (02) 218-2905 *Fax:* (02) 215-3617 *E-mail:* prachak@chulkn.cav.chula.ac.th, pg 1503

Centraal Boekhuis BV (Netherlands) *Tel:* (0345) 475911 *Fax:* (0345) 475343, pg 1254

Central Library (India) *Tel:* (0265) 540133, pg 1473

Central de Publicaciones SA (Mexico) *Tel:* (05) 5104231, pg 1299

Central Africana Ltd (Malawi) *Tel:* 623227 *Fax:* 622236 *E-mail:* africana@sdwp.org.mw, pg 450

Central Agricultural Library, National Agro-industrial Union (Bulgaria) *Tel:* (02) 709168, pg 1455

The Central Archives for the History of the Jewish People (Israel) *Tel:* (02) 635716 *Fax:* (02) 635716 *E-mail:* archives@vms.huji.ac.il *Web Site:* www.sites.huji.ac.il/archives, pg 1476

Central Book Distribution Co, Ltd (Thailand) *Tel:* (02) 367-5565 (direct); (02) 367-5030-41 (ext 181 & 178) *Fax:* (02) 367-5049, pg 1314

Central Bookshop Ltd (Malawi) *Tel:* 623534 *Fax:* 633863, pg 1298

Central Catequistica Salesiana (CCS) (Spain) *Tel:* (091) 7252000 *Fax:* (091) 7262570 *E-mail:* sei@editorialccs.com *Web Site:* www.editorialccs.com, pg 567

Central European University Press (Hungary) *Tel:* (01) 327 3136 *Fax:* (01) 327 3183 *E-mail:* ceupress@ceupress.com *Web Site:* www.ceupress.com, pg 323

Central Medical Library (Bulgaria) *Tel:* (02) 523171 *Fax:* (02) 523171 *E-mail:* medlib@bgcict.bitnet, pg 1455

Central News Agency Ltd (South Africa) *Tel:* (011) 4917500, pg 1310

Central News Agency (CNA) (Namibia) *Tel:* (061) 25625 *Fax:* (061) 227210, pg 1300

Central Reference Library (Uganda) *Tel:* (041) 233633 *Fax:* (041) 348625 *E-mail:* library@imul.com, pg 1504

Central Secretariat Library (India) *Tel:* (011) 3389684 *Fax:* (011) 3384846 *E-mail:* rootofcsl@delnet.ren.nic.in, pg 1473

Central State Archives (Bulgaria) *Tel:* (02) 940 0104 *Fax:* (02) 9801443, pg 1455

Central State Archives (Russian Federation) *Tel:* (095) 1597383, pg 1494

Central Tanganyika Press (United Republic of Tanzania) *Tel:* (061) 22140 *Fax:* (061) 324565, pg 633

Central Technical Library (Bulgaria) *Tel:* (02) 702935 *Fax:* (02) 710157 *E-mail:* ctb@nacid.nat.bg *Web Site:* www.nacid.nat.bg, pg 1455

Central Tibetan Secretariat (India) *Tel:* (01892) 22467 *Fax:* (01892) 23723 *E-mail:* ltwa@ndf.vsnl.net.in, pg 334

Centrala Handlu Zagranicznego ARS Polona SA (Poland) *Tel:* (022) 8261201; (022) 8266248 *Fax:* (022) 8265334; (022) 8264763 *E-mail:* arspolona@arspolona.com.pl *Web Site:* www.arspolona.com.pl, pg 1306

Biblioteca Centrala Universitara Mihail Eminescu (Romania) *Tel:* (032) 316281 *Fax:* (032) 261796 *Web Site:* www.bcu-iasi.ro, pg 1494

Central Books (United Kingdom) *Tel:* (020) 8986 4854 *Fax:* (020) 8533 5821 *E-mail:* orders@centralbooks.com, pg 1318

Istituto Centrale per il Catalogo Unico delle Biblioteche Italiane e per le Informazioni Bibliografiche (Italy) *Tel:* (06) 4454701 *Fax:* (06) 4959302 *E-mail:* depinedo@itcaspur.caspur.it, pg 380

Istituto Centrale per il Catalogo Unico delle Biblioteche Italiane e per le Informazioni Bibliografiche (Italy) *Tel:* (06) 4454701 *Fax:* (06) 4959302, pg 1518

Centralna Narodna Biblioteka SR Crne Gore (Yugoslavia) *Tel:* (086) 31143 *Fax:* (086) 31726 *E-mail:* cnb@cg.yu *Web Site:* www.heritage.cg.yu, pg 1508

Centre Africain d'Animation et d'Echanges Culturels Editions Khoudia (Senegal) *Tel:* 211023 *Fax:* 215109, pg 544

Centre Africain de Formation et de Recherche Administratives pour le Developpement, Centre de Documentation (Morocco) *Tel:* (09) 94-26-52 *Fax:* (09) 94-14-15, pg 1253

Centre Bibliotheque d'Information (Gabon) *Tel:* 21115, pg 1466

Centre Culturel De Differdange (Luxembourg) *Tel:* (352) 587045 *Fax:* (352) 474692, pg 447

Centre Culturel Francais, Bibliotheque (Congo) *Tel:* 832566 *Fax:* 83-25-66, pg 1458

Centre Culturel Francais, Bibliotheque (Cote d'Ivoire) *Tel:* 211599; 225628 *Fax:* 227132 *E-mail:* cef@ci.refer.org, pg 1459

Centre d'Action Laique (Belgium) *Tel:* (02) 6276860 *Fax:* (02) 6266861, pg 66

Centre De Documentation Universitaire (CDU) (Chad) *Tel:* (0235) 51 44 44; (0235) 51 62 68 *Fax:* (0235) 51 40 33 *E-mail:* rectorat@intnet.td, pg 1456

Centre de Librairie et d'Editions Techniques (CLET) (France) *Tel:* (01) 40926500 *Fax:* (01) 40926550, pg 153

Centre de Linguistique Appliquee (Senegal) *Tel:* 230126, pg 544

Centre de Publications Evangeliques (Cote d'Ivoire) *Tel:* 444805 *Fax:* 445817, pg 117

Centre de Recherche des Archives et de Documentation (CRAD) (Chad) *Tel:* (051) 2327, pg 1456

Centre de Recherche, et Pedagogie Appliquee (The Democratic Republic of the Congo), pg 114

Centre de Recherches et d'Etudes Administratives (Tunisia) *Tel:* (01) 846167 *Fax:* (01) 787205, pg 1504

Centre de Vulgarisation Agricole (The Democratic Republic of the Congo) *Tel:* (012) 71165 *Fax:* (012) 21351, pg 115

Centre d'Edition et de Diffusion Africaines (Cote d'Ivoire) *Tel:* 22 20 55; 21 72 62 *Fax:* 21 72 62 *E-mail:* infos@ceda-ci.com *Web Site:* www.ceda-ci.com, pg 117

Centre d'Edition et de Diffusion Africaines (Cote d'Ivoire) *Tel:* 222242; 222055 *Fax:* 217262, pg 1280

Centre d'Edition et de Production pour l'Enseignement et la Recherche (CEPER) (Cameroon) *Tel:* (023) 7 23 12 93, pg 99

Centre d'Enseignement Superieur de Niamey (Niger) *Tel:* 732713 *Fax:* 733862, pg 1488

Centre d'Etudes et Documentation Economique Juridique et Sociale (CEDEJ) (Egypt (Arab Republic of Egypt)) *Tel:* (02) 704641, pg 138

Centre d'Information et de Conservation de l'Universite de Liege (Belgium) *Tel:* (04) 3665206 *Fax:* (04) 3665702, pg 1453

Centre Europeen pour l'Enseignement Superieur (Romania) *Tel:* (01) 3130839 *Fax:* (01) 3123567 *E-mail:* cepes@cepes.ro, pg 1257

Centre for Alternative Technology (United Kingdom) *Tel:* (01654) 705980; (01654) 705959 (mail order); (01654) 705993 (CAT shop) *Fax:* (01654) 702782; (01654) 705999 (mail order); (01654) 703605 (education & courses) *E-mail:* pubs@cat.org.uk *Web Site:* www.cat.org.uk, pg 665

Centre for Basic Research (Uganda) *Tel:* (041) 231228; (041) 235533; (041) 342987 *Fax:* (041) 235413 *E-mail:* cbr@imul.com, pg 642

Centre for Comparative Literature & Cultural Studies (Australia) *Tel:* (03) 9905 4000; (03) 9905 3059 *Fax:* (03) 9905 4007, pg 17

Centre for Conflict Resolution (South Africa) *Tel:* (021) 6502503; (021) 6502750 *Fax:* (021) 6852142; (021) 6504053 *E-mail:* ccr@uctvax.uct.ac.za *Web Site:* www.ccrweb.ccr.uct.ac.za, pg 553

The Centre for Creative Communities (United Kingdom) *Tel:* (020) 7247 5385 *Fax:* (020) 7247 5256 *E-mail:* baaa@easynet.co.uk, pg 1370

Centre for Documentation & Research (United Arab Emirates) *Tel:* (02) 4445400 *Fax:* (02) 4445811, pg 1505

Centre for Educational Technology (Israel) *Tel:* (03) 6460183 *Fax:* (03) 6460821, pg 366

Centre for European Policy Studies (Belgium) *Tel:* (02) 2293911 *Fax:* (02) 2194151; (02) 2293971 *E-mail:* ceps@infoboard.be, pg 1237

Centre for Information on Language Teaching & Research (CILT) (United Kingdom) *Tel:* (20) 7379 5101; (020) 7379 5110 (resources library & information services) *Fax:* (020) 7379 5082 *E-mail:* publications@cilt.org.uk; library@cilt.org.uk (library information) *Web Site:* www.cilt.org.uk, pg 666

Centre for South Asian Studies (Pakistan) *Tel:* (042) 5864014 *Fax:* (042) 5867206, pg 506

Centre International de Recherches 'Primitifs Flamands' ASBL (Belgium) *Tel:* (02) 7396866 *Fax:* (02) 7320105, pg 66

Centre National des Archives (Burkina Faso) *Tel:* 336196 *Fax:* 314926, pg 1456

Centre National du Livre (France) *Tel:* (01) 49546868 *Fax:* (01) 45491021 *Web Site:* www.centrenationaldulivre.fr, pg 1362

Centre National de Documentation (Morocco) *Tel:* (07) 774944 *Fax:* (07) 773134 *E-mail:* magridoc@wizarat-sukkan.sukkan.gov.ma, pg 1485

Centre National de Documentation Pedagogique (CNDP) (France) *Tel:* (01) 55436000 *Fax:* (01) 55436001 *Web Site:* www.cndp.fr/cndp_reseau/enregion/ulm.htm, pg 153

Centre National de Production de Materiel Didactique (CNAPMAD) (Madagascar) *Tel:* (02) 28954 *Fax:* (02) 20053, pg 450

Centre of Legal Information (Lithuania) *Tel:* (02) 617529; (02) 623650 *Fax:* (02) 625940 *E-mail:* webadm@utic.tm.lt, pg 445

Centre Protestant d'Editions et de Diffusion (CEDI) (The Democratic Republic of the Congo) *Tel:* 02 22202, pg 115

Centre Publications (Australia) *Tel:* (03) 8700149, pg 17

Centre Regional pour la Promotion du Livre en Afrique (CREPLA) (Cameroon) *Tel:* 224782; 2936, pg 1239

CentrePolygraph Traders & Publishers Co (Russian Federation) *Tel:* (095) 2817411 *Fax:* (095) 2844074, pg 537

Centro Agronomico Tropical de Investigacion y Ensenanza (CATIE) (Costa Rica) *Tel:* 5560501 *Fax:* 5560858; 5560176; 5568464 *Web Site:* www.catie.ac.cr, pg 115

Centro Ambrosiano di Documentazione e Studi Religiosi (Italy) *Tel:* (02) 6713161 *Fax:* (02) 66984388, pg 380

Centro Biblico (Italy) *Tel:* (081) 8048933 *Fax:* (081) 8048933, pg 380

Centro de Cultura Tradicional (Spain) *Tel:* (0923) 218707 *Fax:* (0923) 293256, pg 567

Centro de Documentacao e Informacao da Camara dos Deputados (Brazil) *Tel:* (061) 3186785 *Fax:* (061) 3182171, pg 1455

Centro de Documentacao e Informao para o Desenvolvimento (Cape Verde) *Tel:* 613969 *Fax:* 1527, pg 99

Centro de Documentacion Bibliotecologica (Argentina) *Tel:* (091) 28035 *Fax:* (091) 551447, pg 1511

Centro De Educacion Popular (Ecuador) *Tel:* (02) 525521 *Fax:* (02) 542818 *E-mail:* cedep@fmlaluna.com *Web Site:* www.jacomenet.com/laluna/cedep.html, pg 137

Centro de Estudios sobre Desarrollo Economico CEDE (Colombia) *Tel:* (01) 3520466 *Fax:* (01) 2841890 *E-mail:* cede@uniandes.edu.co, pg 1458

Centro de Estudios Avanzados en Ciencias Sociales (CEACS) del Instituto Juan March de Estudios e Investigaciones (Spain) *Tel:* (091) 4354240 *Fax:* (091) 5763420 *E-mail:* jackie@ceacs.march.es *Web Site:* www.march.es, pg 567

Centro de Estudios Mexicanos y Centroamericanos (Mexico) *Tel:* (05) 5405921; (05) 5405922 *Fax:* (05) 5405923 *E-mail:* cemca@data.net.mx *Web Site:* www.casadefiancia.org.mx/cemca, pg 458

Centro de Estudios Politicos Y Constitucionales (Spain) *Tel:* (091) 5401950 *Fax:* (091) 5478549, pg 567

Centro de Estudos Juridicosdo Para (CEJUP) (Brazil) *Tel:* (091) 225-0355 *Fax:* (091) 241-3184, pg 80

Centro de Informacion Cientifica y Humanistica (Mexico) *Tel:* (05) 6223966 *Fax:* (05) 6162557, pg 1484

Centro de la Mujer Peruana Flora Tristan (Peru) *Tel:* (01) 4332765; (01) 433 1457; (01) 433 9060 *Fax:* (01) 4339500 *E-mail:* postmast@flora.org.pe, pg 511

Centro de Traducciones y Terminologia Especializada (CTTE) (Cuba) *Tel:* (07) 626531 *Fax:* (07) 626501; (07) 338237 *E-mail:* ctte@ceniai.inf.cu *Web Site:* www.Z.cuba.cu/ciencia/idict/ctte/inicio.html, pg 1125

Centro Di (Italy) *Tel:* (055) 2342668 *Fax:* (055) 2342667, pg 381

Centro Documentazione Alpina (Italy) *Tel:* (011) 3197823 *Fax:* (011) 3197827, pg 381

Centro Editor de America Latina SA (Argentina) *Tel:* (011) 4371-2411, pg 4

Centro Editorial Mexicano Osiris SA (Mexico) *Tel:* (05) 5406902; (05) 2027185 *Fax:* (05) 2027185, pg 458

Centro Editoriale Valtortiano SRL (Italy) *Tel:* (0776) 807032 *Fax:* (0776) 809789 *E-mail:* cev@mariavaltorta.com *Web Site:* www.mariavaltorta.com, pg 381

Centro Estudos Geograficos (Portugal) *Tel:* (021) 7940218 *Fax:* (021) 7938690 *E-mail:* ceg@mail.telepac.pt, pg 523

Centro Italiano Studi Alto Medioevo (Italy) *Tel:* (0743) 23271 *Fax:* (0743) 232701 *E-mail:* cisam@cisam.org *Web Site:* www.cisam.org, pg 381

Centro Latinoamericano de Demografia (CELADE) (Chile) *Tel:* (02) 2087037; (02) 2102023 *Fax:* (02) 2080196; (02) 2080252 *E-mail:* djaspers@eclac.cl *Web Site:* www.eclac.org/Celade-Eng/index.html, pg 1240

Centro Nacional de Documentacion Cientifica, Tecnica y Economics (CNDCTE) (Uruguay) *Tel:* (02) 485030 *Fax:* (02) 496902, pg 1507

Centro Nacional de Documentacion Cientifica y Tecnologica - Universidad Mayor De S an Andres (Bolivia) *Tel:* (02) 359586; (02) 359587 *Fax:* (02) 359491, pg 1513

Centro Nacional de Informacion, Agencia Nacional ISBN (Mexico) *Tel:* (05) 2503900 *Fax:* (05) 2031657; (05) 2307632 *E-mail:* jmarquez@sep.gob.mx, pg 1253

Centro Psicologia Clinica (Portugal) *Tel:* (01) 9211182, pg 523

Centro Regional para el Fomento del Libro en America Latina y el Caribe (Colombia) *Tel:* (01) 2126056; (01) 2495141; (01) 3125690; (01) 3217501; (01) 5402071 *Fax:* (01) 2554614; (01) 3217503 *E-mail:* cerlalc@impsat.net.co; info@cerlalc.org *Web Site:* www.cerlalc.com, pg 111

Centro Regional para el Fomento del Libro en America Latina y el Caribe (Colombia) *Tel:* (01) 2495141; (01) 2126056 *Fax:* (01) 2554614 *E-mail:* cerlalc@impsat.net.co, pg 1240

Centro Scientifico Int (Italy) *Tel:* (011) 3853656 *Fax:* (011) 3853244 *E-mail:* cse@estorinese.inet.it, pg 381

Centro Scientifico Torinese (Italy) *Tel:* (011) 3853656 *Fax:* (011) 3853244 *E-mail:* cse@estorinese.inet.it, pg 381

Edizioni Centro Studi Erickson (Italy) *Tel:* (0461) 950690 *Fax:* (0461) 950698 *E-mail:* info@erickson.it *Web Site:* www.erickson.it, pg 381

Centro Studi Terzo Mondo (Italy) *Tel:* (02) 29409041; (330) 687866 *Fax:* (02) 29409041 *E-mail:* cstm@libero.it, pg 381

YELLOW PAGES

Centro UNESCO de San Sebastian (Spain) *Tel:* (0943) 427003 *Fax:* (0943) 427003 *E-mail:* unescoeskola@retemail.es *Web Site:* www.servicom.es/unesco, pg 567

Centrul National de Numerotare Standardizata Biblioteca Nationala (Romania) *Tel:* (01) 3124990 *Fax:* (01) 3124990 *E-mail:* isbn@bibnat.ro; issn@bibnat.ro, pg 1257

Forlaget Centrum (Denmark) *Tel:* 33 32 12 06 *Fax:* 33 32 12 07 *E-mail:* info@forlaget-centrum.dk, pg 131

Centrum Vedecko-Technickych Informaci SR (Slovakia) *Tel:* (07) 362419 *Fax:* (07) 323527 *E-mail:* cvti@tbb1.sltk.stuba.sk, pg 1496

CEP Editions (France) *Tel:* (01) 42961550 *Fax:* (01) 48243489, pg 153

Cep Kitaplari AS (Turkey) *Tel:* (0212) 5162004; (0212) 5163301; (0212) 4582409 *Fax:* (0212) 5162005; (0212) 5162004 Ext 17, pg 639

CEPA - Centro Editor de Psicologia Aplicada Ltda (Brazil) *Tel:* (021) 2220-6545 *Fax:* (021) 2510-3468 *Web Site:* www.psicocepa.com.br, pg 81

Cepadues Editions SA (France) *Tel:* (05) 61 40 57 36 *Fax:* (05) 61 41 79 89 *E-mail:* cepadues@cepadues.com *Web Site:* www.cepadues.com, pg 153

CEPLAES (Ecuador) *Tel:* (02) 232261; (02) 547854 *Fax:* (02) 566207 *E-mail:* ceplaes@ceplaes.ec, pg 137

Le Cerchio Imigiative Editoriali (Italy) *Tel:* (0541) 21158; (0541) 708190 *Fax:* (0541) 21158 *E-mail:* ilcerchio@iper.net *Web Site:* www.ilcerchio.it, pg 381

Editions Cercle d'Art SA (France) *Tel:* (01) 48879212 *Fax:* (01) 48874779 *E-mail:* info@officieldesarts.com *Web Site:* www.officieldesarts.com/cercledart/, pg 153

Cercle de la Librairie (France) *Tel:* (01) 44412800 *Fax:* (01) 44412865, pg 1243

CERDIC-Publications (France) *Tel:* (0388) 877107 *Fax:* (0388) 877125, pg 153

Ceres Editions (Tunisia) *Tel:* (01) 782033 *Fax:* (01) 787516 *E-mail:* ceres@planet.tm, pg 637

Editura Ceres (Romania) *Tel:* (01) 2224836, pg 532

Editions du Cerf (France) *Tel:* (01) 44181212 *Fax:* (01) 45560427 *Web Site:* www.editionsducerf.fr/html/contact/contact.htm, pg 153

Cesarini Hermanos (Argentina) *Tel:* (011) 4861-1152, pg 4

Ceska Biblicka Spolecnost (Czech Republic) *Tel:* (02) 20181412 *Fax:* (02) 24315723 *E-mail:* cbs@biblenet.cz, pg 123

Ceska Expedice (Czech Republic) *Tel:* (02) 727 612 04, pg 123

Cesky Filmovy ustav (Czech Republic) *Tel:* (02) 894300; (02) 894686-9 *Fax:* (02) 894501, pg 123

Cesky spisovatel (Czech Republic) *Tel:* (02) 6911902; (02) 6911909; (02) 6911897 *Fax:* (02) 6911902, pg 123

Cesoc Ltda (Chile) *Tel:* (02) 6391081; (02) 6336992 *Fax:* (02) 6325382 *E-mail:* cesoc@bellsouth.cl, pg 100

Cetal Ediciones (Chile) *Tel:* (032) 213360 *Fax:* (032) 214851, pg 100

Edicoes Cetop (Portugal) *Tel:* (01) 9263222 *Fax:* (01) 9217940, pg 523

CEU-Press (Hungary) *Tel:* (01) 327-3014 *Fax:* (01) 327-3042 *E-mail:* sales@ceu.hu, pg 323

The Ceylon Chamber of Commerce (Sri Lanka) *Tel:* (01) 412745; (01) 412747 *Fax:* (01) 449352, pg 596

Les Editions du CFPJ (Centre de Formation et de Perfectionnement des Journalistes) - Sarl Presse et Formation (France) *Tel:* (01) 44822000 *Fax:* (01) 44822001 *Web Site:* www.cfpj.com, pg 154

CFW Publications Ltd (Hong Kong) *Tel:* (02) 5543004 *Fax:* (02) 5438007, pg 318

CG Ediz Medico-Scientifiche (Italy) *Tel:* (011) 338507 *Fax:* (011) 3852750, pg 381

Chadwyck-Healey Ltd (United Kingdom) *Tel:* (01223) 215512 *Fax:* (01223) 215513 *E-mail:* mail@chadwyck.co.uk *Web Site:* www.chadwyck.co.uk, pg 666

Chadwyck-Healey France (France) *Tel:* (01) 44838181 *Fax:* (01) 44838183, pg 154

Chalantika (Bangladesh) *Tel:* (02) 7123925 *Fax:* (02) 7115691, pg 62

Editions du Chalet (France) *Tel:* (01) 45443834 *Fax:* (01) 45499392, pg 154

Chalkface Press Pty Ltd (Australia) *Tel:* (061) 8 9385 1923 *Fax:* (061) 8 9385 1922 *E-mail:* info@chalkface.net.au *Web Site:* www.chalkface.net.au, pg 17

Challenge Bookshops (Nigeria) *Tel:* (073) 53897; (073) 52230, pg 1303

Chamaeleon Verlag AG (Switzerland) *Tel:* (01) 2525497 *Fax:* (01) 2725282, pg 611

Chamber of Books (Poland) *Tel:* (022) 6215571; (022) 6254170, pg 1306

Chambers Harrap Publishers Ltd (United Kingdom) *Tel:* (0131) 5565929 *Fax:* (0131) 5565313 *E-mail:* admin@chambersharrap.co.uk; webmanager@chambersharrap.co.uk *Web Site:* www.chambersharrap.co.uk, pg 666

Jacqueline Chambon (France) *Tel:* (04) 66676396 *Fax:* (04) 666739 74, pg 154

Editions de la Chambre de Commerce et d'Industrie SA (Belgium) *Tel:* (04) 344-50-88 *Fax:* (04) 343-05-53 *Web Site:* www.ecci.be, pg 66

Chambre des Employes Prives (Luxembourg) *Tel:* 444091-1 *Fax:* 459440 *E-mail:* info@cepp.pu, pg 447

Chambre Nationale du Livre Agence ISBN (Republic of Moldova) *Tel:* (02) 24 65 11; (02) 24 65 42 *Fax:* (02) 24 65 11 *E-mail:* cameracartii@yahoo.com; cncm@moldova.cc *Web Site:* www.iatp.md/cnc, pg 1253

Editions Champ Vallon (France) *Tel:* (04) 50561551 *Fax:* (04) 50561564 *E-mail:* info@champ-vallon.com *Web Site:* www.champ-vallon.com, pg 154

Editions Honore Champion (France) *Tel:* (01) 46340729 *Fax:* (01) 46346406 *E-mail:* champion@honorechampion.com *Web Site:* www.honorechampion.com, pg 154

Librairie des Champs-Elysees SA (France) *Tel:* (01) 45759602 *Fax:* (01) 43923573, pg 154

Chanakya Publications (India) *Tel:* (011) 711976, pg 334

Chancellor Publications (United Kingdom) *Tel:* (020) 7269 9150 *Fax:* (020) 7269 9151 *E-mail:* mail@chancellorpublication.com *Web Site:* www.chancellorpublication.com, pg 666

Chancerel International Publishers Ltd (United Kingdom) *Tel:* (020) 7240 2811 *Fax:* (020) 7836 4186 *E-mail:* chancerel@chancerel.com *Web Site:* www.chancerel.com, pg 666

Philippe Chancerel Editeur (France) *Tel:* (01) 39656918, pg 154

Nem Chand & Bros (India) *Tel:* (01332) 72258; (01332) 72752; (01322) 74343 *Fax:* (01332) 73258, pg 1288

S Chand & Co Ltd (India) *Tel:* (011) 3672080-81-82 *Fax:* (011) 3677446 *E-mail:* schand@vsnl.com *Web Site:* stepsindia.com/schand/group.html, pg 334

Chang-josa Publishing Co (Republic of Korea) *Tel:* (02) 7380393, pg 435

Editions Chanlis (Belgium) *Tel:* (071) 326394, pg 66

Editions Chantecler (Belgium) *Tel:* (03) 8 77 14 64 *Fax:* (03) 8 77 21 15, pg 66

Chapman (United Kingdom) *Tel:* (0131) 5572207 *Fax:* (0131) 5569565 *E-mail:* admin@chapman-pub.co.uk *Web Site:* www.chapman-pub.co.uk, pg 666

CHEMICAL INDUSTRY PRESS

Chapter Two (United Kingdom) *Tel:* (020) 8316 5389 *Fax:* (020) 8854 5963 *E-mail:* chapter2UK@aol.com *Web Site:* www.chaptertwo.org.uk, pg 666

Chardon Bleu (France) *Tel:* (016) 72390213 *Fax:* (016) 72390403 *E-mail:* chardonbleued@aol.com *Web Site:* www.chardonbleu.com/presentation/presentation.html, pg 154

Le Chariot (France) *Tel:* (02) 37258989 *Fax:* (02) 37258900 *E-mail:* edchariot@aol.com *Web Site:* www.editions-du-chariot.com, pg 154

Deborah Charles Publications (United Kingdom) *Tel:* (0151) 724 2500 *Fax:* (0151) 729 0371 *E-mail:* dcp@legaltheory.demon.co.uk *Web Site:* www.legaltheory.demon.co.uk, pg 666

Editions Charles-Lavauzelle SA (France) *Tel:* (05) 55584545 *Fax:* (05) 55584525, pg 154

The Charlesworth Group (United Kingdom) *Tel:* (01484) 517077 *Fax:* (01484) 517068 *E-mail:* sales@charlesworth.com, pg 1161, 1202

Charotar Publishing House (India) *Tel:* (02692) 56237 *Fax:* (02692) 40089 *E-mail:* charotar@icenet.net *Web Site:* www.charotarpublishinghouse.com, pg 334

Charran Educational Publishers (Trinidad & Tobago) *Tel:* 6223832 *Fax:* 6235829, pg 636

Charran's Bookshop (1978) Ltd (Trinidad & Tobago) *Tel:* (868) 6223832, pg 1314

La Charte Editions juridiques (Belgium) *Tel:* (02) 512 29 49 *Fax:* (02) 512 26 93 *E-mail:* info@lacharte.be *Web Site:* www.lacharte.be, pg 66

The Chartered Institute of Building (United Kingdom) *Tel:* (01344) 630700 *Fax:* (01344) 630777 *E-mail:* reception@ciob.org.uk *Web Site:* www.ciob.org.uk, pg 666

Chartered Institute of Journalists (CIJ) (United Kingdom) *Tel:* (020) 7252 1187 *Fax:* (020) 7232 2302 *E-mail:* memberservices@iojco.uk *Web Site:* www.ioj.co.uk, pg 1264

Chartered Institute of Library & Information Professionals (United Kingdom) *Tel:* (020) 7255 0500; (020) 7255 0505 (textphone) *Fax:* (020) 7255 0501 *E-mail:* info@cilip.org.uk *Web Site:* www.cilip.org.uk, pg 1525

Chartered Institute of Library & Information Professionals in Scotland (United Kingdom) *Tel:* (01698) 458888 *Fax:* (01698) 458899 *E-mail:* sla@slainte.org.uk *Web Site:* www.slainte.org.uk, pg 666

Chartered Institute of Personnel & Development (United Kingdom) *Tel:* (020) 8971 9000 *Fax:* (020) 8263 3333 *E-mail:* publish@cipd.co.uk *Web Site:* www.cipd.co.uk, pg 667

Chase Just Publishing (Australia) *Tel:* (03) 9853-8799, pg 17

Chase Publishing Services (United Kingdom) *Tel:* (01395) 514709 *Fax:* (01395) 514709 *E-mail:* r.addicott@btinternet.com, pg 1140, 1161, 1223

Chasse Maree-Armen (France) *Tel:* (02) 98920919 *Fax:* (02) 98928001 *E-mail:* chasse-maree.armen@wanadoo.fr *Web Site:* www.chasse-maree.com, pg 154

Chatham Publishing (United Kingdom) *Tel:* (01634) 810760 *Fax:* (01634) 810761 *Web Site:* www.chathampublishing.com, pg 667

Chaves Ferreira Publicacoes SA (Portugal) *Tel:* (021) 3871373 *Fax:* (021) 3871396, pg 523

Chef i forvaltning (Sweden) *Tel:* (08) 6909000 *Fax:* (08) 6909470 *E-mail:* export@liber.se *Web Site:* www.liber.se, pg 1232

Chemical Industry Press (China) *Tel:* (010) 64918054 *Fax:* (010) 64918054 *E-mail:* liangh@cip.com.cn *Web Site:* www.cip.com.cn, pg 102

1583

VERLAG FUR CHEMISCHE INDUSTRIE H ZIOLKOWSKY GMBH INDUSTRY

Verlag fur chemische Industrie H Ziolkowsky GmbH (Germany) *Tel:* (0821) 325-830 *Fax:* (0821) 325-8323, pg 209

Editions du Chene (France) *Tel:* (01) 43 92 30 00 *Fax:* (01) 43 92 33 81, pg 154

Cheng Chung Book Co, Ltd (Taiwan, Province of China) *Tel:* (02) 3821147 *Fax:* (02) 3822805, pg 629

Cheng Wen Publishing Company (Taiwan, Province of China) *Tel:* (02) 3628032 *Fax:* (02) 3925428, pg 629

Cheng Yun Publishing Company Ltd (Taiwan, Province of China) *Tel:* (02) 8117798 *Fax:* (02) 8123041, pg 629

Chengdu Maps Publishing House (China) *Tel:* (028) 442512-493 *Fax:* (028) 4852529 *E-mail:* ccph@public.cd.sc.cn, pg 103

Cheong-mun-gag Publishing Co (Republic of Korea) *Tel:* (02) 9851451; (02) 9897423; (02) 9897421 *Fax:* (02) 9828679 *E-mail:* CMGbook@hitel.kol.co.kr, pg 435

Le Cherche Midi Editeur (France) *Tel:* (01) 42227120 *Fax:* (01) 45440838 *E-mail:* infos@cherche-midi.com *Web Site:* www.cherche-midi.com/scripts, pg 154

Cherokee Literary Agency (South Africa) *Tel:* (021) 6714508 *Fax:* (021) 761-4329, pg 1116

Cherrytree Books (United Kingdom) *Tel:* (020) 7487 0920 *Fax:* (020) 7487 0921 *E-mail:* sales@evansbrothers.co.uk *Web Site:* www.evansbooks.co.uk, pg 667

Chetana Private Ltd (India) *Tel:* (022) 284 4968; (022) 282 4983 *Fax:* (022) 262 4316 *E-mail:* kavi@chetana.com *Web Site:* www.chetana.com, pg 334

Chiang Mai University Library (Thailand) *Tel:* (053) 221154 *Fax:* (053) 222766; (053) 221013; (053) 221154 *E-mail:* prasit@lib.cmunet.edu, pg 635

Chien Chen Bookstore Publishing Company Ltd (Taiwan, Province of China) *Tel:* (07) 3820363 *Fax:* (07) 3892816, pg 629

Chijin Shokan Co Ltd (Japan) *Tel:* (03) 32354422 *Fax:* (03) 32358984 *E-mail:* KYY02177@nifty.ne.jp *Web Site:* www.chijishokan.co.jp, pg 415

Chikuma Shobo Publishing Co Ltd (Japan) *Tel:* (03) 5687-2687 *Fax:* (03) 5687-2688 *Web Site:* www.chikumashobo.co.jp, pg 415

Chikyu-sha Co Ltd (Japan) *Tel:* (03) 35850087 *Fax:* (03) 35892902, pg 415

Wilfred Bwalya Chilangwa Publications (Zambia) *Tel:* (01) 282998 *E-mail:* hope@samnet.zm, pg 766

Child Honsha Co Ltd (Japan) *Tel:* (03) 38133781 *Fax:* (03) 38184970, pg 415

Childerset Publishers (Australia) *Tel:* (07) 5474 0242 *Fax:* (07) 5474 4446 *E-mail:* tessgsp@ozemail.com.au, pg 18

Children's Book Circle (United Kingdom) *Tel:* (020) 7739 2929 *Fax:* (020) 7739 2181, pg 1265

Children's Book Council of Australia (Australia) *Tel:* (08) 9371 5018 *Web Site:* www.cbc.org.au, pg 1359

The Children's Book Store Company Ltd (Taiwan, Province of China) *Tel:* (02) 7628222 *Fax:* (02) 7604322, pg 1313

Children's Book Trust (India) *Tel:* (011) 3316974; (011) 3316970 *Fax:* (011) 3721090 *E-mail:* cbtnd@vsnl.com *Web Site:* www.childrensbooktrust.com, pg 334

Children's Books History Society (United Kingdom) *Tel:* (01992) 464885 *Fax:* (01992) 464885 *E-mail:* cbhs@abcgarrelt.demon.co.uk, pg 1370

Children's Literature Association of Nigeria (Nigeria) *Tel:* (022) 400550; (022) 400614 *Fax:* (022) 711254, pg 1255

Children's Literature Documentation & Research Centre, Ibadan (Nigeria) *Fax:* (022) 711254, pg 1255

The Children's Press (Ireland) *Tel:* (01) 4973628, pg 359

Children's Writers & Illustrators Group (United Kingdom) *Tel:* (20) 7373 6642 *Fax:* (20) 7373 5768, pg 1265

Child's Play (International) Ltd (United Kingdom) *Tel:* (01793) 616286 *Fax:* (01793) 512795 *E-mail:* allday@childs-play.com *Web Site:* www.childs-play.com, pg 667

Child's World Education Ltd (United Kingdom) *Tel:* (01753) 647060 *Fax:* (01753) 645522, pg 667

Chin Chin Publications Ltd (Taiwan, Province of China) *Tel:* (02) 3633486 *Fax:* (02) 3636081, pg 629

China National Association of Literature and the Arts (Taiwan, Province of China), pg 1368

Library Association of China (Taiwan, Province of China) *Tel:* (02) 23312475 *Fax:* (02) 23700899 *E-mail:* lac@msg.ncl.edu.tw *Web Site:* www.lac.ncl.edu.tw, pg 1524

China Agriculture Press (China) *Tel:* (010) 5005665 *Fax:* (010) 5005894 *E-mail:* fcap@bj.col.com.cn, pg 103

China Books (Australia) *Tel:* (03) 9663 8822 *Fax:* (03) 9663 8821 *E-mail:* info@chinabooks.com.au *Web Site:* www.chinabooks.com.au, pg 18

China Braille Press (China) *Tel:* (010) 6383 3585 *Fax:* (010) 6383 3585, pg 103

China Cartographic Publishing House (China) *Tel:* (010) 6356 4947 *Fax:* (010) 6352 9403 *E-mail:* fanyi@chinamap.com, pg 103

China Express Media Ltd (Hong Kong) *Tel:* (02) 5757288 *Fax:* (02) 5757088 *E-mail:* ossima@netvigator.com, pg 318

China Film Press (China) *Tel:* (010) 4216761; (010) 4219977 *Fax:* (010) 4219489, pg 103

China Foreign Economic Relations & Trade Publishing House (China) *Tel:* (010) 64263813; (010) 64219742 *Fax:* (010) 64219392 *Web Site:* www.cfertph.com, pg 103

China Forestry Publishing House (China) *Tel:* (010) 6013117; (010) 661884477-2038 *Fax:* (010) 66180373 *E-mail:* cfph@public3.bta.net.cn, pg 103

China International Book Trading Corporation (China) *Tel:* (010) 68412026 *Fax:* (010) 68475199 *E-mail:* cibtc@mail.cibtc.com.cn *Web Site:* www.cibtc.com.cn, pg 1279

China ISBN Agency (China) *Tel:* (010) 65127806 *Fax:* (010) 65127875, pg 1240

China Labour Publishing House (China) *Tel:* (010) 4910448, pg 103

China Law Magazine Ltd (Taiwan, Province of China) *Tel:* (02) 23814211 *Fax:* (02) 23814211 *E-mail:* chinals@hk.china.com, pg 629

China Light Industry Press (China) *Tel:* (010) 5121122-565 *Fax:* (010) 65121371, pg 103

China Machine Press (CMP) (China) *Tel:* (010) 68326677 (trunk line); (010) 68320405 *Fax:* (010) 68320405 *E-mail:* cjhui@mail.machineinfo.gov.cn *Web Site:* www.cmpbooks.com, pg 103

China Materials Management Publishing House (China) *Tel:* (010) 8392745 *Fax:* (010) 8392911, pg 103

China National Publications Import & Export Corp (China) *Tel:* (010) 65066688 *Fax:* (010) 65063101, pg 1279

China Ocean Press (China) *Tel:* (010) 62173322 (ext 212) *Fax:* (010) 62173569 *E-mail:* oceanpress@china.com *Web Site:* www.oceanpress.com.cn, pg 103

China Oil & Gas Periodical Office (China) *Tel:* (010) 4219111, pg 104

China Pictorial Publishing House (China) *Tel:* (010) 68412392; (010) 68414896; (010) 68412665 *Fax:* (010) 68413023 *Web Site:* www.china-pictorial.com, pg 104

China Social Sciences Publishing House (China) *Tel:* (010) 64074509 *Fax:* (010) 64074509, pg 104

China Society for Library Science (China) *Tel:* (010) 68415566 ext 5563; (010) 68417815 *Fax:* (010) 68419271, pg 1513

China Theatre Publishing House (China) *Tel:* (010) 2550255, pg 104

China Tibetology Publishing House (China) *Tel:* (010) 4910088-213 *Fax:* (010) 4917619, pg 104

China Times Publishing Co (Taiwan, Province of China) *Tel:* (02) 23087111 *Fax:* (02) 23027844 *Web Site:* www.chinatimes.com.tw, pg 629

China Translation & Publishing Corp (China) *Tel:* (010) 6022134 *Fax:* (010) 6022734 *E-mail:* ctpc@public.bta.net.cn, pg 104

China Youth Publishing House (China) *Tel:* (010) 4032266-328 *Fax:* (010) 4031803, pg 104

Chinese Christian Literature Council Ltd (Hong Kong) *Tel:* 23678031, pg 318

Chinese Christian Literature Council Taiwan Ltd (Taiwan, Province of China) *Tel:* (02) 7080230 *Fax:* (02) 7551895, pg 629

Chinese Language Society of Hong Kong (Hong Kong) *Tel:* (02) 5284853, pg 1364

Chinese Literature Press (China) *Tel:* (010) 68326678 *Fax:* (010) 68326678 *E-mail:* chinalit@public.east.cn.net, pg 104

Chinese Marketing & Communications (United Kingdom) *Tel:* (0161) 2373821 *Fax:* (0161) 2367558 *E-mail:* info@chinese-marketing.com *Web Site:* www.chinese-marketing.com, pg 1128

Chinese Pedagogics Publishing House (China) *Tel:* (010) 8315599-602 *Fax:* (010) 8317390, pg 104

Chinese University of Hong Kong Library System (Hong Kong) *Tel:* 2609-7301; 2609-7302 *Fax:* 2603-6952 *E-mail:* library@cuhk.edu.hk *Web Site:* www.lib.cuhk.edu.hk/, pg 1471

The Chinese University Press (Hong Kong) *Tel:* 26096508; 26096500 *Fax:* 26036692; 26037355 *E-mail:* cup@cuhk.edu.hk *Web Site:* www.cuhk.edu.hk/cupress.w1.htm; www.chineseupress.com, pg 319

Chingchic Publishers (Australia) *Tel:* (07) 55385945 *Fax:* (07) 55385945 *E-mail:* chingchic@winshop.com.au, pg 18

Editions Chiron (France) *Tel:* (01) 30141930 *Fax:* (01) 34603132 *E-mail:* chiron@wanadoo.fr, pg 154

Chiron Media (Australia) *Tel:* (074) 947311 *Fax:* (074) 947890 *E-mail:* chiron@acslink.net.au, pg 18

Chiron-Verlag Reinhardt Stiehle (Germany) *Tel:* (07071) 8884150 *Fax:* (07071) 8884151 *E-mail:* info@chironverlag.de *Web Site:* www.chironverlag.com, pg 210

Cedric Chivers Ltd (United Kingdom) *Tel:* (0117) 9371910 *Fax:* (0117) 9371920 *E-mail:* info@cedricchivers.co.uk *Web Site:* www.cedricchivers.co.uk, pg 1203

Chmielorz GmbH Verlag (Germany) *Tel:* (0611) 360980 *Fax:* (0611) 301303, pg 210

CHOICE Magazine (Australia) *Tel:* (02) 9577 3399 *Fax:* (02) 9577 3377 *E-mail:* ausconsumer@choice.com.au *Web Site:* www.choice.com.au, pg 18

Chokechai Thewet Co Ltd (Thailand) *Tel:* (02) 2226660, pg 635

An Chomhairle Leabharlanna (Ireland) *Tel:* (01) 6761167 *Fax:* (01) 6766721 *E-mail:* info@librarycouncil.ie *Web Site:* www.librarycouncil.ie, pg 1518

Chong Moh Offset Printing Ltd (Singapore) *Tel:* 8622701 *Fax:* 8624335 *E-mail:* chongmoh@singnet.com.sg, pg 1138, 1159, 1200

Chong No Books Publishing Co Ltd (Republic of Korea) *Tel:* (02) 7325381 *Fax:* (02) 7326202, pg 435

Chongqing Library (China) *Tel:* 54832, pg 1457

Chongqing University Press (China) *Tel:* (023) 6511 1125 *Fax:* (023) 6510 6789 *E-mail:* office@cqup.com.cn *Web Site:* www.cqup.com.cn, pg 104

Chopsons Pte Ltd (Singapore) *Tel:* 64483634 *Fax:* 64481071 *E-mail:* chopsons@singnet.com.sg, pg 545

Chopsticks Publications Ltd (Hong Kong) *Tel:* (02) 3368433; (02) 3368037 *Fax:* (02) 3381462, pg 319

Chorion IP (United Kingdom) *Tel:* (020) 7434 1880 *Fax:* (020) 7434 1882 *E-mail:* info@enidblyton.co.uk *Web Site:* www.chorion-ip.com, pg 667

Chorus-Verlag (Germany) *Tel:* (089) 634 999 60 *Fax:* (089) 634 999 61 *Web Site:* www.chorus-verlag.de, pg 210

The Chosun Ilbo Co, Ltd (Republic of Korea) *Tel:* (02) 7245114 *Fax:* (02) 7246199, pg 435

Chotard et Associes Editeurs (France) *Tel:* (01) 41299605 *Fax:* (01) 41299815, pg 154

Chowkhamba Sanskrit Series Office (India) *Tel:* (0542) 333458 *Fax:* (0542) 333458 *E-mail:* cssoffice@satyam.net.in, pg 335

Chr Belser AG fur Verlagsgeschaefte und Co KG (Germany) *Tel:* (0711) 2191-0 *Fax:* (0711) 2191-355, pg 210

CHRIKER (Bulgaria) *Tel:* (02) 319-217, pg 94

Christchurch City Libraries (New Zealand) *Tel:* (03) 3796914 *Fax:* (03) 3651751, pg 1487

Christian Audio-Visual Action (CAVA) (Zimbabwe) *Tel:* (04) 752233 *Fax:* (04) 727030, pg 768

The Christian Book Centre (Papua New Guinea) *Tel:* 822989 *Fax:* 823313, pg 510

Christian Book Service (Guyana) *Tel:* (02) 52521 *Fax:* (02) 54039, pg 1287

Christian Booksellers Association (United Kingdom) *Tel:* (0161) 434 7000 *Fax:* (0161) 445 2911 *E-mail:* info@cba-ukeurop.org *Web Site:* www.cba-ukeurop.org, pg 1265

Christian Booksellers' Association (NZ Chapter) (New Zealand) *Tel:* (07) 888 6010 *E-mail:* cba@cba.net.nz, pg 1255

Christian Booksellers Association of Nigeria (Nigeria) *Tel:* 53090 *Fax:* 57684, pg 1255

Christian Bookselling Association of Australia Inc (Australia) *Tel:* (02) 95243349 *Fax:* (02) 95403001 *Web Site:* www.christprdoz.com, pg 1236

Christian Bookstore (Thailand) *Tel:* (02) 234-7991, pg 1314

Christian Bourgois Editeur (France) *Tel:* (01) 45 44 09 13 *Fax:* (01) 45 44 87 86 *E-mail:* bourgois-editeur@wanadoo.fr *Web Site:* www.christianbourgois-editeur.fr, pg 155

Christian Communications Ltd (Hong Kong) *Tel:* (02) 7258558 *Fax:* (02) 3861804 *Web Site:* www.ccl.org.hk, pg 319

Christian Education (United Kingdom) *Tel:* (0121) 4724242 *Fax:* (0121) 4727575 *E-mail:* enquiries@christianeducation.org.uk (general enquiries & membership) *Web Site:* www.christianeducation.org.uk/cep/cep_about.htm, pg 667

Christian Focus Publications Ltd (United Kingdom) *Tel:* (01862) 871 011 *Fax:* (01862) 871 699 *E-mail:* info@christianfocus.com *Web Site:* www.christianfocus.com, pg 667

Christian Literature Association in Malawi (Malawi) *Tel:* 620839, pg 450

Christian Literature Crusade (Australia) *Tel:* (02) 8751566 *Fax:* (02) 4818304, pg 18

Christian Literature Crusade (Barbados) *Tel:* (246) 426-9254; (246) 429-5630 *Fax:* (246) 435-6642, pg 1275

The Christian Literature Society (India) *Tel:* (044) 5354296 *Fax:* (044) 5354297, pg 335

The Christian Literature Society of Korea (Republic of Korea) *Tel:* (02) 5530807 *Fax:* (02) 5643532, pg 435

Christian Verlag GmbH (Germany) *Tel:* (089) 381803-17 *Fax:* (089) 38180381 *E-mail:* info@christian-verlag.de *Web Site:* www.christian-verlag.de, pg 210

Christiana-Verlag (Switzerland) *Tel:* (052) 7412092 *Fax:* (052) 7412092 *E-mail:* orders@christiana.ch; info@christiana.ch *Web Site:* www.christiana.ch, pg 611

Hans Christians Druckerei und Verlag GmbH & Co (Germany) *Tel:* (040) 35 60 06-0 *Fax:* (040) 35 60 06-26 *E-mail:* vertag@christians.de *Web Site:* www.christians.de, pg 210

Christliche Verlagsgesellschaft mbH (Germany) *Tel:* (02771) 8302-0 *Fax:* (02771) 8302-30 *E-mail:* 101741.2264@compuserve.com *Web Site:* www.cv-dillenburg.de, pg 210

Christliches Verlagshaus GmbH (Germany) *Tel:* (0711) 830000 *Fax:* (0711) 830003, pg 210

Uitgeverij Christofoor (Netherlands) *Tel:* (030) 6923974 *Fax:* (030) 6914834, pg 475

Christoph Merian Verlag (Switzerland) *Tel:* (061) 221288; (061) 271288 *Fax:* (061) 2711273 *E-mail:* cmsbasel@swissonline.ch, pg 611

Christophorus-Verlag GmbH (Germany) *Tel:* (0761) 27170 *Fax:* (0761) 2717352, pg 210

Christusbruderschaft Selbitz ev, Abt Verlag (Germany) *Tel:* (09280) 68-34 *Fax:* (09280) 68-68 *E-mail:* info@verlag-christusbruderschaft.de *Web Site:* www.verlag-christusbruderschaft.de, pg 210

Chroma Graphics (Overseas) Pte Ltd (Singapore) *Tel:* 67423706 *Fax:* 67486712, pg 1159

Chronicles Publishers Ltd (Israel) *Tel:* (03) 5615052 *Fax:* (03) 5624104 *E-mail:* chronicl@inter.net.il, pg 1136

Chronique Sociale (France) *Tel:* (04) 78372212 *Fax:* (04) 78420318, pg 155

Chronos Verlag (Switzerland) *Tel:* (01) 2654343 *Fax:* (01) 2654344 *E-mail:* loinfo@chronos-verlag.ch *Web Site:* www.chronos-verlag.ch, pg 611

The Chrysalis Press (United Kingdom) *Tel:* (01926) 855223 *Fax:* (01926) 748202 *E-mail:* chrysalis@which.net, pg 667

Chrysi Penna - Golden Pen Books (Greece) *Tel:* (01) 03805672 *Fax:* (01) 03825205 *E-mail:* xpenna@acci.gr; info@chrissipenna.com *Web Site:* www.chrissipenna.com, pg 309

Chrysopolitissa Publishers (Cyprus) *Tel:* (02) 2353929 *Fax:* (02) 2353929, pg 122

Chryssos Typos AE Ekodeis (Greece) *Tel:* (01) 3637945 *Fax:* (01) 3824417, pg 309

Chu Liu Book Company (Taiwan, Province of China) *Tel:* (02) 3711031 *Fax:* (02) 3815823 *E-mail:* chuliu@ms13.hinet.net, pg 629

Chugh Publications (India) *Tel:* (0532) 623561, pg 335

Chung Hwa Book Co (HK) Ltd (Hong Kong) *Tel:* (02) 7150176 *Fax:* (02) 7138202; (02) 7134675 *E-mail:* info@chunghwabook.com.hk *Web Site:* www.chunghwabook.hk, pg 319

Chung Hwa Book Co Ltd (Taiwan, Province of China) *Tel:* (02) 3117365 *Fax:* (02) 7355887, pg 629

Chung Rim Publishing Co Ltd (Republic of Korea) *Tel:* (02) 544-3616 *Fax:* (02) 5468053, pg 435

Chuo-Koron-Sha Inc (Japan) *Tel:* (03) 35631431 *Fax:* (03) 35615922, pg 415

Chuo-Tosho Co Ltd (Japan) *Tel:* (075) 4412174 *Fax:* (075) 4413300, pg 415

Church Archivists Press (Australia) *Tel:* (07) 38650466 *Fax:* (07) 38650458, pg 18

Church House Publishing (United Kingdom) *Tel:* (020) 7898 1306 *Fax:* (020) 7898 1305 *E-mail:* publishing@c-of-e.org.uk *Web Site:* www.chpublishing.co.uk, pg 668

Church Mouse Press (New Zealand) *Tel:* (06) 357-2445, pg 490

Church Society (United Kingdom) *Tel:* (01923) 235111 *Fax:* (01923) 800362 *E-mail:* enquiries@churchsociety.org *Web Site:* www.churchsociety.org, pg 668

Church Union (United Kingdom) *Tel:* (020) 7222 6952 *Fax:* (020) 7976 7180 *E-mail:* churchunion@care4free.net *Web Site:* www.churchunion.care4free.net, pg 668

Churchill Livingstone (United Kingdom) *Tel:* (020) 7424 4200 *Fax:* (020) 7485 4752, pg 668

Jiri Chvojka (Czech Republic) *Tel:* (02) 225 169 65 *Fax:* (02) 225 169 65, pg 123

CIACO (Belgium) *Tel:* (018) 213700 *Fax:* (018) 212372, pg 66

CIAT - Centro Internacional de Agricultura Tropical (Colombia) *Tel:* (02) 675050; (02) 4450000 *Fax:* (02) 4550073 *E-mail:* ciat@cgnet.com; ciat@cgiar.org *Web Site:* www.ciat.cgiar.org, pg 111

CIC Edizioni Internazionali (Italy) *Tel:* (06) 8412673 *Fax:* (06) 8412688 *E-mail:* info@gruppocic.it *Web Site:* www.gruppocic.it, pg 381

Cicada Press (New Zealand) *Tel:* (09) 4180890 *Fax:* (09) 4181142, pg 490

CICC Book House (India) *Tel:* (0484) 353557; (0484) 355658, pg 335

Cicero-Chr Erichsens (Denmark) *Tel:* 33160308 *Fax:* 33160307 *E-mail:* info@cicero.dk *Web Site:* www.cicero.dk, pg 131

Cicero Editeurs (France) *Tel:* (01) 43544757 *Fax:* (01) 40517385, pg 155

Cicero Presse Verlag & Antiquariat (Germany) *Tel:* (04651) 89 03 05 *Fax:* (04651) 89 08 85 *E-mail:* ciceropresse@t-online.de, pg 210

Cicerone Press (United Kingdom) *Tel:* (01539) 562 069 *Fax:* (01539) 563 417 *E-mail:* info@cicerone.co.uk *Web Site:* www.cicerone.co.uk, pg 668

Cidade Nova Editora (Portugal) *Tel:* (01) 2478734 *Fax:* (01) 2476369, pg 523

CIDAP (Ecuador) *Tel:* (07) 829451; (07) 828878 *Fax:* (07) 831450 *E-mail:* cidap1@cidap.org.ec *Web Site:* www.uazuay.edu.ec/cidap/home.htm, pg 137

Cideb Editrice SRL (Italy) *Tel:* (0185) 55803 *Fax:* (0185) 67150 *E-mail:* info@blackcat-cideb.com, pg 381

CIE (International Commission on Illumination Central Bureau) (Austria) *Tel:* (01) 71431870 *Fax:* (01) 713083818 *E-mail:* ciecb@ping.at *Web Site:* www.cie.co.at/cie, pg 1236

Ciela Publishing House (Bulgaria) *Tel:* (02) 9516376; (02) 9549397; (02) 9516697 *Fax:* (02) 9549397 *E-mail:* ciela@bulnet.bg *Web Site:* www.ciela.net, pg 94

Publicacoes Ciencia e Vida Lda (Portugal) *Tel:* (021) 342-7989 *Fax:* (021) 3460224, pg 523

Instituto de Ciencias de la Computacion (NCR) (Paraguay) *Tel:* (021) 490076 *Fax:* (021) 497849, pg 510

Editorial de Ciencias Sociales (Cuba) *Tel:* (07) 23 3959; (07) 23 6090; (07) 23 4801 *Fax:* (07) 2304801, pg 121

Libreria Cientifica SA (Ecuador) *Tel:* (02) 12556, pg 1281

Cientifica Interamericana SACI, Editorial (Argentina) *Tel:* (011) 4822-8883 *Fax:* (011) 4827-0486 *E-mail:* edit@interame.satlink.net, pg 4

Editora Cientifica Medica Latinoamerican SA de CV (Mexico) *Tel:* (05) 5206135; (05) 5405600 *Fax:* (05) 5367579; (05) 5403764, pg 458

Editorial Cientifico Tecnica (Cuba) *Tel:* (07) 236090; (07) 234801 *Fax:* (07) 333441, pg 121

Ediciones Cieplan (Chile) *Tel:* (02) 2323212; (02) 2324558 *Fax:* (02) 3340312 *E-mail:* cieplan@ctcreuna.cl *Web Site:* www.cieplan.cl, pg 100

Marianne Cieslik (Germany) *Tel:* (02461) 51222; (02461) 57661 *Fax:* (02461) 52772, pg 210

CIESPAL (Centro Internacional de Estudios Superiores de Comunicacion para America Latina) (Ecuador) *Tel:* (02) 2548011 *Fax:* (02) 2502487 *E-mail:* info@ciespal.net *Web Site:* www.ciespal.net, pg 137

Il Cigno Galileo Galilei-Edizioni di Arte e Scienza (Italy) *Tel:* (06) 6865493; (06) 68808432; (06) 6873842 *Fax:* (06) 6892109 *E-mail:* lzichic@tin.it, pg 381

Ciirculo de Lectores SA (Colombia) *Tel:* 2173211; 2177720 *Fax:* 2178157, pg 1227

Libreria Cima (Ecuador) *Tel:* (02) 571218; (02) 571318, pg 1282

Cimaise sarl (France) *Tel:* (01) 45437045 *Fax:* (01) 45437045, pg 155

Cinema (Czech Republic) *Tel:* (02) 627 83 95-6 *Fax:* (02) 627 72 39 *E-mail:* schur@comp.cz, pg 123

CIPG Editorial & Translation Research Center (China) *Tel:* (010) 68326681 *E-mail:* ftrchina@public3.bta.net.cn, pg 1125

Cirad (France) *Tel:* (0467) 61 55 23 *Fax:* (0467) 61 55 13 *Web Site:* www.cirad.fr, pg 155

Ciranna e Ferrara (Italy) *Tel:* (0362) 230849 *Fax:* (0362) 326213, pg 381

Ciranna - Roma (Italy) *Tel:* (091) 224499 *Fax:* (091) 311064, pg 381

Circe (France) *Tel:* (01) 48249676, pg 155

Circe Ediciones, SA (Spain) *Tel:* (093) 2040990; (093) 2040659 *Fax:* (093) 2041183 *E-mail:* circe@oceano.com, pg 567

Circle of State Librarians (United Kingdom) *Tel:* (020) 7273 4463, pg 1525

Circle of Wine Writers (United Kingdom) *Tel:* (020) 7486 6563 *Fax:* (020) 7486 5375, pg 1265

Circonflexe (France) *Tel:* (01) 46347777 *Fax:* (01) 43253467 *E-mail:* info@circonflexe.fr *Web Site:* www.circonflexe.fr/nous/centre.php, pg 155

Circulo de Lectores SA (Colombia) *Tel:* (01) 2173211; (01) 2177720 *Fax:* (01) 2178157, pg 1279

Circulo de Lectores SA (Spain) *Tel:* (093) 3660100 *Fax:* (093) 2002220 *Web Site:* www.circulolectores.com, pg 1231

Circulo de Leitores (Portugal) *Tel:* (021) 709221 *Fax:* (021) 707149, pg 1231

Circulo do Livro SA (Brazil) *Tel:* (011) 8513644 *Fax:* (011) 2827273, pg 1227

CIS Publishers (Australia) *Tel:* (03) 92467131 *Fax:* (03) 3470175, pg 18

CISAC (Confederation Internationale des Societes d'Auteurs et de Compesiteurs) (France), pg 1243

Cisalpino - Monduzzi (Italy) *Tel:* (051) 4151111 *Fax:* (051) 370529, pg 382

CISAM (Italy) *Tel:* (0743) 23271 *Fax:* (0743) 232701 *E-mail:* cisam@etcisam.org *Web Site:* www.cisam.org, pg 382

Cisneros (Spain) *Tel:* (091) 5619900 *Fax:* (091) 5613990, pg 567

Editorial CISSPRAXIS SA (Spain) *Tel:* (06) 352 34 61 *Fax:* (06) 352 25 38 *E-mail:* dpto.directories@ciss.es *Web Site:* www.ciss.es, pg 567

Editions Citadelles & Mazenod (France) *Tel:* (01) 53043060 *Fax:* (01) 45220427 *E-mail:* info@citadelles-mazenod.com *Web Site:* www.citadelles-mazenod.com, pg 155

CITIC Publishing House (China) *Tel:* (010) 64661098 *Fax:* (010) 64661098 *E-mail:* citicph@mx.cei.gov.cn *Web Site:* www.citic.com.cn, pg 104

Citta Nuova Editrice (Italy) *Tel:* (06) 3216212 *Fax:* (06) 3207185, pg 382

Cittadella Editrice (Italy) *Tel:* (075) 813595 *Fax:* (075) 813719 *E-mail:* amministrazione@cittadellaeditrice.com *Web Site:* cittadellaeditrice.com, pg 382

City Bookshop Ltd (Kenya) *Tel:* (011) 313149; (011) 225548 *Fax:* (011) 314815, pg 1296

City Library (Mauritius) *Tel:* 212083 ext 161-163 *Fax:* 2124258, pg 1484

Editorial Ciudad Nueva (Spain) *Tel:* (091) 725 95 30; (091) 356 96 12 *Fax:* (091) 713 04 52 *E-mail:* editorial@ciudadnueva.com *Web Site:* www.ciudadnueva.com, pg 567

Livraria Civilizacao (Americo Fraga Lamares & Ca Lda) (Portugal) *Tel:* (02) 20002286 *Fax:* (02) 312382, pg 523

Civitas SA Editorial (Spain) *Tel:* (091) 902 011 787 *Fax:* (091) 725 26 73 *E-mail:* clientes@civitas.es *Web Site:* www.civitas.es, pg 567

Claassen Verlag GmbH (Germany) *Tel:* (089) 5148-0; (089) 5148 20 *Fax:* (089) 5148-2229; (089) 5148 2233 *E-mail:* info@ullstein-heyne-list.de *Web Site:* www.claassen-verlag.de, pg 210

CLAIM Bookshop (Malawi) *Tel:* 620839, pg 1298

Clairefontaine, Editions (Switzerland) *Tel:* (021) 230879, pg 611

The John Clare Society (United Kingdom) *Tel:* (01733) 252678 *Fax:* (01733) 252678 *Web Site:* www.thezone.virgin.net/linda.curry/jclaresoceity.htm, pg 1370

Editorial Claret SA (Spain) *Tel:* (093) 3010887 *Fax:* (093) 3174830 *E-mail:* editorial@clarnet.es; libreria@claret.es *Web Site:* www.claret.es, pg 568

Claretian Communications Inc (Philippines) *Tel:* (02) 9213984 *Fax:* (02) 9217429 *E-mail:* cci@claret.org *Web Site:* www.bible.claret.org, pg 513

Editorial Claretiana (Argentina) *Tel:* (011) 4305-9510; (011) 4305-9597 *Fax:* (011) 4305-6552 *E-mail:* editorial@editorialclaretiana.com.ar *Web Site:* www.editorialclaretiana.com.ar, pg 4

Editorial Claridad SA (Argentina) *Tel:* (011) 4371-5546 *Fax:* (011) 4375-1659 *E-mail:* editorial@heliasta.com.ar *Web Site:* www.editorialclaridad.com.ar, pg 4

Clarion Books (India) *Tel:* (011) 2282332 *Fax:* (011) 2282332, pg 335

Clarke Associates Ltd (United Kingdom) *Tel:* (0117) 968864 *Fax:* (0117) 9226437, pg 1318

James Clarke & Co Ltd (United Kingdom) *Tel:* (01223) 350865 *Fax:* (01223) 366951 *E-mail:* sales@jamesclarke.co.uk *Web Site:* www.jamesclarke.co.uk, pg 668

Clasicos Roxsil Editorial SA de CV (El Salvador) *Tel:* 228-1832; 288-2646; 229-6742 *Fax:* 228-1212, pg 139

Clasicos Roxsil Editorial SA de CV (El Salvador) *Tel:* 228 1832; 229 3621 *Fax:* 228 1212, pg 1282

Class Publishing (United Kingdom) *Tel:* (020) 7371 2119 *Fax:* (020) 7371 2878 *E-mail:* post@class.co.uk *Web Site:* www.class.co.uk, pg 668

Werner Classen Verlag (Switzerland) *Tel:* (01) 2015606, pg 611

E W Classey Ltd (United Kingdom) *Tel:* (01367) 244700 *Fax:* (01367) 244800 *E-mail:* bugbooks@classey.demon.co.uk *Web Site:* www.abebooks.com/home/bugbooks, pg 668

Classic (Pakistan) *Tel:* (042) 323963; (042) 312977 *Fax:* (042) 7238236, pg 506

Editora Classica (Portugal) *Tel:* (021) 372386 *Fax:* (021) 3474729, pg 523

Classical Publishing Co (India) *Tel:* (011) 563689, pg 335

Classikaletet (Israel) *Tel:* (03) 5582080 *Fax:* (03) 5582299 *E-mail:* kimbooks@netvision.net.it, pg 366

Claudiana Editrice (Italy) *Tel:* (011) 6689804 *Fax:* (011) 6504394 *E-mail:* claudiana.editirce@alpcom.it, pg 382

Claudius Verlag (Germany) *Tel:* (089) 121 72-0 *Fax:* (089) 121 72-138 *E-mail:* claudius@csi.com *Web Site:* www.claudius.de, pg 211

De Clauwaert VZW (Belgium) *Tel:* (016) 310-660 *Fax:* (016) 310-608 *E-mail:* uitgeverij@davidsfonds.be, pg 66

Uitgeverij Clavis (Belgium) *Tel:* (011) 28 68 68 *Fax:* (011) 28 68 69 *E-mail:* info@clavis.be *Web Site:* www.clavis.be, pg 66

Clays Ltd (United Kingdom) *Tel:* (01986) 893211 *E-mail:* clays@claysltd.co.uk, pg 1140, 1203, 1214

Clays Ltd (United Kingdom) *Tel:* (01986) 893211 *Fax:* (01986) 895293 *E-mail:* clays@claysltd.co.uk, pg 1223

CLD (France) *Tel:* (02) 47282068 *Fax:* (02) 47288548, pg 155

Editions CLE (Cameroon) *Tel:* (023) 7-22-35-54 *Fax:* (023) 7-23-27-09 *E-mail:* edition@iccnet.cm, pg 99

Cle International (France) *Tel:* (01) 45874400 *Fax:* (01) 45874410, pg 155

CLE: The Irish Book Publishers' Association (Ireland) *Tel:* (01) 670-7393 *Fax:* (01) 670-7642 *E-mail:* info@publishingireland.com *Web Site:* www.publishingireland.com, pg 1249

R J Cleary Publishing (Australia) *Tel:* (02) 2643750, pg 18

Clematis Press Ltd (United Kingdom) *Tel:* (020) 7352 8755, pg 668

Clerestory Press (New Zealand) *Tel:* (03) 3553588 *Fax:* (03) 3553588, pg 490

CLEUP - Cooperative Libraria Editrice dell 'Universita di Padova (Italy) *Tel:* (049) 8753496 *Fax:* (049) 650261, pg 382

The Cleveland Vibrator Co (United States) *Tel:* 216-241-7157 *Fax:* 216-241-3480 *E-mail:* cvc@clevelandvibrators.com *Web Site:* www.clevelandvibrator.com, pg 1224

Clever Books (South Africa) *Tel:* (012) 3424715 *Fax:* (012) 432376 *E-mail:* inlo631@mweb.co.2a, pg 553

Editorial Clie (Spain) *Tel:* (093) 7884262; (093) 7885722 *Fax:* (093) 7800514 *E-mail:* libros@clie.es *Web Site:* www.clie.es, pg 568

Climats (France) *Tel:* (04) 99583091; (04) 67453790 *Fax:* (04) 99583092 *E-mail:* climats.editions@wanadoo.fr *Web Site:* www.editions-climats.com/, pg 155

Climent, Eliseau Editor (Spain) *Tel:* (06) 3516492 *Fax:* (06) 3529872, pg 568

Clipper Distribution Services (United Kingdom) *Tel:* (01705) 200080 *Fax:* (01705) 200090, pg 1318

De Clivo Press (Switzerland) *Tel:* (01) 8201124, pg 611

Clo Iar-Chonnachta Teo (Ireland) *Tel:* (091) 593307 *Fax:* (091) 593362 *E-mail:* cic@iol.ie *Web Site:* www.cic.ie, pg 359

Clodhanna Teoranta (Ireland), pg 359

Cloister Bookstore Ltd (Barbados) *Tel:* (246) 426-2662 *Fax:* (246) 429-7269 *E-mail:* cloisterbookstore@caribsurf.com, pg 1275

Jonathan Clowes Ltd (United Kingdom) *Tel:* (020) 7722 7674 *Fax:* (020) 7722 7677, pg 1118

William Clowes Ltd (United Kingdom) *Tel:* (01502) 712884 *Fax:* (01502) 717003, pg 1140, 1161, 1203, 1214, 1223

Club de Lectores (Argentina) *Tel:* (011) 4342-6251; (011) 4342-3955, pg 4

Club de Lectores Extemporaneos (Mexico) *Tel:* (05) 5875424; (05) 5878785, pg 1230

Club du Livre SA (France) *Tel:* (01) 47638055 *Fax:* (01) 44404865, pg 1228

CLUEB (Cooperativa Libraria Universitaria Editrice Bologna) (Italy) *Tel:* (051) 220736 *Fax:* (051) 237758 *E-mail:* clueb@clueb.com *Web Site:* www.clueb.com, pg 382

Clunies Ross Press (Australia) *Tel:* (03) 9347-6077 *Fax:* (03) 9347-0605 *E-mail:* icr@crnet.com.au, pg 18

Editura Clusium, Casa de Editura Atlas-Clusium SRL (Romania) *Tel:* (095) 116940 *E-mail:* 1060 o.p.1@clug-Napoca, pg 532

CLUT Editrice (Italy) *Tel:* (011) 542192 *Fax:* (011) 542192, pg 382

CMA Edition (Germany) *Tel:* (0941) 23939; (0941) 34003; (08458) 8960 *Fax:* (0941) 8960; (0941) 34003, pg 211

CMC Co Ltd (Japan) *Tel:* (03) 32932065 *Fax:* (03) 32932069, pg 415

CNRS Editions (France) *Tel:* (01) 53102700 *Fax:* (01) 53102727 *Web Site:* www.cnrseditions.fr, pg 155

Co-Fine Production (Hong Kong) *Tel:* 25180383 *E-mail:* cofine@netvigator.com, pg 1221

Co Libri (Slovenia) *Tel:* (061) 1255111 *Fax:* (061) 224454, pg 1309

Coach House Printing (Canada) *Tel:* 416-979-2217 *Fax:* 416-977-1158 *E-mail:* mail@chbooks.com *Web Site:* www.chbooks.com, pg 1153, 1193

Coachwise Ltd (United Kingdom) *Tel:* (0113) 2311310 *Fax:* (0113) 2319606 *Web Site:* www.1st4sport.com, pg 668

La Coccinella Editrice SRL (Italy) *Tel:* (0332) 224690 *Fax:* (0332) 222025, pg 382

Elspeth Cochrane Agency (United Kingdom) *Tel:* (020) 7622 0314 *Fax:* (020) 7622 5815, pg 1118

Cockatoo Press (Schweiz), Thailand-Publikationen (Switzerland) *Tel:* (01) 9841725 *Fax:* (01) 9843420 *E-mail:* cockatoo@thailine.com *Web Site:* www.thailine.com, pg 611

Cockbird Press (United Kingdom) *Tel:* (01435) 830430 *Fax:* (01435) 830027, pg 669

Coconut Productions (Australia) *Tel:* (07) 3854 1350 *Fax:* (07) 3854 1533 *E-mail:* camquinn@cheerful.com, pg 18

Coda (Belgium) *Tel:* (011) 540403 *Fax:* (011) 540403, pg 66

CODE - Europe (United Kingdom) *Tel:* (01865) 202438 *Fax:* (01865) 2024390 *E-mail:* code_europe@compuserve.com, pg 1265

Codes Rousseau (France) *Tel:* (02) 51231100 *Fax:* (02) 51213102 *E-mail:* info@codes-rousseau.fr *Web Site:* www.codesrousseau.fr, pg 155

CODESRIA (Council for the Development of Social Science Research in Africa) (Senegal) *Tel:* 8259814; 8259822 *Fax:* 8241289; 8640143 *E-mail:* codesria@sonatel.senet.net *Web Site:* www.cordesria.org, pg 544

Codice Comercio Distriduicao e Casa Editorial Ltda (Brazil) *Tel:* (011) 2408033 *E-mail:* codice@codicenet.com.br, pg 81

Codra Enterprises Inc (United States) *Tel:* 714-891-5652 *Fax:* 714-891-5642 *E-mail:* codra@codra.com, pg 1143

Rene Coeckelberghs Bokfoerlag AB (Sweden) *Tel:* (08) 7230880 *Fax:* (08) 7230311, pg 601

Rene Coeckelberghs Editions (Switzerland) *Tel:* 515060 *Fax:* 516645, pg 611

Coffee Industry Board (Papua New Guinea) *Tel:* (675) 7321207 *Fax:* (675) 7321351, pg 510

Eric Cohen Books Ltd (Israel) *Tel:* (09) 7478000 *Fax:* (09) 7441497, pg 1292

Mo Cohen (Germany) *Tel:* (040) 273814, pg 1111

Coimbra Editora Lda (Portugal) *Tel:* (039) 25459 *Fax:* (039) 35371, pg 523

Cole Publications (Australia) *Tel:* (03) 815640, pg 18

Colegial Bolivariana CA (Venezuela) *Tel:* (02) 2391055; (02) 2391244 *Fax:* (02) 2396502, pg 762

Colegio de Bibliotecarios de Chile AG (Chile) *Tel:* (02) 222 56 52 *Fax:* (02) 635 50 23 *E-mail:* cdb@transtar.cl *Web Site:* www.bibliotecarios.cl, pg 1513

Ediciones Colegio De Espana (ECE) (Spain) *Tel:* (023) 21 47 88 *Fax:* (023) 21 87 91 *E-mail:* info@colesp.eurart.es *Web Site:* www.eurart.es/emp/colesp/, pg 568

El Colegio de Mexico AC (Mexico) *Tel:* (05) 5686033 ext 388; (05) 5686033 ext 297 *Fax:* (05) 6526233 *E-mail:* biblio@colmex.mx, pg 459

Colegio de Postgraduados en Ciencias Agricolas (Mexico) *Tel:* (0595) 5854555 (ext 5509) *Fax:* (0595) 10275 *E-mail:* difusion@colpos.colpos.mx, pg 459

Libreria del Colegio SA (Argentina) *Tel:* (011) 4362-1616; (011) 4362-1222 *Fax:* (011) 3627364, pg 4

Charles Coleman Verlag GmbH & Co KG (Germany) *Tel:* (0451) 7 99 33-0 *Fax:* (0451) 7 99 33-99 *E-mail:* coleman@rudolf.mueller.de *Web Site:* www.coleman-verlag.de; www.rudolf-mueller.de, pg 211

Nuova Coletti Editore Roma (Italy) *Tel:* (06) 8557981 *Fax:* (06) 8557981, pg 382

Edicoes Colibri (Portugal) *Tel:* (021) 796-4038 *Fax:* (021) 796-4038 *E-mail:* colibri@edi-colibri.pt *Web Site:* www.edi-colibri.pt, pg 523

Armand Colin, Editeur (France) *Tel:* (01) 44395447 *Fax:* (01) 44394343 *E-mail:* infos@armand-colin.com *Web Site:* www.armand-colin.com/pr/infosf.html, pg 155

Rosica Colin Ltd (United Kingdom) *Tel:* (020) 7370 1080 *Fax:* (020) 7244 6441, pg 669, 1118

COLIVRO - Comercio e Distribuicao de Livros Ltda (Brazil) *Tel:* (021) 2243177 *Fax:* (021) 2424517, pg 1277

Collectieve Propaganda van het Nederlandse Boek (CPNB) (Netherlands) *Tel:* (020) 6264971 *Fax:* (020) 6231696, pg 1137, 1254

College International des Traducteurs Litteraires (CITL) (France) *Tel:* (04) 90497252 *Fax:* (04) 90934321, pg 1243

The College of the Bahamas Library (Bahamas) *Tel:* (242) 323-7930 *Fax:* (242) 326-7834 *E-mail:* library@cob.edu.bs *Web Site:* www.cob.edu.bs, pg 1452

College of Careers (Pty) Ltd (South Africa) *Tel:* (021) 4624360 *Fax:* (021) 4619378, pg 553

College of Medicine Library, Arabian Gulf University (Bahrain) *Tel:* 440044 *Fax:* 440002 *E-mail:* suad@mail.agu.edu.bh, pg 1452

College Press Publishers (Pvt) Ltd (Zimbabwe) *Tel:* (04) 754145; (04) 773231; (04) 773236; (04) 757153; (04) 754255 *Fax:* (04) 754256 *E-mail:* nellym@collegepress.co.zw, pg 768

Peter Collin Publishing Ltd (United Kingdom) *Tel:* (020) 7222 1155 *Fax:* (020) 7222 1551 *E-mail:* info@petercollin.com *Web Site:* www.petercollin.com, pg 669

Collins Booksellers Pty Ltd (Australia) *Tel:* (03) 96629472 *Fax:* (03) 96622527 *E-mail:* enquiries@collinsbooks.com.au *Web Site:* www.collinsbooks.com.au, pg 1272

The Collins Press (Ireland) *Tel:* (021) 4347717 *Fax:* (021) 4347720 *E-mail:* enquiries@collinspress.le *Web Site:* www.collinspress.com, pg 359

Colmegna SA (Argentina) *Tel:* (042) 523102; (042) 557345 *Fax:* (042) 4557345, pg 4

Colombo Public Library (Sri Lanka) *Tel:* (01) 691968; (01) 696530; (01) 695156 *Fax:* (01) 691968, pg 1499

Colombo Book Association (Sri Lanka) *Tel:* (01) 686878; (01) 072270652 *Fax:* (01) 696578, pg 596

Librairie des Colonnes (Morocco) *Tel:* (099) 936955 *Fax:* (099) 936955, pg 1300

Colonnese Editore (Italy) *Tel:* (081) 459858; (081) 293900 *Fax:* (081) 455420 *E-mail:* info@colonnese.it *Web Site:* spacee.tin.it/lettura/gacolon, pg 382

Colorcraft Ltd (Hong Kong) *Tel:* 25909033 *Fax:* 25909005; 25909271 *E-mail:* info.cc@colorcraft.com.hk *Web Site:* www.colorcraft.com.hk, pg 1221

Colorprint Offset (Hong Kong) *Tel:* 28967777 *Fax:* 28896606, pg 1133, 1155, 1195

Colorprint Offset Inc (United States) *Tel:* 212-681-9400 *Fax:* 212-681-9362, pg 1143, 1164, 1206

Colour Library Direct (United Kingdom) *Tel:* (01483) 426777 *Fax:* (01483) 426947 *E-mail:* prod@quad-pub.co.uk, pg 669

Colourpoint Books (United Kingdom) *Tel:* (028) 9182 0505 *Fax:* (028) 9182 1900 *E-mail:* info@colourpoint.co.uk; sales@colourpoint.co.uk *Web Site:* www.colourpoint.co.uk, pg 669

Colrick & Associates Ltd (United Kingdom) *Tel:* (07000) 265742 *Fax:* (07000) 265741, pg 1128

Colt Associates (United Kingdom) *Tel:* (0158) 2834292 *Fax:* (0158) 825778, pg 1318

The Columba Book Service (Ireland) *Tel:* (01) 2942556 *Fax:* (01) 2942564 *E-mail:* info@columba.ie *Web Site:* www.columba.ie, pg 359, 1291

The Columba Press (Ireland) *Tel:* (01) 2942556 *Fax:* (01) 2942564 *E-mail:* info@columba.ie *Web Site:* www.columba.ie, pg 359

Columbia Overseas Marketing Pte Ltd (Singapore) *Tel:* 7478607 *Fax:* 7442338, pg 1200

Columbus (Czech Republic) *Tel:* (02) 683 10 17 *Fax:* (02) 683 10 17 *E-mail:* columbus@alpha-net.cz, pg 123

Columbus Cultural Editora Comercial Importacao e Exporta (Brazil) *Tel:* (011) 8648777 *Fax:* (011) 8646531, pg 1277

Columbus Verlag Paul Oestergaard GmbH (Germany) *Tel:* (07576) 96 03-0 *Fax:* (07576) 96 03-29 *E-mail:* info@columbus-verlag.de *Web Site:* www.columbus-verlag.de, pg 211

Columna Edicions, Libres i Comunicacio, SA (Spain) *Tel:* (093) 4264252; (093) 4261995; (093) 2076726 *Fax:* (093) 4238761, pg 568

Combel Editorial SA (Spain) *Tel:* (093) 2449550 *Fax:* (093) 2656895 *E-mail:* combel@editorialcasals.com, pg 568

Combined Academic Publishers (United Kingdom) *Tel:* (01494) 581601 *Fax:* (01494) 581602 *E-mail:* nickesson@combinedacademic.demon.co.uk *Web Site:* www.combinedacademic.co.uk, pg 669

Combined Book Services (United Kingdom) *Tel:* (01892) 837171 *Fax:* (01892) 837272 *E-mail:* orders@combook.co.uk, pg 1318

Editora Comercial de Publicaciones (Spain) *Tel:* (06) 3957293; (06) 3952045 *Fax:* (06) 3952297, pg 568

COMHAIRLE NAN LEABHRAICHEAN - THE GAELIC BOOKS COUNCIL INDUSTRY

Comhairle nan Leabhraichean - The Gaelic Books Council (United Kingdom) *Tel:* (0141) 337 6211 *Fax:* (0141) 341 0515 *E-mail:* fios@gaelicbooks.net *Web Site:* www.gaelicbooks.net, pg 1265

Los Libros del Comienzo (Spain) *Tel:* (091) 5930251 *Fax:* (091) 5931603 *E-mail:* comienzo@teleline.es *Web Site:* www.libroscomienzo.com, pg 568

Comision Nacional Forestal (Mexico) *Tel:* (05) 5349707; (05) 5247862, pg 459

Comissao Nacional de Energia Nuclear (Brazil) *Tel:* (021) 2546 2481 *Fax:* (021) 2546 2447 *E-mail:* macedo@cnen.gov.br *Web Site:* www.cnen.gov.br, pg 81

Comissao para Igualdade e Direitos das Mulheres (Portugal) *Tel:* (021) 7983000 *Fax:* (021) 7983099 *E-mail:* cidm@mail.telepac.pt, pg 524

Editions du Comite des Travaux Historiques et Scientifiques (CTHS) (France) *Tel:* (01) 46 34 47 76 *Fax:* (01) 46 34 47 60, pg 156

Comite Gremial de Editores de Guatemala (Guatemala) *Tel:* (02) 2329053; (02) 2518381 *Fax:* (02) 2329053; (02) 2518381, pg 1247

Comite National d'Evaluation (CNE) (France) *Tel:* (01) 55 55 63 63 *Fax:* (01) 55 55 63 94 *E-mail:* j-c.martin@cne-evaluation.fr *Web Site:* www.cne-evaluation.fr, pg 156

ComMedia & Arte Verlag Bernd Mayer (Germany) *Tel:* (07945) 950719 *Fax:* (07945) 950718, pg 211

Commercial Colorlab Ltd (Hong Kong) *Tel:* 25731833 *Fax:* 28934688, pg 1195

Commercial Press (Hong Kong) Ltd (China) *Tel:* (010) 65241547 *Fax:* (010) 65135899 *E-mail:* comprs@public.gb.com.cn *Web Site:* www.cp.com.cn, pg 104

Commission Belge de Bibliographie et de Bibliologie (Belgium) *Tel:* (080) 510464 *Fax:* (080) 80510465, pg 1360

Commission des Bibliotheques de l'AIDBA (Senegal) *Tel:* 240954, pg 1258

Commission for Racial Equality (United Kingdom) *Tel:* (020) 7828 7022 *Fax:* (020) 7630 7605 *E-mail:* info@cre.gov.uk *Web Site:* www.cre.gov.uk, pg 669

Commonwealth Council for Educational Administration & Management (New Zealand) *Tel:* (09) 307 9999 ext 6879 *Fax:* (09) 307 9984, pg 490

Commonwealth Education Foundation (United Kingdom) *Tel:* (020) 8931 2359; (020) 8959 2137 *Fax:* (0181) 9592137 *E-mail:* roshanbp@aol.com, pg 1233

Commonwealth Education Foundation (United Kingdom) *Tel:* (0208) 9312359 *Fax:* (0208) 9592137 *E-mail:* rushanbp@aol.com, pg 1318

The Commonwealth Library Association (COMLA) (Jamaica) *Tel:* (876) 927-2123 *Fax:* (876) 927-1926, pg 1250

Commonwealth Publishing Company Ltd (Taiwan, Province of China) *Tel:* (02) 2517-3688 *Fax:* (02) 2517-3686 *Web Site:* www.bookzone.com.tw, pg 629

Commonwealth Secretariat (United Kingdom) *Tel:* (020) 7747 6385 *Fax:* (020) 7839 9081 *E-mail:* info@commonwealth.int *Web Site:* www.thecommonwealth.org, pg 669

Bibliotheque de la Communaute Urbaine de Casablanca (Morocco) *Tel:* (02) 314170, pg 1485

Communication Art Design & Printing Ltd (Hong Kong) *Tel:* 28656787 *Fax:* 28663429 *E-mail:* cadesign@pacific.net.hk, pg 1134

Communication Foundation for Asia Media Group (CFAMG) (Philippines) *Tel:* (02) 612342; (02) 607659, pg 513

Community Based Rehabilitation Progeamme (Guyana) *Tel:* (02) 64004 *Fax:* (02) 62615, pg 317

Community Quarterly (Australia) *Tel:* (03) 9654 1595 *Fax:* (03) 9654 1595 *E-mail:* comm_quar@vicnet.net.au, pg 18

COMP'ACT (France) *Tel:* (04) 79 85 27 85 *Fax:* (04) 79 85 29 34 *E-mail:* editionscomp.act@wanadoo.fr *Web Site:* www.theatre-contemporain.net/editions/compact/compact.htm, pg 156

Compact Verlag GmbH (Germany) *Tel:* (089) 7451610 *Fax:* (089) 756095; (089) 7593922 *E-mail:* info@compactverlag.de *Web Site:* www.compactverlag.de, pg 211

Compagnie 12 (France) *Tel:* (01) 43709900 *Fax:* (01) 43708088, pg 156

Compania Editorial Continental SA de CV (Mexico) *Tel:* (05) 5732300 ext 101 *Fax:* (05) 5618155, pg 459

Compania Literaria (Spain) *Tel:* (091) 4015312 *Fax:* (091) 4015312, pg 568

Companion Travel Guide Books (Australia) *Tel:* (02) 9608-1169 *Fax:* (02) 9608-1169 *E-mail:* 6LEI937764@aol.com, pg 18

Compass Equestrian Ltd (United Kingdom) *Tel:* (0156) 479 5136 *Fax:* (0156) 479 5136 *E-mail:* compbook@globalnet.co.uk, pg 669

Compass Maps Ltd (United Kingdom) *Tel:* (01275) 474737 *E-mail:* info@papoutmaps.com *Web Site:* www.mapgroup.net, pg 670

Compass-Verlag GmbH (Austria) *Tel:* (01) 981 16-113 *Fax:* (01) 981 16-113 *E-mail:* hfu@compass.co.at *Web Site:* www.plau.al; www.maskt.al; www.compass.at, pg 50

Compendium Publishing (United Kingdom) *Tel:* (020) 72874570 *Fax:* (020) 74940583 *E-mail:* compendium@compuserve.com, pg 670

Editions Complexe SPRL (France) *Tel:* (01) 4634 6040 *Fax:* (01) 4329 9433, pg 156

Complutense, SA Editorial (Spain) *Tel:* (091) 3946460; (091) 3946461 *Fax:* (091) 3946458 *E-mail:* ecsa@eucemos.sim.ucm.es *Web Site:* www.ucm.es/info/ecsa, pg 568

Ediciones de la Universidad Complutense de Madrid (Spain) *Tel:* (091) 394 64 60; (091) 394 64 61 *Fax:* (091) 394 64 58 *E-mail:* ecsa@rect.ucm.es *Web Site:* www.ucm.es/info/ecsa, pg 568

Editions de Compostelle (France) *Tel:* (01) 64299404, pg 156

Comprehensive Book Service (Pakistan) *Tel:* (021) 214682 *Fax:* (021) 2632131 *E-mail:* shahzad@cbs.khi.sdnpk.undp.org, pg 1304

Computer Bookshops Ltd (United Kingdom) *Tel:* (0121) 7783333 *Fax:* (0121) 6060469 *E-mail:* info@compbook.co.uk *Web Site:* www.compbook.co.uk, pg 1318

Computer Step (United Kingdom) *Tel:* (020) 7010 3000 *Fax:* (020) 7416 3193 *E-mail:* sevanti@computerstep.com, pg 670

Libreria Comuneros (Paraguay) *Tel:* (021) 446176; (021) 444667 *Fax:* (021) 444667, pg 1305

Comunica Press SA (Spain) *Tel:* (091) 5012171 *Fax:* (091) 5514209 *E-mail:* comunica@tsai.es *Web Site:* www.comunica.es, pg 568

Comunidad Autonoma de Madrid, Servicio de Documentacion y Publicaciones (Spain) *Tel:* (091) 319 51 54 *Fax:* (091) 319 85 68, pg 568

Edizioni di Comunita SpA (Italy) *Tel:* (011) 56561 *Fax:* (011) 542903 *E-mail:* novarese@amemail.mondadori.it *Web Site:* www.comunita.einaudi.it, pg 382

Concept Publishing Ltd (New Zealand) *Tel:* (09) 4895330 *Fax:* (09) 4895335 *E-mail:* info@concept-publishing.co.nz, pg 490

Concept Publishing Co (India) *Tel:* (011) 5351460; (011) 5351794 *Fax:* (011) 5357103 *E-mail:* publishing@conceptpub.com, pg 335

Concordia (Czech Republic) *Tel:* (02) 3413751 *Fax:* (02) 7929747, pg 124

Concordia-Buchhandlung & Verlag (Germany) *Tel:* (0375) 21 28 50 *Fax:* (0375) 29 80 80; (0375) 21 28 50 *E-mail:* concordia@t-online.de *Web Site:* www.concordiabuch.de, pg 211

Concordia Editora Ltda (Brazil) *Tel:* (051) 342 2699 *Fax:* (051) 343 5254 *E-mail:* pedido@editoraconcordia.com.br; ediluter@zaz.com.br *Web Site:* www.editoraconcordia.com.br, pg 81

Concraid (Belgium) *Tel:* (065) 34-72-34 *Fax:* (065) 34-72-34, pg 67

Coneco Litho Graphics (United States) *Tel:* 518-793-3823 *Fax:* 518-793-5823 *Web Site:* www.conecolithographics.com, pg 1143, 1164, 1206

Coneco Litho Graphics (United States) *Tel:* 518-793-3823 *Fax:* 518-793-5823, pg 1215

Confederacion de Cooperativas del Caribe y Centro America (Costa Rica) *Tel:* 506-240-4641; 506-240-4592 *Fax:* 506-240-4284; 233-3122 *E-mail:* ccocca@sol.racsa.co.cr, pg 115

Confederation of Information Communication Industries (United Kingdom) *Tel:* (020) 7607 0021 *Fax:* (020) 7607 0415 *Web Site:* www.cici.org.uk, pg 1265

Conference Interpreters Group (United Kingdom) *Tel:* (0208) 9950801 *Fax:* (0208) 7421066 *E-mail:* cig@clara.net, pg 1128

Conference of Directors of National Libraries (CDNL) (South Africa) *Tel:* (012) 218931 *Fax:* (012) 3255984 *E-mail:* therese@statelib.gov.za, pg 1258

Conference of European Churches (Switzerland) *Tel:* (022) 791-6111 *Fax:* (022) 791-6227 *Web Site:* www.cec-kek.org, pg 1260

Editorial Confluencia Lda (Portugal) *Tel:* (021) 663853 *Fax:* (021) 326921, pg 524

Congolese Pen Club (Congo) *Tel:* 813601 *Fax:* 813601, pg 1361

Congregacion Paulinas - Hijas de San Pablo (Chile) *Tel:* (02) 221 2832 *Fax:* (02) 294 3426 *E-mail:* paulinasedit@entelchile.net, pg 100

Biblioteca del Congreso de la Nacion (Argentina) *Tel:* (011) 4761641 *Fax:* (011) 954-1067, pg 1450

Biblioteca del Congreso de la Union (Mexico) *Tel:* (05) 5103866 *Fax:* (05) 5121085, pg 1484

Congress of South-East Asian Librarians IV (CONSAL IV) (Philippines) *Tel:* (02) 590646 *Fax:* (02) 572644, pg 1256

CONICYT (Chile) *Tel:* (02) 3654450 *Fax:* (02) 6551395 *E-mail:* info@conicyt.cl *Web Site:* www.conicyt.cl, pg 1513

Coningsby International Bookshop Services (United Kingdom) *Tel:* (01526) 342231 *Fax:* (01526) 344367 *E-mail:* service@coningsby.com *Web Site:* www.coningsby.com, pg 1318

Connaissance et Pratique du Droit Zairos (CDPZ) (The Democratic Republic of the Congo), pg 115

Connection Medien GmbH (Germany) *Tel:* (08639) 98 34-0 *Fax:* (08639) 1219 *E-mail:* seminare@connection-medien.de *Web Site:* www.connection-medien.de; www.seminar-connection.de, pg 211

Conquista, Empresa de Publicacoes Ltda (Brazil) *Tel:* (021) 569-6752, pg 81

The Joseph Conrad Society (UK) (United Kingdom) *E-mail:* k.carabine@ukc.ac.uk; allansimmons@compuserve.com *Web Site:* www.bathspa.ac.uk/conrad/, pg 1370

Conran Octopus (United Kingdom) *Tel:* (020) 7531 8400 *Fax:* (020) 7531 8627 *E-mail:* info@conran-octopus.co.uk *Web Site:* www.conran-octopus.co.uk, pg 670

Conscious Living Publications (Australia) *Tel:* (02) 66858585 *Web Site:* www.leonardjacobson.com, pg 18

YELLOW PAGES

CORPORACION DE PROMOCION UNIVERSITARIA

Conseil international des Associations de Bibliotheques de Theologie (Germany) *Tel:* (0221) 3382110 *Fax:* (0221) 3382103, pg 1245

Biblioteca Central y Publicaciones del Consejo de Educacion Secundaria (Uruguay) *Tel:* (02) 484273; (02) 483051 *Fax:* (02) 481252, pg 1507

Consejo Episcopal Latinoamericano Celam (Colombia) *Tel:* (01) 6714789; (01) 6578330 *Fax:* (01) 2158990; (01) 6121929 *E-mail:* editora@celam.org; celam@celam.org; itepal@celam.org *Web Site:* www.celam.org, pg 111

Consejo Interamericano de Archiveros (CITA) (Mexico), pg 1253

Consejo Superior de Investigaciones Cientificas (Spain) *Tel:* (091) 5629633 *Fax:* (091) 5629634 *E-mail:* publ@orgc.csic.es *Web Site:* www.csic.es/publica, pg 568

Biblioteca General de Humanidades Consejo Superior de Investigaciones Cientificas (Spain) *Tel:* (091) 4292017; (091) 5854883 *Fax:* (091) 4296823; (091) 5854883 *E-mail:* medina@bib.csic.es *Web Site:* www.csic.es/cbic/BGH/bgh.htm, pg 1499

Consello da Cultura Galega - CCG (Spain) *Tel:* (0981) 56 90 20 *Fax:* (0981) 58 86 99 *E-mail:* consello.cultura.galega@xunta.es, pg 568

Conservart SA (Belgium) *Tel:* (02) 3322538 *Fax:* (02) 3754040, pg 67

Conservation Resources International Inc (United States) *Tel:* 703-321-7730 *Fax:* 703-321-0629 *E-mail:* criusa@conservationresources.com *Web Site:* www.conservationresources.com, pg 1215

Conservative Policy Forum (United Kingdom) *Tel:* (020) 7984 8316 *Fax:* (020) 7984 8320 *E-mail:* cpf@conservatives.com *Web Site:* www.conservativepolicyforum.com, pg 670

Uitgeverij Conserve (Netherlands) *Tel:* (072) 5093693 *Fax:* (072) 5094370, pg 475

Consiglio Nazionale delle Ricerche Rep Pubblicazioni e Informazioni Scientifiche (Italy), pg 383

Consolidated Printers Inc (United States) *Tel:* 510-843-8524 *Fax:* 510-486-0580 *E-mail:* cpi@consoprinters.com *Web Site:* www.consoprinters.com, pg 1143, 1206

Constable & Robinson Ltd (United Kingdom) *Tel:* (020) 8741 3663 *Fax:* (020) 8748 7562 *E-mail:* enquiries@constablerobinson.com *Web Site:* www.constablerobinson.com, pg 670

Constable Publishers (United Kingdom) *Tel:* (020) 8741 3663 *Fax:* (020) 8748 7562, pg 670

Constancia Editores, SA (Portugal) *Tel:* (021) 4246903 *Fax:* (021) 4246909 *E-mail:* info@constancia-editores.pt, pg 524

Editorial Constitucion y Leyes SA - COLEX (Spain) *Tel:* (091) 581.34.85 *Fax:* (091) 581.34.90 *E-mail:* colexeditor@interbook.net *Web Site:* www.colex.es, pg 568

Constitutional Publishing Co Pty Ltd (Australia) *Tel:* (09) 4216216 *Fax:* (09) 2211572, pg 18

Consultor Assessoria de Planejamento Ltda (Brazil) *Tel:* (021) 5893030 *Fax:* (021) 580-2163, pg 81

Ediciones Contables y Administrativas SA (Mexico) *Tel:* (05) 6040140; (05) 6041998; (05) 6040260 *Fax:* (05) 6056730, pg 459

Contact NV (Belgium) *Tel:* (03) 4572024 *Fax:* (03) 4581327, pg 67

Contact Publishers (Netherlands) *Tel:* (020) 5249800 *E-mail:* info@contact-bv.nl, pg 476

Contex Corporation (Japan) *Tel:* (03) 42-522-0051 *Fax:* (03) 42-526-2345; (03) 42-548-2400 *E-mail:* contex@qa2.so-net.ne.jp *Web Site:* contex.co.jp/, pg 415

Contexto Editora (Portugal) *Tel:* (021) 3479769 *Fax:* (021) 3479770, pg 524

Editora Contexto (Editora Pinsky Ltda) (Brazil) *Tel:* (011) 3832-5838 *Fax:* (011) 3832-1043 *E-mail:* contexto@editoracontexto.com.br *Web Site:* www.editoracontexto.com.br, pg 81

Continental Bookshop (Australia) *Tel:* (03) 98247711 *Fax:* (03) 98247855, pg 1272

Continental SRL Editrice (Italy) *Tel:* (035) 237088 *Fax:* (035) 237039, pg 383

The Continuum International Publishing Group Ltd (United Kingdom) *Tel:* (020) 7922 0880 *Fax:* (020) 7922 0881 *Web Site:* www.continuum-books.com, pg 670

Jane Conway-Gordon (United Kingdom) *Tel:* (020) 7494 0148 *Fax:* (020) 7287 9264, pg 1118

Conway Maritime Press (United Kingdom) *Tel:* (020) 7471 1100 *Fax:* (020) 7471 1101 *E-mail:* info@batsford.com, pg 671

Albert Cook Medical Library (Uganda) *Tel:* (041) 534149 *Fax:* (041) 530024 *E-mail:* acook@uga.healthnet.org, pg 1504

Martin Cook Associates Ltd (United States) *Tel:* 845-639-5316 *Fax:* 845-639-5318 *Web Site:* www.mcabooks.com, pg 1143

Martin Cook Associates Ltd (United States) *Tel:* 845-639-5316 *Fax:* 845-639-5318 *E-mail:* mcanewcity@aol.com *Web Site:* www.mcabooks.com, pg 1164, 1206, 1215, 1224

Cookery Book (Australia) *Tel:* (02) 9439 3144 *Fax:* (02) 9439 3405 *E-mail:* answers@cookerybook.com.au *Web Site:* www.cookerybook.com.au, pg 18

Coolabah Publishing (Australia) *Tel:* (02) 6766 4420 *Fax:* (02) 6766 1058 *E-mail:* edubook@mpx.com.au *Web Site:* www.narnia.com, pg 18

Cooper Dale (United Kingdom) *Tel:* (020) 8748 6824 *Fax:* (020) 8748 5689, pg 1161

Leo Cooper (United Kingdom) *Tel:* (01226) 734222 *Fax:* (01226) 734438 *E-mail:* enquiries@pen-sword.demon.co.uk *Web Site:* www.pen-and-sword.co.uk, pg 671

Biblioteca de la Agencia Espanola de Cooperacion Internacional (Spain) *Tel:* (091) 5838524 *Fax:* (091) 5838525, pg 1499

Cooperativa Libraria IULM SCRL (Italy) *Tel:* (02) 89150013 *Fax:* (02) 89150013; (02) 8915002 *E-mail:* coopli-iulm@libezo.it, pg 383

Cooperative Action by Victorian Academic Libraries (CAVAL) (Australia) *Tel:* (03) 94592722 *Fax:* (03) 94592733 *E-mail:* caval@caval.edu.au; richardj@caval.edu.au, pg 1511

Cooperative Regionale de l'Enseignement Religieux (CRER) (France) *Tel:* (02) 41689140 *Fax:* (02) 41689141 *E-mail:* crer49@wanadoo.fr, pg 156

Edizioni Cooperative Scarl (Italy) *Tel:* (06) 442392227 *Fax:* (06) 44238504 *E-mail:* incm@legacoop.it *Web Site:* www.legacoop.it, pg 383

Copenhagen Business School Press (Denmark) *Tel:* (45) 38153960 *Fax:* (45) 38153962 *E-mail:* cbspress@cbs.dk *Web Site:* www.cbspress.dk, pg 131

Copernic (France) *Tel:* (01) 40619767 *Fax:* (01) 40619633, pg 156

Coppenrath Verlag (Germany) *Tel:* (0251) 4 14 11-0 *Fax:* (0251) 4 14 11 20 *E-mail:* info@coppenrath.de *Web Site:* www.coppenrath.de, pg 211

Copper Beech Publishing Ltd (United Kingdom) *Tel:* (01342) 314734 *Fax:* (01342) 314794 *E-mail:* sales@copperbeechpublishing.co.uk *Web Site:* www.btinternet.com/~copperbeechpublishing, pg 671

The Copperbelt University Library (Zambia) *Tel:* (02) 222066; (02) 223972 *Fax:* (02) 222469; (02) 223972 *E-mail:* library@cbu.ac.zm, pg 1509

Copress Verlag (Germany) *Tel:* (089) 1 25 74 14 *Fax:* (089) 12 16 22 82 *E-mail:* info@stiebner.com *Web Site:* www.stiebner.com, pg 211

Editions Coprur (France) *Tel:* (0388) 147241 *Fax:* (0388) 147239 *E-mail:* coprur@editions-coprur.fr, pg 156

Copyright Agency Ltd (Australia) *Tel:* (02) 93947600 *Fax:* (02) 93947601 *E-mail:* info@copyright.com.au *Web Site:* www.copyright.com.au, pg 1236

Copyright International Agency Corina GmbH (Germany) *Tel:* (030) 80902386 *Fax:* (030) 80902388 *E-mail:* info@corina.com *Web Site:* www.corina.com, pg 1111

Copyright Licensing Agency (United Kingdom) *Tel:* (020) 7436 5931 *Fax:* (020) 7436 3986, pg 1265

Copyright Services Systems Centre (CSSC) Nepal, (COSESCEN) (Nepal) *Tel:* (01) 212289; (01) 223036; (01) 224005, pg 1253

Copytrain (United Kingdom) *Tel:* (01844) 279345 *Fax:* (01844) 279345, pg 1118

Casa Editrice Corbaccio srl (Italy) *Tel:* (020) 8692413 *Fax:* (020) 804067 *E-mail:* info@corbaccio.it *Web Site:* www.corbaccio.it, pg 383

Cordee Ltd (United Kingdom) *Tel:* (0116) 254 3579 *Fax:* (0116) 247 1176 *E-mail:* info@cordee.co.uk *Web Site:* www.cordee.co.uk, pg 671

Cordee Ltd (United Kingdom) *Tel:* (0116) 254 3579 *Fax:* (0116) 247 1176, pg 1318

Editorial Cordillera Inc (Puerto Rico) *Tel:* (787) 767-6188 *Fax:* (787) 767-8646, pg 530

Cordinata Ltd (Holy Land 2000) (Israel) *Tel:* (03) 5226885 *Fax:* (03) 5276661 *E-mail:* cordinata@isdn.net.il *Web Site:* www.holy-land2000.com, pg 366

Coresi SRL (Romania) *Tel:* (01) 3127115 *Fax:* (01) 2230177, pg 532

Corian-Verlag Heinrich Wimmer (Germany) *Tel:* (08271) 5951 *Fax:* (08271) 6931 *E-mail:* 082716941-0001@t-online.de; 101374.1022@compuserve.com, pg 211

Corint Verlag (Romania) *Tel:* (01) 2119766 *Fax:* (01) 2119766, pg 532

Cork University Press (Ireland) *Tel:* (021) 4902980 *Fax:* (021) 4273553; (021) 4315329 *E-mail:* corkunip@ucc.ie *Web Site:* www.corkuniversitypress.com, pg 359

Cornelsen und Oxford University Press GmbH & Co (Germany) *Tel:* (030) 827936-0 *Fax:* (030) 827936-36 *Web Site:* www.cornelsen.de, pg 211

Cornelsen Verlag GmbH & Co OHG (Germany) *Tel:* (030) 897 85-0 *Fax:* (030) 897 85-299 *E-mail:* c-mail@cornelsen.de *Web Site:* www.cornelsen.com, pg 211

Cornelsen Verlag Scriptor GmbH & Co KG (Germany) *Tel:* (030) 897 77 4-0 *Fax:* (030) 897 77 4-44 *E-mail:* c-mail@cornelsen.de *Web Site:* www.cornelsen.de, pg 212

Cornford Press (Australia) *Tel:* (03) 6331 9658 *Fax:* (03) 6331 9685 *E-mail:* dadaa_tas@vision.net.au; info@cornfordpress.com *Web Site:* www.cornfordpress.com, pg 19

Cornucopia Press (Australia) *Tel:* (08) 9388 1965 *Fax:* (08) 9388 1852 *E-mail:* cornucop@aoi.com.au, pg 19

Archivo de la Corona de Aragon (Spain) *Tel:* (093) 4854285 *Fax:* (093) 3001252, pg 1499

Corona Publishing Co Ltd (Japan) *Tel:* (03) 39413131 *Fax:* (03) 39413137, pg 415

Corona Verlag (Germany) *Tel:* (040) 6424144 *Fax:* (040) 64221023, pg 212

Corporacion de Estudios y Publicaciones (Ecuador) *Tel:* (02) 221-711 *Fax:* (02) 226-256 *E-mail:* cep@accessinter.net, pg 137

Corporacion de Promocion Universitaria (Chile) *Tel:* (02) 2749022 *Fax:* (02) 2741828, pg 100

Ediciones Corregidor SAICI y E (Argentina) *Tel:* (011) 4374-4959; (011) 4374-5000 *Fax:* (011) 4374-5000 *Web Site:* www.corregidor.com, pg 4

Corsaire Editions (France) *Tel:* (02) 38 53 1500 *Fax:* (02) 38 54 0892 *E-mail:* corsaire.editions@wanadoo.fr, pg 156

Cortez Editora e Livraria Ltda (Brazil) *Tel:* (011) 3864 0111 *Fax:* (011) 3864 4290 *E-mail:* cortez@cortezeditora.com.br *Web Site:* www.cortezeditora.com.br, pg 1277

Librairie Jose Corti (France) *Tel:* (01) 43266300; (01) 43268048 *Fax:* (01) 40468924 *E-mail:* corti@noos.fr *Web Site:* www.jose-corti.fr, pg 156

Libreria Cortina Editrice SRL (Italy) *Tel:* (045) 594177 *Fax:* (045) 597551 *E-mail:* libreriacortina@tin.it; cortinab@tin.it, pg 383

Ediciones Corunda SA de CV (Mexico) *Tel:* (05) 5684741; (05) 5684751; (05) 5684640 *Fax:* (05) 6525211, pg 459

Corvina Books Ltd (Hungary) *Tel:* (01) 3184148 *Fax:* (01) 3184410 *E-mail:* corvina@mail.matav.hu, pg 323

Cosa-Verlag, Giusep Condrau SA (Switzerland) *Tel:* (081) 9476464; (081) 9476352 *Fax:* (081) 947-63-52 *E-mail:* info@casanova.ch *Web Site:* www.casanova.ch, pg 611

Cosmo Publications (India) *Tel:* (011) 3278779; (011) 3280455 *Fax:* (011) 3274597 *E-mail:* genesis.cosmo@axcess.net.in; genesis@ndb.vsnl.net.in, pg 335

Cosmopolita SRL (Argentina) *Tel:* (011) 4361-8925; (011) 4361-8049 *Fax:* (011) 4361-8049; (011) 4361-8925, pg 4

Cosmopolitan Publishers Ltd (Kenya) *Tel:* (02) 22143 *Fax:* (02) 333448, pg 431

Edicoes Cosmos (Portugal) *Tel:* (021) 7955140 *Fax:* (021) 7969713, pg 524

Cosmos Libros SRL (Argentina) *Tel:* (011) 148127364; (011) 148155347 *E-mail:* cosmoslibros@arnet.com.ar, pg 1271

Cosmos-Verlag AG (Switzerland) *Tel:* (31) 9506464 *Fax:* (31) 9506460 *E-mail:* info@cosmosverlag.ch, pg 611

Costa e Nolan SpA (Italy) *Tel:* (010) 873888 *Fax:* (010) 873889, pg 383

Editorial Costa Rica (Costa Rica) *Tel:* 253-5354 *Fax:* 253-5091 *E-mail:* editocr@racsa.co.cr, pg 115

Costaisa, SA (Spain) *Tel:* (093) 2536107 *Fax:* (093) 2057917 *E-mail:* costaisa@costaisa.com *Web Site:* www.costaisa.com, pg 568

Cotidiano Mujer (Uruguay) *Tel:* (02) 4130374; (02) 4024180 *Fax:* (02) 4095651 *E-mail:* cotidian@chasque.apc.org.uy, pg 760

Cottage Publications (United Kingdom) *Tel:* (01247) 888033; (0410) 057990 (mobile) *Fax:* (01247) 888063 *E-mail:* info@cottage-publications.com *Web Site:* www.cottage-publications.com, pg 671

J G Cotta'sche Buchhandlung Nachfolger GmbH (Germany) *Tel:* (0711) 6672-0 *Fax:* (0711) 6672-2000 *E-mail:* info@klett-cotta.de *Web Site:* www.klett-cotta.de, pg 212

Council for British Archaeology (United Kingdom) *Tel:* (01904) 671417 *Fax:* (01904) 671384 *E-mail:* archaeology@compuserve.com; cbabooks@dial.pipex.com *Web Site:* www.britarch.ac.uk, pg 671

Council for Scientific & Industrial Research-Institute for Scientific & Technological Information (Ghana) *Tel:* (021) 778808; (021) 764822 *E-mail:* csir@ghana.com; cemensah@hotmail.com *Web Site:* www.csir.org.gh, pg 1470

Council of Academic & Professional Publishers (United Kingdom) *Tel:* (020) 7565 7474 *Fax:* (020) 7836 4543 *E-mail:* mail@publishers.org.uk *Web Site:* www.publishers.org.uk, pg 1265

Council of Australian State Libraries (Australia) *Tel:* (02) 92731414 *Fax:* (07) 38462421, pg 1511

Council of Europe Publishing (France) *Tel:* (0388) 412581 *Fax:* (0388) 413910 *E-mail:* publishing@coe.int *Web Site:* book.coe.int, pg 156, 1243

Council of Libraries (Albania) *Tel:* (042) 7984; (042) 7823, pg 1511

Counseil International de la Langue Francaise (France) *Tel:* (01) 48787395 *Fax:* (01) 48784928 *E-mail:* cilf@cilf.org *Web Site:* www.cilf.org, pg 157

Countryside Books (United Kingdom) *Tel:* (01635) 43816 *Fax:* (01635) 551004 *Web Site:* www.countrysidebooks.co.uk, pg 671

Countyvise Ltd (United Kingdom) *Tel:* (0151) 6473333 *Fax:* (0151) 6478286 *E-mail:* cv@birkenheadpress.co.uk, pg 671

Cour Internationale de Justice (Netherlands) *Tel:* (070) 302 23 23 *Fax:* (070) 364 99 28 *E-mail:* mail@icj-cij.org *Web Site:* www.icj-cij.org, pg 1254

Courrier du Livre Sarl (France) *Tel:* (01) 43364105 *Fax:* (01) 43310745 *E-mail:* info@tredaniel-courrier.com *Web Site:* www.tredaniel.com/, pg 157

Courseguides International Ltd (Hong Kong) *Tel:* (02) 7373322 *Fax:* (02) 7931188, pg 319

Uitgeverij Coutinho BV (Netherlands) *Tel:* (035) 6949991 *Fax:* (035) 6947165 *E-mail:* info@coutinho.ul *Web Site:* www.coutinho.ul, pg 476

Covenant Publishing Co Ltd (United Kingdom) *Tel:* (020) 8877 9010 *Fax:* (020) 8871 4770 *E-mail:* admin@britishisrael.co.uk *Web Site:* www.britishisrael.co.uk, pg 671

Covenanter Press (Australia) *Tel:* (02) 6351 4611 *Fax:* (02) 6351 4611 *Web Site:* www.covenanterpress.com.au, pg 19

Cover to Cover (United Kingdom) *Tel:* (01993) 893456 *Fax:* (01993) 6039092, pg 1233

Richard & Erika Coward Writing & Publishing Partnership (United Kingdom) *Tel:* (020) 8202 9592 *E-mail:* info@writers.net, pg 671

Cox & Wyman Ltd (United Kingdom) *Tel:* (01189) 530500 *Fax:* (01189) 507222, pg 1140, 1161, 1203, 1214

CPE - Centro Programmazione Editoriale (Italy) *Tel:* (059) 908065 *Fax:* (059) 906029, pg 383

CPE (Conseil Permanent des Ecrivains) (France) *Tel:* (01) 49546880 *Fax:* (01) 42842087, pg 1243

CPL- La Communication Par le Livre (France) *Tel:* (01) 42733047 *Fax:* (01) 42733047, pg 157

Cradley Print Ltd (United Kingdom) *Tel:* (01384) 414100 *Fax:* (01384) 414102 *E-mail:* sales@cradleygp.co.uk, pg 1161, 1203

Cradley Print Ltd (United Kingdom) *Tel:* (01384) 414100 *Fax:* (01384) 414102, pg 1223

Craft Print Pte Ltd (Singapore) *Tel:* 8614040 *Fax:* 8610530 *E-mail:* craftprt@singet.com.sq, pg 1159

Craft Print Pte Ltd (Singapore) *Tel:* 8614040 *Fax:* 8610530 *E-mail:* craftprt@singnet.com.sg, pg 1200, 1222

The Crafts Council (United Kingdom) *Tel:* (020) 7806 2559 *Fax:* (020) 7837 6891, pg 1318

Craig Potton Publishing (New Zealand) *Tel:* (03) 5489009 *Fax:* (03) 5489456 *E-mail:* info@cpp.co.nz *Web Site:* www.craigpotton.co.nz, pg 490

Craig Printing Company Ltd (New Zealand) *Tel:* (03) 2187029 *Fax:* (03) 2184811, pg 490

Otto Cramwinckel Uitgever (Netherlands) *Tel:* (020) 6276609 *Fax:* (020) 6383817 *E-mail:* otto.cram@cram.nl, pg 476

Wendy Crane Books (New Zealand) *Tel:* (04) 5664228, pg 490

Crathern Machinery Group Inc (United States) *Tel:* 603-746-4111 *Fax:* 603-746-4172 *E-mail:* info@crathern.com *Web Site:* www.crathern.com, pg 1224

Crawford House Publishing (Australia) *Tel:* (08) 8340 1411 *Fax:* (08) 8340 1811 *E-mail:* frontdesk@chp.com.au *Web Site:* www.chp.com.au, pg 19

Creaciones Monar Editorial (Spain) *Tel:* (093) 2133928 *Fax:* (093) 2198460 *Web Site:* www.monar.com, pg 569

Creadif (Belgium) *Tel:* (02) 7360630 *Fax:* (02) 7348747, pg 67

Editure Ion Creanga (Romania) *Tel:* (01) 2231112, pg 532

Creation Books (United Kingdom) *Tel:* (020) 7430 9878 *Fax:* (020) 7242 5527 *E-mail:* info@creationbooks.com *Web Site:* www.creationbooks.com, pg 671

Creative Learning Systems (Australia) *Tel:* (03) 3700131 *Fax:* (03) 93701102, pg 19

Creative Monochrome Ltd (United Kingdom) *Tel:* (020) 8686 3282 *Fax:* (020) 8681 0662 *E-mail:* sales@cremono.com *Web Site:* www.cremono.com, pg 672

CREDES - Centre de Recherche d'Etude et de Documentation en Economie de la Sante (France) *Tel:* (01) 53934300 *Fax:* (01) 53934350 *Web Site:* www.credes.fr, pg 157

Cremers (Schoollandkaarten) PVBA (Belgium) *Tel:* (02) 2680345 *Fax:* (02) 2680345, pg 67

Edizioni Cremonese SRL (Italy) *Tel:* (055) 2476371 *Fax:* (055) 2476372 *Web Site:* www.ed-cremonese.it, pg 383

Editeurs Crepin-Leblond (France) *Tel:* (032) 5038748 *Fax:* (032) 5038740 *Web Site:* www.graphycom.com, pg 157

Editora Crescer Ltda (Brazil) *Tel:* (031) 221-9235 *Fax:* (031) 221-7482 *E-mail:* crescer@crescer.com.br *Web Site:* www.crescer.com.br, pg 81

Cressrelles Publishing Company Ltd (United Kingdom) *Tel:* (01684) 540154 *Fax:* (01684) 540154, pg 672

Rupert Crew Ltd (United Kingdom) *Tel:* (020) 7242 8586 *Fax:* (020) 7831 7914 *E-mail:* rupertcrew@compuserve.com, pg 1118

Le Cri Editions (Belgium) *Tel:* (02) 6466533 *Fax:* (02) 6466607 *E-mail:* lecri@shynet.be, pg 67

Crime Writers' Association (United Kingdom) *E-mail:* info@theCWA.co.uk *Web Site:* www.thecwa.co.uk, pg 1265

Crisalide (Italy) *Tel:* (0771) 64463 *Fax:* (0771) 64693 *E-mail:* crisalide@crisalide.com; info@crisalide.com *Web Site:* crisalide.com, pg 383

Crista International (Australia) *Tel:* (07) 5537 2956 *Fax:* (07) 5537 2956, pg 19

Librerias de Cristal, sa de cv (Mexico) *Tel:* (05) 5746499; (05) 5644100 *Fax:* (05) 2640983; (05) 5644100 ext 287 (fax on demand) *E-mail:* biblio10@prodigy.net.mx, pg 1299

Ediciones Cristiandad (Spain) *Tel:* (091) 781 99 70 *Fax:* (091) 781 99 77 *E-mail:* info@kgm.es *Web Site:* www.edicionescristiandad.com, pg 569

Cristy's Atelier (Hong Kong) *Tel:* 25418609 *Fax:* 28540995 *E-mail:* cristys@intercon.net, pg 1155

Editions Criterion (France) *Tel:* (01) 45443834 *Fax:* (01) 45499392, pg 157

Critica (Argentina) *Tel:* (011) 3834940; (011) 3837403 *E-mail:* info@grijalbo.com.ar *Web Site:* www.grijalbo.com.ar, pg 4

Critics' Circle (United Kingdom) *Tel:* (020) 7403 1818 (ext 148) *Fax:* (020) 7357 9287, pg 1370

Critiques Livres Distribution SAS (France) *Tel:* (01) 43603910 *Fax:* (01) 48973706 *E-mail:* critiques.livres@wanadoo.fr, pg 1221, 1283

Croatian ISBN Agency (Croatia) *Tel:* (01) 6164087; (01) 6164288 *Fax:* (01) 6164371 *E-mail:* isbn@nsk.hr *Web Site:* www.nsk.hr, pg 1240

Studia Croatica (Argentina) *Tel:* (011) 4771-4954 *Fax:* (011) 4771-4954, pg 5

Crofthouse Books Ltd (United Kingdom) *Tel:* (01932) 845559 *Fax:* (01932) 849528; (01932) 830006 *E-mail:* croft@croftbook.co.uk *Web Site:* www.crofthouse.co.uk, pg 1318

Comite international de la Croix-Rouge (Switzerland) *Tel:* (022) 7346001 *Fax:* (022) 7384416; (022) 7348280, pg 612

Paul H Crompton Ltd (United Kingdom) *Tel:* (020) 8780 1063 *Fax:* (020) 8780 1063, pg 672

Croner CCH Group Ltd (United Kingdom) *Tel:* (020) 85473333 *Fax:* (020) 85472638 *E-mail:* info@croner.co.uk *Web Site:* www.croner.co.uk, pg 672

Editura Cronos SRL (Romania) *Tel:* (044) 262245; (094) 643310 (mobile phone); (044) 7690952 *Fax:* (01) 2231025 *E-mail:* crons@dial.kappa.rd *Web Site:* www.cronos.roknet.rd, pg 532

Cross Continent Press Ltd (Nigeria) *Tel:* (01) 862437 *Fax:* (01) 685679, pg 498

Crossbridge Books (United Kingdom) *Tel:* (0121) 447 7897 *Fax:* (0121) 445 1063 *E-mail:* em@crossbridgebooks.com *Web Site:* www.crossbridgebooks.com, pg 672

Crossroad Distributors Pty Ltd (Australia) *Tel:* (02) 898-0644 *Fax:* (02) 898-0690 *E-mail:* custserv@crossroad.com.au, pg 19

Crown House Publishing Ltd (United Kingdom) *Tel:* (01267) 211345 *Fax:* (01267) 211882 *E-mail:* books@crownhouse.co.uk *Web Site:* www.crownhouse.co.uk, pg 672

The Crowood Press Ltd (United Kingdom) *Tel:* (01672) 520320 *Fax:* (01672) 520280 *E-mail:* enquiries@crowood.com *Web Site:* www.crowood.com, pg 672

Ediciones Cruilla SA (Spain) *Tel:* (093) 2376344; (093) 2922172 *Fax:* (093) 2380116 *E-mail:* editorial@cruilla.com *Web Site:* www.cruilla.com, pg 569

Publicaciones Cruz O SA (Mexico) *Tel:* (05) 5637544; (05) 5930232 *Fax:* (05) 6806122 *E-mail:* pcosa@infosel.net.mx, pg 459

Crystal Publishing (Australia) *Tel:* (03) 95254549 *E-mail:* minx@alphalink.com.au, pg 19

CS Graphics Pte Ltd (Singapore) *Tel:* 8610100 *Fax:* 8610190, pg 1138

CS Graphics Pte Ltd (Singapore) *Tel:* 8610100 *Fax:* 8610190 *E-mail:* hhlee@singnet.com.sq, pg 1159

CS Graphics Pte Ltd (Singapore) *Tel:* 8610100 *Fax:* 8610190 *E-mail:* hhlee@singnet.com.sg, pg 1200

CS Graphics Pte Ltd (Singapore) *Tel:* 8610100 *Fax:* 8610190 *E-mail:* stlee@csgraphics.com.sg, pg 1213

CS Graphics USA Inc (United States) *Tel:* 916-791-9066 *Fax:* 916-791-9112 *E-mail:* csgraphics@mindspring.com, pg 1143, 1164, 1206, 1215

CSA (Cambridge Scientific Abstracts) (United Kingdom) *Tel:* (01342) 336159 *Fax:* (01342) 336197 *E-mail:* service@csa.com; tjones@csa.com (sales); marketing@bowker.uk.co *Web Site:* www.csa.com, pg 672

Verlag CSA Rosemarie Schneider (Germany) *Tel:* (06082) 970116 *Fax:* (06082) 970123 *E-mail:* csa-europa@csa-activ.de *Web Site:* www.csa-activ.de, pg 212

CSIR Information Services (South Africa) *Tel:* (012) 8412911 *Fax:* (012) 3491154, pg 1497

CSIRO (Commonwealth Scientific & Industrial Research Organization) (Australia) *Tel:* (03) 4187333 *Fax:* (03) 4190459 *Web Site:* www.csiro.au, pg 1450

CSIRO Publishing (Commonwealth Scientific & Industrial Research Organisation) (Australia) *Tel:* (03) 9662 7500 *Fax:* (03) 9662 7582 *E-mail:* publishing@csiro.au *Web Site:* www.publish.csiro.au, pg 19

CSS Bookshops, Agency & Publishing Division (Nigeria) *Tel:* (01) 2633081; (01) 2637009; (01) 2637023; (01) 2633010 *Fax:* (01) 2637089, pg 498, 1303

CTBI Publications (United Kingdom) *Tel:* (020) 7523 2121 *Fax:* (020) 7928 0010 *E-mail:* info@ctbi.org.uk *Web Site:* www.ctbi.org.uk, pg 672

CTE-Centro de Tecnologia Educativa SA (Spain) *Tel:* (093) 217 75 01 *Fax:* (093) 217 62 53 *E-mail:* cte@mx2.redestb.es.com *Web Site:* www.centrocte.com, pg 569

CTIF (Center Technique des Industries de la Fonderie) (France) *Tel:* (01) 41146300 *Fax:* (01) 45341434 *Web Site:* www.ctif.com, pg 157

CTL-Presse Clemens-Tobias Lange (Germany) *Tel:* (040) 39902223 *Fax:* (040) 39902224 *E-mail:* mail@ctl-presse.de *Web Site:* www.ctl-presse.de, pg 212

CTNERHI - Centre Technique National d'Etudes et de Recherches sur les Handicaps et les Inadaptations (France) *Tel:* (01) 45655900 *Fax:* (01) 45654494 *E-mail:* ctnerhi@club-internet.fr *Web Site:* www.perso.club-internet.fr/ctnerhi, pg 157

CTP Book Printers (Pty) Ltd (South Africa) *Tel:* (011) 8890600 *Fax:* (011) 8890922 *E-mail:* ctpjhb@iafrica.com, pg 1159

CTP Book Printers (Pty) Ltd (South Africa) *Tel:* (011) 8890600 *Fax:* (011) 8890922, pg 1201

Editorial Cuarto Propio (Chile) *Tel:* (02) 204 7645 *Fax:* (02) 204 7622 *E-mail:* clic@netup.cl *Web Site:* www.cuartopropio.cl, pg 100

Editora Cuatro Vientos (Chile) *Tel:* (02) 2258381 *Fax:* (02) 3413107 *E-mail:* 4vientos@netline.cl *Web Site:* http//www.cuatrovientos.net, pg 100

Library Association of Cuba (Cuba) *Tel:* (07) 708277, pg 1514

Agencia Cubana del ISBN (Cuba) *Tel:* (07) 36034 *Fax:* (07) 333441 *E-mail:* cclfilh@artsoft.cult.cu, pg 1241

Ediciones Cubanas (Cuba) *Tel:* (07) 631989; (07) 338942 *Fax:* (07) 338943, pg 1281

Cuernavaca Editorial S A (Mexico) *Tel:* (05) 5113619; (05) 5142529; (05) 2867794 *Fax:* (05) 2117112, pg 459

Editions Cujas (France) *Tel:* (01) 44242436; (01) 44242437 *Fax:* (01) 44242438, pg 157

Cultur Prospectiv, Edition (Switzerland) *Tel:* (01) 2718388 *Fax:* (01) 2719788 *E-mail:* cpinstitut@access.ch, pg 612

Cultura (Belgium) *Tel:* (09) 9 369 15 95 *Fax:* (09) 3695925 *E-mail:* cultura@cultura-net.com, pg 67

Edizioni Cultura della Pace (Italy) *Tel:* (055) 580550 *Fax:* (055) 597185, pg 383

Casa de la Cultura Ecuatoriana Benjamin Carrion (Ecuador), pg 1362

Editorial Cultura (Guatemala) *Tel:* (02) 692080 *Fax:* (02) 346135, pg 316

Instituto Colombiano de Cultura Hispanica (Colombia) *Tel:* (01) 3413857 *Fax:* (01) 2811051, pg 1361

Livraria Cultura Editora Ltda (Brazil) *Tel:* (011) 2854033 *Fax:* (011) 2854457 *E-mail:* livros@livcultura.com.br, pg 1277

Editora Cultura Medica Ltda (Brazil) *Tel:* (021) 2567-3888 *Fax:* (021) 2569-5443 *E-mail:* cultmed@terra.com.br *Web Site:* www.culturamedica.com.br, pg 81

Instituto de Cultura Puertorriquena (Puerto Rico) *Tel:* (787) 724-0910, pg 530

Ediciones Cultural Colombiana Ltda (Colombia) *Tel:* (01) 2176529; (01) 2116090 *Fax:* (01) 2176570, pg 111

Editorial Cultural Inc (Puerto Rico) *Tel:* (787) 765-9767 *Fax:* (787) 765-9767 *E-mail:* cultural@coqui.net, pg 530

Cultural Relics Publishing House (China) *Tel:* (010) 64048057 *Fax:* (010) 64010698 *E-mail:* web@wenwu.com *Web Site:* www.wenwu.com, pg 105

La Culturale (Italy) *Tel:* (02) 29409041 *Fax:* (02) 29409041, pg 383

Ediciones Culturales Internacionales SA de CV Edicion Compra y Venta de Libros, Casetes, Videos (Mexico) *Tel:* (05) 2508099 *Fax:* (05) 5311597; (05) 5312454, pg 459

Ediciones Culturales Ver Ltda (Colombia) *Tel:* (01) 2859362; (01) 2859204 *Fax:* (01) 2859362, pg 111

Culture et Bibliotheque pour Tous (France) *Tel:* (01) 45 33 07 07 *Fax:* (01) 45 33 45 76 *E-mail:* uncbpt.services@wanadoo.fr, pg 157

Bibliotheek Cultureel Centrum Suriname (Suriname) *Tel:* 472369; 473309 *Fax:* 476516 *E-mail:* sccs@sr.net; stgccs1947@hotmail.com, pg 1500

Cumann Leabharlann na h-Eireann (Ireland) *Tel:* (01) 6619000 *Fax:* (01) 6761628 *Web Site:* www.libraryassociation.ie, pg 1518

The Mary Cunnane Agency Pty Ltd (Australia) *Tel:* (02) 43859911 *Fax:* (02) 43859922, pg 1109

Ediciones CUPSA, Centro de Comunicacion Cultural CUPSA, AC (Mexico) *Tel:* (05) 5925252; (05) 5662307 *Fax:* (05) 5462100, pg 459

Ediciones la Cupula SL (Spain) *Tel:* (093) 268 28 05 *Fax:* (093) 268 07 65 *E-mail:* lacupula@eix.intercom.es *Web Site:* www.lacupula.com, pg 569

Cura Verlag GmbH (Austria) *Tel:* (01) 7136480 *Fax:* (01) 7126258; (01) 7126219, pg 50

Edizioni Curci SRL (Italy) *Tel:* (02) 794746 *Fax:* (02) 76014504 *E-mail:* curci@iol.it *Web Site:* www.edizionicurci.it, pg 383

Curiad (United Kingdom) *Tel:* (01286) 882166 *Fax:* (01286) 882692 *E-mail:* curiad@curiad.co.uk *Web Site:* www.curiad.co.uk, pg 672

Curial Edicions Catalanes SA (Spain) *Tel:* (093) 4588101 *Fax:* (093) 2077427, pg 569

Currency Press Pty Ltd (Australia) *Tel:* (02) 9319 5877 *Fax:* (02) 9319 3649 *E-mail:* enquiries@currency.com.au *Web Site:* www.currency.com.au, pg 19

Current Technical Literature Co (Pvt) Ltd (India) *Tel:* (033) 331333, pg 1288

Current Books (India) *Tel:* (0487) 335642; (0487) 335292; (0487) 335660 *Web Site:* www.dcbooks.com/currentbooks.htm, pg 335

Current Pacific Limited (New Zealand) *Tel:* (09) 480 1388 *Fax:* (09) 480 1387 *Web Site:* www.cplnz.com, pg 490

Current Science Group (United Kingdom) *Tel:* (020) 7323 0323 *Fax:* (020) 7580 1938 *E-mail:* info@current-science.com *Web Site:* www.current-science-group.com, pg 672

James Currey Ltd (United Kingdom) *Tel:* (01865) 244 111 *Fax:* (01865) 246 454 *E-mail:* editorial@jamescurrey.co.uk *Web Site:* www.jamescurrey.co.uk, pg 673

Curriculum Corporation (Australia) *Tel:* (03) 9207 9600 *Fax:* (03) 9639 1616 *E-mail:* sales@curriculum.edu.au *Web Site:* www.curriculum.edu.au, pg 19

Eleanor Curtain Publishing (Australia) *Tel:* (03) 9822 0344 *Fax:* (03) 9824 8851, pg 19

Distribuidora Cuspide (Argentina) *Tel:* (011) 3228366; (011) 3227434 *Fax:* (011) 3223456; (011) 3223465, pg 1271

Custom Services (United States) *Tel:* 845-365-0414 *Fax:* 845-365-0864, pg 1164

CUTTINGTON UNIVERSITY COLLEGE LIBRARY INDUSTRY

Cuttington University College Library (Liberia) *Tel:* 227413, pg 1481

CVM Publications (Jamaica) *Tel:* (876) 977-3829 *Fax:* (876) 927-4117, pg 413

CyberClub (United Kingdom) *Tel:* (020) 8731 6161 *Fax:* (020) 8905 5050, pg 673

Cyhoeddiadau Barddas (United Kingdom) *Tel:* (01792) 792 829, pg 673

Cyhoeddiadau'r Gair (United Kingdom) *Tel:* (01248) 382947 *Fax:* (01248) 383954 *E-mail:* eds00e@bangor.ac.uk, pg 673

Cymdeithas Lyfrau Ceredigion (United Kingdom) *Tel:* (01970) 617776 *Fax:* (01970) 624049, pg 673

Cynosure Publishing Inc (Taiwan, Province of China) *Tel:* (02) 26573275 *Fax:* (02) 26575300 *E-mail:* cynobook@tpts4.seed.net.tw, pg 629

Library Association of Cyprus (Cyprus), pg 1514

Cyprus Library (Cyprus) *Tel:* (022) 303180; (022) 676118 *Fax:* (022) 304532 *E-mail:* cypruslibrary@cytanet.com.cy, pg 1459

Library of the Cyprus Museum - Dept of Antiquities (Cyprus) *Tel:* (022) 865848 *Fax:* (022) 303148, pg 1459

Cyprus Telecommunications Authority (CYTA) (Cyprus) *Tel:* (02) 22701000 *Fax:* (02) 497155 *E-mail:* enquiries@cyta.com.cy *Web Site:* www.cyta.com.cy, pg 122

Czernin Verlag (Austria) *Tel:* (01) 512 01 32 *Fax:* (01) 512 01 32-15 *E-mail:* office@czernin-verlag.com *Web Site:* www.czernin-verlag.com, pg 50

Spoldzielnia Wydawnicza 'Czytelnik' (Poland) *Tel:* (022) 6281441 *Fax:* (022) 6283178 *E-mail:* sekretariat@czytelnik.pl *Web Site:* www.czytelnik.pl, pg 516

D&B Ltd (United Kingdom) *Tel:* (01494) 422000 *Fax:* (01494) 422260 *E-mail:* customerhelp@dnb.com *Web Site:* www.dnb.com, pg 673

D&B Marketing Pty Ltd (Australia) *Tel:* (02) 9935 2700 *Fax:* (02) 9935 2777 *E-mail:* csc.austral@dnb.com.au *Web Site:* www.dbmarketing.com.au, pg 20

D & D Kommunikation Verlug Dirk Nishen Gmbh & Co KG (Germany) *Tel:* (030) 2173830 *Fax:* (030) 21738393, pg 212

D & K Group (United States) *Tel:* 847-956-0160 *Fax:* 847-956-8214 *E-mail:* info@dkgroup.net *Web Site:* www.dkgroup.com, pg 1206, 1215, 1224

D C Thomson & Co Ltd (United Kingdom) *Tel:* ((01382) 223131 *Fax:* (01382) 462097 *Web Site:* www.dcthomson.co.uk, pg 673

D Services (United Kingdom) *Tel:* (0116) 2547671 *Fax:* (0116) 2544670, pg 1318

Universite d' Abidjan (Cote d'Ivoire) *Tel:* 441285 *Fax:* 434254 *E-mail:* puci@africaonline.co.ci, pg 118

DA Information Services Pty Ltd (Australia) *Tel:* (03) 9210-7777 *Fax:* (03) 9210-7788 *E-mail:* service@dadirect.com.au, pg 1272

DA-Izdatelstvo Publishers (Bulgaria) *Tel:* (02) 988 1208 *Fax:* (02) 986 6290, pg 95

Ediciones Dabar, SA de CV (Mexico) *Tel:* (05) 6550396 *Fax:* (05) 6550396, pg 459

Dabill Publications (Australia) *Tel:* (02) 4228 8836 *Fax:* (02) 4226 9367 *Web Site:* www.dabill.com.au, pg 20

Dachs-Verlag GmbH (Austria) *Tel:* (01) 285 22 05-0 *Fax:* (01) 285 22 05-15 *E-mail:* office@dachs.at *Web Site:* www.dachs.at, pg 50

Editura Dacia (Romania) *Tel:* (064) 194 912 *Fax:* (064) 11665 *E-mail:* dacia@multiarea.ro *Web Site:* www.edituradacia.ro; www.cjnet.ro, pg 532

Daco Verlag Guenter Blase oHG (Germany) *Tel:* (0711) 96421-0 *Fax:* (0711) 96421-10 *E-mail:* info@daco-verlag.de *Web Site:* www.daco-verlag.de, pg 212

Les Editions Roger Dacosta (France) *Tel:* (01) 45441491, pg 157

Edizioni Armando Dado, Tipografia Stazione (Switzerland) *Tel:* (091) 7514802 *Fax:* (091) 7521026, pg 612

Dae Won Sa Co Ltd (Republic of Korea) *Tel:* (02) 7576717 *Fax:* (02) 7758043, pg 435

Daedalus Verlag (Germany) *Tel:* (0251) 231 355 *Fax:* (0251) 232 631 *E-mail:* info@daedalus-verlag.de *Web Site:* www.daedalus-verlag.com, pg 212

Daehan Printing & Publishing Co Ltd (Republic of Korea) *Tel:* (031) 730-3830 (i-3) *Fax:* (031) 735-8104 *Web Site:* www.dhpop.com, pg 435, 1137

Daehan Printing & Publishing Co Ltd (Republic of Korea) *Tel:* (031) 730-3830 (i-3) *Fax:* (031) 735-8104 *E-mail:* mschung@dhpop.com *Web Site:* www.dhpop.com, pg 1158

Daehan Printing & Publishing Co Ltd (Republic of Korea) *Tel:* (031) 730-3830 (i-3) *Fax:* (031) 735-8104 *Web Site:* www.dhpop.com, pg 1199, 1213

Daejon Trading Co Ltd (Republic of Korea) *Tel:* (02) 536-9555 *Fax:* (02) 536-0025, pg 1296

Daeyoung Munhwasa (Republic of Korea) *Tel:* (02) 716-3883 *Fax:* (02) 703-3839 *E-mail:* spotto29@hotmail.com, pg 435

Dafolo Forlag (Denmark) *Tel:* 96206666 *Fax:* 98431388 *E-mail:* dafolo@dafolo.dk *Web Site:* www.dafolo.dk, pg 131

DAFSA (France) *Tel:* (01) 44372600 *Fax:* (01) 44372635 *E-mail:* dorra.medjani@dri-wefa.com *Web Site:* www.dafsa.fr/contact/contact.cfm, pg 157

Institut Dagang Muchtar (Indonesia) *Tel:* (031) 42973, pg 355

Dagmar Dreves Verlag (Germany) *Tel:* (04108) 6866, pg 212

Dagraja Press (Australia) *Tel:* (02) 62470782; (02) 62627533 *E-mail:* granorab@ozemail.com.au, pg 20

Dahlia Books, International Publishers & Booksellers (Sweden) *Tel:* (018) 101098 *Fax:* (018) 100525 *E-mail:* dahlia@telia.com, pg 601

Dai Hak Publishing Co (Republic of Korea) *Tel:* (02) 364-9788 *Fax:* (02) 393-9045, pg 436

Dai Nippon Printing Co (Hong Kong) Ltd (Hong Kong) *Tel:* 24080188 *Fax:* 24076201, pg 1134

Dai Nippon Printing Co (Hong Kong) Ltd (Hong Kong) *Tel:* 24080188 *Fax:* 24076201 *Web Site:* www.dnp.co.jp, pg 1155, 1196, 1212

Dai Nippon Printing Co Ltd (Japan) *Tel:* (03) 53608602 *Fax:* (03) 53608222, pg 1198

Daiichi Media Pte Ltd (Singapore) *Tel:* 2563722 *Fax:* 2565922 *E-mail:* info@daiichimedia.com.sg; sales@daiichimedia.com.sg *Web Site:* www.daiichimedia.com, pg 545

Daiichi Shuppan Co Ltd (Japan) *Tel:* (03) 32914577 *Fax:* (03) 32914579 *E-mail:* ishikawa@japan.email.ne.jp, pg 415

Le Daily-Bul (Belgium) *Tel:* (064) 222973 *Fax:* (064) 222973, pg 67

Daily Times of Nigeria Ltd (Publication Division) (Nigeria) *Tel:* (01) 900850-9, pg 498

Daimon Verlag AG (Switzerland) *Tel:* (055) 4122266 *Fax:* (055) 412-2231 *E-mail:* daimon@compuserve.com *Web Site:* www.daimon.ch, pg 612

Dainippon Tosho Publishing Co, Ltd (Japan) *Tel:* (03) 35618672 *Fax:* (03) 35635596, pg 416

Dalesman Publishing Co Ltd (United Kingdom) *Tel:* (01756) 701381 *Fax:* (01756) 701326 *E-mail:* editorial@dalesman.co.uk *Web Site:* www.dalesman.co.uk, pg 673

Dalia Peled Publishers, Division of Modan (Israel) *Tel:* (08) 4221821 *Fax:* (08) 4221299, pg 366

Dalian Maritime University Press (China) *Tel:* (0411) 4729605 *Fax:* (0411) 4727996 *E-mail:* dmup@dmupress.com; cbs@dmupress.com *Web Site:* www.dmupress.com, pg 105

Dalian University of Technology (China) *Tel:* (0411) 4708620 *Fax:* (0411) 4671872 *E-mail:* lib@dlut.edu.cn *Web Site:* www.dlut.edu.cn, pg 1457

Editions Dalloz Sirey (France) *Tel:* (01) 40645454 *Fax:* (01) 40645460 *E-mail:* ventes@dalloz.fr *Web Site:* www.dalloz.fr, pg 157

Rafael Dalmau, Editor (Spain) *Tel:* (093) 3173338 *Fax:* (093) 3173338, pg 569

Terence Dalton Ltd (United Kingdom) *Tel:* (01787) 249290 *Fax:* (01787) 248267 *E-mail:* tdl@lavenhamgroup.cp.uk *Web Site:* www.terencedalton.co.uk, pg 673

Daltons Books (Australia) *Tel:* (062) 491844 *Fax:* (062) 2475753, pg 1272

Ediciones Daly S L (Spain) *Tel:* (095) 2582569 *Fax:* (095) 2583619 *E-mail:* daly@edicionesdaly.com *Web Site:* edicionesdaly.com, pg 569

Damascus University Library (Syrian Arab Republic) *Tel:* (011) 2119840, pg 1502

Damascus University Press (Syrian Arab Republic) *Tel:* (011) 2215100 *Fax:* (011) 2236010, pg 628

Dami Editore SRL (Italy) *Tel:* (02) 76005497 *Fax:* (02) 784010 *E-mail:* damieditore@damieditore.it, pg 383

N W Damm og Son A/S (Norway) *Tel:* 22 47 11 00 *Fax:* 22 47 11 49; 22 47 11 42 *E-mail:* nwd@egmont.no *Web Site:* www.damm.no, pg 503

Damms Junior Bokklubb (Norway) *Tel:* 22471000 *Fax:* 22471098 *E-mail:* egmont@egmont.com *Web Site:* www.egmont.com, pg 1230

Bokklubben Damms Leselover (Norway) *Tel:* 22471000 *Fax:* 22471098 *E-mail:* egmont@egmont.com *Web Site:* www.egmont.com, pg 1230

Dana Verlag (Germany) *Tel:* (05468) 1813 *Fax:* (05468) 239, pg 212

Dance Books Ltd, The Old Bakery (United Kingdom) *Tel:* (01420) 86138 *Fax:* (01420) 86142 *E-mail:* dl@dancebooks.co.uk *Web Site:* www.dancebooks.co.uk, pg 673

Youl Hwa Dang Publisher (Republic of Korea) *Tel:* (02) 5153141; (02) 5153143; (02) 5153142 *Fax:* (02) 5153144 *E-mail:* yhdp@hitel.net; horang2@unitel.co.kr, pg 436

Dangaroo Press (Australia) *Tel:* (02) 49545938 *Fax:* (02) 49546531, pg 20

Editions Dangles SA (France) *Tel:* (02) 38864180 *Fax:* (02) 38837234 *E-mail:* dangles@wanadoo.fr *Web Site:* www.editions-dangles.com, pg 157

The C W Daniel Co Ltd (United Kingdom) *Tel:* (01799) 521909; (01799) 526216 *Fax:* (01799) 513462 *E-mail:* cwdaniel@ukonline.co.uk *Web Site:* www.cwdaniel.com, pg 673

Ann-Christine Danielsson Agency (Sweden) *Tel:* (040) 482380 *Fax:* (040) 482190 *E-mail:* acd.agency@swipnet.se, pg 1116

The Danish Literature Centre (Denmark) *Tel:* 33744500 *Fax:* 33911545 *E-mail:* danlit@danlit.dk *Web Site:* www.danlit.dk; www.literaturenet.dk, pg 131

Danish National Library Authority (Denmark) *Tel:* 44867777 *Fax:* 44867891 *E-mail:* dbc@dbc.dk *Web Site:* www.dbc.dk, pg 131

Beate Danker-Verlag (Germany) *Tel:* (06036) 9430 *Fax:* (06036) 6270, pg 212

DanKook University Press (Republic of Korea) *Tel:* (02) 793-5034 *Fax:* (02) 792-5814, pg 436

Danmar Publishers (Kenya) *Tel:* (02) 504818, pg 431

Danmarks BlindeBibliotek (Denmark) *Tel:* 39274444 *Fax:* 39274454 *E-mail:* dbb@dbb.dk *Web Site:* www.dbb.dk, pg 1460

Danmarks Biblioteksforening (Denmark) *Tel:* 33250935 *Fax:* 33257900, pg 1514

Danmarks Forskningsbiblioteksforening (Denmark) *Tel:* 33936222 *Fax:* 33919596 *E-mail:* df@kb.dk, pg 1514

Danmarks Forvaltningshojskole Forlaget (Denmark) *Tel:* 38 14 52 00 *Fax:* 38 14 53 45 *E-mail:* le@dkdfh.dk, pg 131

Danmarks Natur-og Laegevidenskabelige Bibliotek, Universitet sbiblioteket (Denmark) *Tel:* 35396523 *Fax:* 35398533 *E-mail:* dnlb@dnlb.dk *Web Site:* www.dnlb.dk, pg 1460

Danmarks Paedagogiske Bibliotek (Denmark) *Tel:* 39696633 *Fax:* 39551000 *E-mail:* dpb@dpb.dpu.dk *Web Site:* www.dpb.dpu.dk/, pg 1460

Danmarks Statistik Biblioteket (Denmark) *Tel:* 39173030 *Fax:* 39173003 *E-mail:* bib@dst.dk, pg 1460

Danmarks Tekniske Videncenter (DTV) (Denmark) *Tel:* 45257200 *Fax:* 45883040 *E-mail:* dtv@dtv.dk *Web Site:* www.dtv.dk, pg 1461

D'Anna (Italy) *Tel:* (055) 242800 *Fax:* (055) 2480781 *E-mail:* gdanna@tin.it, pg 383

Hristo G Danov State Publishing House (Bulgaria) *Tel:* (032) 231201; (032) 265421 *Fax:* (032) 260560, pg 95

Dansk Forfatterforening (Denmark) *Tel:* 32955100 *Fax:* 32540115 *E-mail:* danskforfatterforening@danskforfatterforening.dk *Web Site:* www.danskforfatterforening.dk, pg 1362

Dansk Historisk Handbogsforlag ApS (Denmark) *Tel:* 45 93 48 00 *Fax:* 45 93 47 47 *E-mail:* genos@worldonline.dk, pg 131

Dansk ISBN - Kontor (the Danish ISBN Agency) (Denmark) *Tel:* 44867777 *Fax:* 44867853 *E-mail:* isbn@dbc.dk *Web Site:* www.isbn.kontoret.dk, pg 1241

Dansk Musikbiblioteksforening (Denmark) *Tel:* 33474316 *Fax:* 33474710 *E-mail:* dmbf@kb.dk *Web Site:* www.dmbf.sb.aau.dk, pg 1514

Dansk Psykologisk Forlag (Denmark) *Tel:* 35381655 *Fax:* 35381655 *E-mail:* dk-psych@dpf.dk *Web Site:* www.dpf.dk, pg 131

Dansk Teknologisk Institut, Forlaget (Denmark) *Tel:* 72 20 20 00 *Fax:* 72 20 20 19 *E-mail:* info@teknologisk.dk *Web Site:* www.teknologisk.dk, pg 131

Den Danske Boghandlerforening (Denmark) *Tel:* 32542255 *Fax:* 32540041 *E-mail:* ddb@bogpost.dk *Web Site:* www.bogguide.dk, pg 1241

Den Danske Forlaeggerforening (Denmark) *Tel:* 33156688 *Fax:* 33156588 *E-mail:* publassn@webpartner.dk, pg 1241

Det Danske Sprog - og Litteraturselskab (Denmark) *Tel:* 33130660 *Fax:* 33140608 *E-mail:* sekretariat@dsl.dk *Web Site:* www.dsl.dk, pg 1362

Libreria Dante di A M Longo (Italy) *Tel:* (0544) 33500 *Fax:* (0544) 217554 *E-mail:* longo-ra@linknet.it, pg 1293

Danubia Werbung und Verlagsservice (Austria) *Tel:* (01) 792666 *Fax:* (01) 792666443, pg 50

Danubiaprint (Slovakia) *Tel:* (07) 309167 *Fax:* (07) 362613, pg 549

Danuma Prakashakayo (Sri Lanka) *Tel:* (01) 686878 *Fax:* (01) 696578, pg 596

Daphne Diffusion SA (Belgium) *Tel:* (09) 221 45 91 *Fax:* (09) 220 16 12 *E-mail:* info@daphne.be, pg 67

Daphnis-Verlag (Switzerland) *Tel:* (01) 9153639 *Fax:* (01) 2014231, pg 612

Dar Al-Kitab Al-Masri (Egypt (Arab Republic of Egypt)) *Tel:* (02) 3922168; (02) 3934301; (02) 3924614 *Fax:* (02) 3924657 *E-mail:* hlelzein@datum.com.eg, pg 138

Dar Al-Kitab Alloubnani (Lebanon) *Tel:* (01) 861563 *Fax:* (01) 351433, pg 443

Dar Al-Maaref-Liban Sarl (Lebanon) *Tel:* (01) 931243, pg 443

Dar Al Maarifah (Syrian Arab Republic) *Tel:* (011) 2210269 *Fax:* (011) 2241615 *E-mail:* staha@net.sy *Web Site:* www.easyquram.com, pg 628

Dar Al-Matbo at Al-Gadidah (Egypt (Arab Republic of Egypt)) *Tel:* (03) 4825508 *Fax:* (03) 4833819, pg 138

Dar Al-Mirrikh (Mars Publishing House) (Saudi Arabia) *Tel:* (01) 4647531; (01) 4658523 *Fax:* (01) 4657939, pg 543

Dar al-Nahda al Arabia (Egypt (Arab Republic of Egypt)), pg 138

Dar Al Raed Al Lubnani (Lebanon) *Tel:* (01) 450757; (01) 451581, pg 443

Dar Al-Rayah for Publishing & Distribution (Saudi Arabia) *Tel:* (01) 4931869 *Fax:* (01) 4911985, pg 543

Dar Al-Shareff for Publishing & Distribution (Saudi Arabia) *Tel:* (01) 4034931 *Fax:* (01) 4052234, pg 543

Dar Al-Thakafah Al-Gadidah (Egypt (Arab Republic of Egypt)) *Tel:* (02) 42718, pg 138

Dar Al-Ulum Publishers, Booksellers & Distributors (Saudi Arabia) *Tel:* (01) 4777121 *Fax:* (01) 4793446, pg 1308

Dar an-Nahar Sal (Lebanon) *Tel:* (01) 340044; (01) 340960, pg 443

Dar Arabia Lil Kitab (Tunisia) *Tel:* (01) 888255, pg 637

SARL DAR-Echihab (Algeria) *Tel:* (02) 626727; (02) 626734 *Fax:* (02) 574632, pg 2

Dar El Afaq (Tunisia) *Tel:* (01) 265904 *Fax:* (01) 569035, pg 637

Dar El Kitab (Morocco) *Tel:* (02) 304581; (02) 305419 *Fax:* (02) 304581, pg 469

Dar El Shorouk (Egypt (Arab Republic of Egypt)) *Tel:* (02) 4023399; (02) 4037567 *Fax:* (02) 3934814 *E-mail:* dar@sharouk.com *Web Site:* www.shorouk.com, pg 138

Dar El Shorouk Publishing & Distributing House (Egypt (Arab Republic of Egypt)) *Tel:* (02) 4023399 *Fax:* (02) 4037567 *E-mail:* dar@shorouk.com *Web Site:* www.shorouk.com, pg 138

The Dar Es Salaam Bookshop (United Republic of Tanzania) *Tel:* (051) 23416, pg 1314

Dar Nachr Al Maarifa Pour L'Edition et La Distribution (Morocco) *Tel:* (07) 795702; (07) 796914 *Fax:* (07) 790343, pg 469

Typothito G Dardanos (Greece) *Tel:* (010) 3642003 *Fax:* (010) 3642030 *E-mail:* info@dardanosnet.gr *Web Site:* www.dardanosnet.gr, pg 1286

Daresbury Lewis Carroll Society (United Kingdom) *Tel:* (01606) 891303, pg 1370

Darf Publishers Ltd (United Kingdom) *Tel:* (020) 7431 7009 *Fax:* (020) 7431 7655 *E-mail:* darf@freeuk.com *Web Site:* home.freeuk.net/darf, pg 674

Dargaud (France) *Tel:* (01) 53 26 32 32 *Fax:* (01) 53 26 32 00 *E-mail:* contact@dargaud.fr *Web Site:* www.dargaud.fr, pg 157

Dargenis Publishers (Lithuania) *Tel:* (037) 745271 *Fax:* (037) 745271 *E-mail:* dargenis@kaunas.omnitel.net, pg 445

Ediciones de Juan Darien (Uruguay) *Tel:* (02) 2090223 *E-mail:* dayraq@chasque.apc.org, pg 760

Verlag Darmstaedter Blaetter Schwarz und Co (Germany) *Tel:* (06151) 48196, pg 212

D'Artagnan Publishing (Australia) *Tel:* (08) 2726718, pg 20

Darton, Longman & Todd Ltd (United Kingdom) *Tel:* (020) 8875 0155 *Fax:* (020) 8875 0133 *E-mail:* tradesales@darton-longman-todd.co.uk, pg 674

Darulfikir (Malaysia) *Tel:* (03) 2981636; (03) 26913892 *Fax:* (03) 26928757 *E-mail:* emel@darulfikir.com.my, pg 451

Darzavno Izdatelstvo Narodna Kultura (Bulgaria) *Tel:* (02) 9872722; (02) 9878063 *Fax:* (02) 894946, pg 95

Darzhavno Izdatelstvo Zemizdat (Bulgaria) *Tel:* (02) 441829 *Fax:* (02) 442319, pg 95

Das Arsenal, Verlag fuer Kultur und Politik GmbH (Germany) *Tel:* (030) 3441827; (030) 34651360 *Fax:* (030) 3441827, pg 212

D'Assis Books (Australia) *Tel:* (0754) 482145 *Fax:* (0754) 475200, pg 20

Dastane Ramchandra & Co (India) *Tel:* (020) 4478193; (020) 4485950; (020) 5511964 *Fax:* (020) 4478193, pg 335

DAT Publications (Israel) *Tel:* (03) 5071239 *Fax:* (03) 5070458 *E-mail:* DAT@y-dat.co.il *Web Site:* www.y-dat.co.il, pg 366

Data Becker GmbH & Co KG (Germany) *Tel:* (0211) 9331 800; (0211) 9334 900 (orders) *Fax:* (0211) 9331 444; (0211) 9334 999 (orders) *E-mail:* info@databecker.de *Web Site:* www.databecker.de, pg 212

Datacom Buchverlag GmbH (Germany) *Tel:* (02271) 6080 *Fax:* (02271) 608290, pg 212

DATAMAP - Europe (Bulgaria) *Tel:* (02) 510090 *Fax:* (02) 510090 *E-mail:* datamap@mail.techno-linek.com *Web Site:* www.datamap.dir.bg, pg 95

Datanews (Italy) *Tel:* (06) 70450318 *Fax:* (06) 70450320 *E-mail:* datanews.edit@mclink.it, pg 384

Datapage Technologies International Inc (United States) *Tel:* 636-278-8888 *Fax:* 636-278-2180 *Web Site:* www.datapage.com, pg 1164

Editions du Dauphin (France) *Tel:* (01) 43277631, pg 158

M d'Auria Editore SAS (Italy) *Tel:* (081) 5518963 *Fax:* (081) 5493827 *E-mail:* info@dauria.it *Web Site:* www.dauria.it, pg 384

Verlag Werner Dausien (Germany) *Tel:* (06181) 92810; (06181) 259052 (orders) *Fax:* (06181) 257387, pg 212

Davaco Publishers (Netherlands) *Tel:* (0525) 661823 *Fax:* (0525) 662153, pg 476

David & Charles Ltd (United Kingdom) *Tel:* (01626) 323200 *Fax:* (01626) 323319; (01626) 364463 *E-mail:* postermaster@davidandcharles.co.uk *Web Site:* www.davidandcharles.co.uk, pg 674

David Bennett Books (United Kingdom) *Tel:* (020) 7738 0314 *Fax:* (020) 7223 4936 *Web Site:* www.illustratedlibrary.com, pg 674

David Godwin Associates (United Kingdom) *Tel:* (020) 7240 9992 *Fax:* (020) 7395 6110 *Web Site:* www.davidgodwinassociates.co.uk, pg 1118

David's Marine Books (New Zealand) *Tel:* (09) 3031459 *Fax:* (09) 3078170 *E-mail:* sales@transpacific.co.nz, pg 490

Davidsfonds - Infodok NV (Belgium) *Tel:* (016) 310-600 *Fax:* (016) 310-608 *E-mail:* informatie@davidsfonds.be *Web Site:* www.davidsfonds.be, pg 67

Davidsfonds VZW (Belgium) *Tel:* (016) 310-600 *Fax:* (016) 310-608 *E-mail:* informatie@davidsfonds.be *Web Site:* www.davidsfonds.be, pg 67

Christopher Davies Publishers Ltd (United Kingdom) *Tel:* (01792) 648825 *Fax:* (01792) 648825 *E-mail:* sales@cdaviesbookswales.com *Web Site:* www.cdaviesbookswales.com, pg 674

Wendy Davies (Australia) *Tel:* (0746) 622-595 *Fax:* (0746) 625-994, pg 20

DAWSON HOLDINGS PLC

Dawson Holdings PLC (United Kingdom) *Tel:* (0181) 6670770 *Fax:* (0181) 7743010 *Web Site:* dawson.investor-relations.co.uk, pg 674

Dawson UK Ltd, Books Division (United Kingdom) *Tel:* (01933) 274444 *Fax:* (01933) 225993 *E-mail:* bksales@dawson.co.uk, pg 1318

Daya Publishing House (India) *Tel:* (011) 3245578; (011) 3244987 *Fax:* (011) 7199029 *E-mail:* dayabooks@vsnl.com *Web Site:* www.dayabooks.com, pg 336

Dayi Information Co (Taiwan, Province of China) *Tel:* (02) 5796800 *Fax:* (02) 5796805, pg 629

Daystar Press (Publishers) (Nigeria) *Tel:* (022) 412670, pg 498

dbv-Druck Beratungs-und Verlags GmbH Verlag fur die Technische Universitat Graz (Austria) *Tel:* (0316) 38 30 33 *Fax:* (0316) 38 30 43 *E-mail:* office@dbv.at *Web Site:* www.dbv.at, pg 51

DC Book Club (India) *Tel:* 0481 3114; 0481 3226; 0481 8214, pg 1229

DC Books (India) *Tel:* 0481 3114; 0481 3226; 0481 8214 *E-mail:* dcbooks@sancharnet.com *Web Site:* www.dcbooks.com, pg 336

Editions De Boeck-Larcier SA (Belgium) *Tel:* (02) 482511 *Fax:* (02) 482650 *Web Site:* www.deboeck.be, pg 67

G De Bono Editore (Italy) *Tel:* (055) 570670 *Fax:* (055) 5001665, pg 384

De Cervantes Ediciones SA (Ecuador) *Tel:* (02) 223062 *Fax:* (02) 523452, pg 1282

Maria Esther De Fleischmann (Mexico) *Tel:* (05) 5852698; (05) 5852698 *Fax:* (05) 5854296 *E-mail:* fleischmann1@compuserve.com.mx, pg 459

De La Salle University (Philippines) *Tel:* (02) 7419271; (02) 594832 *Fax:* (02) 5264237 *E-mail:* mcovatg@dlsu.edu.ph, pg 513

Michel De Maule Editions (France) *Tel:* (01) 56249874, pg 158

De Plukvogel nv (Belgium) *Tel:* (02) 253-06-58 *Fax:* (02) 253-06-58, pg 1276

De Vecchi Editions SA (France) *Tel:* (01) 47204041 *Fax:* (01) 40701336, pg 158

Giovanni De Vecchi Editore SpA (Italy) *Tel:* (02) 66984851 *Fax:* (02) 6701548, pg 384

Editorial De Vecchi SA (Spain) *Tel:* (093) 272 46 70 *Fax:* (093) 487 74 94, pg 569

De Walburg Pers (Netherlands) *Tel:* (0575) 510522 *Fax:* (0575) 541025, pg 476

De Wit Stores NV (Netherlands Antilles) *Tel:* (0297) 823500 *Fax:* (0297) 821575 *E-mail:* dewitstores@sctarnet.aw, pg 488

De WitAruba Boekhandel (Netherlands Antilles) *Tel:* (0297) 823500 *Fax:* (0297) 821575, pg 1302

DEA Diffusione Edizioni Anglo-Americane (Italy) *Tel:* (06) 8551441 *Fax:* (06) 8543228 *E-mail:* deanet@deanet.it *Web Site:* www.deanet.com, pg 384

DEA Diffusione Edizioni Anglo-Americane (Italy) *Tel:* (06) 8551441 *Fax:* (06) 8543228, pg 1293

Deakin University Press (Australia) *Tel:* (03) 5227 1100 *Fax:* (03) 5227 2001 *E-mail:* lynnew@deakin.edu.au *Web Site:* www.deakin.edu.au, pg 20

Nouvelles Editions Debresse (France) *Tel:* (01) 45481047, pg 158

Debrett's Peerage Ltd (United Kingdom) *Tel:* (020) 7915 9633 *Fax:* (020) 7753 4212 *E-mail:* people@debretts.co.uk *Web Site:* www.debretts.co.uk, pg 674

Decanord (France) *Tel:* (03) 20 09 90 60 *Fax:* (03) 20 09 92 75, pg 158

La Decouverte et Syros (France) *Tel:* (01) 44 08 84 00 *Fax:* (01) 44 08 84 19 *E-mail:* ladecouverte@ladecouverte-syros.com, pg 158

Dedalo Litostampa SRL (Italy) *Tel:* (080) 5311400 *Fax:* (080) 5311414, pg 1136, 1158, 1198, 1213

Edizioni Dedalo SRL (Italy) *Tel:* (080) 5311413 *Fax:* (080) 5311414 *E-mail:* info@edizionidedalo.it *Web Site:* www.edizionidedalo.it, pg 384

Dedalus Ltd (United Kingdom) *Tel:* (01487) 832382 *Fax:* (01487) 832382 *E-mail:* sales@dedalusbooks.com *Web Site:* www.dedalusbooks.com, pg 674

Dee-Jay Publications (Ireland) *Tel:* (0402) 39125 *Fax:* (0402) 39064, pg 359

DEF (De Blauwe Vogel) NV/SA (Belgium) *Tel:* (011) 68-57-51 *Fax:* (011) 67-21-70, pg 67

Association d'Information et de Defense des Auteurs - Calcre (France) *E-mail:* secr@calcre.com *Web Site:* www.calcre.com, pg 1362

Defiant Publications (United Kingdom) *Tel:* (0121) 745 8421 *E-mail:* info@defiantpublications.co.uk *Web Site:* www.defiantpublications.co.uk, pg 675

Degener & Co, Manfred Dreiss Verlag (Germany) *Tel:* (09161) 886039 *Fax:* (09161) 1378 *E-mail:* degener@degener-verlag.com *Web Site:* www.degener-verlag.com, pg 213

Edizioni Dehoniane (Italy) *Tel:* (06) 6624996 *Fax:* (06) 6628326, pg 384

Edizioni Dehoniane Bologna (EDB) (Italy) *Tel:* (051) 306811 *Fax:* (051) 341706 *E-mail:* ced-amm@dehoniane.it, pg 384

Editorial DEI (Departamento Ecumenico de Investigaciones) (Costa Rica) *Tel:* 2530229; 2539124; 2533713; 2539142 *Fax:* 2531541 *E-mail:* asodei@sol.racsaco.cr *Web Site:* www.dei-cr.org, pg 116

Deichmanske Bibliotek (Norway) *Tel:* 22032900 *Fax:* 22113389, pg 1489

Verlag Horst Deike KG (Germany) *Tel:* (07531) 81550 *Fax:* (07531) 815581 *E-mail:* deike@deike-verlag.de *Web Site:* www.deike-verlag.de, pg 213

Editorial Deimos, SL (Spain) *Tel:* (091) 479-23-42 *Fax:* (091) 5438214 *E-mail:* editorial@deimos-es.com *Web Site:* www.deimos-es.com, pg 569

DEI Tipographia del Genio Civile (Italy) *Tel:* (06) 4402046 *Fax:* (06) 4403307 *E-mail:* dei@aec2000.it, pg 384

Maison d'Editions Cl Dejaie (Belgium) *Tel:* (081) 460748, pg 67

Dekel Publishing House (Israel) *Tel:* (03) 5230063 *Fax:* (03) 5273011 *E-mail:* dekelpbl@netvision.net.il *Web Site:* www.dekelpublishing.com, pg 366

Marcel Dekker AG (Switzerland) *Tel:* (061) 258484 *Fax:* (061) 2618896, pg 612

Dekker v d Vegt (Netherlands) *Tel:* (024) 3221010 *Fax:* (024) 3242111 *E-mail:* mariken@dekker.nl, pg 1301

Edizioni del Capricorno (Italy) *Tel:* (011) 386500 *Fax:* (011) 3853244 *E-mail:* cse@estorinese.inet.it, pg 384

Edizioni del Centro (Italy) *Tel:* (0364) 42091 *Fax:* (0364) 42572 *E-mail:* ccspriest@tin.it *Web Site:* www.rockart-ccsp.com, pg 384

Edizioni del Riccio SAS di G Bernardi (Italy) *Tel:* (055) 702020 *Fax:* (055) 716362, pg 384

Instituto del Tercer Mundo (Uruguay) *Tel:* (02) 496192 *Fax:* (02) 419222, pg 760

Del Verbo Emprender SA de CV (Mexico) *Tel:* (05) 2941160 *Fax:* (05) 2948633, pg 459

Guy Delabergerie Editions Sarl (French Guiana) *Tel:* 311162 *Fax:* 311759, pg 190

Delabie Europrint SA (Belgium) *Tel:* (056) 841306 *Fax:* (056) 840962, pg 1193

Editions Delachaux et Niestle SA (Switzerland) *Tel:* (021) 6533044 *Fax:* (021) 6534095 *E-mail:* contact@delachaux-niestle.com, pg 612

Delagrave Edition SA (France) *Tel:* (01) 44 41 89 30 *Fax:* (01) 44 41 89 39 *E-mail:* delagrave@delagrave-editions.fr *Web Site:* www.delagrave-edition.fr, pg 158

Editions Andre Delcourt & Cie (Switzerland) *Tel:* (021) 6479772; (021) 721294 *Fax:* (021) 6478831, pg 612

Guy Delcourt Productions (France) *Tel:* (01) 56-03-92-20 *Fax:* (01) 56-03-92-30 *Web Site:* www.editions-delcourt.fr, pg 158

Delectus Books (United Kingdom) *Tel:* (020) 8963 0979 *Fax:* (020) 8963 0502 *Web Site:* abebooks.com/home/DELECTUS/, pg 675

Delft University Press (Netherlands) *Tel:* (015) 2783254 *Fax:* (015) 2781661 *E-mail:* dup@dup.tudelft.nl, pg 476

Delhi Public Library (India) *Tel:* (011) 2916881, pg 1473

Delhi University Library System (India) *Tel:* (011) 7667848 *Fax:* (011) 7666404 *E-mail:* crl@delnet.ven.nic.in, pg 1473

Delhi State Booksellers' & Publishers' Association (India) *Tel:* (011) 231867; (011) 2515726 *Fax:* (011) 2936758, pg 1248

La Delirante (France) *Tel:* (01) 45 08 86 65 *Fax:* (01) 55 42 12 67, pg 158

Delius, Klasing und Co (Germany) *Tel:* (0521) 55 90 *Fax:* (0521) 55 91 13 *E-mail:* info@delius-klasing.de *Web Site:* www.delius-klasing.de, pg 213

Delius Klasing Verlag (Germany) *Tel:* (0521) 55 90 *Fax:* (0521) 55 91 13 *E-mail:* info@delius-klasing.de *Web Site:* www.delius-klasing.de, pg 213

Istituto della Enciclopedia Italiana (Italy) *Tel:* (06) 68981 *Fax:* (06) 68982175 *E-mail:* treccani5@pop.inet.it, pg 384

Casa Editrice Istituto della Santa (Italy) *Tel:* (0321) 22371, pg 384

Edizioni Della Torre di Salvatore Fozzi & C SAS (Italy) *Tel:* (070) 270507 *Fax:* (070) 270507, pg 384

Dellasta Publishing (Australia) *Tel:* (03) 9888 9188 *Fax:* (03) 9888 7806 *E-mail:* dellasta@publishaust.net.au *Web Site:* www.dellasta.com.au, pg 20

Edizioni dell'Orso SAS (Italy) *Tel:* (0131) 252349 *Fax:* (0131) 257567, pg 385

Editions Delmas (France) *Tel:* (08) 20 80 00 17 *Fax:* (01) 40 64 89 90 *E-mail:* delmas@dalloz.fr *Web Site:* www.editions-delmas.com, pg 158

Delphin Verlag GmbH (Germany) *Tel:* (02236) 39990 *Fax:* (02236) 399997, pg 213

Delp'sche Verlagsbuchhandlung (Germany) *Tel:* (09841) 9030 *Fax:* (09841) 90315, pg 213

Libreria DELSA (Spain) *Tel:* (091) 5751541 *Fax:* (091) 5758414, pg 1311

Delta Books Worldwide (United Kingdom) *Tel:* (01932) 854776 *Fax:* (01932) 849528, pg 1318

Delta Books (Pty) Ltd (South Africa) *Tel:* (011) 622-2900 *Fax:* (011) 622-7610, pg 553

Editions Delta SA (Belgium) *Tel:* (02) 217 55 55 *Fax:* (02) 217 93 93 *E-mail:* editions.delta@skynet.be, pg 67

Delta Forlags AB (Sweden) *Tel:* (08) 25 11 18, pg 601

Delta Publications (Nigeria) Ltd (Nigeria) *Tel:* (042) 3606, pg 498

Delta Science Fiction Bok Klubb (Sweden) *Tel:* (08) 254781, pg 1232

Editions Delville (France) *Tel:* (01) 42 22 72 90 *Fax:* (01) 42 22 65 62 *E-mail:* editions.delville@wanadoo.fr, pg 158

Georges-Charles Demay (France) *Tel:* (01) 69 48 92 54 *Fax:* (01) 69 49 56 08, pg 158

Demeter (Tunisia) *Tel:* (01) 893083; (01) 283579 *Fax:* (01) 787516, pg 637

Demetra SRL (Italy) *Tel:* (045) 6174111 *Fax:* (045) 6174100, pg 385

Editions du Demi-Cercle (France) *Tel:* (01) 42330685 *Fax:* (01) 42330862, pg 158

Demonvamp Publications (Australia) *Tel:* (03) 98023875, pg 20

Den Norske Bokhandlerforening (Norway) *Tel:* 22007580 *Fax:* 22333830 *E-mail:* dfn@forleggerforeningen.no *Web Site:* www.forleggerforeningen.no, pg 1256

Fundacion Omar Dengo (Costa Rica) *Tel:* 257 6263 *Fax:* 2221654 *E-mail:* info@fod.ac.cr *Web Site:* www.fod.ac.cr, pg 116

Denkmayr GmbH Druck & Verlag (Austria) *Tel:* (0732) 654511 *Fax:* (0732) 65612417, pg 51

Editions Denoel Sarl (France) *Tel:* (01) 44 39 73 72 *Fax:* (01) 44397390, pg 158

Denor Press (United Kingdom) *Tel:* (020) 8343 7368 *Fax:* (020) 8446 4504 *E-mail:* denor@dial.pipex.com *Web Site:* www.xhf37.dial.pipex.com, pg 675

Verlag Harald Denzel, Auto- und Freizeitfuehrer (Austria) *Tel:* (0512) 586880 *Fax:* (0512) 586880, pg 51

Depalma SRL (Argentina) *Tel:* (011) 371-7306 *Fax:* (011) 371-6913 *E-mail:* info@ed-depalma.com *Web Site:* www.ed-depalma.com, pg 5

Departamento de Documentacion y Bibliotecas (Dominican Republic), pg 1514

Departamento Nacional do Livro (Brazil) *Tel:* (021) 2544 85 97; (021) 2544 85 14; (021) 2544 87 03 *Fax:* (021) 2220 10 09; (021) 2240 79 29 *E-mail:* dnl@bn.br *Web Site:* www.bn.br, pg 1239

Departemento de Publicaciones de la Universidad de la Republica (Uruguay) *Tel:* (02) 485714 *Fax:* (02) 480303, pg 760

Department for Education & Children's Services, South Australia (Australia) *Tel:* (08) 3770399 *Fax:* (08) 3770341, pg 20

Department of Arts, Culture, Science and Technology (South Africa) *Tel:* (012) 3146033; (012) 3146032; (012) 3146031 *Fax:* (012) 3232720 *E-mail:* ab02@acts1.pwv.gov.2a, pg 1497

Department of Census & Statistics (Sri Lanka) *Tel:* (01) 692988; (01) 595291 *Fax:* (01) 687931, pg 596

Department of Culture & Information Government of Sharjah (United Arab Emirates) *Tel:* (06) 541116 *Fax:* (06) 362126 *E-mail:* shjbookfair@shariah-welcome.com, pg 643

Department of Energy (NSW) (Australia) *Tel:* (02) 9901 8888 *Fax:* (02) 9901 8777 *Web Site:* www.doe.nsw.gov.au, pg 20

Department of National Museums (Sri Lanka) *Tel:* (01) 595366, pg 597

Department of Primary Industries, Queensland (Australia) *Tel:* (07) 32393772 *Fax:* (07) 32396509 *E-mail:* books@dpi.qld.gov.au *Web Site:* www.dpi.qld.gov.au, pg 20

The Department of the National Library (Jordan) *Tel:* (06) 610311 *Fax:* (06) 616832, pg 1479

Dervy-Livres (France) *Tel:* (01) 42 79 10 89 *Fax:* (01) 42 79 19 37, pg 158

Derzhavne Naukovo-Vyrobnyche Pidpryemstro Kartografia (Ukraine) *Tel:* (044) 5524033 *Fax:* (044) 2388314 *E-mail:* admin@ukrmap.com.ua *Web Site:* www.ukrmap.com.ua, pg 643

Editorial Desarrollo SA (Peru) *Tel:* (01) 285380; (01) 286628 *Fax:* (01) 286628, pg 511

Desbooks Pty Ltd (Australia) *Tel:* (03) 94842465 *Fax:* (03) 94843877 *E-mail:* desb@alphalink.com.au, pg 20

Deschamps Imprimerie (Haiti) *Tel:* 57-8999; 57-3596; 56-3853; 56-2253 *E-mail:* henrid@acn2.net, pg 317

Desclee de Brouwer SA (France) *Tel:* (01) 45 49 61 92 *Fax:* (01) 42 22 61 41 *E-mail:* direction@descleedebrouwer.com *Web Site:* www.descleedebrouwer.com, pg 158

Espanola Desclee De Brouwer SA (Spain) *Tel:* (094) 4233045; (094) 4246843 *Fax:* (094) 4237594 *E-mail:* desclee@tsai.es *Web Site:* www.desclee.com, pg 569

Desclee et Cie, Editeurs (France) *Tel:* (01) 45443834 *Fax:* (01) 45499392, pg 159

Desert Research Foundation of Namibia (DRFN) (Namibia) *Tel:* (061) 229855 *Fax:* (061) 230172 *E-mail:* drfn@drfn.org.na, pg 471

Design & Artists Copyright Society (DACS) (United Kingdom) *Tel:* (020) 7336 8811 *Fax:* (020) 7336 8822 *E-mail:* info@dacs.co.uk *Web Site:* www.dacs.co.uk, pg 1265

Design Human Resources Training & Development (Hong Kong) *Tel:* (02) 29877018 *Fax:* (02) 29877018, pg 319

Designer Publisher Inc (Taiwan, Province of China) *Tel:* (02) 23656268 *Fax:* (02) 23676500, pg 629

Desktop Miracles Inc (United States) *Tel:* 802-253-7900 *Fax:* 802-253-1900 *Web Site:* www.desktopmiracles.com, pg 1164, 1215, 1224

Deslogish-Lacoste (France) *Tel:* (01) 53 40 53 53 *Fax:* (01) 42 33 82 47 *Web Site:* www.bertrand-lacoste.fr, pg 159

Ediciones Desnivel, SL (Spain) *Tel:* (091) 3602242 *Fax:* (091) 3602263 *E-mail:* direccion.desnivel@desnivel.com *Web Site:* www.desnivel.com, pg 569

Dessain - Departement de De Boeck & Larcier SA (Belgium) *Tel:* (02) 48 25 11 *Fax:* (02) 48 26 50 *E-mail:* dbw@deboeck.be *Web Site:* www.adeb.irisnet.be, pg 68

Dessain et Tolra SA (France) *Tel:* (01) 44 39 44 00 *Fax:* (01) 44 39 43 43, pg 159

Destarte, Lda (Portugal) *Tel:* (021) 3465155 *Fax:* (021) 3475811 *E-mail:* destarte@esoterica.pt, pg 1307

Ediciones Destino SA (Spain) *Tel:* (093) 496 70 01 *Fax:* (093) 496 70 02 *E-mail:* edicionesdestino@stl.logiccontrol.es *Web Site:* www.edestino.es, pg 569

Editions Desvigne (France) *Tel:* (01) 30 14 19 30 *Fax:* (01) 34 60 31 32 *E-mail:* info@casteilla.fr *Web Site:* www.casteilla.fr, pg 159

Det Norske Samlaget (Norway) *Tel:* 22687600 *Fax:* 22687502 *E-mail:* det.norske@samlaget.no *Web Site:* www.samlaget.no, pg 503

Detska radost (The Former Yugoslav Republic of Macedonia) *Tel:* (091) 112394; (091) 213059 *Fax:* (091) 225830; (091) 213059, pg 448

Izdatelstvo Detskaya Literatura (Russian Federation) *Tel:* (095) 9280803 *Fax:* (095) 9213007, pg 537

Franz Deuticke Verlagsges mbH (Austria) *Tel:* (01) 51405210 *Fax:* (01) 51405289 *Web Site:* www.deuticke.at, pg 51

Andre Deutsch Ltd (United Kingdom) *Tel:* (020) 7316 4450 *Fax:* (020) 7316 4499, pg 675

Verlag fuer Deutsch GmbH (Germany) *Tel:* (089) 9602-0 *Fax:* (089) 9602-358, pg 213

Verlag Harri Deutsch (Switzerland) *Tel:* (033) 2223975 *Fax:* (033) 2223950 *E-mail:* verlag@harri-deutsch.de, pg 612

Verlag Harri Deutsch (Germany) *Tel:* (069) 77015860 *Fax:* (069) 77015869 *E-mail:* verlag@harri-deutsch.de *Web Site:* www.harri-deutsch.de, pg 213

Deutsche Akademie fuer Sprache und Dichtung (Germany) *Tel:* (06151) 40920 *Fax:* (06151) 409299 *E-mail:* Deutsche.Akademie@T-Online.de *Web Site:* www.deutscheakademie.de, pg 1363

Deutsche Bibelgesellschaft (Germany) *Tel:* (0711) 7181-0 *Fax:* (0711) 7181-250 *E-mail:* infoabt@dbg.de *Web Site:* www.dbg.de, pg 213

Die Deutsche Bibliothek (Germany) *Tel:* (069) 15250 *Fax:* (069) 15251010 *E-mail:* info@dma.ddb.de *Web Site:* www.ddb.de, pg 1466

Die Deutsche Bibliothek/Deutsche Buecherei Leipzig (Germany) *Tel:* (069) 15250 *Fax:* (069) 15251010 *E-mail:* info@dbf.ddb.de *Web Site:* www.ddb.de, pg 213

Deutsche Blinden-Bibliothek (Germany) *Tel:* (06421) 6060 *Fax:* (06421) 606229 *E-mail:* info@blista.de *Web Site:* www.blista.de, pg 213

Deutsche Buch-Gemeinschaft C A Koch's Verlag Nachfolger (Austria) *Tel:* (01) 8123730 *Fax:* (01) 811024, pg 1227

Deutsche Exlibris Gesellschaft ev (Germany) *Tel:* (0261) 57885 *Fax:* (0261) 9523494 *Web Site:* www.exlibris-gesellschaft.de, pg 1516

Deutsche Gesellschaft fuer Eisenbahngeschichte eV (Germany) *Tel:* (02922) 84970 *Fax:* (02922) 84927 *E-mail:* gs@dgeg.de *Web Site:* www.dgeg.de, pg 213

Deutsche Gesellschaft fuer Luft-und Raumfahrt Lilienthal Oberth eV (Germany) *Tel:* (0228) 30 80 5-0 *Fax:* (0228) 30 80 5-24 *E-mail:* geschaeftsstelle@dglr.de *Web Site:* www.dglr.de, pg 213

Deutsche Gesellschaft fur Informationswissenschaft und informationspraxis eV (Germany) *Tel:* (069) 430313 *Fax:* (069) 4909096 *E-mail:* dgd@darmstadt.gmd.de *Web Site:* www.dgd.de, pg 1516

Deutsche Landwirtschaft-Gesellschaft VerlagsgesGmbH (Germany) *Tel:* (069) 24788-0 *Fax:* (069) 24788-480 *E-mail:* dlg-verlag@dlg-frankfurt.de *Web Site:* www.dlg-verlag.de, pg 214

Verlag Deutsche Unitarier (Germany) *Tel:* (0751) 6 25 96 *Fax:* (0751) 6 72 01 *E-mail:* verlag@unitarier.de *Web Site:* www.unitarier.de, pg 214

Deutsche Verlags-Anstalt GmbH (DVA) (Germany) *Tel:* (0711) 2631-0 *Fax:* (0711) 2631-292 *E-mail:* info@dva.de *Web Site:* www.dva.de, pg 214

Deutsche Zentralbibliothek fuer Wirtschaftswissenschaften (ZBW)/Bibliothek des Instituts fuer Weltwirtschaft (Germany) *Tel:* (0431) 8814-383 *Fax:* (0431) 8814520 *E-mail:* info@zbw.ifw-kiel.de, pg 1467

Deutscher Adressbuch-Verlag fuer Wirtschaft und Verkehr GmbH (Germany) *Tel:* (06154) 699500 *Fax:* (06154) 6995480; (06154) 6995490 *E-mail:* info@businessdeutschland.de *Web Site:* www.businessdeutschland.de, pg 214

Deutscher Aerzte-Verlag GmbH (Germany) *Tel:* (02234) 7011-0 *Fax:* (02234) 7011-398; (02234) 7011-475 *E-mail:* zielinka@aerzteverlag.de *Web Site:* www.aerzteverlag.de, pg 214

Deutscher Apotheker Verlag (Germany) *Tel:* (0711) 2582-0 *Fax:* (0711) 2582-290 *E-mail:* service@deutscher-pharmacist-verlag.de *Web Site:* www.deutscher-apotheker-verlag.de, pg 214

Deutscher Betriebswirte-Verlag GmbH (Germany) *Tel:* (07224) 9397-151 *Fax:* (07224) 9397-251 *E-mail:* info@betriebswirte-verlag.de *Web Site:* www.betriebswirte-verlag.de, pg 214

Deutscher Bibliotheksverband eV (DBV) (Germany) *Tel:* (030) 39001480 *Fax:* (030) 39001484 *E-mail:* dbv@bdbibl.de *Web Site:* www.bdbibl.de/bv, pg 1516

Deutscher Buchkreis (Germany) *Tel:* (07071) 96590 *Fax:* (07071) 965965, pg 1228

Deutscher Bundestag Bibliothek (Germany) *Tel:* (030) 22732372 *Fax:* (030) 22736087 *Web Site:* www.bundestag.de, pg 1467

DEUTSCHER DRUCKER VERLAGSGESELLSCHAFT INDUSTRY

Deutscher Drucker Verlagsgesellschaft (Germany) *Tel:* (0711) 448170 *Fax:* (0711) 442099 *E-mail:* info@publish.de *Web Site:* www.publish.de, pg 214

Deutscher EC-Verband (Germany) *Tel:* (0561) 40950 *Fax:* (0561) 4095112 *E-mail:* info.dv@ec-jugend.de *Web Site:* www.ec-jugend.de, pg 214

Deutscher Fachverlag GmbH (Germany) *Tel:* (069) 7595-01 *Fax:* (069) 75952999 *E-mail:* zilling@dfu.de *Web Site:* www.dfv.de, pg 214

Deutscher Gemeindeverlag GmbH (Germany) *Tel:* (02234) 1060 *Fax:* (02234) 106284, pg 214

Deutscher Instituts-Verlag GmbH (Germany) *Tel:* (0221) 49 81-0 *Fax:* (0221) 49 81 *E-mail:* div@iwkoeln.de *Web Site:* www.divkoeln.de, pg 215

Deutscher Klassiker Verlag (Germany) *Tel:* (069) 75601-0 *Fax:* (069) 75601-522 *Web Site:* www.suhrkamp.de, pg 215

Deutscher Komponisten-Interessenverband eV (Germany) *Tel:* (030) 84 31 05 80 *Fax:* (030) 84 31 05 82 *Web Site:* www.dkiv.allmusic.de, pg 1245

Deutscher Kunstverlag GmbH (Germany) *Tel:* (089) 121516-0; (089) 12516-22; (089) 12516-24 *Fax:* (089) 121516-10; (089) 121516-16 *E-mail:* vertrieb@deutscher-kunstverlag.ccn.de, pg 215

Deutscher Literatur-Verlag (Germany) *Tel:* (040) 6 28 95-0 *Fax:* (040) 68 28 95 50 *E-mail:* info@kelter.de *Web Site:* www.kelter.de, pg 215

Deutscher Literaturfonds eV (Germany) *Tel:* (06151) 40930 *Fax:* (06151) 409333 *Web Site:* stadt.darmstadt.gmd.de/kultur/literatur/lit-fond.html, pg 1363

Deutscher Psychologen Verlag GmbH (DPV) (Germany) *Tel:* (0228) 987310 *Fax:* (0228) 641023 *E-mail:* service@bdp-verband.org *Web Site:* www.bdp-verband.org, pg 215

Deutscher Sparkassenverlag GmbH (Germany) *Tel:* (0711) 782-21 02 *Fax:* (0711) 782-16 35 *Web Site:* www.dsv-gruppe.de, pg 215

Deutscher Studien Verlag (Germany) *Tel:* (06201) 60070 *Fax:* (06201) 6007-310 *E-mail:* info@beltz.de *Web Site:* www.beltz.de, pg 215

Deutscher Taschenbuch Verlag GmbH & Co KG (dtv) (Germany) *Tel:* (089) 38167-0 *Fax:* (089) 346428 *E-mail:* info@dtv.de *Web Site:* www.dtv.de, pg 215

Deutscher Universitats-Verlag (Germany) *Tel:* (0611) 7878-239 *Fax:* (0611) 7878-411 *Web Site:* www.duv.de, pg 215

Deutscher Verband Evangelischer Buchereien eV (Germany) *Tel:* (0551) 5007590 *Fax:* (0551) 704415 *E-mail:* dveb@evlka.de, pg 1516

Deutscher Verlag fur Grundstoffindustrie GmbH (Germany) *Tel:* (0711) 8931-0 *Fax:* (0711) 8931-410 *E-mail:* custserv@thieme.de *Web Site:* www.thieme.de, pg 215

Deutscher Verlag fur Kunstwissenschaft GmbH (Germany) *Tel:* (030) 25913864; (030) 25913865 *Fax:* (030) 25913537, pg 215

Deutscher Wanderverlag Dr Mair & Schnabel & Co (Germany) *Tel:* (0711) 455005 *Fax:* (0711) 4569952, pg 215

Deutscher Wirtschaftsdienst John von Freyend GmbH (Germany) *Tel:* (0221) 93763-0 *Fax:* (0221) 93763-99 *E-mail:* box@dwd-verlag.de *Web Site:* www.dwd-verlag.de, pg 216

Deutsches Bibliotheksinstitut (Germany) *Tel:* (030) 41034-0 *Fax:* (030) 403410-0 *E-mail:* www@dbi-berlin.de, pg 1516

Deutsches Bucharchiv Munchen, Institut fur Buchwissenschaften (Germany) *Tel:* (089) 7901220 *Fax:* (089) 7901419 *E-mail:* kontakt@bucharchiv.de *Web Site:* www.bucharchiv.de, pg 1467

Deutsches Bucharchiv Muenchen, Institut fur Buchwissenschaften (Germany) *Tel:* (089) 291951-0 *Fax:* (089) 291951-95 *E-mail:* kontakt@bucharchiv.de *Web Site:* www.bucharchiv.de, pg 216

Deutsches Jugendinstitut (DJI) (Germany) *Tel:* (089) 62306-241 *Fax:* (089) 62306-265 *Web Site:* www.dji.de, pg 216

Deutsches PEN-Zentrum (Ost) (Germany) *Tel:* (030) 304413904 *Fax:* (030) 304413904, pg 1363

Deutschklub (United Kingdom) *Tel:* (01642) 813467 *Fax:* (01642) 865943, pg 1128

Les Editions des Deux Coqs d'Or (France) *Tel:* (01) 43923334 *Fax:* (01) 43923338, pg 159

Deva Wings Publications (Australia) *Tel:* (03) 5348 1414 *Fax:* (03) 5348 1414 *E-mail:* devawings@netconnect.com.au *Web Site:* www.spacountry.net.au/devawings/, pg 20

Development News Ltd (Austria) *Tel:* (01) 3880324, pg 51

Development Study Center (Israel) *Tel:* (08) 474111 *Fax:* (08) 475884 *E-mail:* dsc@netvision.net.il, pg 1476

Institut pour le Developpement Forestier (France) *Tel:* (01) 40622280 *Fax:* (01) 45559854 *E-mail:* paris@association-idf.com, pg 159

Devenirs Visuels SA (France) *Tel:* (01) 47 70 60 02 *Fax:* (01) 47 70 60 03, pg 159

Librairie Deves et Chaumet (Mali), pg 1298

Perpustakaan Dewan Perwakilan Rakyat - RI (Indonesia) *Tel:* (021) 5715220 *Fax:* (021) 5715884, pg 1474

Dewan Bahasa dan Pustaka (Malaysia) *Tel:* (03) 21481011; (03) 2481820 *Fax:* (03) 21443875 *Web Site:* www.dbp.gov.my, pg 451

Dewan Bahasa dan Pustaka (Malaysia) *Tel:* (03) 21481011; (03) 2481820 *Fax:* (03) 21443875, pg 1366

Dewan Pustaka Islam (Malaysia) *Tel:* (03) 7557225 *Fax:* (03) 7586439, pg 451

Dexia Bank (Belgium) *Tel:* (02) 222 54 89 *Fax:* (02) 222 57 52, pg 68

Dhaka Book Mart (Bangladesh) *Tel:* (02) 259173, pg 1275

Dhaka University Library (Bangladesh) *Tel:* (02) 505789 *Fax:* (02) 865583, pg 1452

Dharma Edition, Tibetisches Zentrum (Germany) *Tel:* (040) 6443585 *Fax:* (040) 6443515 *E-mail:* tz@tibet.de *Web Site:* www.tibet.de, pg 216

The Dharmasthiti Buddist Institute Ltd (Hong Kong) *Tel:* (02) 7608878 *Fax:* (02) 7610825 *E-mail:* dharma@glink.nethk *Web Site:* www.glink.net.hk/~dharma, pg 319

Dhillon Publishers Ltd, Paa Crescent (Kenya) *Tel:* (02) 505393, pg 431

di animali V (Germany) *Tel:* (0911) 951 9490 *Fax:* (0911) 951 9489 *E-mail:* di.animali@web.de, pg 216

Di Baio Editore SpA (Italy) *Tel:* (02) 6692254 *Fax:* (02) 6709257, pg 385

Edition Dia (Germany) *Tel:* (030) 6235021; (030) 6235022 *Fax:* (030) 6235023 *E-mail:* info@editiondia.de *Web Site:* www.editiondia.de, pg 216

Diachronikes Ekdoseis (Greece) *Tel:* (01) 7213225 *Fax:* (01) 7246180, pg 309

Editorial Diagonal (Spain) *Tel:* (093) 443 71 00 *Fax:* (093) 443 71 30 *E-mail:* correu@grup62.com *Web Site:* www.grup62.com, pg 569

Diagonal-Verlag GbR Rink-Schweer (Germany) *Tel:* (06421) 681936 *Fax:* (06421) 681944 *E-mail:* info@diagonal-verlag.de *Web Site:* www.diagonal-verlag.de, pg 216

The Diagram Group (United Kingdom) *Tel:* (020) 7482 3633 *Fax:* (020) 7482 4932 *E-mail:* diagramuis@aol.com, pg 1161

Diagram Visual Information Ltd (United Kingdom) *Tel:* (020) 74823633 *Fax:* (020) 74824932 *E-mail:* diagramuis@aol.com, pg 675, 1118

Diakronia (Italy) *Tel:* (0381) 83034 *Fax:* (0381) 690576, pg 385

Dialog-Verlag GmbH (Germany) *Tel:* (040) 7111424 *Fax:* (040) 7101267, pg 216

Diamond Comics (P) Ltd (India) *Tel:* 4580372; 4580834; 4583939 *Fax:* 4580372, pg 336

Diamond Inc (Japan) *Tel:* (03) 35046505 *Fax:* (03) 35046397, pg 416

PT Dian Rakyat (Indonesia) *Tel:* (021) 4604444, pg 355

Diana Argentina SA, Editorial (Argentina) *Tel:* (011) 4922-5035; (011) 4922-5036 *Fax:* (011) 4922-5035; (011) 4922-5036 *E-mail:* todianaarg@sinectis.com.ar, pg 5

Editorial Diana SA de CV (Mexico) *Tel:* (055) 5089-1220 *Fax:* (052) 5089-1230 *E-mail:* 4sales@diana.com.mx; editors@diana.com.mx, pg 459

Diario la Voz del Interior (Argentina) *Tel:* (011) 4382-2267 *Fax:* (011) 3822508 *E-mail:* info@nueva.com.ar, pg 5

Diavlos (Greece) *Tel:* (01) 3631169 *Fax:* (01) 3617473 *E-mail:* info@diavlos-books.gr *Web Site:* www.diavlos-books.gr, pg 309

Diavlos (Greece) *Tel:* (01) 3631169 *Fax:* (01) 3617473 *E-mail:* info@diavlos-books.gr *Web Site:* www.otenet.gr/diavlos, pg 1286

Ediciones Diaz de Santos SA (Spain) *Tel:* (091) 431-24-82 *Fax:* (091) 575-55-63, pg 569

Diaz de Santos SA - Libreria Cientifico-Tecnica (Spain) *Tel:* (091) 4312482 *Fax:* (091) 5755563, pg 1311

Editorial Ruy Diaz SAEIC (Argentina) *Tel:* (011) 4567-4055; (011) 4567-2865 *Fax:* (011) 4567-4918 *E-mail:* ruydiaz@pinos.com *Web Site:* www.ruydiaz.com.ar, pg 5

The Dickens Fellowship (United Kingdom) *Tel:* (020) 7405 2127 *Fax:* (020) 7831 5175, pg 1370

Dickson Price Publishers Ltd (United Kingdom) *Tel:* (01797) 344626 *Fax:* (01797) 344668, pg 675

Dictionnaires Le Robert (France) *Tel:* (01) 45 87 43 20 *Fax:* (01) 45 87 32 33 *Web Site:* www.lerobert.com.fr, pg 159

Didaco Comunicacion y Didactica, SA (Spain) *Tel:* (093) 237 64 00 *Fax:* (093) 218 92 77 *E-mail:* didaco@cambrabcn.es *Web Site:* www.didaco.es, pg 569

Didactica Editora (Portugal) *Tel:* (021) 3011731 *Fax:* (021) 3014887, pg 524

Editura Didactica si Pedagogica (Romania) *Tel:* (01) 3122885 *Fax:* (01) 3122885 *E-mail:* edpdirector@mail.codecnet.ro, pg 532

Organizzazione Didattica Editoriale Ape (Italy) *Tel:* (055) 392670; (055) 689295 *Fax:* (055) 343485; (055) 683760, pg 385

Diderot sro (Czech Republic) *Tel:* (02) 66035757; (02) 21841004 *Fax:* (02) 66035381; (02) 21841001 *E-mail:* fialkovam@bp.diderot.cz *Web Site:* www.diderot.cz, pg 124

Die Deutsche Bibliothek/Deutsche Bucherei Leipzig (Germany) *Tel:* (0341) 22710 *Fax:* (0341) 2271444 *E-mail:* info@dbl.ddb.de *Web Site:* www.ddb.de, pg 1467

Die Verlag H Schafer GmbH (Germany) *Tel:* (06172) 95830 *Fax:* (06172) 71288 *E-mail:* dieverlag@t-online.de, pg 216

Eugen Diederichs Verlag GmbH & Co KG (Germany) *Tel:* (089) 51480 *Fax:* (089) 5148111, pg 216

Dienst Bibliotheek en Archief (Netherlands) *Tel:* (070) 3534455 *Fax:* (070) 3534504 *E-mail:* sear@dbadenhaag.nl, pg 1486

Diesterweg, Moritz Verlag (Germany) *Tel:* (069) 42081-0 *Fax:* (069) 42081-200 *Web Site:* www.diesterweg.de, pg 216

Sammlung Dieterich Verlagsgesellschaft mbH (Germany) *Tel:* (0341) 9954600 *Fax:* (0341) 9954620 *E-mail:* info@aufbau-verlag.de *Web Site:* www.aufbau-verlag.de, pg 216

Dieterichsche Verlagsbuchhandlung Mainz (Germany) *Tel:* (06131) 573276 *Fax:* (06131) 571061 *E-mail:* DVB-mainz@t-online.de, pg 216

Maximilian Dietrich Verlag (Germany) *Tel:* (08331) 2853 *Fax:* (08331) 490364, pg 216

Dietrich zu Klampen Verlag (Germany) *Tel:* (04131) 733030 *Fax:* (04131) 733033 *E-mail:* info@zuklampen.de *Web Site:* www.dan4u.de/zuklampen, pg 216

Dietz GmbH (Austria) *Tel:* (0222) 5875772 *Fax:* (02236) 47127, pg 1274

Verlag J H W Dietz Nachf GmbH (Germany) *Tel:* (0228) 23 80 83 *Fax:* (0228) 23 41 04 *E-mail:* info@dietz-verlag.de *Web Site:* www.dietz-verlag.de, pg 217

Dietz Verlag Berlin GmbH (Germany) *Tel:* (030) 248409290 *Fax:* (030) 28409590, pg 217

DIFEL - Difusao Editorial SA (Portugal) *Tel:* (021) 4120848 *Fax:* (021) 4120849 *E-mail:* difel.sa@netc.pt, pg 524

Editions de la Difference (France) *Tel:* (01) 53 38 85 38 *Fax:* (01) 42 45 34 94 *E-mail:* editions-de-la-difference@wanadoo.fr *Web Site:* www.ladifference.fr, pg 159

Difros Publications (Greece) *Tel:* (01) 3610811, pg 309

Difusao Cultural (Portugal) *Tel:* (021) 3173620 *Fax:* (021) 3528215, pg 524

Digital Publishing (Germany) *Tel:* (089) 747482-0 *Fax:* (089) 74792308 *E-mail:* info@digitalpublishing.de *Web Site:* www.digitalpublishing.de, pg 217

Digma Publications (South Africa) *Tel:* (011) 8834854 *Fax:* (011) 8836540, pg 554

Dilagro SA (Spain) *Tel:* (0973) 24 51 00; (0973) 23 34 80 *Fax:* (0973) 23 64 13 *Web Site:* www.dilagro.com, pg 569

Le Dilettante (France) *Tel:* (01) 43-37-98-98 *Fax:* (01) 43-37-06-10 *E-mail:* info@ledilettante.com *Web Site:* www.ledilettante.com, pg 159

DILIA (Czech Republic) *Tel:* (02) 826444; (02) 8268418 *Fax:* (02) 824009, pg 1110

Dilicom (France) *Tel:* (01) 43254335 *Fax:* (01) 43297688 *E-mail:* dilicom@edilectre.fr *Web Site:* www.dilicom.net, pg 159

Dilicom (France) *Tel:* (01) 43254335 *Fax:* (01) 43297688 *E-mail:* bf@edilectre.fr *Web Site:* www.dilicom.net, pg 1243

Diligentia-Uitgeverij (Belgium) *Tel:* (052) 44 45 11 *Fax:* (052) 44 45 22 *E-mail:* diligentia.book@planetinternet.be, pg 68

Dillons, The Bookstore (United Kingdom) *Tel:* (0121) 6314333, pg 1318

Dillons City Business Book Store (United Kingdom) *Tel:* (020) 7628 7479 *Fax:* (020) 7628 7871 *E-mail:* loncbus@dillons.eunet.co.uk, pg 1319

Editorial Dimensao Ltda (Brazil) *Tel:* (021) 2263-3077 *Fax:* (021) 2263-3123 *E-mail:* memoria@ig.com.br, pg 81

Dimension World Ltd (Switzerland) *Tel:* (061) 3225214 *Fax:* (061) 3133862, pg 612

Dimenze 2 Plus 2 Praha (Czech Republic) *Tel:* (02) 231 11 41 *Fax:* (02) 231 11 41, pg 124

Dinalivro (Portugal) *Tel:* (021) 670348 *Fax:* (021) 3908489 *E-mail:* dinalivro@ip.pt, pg 524

Dinapress (Portugal) *Tel:* (021) 608992 *Fax:* (021) 608992 *E-mail:* dinalivro@ip.pt, pg 1307

Dinastindo (Indonesia) *Tel:* (021) 7250002; (021) 72799307 *Fax:* (021) 7262145 *E-mail:* dinastindo@yahoo.com *Web Site:* www.dinastindo.net, pg 355

Dingfelder-Verlag Inh Gerd Gmelin (Germany) *Tel:* (08152) 6671 *Fax:* (08152) 5120 *Web Site:* www.gmelin-verlag.de, pg 217

Dinsic Publicacions Musicals (Spain) *Tel:* (093) 3180605 *Fax:* (093) 4120501 *E-mail:* dinsic@dinsic.com *Web Site:* www.dinsic.com/, pg 570

Diogenes Verlag AG (Switzerland) *Tel:* (01) 254 85 11 *Fax:* (01) 252 84 07 *E-mail:* info@diogenes.ch *Web Site:* www.diogenes.ch, pg 612

Dion (Greece) *Tel:* (031) 265042 *Fax:* (031) 265083 *E-mail:* dionbook@otenet.gr *Web Site:* www.psarasbooks.gr, pg 1286

Dionysis Noti Karavias (Greece) *Tel:* (01) 3620465 *Fax:* (01) 3620465, pg 309

Dioptra Publishing (Greece) *Tel:* (01) 33 02 828 *Fax:* (01) 3302882 *E-mail:* info@dioptra.gov *Web Site:* www.dioptra.gr/english/main.htm, pg 309

Diotima Presse (Austria) *Tel:* (043) 2747-8528 *Fax:* (043) 2747-8528 *E-mail:* diotimapresse@utanet.at, pg 51

Dipa-Verlag GmbH (Germany) *Tel:* (069) 95732044 *Fax:* (069) 576128, pg 217

Dipak Kumar Guha (India) *Tel:* (011) 5500998 *Fax:* (011) 6880198; (011) 6117058 *E-mail:* dkginfo@bol.net.in, pg 1112

Diponegoro CV (Indonesia) *Tel:* (022) 5201215 *Fax:* (022) 5201215, pg 355

Ediciones Diputacion de Salamanca (Spain) *Tel:* (0923) 29 31 00 *Fax:* (0923) 29 31 29 *E-mail:* ediciones@dipsanet.es *Web Site:* www.dipsanet.es, pg 570

Diputacion Provincial de Cordoba (Spain) *Tel:* (0957) 329646 *Fax:* (057) 211308, pg 570

Diputacion Provincial de Malaga (Spain) *Tel:* (0952) 069 207 *Fax:* (0952) 069 215 *E-mail:* cedma@cedma.com *Web Site:* cedma.com, pg 570

Diputacion Provincial de Sevilla, Servicio de Publicaciones (Spain) *Tel:* (095) 4550029 *Fax:* (095) 4550050 *E-mail:* caba174@dipusevilla.es *Web Site:* www.dipusevilla.es, pg 570

Direccao Provincial Servicos de Geologia e Minas de Angola Biblioteca (Angola) *Tel:* (02) 322766, pg 1449

Direccao Geral Familia (Portugal) *Tel:* (021) 8470430 *Fax:* (021) 8491516, pg 524

Direccao Nacional de Geologia (Centro de Documentacao) (Mozambique) *Tel:* (01) 424031-4; (01) 420797 *Fax:* (01) 429216 *E-mail:* geologia@zebra.uem.mz, pg 1485

Biblioteca de la Direccion de Cultura (Bolivia), pg 1454

Direccion General de Publicaciones CNCA Coordinacion Juridica (Mexico) *Tel:* (05) 6056565; (05) 6058589 *Fax:* (05) 6058731, pg 460

Direction de la Recherche Scientifique et Techniques (Guinea) *Tel:* (04) 461010, pg 1517

Direction des Archives Nationales, Bibliotheque Publique et Centre du Documentation (Mauritania) *Tel:* 52317 (ext 32), pg 1484

Direction des Archives Nationales du Benin (Benin) *Tel:* 213079 *Fax:* 213079, pg 1454

Direction du Patrimoine (France) *Tel:* (01) 40-15-80-00 *Fax:* (01) 42606673 *Web Site:* www.culture.gouv.fr, pg 159

Direction Generale des Archives Nationales, de la Bibliotheque Nationale et de la Documentation Gabonaise (DGABD) (Gabon) *Tel:* 736310 *Fax:* 730972, pg 1466

Direction Generale des Services de Bibliotheques, Archives et Documentation (Congo) *Tel:* 833485, pg 1513

The Director State Library (South Africa) *Tel:* (012) 218931 *Fax:* (012) 3255984 *E-mail:* rhona@statelib.pwv.gov.za, pg 1258

Directory & Database Publishers Association (United Kingdom) *Tel:* (020) 8846 9707 *Fax:* (020) 0870 168 0552 *Web Site:* www.directory-publisher.co.uk, pg 1265

Direzione Generale Archivi (Italy) *Tel:* (06) 4742177 *Fax:* (06) 4742177 *E-mail:* studi@archivi.beniculturali.it *Web Site:* www.archivi.beniculturali.it, pg 385

Editions Dis Voir (France) *Tel:* (01) 48 87 07 09 *Fax:* (01) 48 87 07 14 *E-mail:* disvoir@aol.com *Web Site:* www.disvoir.com, pg 159

Disal S/A Distribuidores Asssociados de Livros (Brazil) *Tel:* (011) 2211011 *Fax:* (011) 2230306 *E-mail:* disal@disal.com.br *Web Site:* www.disal.com.br, pg 1277

Discordia Verlagsgesellschaft mbH (Germany) *Tel:* (02291) 911024 *Fax:* (02291) 911925, pg 217

Discovery Walking Guides Ltd (United Kingdom) *Tel:* (01604) 752576 *Web Site:* www.walking.demon.co.uk, pg 675

Diseno Editorial SA (Spain) *Tel:* (091) 918903936 *Fax:* (091) 918903936, pg 570

Disha Prakashan (India), pg 336

Edition Diskord (Germany) *Tel:* (07071) 40102 *Fax:* (07071) 44710 *E-mail:* ed.diskord@t-online.de *Web Site:* www.edition-diskord.de, pg 217

Editorial Dismar (Uruguay) *Tel:* (02) 407946, pg 760

Disney Hachette Edition (France) *Tel:* (01) 53898500 *Fax:* (01) 45632201, pg 159

Disney Junior Bokklubb (Norway) *Tel:* 22471000 *Fax:* 22471098, pg 1231

Distique (France) *Tel:* 37305700 *Fax:* 37305712, pg 1283

Distri Cultural Lda (Portugal) *Tel:* (01) 9425394 *Fax:* (01) 9425214, pg 524, 1307

Distri Editora Lda (Portugal) *Tel:* (01) 9425394 *Fax:* (01) 9425214, pg 524

Distri Lojas-Sociedade Livreira Lda (Portugal) *Tel:* (01) 9425394 *Fax:* (01) 9425214, pg 1307

Distribuidora Editora Vral, Lda (Portugal) *Tel:* (01) 4393978 *Fax:* (01) 4373558, pg 1307

Distribuidora Importadora Durand SA (Peru) *Tel:* (014) 4452113 *Fax:* (014) 4463190, pg 1305

Editora e Distribuidora Irradiacao Cultural Ltda (Brazil) *Tel:* (021) 5773522 *Fax:* (021) 5771249, pg 81

Distribuidoras Unidas SA (Colombia) *Tel:* 4139300 *Fax:* 4138502, pg 1279

Distripress (Switzerland) *Tel:* (0411) 2024121 *Fax:* (0411) 2021025 *E-mail:* info@distripress.ch *Web Site:* www.distripress.ch, pg 1260

Divadelni Ustav (Czech Republic) *Tel:* (02) 24809141 *Fax:* (02) 24811452 *E-mail:* info@theatre.cz *Web Site:* institute.theatre.cz, pg 124

Diversity Management (Australia) *Tel:* (02) 9130 4305 *Fax:* (02) 9365 1426, pg 1109

Divyanand Verlags GmbH (Germany) *Tel:* (07764) 93 97-0 *Fax:* (07764) 93 97-39 *E-mail:* sandila@t-online.de *Web Site:* www.sandila.de, pg 217

The Diwan Library, Ministry of Education (Iraq) *Tel:* (01) 8860000-2178, pg 1475

DIY Publishing (United Kingdom) *Tel:* (020) 7266 2202 *Fax:* (020) 7266 2314 *E-mail:* info@diypublishing.com *Web Site:* www.diypublishing.com, pg 675

Djambatan PT (Indonesia) *Tel:* (021) 3908790; (021) 7203199; (021) 7208562 *Fax:* (021) 7227989, pg 355

DJOF PUBLISHING JURIST-OG OKONOMFORBUNDETS FORLAG INDUSTRY

Djof Publishing Jurist-og Okonomforbundets Forlag (Denmark) *Tel:* 39 13 55 00 *Fax:* 39 13 55 55 *E-mail:* fl@djoef.dk *Web Site:* www.djoef-forlag.dk, pg 131

DK Agencies (P) Ltd (India) *Tel:* (011) 535-7104; (011) 535-7105 *Fax:* (011) 535-7103 *E-mail:* custserv@dkagencies.com *Web Site:* www.dkagencies.com, pg 1288

DK Book House (Thailand) *Tel:* (02) 2516335 *Fax:* (02) 2471033, pg 635

DK Printworld (P) Ltd (India) *Tel:* (011) 5453975; (011) 5466019 *Fax:* (011) 5465926 *E-mail:* dkprintworld@vsnl.net, pg 336

DLV Deutscher Landwirtschaftsverlag Berlin (Germany) *Tel:* (0511) 678 06-0 *Fax:* (0511) 678 06-200 *E-mail:* dlv-berlin@t-online.de *Web Site:* www.dlv.de, pg 217

DMG Business Media Ltd (United Kingdom) *Tel:* (01737) 768611 *Fax:* (01737) 855477 *Web Site:* www.dmg.co.uk, pg 675

DMK-Verlag (Germany) *Tel:* (0911) 203946; (0911) 227698 *Fax:* (0911) 208897, pg 1111

Dnipro (Ukraine) *Tel:* (044) 2243182 *Fax:* (044) 2244157, pg 643

DNP America LLC (United States) *Tel:* 212-503-1074; 212-503-1060 *Fax:* 212-286-1505 *Web Site:* www.dnp.co.jp/, pg 1143, 1164, 1206, 1215

Doaba House (India) *Tel:* (011) 3274669 *Fax:* (011) 6968735, pg 336

Ludwig Doblinger (Bernhard Herzmansky) Musikverlag KG (Austria) *Tel:* (01) 515 03-0 *Fax:* (01) 515 03-51 *E-mail:* music@doblinger.at *Web Site:* www.doblinger.at, pg 51

Dobro Publishing (United Kingdom) *Tel:* (020) 8346 4010 *E-mail:* dobropublishing@aol.com *Web Site:* www.drsandradelroy.com, pg 675

Dobun Shoin (Japan) *Tel:* (03) 38127777 *Fax:* (03) 38127792, pg 416

DOC 6, SA (Spain) *Tel:* (093) 215 43 13 *Fax:* (093) 488 36 21 *E-mail:* mail@doc6.es *Web Site:* www.doc6.es, pg 570

Ediciones Doce Calles SL (Spain) *Tel:* (091) 300 33 83; (091) 892 4218 *Fax:* (091) 892 5149 *E-mail:* docecalles@infonegocio.com *Web Site:* www.infonegocio.com/docecalles, pg 570

Doctrine & Life Book Club (Ireland) *Tel:* (01) 8721611 *Fax:* (01) 8731760, pg 1229

Documenta CV (Belgium) *Tel:* (02) 7068181 *Fax:* (02) 7068170, pg 68

Documentation Research and Training Centre (India) *Tel:* (080) 604648 *Fax:* (080) 8430265 *E-mail:* drtc@isibang.ernet.in, pg 1517

La Documentation Francaise (France) *Tel:* (01) 40157000 *Fax:* (01) 40 15 68 00 *E-mail:* postmaster@ladocfrancaise.gouv.fr *Web Site:* www.ladocfrancaise.gouv.fr, pg 159

La Documentation Francaise (France) *Tel:* (01) 40157000 *Fax:* (01) 40 15 68 00, pg 1465

Bibliotheque de Documentation Internationale Contemporaine (France) *Tel:* (01) 40977900 *Fax:* (01) 40977940 *E-mail:* courrier.bdic@u-paris10.fr, pg 1465

Dodoni Publications (Greece) *Tel:* (01) 3637973; (01) 3630312; (01) 3641787 *Fax:* (01) 36 37 067, pg 310

Docker Verlag GmbH & Co KG (Austria) *Tel:* (01) 7159200 *Fax:* (01) 715920076 *E-mail:* vgkritik@ping.at, pg 51

Dogakusha Inc (Japan) *Tel:* (03) 38167011 *Fax:* (03) 38167044, pg 416

Daniel Doglioli (Italy) *Tel:* (0382) 529317 *Fax:* (0382) 529317 *Web Site:* www.filastrocche.it/contempo/daniele/daniele.asp, pg 1113

Dohosha Publishing Co Ltd (Japan) *Tel:* (075) 255-9801 *Fax:* (075) 255-9811, pg 416

Christoph Dohr (Germany) *Tel:* (0221) 70 70 02 *Fax:* (0221) 70 43 95 *E-mail:* info@dohr.de *Web Site:* www.dohr.de, pg 217

Doin Editeurs (France) *Tel:* (01) 34633333 *Fax:* (01) 34653985, pg 160

Editura DOINA SRL (Romania) *Tel:* (01) 3228107 *Fax:* (01) 3227541, pg 533

Doko Video Ltd (Israel) *Tel:* (03) 5753555; (03) 2721771 *Fax:* (03) 5753189 *E-mail:* dokoa@ibm.net, pg 366

Pusat Dokumentasi dan Informasi Ilmiah (Indonesia) *Tel:* (021) 5733465 *Fax:* (021) 5733467, pg 1474

Dokumentationsstelle fur neuere Osterreichische Literatur (Austria) *Tel:* (01) 5262044 *Fax:* (01) 526204430 *E-mail:* hl@literaturhans.at *Web Site:* www.literaturhans.at, pg 1511

Dokumente Verlag Versandbuchhandlung Librairie (Germany) *Tel:* (0781) 923699-0 *Fax:* (0781) 923699-70 *E-mail:* info@dokumente-verlag.de *Web Site:* www.dokumente-verlag.de, pg 1283

Dokuz Eylul Universitesi (Turkey) *Tel:* (0232) 4204180 *Fax:* (0232) 4201789, pg 639

Dolling und Galitz Verlag GmbH (Germany) *Tel:* (040) 3893515 *Fax:* (040) 388587 *E-mail:* doellingundgalitzverlag@compuserve.com, pg 217

Dolmen Ediciones SA (Chile) *Tel:* (02) 235 8295 *Fax:* (02) 235 8812, pg 100

Wydawnictwo Dolnoslaskie (Poland) *Tel:* (071) 3288954; (071) 3288952 *Fax:* (071) 3288951 *E-mail:* sekretariat@wd.wroc.pl, pg 516

Nuove Edizioni Dolomiti SRL (Italy) *Tel:* (0437) 989216 *Fax:* (0437) 989099, pg 385

Dolphin Books (China) *Tel:* (010) 8315599-353 *Fax:* (010) 8317390, pg 105

Dolphin Press Group Ltd (Bulgaria) *Tel:* (056) 844044 *Fax:* (056) 844077 *Web Site:* www.dolphin-press.com, pg 95

Dolphin Publications (India) *Tel:* (022) 6490184 *Fax:* (022) 6233674, pg 336

Dom, Izdatel'stvo sovetskogo deskkogo fonda im & I Lenina (Russian Federation) *Tel:* (095) 9236661 *Fax:* (095) 9285322, pg 537

Dom Ksiazki, Panstwowe Przedesiebiorstwo (Poland) *Tel:* (012) 4225472; (012) 4228202 *Fax:* (012) 4228202, pg 1306

Dom Techniky Zvazu Slovenskych Vedeckotechnickych Spolocnosti Ltd (Slovakia) *Tel:* (088) 533512 *Fax:* (088) 42351, pg 549

Dom Wydawniczy Bellona (Poland) *Tel:* (022) 620-20-44 *Fax:* (022) 652 26 95 *E-mail:* biuro@bellona.pl *Web Site:* www.bellona.pl, pg 516

Ekdoseis Domi AE (Greece) *Tel:* (01) 3637389; (01) 3672056; (01) 03646014 *Fax:* (01) 3601782; (01) 3601786, pg 310

Domingos Castro (Portugal) *Tel:* (043) 332920 *Fax:* (043) 27406, pg 1307

Dominican Publications (Ireland) *Tel:* (01) 8721611 *Fax:* (01) 8731760 *E-mail:* dompubs@iol.ie, pg 359

Dominie (Australia) *Tel:* (02) 9050201 *Fax:* (02) 9055209, pg 1273

agenda Verlag Thomas Dominikowski (Germany) *Tel:* (0251) 79 96 10 *Fax:* (0251) 79 95 19 *E-mail:* info@agenda.de, pg 217

Domino Verlag, Guenther Brinek GmbH (Germany) *Tel:* (089) 17 91 30 *Fax:* (089) 17 91 34 13 *Web Site:* www.domino-verlag.de, pg 217

Domowina Verlag GmbH (Germany) *Tel:* (03591) 5770 *Fax:* (03591) 577243 *E-mail:* DomowinaVerlag@t-online.de *Web Site:* www.buchhandel.de/domowinaverlag, pg 217

Domus Academy (Italy) *Tel:* (02) 47719155 *Fax:* (02) 4222525 *E-mail:* info@domac.it *Web Site:* www.domac.it, pg 385

Editoriale Domus Spa (Italy) *Tel:* (02) 824721 *Fax:* (02) 26863123; (02) 57500132 *E-mail:* editorialedomus@edidomus.it, pg 385

Editorial Don Bosco (Bolivia) *Tel:* (02) 357755; (02) 371149 *Fax:* (02) 362822, pg 76

Ediciones Don Bosco Argentina (Argentina) *Tel:* (011) 4981-7314; (011) 4981-1388 *Fax:* (011) 4958-1506, pg 5

Ediciones Don Bosco SA de C (Mexico) *Tel:* (05) 3963349, pg 460

Don Bosco Verlag (Germany) *Tel:* (089) 48008300 *Fax:* (089) 48008309, pg 217

Editorial Don Quijote (Spain) *Tel:* (05) 4235080, pg 570

Donald Duck's Bokklubb (Norway) *Tel:* 22471000 *Fax:* 22471098 *E-mail:* egmont@egmont.com *Web Site:* www.egmont.com, pg 1231

John Donald Publishers Ltd (United Kingdom) *Tel:* (0131) 668 4371 *Fax:* (0131) 668 4466 *E-mail:* info@birlinn.co.uk *Web Site:* www.birlinn.co.uk, pg 675

Donat Verlag (Germany) *Tel:* (0421) 274886 *Fax:* (0421) 275106 *E-mail:* donatverlag@excite.de, pg 217

Buchgemeinschaft Donauland Kremayr & Scheriau (Austria) *Tel:* (01) 81102297 *Fax:* (01) 81102315, pg 1227

Dong-A Publishing & Printing Co Ltd (Republic of Korea) *Tel:* (02) 8668800 *Fax:* (02) 8620410, pg 436

Dong Hwa Publishing Co (Republic of Korea) *Tel:* (02) 7135411; (02) 7135415 *Fax:* (02) 7017041, pg 436

Dongguk University Central Library (Republic of Korea) *Tel:* (02) 2603114 *Fax:* (02) 2771274, pg 1480

Donhead Publishing Ltd (United Kingdom) *Tel:* (01747) 828422 *Fax:* (01747) 828522 *E-mail:* sales@donhead.com *Web Site:* www.donhead.com, pg 675

Uitgeversmaatschappij Ad Donker BV (Netherlands) *Tel:* (010) 436 30 09 *Fax:* (010) 436 29 63 *Web Site:* www.uitgeverijdonker.nl, pg 476

Ad Donker (Pty) Ltd (South Africa) *Tel:* (011) 622-2900 *Fax:* (011) 622-7610, pg 554

R R Donnelley (United Kingdom) *Tel:* (01904) 798241 *Fax:* (01904) 791017, pg 1203

Editorial Donostiarra SA (Spain) *Tel:* (0943) 215 737; (0943) 213 011 *Fax:* (0943) 219 521 *E-mail:* info@donostiarra.com *Web Site:* www.donostiarra.com, pg 570

Doplnek (Czech Republic) *Tel:* (05) 452-424-55 *Fax:* (05) 546346 *E-mail:* doplnek.brno@quick.cz *Web Site:* www.sky.cz; www.doplnek.cz, pg 124

Dorikos Publishing House (Greece) *Tel:* (01) 6854726 *Fax:* (01) 3301866, pg 310

Dorleta SA (Spain) *Tel:* (04) 4448573 *Fax:* (04) 4223222 *E-mail:* dorletoi@sarenet.es, pg 570

Dorling Kindersley Ltd (United Kingdom) *Tel:* (020) 7010 3000 *Fax:* (020) 7010 6060 *E-mail:* onlineDKcustomer.service@dk.com *Web Site:* www.dk.com, pg 676

Verlagsgruppe Dornier (Germany) *Tel:* (030) 28447-101 *Fax:* (030) 28447-103 *E-mail:* info@dornier-verlage.de *Web Site:* www.dornier-verlage.de, pg 218

The Dorothy L Sayers Society (United Kingdom) *Tel:* (01273) 833444 *Fax:* (01273) 835988 *E-mail:* jasmine@bredon.demon.co.uk, pg 1370

Dorriston Publishers Ltd (United Kingdom) *Tel:* (020) 7272 2722 *Fax:* (020) 7272 7274, pg 1140

Universitaet Dortmund (Germany) *Tel:* (0231) 7554029; (0231) 7554001; (0231) 4554030 *Fax:* (0231) 7554032, pg 1467

Dosmil Editora (Colombia) *Tel:* (01) 2699698; (01) 2694800, pg 111

Editorial Dossat SA (Spain) *Tel:* (091) 3694011 *Fax:* (091) 3691398, pg 570

Les Dossiers d'Aquitaine (France) *Tel:* (05) 56 91 84 98 *Fax:* (05) 56916492 *E-mail:* ddabx@wanadoo.fr, pg 160

Dost Kitabevi Yayinlari (Turkey) *Tel:* (0312) 4188772 *Fax:* (0312) 4199397 *E-mail:* raulman@domi.net.tr; levent@easynet.fr, pg 639

Dost Yayinlari San Ve Tic Ltd (Turkey) *Tel:* (0212) 2453141 *Fax:* (0212) 2430278, pg 639

Doubleday New Zealand Ltd, Book Club Division (New Zealand) *Tel:* (09) 4782846 *Fax:* (09) 4781609, pg 1230

Doubleday New Zealand Ltd (New Zealand) *Tel:* (09) 4782846, pg 490

Doyle Graphics (Ireland) *Tel:* (0506) 21970 *Fax:* (0506) 51323, pg 1157

Ediciones Doyma SA (Spain) *Tel:* (093) 2000 711 *Fax:* (093) 2091 136 *Web Site:* www.doyma.es, pg 570

Dr Oetker Verlag KG (Germany) *Tel:* (0521) 521 155-0 *Fax:* (0521) 521 155-2995 *E-mail:* presse@oetker.de *Web Site:* www.oetker-gruppe.de, pg 218

Dr Sun Yat-sen Library (Taiwan, Province of China) *Tel:* (02) 27297030 *Fax:* (02) 27582460, pg 1502

Edicions del Drac SA (Spain) *Tel:* (093) 2171762 *Fax:* (093) 2171766, pg 570

Dragon Press (Australia) *Tel:* 09 3412004, pg 20

Drake Educational Associates Ltd (United Kingdom) *Tel:* (029) 2056 0333 *Fax:* (029) 2055 4909 *E-mail:* drakegroup@btinternet.com *Web Site:* www.drakegroup.co.uk, pg 676

Drake Educational Associates Ltd (United Kingdom) *Tel:* (01222) 2056 0333 *Fax:* (01222) 29 20554909 *E-mail:* drakegroup@btinternet.com *Web Site:* www.drakegroup.co.uk, pg 1118

Dramatic Lines Publishers (United Kingdom) *Tel:* (020) 8296 9502 *Fax:* (020) 8296 9503 *E-mail:* mail@dramaticlines.co.uk *Web Site:* www.dramaticlines.co.uk, pg 676

Drammen Folkebibliotek (Norway) *Tel:* 32806300 *Fax:* 32806453 *E-mail:* magne@drmbib.bibsyst.no, pg 1489

Dreamland Editeur (France) *Tel:* (01) 53204666 *Fax:* (01) 53204667 *E-mail:* dreamland@nous.fr, pg 160

Dreamland Publications (India) *Tel:* (011) 5121050; (011) 5435657; (011) 5455657 *Fax:* (011) 5428283 *E-mail:* dreamland@vsnl.com, pg 336

Drei Brunnen Verlag GmbH & Co (Germany) *Tel:* (0711) 86020 *Fax:* (0711) 860229 *E-mail:* mail@drei-brunnen-verlag.de *Web Site:* www.drei-brunnen-verlag.de, pg 218

Drei Eichen Verlag Manuel Kissener (Germany) *Tel:* (09732) 9142-0 *Fax:* (09732) 9142-20 *E-mail:* info@drei-eichen.de *Web Site:* www.drei-eichen.de, pg 218

Drei Ulmen Verlag GmbH (Germany) *Tel:* (089) 3087911; (089) 3088343 (orders), pg 218

Dreisam Ratgeber in der Rutsker Verlag GmbH (Germany) *Tel:* (0221) 921635-0 *Fax:* (0221) 921635-24 *E-mail:* kontakt@hayit.com *Web Site:* www.hayit.com, pg 218

Cecilie Dressler Verlag (Germany) *Tel:* (040) 607909-03 *Fax:* (040) 6072326 *Web Site:* www.cecilie-dressler.de, pg 218

De Driehoek BV (Netherlands) *Tel:* (020) 6246426 *Fax:* (020) 6387155, pg 476

Droemersche Verlagsanstalt Th Knaur Nachfolger GmbH & Co (Germany) *Tel:* (089) 92710 *Fax:* (089) 9271168 *E-mail:* info@dioemer-weltbilt.de *Web Site:* www.dioemer-weltbild.de, pg 218

Droguet et Ardant (France) *Tel:* (01) 45443834 *Fax:* (01) 45499392, pg 160

Librairie Generale de Droit et de Jurisprudence (LGDJ) - Montchrestien (France) *Tel:* (01) 56541600 *Fax:* (01) 56541649, pg 160

Literature Verlag Droschl (Austria) *Tel:* (0316) 32-64-04 *Fax:* (0316) 32-40-71 *E-mail:* literaturverlag@droschl.com *Web Site:* www.droschl.com, pg 51

Droste Verlag GmbH (Germany) *Tel:* (0211) 5050 *Fax:* (0211) 5052671, pg 218

Librairie Droz SA (Switzerland) *Tel:* (022) 3466666 *Fax:* (022) 3472391 *E-mail:* droz@droz.org *Web Site:* www.droz.org, pg 612

Drs F H R Oedayrajsingh Varma (Suriname), pg 599

DRT International (Republic of Korea) *Tel:* (02) 7453350 *Fax:* (02) 7453612 *E-mail:* drt@chollian.dacom.co.kr, pg 1114

Dru-stvo na Pisatelite na Makedonija (The Former Yugoslav Republic of Macedonia) *Tel:* (091) 117668 *Fax:* (091) 228345, pg 1366

Druck & Verlagshaus Fromm GmbH & Co KG (Germany) *Tel:* (0541) 3100 *Fax:* (0541) 310315 *E-mail:* druckhaus@fromm-os.de, pg 1133

Karl Elser Druck GmbH (Germany) *Tel:* (07041) 805-41 *Fax:* (07041) 805-50 *E-mail:* info@elserdruck.de *Web Site:* www.elserdruck.de, pg 218

Druckerei u Verlagsanstalt Bayerland GmbH (Germany) *Tel:* (08131) 7 20 66 *Fax:* (08131) 73 53 99 *E-mail:* zentrale@bayerland-amperbote.de *Web Site:* www.bayerland.de, pg 219

Druffel-Verlag (Germany) *Tel:* (08151) 50024 *Fax:* (08151) 51856, pg 219

Drukarnia I Ksiegarnia Swietego Wojciecha, Dziat Wydawniczy (Poland) *Tel:* (061) 8529186 *Fax:* (061) 8523746 *E-mail:* wydawnictwo.ksw@archpoznan.org.pl, pg 516

Drukkerij Lannoo NV (Belgium) *Tel:* (051) 424211 *Fax:* (051) 407070 *E-mail:* lannoo@lannooprint.be *Web Site:* www.lannooprint.be, pg 1131, 1153, 1193

The Drummond Agency (Australia) *Tel:* (03) 5427 3644 *Fax:* (03) 5427 3655, pg 1109

Drustvo Bibliotekara Bosne i Hercegovine (Bosnia and Herzegovina) *Tel:* (071) 212-435 *Fax:* (071) 212-435, pg 1513

Druzhba Narodov (Russian Federation) *Tel:* (095) 9258671, pg 537

DRW-Verlag Weinbrenner-GmbH & Co (Germany) *Tel:* (0711) 75 91-0 *Fax:* (0711) 75 91-333 *Web Site:* www.drw-verlag.de; www.weinbrenner.de, pg 219

Dryden Press (Australia) *Tel:* (02) 331-4571 *Fax:* (02) 398-9782, pg 21

Drzavna Uprava za Zastitu Prirode i Okolisa (State Directorate for the Protection of Nature & Environment) (Croatia) *Tel:* (01) 610 6555; (01) 610 6556; (01) 610 6578 *Fax:* (01) 6118 388; (01) 611 2073 *E-mail:* duzo@ring.net *Web Site:* www.mzopu.hr, pg 118

DSI Data Service & Information (Germany) *Tel:* 2843 3220 *Fax:* 2843 3230 *E-mail:* dsi@dsidata.com *Web Site:* www.dsidata.com, pg 219

Du May (France) *Tel:* (01) 46992424 *Fax:* (01) 48255692, pg 160

Duang Kamon (Thailand) *Tel:* (02) 2516335, pg 635

Livraria Duas Cidades Ltda (Brazil) *Tel:* (011) 220-5134; (011) 220-5813, pg 81

Livraria Duas Cidades Ltda (Brazil) *Tel:* (011) 220-5134, pg 1277

Dublin Institute for Advanced Studies (Ireland) *Tel:* (01) 6680748 *Fax:* (01) 6680561, pg 360

Dublin Public Libraries (Ireland) *Tel:* (01) 6644800 *Fax:* (01) 6761628 *E-mail:* dublin.city.libs@iol.ie, pg 1475

Dubois Publishing (Australia) *Tel:* (02) 92111178 *Fax:* (02) 92111868, pg 21

Duboux Editions SA (Switzerland) *Tel:* (033) 2256060 *Fax:* (033) 2256066 *E-mail:* duboux-editions@duboux.ch *Web Site:* www.duboux.ch, pg 612

Gerald Duckworth & Co Ltd (United Kingdom) *Tel:* (020) 7434 4242 *Fax:* (020) 7434 4420 *E-mail:* info@ducknet.co.uk *Web Site:* www.duckw.com, pg 676

Verlag Duerr & Kessler GmbH (Germany) *Tel:* (0941) 568940 *Fax:* (0941) 568999 *E-mail:* info@wolfverlag.de *Web Site:* www.wolfverlag.de, pg 219

Archibook Verlag Martina Duettmann (Germany) *Tel:* (030) 3046578 *Fax:* (030) 3049902, pg 219

Dumara Distribuidora de Publicacoes Ltda (Brazil) *Tel:* (021) 5420248 *Fax:* (021) 2750294, pg 81

Dumjahn Verlag (Germany) *Tel:* (06131) 330810 *Fax:* (06131) 330811 *E-mail:* railway@dumjahn.de *Web Site:* www.dumjahn.de, pg 219

DuMont Buchverlag GmbH & Co KG (Germany) *Tel:* (0221) 2 24 18-0 *Fax:* (0221) 2 24 18-12 *E-mail:* info@dumontverlag.de *Web Site:* www.dumontverlag.de/dumont, pg 219

DuMont Monte (Germany) *Tel:* (0221) 224-180 *Fax:* (0221) 224-1828 *E-mail:* info@dumontverlag.de *Web Site:* www.dumontverlag.de/monte, pg 219

Dorothy Duncan Braille & Transcription Library (Zimbabwe) *Tel:* (04) 251116 *Fax:* (04) 251117 *E-mail:* chiedza@samara.co.zw, pg 768

Duncker und Humblot GmbH (Germany) *Tel:* (030) 79 00 06-0 *Fax:* (030) 79 00 06-31 *E-mail:* info@duncker-humblot.de *Web Site:* www.duncker-humblot.de, pg 219

Dunedin Public Libraries (New Zealand) *Tel:* (03) 4743690 *Fax:* (03) 4743660 *E-mail:* library@dcc.govt.nz, pg 1487

Dunedin Academic Press (United Kingdom) *Tel:* (0131) 473 2397, pg 676

Dunia Pustaka Jaya (Indonesia) *Tel:* (021) 3909322; (021) 3909284 *Fax:* (021) 3909320, pg 355

Martin Dunitz Ltd (United Kingdom) *Tel:* (020) 7482 2202 *Fax:* (020) 7267 0159 *E-mail:* info@dunitz.co.uk *Web Site:* www.dunitz.co.uk, pg 676

Dunmore Press Ltd (New Zealand) *Tel:* (06) 3587169 *Fax:* (06) 3579242 *E-mail:* books@dunmore.co.nz *Web Site:* www.dunmore.co.nz, pg 490

Dunod Editeur (France) *Tel:* (01) 40 46 35 00 *Fax:* (01) 40 46 49 95 *E-mail:* infos@dunod.com *Web Site:* www.dunod.com, pg 160

DUP (1996) Ltd (United Republic of Tanzania) *Tel:* (051) 49106; (051) 49107; (051) 49108 *Fax:* (051) 49106 *E-mail:* director@dup.udsm.ac.tz, pg 633

Editions Dupuis SA (Belgium) *Tel:* (071) 600 500 *Fax:* (071) 600 519 *Web Site:* www.dupuis-entertainment.com, pg 68

Editions J Dupuis (France) *Tel:* (01) 44 84 40 80 *Fax:* (01) 44 84 40 99 *Web Site:* www.dupuis-entertainment.com, pg 160

Durban Metropolitan Library (South Africa) *Tel:* (031) 300-6911 *Fax:* (031) 300-6301 *E-mail:* michelej@durban.gov.2a, pg 1497

Durham Chapter Library (United Kingdom) *Tel:* (0191) 386-2489 *Fax:* (0191) 386-4267 *Web Site:* www.durhamcathedral.co.uk/, pg 1506

Durham University Library (United Kingdom) *Tel:* (0191) 3743018 *Fax:* (0191) 3747481, pg 1506

Durieux d o o (Croatia) *Tel:* (01) 23 00 337; (01) 23 21 178 *Fax:* (01) 23 00 337 *E-mail:* durieux@zg.tel.hr *Web Site:* www.durieux.hr, pg 118

Durvan SA de Ediciones (Spain) *Tel:* (094) 4230777; (094) 4236263 *Fax:* (094) 4243832 *E-mail:* editorial@durvan.com *Web Site:* www.durvan.com, pg 570

Dustri-Verlag Dr Karl Feistle (Germany) *Tel:* (089) 61 38 61-0 *Fax:* (089) 613 54 12 *E-mail:* info@dustri.de *Web Site:* www.dustri.de, pg 219

Duta Wacana University Press (Indonesia) *Tel:* (0274) 563929 *Fax:* (0274) 513235 *E-mail:* humas@ukdw.ac.id *Web Site:* www.ukdw.ac.id, pg 355

Dutch Connection (United Kingdom) *Tel:* (01625) 610613 *Fax:* (01625) 610613 *E-mail:* 100345.14@compuserve.com, pg 1128

Dutta Baruah Publishing Co Pvt Ltd (India) *Tel:* (0361) 543995, pg 336

Gottlieb Duttweiler Institute for Trends & Futures (Switzerland) *Tel:* (01) 7240020 *Fax:* (01) 7246262 *E-mail:* biblio@gdi.ch, pg 612

Klaus D Dutz (Germany) *Tel:* (0251) 65514 *Fax:* (0251) 66 16 92 *E-mail:* dutz.nodus@t-online.de, pg 219

DVG-Deutsche Verlagsgesellschaft mbH (Germany) *Tel:* (08031) 15643 *Fax:* (08031) 380662, pg 219

Dvir Bialik Municipal Central Public Library (Israel) *Tel:* (03) 786375, pg 1476

Dvir Publishing Ltd (Israel) *Tel:* (08) 9246565 *Fax:* (08) 9251770 *E-mail:* info@zmora.co.il, pg 366

E J Dwyer (Australia) Pty Ltd (Australia) *Tel:* (02) 9550 2355 *Fax:* (02) 9519 3218, pg 21

Gwasg Dwyfor (United Kingdom) *Tel:* (01236) 881 911 *Fax:* (01236) 880 120 *E-mail:* argraff@gwasgdwyfor.demon.co.uk, pg 676

Dykinson SL (Spain) *Tel:* (091) 544 28 46 *Fax:* (091) 544 60 40 *E-mail:* dykinson@telefonica.net *Web Site:* www.dykinson.es; www.dykinson.com, pg 571

Dymocks Pty Ltd (Australia) *Tel:* (02) 9235 0155 *Fax:* (02) 9233 7009 *E-mail:* service@dymocks.com.au *Web Site:* www.dymocks.com.au, pg 1273

Dynamo House P/L (Australia) *Tel:* (03) 9427 0955; (03) 9428 3636 *Fax:* (03) 9429 8036 *E-mail:* info@dynamoh.com.au, pg 21

Dyonon/Papyrus Publishing House of the Tel-Aviv (Israel) *Tel:* (03) 6410351; (03) 6410352; (03) 6427545 (head office) *Fax:* (03) 6423149, pg 367

Dyonon/Papyrus Publishing House of the Tel-Aviv (Israel) *Tel:* (03) 6410351; (03) 6410352; (03) 6427545 (head office); (03) 6422667 (import office) *Fax:* (03) 6423149, pg 1292

Dzuka Publishing Company Ltd (Malawi) *Tel:* 01670855; 01670880 *Fax:* 67111433; 670021, pg 450

Edizioni E - Elle SRL (Italy) *Tel:* (040) 637969 *Fax:* (0406) 378660, pg 385

E Lopfe-Benz AG Rorschach, Graphische Anstalt und Verlag (Switzerland) *Tel:* (071) 8440444 *Fax:* (071) 8440445, pg 612

Edizioni E/O (Italy) *Tel:* (06) 3722829 *Fax:* (06) 7351096, pg 385

E P U Editora Pedagogica e Universitaria Ltd (Brazil) *Tel:* (011) 3168-6077 *Fax:* (011) 3078-5803 *E-mail:* vendas@epu.com.br *Web Site:* www.epu.com.br, pg 81

E Schweizerbart'sche Verlagsbuchhandlung (Nagele und Obermiller) (Germany) *Tel:* (0711) 625001 *Fax:* (0711) 625005 *E-mail:* mail@schweizerbart.de *Web Site:* www.schweizerbart.de, pg 220

EA Books (Australia) *Tel:* (02) 9438 1533 *Fax:* (02) 9438 5934 *E-mail:* eabooks@engaust.com *Web Site:* www.engaust.com.au, pg 21

EA Publishing House (Bulgaria) *Tel:* (064) 800974 *Fax:* (064) 22528 *E-mail:* ea@famahold.com, pg 95

Toby Eady Associates Ltd (United Kingdom) *Tel:* (020) 7792 0092 *Fax:* (020) 7792 0879 *E-mail:* toby@tobyeady.demon.co.uk, pg 1119

Eagle/Inter Publishing Service (IPS) Ltd (United Kingdom) *Tel:* (01483) 306309 *Fax:* (01483) 579196 *E-mail:* eagle_ips@compuserve.com, pg 676

Eagle Press (United Kingdom) *Tel:* (0115) 9552335 *Fax:* (0115) 9552336, pg 1203

Eaglemoss Publications Ltd (United Kingdom) *Tel:* (020) 7590 8300 *Fax:* (020) 7590 8301 *E-mail:* enquiries@eaglemoss.co.uk *Web Site:* www.eaglemoss.co.uk, pg 676

EAIS Literary Agents (France) *Tel:* (01) 47880840 *Fax:* (01) 47880840, pg 1110

Early English Text Society (United Kingdom) *Web Site:* eets.org.uk, pg 1370

Earthscan Publications Ltd (United Kingdom) *Tel:* (020) 7278 0433 *Fax:* (020) 7278 1142 *E-mail:* earthinfo@earthscan.co.uk *Web Site:* www.earthscan.co.uk, pg 677

Eason & Son Ltd (Ireland) *Tel:* (01) 8733811 *Fax:* (01) 8730620, pg 360, 1291

East African Publishing House (United Republic of Tanzania) *Tel:* (02) 557417; (02) 557788, pg 633

East & West Publishing Co (Pakistan) *Tel:* (021) 212036 *Fax:* (021) 7784362, pg 506

The Centre for East Asian Cultural Studies for UNESCO (Japan) *Tel:* (03) 39420124 *Fax:* (03) 39420120 *E-mail:* nad03367@niftyserve.or.jp., pg 1250

East China Normal University Press (China) *Tel:* (021) 62863896 *Fax:* (021) 62864922 *E-mail:* lxb@ecnu.edu.cn *Web Site:* www.ecnu.edu.cn, pg 105

East China University of Science & Technology Press (China) *Tel:* (021) 64252769 *Fax:* (021) 64250735 *Web Site:* www.ecust.edu.cn, pg 105

East London Municipal Library (South Africa) *Tel:* (0431) 24991 *Fax:* (431) 431729, pg 1497

East West Operation (EWO) Ltd (Slovenia) *Tel:* (061) 217124; (061) 1264124; (061) 161181 *Fax:* (061) 217348 *E-mail:* ewo-arkadna@siol.net, pg 551

East-West Publications Fonds BV (Netherlands) *Tel:* (70) 3644590 *Fax:* (70) 3614864, pg 476

East-West Publications (UK) Ltd (United Kingdom) *Tel:* (020) 7837 5061 *Fax:* (020) 7278 4429, pg 677

East Word (United Kingdom) *Tel:* (020) 7582 9349 *Fax:* (020) 7793 0474 *E-mail:* info@eastword.uk.com, pg 1128

Eastern Book Centre (India) *Tel:* (011) 3314191, pg 336

Eastern Africa Publications Ltd (United Republic of Tanzania) *Tel:* (057) 3176; (057) 26708, pg 633

Eastern and Southern Africa Regional Branch of the International Council on Archives (ESARBICA) (Kenya) *Tel:* (02) 228959 *Fax:* (02) 228020 *E-mail:* knarchives@form-net.com, pg 1251

Eastern & Southern African Management Institute (ESAMI) (United Republic of Tanzania) *Tel:* 8383; 8388 *Fax:* 8285 *E-mail:* esamihg@yako.habar.co.tz, pg 1502

Eastern Book Co (India) *Tel:* (0522) 223171; (0522) 226517; (0522) 214218 *Fax:* (0522) 224328 *E-mail:* sales@ebc-india.com *Web Site:* www.ebc-india.com, pg 336

Eastern Law House Pvt Ltd (India) *Tel:* (033) 237 4989; (033) 237 2301 *Fax:* (033) 215 0491 *E-mail:* elh@cal.vsnl.net.in *Web Site:* easternlawhouse.com, pg 336

Eastview Productions Sdn Bhd (Malaysia) *Tel:* (03) 7762669; (03) 7762614; (03) 7556639 *Fax:* (03) 7550731, pg 452

Easy Computing NV (Belgium) *Tel:* (02) 346 52 52 *Fax:* (02) 346 01 20 *E-mail:* info@easycomputing.com, pg 68

Easy Finder Ltd (Hong Kong) *Tel:* (02) 29907100 *Fax:* (02) 9907212, pg 319

Editions l'Eau Vive (Switzerland) *Tel:* (022) 7329847 *Fax:* (022) 7410482, pg 613

Edizioni EBE (Italy) *Tel:* (0766) 858878 *Fax:* (0766) 858877, pg 385

Ediciones Ebenezer (Spain) *Tel:* (093) 213669 *E-mail:* 101745.1635@compuserve.com, pg 571

EBG Verlags GmbH (Germany) *Tel:* (07154) 1340, pg 1228

Eboris-Coda-Bompiani (Switzerland) *Tel:* (022) 9092840 *Fax:* (022) 7381425, pg 613

Ebury Press (United Kingdom) *Tel:* (020) 7840 8400 *Fax:* (020) 7233 7398 *Web Site:* www.randomhouse.co.uk, pg 1119

ECA Bookshop Co-op Society (Ethiopia) *Tel:* (01) 447200, pg 1282

ECA (Ediciones Culturales Argentinas) (Argentina) *Tel:* (011) 49232579; (011) 49232658, pg 5

Ediciones Eca SA de CV (Mexico) *Tel:* (05) 5787325 *Fax:* (05) 5449561; (05) 6899935, pg 460

Biblioteca Jose Antonio Echeverria (Cuba) *Tel:* (07) 552705 *Fax:* (07) 334554 *E-mail:* casa@tinored cu, pg 1459

Echo Publishing Company Ltd (Taiwan, Province of China) *Tel:* (02) 27361452 *Fax:* (02) 27568712, pg 629

Echo Verlag (Germany) *Tel:* (0551) 796824 *Fax:* (0551) 74035 *E-mail:* clages.echoverlag@t-online.de *Web Site:* www.echoverlag.de, pg 220

Echter Wurzburg Frankische Gesellschaftsdruckerei und Verlag GmbH (Germany) *Tel:* (0931) 66068-0; (0931) 6671252; (0931) 6671253 *Fax:* (0931) 66068-23 *E-mail:* info@echterverlag.de *Web Site:* www.echter-verlag.de, pg 220

ECI voor Boeken en Grammofoonplaten BV (Netherlands) *Tel:* (03473) 79214 *Fax:* (03471) 79380, pg 476, 1230

ECIG (Italy) *Tel:* (010) 2512399 *Fax:* (010) 2512398, pg 385

Frank P van Eck Publishers (Liechtenstein) *Tel:* (075) 29557 *Fax:* (075) 29557, pg 444

Eckardt & Messtorff GmbH (Germany) *Tel:* (040) 374842-0 *Fax:* (040) 37500768 *E-mail:* e&m-sales@eum.hh.eunet.de *Web Site:* www.em-seacharts.de, pg 220

ECL (Portugal) *Tel:* (02) 600-40-01 *Fax:* (02) 609-96-15 *E-mail:* ecl@mail.telepac.pt, pg 1307

Editions de l'Eclat (France) *Tel:* (04) 66 21 17 50 *Fax:* (04) 66 21 03 42 *E-mail:* eclat@lyber-eclat.net *Web Site:* www.lyber-eclat.net, pg 160

Ediciones del Eclipse (Argentina) *Tel:* (011) 4771-3583 *Fax:* (011) 4771-3583 *E-mail:* deleclipse@overnet.com.ar *Web Site:* www.deleclipse.com, pg 5

Eco Verlags AG (Switzerland) *Tel:* (01) 440400, pg 613

Ecobooks (Belgium) *Tel:* (052) 37 11 38 *Fax:* (052) 37 11 51 *E-mail:* ecobooks@ping.be, pg 68

Ecoe Ediciones Ltda (Colombia) *Tel:* (01) 2882556; (01) 2433949; (01) 2889821; (01) 2889871 *Fax:* (01) 3201377 *E-mail:* ecoe@col1.telecom.com.co *Web Site:* www.ecoediciones.com, pg 111

Ecole normale superieure (Mali) *Tel:* 222189, pg 1483

Biblioteqe l'Ecole nationale d'administration du Niger (Niger) *Tel:* 723183, pg 1488

Ecole de Traducteurs et d'Interpretes de Beyrouth-Universite Saint-Joseph (ETIB) (France) *Tel:* (01) 201617 *Fax:* (01) 423369; (01) 200631 *Web Site:* www.usj.edu.1b/ecolede, pg 1125

Ecole des Bibliothecaires, Archivistes et Documentalistes de l'Universite Cheikh Anta Diop de Dakar (Senegal) *Tel:* 8240542; 8257660 *Fax:* 252883; 8240542, pg 1496

Editions de l'Ecole des Hautes Etudes en Sciences Sociales (EHESS) (France) *Tel:* (01) 40 46 70 80 *Fax:* (01) 44 07 08 89 *E-mail:* editions@ehess.fr *Web Site:* www.ehess.fr, pg 160

L'Ecole/L'Ecole des Loisirs Sarl (France) *Tel:* (01) 42 22 94 10 *Fax:* (01) 45 48 04 99 *Web Site:* www.ecoledesloisirs.fr, pg 160

Ecole francaise d'Athenes (Greece) *Tel:* (010) 36 79 900 *Fax:* (010) 36 32 101 *E-mail:* efa@efa.gr *Web Site:* www.efa.gr, pg 310

Ecole Francaise de Rome (Italy) *Tel:* (06) 688851 *Fax:* (06) 68885405 *E-mail:* publ@ecole-francaise.it; secr@ekole-francaise.it *Web Site:* www.ecole-francaise.it, pg 385

Ecole nationale polytechnique, Bibliotheque (Algeria) *Tel:* (052) 1027 *Fax:* (052) 2973 *E-mail:* enp@ist.cerist.dz, pg 1449

Ecole Nationale Superieure des Beaux-Arts (France) *Tel:* (01) 47035055 *Fax:* (01) 47035086 *E-mail:* info@ensba.fr *Web Site:* www.ensba.fr, pg 160

Ecole Nationale Superieure des Sciences de l'information et des bibliotheques (ENSSIB) (France) *Tel:* (04) 72444343; (04) 72444307 *Fax:* (04) 72442788 *E-mail:* com@enssib.fr; dupuigre@enssib.fr, pg 1465

Presses de l'Ecole Normale Superieure (France) *Tel:* (01) 44 32 30 00 *Fax:* (01) 44 32 20 99 *Web Site:* www.ens.fr, pg 160

Librairie des Ecoles (Morocco) *Tel:* (02) 266742; (02) 266743; (02) 266741 *Fax:* (02) 201003, pg 1300

Ecomed Verlagsgesellschaft AG & Co KG (Germany) *Tel:* (08191) 125 0 *Fax:* (08191) 125 492 *E-mail:* medicine@ecomed.de *Web Site:* www.ecomed.de, pg 220

Econ Taschenbuchverlag (Germany) *Tel:* (0211) 43596, pg 220

Econ Verlag GmbH (Germany) *Tel:* (089) 5148-0 *Fax:* (089) 5148-2229 *Web Site:* www.econ-verlag.de, pg 220

Economic & Business Research (Trinidad & Tobago) *Tel:* 624-5064 *Fax:* 623-4137 *E-mail:* maxifill@opus.co.tt *Web Site:* www.opus.co.tt/maxifill, pg 637

The Economic & Social Research Institute (Ireland) *Tel:* (01) 6671525 *Fax:* (01) 6686231 *E-mail:* brendan.whelan@esri.ie *Web Site:* www.esri.ie, pg 360

The Economist Intelligence Unit (United Kingdom) *Tel:* (020) 7830 1007 *Fax:* (020) 7830 1023 *E-mail:* london@eiu.com *Web Site:* www.eiu.com, pg 677

The Economists' Bookshop (United Kingdom) *Tel:* (020) 7405 5531 *Fax:* (020) 7430 1584 *E-mail:* economists@waterstones.co.uk, pg 1319

Economy and Press (Hong Kong) *Tel:* (02) 28917556, pg 319

Association des Ecrivains de Langue Francaise (ADELF) (France) *Tel:* (01) 43219599 *Fax:* (01) 43201222, pg 1243

Academia Ecuatoriana de la Lengua (Ecuador) *Tel:* (02) 226-870, pg 1362

Ecuazeta De Publicacioes Cia Ltda (Ecuador) *Tel:* (02) 443074 *Fax:* (02) 443074, pg 1282

ECWA Productions Ltd (Nigeria) *Tel:* (073) 53897; (073) 52230, pg 498

Verlag ED Emmentaler Druck AG (Switzerland) *Tel:* (035) 21911 *Fax:* (035) 0524642, pg 613

Editorial EDAF SA (Spain) *Tel:* (091) 435 82 60 *Fax:* (091) 431 52 81 *E-mail:* edaf@edaf.net *Web Site:* www.edaf.es, pg 571

Edagricole - Edizioni Agricole (Italy) *Tel:* (051) 62267 *Fax:* (051) 490200 *E-mail:* comm@calderini.agriline.it *Web Site:* www.edagricole.it, pg 385

Edamex SA de CV (Mexico) *Tel:* (05) 55598588 *Toll Free Tel:* 800 024 8588 *Fax:* (05) 55750555; (05) 55757035 *E-mail:* info@edamex.com *Web Site:* www.edamex.com, pg 460

Edanim Publishers Ltd (Israel) *Tel:* (03) 688-8466 *Fax:* (03) 537-7820, pg 367

EDAS (Italy) *Tel:* (090) 675653 *Fax:* (090) 675653, pg 386

EDC -Empresa De Divulgacao Cultural, SA (Portugal) *Tel:* (021) 562131 *Fax:* (021) 562139, pg 1307

Editions Eddif Maroc (Morocco) *Tel:* (02) 442375; (02) 442376 *Fax:* (02) 313565, pg 469

Eddison Sadd Editions Ltd (United Kingdom) *Tel:* (020) 7837 1968 *Fax:* (020) 7837 6844 *E-mail:* langel@eddisonsadd.co.uk, pg 677

Ede Vau Verlag GmbH (Germany) *Tel:* (02154) 490080 *Fax:* (02154) 490081 *E-mail:* evvgmbh@tonline.de, pg 220

Edebe (Spain) *Tel:* (093) 2037408 *Fax:* (093) 2054670 *E-mail:* editorial@edebe.com *Web Site:* www.edebe.com, pg 571

EDERSA (Editoriales de Derecho Reunidas SA) (Spain) *Tel:* (0902) 22 66 00 *Fax:* (091) 314 93 07 *E-mail:* dijusa@retemail.es *Web Site:* www.edersa.com, pg 571

Edeval (Universidad de Valparaiso) (Chile) *Tel:* (02) 250792 *Fax:* (02) 252125 *E-mail:* rrpp@uv.cl *Web Site:* www.uv.cl, pg 100

Edex, Centro de Recursos Comunitarios (Spain) *Tel:* (094) 442 57 84 *Fax:* (094) 427 64 20 *E-mail:* edex@jet.es *Web Site:* www.edex.es, pg 571

EDHASA (Editora y Distribuidora Hispano-Americana SA) (Spain) *Tel:* (093) 4949720 *Fax:* (093) 4194584 *E-mail:* info@edhasa.es *Web Site:* www.edhasa.es, pg 571, 1311

Edi Ermes SRL (Italy) *Tel:* (02) 70209911 *Fax:* (02) 70209919, pg 386

Edi-Liber Irlan SA (Spain) *Tel:* (093) 4161452 *Fax:* (093) 4160663 *E-mail:* ediliber@mx3.redestb.es, pg 571

Ediart Editrice (Italy) *Tel:* (075) 8943594 *Fax:* (075) 8942411 *E-mail:* ediart@ediart.it, pg 386

Ediblanchart sprl (Belgium) *Tel:* (02) 4783706 *Fax:* (02) 4786429, pg 68

Edicart (Italy) *Tel:* (0331) 465662 *Fax:* (0331) 465663 *E-mail:* edicart@galctica.it, pg 386

Edicef - Editions Classiques d'Expression Francaise (France) *Tel:* (01) 46 62 10 10 *Fax:* (01) 40 95 10 74 *E-mail:* infos@foliesdencre.com *Web Site:* www.foliesdencre.com/afr/edicef.html, pg 161

Edicial SA (Argentina) *Tel:* (011) 342 84 81; (011) 342 84 82; (011) 342 84 83 *Fax:* (011) 343 11 51 *E-mail:* edicial@ssdnet.com.ar *Web Site:* www.ssdnet.com.ar/edicial, pg 5

Ediciclo Editore SRL (Italy) *Tel:* (0421) 74475 *Fax:* (0421) 282070 *E-mail:* posta@ediciclo.it, pg 386

Ediciones Deusto SA (Spain) *Tel:* (094) 4356177 *Fax:* (094) 4356173 *E-mail:* edicio01@sarenet.es *Web Site:* www.ediciones-deusto.es, pg 571

Ediciones El Almendro de Cordoba (Spain) *Tel:* (0957) 082 789; (0957) 274 692 *Fax:* (0957) 274 692 *E-mail:* ediciones@elalmendro.com *Web Site:* www.elalmendro.com, pg 571

Ediciones Euroamericanas SA (Peru) *Tel:* (014) 4274686 *Fax:* (014) 4280545, pg 1305

Ediciones l'Isard, S L (Spain) *Tel:* (093) 436 81 18 *Fax:* (093) 436 03 41 *E-mail:* isard@isard.net *Web Site:* www.isard.net, pg 571

Ediciones Union, Union de Escritores y Artistas de Cuba (Cuba) *Tel:* (07) 324571 *Fax:* (07) 333158, pg 1241

Ediciones Universidad Technologica Metropolitana (Chile) *Tel:* (02) 7877962 *Fax:* (02) 7877925, pg 1456

Ediciones y Distribuciones Universitarias SA (Spain) *Tel:* (093) 4101727 *Fax:* (093) 4399429, pg 571

Ediciones Zeta SCR Ltda (Peru) *Tel:* (014) 4729890; (014) 4720781 *Fax:* (014) 4725942; (014) 4750094, pg 1305

Edicions Camacuc (Spain) *Tel:* (096) 357 28 56 *Fax:* (096) 357 28 56, pg 571

Institut d'Edicions de la Diputacio de Barcelona (Spain) *Tel:* (093) 4022 116 *Fax:* (093) 4022 290 *E-mail:* godovx@diba.es *Web Site:* www.diba.es, pg 571

Edicoes 70, Lda (Portugal) *Tel:* (0351) 21 319 02 40 *Fax:* (0351) 21 319 02 49 *E-mail:* edi.70@mail.telepac.pt *Web Site:* www.edicoes70.pt, pg 524

Editorial Edicol SA (Mexico) *Tel:* (05) 5636990; (05) 5981512 *Fax:* (05) 5636966, pg 460

Edicomunicacion SA (Spain) *Tel:* (093) 3590866 *Fax:* (093) 3590004, pg 572

Edicon Editora e Consultorial Ltda (Brazil) *Tel:* (011) 3255-1002 *Fax:* (011) 2559828 *E-mail:* edicon@edicon.com.br *Web Site:* www.edicon.com.br, pg 81

EDIFIR SRL (Italy) *Tel:* (055) 289506 *Fax:* (055) 289478 *E-mail:* edifir@cibernet.it, pg 386

Edigol Ediciones SA (Spain) *Tel:* (093) 372 63 04 *Fax:* (093) 371 76 32 *E-mail:* info@edigol.com *Web Site:* www.edigol.com, pg 572

Edika-Med, SA (Spain) *Tel:* (093) 454 96 00 *Fax:* (093) 323 48 03 *E-mail:* edikamed@edikamed.com *Web Site:* www.edikamed.com, pg 572

Ediles-Ediciones Leonesas SA (Spain) *Tel:* (0987) 22 10 66 *Fax:* (0987) 22 54 60, pg 572

Edilux (Spain) *Tel:* (0958) 08 20 00 *Fax:* (0958) 08 20 00 *E-mail:* ediluxsl@supercable.es, pg 572

EDIM SA (Mali) *Tel:* 225522 *Fax:* 238503, pg 455

Edimecien Cia Ltda (Ecuador) *Tel:* (02) 502-427 *Fax:* (02) 502-429, pg 1282

EDIMSA - Editores Medicos SA (Spain) *Tel:* (091) 376 81 40 *Fax:* (091) 373 99 07 *E-mail:* edimsa@edimsa.es *Web Site:* www.edimsa.es, pg 572

Edinburgh Bibliographical Society (United Kingdom) *Tel:* (0131) 6503412 *Fax:* (0131) 6506863 *E-mail:* exkb33@srv1.lib.ed.ac.uk, pg 1370

Edinburgh University Library (United Kingdom) *Tel:* (0131) 650 3384; (0131) 650 3374 (reference & information services) *Fax:* (0131) 667 9780; (0131) 650 3380 (administration); (0131) 650 6863 (special collections) *E-mail:* library@ed.ac.uk *Web Site:* www.lib.ed.ac.uk, pg 1506

Edinburgh City Library & Information Services (United Kingdom) *Tel:* (0131) 242 8000 *Fax:* (0131) 242 8007 *E-mail:* eclis@edinburgh.gov.uk *Web Site:* www.edinburgh.gov.uk/libraries, pg 1506

Edinburgh University Press Ltd (United Kingdom) *Tel:* (0131) 650 4218; (0131) 650-6220 (Orders) *Fax:* (0131) 662 0053; (0131) 662-0053 (Orders) *E-mail:* marketing@eup.ed.ac.uk; journals@eup.ed.ac.uk (Orders) *Web Site:* www.eup.ed.ac.uk, pg 677

Ediciones Edinford SA (Spain) *Fax:* (095) 254689, pg 572

Ediouro Publicacoes, SA (Brazil) *Tel:* (021) 5606122 *Fax:* (011) 55893300 *E-mail:* ediourolivrosp@openlink.com.br; livros@ediouro.com.br *Web Site:* www.ediouro.com.br, pg 81

Edipro-Edicoes Profissionais Ltda (Brazil) *Tel:* (014) 232-3375 *Fax:* (014) 232-4684, pg 81

Edipuglia (Italy) *Tel:* (080) 5333056 *Fax:* (080) 5333057 *E-mail:* edipugli@tin.it *Web Site:* www.edipuglia.it, pg 386

Edirisooriya & Company (Sri Lanka) *Tel:* (01) 522555; (01) 523216 *Fax:* (01) 446380; (01) 074618905, pg 597

Editrice Edisco (Italy) *Tel:* (011) 54 78 80 *Fax:* (011) 51 75 396 *E-mail:* info@edisco.it *Web Site:* www.edisco.it, pg 386

Editorial Ediseis SA (Spain) *Tel:* (091) 4165511; (091) 4165218 *Fax:* (091) 4165411, pg 572

Edisport Editoriale SpA (Italy) *Tel:* (02) 380851 *Fax:* (02) 38010393, pg 386

Edisud (France) *Tel:* (04) 42 21 61 44 *Fax:* (04) 42 21 56 20 *E-mail:* info@edisud.com *Web Site:* www.edisud.com, pg 161

Editions Edita (Switzerland) *Tel:* (021) 6251392 *Fax:* (021) 6254291, pg 613

Editalia (Edizioni d'Italia) (Italy) *Tel:* (06) 8546146 *Fax:* (06) 8411225, pg 386

Editest, SPRL (Belgium) *Tel:* (02) 6476284 *Fax:* (02) 7325629, pg 68

Les Editeurs Reunis (France) *Tel:* (01) 43 54 74 46; (01) 43 54 43 81 *Fax:* (01) 43 25 34 79, pg 161

Editorial Editex SA (Spain) *Tel:* (091) 505 10 35 *Fax:* (091) 798 19 80 *E-mail:* correo@editex.es *Web Site:* www.editex.es, pg 572

Edition (United Kingdom) *Tel:* (01683) 220808 *Fax:* (01683) 220012, pg 1140

Edition (United Kingdom) *Tel:* (01683) 220808 *Fax:* (01683) 220012 *E-mail:* editorial@cameronbooks.co.uk *Web Site:* www.cameronbooks.co.uk, pg 1161

Edition Aragon-Verlagsgesellschaft mbH (Germany) *Tel:* (02841) 16561 *Fax:* (02841) 24336, pg 220

Edition Epoca (Switzerland) *Tel:* (01) 4511717 *Fax:* (01) 4511717 *E-mail:* info@epoca.ch *Web Site:* www.epoca.ch, pg 613

Edition Klaus Blahak Dr Fredric Kroll (Germany) *Tel:* (049) 761-244-73 *Fax:* (049) 761-244-73, pg 220

Edition Mariannepresse (Germany) *Tel:* (04864) 660 *E-mail:* quehilie@onlinehome.de, pg 220

Edition1 (France) *Tel:* (01) 43923587 *Fax:* (01) 43923585, pg 161

edition q Berlin Edition in der Quintessenz Verlags-GmbH (Germany) *Tel:* (030) 7 61 80-5 *Fax:* (030) 7 61 80-693 *E-mail:* info@quintessenz.de *Web Site:* www.quintessenz.de, pg 221

Edition S der OSD (Austria) *Tel:* (01) 79789295 *Fax:* (01) 79789455, pg 51

Edition Solitude - Akademie Schloss Solitude (Germany) *Tel:* (0711) 996190 *Fax:* (0711) 99619-50 *E-mail:* mail@akademie-solitude.de *Web Site:* www.akademie-solitude.de, pg 221

Editon XII (United Kingdom) *Tel:* (020) 7833 0120 *Fax:* (020) 7923 5500; (020) 7923 5505 *E-mail:* info@editionxii.co.uk, pg 677

Editions Ad Solem (Switzerland) *Tel:* (022) 321 19 30 *Fax:* (022) 321 19 31 *E-mail:* office@adsolem.ch, pg 613

Editions d'Organisation (France) *Tel:* (01) 44 41 46 41 *Fax:* (01) 44 41 46 00 *E-mail:* service-lecteurs@editions-organisation.com *Web Site:* www.editions-organisation.com, pg 161

Les Editions ESF (France) *Tel:* (01) 44691500 *Fax:* (01) 44692107 *Web Site:* www.pratique.fr/prat/, pg 161

Editions Grund (France) *Tel:* (01) 53103600 *Fax:* (01) 43294986 *E-mail:* grund@grund.fr *Web Site:* www.grund.fr, pg 161

Editions Recherche sur les Civilisations (ERC) (France) *Tel:* (01) 43 13 11 00 *Fax:* (01) 43 13 11 25 *Web Site:* www.france.diplomatie.fr; www.adpf.asso.fr, pg 161

Editions Tarmeye (France) *Tel:* (0471) 650153; (0477) 435814 *Fax:* (0471) 650154; (0477) 435899, pg 161

Editogo (Togo) *Tel:* 213718, pg 636

Editora Artes Medicas Ltda (Brazil) *Tel:* (011) 221-9033 *Fax:* (011) 223-6635 *E-mail:* artesmedicas@artesmedicas.com.br *Web Site:* www.artesmedicas.com.br, pg 82

Editora Brasil-America (EBAL) SA (Brazil) *Tel:* (021) 5800303 *Fax:* (021) 5801637, pg 82

Editora Cidade Nova Socieda de Movimentodos Focolari (Brazil) *Tel:* (011) 7960 2252 *Fax:* (011) 7960 2252 *E-mail:* editoria@cidadenova.org.br *Web Site:* www.cidadenova.org.br, pg 82

Editora Companhia das Letras/Editora Schwarcz Ltda (Brazil) *Tel:* (011) 3846-0801 *Fax:* (011) 3846-0814 *E-mail:* editora@companhiadasletras.com.br *Web Site:* www.companhiadasletras.com.br, pg 82

Editora Elevacao (Brazil) *Tel:* (011) 3225-4800; (011) 3225-4780; (011) 3225-4778 *Fax:* (011) 220-5803 *E-mail:* info@elevacao.com.br *Web Site:* www.elevacao.com.br, pg 82

Companhia Editora Forense (Brazil) *Tel:* (021) 2533-5537 *Fax:* (021) 2533-4752 *E-mail:* forense@forense.com.br; gryphus@gryphus.com.br *Web Site:* www.forense.com.br; www.gryphus.com.br, pg 82

Cia Editora Nacional (Brazil) *Tel:* (011) 2912355 *Fax:* (011) 2918614, pg 82

Corporacion Editora Nacional (Ecuador) *Tel:* (02) 554358; (02) 554558; (02) 554658 *Fax:* (02) 566340 *E-mail:* cen@accessinter.net, pg 137

Editora Paideia (Romania) *Tel:* (01) 3308006; (01) 3301678 *Fax:* (01) 3301677 *E-mail:* paideia@fx.ro, pg 1138

Editora Universidade De Brasilia (Brazil) *Tel:* (061) 2266874 *Fax:* (061) 2255611 *E-mail:* editora@unb.br, pg 1227

Editorama SA (Dominican Republic) *Tel:* (809) 5966669 (ext 4274) *Fax:* (809) 5941421 *E-mail:* editorama@codetel.net.do *Web Site:* www.editorama.com, pg 136

Editori Laterza (Italy) *Tel:* (06) 3223550; (06) 3218393 *Fax:* (06) 3223853 *E-mail:* laterza@laterza.it *Web Site:* www.laterza.it, pg 386

Editorial Ciudad Nueva de la Sefoma (Argentina) *Tel:* (011) 4981-4885 *Fax:* (011) 4981-3719, pg 5

Editorial Everest SA (Spain) *Tel:* (087) 844200 *Fax:* (087) 844202 *E-mail:* publicaciones@everest.es *Web Site:* www.everest.es, pg 572

Editorial Idearium de la Universidad de Mendoza (EDIUM) (Argentina) *Tel:* (0261) 420-2017 *Fax:* (0261) 420-1100 *E-mail:* umimen@um.edu.ar *Web Site:* www.um.edu.ar/um/, pg 5

Editoriale Bortolazzi-Stei srl (United States) *Tel:* 914-834-9594 *Fax:* 914-833-9106 *E-mail:* fulvioforcellini@ebs-bortolazzi.com, pg 1164

Editoriale Bortolazzi-Stei srl (United States) *Tel:* 914-834-9594 *Fax:* 914-833-9106, pg 1206

Editpress (Luxembourg) *Tel:* 547131 *Fax:* 547130 *E-mail:* tageblatt@tageblatt.lu, pg 447

Editrice Bibliografica SpA (Italy) *Tel:* (02) 28315996 *Fax:* (02) 28315906 *E-mail:* bibliografica@bibliografica.it *Web Site:* www.bibliografica.it, pg 386

Editrice la Giuntina (Italy) *Tel:* (055) 268684 *Fax:* (055) 219718 *E-mail:* giuntina@fol.it *Web Site:* www.giuntina.it, pg 386

Editrice la Scuola SpA (Italy) *Tel:* (030) 29931 *Fax:* (030) 2993299, pg 386

Edizioni Associate/Editrice Internazionale Srl (Italy) *Tel:* (06) 8841076 *Fax:* (06) 8841066, pg 386

Edizioni d'Arte e Moderna, Edam (Italy) *Tel:* (055) 2298578 *Fax:* (055) 2208837, pg 386

Edizioni Il Punto d'Incontro SAS (Italy) *Tel:* (0444) 928793 *Fax:* (0444) 928459 *E-mail:* edpunto@cdc.it, pg 386

Edizioni la Scala (Italy) *Tel:* (080) 4975838 *Fax:* (080) 4975839, pg 387

Edizioni l'Arciere SRL (Italy) *Tel:* (0171) 693174 *Fax:* (0171) 697729, pg 387

Edizioni l'eta Dell'Acquario Di I Bresci & C Sas (Italy) *Tel:* (0163) 418978 *Fax:* (0163) 411095, pg 387

Edizioni Mediterranee SRL (Italy) *Tel:* (06) 3235433 *Fax:* (06) 3236277 *E-mail:* info@ediz-mediterranee.com *Web Site:* www.ediz-mediterranee.com, pg 387

Edizioni Qiqajon (Italy) *Tel:* (015) 679264 *Fax:* (015) 679290 *E-mail:* edizioni@qiqajon.it *Web Site:* www.qiqajon.it, pg 387

Edizioni Studio Domenicano (ESD) (Italy) *Tel:* (051) 582034 *Fax:* (051) 331583 *E-mail:* esd@alinet.it *Web Site:* www.esd-domenicani.it, pg 387

EDP Sciences (France) *Tel:* (01) 69 18 75 75 *Fax:* (01) 69 28 84 91 *E-mail:* edps@edpsciences.org *Web Site:* www.edpsciences.org, pg 161

EDT Edizioni di Torino (Italy) *Tel:* (011) 5591811 *Fax:* (011) 5591824, pg 387

Educatieve Uitgeverij Edu'Actief BV (Netherlands) *Tel:* (0522) 262222 *Fax:* (0522) 263052, pg 476

EDUC - Editora da PUC-SP (Brazil) *Tel:* (011) 38733359 *Fax:* (011) 38733359 *E-mail:* educsp@puc001.pucsp.ansp.br, pg 82

Educatieve Partners Nederland bv (Netherlands) *Tel:* (030) 6359777 *Fax:* (030) 6359700, pg 476

Education Science Publishing House (China) *Tel:* (010) 2011177-365 *Fax:* (010) 62012454 *E-mail:* esph@public.net.china.com.cn, pg 105

Educational Advantage (Australia) *Tel:* (03) 5480 9466 *Fax:* (03) 5480 9462 *E-mail:* info@mathsmate.net *Web Site:* www.mathsmate.net, pg 21

Educational Books Publishing House (Democratic People's Republic of Korea), pg 434

The Educational Company of Ireland (Ireland) *Tel:* (01) 4500611 *Fax:* (01) 4500993 *E-mail:* info@edco.ie, pg 360

Educational Distributors Ltd (New Zealand) *Tel:* (09) 8184473 *Fax:* (09) 8362399 *E-mail:* 100241.222@compuserve.com, pg 490

Educational Explorers (Publishers) Ltd (United Kingdom) *Tel:* (0118) 987 3101 *Fax:* (0118) 987 3103 *E-mail:* explorers@cuisenaire.co.uk *Web Site:* www.cuisenaire.co.uk, pg 677

Educational Press & Manufacturers Ltd (Ghana) *Tel:* (051) 5003; (051) 5845 *Fax:* (051) 227572, pg 307

Educational Publishers Council (United Kingdom) *Tel:* (020) 7565 7474 *Fax:* (020) 7836 4543 *E-mail:* mail@publishers.org.uk *Web Site:* www.publishers.org.uk, pg 1265

Educational Publishers Ltd (Ghana) *Tel:* (021) 220395 *Fax:* (021) 227572, pg 307

The Educational Publishing House Ltd (Hong Kong) *Tel:* (02) 4088801 *Fax:* (02) 4080174, pg 319

Educational Research & Study Group (Nigeria), pg 499

Educational Supplies Pty Ltd (The Dominie Group) (Australia) *Tel:* (02) 99050201 *Fax:* (02) 99055209, pg 21

Educational Writers' Group (United Kingdom) *Tel:* (020) 7373 6642 *Fax:* (020) 7373 5768 *E-mail:* info@societyofauthors.org *Web Site:* www.societyofauthors.org, pg 1265

Educum Publishers Ltd (South Africa) *Tel:* (011) 3153647 *Fax:* (011) 3152757, pg 554

EDULIS (Education Library & Information Services) (South Africa) *Tel:* (021) 4835265; (021) 4835266; (021) 4835267 *Fax:* (021) 4835747, pg 1497

EDUSC - Editora da Universidade do Sagrado Coracao (Brazil) *Tel:* (014) 235 7111 *Fax:* (014) 235 7219 *E-mail:* edusc@usc.br *Web Site:* www.usc.br/edusc, pg 82

Eduskunnan Kirjasto (Finland) *Tel:* (00) 4321 *Fax:* (00) 4323495 *E-mail:* library@eduskunta.fi *Web Site:* www.eduskunta.fi/kirjasto/, pg 1463

Edwina Publishing (Australia) *Tel:* (03) 9836 3810 *Fax:* (03) 9830 1356, pg 21

Eekhoorn BV Uitgeverij (Netherlands) *Tel:* (036) 5227545 *Fax:* (036) 5226986, pg 476

Eenhoorn BVBA (Belgium) *Tel:* (056) 605460 *Fax:* (056) 616981 *E-mail:* info@eenhoorn.be *Web Site:* users.skynet.be/eenhoorn, pg 68

Oue Eesti Raamat (Estonia) *Tel:* (02) 6587885; (02) 6587886; (02) 6587887; (02) 6587889 *Fax:* (02) 6587889, pg 139

EFE Tres D-Pub Juridicas Ltda (Brazil) *Tel:* (084) 2233394 *Fax:* (084) 2232263 *E-mail:* f3dsat@truenetrn.com.br, pg 83

eFeF-Verlag/Edition Ebersbach (Switzerland) *Tel:* (031) 3822004 *Fax:* (031) 3824555, pg 613

Effata Editrice (Italy) *Tel:* (0121) 353452 *Fax:* (0121) 353839 *E-mail:* info@effata.it *Web Site:* www.effata.it, pg 387

Effective Publishing (United Kingdom) *Tel:* (01926) 812110, pg 1265

Effendi Harahap Bookstore (Indonesia), pg 1290

EFR-Editrici Francescane (Italy) *Tel:* (049) 8225702 *Fax:* (049) 8225713 *E-mail:* ebf@biblia.it, pg 387

Efstathiadis Group SA (Greece) *Tel:* (01) 8131593 *Fax:* (01) 8142915, pg 1286

Ediciones Ega (Spain) *Tel:* (04) 4216787 *Fax:* (04) 4213010, pg 572

Egales (Editorial Gai y Lesbiana) (Spain) *Tel:* (093) 4127283 *Fax:* (093) 4127283 *E-mail:* complices@retemail.es, pg 572

Egan Publishing Pty Ltd (Australia) *Tel:* (03) 5923451 *Fax:* (03) 95931026, pg 21

Egan-Reid Ltd (New Zealand) *Tel:* (09) 3784100 *Fax:* (09) 3784300 *E-mail:* books@eganreid.co.nz, pg 1158, 1222

Editions EGC (Monaco) *Tel:* (093) 92057433 *Fax:* (093) 92052422 *E-mail:* multip@webstore.mc, pg 468

EGEA (Edizioni Giuridiche Economiche Aziendali) (Italy) *Tel:* (02) 58362034; (02) 89401158; (02) 89402431 *Fax:* (02) 58362033; (02) 89402431 *E-mail:* egea.edizioni@egea.uni-bocconi.it, pg 387

Egerton University (Kenya) *Tel:* (037) 61620; (037) 61031; (037) 61032 *Fax:* (037) 61527; (037) 61442; (037) 61389, pg 431

Egerton University Library (Kenya) *Tel:* (037) 61620 *Fax:* (037) 61527 *E-mail:* eu-vc@net2000kc.com, pg 1479

Egmont-Easy Readers (Denmark) *Tel:* 33305830 *E-mail:* um@ash.egmont.com *Web Site:* www.easyreader.dk, pg 131

Egmont EHAPA Verlag GmbH (Germany) *Tel:* (030) 24008-0 *Fax:* (030) 24008-599, pg 221

Egmont Franz Schneider Verlag GmbH (Germany) *Tel:* (089) 3 58 11-6 *Fax:* (089) 3 58 11-7 55 *E-mail:* postmaster@schneiderbuch.de *Web Site:* schneiderbuch.funonline.de, pg 221

Egmont Group (Denmark) *Tel:* 33305550 *Fax:* 33321902 *E-mail:* egmont@egmont.com; info@egt.egmont.com *Web Site:* www.egmont.com, pg 131

Egmont Lademann A/S (Denmark) *Tel:* 36 15 66 00 *Fax:* 36 44 11 62 *Web Site:* www.egmont.com; www.egmontbogklub.dk (Book Club), pg 131

Egmont Latvia Ltd (Latvia) *Tel:* (02) 2468671 *Fax:* (02) 7860049, pg 442

Egmont Lietuva (Lithuania) *Tel:* (02) 231265; (02) 231266; (02) 231267 *Fax:* (02) 231269, pg 445

Egmont Neografia spol sro (Slovakia) *Tel:* (07) 238064; (07) 233933; (07) 295966 *Fax:* (07) 238755 *E-mail:* egmont@netlab.sk, pg 549

Egmont Pestalozzi-Verlag (Germany) *Tel:* (089) 3 58 11-8 62 *Fax:* (089) 58 11-8 69 *E-mail:* postmaster@pestalozzi-verlag.de *Web Site:* pestalozzi-verlag.funonline.de, pg 221

Egmont Serieforlaget A/S (Denmark) *Tel:* 33305000 *Fax:* 33305510 *Web Site:* www.serieforlaget.dk, pg 131

Egmont Serieforlaget (Sweden) *Tel:* (040) 6399400 *Fax:* (040) 939325, pg 601

Egmont vgs verlagsgesellschaft mbH (Germany) *Tel:* (0221) 20811-0 *Fax:* (0221) 20811-66 *E-mail:* info@vgs.de *Web Site:* www.vgs.de, pg 221

Egmont Wangel A/S (Denmark) *Tel:* 36156600 *Fax:* 36441162 *Web Site:* www.bogklubber.dk, pg 1227

Egyptian Association for Library & Information Science (Egypt (Arab Republic of Egypt)) *Tel:* (02) 5676365 *Fax:* (02) 5729659, pg 1515

Egyptian National Library (Dar-ul-Kutub) (Egypt (Arab Republic of Egypt)) *Tel:* (02) 900232, pg 1462

The Egyptian Society for the Dissemination of Universal Culture and Knowledge (ESDUCK) (Egypt (Arab Republic of Egypt)) *Tel:* (02) 35425079; (02) 35420295 *Fax:* (02) 3540295, pg 138

The Egyptian Society for the Dissemination of Universal Culture and Knowledge (ESDUCK) (Egypt (Arab Republic of Egypt)) *Tel:* (02) 3545079 *Fax:* (02) 3540295, pg 1110

The Egyptian Society for the Dissemination of Universal Culture and Knowledge (ESDUCK) (Egypt (Arab Republic of Egypt)) *Tel:* (02) 3545079; (02) 3540295, pg 1125

Ehrenwirth Verlag (Germany) *Tel:* (02202) 121-0 *Fax:* (02202) 121-920 *E-mail:* info@luebbe.de *Web Site:* www.luebbe.de, pg 221

Ehrenwirth Verlag GmbH (Germany) *Tel:* (089) 54 43 35-0 *Fax:* (089) 534739 *Web Site:* www.ehrenwirth.de, pg 221

Eichborn AG (Germany) *Tel:* (069) 2560030 *Fax:* (069) 25600330 *E-mail:* rights@eichborn.de *Web Site:* www.eichborn.de, pg 222

Eichosha Company Ltd (Japan) *Tel:* (03) 32636171 *Fax:* (03) 32636155, pg 416

Universitaetsbibliothek Eichstaett (Germany) *Tel:* (08421) 931330 *Fax:* (08421) 931791 *E-mail:* ub-direktion@ku-eichstaett.de, pg 1467

J W Eides Forlag A/S (Norway) *Tel:* 55329040 *Fax:* 55319018, pg 503

Drei Eidgenossen Verlag (Switzerland) *Tel:* (061) 475166 *Fax:* (061) 475166, pg 613

Eiffes Romain (Luxembourg) *Tel:* (023) 65 10 52 *E-mail:* rend@pt.lu, pg 447

The Eighteen Nineties Society (United Kingdom) *Tel:* (020) 7582 4690, pg 1370

The Eihosha Ltd (Japan) *Tel:* (03) 32920167 *Fax:* (03) 32196095, pg 416

Eike-Boekklub (South Africa) *Tel:* (012) 401 0700 *Fax:* (012) 3255498 *E-mail:* lapa@atkv.org.za, pg 1231

Eiland-Verlag Sylt Frank Roseman (Germany) *Tel:* (04651) 936212 *Fax:* (04651) 936214 *E-mail:* info@eiland-verlag.de *Web Site:* www.eiland-verlag.de, pg 222

Ein Fach-Verlag (Germany) *Tel:* (0241) 405501 *Fax:* (0241) 400 96 67 *E-mail:* einfachverlag@gmx.de *Web Site:* www.philosophinnen.de/verlag/index.htm, pg 222

Ein Shams University Library (Egypt (Arab Republic of Egypt)) *Tel:* (02) 2847827 *Fax:* (02) 2847824, pg 1462

Giulio Einaudi Editore SpA (Italy) *Tel:* (011) 56561 *Fax:* (011) 542903; (011) 5626220, pg 387

Bibliotheek Technische Universiteit Eindhoven (Netherlands) *Tel:* (040) 2472381 *Fax:* (040) 2447015 *E-mail:* helpdesk.bib@tue.nl, pg 1486

EinfallsReich Verlagsgesellschaft MbH (Germany) *Tel:* (05533) 2017 *Fax:* (0531) 791507, pg 222

Eironeia-Verlag (Germany) *Tel:* (0761) 581617 *Fax:* (0761) 581617, pg 222

Editions Eisele SA (Switzerland) *Tel:* (021) 6256324 *Fax:* (021) 6256374 *E-mail:* editions.eisele@worldcom.ch, pg 613

Verlag Eisenbahn (Switzerland) *Tel:* (056) 2845584; 441595 *Fax:* (056) 2845884, pg 613

Christian Ejlers' Forlag aps (Denmark) *Tel:* 33122114 *Fax:* 33122884 *E-mail:* liber@ce-publishers.dk *Web Site:* www.ejlers.dk, pg 131

EK Press (Australia) *Tel:* (07) 4097 6474 *Fax:* (07) 4097 6474, pg 21

EK-Verlag GmbH (Germany) *Tel:* (0761) 70310-0 *Fax:* (0761) 70310-50, pg 222

Ekab Business Ltd (Ghana) *Tel:* (021) 225318, pg 307

Ediciones Ekare (Venezuela) *Tel:* (02) 2630080; (02) 2636170; (02) 2630091 *Fax:* (02) 2633291, pg 762

Ekdoseis Kazantzaki (Kazantzakis Publications) (Greece) *Tel:* (01) 3642829 *Fax:* (01) 3642829, pg 310

Ekdotike Athenon SA (Greece) *Tel:* (01) 360-8911; (01) 3606666 *Fax:* (01) 3606157 *Web Site:* www.addgr.com/comp/ekdotiki/index.html, pg 310

Ekelunds Forlag AB (Sweden) *Tel:* (08) 821320 *Fax:* (08) 832956 *E-mail:* education@ekelunds.se, pg 601

Ekenas Tryckeri AB (Finland) *Tel:* (09) 222800 *Fax:* (09) 222813 *E-mail:* leif.rex@eta.fi, pg 142

Izdatelstvo Ekologija (Russian Federation) *Tel:* (095) 9287860, pg 537

Ekonomibok Forlag AB (Sweden) *Tel:* (042) 92950 *Fax:* (042) 92950, pg 601

Polskie Wydawnictwo Ekonomiczne PWE SA (Poland) *Tel:* (022) 8278001 *Fax:* (022) 8275567 *E-mail:* pwe@pwe.com.pl *Web Site:* www.pwe.com.pl, pg 516

Izdatelstvo 'Ekonomika' (Russian Federation) *Tel:* (095) 2404877 *Fax:* (095) 2404869, pg 537

EL Ciervo 96 (Spain) *Tel:* (093) 200 51 45; (093) 201 00 96 *Fax:* (093) 201 10 15 *E-mail:* redaccion@elciervo.es *Web Site:* www.elciervo.es, pg 572

El Colegio de Michoacan A C (Mexico) *Tel:* (0351) 515 71 00 *Fax:* (0351) 5157100, Ext 1712 *E-mail:* publica@colmich.cmich.udg.mx; publica@colmich.edu.mx *Web Site:* www.colmich.edu.mx, pg 460

El Hogar y la Moda SA (Spain) *Tel:* (093) 508 70 00 *Fax:* (093) 454 87 72 *E-mail:* hymsa@hymsa.com *Web Site:* www.hymsa.com, pg 572

El-M'aaref Editions (Tunisia) *Tel:* (03) 256235 *Fax:* (03) 256530, pg 638

Darl el-Machreq Sarl (Lebanon) *Tel:* (01) 202423; (01) 202424 *Fax:* (01) 329348 *E-mail:* machreq@cyberia.net.lb, pg 443

Editorial El Manual Moderno SA de CV (Mexico) *Tel:* (05) 5648979; (05) 5642321 *Fax:* (05) 2641701; (05) 2651162 *E-mail:* mmoderuo@compuserve.com.ux, pg 460

El Viso, SA Ediciones (Spain) *Tel:* (091) 5196576; (091) 5196583 *Fax:* (091) 5196583 *E-mail:* lvisoh@anexo.es, pg 572

Elafaki (Greece) *Tel:* (01) 7239476 *Fax:* (01) 7239483, pg 310

Eland (United Kingdom) *Tel:* (020) 7833 0762 *Fax:* (020) 7833 4434 *E-mail:* feedback@travelbooks.co.uk *Web Site:* www.travelbooks.co.uk, pg 677

Elanders Publishing AS (Norway) *Tel:* 22636400 *Fax:* 22636594 *Web Site:* www.elanders.no, pg 503

ELC International (United Kingdom) *Tel:* (01865) 513186; (01865) 26520284 *Fax:* (01865) 513186; (01865) 26530180 *E-mail:* snyderpub@aol.com, pg 678

ELCE Editeurs et Libraires Catholiques d'Europe (Switzerland) *Tel:* (071) 279580 *Fax:* (071) 279580 *E-mail:* hawas@mhs.ch, pg 613

ELCIN Book Depot (Namibia) *Tel:* (06756) 40211 *Fax:* (06756) 40211, pg 1300

NV Drukkerij Eldorado (Suriname) *Tel:* 472362, pg 599

Electa (Italy) *Tel:* (02) 215631 *Fax:* (02) 26413121, pg 387

Electre Editions du Cercle de la Librairie (France) *Tel:* (01) 44 41 28 00 *Fax:* (01) 44 41 28 65 *Web Site:* www.imaginet.fr/electre, pg 161

Electroliber Lda (Portugal) *Tel:* (01) 9425394 *Fax:* (01) 9425214, pg 1307

Electronic Publishing Services Ltd (United Kingdom) *Tel:* (020) 7837 3345 *Fax:* (020) 7837 8901 *E-mail:* eps@epsltd.com *Web Site:* www.epsltd.com, pg 678

Electronic Technology Publishing Co Ltd (Hong Kong) *Tel:* 2342 8297 *Fax:* 2341 4247 *E-mail:* info@electronictechnology.com *Web Site:* www.electronictechnology.com, pg 319

Electronica Books & Media Ltd (United Kingdom) *Tel:* (01932) 765119 *Fax:* (01932) 765429, pg 1319

Electronics Industry Publishing House (China) *Tel:* (010) 8212233-3462 *Fax:* (010) 86106821-4062, pg 105

Edizioni dell'Elefante (Italy) *Tel:* (06) 68803710 *Fax:* (06) 6832526, pg 388

Elefanten Press Verlag GmbH (Germany) *Tel:* (01805) 99 05 05 *Web Site:* www.randomouse.de/elefantenpress/, pg 222

Eleftheri Skepsis (Greece) *Tel:* (01) 3614736; (01) 3630697, pg 1286

G C Eleftheroudakis Co Ltd (Greece) *Tel:* (01) 3222255; (01) 3229388 *Fax:* (01) 3231401; (01) 3229388, pg 1286

Eleftheroudakis, GCSA International Bookstore (Greece) *Tel:* (01) 322 63 23 *Fax:* (01) 325 48 89 *E-mail:* elebooks@netor.gr, pg 310

Elegance Finance Printing Services Ltd (Hong Kong) *Tel:* 25212200 *Fax:* 25213616 *E-mail:* saledept@elegancefinptg.com, pg 1155, 1221

Elegance Printing & Book Binding (USA) (United States) *Tel:* 516-676-5941 *Fax:* 516-676-5973 *Web Site:* www.elegancebooks.com, pg 1143, 1164, 1206, 1215

Elektor-Verlag GmbH (Germany) *Tel:* (0241) 889090 *Fax:* (0241) 8890988 *E-mail:* redaktion@elektor.de *Web Site:* www.elektor.de, pg 222

Elektrowirtschaft Verlag (Switzerland) *Tel:* (01) 2910102 *Fax:* (01) 2910903, pg 613

Element Books Ltd (United Kingdom) *Tel:* (01747) 851448 *Fax:* (01747) 855721, pg 678

Element Uitgevers (Netherlands) *Tel:* (035) 6941750 *Fax:* (035) 6945824 *E-mail:* element@wxs.nl, pg 476

Elephas Books Pty Ltd (Australia) *Tel:* (09) 3701461 *Fax:* (09) 3418952, pg 21

Selecoes Eletronicas Editora Ltda (Brazil) *Tel:* (021) 2539268 *Fax:* (021) 2638840, pg 83

Elf Exploration Production (France) *Tel:* (05) 59 83 65 80 *Fax:* (05) 59 83 57 88 *Web Site:* www.cgt-totalfina-elf.org, pg 161

Elfande Ltd (United Kingdom) *Tel:* (01372) 220330 *Fax:* (01372) 220340 *E-mail:* sales@contact-uk.com *Web Site:* www.contact-uk.com, pg 678

Ediciones Elfos SL (Spain) *Tel:* (093) 4069479 *Fax:* (093) 4069006 *E-mail:* eltos-ed@teleline.es *Web Site:* www.edicioneselfos.com, pg 572

Edward Elgar Publishing Ltd (United Kingdom) *Tel:* (01242) 226934 *Fax:* (01242) 262111 *E-mail:* info@e-elgar.co.uk *Web Site:* www.e-elgar.co.uk, pg 678

Elgin Consultants Ltd (Hong Kong) *Tel:* 28151680, pg 1134

Elias Modern Publishing House (Egypt (Arab Republic of Egypt)) *Tel:* (02) 903756 B *Fax:* (02) 2490736; (02) 938003, pg 138

The George Eliot Fellowship (United Kingdom) *Tel:* (024) 7659 2231, pg 1370

Elite Printing Company Ltd (Hong Kong) *Tel:* 25580119 *Fax:* 28972675 *E-mail:* elitemkt@elite.com.hk; sales@elite.com.hk *Web Site:* www.elite.com.hk, pg 1134

Elkar, Euskal Liburu eta Kantuen Argitaldaria, SL (Spain) *Tel:* (043) 310267 *Fax:* (043) 310216, pg 573

David Ell Press Pty Ltd (Australia) *Tel:* (02) 5551634 *Fax:* (02) 5557067, pg 21

Elle Di Ci - Libreria Dottrina Cristiana (Italy) *Tel:* (011) 9552111 *Fax:* (011) 9572900; (011) 9574048 *E-mail:* mail@elledici.org *Web Site:* www.elledici.org, pg 388

Ellebore (France) *Tel:* (01) 40 01 09 49 *Fax:* (01) 40 01 09 94 *E-mail:* ellebore@wfi.fr *Web Site:* www.wfi.fr/ellebore, pg 161

Verlag Heinrich Ellermann GmbH & Co KG (Germany) *Tel:* (040) 60790901 *Fax:* (040) 6072326 *E-mail:* ellermann@vsg-hamburg.de *Web Site:* www.ellermann.de, pg 222

Ellerstroms (Sweden) *Tel:* 323295 *Fax:* 323295 *E-mail:* info@ellerstroms.se *Web Site:* www.ellerstroms.se, pg 602

Ellert & Richter Verlag GmbH (Germany) *Tel:* (040) 39 84 77-0 *Fax:* (040) 39 84 77-23 *E-mail:* info@ellert-richter.de *Web Site:* www.ellert-richter.de, pg 222

Elliniki Etaireia Metafraston Logotechnias (Greece) *Tel:* (01) 6717466 *Fax:* (01) 6776912, pg 1126

Elliniki Leschi Tou Vivliou (Greece) *Tel:* (01) 6463888 *Fax:* (01) 6463263 *E-mail:* elli@gezmanosnet.gz, pg 310

Elliot Right Way Books (United Kingdom) *Tel:* (01737) 832202 *Fax:* (01737) 830311 *E-mail:* info@right-way.co.uk *Web Site:* www.right-way.co.uk, pg 678

Ellipses - Edition Marketing SA (France) *Tel:* (01) 56 56 64 10 *Fax:* (01) 45 31 07 67 *E-mail:* infos@editions-ellipses.com *Web Site:* www.editions-ellipses.com, pg 162

Aidan Ellis Publishing (United Kingdom) *Tel:* (01548) 842755 *Fax:* (01548) 844356 *E-mail:* aidan@aepub.demon.co.uk *Web Site:* www.demon.co.uk/aepub, pg 678

Thomas Ellis Memorial Fund (United Kingdom) *Tel:* (029) 2038 2656 *Fax:* (029) 2078 6259 *E-mail:* awards@wales.ac.uk, pg 1370

ELLUG (Editions Litteraires et Linguistiques de l'Universite de Grenoble III) (France) *Tel:* (04) 76 82 43 72; (04) 76 82 77 74 *Fax:* (04) 76 82 41 12 *E-mail:* ellug@u-grenoble3.fr *Web Site:* www-ellug.u-grenoble3.fr, pg 162

Elm Publications (United Kingdom) *Tel:* (01487) 773254; (01487) 773238 *Fax:* (01487) 773359 *E-mail:* elm@elm-training.co.uk *Web Site:* www.elm-training.co.uk, pg 678

Elmar BV (Netherlands) *Tel:* (015) 2153232 *Fax:* (015) 2153230 *E-mail:* elmar@elmar.nl, pg 476

Edicoes ELO (Portugal) *Tel:* (061) 812143 *Fax:* (061) 812820 *E-mail:* eloag@elografica.pt *Web Site:* www.elografica.pt, pg 524

Elpis Verlag GmbH (Germany) *Tel:* (06221) 165789, pg 222

Buchhandlung zum Elsasser AG (Switzerland) *Tel:* (01) 2610847; (01) 2511612 *Fax:* (01) 2610897, pg 1313

Elsevier Advanced Technology (United Kingdom) *Tel:* (01865) 843848 *Fax:* (01865) 843010 *E-mail:* eatsales@elsevier.co.uk (sales) *Web Site:* www.nepcon.co.uk/ex0210g.htm, pg 678

Elsevier Science (Japan) *Tel:* (03) 5561 5033 *Fax:* (03) 5561 5047 *E-mail:* info@elsevier.co.jp *Web Site:* www.elsevier.co.jp, pg 416

Elsevier Science SA (Switzerland) *Tel:* (021) 3207381 *Fax:* (021) 3235444, pg 613

Elsevier Science BV (Netherlands) *Tel:* (020) 5862911 *Fax:* (020) 4852457 *E-mail:* nlinfo-f@elsevier.nl, pg 477

Elsevier Science Ltd (United Kingdom) *Tel:* (01865) 843000 *Fax:* (01865) 843010 *E-mail:* initial.lastname@elsevier.com *Web Site:* www.elsevier.com, pg 678

Elstead Maps (United Kingdom) *Tel:* (01252) 703472 *Fax:* (01252) 703971 *E-mail:* maps@elstead.co.uk *Web Site:* www.elstead.co.uk, pg 1319

Elton Publications (Australia) *Tel:* (08) 9 446 1328 *Fax:* (08) 9 445 8229 *E-mail:* elton@iinet.net.au *Web Site:* www.elton.iinet.net.au, pg 21

Elvetica Edizioni SA (Switzerland) *Tel:* (091) 6839920; (091) 6835056 *Fax:* (091) 6837605 *E-mail:* info@swissfinance.com *Web Site:* www.swissfinance.com, pg 613

N G Elwert Verlag (Germany) *Tel:* (06421) 17090 *Fax:* (06421) 15487 *E-mail:* elwertmail@elwert.de *Web Site:* www.elwert.de, pg 222

Uitgeverij Hans Elzenga BV (Netherlands) *Tel:* (020) 5511262 *Fax:* (020) 6203509, pg 477

Gholam EMAMI (Germany) *Tel:* (0911) 288356 *Fax:* (0911) 288356, pg 222

Emece Editores (Spain) *Tel:* (093) 2151199 *Fax:* (093) 2154636 *E-mail:* emece@ran.es, pg 573

Emece Editores SA (Argentina) *Tel:* (011) 4954-0105; (011) 4954-0120 *Fax:* (011) 4953-4200 *E-mail:* editorial@emece.com.ar *Web Site:* www.emece.com.ar, pg 5

Emerald City Books (Australia) *Tel:* (02) 7641115 *Fax:* (02) 7641115 *E-mail:* emeraldcitybooks@hotmail.com, pg 22

Emerald Publications (Ireland) *Tel:* (021) 962853 *Fax:* (021) 310983 *E-mail:* alongk@iol.ie, pg 360

Editura Eminescu (Romania) *Tel:* (01) 2228540, pg 533

Emirates Printing Press (LLC) (United Arab Emirates) *Tel:* (04) 347 5550; (04) 347 5544 *Fax:* (04) 347 5959 *E-mail:* eppdubai@emirates.net.ae *Web Site:* www.eppdubai.com, pg 1202

Emmaus Bible School (United Republic of Tanzania) *Tel:* (026) 2354500 *Fax:* (026) 2350911 *E-mail:* cmml-dar@maf.or.tz, pg 633

Emons Verlag (Germany) *Tel:* (0221) 569 77-0 *Fax:* (0221) 52 49 37 *E-mail:* info@emons-verlag.de *Web Site:* www.emons-verlag.de, pg 222

Editorial Empeno 14 (Spain) *Tel:* (091) 3079386 *Fax:* (091) 3079384, pg 573

Emperor Publishing (Australia) *Tel:* (02) 9261-4055 *Fax:* (02) 9264-9435 *E-mail:* pa@oxfordsquare.com.au, pg 22

Empire Printing Ltd (Hong Kong) *Tel:* 26655193 *Fax:* 26617722, pg 1134

Emporio de Promocao Artistica Cultural e Editora Ltda (Brazil) *Tel:* (011) 8262992 *Fax:* (011) 661135, pg 83

Empresa Brasileira de Pesquisa Agropecaria (Brazil) *Tel:* (061) 448-4433 *Fax:* (061) 347-1041 *E-mail:* web@spi.embrapa.br *Web Site:* www.embrapa.br, pg 83

Empresa Moderna Lda (Mozambique) *Tel:* (01) 424594, pg 470

Empresas Editoriales SA (Mexico) *Tel:* (05) 5288979; (05) 5288417 *Fax:* (05) 5288417, pg 460

Editorial Empuries (Spain) *Tel:* (093) 443 71 00 *Fax:* (093) 443 71 30 *E-mail:* correu@grup62.com *Web Site:* www.grup62.com, pg 573

Enalios (Greece) *Tel:* (01) 2531614 *Fax:* (01) 2184854, pg 1286

Enciclopedia Catalana, SA (Spain) *Tel:* (093) 412 0030 *Fax:* (093) 301 4863 *E-mail:* secedit@grec.com *Web Site:* www.enciclopedia-catalana.com, pg 573

Encres Vives (France) *Tel:* (05) 62740787 *E-mail:* encres@mygale.org, pg 162

Ediciones Encuentro SA (Spain) *Tel:* (091) 532 26 07 *Fax:* (091) 532 23 46 *E-mail:* encuentro@ediciones-encuentro.es *Web Site:* www.ediciones-encuentro.es, pg 573

Encyclopaedia Publishing House (Albania) *Tel:* (042) 28064 *Fax:* (042) 28064, pg 1

Encyclopaedia Britannica (Australia) Inc (Australia) *Tel:* (02) 96805666 *Fax:* (02) 98993231, pg 22

Encyclopaedia Britannica (Philippines) Inc (Philippines) *Tel:* (02) 895816 *Fax:* (02) 8102144, pg 513

Encyclopaedia Britannica (UK) International Ltd (United Kingdom) *Tel:* (020) 7500 7800; (0845) 075 700 (orders CD or DVD inside UK); (0177) 901 3948 (orders CD or DVD outside UK); (0845) 075 8000 (order bks inside UK); (0845) 901 3948 (order bks outside UK) *Fax:* (020) 7500 7875 *E-mail:* enquiries@brittanica.co.uk *Web Site:* corporate.britannica.co.uk, pg 679

Encyclopedia Britannica (Germany) *Tel:* (0251) 48 227-0 *Fax:* (0251) 48 227-27 *E-mail:* lexikadienst@aol.com *Web Site:* www.britannica.de, pg 222

Encyclopedia Judaica (Israel) *Tel:* (02) 6557822 *Fax:* (02) 6528962 *E-mail:* info@keter-books.co.il *Web Site:* www.keter-books.co.il, pg 367

Encyclopedia of China Publishing House (China) *Tel:* (010) 68345014 *Fax:* (010) 68316510 *E-mail:* ygh@bj.col.com.cn, pg 105

Encyclopedia Universalis France SA (France) *Tel:* (01) 45 72 72 72 *Fax:* (01) 45 72 03 43 *E-mail:* communication@universalis.fr *Web Site:* www.universalis.fr, pg 162

Enda Tiers Monde (Senegal) *Tel:* (0221) 216027; (0221) 224229 *Fax:* (0221) 222695, pg 544

Ediciones Endymion (Spain) *Tel:* (01) 5223668; (01) 5222210, pg 573

EnEffect, Center for Energy Efficiency (Bulgaria) *Tel:* (02) 963 1714; (02) 9630723; (02) 9632169 *Fax:* (02) 9632574 *E-mail:* eneffect@mail.orbitel.bg *Web Site:* www.eneffect.bg, pg 95

Energeia sp zoo Wydawnictwo (Poland) *Tel:* (022) 847-00-53 *Fax:* (022) 847-00-53, pg 516

Energica Foerlags AB/Halsabocker (Sweden) *Tel:* (0250) 552000 *Fax:* (0250) 43191 *Web Site:* www.energica.com, pg 602

Energoatomizdat (Russian Federation) *Tel:* (095) 9259993 *Fax:* (095) 2356585, pg 537

The Energy Information Centre (United Kingdom) *Tel:* (01638) 751 400 *Fax:* (01638) 751 801 *E-mail:* info@eic.co.uk *Web Site:* www.eic.co.uk, pg 679

Engel & Bengel Verlag (Germany) *Tel:* (06353) 8107 *Fax:* (06353) 507057 *E-mail:* verlag@engelundbengel.de *Web Site:* www.engelundbengel.de, pg 222

Engelhorn Verlag (Germany) *Tel:* (0711) 2631-0 *Fax:* (0711) 2631-292, pg 222

Englisch Verlag GmbH (Germany) *Tel:* (0611) 9 427 2-0 *Fax:* (0611) 9 42 72-40 *E-mail:* englisch@englisch-verlag.de *Web Site:* www.englisch-verlag.de, pg 222

The English Agency (Japan) Ltd (Japan) *Tel:* (03) 34065385 *Fax:* (03) 34065387 *E-mail:* info@eaj.co.jp, pg 1113

English Association (United Kingdom) *Tel:* (0116) 2523982 *Fax:* (0116) 2522301 *E-mail:* engassoc@le.ac.uk *Web Site:* www.le.ac.uk/engassoc/, pg 1370

English Book Store (India) *Tel:* (011) 3329126 *Fax:* (011) 3321731, pg 1288

English Language Editors' Association (ELEAS) (Israel) *Tel:* (02) 586-5772 *Fax:* (02) 586-6411 *Web Site:* www.geocities.com/jewishgroups/8Eleas.html, pg 1365

The English-Speaking Union of the Commonwealth (United Kingdom) *Tel:* (020) 7529 1550 *Fax:* (020) 7495 6108 *E-mail:* esu@esu.org *Web Site:* www.esu.org, pg 1371

English Teaching Professional (United Kingdom) *E-mail:* etp@etprofessional.com *Web Site:* www.etprofessional.com, pg 679

Verlag Peter Engstler (Germany) *Tel:* (09774) 858490 *Fax:* (09774) 858491 *E-mail:* engstler-verlag@t-online.de *Web Site:* www.engstler-verlag.de, pg 223

Enkay Publishers Pvt Ltd (India) *Tel:* (011) 301-6994; (011) 301-2314 *Fax:* (011) 301-2314, pg 336

Enne (Italy) *Tel:* (0874) 412357 *Fax:* (0874) 412357, pg 388

Ennsthaler GesmbH & Co KG (Austria) *Tel:* (07252) 52053 26 *Fax:* (07252) 52053 3 *E-mail:* buero@ennsthaler.at *Web Site:* www.ennsthaler.at, pg 51

Enosis Hellinon Bibliothekarion (Greece) *Tel:* (01) 3226625, pg 1517

Enrique Libreria (Spain) *Tel:* (091) 5228088, pg 1311

Enschede en Zonen (Netherlands) *Tel:* (020) 5858600 *Fax:* (020) 5858605, pg 477

Ensiklopedie Afrikana (South Africa) *Tel:* (011) 4021400; (011) 297093, pg 554

Enso Oy (Finland) *Tel:* (0204) 6121 *Fax:* (02046) 24701, pg 1132

Ensslin und Laiblin Verlag GmbH & Co KG (Germany) *Tel:* (01721) 98 98 0 *Fax:* (01721) 98 98 44 *E-mail:* ensslin-verlag@t-online.de *Web Site:* www.ensslin-verlag.de, pg 223

Editions Entente (France) *Tel:* (01) 42 22 80 70 *Fax:* (01) 40 49 01 02, pg 162

Enterprise International (Hong Kong) *Tel:* 25734161 *Fax:* 28383469 *E-mail:* hernad@netvigator.com, pg 1287

Enterprise Nationale du Livre (ENAL) (Algeria) *Tel:* (02) 639712; (02) 639643, pg 2

Enterprise Publications (Australia) *Tel:* (08) 2619528 *Fax:* (08) 2619528, pg 22

Entretenlibro SA de CV (Mexico) *Tel:* (09183) 425570, pg 460

Envirobook (Australia) *Tel:* (02) 96606397 *E-mail:* trekaway@sia.net.au, pg 22

Environmental Research Unit (Ireland) *Tel:* (01) 764211, pg 360

Enzyklopadie Verlag (Romania) *Tel:* (01) 2223322 *Fax:* (01) 2243667, pg 533

EOS Gabinete de Orientacion Psicologica (Spain) *Tel:* (091) 554 12 04 *Fax:* (091) 554 12 03 *E-mail:* eos@eos.es *Web Site:* www.eos.es, pg 573

EOS Verlag der Benefiktiner der Erzabtei St. Ottilien (Germany) *Tel:* (08193) 71261 *Fax:* (08193) 6844 *E-mail:* mail@eos-verlag.de *Web Site:* www.eos-verlag.de, pg 223

EP Graphics (United States) *Tel:* 260-589-2145 *Fax:* 260-589-2810 *Web Site:* www.epgraphics.com, pg 1206

EPA SA (Editions Presse Audiovisuel) (France) *Tel:* (01) 43 92 30 00 *Fax:* (01) 43 92 33 81, pg 162

Les Editions de l'Epargne (France) *Tel:* (01) 44169580 *Fax:* (01) 44169590, pg 162

EPB Publishers Pte Ltd (Singapore) *Tel:* (065) 2780881 *Fax:* (065) 2782456 *Web Site:* www.epb.com.sg, pg 546

EPEL (France) *Tel:* (06) 81 06 02 52 *Fax:* (01) 45 44 22 85 *Web Site:* www.ecole-lacanienne.net/popup-epel.html, pg 162

EPER (United Kingdom) *Tel:* (0131) 650 8211; (0131) 650 6200 *Fax:* (0131) 667 5927 *E-mail:* eper.enquiries@ed.ac.uk *Web Site:* www.ials.ed.ac.uk, pg 679

Editions les eperonniers (Belgium) *Tel:* (02) 4283033 *Fax:* (02) 4283525, pg 68

Epikerotita (Greece) *Tel:* (01) 3636083, pg 310

EPLS - ACLA Edition (France) *Tel:* (01) 48040075 *Fax:* (01) 42777298, pg 162

EPO Publishers, Printers, Booksellers (Belgium) *Tel:* (03) 2396874 *Fax:* (03) 2184604 *E-mail:* vitgevery@epo.be *Web Site:* www.epo.be, pg 68

EPP Books Services (Ghana) *Tel:* (021) 778853; (021) 778347 *Fax:* (021) 779099 *E-mail:* epp@africaonline.com.gh *Web Site:* www.eppbooks.com, pg 307

Eppinger-Verlag OHG (Germany) *Tel:* (0791) 95061-0 *Fax:* (0791) 95061-40 *E-mail:* info@eppinger-verlag.de, pg 223

Epworth Press (United Kingdom) *Tel:* (01733) 325002 *Fax:* (01733) 384180 *E-mail:* sales@mph.org.uk *Web Site:* www.mph.org.uk, pg 679

EQ Opciones en Educacion (Uruguay) *Tel:* (02) 4808720; (02) 9009934 *Fax:* (02) 4873965 *E-mail:* opciones@adinet.com.uy, pg 760

Era Book Enterprises (India) *Tel:* (011) 473993; (022) 5741764, pg 336

Ediciones Era SA de CV (Mexico) *Tel:* (055) 55 28 1221 *Fax:* (055) 56 06 2904 *E-mail:* edicionesera@laneta.apc.org *Web Site:* www.edicionesera.com.mx, pg 460

Era Publications (Australia) *Tel:* (08) 8352 4122 *Fax:* (08) 8234 0023 *E-mail:* admin@erapublications.com *Web Site:* www.erapublications.com, pg 22

ERA Technology Ltd (United Kingdom) *Tel:* (01372) 36 74 38 *Fax:* (01372) 36 71 02 *E-mail:* 264045pub.sales@era.co.uk *Web Site:* www.era.co.uk, pg 679

Editrice Eraclea (Italy) *Tel:* (02) 8693635 *Fax:* (02) 86453613 *E-mail:* cinquevie@libero.it, pg 388

Erasmus Grasser-Verlag GmbH (Germany) *Tel:* (08861) 241900 *Fax:* (08861) 241901, pg 223

ERB (Czech Republic) *Tel:* (02) 24009111 *Fax:* (02) 2320989, pg 1227

Verlag Peter Erd GmbH (Germany) *Tel:* (089) 725 30 04 *Fax:* (089) 725 01 41, pg 223

Ere Nouvelle (France) *Tel:* (0493) 99-30-13 *E-mail:* lerenouvelle@wanadoo.fr *Web Site:* assoc.wanadoo/fr/lerenouvelle/pub, pg 162

Erein (Spain) *Tel:* (0943) 218300; (0943) 218211 *Fax:* (0943) 218311 *E-mail:* erein@erein.com *Web Site:* www.erein.com, pg 573

Eremiten-Presse und Verlag GmbH (Germany) *Tel:* (0211) 66 05 90 *Fax:* (0211) 698 94 70, pg 223

Eren Yayincilik ve Kitapcilik Ltd Sti (Turkey) *Tel:* (0212) 2520560; (0212) 2512858 *Fax:* (0212) 2433016 *E-mail:* eren@turk.net, pg 639

Editions Eres (France) *Tel:* (05) 61 75 15 76 *Fax:* (05) 61 73 52 89 *E-mail:* eres@edition-eres.com *Web Site:* www.edition-eres.com, pg 162

Eres Editions-Horst Schubert Musikverlag (Germany) *Tel:* (04298) 1676 *Fax:* (04298) 5312 *E-mail:* info@eres-musik.de *Web Site:* www.eres-musik.de, pg 223

Eresco PT (Indonesia) *Tel:* (022) 5205985 *Fax:* (022) 5205984, pg 355

Eretz Hemdah Institute for Advanced Jewish Studies (Israel) *Tel:* (02) 371-485; (02) 371-940 *Fax:* (02) 371-940 *E-mail:* eretzhemdah@ou.org, pg 367

Erevnites (Greece) *Tel:* (01) 5241862; (01) 3622948 *E-mail:* erevnite@otenet.gr, pg 1286

ERF-Verlag GmbH (Germany) *Tel:* (06441) 9570 *Fax:* (06441) 957120 *E-mail:* info@erf.de *Web Site:* www.erf.de, pg 223

ERGA SNC di Carla Ottino Merli & C (Edizioni Realizzazioni Grafiche - Artigiana) (Italy) *Tel:* (010) 8328441 *Fax:* (010) 8328799, pg 388

Ergebnisse Verlag GmbH (Germany) *Tel:* (040) 4801027 *Fax:* (040) 4801592, pg 223

Ergon Verlag Dr H J Dietrich (Germany) *Tel:* (0931) 280084 *Fax:* (0931) 282872 *E-mail:* service@ergon-verlag.de *Web Site:* www.ergon-verlag.de, pg 223

Erich-Weinert Universitatsbuchhandlung (Germany) *Tel:* (0391) 568590 *Fax:* (0391) 5685923 *E-mail:* e.angerer@weinert.de *Web Site:* www.weinert.de, pg 1284

Erika (Czech Republic) *Tel:* (02) 7950452 *Fax:* (02) 7929351, pg 124

Eriksson & Lindgren Bokforlag (Sweden) *Tel:* (08) 6523226; (08) 6523227 *Fax:* (08) 6523223 *E-mail:* info@eriksson-lindgren.se, pg 602

Erker-Verlag (Switzerland) *Tel:* (071) 2227979 *Fax:* (071) 2227919, pg 613

Erlanger Verlag Fuer Mission und Okumene (Germany) *Tel:* (09131) 33064 *Fax:* (09131) 39481 *E-mail:* erlanger.verlag@gmx.de, pg 223

Ernest Press (United Kingdom) *Tel:* (0141) 637 5492 *Fax:* (0141) 637 5492 *E-mail:* sales@ernest-press.co.uk *Web Site:* www.ernest-press.co.uk, pg 679

Ernesto Reichmann Distribuidores de Livros LTDA (Brazil) *Tel:* (011) 2182122 *Fax:* (011) 2182122 *E-mail:* rrr@lb.com, pg 1277

Ernst & Young (United Kingdom) *Tel:* (020) 7951 2000 *Fax:* (020) 7951 1345, pg 679

Ernst Kabel Verlag GmbH (Germany) *Tel:* (089) 381801-0 *Fax:* (089) 338704 *E-mail:* info@piper.de *Web Site:* www.kabel-verlag.de, pg 223

Ernst-Moritz-Arndt Universitat Greifswald, Universitatsbibliothek (Germany) *Tel:* (03834) 861502 *Fax:* (03834) 861501 *E-mail:* ub@rz.uni-greifswald.de, pg 1467

Ernst, Wilhelm & Sohn, Verlag Architektur und technische Wissenschaft GmbH & Co (Germany) *Tel:* (030) 47031-200 *Fax:* (030) 47031-270 *E-mail:* info@ernst-und-sohn.de *Web Site:* www.ernst-und-sohn.de, pg 224

Ernster Sarl (Luxembourg) *Tel:* 225077-1 *Fax:* 225073 *E-mail:* librairie@ernster.com *Web Site:* www.ernster.com, pg 1297

Edition Hans Erpf Verlagsgenossenschaft (Switzerland) *Tel:* (031) 3054410 *Fax:* (031) 3054410, pg 613

Editions Errance (France) *Tel:* (01) 43 26 40 41 *Fax:* (01) 43 29 34 88, pg 162

Errepar SA (Argentina) *Tel:* (011) 4300-3942; (011) 4300-0549 *Fax:* (011) 4307-9541 *E-mail:* libros@errepar.com *Web Site:* www.errepar.com, pg 5

The Erskine Press (United Kingdom) *Tel:* (01953) 88 72 77 *Fax:* (01953) 88 83 61 *E-mail:* erskpres@aol.com *Web Site:* www.erskine-press.com, pg 679

Erudita Publications (Pty) Ltd (South Africa) *Tel:* (011) 7264350 *Fax:* (011) 4821279, pg 554

Verlagsgesellschaft des Erziehungsvereins GmbH (Germany) *Tel:* (02845) 392-222 *Fax:* (02845) 33689 *E-mail:* info@neukirchener-verlag.de *Web Site:* www.neukirchener-verlag.de, pg 224

ESA Publications (NZ) Ltd (New Zealand) *Tel:* (09) 579 3126 *Fax:* (09) 579 4713 *Web Site:* www.esa.co.nz, pg 490

ESAN - Escuela de Administracion de Negocios para Graduados, Direccion de Investigacion (Peru) *Tel:* (01) 3451565 *Fax:* (01) 3451328 *E-mail:* cendoc@esan.edu.pe, pg 1491

Escala Ltda (Colombia) *Tel:* (01) 2878200 *Fax:* (01) 2325148, pg 111

Verlag am Eschbach GmbH (Germany) *Tel:* (07634) 1088 *Fax:* (07634) 3796 *E-mail:* e-mail@verlag-am-eschbach.de *Web Site:* www.verlag-am-eschbach.de, pg 224

Esco BVBA (Belgium) *Tel:* (03) 2223800 *Fax:* (03) 2223838, pg 68

Escrituras Editora e Distribuidora de Livros Ltda (Brazil) *Tel:* (011) 5082-4190 *Fax:* (011) 5082-4190 *E-mail:* vendas@escrituras.com.br *Web Site:* www.escrituras.com.br, pg 83

Escuela Nacional de Biblioteconomia y Archivonomia (Mexico), pg 1520

Asocicion Escuela Para Todos (Costa Rica) *Tel:* 2255438; 2255338; 2340530; 2341339 *Fax:* 2243014, pg 116

Escutcheon Press (Australia) *Tel:* (02) 4344-2304 *Fax:* (02) 4341-1248, pg 22

Ediciones Eseuve SA (Spain) *Tel:* (091) 539-01-03 *Fax:* (091) 528-87-59, pg 573

Editorial Esfinge SA de CV (Mexico) *Tel:* (05) 3591313; (05) 3591111 *Fax:* (05) 5761343, pg 460

Eshkol Books Publishers & Printing Ltd (Israel) *Tel:* (02) 5370451; (02) 5370179 *Fax:* (02) 5372732, pg 367

Esic Editorial (Spain) *Tel:* (091) 4524100 *Fax:* (091) 3528534 *E-mail:* info.madrid@esic.es *Web Site:* www.esic.es, pg 573

Editorial Esin, SA (Spain) *Tel:* (093) 244 95 50 *Fax:* (093) 265 68 95 *E-mail:* combel@editorialcasals.com *Web Site:* www.editorialcasals.com, pg 573

Editions Eska (France) *Tel:* (01) 42 86 56 00 *Fax:* (01) 42 86 55 95 *E-mail:* eska@multimediart.fr *Web Site:* www.sybex.fr, pg 162

Esogetics GmbH (Germany) *Tel:* (07251) 8001-30 *Fax:* (07251) 8001-55 *E-mail:* info-de@esogetics.com *Web Site:* www.esogetics.com, pg 224

Esoptron (Greece) *Tel:* (01) 6441169, pg 1286

Libreria Esoterica (Chile) *Tel:* (02) 6338430 *Fax:* (02) 6397933 *E-mail:* wzzdarmd@entelchile.net, pg 1279

Verlag Esoterische Philosophie GmbH (Germany) *Tel:* (0511) 755331 *Fax:* (0511) 755334 *E-mail:* info@esoterische-philosophie.de *Web Site:* www.esoterische-philosophie.de, pg 224

Editions Espaces 34 (France) *Tel:* (04) 67 84 11 23 *Fax:* (04) 67 84 00 74 *E-mail:* chesp34@club-internet.fr, pg 162

Editorial Espasa-Calpe SA (Spain) *Tel:* (091) 3589689 *Fax:* (091) 3588679; (091) 3589505 *E-mail:* info@espasa.es *Web Site:* www.espasa.com, pg 573

Espasa-Calpe Argentina SA (Argentina) *Tel:* (011) 4382-4043; (011) 4382-4045 *Fax:* (011) 4383-3793 *E-mail:* info@eplaneta.com.ar, pg 5

Casa del Libro Espasa-Calpe SA (Spain) *Tel:* (091) 3589689 *Fax:* (091) 3589505, pg 1311

Espasa-Calpe Mexicana SA (Mexico) *Tel:* (05) 5752894; (05) 5755022, pg 460

Editorial Espaxs SA (Spain) *Tel:* (093) 454 06 52 *Fax:* (093) 4510149, pg 573

Universala Esperanto-Asocio (Netherlands) *Tel:* (010) 4361044; (010) 4361539 *Fax:* (010) 4361751 *E-mail:* uea@inter.nl.net *Web Site:* www.uea.org, pg 1254

Esperanto Translating Service (United Kingdom) *Tel:* (0181) 4282829 *Fax:* (0181) 4282829 *E-mail:* espero@moose.co.uk, pg 1128

Espiritualidad (Spain) *Tel:* (091) 350-49-22 *Fax:* (091) 350-49-22 *E-mail:* ede@edespiritualidad.org *Web Site:* www.edespiritualidad.org, pg 573

L'Esprit Du Temps (France) *Tel:* (056) 02 84 19 *Fax:* (056) 02 91 31, pg 162

Editions Esprit Ouvert (Switzerland) *Tel:* (021) 2308844 *Fax:* (021) 3235403, pg 613

Esquina-Livraria e Papelaria Lda (Portugal) *Tel:* (022) 6065234 *Fax:* (022) 6053878 *E-mail:* livrariaesquina@mail.telepac.pt, pg 1307

Ess Ess Publications (India) *Tel:* (011) 3260807 *Fax:* (011) 3274173, pg 337

Essay und Zeitgeist Verlag (Luxembourg) *Fax:* 425227, pg 447

Essegi (Italy) *Tel:* (0544) 218849 *Fax:* (0544) 217358, pg 388

Esselibri (Italy) *Tel:* (081) 5757255 *Fax:* (081) 5757944, pg 388

Essex Colour Services Ltd (United Kingdom) *Tel:* (01702) 541311 *Fax:* (01702) 540094 *Web Site:* www.goodspeed.co.uk, pg 1161

Essex Colour Services Ltd (United Kingdom) *Tel:* (01702) 541311 *Fax:* (01702) 540094, pg 1203

Esslinger Verlag J F Schreiber GmbH (Germany) *Tel:* (0711) 310594-6 *Fax:* (0711) 310594-77 *E-mail:* esslinger@klett-mail.de, pg 224

Editions de L'Est (France) *Tel:* (016) 83567677 *Fax:* (016) 83533456, pg 162

estamp (United Kingdom) *Tel:* (020) 8994 2379 *Fax:* (020) 8994 2379 *E-mail:* st@estamp.demon.co.uk, pg 679

Editorial Estampa, Lda (Portugal) *Tel:* (021) 3555663 *Fax:* (021) 521911 *E-mail:* estampa@mail.telepac.pt *Web Site:* www.editorialestampa.pt, pg 524

Estates Gazette (United Kingdom) *Tel:* (020) 8652 3500; (020) 7411 2540 (Edit); (020) 7411 2626 (Adv); (01444) 445335 (Subns) *Fax:* (020) 7437 2432; (020) 7437 0294 (Edit); (020) 7437 2432 (Adv); (01444) 445567 (Subns), pg 679

Libreria del Este (Venezuela) *Tel:* (02) 9511297; (02) 9512307; (02) 9511705, pg 1324

Biblioteca Estense Universitaria (Italy) *Tel:* (059) 222248 *Fax:* (059) 230195 *E-mail:* estense@kril.cedoc.unimo.it; biblio.estense@cedoc.mo.it *Web Site:* www.cedoc.mo.it/estense, pg 1477

Estonian Academic Library (Estonia) *Tel:* (02) 6659401; (02) 6659402 *Fax:* (02) 6659400 *E-mail:* ear@ear.ee *Web Site:* www.ear.ee, pg 139

Estonian Academy Publishers *Tel:* (02) 6454504 *Fax:* (02) 6466026 *Web Site:* www.kirj.ee/, pg 139

Estonian Bible Society (Estonia) *Tel:* (02) 6311671 *Fax:* (02) 6311438 *E-mail:* eps@eps.ee, pg 140

Estonian Encyclopaedia Publishers Ltd (Estonia) *Tel:* (02) 6259413 *Fax:* (02) 6566542 *E-mail:* encyclo@online.ee, pg 140

Estonian ISBN Agency (Estonia) *Tel:* (02) 6307372 *Fax:* (02) 6311200 *E-mail:* eraamat@nlib.ee, pg 140

Estonian Publishers Association (Estonia) *Tel:* (02) 443937 *Fax:* (02) 445720, pg 1242

Angel Estrada y Cia SA (Argentina) *Tel:* (011) 4344-5589 *Fax:* (011) 4331-6527 *E-mail:* editocom@estrada.com.ar *Web Site:* www.estrada.com.ar, pg 6

Estragon Press Ltd (Ireland) *Tel:* (027) 61186 *Fax:* (027) 61186, pg 360

Estrella Publishing (Philippines), pg 513

Estudio de Bioinformacion, S L (Spain) *Tel:* (096) 351 46 27 *Fax:* (096) 394 37 27 *E-mail:* bioinformacion@bioinformacion.com *Web Site:* www.bioinformacion.com, pg 574

Instituto de Estudios Fiscales (Spain) *Tel:* (091) 5273951 *Fax:* (091) 5273951 *Web Site:* www.minhac.es/ief, pg 574

Centro de Estudios Monetarios Latinoamericanos (CEMLA) (Mexico) *Tel:* (05) 5330300 *Fax:* (05) 5146554 *E-mail:* cemlasub@mail.internet.com.mx, pg 460

Instituto de Estudios Peruanos (Peru) *Tel:* (014) 323070; (014) 244856 *Fax:* (014) 4324981 *E-mail:* libreria@iep.org.pe, pg 511

Instituto de Estudios Riojanos (Spain) *Tel:* (0941) 262064; (0941) 262065 *Fax:* (0941) 246667, pg 574

Institut d'Estudis Metropolitans de Barcelona (Spain) *Tel:* (093) 691 83 61; (093) 691 97 97; (093) 691 91 82 *Fax:* (093) 580 65 72 *E-mail:* iermb@uab.es *Web Site:* www.uab.es/iemb/, pg 574

Institut d'Estudis Vallencs (IEV) (Spain) *Tel:* (0977) 600 660 *Fax:* (0977) 606 109 *E-mail:* iev@iev.es *Web Site:* www.iev.es, pg 574

Centro De Estudos Africanos (Mozambique) *Tel:* (01) 490828 *Fax:* (01) 491896, pg 470

Etaireia Spoudon Neoellinikou Politismou Kai Genikis Paideias (Greece) *Tel:* (01) 06795 000 *Fax:* (01) 06795 090 *E-mail:* admin@moraitis.edu.gr *Web Site:* www.moraitis.edu.gr, pg 310

Etas Libri (Italy) *Tel:* (02) 50952309 *Fax:* (02) 50952898 *Web Site:* www.etas.it, pg 388

Publicaciones Etea (Spain) *Tel:* (0957) 222121 *Fax:* (0957) 222101 *E-mail:* webadmin@etea.com *Web Site:* www.etea.com, pg 574

ETH- Bibliothek (Eidgenossische Technische Hochschule Bibliothek) (Switzerland) *Tel:* (01) 6322549 *Fax:* (01) 6321357, pg 1501

Ethiope Publishing Corporation (Nigeria) *Tel:* (052) 243036, pg 499

Ethiopian Library & Information Association (Ethiopia) *Tel:* (01) 518020 *Fax:* (01) 552544, pg 1515

Ethiopian Nutrition Institute (ENI) (Ethiopia) *Tel:* (01) 151600 *Fax:* (01) 754744, pg 141

Ethnikon Idryma Erevnon (Greece) *Tel:* (01) 722981115 *Fax:* (01) 7246618, pg 1470

Institut d'Ethnologie du Museum National d'Histoire Naturelle (France) *Tel:* (01) 4079 48 38 *Fax:* (01) 4079 38 58 *E-mail:* diff.pub@mnhn.fr *Web Site:* www.mnhn.fr/publication, pg 163

L'Etoile/Cahiers du Cinema (France) *Tel:* (01) 53 44 75 75 *Fax:* (01) 43 43 95 04, pg 163

Eton Press (Auckland) Ltd (New Zealand) *Tel:* (09) 4183635 *Fax:* (09) 4806488 *E-mail:* info@eton.co.nz, pg 490

ETR (Editrice Trasporti su Rotaie) (Italy) *Tel:* (03) 6541092 *Fax:* (03) 6541092 *Web Site:* www.itreni.com, pg 388

Etu Ediciones SL (Spain) *Tel:* (093) 2741671 *Fax:* (093) 2741671 *E-mail:* etu@arrakis.es, pg 574

Institut d'Etudes Augustiniennes (France) *Tel:* (01) 43-54-80-25 *Fax:* (01) 43 54 39 55 *E-mail:* iea@wanadoo.fr, pg 163

Institut d'Etudes Slaves (France) *Tel:* (01) 43 26 50 89; (01) 43 26 79 18 *Fax:* (01) 43 26 16 23 *E-mail:* etudes.slaves@paris4.sorbonne.fr, pg 163

EUDEBA (Editorial Universitaria de Buenos Aires) (Argentina) *Tel:* (011) 4383-8025 *Fax:* (011) 4383-2202 *E-mail:* eudela@eudeba.com *Web Site:* www.eudeba.com.ar, pg 6

Eugenides Foundation Technical Library (Greece) *Tel:* (01) 9411181 *Fax:* (01) 9417372 *E-mail:* library@eugenides_found.edu.gr, pg 1470

Biblioteca Nacional Eugenio Espejo de la Casa de la Cultura Ecuatoriana (Ecuador) *Tel:* (02) 528840, pg 1461

Eugrimas (Lithuania) *Tel:* (02) 300075 *Fax:* (02) 300075 *E-mail:* eugrimas@post.5ci.lt, pg 445

Eulama Literary Agencies (Italy) *Tel:* (06) 5407309 *Fax:* (06) 5408772, pg 1113

EULAR Publishers (Switzerland) *Tel:* (061) 251317 *Fax:* (061) 251286 *E-mail:* eular@reinhardt.ch, pg 613

Eulen Verlag (Germany) *Tel:* (0761) 2 62 67 *Fax:* (0761) 2 58 61 *E-mail:* info@eulenverlag.de *Web Site:* www.eulen-verlag.de, pg 224

Eulenhof-Verlag Wolfgang Ehrhardt Heinold (Germany) *Tel:* (040) 49 00 05-0 *Fax:* (040) 49 00 05-15 *E-mail:* eulenwolf@compuserve.com *Web Site:* www.eulenhof.de, pg 224

Eulyu Publishing Co Ltd (Republic of Korea) *Tel:* (02) 7338150; (02) 7338151; (02) 7338152; (02) 7338153 *Fax:* (02) 7329154, pg 436

Eumo Editorial (Spain) *Tel:* (093) 889 28 18; (093) 889 29 61 *Fax:* (093) 889 35 41 *E-mail:* eumo.editorial@uvrc.es *Web Site:* www.eumoeditorial.com, pg 574

Ediciones Eunate (Spain) *Tel:* (0948) 272352 *Fax:* (0948) 172636 *E-mail:* eunate@cin.es *Web Site:* www.cin.es, pg 574

EUNSA (Ediciones Universidad de Navarra SA) (Spain) *Tel:* (0948) 256850 *Fax:* (0948) 256854 *E-mail:* eunsa@cin.es *Web Site:* www.eunsa.es, pg 574

Eurasia Academic Publishers (Bulgaria) *Tel:* (02) 252547 *E-mail:* eurasia@realsci.com *Web Site:* www.biblio.hit.bg, pg 95

Eurasia Press Pte Ltd (Singapore) *Tel:* 2805522 *Fax:* 2800593; 3825458 *E-mail:* eurasia@mbox3.singnet.com.sg, pg 1138, 1159, 1200, 1213, 1222

Eurasia Publishing House Pvt Ltd (India) *Tel:* (011) 7772080; (011) 7779891 *Fax:* (011) 7777446, pg 337

Eureka Press Ltd (Jamaica) *Tel:* (876) 962-3947 *Fax:* (876) 961-5383 *E-mail:* eurekapr@cwjamaica.com, pg 413

Euro Translations (United Kingdom) *Tel:* (0208) 6686133 *Fax:* (0208) 6686133 *E-mail:* eurotrans@lineone.net, pg 1128

Euro Print Verlag (Romania) *Tel:* (01) 745-20-11 *Fax:* (01) 312-42-25, pg 533

Ediciones Euroamericanas (Mexico) *Tel:* (05) 610-01-33 *Fax:* (05) 610-01-33 *E-mail:* thielemedina@prodigy.net.mx, pg 461

Eurobook Ltd (United Kingdom) *Tel:* (01865) 749033 *Fax:* (01865) 749044 *E-mail:* eurobook@compuserve.com, pg 679

Eurodiastasi (Greece) *Tel:* (01) 8610071 *Fax:* (01) 8611303, pg 1286

EuroGeoGrafiche Mencattini SRL (Italy) *Tel:* (0575) 900010 *Fax:* (0575) 911161, pg 388

Eurohueco SA (Spain) *Tel:* (093) 7730700 *Fax:* (093) 7730708, pg 1201

Eurolibros Ltda (Colombia) *Tel:* (01) 2886400; (01) 3401837 *Fax:* (01) 2450291; (01) 2886400, pg 111

Eurolibros (Colombia) *Tel:* (01) 2886400 *Fax:* (01) 2450291; (01) 3401811; (01) 3401830; (01) 2886400, pg 1279

Euromonitor PLC (United Kingdom) *Tel:* (020) 7251 8024 *Fax:* (020) 7608 3149 *E-mail:* info@euromonitor.com *Web Site:* www.euromonitor.com, pg 680

Europ Export Edition GmbH (Germany) *Tel:* (06151) 51-38 92 0 *Fax:* (06151) 51-3 31 64; (06151) 38 92 80 *E-mail:* info@abconline.de *Web Site:* www.abconline.de, pg 224

Publicacoes Europa-America Lda (Portugal) *Tel:* (01) 9211461; (01) 9211462 *Fax:* (01) 9217940, pg 524

Edizioni Europa (Italy) *Tel:* (06) 8419124, pg 388

Europa Konyvkiado (Hungary) *Tel:* (01) 1312700; (01) 1312708 *Fax:* (01) 1314162, pg 323

Verlag Europa-Lehrmittel, Nourney, Vollmer GmbH & Co (Germany) *Tel:* (02104) 6916-0 *Fax:* (02104) 6916-27 *Web Site:* www.europa-lehrmittel.de, pg 224

Europa Publications (United Kingdom) *Tel:* (020) 7822 4300; (020) 7842 2110 (marketing & sales) *Fax:* (020) 7822 4329; (020) 7842 2249 (marketing & sales) *E-mail:* info.europa@tandf.co.uk *Web Site:* www.europapublications.com, pg 680

Europa Star, Bill Communication SA (Switzerland) *Tel:* (022) 307 78 37 *Fax:* (022) 300 37 48 *Web Site:* www.europastar.com, pg 614

Europa Union Verlag GmbH (Germany) *Tel:* (0228) 7 29 00 10 *Fax:* (0228) 7 29 00 13 *E-mail:* Service@euverlag.de *Web Site:* www.europa-union-verlag.de, pg 224

Europa Verlag AG (Switzerland) *Tel:* (01) 4711629 *Fax:* (01) 2516081, pg 614

Europa Verlag GmbH (Germany) *Tel:* (040) 355434-0 *Fax:* (040) 355434-66 *E-mail:* info@europaverlag.de *Web Site:* www.europaverlag.de, pg 224

Europaeische Verlagsanstalt GmbH & Rotbuch Verlag GmbH & Co KG (Germany) *Tel:* (040) 45 01 94-0 *Fax:* (040) 45 01 94 55 *E-mail:* info@rotbuch.de *Web Site:* www.rotbuch.de; www.europaeische-verlagsanstalt.de, pg 225

Verlag Europaeische Wehrkunde (Germany) *Tel:* (0228) 340884 *Fax:* (040) 79713304, pg 225

Europaring der Buch- und Schallplattenfreunde (Switzerland) *Tel:* (031) 584466, pg 1232

European University Institute Library (Italy) *Tel:* (055) 4685379 *Fax:* (055) 468544 *E-mail:* biblio@iue.it, pg 1477

European Book Service (Netherlands) *Tel:* (030) 6660211 *Fax:* (030) 6662674, pg 1301

European Association for Health Information & Libraries (Netherlands) *Tel:* (030) 2619663 *Fax:* (030) 2311830 *E-mail:* EAHIL-secr@nic.surfnet.nl *Web Site:* www.eahil.org, pg 1254

European Association of Directory & Database Publishers (Belgium) *Tel:* (02) 6463060 *Fax:* (02) 6463637 *E-mail:* mailbox@eadp.org *Web Site:* www.eadp.org, pg 1238

European Booksellers Federation (EBF) (Belgium) *Tel:* (02) 2420957 *Fax:* (02) 2420957 *E-mail:* eurobooks@skynet.be *Web Site:* www.editeur.org/ebf.html, pg 1238

European Foundation for the Improvement of Living & Working Conditions (Ireland) *Tel:* (01) 2043100 *Fax:* (01) 2826456 *E-mail:* postmaster@eurofound.eu.int, pg 360

European Healthcare Management Association (Ireland) *Tel:* (01) 2839299 *Fax:* (01) 2838653 *E-mail:* ehma@iol.le, pg 360

European Information Association (United Kingdom) *Tel:* (0161) 2283691 *Fax:* (0161) 2366547 *E-mail:* eia@manchestergb.demon.co.uk, pg 1265

European Schoolbooks Ltd (United Kingdom) *Tel:* (01242) 245252 *Fax:* (01242) 224137 *E-mail:* direct@esb.co.uk *Web Site:* www.eurobooks.co.uk, pg 680

European Schoolbooks Ltd (United Kingdom) *Tel:* (01242) 245252 *Fax:* (01242) 224137, pg 1319

European Society for Opinion & Marketing Research (Netherlands) *Tel:* (020) 6642141 *Fax:* (020) 6642922 *E-mail:* email@esomar.nl *Web Site:* www.esomar.nl, pg 1254

Europhone Language Institute (Pte) Ltd (Singapore) *Tel:* 3373617; 3363992 *Fax:* 3374506, pg 546

Europress Editores e Distribuidores de Publicacoes Lda (Portugal) *Tel:* (01) 9387180; (01) 9387190; (01) 9387317; (01) 9877560 *Fax:* (01) 9381452; (01) 9877560 *E-mail:* europress@mail.telepac.pt, pg 525

Eurospan Distribution Center Ltd (United Kingdom) *Tel:* (0161) 7642296 *Fax:* (0161) 7648213 *E-mail:* chris@e.d.c.co.uk, pg 1319

The Eurospan Group (United Kingdom) *Tel:* (020) 7240 0856 *Fax:* (020) 7379 0609 *E-mail:* info@eurospan.co.uk, pg 680

Eusidic (European Association of Information Services) (United Kingdom), pg 1265

Evagean Publishing (New Zealand) *Tel:* (09) 856-6639 *Fax:* (09) 856-6649 *E-mail:* evagean@iconz.co.nz *Web Site:* www.evagean.co.nz, pg 491

Evangel Publishing House (Kenya) *Tel:* (02) 802033; (02) 802034 *Fax:* (02) 860840 *E-mail:* evanglit@maf.or.ke, pg 431

Evangelical Press & Services Ltd (United Kingdom) *Tel:* (01325) 380232; 866-588-6778 *Fax:* (01325) 466153; 866-588-6778 *E-mail:* sales@evangelicalpress.org *Web Site:* www.evangelicalpress.org, pg 680

Maison d'Edition de la Librairie-Imprimerie Evangelique du Togo (Togo) *Tel:* 214582 *Fax:* 212967, pg 636

Evangelische Haupt-Bibelgesellschaft und von Cansteinsche Bibelanstalt (Germany) *Tel:* (030) 2827573 *Fax:* (030) 2824266 *E-mail:* kontakt@ehbg.de *Web Site:* www.bibelgesellschaftberlin.de, pg 225

Evangelische Verlagsanstalt GmbH (Germany) *Tel:* (0341) 7 11 41-0 *Fax:* (0341) 7 11 41 40 *E-mail:* info@eva-leipzig.de *Web Site:* www.eva-leipzig.de, pg 225

Evangelischer Presseverband fur Bayern eV (Germany) *Tel:* (089) 121 72-111; (089) 121 72-110; (089) 121 72-0 *Fax:* (089) 121 72-138 *E-mail:* verlag@epv.de *Web Site:* www.epv.de, pg 225

Evangelischer Presseverband in Osterreich (Austria) *Tel:* (01) 712 54 61 *Fax:* (01) 712 54 75 *E-mail:* epd@evang.at, pg 51

Evangelischer Presseverband STET Baden eVerlag (Germany) *Tel:* (0721) 932750 *Fax:* (0721) 9175950, pg 225

Evans Brothers Ltd (United Kingdom) *Tel:* (020) 7487 0920 *Fax:* (020) 7487 0921 *E-mail:* sales@evansbrothers.co.uk *Web Site:* www.evansbooks.co.uk, pg 680

Evans Brothers (Nigeria Publishers) Ltd (Nigeria) *Tel:* (02) 2417570; (02) 2417601; (02) 2417626, pg 499

Faith Evans Associates (United Kingdom) *Tel:* (020) 8340 9920 *Fax:* (020) 8340 9410, pg 1119

EVD eenheid Bibliotheek (Netherlands) *Tel:* (070) 3797210 *Fax:* (070) 3797878, pg 1486

Events of the Week (Ireland) *Tel:* (01) 2954962 *Fax:* (01) 2954963 *Web Site:* www.eventoftheweek.com, pg 360

Everbest Printing Co Ltd (Hong Kong) *Tel:* (02) 7274433 *Fax:* (02) 7727687 *E-mail:* sales@everbest.com.hk, pg 1134

Everbest Printing Co Ltd (Hong Kong) *Tel:* (02) 7274433 *Fax:* (02) 7727687 *E-mail:* everbest@hk.super.net; sales@everbest.com.hk, pg 1156, 1196, 1212

Everest Editora (Portugal) *Tel:* (021) 8139554 *Fax:* (021) 8152345 *E-mail:* everesteditora@mail.telepac.pt, pg 525

Evrodiastasi (Greece) *Tel:* (01) 8611303, pg 310

EVT Energy Video Training & Verlag GmbH (Germany) *Tel:* (069) 431575 *Fax:* (069) 2169852, pg 225

Ewha Womans University Central Library (Republic of Korea) *Tel:* (02) 3602114 *Fax:* (02) 3935903 *E-mail:* libacq@mm.ewha.ac.kr, pg 1480

Ewha Womans University Press (Republic of Korea) *Tel:* (02) 3626076 *Fax:* (02) 3124312, pg 436

Ewing Memorial Library (Pakistan), pg 1489

Ex Libris Forlag A/S (Norway) *Tel:* 22809500 *Fax:* 22385160 *E-mail:* office@exlibris.no, pg 503

Ex Libris Press (United Kingdom) *Tel:* (01225) 863595 *Fax:* (01225) 863595 *Web Site:* www.ex-librisbooks.co.uk, pg 680

Exandas Publishers (Greece) *Tel:* (01) 3822064; (01) 3084885 *Fax:* (01) 3813065 *E-mail:* exandas@otenet.gr *Web Site:* www.exandasbooks.gr, pg 310

Excel United Company Ltd (Hong Kong) *Tel:* 28891078 *Fax:* 28891721, pg 1196

Editura Excelsior (Romania) *Tel:* (056) 201078 *Fax:* (056) 201078 *E-mail:* excelsior@mail.dmltm.ro, pg 533

Ediciones Exclusivas SA (Mexico) *Tel:* (05) 815878, pg 461

University of Exeter (United Kingdom) *Tel:* (01392) 263869 *Fax:* (01392) 263871 *E-mail:* library@exeter.ac.uk *Web Site:* www.ex.ac.uk/library/, pg 1506

Exhibitions International NV/SA (Belgium) *Tel:* (016) 296900 *Fax:* (016) 296129, pg 1276

Exil Verlag (Germany) *Tel:* (069) 751102 *Fax:* (069) 751547 *E-mail:* fs7a020@uni-hamburg.de, pg 225

Exisle Publishing Ltd (New Zealand) *Tel:* (09) 520 1162 *Fax:* (09) 520 1146 *E-mail:* mail@exisle.co.nz *Web Site:* www.exisle.co.nz, pg 491

Exley Publications Ltd (United Kingdom) *Tel:* (01923) 250505 *Fax:* (01923) 818733 *Toll Free Fax:* 800-440 *E-mail:* enquiry@exleypublications.co.uk, pg 681

Edition Exodus (Switzerland) *Tel:* 4108767 *Fax:* 4108741 *E-mail:* editionexodus@compuserve.com, pg 614

L'Expansion Scientifique Francaise (France) *Tel:* (01) 45 48 42 60 *Fax:* (01) 45 44 81 55 *E-mail:* expansionscientifiquefrancaise@wanadoo.fr *Web Site:* www.expansionscientifique.com, pg 163

Experimental Art Foundation (Australia) *Tel:* (08) 8211 7505 *Fax:* (08) 8211 7323 *E-mail:* eaf@eaf.asn.au *Web Site:* www.eaf.asn.au, pg 22

expert verlag GmbH, Fachverlag fur Wirtschaft & Technik (Germany) *Tel:* (07159) 92 65-0 *Fax:* (07159) 92 65-20 *E-mail:* expert@expertverlag.de *Web Site:* www.expertverlag.de, pg 225

Expolibri GmbH (Germany) *Tel:* (0341) 2113 231 *Fax:* (0341) 2115 996, pg 225

Export Booksellers Group (United Kingdom) *Tel:* (020) 7834 5477 *Fax:* (020) 7834 8812 *E-mail:* mail@booksellers.org.uk, pg 1140

Exportradet Spraktjanst AB (Sweden) *Tel:* (08) 7838500 *Fax:* (08) 7838550 *E-mail:* sed@swedishtrade.se *Web Site:* www.swedishtrade.com, pg 1127

Express Media Corp (United States) *Tel:* 615-360-6400 *Fax:* 615-360-3140 *E-mail:* info@expressmedia.com *Web Site:* www.expressmedia.com, pg 1143, 1165, 1206, 1224

Express Newspapers (United Kingdom) *Tel:* (020) 7928 8000 *Fax:* (020) 7922 7966, pg 681

Editora Expressao e Cultura Exped Ltda (Brazil) *Tel:* (021) 2444 0650 *Fax:* (021) 2444 0651, pg 83

Editorial Extemporaneos SA (Mexico) *Tel:* (05) 5875424; (05) 5878785, pg 461

Extent Verlag und Service Wolfgang M Flamm (Germany) *Tel:* (030) 3279805-11 *Fax:* (030) 3279805-35 *E-mail:* extent@t-online.de, pg 225

Universidad Externado de Colombia (Colombia) *Tel:* (01) 3419900; (01) 3420288; (01) 3452500 (ext 3151); (01) 2826066 *Fax:* (01) 2843769 *E-mail:* publicaciones@uexternado.edu.co; sitioweb@uexternado.edu.co *Web Site:* www.uexternado.edu.co, pg 112

Extraordinary People Press (United Kingdom) *Tel:* (020) 7935 4490 *Fax:* (020) 7486 5998, pg 681

Editions Eyrolles (France) *Tel:* (01) 44 41 11 11 *Fax:* (01) 44 41 11 85 *E-mail:* service-lecteurs@editions-eyrolles.com *Web Site:* www.editions-eyrolles.com, pg 163

Ezel Erverdi (Dergah Yayinlari AS) Muessese Muduru (Turkey) *Tel:* (0212) 5161262; (0212) 5160047 *Fax:* (0212) 5161921, pg 640

F A Brockhaus, GmbH (Germany) *Tel:* (0341) 9786-30 *Fax:* (0341) 9786-560 *Web Site:* www.brockhaus.de, pg 225

F Bruckmann Munchen Verlag & Druck GmbH & Co Produkt KG (Germany) *Tel:* (089) 13 06 99 11 *Fax:* (089) 13 06 99 10 *E-mail:* info@bruckmann.de *Web Site:* www.bruckmann-verlag.de, pg 225

FAB (France) *Tel:* (0238) 70 84 44 *Fax:* (0238) 70 56 76 *E-mail:* fab45.paradigme@wanadoo.fr *Web Site:* pradigme.com, pg 163

FAB-Verlag (Germany) *Tel:* (030) 88 92 16 42 *Fax:* (030) 88 92 16 50 *E-mail:* e-mail@fab-berlin.de *Web Site:* www.fab-berlin.de, pg 226

Fabbri (GE) Ltd (United Kingdom) *Tel:* (020) 7836 0519; (020) 7468 5600 *Fax:* (020) 7836 0280 *E-mail:* mailbox@gefabbri.co.uk *Web Site:* www.geffabbri.co.uk, pg 681

Fabel-Verlag Gudrun Liebchen (Germany) *Tel:* (09701) 1463 *Fax:* (09701) 1463, pg 226

Faber & Faber Ltd (United Kingdom) *Tel:* (020) 7465 0045 *Fax:* (020) 7465 0034 *Web Site:* www.faber.co.uk, pg 681

Fabian Society (United Kingdom) *Tel:* (020) 7227 4900 *Fax:* (020) 7976 7153 *E-mail:* info@fabian-society.org.uk *Web Site:* www.fabian-society.org.uk, pg 681

Fabylon-Verlag (Germany) *Tel:* (089) 8110881 *Fax:* (089) 8110882, pg 226

Fac Editions (France) *Tel:* (01) 45487651 *Fax:* (01) 42222231, pg 163

Facet NV (Belgium) *Tel:* (03) 227 40 28 *Fax:* (03) 227 37 92 *E-mail:* Facet@village.uunet.be, pg 68

Facet Publishing (United Kingdom) *Tel:* (020) 7255 0594 *Fax:* (020) 7255 0591 *E-mail:* info@facetpublishing.co.uk *Web Site:* www.facetpublishing.co.uk, pg 681, 1525

Fachbuchhandlung fur Wirtschaft und Recht Dr Karl Stropek GmbH (Austria) *Tel:* (0222) 4795495 *Fax:* (0222) 4796230, pg 1274

Fachbuchverlag Leipzig im Carl Hanser Verlag (Germany) *Tel:* (089) 9 98 30 0 *Fax:* (089) 98 48 09 *E-mail:* info@hanser.de *Web Site:* www.hanser.de, pg 226

Fachbuchverlag Pfanneberg & Co (Germany) *Tel:* (02104) 6916-0 *Fax:* (02104) 6916-27 *E-mail:* gero.pfanneberg@giessen.netsurf.de *Web Site:* www.pfanneberg.de, pg 226

Fachhochschule Dortmund (Germany) *Tel:* (0231) 7554047 *Fax:* (0231) 7554604 *E-mail:* bibliothek@fhb.fh-dortmund.de *Web Site:* www.fhb.fh.dortmund.de, pg 1467

Fachhochschule Fur Druk, Studiengang Verlagswirtschaft und Verlagsherstellung (Germany) *Tel:* (0711) 6852807 *Fax:* (0711) 6852834 *Web Site:* www.fhd.stuttgart.de, pg 1154

Fachhochschule Fur Druk, Studiengang Verlagswirtschaft und Verlagsherstellung (Germany) *Tel:* (0711) 6852807 *Fax:* (0711) 6852834 *Web Site:* www.fhd-stuttgart.de, pg 1195

Fachhochschule Stuttgart Hochschule der Medien (Germany) *Tel:* (0711) 257060 *Fax:* (0711) 25706300 *E-mail:* info@hdm-stuttgart.de; friedling@hdm-stuttgart.de *Web Site:* www.hdm-stuttgart.de, pg 1467

Fachmedien Verlag Winfried Ruf (FMV) (Germany) *Tel:* (08233) 4924 *Fax:* (08233) 4789, pg 226

Fachverband der Buch und Medienwirtschaft (Austria) *Tel:* (01) 50105 DW 3331; (01) 50105 DW 3333 *Fax:* (01) 50105 DW 3043 *E-mail:* fbuchwirtschaft@wko.at *Web Site:* www.buchwirtschaft.at, pg 1236

Fachverlag fur das graphische Gewerbe GmbH (Germany) *Tel:* (089) 332568; (089) 399061 *Fax:* (089) 3401396, pg 226

Fachverlag Schiele & Schoen GmbH (Germany) *Tel:* (030) 253 75 20 *Fax:* (030) 251 72 48 *E-mail:* service@schiele-schoen.de *Web Site:* www.schiele-schoen.de, pg 226

Fackeltrager-Verlag GmbH (Germany) *Tel:* (0441) 980 66-0 *Fax:* (0441) 980 66-34 *E-mail:* info@lappan.de *Web Site:* www.lappan.de, pg 226

Factor-Alias (Bulgaria) *Tel:* (02) 747-891 *E-mail:* factoral@omega.bg, pg 95

The Factory Shop Guide (United Kingdom) *Tel:* (020) 8678 0593 *Fax:* (020) 8674 1594 *E-mail:* factshop@macline.co.uk, pg 681

Facts On File (United Kingdom) *Tel:* (020) 7720 8643 *Fax:* (020) 76278953; (020) 76273041 (foreign sales); (020) 7622 6956 (UK sales & publicity) *Web Site:* www.factsonfile.com, pg 681

Biblioteca Facultad de Humanidades y Ciencias de la Educacion (Uruguay) *Tel:* (02) 488185 *Fax:* (02) 484303 *E-mail:* biblio@fhudec.edu.uy, pg 1508

Bibliotheque de la Faculte des Sciences de Tunis (Tunisia) *Tel:* (01) 873366, pg 1504

Faculte des Sciences Humaines et Sociales de Tunis (Tunisia) *Tel:* (01) 260858; (01) 262252; (01) 260950; (01) 260960; (01) 560840; (01) 560950 *Fax:* (01) 567551, pg 638

Faculte des Sciences Medicales, Bibliotheque (Lebanon) *Tel:* (01) 614001-2-3 *Fax:* (01) 614054 *E-mail:* msamaha@usj.edu.lb *Web Site:* www.usj.edu.lb, pg 1481

Facultes catholiques de Kinshasa c/o Prof Dr L Bertsch S J (The Democratic Republic of the Congo) *Tel:* (0243) 88 46 965 *Fax:* (0243) 88 46 965 *E-mail:* facakin@yahoo.fr, pg 115

Facultes Catoliques de Kinshasa (The Democratic Republic of the Congo) *Tel:* (012) 78476 *Fax:* (012) 46965, pg 115

Library of the Faculty of Engineering (Lebanon) *Tel:* (01) 395606, pg 1481

Library of the Faculty of Law (Lebanon) *Tel:* (01) 426 456 *Fax:* (01) 423 369, pg 1481

FADL's Forlag A/S (Foreningen af danske Laegestuderendes Forlag) (Denmark) *Tel:* 35356287 *Fax:* 35366229 *E-mail:* forlag@fadl.dk *Web Site:* forlag.fadl.dk, pg 132

Forlaget Fag og Kultur (Norway) *Tel:* 22683630 *Fax:* 22680625 *E-mail:* fffk@online.no, pg 503

Olaiya Fagbamigbe Ltd (Publishers) (Nigeria) *Tel:* (034) 2075, pg 499

Forlaget for Faglitteratur A/S (Denmark) *Tel:* 33137900 *Fax:* 33145156, pg 132

Fahrner & Fahrner (Germany) *Tel:* (069) 584777, pg 226

Fairfield Marketing Group Inc (United States) *Tel:* 203-261-5585; 203-261-5568 *Fax:* 203-261-0884 *E-mail:* ffldmktgrp@aol.com, pg 1165, 1206

Fairfield Marketing Group Inc (United States) *Tel:* 203-261-5585; 203-261-5568 *Fax:* 203-261-0884 *E-mail:* ffijmktgrp@aol.com, pg 1224

Faksimile Verlag AG (Switzerland) *Tel:* (041) 511571 *Fax:* (041) 516902 *E-mail:* fvl@faksimile, pg 614

Christa Falk-Verlag (Germany) *Tel:* (08667) 14 13 *Fax:* (08667) 14 17 *E-mail:* email@chfalk-verlag.de *Web Site:* www.chfalk-verlag.de, pg 226

Falk Verlag AG (Germany) *Tel:* (089) 431890; (089) 43146; (089) 43256 *Fax:* (089) 43189-160; (089) 43189-783, pg 226

Falken-Verlag GmbH (Germany) *Tel:* (06127) 702-0 *Fax:* (06127) 702-133 *E-mail:* vertrieb.verlagsgruppe@bertelsmann.de *Web Site:* www.randomhouse.de/falken, pg 227

Falkplan-Suurland BV (Netherlands) *Tel:* (040) 264221 *Fax:* (040) 2417635, pg 477

Bernard de Fallois (France) *Tel:* (01) 42669195 *Fax:* (01) 49240637, pg 163

C J Fallon (Ireland), pg 360

Fama (Bulgaria) *Tel:* (02) 881175, pg 95

Famedram Publishers Ltd (United Kingdom) *Tel:* (01651) 842429 *Fax:* (01651) 842180 *E-mail:* famedram@artwork.co.uk, pg 681

Family Health Publications (Australia) *Tel:* (08) 9389 8777 *Fax:* (08) 9389 8444 *Web Site:* www.familyhealth.info/fhp.php, pg 22

Family Reading Publications (Australia) *Tel:* (03) 5334 3244 *Fax:* (03) 5334 3299 *E-mail:* info@familyreading.com.au *Web Site:* www.familyreading.com.au, pg 22

Fan Noli Verlag Rexhep Hida (Albania) *Tel:* (042) 61673 *E-mail:* fannoli2002@yahoo.com, pg 1

Editions Fanlac (France) *Tel:* (05) 53-53-41-90 *Fax:* (05) 53-08-05-85 *E-mail:* fanlac-edition@aquinet.tm.fr *Web Site:* www.fanlac.com, pg 163

Fannei & Walz Verlag (Germany) *Tel:* (030) 88 92 16 42 *Fax:* (030) 88 92 16 50 *E-mail:* mail@fab-berlin.de *Web Site:* www.fab-berlin.de/Verlage, pg 227

Fanucci (Italy) *Tel:* (06) 393366384 *Fax:* (06) 6382998, pg 388

Far East Book Co Ltd (Taiwan, Province of China) *Tel:* (02) 3118740 *Fax:* (02) 3114184, pg 630

Far Eastern University Library (Philippines) *Tel:* (02) 7413421, pg 1491

Faradawn cc (South Africa) *Tel:* (011) 8851787; (011) 8851847 *Fax:* (011) 8851829, pg 1310

Clive Farahar & Sophie Dupre Booksellers (United Kingdom) *Tel:* (01249) 821121 *Fax:* (01249) 821202 *E-mail:* post@farahardupre.co.uk *Web Site:* www.farahardupre.co.uk, pg 1319

Editions Farel (France) *Tel:* (01) 64 68 46 44 *Fax:* (01) 64 68 39 90 *E-mail:* lire@editionsfarel.com *Web Site:* www.editionsfarel.com, pg 163

Farmesa Regional Prog on Farm Research Methods (Zimbabwe) *Tel:* (04) 791407; (04) 791485; (04) 791495 *Fax:* (04) 703497 *E-mail:* makradho@havare.iafrica.com *Web Site:* www.farmesa.co.zw, pg 768

T C Farries & Co Ltd (United Kingdom) *Tel:* (01387) 720755 *Fax:* (01387) 721105, pg 1319

Farseeing Publishing Company Ltd (Taiwan, Province of China) *Tel:* (02) 3932166 *Fax:* (02) 3225455 *E-mail:* fars@msb.ninet.net, pg 630

Farsight Press (United Kingdom) *Tel:* (020) 8675 1693, pg 682

Fassbaender Verlag (Austria) *Tel:* (01) 8923546 *Fax:* (01) 8923546-22 *E-mail:* mail@fassbaender.com *Web Site:* www.fassbaender.com, pg 51

Fata Morgana (France) *Tel:* (04) 67 54 40 40 *Fax:* (04) 67 04 14 91 *E-mail:* fatamorgan@wanadoo.fr, pg 163

Editorial Fata Morgana SA de CV (Mexico) *Tel:* (055) 52 80 08 29 *Fax:* (055) 52 80 81 37 *E-mail:* editorial@fatamorgana.com.mx *Web Site:* www.fatamorgana.com.mx, pg 461

Fatatrac (Italy) *Tel:* (055) 669102 *Fax:* (055) 679289 *Web Site:* www.fatatrac.com, pg 388

Al- Fateh University, The Central Library (Libyan Arab Jamahiriya) *Tel:* (022) 605441 *Fax:* (022) 605460, pg 1481

Ekkehard Faude Verlag (Germany) *Tel:* (0041) 6883555 *Fax:* (0041) 6883565, pg 227

Faust Vrani (Croatia) *Tel:* (01) 213646; (01) 2332 302 *Fax:* (01) 213646; (01) 2332 302 *E-mail:* faust.vrancic@zg.tel.hr *Web Site:* www.pontes.com; www.nomad.hr, pg 118

Ediciones Librerias Fausto (Argentina) *Tel:* (011) 4372-4919 *Fax:* (011) 4372-3914 *E-mail:* fausto@fausto.com *Web Site:* www.fausto.com, pg 6

Librerias Fausto (Argentina) *Tel:* (011) 3724919, pg 1271

Favorit-Verlag Huntemann und Markus & Co GmbH (Germany) *Tel:* (07222) 2 22 54 *Fax:* (07222) 2 98 38 *E-mail:* info@favorit-verlag.de *Web Site:* www.favorit-verlag.de, pg 227

Librairie Artheme Fayard (France) *Tel:* (01) 45498200 *Fax:* (01) 42224017 *Web Site:* www.editions-fayard.fr, pg 163

Fazlee Sons (Pvt) Ltd (Pakistan) *Tel:* (021) 214585; (021) 212289 *Fax:* (021) 6640522 *E-mail:* fazlee@tarique.khi.sdnpk.undp.org, pg 506

FBT de R Editions/Editions des Limbes d'Or (France) *Tel:* (01) 41151969; (06) 07683371 *Fax:* (01) 41151969, pg 163

FCA Editora de Informatica (Portugal) *Tel:* (021) 3151218 *Fax:* (021) 577827, pg 525

Editora FCO Ltda (Brazil) *Tel:* (031) 2131288 *Fax:* (031) 2243825 *E-mail:* ottomi@fco.org.br, pg 83

Feakle Press (Australia) *Tel:* (02) 95573248, pg 22

FEDA SA (Italy) *Tel:* (091) 9235677 *Fax:* (091) 220171, pg 388

Federacao Brasileira de Associacoes de Bibliotecarios - Comissao Brasileira de Documentacao Juridica (FEBAB/CBDJ) (Brazil) *Tel:* (011) 2579979 *Fax:* (011) 2830747, pg 1513

Federacion de Gremios de Editores de Espana (FGEE) (Spain) *Tel:* (091) 5345195 *Fax:* (09) 5352625 *E-mail:* fgee@fge.es *Web Site:* www.federacioneditores.org, pg 1259

Federal Publications Ltd (Hong Kong) *Tel:* (02) 3342421 *Fax:* (02) 7645095, pg 319

Federal Publications (S) Pte Ltd (Singapore) *Tel:* 62139288 *Fax:* 62889254 *E-mail:* fps@tpl.com.sg *Web Site:* www.tpl.com.sg, pg 546

Federal Publications Sdn Bhd (Malaysia) *Tel:* (03) 7351511 *Fax:* (03) 7364620 *E-mail:* kesoon@pc.jaring.my, pg 452

Federation de l'Imprimerie et de la Communaute Graphique-FICG (France) *Tel:* (01) 46342115 *Fax:* (01) 46337334, pg 1243

Federation des Enseignants Documentalistes de l'Education nationale (France) *Tel:* (01) 43724560; (03) 8588898 *Fax:* (03) 8588898 *E-mail:* fadben@insat.com, pg 1515

Federation Francaise de la Randonnee Pedestre (France) *Tel:* (01) 44 89 93 93 *Fax:* (01) 40 35 85 67 *E-mail:* info@ffrp.asso.fr *Web Site:* asp.ffrp.asso.fr, pg 164

Federation Internationale des Traducteurs (FIT) (Austria) *Tel:* (01) 4403607; (01) 4709819 *Fax:* (01) 4403756; (01) 4708194 *E-mail:* info@fit.org *Web Site:* www.fit.ift.org, pg 1237

Federation Luxembourgeoise des Editeurs de Livres, ASBL (Luxembourg) *Tel:* 439444 *Fax:* 439450 *E-mail:* promoculture@ibm.net, pg 1251

Federation of Children's Book Groups (United Kingdom) *Tel:* (0113) 4442105, pg 1265

Federation of European Publishers (FEP) (Belgium) *Tel:* (02) 7701110 *Fax:* (02) 7712071 *E-mail:* fep.Alemann@brutele.be *Web Site:* www.editeur.org/FEP.html, pg 1238

Federation of Indian Publishers (India) *Tel:* (011) 6964847; (011) 6852263 *Fax:* (011) 6864054, pg 1248

The Federation Press (Australia) *Tel:* (02) 9552-2200 *Fax:* (02) 9552-1681 *E-mail:* info@federationpress.com.au *Web Site:* www.federationpress.com.au, pg 22

Federico Motta Editore SpA (Italy) *Tel:* (02) 300761 *Fax:* (02) 38010046 *E-mail:* editor@mottaeditore.it *Web Site:* www.mottaeditore.it, pg 389

Libreria Universal Carlos Federspiel (Costa Rica), pg 1280

Feguagiskia' Studios (Italy) *Tel:* (010) 2757544 *Fax:* (010) 2510838, pg 389

Frank Fehmers Productions (Netherlands) *Tel:* (020) 6238766 *Fax:* (020) 6246262, pg 477

Fehr'sche Buchhandlung AG (Switzerland) *Tel:* (075) 221152; (075) 231381, pg 1313

Editions Francois Feij (Switzerland) *Tel:* (021) 8254675, pg 614

Felag Islenskra Bokautgefenda (Iceland) *Tel:* 5118020 *Fax:* 5115020 *E-mail:* baekur@mmedia.is *Web Site:* www.bokautgefa.is, pg 1248

Feldheim Publishers Ltd (Israel) *Tel:* (02) 6513947 *Fax:* (02) 6536061 *E-mail:* feldheim@netvision.net.il *Web Site:* www.feldheim.com, pg 367

Fellowship of Australian Writers (Australia), pg 1359

Fellowship of Australian Writers (Vic) Inc (Australia) *Tel:* (03) 93493722 *Fax:* (02) 93493722, pg 1359

Felta Book Sales Inc (Philippines) *Tel:* (02) 8178155; (02) 8177773 *Fax:* (02) 8181188; (02) 9114103, pg 1306

Libreria Feltrinelli (Italy) *Tel:* (02) 86463485 *Fax:* (02) 72001064, pg 1293

Giangiacomo Feltrinelli SpA (Italy) *Tel:* (02) 86463485 *Fax:* (02) 72001064, pg 389

Feltron-Elektronik Zeissler & Co GmbH (Germany) *Tel:* (02241) 48670 *Fax:* (02241) 404241, pg 227

Bokklubben Feminina (Norway) *Tel:* 22471000 *Fax:* 22471098, pg 1231

Des Femmes (France) *Tel:* (01) 4548 8380 *Fax:* (01) 40358548 *E-mail:* adfemmes@iway.fr, pg 164

Fen Kitabevi (Turkey) *Tel:* (0312) 4253111 *Fax:* (0312) 4185109; (0312) 4171733, pg 1315

Fenda Edicoes (Portugal) *Tel:* (021) 8823650 *Fax:* (021) 8823659 *E-mail:* info@fenda.pt *Web Site:* www.fenda.pt, pg 525

La Fenice SRL (Italy) *Tel:* (06) 5565954 *Fax:* (06) 5565954, pg 389

Fenice 2000 (Italy) *Tel:* (02) 66984638; (02) 67075155 *Fax:* (02) 67074283, pg 389

Fenix-Kustannus Oy (Finland) *Tel:* (09) 420 8190 *Fax:* (09) 420 8045, pg 142

Editions Le Fennec (Morocco) *Tel:* (02) 209268; (02) 209314 *Fax:* (02) 277702 *E-mail:* fennec@techno.net.ma, pg 470

FEP International Private Ltd (Singapore) *Tel:* 4743135 *Fax:* 4752389, pg 546

FEP International Sdn Bhd (Malaysia) *Tel:* (03) 7036150; (03) 7036152; (03) 7036154 *Fax:* (03) 7036989, pg 452

Ferd Dummler's Verlag (Germany) *Tel:* (0228) 91340 *Fax:* (0228) 213040, pg 227

Ferdinand Berger und Sohne (Austria) *Tel:* (02982) 4161-332 *Fax:* (02982) 4161-382 *E-mail:* druckerei.office@berger.at *Web Site:* www.berger.at, pg 51

Ferdinand Enke Verlag (Germany) *Tel:* (0711) 8931-0 *Fax:* (0711) 8931-706 *Web Site:* www.enke.de, pg 227

Ferdowsi University of Mashhad Central Library & Documentation Centre (Islamic Republic of Iran) *Tel:* (051) 818113-14 *Fax:* (051) 818113, pg 1474

Feria del Libro (Uruguay) *Tel:* (02) 902070 *Fax:* (02) 902070, pg 1324

Feria Chilena del Libro Ltda (Chile) *Tel:* (02) 6396621 *Fax:* (02) 6339374 *Web Site:* www.feriachilenadellibro.cl, pg 1279

Livraria Ferin, Lda (Portugal) *Tel:* (01) 213424422; (01) 213469033 *Fax:* (01) 213471101 *E-mail:* livraria.ferin@mail.telepac.pt, pg 1307

Fern House (United Kingdom) *Tel:* (01353) 740222 *Fax:* (01353) 741987 *E-mail:* info@fernhouse.com, pg 1161

Libreria Amalio M Fernandez SRL (Uruguay) *Tel:* (02) 852684 *Fax:* (02) 852684, pg 1324

Libreria Amalio M Fernandez, Editorial (Uruguay) *Tel:* (02) 9151782; (02) 852684 *Fax:* (02) 9151782, pg 760

Fernandez Editores SA de CV (Mexico) *Tel:* (05) 5244600; (05) 5342285 *Fax:* (05) 6889173, pg 461

Fernfawn Publications (Australia) *Tel:* (07) 3202 6157 *Fax:* (07) 3202 6157, pg 22

Fernhurst Books (United Kingdom) *Tel:* (01903) 882277 *Fax:* (01903) 882715 *E-mail:* sales@fernhurstbooks.co.uk *Web Site:* fernhurstbooks.co.uk, pg 682

Fernwood Press (Pty) Ltd (South Africa) *Tel:* (021) 6833784 *Fax:* (021) 6718574 *E-mail:* ferpress@iafrica.com *Web Site:* www.fernwoodpress.co.za, pg 554

Ferozsons (Private) Ltd (Pakistan) *Tel:* (042) 6301196; (042) 6301197; (042) 6301198 *Fax:* (042) 6369204 *E-mail:* ferozsons@showroom.edunet.sdnpk.undp.org, pg 506

Ferozsons (Private) Ltd (Pakistan) *Tel:* (042) 111626262 *Fax:* (042) 6369204 *E-mail:* support@ferozsons.com.pk, pg 1304

Franz Ferzak World & Space Publications (Germany) *Tel:* (09446) 1403 *Fax:* (089) 7293 9737, pg 227

Festina Lente Edizioni (Italy) *Tel:* (055) 2313506; (055) 292612 *Fax:* (055) 292612, pg 389

Festland Verlag GmbH (Germany) *Tel:* (0228) 36 20 21 *Fax:* (0228) 35 17 71 *E-mail:* festland@t-online.de, pg 227

Festo Didactic GmbH & Co (Germany) *Tel:* (0711) 3467-0 *Fax:* (0711) 3467-1318 *E-mail:* did@festo.com *Web Site:* www.festo.com, pg 227

Editions du Feu Nouveau (France) *Tel:* (01) 44844797, pg 164

FF Press (Romania) *Tel:* (01) 6191544 *Fax:* (01) 3129694, pg 533

FFSL (Federation francaise des syndicats de libraires) (France) *Tel:* (01) 42820003 *Fax:* (01) 42821051, pg 1243

FGUP Izdatelstvo Mashinostroenie (Russian Federation) *Tel:* (095) 2683858 *Fax:* (095) 2694897 *E-mail:* mashpubl@mashin.ru *Web Site:* www.mashin.ru, pg 538

FHB Exporter (Egypt (Arab Republic of Egypt)) *Tel:* (02) 5083898 *Fax:* (02) 5083898 *E-mail:* fhb@link.net, pg 1282

FHG Publications Ltd (United Kingdom) *Tel:* (0141) 8870428 *Fax:* (0141) 8897204 *E-mail:* fhg@ipcmedia.com *Web Site:* www.holidayguides.com, pg 682

FIAF (International Federation of Film Archives) (Belgium) *Tel:* (02) 5383065 *Fax:* (02) 5344774 *E-mail:* fiaf@mail.interpac.be *Web Site:* www.cinema.ucla.edu/fiaf, pg 1238

Fibre Leather Manufacturing Corp (United States) *Tel:* 508-997-4557 *Fax:* 508-997-7268 *E-mail:* fibreleather@earthlink.net, pg 1215

Fibre Verlag (Germany) *Tel:* (0541) 431838 *Fax:* (0541) 432786 *E-mail:* info@fibre-verlag.de *Web Site:* www.fibre-verlag.de, pg 227

Fiction Factory International Ltd (Denmark) *Tel:* (043) 33 75 55 09 *Fax:* (043) 33 75 55 44, pg 1227

Sadie Fields Productions Ltd (United Kingdom) *Tel:* (020) 8746 1171 *Fax:* (020) 8746 1170 *E-mail:* sales@tangobooks.co.uk, pg 682

Wolfgang Fietkau Verlag (Germany) *Tel:* (033203) 71 105 *Fax:* (033203) 71 109 *E-mail:* fietkau@fietkau.de *Web Site:* www.fietkau.de, pg 227

Julio de Figueiredo, Lda (Portugal) *Tel:* (021) 8460784 *Fax:* (021) 8464164 *E-mail:* jlfig@individual.eunet.pt, pg 1307

Figueirinhas, Lda (Portugal) *Tel:* (021) 8879268 *Fax:* (021) 8879639 *E-mail:* correio@liv_figueirinhas.pt, pg 1307

Livraria Editora Figueirinhas Lda (Portugal) *Tel:* (022) 3325300 *Fax:* (022) 3325907 *E-mail:* correio@liv-figueirinhas.pt, pg 525

Filadelfia forlag (Iceland) *Tel:* 5525155 *Fax:* 5620735, pg 327

Filef Italo-Australian Publications (Australia) *Tel:* (02) 9568-3776 *Fax:* (02) 9568-3776, pg 22

Editions Filipacchi-Sonodip (France) *Tel:* (01) 41349069; (01) 41349055 *Fax:* (01) 41349070, pg 164

Filistor Publishing (Greece) *Tel:* (01) 3818457, pg 1286

Filmfaust Verlag - Internationale Filmzeitschrift (Germany) *Tel:* (069) 748305 *Fax:* (069) 564321, pg 227

Ekdoseis Filon (Greece) *Tel:* (01) 3618705 *Fax:* (01) 3618705, pg 310

Filozofski Fakultet Sveucilista u Zagrebu (Croatia) *Tel:* (01) 6120 111 *Fax:* (01) 6156 879 *Web Site:* www.ffzg.hr, pg 118

Financial Training Co (United Kingdom) *Tel:* (020) 7481 6050 *Fax:* (020) 7265 0337, pg 682

Financial World Publishing (United Kingdom) *Tel:* (01227) 762 600 *Fax:* (01227) 763 788 *E-mail:* institute@ifslearning.com, pg 682

Finansy i Statistika Publishing House (Russian Federation) *Tel:* (095) 925 4708 *Fax:* (095) 925 0957 *E-mail:* mail@finstat.ru *Web Site:* www.finstat.ru, pg 538

Finch Publishing (Australia) *Tel:* (02) 9418 6247 *Fax:* (02) 9418 8878 *E-mail:* info@finch.com.au *Web Site:* www.finch.com.au, pg 22

Findhorn Press Inc (United Kingdom) *Tel:* (01309) 690582 *Fax:* (01309) 690036 *E-mail:* books@findhorn.org *Web Site:* www.findhornpress.com, pg 682

Fine Arts Press Pty Ltd (Australia) *Tel:* (02) 9966 8400 *Fax:* (02) 9906 0355 *E-mail:* sacret@gbpub.com.au *Web Site:* www.artasiapacific.com, pg 23

Bokforlaget Fingraf AB (Sweden) *Tel:* (08) 55030023 *Fax:* (08) 55069570, pg 602

Emil Fink Verlag (Germany) *Tel:* (0711) 814646 *Fax:* (0711) 8106070 *E-mail:* info@fink-verlag.de, pg 227

Fink - Kummerly und Frey Verlag GmbH (Germany) *Tel:* (0711) 4506400 *Fax:* (0711) 4506456, pg 227

Wilhelm Fink GmbH & Co Verlags-KG (Germany) *Tel:* (089) 348017; (089) 348018 *Fax:* (089) 341378 *E-mail:* kontakt@fink.de *Web Site:* www.fink.de, pg 228

Finken Verlag GmbH (Germany) *Tel:* (06171) 6388-18 *Fax:* (06171) 6388-44 *E-mail:* info@finken.de *Web Site:* www.finken.de, pg 228

The Arnold & Leona Finkler Institute of Holocaust Research (Israel) *Tel:* (03) 5340333 *Fax:* (03) 5351233 *E-mail:* michmad@mail.biu.ac.il, pg 367

Finlands svenska forfattareforening (Finland) *Tel:* (09) 446266 *Fax:* (09) 446871, pg 1362

Finnish Building Centre Ltd (Finland) *Tel:* (09) 5495570 *Web Site:* www.rakennustieto, pg 142

Finnish ISBN Agency (Finland) *Tel:* (09) 19144327; (09) 19144329 *Fax:* (09) 19144341 *E-mail:* marrit.hutunen@helsinki.fi *Web Site:* hul.helsinki.fi/hyk/kt/kustantajat/isbn/html, pg 1242

Libreria Editrice Fiorentina di Vittorio Zani e C SAS (Italy) *Tel:* (055) 579921 *Fax:* (055) 579921, pg 389

Firebird Books Ltd (United Kingdom) *Tel:* (01202) 715349 (sales); (01258) 454675 (editorial) *Fax:* (01202) 736191, pg 682

Firefly (United Kingdom) *Tel:* (01926) 887799 *Fax:* (01926) 883331, pg 1233

Firma KLM Privatee Ltd, Publishers & International Booksellers (India) *Tel:* (033) 274391; 4681209 *Fax:* (033) 274391; (033) 276544, pg 337

First & Best in Education Ltd (United Kingdom) *Tel:* (01536) 399004 (editorial); (01536) 399005 (accounts) *Fax:* (01536) 399012 *E-mail:* firstandbest@themail.co.uk *Web Site:* www.firstandbest.co.uk, pg 682

First Edition Translations Ltd (United Kingdom) *Tel:* (01223) 356733 *Fax:* (01223) 321488 *E-mail:* info@firstedit.co.uk, pg 1128

Librairie Fischbacher, International Art Book Distribution (import-export) (France) *Tel:* (01) 43 26 84 87 *Fax:* (01) 43 26 48 87, pg 164

F Fischer Book Service (Israel) *Tel:* (04) 255830 *Fax:* (04) 244970, pg 1292

Fischer & Co (Sweden) *Tel:* (08) 242160 *Fax:* (08) 247825 *E-mail:* bokforlaget@fischer-co.se *Web Site:* www.fischer.co.se, pg 602

Harald Fischer Verlag GmbH (Germany) *Tel:* (09131) 205620 *Fax:* (09131) 206028 *E-mail:* info@haraldfischerverlag.de *Web Site:* www.haraldfischerverlag.de, pg 228

Verkehrs-Verlag J Fischer GmbH & Co KG (Germany) *Tel:* (0211) 99193-0 *Fax:* (0211) 6801544 *E-mail:* vvf@verkehrsverlag-fischer.de *Web Site:* www.verkehrsverlag-fischer.de, pg 228

Karin Fischer Verlag GmbH (Germany) *Tel:* (0241) 960 90 90 *Fax:* (0241) 960 90 99 *Web Site:* www.karin-fischer-verlag.de, pg 228

Fischer Media AG fur Verlag und Publishing (Switzerland) *Tel:* (031) 922211 *Fax:* (031) 7205112 *E-mail:* all@fischermedia.ch, pg 614

Verlag Reinhard Fischer (Germany) *Tel:* (089) 791 88 92 *Fax:* (089) 791 83 10 *E-mail:* verlagfischer@compuserve.de *Web Site:* www.verlag-reinhard-fischer.de, pg 228

Rita G Fischer Verlag (Germany) *Tel:* (069) 941942-0 *Fax:* (069) 941942-99; (069) 941942-98 *E-mail:* r.g.fischer.verlag@t-online.de *Web Site:* www.buchhandel.de/r.g.fischer/, pg 228

S Fischer Verlag GmbH (Germany) *Tel:* (069) 6062-0 *Fax:* (069) 6062-214 *Web Site:* www.s-fischer.de, pg 228

Fischer Taschenbuch Verlag GmbH (Germany) *Tel:* (069) 60620 *Fax:* (069) 606214 *Web Site:* www.s-fischer.de, pg 228

FISH Publishing (Ireland) *Tel:* (027) 61246 *Fax:* (027) 61246 *E-mail:* info@fishpublishing.com *Web Site:* www.fishpublishing.com, pg 360

Anne-Louise Fisher (United Kingdom) *Tel:* (020) 7494 4609 *Fax:* (020) 7494 4611, pg 1119

Fishing News Books Ltd (United Kingdom) *Tel:* (01865) 206206 *Fax:* (01865) 721205 *E-mail:* fnb@blacksci.co.uk *Web Site:* www.fishknowledge.com, pg 682

Fitzwilliam Publishing Co Ltd (Ireland) *Tel:* (01) 614575 *Fax:* (01) 614575, pg 360

The Five Mile Press Pty Ltd (Australia) *Tel:* (03) 9790 5000 *Fax:* (03) 9790 6688 *E-mail:* info@fivemile.com.au *Web Site:* www.fivemile.com.au, pg 23

Editions Fivedit (France) *Tel:* (0450) 663378 *Fax:* (0450) 233308, pg 164

Fixot (France) *Tel:* (01) 53 67 15 22 *Fax:* (01) 53 67 14 14, pg 164

Izdatelstvo Fizkultura i Sport (Russian Federation) *Tel:* (095) 2582690 *Fax:* (095) 2001217, pg 538

Fizmatlit Publishing Co (Russian Federation) *Tel:* (095) 3347151 *Fax:* (095) 9550597, pg 538

Fjolvi (Iceland) *Tel:* 5688433 *Fax:* 5688142, pg 327

Flaccovio Dario (Italy) *Tel:* (091) 6700453 *Fax:* (091) 528100, pg 389

Flaccovio Editore (Italy) *Tel:* (091) 589442 *Fax:* (091) 331992, pg 389

Libreria S F Flaccovio (Italy) *Tel:* (091) 589442 *Fax:* (091) 331992 *E-mail:* flaccovio@lycosmail.com *Web Site:* www.flaccovio.com, pg 1293

Werner Flach Internationale Fachbuchhandlung (Germany) *Tel:* (069) 9591750 *Fax:* (069) 95917522 *E-mail:* fadibuch@flachbuch.com *Web Site:* www.flachbuch.com, pg 1284

Ediciones FLACSO Costa Rica (Costa Rica) *Tel:* 2346890; 2248059 *Fax:* 2256779, pg 116

Flactem (Australia) *Tel:* (03) 98083444 *Fax:* (03) 98888948, pg 23

Les Editions du Flamboyant (Benin) *Tel:* 312517 *E-mail:* IPEC@leland.bj, pg 76

Flammarion SA (France) *Tel:* (01) 40513008 *Fax:* (01) 43250118, pg 164

Flammarion (France) *Tel:* (01) 78380157; (01) 40513041 *Fax:* (01) 43292148, pg 1283

Flechsig Buchvertrieb (Germany) *Tel:* (0931) 385235 *Fax:* (0931) 385305 *E-mail:* info@verlagshaus.com *Web Site:* www.verlagshaus.com, pg 228

Erich Fleischer Verlag (Germany) *Tel:* (04202) 517-0 *Fax:* (04202) 517-41 *E-mail:* info@efv-online.de *Web Site:* www.efv-online.de, pg 228

Fleischhauer & Spohn GmbH & Co (Germany) *Tel:* (07142) 596161 *Fax:* (07142) 596280 *E-mail:* verlag-fleischhauer@t-online.de *Web Site:* www.verlag-fleischhauer.de, pg 228

Flensburger Hefte Verlag GmbH (Germany) *Tel:* (0461) 2 63 63; (0461) 2 14 72 *Fax:* (0461) 2 69 12 *E-mail:* flensburgerhefte@t-online.de *Web Site:* www.flensburgerhefte.de, pg 228

Flesch Financial Publications (Pty) Ltd (South Africa) *Tel:* (021) 4617472 *Fax:* (021) 4613758 *E-mail:* sflesch@aztec.co.za, pg 554

Robert Fletcher (Stoneclough) Ltd (United Kingdom) *Tel:* (01204) 571241 *Fax:* (01204) 572919, pg 1140

Groupe Fleurus-Mame (France) *Tel:* (01) 53 26 33 35 *Fax:* (01) 53 26 33 36, pg 164

Flicks Books (United Kingdom) *Tel:* (01225) 767 728 *Fax:* (01225) 760 418 *E-mail:* flicks.books@pipex.com, pg 683

Flo Enterprise Sdn Bhd (Malaysia) *Tel:* (03) 7187770; (03) 7187790 *Fax:* (03) 7931066, pg 1298

La Flor del Itapebi (Uruguay) *Tel:* (02) 7115847 *Fax:* (02) 4090191, pg 760

Ediciones de la Flor SRL (Argentina) *Tel:* (011) 4963-7950 *Fax:* (011) 4963-5616 *E-mail:* edic-flor@datamarkets.com.ar *Web Site:* www.edicionesdelaflor.com.ar, pg 6

Flora Publications International Pty Ltd (Australia) *Tel:* (07) 3229 6366 *Fax:* (07) 3229 8782 *E-mail:* info@flora.com.au, pg 23

Florilegium (Australia) *Tel:* (02) 95558589 *Fax:* (02) 98184409 *E-mail:* florileg@ozemail.com.au, pg 23

Floris Books (United Kingdom) *Tel:* (0131) 337 2372 *Fax:* (0131) 346 7516 *E-mail:* floris@floris.demon.co.uk, pg 683

Flugzeug Publikations GmbH (Germany) *Tel:* (07303) 964220 *Fax:* (07303) 964141 *E-mail:* online@flugzeug-publikation.de *Web Site:* www.flugzeug-publikation.de, pg 229

Empresa Literaria Fluminense, Lda (Portugal) *Tel:* (021) 601138 *Fax:* (021) 3963371, pg 525

Flyleaf Press (Ireland) *Tel:* (01) 2806231 *E-mail:* flyleaf@indigo.ie *Web Site:* www.flyleaf.ie, pg 360

FMR Ricci (Italy) *Tel:* (02) 414101 *Fax:* (02) 48301473 *E-mail:* ricci@fmrmagazine.it, pg 1293

FN-Verlag der Deutschen Reiterlichen Vereinigung GmbH (Germany) *Tel:* (02581) 63 62-115 *Fax:* (02581) 63 31 46 *E-mail:* fnverlag@fn-dokr.de *Web Site:* www.fnverlag.de, pg 229

FNPS (Federation nationale depresse d'information specialisee) (France) *Tel:* (01) 44904360 *Fax:* (01) 44904372 *Web Site:* www.fnps.fr/main.asp, pg 1243

Focus Publications International SA (Panama) *Tel:* 225 6638 *Fax:* 225 0466 *E-mail:* focusint@sinfo.net *Web Site:* focuspublicationsint.com, pg 509

Focus Publications Ltd (Kenya) *Tel:* (02) 48233, pg 431

Focus-Verlag Gesellschaft mbH (Germany) *Tel:* (0641) 76031 *Fax:* (0641) 76031 *E-mail:* info@focus-verlag.de *Web Site:* www.focus-verlag.de, pg 229

Foldmuvelesugyi Miniszterium Muszaki Intezet (Hungary) *Tel:* (028) 320644 *Fax:* (028) 320960 *E-mail:* dekani@eng.gau.hu, pg 323

Foereningen Auktoriserade Translatorer (Sweden) *Tel:* (018) 858 355869 *Fax:* (018) 858 355869, pg 1127

Forlaget By och Bygd (Sweden) *Tel:* (08) 6520955, pg 602

Forlaget Sanctus (Metodistkyrkans Forlag) (Sweden) *Tel:* (08) 315570 *Fax:* (08) 315579, pg 602

Forlagshuset Norden AB (Sweden) *Tel:* (040) 934250 *Fax:* (040) 930156, pg 602

Foersamlingsfoerbundets Foerlags AB (Finland) *Tel:* (09) 6126150; (09) 61261535 *Fax:* (09) 603963, pg 142

Foszekesegyhazi Konyvtar (Hungary) *Tel:* 33411891 *E-mail:* bibliotheca@ehf.hu, pg 1472

Maurice et Pierre Foetisch SA (Switzerland) *Tel:* (021) 3239444; (021) 3239445 *Fax:* (021) 3115011, pg 614

Fovarosi Szabo Ervin Konyvtar (Hungary) *Tel:* (01) 1185815 *Fax:* (01) 1185914 *E-mail:* h7448kis@huelia.bitnet, pg 1472

Fogarty's Bookshop (South Africa) *Tel:* (041) 3681425; (041) 3681454 *Fax:* (041) 3681279, pg 1310

Fogola Editore in Torino (Italy) *Tel:* (011) 541512 *Fax:* (011) 530305, pg 389

Foi-Commerce (Bulgaria) *Tel:* (02) 227116 *Fax:* (02) 227116 *E-mail:* foi@nlcv.net, pg 95

Foibe Filan-Kevitry NY Mpampianatra (FOFIPA) (Madagascar) *Tel:* (02) 27500 *Fax:* (02) 35788, pg 450

Fola Abbey Educational Book Services, Fola Abbey Bookshops Ltd (Nigeria) *Tel:* (01) 2636679 *Fax:* (01) 825268, pg 1303

Folens Ltd (United Kingdom) *Tel:* (01582) 470821 *Fax:* (01582) 470818 *E-mail:* folens@folens.com *Web Site:* www.folens.com, pg 683

Folens Publishers (Ireland) *Tel:* (01) 451-5311 *Fax:* (01) 451-5308, pg 360

Folhenuniversitetets Forlag (Norway) *Tel:* 22575307 *Fax:* 22575310, pg 503

Folini (Italy) *Tel:* (0131) 807001 *Fax:* (0131) 807001 *E-mail:* edifolini@edifolini.com *Web Site:* www.edifolini.com, pg 389

The Folio Society (United Kingdom) *Tel:* (020) 7400 4242 *Fax:* (020) 7400 4242 *Web Site:* www.foliosoc.co.uk, pg 1233

Folio Verlagsgesellschaft mbH (Austria) *Tel:* (01) 5813708-0 *Fax:* (01) 5813708-20 *E-mail:* office@folioverlag.com *Web Site:* www.folioverlag.com/books.php, pg 51

Folklore Comtois (France) *Tel:* 81552977 *Fax:* 81552397, pg 164

The Folklore Society (United Kingdom) *Tel:* (020) 7387 5894, pg 1265

Folkuniversitetets foerlag (Sweden) *Tel:* 148720 *Fax:* 132904 *E-mail:* info@fu-forlag.m.se *Web Site:* www.fu-forlag.m.se, pg 602

Editions Foma SA (Switzerland) *Tel:* (021) 6351361 *Fax:* (021) 6351704, pg 614

Fondacija Zlatno Kljuce (Bulgaria) *Tel:* (02) 760-671; (02) 623517 *Fax:* (02) 623517 *E-mail:* ynfirst@mat.bg, pg 95

Institut Fondamental d'Afrique Noire, Cheikh Anta Diop (Senegal) *Tel:* (0221) 250090; (0221) 241652; (0221) 251990; (0221) 259890 *Fax:* (0221) 244918, pg 544

Fondation de l'Encyclopedie de Geneve (Switzerland) *Fax:* (022) 3273391; (022) 3273365, pg 614

Presses de la Fondation Nationale des Sciences Politiques (France) *Tel:* (01) 44 39 39 60 *Fax:* (01) 45 48 04 41 *Web Site:* www.sciences.po.fr, pg 164

Fondazzjoni Patrimonju Malti (Malta) *Tel:* 21 231515 *Fax:* 21 250118 *E-mail:* patrimonju@keyworld.net *Web Site:* www.patrimonju.org.mt, pg 456

Fondo de Cultura Economica SA (Chile) *Tel:* (02) 6990189 *Fax:* (02) 6962329, pg 1279

Fondo de Cultura Economica (Mexico) *Tel:* (05) 5242240; (05) 5243840; (05) 5246664 *Fax:* (05) 2274640; (05) 2274683; (05) 2274694 *E-mail:* fceedi@infoabc.com(fceedi), pg 461

Fondo de Cultura Economica de Espana, SL (Spain) *Tel:* (091) 7632800; (091) 7632766 *Fax:* (091) 7635133, pg 574

Fondo Editorial de la Plastica Mexicana (Mexico) *Tel:* (05) 56-88-30-67 *Fax:* (05) 56-88-11-68, pg 461

Fondo Editorial de la Pontificia Universidad Catolica del Peru (Peru) *Tel:* (01) 4622540 (ext 220) *Fax:* (01) 4626390 (direct), pg 511

Fondo Educativo Interamericano SA (Colombia) *Tel:* (01) 2459279; (01) 2852773; (01) 2852542; (01) 2859180; (01) 3382877 *Fax:* (01) 2852891 *E-mail:* eeducativa@multi.net.co, pg 112

Fondo Educativo Interamericano (Panama) *Tel:* 2691511; 2230210, pg 509

Fong & Sons Printers Pte Ltd (Singapore) *Tel:* 2663688 *Fax:* 2664988, pg 1200

Fonna Forlag L/L (Norway) *Tel:* 22201303 *Fax:* 22201201, pg 503

Fono Forlag (Norway) *Tel:* 66846490 *Fax:* 66847507 *E-mail:* mail@fonoforlag.no, pg 503

The Font Bureau (United States) *Tel:* 617-423-8770 *Fax:* 617-423-8771 *E-mail:* typesales@fontbureau.com *Web Site:* www.fontbureau.com, pg 1165

Miguel Font Editor (Spain) *Tel:* (071) 477300 *Fax:* (071) 476805 *E-mail:* miquel@globalnet.es, pg 574

Uitgeverij De Fontein BV (Netherlands) *Tel:* (035) 5422141 *Fax:* (035) 5423855, pg 477

Livraria Martins Fontes Editora Ltda (Brazil) *Tel:* (011) 3241 3677 *Fax:* (0800) 11 3619 *E-mail:* info@martinsfontes.com.br *Web Site:* www.martinsfontes.com.br, pg 83

Food and Agriculture Organization of the United Nations (FAO) (Italy) *Tel:* (06) 52251 *Fax:* (06) 52253152 *E-mail:* telex-room@fao.org, pg 1249

Food Trade Press Ltd (United Kingdom) *Tel:* (01959) 563944 *Fax:* (01959) 561285 *E-mail:* foodtradereview@aol.com *Web Site:* foodbooks.net, pg 683

Forbes Publications Ltd (United Kingdom) *Tel:* (020) 7495 7945 *Fax:* (020) 7495 7916 *E-mail:* editorial@rapportgroup.com, pg 683

Foreign Language Bookshop (Australia) *Tel:* (03) 96542883 *Fax:* (03) 96507664 *E-mail:* flb@ozonline.com.au *Web Site:* www.languages.com.au, pg 1273

The Foreign Language Press Group (Democratic People's Republic of Korea) *Tel:* (02) 841342 *Fax:* (02) 812100, pg 434

Foreign Language Teaching & Research Press (China) *Tel:* (010) 6891 7641 *Fax:* (010) 6842 0956, pg 105

Foreign Languages Press (China) *Tel:* (010) 8320579 *Fax:* (010) 8317390 *E-mail:* flpcn@public3.bta.net.cn *Web Site:* www.flp.com.cn, pg 105

Foreign Languages Publishing House (Democratic People's Republic of Korea) pg 434

Forening for Boghaandvaerk, Nordjysk afdeling (Denmark) *Tel:* 98127933 *Web Site:* www.boghaandvaerk.dle, pg 1241

Foreningen Svenska Laromedelsproducenter (The Swedish Association of Educational Publishers (Sweden) *Tel:* (08) 7361940 *Fax:* (08) 7361944 *E-mail:* fsl@forlagskansli.se, pg 1259

Foreningen Svenska Laromedelsproducenter (The Swedish Association of Educational Publishers) (Sweden) *Tel:* (08) 7361940 *Fax:* (08) 7361944 *E-mail:* fsl@forlagskansli.se *Web Site:* www.fsl.se, pg 602

Editora Forense (Brazil) *Tel:* (021) 2533-5537 *Fax:* (021) 5334931 *E-mail:* forense@forense.com.br *Web Site:* www.forense.com, pg 83

Forense Universitaria Editora (Brazil) *Tel:* (011) 580-0776 *Fax:* (011) 589-2084 *E-mail:* foruniv@unisys.com.br, pg 83

Forlagid (Iceland) *Tel:* 5525188 *Fax:* 5527937 *E-mail:* forlag@mm.is, pg 327

Forlagsaktiebolaget Scriptum (Finland) *Tel:* (06) 3242228 *Fax:* (06) 3242210 *E-mail:* scriptum@svof.fi *Web Site:* www.syh.fi/scriptum/, pg 142

Forlagshuset Gothia (Sweden) *Tel:* (08) 4622660 *Fax:* (08) 4620322, pg 602

Forma Publications Ltd (Greece) *Tel:* (01) 8327008 *Fax:* (01) 8325650, pg 310

FormAsia Books Ltd (Hong Kong) *Tel:* (02) 5226422 *Fax:* (02) 5224234 *E-mail:* info@formasiabooks.com *Web Site:* www.formasiabooks.com, pg 320

Formato Editorial ltda (Brazil) *Tel:* (031) 4211588 *Fax:* (031) 4211803 *E-mail:* editorial@formatoeditorial.com.br *Web Site:* www.formatoeditorial.com.br, pg 83

Arnaldo Forni Editore SRL (Italy) *Tel:* (051) 6814142 *Fax:* (051) 6814672 *E-mail:* info@fornieditore.com *Web Site:* www.fornieditore.com, pg 389

Foroya Landsbokasavn (Faroe Islands) *Tel:* (031) 311626 *Fax:* (031) 318895 *E-mail:* fonalib@flb.fo *Web Site:* www.flb.fo, pg 1242

Foroya Landsbokasavn (Faroe Islands) *Tel:* 29811626 *Fax:* 29818895 *E-mail:* fonalib@flb.fo, pg 1463

Bengt Forsbergs Foerlag AB (Sweden) *Tel:* (040) 76320 *Fax:* (040) 303939 *E-mail:* info@forsbergsforlag.se *Web Site:* www.forsbergsforlag.se, pg 602

Forth Naturalist & Historian (United Kingdom) *Tel:* (01786) 467755 *Fax:* (01786) 464994 *Web Site:* www.stir.ac.uk/departments/naturalsciences/Forth_naturalist/index.htm, pg 683

Fortuna Finanz-Verlag AG (Switzerland) *Tel:* (01) 9803622 *Fax:* (01) 9103353, pg 614

Fortuna Print spol sra (Slovakia) *Tel:* (07) 5723140-3; (07) 5269295; (07) 5268727 *Fax:* (07) 5723145-6; (07) 5268561, pg 549

Fortunajaya (Indonesia) *Tel:* (0272) 22030 *Fax:* (0272) 22543, pg 355

Fortune Publications (Australia) *Tel:* (03) 9890-7731, pg 23

Forum (Yugoslavia) *Tel:* (021) 57216 *Fax:* (021) 57216, pg 764, 1324

Forum Artis, SA (Spain) *Tel:* (091) 4353180; (091) 4350548 *Fax:* (091) 4355124 *E-mail:* forum@adenet.es, pg 574

Bokforlaget Forum AB (Sweden) *Tel:* (08) 6968440; (08) 6968410 (Orders) *Fax:* (08) 6968367, pg 602

Forum Publications (Malaysia) *Tel:* (03) 7554007 *Fax:* (03) 7561879 *E-mail:* g2jomo@umcsd.um.edu.my, pg 452

Forum Publishers (Denmark) *Tel:* 33411830 *Fax:* 33411831 *E-mail:* gyldendal@gyldendal.dk *Web Site:* www.gyldendal.dk, pg 132

Forum Verlag GmbH & Co (Germany) *Tel:* (0711) 76727-0 *Fax:* (0711) 76727-28 *E-mail:* info@forumverlag.de *Web Site:* www.forumverlag.de, pg 229

Forum Verlag Leipzig Buch-Gesellschaft (Germany) *Tel:* (0341) 980 50 08 *Fax:* (0341) 980 50 07 *Web Site:* www.leipzig-plus.de, pg 229

Les Editions Foucher SA (France) *Tel:* (01) 49 54 35 35 *Fax:* (01) 49 54 35 00 *E-mail:* contact@foucher.fr *Web Site:* www.ecodroit.editions-foucher.fr, pg 164

Foulsham Publishers (United Kingdom) *Tel:* (01753) 526769 *Fax:* (01753) 535003, pg 683

Foundation Books (Kenya) *Tel:* (02) 765485, pg 431

Foundation for the Production & Translation of Dutch Literature (Netherlands) *Tel:* (020) 6206261 *Fax:* (020) 6207179 *E-mail:* bp@nlpvf.xs4all.nl *Web Site:* www.nlpvf.nl, pg 1115

The Foundational Book Company for the John W Doorly Trust (United Kingdom), pg 683

Lora Fountain & Associates Literary Agency (France) *Tel:* (01) 43562196 *Fax:* (01) 43482272 *E-mail:* FountLit@aol.com, pg 1110

Fountain Publishers Ltd (Uganda) *Tel:* (041) 259163; (041) 251112 *Fax:* (041) 251160 *E-mail:* fountain@starcom.co.ug *Web Site:* www.fountainpublishers.com, pg 642

Four Courts Press Ltd (Ireland) *Tel:* (01) 453-4668 *Fax:* (01) 453-4672 *E-mail:* info@four-courts-press.ie *Web Site:* www.four-courts-press.ie, pg 360

Four Seasons Publishing Ltd (United Kingdom) *Tel:* (020) 8942 4445 *Fax:* (020) 8942 4446 *E-mail:* info@fourseasons.net, pg 683

Fourah Bay College Library (Sierra Leone) *Tel:* (022) 229471, pg 1496

Naipes Heraclio Fournier SA (Spain) *Tel:* (0945) 465525 *Fax:* (0945) 465543 *E-mail:* fournier@nhfournier.es *Web Site:* www.nhfournier.es, pg 574

Fourth Dimension Publishing Co Ltd (Nigeria) *Tel:* (042) 459969 *Fax:* (042) 456904 *E-mail:* info@fdpbooks.com; fdpbook@aol.com *Web Site:* www.fdpbooks.com, pg 499

Fourth Estate Ltd (United Kingdom) *Tel:* (020) 7727 8993 *Fax:* (020) 7792 3176 *E-mail:* general@4thestate.co.uk, pg 683

W & G Foyle Ltd (United Kingdom) *Tel:* (020) 7437 5660, pg 1319

W & G Foyle Ltd (United Kingdom) *Tel:* (020) 7437 5660 *Fax:* (020) 7434 1574 *E-mail:* administration@foyles.co.uk *Web Site:* www.foyles.co.uk, pg 684

Fragment Cooperatieve Vereniging UA, Uitgeverij (Netherlands) *Tel:* (020) 6267133 *Fax:* (020) 6207989, pg 477

Editions Fragments (France) *Tel:* (01) 47 00 76 48 *Fax:* (01) 47 00 22 04 *E-mail:* art@fragmentseditions.com *Web Site:* www.fragmentseditions.com, pg 164

Fragua Editorial (Spain) *Tel:* (091) 544 22 97; (091) 549 18 06 *Fax:* (091) 549 18 06 *E-mail:* fragua@fragua.com *Web Site:* www.fragua.com, pg 574

Franc-Franc podjetje za promocijo kulture Murska Sobota d o o (Slovenia) *Tel:* (069) 22501 *Fax:* (069) 22501 *E-mail:* franc.franc@siol.net, pg 551

Institut Francais de Recherche pour l'Exploitation de la Mer (IFREMER) (France) *Tel:* (02) 98 22 40 13 *Fax:* (02) 98 22 45 86 *E-mail:* editions@ifremer.fr *Web Site:* www.ifremer.fr, pg 165

Institut Francais d'Etudes Arabes de Damas (Syrian Arab Republic) *Tel:* (011) 3330214; (011) 3331962; (011) 3334959 *Fax:* (011) 3327887 *E-mail:* ifead@net.sy *Web Site:* www.univ-aioc.fr/iflead, pg 628

Edition Francaise pour le Monde Arabe (EDIFRAMO) (Lebanon) *Tel:* (01) 862437; (01) 341650; (01) 341614, pg 443

France Edition (France) *Tel:* (01) 44411313 *Fax:* (01) 46346383 *E-mail:* info@franceedition.org *Web Site:* www.franceedition.org, pg 1243

France Edition Office de Promotion Internationale (France) *Tel:* (01) 44 41 13 13 *Fax:* (01) 46 34 63 83 *E-mail:* info@franceedition.com *Web Site:* www.franceedition.com, pg 165

France-Empire (France) *Tel:* (01) 45 00 33 00 *Fax:* (01) 45 00 20 77 *E-mail:* france-empire@france-empire.fr *Web Site:* www.france-empire.fr, pg 165

France-Loisirs (France) *Tel:* (01) 45 68 60 00 *Fax:* (01) 42 73 14 38 *Web Site:* www.franceloisirs.com, pg 165

France Tosho (Japan) *Tel:* (03) 3346-0396 *Fax:* (03) 3346-9154 *E-mail:* frtosho@blue.ocn.ne.jp, pg 1294

Instituto Frances de Estudios Andinos, IFEA (Peru) *Tel:* (01) 4476070 *Fax:* (01) 4457650 *E-mail:* postmast@ifea.org.pe, pg 511

Editorial Francesa Espanola SA (Chile) *Tel:* (02) 235-0911; (02) 235-9734 *Fax:* (02) 236-0900, pg 1279

Biblioteca Francescana (Italy) *Tel:* (02) 29002736 *Fax:* (02) 29002736 *E-mail:* ebf@biblia.it, pg 389

Francis Balsom Associates (United Kingdom) *Tel:* (01970) 636400 *Fax:* (01970) 636414 *E-mail:* publishing@fbagroup.co.uk *Web Site:* www.fbagroup.co.uk, pg 684

Les Editions Franciscaines SA (France) *Tel:* (01) 45407351 *Fax:* (01) 40447504 *E-mail:* editofm@club-internet.fr, pg 165

Editorial Franciscana (Portugal) *Tel:* (053) 22490 *Fax:* (052) 053519735, pg 525

Verlag der Francke Buchhandlung GmbH (Germany) *Tel:* (06421) 17 25-0 *Fax:* (06421) 17 25-30 *E-mail:* info@francke-buch.de *Web Site:* www.francke-buch.de, pg 229

Franco-English Bureau (United Kingdom) *Tel:* (020) 7603 5390 *Fax:* (020) 7602 1592, pg 1129

Association Frank (France) *Tel:* (01) 43656405 *Fax:* (01) 48596668, pg 165

Frank Brothers & Co (Publishers) Ltd (India) *Tel:* (011) 3263393; (011) 3279963; (011) 278150; (011) 260796; (011) 3279963 *Fax:* (011) 3269032 *E-mail:* fbros@ndb.vsnl.net.in, pg 337

Frank Publishing Ltd (Ghana) *Tel:* (21) 240711, pg 307

FVA-Frankfurter Verlagsanstalt GmbH (Germany) *Tel:* (069) 96220610 *Fax:* (069) 96220630 *E-mail:* info@frankfurter-verlagsanstalt.de *Web Site:* www.frankfurter-verlagsanstalt.de, pg 229

Franklin Book Programs Inc (Afghanistan), pg 1

Rodney Franklin Agency (Israel) *Tel:* (03) 5600724 *Fax:* (03) 5600479 *E-mail:* rodneyf@netvision.net.il, pg 367

Leanne Franson (Canada) *Tel:* 514-526-4236 *Fax:* 514-526-0972 *E-mail:* inksports@videotron.ca, pg 1153

Franz-Sales-Verlag (Germany) *Tel:* (08421) 93 489-31 *Fax:* (08421) 934 89-35 *E-mail:* info@franz-sales-verlag.de *Web Site:* www.franz-sales-verlag.de, pg 229

Verlag Franz Vahlen GmbH (Germany) *Tel:* (089) 38189-0 *Fax:* (089) 38189-402 *E-mail:* info@vahlen.de *Web Site:* www.vahlen.de, pg 229

Franzis-Verlag GmbH (Germany) *Tel:* (08121) 95 14 44 *Fax:* (08121) 95 16 96 *Web Site:* www.franzis.de, pg 229

Fraser Books (New Zealand) *Tel:* (06) 3771359 *Fax:* (06) 3771359, pg 491

The Fraser Press (United Kingdom) *Tel:* (0141) 3331992 *Fax:* (0141) 3331992, pg 684

Fraser Publications (Australia) *Tel:* (018) 039845 *Fax:* (018) 261775 *E-mail:* fraspub@albury.net.au, pg 23

Edizioni Frassinelli SRL (Italy) *Tel:* (02) 217211 *Fax:* (02) 21721277, pg 389

Fratelli Conte Editori SRL (Italy) *Tel:* (081) 7613667 *Fax:* (081) 669771, pg 389

Frauenoffensive Verlagsgesellschaft MbH (Germany) *Tel:* (089) 489500-48 *Fax:* (089) 489500-49, pg 229

Fraunhofer IRB Verlag Fraunhofer Informationszentrum Raum und Bau (Germany) *Tel:* (0711) 9 70-25 00 *Fax:* (0711) 9 70-25 08 *E-mail:* info@irb.fhg.de *Web Site:* www.irbdirekt.de, pg 229

Frech-Verlag GmbH und Co Druck KG (Germany) *Tel:* (0711) 83086-0 *Fax:* (0711) 8 30 86-56 *Web Site:* www.frech.de, pg 229

Fredebeul und Koenen GmbH (Germany) *Tel:* (0201) 49821 *Fax:* (0201) 8492415, pg 229

Frederiksberg Kommunes Biblioteker (Denmark) *Tel:* (045) 38211800 *Fax:* (045) 38211799 *E-mail:* bib@fkb.dk *Web Site:* www.fkb.dk, pg 1461

Frederking & Thaler Verlag GmbH (Germany) *Tel:* (089) 12113 0 *Fax:* (089) 12113 14, pg 230

Free Association Books Ltd (United Kingdom) *Tel:* (020) 7388 3182 *Fax:* (020) 7388 3187 *E-mail:* fab@fa-b.com *Web Site:* www.fa-b.com, pg 684

National Free Library of Zimbabwe (Zimbabwe) *Tel:* (09) 62359 *Fax:* (09) 77662, pg 1509

Free State Provincial Library & Information Services (South Africa) *Tel:* (051) 4054680 *Fax:* (051) 4033567 *E-mail:* jacomien@majuba.ofs.gov.za *Web Site:* mangaung.ofs.gov.za/library/index/htm, pg 1497

Freedom Press (United Kingdom) *Tel:* (020) 7247 9249 *Fax:* (020) 7377 9526, pg 684

Freelance Market News Ltd (United Kingdom) *Tel:* (0161) 2282362 *Fax:* (0161) 2283533 *E-mail:* fmn@writersbureau.com *Web Site:* www.writersbureau.com, pg 1319

W H Freeman & Co Ltd (United Kingdom) *Tel:* (01256) 332807 *Fax:* (01256) 330688, pg 684

Erika G Freese Verlag (Germany) *Tel:* (030) 8333077 *Fax:* (030) 8333077, pg 230

Freie Universitaet Berlin (Germany) *Tel:* (030) 83854224; (030) 83854093 *Fax:* (030) 83853738 *E-mail:* leitung@ub.fu-berlin.de *Web Site:* www.ub.fu-berlin.de, pg 1467

Verlag Freies Geistesleben (Germany) *Tel:* (0711) 28532 00 *Fax:* (0711) 28532 10 *E-mail:* info@geistesleben.com *Web Site:* www.geistesleben.com, pg 230

Freimund-Verlag der Gesellschaft fur Innere und Aeussere Mission im Sinne der Lutherischen Kirche eV (Germany) *Tel:* (09874) 6 89 39 80 *Fax:* (09874) 6 89 39 99 *E-mail:* info@freimund-verlag.de *Web Site:* www.freimund-buchhandlung.de/verlag, pg 230

Livraria Freitas Bastos Editora SA (Brazil) *Tel:* (021) 2573-8949 *Fax:* (021) 2573-8949 *E-mail:* fbastos@netfly.com.br; freitasbastos@freitasbastos.com.br, pg 83

Fremad A/S (Denmark) *Tel:* 33411810 *Fax:* 33411811 *Web Site:* www.fremad.dk, pg 132

Fremantle Arts Centre Press (Australia) *Tel:* (08) 9430 6331 *Fax:* (08) 9430 5242 *E-mail:* facp@iinet.net.au *Web Site:* members.iinet.au/~facp/, pg 23

Samuel French Ltd (United Kingdom) *Tel:* (020) 7387 9373 *Fax:* (020) 7387 2161 *E-mail:* theatre@samuelfrench-london.co.uk *Web Site:* www.samuelfrench-london.co.uk, pg 684

French's (United Kingdom) *Tel:* (020) 74834269 *Fax:* (020) 77220574, pg 1119

Frenckell Printing Work Ltd (Finland) *Tel:* (09) 8036044 *Fax:* (09) 8036090, pg 142

Freshet Press (Australia) *Tel:* (03) 53483085, pg 23

Sigmund Freud Copyrights (United Kingdom) *Tel:* (01206) 825433 *Fax:* (01206) 822990 *E-mail:* info@markpaterson.co.uk *Web Site:* www.markpaterson.co.uk/sigmund.htm, pg 684

Margarethe Freudenberger - selbstverlag fur jedermann (Germany) *Tel:* (09392) 8449, pg 230

Freund Publishing House Ltd (Israel) *Tel:* (03) 562-8540 *Fax:* (03) 562-8538, pg 367

Freund Publishing House Ltd (Israel) *Tel:* (03) 562-8540 *Fax:* (03) 562-8538 *E-mail:* h_freund@netvision.net.il *Web Site:* www.angelfire.com/il/feund/, pg 1127

Verlag Walter Frey (Germany) *Tel:* (030) 883 25 61 *Fax:* (030) 883 25 61 *E-mail:* tranvia@aol.com, pg 230

Freytag-Berndt und Artaria, Kartographische Anstalt (Austria) *Tel:* (01) 869 90 90 *Fax:* (01) 869 88 55 *E-mail:* office@freytagberndt.at, pg 52

FRICK Verlag-GmbH (Germany) *Tel:* (07231) 102842 *Fax:* (07231) 357744 *E-mail:* info@frickverlag.de *Web Site:* www.frickverlag.de, pg 230

Friedemann von Engel Verlag (Germany) *Tel:* (030) 3233145, pg 230

R Friedlaender & Sohn GmbH Buchhaunlung & Antiquariat (Germany) *Tel:* (030) 2622328, pg 1284

Russel Friedman Books (South Africa) *Tel:* (011) 7022300 *Fax:* (011) 7021403 *E-mail:* rvulture@iafrica.com, pg 554

S Friedman Publishing House Ltd (Israel) *Tel:* (03) 5176091 *Fax:* (03) 5179756, pg 367

Blake Friedmann Literary Agency Ltd (United Kingdom) *Tel:* (020) 7284 0408 *Fax:* (020) 7284 0442 *Web Site:* www.blakefriedmann.co.uk, pg 1119

Erhard Friedrich Verlag (Germany) *Tel:* (0511) 400040 *Fax:* (0511) 40004-119 *Web Site:* www.friedrich-verlagsgruppe.de, pg 230

Friedrich Kiehl Verlag GmbH (Germany) *Tel:* (0621) 6 35 02-0 *Fax:* (0621) 6 35 02-22 *E-mail:* hotline@kiehl.de *Web Site:* www.kiehl.de, pg 230

Frieling & Partner GmbH (Germany) *Tel:* (030) 7 66 99 90 *Fax:* (030) 7 74 41 03 *Web Site:* www.frieling.de, pg 230

The Friendly Press (United Kingdom) *Tel:* (0117) 908-2281 *Fax:* (0117) 908-2282 *E-mail:* phgassoc@aol.com, pg 684

Friends of the National Libraries (United Kingdom) *Tel:* (020) 7412 7559, pg 1525

Friends of Antiquity (Czech Republic) *Tel:* (02) 24811549; (02) 24225143 *Fax:* (02) 24226026, pg 1227

Friends of the Earth (Charity) Ltd (Hong Kong) *Tel:* (02) 5285588 *Fax:* (02) 5292777 *E-mail:* foehk@hk.super.net, pg 320

Friesens Corp (Canada) *Tel:* 204-324-6401 *Fax:* 204-324-1333 *E-mail:* friesens@friesens.com, pg 1131

J Frimodts Forlag (Denmark) *Tel:* 75334455 *Fax:* 75924275 *E-mail:* lohse@imh.dk, pg 132

Paul und Peter Fritz AG Literary Agency (Switzerland) *Tel:* (01) 3884140 *Fax:* (01) 3884130 *E-mail:* info@fritzagency.com *Web Site:* www.fritzagency.com, pg 1117

Fritzes Booksellers (Sweden) *Tel:* (08) 6909090 *Fax:* (08) 8205021, pg 1312

C E Fritzes AB (Sweden) *Tel:* (08) 6909090 *Fax:* (08) 205021, pg 602

Frjals fjolmiolun hf-Urvalsbaekur (Iceland) *Tel:* 5632700; 5227022 *Fax:* 9127079, pg 327

Frobenius AG (Switzerland) *Tel:* (061) 7715677 *Fax:* (061) 7116218, pg 614

Frodi Ltd (Iceland) *Tel:* 5155500 *Fax:* 515-5599 *E-mail:* frodi@frodi.is *Web Site:* www.frodi.is, pg 328

Froebel-Kan Co Ltd (Japan) *Tel:* (03) 53956614; (03) 53956600 *Fax:* (03) 53956627 *Web Site:* www.froebel-kan.co.jp, pg 416

Verlag A Fromm im Druck- u Verlagshaus Fromm GmbH & Co KG (Germany) *Tel:* (0541) 3100 *Fax:* (0541) 310315; (0541) 310440, pg 230

Friedrich Frommann Verlag (Germany) *Tel:* (0711) 955969-0 *Fax:* (0711) 955969-1 *E-mail:* info@frommann-holzboog.de *Web Site:* www.frommann-holzboog.de, pg 230

Georg Fromme und Co (Austria) *Tel:* (01) 5445641 *Fax:* (01) 544564166, pg 52

Frontier Publishing (United Kingdom) *Tel:* (01508) 558174 *Fax:* frontier.pub@macunlimited.net *Web Site:* www.frontierpublishing.co.uk, pg 684

The FruitMarket Gallery (United Kingdom) *Tel:* (0131) 225 2383 *Fax:* (0131) 220 3130 *E-mail:* fruitmarket@fruitmarket.co.uk *Web Site:* www.fruitmarket.co.uk, pg 685

Forlaget FSR A/S (ITID A/S) (Denmark) *Tel:* 33740700 *Fax:* 33933077 *E-mail:* thomson@thi.dk, pg 132

FT Caribbean (BVI) Ltd (Antigua & Barbuda) *Tel:* 462-3392; 462-3692 *Fax:* 462-3492 *E-mail:* ftcarib@candw.ag, pg 2

Editora FTD SA (Brazil) *Tel:* (011) 3284-8500 *Fax:* (011) 3283-5011 *E-mail:* ftd@dial&ta.com.br *Web Site:* www.ftd.com.br, pg 83

Fu Ssu-Nien Library, Institute of History & Philology, Academia Sinica (Taiwan, Province of China) *Tel:* (02) 27829555 (ext 136) *Fax:* (02) 27868834, pg 1502

Edition Dr Heinrich Fuchs (Austria) *Tel:* (01) 4792381 *Fax:* (01) 4792381 *E-mail:* edition.h.fuchs@aon.at, pg 52

Fudan University Library (China) *Tel:* (021) 65492222 (ext 3162) *Fax:* (021) 65649814 *E-mail:* zfqin@fudan.edu.cn.f, pg 1457

Fudan University Press (China) *Tel:* (021) 5484906-2842 *Fax:* (021) 65104812; (021) 65642840 *E-mail:* fupirc@fudan.edu.cn, pg 105

Fuh-Wen Book Co (Taiwan, Province of China) *Tel:* (06) 2386935 *Fax:* (06) 2347222, pg 630

Fuji Keizai Company Ltd (Japan) *Tel:* (03) 36445811 *Fax:* (03) 36610165, pg 416

Fujian Children's Publishing House (China) *Fax:* (0591) 7606554 *E-mail:* fcph@163.net, pg 106

Fujian Science & Technology Publishing House (China) *Tel:* (0591) 7538472 *Fax:* (0591) 7538472 *Web Site:* www.fjbook.com, pg 106

Fukuinkan Ehon Library (Japan) *Tel:* (03) 39421226 *Fax:* (03) 39429691, pg 1230

Fukuinkan Shoten Publishers Inc (Japan) *Tel:* (03) 39420032 *Fax:* (03) 39421401 *Web Site:* www.fukuinkan.co.jp, pg 416

Fukumura Shuppan Inc (Japan) *Tel:* (03) 38133981 *Fax:* (03) 38182786, pg 416

Fuldaer Verlagsanstalt GmbH (Germany) *Tel:* (0661) 295-0 *Fax:* (0661) 295-71 *E-mail:* info@fva.de *Web Site:* www.fva.de, pg 231

Full Circle Publications Co-Operative (Australia) *Tel:* (03) 98304253, pg 23

David Fulton Publishers Ltd (United Kingdom) *Tel:* (020) 7405 5606 *Fax:* (020) 7831 4840 *E-mail:* mail@fultonpublishers.co.uk *Web Site:* www.fultonbooks.co.uk, pg 685

Michael Fulton Partners (United Kingdom) *Tel:* (01491) 680042 *Fax:* (01491) 680085, pg 1129

Fumaido Publishing Company Ltd (Japan) *Tel:* (03) 39462345 *Fax:* (03) 39470110 *E-mail:* fumaido@tkd.att.ne.jp, pg 416

Fundacao Biblioteca Nacional (Brazil) *Tel:* (021) 22408079 *Fax:* (021) 2204173 *E-mail:* portella@bn.br *Web Site:* www.bn.br, pg 1455

Fundacao Cultural Avatar (Brazil) *Tel:* (021) 621-0217 *Fax:* (021) 2719-1574 *E-mail:* fcavatar@nitnet.com.br *Web Site:* www.nitnet.com.br/~fcavatar, pg 83

Fundacao de Assistencia ao Estudante (Brazil) *Tel:* (061) 212-4150; (061) 225-6603 *Fax:* (061) 226-7712, pg 83

Fundacao Instituto Brasileiro de Geografia e Estatistica (IBGE - CDDI/DECOP) (Brazil) *Tel:* (021) 2514-4732 *Fax:* (021) 2234-8400 *Web Site:* www.ibge.gov.br, pg 84

Fundacao Joaquim Nabuco Editora (Brazil) *Tel:* (081) 4415900 R298 *Fax:* (081) 4414201 *E-mail:* joanildo@fundaj.gov.br *Web Site:* www.fundaj.gov.br, pg 84

Fundacao para a Ciencia e a Tecnologia/Servico de Informacao e Documentacao(SID) (Portugal) *Tel:* (01) 3924440 *Fax:* (01) 3957284, pg 1493

Fundacio La Caixa (Spain) *Tel:* (093) 404 6079 *Fax:* (093) 3395703 *E-mail:* info@lacaixa.es *Web Site:* portal1.lacaixa.es, pg 574

Fundacion Biblioteca Alemana Gorres (Spain) *Tel:* (091) 3668508; (091)3668509, pg 574

Fundacion Centro de Investigacion y Educacion Popular (CINEP) (Colombia) *Tel:* (01) 2858977 *Fax:* (01) 2879089 *E-mail:* info@cinep.org.co *Web Site:* www.cinep.org.co, pg 112

Fundacion Centro Gumilla (Venezuela) *Tel:* (02) 5649803; (02) 5644757 *Fax:* (02) 5647557, pg 762

Fundacion Coleccion Thyssen-Bornemisza (Spain) *Tel:* (091) 420 39 44 *Fax:* (091) 4202780 *E-mail:* umseo.thyssen-bornemisza@offcampus.es, pg 575

Fundacion de Cultura Universitaria (Uruguay) *Tel:* (02) 9161152; (02) 959038 *Fax:* (02) 952549 *E-mail:* fcuedit@adinet.com.uy, pg 760

Fundacion de Estudios Libertarios Anselmo Lorenzo (Spain) *Tel:* (091) 7970424 *Fax:* (091) 5052183 *E-mail:* fal@cnt.es *Web Site:* www.cnt.es/fal, pg 575

Fundacion de los Ferrocarriles Espanoles (Spain) *Tel:* (091) 511 071 *Fax:* (091) 5284822; (091) 5391415 *E-mail:* fudou01@ffe.es *Web Site:* www.ffe.es, pg 575

Fundacion El Libro (Argentina) *Tel:* (011) 43743288 *Fax:* (011) 43750268 *E-mail:* fund@libro.satlink.net *Web Site:* www.el-libro.com.ar, pg 1235

Fundacion Esade (Spain) *Tel:* (093) 2806162 *Fax:* (093) 2048105 *Web Site:* www.esade.es/biblio, pg 1499

Fundacion Gratis Date (Spain) *Tel:* (0948) 1233612 *Fax:* (0948) 123612 *E-mail:* fundacion@gratisdate.org *Web Site:* www.gratisdate.org, pg 575

Fundacion Juan March (Spain) *Tel:* (091) 435 42 40 *Fax:* (091) 576 34 20 *E-mail:* webmast@mail.march.es *Web Site:* www.march.es, pg 575

Fundacion Kuai-Mare (Venezuela) *Tel:* (02) 938535 ext 213; (02) 9418011 (ext 227) *Fax:* (02) 9415219, pg 1324

Fundacion Marcelino Botin (Spain) *Tel:* (0942) 226072 *Fax:* (0942) 226045 *E-mail:* fmabotin@fundacionmbotin.org *Web Site:* www.fundacionmbotin.org, pg 575

Fundacion para la Cultura y el Desarrollo (Guatemala) *Tel:* (02) 500216 *Fax:* (02) 325508, pg 316

Fundacion Rosacruz (Spain) *Tel:* (076) 589100 *Fax:* (076) 589161 *E-mail:* correo@fundacionrosacruz.org *Web Site:* www.fundacionrosacruz.org, pg 575

Fundacion Servicio para el Agricultor (Venezuela) *Tel:* (02) 2843089; (02) 2841134; (02) 2852016 *Fax:* (02) 2853946 *E-mail:* izamora@etheron.net, pg 762

Fundacion Universidad Externado de Colombia (Colombia) *Tel:* (01) 2826066 *Fax:* (01) 2847769 *E-mail:* uextpub3@impsat.net.co, pg 1458

Fundacion Universidad de la Sabana Ediciones Udes (Colombia) *Tel:* (01) 6760867 *E-mail:* susabana@coll.telcom.com.co, pg 112

Editorial Fundamentos (Spain) *Tel:* (091) 319 96 19 *Fax:* (091) 319 55 84 *E-mail:* fundamentos@editorialfundamentos.es *Web Site:* www.editorialfundamentos.es, pg 575

Funfax Ltd (United Kingdom) *Tel:* (020) 7836 5411 *Fax:* (020) 7836 7570 *E-mail:* clairrey@dk-uk.com, pg 685

Furnival Press (United Kingdom) *Tel:* (020) 7274 2067 *Fax:* (020) 7274 6984 *E-mail:* furnprint@aol.com, pg 1203, 1214

Vernon Futerman Associates (United Kingdom) *Tel:* (020) 7625 9601 *Fax:* (020) 7625 9601, pg 1119

Editorial Futura (Portugal) *Tel:* (021) 155848 *Fax:* (021) 155848, pg 525

Futuribles SARL (France) *Tel:* (01) 53633770 *Fax:* (01) 42226554 *E-mail:* revue@futuribles.com *Web Site:* www.futuribles.com, pg 165

Edizioni Futuro SRL (Italy) *Tel:* (045) 915622 *Fax:* (045) 8300261, pg 389

Fuzambo Publishing Co (Japan) *Tel:* (03) 32912171 *Fax:* (03) 32912179, pg 416

FVerlag Anke Schaefer (Germany) *Tel:* (0611) 371515 *Fax:* (0611) 371913, pg 231

G+B Arts International (Switzerland) *Tel:* (061) 2610138 *Fax:* (061) 2610173, pg 614

G Braun (vormals G Braun'sche Hofbuchdruckerei und Verlag) (Germany) *Tel:* (0721) 165-195 *Fax:* (0721) 165-855 *E-mail:* volpp@gbraun-fachverlage.de, pg 1195

G Braun (vormals G Braun'sche Hofbuchdruckerei und Verlag) Gmbh (Germany) *Tel:* (0721) 165-195 *Fax:* (0721) 165-855 *E-mail:* buchverlag@gbraun.de *Web Site:* www.gbraun.de, pg 231

Gaanetgetal Books (Australia) *Tel:* (02) 9550-0431 *Fax:* (02) 4234-0875 *E-mail:* galong@ozemail.com.au, pg 1273

Gaba Publications Amecea, Pastoral Institute (Kenya) *Tel:* (0321) 61218; (0321) 62153 *Fax:* (0321) 62570 *E-mail:* gabapubs@africaonline.co.ke, pg 431

Gabal-Verlag GmbH (Germany) *Tel:* (069) 84 000 3-0 *Fax:* (069) 84 000 3-33 *E-mail:* info@juenger.de *Web Site:* www.juenger.de/gabal.htm, pg 231

J Gabalda et Cie (Librairie Lecoffre) SA (France) *Tel:* (01) 43 26 53 55 *Fax:* (01) 43 25 04 71 *E-mail:* editions@gabalda.com *Web Site:* www.gabalda.com, pg 165

Editions Jacques Gabay (France) *Tel:* (01) 43 54 64 64 *Fax:* (01) 43 54 87 00 *E-mail:* infos@gabay.com *Web Site:* www.gabay.com, pg 165

Verlagsbuchhandlung Megapress, Franz-J Gaber (Germany) *Tel:* (0610) 225951; (0610) 2327044 *Fax:* (0610) 231018, pg 231

Gaberbocchus Press (Netherlands) *Tel:* (020) 6245181 *Fax:* (020) 6230672, pg 477

Betriebswirtschaftlicher Verlag Dr Th Gabler GmbH (Germany) *Tel:* (0611) 7878615 *Fax:* (0611) 7878470 *Web Site:* www.gabler.de, pg 231

Verlag Gachnang & Springer, Bern-Berlin (Switzerland) *Tel:* (031) 211780 *Fax:* (031) 3518385, pg 614

Gad (Denmark) *Tel:* (033) 150558 *Fax:* (033) 154232, pg 1281

Editions Victor Gadoury (Monaco) *Tel:* (093) 251296 *Fax:* (093) 501339 *E-mail:* contact@gadoury.com *Web Site:* www.gadoury.com, pg 469

Ediciones de Arte Gaglianone (Argentina) *Tel:* (011) 4923-2579; (011) 4923-2658 *Fax:* (011) 4923-0150 *E-mail:* webmaster@gaglianone.com.ar *Web Site:* www.gaglianone.com.ar, pg 6

Gaia Books Ltd (United Kingdom) *Tel:* (020) 7323 4010 *Fax:* (020) 7323 0435 *E-mail:* info@gaiabooks.com *Web Site:* www.gaiabooks.co.uk, pg 685

Editora Gaia Ltda (Brazil) *Tel:* (011) 32777999 *Fax:* (011) 32778141 *E-mail:* gaia@dialdata.com.dr, pg 84

Gaia Media AG/Literary & Media Agency (Switzerland) *Tel:* (061) 2619119 *Fax:* (061) 2619117 *E-mail:* gaiamediaag@access.ch, pg 1117

Imprimerie Gaignault (France), pg 1194

Gairm Publications (United Kingdom) *Tel:* (0141) 221 1971 *Fax:* (0141) 221 1971, pg 685

Gakken Co Ltd (Japan) *Tel:* (03) 34933331 *Fax:* (03) 34933338, pg 416

Gakujutsu Bunken Fukyu-Kai (Japan), pg 1518

GakuseiSha Publishing Co Ltd (Japan) *Tel:* (03) 38573031 *Fax:* (03) 38573037 *E-mail:* info@gakusei.co.jp *Web Site:* www.gakusei.co.jp, pg 416

Galago Publishing Pty Ltd (South Africa) *Tel:* (011) 9072029 *Fax:* (011) 8690890 *E-mail:* lemur@mweb.co.za *Web Site:* www.galago.co.za, pg 554

Galaktika Publishing House (Bulgaria) *Tel:* (052) 225077; (052) 241132; (052) 241156 *Fax:* (052) 234750, pg 95

Izdatelstvo Galart (Russian Federation) *Tel:* (095) 1512502; (095) 1514513 *Fax:* (095) 1513761, pg 538

Galaxia SA Editorial (Spain) *Tel:* (0986) 432100 *Fax:* (0986) 223205 *E-mail:* galaxia@editorialgalaxia.es *Web Site:* www.editorialgalaxia.es, pg 575

Galaxie, vydavatelelstvi a nakladatelstvi (Czech Republic) *Tel:* (02) 2317801; (02) 2317875 *Fax:* (02) 2311351, pg 124

Gale Research (United Kingdom) *Tel:* (01264) 342962 *Fax:* (01264) 342763 *E-mail:* sales@psmedia.co.uk *Web Site:* www.gale.com, pg 685

El Galeon (Uruguay) *Tel:* (02) 9156139; (02) 9157909 *Fax:* (02) 9157909 *E-mail:* elgaleon@netgate.com.uy *Web Site:* www.elgaleonlibros.com, pg 1324

La Galera, SA Editorial (Spain) *Tel:* (093) 4120030 *Fax:* (093) 3173277 *E-mail:* lagalera@grec.com *Web Site:* www.enciclopedia-catalana.com, pg 575

Galerie Der Spiegel-Dr E Stunke Nachfolge GmbH (Germany) *Tel:* (0221) 25 55 52 *Fax:* (0221) 25 55 53 *E-mail:* thatspiegel@galerie.de *Web Site:* www.galerie.de/der-spiegel, pg 231

Galerie Editions Kutter (Luxembourg) *Tel:* 23571 *Fax:* 471884, pg 447

Editorial Galerna SRL (Argentina) *Tel:* (011) 4867 1661 *Fax:* (011) 4862-5031 *E-mail:* galerna@overnet.com.ar, pg 6

E D Galgotia & Sons (India) *Tel:* (011) 589334, pg 1288

Galgotia Publications Pvt Ltd (India) *Tel:* (011) 3263334; (011) 3288134 *Fax:* (011) 3281909; (011) 321909 *E-mail:* gppl.galgtia@axcess.net.in, pg 337

Galician Pen Club (Spain) *Tel:* (081) 587750 *E-mail:* rabade@ctv.esp, pg 1368

Edition Galilee (France) *Tel:* (01) 43 31 23 84 *Fax:* (01) 45 35 53 68 *E-mail:* editions.galilee@free.fr, pg 165

Galleon Publications (Philippines) *Tel:* (632) 523-1825 *Fax:* (632) 525-6129, pg 513

Gallery Books, Ireland (Ireland) *Tel:* (049) 8541779 *Fax:* (049) 8541779 *E-mail:* gallery@indigo.ie, pg 360

Galley Press Publishing (Australia) *Tel:* (02) 9360 5312 *Fax:* (02) 9360 1968 *E-mail:* galleypr@ozemail.com.au, pg 23

Editions Gallimard (France) *Tel:* (01) 49 54 42 00 *Fax:* (01) 45 44 94 03 *Web Site:* www.gallimard.fr, pg 165

Adriano Gallina Editore sas (Italy) *Tel:* (081) 5496730 *Fax:* (081) 5448747, pg 389

Galrev Druck-und Verlagsgesellschaft Hesse & Partner OHG (Germany) *Tel:* (030) 44 65 01 83 *Fax:* (030) 44 65 01 84 *E-mail:* galrev@galrev.com *Web Site:* www.galrev.com, pg 231

Galzerano Editore (Italy) *Tel:* (0974) 62028 *Fax:* (0974) 62028, pg 390

GAMA (United States) *Tel:* 603-898-2822 *Fax:* 603-898-3393, pg 1206

Gamberetti Editrice SRL (Italy) *Tel:* (06) 3728394 *Fax:* (06) 3728394; (06) 535469 *E-mail:* schiarim@ilmanifesto.it, pg 390

The Gambia Methodist Bookshop Ltd (Gambia) *Tel:* 28179, pg 1283

Gambia College Library (Gambia) *Tel:* 84812, pg 1466

The Gambia National Library (Gambia) *Tel:* 28312 *Fax:* 223776, pg 1466

Ediciones Gamma (Colombia) *Tel:* (01) 2122873; (01) 2128966; (01) 3460800 *Fax:* (01) 2128931 *E-mail:* r-diners@colomsat.net.co, pg 112

Editions Gamma (France) *Tel:* (03) 44806868 *Fax:* (03) 44806860, pg 165

Gamma Medya Agency (Turkey) *Tel:* (212) 663 96 80 *Fax:* (212) 663 96 81 *E-mail:* web@gammamedya.net *Web Site:* www.gammamedya.net, pg 1117

Editions Gammaprim (France) *Tel:* (01) 49959492 *Fax:* (01) 40230134 *E-mail:* fgosselin@gammaprim.fr, pg 166

Gamsberg Macmillan Publishers (Pty) Ltd (Namibia) *Tel:* (061) 232165 *Fax:* (061) 233538 *E-mail:* gmp@iafrica.com.na, pg 471

Gandon Editions (Ireland) *Tel:* (021) 770830 *Fax:* (021) 770755, pg 360

Ganesh & Co (India) *Tel:* (044) 4344519 *Fax:* (044) 4342009 *E-mail:* ksm@md2.vsnl.net.in; service@kkbooks.com, pg 337

Gangan Publishing (Australia) *Tel:* (02) 9280 2120 *Fax:* (02) 9280 2130 *E-mail:* books@gangan.com *Web Site:* www.gangan.com, pg 23

Gangan Verlag (Austria) *Web Site:* www.gangan.com, pg 52

Gangemi Editore (Italy) *Tel:* (06) 6872774; (06) 6872775 *Fax:* (06) 68806189 *E-mail:* gangemi@jnet.it, pg 390

A R Gantner Verlag KG (Liechtenstein) *Tel:* (0423) 3771808 *Fax:* (0423) 3771802, pg 444

Ganymede (France) *Tel:* (01) 48945232 *Fax:* (02) 64 42 86 68 *Web Site:* www.hatem.com, pg 166

Garbe Verlag Ellen Vogt (Germany) *Tel:* (0911) 5430983 *Fax:* (0911) 5430983, pg 231

Garcia Hermanos Imprentay Litografia (Costa Rica) *Tel:* 2202003 *Fax:* 2310675 *E-mail:* garcia@sol.racsa.co.cr *Web Site:* www.novanet.co.cr/garcia/main.html, pg 116

Vicent Garcia Editores, SA (Spain) *Tel:* (096) 369 32 46 *Fax:* (096) 393 00 57 *E-mail:* vgesa@combios.es *Web Site:* www.vgesa.com, pg 575

Editions du Garde-Temps (France) *Tel:* (01) 44788477 *Fax:* (01) 44788479 *E-mail:* studio-magnet@calva.net, pg 166

Garden Art Press Ltd (United Kingdom) *Tel:* (01394) 385501 *Fax:* (01394) 384434, pg 685

Gardenhouse Editions (United Kingdom) *Tel:* (020) 76221720 *Fax:* (020) 7720 9114, pg 1140

Imprimerie Librairie Gardet (France) *Tel:* (04) 50 47 58 10 *Fax:* (04) 50 47 58 11 *E-mail:* edimontagne@wanadoo.fr, pg 166

Walter H Gardner & Co (United Kingdom) *Tel:* (20) 8458 3202 *Fax:* (20) 8458 8499, pg 685, 1319

Gardners Books (United Kingdom) *Tel:* (01323) 521555 *Fax:* (01323) 521666 *E-mail:* export@gardners.com *Web Site:* www.gardners.com, pg 1319

Gardum A/S (Norway) *Tel:* 04520200; 04520400 *Fax:* 04520680, pg 1304

Editrice Garigliano SRL (Italy) *Tel:* (0776) 21869 *Fax:* (0776) 21869, pg 390

Garnet Publishing Ltd (United Kingdom) *Tel:* (0118) 959 7847 *Fax:* (0118) 959 7356 *E-mail:* enquiries@garnet-ithaca.demon.co.uk (general enquiries); orders@garnet-ithaca.demon.co.uk (ordering) *Web Site:* www.garnet-ithaca.co.uk, pg 685

Garolla (Italy) *Tel:* (02) 48005574 *Fax:* (02) 48003915, pg 390

Garotech (Philippines) *Tel:* (02) 993286, pg 513

Garr Publishing (Australia) *Tel:* (02) 43677223 *Fax:* (02) 43670762 *E-mail:* garrpub@ozemail.com.au *Web Site:* www.ozemail.com.au/~garrpub/, pg 23

Garradunga Press (Australia) *Tel:* (0409) 320 619 (mobile) *Fax:* (07) 4032 5918 *E-mail:* bolton@iig.com.au, pg 23

John Garratt Publishing (Australia) *Tel:* (03) 9545 3111 *Fax:* (03) 9545 3222 *E-mail:* sales@johngarratt.com.au *Web Site:* www.johngarratt.com.au, pg 24

Ediciones Garriga SA (Spain) *Tel:* (093) 4392204 *Fax:* (093) 4107314, pg 575

Gartaganis D (Greece) *Tel:* (031) 209680 *Fax:* (031) 209680, pg 310

Garuda-Verlag (Switzerland) *Tel:* (01) 7411287 *Fax:* (056) 6401012 *E-mail:* garuda@bluewin.ch, pg 614

Garzanti Editore (Italy) *Tel:* (02) 487941 *Fax:* (02) 48794292, pg 390

Verlag HP Gassner AG (Liechtenstein) *Tel:* (075) 2327253 *Fax:* (075) 2323720, pg 444

Gateway Books (United Kingdom) *Tel:* (01225) 835 127 *Fax:* (01225) 840 012 *E-mail:* sales@gatewaybooks.com, pg 686

Gatidhara (Bangladesh) *Tel:* (02) 7392077 (press); (02) 7113117 (res); (02) 7115630 (res); (02) 7117515 (showroom); (02) 7118273 (showroom) *Fax:* (02) 9134617; (02) 9566456 *E-mail:* akter@aitlbd.net; gatidara@bdonline.com, pg 62

Gatzanis Verlags GmbH (Germany) *Tel:* (0711) 9640570 *Fax:* (0711) 9640572 *E-mail:* info@gatzanis.de *Web Site:* www.gatzanis.de, pg 231

Gaulitana (Malta) *Tel:* 554212 *Fax:* 554598 *E-mail:* joseph.bezzina@magnet.mt, pg 456

Ediciones Gaviota SA (Spain) *Tel:* (091) 358 01 08 *Fax:* (091) 729 38 58 *E-mail:* publicaciones@ediciones-gaviota.es *Web Site:* www.everest.es, pg 575

Gaya Favorit Press (Indonesia) *Tel:* (021) 4604444; (021) 5209370; (021) 5253816; (021) 5209366 *Fax:* (021) 5209366; (021) 5262131 *E-mail:* ptgfp1@rad.net.id, pg 355

Gazelle Book Services Ltd (United Kingdom) *Tel:* (01524) 68765 *Fax:* (01524) 63232 *E-mail:* gazellebooks@talk21.com *Web Site:* www.gazellebook.co.uk, pg 1319

Edizioni GB (Italy) *Tel:* (049) 772252 *Fax:* (049) 772252, pg 390

Gbabeks Publishers Ltd (Nigeria) *Tel:* (062) 217976, pg 499

GCL Publishing (1997) Ltd (New Zealand) *Tel:* (09) 3092444 *Fax:* (09) 3092449 *E-mail:* info@gcl.co.nz *Web Site:* www.gcl.co.nz; www.auto.co.nz, pg 491

Politechnika Gdanska (Poland) *Tel:* (058) 3415791 *Fax:* (058) 3415821 *E-mail:* mainlibr@sunrise.pg.gda.pl; jligman@sunrise.pg.gda.pl *Web Site:* www.pg.gda.pl, pg 1492

Biblioteka Gdanska PAN (Poland) *Tel:* (058) 312251-54 *Fax:* (058) 312970 *E-mail:* bgpan@task.gda.pl, pg 1492

Gdanskie Wydawnictwo Psychologiczne SC (Poland) *Tel:* (058) 551-61-04; (058) 550-16-04; (058) 551-11-01 *Fax:* (058) 551-61-04; (058) 550-16-04 *Web Site:* www.gwp.pl, pg 516

Gea-Libris Publishing House (Bulgaria) *Tel:* (02) 986-31-71; (02) 986-46-04 *Fax:* (02) 986-69-00 *E-mail:* emilgea@techno-link.com *Web Site:* www.gea-libris.search.bg, pg 95

Gebrueder Borntraeger Science Publishers (Germany) *Tel:* (0711) 3514560 *Fax:* (0711) 35145699 *E-mail:* mail@schweizerbart.de *Web Site:* www.schweizerbart.de, pg 231

GEC Gads Forlag Aktieselskab af 1994 (Denmark) *Tel:* 33150558 *Fax:* 33110800 *E-mail:* marketing@gads-forlag.dk *Web Site:* www.gads-forlag.dk, pg 132

GECTI (Gabinete de Especializacao e Cooperacao Tecnica Internacional L) (Portugal) *Tel:* (021) 768833 *Fax:* (021) 7963465, pg 525

Geddes & Grosset (United Kingdom) *Tel:* (01555) 665000 *Fax:* (01555) 665694 *E-mail:* info@gandg.sol.co.uk, pg 686

Gedins Forlag (Sweden) *Tel:* (08) 6621551 *Fax:* (08) 6637073 *E-mail:* gedins@perigab.se, pg 602

Editorial Gedisa SA (Spain) *Tel:* (093) 253 09 04 *Fax:* (093) 253 09 05 *E-mail:* gedisa@gedisa.com *Web Site:* www.gedisa.com, pg 575

Gee & Son (Denbigh) Ltd-Gwasg Gee-Gee's Press (United Kingdom) *Tel:* (01745) 812020 *Fax:* (01745) 812825, pg 1140

Uitgeverij Vrij Geestesleven (Netherlands) *Tel:* (030) 6924953 *Fax:* (030) 6932304, pg 477

Geeta Prakasham (India) *Tel:* (0821) 33589, pg 337

Geetha Publishers Sdn Bhd (Malaysia) *Tel:* (03) 4417073, pg 452

Gefen Publishing House Ltd (Israel) *Tel:* (02) 5380247 *Fax:* (02) 5388423 *E-mail:* info@gefenpublishing.com *Web Site:* www.gefenpublishing.com; www.israelbooks.com, pg 367

Konkursbuch Verlag Claudia Gehrke (Germany) *Tel:* (07071) 66551; (07071) 78779 *Fax:* (07071) 63539; (07071) 763780 *E-mail:* gehrke@konkursbuch.com *Web Site:* www.konkursbuch.com, pg 231

SK-Gehrmans Musikforlag AB (Sweden) *Tel:* (08) 6100600 *Fax:* (08) 6100628 *E-mail:* order@sk-gehrmans.se *Web Site:* www.sk-gehrmans.se, pg 602

Geiser Productions (United Kingdom) *Tel:* (020) 8579 4653 *Fax:* (020) 8567 6593 *E-mail:* geiser@globalnet.co.uk *Web Site:* www.geiserproductions.com; www.sidsjournal.com, pg 686

Uitgevery Gelbis NV (Belgium) *Tel:* (03) 2410202 *Fax:* (03) 2410200 *E-mail:* gelbis.boeken@lequana.com, pg 68

Gembooks (United Kingdom) *Tel:* (01202) 399729 *Fax:* (01202) 399729 *E-mail:* readbooks@onmail.co.uk, pg 686

Verlag Junge Gemeinde E Schwinghammer GmbH & Co KG (Germany) *Tel:* (0711) 7978994 *Fax:* (0711) 7970660, pg 231

General Book Depot (India) *Tel:* (011) 3263695; (0110 3250635 *Fax:* (011) 2940861; (011) 3712710, pg 337

General Book Depot (India) *Tel:* (011) 3263695 *Fax:* (011) 2940861, pg 1288

General Department of Archives of the Republic of Bulgaria (Bulgaria) *Tel:* (02) 9400101 *Fax:* (02) 980 14 43 *E-mail:* gua@mail.orbitel.bg, pg 1455

General Egyptian Book Organization (Egypt (Arab Republic of Egypt)) *Tel:* (02) 775371; (02) 775649; (02) 5775109 *Fax:* (02) 754213, pg 138, 1242

General Printers & Publishers (India) *Tel:* (022) 3873113; (022) 3826854 *Fax:* (022) 3827197, pg 337

General Publications Ltd (United Republic of Tanzania) *Tel:* (051) 68240; (051) 68249, pg 633

General Scientific Library of Ho Chi Minh City (Viet Nam) *Tel:* (08) 225055 *Fax:* (08) 299318, pg 1508

Bibliotheque Generale et Archives (Morocco) *Tel:* (096) 3258, pg 1485

Librairie Generale Francaise SA (France) *Tel:* (01) 43 92 30 00 *Fax:* (01) 43 92 35 90, pg 166

Librairie Generale JASOR (Guadeloupe) *Tel:* (590) 821770 *Fax:* (590) 917599, pg 316

Editions Generales First (France) *Tel:* (01) 40 21 46 46 *Fax:* (01) 40 21 46 20 *E-mail:* firstinfo@efirst.com *Web Site:* www.efirst.com, pg 166

Generalitat de Catalunya Diari Oficial de la Generalitat vern (Spain) *Tel:* (093) 302 64 62 *Fax:* (093) 318 62 21 *E-mail:* llibrbcn@correu.cattel.com *Web Site:* www.gencat.es/diari/, pg 575

Genesis Forlag (Norway) *Tel:* 22310310 *Fax:* 22310305, pg 503

Genesis Publications Ltd (United Kingdom) *Tel:* (01483) 540970 *Fax:* (01483) 304709 *E-mail:* postmaster@genesiseditions.demon.co.uk *Web Site:* www.genesis-publications.com, pg 686

Genius Verlag (Germany) *Tel:* (08386) 960401 *Fax:* (08386) 960402 *E-mail:* contact@genius-verlag.de *Web Site:* www.genius-verlag.de, pg 231

Genko-Sha (Japan) *Tel:* (03) 32633515 *Fax:* (03) 32633045 *E-mail:* gks@genkosha.co.jp *Web Site:* www.genkosha.co.jp, pg 416

Gennadius Library (Greece) *Tel:* (01) 7210536 *Fax:* (01) 7237767 *E-mail:* djord@leon.nrcps.ariadne-t.gr, pg 1470

Van Gennep Ltd (Netherlands) *Tel:* (20) 6247033 *Fax:* (20) 6247035 *E-mail:* vangennep@wxs.nl, pg 477

Editora Gente Livraria e Editora Ltda (Brazil) *Tel:* (011) 3675 2505 *Fax:* (011) 36750430 *E-mail:* gentedit@mandic.com.br, pg 84

Editorial Gente Nueva (Cuba) *Tel:* (07) 624753 *Fax:* (07) 338187, pg 121

Alfons W Gentner Verlag GmbH & Co KG (Germany) *Tel:* (0711) 63672-0 *Fax:* (0711) 63672747 *E-mail:* gentner@gentnerverlag.de *Web Site:* www.gentnerverlag.de, pg 231

Gentofte Bibliotekerne (Denmark) *Tel:* 39627500 *Fax:* 39627507, pg 1461

Geocart Uitg Cartogr AG Claus BVBA (Belgium) *Tel:* (03) 760 14 60 *Fax:* (03) 760 15 28 *E-mail:* site@geocart.be *Web Site:* www.geocart.be, pg 68

Geocarto International Centre (Hong Kong) *Fax:* 25464262 *E-mail:* geocanto@hkstan.com, pg 320

GeoCenter Touristik Medienservice GmbH (Germany) *Tel:* (0711) 781946 10 *Fax:* (0711) 781946 54 *E-mail:* geocenterilh@t-online.de, pg 231

Geodeticky a kartograficky podnik v Praha, sp (Czech Republic) *Tel:* (02) 204 121 11; (02) 204 121 51; (02) 204 121 50 *Fax:* (02) 204 121 17; (02) 333 747 25 *E-mail:* digiteam@kartografie.cz, pg 124

Istituto Geografico de Agostini SpA (Italy) *Tel:* (0321) 4241 *Fax:* (0321) 471286, pg 390

Instituto Geografico Militar (Chile) *Tel:* (02) 4606800 *Fax:* (02) 4608294 *E-mail:* ventas@igm.cl; informaciones@igm.cl *Web Site:* www.igm.cl, pg 100

Geographers' A-Z Map Company Ltd (United Kingdom) *Tel:* (01732) 781000 *Fax:* (01732) 780677 *E-mail:* tradesales@a-zmaps.co.uk *Web Site:* www.azmaps.co.uk, pg 686

The Geographical Association (United Kingdom) *Tel:* (0114) 296 0088 *Fax:* (0114) 296 7176 *E-mail:* ga@geography.org.uk *Web Site:* www.geography.org.uk, pg 686

Bibliotheque de Geographie (France) *Tel:* (01) 44324461; (01) 44321463 *Fax:* (01) 44321467, pg 1465

Geological Survey Department Library (Botswana) *Tel:* (0330) 330327 *Fax:* (0330) 332013, pg 1454

Geological Survey Department Reference Library (Ghana) *Tel:* (021) 228093 *Fax:* (021) 228063, pg 1470

Geological Publishing House (China) *Tel:* (010) 4219994-268; (010) 4221120 *Fax:* (010) 6024523, pg 106

Geological Society Publishing House (United Kingdom) *Tel:* (01225) 445046 *Fax:* (01225) 442836 *E-mail:* rebecca.toop@geolsoc.org.uk *Web Site:* www.geolsoc.org.uk, pg 686

Geological Survey Department (Zimbabwe), pg 768

Geological Survey of Zimbabwe (Zimbabwe) *Tel:* (04) 726342 *Fax:* (04) 739601, pg 1509

Wydawnictwa Geologiczne (Poland) *Tel:* (022) 495351 ext 518, pg 516

Geoprojects Sarl (Lebanon) *Tel:* (01) 350721; (01) 344236 *Fax:* (01) 353000, pg 443

Georeto-Geogidsen (Belgium) *Tel:* (011) 37 52 54 *Fax:* (011) 37 52 54 *E-mail:* georeto@pandora.be *Web Site:* www.geogidsen.be, pg 68

Georg Editeur SA (Switzerland) *Tel:* (022) 8690029 *Fax:* (022) 8690015 *E-mail:* livres@medecinehygiene.ch *Web Site:* www.medecinehygiene.ch, pg 614

George Gregory Bookseller (United Kingdom) *Tel:* (01225) 466000 *Fax:* (01225) 482122, pg 1319

George Mann Publications (United Kingdom) *Tel:* (01622) 759591 *Fax:* (01622) 209193 *Web Site:* www.gmp.co.uk, pg 687

George Padmore Research Library on African Affairs (Ghana) *Tel:* (021) 228402, pg 1470

William George's Sons Ltd (United Kingdom) *Tel:* (0117) 9276602, pg 1319

Georgi GmbH (Germany) *Tel:* (08105) 3763-0 *Fax:* (08105) 3763-772 *Web Site:* www.korsch-verlag.de, pg 232

Georgian Encyclopedia Main Science Editorial Board (Georgia) *Tel:* (0995) 32-998891 *Fax:* (0995) 32-998823 *E-mail:* frg@gas.acnet.ge *Web Site:* www.acnet.ge/index.html, pg 190

Gerald Griffin Press (Australia) *Tel:* (03) 93475723; (03) 93475065 *Fax:* (03) 93494595, pg 24

Editions Gerard de Villiers (France) *Tel:* (01) 43 92 30 00 *Fax:* (01) 43 92 30 30 *Web Site:* www.editionsgerarddevilliers.com, pg 166

Gerhard Wolf Janus-Press GmbH (Germany) *Tel:* (030) 47535220 *Fax:* (030) 47533790, pg 232

German Book Centre (India) *Tel:* (044) 4346244 *Fax:* (044) 4346529 *E-mail:* germanbk@vsnl.com *Web Site:* germanbookcentre.com, pg 1288

Germanisches Nationalmuseum (Germany) *Tel:* (0911) 13310; (0911) 1331 165 (orders) *Fax:* (0911) 1331 200 *E-mail:* verlag@gnm.de; j.hofmann@gnm.de (orders) *Web Site:* www.gnm.de, pg 232

Germinal Press (Australia), pg 24

Gerold & Co (Austria) *Tel:* (01) 521 4731 *Fax:* (1) 512 473129 *E-mail:* buch@gerold.at, pg 52

Gerold & Co (Austria) *Tel:* (01) 521 4731, pg 1274

Gerstenberg Verlag (Germany) *Tel:* (05121) 1060 *Fax:* (05121) 106498; (05121) 106499 *E-mail:* verlag@gerstenberg-verlag.de *Web Site:* www.gerstenberg-verlag.de, pg 232

Gerth, Klaus, Verlag GmbH (Germany) *Tel:* (06443) 68-0 *Fax:* (06443) 6849 *E-mail:* info@gerth.de *Web Site:* www.gerth.de, pg 232

Verlag fuer Geschichte der Naturwissenschaften und der Technik (Germany) *Tel:* (05441) 92 71 29 *Fax:* (05441) 92 71 27 *E-mail:* service@gnt-verlag.de *Web Site:* www.gnt-verlag.de, pg 232

Verlag fuer Geschichte und Politik (Austria) *Tel:* (01) 712 62 58 0 *Fax:* (01) 712 62 58 19, pg 52

Gesellschaft fur Bibliothekswesen und Dokumentation des Landbaues (GBDL) (Germany) *Tel:* (08161) 714029 *Fax:* (08161) 715093, pg 1516

Gesellschaft fur deutsche Sprache und Literatur in Zurich (Switzerland) *Tel:* (01) 6342571 *Fax:* (01) 6344905 *E-mail:* uguenthe@ds.unizh.ch, pg 1368

Gesellschaft fur Interkulturelle Germanistik eV (GIG) (Germany) *Tel:* (0721) 6080 *Fax:* (0721) 6084290, pg 1363

Gesellschaft fur Organisationswissenschaft e V (Germany) *Tel:* (9206) 480 *Fax:* (9206) 628, pg 232

Verlag Lynkeus/H Hakel Gesellschaft (Austria) *Tel:* (01) 7342294, pg 52

Gesellschaft zur Foerderung der Literatur aus Afrika Asien und Lateinamerika eV (Germany) *Tel:* (069) 2102247 *Fax:* (069) 2102227 *E-mail:* litprom@bookfair.com *Web Site:* www.litprom.de, pg 1363

Ediciones Gestio 2000 SA (Spain) *Tel:* (093) 4106767 *Fax:* (093) 4109645 *E-mail:* info@gestion2000.com *Web Site:* www.gestion2000.com, pg 575

Gesundheits-Dialog Verlag GmbH (Germany) *Tel:* (089) 6 13 40 24 *Fax:* (089) 6 13 37 87 *E-mail:* dialog.top@t-online.de *Web Site:* www.gesundheit-naturheilkunde.de, pg 232

Uitgeverij De Geus BV (Netherlands) *Tel:* (076) 5228151 *Fax:* (076) 5222599, pg 477

Paul Geuthner Librairie Orientaliste (France) *Tel:* (01) 43297564 *Fax:* (01) 46347130 *E-mail:* geuthner@geuthner.com *Web Site:* www.geuthner.com, pg 166

Ghana Publishing Corporation, Distribution and Sales Division (Ghana) *Tel:* (022) 812921, pg 1285

Ghana Library Board (Ghana) *Tel:* (021) 662795, pg 1470

Ghana Academy of Arts & Sciences (Ghana) *Tel:* (021) 772002; (021) 772032 *Fax:* (021) 777655 *E-mail:* gaas@ghastinet.gn.apc.org, pg 307

Ghana Institute of Linguistics Literacy & Bible Translation (GILLBT) (Ghana) *Tel:* (021) 777525, pg 307

Ghana Institute of Management & Public Administration, Library & Documentation Centre (Ghana) *Tel:* 4016813 ext 224 1 *Fax:* 667681, pg 1470

Ghana Library Association (Ghana) *Tel:* (02) 668 731, pg 1517

Ghana Publishing Corporation (Ghana) *Tel:* (021) 664338 *Fax:* (021) 664330 *E-mail:* asspcom@africaonline.com.gh *Web Site:* www.africaonline.com/assembly/intro.html, pg 307

Ghana Universities Press (GUP) (Ghana) *Tel:* (021) 22532, pg 307

Bruno Ghigi Editore (Italy) *Tel:* (0541) 781269, pg 390

Ghisetti e Corvi Editori SpA (Italy) *Tel:* (02) 76006232 *Fax:* (02) 76009468, pg 390

Giampiero Casagrande Editore (Switzerland) *Tel:* (091) 9235677 *Fax:* (091) 9220171, pg 614

Giancarlo Politi Editore (Italy) *Tel:* (02) 6887341 *Fax:* (02) 66801290, pg 390

Editrice Giannotta di Sebastiano Pace Giannotta (Italy) *Tel:* (095) 447629, pg 390

Boekhandel Gianotten BV (Netherlands) *Tel:* (013) 4651111 *Fax:* (013) 4635390, pg 1301

Giao Duc Publishing House (Viet Nam) *Tel:* (04) 262011, pg 763

G Giappichelli Editore SRL (Italy) *Tel:* (011) 8153511 *Fax:* (011) 8125100, pg 390

E J W Gibb Memorial Trust (United Kingdom) *Tel:* (01985) 213409 *Fax:* (01985) 212910 *Web Site:* www.arisandphillips.com, pg 687

Stanley Gibbons Publications (United Kingdom) *Tel:* (01425) 472363 *Fax:* (01425) 470247 *E-mail:* sales@stangib.demon.co.uk *Web Site:* www.stanleygibbons.com, pg 687

Gibraltar Bookshop (Gibraltar) *Tel:* 71894 *Fax:* 75554, pg 1285

Gibraltar Garrison Library (Gibraltar) *Tel:* 77418 *Fax:* 79927, pg 1470

Gibson Golubov & Associates, Translation Services (Mexico) *Tel:* (05) 5686240 *E-mail:* mexlon@compuserve.com, pg 1127

Gibson Golubov & Associates, Translation Services (United Kingdom) *Tel:* (020) 7241 6101, pg 1129

Gidlunds Bokforlag (Sweden) *Tel:* (0225) 771155 *Fax:* (0255) 771165 *E-mail:* hedemora@gidlunds.se *Web Site:* www.gidlunds.sc, pg 602

Gidrometeoizdat (Russian Federation) *Tel:* (0812) 3520815 *Fax:* (0812) 3522688, pg 538

Gieck Reiner v Ursel Gieck (Germany) *Tel:* (089) 8415906 *Fax:* (089) 8403310, pg 232

Verlag Ernst und Werner Giesseking GmbH (Germany) *Tel:* (0521) 1 46 74 *Fax:* (0521) 14 37 15 *Web Site:* www.giesseking.de, pg 232

H Gietl Verlag & Publikationsservice GmbH (Germany) *Tel:* (09402) 93 37-0 *Fax:* (09402) 93 37-24 *E-mail:* gietl-verlag@t-online.de *Web Site:* www.gietl-verlag.de, pg 232

Michael Gifkins & Associates (New Zealand) *Tel:* (09) 5235032 *Fax:* (09) 5235033, pg 1115

Gifu Diagaku Fuzoku Toshokan (Japan) *Tel:* (0582) 801111, pg 1478

Gihan Book Shop (Sri Lanka), pg 597

Instituto de Cultura Juan Gil-Albert (Spain) *Tel:* (096) 5121 216; (096) 5121 300 *Fax:* (096) 5121 216 *E-mail:* galbert@dip-alicante.es *Web Site:* www.dip-alicante.es/galbert/, pg 576

Gildefachverlag GmbH & Co KG (Germany) *Tel:* (05181) 8004-0 *Fax:* (05181) 800490, pg 232

Editorial Gustavo Gili SA (Spain) *Tel:* (093) 3228161 *Fax:* (093) 3229205 *E-mail:* info@ggili.com *Web Site:* www.ggili.com, pg 576

Ediciones Gili SA de CV (Mexico) *Tel:* (05) 5606121; (05) 5606011 *Fax:* (05) 3601453, pg 461

Giliukas Ltd (Lithuania) *Tel:* (07) 715950 *Fax:* (07) 709560 *E-mail:* giliukas@isi.kvn.lt, pg 1297

Gill & Macmillan Distribution (Ireland) *Tel:* (01) 500 9500 *Fax:* (01) 500 9599, pg 1291

Gill & Macmillan Ltd (Ireland) *Tel:* (01) 500 9500 *Fax:* (01) 500 9599 *Web Site:* www.gillmacmillan.ie, pg 361

Gilles und Francke Verlag (Germany) *Tel:* (0203) 362787 *Fax:* (0203) 355520 *E-mail:* gilles-francke@t-online.de *Web Site:* www.gilles-francke.de, pg 232

Gim-Yeong Co (Republic of Korea) *Tel:* (02) 7454823; (02) 7454825 *Fax:* (02) 7454826, pg 436

Gina Schlenz Literatur-Agentur Koln (Germany) *Tel:* (02206) 81125 *Fax:* (02206) 81125 *E-mail:* litschleuz@aol.com, pg 1111

Ginn & Co Ltd (United Kingdom) *Tel:* (01865) 888000 *Fax:* (01865) 314222 *E-mail:* services@ginn.co.uk *Web Site:* www.ginn.co.uk, pg 687

A Van Ginneken (France) *Tel:* (03) 80740506 *Fax:* (03) 80740700 *E-mail:* hexalivre@axnet.fr, pg 1283

Ginninderra Press (Australia) *Tel:* (02) 6258-9060 *Fax:* (02) 6258-9069 *Web Site:* www.ginninderrapress.com.au, pg 24

Ginsberg Univ Boekhandel (Netherlands) *Tel:* (071) 124642; (071) 141773 *Fax:* (071) 127505 *E-mail:* ginsberg@euronet.nl, pg 1301

Giourdas Moschos (Greece) *Tel:* (01) 3624947 *E-mail:* mgiurdas@acci.gr *Web Site:* www.mgiurdas.gr, pg 310

Giovanis Publications, Pangosmios Ekdotikos Organismos (Greece) *Tel:* (01) 3825798; (01) 3301511 *Fax:* (01) 3824417 *E-mail:* giovani1@otenet.gr *Web Site:* www.geocities.com/giovanis_pub/en_main1.htm, pg 310

Gippe-Marche Du Livre Ancien (France) *Tel:* (01) 45 32 12 75 *Fax:* (01) 45 32 12 75 *E-mail:* gippe@free.fr, pg 166

Edizioni del Girasole srl (Italy) *Tel:* (0544) 212830 *Fax:* (0544) 38432 *E-mail:* info@europart.it, pg 390

Girassol Edicoes, LDA (Portugal) *Tel:* (021) 9151540 *Fax:* (021) 9151548 *E-mail:* girassol@mail.telepac.pt, pg 525

Girault Gilbert bvba (Belgium) *Tel:* (02) 2171430; (02) 2175880 *Fax:* (02) 2173375, pg 69

Giri Trading Agency Pvt. Ltd (India) *Tel:* (044) 4943551; (044) 4940376 (Showroom); (044) 4942530 (Showroom); (044) 4953817; (044) 4953823; (044) 4611610 *Fax:* (044) 4953821 *E-mail:* giritrading@vsnl.com *Web Site:* www.giritrading.com, pg 1288

Girol Books Inc (Canada) *Tel:* 613-233-9044 *Fax:* 613-233-9044 *E-mail:* info@girol.com *Web Site:* www.girol.com, pg 1153

Gisbert y Cia SA (Bolivia) *Tel:* (02) 20 26 26 *Fax:* (02) 20 29 11 *E-mail:* libgis@ceibo.entelnet.bo *Web Site:* www.sonnegocios.com, pg 76

Gisbert y Cia SA (Bolivia) *Tel:* (02) 220 26 26 *Fax:* (02) 220 29 11 *E-mail:* libgis@ceibo.entelnet.bo, pg 1276

Editions Jean Paul Gisserot (France) *Tel:* (01) 43 31 88 25 *Fax:* (01) 43 31 88 15 *E-mail:* editions@editions-gisserot.com, pg 166

Gitanjali Publishing House (India) *Tel:* (011) 621991; (011) 6237555, pg 337

Promociones Culturales Gitral SA (Ecuador) *Tel:* (02) 510510; (02) 532060; (02) 32644 *Fax:* (02) 510510; (02) 326733, pg 1282

A Giuffre Editore SpA (Italy) *Tel:* (02) 380891 *Fax:* (02) 38009582, pg 390

Giunti (Gruppo Editoriale) (Italy) *Tel:* (055) 5062-1 *Fax:* (055) 5062274 *E-mail:* estero@giunti.it, pg 390

Giunti Publishing Group (Italy) *Tel:* (055) 66791 *Fax:* (055) 6679298, pg 391

Edizioni Giuridico Scientifiche (SRL) (Italy) *Tel:* (02) 55192219 *Fax:* (02) 76009444, pg 391

Gius Laterza e Figli SpA (Italy) *Tel:* (080) 5216713 *Fax:* (080) 5243461 *E-mail:* laterza@laterza.it, pg 391

Giuseppe Laterza Editore Snc (Italy) *Tel:* (080) 5237936 *Fax:* (080) 5237360, pg 391

Gjurgja Journalistic & Publishing Firm (The Former Yugoslav Republic of Macedonia) *Tel:* (091) 228076, pg 449

Glad Sounds Sdn Bhd (Malaysia) *Tel:* (03) 7187070 *Fax:* (03) 7189948, pg 452

Glas New Russian Writing (Russian Federation) *Tel:* (095) 4419157 *Fax:* (095) 4419157 *Web Site:* www.bham.ac.uk/glas; www.glas.msk.su, pg 538

Glasgow City Libraries and Archives, the Mitchell Library (United Kingdom) *Tel:* (0141) 287-2999 *Fax:* (0141) 287-2815, pg 1506

Glasgow City Libraries Publications (United Kingdom) *Tel:* (0141) 287 2999 *Fax:* (0141) 287 2815, pg 687

University of Glasgow (United Kingdom) *Tel:* (0141) 3306704 *Fax:* (0141) 3304952 *E-mail:* library@lib.gla.ac.uk *Web Site:* www.lib.gla.ac.uk, pg 1506

Eric Glass Ltd (United Kingdom) *Tel:* (020) 7229 9500 *Fax:* (020) 7229 6220, pg 1119

GLB Parkland Verlags-und Vertriebs GmbH (Germany) *Tel:* (0221) 9364380 *Fax:* (0221) 9364383, pg 232

Gleaner Co Ltd (Jamaica) *Tel:* (876) 922-2340 *Fax:* (876) 922-2319; (876) 922-6297; (876) 922-6223, pg 413

AB Gleerups Universitetsbokhandeln (Sweden) *Tel:* (046) 196000 *Fax:* (046) 184247; (046) 196027, pg 1312

Verlag Gleitschirm (Switzerland) *Tel:* (081) 235241 *Fax:* (081) 221452, pg 614

Glenat Benelux SA (Belgium) *Tel:* (02) 7612640 *Fax:* (02) 7612645 *E-mail:* glenat@glenat.be, pg 69

Editions J Glenat SA (France) *Tel:* (04) 76 88 75 75 *Fax:* (04) 76 88 75 70 *Web Site:* www.glenat.com, pg 166

Gloatz, Hille GmbH & Co KG fur Mehrfarben und Zellglasdruck (Germany) *Tel:* (030) 721 99 12; (030) 723 254 93 *Fax:* (030) 721 95 65 *E-mail:* gloatz.hille.gmbh@gmx.de; info@gloatz-hille.de *Web Site:* www.gloatz-hille.de, pg 233

Global Editora e Distribuidora Ltda (Brazil) *Tel:* (011) 3277-7999, pg 1277

Global Books Ltd (United Kingdom) *Tel:* (1303) 226799 *Fax:* (1303) 243087 *E-mail:* globook@aol.com *Web Site:* simplyglobalbooks.com, pg 687

Global Editora e Distribuidora Ltda (Brazil) *Tel:* (011) 32777999 *Fax:* (011) 32778141 *E-mail:* global@dialdata.com.br, pg 84

Global Educational Services Pte Ltd (Singapore) *Tel:* 2896351 *Fax:* 2896086, pg 546

Global Kontakts Balgarija (Bulgaria) *Tel:* (02) 540636 *Fax:* (02) 528790 *Web Site:* www.m3.bulgaria.com, pg 95

Globi Verlag AG (Switzerland) *Tel:* (01) 4634135 *Fax:* (01) 4633502; (01) 4613971, pg 614

Editora Globo SA (Brazil) *Tel:* (011) 37677890 *Fax:* (011) 37677870 *E-mail:* wcarelli@edglobo.com.br *Web Site:* www.editoraglobo.com.br, pg 84

Globus Buchvertrieb (Austria) *Tel:* (01) 513 96 92 0 *Fax:* (01) 513 96 92 9, pg 52

Casa de editura Globus (Romania) *Tel:* (01) 2231510; (01) 2231530 *Fax:* (01) 6664265, pg 533

Globus-Nakladni zavod (Croatia) *Tel:* (01) 4628 400 *Fax:* (01) 4551 146, pg 118

Verlagsgesellschaft R Gloess & Co (Germany) *Tel:* (040) 890 5202 *Fax:* (040) 890 5193, pg 233

Glossa (Italy) *Tel:* (02) 877609 *Fax:* (02) 72003162 *E-mail:* informazioni@glossaeditrice.it, pg 391

Glowna Biblioteka Lekarska (Poland) *Tel:* (022) 497851 *Fax:* (022) 497802 *E-mail:* gbl@atos.warman.com.pl, pg 1492

Biblioteka Glowna Politechniki Warszawskiej (Poland) *Tel:* (022) 6211370 *Fax:* (022) 6287184 *E-mail:* bgpw@bg.pw.edu.pl, pg 1492

Glowworm Books Ltd (United Kingdom) *Tel:* (01506) 857570 *Fax:* (01506) 858100 *E-mail:* admin@GlowwormBooks.co.uk; sales@amaising.co.uk (packaging); sales@glowwormbooks.co.uk (publishing & schools division) *Web Site:* www.GlowwormBooks.co.uk, pg 687

GLS Language Services (United Kingdom) *Tel:* (0141) 2268440 *Fax:* (0141) 2268441 *E-mail:* glslanguageservices@compuserve.com, pg 1129

Verlag Glueckauf GmbH (Germany) *Tel:* (02054) 924121 *Fax:* (02054) 924129 *E-mail:* vge-vertrieb@t-online.de *Web Site:* www.vge.de, pg 233

Glydendal Akademisk (Norway) *Tel:* (022) 034300 *Fax:* (022) 034305, pg 503

GMC Publications Ltd (United Kingdom) *Tel:* (01273) 477374; (01273) 488005 *Fax:* (01273) 486300 *E-mail:* pubs@thegmcgroup.com, pg 687

GMP Publishers Ltd (United Kingdom) *Tel:* (01366) 328101 *Fax:* (01366) 328102 *E-mail:* davidoraubrey@gmpub.demon.co.uk *Web Site:* www.gmppubs.co.uk; www.gaymenspress.co.uk, pg 687

Forlaget GMT (Denmark) *Tel:* 86386095, pg 132

Bruno Gmuender Verlag GmbH (Germany) *Tel:* (030) 6150030 *Fax:* (030) 6159007 *E-mail:* info@brunogmuender.com *Web Site:* www.brunogmuender.com, pg 233

Gnocchi Editore (Italy) *Tel:* (081) 5524733 *Fax:* (081) 5518295 *E-mail:* idelgno@tin.it, pg 391

Gnostic Editions (Australia) *Tel:* (03) 9853 1401 *Fax:* (03) 9853 1481 *E-mail:* mail@gnoticeditions.com *Web Site:* www.gnosticeditions.com, pg 24

Gnostic Press (New Zealand) *Tel:* (09) 4127054 *Fax:* (09) 4126476 *E-mail:* gnostic.press.nz@xtra.co.nz, pg 491

Godfrey Cave Associates (United Kingdom) *Tel:* (020) 7416 3000 *Fax:* (020) 7416 3289, pg 1233

Godfrey Cave Associates Ltd (United Kingdom) *Tel:* (020) 7416 3000 *Fax:* (020) 7416 3289, pg 1319

Godfrey Cave Holdings Ltd (United Kingdom) *Tel:* (020) 7416 3000 *Fax:* (020) 7416 3099, pg 1319

Godord (Iceland) *Tel:* 5516998, pg 328

Godsfield Press Ltd (United Kingdom) *Tel:* (01626) 323200 *Fax:* (01626) 323231 *E-mail:* mail@davidandcharles.co.uk *Web Site:* www.davidandcharles.co.uk, pg 688

Godwit Publishing Ltd (New Zealand) *Tel:* (09) 4805410 *Fax:* (09) 4805930 *E-mail:* godwit@godwit.co.nz, pg 491

BV Uitgeversbedryf Het Goede Boek (Netherlands) *Tel:* (35) 5253508 *Fax:* (35) 5254013, pg 477

Goel Prakashen (India) *Tel:* (0121) 642946; (0121) 644766 *Fax:* (0121) 645855, pg 337

Alois Goschl & Co (Austria) *Tel:* (01) 321180 *Fax:* (01) 651899, pg 52

Goteborgs Stadsbibliotek (Sweden) *Tel:* (031) 61-65-00 *Fax:* (031) 61-66-93, pg 1500

Goteborgs Universitetsbibliotek (Sweden) *Tel:* (031) 7731000 *Fax:* (031) 163797 *E-mail:* library@ub.gu.se, pg 1500

Cornelia Goethe Literaturverlag (Germany) *Tel:* (069) 40894-0 *Fax:* (069) 40894-194 *E-mail:* literatur@fouque-verlag.de *Web Site:* www.cornelia-goethe.de; www.fouque-verlag.de, pg 233

Goethe-Gesellschaft in Weimar eV (Germany) *Tel:* (3643) 202050 *Fax:* (3643) 202061 *E-mail:* goetheges@aol.com *Web Site:* www.goethe-gessellschaft.de, pg 1363

Goethe-Institut (Belgium) *Tel:* (02) 2303970 *Fax:* (02) 2307725 *E-mail:* goethe.library@infoboard.be, pg 1453

Goethe-Verlag, Godhard von Heydebrand (Switzerland) *Tel:* (031) 8333248, pg 615

Golden Books Publishing Company, Inc (United Kingdom) *Tel:* (020) 7973 9000 *Fax:* (020) 7233 6125, pg 688

Golden Cockerel Press Ltd (United Kingdom) *Tel:* (020) 7405 7979 *Fax:* (020) 7404 3598, pg 688

Golden Cup Printing Co Ltd (Hong Kong) *Tel:* 23434254 *Fax:* 23415426 *E-mail:* sales@goldencup.com.hk *Web Site:* www.goldencup.com.hk, pg 1134, 1156, 1196, 1212, 1222

Golden Publications (Mauritius) *Tel:* 2416640, pg 457

Goldland Business Co Ltd (Nigeria) *Tel:* (01) 8023179087; (01) 821203 *E-mail:* goldland@consultant.com, pg 499

Wilhelm Goldmann Verlag GmbH (Germany) *Tel:* (089) 4372-0 *Fax:* (089) 43722812 *E-mail:* vertrieb.verlagsgruppe@bertelsmann.de, pg 233

Victor Goldschmidt Verlagsbuchhandlung (Switzerland) *Tel:* (061) 236565 *Fax:* (061) 2616123, pg 615

Goldschneck Verlag (Germany) *Tel:* (07151) 66 01 19 *Fax:* (07151) 66 07 78 *E-mail:* goldschneck@t-online.de *Web Site:* www.goldschneck.de, pg 233

Goldshield Communications Ltd (United Kingdom) *Tel:* (0114) 2431000 *Fax:* (0114) 2433000, pg 1140, 1161, 1203, 1214, 1223

The Goldsmith Press Ltd (Ireland) *Tel:* (045) 433613 *Fax:* (045) 434648 *E-mail:* de@iol.ie, pg 361

Goll Bruno Verlag fur Aussergewoehnliche Perspektiven (VAP) (Germany) *Tel:* (05742) 93 04 44 *Fax:* (05742) 93 04 55 *Web Site:* www.vap-buch.de, pg 233

Gollancz/Witherby (United Kingdom) *Tel:* (020) 7240 3444 *Fax:* (020) 7240 4822 *Web Site:* www.orionbooks.co.uk, pg 688

Gomer Press (J D Lewis & Sons Ltd) (United Kingdom) *Tel:* (01559) 362371 *Fax:* (01559) 363758 *E-mail:* gwasg@gomer.co.uk *Web Site:* www.gomer.co.uk, pg 688

Gomez Gomez Hermanos Editores S de RL Edicion de Libros y Revistas (Mexico) *Tel:* (05) 6123946; (05) 6123906 *Fax:* (05) 633786, pg 461

Gondolat Kiado (Hungary) *Tel:* (01) 138-3358 *Fax:* (01) 138-4540, pg 324

Gondrom Verlag GmbH & Co KG (Germany) *Tel:* (09208) 51-0 *Fax:* (09208) 51-21 *E-mail:* service@gondrom.de *Web Site:* www.gondrom.de, pg 233

Editions Gondwana (Martinique) *Tel:* 583676 *Fax:* 580014, pg 456

Gondwanaland Press (New Zealand) *Tel:* (04) 4758092 *Fax:* (04) 4756194, pg 491

Pierre Gonin Editions d'Art (Switzerland) *Tel:* (021) 3129996 *Fax:* (021) 3129996, pg 615

Gono Prakashani, Gono Shasthya Kendra (Bangladesh) *Tel:* (02) 500406; (02) 839366 *Fax:* (02) 863567; (02) 833182 *E-mail:* gk.mail@drik.bgd.toolnet.org, pg 62

Librerias Gonvill SA de CV (Mexico) *Tel:* (03) 6141946 *Fax:* (03) 6132282, pg 1299

Good Earth Publishing Co Ltd (Hong Kong) *Tel:* (02) 3386103 *Fax:* (02) 3383610, pg 320

Goodbooks Publishing Co (Ghana) *Tel:* (021) 665629 *Fax:* (021) 302993 *E-mail:* allgoodbooks@hotmail.com, pg 307

Goodwill Trading Co Inc (Philippines) *Tel:* (02) 403610, pg 1306

Van Goor BV (Netherlands) *Tel:* (020) 5353135 *Fax:* (020) 5353130 *E-mail:* boekerij@boekery.nl, pg 477

Uitgeverij CJ Goossens BV (Netherlands) *Tel:* (015) 2123623 *Fax:* (015) 2124295, pg 477

A H Gordon (United Kingdom) *Tel:* (01408) 622660, pg 688

The Robert Gordon University (United Kingdom) *Tel:* (01224) 262000 *Fax:* (01224) 263636 *E-mail:* sim@rgu.ac.uk *Web Site:* www.rgu.ac.uk, pg 688

Gorenjski Tisk Printing Co (Slovenia) *Tel:* (064) 2630 *Fax:* (064) 241323, pg 1139, 1159, 1201, 1213, 1222

Biblioteca Bio-Medica del Laboratorio Conmemorativo Gorgas (Panama) *Tel:* (02) 274111 *Fax:* (02) 254366 *E-mail:* igorgas@sin.fonet, pg 1490

Gosudarstvennaya publichnaya istoricheskaya biblioteka Rossii (Russian Federation) *Tel:* (095) 9256514 *Fax:* (095) 9284332; (095) 9256514 *E-mail:* maf@shpl.ru, pg 1495

Gosudarstvennaya publichnaya nauchno-tekhnicheskaya biblioteka SSSR (Russian Federation) *Tel:* (095) 9259288 *Fax:* (095) 9219862 *E-mail:* root@gpntb.msk.su, pg 1495

Gosudarstvennaya Respublikanskaya biblioteka Gruzinskoi SSR im K Marksai (Georgia) *Tel:* (08832) 999286 (Director's Office) *Fax:* (08832) 998095, pg 1466

Gosudarstvenny Komitet Armjamskoj SSR po delam izdatel'stv, poligrafii, kniznoj targovli (Armenia) *Tel:* (02) 527595 *E-mail:* grapalat@arminco.com, pg 1235

Gothia AB, Forlagshuset (Sweden) *Tel:* (08) 4622660; (08) 7576270 *Fax:* (08) 4620322, pg 603

Gothia Publishing House (Sweden) *Tel:* (08) 4622660 *Fax:* (08) 4620322 *E-mail:* info.gothia@verbum.se *Web Site:* www.gothia.nu, pg 603

Gotthelf-Verlag (Switzerland) *Tel:* (061) 2428155 *Fax:* (061) 2646486 *E-mail:* rms@reinhardt.ch, pg 615

Gottmer Uitgevers Groop (Netherlands) *Tel:* (23) 5411190 *Fax:* (23) 5274404 *E-mail:* post@gottmer.nl *Web Site:* www.gottmer.nl, pg 477

Gould Books (Australia) *Tel:* (08) 8389 1611 *Fax:* (08) 8389 1599 *E-mail:* inquiries@gould.com.au *Web Site:* www.gould.com.au, pg 24

Gousudarstvennaja Biblioteka Respublika Tadzkistan im Firdousi (Tajikistan) *Tel:* (03772) 27-47-26, pg 1502

Government Public Library (Liberia), pg 1481

Government Library (Libyan Arab Jamahiriya), pg 1481

Government Information Services (Hong Kong) *Tel:* (852) 2842-8728 *Web Site:* www.info.gov.hk/isd, pg 1248

Government of Pakistan Department of Libraries (Pakistan) *Tel:* (051) 9214523 *Fax:* (051) 9221375 *E-mail:* nlpiba@paknet2.ptc.pk, pg 1521

Government Press (Afghanistan) *Tel:* 26851, pg 1

Government Printer (Ethiopia), pg 141

Government Printer (Gambia) *Tel:* 227399, pg 190

The Government Printer (Israel) *Tel:* (02) 5685111; (02) 5685200 *Fax:* (02) 5685226, pg 1136

Government Printer (Kenya), pg 431

Government Printer (Lesotho) *Tel:* 313023, pg 444

Government Printer (South Africa) *Tel:* (012) 3239731 *Fax:* (012) 4614404, pg 554

Government Printer (United Republic of Tanzania), pg 633

Government Printer (Zambia) *Tel:* (01) 215401; (01) 215805; (01) 215685; (01) 216972, pg 766

Government Printer (Imprimerie National du Rwanda) (Rwanda) *Tel:* 75350 *Fax:* 75820, pg 543

Government Printer (Imprimerie National Du Tchad) (Chad), pg 99

Government Printer (Imprimerie Nationale) (Madagascar) *Tel:* (02) 23675, pg 450

Government Printer (Imprimerie Nationale) (Malawi) *Tel:* (050) 523155 *Fax:* (050) 52230133, pg 450

Government Printer (Imprimerie Nationale) (Mauritius) *Tel:* 2345284, pg 457

Government Printer (Imprimerie Officielle) (Morocco) *Tel:* (077) 65024, pg 470

Government Printer (Imprimerie Officielle de la Republique Tunisienne - IORT) (Tunisia) *Tel:* (01) 299914, pg 638

Government Printer (INABU) (Burundi) *Tel:* (02) 22214; (02) 24046, pg 98

Government Printer (Societe De L'Imprimerie Nationale Du Niger) (Niger) *Tel:* 734798, pg 497

Government Publications Ireland (Ireland) *Tel:* (01) 6476000 *Fax:* (01) 6476843 *E-mail:* opw@sol.ie *Web Site:* www.opw.ie, pg 361

The Government Supplies Agency, Publications Branch (Ireland) *Tel:* (01) 6476000 *Fax:* (01) 6476843 *E-mail:* opw@iol.ie *Web Site:* www.opw.ie, pg 1112

Govi-Verlag Pharmazeutischer Verlag GmbH (Germany) *Tel:* (06196) 928 250 *Fax:* (06196) 928 259 *E-mail:* service@govi.de *Web Site:* www.govi.de, pg 233

Govinda-Verlag (Switzerland) *Tel:* (052) 6726677 *Fax:* (052) 6726678 *E-mail:* info@govinda.ch *Web Site:* www.govinda.ch, pg 615

Govostis Publishing SA (Greece) *Tel:* (010) 3816661, pg 311

James Gowans Ltd (United Kingdom) *Tel:* (0141) 4293337 *Fax:* (0141) 4201694 *E-mail:* info@skipper.co.uk *Web Site:* www.skipper.co.uk, pg 1140, 1161

Gower Publishing Ltd (United Kingdom) *Tel:* (01252) 331551 *Fax:* (01252) 344405 *E-mail:* info@gowerpub.com *Web Site:* www.gowerpub.com, pg 688

Gozo Press (Malta) *Tel:* 551534; 564395 *Fax:* 560857 *E-mail:* gozopress@orbit.net.mt, pg 456

Gozo Public Library (Malta) *Tel:* 556200 *Fax:* 555944, pg 1483

De Graaf Publishers (Netherlands) *Tel:* (0172) 571461 *Fax:* (0172) 572231 *E-mail:* degraaf.books@xws.nl, pg 478

Edicoes Graal Ltda (Brazil) *Tel:* (011) 7961-0006 *Fax:* (011) 7961-0006, pg 84

Ordem do Graal na Terra (Brazil) *Tel:* (011) 4781-0006 *Fax:* (011) 4781-0006 ext 217 *E-mail:* graal@graal.org.br *Web Site:* www.graal.org.br, pg 84

Grabert-Verlag (Germany) *Tel:* (07071) 40700 *Fax:* (07071) 407026, pg 233

Brigitte Grabitz - ikoo Buchverlag (Germany) *Tel:* (09234) 1295, pg 233

Gracewing/Fowler Wright Books (United Kingdom) *Tel:* (0568) 616835 *Fax:* (0568) 613289, pg 1319

Gracewing Publishing (United Kingdom) *Tel:* (01568) 616835 *E-mail:* gracewingx@aol.com *Web Site:* www.gracewing.co.uk, pg 688

Grada Publishing sro (Czech Republic) *Tel:* (02) 20386401; (02) 20386402 *Fax:* (02) 20386400 *E-mail:* info@gradapublishing.cz *Web Site:* www.grandpublishing.cz, pg 124

Gradevinska Knjiga (Yugoslavia) *Tel:* (011) 3233-565; (011) 3244-345; (011) 3244-359 *Fax:* (011) 3233-565, pg 764

Izdavacka preduzece Gradina (Yugoslavia) *Tel:* (018) 25-864 *Fax:* (018) 25-456, pg 764

Gradiva-Publicacnoes Lda (Portugal) *Tel:* (021) 3974067 *Fax:* (021) 3953471 *E-mail:* gradiva@ip.pt *Web Site:* www.gradiva.pt, pg 525

Graduate Institute of International Studies (Switzerland) *Tel:* (022) 7311730 *Fax:* (022) 7384306 *E-mail:* info@hei.unige.ch *Web Site:* heiwww.unige.ch, pg 615

Graefe und Unzer Verlag GmbH (Germany) *Tel:* (089) 4 19 81-0 *Fax:* (089) 4 19 81-113 *Web Site:* www.graefe-und-unzer.de, pg 233

Graf Editions (Germany) *Tel:* (089) 27 159 57 *Fax:* (089) 27 159 97 *Web Site:* www.grafeditions.de, pg 234

Graff Buchhandlung (Germany) *Tel:* (0531) 480890 *Fax:* (0531) 46531 *E-mail:* infos@graff.de *Web Site:* www.graff.de, pg 1284

Graffiti Publications (Australia) *Tel:* (03) 5472-3653 *Fax:* (03) 5472-3805 *E-mail:* graffiti@netcon.net.au *Web Site:* www.graffitipub.com.au, pg 24

Editora e Grafica Carisio Ltda (Brazil) *Tel:* (034) 2413557 *Fax:* (034) 2413310, pg 84

Grafica e Arte SRL (Italy) *Tel:* (035) 255014 *Fax:* (035) 250164 *E-mail:* info@graficaearte.it *Web Site:* www.graficaearte.it, pg 391

Grafica Editora Primor Ltda (Brazil) *Tel:* (021) 4744966, pg 84

Marchesi Grafiche Editoriali SpA (Italy) *Tel:* (06) 331359 *Fax:* (06) 3336505, pg 391

Graficki zavod Hrvatske (Croatia) *Tel:* (01) 240-4444; (01) 240-7166 *Fax:* (041) 430331, pg 118

Grafis Edizioni (Italy) *Tel:* (051) 6165611 *Fax:* (051) 6167095, pg 391

Grafit Verlag GmbH (Germany) *Tel:* (0231) 7 21 46 50 *Fax:* (0231) 7 21 46 77 *E-mail:* info@grafit.de *Web Site:* www.grafit.de, pg 234

Grafo Edizioni (Italy) *Tel:* (030) 393221 *Fax:* (030) 3701411, pg 391

Grafos SA Arte Sobre Papel (Spain) *Tel:* (093) 2618750 *Fax:* (093) 2631004, pg 1201, 1213

Graham Brash Pte Ltd (Singapore) *Tel:* 8311336 *Fax:* 8614815, pg 546

Graham-Cameron Publishing & Illustration (United Kingdom) *Tel:* (01263) 821 333 *Fax:* (01263) 821 334 *E-mail:* enquiry@graham-cameron-illustration.com *Web Site:* www.graham-cameron-illustration.com, pg 688

The Graham Publishing Company (Pvt) Ltd (Zimbabwe) *Tel:* (04) 706207 *Fax:* (04) 752439, pg 768

W F Graham (Northampton) Ltd (United Kingdom) *Tel:* (01604) 645537 *Fax:* (01604) 648414, pg 688

Grahames Bookshop (Australia) *Tel:* (02) 9296144 *Fax:* (02) 9571814, pg 1273

Grainger Museum (Australia) *Tel:* (03) 9344 5270 *Fax:* (03) 9349 1707 *E-mail:* grainger@unimelb.edo.au *Web Site:* www.lib.unimelb.edu.au/collections/grainger/introduction/intro.html, pg 24

Verlag der Stiftung Gralsbotschaft GmbH (Germany) *Tel:* (07156) 5096 *Fax:* (07156) 18663 *E-mail:* info@gral.de *Web Site:* www.gral.de, pg 234

Gram Editora (Argentina) *Tel:* (011) 4304-4833; (011) 4305-8397 *Fax:* (011) 4304-5692 *E-mail:* grameditora@infovia.com.ar *Web Site:* www.grameditora.com.ar, pg 6

Gramedia (Indonesia) *Tel:* (021) 5483008; (021) 5490666 *Fax:* (021) 5300545 *E-mail:* elex@elexmedia.com, pg 355

Gramedia Bookshop (Indonesia) *Tel:* (021) 5300545 *Fax:* (021) 5486085, pg 1290

Gran Enciclopedia-Asturiana Silverio Canada (Spain) *Tel:* (085) 5349684 *Fax:* (098) 5356879, pg 576

Editions Grancher (France) *Tel:* (01) 42 22 64 80 *Fax:* (01) 45 48 25 03 *E-mail:* info@grancher.com *Web Site:* www.grancher.com, pg 166

The Grand National Assembly of Turkey Library & Documentation TBMM (Turkey) *Tel:* (0312) 4206835 *Fax:* (0312) 4207548 *E-mail:* library@tbmm.gov.tr *Web Site:* www.tbmm.gov.tr, pg 1504

Grand People's Study House (Democratic People's Republic of Korea) *Tel:* (08502) 321 5614 *Fax:* (08502) 381-4427; (08502) 381-2100, pg 434

Editions du Grand-Pont (Switzerland) *Tel:* (021) 3123222 *Fax:* (021) 3113222, pg 615

Grande Loge de Luxembourg (Luxembourg) *Tel:* 229451 *Fax:* 463566, pg 447

Grandi & Associati SRL (Italy) *Tel:* (02) 4695541; (02) 4818962 *Fax:* (02) 48195108 *E-mail:* agenzia@grandieassociati.it, pg 1113

Editions Grandir (France) *Tel:* (04) 66 84 01 19; (04) 66 84 01 79 (showroom) *Fax:* (04) 66 26 14 50; (04) 66 26 14 50 (showroom), pg 166

Grandreams Ltd (United Kingdom) *Tel:* (01225) 485923 *Fax:* (01225) 485928 *E-mail:* wrrake@robertfrederick.co.uk, pg 689

Grange Books PLC (United Kingdom) *Tel:* (01634) 256 000 *Fax:* (01634) 255 500 *E-mail:* grangebooks@aol.com *Web Site:* www.grangebooks.co.uk, pg 689, 1319

Granit (France) *Tel:* (01) 40 71 98 75 *Fax:* (01) 46 51 30 06, pg 166

Granit SRO (Czech Republic) *Tel:* (00420) 57018357; (00420) 57018356; (00420) 57018361 *Fax:* (00420) 57018361 *E-mail:* info@granit-publishing.cz *Web Site:* www.granit-publishing.cz, pg 124

Granrott Press (Australia) *Tel:* (08) 8383-6081 *Fax:* (08) 8383 6067, pg 24

Grant & Cutler Ltd (United Kingdom) *Tel:* (020) 7734 2012 *Fax:* (020) 7734 9272 *E-mail:* contactus@grantandcutler.com *Web Site:* www.grant-c.demon.co.uk, pg 689

Granta Books (United Kingdom) *Tel:* (020) 7704 9776 *Fax:* (020) 7354 3469 *E-mail:* info@granta.com *Web Site:* www.granta.com, pg 689

Grantham Book Services Ltd (United Kingdom) *Tel:* (01476) 541000; (01476) 541 080 (orders) *Fax:* (01476) 541061 *E-mail:* orders@gbs.tbs-ltd.co.uk, pg 1319

Grantham House Publishing (New Zealand) *Tel:* (04) 3813071 *Fax:* (04) 3813067 *E-mail:* gstewart@iconz.co.nz, pg 491

Grao Editorial (Spain) *Tel:* (093) 4080464; (093) 4050455 *Fax:* (093) 3524337 *E-mail:* grao@grao.com; editorial@grao.com *Web Site:* www.grao.com, pg 576

Graphic Art Publishing (Thailand) *Tel:* (02) 2330302, pg 635

Graphic Educational Publications (New Zealand) *Tel:* (09) 6300488 *Fax:* (09) 6221559 *Web Site:* www.ak.planet.gen.nz/~com, pg 491

Graphic Reproductions Ltd (Ireland) *Tel:* (01) 6230101 *Fax:* (01) 6166598; (01) 6166599, pg 1157

Graphic Services Corp (United States) *Tel:* 203-270-7578 *Fax:* 203-270-1578 *Web Site:* www.independentcartongroup.com, pg 1215

Edition Graphischer Zirkel (Austria) *Tel:* (01) 0277346615, pg 52

GRASPO CZ AS - Druckerei und Buchbinderei (Czech Republic) *Tel:* (067) 7606111; (067) 7606246 *Fax:* (067) 7104052 *E-mail:* graspo@graspo.com; mp@graspo.com *Web Site:* www.graspo.com, pg 1194

Grass-Verlag (Germany) *Tel:* (02173) 51305 *Fax:* (02224) 79671, pg 234

Sarl Editions Jean Grassin (France) *Tel:* (02) 97 52 93 63 *Fax:* (02) 97 52 83 90 *E-mail:* j.grassin@wanadoo.fr *Web Site:* perso.wanadoo.fr/j.grassin/contact.htm, pg 167

Graton Editeur SA (Belgium) *Tel:* (02) 6756 666 *Fax:* (02) 6756 363 *E-mail:* graton.sa@skynet.be, pg 69

Graz Stadtmuseum (Austria) *Tel:* (0316) 822580 *Fax:* (0316) 822580-6 *Web Site:* homepage.sime.com, pg 52

Universitaetsbibliothek Graz (Austria) *Tel:* (0316) 380 3101; (0316) 380 3102; (0316) 380 3100 *Fax:* (0316) 384 987 *Web Site:* www.ub.kfunigtaz.ac.at, pg 1451

Great China Book Corporation (Taiwan, Province of China) *Tel:* (02) 23311433 *Fax:* (02) 23895866, pg 630

Library of the Great Mosque of Sana'a (Yemen), pg 1508

Great Wall Graphics Ltd (Hong Kong) *Tel:* 25240014 *Fax:* 28453588, pg 1134

Great Western Press Pty Ltd (Australia) *Tel:* (02) 94497929 *Fax:* (02) 91445566, pg 24

Greater Glider Productions Australia Pty Ltd (Australia) *Tel:* (07) 5494 3000 *Fax:* (07) 5494 3284 *E-mail:* greaterglide@publishaust.apc.org *Web Site:* www.greaterglider.com, pg 24

Editorial Gredos SA (Spain) *Tel:* (091) 7444920 *Fax:* (091) 5192033 *E-mail:* comercial@editorialgredos.com *Web Site:* www.editorialgredos.com, pg 576

The Greek Bookshop (United Kingdom) *Tel:* (020) 8446 1985 *Fax:* (020) 8446 1998 *E-mail:* info@thegreekbookshop.com *Web Site:* www.thegreekbookshop.com, pg 689

Greek Institute (United Kingdom) *Tel:* (020) 8360 7968 *Fax:* (020) 8360 7968, pg 1129

Greek Translations (United Kingdom) *Tel:* (020) 8445 3324 *Fax:* (020) 8446 1448, pg 1129

Green Books Ltd (United Kingdom) *Tel:* (01803) 863260 *Fax:* (01803) 863843 *E-mail:* greenbooks@gn.apc.org *Web Site:* www.greenbooks.co.uk, pg 689

Christine Green Authors' Agent (United Kingdom) *Tel:* (020) 7401 8844 *Fax:* (020) 7401 8860, pg 1119

The Green Pagoda Press Ltd (Hong Kong) *Tel:* 25611924 *Fax:* 28110946 *E-mail:* gpinfo@gpp.com.hk, pg 1156, 1196, 1212

Green Street Bindery (United Kingdom) *Tel:* (01865) 243540 *Fax:* (01865) 791329, pg 1203

Green Street Bookshop (Mail Order) (United Kingdom) *Tel:* (01371) 831449 *Fax:* (01371) 831599 *E-mail:* info@gsb.org.uk *Web Site:* www.gsb.org.uk, pg 1319

W Green The Scottish Law Publisher (United Kingdom) *Tel:* (0131) 225 4879 (orders); (0131) 225 4879 (marketing); (0207) 449 1104 (trade customers); (264) 342 828 (international book orders & information); (264) 342 766 (international subscription orders & information) *Fax:* (0131) 225 2104 (orders); (0131) 225 2104 (marketing); (0207) 449 1144 (trade customers); (264) 342 761 (international book orders & information); (264) 342 761 (international subscription orders & information) *E-mail:* enquiries@wgreen.co.uk; trade.sales@sweetandmaxwell.co.uk (trade customers) *Web Site:* www.wgreen.co.uk, pg 689

Greene & Heaton Ltd (United Kingdom) *Tel:* (020) 8749 0315 *Fax:* (020) 8749 0318, pg 1119

Greene's Bookshop Ltd (Ireland) *Tel:* (01) 6762554 *Fax:* (01) 6789091 *E-mail:* greenes@iol.ie, pg 1291

Greenhill Books/Lionel Leventhal Ltd (United Kingdom) *Tel:* (020) 8458 6314 *Fax:* (020) 8905 5245 *E-mail:* info@greenhillbooks.com; sales@greenhillbooks.com *Web Site:* www.greenhillbooks.com, pg 689

Greger-Delacroix (Hungary) *Tel:* (01) 1608936 *E-mail:* gregerdelacroix@compuserve.com, pg 324

Gregg Publishing Co (United Kingdom) *Tel:* (01444) 445070 *Fax:* (01444) 445050 *E-mail:* Rdowling@gowerpub.com, pg 690

Libreria Editrice Gregoriana (Italy) *Tel:* (049) 657493 *Fax:* (049) 662089, pg 391

Gregoriana Libreria Editrice (Italy) *Tel:* (049) 657493 *Fax:* (049) 662089, pg 1293

Gregory & Radice Authors' Agents (United Kingdom) *Tel:* (020) 7610 4676 *Fax:* (020) 7610 4686 *E-mail:* info@gregoryradice.co.uk *Web Site:* www.gregoryradice.co.uk, pg 1119

Ernesto Gremese Editore SRL (Italy) *Tel:* (06) 65740507 *Fax:* (06) 65740509 *E-mail:* gremese@gremese.com *Web Site:* www.gremese.com, pg 391

Gremese International Srl (Italy) *Tel:* (06) 65746320 *Fax:* (06) 65740509, pg 391

Gresham Books Ltd (United Kingdom) *Tel:* (01865) 513582 *Fax:* (01865) 512718 *E-mail:* info@gresham-books.co.uk *Web Site:* www.gresham-books.co.uk, pg 690

Groupe de Recherche et d'Echanges Technologiques (GRET) (France) *Tel:* (01) 40 05 61 61 *Fax:* (01) 40 05 61 10 *E-mail:* gret@gret.org; librairie@gret.org *Web Site:* www.gret.org, pg 167

Greuthof Verlag und Vertrieb GmbH (Germany) *Tel:* (07681) 6025 *Fax:* (07681) 6027, pg 234

Grevas Forlag (Denmark) *Tel:* 86997065, pg 132

Greven Verlag Koeln GmbH (Germany) *Tel:* (0221) 20 33-161 *Fax:* (0221) 20 33-162 *E-mail:* greven.verlag@greven.de *Web Site:* www.greven-verlag.de, pg 234

Piero Gribaudi Editore (Italy) *Tel:* (02) 89302244 *Fax:* (02) 89302376 *E-mail:* info@gribaudi.it *Web Site:* www.gribaudi.it, pg 391

John Grieg Forlag AS (Norway) *Tel:* 55213181 *Fax:* 55218180, pg 503

Griese Ingolf Wipe Griese (Germany) *Tel:* (0231) 417412 *Fax:* (0231) 418461; (0231) 417418, pg 234

Editions du Griffon (Neuchatel) (Switzerland) *Tel:* (032) 7252204, pg 615

Grijalbo SA (Venezuela) *Tel:* (02) 2381542; (02) 2381732 *Fax:* (02) 2390308, pg 762

Editorial Grijalbo SA de CV (Mexico) *Tel:* (05) 3584355 *Fax:* (05) 3584312, pg 461

Grijalbo Mondadori SA (Spain) *Tel:* (093) 4767110 *Fax:* (093) 4767119 *E-mail:* marketing@grijalbo.com *Web Site:* www.grijalbo.com, pg 576

Grijalbo y Cia Ltda (Chile) *Tel:* (02) 696-5152; (02) 696-1154 *Fax:* (02) 672-1850 *E-mail:* ramiro@senderos.cl *Web Site:* www.senderos.cl, pg 100

Grimm Press Ltd (Taiwan, Province of China) *Tel:* (02) 23517251 *Fax:* (02) 23517244 *E-mail:* grimm@gmail.gcn.net.tw, pg 630

Grivas Publications (Greece) *Tel:* (01) 5573470 *Fax:* (01) 5573076 *E-mail:* info@grivas.gr *Web Site:* www.grivas.gr, pg 1286

Groeninghe NV (Belgium) *Tel:* (056) 22-22-62 *Fax:* (056) 22-82-86 *Web Site:* www.groeninghebe.com, pg 69

David Grossman Literary Agency Ltd (United Kingdom) *Tel:* (020) 7221 2770 *Fax:* (020) 7221 1445, pg 1119

Grote'sche Verlagsbuchhandlung GmbH & Co KG (Germany) *Tel:* (02234) 1060 *Fax:* (02234) 106284, pg 234

Groto Publikasi (Suriname) *Tel:* 493569, pg 599

Editions Francois Grounauer (Switzerland) *Tel:* (022) 447948, pg 615

Editora Ground Ltda (Brazil) *Tel:* (011) 5031 1500 *Fax:* (011) 5031 3462 *E-mail:* editora@ground.com.br *Web Site:* www.ground.com.br, pg 84

Groupe des Editions du Rocher (France) *Tel:* (01) 40 46 54 00 *Fax:* (01) 40 46 91 36 *E-mail:* jpb@post.club-internet.fr, pg 167

Groupe Expansion (France) *Tel:* (01) 40604060 *Fax:* (01) 40604116, pg 167

Groupe Hatier International (France) *Tel:* (01) 44-39-28-84 *Fax:* (01) 42-84-03-19 *E-mail:* hatier@intl.com, pg 167

Groupe Moniteur -L'Argus (France) *Tel:* (01) 40-13-30-30 *Fax:* (01) 40-13-51-06 *E-mail:* infos@collectiviteslocales.com, pg 167

Groupements Francais des Fabricants de Papiers d'Impression-Ecriture (COPACEL) (France) *Tel:* (01) 45628707 *Fax:* (01) 45628247, pg 1243

Grub Street (United Kingdom) *Tel:* (020) 7924 3966; (020) 7738 1008 *Fax:* (020) 7738 1009 *E-mail:* post@grubstreet.co.uk *Web Site:* www.grubstreet.co.uk, pg 690

Verlag Grundlagen und Praxis GmbH & Co (Germany) *Tel:* (0491) 6 18 86 *Fax:* (0491) 36 34 *E-mail:* grundlagen-praxis@t-online.de *Web Site:* www.grundlagen-praxis.de, pg 234

Gruner + Jahr AG & Co (Germany) *Tel:* (040) 37030 *Fax:* (040) 37036000 *E-mail:* oeffentlichkeiharbeit@guj.de, pg 234

Grupo Bibliografico Nacional de la Republica Dominicana (Dominican Republic), pg 1514

Editorial Grupo Cero (Spain) *Tel:* (091) 542 33 49 *Fax:* (091) 8700944 *E-mail:* pedidos@editorialgrupocero.com *Web Site:* www.editorialgrupocero.com, pg 576

Grupo Comunicar (Spain) *Tel:* (0959) 248380 *Fax:* (0959) 248380 *E-mail:* info@grupocomunicar.com *Web Site:* www.grupo-comunicar.com, pg 576

Grupo Cultural Especializado, SA (Mexico) *Tel:* (05) 6889831 *Fax:* (05) 6889965, pg 1299

Grupo Editorial CEAC SA (Spain) *Tel:* (093) 2472424 *Fax:* (093) 2315115 *E-mail:* atencioncliente@ceacedit.com *Web Site:* www.ceacedit.com; www.editorialceac.com, pg 576

Grupo Editorial Iberoamerica, SA de CV (Mexico) *Tel:* (05) 55230994, pg 461

Grupo Editorial Iberoamerica de Colombia SA (Colombia) *Tel:* (01) 3106553 *Fax:* (01) 3106553 *E-mail:* geicol@colomsat.net.co, pg 1279

Grupo Editorial RIN-78 (Guatemala) *Tel:* (02) 692080 *Fax:* (02) 601834, pg 316

Grupo Editorial Z Zeta SA de CV (Mexico) *Tel:* (05) 6705627; (05) 5817929 *Fax:* (05) 5758280, pg 461

Grupo Noriega Editores de Colombia Ltda (Colombia) *Tel:* (01) 2328336; (01) 2344929 *Fax:* (01) 2858905 *E-mail:* gnoriega@openway.com.co, pg 1280

Grupo Santillana de Ediciones SA (Spain) *Tel:* (091) 7449060 *Fax:* (091) 7449019 *E-mail:* grupo@santillana.es *Web Site:* www.gruposantillana.com, pg 576

Schweizer Autorinnen und Autoren Gruppe Olten (Switzerland) *Tel:* (052) 7288933 *Fax:* (052) 7288932 *E-mail:* sekretariate@gruppe.olten, pg 1368

Gruppe 21 GmbH (Germany) *Tel:* (02054) 1048-90 *Fax:* (02054) 1048-929 *E-mail:* marketing@gruppe21.de *Web Site:* www.gruppe21.de, pg 234

Verlag Gruppenpaedagogischer Literatur (Germany) *Tel:* (06081) 5 67 40 *Fax:* (06081) 5 74 38 *E-mail:* info@vglw.de *Web Site:* vglw.de, pg 234

Gruppo Calderini Edagricole (Italy) *Tel:* (051) 62267 *Fax:* (051) 490200 *E-mail:* comunica@calderini.agriline.it *Web Site:* www.calderini.it, pg 392

Gruppo Editoriale Faenza Editrice SpA (Italy) *Tel:* (0546) 670411 *Fax:* (0546) 660440 *E-mail:* info@faenza.com *Web Site:* www.faenza.com, pg 392

Walter de Gruyter GmbH & Co KG (Germany) *Tel:* (030) 260 05-0 *Fax:* (030) 260 05-222 *E-mail:* wdg-info@degruyter.de *Web Site:* www.degruyter.de, pg 234

Editura Gryphon (Romania) *Tel:* (068) 68313642; (068) 68314049 *Fax:* (068) 68312888 *E-mail:* gryphon@gryphon.ro *Web Site:* www.gryphon.ro, pg 533

GSB (Ghana Standards Board) (Ghana) *Tel:* (021) 500065; (021) 500066 *Fax:* (021) 500092; (021) 500231, pg 307

GSMBA, Edition Bruno Gasser (Switzerland) *Tel:* (061) 6811103 *Fax:* (061) 6811103 *E-mail:* gasser@dial-switch.ck, pg 615

Guadalquivir SL Ediciones (Spain) *Tel:* (095) 422 19 76; (095) 422 19 17 *Fax:* (095) 421 33 20 *E-mail:* guadalquivir.ed@svq.servicom.es, pg 576

Editorial Guadalupe (Argentina) *Tel:* (011) 4826-8587 *Fax:* (011) 4823-6672 *E-mail:* ventas@editorialguadalupe.com.ar *Web Site:* www.editorialguadalupe.com.ar, pg 6

Editora Guadalupe Ltda (Colombia) *Tel:* (01) 2690788; (01) 2690211 *Fax:* (01) 2685308, pg 112

Editora Guanabara Koogan SA (Brazil) *Tel:* (021) 2217106 *Fax:* (021) 2215744 *E-mail:* norengbk@unisys.com.br, pg 84

Ugo Guanda Editore (Italy) *Tel:* (02) 8693072 *Fax:* (02) 76000306 *E-mail:* info@guanda.it, pg 392

Guangdong Science & Technology Press (China) *Tel:* (020) 87768688; (020) 87618870 (Directorial Office); (020) 87769412 (Foreign Cooperation Editorial Office) *Fax:* (020) 87764169 *E-mail:* gdkjwb@ns.guangzhou.gb.com.cn *Web Site:* www.gdpress.gov.cn, pg 106

Guarro Casas SA (Spain) *Tel:* (093) 7767676 *Fax:* (093) 7767630 *E-mail:* guarro@guarro.com *Web Site:* www.guarro.com, pg 1214

Editorial Guaymuras (Honduras) *Tel:* 237 49 31 *Fax:* 238 42 45 *E-mail:* editorial@sigmanet.hn, pg 318

Librairie Guenegaud Sarl (France) *Tel:* (01) 43260791 *Fax:* (01) 40468872 *E-mail:* libraire.guenegaud@wanadoo.fr *Web Site:* www.guenegaud.com, pg 167

Gunter Olzog Verlag GmbH (Germany) *Tel:* (089) 71 04 66 60 *Fax:* (089) 71 04 66 61 *E-mail:* olzog.verlag@t-online.de *Web Site:* www.olzog.de, pg 235

Guenther Butkus (Germany) *Tel:* (0521) 69689 *Fax:* (0521) 174470 *E-mail:* pendragon.verlag@t-online.de *Web Site:* www.pendragon.de, pg 235

Edizioni Guerini e Associati SpA (Italy) *Tel:* (02) 582980 *Fax:* (02) 58298030 *E-mail:* guerini@iol.it; info@guerini.it *Web Site:* www.guerini.it, pg 392

The Guernsey Press Co Ltd (United Kingdom) *Tel:* (01481) 240240; (01481) 243657 (ISDN) *Fax:* (01481) 240290; (01481) 249147 *E-mail:* books@guernsey-press.com, pg 1140

The Guernsey Press Co Ltd (United Kingdom) *Tel:* (01481) 240240; (01481) 243657 (ISDN) *Fax:* (01481) 240290; (01481) 249147 *E-mail:* books@guernsey-press.com *Web Site:* www.gp.guernsey-press.com, pg 1161, 1203

The Guernsey Press Co Ltd (United Kingdom) *Tel:* (01481) 240240; (01481) 243657 (ISDN) *Fax:* (01481) 240290; (01481) 249147 *E-mail:* books@guernsey-press.com, pg 1214

Guerra Edizioni Guru Azp (Italy) *Tel:* (075) 5289090 *Fax:* (075) 5288244 *E-mail:* guerra@tecnonet.it *Web Site:* www.guru.it, pg 392

Guetersloher Verlagshaus Gerd Mohn (Germany) *Tel:* (05241) 74050 *Fax:* (05241) 740548 *E-mail:* info@guetersloher-vh.de *Web Site:* www.guetersloher-vh.de, pg 235

Verlag Klaus Guhl (Germany) *Tel:* (030) 3213062 *Fax:* (030) 3215549, pg 235

Guildhall Library (United Kingdom) *Tel:* (020) 7332 1868 (ext 1870) *Fax:* (020) 7600 3384, pg 1506

Editions d'Art Albert Guillot (France) *Tel:* (04) 78521026, pg 167

Livraria Guimaraes (Portugal) *Tel:* (021) 3462436 *Fax:* (021) 3462620, pg 1307

Guimaraes Editores, Lda (Portugal) *Tel:* (021) 3432619; (021) 3462436 *Fax:* (021) 3432620 *E-mail:* guimaraes.ed@mail.telepac.pt *Web Site:* www.guimaraes-ed.pt, pg 525

Guinness Publishing Ltd (United Kingdom) *Tel:* (020) 7891 4567 *Fax:* (020) 7891 4501 *E-mail:* guinness-publishing@guinness.com, pg 690

Guizhou Education Publishing House (China) *Tel:* (0851) 627904; (0851) 524211, pg 106

Gujarat Vidyapith Granthalaya (India) *Tel:* (079) 7541148 *Fax:* (079) 7542547 *E-mail:* gujvi@adinet.emet.in, pg 1473

Gujarat Book Trade Federation (India) *Tel:* (079) 447 634; (079) 447 635, pg 1248

Editorial Gulaab (Spain) *Tel:* (071) 61 86 55 *Fax:* (071) 61 86 55 *E-mail:* osho@arrakis.es, pg 577

Gulur Raudur Grenn og Blar Childrens Bookclub (Iceland) *Tel:* 5102525 *Fax:* 5102525 *E-mail:* klubbar@mm.is, pg 1229

Gummerus Printing (Finland) *Tel:* (014) 683525 *Fax:* (014) 676770; (014) 685166, pg 1154, 1194

Gummerus Publishers (Finland) *Tel:* (09) 584 301 *Fax:* (09) 5843 0200 *Web Site:* www.gummerus.fi/kustannus, pg 142

M D Gunasena & Co Ltd (Sri Lanka) *Tel:* (01) 323981; (01) 323982; (01) 323983; (01) 323984; (01) 544840; (01) 544841; (01) 544824 *Fax:* (01) 323336 *E-mail:* mdgunasena@mail.ewisl.net *Web Site:* mdgunasena.com, pg 597

Gunnar Lie & Associates Ltd (United Kingdom) *Tel:* (020) 8487 9020 *Fax:* (020) 8878 2832, pg 1119

PT BPK Gunung Mulia (Indonesia) *Tel:* (021) 3901208 *Fax:* (021) 3901633 *E-mail:* bpkgm@centrin.net.id *Web Site:* www.bpkgm.com, pg 355

PT BPK Gunung Mulia (Indonesia) *Tel:* (021) 3901208 *E-mail:* trade@bpkgm.com *Web Site:* www.bpkgm.com, pg 1291

Guru Publishers Ltd (Kenya) *Tel:* (02) 764146, pg 431

Verlag des Gustav-Adolf-Werks (Germany) *Tel:* (0341) 490 62 18 *Fax:* (0341) 49 62 66 *E-mail:* gaw-verlag@t-online.de, pg 235

Th Gut Verlag (Switzerland) *Tel:* (01) 9281101 *Fax:* (01) 9285200 *Web Site:* www.gutverlag.ch/, pg 615

Gutenberg-Gesellschaft eV (Germany) *Tel:* (06131) 22 64 20 *Fax:* (06131) 23 35 30 *E-mail:* gutenberg-gesellschaft@freenet.de *Web Site:* www.gutenberg-gesellschaft.uni-mainz.de, pg 235

Gutenberg-Gesellschaft eV (Germany) *Tel:* (06131) 22 64 20 *Fax:* (06131) 23 35 30, pg 1245

GUTENBERG-GESELLSCHAFT-INTERNATIONALE VEREINIGUNG FUR INDUSTRY

Gutenberg-Gesellschaft-Internationale Vereinigung fur Geschichte und Gegenwart der Druckkunst eV (Germany) *Tel:* (06131) 22 64 20 *Fax:* (06131) 23 35 30, pg 1363

Gutenberg Publications (Greece) *Tel:* (01) 3808334 *Fax:* (01) 3642030 *E-mail:* gut_ub@otenet.gr, pg 311

Gutersloher Verlaghaus GmbH /Chr Kaiser/Kiefel/Quell (Germany) *Tel:* (05241) 74050 *Fax:* (05241) 740550 *E-mail:* info@guetersloher-vh.de *Web Site:* www.gtv.de, pg 235

Guthmann & Peterson Liber Libri, Edition (Austria) *Tel:* (01) 877 04 26 *Fax:* (01) 876 40 04 *E-mail:* verlag@guthmann-peterson.at *Web Site:* www.guthmann-peterson.de, pg 52

Guyana Library Association (Guyana) *Tel:* (02) 62690; (02) 62699, pg 1517

Guyana Medical Science Library (Guyana), pg 1471

GVA Publishers Ltd (Switzerland) *Tel:* (022) 3112424 *Fax:* (022) 3112556, pg 615

Gvanim Publishing House (Israel) *Tel:* (03) 5281044; (03) 5283648 *Fax:* (03) 5283648 *E-mail:* traklinm@zahav.net.il, pg 367

Gwasg Carreg Gwalch (United Kingdom) *Tel:* (01492) 642 031 *Fax:* (01492) 641 502 *E-mail:* books@carreg-gwalch.co.uk *Web Site:* www.carreg-gwalch.co.uk, pg 690

Gwasg Prifysgol Cymru (United Kingdom) *Tel:* (029) 2049 6899 *Fax:* (029) 2049 6108 *E-mail:* press@press.wales.ac.uk *Web Site:* www.uwp.co.uk; www.wales.ac.uk/press, pg 690

Gwasg y Dref Wen (United Kingdom) *Tel:* (01222) 617860 *Fax:* (01222) 610507 *E-mail:* gwil-drefwen@btinternet.com, pg 690

Gwasg Gwenffrwd (United Kingdom) *Tel:* (01490) 420 560, pg 690

Gyan Publishing House (India) *Tel:* (011) 3261060; (011) 3282060 *Fax:* (011) 3285914 *E-mail:* gyanbook@del2.vsnl.net.in *Web Site:* www.gyanbooks.com, pg 338

Gyeom-jisa (Republic of Korea) *Tel:* (02) 3351985 *Fax:* (02) 3351986, pg 436

Gyldendal Norsk Forlag A/S (Norway) *Tel:* 22034100 *Fax:* 22034105 *E-mail:* gnf@gyldendal.no *Web Site:* www.gyldendal.no, pg 503

Gyldendals Bornebogklub (Denmark) *Tel:* 33755555 *Fax:* 33755556 *Web Site:* www.gyldendal.dk, pg 1228

Gyldendals Bogklub (Denmark) *Tel:* 33110775 *Fax:* 33110323 *Web Site:* www.glydendal.dk, pg 1228

Gyldendalske Boghandel - Nordisk Forlag A/S (Denmark) *Tel:* 33755555 *Fax:* 33755556 *E-mail:* gyldendal@gyldendal.dk *Web Site:* www.gyldendal.dk, pg 132

Gylym, Izd-Vo (Kazakstan) *Tel:* (03272) 618005; (03272) 618845 *Fax:* (03272) 618845; (03272) 618005, pg 430

Gyosei Corporation (Japan) *Tel:* (03) 53496666 *Fax:* (03) 53496677 *E-mail:* ldz06555@niftyserve.or.jp, pg 417

H & Y Printing Ltd (Hong Kong) *Tel:* 28702379 *Fax:* 25550028 *E-mail:* hyphk@netvigator.com, pg 1134

H B Verlags und Vertriebs-Gesellschaft mbH (Germany) *Tel:* (040) 4151-04 *Fax:* (040) 41513231, pg 235

H I Jaffari & Co Publishers (Pakistan) *Tel:* (051) 811153, pg 506

H K Scanner Arts International Ltd (Hong Kong) *Tel:* 29760302 *Fax:* 29760292, pg 1156

H L Schlapp Buch- und Antiquariatshandlung GmbH und Co KG Abt Verlag (Germany) *Tel:* (06151) 17 90-0 *Fax:* (06151) 17 90 40 *E-mail:* hlschlapp@aol.com *Web Site:* www.schlapp.de, pg 235

Verlag H M Hauschild GmbH (Germany) *Tel:* (0421) 1785-0; (0421) 407040 *Fax:* (0421) 1785-285 *E-mail:* info@hauschild-werbedruck.de *Web Site:* www.hauschild.werbedruck.de, pg 235

Haag und Herchen Verlag GmbH (Germany) *Tel:* (069) 550911-13 *Fax:* (069) 552601; (069) 554922 *E-mail:* verlag@haagundherchen.de *Web Site:* www.haagundherchen.de, pg 235

C W Haarfeld GmbH & Co (Germany) *Tel:* (0201) 720950 *Fax:* (0201) 7209533, pg 235

Wolfgang G Haas - Musikverlag Koeln ek (Germany) *Tel:* (02203) 98 88 3-0 *Fax:* (02203) 98 88 3-50 *E-mail:* info@haas-koeln.de *Web Site:* www.haas-koeln.de, pg 235

P Haase & Sons Forlag A/S (Denmark) *Tel:* 33144175 *Fax:* 33115959 *E-mail:* haase@haase.dk *Web Site:* www.haase.dk, pg 132

Dr Rudolf Habelt GmbH (Germany) *Tel:* (0228) 9 23 83-0 *Fax:* (0228) 9 23 83-6 *E-mail:* info@habelt.de *Web Site:* www.habelt.de, pg 235

Habermann Institute for Literary Research (Israel) *Tel:* (08) 9244569; (08) 9229384 *Fax:* (08) 9249466 *E-mail:* zmalachi@post.tau.ac.il, pg 367

Hachette Livre SA - H E D (France) *Tel:* (01) 43923000 *Fax:* (01) 43923030, pg 1283

Hachette Education (France) *Tel:* (01) 43923000; (01) 43923516 *Fax:* (01) 43923501, pg 167

Hachette francais langue etrangere - FLE (France) *Tel:* (01) 46 62 10 10 *Fax:* (01) 40 95 10 39 *E-mail:* fle@hachette-livre.fr *Web Site:* www.fle.hachette.livre.fr, pg 167

Hachette Jeunesse Image (France) *Tel:* (01) 43923000 *Fax:* (01) 43923030, pg 167

Hachette JeunesseRoman (France) *Tel:* (01) 43923000 *Fax:* (01) 43923222, pg 167

Hachette Livre (France) *Tel:* (01) 43923000; (01) 43923587 *Fax:* (01) 43923030; (01) 43923585, pg 167

Hachette Pratiques (France) *Tel:* (01) 43923238 *Fax:* (01) 43923030, pg 167

Hachmeister Verlag (Germany) *Tel:* (0251) 51210 *Fax:* (0251) 57217 *E-mail:* hachmeister.galerie@t-online.de *Web Site:* www.hachmeister-galerie.de, pg 236

Hadar Publishing House Ltd (Israel) *Tel:* (08) 9246565 *Fax:* (08) 9251770 *E-mail:* info@zmora.co.il, pg 367

Peter Haddock Ltd (United Kingdom) *Tel:* (01262) 678121 *Fax:* (01262) 400043 *E-mail:* enquiries@peterhaddock.com *Web Site:* phaddock.sslserver.co.uk, pg 690

Walter Haedecke Verlag (Germany) *Tel:* (07033) 13 80 80 *Fax:* (07033) 13 80 813 *E-mail:* haedecke_vlg@t-online.de, pg 236

Haedong (Republic of Korea) *Tel:* (02) 953707 (Source lists phone w/o 1st digit) *Fax:* (02) 953707, pg 436

Dr Curt Haefner-Verlag GmbH (Germany) *Tel:* (06221) 64 46-0 *Fax:* (06221) 64 46-40 *E-mail:* info@haefner-verlag.de *Web Site:* www.haefner-verlag.de, pg 236

Dr Haensel-Hohenhausen AG (Germany) *Tel:* (069) 40894-0 *Fax:* (069) 40894-194 *E-mail:* info@haensel-hohenhausen.de *Web Site:* www.german-library.com, pg 236

Haenssler Verlag GmbH (Germany) *Tel:* (07158) 1770 *Fax:* (07158) 177119; (07158) 177100 *E-mail:* info@haenssler.de *Web Site:* www.haenssler.de, pg 236

Haere Po No Tahiti (French Polynesia) *Tel:* 582636 *Fax:* 582333, pg 190

Haering, Siegfried, Literaten-Verlag Ulm (Germany) *Tel:* (0731) 9806040 *Fax:* (0731) 9806042 *E-mail:* ratart.edition@t-online.de, pg 236

Heinz-Jurgen Hausser (Germany) *Tel:* (06151) 22824 *Fax:* (06151) 26854, pg 236

Haffmans Verlag AG (Switzerland) *Tel:* (01 386 4000 *Fax:* (01) 386 4001 *E-mail:* verlag@haffmans.ch, pg 615

Hagaberg AB (Sweden) *Tel:* (08) 6909000 *Fax:* (08) 7021940, pg 603

Lehrmittelverlag Wilhelm Hagemann GmbH (Germany) *Tel:* (0211) 17 92 70-0 *Fax:* (0211) 17 92 70-70 *E-mail:* aktuell@hagemann.de *Web Site:* www.hagemann.de, pg 236

Hagen & Stam Uitgeverij Ten (Netherlands) *Tel:* (070) 3045888; (070) 3045700 *Fax:* (070) 3045800; (070) 3045806, pg 478

Hagenbach & Bender GMBH (Switzerland) *Tel:* (31) 3816666 *Fax:* (31) 3816677 *E-mail:* rights@hagenbach-bender.com *Web Site:* www.hagenbach-bender.com, pg 615

Hahndorf Academy Foundation Inc (Australia) *Tel:* (08) 3887250 *E-mail:* info@postcards.sa.com.au, pg 24

Hahner Verlagsgesellschaft mbH (Germany) *Tel:* (02408) 55 05 *Fax:* (02408) 58081 *E-mail:* office@hvg.de, pg 236

Mary Hahn's Kochbuchverlag (Germany) *Tel:* (089) 2 90 88-0 *Fax:* (089) 29088154 *E-mail:* l.eggs@herbig.net *Web Site:* www.herbig.net, pg 236

Hahnsche Buchhandlung (Germany) *Tel:* (0511) 80 71 80 40 *Fax:* (0511) 36 36 98 *E-mail:* verlag-hahnsche-buchhandlung@t-online.de, pg 236

Chu Hai Publishing (Taiwan) Co Ltd (Taiwan, Province of China) *Tel:* (02) 7039867 *Fax:* (02) 7084804, pg 630

Haifa University Press (Israel) *Tel:* (04) 8240111 *Fax:* (04) 8342245 *Web Site:* www.haifa.ac.il, pg 368

Haigh & Hochland Ltd (United Kingdom) *Tel:* (061) 2734156 *Fax:* (061) 2734340, pg 1320

Hainaim Publishing Co Ltd (Republic of Korea) *Tel:* (02) 326-1600; (02) 701-6819 *Fax:* (02) 326-1625, pg 436

Hak Won Publishing Co (Republic of Korea) *Tel:* (02) 7414621; (02) 7414623 *Fax:* (02) 7654584, pg 436

Hakgojae Publishing Inc (Republic of Korea) *Tel:* (02) 7361713 *Fax:* (02) 7398592 *E-mail:* hkjass@hitel.kol.co.kr, pg 436

Hakibbutz Hameuchad Publishing House Ltd (Israel) *Tel:* (03) 5785810 *Fax:* (03) 5785811, pg 368

Hakluyt Society (United Kingdom) *Tel:* (01428) 641850 *Fax:* (01428) 641933 *E-mail:* office@hakluyt.com *Web Site:* www.hakluyt.com, pg 691, 1371

Hakmun Publishing, Co (Republic of Korea) *Tel:* (02) 733-1340 *Fax:* (02) 733-1350 *E-mail:* hakmun97@soback.kornet.nm.kr, pg 436

Hakubunkan-Shinsha Publishers Ltd (Japan) *Tel:* (03) 38114721 *Fax:* (03) 38181431, pg 417

Hakusui-Sha Co Ltd (Japan) *Tel:* (03) 32917811 *Fax:* (03) 32918448, pg 417

Hakutei-Sha (Japan) *Tel:* (03) 39863271 *Fax:* (03) 39863272, pg 417

Hakuyo-Sha (Japan) *Tel:* (03) 5281-9772 *Fax:* (03) 5281-9886 *E-mail:* hakuyo@mars.dti.ne.jp *Web Site:* www.hakuyo-sha.co.jp, pg 417

Hakuyu-Sha (Japan) *Tel:* (03) 32688271 *Fax:* (03) 32688273, pg 417

Peter Halban Publishers Ltd (United Kingdom) *Tel:* (020) 7437 9300 *Fax:* (020) 7431 9512 *E-mail:* books@halbanpublishers.com *Web Site:* www.halbanpublishers.com, pg 691

Halbooks Publishing (Australia) *Tel:* (02) 9918 7043 *Fax:* (02) 9973 1081, pg 24

Halcyon Publishing Ltd (New Zealand) *Tel:* (09) 4895337 *Fax:* (09) 4895218 *E-mail:* info@halcyonpublishing.co.nz, pg 491

Haldane Mason (United Kingdom) *Tel:* (020) 8459 2131 *Fax:* (020) 8728 1216 *E-mail:* syd.hm@gtclick.com, pg 691

Hale & Iremonger Pty Ltd (Australia) *Tel:* (02) 9560 0470 *Fax:* (02) 9550 0097 *E-mail:* info@haleiremonger.com *Web Site:* www.haleiremonger.com, pg 24

Robert Hale Ltd (United Kingdom) *Tel:* (020) 7251 2661 *Fax:* (020) 7490 4958 *E-mail:* enquire@halebooks.com *Web Site:* www.halebooks.com, pg 691

Robert Hale Ltd (United Kingdom) *Tel:* (020) 7251 2661 *Fax:* (020) 7490 4958 *E-mail:* english@halebooks.com *Web Site:* www.halebooks.com, pg 1141

Halldale Publishing & Media Ltd (United Kingdom) *Tel:* (01252) 532000 *Fax:* (01252) 512714, pg 691

Hallgren och Fallgren Studieforlag AB (Sweden) *Tel:* (018) 507100 *Fax:* (018) 127270 *E-mail:* info@hallgren-fallgren.se, pg 603

Hallwag AG (Switzerland) *Tel:* (031) 423131 *Fax:* (031) 414133 *E-mail:* office@hallweb.ch *Web Site:* www.hallweb.ch, pg 615

Hallwag AG (Switzerland) *Tel:* (031) 423131 *Fax:* (031) 414133, pg 1139

Hallwag AG (Switzerland) *Tel:* (031) 423131 *Fax:* (031) 414133 *E-mail:* kartenverlag@hallwag.com, pg 1160

Hallwag AG (Switzerland) *Tel:* (031) 423131 *Fax:* (031) 414133 *E-mail:* kartenverlag@hallwag.ch, pg 1201

Hallwag Verlag GmbH (Germany) *Tel:* (0711) 449840 *Fax:* (0711) 4498460, pg 236

F H Halpern (Australia) *Tel:* (03) 9534 6033 *Fax:* (03) 9534 3998, pg 25

The Hambledon Press (United Kingdom) *Tel:* (020) 7586 0817 *Fax:* (020) 7586 9970 *E-mail:* office@hambledon.co.uk *Web Site:* www.hambledon.co.uk, pg 691

Hamburger Lesehefte Verlag Iselt & Co Nfl mbH (Germany) *Tel:* (04841) 8352-0 *Fax:* (04841) 8352-10 *E-mail:* verlagsgruppe.husum@t-online.de *Web Site:* www.verlagsgruppe.de, pg 236

Hamburgh Press (Guyana) *Tel:* (02) 58486 *Fax:* (02) 58511, pg 317

Hamburgisches Welt-Wirtschafts-Archiv (HWWA) Bibliothek (Germany) *Tel:* (040) 42834 242 *Fax:* (040) 42834 550 *E-mail:* biblio@hwwa.de *Web Site:* www.hwwa.de, pg 1467

Libreria Hamburgo SA (Mexico) *Tel:* (05) 5126796; (05) 5218265, pg 1299

Hamdard Foundation (Pakistan) *Tel:* (021) 6616001; (021) 6616002; (021) 6616003; (021) 6616004; (021) 641766 *Fax:* (021) 6611755 *E-mail:* hlpak@net3.ptc.pk, pg 507

Liselotte Hamecher (Germany) *Tel:* (0561) 16611 *Fax:* (0561) 775262, pg 236

Kerri Hamer (Australia) *Tel:* (02) 93495170 *Fax:* (02) 93495170, pg 25

Hamilton Printing Co (United States) *Tel:* 518-732-4491 *Fax:* 518-732-7714, pg 1143, 1206, 1224

Hamish Hamilton Ltd (United Kingdom) *Tel:* (020) 7416 3000 *Fax:* (020) 7416 3099 *Web Site:* www.penguin.co.uk, pg 691

Hamlyn (United Kingdom) *Tel:* (020) 7531 8400 *Fax:* (020) 7531 8650 *Web Site:* www.hamlyn.co.uk, pg 691

Geoffrey Hamlyn-Harris (Australia) *Tel:* (0746) 811450; (018) 063662 *Fax:* (018) 063662, pg 25

Hammarskjold Memorial Library (Zambia) *Tel:* (02) 214572; (02) 219012; (02) 211488 *Fax:* (02) 211001, pg 1509

Alfred Hammer (Germany) *Tel:* (06078) 71622 *Fax:* (06078) 71655, pg 236

Peter Hammer Verlag GmbH (Germany) *Tel:* (0202) 505066; (0202) 505067 *Fax:* (0202) 509252 *E-mail:* peter-hammer-verlag@t-online.de *Web Site:* www.peter-hammer-verlag.de, pg 237

Maison d'Edition Mohamed Ali Hammi (Tunisia) *Tel:* (04) 224534 *Fax:* (04) 211552, pg 638

Hammicks Bookshops Ltd (United Kingdom) *Tel:* (0181) 8995060 (head office & general inquiries) *Fax:* (0181) 8995075, pg 1320

Hammond Bindery Ltd (United Kingdom) *Tel:* (01924) 369598 *Fax:* (01924) 364108, pg 1203, 1214, 1223

Hammond Packaging Ltd (United Kingdom) *Tel:* (0113) 2423548 *Fax:* (0113) 2445442 *E-mail:* hammpack@dial.pipex.com *Web Site:* www.hammpack.co.uk, pg 1141, 1161, 1203

Hammonia-Verlag GmbH Fachverlag der Wohnungswirtschaft (Germany) *Tel:* (040) 520 103-0 *Fax:* (040) 520 103-30 *E-mail:* info@hammonia.de *Web Site:* www.hvh.de, pg 237

Otzar Hamore (Israel) *Tel:* (03) 6922983 *Fax:* (03) 6922903, pg 368

Hampden Press (Australia) *Tel:* (02) 9712 5755 *Fax:* (02) 9712 5756, pg 25

Hanjin Publishing Co (Republic of Korea) *Tel:* (02) 7137453 *Fax:* (02) 7135510, pg 436

Hand-Presse (Austria) *Tel:* (0512) 87975, pg 52

H&H Publishing (Australia) *Tel:* (03) 6307 624 *Fax:* (03) 9877 4222 *E-mail:* mvent@iaccess.com.au, pg 25

The Handsel Press (United Kingdom) *E-mail:* handsel@dial.pipex.com *Web Site:* www.handselpress.co.uk, pg 691

Verlag Handwerk und Technik GmbH (Germany) *Tel:* (040) 5 38 08-0 *Fax:* (040) 5 38 08-101 *Web Site:* www.handwerk-technik-shop.de, pg 237

Hangil Art Vision (Republic of Korea) *Tel:* (02) 5154811 *Fax:* (02) 5154816, pg 436

Hanguk Seoji Hakhoe (Republic of Korea) *Tel:* (02) 784-3561 *Fax:* (02) 788-3385, pg 1519

Hanguk Tosogwan Hakhoe (Republic of Korea) *Tel:* (02) 7600114 *Fax:* (02) 7442453, pg 1519

Hanitzotz A-Sharara Publishing House (Israel) *Tel:* (03) 6839145 *Fax:* (03) 6839148 *E-mail:* oda@netvision.net.il *Web Site:* www.odaction.org; www.hanitzotz.com/challenge, pg 368

Fred Hanna Ltd (Ireland) *Tel:* (01) 6771255; (01) 8720797 *Fax:* (01) 6714330 *E-mail:* hannas@indigo.ie, pg 1291

Hannibal-Verlag (Germany) *Tel:* (089) 857 95-0 *Fax:* (089) 857 95 294 *E-mail:* info@hannibal-verlag.de *Web Site:* www.hannibal-verlag.de, pg 237

The Hannon Press (Ireland) *Tel:* (0405) 46089 *Fax:* (0405) 46089, pg 361

Universitaetsbibliothek Hannover und Technische Informationsbibliothek (Germany) *Tel:* (0511) 7622268 *Fax:* (0511) 715936 *E-mail:* ubtib@tib.uni-hannover.de *Web Site:* www.tib.uni-hannover.de, pg 1467

Hans Furstelberger (Austria) *Tel:* (0732) 773177 *Fax:* (0732) 784485, pg 1274

Hans Prakashan (India) *Tel:* (0532) 623077 *E-mail:* ar@nde.vsnl.net.in, pg 338

Hansa Verlag Ingwert Paulsen Jr (Germany) *Tel:* (04841) 8352-0 *Fax:* (04841) 8352-10 *E-mail:* verlagsgruppe.husum@t-online.de *Web Site:* www.verlagsgruppe.de, pg 237

Hanse Production AB (Sweden) *Tel:* 0498 249318 *Fax:* 0498 249318, pg 603

Edition Wilhelm Hansen AS (Denmark) *Tel:* 33117888 *Fax:* 33148178 *E-mail:* ewh@ewh.dk *Web Site:* www.ewh.dk; www.wilhelm-hansen.dk, pg 132

Carl Hanser Verlag (Germany) *Tel:* (089) 9 98 30 0 *Fax:* (089) 98 48 09 *E-mail:* info@hanser.de *Web Site:* www.hanser.de/verlag/, pg 237

Soederbokhandeln Hansson och Bruce AB (Sweden) *Tel:* (08) 405432; (08) 6405433 *Fax:* (08) 6441315, pg 1312

Hanthawaddy Bookshop (Myanmar), pg 1300

Hanthawaddy Book House (Myanmar), pg 471

Hanul Publishing Co (Republic of Korea) *Tel:* (02) 3260095; (02) 3366183 *Fax:* (02) 3337543 *E-mail:* newhanul@nuri.net, pg 436

Happy Books (Zimbabwe) *Tel:* (04) 8871414, pg 768

Happy Cat Books Ltd (United Kingdom) *Tel:* (01255) 870902 *Fax:* (01255) 870902 *E-mail:* mcwest@happycat.co.uk, pg 691

Happy Mental Buch- und Musik Verlag (Germany) *Tel:* (08158) 993303 *Fax:* (08158) 993305, pg 237

Har-El Printers & Publishers (Israel) *Tel:* (03) 6816834 *Fax:* (03) 6813563 *Web Site:* www.interart.co.il/harel, pg 1136

Har-El Printers & Publishers (Israel) *Tel:* (03) 6816834 *Fax:* (03) 6813563 *E-mail:* mharel@harelart.co.il *Web Site:* www.interart.co.il/harel, pg 1157, 1198

Harare City Library (Zimbabwe) *Tel:* (04) 751834; 751835, pg 1509

Harare Polytechnic Library (Zimbabwe) *Tel:* (04) 752311, pg 1509

Editora Harbra Ltda (Brazil) *Tel:* (011) 5084-2403; (011) 5084-2482; (011) 5571-1122; (011) 5549-2244; (011) 5571-0276 *Fax:* (011) 5575-6876; (011) 5571-9777 *E-mail:* editorial@harbra.com.br *Web Site:* www.harbra.com.br, pg 84

Harcourt Australia Pty Ltd (Australia) *Tel:* (02) 5178999 *Fax:* (02) 5172249, pg 25

Harcourt Publishers Ltd (United Kingdom) *Tel:* (0171) 7424 4200 Toll Free *Tel:* 888-677-7357 *Fax:* (0171) 7482 2293 *E-mail:* ecare@harcourt.com *Web Site:* www.harcourt.com, pg 691

Harden's Ltd (United Kingdom) *Tel:* (020) 7839 4763 *Fax:* (020) 7839 7561 *E-mail:* mail@hardens.com *Web Site:* www.hardens.com, pg 692

Hardt und Worner Marketing fur das Buch (Germany) *Tel:* (06172) 7005 *Fax:* (01672) 71547 *E-mail:* hardt.woerner@t-online.de, pg 237

Norman Hardy Printing Group (United Kingdom) *Tel:* (020) 7378 1579 *Fax:* (020) 7378 6421 *E-mail:* info@normanwhardy.co.uk *Web Site:* www.normanwhardy.com, pg 1203

Patrick Hardy Books (United Kingdom) *Tel:* (01223) 350865 *Fax:* (01223) 366951 *E-mail:* sales@lutterworth.com; publishing@lutterworth.com *Web Site:* www.lutterworth.com, pg 692

Thomas Hardy Society (United Kingdom) *Tel:* (01305) 251501 *Fax:* (01305) 251501 *E-mail:* info@hardysociety.org *Web Site:* hardysociety.org, pg 1371

Harenberg Kommunikation Verlags- und Medien GmbH & Co KG (Germany) *Tel:* (0231) 9056-0 *Fax:* (0231) 9056-110 *E-mail:* post@harenberg.de *Web Site:* www.harenberg.de, pg 237

Hargreen Publishing Co (Australia) *Tel:* (03) 9329 9714 *Fax:* (03) 3295295, pg 25

Harlenic Hellas Publishing SA (Greece) *Tel:* (01) 3609438 *Fax:* (01) 3614846 *E-mail:* harlenic@otenet.gr *Web Site:* www.harlenic.gr, pg 311

Harlequin Books (Australia) *Tel:* (02) 9415 9200 *Fax:* (02) 417-5232 *E-mail:* bhobbs@romance.net.au, pg 25

Harlequin Iberica SA (Spain) *Tel:* (091) 4358712 *Fax:* (091) 4310484, pg 577

Harlequin SA (France) *Tel:* (01) 42166363 *Fax:* (01) 45828694, pg 167

Harley Books (United Kingdom) *Tel:* (01206) 271216 *Fax:* (01206) 271182 *E-mail:* harley@keme.co.uk *Web Site:* www.harleybooks.com, pg 692

L'Harmattan (France) *Tel:* (01) 40 46 79 11; (01) 40 46 79 20 *Fax:* (01) 43 25 82 03 *E-mail:* harmat@ worldnet.fr *Web Site:* www.editions-harmattan.fr, pg 168

Harmi-Press Publications, Haroula D Papadimitriou G P (Greece) *Tel:* (01) 3456734 *Fax:* (01) 3474732, pg 311

De Harmonie (Netherlands) *Tel:* (020) 6245181 *Fax:* (020) 6230672 *E-mail:* info@deharmonie.nl *Web Site:* www.deharmonie.nl, pg 478

HarperCollins Publishers (New Zealand) Ltd (New Zealand) *Tel:* (09) 4439400 *Fax:* (09) 4439403 *E-mail:* editors@harpercollins.co.nz *Web Site:* www.harpercollins.co.nz, pg 491

HarperCollins Publishers (United Kingdom) *Tel:* (020) 8741 7070 *Toll Free Tel:* (0870) 900 2050 (cust serv) *Fax:* (020) 8307 4440 *Toll Free Fax:* (0141) 306 3767 (cust serv) *Web Site:* www.harpercollins.com, pg 692

HarperCollins Publishers (Australia) Pty Limited (Australia) *Tel:* (02) 9952 5445 *Fax:* (02) 9952 5544 *Web Site:* www.harpercollins.com.au, pg 25

HarperCollins Publishers India Pty Ltd (India) *Tel:* (011) 3278586; (011) 3272161 *Fax:* (011) 3277294, pg 338

HarperCollins Publishers Zimbabwe Pvt Ltd (Zimbabwe) *Tel:* (04) 721413; (04) 727516 *Fax:* (04) 721413, pg 768

HarperCollins Religious (South Africa) *Tel:* (011) 6222900 *Fax:* (011) 6223553, pg 554

Otto Harrassowitz Wissenschaftliche Buchhandlung & Zeitschriftenagentur (Germany) *Tel:* (0611) 5300 *Fax:* (0611) 530560 *E-mail:* service@harrassowitz.de *Web Site:* www.harrassowitz.de, pg 1284

Harrassowitz Verlag (Germany) *Tel:* (0611) 530-0 *Fax:* (0611) 530-570; (0611) 530-560 (orders) *E-mail:* verlag@harrassowitz.de; service@ harrassowitz.de *Web Site:* www.harrassowitz.de, pg 237

Harris (Indonesia) *Tel:* (061) 22272, pg 355

Harris-Elon Agency (Israel) *Tel:* (02) 672 2143/5 *Fax:* (02) 672 5797 *E-mail:* litagent@netvision.net.il, pg 1113

Harry Joe Patsis' European Publications' Center Ltd (Greece) *Tel:* (01) 3841040; (01) 3841050 *Fax:* (01) 6232194, pg 1286

Hart Publishing (United Kingdom) *Tel:* (01865) 245533 *Fax:* (01865) 794882 *E-mail:* mail@hartpub.co.uk *Web Site:* www.hartpub.co.uk, pg 692

Harth Musik Verlag-Pro musica Verlag GmbH (Germany) *Tel:* (02204) 2003-0 *Fax:* (02204) 2003-33, pg 237

A Hartleben Inhaber Dr Walter Rob (Austria) *Tel:* (0222) 5126236, pg 1274

Litteraturverlag Karlheinz Hartmann (Germany) *Tel:* (06007) 7622 *Fax:* (069) 614606, pg 237

Hartys Creek Press (Australia) *Tel:* (02) 65871100, pg 25

Harvard University Press (United Kingdom) *Tel:* (020) 7306 0603 *Fax:* (020) 7306 0604 *E-mail:* info@hup-mitpress.co.uk *Web Site:* www.hup.harvard.edu, pg 692

Denise Harvey (Greece) *Tel:* (02270) 31154 *Fax:* (02270) 31154, pg 311

Harvey Map Services Ltd (United Kingdom) *Tel:* (01786) 841202 *Fax:* (01786) 841098 *E-mail:* sales@harveymaps.co.uk *Web Site:* www.harveymaps.co.uk, pg 692

Roland Harvey Studios (Australia) *Tel:* (03) 9646 8711 *Fax:* (03) 9646 2245, pg 25

Harveys Ltd (United Kingdom) *Tel:* (0131) 4400074 *Fax:* (0131) 4403478 *E-mail:* sales@harveys.ltd.uk, pg 1203, 1214

The Harvill Press Ltd (United Kingdom) *Tel:* (020) 7704 8766 *Fax:* (020) 7704 8805 *E-mail:* info@harvill-press.com *Web Site:* www.harvill-press.com, pg 693

Library of Hasanuddin University (Indonesia) *Tel:* (0411) 512026 *Fax:* (0411) 510088, pg 1474

Haschemi Edition Cologne Kunstverlag (Germany) *Tel:* (0221) 561007; (0221) 561008 *Fax:* (0221) 529282 *E-mail:* info@haschemi.de *Web Site:* www.haschemi.de, pg 237

von Hase & Koehler Verlag KG (Germany) *Tel:* (06131) 232334 *Fax:* (06131) 227952, pg 238

Hasefer (Romania) *Tel:* (021) 312 22 84 *Fax:* (021) 312 22 84 *E-mail:* hasefer@fx.ro, pg 533

Haseo Publishing Co (Republic of Korea) *Tel:* (02) 2378161; (02) 2378165 *Fax:* (02) 2376575, pg 436

Drukkerij Scherpenheuvel Haseth (Netherlands Antilles) *Tel:* (09) 7671134, pg 488

Haskolautgafan - University of Iceland Press (Iceland) *Tel:* 5694361; 5694300 *Fax:* 5521331 *E-mail:* jorig@ rhi.hi.is, pg 328

Hastings Publishing Co (United Kingdom) *Tel:* (01424) 712 765, pg 1203

Hat Box Press (Australia) *Tel:* (03) 97492510, pg 25

Hatagu Sip Alapitvany (Hungary) *Tel:* (01) 140-3728; (01) 140-1717; (01) 111-3033, pg 324

Hatchards Ltd (United Kingdom) *Tel:* (020) 7439 9921 *Fax:* (020) 7494 1313 *E-mail:* books@hatchards.co.uk *Web Site:* www.hatchards.co.uk, pg 1320

Beth Hatefutsoth (Israel) *Tel:* (03) 646 2020 *Fax:* (03) 646 2134 *E-mail:* bhwebmas@post.tau.ac.il *Web Site:* www.bh.org.il/General/index.asp, pg 368

Editions Hatier SA (France) *Tel:* (01) 49 54 49 54 *Fax:* (01) 40 49 00 45 *Web Site:* www.editions-hatier.fr, pg 168

Hatje Cantz Verlag (Germany) *Tel:* (0711) 44 05-0 *Fax:* (0711) 44 05-220 *E-mail:* contact@hatjecantz.de *Web Site:* www.hatjecantz.de, pg 238

Hatta Foundation Library (Indonesia) *Tel:* (0274) 87747 *Fax:* (0274) 87747, pg 1474

Hatter Lap- es Konyvkiado Kft (Hungary) *Tel:* (01) 1315101 *Fax:* (01) 1315101, pg 324

Haude und Spenersche Verlagsbuchhandlung (Germany) *Tel:* (030) 6917073 *Fax:* (030) 6914067, pg 238

Haufe Mediengruppe (Germany) *Tel:* (0761) 3683-0 *Fax:* (0761) 3683-195 *E-mail:* online@information-verlag.de *Web Site:* www.haufe.de, pg 238

Rudolf Haufe Verlag GmbH & Co KG (Germany) *Tel:* (0761) 3683-0 *Fax:* (0761) 3683-195 *E-mail:* online@haufe.de *Web Site:* www.haufe.de, pg 238

Karl F Haug Verlag GmbH & Co (Germany) *Tel:* (00711) 8931-0 *Fax:* (0711) 8931-706 *Web Site:* www.haug-verlag.de/, pg 238

HAUM Booksellers (South Africa) *Tel:* (012) 3228474, pg 1310

HAUM - Daan Retief Publishers (Pty) Ltd (South Africa) *Tel:* (012) 3228474 *Fax:* (012) 3222424, pg 555

HAUM - De Jager Publishers (South Africa) *Tel:* (012) 3284620 *Fax:* (012) 3284706; (012) 3283809, pg 555

HAUM (Hollandsch Afrikaansche Uitgevers Maatschappij) (South Africa) *Tel:* (012) 32284620 *Fax:* (012) 3284706; (012) 3283809, pg 555

Paul Haupt Berne (Switzerland) *Tel:* (031) 3012345 *Fax:* (031) 3014669 *E-mail:* verlag@haupt.ch *Web Site:* www.haupt.ch, pg 615

Hauptverband des Oesterreichischen Buchhandels (Austria) *Tel:* (01) 5121535 *Fax:* (01) 5128482 *Web Site:* www.buecher.at, pg 1237

Dr Ernst Hauswedell & Co Verlag (Germany) *Tel:* (0711) 54 99 71-0; (0711) 54 99 71-11 *Fax:* (0711) 54 99 71-21, pg 238

Pierre Hautot SA (France) *Tel:* (01) 42 61 10 15 *Fax:* (01) 49 27 00 06, pg 168

Uitgeverij Ten Have (Netherlands) *Tel:* (038) 3392555 *Fax:* (038) 3327331, pg 478

Hawk Books (United Kingdom) *Tel:* (01326) 376633 *Fax:* (01326) 376669, pg 693

Hawker Brownlow (Australia) *Tel:* (03) 9555-1344 *Fax:* (03) 9553-4538 *E-mail:* brown@hbe.com.au *Web Site:* www.hbe.com.au/custserv.html, pg 25

Hawker Publications Ltd (United Kingdom) *Tel:* (020) 7720 2108 *Fax:* (020) 7498 3023 *E-mail:* hawker@ hawkerpubs.demon.co.uk *Web Site:* www.careinfo.org, pg 693

Hawthorn Press (United Kingdom) *Tel:* (01453) 757040 *Fax:* (01453) 751138 *E-mail:* hawthornpress@ hawthornpress.com *Web Site:* www.hawthornpress.com, pg 693

Hawthorns Publications Ltd (United Kingdom) *Tel:* (01959) 522368 *Fax:* (01959) 522368, pg 693

Hayakawa Publishing Inc (Japan) *Tel:* (03) 32541551 *Fax:* (03) 32541550, pg 417

Hayes Publishing (Australia) *Tel:* (07) 3379 4137 *Fax:* (07) 3379 4137, pg 26

Imprimerie Hayez SPRL (Belgium) *Tel:* (02) 413 02 00 *Fax:* (02) 411 23 78 *E-mail:* com@hayez.be *Web Site:* www.hayez.be, pg 69

Hayit Nederland BV (Netherlands) *Tel:* (020) 6384980 *Fax:* (020) 6384975, pg 478

Hayit Reisefuhrer in der Rutsker Verlag GmbH (Germany) *Tel:* (0221) 921635-0 *Fax:* (0221) 921635-24 *E-mail:* kontakt@hayit.com *Web Site:* www.hayit.com, pg 238

Haymon-Verlag GesmbH (Austria) *Tel:* (0512) 576300 *Fax:* (0512) 576300-14 *E-mail:* office@haymonverlag.at *Web Site:* www.haymonverlag.at, pg 52

Haynes Publishing (United Kingdom) *Tel:* (01963) 442030; (01963) 442080 (trade) *Fax:* (01963) 440001 (trade) *E-mail:* sales@haynes-manuals.co.uk *Web Site:* www.haynes.co.uk, pg 693

Fernand Hazan Editeur SA (France) *Tel:* (01) 44 41 17 00 *Fax:* (01) 44 41 17 09, pg 168

Hazard Press Ltd (New Zealand) *Tel:* (03) 3770370 *Fax:* (03) 3770390 *E-mail:* quentinw@hazard.co.nz, pg 491

Hazleton Publishing Ltd (United Kingdom) *Tel:* (020) 8948 5151 *Fax:* (020) 8948 4111 *E-mail:* info@hazletonpublishing.com *Web Site:* www.hazletonpublishing.com, pg 693

HB Media Holdings Pte Ltd (Singapore) *Tel:* 2591919 *Fax:* 3532616, pg 1138

HB Publications (United Kingdom) *Tel:* (020) 8769 1585 *Fax:* (020) 8769 2320 *E-mail:* sales@hbpublications.com *Web Site:* www.hbpublications.com, pg 693

Headley Brothers Ltd (United Kingdom) *Tel:* (01233) 623131 *Fax:* (01233) 622704; (01233) 612345 *E-mail:* rpitt@headley.co.uk, pg 1161

Headley Brothers Ltd (United Kingdom) *Tel:* (01233) 623131 *Fax:* (01233) 622704; (01233) 612345 *E-mail:* printing@headley.co.uk *Web Site:* www.headley.co.uk, pg 1203

Headley Brothers Ltd (United Kingdom) *Tel:* (01233) 623131 *Fax:* (01233) 622704; (01233) 612345, pg 1223

Headline Book Publishing Ltd (United Kingdom) *Tel:* (020) 7873 6000 *Fax:* (020) 7873 6124 *E-mail:* headline.books@headline.co.uk *Web Site:* www.madaboutbooks.com, pg 693

Health Development Agency (United Kingdom) *Tel:* (020) 7430 0850 *Fax:* (020) 7061 3390 *E-mail:* hda.enquirydesk@hda-online.org.uk *Web Site:* www.hda-online.org.uk, pg 694

Health Sciences Associates International (United Kingdom) *Tel:* (020) 8876 2340 *Fax:* (020) 8392 9845, pg 1320

Heartland Publishing Ltd (United Kingdom) *Tel:* (01622) 843040 *Fax:* (01622) 843040 *E-mail:* publish@heartland.co.uk *Web Site:* www.heartland.co.uk, pg 694

A M Heath & Co Ltd (United Kingdom) *Tel:* (020) 7836 4271 *Fax:* (020) 7497 2561 *E-mail:* amheath@demon.co.uk, pg 1119

Heavenly Lotus Publishing Co, Ltd (Taiwan, Province of China) *Tel:* (02) 8736629 *Fax:* (02) 8736709, pg 630

Hebrew University of Jerusalem (Israel) *Tel:* (02) 6585017 *Fax:* (02) 6511771 *Web Site:* jnul.huji.ac.il/rambi, pg 1476

Hebrew Writers Association of Israel (Israel) *Tel:* (03) 6953256 *Fax:* (03) 6919681, pg 1249

Heckners Verlag (Germany) *Tel:* (05331) 8008-0 *Fax:* (05331) 8008-58, pg 238

Hedley's Bookshop Ltd (New Zealand) *Tel:* (06) 3782875 *Fax:* (06) 3782570, pg 1302

Heel Verlag GmbH (Germany) *Tel:* (02223) 92 30-0 *Fax:* (02223) 92 30-13; (02223) 92-30-26 *E-mail:* info@heel-verlag.de *Web Site:* www.heel-verlag.de, pg 238

Heffers Booksellers & Library Suppliers (United Kingdom) *Tel:* (01223) 568568 *Fax:* (01223) 568591 *E-mail:* heffers@heffers.co.uk *Web Site:* www.heffers.co.uk, pg 1320

Bokforlaget Hegas AB (Sweden) *Tel:* (042) 330 340 *Fax:* (042) 330 141 *E-mail:* info@hegas.se, pg 603

June Heggenhougen (Norway) *Tel:* 32832125 *Fax:* 32832125, pg 1115

Heibonsha Ltd, Publishers (Japan) *Tel:* (03) 57211241 *Fax:* (03) 57211249 *Web Site:* www.heibonsha.co.jp/, pg 417

Heideland-Orbis NV (Belgium) *Tel:* (03) 3247890 *Fax:* (03) 3600212, pg 69

Joh Heider Verlag GmbH (Germany) *Tel:* (02202) 95 40-35 *Fax:* (02202) 2 15 31 *E-mail:* 101447.1712@compuserve.com *Web Site:* www.heider-verlag.de/mb/mediadaten/, pg 239

Heidrich, Leopold, Buchhandlung u Verlagsgesellschaft (Austria) *Tel:* (0222) 5123701 *Fax:* (0222) 512370214, pg 1274

Heigl Verlag, Horst Edition (Germany) *Tel:* (07554) 283 *Fax:* (07552) 4280, pg 239

Yozmot Heiliger Ltd (Israel) *Tel:* (03) 528 4851 *Fax:* (03) 5285397, pg 1292

Heilongjiang Science & Technology Press (China) *Tel:* (0451) 332486 *Fax:* (0451) 3642127, pg 106

Institut fuer Heilpaedagogik (Switzerland) *Tel:* (041) 415765, pg 615

Heilpaedagogisches Institut der Universitaet Freiburg (Switzerland) *Tel:* (026) 3007700 *Fax:* (026) 3009749, pg 615

Heima er Bezt Book Club (Iceland) *Tel:* 5531599; 5882400 *Fax:* 5888994, pg 1229

Heimskringla (Iceland) *Tel:* 5515199; 5524040; 5689519 *Fax:* 5623523 *E-mail:* mm@centrum.is, pg 328

Heinemann Educational Botswana (Botswana) *Tel:* 372305 *Fax:* 371832, pg 77

Heinemann Educational Publishers Southern Africa (South Africa) *Tel:* (011) 322 8600 *Fax:* (011) 322 8717; (011) 322 8718 *E-mail:* customerliaison@heinemann.co.za *Web Site:* ww.heinemann.co.za, pg 555

Heinemann Educational Publishing (United Kingdom) *Tel:* (01865) 888130 (General Inquiries) *Fax:* (01865) 314290 (General inquiries) *Web Site:* www.heinemann.co.uk, pg 694

Heinemann Kenya Limited (EAEP) (Kenya) *Tel:* (02) 222057; (02) 222144; (02) 228947 *Fax:* (02) 448753; (02) 226286, pg 431

Heinemann Library (Australia) *Tel:* (03) 9245 7111, pg 26

Heinemann Publishers (Pty) Ltd (South Africa) *Tel:* (011) 9741181 *Fax:* (011) 974311, pg 555

William Heinemann Ltd (United Kingdom) *Tel:* (020) 7840 8628 *Fax:* (020) 7233 6127, pg 694

Verlag Otto Heinevetter Lehrmittel GmbH (Germany) *Tel:* (040) 25 90 19 *Fax:* (040) 251 2128 *E-mail:* info@heinevetter-verlag.de *Web Site:* www.heinevetter-verlag.de, pg 239

Arnold Heinman Publishers (India) Pvt Ltd (India) *Tel:* (011) 6883422; (011) 607806; (011) 664256 *Fax:* (011) 6877571, pg 338

Heinrichshofen's Verlag GmbH & Co KG (Germany) *Tel:* (04421) 92 67 0 *Fax:* (04421) 20 20 07 *E-mail:* info@heinrichshofen.de; heinrichshofen@t-online.de *Web Site:* www.heinrichshofen.de, pg 239

Heinz-Theo Gremme Verlag (Germany) *Tel:* (02592) 984200 *E-mail:* theo.gremme@epost.de *Web Site:* www.gremme-verlag.de, pg 239

Heinze GmbH (Germany) *Tel:* (05141) 500 *Fax:* (05141) 50104 *E-mail:* info@heinze.de *Web Site:* www.heinze.de/, pg 239

Hekla Forlag (Denmark) *Tel:* 36 15 36 15 *Fax:* 36 15 36 16, pg 132

Helbing und Lichtenhahn Verlag AG (Switzerland) *Tel:* (061) 231116; (061) 2721117 *Fax:* (061) 2721150 *E-mail:* helbing@access.ch *Web Site:* www.helbing.ch, pg 615

Edition Helbling Verlags-Gesellschaft mbH (Austria) *Tel:* (512) 262333-0 *Fax:* (512) 262333-111 *E-mail:* office@helbling.co.at *Web Site:* www.helbling.com, pg 52

HelfRecht Verlag und Druck (Germany) *Tel:* (09232) 6010 *Fax:* (09232) 601280 *E-mail:* info@helfrecht.de *Web Site:* www.helfrecht.de, pg 239

Editorial Heliasta SRL (Argentina) *Tel:* (011) 4371-5546 *Fax:* (011) 4375-1659 *E-mail:* editorial@heliasta.com.ar *Web Site:* www.heliasta.com.ar, pg 6

Helicon Publishing Ltd (United Kingdom) *Tel:* (08709) 200200 *Fax:* (01235) 826999 *E-mail:* admin@helicon.co.uk *Web Site:* www.helicon.co.uk, pg 694

Helikon Kiado (Hungary) *Tel:* (01) 1174756; (01) 1174678; (01) 1174865 *Fax:* (01) 1174865, pg 324

Helion & Co (United Kingdom) *Tel:* (0121) 705 3393 *Fax:* (0121) 711 4075 *E-mail:* info@helion.co.uk *Web Site:* www.helion.co.uk, pg 694

Heliopol (Bulgaria) *Tel:* (02) 746-850; (02) 718513, pg 95

Heliopolis-Verlag (Germany) *Tel:* (07473) 5427 *Fax:* (07473) 5427, pg 239

Uitgeverij Helios (Belgium) *Tel:* (03) 6645320, pg 69

Hellenic Bookservice (United Kingdom) *Tel:* (020) 72679499 *Fax:* (020) 72679498 *E-mail:* hellenicbooks@btinternet.com *Web Site:* www.hellenicbookservice.com, pg 1320

Hellenic Federation of Publishers & Booksellers (Greece) *Tel:* (01) 3300924; (01) 3804760 *Fax:* (01) 3301617 *E-mail:* poev@otenet.gr, pg 1247

Hellerau-Verlag Dresden GmbH (Germany) *Tel:* (0351) 803 5293 *Fax:* (0351) 826 0130 *E-mail:* info@hellerau-verlag.de *Web Site:* www.hellerau-verlag.de/, pg 239

Christopher Helm (Publishers) Ltd (United Kingdom) *Tel:* (020) 7758 0200 *Fax:* (020) 7758 0222 *E-mail:* enquiries@acblack.com, pg 694

Helm Information Ltd (United Kingdom) *Tel:* (01580) 880 561 *Fax:* (01580) 880 541 *Web Site:* www.helm-information.co.uk, pg 694

Helmond B. V. Uitgeverij (Netherlands) *Tel:* (035) 5417241 *Fax:* (035) 5418366 *E-mail:* pivo@knoware.nl, pg 478

Helsingin Kaupunginkirjasto - yleisten kirjastojen keskuskirjasto (Finland) *Tel:* (09) 3108511 *Fax:* (09) 31085517 *E-mail:* city.library@hel.fi, pg 1463

Helsinki University Library (Finland) *Tel:* (09) 19122709 *Fax:* (09) 19122719 *E-mail:* hyk.palvelu@helsinki.fi, pg 1463

Verlag Helvetica Chimica Acta (Switzerland) *Tel:* (061) 2724973 *Fax:* (061) 2724089, pg 615

Helyode Editions (SA-ADN) (Belgium) *Tel:* (02) 2112733 *Fax:* (01) 2112762, pg 69

Hema Maps Pty Ltd (Australia) *Tel:* (07) 3340 0000 *Fax:* (07) 3340 0099 *E-mail:* manager@hemamaps.com.au *Web Site:* www.hemamaps.com, pg 26

Hemco Publications (Mauritius) *Tel:* 4643141, pg 457

Van Hemeldonck NV (Belgium) *Tel:* (014) 611034 *Fax:* (014) 620288 *E-mail:* booksell@innet.be, pg 69

Hemeroteca Municipal de Madrid (Spain) *Tel:* (091) 5885771, pg 1499

Hemeroteca Nacional de Mexico (Mexico) *Tel:* (05) 6226808 *Fax:* (065) 665-0951, pg 1484

Hemisferio Sur Edicion Agropecuaria (Uruguay) *Tel:* (02) 964515 *Fax:* (02) 964520, pg 760

Editorial Hemisferio Sur SA (Argentina) *Tel:* (011) 49529825 *Fax:* (011) 49528454 *E-mail:* informe@hemisferiosur.com.ar *Web Site:* www.hemisferiosur.com.ar, pg 6

Editions Hemma (Belgium) *Tel:* (086) 43 01 01 *Fax:* (086) 43 36 40 *Web Site:* www.hemma.be, pg 69

Hemma Holland (Netherlands) *Tel:* (020) 6755326 *Fax:* (020) 6796254, pg 478

Hemma Joven, SA (France) *Tel:* 01 48 10 34 86 *E-mail:* hemma@libronet.es, pg 168

Hemming Information Services (United Kingdom) *Tel:* (020) 7973 6402 *Fax:* (020) 7233 5057 *E-mail:* h-info@hemming-group.co.uk *Web Site:* www.h-info.co/uk/about_us.asp, pg 695

Hemus Co Inc (Bulgaria) *Tel:* (02) 875902 *Fax:* (02) 870186, pg 1278

Hemus Editora Ltda (Brazil) *Tel:* (011) 2799911 *Fax:* (011) 2799721, pg 85

Wissenschaft und Technik Verlag Henan Henan Scientific & Technological Publishing House (China) *Tel:* (0371) 551756-565 *Fax:* (0371) 5720158 *E-mail:* hnkj565@public2.22.ha.cn, pg 106

Hendon Publishing Co Ltd (United Kingdom) *Tel:* (01282) 613129; (01282) 697725 *Fax:* (01282) 870215, pg 695

Thomas Heneage Art Books (United Kingdom) *Tel:* (020) 7930 9223 *Fax:* (020) 7839 9223 *E-mail:* artbooks@heneage.com, pg 1320

G Henle Verlag (Germany) *Tel:* (089) 759820 *Fax:* (089) 7598240 *E-mail:* info@henle.de *Web Site:* www.henle.de, pg 239

Ian Henry Publications Ltd (United Kingdom) *Tel:* (01708) 749119 *Fax:* (01621) 850862, pg 695

Edition Hentrich Druck & Verlag Gebr Hentrich und Tank GmbH & Co KG (Germany) *Tel:* (030) 7927011 *Fax:* (030) 7929428, pg 239

Heraldry Today (United Kingdom) *Tel:* (01672) 520617 *Fax:* (01672) 520183 *E-mail:* heraldry@heraldrytoday.co.uk *Web Site:* www.heraldrytoday.co.uk, pg 695

Herattaja-yhdistys Ry (Finland) *Tel:* (06) 438 8911 *Fax:* (06) 438 7430, pg 142

Editions Herault (France) *Tel:* (02) 41554590 *Fax:* (02) 41586228, pg 168

Herbert Press Ltd (United Kingdom) *Tel:* (020) 7758 0200 *Fax:* (020) 7758 0222 *Web Site:* www.acblack.com, pg 695

F A Herbig Verlagsbuchhandlung GmbH (Germany) *Tel:* (089) 290880 *Fax:* (089) 29088144 *E-mail:* l.eggs@herbig.net, pg 239

Herbita Editrice di Leonardo Palermo (Italy) *Tel:* (091) 6167732 *Fax:* (091) 6167716, pg 392

Hans-Alfred Herchen & Co Verlag KG (Germany) *Tel:* (069) 550911 *Fax:* (069) 552601; (069) 554922, pg 239

Hercules de Ediciones, SA (Spain) *Tel:* (0981) 220585; (0981) 226443 *Fax:* (0981) 220717 *E-mail:* empg05052@empresas-galicia.com, pg 577

Editorial y Libreria Herder Ltda (Colombia) *Tel:* (01) 3344853 *Fax:* (01) 2832272, pg 1280

Herder AG (Switzerland) *Tel:* (031) 8210900; (031) 2720818 *Fax:* (061) 8210907, pg 616

Herder-Buchgemeinde (Germany) *Tel:* (0761) 27170 *Fax:* (0761) 2717520, pg 1228

Editorial Herder SA (Spain) *Tel:* (093) 476 26 26 *Fax:* (093) 207 34 48 *E-mail:* editorialherder@herder-sa.com *Web Site:* www.herder-sa.com, pg 577

Herder Editrice e Libreria (Italy) *Tel:* (06) 6795304; (06) 6794628 *Fax:* (06) 6784751 *E-mail:* bookcenter@herder.it *Web Site:* www.herder.it, pg 392

Herder Editrice e Libreria (Italy) *Tel:* (06) 6795304; (06) 6794628 *Fax:* (06) 6784751 *E-mail:* bookcenter@herder.it; distr@herder.it *Web Site:* www.herder.it, pg 1293

Verlag Herder GmbH & Co KG (Germany) *Tel:* (0761) 2717440 *Fax:* (0761) 2717360 *E-mail:* kundenservice@herder.de *Web Site:* www.herder.de/, pg 239

Heretic Books Ltd (United Kingdom) *Tel:* (01366) 328101 *Fax:* (01366) 328102 *E-mail:* davidoraubrey@gmpubs.demon.co.uk, pg 695

Heritage Books (Nigeria) *Tel:* (01) 5871333 *E-mail:* obw@infoweb.abs.net, pg 499

Heritage House Group Ltd (United Kingdom) *Tel:* (01332) 347087 *Fax:* (01332) 290688 *E-mail:* sales@hhgroup.co.uk *Web Site:* www.hhgroup.co.uk, pg 695

Heritage Press (United Kingdom) *Tel:* (01273) 731296 *Fax:* (01273) 731296, pg 695

Heritage Press Ltd (New Zealand) *Tel:* (09) 4137503 *Fax:* (09) 4137503 *E-mail:* heritage.press@xtra.co.nz *Web Site:* www.heritagepress.co.nz, pg 492

Heritage Publishers (India) *Tel:* (011) 3266258; (011) 3288283; (011) 3241513 *Fax:* (011) 3263050 *E-mail:* heritage@nda.vsnl.net.in, pg 338

Heritage Publishing Co (Cote d'Ivoire) *Tel:* 433056 *Fax:* 433056, pg 118

Heritage Publishing House (Philippines) *Tel:* (02) 799484 *Fax:* (02) 7221484, pg 513

Hermagoras/Mohorjeva (Austria) *Tel:* (0463) 56515 21 *Fax:* (0463) 514189 *E-mail:* office@mohorjeva.at *Web Site:* www.mohorjeva.at, pg 52

Hermann editeurs des Sciences et des Arts SA (France) *Tel:* (01) 45 57 45 40 *Fax:* (01) 40 60 12 93 *E-mail:* hermann.sa@wanadoo.fr, pg 168

Helmut Hermann (Germany) *Tel:* (07145) 8278 *Fax:* (07145) 26736, pg 240

Editorial Hermes SA (Mexico) *Tel:* (05) 6741425; (05) 6741894; (05) 6744385 (ext 71) *Fax:* (05) 6743949, pg 461

Hermes Edizioni SRL (Italy) *Tel:* (06) 3222797 *Fax:* (06) 3236277 *E-mail:* edimedit@flashnet.it *Web Site:* www.ediz-mediterranee.com, pg 392

Hermes Publishing House (Bulgaria) *Tel:* (032) 630630 *Fax:* (032) 634095 *E-mail:* hermes@plovdiv.technolink.com, pg 95

Hermes Science Publications (France) *Tel:* (01) 53 10 15 20 *Fax:* (01) 53 10 15 21 *E-mail:* hermes@iway.fr *Web Site:* www.hermes-science.com; www.editions-hermes.fr, pg 168

Hermess Ltd (Latvia) *Tel:* (02) 7216801 *Fax:* (02) 7221290, pg 442

Hermetische Truhe Buchhandlung fuer Esoterische Literatur Barbara Dethlefsen (Germany) *Tel:* (089) 2710650 *Fax:* (089) 2724627, pg 240

Nick Hern Books Ltd (United Kingdom) *Tel:* (020) 8749 4953 *Fax:* (020) 8735 0250 *E-mail:* info@nickhernbooks.demon.co.uk *Web Site:* www.nickhernbooks.co.uk, pg 695

Editions de l'Herne (France) *Tel:* (01) 42 61 25 06 *Fax:* (01) 42 60 10 00 *E-mail:* lherne@freesurf.fr, pg 168

Hernovs Book Club (Denmark) *Tel:* 32963314 *Fax:* 32960446 *E-mail:* admin@hernov.dk, pg 1228

Hernovs Forlag (Denmark) *Tel:* 32963314 *Fax:* 32960446 *E-mail:* admin@hernov.dk *Web Site:* www.hernov.dk, pg 132

Herodotus Press (Ireland) *Tel:* (01) 4540120 *Fax:* (01) 4541134, pg 361

Herold Business Data AG (Austria) *Tel:* (02236) 401-133 *Fax:* (02236) 401-8 *E-mail:* kundendienst@herold.at *Web Site:* www.herold.co.at, pg 52

Herold Druck-und Verlagsgesellschaft mbH (Austria) *Tel:* (01) 795 94-115 *Fax:* (01) 79594115, pg 52

Herold Verlag Dr Wetzel (Germany) *Tel:* (089) 7915774 *Web Site:* www.herold-verlag.de, pg 240

Heron Press Publishing House (Bulgaria) *Tel:* (02) 443368 *Fax:* (02) 443368 *E-mail:* heron_press@attglobal.net, pg 96

Editorial Herrero SA (Mexico) *Tel:* (05) 5664900 *Fax:* (05) 5664900, pg 462

Herron Book Distributors (Australia) *Tel:* (07) 3257 1711 *Fax:* (07) 3257 1686 *E-mail:* herronbooks@bigpond.com, pg 1273

Herscher (France) *Tel:* (01) 55 42 84 00 *Fax:* (01) 43 25 18 29 *Web Site:* www.editions-belin.fr, pg 168

Hertenstein, Axel, Hernstein-Presse (Germany) *Tel:* (07231) 27084 *Fax:* (07231) 27084, pg 240

Hervas (France) *Tel:* (01) 43 79 12 54 *Fax:* (01) 43797710, pg 168

Herzig Somerville Ltd (Canada) *Tel:* 416-681-1200 *Fax:* 416-681-1241 *Web Site:* www.herzig.com, pg 1153, 1193

Herzog August Bibliothek (Germany) *Tel:* (05331) 8080 *Fax:* (05331) 808173; (05331) 808134 *E-mail:* direktor@hab.de, pg 1467

Herzogin Anna Amalia Bibliothek (Germany) *Tel:* (03643) 545200 *Fax:* (03643) 545220 *E-mail:* haab@weimar-klassik.de, pg 1467

HES & De Graaf Publishers BV (Netherlands) *Tel:* (030) 6011955 *Fax:* (030) 6011813 *E-mail:* HES@forum-hes.nl *Web Site:* www.forum-hes.nl, pg 478

Hessische Landes und Hochschulbibliothek Darmstadt (Germany) *Tel:* (06151) 165800 *Fax:* (06151) 165897 *E-mail:* auskunft@lhb.tu-darmstadt.de *Web Site:* elib.tu-darmstadt.de/lhb, pg 1467

Hessischer Verleger- und Buchhandler-Verband eV (Germany) *Tel:* (0611) 16660-0 *Fax:* (0611) 16660-59 *E-mail:* buchhandelgverband.hs@t-online.de, pg 1245

Hessisches Ministerium fuer Umwelt, Landwirtschaft und Forsten (Germany) *Tel:* (0611) 8150 *Fax:* (0611) 8151941 *E-mail:* poststelle@mulf.hessen.de *Web Site:* www.mulf.hessen.de, pg 240

Hestia-I D Hestia-Kollaros & Co Corporation (Greece) *Tel:* (01) 3635970; (01) 3615077; (01) 360574 *Fax:* (01) 3606758; (01) 3606759, pg 311

Hestra-Verlag Hernichel & Dr Strauss GmbH & Co KG (Germany) *Tel:* (06151) 390700 *Fax:* (06151) 390777, pg 240

Uitgeverij Het-Volk (Belgium) *Tel:* (09) 2656424; (09) 2656420 *Fax:* (09) 2258406, pg 1276

Uitgeverij Heuff Nieuwkoop (Netherlands) *Tel:* (020) 6204625 *Fax:* (020) 6204625, pg 478

Heureka Uitgeverij (Netherlands) *Tel:* (0294) 450972 *Fax:* (0294) 415183, pg 478

Uitgeverij Heureka (Netherlands) *Tel:* (0294) 450972 *Fax:* (0294) 415183, pg 478

Hexaglot Holding GmbH (Germany) *Tel:* (040) 514560 *Fax:* (040) 51456991 *E-mail:* info@hexaglot.de *Web Site:* www.hexaglot.de/, pg 240

Heyden & Son (United Kingdom) *Tel:* (020) 8266 3300 *Fax:* (020) 8203 1027 *E-mail:* sales@heyden.com, pg 1162

Erika Heydick Sax-Verlag Beucha (Germany) *Tel:* (034292) 75210 *Fax:* (034292) 75220 *E-mail:* info@sax-verlag.de *Web Site:* www.sax-verlag.de, pg 240

Friedrich W Heye Verlag GmbH (Germany) *Tel:* (089) 66532101 *Fax:* (089) 66532210 *E-mail:* verlag@heye.de *Web Site:* www.heye-verlag.de, pg 240

Carl Heymanns Verlag KG (Germany) *Tel:* (0221) 94373-0 *Fax:* (0221) 94373-901 *E-mail:* welb@heymanns.com; bestellung@heymanns.com; service@heymanns.com *Web Site:* www.heymanns.com, pg 240

Johannes Heyn, Gert und Volkmar Zechner (Austria) *Tel:* (0463) 33631 *Fax:* (0463) 33631-33, pg 52

Verlag Johannes Heyn (Austria) *Tel:* (0463) 33631 *Fax:* (0463) 3363133, pg 1274

Wilhelm Heyne Verlag (Germany) *Tel:* (089) 51480 *Fax:* (089) 51482103 *E-mail:* verlag@heyne.de *Web Site:* www.heyne.de/, pg 240

Monica Heyum Agency (Sweden) *Tel:* (08) 7451934 *Fax:* (08) 7771470, pg 1116

Hid Islenzka Bokmenntafelag (Iceland) *Tel:* 5889060 *Fax:* 5889095 *E-mail:* hib@islandia.is *Web Site:* www.arctic.is/hib, pg 328

Hid Islenzka Bokmenntafelag (Iceland) *E-mail:* hib@islandia.is, pg 1364

Max Hieber KG (Germany) *Tel:* (089) 29008023; (089) 227045 *Fax:* (089) 229782 *E-mail:* info@eminent-orgeln.de *Web Site:* www.eminent-orgeln.de/kontakte.htm, pg 240

Anton Hiersemann, Verlag (Germany) *Tel:* (0711) 5499710; (0711) 5499711 *Fax:* (0711) 54997121 *E-mail:* hiersemann.hauswedell.verlage@t-online.de *Web Site:* www.hiersemann.de/hiersemann.html, pg 240

Anton Hiersemann, Verlag (Germany) *Tel:* (0711) 638264; (0711) 638265 *Fax:* (0711) 6369010, pg 1284

Higginbothams Ltd (India) *Tel:* (044) 831-8413 *Fax:* (044) 834-590, pg 1289

High Council of Arts & Literature (Egypt (Arab Republic of Egypt)), pg 1362

High Resolution Inc (United States) *Tel:* 207-236-3777 *Fax:* 207-236-2500 *Web Site:* www.highres.com, pg 1165

David Higham Associates Ltd (United Kingdom) *Tel:* (020) 7434 5900 *Fax:* (020) 7437 1072 *E-mail:* dha@davidhigham.co.uk, pg 1119

Higher Education Press (China) *Tel:* (10) 64014043 *Fax:* (10) 64054602 *Web Site:* www.hep.edu.cn; www.hep.com.cn, pg 106

Central Library of the Higher Technical Institutes (Bulgaria) *Tel:* (02) 665274 *Fax:* (02) 656863 *E-mail:* lib@vaeg.acad.bg, pg 1455

Highland Books Ltd (United Kingdom) *Tel:* (0148) 342 4560 *Fax:* (0148) 342 4388 *E-mail:* highlandbooks@compuserve.com, pg 695

Highlight Publishing Company Ltd (Taiwan, Province of China) *Tel:* (02) 6984565; (02) 26984633 *Fax:* (02) 6984980 *E-mail:* hilit@tpts5.seed.net.tw *Web Site:* www.ptri.org.tw/hilit, pg 630

Hihorse Publishing Pty Ltd (Australia) *Tel:* (03) 9397 3084 *Fax:* (03) 9397 3084 *E-mail:* hihorse@c031.aone.net.au, pg 26

Hikarinokuni Ltd (Japan) *Tel:* (06) 7681151 *Fax:* (06) 7686910, pg 417

Al Hilal Publications (Bahrain) *Tel:* 231122, pg 61

Dar Al Hilap Publishing Institution (Egypt (Arab Republic of Egypt)) *Tel:* (02) 20610, pg 139

AIG I Hilbinger Verlag GmbH (Germany) *Tel:* (06124) 77704 *Fax:* (06124) 77704, pg 241

Edition E Hilger (Austria) *Tel:* (01) 512 53 15 *Fax:* (01) 513 91 26 *E-mail:* hilger@hilger.at, pg 53

Hilit Publishing Co Ltd (Taiwan, Province of China) *Tel:* (02) 26984565; (02) 26984633 *Fax:* (02) 6984980 *E-mail:* hilit@tpts5.seed.net.tw, pg 630

Hill & Knowlton Asia Ltd (Hong Kong) *Tel:* 28946321, pg 1134

Hillelforlaget (Sweden) *Tel:* (08) 6633866 *Fax:* (08) 6619366, pg 603

Hillview Publications Pte Ltd (Singapore) *Tel:* 2241955 *Fax:* 3245103, pg 546

Hilmarton Manor Press (United Kingdom) *Tel:* (01249) 760208 *Fax:* (01249) 760379 *E-mail:* mailorder@hilmartonpress.co.uk *Web Site:* www.hilmartonpress.co.uk, pg 696

Hilt & Hansteen A/S (Norway) *Tel:* 22384010 *Fax:* 22374015, pg 504

Himalaya Publishing House (India) *Tel:* (011) 3860170; (011) 3863863; (011) 3270329 *Fax:* (022) 2080404; 3256286, pg 338

Himalayan Books (India) *Tel:* (011) 3329126; (011) 3722031 *Fax:* (011) 3321731, pg 338

Himmelsturmer Verlag (Germany) *Tel:* (040) 48061717 *Fax:* (040) 48061799 *E-mail:* himmelstuermer@gmx.de, pg 241

Himpunan Masyarakat Pencinta Buku (Indonesia) *Tel:* (022) 470821; (022) 470287, pg 1229

Hind Pocket Books Private Ltd (India) *Tel:* (011) 2282467 *Fax:* (011) 2282332, pg 338

Verlag Hinder und Deelmann (Germany) *Tel:* (06462) 1301 *Fax:* (06462) 3307 *Web Site:* www.hinderunddeelmann.de/, pg 241

Hindi Book Centre (India) *Tel:* (011) 3286757; (011) 3274874; (011) 3257220 *Fax:* (011) 3273335; (011) 6481565 *E-mail:* del.starpub@axcess.net.in, pg 1289

Hindi Pracharak Sansthan (India) *Tel:* (0542) 54470; (0542) 52425; (0542) 52670; (0542) 355168; (0542) 56850; (0542) 361452, pg 338

Hindustan Book Agency (India) *Tel:* (011) 6163294; (011) 6193295; (011) 6163296 *Fax:* (011) 6193297 *E-mail:* hba@vsnl.com *Web Site:* www.hindbook.com, pg 1289

Hindy's Enterprise (United States) *Tel:* 845-735-4666 *Fax:* 617-344-5905, pg 1143, 1165, 1207, 1216

Hindy's Enterprise Co Ltd (Hong Kong) *Tel:* 25166318 *Fax:* 25165161, pg 1156, 1196

Hing Yip Printing Co Ltd (Hong Kong) *Tel:* 28147287 *Fax:* 28735317, pg 1196

Hinoki Publishing Company Ltd (Japan) *Tel:* (03) 32912488 *Fax:* (03) 32953554 *Web Site:* www.hinoki-shoten.co.jp, pg 417

Hinstorff Verlag GmbH (Germany) *Tel:* (0381) 49690 *Fax:* (0381) 4969103 *E-mail:* sekretariat@hinstorff.de *Web Site:* www.hinstorff.de/, pg 241

Hiotellis P (Greece) *Tel:* (01) 3638066; (01) 3611159 *Fax:* (01) 2113112 *E-mail:* panos-x@otenet.gr, pg 311

Ediciones Hiperion SL (Spain) *Tel:* (091) 577 60 15; (091) 577 60 16 *Fax:* (091) 435 86 90 *E-mail:* info@hiperion.com *Web Site:* www.hiperion.com, pg 577

Hipocrates - Livros Tecnicos, Lda (Portugal) *Tel:* (021) 3571247 *Fax:* (021) 3571247, pg 1307

The Hippogriff Press CC (South Africa) *Tel:* (011) 6464229 *Fax:* (011) 6464229, pg 555

Hippokrates-Verlag GmbH (Germany) *Tel:* (0711) 89310 *Fax:* (0711) 8931706 *Web Site:* www.hippokrates.de/, pg 241

Hiralal Printing Works Ltd (India) *Tel:* (022) 7672726; (022) 7683012 *Fax:* (022) 7631191, pg 1136, 1157, 1197

Hirmer Verlag GmbH (Germany) *Tel:* (089) 1215160 *Fax:* (089) 12151610; (089) 12151616 (distribution) *E-mail:* vertrieb@hirmer-verlag.ccn.de, pg 241

Hirokawa Publishing Co (Japan) *Tel:* (03) 38153652 *Fax:* (03) 38153650, pg 417

Carlos Hirsch SRL (Argentina) *Tel:* (011) 3312391; (011) 3311787 *Fax:* (011) 3311787, pg 1271

Harro V Hirschheydt (Germany) *Tel:* (05130) 36758 *Fax:* (05130) 36799 *E-mail:* hirschheydt.antiquariatverlag@t-online.de, pg 241

Ferdinand Hirt mbH & Co KG (Austria) *Tel:* (01) 343558, pg 53

F Hirthammer Verlag GmbH (Germany) *Tel:* (089) 3233360 *Fax:* (089) 3241728 *E-mail:* hirthammerverlag@t-online.de, pg 241

S Hirzel Verlag GmbH und Co (Germany) *Tel:* (0711) 2582206 *Fax:* (0711) 2582290 *E-mail:* service@hirzel.de *Web Site:* www.hirzel.de, pg 241

Libreria Hispano Americana (Spain) *Tel:* (093) 3175337; (093) 3180079 *Fax:* (093) 3189339, pg 1311

Editorial Hispano Europea SA (Spain) *Tel:* (093) 2013709; (093) 2018500 *Fax:* (093) 4142635 *E-mail:* hispaneuropea@mx3.redestb.es, pg 577

Editorial Hispanoamerica (Colombia) *Tel:* (01) 2492929; (01) 2489682; (01) 2216694 *Fax:* (01) 2213020, pg 112

Histec Publications (Australia) *Tel:* (03) 95923787 *Fax:* (03) 95922823, pg 26

Editions d'Histoire Sociale (EDHIS) (France) *Tel:* (01) 42614778, pg 168

Historical Association of Zambia (Zambia), pg 766

Historical Society of Afghanistan (Afghanistan) *Tel:* 30370, pg 1

Historicky ustav Akademie ved Ceske republiky (Czech Republic) *Tel:* (02) 884190 *Fax:* (02) 887513, pg 124

Arquivo Historico de Mocambique (Mozambique) *Tel:* (01) 421177; (01) 421178 *Fax:* (01) 423428 *E-mail:* ahm@ahm.mz *Web Site:* www.ahm.mz, pg 1485

Institutum Historicum S I (Italy) *Tel:* (06) 6869357 *Fax:* (06) 6861342 *E-mail:* archivum@tin.it; ihsiroma@tin.it, pg 392

Instytut Historii Nauki PAN (Poland) *Tel:* (022) 8268754; (022) 6572746 *Fax:* (022) 8266137 *E-mail:* mah01@plearn.bitnet, pg 516

Historische Uitgeverij (Netherlands) *Tel:* (050) 3181700 *Fax:* (050) 3146383 *E-mail:* info@histuitg.ne *Web Site:* www.histuitg.ne, pg 478

Historischer Verein fur das Furstentum Liechtenstein (Liechtenstein) *Tel:* (0423) 8921747 *Fax:* (0423) 3921961 *E-mail:* hvfl@hvfl.li *Web Site:* www.hvfl.li, pg 444

History House Publishing (Ireland) *Tel:* (065) 24066 *Fax:* (065) 20388, pg 361

Publishing House Hristo Botev (Bulgaria) *Tel:* (02) 441408; (02) 443503 *Fax:* 441490, pg 96

Hjemmenes Forlag (Norway) *Tel:* 22143151 *Fax:* 22920738, pg 504

Hjemmets Bokklubb (Norway) *Tel:* 22471000 *Fax:* 22471098 *E-mail:* egmont@egmont.com *Web Site:* www.egmont.com, pg 1231

Egmont Hjemmets Bokforlag AS (Norway) *Tel:* 22471000 *Fax:* 22471098 *E-mail:* egmont@egmont.com *Web Site:* www.egmont.com, pg 504

Forlaget Hjulet (Denmark) *Tel:* 31310900 *Fax:* 31310900 *E-mail:* aloa@gte2net.dk, pg 132

Galerie Hlavniho Mesta Prahy (Czech Republic) *Tel:* (02) 3332 1200 *Fax:* (02) 3332 3664 *Web Site:* www.citygalleryprague.cz, pg 124

HLT Publications (United Kingdom) *Tel:* (020) 7385 3377; (020) 7381 7404 *Fax:* (020) 7381 3377 *E-mail:* obp@hltpublications.co.uk *Web Site:* www.holborncollege.ac.uk/OldbaileyPress.cfm, pg 696

HMR Publishing Co (Pakistan) *Tel:* (042) 7588972; (042) 7588967 *Fax:* (042) 7581212, pg 507

Ho-Chi Book Publishing Co (Taiwan, Province of China) *Tel:* (02) 2974-0168 *Fax:* (02) 2792-4702 *E-mail:* hochi@ms12.hinet.net; hochi@email.gcn.net.tw, pg 630

Ho Printing Singapore Pte Ltd (Singapore) *Tel:* 5429322 *Fax:* 2896065, pg 1138, 1159, 1200, 1213, 1222

Hobbs The Printers Ltd (United Kingdom) *Tel:* (023) 8066 4800 *Fax:* (023) 8066 4801 *E-mail:* htp@tcp.co.uk, pg 1162, 1203

Hobbs The Printers Ltd (United Kingdom) *Tel:* (023) 8066 4800 *Fax:* (023) 8066 4801 *Web Site:* www.hobbs.uk.com, pg 1214

Hobbs The Printers Ltd (United Kingdom) *Tel:* (023) 8066 4800 *Fax:* (023) 8066 4801 *E-mail:* htp@tcp.co.uk, pg 1223

Hobsons (United Kingdom) *Tel:* (020) 7336 6633 *Fax:* (020) 7608 1034 *Web Site:* www.hobsons.com, pg 696

Technische Hochschule Aachen (Germany) *Tel:* (0241) 804445 *Fax:* (0241) 8888273, pg 1467

Hod-Ami, Computer Books Ltd (Israel) *Tel:* (09) 9564716 *Fax:* (09) 9571582 *E-mail:* info@hod-ami.co.il *Web Site:* www.hod-ami.co.il, pg 368

Hodder & Stoughton Educational (United Kingdom) *Tel:* (020) 7873 6272 *Fax:* (020) 7873 6299 *E-mail:* joanne.symmonds@hodder.co.uk *Web Site:* www.hodderheadline.co.uk, pg 696

Hodder & Stoughton General (United Kingdom) *Tel:* (020) 7873 6000 *Fax:* (020) 7873 6024, pg 696

Hodder & Stoughton Religious (United Kingdom) *Tel:* (020) 7873 6000 *Fax:* (020) 7873 6059 *E-mail:* firstname.surname@hodder.co.uk, pg 696

Hodder Children's Books (United Kingdom) *Tel:* (020) 7873 6000 *Fax:* (020) 7873 6225 *Web Site:* www.hodderheadline.co.uk, pg 696

Hodder Headline Australia (Australia) *Tel:* (02) 82480800; (02) 43901300 (customer service) *Fax:* (02) 82480810 *E-mail:* Auspub@hha.com.au (Australian publishing); hsales@alliancedist.com.au; adscs@alliancedist.com.au (customer service) *Web Site:* www.hha.com.au; www.hodderheadline.co.us, pg 26

Hodder Headline Ltd (United Kingdom) *Tel:* (020) 7873 6000 *Fax:* (020) 7873 6024 *Web Site:* www.hodderheadline.co.uk, pg 696

Hodder Moa Beckett Publishers Ltd (New Zealand) *Tel:* (09) 4443640 *Fax:* (09) 4443646, pg 492

Hodges Figgis & Co (Ireland) *Tel:* (01) 6774754 *Fax:* (01) 6792810; (01) 6793402 *E-mail:* books@hfiggis.ir, pg 1291

Editions Hoebeke (France) *Tel:* (01) 42 22 83 81 *Fax:* (01) 45 44 04 96, pg 168

Lars Hoekerbergs Bokfoerlag (Sweden) *Tel:* (08) 244360 *Fax:* (08) 6503984 *E-mail:* hokerbook@ebox.tninet.se, pg 603

Verlag Hoelder-Pichler-Tempsky (Austria) *Tel:* (01) 401 36-0 *Fax:* (01) 401 35-85, pg 53

Verlag Wolfgang Hoelker (Germany) *Tel:* (0251) 414110 *Fax:* (0251) 4141120 *E-mail:* info@coppenrath.de, pg 241

Verlag Peter Hoell (Germany) *Tel:* (06167) 912220 *Fax:* (06167) 912221 *E-mail:* hoell.verlag@t-online.de, pg 241

Ing W Hofacker GmbH Verlag (Germany) *Tel:* (08024) 7331 *Fax:* (08024) 7580 *E-mail:* hofacker@t-online.de *Web Site:* www.hofacker.de/, pg 241

Hofbauer, Christoph und Trojanow Ilia, Akademischer Verlag Muenchen (Germany) *Tel:* (089) 51616151 *Fax:* (089) 51616199 *E-mail:* avm@druckmedien.de, pg 241

Buchhandlung Karl Hofbauer KG (Austria) *Tel:* (03452) 82793; (03452) 82177 *Fax:* (03452) 71218 *E-mail:* hofbauer.buch@nextra.at *Web Site:* members.nextra.at/hofbauer.buch/hofbauer.buch, pg 1274

Agence Hoffman (France) *Tel:* (01) 43265694 *Fax:* (01) 43263407, pg 1110

Edition Hoffmann & Co (Germany) *Tel:* (06031) 2443 *Fax:* (06031) 62965, pg 242

Dieter Hoffmann Verlag (Germany) *Tel:* (06136) 95100 *Fax:* (06136) 951037, pg 242

H Hoffmann GmbH (Germany) *Tel:* (033203) 305810 *Fax:* (033203) 305820 *E-mail:* hhvberlin@t-online.de, pg 242

Hoffmann und Campe Verlag GmbH (Germany) *Tel:* (040) 441880 *Fax:* (040) 44188202 *E-mail:* email@hoca.de *Web Site:* www.hoffmann-und-campe.de/, pg 242

Verlag Karl Hofmann GmbH & Co (Germany) *Tel:* (07181) 4020 *Fax:* (07181) 402111 *E-mail:* info@hofmann-verlag.de *Web Site:* www.hofmann-verlag.de, pg 242

Friedrich Hofmeister-Figaro Verlag Grossortiment und Musikalienhandlung GesmbH (Austria) *Tel:* (01) 50576510 *Fax:* (01) 5059185, pg 1274

Friedrich Hofmeister Musikverlag GmbH (Germany) *Tel:* (0341) 9600750 *Fax:* (0341) 9603055 *E-mail:* f.hofmeister.musikverlag@t-online.de *Web Site:* www.friedrich-hofmeister.de/, pg 242

Dr Verena Hofstaetter (Austria) *Tel:* (01) 370 33 02 *Fax:* (01) 370 59 34 *E-mail:* verlag@vh-communications.at, pg 53

Hogar del Libro, SA (Spain) *Tel:* (093) 3182700 *Fax:* (093) 3010399, pg 577, 1311

Hogrefe Verlag GmbH & Co Kg (Germany) *Tel:* (0551) 496090 *Fax:* (0551) 4960988 *E-mail:* verlag@hogrefe.de *Web Site:* www.hogrefe.de/, pg 242

Hohenrain-Verlag GmbH (Germany) *Tel:* (07071) 40700 *Fax:* (07071) 407026, pg 242

Matth Hohner AG Verlag (Germany) *Tel:* (07425) 200 *Fax:* (07425) 249 *E-mail:* info@hohner.de *Web Site:* www.matth-hohner-ag.de/, pg 242

Hoi Kwong Printing Co Ltd (Hong Kong) *Tel:* 2562 1641 *Fax:* 2564 2142, pg 1134

Hoi Kwong Printing Co Ltd (Hong Kong) *Tel:* 2562 1641 *Fax:* 2564 2142 *E-mail:* sales@hoikwong.com *Web Site:* www.hoikwong.com, pg 1196

Hoi Thu-Vien Viet Nam (Viet Nam) *Tel:* (04) 8252643, pg 1526

Hoikusha Publishing Co Ltd (Japan) *Tel:* (06) 788 4470 *Fax:* (06) 788 4970, pg 417

Hoja Casa Editorial SA de CV (Mexico) *Tel:* (05) 6884828; (05) 6880318 *Fax:* (05) 6057600, pg 462

Ediciones Mil Hojas Ltda (Chile) *Tel:* (02) 2743172 *Fax:* (02) 2250261, pg 100

Hokkaido University Library (Japan) *Tel:* (011) 7162111 *Fax:* (011) 7464595, pg 1478

Hokkaido University Press (Japan) *Tel:* (011) 7472308 *Fax:* (011) 7368605, pg 417

Hokuryukan Co Ltd (Japan) *Tel:* (03) 54494591 *Fax:* (03) 54494950, pg 417

The Hokuseido Press (Japan) *Tel:* (03) 38270511 *Fax:* (03) 38270567, pg 417

Holbrook Design (United Kingdom) *Tel:* (01865) 459000 *E-mail:* info@holbrook-design.co.uk, pg 1162

Holguin, Ediciones (Cuba) *Tel:* (24) 424974 *E-mail:* cpllhlg@tauronet.cult.cu, pg 121

Holkenfeldt 3 (Denmark) *Tel:* 93 12 21 *Fax:* 93 82 41, pg 133

Holland & Josenhans GmbH & Co (Germany) *Tel:* (0711) 614390 *Fax:* (0711) 6143922 *Web Site:* www.holland-josenhans.de/, pg 242

Holland B V Uitgeversmaatschappij (Netherlands) *Tel:* (023) 5323061 *Fax:* (023) 5342908, pg 478

Holland Enterprises Ltd (United Kingdom) *Tel:* (020) 8551 7711 *Fax:* (020) 8551 1266 *E-mail:* enquires@holland-enterprises.co.uk *Web Site:* www.holland-enterprises.co.uk, pg 697

Holland University Press BV (APA) (Netherlands) *Tel:* (020) 6265544 *E-mail:* info@apa-publishers.com, pg 478

Uitgeverij Hollandia BV (Netherlands) *Tel:* (033) 2996899 *Fax:* (033) 2996980, pg 478

Hollinek Bruder & Co mbH Gesellschaftsdruckerei & Verlagsbuchhandring (Austria) *Tel:* (02231) 67365 *Fax:* (02231) 67365 *E-mail:* hollinek@via.at, pg 53

Hollis Publishing Ltd (United Kingdom) *Tel:* (020) 8977 7711 *Fax:* (020) 8977 1133 *E-mail:* hollis@hollis-pr.co.uk; orders@hollis-pr.co.uk *Web Site:* www.hollis-pr.co.uk, pg 697

Hollym Corporation Publishers (Republic of Korea) *Tel:* (02) 735-75514 *Fax:* (02) 7305149; (02) 7308192 *E-mail:* hollym@cholltan.net; info@hollym.co.kn, pg 437

Holnap Kiado Vallalat (Hungary) *Tel:* (01) 1656624; (01) 1666928, pg 324

Holograms (M) Sdn Bhd (Malaysia) *Tel:* (03) 2824002 *Fax:* (03) 2822751, pg 452

Holos Verlag (Germany) *Tel:* (0228) 263020; (0228) 262332 *Fax:* (0228) 212435, pg 242

Holp Book Co Ltd (Japan) *Tel:* (03) 5285-5011 *Fax:* (03) 3225-1663 *E-mail:* holp@holp.co.jp *Web Site:* www.holp.co.jp, pg 417

The Holt Jackson Book Co Ltd (United Kingdom) *Tel:* (01253) 737464 *Fax:* (01253) 733361 *E-mail:* info@holtjackson.co.uk *Web Site:* www.holtjackson.co.uk, pg 1320

Vanessa Holt Ltd (United Kingdom) *Tel:* (01702) 473787 *Fax:* (01702) 471890, pg 1119

Holyoake Books (United Kingdom) *Tel:* (0161) 832 4300 *Fax:* (0161) 831 7684 *E-mail:* info@co-opu.demon.co.uk, pg 697

Hans Holzmann Verlag GmbH und Co KG (Germany) *Tel:* (08247) 35401 *Fax:* (08247) 354170 *Web Site:* www.holzmannverlag.de/, pg 242

Home Health Education Service (United Kingdom) *Tel:* (01476) 591800; (01476) 591700; (01476) 590866 (orders) *Fax:* (01476) 577144 *E-mail:* 101654.543@compuserve.com, pg 697

Uitgeverij Homeovisie BV (Netherlands) *Tel:* (072) 5661133 *Fax:* (072) 5661295, pg 478

Homestead Books (Australia) *Tel:* (03) 9873 7202 *Fax:* (03) 9873-0542 *E-mail:* service@theruralstore.com.au *Web Site:* www.theruralstore.com.au, pg 26

Evelyn Hone College Library (Zambia) *Tel:* 211557, pg 1509

Honeyglen Publishing Ltd (United Kingdom) *Tel:* (020) 7602 2876 *Fax:* (020) 7602 2876, pg 697

Hong Kong Book Centre Ltd (Hong Kong) *Tel:* 2522 3669 *Fax:* 2868 5079 *E-mail:* orders@hkbookcentre.com.hk *Web Site:* www.swindonbooks.com, pg 1287

Hong Kong China Tourism Press (Hong Kong) *Tel:* (02) 25618196 *Fax:* (02) 25618196, pg 320

Hong Kong Chinese PEN Centre (Hong Kong), pg 1364

Hong Kong Christian Service (China) *Tel:* 27316316 *Fax:* 27316333 *E-mail:* corpaffairs@hkcs.org *Web Site:* www.hkcs.org, pg 1132

Hong Kong Christian Service (China) *Tel:* 27316316 *Fax:* 27316333, pg 1221

Hong Kong Library Association (Hong Kong) *E-mail:* hklib@hklib.org.hk *Web Site:* www.hklib.org.hk, pg 1517

The Hong Kong Polytechnic University Library (Hong Kong) *Tel:* 2766 6857 *Fax:* 2765 8274, pg 1471

Hong Kong Public Libraries (Hong Kong) *Tel:* 2921 0208 *Fax:* 2415 8211 *E-mail:* enquiries@lcsd.gov.hk *Web Site:* www.hkpl.gov.hk, pg 1471

Hong Kong Publishing Co Ltd (Hong Kong) *Tel:* (02) 5259053, pg 320

Hong Kong University Press (Hong Kong) *Tel:* 25502703 *Fax:* 28750734 *E-mail:* hkupress@hkucc.hku.hk *Web Site:* www.hkupress.org, pg 320

Hongik Media Plus Ltd (Republic of Korea) *Tel:* (02) 786-1016 *Fax:* (02) 786-1709 *E-mail:* hongikcb@soback.kornet.nm.kr, pg 437

Honno Welsh Women's Press (United Kingdom) *Tel:* (01970) 623 150 *Fax:* (01970) 623 150 *E-mail:* post@honno.co.uk *Web Site:* www.honno.co.uk, pg 697

Hook & Hatton Ltd (United Kingdom) *Tel:* (01604) 847278 *Fax:* (01604) 821486 *E-mail:* hook_hatton@compuserve.com, pg 1129

Hoover's Business Press (United Kingdom) *Tel:* (01865) 513186 *Fax:* (01865) 513186 *Web Site:* www.hoovers-europe.com, pg 697

Hopeful Monster Editore (Italy) *Tel:* (011) 4367197; (011) 4358519 *Fax:* (011) 4369025 *E-mail:* hopmonst@tin.it *Web Site:* www.hopefulmonster.net, pg 392

Verlag Hoppenstedt GmbH (Germany) *Tel:* (06151) 380100 *Fax:* (06151) 380101 *E-mail:* info@hopp.de *Web Site:* www.hoppenstedt.de, pg 242

Hora (Italy) *Tel:* (02) 2155589 *Fax:* (02) 26412203, pg 392

Horan Wall & Walker (Australia) *Tel:* (02) 8268 8268 *Fax:* (02) 8268 8267 *E-mail:* info@hww.com.au *Web Site:* www.hww.com.au, pg 26

Pierre Horay Editeur (France) *Tel:* (01) 43 54 53 90 *Fax:* (01) 43 54 63 50 *E-mail:* editions@horay-editeur.fr *Web Site:* www.horay-editeur.fr, pg 168

Kate Hordern (United Kingdom), pg 1119

Horitsu Bunka-Sha (Japan) *Tel:* (075) 7025831, pg 417

Horizon Scientific Press (United Kingdom) *Tel:* (01953) 601106 *Fax:* (01953) 603068 *E-mail:* mail@horizonpress.com *Web Site:* www.horizonpress.com, pg 697

Editorial Horizonte (Peru) *Tel:* (01) 279364; (01) 274341, pg 511

Horlemann Verlag (Germany) *Tel:* (02224) 5984; (02224) 5589 *Fax:* (02224) 5429 *E-mail:* horlemann@aol.com *Web Site:* www.horlemann-verlag.de/, pg 243

YELLOW PAGES

Editions Hors Collection (France) *Tel:* (01) 44 16 05 00 *Fax:* (01) 44 16 05 05, pg 168

Editorial Horsori SL (Spain) *Tel:* (093) 2322755 *Fax:* (093) 2651776 *E-mail:* horsori@retemail.es *Web Site:* www.horsori.com, pg 577

Horus (Italy) *Tel:* (011) 511705 *Fax:* (011) 511705, pg 393

Horus Editora Ltda (Brazil) *Tel:* (011) 288-7681 *Fax:* (011) 288-7681 *E-mail:* horus@horuseditora.com.br *Web Site:* www.horuseditora.com.br, pg 85

Hospitality Books (Australia) *Tel:* (02) 9809 5793 *Fax:* (02) 9809 4884 *Web Site:* www.hospitalitybooks.com.au, pg 26

Hospitality Press Pty Ltd (Australia) *Tel:* (03) 9528 5021 *Fax:* (03) 9528 2645 *E-mail:* hosppress@access.net.au, pg 26

Hospitality Training Foundation (United Kingdom) *Tel:* (020) 8579 2400 *Fax:* (020) 8840 6217 *E-mail:* info@htf.org.uk *Web Site:* www.htf.org.uk, pg 697

Host & Son Publishers Ltd (Denmark) *Tel:* 33382888 *Fax:* 33382898 *E-mail:* host@euroconnect.dk, pg 133

Hotei Publishing (Netherlands) *Tel:* (071) 5663190 *Fax:* (071) 5663191 *E-mail:* info@hotei-publishing.com *Web Site:* www.hotei-publishing.com, pg 478

House of Lochar (United Kingdom) *Tel:* (01951) 200232 *Fax:* (01951) 200232 *E-mail:* lochar@colonsay.org.uk *Web Site:* www.colosay.org.uk, pg 697

Uitgeverij Houtekiet (Netherlands) *Tel:* (035) 5422141 *Fax:* (035) 5423855, pg 479

Forlaget Hovedland (Denmark) *Tel:* 86276500 *Fax:* 86276537 *E-mail:* mail@hovedland.dk *Web Site:* www.hovedland.dk, pg 133

How To Books Ltd (United Kingdom) *Tel:* (01865) 793806 *Fax:* (01865) 248780 *E-mail:* info@howtobooks.co.uk *Web Site:* www.howtobooks.co.uk, pg 697

Nakladatelstvi Josef Hribal (Czech Republic) *Tel:* (02) 542731, pg 124

Izdavacka Delatnost Hrvatske Akademije Znanosti I Umjetnosti (Croatia) *Tel:* (01) 49 22 373; (01) 48 72 902 *Fax:* (01) 48 19 979 *E-mail:* izddjel@hazu.hr, pg 118

Hrvatsko filozofsko drustvo (Croatia) *Tel:* (01) 6111808 *Fax:* (01) 6170682 *E-mail:* filozofska-istrazivanja@zg.tel.hr, pg 119

Hrvatsko knjiznicarsko drustvo (Croatia) *Tel:* (41) 6164 037; (41) 6164 210; (41) 6159 320 *Fax:* (41) 6164 186 *E-mail:* hbd@nsk.hr *Web Site:* pubwww.srce.hr/hkd, pg 1514

Hsiao Yuan Publication Co, Ltd (Taiwan, Province of China) *Tel:* (02) 3949931 *Fax:* (02) 3417931, pg 630

Hsin Yi Publications (Taiwan, Province of China) *Tel:* (02) 23965303 *Fax:* (02) 23910799 *Web Site:* www.hsin-yi.org.tw//, pg 630

Hua Yang Printing Holding Co Ltd (Hong Kong) *Tel:* 24167591 *Fax:* 24110235; 24166318, pg 1196

Hubei Publications Import & Export Corporation (China) *Tel:* (027) 87825561 *Fax:* (027) 87815557 *E-mail:* hbwsdjkb@lbs.com, pg 1279

Verlag Huber & Co AG (Switzerland) *Tel:* (052) 7235617 *Fax:* (052) 7235619 *E-mail:* buchverlag@huber.ch *Web Site:* www.huber.ch, pg 616

Hans Huber (Germany) *Tel:* (031) 3004500 *Fax:* (031) 3004590 *E-mail:* verlag@hanshuber.com *Web Site:* www.hanshuber.com, pg 243

Hans Huber (Switzerland) *Tel:* (031) 3004500 *Fax:* (031) 3004590 *E-mail:* admin@hanshuber.com *Web Site:* verlag.hanshuber.com, pg 1313

Volker Huber Edition & Galerie (Germany) *Tel:* (069) 814523 *Fax:* (069) 880155 *E-mail:* edition-huber@t-online.de, pg 243

Hubsch (Luxembourg) *E-mail:* 101755.3213@compuserve.com, pg 447

Hudanuda Publishing Co Ltd (Nigeria) *Tel:* (069) 5141, pg 499

Angus Hudson Ltd (United Kingdom) *Tel:* (020) 8959 3668 *Fax:* (020) 8959 3678 *E-mail:* sales@angushudson.com, pg 697

Hudson Publishing (Australia) *Tel:* (03) 9853 7753 *Fax:* (03) 9853 7290 *E-mail:* hudson@c031.aone.net.au, pg 27

Max Hueber Verlag GmbH & Co KG (Germany) *Tel:* (089) 96020 *Fax:* (089) 9602358 *Web Site:* www.hueber.de/, pg 243

Huebner Felicitas Verlag (Germany) *Tel:* (05695) 1028 *Fax:* (05695) 1027, pg 243

Verlag Uta Huelsey (Germany) *Tel:* (0281) 27227 *Fax:* (0281) 24682 *E-mail:* uta.hulsey@t-online.de, pg 243

Libreria Huemul SA (Argentina) *Tel:* (011) 825-2290 *Fax:* (011) 822-1666, pg 6, 1271

Hug & Co (Switzerland) *Tel:* (01) 2212652 *Fax:* (01) 5121213, pg 616

Heinrich Hugendubel (Germany) *Tel:* (089) 2355860 *Fax:* (089) 23558611, pg 1284

Heinrich Hugendubel Verlag GmbH (Germany) *Tel:* (089) 23 55 86-0 *Fax:* (089) 23 55 86-111, pg 243

Editions Charles Hugenin Pro Arte (Switzerland) *Tel:* (032) 612727 *Fax:* (032) 8612727, pg 616

Hugo's Language Books Ltd (United Kingdom) *Tel:* (01491) 572656 *Fax:* (01491) 573590 *E-mail:* danadde@dk.com, pg 697

Huia Publishers (New Zealand) *Tel:* (04) 473-9262 *Fax:* (04) 473-9265 *E-mail:* huiapubs@huia.co.nz *Web Site:* www.huia.co.nz, pg 492

Huis Van Het Boek (Belgium) *Tel:* (03) 230 89 23 *Fax:* (03) 281 22 40 *E-mail:* info@boek.be *Web Site:* www.boek.be, pg 69

Human & Rousseau (Pty) Ltd (South Africa) *Tel:* (021) 251280 *Fax:* (021) 4192619 *E-mail:* rhauman@nbh.naspers.co.za, pg 555

Human Sciences Research Council (South Africa) *Tel:* (012) 2022004; (012) 2022978 *Fax:* (012) 2022891 *Web Site:* www.hsrc.ac.za, pg 555

Human Wissenschafilicher Verlag (Germany) *Tel:* (0611) 3082096 *Fax:* (0611) 3082096, pg 243

Edition Humanistische Psychologie (EHP) (Germany) *Tel:* (02202) 981236 *Fax:* (02202) 981237 *E-mail:* info@ehp-koeln.com *Web Site:* www.ehp-koeln.com; www.ehp.biz, pg 243

Humanistischer Verband Deutschlands, Landesverband Berlin eV (Germany) *Tel:* (030) 613904-0 *Fax:* (030) 61390450 *E-mail:* hvd@humanismus.de *Web Site:* www.humanismus.de/, pg 243

Editura Humanitas (Romania) *Tel:* (01) 2228546 *Fax:* (01) 2229061; (01) 2228252 *E-mail:* editors@agora.humanitas.ro, pg 533

Humanitas Ltd (Lithuania) *Tel:* 07 423664 *E-mail:* info@humanitas.lt, pg 1297

Humanitas Publishing House (Romania) *Tel:* (01) 2228546 *Fax:* (01) 2243632 *E-mail:* editors@agora.humanitas.ro *Web Site:* www.humanitas.ro, pg 533

Humboldt Universitaet zu Berlin (Germany) *Tel:* (030) 20933212 *Fax:* (030) 20933207 *E-mail:* info@ub.hu-berlin.de *Web Site:* www.ub.hu-berlin.de, pg 1467

Humboldt-Taschenbuchverlag Jacobi KG (Germany) *Tel:* (089) 360960 *Fax:* (089) 36096-222 (general); (089) 36096-258 (orders) *E-mail:* redaktion@humboldt.de, pg 243

Edition Hundertmark (Germany) *Tel:* (0221) 237944 *Fax:* (0221) 249146 *E-mail:* info@hundertmark-gallery.com *Web Site:* www.hundertmark-gallery.com, pg 243

Hundskolan i Solleftea AB (Sweden) *Tel:* (0620) 83200 *Fax:* (0620) 83229, pg 603

Hung Hing Off-set Printing Co Ltd (Hong Kong) *Tel:* 26648682 *Fax:* 26642070 *E-mail:* info@hhop.com.hk, pg 1134, 1156, 1196

John Hunt Publishing Ltd (United Kingdom) *Tel:* (01962) 736880; (01962) 736888 (orders) *Fax:* (01962) 736881 *E-mail:* office@johnhunt-publishing.com *Web Site:* www.johnhunt-publishing.com, pg 698

Hunter Books (Australia), pg 27

Hunter & Foulis Ltd (United Kingdom) *Tel:* (0131) 5567947 *Fax:* (0131) 5573911 *E-mail:* mail@hunterfoulis.co.uk, pg 1203, 1214

Hunter House Publications (Australia) *Tel:* (02) 4988-6401 *Fax:* (02) 4988-6401 *E-mail:* wf&mc@hunterlink.net.au, pg 27

Huntsmen Offset Printing Pte Ltd (Singapore) *Tel:* 2650600 *Fax:* 2658575, pg 1200

Ediciones Huracan Inc (Puerto Rico) *Tel:* (787) 763-7407 *Fax:* (787) 763-7407, pg 530

Huron Valley Graphics Inc (United States) *Tel:* 734-477-0448 *Fax:* 734-477-0393 *E-mail:* custserv@hvg.com *Web Site:* www.hvg.com, pg 1165

C Hurst & Co (Publishers) Ltd (United Kingdom) *Tel:* (020) 7240 2666 *Fax:* (020) 7240 2667 *E-mail:* hurst@atlas.co.uk *Web Site:* www.hurstpub.co.uk, pg 698

Dr Mahmud Husain Library (Pakistan) *Tel:* (021) 474953 *Fax:* (021) 4969277, pg 1489

Huss-Medien GmbH (Germany) *Tel:* (030) 42151438 *Fax:* (030) 42151300 *E-mail:* huss.medien@hussberlin.de, pg 243

Huss-Verlag GmbH (Germany) *Tel:* (089) 323910 *Fax:* (089) 32391416 *E-mail:* 101742.3244@compuserve.com *Web Site:* www.huss-verlag.de/, pg 244

Husum Druck- und Verlagsgesellschaft mbH Co KG (Germany) *Tel:* (04841) 83520 *Fax:* (04841) 835210 *E-mail:* verlagsgruppe.husum@t-online.de *Web Site:* www.verlagsgruppe.de/, pg 244

Alan Hutchison Ltd (United Kingdom) *Tel:* (020) 7221 0129, pg 698

Huthig GmbH & Co KG (Germany) *Tel:* (06221) 4890 *Fax:* (06221) 489279 *Web Site:* www.huethig.de/, pg 244

Hutton Press Ltd (United Kingdom) *Tel:* (01964) 550573 *Fax:* (01964) 550573, pg 698

Hutton-Williams Agency (United Kingdom) *Tel:* (020) 8879 0237 *Fax:* (020) 8879 3831, pg 1119

Hw Moon Publishing Co (Republic of Korea) *Tel:* (02) 724897, pg 437

Hyangmunsa Publishing Co (Republic of Korea) *Tel:* (02) 5385671; (02) 5385672 *Fax:* (02) 5385673, pg 437

Hyden House Ltd (United Kingdom) *Tel:* (01730) 823311 *Fax:* (01730) 823322 *E-mail:* info@permaculture.co.uk *Web Site:* www.permaculture.co.uk, pg 698

Hyein Publishing House (Republic of Korea) *Tel:* (02) 3836928 *Fax:* (02) 3836929 *E-mail:* vvh103@chollian, pg 437

Hyland House Publishing Pty Ltd (Australia) *Tel:* (03) 9376 4461 *Fax:* (03) 9376 4461 *E-mail:* hyland3@netspace.net.au, pg 27

Hymns Ancient & Modern Ltd (United Kingdom) *Tel:* (01603) 612914 *Fax:* (01603) 624483 *E-mail:* admin@scm-canterburypress.co.uk *Web Site:* www.scm-canterburypress.co.uk, pg 698

HYORONSHA PUBLISHING CO LTD

Hyoronsha Publishing Co Ltd (Japan) *Tel:* (03) 32609406 *Fax:* (03) 32609408, pg 417

Editura Hyperion (Republic of Moldova) *Tel:* (02) 244259, pg 468

Hyperion - Verlag (Germany) *Tel:* (089) 32954165 *Fax:* (089) 32954175 *E-mail:* mail@hyperion-verlag.de *Web Site:* www.hyperion-verlag.de, pg 244

HYS Culture Co Ltd (Taiwan, Province of China) *Tel:* (07) 6914310 *Fax:* (02) 6914311 *E-mail:* hysccl@msl.hinet.net, pg 630

Hyun Am Publishing Co (Republic of Korea) *Tel:* (02) 877-2565 *Fax:* (02) 877-2566, pg 437

I Prooptiki (Greece) *Tel:* (01) 2014872; (01) 8655413 *Fax:* (01) 8226254 *E-mail:* hronis@otenet.gr, pg 311

IAEA - International Atomic Energy Agency (Austria) *Tel:* (01) 2600 0 *Fax:* (01) 2600-29302 *E-mail:* sales.publications@iaea.org *Web Site:* www.iaea.org/worldatom/Books, pg 53

Iaith Cyf (United Kingdom) *Tel:* (01239) 711668 *Fax:* (01239) 711698 *E-mail:* ymhol@cwmni-iaith.com *Web Site:* www.cwmni-iaith.com, pg 698

Iamvlichos (Greece) *Tel:* (01) 5227678 *Fax:* (01) 5226581, pg 1286

Ianos (Greece) *Tel:* (031) 277004 *Fax:* (031) 284832 *Web Site:* www.ianos.gr, pg 311

IBA International Book Agency Schmidt-Braul & Partner (Germany) *Tel:* (069) 9441 4744 *Fax:* (069) 9441 4746 *E-mail:* iba.media@t-online.de, pg 1111

Ibadan University Press (Nigeria) *Tel:* (022) 400550; (022) 400614 (ext 1244, 1042, 1032, 1093), pg 499

Ibaizabal Edelvives SA (Spain) *Tel:* (094) 6308036 *Fax:* (094) 6308028 *E-mail:* ibaizabal@euskalnet.net, pg 577

Ibcon SA (Mexico) *Tel:* (05) 5665700 *Fax:* (05) 2554577 *E-mail:* ibcon@infosel.net.mx *Web Site:* www.ibcom.com.mx, pg 462

IBD Publisher & Distributors (India) *Tel:* (011) 3251094 *Fax:* (011) 3259102 *E-mail:* piyush_gahlot@rediffmail.com, pg 338

Ibera VerlagsgesmbH (Austria) *Tel:* (01) 513 19 72 *Fax:* (01) 513 19 72-28 *E-mail:* strobele@ibera.at *Web Site:* www.ibera.at, pg 53

Editorial Iberia, SA (Spain) *Tel:* (093) 2010599; (093) 2013807 *Fax:* (093) 2097362 *E-mail:* omega@ediciones-omega.es *Web Site:* www.ediciones-omega.es, pg 577

Iberico Europea de Ediciones SA (Spain) *Tel:* (091) 4357243, pg 577

Livro Ibero-Americano Ltda (Brazil) *Tel:* (021) 221-2026 *Fax:* (021) 2252-8814 *Web Site:* www.livroiberoamericano.hpg.ig.com.br, pg 85

Livro Ibero-Americano Ltda (Brazil) *Tel:* (021) 221-2026; (021) 2325248; (021) 2329048 *Fax:* (065) 2528814, pg 1277

Ibero-Amerikanisches Institut Preussischer Kulturbesitz (Germany) *Tel:* (030) 2662520 *Fax:* (030) 2662503 *E-mail:* iai@iai.spk-berlin.de *Web Site:* www.iai.spk-berlin.de, pg 1467

Iberoamericana Editorial Vervuert (Germany) *Tel:* (069) 5974617 *Fax:* (069) 5978743 *E-mail:* info@iberoamericanalibros.com *Web Site:* www.iberoamericana.net, pg 1284

IBIS (Denmark) *Tel:* 35358788 *Fax:* 35350696 *E-mail:* ibis@ibis.dk *Web Site:* www.ibis.dk, pg 133

Ibis (Italy) *Tel:* (031) 3371367 *Fax:* (031) 306829 *E-mail:* ibisedizioni@galactica.it *Web Site:* www.ibisedizioni.it, pg 393

IBRASA (Instituicao Brasileira de Difusao Cultural Ltda) (Brazil) *Tel:* (011) 3107 41 00 *Fax:* (011) 3107 35 13 *E-mail:* editora.ibrasa@uol.com.br *Web Site:* www.ibrasa.com.br, pg 85

IBS Buku Sdn Bhd (Malaysia) *Tel:* (03) 7751763; (03) 7751566; (03) 7760514 *Fax:* (03) 7765551 *E-mail:* ibsbuku@po.jaring.my, pg 452

IBS Buku Sdn Bhd (Malaysia) *Tel:* (03) 7760514; (03) 775166; (03) 7751763 *Fax:* (03) 7765551 *E-mail:* ibss@ibsbuku.po.my, pg 1298

ICA bokforlag (Sweden) *Tel:* (021) 194278 *Fax:* (021) 194283 *E-mail:* bok@forlaget.ica.se *Web Site:* www.forlaget.ica.se/bok, pg 603

Icaria Editorial SA (Spain) *Tel:* (093) 3011723 *Fax:* (093) 3178242 *Web Site:* www.icariaeditorial.com, pg 577

ICBS/IBIS ApS (Denmark) *Tel:* 33114255 *Fax:* 33911167 *E-mail:* icbs@get2net.dk, pg 1110

ICC United Kingdom (United Kingdom) *Tel:* (020) 7823 2811 *Fax:* (020) 7235 5447 *E-mail:* katharinehedger@iccorg.co.uk *Web Site:* www.iccwbo.org; www.iccuk.net, pg 698

Publicaciones ICCE (Spain) *Tel:* (091) 725 72 00 *Fax:* (091) 361 10 52 *E-mail:* info@ciberaula.net *Web Site:* www.ciberaula.net, pg 577

Iceland Review (Iceland) *Tel:* 522 2000 *Fax:* 522 2022 *E-mail:* info@edda.is, pg 328

ICG/Holliston (United States) *Tel:* 423-357-6141 *Fax:* 423-357-8840 *E-mail:* custserv@icg-online.com *Web Site:* www.icg-online.com, pg 1216

ICG Publications Holland (Netherlands) *Tel:* (078) 6510454 *Fax:* (078) 6510972, pg 479

Ichiryu-Sha (Japan) *Tel:* (03) 38213916 *Fax:* (03) 38213964, pg 417

Ichtiar Baru I Van Hoeve (Indonesia) *Tel:* (021) 354533, pg 1157, 1198, 1212

Ici et Ailleurs-Vents des Iles (France) *Tel:* (04) 42533087 *Fax:* (04) 42533097 *E-mail:* mail@kaona.com *Web Site:* www.kaona.com, pg 169

ICOB/Atrium (Netherlands) *Tel:* (0172) 437231 *Fax:* (01720) 39379, pg 1301

Icon Press (United Kingdom) *Tel:* (01323) 507270 *Fax:* (01323) 507270 *E-mail:* iconpress@philipbrown.screaming.net *Web Site:* www.iconpress.co.uk, pg 698

Icone Editora Ltda (Brazil) *Tel:* (011) 826-7074; (021) 826-9510 *Fax:* (011) 826-9510, pg 85

ICPC Ltd (Ireland) *Tel:* (01) 8474711 *Fax:* (01) 8474546, pg 1157

ICSI Corp (United States) *Tel:* 330-645-0004; 330-786-0002 *Fax:* 330-786-0056 *Web Site:* www.equidataservice.com, pg 1165

Edition ID-Archiv/ID-Verlag (Germany) *Tel:* (030) 6947703 *Fax:* (030) 6947808 *E-mail:* id-verlag@mail.nadir.org *Web Site:* www.txt.de/id-verlag/, pg 244

Idara-e-Tehqiqat-e-Islami (Pakistan) *Tel:* (051) 850751-5; (051) 850755, pg 507

Idara Ishaat-E-Diniyat Ltd (India) *Tel:* (011) 6926832; (011) 6926833 (office); (011) 461676; (011) 4631786 (showroom) *Fax:* (011) 6932787; (011) 4632786 *E-mail:* idara@del2.vsnl.net.in; sales@idara.com *Web Site:* www.idara.com, pg 339

Idara Siqafat-e-Islamia (Pakistan) *Tel:* (042) 53908, pg 507

Idea Verlag GmbH (Germany) *Tel:* (08141) 80939 *Fax:* (08141) 80939 *E-mail:* idea-verlag@freepage.de *Web Site:* www.idea-verlag.de, pg 244

Idea Books (Italy) *Tel:* (02) 89010670 *Fax:* (02) 86462515, pg 393

Idea (Italy) *Tel:* (02) 8373949 *Fax:* (02) 8357776, pg 1293

Idea Books, SA (Spain) *Tel:* (093) 4533002 *Fax:* (093) 4541895 *E-mail:* ideabooks@ideabooks.es *Web Site:* www.ideabooks.es, pg 578

The Ideal Bookshop (Malta) *Tel:* 553944, pg 1299

Idegenforgalmi Propaganda es Kiado Vallalat (Hungary) *Tel:* (01) 1363652; (01) 363653 *Fax:* (01) 1837320, pg 324

Idegraf SA, Editions (Switzerland) *Tel:* (022) 7920395 *Fax:* (022) 7936330 *E-mail:* 101512.3363@compuserve.com, pg 616

Casa Editrice Libraria Idelson di G Gnocchi (Italy) *Tel:* (081) 5524733 *Fax:* (081) 5518295 *E-mail:* idelgno@tin.it *Web Site:* www.idelson-gnocchi.com, pg 393

Editions Ides et Calendes SA (Switzerland) *Tel:* (32) 7253861 *Fax:* (32) 7255880 *E-mail:* artides@artides.com; ides@livre.net *Web Site:* www.artides.com; www.livre.net/ides, pg 616

Idmon Publications (Greece) *Fax:* (01) 5015550 *E-mail:* idmon@in.gr, pg 311

Istituto Idrografico della Marina (Italy) *Tel:* (010) 24431 *Fax:* (010) 261400 *E-mail:* maridrografico.ge.sre@marina.difesa.it, pg 393

Idryma Meleton Chersonisou tou Aimou (Greece) *Tel:* (0310) 832143 *Fax:* (0310) 831429 *E-mail:* imxa@imxa.gr, pg 311

Idunn (Iceland) *Tel:* 5528555 *Fax:* 5528380 *E-mail:* idunn@vortex.is, pg 328

IDW-Verlag GmbH (Germany) *Tel:* (0211) 45610 *Fax:* (0211) 4541206 *Web Site:* www.idw-verlag.de, pg 244

Ie-No-Hikari Association (Japan) *Tel:* (03) 32669028 *Fax:* (03) 52612307, pg 418

Ifjusagi Lap-eskonyvkiado Vallalat (Hungary) *Tel:* (01) 1116660 *Fax:* (01) 1530959, pg 324

IFLA International Programme for UAP (United Kingdom) *Tel:* (01937) 546123 *Fax:* (01937) 546478 *E-mail:* ifla@bl.uk *Web Site:* www.ifla.org/VI/2/uap.htm, pg 698

IG Autorinnen Autoren (Austria) *Tel:* (01) 526 20 44-13 *Fax:* (01) 526 20 44-55 *E-mail:* ig@literaturhaus.at *Web Site:* www.literaturhaus.at/lh/ig, pg 53

Igaku-Shoin Ltd (Japan) *Tel:* (03) 38175664 *Fax:* (03) 38157804, pg 418

Igbo Language Translation Agency (Nigeria) *Tel:* (046) 230013, pg 1127

Igel Verlag Literatur Michael Matthias Schardt (Germany) *Tel:* (0441) 6640262 *Fax:* (0441) 6640263, pg 244

Editorial Pablo Iglesias (Spain) *Tel:* (091) 3 104 313 *Fax:* (091) 3 194 585 *Web Site:* www.fpabloiglesias.es, pg 578

Iglu Editora Ltda (Brazil) *Tel:* (011) 3873-0227 *Fax:* (011) 872-9907, pg 85

IGN (Institut Geographique National) (France) *Tel:* (01) 43988000 *Fax:* (01) 43988400 *Web Site:* www.ign.fr/fr/pi/adresse, pg 169

IHT Gruppo Editoriale SRL (Italy) *Tel:* (02) 794181 *Fax:* (02) 784021 *E-mail:* info@iht.it *Web Site:* www.iht.it, pg 393

Il Pensiero Scientifico Editore SRL (Italy) *Tel:* (06) 86282334 *Fax:* (06) 86282250 *E-mail:* pensiero@pensiero.it *Web Site:* www.pensiero.it, pg 393

Ikaros (Greece) *Tel:* (01) 3225152, pg 1286

Ikaros Ekdotiki (Greece) *Tel:* (01) 3225152 *Fax:* (01) 3235262, pg 311

Ikarus - Buchverlag (Germany) *Tel:* (06682) 919383 *Fax:* (06682) 919385 *E-mail:* ikarus-verlag@t-online.de *Web Site:* www.ikarus-verlag.de, pg 244

Ikatan Pustakawan Indonesia (Indonesia) *Tel:* (021) 342529 *Fax:* (021) 3103554, pg 1518

Ikatan Penerbit Indonesia (IKAPI) (Indonesia) *Tel:* (021) 3141907; (021) 3146050 *Fax:* (021) 3146050 *E-mail:* sekretariat@ikapi.or.id *Web Site:* www.ikapi.or.id, pg 1249

IKI NOKTA Research Press & Publications Industry & Trade Ltd (Turkey) *Tel:* (0216) 4180319; (0216) 4180320 *Fax:* (0216) 3376756 *E-mail:* ikinokta@superonline.com; ikinokta@turkinfo.com; ikinokta@gisoturkey.com; ikinokta@turkgis.com; ikinokta@infoturk.com *Web Site:* www.ikinekta.com, pg 640

IKO Verlag fur Interkulturelle Kommunikation (Germany) *Tel:* (069) 784808 *Fax:* (069) 7896575 *E-mail:* ikoverlag@t-online.de *Web Site:* www.iko-verlag.de, pg 244

Ikon Document Services (United States) *Tel:* 978-562-9131 *Fax:* 978-562-4304, pg 1165

Ikon Document Services (United States) *Tel:* 978-562-9131 *Fax:* 978-562-4304 *Web Site:* www.tecdoc.com, pg 1207

Ikon Document Services Ltd (United Kingdom) *Tel:* (0118) 9770510 *Fax:* (0118) 9770513, pg 1141

Ikon Document Services Ltd (United Kingdom) *Tel:* (0118) 9770510 *Fax:* (0118) 9770513 *E-mail:* pamh@ikonds.co.uk *Web Site:* www.ikon.com, pg 1162, 1203

Ikon Document Services Ltd (United Kingdom) *Tel:* (0118) 9770510 *Fax:* (0118) 9770513 *E-mail:* marcb@ikonds.co.uk, pg 1223

Ikon Publishing Ltd (Hungary) *Tel:* (01) 1761404 *Fax:* (01) 1158089, pg 324

Ikubundo Publishers Co (Japan) *Tel:* (03) 8145571 *Fax:* (03) 38145576, pg 1294

Il Minotauro (Italy) *Tel:* (06) 5591864 *Fax:* (06) 5592337 *E-mail:* ilminotauro@tin.it *Web Site:* www.ilminotauroeditore.it, pg 393

Il Polifilo (Italy) *Tel:* (02) 6551549 *Fax:* (02) 6598045, pg 393

Il Poligrafo (Italy) *Tel:* (049) 776986 *Fax:* (049) 8070910, pg 393

Il Quadrante SRL (Italy) *Tel:* (011) 6693910 *Fax:* (011) 6693929, pg 393

Il Saggiatore (Italy) *Tel:* (02) 29403460 *Fax:* (02) 29513061 *E-mail:* info@saggiatore.it *Web Site:* www.saggiatore.it, pg 393

ILA (International Literary Agency) USA (Italy) *Tel:* (0184) 484048; (0347) 9334966 *Fax:* (0184) 487292 *E-mail:* libri.gg@dmw.it, pg 1113

Ila - Palma, Tea Nova (Italy) *Tel:* (091) 332051 *Fax:* (091) 6259260, pg 393

Ilesanmi Press (Educational Publishers) Ltd (Nigeria) *Tel:* (034) 232762; (034) 232044, pg 499

Iletisim Yayinlari (Turkey) *Tel:* (0212) 5162263; (0212) 5162260; (0212) 5162264; (0212) 5162265 *Fax:* (0212) 5161258 *E-mail:* editors@iletisim.com.tr, pg 640

Ilisso Edizioni di Vanna Fois & CSNC (Italy) *Tel:* (0784) 33033 *Fax:* (0784) 35413 *E-mail:* ilisso@ilisso.it *Web Site:* www.ilisso.it, pg 1293

Iljisa Publishing House (Republic of Korea) *Tel:* (02) 7329320 *Fax:* (02) 7222807, pg 437

Iljo-gag Publishers (Republic of Korea) *Tel:* (02) 733543011 *Fax:* (02) 7385857 *E-mail:* ilchokak@hitel.kol.co.kr; ilchokak@chollian.dacom.co.kr, pg 437

Illert Publications (Australia) *Tel:* (0242) 83-3009 (international); (0242) 833009 (within Australia) *Fax:* (0242) 833009 (within Australia), pg 27

Ilmamaa (Estonia) *Tel:* (07) 427320; (07) 427290 *Fax:* (07) 427320 *E-mail:* ilmamaa@ilmamaa.ee *Web Site:* www.ilmamaa.ee, pg 140

Iluminuras - Projetos e Producoes Editoriais Ltda (Brazil) *Tel:* (011) 3068-9433 *Fax:* (011) 2825317, pg 85

Image & Print Group Ltd (United Kingdom) *Tel:* (0141) 3531900 *Fax:* (0141) 3532472 *E-mail:* imageandprint@dial.pipex.com *Web Site:* www.imageandprint.co.uk, pg 1162, 1203, 1214

Image/Magie (France) *Tel:* (01) 66803402 *Fax:* (01) 66803456, pg 169

Image Printing Company Ltd (Hong Kong) *Tel:* 28732633 *Fax:* 25583044 *E-mail:* imageprt@pop3.hknet.com, pg 1134, 1156, 1196, 1212

Imagen y Deporte, SL (Spain) *Tel:* (0976) 754000 *Fax:* (0976) 754000 *E-mail:* internocional@imagenydeporte.com *Web Site:* www.imagenydeporte.com, pg 578

The Images Publishing Group Pty Ltd (Australia) *Tel:* (03) 9561 5544 *Fax:* (03) 9561 4860 *E-mail:* books@images.com.au *Web Site:* www.imagespublishinggroup.com, pg 27

Imago (United States) *Tel:* 847-358-3047 *Fax:* 212-921-8226 *E-mail:* imagousa@imagousa.com *Web Site:* www.imagousa.com, pg 1143, 1207, 1216

Imago Editora Importacao e Exportacao Ltda (Brazil) *Tel:* (021) 5029092 *Fax:* (021) 5025435 *E-mail:* imago@imagoeditora.com.br, pg 85

Editions Imago (France) *Tel:* (01) 46-33-15-33 *Fax:* (01) 60-23-87-51 *E-mail:* info@editions-imago.fr *Web Site:* www.editions-imago.fr, pg 169

Imago Productions (Far East) Pte Ltd (Singapore) *Tel:* 7484433 *Fax:* 7486082, pg 1222

Imago Publishing Ltd (United Kingdom) *Tel:* (01844) 337000 *Fax:* (01844) 339935 *E-mail:* sales@imago.co.uk *Web Site:* www.imago.co.uk, pg 698

Imago Services (HK) Ltd (Hong Kong) *Tel:* 28113316 *Fax:* 25975253, pg 1134

Imam Mohamed Bin Saud University Library (Saudi Arabia) *Tel:* (01) 2580812 *Fax:* (01) 4020886, pg 1495

IMEC (France) *Tel:* (01) 53 34 23 23 *Fax:* (01) 53 34 23 00 *E-mail:* bibliotheque@imec-archives.com *Web Site:* www.imec-archives.com, pg 169

Imge Kitabevi (Turkey) *Tel:* (0312) 4181942 *Fax:* (0312) 4256532 *E-mail:* imge@www.imge.com.tr, pg 640

Immediate Publishing (United Kingdom) *Tel:* (01865) 200422 *Fax:* (01865) 200355, pg 699

Impact (United Kingdom) *Tel:* (020) 7222 7777; (020) 7636 7543 *Fax:* (020) 7222 2782; (020) 7436 7218, pg 1525

Impala (Portugal) *Tel:* (01) 4364401; (01) 4363860 *Fax:* (01) 4366572, pg 525

Imparudi (Imprimerie et Papeterie du Burundi) (Burundi) *Tel:* (02) 3125; (02) 7381 *Fax:* (02) 2572, pg 1278

Imperial College Press (United Kingdom) *Tel:* (020) 7836 3954 *Fax:* (020) 7836 2002 *E-mail:* edit@icpress.co.uk *Web Site:* www.icpress.co.uk, pg 699

IMPF BV BA (Belgium) *Tel:* (09) 2254429 *Fax:* (09) 2331338 *E-mail:* IMPF@xs4all.be, pg 1153

IMPF BV BA (Belgium) *Tel:* (09) 2254429 *Fax:* (09) 2331338, pg 1193, 1221

Impredisur, SL (Spain) *Tel:* (058) 290577, pg 578

Imprensa Nacional-Casa da Moeda (Portugal) *Tel:* (021) 658325 *Fax:* (021) 693166, pg 526

Imprenta de la Universidad Nacional (Colombia) *Tel:* (01) 2686965; (01) 2699111 (ext 860) *Fax:* (01) 2441035, pg 112

Imprenta y Litografia Trejos SA (Costa Rica) *Tel:* 2242411 *Fax:* 2241528, pg 116

Imprima Korea Agency (Republic of Korea) *Tel:* (02) 714 9154 *Fax:* (02) 714 9150 *E-mail:* imprima@bora.dacom.co.kr; imprima@chollian.net, pg 1114

Imprimerie Bene (France) *Tel:* (04) 66294897 *Fax:* (04) 66382146, pg 1132, 1194

Imprimerie Bietlot Freres SA (Belgium) *Tel:* (071) 283611 *Fax:* (071) 283620, pg 1211

Imprimerie Commerciale et Administrative de Mauritanie (Mauritania), pg 456

Imprimerie de Kabgayi (Rwanda) *Tel:* 62252; 62877 *Fax:* 62345, pg 543

Imprimerie Descamps SA (France) *Tel:* (03) 27400208 *Fax:* (03) 27405683, pg 1132

Imprimerie et Papeterie Commerciale, IPC (Mauritius) *Tel:* 2124190 *Fax:* 2083523, pg 457

IMPS Research Pty Ltd (Papua New Guinea) *Tel:* 3213283 *Fax:* 3217360 *E-mail:* slandon@dotec.com.pg, pg 510

Impuls (Poland) *Tel:* (012) 4225947 *Fax:* (012) 4224180; (012) 4225947, pg 517

Impuls-Theater-Verlag (Germany) *Tel:* (089) 8597577 *Fax:* (089) 8593044 *E-mail:* info@buschfunk.de *Web Site:* www.buschfunk.de, pg 244

Imrie & Dervis Literary Agency (United Kingdom) *Tel:* (020) 8809 3282 *Fax:* (020) 8880 2086 *E-mail:* info@imriedervis.com, pg 1119

In Dialogo (Italy) *Tel:* (02) 8052529 *Fax:* (02) 58391345 *E-mail:* indial@tin.it, pg 393

In-Tune Books (Australia) *Tel:* (02) 9974 5981 *Fax:* (02) 9974 4552, pg 27

INADES (Institut Africain pour le Developpment Economique et Social) (Cote d'Ivoire) *Tel:* 224404720 *Fax:* 22448438 *E-mail:* inades@ci.refer.org; inades@africaonline.co.ci *Web Site:* www.inades.ci.refer.org, pg 1459

INADES (Institut Africain pour le Developpment Economique et Social) (Rwanda), pg 543

Inbal Publishers (Israel) *Tel:* (03) 9030111 *Fax:* (03) 9030888 *E-mail:* inbalpub@internet-zahav.net, pg 368

Inbal Travel Information (Israel) *Tel:* (03) 5753032 *Fax:* (03) 5753130, pg 368

Editorial Incafo SA (Spain) *Tel:* (091) 4313460; (091) 5780961 *Fax:* (091) 4313589, pg 578

Incorporated Catholic Truth Society (United Kingdom) *Tel:* (020) 7640 0042 *Fax:* (020) 7640 0046 *E-mail:* info@cts-online.org.uk *Web Site:* www.cts-online.org.uk, pg 699

Incunabula Press (Australia) *Tel:* (03) 93811559, pg 27

Independence (United Kingdom) *Tel:* (01223) 566 130 *Fax:* (01223) 566 131 *E-mail:* issues@independence.co.uk *Web Site:* www.independence.co.uk, pg 699

Independent Publishers Guild (United Kingdom) *Tel:* (01767) 677753 *Fax:* (01767) 677069, pg 1266

Independent Writers Publications Ltd (United Kingdom) *Tel:* (020) 8438 0179 *Fax:* (020) 8438 0179, pg 699

Editora Index Ltda (Brazil) *Tel:* (021) 5162336 *Fax:* (021) 2533507 *E-mail:* editoraindex@ax.ibase.org.br, pg 85

India Book House Pvt Ltd (India) *Tel:* (022) 2840165 *Fax:* (022) 2835099 *E-mail:* padmini@ibhindia.com, pg 339

Indian Association of Academic Librarians (India) *Tel:* (011) 6831717, pg 1517

Indian Association of Special Libraries & Information Centres (IASLIC) (India) *Tel:* (033) 334-9651, pg 1517

Indian Book Depot (Map House) (India) *Tel:* (011) 3673927; (011) 3523635 *Fax:* (011) 3552096 *E-mail:* ibdmaps@ndb.vsnl.net.in; ibd@indiabookfair.net *Web Site:* www.indiabookfair.net, pg 339

Indian Council for Cultural Relations (India) *Tel:* (011) 3319309 *Fax:* (011) 3712639 *Web Site:* education.vsnl.com/iccr/index.html, pg 339

Indian Council of Agricultural Research (India) *Tel:* (011) 388991 *Fax:* (011) 387293 *Web Site:* www.icar.org.in, pg 339

INDIAN COUNCIL OF WORLD AFFAIRS LIBRARY INDUSTRY

Indian Council of World Affairs Library (India) *Tel:* (011) 3317246 *Fax:* (011) 3317248, pg 1473

Indian Documentation Service (India) *Tel:* (0124) 6322005; (0124) 6322779 *Fax:* (0124) 6324782 *E-mail:* indoc@indiatimes.com *Web Site:* www.indocservice.com, pg 339

Indian Institute of Advanced Study (India) *Tel:* (0177) 72303; (0177) 75139 *Fax:* (0177) 75139 *E-mail:* info@iias.org *Web Site:* www.iias.org, pg 339

Indian Institute of Management (India) *Tel:* (079) 6307241; (079) 6324980 *Fax:* (079) 6306896, pg 1473

Indian Institute of Technology Central Library (India) *Tel:* (044) 2351365 *Fax:* (044) 2350509 *E-mail:* lib@iitm.ernet.in, pg 1473

Indian Institute of World Culture (India) *Tel:* (080) 6678581 *Web Site:* www.ultindia.org, pg 339

Indian Library Association (India) *Tel:* (011) 7117743, pg 1517

Indian Museum (India) *Tel:* (033) 2499902; (033) 2499904; (033) 249 9979; (033) 249 8948; (033) 249 8931 *Fax:* (033) 249 5699 *E-mail:* imbot@cal2.vsnl.net.in *Web Site:* www.indianmuseum-calcutta.org, pg 339

Indian National Scientific Documentation Centre (INSDOC) (India) *Tel:* (011) 660141 *Fax:* (011) 6862228 *E-mail:* mcs@sirnet.ernet.in *Web Site:* www.insdoc.org, pg 1126

Indian Society for Promoting Christian Knowledge (ISPCK) (India) *Tel:* (011) 2966323 *Fax:* (011) 2965490 *E-mail:* ispck@nde.vsnl.net.in *Web Site:* www.acpl.com, pg 339

Instituto Indigenista Interamericano (Mexico) *Tel:* (05) 6600007; (05) 6600132 *Fax:* (05) 6521274, pg 462

Indigo & Cote-Femmes Editions (France) *Tel:* (1) 43797479 *Fax:* (1) 43794687 *E-mail:* indigo.cote-femmes.edition@wanadoo.fr *Web Site:* www.indigo-cf.com, pg 169

PT Indira (Indonesia) *Tel:* (021) 3904290; (021) 3148868 *Fax:* (021) 3929373 *E-mail:* indirawb@mweb.co.id, pg 355

PT Indira (Indonesia) *Tel:* (021) 3148868; (021) 3904290 *Fax:* (021) 3929373 *E-mail:* indirawb@mweb.co.id, pg 1291

Indo Lingua Services Ltd (United Kingdom) *Tel:* (0171) 4822666 *Fax:* (0171) 4852667 *E-mail:* indolingua@compuserve.com, pg 1129

Indonesian ISBN Agency (Indonesia) *Tel:* (021) 3101411 *Fax:* (021) 3103554 *E-mail:* sauliah@pnri.go.id, pg 1249

Indra Publishing (Australia) *Tel:* (03) 9439 7555 *Fax:* (03) 9439 7555 *Web Site:* www.indra.com.au, pg 27

Indrajaya CV (Indonesia) *Tel:* (021) 3457039; (021) 3457041 *Fax:* (021) 3457039, pg 355

Indus Publishing Co (India) *Tel:* (011) 5935289; (011) 5151333 *Fax:* (011) 5449682 *E-mail:* mail@indusbooks.com; indusbooks@vsnl.com *Web Site:* www.indusbooks.com, pg 339

Industria-Verlagsbuchhandlung GmbH (Germany) *Tel:* (02323) 1410 *Fax:* (02323) 141123, pg 244

Industrial Publishing House (Democratic People's Republic of Korea), pg 434

Industrial Technology Institute Information Services Centre (Sri Lanka) *Tel:* (01) 698624 *Fax:* (01) 697994; (01) 686567; (01) 698624, pg 1499

Industrias del Envase SA (Peru) *Tel:* (01) 5741150 *Fax:* (01) 5741787 *E-mail:* postmast@envase.com.pe *Web Site:* www.envase.com.pe, pg 1199

Industrie- und Handelsverlag GmbH & Co KG (Germany) *Tel:* (0511) 98489957 *Fax:* (0511) 98489952 *E-mail:* info@fhb-online.de *Web Site:* www.fhb-online.de/, pg 244

Verlag Industrielle Organisation (Switzerland) *Tel:* (01) 4667711 *Fax:* (01) 4667412 *E-mail:* info@ofv.ch *Web Site:* www.ofv.ch, pg 616

Styret for det Industrielle Rettsvern Information Department (Norway) *Tel:* 22387300 *Fax:* 22387301, pg 1489

Industrieschau Verlagsgesellschaft mbH (Germany) *Tel:* (06151) 38920 *Fax:* (06151) 33164 *E-mail:* info@abconhine.de *Web Site:* www.abconline.de, pg 244

Industrilitteratur Vindex, Forlags AB (Sweden) *Tel:* (08) 7838100 *Fax:* (08) 6605911, pg 603

Info Access & Distribution (Singapore) *Tel:* 7418422 *Fax:* 7418821 *E-mail:* andrew@accesshost.com.sg, pg 1309

Infoa (Czech Republic) *Tel:* (0648) 449-091 *Fax:* (0648) 449-091 *E-mail:* infoa@ova.pvtnet.cz *Web Site:* www.infoa.cz, pg 124

Infoboek NV (Belgium) *Tel:* (014) 30 04 77 *Fax:* (014) 30 32 43 *E-mail:* info@infoboek.be, pg 69

Centre National Infor Jeunes (Belgium) *Tel:* (02) 537 64 63 *Fax:* (081) 228264, pg 69

Informa Publishing Group Ltd (United Kingdom) *Tel:* (020) 7453 2222 *Fax:* (020) 7436 2450 *Web Site:* www.informa.com, pg 699

Instituto de Informacion Cientifica y Tecnologica (IDICT) (Cuba) *Tel:* (07) 626501 *Fax:* (07) 338237 *E-mail:* decoreli@ceniai.inf.cu; garriga@ceniai.inf.cu *Web Site:* www.idict.cu, pg 121

Informatica Cosmos SA de CV (Mexico) *Tel:* (05) 6774868; (05) 6776043 *Fax:* (05) 6793575 *E-mail:* online@cosmos.com.mx *Web Site:* www.cosmos.com.mx, pg 462

Mediteg-Gesellschaft fuer Informatik Technik und Systeme Verlag (Germany) *Tel:* (06081) 5171 *Fax:* (06081) 56017, pg 245

Information Agents Ltd (United Kingdom) *Tel:* (020) 7837 3345 *Fax:* (020) 7837 8901 *E-mail:* eps@epsltd.com *Web Site:* www.epsltd.com, pg 1119

Information Processing Society of Japan (Japan) *Tel:* (03) 54843535 *Fax:* (03) 54843534 *E-mail:* Iizuka@ipsj.or.jp; tsuchi@ipsj.or.jp; somo@ipsj.or.jp, pg 1518

Informationsfoerlaget AB (Sweden) *Tel:* (08) 340915 *Fax:* (08) 313903 *E-mail:* red@informationsforlaget.se, pg 603

Informationsstelle Suedliches Afrika eV (ISSA) (Germany) *Tel:* (0228) 464369 *Fax:* (0228) 468177 *E-mail:* issa@comlink.org *Web Site:* www.issa-bonn.org, pg 245

Informationszentrum fuer Informationswissenschaft und -praxis (IZ) (Germany) *Tel:* (0331) 5802210 *Fax:* (0331) 5802229 *E-mail:* iz@fh-potsdam.de, pg 1516

Informator dd (Croatia) *Tel:* (01) 6111-500 *Fax:* (01) 6111-446 *E-mail:* info@informator.hr *Web Site:* www.informator.hr, pg 119

Infostelle Industrieverband Deutscher Schmieden e V (Germany) *Tel:* (02331) 95 88 28 *Fax:* (02331) 95 87 28 *E-mail:* oders@metalform.de *Web Site:* www.metalform.de, pg 245

INFRA-M Izdatel 'skij dom (Russian Federation) *Tel:* (095) 4855936 *Fax:* (095) 4855318 *E-mail:* books@orc.ru, pg 538

Editions Infrarouge (France) *Tel:* (01) 49950874 *Fax:* (01) 49950874 *E-mail:* editionsinfrarouge@libertysurf.fr; editions.infrarouge@caramail.com *Web Site:* www.chez.com/editinfrarouge, pg 169

Ingenioeren/Boger (Denmark) *Tel:* 33265300 *Fax:* 33265390 *E-mail:* bogservice@ing.dk *Web Site:* www.bog.ing.dk, pg 133

Ingenioeren/Boger (Denmark) *Tel:* 33265454 *Fax:* 33265545, pg 1132

Ingenjoersforlaget AB (Sweden) *Tel:* (08) 7966500 *Fax:* (08) 7896224, pg 603

Inkilap Publishers Ltd (Turkey) *Tel:* (0212) 5140611; (0212) 5140610 *Fax:* (0212) 5140612 *Web Site:* www.inkilap.com, pg 640

Inland Publishers (United Republic of Tanzania) *Tel:* (068) 40064, pg 633

Inn-Verlag, DrieBlein & Co KG (Austria) *Tel:* (0512) 34 53 31 *Fax:* (0512) 34 12 90 *E-mail:* office@innverlag.at; innverlag@tirol.com *Web Site:* www.innverlag.at, pg 53

Inn-Verlag, DrieBlein & Co KG (Austria) *Tel:* (0512) 34 53 31 *Fax:* (0512) 34 12 90 *E-mail:* office@innverlag.at *Web Site:* www.innverlag.at, pg 1274

Inner Mongolia Science & Technology Publishing House (China) *Tel:* (0476) 22942, pg 106

Inno Vatio Verlags AG (Germany) *Tel:* (0228) 2433180 *Fax:* (0228) 319471 *E-mail:* medien-tenor@innovatio.de *Web Site:* www.innovatio.de; www.medien-tenor.de, pg 245

Editrice Innocenti SNC (Italy) *Tel:* (0461) 36521 *Fax:* (0461) 30115, pg 393

Innodata Corp (United States) *Tel:* 201-488-1200 *Fax:* 201-488-9099 *E-mail:* solutions@innodata.com *Web Site:* www.innodata.com, pg 1165

Brian Inns Booksales & Services (United Kingdom) *Tel:* (01926) 498428 *Fax:* (01926) 498428, pg 1320

Universitaetsbibliothek Innsbruck (Austria) *Tel:* (0512) 5072401 *Fax:* (0512) 5072864, pg 1451

Inprint Caribbean Ltd (Trinidad & Tobago) *Tel:* 6271569; 6231711 *Fax:* 6271451, pg 637

Editorial Inquerito Lda (Portugal) *Tel:* (021) 917 0096 *Fax:* (021) 917 0130 *E-mail:* inquerito@iol.pt, pg 526

INRA Editions (Institut National de la Recherche Agronomique) (France) *Tel:* (01) 30833406 *Fax:* (01) 30833449 *E-mail:* inra_editions@versailles.inra.fr *Web Site:* www.inra.fr/editions, pg 169

Insel Verlag (Germany) *Tel:* (069) 756010 *Fax:* (069) 75601522 *Web Site:* www.suhrkamp.de, pg 245

Editions INSERM (France) *Tel:* (01) 44 23 60 82 *Fax:* (01) 44 23 60 99 *Web Site:* www.inserm.fr, pg 169

Insituto Centroamericano de Administracion de Empresas (INCAE) (Costa Rica) *Tel:* 506-433-9908; 433-9961; 433-9269; 443-0506 *Fax:* 506-433-9955; 433-9983; 433-9101 *Web Site:* www.incae.ac.cr, pg 116

Inspirace (Czech Republic) *Tel:* (02) 7356615, pg 124

Editions l'Instant Durable (Soprep) (France) *Tel:* (04) 73 92 07 89 *Fax:* (04) 73 91 13 87 *E-mail:* art@instantdurable.com *Web Site:* www.instantdurable.com, pg 169

Instauratio Press (Australia) *Tel:* (03) 59666217 *Fax:* (03) 59666447 *E-mail:* catholic@scservnet.com, pg 27

Institucion Fernando el Catolico de la Excma Diputacion de Zaragoza (Spain) *Tel:* (0976) 28 88 78; (0976) 28 88 79 *Fax:* (0976) 28 88 69 *E-mail:* info@ifc.dpz.es *Web Site:* www.dpz.es, pg 578

Editorial Institucional y Desarrollo Humanistico SA de CV Edicion de Libros (Mexico) *Tel:* (05) 5215060; (05) 5215009, pg 462

Institut Africain de Developpement Economique et de Planification (IDEP), Bibliotheque (Senegal) *Tel:* 8231020 *Fax:* 8222964 *E-mail:* idep@sonatel.senet.net, pg 1496

Institut de Bibliotheconomie et des Sciences Documentaires (Algeria) *Tel:* 647971, pg 1511

Institut de Formation et de Recherche Demographiques (IFORD) (Cameroon) *Tel:* (023) 222471; (023) 231917 *Fax:* (023) 226793, pg 1239

Bibliotheque de l'Institut de France (France) *Tel:* (01) 44414410 *Fax:* (01) 44414411, pg 1465

Institut de l'Information Scientifique et Technique (INIST) (France) *Tel:* (03) 83504600 *Fax:* (03) 83504650 *E-mail:* infoclient@inist.fr *Web Site:* www.inist.fr, pg 1465

Institut de Presse & des Sciences de l'Information Universite La Manouba (Tunisia) *Tel:* (01) 600 831; (01) 600 981 *Fax:* (01) 600 465, pg 1504

Institut de Recherche en Sciences Humaines (Niger) *Tel:* 735141, pg 1488

Institut de Recursos I investigacio per a la Formacio SL (IRIF) (Spain) *Tel:* (093) 4080464 *Fax:* (093) 3524337 *E-mail:* grao@grao.com *Web Site:* www.grao.com, pg 578

Institut des Belles Lettres Arabes (Tunisia) *Tel:* (01) 560133 *Fax:* (01) 572683 *E-mail:* ibla@gnet.tn, pg 1369

Institut Fondamental d'Afrique Noire, Bibliotheque (Senegal) *Tel:* (0221) 250090 *E-mail:* bibifan@ifan.refer.sn, pg 1496

Bibliotheque de l'Institut Francais d'Archeologie du Proche Orient (Lebanon) *Tel:* (01) 615 844 *Fax:* (01) 615 866 *E-mail:* ifapo@lb.refer.org, pg 1481

Institut Francais de Recherche Scientifique pour le Developpement en Cooperation (French Guiana) *Tel:* 302785 *Fax:* 319855, pg 1466

Institut National Agronomique, Bibliotheque (Algeria) *Tel:* (052) 1987 *Fax:* (052) 3547, pg 1449

Institut Nauchnoy Informatsii po Obschestvennym Naukam, Rossijskoj Akademii Nauk RF (Russian Federation) *Tel:* (095) 1288881; (095) 1288930 *Fax:* (095) 4202261, pg 1495

Institut Pasteur d'Algerie, Bibliotheque (Algeria) *Tel:* (065) 8860 *Fax:* (067) 2503, pg 1449

Institut Pedagogique National (The Democratic Republic of the Congo) *Tel:* (012) 80573, pg 1458

Institut pour la Recherche Scientifique en Afrique Centrale (IRSAC) (The Democratic Republic of the Congo), pg 1458

Institut Royal des Relations Internationales (Belgium) *Tel:* (02) 2234114 *Fax:* (02) 2234116 *E-mail:* info@irri-kiib.be *Web Site:* www.irri-kiib.be, pg 69

Institut Royal des Sciences Naturelles de Belgique, Bibliotheque (Belgium) *Tel:* (02) 627 41 89 *Fax:* (02) 627 41 13 *E-mail:* bib@naturalsciences.be *Web Site:* www.naturalsciences.be, pg 1453

Institut Scientifique (Morocco) *Tel:* (07) 774548 *Fax:* (07) 774540, pg 1485

Perpustakaan Pusat Institut Teknologi Bandung (Indonesia) *Tel:* (022) 2500089 *Fax:* (022) 2500089, pg 1474

Institut Teknologi Bandung (Indonesia) *Tel:* (022) 2504048; (022) 2503147 *Fax:* (022) 431792 *E-mail:* itbpress@melsa.net.id; sofia@penerbit.itb.ac.id *Web Site:* www.itb.ac.id, pg 355

Institute (France) *Tel:* (01) 0871717 *Fax:* (01) 40871718 *E-mail:* graphite@wandadoo.fr, pg 169

Institute of Aboriginal Development (IAD Press) (Australia) *Tel:* (089) 8951 1331 *Fax:* (089) 8952 2527 *E-mail:* press@iad.edu.au, pg 28

Institute for Agricultural Research (IAR) (Nigeria) *Tel:* (069) 50681 *Fax:* (069) 50563, pg 1488

Institute for Financial Affairs Inc-KINZAI (Japan) *Tel:* (03) 33580011 *Fax:* (03) 33580036, pg 418

Institute for Fiscal Studies (United Kingdom) *Tel:* (020) 7291 4800 *Fax:* (020) 7323 4780 *E-mail:* mailbox@ifs.org.uk *Web Site:* www.ifs.org.uk, pg 699

The Institute for Israeli Arabs Studies (Israel) *Tel:* (09) 7486738 *Fax:* (09) 7486341, pg 368

Institute for Palestine Studies, Publishing & Research Organization (IPS) (Lebanon) *Tel:* (01) 868387 *Fax:* (01) 868387, pg 443

Institute for Reformational Studies CHE (South Africa) *Tel:* (0148) 2992826 *Fax:* (0148) 2992824 *E-mail:* irsmcs@puknet.puk.ac.za, pg 555

Institute for Research Extension and Training in Agriculture (IRETA) (Samoa) *Tel:* (0685) 21882 *Fax:* (0685) 21671, pg 543

Institute for Social & Economic Change Library (India) *Tel:* (080) 3355468; (080) 3387010 *Fax:* (080) 3387008 *E-mail:* ssisec@ren.nic.in, pg 1473

The Institute for the Translation of Hebrew Literature (Israel) *Tel:* (03) 5796830 *Fax:* (03) 5796832 *E-mail:* hamachon@inter.net.il *Web Site:* www.ithl.org.il, pg 368

The Institute for the Translation of Hebrew Literature (Israel) *Tel:* (03) 5796830 *Fax:* (03) 5796832 *E-mail:* litscene@ithl.org.il *Web Site:* www.ithl.org.il, pg 1113, 1127, 1249

Institute of African Studies Library (Ghana) *Tel:* (021) 500512 *Fax:* (021) 667701; (021) 500512; (021) 502397 *E-mail:* africans@africanline.com.gh, pg 1470

Institute of African Studies, Onyeka, A (Nigeria) *Tel:* (022) 400550; (022) 400614 ext 12444, pg 500

Institute of Arab Research & Studies Library (Egypt (Arab Republic of Egypt)) *Tel:* (02) 3551648 *Fax:* (02) 3562543, pg 1462

Institute of Development Management Library (United Republic of Tanzania) *Tel:* (023) 260-4380-4 *Fax:* (023) 260-4382 *E-mail:* idm@raha.com, pg 1502

Institute of Development Studies (United Kingdom) *Tel:* (01273) 606261 *Fax:* (01273) 621202; (01273) 691647 *E-mail:* idsbtng.ids.books@sussex.au.uk *Web Site:* www.ids.ac.uk/ids/publicat, pg 699

Institute of Development Studies (United Kingdom) *Tel:* (01273) 606261 *Fax:* (01273) 621202; (01273) 691647, pg 1506

Institute of Economic Affairs (United Kingdom) *Tel:* (020) 7799 8900 *Fax:* (020) 7799 2137 *E-mail:* enquiries@iea.org.uk; iea@iea.org.uk *Web Site:* www.iea.org.uk, pg 699

Institute of Economics Library (Myanmar) *Tel:* (01) 532433, pg 1485

Institute of Education Library, Kabul University (Afghanistan) *Tel:* 42594, pg 1449

Institute of Education Library (Myanmar) *Tel:* (01) 31345, pg 1485

Institute of Education, University of London (United Kingdom) *Tel:* (020) 7580 1122 *Fax:* (020) 7612 6560 *Web Site:* www.ioe.ac.uk/publications, pg 699

Institute of Ethiopian Studies Library (Ethiopia) *Tel:* (01) 550844; (01) 119469 *Fax:* (01) 552688 *E-mail:* ies.aau@telecom.net.et, pg 1463

Institute of Irish Studies, The Queens University of Belfast (United Kingdom) *Tel:* (028) 9027 3386 *Fax:* (028) 9043 9238 *E-mail:* iispubs@qub.ac.uk *Web Site:* www.qub.ac.uk/iis, pg 699

Institute of Islamic Culture (Pakistan) *Tel:* (042) 305920; (042) 6363127, pg 507

Institute of Jamaica Publications (Jamaica) *Tel:* (876) 926-5683; (876) 929-4786; (876) 929-4785 *Fax:* (876) 926-8817, pg 413

Institute of Kiswahili Research (United Republic of Tanzania) *Tel:* (051) 49106 ext 2647, pg 633

Institute of Linguists (United Kingdom) *Tel:* (020) 7940 3100 *Fax:* (020) 7940 3101 *E-mail:* info@iol.orgk.uk, pg 1129

Papua New Guinea Institute of Medical Research (Papua New Guinea) *Tel:* 7322800; 712200 *Fax:* 7321998, pg 510

Institute of Neohellenic Studies, Manolis Triantaphyllidis Foundation (Greece) *Tel:* (031) 279695 *Fax:* (031) 997122, pg 311

Institute of Physics Publishing (United Kingdom) *Tel:* (0117) 929 7481 *Fax:* (0117) 929 4318 *E-mail:* custserv@iop.org *Web Site:* www.iop.org, pg 700

Institute of Printing (United Kingdom) *Tel:* (01892) 538118; (01892) 518028 *Fax:* (01892) 518028 *E-mail:* iop@globalprint.com *Web Site:* www.globalprint.com/uk/iop, pg 1266

Institute of Public Administration (Ireland) *Tel:* (01) 2697011 *Fax:* (01) 2698644 *E-mail:* information@ipi.ie *Web Site:* www.ipa.ie, pg 361

Institute of Public Administration Library (Saudi Arabia) *Tel:* (01) 4768888 *Fax:* (01) 4792136 *E-mail:* library@ipa.edu.sa, pg 1495

Institute of Scientific & Technical Communicators (ISTC) (United Kingdom) *Tel:* (1480) 211550 *Fax:* (1480) 211560 *E-mail:* istc@istc.org.uk *Web Site:* www.istc.org.uk, pg 1266

Institute of Southeast Asian Studies (Singapore) *Tel:* 6778 0955 *Fax:* 6775 6259 *E-mail:* pubsunit@iseas.edu.sg *Web Site:* www.iseas.edu.sg/pub.html, pg 546

Institute of Translation & Interpreting (United Kingdom) *Tel:* (020) 7713 7600 *Fax:* (020) 7713 7650 *E-mail:* info@iti.org.uk *Web Site:* www.iti.org.uk, pg 1129

Instituti Editoriali E Poligrafici Internazionali SRL (Italy) *Tel:* (050) 878066 *Fax:* (050) 878732 *E-mail:* iepi@iepi.it, pg 393

Institution of Chemical Engineers (United Kingdom) *Tel:* (01788) 578214 *Fax:* (01788) 560833 *E-mail:* jcressey@icheme.org.uk *Web Site:* www.icheme.org, pg 700

Institution of Electrical Engineers (United Kingdom) *Tel:* (01438) 313311 *Fax:* (01438) 313465 *E-mail:* postmaster@iee.org.uk *Web Site:* www.iee.org.uk/publish, pg 700

Biblioteca del Instituto Anglo-Mexicano de Cultura (Mexico) *Tel:* (05) 5664500 *Fax:* (05) 5666739, pg 1484

Instituto Autonomo, Biblioteca Nacional y de Servicios de Bibliotecas (Venezuela) *Tel:* (02) 5059141 *Fax:* (02) 5059159, pg 1508

Instituto Caro y Cuervo (Colombia) *Tel:* (01) 255-82-89; (01) 248-84-66 *Fax:* (01) 217-02-43; (01) 342-21-21 *E-mail:* carocuer@gaitana.interred.net.co *Web Site:* www.caroycuervo.gov.co; www.caroycuervo.edu.co, pg 112

Instituto Caro y Cuervo (Colombia) *Tel:* (01) 2557753 *Fax:* (01) 217-02-43 *E-mail:* carocuer@interred.gov.co, pg 1361

Instituto Centroamericano de Administracion de Empresas (INCAE) Library (Nicaragua) *Tel:* (02) 58446-8, pg 1488

Instituto de Bibliografia del Ministerio de Educacion de la Provincia de Buenos Aires (Argentina) *Tel:* (021) 35915, pg 1511

Instituto de Estudios Economicos (Spain) *Tel:* (091) 782 05 80 *Fax:* (091) 562 36 13 *E-mail:* iee@ieemadrid.com, pg 578

Instituto de Informacion Cientifica y Tecnologica (IDICT) Ministerio de Ciencia, Technolia y Medio Ambiente (CITMA) (Cuba) *Tel:* (07) 62-6501; 60-3411 *Fax:* (07) 33-8237 *E-mail:* garriga@ceniai.inf.cu, pg 1459

Instituto de Investigaciones Bibliograficas (Mexico) *Tel:* (05) 6226808 *Fax:* (05) 6650951, pg 1520

Instituto de Investigaciones Electricas (Mexico) *Tel:* (073) 183811 *Fax:* (073) 182521 *E-mail:* postmaster@iie.org.mx, pg 1484

Instituto de Literatura y Lingueistica (Cuba) *Tel:* (07) 785405 *Fax:* (07) 338054; (07) 331325, pg 1459

Instituto dos Arquivos Nacionais/Torre do Tombo (Portugal) *Tel:* (01) 7811500 *Fax:* (01) 7937230 *E-mail:* dc@iantt.pt, pg 1493

Instituto Interamericano de Cooperacion para la Agricultura (IICA) (Costa Rica) *Tel:* (0506) 2290222 *Fax:* (0506) 2294741, pg 1240

Instituto Nacional de Estadistica (Spain) *Tel:* (091) 583 91 00 *E-mail:* info@ine.es *Web Site:* www.ine.es, pg 578

Biblioteca del Instituto Panamericano de Geografia e Historia (Mexico) *Tel:* (05) 2775888 *Fax:* (05) 2716172, pg 1485

Instituto Portugues da Sociedade Cientifica de Goerres (Portugal) *Tel:* (021) 7265554 *Fax:* (021) 7260546 *E-mail:* mrato@reitoria.ucp.pt, pg 1367

Instituto Tecnologico y de Estdios Superiores de Monterrey Biblioteca (Mexico) *Tel:* (081) 8328-4096 *Fax:* (081) 8328-4067 *Web Site:* cib.mty.itesm.mx, pg 1485

Instituto Vasco de Criminologia (Spain) *Tel:* (0943) 321411; (0943) 321412 *Fax:* (0943) 321272 *E-mail:* szoivac@sc.ehu.es *Web Site:* www.sc.edu.es, pg 578

Editura Institutul European (Romania) *Tel:* (032) 127311 *Fax:* (032) 230197 *E-mail:* rtvnova@mail.cccis.ro, pg 533

Institutul National de Informare si Documentare (INID) (Romania) *Tel:* (01) 6134010 *Fax:* (01) 3126734 *E-mail:* inid@iniduw.inid.ro, pg 1494

Instytut Badan Literackich PAN (Poland) *Tel:* (022) 8269945, pg 1367

Instytut Bibliograficzny (Poland) *Tel:* (022) 6082946 *Fax:* (022) 8255251 *E-mail:* sadowska@bn.org.pl, pg 1492

Instytut Wydawniczy Pax, Inco-Veritas (Poland) *Tel:* (022) 6257795; (022) 6253398; (022) 6251378 *Fax:* (022) 6253398; (022) 6251378; (022) 6257795 *E-mail:* iwpax@com.pl *Web Site:* www.iwpax.com.pl, pg 517

Int Press (Australia) *Tel:* (03) 93262416 *Fax:* (03) 93262413 *E-mail:* intpress@ozemail.com.au *Web Site:* www.intpress.com.au, pg 28

Integrated Book Technology Inc (United States) *Tel:* 518-271-5117 *Fax:* 518-266-9422 *E-mail:* mail@integratedbooktechnology.com *Web Site:* www.integratedbooktechnology.com, pg 1145, 1165, 1207, 1216, 1224

Intellect Ltd (United Kingdom) *Tel:* (0117) 955 6811 *E-mail:* mail@intellectbooks.com *Web Site:* www.intellectbooks.com, pg 700

Intellectual Publishing Co (Singapore) *Tel:* 7466025 *Fax:* 7489108, pg 546

Intellectual Publishing House (India) *Tel:* (011) 279911, pg 339

Inter American University of Puerto Rico Library (Puerto Rico) *Tel:* (787) 878-5475 (ext 320) *Fax:* (787) 880-1624 *E-mail:* sabreu@uiprl.inter.edu, pg 1493

Inter-Cultural Book Promoters (Sri Lanka) *Tel:* 925359 *Fax:* 925359 *E-mail:* inculture@eureka.lk, pg 597

Inter-India Publications (India) *Tel:* (011) 5441120; (011) 5467082, pg 340

Inter-Medica (Argentina) *Tel:* (011) 4961-9234 *Fax:* (011) 4961-5572 *E-mail:* intervet@satlink.com, pg 6

Inter-Parliamentary Union (Switzerland) *Tel:* (022) 9194150 *Fax:* (022) 9194160 *E-mail:* postbox@mail.ipu.org *Web Site:* www.ipu.org, pg 1260

Inter-Varsity Press (United Kingdom) *Tel:* (0116) 2551754 *Fax:* (0116) 2542044 *E-mail:* ivp@uccf.org.uk, pg 700

Libreria Interacademica SA de CV (Mexico) *Tel:* (05) 265-1165 *Fax:* (05) 265-1164, pg 1299

Instituto Interamericano de Cooperacion para la Agricultura (IICA) (Costa Rica) *Tel:* (02) 2443680 *Fax:* (02) 2469175 *E-mail:* iicahq@iica.ac.cr *Web Site:* www.iica.int, pg 116

Interbook-Business AO (Russian Federation) *Tel:* (095) 2006469; (095) 2006462 *Fax:* (095) 9563752, pg 538

Intercept Ltd (United Kingdom) *Tel:* (01264) 334748 *Fax:* (01264) 334058 *E-mail:* intercept@andover.co.uk *Web Site:* www.intercept.co.uk, pg 700

Editora Interciencia Ltda (Brazil) *Tel:* (021) 2241-6916 *Fax:* (021) 2501-4760, pg 85

Interconnections Reisen und Arbeiten Georg Beckmann (Germany) *Tel:* (0761) 2000 *Fax:* (0761) 200572, pg 245

Intercontinental Editora (Paraguay) *Tel:* (021) 496991 *Fax:* (021) 449738, pg 510

Intercontinental Literary Agency (United Kingdom) *Tel:* (020) 7351 4763 *Fax:* (020) 7351 4809 *E-mail:* mesdaile@pfd.co.uk, pg 1119

Intercultural Networking Ltd (ICN) (United Kingdom) *Tel:* (020) 7628 5876 *Fax:* (020) 7628 9147 *E-mail:* icn@dircon.co.uk *Web Site:* www.users.dircon.co.uk/~icn/, pg 1129

Interculture (Sweden) *Tel:* (08) 6427804 *Fax:* (08) 6423591, pg 603

Interdigets Publishing House (Belarus) *Tel:* (0172) 847888; (0172) 843778 *Fax:* (0172) 133073, pg 63

InterEditions Paris (France) *Tel:* (01) 40463500 *Fax:* (01) 40466111, pg 169

Editions Interferences (France) *Tel:* (01) 45 67 33 56 *E-mail:* interferences@editions-interferences.com *Web Site:* www.editions-interferences.com, pg 169

Interfisc Publishing (United Kingdom) *Tel:* (020) 7610 2722 *Fax:* (020) 7610 3373 *E-mail:* editor@interfisc.com *Web Site:* www.interfisc.com, pg 700

Interfrom AG Editions (Switzerland) *Tel:* (01) 2020900, pg 616

Interlivros Edicoes Ltda (Brazil) *Tel:* (021) 3913134 *Fax:* (021) 3521005 *E-mail:* interlivros@ibm.net, pg 85

Intermedia Audio, Video Book Publishing Ltd (Israel) *Tel:* (03) 5608501 *Fax:* (03) 5608513 *E-mail:* freed@inter.net.il, pg 368

Intermediate Technology Publications Ltd (United Kingdom) *Tel:* (020) 7436 9761 *Fax:* (020) 7436 2013 *E-mail:* marketing@itpubs.org.uk *Web Site:* www.itdgpublishing.org.uk, pg 700

Libreria Internacional Estudio (Chile) *Tel:* (041) 225533 *Fax:* (041) 244542, pg 1279

Ediciones Internacionales Universitarias SA (Spain) *Tel:* (091) 5193907 *Fax:* (091) 4136808 *Web Site:* www.eunsa.es, pg 578

Internationaal Instituut voor Sociale Geschiedenis (Netherlands) *Tel:* (020) 6685866 *Fax:* (020) 6654181 *E-mail:* inf.gen@iisg.nl *Web Site:* www.iisg.nl, pg 1486

International Book House Pvt Ltd (India) *Tel:* (0812) 2021634; (0812) 2021795, pg 1289

International Book Centre (Portugal), pg 1307

International Bookshops (Saudi Arabia) *Tel:* (03) 4641851 *Fax:* (03) 4641851, pg 1308

International Bookshop (United Republic of Tanzania) *Tel:* (051) 21930; (051) 27458, pg 1314

International Academic Publishers (China) *Tel:* (010) 8316677-530 *Fax:* (010) 4015664, pg 106

International African Institute (United Kingdom) *Tel:* (020) 7898 4420 *Fax:* (020) 7898 4419 *E-mail:* ed2@soas.ac.uk; iai@soas.ac.uk, pg 1266

International Association for Mass Communication Research (Netherlands) *Tel:* (020) 6101581 *Fax:* (020) 6104821, pg 1254

International Association for the Evaluation of Educational Achievement (IEA) (Netherlands) *Tel:* (020) 6253625 *Fax:* (020) 4207136 *E-mail:* department@iea.nl *Web Site:* www.iea.nl, pg 1254

International Association of Agricultural Information Specialists (United Kingdom), pg 1266

International Association of Law Libraries (IALL) (United States) *Tel:* 804-924-3384 *Fax:* 804-982-2232 *E-mail:* lbw@virginia.edu *Web Site:* www.iall.org, pg 1268

International Association of Literary Critics (France) *Tel:* (01) 53101200 *Fax:* (01) 53101212, pg 1244

International Association of Music Libraries, New Zealand Branch, Inc (New Zealand) *Tel:* (04) 8014040 *Fax:* (04) 8014047, pg 1521

International Association of Music Libraries, Archives & Documentation Centres (IAML) (Canada) *Tel:* 613-520-2600 (ext 8150) *Fax:* 613-520-3583, pg 1239

International Association of Music Libraries, Archives & Documentation Centres (Canada) *Tel:* 613-520-2600 (ext 8150) *Fax:* 613-520-3583, pg 1513

International Association of Music Libraries, Archives & Documentation Centres (UK & Irl Branch) (United Kingdom) *Tel:* (0131) 242 8053 *Fax:* (0131) 242 8009, pg 1525

International Association of Orientalist Librarians (Belgium) *Tel:* (016) 16324698 *Fax:* (016) 16324703 *Web Site:* www.-01.uchicago.edu/01/1aol, pg 1238

International Association of Scholarly Publishers (IASP) (United States) *Tel:* 517-355-9543 *Fax:* 517-432-2611 *E-mail:* bohm@pilot.msu.edu, pg 1268

International Association of School Librarianship (United States) *Tel:* 604-925-0266 *Fax:* 604-925-0566 *E-mail:* iasl@rockland.com, pg 1268

International Association of Scientific, Technical and Medical Publishers (STM) (Netherlands) *Tel:* (033) 4656060 *Fax:* (033) 4656538 *E-mail:* lefebvre@stm.nl *Web Site:* www.stm-assoc.org, pg 1254

International Association of Sound & Audiovisual Archives (Germany) *Tel:* (07221) 9293487 *Fax:* (07221) 9294199 *Web Site:* www.llgc.org.uk/iasa/, pg 1245

International Association of Technological University Libraries (IATUL) (United Kingdom) *Tel:* (0131) 451 3570 *Fax:* (0131) 451 3164, pg 1266

International Association of Universities (France) *Tel:* (01) 45 6825 45 *Fax:* (01) 47 3476 05 *E-mail:* iau@unesco.org *Web Site:* www.unesco.org/iau, pg 1244

International Atomic Energy Agency (IAEA) (Austria) *Tel:* (0222) 2600-0 *Fax:* (0222) 2600-7 *E-mail:* official.mail@iaea.org *Web Site:* www.iaea.org, pg 1237

International Bee Research Association (United Kingdom) *Tel:* (02920) 372409 *Fax:* (02920) 665522 *E-mail:* mail@cardiff.ac.uk *Web Site:* www.cf.ac.uk/ibra, pg 701

International Bible Society (Sweden) *Tel:* (0513) 21930 *Fax:* (0513) 21501, pg 603

International Board on Books for Young People (IBBY) (Switzerland) *Tel:* (061) 2722917 *Fax:* (061) 2722757 *E-mail:* ibby@eye.ch *Web Site:* www.ibby.org, pg 1139

International Board on Books for Young People (IBBY) (Switzerland) *Tel:* (061) 2722917 *Fax:* (061) 2722757 *E-mail:* ibby@eye.ch; ibby@ibby.org, pg 1260

International Book Development (United Kingdom) *Tel:* (020) 8742 7474 *Fax:* (020) 8747 8715, pg 1266

International Book Distributors (India) *Tel:* (0135) 656526; (0135) 657497; (0135) 650949; (0135) 9897003322 *Fax:* (0135) 656554 *E-mail:* ibdbooks@sancharnet.in *Web Site:* ibdbooks.com, pg 340

International Booksellers Federation (IBF) (Belgium) *Tel:* (02) 2234940 *Fax:* (02) 2234941 *E-mail:* eurobooks@skynet.be, pg 1238

International Catholic Organization for Cinema & Audiovisual (OCIC) (Belgium) *Tel:* (02) 7344294 *Fax:* (02) 7343207 *E-mail:* sg@ocic.org *Web Site:* www.ocic.org, pg 1238

International Centre for Ethnic Studies (Sri Lanka) *Tel:* (08) 23095 *Fax:* (08) 234892 *E-mail:* ices@slt.lk, pg 597

International Centre for Research in Agroforestry (ICRAF) (Kenya) *Tel:* (02) 524000 *Fax:* (02) 524001 *E-mail:* icraf@cgiar.org *Web Site:* cgiar.org/ICRAF, pg 432

International Centre Study Preservation & Restoration of Cultural Property (ICCROM) (Italy) *Tel:* (06) 585531 *Fax:* (06) 58553349 *E-mail:* iccrom@iccrom.org *Web Site:* www.iccrom.org, pg 1250

International Chamber of Commerce (France) *Tel:* (01) 49532828 *Fax:* (01) 49532942 *E-mail:* icclib@ibnet.com; icc@iccwbo.org *Web Site:* www.iccwbo.org, pg 1244

International Commission of Jurists (Switzerland) *Tel:* (022) 7884747 *Fax:* (022) 7884880 *E-mail:* icjch@gn.apc.org, pg 1260

International Communications (United Kingdom) *Tel:* (020) 7713 7711 *Fax:* (020) 7713 7898; (020) 7713 7970 *E-mail:* icpubs@africasia.com *Web Site:* www.africasia.com, pg 701

International Community of Writers' Unions (Russian Federation) *Tel:* (095) 2916307 *Fax:* (095) 2919760, pg 1257

International Comparative Literature Association (United States) *Tel:* 416-487-6727 *Fax:* 416-487-6786, pg 1268

International Council on Archives (France) *Tel:* (01) 40276306 *Fax:* (01) 42722065 *E-mail:* ica@ica.org *Web Site:* www.ica.org, pg 1244

International Crops Research Institute for the Semi-Arid Tropics (ICRISAT) (India) *Tel:* 40596161 *Fax:* 40241239 *E-mail:* icrisat@cgnet.com, pg 1248

International Culture Publishing Corp (China) *Tel:* (010) 4013415; (010) 4010830 *Fax:* (010) 4013437, pg 106

Institut International de la Marionnette (France) *Tel:* (03) 24337250 *Fax:* (03) 24337269 *E-mail:* inst.marionnette@ardennes.com *Web Site:* perso.wanadoo.fr/institut; www.marionnette.com, pg 170

The International Documentary Centre of Arab Manuscripts (Lebanon), pg 443

International Documentation Center, The University of Tokyo (Japan) *Tel:* (03) 38122111 ext 2645 *Fax:* (03) 58002426 *E-mail:* kokusai@lib.u-tokyo.ac.jp, pg 1478

International Ediemme (Italy) *Tel:* (06) 39378788 *Fax:* (06) 6380839 *E-mail:* iscd@colosseum.it, pg 394

International Editors' Co (Argentina) *Tel:* (011) 4788-2992; (011) 4786-0888 *Fax:* (011) 4786-0888 *E-mail:* costa@lvd.com.ar, pg 1109

International Editors' Co SL (Spain) *Tel:* (093) 2158812 *Fax:* (093) 4873583 *E-mail:* ieco@internationaleditors.com, pg 1116

International Educational Services (Pakistan) *Tel:* (021) 521540, pg 507

International Federation for Information & Documentation (FID) (Netherlands) *Tel:* (070) 3140671 *Fax:* (070) 3140667 *E-mail:* fid@fid.nl *Web Site:* www.fid.nl, pg 1254

International Federation for Information Processing (IFIP) (Austria) *Tel:* (02236) 73616 *Fax:* (02236) 736169 *E-mail:* ifip@ifip.or.at *Web Site:* www.ifip.or.at, pg 1237

International Federation of Library Associations & Institutions (IFLA) (Netherlands) *Tel:* (070) 3140884 *Fax:* (070) 3834827 *E-mail:* ifla@ifla.org *Web Site:* www.ifla.org, pg 1254, 1520

International Federation of Reproduction Rights Organisations (IFRRO) (Belgium) *Tel:* (02) 551 08 99 *Fax:* (02) 551 08 95 *E-mail:* iffro@skynet.be; secretariat@ifrro.be *Web Site:* www.ifrro.org, pg 1238

International Fiction Review (Canada) *Tel:* 506-453-4636 *Fax:* 506-447-3166 *E-mail:* ifr@unb.ca *Web Site:* www.lib.unb.ca/Texts/IFR, pg 1239

International Holographic Paper (United States) *Tel:* 215-997-8006 *Fax:* 215-997-9005 *E-mail:* sales@itwholographics.com *Web Site:* www.itwholographics.com, pg 1216

International Institute for Applied Systems Analysis (IIASA) (Austria) *Tel:* (02236) 807 433 *Fax:* (02236) 71313 *E-mail:* info@iiasa.ac.at; publications@iiasa.ac.at *Web Site:* www.iiasa.ac.at, pg 53

International Institute for Children's Literature & Reading Research (UNESCO category C) (Austria) *Tel:* (01) 5050359; (01) 5052831 *Fax:* (01) 5050359-17; (01) 5052831-17 *E-mail:* office@jupendliturature.net *Web Site:* www.jugendliteratur.net, pg 1237

International Institute for Educational Planning (IIEP) (France) *Tel:* (01) 45037700 *Fax:* (01) 40728366, pg 1244

International Institute for Labour Studies (Switzerland) *Tel:* (022) 7996128 *Fax:* (022) 7998542 *E-mail:* info@ils.org *Web Site:* www.ils.org/inst, pg 1260

International Institute for Strategic Studies (United Kingdom) *Tel:* (020) 7379 7676 *Fax:* (020) 7836 3108 *E-mail:* iiss@iiss.org *Web Site:* www.iiss.org, pg 701

International Institute of Iberoamerican Literature (United States) *Tel:* 412-624-5246 *Fax:* 412-624-0829 *E-mail:* iilit@pitt.edu *Web Site:* www.pitt.edu/~illi, pg 1268

International Institute of Islamic Thought (Pakistan) *Tel:* (051) 851621 *Fax:* (051) 280489 *E-mail:* iiipak@paknet1.ptc.pk, pg 507

International Institute of Tropical Agriculture Library (Nigeria) *Tel:* (02) 2412626 *Fax:* (02) 8741772276 via INMARSAT *E-mail:* iita@cgnet.com, pg 1488

The International Irrigation Management Institute (Sri Lanka) *Tel:* (01) 867404 *Fax:* (01) 866854, pg 1259

International ISBN Agency, International ISMN Agency (Germany) *Tel:* (030) 266 2498 *Fax:* (030) 2662378 *E-mail:* isbn@sbb.spk-berlin.de; ismn@sbb.spk.berlin.de *Web Site:* isbn-international.org; ismn-international.org, pg 1246

International ISMN Agency (Germany) *Tel:* (030) 266 2496; (030) 266 2498; (030) 266 2338 *Fax:* (030) 266-2378 *E-mail:* ismn@sbb.spk-berlin.de *Web Site:* ismn-international.org, pg 1246

International Labour Office (United Kingdom) *Tel:* (020) 7828 6401 *Fax:* (020) 7233 5925 *E-mail:* ipu@ilo-london.org.uk *Web Site:* www.ilo.org, pg 701

International Labour Office, Bureau of Library & Information Services (Switzerland) *Tel:* (022) 7998675 *Fax:* (022) 7996516 *E-mail:* bibl@ilo.org, pg 1501

International Labour Organization (ILO) (Switzerland) *Tel:* (022) 7996111 *Fax:* (022) 7998578 *E-mail:* pubvente@ilo.org, pg 1260

International Languages & Translations School (United Kingdom) *Tel:* (020) 8882 3362 *Fax:* (020) 8882 3362, pg 1129

International Law Book Services (Malaysia) *Tel:* (03) 2939864; (03) 2939862; (03) 2933661; (03) 2931661 *Fax:* (03) 2928035 *E-mail:* gbc@pc.jaring.my *Web Site:* bookgold.com, pg 452

International League of Antiquarian Booksellers (ILAB) (United States) *Tel:* 800-441-0076; 612-290-0700 *Fax:* 612-290-0646 *E-mail:* rulon@winternet.com *Web Site:* www.ilab.org, pg 1268

International Literatuur Bureau BV (Netherlands) *Tel:* (035) 6213500 *Fax:* (035) 6215771 *Web Site:* www.ilb.nu, pg 1115

International Livestock Research Institute (Kenya) *Tel:* (02) 632311 *Fax:* (02) 631499, pg 1251

International Map Trade Association (United Kingdom) *Tel:* 01425) 620532 *Fax:* (01425) 620532 *E-mail:* imtaeurope@compuserve.com *Web Site:* www.maptrade.org, pg 701

International Maritime Organization (IMO) (United Kingdom) *Tel:* (020) 7735 7611 *Fax:* (020) 7587 3210, pg 1266

The International Molinological Society (United Kingdom) *Tel:* (1923) 232980, pg 1266

International Monetary Fund (United States) *Tel:* 202-623-7430 *Fax:* 202-623-7201, pg 1268

International Organization for Standardization (ISO) (Switzerland) *Tel:* (022) 7490111 *Fax:* (022) 7333430 *E-mail:* central@iso.org *Web Site:* www.iso.org (online catalogue provides full listing), pg 1261

International PEN (United Kingdom) *Tel:* (020) 7253 4308 *Fax:* (020) 7253 5711 *E-mail:* intpen@dircon.co.uk *Web Site:* www.internatpen.org, pg 1266

The International Press Agency (United Kingdom) *Tel:* (0181) 3904414 *Fax:* (0181) 3904414, pg 1119

The International Press Agency (Pty) Ltd (South Africa) *Tel:* (021) 5311926 *Fax:* (021) 5318789 *E-mail:* inpra@iafrica.com, pg 1116

International Press Co Pte Ltd (Singapore) *Tel:* 2983800 *Fax:* 2971668, pg 1138, 1200, 1213

International Publications Agency (IPA) (Saudi Arabia) *Tel:* (03) 8954925, pg 543

International Publications Service Inc (IPS) (Republic of Korea) *Tel:* (02) 7342666; (02) 7342669 *Fax:* (02) 7336936, pg 1296

International Publishers Association (Switzerland) *Tel:* (022) 3463018 *Fax:* (022) 3475717 *E-mail:* secretariat@ipa-uie.org *Web Site:* www.ipa-uie.org, pg 1261

International Publishers Distributor (S) Pte Ltd (Singapore) *Tel:* 7416933 *Fax:* 7416922, pg 546

International Reading Association (United States) *Tel:* 302-731-1600 *Fax:* 302-731-1057, pg 1268

International Rice Research Institute (IRRI) (Philippines) *Tel:* (02) 884669; (02) 884511 *Fax:* (02) 7612404; (02) 8911292 *E-mail:* postmaster@irri.cgnet.com, pg 513

International Road Federation (Switzerland) *Tel:* (022) 3060260 *Fax:* (022) 3060270 *E-mail:* info@irfnet.org *Web Site:* www.irfnet.org, pg 1261

International Scripts Ltd (United Kingdom) *Tel:* (020) 8319 8666 *Fax:* (020) 8319 0801, pg 1120

International Society for Educational Information (ISEI) (Japan) *Tel:* (03) 33581138 *Fax:* (03) 33597188 *E-mail:* kaya@isei.or.jp *Web Site:* www.isei.or.jp, pg 418

International Standard Book Numbering Agency (South Africa) *Tel:* (012) 218931 *Fax:* (012) 3255984 *E-mail:* therese@statelib.pwv.gov.za, pg 1258

International Standards Books & Periodicals (P) Ltd (Nepal) *Tel:* (01) 212289; (01) 224005; (01) 223036 *Fax:* (01) 223036, pg 471

International Telecommunication Union (ITU) (Switzerland) *Tel:* (022) 7306161 *Fax:* (022) 7306444, pg 1261

Uitgevery International Theatre & Film Books (Netherlands) *Tel:* (020) 60 60 911 *Fax:* (020) 60 60 914 *E-mail:* info@itfb.nl *Web Site:* www.itfb.nl, pg 479

International Thomson Publishing (ITP) (Germany) *Tel:* (0228) 970240 *Fax:* (0228) 441342 *E-mail:* mitp@mitp.de *Web Site:* www.mitp.de, pg 245

International Union Against Cancer (Switzerland) *Tel:* (022) 8091811 *Fax:* (022) 8091810 *E-mail:* info@uicc.org *Web Site:* www.uicc.org, pg 1261

INTERNATIONAL UNION OF GEOLOGICAL SCIENCES (IUGS)

International Union of Geological Sciences (IUGS) (Norway) *Tel:* 73921500 *Fax:* 73502230, pg 1256

International University Press Srl (Italy) *Tel:* (06) 86211027; (06) 86211028 *Fax:* (06) 86211026, pg 394

Internationale Jugendbibliothek (Germany) *Tel:* (089) 891211-0 *Fax:* (089) 8117553 *E-mail:* bib@ijb.de *Web Site:* www.ijb.de, pg 1246

Internationale Jugendbibliothek (Germany) *Tel:* (089) 8912110 *Fax:* (089) 8117553 *E-mail:* bib@ijb.de, pg 1468

Verlag fuer Internationale Politik GmbH (Germany) *Tel:* (0228) 7290010 *Fax:* (0228) 695734, pg 245

Edizioni Internazionali di Letteratura e Scienze (Italy) *Tel:* (06) 6241563 *Fax:* (06) 61520253, pg 394

Internews Distribution Co (Australia) *Tel:* (02) 97074577 *Fax:* (02) 97086025, pg 1273

Internos Books (United Kingdom) *Tel:* (020) 7637 4255 *Fax:* (020) 7637 4251, pg 1320

Interpet Publishing (United Kingdom) *Tel:* (01306) 881033 *Fax:* (01306) 885009 *E-mail:* publishing@interpet.co.uk, pg 701

InterPost North America (United States) *E-mail:* exo@tnt.com *Web Site:* www.tnt.com, pg 1225

Interpres (Bulgaria) *Tel:* (02) 517915 *Fax:* (02) 517915 *E-mail:* interpres@bis.bg; intrpres@usa.net, pg 96

Interpress (Poland) *Tel:* (022) 6214876; (022) 6289331; (022) 6289202 *Fax:* (022) 6289331; (022) 6289202, pg 517

Interpress Aussenhandels GmbH (Hungary) *Tel:* (01) 3027525; (01) 2508267 *Fax:* (01) 3027530, pg 1136

Interpress Aussenhandels GmbH (Hungary) *Tel:* (01) 3027525 *Fax:* (01) 3027530 *E-mail:* office@interpress.hu *Web Site:* www.interpress.hu, pg 1197, 1212

Interpresse A/S (Denmark) *Tel:* 33337535 *Fax:* 33337505, pg 133

Interprint Ltd - Malta (Malta) *Tel:* 240169; 222720 *Fax:* 243780; 249712 *E-mail:* interprintjb@camline.net.mt, pg 1137, 1199

Interpublications (France) *Tel:* (01) 40921221 *Fax:* (01) 42310729, pg 170

Intersentia Uitgevers NV (Belgium) *Tel:* (03) 680 15 50 *Fax:* (03) 658 71 21 *E-mail:* mail@intersentia.be *Web Site:* www.intersentia.com, pg 69

Intersistemas SA de CV (Mexico) *Tel:* (05) 2028243; (05) 5405600; (05) 5400798 *Fax:* (05) 5403764; (05) 5403464, pg 462

Interskol Forlag AB (Sweden) *Tel:* (040) 510195 *Fax:* (040) 150625 *E-mail:* info@interskol.se *Web Site:* www.interskol.se, pg 603

Uitgeverij Intertaal BV (Netherlands) *Tel:* (020) 5756750 *Fax:* (020) 6752686 *E-mail:* int@intertaal.nl, pg 479

Intertrade Publications (India) *Tel:* (033) 474872; (033) 475069, pg 340

Intertrans-Verlag GmbH (Germany) *Tel:* (069) 871500 *Fax:* (069) 852894, pg 245

Intext Book Company Pty Ltd (Australia) *Tel:* (03) 9819-4500 *Fax:* (03) 9819-4511 *E-mail:* customerservice@intextbook.com.au *Web Site:* www.intextbook.com.au, pg 28

Editions Intore (Burundi) *Tel:* (02) 225167, pg 98

Les Introuvables-Editions L'Harmattan (France) *Tel:* (01) 40467910 *Fax:* (01) 43298620 *E-mail:* harmat@worldnet.fr *Web Site:* www.editions-harmattan.fr, pg 170

Intype London Ltd (United Kingdom) *Tel:* (020) 8947 7863 *Fax:* (020) 8947 3652 *E-mail:* intype@btconnect.com *Web Site:* www.intype.co.uk, pg 1141

Intype London Ltd (United Kingdom) *Tel:* (020) 8947 7863 *Fax:* (020) 8947 3652 *E-mail:* intype@btconnect.com, pg 1162, 1204, 1214

Invandrarfoerlaget (Sweden) *Tel:* (033) 136070 *Fax:* (033) 136075 *E-mail:* migrant@immi.se *Web Site:* www.immi.se, pg 603

El Inversionista Mexicano SA de CV (Mexico) *Tel:* (05) 5243131; (05) 5245346; (05) 5349297 *Fax:* (05) 5243794 *E-mail:* elimmbi@iserve.net.mx, pg 462

Instituto de Investigacao Cientifica Tropical (Portugal) *Tel:* (021) 362 2621; (021) 362 2622; (021) 362 2623; (021) 362 2624; (021) 362 2625; (021) 3645031 *Fax:* (021) 362 2626 *E-mail:* cdi@iict.pt; iictcdi@sapo.pt *Web Site:* www.iict.pt, pg 526

Inwardpath Publishers (Australia) *Tel:* (03) 9499 3405 *Fax:* (03) 94975656, pg 28

IOM Communications Ltd (United Kingdom) *Tel:* (020) 7451 7300 *Fax:* (020) 7839 1702 *E-mail:* admin@materials.org.uk *Web Site:* www.materials.org.uk, pg 701

IOS Press BV (Netherlands) *Tel:* (020) 688 33 55 *Fax:* (020) 620 3419 *E-mail:* market@iospress.nl *Web Site:* www.iospress.nl, pg 479

IP Oslobodenje (Bosnia and Herzegovina) *Tel:* (071) 205-488 *Fax:* (071) 442-500 *E-mail:* redaction@oslobodjenje.com.ba *Web Site:* www.oslobodjenje.com.ba//, pg 77

Iperborea (Italy) *Tel:* (02) 706684 *Fax:* (02) 798919 *E-mail:* iperborea@iol.it, pg 394

Ipis VZW (International Peace Information Service) (Belgium) *Tel:* (03) 225-0022 *Fax:* (03) 231-01-51 *E-mail:* ipis@skynet.be *Web Site:* www.skynet.be/ipis/, pg 69

IPL - Istituto Propaganda Libraria (Italy) *Tel:* (02) 58301960 *Fax:* (02) 58301960, pg 1250

IPL Publishing Group (New Zealand) *Tel:* (04) 499-3032 *Fax:* (04) 499-3032, pg 492

IPS Copyright Agency (International Publications Service (Republic of Korea) *Tel:* (02) 7342666 *Fax:* (02) 7336936 *E-mail:* copyright@ips-korea.com, pg 1114

IR Indo Edicions (Spain) *Tel:* (0986) 21 48 34 *Fax:* (0986) 21 11 33 *E-mail:* correo@irindo.com *Web Site:* www.irindo.com; irindo.net, pg 578

Iralka Editorial SL (Spain) *Tel:* (0943) 32 30 14 *Fax:* (0943) 32 30 22 *E-mail:* iralka@euskalnet.net *Web Site:* www.euskalnet.net/iralka, pg 578

Iranian Information Documentation Centre (Islamic Republic of Iran) *Tel:* (021) 6494954; (021) 6462548 *Fax:* (021) 6462254 *E-mail:* info@irandoc.ac.ir *Web Site:* www.irandoc.ac.ir, pg 1474

Iraq Library Association (Iraq) *Tel:* (01) 4164190, pg 1518

Library of the Iraq Museum (Iraq) *Tel:* (01) 8879687, pg 1475

IRD Editions (France) *Tel:* (01) 48037602 *Fax:* (01) 48037612 *E-mail:* editions@paris.ird.fr *Web Site:* www.ird.fr, pg 170

Ireland Literature Exchange (Ireland) *Tel:* (01) 8727900 *Fax:* (01) 8727875 *E-mail:* info@irelandliterature.com *Web Site:* www.irelandliterature.com, pg 1126

Irfon (Tajikistan) *Tel:* (03772) 33-39-06; (03772) 33-62-54, pg 632

Irini Publishing House - Vassilis G Katsikeas SA (Greece) *Tel:* (01) 3839259; (01) 3810465 *Fax:* (01) 3600651, pg 311

Iris Verlag AG (Switzerland) *Tel:* (031) 947744, pg 616

Irish Academy of Letters (Ireland), pg 1365

Irish Academic Press (Ireland) *Tel:* (01) 668 8244 *Fax:* (01) 660 1610 *E-mail:* info@iap.ie *Web Site:* www.iap.ie, pg 361

Irish Educational Publishers' Association (Ireland) *Tel:* (01) 500 9509 *Fax:* (01) 500 9598, pg 1249

INDUSTRY

Irish Management Institute (Ireland) *Tel:* (01) 2078400 *Fax:* (01) 2955147 *E-mail:* 3025reception@imi.ie *Web Site:* www.imi.ie, pg 361

Irish Texts Society (Cumann Na Scribeann nGaedhilge) (United Kingdom) *E-mail:* shuttonseanfile@aol.com, pg 701

Irish Times Ltd (Ireland) *Tel:* (01) 6758000 *Fax:* (01) 6773282 *E-mail:* b.mcniff@irish-times.ie *Web Site:* www.ireland.com, pg 361

Irish Translators' Association (Ireland) *Tel:* (01) 8721302 *Fax:* (01) 8726282 *E-mail:* translation@eircom.net *Web Site:* www.homepage.eircom.net/~translation; www.translatorsassociation.ie, pg 1127

Irish YouthWork Press (Ireland) *Tel:* (010) 8729933 *Fax:* (010) 8724183 *E-mail:* info@nyf.ie *Web Site:* www.nyf.ie, pg 362

Irmaos Vitale S/A Industria e Comercio (Brazil) *Tel:* (011) 5574-7001 *Fax:* (011) 5574-7388 *E-mail:* irmaos@vitale.com.br *Web Site:* www.vitale.com.br, pg 85

Ediciones Irusa (Spain) *Tel:* (093) 2318032 *Fax:* (093) 2653670, pg 578

Isafoldarprentsmidja hf (Iceland) *Tel:* 5517165 *Fax:* 5517226, pg 328

ISAL (Ist Storia Arte Lombarda) (Italy) *Tel:* (02) 878475 *Fax:* (02) 86463412 *E-mail:* isalbibl@tin.it, pg 394

ISBN Agency (International Standard Book Number National Agency) (Malawi) *Tel:* (050) 525240; (050) 524184 *Fax:* (050) 525 362 *E-mail:* archives@sdnp.org.mw *Web Site:* www.sdnp.org.nw/~archives/index.html, pg 1252

ISBN Agency Australia (Australia) *Tel:* (03) 9245 7385 *Fax:* (03) 9245 7393 *E-mail:* isbn.agency@thorpe.com.au *Web Site:* www.thorpe.com.au, pg 1236

ISBN Agency - Korea (Republic of Korea) *Tel:* (02) 5900627 *Fax:* (02) 5900622; (02) 5900621 *E-mail:* ISSNKC@sun.nl.go.kr, pg 1251

ISBN Agency - Luxembourg (Luxembourg) *Tel:* 229755-225 *Fax:* 475672 *Web Site:* www.bnl.lu, pg 1251

ISBN Agency - Namibia (Namibia) *Tel:* (061) 2935305; (061) 2935301 *Fax:* (061) 2935321 *E-mail:* werner@yaotto.natlib.mec.gov.na, pg 1253

ISBN/BNQ (Canada) *Tel:* 514-873-1100 (ext 319) *Fax:* 514-873-4310 *E-mail:* isbn@bnquebec.ca *Web Site:* www.bnquebec.ca, pg 1240

Bureau ISBN (Netherlands) *Tel:* (0345) 475855 *Fax:* (0345) 475895 *E-mail:* ISBN@centraal.boekhuis.nl, pg 1254

ISBN-Kontoret Norge (Norway) *Tel:* 23276217 *Fax:* 23276010 *E-mail:* isbn-kontoret@nb.no *Web Site:* www.nb.no/html/isbn_eng.html, pg 1256

ISBN National Agency (Slovakia) *Tel:* (842) 4134035 *Fax:* (842) 4734035 *E-mail:* isbn@snk.sk; snk@snk.sk *Web Site:* www.snk.sk, pg 1258

ISCAH Fructuoso Rodriguez (Cuba) *Tel:* (07) 62936 *Fax:* (07) 330942 *E-mail:* athena.isch.cu, pg 121

Klaus Isele (Germany) *Tel:* (07746) 91116 *Fax:* (07746) 91117 *E-mail:* klaus.isele@t-online.de, pg 245

R Ishaak (Suriname) *Tel:* 031917 *Fax:* 0231917, pg 599

Ishihara Publishing Company Ltd (Japan) *Tel:* (0992) 391200 *Fax:* (0992) 391202, pg 418

Ishiyaku Publishers Inc (Japan) *Tel:* (03) 39443131 *Fax:* (03) 53957611, pg 418

Editorial Isidoriana, Libreria (Spain) *Tel:* (0987) 876161 *Fax:* (0987) 876162 *E-mail:* sanisidoro@infonegocio.com, pg 578

ISIOM Verlag fur Tondokumente, Weinreb Tonarchiv (Switzerland) *Tel:* (091) 7513524 *Fax:* (091) 7433913 *E-mail:* isiom@bluewin.ch, pg 616

Isis Publishing Ltd (United Kingdom) *Tel:* (01865) 250 333 *Fax:* (01865) 790 358 *E-mail:* sales@isis-publishing.co.uk *Web Site:* www.isis-publishing.co.uk, pg 701

Isis Yayin Tic ve San Ltd (Turkey) *Tel:* (0216) 3213851; (0216) 3213847; (0216) 3213847 *Fax:* (0216) 3218666 *E-mail:* isis@turk.net, pg 640

Iskry - Publishing House Ltd spotka zoo (Poland) *Tel:* (022) 8279415 *Fax:* (022) 8279415, pg 517

Perpustakaan Islam (Indonesia) *Tel:* (0274) 2078, pg 1474

Islam International Publications Ltd (United Kingdom) *Tel:* (01252) 783155 *Fax:* (01252) 783155, pg 701

Verlag der Islam (Germany) *Tel:* (069) 681485; (069) 681062 *Fax:* (069) 686504, pg 245

Islamic University Central Library (Saudi Arabia) *Tel:* (04) 8474080 *Fax:* (04) 8474560, pg 1495

Islamic Book Centre (Pakistan) *Tel:* (042) 6316803 *Fax:* (042) 6360955, pg 507

Islamic Foundation Publications (United Kingdom) *Tel:* (01530) 244 944; (01530) 249 230 *Fax:* (01530) 244 946; (01530) 249 230 *E-mail:* info@islamic-foundation.org.uk; publication@islamic-foundation.com *Web Site:* www.islamic-foundation.com, pg 701

Islamic Publications (Pvt) Ltd (Pakistan) *Tel:* (042) 7325243; (042) 7664504; (042) 325243; (042) 3664504 *Fax:* (042) 7658674 *E-mail:* islamic@ms.net.pk, pg 507

Islamic Publishing House (India) *Tel:* (0495) 720092; (0495) 724618 *Fax:* (0495) 724524 *E-mail:* iphcalicut@eth.net, pg 340

The Islamic Republic of Iran Parliament Library, No 2 (Ketab-Khane-ye Majles-e Shora-ye Eslami, no 2) (Islamic Republic of Iran) *Tel:* (021) 6135429; (021) 6135335 *Fax:* (021) 3130919; (021) 3129385 *E-mail:* webmaster@majlislib.com *Web Site:* www.majlislib.org, pg 1474

The Islamic Republic of Iran Parliament Library, No 1 (Ketabkhane-ye Majles-e Shora-ye Elsami, No 1) (Islamic Republic of Iran) *Tel:* (021) 3130919; (021) 3126092 *Fax:* (021) 3130919; (021) 3129385; (021) 3124339 *E-mail:* frelations@majlislib.com; irparlib@majlislib.com; info@majlislib.com *Web Site:* www.majlislib.org, pg 1475

Islamic Research Institute Library (Pakistan) *Tel:* (051) 9261761-5; (051) 2252816, pg 1489

Islamic Research Institute (Pakistan) *Tel:* (051) 851621 *Fax:* (051) 853360 *E-mail:* dg-iri@iri-iiu.sdnpd.undp.org, pg 507

The Islamic Texts Society (United Kingdom) *Tel:* (01223) 314387 *Fax:* (01223) 324342 *E-mail:* mail@its.org.uk *Web Site:* www.its.org.uk, pg 701

Islamiyah (Indonesia) *Tel:* (061) 25421, pg 355

Island Press (Australia) *Tel:* (02) 98956119 *Fax:* (02) 98957077, pg 28

Island Press (Hong Kong) *Tel:* 8588176 *Fax:* 4829889, pg 320

Islands Business International Ltd (Fiji) *Tel:* 303108; 303616 *Fax:* 301423 *E-mail:* editor@ibi.com.fj, pg 141

Islendingasagnautgafan (Iceland) *Tel:* 898 5868 *Fax:* 565 5868 *E-mail:* muninn@isl.is, pg 328

Isoete (France) *Tel:* (0233) 533409 *Fax:* (0233) 534731, pg 170

Isper Club (Italy) *Tel:* (011) 6647803 *Fax:* (011) 6670829, pg 1229

Isper SRL (Italy) *Tel:* (011) 633950 *Fax:* (011) 6670829, pg 394

Israbook (Israel) *Tel:* (02) 5380247 *Fax:* (02) 5388423 *E-mail:* isragefen@netmedia.net.il *Web Site:* www.israelbooks.com, pg 1292

Israel State Archives (Israel) *Tel:* (02) 5680680 *Fax:* (02) 6793375, pg 1476

The Israel Academy of Sciences & Humanities (Israel) *Tel:* (02) 636 211 *Fax:* (02) 666 059 *E-mail:* isracad2@vms.huji.ac.il, pg 368

Israel Antiquities Authority (Israel) *Tel:* (02) 5638421 *Fax:* (02) 6289066 *Web Site:* www.israntique.org.il, pg 368

Israel Book and Printing Centre (Israel) *Tel:* (03) 5142895 *Web Site:* www.expot.gov.il, pg 368

Israel Exploration Society (Israel) *Tel:* (02) 6257991 *Fax:* (02) 6247772 *E-mail:* ies@vms.huji.ac.il *Web Site:* www.hum.huji.ac.il/ies, pg 368

The Israel Institute for Occupational Safety & Hygiene (Israel) *Tel:* (03) 6875037 *Fax:* (03) 6875038, pg 368

Israel ISBN Group Agency (Israel) *Tel:* (03) 6180151 *Fax:* (03) 5798048 *E-mail:* id@icl.org.il *Web Site:* www.icl.org.il, pg 1249

Israel Librarians & Information Specialists Association (Israel) *Tel:* (02) 62072868 *Fax:* (02) 625628, pg 1518

Israel Museum Products, Ltd (Israel) *Tel:* (02) 6708811 *Fax:* (02) 5631833 *Web Site:* www.imj.org.il, pg 369

Israel Music Institute (IMI) (Israel) *Tel:* (03) 6811010 *Fax:* (03) 6816070 *E-mail:* musicinst@bezeqint.net *Web Site:* aquanet.co.il/vip/imi, pg 369

Israel Society of Libraries & Information Centers (ASMI) (Israel) *Tel:* (02) 6249421 *Fax:* (02) 6249421 *E-mail:* asmi@asmi.org.il *Web Site:* www.asmi.org.il, pg 1518

Israel Translators' Association (Israel) *Tel:* (02) 412821, pg 1127

Israel Universities Press (Israel) *Tel:* (02) 6557822 *Fax:* (02) 6528962, pg 369

The Israeli Center for Libraries (Israel) *Tel:* (03) 6180151 *Fax:* (03) 5798048 *E-mail:* icl@icl.org.il *Web Site:* www.icl.org.il, pg 1518

Israeli Music Publications Ltd (Israel) *Tel:* (02) 625-1370 *Fax:* (02) 624-1378 *E-mail:* khanukaev@pop.isracom.net.il, pg 369

ISSN International Centre (France) *Tel:* (01) 44882220 *Fax:* (01) 40263243 *E-mail:* issnic@issn.org *Web Site:* www.issn.org, pg 1244

ISSN Norway (Norway) *Tel:* 22859181 *Fax:* 22859050 *E-mail:* issn-norge@nb.no, pg 1137

ISSN UK Centre (United Kingdom) *Tel:* (01937) 546959 *Fax:* (01937) 546562 *E-mail:* issn-uk@bl.uk, pg 1266

Ist Patristico Augustinianum (Italy) *Tel:* (06) 6800069 *Fax:* (06) 68006298 *E-mail:* pubblic.augnum@pcn.net, pg 394

Istanbul Universitesi Merkez Kuetuephanesi (Turkey) *Tel:* (0212) 5140380 *Fax:* (0212) 5111219 *E-mail:* acpay-ed@mam.net.tr, pg 1504

Istituto Lombardo Accademia di Scienze e Lettere (Italy) *Tel:* (02) 864087 *Fax:* (02) 86461388 *E-mail:* istituto.lombardo@unimi.it, pg 1365

Ediciones Istmo SA (Spain) *Tel:* (091) 3454101; (091) 6568818 *Fax:* (091) 3592412; (091) 6564995, pg 579

Istytut Bibliograficzny Biblioteka Narodowa, Krajowe Biuro ISBN (Poland) *Tel:* (022) 6082410 *Fax:* (022) 6082433 *E-mail:* bnisbn@bn.org.pl; sadowska@bn.org.pl *Web Site:* www.bn.org.pl, pg 1256

Italia Shobo Ltd (Japan) *Tel:* (03) 32621656 *Fax:* (03) 32346469, pg 418

Istituto Italiano Edizioni Atlas (Italy) *Tel:* (035) 249711 *Fax:* (035) 216047 *E-mail:* edatlas@tin.it, pg 394

Istituto Italiano Per Il Medio Ed Estremo Oriente (ISMEO) (Italy) *Tel:* (06) 732742 *Fax:* (06) 4873138, pg 394

Edicoes ITAU (Instituto Tecnico de Alimentacao Humana) Lda (Portugal) *Tel:* (01) 9661603 *Fax:* (01) 9661227, pg 526

ITC (United States) *Tel:* 954-623-3101 *Fax:* 954-623-3122 *E-mail:* team@inttype.com *Web Site:* www.inttype.com, pg 1165

ITD (United Kingdom) *Tel:* (01296) 427211 *Fax:* (01296) 4392019, pg 1141

Ithaca (Italy) *Tel:* (02) 48009484 *Fax:* (02) 48009493, pg 394

Ithemba! Publishing (South Africa) *Tel:* (011) 7266529 *Fax:* (011) 4824258 *E-mail:* firechildren@icon.co.za *Web Site:* www.icon.co.za/~firechildren, pg 555

ITK Laromedel AB (Sweden) *Tel:* (08) 244360 *Fax:* (08) 6503984, pg 603

ITpress Verlag (Germany) *Tel:* (07251) 300575 *Fax:* (07251) 14823 *E-mail:* itpress@acm.org *Web Site:* www.itpress.com, pg 245

IUCN-The World Conservation Union (United Kingdom) *Tel:* (01223) 277894 *Fax:* (01223) 277175 *E-mail:* info@books.iucn.org *Web Site:* www.iucn.org, pg 702

Iudicium Verlag GmbH (Germany) *Tel:* (089) 718747 *Fax:* (089) 7142039 *E-mail:* info@iudicium.de *Web Site:* www.iudicium.de, pg 245

Iustus Forlag AB (Sweden) *Tel:* (018) 693091 *Fax:* (018) 693099 *E-mail:* iustus@iustus.se *Web Site:* www.iustus.se, pg 603

Iuventus (Czech Republic) *Tel:* (02) 7817314, pg 124

Editions Ivrea (France) *Tel:* (01) 43260621 *Fax:* (01) 43261168, pg 170

Ivy Publications (South Africa) *Tel:* (012) 218931 *Fax:* (012) 3255984 *E-mail:* therese@statelib-pww.gov.za, pg 555

Iwanami Shoten, Publishers (Japan) *Tel:* (03) 52104000 *Fax:* (03) 52104039 *E-mail:* rights@iwanami.co.jp (foreign rights) *Web Site:* www.iwanami.co.jp/, pg 418

Reisebuchverlag Iwanowski GmbH (Germany) *Tel:* (02133) 26030 *Fax:* (02133) 260333 *E-mail:* info@iwanowski.de *Web Site:* www.iwonowski.de, pg 246

Iwasaki Shoten Publishing Co Ltd (Japan) *Tel:* (03) 38129131 *Fax:* (03) 38166033 *E-mail:* xlb02240@niftyserve.or.jp, pg 418

Izdatel 'stvo Kazanskago Universiteta (Russian Federation) *Tel:* 325363 *E-mail:* kacimov@niimm.kazan.su, pg 538

Izdatel 'stvo Mordovskogo gosudar stvennogo (Russian Federation) *Tel:* 74771 *Fax:* 74771, pg 538

Izdatel 'stvo Ural' skogo (Russian Federation) *Tel:* (03432) 515448 *Fax:* (03432) 51-54-48 *E-mail:* info@idc.e-burg-ru, pg 538

Izdatelska kasta JA (Bulgaria) *Tel:* (046) 26166; (046) 20077, pg 96

Izdatel'stovo Dal'nevostonogo Gosudarstvennogo Universite (Russian Federation) *Tel:* 57779 (Director) *Fax:* 257200, pg 538

Izdatelstvo Bolshaya Rossiyskaya Entsiklopedia (Russian Federation) *Tel:* (095) 9177582; (095) 9179009 *Fax:* (095) 9177139, pg 538

Izdatelstvo Iskusstvo (Russian Federation) *Tel:* (095) 2035872 *Fax:* (095) 2918882, pg 538

Izdatelstvo Literatury i isskustva (Uzbekistan) *Tel:* (0371) 445172, pg 761

Izdatelstvo Moskovskii Rabochii (Russian Federation) *Tel:* (095) 2210735 *Fax:* (095) 9254274, pg 539

Editorial Iztaccihuatl SA (Mexico) *Tel:* (05) 7050938; (05) 7051063 *Fax:* (05) 5352321, pg 462

Izvestia Sovetov Narodnyh Deputatov Russian Federation (RF) (Russian Federation) *Tel:* (095) 2093738 *Fax:* (095) 2095394, pg 539

J C Palabay Enterprises (Philippines) *Tel:* (02) 9478282 *Fax:* (02) 9424512, pg 513

J Ch Mellinger Verlag GmbH (Germany) *Tel:* (0711) 543787 *Fax:* (0711) 556889 *E-mail:* mellinger@sambo.de, pg 246

J Film Process Co Ltd (Thailand) *Tel:* (02) 2486888 *Fax:* (02) 2464620; (02) 2474719, pg 1139, 1201, 1223

J K Publications (Sri Lanka) *Tel:* (01) 518954, pg 597

Verlag J P Peter, Gebr Holstein GmbH & Co KG (Germany) *Tel:* (09861) 4 00 384 *Fax:* (09861) 4 00 79 *E-mail:* peter-verlag@rotabene.de *Web Site:* www.peter-verlag.de, pg 246

J Story-Scientia BVBA (Belgium) *Tel:* (09) 2255757 *Fax:* (09) 2331409 *E-mail:* bookshop@story.be *Web Site:* www.story.be, pg 1276

Uitgeverij J van In (Belgium) *Tel:* (03) 4805511 *Fax:* (03) 4807664, pg 70

J Whitaker & Sons Ltd (United Kingdom) *Tel:* (01252) 742525; (01252) 742542 *Fax:* (01252) 742526; (01252) 742543 *E-mail:* custserv@whitaker.co.uk; help@whitaker.co.uk *Web Site:* www.whitaker.co.uk, pg 702

Jabiru Press (Australia) *Tel:* (03) 9857-7362 *Fax:* (03) 9857-9110, pg 28

Jabotinsky Institute in Israel (Israel) *Tel:* (03) 6210611; (03) 5287320 *Fax:* (03) 5285587 *E-mail:* jabo@actcom.co.il *Web Site:* www.jabotinsky.org, pg 369

Editoriale Jaca Book SpA (Italy) *Tel:* (02) 48561520-29 *Fax:* (02) 48193361 *E-mail:* jacabook@jacabook.it *Web Site:* www.jacabook.it, pg 394

Jacana Education (South Africa) *Tel:* (011) 4831294 *Fax:* (011) 4833441 *E-mail:* jacedu@iafrica.com, pg 555

Jacaranda Designs Ltd (Kenya) *Tel:* (02) 569736; (02) 568353 *Fax:* (02) 740524, pg 432

Jacklin Enterprises (Pty) Ltd (South Africa) *Tel:* (011) 6521800 *Fax:* (011) 3142984 *E-mail:* mjacklin@jacklin.co.za, pg 556

Gruppo Editoriale Jackson SpA (Italy) *Tel:* (02) 665261 *Fax:* (02) 66526222 *E-mail:* ordini@futura-ge.com, pg 394

JAD Publishers Ltd (Nigeria), pg 500

Jade Publishers (United Kingdom) *Tel:* (01428) 644846, pg 702

Editions du Jaguar (France) *Tel:* (01) 44301970 *Fax:* (01) 44301979, pg 170

Jahreszeiten-Verlag GmbH (Germany) *Tel:* (040) 2717-0; (040) 2493; (040) 2412 *Fax:* (040) 2063; (040) 2717 *E-mail:* press@jalag.de *Web Site:* www.jalag.de, pg 246

Editions J'ai Lu (France) *Tel:* (01) 44393470 *Fax:* (01) 44393260 *Web Site:* www.flammarion.com, pg 170

JAI Press Ltd (United Kingdom) *Tel:* (020) 7379 8834 *Fax:* (020) 7379 8835 *Web Site:* www.jaipress.com, pg 702

Jaico Publishing House (India) *Tel:* (022) 270621; (022) 2676702; (022) 2676802; (022) 2674501 *Fax:* (022) 2041673; (022) 2656412 *E-mail:* jaicoborn@bom5.vsnl.net.in *Web Site:* www.jaicobooks.com, pg 340

Jaicos (India) *Tel:* (022) 270621 *Fax:* (022) 264-6412 *E-mail:* jaicopub@giasbm01.vsnl.net.in, pg 1289

B Jain Publishers Overseas (India) *Tel:* (011) 3670430; (011) 3683200; (011) 3683300 *Fax:* (011) 3610471; (011) 3683400 *E-mail:* bjain@vsnl.com; info@bjainbooks.com *Web Site:* www.bjainbooks.com; www.bjainindia.com, pg 340

B Jain Publishers Overseas (India) *Tel:* (011) 7536418; (011) 3670430; (011) 3670572 *Fax:* (011) 7536420; (011) 3610471 *E-mail:* bjain@vsnl.com *Web Site:* www.bjainbooks.com, pg 1289

B Jain Publishers (P) Ltd (India) *Tel:* (011) 3670430; (011) 3670572; (011) 3683100 *Fax:* (011) 3610471; (011) 3683400 *E-mail:* bjain@vsnl.com *Web Site:* www.bjainbooks.com, pg 340

Jaipur Publishing House (India) *Tel:* (0141) 62257, pg 340

Jamaica Archives (Jamaica) *Tel:* (876) 984-2581 *Fax:* (876) 984-8254, pg 1478

Jamaica Library Service (Jamaica) *Tel:* (876) 926-3310; (876) 926-3312 *Fax:* (876) 926-2188, pg 1478

The Jamaica Bauxite Institute (Jamaica) *Tel:* (876) 927-2073; (876) 927-2079 *Fax:* (876) 927-1159 *E-mail:* info@jbi.org.jm, pg 413

Jamaica Bureau of Standards (Jamaica) *Tel:* (876) 926-3140 *Fax:* (876) 929-4736, pg 413

Jamaica Information Service (Jamaica) *Tel:* (876) 926-3740; (876) 926-3749 *Fax:* (876) 926-6715 *E-mail:* jis@jis.gov.jm; jis@researchjis.gov.jm *Web Site:* www.jis.gov.jm, pg 413

Jamaica Library Association (Jamaica) *Tel:* (876) 63310 *Fax:* (876) 62188, pg 1518

Jamaica Printing Services (Jamaica) *Tel:* (876) 967-2250 *Fax:* (876) 967-2225, pg 413

Jamaica Publishing House Ltd (Jamaica) *Tel:* (876) 922-1385; (876) 967-3866 *Fax:* (876) 922-5412 *E-mail:* jph@jol.com.jm, pg 413

James & James (Publishers) Ltd (United Kingdom) *Tel:* (020) 7482 8888 *Fax:* (020) 7482 8889 *E-mail:* jxj@jamesxjames.co.uk *Web Site:* www.jamesxjames.co.uk, pg 702

James & James (Science Publishers) Ltd (United Kingdom) *Tel:* (020) 7387 8558 *Fax:* (020) 7387 8998 *E-mail:* jxj@jxj.com *Web Site:* www.jxj.com, pg 702

James Nicholas Publishers Pty Ltd (Australia) *Tel:* (03) 9696 5545; (03) 9690 5955 *Fax:* (03) 9699 2040 *E-mail:* custservice@jamesnicholaspublishers.com.au *Web Site:* www.jamesnicholaspublishers.com.au, pg 28

Jamrite Publications (Jamaica) *Tel:* (876) 926-1180; (876) 926-1181 *Fax:* (876) 968-4519 *E-mail:* blackolive@cwjamaica.com, pg 413

Jan Thorbecke Verlag GmbH & Co (Germany) *Tel:* (07571) 728100 *Fax:* (07571) 728280; 728287 (distribution) *Web Site:* www.thorbecke.de, pg 246

Jan Vasut Publishing (Czech Republic) *Tel:* (02) 2319318; (02) 2319319 *Fax:* (02) 2481 1059 *E-mail:* vasut@mbox.vol.cz *Web Site:* www.vasut.cz, pg 124

Karel Janak Amosium Servis (Czech Republic) *Tel:* (069) 624 55 01, pg 125

Jandi-Sapi Editori (Italy) *Tel:* (06) 68805509-15; (06) 6876054 *Fax:* (06) 6832612 *E-mail:* mail@jandisapi.com *Web Site:* www.jandisapi.com, pg 394

Janeff Books (JM & MJ Books Ltd) (New Zealand) *Tel:* (070) 777783, pg 1302

Jane's Information Group (United Kingdom) *Tel:* (020) 8700 3700 *Fax:* (020) 8763 1005 *E-mail:* info@janes.co.uk *Web Site:* www.janes.com, pg 702

Jang Publishers (Pakistan) *Tel:* (042) 6367480-83 *Fax:* (042) 6361026; (042) 6362316 *E-mail:* thenewslhr@jang.group.com *Web Site:* www.jang-group.com, pg 507

Janibi Editores SA de CV (Mexico) *Tel:* (05) 6046160 *Fax:* (05) 6882848, pg 462

Jannersten Forlag AB (Sweden) *Tel:* (0226) 61900 *Fax:* (0226) 10927 *E-mail:* bridge@jannersten.se, pg 604

Editions Jannink (France) *Tel:* (01) 45 89 14 02 *Fax:* (01) 45 89 14 02 *E-mail:* jannink@cybercable.fr *Web Site:* www.parissimo.com/pages/jannink.htm, pg 170

Janssen Publishers CC (South Africa) *Tel:* (021) 7861548 *Fax:* (021) 7862468 *E-mail:* janssenp@iafrica.com *Web Site:* www.janssenbooks.co.za, pg 556

Janus Pannonius Tudomanyegyetem (Hungary) *Tel:* (072) 411433 *Fax:* (072) 15738, pg 324

Janus Publishing Company Ltd (United Kingdom) *Tel:* (020) 7580 7664 *Fax:* (020) 7636 5756 *E-mail:* sales@januspublishing.co.uk *Web Site:* www.januspublishing.co.uk, pg 702

Editrice Janus SpA (Italy) *Tel:* (035) 247180 *Fax:* (035) 247092, pg 394

Janus Verlagsgesellschaft, Dr Norbert Meder & Co (Germany) *Tel:* (0221) 5996035 *Fax:* (0221) 9725519, pg 246

L Japadre Editore (Italy) *Tel:* (0862) 26025 *Fax:* (0862) 25587, pg 394

Japan Publications Trading Co Ltd (Import and Export) (Japan) *Tel:* (03) 3292-3751 *Fax:* (03) 3290410 *E-mail:* jpt@po.iijnet.or.jp, pg 1294

Japan Association of International Publications (Japan) *Tel:* (03) 32716901 *Fax:* (03) 32716920 *Web Site:* www.jaip.gr.jp, pg 1250

Japan Bible Society (Japan) *Tel:* (03) 35670386 *E-mail:* info@bible.or.jp *Web Site:* www.bible.or.jp, pg 418

Japan Book Publishers Association (Japan) *Tel:* (03) 32681303 *Fax:* (03) 32681196 *E-mail:* onuki@jbpa.or.jp, pg 1250

Japan Broadcast Publishing Co Ltd (Japan) *Tel:* (03) 3780-3356 *Fax:* (03) 34960123, pg 418

Japan Electronic Publishing Association (Japan) *Tel:* (03) 3219-2958 *Fax:* (03) 3219-2940 *Web Site:* www.jepa.or.jp, pg 1250

Japan Foreign-Rights Centre (JFC) (Japan) *Tel:* (03) 59960321 *Fax:* (03) 59960323, pg 1113

Japan Industrial Publishing Co Ltd (Japan) *Tel:* (03) 34561827, pg 418

Japan ISBN Agency (Japan) *Tel:* (03) 32672301 *Fax:* (03) 32672304, pg 1250

Japan PEN Club (Japan) *Tel:* (03) 34021171; (03) 34021172 *Fax:* (03) 34025951, pg 1365

Japan Publications Inc (Japan) *Tel:* (03) 32958411 *Fax:* (03) 32958416, pg 418

The Japan Times (Japan) *Tel:* (03) 34532013 *Fax:* (03) 34538023, pg 418

Japan Travel Bureau Inc (Japan) *Tel:* (03) 34779525 *Fax:* (03) 34779538, pg 418

Japan UNI Agency Inc (Japan) *Tel:* (03) 32950301 *Fax:* (03) 32945173 *E-mail:* info@japanuni.co.jp, pg 1113

Jardine Wenwu Printing Co (China), pg 1132

Jared Publishing (Australia) *Tel:* (03) 9874-2415, pg 28

Jarrah Publications (Australia) *Tel:* (09) 4954569 *Fax:* (09) 4954569 *Web Site:* www.jarpub73.com.au, pg 28

Jarrold Publishing (United Kingdom) *Tel:* (01603) 763300 *Fax:* (01603) 662748 *E-mail:* publishing@jarrold.com *Web Site:* www.jarrold-publishing.co.uk, pg 703

Java Books (Indonesia) *Tel:* (021) 4515351 (Hunting) *Fax:* (021) 4534987 *E-mail:* mndl@indo.net.id, pg 1291

Dayawansa Jayakody & Co (Sri Lanka) *Tel:* (01) 695773 *Fax:* (01) 696653 *E-mail:* dayawansa@eureka.lk, pg 597

Jayantilal Jamnadas, Lda (Portugal) *Tel:* (01) 4960951, pg 1307

Jaypee Brothers Medical Publishers Pvt Ltd (India) *Tel:* (011) 3272143; (011) 3282021 *Fax:* (011) 3276490, pg 340

Al Jazirah Organization for Press, Printing, Publishing (Saudi Arabia) *Tel:* (01) 4419999 *Fax:* (01) 4412536, pg 543

(JDC) Brookdale Institute of Gerontology & Adult Human Development in Israel (Israel) *Tel:* (02) 6557400 *Fax:* (02) 5612391 *E-mail:* brook@jdc.org.il *Web Site:* www.jdc.org.il/brookdale/, pg 369

JEAG (Madagascar) *Tel:* (02) 24141 *Fax:* (02) 20397, pg 450

Editions Jean-Claude Lattes (France) *Tel:* (01) 44417400 *Fax:* (01) 43253047 *E-mail:* jpeguillam@editions-jclattes.fr, pg 170

Jednota Ceskych Matematiku A Fysiku (Czech Republic) *Tel:* (02) 24230877; (02) 242139, pg 125

Jednota Tlumocniku a Prekladatelu (Czech Republic) *Tel:* (02) 24142517 *Fax:* (02) 24142312 *E-mail:* JTP@4u.net *Web Site:* www.JTPunion.org, pg 1125

The Richard Jefferies Society (United Kingdom) *Tel:* 01865 735678 *Web Site:* web.sirius.com/~treitel/jefferies.html, pg 1371

Jelenkor Verlag (Hungary) *Tel:* (072) 314782 *Fax:* (072) 336803 *E-mail:* jelenkor@mail.datanet.hu, pg 324

Jenelle Press (Australia) *Tel:* (02) 4281531 *Fax:* (02) 4284144, pg 28

Verlag Winfried Jenior (Germany) *Tel:* (0561) 7391621 *Fax:* (0561) 774148 *E-mail:* jenior@aol.com *Web Site:* www.jenior.de, pg 246

Jeong-eum Munhwasa (Republic of Korea) *Tel:* (02) 5680070 *Fax:* (02) 5650352, pg 437

Jerusalem City (Public) Library (Israel) *Tel:* (02) 226785 *Fax:* (02) 255785, pg 1476

Jerusalem Books Ltd (Israel) *Tel:* (02) 5321973 *Fax:* (02) 5321973 *E-mail:* jerbooks@netmedia.co.il *Web Site:* www.jerusalembooks.co.il/index.html, pg 1292

Jerusalem Center for Public Affairs (Israel) *Tel:* (02) 5619281 *Fax:* (02) 5619112 *E-mail:* jcpa@netvision.net.il *Web Site:* www.jcpa.org, pg 369

The Jerusalem Publishing House Ltd (Israel) *Tel:* (02) 5617744 *Fax:* (02) 5634266 *E-mail:* jphgagi@netvision.net.il, pg 369

Jesuit Publications (Australia) *Tel:* (03) 9427-7311 *Fax:* (03) 9428-4450 *E-mail:* paul-jp@jespub.jesuit.org.au *Web Site:* www.openplanet.com.au, pg 28

Jett Samm Publishing Ltd (Trinidad & Tobago) *Tel:* 637-9548, pg 637

Editions du Jeu de Paume (France) *Tel:* (01) 47 03 12 50 *Fax:* (01) 42 61 26 10, pg 170

JF Printhaus (Philippines) *Tel:* (049) 562-0916, pg 1199

Jiangsu People's Publishing House (China) *Tel:* (025) 6634309 *Fax:* (025) 3379766 *Web Site:* www.book-wind.com, pg 106

Jiangsu Science & Technology Publishing House (China) *Tel:* (025) 6633121; (025) 3273012; (025) 3273033 *Fax:* (025) 3273111 *E-mail:* cnjsstph@public1.ptt.js.cn, pg 106

Jigyungsa Ltd (Republic of Korea) *Tel:* (02) 5576351 *Fax:* (02) 5576352 *E-mail:* jigyung@nextell.net, pg 437

Jika Publishing (Australia) *Tel:* (03) 9467-3295 *Fax:* (03) 9467-1770, pg 28

Editorial Jilguero, SA de CV (Mexico) *Tel:* (05) 2026585 *Fax:* (05) 5401771 *E-mail:* mexdesco@compuserve.com.mx, pg 462

Jilin Science & Technology Publishing House (China) *Tel:* (431) 845184; (431) 845175 *Fax:* (431) 5635185 *E-mail:* jlkjcbs@public.ec.jl.cn, pg 106

Jillion Publishing Co (Taiwan, Province of China) *Tel:* (02) 5432682 *Fax:* (02) 5231891, pg 630

Jinan Publishing House (China) *Tel:* (0531) 613006, pg 107

Jinno International Group (United States) *Tel:* 845-735-4666 *Fax:* 617-344-5905 *E-mail:* jinno@hotmail.com, pg 1145, 1165, 1207, 1216

Ediciones JJB (Spain) *Tel:* (041) 236429 *Fax:* (041) 226127, pg 579

JKL Publikationen GmbH (Germany) *Tel:* (030) 74104625 *Fax:* (030) 74104626 *E-mail:* info@zeitgut.com *Web Site:* www.zeitgut.com, pg 246

JL Publications (Australia) *Tel:* (03) 98860200 *Fax:* (03) 98860200 *E-mail:* jlpubs@c031.aone.net.au, pg 28

Ediciones JLA (Spain) *Tel:* (091) 3158577 *Fax:* (091) 7336239, pg 579

Biblioteca Municipal Dr Joaquin de Salterain (Uruguay), pg 1508

Editorial Joaquin Mortiz SA de CV (Mexico) *Tel:* (05) 5598781; (05) 5758585; (05) 5758019 *Fax:* (05) 5758980; (05) 5752426, pg 462

JOC Internacional, SA (Spain) *Tel:* (093) 3458565; (093) 2741954 *Fax:* (093) 3465362 *Web Site:* www.jocicw.net, pg 579

Joensuun Yliopisto (Finland) *Tel:* (013) 2511 *Fax:* (0251) 2050 *E-mail:* joyle@joyl.joensuun.ti, pg 1463

Johann Wolfgang Goethe Universitat (Germany) *Tel:* (069) 798-23590 *Fax:* (069) 798-28313 *E-mail:* hrz@rz.uni-frankfurt.de *Web Site:* www.rz.uni-frankfurt.de, pg 246

Johannes Berchmans Verlagsbuchhandlung GmbH (Germany) *Tel:* (089) 38185-244 *Fax:* (089) 2386-2342, pg 246

Johannes Verlag Einsiedeln, Freiburg (Germany) *Tel:* (0761) 640168 *Fax:* (0761) 640169 *E-mail:* johverlag@aol.com, pg 246

Johannesburg Art Gallery (South Africa) *Tel:* (011) 7253130; (011) 7253180 *Fax:* (011) 7206000, pg 556

Johannesburg College of Education, Harold Holmes Library (South Africa) *Tel:* (011) 6421417 *Fax:* (011) 6436312, pg 1497

Johannesburg Public Library (South Africa) *Tel:* (011) 8363787 *Fax:* (011) 8366607 *E-mail:* library@mj.org.za, pg 1497

Johannis (Germany) *Tel:* (07821) 5810 *Fax:* (07821) 581-26 *E-mail:* johannis-druck@t-online.de *Web Site:* www.johannis-verlag.de, pg 246

John Blake Publishing Ltd (United Kingdom) *Tel:* (020) 7381 0666 *Fax:* (020) 7381 6868 *E-mail:* words@blake.co.uk, pg 703

John Mackintosh Hall Library (Gibraltar) *Tel:* 78000 *Fax:* 40843, pg 1470

John Wiley & Sons Australia Ltd (Australia) *Tel:* (07) 3859 9755 *Fax:* (07) 3859 9715 *E-mail:* brisbane@johnwiley.com.au *Web Site:* www.johnwiley.com.au, pg 28

Johnson Publications Ltd (United Kingdom) *Tel:* (020) 7486 6757 *Fax:* (020) 7487 5436, pg 703

Johnston & Streiffert Editions (Sweden) *Tel:* (031) 826160 *Fax:* (031) 825150, pg 604

Joho Kagaku Gijutsu Kyokai (Japan), pg 1518

The Joint Board of Christian Education (New Zealand) *Tel:* (04) 3850352 *Fax:* (04) 3856114, pg 492

Joint Publishing (HK) Co Ltd (Hong Kong) *Tel:* (02) 5230105 *Fax:* (02) 8104201 *E-mail:* jpchk@hk.super.net, pg 320

Joly Editions (France) *Tel:* (01) 56 54 16 29 *Fax:* (01) 56 54 16 49 *E-mail:* sandrine.jacques@editions-joly.com *Web Site:* www.editions-joly.com, pg 170

Jonas Verlag fuer Kunst und Literatur GmbH (Germany) *Tel:* (06421) 25132 *Fax:* (06421) 210572 *E-mail:* jonas@jonas-verlag.de, pg 246

Jones & Bartlett International (United Kingdom) *Tel:* (01892) 539356 *Fax:* (01892) 614944 *E-mail:* j&b@class.co.uk *Web Site:* www.jbpub.com, pg 703

John Jones Publishing Ltd (United Kingdom) *Tel:* (01824) 707255 *Fax:* (01824) 705272 *E-mail:* johnjonespublishing.ltd@virgin.net *Web Site:* www.johnjonespublishing.ltd.uk, pg 703

Dr Werner Jopp Verlag (Germany) *Tel:* (0611) 547116 *Fax:* (0611) 542762, pg 246

Jordan Book Centre Co Ltd (Jordan) *Tel:* (06) 5151882; (06) 5156882; (06) 5155882; (06) 606882; 06 676882 *Fax:* (06) 602016 *E-mail:* jbc@nets.com.jo; jbc@go.com.jo, pg 430

Jordan Book Centre Co Ltd (Jordan) *Tel:* (06) 676882; (06) 606882 *Fax:* (06) 602016, pg 1296

Jordan Distribution Agency Co Ltd (Jordan) *Tel:* (06) 4630191; (06) 4630192 *Fax:* (06) 463152 *E-mail:* jda@go.com.jo, pg 430

Jordan Distribution Agency Co Ltd (Jordan) *Tel:* (06) 4630191; (06) 4630192 *Fax:* (06) 4635152 *E-mail:* jda@go.com.jo, pg 1296

Jordan House for Publication (Jordan) *Tel:* (06) 24224 *Fax:* (06) 51062, pg 430

Jordan Library Association (Jordan) *Tel:* (06) 629412, pg 1519

Jordan Publishing Ltd (United Kingdom) *Tel:* (0117) 923 0600 *Fax:* (0117) 925 0486 *E-mail:* customerservice@jordanpublishing.co.uk *Web Site:* www.jordanpublishing.co.uk, pg 703

Jordan University of Science and Technology Library (Jordan) *Tel:* (06) 843555 *Fax:* (06) 832318, pg 1479

Jordanverlag AG (Switzerland) *Tel:* (01) 3023676, pg 616

University of Jos Library (Nigeria) *Tel:* (073) 610514 *Fax:* (073) 610514 *E-mail:* library@unijos.edu.ng, pg 1488

Jose Alfonso Sandoval Nunez (Costa Rica) *Tel:* 2252331 *E-mail:* asandova@alpha.emate.ucr.ac.cr; k_sanny@hotmail.com, pg 116

Michael Joseph Ltd (United Kingdom) *Tel:* (020) 7416 3000 *Fax:* (0201) 7416 3099, pg 703

Richard Joseph Publishers Ltd (United Kingdom) *Tel:* (01256) 811314 *Fax:* (01256) 336362 *E-mail:* rjoe01@aol.com *Web Site:* www.sheppardsdirectories.co.uk, pg 703, 1320

Joszoveg Muhely Kiado (Hungary) *Tel:* (01) 3326467 *Fax:* (01) 3173536 *E-mail:* joszoveg@euroweb.hu, pg 324

Jota (Czech Republic) *Tel:* (05) 4353 0210; (05) 4353 0203 *Fax:* (05) 4353 0203 *E-mail:* jota@netbrno.cz; books@bm.cesnet.cz *Web Site:* www.jota.cz, pg 125

Le Jour, Editeur (France) *Tel:* (01) 49591189 *Fax:* (01) 49591196 *Web Site:* www.edjour.com, pg 170

Les Editions du Journal L' Unite Maghrebine (Morocco) *Tel:* 780169 *Fax:* 780169, pg 470

Journal on Social Change (Zimbabwe) *Tel:* (04) 720417; (04) 700047 *Fax:* (04) 730808 *E-mail:* schange@africaonline.co.zw, pg 768

Jouvence (Italy) *Tel:* (06) 3202897 *Fax:* (06) 3202897 *E-mail:* ed.jouvence@flashnet.it, pg 394

Editions Jouvence (Switzerland) *Tel:* (022) 7576220 *Fax:* (0450) 432924 *E-mail:* jouvence@wanadoo.fr, pg 616

Joval Publications (Australia) *Tel:* (053) 674593, pg 29

Casa Editrice Dott Eugenio Jovene SpA (Italy) *Tel:* (081) 5521019 *Fax:* (081) 5520687, pg 394

Jovis Verlag GmbH (Germany) *Tel:* (030) 261 12 07 *Fax:* (030) 261 15 42 *E-mail:* jovis@jovis.de *Web Site:* www.jovis.de, pg 246

Jowi-Verlag (Germany) *Tel:* (09353) 2921, pg 246

Joy Verlag GmbH (Germany) *Tel:* (08376) 8922 *Fax:* (08376) 8845 *E-mail:* joy_verlag@compuserve.com, pg 247

Joyas Bibliograficas SA (Spain) *Tel:* (091) 5470220, pg 579

Jozsef Attila Tudomanyegyetem Egyetemi Koenyvtar (Hungary) *Tel:* (062) 454036 *Fax:* (062) 312718 *E-mail:* mader@bibl.u-szeged.hu, pg 1472

JPM Publications SA (Switzerland) *Tel:* (021) 6177561 *Fax:* (021) 6161257 *E-mail:* information@jpmguides.com *Web Site:* www.jpmguides.com, pg 616

Ediciones Jucar (Spain) *Tel:* (08) 5170921; (08) 5349684 *Fax:* (08) 5349542, pg 579

Gerald Judd Sales Ltd (United Kingdom) *Tel:* (020) 7828 8821 *Fax:* (020) 7828 0840, pg 1141

Jane Judd Literary Agency (United Kingdom) *Tel:* (020) 7607 0273 *Fax:* (020) 7607 0623, pg 1120

Juedischer Verlag GmbH (Germany) *Tel:* (069) 75601-0 *Fax:* (069) 75601-522 *Web Site:* www.suhrkamp.de, pg 247

Juegos & Co SRL (Argentina) *Tel:* (011) 4374-7903; (011) 4371-1825 *Fax:* (011) 4372-3829 *E-mail:* comercial@demente.com *Web Site:* www.demente.com, pg 6

Jugend mit einer Mission Verlag (Switzerland) *Tel:* (032) 418988 *Fax:* (032) 418920, pg 616

Jugoslavijapublik (Yugoslavia) *Tel:* (011) 633266 *Fax:* (011) 622858; (011) 622669, pg 764

Jugoslovenska Knjiga (Yugoslavia) *Tel:* (011) 3340025 *Fax:* (011) 3231079, pg 1324

Jugoslovenska Revija (Yugoslavia) *Tel:* (011) 625-829, pg 764

Jugoslovenski Bibliografsko-Informacijski Institut (Yugoslav Institute for Bibliography & Information) (Yugoslavia) *Tel:* (011) 687836; (011) 688927 *Fax:* (011) 687760; (011) 38111, pg 1526

Jugoslovenski Bibliografsko-informacijski institut, Yubin, Agencija za ISBN (Yugoslavia) *Tel:* (011) 687836; (011) 688927 *Fax:* (011) 687760 *E-mail:* yubin@jbi.bg.ac.yu *Web Site:* www.yugoslavia.com/Culture/yubin.htm, pg 1269

Julius Klinkhardt Verlagsbuchhandlung (Germany) *Tel:* (08046) 9304; (08046) 9305 *Fax:* (08046) 9306 *E-mail:* info@klinkhardt.de, pg 247

Junactva, Vydavectva (Belarus) *Tel:* (0172) 23326 *Fax:* (0172) 266616, pg 63

Junfermann-Verlag (Germany) *Tel:* (05251) 1 34 40 *Fax:* (05251) 13 44 44 *E-mail:* ju@junfermann.de *Web Site:* www.junfermann.de, pg 247

Jung-ang Munhwa Sa (Republic of Korea) *Tel:* (02) 7172114 *Fax:* (02) 7161369, pg 437

Verlag Jungbrunnen - Wiener Spielzeugschachtel GesellschaftmbH (Austria) *Tel:* (01) 512-1299 *Fax:* (01) 512-1299-75 *E-mail:* office@jungbrunnen.co.at, pg 53

Editura Junimea (Romania) *Tel:* (032) 117290, pg 534

Junior Publications Ltd (New Zealand) *Tel:* (09) 6205459 *Fax:* (09) 6205459, pg 492

Ediciones Junior SA (Spain) *Tel:* (093) 4767100 *Fax:* (093) 4767121, pg 579

Junius Verlag GmbH (Germany) *Tel:* (040) 89 25 99 *Fax:* (040) 89 12 24 *E-mail:* junius-verlag@t-online.de *Web Site:* www.junius-verlag.de, pg 247

Junius Verlags- und Vertriebs GmbH (Austria) *Tel:* (01) 4921272, pg 53

Junod Nicholas (Switzerland) *Tel:* (022) 3470242 *Fax:* (022) 3470242, pg 616

Junta de Castilla y Leon Consejeria de Educacion y Cultura (Spain) *Tel:* (0983) 411586 *Fax:* (0983) 403070 *Web Site:* www.jcyl.es, pg 579

Junta de Educacao Religiosa e Publicacoes da Convencao Batista Brasileira (JUERP) (Brazil) *Tel:* (021) 2690772 *Fax:* (021) 2690296 *E-mail:* juerp@openlink.com.br *Web Site:* www.juerp.org.br, pg 85

Jupiter Verlagsgesellschaft mbH (Austria) *Tel:* (01) 21422940 *Fax:* (01) 2160720, pg 53

Juricom (Costa Rica) *Tel:* 2836942 *Fax:* 2253800 *E-mail:* juricom@sol.racsa.co.cr, pg 116

Juridica Verlag GmbH (Austria) *Tel:* (01) 533 37 47-398 *Fax:* (01) 533 37 47-399 *E-mail:* juridica@manz.at *Web Site:* www.juridica.at, pg 53

Editions Juridiques Associees - LGDJ/Montchrestien (France) *Tel:* (01) 56 54 16 00 *Fax:* (01) 56 54 16 47, pg 170

Editions Juridiques Africaines (France) *Tel:* (01) 43370401 *Fax:* (01) 43370401, pg 171

Editions Juridiques et Techniques Lamy SA (France) *Tel:* (01) 44721200 *Fax:* (01) 44721389, pg 171

SDU Juridische en Fiscale Uitgeverij (Netherlands) *Tel:* (070) 3789860 *Fax:* (070) 3458068 *E-mail:* sdu@sdu.nl *Web Site:* www.sdu.nl, pg 479

Editions du Juris-Classeur (France) *Tel:* (01) 45 58 93 79 *Fax:* (01) 45 58 94 00 *E-mail:* editorial@juris-classeur.com *Web Site:* www.ed-juris-classeur.fr, pg 171

Juris Druck & Verlag AG (Switzerland) *Tel:* (01) 7409038; (01) 2117727; (01) 2117747 *Fax:* (01) 7409019 *E-mail:* juris@swissonline.ch, pg 616

Juris Editorial (Argentina) *Tel:* (0341) 4267301; (0341) 4267302 *Fax:* (0341) 4267301; (0341) 4267302 *E-mail:* editorialjuris@arnet.com.ar, pg 6

Editions Juris Service (France) *Tel:* (04) 72 10 10 03 *Fax:* (04) 78 28 93 83 *E-mail:* info@editionsjuris.com *Web Site:* www.editionsjuris.com, pg 171

Editorial Jus SA de CV (Mexico) *Tel:* (05) 5260538; (05) 5260540 *Fax:* (05) 5291444, pg 462

Justus-Liebig-Universitat Giessen (Germany) *Tel:* (0641) 99-0 *Fax:* (0641) 99-12259 *E-mail:* michael.kost@admin.uni-giessen.de *Web Site:* www.uni-giessen.de, pg 247

Juta & Co Ltd (South Africa) *Tel:* (021) 7975101 *Fax:* (021) 7970121, pg 1310

Juta & Co (South Africa) *Tel:* (021) 7975101 *Fax:* (021) 7975569 (orders only); (021) 7970121 *E-mail:* books@juta.co.za *Web Site:* www.juta.co.sa, pg 556

Jutta Pohl Verlag (Germany) *Tel:* (07202) 2239 *Fax:* (07202) 3879 *E-mail:* jutta@pohlverlag.de *Web Site:* www.pohl-verlag.de, pg 247

Juvenile & Childrens Books Publishing House (China) *Tel:* (021) 2512851 *Fax:* (021) 2512851, pg 107

Juventa Verlag GmbH (Germany) *Tel:* (06201) 9020-0 *Fax:* (06201) 9020-13 *E-mail:* juventa@juventa.de *Web Site:* www.juventa.de, pg 247

Libreria Juventud (Bolivia) *Tel:* (02) 2406248 *Fax:* (02) 2406248, pg 1277

Editorial Juventud Colombiana Ltda (Colombia) *Tel:* (01) 2557485; (01) 2490543; (01) 2557416 *Fax:* (01) 2557416, pg 112

Editorial Juventud SA (Spain) *Tel:* (093) 444 18 00 *Fax:* (093) 444 18 02 *E-mail:* juventud@bcn.servicom.es *Web Site:* www.editorialjuventud.es, pg 579

Juventus/Femina Publishers (South Africa) *Tel:* (012) 3284620 *Fax:* (012) 3283809, pg 556

Jyvaskylan Yliopiston Kirjasto (Finland) *Tel:* (014) 2603373 *Fax:* (014) 2603371 *E-mail:* jyk@Library.jyu.fi, pg 1463

K C Ang Publishing Pte Ltd (Singapore) *Tel:* 4741680 *Fax:* 2542002, pg 547

K L V Konkret Literatur Verlag GmbH (Germany) *Tel:* (040) 47 52 34 *Fax:* (040) 47 84 15 *E-mail:* info@konkret-literatur-verlag.de *Web Site:* www.konkret-verlage.de, pg 247

K Publishing & Distributors Sdn Bhd (Malaysia) *Tel:* (03) 5501755; (03) 5501442 *Fax:* (03) 5501826, pg 452

Kaantopiiri Oy (Finland) *Tel:* (09) 1351385 *Fax:* (09) 1351372, pg 142

Kabardino-Balkarskoye knizhnoye izdatelstvo (Russian Federation) *Tel:* 54184, pg 539

Kabete Library (Kenya) *Tel:* (02) 334244 *Fax:* (02) 336885, pg 1479

Kadena Press (Philippines) *Tel:* (02) 9217429; (02) 9213984, pg 513

Kadokawa Shoten Publishing Co (Japan) *Tel:* (03) 32388431 *Fax:* (03) 32627734, pg 419

Library Board of Kaduna State (Nigeria) *Tel:* (062) 242590, pg 1488

Kaerntner Druck- und Verlags-GmbH (Austria) *Tel:* (0463) 5866 *Fax:* (0463) 5866-321 *E-mail:* info@kaerntner-druckerei.at *Web Site:* www.kaerntner-druckerei.at, pg 53

Lonnie Kahn Ltd (Israel) *Tel:* (03) 9518418 *Fax:* (03) 9518415; (03) 9518416, pg 1292

Kahn & Averill (United Kingdom) *Tel:* (020) 8743 3278 *Fax:* (020) 8743 3278, pg 703

Kaibundo Publishing Co Ltd (Japan) *Tel:* (03) 38153291 *Fax:* (03) 38153953, pg 419

Kaigai Publications Ltd (Kaigai Shuppan Boeki Kabushiki Kaisha) (Japan) *Tel:* (03) 32924271 *Fax:* (03) 32924278 *E-mail:* admin@kaigai-pub.co.jp, pg 1294

Kailash Editions (France) *Tel:* (01) 43.29.52.52 *Fax:* (01) 46.34.03.29 *E-mail:* kailash@imaginet.fr, pg 171

Kairali Children's Book Trust (India) *Tel:* (0481) 563226 *Fax:* (0481) 564758, pg 340

Kairalee Mudralayam (India) *Tel:* (0481) 56314 *Fax:* (0481) 564758, pg 341

Editorial Kairos SA (Spain) *Tel:* (093) 430 3746 *Fax:* (093) 410 5166 *E-mail:* kairos@sendanet.es, pg 579

Kaisei-Sha Publishing Co Ltd (Japan) *Tel:* (03) 32603229 *Fax:* (03) 32603540 *E-mail:* foreign@kaiseisha.co.jp *Web Site:* www.kaiseisha.co.jp, pg 419

Kaitakusha (Japan) *Tel:* (03) 58428900 *Fax:* (03) 58425560 *E-mail:* kaitakusha@kaitakusha.co.jp *Web Site:* www.kaitakusha.co.jp, pg 419

Kajima Institute Publishing Co Ltd (Japan) *Tel:* (03) 55612554 *Fax:* (03) 55612561, pg 419

KaJo Verlag (Germany) *Tel:* (0931) 385235 *Fax:* (0931) 385305 *E-mail:* info@verlagshaus.com *Web Site:* www.verlagshaus.com, pg 247

Kajura Publications (United Republic of Tanzania) *Tel:* (051) 866181, pg 633

Kaleidoscope (France) *Tel:* (01) 45440708 *Fax:* (01) 45445371 *E-mail:* infos@editions-kaleidoscope.com *Web Site:* www.editions-kaleidoscope.com, pg 171

Kaleidoscope Publishers Ltd (Denmark) *Tel:* 33755555 *Fax:* 33755544 *E-mail:* gujbt@gyldendal.dk *Web Site:* www.kaleidoscope.publishers.dk; www.gyldendal.dk, pg 133

Editions Kalentis (Greece) *Tel:* (01) 36-01-551 *Fax:* (01) 36-23-553, pg 312

Kali For Women (India) *Tel:* (011) 6864497; (011) 6964947; (011) 6521008 *Fax:* (011) 6864497 *E-mail:* kaliw@del2.vsnl.net.in, pg 341

Kalich SRO (Czech Republic) *Tel:* (02) 24947505; (02) 24220296 *Fax:* (02) 24947504; (02) 24220296, pg 125

Kalle Ankas Bokklubb (Sweden) *Tel:* (040) 380600 *Fax:* (040) 933708, pg 1232

Kalligram Kiado spol sro (Slovakia) *Tel:* (07) 54411-801 *Fax:* (07) 54411-801 *Web Site:* www.kalligram.sk, pg 549

Kallmeyer'sche Verlagsbuchhandlung GmbH (Germany) *Tel:* (0511) 4 00 04-1 75 *Fax:* (0511) 4 00 04-1 76 *E-mail:* info@kallmeyer.de *Web Site:* www.kallmeyer.de, pg 247

Kalos-Verlag (Switzerland) *Tel:* (01) 3022751 *Fax:* (01) 3022751, pg 616

Kalyani Publishers (India) *Tel:* (011) 3278689; (011) 3274393; (011) 3271469, pg 341

Ilias Kambanas Publishing Organization, SA (Greece) *Tel:* (01) 5762791 *Fax:* (01) 5743988 *E-mail:* info@kambanas.gr, pg 312

Kamenyar (Ukraine) *Tel:* (0322) 721949 *Fax:* (0322) 727922, pg 643

KAMS Information & Publishing Ltd (Hong Kong) *Tel:* 23889172 *Fax:* 27716403 *E-mail:* kamsinfo@hkstar.com *Web Site:* kamsinfo.com, pg 1126

Kanakis Publications & Bookshop (Greece) *Tel:* (01) 3302385 *Fax:* (01) 3811902, pg 1286

Kanda Bookshop (Japan) *Tel:* (03) 32553497 *Fax:* (03) 2938005; (03) 32553495, pg 1294

Kanehara & Co Ltd (Japan) *Tel:* (03) 38117162 *Fax:* (03) 38130288, pg 419

Kangaroo Press (Australia) *Tel:* (02) 6541502 *Fax:* (02) 6541338, pg 29

Kanisa la Biblia Publishers (KLB) (United Republic of Tanzania) *Tel:* (061) 354500 *Fax:* (061) 350911 *E-mail:* cmml-dodoma@maf.org, pg 633

Kanisius Verlag (Switzerland) *Tel:* (037) 243128 *Fax:* (026) 4258738, pg 616

Kano State Library Board (Nigeria) *Tel:* (064) 645614, pg 1488

Kansai University Press (Japan) *Tel:* (06) 3681121 *Fax:* (06) 3377078, pg 419

Kansallisarkisto Kirjasto (Finland) *Tel:* (09) 228521 *Fax:* (09) 176302 *E-mail:* national_archives@narc.fi *Web Site:* www.narc.fi, pg 1464

Jan Kanzelsberger (Czech Republic) *Tel:* (02) 22 51 42 40; (02) 22 52 02 64 *Fax:* (02) 22 51 15 73 *E-mail:* masarykova@volny.cz, pg 125

Kaos Edizioni SRL (Italy) *Tel:* (02) 29523063 *Fax:* (02) 29524822, pg 395

Kapelusz Editora SA (Argentina) *Tel:* (011) 4382-7400 *Fax:* (011) 4383-8020 *E-mail:* empresa@kapelusz.com.ar *Web Site:* www.kapelusz.com.ar, pg 6

Kapelusz Ltda Editorial (Colombia) *Tel:* (01) 2482235; (01) 2359291; (01) 2442035; (01) 3350031 *Fax:* (01) 3350042, pg 112

Editorial Kapelusz Venezolana SA (Venezuela) *Tel:* (02) 517601; (02) 526281, pg 762

Kapon Editions (Greece) *Tel:* (01) 92-35-098 *Fax:* (01) 92-14-089 *Web Site:* www.kaponeditions.gr, pg 1286

Karachi University Library Science Alumni Association (Pakistan) *Tel:* (021) 479001, pg 1521

Karas-Sana Oy (Finland) *Tel:* (09) 68155640 *Fax:* (09) 68155611 *E-mail:* kirjat@karas-sana.fi, pg 142

Karatzas Charis (Greece) *Tel:* (010) 3678800 *Fax:* (01) 3678857 *E-mail:* info@nb.org, pg 312

Kardamitsa A (Greece) *Tel:* (01) 36 15 156 *Fax:* (01) 36 31 100 *E-mail:* info@kardamitsa.gr *Web Site:* 194.219.182.214/kardamitsa/en/, pg 312

S Karger GmbH Verlag fuer Medizin und Naturwissenschaften (Germany) *Tel:* (0761) 45 20 70 *Fax:* (0761) 45 20 714 *E-mail:* karger@karger.de, pg 247

S Karger AG, Medical and Scientific Publishers (Switzerland) *Tel:* (061) 3061111 *Fax:* (061) 3061234 *E-mail:* karger@karger.ch *Web Site:* www.karger.com, pg 617

Karisto Oy (Finland) *Tel:* (03) 6161 551 *Fax:* (03) 6161 565, pg 142

Verlag Karl Baedeker GmbH (Germany) *Tel:* (0711) 4502262 *Fax:* (0711) 4502343 *E-mail:* baedeker@mairs.de, pg 248

Karl-May-Verlag Lothar Schmid GmbH (Germany) *Tel:* (0951) 98 20 60 *Fax:* (0951) 2 43 67 *E-mail:* info@karl-may.de *Web Site:* www.karl-may.de, pg 248

Karmelitanske Nakladatelstvi (Czech Republic) *Tel:* (0332) 420295 *Fax:* (0332) 420295 *E-mail:* karmelnakl@da.bohem-net.cz *Web Site:* www.karmelitanske-nakladatelstvi.cz, pg 125

Karnac Books Ltd (United Kingdom) *Tel:* (020) 7584 3303 *Fax:* (020) 7823 7743 *E-mail:* books@karnac.demon.co.uk *Web Site:* www.karnacbooks.com, pg 703

Karnak House (United Kingdom) *Tel:* (020) 7243 3620 *Fax:* (020) 7243 3620 *E-mail:* karnakhouse@aol.com, pg 703

Karni Publishers Ltd (Israel) *Tel:* (08) 9246565 *Fax:* (08) 9251770 *E-mail:* info@zmora.co.il, pg 369

Karolinger Verlag GmbH & Co KG (Austria) *Tel:* (0222) 4302093 *Fax:* (0222) 4302093, pg 53

Karolinum, nakladatelstvi (Czech Republic) *Tel:* (02) 24491276 *Fax:* (02) 24212041 *E-mail:* cupress@ruk.cuni.cz *Web Site:* www.cupress.cuni.cz, pg 125

The Harry Karren Institute for the Analysis of Propaganda, Yad Labanim (Israel) *Tel:* (09) 500762 *Fax:* (09) 500043, pg 369

Karthala Editions-Diffusion (France) *Tel:* (01) 43 31 15 59 *Fax:* (01) 45 35 27 05 *E-mail:* karthala@wanadoo.fr, pg 171

Izdatelstvo Kartia Moldoveniaske (Republic of Moldova) *Tel:* (02) 244022, pg 468

Karto + Grafik Verlagsgesellschaft (K & G Verlagsgesellschaft) (Germany) *Tel:* (069) 76 20 31 *Fax:* (069) 76 91 06 *E-mail:* kugverlag@aol.com *Web Site:* www.hildebrands.de, pg 248

Kartoen (Netherlands) *Tel:* (050) 3110505 *Fax:* (050) 3112299 *E-mail:* mondria@worldonline.nl, pg 479

Panstwowe Przedsiebiorstwo Wydawnictw Kartograficznych (Poland) *Tel:* (022) 6283251; (022) 6214850 *Fax:* (022) 6280236; (022) 6214850 *E-mail:* ppwk@pdsox.com, pg 517

Kartographischer Verlag Reinhard Ryborsch (Germany) *Tel:* (06104) 79039 *Fax:* (06104) 75356, pg 248

Karunaratne & Sons Ltd (Sri Lanka) *Tel:* 692295 *Fax:* 855520; 850256 *E-mail:* karusons@sri.lanka.net, pg 597

Karunia CV (Indonesia) *Tel:* (031) 5344120 *Fax:* (031) 5343409, pg 355

Karya Anda, CV (Indonesia) *Tel:* (031) 5344215; (031) 522580; (031) 5315402 *Fax:* (031) 5310594, pg 356

Main Library, Kasetsart University (Thailand) *Tel:* (02) 5611369, pg 1503

Kastaniotis Editions SA (Greece) *Tel:* (01) 3301208; (01) 3803234 *Fax:* (01) 3822530 *E-mail:* kastaniotis@ath.forthnet.gr, pg 312

Kastell Verlag GmbH (Germany) *Tel:* (089) 33 21 75 *Fax:* (089) 340 11 78 *E-mail:* kastell-verlag@t-online.de, pg 248

Katai & Bolza Irodalmi Ugynokseg (Hungary) *Tel:* (01) 456-0313 *Fax:* (01) 215-4420 *Web Site:* www.kataibolza.hu, pg 1112

Katalis PT Bina Mitra Plaosan (Indonesia) *Tel:* (021) 7510477, pg 356

Kathakali (Bangladesh) *Tel:* (031) 619476; (031) 619006; (031) 612625, pg 1275

Katholieke Bijbelstichting (Netherlands) *Tel:* (073) 6133220 *Fax:* (073) 6910140, pg 479

Katholieke Universiteit Leuven (Belgium) *Tel:* (016) 324660; (016) 324601 *Fax:* (016) 324616 *Web Site:* www.bib.kuleuven.ac.be, pg 1453

Verlag Katholisches Bibelwerk GmbH (Germany) *Tel:* (0711) 61920-0 *Fax:* (0711) 61920-44 *E-mail:* verlag@bibelwerk.de *Web Site:* www.bibelwerk.de, pg 248

Katholska kirkjan a Islandi - Landakot Publishers Thorlakssjodur (Iceland) *Tel:* 550188, pg 328

Katolicki Uniwersytet Wydawniczo -Redakcja (Poland) *Tel:* (081) 5257151; (081) 5251809 *Fax:* (081) 541246 *E-mail:* sekret@kul.lublin.pl, pg 517

Katoptro Publications (Greece) *Tel:* (01) 9244827; (01) 9244852 *Fax:* (01) 9244756 *E-mail:* info@katoptro.gr *Web Site:* www.katoptro.gr, pg 312

Katzmann Verlag KG (Germany) *Tel:* (07473) 5427 *Fax:* (07473) 5427, pg 248

Kaufmann SA (Greece) *Tel:* (01) 3230320 *Fax:* (01) 3633967, pg 1286

Verlag Ernst Kaufmann GmbH (Germany) *Tel:* (07821) 93 90-0 *Fax:* (07821) 9390-11 *Web Site:* www.kaufmann-verlag.de, pg 248

Kauppakaari Oyj Lakimiesliiton Kustannus, Yrityksen Tietokirjat (Finland) *Tel:* (09) 647 101 *Fax:* (09) 602 127 *E-mail:* kustannus@kauppakaari.fi *Web Site:* www.kauppakaari.fi, pg 142

Kavaler Publishers (Belarus) *Tel:* (0172) 238041; (0172) 548198 *Fax:* (0172) 238041 *E-mail:* Kavaler@inbox.ru, pg 63

Jennifer Kavanagh (United Kingdom) *Tel:* (020) 7636 2477 *Fax:* (020) 7636 2479, pg 1120

Kavkazskaya Biblioteka Publishing House (Russian Federation) *Tel:* (8652) 32314, pg 539

KAW Krajowa Agencja Wydawnicza (Poland) *Tel:* (022) 32336, pg 517

Kawade Shobo Shinsha (Japan) *Tel:* (03) 34041201 *Fax:* (03) 34046386, pg 419

Kazakh Al-Farabi State National University (Kazakstan) *Tel:* (03272) 472517 *E-mail:* evgenyaakazgu@ksisti.alma-ata.su, pg 430

Kazakhstan Academy of Sciences (Kazakstan) *Tel:* (03272) 628341 (voice & fax), pg 1479

Kazakhstan, Izd-Vo (Kazakstan) *Tel:* (03272) 422929; (03272) 428562 *Fax:* (03272) 422929, pg 430

Kazama Shobo (Japan) *Tel:* (03) 32915729 *Fax:* (03) 32915757, pg 419

KBV-Verlags-und Mediengesellschaft mbH (Germany) *Tel:* (0221) 28 26 92 0 *Fax:* (0221) 28 26 91 9 *E-mail:* info@kbv-verlag.de *Web Site:* www.kbv-verlag.de, pg 248

KCL Language Consultancy Ltd (Hong Kong) *Tel:* (02) 8811368 *Fax:* (02) 8080389 *E-mail:* kcl@iohk.com, pg 1126

KD - Consult A/S (Denmark) *Tel:* 35373533 *Fax:* 35373299, pg 133

Keats-Shelley Memorial Association (United Kingdom) *Tel:* (01892) 533452 *Fax:* (01892) 519142, pg 1371

Keats-Shelley Memorial Association (Italy) *Tel:* (06) 6784235 *Fax:* (06) 6784167 *E-mail:* info@keats-shelley-house.org *Web Site:* www.keats-shelley-house.org, pg 1365

Kedros Publishers (Greece) *Tel:* (01) 3802007; (01) 3089712 *Fax:* (01) 3831981 *E-mail:* kedros@ermis.accl.gr, pg 312

Gregory Kefalas Publishing (Australia) *Tel:* (02) 9789 6049 *Fax:* (02) 97876181, pg 29

Kegan Paul International Ltd (United Kingdom) *Tel:* (020) 7580 5511 *Fax:* (020) 7436 0899 *E-mail:* books@keganpaul.com *Web Site:* www.keganpaul.com, pg 703

Keigaku Publishing Co Ltd (Japan) *Tel:* (03) 32333731 *Fax:* (03) 32333730, pg 419

Keil & Keil Literary Agency (Germany) *Tel:* (040) 27166892 *Fax:* (040) 27166896 *E-mail:* anfragen@keil-keil.com *Web Site:* www.keil-keil.com, pg 1111

Keisuisha Publishing Company Ltd (Japan) *Tel:* (082) 2467909 *Fax:* (082) 2467876 *E-mail:* info@keisui.co.jp *Web Site:* www.keisui.co.jp, pg 419

Verlag Walter Keller, Dornach (Switzerland) *Tel:* (061) 7015713 *Fax:* (061) 7015716 *E-mail:* info@verlag-walterkeller.ch *Web Site:* www.verlag-walterkeller.ch, pg 617

SachBuchVerlag Kellner (Germany) *Tel:* (421) 77866 *Fax:* (421) 704058 *E-mail:* kellner-verlag@t-online.de *Web Site:* kellner-verlag.de, pg 248

Kells Publishing Company Ltd (Ireland) *Tel:* (046) 40117; (046) 40255 *Fax:* (046) 41522, pg 362

The Frances Kelly Agency (United Kingdom) *Tel:* (0181) 5497830 *Fax:* (0181) 5470051, pg 1120

Kelly's (United Kingdom) *Tel:* (01342) 335699 *Fax:* (01342) 335825 *E-mail:* kellys.mktg@reedinfo.co.uk *Web Site:* www.kellysearch.com, pg 704

Martin Kelter Verlag GmbH u Co (Germany) *Tel:* (040) 68 28 95-0 *Fax:* (040) 68 28 95 50 *Web Site:* www.kelter.de, pg 248

Kemongsa Publishing Co Ltd (Republic of Korea) *Tel:* (02) 723-9367 *Fax:* (02) 561-0910, pg 437

Kemps Publishing Ltd (United Kingdom) *Tel:* (0121) 765 4144 *Fax:* (0121) 706 1408 *E-mail:* info@kempsgold.co.uk *Web Site:* www.kempsgold.co.uk, pg 704

Kempton Park Public Library (South Africa) *Tel:* (011) 9212150 *Fax:* (011) 9750921, pg 1497

Kenek Ltd (Cyprus) *Tel:* (02) 365842 *Fax:* (02) 475150, pg 122

The Kenilworth Press Ltd (United Kingdom) *Tel:* (01296) 715101 *Fax:* (01296) 715148 *E-mail:* mail@kenilworthpress.co.uk *Web Site:* www.kenilworthpress.co.uk, pg 704

Kenkyusha Ltd (Japan) *Tel:* (03) 32887775 *Fax:* (03) 32694155, pg 419

Kennarahaskoli Islands (Iceland) *Tel:* 5633800; 5633863 *Fax:* 5633914 *Web Site:* www.khi.is/bok, pg 1472

Albertine Kennedy Publishing (Ireland) *Tel:* (01) 6607090 *Fax:* (01) 6607090, pg 362

Kenneth Dike Library (Nigeria) *Tel:* (02) 8103118 *Fax:* (02) 8103118 *E-mail:* library@kdl.ui.edu.ng, pg 1488

Kennys Bookshop & Art Galleries (Ireland) *Tel:* (091) 562739 *Fax:* (091) 568544 *E-mail:* queries@kennys.ie *Web Site:* www.kennys.ie, pg 362

Kentro Byzantinon Erevnon (Greece) *Tel:* (031) 270941 *Fax:* (031) 228922, pg 312

Kentron Ekdoseos Ellinon Syngrafeon (Greece) *Tel:* (01) 3612541 *Fax:* (01) 3602691, pg 1364

Kenway Publications Ltd (Kenya) *Tel:* (02) 444700 *Fax:* (02) 448753; (02) 532095 *E-mail:* eaep@africaonline.co.ke *Web Site:* www.eastafricanpublishers.com, pg 432

Kenya Agricultural Research Institute (Kenya) *Tel:* (02) 32880 *Fax:* (0154) 583384, pg 1479

Kenya Energy & Environment Organisation, Kengo (Kenya) *Tel:* (02) 749747; (02) 748281 *Fax:* (02) 749382, pg 432

Kenya Library Association (Kenya) *Tel:* (02) 214917 *Fax:* (02) 336885, pg 1519

Kenya Literature Bureau (Kenya) *Tel:* (02) 506142; (02) 506143; (02) 506148; (02) 506156; (02) 506158; (02) 722657 *Fax:* (02) 505903; (02) 601474, pg 432

Kenya Literature Bureau (Kenya) *Tel:* (02) 722657, pg 1251

Kenya Medical Research Institute (KEMRI) (Kenya) *Tel:* (02) 722541; (02) 722672; (02) 722532 *Fax:* (02) 720030 *E-mail:* kemrilib@ken.healthnet.org, pg 432

Kenya Meteorological Department (Kenya) *Tel:* (02) 567880 *Fax:* (02) 576955 *E-mail:* director@lion.meteo.go.ke; imtr@lion.meteo.go.ke *Web Site:* www.meteo.go.ke, pg 432

Kenya National Archives & Documentation Service (Kenya) *Tel:* (02) 228959 *Fax:* (02) 228020 *E-mail:* knarchives@kenyaweb.com, pg 1479

Kenya National Library Service (Kenya) *Tel:* (02) 725550 *Fax:* (02) 721749 *E-mail:* knls@nbnet.co.ke *Web Site:* www.knls.or.ke, pg 1479

Kenya Polytechnic Library (Kenya) *Tel:* (02) 338231, pg 1479

Kenya Publishers Association (Kenya) *Tel:* (02) 222309; (02) 223262 *Fax:* (02) 339875, pg 1251

Kenya Quality & Productivity Institute (Kenya), pg 432

Kenya School of Law (Kenya), pg 1479

Kenya Technical Teachers' College Library (Kenya) *Tel:* (02) 520211 *Fax:* (02) 520037, pg 1479

Kenyatta University Library (Kenya) *Tel:* (02) 810901 *Fax:* (02) 810759, pg 1479

The Jomo Kenyatta Foundation (Kenya) *Tel:* (02) 557222; (02) 557223; (02) 557224 *Fax:* (02) 531966, pg 432

Kenyon-Deane (United Kingdom) *Tel:* (01684) 540154 *Fax:* (01684) 540154, pg 704

P Keppler Verlag GmbH & Co KG (Germany) *Tel:* (06104) 606 0 *Fax:* (06104) 606 121 *E-mail:* info@kepplermediengruppe.de, pg 248

Kepzoemueveszeti Kiado (Hungary) *Tel:* (01) 2522177; (01) 251-1677; (01) 1176222 *Fax:* (01) 2522177, pg 324

Kerala University, Department of Publications (India) *Tel:* (0471) 445631 *Fax:* (0471) 447158, pg 341

Kerber Christof Verlag (Germany) *Tel:* (0521) 95008-10 *Fax:* (0521) 95008-88 *E-mail:* info@kerber-verlag.de *Web Site:* www.kerber-verlag.de, pg 248

Alexander Kerbiser KG (Austria) *Tel:* (03852) 4807 *Fax:* (03852) 5349, pg 1274

Verlag Kerle im Verlag Herder (Germany) *Tel:* (0761) 2717-0 *Fax:* (0761) 2717-352 *E-mail:* info@kerle.de *Web Site:* www.kerle.de, pg 248

Verlag Kerle im Verlag Herder & Co (Austria) *Tel:* (01) 521413; (01) 521414 *Fax:* (01) 28828180, pg 53

Uitgeverij De Kern (Netherlands) *Tel:* (035) 5486345 *Fax:* (035) 5420210, pg 479

Kernerman Publishing Ltd (Israel) *Tel:* (03) 6492715 *Fax:* (03) 6493712 *E-mail:* kp@internet-zahav.net, pg 369

Kerryman Ltd (Ireland) *Tel:* (071) 45500 *Fax:* (071) 45570 *E-mail:* ads@kerryman.ie *Web Site:* www.kerryman.ie, pg 362

Kershaw Publishing Co Ltd (United Kingdom) *Tel:* (020) 7240 0856 *Fax:* (020) 7764 8218 *E-mail:* chris@e-d-c.co.uk, pg 704

C Kersten & Co (Suriname) *Tel:* 471133, pg 599

Kesaint Blanc (Indonesia) *Tel:* (021) 4204847; (021) 4204851; (021) 8207555 *Fax:* (021) 4216792; (021) 8207557, pg 356

Nurcihan Kesim Literary Agency, Inc (Turkey) *Tel:* (0212) 5111078; (0212) 5285797 *Fax:* (0212) 5285791 *E-mail:* kesim@superonline.com *Web Site:* www.nurcihankesim.com, pg 1117

Simona Kessler International Copyright Agency Ltd (Romania) *Tel:* (01) 2318150 *Fax:* (01) 2314522, pg 1115

Keswick Books & Gifts Ltd (Kenya) *Tel:* (02) 226047; (02) 331692 *Fax:* (02) 331692 *E-mail:* keswick@swiftkenya.com, pg 1296

Keter Publishing House Ltd (Israel) *Tel:* (02) 6557822 *Fax:* (02) 6528962, pg 369

Keterpress Enterprises Jerusalem (Israel) *Tel:* (02) 6557822 *Fax:* (02) 6527956 *E-mail:* keterprs@isdn.net.il, pg 1136, 1157

Keterpress Enterprises Jerusalem (Israel) *Tel:* (02) 6557822 *Fax:* (02) 6528962 *E-mail:* keterprs@isdn.net.il, pg 1198

Keterpress Enterprises Jerusalem (Israel) *Tel:* (02) 6557822 *Fax:* (02) 6528962, pg 1213

Editions Ketty & Alexandre (Switzerland) *Tel:* (021) 9051111 *Fax:* (021) 9056050, pg 617

Keurbiblioteek (South Africa) *Tel:* (012) 401-0700 *Fax:* (012) 3255498 *E-mail:* lapa@atkv.org.za, pg 1231

Die Keure (Belgium) *Tel:* (050) 47 12 72 *Fax:* (050) 33 51 54 *E-mail:* die.keure@pophost.eunet.be *Web Site:* www.diekeure.be, pg 70

Key Language Services (United Kingdom) *Tel:* (01908) 232101 *Fax:* (01908) 232815 *E-mail:* keylanguages@btinternet.com, pg 1129

Keysersche Verlagsbuchhandlung GmbH (Germany) *Tel:* (089) 4554-0 *Fax:* (089) 4554-111, pg 248

Keytec Typesetting Ltd (United Kingdom) *Tel:* (01308) 427580 *Fax:* (01308) 421961 *E-mail:* all@keytectype.co.uk *Web Site:* www.keytectype.co.uk, pg 1162

Keyware sarl (Luxembourg) *Tel:* 358660 *E-mail:* texthaus@webcom.com, pg 447

Khai Wah-Ferco Pte Ltd (Singapore) *Tel:* 7583313 *Fax:* 7582038 *E-mail:* kwfppi@pacific.net.sg, pg 1138

Khanna Publishers (India) *Tel:* (011) 2912380; (011) 7224179, pg 341

Kharisma Publications Sdn Bhd (Malaysia) *Tel:* (03) 724660 *Fax:* (03) 724602, pg 452

Khartoum Polytechnic Library (Sudan) *Tel:* 78922, pg 1500

Khartoum University Press (Sudan) *Tel:* (011) 80558; (011) 81806, pg 598

Khayat Book and Publishing Co Sarl (Lebanon), pg 443

Khlang Withaya Pub (Thailand) *Tel:* (02) 224546; (02) 2219331, pg 635

Izdatelstvo Khudozhestvennaya Literatura (Russian Federation) *Tel:* (095) 268865; (095) 2613864 *Fax:* (095) 2618300, pg 539

Ki Moon Dang (Republic of Korea) *Tel:* (02) 2995496; (02) 2956175 *Fax:* (02) 2968188, pg 437

Kibea Publishing Co *Tel:* (02) 24 10 20; (02) 925 01 52 *Fax:* (02) 925 07 48 *E-mail:* kibea@internet-bg.net; office@kibea.net *Web Site:* www.kibea.net, pg 96

Kidemus Verlag GmbH (Germany) *Tel:* (0221) 84 20 97 *Fax:* (0221) 84 20 98 *E-mail:* info@kidemus.de *Web Site:* www.kidemus.de, pg 248

Gustav Kiepenheuer Verlag GmbH (Germany) *Tel:* (0341) 99 54 60 0 *Fax:* (0341) 9954 620 *E-mail:* info@aufbau-verlag.de *Web Site:* www.aufbau-verlag.de, pg 249

Verlag Kiepenheuer und Witsch GmbH & Co KG (Germany) *Tel:* (0221) 376 85-0 *Fax:* (0221) 376 85-70 *E-mail:* verlag@kiwi-koeln.de *Web Site:* www.kiwi-koeln.de, pg 249

Libreria Kier (Argentina) *Tel:* (011) 8110507; (011) 8118243; (011) 8132668 *Fax:* (011) 8132668, pg 1271

Editorial Kier SACIFI (Argentina) *Tel:* (011) 4811-0507 *Fax:* (011) 4811-3395 *E-mail:* ediciones@kier.com.ar *Web Site:* www.kier.com.ar, pg 7

Kierdorf Ute Verlag (Germany) *Tel:* (02267) 4495 *Fax:* (02267) 4458 *E-mail:* Kierdorfverlag@t-online.de *Web Site:* www.kierdorfverlag.de, pg 249

Kiiarat Konyvdiado (Hungary) *Tel:* (01) 3886312, pg 324

Kilda Verlag (Germany) *Tel:* (02571) 52115 *Fax:* (02571) 97098, pg 249

Verlag im Kilian GmbH (Germany) *Tel:* (06421) 2 93 30 *Fax:* (06421) 16 38 94 *Web Site:* www.kilian-verlag.de, pg 249

Kilkenny People/Wellbrook Press (Ireland) *Tel:* (056) 21015 *Fax:* (056) 21414, pg 1157, 1198

Killara Press (Australia) *Tel:* (07) 5499-7717 *Fax:* (07) 4168-0244 *Web Site:* www.gippsnet.com.au/sylvia/kettle/kettle.htm, pg 29

Kim Hup Lee Printing Co Pte Ltd (Singapore) *Tel:* 2833306 *Fax:* 2889222, pg 1138

Kima Global Publishers (South Africa) *Tel:* (021) 686-7154 *Fax:* (021) 686-9066 *E-mail:* kima@global.co.za *Web Site:* www.kimaglobal.co.za, pg 556

Kimberley Public Library (South Africa) *Tel:* (053) 8306241 *Fax:* (053) 8331954 *E-mail:* fritz@kbymun.org.za, pg 1498

Kimio Uitgeverij bv (Netherlands) *Tel:* (035) 6950760 *Fax:* (035) 6951548, pg 479

Kin no Hoshi-Sha Co Ltd (Japan) *Tel:* (03) 38611861 *Fax:* (03) 38611507, pg 419

Kindai Kagaku Sha Co, Ltd (Japan) *Tel:* (03) 32606101 *Fax:* (03) 32606102, pg 419

Der Kinderbuch Verlag GmbH (Germany) *Tel:* (030) 89 38 84-0 *Fax:* (030) 89 38 84-20; (030) 885722, pg 249

Kinderbuchfonds Baobab (Switzerland) *Tel:* (061) 3332727 *Fax:* (061) 3332726 *E-mail:* baobab@access.ch, pg 617

Kinderbuchverlag Luzern (Switzerland) *Tel:* (041) 516861 *Fax:* (062) 8245780, pg 617

Kindler Verlag AG (Switzerland) *Tel:* (01) 3633007, pg 617

Kindler Verlag GmbH (Germany) *Tel:* (089) 92710 *Fax:* (089) 9271168 *E-mail:* presse@rowohlt.de, pg 249

King Abdulasiz University Library (Saudi Arabia) *Tel:* (02) 6879033 *Fax:* (02) 6405974, pg 1495

King Abdulaziz Public Library (Saudi Arabia) *Tel:* (01) 4911300; (01) 4911304 *Fax:* (01) 4911949 *E-mail:* kapl@anet.net.sa, pg 1495

King Baudouin Foundation (Belgium) *Tel:* (02) 511 18 40 *Fax:* (02) 511 52 21 *E-mail:* publi@kbs-frb.be *Web Site:* www.kbs-frb.be, pg 70

King Faisal University Library (Saudi Arabia) *Tel:* (03) 8574456 *Fax:* (03) 8576748, pg 1495

Hilda King Educational (United Kingdom) *Tel:* (01494) 813947; (01494) 817947 *Fax:* (01494) 813947 *E-mail:* hildaking@clara.co.uk; orders@hilda-king.co.uk *Web Site:* www.hildaking.clara.net, pg 704

Laurence King Publishing Ltd (United Kingdom) *Tel:* (020) 7430 8850 *Fax:* (020) 7430 8880 *E-mail:* enquiries@laurenceking.co.uk *Web Site:* www.laurenceking.co.uk, pg 704

King Saud University (Saudi Arabia) *Tel:* (01) 4675634 *Fax:* (01) 4678633, pg 543

King Saud University Library (Saudi Arabia) *Tel:* (01) 4676148 *Fax:* (01) 4676162 *Web Site:* www.ksu.edu.sa, pg 1496

Kingfisher Books (Australia), pg 29

Kingfisher Publications Plc (United Kingdom) *Tel:* (020) 7903 9999 *Fax:* (020) 7242 4979 *E-mail:* sales@kingfisherpub.com *Web Site:* www.kingfisherpub.com, pg 704

King's Fund Publishing (United Kingdom) *Tel:* (020) 7307 2400 *Fax:* (020) 7307 2801 *E-mail:* libweb@kingsfund.org.uk *Web Site:* www.kingsfund.org.uk, pg 704

Kingsclear Books (Australia) *Tel:* (02) 95574367 *Fax:* (02) 95572337 *E-mail:* kingsclear@wr.com.au *Web Site:* www.kingsclearbooks.com.au, pg 29

Jessica Kingsley Publishers (United Kingdom) *Tel:* (020) 7833 2307 *Fax:* (020) 7837 2917 *E-mail:* post@jkp.com *Web Site:* www.jkp.com, pg 704

Kingston Bookshop Ltd (Jamaica) *Tel:* (876) 927-8899, pg 1294

Kingston Publishers Ltd (Jamaica) *Tel:* (876) 927-8899 *Fax:* (876) 928-5719, pg 413

Kingstons Ltd (Zimbabwe) *Tel:* (04) 750547; (04) 750548; (04) 750549; (04) 750550 *Fax:* (04) 723697, pg 1325

Kingsway Publications (United Kingdom) *Tel:* (01323) 437700 *Fax:* (01323) 411970 *E-mail:* books@kingsway.co.uk *Web Site:* www.kingsway.co.uk, pg 705

Kino Verlag GmbH (Germany) *Tel:* (040) 4131-1455 *Fax:* (040) 4131-2045 *Web Site:* www.vgm.de, pg 249

Kinokuniya Co Ltd (Japan) *Tel:* (03) 3354-0131 *Fax:* (03) 3439-3955, pg 1294

Kinokuniya Co Ltd (Publishing Department) (Japan) *Tel:* (03) 54695919 *Fax:* (03) 54695959 *E-mail:* publish@kimokunya.co.jp *Web Site:* www.kimokuniya.co.jp, pg 420

Kinpodo (Japan) *Tel:* (075) 7511111 *Fax:* (075) 7516858 *E-mail:* kkimpodo@kb3.so-net.or.jp, pg 420

Kinta CV (Indonesia) *Tel:* (021) 5494751, pg 356

KINZAI Corporation (Japan) *Tel:* (03) 33580011 *Fax:* (03) 33580036 *E-mail:* jdi04072@nifty.ne.jp, pg 420

Kipling Society (United Kingdom) *Tel:* (020) 7286 0194 *Fax:* (020) 7286 0194 *Web Site:* www.kipling.org.uk, pg 1371

Kirby Book Co Pty Ltd (Australia) *Tel:* (02) 9698 2377 *Toll Free Tel:* 800 225271 *Fax:* (02) 9698 8748, pg 1273

Peter Kirchheim Verlag (Germany) *Tel:* (089) 267474 *Fax:* (089) 2605528 *Web Site:* www.kirchheimverlag.de, pg 249

Kirja-Leitzinger (Finland) *Tel:* (09) 3493850 *Fax:* (09) 3421853, pg 143

Kirjakauppaliitto Ry (Finland) *Tel:* (09) 68599110 *Fax:* (09) 68599119 *E-mail:* toimisto@kirjakauppaliitto.fi, pg 1242

Kirjallisuudentutkijain Seura (Finland) *Tel:* (09) 19122658 *Fax:* (09) 19123008 *Web Site:* www.helsinki.fi/jarj/skts, pg 1362

Kirjatoimi (Finland) *Tel:* (03) 3611200 *Fax:* (03) 3600454 *E-mail:* kirjatoimi@sdafin.org, pg 143

Kirjayhtymae Oy (Finland) *Tel:* (09) 6937641 *Fax:* (09) 69376366 *E-mail:* oppikirjat@kirjayhtyma.fi *Web Site:* www.kirjayhtyma.fi, pg 143

Kirschbaum Verlag GmbH (Germany) *Tel:* (0228) 9 54 53-0 *Fax:* (0228) 9 54 53-27 *E-mail:* info@kirschbaum.de *Web Site:* www.kirschbaum.de, pg 249

Kiryat Sefer (Israel) *Tel:* (03) 5178922 *Fax:* (03) 5100227, pg 369

Kisambo Publishers Ltd (United Republic of Tanzania) *Tel:* (051) 114876; (051) 131382 *Fax:* (051) 112351, pg 633

KIT Press - Royal Tropical Institute (United Kingdom) *Fax:* (020) 7236 9761, pg 705

Kitab Ghar (India) *Tel:* (011) 213206, pg 341

KITLV Press Royal Institute of Linguistics & Anthropology (Netherlands) *Tel:* (071) 5272295 *Fax:* (071) 5272638 *E-mail:* kitlvpress@kitlv.nl *Web Site:* www.iias.leidenuniv.nl/institutes/kitlv, pg 479

Kitwe Public Library (Zambia) *Tel:* 213685, pg 1509

Kivukoni College Library (United Republic of Tanzania) *Tel:* (051) 820047, pg 1503

Kivunim-Arsan Publishing House (Israel) *Tel:* (08) 9470791 *Fax:* (08) 9469740, pg 369

Kiyi Yayinlari (Turkey) *Tel:* (0212) 2455845 *Fax:* (0212) 2454009, pg 640

KJK-Keaszov (Hungary) *Tel:* (01) 1126430 *Fax:* (01) 464-5607 *E-mail:* vevoszolg@kjk.hn *Web Site:* www.kerszov.hn (or kjk.hn), pg 324

Klages-Verlag (Germany) *Tel:* (0511) 5358936 *Fax:* (0511) 5358928 *E-mail:* kv@lsz.de, pg 249

Klaipedos Universiteto Leidykla (Lithuania) *Tel:* (06) 398890 *Fax:* (06) 398999 *E-mail:* leidykla@rekt.ku.lt *Web Site:* www.ku.lt, pg 445

Klartext Verlagsgesellschaft mbH (Germany) *Tel:* (0201) 86 206-0 *Fax:* (0201) 86 206-22 *E-mail:* info@klartext-verlag.de, pg 249

Klassikerfoerlaget (Sweden) *Tel:* (08) 4570300 *Fax:* (08) 4570334 *E-mail:* klassikerforlaget@raben.se, pg 604

Kleidarithmos (Greece) *Tel:* (01) 3832044 *Fax:* (01) 3617950, pg 312

Ingrid Anna Kleihues Verlags und Autorenagentur (Germany) *Tel:* (0711) 6788800 *Fax:* (0711) 6788801 *E-mail:* info@agentur-kleihues.de, pg 1111

Ingrid Klein Verlag GmbH (Germany) *Tel:* (089) 3818010 *Fax:* (089) 338704 *E-mail:* info@piper.de *Web Site:* www.piper.de, pg 249

Verlag Kleine Schritte Ursula Dahm & Co (Germany) *Tel:* (0651) 300 698 *Fax:* (0651) 300 699 *E-mail:* mail@kleine-schritte.de *Web Site:* www.kleine-schritte.de, pg 249

Kleiner Bachmann Verlag fur Kinder und Umwelt (Germany) *Tel:* (06251) 78 98 22 *Fax:* (06251) 78 98 24 *E-mail:* mail@kleinerbachmann.de *Web Site:* www.kleinerbachmann.de, pg 250

Unterwegs Verlag, Manfred Klemann (Germany) *Tel:* (07731) 63544 *Fax:* (07731) 62401 *E-mail:* uv@reisefuehrer.com, pg 250

Forlaget Klematis A/S (Denmark) *Tel:* 86175455 *Fax:* 86175959 *E-mail:* klematis@klematis.dk; production@klematis.dk *Web Site:* www.klematis.dk, pg 133

Klens Verlag GmbH (Germany) *Tel:* (0211) 4499251 *Fax:* (0211) 4499277, pg 250

Ernst Klett Verlag GmbH (Germany) *Tel:* (0711) 66 72-13 33 *Fax:* (0711) 66 72-20 00 *E-mail:* klett-kundenservice@klett-mail.de *Web Site:* www.klett-verlag.de, pg 250

Klett und Balmer & Co Verlag (Switzerland) *Tel:* (042) 214131 *Fax:* (042) 214131 *E-mail:* info@sklett.ch *Web Site:* www.klett.ch, pg 617

Klett-Cotta (Germany) *Tel:* (0711) 66721256 *Fax:* (0711) 66722031 *E-mail:* info@klett-cotta.de *Web Site:* www.klett-cotta.de, pg 250

Kley, Werner, Beteiligungs GmbH (Germany) *Tel:* (02381) 95040-0 *Fax:* (02381) 9504019, pg 250

Kliemand Verlag (Liechtenstein) *Tel:* (075) 21177 *Fax:* (075) 2321048, pg 444

Johann Kliment KG Musikverlag (Austria) *Tel:* (01) 317 51 47 *Fax:* (01) 310 08 27 *E-mail:* office@kliment.at *Web Site:* www.kliment.at, pg 54

Narodna i univerzitetska biblioteka Kliment Ohridski (The Former Yugoslav Republic of Macedonia) *Tel:* (091) 115177 *Fax:* (091) 226846 *E-mail:* kliment@nubski.edu.mk, pg 1482

Editions Klincksieck (France) *Tel:* (01) 43.54.59.53 *Fax:* (01) 43.25.25.53, pg 171

Klink, Vincent, Edition, Stecknadel (Germany) *Tel:* (0711) 65863-51 *Fax:* (0711) 65863-53, pg 250

Klinkhardt & Biermann Verlagsbuchhandlung GmbH (Germany) *Tel:* (089) 38 17 9-0 *Fax:* (089) 38 17 09-35 *E-mail:* info@prestel.de *Web Site:* www.prestel.de, pg 250

Erika Klopp Verlag GmbH (Germany) *Tel:* (040) 607 90 902 *Fax:* (040) 607 20 326 *E-mail:* klopp@vsg.hamburg.de *Web Site:* www.erika-klopp.de, pg 250

Klosterhaus-Verlagsbuchhandlung Dr Grimm KG (Germany) *Tel:* (05572) 7310 *Fax:* (05572) 999823, pg 250

Vittorio Klostermann GmbH (Germany) *Tel:* (069) 97 08 16-0 *Fax:* (069) 70 80 38 *E-mail:* verlag@klostermann.de *Web Site:* www.klostermann.de, pg 250

Klub-Dagbreek (South Africa) *Tel:* (011) 6736725 *Fax:* (011) 6736719, pg 1231

Walter Klugel (Austria) *Tel:* (0222) 581 84 28, pg 1274

Uitgeverij Kluitman Alkmaar BV (Netherlands) *Tel:* (072) 5710542 *Fax:* (072) 5743348, pg 479

Kluwer Academic/Plenum Publishers (United Kingdom) *Tel:* (020) 7940 7494 *Fax:* (020) 7940 7495 *E-mail:* mail@plenum.co.uk *Web Site:* www.wkap.nl, pg 705

Kluwer Academic Publishers (Netherlands) *Tel:* (078) 6392 392 *Fax:* (078) 6392 254, pg 479

Kluwer Bedrijfswetenschappen (Netherlands) *Tel:* (0172) 466321 *Fax:* (0172) 435527, pg 479

Editions Juridiques Kluwer a Deurne Anvers (Belgium) *Tel:* (02) 300 3000 *Fax:* (03) 360-04 *E-mail:* custumer.kejb@wkb.be *Web Site:* www.editionskluwer.be, pg 70

Kluwer Law International (Netherlands) *Tel:* (070) 30 81 500 *Fax:* (070) 30 81 515, pg 479

Kluwer Technische Boeken BV (Netherlands) *Tel:* (0172) 466321 *Fax:* (0172) 435527, pg 480

KM C (Czech Republic) *Tel:* (02) 24810704; (02) 2311156; (02) 2314289 *Fax:* (02) 24810850, pg 1227

Verlag Fritz Knapp GmbH (Germany) *Tel:* (069) 97 08 33-0 *Fax:* (069) 7 07 84 00 *E-mail:* kreditwesen@t-online.de *Web Site:* www.kreditwesen.de, pg 250

Horst Knapp Finanznachrichten (Austria) *Tel:* (01) 7154460-0 *Fax:* (01) 7154460-22, pg 54

Albrecht Knaus Verlag GmbH (Germany) *Tel:* (089) 4372-0 *Fax:* (089) 4372-2790, pg 250

Knesebeck Verlag (Germany) *Tel:* (089) 264059 *Fax:* (089) 269258 *E-mail:* vertrieb@knesebeck-verlag.de; presse@knesebeck-verlag.de *Web Site:* www.knesebeck-verlag.de, pg 250

Knesset Library (Israel) *Tel:* (02) 753333 *Fax:* (02) 5662733 *E-mail:* sifriaz@netvision.net.il, pg 1477

KNI Inc (United States) *Tel:* 714-956-7300 *Fax:* 714-635-1744 *E-mail:* epp@kniinc.com *Web Site:* www.kniinc.com, pg 1145, 1207

Izdatelstvo Kniga (Russian Federation) *Tel:* (095) 2516003 *Fax:* (095) 2500489, pg 539

Knight Features (United Kingdom) *Tel:* (020) 7622 1522 *Fax:* (020) 7622 1522 *E-mail:* peter@knightfeatures.co.uk *Web Site:* www.knightfeatures.co.uk, pg 705

Knight Features (United Kingdom) *Tel:* (020) 7622 1522 *Fax:* (020) 7622 1522, pg 1120

Knihkupectvi - Antikvariat Galerie (Czech Republic) *Tel:* (0417) 23966 (voice & fax), pg 1281

Knihovna A Tiskarna Pro Nevidome (Czech Republic) *Tel:* (02) 22 21 04 92; (02) 22 21 15 23 *Fax:* (02) 22 21 04 94 *Web Site:* www.ktn.cz, pg 125

Knihovna Narodniho muzea (Czech Republic) *Tel:* (02) 24497111 *Fax:* (02) 24226488 *E-mail:* nm@nm.cz, pg 1460

Izdatelstvo Knizhnaya Palata (Russian Federation) *Tel:* (095) 2889247 *Fax:* (095) 1635827, pg 539

Univerzitna Kniznica (Slovakia) *Tel:* (07) 5333247 *Fax:* (07) 5334246, pg 1496

Tehnicka Knjiga (Yugoslavia) *Tel:* (011) 468596 *Fax:* (011) 473442 *E-mail:* tkmjiga@eumet.yu, pg 764

Knockabout Comics (United Kingdom) *Tel:* (020) 8969 2945 *Fax:* (020) 8968 7614 *E-mail:* knockcomic@aol.com, pg 705

Karl Knoll Verlag Alte Uni (Germany) *Tel:* (07262) 4417 *Fax:* (07262) 7942 *E-mail:* alteuni@aol.com, pg 250

Doris Knop-Verlag (Germany) *Tel:* (0421) 451743 *Fax:* (0421) 455406, pg 251

Knossos Publications (Greece) *Tel:* (01) 3610108; (01) 3804681 *Fax:* (01) 3804681, pg 312

Druckerei & Verlag Ernst Knoth GmbH (Germany) *Tel:* (05422) 94320 *Fax:* (05422) 9432-20, pg 251

Knowledge Book House (Myanmar), pg 1300

Knowledge Media International (Germany) *Tel:* (089) 4136-8433 *Fax:* (089) 4136-8411 *Web Site:* www.k-m-i.com, pg 251

Knowledge Press (China) *Tel:* (010) 8315533 *Fax:* (010) 8316510 *E-mail:* ecphtdb@public3.bta.net.cn, pg 107

Knowledge Printing & Publishing House (Myanmar), pg 471

Verlag Knut Reim, Jugendpresseverlag (Germany) *Tel:* (040) 34 26 41 *Fax:* (040) 34 46 87, pg 251

Koala-Kustannus/Oy Greenbay House Publishing Ltd (Finland) *Tel:* (09) 4111 7177 *Fax:* (09) 684 5034 *E-mail:* info@koalakustannus.fi *Web Site:* www.koalakustannus.fi, pg 143

Kobenhavns Kommunes Biblioteker (Denmark) *Tel:* 33664650 *Fax:* 33667061 *E-mail:* ibertelsen.kff@ipost.kk.dk, pg 1461

Kobenhavns Stadsarkiv (Denmark) *Tel:* 33662370 *Fax:* 33667039 *E-mail:* stadsarkiv@kff.kk.dk *Web Site:* www.ksa.kk.dk, pg 1461

Kober Verlag AG (Switzerland) *Tel:* (031) 554433 *Fax:* (055) 535181, pg 617

Verlagsanstalt Alexander Koch GmbH (Germany) *Tel:* (0711) 7591-0 *Fax:* (0711) 7591-380, pg 251

Koch, Neff und Oetinger & Co (Germany) *Tel:* (0711) 7860-0, pg 1284

Kochbuch Verlag Olga Leeb (Germany) *Tel:* (089) 171690; (089) 58998303 *Fax:* (089) 560208; (089) 71690, pg 251

Kodansha (Japan) *Tel:* (03) 53953419 *Fax:* (03) 39444441 *Web Site:* www.kodansha.co.jp, pg 420

Kodansha Disney Children's Book Club (Japan) *Tel:* (03) 39446491 *Fax:* (03) 39446323, pg 1230

Kodansha International (Japan) *Tel:* (03) 39446491 *Fax:* (03) 39446394 *Web Site:* www.thejapanpage.com, pg 420

Kodansha Scientific Ltd (Japan) *Tel:* (03) 39466201 *Fax:* (03) 39449915, pg 420

Eric Koehler (France) *Tel:* (01) 49270637 *Fax:* (01) 47033986, pg 171

K F Koehler Verlag (Germany) *Tel:* (0711) 7892 130; (0711) 7892 149 *Fax:* (0711) 7892 132 *E-mail:* info@kfk.de; sabine.haegele@kfk.de *Web Site:* www.buchkatalog.de, pg 251

Verlagsgruppe Koehler/Mittler (Germany) *Tel:* (040) 7971303 *Fax:* (040) 79713324 *Web Site:* www.koehler-mittler.de/, pg 251

Koehler und Amelang Verlagsgesellschaft mbH (Germany) *Tel:* (089) 45554-0 *Fax:* (089) 45554110 *E-mail:* info@dva.de *Web Site:* www.dva.de, pg 251

Koehlers Verlagsgesellschaft mbH (Germany) *Tel:* (040) 7 97 13-03 *Fax:* (040) 79713324 *Web Site:* www.koehler-mittler.de/, pg 251

Koelner Universitaets-Verlag GmbH (Germany) *Tel:* (0221) 48 81 452 *Fax:* (0221) 49 81 445 *E-mail:* div@iwkoeln.de *Web Site:* www.iwkoeln.de/, pg 251

Koenemann Verlagesellschaft mbH (Germany) *Tel:* (01149) 221-3799-0 *Fax:* (01149) 3799-288, pg 251

R Koenig GmbH (Germany) *Tel:* (089) 724970 *Fax:* (089) 7238813 *E-mail:* info@koenig-specials.com *Web Site:* www.koenig-specials.com, pg 251

Koenigsfurt Verlag, Evelin Burger et Johannes Fiebig (Germany) *Tel:* (04334) 18 99 02; (04334) 18 22 010 *Fax:* (04334) 18 22 011 *E-mail:* info@koenigsfurt.com *Web Site:* www.koenigsfurt.com, pg 251

Verlag Koenigshausen und Neumann GmbH (Germany) *Tel:* (0931) 78 40-7 00 *Fax:* (0931) 8 36 20 *E-mail:* info@koenigshausen-neumann.de *Web Site:* www.koenigshausen-neumann.de/, pg 251

Edition Koenigstein (Austria) *Tel:* (02243) 26046 *Fax:* (02243) 26046 *E-mail:* edition.koenigstein@aon.at *Web Site:* members.aon.at/edition_koenigstein, pg 54

Officina Nova, Koenyv-es Lapkiado/Bertelsmann Media Kft (Hungary) *Tel:* (01) 1887989 *Fax:* (01) 1686674, pg 324

Koenyveshaz Kft (Hungary) *Tel:* (01) 1311566 *Fax:* (01) 1311566, pg 324

Koepel van de Vlaamse Noord - Zuidbeweging 11.11.11 (Belgium) *Tel:* (02) 536-11-13 *Fax:* (02) 536-19-10 *E-mail:* info@11.be *Web Site:* www.11.be, pg 70

Lucy Koerner Verlag (Germany) *Tel:* (0711) 588472 *Fax:* (0711) 5789634, pg 252

Ute Koerner Literary Agent (Spain) *Tel:* (093) 4550414 *Fax:* (093) 4365548, pg 1116

Verlag Valentin Koerner GmbH (Germany) *Tel:* (07221) 22423 *Fax:* (07221) 38697 *E-mail:* info@koernerverlag.de *Web Site:* www.koernerverlag.de/, pg 252

Koesel-Verlag GmbH & Co (Germany) *Tel:* (089) 17801-0 *Fax:* (089) 17801-111 *E-mail:* leserservice@koesel.de *Web Site:* www.koesel.de/, pg 252

Koesler Verlag GmbH (Germany) *Tel:* (02263) 951650-51 *Fax:* (02263) 951691, pg 252

Magyar Tudomanyos Akademia Koezponti Fizikai Kutato Intezet Koenyvtara (Hungary) *Tel:* (01) 1699499 *E-mail:* kolcs@sunserv.kfki.hu, pg 325

Koezponti Statisztikai Hivatal Koenyvtar es Dokumentacios Szolgalat (Hungary) *Tel:* (01) 3456105 *Fax:* (01) 3456112, pg 1472

Kogan Page Ltd (United Kingdom) *Tel:* (020) 7278 0433 *Fax:* (020) 7278 0433 *E-mail:* kpinfo@kogan-page.co.uk; kpsales@kogan-page.co.uk; orders@kogan-page.co.uk *Web Site:* www.kogan-page.co.uk, pg 705

Kogyo Chosakai Publishing Co, Ltd (Japan) *Tel:* (03) 38174701 *Fax:* (03) 38174709 *E-mail:* mya34844@pcvah.or.jp, pg 420

W Kohlhammer GmbH, abt Haussortiment (Germany) *Tel:* (0711) 7863-7261 *Fax:* (0711) 7863-8204 *E-mail:* redaktion@kohlhammer.de *Web Site:* www.kohlhammer.de, pg 252

Koinonia Comunidade Edicoes Ltda (Editora Koinonia Ltda) (Brazil) *Tel:* (061) 223 3070 *Fax:* (061) 3228377, pg 86

Uitgeefmaatschappij J H Kok BV (Netherlands) *Tel:* (038) 3392555 *Fax:* (038) 3327331 *E-mail:* algemeen@kok.nl, pg 480

Kok Yayincilik (Turkey) *Tel:* (0312) 4302622 *Fax:* (0312) 4350497 *E-mail:* kokbilgi@kokyayincilik.com.tr *Web Site:* www.kokyayincilik.com.tr, pg 640

Kokbokskklubben God Mat (Sweden) *Tel:* (040) 380600 *Fax:* (040) 933708, pg 1232

Kokudo-Sha (Japan) *Tel:* (03) 5996-3101 *Fax:* (03) 5983-7434, pg 420

Kokuritsu Kobunshokan (Japan) *Tel:* (03) 32140621 *Fax:* (03) 32128806, pg 1478

Kokusho Kankokai Co Ltd (Japan) *Tel:* (03) 59707421 *Fax:* (03) 59707427, pg 420

Kola Sanya Publishing Enterprise (Nigeria) *Tel:* (037) 432638, pg 500

Kolibri Forlag A/S (Norway) *Tel:* 22438778 *Fax:* 22447740, pg 504

Kolibri Publishing Group (Bulgaria) *Tel:* (02) 814728; (02) 813625 *Fax:* (02) 814728, pg 96

Kolibri-Verlags GmbH (Germany) *Tel:* (040) 2202258 *Fax:* (040) 2276368 *E-mail:* daomagazin@aol.com, pg 252

Kolumbus-Verlag (Switzerland) *Tel:* (062) 7711370, pg 617

Komine Shoten Publishing Co Ltd (Japan) *Tel:* (03) 33573521 *Fax:* (03) 33571027, pg 420

Kommissionsverlag Leobuchhandling (Switzerland) *Tel:* (071) 22917 *Fax:* (071) 220587, pg 617

Kommunernes Skolebiblioteksforening (Denmark) *Tel:* 33253222 *Fax:* 33253223 *E-mail:* komskolbib@internet.dk *Web Site:* www.ksbk.dk, pg 1514

Kompass Fleischmann (Italy) *Tel:* (0461) 961240 *Fax:* (0461) 961203, pg 395

Izdatelskii Dom Kompositor (Russian Federation) *Tel:* (095) 2092980; (095) 2094105 *Fax:* (095) 2095498 *E-mail:* music@sumail.ru, pg 539

Komputerowa Oficyna Wydawnicza Help (Poland) *Tel:* (022) 723 89 21 *Fax:* (022) 723 87 64 *Web Site:* www.besthelp.pl, pg 517

Wydawnictwa Komunikacji i Lacznosci Co Ltd (Poland) *Tel:* (022) 492751-56; (022) 492314; (022) 492324; (022) 492345 *Fax:* (022) 492322 *E-mail:* wkl@wkl.com.pl *Web Site:* www.wkl.com.pl, pg 517

Konark Publishers, Pvt, Ltd (India) *Tel:* (011) 2207103; (011) 2204101 *Fax:* (011) 2207103 *E-mail:* kprn07@hotmail.com; kprn@aol.net.in, pg 341

Det Kongelige Bibliotek (Denmark) *Tel:* 33474747 *Fax:* 3332 9846 *E-mail:* kb@kb.dk *Web Site:* www.kb.dk, pg 1461

Det Kongelige Danske Videnskabernes Selskab (Denmark) *Tel:* 33435300 *Fax:* 33435301 *E-mail:* kvds@royalacademy.dk *Web Site:* www.royalacademy.dk, pg 1362

Konias (Czech Republic) *Tel:* (019) 738 06 90 *Fax:* (019) 285879, pg 125

Koninklijk Instituut Voor de Tropen (Netherlands) *Tel:* (020) 5688272 *Fax:* (020) 5688286 *E-mail:* kitpress@kit.nl *Web Site:* www.kit.nl, pg 480

Koninklijke Academie voor Nederlandse Taal- en Letterkunde (Belgium) *Tel:* (09) 265 93 40 *Fax:* (09) 265 93 49 *E-mail:* secretariaat@kantl.be *Web Site:* www.kantl.be, pg 1360

Koninklijke Bibliotheek (Netherlands) *Tel:* (070) 3140911 *Fax:* (070) 3140651 *E-mail:* secretariaat@konbib.nl, pg 1486

Koninklijke Academie voor Wetenschappen Letteren en Schone Kunsten Van Belgie (Belgium) *Tel:* (02) 550 23 23 *Fax:* (02) 550 23 25; (02) 5502325, pg 1360

Koninklijke Vermande bv (Netherlands) *Tel:* (070) 3789860 *Fax:* (070) 3789783, pg 480

Koninklijke Vlaamse Academie van Belgie voor Wetenschappen en Kunsten (Belgium) *Tel:* (02) 550 23 23 *Fax:* (02) 550 23 25 *E-mail:* info@kvab.be *Web Site:* www.kvab.be, pg 70

Konkordia Verlag GmbH (Germany) *Tel:* (07223) 98 89-0 *Fax:* (07223) 98 89-45 *E-mail:* verlag@konkordia.de, pg 252

Anton H Konrad Verlag (Germany) *Tel:* (07309) 26 57 *Fax:* (07309) 60 69 *E-mail:* info@konrad-verlag.de *Web Site:* www.konrad-verlag.de/, pg 252

Konradin-Verlagsgruppe (Germany) *Tel:* (0711) 7594-0 *Fax:* (0711) 7594-390 *E-mail:* info@konradin.de *Web Site:* www.konradin.de/, pg 252

Konst-Bibliofilen (Sweden) *Tel:* (08) 6407868, pg 1312

Universitat Konstanz (Germany) *Tel:* (07531) 882800 *Fax:* (07531) 883082, pg 1468

Konsultace (Czech Republic) *Tel:* (02) 2310363 *Fax:* (02) 2310363, pg 125

Konsultforlaget AB (Sweden) *Tel:* (018) 555080 *Fax:* (018) 155081 *E-mail:* info@konsultforlaget.se, pg 604

KONTEXTverlag (Germany) *Tel:* (030) 94415444 *Fax:* (030) 94415445 *E-mail:* service@kontextverlag.de *Web Site:* www.kontextverlag.de, pg 252

Kookaburra Technical Publications Pty Ltd (Australia) *Tel:* (03) 9560 0841 *Fax:* (03) 95451121 *E-mail:* kookaburra@boundy39.com, pg 29

Koolibri (Estonia) *Tel:* (02) 445223; (02) 441975 *Fax:* (02) 446813, pg 140

Koorong Books Pty Ltd (Australia) *Tel:* (02) 98574477 *Fax:* (02) 98574499 *E-mail:* west_ryde@koorong.com.au; koorong@koorong.com.au *Web Site:* www.koorong.com.au, pg 1273

kopaed verlagsgmbh (Germany) *Tel:* (089) 68890098 *Fax:* (089) 6891912 *E-mail:* info@kopaed.de *Web Site:* www.kopaed.de, pg 252

Koptisch-Orthodoxes Zentrum (Germany) *Tel:* (06085) 23 17 *Fax:* (06085) 26 66 *Web Site:* www.kopten.de, pg 252

Korea University Library (Republic of Korea) *Tel:* (02) 942641; (02) 942649; (02) 944381; (02) 944389 *Fax:* (02) 9225820, pg 1480

Korea Britannica Corp (Republic of Korea) *Tel:* (02) 2789981; (02) 2789982 *Fax:* (02) 2789983, pg 437

Korea Development Institute Library (Republic of Korea) *Tel:* (02) 958 4262 *Fax:* (02) 958 4261 *E-mail:* libyhj@kdiux.kdi.re.kr *Web Site:* www.kdi.re.kr, pg 1480

Korea Local Authorities Foundation for International Relations (Republic of Korea) *Tel:* 02 378973 *Fax:* 02 378970 *E-mail:* klfool@bova.dacom.co.kr, pg 437

Korea Psychological Testing Institute (Republic of Korea) *Tel:* (02) 558-0286; (02) 558-0287 *Fax:* (02) 567-4877 *E-mail:* SHLK@hitel.kol.co.kr, pg 437

Korea Publications Export & Import Corporation (Democratic People's Republic of Korea) *Tel:* (02) 3818536 *Fax:* (02) 3814410, pg 1296

Korea Science and Encyclopedia Publishing House (Democratic People's Republic of Korea) *Tel:* (02) 381 8091 (Call between 18 & 21 hours Pyongyang local time, Mon, Wed & Fri only) *Fax:* (02) 381 4550 (24 hours), pg 434

Korea Textbook Co Ltd (Republic of Korea) *Tel:* (02) 3920996 *Fax:* (02) 3127415, pg 437

Korea University Press (Republic of Korea) *Tel:* (02) 9201720 *Fax:* (02) 9236311, pg 437

Korean Library Association (Republic of Korea) *Tel:* (02) 5354868 *Fax:* (02) 5355616 *E-mail:* klanet@hitel.net, pg 1519

Korean PEN Centre (Republic of Korea) *Tel:* (02) 782 1337; (02) 782 1338 *Fax:* (02) 786 1090 *E-mail:* penkon2001@yahoo.co.kr, pg 1365

Korean Publishers Association (Republic of Korea) *Tel:* (02) 735 2702 *Fax:* (02) 738 5414 *E-mail:* kpa@kpa21.or.kr *Web Site:* www.kpa21.or.kr, pg 437

Korean Publishers Association (Republic of Korea) *Tel:* (02) 735 2702 *Fax:* (02) 738 5414 *E-mail:* kpa@kpa21.or.kr *Web Site:* www.ifrro.org/members/kpa.html, pg 1251

Korean Publishing Research Institute (Republic of Korea) *Tel:* (02) 7399040 *Fax:* (02) 7376187 *E-mail:* p715@chollian.net, pg 1251

Korean Research & Development Library Association (KORDELA) (Republic of Korea) *Tel:* (02) 9673692 *Fax:* (02) 29634013, pg 1519

Koreaone Press Inc (Republic of Korea) *Tel:* (02) 7391156 *Fax:* (02) 7343512, pg 438

Koren Publishers Jerusalem Ltd (Israel) *Tel:* (02) 5660188 *Fax:* (02) 5666658, pg 369

Galerie Kornfeld & Co (Switzerland) *Tel:* (031) 254673 *Fax:* (031) 261891, pg 617

Kosei Publishing Co Ltd (Japan) *Tel:* (03) 5385-2319 *Fax:* (03) 5385-2331 *E-mail:* dharmaworld@mail.kosei-shuppan.co.jp *Web Site:* www.kosei-shuppan.co.jp/english/, pg 420

Koseisha-Koseikaku Co Ltd (Japan) *Tel:* (03) 33597371 *Fax:* (03) 33597375, pg 420

Kosik (Czech Republic) *Tel:* (02) 670929 *Fax:* (02) 2359403, pg 125

Verlag A F Koska (Austria) *Tel:* (0222) 5874344, pg 54

Franckh-Kosmos Verlags-GmbH & Co (Germany) *Tel:* (0711) 2191-0 *Fax:* (0711) 2191-422 *E-mail:* info@kosmos.de *Web Site:* www.kosmos.de, pg 252

Kossodo Verlag AG (Switzerland) *Tel:* (022) 962230, pg 617

Kossuth Kiado RT (Hungary) *Tel:* (01) 3700607 *Fax:* (01) 3700602 *E-mail:* rt@kossuted.hu *Web Site:* www.kossuth.hu, pg 325

Kossuth Lajos Tudomanyegyetem Egyetemi Koenyvtar (Hungary) *Tel:* (052) 410443 *Fax:* (052) 316835 *E-mail:* ilevay@giant.lib.klte.hu, pg 1472

Kotuku Media Ltd (New Zealand) *Tel:* (04) 2331842 *E-mail:* kotuku.media@xtra.co.nz *Web Site:* www.kotuku.media.co.nz, pg 492

Dr Anton Kovac Slavica Verlag (Germany) *Tel:* (089) 2725612 *Fax:* (089) 2716594 *E-mail:* 101566.2450@compuserve.com, pg 253

Roman Kovar Verlag (Germany) *Tel:* (08206) 961977 *Fax:* (08206) 961978 *E-mail:* romankovar@gmx.net *Web Site:* www.kovar-verlag.com, pg 253

Kowhai Publishing Ltd (New Zealand) *Tel:* (09) 5759126 *Fax:* (09) 5753178, pg 492

Koyo Shobo (Japan) *Tel:* (075) 3120788 *Fax:* (075) 3127447, pg 420

KPI (Indonesia) *Tel:* (021) 361701; (021) 41701, pg 1229

KPT InfoTrader Inc (Japan) *Tel:* (06) 6203 5961 *Fax:* (06) 6222 3590 *E-mail:* osaka@kpt-infotrader.co.jp, pg 1294

Karl Kraemer Verlag GmbH und Co (Germany) *Tel:* (0711) 7 84 96-0 *Fax:* (0711) 7 84 96-20 *E-mail:* info@kraemerverlag.com *Web Site:* www.kraemerverlag.de, pg 253

Verlag Karl Kraemer & Co (Switzerland) *Tel:* (0711) 78 49 60 (Germany) *Fax:* (0711) 78 49 620 (Germany) *E-mail:* info@kraemerverlag.com *Web Site:* www.kraemerverlag.com, pg 617

Reinhold Kraemer Verlag (Germany) *Tel:* (040) 4101429 *Fax:* (040) 455770 *E-mail:* info@kraemer-verlag.de *Web Site:* www.kraemer-verlag.de, pg 253

Adam Kraft Verlag (Germany) *Tel:* (0931) 385235 *Fax:* (0931) 385305 *E-mail:* info@verlagshaus.com *Web Site:* www.verlagshaus.com, pg 253

Krafthand Verlag Walter Schultz GmbH (Germany) *Tel:* (08247) 30070 *Fax:* (08247) 300770 *Web Site:* www.krafthand.de, pg 253

Edition Kraftpunkt Toni Fedrigotti (Germany) *Tel:* (0821) 705011 *Fax:* (0821) 705008, pg 253

Krajowe Biuro Miedzynarodowego Numeru Ksiazki ISBN (Poland) *Tel:* (022) 256877; (022) 6082999 *Fax:* (022) 6082433; (022) 8255251 *E-mail:* bnisbn@bn.org.pl, pg 1256

Kraks Forlag AS (Denmark) *Tel:* 956500 *Fax:* 956565 *E-mail:* krak@krak.dk *Web Site:* www.krak.dk, pg 133

Kralica MAB (Bulgaria) *Tel:* (02) 767357 *Fax:* (02) 767357 *Web Site:* www.mab.hit.bg, pg 96

Kramds-reklama Publishing & Advertising (Kazakstan) *Tel:* (03272) 453968 *Fax:* (03272) 696753, pg 430

Karin Kramer Verlag (Germany) *Tel:* (030) 6845055; (030) 6842598 *Fax:* (030) 6858577 *E-mail:* kramer@virtualitas.com *Web Site:* www.anares.org/kramer/, pg 253

Verlag Rene Kramer AG (Switzerland) *Tel:* (091) 518941, pg 617

Verlag Waldemar Kramer (Germany) *Tel:* (069) 449045 *Fax:* (069) 449064 *E-mail:* kramerverlag@frankfurtbuecher.de, pg 253

Kranich-Verlag, Dres AG & H R Bosch-Gwalter (Switzerland) *Tel:* (01) 3918484 *Fax:* (01) 3920884, pg 617

Nara Verlag Josef Krauthaeuser (Germany) *Tel:* (08166) 8530; (08166) 8531 *Fax:* (08166) 8530 *E-mail:* j.krauthaeuser@nara-verlag.de *Web Site:* www.nara-international.de, pg 253

Kremayr & Scheriau Verlag (Austria) *Tel:* (01) 713 8770 *Fax:* (01)713 8770-20, pg 54

Kretschmar Hubert Leipziger Verlagsgesellschaft (Germany) *Tel:* (0341) 8789644 *Fax:* (0341) 8789644, pg 253

Verlag Hubert Kretschmer (Germany) *Tel:* (089) 1234530 *Fax:* (089) 1238638 *E-mail:* hubert.kretschmer@t-online.de, pg 253

Kreuz Verlag GmbH & Co KG (Germany) *Tel:* (0711) 7880321 *Fax:* (0711) 7880310 *E-mail:* service@kreuzverlag.de *Web Site:* www.kreuzverlag.de, pg 1284

Svet Kridel (Czech Republic) *Tel:* (0166) 430371 *Fax:* (0166) 23395, pg 125

Kriebel Verlag GmbH (Germany) *Tel:* (08806) 9360 *Fax:* (08806) 9361 *E-mail:* info@kriebel-sat.de *Web Site:* www.kriebel-sat.de, pg 253

Antiquariat Walter Krieg Verlag (Austria) *Tel:* (01) 5121083, pg 1274

De Krijger (Belgium) *Tel:* (053) 808449 *Fax:* (053) 808453 *E-mail:* de.krijger@primemedia.be, pg 70

Bokklubben Ny Krim (Norway) *Tel:* 22471000 *Fax:* 22471098 *E-mail:* egmont@egmont.com *Web Site:* www.egmont.com, pg 1231

Krishnamurthy K (India) *Tel:* (044) 4344519 *Fax:* (044) 4342009 *E-mail:* ksm@md2.vsnl.net.in; service@kkbooks.com, pg 1289

Kristen Pres (Papua New Guinea) *Tel:* (675) 822989 *Fax:* (675) 823313, pg 510

Kristiansand Folkebibliotek (Norway) *Tel:* 38124910 *Fax:* 38124949, pg 1489

Kritak Uitgeverij (Belgium) *Tel:* (016) 231264 *Fax:* (016) 223310, pg 70

Editura Kriterion SA (Romania) *Tel:* (01) 2243638 *Fax:* (01) 2243628 *E-mail:* krit@dnt.ro, pg 534

Kritiki (Greece) *Tel:* (01) 3836460 *E-mail:* kritiki@hol.gr, pg 1286

Kritiki Publishing (Greece) *Tel:* (01) 3622390; (01) 3836460 *Fax:* (01) 3621367 *E-mail:* kritiki@hol.gr, pg 312

Alfred Kroner Verlag (Germany) *Tel:* (0711) 6155363 *Fax:* (0711) 61553646 *E-mail:* a.kroner@z.zgv.de *Web Site:* www.kroener-verlag.de, pg 253

Krscanska sadasnjost (Croatia) *Tel:* (01) 48 28 219; (01) 48 28 222 *Fax:* (01) 48 28 227 *E-mail:* ks@zg.tel.hr *Web Site:* www.ks.hr, pg 119

Wolfgang Krueger Verlag GmbH (Germany) *Tel:* (069) 60620 *Fax:* (069) 6062352 *Web Site:* www.krugschadenberg.de, pg 254

Krug & Schadenberg (Germany) *Tel:* (030) 6941243; (030) 61625750 *Fax:* (030) 6941231 *E-mail:* info@krugschadenberg.de *Web Site:* www.krugschadenberg.de, pg 254

Knjizevni Krug Split (Croatia) *Tel:* (021) 342 226; (021) 361 081 *Fax:* (021) 342 226 *E-mail:* bratislav.lucin@public.srce.hr, pg 119

'Ksiazka i Wiedza' Spotdzielnia Wydawniczo-Handlowa (Poland) *Tel:* (022) 8275401; (022) 8279416 *Fax:* (022) 8279416 *E-mail:* publisher@kiw.com.pl *Web Site:* www.kiw.com.pl, pg 517

Ksiaznica Publishing Ltd (Poland) *Tel:* (032) 2572216 *Fax:* (032) 2572217 *E-mail:* ksiaznica@domnet.com.pl, pg 517

Ktitor (The Former Yugoslav Republic of Macedonia) *Tel:* (092) 21903; (092) 34746 *Fax:* (092) 34746, pg 449

Kuang Fu Book Co Ltd (Taiwan, Province of China) *Tel:* (02) 7716622 *Fax:* (02) 7315982 *E-mail:* lolatiao@kfgroup.com.tw *Web Site:* www.kfgroup.com.tw, pg 630

Editora Kuarup Ltda (Brazil) *Tel:* (051) 361-6044 *Fax:* (051) 3613550 *E-mail:* kuarup@conex.com.br, pg 86

Kubbealti Akademisi Kultur ve Sasat Vakfi (Turkey) *Tel:* (0212) 5162356; (0212) 5189209 *Fax:* (0212) 5171460, pg 640

KUbK Publishing House (Russian Federation) *Tel:* (095) 1640910; (095) 3679473 *Fax:* (095) 1528689, pg 539

Kubon & Sagner Buchexport-Import GmbH (Germany) *Tel:* (089) 542180 *Fax:* (089) 54218218 *E-mail:* postmaster@kubon-sagner.de *Web Site:* www.kubon-sagner.de, pg 254

Kubon Und Sagner (Germany) *Tel:* (089) 54 218-0 *Fax:* (089) 54 218-218 *E-mail:* postmaster@kubon-sagner.de *Web Site:* www.kubon-sagner.de, pg 254

Kuemmerly & Frey (Geographischer Verlag) (Switzerland) *Tel:* (031) 235111 *Fax:* (031) 9152220, pg 617

Kuemmerly und Frey Verlags GmbH (Austria) *Tel:* (01) 545 14 45 *Fax:* (01) 545 10 80-83 *E-mail:* kuemmerly-frey@xpoint.at, pg 54

Imprimerie A Kuendig (Switzerland) *Tel:* (022) 966013, pg 617

Kugler Publications (Netherlands) *Tel:* (070) 33-00253 *Fax:* (070) 33-00254 *E-mail:* kuglerspb@wxs.nl *Web Site:* www.kuglerpublications.com, pg 480

Verlag Ernst Kuhn (Germany) *Tel:* (030) 44342230 *Fax:* (030) 4424732 *E-mail:* ernst-kuhn-verlag@t-online.de *Web Site:* www.vek.de, pg 254

Kuiseb-Verlag (Namibia) *Tel:* (061) 225372 *Fax:* (061) 226846 *E-mail:* nwg@iafrica.com.na, pg 471

Kukmin Doseo Publishing Co Inc (Republic of Korea) *Tel:* (02) 858-2461; (02) 858-2463 *Fax:* (02) 858-2464 *E-mail:* younhlee@chollian.net, pg 438

Kukminseokwan Publishing Co Ltd (Republic of Korea) *Tel:* (02) 7107722; (02) 7107724 *Fax:* (02) 7155771, pg 438

Kultura (Hungary) *Tel:* (01) 2501194 *Fax:* (01) 2500233, pg 1197

Kultura (The Former Yugoslav Republic of Macedonia) *Tel:* (091) 111332 *Fax:* (091) 228608, pg 1297

Kultura (Yugoslavia) *Tel:* (021) 780-156 *Fax:* (021) 780-291, pg 764

Kul'tura redakcionno-izdatel skij kompleks (Russian Federation) *Tel:* (095) 2481151 *Fax:* (095) 2302180, pg 539

Kulturbuch-Verlag GmbH (Germany) *Tel:* (030) 6618484; (030) 6614002 *Fax:* (030) 6617828; (030) 6614002 *E-mail:* kbvinfo@kulturbuch-verlag.de *Web Site:* www.kulturbuch-verlag.de, pg 254

Kulturstiftung der deutschen Vertriebenen (Germany) *Tel:* (0228) 915120 *Fax:* (0228) 218397 *E-mail:* kulturstiftung@t-online.de *Web Site:* www.kulturstiftung-der-deutschen-vertriebenen.de/home.html, pg 254

Kulturtrade (Hungary) *Tel:* (01) 3757288 *Fax:* (01) 2027145 *E-mail:* hl2618vin@ella.hu, pg 325

Kum Sung Publishing Co Ltd (Republic of Korea) *Tel:* (02) 7139651 *Fax:* (02) 7041979, pg 438

Kungl Ingenjoersvetenskapsakademien (IVA) (Sweden) *Tel:* (08) 7912900 *Fax:* (08) 6115623 *E-mail:* info@iva.se *Web Site:* www.iva.se, pg 604

Kungl Tekniska Hoegskolan (Royal Institute of Technology Library) (Sweden) *Tel:* (08) 7906000 *Fax:* (08) 109199, pg 1500

Kungl Vitterhets Historie och Antikvitets Akademien (Sweden) *Tel:* (08) 4404280 *Fax:* (08) 4404290 *E-mail:* kansli@vitterhetsakad.se *Web Site:* www.vitterhetsakad.se, pg 1368

Kungliga Biblioteket (Sweden) *Tel:* (08) 4634000 *Fax:* (08) 4634004 *E-mail:* kungl.biblioteket@kb.se *Web Site:* www.kb.se, pg 1500

Kunlun Publishing House (China) *Tel:* (010) 6732721 *Fax:* (010) 62183683; (010) 66847703, pg 107

Kunnskapsforlaget ANS (Norway) *Tel:* 22036600 *Fax:* 22036605 *E-mail:* gunnar.sveen@Kunnskapsforlaget.no, pg 504

Kunst Publishers Ltd (Estonia) *Tel:* (02) 6411764 *Fax:* (02) 6411762 *E-mail:* helme@skkke.ee, pg 140

Archiv fur Kunst & Geschichte Bilderdienst & Verlagsgesellschaft mbH (Germany) *Tel:* (030) 804850 *Fax:* (030) 80485500 *E-mail:* info@akg.de *Web Site:* www.akg.de, pg 254

Verlag der Kunst/G+B Fine Arts Verlag GmbH (Germany) *Tel:* (0351) 3360742; (0351) 3100052 *Fax:* (0351) 3105245 *E-mail:* verlag-der-kunst@t-online.de *Web Site:* www.verlag-der-kunst.de, pg 254

Verlag Antje Kunstmann GmbH (Germany) *Tel:* (089) 121193-0 *Fax:* (089) 12193-20 *E-mail:* info@kunstmann.de *Web Site:* www.kunstmann.de, pg 254

Kunstmuseum Liechtenstein Vaduz (Liechtenstein) *Tel:* (00423) 235 03 00 *Fax:* (00423) 235 03 29 *E-mail:* mail@kunstmuseum.li *Web Site:* www.kunstmuseum.li, pg 444

Kunstverlag Maria Laach (Germany) *Tel:* (0751) 561290 *Fax:* (0751) 5612920 *E-mail:* kunstverlag@weingarten-verlag.de *Web Site:* www.maria-laach.de/verlag/, pg 254

Kunstverlag Weingarten GmbH (Germany) *Tel:* (0751) 561290 *Fax:* (0751) 5612920 *E-mail:* kunstverlag@kv-weingarten.de *Web Site:* www.kv-weingarten.de, pg 254

Edition Kunzelmann GmbH (Switzerland) *Tel:* (01) 7103681 *Fax:* (01) 7103817, pg 617

Kupar Publishers (Estonia) *Tel:* (02) 6286173 *Fax:* (02) 6462076 *E-mail:* kupar@netexpress.ee, pg 140

Kuperard (United Kingdom) *Tel:* (020) 8446 2440 *Fax:* (020) 8446 2441 *Web Site:* www.kuperard.co.uk, pg 705

Kuperard (United Kingdom) *Tel:* (020) 8446 2440 *Fax:* (020) 8446 2441 *E-mail:* kuperard@bravo.clara.net *Web Site:* www.kuperard.co.uk, pg 1320

Kupfergraben Verlagsgesellschaft mbH (Germany) *Tel:* (030) 2622097 *Fax:* (030) 2621990, pg 254

Kurlana Publishing (Australia) *Tel:* (08) 3886619, pg 29

Kurnia Esanata (Indonesia) *Tel:* (021) 361974; (021) 3104948, pg 356

Kustannus Oy Duodecim (Finland) *Tel:* (09) 618 851 *Fax:* (09) 6188 5400 *Web Site:* www.duodecim.fi, pg 143

Kustannus Oy Kolibri (Finland) *Tel:* (09) 7019443 *Fax:* (09) 7019351, pg 143

Rakentajain Kustannus Oy (Building Publications Ltd) (Finland) *Tel:* (09) 142855 *Fax:* (09) 5032542, pg 143

Kustannus Oy Semic (Finland) *Tel:* (031) 2738700 *Fax:* (031) 2438287 *E-mail:* jaana.huttunen@semic.fi, pg 143

Kustannus Oy Uusi Tie (Finland) *Tel:* (01) 977820 *Fax:* (01) 9757055 *E-mail:* uusitie@sci.fi, pg 143

Kustannuskiila Oy (Finland) *Tel:* (017) 303551 *Fax:* (017) 303243, pg 143

Kuva ja Sana (Finland) *Tel:* (09) 4774920 *Fax:* (09) 550892, pg 143

Kuwait University Library (Kuwait) *Tel:* 4813182 *Fax:* 4816095, pg 1480

Kuwait University Library (Kuwait), pg 1519

The Kuwait Book Shop Company Ltd (Kuwait) *Tel:* 2424687 *Fax:* 2420558, pg 1297

Kuwait Publishing House (Kuwait) *Tel:* 2414697, pg 441

KVB Koninklijke Vereeniging van het Boekenvak (Netherlands) *Tel:* (020) 6240212 *Fax:* (020) 6208871 *E-mail:* info@kvb.nl *Web Site:* www.kvb.nl, pg 1254

KVG de Silva & Sons (Sri Lanka) *Tel:* (01) 84146 *Fax:* (01) 586598, pg 597

KVG de Silva & Sons (Sri Lanka) *Tel:* (01) 84146 *Fax:* (01) 588875, pg 1312

Kerstin Kvint Literary & Co-Production Agency (Sweden) *Tel:* (08) 107014 *Fax:* (08) 107606, pg 1116

Kwa-Zulu Natal Provincial Library Service (South Africa) *Tel:* (0331) 3940241 *Fax:* (0331) 3942237 *E-mail:* bawar@kzntl.gov.za, pg 1498

Kwame Nkrumah University of Science & Technology Library (Ghana) *Tel:* (051) 60199; (051) 60133 *Fax:* (051) 60358 *E-mail:* ustlib@libr.ug.edu.gh, pg 1470

Kwamfori Publishing Enterprise (Ghana), pg 307

Kwangmyong Publishing Co (Republic of Korea) *Tel:* (02) 3923081; (02) 3920996; (02) 3925855 *Fax:* (02) 3127415, pg 438

Kwong Fat Offset Printing Company Ltd (Hong Kong) *Tel:* 25622144 *Fax:* 25657736, pg 1196

KY KE M (Cyprus) *Tel:* (02) 450302 *Fax:* (02) 463624, pg 122

Kydds Paper Plus (New Zealand) *Tel:* (07) 8957430 *Fax:* (07) 8957977, pg 1302

Kyi-Pwar-Ye Book House (Myanmar) *Tel:* (02) 21003, pg 471

Kynos Verlag Dr Dieter Fleig GmbH (Germany) *Tel:* (06) 594-653 *Fax:* (06) 594-452 *E-mail:* info@kynos-verlag.de *Web Site:* www.kynos-verlag.de, pg 254

Kyobo Book Centre Co Ltd (Republic of Korea) *Tel:* (02) 333-4570 *Fax:* (02) 735-0030, pg 1296

Kyobo Book Centre (Republic of Korea) *Tel:* (02) 3973521; (02) 3973509 *Fax:* (02) 7362361, pg 438

Kyobunkan Inc (Christian Literature Society of Japan) (Japan) *Tel:* (03) 35615549 *Fax:* (03) 35355033 *E-mail:* kbk_fbd@msn.com, pg 1294

Kyodo-Isho Shuppan Co Ltd (Japan) *Tel:* (03) 38182361 *Fax:* (03) 38182368 *E-mail:* kyodo-ed@fd5.so-net.ne.jp *Web Site:* www.kyodo-isho.co.jp, pg 420

Kyodo Printing Co (S'pore) Pte Ltd (Singapore) *Tel:* 2652955 *Fax:* 2644939; 2610891, pg 1200

Kyohaksa Publishing Co Ltd (Republic of Korea) *Tel:* (02) 7174561; (02) 8592017 *Fax:* (02) 7183976, pg 438

Kyoritsu Shuppan Co Ltd (Japan) *Tel:* (03) 39472511 *Fax:* (03) 39446043, pg 420

Kyoto Sangyo University Library (Japan) *Tel:* (075) 7012151 *Fax:* (075) 7051447, pg 1478

Kyrenia Municipality (Cyprus) *Tel:* (02) 351460, pg 122

Kyriakidis (Greece) *Tel:* (031) 208540; (031) 210360; (031) 210067 *Fax:* (031) 245541, pg 312

Kyriakidis Brothers sa (Greece) *Tel:* (031) 210-067 *E-mail:* johukyr@the.forthnet.gr, pg 1286

Kyriakidis Vasileios (Greece) *Tel:* (01) 3609126 *E-mail:* bkyriakid@otenet.gr, pg 312

K P Kyriakou (Books - Stationery) Ltd (Cyprus) *Tel:* (05) 747555 *Fax:* (05) 747047 *E-mail:* cybooks@logosnet.cy, pg 1281

Kyungnam University Press (Republic of Korea) *Tel:* (0551) 2432330 *Fax:* (0551) 2492073, pg 438

Kyungpook National University Central Library (Republic of Korea) *Tel:* (053) 9555516 *Fax:* (053) 9506533, pg 1480

Kyushu University Library (Japan) *Tel:* (092) 6411101; (092) 6422111, pg 1478

L'Airone Editrice (Italy) *Tel:* (06) 6570758 *Fax:* (06) 65740509 *E-mail:* gremese@gremese.com *Web Site:* www.gremese.com, pg 395

L B Publishing Co (Israel) *Tel:* (02) 664 637 *Fax:* (02) 290 774, pg 369

Laaber-Verlag (Germany) *Tel:* (09498) 2307 *Fax:* (09498) 2543 *E-mail:* info@laaber-verlag.de *Web Site:* www.laaber.de, pg 255

Laams Publications (Australia) *Fax:* (02) 9369 1812 *E-mail:* cle@laams.com.au *Web Site:* www.laams.com.au, pg 29

Editorial Labor de Venezuela SA (Venezuela) *Tel:* (02) 7811398; (02) 7815819, pg 762

Editions Labor (Belgium) *Tel:* (02) 250-06-70 *Fax:* (02) 217-71-97 *E-mail:* labor@labor.be *Web Site:* www.labor.be, pg 70

Editorial Labor SA (Spain) *Tel:* (093) 5808124 *Fax:* (093) 6921851, pg 579

Labor et Fides SA (Switzerland) *Tel:* (022) 3113290; (022) 3113269 *Fax:* (022) 7813051, pg 618

Labyrint (Czech Republic) *Tel:* (02) 2321934 *Fax:* (02) 2321934 *E-mail:* labyrint@wo.cz *Web Site:* labyrint.net, pg 125

Labyrinth Verlag Gisela Ottmer (Germany) *Tel:* (0531) 64259 *Fax:* (0531) 681358 *E-mail:* labyrinthbraunschweig@t-online.de *Web Site:* www.frauenart.de/labyrinthbraunschweig, pg 255

LAC - Litografia Artistica Cartografica Srl (Italy) *Tel:* (055) 483557 *Fax:* (055) 483690, pg 395

Lachlan Publishing (Australia) *Tel:* (060) 216933 *Fax:* (060) 412950, pg 29

Lacour-Olle (France) *Tel:* (04) 66 67 33 06 *Fax:* (04) 66 21 11 23, pg 171

Ambro Lacus, Buch- und Bildverlag Walter Kremnitz (Germany) *Tel:* (8152) 1332 *Fax:* (8152) 40186, pg 255

Ladomir Publishing House (Russian Federation) *Tel:* (095) 5309833; (095) 5304742 *Fax:* (095) 5374742, pg 539

L'Adret editions (France), pg 171

Ladybird Books (United Kingdom) *Tel:* (020) 7010 2900 *Fax:* (01509) 234672 *Web Site:* www.ladybird.co.uk, pg 705

Laertes SA de Ediciones (Spain) *Tel:* (093) 2376869; (093) 2376944 *Fax:* (093) 2170384 *E-mail:* laertes@jet.es, pg 579

Laffitte Reprints (France) *Tel:* (0491) 59 80 43 *Fax:* (0491) 54 25 64 *Web Site:* www.jeanne-laffitte.com, pg 171

Laffont Ediciones Electronicas SA (Argentina) *Tel:* (011) 4302-8668 *Fax:* (011) 4301-2525 *E-mail:* cliente@laffont.com.ar *Web Site:* www.laffont.com.ar, pg 7

Verlag Lafite (Austria) *Tel:* (01) 5126869 *Fax:* (01) 51268699 *E-mail:* redaktion@musikzeit.at *Web Site:* www.musikzeit.at, pg 54

Editions Jacques Lafitte - Who's Who in France (France) *Tel:* (0141) 272 830 *Fax:* (0141) 272 840 *E-mail:* whoswho@whoswho.fr *Web Site:* www.whoswho.fr, pg 171

Editions Michel Lafon SA (France) *Tel:* (01) 40 71 11 11 *Fax:* (01) 46 51 01 31, pg 171

Librairie Leonce Laget (France) *Tel:* (01) 43 29 90 04 *Fax:* (01) 43 26 89 68 *E-mail:* liblaget@wanadoo.fr *Web Site:* www.franceantiq.fr/slam/laget/uk.htm, pg 171

Lagos City Council Libraries (Nigeria) *Tel:* (01) 50246, pg 1488

Lahn-Verlag GmbH (Germany) *Tel:* (06431) 9474-10 *Fax:* (06431) 9474-11 *E-mail:* lahn-verlag@lahnverlag.de *Web Site:* www.lahn-verlag.de, pg 255

Editorin Laiovento SL (Spain) *Tel:* (0981) 564767; (0981) 589199 *Fax:* (0981) 572239 *E-mail:* laiovento@laiovento.com *Web Site:* www.laiovento.com, pg 579

Francisco J Laissue Livraria (Brazil) *Tel:* (021) 509-7298, pg 86

Lake House Bookshop (Sri Lanka) *Tel:* (01) 32104; (01) 432105, pg 1312

Lake House Investments Ltd (Sri Lanka) *Tel:* (01) 33271; (01) 35175 *Fax:* (01) 447848 *E-mail:* lhl@sri.lanka.net, pg 597

Lake-Livraria Allan Kardec Editora (Brazil) *Tel:* (011) 229-0526; (011) 229-1227; (011) 227-1396; (011) 229-0937; (011) 229-4592; (011) 229-0514 *Fax:* (011) 229-0935; (011) 227-5714 *E-mail:* lake@lake.com.br *Web Site:* www.lakelivraria.com.br, pg 86

Lake Publishers & Enterprises Ltd (Kenya) *Tel:* (035) 22707; (035) 22291 *Fax:* (035) 22291, pg 432

Lalit Kala Akademi (India) *Tel:* (011) 387241; (011) 387243 *Fax:* (011) 383 450, pg 341

Lalli Editore SRL (Italy) *Tel:* (0577) 933305 *Fax:* (0577) 983308, pg 395

Editions Lamarre SA (France) *Tel:* (01) 41.29.97.27; (01) 41.29.97.34 *Fax:* (01) 41.29.77.35 *E-mail:* vpc@espaceinfirmier.com, pg 171

Charles Lamb Society (United Kingdom), pg 1371

Lambda Edition GmbH (Germany) *Tel:* (040) 312836 *Fax:* (040) 3192096, pg 255

Lambertus Verlag GmbH (Germany) *Tel:* (0761) 368250 *Fax:* (0761) 3682533 *E-mail:* info@lambertus.de *Web Site:* www.lambertus.de, pg 255

Lammar Offset Printing Co (Hong Kong) *Tel:* 25631068 *Fax:* 28113375, pg 1196

Editions Lampe d'Or ASBL (Belgium) *Tel:* (02) 427-92-77 *Fax:* (02) 428-82-06 *E-mail:* llb_ibb@freegates.be, pg 70

Lamuv Verlag GmbH (Germany) *Tel:* (0551) 44024 *Fax:* (0551) 41392 *E-mail:* rabe@lamuv.de *Web Site:* www.lamuv.de, pg 255

Lancashire Authors' Association (United Kingdom) *Tel:* (01942) 791390, pg 1371

Lancer Publisher's & Distributors (India) *Tel:* (011) 6867339; (011) 6854691 *Fax:* (011) 6862077, pg 341

Landarc Publications (Australia) *Tel:* (03) 93801276 *Fax:* (03) 93801276 *E-mail:* carmar@bigpond.com, pg 29

Landbuch-Verlagsgesellschaft mbH (Germany) *Tel:* (0511) 27046230 *Fax:* (0511) 27046220 *E-mail:* info@landbuch.de *Web Site:* www.landbuch.de, pg 255

Landcare Research NZ (New Zealand) *Tel:* (03) 3256700 *Fax:* (03) 3252127 *E-mail:* mwpress@landcare.cri.nz *Web Site:* www.landcare.cri.nz/mwpress/, pg 492

Institut fuer Landes- und Stadtentwicklungsforschung, ILS Nordrhein-Westfalen (Germany) *Tel:* (0231) 90510 *Fax:* (0231) 90515155 *E-mail:* ils@ils.nrw.de *Web Site:* www.ils.nrw.de, pg 255

Jay Landesman (United Kingdom) *Tel:* (020) 7837 7290 *Fax:* (020) 7833 1925, pg 706

Landesverband der Verleger und Buchhaendler Rheinland-Pfalz eV (Germany) *Tel:* (06131) 234035 *Fax:* (06131) 230364, pg 1246

Landmark Education Supplies Pty Ltd (Australia) *Tel:* (056) 251701, pg 1273

Lands Department, Survey & Mapping Office (Hong Kong) *Tel:* (02) 28482267; (02) 28482182 *Fax:* (02) 25218726, pg 320

Landsberger (Israel) *Tel:* (03) 5176330 *Fax:* (03) 5222646, pg 1292

Landsbokasafn Islands-Haskolabokasafn (Iceland) *Tel:* 5255600 *Fax:* 5255615 *E-mail:* lbs@bok.hi.is *Web Site:* www.bok.hi.is, pg 1472

Landy Publishing (United Kingdom) *Tel:* (01253) 895678 *Fax:* (01253) 895678, pg 706

Lanfranchi (Italy) *Tel:* (02) 8056083 *Fax:* (02) 8056083, pg 395

Herbert Lang & Cie AG, Buchhandlung, Antiquariat (Switzerland) *Tel:* (031) 3108484 *Fax:* (031) 3108494 *E-mail:* ius@buchlang.com *Web Site:* www.buchlang.com, pg 618

Lang Kiado (Hungary) *Tel:* (01) 1534805; (01) 2695264 *Fax:* (01) 1112230, pg 325

Peter Lang GmbH Europaeischer Verlag der Wissenschaften (Germany) *Tel:* (069) 7807050 *Fax:* (069) 780705-50 *E-mail:* zentrale.frankfurt@peterlang.com *Web Site:* www.peterlang.de, pg 255

Lang Syne Publishers Ltd (United Kingdom) *E-mail:* enquiries@scottish-memories.co.uk *Web Site:* www.scottish-memories.co.uk/langsyne/, pg 706

Lange & Springer Antiquariat (Germany) *Tel:* (030) 340050; (030) 3422011 *Fax:* (030) 3405140 *Web Site:* www.lange-springer-antiquariat.de, pg 1284

Langenscheidt-Verlag GmbH (Austria) *Tel:* (01) 6887133 *Fax:* (01) 68014140, pg 54

Langenscheidt AG Zuerich-Zug (Switzerland) *Tel:* (01) 2115000 *Fax:* (01) 2122149, pg 618

Langenscheidt Fachverlag GmbH (Germany) *Tel:* (089) 36096-476 *Fax:* (089) 36096-479 *E-mail:* fachverlag@langenscheidt.de, pg 255

The Langenscheidt Group (Germany) *Tel:* (089) 36096-0; (089) 36096-258 (Orders) *Fax:* (089) 36096-376; (089) 36096-258 *E-mail:* mail@langenscheidt.de *Web Site:* www.langenscheidt.de, pg 255

Langenscheidt-Hachette (Germany) *Tel:* (089) 360960 *Fax:* (089) 36096-222; (089) 36096-472 (general); (089) 36096-258 (orders), pg 255

Langenscheidt KG (Germany) *Tel:* (089) 36096-0; (089) 36096-258 (Orders) *Fax:* (089) 36096-222, pg 256

Verlag Langewiesche-Brandt KG (Germany) *Tel:* (08178) 4857 *Fax:* (08178) 7388 *E-mail:* textura@langewiesche-brandt.de *Web Site:* www.langewiesche-brandt.de, pg 256

Karl Robert Langewiesche Nachfolger Hans Koester KG (Germany) *Tel:* (06174) 7333 *Fax:* (06174) 933-039 *E-mail:* info@langewiesche-verlag.de *Web Site:* www.langewiesche-verlag.de, pg 256

Ingrid Langner (Germany) *Tel:* (04123) 7780 *Fax:* (04123) 7885, pg 256

Language Book Centre (Australia) *Tel:* (02) 92671397 *Fax:* (02) 92648993 *E-mail:* language@abbeys.com.au *Web Site:* www.languagebooks.com.au, pg 1273

Language Consultancy Services (United Kingdom) *Tel:* (020) 8450 5344 *Fax:* (020) 8452 9005, pg 1129

Language Publishing House (China) *Tel:* (010) 550075, pg 107

Language Teaching Publications (United Kingdom) *Tel:* (01273) 736344 *Fax:* (01273) 775361 *E-mail:* ltp@ltpwebsite.com *Web Site:* www.ltpwebsite.com, pg 706

Langues & Mondes/L'Asiatheque (France) *Tel:* (01) 42620400 *Fax:* (01) 42621234 *E-mail:* info@asiatheque.com *Web Site:* www.asiatheque.com, pg 171

Bibliotheque Interuniversitaire des Langues Orientales (France) *Tel:* (01) 44778720 *Fax:* (01) 44778730 *E-mail:* biulo@idf.ext.jussieu.fr, pg 1465

Uitgeverij Lannoo NV (Belgium) *Tel:* (051) 42 42 11 *Fax:* (051) 40 11 52 *E-mail:* lannoo@lannoo.be *Web Site:* www.lannoo.be, pg 70

Editions Fernand Lanore Sarl (France) *Tel:* (01) 43256661 *Fax:* (01) 43296981, pg 172

LT Editions-J Lanore-H Laurens (France) *Tel:* (01) 55580540 *Fax:* (01) 46542193, pg 172

Lansdowne Publishing Pty Ltd (Australia) *Tel:* (02) 9240 9222 *Fax:* (02) 9241 4818 *E-mail:* sales@lanspub.com.au, pg 29

Lansman Editeur (Belgium) *Tel:* (064) 23-78-40 *Fax:* (064) 44-31-02; (064) 23-78-49 *E-mail:* lansman.editeur@freeworld.be *Web Site:* www.lansman.org, pg 70

Lanzhou University Press (China) *Tel:* (0931) 22991-272 *Fax:* (0931) 8615095 *E-mail:* press@lzu.edu.cn, pg 107

Lao Dong (Labor) Publishing House (Viet Nam) *Tel:* (04) 253972, pg 763

Lao-phanit (Laos People's Democratic Republic), pg 441

LAPA Publishers (Pty) Ltd (South Africa) *Tel:* (012) 401 0700 *Fax:* (012) 3255498 *E-mail:* lapa@atkv.org.za, pg 556

Michelle Lapautre (France) *Tel:* (01) 47348241 *Fax:* (01) 47340090 *E-mail:* lapautre@club_internet.fr, pg 1110

Lappan Verlag GmbH (Germany) *Tel:* (0441) 980660 *Fax:* (0441) 9806622; (0441) 9806624; (0441) 9806634 *Web Site:* www.lappan.de, pg 256

Editions du Laquet (France) *Tel:* (05) 65 37 43 54 *Fax:* (05) 65 37 43 55 *E-mail:* contact@editions-dulaquet.fr *Web Site:* editions-dulaquet.fr, pg 172

Leandro Lara Editor (Spain) *Tel:* (093) 6970036; (093) 6970364 *E-mail:* leandro@bbvnet.co, pg 579

Les Editions de l'Arbre (Tunisia) *Tel:* (01) 887 927 *Fax:* (01) 887 927, pg 638

Larcier-Department of De Boeck & Larcier SA (Belgium) *Tel:* (02) 548 07 11 *Fax:* (02) 513 90 09 *E-mail:* deboeck.larcier@deboeck.be *Web Site:* www.larcier.be, pg 71

Hans Richter Laromedel (Sweden) *Tel:* (0152) 150 60; (0200) 11 55 30 (orders) *Fax:* (0152) 151 40; (0200) 11 55 31 (orders) *E-mail:* info@richter.d.se *Web Site:* www.richter.d.se, pg 604

Ediciones Larousse Argentina SA (Argentina) *Tel:* (011) 4865-9581; (011) 4865-9582; (011) 4865-9583 *E-mail:* editorial@aique.com.ar; comercial@aique.com.ar *Web Site:* www.larousse.com.ar, pg 7

Librairie Larousse (France) *Tel:* (01) 44394343 *Fax:* (01) 44394107, pg 172

Larousse Nathan International (France) *Tel:* (01) 45874300 *Fax:* (01) 45870553, pg 172

Larousse Planeta SA (Spain) *Tel:* (093) 908 99 10 54 *E-mail:* larousse@larousse.es, pg 579

Ediciones Larousse SA de CV (Mexico) *Tel:* (05) 5330469 al 73; (05) 5330530 *Fax:* (05) 208-6225; (05) 208-0775 *E-mail:* larousse@compuserve.com, pg 462

Larousse (Suisse) SA (Switzerland) *Tel:* (021) 335336, pg 618

Bokforlaget Robert Larson AB (Sweden) *Tel:* (08) 7328460 *Fax:* (08) 7327176 *E-mail:* info@larsonforlag.se *Web Site:* www.larsonforlage.se, pg 604

Laruffa Editore SRL (Italy) *Tel:* (0965) 814948 *Fax:* (0965) 814954 *E-mail:* laruffa@tin.it; laruffa@libero.it *Web Site:* www.laruffaeditore.com, pg 395

Editrice LAS (Italy) *Tel:* (06) 87290626 *Fax:* (06) 87290629, pg 395

Roger Lascelles (United Kingdom) *Tel:* (0181) 8470935 *Fax:* (0181) 5683886, pg 706

Lasser Press Mexicana SA de CV (Mexico) *Tel:* (05) 5332097; (05) 5112312; (05) 5142705 *Fax:* (05)2076361; (05) 5148038, pg 462

Michael Lassleben Verlag (Germany) *Tel:* (09473) 205 *Fax:* (09473) 8357 *E-mail:* druckerei@oberpfalzverlag-lassleben.de *Web Site:* www.oberpfalzverlag-lassleben.de, pg 256

L'Association des Professionnels de l'Information et de la Documentation (ADBS) (France) *Tel:* (01) 43722525 *Fax:* (01) 43723041 *E-mail:* adbs@adbs.fr *Web Site:* www.adbs.fr, pg 1515

Lasten Keskus Oy (Finland) *Tel:* (09) 6926344 *Fax:* (09) 6926393, pg 143

The Latchmere Press (United Kingdom) *Tel:* (020) 7639 7282, pg 706

Verlag Laterna magica GmbH & Co KG (Germany) *Tel:* (089) 43 6005 162 *Fax:* (089) 43 6005 113 *E-mail:* info@laterna-magica.de *Web Site:* www.laterna-magica.de, pg 256

Latin America Bureau (United Kingdom) *Tel:* (020) 7278 2829 *Fax:* (020) 7278 0165 *E-mail:* lab@gn.apc.org, pg 1266

Latina Livraria (Portugal) *Tel:* (02) 2001294 *Fax:* (02) 2086053, pg 526

J Latka Verlag GmbH (Germany) *Tel:* (0228) 919320 *Fax:* (0228) 9193217 *E-mail:* info@latka.de *Web Site:* www.latka.de, pg 256

Library Association of Latvia (Latvia) *Tel:* (0132) 728-98-74 *Fax:* (0132) 728-08-51 *E-mail:* lnb@com.latnet.lv, pg 1519

Latvian Publishers Association (Latvia) *Tel:* (0371) 7282392 *Fax:* (0371) 7280549 *E-mail:* lga@gramatizdeveji.lv *Web Site:* www.gramatizdeveji.lv, pg 1251

Laumann-Polska (Poland) *Tel:* (075) 7617182 *Fax:* (075) 7617192, pg 517

Laureate Book Co Ltd (Taiwan, Province of China) *Tel:* (02) 2193338 *Fax:* (02) 2182859 *E-mail:* laureate@ms10.hinet.net, pg 631

Laurel Press (Australia) *Tel:* (03) 62391139 *Fax:* (03) 62391139, pg 29

Le Laurier (France) *Tel:* (01) 45.51.55.08 *Fax:* (01) 45.51.81.83 *E-mail:* web@lelaurier.fr *Web Site:* www.lelaurier.fr, pg 172

Lavenham Press Ltd (United Kingdom) *Tel:* (01787) 247436 *Fax:* (01787) 248267 *E-mail:* postmaster@lavenhamgroup.co.uk, pg 1141, 1204

Les Presses Lavigerie (Burundi) *Tel:* (02) 22368 *Fax:* (02) 220318 *E-mail:* lpl~bujumbura@cbinf.com, pg 99

Lavis Marketing (United Kingdom) *Tel:* (01865) 767575 *Fax:* (01865) 750079 *E-mail:* orders@lavismarketing.co.uk, pg 1320

Lavoisier (France) *Tel:* (01) 42 65 39 95 *Fax:* (01) 42 65 02 46 *E-mail:* editions@lavoisier.fr *Web Site:* www.lavoisier.fr, pg 172

Lavoisier (France) *Tel:* (01) 42 65 39 95 *Fax:* (01) 42650246 *E-mail:* besnault@lavoisier.fr, pg 1283

Edizioni Lavoro SRL (Italy) *Tel:* (06) 44251174 *Fax:* (06) 44251177, pg 395

Il Lavoro Editoriale (Italy) *Tel:* (071) 2072210 *Fax:* (071) 2081342 *E-mail:* transeuropa@logica.it *Web Site:* www.illavoreditoriale.com, pg 395

Law Book Co Information Services (Australia) *Tel:* (02) 99366444 *Fax:* (02) 98882229, pg 29

Law Pack Publishing Ltd (United Kingdom) *Tel:* (020) 7394 4040 *Fax:* (020) 7394 4041 *E-mail:* mailbox@lawpack.co.uk *Web Site:* www.lawpack.co.uk, pg 706

Law Publishers (India) *Tel:* (0532) 4094; (0532) 2835; (0532) 3716; (0532) 2298 *Fax:* (0532) 622781; (0532) 609943 *E-mail:* lawpubxd@nde.vsnl.net.in, pg 341

Law Publishers Association (Sri Lanka) *Tel:* (01) 330363 *Fax:* (01) 436629, pg 597

The Law Publishing House (China) *Tel:* (010) 3266792, pg 107

Lawrence & Wishart (United Kingdom) *Tel:* (020) 8533 2506 *Fax:* (020) 8533 7369 *E-mail:* office@l-w-bks.demon.co.uk *Web Site:* www.l-w-bks.co.uk, pg 706

Laxmi Publications Pvt Ltd (India) *Tel:* (011) 3252574 *Fax:* (011) 3252572 *E-mail:* colaxmi@hotmail.com *Web Site:* www.laxmipublications.com, pg 341

Phillip Richard Conover Lazo (Mexico) *Tel:* (05) 5509705 *Fax:* (05) 5500641 *E-mail:* mel778@latinmail.com, pg 462

Editions Universitaires LCF (France) *Tel:* (0556) 81.89.82, pg 172

LCG Malmberg BV (Netherlands) *Tel:* (073) 6288811 *Fax:* (073) 6210512, pg 480

LDA Editores Ltda (Brazil) *Tel:* (041) 362-9173 *Fax:* (041) 262-3439 *E-mail:* lda.editores@uol.com.br, pg 86

LDA-Living & Learning (Cambridge) Ltd (United Kingdom) *Tel:* (01223) 357788 *Fax:* (01223) 460557 *E-mail:* internationalsales@mcgraw-hill.com, pg 706

Lea Publications Ltd (Hong Kong) *Tel:* 25620121 *Fax:* 25650187, pg 320

Lead Wave Publishing Company Ltd (Taiwan, Province of China) *Tel:* (02) 23650177 *Fax:* (02) 23656407 *Web Site:* www.liwil.com.tw, pg 631

Learners Press Private Ltd (India) *Tel:* (011) 6313023; (011) 6916209; (011) 6966165 *Fax:* (011) 6331241 *E-mail:* ghai@nde.vsnl.net.in, pg 341

Learning Development Aids (United Kingdom) *Tel:* (01223) 365445 *Fax:* (01223) 460557 *E-mail:* ldaorders@compuserve.com, pg 706

Learning Guides (Writers & Publishers Ltd) (New Zealand) *Tel:* (04) 23399400 *Fax:* (04) 2399400 *E-mail:* learning.guides@xtra.co.nz, pg 492

Learning Matters Ltd (United Kingdom) *Tel:* (01392) 215560 *Fax:* (01392) 215561 *E-mail:* info@learningmatters.co.uk *Web Site:* www.learningmatters.co.uk, pg 706

Learning Media Ltd (New Zealand) *Tel:* (04) 4962482 *E-mail:* info@learningmedia.co.nz *Web Site:* www.learningmedia.co.nz; www.learningmedia.com, pg 492

Learning Together (United Kingdom) *Tel:* (028) 90402086 *Fax:* (2890) 402086 *E-mail:* info@learningtogether.co.uk *Web Site:* www.learningtogether.co.uk, pg 706

The Lebanese Library Association (Lebanon) *Tel:* (01) 374374 ext 2606 *Fax:* (01) 351 706, pg 1519

Lebensbaum Verlags-GmbH (Germany) *Tel:* (0521) 172875 *Fax:* (0521) 68771, pg 256

Lebenshilfe-Verlag Marburg, Verlag der Bundesvereinigung Lebenshilfe fuer Menschen mit geistiger Behinderung eV (Germany) *Tel:* (06421) 491150; (06421) 491153 *Fax:* (06421) 491167 *E-mail:* bvlh-verlag@t-online.de *Web Site:* www.lebenshilfe.de, pg 256

Gerda Leber Buch-Kunst-und Musikverlag Proscenium Edition (Austria) *Tel:* (01) 5332858; (01) 6390025, pg 54

Lecce Spazio Vivo Srl (Italy) *Tel:* (0832) 308885 *Fax:* (0832) 308885; (0832) 241562, pg 395

LED - Edizioni Universitarie di Lettere Economia Diritto (Italy) *Tel:* (02) 59902055 *Fax:* (02) 55193636, pg 395

LEDA (Las Ediciones de Arte) (Spain) *Tel:* (093) 2379389; (093) 2155273, pg 579

Ledory Publishing House (Israel) *Tel:* (03) 5178555 *Fax:* (03) 9612182, pg 370

Lee & Lee Communications (Taiwan, Province of China) *Tel:* (02) 7068833 *Fax:* (02) 7066205 *E-mail:* leelee@tpts1.seed.net.tw, pg 631

Sandra Lee Agencies (Australia) *Tel:* (03) 95925235 *Fax:* (03) 95927608 *E-mail:* winston@ozonline.com.au, pg 29

Leeds University Library (United Kingdom) *Tel:* (0113) 2336388; (0113) 2335501 *Fax:* (0113) 2335561 *E-mail:* library@library.novell.leeds.ac.uk, pg 1506

Leefung-Asco Printers Ltd (Hong Kong) *Tel:* 24216708 *Fax:* 28105530; 28105612, pg 1134

Editions Francis Lefebvre (France) *Tel:* (01) 41 05 22 00 *Fax:* (01) 41 05 22 30, pg 172

Claude Lefrancq Editeur (Belgium) *Tel:* (02) 344-49-34 *Fax:* (02) 347-55-34 *E-mail:* claude.lefrancq@skynet.be, pg 78

Legal Action Group (United Kingdom) *Tel:* (020) 7833 2931 *Fax:* (020) 7837 6094 *E-mail:* lag@lag.org.uk *Web Site:* www.lag.org.uk, pg 706

Legal & Technical Translation Services (United Kingdom) *Tel:* (01622) 751537 *Fax:* (01622) 754431 *E-mail:* ltts@compuserve.com, pg 1129

Legal Resources Foundation Publications Unit (Zimbabwe) *Tel:* (04) 790947; (04) 728211; (04) 728212 *Fax:* (04) 728213, pg 768

Ediciones Legales SA (Ecuador) *Tel:* (02) 548422 *Fax:* (02) 554954, pg 137

LEGIS - Editores SA (Colombia) *Tel:* (01) 2634100; (01) 2957387 *Fax:* (01) 2952650, pg 112

Legislation Direct (New Zealand) *Tel:* (04) 4965655 *Fax:* (04) 4965698 *E-mail:* lorders@legislationdirect.co.nz *Web Site:* gplegislation.co.nz, pg 492

Editions Legislatives (France) *Tel:* (01) 40 92 36 36 *Fax:* (01) 46 56 00 15 *E-mail:* info@editions-legislatives.fr *Web Site:* www.editions-legislatives.fr, pg 172

Legprombytizdat (Russian Federation) *Tel:* (095) 2330947, pg 539

Libreria Imprenta y Litografia Lehmann SA (Costa Rica) *Tel:* 2231212, pg 116, 1280

Lehnert & Landrock Bookshop (Egypt (Arab Republic of Egypt)) *Tel:* (02) 3927606 *Fax:* (02) 3934421, pg 139

Lehnert & Landrock, Bookshop and Art Publishers (Egypt (Arab Republic of Egypt)) *Tel:* (02) 3927606; (02) 3935324 *Fax:* (02) 3934421, pg 1282

Verlag fuer Lehrmittel Poessneck GmbH (Germany) *Tel:* 03647 425020 *Fax:* (03647) 425020, pg 256

Lehrmittelverlag des Kantons Zurich (Switzerland) *Tel:* (01) 4658585 *Fax:* (01) 4658583 *E-mail:* lehrmiHelverlag@lmv.zh.ch *Web Site:* www.access.ch/lmvzh, pg 618

Leibniz Verlag (Germany) *Tel:* (06741) 1720 *Fax:* (06741) 1749 *E-mail:* reichl-verlag@telda.net, pg 256

Leibniz-Buecherwarte (Germany) *Tel:* (05042) 1528 *Fax:* (05042) 1528 *E-mail:* leibniz-buecherwarte@t-online.de *Web Site:* www.leibniz-buecherwarte.de/.com, pg 257

University of Leicester (United Kingdom) *Tel:* (0116) 2522042 *Fax:* (0116) 2522066 *E-mail:* library@lx.ac.uk, pg 1506

Leipziger Staedtische Bibliotheken (Germany) *Tel:* (0341) 123 53 43 *Fax:* (0341) 123 53 05 *E-mail:* stadtbib@leipzig.de *Web Site:* www.leipzig.de/stadtbib.htm, pg 1468

Leipziger Universitaetsverlag GmbH (Germany) *Tel:* (0341) 9900440 *Fax:* (0341) 9900440 *E-mail:* info@univerlag-leipzig.de, pg 257

Leitfadenverlag Verlag Dieter Sudholt (Germany) *Tel:* (08151) 51045 *Fax:* (08151) 50357, pg 257

Anton G Leitner Verlag (AGLV) (Germany) *Tel:* (08153) 9525-22 *Fax:* (08153) 9525-24 *E-mail:* info@aglv.com *Web Site:* www.dasgedicht.de, pg 257

Editora Leitura Ltda (Brazil) *Tel:* (031) 3371-4902 *Fax:* (031) 3714902 *E-mail:* leitura@editoraleitura.com.br *Web Site:* www.editoraleitura.com.br/, pg 86

Edicions de l'Eixample, SA (Spain) *Tel:* (093) 4589405 *Fax:* (093) 2076248, pg 580

Leksikografski Zavod Miroslav Krleza (Croatia) *Tel:* (01) 4800 492; (01) 4800 300 *Fax:* (01) 4800 399 *E-mail:* lzmk@hlz.hr *Web Site:* www.hlz.hr, pg 119

Lembaga Demografi Fakultas Ekonomi Universitas Indonesia (Indonesia) *Tel:* (021) 3900703; (021) 336434; (021) 336539 *Fax:* (021) 3102457 *E-mail:* demofeui@indo.net.id, pg 356

Verlag Otto Lembeck (Germany) *Tel:* (069) 5970988 *Fax:* (069) 5975742 *E-mail:* verlag@lembeck.de *Web Site:* www.lembeck.de, pg 257

Uitgeverij Lemma BV (Netherlands) *Tel:* (30) 2545652 *Fax:* (30) 2586975 *E-mail:* infodesk@lemma.nl *Web Site:* www.lemma.nl, pg 480

Lemniscaat (Netherlands) *Tel:* (010) 2062929 *Fax:* (010) 1141560 *E-mail:* info@lemniscaat.nl, pg 480

Lemos & Crane (United Kingdom) *Tel:* (020) 8348 8263 *Fax:* (020) 8347 5740 *E-mail:* paulc@lemos.demon.co.uk *Web Site:* www.lemosandcrane.co.uk, pg 707

Edicoes Manuel Lencastre (Portugal) *Tel:* 4688328, pg 526

Izdatelstvo Lenizdat (Russian Federation) *Tel:* (0812) 3111451 *Fax:* (0812) 3151295, pg 539

Lenos Verlag (Switzerland) *Tel:* (061) 253414 *Fax:* (061) 2613518, pg 618

Lentz Verlag (Germany) *Tel:* (089) 290880 *Fax:* (089) 29088-144 *E-mail:* l.eggs@herbig.net *Web Site:* www.herbig.net, pg 257

Lenz & Riecker Inc (United States) *Tel:* 973-256-2456 *Fax:* 973-256-3433; 973-256-2459 *E-mail:* info@l-r.com *Web Site:* www.l-r.com, pg 1145, 1165, 1207, 1216, 1225

Lenz-Mulligan Rights & Co-editions (United Kingdom) *Tel:* (020) 8543 7846 *Fax:* (020) 8543 8909, pg 1120

Leo Books (South Africa) *Tel:* (021) 406-3315 *Fax:* (021) 406-2926 *E-mail:* leobooks@nbh.nasper.co.za, pg 1310

Leo Paper Products Ltd (Hong Kong) *Tel:* 25696293 *Fax:* 25138400 *E-mail:* lrg@leo.com.hk *Web Site:* www.leo.com.hk, pg 1134, 1156

Leo Paper Products Ltd (Hong Kong) *Tel:* (852) 28841374 *Fax:* (852) 25130698 *E-mail:* lpp@leo.com.hk *Web Site:* www.leo.com.hk, pg 1196

Leo Paper USA (United States) *Tel:* 425-646-8801 *Fax:* 425-646-8805 *E-mail:* leo@leousa.com *Web Site:* www.leousa.com, pg 1145, 1165, 1207

Leo Reprographic Ltd (Hong Kong) *Tel:* (02) 569-6293 *Fax:* (02) 513-8400 *E-mail:* lrg@leo.com.hk *Web Site:* www.leo.com.hk, pg 1156

Leong Brothers (Brunei Darussalam) *Tel:* (03) 225193 *Fax:* (03) 222223, pg 93

Leonhardt & Hoier Literary Agency aps (Denmark) *Tel:* 33132523 *Fax:* 33134992, pg 1110

Leonis Verlag (Switzerland) *Tel:* (01) 475565 *Fax:* (01) 2624881, pg 618

Uitgeverij Leopold BV (Netherlands) *Tel:* (020) 5511250 *Fax:* (020) 4204699, pg 480

Leopold Stocker Verlag (Austria) *Tel:* (0316) 82 16 36 *Fax:* (0316) 83 56 12 *E-mail:* landwirt@stocker-verlag.com *Web Site:* www.stocker-verlag.com; www.oezv.or.at, pg 54

Leopold Stocker Verlag (Austria) *Tel:* (0316) 82 16 36 *Fax:* (0316) 83 56 12, pg 1274

L'Erma di Bretschneider SRL (Italy) *Tel:* (06) 6874127 *Fax:* (06) 6874129 *E-mail:* edizioni@lerma.it *Web Site:* www.lerma.it, pg 395

Dr Gisela Lermann (Germany) *Tel:* (06131) 31149 *Fax:* (06131) 387945 *Web Site:* www.lermann-verlag.de, pg 257

Libreria y Distribuidora Lerner Ltda (Colombia) *Tel:* (01) 2430567 *Fax:* (01) 2814319, pg 1280

Lerner Limitada (Colombia) *Tel:* (01) 2628200; (01) 2624224 *Fax:* (01) 2624459, pg 112

Editions Dominique Leroy (France) *Tel:* (01) 44 41 68 40 *Fax:* (01) 44 41 68 42 *E-mail:* curiosa@enfer.com *Web Site:* www.enfer.com, pg 172

Verlag Leske plus Budrich GmbH (Germany) *Tel:* (02171) 4907-0 *Fax:* (02171) 4907-11 *E-mail:* leske-budrich@t-online.de *Web Site:* www.leske-budrich.de, pg 257

Lesotho Library Association (Lesotho), pg 1519

Lesotho National Library Service (Lesotho) *Tel:* 323100 *Fax:* 327890, pg 1481

Editions Lessius ASBL (Belgium) *Tel:* (02) 739 34 90 *Fax:* (02) 739 34 91 *E-mail:* info@editions-lessius.be, pg 71

P Lethielleux Editions (France) *Tel:* (01) 44 32 05 60 *Fax:* (01) 44 32 05 61, pg 172

Letouzey et Ane Sarl (France) *Tel:* (01) 45 48 80 14 *Fax:* (01) 45 49 03 43, pg 172

Editorial Letras Cubanas (Cuba) *Tel:* (07) 626864 *Fax:* (07) 338187 *E-mail:* elc@icl.cult.cu, pg 121

Editora Letraviva Importacao Distribuidora Livros Ltd (Brazil) *Tel:* (011) 2807992 *Fax:* (011) 2807780 *E-mail:* letraviva@letraviva.com.br *Web Site:* www.letraviva.com.br, pg 1277

Lettera (Bulgaria) *Tel:* (032) 600 930 *Fax:* (032) 600 940 *E-mail:* lettera@plovdiv.techno-link.com *Web Site:* www.lettera.bg, pg 96

Letterbox Library (United Kingdom) *Tel:* (020) 7503 4801 *Fax:* (020) 7503 4800 *E-mail:* info@letterboxlibrary.com *Web Site:* www.letterboxlibrary.com, pg 707

Letterbox Library (United Kingdom), pg 1233

Casa Editrice Le Lettere SRL (Italy) *Tel:* (055) 2342710 *Fax:* (055) 2346010, pg 395

Letterland International Ltd (United Kingdom) *Tel:* (01223) 262675 *Fax:* (01223) 264126 *E-mail:* info@letterland.com *Web Site:* www.letterland.com, pg 707

Lettre International Kulturzeitung (Germany) *Tel:* (030) 30870440; (030) 30870462 *Fax:* (030) 2833128 *E-mail:* lettre@lettre.de *Web Site:* www.lettre.de, pg 257

Lettres Modernes (France) *Tel:* (01) 43362583 *E-mail:* editorat.lettresmodernes@wanadoo.fr, pg 172

Lettres Vives (France) *Tel:* (01) 42781379 *Fax:* (01) 42783761 *E-mail:* lettresvives@mic.fr, pg 173

Charles Letts & Co Ltd (United Kingdom) *Tel:* (0131) 6631971 *Fax:* (0131) 6603225, pg 1141, 1204

Letts Educational (United Kingdom) *Tel:* (020) 8996 3333 *Fax:* (020) 8742 8390 *E-mail:* mail@lettsed.co.uk *Web Site:* www.lettsed.co.uk, pg 707

Letture Mensile di Informazione Culturale, Letteratura e Spettacolo (Italy) *Tel:* (02) 48071 *Fax:* (02) 48072568 *E-mail:* letture@stpauls.it, pg 395

Bernard Letu Editeur (Switzerland) *Tel:* (022) 204757 *Fax:* (022) 208492, pg 618

LEU-VERLAG Wolfgang Leupelt (Germany) *Tel:* (02204) 981141 *Fax:* (02204) 981143 *E-mail:* info@leu-verlag.net; leuverlag@aol.com *Web Site:* www.leu-verlag.net, pg 257

Leuchter-Verlag EG (Germany) *Tel:* (06150) 97 36 20 *Fax:* (06150) 6155, pg 257

Verlag Gerald Leue (Germany) *Tel:* (030) 7865020 *Fax:* (030) 78913876 *E-mail:* vertrieb@leue-verlag.de *Web Site:* www.leue.purespace.de, pg 257

Leuven University Press (Belgium) *Tel:* (016) 32 53 45 *Fax:* (016) 32 53 52 *E-mail:* university.press@upers.kuleuven.ac.be; universitaire.pers@upers.kuleuven.ac.be *Web Site:* www.lup.be, pg 71

Levante (Italy) *Tel:* (080) 5213778 *Fax:* (080) 5213778 *E-mail:* levanted@tin.it *Web Site:* www.levantebari.com, pg 395

Levanter Publishing & Associates (Australia) *Tel:* (02) 93717824, pg 30

A G Leventis Foundation (Cyprus) *Tel:* (01) 729 3015-18 *Fax:* (01) 725 1951 *E-mail:* leventcy@zenon.logos.cy.net *Web Site:* www.leventisfoundation.org, pg 1120

Editions Liana Levi Sarl (France) *Tel:* (01) 43262961 *Fax:* (01) 46336956, pg 173

Levrotto e Bella Libreria Editrice Universitaria SAS (Italy) *Tel:* (011) 8121205 *Fax:* (011) 8124025 *E-mail:* levrotto@ipsnet.it, pg 395

Barbara Levy Literary Agency (United Kingdom) *Tel:* (020) 7435 9046 *Fax:* (020) 7431 2063 *E-mail:* blevy@dircon.co.uk, pg 172

The Lewis Carroll Society (United Kingdom) *E-mail:* aztec@compuserve.com, pg 1266

The Lexicon Bookshop (United Kingdom) *Tel:* (01624) 673004 *Fax:* (01624) 661959, pg 1320

LexisNexis (Singapore) *Tel:* 6336 9661 *Fax:* 6336 9662 *Web Site:* www.lexisnexis.com.sg, pg 547

LexisNexis Butterworths (India) (India) *Tel:* (011) 373 9614; (011) 373 9615; (011) 373 9616; (011) 332 6454; (011) 332 6455 *Fax:* (011) 332 6456 *E-mail:* info@lexisnexis.co.on *Web Site:* www.lexisnexis.co.in, pg 341

Lexus Ltd (United Kingdom) *Tel:* (0141) 2215266 *Fax:* (0141) 2263139 *E-mail:* pt@lexus.win-uk.net, pg 1129

La Ley SA Editora e Impresora (Argentina) *Tel:* (011) 4378-4841 *Fax:* (011) 4372-0953 *E-mail:* bausilic@la-ley.com.ar *Web Site:* www.la-ley.com.ar, pg 7

Leykam Buchverlagsges mbH (Austria) *Tel:* (0316) 80 76-31 *Fax:* (0316) 81 66-39 *E-mail:* verlag@leykam.com *Web Site:* www.leykam.com; www.leykamverlag.at, pg 54

Lia rumantscha (Switzerland) *Tel:* (081) 22442 *Fax:* (081) 2583223 *E-mail:* liarum@spin.ch, pg 618

Liang Yu Printing Factory Ltd (Hong Kong) *Tel:* 25604453 *Fax:* 28858099 *E-mail:* liangyup@netvigator.com, pg 1196

Liaoning Library (China), pg 1457

Liaoning People's Publishing House (China) *Tel:* (024) 363316; (024) 363541 *Fax:* (024) 371472, pg 107

Librairie du Liban (Lebanon) *Tel:* (0357) 862957 *Fax:* (0357) 9512906, pg 443, 1297

Bibliotheque Nationale du Liban (Lebanon) *Tel:* (01) 862957 *Fax:* (01) 374079, pg 1481

John Libbey & Co Ltd (United Kingdom) *Tel:* (020) 8947 2777 *Fax:* (020) 8947 2664 *E-mail:* johnlibbey@aol.com *Web Site:* www.johnlibbey.com, pg 707

John Libbey Eurotext (France) *Tel:* (01) 46 73 06 60 *Fax:* (01) 40 84 09 99 *E-mail:* contact@jle.com *Web Site:* www.john-libbey-eurotext.fr, pg 173

Die Libelle Verlag Ag Libellen Haus (Switzerland) *Tel:* (072) 753555 *Fax:* (072) 753565 *E-mail:* libelleverlag@bluewin.ch, pg 618

Liber AB (Sweden) *Tel:* (08) 6909200 *Fax:* (08) 6909470 *E-mail:* export@liber.se; infomaster@liber.se *Web Site:* www.liber.se, pg 604

Liber Ediciones, SA (Spain) *Tel:* (0948) 177 488 *Fax:* (0948) 176 667 *E-mail:* info@arsliber.com *Web Site:* www.arsliber.com, pg 580

Liber Hermods AB (Sweden) *Tel:* (040) 258600 *Fax:* (040) 304600, pg 604

Liberia Editorial Minerva-Miraflores (Peru) *Tel:* (014) 4475499 *Fax:* (014) 4458583 *E-mail:* minerva@chavin-rcp-net-pe, pg 1305

Ediciones Libertarias/Prodhufi SA (Spain) *Tel:* (091) 593 33 93 *Fax:* (091) 594 16 96 *E-mail:* libertarias@libertarias.com *Web Site:* www.libertarias.com, pg 580

Libertas- Europaeisches Institut GmbH (Germany) *Tel:* (07031) 6186-80 *Fax:* (07031) 6186-86 *E-mail:* info@libertas-institut.com *Web Site:* www.libertas-institut.com, pg 257

Libertatea (Yugoslavia) *Tel:* (013) 33-51; (013) 46-447 *Fax:* (013) 46-447, pg 764

Liberty Books (Pvt) Ltd (Pakistan) *Tel:* (021) 111311113 *Fax:* (021) 5684319 *E-mail:* libertybooks@libertybooks.com *Web Site:* www.libertybooks.com, pg 1304

Liberty (United Kingdom) *Tel:* (020) 7403 3888 *Fax:* (020) 7407 5354 *E-mail:* info@liberty-human-rights.org.uk *Web Site:* www.liberty-human-rights.org.uk, pg 707

Libiosy Libres, Editorial (Colombia) *Tel:* (01) 2907145; (01) 2907862; (01) 2886188 *Fax:* (01) 2696830, pg 112

Libra Books Pty Ltd (Australia) *Tel:* (03) 6225 1479 *Fax:* (03) 6225 0900, pg 30

Libra House Ltd (Ireland) *Tel:* (01) 542-717, pg 362

Ediciones Libra, SA de CV (Mexico) *Tel:* (05) 6045952 *Fax:* (05) 68828486, pg 463

Libra Editorial SA de CV (Mexico) *Tel:* (05) 6641454; (05) 6514156 *Fax:* (05) 6641454, pg 463

Librairie Bilingue/The Bilingual Bookshop (Cameroon) *Tel:* 224899 *Fax:* 232903, pg 1278

Librairie Clairafrique (Senegal) *Tel:* 222169 *Fax:* 218409, pg 1309

La Librairie de Madagascar (Madagascar) *Tel:* (020) 22454, pg 1297

Librairie des Champs-Elysees, Groupe Hachette (France) *Tel:* (01) 43923577 *Fax:* (01) 43923573, pg 173

Librairie des Presses Universitaires (The Democratic Republic of the Congo) *Tel:* (012) 30652, pg 1280

Librairie des Presses Universitaires de Bruxelles (Belgium) *Tel:* (02) 6499780 *Fax:* (02) 6477962, pg 1276

Librairie FNAC (France) *Tel:* 01 55215053, pg 1283

Librairie Generale des PUF (France) *Tel:* (01) 43267741 *Fax:* (01) 46332194, pg 1283

Librairie Internationale (Morocco) *Tel:* (07) 750183 *Fax:* (07) 758661, pg 1300

Librairie la Hune (France) *Tel:* (01) 43255406, pg 1283

Librairie les Volcans (The Democratic Republic of the Congo) *Tel:* 366, pg 1280

Librairie Luginbuhl (France) *Tel:* (01) 45 51 42 58 *Fax:* (01) 45 56 07 80 *E-mail:* liblug@club-internet.fr, pg 173

Librairie Mixte Sarl (Madagascar) *Tel:* (020) 25130, pg 1297

YELLOW PAGES

Librairie Orientale sal (Lebanon) *Tel:* (01) 485793; (01) 485794; (01) 485795 *Fax:* (01) 485796 *E-mail:* libor@cyberia.net.lb, pg 443

Librairie Scientifique et Technique Albert Blanchard (France) *Tel:* (01) 43 26 90 34 *Fax:* (01) 43 29 97 31 *E-mail:* librairie.blanchard@wanadoo.fr *Web Site:* www.blanchard75.fr, pg 173

Librairie Universitaire (Madagascar) *Tel:* (020) 24114, pg 1298

Librairie Universitaire (Rwanda) *Tel:* 30272; 30273, pg 1308

Office national des Librairies Populaires (ONLP) (Congo) *Tel:* 833485 *Fax:* 831879, pg 1280

Libraria Universitatii (Romania) *Tel:* (064) 18107; (064) 14267, pg 1308

The Librarian, University College of Swaziland (Swaziland) *Tel:* 5184011 *Fax:* 5185276 *E-mail:* mmavuso@uniswac1.uniswa.sz *Web Site:* library.uniswa.sz, pg 1259

Librarie Mixte (Madagascar) *Tel:* (02) 25130 *Fax:* (02) 25130, pg 450

Library & Information Association of New Zealand Aotearoa (LIANZA) (New Zealand) *Tel:* (04) 4735834 *Fax:* (04) 4991480, pg 1521

Library & Information Association of South Africa (LIASA) (South Africa) *Tel:* (012) 481 2870; (012) 481 2871; (012) 481 2872; (012) 481 2875 *Fax:* (012) 481 2873 *E-mail:* liasa@liasa.org.za *Web Site:* www.liasa.org.za, pg 1523

School of Library & Information Science (Japan) *Tel:* (03) 34534511, pg 1478

Library & Information Science Society (Zimbabwe) *Tel:* (04) 752311, pg 1526

Library & Information Statistics Unit (United Kingdom) *Tel:* (01509) 223071 *Fax:* (01509) 223072 *E-mail:* lisu@lboro.ac.uk *Web Site:* www.lboro.ac.uk/departments/dis/lisu/lisuhp.html, pg 707

The Library Association of Bangladesh (Bangladesh) *Tel:* (02) 504269; (02) 8619408 *E-mail:* msik@icddrb.org, pg 1512

Library Association of Barbados (Barbados), pg 1512

Library Association of Singapore (Singapore), pg 1523

The Asiatic Society of Bombay (India) *Tel:* (022) 2860956 *E-mail:* asbl@giasbom2.vsnl.net.in, pg 1473

Library of Australian History (Australia) *Tel:* (02) 9929 5087 *Fax:* (02) 9929 5087 *E-mail:* grdxxx@ozemail.com.au, pg 30

Library of Chinese Academy of Sciences (China) *Tel:* (010) 62566847 *Fax:* (010) 62566846 *E-mail:* office@mail.las.ac.cn, pg 1457

Library of Parliament (South Africa) *Tel:* (021) 4032140 *Fax:* (021) 4614331, pg 1498

Library of the Near East School of Theology (Lebanon) *Tel:* (01) 354194 *Fax:* (01) 347129 *E-mail:* nest.lib@inco.com.lb, pg 1481

Library of the Press & Information Department (Afghanistan), pg 1449

Library Promotion Bureau (Pakistan) *Tel:* (021) 6335605, pg 507

Library Promotion Bureau (Pakistan), pg 1521

Library Service of Fiji (Fiji) *Tel:* 315303; 315344 *Fax:* 314994, pg 141

Library Service of Fiji (Fiji) *Tel:* 315303 *Fax:* 314994, pg 1463

The Library Shop (Ireland) *Tel:* (01) 6081171 *Fax:* (01) 6081016 *Web Site:* www.tcd.ie/library/shop/, pg 1291

Libreria Cultural Panamena SA (Panama) *Tel:* 2235628; 2236267 *Fax:* 2237280, pg 1305

Libreria Editora Ltda (Brazil) *Tel:* (011) 6085411 *Fax:* (011) 6085411 *E-mail:* libreria@libreria.com.br *Web Site:* www.libreria.com.br, pg 86

Libreria Internacional SA (Paraguay) *Tel:* (021) 491423 *Fax:* (021) 449730, pg 1305

Libreria la Paz (Bolivia) *Tel:* (02) 353323; (02) 357109 *Fax:* (02) 391513, pg 1277

Libreria l'Universidad, Nicolas Ojeda Fierro e Hijos SRL Ltda (Peru) *Tel:* (014) 282461; (014) 282036, pg 1305

Libreria Libertad SA (Chile) *Tel:* (02) 695 7777 *Fax:* (02) 672 6314, pg 100

Libreria Nacional Ltda (Colombia) *Tel:* (01) 825829; (01) 833849; (01) 2139842; (01) 2139882 *Fax:* (01) 822404; (01) 2138404, pg 1280

Libreria Panamericana (Colombia) *Tel:* (01) 2770100 *Fax:* (01) 2773599, pg 1280

Libreria Parroquial de Claveria SA Edicion Compra y Venta de Libros (Mexico) *Tel:* (05) 3967027; (05) 3967718 *Fax:* (05) 3991243, pg 463

Libreria Tecnologica Universitaria (Nicaragua) *Tel:* (02) 773026 *Fax:* (02) 670106, pg 1303

Libreria Universitaria (Chile) *Tel:* (02) 2234555; (02) 2236980 *Fax:* (02) 2099455; (02) 499455, pg 1279

Libreria Universitaria (Ecuador) *Tel:* (02) 212521, pg 1282

Libreria Universitaria (Nicaragua) *Tel:* (0311) 2612; (0311) 2613, pg 1303

Libreria Universitaria de l'Universidad de El Salvador (El Salvador) *Tel:* 259427; 256604 *Fax:* 259427, pg 1282

Libresa S A (Ecuador) *Tel:* (02) 230925 *Fax:* (02) 502992, pg 137

Libresso Berlin (Germany) *Tel:* (030) 2826346 *Fax:* (030) 2834494, pg 1111

Libretto Forlag (Norway) *Tel:* (022) 443011 *Fax:* (022) 443012, pg 504

Edizioni Librex (Italy) *Tel:* (02) 58302006, pg 396

Edition Libri Illustri GmbH (Germany) *Tel:* (07141) 84720 *Fax:* (07141) 875117 *E-mail:* libri.illustri@t-online.de *Web Site:* www.edition-libri-illustri.de, pg 257

Libri s r o (Czech Republic) *Tel:* (02) 5161 3113 *Fax:* (02) 5161 1013 *E-mail:* libri@libri.cz *Web Site:* www.libri.cz, pg 125

Libris Bokforlaget (Sweden) *Tel:* (019) 208400 *Fax:* (019) 208430 *E-mail:* info@libris.se *Web Site:* www.libris.se, pg 604

Libris Emo AS (Norway) *Tel:* 63849200 *Fax:* 63849345, pg 1304

Libris Ltd (United Kingdom) *Tel:* (020) 7482 2390 *Fax:* (020) 7485 4220, pg 707

Libro Ltd (Greece) *Tel:* (01) 7247116 *Fax:* (01) 7232066, pg 312

Librograf (Argentina) *Tel:* (011) 4300-5662; (011) 4300-1466 *Fax:* (011) 4300-3670, pg 7

Librolandia del Centro SA de CV (Mexico) *Tel:* (062) 135646; (062) 170236 *Fax:* (062) 170236, pg 1299

Libros-Ediciones Homines (Puerto Rico) *Tel:* (787) 250-1912 (ext 2347) *Web Site:* coqui.ice.org/homines; coqui.metro.inter.edu.homines, pg 530

Editorial Libros y Libres SA (Colombia) *Tel:* (01) 2907145; (01) 2907862; (01) 2886188 *Fax:* (01) 2696830 *E-mail:* edilibro@colomsat.net.co, pg 112

Libros y Revistas SA de CV (Mexico) *Tel:* (05) 5437295, pg 463

Libsa Editorial SA (Spain) *Tel:* (091) 657 25 80 *Fax:* (091) 657 25 83 *E-mail:* libsa@libsa.es *Web Site:* www.libsa.es, pg 580

Licap CVBA (Belgium) *Tel:* (02) 509 97 03 *Fax:* (02) 509 97 04, pg 71

Licap CVBA (Belgium) *Tel:* (02) 5099670; (02) 5099703 *Fax:* (02) 5099606, pg 1276

Licht & Licht Literary Agency (Denmark) *Tel:* 39610908 *Fax:* 39611105, pg 1110

Lid Editorial Empresarial, SL (Spain) *Tel:* (091) 372 90 03 *Fax:* (091) 372 85 14 *E-mail:* consejeros-lid@nexo.es, pg 580

Editora Lidador Ltda (Brazil) *Tel:* (021) 25690594 *Fax:* (021) 22040684 *E-mail:* lidador@terra.com.br, pg 86

Lidel Edicoes Tecnicas, Lda (Portugal) *Tel:* (021) 3151218 *Fax:* (021) 3577827, pg 526

Lider Verlag (Romania) *Tel:* (01) 4102214 *Fax:* (01) 3374822, pg 534

Lidhja e Shkrimtareve dhe e Artisteve toe Shqiperise (Albania) *Tel:* (042) 23843 *Fax:* (042) 23843 *E-mail:* isbn@natlib.tirana.al, pg 1235

Edition Lidiarte (Germany) *Tel:* (030) 3137420 *Fax:* (030) 3127117 *E-mail:* edition@lidiarte.de *Web Site:* www.lidiarte.de, pg 258

Ediciones Lidiun (Argentina) *Tel:* (011) 4942-9002 *Fax:* (011) 4942-9162 *E-mail:* info@ateneo.com *Web Site:* www.ateneo.com, pg 7

Ediciones Lidiun (Argentina) *Tel:* (011) 4942 9002 *Fax:* (011) 942-9162 *E-mail:* info@ateneo.com *Web Site:* www.yenny.com; www.ateneo.com, pg 1271

Lidman Production AB (Sweden) *Tel:* (08) 6633615 *Fax:* (08) 6633615, pg 604

Lidove noviny Nakladatelstvi (Czech Republic) *Tel:* (02) 225 140 12; (02) 225 223 50 *Fax:* (02) 225 120 79 *E-mail:* nlnpress@iol.cz, pg 125

Hildegard Liebaug-Dartmann (Germany) *Tel:* (02225) 909343 *Fax:* (02225) 909345 *E-mail:* liebaug-dartmann@t-online.de *Web Site:* www.liebaug-dartmann.de, pg 258

Liebenzeller Mission, GmbH, Abt. Verlag (Germany) *Tel:* (07052) 17-163 *Fax:* (07052) 17-170, pg 258

Liechtenstein Verlag AG (Liechtenstein) *Tel:* 23 224 14 *Fax:* 23 243 40 *E-mail:* flbooks@verlag_ag.LOL.li, pg 444

Liechtenstein Verlag AG (Liechtenstein) *Tel:* (00423) 2322414 *Fax:* (00423) 2324340 *E-mail:* flbooks@verlag_ag.LOL.li, pg 1114

Liechtensteinische Landesbibliothek (Liechtenstein) *Tel:* 2366362 *Fax:* 2331419 *E-mail:* labibl@firstlink.li *Web Site:* www.lbfl.li, pg 1481

Verlag der Liechtensteinischen Akademischen Gesellschaft (Liechtenstein) *Tel:* (0423) 2323028 *Fax:* (0423) 2331449, pg 444

Lielvards Ltd (Latvia) *Tel:* (050) 53824 *Fax:* (050) 54310 *E-mail:* info@lielvards.lv *Web Site:* www.lielvards.lv, pg 442

Robert Lienau GmbH & Co KG (Germany) *Tel:* (069) 9782866 *Fax:* (069) 97828689 *E-mail:* info@lienau-frankfurt.de *Web Site:* www.lienau-frankfurt.de, pg 258

Lienhard Pallast Verlag (Germany) *Tel:* (02244) 5863 *Web Site:* www.pallast-publisher.com, pg 258

Liepman AG (Switzerland) *Tel:* (01) 2617660 *Fax:* (01) 2610124 *E-mail:* info@liepmanagency.com, pg 1117

Lierre et Coudrier (France) *Tel:* (01) 42550027 *Fax:* (01) 42570497, pg 173

Liesma Publishers (Latvia) *Tel:* (02) 7223063 *Fax:* (02) 7223063, pg 442

Lietus Ltd (Lithuania) *Tel:* (02) 312298; (02) 8299 35423; (02) 745720 *Fax:* (02) 312298, pg 445

Lietuvos Informacijos Institutas (Lithuania) *Tel:* (02) 752284; (02) 753590; (02) 753382; (02) 752429 *Fax:* (02) 723017 *E-mail:* lii@lii.lt, pg 446

Lietuvos Rasytoju Sajungos Leidykla (Lithuania)
Tel: (02) 628945; (02) 626154 *Fax:* (02) 628945
E-mail: zsleidykla@is.lt *Web Site:* www.rsleidykla.lt,
pg 446

Life Challenge AFRICA (Kenya) *Tel:* (02) 561121; (02) 722314 *Fax:* (02) 721644 *E-mail:* lca@umsg.org, pg 433

Life Planning Foundation of Australia, Inc (Australia) *Tel:* (03) 9670 4417 *Fax:* (03) 9640 0094 *E-mail:* lifeclub@vicnet.net.au, pg 30

Lightbild PTY Ltd (Australia) *Tel:* (03) 95849638 *Fax:* (03) 95849638 *E-mail:* lightbild@compuserve.com, pg 30

Ligue des Bibliotheques Europeennes de Recherche (LIBER) (Germany) *Tel:* (0421) 2183361, pg 1246

Liguori Editore SRL (Italy) *Tel:* (081) 7206111; (081) 7206202 (orders) *Fax:* (081) 7206244 *E-mail:* liguori@liguori.it, pg 396

Editrice Liguria SNC di Norberto Sabatelli & C (Italy) *Tel:* (019) 829917 *Fax:* (019) 8387798, pg 396

Lijnkamp Literary Agents (Netherlands) *Tel:* (020) 6207742 *Fax:* (020) 6385298 *E-mail:* lijnkamp@xs4all.nl *Web Site:* www.lijnkamp.nl, pg 1115

LIK IZDANIJA (Bulgaria) *Tel:* (02) 444121 *Fax:* (02) 444 121 *E-mail:* lik@ttm.bg, pg 96

Likuni Press (Malawi) *Tel:* 721135; 721388 *Fax:* 72114133, pg 1137

Lila Libreria de Mujeres (Chile) *Tel:* (02) 2361725 *Fax:* (02) 2361725, pg 1279

The Lilliput Press Ltd (Ireland) *Tel:* (01) 6711647 *Fax:* (01) 671123 *E-mail:* info@lilliputpress.ie, pg 362

LIM Editrice SRL (Italy) *Tel:* (0583) 394464 *Fax:* (0583) 394469 *E-mail:* lim@lim.it, pg 396

Editorial Lima 2000 SA (Peru) *Tel:* (01) 4403486 *Fax:* (01) 4403480 *E-mail:* oliver@amanta.rcp.net.pe, pg 511

Waldyr Lima Editora (Brazil) *Tel:* (05521) 501-5000 *Fax:* (05521) 581-8900 *E-mail:* geapo@ccaa.com.br *Web Site:* www.ccaa.com.br, pg 86

Editions des Limbes d'Or/FBT de R Editions (France) *Tel:* (01) 41151969; (06) 07683371 *Fax:* (01) 41151969, pg 173

Publishing House Limbus Press (Russian Federation) *Tel:* (0812) 1126547 *Fax:* (0812) 1126706 *E-mail:* limbuspr@rol.ru; limbus@limbuspress.ru *Web Site:* www.limbuspress.ru, pg 539

Liming Cultural Enterprise Co Ltd (Taiwan, Province of China) *Tel:* (02) 3821146 *Fax:* (02) 3821240, pg 631

Limmat Verlag (Switzerland) *Tel:* (01) 445 80 80 *Fax:* (01) 445 80 88 *E-mail:* mail@limmatverlag.ch *Web Site:* www.limmatverlag.ch, pg 618

Limpert Verlag (Germany) *Tel:* (06766) 903160 *Fax:* (06766) 903320 *E-mail:* vertrieb@limpert.de, pg 258

Editorial Limusa SA de CV (Mexico) *Tel:* (05) 512 6858; (05) 585 3500 *Fax:* (05) 512 2903 *E-mail:* limusa@noriega.com.mx *Web Site:* www.noriega.com.mx, pg 463

Lin Pai Press Company Ltd (Taiwan, Province of China) *Tel:* (02) 7765889 *Fax:* (02) 7712568, pg 631

Libreria Linardi y Risso (Uruguay) *Tel:* (02) 915 7129 *Fax:* (02) 915 7328 *E-mail:* lyrbooks@linardiyrisso.com, pg 1324

Linardi y Risso Libreria (Uruguay) *Tel:* (02) 957129 *Fax:* (02) 957328; (02) 957431; (02) 957598 *E-mail:* lyrbooks@chasque.apc.org, pg 760

Lincoln College Centre for Resource Management (New Zealand) *Tel:* (03) 3252811 *Fax:* (03) 3252944 *Web Site:* www.lincoln.ac.nz, pg 492

Frances Lincoln Ltd (United Kingdom) *Tel:* (020) 7284 4009 *Fax:* (020) 7485 0490 *E-mail:* rowans@frances-lincoln.com, pg 707

Lincoln University Bookshop (New Zealand) *Tel:* (03) 3253892 *Fax:* (03) 3253615, pg 1302

Lincoln University Press (New Zealand) *Tel:* (04) 4710601 *Fax:* (04) 4710489 *E-mail:* braselld@lincoln.ac.nz *Web Site:* www.learn.lincoln.ac.nz, pg 492

Lindau (Italy) *Tel:* (011) 6693910 *Fax:* (011) 6693929 *E-mail:* lindau@lindau.it *Web Site:* www.lindau.it, pg 396

J Lindauer Verlag (Germany) *Tel:* (089) 223041 *Fax:* (089) 224315 *E-mail:* lindauerverlag@t-online.de *Web Site:* www.lindauer-verlag.de, pg 258

Linde Verlag Wien GmbH (Austria) *Tel:* (01) 2780526 *Fax:* (01) 2780523 *E-mail:* office@linde-verlag.at; presse@linde-verlag.at *Web Site:* www.linde-verlag.at, pg 54

Lindemann, H, Buchhandlung (Germany) *Tel:* (0711) 24899977 *Fax:* (0711) 2369672 *Web Site:* www.lindemanns-buchhandlung.de, pg 258

Linden Artists Ltd (United Kingdom) *Tel:* (020) 7738 2505 *Fax:* (020) 7738 2513, pg 1162

Linden-Verlag (Germany) *Tel:* (0341) 5902024 *Fax:* (0341) 5904436 *E-mail:* lindenbuch@aol.com *Web Site:* www.linden-buch.de, pg 258

De Lindenboom/INOR Publikaties (Netherlands) *Tel:* (05427) 40004 *Fax:* (05427) 29296 *E-mail:* lindeboo@worldonline.nl, pg 1115

Lindhardt og Ringhof (Denmark) *Tel:* 33695000 *Fax:* 33695001 *E-mail:* lr@lrforlag.dk *Web Site:* www.logr.dk, pg 133

Martha Lindner Verlags-GmbH (Germany) *Tel:* (0721) 843965 *Fax:* (0721) 843965, pg 258

Linea d'Ombra Libri (Italy) *Tel:* (0438) 412647 *Fax:* (0438) 412690 *E-mail:* info@lineadombra.it *Web Site:* www.lineadombra.it, pg 396

Linen Hall Library (United Kingdom) *Tel:* (028) 9032 1707 *Fax:* (028) 9043 8586 *E-mail:* info@linenhall.com *Web Site:* www.linenhall.com, pg 707

David Ling Publishing (New Zealand) *Tel:* (09) 4182785 *Fax:* (09) 4182785, pg 493

Ling Kee Publishing Group (Hong Kong) *Tel:* (02) 5616151 *Fax:* (02) 8111980, pg 320

Georg Lingenbrink GmbH & Co, Libri (Germany) *Tel:* (040) 853 98 0 *Fax:* (040) 853 98 300 *E-mail:* libri@libri.de *Web Site:* www.libri.de, pg 1284

Linguaphone Institute Ltd (United Kingdom) *Tel:* (020) 8687 6000 *Fax:* (020) 8687 6310 *E-mail:* ads@linguaphone.co.uk (Advertising); cst@linguaphone.co.uk (Customer Support) *Web Site:* www.linguaphone.co.uk, pg 708

Linick International Inc (United States) *Tel:* 631-924-3888 *Fax:* 631-924-3890 *E-mail:* linickgrp@att.net *Web Site:* www.lgroup.addr.com; www.linickgroup.com, pg 1166

Linick International Inc (United States) *Tel:* 631-924-3888 *Fax:* 631-924-3890 *E-mail:* linickgrp@att.net *Web Site:* www.lgroup.addr.com; www.linickgroup.com, pg 1207

Linick International Inc (United States) *Tel:* 631-924-3888 *E-mail:* linickgrp@att.net *Web Site:* www.lgroup.addr.com; www.linickgroup.com, pg 1216, 1225

Link Up Mitaka Ltd (United Kingdom) *Tel:* (01926) 311126 *Fax:* (01926) 332990 *E-mail:* trans@leamington.linkup.co.uk *Web Site:* www.mitaka.co.uk, pg 1129

Linking Publishing Company Ltd (Taiwan, Province of China) *Tel:* (02) 7634300-5052 *Fax:* (02) 27634590, pg 631

Linking Up Publishing (Australia) *Tel:* (02) 9712-5576 *Fax:* (02) 9712-1963, pg 30

Christoph Links Verlag - LinksDruck GmbH (Germany) *Tel:* (030) 440232-0 *Fax:* (030) 44023229 *E-mail:* mail@linksverlag.de *Web Site:* www.linksverlag.de, pg 258

Siegbert Linnemann Verlag (Germany) *Tel:* (05241) 14061 *Fax:* (05241) 26439 *E-mail:* info@linnemann-verlag.com; slinnem477@aol.com; sl@linnemann-verlag.com *Web Site:* www.linnemann-verlag.com, pg 258

Lion Publishing PLC (United Kingdom) *Tel:* (01865) 302750 *Fax:* (01865) 302757 *E-mail:* international@lion-publishing.co.uk *Web Site:* www.lion-publishing.co.uk, pg 708

Lippincott Williams & Wilkins (United Kingdom) *Tel:* (020) 7940 7500 *Fax:* (020) 7940 7575 *Web Site:* www.llw.co.uk, pg 708

LISA (Livros Irradiantes SA) (Brazil) *Tel:* (011) 32563755 *Fax:* (011) 32575776 *E-mail:* lerlisalivros@ig.com.br, pg 86

George Lise-Huyghes des Etages (Martinique) *Tel:* 736819, pg 456

Lister Art Books of Southport (United Kingdom) *Tel:* (01704) 232033 *Fax:* (01704) 505926 *E-mail:* sales@laboox.demon.co.uk, pg 1320

Editora Listin Diario (Dominican Republic) *Tel:* (809) 6866688; (809) 6897171 *Fax:* (809) 6866595, pg 136

Liston Translations (United Kingdom) *Tel:* (020) 7732 9431 *Fax:* (020) 7277 6862, pg 1129

LIT Verlag (Germany) *Tel:* (0251) 235091 *Fax:* (0251) 231972 *E-mail:* lit@lit-verlag.de *Web Site:* www.lit-verlag.de, pg 258

LITA Ochranna Autorska Spolocnost' Agentura (Slovakia) *Tel:* (07) 311719 *Fax:* (07) 3136458, pg 550

LITA Ochranna Autorska Spolocnost' Agentura (Slovakia) *Tel:* (07) 313623; (07) 580 2248; (07) 580 2251 *Fax:* (07) 580 2246, pg 1115

Litag Anstalt- Literarische, Medien und Kuenstler Agentur (Liechtenstein) *Tel:* (0423) 3771809 *Fax:* (0423) 3771802, pg 445

LITEC (Livraria Editora Tecnica) Ltda (Brazil) *Tel:* (011) 2220477 *Fax:* (011) 2220477 *E-mail:* livraria@litec.net *Web Site:* www.litec.com.br, pg 1278

LiTec (Librairies Techniques SA) (France) *Tel:* (01) 43 26 60 90 *Fax:* (01) 46 34 22 98, pg 173

Litera Prima (Bulgaria) *Tel:* (02) 423698 *E-mail:* mmihales@vmei.acad.bg, pg 96

Litera Publishing House (Romania) *Tel:* (01) 3303502 *Fax:* (01) 3303502 *E-mail:* info@litera.ro, pg 534

Wydawnictwo Literackie (Poland) *Tel:* (012) 4225423 *Fax:* (012) 4225423 *E-mail:* redakcja@wl.interkom.pl, pg 517

Literamed Publications Nigeria Ltd (Nigeria) *Tel:* (01) 4962512; (01) 4935258 *Fax:* (01) 4972217 *E-mail:* literamed@infoweb.abs.net *Web Site:* www.lantern-books.com, pg 500

Literar-Mechana, Wahrnehmungsgesellschaft fuer Urheberrechte GmbH (Austria) *Tel:* (01) 5872161 *Fax:* (01) 58721619, pg 1237

Literarischer Verein in Stuttgart eV (Germany) *Tel:* (0711) 5499710 *Fax:* (0711) 54997121, pg 1363

Literarisches Colloquium Berlin (Germany) *Tel:* (030) 8169960 *Fax:* (030) 81699619 *Web Site:* www.lcb.de, pg 1364

Literary Dynamics (South Africa) *Tel:* (031) 2016919 *Fax:* (031) 2016919 *E-mail:* literary@saol.com *Web Site:* www.enterest.co.za/literarydynamics, pg 1116

Literas-Verlag GmbH (Austria) *Tel:* (01) 31565925 *Fax:* (01) 34368521, pg 54

Literature Academy (Republic of Korea) *Tel:* (02) 7645057 *Fax:* (02) 7458516 *E-mail:* munhac@ppp.kornet4.net *Web Site:* www.munhakac.co.kr, pg 438

Literature and Art Publishing House (Democratic People's Republic of Korea), pg 434

The Literature Bureau (Zimbabwe) *Tel:* (04) 726929; (04) 729120, pg 768

The Literature Bureau (Zimbabwe) *Tel:* (04) 333812, pg 1270

The Literature Bureau (Zimbabwe) *Tel:* (04) 726929, pg 1325

The Literature Bureau (Zimbabwe) *Tel:* (04) 333812, pg 1372

Literature Ministry Department (Hong Kong) *Tel:* 27258558 *Fax:* 23862304 *E-mail:* hkccllmd@hkstar.com, pg 1135

Lithuanian ISBN Agency (Lithuania) *Tel:* (02) 496066 *Fax:* (02) 496055 *E-mail:* isbnltu@lnb.lt *Web Site:* www.lnb.lt, pg 1251

Lithuanian Librarians Association (Lithuania) *Tel:* (02) 750340 *Fax:* (02) 750340 *E-mail:* lbd@vpu.lt *Web Site:* www.lbd.lt, pg 1520

Lithuanian National Museum Publishing House (Lithuania) *Tel:* (02) 627774 *Fax:* (02) 611023 *E-mail:* muziejus@lnm.lt *Web Site:* www.lnm.lt, pg 446

Lithuanian Publishers' Association (Lithuania) *Tel:* (02) 332943 *Fax:* (02) 263197, pg 446

Lithuanian Publishers' Association (Lithuania) *Tel:* (02) 332943; (02) 332943 *Fax:* (02) 330519; (02) 263157, pg 1251

LITkom Elisabeth Falk Agentur fur Literatur und Kommunikation (Germany) *Tel:* (221) 885413 *Fax:* (221) 885433 *Web Site:* www.litkom.de, pg 1111

Lito Technion Ltda (Colombia) *Tel:* (01) 2443502; (01) 2443177; (01) 2441538, pg 112

Editions Lito (France) *Tel:* (01) 45161700 *Fax:* (01) 48820085 *E-mail:* annick.cabrelli@editionslito.com, pg 173

Litografia Artex, SA (Costa Rica) *Tel:* 2373144 *Fax:* 2379568, pg 116

Litografia e Imprenta LIL SA (Costa Rica) *Tel:* 2350011; 2213622 *Fax:* 2407814, pg 116

Litopia Corp Ltd (United Kingdom) *Tel:* (020) 7224 1748 *Fax:* (020) 7224 1802; 212-202-4236 (N.Y.) *E-mail:* info@litopia.com *Web Site:* www.litopia.com, pg 1120

Littera Scripta Manet (Netherlands) *Tel:* (0575) 491950, pg 480

Editeurs de Litterature Biblique (Belgium) *Tel:* (02) 384-54-02; (02) 384-52-12 *Fax:* (02) 384-98-66 *E-mail:* elb@elbeurope.org *Web Site:* www.elbeurope.org, pg 71

Christopher Little Literary Agency (United Kingdom) *Tel:* (020) 7736 4455 *Fax:* (020) 7736 4490, pg 1120

Little Hills Press (Australia) *Tel:* (02) 9838 4373 *Fax:* (02) 9838 7929 *E-mail:* lhills@idx.com.au *Web Site:* www.littlehills.com, pg 30

Little Red Apple Publishing (Australia) *Tel:* (02) 9430 6867 *Fax:* (02) 9440 3771 *E-mail:* littleredapple@hotmail.com, pg 30

Littlehampton Book Services Ltd (United Kingdom) *Tel:* (01903) 828500 *Fax:* (01903) 828625 *E-mail:* rcm@lbsltd.co.uk, pg 1320

The Littman Library of Jewish Civilization (United Kingdom) *Tel:* (01865) 514688 *Fax:* (01865) 514688 *E-mail:* enquiries@littman.co.uk; editorial@littman.co.uk; marketing@littman.co.uk *Web Site:* www.littman.co.uk, pg 708

Liverpool Libraries & Information Services (United Kingdom) *Tel:* (0151) 2255429 *Fax:* (0151) 2335886, pg 1506

Liverpool University Press (United Kingdom) *Tel:* (0151) 794 2233; (0151) 794 2237 *Fax:* (0151) 794 2235 *E-mail:* j.m.smith@liverpool.ac.uk *Web Site:* www.liverpool-unipress.co.uk, pg 708

Living Literary Agency (Italy) *Tel:* (02) 33100584 *Fax:* (02) 33100618 *E-mail:* living@galactica.it, pg 1113

Living Word Distribution (New Zealand) *Tel:* (07) 839 5607 *Fax:* (07) 834 3916 *E-mail:* livingword.ltd@xtra.co.nz, pg 1302

Livraria Apostolado da Imprensa (Portugal) *Tel:* (053) 22485 *Fax:* (053) 615631, pg 526

Livraria Barata, Antonio D M Barata (Portugal) *Tel:* (021) 8481631 *Fax:* (021) 8403344, pg 1307

Livraria Buchholz, Lda (Portugal) *Tel:* (021) 3170580 *Fax:* (021) 3522634 *E-mail:* buchholz@mail.telepac.pt *Web Site:* www.buchholz.pt, pg 1307

Livraria Buecherstube Brooklin Ltda (Brazil) *Tel:* (011) 2403735; (011) 1543-38-29 *Fax:* (011) 2414315, pg 1278

Livraria Caravana (Portugal) *Tel:* (089) 462879 *Fax:* (089) 462871, pg 1307

Livraria Dos Advogados Editora Ltda (Brazil) *Tel:* (011) 3107-3979 *Fax:* (011) 3107-6878 *E-mail:* lael@lael.com.br *Web Site:* www.lael.com.br, pg 86

Livraria Editora Infobook SA (Brazil) *Tel:* (021) 2633807 *Fax:* (021) 2633807, pg 86

Livraria Latina (Portugal) *Tel:* (022) 2001294 *Fax:* (022) 2086053, pg 1307

Livraria Ler, Lda (Portugal) *Tel:* (021) 3888371, pg 1308

Livraria Luzo-Espanhola Lda (Portugal) *Tel:* (021) 3424917, pg 526

Livraria Manuel Ferreira (Portugal) *Tel:* (02) 563237 *E-mail:* manuelferreira@ip.pt, pg 1308

Livraria Minerva Editora (Portugal) *Tel:* (039) 26259 *Fax:* (039) 717267 *E-mail:* livrariaminerva@mail.telepac.pt, pg 526

Livraria Nobel S/A (Brazil) *Tel:* (011) 3933 2822; (011) 3933 2811 *Fax:* (011) 3931 3988 *E-mail:* ednobel@livrarianobel.com.br *Web Site:* www.livrarianobel.com.br, pg 86

Livraria Nobel S/A (Brazil) *Tel:* (011) 3933 2822; (011) 3933 2811 *Fax:* (011) 3931 3988 *E-mail:* ednobel@livrarianobel.com.br, pg 1278

Livraria Teorema 1-Cogitum Livrarias Lda (Portugal) *Tel:* 4304430 *Fax:* 4394909; 4394431 *E-mail:* cogitum@ip.pt, pg 1308

Le Livre de Paris (France) *Tel:* (01) 41 23 60 00 *Fax:* (01) 41 45 34 42 *Web Site:* www.livre-de-paris.com; www.livredeparis.com, pg 173

Le Livre de Poche-L G F (Librairie Generale Francaise) (France) *Tel:* (01) 43923555 *Fax:* (01) 43923590, pg 173

Librairie Livre-Service (Morocco) *Tel:* (037) 724495 *Fax:* (037) 701963, pg 1300

Livres de France (Egypt (Arab Republic of Egypt)) *Tel:* (02) 51512, pg 1282

Les Livres du Dragon d'Or (France) *Tel:* (01) 53 10 36 37 *Fax:* (01) 53 10 36 39 *E-mail:* dragondor@gruend.fr, pg 173

Editora Livros do Brasil Sarl (Portugal) *Tel:* (021) 3426113 *Fax:* (021) 3428487, pg 526

Livros Do Oriente (Macau) *Tel:* 518063 *Fax:* 518064, pg 448

Livros Horizonte Lda (Portugal) *Tel:* (021) 3466917 *Fax:* (021) 326921, pg 526

Oficina de Livros Ltda (Brazil) *Tel:* (031) 2221577 *Fax:* (031) 2244473, pg 86

Univerza Ljubljana (Slovenia) *Tel:* (061) 1254055 *Fax:* (061) 1254053, pg 1497

LK Litho (United States) *Tel:* 631-924-8555 *E-mail:* linickgrp@att.net *Web Site:* www.lgroup.addr.com; www.linickgroup.com, pg 1145

LK Litho (United States) *Tel:* 631-924-3888 *E-mail:* linickgrp@att.net *Web Site:* www.lgroup.addr.com; www.linickgroup.com, pg 1166

LK Litho (United States) *Tel:* 631-924-3888 *E-mail:* linickgrp@att.net *Web Site:* www.lgroup.addr.com/lklitho.htm, pg 1207

LK Litho (United States) *Tel:* 631-924-3888 *E-mail:* linickgrp@att.net *Web Site:* www.lgroup.addr.com; www.linickgroup.com, pg 1216, 1225

LKG (Leipziger Kommissions- und Grossbuchhandelsgesellschaft mbH) (Germany) *Tel:* (034206) 650 *Fax:* (034206) 72361 *E-mail:* lkg.verlagsauslieferung@t-online.de, pg 1284

LLB France (Ligue pour la Lecture de la Bible) (France) *Tel:* (04) 75 56 02 68 *Fax:* (04) 75 56 02 97 *E-mail:* contact@llbfrance.com *Web Site:* www.llbfrance.com, pg 173

Llibres del Segle (Spain) *Tel:* (0972) 795079 *Fax:* (0972) 210354 *E-mail:* costapau@releline.es, pg 580

Chris Lloyd Sales & Marketing Services (United Kingdom) *Tel:* (01202) 649930 *Fax:* (01202) 649950 *E-mail:* chrlloyd@globalnet.co.uk, pg 1320

LLP Ltd (United Kingdom) *Tel:* (020) 7553 1000 *Fax:* (020) 7553 1109 *E-mail:* info@lloydslist.com *Web Site:* www.lloydslist.com, pg 708

Lluvia Editores Srl (Peru) *Tel:* (01) 4320732 *Fax:* (01) 4320732, pg 511

Vincenzo Lo Faro Editore (Italy) *Tel:* (06) 70451187 *Fax:* (06) 70451641, pg 396

Local Consumption Publications (Australia) *Tel:* (02) 9519-7503 *Fax:* (02) 95197503 *E-mail:* s.muecke@hum.uts.edu.au *Web Site:* www.hss.uts.edu.au, pg 30

Editrice la Locusta (Italy) *Tel:* (0444) 324051, pg 396

Lodenek Press (United Kingdom) *Tel:* (01208) 880850, pg 708

Wydawnictwo Lodzkie (Poland) *Tel:* (042) 6360331; (042) 6366189 *Fax:* (042) 6368524, pg 517

Loecker Verlag (Austria) *Tel:* (01) 512 02 82 *Fax:* (01) 512 02 82-22 *E-mail:* lverlag@loecker.at *Web Site:* www.loecker.at, pg 54

Uitgeverij Loempia (Belgium) *Tel:* (03) 2184292, pg 71

Loescher Editore SRL (Italy) *Tel:* (011) 5654111 *Fax:* (011) 5625822 *E-mail:* Loescher@inrete.it, pg 396

Rainer Loessl Verlag (Germany) *Tel:* (089) 362646, pg 258

Loewe Verlag GmbH & Co KG (Germany) *Tel:* (0920) 8510 *Fax:* (0920) 8309 *Web Site:* www.loewe-verlag.de, pg 258

Loffredo Editore Napoli SpA® (Italy) *Tel:* (081) 5937073 *Fax:* (081) 5936953, pg 396

LOG-Internationale Zeitschrift fuer Literatur (Austria) *Tel:* (01) 2313433 *Fax:* (01) 2313433, pg 54

Logans University Bookshop (Pty) Ltd (South Africa) *Tel:* (031) 3076530 *Fax:* (031) 3073230, pg 1310

Logical Products (HK) Ltd (Hong Kong) *Tel:* 8592797 *Fax:* 5598452 *E-mail:* fctmoore@hkuxa.hku.hk, pg 320

Logophon Lehrmittelverlag GmbH (Germany) *Tel:* (06131) 71645 *Fax:* (06131) 72596 *E-mail:* verlag@logophon.de *Web Site:* www.logophon.de, pg 258

Logos (Greece) *Tel:* (01) 3620989 *Fax:* (01) 4834000 *E-mail:* amglogos@otenet.gc, pg 312

Logos Consorcio Editorial SA (Mexico) *Tel:* (05) 5151633, pg 463

Logos (Divine Word) Publications Inc (Philippines) *Tel:* (02) 7111323 *Fax:* (02) 7322736 *E-mail:* dwpsvd@rp1.net, pg 513

Logos Verlag GmbH (Germany) *Tel:* (05232) 960120 *Fax:* (05232) 960121, pg 258

Logos-Verlag Literatur & Layout GmbH (Germany) *Tel:* (06893) 986096 *Fax:* (06893) 986095; (06893) 374443, pg 258

Editora Logosofica (Brazil) *Tel:* (011) 8851476; (011) 8856574 *Fax:* (011) 8879480, pg 86

Loguez Ediciones (Spain) *Tel:* (0923) 138541 *Fax:* (0923) 138586 *E-mail:* loguezediciones@eresmas.com, pg 580

Ulla Lohren Literary Agency (Denmark) *Tel:* 44494515 *Fax:* 44493515, pg 1110

Lohses Forlag (Denmark) *Tel:* 75934455 *Fax:* 75924275 *E-mail:* lohse@imh.dk *Web Site:* www.lohse.dk, pg 133

Lojas Europa-America (Portugal) *Tel:* (01) 9211461 *Fax:* (01) 9217940, pg 1308

Lokrundschau Verlag GmbH (Germany) *Tel:* (04151) 8 28 89 *Fax:* (04151) 8 28 89 *E-mail:* verlag@lokrundschau.de *Web Site:* www.lokrundschau.de, pg 258

Y Lolfa Cyf (United Kingdom) *Tel:* (01970) 832 304 *Fax:* (01970) 832 782 *E-mail:* ylolfa@ylolfa.com *Web Site:* www.ylolfa.com, pg 708

Les Editions du Lombard SA (Belgium) *Tel:* (02) 5266811 *Fax:* (02) 5204405 *E-mail:* info@lombard.be *Web Site:* www.lelombard.com, pg 71

Lomond Books (United Kingdom) *Tel:* (0131) 5512261 *Toll Free Tel:* 800 0286943 (orders only) *Fax:* (0131) 5521703 *E-mail:* sales@lomand-books.co.uk, pg 1320

London Chamber of Commerce & Industry Examinations Board (United Kingdom) *Tel:* (020) 7793 3850 *Fax:* (020) 7582 1806 *Web Site:* www.lccieb.org.uk, pg 709

London Independent Books (United Kingdom) *Tel:* (020) 7706 0486 *Fax:* (020) 7724 3122, pg 1120

Lonely Planet (France) *Tel:* (01) 55 25 33 00 *Fax:* (01) 55 25 33 01 *E-mail:* 100560.415@compuserve.com *Web Site:* www.lonelyplanet.fr, pg 174

Lonely Planet Publications Pty Ltd (Australia) *Tel:* (03) 8379 8000 *Fax:* (03) 8379 8111 *E-mail:* talk2us@lonelyplanet.com.au *Web Site:* www.lonelyplanet.com, pg 30

Lonely Planet, UK (United Kingdom) *Tel:* (020) 7428 4800 *Fax:* (020) 7428 4828 *E-mail:* go@lonelyplanet.co.uk *Web Site:* www.lonelyplanet.com, pg 709

Barry Long Books (Australia), pg 30

Longacre Press (New Zealand) *Tel:* (03) 4772911 *Fax:* (03) 4777222 *E-mail:* longacre.press@clear.net.nz, pg 493

Longanesi & C (Italy) *Tel:* (02) 8692640; (02) 8692144 *Fax:* (02) 72000306 *E-mail:* info@longanesi.it *Web Site:* www.longanesi.it, pg 396

Longman Italia srl (Italy) *Tel:* (02) 67397 6390 *Fax:* (02) 67397 6500 *E-mail:* firstname.lastname@pearsonedema.com, pg 396

Longman Nigeria Plc (Nigeria) *Tel:* (01) 497 89259 *Fax:* (01) 496 4370 *E-mail:* longman@infoweb.abs.net, pg 500

Longman Zimbabwe (Pvt) Ltd (Zimbabwe) *Tel:* (04) 621 661; (04) 621 670 *Fax:* (04) 62716, pg 768

Angelo Longo Editore (Italy) *Tel:* (0544) 217026 *Fax:* (0544) 217554 *E-mail:* longo-ra@linknet.it *Web Site:* www.longo-editore.it, pg 396

La Longue Vue (Belgium) *Tel:* (02) 3582012 *Fax:* (02) 3581737 *E-mail:* longuevue@skynet.be, pg 71

Stefan Loose Verlag (Germany) *Tel:* (030) 6 91 37 89 *Fax:* (030) 6 93 01 71 *E-mail:* info@loose-verlag.de *Web Site:* www.loose-verlag.de, pg 259

Livraria Lopes Da Silva-Editora de M Moreira Soares Rocha Lda (Portugal) *Tel:* (02) 21678 *Fax:* (02) 2006017, pg 527

Lopez Libreros Editores S R L (Argentina) *Tel:* (011) 4963-9646, pg 7

Lorber-Verlag & Turm-Verlag Otto Zluhan (Germany) *Tel:* (07142) 940843 *Fax:* (07142) 940844, pg 259

Lorenz Books (United Kingdom) *Tel:* (020) 7401 2077 *Fax:* (020) 7633 9499 *E-mail:* info@anness.com, pg 709

Carlo Lorenzini Editore (Italy) *Tel:* (0432) 678712 *Fax:* (0432) 678730, pg 397

Lorenzo Editore (Italy) *Tel:* (011) 2485387 *Fax:* (011) 2485387, pg 397

Johannes Loriz Verlag der Kooperative Duernau (Germany) *Tel:* (07582) 93000 *Fax:* (07582) 930020 *E-mail:* kooperative-duernau.rt@eunet.de *Web Site:* www.kooperative.de, pg 259

Editorial Losada SA (Argentina) *Tel:* (011) 4373-4006; (011) 4375-5001 *Fax:* (011) 4373-4006; (011) 4375-5001, pg 7

Thomas C Lothian Pty Ltd (Australia) *Tel:* (03) 9694 4900 *Fax:* (03) 9645 0705 *E-mail:* books@lothian.com.au *Web Site:* www.lothian.com.au, pg 30

Verlag an der Lottbek (Germany) *Tel:* (0241) 873434 *Fax:* (0241) 875577, pg 259

Lotu Pacifika Productions (Fiji) *Tel:* 301314 *Fax:* 301183, pg 141

Editions Loubatieres (France) *Tel:* (05) 61 72 83 53 *Fax:* (05) 61 72 83 50, pg 174

Loughborough University (United Kingdom) *Tel:* (01509) 263171; (01509) 223052 *Fax:* (01509) 223053 *E-mail:* dis@lboro.ac.uk *Web Site:* www.lboro.ac.uk, pg 709

Lowden Publishing Co (Australia) *Tel:* (03) 9873 7202 *Fax:* (03) 9873 0542 *E-mail:* service@theruralstore.com.au *Web Site:* www.theruralstore.com.au, pg 31

Antiquariat Oskar Loewe (Germany) *Tel:* (02361) 960813 *Fax:* (02361) 960815 *E-mail:* loewe.bochum@t-online.de *Web Site:* www.antiquariat.net/loewe, pg 259

Lowfield Printing Co Ltd (United Kingdom) *Tel:* (01322) 522216 *Fax:* (01322) 555362 *E-mail:* lowfield@compuserve.com, pg 1162, 1204

Andrew Lownie Literary Agency (United Kingdom) *Tel:* (020) 7828 1274 *Fax:* (020) 7828 7608 *E-mail:* lownie@globalnet.co.uk *Web Site:* www.andrewlownie.co.uk, pg 1120

Edicoes Loyola SA (Brazil) *Tel:* (011) 69141922 *Fax:* (011) 61634275 *E-mail:* editorial@loyola.com.br *Web Site:* www.loyola.com.br, pg 87

Ediciones LR SA (Argentina) *Tel:* (011) 4326-3725; (011) 4326-3826, pg 7

LTC-Livros Tecnicos e Cientificos Editora S/A (Brazil) *Tel:* (021) 2221-7106 *Fax:* (021) 2252-2732; (021) 2221-5744, pg 87

LTR Editora Ltda (Brazil) *Tel:* (011) 8262788; (011) 663289; (011) 675499 *Fax:* (011) 3667-7172 *E-mail:* livtr@mandic.com.br *Web Site:* www.ltr.com.br/web/home.htm, pg 87

Steve Lu Publishing Ltd (Hong Kong) *Tel:* (02) 5210681 *Fax:* (02) 8450492 *E-mail:* ltlahk@netvigator.com, pg 320

Lua Viajante-Edicao e Distribuicao de Livros e Material Audiovisual, Lda (Portugal) *Tel:* (01) 9376180 *Fax:* (01) 9381452; (01) 9377560 *E-mail:* europress@mail.telepac.pt, pg 527

Luath Press Ltd (United Kingdom) *Tel:* (0131) 225 4326 *Fax:* (0131) 225 4324 *Web Site:* www.luath.co.uk, pg 709

Wydawnictwo Lubelskie (Poland) *Tel:* (081) 7436130, pg 518

Lubrina Editore Srl (Italy) *Tel:* (035) 360782 *Fax:* (035) 241547 *E-mail:* obramas@spm.it, pg 397

Luc vydavatelske druzstvo (Slovakia) *Tel:* (07) 65730331 *Fax:* (07) 65730331, pg 550

Edizioni de Luca SRL (Italy) *Tel:* (06) 32650712 *Fax:* (06) 32650715, pg 397

Lucas, Alexander, Whitley (United Kingdom) *Tel:* (020) 7471 7900 *Fax:* (020) 7471 7910, pg 1120

Lucasville Press (Australia) *Tel:* (03) 93951446, pg 31

Hermann Luchterhand Verlag GmbH (Germany) *Tel:* (02631) 8010 *Fax:* (02631) 801210 *E-mail:* info@luchterhand.de *Web Site:* www.luchterhand.de, pg 259

Luchterhand Literaturverlag GmbH/Verlag Volk & Welt GmbH (Germany) *Tel:* (089) 4372-2751 *Fax:* (089) 21215250 *E-mail:* info@luchterhand.com, pg 259

Ediciones Luciernaga (Spain) *Tel:* (093) 443 71 00 *Fax:* (093) 443 71 30 *E-mail:* correu@grup62.com *Web Site:* www.grup62.com, pg 580

Lucis Press Ltd (United Kingdom) *Tel:* (020) 7839 4512; (020) 7839 4513 *Fax:* (020) 7839 5575 *E-mail:* lucis@lucistrust.org *Web Site:* www.lucistrust.org, pg 709

Lucius & Lucius Verlagsgesellschaft mbH (Germany) *Tel:* (0711) 242060 *Fax:* (0711) 242088 *E-mail:* lucius@luciusverlag.com *Web Site:* www.luciusverlag.com, pg 259

Editora Lucre Comercio e Representacoes (Brazil) *Tel:* (019) 287-8593 *Fax:* (019) 287 8593 *E-mail:* lucre@mute.net.br, pg 87

Ludowa Spoldzielnia Wydawnicza (Poland) *Tel:* (022) 6205718; (022) 6205719 *Fax:* (022) 6207277, pg 518

Gustav Luebbe Verlag (Germany) *Tel:* (02202) 121-0 *Fax:* (02202) 121-920 *E-mail:* info@luebbe.de *Web Site:* www.luebbe.de, pg 259

Verlagsgruppe Luebbe GmbH & Co KG (Germany) *Tel:* (02202) 121-0 *Fax:* (02202) 121-920; (02202) 121-933 *E-mail:* info@luebbe.de; info@bastei.de *Web Site:* www.luebbe.de; www.bastei.de, pg 259

Editorial Luis Vives (Edelvives) (Spain) *Tel:* (091) 334 48 83 *Fax:* (091) 334 48 92; (091) 334 48 94 *E-mail:* jmarketing@edelvives.es *Web Site:* www.edelvives.es, pg 580

Lukas Verlag fur Kunst- und Geistesgeschichte (Germany) *Tel:* (030) 44049220 *Fax:* (030) 4428177 *E-mail:* lukas.verlag@t-online.de *Web Site:* www.lueasverlag.com, pg 259

Josef Lukasik A Spol (Czech Republic) *Tel:* (02) 80 31 05, pg 125

Editorial Lumen SA (Spain) *Tel:* (093) 2043496 *Fax:* (093) 2055619 *E-mail:* mbusquets.plaza@asertel.es, pg 580

Editions Lumen Vitae ASBL (Belgium) *Tel:* (02) 3490399; (02) 3490370 *Fax:* (02) 3490385 *E-mail:* lumen.vitae.editions@euronet.be *Web Site:* www.catho.be/lumen, pg 71

Lumina Publishing House (Republic of Moldova) *Tel:* (02) 246397, pg 468

La Luna (Italy) *Tel:* (091) 301650 *Fax:* (091) 302075, pg 397

Lund Humphries (United Kingdom) *Tel:* (01252) 331551 *Fax:* (01252) 368595 *E-mail:* info@lundhumphries.com *Web Site:* www.lundhumphries.com, pg 709

Lunde Forlag og Bokhandel A/S (Norway) *Tel:* 22007365 *Fax:* 22007373 *E-mail:* lunde@nlm.no, pg 504

Esselte Bokhandel Lundequistska (Sweden) *Tel:* (018) 139830 *Fax:* (018) 695837, pg 1313

Lunds Universitets Bibliotek (Sweden) *Tel:* (046) 222 00 00 *Fax:* (046) 222 36 82 *E-mail:* lub@lub.lu.se *Web Site:* www.lub.lu.se, pg 1500

Lundula Publishing House (Zambia) *Fax:* (01) 26012; (01) 26200, pg 766

Luni (Italy) *Tel:* (02) 796040 *Fax:* (02) 780384, pg 397

Lunwerg Editores, SA (Spain) *Tel:* (091) 5930058 *Fax:* (091) 5930070 *E-mail:* lunwerg.mad@retemail.es, pg 580

Lusaka City Library (Zambia) *Tel:* (01) 227282, pg 1509

Lusatia Verlag-Dr Stuebner & Co KG (Germany) *Tel:* (049) 532400; (049) 532401 *Fax:* (049) 532400 *E-mail:* lusatiaverlag@t-online.de, pg 259

Lusva Editrice (Italy) *Tel:* (02) 4985386, pg 397

Lutchman, Drs LFS (Suriname) *Tel:* 465558; 44/453419, pg 599

Luther Forlag A/S (Norway) *Tel:* 22330608 *Fax:* 22421000 *E-mail:* post@lutherforlag.no, pg 504

Luther-Verlag GmbH (Germany) *Tel:* (0521) 94 40-137 *Fax:* (0521) 94 40-136 *E-mail:* vertrieb@luther-verlag.de *Web Site:* www.ekvw.de/pressehaus/lv/, pg 259

Lutherische Verlagsgesellschaft mbH (Germany) *Tel:* (0431) 51970 *Fax:* (0431) 5197292, pg 259

Lutherisches Verlagshaus GmbH (Germany) *Tel:* (0511) 1241-716 *Fax:* (0511) 1241-705 *E-mail:* lvh@lvh.de *Web Site:* www.lvh.de, pg 260

The Lutterworth Press (United Kingdom) *Tel:* (01223) 350865 *Fax:* (01223) 366951 *E-mail:* publishing@lutterworth.com *Web Site:* www.lutterworth.com, pg 709

Lutyens & Rubinstein (United Kingdom) *Tel:* (020) 7792 4855 *Fax:* (020) 7792 4833 *E-mail:* name@lutyensrubinstein.co.uk, pg 1120

Verlag Waldemar Lutz (Germany) *Tel:* (07621) 8812 *Fax:* (07621) 12599 *E-mail:* wlutz@lutz-die-buchhandlung.de *Web Site:* www.verlag-lutz.de, pg 260

Lux Verbi (Pty) Ltd (South Africa) *Tel:* (021) 4215540 *Fax:* (021) 4191865 *E-mail:* luxverbi.publ@kinglsey.co.za, pg 556

Luxpress VOS (Czech Republic) *Tel:* (02) 203 972 60 *Fax:* (02) 203 972 60 *E-mail:* ibs.czech@iol.cz, pg 126

Sagra-D C Luzzatto Livreiros, Editores e Distribuidores Ltda (Brazil) *Tel:* (0512) 2275222 *Fax:* (0512) 2274438, pg 1278

Lybid (University of Kyyiv Press) (Ukraine) *Tel:* (044) 2291171 *Fax:* (044) 2287272, pg 643

Lybra Immagine (Italy) *Tel:* (02) 48000818 *Fax:* (02) 48012748 *E-mail:* lybra@galactica.it *Web Site:* www.lybra.it, pg 397

Lycabettus Lycabettus Press (Greece) *Tel:* (01) 6471788 *Fax:* (01) 6710666, pg 1286

Lyle Publications Ltd (United Kingdom) *Tel:* (01750) 23355 *Fax:* (01750) 23388 *E-mail:* lyle.publications@talk21.com, pg 709

Lyngs Bokhandel A/S (Norway) *Tel:* 73512544 *Fax:* 73512544, pg 1304

Lynx Edicions (Spain) *Tel:* (093) 594 77 10 *Fax:* (093) 592 09 69 *E-mail:* pruizolalla@hbw.com *Web Site:* www.hbw.com, pg 580

Editions Josette Lyon (France) *Tel:* (01) 40 44 81 60 *Fax:* (01) 45 42 30 99 *E-mail:* editions.josette.lyon@wanadoo.fr *Web Site:* www.editions-josette-lyon.com, pg 174

Editions Lyonnaises d'Art et d'Histoire (France) *Tel:* (04) 78 72 49 00 *Fax:* (04) 78 69 00 48 *E-mail:* editions.lyonnaises@wanadoo.fr *Web Site:* www.perso.wandoo.fr/editions.lyonnaises, pg 174

Lyra Libri SAS (Italy) *Tel:* (031) 279146 *Fax:* (031) 300135, pg 397

Thomas Lyster Ltd (United Kingdom) *Tel:* (01695) 575112 *Fax:* (01695) 570120 *E-mail:* books@tlyster.co.uk *Web Site:* www.tlyster.co.uk, pg 709

M & M Management & Labour Consultants Ltd (Zambia) *Tel:* (01) 217218 *Fax:* (01) 224495, pg 766

M & P Publishing House (Netherlands) *Tel:* (030) 6377736 *Fax:* (030) 6377764; (030) 6377736, pg 480

Maaliyot-Institute for Research Publications (Israel) *Tel:* (02) 5353655 *Fax:* (02) 5353947 *E-mail:* ybm@virtual.co.il, pg 370

Ma'alot Publishing Company Ltd (Israel) *Tel:* (03) 5614121 *Fax:* (03) 5611996 *E-mail:* maalot@tbpai.co.il, pg 370

Dar Al Maaref (Egypt (Arab Republic of Egypt)) *Tel:* (02) 759411; (02) 759552 *Fax:* (02) 5744999, pg 139

Ma'ariv Book Guild (Sifriat Ma'ariv) (Israel) *Tel:* (03) 5333333 *Fax:* (03) 5333619, pg 370, 1229

Maatschappij der Nederlandse Letterkunde (Netherlands) *Tel:* (071) 5144962 *Fax:* (071) 5272836 *E-mail:* mnl@library.leidenuniv.nl, pg 1366

The MAB Cookery Book Club (Iceland) *Tel:* 5643170 *Fax:* 5643190, pg 1229

Mabrochi International Co Ltd (Nigeria) *Tel:* (01) 2662275 *E-mail:* mabrochiadol@yahoo.com, pg 1303

Casa Editrice Maccari (CEM) (Italy) *Tel:* (0521) 771268 *Fax:* (0521) 771268 *E-mail:* maccarieditore@tin.it, pg 397

Ediciones Macchi (Argentina) *Tel:* (011) 4375-1195 *Fax:* (011) 4375-1870; (011) 4374-2506 *E-mail:* info@macchi.com.ar *Web Site:* www.macchi.com, pg 7

Macedonia Prima Publishing House (The Former Yugoslav Republic of Macedonia) *Tel:* (096) 37109 *Fax:* (096) 31478, pg 449

Antonio Machado, SA (Spain) *Tel:* (091) 4681398 *Fax:* (091) 4681098 *E-mail:* editorial@visordis.es *Web Site:* www.visordis.es, pg 580

Machbarot Lesifrut (Israel) *Tel:* (08) 9246565 *Fax:* (08) 9251770 *E-mail:* info@zmora.co.il, pg 370

Friends of Arthur Machen (United Kingdom) *Tel:* (01633) 422520 *Fax:* (0633) 421055 *Web Site:* www.machensoc.demon.co.uk, pg 1371

MacKays of Chatham PLC (United Kingdom) *Tel:* (01634) 864381 *Fax:* (01634) 867742 *E-mail:* mackays@mackayschatham.co.uk, pg 1204

MacLean Dubois Ltd (Writers & Agents) (United Kingdom) *Tel:* (0131) 4455885 *Fax:* (0131) 4455898 *E-mail:* whisteymac@clearut.com, pg 1120

MacLennan & Petty Pty Ltd (Australia) *Tel:* (02) 9349 5811 *Fax:* (02) 9349 5911 *E-mail:* macpetty@zip.com.au *Web Site:* www.maclennanpetty.com.au, pg 31

Macmillan Audio Books (United Kingdom) *Tel:* (020) 7373 6070 *Fax:* (020) 7244 6379, pg 710

Macmillan Boleswa Publishers (Pty) Ltd (Swaziland) *Tel:* 84533 *Fax:* 85247 *E-mail:* macmillan@iafrica.sz *Web Site:* www.macmillansa.co.za; www.macmillan-africa.com, pg 599

Macmillan Children's Books (United Kingdom) *Tel:* (020) 7014 6000 *Fax:* (020) 7014 6001 *Web Site:* www.panmacmillan.com, pg 710

Macmillan Editores SA de CV (Mexico) *Tel:* (05) 482 2200 *Fax:* (05) 482 2202, pg 463

Editorial Macmillan de Mexico SA de CV (Mexico) *Tel:* (05) 482 2200 *Fax:* (05) 482 2202 *Web Site:* www.macmillan.com.mx, pg 463

Macmillan Education (Sierra Leone) *Tel:* (022) 225683 *Fax:* (022) 229186 *E-mail:* macmillan@sierratel.sl *Web Site:* www.macmillan-africa.com, pg 544

Macmillan Education Australia (Australia) *Tel:* (03) 9825 1025 *Fax:* (03) 9825 1010 *E-mail:* mea@macmillan.com.au *Web Site:* www.macmillan.com.au, pg 31

Macmillan Heinemann ELT (Greece) *Tel:* (01) 748 2828 *Fax:* (01) 748 8735 *E-mail:* mhelt@ath.forthnet.gr *Web Site:* www.mhelt.com, pg 313

Macmillan Heinemann ELT (Italy) *Tel:* (055) 649 1289 *Fax:* (055) 649 1501 *E-mail:* mheltinfo@dada.it *Web Site:* www.mhelt.com, pg 397

Macmillan Heinemann ELT (Spain) *Tel:* (091) 517 85 40 *Fax:* (091) 517 85 54 *E-mail:* madrid@mad.heinemann.es *Web Site:* www.heinemann.es, pg 581

Macmillan Heinemann ELT (United Kingdom) *Tel:* (01865) 405700 *Fax:* (01865) 405701 *E-mail:* elt@mhelt.com *Web Site:* www.mhelt.com, pg 710

Macmillan Kenya Publishers Ltd (Kenya) *Tel:* (02) 220 012; (02) 224 485 *Fax:* (02) 212 179 *Web Site:* www.macmillan-africa.com, pg 433

Macmillan Ltd (United Kingdom) *Tel:* (020) 7843 3600 *Fax:* (020) 7843 4640 *E-mail:* books@macmillan.com *Web Site:* www.macmillan.com, pg 710

Macmillan Publishers (China) Ltd (Hong Kong) *Tel:* 2811 8781 *Fax:* 2811 0743 *Web Site:* www.macmillan.com.hk, pg 321

Macmillan Publishers New Zealand Ltd (New Zealand) *Tel:* (09) 414 0350; (09) 414 0356 (customer service); (09) 414 0352 (trade sales) *Fax:* (09) 414 0351 *Web Site:* www.macmillan.co.nz, pg 493

Macmillan Publishers (UK) Ltd (United Kingdom) *Tel:* (020) 7881 8000 *Fax:* (020) 7881 8001 *E-mail:* books@macmillan.com *Web Site:* www.macmillan.com, pg 710

Macmillan Publishers (Zambia) Ltd (Zambia) *Tel:* (01) 223 669 *Fax:* (01) 223 657; (01) 641 018 *E-mail:* macpub@zamnet.zm *Web Site:* www.macmillan-africa.com, pg 766

Macmillan Reference Ltd (United Kingdom) *Tel:* (020) 7881 8000 *Fax:* (020) 7881 8001 *E-mail:* books@macmillan.co.uk *Web Site:* www.macmillan-reference.co.uk, pg 710

The Macquarie Library Pty Ltd (Australia) *Tel:* (02) 98059800 *Fax:* (02) 9888 2984 *E-mail:* alison@dict.mq.edu, pg 31

Macro Edizioni (Italy) *Tel:* (0547) 346290 *Fax:* (0547) 345091 *E-mail:* ordini@macroed12oni.it, pg 397

Macula (France) *Tel:* (01) 45 48 58 70 *Fax:* (01) 45 44 45 89, pg 174

Mad Dog Design Connection Inc (Canada) *Tel:* 416-467-0090 *Fax:* 416-484-1140 *E-mail:* maddogs9@rogers.com, pg 1131

Mad SL Editorial (Spain) *Tel:* (095) 5630820 *Fax:* (095) 5630713 *E-mail:* info@mad.es *Web Site:* www.mad.es, pg 581

Madagascar Print & Press Company (Madagascar) *Tel:* (02) 2222536 *Fax:* (02) 2234534 *E-mail:* roi@dts.mg, pg 450

Madan Puraskar Library (Nepal) *Tel:* (01) 521014 *Fax:* (01) 536390 *E-mail:* kmldxt@wlink.com.np, pg 1486

Karin Mader (Germany) *Tel:* (04208) 556 *Fax:* (04208) 3429 *E-mail:* mader@mader-verlag.de *Web Site:* www.mader-verlag.de, pg 260

Madju FA (Indonesia) *Tel:* (061) 711990; (061) 710430 *Fax:* (061) 717753, pg 356

Madras Editora (Brazil) *Tel:* (011) 6959-1127 *Fax:* (011) 6959-3090 *E-mail:* editor@madras.com.br *Web Site:* www.madras.com.br, pg 87

Madras Literary Society Library (India), pg 1473

Madris (Latvia) *Tel:* 7374000; 7374700 *Fax:* 7374000 *E-mail:* madris@latnet.lv, pg 442

Maeander Verlag GmbH (Germany) *Tel:* (08727) 1657 *Fax:* (08727) 1569, pg 260

Annemarie Maeger (Germany) *Tel:* (040) 8992480 *Fax:* (040) 8904475 *E-mail:* re@a-maeger-verlag.de *Web Site:* www.a-maeger-verlag.de, pg 260

Maeil Gyeongje (Republic of Korea) Tel: (02) 276-0210; (02) 2760211; (02) 2760212; (02) 2760213; (02) 2760214; (02) 2760215 Fax: (02) 271-0463 E-mail: mpd@unitel.co.kv, pg 438

Ediciones Maeva (Spain) Tel: (091) 355 95 69 Fax: (091) 355 19 47 E-mail: maeva@infornet.es Web Site: www.maeva.es, pg 581

Magabala Books Aboriginal Corporation (Australia) Tel: (091) 921991 Fax: (091) 935254 E-mail: info@magabala.com, pg 31

Magari Publishing (New Zealand) Tel: (07) 3770169 Fax: (07) 3773134 E-mail: frontdesk@magari.co.nz Web Site: www.magari.co.nz, pg 493

Magasin du Nord A/S (Denmark) Tel: 33114433, pg 1281

Magdalenen-Verlag GmbH (Germany) Tel: (08024) 5051 Fax: (08024) 7064 E-mail: info@magdalenen-verlag.de Web Site: www.magdalenen-verlag.de, pg 260

Magenta Lithographic Consultants (Singapore) Tel: 2746288, pg 1138

Les Editions Maghrebines, EDIMA (Morocco) Tel: (02) 351797; (02) 353230; (02) 353249 Fax: (02) 355541, pg 470

Magi Publications (United Kingdom) Tel: (020) 7385 6333 Fax: (020) 7385 7333 E-mail: info@littletiger.co.uk Web Site: www.littletigerpress.com, pg 710

Editorial Magisterio Espanol SA (Spain) Tel: (093) 5776653 Fax: (093) 6420086 Web Site: www.editorialcasals.com, pg 581

Magna Large Print Books (United Kingdom) Tel: (01729) 840 225; (01729) 840 526; (01729) 840 251 Fax: (01729) 840 683 Web Site: www.ulverscroft.co.uk, pg 710

Magnard SA (France) Tel: (01) 44088585 Fax: (01) 44084979, pg 174

The Magnes Press (Israel) Tel: (02) 6586656 Fax: (02) 5633370 E-mail: magnes@vms.huji.ac.il, pg 370

Magnum Publishing House Ltd (Poland) Tel: (022) 6460085; (022) 485505 E-mail: magnum@it.com.pl, pg 518

Magnus Verlag (Germany) Tel: (02054) 5080; (02054) 5094; (02327) 292 0 Fax: (02054) 83762, pg 260

Magnus Edizioni SpA (Italy) Tel: (0432) 800081 Fax: (0432) 810071, pg 397

Magpie Books (Australia) Tel: (0613) 9592 9931 Fax: (0613) 9592 2045 E-mail: admin01@magpiebooks.com.au Web Site: www.magpiebooks.com.au, pg 31

Magpie Books (Australia) Tel: (08) 85642309, pg 1273

Magpie Publications (Australia) Tel: 06 2509442, pg 31

Magpies Magazine (Australia) Tel: (07) 3356 4503 Fax: (07) 3356 4649 E-mail: james@magpies.net.au, pg 31

Edicions de la Magrana SA (Spain) Tel: (093) 4173000 Fax: (093) 4170106 E-mail: magrana@essi.es, pg 581

Magveto Koenyvkiado (Hungary) Tel: (01) 1176222 Fax: (01) 1185219, pg 325

Magwe Degree College Library (Myanmar) Tel: (63) 21030, pg 1485

Magyar Iroszoevetseg Koenyvtara (Hungary) Tel: (01) 3228840 Fax: (01) 213419, pg 1126

Magyar Irodalomtoerteneti Tarsasag (Hungary) Tel: (01) 377819 Fax: (01) 3377819, pg 1364

Magyar Iroszoevetseg (Hungary) Tel: (01) 3228840 Fax: (01) 213419, pg 1248

Magyar Kemikusok Egyesulete (Hungary) Tel: (01) 2016883; (01) 2012535 Fax: (01) 2018056 E-mail: mail.mke@mtesz.hu Web Site: www.mtesz.hu, pg 325

Magyar Koenyvkiadok es Koenyvterjesztoek Egyesuelese (Hungary) Tel: (01) 3432540 Fax: (01) 3432541, pg 1248

Magyar Koenyvkiadok es Koenyvterjesztoek Egyesuelese Vereinigung der Ungarischen Buchverlage & Vertriebsunternehmen (Hungary) Tel: (01) 1176222, pg 325

Magyar Koenyvtarosok Egyesuelete (Hungary) Tel: (01) 311 8634 Fax: (01) 311 8634 E-mail: mke@oszk.hu Web Site: www.mke.oszk.hu, pg 1517

Magyar Orszagos Leveltar (MOL) (Hungary) Tel: (01) 3565811 Fax: (01) 2121619 E-mail: mail@natarch.hu Web Site: www.natarch.hu, pg 1472

Magyar Tudomanyos Akademia Irodalomtudomanyi Intezete (Hungary) Tel: (01) 3858790 Fax: (01) 3853876, pg 1364

Magyar Tudomanyos Akademia Koenyvtara (Hungary) Tel: (01) 411 6100 Fax: (01) 311 6954 E-mail: mtak@vax.mtak.hu Web Site: w3.mtak.hu, pg 1472

Mahajan Publishers Private Limited (India) Tel: (079) 6588537 Fax: (079) 6589101 E-mail: mahajan2000@hotmail.com, pg 342

Mahir Marketing Services Sdn Bhd (Malaysia) Tel: (088) 2827372 Fax: (088) 718067, pg 1298

Mahir Publications Sdn Bhd (Malaysia) Tel: (03) 5501826; (03) 5501442; (03) 5501755 Fax: (03) 5501826, pg 452

Karl Mahnke, Dierk Mahnke (Germany) Tel: (04231) 3011-0 Fax: (04231) 3011-11 E-mail: info@mahnke-verlag.de Web Site: www.mahnke-verlag.de, pg 260

Otto Maier Benelux BV (Netherlands) Tel: (049) 0751860 Fax: (049) 075186 1289 E-mail: anja.fahs@ravensburger.de Web Site: www.ravensburger.de, pg 481

Maihof Verlag (Switzerland) Tel: 395170 Fax: 4295367 E-mail: maihofdruck@logon.ch Web Site: www.maihofdruck.ch, pg 618

Giuseppe Maimone Editore (Italy) Tel: (095) 310315 Fax: (095) 310315, pg 397

Mainstream Publishing Co (Edinburgh) Ltd (United Kingdom) Tel: (0131) 557 2959 Fax: (0131) 556 8720 E-mail: mainstream.pub@btinternet.com, pg 711

Mairs Geographischer Verlag (Germany) Tel: (0711) 45020 Fax: (0711) 4502340 E-mail: info@mairs.de Web Site: www.mairs.de, pg 260

Mais Verlag GmbH und Reisefuehrer (Germany) Tel: (06103) 62933 Fax: (06103) 64885, pg 260

La Maison de la Bible (Switzerland) Tel: (021) 867 10 10 Fax: (021) 867 10 15 E-mail: cmd@bible.ch Web Site: www.bible.ch, pg 618

Maison de la Revelation (France) Tel: (05) 56602477 Fax: (05) 56931631, pg 174

Maison des Ecrivains (France) Tel: (01) 49546880 Fax: (01) 42842087 E-mail: courrier@maison-des-ecrivains.asso.fr Web Site: www.maison-des-ecrivains.asso.fr, pg 1363

Maison des Langues Vivantes-Intertaal SA (Belgium) Tel: (02) 5117117 Fax: (02) 5145820, pg 1276

Editions de la Maison des Sciences de l'Homme, Paris (France) Tel: (01) 49 54 20 30; (01) 49 54 20 31 Fax: (01) 49 54 21 33 Web Site: www1.msh-paris.fr, pg 174

La Maison du Dictionnaire (France) Tel: (01) 43 22 12 93 Fax: (01) 43 22 01 77 E-mail: lamaison@artinternet.fr Web Site: www.lmdd.com, pg 174

Maison Tunisienne de l'Edition (Tunisia) Tel: (01) 345333 Fax: (01) 353992, pg 638

Maisonneuve (France) Tel: (03) 34 63 33 80 Fax: (03) 34 65 93 08, pg 174

Editions Maisonneuve (France) Tel: (01) 43 26 86 35 Fax: (01) 43 54 59 54 E-mail: maisonneuve@maisonneuve-adrien.com, pg 174

Editions G P Maisonneuve et Larose (France) Tel: (01) 44414930 Fax: (01) 43257741, pg 174

Makedonska kniga (The Former Yugoslav Republic of Macedonia) Tel: (091) 224055 Fax: (091) 236951, pg 1297

Makedonska kniga (Knigoizdatelstvo) (The Former Yugoslav Republic of Macedonia) Tel: (091) 224055; (091) 231610; (091) 235524 Fax: (091) 236951, pg 449

Makerere University Library (Uganda) Tel: (041) 31041; (041) 31042, pg 1505

Makerere Institute of Social Research Library (Uganda) Tel: (041) 554582 Fax: (041) 532821 E-mail: misrlib@imul.com, pg 1505

Maklu (Belgium) Tel: (03) 231-29-00 Fax: (03) 233-26-59 E-mail: info@maklu.be Web Site: www.maklu.be, pg 71

Makron Books do Brasil Editora Ltda (Brazil) Tel: (011) 829-1518 Fax: (011) 829-4970 E-mail: makron@books.com.br Web Site: www.makron.com.br, pg 87

Makros 2000 - Plovdiv (Bulgaria) Tel: (032) 828391, pg 96

Makumira Lutheran Theological College Library (United Republic of Tanzania), pg 1503

MM Mal og menning (Iceland) Tel: 5152500 Fax: 5152505 E-mail: thorai@mm.is Web Site: www.mm.is, pg 1229

Mal og menning (Iceland) Tel: 522 2000 Fax: 522 2022 E-mail: edda@edda.is Web Site: www.edda.is, pg 328

Bibliotheque Nationale Malagasy (Madagascar) Tel: (02) 25872 Fax: (02) 29448, pg 1482

Biblioteca Comunale Malatestiana (Italy) Tel: (0547) 610892 Fax: (0547) 21237, pg 1477

Malawi National Library Service (Malawi) Tel: 783700, pg 1482

The Malawi Library Association (Malawi) Tel: (050) 522222 Fax: (050) 523225, pg 1520

Malaya Books Suppliers Co (Malaysia) Tel: (03) 7910420, pg 452

Malaya Educational Supplies Sdn Bhd (Malaysia) Tel: (03) 7046628 Fax: (03) 7046629, pg 453

The Malaya Press Sdn Bhd (Malaysia) Tel: (03) 5755890; (03) 5757817 Fax: (03) 5757194, pg 453

Malayan Law Journal Sdn Bhd (Malaysia) Tel: (03) 2162 2822 Fax: (03) 2162 3811 Web Site: www.mlj.com.my, pg 453

Malaysian Book Importers & Distributors Association (Malaysia) Tel: (03) 7193485 Fax: (03) 7181664, pg 1252

Malaysian Book Publishers' Association (Malaysia) Tel: (03) 8292840; (03) 8253485 Fax: (03) 8254515, pg 1252

The Malaysian Current Law Journal Sdn Bhd (Malaysia) Tel: (03) 4081400 Fax: (03) 4081451, pg 453

Societe Malgache d'Edition (Madagascar) Tel: (020) 2222635 Fax: (020) 2222254 E-mail: tribune@bow.dts.mg, pg 450

Societe Malgache d'Edition (Madagascar) Tel: (020) 2222635 Fax: (020) 2222254 E-mail: tribune@bow.dts.mg Web Site: www.madagascar-tribune.com, pg 1137, 1158

Societe Malgache d'Edition (Madagascar) Tel: (020) 2222635 Fax: (020) 2222254 E-mail: tribune@bow.dts.mg; tribune@blanbir.mg Web Site: www.madagascar-tribune.com, pg 1199

Societe Malgache d'Edition (Madagascar) Tel: (020) 2222635 Fax: (020) 2222254 E-mail: tribune@bow.dts.mg Web Site: www.madagascar-tribune.com, pg 1298

Malik Sirajuddin & Sons (Pakistan) *Tel:* (042) 7657527 *Fax:* (042) 7657490 *E-mail:* sirajco@brain.net.pk, pg 507

Malliaris - Pedia (Greece) *Tel:* (031) 278707; (031) 277113 *Fax:* (031) 264856 *E-mail:* info@mailiaris.gr; mailiaris@classic.diavlos.gr *Web Site:* www.malliaris.gr, pg 1286

Mallings ApS (Denmark) *Tel:* 44443233 *Fax:* 44443633 *E-mail:* carlsen@carlsen.dk *Web Site:* www.carlsen.dk, pg 133

Mallinson Rendel Publishers Ltd (New Zealand) *Tel:* (04) 802 5012 *Fax:* (04) 802 5013, pg 493

Mallory International Ltd (United Kingdom) *Tel:* (01404) 815310 *Fax:* (01404) 812245 *E-mail:* sales@malloryint.co.uk *Web Site:* www.malloryint.co.uk, pg 1321

Malmoe Stadsbibliotek (Sweden) *Tel:* (040) 6608500 *Fax:* (040) 6608681 *Web Site:* www2.malmo.stadsbibliotek.org, pg 1500

Editions Maloine (France) *Tel:* (01) 43 25 60 45; (01) 43 29 54 50 *Fax:* (03) 44 23 02 27 *E-mail:* vpc@vigot.fr *Web Site:* www.vigotmaloine.fr, pg 174

Bokabud Mals og menningar (Iceland) *Tel:* 5515199 *Fax:* 5623523 *E-mail:* mm@centrum.is, pg 1288

Malta Library & Information Association (MaLIA) (Malta) *Tel:* (0356) 21322054 *Web Site:* www.malia-malta.org, pg 1520

The Malvern Press Ltd (United Kingdom) *Tel:* (0171) 2492991 *Fax:* (0171) 2541720, pg 1204, 1214

Izdatelstvo Malysh (Russian Federation) *Tel:* (095) 4430654 *Fax:* (095) 4430655, pg 539

MAM (The House of the Cyprus & Cyprological Publications) (Cyprus) *Tel:* (02) 464698; (02) 472744 *Fax:* (02) 465411 *E-mail:* mam@mam.cy.net *Web Site:* www.mam.cy.net, pg 122

MAM (The House of the Cyprus & Cyprological Publications) (Cyprus) *Tel:* (022) 753536 *Fax:* (022) 375802 *E-mail:* mam@mam.cy.net *Web Site:* www.mam.cy.net, pg 1281

Mambo Press (Zimbabwe) *Tel:* (054) 24016; (054) 25807 *Fax:* (054) 21991 *E-mail:* mambo@icon.co.zw, pg 768

Mambo Bookshop (Zimbabwe) *Tel:* (0154) 4016; (0154) 4017 *Fax:* (0154) 51991 *E-mail:* mambo@icon.co.zw, pg 1325

Mamuth Comix Ltd (Greece) *Tel:* (01) 3625055 *Fax:* (01) 3625054 *E-mail:* themask@athena.gr, pg 313

Manadens Bok (Sweden) *Tel:* (08) 6968520 *Fax:* (08) 6968372 *E-mail:* mpocket@manbok.se, pg 1232

Management Books 2000 Ltd (United Kingdom) *Tel:* (01285) 771441 *Fax:* (01285) 771055 *E-mail:* m.b.2000@virgin.net *Web Site:* www.mb2000.com, pg 711

Management Pocketbooks Ltd (United Kingdom) *Tel:* (01962) 735 573 *Fax:* (01962) 733 637 *E-mail:* sales@pocketbook.ca.uk *Web Site:* www.pocketbook.co.uk, pg 711

Manama Central Library (Bahrain) *Tel:* 231105 *Fax:* 274036, pg 1452

Manchester University Press (United Kingdom) *Tel:* (0161) 273 5539 *Fax:* (161) 274 3346 *E-mail:* mup@man.ac.uk *Web Site:* www.manchesteruniversitypress.co.uk, pg 711

Mandala Ediciones (Spain) *Tel:* (091) 5840954 *Fax:* (091) 5480326 *E-mail:* fcabal@lander.es *Web Site:* www.lander.es:800/~fcabal, pg 581

Mandalay University Library (Myanmar) *Tel:* (02) 21211, pg 1486

Mandrake of Oxford (United Kingdom) *Tel:* (01865) 243671 *E-mail:* mandrake@mandrake.uk.net *Web Site:* www.mandrake.uk.net, pg 711

Manesse Verlag GmbH (Switzerland) *Tel:* (01) 2525707; (01) 2525551 *Fax:* (01) 2625347, pg 618

Maney Publishing (United Kingdom) *Tel:* (0113) 249 7481 *Fax:* (0113) 248 6983 *E-mail:* maney@maney.co.uk *Web Site:* www.maney.co.uk, pg 711

Maney Publishing (United Kingdom) *Tel:* (0113) 249 7481 *Fax:* (0113) 248 6983 *E-mail:* maney@maney.co.uk, pg 1162

Manfrini Editori (Italy) *Tel:* (0464) 839111 *Fax:* (0464) 85086, pg 397

Editions Mango (France) *Tel:* (01) 49 70 15 55 *Fax:* (01) 49 70 15 49, pg 174

Mango Publishing (United Kingdom) *Tel:* (020) 7751 2070 *Fax:* (020) 7751 2071 *Web Site:* www.mangopublishing.net, pg 711

Mangold Verlag GmbH (Austria) *Tel:* (0316) 47142419 *Fax:* (0316) 47142440, pg 54

Manhattan Publications (Zimbabwe) *Tel:* (04) 781805 *Fax:* (04) 496292 *E-mail:* nchudy@mweb.co.zw, pg 769

Manholt Verlag (Germany) *Tel:* (0421) 32 35 94 *Fax:* (0421) 3 36 54 63 *E-mail:* manholtverlag@t-online.de *Web Site:* www.manholt.de, pg 260

Manifestolibri (Italy) *Tel:* (06) 5881496 *Fax:* (06) 5882839 *E-mail:* redazione@manifestolibri.it *Web Site:* www.manifestolibri.it, pg 397

Manila City Library (Philippines), pg 1491

Gebr Mann Verlag GmbH & Co (Germany) *Tel:* (030) 25913864; (030) 25913865 *Fax:* (030) 25913537 *E-mail:* vertrieb-kunstverlage@reimer-verlag.de, pg 260

Wolfgang Mann-Verlag GmbH (Germany) *Tel:* (030) 8857210 *Fax:* (030) 89388420, pg 260

Mannerschwarm Skript Verlag Bartholomae & Co OHG (Germany) *Tel:* (040) 4302650 *Fax:* (040) 4302932 *E-mail:* verlag@maennerschwarm.de *Web Site:* www.maennerschwarm.de, pg 260

Manohar Publishers & Distributors (India) *Tel:* (011) 275162 *Fax:* (011) 3265162, pg 342

Editora Manole Ltda (Brazil) *Tel:* (011) 4196-6000 *Fax:* (011) 2872853 *E-mail:* manole@virtual-net.com.br *Web Site:* www.linux.manole.com.br, pg 87

The Mansk Svenska Publishing Co Ltd (United Kingdom) *Tel:* (0162) 4842855 *Fax:* (0162) 844241 *E-mail:* hanneke@advsys.co.uk, pg 711

Manson Publishing Ltd (United Kingdom) *Tel:* (020) 8905 5150 *Fax:* (020) 8201 9233 *E-mail:* manson@man-pub.demon.co.uk *Web Site:* www.manson-publishing.co.uk, pg 711

Editora Mantiqueira de Ciencia e Arte (Brazil) *Tel:* (0122) 621832 *Fax:* (0122) 622126, pg 87

Editora Manuais Tecnicos de Seguros Ltda (Brazil) *Tel:* (011) 8260844 *Fax:* (011) 8250833, pg 87

Biblioteca Manuel Sanguily (Cuba), pg 1459

Manus Verlag (Switzerland) *Tel:* (01) 9202727 *Fax:* (01) 9202740, pg 618

Manutius Verlag (Germany) *Tel:* (06221) 16 32 90 *Fax:* (06221) 16 71 43 *E-mail:* order@manutius-verlag.de *Web Site:* www.manutius-verlag.de, pg 260

Manz G J Verlag und Druckerel (Germany) *Tel:* (0711) 6151790 *Fax:* (0711) 6151791, pg 261

Manz'sche Verlags- und Universitaetsbuchhandlung (Austria) *Tel:* (01) 531 61-0 *Fax:* (01) 531 61-181 *E-mail:* redaktion@manz.co.at *Web Site:* www.manz.at, pg 54

Manz'sche Verlags- und Universitaetsbuchhandlung (Austria) *Tel:* (01) 531 61-0 *Fax:* (01) 531 61-181 *E-mail:* redaktion@manz.co.at, pg 1274

Maori Publications Unit (New Zealand) *Tel:* (07) 3087254 *Fax:* (07) 3085098, pg 493

MAP-Mapping & Publishing Ltd (Israel) *Tel:* (03) 6210500 *Fax:* (03) 5257725 *E-mail:* info@mapa.co.il *Web Site:* www.mapa.co.il, pg 370

Editorial Mapfre SA (Spain) *Tel:* (091) 581 53 57 *Fax:* (091) 581 18 83 *E-mail:* edimap@mapfre.com *Web Site:* www2.mapfre.com, pg 581

Mapin Publishing Pvt Ltd (India) *Tel:* (079) 755-1793; (079) 755-1833 *Fax:* (079) 755-0955 *E-mail:* mapin@icenet.net *Web Site:* www.mapinpub.com, pg 342

MapQuest (United States) *Tel:* 717-285-8500 *Fax:* 717-285-8456 *E-mail:* infodms@mapquest.com *Web Site:* www.oneworldmapping.com, pg 1123

Maqbool Academy (Pakistan) *Tel:* (042) 7233165 *Fax:* (042) 7324164, pg 508

Marabout (Belgium) *Tel:* (04) 246 3863; (04) 4146 3815 *Fax:* (04) 246 3635, pg 72

Maracle Press Ltd (Canada) *Tel:* 905-723-3438 *Fax:* 905-428-6024 *E-mail:* maracle@maraclepress.com *Web Site:* www.maraclepress.com, pg 1131, 1153, 1193

Peter Marcan Publications (United Kingdom) *Tel:* (020) 7357 0368, pg 711

Biblioteca Marcel Roche del Instituto Venezolano de Investigaciones Cientificas (Venezuela) *Tel:* (02) 5041512 *Fax:* (02) 5041423 *E-mail:* xjayaro@ivic.ivic.ve, pg 1508

Marcham Books (United Kingdom) *Tel:* (01235) 848319, pg 711

Marcial Pons Librero (Spain) *Tel:* (091) 3043303 *Fax:* (091) 7541218 *E-mail:* ediciones@marcialpons.es, pg 1311

Marcial Pons Ediciones Juridicas SA (Spain) *Tel:* (091) 304 33 03 *Fax:* (091) 754 12 18 *Web Site:* www.marcialpons.es, pg 581

Editora Marco Zero Ltda (Brazil) *Tel:* (011) 876-2822 *Fax:* (011) 257-2744 *E-mail:* marcozero@mutecnet.com.br, pg 87

Marcombo SA (Spain) *Tel:* (093) 3180079 *Fax:* (093) 3189339 *E-mail:* marcombo.boixareu@marcombo.es, pg 1116

Marcombo SA de Boixareu Editores (Spain) *Tel:* (093) 3180079 *Fax:* (093) 3189339 *E-mail:* marcombo.boixareu@marcombo.es *Web Site:* www.marcombo.es, pg 581

Editions Marcus (France) *Tel:* (01) 45770404 *Fax:* (01) 45759251, pg 174

Mardaga, Pierre 12 (Belgium) *Tel:* (04) 3684242 *Fax:* (04) 3684240, pg 72

Mardev (Australia) *Tel:* (02) 9422 2644 *Fax:* (02) 9422 2633 *E-mail:* mardevlists@reedbusiness.com.au *Web Site:* www.mardevlists.com, pg 1236

Mardev (United Kingdom) *Tel:* (020) 8643 0955 *Fax:* (020) 8652 4580 *E-mail:* mardevlists@rbi.co.uk *Web Site:* www.mardevlists.com, pg 1266

Marfiah, CV (Indonesia) *Tel:* (031) 46023, pg 356

Editorial Marfil SA (Spain) *Tel:* (096) 5523311 *Fax:* (096) 5523496 *E-mail:* editorialmarfil@editorialmerfil.com *Web Site:* www.editorialmarfil.com, pg 581

Marg Publications (India) *Tel:* (022) 2821151 *Fax:* (022) 2047102 *E-mail:* margpub@bom5.vsnl.net.in *Web Site:* www.tata.com/marg, pg 342

Margaret Hamilton Books (Australia) *Tel:* (02) 98162561 *Fax:* (02) 98175144 *Web Site:* www.scholastic.com.au, pg 31

La Marge (France) *Tel:* (04) 95215301 *Fax:* (04) 95215721, pg 174

Margraf Verlag (Germany) *Tel:* (07934) 3071 *Fax:* (07934) 8156 *E-mail:* info@margraf-verlag.de *Web Site:* www.margraf-verlag.de, pg 261

Librairie-Editions J Marguerat (Switzerland) *Tel:* (021) 3237717 *Fax:* (021) 3126732, pg 618

Edition Marhold (Germany) *Tel:* (030) 6917073 *Fax:* (030) 6914067, pg 261

Mariadan (Czech Republic) *Tel:* (02) 41 40 83 91, pg 126

Mariani Ritti Grafiche SRL (Italy) *Tel:* (02) 58310004 *Fax:* (02) 58310408 *E-mail:* ritti@tiw.it, pg 1198

Marican Sdn Bhd (Malaysia) *Tel:* (03) 2981133, pg 1298

Editions Marie-Noelle (France) *Tel:* (03) 81877500; (03) 84812891 *Fax:* (03) 81875669, pg 175

Casa Editrice Marietti SpA (Italy) *Tel:* (010) 6984226 *Fax:* (010) 667092 *E-mail:* marietti1820@split.it, pg 397

Editorial Marin SA (Spain) *Tel:* (093) 8468101 *Fax:* (093) 8468107, pg 581

Aldo Marino Editore (Italy) *Tel:* (095) 438064 *Fax:* (095) 438064, pg 398

Edition Maritim GmbH (Germany) *Tel:* (040) 3396670; (040) 339667-10 *Fax:* (040) 33966777 *E-mail:* edmaritim@aol.com, pg 261

Maritime Books (United Kingdom) *Tel:* (01579) 343663 *Fax:* (01579) 346747 *E-mail:* warshipworld. marbooks@virgin.net *Web Site:* www.navybooks.com, pg 712

Maritime Information Association (United Kingdom) *Tel:* (020) 7261 9535 *Fax:* (020) 7401 2537, pg 1266

Editions Maritimes et d'Outre-Mer SA (France) *Tel:* (04) 91 54 79 40 *Fax:* (04) 91 54 79 49 *E-mail:* webmaster@librairie-outremer.com *Web Site:* www.librairie-outremer.com, pg 175

Biblioteca Mark Twain, Centro Cultural Costarricense-Norteamericano (Costa Rica) *Tel:* 2259433 *Fax:* 2241480 *E-mail:* bncsjcr@sol.racsa.co.cr, pg 1458

Market House Books Ltd (United Kingdom) *Tel:* (01296) 484911 *Fax:* (01296) 437073 *E-mail:* information@mhbref.com *Web Site:* www.mhbref.com, pg 712

Marketasia Distributors (S) Pte Ltd (Singapore) *Tel:* 67448483; 67448486 *Fax:* 67448497 *E-mail:* marketasia@pacific.net.sg *Web Site:* www.marketasia.com.sg, pg 1309

Marketing & Wirtschaft Verlagsges, Flade & Partner mbH (Germany) *Tel:* (089) 2713021; (089) 278134-0 *Fax:* (089) 2710156, pg 261

Marketing Focus (Australia) *Tel:* (08) 92571777 *Fax:* (08) 92571888 *Web Site:* www.marketingfocus.net.au, pg 31

Markono Print Media Pte Ltd (Singapore) *Tel:* 62811118 *Fax:* 62866663 *E-mail:* sales@markono.com.sg, pg 1138, 1159, 1200, 1213, 1222

Maro Verlag und Druck, Benno Kasmayr (Germany) *Tel:* (0821) 416034 *Fax:* (0821) 416036 *E-mail:* maro.augsburg@gmx.de *Web Site:* www.maroverlag.de, pg 261

Tommaso Marotta Editore Srl (Italy) *Tel:* (081) 418881 *Fax:* (081) 418411, pg 398

Ediciones Marova SL (Spain) *Tel:* (091) 5322606 *Fax:* (091) 5322346 *E-mail:* glanzas@infornet.es, pg 581

Marque Publishing (Australia) *Tel:* (02) 9546 5521 *Fax:* (02) 9547 2061 *E-mail:* books@marque.com.au *Web Site:* www.marque.com.au, pg 31

Marrakech Express Inc (United States) *Tel:* 727-942-2218 *Fax:* 727-937-4758 *E-mail:* print@marrak.com *Web Site:* www.marrak.com, pg 1145, 1207, 1225

Marren Publishing House, Inc (Philippines) *Tel:* (02) 3728937; (02) 3728938; (02) 3728939; (02) 3728940; (02) 3728441; (02) 4153116; (02) 4153117; (02) 4153118; (02) 4153119; (02) 7115829 *Fax:* (02) 9286611, pg 513

Mars Business Associates Ltd (United Kingdom) *Tel:* (01367) 252 506 *Fax:* (01367) 252 506 *E-mail:* sales@marspub.co.uk *Web Site:* www.marspub.co.uk, pg 712

The Marsh Agency (United Kingdom) *Tel:* (020) 7399 2800 *Fax:* (020) 7399 2801 *E-mail:* enquiries@marsh-agency.co.uk *Web Site:* www.marsh-agency.co.uk, pg 1120

Tracy Marsh Publications Pty Ltd (Australia) *Tel:* (08) 8355 4716 *Fax:* (08) 8355 4916 *E-mail:* enquires@tracymarsh.com *Web Site:* www.tracymarsh.com, pg 32

Marshall Editions Ltd (United Kingdom) *Tel:* (020) 72948222 *Fax:* (020) 72918233 *Web Site:* www.marshalleditions.com, pg 712

Marsilio Editori SpA (Italy) *Tel:* (041) 2406511 *Fax:* (041) 5238352, pg 398

Marston Book Services Ltd (United Kingdom) *Tel:* (01235) 46550 *Fax:* (01235) 46555, pg 1321

Marston House (United Kingdom) *Tel:* (01935) 851331 *Fax:* (01935) 851372, pg 712

Marsu Productions SAM (Monaco) *Tel:* (093) 92056111 *Fax:* (093) 92057660, pg 469

Martelle (France) *Tel:* (03) 22715454 *Fax:* (03) 22928933, pg 175

Horwitz Martin Education (Australia) *Tel:* (02) 9901 6100 *Fax:* (02) 9901 6155, pg 32

John Martin Press (New Zealand) *Tel:* (09) 6255850 *Fax:* (09) 6255850 *E-mail:* nataliem@ihug.co.nz, pg 493

H F Martinez de Murguia SAC y E (Argentina) *Tel:* (011) 9526173; (011) 9521088, pg 1271

H F Martinez de Murguia SA (Spain) *Tel:* (091) 5227053 *Fax:* (091) 5313786, pg 1311

Ediciones Martinez-Roca SA (Spain) *Tel:* (093) 496 70 12 *Fax:* (093) 496 70 14 *E-mail:* info@ediciones-martinez-roca.es *Web Site:* www.edicionesmartinezroca.com, pg 581

Editions de la Martiniere (France) *Tel:* (01) 40515200 *Fax:* (01) 40515205, pg 175

Martins Printing Group Ltd (United Kingdom) *Tel:* (01483) 757501 *Fax:* (01483) 724629 *E-mail:* chandler@martins-print.co.uk, pg 1162, 1204

Livraria Tavares Martins (Portugal) *Tel:* (022) 23459, pg 527

Marton Aron Kiado Publishing House (Hungary) *Tel:* (01) 368 9584 *Fax:* (01) 367 8415 *E-mail:* olimak@freemail.hu, pg 325

Martynas Mazvydas National Library of Lithuania (Lithuania) *Tel:* 52496044 *Fax:* 52496055 *E-mail:* isbnetu@lnb.lt, pg 446

Martynas Mazvydas National Library of Lithuania (Lietuvos Nacionaline Martyno Mazvydo Biblioteka) (Lithuania) *Tel:* (02) 497023 *Fax:* (02) 496129 *E-mail:* biblio@lnb.lt *Web Site:* www.lnb.lt, pg 1482

Maruzen Asia (Pte) Ltd (Singapore) *Tel:* 7751577, pg 547

Maruzen Co Ltd (Japan) *Tel:* (03) 32720514 *Fax:* (03) 32740579 *Web Site:* www.maruzen.co.jp, pg 421

Maruzen Co Ltd (Japan) *Tel:* (03) 3275-8582 *Fax:* (03) 3275-9072, pg 1294

Marval (France) *Tel:* (01) 43 25 33 33 *Fax:* (01) 43 25 88 88 *E-mail:* info@marval.com *Web Site:* www.marval.com, pg 175

Blanche Marvin Agency (United Kingdom) *Tel:* (020) 7722 2313 *Fax:* (020) 7722 2313, pg 1120

Institut fuer Marxistische Studien und Forschungen eV (IMSF) (Germany) *Tel:* (069) 7392934, pg 261

Marymar Ediciones SA (Argentina) *Tel:* (011) 4988-0200, pg 7

Marzorati Editore SRL (Italy) *Tel:* (02) 8546146 *Fax:* (02) 8411225, pg 398

Masagung Books Pte Ltd (Singapore) *Tel:* 4683276 *Fax:* 345000, pg 547

Masagung Books Pte Ltd (Singapore) *Tel:* 4683276, pg 1309

La Mascara, SL Editorial (Spain) *Tel:* (096) 3486500 *Fax:* (096) 3487440, pg 581

Maskew Miller Longman (Botswana) *Tel:* 322969 *Fax:* 322682 *E-mail:* firstname@longman.info.bw, pg 77

Maskew Miller Longman (South Africa) *Tel:* (021) 531 7750 *Fax:* (021) 531 4877 *E-mail:* firstname@mml.co.za, pg 557

Maskew Miller Longman (South Africa) *Tel:* (021) 531 7750 *Fax:* (021) 5314049 *E-mail:* firstname@mml.co.za, pg 1310

Veselin Maslesa (Bosnia and Herzegovina) *Tel:* (071) 214633; (071) 218636 *Fax:* (071) 41154, pg 77

Veselin Maslesa (Bosnia and Herzegovina) *Tel:* (071) 214633, pg 1277

Masmedia (Croatia) *Tel:* (01) 45.77.400 *Fax:* (01) 45.77.769 *E-mail:* masmedia@zg.tel.hr *Web Site:* www.masmedia.hr, pg 119

Kenneth Mason Publications Ltd (United Kingdom) *Tel:* (01243) 377977; (01243) 377978 *Fax:* (01243) 379136 *E-mail:* boatswain@dial.pipex.com, pg 712

Mason's Book Centre (Australia) *Tel:* (03) 93383044 *Fax:* (03) 93382225, pg 1273

Masons Design & Print (United Kingdom) *Tel:* (01244) 674433 *Fax:* (01244) 674274 *E-mail:* 100612.3105@compuserve.com, pg 1141

Massada Press Ltd (Israel) *Tel:* (02) 6719441, pg 370

Massada Publishers Ltd (Israel) *Tel:* (03) 5716659 *Fax:* (03) 5716639, pg 370

Editrice Massimo SAS di Crespi Cesare e C (Italy) *Tel:* (02) 55210800; (02) 55211220 *Fax:* (02) 55211315, pg 398

Editions Charles Massin et Cie (France) *Tel:* (01) 45 65 48 48 *Fax:* (01) 45 65 47 00 *E-mail:* info@massin.fr *Web Site:* www.massin.fr, pg 175

Masson Editores (Mexico) *Tel:* (05) 6870933, pg 463

Masson SA (France) *Tel:* (01) 40 46 60 00 *Fax:* (01) 40 46 60 01 *E-mail:* infos@masson.fr *Web Site:* www.masson.fr; www.e2med.com, pg 175

Masson SpA (Italy) *Tel:* (02) 270741 *Fax:* (02) 27074510 *E-mail:* info@masson.it, pg 398

Masson-Williams et Wilkins (France) *Tel:* (01) 40466000 *Fax:* (01) 40466126 *E-mail:* pradel@lsicom.fr, pg 175

MAST Verlag (Romania) *Tel:* (01) 7786950 *Fax:* (01) 4104588, pg 534

Izdatelstvo Mastatskaya Litaratura (Belarus) *Tel:* (0172) 234809 *Fax:* (0172) 269112; (0172) 238363, pg 63

Master Flo Technology Inc (Canada) *Tel:* 613-636-0539 *Fax:* 613-636-0762 *E-mail:* info@mflo.com *Web Site:* www.mflo.com, pg 1221

Matar - Triwacks Enterprises (Israel) *Tel:* (03) 5463433 *Fax:* (03) 5461679, pg 370

MATEX (Bulgaria) *Tel:* (02) 430177 *E-mail:* mmk_fte@uacg.acad.bg, pg 96

Sri Ramakrishna Math (India) *Tel:* (044) 4941231; (044) 4941959 *Fax:* (044) 4934589 *E-mail:* srkmath@giasmd01.vsnl.net.in, pg 342

Matica hrvatska (Croatia) *Tel:* (01) 4819-310; (01) 4819-325; (01) 4819-313; (01) 4819-321 *Fax:* (01) 4819-319 *E-mail:* matica@matica.hr *Web Site:* www.matica.hr, pg 119

Matice moravska (Czech Republic) *Tel:* (05) 750050 *Fax:* (05) 753050, pg 1361

Biblioteka Matice Srpske (Yugoslavia) *Tel:* (021) 420199 *Fax:* (021) 28574 *E-mail:* bms@bms.nsac.yu, pg 1508

Matrice (France) *Tel:* (01) 69 42 13 02 *Fax:* (01) 69 40 21 57, pg 175

Mats Publishers Ltd (Estonia) *Tel:* (O2) 6563589, pg 140

Mattes Verlag GmbH (Germany) *Tel:* (06221) 459321 *Fax:* (06221) 459322 *E-mail:* mattes@mattes.de *Web Site:* www.mattes.de, pg 261

Hugo Matthaes Druckerei und Verlag GmbH & Co KG (Germany) *Tel:* (0711) 21 33 2 00 *Fax:* (0711) 2133 4 44 *Web Site:* www.matthaesdruck.de, pg 261

Matthes und Seitz Verlag GmbH (Germany) *Tel:* (089) 1232510 *Fax:* (089) 187534, pg 261

Adam Matthew Publications (United Kingdom) *Tel:* (01672) 511921 *Fax:* (01672) 511663 *Web Site:* www.adam-matthew-publications.co.uk, pg 712

Matthias-Gruenewald-Verlag GmbH (Germany) *Tel:* (06131) 92860 *Fax:* (06131) 928626 *E-mail:* mail@gruenewaldverlag.de *Web Site:* members.aol.com/matthgruen/, pg 261

Matthias Media (Australia) *Tel:* (02) 3100813; (02) 9663-1478 (overseas) *Toll Free Tel:* 800 814 360 *Fax:* (02) 9663-3265; (02) 9663-3265 *E-mail:* info@matthiasmedia.com.au *Web Site:* www.matthiasmedia.com.au, pg 32

Matthiesen Verlag Ingwert Paulsen Jr (Germany) *Tel:* (04841) 83520 *Fax:* (04841) 835210 *E-mail:* info@verlagsgruppe.de *Web Site:* www.verlagsgruppe.de, pg 261

Hans K Matussek Buchhandlung & Antiquariat (Germany) *Tel:* (02153) 91 64 30 *Fax:* (02153) 1 33 63 *Web Site:* www.buchkatalog.de/matussek, pg 261

Les Editions la Matze (Switzerland) *Tel:* (027) 3231652 *Fax:* (027) 3231652, pg 618

Matzker Verlag DiA (Germany) *Tel:* (030) 80604797, pg 261

Verlag Wilhelm Maudrich (Austria) *Tel:* (01) 4024712 *Fax:* (01) 4085080 *E-mail:* medbook@maudrich.com *Web Site:* www.maudrich.com, pg 54

C Maurer Druck und Verlag (Germany) *Tel:* (07331) 9300 *Fax:* (07331) 930190, pg 1154

C Maurer Druck und Verlag (Germany) *Tel:* (07331) 9300 *Fax:* (07331) 930190 *Web Site:* www.maurer.oupiuke.de, pg 1195

Mauritius Archives (Mauritius) *Tel:* 088469, pg 1484

Mauritius Institute Public Library (Mauritius) *Tel:* 2120639 *Fax:* 2125717, pg 1484

Mauritius Library Association (Mauritius) *Tel:* 4549550; 4549551; 4549552 *Fax:* 4549553 *E-mail:* bcouncil@intnet.mu *Web Site:* www.britishcouncil.org/mauritius/, pg 1520

Mavisu International Co Ltd (Thailand) *Tel:* (02) 2711148 *Fax:* (02) 2711168, pg 1201

Mavrogianni Publications (Greece) *Tel:* (01) 3304628 *Fax:* (01) 3838228, pg 313

Mavrogianni Publications (Greece) *Tel:* (01) 3304628 *Fax:* (01) 3304628, pg 1286

Mawaddah Enterprise Sdn Bhd (Malaysia) *Tel:* (06) 711062; (06) 722062 *Fax:* (06) 733062 *E-mail:* azhari@mawadah.pc.my, pg 1298

Max Schimmel Verlag (Germany) *Tel:* (0931) 27 91 400 *Fax:* (0931) 27 91 444 *E-mail:* info@schimmelverlag.de *Web Site:* www.schimmelverlag.de, pg 261

Maxdorf Ltd (Czech Republic) *Tel:* (02) 4171 0243; (02) 4171 0244 *Fax:* (02) 4171 0245 *E-mail:* maxdorf@maxdorf.cz *Web Site:* www.maxdorf.cz, pg 126

Maxima Laurent du Mesnil Editeur (France) *Tel:* (01) 44397400 *Fax:* (01) 45484688 *Web Site:* www.maxima.fr, pg 175

Maximilian-Gesellschaft eV (Germany) *Tel:* (0711) 5499711 *Fax:* (0711) 54997121 *E-mail:* hiersemann.hauswedell.verlage@t-online.de *Web Site:* www.maximilian-gesellschaft.de, pg 1364

Maxwell Macmillan Publishing (Australia) Pty Ltd (Australia) *Tel:* (03) 9825 1000 *Fax:* (03) 9825 1010 *Web Site:* www.macmillan.co.uk, pg 32

Maya Publishers Pvt Ltd (India) *Tel:* (011) 6490959; (011) 6494850 *Fax:* (011) 6491039 *E-mail:* surit@del2.vsnl.net.in, pg 342

Ludwig Mayer Jerusalem Ltd (Israel) *Tel:* (02) 6252628 *Fax:* (02) 6232640 *E-mail:* mayerbks@netvision.net.il *Web Site:* www.mayer-books.co.il, pg 1292

J A Mayersche Buchhandlung GmbH & Co KG Abt Verlag (Germany) *Tel:* (0241) 47770 *Fax:* (0241) 4777167 *E-mail:* info@mayersche.de, pg 1284

J A Mayersche Buchhandlung GmbH & Co KG Abt Verlag (Germany) *Tel:* (0241) 4777 499 *Fax:* (0241) 4777 467 *E-mail:* info@mayersche.de *Web Site:* www.mayersche.de, pg 261

Mayibuye Books (South Africa) *Tel:* (021) 9592529 *Fax:* (021) 9593411 *E-mail:* mayibuye@mweb.co.za, pg 557

Mayne Publishing (Australia) *Tel:* (076) 973558, pg 32

Mayr Miesbach Druckerei und Verlag GmbH (Germany) *Tel:* (08025) 294-0 *Fax:* (08025) 294-235 *E-mail:* gl@mayrmiesbach.de *Web Site:* www.mayrmiesbach.de, pg 262

Bibliotheque Mazarine (France) *Tel:* (01) 44414406 *Fax:* (01) 44414407, pg 1465

Mazenod Book Centre (Lesotho) *Tel:* 350224, pg 444, 1297

Mazer Publishing Services (United States) *Tel:* 937-264-2600 *Fax:* 937-264-2624 *E-mail:* info@mazer.com *Web Site:* www.mazer.com, pg 1145, 1166, 1208, 1216, 1225

Edizioni Gabriele Mazzotta SRL (Italy) *Tel:* (02) 8055803 *Fax:* (02) 8693046, pg 398

MBA Literary Agents Ltd (United Kingdom) *Tel:* (020) 7387 2076 *Fax:* (020) 7387 2042 *E-mail:* agent@mbalit.co.uk, pg 1120

MBEU Christian Bookshop (South Africa) *Tel:* (015) 58147 *Fax:* (015) 932258, pg 1310

MBMS-Bibliography and Management Service (Germany) *Tel:* (02733) 7657 *Fax:* (02733) 8492 *E-mail:* iurlea@wolnet.de, pg 1111

MCB University Press Ltd (United Kingdom) *Tel:* (01274) 777700 *Fax:* (01274) 785201 *E-mail:* info@emeraldinsight.com; help@emeraldinsight.com (academic sales); editorial@emeraldinsight.com (editorial) *Web Site:* www.mcb.co.uk, pg 712

Yvonne McBurney (Australia) *Tel:* (02) 7467962, pg 32

McCrimmon Publishing Co Ltd (United Kingdom) *Tel:* (01702) 218956 *Fax:* (01702) 216082 *E-mail:* sales@mccrimmons.com (Sales); orders@mccrimmons.com (Orders); perms@mccrimmons.com (Permission-related inquiries); clipart@mccrimmons.com (Clip Art) *Web Site:* www.mccrimmons.com, pg 712

McDonald-Kirkwood Pty Ltd (Australia) *Tel:* (08) 8221 6111 *Fax:* (08) 8221 6211, pg 32

McGraw-Hill Australia Pty Ltd (Australia) *Tel:* (02) 9415 9899 *Fax:* (02) 9417 8872 *E-mail:* cservice_sydney@mcgraw-hill.com.au *Web Site:* www.mcgraw-hill.com.au, pg 32

McGraw-Hill Book NZ (New Zealand) *Tel:* (09) 2622537 *Fax:* (09) 2622540, pg 493

McGraw-Hill Editora de Portugal (Portugal) *Tel:* (021) 4718964; (021) 14728500 *Fax:* (021) 14718981, pg 527

McGraw-Hill Interamericana de Mexico, SA de CV (Mexico) *Tel:* (05) 5767304; (05) 5769044 ext 156; 5413155 al 59 (Mexico City) *Fax:* (05) 6285367 *E-mail:* mcgraw-hill@infosel.net.mx *Web Site:* www.mcgraw-hill.com.mx, pg 463

McGraw-Hill/Interamericana de Venezuela CA (Venezuela) *Tel:* (02) 2383494; (02) 7618181; (02) 7616992 *Fax:* (02) 2382374; (02) 7616993 *E-mail:* mikan@attmail.com, pg 762

McGraw-Hill InterAmericana SA (Colombia) *Tel:* (01) 3682700 *Fax:* (01) 3687484; (01) 3686460, pg 113

McGraw-Hill Intermericana del Caribe, Inc (Puerto Rico) *Tel:* (787) 751-2451 *Fax:* (787) 764-1890 *E-mail:* c-davila@spiderlink.net, pg 530

McGraw-Hill Libri Italia Srl (Italy) *Tel:* (02) 701601 *Fax:* (02) 733643, pg 398

McGraw-Hill Publishing Company (United Kingdom) *Tel:* (01628) 502500 *Fax:* (01628) 635895, pg 712

McGraw-Hill Iberic/Brazil Group (Spain) *Tel:* (01) 3728193; (01) 3728409 (customer service) *Fax:* (01) 3728513 *Web Site:* www.mcgraw-hill.es, pg 581

J M McGregor Pty Ltd (Australia) *Tel:* (02) 91351923, pg 32

McGregor Publishers (Namibia) *Tel:* (061) 62155 *Fax:* (061) 63059 *E-mail:* gmcgregor@unam.na, pg 471

John McIndoe Ltd (New Zealand) *Tel:* (03) 4770355 *Fax:* (03) 4771982 *E-mail:* jmcindoe@earthlight.co.nz, pg 1137, 1158, 1199, 1213, 1222

McLaren Morris & Todd Ltd (Canada) *Tel:* 905-677-3592 *Fax:* 905-677-3675 *Web Site:* www.mmt.ca, pg 1131, 1193, 1211

McLeods Booksellers (New Zealand) *Tel:* (07) 3485388 *Fax:* (07) 3490288 *E-mail:* mcleods@clear.net.nz *Web Site:* www.mcleodsbooks.co.nz, pg 1302

McMillan Memorial Library (Kenya) *Tel:* (02) 21844, pg 1480

McRae Books (Italy) *Tel:* (055) 264384 *Fax:* (055) 212573, pg 398

MDC Publishers Printers (Malaysia) *Tel:* (03) 4086600 *Fax:* (03) 4081506 *E-mail:* mdcpp@2mws.com.my *Web Site:* www.2mws.com.my/mdc, pg 453

Editions MDI (La Maison des Instituteurs) (France) *Tel:* (01) 45 87 58 20 *Fax:* (01) 43 31 39 60 *E-mail:* serviceclient@mdi-editions.com *Web Site:* www.mdi-editions.com, pg 175

ME Editores, SL (Spain) *Tel:* (091) 3151008 *Fax:* (091) 3230844, pg 582

Meander Uitgeverij BV (Netherlands) *Tel:* (071) 5601040 *Fax:* (071) 5619741 *E-mail:* info@vierwindstreken.com *Web Site:* www.vierwindstreken.com, pg 481

Meandre (Switzerland) *Tel:* (026) 322174 *Fax:* (026) 323287, pg 618

Editora Meca Ltda (Brazil) *Tel:* (011) 2599049; (011) 2599034; (011) 2575346 *Fax:* (011) 2570312, pg 87

Landesbibliothek Mecklenburg-Vorpommern (Germany) *Tel:* (0385) 558440 *Fax:* (0385) 5584424 *E-mail:* lb@lbmv.de *Web Site:* www.lbmv.de, pg 1468

Mecron Sdn Bhd (Malaysia) *Tel:* (03) 6269326 *Fax:* (03) 6219869, pg 453

Med Info Publishing Co (Hong Kong) *Tel:* (02) 5222713, pg 321

Medcom Ltd (Israel) *Tel:* (03) 9342852; (03) 9342853 *Fax:* (03) 9343850, pg 370

Bibliotheque Interuniversitaire de Medecine (France) *Tel:* (01) 40461616 *Fax:* (01) 44411020, pg 1465

Faculte de Medecine de Pharmuacie et d'Odonto-Stomatologie (Mali) *Tel:* 225277 *Fax:* 228109; 229658 *E-mail:* diawara@mrtcbko.malinet.ml, pg 1483

Medecine et Hygiene (Switzerland) *Tel:* (022) 7029311 *Fax:* (022) 7029355 *E-mail:* direction@medecinehygiene.dr, pg 619

Stichting Evangelische Uitgeverij H Medema (Netherlands) *Tel:* (0578) 574995 *Fax:* (0578) 573099 *E-mail:* medema@pi.net, pg 481

Media Centre (Malta) *Tel:* 249005; 223047; 247460; 224018; 220538; 244913 *Fax:* 243508, pg 456

Media East Press (Australia) *Tel:* (02) 9349-6683 *Fax:* (02) 9349-6683, pg 33

Media House Publications (South Africa) *Tel:* (011) 8826237 *Fax:* (011) 8829652, pg 557

Media House Publications Pty Ltd (South Africa) *Tel:* (011) 8826237 *Fax:* (011) 8829652, pg 1310

Media Institute of Southern Africa (MISA) (Namibia) *Tel:* (061) 32975 *Fax:* (061) 248016 *E-mail:* dush@ingrid.misa.org.na, pg 471

Media-Print Informationstechnologie GmbH (Germany) *Tel:* (05251) 522300 *Fax:* (05251) 522480 *E-mail:* contact@mediaprint.de *Web Site:* www.mediaprint.de, pg 1133, 1154, 1195

Media Research Publishing Ltd (United Kingdom) *Tel:* (01934) 644 309 *Fax:* (01934) 644 402, pg 712

Mediabank (Republic of Korea) *Tel:* (02) 7420425 *Fax:* (02) 7452174 *Web Site:* mediabank.pe.kr, pg 1114

Editions Medianes (France) *Tel:* (02) 35 88 85 71 *Fax:* (02) 35 15 28 44 *E-mail:* medianesconseil@wanadoo.fr, pg 175

Mediapress GmbH (Germany) *Tel:* (02151) 79553334, pg 262

Editions Mediaspaul (France) *Tel:* (01) 64 90 88 07, pg 175

Mediatheque de Saint Pierre (Reunion) *Tel:* 96 71 91 *Fax:* 25 74 10 *Web Site:* www.mediatheque-saintpierre.fr, pg 1494

Medica Paris Libreria (Venezuela) *Tel:* (02) 7816044; (02) 7821464; (02) 78190452709; (02) 727425 *Fax:* (02) 7931753, pg 1324

Editorial Medica JIMS, SL (Spain) *Tel:* (093) 2188800 *Fax:* (093) 2188928, pg 582

Editorial Medica Panamericana (Argentina) *Tel:* (091) 4570203 *Fax:* (091) 4570919 *E-mail:* edmedpan@emp.es *Web Site:* www.medicapanamericana.com, pg 7

Editorial Medica, Panamericana SA (Argentina) *Tel:* (011) 4821-5520; (011) 4821-0175 *Fax:* (011) 4821-1214 *E-mail:* postmaster@edmedpan.satlink.net, pg 7

Medical Sciences International Ltd (Japan) *Tel:* (03) 5804-6051 *Fax:* (03) 5804-6055, pg 421

Medical Writers Group (United Kingdom) *Tel:* (020) 7373 6642 *Fax:* (020) 7373 5768 *E-mail:* info@societyofauthors.org *Web Site:* www.societyofauthors.org, pg 1371

Editura Medicala (Romania) *Tel:* (01) 25 25 186 *Fax:* (01) 25 25 189 *E-mail:* edmedicala@fx.ro *Web Site:* www.edmedicala.ro, pg 534

Editions Medicales et Paramedicales de Charleroi (EMPC) (Belgium) *Tel:* (071) 324689 *Fax:* (071) 324689, pg 72

Ediciones Medicas SA (Argentina) *Tel:* (011) 4384-0750 *Fax:* (011) 4384-0750 *E-mail:* emsa@havasmedimedia.com.ar, pg 7

Edizioni Medicea SRL (Italy) *Tel:* (055) 363057 *Fax:* (055) 333862, pg 398

Ediciones Medici SA (Spain) *Tel:* (093) 2 010 599; (093) 2 013 807; (093) 2 012 144 *Fax:* (093) 2 097 362 *E-mail:* omega@ediciones-omega.es *Web Site:* www.ediciones-medici.es; www.ediciones-omega.es, pg 582

The Medici Society Ltd (United Kingdom) *Tel:* (020) 8205 2500 *Fax:* (020) 8205 2552 *E-mail:* export@medici.co.uk *Web Site:* www.medici.co.uk, pg 713

AS Medicina (Estonia) *Tel:* (02) 42 1474 *Fax:* (02) 42 5098, pg 140

Medicina i Fizkultura EOOD (Bulgaria) *Tel:* (02) 871308; (02) 884068 *Fax:* (02) 897165, pg 96

Izdatelstvo Medicina (Russian Federation) *Tel:* (095) 9248785 *Fax:* (095) 9286003, pg 539

Medicina Koenyvkiado (Hungary) *Tel:* (01) 1122650 *Fax:* (01) 1122450, pg 325

Medicina Panamericana Editora Do Brasil Ltda (Brazil) *Tel:* (011) 222-0366 *Fax:* (011) 222-0542, pg 87

Bibliothecarii Medicinae Fenniae (Finland) *Tel:* (09) 19126645 *Fax:* (09) 19126652, pg 1515

Medico International eV (Germany) *Tel:* (069) 94438-0 *Fax:* (069) 436002 *E-mail:* info@medico.de *Web Site:* www.medico.de, pg 262

Medien & Recht (Austria) *Tel:* (01) 5052766 *Fax:* (01) 5052766-15 *E-mail:* verlag@medien-recht.ccom *Web Site:* www.medien-recht.com, pg 55

Medien-Verlag Bernhard Gregor GmbH (Germany) *Tel:* (06625) 5011; (0171) 7723972 *Fax:* (06625) 919743 *E-mail:* gregor-medien@t-online.de; mail@gregor-medien.de *Web Site:* www.gregor-medien.de, pg 262

Medienbuero Muenchen (Germany) *Tel:* (089) 299975 *Fax:* (089) 299975 *E-mail:* info@philosophiaverlag.com *Web Site:* www.philosophiaverlag.com, pg 1111

Medios Publicitarios Mexicanos SA de CV Editora de Directorios de Medios (Mexico) *Tel:* (05) 5742858 *Fax:* (05) 5742668 *E-mail:* mpmdirec@data.net.mx, pg 464

Medios y Medios, Sa de CV (Mexico) *Tel:* (05) 56-01-85-11 *Fax:* (05) 56-88-59-85 *E-mail:* mass+medios@fc.camoapa.com.mx, pg 464

Medis, Skopje (The Former Yugoslav Republic of Macedonia) *Tel:* (091) 118-104 *Fax:* (091) 272-253 *E-mail:* medis@informa.mk *Web Site:* www.medis.com.mk, pg 449

Mediserve SRL (Italy) *Tel:* (081) 5452717 *Fax:* (081) 5462026, pg 398

Editorial Mediterrania SL (Spain) *Tel:* (093) 218 34 58; (093) 237 86 65 *Fax:* (093) 237 22 10, pg 582

Medium-Buchmarkt (Germany) *Tel:* (0251) 46 000 *Fax:* (0251) 46 745 *E-mail:* info@mediumbooks.com *Web Site:* www.mediumbooks.com, pg 262

Medizinisch-Literarische Verlagsgesellschaft mbH (Germany) *Tel:* (0581) 808-150 *Fax:* (0581) 808-158 *E-mail:* ml.verlag.uelzen@t-online.de *Web Site:* www.mlverlag.de, pg 262

Medpharm Scientific Publishers (Germany) *Tel:* (0711) 2582-0 *Fax:* (0711) 2582-290 *E-mail:* service@medpharm.de *Web Site:* www.dav-buchhandlung.de, pg 262

Medsi - Editora Medica e Cientifica Ltda (Brazil) *Tel:* (021) 5694342 *Fax:* (021) 2646392, pg 87

Medusa/Selas (Greece) *Tel:* (01) 3608088; (01) 3608168 *Fax:* (01) 3808970 *E-mail:* medusa@otenet.gr, pg 313

Wydawnictwo Medyczne Urban & Partner (Poland) *Tel:* (071) 3285487; (071) 223061; (071) 223068; (071) 223069; (071) 223065; (071) 3283068 *Fax:* (071) 3284391, pg 518

Meerut Publishers' Association (India) *Tel:* (0121) 510688; (0121) 516080 *Fax:* (0121) 512545, pg 1248

Willem A Meeuws Publisher (United Kingdom) *Tel:* (01865) 242939 *Fax:* (01865) 204021 *E-mail:* thorntons@booknews.demon.co.uk *Web Site:* www.thorntonsbooks.co.uk, pg 713

Megatrade AG (Liechtenstein) *Tel:* (075) 279976 *Fax:* (075) 20064 *E-mail:* wanger@wanger.net *Web Site:* www.wanger.net, pg 445

Mehanograf (Croatia) *Tel:* (01) 2408567 *Fax:* (01) 2408563, pg 1132

Mehta Publishers (India) *Fax:* (011) 5700644 *E-mail:* mopl@vsnl.com, pg 342

Mei Ka Printing & Publish Enterprise Ltd (Hong Kong) *Tel:* 25401131 *Fax:* 25598718, pg 1135, 1156, 1212

Mei Ya Publications Inc (Sueling Inc) (Taiwan, Province of China) *Tel:* (02) 7037481 *Fax:* (02) 7033847, pg 1314

Meiji Shoin Co Ltd (Japan) *Tel:* (03) 32923741 *Fax:* (03) 32924429, pg 421

Buchhandlung Meili & Co (Switzerland) *Tel:* (053) 254144 *Fax:* (053) 254746, pg 1313

Peter Meili & Co, Buchhandluna (Switzerland) *Tel:* (053) 254144 *Fax:* (053) 254746, pg 619

Meinema (Netherlands) *Tel:* (079) 3615481 *Fax:* (079) 3615489 *E-mail:* info@boekencentrum.nl, pg 481

Felix Meiner Verlag GmbH (Germany) *Tel:* (040) 29 87 56-0 *Fax:* (040) 29 93 61-4 *E-mail:* info@meiner.de *Web Site:* meiner.de, pg 262

Meisenbach Verlag GmbH (Germany) *Tel:* (0951) 861-0 *Fax:* (0951) 861-158 *Web Site:* www.meisenbach.de, pg 262

Otto Meissner Verlag (Germany) *Tel:* (030) 8249558 *Fax:* (030) 8233338, pg 262

Mejikaru Furendo-sha (Japan) *Tel:* (03) 32646611 *Fax:* (03) 32616602 (distribution); (03) 32640704 (editorial affairs) *E-mail:* mfhensyu@mb.infoweb.ne.jp; mfeigyou@mb.infoweb.ne.jp; mfsoumu@mb.infoweb.ne.jp *Web Site:* www.web.infoweb.ne.jplmedical-friend/, pg 421

Mekise Nirdamim Society (Israel) *Tel:* (02) 636072, pg 1365

Melanesian Institute (Papua New Guinea) *Tel:* 7321777 *Fax:* 72-1214, pg 510

Il Melangolo (Italy) *Tel:* (010) 2514002 *Fax:* (010) 2514037, pg 398

Melantrich (Czech Republic) *Tel:* (02) 24227258 *Fax:* (02) 24213176, pg 126

Pustaka Melayu Baru (Malaysia) *Tel:* (03) 2985281 *Fax:* (03) 2414457, pg 453

Melbourne Institute of Applied Economic & Social Research (Australia) *Tel:* (03) 8344 5330 *Fax:* (03) 8344 5630 *E-mail:* melb.inst@iaesr.unimelb.edu.au *Web Site:* www.melbourneinstitute.com, pg 33

Melbourne University Press (Australia) *Tel:* (03) 9342 0300 *Fax:* (03) 9342 0399 *E-mail:* info@mup.unimelb.edu.au *Web Site:* www.mup.unimelb.edu.au, pg 33

Melhoramentos de Portugal Editora, Lda (Portugal) *Tel:* (021) 3963225 *Fax:* (021) 678254, pg 527

Editora Melhoramentos Ltda (Brazil) *Tel:* (011) 3874 0854 *Fax:* (011) 3874 0855 *E-mail:* blerner@melhoramentos.com.br *Web Site:* melhoramentos.com.br, pg 87

Melissa Publishing House (Greece) *Tel:* (010) 3611692 *Fax:* (010) 3600865 *Web Site:* www.melissabooks.com, pg 313

Melissa Publishing House (Greece) *Tel:* (010) 3611692 *Fax:* (010) 3600865 *E-mail:* melissa@compulink.gr, pg 1286

Mellemfolkeligt Samvirke (Denmark) *Tel:* 77310000 *Fax:* 77310101 *E-mail:* ms@ms-dan.dk *Web Site:* www.ms.dk, pg 133

Ediciones y Publicidad Melquiades (Chile) *Tel:* (02) 2731545 *Fax:* (02) 2266602, pg 100

Melrose Press Ltd (United Kingdom) *Tel:* (01353) 646600 *Fax:* (01353) 646601 *E-mail:* tradesales@melrosepress.co.uk, pg 713

Melting Pot Press (Australia) *Tel:* (02) 9211 1660 *Fax:* (02) 9211 1868 *E-mail:* books@elt.com.au *Web Site:* www.elt.com.au, pg 33

Melway Publishing Pty Ltd (Australia) *Tel:* (03) 98859900 *Fax:* (03) 98854254 *E-mail:* melway@ausway.com *Web Site:* www.ausway.com, pg 33

Idime Verlag Inge Melzer (Germany) *Tel:* (07541) 55220 *Fax:* (07541) 55201 *E-mail:* idime@t-online.de, pg 262

Editions Memo (France) *Tel:* (02) 40 47 98 19 *Fax:* (02) 40 47 98 21, pg 175

Editions Memoire des Arts (France) *Tel:* (04) 78 83 22 62 *Fax:* (04) 72 19 48 74 *Web Site:* www.editions-memory-of-arts.fr, pg 175

Editions Memor (Belgium) *Tel:* (02) 644-04-43 *Fax:* (02) 644-04-43 *Web Site:* www.memor.cjb.net, pg 72

Memorias Futuras Edicoes Ltda (Brazil) *Tel:* (021) 205-3549 *Fax:* (021) 2252518 *E-mail:* memorias@br.homeshopping.com.br, pg 88

Memorie Domenicane (Italy) *Tel:* (0573) 28158 *Fax:* (0573) 975808, pg 398

Memory/Cage Editions (Switzerland) *Tel:* (01) 2410445 *Fax:* (01) 2410445 *E-mail:* mail@memorycage.com *Web Site:* www.memorycage.com, pg 619

Mendelova zemedelska a lesnicka univerzita v Brne (Czech Republic) *Tel:* (05) 4513 1111; (05) 4513 2678 *Fax:* (05) 4513 5008 *Web Site:* www.mendelu.cz, pg 126

Sonny A Mendoza (Philippines) *Tel:* (02) 8691111, pg 513

Libreria Menendez (Panama) *Tel:* 2258996, pg 1305

Biblioteca de Menendez Pelayo (Spain) *Tel:* (042) 234534, pg 1499

Societe des Editions Menges (France) *Tel:* (01) 44 55 37 50 *Fax:* (01) 40 20 99 74, pg 175

Edition Axel Menges (Germany) *Tel:* (0711) 574759 *Fax:* (0711) 574784, pg 262

Casa Editrice Menna di Sinisgalli Menna Giuseppina (Italy) *Tel:* (0825) 24080 *Fax:* (0825) 24080, pg 398

Menora Publishing House (The Former Yugoslav Republic of Macedonia) *Tel:* (091) 418872 *Fax:* (091) 418872 *E-mail:* memoya@unet.com.mk *Web Site:* members.xoom.com/menora, pg 449

Menoshire Ltd (United Kingdom) *Tel:* (0181) 5667344 *Fax:* (0181) 9912439, pg 1321

Ediciones Mensajero (Spain) *Tel:* (094) 4 470 358 *Fax:* (094) 4 472 630 *E-mail:* mensajero@mensajero.com *Web Site:* www.mensajero.com, pg 582

Menschenkinder Verlag und Vertrieb GmbH (Germany) *Tel:* (0251) 9 32 52-0 *Fax:* (0251) 32 84 37 *E-mail:* info@menschenkinder.de *Web Site:* www.menschenkinder.de, pg 262

mentis Verlag GmbH (Germany) *Tel:* (05251) 687902; (05251) 6879004 *Fax:* (05251) 687905 *E-mail:* info@mentis.de *Web Site:* www.mentis.de, pg 262

Mentor Kiado (Romania) *Tel:* (01) 2232652 *Fax:* (01) 2232652, pg 534

Mentor Publications (Ireland) *Tel:* (01) 2952112 *Fax:* (01) 2952114 *E-mail:* admin@mentorbooks.ie *Web Site:* www.mentorbooks.ie, pg 362

Mentor-Verlag Dr Ramdohr KG (Germany) *Tel:* (089) 360960 *Fax:* (089) 36096-222 (general); (089) 36096-258 (orders) *E-mail:* mentor@langenscheidt.de, pg 262

Merani Publishing House (Georgia) *Tel:* (099532) 996492 *Fax:* (099532) 935514; (099532) 934675, pg 190

La Spiga Meravigli (Italy) *Tel:* (02) 2157240 *Fax:* (02) 2157833, pg 398

Merbod Verlag (Austria) *Tel:* (02622) 81724 *Fax:* (02622) 817244, pg 55

Editora Mercado Aberto Ltda (Brazil) *Tel:* (051) 3337-4833 *Fax:* (051) 3337-4905 *E-mail:* mercado@mercadoaberto.com.br *Web Site:* www.mercadoaberto.com.br, pg 88

Mercametrica Ediciones SA Edicion de Libros (Mexico) *Tel:* (05) 6616293 *Fax:* (05) 6616293, pg 464

Mercantila Publishers A/S (Denmark) *Tel:* 35436222 *Fax:* 35435151 *E-mail:* info@mercantila.dk *Web Site:* www.mercantila.dk, pg 133

Mercat Press (United Kingdom) *Tel:* (0131) 225 5324 *Fax:* (0131) 226 6632 *E-mail:* enquiries@mercatpress.com *Web Site:* www.mercatpress.com, pg 713

Mercatorfonds NV (Belgium) *Tel:* (03) 2027260 *Fax:* (03) 2311319 *E-mail:* artbooks@mercatorfonds.be *Web Site:* www.mercatorfonds.be, pg 72

Merchandising Muenchen KG (Germany) *Tel:* (089) 95078600 *Fax:* (089) 95078600 *E-mail:* jens.puppe@pro-sieben.de, pg 1111

Merchiston Publishing (United Kingdom) *Tel:* (0131) 455 6150 *Fax:* (0131) 455 6193, pg 713

The Mercier Bookshop Ltd (Ireland) *Tel:* (021) 275040 *Fax:* (021) 274969, pg 1291

Editions Franck Mercier (France) *Tel:* (04) 50 57 16 50 *Fax:* (04) 450579301 *E-mail:* franck@mercier.com.ch, pg 176

Mercier Press Ltd (Ireland) *Tel:* (021) 4275040 *Fax:* (021) 4274969 *E-mail:* books@mercier.ie *Web Site:* www.mercier.ie, pg 362

Mercure de France SA (France) *Tel:* (01) 55 42 61 90 *Fax:* (01) 43 54 49 91 *E-mail:* mercure@mercure.fr *Web Site:* www.gallimard.fr, pg 176

Mercury Press Pvt Ltd (Zimbabwe) *Tel:* (04) 751515; (04) 751516 *Fax:* (04) 737670, pg 769

Editora Mercuryo Ltda (Brazil) *Tel:* (011) 5531-8222 *Fax:* (011) 5093-3265 *E-mail:* diretoraeditorial@mercuryo.com.br *Web Site:* www.mercuryo.com.br/, pg 88

Merehurst Publishers (United Kingdom) *Tel:* (020) 8355 1480 *Fax:* (020) 8355 1499 *E-mail:* intsales@merehurst.co.uk, pg 713

Meresborough Books (United Kingdom) *Tel:* (01634) 371591 *Fax:* (01634) 262114 *E-mail:* shop@rainhambookshop.co.uk, pg 713

Meresborough Books (United Kingdom) *Tel:* (01634) 371591 *Fax:* (01634) 262114 *E-mail:* shop@rainhambookshop.co.uk *Web Site:* www.rainhambookshop.co.uk, pg 1321

Mergus Verlag GmbH Hans A Baensch (Germany) *Tel:* (05422) 3636 *Fax:* (05422) 1404 *E-mail:* mergus@t-online.de *Web Site:* www.mergus.com, pg 263

Meriberica/Liber (Portugal) *Tel:* (021) 8583849 *Fax:* (021) 8581536, pg 527

Meridian Books (United Kingdom) *Tel:* (0121) 429 4397, pg 713

Editura Meridiane (Romania) *Tel:* (01) 2243623 *Fax:* (01) 2223037, pg 534

Merlin Library Ltd (Malta) *Tel:* 221205; 234438 *Fax:* 221135, pg 456

Merlin Library Ltd (Malta) *Tel:* 221205; 234438 *Fax:* 221135 *E-mail:* chrigrup@keyworld.net, pg 1299

The Merlin Press Ltd (United Kingdom) *Tel:* (020) 7836 3020 *Fax:* (020) 7497 0309 *E-mail:* info@merlinpress.co.uk *Web Site:* www.merlinpress.co.uk, pg 713

Merlin Verlag Andreas Meyer Verlags GmbH und Co KG (Germany) *Tel:* (04137) 7207 *Fax:* (04137) 7948 *E-mail:* info@merlin-verlag.de *Web Site:* www.merlin-verlag.de, pg 263

Merrell Publishers Ltd (United Kingdom) *Tel:* (020) 7403 2047 *Fax:* (020) 7407 1333 *E-mail:* mail@merrellpublishers.com; sales@merrellpublishers.com, pg 713

Merrion Press (United Kingdom) *Tel:* (020) 7735 7791 *Fax:* (020) 77357 059, pg 713

Merrow Publishing Co Ltd (United Kingdom) *Tel:* (01325) 351661 *Fax:* (01325) 351661, pg 714

Verlag Merseburger Berlin GmbH (Germany) *Tel:* (0561) 789809-0 *Fax:* (0561) 789809-16 *E-mail:* info@merseburger.de; order@merseburger.de *Web Site:* www.merseburger.de, pg 263

Dr Ray-Gude Mertin Literarische Agentur (Germany) *Tel:* (06172) 29842 *Fax:* (06172) 29771 *E-mail:* mertin@em.uni-frankfurt.de, pg 1111

Merve Verlag (Germany) *Tel:* (030) 784 8433 *Fax:* (030) 788 1074 *E-mail:* merve@compuserve.com *Web Site:* www.merve.de, pg 263

The Mervyn Peake Society (United Kingdom) *Tel:* (01206) 396 130, pg 1371

Messaggero di San Antonio (Italy) *Tel:* (049) 8225000 *Fax:* (049) 8225688, pg 398

Editions H Messeiller SA (Switzerland) *Tel:* (032) 7251296 *Fax:* (032) 7241937, pg 619

Messenger Publications (Ireland) *Tel:* (01) 6767 491; (01) 6767 492 *Fax:* (01) 661 16 06 *E-mail:* sales@messenger.ie *Web Site:* www.messenger.ie, pg 362

Mestska knihovna v Praze (Czech Republic) *Tel:* (02) 22113300 *Fax:* (02) 22113305 *E-mail:* bimkovaa@mlp.czi, pg 1460

Metallurgical Industry Press (MIP) (China) *Tel:* (010) 64013877; (010) 4015599 *Fax:* (010) 64013877, pg 107

Izdatelstvo Metallurgiya (Russian Federation) *Tel:* (095) 2025532 *Fax:* (095) 2025752, pg 540

Instytut Meteorologii i Gospodarki Wodnej (Poland) *Tel:* (022) 56-94-100 *Fax:* (022) 834-54-66 *E-mail:* sekretariat@imgw.pl *Web Site:* www.imgw.pl, pg 518

The Methodist Publishing House (South Africa) *Tel:* (021) 4483640 *Fax:* (021) 4483716 *E-mail:* methpub@iafrica.com, pg 557

Methodist Publishing House (United Kingdom) *Tel:* (01733) 335002 *Fax:* (01733) 384180 *E-mail:* sales@mph.org.uk; chief.exec@mph.org.uk *Web Site:* www.mph.org.uk, pg 714

Methuen Publishing Ltd (United Kingdom) *Tel:* (020) 7798 1600 *Fax:* (020) 7828 2098 *Web Site:* www.methuen.co.uk, pg 714

Metis Yayinlari (Turkey) *Tel:* (0212) 2454509; (0212) 2454696 *Fax:* (0212) 2454519 *E-mail:* metis@turk.net *Web Site:* www.metisbooks.com, pg 640

Metrica Fachverlag u Versandbuchhandlung Ing Bartak (Austria) *Tel:* (01) 7695160; (01) 7485448, pg 55

Metro Publishing Ltd (United Kingdom) *Tel:* (020) 7734 1411 *Fax:* (020) 7734 1811 *E-mail:* metro@metro.books.demon.co.uk, pg 714

Metropolis- Verlag fur Okonomie, Gesellschaft und Politik GmbH (Germany) *Tel:* (06421) 67377 *Fax:* (06471) 681918 *E-mail:* info@metropolis-verlag.de *Web Site:* www.metropolis-verlag.de, pg 263

Metropolitan Verlag (Germany) *Tel:* (0941) 5684132 *Fax:* (0941) 5684111 *E-mail:* metropolitan@walhalla.de *Web Site:* www.metropolitan.de, pg 263

Mets & Schilt Uitgevers en Distributeurs (Netherlands) *Tel:* (020) 6256087 *Fax:* (020) 6270242 *E-mail:* info@metsenschilt.com *Web Site:* www.metsenschilt.com, pg 481

Karl-Heinz Metz (Germany) *Tel:* (07225) 74098 *Fax:* (07225) 74098 *E-mail:* metzverlag@aol.com *Web Site:* www.metz-verlag.de, pg 263

J B Metzler'sche Verlagsbuchhandlung (Germany) *Tel:* (0711) 2194 0 *Fax:* (0711) 21942 49 *E-mail:* info@metzelerverlag.de *Web Site:* www.metzlerverlag.de, pg 263

J M Meulenhoff BV (Netherlands) *Tel:* (020) 5533500 *Fax:* (020) 6258511 *E-mail:* j.m.meulenhoff@meulenhoff.nl, pg 481

Preubmpassling Verlag Gisela Meussling (Germany) *Tel:* (0228) 466347 *Fax:* (0228) 466347, pg 263

Mexican Academic Clearing House (MACH) (Mexico) *Tel:* (0915) 6740779; (0915) 6740567 *E-mail:* hpadilla@spin.com.mx, pg 1299

Editores Mexicanos Unidos SA (Mexico) *Tel:* (05) 5217596; (05) 5218870 al 74; (05) 5211874 *Fax:* (05) 5128516, pg 464

Meyer & Meyer Fachverlag und Buchhandel GmbH (Germany) *Tel:* (0241) 95810-0 *Fax:* (0241) 95810-10 *E-mail:* verlag@m-m-sports.com *Web Site:* www.m-m-sports.com, pg 263

Mezdunarodnye Otno Denija (Russian Federation) *Tel:* (095) 2076793 *Fax:* (095) 2002204, pg 540

Mezhdunarodnaya Kniga (Russian Federation) *Tel:* (095) 2384600, pg 1308

Izdatelstvo Mezhdunarodnye Otnoshenia (Russian Federation) *Tel:* (095) 2076793 *Fax:* (095) 2002204, pg 540

Mezoegazda Kiado (Hungary) *Tel:* (01) 4076575 *Fax:* (01) 4071787 *E-mail:* mezogazda@matavnet.hu, pg 325

Mezoegazdasagi Koenyvkiado Vallalat (Hungary) *Tel:* (01) 1317330 *Fax:* (01) 1117270, pg 325

Mezopotamya Publishing & Distribution (Sweden) *Tel:* (08) 7747354 *Fax:* (08) 7110836, pg 604

MFK Management Consultants Services (Zambia) *Tel:* (01) 223530; (01) 252934, pg 766

MG Editores Associados Ltda (Brazil) *Tel:* (011) 8890861 *Fax:* (011) 8858646, pg 88

MGM (United Kingdom) *Tel:* (020) 7262 8386, pg 714

Mi-An Knigoizdatelstvo (The Former Yugoslav Republic of Macedonia) *Tel:* (091) 252565 *E-mail:* mtimes@soros.org.mk, pg 449

Micelle Press (United Kingdom) *Tel:* (01305) 781574 *Fax:* (01305) 781574 *E-mail:* tony@wdi.co.uk *Web Site:* www.wdi.co.uk/micelle, pg 714

Michalis Sideris (Greece) *Tel:* (01) 3301161; (01) 3301163 *Fax:* (01) 3301164, pg 313

Michelin Editions des Voyages (Belgium) *Tel:* (02) 274 45 03 *Fax:* (02) 274 43 62 *E-mail:* kontakt@viamichelin.com *Web Site:* www.viamichelin.com, pg 72

Michelin et Cie (Services de Tourisme) (France) *Tel:* (01) 45661234 *Fax:* (01) 45661163, pg 176

Michelin Tyre PLC, Tourism Dept, Maps & Guides Division (United Kingdom) *Tel:* (01923) 415000 *Fax:* (01923) 415250 *Web Site:* www.michelin.co.uk, pg 714

Michlol Ltd (Israel) *Tel:* (04) 8322970 *Fax:* (04) 8223854 *E-mail:* ws2@isdn.net.il, pg 1292

Microsoft Press France (France) *Tel:* (0825) 827 8291 *Fax:* (01) 69 86 47 55 *E-mail:* msfrance@microsoft.com *Web Site:* www.microsoft.com/france, pg 176

Midas Printing Ltd (Hong Kong) *Tel:* 24076888 *Fax:* 24065800 *E-mail:* midas@hkstar.com, pg 1135

Midas Printing Ltd (Hong Kong) *Tel:* 24076888 *Fax:* 24065800; 24096875 *E-mail:* midas@hkstar.com, pg 1156, 1197

Gertraud Middelhauve Verlag GmbH & Co KG (Germany) *Tel:* (089) 41 94 02-0 *Fax:* (089) 47 01 08-1, pg 263

Literaturbetreuung Klaus Middendorf (LKM) (Germany) *Tel:* (08232) 78463 *Fax:* (08232) 78468 *E-mail:* lkm@compuserve.com, pg 1111

Middle East Technical University Library (Turkey) *Tel:* (0312) 2102780; (0312) 2102782 *Fax:* (0312) 2101119 *E-mail:* lib-hot-line@metu.edu.tr, pg 1504

Middle East Book Centre (Egypt (Arab Republic of Egypt)) *Tel:* (02) 910980, pg 139

Middle East Librarians Association (United States) *Tel:* (206) 543-8407 *Fax:* (206) 685-8049 *Web Site:* www.depts.washington.edu/wsx9/melahp.html, pg 1269

Middleton Press (United Kingdom) *Tel:* (01730) 813169 *Fax:* (01730) 812601, pg 714

Midena Verlag (Germany) *Tel:* (0821) 70040 *Fax:* (0821) 700479 *Web Site:* www.droemer.de, pg 264

Midi Teki Publishers (Kenya) *Tel:* (02) 506993, pg 433

Midland Publishing (United Kingdom) *Tel:* (01455) 254490 *Fax:* (01455) 254495 *E-mail:* midlandbooks@compuserve.com *Web Site:* www.ianallan.com/publishing, pg 714

Midrashiat Naom, Pardess Hanna (Israel) *Tel:* (09) 5172637 *Fax:* (09) 5100594, pg 370

Migema Ediciones Ltda (Colombia) *Tel:* (01) 2873158; (01) 2858538 *Fax:* (01) 2858538; (01) 2858224 *E-mail:* emigema@cc-net.net, pg 113

Miland Publishers (Netherlands) *Tel:* (0172) 571461 *Fax:* (0172) 572231 *E-mail:* degraaf.books@wxs.nl, pg 481

Milano Libri (Italy) *Tel:* (02) 50951 *Fax:* (02) 5065361, pg 398

Nicola Milano Editore (Italy) *Tel:* (051) 239060 *Fax:* (051) 239286 *E-mail:* scuola@nicolamilano.com *Web Site:* www.nicolamilano.com, pg 398

Milanostampa/New Interlitho USA Inc (United States) *Tel:* 212-964-2430 *Fax:* 212-964-2497 *Web Site:* www.milanostampa.com, pg 1145, 1166, 1208, 1216

Milanostampa SPA (Italy) *Tel:* (0173) 746111 *Fax:* (0173) 746248 *E-mail:* milanostamp@areacom.it, pg 1158

Milanostampa SPA (Italy) *Tel:* (0173) 746111 *Fax:* (0173) 746248 *E-mail:* milanostampa@areacom.it, pg 1198, 1213

Milella di Lecce Spazio Vivo SRL (Italy) *Tel:* (0832) 308885 *Fax:* (0832) 308885 *E-mail:* leccespaziovivo@tiscalinet.it *Web Site:* www.milellaeditore.com, pg 399

Milena Verlag (Austria) *Tel:* (01) 402 59 90 *Fax:* (01) 408 88 58 *E-mail:* frauenverlag@milena-verlag.at, pg 55

Editorial Milenio Arts Grafiques Bobala, SL (Spain) *Tel:* (0973) 236 611 *Fax:* (0973) 240 795 *E-mail:* editorial.milenio@cambrescat.es *Web Site:* www.edmilenio.com, pg 582

Miles Kelly Publishing Ltd (United Kingdom) *Tel:* (01371) 811309 *Fax:* (01371) 811393 *E-mail:* info@mileskelly.net *Web Site:* www.mileskelly.net, pg 714

Editura Militara (Romania) *Tel:* (01) 6138924; (01) 3237822, pg 534

Militzke Verlag (Germany) *Tel:* (0341) 42643-0 *Fax:* (0341) 42643-99 *E-mail:* info@militzke.de *Web Site:* www.militzke.de, pg 264

Millbank Books Ltd (United Kingdom) *Tel:* (01279) 655233 *Fax:* (01279) 655244 *E-mail:* caw@millbank.demon.co.uk, pg 1321

Mille et Une Nuits (France) *Tel:* (01) 45 4982 00 *Fax:* (01) 45 4979 96, pg 176

Cathy Miller Foreign Rights Agency (United Kingdom) *Tel:* (020) 7386 5473 *Fax:* (020) 7385 1774, pg 1120

J Garnet Miller (United Kingdom) *Tel:* (01684) 540154 *Fax:* (01684) 540154, pg 714

Harvey Miller Publishers (United Kingdom) *Tel:* (020) 7284 4359 *Fax:* (020) 7267 8764 *E-mail:* harvey.miller@brepols.com, pg 714

Miller's Publications (United Kingdom) *Tel:* (020) 7531 8400 *Fax:* (020) 7531 8650, pg 715

Milliii Kuetuephane (Turkey) *Tel:* (0312) 2223812 (ext 4148) *Fax:* (0312) 2230451, pg 1504

Mills Group (New Zealand) *Tel:* (04) 5696744 *Fax:* (04) 5697464, pg 493

Millwood Press Ltd (New Zealand) *Tel:* (04) 4735176 *Fax:* (04) 4735177, pg 493

Richard Milne Ltd (United Kingdom) *Tel:* (020) 8883 3987 *Fax:* (020) 8883 0323 *E-mail:* dsharp121@aol.com, pg 1120

Milton Margai Teachers' College Library (Sierra Leone) *Tel:* (022) 024305, pg 1496

Mimosa Publications Pty Ltd (Australia) *Tel:* (03) 9819 0511 *Fax:* (03) 9819 0524 *E-mail:* info@mimosa.pub.com.au, pg 33

Min Jung Seo Rim Publishing Co (Republic of Korea) *Tel:* (02) 7036541; (02) 7036547 *Fax:* (02) 7036549 *E-mail:* editmin@minjungdic.co.kr *Web Site:* www.minjumgdic.co.kr, pg 438

Librairie Minard (France) *Tel:* (02) 31844706 *Fax:* (02) 31844809, pg 176

MIND Publications (United Kingdom) *Tel:* (020) 8519 2122 *Fax:* (020) 8522 1725; (020) 8534 6399 (orders) *E-mail:* contact@mind.org.uk; publications@mind.org.uk (mail order) *Web Site:* www.mind.org.uk, pg 715

Mindanao State University - Mamitua Saber Research Center (Philippines), pg 513

Library of the Mineral Research and Exploration General Directorate (Turkey) *Tel:* (0312) 2873430 *Fax:* (0310) 2879188 *Web Site:* www.mta.gov.tr, pg 1504

Minerva (France) *Tel:* (01) 40 51 52 00 *Fax:* (01) 40 51 52 05 *Web Site:* www.lamartiniere.net, pg 176

Minerva KG Internationale Fachliteratur fur Medizin und Naturwissens ften Neue Medien (Germany) *Tel:* (06151) 98R0 *Fax:* (06151) 98839, pg 1284

Libreria Editrice Minerva (Italy) *Tel:* (075) 812381 *Fax:* (075) 816564, pg 1293

Minerva (Yugoslavia) *Tel:* (024) 28834; (024) 25712 *Fax:* (024) 23-208, pg 764

Minerva Associates (Publications) Pvt Ltd (India) *Tel:* (033) 4763783, pg 342

Editora Minerva Central (Mozambique) *Tel:* (01) 22092; (01) 22093; (01) 26114; (01) 23637, pg 470

Editorial Minerva (Portugal) *Tel:* (021) 3422535 *Fax:* (021) 3464720, pg 527

Editura Minerva (Romania) *Tel:* (01) 2224823, pg 534

Minerva Italica SpA (Italy) *Tel:* (02) 215631 *Fax:* (02) 21213699, pg 399

Minerva Medica (Italy) *Tel:* (011) 678282 *Fax:* (011) 674502, pg 1137, 1198

Minerva Publications (Malaysia) *Tel:* (06) 734439 *Fax:* (06) 734439, pg 453

Minerva Shobo Co Ltd (Japan) *Tel:* (075) 5815191 *Fax:* (075) 5810589 *E-mail:* info@minervashobo.co.jp *Web Site:* www.minervashoboco.jp, pg 421

Minervaverlag Bern (Switzerland) *Tel:* (031) 3726223 *Fax:* (031) 3726223, pg 619

Mines & Geological Department Library (Kenya) *Tel:* (02) 29621, pg 1480

Ming Pao Publications Ltd (Hong Kong) *Tel:* 2595 3111; 2595 3318 *Fax:* 2898 2646 *Web Site:* security.mingpao.com/books, pg 321

Uitgeverij Mingus (Netherlands) *Tel:* (0348) 425507 *Fax:* (0348) 425507, pg 481

Ministere des Affaires Culturelles (Luxembourg) *Tel:* 4781 *Fax:* 402427, pg 447

Ministere des Affaires Etrangeres Division de L'Ecrit et des Mediatheques (France) *Tel:* (01) 43178688 *Fax:* (01) 43178883, pg 1244

Ministerie van Verkeer en Waterstaat (Netherlands) *Tel:* (070) 3517086 *Fax:* (070) 3516430 *Web Site:* www.minverw.nl, pg 481

Ministerio da Marinha Diretoria de Hidrografia Navegacao (Brazil) *Tel:* (021) 613 8001; (021) 719 4824 *Fax:* (021) 6138063; (021) 719 4824 *E-mail:* 01@dhm.mar.mil.sr, pg 88

Ministerio de Economia y Hacienda Secretario General Tecnica Centro de Publicaciones (Spain) *Tel:* (091) 3493592 *Fax:* (091) 3493502, pg 582

Ministerio de Educacion Biblioteca Central (Venezuela) *Tel:* (02) 5628970 (ext 8149); (02) 5621767; (02) 5640025 *Fax:* (02) 5641224, pg 762

Ministerio de Educacion y Culture Centro de Publicaciones (Spain) *Tel:* (091) 453 98 00 *Fax:* (091) 453 98 00, pg 582

Editorial del Ministerio de Educacion (Guatemala), pg 316

Ministerio de Justicia e Interior, Centro de Publicaciones (Spain) *Tel:* (091) 390 44 29; (091) 390 20 83; (091) 390 20 97 *Fax:* (091) 390 20 92 *Web Site:* www.mju.es, pg 582

Ministerio de Trabajo y Asuntos Sociales (Spain) *Tel:* (091) 4037000 *Fax:* (091) 4030050 *E-mail:* gprensa@mtas.es *Web Site:* www.mtas.es, pg 582

Ministerstvo Kul'tury RF (Russian Federation) *Tel:* (0812) 2204500 *E-mail:* rnb@q1as.apc.org, pg 540

Ministerstvo Kultury C R, Oddeleni Tisku Oddeleni Knizi Kultury (Czech Republic) *Tel:* (02) 24510452 *Fax:* (02) 57311376, pg 1241

Izdatelstvo na Ministerstvoto na Otbranata (Bulgaria) *Tel:* (02) 878188; (02) 9885570 *Fax:* (02) 881568, pg 96

Ministry of Agriculture Library (Malaysia) *Tel:* (03) 2982011 *Fax:* (03) 2913758, pg 1483

Ministry of Agriculture & Livestock Development Library (Kenya) *Tel:* (02) 718870 *Fax:* (02) 725774, pg 1480

Ministry of Cultural Affairs (Sri Lanka) *Tel:* (01) 437328, pg 597

Book Club of the Ministry of Cultural Affairs of Sri Lanka (Sri Lanka) *Tel:* (01) 437328, pg 1231

Ministry of Defence Publishing House (Israel) *Tel:* (03) 5655900; (03) 6917940 *Fax:* (03) 5655994; (03) 6375509, pg 370

Ministry of Education Library (Afghanistan), pg 1449

Ministry of Education Library (Egypt (Arab Republic of Egypt)) *Tel:* (02) 8544805, pg 1462

Ministry of Education (Sri Lanka) *Tel:* 565141; 565150, pg 597

Ministry of Education, Department of Educational Publications (Afghanistan) *Tel:* 25151, pg 1

Ministry of Environment & Public Health, Library Division (Malaysia) *Tel:* (082) 242911 *Fax:* (082) 246552, pg 1483

Ministry of Information (Kuwait) *Tel:* 2415300 *Fax:* 2421926, pg 441

Ministry of Information & Broadcasting (India) *Tel:* (011) 386879, pg 342

Ministry of Justice Library (Egypt (Arab Republic of Egypt)) *Tel:* (02) 20806, pg 1462

Minjisa Publishing Co (Republic of Korea) *Tel:* (02) 9806382 *Fax:* (02) 9861531 *E-mail:* minjisa@nownuri.net *Web Site:* www.minjisa.co.kr, pg 438

Editions Minkoff (Switzerland) *Tel:* (022) 3104660 *Fax:* (022) 3102857 *E-mail:* minkoff@minkoff-editions.com *Web Site:* www.minkoff-editions.com, pg 619

Minoas SA (Greece) *Tel:* (010) 2711222 *Fax:* (010) 2711056 *E-mail:* info@minoas.ge *Web Site:* www.minoas.ge, pg 313

Ediciones Minotauro (Spain) *Tel:* (093) 487 1089 *Fax:* (093) 487 1849 *E-mail:* edicionesminotauro@arrakis.es *Web Site:* www.edicionesminotauro.com, pg 582

Ediciones Minotauro SRL (Argentina) *Tel:* (011) 4362-1616; (011) 4362-1222 *Fax:* (011) 4362-7364, pg 7

Les Editions de Minuit SA (France) *Tel:* (01) 44 39 39 20 *Fax:* (01) 45 44 82 36 *Web Site:* www.leseditionsdeminuit.fr, pg 176

Minumsa Publishing Co Ltd (Republic of Korea) *Tel:* (02) 515-2000; (02) 515-2005; (02) 515-9108 *Fax:* (02) 515-2007; (02) 3444-5185 *Web Site:* www.minumsa.com, pg 438

Editorial Minutiae Mexicana SA (Mexico) *Tel:* (052) 55-5535-9488 *Fax:* (052) 722-232-0662, pg 464

Izdatelstvo Mir (Russian Federation) *Tel:* (095) 286-17-83 *Fax:* (095) 288-95-22 *Web Site:* www.mir-pubs.dol.ru, pg 540

Mir Knigi Ltd (Russian Federation) *Tel:* (095) 2083879 *Fax:* (095) 7428579, pg 540

Editores Mira, SA (Spain) *Tel:* (0976) 460505 *Fax:* (0976) 460446 *E-mail:* miraeditores@ctv.es *Web Site:* www.miraeditores.com, pg 582

Mirabel Books Ltd (United Kingdom) *Tel:* (0171) 385 2515 *Fax:* (0171) 386 5027, pg 715

Mirai-Sha (Japan) *Tel:* (03) 38145521 *Fax:* (03) 38148600, pg 421

Presses Universitaires du Mirail (France) *Tel:* (0561) 503808 *Fax:* (0561) 503800 *E-mail:* pum@univ-tlse2.fr *Web Site:* www.crlmidipyrenees.asso.fr/editeurs/pum.htm, pg 176

Mirananda Publishers BV (Netherlands) *Tel:* (070) 3585943 *Fax:* (070) 3586843 *E-mail:* info@mirananda.nl *Web Site:* www.mirananda.nl, pg 481

G Miranda & Sons (Philippines) *Tel:* (02) 7121620 *Fax:* (02) 7120502, pg 1306

Miranda-Verlag Stefan Ehlert (Germany) *Tel:* (0421) 7943226 *Fax:* (0421) 7943226 *E-mail:* miranda-verlag@t-online.de, pg 264

Mirinae (Republic of Korea) *Tel:* (02) 2279-2669 *Fax:* (02) 2234-1450 *E-mail:* mrn@lycos.co.kr, pg 438

Mirkam Publishers (Israel) *Tel:* (06) 6900967 *Fax:* (06) 6900967, pg 370

Mirran (Netherlands) *Tel:* (013) 5169534 *E-mail:* post@mirran.com *Web Site:* www.mirran.com, pg 481

Mirza Book Agency (Pakistan) *Tel:* (042) 7353601 *Fax:* (042) 5763714, pg 1115

Misgav Yerushalayim (Israel) *Tel:* (02) 5883962 *Fax:* (02) 5815460 *E-mail:* misgav@h2.hum.huji.ac.il *Web Site:* www.hum.huji.ac.il/misgav, pg 370

Instituto Misionerao Hijas De San Pablo (Colombia) *Tel:* (01) 2435885; (01) 6 71 89 74 *Fax:* (01) 670 6378, pg 113

Miskal Publishing Ltd (Israel) *Tel:* (03) 9246980 *Fax:* (03) 9246985, pg 370

Misr Bookshop (Egypt (Arab Republic of Egypt)) *Tel:* (02) 908920, pg 1282

Galeria de Arte Misrachi SA (Mexico) *Tel:* (05) 5334551 *Fax:* (05) 5257187, pg 464

Missio eV Aachen (Germany) *Tel:* (0241) 75 07-00 *Fax:* (0241) 75 07-335 *E-mail:* info@missio-aachen.de *Web Site:* www.missio-aachen.de, pg 264

Mission Publications of Australia (Australia) *Tel:* (02) 4759 1003 *Fax:* (02) 4759 1101, pg 33

Editrice Missionaria Italiana (EMI) (Italy) *Tel:* (051) 326027 *Fax:* (051) 327552, pg 399

Missionshandlung (Germany) *Tel:* (05052) 471 *Fax:* (05052) 30 82 *E-mail:* m-druckerei@t-online.de, pg 264

Pietro Missorini & Co - Libreria Commissionaria (Italy) *Tel:* (0521) 993919 *Fax:* (0521) 993929 *Web Site:* www.rsadvnet.it/missorini/, pg 1113

Misuzu Shobo Ltd (Japan) *Tel:* (03) 3815-9181 *Fax:* (03) 3818-8497 *E-mail:* nakagawa@msz.co.jp *Web Site:* www.msz.co.jp, pg 421

Miswat Library (Yemen), pg 1508

MIT Press Ltd (United Kingdom) *Tel:* (020) 7306 0603 *Fax:* (020) 7306 0604 *E-mail:* info@hup-mitpress.co.uk *Web Site:* www-mitpress.mit.edu, pg 715

Mita Press, Mita Industrial Co, Ltd (Japan) *Tel:* (03) 38177200 *Fax:* (03) 38177207, pg 421

Mita Society for Library & Information Science (Japan) *Tel:* (03) 34533920, pg 1518

Mitt foeretag (Sweden) *Tel:* (08) 6909000 *Fax:* (08) 320851, pg 1232

Mittal Publications (India) *Tel:* (011) 5552070; (011) 5592070, pg 343

Mitteldeutscher Verlag GmbH (Germany) *Tel:* (0345) 2 33 22-0 *Fax:* (0345) 2 33 22-66 *E-mail:* mitteldeutscher.verlag@t-online.de *Web Site:* www.buecherkisten.de, pg 264

E S Mittler und Sohn GmbH (Germany) *Tel:* (040) 7 97 13-03 *Fax:* (040) 79713324, pg 264

Mizan (Indonesia) *Tel:* (022) 7200931 *Fax:* (022) 72070238 *E-mail:* info@mizan.com *Web Site:* www.mizan.com, pg 356

M Mizrahi Publishers (Israel) *Tel:* (03) 6870936 *Fax:* (03) 5475399, pg 370

MK Ediciones y Publicaciones (Spain) *Tel:* (091) 4316305 *Fax:* (091) 5754978, pg 582

Mlada fronta (Czech Republic) *Tel:* (02) 2527 6120, pg 126

Mlade leta Spd sro (Slovakia) *Tel:* (07) 5664512; (07) 5664293 *Fax:* (07) 215714, pg 550

Mladezh (Bulgaria) *Tel:* (02) 882137 *Fax:* (02) 876135, pg 96

Mladinska Knjiga International (Slovenia) *Tel:* (061) 1261300; (061) 1252796; (061) 1252798 *Fax:* (061) 215320, pg 552

Mladost d d Izdavacku graficku i informaticku djelatnost (Croatia) *Tel:* (01) 215-853; (01) 229-811 *Fax:* (01) 239-5336, pg 119

Thomas Mlakar Verlag (Austria) *Tel:* (03579) 2258 *Fax:* (03579) 2258, pg 55

MM-Verlagsgesellschaft mbH (Germany) *Tel:* (07158) 940 800 *Fax:* (07158) 940 802 *E-mail:* mm@ebb.de, pg 264

MMV Medizin Verlag GmbH Munich (Germany) *Tel:* (089) 4372-1300 *Fax:* (089) 4372-1399 *Web Site:* www.urban-vogel.de, pg 264

mnemes - Alfieri & Ranieri Publishing (Italy) *Tel:* (091) 588813 *Fax:* (091) 588813 *E-mail:* alfieri@mnemes.com *Web Site:* www.mnemes.com, pg 399

Moby Dick Verlag (Germany) *Tel:* (0431) 640110 *Fax:* (0431) 6401112 *E-mail:* mobybook@aol.com, pg 264

Modan Publishers Ltd (Israel) *Tel:* (08) 9221821 *Fax:* (08) 9221299 *E-mail:* modan@modan.co.il, pg 371

mode information Heinz Kramer GmbH (Germany) *Tel:* (02206) 60070 *Fax:* (02206) 600717 *E-mail:* info@modeinfo.com *Web Site:* www.modeinfo.com, pg 264

Modellsport Verlag GmbH (Germany) *Tel:* (07221) 95210 *Fax:* (07221) 9521-45 *E-mail:* mfiredaktion@modellsport.de *Web Site:* www.modellsport.de, pg 264

The Modern Book Depot (India) *Tel:* (033) 2493102; (033) 2490933 *Fax:* (033) 2497455 *E-mail:* modcal@vsnl.com, pg 1289

Modern Electronic & Computing Publishing Co Ltd (Hong Kong) *Tel:* 23428297 *Fax:* 23414247 *E-mail:* info@computertoday.com.hk *Web Site:* www.computertoday.com.hk, pg 321

Modern Guides Company (Puerto Rico) *Tel:* (787) 723-9105 *Fax:* (787) 723-4380, pg 530

Modern Press (China) *Tel:* (010) 4215031-383 *Fax:* (010) 4214540, pg 107

Moderna galerija Ljubljana/Museum of Modern Art (Slovenia) *Tel:* (001) 2416800 *Fax:* (001) 2514120 *Web Site:* www.mg-lj.si, pg 552

Editora Moderna Ltda (Brazil) *Tel:* (011) 6090-1500 *Fax:* (011) 6090-1501 *E-mail:* moderna@moderna.com.br *Web Site:* www.moderna.com.br, pg 88

Editions Modernes Media (France) *Tel:* (01) 43268384 *Fax:* (01) 42333535, pg 176

modo verlag GmbH (Germany) *Tel:* (0761) 2022875 *Fax:* (0761) 2022876 *E-mail:* info@modoverlag.de *Web Site:* www.modoverlag.de, pg 264

Forlaget Modtryk AMBA (Denmark) *Tel:* 87317600 *Fax:* 87317601 *E-mail:* forlaget@modtryk.dk *Web Site:* www.modtryk.dk, pg 133

Modulo Editora e Desenvolvimento Educacional Ltda (Brazil) *Tel:* (041) 2530077 *Fax:* (041) 2530103 *E-mail:* moduloed@moduloeditora.com.br, pg 88

Modulverlag (Austria) *Tel:* (01) 5129892 *Fax:* (01) 5129893, pg 55

Moeck Verlag und Musikinstrumentenwerk, Inhaber Dr Hermann Moeck (Germany) *Tel:* (05141) 88 53-0 *Fax:* (05141) 88 53-42 *E-mail:* info@moeck-music.de *Web Site:* www.moeck-music.de, pg 264

Moench Verlagsgesellschaft mbH (Germany) *Tel:* (0228) 64830 *Fax:* (0228) 6483109 *E-mail:* 101336.245@compuserve.com, pg 264

Karl Heinrich Moeseler Verlag (Germany) *Tel:* (05331) 95970 *Fax:* (05331) 9597-20, pg 264

Moggy Publications (Australia) *Tel:* (03) 9867-2347 *E-mail:* rose-1@rocketmail.com, pg 33

Mohndruck Graphische Betriebe GmbH (Germany) *Tel:* (05241) 802095 *Fax:* (05241) 78329, pg 1133, 1154, 1195, 1211

Mohr Siebeck (Germany) *Tel:* (07071) 923-0 *Fax:* (07071) 5 11 04 *E-mail:* info@mohr.de *Web Site:* www.mohr.de, pg 264

Mohr-ZA Verlagsauslieferungen Ges mbH (Austria) *Tel:* (01) 5121676; (01) 5125711; (01) 5126994 *Fax:* (01) 111859, pg 1274

MOHRBOOKS AG, Literary Agency (Switzerland) *Tel:* (01) 2511610 *Fax:* (01) 2625213, pg 1117

Moksha Institute of Caribbean Arts & Letters (Trinidad & Tobago) *Tel:* 6374516, pg 637

Mokslo ir enciklopediju leidybos institutas (Lithuania) *Tel:* (02) 458526; (02) 457980; (02) 458528 *Fax:* (02) 458537 *E-mail:* meli@meli.taide.lt, pg 446

M Moleiro Editor, SA (Spain) *Tel:* (093) 240 20 91 *Fax:* (093) 201 50 62 *E-mail:* mmoleiro@moleiro.com *Web Site:* www.moleiro.com, pg 582

Editorial Molino (Spain) *Tel:* (093) 226 06 25 *Fax:* (093) 226 69 98 *E-mail:* molino@menta.net *Web Site:* www.editorialmolino.com, pg 582

Editorial Moll SL (Spain) *Tel:* (0971) 724472 *Fax:* (0971) 726252 *E-mail:* info@editorialmoll.es; editorial.moll@ocesa.es *Web Site:* www.editorialmoll.es, pg 582

Librairie Mollat (France) *Tel:* (0556) 564040 *Fax:* (0556) 564088, pg 1283

Izdatelstvo Molodaya Gvardia (Russian Federation) *Tel:* (095) 9722288 *Fax:* (095) 9720582, pg 540

Mombasa Polytechnic Library (Kenya) *Tel:* (011) 492222, pg 1480

Pavla Momcilova (Czech Republic) *Tel:* (02) 677 101 28 *Fax:* (02) 677 101 28, pg 126

Monarch Books (United Kingdom) *Tel:* (020) 8959 3668 *Fax:* (020) 8959 3678 *E-mail:* monarch@angushudson.com, pg 715

Monash University Library (Australia) *Tel:* (03) 99052662 *Fax:* (03) 99052610 *E-mail:* equery@lib.monash.edu.au, pg 1450

Library of the Monastery of St-Saviour (Basilian Missionary Order of St-Saviour) (Lebanon), pg 1481

Arnoldo Mondadori Editore SpA (Italy) *Tel:* (02) 75421 *Fax:* (02) 75422302 *Web site:* www.mondadori.com, pg 399

Giorgio Mondadori & Associati (Italy) *Tel:* (02) 891661 *Fax:* (02) 89125880, pg 399

Edizioni del Mondo Giudiziario (Italy) *Tel:* (06) 3721071 *Fax:* (06) 3250961, pg 399

Mondo SA (Editions-Verlag-Edizioni) (Switzerland) *Tel:* (021) 9241450 *Fax:* (021) 9244662, pg 619

Mondolibro Editore SNC (Italy) *Tel:* (055) 8546097 *Fax:* (055) 8546097 *Web Site:* www.mondolibraeditore.com, pg 399

Mondria Publishers (Netherlands) *Tel:* (050) 3110505 *Fax:* (050) 3112299, pg 481

Monduzzi Editore SpA (Italy) *Tel:* (051) 4151123 *Fax:* (051) 370529, pg 399

Gerard Monfort Editeur Sarl (France) *Tel:* (01) 40 27 95 54 *Fax:* (01) 40 27 95 60 *E-mail:* contact@gerard-monfort.com *Web Site:* www.gerard-monfort.com, pg 176

Mongolgosknigotorg (Mongolia), pg 469

Monia Verlag (Germany) *Tel:* (6331) 41425 *Fax:* (6331) 41425, pg 265

Edition Monika (Germany) *Tel:* (06848) 7 21 52 *Fax:* (06848) 7 21 59 *E-mail:* edmb@mathbeck.de; jphilippi@mathbeck.de *Web Site:* www.mathbeck.de/edmb/, pg 265

Editions du Moniteur (France) *Tel:* (01) 40 13 33 72 *Fax:* (01) 40 41 08 87 *E-mail:* clients@editionsdumoniteur.com *Web Site:* www.editionsdumoniteur.com, pg 176

Monitor (Portugal) *Tel:* (021) 894893 *Fax:* (021) 7934551 *E-mail:* monitor@esoterica.pt, pg 527

Monitor-Projectos e Edicoes, LDA (Portugal) *Tel:* (021) 849-48-93 *Fax:* (021) 793-45-51 *E-mail:* monitor@esoterica.pt, pg 527

Monitorul Oficial, Editura (Romania) *Tel:* (01) 6142429; (01) 6145759 *Fax:* (01) 3124703; (01) 3120901, pg 534

Monograma Ediciones (Spain) *Tel:* (071) 754124; (071) 712593 *Fax:* (071) 712593 *E-mail:* totem@atlas-iap.es, pg 583

Monoline Ltd (Israel) *Tel:* (08) 9741456 *Fax:* (08) 9741454, pg 1157, 1198, 1222

Ediciones Monserrat (Ecuador) *Tel:* (0222) 567 *Fax:* (0222) 541294 *E-mail:* edimon@uio.stnet.net, pg 1282

Ediciones Monserrate (Colombia) *Tel:* (01) 2531347; (01) 6130343; (01) 2713049 *Fax:* (01) 2534300; (01) 2534300 *E-mail:* edimonse@cable.net.co *Web Site:* www.edimonserrate.com, pg 113

Editorial Monte Carmelo (Spain) *Tel:* (0947) 25 60 61 *Fax:* (0947) 25 60 62 *E-mail:* editorial@montecarmelo.com *Web Site:* www.montecarmelo.com, pg 583

Verlag Monte Verita (Austria) *Tel:* (01) 315222 *Web Site:* www.anares.org, pg 55

Editions Paul Montel (France) *Tel:* (01) 46565266, pg 176

A Monteverde y Cia SA (Uruguay) *Tel:* (02) 952012 *Fax:* (02) 952012, pg 760

The Monthly Magazine for Ceramics Co, Ltd (Republic of Korea) *Tel:* (02) 832747 *Fax:* (02) 978639, pg 438

Montreal-Contacts/The Rights Agency (France) *Tel:* (01) 43 40 06 10 *Fax:* (01) 43 40 02 12, pg 1110

Gabriel Mony (France) *Tel:* (04) 94472832 *Fax:* (04) 94472832, pg 176

Moon Jin Media Co Ltd (Republic of Korea) *Tel:* (02) 792-7611 *Fax:* (02) 7928885 *E-mail:* mjmedia@hitel.kol.co.kr, pg 438

Moon-Ta-Gu Books (Australia) *Tel:* (02) 6336 0317 *Fax:* (02) 6336 1319 *E-mail:* taiji@ozemail.com.au, pg 33

Moonlight Publishing (Australia) *Tel:* 03 5447 8221 *E-mail:* moonlight@impulse.net.au, pg 33

Moonlight Publishing Ltd (United Kingdom) *Tel:* (01235) 821 821 *Fax:* (01235) 821 155 *E-mail:* moonlight.publishing@virgin.net, pg 715

Moorley's Print & Publishing Ltd (United Kingdom) *Tel:* (0115) 9320643 *Fax:* (0115) 9320643 *E-mail:* info@moorleys.co.uk, pg 715

Mora Ferenc Ifjusagi Koenyvkiado Rt (Hungary) *Tel:* (01) 2523284 *Fax:* (01) 1115003, pg 325

Ediciones Morata SL (Spain) *Tel:* (091) 448 09 26 *Fax:* (091) 448 09 25 *E-mail:* morata@infornet.es *Web Site:* www.edmorata.es, pg 583

Editio Moravia-Moravske hudebni vydavatelstvi (Czech Republic) *Tel:* (05) 41220025 *E-mail:* emdl@vtx.cz, pg 126

Moravska Galerie v Brne (Czech Republic) *Tel:* (05) 42 215 753; (05) 32 169 111 *Fax:* (05) 32 169 180 *E-mail:* m-gal@moravska-galerie.cz *Web Site:* www.moravska-galerie.cz, pg 126

Moravska Zemska Knihovna (Czech Republic) *Tel:* (05) 41646111 *Fax:* (05) 41646101 *E-mail:* mzk@mzk.cz *Web Site:* www.mzk.cz, pg 1460

Moravska Zemska Knihovna-Technicka Knihovna (Czech Republic) *Tel:* (05) 42162150 *Fax:* (05) 747758 *E-mail:* pokorna@mzk.cz, pg 1460

Editrice Morcelliana SpA (Italy) *Tel:* (030) 46451 *Fax:* (030) 2400605 *E-mail:* edit.morcelliana@agora.stm.it, pg 399

Editions Moressopoulos (Greece) *Tel:* (01) 3234217 *Fax:* (01) 3232082 *E-mail:* mores.s@altavista.net, pg 313

Moretti & Vitali editori srl (Italy) *Tel:* (035) 321588 *Fax:* (035) 321647, pg 400

Bibliotheque Universitaire Moretus Plantin (Belgium) *Tel:* (081) 724630 *Fax:* (081) 724645 *E-mail:* bump@fundp.ac.be *Web Site:* www.fundp.ac.be/bump, pg 1453

Morfotiki Estia AE (Greece) *Tel:* (01) 3621180 *Fax:* (01) 3627706, pg 313

Morfotiko Idryma Ethnikis Trapezas (Greece) *Tel:* (01) 3230841; (01) 3221335 *Fax:* (01) 3245089; (01) 3227057, pg 313

Morija Sesuto Book Depot (Lesotho) *Tel:* 76204 *Fax:* 360009, pg 1297

Morikita Shuppan Co Ltd (Japan) *Tel:* (03) 32658341 *Fax:* (03) 32648709, pg 421

Moritz Verlag (Germany) *Tel:* (069) 4305084 *Fax:* (069) 4305083 *E-mail:* MoritzVerlag@t-online.de, pg 265

Morley Books (United Kingdom) *Tel:* (0113) 2012900 *Fax:* (0113) 2012929 *E-mail:* frank_schubert@cyphergroup.com *Web Site:* www.cyphergroup.com, pg 1321

Morning Glory Publishers (China) *Tel:* (010) 68411973; (010) 68433187 *Fax:* (010) 68412023; (010) 68485739 *E-mail:* zh@mail.cibtc.com.cn; zh1@mail.cibtc.com.cn, pg 107

Morning Star Publisher Inc (Taiwan, Province of China) *Tel:* (04) 3595820 *Fax:* (04) 3597123, pg 631

Morrigan Book Co (Ireland) *Tel:* (096) 32555 *E-mail:* morrigan@online.ie, pg 362

Morris Press Ltd (Hong Kong) *Tel:* 28892168 *Fax:* 28892180, pg 1135, 1197

William Morris Agency (UK) Ltd (United Kingdom) *Tel:* (020) 7534 6800 *Fax:* (020) 7534 6900, pg 1120

William Morris Society (United Kingdom) *Tel:* (020) 8741 3735 *Fax:* (020) 8748 5207, pg 1371

Morsak Verlag (Germany) *Tel:* (08552) 4200 *Fax:* (08552) 42050 *E-mail:* info@morsak.de *Web Site:* www.morsak.de, pg 265

E J Morten (Publishers) (United Kingdom) *Tel:* (0161) 445 7629 *Fax:* (0161) 448 1323 *E-mail:* timlovat@aol.com, pg 715

Ernst G Mortensens Forlag A/S (Norway) *Tel:* 22941000 *Fax:* 22113040, pg 504

Morula Press, Business School of Botswana (Botswana) *Tel:* 353499 *Fax:* 304809, pg 77

Morus-Verlag GmbH (Germany) *Tel:* (030) 89 79 37-0 *Fax:* (030) 75 70 81 12 *E-mail:* mail@morusverlag.de *Web Site:* www.morusverlag.de, pg 265

Mosaico Editores, LDA (Portugal) *Tel:* (021) 388-19-02 *Fax:* (021) 387-10-81 *E-mail:* mosaico@mail.telepac.pt, pg 527

Mosaik Verlag GmbH (Germany) *Tel:* (089) 4372-0 *Fax:* (089) 4372-2812, pg 265

Mosby Lifeline (Australia) *Tel:* (02) 4383155 *Fax:* (02) 4383284, pg 33

Mosca Hermanos (Uruguay) *Tel:* (02) 489671 *Fax:* (02) 489671, pg 760

Moscow University Press (Russian Federation) *Tel:* (095) 2295091, pg 540

The Moshe Dayan Center for Middle Eastern & African Studies (Israel) *Tel:* (03) 640-9646 *Fax:* (03) 641-5802 *E-mail:* dayancen@ccsg.tau.ac.il *Web Site:* www.dayan.org, pg 371

Moss Associates Ltd (New Zealand) *Tel:* (04) 4728226 *Fax:* (04) 4728226 *E-mail:* moss@xtra.co.nz, pg 493

K & Z Mostafanejad (Australia) *Tel:* (099) 233741 *Fax:* (099) 233741 *E-mail:* mostak@grton.training.wa.gov.au, pg 33

Mostly Unsung (Australia) *Tel:* (03) 9555 5401 *Fax:* (03) 9555 5401 *E-mail:* milhis@alphalink.com.au, pg 33

Library of the Mosul Museum (Iraq), pg 1475

Mosul Public Library (Iraq) *Tel:* (060) 810162 *Fax:* (060) 814765, pg 1475

Motilal Banarsidass (India) *Tel:* (011) 391 1985; (011) 391 8335; (011) 397 4826; (011) 393 2747; (11) 393 0689; (11) 579 7221 *Fax:* (011) 393 0689; (011) 579 7221 *E-mail:* gloryindia@poboxes.com/mlbd@vsnl.com *Web Site:* www.mlbdbooks.com, pg 1289

Motilal Banarsidass Publishers Pvt Ltd (India) *Tel:* (011) 391 1985; (011) 391 8335; (011) 397 4826 *Fax:* (011) 393 0689; (011) 5452771, pg 343

Motilal (UK) Books of India (United Kingdom) *Tel:* (0208) 9051244 *Fax:* (0208) 9051108 *E-mail:* info@mlbduk.com *Web Site:* www.mlbduk.com, pg 715, 1321

Motivate Publishing (United Arab Emirates) *Tel:* (04) 282 4060 *Fax:* (04) 282 4436 *E-mail:* books@motivate.co.ae *Web Site:* www.booksarabia.com, pg 644

Michael Motley Ltd (United Kingdom) *Tel:* (020) 7723 2973 *Fax:* (020) 7262 4566, pg 1120

Motor Racing Publications Ltd (United Kingdom) *Tel:* (0208) 681 3363 *Fax:* (0208) 760 5117 *E-mail:* mrp.books@virgin.net *Web Site:* www.oberon.co.uk/mrp, pg 716

Motorbuch-Verlag (Germany) *Tel:* (0711) 210 80 65 *Fax:* (0711) 210 80 70 *E-mail:* versand@motorbuch.de *Web Site:* www.motorbuch-versand.de, pg 265

Motovun Book GmbH (Switzerland) *Tel:* (041) 4109515 *Fax:* (041) 4109516 *E-mail:* motovun@bluewin.ch, pg 619

Motovun Co Ltd, Tokyo (Japan) *Tel:* (03) 32614002 *Fax:* (03) 32641443, pg 1114

Motta Junior Srl (Italy) *Tel:* (02) 300761 *Fax:* (02) 38010046 *E-mail:* editor@mottaeditore.it *Web Site:* www.mottaeditore.it, pg 400

Motta Periodici Srl (Italy) *Tel:* (02) 33400491 *Fax:* (02) 38010046, pg 400

Mount Eagle Publications Ltd (Ireland) *Tel:* (066) 9151463 *Fax:* (066) 9151234 *Web Site:* www.brandonbooks.com, pg 362

Mountain House Press (Australia) *Tel:* (02) 66886318 *Fax:* (02) 66886318, pg 33

Mouse House Press (Australia) *Tel:* (047) 82-2929 *Fax:* (047) 82-5534 *E-mail:* mouhoupr@pnc.com.au, pg 34

Mousio Benaki (Greece) *Tel:* (01) 3611617; (01) 3612694 *Fax:* (01) 3622547, pg 313

Movement for Multi-Party Democracy (Zambia) *Tel:* (01) 224850; (01) 224851; (01) 224852; (01) 224853 *Fax:* (01) 224855, pg 767

Moxon Paperbacks (Ghana) *Tel:* (021) 665397, pg 307

MPG Books Ltd (United Kingdom) *Tel:* (01208) 73266 *Fax:* (01208) 73603 *E-mail:* print@mpg-books.co.uk, pg 1141, 1204

MPG Colour Ltd (United Kingdom) *Tel:* (01536) 483401 *Fax:* (01536) 481102 *E-mail:* print@mpg-colour.co.uk, pg 1162, 1204

MPH Distributors Sdn Bhd (Malaysia) *Tel:* (03) 7581688 *Fax:* (03) 7565995, pg 1298

MPH Bookstores (S) Pte Ltd (Singapore) *Tel:* 7485050; 7471088 *Fax:* 7440620; 7472630, pg 1309

MQ Publications Ltd (United Kingdom) *Tel:* (020) 7359 2244 *Fax:* (020) 7253 7358 *E-mail:* mqp@btinternet.com, pg 716

Mucchi Editore SRL (Italy) *Tel:* (059) 374094 *Fax:* (059) 282628 *E-mail:* info@mucchieditore.it *Web Site:* www.mucchieditore.it, pg 400

Anaya & Mario Muchnik (Spain) *Tel:* (091) 393 89 00 *Fax:* (091) 742 66 31 *E-mail:* cga@anaya.es *Web Site:* www.anaya.es, pg 583

Mudgala Trust (India) *Tel:* (044) 837257, pg 343

Mudrak Publishers & Distributors (India) *Tel:* (011) 3730818; (011) 3738319; (011) 6416317, pg 343

Verlag Rudolf Muehlemann (Switzerland) *Tel:* (072) 225353 *Fax:* (072) 223004, pg 619

Mueller & Schindler Verlag (Germany) *Tel:* (0711) 233204 *Fax:* (0711) 2369977, pg 265

C F Mueller Verlag, Huethig Gmb H & Co (Germany) *Tel:* (06221) 489 395 *Fax:* (06221) 489623 *E-mail:* cfmueller@huethig.de *Web Site:* www.huethig.de, pg 265

Lars Mueller Publishers (Switzerland) *Tel:* (056) 4301740 *Fax:* (056) 4301741 *E-mail:* books@lars-muller.ch *Web Site:* www.lars-mueller-publishers.com, pg 619

Norbert Mueller AG & Co KG Verlag (Germany) *Tel:* (089) 350 93-02 *Fax:* (089) 350 93-218 *E-mail:* info@vnm.de *Web Site:* www.vnm.de, pg 265

Otto Mueller Verlag GesmbH & Co KG (Austria) *Tel:* (0662) 881974; (0662) 881970 *Fax:* (0662) 872387, pg 55

Verlagsgesellschaft Rudolf Mueller GmbH & Co KG (Germany) *Tel:* (0221) 5497-0 *Fax:* (0221) 5497-326 *E-mail:* service@rudolf-mueller.de *Web Site:* www.rudolf-mueller.de, pg 265

Mueller Rueschlikon Verlags AG (Switzerland) *Tel:* (041) 740 30 40 *Fax:* (041) 741 71 15, pg 619

Mueller-Speiser Wissenschaftlicher Verlag (Austria) *Tel:* (06246) 73166 *Fax:* (06246) 73166 *E-mail:* mueller-speiser@salzburg.co.at *Web Site:* salzburg.co.at/mueller-speiser, pg 55

Mueller und Steinicke Verlag (Germany) *Tel:* (089) 74 99 156 *Fax:* (089) 74 99 157 *E-mail:* info@mueller-und-steinicke.de *Web Site:* www.mueller-und-steinicke.de, pg 266

Verlag Mueller und Kiepenheuer (Germany) *Tel:* (0618) 92810 *Fax:* (06181) 257387, pg 265

Mueszaki Koenyvkiado Ltd (Hungary) *Tel:* (01) 563458; (01) 1557122 *Fax:* (01) 755713 *E-mail:* lakatosz@muszakikiado.hu, pg 325

De Muiderkring BV (Netherlands) *Tel:* (0294) 450460 *Fax:* (0294) 412782, pg 481

Robert Muir Old & Rare Books (Australia) *Tel:* (08) 9386 5842 *Fax:* (09) 3868211 *E-mail:* muir@merriweb.com.au *Web Site:* www.muirbooks.com, pg 1273

Instituto de la Mujer (Miniterio de Trabajo y Asuntos Sociales) (Spain) *Tel:* (091) 363 80 00 *E-mail:* inmujer@mtas.es *Web Site:* www.mtas.es/mujer, pg 583

A Mukherjee & Co Pvt Ltd (India) *Tel:* (033) 341606; (033) 341499, pg 343

Mulavon Press Pty Ltd (Australia) *Tel:* (02) 808 3662 *Fax:* (02) 9552-1608, pg 34

Mulder Holland BV (Netherlands) *Tel:* (020) 442022; (020) 441682; (020) 824805 *Fax:* (020) 465228, pg 481

Mulini Press (Australia) *Tel:* (02) 6251 2519 *Fax:* (02) 6251 2519, pg 34

Societa Editrice Il Mulino (Italy) *Tel:* (051) 256011 *Fax:* (051) 256034 *E-mail:* info@mulino.it *Web Site:* www.mulino.it, pg 400

Muller Edition (France) *Tel:* (01) 40 90 0965 *Fax:* (01) 47 76 3397 *E-mail:* courrier@muller-edition.com *Web Site:* www.muller-edition.com, pg 176

Karl Muller Verlag (Germany) *Tel:* (09131) 30040 *Fax:* (09131) 300466, pg 266

Mullick Bros (Bangladesh) *Tel:* (02) 280728, pg 62, 1275

Mult es Jovo Kiado (Hungary) *Tel:* (01) 316 70 19 *Fax:* (01) 316 70 19 *E-mail:* mandj@multesjovo.hu *Web Site:* www.multesjovo.hu, pg 325

Multi-Disciplinary Research Centre Library (Namibia) *Tel:* (061) 2063907 *Fax:* (061) 2063050 *E-mail:* root@ssdgate.ssd.mrc.unam.na, pg 471

Multi Media Kunst Verlag Dresden (Germany) *Tel:* (0351) 8041291 *Fax:* (0351) 8041291, pg 266

Multi-Media Ltd (Trinidad & Tobago) *Tel:* 6288637; 6226774 *Fax:* 6281903, pg 637

Multilingual Matters Ltd (United Kingdom) *Tel:* (01275) 876519 *Fax:* (01275) 871673 *E-mail:* info@multilingual-matters.com *Web Site:* www.multilingual-matters.com, pg 716

Multimedia Zambia (Zambia) *Tel:* (01) 253666 *Fax:* (01) 363050, pg 767

Multinova (Portugal) *Tel:* (021) 8483365 *Fax:* (021) 8483436, pg 527

Ass Italiana Sclerosi Multipla (Italy) *Tel:* (010) 27131 *Fax:* (010) 2470226, pg 400

Multiplex Medway Ltd (United Kingdom) *Tel:* (01634) 684371 *Fax:* (01634) 683840 *E-mail:* enquiries@multiplex-medway.co.uk *Web Site:* www.multiplex-medway.co.uk, pg 1162, 1204

Multiplex Medway Ltd (United Kingdom) *Tel:* (01634) 684371 *Fax:* (01634) 683840, pg 1223

Multitech Publishing Co (India) *Tel:* (022) 5118820; (022) 513-0147 *Fax:* (022) 5115904, pg 343

Mun Un Dang (Republic of Korea) *Tel:* (02) 7433504; (02) 7433505 *Fax:* (02) 7450265, pg 438

Mundi-Prensa Libros SA (Spain) *Tel:* (091) 4 36 37 00 *Fax:* (091) 5 75 39 98 *E-mail:* liberia@mundiprensa.es *Web Site:* www.mundiprensa.com, pg 583

Mundi-Prensa Libros, SA (Spain) *Tel:* (091) 4363700 *Fax:* (091) 5753998 *E-mail:* libreria@mundiprensa.es *Web Site:* www.mundiprensa.com, pg 1311

Mundici & Zanetti srl (Italy) *Tel:* (051) 325347 *Fax:* (051) 326109, pg 400

Editora Mundo Cristao (Brazil) *Tel:* (011) 566-64829 *Fax:* (011) 566-65011 *E-mail:* editora@mundocristao.com.br, pg 88

Mundo Medico SA de CV Edicion y Distribucion de Revistas Medicas (Mexico) *Tel:* (05) 2038111; (05) 2038547; (05) 2036634; (05) 2554669; (05) 5592755 *Fax:* (05) 2036418, pg 464

Mundo Negro Editorial (Spain) *Tel:* (091) 4158115; (091) 4152412 *Fax:* (091) 5192550 *E-mail:* 100623.1651@compuserve.com, pg 583

Mundo Verlag GmbH (Germany) *Tel:* (0180) 9216350 *Fax:* (0180) 921635-24 *E-mail:* info@mundo-media.de *Web Site:* www.mundo-text.de, pg 266

Munhag-gwan (Republic of Korea) *Tel:* (02) 7186810 *Fax:* (02) 7062225, pg 438

Municipal Library (Cyprus), pg 1459

Biblioteca Municipal de Luanda (Angola) *Tel:* (02) 392297 *Fax:* (02) 33902, pg 1449

Bibliotheque Municipale (Madagascar) *Tel:* (04) 21176, pg 1482

Bibliotheque Municipale de Nancy (France) *Tel:* (03) 83373883 *Fax:* (03) 83379182 *E-mail:* bmnancy@mairie-nancy.fr, pg 1465

Munoz Moya Editor (Spain) *Tel:* (05) 4797251 *Fax:* (05) 4796650 *E-mail:* editorial@mmoya.com *Web Site:* www.mmoya.com, pg 583

James Munro & Co (United Kingdom) *Tel:* (0141) 429 1234 *Fax:* (0141) 420 1694 *E-mail:* enquiry@skipper.co.uk (general enquiries); sales@skipper.co.uk (orders) *Web Site:* www.skipper.co.uk, pg 716

Munshiram Manoharlal Publishers Pvt Ltd (India) *Tel:* (011) 3671668; (011) 3673650 *Fax:* (011) 3612745 *E-mail:* mrml@mantraonline.com *Web Site:* mrmlbooks.com, pg 343

Munshiram Manoharlal Publishers Pvt Ltd (India) *Tel:* (011) 3671668; (011) 2673750; (011) 7538992; (011) 7536097 *Fax:* (011) 3612745 *E-mail:* mml@mantraonline.com, pg 1289

Uitgeverij Maarten Muntinga (Netherlands) *Tel:* (020) 5216767 *Fax:* (020) 6260596 *E-mail:* info@rainbow.nl, pg 481

Munye Publishing Co (Republic of Korea) *Tel:* (02) 3935681; (02) 3935684 *Fax:* (02) 3935685, pg 439

Munzinger-Archiv GmbH Archiv fuer publizistische Arbeit (Germany) *Tel:* (0751) 76931-0 *Fax:* (0751) 65 24 24 *E-mail:* box@munzinger.de *Web Site:* www.munzinger.de, pg 266

Editorial la Muralla SA (Spain) *Tel:* (091) 415 36 87; (091) 416 13 71 *Fax:* (091) 413 59 07 *E-mail:* muralla@arcomuralla.com *Web Site:* www.arcomuralla.com, pg 583

Murchison's Pantheon Ltd (United Kingdom) *Tel:* (020) 7628 1492 *Fax:* (020) 7628 6270 *E-mail:* 100450.1105@compuserve.com, pg 716

Murdoch Books (Australia) *Tel:* (02) 8220 2000 *Fax:* (02) 8220 2558 *Web Site:* www.mm.com.au, pg 34

Murgorski Zoze (The Former Yugoslav Republic of Macedonia) *Tel:* (091) 241340, pg 449

John Murray (Publishers) Ltd (United Kingdom) *Tel:* (020) 7493 4361 *Fax:* (020) 7499 1792 *E-mail:* johnmurray@dial.plpex.com *Web Site:* www.johnmurray.co.uk, pg 716

Gruppo Ugo Mursia Editore SpA (Italy) *Tel:* (02) 67378500 *Fax:* (02) 67378605, pg 400

Musa Editora Ltda (Brazil) *Tel:* (011) 62-2586 *Fax:* (011) 62-2586 *E-mail:* musaeditora@vol.com.br, pg 88

Giov Muscat & Co Ltd (Malta) *Tel:* 237668; 233879; 247380 *Fax:* 240496, pg 1299

Musee d'Art et d'Archaeologie (Madagascar) *Tel:* (02) 21047 *Fax:* (02) 28218 *E-mail:* musedar@syfed.refer.mg, pg 450

Bibliotheque du Musee de l'Homme (France) *Tel:* (01) 44057203; (01) 44057272 *Fax:* (01) 44057212, pg 1465

Editions de la Reunion des Musees Nationaux (France) *Tel:* (01) 40 13 48 37 *Fax:* (01) 40 13 48 61 *E-mail:* communication@rmn.fr *Web Site:* www.rmn.fr, pg 176

Museo y Biblioteca Municipal (Ecuador) *Tel:* (04) 515738, pg 1462

Biblioteca del Museo Historico Nacional (Uruguay) *Tel:* (02) 951051, pg 1508

Museo Chileno de Arte Precolombino (Chile) *Tel:* (02) 6953851; (02) 6953627 *Fax:* (02) 6972779 *E-mail:* lcb.mchap@huelen.renna.cl *Web Site:* www.precolombino.cl, pg 100

Museo Historico Cultural Juan Santamaria (Costa Rica) *Tel:* 441-4775; 442-1838 *Fax:* 441-6926 *E-mail:* mhcjscr@racsa.co.cr *Web Site:* www.museojuansantamaria.go.cr, pg 116

Museo Storico in Trento (Italy) *Tel:* (0461) 230482 *Fax:* (0461) 237418 *E-mail:* info@museostorico.tn.it *Web Site:* www.museostorico.tn.it/editoria_ricerca, pg 400

Museu Maritimo (Macau) *Tel:* (0853) 595481; (0853) 595483 *Fax:* (0853) 512160 *E-mail:* museumaritimo@marine.gov.mo *Web Site:* www.museumaritime.gov.mo, pg 448

Museum of Victoria (Australia) *Tel:* (03) 8341 7777 *Fax:* (03) 9651 6321 *Web Site:* www.museum.vic.gov.au, pg 34

Museum Tusculanum Press (Denmark) *Tel:* 35329109 *Fax:* 35329113 *E-mail:* mtp@mtp.dk *Web Site:* www.mtp.dk, pg 134

Museum Van Het Boek/Museum Meermanno-Westreenianum (Netherlands) *Tel:* (070) 3462700 *Fax:* (070) 3630350, pg 1486

Music Book Distributors Ltd (United Kingdom) *Tel:* (0181) 5591522 *Fax:* (0181) 5591522, pg 1321

Music Publishers Association (United Kingdom) *Tel:* (020) 7839 7779 *Fax:* (020) 7839 7776 *E-mail:* mpa@mcps.co.uk *Web Site:* www.mpaonline.org.uk, pg 1266

Editorial Musica Moderna (Spain) *Tel:* (091) 416 91 81; (091) 415 37 78, pg 583

Musica Publishing House Ltd (Bulgaria) *Tel:* (02) 9877963; (02) 9802256 *Fax:* (02) 9877965 *E-mail:* mphsofia@hotmail.com *Web Site:* www.geocities.com/musicapublishinghouse, pg 96

Editions Musicales De La Schola Cantorum (Switzerland) *Tel:* (024) 485 24 80 *Fax:* (024) 485 24 80 *E-mail:* labatiaz@bluewin.ch, pg 619

Musicoteca Lda (Portugal) *Tel:* (021) 3220130 *Fax:* (021) 3476957 *E-mail:* musicoteca@mail.telepac.pt, pg 527

Musikantiquariat und Dr Hans Schneider Verlag GmbH (Germany) *Tel:* (08158) 3050; (08158) 6967 *Fax:* (08158) 7636 *E-mail:* musikbuch@aol.com; musikantiquar@aol.com, pg 266

Musikverlag Zimmermann (Germany) *Tel:* (069) 978286-6 *Fax:* (069) 978286-89 *E-mail:* info@musikverlag-zimmerman.de; info@lienau-frankfurt.de *Web Site:* www.zimmermann-frankfurt.de, pg 266

Musimed Edicoes Musicais Importacao E Exportacao Ltda (Brazil) *Tel:* (061) 226-0478 *Fax:* (061) 226-0478 *E-mail:* cartas@musimed.com.br *Web Site:* www.musimed.com.br, pg 88

Muslim Architecture Research Program (MARP) (Switzerland) *Tel:* (02) 4711228 *Fax:* (02) 4711228, pg 619

Muster-Schmidt Verlag (Germany) *Tel:* (551) 71741; (551) 597690 *Fax:* (551) 7702774 *E-mail:* info@muster-schmidt.de *Web Site:* www.muster-schmidt.de, pg 266

Musumeci SpA (Italy) *Tel:* (0165) 761216 *Fax:* (0165) 761112, pg 400

MUT Verlag (Germany) *Tel:* (04253) 566; (04253) 672 *Fax:* (04253) 16 03, pg 266

Mu'tah University Library (Jordan) *Tel:* (06) 617860 *Fax:* (03) 654061, pg 1479

Mutiara Sumber Widya PT (Indonesia) *Tel:* (021) 3909864; (021) 3908651; (021) 3904247 *Fax:* (021) 3160313, pg 356

Mutual Books Inc (Philippines) *Tel:* (02) 796050, pg 513

Muza SA (Poland) *Tel:* (022) 621-17-75; (022) 621-50-58; (022) 629-50-83 *Fax:* (022) 629-23-49 *E-mail:* muza@muza.com.pl, pg 518

Muze UK Ltd (United Kingdom) *Tel:* (0870) 7277 256 *Fax:* (0870) 7277 257 *E-mail:* colin@muze.co.uk *Web Site:* www.muze.com, pg 716

Editura Muzicala (Romania) *Tel:* (01) 3129867 *Fax:* (01) 3129867 *E-mail:* editura_muzicala@hotmail.com, pg 534

Muzicka Naklada (Croatia) *Tel:* (01) 424099, pg 119

Polskie Wydawnictwo Muzyczne (Poland) *Tel:* (012) 4227171 *Fax:* (012) 4227044 *E-mail:* pwm@pwm.com.pl, pg 518

Izdatelstvo Muzyka (Russian Federation) *Tel:* (095) 9230497 *Fax:* (095) 9283304 *E-mail:* muzyka@insar.ru, pg 540

Franco Muzzio & C Editore SpA (Italy) *Tel:* (049) 8712477 *Fax:* (049) 8713851, pg 400

MWH London Publishers (United Kingdom) *Tel:* (020) 7272 5170 *Fax:* (020) 7272 3214, pg 716

Myanmar Library Association (Myanmar), pg 1520

Myrtos Inc (Japan) *Tel:* (03) 32882200 *Fax:* (03) 32882225 *E-mail:* pub@myrtos.co.jp *Web Site:* www.myrtos.co.jp, pg 421

Izdatelstvo Mysl (Russian Federation) *Tel:* (095) 2324248; (095) 952-5065; (095) 955-0458, pg 540

Mystetstvo Publishers (Ukraine) *Tel:* (044) 2255392; (044) 2290564 *Fax:* (044) 2290564, pg 643

Mzuzu Publishing Co (Malawi) *Tel:* 352353 *Fax:* 352353 *E-mail:* kchiume@hotmail.com, pg 451

Instituto Nacional de Administracion Publica (Spain) *Tel:* (091) 349 32 41 *Fax:* (091) 349 32 70 *Web Site:* www.inap.map.es, pg 583

Biblioteca Nacional de Angola (Angola) *Tel:* (02) 326299 *Fax:* (02) 326299 *E-mail:* biblioteca@netangola.com, pg 1449

Instituto Nacional de Antropologia e Historia (Mexico) *Tel:* (05) 5335246; (05) 5332272; (05) 2074559; (05) 2074584 *Fax:* (05) 2074633 *E-mail:* difusion@inah.gob.mx, pg 464

Instituto Nacional de Ciencia y Tecnica Hidrica (INCYTH) (Argentina) *Tel:* (011) 4295-1503 *Fax:* (011) 4800094, pg 7

Instituto Nacional del Educacion Fisica Madrid (INEF-Madrid) (Spain) *Tel:* (091) 589 4057; (091) 589 4059 *Web Site:* www.inef.com, pg 583

Instituto Nacional de Estadistica, Geographia e Informatica (Mexico) *Tel:* (05) 5631602; (05) 5638904 *Fax:* (05) 180739 *E-mail:* adconde@cis.inegi.gob.mx, pg 464

Instituto Nacional de Estudos e Pesquisa (Guinea-Bissau) *Tel:* (0245) 223032 *Fax:* (0245) 251125 *E-mail:* inep@sol.gtelecom.gw, pg 316

Instituto Nacional de la Salud (Spain) *Tel:* (091) 338 00 03 *Web Site:* www.msc.es, pg 583

Editorial Nacional de Salud y Seguridad Social Ednass (Costa Rica) *Tel:* 2905744 *Fax:* 2327451 *E-mail:* cendeiss@info.ccss.sa.cr *Web Site:* www.ccss.sa.cr, pg 116

Nacionalna i Sveucilisna Biblioteka (Croatia) *Tel:* (041) 6164009 *Fax:* (041) 6164186, pg 1459

Giorgio Nada Editore SRL (Italy) *Tel:* (02) 27301126 *Fax:* (02) 27301454 *E-mail:* info@giorgionadaeditore.it *Web Site:* www.giorgionadaeditore.it, pg 400

Nadace Lyry Pragensis (Czech Republic) *Tel:* (02) 222 202 89 *Fax:* (02) 222 212 67, pg 126

Editions Maurice Nadeau, Les Lettres Nouvelles (France) *Tel:* (01) 48 87 48 58 *Fax:* (01) 48 87 13 01, pg 177

Edito Georges Naef SA (Switzerland) *Tel:* (022) 7380502 *Fax:* (022) 7384224 *E-mail:* edito@kister.ch, pg 619

Nafees Academy (Pakistan), pg 508

NAG Press (United Kingdom) *Tel:* (20) 7251 2661 *Fax:* (20) 7490 4958 *E-mail:* enquire@halebooks.com *Web Site:* www.halebooks.com/n_a_g_press_files.html, pg 716

Nagai Shoten Co Ltd (Japan) *Tel:* (06) 4521881 *Fax:* (06) 4521882, pg 421

Nagaoka Shoten Company Ltd (Japan) *Tel:* (03) 39925155 *Fax:* (03) 39483021, pg 421

Nagard (Italy) *Tel:* (02) 58371400 *Fax:* (02) 58304790, pg 400

Nagare Press (New Zealand) *Tel:* (06) 3272531, pg 493

Les Editions Nagel SA (Paris) (Switzerland) *Tel:* (022) 734 17 30 *Fax:* (022) 7337424 *E-mail:* admi@nagel.ch; rights@nagel.ch *Web Site:* www.nagel.ch, pg 619

Verlag Nagel & Kimche AG, Zurich (Switzerland) *Tel:* (01) 366 66 80 *Fax:* (01) 366 66 88 *E-mail:* info@nagel-kimche.ch *Web Site:* www.nagel-kimche.ch, pg 619

Verlag Stephanie Naglschmid (Germany) *Tel:* (0711) 62 68 78 *Fax:* (0711) 61 23 23 *E-mail:* naglschmid.vsn@t-online.de *Web Site:* www.naglschmid.de, pg 266

Nahanni Publishing Ltd (New Zealand) *Tel:* (09) 419 0681 *Fax:* (09) 419 0695 *E-mail:* info@nahanni-publishing.com; sales@nahanni.co.nz (for orders), pg 493

Nai Publishers (Netherlands) *Tel:* (010) 2010133 *Fax:* (010) 2010130 *E-mail:* info@naipublishers.nl *Web Site:* www.naipublishers.nl, pg 481

Nairobi University Press (Kenya) *Tel:* (02) 334244 (ext 2258) *Fax:* (02) 336885 *E-mail:* nup@uonbi.ac.ke, pg 433

Nakas Music House (Greece) *Tel:* (01) 364711; (01) 364716 *Fax:* (01) 3642521, pg 313

Nakayama Shoten Company Ltd (Japan) *Tel:* (03) 38131101 *Fax:* (03) 38133270, pg 421

Nakladatelstvi Svoboda (Czech Republic) *Tel:* (02) 449 132 58; (02) 23 06 14 *Fax:* (02) 449 132 58, pg 126

Nakladni zavod Matice hrvatske (Croatia) *Tel:* (01) 272143 *Fax:* (01) 432430 *E-mail:* nzmh@zg.tel.hr, pg 119

Naldoza Printers (Philippines) *Tel:* (032) 261-7326 *Fax:* (032) 261-7326 *E-mail:* naldoza@ebu.skyinet.net, pg 1158, 1199

Nam Hing Holdings Limited (Hong Kong) *Tel:* (02) 4759105 *Fax:* (02) 4732001 *E-mail:* nhillhkg@nh-laminate.com.hk, pg 321

Namibian Information Workers Association (NIWA) (Namibia) *Tel:* (061) 293382 *Fax:* (061) 229808 *E-mail:* e.namhila@parliment.gov.na; geikhoibes@unam.na, pg 1253

Namsgagnastofnun (Iceland) *Tel:* 5528088 *Fax:* 5624137 *E-mail:* simi@nams.is, pg 328

Nanam Publishing House (Republic of Korea) *Tel:* (02) 3413-1711; (02) 552-8537 *Fax:* (02) 552-0711 *E-mail:* nanamcom@soback.kornet21.net; edit@nanamcom.co.kr; post@nanamcom.co.kr *Web Site:* www.nanamcom.co.kr, pg 439

M/S Gulshan Nanda Publications (India) *Tel:* (022) 6406994 *Fax:* (022) 4303696, pg 343

Nanga (France) *Tel:* (06) 11 19 47 53 *Fax:* (02) 31 87 05 92 *E-mail:* nanga@nanga.fr *Web Site:* nanga.fr; feugereux.com, pg 177

Nanjing tushuguan (China) *Tel:* 7717619, pg 1457

Nanjing University Press (China) *Tel:* (025) 302695; (025) 3593642, pg 107

Nankodo Co Ltd (Japan) *Tel:* (03) 38117239 *Fax:* (03) 38117230, pg 421, 1295

Nan'un-Do Company Ltd (Japan) *Tel:* (03) 32682311 *Fax:* (03) 32605425, pg 422

Nanzando Co Ltd (Japan) *Tel:* (03) 56897855 *Fax:* (03) 56897857, pg 422

Naouka i Izkoustvo, Ltd (Bulgaria) *Tel:* (02) 9874790; (02) 9872496 *Fax:* (02) 9872496 *E-mail:* nauk_izk@sigma-bg.com, pg 97

Napier Public Library (New Zealand) *Tel:* (06) 8344180 *E-mail:* library@napier.govt.nz, pg 1487

Casa Editrice Roberto Napoleone (Italy) *Tel:* (06) 37515191 *Fax:* (06) 37515143, pg 400

Naprijed d d Naklada (Croatia) *Tel:* (01) 4873-296 *Fax:* (01) 4873-313 *E-mail:* info@croatian-book.com; naklada-naprijed@zg.tel.hr *Web Site:* www.naklada-ljevak.hr, pg 119

Naque Editora (Spain) *Tel:* (0926) 216714 *Fax:* (0926) 216714 *E-mail:* naque@cim.es *Web Site:* www.naque.es, pg 583

Narcea SA de Ediciones (Spain) *Tel:* (091) 554 64 84; (091) 554 61 02 *Fax:* (091) 554 64 87 *E-mail:* narcea@narceaediciones.es *Web Site:* www.narceaediciones.es, pg 583

Nardini Editore srl (Italy) *Tel:* (055) 598923 *Fax:* (055) 597185, pg 400

Naresh Publishers (India) *Tel:* (011) 5723235; (011) 5754442 *Fax:* (011) 574-6485, pg 343

Narkaling Inc (Australia) *Tel:* (08) 9274 8022 *Fax:* (08) 9274 8362 *E-mail:* info@narkaling.com.au *Web Site:* www.narkaling.com.au, pg 34

Narodna Biblioteka Srbije (Yugoslavia) *Tel:* (011) 431-083; (011) 451-242, pg 764

Narodna Biblioteka Srbije (Yugoslavia) *Tel:* (011) 451242 *Fax:* (011) 451289 *Web Site:* www.nbs.bg.ac.yu, pg 1508

Narodna i univerzitetska biblioteka Bosne i Hercegovine (Bosnia and Herzegovina) *Tel:* (071) 533204, pg 1454

Narodna in Univerzitetna Knjiznica, Ljubljana (Slovenia) *Tel:* (01) 2001-100 *Fax:* (01) 4257-293, pg 1497

Narodna Kultura (Bulgaria) *Tel:* (02) 981 4739 *Fax:* (02) 987 2722 *E-mail:* peepcult@intemet-bg.net *Web Site:* web.narodnakultura.hit.bg, pg 97

Narodnaya Asveta (Belarus) *Tel:* (0172) 264-62-68, 264-02-86, 264-64-69, 264-33-97 *Fax:* (0172) 236184 *E-mail:* ngpna@asveta.belpak.minsk.by., pg 63

Narodne Novine (Croatia) *Tel:* (01) 416-404 *Fax:* (01) 449-629 *Web Site:* www.nn.hr, pg 119

Narodni agentura ISBN v CR (Czech Republic) *Tel:* (02) 21663306 *Fax:* (02) 21663306 *E-mail:* isbn@nkp.cz *Web Site:* www.nkp.cz, pg 1241

Narodni knihovna Ceske republiky (Czech Republic) *Tel:* (02) 21663277 *Fax:* (02) 21663277 *Web Site:* www.nkp.cz, pg 1460

Narodni Knihovna CR (Czech Republic) *Tel:* (02) 81013316 *Fax:* (02) 81013333 *E-mail:* mirosovsky.ivo@cdh.nkp.cz *Web Site:* www.nkp.cz, pg 126

Narodni Muzeum (Czech Republic) *Tel:* (02) 24497111; (02) 24226488 *Fax:* (02) 264919 *E-mail:* ais@nm.anet.cz *Web Site:* www.nm.cz/, pg 126

Publishing House Narodno delo OOD (Bulgaria) *Tel:* (052) 230241; (052) 288516, pg 97

Narosa Book Distributors Pvt Ltd (India) *Tel:* (011) 6433992; (011) 6433818 *E-mail:* dlh.narosa@axcess.net.in, pg 1289

Narosa Publishing House (India) *Tel:* (011) 6433992; (011) 6433818 *Fax:* (011) 6468717, pg 343

Gunter Narr Verlag (Germany) *Tel:* (07071) 97970 *Fax:* (07071) 75288 *E-mail:* narr-francke@t-online.de *Web Site:* www.geist.de, pg 266

Narratio Theologische Uitgeverij (Netherlands) *Tel:* (0183) 628188 *Fax:* (0183) 628188 *E-mail:* narratio@worldonline.nl, pg 482

Nasa Djeca Publishing (Croatia) *Tel:* (01) 423550 *Fax:* (01) 423550, pg 119

Nase vojsko, nakladatelstvi a knizni obchod (Czech Republic) *Tel:* (02) 24915288; (02) 24917147 *Fax:* (02) 24915288, pg 126

Nashiran-e-Quran Pvt Ltd (Pakistan) *Tel:* (042) 58581; (042) 58581, pg 508

Perpustakaan Nasional (Indonesia) *Tel:* (021) 3101411 *Fax:* (021) 3103551, pg 1474

Nasionale Boekhandel Ltd (South Africa) *Tel:* (021) 5911131, pg 557

Nasou - Oudiovista (South Africa) *Tel:* (012) 4063001; (012) 3429971 *Fax:* (012) 4062922 *E-mail:* nasouhk@nbh.naspers.co.za, pg 557

Nasou Via Afrika (South Africa) *Tel:* (021) 406-3314 *Fax:* (021) 406-2922; (021) 406-3086 *E-mail:* MdeWitt@nasou.com *Web Site:* www.nasouviaafrika.com, pg 557

Nasou Via Afrika (South Africa) *Tel:* (021) 4063001 *Fax:* (021) 4062922 *E-mail:* nasouhk@nbh.naspers.co.za, pg 1310

Nassau Public Library (Bahamas) *Tel:* (242) 322-4907, pg 1452

Wydawnictwo Nasza Ksiegarnia Sp zoo (Poland) *Tel:* (022) 6439389 *Fax:* (022) 6437028, pg 518

Natal Society Library (South Africa) *Tel:* (033) 3452383 *Fax:* (033) 3940095 *E-mail:* nsl@alphafuturenet.co.za, pg 1498

Fernand Nathan (France) *Tel:* (01) 45 87 50 00 *Fax:* (01) 45 87 57 57 *Web Site:* www.nathan.fr, pg 177

National Bookseller (Guyana) *Tel:* (02) 71244 *Fax:* (02) 57309, pg 1287

National Books of Zimbabwe (Zimbabwe) *Tel:* (04) 703257; (04) 703258, pg 1325

National Acquisitions Group (United Kingdom) *Tel:* (01782) 750462 *E-mail:* nag@psilink.co.uk, pg 1266

National Agency for ISBN (India) *Tel:* (011) 3381739 *Fax:* (011) 3381355; (011) 3382947, pg 1248

National Archives (Egypt (Arab Republic of Egypt)), pg 1462

National Archives of Fiji (Fiji) *Tel:* 304144, pg 1463

National Archives of India (India) *Tel:* (011) 383436, pg 1473

NATIONAL ARCHIVES

National Archives (Ireland) *Tel:* (01) 4072 300 *Fax:* (01) 4072 333 *E-mail:* mail@nationalarchives.ie *Web Site:* www.nationalarchives.ie, pg 1476

National Archives (Libyan Arab Jamahiriya) *Tel:* (02133) 40166, pg 1481

National Archives of Malawi (Malawi) *Tel:* 522922 *Fax:* 522148, pg 1482

National Archives of Malaysia (Malaysia) *Tel:* (03) 2543244 *Fax:* (03) 2555679, pg 1483

National Archives of Nigeria Library (Nigeria) *Tel:* (022) 415000, pg 1488

National Archives of Singapore (Singapore) *Tel:* 3380000 *Fax:* 3393583, pg 1496

Department of National Archives (Sri Lanka) *Tel:* (01) 694523, pg 1499

National Archives Division (Thailand) *Tel:* (02) 2811599 *Fax:* (02) 28115341, pg 1503

National Archives (Trinidad & Tobago) *Tel:* (868) 6252689 *Fax:* (868) 6252629 *E-mail:* natt@tstt.neth, pg 1503

National Archives, Cape Town Archives Repository, Library (South Africa) *Tel:* (021) 4624050 *Fax:* (021) 4652960 *E-mail:* capearch01@hotmail.com *Web Site:* www.national.archives.gov.za, pg 1498

National Archives of Namibia (Namibia) *Tel:* (061) 2934308 *Fax:* (061) 239042 *E-mail:* natarch@witbooi.natarch.mec.gov.na, pg 1486

National Archives of Pakistan (Pakistan) *Tel:* (051) 9202044; (051) 9214569 *Fax:* (051) 817323; (051) 9203545 *Web Site:* www.unesco.org/web.world/mdm/1999/eng/pakistan, pg 1489

National Archives of Scotland (United Kingdom) *Tel:* (0131) 5351314 *Fax:* (0131) 5351360 *E-mail:* publications@nas.gov.uk *Web Site:* www.nas.gov.uk, pg 716

National Archives of South Africa, Orange Free State Archives Repository, Library/Free State Provincial Archives (South Africa) *Tel:* (051) 5226762 *Fax:* (051) 5226765 *E-mail:* fsarch01@hotmail.com *Web Site:* www.national.archives.gov.za, pg 1498

National Archives of Zambia (Zambia) *Tel:* (01) 254081 *Fax:* (01) 254080 *E-mail:* naz@zamnet.zm, pg 1509

National Archives of Zimbabwe (Zimbabwe) *Tel:* (04) 792741 *Fax:* (04) 792398, pg 769, 1509

National Archives Repository, Library (South Africa) *Tel:* (012) 3235300 *Fax:* (012) 3235287 *E-mail:* arg50@acts4.pwv.gov.za *Web Site:* www.national.archives.gov.za, pg 1498

National Assembly Library (Egypt (Arab Republic of Egypt)) *Tel:* (02) 3540279 *Fax:* (02) 3548977, pg 1462

National Assembly for Wales (United Kingdom) *Tel:* (029) 20 825111 *Fax:* (029) 20 825350 *E-mail:* stats.pubs@wales.gsi.gov.uk *Web Site:* www.wales.gov.uk, pg 717

National Assembly Library (Republic of Korea) *Tel:* (02) 7884101; (02) 7843565 *Fax:* (02) 7884301; (02) 7884193 *E-mail:* cdcol@nanet.go.jp, pg 1480

National Association for the Teaching of English (NATE) (United Kingdom) *Tel:* (0114) 255 5419 *Fax:* (0114) 255 5296 *E-mail:* natehq@btconnect.com *Web Site:* www.nate.org.uk, pg 717

National Association of Forest Industries Ltd (Australia) *Tel:* (02) 6285 3833 *Fax:* (02) 6285 3855 *E-mail:* enquiries@nafi.com.au *Web Site:* www.nafi.com.au, pg 34

Library of the National Bank (Afghanistan), pg 1449

National Bibliographic Agency (United Republic of Tanzania) *Tel:* (051) 150048; (051) 110573 *Fax:* (022) 2151100 *E-mail:* tlsb@africaonline.co.tz, pg 1263

National Book Chamber of Belarus (Belarus) *Tel:* (172) 2893396 *Fax:* (172) 28933963 *E-mail:* palata@palata.belpak.minsk.by, pg 1237

National Book Council Inc (Australia) *Tel:* (03) 6638043 *Fax:* (03) 6638658, pg 1236

National Book Foundation (Pakistan) *Tel:* (051) 9261533; (051) 9261534 *Fax:* (051) 2264283; (051) 2264283 *E-mail:* nbf@paknet2.ptc.pk *Web Site:* nbf.org.pk, pg 508

National Book Organization (India) *Tel:* (011) 669962 *Fax:* (011) 6851795, pg 343

National Book Store Inc (Philippines) *Tel:* (02) 6318061; (02) 6318062; (02) 6318063; (02) 6318064; (02) 6318065; (02) 6318066 *E-mail:* purchbooks@nationalbookstore.com.ph, pg 514

National Book Store Inc (Philippines) *Tel:* (02) 6318061; (02) 6318062; (02) 6318063; (02) 6318064; (02) 6318065; (02) 6318066, pg 1306

National Book Trust India (India) *Tel:* (011) 669962; (011) 664540; (011) 664667 *Fax:* (011) 6851795, pg 343

National Botanical Institute (South Africa) *Tel:* (012) 804-3200 *Fax:* (012) 804-3211 *E-mail:* rpub@nbipre.nbi.ac.za *Web Site:* www.nbi.ac.za, pg 557

National Central Library (Taiwan, Province of China) *Tel:* (02) 23619132 *Fax:* (02) 23110155, pg 1502

Centre National de la Photographie (France) *Tel:* (01) 53 76 12 31 *Fax:* (01) 53 76 12 33 *E-mail:* centre.national.de.la.photographie@wanadoo.fr *Web Site:* www.cnp-photographie.com/cnp_version_fr/lieux/page_liste.html, pg 177

Centre National de la Recherche Scientifique (France) *Tel:* (03) 83 96 21 76 *Fax:* (03) 83 97 24 56 *Web Site:* www.inalf.fr, pg 177

National Centre of Archives (Iraq) *Tel:* (01) 4164190, pg 1475

National Children's Educational Foundation (Sri Lanka) *Tel:* 578090 *Fax:* 578090, pg 597

National Council of Applied Economic Research, Publications Division (India) *Tel:* (011) 3379861 *Fax:* (011) 3370164 *E-mail:* infor@ncaer.org *Web Site:* www.ncaer.org, pg 344

National Council of Educational Research & Training, Publication Department (India) *Tel:* (011) 6851070; (011) 662708 *Fax:* (011) 6868419, pg 344

Institut National de Recherche Pedagogique (France) *Tel:* (01) 46 34 90 00 *Fax:* (01) 43 54 32 01 *Web Site:* www.inrp.fr, pg 177

Office National d'Edition de Presse et d'Imprimerie (ONEPI) (Benin) *Tel:* 300299; 301152 *Fax:* 303463, pg 76

National Defence Industry Press (China) *Tel:* (010) 8412244-214 *Fax:* (010) 68413125; (010) 68427707 *E-mail:* ndip@public3.bta.net.cn *Web Site:* www.ndip.com.cn, pg 107

National Diet Library (Japan) *Tel:* (03) 35812331 *Fax:* (03) 35082934 *E-mail:* kokusai@ndl.go.jp *Web Site:* www.ndl.go.jp, pg 1478

National Extension College (United Kingdom) *Tel:* (01223) 400 200 *Fax:* (01223) 400 399 *E-mail:* info@nec.ac.uk *Web Site:* www.nec.ac.uk, pg 717

National Federation of Retail Newsagents (United Kingdom) *Tel:* (020) 7353 6816 *Fax:* (020) 7250 0927, pg 1267

National Federation of Standard Editor's Association in Nepal (NAFSEEN) (Nepal) *Tel:* (01) 212289; (01) 223036; (01) 224005 *Fax:* (01) 223036, pg 1253

National Federation of Standard Periodicals Publishers Association of Nepal (Nepal) *Tel:* 212289; 223036; 224005 *Fax:* (9771) 223036 ISB-ASS, pg 1253

INDUSTRY

National Federation of Standard Translator's Association in Nepal (Nepal) *Tel:* (01) 212289; (01) 223036; (01) 224005 *Fax:* (01) 223036 ISB-ASS, pg 1253

National Foster Care Association (United Kingdom) *Tel:* (020) 7620 6400 *Fax:* (020) 7620 6401 *E-mail:* nfca@fostercare.org.uk, pg 717

National Foundation for Educational Research (United Kingdom) *Tel:* (01753) 574123 *Fax:* (01753) 691632 *E-mail:* enquiries@nfer.ac.uk *Web Site:* www.nfer.ac.uk, pg 717

National Galleries of Scotland (United Kingdom) *Tel:* (0131) 624 6257; (0131) 624 6261 *Fax:* (0131) 315 2963 *E-mail:* enquiries@nationalgalleries.org *Web Site:* www.nationalgalleries.org, pg 717

National Gallery of Australia (Australia) *Tel:* (02) 6240 6501; (02) 6240 6502 *Fax:* (06) 6240 6427 *E-mail:* information@nga.gov.au *Web Site:* www.nga.gov.au, pg 34

National Gallery of Victoria (Australia) *Tel:* (03) 9208 0222 *Fax:* (03) 9208 0245 *E-mail:* enquiries@ngv.vic.gov.au *Web Site:* www.ngv.vic.gov.au, pg 34

National Historical Institute (Philippines) *Tel:* (0632) 590646; (0632) 572644, pg 514

National House for Publishing, Distributing and Advertising (Iraq) *Tel:* (01) 4251846, pg 358

National Information & Documentation Centre (Egypt (Arab Republic of Egypt)) *Tel:* (02) 3371696, pg 1242, 1462

National Institute for Compilation and Translation (Taiwan, Province of China) *Fax:* (02) 23629256, pg 1127

National Institute of Adult Continuing Education (United Kingdom) *Tel:* (0116) 204 4200; (0116) 204 4201 *Fax:* (0116) 285 4514 *E-mail:* enquiries@niace.org.uk; niace@niace.org.uk *Web Site:* www.niace.org.uk, pg 717

The National Institute of Development Research & Documentation (Botswana) *Tel:* 351151 *Fax:* 356591 *E-mail:* nir@wn.apc.org, pg 1454

National Institute of Historical & Cultural Research (Pakistan) *Tel:* (051) 218535, pg 508

National Institute of Industrial Research (NIIR) (India) *Tel:* (011) 3923955; (011) 3935654 *Fax:* (011) 3941561 *E-mail:* niir@niir.org *Web Site:* www.nexusindia.com/niir.htm, pg 344

National Institute of Public Administration Library (Zambia) *Tel:* (01) 228802, pg 1509

National ISBN Agency (Bulgaria) *Tel:* (02) 982811 *Fax:* (02) 435495 *E-mail:* nbkm@nl.otel.net, pg 1239

National ISBN Agency (Mauritius) *Tel:* (0230) 4646761; (0230) 4643959; (0230) 4643452 *Fax:* (0230) 4643445 *E-mail:* eoibooks@intnet.mu, pg 1252

National Library (Bangladesh) *Tel:* (02) 326578 *Fax:* (02) 833212, pg 1237

National Library of Belarus (Belarus) *Tel:* (0172) 275463 *Fax:* (0172) 292494 *E-mail:* sol@nacbibl.minsk.by, pg 1453

National Library 'Ivan Vazov' (Bulgaria) *Tel:* (032) 62 29 15 *E-mail:* nbiv@plovdiv.techno-link.com *Web Site:* fobos.primasoft.bg/libplovdiv, pg 1455

The National Library of China (China) *Tel:* (010) 68415566 *Fax:* (010) 68419271 *E-mail:* cjsun@sun.ihep.ac.cn, pg 1457

National Library of Greece (Greece) *Tel:* (01) 3614413 *Fax:* (01) 3608495 *E-mail:* nikolopoulos@sysa.nlg.ariaolne-t.gr, pg 1470

National Library (Guyana) *Tel:* (02) 62699, pg 1471

The National Library, Government of India (India) *Tel:* (033) 4791381 *Fax:* (033) 4791462, pg 1473

National Library (Iraq) *Tel:* (01) 4164190, pg 1475

National Library (Libyan Arab Jamahiriya) *Tel:* (061) 90509 *Fax:* (061) 96379, pg 1481

National Library of Malaysia (Gift & Exchange Unit) (Malaysia) *Tel:* (03) 2943488 *Fax:* (03) 2927899 *E-mail:* pnmweb@www.pnm.my, pg 1483

National Library of Malta (Malta) *Tel:* 224338 *Fax:* 235992 *E-mail:* joseph.boffa@magnet.mt, pg 1483

National Library (Myanmar) *Tel:* (01) 272058, pg 1486

National Library (Namibia) *Tel:* (061) 2934490 *Fax:* (061) 229808 *E-mail:* johan@natlib.mec.gov.na, pg 1486

National Library (Saudi Arabia), pg 1496

National Library (Thailand) *Tel:* (02) 6285183 *Fax:* (02) 2810263 *E-mail:* suwksir@emisc.moe.go.th *Web Site:* www.span.com.au/nlt, pg 1263

The National Library of Thailand (Thailand) *Tel:* (02) 2815212 *Fax:* (02) 2810263 *E-mail:* suwaksir@emisc.moc, pg 1503

National Library of Turkmenistan (Turkmenistan) *Tel:* (03632) 253254, pg 1504

National Library (United Arab Emirates) *Tel:* (02) 215300 *Fax:* (02) 217472, pg 1505

National Library and Archives of Ethiopia (Ethiopia) *Tel:* (01) 512241, pg 1463

National Library & Documentation Services Board (Sri Lanka) *Tel:* (01) 685198; (01) 685199; (01) 698847; (01) 685197 *Fax:* (01) 685201 *E-mail:* nldsb@mail.natlib.lk *Web Site:* natlib.lk, pg 597

National Library & Documentation Services Board (Sri Lanka) *Tel:* (01) 6852003; (01) 685199; (01) 698847 *Fax:* (01) 685201 *E-mail:* nldsb@mail.natlib.lk, pg 1499

National Library & Information System Authority (NALIS) (Trinidad & Tobago) *Tel:* (0868) 624-5835; (0868) 623-6137; (0868) 623-4844; (0868) 627-2319 *Fax:* (0868) 625-5369 *E-mail:* nalis@nalis.gov.tt *Web Site:* www.nalis.gov.tt, pg 1503

National Library for the Blind (United Kingdom) *Tel:* (0161) 355 2000 *Fax:* (0161) 355 2098 *E-mail:* enquiries@nlbuk.org *Web Site:* www.nlbuk.org, pg 1506

The National Library of the Islamic Republic of Iran (Islamic Republic of Iran) *Tel:* (021) 2288680 (voice & fax) *Fax:* (021) 8088950 *E-mail:* natlibir@neda.net, pg 1475

National Library of Australia (Australia) *Tel:* (062) 62 1593 *Fax:* (062) 73 4493 *E-mail:* nlasales@nla.gov.au *Web Site:* www.nla.gov.au, pg 34

National Library of Australia (Australia) *Tel:* (06) 2621111 *Fax:* (06) 62571703 *Web Site:* www.nla.gov.au, pg 1511

National Library of Burundi (Burundi) *Tel:* 021 62 73 *Fax:* 021 92 95 *E-mail:* biefbdi@cbinf.com, pg 1456

National Library of Estonia (Estonia) *Tel:* (02) 6307500; (06) 307501 *Fax:* (02) 6311410 *E-mail:* nlib@nlib.ee *Web Site:* www.nlib.ee, pg 140

National Library of Estonia (Estonia) *Tel:* (02) 6307500 *Fax:* (02) 6311410 *E-mail:* nlib@venus.nlib.ee, pg 1462

National Library of Ireland (Ireland) *Tel:* (01) 6030200 *Fax:* (01) 6766690 *E-mail:* info@nli.ie *Web Site:* www.nli.ie, pg 362

National Library of Ireland (Ireland) *Tel:* (01) 6618811 *Fax:* (01) 6766690, pg 1476

National Library of Ireland Society (Ireland) *Tel:* (01) 6030200 *Fax:* (01) 6766690, pg 1518

National Library of Izmir (Turkey) *Tel:* (0232) 4842002 *Fax:* (0232) 4821703, pg 1504

National Library of Jamaica (Jamaica) *Tel:* (876) 967-1526 *Fax:* (876) 922-5567 *E-mail:* nlj@infochan.com *Web Site:* www.nlj.org.jm, pg 1478

The National Library of Korea (Republic of Korea) *Tel:* (02) 5354142; (02) 5900548 *Fax:* (02) 5965749 *E-mail:* nlkpc@sun.nl.or.kr, pg 1480

National Library of Kuwait (Kuwait) *Tel:* 2415192; 2415190 *Fax:* 2415195 *E-mail:* nccalknl@ncc.moc.kw, pg 1480

National Library of Latvia (Latvia) *Tel:* (02) 7289874 *Fax:* (02) 7280851 *E-mail:* lnb@lbi.lnb.lv *Web Site:* www.latnet.lv/lnb, pg 1481

National Library of New Zealand (Te Puna Matauranga o Aotearoa) (New Zealand) *Tel:* (04) 4743000 *Fax:* (04) 4743035; (04) 858077, pg 1487

National Library of Nigeria-Reserch & Development Dept (Nigeria) *Tel:* (01) 2600220 *Fax:* (09) 2347517, pg 1488

National Library of Pakistan (Pakistan) *Tel:* (051) 9214523 *Fax:* (051) 92213754 *E-mail:* nlpiba@isb.paknet.com.pk, pg 1490

National Library (Philippines) *Tel:* (02) 5253196 (Filipiniana); (02) 582271 (Reference); (02) 582660 (Public Documents) *Fax:* (02) 5242329 *E-mail:* amb@max.ph.net, pg 1491

National Library of Scotland (United Kingdom) *Tel:* (0131) 226 4531 *Fax:* (0131) 622 4803 *E-mail:* enquiries@nls.uk *Web Site:* www.nls.uk, pg 717

National Library of Scotland (United Kingdom) *Tel:* (0131) 2264531 *Fax:* (0131) 6224803 *E-mail:* enquiries@nls.uk *Web Site:* www.nls.uk, pg 1506

National Library of Sri Lanka Library Services Board (Sri Lanka) *Tel:* (01) 685203; (01) 685199; (01) 698847 *Fax:* (01) 685201 *E-mail:* nldsb@mail.natlib.lk, pg 1523

National Library of Vietnam (Viet Nam) *Tel:* (04) 8252643 *Fax:* (04) 253357 *E-mail:* tdung@nlv01.gov.vn, pg 1508

National Library of Wales (United Kingdom) *Tel:* (01970) 632 800 *Fax:* (01970) 615 709 *E-mail:* holi@llgc.org.uk *Web Site:* www.llgc.org.uk, pg 717

National Library of Wales (United Kingdom) *Tel:* (01970) 632800 *Fax:* (01970) 615709 *E-mail:* holi@llgc.org.uk *Web Site:* www.llgc.org.uk, pg 1506

National Library Service (Barbados) *Tel:* (0246) 436-6081 *Fax:* (0246) 436-1501, pg 1452

National Library Service of Belize (Belize) *Tel:* (02) 2234248; (02) 2234249 *Fax:* (02) 2234246 *E-mail:* nls@btl.net *Web Site:* www.nlsbze.bz, pg 1453

National Library Service (Botswana) *Tel:* 352288; 352397 *Fax:* 301149, pg 77

National Museum (India) *Tel:* (011) 3018159; (011) 3833436, pg 344

National Museum Library of Sri Lanka (NMLSL) (Sri Lanka) *Tel:* (01) 693314 *Fax:* (01) 693314, pg 1500

National Museum & Gallery (United Kingdom) *Tel:* (029) 2039 7951 *Fax:* (029) 2037 3219 *E-mail:* post@nmgw.ac.uk *Web Site:* www.nmgw.ac.uk, pg 717

National Museum of History (Taiwan, Province of China) *Tel:* (02) 3610270-514 *Fax:* (02) 3610171, pg 631

National Museum of the Philippines (Philippines) *Tel:* (02) 494450 *Fax:* (02) 5270306 *E-mail:* nmuseum@i-next.net *Web Site:* nmuseum.tripod.com, pg 514

National Palace Museum (Taiwan, Province of China) *Tel:* (02) 8821230 *Fax:* (02) 8821440 *E-mail:* service@npm.gov.tw *Web Site:* www.npm.gov.tw, pg 631

National Portrait Gallery Publications (United Kingdom) *Tel:* (020) 7306 0055 (ext 253) *Fax:* (020) 7306 0092 *E-mail:* publications@npg.org.uk *Web Site:* www.npg.org.uk, pg 717

National Public Health Laboratory Services (Medical Department) (Kenya) *Tel:* (02) 725601 *Fax:* (02) 729504, pg 1480

National Publishing House (India) *Tel:* (011) 3274161; (011) 3275267, pg 344

National Records Office Library (Sudan) *Tel:* 76082, pg 1500

National Reference Library (Singapore) *Tel:* 3377355 *Fax:* 3309611, pg 1496

National Research Institute of Papua New Guinea (Papua New Guinea) *Tel:* (675) 3263200, pg 510

National Scientific and Technical Information Center (NSTIC) (Kuwait) *Tel:* 4818713 *Fax:* 4836097, pg 1480

National Social Science Documentation Centre (India) *Tel:* (011) 3383091; (011) 3385959; (011) 3073437; (011) 3073438; (011) 3073563 *Fax:* (011) 3381571 *E-mail:* nassdocigss@hotmail.com *Web Site:* www.icssr.org/nassdoc.htm, pg 1126

National Standards Publisher's and Bookseller's Association Nepal (NASPUBAN) (Nepal) *Tel:* (01) 212289; (01) 223036; (01) 224005 *Fax:* (01) 223036, pg 1300

National Standards Wholesaler's Distributor's and Subscriber's Association of Nepal (NASWDISAN) (Nepal) *Tel:* (01) 212289; (01) 223036; (01) 224005 *Fax:* (01) 223036, pg 1253

National Taiwan University Library (Taiwan, Province of China) *Tel:* (02) 2363-6810 *Fax:* (02) 23634344 *E-mail:* ntulib@ms.cc.ntu.edu.tw *Web Site:* www.lib.ntu.edu.tw, pg 1502

Library of the National Technological University of Athens (Greece), pg 1471

National Trust (United Kingdom) *Tel:* (020) 7222 9251 *Fax:* (020) 7222 5097, pg 717

National Union of Journalists (Book Branch) (United Kingdom) *Tel:* (020) 7278 7916 *Fax:* (020) 7837 8143 *E-mail:* book_branch@hotmail.com *Web Site:* www.nujbook.org, pg 1267

National University of Lesotho Library (Lesotho) *Tel:* 340601 *Fax:* 340000, pg 1481

National University of Malaysia Library (Malaysia) *Tel:* (03) 8250001 *Fax:* (03) 8256484, pg 1483

National University of Singapore Library (Singapore) *Tel:* 7722069 *Fax:* 7771272 *E-mail:* clbsec@nus.edu.sg, pg 1496

National University of Ireland Galway (NUI, Galway) (Ireland) *Tel:* (091) 524809 *Fax:* (091) 522394 *Web Site:* www.library.nuigalway.ie, pg 1476

National War College Library (Taiwan, Province of China) *Tel:* (02) 3619132 *Fax:* (02) 3110155, pg 1502

Bibliotheque Nationale (Laos People's Democratic Republic) *Tel:* (021) 212452; (021) 222485 *Fax:* (021) 213029 *E-mail:* pfd-mill@pan.laos.net.la, pg 1481

Bibliotheque Nationale (Luxembourg) *Tel:* 229755-1 *Fax:* 475672, pg 1482

Bibliotheque Nationale Populaire (Congo) *Tel:* 833485, pg 1458

Archives nationales (Algeria) *Tel:* (054) 2160 *Fax:* (054) 1616, pg 1449

Archives Nationales (Luxembourg) *Tel:* 4786660 *Fax:* 474692, pg 1482

Archives Nationales de Madagascar (Madagascar), pg 1482

The Nationalities Publishing House (China) *Tel:* (010) 4212794; (010) 4212031, pg 107

Natoli Stefan & Oliva Literary Agency (Italy) *Tel:* (02) 7000 1645 *Fax:* (02) 741277 *E-mail:* natoli.oliva@tiscalinet.it, pg 1113

Natraj Prakashan (India), pg 344

Verlag Natur & Wissenschaft Harro Hieronimus & Dr Jurgen Schmidt (Germany) *Tel:* (0212) 819878 *Fax:* (0212) 816216 *E-mail:* info@verlagnw.de, pg 266

Natur och Kultur/LTs foerlag (Sweden) *Tel:* (08) 4538725 *Fax:* (08) 4538798 *E-mail:* lt@nok.se *Web Site:* www.nok.se/lt, pg 604

Bokklubben Natur og Kultur (Norway) *Tel:* 22985600 *Fax:* 22985630, pg 1231

Natura-Verlag Arlesheim (Switzerland) *Tel:* (061) 717111 *Fax:* (061) 7064201, pg 619

The Natural History Museum Library (United Kingdom) *Tel:* (020) 7942 5460 *Fax:* (020) 7942 5559, pg 1506

Natural Resources Development College Library (Zambia) *Tel:* (01) 281328 *Fax:* (01) 224639, pg 1509

NaturaViva Verlags GmbH (Germany) *Tel:* (07033) 13 80 816 *Fax:* (07033) 13 80 817 *E-mail:* naturaviva@t-online.de, pg 266

Naturegraph Publishers Inc (United States) *Tel:* 530-493-5353 *Fax:* 530-493-5240 *E-mail:* nature@sisqtel.net *Web Site:* www.naturegraph.com, pg 1208

Bokfoerlaget Naturoch Kultur (Sweden) *Tel:* (08) 4538600 *Fax:* (08) 4538790 *E-mail:* info@nok.se *Web Site:* www.nok.se, pg 604

Nauchnaya biblioteka im M Gor'kogo Sankt-Petersburgskogo (Russian Federation) *Tel:* (0812) 328 27 41; (0812) 218955 (Reference & Information) *Fax:* (0812) 328 27 41 *E-mail:* info@mail.lib.pu.ru *Web Site:* www.lib.pu.ru, pg 1495

Naucna Knjiga (Yugoslavia) *Tel:* (011) 637230; (011) 186585; (011) 623922; (011) 621342 *Fax:* (011) 638070, pg 764

Naufal Group Sarl (France) *Tel:* (01) 40701280 *Fax:* (01) 40701298, pg 177

Nauka Ltd (Japan) *Tel:* (03) 3981-5266 *Fax:* (03) 3981-5313 *E-mail:* imp@nauka.co.jp *Web Site:* www.nauka.co.jp, pg 1295

Nauka Publishers (Russian Federation) *Tel:* (095) 3347151 *Fax:* (095) 4202220 *E-mail:* nauka@nauka.msk.ru, pg 540

Naukova Dumka Publishers (Ukraine) *Tel:* (044) 2244068; (044) 2251042; (044) 2254170 *Fax:* (044) 2247060 *E-mail:* ndumka@ukrpost.net, pg 643

Naumann & Goebel Verlagsgesellschaft mbH (Germany) *Tel:* (02236) 39990 *Fax:* (02236) 399999 *E-mail:* einstieg@aol.com; fdvemag@netcologne.de, pg 267

Ediciones Nauta Credito SA (Spain) *Tel:* (093) 4392204 *Fax:* (093) 4107314, pg 584

Edition Nautilus Verlag (Germany) *Tel:* (040) 7213536 *Fax:* (040) 7218399 *E-mail:* edition-nautilus@t-online.de *Web Site:* www.edition-nautilus.de, pg 267

Nautiska Foerlaget AB (Sweden) *Tel:* (08) 6770000 *Fax:* (08) 6770010 *E-mail:* nautiska.ab@nautiskamf.se, pg 605

Nauwelaerts Edition SA (Belgium) *Tel:* (010) 861655 *Fax:* (010) 7517408, pg 72

Nava (Czech Republic) *Tel:* (019) 7235633; (019) 7235721; (019) 7223294; (019) 7223251; (019) 7235509 *Fax:* (019) 223143, pg 127

Navajivan Trust (India) *Tel:* (079) 7541329, pg 344

Navakarnataka Publications (P) Ltd (India) *Tel:* (080) 203580; (080) 2203581; (080) 2251382, pg 1289

Instituto de Publicaciones Navales (Argentina) *Tel:* (011) 4311-0042; (011) 4311-0043 *Fax:* (011) 4312-8461; (011) 4312-8462; (011) 4312-8463, pg 7

Navarine Publishing (Australia) *Tel:* (02) 62824602, pg 34

Navarra, Comunidad Autonoma, Servicio de Prensa, Publica Pamplona (Spain) *Tel:* (0948) 427121 *Fax:* (0948) 427123 *E-mail:* fpublio01@cfnavarra.es *Web Site:* www.cfnavarra.es, pg 584

Naves Internacional de Ediciones SA (Mexico) *Tel:* (05) 6690595; (05) 9180055595 *Fax:* (05) 6823728 *E-mail:* niesa@mpsnet.com.mx, pg 464

Navrang Booksellers & Publishers (India) *Tel:* (011) 5835914; (011) 5836197 *Fax:* (011) 5836113; (011) 5836761 *E-mail:* navrang@del2.vsn.net.in, pg 344

Navyug Publishers (India) *Tel:* (011) 278370, pg 344

Naya Prokash (India) *Tel:* (033) 349566 *Fax:* (033) 5523366; (033) 5524053, pg 344

Nayiri Bookshop (Islamic Republic of Iran) *Tel:* (021) 677578; (021) 7536802; (021) 7537029 *Fax:* (021) 677578, pg 1291

Accademia Naz dei Lincei (Italy) *Tel:* (06) 6838831 *Fax:* (06) 6893616, pg 400

Nazarene Publications (Papua New Guinea) *Tel:* (675) 546 2255 *Fax:* (675) 546 2255 *E-mail:* bcbes@datec.com.pg, pg 510

Istituto Nazionale di Archeologia e Storia dell'Arte (Italy) *Tel:* (06) 6798804 *Fax:* (06) 6798804, pg 400

Istituto Nazionale di Studi Romani (Italy) *Tel:* (06) 5743442; (06) 5743445 *Fax:* (06) 5743447 *E-mail:* studiromani@studiromani.it *Web Site:* www.studiromani.it, pg 400

NBLC Vereniging van Openbare Bibliotheken (Netherlands) *Tel:* (070) 3090100 *Fax:* (070) 3090200, pg 1521

NCLC Publishing Society Ltd (United Kingdom) *Tel:* (020) 7222 8877 *Fax:* (020) 7976 7153 *E-mail:* fabian-society@geo2.poptel.org.uk, pg 718

NCVO (United Kingdom) *Tel:* (020) 7713 6161 *Fax:* (020) 7713 6300 *E-mail:* ncvo@ncvo-vol.org.uk *Web Site:* www.ncvo-vol.org.uk, pg 718

Ndanda Mission Press (United Republic of Tanzania), pg 634

Ndermarrja Perhapjes se Librit (Albania) *Tel:* (042) 3323 *Fax:* (042) 3323, pg 1271

Ndermarrja e Botimeve Ushtarake (Albania), pg 1

Ndola Public Library (Zambia) *Tel:* 617173, pg 1509

NDV Neue Darmstadter Verlagsanstalt (Germany) *Tel:* (02224) 3232 *Fax:* (02224) 78639 *E-mail:* info@ndv-verlag.de *Web Site:* www.ndv-verlag.de, pg 267

Ed Nea Acropolis (Greece) *Tel:* (01) 8231301 *Fax:* (01) 8810830, pg 313

Nea Synora (Greece) *Tel:* (01) 3610589; (01) 3600398 *Fax:* (01) 3617791, pg 313

Nea Thesis - Evrotas (Greece) *Tel:* (01) 3634932 *Fax:* (01) 3604665, pg 313

Nebel Verlag GmbH (Germany) *Tel:* (09131) 34042 *Fax:* (09131) 300466, pg 267

Nebelspalter-Verlag (Switzerland) *Tel:* (071) 8440444 *Fax:* (071) 8440445, pg 620

Neckar Verlag GmbH (Germany) *Tel:* (07721) 89 87-0 *Fax:* (07721) 89 87-50 *E-mail:* service@neckar-verlag.de *Web Site:* www.neckar-verlag.de, pg 267

Nederlands Bureau voor Bibliotheekwezen en Informatieverzorging (NBBI) (Netherlands) *Tel:* (070) 3607833 *Fax:* (070) 3615011, pg 1521

Nederlands Instituut voor Wetenschappelijke Informatiediensten (Netherlands) *Tel:* (020) 4628628 *Fax:* (020) 6685079 *E-mail:* info@niwi.knaw.nl *Web Site:* www.niwi.knaw.nl, pg 1486

Nederlands Literair Produktie-en Vertalingenfonds (Netherlands) *Tel:* (020) 6206261 *Fax:* (020) 6207179 *E-mail:* nlpvf@xs4all.nl *Web Site:* www.nlpvf.nl, pg 482

Nederlands Uitgeverbond (Netherlands) *Tel:* (020) 4309150 *Fax:* (020) 4309179 *E-mail:* info@uitgeversverbond.nl *Web Site:* www.uitgeversverbond.nl, pg 1254

Nederlandsche Vereeniging van Antiquaren (Netherlands) *Tel:* (030) 2319286 *Fax:* (030) 2343362 *E-mail:* bestbook@wxs.nl *Web Site:* www.nvva.nl, pg 1254

Nederlandsche Vereeniging voor Druk- en Boekkunst (Netherlands) *Tel:* (071) 5809634, pg 1255

Nederlandse Boekenclub (Netherlands) *Tel:* (03473) 79214 *Fax:* (03473) 79380, pg 1230

Nederlandse Boekverkopersbond (Netherlands) *Tel:* (070) 2287956 *Fax:* (070) 2284566, pg 1255

Nederlandse Lezerskring Boek en Plaat BV (Netherlands) *Tel:* (03473) 79214 *Fax:* (03473) 79380, pg 1230

Nederlandse Vereniging voor beroepsbeoefenaren in de bibliotheeck-informatie-en kennissector (Netherlands) *Tel:* (030) 2311263 *Fax:* (030) 2311830 *E-mail:* nvbinfo@wxs.nl *Web Site:* www.kb.b.nl/nvb, pg 1521

Izdatelstvo Nedra (Russian Federation) *Tel:* (095) 2505255 *Fax:* (095) 2502772, pg 540

Neelain University (Sudan) *Tel:* (011) 776433 *E-mail:* alageedseed Ahmed@hotmail.com, pg 1500

Neeta Prakashan (India) *Tel:* (011) 692013; (011) 692014; (011) 692015 *Fax:* (011) 4636011, pg 344

Paul Neff Verlag KG (Austria) *Tel:* (01) 94061115 *Fax:* (01) 947641288, pg 55

Negotiate Ltd (United Kingdom) *Tel:* (0131) 445 7571; (0131) 477 7858 *Fax:* (0131) 445 7572 *E-mail:* florence@negweb.com *Web Site:* www.negotiate.co.uk, pg 718

Negotiate Ltd (United Kingdom) *Tel:* (0131) 445 7571 *Fax:* (0131) 445 7572 *E-mail:* gavin@neg1.demon.co.uk *Web Site:* www.negotiate.co.uk, pg 1120

Nehanda Publishers (Zimbabwe) *Tel:* (04) 708165 *Fax:* (04) 707698, pg 769

Nehora Press (Israel) *Tel:* (04) 6970255 *Fax:* (o4) 6970255 *E-mail:* nehora@canaan.co.il *Web Site:* www.nehorapress.com, pg 371

Nehru Memorial Museum and Library (NMML) (India) *Tel:* (011) 3015333; (011) 3017089 *Fax:* (011) 37923296, pg 1473

Uitgeverij H Nelissen BV (Netherlands) *Tel:* (035) 5412386 *Fax:* (035) 5423877 *E-mail:* service@nelissen.nl, pg 482

Nelles Verlag GmbH (Germany) *Tel:* (089) 357 194-0 *Fax:* (089) 357 194-30 *E-mail:* info@nelles-verlag.de *Web Site:* www.nelles-verlag.de, pg 267

Nelson Memorial Public Library (Samoa) *Tel:* (0685) 21028 *Fax:* (0685) 21028 *Web Site:* www.samoa.com, pg 1495

Thomas Nelson (Nigeria) Ltd (Nigeria) *Tel:* (01) 961452, pg 500

Nelson Thornes Ltd (United Kingdom) *Tel:* (01242) 267100; (01242) 267311 *Fax:* (01242) 221914 *E-mail:* cservices@nelsonthornes.com *Web Site:* www.nelsonthornes.com, pg 718

Nem Chand & Brothers (India) *Tel:* (01332) 72258; (01332) 72752; (01332) 74343 *Fax:* (01332) 73258, pg 344

Nemira Verlag (Romania) *Tel:* (01) 2116560 *Fax:* (01) 2228916 *E-mail:* nemira@dnt.ro, pg 534

Nemzeti Tankoenyvkiado (Hungary) *Tel:* (01) 1291496; (01) 1530600 *Fax:* (01) 363 2423 *E-mail:* ntk@mail.datanet.hu, pg 326

Nemzetkozi Szinhazi Intezet Magyar Kozpontja (Hungary) *Tel:* (01) 1752372 *Fax:* (01) 1751184, pg 326

Nensho-Sha (Japan) *Tel:* (06) 7719223 *Fax:* (06) 7719424, pg 422

Nepal Library Association (Nepal) *Tel:* (01) 521132, pg 1520

Nepal National Library (Nepal) *Tel:* (01) 521132 *E-mail:* nnl@nnl.wlink.com.np, pg 1486

Nepal PEN Centre (Nepal) *Fax:* (01) 522346 *E-mail:* archana@icimod.org.np; grana@saligram.mos.com.np, pg 1366

Neptun-Verlag (Switzerland) *Tel:* (072) 727262 *Fax:* (072) 6642023, pg 620

Editorial Nerea SA (Spain) *Tel:* (0943) 64 57 43 *Fax:* (0943) 64 60 27 *E-mail:* nerea@nerea.net *Web Site:* www.nerea.editores-euskadi.com, pg 584

NES Arnold Ltd (United Kingdom) *Tel:* (0870) 6000 192 *Fax:* (01530) 418268, pg 1141

Nestegg Books (New Zealand) *Tel:* (04) 3836645, pg 493

Network Promotions P/L (Australia) *Tel:* (018) 82-1848, pg 34

Neue Dimension Buch-und Musik-Verlag (Germany) *Tel:* (0911) 97987-25 *Fax:* (0171) 7906310 *E-mail:* mail@neue-dimension.com, pg 267

Neue Erde Verlags GmbH (Germany) *Tel:* (0681) 372313 *Fax:* (0681) 3904102 *E-mail:* info@neueerde.de, pg 267

Verlag Neue Kritik KG (Germany) *Tel:* (069) 727576 *Fax:* (069) 726585 *E-mail:* neuekritik@compuserve.com, pg 267

Verlag Neue Musik GmbH (Germany) *Tel:* (030) 616981-0 *Fax:* (030) 616981-21 *E-mail:* vnm@verlag-neue-musik.de *Web Site:* www.verlag-neue-musik.de, pg 267

Verlag Neue Musikzeitung GmbH (Germany) *Tel:* (0941) 94 59 30 *Fax:* (0941) 94 59 350 *E-mail:* nmz@nmz.de *Web Site:* www.nmz.de, pg 267

Verlag Neue Stadt GmbH (Germany) *Tel:* (08093) 2091 *Fax:* (08093) 2096, pg 267

Verlag Neue Wirtschafts-Briefe GmbH & Co (Germany) *Tel:* (02323) 141-900; (02361) 9142-0 (edtorial staff) *Fax:* (02323) 141-123 *E-mail:* info@nwb.de *Web Site:* www.nwb.de, pg 267

Neue Zeitschrift Missionswissenschaft Verlag (Switzerland) *Tel:* (041) 8541192 *Fax:* (041) 8504209 *E-mail:* nzmred@bluewin.ch *Web Site:* www.mypage.bluewin.ch/nzm, pg 620

Neue Zuercher Zeitung AG Buchverlag (Switzerland) *Tel:* (01) 2581505 *Fax:* (01) 2581399 *E-mail:* buch.bestellung@nzz.ch *Web Site:* www.nzz-buchverlag.ch, pg 620

Neuer Honos Verlag GmbH (Germany) *Tel:* (0221) 3 36 20-0 *Fax:* (0221) 3 36 20-99 *E-mail:* nhonos@netcologne.de, pg 267

Neuer ISP Verlag GmbH (Germany) *Tel:* (0721) 31 183 *Fax:* (0721) 31 250 *E-mail:* alive@sterneck.net *Web Site:* www.sterneck.net/alive/isp, pg 268

Neuer Weg Verlag und Druck GmbH (Germany) *Tel:* (0201) 2 59 15 *Fax:* (0201) 6 14 44 62 *E-mail:* neuerweg@neuerweg.de *Web Site:* www.neuerweg.de, pg 268

Verlag Neues Leben GmbH (Germany) *Tel:* (030) 284630 *Fax:* (030) 28388075, pg 268

Verlag Neues Leben (Austria) *Tel:* (05550) 3979, pg 55

Neues Literaturkontor (Germany) *Fax:* (0251) 4 05 65 *E-mail:* neues-literaturkontor@t-online.de *Web Site:* www.neues-literaturkontor.de, pg 268

Edition Neues Marchen (Austria) *Tel:* (03184) 2417 *Fax:* (03183) 7400, pg 55

Neufeld-Verlag und Galerie (Austria) *Tel:* (05577) 4657-0, pg 55

Wolfgang Neugebauer Verlag GmbH (Austria) *Tel:* (0316) 05522 4770 *Fax:* (0316) 05522 4770 *E-mail:* wnverlag@utanet.at, pg 55

Buchhandlung Wolfgang Neugebauer (Austria) *Tel:* (05522) 74770 *Fax:* (05522) 74770 *E-mail:* bayer.buch@utanet.at, pg 1274

Neuland-Verlagsgesellschaft mbH (Germany) *Tel:* (04152) 8 13 42 *Fax:* (04152) 8 13 43 *E-mail:* vertrieb@neuland.com *Web Site:* www.neuland.com, pg 268

Neumann Verlag (Germany) *Tel:* (0711) 4507-0 *Fax:* (0711) 4507-120 *E-mail:* info@ulmer.de *Web Site:* www.ulmer.de, pg 268

Verlag J Neumann-Neudamm GmbH & Co KG (Germany) *Tel:* (05661) 52222 *Fax:* (05661) 6008 *E-mail:* info@neumann-neudamm.de *Web Site:* www.neumann-neudamm.de, pg 268

Verlag fuer Messepublikationen Thomas Neureuter KG (Germany) *Tel:* (089) 99 30 91-0 *Fax:* (089) 93 78 96 *E-mail:* info@neureuter.de *Web Site:* www.neureuter.de, pg 268

Neuthor - Verlag (Germany) *Tel:* (06061) 40 79 *Fax:* (06061) 26 46 *Web Site:* www.neuthor-verlag.de, pg 268

Dr Waltraud Neuwirth Selbstverlag (Austria) *Tel:* (01) 3207323 *Fax:* (01) 3200225 *E-mail:* waltraud.neuwith@eunet.at, pg 55

New Africa Books (Pty) Ltd (South Africa) *Tel:* (021) 6744136 *Fax:* (021) 6743358 *E-mail:* newafrica@naep.co.za; orders@dpp.co.za (ordering) *Web Site:* www.dpp.co.za, pg 557

New Africa Publishing Company Ltd (Nigeria) *Tel:* (083) 231891, pg 500

New Albion Press (Australia) *Tel:* (03) 62202223, pg 34

New Aqua Press (Indonesia) *Tel:* (021) 4897566, pg 356

New Arts Graphic Reproduction Co Ltd (Hong Kong) *Tel:* 25641323; 25618161 *Fax:* 25658262 *E-mail:* newarts@writeme.com, pg 1156

New Books/Connolly Books (Ireland) *Tel:* (01) 6711943 *Web Site:* connollybookshop.1accesshost.com, pg 362

The New Bookshop (Sudan) *Tel:* (011) 774425, pg 1312

New Cavendish Books (United Kingdom) *Tel:* (020) 7229 6765 *Fax:* (020) 7792 0027 *Web Site:* www.newcavendishbooks.co.uk, pg 718

New Creation Publications Ministries & Resource Centre (Australia) *Tel:* (08) 8270-1497 *Fax:* (08) 8270-1861 *E-mail:* sales@newcreation.org.au *Web Site:* www.newcreation.org.au, pg 34

New Day Publishers (Philippines) *Tel:* (02) 9988046; (02) 9275982 *Fax:* (02) 9246544 *E-mail:* newday@pworld.net.ph; newdayorders@edsamail.com.ph, pg 514

New Day Readers Circle (South Africa) *Tel:* (021) 215540 *Fax:* (021) 4191865, pg 1231

New Endeavour Press (Australia) *Tel:* (02) 3182384 *Fax:* (02) 3103613, pg 34

New Era Publications Australia Pty Ltd (Australia) *Tel:* (02) 9211-0692 *Fax:* (02) 9211-0686 *Web Site:* www.newerapublications.com, pg 34

New Era Publications Deutschland GmbH (Germany) *Tel:* (04105) 68330 *Fax:* (04150) 683322 *E-mail:* buch@newerapublications.de *Web Site:* www.newerapublications.com, pg 268

New Era Publications International ApS (Denmark) *Tel:* (045) 33736666 *Fax:* (045) 33736633 *E-mail:* books@newerapublications.com *Web Site:* www.newerapublications.com, pg 134

New Era Publications UK Ltd (United Kingdom) *Tel:* (01342) 314 846 *Fax:* (01342) 314 857 *E-mail:* books@newerapublications.com *Web Site:* www.newerapublications.com, pg 718

New Era Publishers (Nigeria) *Tel:* (022) 715706, pg 500

New European Publications Ltd (United Kingdom) *Tel:* (020) 7582 3996 *Fax:* (020) 7582 7021, pg 718

New Generation Publishing Co Ltd (Thailand) *Tel:* (02) 2150674; (02) 2150677 *Fax:* (02) 2150676, pg 635

New Guyana Co Ltd (Guyana) *Tel:* (02) 262471; (02) 262473 *Fax:* (02) 262472, pg 317

New Holland Publishers (UK) Ltd (United Kingdom) *Tel:* (020) 7724 7773 *Fax:* (020) 7724 6184 *E-mail:* postmaster@nhpub.co.uk, pg 718

New Horn Press Ltd (Nigeria), pg 500

New House Publishers Ltd (New Zealand) *Tel:* (09) 4106517 *Fax:* (09) 4106329 *E-mail:* service@newhouse.co.nz *Web Site:* www.newhouse.co.nz, pg 493

New Island Printing Co Ltd (Hong Kong) *Tel:* 24428282 *Fax:* 24439882 *E-mail:* info@newisland.com *Web Site:* www.newisland.com, pg 1135

New Leaf Books Ltd (United Kingdom) *Tel:* (020) 7435 3056 *Fax:* (020) 7431 3625 *E-mail:* newleafbooks@btinternet.com, pg 719

New Light Publishers (India) *Tel:* (011) 5737448 *Fax:* (011) 5812385 *E-mail:* newlight@vsnl.net, pg 344

New Magazine (Italy) *Tel:* (0461) 925007 *Fax:* (0461) 925007 *E-mail:* newmagaz@tin.it *Web Site:* www.newmagazine.it; www.rivistamedica.it, pg 400

New Playwrights' Network (United Kingdom) *Tel:* (01684) 540154 *Fax:* (01684) 540154, pg 719

New Times Press (China) *Tel:* (010) 8412244 *Fax:* (010) 68413125, pg 107

New Women's Press Ltd (New Zealand) *Tel:* (09) 767150 *Fax:* (09) 767150, pg 494

New Writers' Press (Ireland), pg 362

New Zealand Book Council (New Zealand) *Tel:* (04) 4991569 *Fax:* (04) 4991424 *Web Site:* www.vuw.ac.n3/n3bookcouncil, pg 1366

New Zealand Council for Educational Research (New Zealand) *Tel:* (04) 3847939 *Fax:* (04) 3847933 *E-mail:* peter.ridder@nzcer.org.ns, pg 494

New Zealand Council for Educational Research (New Zealand) *Tel:* (04) 3847939 *Fax:* (04) 3847933, pg 1255, 1366

New Zealand Press Council (New Zealand) *Tel:* (04) 4735220 *Fax:* (04) 4711785 *E-mail:* presscouncil@asa.co.nz *Web Site:* www.presscouncil.org.nz, pg 1255

New Zealand Society of Authors (New Zealand) *E-mail:* nzsa@clear.net.nz *Web Site:* www.authors.org.nz, pg 1366

New Zealand Writers Guild (New Zealand) *Tel:* (09) 360 1408 *Fax:* (09) 360-1409 *E-mail:* info@nzwritersguild.org.nz *Web Site:* www.nzwritersguild.org.nz, pg 1366

Newark International Enterprises (Philippines) *Tel:* (02) 2432077 *Fax:* (02) 2414893, pg 514

Newman Centre Publications (Australia) *Tel:* (02) 9637-9406 *Fax:* (02) 9637-3351, pg 35

Newpro UK Ltd (United Kingdom) *Tel:* (01367) 242411 *Fax:* (01367) 241124 *E-mail:* sales@newprouk.co.uk, pg 719

Newscom Pte Ltd (Singapore) *Tel:* 6291 9861 *Fax:* 6293 1445 *E-mail:* circulation@newscom-mail.com *Web Site:* www.newscomonline.com, pg 547

Newspread International (India) *Tel:* (011) 2331402 *Fax:* (011) 2607252, pg 344

Newton Compton Editori SRL (Italy) *Tel:* (06) 6892045 *Fax:* (06) 6893076, pg 401

Newton Publishing Company Ltd (Taiwan, Province of China) *Tel:* (02) 9159500 *Fax:* (02) 9159486, pg 631

Next Magazine Publishing Ltd (Hong Kong) *Tel:* (02) 7442733 *Fax:* (02) 7907240 *E-mail:* editorial@nextmedia.com.hk *Web Site:* www.nextmedia.com.hk, pg 321

NEXUS SPECIAL INTERESTS INDUSTRY

Nexus Special Interests (United Kingdom) *Tel:* (01322) 660070 *Fax:* (01322) 617633 *Web Site:* www.nexusonline.com, pg 719

The NFER-NELSON Publishing Co Ltd (United Kingdom) *Tel:* (01753) 858961; (01753) 827249 (customer service) *Fax:* (01753) 856830; (01753) 620160 (customer service) *E-mail:* information@nfer-nelson.co.uk; edu&hsc@nfer-Nelson.co.uk (customer service) *Web Site:* www.nfer-nelson.co.uk, pg 719

NGM Communication (Pakistan) *Tel:* (042) 5713849 *E-mail:* ngm@shoa.net; anjeeam@anjeeam.com *Web Site:* www.ngm.web-page.net, pg 1304

Nibhondh Co Ltd (Thailand) *Tel:* (02) 2212611; (02) 2211553, pg 1314

Nicholas Enterprises Ltd (United Kingdom) *Tel:* (020) 7323 3319 *Fax:* (020) 7323 4829 *E-mail:* aladdin@duron.co.uk, pg 719

Nico Israel (Netherlands) *Tel:* (020) 6222255 *Fax:* (020) 6382666, pg 482

Nicolaische Verlagsbuchhandlung Beuermann GmbH (Germany) *Tel:* (030) 253738-0 *Fax:* (030) 253738-39 *E-mail:* info@nicolai-verlag.de *Web Site:* www.nicolai-verlag.de, pg 268

Piergiorgio Nicolazzini Literary Agency (Italy) *Tel:* (02) 48713365 *Fax:* (02) 48713365, pg 1113

Editura Niculescu (Romania) *Tel:* (01) 224-47-53; (01) 666-72-13 *Fax:* (01) 224-28-98; (01) 222-03-72 *E-mail:* editura@niculescu.ro; Mayibuye@mweb.co.za *Web Site:* www.niculescu.ro, pg 534

Nie/Nie/Sagen-Verlag (Germany) *Tel:* (07531) 5 35 70 *Fax:* (07531) 6 44 96 *E-mail:* haberkern-imz@t-online.de *Web Site:* www.nie-nie-sagen-verlag.de, pg 268

Niederland-Verlag Helmut Michel (Germany) *Tel:* (07191) 3277-200 *Fax:* (07191) 3277-15 *E-mail:* micheldruck@t-online.de, pg 268

Niederosterreichisches Pressehaus Druck- und Verlagsgesellschaft mbH (Austria) *Tel:* (02742) 802-1412 *Fax:* (02742) 802-1431 *E-mail:* verlag@np-buch.at *Web Site:* www.np-buch.at, pg 55

Niedersaechsische Landesbibliothek (Germany) *Tel:* (0511) 12670 *Fax:* (0511) 12 67202 *E-mail:* nlb@zb.nlb-hannover.de *Web Site:* www.nlb-hannover.de, pg 1468

Niedersaechsische Staats- und Universitaetsbibliothek Goettingen (Germany) *Tel:* (0551) 395212 (Secretariat); (0551) 393079 (Chemie); (0551) 392360 (Physik) *Fax:* (0551) 395222; (0551) 395220 (Bereichsbibliothek Medizin) *E-mail:* sub@mail.sub.uni-goettingen.de *Web Site:* www.sub.uni-goettingen.de, pg 1468

Niedieck Linder AG (Switzerland) *Tel:* (01) 3816592 *Fax:* (01) 3816513 *E-mail:* info@nlagency.ch, pg 1117

C W Niemeyer Buchverlage GmbH (Germany) *Tel:* (05151) 200-312 *Fax:* (05151) 200-319 *E-mail:* info@niemeyer-buch.de; telefonbuch@niemeyer.buch.de *Web Site:* www.niemeyer-buch.de, pg 268

Max Niemeyer Verlag GmbH (Germany) *Tel:* (07071) 98 94 0 *Fax:* (07071) 98 94 50 *E-mail:* max@niemeyer.de; info@niemeyer.de *Web Site:* www.niemeyer.de, pg 269

Nieswand-Verlag GmbH (Germany) *Tel:* (0431) 7028 200 *Fax:* (0431) 7028 228 *E-mail:* vertrieb@nieswandverlag.de *Web Site:* www.nieswand-verlag.de, pg 269

Hans-Nietsch-Verlag (Germany) *Tel:* (0761) 2966930 *Fax:* (0761) 2966966 *E-mail:* info@nietsch.de *Web Site:* www.nietsch.de, pg 269

Nieuwe Stad (Netherlands) *Tel:* (033) 4614615 *Fax:* (033) 4635885, pg 482

Nigensha Publishing Co Ltd (Japan) *Tel:* (03) 5395-2043 *Fax:* (03) 5210-4723, pg 422

Nigerian Book Suppliers Ltd (Nigeria) *Tel:* (01) 22407, pg 1303

Nigerian Book Development Council (Nigeria) *Tel:* (01) 862269; (01) 862272, pg 1255

Nigerian Environmental Study Team (Nigeria) *Fax:* (022) 410588; (022) 412644, pg 500

Nigerian Institute of Advanced Legal Studies (Nigeria) *Tel:* (01) 821752; (01) 821711; (01) 821753, pg 500

Nigerian Institute of International Affairs (Nigeria) *Tel:* (01) 611122; (01) 615606-10 *Fax:* (01) 611360 *E-mail:* niia@ric.nig.com, pg 500

Nigerian ISBN Agency (Nigeria) *Tel:* (01) 5850657 *Fax:* (01) 2631563, pg 1255

Nigerian Library Association (Nigeria) *Tel:* (01) 2600220 *Fax:* (01) 631563, pg 1521

Nigerian Publishers Association (Nigeria) *Tel:* (02) 4963007 *Fax:* (02) 4964370, pg 1255

Nigerian Trade Review (Nigeria) *Tel:* (01) 961147, pg 500

Verlag Arthur Niggli AG (Switzerland) *Tel:* (071) 6449111 *Fax:* (071) 6449190 *E-mail:* info@niggli.ch *Web Site:* www.niggli.ch, pg 620

Night Owl Publishers Pty Ltd (Australia) *Tel:* (057) 947 256 *Fax:* (057) 947 285, pg 35

Nihon Toshokan Kyokai (Japan) *Tel:* (03) 35230841 *Fax:* (03) 34217588 *E-mail:* info@jla.or.jp, pg 1518

Nihon Bunka Kagakusha Co Ltd (Japan) *Tel:* (03) 39463131 *Fax:* (03) 39463567, pg 422

Nihon-Bunkyo Shuppan (Japan Educational Publishing Co Ltd) (Japan) *Tel:* (06) 6921261 *Fax:* (06) 6065172 *E-mail:* sskjep@po.iijnet.or.jp, pg 422

Nihon Dokubungakkai (Japan), pg 1365

Nihon Eibungakkai (Japan) *Tel:* (03) 32937528 *Fax:* (03) 323937539, pg 1365

Nihon Keizai Shimbun Inc Publications Bureau (Japan) *Tel:* (03) 5255-2827 *Fax:* (03) 3246-2861 *Web Site:* www.nikkei.co.jp, pg 422

Nihon Rodo Kenkyu Kiko (Japan) *Tel:* (03) 53213074 *Fax:* (03) 53213015 *E-mail:* hom@po.iijner.or.jp, pg 422

Nihon-Shoseki Ltd (Japan) *Tel:* (06) 6386-8601 *Fax:* (06) 6386-8620 *E-mail:* nihonsho@mtci.ne.jp, pg 1295

Nihon Shoten Shogyo Kumiai Rengokai (Japan) *Tel:* (03) 32940388, pg 1250

Nihon Tosho Center Co Ltd (Japan) *Tel:* (03) 39479387 *Fax:* (02) 39471774 *E-mail:* info@nihontosho.co.jp *Web Site:* www.nihontosho.co.jp, pg 422

Nihon Toshokan Joho Gakka: Nihon Toshok Johogakkai (Japan) *Tel:* (03) 561624111, pg 1519

Nihon Vogue Co Ltd (Japan) *Tel:* (03) 5261 5081 *Fax:* (03) 32698726 *E-mail:* wada-t@tezukuritown.com *Web Site:* tezukuritown.com, pg 422

Nijgh & Van Ditmar Amsterdam (Netherlands) *Tel:* (020) 5511262 *Fax:* (020) 6203509, pg 482

Martinus Nijhoff International BV (Netherlands) *Tel:* (050) 5226286 *Fax:* (079) 615698 *E-mail:* 100137.3636@compuserve.com, pg 1301

Nikas (Greece) *Tel:* (01) 3634686; (01) 3633754, pg 313

Nikkagiren Shuppan-Sha (JUSE Press Ltd) (Japan) *Tel:* (03) 33522231 *Fax:* (03) 33563419, pg 422

The Nikkan Kogyo Shimbun Ltd (Japan) *Tel:* (03) 32227131 *Fax:* (03) 32348504 *Web Site:* www.nikkan.co.jp, pg 422

Nikoklis Publishers (Cyprus) *Tel:* (02) 456544 *Fax:* (02) 360668, pg 122

Nil Editions (France) *Tel:* (01) 53 67 14 00 *Fax:* (01) 53 67 14 90 *Web Site:* www.laffont.fr, pg 177

Nile & Mackenzie Ltd (United Kingdom) *Tel:* (020) 7493 0351 *Fax:* (020) 7495 0128, pg 719

The Nile Bookshop (Sudan) *Tel:* (011) 43737; (011) 44189, pg 1312

Nilsson & Lamm BV, Algemene Import Boekhandel (Netherlands) *Tel:* (0294) 465044 *Fax:* (0294) 415054 *E-mail:* nilam@euronet.nl, pg 1301

Nimaroo Publishers (Australia) *Tel:* (042) 292297, pg 35

Nimrod Publications (Australia) *Tel:* (02) 4957 5562; (02) 4921 5173 *Fax:* (02) 4950 9658 *E-mail:* nimrod@hunterlink.com.au, pg 35

9-12 Club (United Kingdom) *Tel:* (01993) 893456 *Fax:* (0845) 6039092, pg 1233

Editorial 92 SA (Spain) *Tel:* (093) 3009092 *Fax:* (093) 3009109, pg 584

Nio Pobjeda - Oour Izdavacko-Publicisticka Djelatnost (Yugoslavia) *Tel:* (081) 45955; (081) 44433; (081) 44474 *Fax:* (081) 52803, pg 765

Nippon Hikaku Bungakukai (Japan), pg 1365

Nippon Hoso Shuppan Kyokai (NHK Publishing) (Japan) *Tel:* (03) 37803356 *Fax:* (03) 34960123, pg 422

Nippon Igaku Toshokan Kyokai (Japan) *Tel:* (03) 38151942 *Fax:* (03) 38151608 *E-mail:* jmlahq@nisiq.net, pg 1519

Nippon Jitsugyo Publishing Co, Ltd (Japan) *Tel:* (03) 38145161 *Fax:* (03) 38181881 *E-mail:* nipojits@po.iijnet.or.jp, pg 423

Nippon Rosiya Bungakkai (Japan), pg 1365

Nippon Shuppan Hanbai Inc (Japan) *Tel:* (03) 32331111 *Fax:* (03) 32928571, pg 1295

Nippon Yakugaku Toshokan Kyogikai (Japan) *Tel:* (03) 38122111, pg 1519

Niro Decje Novine (Yugoslavia) *Tel:* (032) 712246; (032) 712247; (032) 714970; (032) 711256; (032) 711248; (011) 3221476; (011) 342010 *Fax:* (032) 711248, pg 765

Edit Niro (Novinska-izdavacka radna organizacija) (Croatia) *Tel:* (051) 672 107; (051) 672 119 *Fax:* (051) 672 112 *E-mail:* niro-edit@ri.tel.hr, pg 119

James Nisbet & Co Ltd (United Kingdom) *Tel:* (01462) 438331 *Fax:* (01462) 431528, pg 719

Nishimura Co Ltd (Japan) *Tel:* (025) 2232388 *Fax:* (025) 2247165, pg 423

Nissha Printing Co Ltd (Japan) *Tel:* (075) 756822000 *Fax:* (075) 8235322, pg 1198

Nistri - Lischi Editori (Italy) *Tel:* (050) 563371 *Fax:* (050) 562726, pg 401

Rainar Nitzsche Verlag (Germany) *Tel:* (0631) 61305 *Fax:* (0631) 61305 *E-mail:* rainar.nitzscheverlag@t-online.de *Web Site:* home.t-online.de/home/Rainar.NitzscheVerlag/nitzscheb.htm, pg 269

Niyo Software (India) *Tel:* (020) 445 8742; (020) 400 1603 *Fax:* (020) 400 1603 *E-mail:* info@niyoindia.com *Web Site:* www.niyoindia.com, pg 344

Niyom Vidhya (Thailand) *Tel:* (02) 217661, pg 635

Librairie A-G Nizet Sarl (France) *Tel:* (02) 47455041 *Fax:* (02) 47455015 *E-mail:* librairie-a.g-nizet@wanadoo.fr, pg 177

Izdatel'stvo Nizhegorodskogo Gosudarstvennogo Univ (Russian Federation) *Tel:* (08312) 65 78 25 *Fax:* (08312) 65 85 92, pg 540

Agencia de Librerias Nizza SA (Paraguay) *Tel:* (021) 47160, pg 1305

Njala University College Bookshop (Sierra Leone), pg 1309

Njala University College Library (University of Sierra Leone) (Sierra Leone), pg 1496

Njala Educational Publishing Centre (Sierra Leone), pg 544

NKI Forlaget (Norway) *Tel:* 67588800 *Fax:* 67581902, pg 504

NL SH (Albania) *Tel:* (042) 34207 *Fax:* (042) 34207, pg 1

NLN, Ltd The Lidove noviny Publishing House (Czech Republic) *Tel:* (02) 22510843 *Fax:* (02) 22514012 *E-mail:* nlnpress@iol.cz; nln@iol.cz, pg 127

NMA Publications (Australia) *Tel:* (03) 9428 2405 *Web Site:* www.rainerlinz.net/NMA/, pg 35

NMS Publishing Ltd (United Kingdom) *Tel:* (0131) 247 4026 *Fax:* (0131) 247 4012 *E-mail:* publishing@nms.ac.uk *Web Site:* www.nms.ac.uk, pg 719

Nnamdi Azikiwe Library (Nigeria) *Tel:* (042) 771444 *Fax:* (042) 770644; (042) 771500 *E-mail:* misunn@aol.com, pg 1489

The Maggie Noach Literary Agency (United Kingdom) *Tel:* (020) 8748 2926 *Fax:* (020) 8748 8057 *E-mail:* m-noach@dircon.co.uk, pg 1121

Nobel-Verlag GmbH Vertrieb Neue Medien (Germany) *Tel:* (0201) 81300 *Fax:* (0201) 8130288 *E-mail:* mplatzkoester@beleke.de *Web Site:* www.gewusst-wo.de; www.nobel.de, pg 269

F De Nobele (France) *Tel:* (01) 43 26 08 62 *Fax:* (01) 40 46 85 96, pg 177

Nobelinstituttet (Norway) *Tel:* 22129320 *Fax:* 22129310 *Web Site:* www.nobel.no, pg 1489

Nobunkyo (Rural Village Culture Association) (Japan) *Tel:* (03) 35851141 *Fax:* (03) 35891387 *E-mail:* mbk@mail.ruralnet.or.jp, pg 423

NodoLibri (Italy) *Tel:* (031) 306771 *Fax:* (031) 300554, pg 401

Florian Noetzel Verlag (Germany) *Tel:* (04421) 4 30 03 *Fax:* (04421) 4 29 85 *E-mail:* florian.noetzel@t-online.de, pg 269

Noguer y Caralt Editores SA (Spain) *Tel:* (093) 280 13 99 *Fax:* (093) 280 19 93 *E-mail:* noguer-caralt@mx2.redestb.es, pg 584

NOI - Verlag (Austria) *Tel:* (0463) 22474 *Fax:* (0463) 224744, pg 55

Noir Sur Blanc (France) *Tel:* (01) 42 86 07 10 *Fax:* (01) 42 86 08 90 *E-mail:* noirsurblanc@noirsurblanc.com *Web Site:* www.noirsurblanc.com, pg 177

Les Editions Noir sur Blanc (Switzerland) *Tel:* (021) 8645931 *Fax:* (021) 8644026, pg 620

Nolit Publishing House (Yugoslavia) *Tel:* (011) 3245017; (011) 3228872 *Fax:* (011) 3221365; (011) 627285, pg 765

Nolit Publishing House (Yugoslavia) *Tel:* (011) 3245017; (011) 3228872 *Fax:* (011) 627285, pg 1324

Nomos Verlagsgesellschaft mbH und Co KG (Germany) *Tel:* (07221) 2104-0 *Fax:* (07221) 210427 *E-mail:* nomos@nomos.de *Web Site:* www.nomos.de, pg 269

Non (Thailand) *Tel:* (02) 90130, pg 635

Non-Formal Education Centre (Maldive Islands) *Tel:* 328772; 324622, pg 455

Mavis A Noordwijk (Suriname) *Tel:* 479402, pg 599

Editorial Noray (Spain) *Tel:* (093) 280 59 66 *Fax:* (093) 280 61 90 *E-mail:* noray@europe.com *Web Site:* www.noray.es, pg 584

Norbertinum (Poland) *Tel:* (081) 5333895 *Fax:* (081) 5341243 *E-mail:* norbertinum@norbertinum.com.pl *Web Site:* www.norbertinum.com.pl, pg 518

Casa Editrice Nord SRL (Italy) *Tel:* (02) 405708 *Fax:* (02) 4042207 *E-mail:* editrice.nord@agora.stm.it, pg 401

Editions Nord-Sud (France) *Tel:* (01) 39 21 90 40 *Fax:* (01) 39 21 90 42 *E-mail:* nord-sug@editions-nord-sud.com *Web Site:* www.ldj.tm.fr, pg 177

Nord-Sued Verlag (Switzerland) *Tel:* (01) 9366868 *Fax:* (01) 9366800, pg 620

Nordan-Comunidad (Uruguay) *Tel:* (02) 305 6265 *Fax:* (02) 308 1640 *E-mail:* nordan@chasque.net *Web Site:* www.nordan.com.uy, pg 760

Norddeutscher Verleger- und Buchhaendler-Verband eV (Germany) *Tel:* (040) 4103161 *Fax:* (040) 2298514, pg 1246

Nordic Council of Ministers Publications (Denmark) *Tel:* 33960200 *Fax:* 33960202 *E-mail:* nmr@nmr.dk *Web Site:* www.norden.org, pg 1241

Nordica Printing Co Ltd (Hong Kong) *Tel:* 25659234 *Fax:* 25656445, pg 1197

Nordik/Tapals Publishers Ltd (Latvia) *Tel:* (02) 7602672; (02) 7602617 *Fax:* (02) 7602818 *E-mail:* nordik@nordik.lv *Web Site:* www.nordik.lv, pg 442

Bengt Nordin Agency (Sweden) *Tel:* (08) 57168525 *Fax:* (08) 57168524 *E-mail:* info@nordinagency.se *Web Site:* www.nordinagency.se, pg 1116

AB Nordiska Bokhandeln (Sweden) *Tel:* (08) 269809 *Fax:* (08) 254246, pg 1313

Nordiska Bokhandelns (Sweden) *Tel:* (08) 269809 *Fax:* (08) 254246, pg 605

Det nordjyske Landsbibliotek (Denmark) *Tel:* 99314400 *Fax:* 99314433 *E-mail:* njl@njl.dk, pg 1461

Norges Landbrukshogskoles Bibliotek (Norway) *Tel:* 64947500 *Fax:* 64947670 *E-mail:* biblutl@bibl.nlh.no, pg 1489

NORLA (Information Office for Norwegian Literature Abroad) (Norway) *Tel:* 22122540 *Fax:* 22122544 *E-mail:* firmapost@norla.no *Web Site:* www.norla.no, pg 1366

Olaf Norlis Bokhandel A/S (Norway) *Tel:* 22004300 *Fax:* 22422651, pg 1304

Norma de Chile (Chile) *Tel:* (02) 236 3355 *Fax:* (02) 236 3362 *Web Site:* www.norma.com, pg 101

Editions Norma (France) *Tel:* (01) 40430498 *Fax:* (01) 40439875, pg 177

Editorial Norma SA (Colombia) *Tel:* (01) 410 6355 ext 1754; (01) 2853297 *Fax:* (01) 410 5414, pg 113

Cesky normalizacni institut (Czech Republic) *Tel:* (02) 21 80 21 11 *Fax:* (02) 21 80 23 10 *E-mail:* u30-csni@login.cz, pg 127

Ediciones Norma SA (Spain) *Tel:* (091) 6370760 *Fax:* (091) 5470133; (091) 6370760, pg 584

Normenausschuss Bibliotheks- und Dokumentationswesen (NABD) im DIN Deutsches Institut fuer Normung eV (Germany) *Tel:* (030) 26012791 *Fax:* (030) 26011231 *Web Site:* www.din.de/set/gremien/nas/, pg 1516

Norsk Bibliotekforening (Norway) *Tel:* 22688550 *Fax:* 22672368, pg 1521

Norsk Bokdistribusjon (Norway) *Tel:* 66983980 *Fax:* 66845590 *E-mail:* vv@vettviten.no *Web Site:* www.vettviten.no, pg 1304

Norsk Bokreidingslag L/L (Norway) *Tel:* 55301899 *Fax:* 55320356 *E-mail:* post@bodonihus.no, pg 504

Norsk Musikkforleggerforening (Norway) *Tel:* 22425090 *Fax:* 22425541, pg 1256

Norske Akademi for Sprog og Litteratur (Norway), pg 1366

Den Norske Forfatterforening (Norway) *Tel:* 22424077 *Fax:* 22421107 *E-mail:* dnf@sn.no, pg 1256

Den Norske Forleggerforening (Norway) *Tel:* 22007580 *Fax:* 22333830 *E-mail:* dnf@forleggerforeningen.no, pg 1256

Det Norske Videnskaps-Akademi (Norway) *Tel:* 22121090 *Fax:* 22121099 *E-mail:* dnva@online.no *Web Site:* www.dnva.no, pg 1366

Norstedt (Sweden) *Tel:* (08) 7893000 *Fax:* (08) 7983038, pg 605

P A Norstedt & Soener AB (Sweden) *Tel:* (08) 7893000 *Fax:* (08) 214006, pg 605

Norstedts Foerlag (Sweden) *Tel:* (08) 769 87 00 *Fax:* (08) 769 88 64 *Web Site:* www.norstedts.sc, pg 605

Norstedts Juridik (Sweden) *Tel:* (08) 6909100 *Fax:* (08) 6909070, pg 605

Norstedts Ordbok (Sweden) *Tel:* (08) 7698950 *E-mail:* info.orabok@norstedtordbok.se *Web Site:* www.norstedtsordbok.se, pg 605

Editorial Norte SA (Argentina) *Tel:* (011) 4921-1440 *Fax:* (011) 4921-1440, pg 8

North Shore City Libraries (New Zealand) *Tel:* (09) 4868460 *Fax:* (09) 4868519 *Web Site:* www.shorelibraries.govt.nz, pg 1487

Northcote House Publishers Ltd (United Kingdom) *Tel:* (01822) 810066 *Fax:* (01822) 810034 *E-mail:* northcote.house@virgin.net *Web Site:* www.northcotehouse.com, pg 719

Northern Carribean University (Jamaica) *Tel:* (876) 962-2204 *Fax:* (876) 962-0075 *E-mail:* hswalters@netscape.net *Web Site:* www.w.college.edu, pg 1478

Northern Map Distributors (United Kingdom) *Tel:* (01142) 582660 *Toll Free Tel:* 800 834920, pg 1321

Northern Nigerian Publishing Co Ltd (Nigeria) *Tel:* (069) 32087, pg 500

Northern Technical College Library (Zambia) *Tel:* (02) 680142 *Fax:* (02) 680423 *E-mail:* nortec@zamtel.zm, pg 1509

Northland Historical Publications Society (New Zealand) *Tel:* (09) 4028244 *Fax:* (09) 4028296, pg 494

Northwestern Publishers (United Republic of Tanzania), pg 634

W W Norton & Company Ltd (United Kingdom) *Tel:* (020) 7323 1579 *Toll Free Tel:* 800-233-4830 (orders) *Fax:* (020) 7436 4553 *Toll Free Fax:* 800-458-6515 (orders) *E-mail:* office@wwnorton.co.uk *Web Site:* www.wwnorton.co.uk, pg 720

The Norwegian Association of Literary Translators (Norway) *Tel:* 22478090 *Fax:* 22420356 *Web Site:* www.boknett.no/no, pg 1127

Norwood Publishers (United Kingdom) *Tel:* (01274) 602454, pg 720

Mare Nostrum (France) *Tel:* (04) 68511750 *Fax:* (05) 61411543, pg 177

Editorial Noticias (Portugal) *Tel:* (021) 3552130 *Fax:* (021) 3552168; (021) 3552169 *E-mail:* editnoticias@mail.telepac.pt *Web Site:* www.editorialnoticias.pt, pg 527

Editorial Noticias (Portugal) *Tel:* (021) 3552130 *Fax:* (021) 3552168, pg 1308

Notos (Greece) *Tel:* (01) 3636577; (01) 3629746 *Fax:* (01) 3636737, pg 313

Nour E-Sham Book Centre (Syrian Arab Republic) *Tel:* (11) 4457458 *Fax:* (11) 3324913 *E-mail:* nouresham@mail.sy *Web Site:* www.nouresham.com, pg 1117

Nouveau Cercle Parisien du Livre (France) *Tel:* (01) 43547195 *Fax:* (01) 40518288, pg 1228

La Nouvelle Agence (France) *Tel:* (01) 43258560 *Fax:* (01) 43254798, pg 1111

Nouvelle Cite (France) *Tel:* (01) 40927085 *Fax:* (01) 40921168 *Web Site:* www.perso.wanadoo.fr/nouvelle.cite/commcpe.html, pg 178

Les Nouvelles Editions Africaines (Cote d'Ivoire) *Tel:* 32-12-51; 32-16-22; 32-60-09, pg 118

Les Nouvelles Editions Africaines du Senegal NEAS (Senegal) *Tel:* (08) 211381; (08) 221580 *Fax:* (08) 223604 *E-mail:* neas@sentoo.sn, pg 544

Librairie/Editions Nouvelles Editions Africaines du TOGO (Togo) *Tel:* 216761 *Fax:* 221003, pg 1314

Les Nouvelles Editions Africaines du TOGO (NEA-TOGO) (Togo) *Tel:* 216761; 221019 *Fax:* 221019 *E-mail:* ctce@cafe.tg, pg 636

Nouvelles Editions Fiduciaires (France) *Tel:* (01) 46 39 47 13; (01) 46 39 47 00 *Fax:* (01) 47 58 00 63, pg 178

Nouvelles Editions Francaises (France) *Tel:* (01) 44 74 16 00 *Fax:* (01) 44 04 98 03, pg 178

Les Nouvelles Editions Ivoiriennes (NEI) (Cote d'Ivoire) *Tel:* (021) 240766; (021) 240825 *Fax:* (021) 242456, pg 118

Nouvelles Editions Latines (France) *Tel:* (01) 43 54 77 42 *Fax:* (01) 43 29 69 81, pg 178

Nov Covek Publishing House (Bulgaria) *Tel:* (02) 9863766 *Fax:* (02) 9863772 *E-mail:* newman@mbox.cit.bg, pg 97

Nov svet (New World) (The Former Yugoslav Republic of Macedonia) *Tel:* (02) 378-662, pg 449

Nova Acropole (Portugal) *Tel:* (021) 827097 *Fax:* (021) 8150401, pg 527

Editora Nova Aguilar SA (Brazil) *Tel:* (021) 537-7189 *Fax:* (021) 537-8275, pg 88

Editora Nova Alexandria Ltda (Brazil) *Tel:* (011) 5571-5637 *Fax:* (011) 5571-5637 *E-mail:* novaalexandria@novaalexandria.com.br *Web Site:* www.novaalexandria.com.br, pg 88

Nova Arrancada Sociedade Editora SA (Portugal) *Tel:* (021) 3470096; (021) 3472220 *Fax:* (021) 3472220 *E-mail:* novaarrancada@mail.telepac.pt, pg 527

Editora Nova Fronteira SA (Brazil) *Tel:* (021) 25 37 87 70; (021) 22 66 51 84 *Fax:* (021) 22 86 67 55 *Web Site:* www.novafronteira.com.br, pg 88

Nova Grupo Editorial SA de CV (Mexico) *Tel:* (05) 5320946 *Fax:* (05) 6050879, pg 464

Editorial Nova, SA de CV (Mexico) *Tel:* (05) 2806080 *Fax:* (05) 2803194 *E-mail:* bolind@viernes.iwm.com.mx, pg 464

Novalis Media AG (Switzerland) *Tel:* (052) 633212 *Fax:* (052) 6201491 *E-mail:* novalis@spectraweb.ch, pg 620

Novartis Edizioni - Novartis Farma SpA (Italy) *Tel:* (02) 96542736 *Fax:* (02) 96543320, pg 401

Novecento Editrice Srl (Italy) *Tel:* (091) 587417 *Fax:* (091) 585702 *E-mail:* novedi@mbox.vol.it, pg 401

Novello & Co Ltd (United Kingdom) *Tel:* (020) 7434 0066 *Fax:* (020) 7287-6329 *E-mail:* music@musicsales.co.uk *Web Site:* www.musicsales.co.uk, pg 720

Novelty Printers & Publishers (Maldive Islands) *Tel:* 322474; 318844 *Fax:* 322490 *E-mail:* novelty@dhivehinet.net.mv, pg 455

Novorg Kiado (Hungary) *Tel:* (01) 1603790; (01) 1603596; (01) 1602300 *Fax:* (01) 145581 *E-mail:* novorged@kjk.hu, pg 326

Novosti Izdatel 'stvo (Russian Federation) *Tel:* (095) 2655008 *Fax:* (095) 2655208; (095) 2653880; (095) 9752065, pg 541

Novus Forlag (Norway) *Tel:* (022) 717450 *Fax:* (022) 718107 *E-mail:* novus@novus.no *Web Site:* www.novus.no, pg 504

NPA (Neue Presse Agentur) (Switzerland) *Tel:* (052) 7214374, pg 1117

NPS Educational Publishers Ltd (Nigeria Publishers Services) (Nigeria) *Tel:* (032) 316006; (032) 316008, pg 500

NSB Buch- und Phonoclub (Switzerland) *Tel:* (01) 3833622, pg 1232

NSW Agriculture (Australia) *Tel:* (02) 6391 3100 *Fax:* (02) 6391 3336 *Web Site:* www.agric.nsw.gov.au, pg 35

NSW Writers' Centre (Australia) *Tel:* (02) 95559757 *Fax:* (02) 98181327 *E-mail:* nswwc@ozemail.com.au *Web Site:* www.nswwriterscentre.org.au, pg 1359

NTC Publications Ltd (United Kingdom) *Tel:* (01491) 411000 *Fax:* (01491) 571188 *E-mail:* info@ntc.co.uk, pg 720

La Nuee Bleue - Dernieres Nouvelles d'Alsace (France) *Tel:* (03) 88 15 77 27 *Fax:* (03) 88 75 16 21 *Web Site:* www.sdv.fr/nuee-bleue/, pg 178

Nuer Ediciones (Spain) *Tel:* (091) 310 05 99; 902 118 298 *Fax:* (091) 310 04 59 *E-mail:* nuer@pasadizo.com *Web Site:* www.pasadizo.com, pg 584

Editorial Nuestro Tiempo SA (Mexico) *Tel:* (05) 5503165; (05) 5503170, pg 464

Nueva Acropolis (Spain) *Tel:* (091) 5228730 *Fax:* (091) 5312952 *E-mail:* oinaes@jet.es *Web Site:* www.acropolis.org, pg 584

Editora Nueva Generacion (Chile) *Tel:* (02) 2183974 *Fax:* (02) 2182281, pg 101

Editorial Nueva Imagen SA (Mexico) *Tel:* (05) 2714524; (05) 2711980, pg 464

Editorial Nueva Nicaragua (Nicaragua) *Tel:* (02) 666520, pg 497

Editorial Nueva Sociedad (Venezuela) *Tel:* (02) 2659975; (02) 2650593; (02) 2651265 *Fax:* (02) 313397 *E-mail:* nuso@nuevasoc.org.ve *Web Site:* nuevasoc.org.ve, pg 762

Nueva Vision (Argentina) *Tel:* (011) 8631461; (011) 8635980, pg 1271

Ediciones Nueva Vision SAIC (Argentina) *Tel:* (011) 4863-1461; (011) 4863-5980 *Fax:* (011) 4863-5980, pg 8

Editorial Nuevo Continente (Honduras) *Tel:* 22-5073, pg 318

Nuova Alfa Editoriale (Italy) *Tel:* (02) 215631 *Fax:* (02) 26413121, pg 401

Nuova Ipsa Editore srl (Italy) *Tel:* (091) 6819025 *Fax:* (091) 6816399, pg 401

La Nuova Italia Editrice SpA (Italy) *Tel:* (055) 75901 *Fax:* (055) 7590208, pg 401

Nuove Autonomie (Italy) *Tel:* (06) 36002539 *Fax:* (06) 3240145, pg 401

Editrice Nuovi Autori (Italy) *Tel:* (02) 89409338 *Fax:* (02) 58107048 *E-mail:* faglier@tin.it *Web Site:* www.paginegialle.it/ednuoviaut, pg 401

Nuovi Sentieri Editore (Italy) *Tel:* (0437) 590308, pg 401

Nuovo Instituto Italiano d'Arti Grafiche (Italy) *Tel:* (035) 311311 *Fax:* (035) 311349 *E-mail:* artigraf@bertelsmann.de, pg 1158

Nuovo Instituto Italiano d'Arti Grafiche (Italy) *Tel:* (035) 311311 *Fax:* (035) 311349, pg 1198

Nurdan YayinlariSanayi ve Ticaret Ltd Sti (Turkey) *Tel:* (0212) 5225504; (0212) 5138653 *Fax:* (0212) 5126329; (0212) 5125186, pg 640

Andrew Nurnberg Associates Ltd (United Kingdom) *Tel:* (020) 7417 8800 *Fax:* (020) 7417 8812 *E-mail:* 100663.727@compuserve.com, pg 1121

Nusser Verlag (Germany) *Tel:* (089) 146788 *Fax:* (089) 1493206 *Web Site:* www.nusserverlag.de, pg 269

Nwamife Publishers Ltd (Nigeria) *Tel:* (042) 338454, pg 500

Bokforlaget Nya Doxa AB (Sweden) *Tel:* (0587) 10416; (0587) 12905 *Fax:* (0587) 14257 *E-mail:* info@nya-doxa.se *Web Site:* www.aim.se/doxa, pg 605

nymphenburger (Germany) *Tel:* (089) 290880 *Fax:* (089) 29088144 *E-mail:* nymphenburger@herbig.net *Web Site:* www.herbig.net, pg 269

Nyota Publishers Ltd (United Republic of Tanzania) *Tel:* (051) 25547; (051) 25549, pg 634

Nyt Dansk Literaturselskab (Denmark) *Tel:* 4659 5520 *Fax:* 4659 5520 *E-mail:* ndl@ndl.dk, pg 1362

Nyt Nordisk Forlag Arnold Busck A/S (Denmark) *Tel:* (045) 33733575 *Fax:* (045) 33733576 *E-mail:* nnf@nytnordiskforlag.dk *Web Site:* www.nytnordiskforlag.dk, pg 134

NZN Buchverlag AG (Switzerland) *Tel:* (01) 266 12 92 *Fax:* (01) 266 12 93 *E-mail:* nzn@nzn.ch *Web Site:* www.nzn.ch, pg 620

O Gracklauer Verlag und Bibliographische Agentur GmbH (Germany) *Tel:* (030) 8258139 *Fax:* (030) 8262039 *E-mail:* info@gracklauer.de *Web Site:* www.gracklauer.de, pg 1246

Editorial O Livro Lda (Portugal) *Tel:* (021) 704749 *Fax:* (021) 7783536, pg 528

Editorial O Livro Lda (Portugal) *Tel:* (021) 704709 *Fax:* (021) 7783536, pg 1308

O Neul Publishing Co (Republic of Korea) *Tel:* (02) 716-2811 *Fax:* (02) 712-7392, pg 439

Oak Tree Press (Ireland) *Tel:* (021) 431 3855 *Fax:* (021) 431 3496 *E-mail:* info@oaktreepress.com *Web Site:* www.oaktreepress.com, pg 362

Oakwood Press (United Kingdom) *Tel:* (01291) 650444 *Fax:* (01291) 650484 *E-mail:* oakwood-press@dial.pipex.com *Web Site:* www.oakwood-press.dial.pipex.com, pg 720

OASIS, Producciones Generales de Comunicacion (Spain) *Tel:* (093) 2372020 *Fax:* (093) 2177378, pg 584

Obafemi Awolowo University Library (Nigeria) *Tel:* (036) 230291 ext 2287; (036) 230290 *Fax:* (036) 230291 (ext 2287) *E-mail:* ul@libraryoauife.edu.ng, pg 1489

Obafemi Awolowo University Press Ltd (Nigeria) *Tel:* (036) 230290-9; (036) 230284, pg 501

Obdeestro Znanie (Russian Federation) *Tel:* (095) 9281531, pg 541

Obelisco Ediciones S (Spain) *Tel:* (093) 3098525 *Fax:* (093) 3098523 *E-mail:* obelisco@airtel.net; obelisco@edicionesobelisco.com *Web Site:* www.edicionesobelisco.com, pg 584

Obelisk-Verlag (Austria) *Tel:* (0512) 58 07 33 *Fax:* (0512) 58 07 33 13 *E-mail:* obelisk-verlag@utanet.at *Web Site:* www.obelisk-verlag.at, pg 56

Oberbaum Verlag GmbH (Germany) *Tel:* (030) 624 69 21 *Fax:* (030) 624 69 21, pg 269

Oberoesterreichische Landesbibliothek (Austria) *Tel:* (0732) 6640710 *Fax:* (0732) 664071-44 *E-mail:* landesbibliothek@ooe.gv.at *Web Site:* www.landesbibliothek.at, pg 1451

Edition Objectif Lune (Luxembourg) *Tel:* 335230 *Fax:* 335230 *E-mail:* objectif.lune@cmdnet.lu, pg 447

Editora Objetiva Ltda (Brazil) *Tel:* (021) 2556-7824 *Fax:* (021) 2556-3322 *Web Site:* www.objetiva.com.br, pg 88

Obobo Books (Nigeria) *Tel:* (01) 5871333 *E-mail:* obw@infoweb.abs.net, pg 501

Obod (Yugoslavia) *Tel:* (086) 21953; (086) 21331 *Fax:* (086) 21953; (086) 21649; (086) 33951, pg 765

O'Brien Educational (Ireland) *Tel:* (01) 4923333 *Fax:* (01) 4922777 *E-mail:* books@obrien.ie *Web Site:* www.obrien.ie, pg 363

The O'Brien Press Ltd (Ireland) *Tel:* (01) 4923333 *Fax:* (01) 4922777 *E-mail:* books@obrien.ie *Web Site:* www.obrien.ie, pg 363

Observatorio Astronomico de Lisboa (Portugal) *Tel:* (021) 3637351 *Fax:* (021) 3621722, pg 528

Editions Obsidiane (France) *Tel:* (01) 86965218 *Fax:* (01) 86870112 *E-mail:* genevieve.bigant@wanadoo.fr, pg 178

Obunsha Co Ltd (Japan) *Tel:* (03) 32666351 *Fax:* (03) 32666011, pg 423

Vydavatelstvo Obzor (Slovakia) *Tel:* (07) 368395; (07) 55695; (07) 57015 *Fax:* (07) 368395, pg 550

Edizioni OCD (Italy) *Tel:* (06) 79847482 *Fax:* (06) 79845387, pg 401

Editions Ocean (Reunion) *Tel:* (0262) 588400 *Fax:* (0262) 588410 *E-mail:* ocean@guetali.fr, pg 531

Editions de l'Ocean Indien Ltd (Mauritius) *Tel:* 4646761 *Fax:* 4643445 *E-mail:* eoibooks@intnet.me, pg 457

Editions de l'Ocean Indien (Mauritius) *Tel:* 4642955; 4643952; 4643959; 4646761 *Fax:* 4643445, pg 1299

Ocean Press (Australia) *Tel:* (03) 9326 4280 *Fax:* (03) 9329 5040 *E-mail:* edit@oceanpress.com.au *Web Site:* www.oceanbooks.com.au, pg 35

Ediciones Oceano Grupo SA (Spain) *Tel:* (093) 280 20 20 *Fax:* (093) 204 10 73 *E-mail:* info@oceano.com *Web Site:* www.oceano.com, pg 584

Oceanographic Research Institute (South Africa) *Tel:* (031) 3373536 *Fax:* (031) 3372132 *E-mail:* seaworld@dbn.lia.net; ori@superbowl.und.ac.za; seaworld@neptune.lia.co.za, pg 558

Oceans Enterprises (Australia) *Tel:* (03) 5182 5108 *Fax:* (03) 5182 5823 *E-mail:* oceans@netspace.net.au *Web Site:* www.oceans.com.au, pg 35

OCEI (Oficina Central de Estadistica e Informatica) (Venezuela) *Tel:* (02) 7821133; (02) 7821167; (02) 7825756; (02) 7821156 *Fax:* (02) 7930428, pg 763

Universitetsko Izdatelstvo 'Kliment Ochridski' (Bulgaria) *Tel:* (02) 71288; (02) 71265; (02) 704271; (02) 71151 *Fax:* (02) 704271 *E-mail:* gzisha@ns.sclg.uni-sofia.bg, pg 97

The Octagon Press Ltd (United Kingdom) *Tel:* (020) 8341 5971 *Fax:* (020) 8348 9392 *E-mail:* octagon@schredds.demon.co.uk *Web Site:* www.octagonpress.com, pg 720

OCTAVO Franco Cantini Editore (Italy) *Tel:* (055) 2346022 *Fax:* (055) 2346109, pg 401

Edition Octopus & Okeanos Presse (Germany) *Tel:* 02226 915168 *Fax:* (02226) 915165; (040) 3603561585 *E-mail:* octopusokeanos@aol.com *Web Site:* www.hometown.aol.delanveshaka/homepage/firma.html, pg 269

Octopus Publishing Group (United Kingdom) *Tel:* (020) 7531 8400 *Fax:* (020) 7531 8650 *Web Site:* www.octopus-publishing.co.uk, pg 720

Octopus Verlag (Switzerland) *Tel:* (081) 221029 *Fax:* (081) 2529466, pg 620

Odense Centralbibliotek (Denmark) *Tel:* 66131372 *Fax:* 66137337, pg 1461

Odense Universitetsbibliotek (Denmark) *Tel:* 65501000 *Fax:* 66158162 *E-mail:* sdub@bib.sdu.dk, pg 1461

Odeon Book Store Lp (Thailand) *Tel:* (02) 2210742; (02) 2216567 *Fax:* (02) 2253300; (02) 2548806, pg 1314

Odeon Buch- und Phonoclub (Czech Republic) *Tel:* (02) 264100 *Fax:* (02) 24225254 *E-mail:* odeon@comp.cz, pg 1227

Odeon, nakladatelstvi krasne literatury a umeni (Czech Republic) *Tel:* (02) 241 625 21-6 *Fax:* (02) 241 623 28 *E-mail:* odeon@comp.cz, pg 127

Odeon Store LP (Thailand) *Tel:* (02) 2210742; (02) 2216567, pg 635

Editions Odile Jacob (France) *Tel:* (01) 44 41 64 84 *Fax:* (01) 44 41 64 99; (01) 43 29 88 77 *Web Site:* www.odilejacob.fr, pg 178

Anne O'Donovan Pty Ltd (Australia) *Tel:* (03) 9819 2203 *Fax:* (03) 9818 6849 *E-mail:* odonovan@netspace.net.au, pg 35

Odusote Bookstores Ltd (Nigeria) *Tel:* (02) 316451 *Fax:* (02) 315654, pg 1303

Odysseas Publications Ltd (Greece) *Tel:* (01) 3624326; (01) 3625575 *Fax:* (01) 3648030, pg 313

oebv & hpt Verlagsgesellschaft mbH & Co KG (Austria) *Tel:* (01) 40136-0 *Fax:* (01) 40136-185 *E-mail:* office@oebvhpt.at *Web Site:* www.oebvhpt.at, pg 56

OECD (France) *Tel:* (01) 45 24 82 00 *Fax:* (01) 45 24 83 00 *Web Site:* www.oecd.org; www.oecd.org/bookshop, pg 178

Oeko-Test Verlag GmbH & Co KG Betriebsgesellschaft (Germany) *Tel:* (069) 9 77 77-0 *Fax:* (069) 9 77 77-139 *E-mail:* oet.verlag@oekotest.de, pg 269

Oekobuch Verlag & Versand GmbH (Germany) *Tel:* (07633) 50613 *Fax:* (07633) 50870 *E-mail:* oekobuch@t-online.de *Web Site:* www.oekobuch.de, pg 269

Oekotopia Verlag, Wolfgang Hoffman (Germany) *Tel:* (0251) 661035 *Fax:* (0251) 48198-0 *E-mail:* info@oekotopia-verlag.de *Web Site:* www.oekotopia-verlag.de, pg 270

Oekumenischer Verlag Dr R-F Edel (Germany) *Tel:* (02351) 21319 *Fax:* (02351) 568908, pg 270

OEMF srl International (Italy) *Tel:* (02) 332101 *Fax:* (02) 33210200, pg 401

Martina M Oepping Literary Agency (Germany) *Tel:* (069) 59790011 *Fax:* (069) 59790012 *E-mail:* litag@oepping.de, pg 1112

Oertel & Sporer GmbH & Co (Germany) *Tel:* (07121) 302 555; (07121) 302 553 *Fax:* (07121) 302 558, pg 270

Oertel & Sporer GmbH & Co (Germany) *Tel:* (07121) 302555 *Fax:* (07121) 302558, pg 1154, 1195

Oesch Verlag AG (Switzerland) *Tel:* (01) 305 70 60 *Fax:* (01) 305 70 66 *E-mail:* info@oeschverlag.ch *Web Site:* www.oeschverlag.ch, pg 620

Verlag Oesterreich GmbH (Austria) *Tel:* (01) 610771333 *Fax:* (01) 6100771502 *E-mail:* office@verlagoesterreich.at *Web Site:* www.verlagoesterreich.at, pg 56

Oesterreichische Gesellschaft fuer Literatur (Austria) *Tel:* (01) 5338159; (01) 5338159 *Fax:* (01) 5334067 *E-mail:* office@ogl.at *Web Site:* www.ogl.at, pg 1360

Oesterreichische Gesellschaft fuer Dokumentation und Information (Austria) *Tel:* (01) 74040280 *Fax:* (01) 74040281 *E-mail:* oegdi@oegdi.at *Web Site:* www.oegdi.at, pg 1511

Oesterreichische Staatsdruckerei (Austrian State Printing Office) (Austria) *Tel:* (01) 206 66-0 *Fax:* (01) 206 66-105 *E-mail:* office@staatsdruckerei.at *Web Site:* www.oesd.co.at, pg 56

Oesterreichische Verlagsanstalt GmbH (Austria) *Tel:* (01) 5445641 *Fax:* (01) 544564166, pg 56

Verlag der Oesterreichischen Akademie der Wissenschaften (OEAW) (Austria) *Tel:* (01) 51581; (01) 5129050 *Fax:* (01) 515813400 *E-mail:* verlag@oeaw.ac.at *Web Site:* verlag.oeaw.ac.at, pg 56

Verlag des Oesterreichischen Gewerkschaftsbundes GmbH (Austria) *Tel:* (01) 662 32 96-62 36 *Fax:* (01) 662 32 96-63 85 *E-mail:* office@verlag-oegb.co.at *Web Site:* www.verlag-oegb.co.at, pg 56

Oesterreichischer Agrarverlag, Druck- und Verlags-GmbH (Austria) *Tel:* (02235) 929-0 *Fax:* (02235) 929-929 *E-mail:* office@agrarverlag.at *Web Site:* www.agrarverlag.at, pg 56

Oesterreichischer Bundesverlag GmbH (Austria) *Tel:* (01) 51405, pg 56

Oesterreichischer Gewerbeverlag GmbH (Austria) *Tel:* (01) 53307680 *Fax:* (01) 5330768030 *E-mail:* gewerbeverlag@tbxa.telecom.at, pg 56

Oesterreichischer Jagd-und Fischerei-Verlag der JFB GmbH (Austria) *Tel:* (01) 421636 *Fax:* (01) 421636 *E-mail:* verlag@jagd.at *Web Site:* members.ping.at, pg 56

Oesterreichischer Kunst und Kulturverlag (Austria) *Tel:* (01) 587 85 51 *Fax:* (01) 587 85 82, pg 56

Oesterreichischer Uebersetzer- und Dolmetscherverband Universitas (Austria) *Tel:* (01) 3686060 *Fax:* (01) 3686008 *E-mail:* info@universitas.org *Web Site:* www.univeritas.org, pg 1125

Oesterreichisches Institut fuer Bibliotheksforschung, Dokumentations- und Informationswesen (Austria), pg 1512

Oesterreichisches Katholisches Bibelwerk (Austria) *Tel:* (02243) 2938 *Fax:* (02243) 2939, pg 56

Oesterreichisches Staatsarchiv (Austria) *Tel:* (01) 79540-0 *Fax:* (01) 79540 (ext 109) *E-mail:* gdpost@oesta.gv.at *Web Site:* www.oesta.gv.at, pg 1451

Institut fur Oesterreichkunde (Austria) *Tel:* (01) 512-79-32 *Fax:* (01) 512-79-32 *E-mail:* loek.wirtschaftsgeschichte@univie.ac.at, pg 1360

Verlag Friedrich Oetinger GmbH (Germany) *Tel:* (040) 607909-03 *Fax:* (040) 60723-26 *E-mail:* oetinger@vsg-hamburg.de *Web Site:* www.oetinger.de, pg 270

Off the Shelf Publishing (Australia) *Tel:* (02) 4443 7555 *Fax:* (02) 4443 7666 *E-mail:* offshelf@ozemail.com.au, pg 35

Verlag Offene Worte (Germany) *Tel:* (040) 7 97 13-03 *Fax:* (040) 7 97 13-304 *Web Site:* www.koehler-mittler.de, pg 270

Office des Publications Officielles des Communautes Europeenes (Luxembourg) *Tel:* 29291 42451 *Fax:* 488857, pg 447

Office des Publications Officielles des Communautes Europeenes (Luxembourg) *Tel:* 292942053 *Fax:* 292942025 *E-mail:* idea@opoce.cec.be *Web Site:* www.eur-op.eu.int, pg 1252

Office du Livre SA (Buchhaus AG) (Switzerland) *Tel:* (026) 4675111 *Fax:* (026) 4675466, pg 620

Office du Livre Malagasy (OLM) (Madagascar) *Tel:* (02) 24449, pg 1252

Office International de Documentation et Librairie (OFFILIB) (France) *Tel:* (01) 43290408 *Fax:* (01) 43290612, pg 1283

Office International des Epizooties (France) *Tel:* (01) 44151888 *Fax:* (01) 42670987 *E-mail:* oie@oie.int; pub.sales@oie.int *Web Site:* www.oie.int, pg 1244

Office Marocain D'Annonces-OMA (Morocco) *Tel:* (02) 234891; (02) 232342 *Fax:* (02) 234892, pg 470

Office National du Tourisme (ONT) (Burundi) *Tel:* (02) 2202; (02) 2023; (02) 4208 *Fax:* (02) 9390, pg 1456

Office of Libraries and Archives, Papua, New Guinea (Papua New Guinea) *Tel:* 3256200 *Fax:* 3251331 *E-mail:* ola@datec.com.pg, pg 1490

Office of Libraries and Archives, Papua New Guinea (Papua New Guinea) *Tel:* (675) 325-6200 *Fax:* (675) 325-1331 *E-mail:* ola@datec.com.pg, pg 510

Officina Edizioni di Aldo Quinti (Italy) *Tel:* (06) 3215293 *Fax:* (06) 65740514 *E-mail:* officinaedizioni@yahoo.com, pg 401

Ediciones Offo, SA (Spain) *Tel:* (091) 5514214 *Fax:* (091) 5010699, pg 584

Offo SL (Spain) *Tel:* (01) 5514214 *Fax:* (01) 5010699, pg 1139

Ogunsanya Press, Publishers and Bookstores Ltd (Nigeria) *Tel:* (022) 310924, pg 501

Oguz Yayinlari (Turkey) *Tel:* (0212) 5264745; (0212) 5113418 *Fax:* (0212) 5114695, pg 640

Ohmsa (Republic of Korea) *Tel:* (02) 7764868 *Fax:* (02) 7796757, pg 439

Ohmsha Ltd (Japan) *Tel:* (03) 3233-0641 *Fax:* (03) 3293-6224 *E-mail:* kaigaika@ohmsha.co.jp *Web Site:* www.ohmsha.co.jp, pg 423

Oidium Books (Australia) *Tel:* (052) 757045 *E-mail:* tecnilab@ozemail.com.au, pg 35

Oikos (Argentina) *Tel:* (011) 4951-9489; (011) 4951-8129 *E-mail:* postmaster@atlas.edu.ar, pg 8

Oikos-Tau SA Ediciones (Spain) *Tel:* (093) 7590791 *Fax:* (093) 7506825, pg 584

Oilfield Publications Ltd (United Kingdom) *Tel:* (01531) 634563 *Fax:* (01531) 634239; (01531) 633744 *E-mail:* opl@dial.pipex.com *Web Site:* www.oilpubs.com, pg 720

Oireachtas Library (Ireland) *Tel:* (01) 6183412 *Fax:* (01) 6184376, pg 1476

Editions de l'Oiseau-Lyre SAM (Monaco) *Tel:* (093) 300944 *Fax:* (093) 301915 *E-mail:* oiseau_lyre@compuserve.com, pg 469

Ediciones Ojeda (Spain) *Tel:* (093) 2120254; (093) 2370009 *Fax:* (093) 4159845 *E-mail:* lib.europa@mx3.redestb.es, pg 584

Editions Okad (Morocco) *Tel:* (07) 796970; (07) 796971; (07) 796973; (07) 798589 *Fax:* (07) 798556, pg 470

Okapi Centre de Diffusion (The Democratic Republic of the Congo) *Tel:* (012) 31457, pg 1280

Okeanida (Greece) *Tel:* (01) 3827341 *Fax:* (01) 3805531 *E-mail:* oceanida@internet.gr, pg 313

OKKER Oktatasi, Kereskedelmi es Szervezesi Iroda (Hungary) *Tel:* 01 332 4587, pg 326

Okoshko Ltd Publishers (Izdatelstvo) (Russian Federation) *Tel:* (095) 2450998 *Fax:* (095) 2053424, pg 541

Oktagon Verlagsgesellschaft mbH (Germany) *Tel:* (0221) 2059654 *Fax:* (0221) 2059660 *E-mail:* oktagon@buchhandlung-walterkoenig.de *Web Site:* www.oktagon.de, pg 270

Forlaget Oktober A/S (Norway) *Tel:* 22207760 *Fax:* 22207765 *E-mail:* oktober@aschehoug.no, pg 504

Old Vicarage Publications (United Kingdom) *Tel:* (01260) 279276 *Fax:* (01260) 298913, pg 720

Oldcastle Books Ltd (United Kingdom) *Tel:* (01582) 761264 *Fax:* (01582) 712244 *E-mail:* info@noexit.co.uk *Web Site:* www.noexit.co.uk, pg 720

Verlag Oldenbourg (Austria) *Tel:* (01) 712 62 58-17 *Fax:* (01) 712 62 58-19 *E-mail:* gala@oldenbourg.co.at, pg 56

The Oleander Press (United Kingdom) *Tel:* (01223) 357768 *E-mail:* editor@oleanderpress.com *Web Site:* oleanderpress.com, pg 721

David O'Leary Literary Agents (United Kingdom) *Tel:* (020) 7229 1623 *Fax:* (020) 7727 9624 *E-mail:* d.o'leary@virgin.net, pg 1121

Olho D'Agua Comercio e Servicos Editoriais Ltda (Brazil) *Tel:* (011) 2631287 *Fax:* (011) 2631287 *E-mail:* editora@olhodaguo.com.br *Web Site:* www.olhodaguo.com.br, pg 88

Editoriale Olimpia SpA (Italy) *Tel:* (055) 50161 *Fax:* (055) 5016280 *E-mail:* info@edolimpia.it *Web Site:* www.edolimpia.it, pg 401

Ediciones Olimpic, SL (Spain) *Tel:* (093) 977650885 *Fax:* (093) 977650885 *E-mail:* edolimpic@worldonline.es, pg 585

Olion Publishers (Estonia) *Tel:* (02) 6445403 *Fax:* (02) 6443488 *E-mail:* olin@eol.ee, pg 140

Edizioni Olivares (Italy) *Tel:* (02) 76001753 *Fax:* (02) 76002579, pg 402

Oliveira Rocha-Comercio e Servics Ltda (Brazil) *Tel:* (011) 2845527; (011) 2886440 *Fax:* (011) 2845362; (011) 2842096 *E-mail:* dialetic@virtual.net.com.br, pg 89

Oliver Books Ltd (United Kingdom) *Tel:* (020) 8879 3949 *Fax:* (020) 8879 0792 *E-mail:* info@oliverbooks.co.uk; sales@oliverbooks.co.uk *Web Site:* www.oliverbooks.co.uk, pg 721

Olivia - det gronne forlag (Denmark) *Tel:* 33 15 67 44 *Fax:* 33 15 67 45 *E-mail:* books@olivia.dk *Web Site:* www.olivia.dk, pg 134

Editions Olizane (Switzerland) *Tel:* (022) 3285252 *Fax:* (022) 3285796 *E-mail:* guides@olizane.ch, pg 620

Olkos (Greece) *Tel:* (01) 3224131 *Fax:* (01) 3253972, pg 1287

Ollif Publishing (Australia) *Tel:* (02) 9477-3496, pg 35

Edition Olms AG (Switzerland) *Tel:* (01) 2610270 *Fax:* (01) 2617103, pg 620

Georg Olms Verlag AG (Germany) *Tel:* (05121) 15010 *Fax:* (05121) 150150; (05121) 32007 *E-mail:* info@olms.de *Web Site:* www.olms.de, pg 270

Leo S Olschki (Italy) *Tel:* (055) 6530684 *Fax:* (055) 6530214 *E-mail:* celso@olschki.it *Web Site:* www.olschki.it, pg 402

Nakladatelstvi Olympia AS (Czech Republic) *Tel:* (02) 24810146 *Fax:* (02) 2312137; (02) 2315136 *E-mail:* olympia@mbox.vo.cz *Web Site:* olympia.gcomp.cz, pg 127

O'Mahony & Co Ltd (Ireland) *Tel:* (061) 418155 *Fax:* (061) 414558 *Web Site:* www.omahonys.ie, pg 1291

Michael O'Mara Books Ltd (United Kingdom) *Tel:* (020) 7720 8643 *Fax:* (020) 7627 8953 (Editorial); (020) 7627 4900 (Foreign Sales) *E-mail:* foreignsales@michaelomarabooks.com *Web Site:* www.michaelomarabooks.com, pg 721

Omdurman Islamic University (Sudan) *Tel:* 51489, pg 1500

Omega Boek BV (Netherlands) *Tel:* (020) 6905997 *Fax:* (020) 6957428, pg 482

Omega Distributors Ltd (New Zealand) *Tel:* (09) 2570081 *Fax:* (09) 2570082 *E-mail:* books@omegavision.co.nz, pg 1302

Ediciones Omega SA (Spain) *Tel:* (093) 2010599; (093) 2013807; (093) 2012144 *Fax:* (093) 2097362 *E-mail:* omega@ediciones-omega.es *Web Site:* www.ediciones-omega.es, pg 585

Omilos Pnevmatikis Ananeoseos (Cyprus) *Tel:* (02) 775854 *Fax:* (02) 311931, pg 122

Omnibus Books (Australia) *Tel:* (08) 8363 2333 *Fax:* (08) 8363 1420, pg 35

Omnibus Press (United Kingdom) *Tel:* (020) 7434 0066 *Fax:* (020) 7439 2848 *E-mail:* music@musicsales.co.uk *Web Site:* www.musicsales.com, pg 721

Omnicon, SA (Spain) *Tel:* (091) 5278249 *Fax:* (091) 5281348 *E-mail:* omnicon@skios.es *Web Site:* www.omnicon.es, pg 585

Omnipress Praha (Czech Republic) *Tel:* (02) 61211406 *Fax:* (02) 61211856 *E-mail:* dcf.clock@omnipress.cz *Web Site:* www.omnipress.cz, pg 127

Omsons Publications (India) *Tel:* (011) 5412452 *Fax:* (011) 3289353 *E-mail:* omsons@satyam.net.in, pg 345

Omun Gak (Republic of Korea) *Tel:* (02) 3453-8278 *Fax:* (02) 508-5210, pg 439

On Stream Publications Ltd (Ireland) *Tel:* (021) 4385798 *Fax:* (021) 4385798 *E-mail:* info@onstream.ie *Web Site:* www.onstream.ie, pg 363

On The Stone (Australia) *Tel:* (06) 62576267 *Fax:* (06) 2497323 *E-mail:* thestone@dynamite.com.au, pg 35

Oncken Verlag KG (Germany) *Tel:* (02104) 968600; (02104) 968620 (sales) *Fax:* (02104) 968601 *E-mail:* edit@brockhaus-verlag.de; info@brockhaus-verlag.de *Web Site:* www.brockhaus-verlag.de, pg 270

Ondorisha Publishers Ltd (Japan) *Tel:* (03) 32683101 *Fax:* (03) 32353530, pg 423

One Way Book Centre (New Zealand) *Tel:* (03) 3663657 *Fax:* (03) 3664445, pg 1302

One Way Medien OHG (Germany) *Tel:* (0202) 309 9946 *Fax:* (0202) 314113 *E-mail:* one_way@t-online.de, pg 270

Oneindige Verhaal, t bvba (Belgium) *Tel:* (03) 7765225 *Fax:* (03) 7765225 *E-mail:* oneindigeverhaal@boekenbank.be, pg 1276

Oneworld Publications (United Kingdom) *Tel:* (01865) 310597 *Fax:* (01865) 310598 *E-mail:* info@oneworld-publications.com *Web Site:* www.oneworld.publications.com, pg 721

Ongaku No Tomo Sha Corporation (Japan) *Tel:* (03) 32352111 *Fax:* (03) 32352119, pg 423

Onibon-Oje Book Club (Nigeria) *Tel:* (022) 313956, pg 1230

Onibon-Oje Publishers (Nigeria) *Tel:* (022) 313956, pg 501

ONK Agency Ltd (Turkey) *Tel:* (0212) 2498602; (0212) 2498603 *Fax:* (0212) 2525153 *E-mail:* info@onkagency.com *Web Site:* www.onkagency.com, pg 1117

Online Information Resources Pty Ltd (Australia) *Tel:* (03) 98503361 *Fax:* (03) 98503641, pg 35

Dr C D Ooft (Suriname) *Tel:* 499139, pg 599

Ooievaar (Netherlands) *Tel:* (020) 624 19 34 *Fax:* (020) 622 54 61 *E-mail:* pbo@pbo.nl *Web Site:* www.pbo.nl, pg 482

Op der Lay (Luxembourg) *Tel:* 839742 *Fax:* 899350 *E-mail:* opderlay@pt.lu *Web Site:* //webplaza.pt.lu/public/opderlay, pg 447

The Open Book (Australia) *Tel:* (08) 82235468 *Toll Free Tel:* 800-888-261 *Fax:* (08) 82234552 *E-mail:* openbook@openbook.com.au *Web Site:* www.openbook.com.au; www.lca.org.au/openbook.html, pg 1273

Open Books Publishing Ltd (United Kingdom) *Tel:* (01460) 52565 *Fax:* (01460) 52565, pg 721

Open Gate Press (United Kingdom) *Tel:* (020) 7431 4391 *Fax:* (020) 7431 5129 *E-mail:* books@opengatepress.co.uk *Web Site:* www.opengatepress.co.uk, pg 721

Open University of Israel (Israel) *Tel:* (03) 6460460 *Fax:* (03) 6419279 *Web Site:* www.openu.ac.il, pg 371

Open University Press (United Kingdom) *Tel:* (01280) 823388 *Fax:* (01280) 823233 *E-mail:* enquiries@openup.co.uk *Web Site:* www.openup.co.uk, pg 721

Open University Worldwide (United Kingdom) *Tel:* (01908) 858785 *Fax:* (01908) 858787 *E-mail:* ouwenq@open.ac.uk *Web Site:* www.open.ac.uk, pg 721

Openbare Bibliotheek (Netherlands Antilles) *Tel:* (09) 4617055 *Fax:* (09) 4656247, pg 1487

Openbook Publishers (Australia) *Tel:* (08) 8223 5468 *Fax:* (08) 8223 4552 *E-mail:* enquiries@openbook.com.au *Web Site:* www.openbook.com.au, pg 35

Opera (Greece) *Tel:* (01) 6527516 *Fax:* (01) 3303634 *E-mail:* opera@acci.gr, pg 314

Opera Tres Ediciones Musicales (Spain) *Tel:* (091) 542 4320 *Fax:* (091) 541 0580; (091) 680 76 26, pg 585

Editions Ophrys (France) *Tel:* (04) 92 53 85 72 *Fax:* (04) 92 53 35 60 *E-mail:* edition.ophrys@wanadoo.fr *Web Site:* www.ophrys-editions.com, pg 178

Opsys Operating System (France) *Tel:* (04) 76 84 34 20 *Fax:* (04) 76 84 34 21 *E-mail:* opsys@opsys.fr *Web Site:* www.opsys.fr, pg 178

Opus Libri SRL (Italy) *Tel:* (055) 660833 *Fax:* (055) 670604 *E-mail:* opuslib@dada.it, pg 1293

Opus Book Publishing Ltd (United Kingdom) *Tel:* (01206) 383629 *Fax:* (01206) 383629 *E-mail:* opus@mac.co.uk, pg 722

Opus Publishing Ltd (United Kingdom) *Tel:* (020) 7267 1034 *Fax:* (020) 7267 6026 *E-mail:* opuspub@dircon.co.uk, pg 722

Opus Records & Publishing House (Slovakia) *Tel:* (07) 222680; (07) 61783 *Fax:* (07) 92219, pg 550

Edicoes Ora & Labora (Portugal) *Tel:* (252) 94 11 76 *Fax:* (252) 87 29 47 *E-mail:* msingeverga@net.sapo.pt, pg 528

Verlag Orac im Verlag Kremayr & Scheriau (Austria) *Tel:* (01) 713 8770-11 *Fax:* (01) 713 8770-20, pg 56

Or'am Publishers (Israel) *Tel:* (03) 5372277 *Fax:* (03) 5372281 *E-mail:* orampub@netvision.net.il *Web Site:* www.oram.co.il, pg 371

Editions de l'Orante (France) *Tel:* (01) 47 83 55 02 *Fax:* (01) 45 66 00 16, pg 178

Orbis Books (London) Ltd (United Kingdom) *Tel:* (020) 7602 5541 *Fax:* (020) 8742 7686 *E-mail:* bookshop@orbis-books.co.uk, pg 1321

Ediciones Orbis SA (Spain) *Tel:* (093) 280 05 12 *Fax:* (093) 280 14 72 *E-mail:* orbis@edorbis.es *Web Site:* www.edorbis.es, pg 585

Orbis Verlag fur Publizistik GmbH (Germany) *Tel:* (089) 431890 *Fax:* (089) 43189113, pg 270

Orca Publishing Services Ltd (New Zealand) *Tel:* (03) 3777770 *Fax:* (03) 3770390, pg 494

Orchid Press (Suriname), pg 599

Ordfront Foerlag AB (Sweden) *Tel:* (08) 4624420 *Fax:* (08) 4624490 *E-mail:* forlaget@ordfront.se *Web Site:* www.ordfront.se, pg 605

Ordnance Survey (United Kingdom) *Tel:* (08456) 05 05 05 (customer information); (023) 8079 5519 (trade orders) *Fax:* (023) 8079 2615 (trade customer information); (023) 8079 2388 (trade orders) *E-mail:* enquiries@ordsvy.gov.uk *Web Site:* www.ordnancesurvey.co.uk, pg 722

Orell Fuessli Verlag (Switzerland) *Tel:* (01) 2113630 *Fax:* (01) 4667412 *E-mail:* info@orell-fuessli-verlag.ch *Web Site:* www.orell-fuessli-verlag.ch, pg 620

Orell Fuessli Verlag (Switzerland) *Tel:* (01) 2113630 *Fax:* (01) 4667412, pg 1313

Oreos Verlag GmbH (Germany) *Tel:* (08021) 86 68 *Fax:* (08021) 17 50 *E-mail:* info@oreos.de *Web Site:* www.oreos.de, pg 270

Orfanidis Publications (Greece) *Tel:* (01) 3836925 *Fax:* (01) 3845623, pg 314

Verlag Organisator AG (Switzerland) *Tel:* (01) 2118155 *Fax:* (01) 4010815; (01) 4928758, pg 620

Organizacao Andrei Editora Ltda (Brazil) *Tel:* (011) 223-5111 *Fax:* (011) 221-0246 *E-mail:* andrei@cepa.com.br *Web Site:* www.editora-andrei.com.br, pg 89

Izdavacka Organizacija Rad (Yugoslavia) *Tel:* (011) 3239-758; (011) 3239-998 *Fax:* (011) 3230-923, pg 765

Organizacion Cultural LP SA de CV (Mexico) *Tel:* (05) 5112312; (05) 5147608 *Fax:* (05) 3584761, pg 465

Organizacion de Bienestar Estudiantil (OBE) (Venezuela) *Tel:* (02) 6054050 (ext 4200, 4201 & 4202) *Fax:* (02) 6930638, pg 1324

Organization for African Unity Library (Ethiopia) *Tel:* (01) 517700 (ext 211) *Fax:* (01) 513036, pg 1463

Organization for Economic Cooperation & Development (OECD) (France) *Tel:* (01) 45248200 *Fax:* (01) 45248500 *E-mail:* news.contact@oecd.org *Web Site:* www.oecd.org, pg 1244

Organizations of Libraries, Museums & Documentation Centre of Astan Quds (Islamic Republic of Iran) *Tel:* (098511) 2216009 *Fax:* (098511) 2220845 *E-mail:* radad@imamreza.or.ir; astanlib@imamreza.or.ir *Web Site:* www.aqlibrary.org, pg 1475

The Organizing Committee of the 11th Int-l Zeolite Conference (Republic of Korea) *Tel:* (042) 69-8161 *Fax:* (042) 69-8170 *E-mail:* skihm@sorak.kaist.ac.kr, pg 439

Orient Book Club (India) *Fax:* (011) 386-2935 *E-mail:* orientpbk@vsnl.com, pg 1229

Orient Paperbacks (India) *Tel:* (011) 3862267; (011) 3862201 *Fax:* (011) 3862935 *E-mail:* orientpbk@vsnl.com *Web Site:* www.orientpaperbacks.com, pg 345

Oriental Books (Republic of Korea) *Tel:* (02) 371737 *Fax:* (02) 346624, pg 439

Oriental Press BV (APA) (Netherlands) *Tel:* (020) 6265544 *E-mail:* info@apa-publishers.com, pg 482

Oriental Publications (Australia) *Tel:* (08) 8210 0863 *Fax:* (08) 8410 0863 *E-mail:* oriental@dove.net.au, pg 36

Bibliotheque Orientale (Lebanon) *Tel:* (01) 200297 *E-mail:* bibor@cyberia.net.lb, pg 1481

Editorial Oriente (Cuba) *Tel:* (0226) 22496; (0226) 28096 *Fax:* (0226) 86111 *E-mail:* edoriente@cultstgo.cult.cu *Web Site:* www.amafra.com.ar/oriente/, pg 121

Ediciones del Oriente y del Mediterraneo (Spain) *Tel:* (091) 8543428 *Fax:* (091) 8548352 *E-mail:* sicamor@teleline.es *Web Site:* www.webdoce.com/orienteymediterraneo, pg 585

Origen Editorial SA (Mexico) *Tel:* (05) 5750711 ext 30; (05) 5750711 ext 31, pg 465

L'Originel - Editions Accarias (France) *Tel:* (01) 43 48 73 07 *Fax:* (01) 43 48 73 07 *E-mail:* originel-accarias@club-internet.fr, pg 178

Origo Verlag (Switzerland) *Tel:* (031) 224480 *Fax:* (031) 3114470, pg 621

Origo Forlag (Norway) *Tel:* 22160769 *Fax:* 22164837, pg 504

Orin Books (Australia) *Tel:* (03) 9534 5680; (03) 9534 4746 *Fax:* (03) 9527 3308, pg 36

Orion Children's Books (United Kingdom) *Tel:* (020) 7240 3444 *Fax:* (020) 7240 4822 *Web Site:* www.orionbooks.co.uk, pg 722

Editorial Orion (Mexico) *Tel:* (05) 5200224 *Fax:* (05) 5200224, pg 465

Editura Orion (Romania) *Tel:* (01) 6146151; (01) 6594697, pg 534

Orion Publishing Group Ltd (United Kingdom) *Tel:* (020) 7240 3444 *Fax:* (020) 7240 4822 *E-mail:* info@orionbooks.co.uk *Web Site:* orionbooks.co.uk, pg 722

The Orkney Press Ltd (United Kingdom) *Tel:* (1856) 875747 *Fax:* (1856) 876284, pg 722

Orlanda Frauenverlag (Germany) *Tel:* (030) 216-3566; (030) 216-2960 *Fax:* (030) 2153958 *E-mail:* post@orlanda.de *Web Site:* www.orlanda.de, pg 270

Ormstunga (Iceland) *Tel:* 561-0055 *Fax:* 561-0025 *E-mail:* ormstunga@mmedia.is, pg 328

Oros Verlag (Germany) *Tel:* (02505) 3534 *Fax:* (02505) 3534, pg 271

Orpheus Books Ltd (United Kingdom) *Tel:* (01993) 774949 *Fax:* (01993) 700330 *E-mail:* info@orpheusbooks.com *Web Site:* www.orpheusbooks.com, pg 722

Orszagos Mueszaki, Informacios Koezpont es Koenyvtar (Hungary) *Tel:* (01) 1336300; (01) 1137439 *Fax:* (01) 1382414, pg 326

Orszagos Muoszaki, Informacios Koozpont es Koonyvtar (OMIKK) (Hungary) *Tel:* (01) 3384074; (01) 3382300 *Fax:* (01) 3382414 *E-mail:* fotik@omk.omikkh.hu, pg 1472

Orszagos Szechenyi Koenyvtar (Hungary) *Tel:* (01) 2243700 *Fax:* (01) 202-0804 *E-mail:* viki@oszk.hu, pg 1472

Orszagos Szechenyi Koenyvtar Magyar ISBN Iroda (Hungary) *Tel:* (01) 224 3748 *Fax:* (01) 202-0804, pg 1248

Orte-Verlag (Switzerland) *Tel:* (01) 3630234; (01) 559751, pg 621

Editorial Alfredo Ortells SL (Spain) *Tel:* (06) 347 10 00 *Fax:* (06) 347 39 10 *E-mail:* editorial@ortells.com *Web Site:* www.ortells.com, pg 585

Editora Ortiz SA (Brazil) *Tel:* (051) 225-3026 *Fax:* (051) 225-3026, pg 89

Oruem Publishing House (Republic of Korea) *Tel:* (02) 5859122; (02) 5859123 *Fax:* (02) 5847952, pg 439

OS (Organizzazioni Speciali SRL) (Italy) *Tel:* (055) 6236501 *Fax:* (055) 669446, pg 402

Osaka University Library (Japan) *Tel:* (06) 8505045 *Fax:* (06) 8505052, pg 1478

Osaka Oviss Inc (Japan) *Tel:* (06) 3527090 *Fax:* (06) 3528898, pg 1295

Osaka Prefectural Nakanoshima Library (Japan) *Tel:* (06) 2030474 *Fax:* (06) 2034914, pg 1478

Osanna Venosa (Italy) *Tel:* (0972) 35952 *Fax:* (0972) 35723, pg 402

Osborne Books Ltd (United Kingdom) *Tel:* (01905) 748071 *Fax:* (0190) 748952 *E-mail:* books@osborne.u-net.com *Web Site:* www.osbornebooks.co.uk, pg 722

Oscar Book International (Malaysia) *Tel:* (03) 78753515; (03) 78762797 *Fax:* (03) 78762797, pg 453

Osho Verlag GmbH (Germany) *Tel:* (0221) 278 04-0 *Fax:* (0221) 278 04-66 *E-mail:* info@oshoverlag.de *Web Site:* www.oshoverlag.de, pg 271

Osimpam Educational Books (Ghana), pg 307

Osiris Kiado (Hungary) *Tel:* (01) 266-6560 *Fax:* (01) 267-0935 *E-mail:* osiriskiado@mail.datanet.hu *Web Site:* www.osiriskiado.hu, pg 326

Osnova, Kharkov State University Press (Ukraine) *Tel:* (057) 224647, pg 643

Osnovy Publishers (Ukraine) *Tel:* (044) 2952582; (044) 2958636 *Fax:* (044) 2952582, pg 643

Osprey Publishing Ltd (United Kingdom) *Tel:* (01865) 727022 *Fax:* (01865) 727017 *E-mail:* info@ospreydirect.co.uk *Web Site:* www.ospreypublishing.com, pg 722

Ossian Publications (Ireland) *Tel:* (021) 4502040 *Fax:* (021) 4502025 *E-mail:* ossian@iol.ie *Web Site:* www.ossian.ie, pg 363

Ossolineum Zaklad Narodowy im Ossolinskich - Wydawnictwo (Poland) *Tel:* (071) 3436961 *Fax:* (071) 448103 *Toll Free Fax:* 800 0712771 *E-mail:* ossobn@pwr.wroc.pl, pg 518

Verlag des Osterr Kneippbundes GmbH (Austria) *Tel:* (03842) 21682; (03842) 21718; (03842) 24094 *Fax:* (03842) 2171832 *E-mail:* office@kneippverlag.com *Web Site:* www.kneippverlag.com, pg 57

Osterreichische Bibelgesellschaft (Austria) *Tel:* (0222) 938240, pg 1275

Osterreichische Nationalbibliothek (Austria) *Tel:* (01) 534100 *Fax:* (01) 533704983, pg 1451

Osterreichischer Alpenverein Sektion Weiner Lehrer (Austria) *Tel:* (02244) 3536 *Fax:* (02244) 3536, pg 57

Osterreichischer Bundesveilag Ges.mbh (Austria) *Tel:* (02236) 635 35-290 *Fax:* (02236) 635 35-243 *E-mail:* oebz@oebv.co.at, pg 57

Osterreichischer Wirtschaftsverlag Druck-und Verlagsgesellschaft mbH (Austria) *Tel:* (01) 54664-336 *Fax:* (01) 54664-360 *E-mail:* s.drabosenig@oewv.at, pg 57

Ostfalia-Verlag Jurgen Schierer (Germany) *Tel:* (05171) 41763 *Fax:* (05171) 41769 *E-mail:* 0517141763-001@t-online.de *Web Site:* www.ostfalia-verlag.de, pg 271

Ostschweiz Druck und Verlag (Switzerland) *Tel:* (071) 208585 *Fax:* (071) 236577, pg 621

Osvita (Ukraine) *Tel:* (044) 216-58-02 *Fax:* (044) 216-98-15; (044) 216-54-44 *E-mail:* osvita@ukrpack.net, pg 643

Otago Heritage Books (New Zealand) *Tel:* (03) 4771500, pg 494

Otava Publishing Co Ltd (Finland) *Tel:* 19961 *Fax:* 643136 *E-mail:* otava@otava.fi *Web Site:* www.otava.fi, pg 143

OTEN (Open Training & Education Network) (Australia) *Tel:* (02) 9715 8000; (02) 9715 8222 *Fax:* (02) 9715 8111; (02) 9715 8174 *E-mail:* oten.dir@tafensw.edu *Web Site:* www.oten.edu.au, pg 36

Otokar Kersovani (Croatia) *Tel:* (051) 338 558; (051) 338 016 *Fax:* (051) 331 690 *E-mail:* otokar-kersovani@ri.tel.hr, pg 120

Otsuki Shoten Publishers (Japan) *Tel:* 03 38134651 (Sales) *Fax:* 03 38134656 *E-mail:* otsuki@meibun.or.jp, pg 423

Ott Verlag AG (Switzerland) *Tel:* (033) 221622 *Fax:* (033) 2253939 *E-mail:* info@ott-verlag.ch, pg 621

Ott Verlag AG (Switzerland) *Tel:* (033) 221622 *Fax:* (033) 2253939, pg 1139

Otto-Friedrich Universitat Bamberg (Germany) *Tel:* (0951) 863-1020; (0951) 863-1021 *Fax:* (0951) 863-1005 *E-mail:* pressestelle@zuv.uni-bamberg.de *Web Site:* www.uni-bamberg.de/zuv/presse/mitarbeiter, pg 271

Ouest Editions (France) *Tel:* (02) 40 14 34 34 *Fax:* (02) 40 14 36 36, pg 178

Editions Ouest-France (France) *Tel:* (016) 99 32 58 27 *Fax:* (016) 99 32 58 30 *Web Site:* www.edilarge.com, pg 178

Oulun Yliopiston Kirjasto (Finland) *Tel:* (081) 5531011 *Fax:* (081) 5569135, pg 1464

Editions Oum (Morocco) *Tel:* (02) 274972 *Fax:* (02) 208882, pg 470

Our Lady of Manaoag Publisher (Philippines) *Tel:* (02) 610214; (02) 610219 *Fax:* (06) 610219, pg 514

Outback Books - CQU Press (Australia) *Tel:* (07) 4923 2520 *Fax:* (07) 4923 2525 *E-mail:* cqupress@cqu.edu.au *Web Site:* www.outbackbooks.com, pg 36

Outdoor Press Pty Ltd (Australia) *Tel:* (03) 57905226 *Fax:* (03) 57905393 *Web Site:* www.goldexpeditions.com, pg 36

Outrigger Publishers (New Zealand) *Tel:* (07) 856 6981, pg 494

Editorial Oveja Negra (Colombia) *Tel:* (01) 2577900; (01) 2368198 *Fax:* (01) 6100931, pg 113

George Over Ltd (United Kingdom) *Tel:* (01788) 573621 *Fax:* (01788) 578738 *E-mail:* xuz23@dial.pinex.com, pg 1204

Deborah Owen Ltd (United Kingdom) *Tel:* (020) 7987 5119; (020) 7987 5441 *Fax:* (020) 7538 4004 *E-mail:* debowen@dial.pipex.com, pg 1121

Peter Owen Ltd (United Kingdom) *Tel:* (020) 7373 5628; (020) 7370 6093 *Fax:* (020) 7373 6760. *E-mail:* admin@peterowen.u-net.com *Web Site:* www.peterowen.com, pg 722

Owl Books (United Kingdom) *Tel:* (01695) 622022 *Fax:* (01542) 821819, pg 722

Owl Publishing (Australia) *Tel:* (03) 95966064 *Fax:* (03) 95966942, pg 36

Oxfam (United Kingdom) *Tel:* (01865) 312610 *Fax:* (01865) 313925 *E-mail:* oxfam@oxfam.org.uk *Web Site:* www.oxfam.org.uk, pg 722

Oxfam Community Aid Abroad (Australia) *Tel:* (03) 9289 9444 *Fax:* (03) 9419 5895 *E-mail:* enquire@caa.org.au *Web Site:* www.caa.org.au, pg 36

Oxford Bibliographical Society (United Kingdom) *Tel:* (01865) 277102 *Fax:* (01865) 277182, pg 1371

Oxford & IBH Publishing Co Pvt Ltd (India) *Tel:* (011) 332 45 78; (011) 332 05 18 *Fax:* (011) 371 32 75 *E-mail:* oxford@vsnl.com, pg 345

Oxford & IBH Publishing Co Pvt Ltd (India) *Tel:* (011) 3314957; (011) 3320518; (0121) 3313584 *Fax:* (011) 3322639; (011) 3713275 *E-mail:* oxfordpubl@axcess.net.in, pg 1289

Oxford International Centre for Publishing Studies (United Kingdom) *Tel:* (01865) 484951 *Fax:* (01865) 484952 *E-mail:* apm@brookes.ac.uk *Web Site:* www.brookes.ac.uk/schools/apm/publishing, pg 722

Oxford University Press (India) *Tel:* (011) 2021029; (011) 2021198; (011) 2021396 *Fax:* (011) 3732312; (011) 3360897 *E-mail:* ibho@oup.wiprobt.ems.vsnl.net.in, pg 345

Oxford University Press (New Zealand) *Tel:* (09) 5233134 *Fax:* (09) 5233134, pg 494

Oxford University Press (United Republic of Tanzania) *Tel:* (051) 29209 *Fax:* (051) 46822, pg 634

Oxford University Press (United Kingdom) *Tel:* (01865) 556767 *Fax:* (01865) 556646 *Web Site:* www.oup.co.uk, pg 723

Oxford University Press Children's Books (United Kingdom) *Tel:* (01865) 556767 *Fax:* (01865) 267732 *E-mail:* enquiry@oup.co.uk *Web Site:* www.oup.co.uk, pg 723

Oxford University Press Espana SA (Spain) *Tel:* (091) 6775053, pg 585

Oxford University Press KK (Japan) *Tel:* (03) 59953801 *Fax:* (03) 59953919, pg 423

Oxford University, Taylor Institution Library (United Kingdom) *Tel:* (01865) 278158 (issue desk); (01865) 278161; (01865) 278154 (office) *Fax:* (01865) 278165 *E-mail:* enquiries@taylib.ox.ac.uk *Web Site:* www.taylib.ox.ac.uk, pg 1507

Oxonian Press (P) Ltd (India) *Tel:* (011) 44957; (011) 3313584 *Fax:* (011) 3322639 *E-mail:* oxford.publ@axcess.net.in, pg 345

Jill Oxton Publications Pty Ltd (Australia) *Tel:* (08) 2762722 *Fax:* (08) 3743494 *E-mail:* jill@jilloxtonxstitch.com *Web Site:* www.jilloxtonxstitch.com, pg 36

Oy Edita AB (Finland) *Tel:* (09) 56601 *Fax:* (00) 5660396, pg 143

Oy LIKE Kustannus Ltd (Finland) *Tel:* (09) 1351385 *Fax:* (09) 1351372 *Web Site:* www.likekustannus.fi, pg 144

Oyster Books (United Kingdom) *Tel:* (01934) 732251 *Fax:* (01934) 732123 *E-mail:* pearls@oysterbooks.co.uk *Web Site:* www.oysterbooks.co.uk, pg 723

Oz Publishing Co Pty Ltd (Australia) *Tel:* (07) 8922313 *Fax:* (07) 8462491, pg 36

P P H Penta (Poland) *Tel:* (022) 6390465 *Fax:* (022) 6390465 *E-mail:* penta@penta.pol.pl, pg 518

Pabel-Moewig Verlag KG (Germany) *Tel:* (07222) 13 0 *Fax:* (07222) 13 218 *E-mail:* kontakt@moewig.de *Web Site:* www.vpm-online.de, pg 271

Pacific Book Centre (S) Pte Ltd (Singapore) *Tel:* 2616288 *Fax:* 2616088, pg 1309

Pacific Publications (Australia) Pty Ltd (Australia) *Tel:* (02) 20231 *Fax:* (02) 2883322, pg 36

Maria Pacini Fazzi Editore (Italy) *Tel:* (0583) 55530 *Fax:* (0583) 418245 *E-mail:* pacini.fazzi@lunet.it, pg 402

Packard Publishing Ltd (United Kingdom) *Tel:* (01243) 537977 *Fax:* (01243) 537977 *E-mail:* info@packardpublishing.co.uk *Web Site:* www.packardpublishing.com, pg 723

Packer-Evans and Associates Ltd (Jamaica) *Tel:* 924-1270 *Fax:* 926-3487, pg 413

PacPress Media Pte Ltd (Singapore) *Tel:* 2768090; 2730756 *Fax:* 2730060, pg 1200

Pademelon Press (Australia) *Tel:* (02) 9634-4655 *Fax:* (02) 9680-4634 *E-mail:* info@pademelonpress.com.au *Web Site:* www.pademelonpress.com.au, pg 36

Editorial Padilla (Dominican Republic) *Tel:* (809) 682-0111; (809) 688-0303, pg 1281

Biblioteca Universitaria di Padua (Italy) *Tel:* (049) 8240211; (049) 8240241 *Fax:* (049) 8762711 *E-mail:* bupd@librari.beniculturali.it *Web Site:* www.unipd.it/bibliotecauniversitaria, pg 1477

Library of the Paedagogiki Institute Academia (College of Education) (Cyprus) *Tel:* (02) 305933, pg 1460

Paerangi Books (New Zealand) *Tel:* (04) 4787789, pg 494

Pagano Editore (Italy) *Tel:* (081) 5523840 *Fax:* (081) 54242949, pg 402

Page Bros Ltd (Norwich) (United Kingdom) *Tel:* (01603) 429141 *Fax:* (01603) 485126, pg 1141, 1162, 1204, 1214

Page Bros Ltd (Norwich) (United Kingdom) *Tel:* (01603) 429141 *Fax:* (01603) 485126 *E-mail:* sco@pagesales.co.uk, pg 1223

Pages Editors, SL (Spain) *Tel:* (0973) 23 66 11 *Fax:* (0973) 24 07 95 *E-mail:* ed.pages.editors@cambrescat.es, pg 585

Pageworks (United States) *Tel:* 860-395-2022 *Fax:* 860-388-4353, pg 1166

Pagina da Cultura Agencia Literaria Ideias sobre Linhas Ltda (Brazil) *Tel:* (011) 3266 4299 *Fax:* (011) 3266 4299 *E-mail:* paginadacultura@pobox.com *Web Site:* www.pagina-da-cultura.com.br, pg 1109

Pagina Forlags AB (Sweden) *Tel:* (08) 56421800 *Fax:* (08) 56421819 *E-mail:* pagina@pagina.se, pg 605

Pagoulatos Bros (Greece) *Tel:* (01) 03818780; (01) 03801485 *Fax:* (01) 03838028 *E-mail:* pagoulatos_publ@ath.forthnet.gr, pg 314

Pagoulatos G-G P Publications (Greece) *Tel:* (01) 3604895; (01) 3624624 *Fax:* (01) 3604897, pg 314

Pahl-Rugenstein Verlag Nachfolger-GmbH (Germany) *Tel:* (0228) 632306 *Fax:* (0228) 634968 *E-mail:* prv@che-chandler.com, pg 271

Paico Publishing House (India) *Tel:* (0484) 355835, pg 345

Paideia Editrice (Italy) *Tel:* (030) 3582434 *Fax:* (030) 3582691 *E-mail:* paideiaeditrice@tin.it, pg 402

Editura Paideia (Romania) *Tel:* (01) 3308006; (01) 3301678 *Fax:* (01) 3301677 *E-mail:* paideia@fx.ro, pg 535

Ediciones Paidos Iberica SA (Spain) *Tel:* (093) 2002804; (093) 241 9250 *Fax:* (093) 2022954 *E-mail:* paidos@paidos.com, pg 585

Editorial Paidos Mexicana, SA (Mexico) *Tel:* (05) 5645607; (05) 5647908 *Fax:* (05) 5904361 *E-mail:* paimex@iserve.net.mx, pg 465

Editorial Paidos SAICF (Argentina) *Tel:* (011) 4331-2275; (011) 4331-9399 *Fax:* (011) 4331-2275 *E-mail:* paidos@internet.siscotel.com, pg 8

Editorial Paidotribo SL (Spain) *Tel:* (093) 3233311 *Fax:* (093) 4535033 *E-mail:* paidotribo@paidotribo.com *Web Site:* www.paidotribo.com, pg 585

Editions J H Paillet et B Drouaud (France) *Tel:* 54704303, pg 178

Charles Paine Pty Ltd (Australia) *Tel:* (02) 9890-1388 *Fax:* (02) 9890-1915, pg 36

Ediciones El Pais SA (Spain) *Tel:* (091) 7449060 *Fax:* (091) 7449093 *E-mail:* elpaisaguilar@santillana.es *Web Site:* www.elpaisaguilar.es, pg 585

YELLOW PAGES

Pais Vasco Servicio Central de Publicaciones (Spain) *Tel:* (0945) 018656 *Fax:* (0945) 018709 *E-mail:* hacsabd@ej-gv.es *Web Site:* www.ej-gv.net, pg 585

El Paisaje Editorial (Spain) *Tel:* (04) 6390774, pg 585

Paiva Osakeyhtio (Finland) *Tel:* (01) 976446113 *Fax:* (09) 176122109 *E-mail:* paivaoy@svk.fi *Web Site:* www.svk.fi/paivaoy/, pg 144

Pak American Commercial (Pvt) Ltd (Pakistan) *Tel:* (042) 563709 *Fax:* (021) 565190, pg 508

Pak American Commercial (Pvt) Ltd (Pakistan) *Tel:* (021) 563709 *Fax:* (021) 565190, pg 1304

Pak Book Corporation (Pakistan) *Tel:* (042) 111 636 636 *Fax:* (042) 6362328 *E-mail:* pbc@brain.net.pk, pg 1304

Pakistan Library Association (PLA) (Pakistan) *Tel:* (051) 9214041 *Fax:* (051) 9210886, pg 1522

Pakistan Institute of Development Economics (Pakistan) *Tel:* (051) 9206610-27 *Fax:* (051) 9210886 *E-mail:* pide@apollo.net.pk *Web Site:* www.pide.org.pk, pg 508

Pakistan Institute of Development Economics (Pakistan) *Tel:* (051) 9206616 *Fax:* (051) 9210886 *E-mail:* pide@isb.paknet.com.pk *Web Site:* www.pide.org.pk, pg 1490

Pakistan Institute of Nuclear Science & Technology Library, Science Information Division (Pakistan) *Tel:* (051) 452350 *Fax:* (051) 429533 *E-mail:* ctc@shell.portal.com, pg 1490

Pakistan Publishing House (Pakistan) *Tel:* (021) 5681457, pg 508

Pakistan Scientific and Technological Information Centre (PASTIC) (Pakistan) *Tel:* (051) 824161 *Fax:* (051) 9201341 *E-mail:* pnc%pastic@sdnpk.undp.org.pk, pg 1490

Pakistan Writers' Guild (Pakistan), pg 1367

Pakpassak Kanphin (Laos People's Democratic Republic), pg 441

Pal Verlagsgesellschaft mbH (Germany) *Tel:* (0621) 415741 *Fax:* (0621) 415101 *E-mail:* palverlag@aol.com *Web Site:* www.pal-verlag.de, pg 271

Pala-Verlag GmbH (Germany) *Tel:* (06151) 23028 *Fax:* (06151) 292713 *E-mail:* info@pala-verlag.de *Web Site:* www.pala-verlag.de, pg 271

Ediciones Palabra SA (Spain) *Tel:* (091) 350 7720 *Fax:* (091) 359 02 30 *E-mail:* epalsa@edicionespalabra.es *Web Site:* www.edicionespalabra.es, pg 585

Palabra Ediciones Verlagsgesellschaft mbH (Mexico) *Tel:* (05) 5730985 *Fax:* (05) 5730985, pg 465

Palace Press International (Hong Kong) *Tel:* (02) 3579019 *Fax:* (02) 5613616 *E-mail:* palacehk@palacepress.ocm *Web Site:* www.palacepress.com, pg 1135

Palace Press International (United States) *Tel:* 415-626-1080 *Fax:* 415-626-1510 *E-mail:* ppisfo@palacepress.com *Web Site:* www.palacepress.com, pg 1145, 1166, 1208

Palacio del Libro (Uruguay) *Tel:* (02) 959019 *Fax:* (02) 957543, pg 1324

Biblioteca do Palacio Nacional de Mafra (Portugal) *Tel:* (0261) 817550 *Fax:* (0261) 811947, pg 1493

Palas Editores Lda (Portugal) *Tel:* (021) 574903 *Fax:* (021) 795-4019, pg 528

Palatina Editrice (Italy) *Tel:* (0521) 282388 *Fax:* (0521) 282388, pg 402

Edit Palavra Magica (Brazil) *Tel:* (016) 6100074 *Fax:* (016) 610-0204 *E-mail:* editora@palavramagica.com.br *Web Site:* www.palavramagica.com.br, pg 89

Palazzi Verlag GmbH (Germany) *Tel:* (0421) 321100 *Fax:* (0421) 321300, pg 271

Palestinian PEN Centre (Israel) *Tel:* (02) 6262970 *Fax:* (02) 6264620, pg 1365

Palgrave Publishers Ltd (United Kingdom) *Tel:* (01256) 329242 *Fax:* (01256) 479476 *E-mail:* orders@palgrave.com (ordering online); catalogue@palgrave.com (catalogue requests); conferences@palgrave.com (conference & exhibition information); rights@palgrave.com (copyright & permissions); lectureservices@palgrave.com (inspection copy service); reviews@palgrave.com (review copy requests); booksellers@palgrave.com (bookseller queries) *Web Site:* www.palgrave.com, pg 723

Pallas-Akademia Koenyvkiadoes Koenyvkereskedes (Romania) *Tel:* (066) 171036; (066) 171955 *Fax:* (066) 171955 *E-mail:* pallas@nextra.ro, pg 535

Pallas Athene (United Kingdom) *Tel:* (020) 7229 2798 *Fax:* (020) 7792 1067, pg 723

Pallas Editora e Distribuidora Ltda (Brazil) *Tel:* (021) 270-0186 *Fax:* (021) 590-6996; (21) 5618007 *E-mail:* pallas@alternex.com.br *Web Site:* www.pallaseditora.com.br/, pg 89

Vydavatel'stvo SFVU Pallas (Slovakia) *Tel:* (07) 296627 *Fax:* (07) 294229; (07) 292820, pg 550

Palle Fogtdal A/S (Denmark) *Tel:* 33153915 *Fax:* 33933505, pg 134

Pallottinum Wydawnictwo Stowarzyszenia Apostolstwa Katolickiego (Poland) *Tel:* (061) 8675233 *Fax:* (061) 8675238 *E-mail:* pallottinum@pallottinum.pl *Web Site:* pallottinum.poznan.pl, pg 518

Palm Beach Press (Australia) *Tel:* (066) 46-1622 *Fax:* (02) 9946-1515, pg 36

Palmerston North Public Library (New Zealand) *Tel:* (06) 3583076 *Fax:* (06) 3568869 *E-mail:* library@pnlibrary.manawatan.planet.co.nz, pg 1487

Palms Press (Australia) *Tel:* (049) 731236, pg 36

Palmyra Verlag (Germany) *Tel:* (06221) 165409 *Fax:* (06221) 167310 *E-mail:* palmyra-verlag@t-online.de *Web Site:* www.palmyra-verlag.de, pg 271

Fratelli Palombi SRL (Italy) *Tel:* (06) 3214150 *Fax:* (06) 3214752, pg 402

Palphot Ltd (Israel) *Tel:* (09) 9555238 *Fax:* (09) 9555238 *E-mail:* palphot@palphot.com *Web Site:* www.palphot.com, pg 1292

Joergen Paludans Forlag ApS (Denmark) *Tel:* 49751556 *Fax:* 49751537, pg 134

G B Palumbo & C Editore SpA (Italy) *Tel:* (091) 588850 *Fax:* (091) 6111848, pg 402

Pamatnik narodniho pisemnictvi (Czech Republic) *Tel:* (02) 20516695 *Fax:* (02) 20517277, pg 1460

Pan African Institute for Development (PAID) (Cameroon) *Tel:* 421061; 424335; 428030; 433316 *Fax:* 424335 *E-mail:* ipd.sg@cmnet.cm, pg 1239

Pan Korea Book Corporation (Republic of Korea) *Tel:* (02) 7332011; (02) 7332018 *Fax:* (02) 7368696, pg 439

Pan Macmillan (United Kingdom) *Tel:* (020) 7881 8000 *Fax:* (020) 7881 8001 *Web Site:* www.panmacmillan.com, pg 723

Pan Macmillan Australia Pty Ltd (Australia) *Tel:* (02) 9285 9100 *Fax:* (02) 9285 9100 *E-mail:* pansyd@macmillan.com.au (General); panpublicity@macmillan.com.au (Publicity) *Web Site:* www.panmacmillan.com.au, pg 36

Pan Malayan Publishing Co Sdn Bhd (Malaysia) *Tel:* (603) 92218377 *Fax:* (603) 92214333, pg 453

Pan Pacific Publications (Australia) *Tel:* (07) 38480350 *Fax:* (07) 38484945, pg 37

Pan Pacific Publications (S) Pte Ltd (Singapore) *Tel:* 2616288 *Fax:* 2616088 *E-mail:* ppps@pacific.net.sg, pg 547

PANTHER PUBLISHING

Pan Yayincilik (Turkey) *Tel:* (0212) 2618072 *Fax:* (212) 2275674 *E-mail:* pankitap@superonline.com, pg 640

Editorial Panamericana (Colombia) *Tel:* (01) 277 46 13; (01) 360 30 77 *Fax:* (01) 2774991 *Web Site:* www.panamericanaeditorial.com, pg 113

Instituto Panamericano de Geografia e Historia (Mexico) *Tel:* (05) 2775888; (05) 5151910 *Fax:* (05) 2716172 *E-mail:* ipgh@laneta.apc.org, pg 465

Libreria Commissionaria Internazionale di Raffaele Pancaldi (Italy) *Tel:* (051) 229466 *Fax:* (051) 229466, pg 1293

Panchasheel Prakashan (India) *Tel:* (0141) 65072, pg 345

Pandani Press (Australia) *Tel:* (03) 62349925 *E-mail:* pandani@iprimus.com.au, pg 37

Pandion-Verlag, Ulrike Schmoll (Germany) *Tel:* (06761) 7142 *Fax:* (06761) 77172 *E-mail:* pandion@t-online.de; info@pandion-verlag.de *Web Site:* www.pandion-verlag.de, pg 271

Pandora (Belgium) *Tel:* (03) 475730978 *Fax:* (03) 32333399, pg 72

Pandora Publishing House (Romania) *Tel:* (021) 243 3739 *Fax:* (021) 243 3739, pg 535

Panem (Hungary) *Tel:* (01) 120-8303 *Fax:* (01) 344-3923 *E-mail:* panem@mail.datanet.hu, pg 326

Panepistimio Ioanninon (Greece) *Tel:* (06510) 97105-7 *Fax:* (06510) 97024 *E-mail:* intlrel@uoi.gr *Web Site:* www.uoi.gr, pg 314

Pangea Editores, Sa de CV (Mexico) *Tel:* (05) 6813035; (05) 6813160 *E-mail:* pangea@data.net.mx, pg 465

Franco Cosimo Panini Editore SpA (Italy) *Tel:* (059) 343572 *Fax:* (059) 344274 *E-mail:* info@fcp.it *Web Site:* www.fcp.it; www.francopanini.com, pg 402

Franco Panini SPA Editore in Bologna (Italy) *Tel:* (059) 343572 *Fax:* (059)344274, pg 402

Edizioni Panini SpA (Italy) *Tel:* (059) 343572 *Fax:* (059) 344274, pg 402

Panjab University Publication Bureau (India) *Tel:* (0172) 541782; (0172) 534373, pg 345

Pankaj Publications (India) *Tel:* (011) 3363395; (011) 3348805 *Fax:* (011) 5448265; (01) 3348805 *E-mail:* book@vsnl.in, pg 345

Panmun Book Co Ltd (Republic of Korea) *Tel:* (02) 7338688; (02) 7338501; (02) 720-2859 *Fax:* (02) 7205756; (02) 953-2456, pg 439

Panmun Book Co Ltd (Republic of Korea) *Tel:* (02) 720-2859; (02) 733-5300; (02) 924-0733 *Fax:* (02) 735-0376; (02) 953-2456, pg 1297

Editions du Panorama (Switzerland) *Tel:* (032) 3581665 *Fax:* (032) 3581665, pg 621

Panorama Editorial, SA (Mexico) *Tel:* (05) 5355135; (05) 5359074; (05) 5350377 *Fax:* (05) 5359202; (05) 5351217, pg 465

Nakladatelstvi a vydavatelstvi Panorama (Czech Republic) *Tel:* (02) 24222509; (02) 24222762; (02) 2422392630 *Fax:* (02) 22422474, pg 127

Panorama NIJP/ID Grigorije Bozovic (Yugoslavia) *Tel:* (038) 24-619; (038) 24-618 *Fax:* (038) 29637, pg 765

Panorama Publishing House (Russian Federation) *Tel:* (095) 2053707 *Fax:* (095) 2053708, pg 541

Panos Institute (United Kingdom) *Tel:* (020) 7278 1111 *Fax:* (020) 7278 0345 *E-mail:* panos@panoslondon.org.uk *Web Site:* www.panos.org.uk, pg 723

Panstwowy Instytut Wydawniczy (PIW) (Poland) *Tel:* (022) 8260201; (022) 8260202; (022) 8260203; (022) 8260204; (022) 8260205 *Fax:* (022) 8261536 *E-mail:* piw@piw.pl *Web Site:* www.piw.pl, pg 518

J M Pantelides Booksellers Ltd (Greece) *Tel:* (01) 3645608 *Fax:* (01) 3636453, pg 1287

Panther Publishing (Malaysia) *Tel:* (03) 2749854, pg 453

1679

Panton (Czech Republic) *Tel:* (02) 515 539 52; (02) 515 545 11 *Fax:* (02) 515 559 94 *E-mail:* panton@panton.cz *Web Site:* www.panton.cz, pg 127

D Papadimas (Greece) *Tel:* (01) 3627318; (01) 3642692 *Fax:* (01) 3610271, pg 314

Kyr I Papadopoulos E E (Greece) *Tel:* (01) 2816234; (01) 2846074; (01) 2846075 *Fax:* (01) 2817127, pg 314

Papazissis Publishers SA (Greece) *Tel:* (01) 3609150; (01) 3838020; (01) 3808173 *Fax:* (01) 3809150, pg 314

Paper Art Product Ltd (Hong Kong) *Tel:* 24812929 *Fax:* 24892255, pg 1135

Paper Art Product Ltd (Hong Kong) *Tel:* 24812929 *Fax:* 24892255 *E-mail:* paperart@netvigator.com, pg 1197

Paper Communication Printing Express Ltd (Hong Kong) *Tel:* 27864191 *Fax:* 27864498 *E-mail:* pcpe@papercom.com.hk, pg 1135

Paper Communication Printing Express Ltd (Hong Kong) *Tel:* 27864191 *Fax:* 27864498 *E-mail:* pcpc@papercom.com.hk, pg 1156

Paper Communication Printing Express Ltd (Hong Kong) *Tel:* 27864191 *Fax:* 27864498, pg 1197

Paperback Publishers Ltd (Nigeria) *Tel:* (022) 317363, pg 501

Papirus Editora (Brazil) *Tel:* (0192) 313500 *Fax:* (0192) 22578, pg 1278

Papua New Guinea Institute of Public Administration Library (PNGIPA) (Papua New Guinea) *Tel:* 3260433 *Fax:* 3261654, pg 1490

PapyRossa Verlags GmbH & Co Kommanditgesellschaft KG (Germany) *Tel:* (0221) 44 85 45 *Fax:* (0221) 44 43 05 *E-mail:* mail@papyrossa.de *Web Site:* www.papyrossa.de, pg 271

Editions du Papyrus (France) *Tel:* (01) 4 85 27 05 *Fax:* (01) 48 57 26 79 *E-mail:* papyrus@netfly.fr *Web Site:* www.editions-papyrus.com, pg 179

Papyrus Publishing (Australia) *Tel:* (03) 9758 9395 *Fax:* (03) 9752 4032 *Web Site:* www.papyrus.com, pg 37

Parabel Place (Australia) *Tel:* (03) 97271894 *Fax:* (03) 97271857, pg 37

Edition Parabolis (Germany) *Tel:* (030) 44 65 10 65 *Fax:* (030) 444 10 85 *E-mail:* info@emz-berlin.de *Web Site:* www.emz-berlin.de, pg 271

Editions Paradigme (France) *Tel:* (02) 38 70 84 44 *Fax:* (02) 38 70 56 76 *E-mail:* fab45.paradigme@wanadoo.fr *Web Site:* paradigme.com, pg 179

Paradox Pers vzw (Belgium) *Tel:* (03) 2322313 *Fax:* (03) 2322313 *E-mail:* paradox@glo.be; paradoxpers@belgacom.be, pg 72

Paragon Prepress Inc (India) *Tel:* (011) 622 44 51 *Fax:* (011) 643 73 43 *Web Site:* www.paragonprepress.com, pg 1157

Ediciones Paraiso, SL (Spain) *Tel:* (985) 203 789 *E-mail:* paraiso@seteas.com, pg 586

Paramount Books (Pvt) Ltd (Pakistan) *Tel:* (021) 4550661; (021) 4551630, pg 1305

Paramount Commercial Press Ltd (Hong Kong) *Tel:* 28958688 *Fax:* 28978942, pg 1135

Paramount Publishing Group Limited (Hong Kong) *Tel:* 28968688 *Fax:* 28978942 *E-mail:* paramountprin@navigator.com *Web Site:* www.paramount.com.hk, pg 1135, 1197

Paramount Sales (India) Pvt Ltd (India) *Tel:* (011) 5723235; (011) 5754442 *Fax:* (011) 5746485, pg 345

Editorial Paraninfo SA (Spain) *Tel:* (091) 4463350 *Fax:* (091) 4456218; (091) 14478892 *Web Site:* www.paraninfo.es, pg 586

Parantez Yayinlari Ltd (Turkey) *Tel:* (0212) 5168280 *Fax:* (0212) 5168280 *E-mail:* parantezyay@superonline.com.tr, pg 640

Paranus Verlag - Bruecke Neumuenster GmbH (Germany) *Tel:* (04321) 2004-500 *Fax:* (04321) 2004-411 *E-mail:* verlag@paranus.de *Web Site:* www.paranus.de, pg 271

Parapress Ltd (United Kingdom) *Tel:* (01892) 512118 *Fax:* (01892) 512118 *E-mail:* office@parapress.co.uk *Web Site:* www.parapress.co.uk, pg 724

PARAS (United Kingdom) *Tel:* (020) 8342 9600 *Fax:* (020) 8342 9600, pg 724

Parasol NV (Belgium) *Tel:* (03) 460 1880 *Fax:* (03) 460 1881 *E-mail:* info@parasol.be, pg 72

Paravia Bruno Mondadori Editori (Italy) *Tel:* (02) 748231 *Fax:* (02) 74823362 *Web Site:* paravia.it; paramond.it; langedizoni.it; edizioniscolastichebrunomondadori.it, pg 402

G B Paravia & C SpA (Italy) *Tel:* (011) 7710166 *Fax:* (011) 752812, pg 402

Pardes (France) *Tel:* (02) 38 33 53 28 *Fax:* (02) 38 33 58 99 *Web Site:* perso.wanadoo.fr/mackadam/livre/Editeurs/pardes.htm, pg 179

Libreria General de Tomas Pardo SRL (Argentina) *Tel:* (011) 4322-0496 *Fax:* (011) 4393-6759, pg 1271

Editions Parentheses (France) *Tel:* (0496) 08 18 20 *Fax:* (0495) 08 18 24, pg 179

Parfitts Book Services (United Kingdom) *Tel:* (01985) 216371 *Fax:* (01985) 212982 *E-mail:* parfitts@cix.compulink.co.uk, pg 1321

Parimal Prakashan (India) *Tel:* (0240) 323887, pg 345

Paris Musees (France) *Tel:* (01) 44 58 99 41 *Fax:* (01) 47 03 36 44, pg 179

Park Konyvkiado Kft (Park Publisher) (Hungary) *Tel:* (01) 1315767 *Fax:* (01) 2124363 *E-mail:* park@mail.matav.hu, pg 326

Parkett Publishers Inc (Switzerland) *Tel:* (01) 2718140 *Fax:* (01) 2724301 *E-mail:* parkettmag@aol.com, pg 621

Parlamentni Knihovna (Czech Republic) *Tel:* (02) 57534409 *Fax:* (02) 57534408 *Web Site:* www.psp.ez/kps/knih/, pg 1460

Bibliotheque du Parlement (Belgium) *Tel:* (02) 5499200 *Fax:* (02) 5499497, pg 1453

Library of Parliament (Zimbabwe) *Tel:* (04) 700181 ext 2131; (04) 700181 ext 132 *Fax:* (04) 795548, pg 1509

Parliamentary Library (New Zealand) *Tel:* (04) 4719623 *Fax:* (04) 4711250 *E-mail:* moira.fraser@parliament.govt.nz, pg 1487

Editions Parole et Silence (Switzerland) *Tel:* (024) 6982301 *Fax:* (024) 6982311, pg 621

Parramon Ediciones SA (Spain) *Tel:* (093) 289 27 20 *Fax:* (093) 426 37 30 *E-mail:* sales@parramon.es, pg 586

Editorial Libreria Parroquial de Claveria SA de CV (Mexico) *Tel:* (05) 3967027; (05) 3967718 *Fax:* (05) 3967718, pg 465

Parry's Book Center Sdn Bhd (Malaysia) *Tel:* (03) 4079179; (03) 4087235; (03) 4079176 *Fax:* (03) 4079180, pg 1298

Parry's Press (Malaysia) *Tel:* (03) 4079179 *Fax:* (03) 4079180 *E-mail:* haja@pop.3.jaring.my, pg 453

Parsifal BVBA (Belgium) *Tel:* (050) 339516 *Fax:* (050) 333386 *E-mail:* info@parsifal.be *Web Site:* www.parsifal.be, pg 72

La Part de L'Oeil (Belgium) *Tel:* (02) 514 18 41 *Fax:* (02) 514 18 41 *E-mail:* lapartdeloeil@brunette.brucity.be *Web Site:* aca-bxl.be/intro/index.htm, pg 72

Ediciones Partenon (Spain) *Tel:* (091) 5634450 *Fax:* (091) 5628405, pg 586

Partenon MAM Sistem (Yugoslavia) *Tel:* (011) 632535; (011) 625942; (011) 633465 *Fax:* (011) 632535; (011) 623980 *E-mail:* partenon@infosky.net, pg 765

Editorial Parthenon Communication, SL (Spain) *Tel:* (093) 7952008 *Fax:* (093) 7952008, pg 586

The Parthenon Publishing Group Ltd (United Kingdom) *Tel:* (01524) 585700 *Fax:* (01524) 66882 *E-mail:* mail@parthpub.com *Web Site:* www.parthpub.com, pg 724

Parthian Books (United Kingdom) *Tel:* (2920) 341314 *Fax:* (2920) 341314 *E-mail:* parthianbooks@yahoo.co.uk *Web Site:* www.parthianbooks.co.uk, pg 724

Partners Training & Innovatie (Netherlands) *Tel:* (010) 4071563 *E-mail:* partners@ced.nl, pg 482

Editions du Parvis (Switzerland) *Tel:* (026) 915 93 93 *Fax:* (026) 915 93 99 *E-mail:* book@parvis.ch *Web Site:* www.parvis.ch, pg 621

Verlag Parzeller GmbH & Co KG (Germany) *Tel:* (0661) 280-663 *Fax:* (0661) 280-285 *E-mail:* verlag@parzeller.de *Web Site:* www.buchkatalog.de/parzeller, pg 271

Pascal Press (Australia) *Tel:* (02) 8585 4044 *Fax:* (02) 8585 4001 *Web Site:* www.askblake.com.au, pg 37

Pascoe Publishing (Australia) *Tel:* (052) 379227 *Fax:* (052) 376559 *Web Site:* www.bruce-pascoe.pho-online.net, pg 37

Paseka (Czech Republic) *Tel:* (02) 22710752; (02) 22718887 *Fax:* (02) 22718886 *E-mail:* paseka@mbox.vol.cz *Web Site:* www.paseka.cz, pg 127

Passage, Uitgeverij (Netherlands) *Tel:* (050) 5271332 *E-mail:* passuit@xs4all.nl *Web Site:* www.uitgeverijpassage.nl, pg 482

Passagen Verlag GmbH (Austria) *Tel:* (01) 513 77 61 *Fax:* (01) 512 63 27 *E-mail:* office@passagen.at *Web Site:* www.passagen.at, pg 57

Passavia Druckerei GmbH, Verlag (Germany) *Tel:* (0851) 802670 *Fax:* (0851) 802680 *Web Site:* www.passavia.de, pg 271

Passavia Universitaetsverlag und -Druck GmbH (Germany) *Tel:* (0851) 700226 *Fax:* (0851) 700277, pg 272

Passigli Editori srl (Italy) *Tel:* (055) 640265 *Fax:* (055) 644627, pg 403

Libreria Passim SA (Spain) *Tel:* (093) 4574757 *Fax:* (093) 4574757 *E-mail:* passim@intercom.es, pg 1311

Password Publishers Ltd (Israel) *Tel:* (03) 6833566 *Fax:* (03) 6833702 *E-mail:* pass@password.co.il *Web Site:* password.co.il, pg 371

PasTest (United Kingdom) *Tel:* (01565) 752000 *Fax:* (01565) 650264 *E-mail:* enquiries@pastest.co.uk *Web Site:* www.pastest.co.uk, pg 724

Centre de Pastoral Liturgica (Spain) *Tel:* (093) 3022235 *Fax:* (093) 3184218 *Web Site:* www.cpl.es/, pg 586

Patakis Publishers (Greece) *Tel:* (01) 36 500 00 *Fax:* (01) 36 500 69 *E-mail:* info@patakis.gr *Web Site:* www.patakis.gr, pg 314

PATCO (Indonesia) *Tel:* (031) 310021, pg 356

Patent Documentation Publishing House (China) *Tel:* (010) 2013103; (010) 2026893 *Fax:* (010) 2019307, pg 107

Paternoster Publishing (United Kingdom) *Tel:* (01228) 512512 *Fax:* (01228) 514949 *E-mail:* orderline@stl.org *Web Site:* www.paternoster-publishing.com, pg 724

Paternoster Publishing (United Kingdom) *Tel:* (01228) 512512 *Fax:* (01228) 514949 *E-mail:* info@Paternoster-Publishing.com *Web Site:* www.paternoster-publishing.com, pg 1141

Mark Paterson & Associates, Authors & Publishers Literary Agents (United Kingdom) *Tel:* (01206) 825433 *Fax:* (01206) 822990 *E-mail:* info@markpaterson.co.uk, pg 1121

Pathfinder Bookshop (New Zealand) *Tel:* (09) 3790147 *Fax:* (09) 3098167, pg 1302

Pathfinder London (United Kingdom) *Tel:* (020) 7261 1354 *Fax:* (020) 7261 1354 *E-mail:* pathfinderlondon@compuserve.com *Web Site:* www.pathfinderpress.com, pg 724

Editions Patino (Switzerland) *Tel:* (022) 3470211 *Fax:* (022) 7891829, pg 621

Patio, Galerie und Druckwerkstatt (Germany) *Tel:* (06150) 84566, pg 272

Patio-Livraria Inglesa (Portugal) *Tel:* (0291) 224490 *Fax:* (0291) 232077 *E-mail:* patiolivros@mail.pt, pg 1308

Patmos (Latvia) *Tel:* (02) 7289674 *Fax:* (02) 7820437 *E-mail:* bauc@mail.bkc.lv, pg 442

Patmos Verlag GmbH & Co KG (Germany) *Tel:* (0211) 16795-0 *Fax:* (0211) 16795-75 *E-mail:* service@patmos.de *Web Site:* www.patmos.de, pg 272

Editorial Patria SA de CV (Mexico) *Tel:* (05) 6704712; (05) 6704887 *Fax:* (05) 5613218; (05) 5614063, pg 465

Editora Patria Grande (Argentina) *Tel:* (011) 4631-6446, pg 8

Libreria Patria (Mexico) *Tel:* (05) 5613446, pg 1299

Libreria Patria SA (Mexico) *Tel:* (05) 6704712; (05) 6704887 *Fax:* (05) 5109417, pg 465

Patrimonio Nacional, Real Biblioteca (Spain) *Tel:* (091) 4548733; (091) 4548732; (091) 4548732 *Fax:* (091) 4548867, pg 1499

Izdatel'stvo Patriot (Russian Federation) *Tel:* (095) 2844904, pg 541

Editorial Patris SA (Chile) *Tel:* (02) 2351343 *Fax:* (02) 2351343 *E-mail:* edit.patris@entelchile.net *Web Site:* www.patris.cl, pg 101

Libreria Internazionale Patron (Italy) *Tel:* (051) 767003 *Fax:* (051) 768252, pg 1293

Patron Editore SrL (Italy) *Tel:* (051) 767003 *Fax:* (051) 768252, pg 403

Pattloch Verlag GmbH & Co KG (Germany) *Tel:* (089) 9271-0 *Fax:* (089) 9271-168 *Web Site:* www.droemer-weltbild.de, pg 272

Paul Ntem Maanoh (Ghana) *Tel:* (021) 508251 *Fax:* (021) 669078, pg 307

Ediciones Paulinas (Libreria San Pablo) (Colombia) *Tel:* (01) 2444516 *Fax:* (01) 2684288, pg 1280

Paulinas (Portugal) *Tel:* (021) 8484355 *Fax:* (021) 8474151, pg 528

Paulinas Editorial (Brazil) *Tel:* (011) 50855199 *Fax:* (011) 50855198 *E-mail:* editora@paulinas.org.br, pg 89

Paulines Publications-Africa (Kenya) *Tel:* (02) 447202; (02) 447203 *Fax:* (02) 442319 *E-mail:* paulines@iconnect.co.uk, pg 433

Paulinus Verlag GmbH (Germany) *Tel:* (0651) 4608-100 *Fax:* (0651) 4608-221 *E-mail:* verlag@paulinus.de *Web Site:* www.paulinus.de, pg 272

Paulus Editora (Brazil) *Tel:* (011) 50843066; (011) 5757362 *Fax:* (011) 5703627 *E-mail:* dir.editorial@paulus.org.br *Web Site:* www.paulus.org.br, pg 89

Pavilion Books Ltd (United Kingdom) *Tel:* (020) 7350 1230 *Fax:* (020) 7350 1260; (020) 7801 0315 *E-mail:* info@pavilionbooks.co.uk *Web Site:* www.pavilionbooks.co.uk, pg 724

Pavilion Publishing (Brighton) Ltd (United Kingdom) *Tel:* (01273) 623222 *Fax:* (01273) 625526 *E-mail:* info@pavpub.com *Web Site:* www.pavpub.com, pg 725

Pawel Panpresse (Germany) *Tel:* (06041) 5822, pg 272

John Pawsey (United Kingdom) *Tel:* (01903) 205167 *Fax:* (01903) 205167, pg 1121

Pax Forlag A/S (Norway) *Tel:* (023) 136900 *Fax:* (023) 136919, pg 504

Editorial Pax Mexico (Mexico) *Tel:* (05) 605 7677 *Fax:* (05) 605 7600 *E-mail:* editorialpax@editorialpax.com *Web Site:* www.editorialpax.com, pg 465

Payel Yayinevi (Turkey) *Tel:* (0212) 5284409; (0212) 5118233 *Fax:* (0212) 5124353, pg 641

Editions Payot & Rivages (France) *Tel:* (01) 44 41 39 90 *Fax:* (01) 44 41 39 69 *E-mail:* payotrivages@wanadoo.fr, pg 179

Editions Payot Lausanne (Switzerland) *Tel:* (021) 3290264 *Fax:* (021) 3290266 *E-mail:* ed.payot.nadir@bluewin.ch, pg 621

Editora Paz e Terra (Brazil) *Tel:* (011) 3337-8399 *Fax:* (011) 223-6290 *E-mail:* vendas@pazeterra.com.br *Web Site:* www.pazeterra.com.br, pg 89

Paz-Editora de Multimedia, LDA (Portugal) *Tel:* (021) 8101282 *Fax:* (021) 8101287 *E-mail:* paz@esoterica.pt *Web Site:* www.paseditora.pt, pg 528

PC Publishing (United Kingdom) *Tel:* (01732) 770893 *Fax:* (01732) 770268 *E-mail:* info@pc-publishing.com *Web Site:* www.pc-publishing.co.uk, pg 725

PCE Press (Australia) *Tel:* (07) 3252 1114 *Fax:* (07) 3852 1564 *E-mail:* webmaster@pcq.org.au *Web Site:* www.pcq.org.au, pg 37

Peace Book Co Ltd (Hong Kong) *Tel:* (02) 8046687; (02) 25222130 *Fax:* (02) 8046409, pg 321

Peaceful Living Publications (New Zealand) *Tel:* (071) 5718105 *Fax:* (071) 5718513 *E-mail:* books@peaceful-living.co.nz, pg 1302

Peak Technologies UK Ltd (United Kingdom) *Tel:* (0) 1344-290000 *Fax:* (0) 1344 290001 *E-mail:* nreed@peakeurope.com *Web Site:* www.peakeurope.com, pg 1204

Peak Translations (United Kingdom) *Tel:* (01663) 732074 *Fax:* (01663) 735499 *E-mail:* info@peak-translations.co.uk *Web Site:* www.peak-translations.co.uk, pg 1129

Peake Associates Tony Peake (United Kingdom) *Tel:* (020) 7267 8033 *Fax:* (020) 7284 1876, pg 1121

Pearl River Printing Co Ltd (Hong Kong) *Tel:* 28732909 *Fax:* 28730784; 25597042, pg 1135

Maggie Pearlstine Associates Limited (United Kingdom) *Tel:* (020) 7828-4212 *Fax:* (020) 7834-5546 *E-mail:* post@pearlstine.co.uk, pg 1121

Pearson Educacion de Argentina (Argentina) *Tel:* 011 4 309 6100 *Fax:* 011 4 309 6199 *E-mail:* firstnamelastinitial@pearsoned.com.ar, pg 8

Pearson Educacion de Colombia LTDA (Colombia) *Tel:* (01) 405 9300 *Fax:* (01) 405 9330 *E-mail:* firstname.lastname@pearsoned.com *Web Site:* www.pearsoned.com.mx, pg 113

Pearson Educacion de Mexico, SA de CV (Mexico) *Tel:* (05) 387-0700 *Fax:* (05) 358-6445 *E-mail:* firstname.lastname@pearsoned.com *Web Site:* www.pearson.com.mx, pg 465

Pearson Educacion S A (Spain) *Tel:* (091) 5903432 *Fax:* (091) 5903448 *E-mail:* firstname.lastname@pearsoned-ema.com, pg 586

Pearson Education (Malaysia) *Tel:* (03) 7782 0466 *Fax:* (03) 7781 8005 *E-mail:* name@pearsoned.com.my, pg 453

Pearson Education (Malaysia) *Tel:* (03) 7920466 *Fax:* (030) 7918005, pg 1298

Pearson Education (New Zealand) *Tel:* (09) 444 4968 *Fax:* (09) 444 4957 *E-mail:* firstname.lastname@pearsoned.co.nz, pg 494

Pearson Education (Switzerland) *Tel:* 747 4747 *Fax:* 747 4777 *E-mail:* firstname.lastname@pearson.ch *Web Site:* www.pearson.ch, pg 621

Pearson Education (Taiwan, Province of China) *Tel:* (02) 2736 5155 *Fax:* (02) 2738 1970 *E-mail:* firstname@pearsoned.com.tw, pg 631

Pearson Education (United Kingdom) *Tel:* (020) 7447 2000 *Fax:* (020) 7240 5771 *E-mail:* firstname.lastname@pearsoned-ema.com, pg 725

Pearson Education Asia (Philippines) *Tel:* (02) 434 5501 *Fax:* (02) 433 9757 *E-mail:* custserv@pearsoned.com.ph *Web Site:* www.pearsoned.com, pg 514

Pearson Education Asia (Singapore) *Tel:* 476 4688 *Fax:* 268 0370 *E-mail:* firstname.lastname@pearsoned.com.sg *Web Site:* www.pearsoned.com, pg 547

Pearson Education Asia Pte Ltd (Singapore) *Tel:* 0268 2666 *Fax:* 0264 1740 *E-mail:* firstname.lastname@pearsoned.com.sg, pg 547

Pearson Education Australia (Australia) *Tel:* (02) 9454 2200 *Fax:* (02) 9453 0089 *E-mail:* firstname.lastname@pearsoned.com.au *Web Site:* www.pearson.com.au, pg 37

Pearson Education China Ltd (Hong Kong) *Tel:* 3181 0000 *Fax:* 2565 7440 *E-mail:* firstnamelastinitial@pearsoned.com.hk, pg 321

Pearson Education Deutschland GmbH (Germany) *Tel:* (089) 46003-0 *Fax:* (089) 46003-120 *E-mail:* firstinitiallastname@pearson.de, pg 272

Pearson Education Do Brasil (Brazil) *Tel:* (011) 3611 0740 *Fax:* (011) 3611 0444 *E-mail:* firstname.lastname@pearsoned.com.br, pg 89

Pearson Education Europe, Mideast & Africa (United Kingdom) *Tel:* (01279) 62 3623 *Fax:* (01279) 43 1059 *E-mail:* firstname.lastname@pearsoned-ema.com *Web Site:* www.pearsoned-ema.com, pg 725

Pearson Education France (France) *Tel:* (01) 4454 5110 *Fax:* (01) 4804 5361 (sales); (01) 4887 7130 (finance) *E-mail:* firstname.lastname@pearson.fr *Web Site:* www.pearsoned.fr, pg 179

Pearson Education Hellas SA (Greece) *Tel:* (01) 937 3170 *Fax:* (01) 937 3194 *Web Site:* www.pearsoneduc.com, pg 314

Pearson Education Indochina, Ltd (Thailand) *Tel:* (02) 722 7301 *Fax:* (02) 722 7307 *E-mail:* firstname@pearsoned.th.com, pg 635

Pearson Education Japan (Japan) *Tel:* (03) 3365 9001 *Fax:* (03) 3365 9009 *E-mail:* firstname.lastname@pearsoned.co.jp *Web Site:* pearsoned.co.jp, pg 423

Pearson Education Korea Ltd (Republic of Korea) *Tel:* (02) 332 0841 *Fax:* (02) 332 0843 *E-mail:* firstname.lastname@pearsoned.co.kr, pg 439

Pearson Education Netherlands (Netherlands) *Tel:* (020) 575-5800 *Fax:* (020) 664-5334 *E-mail:* firstname.lastname@mail.aw.nl, pg 482

Pearson Education Polska Sp z oo (Poland) *Tel:* (022) 533 1533 *Fax:* (022) 533 1534 *E-mail:* firstname.lastname@longman.com.pl, pg 518

Pearson Education (Prentice Hall) (South Africa) *Tel:* (021) 686 6356 *Fax:* (021) 686 4590 *E-mail:* firstname@mml.co.za, pg 558

Pearson Education Turkey (Turkey) *Tel:* (0212) 288 6941 *Fax:* (0212) 267 1851 *E-mail:* firstname.lastname@pearsoned-ema.com, pg 641

Peartree Publications (United Kingdom) *Tel:* 01424 844274, pg 725

Pedagogika Press (Russian Federation) *Tel:* (095) 2465969 *Fax:* (095) 2465969, pg 541

Editions Pedone (France) *Tel:* (01) 43 54 05 97 *Fax:* (01) 46 34 07 60 *E-mail:* editions-pedone@wanadoo.fr *Web Site:* www.franceedition.org/Pedone, pg 179

Pedrazzini Tipografia (Switzerland) *Tel:* (093) 317735; (093) 317734 *Fax:* (093) 315118, pg 621

Universidad Nacional Pedro Henriquez Urena (Dominican Republic) Tel: (0809) 542-6888 (ext 2301-2315) Fax: (0809) 566-2206; (0809) 540-3803 E-mail: biblioteca@unphu.edu.do Web Site: www.unphu.edu.do/biblioteca.html, pg 1461

Peepal Tree Press (United Kingdom) Tel: (0113) 2451703 Fax: (0113) 2468368, pg 725

Peeters-France (France) Tel: (016) 244000 Fax: (016) 228500 Web Site: www.peeters-leuven.be, pg 179

Uitgeverij Peeters Leuven (Belgie) (Belgium) Tel: (016) 23 51 70 Fax: (016) 22 85 00 E-mail: peeters@peeters-leuven.be Web Site: www.peeters-leuven.be, pg 72

Editoriale PEG (Italy) Tel: (02) 4859181 Fax: (02) 485918220, pg 403

Pegasus Publishers & Booksellers (Netherlands) Tel: (020) 6231138 Fax: (020) 6203478 E-mail: pegasus@pegasusboek.nl Web Site: www.pegasusboek.nl, pg 1301

Pehuen Editores Ltda (Chile) Tel: (02) 204 93 99 Fax: (02) 204 93 99 E-mail: pehuen@cmet.net, pg 101

Ediciones Peisa (Promocion Editorial Inca SA) (Peru) Tel: (01) 4404603; (01) 4410473 Fax: (01) 4425906 E-mail: peisa@terro.com.pe, pg 511

Peking University Library (China) Tel: (010) 62751051 Fax: (010) 62761008 E-mail: office@lib.pku.edu.cn, pg 1457

Pelanduk Publications (M) Sdn Bhd (Malaysia) Tel: (03) 7761414; (03) 7761613 E-mail: pelpub@tm.net.my Web Site: www.pelanduk.com, pg 453

Pelckmans NV, De Nederlandsche Boekhandel (Belgium) Tel: (03) 664-53-20 Fax: (03) 664-70-80, pg 73

Uitgeverij Pelckmans N V (Belgium) Tel: (03) 660 27 00 Fax: (03) 660 27 00 E-mail: uitgeverij@pelckmans.be Web Site: www.pelckmans.be, pg 73

Pelikan Vertriebsgesellschaft mbH & Co KG (Germany) Tel: (0511) 6969-0 Fax: (0511) 6969-212 Web Site: www.pelikan.de, pg 272

Pelita Masa PT (Indonesia) Tel: (022) 50823, pg 356

Luigi Pellegrini Editore (Italy) Tel: (0984) 454237 Fax: (0984) 454392, pg 403

Pembimbing Masa PT (Indonesia) Tel: (021) 367645; (021) 366042, pg 356

Pembimbing Masa PT (Indonesia) Tel: (021) 367645, pg 1291

International PEN (Melbourne Centre) (Australia) Tel: (03) 95097257 Fax: (03) 95097257, pg 1359

International PEN Sydney Centre (Australia) Tel: (02) 95559931 Fax: (02) 96928836, pg 1359

China PEN Centre (China) Fax: 8610 64221704, pg 1361

Czech PEN Centre (Czech Republic) Tel: (02) 24235546 Fax: (02) 24221926 E-mail: centrum@pen.cz Web Site: www.pen.cz, pg 1361

Finnish PEN Center (Finland) Tel: (09) 1996448 Fax: (09) 1996540, pg 1362

PEN Zentrum Bundesrepublik Deutschland (Germany) Tel: (06151) 23120 Fax: (06151) 293414, pg 1364

Hong Kong English PEN Centre (Hong Kong) Tel: 25774168 Fax: 25774168, pg 1364

International PEN Centre (Iceland), pg 1364

PEN Centre (Indonesia) Tel: (093) 3905837 Fax: (093) 325890, pg 1364

Irish PEN (Ireland), pg 1365

Israeli PEN Centre (Israel) Tel: (03) 6964937 Fax: (03) 6964937, pg 1365

PEN International Centre (Italy), pg 1365

Macedonian PEN - Skopje (The Former Yugoslav Republic of Macedonia) Tel: (091) 130054 Fax: (091) 117668, pg 1366

Mexican PEN Centre (Mexico) Tel: (05) 574-4882 Fax: (05) 264-0813, pg 1366

Netherlands Centre of the International PEN (Netherlands) Tel: (043) 433498 Fax: (043) 433498, pg 1366

Norwegian PEN Centre (Norway) Tel: 22194551 Fax: 22194551, pg 1367

International PEN Centre, Philippine Chapter (Philippines) Tel: (02) 5230870 Fax: (02) 5255038, pg 1367

Polish PEN Club (Poland) Tel: (022) 8265784 Fax: (022) 8260589, pg 1367

Romanian PEN Centre (Romania) Tel: (01) 3111112 Fax: (01) 3125854, pg 1367

Centro Uruguayo PEN (Sweden) Fax: (08) 155320, pg 1368

Svenska Penklubben (Swedish Centre of International PEN) (Sweden) Tel: (08) 4538677 Fax: (08) 4538794, pg 1368

PEN Internazionale - Centro della Svizzera Italiana e Romancia (Switzerland) Tel: (091) 8039325 Fax: (091) 8039300, pg 1368

The Taipei Chinese PEN Centre (Taiwan, Province of China) Tel: (02) 23693609 Fax: (02) 23699948, pg 1368

Thailand PEN Centre (Thailand) Tel: (02) 6685147; (02) 2792621, pg 1369

PEN Yazarlar Dernegi (Turkey) Tel: (0212) 2920026 Fax: (0212) 2526314; (0212) 2920026, pg 1369

Centro Venezolano del PEN Internacional (Venezuela) Tel: (02) 5616691; (02) 5617589; (02) 5617287 Fax: (02) 5718064, pg 1372

Serbian PEN Centre (Yugoslavia) Tel: (011) 626081 Fax: (011) 635979, pg 1372

The PEN All-India Centre (India) Tel: (022) 2032175 E-mail: ambika.sirkar@gems.vsnl.net.in, pg 1364

Pen & Sword Books Ltd (United Kingdom) Tel: (01226) 734222 Fax: (01226) 734438 E-mail: ps-it@pen-and-sword.co.uk Web Site: www.pen-and-sword.co.uk, pg 725

PEN Club Argentino-Centro Internacional de la Asociacion PEN (Argentina), pg 1359

Oesterreichischer PEN-Club (Austria) Tel: (01) 5334459 Fax: (01) 5328749, pg 1360

International PEN Club, Belgian French-Speaking Centre (Belgium) Tel: (02) 7314847 Fax: (02) 7314847, pg 1360

PEN Club-Belgian (Belgium) Tel: (052) 351118 Fax: (052) 351119, pg 1360

PEN Club de Bolivia (Centro Internacional de Escritores) (Bolivia), pg 1361

PEN Club de Suisse romande (France) Tel: (022) 50-43-69-35, pg 1363

PEN Club Francais (France) Tel: (01) 42773787 Fax: (01) 42786487, pg 1363

PEN Club del Paraguay (Paraguay), pg 1367

PEN Club du Senegal (Senegal) Tel: 210471; 258009 Fax: 211632, pg 1367

Swiss-German PEN Club Centre (Switzerland) Tel: (031) 3724085 Fax: (031) 3723032, pg 1368

PEN Club-German Speaking Writers Abroad (United Kingdom) Tel: (020) 8946 0178, pg 1267

PEN Club Liechtenstein (Liechtenstein) Tel: (0423) 2327271 Fax: (0423) 2328071 E-mail: pen@schlapp.li, pg 1366

Magyar PEN Club (Hungary) Tel: (01) 3184143 Fax: (01) 1171722, pg 1364

PEN Club-Panamanian (Panama) Tel: 263-8822 Fax: 263-9918, pg 1367

PEN Club-Russian (Russian Federation) Tel: (095) 2094589; (095) 2093171 Fax: (095) 2000293 E-mail: 7416.g23@g23.relcom.ru, pg 1367

PEN Club-Writers in Exile London Branch (United Kingdom) Tel: (020) 8340 5279, pg 1267

PEN Clube do Brasil (Associacao Universal de Escritores) (Brazil), pg 1361

PEN Clube Portugues (Portugal) Tel: (021) 7573452 Fax: (021) 7573452 E-mail: penclube@mail.telepac.pt, pg 1367

English Centre of International PEN (United Kingdom) Tel: (020) 7267 9444 Fax: (020) 7267 9304 E-mail: enquiries@pen.org.uk Web Site: www.pen.org.uk, pg 1371

PEN Internacional de Colombia (Colombia) Tel: (01) 2846761; (01) 2561540 Fax: (01) 2184236, pg 1361

PEN Scottish Centre (United Kingdom) Tel: (01436) 672010, pg 1371

Pendo Verlag GmbH (Switzerland) Tel: (01) 3897030 Fax: (01) 3897035 E-mail: pendo-verlag@pendo.ch, pg 621

Pendragon Verlag (Germany) Tel: (0521) 69689 Fax: (0521) 174470 E-mail: pendragon.verlag@t-online.de Web Site: www.pendragon.de, pg 272

Penerbit Erlangga (Indonesia) Tel: (021) 8717006 Fax: (021) 8708660 E-mail: eriprom@rad.net.id Web Site: www.erlangga.com, pg 356

Penerbit Fajar Bakti Sdn Bhd (Malaysia) Tel: (03) 7047011 Fax: (03) 7047010, pg 454

Penerbit Jayatinta Sdn Bhd (Malaysia) Tel: (03) 7764036, pg 454

Penerbit Nusa Indah (Indonesia) Tel: (0381) 21502 Fax: (0381) 21645; (0381) 22373, pg 356

Penerbit Prisma Sdn Bhd (Malaysia) Tel: (03) 7034393 Fax: (03) 7039367, pg 454

Penerbit Universiti Sains Malaysia (Malaysia) Tel: (04) 6577888 Fax: (04) 6571526 E-mail: penerbitusm@notes.usm.my or rashidah@usm.my Web Site: www.lib.usm.my:8080/katalog2000.nsf/tajukl, pg 454

Penerbitan Jaya Bakti (Malaysia) Tel: (03) 6219399 Fax: (03) 6219585, pg 454

Penerbitan Pelangi Sdn Bhd (Pelangi Publishing Pte Ltd) (Malaysia) Tel: (07) 3316288; (07) 3327938; (07) 3326805 Fax: (07) 3329201, pg 454

Penerbitan Tinta (Malaysia) Tel: (03) 4424163 Fax: (03) 4424640, pg 454

Penguin Books Australia Ltd (Australia) Tel: (03) 9811 2400 Fax: (03) 9811 2620 Web Site: www.penguin.com.au, pg 37

Penguin Books Ltd (United Kingdom) Tel: (020) 7416 3000 Fax: (020) 7416 3099; (020) 7416 3293 Web Site: www.penguin.com, pg 725

Penguin Books Netherlands BV (Netherlands), pg 482

Penguin Books Netherlands BV (Netherlands) Tel: (020) 6259566 Fax: (020) 6258676, pg 482

Penguin Books (NZ) Ltd (New Zealand) Tel: (09) 4444965 Fax: (09) 4441470, pg 494

The Penguin Group UK (United Kingdom) Tel: (020) 7010 3000 Web Site: www.penguin.co.uk, pg 726

Penguin Publishing Co Ltd (United Kingdom) Tel: (020) 7010 3000 Fax: (020) 7010 6060, pg 726

Ediciones Peninsula (Spain) Tel: (093) 443 71 00 Fax: (093) 443 71 30 E-mail: correu@grup62.com Web Site: www.grup62.com, pg 586

Penki Kontinentai (Lithuania) *Tel:* (02) 1481; (02) 221482 *Fax:* (02) 226115 *E-mail:* info@post.5ci.lt *Web Site:* www.5ci.lt, pg 1114

The Penman Club (United Kingdom) *Tel:* (01702) 557431, pg 1267

The Penman Literary Service-Agency Department (United Kingdom) *Tel:* (01702) 557431, pg 1121

The Pensions Management Institute (United Kingdom) *Tel:* (020) 7247 1452 *Fax:* (020) 7375 0603 *E-mail:* enquiries@pensions-pmi.org.uk *Web Site:* www.pensions-pmi.org.uk, pg 726

Pensoft Publishers (Bulgaria) *Tel:* (02) 716451 *Fax:* (02) 704508 *E-mail:* pensoft@mbox.infotel.bg *Web Site:* www.pensoft.net, pg 97

Pensord Press Ltd (United Kingdom) *Tel:* (01495) 223721 *Fax:* (01495) 222157, pg 1141

Pentalfa Ediciones (Spain) *Tel:* (0985) 985 386 *Fax:* (0985) 985 512 *E-mail:* pentalfa@helicon.es *Web Site:* www.helicon.es/pentalfa.htm, pg 586

Pentathol Publishing (United Kingdom), pg 726

Institut Penyelidikan Minyak Kelapa Sawit Malaysia (Malaysia) *Tel:* (03) 8335155 *Fax:* (03) 8259446 *E-mail:* pub@porim.gov.my, pg 454

The People's Communications Publishing House (China) *Tel:* (010) 4214479 *Fax:* (010) 4213713, pg 107

People's Education Press (China) *Tel:* (010) 6402 4555 *Fax:* (010) 6401 0370 *E-mail:* yaod@pep.com.cn (English); dongyj@pep.com.cn (Japanese), pg 107

People's Fine Arts Publishing House (China) *Tel:* (010) 5122371 *Fax:* (010) 5122370, pg 108

People's Literature Publishing House (China) *Tel:* (010) 65138394 *Fax:* (010) 65138394, pg 108

People's Medical Publishing House (PMPH) (China) *Tel:* (010) 67015802 *Fax:* (010) 67025429, pg 108

The People's Posts & Telecommunication Publishing House (China) *Tel:* (010) 5138139; (010) 5138129 *Fax:* (010) 5138139, pg 108

People's Publishing House (P) Ltd (India) *Tel:* (011) 529365, pg 346

People's Sports Publishing House (China) *Tel:* (010) 754525 *Fax:* (010) 67116129, pg 108

PEP Buchhandlung & No Name Photo Gallery (Switzerland) *Tel:* (061) 352065, pg 1313

The Pepin Press (Netherlands) *Tel:* (020) 4202021 *Fax:* (020) 4201152, pg 482

Peramiho Publications (United Republic of Tanzania) *Tel:* (054) 2730 *Fax:* (054) 2917, pg 634, 1139, 1160, 1201, 1223

Perea Ediciones (Spain) *Tel:* (026) 568261 *Fax:* (026) 586386, pg 586

Editorial Peregrino SL (Spain) *Tel:* (0926) 338 245 *Fax:* (0926) 338 002 *E-mail:* eplibros@teleline.es *Web Site:* www.editorialperegrino.net, pg 586

Perfect Frontier Sdn Bhd (Malaysia) *Tel:* (03) 7832926 *Fax:* (03) 7816448, pg 454

Editorial Perfils (Spain) *Tel:* (0973) 242160 *Fax:* (0973) 221670 *E-mail:* perfils@arrakis.es *Web Site:* www.arrakis.es/~cvlmallorca/perfils-e.htm, pg 586

Editora Pergaminho Lda (Portugal) *Tel:* (021) 4847500 *Fax:* (021) 4836077 *E-mail:* pergaminho@mail.telepac.pt, pg 528

Pergamon Flexible Learning (United Kingdom) *Tel:* (01865) 310366; (01865) 388190 *Fax:* (01865) 314290 *E-mail:* bhmarketing@repp.co.uk *Web Site:* www.bh.com/pergamonfl, pg 726

Peribo Pty Ltd (Australia) *Tel:* (02) 4457 0011 *Fax:* (02) 9457 0022 *E-mail:* peribo@bigpond.com, pg 37

Periodical & Book Publishers Association (Malta) *Tel:* 9882033 *Fax:* 871 2229; 169 5132 *E-mail:* bookpub@cwebdesign.com *Web Site:* www.cwebdesign.com/pbpa.html, pg 1252

Perioodika (Estonia) *Tel:* (02) 644 3158 *Fax:* (02) 644 2484, pg 140

E Perlinger Naturprodukte Handelsgesellschaft mbH (Austria) *Tel:* (05332) 75 654 *Fax:* (05332) 75 656 *E-mail:* engelberts.naturprodukte@tirol.com, pg 57

Permanyer Publications (Spain) *Tel:* (093) 207 59 20 *Fax:* (093) 457 66 42 *E-mail:* permanyer@permanyer.com *Web Site:* www.dolor.es; www.aidsreviews.com, pg 586

Permission & Rights, Moscow (Russian Federation) *Tel:* (095) 2092263 *Fax:* (095) 8836050, pg 1115

Permskaja Kniga (Russian Federation) *Tel:* (03422) 324245, pg 541

Perpetuity Press (United Kingdom) *Tel:* (0116) 217778 *Fax:* (0116) 217171 *E-mail:* info@perpetuitypress.com *Web Site:* www.perpetuitypress.com, pg 726

Editorial Perpetuo Socorro (Portugal) *Tel:* (02) 564251 *Fax:* (02) 564251, pg 528

Editorial El Perpetuo Socorro (Spain) *Tel:* (091) 445 51 26 *Fax:* (091) 445 51 27 *E-mail:* ed-ps@planalfa.es, pg 586

Perpustakaan Dewan Bahasa dan Pustaka Brunei, Kementerian Kebudayaan, Belia dan Sukan (Brunei Darussalam) *Tel:* (02) 235501 *Fax:* (02) 224763, pg 1455

Perret Edition (Switzerland) *Tel:* (01) 2627357 *Fax:* (01) 2627357, pg 621

Persatuan Perpustakaan Kebangsaan Negara Brunei (Brunei Darussalam) *Tel:* (02) 235501, pg 1513

Persatuan Perpustakaan Malaysia (Malaysia) *Tel:* (03) 273114 *Fax:* (03) 2731167, pg 1520

Verlag Sigrid Persen (Germany) *Tel:* (04163) 81 40 0 *Fax:* (04163) 8140 50 *Web Site:* www.persen.de, pg 272

Perskor Books (Pty) Ltd (South Africa) *Tel:* (011) 3153647 *Fax:* (011) 3152757, pg 558

Editora Perspectiva (Brazil) *Tel:* (011) 8858388 *Fax:* (011) 3885-8388 *E-mail:* editora@editoraperspectiva.com.br *Web Site:* www.editoraperspectiva.com.br/, pg 89

Perspectivas e Realidades, Artes Graficas, Lda (Portugal) *Tel:* (021) 3471371 *Fax:* (021) 3471372, pg 528

Justus Perthes Verlag Gotha GmbH (Germany) *Tel:* (03621) 385-0 *Fax:* (03621) 385-102 *E-mail:* perthes@klett-mail.de *Web Site:* www.klett-verlag.de/klett-perthes, pg 272

Pet Plus (Bulgaria) *Tel:* (02) 9874188 *Fax:* (02) 9809726 *E-mail:* fiveplus@bulgaria.net; petplus@bnc.bg, pg 97

Verlag Sankt Peter (Austria) *Tel:* (0662) 842166-82 *Fax:* (0662) 842166-80 *E-mail:* verlag-st.peter@magnet.at *Web Site:* www.stift-stpeter.at, pg 57

C F Peters Musikverlag GmbH & Co KG (Germany) *Tel:* (069) 6300990 *Fax:* (069) 635401 *E-mail:* info@musia.de *Web Site:* www.musia.de, pg 272

The Peters Fraser & Dunlop Group Ltd (United Kingdom) *Tel:* (020) 7344 1000 *Fax:* (020) 7836 9541 *E-mail:* rscoular@pfd.co.uk, pg 1121

Jens Peters Publikationen (Germany) *Tel:* (030) 7847265 *Fax:* (030) 7883127 *Web Site:* www.jenspeters.com, pg 272

Heinrich Petersen Hans Buchimport GmbH (Germany) *Tel:* (040) 8338801 *Fax:* (040) 83388130, pg 1284

Petit Editora e Distribuidora Ltda (Brazil) *Tel:* (011) 6684 6000; (011) 6917 165 *Fax:* (011) 2924616 *E-mail:* petit@dialdata.com.br *Web Site:* www.petit.com.br, pg 89

Petrion Verlag (Romania) *Tel:* (01) 637-23-34 *Fax:* (01) 312-45-25 *E-mail:* petrion@stranets.ro, pg 535

Petroc Press (United Kingdom) *Tel:* (01635) 522651 *Fax:* (01635) 36294 *E-mail:* petroc@librapharm.com *Web Site:* www.librapharm.com, pg 726

Petroleum Information Publishing Co (Taiwan, Province of China) *Tel:* (02) 9042387 *Fax:* (02) 9021060 *E-mail:* pip@tptsl.seed.net.tw, pg 631

Petrony Livraria (Portugal) *Tel:* (021) 3422911 *Fax:* (021) 3431602, pg 528

Galousis P Petros (Greece) *Tel:* (01) 360 5004, pg 314

Petrozavodskij Gosudarstvennyj Universitet (Russian Federation) *Tel:* (08142) 775148 *Fax:* (08142) 71021 *E-mail:* postmaster@mainpgn.kardia.su, pg 1495

Pevsner Public Library (Israel) *Tel:* (04) 667766, pg 1477

Pfaffenweiler Presse (Germany) *Tel:* (07664) 8999 *Fax:* (07664) 8999 *E-mail:* info@pfaffenweiler-presse.de *Web Site:* www.pfaffenweiler-presse.de, pg 272

Pfalzische Verlagsanstalt GmbH (Germany) *Tel:* (06341) 142-0 *Fax:* (06341) 142-265, pg 272

J Pfeiffer Verlag (Germany) *Tel:* (089) 4130010 *Fax:* (089) 41300138, pg 273

Verlag Dr Friedrich Pfeil (Germany) *Tel:* (089) 7428270 *Fax:* (089) 7242772 *E-mail:* 100417.1722@compuserve.com *Web Site:* www.pfeil-verlag.de, pg 273

Richard Pflaum Verlag GmbH & Co KG (Germany) *Tel:* (089) 12607-0 *Fax:* (089) 12607-202 *E-mail:* hoefer-heyne@pflaum.de *Web Site:* www.pflaum.de, pg 273

Verlag Die Pforte im Rudolf Steiner Verlag (Switzerland) *Tel:* (061) 7012240 *Fax:* (061) 7012534 *E-mail:* steiner-verlag@magnet.ch, pg 621

PG Publishing Pte Ltd (Singapore) *Tel:* 4726339 *Fax:* 4728279, pg 547

Phaidon Press Ltd (United Kingdom) *Tel:* (020) 7843 1231 *Fax:* (020) 7843 1111 *E-mail:* esales@phaidon.com *Web Site:* www.phaidon.com, pg 726

Phantom Publishers (Zimbabwe) *Tel:* (04) 737241, pg 769

Pharmaceutical Press (United Kingdom) *Tel:* (01491) 829 272 *Fax:* (01491) 829 292 *E-mail:* rpsgb@cabi.org *Web Site:* www.pharmpress.com, pg 726

Bibliotheque Interuniversitaire de Pharmacie (France) *Tel:* (01) 53739517 (ext 9523) *Fax:* (01) 53739520 *E-mail:* piketty@pharmacie.univ_paris5.fr, pg 1465

Pharos-Verlag, Hansrudolf Schwabe AG (Switzerland) *Tel:* (061) 541021 *Fax:* (061) 2797972, pg 621

Editions Phebus (France) *Tel:* (01) 46332929 *Fax:* (01) 43256769, pg 179

Pheljna Edizioni d'Arte e Suggestione (Italy) *Tel:* (0125) 234114 *Fax:* (0125) 230085, pg 403

Editions Phi (Luxembourg) *Tel:* (00352) 541382-220 *Fax:* (00352) 541387 *E-mail:* editions.phi@editpress.lu, pg 448

Philip & Tacey Ltd (United Kingdom) *Tel:* (01264) 332171 *Fax:* (01264) 332226 *E-mail:* info@philipandtacey.co.uk *Web Site:* www.philipandtacey.co.uk, pg 726

Philipp Reclam Jun Verlag GmbH (Germany) *Tel:* (07156) 163 0 *Fax:* (07156) 163 197 *E-mail:* info@reclam.de *Web Site:* www.reclam.de, pg 273

Philippine Normal College Library & Library Science Departments (Philippines) *Tel:* (02) 5270372 *Fax:* (02) 5270372, pg 1491

Philippine Librarians Association Inc (Philippines) *Tel:* (02) 590177, pg 1522

Philippine Baptist Mission SBC FMB Church Growth International (Philippines) *Tel:* (02) 599256; (02) 599257 *Fax:* (02) 512-1499 *E-mail:* csm@i-manila.com.ph, pg 514

Philippine Education Co Inc (Philippines) *Tel:* (02) 487215; (02) 487317, pg 514, 1306

Philippine Educational Publishers' Association (Philippines) *Tel:* (02) 7402698 *Fax:* (02) 7115702, pg 1256

Philippine Graphic Arts Inc (Philippines) *Tel:* (02) 364-4591 *Fax:* (02) 631-9733 *E-mail:* philippinegraphicarts@yahoo.com, pg 1199

Philippka-Sportverlag (Germany) *Tel:* (0251) 230050 *Fax:* (0251) 2300599 *E-mail:* info@philippka.de *Web Site:* www.philippka.de, pg 273

Philipps-Universitaet Marburg (Germany) *Tel:* (06421) 28-20 *Fax:* (06421) 28-22500 *E-mail:* verwaltung@ub.uni.marburg.de *Web Site:* www.uni-marburg.de, pg 273

Philip's (United Kingdom) *Tel:* (020) 7531 8459; (020) 7531 8439 (rights & data sales) *Fax:* (020) 7531 8460; (020) 7531 8464 (rights & data sales) *E-mail:* george.philip@philips-maps.co.uk *Web Site:* www.philips-maps.co.uk, pg 727

Phillimore & Co Ltd (United Kingdom) *Tel:* (01243) 787636 *Fax:* (01243) 787639 *E-mail:* bookshop@phillimore.co.uk *Web Site:* www.phillimore.co.uk, pg 727

Philo Press-Van Heusden-Hissink & Co CV (APA) (Netherlands) *Tel:* (020) 6265544 *E-mail:* info@apa-publishers.com, pg 482

Philograph Publications Ltd (United Kingdom) *Tel:* (01271) 45061 *Fax:* (01271) 23076, pg 727

Philopsychy Press (Hong Kong) *Tel:* (02) 6044403 *Fax:* (02) 6044403 *E-mail:* ppp@hkbu.edu.hk, pg 321

Philosophia Verlag GmbH (Germany) *Tel:* (089) 299975 *Fax:* (089) 299975 *E-mail:* info@philosophiaverlag.com *Web Site:* www.philosophiaverlag.com, pg 273

Philosophisch-Anthroposophischer Verlag am Goetheanum (Switzerland) *Tel:* (061) 7211116; (061) 7064200 *Fax:* (061) 7011436; (061) 7064201, pg 621

Pho Thong (Popularization) Publishing House (Viet Nam), pg 763

Phoenix Education Pty Ltd (Australia) *Tel:* (03) 9699 8377; (02) 9809 3579 *Fax:* (03) 9699 9242; (02) 9808 1430, pg 38

Phoenix Publishers (Kenya) *Tel:* (02) 222309; (02) 223262 *Fax:* (02) 339875, pg 433

Phongwarin Printing Company Ltd (Thailand) *Tel:* (02) 7498934-45; (02) 3994525-31 *Fax:* (02) 3994524; (02) 3994255 *E-mail:* somphong@mozart.inet.co.th *Web Site:* www.phongwarin.com, pg 1139

Phongwarin Printing Company Ltd (Thailand) *Tel:* (02) 7498934-45; (02) 3994525-31; (02) 7498275-79 *Fax:* (02) 3994524; (02) 3994255 *Web Site:* www.phongwarin.com, pg 1160, 1201

Photoart Ltd (Hong Kong) *Tel:* (02) 23617782 *Fax:* (02) 8669230, pg 321

Photoengraving Inc (United States) *Tel:* 813-253-3427 *Fax:* 813-253-5491, pg 1166

Photolitho AG (Switzerland) *Tel:* (01) 9352676 *Fax:* (01) 9353247, pg 1160, 1201

PHP Kenkyujo (Japan) *Tel:* (03) 32396221 *Fax:* (03) 32396263, pg 423

Physica-Verlag (Germany) *Tel:* (06221) 4878-0 *Fax:* (06221) 4878-177 *E-mail:* physica@springer.de *Web Site:* www.springer.de, pg 273

Piatkus Books (United Kingdom) *Tel:* (020) 7631 0710 *Fax:* (020) 7436 7137 *E-mail:* info@piatkus.co.uk *Web Site:* www.piatkus.co.uk, pg 727

Daniela Piazza Editore (Italy) *Tel:* (011) 4342706 *Fax:* (011) 4342471, pg 403

Pica Overseas Color Separation Ltd (Singapore) *Tel:* 7761311 *Fax:* 7793055, pg 1159

Editions A et J Picard SA (France) *Tel:* (01) 43 26 96 73 *Fax:* (01) 43 26 42 64 *E-mail:* livres@librairie-picard.com *Web Site:* www.abebooks.com/home/libpicard, pg 179

Picaron Editions (Netherlands) *Tel:* (020) 6201484, pg 482

Piccadilly Press (United Kingdom) *Tel:* (020) 7267 4492 *Fax:* (020) 7267 4493 *E-mail:* books@piccadillypress.co.uk *Web Site:* www.piccadillypress.co.uk, pg 727

Piccin Nuova Libraria SpA (Italy) *Tel:* (049) 655566 *Fax:* (049) 8750693 *E-mail:* info@piccinonline.com *Web Site:* www.piccinonline.com, pg 403

Anna Pichler Verlag GmbH (Austria) *Tel:* (0043) 2238-77078 *Fax:* (0043) 2238-77076 *E-mail:* apverlag@magnet.at, pg 57

Pichler Verlag GmbH & Co KG (Austria) *Tel:* (01) 203 28 28-0 *Fax:* (01) 203 28 28-6875 *E-mail:* office@pichlerverlag.at *Web Site:* www.pichlerverlag.at, pg 57

Pickering & Chatto (Publishers) Ltd (United Kingdom) *Tel:* (020) 7405 1005 *Fax:* (020) 7405 6216 *E-mail:* info@pickeringchatto.co.uk *Web Site:* www.pickeringchatto.com, pg 727

Editions Jean Picollec (France) *Tel:* (01) 45 89 73 04 *Fax:* (01) 45 89 40 72 *E-mail:* jean.picollec@noos.fr, pg 179

Editions Philippe Picquier (France) *Tel:* (04) 90496156 *Fax:* (04) 90499614, pg 180

Picton Publishing (Chippenham) Ltd (United Kingdom) *Tel:* (01249) 443430 *Fax:* (01249) 443430, pg 727

Picture Research Assoc (United Kingdom) *Tel:* (020) 7431 9886 *Fax:* (020) 7431 9887, pg 1267

PIE-Peter Lang SA (Switzerland) *Tel:* (031) 9402121 *Fax:* (031) 9402131 *E-mail:* peterlang@datacomm.ch, pg 622

Piedra Santa (Guatemala) *Tel:* (02) 2329053; (02) 2201524; (02) 2201526 *Fax:* (02) 2329053 *E-mail:* editorialps@yahoo.com, pg 1287

Editorial Piedra Santa (Guatemala) *Tel:* (02) 29053; (02) 851524; (02) 851526; (02) 328603 *Fax:* (02) 329053 *E-mail:* piedrasanta.sal@salnet.net, pg 316

Piedras Press, Inc (Puerto Rico) *Tel:* (787) 731-9215, pg 531

Edizioni Piemme SpA (Italy) *Tel:* (0141) 3361 *Fax:* (0142) 74223 *E-mail:* dirgen@edizpiemme.it *Web Site:* www.edizpiemme.it, pg 403

Heinz Pier (Germany) *Tel:* (02235) 3998 *Fax:* (02235) 41654, pg 273

Pierides Foundation (Cyprus) *Tel:* (02) 444486 *Fax:* (02) 466412, pg 122

Piero Lacaita Editore (Italy) *Tel:* (099) 9711124 *Fax:* (099) 9711124, pg 403

Piero Manni srl (Italy) *Tel:* (0832) 387057 *Fax:* (0832) 387057, pg 403

Editions Pierron (France) *Tel:* (03) 87951089 *Fax:* (03) 87956095, pg 180

Libreria Gozzini di Pietro e Francesco Chellini (SNC) (Italy) *Tel:* (055) 212433 *Fax:* (055) 211105 *E-mail:* gozzini@gozzini.it; info@gozzini.com *Web Site:* www.gozzini.com, pg 403

Paul Pietsch Verlage GmbH & Co (Germany) *Tel:* (0711) 2 10 80-0 *Fax:* (0711) 2 10 80-82; (0711) 2 36 04-15 *E-mail:* ppv@motorbuch.de, pg 273

Pijl Boekbedrijf nv (Belgium) *Tel:* (03) 236-98-30; (03) 270-02-70 *Fax:* (03) 235-90-02 *E-mail:* booksell@innet.be, pg 1276

Pikkhanet Kanphim (Thailand) *Tel:* (02) 222850, pg 635

Pilgermission Buch & Brunnen-Verlag Basel (Switzerland) *Tel:* (061) 234406 *Fax:* (061) 2646010, pg 1313

Pillar Publications Ltd (United Kingdom) *Tel:* (01932) 847629 *Fax:* (01932) 821610 *E-mail:* hu@bjhc.demon.co.uk, pg 1223

La Pilotta Editrice Coop RL (Italy) *Tel:* (0521) 771268 *Fax:* (0521) 771268, pg 403

Richard Pils Publication P (Austria) *Tel:* (02815) 635594 *Fax:* (02815) 635592, pg 57

Pinchgut Press (Australia) *Tel:* (02) 9908-2402 *Fax:* (02) 9960-4689, pg 38

Pinevale Publications (Australia) *Tel:* (07) 93-3169, pg 38

Pinguin-Verlag, Pawlowski GmbH (Austria) *Tel:* (0512) 281183-0 *Fax:* (0512) 293243 *Web Site:* www.worldport.at, pg 57

Editora Pini Ltda (Brazil) *Tel:* (011) 224-8811 *Fax:* (011) 224-0314; (011) 224-8541 *E-mail:* construcao@pini.com.br *Web Site:* www.piniweb.com.br, pg 89

Pinwheel Ltd (United Kingdom) *Tel:* (020) 7586 5100 *Fax:* (020) 7483 1999 *E-mail:* sales@pinwheel.co.uk *Web Site:* www.pinwheel.co.uk, pg 728

Pion Ltd (United Kingdom) *Tel:* (020) 8459 0066 *Fax:* (020) 8451 6454 *E-mail:* admin@pion.co.uk *Web Site:* www.pion.co.uk, pg 728

Pioneer Design Studio Pty Ltd (Australia) *Tel:* (03) 9735 5505, pg 38

Pioneer Graphic Scanning (United States) *Tel:* 845-735-4666 *Fax:* 617-344-5905, pg 1146, 1166

Livraria Pioneira Editora/Enio Matheus Guazzelli e Cia Ltd (Brazil) *Tel:* (011) 8583199 *Fax:* (011) 8580443 *E-mail:* pioneira@virtual-net.com.br, pg 89

Piper Verlag GmbH (Germany) *Tel:* (089) 381801-0 *Fax:* (089) 338704 *E-mail:* info@piper.de *Web Site:* www.piper.de, pg 274

PIRA Intl (United Kingdom) *Tel:* (01372) 802080 *Fax:* (01372) 802079 *E-mail:* publications@pira.co.uk *Web Site:* www.piranet.com, pg 728

Publicaciones Piramide, SA de CV (Mexico) *Tel:* (05) 5313215 *Fax:* (05) 2725883, pg 465

Ediciones Piramide SA (Spain) *Tel:* (091) 393 89 89 *Fax:* (091) 742 36 61 *E-mail:* infopiramide@piramide.es *Web Site:* www.edicionespiramide.es, pg 586

Francesco Pirella Editore (Italy) *Tel:* (010) 363628 *Fax:* (010) 363644 *E-mail:* fpirella@split.it, pg 403

Pirene Editorial, sal (Spain) *Tel:* (093) 3178682 *Fax:* (093) 3178242, pg 587

Pirola (Italy) *Tel:* (02) 30221 *Fax:* (02) 38011205, pg 403

Editions Christian Pirot (France) *Tel:* (02) 47 54 54 20 *Fax:* (02) 47 51 57 96 *Web Site:* www.friendship-first.com, pg 180

Pitagora Editrice SRL (Italy) *Tel:* (051) 530003 *Fax:* (051) 535301 *E-mail:* pited@pitagoragroup.it *Web Site:* www.pitagoragroup.it, pg 403

Pitambar Publishing Co (P) Ltd (India) *Tel:* (011) 367 0067; (011) 352 2997; (011) 367 3608 *Fax:* (011) 367 6058 *E-mail:* pitambar@bol.net.in *Web Site:* www.pitambar.com, pg 346

Pitkin Unichrome Ltd (United Kingdom) *Tel:* (01264) 409200 *Fax:* (01264) 334110 *E-mail:* enquiries@pitkin-unichrome.com *Web Site:* www.britguides.com, pg 728

Pitspopany Press (Israel) *Tel:* (02) 6233507 *Fax:* (02) 6233510 *E-mail:* pitspop@netvision.net.il *Web Site:* www.pitspopany.com, pg 371

Amilcare Pizzi SpA (Italy) *Tel:* (02) 618361 *Fax:* (02) 61836283 *E-mail:* mapizzi@tin.it, pg 1158, 1198

Amilcare Pizzi SpA (Italy) *Tel:* (02) 618361 *Fax:* (02) 61836283, pg 403

Pizzicato Edizioni Musicali (Italy) *Tel:* (0432) 45288 *Fax:* (0432) 45288 *E-mail:* pizzikat@tin.it *Web Site:* www.pizzicato.ch, pg 403

PJ Publishing (Australia) *Tel:* (06723) 22-368 *Fax:* (06723) 22-218, pg 38

Jean-Michel Place (France) *Tel:* (01) 44 32 05 90 *Fax:* (01) 44 32 05 91 *E-mail:* place@jmplace.com *Web Site:* www.jmplace.com, pg 180

Planet (United Kingdom) *Tel:* (01970) 611255 *Fax:* (01970) 611197 *E-mail:* planet.enquiries@planetmagazine.org.uk *Web Site:* www.planetmagazine.org.uk, pg 728

Planeta SA (Chile) *Tel:* (02) 6962374 *Fax:* (02) 6957260, pg 101

Editorial Planeta Argentina SAIC (Argentina) *Tel:* (011) 4382-4045; (011) 4382-4043 *Fax:* (011) 4383-3793 *E-mail:* info@eplaneta.com.ar, pg 8

Planeta Editora, LDA (Portugal) *Tel:* (021) 397-87-56 *Fax:* (021) 395-10-26, pg 528

Grupo Editorial Planeta (Mexico) *Tel:* (05) 5331250, pg 465

Planeta Publishers (Russian Federation) *Tel:* (095) 9230470 *Fax:* (095) 2005246, pg 541

Editorial Planeta SA (Spain) *Tel:* (093) 228 58 00 *Fax:* (093) 2177140; (093) 2177748, pg 587

Editorial Planeta Venezolana (Venezuela) *Tel:* (02) 913982; (02) 924872 *Fax:* (02) 913792, pg 763

Planetas Kiadoi es Kereskedelmi Kft (Hungary) *Tel:* (01) 1315767, pg 326

Plantagenet Press (Australia) *Tel:* (09) 4304466 *Fax:* (09) 4305217 *E-mail:* 100240.3406rogergarwood@compuserve.com, pg 38

Plantain Park (Australia), pg 38

Museum Plantin-Moretus (Belgium) *Tel:* (03) 221 14 50; (03) 221 14 51 *Fax:* (03) 221 14 71 *E-mail:* museum.plantin.moretus@antwerpen.be *Web Site:* www.antwerpen.be/cultuur/museum_plantinmoretus/, pg 1453

Plantin Publishers (United Kingdom) *Tel:* (029) 2056 0333 *Fax:* (029) 2055 4909 *E-mail:* drakegroup@btinternet.com *Web Site:* www.drakegroup.co.uk, pg 728

Plastic Comunicacion SL (Spain) *Tel:* (093) 4019833 *Fax:* (093) 4019830 *E-mail:* plastunivers@app.es *Web Site:* www.plastunivers.es, pg 587

Platano Editora SA (Portugal) *Tel:* (021) 7979278 *Fax:* (021) 7954019, pg 528

Platform 5 Publishing Ltd (United Kingdom) *Tel:* (0114) 255 2625 *Fax:* (0114) 255 2471 *E-mail:* platform5@platfive.freeserve.co.uk, pg 728

Plawerg SA (Spain) *Tel:* (093) 414 72 26 *Fax:* (093) 209 50 01 *E-mail:* info@plawerg.es *Web Site:* www.plawerg.com, pg 587

Playbox Theatre Co (Australia) *Tel:* (03) 9685 5100 *Fax:* (03) 9685 5112 *E-mail:* playbox@netspace.net.au, pg 38

Playlab Press (Australia) *Tel:* 3236 1396 *Fax:* 3236 1026 *E-mail:* cluster@thehub.com.au *Web Site:* www.thehub.com.au/~cluster/playlab, pg 38

Playmarket (New Zealand) *Tel:* (04) 3828461 *Fax:* (04) 3854279, pg 1115

Editorial Playor SA (Spain) *Tel:* (091) 4340201 *Fax:* (091) 5011342 *E-mail:* playor@attglobal.net, pg 587

Plaza y Janes Editores SA (Spain) *Tel:* (093) 45110 *Fax:* (093) 4156976, pg 587

Plaza y Valdes SA de CV (Mexico) *Tel:* (05) 5359851; (05) 5664055 *Fax:* (05) 7050030 *E-mail:* pyvedito@servidor.unam.mx, pg 465

Editorial Pleamar (Argentina) *Tel:* (011) 485-6597, pg 8

Plein Chant (France) *Tel:* (05) 45819326 *Fax:* (05) 45819283, pg 1133, 1194

Pleniluni Edicions (Spain) *Tel:* (093) 301 08 87 *Fax:* (093) 3174830, pg 587

Jurriaan Plesman (Australia) *Tel:* (02) 91306202 *Fax:* (02) 91306202, pg 38

Plexus Publishing Ltd (United Kingdom) *Tel:* (020) 7662 2440 *Fax:* (020) 7622 2441 *E-mail:* info@plexusuk.demon.co.uk *Web Site:* www.plexusbooks.com, pg 728

Editorial Pliegos (Spain) *Tel:* (091) 4291545 *Fax:* (091) 4291545, pg 587

Uitgeverij Ploegsma BV (Netherlands) *Tel:* (020) 6262907 *Fax:* (020) 6242994, pg 483

Librairie Plon SA (France) *Tel:* (01) 44 41 35 00 *Fax:* (01) 44 41 35 02, pg 180

Plough Publishing House of Bruderhof Communities in the UK (United Kingdom) *Tel:* (01580) 883 344 *Fax:* (01580) 883 317 *Toll Free Fax:* 800-018-3347 *E-mail:* ploughuk@plough.com *Web Site:* www.plough.com, pg 728

Plum Press (Australia) *Tel:* (07) 3870 2964 *Fax:* (07) 3870 2860 *Web Site:* www.justasktom.com, pg 38

Editions Plume (France) *Tel:* (01) 40 29 96 09 *Fax:* (01) 40 29 96 11, pg 180

Plurigraf SPA (Italy) *Tel:* (0744) 715946 *Fax:* (0744) 722540, pg 404

Editorial Plus Ultra SA (Argentina) *Tel:* (011) 4374-2973 *Fax:* (011) 4374-2973 *E-mail:* plus_ultra@epu.virtual.ar.net, pg 8

Pluto Press (United Kingdom) *Tel:* (020) 8348 2724 *Fax:* (020) 8348 9133 *E-mail:* pluto@plutobooks.com *Web Site:* www.plutobooks.com, pg 728

Pluto Press Australia (Australia) *Tel:* (02) 9692 5111 *Fax:* (02) 9692 5192 *E-mail:* info@socialchange.net.au *Web Site:* www.plutoaustralia.com, pg 38

Plymbridge Distributors Ltd (United Kingdom) *Tel:* (01752) 202300 *Fax:* (01752) 202330 *E-mail:* orders@plymbridge.com *Web Site:* www.plymbridge.com, pg 1321

pmi Verlag (Germany) *Tel:* (069) 54 80 00-0 *Fax:* (069) 54 80 00 66 *E-mail:* pmiverlag@aol.com *Web Site:* www.pmi-verlag.de, pg 274

Pochinchai Printing Co Ltd (Republic of Korea) *Tel:* (02) 679-2351 *Fax:* (02) 676-2821, pg 439

Pociao's Books (Germany) *Tel:* (228) 229583 *Fax:* (228) 219507 *E-mail:* pociao@t-online.de *Web Site:* pociaos-books.de, pg 1284

Max Pock, Universitaetsbuchhandlung (Austria) *Tel:* (0316) 825254 *Fax:* (0316) 825258; (0316) 825254-8, pg 1275

Biblioteca del Poder Legislativo (Uruguay) *Tel:* (02) 409111 *Fax:* (02) 235538, pg 1508

Podium Uitgeverij (Netherlands) *Tel:* (020) 4213830 *E-mail:* post@uitgeverijpodium.nl, pg 483

Wydawnictwo Podsiedlik-Raniowski i Spolka (Poland) *Tel:* (061) 8679546 *Fax:* (061) 8676850 *E-mail:* office@priska.com.pl, pg 519

Verlag Walter Podszun Burobedarf-Bucher Abt (Germany) *Tel:* (02961) 53213 *Fax:* (02961) 2508 *E-mail:* verlag.podszun@t-online.de *Web Site:* podszun.com, pg 274

Podzun-Pallas Verlag GmbH (Germany) *Tel:* (06036) 9436 *Fax:* (06036) 6270 *Web Site:* www.podzun-pallas.de, pg 274

Poetes Presents (France) *Tel:* (02) 97529363 *Fax:* (02) 97528390, pg 1228

Poetry Society of Australia (Australia) *Tel:* (02) 423861, pg 1359

The Poetry Book Society Ltd (United Kingdom) *Tel:* (020) 8870 8403 *Fax:* (020) 8877 1615 *E-mail:* info@poetrybooks.co.uk *Web Site:* www.poetrybooks.co.uk, pg 1233

The Poetry Society Inc (United Kingdom) *Tel:* (020) 7420 9880 *Fax:* (020) 7240 4818 *E-mail:* poetryreview@poetrysociety.org.uk *Web Site:* www.poetrysociety.org.uk, pg 1371

Poetry Wales Press Ltd (United Kingdom) *Tel:* (01656) 663018 *Fax:* (01656) 649226 *E-mail:* enquiries@seren.force9.co.uk *Web Site:* www.seren-books.com, pg 729

Poeziecentrum (Belgium) *Tel:* (09) 225 22 25 *Fax:* (09) 225 90 54 *E-mail:* info@poeziecentrum.be *Web Site:* www.poeziecentrum.be, pg 73

Pohjoinen (Finland) *Tel:* (09) 815377570 *Fax:* (09) 815377572 *E-mail:* annariitta.lankela@kaleva.fi, pg 144

Point Hors Ligne (France) *Tel:* (01) 43544964 *Fax:* (01) 43253032, pg 180

Editions du Point Veterinaire (France) *Tel:* (01) 45 17 02 25 *Fax:* (01) 42 07 93 88 *Web Site:* www.pointveterinaire.com, pg 180

Pointer Publishers (India) *Tel:* (0141) 568159 *Fax:* (0141) 562000, pg 346

POL Editeur (France) *Tel:* (01) 43 54 21 20 *Fax:* (01) 43 54 11 31 *Web Site:* www.pol-editeur.fr, pg 180

The Polding Press (Australia) *Tel:* (03) 675157; (03) 671740 *Fax:* (03) 96390879, pg 38

Literatur-Agentur Axel Poldner-Verlagsbuero (Germany) *Tel:* (089) 574824 *Fax:* (089) 5707640, pg 1112

Le Pole Nord ASBL (Belgium) *Tel:* (02) 2184576 *Fax:* (02) 2184576 *E-mail:* pole.nord@skynet.be, pg 73

Polemos SA (Argentina) *Tel:* (011) 4383-5291 *Fax:* (011) 4382-4181 *E-mail:* editorial@polemos.com.ar *Web Site:* www.polemus.com.ar, pg 8

Polestar Purnell Ltd (United Kingdom) *Tel:* (01761) 404142 *Fax:* (01761) 404198, pg 1141

Polgar Citizen Press (Hungary) *Tel:* (01) 1752854; (01) 1568358, pg 326

Police Review Publishing Company Ltd (United Kingdom) *Tel:* (020) 7440 4700 *Fax:* (020) 7405 7167; (020) 7405 7163, pg 729

The Policy Press (United Kingdom) *Tel:* (0117) 954 6800 *Fax:* (0117) 973 7308 *E-mail:* tpp-info@bristol.ac.uk *Web Site:* www.policypress.org.uk, pg 729

Policy Studies Institute (United Kingdom) *Tel:* (020) 7468 0468 *Fax:* (020) 7388 0914 *E-mail:* postmaster@psi.org.uk *Web Site:* www.psi.org.uk, pg 729

Polifemo, Ediciones (Spain) *Tel:* (091) 7257101 *Fax:* (091) 3556811 *E-mail:* libros@polifemo.com *Web Site:* www.polifemo.com, pg 587

Istituto Poligrafico e Zecca Dello Stato (Italy) *Tel:* (06) 85081 *Fax:* (06) 85082517, pg 1137

Istituto Poligrafico e Zecca dello Stato (Italy) *Tel:* (06) 85081 *Fax:* (06) 85082517 *E-mail:* infoipzs@ipzs.it, pg 404

Polirom Verlag (Romania) *Tel:* (032) 217-440 *Fax:* (032) 214-100 *E-mail:* polirom@olntis.ro, pg 535

Polish Chamber of Books (Poland) *Tel:* (022) 8261201 *Fax:* (022) 8266240 *E-mail:* rg.pik@arspolona.com.pl, pg 1257

Polish Scientific Publishers PWN (Poland) *Tel:* (022) 6954321; (022) 080020145 *Fax:* (022) 8267163, pg 519

Politechnika Krakowska im Tadeusza Kosciuszki (Poland) *Tel:* (12) 6282014 *Fax:* (12) 6332909; (12) 6282014 *E-mail:* listy@biblos.pk.edu.pl *Web Site:* www.biblios.pk.edu.pl, pg 1492

Politechnika Slaska (Poland) *Tel:* (032) 23412 69 *Fax:* (032) 23715 51 *E-mail:* info@bibgl.polsl.gliwice.pl, pg 1492

Politechnika Wroclawska/Biblioteka Glowna i OINT (Poland) *Tel:* (071) 3202305 *Fax:* (071) 3282960 *E-mail:* bg@bg.pwr.wroc.pl, pg 1492

Oficyna Wydawnicza Politechniki Wroclawskiej (Poland) *Tel:* (071) 3202304; (071) 3282940 *Fax:* (071) 3282940, pg 519

Editora Politica (Cuba) *Tel:* (07) 79 8553-59 *Fax:* (07) 811024 *Web Site:* www.cuba.cu/politica/webpcc/editora.htm, pg 121

Library of Political and Social History (Indonesia) *Tel:* (021) 360136, pg 1474

Politisk Revy (Denmark) *Tel:* 33 91 41 41 *Fax:* 33 91 51 15 *E-mail:* politiskrevy@forlagene.dk *Web Site:* www.forlagene.dk/politiskrevy, pg 134

Galerie Eva Poll (Germany) *Tel:* (030) 261 70 91 *Fax:* (030) 261 70 92 *E-mail:* galerie@poll-berlin.de *Web Site:* www.germangalleries.com/poll, pg 274

Pollinger Ltd (United Kingdom) *Tel:* (020) 7025 7820 *Fax:* (020) 7025 7829 *Web Site:* www.pollingerltd.com, pg 1121

Pollitecon Publications (Australia) *Tel:* (02) 9713 7608 *Fax:* (02) 9713 1004 *Web Site:* members.ozemail.com.au/~pollitec/, pg 38

Pollner Verlag (Germany) *Tel:* (089) 3151890 *Fax:* (089) 3151890 *E-mail:* info@pollner-verlag.de *Web Site:* www.pollner-verlag.de, pg 274

Polo Publishing (United Kingdom) *Tel:* (0181) 783-1903 *Fax:* (0181) 979-9425, pg 729

Polska Fundacja Spraw Miedzynarodowych (Poland) *Tel:* (022) 8278888; (022) 5239086 *Fax:* (022) 5239027 *E-mail:* warecka@qdnet.pl, pg 1492

Polskie Towarzystwo Wydawcow Ksiazek (Poland) *Tel:* (022) 8260735 *Fax:* (022) 8260735, pg 1257

Wydawnictwo Polskiego Towarzystwa Wydawcow Ksiazek (Poland) *Tel:* (035) 260735 *Fax:* (035) 260735, pg 519

POLTE (Pancyprian Organization of Tertiary Education) (Cyprus) *Tel:* (02) 305030 *Fax:* (02) 494953, pg 122

Polyband Gesellschaft fur Bild Tontraeger mbH & Co Betriebs KG (Germany) *Tel:* (089) 420 03-0 *Fax:* (089) 420 03-42 *E-mail:* contact@polyband.de *Web Site:* www.polyband.de, pg 274

Polybooks Ltd (United Kingdom) *Tel:* (020) 7351 4995 *Fax:* (020) 7351 4995, pg 729

Polyglot Translation (China) *Tel:* (020) 8657-3608 *Fax:* (020) 8657-3965 *E-mail:* info@polyglot.com.cn *Web Site:* www.polyglot.com.cn; www.chinapolyglot.com, pg 1125

Polyglott-Verlag (Germany) *Tel:* (089) 360960 *Fax:* (089) 36096-222 (general); (089) 36096-258 (orders), pg 274

Polygon (United Kingdom) *Tel:* (0131) 650 8436 *Fax:* (0131) 662 0038 *E-mail:* polygon.press@eup.ed.ac.uk *Web Site:* www.eup.ed.ac.uk, pg 729

Polygon (United Kingdom) *Tel:* (0131) 6504223 *Fax:* (0131) 662053 *E-mail:* editorial@eup.ed.ac.uk, pg 1121

Polygraf Print, s r o (Slovakia) *Tel:* (051) 44 13 280 *Fax:* (051) 77 13 241; (051) 77 13 270 *E-mail:* polygrafprint@polygrafprint.sk, pg 550

Polygraph Verlag GmbH (Germany) *Tel:* (069) 630086-0 *Fax:* (069) 630086-50, pg 274

Polygraphics Trading (Philippines) *Tel:* (02) 817-95-56; (02) 728-43-65; (02) 728-43-66 *Fax:* (02) 817-95-56; (02) 817-95-64, pg 1137

Polynesian Press (New Zealand) *Tel:* (09) 3032349 *Fax:* (09) 3779528, pg 494

Polytechnica (France) *Tel:* (01) 47074079 *Fax:* (01) 45350619, pg 180

Polyteknisk Boghandel og Forlag (Denmark) *Tel:* 77424344 *Fax:* 77424354 *E-mail:* polybog@pb.dtu.dk, pg 1281

Polyteknisk Forlag (Denmark) *Tel:* 77424344 *Fax:* 77424354 *E-mail:* poly@poly.dtu.dk *Web Site:* www.polyteknisk.dk, pg 134

Editorial Pomaire Venezuela SA (Venezuela) *Tel:* (02) 2622122; (02) 2621253 *Fax:* (02) 2616962, pg 763

Ediciones Pomares-Corredor (Spain) *Tel:* (093) 2652950 *Fax:* (093) 2653010 *E-mail:* edpomazes@mx3.zedestb.es, pg 587

Pomegranate Europe Ltd (United Kingdom) *Tel:* (01621) 851646 *Fax:* (01621) 852426 *E-mail:* sales@pomeurope.co.uk, pg 729

Il Pomerio (Italy) *Tel:* (0371) 420381 *Fax:* (0371) 422080, pg 404

POMORZE-Pomorskie Wydawnictwo Prasowe (Poland) *Tel:* (052) 220237; (052) 211396; (052) 210452, pg 519

Pomorze Wydawnictwo Spoldzielnia Pracy (Poland) *Tel:* (052) 220237; (052) 211396; (052) 210452, pg 519

Editions du Centre Pompidou (France) *Tel:* (01) 44 78 12 33 *Fax:* (01) 44 78 12 05 *Web Site:* www.centrepompidou.fr, pg 180

Pomurska zalozba (Slovenia) *Tel:* (069) 32420 *Fax:* (069) 31086, pg 552

Libreria Pons SL (Spain) *Tel:* (0976) 359037 *Fax:* (0976) 356072 *E-mail:* promedit@libreriapons-zaragoza.com *Web Site:* www.libreriapons-zaragoza.com, pg 1311

Pontificia Academia Scientiarum (Holy See (Vatican City State)) *Tel:* 0669883195 *Fax:* 0669885218 *E-mail:* academy.sciences@acdscience.va *Web Site:* www.vatican.va/roman_curia/pontifical_academies/index_it.htm, pg 317

Pontificia Universidad Catolica de Chile Sistema de Bibliotecas (Chile) *Tel:* (02) 6864615 *Fax:* (02) 6865852, pg 1456

Biblioteca Central de la Pontificia Universidad Catolica del Peru (Peru) *Tel:* (01) 4602870 (ext 176) *Fax:* (01) 4633773 *E-mail:* biblio@pucp.edu.pe, pg 1491

Pontificia Universidad Catolica de Chile (Chile) *Tel:* (02) 2224516 (ext 2417) *Fax:* (02) 2225515 *Web Site:* www.puc.cl, pg 101

Pontificia Universidad Catolica de Ecuador, Centro de Publicaciones (Ecuador) *Tel:* (02) 529240 *Fax:* (02) 567117, pg 137

Pontificia Universidad Catolica Madre y Maestra (Dominican Republic) *Tel:* (809) 5801962; (809) 5350111 *Fax:* (809) 5824549; (809) 5350053, pg 136

Pontificia Universidad Javeriana, Facultad de Comunicacion y Lenguaje (Colombia) *Tel:* (01) 2858177 *Fax:* (01) 2887896; (01) 2850973 *E-mail:* incabarc@javercol.javeriana.edu.co, pg 1458

Pontificio Istituto di Archeologia Cristiana (Italy) *Tel:* (06) 4465574 *Fax:* (06) 4469197 *E-mail:* piac@piac.it; piac.biblio@piac.it *Web Site:* www.piac.it, pg 404

Pontifico Istituto Orientale (Italy) *Tel:* (06) 447417104 *Fax:* (06) 4465576 *Web Site:* www.pio.urbe.it, pg 404

Pontiki Publications SA (Greece) *Tel:* (01) 3609531; (01) 3609533 *Fax:* (01) 3645406, pg 314

Pookie Productions Ltd (United Kingdom) *Tel:* (0131) 221868 *Fax:* (0131) 221868, pg 729

Pool Editorial Ltda (Brazil) *Tel:* (081) 2215355; (081) 2215150; (081) 2215096, pg 90

Poolbeg Press Ltd (Ireland) *Tel:* (01) 8321477 *Fax:* (01) 8321430 *E-mail:* poolbeg@poolbeg.com *Web Site:* www.poolbeg.com, pg 363

Pop Plus Rock Centrum (Czech Republic) *Tel:* (02) 51555598 *Fax:* (02) 51554485 *E-mail:* olda@katapult.cz, pg 127

Poplar Publishing Co Ltd (Japan) *Tel:* (03) 33572211 *Fax:* (03) 39245341, pg 423

Popular Army Publishing House (Viet Nam), pg 763

Popular Book Depot (India) *Tel:* (022) 382 9401; (022) 382 6762, pg 1289

Popular Book Store (Philippines) *Tel:* (02) 372-2162 *Fax:* (02) 372-2050 *E-mail:* popular@pworld.net.ph, pg 1306

Biblioteca Popular Judia (Argentina) *Tel:* (011) 4961-4534 *Fax:* (011) 4963-7056 *E-mail:* cjl@mayo.com.ar *Web Site:* www.counsnet.com/ojicjl, pg 8

Popular Prakashan Pvt Ltd (India) *Tel:* (022) 4941656 *Fax:* (022) 4938049, pg 346

Popular Publications (Malawi) *Tel:* 641126 *Fax:* 651171 *E-mail:* mpp@malawi.net, pg 451

Editorial Popular SA (Spain) *Tel:* (091) 409 35 73 *Fax:* (091) 573 41 73 *E-mail:* epopular@infornet.es *Web Site:* www.editorialpopular.com, pg 587

Popular Science Press (China) *Tel:* (010) 8023226; (010) 8318877, pg 108

H Pordes Ltd (United Kingdom) *Tel:* (020) 8445 1273 *Fax:* (020) 8445 5510, pg 1321

Frederique Porretta (France) *Tel:* (01) 45448868 *Fax:* (01) 45446936, pg 1111

Libreria de Porrua Hermanos y Cia, SA (Mexico) *Tel:* (05) 7025467; (05) 7024574 *Fax:* (05) 7024574; (05) 7024315 *E-mail:* servicios@porrua.com, pg 1299

Editorial Porrua SA (Mexico) *Tel:* (05) 7025467; (05) 7024574 *Fax:* (05) 7026529, pg 466

Portal Ltd (Czech Republic) *Tel:* (02) 83028111 *Fax:* (02) 83028112 *E-mail:* naklad@portal.cz *Web Site:* www.portal.cz, pg 127

Editions La Porte (Morocco) *Tel:* (07) 709958; (07) 706476 *Fax:* (07) 709958; (07) 706478, pg 470

David Porteous Editions (United Kingdom) *Tel:* (01626) 853310 *Fax:* (01626) 853663 *E-mail:* dp@davidporteous.com *Web Site:* www.davidporteous.com, pg 729

Porthill Publishers (United Kingdom) *Tel:* (020) 89586783 *Fax:* (020) 89054516, pg 730

Editorial Portic SA (Spain) *Tel:* (093) 412 00 30 *Fax:* (093) 301 48 63 *E-mail:* secedit@grec.com *Web Site:* www.enciclopedia-catalana.com, pg 587

Portikus (Germany) *Tel:* (069) 219 987-60; (069) 219 987-59 *Fax:* (069) 219 987-61 *E-mail:* portikus@pop.stadt-frankfurt.de *Web Site:* www.portikus.de, pg 274

Portland Press Ltd (United Kingdom) *Tel:* (020) 7580 5530 *Fax:* (020) 7323 1136 *E-mail:* editorial@portlandpress.com *Web Site:* www.portlandpress.com, pg 730

Porto Editora Lda (Portugal) *Tel:* (02) 2005813 *Fax:* (02) 313072 *E-mail:* pe@portoeditora.pt, pg 528

Livraria Portugal (Dias e Andrade Lda) (Portugal) *Tel:* (021) 3474982, pg 1308

Portugalmundo (Portugal) *Tel:* (021) 8155351 *Fax:* (021) 8144746, pg 528

Instituto Portugues Oriente (Macau) *Tel:* 370642 *Fax:* 305426, pg 448

Editorial Porvenir (Costa Rica) *Tel:* 224-8119; 224-1052; 225-3115 *Fax:* 283-8893; 224-8119 *E-mail:* porvenir@racsa.co.cr, pg 116

Possev-Verlag GmbH (Germany) *Tel:* (069) 34-12-65 *Fax:* (069) 34-38-41 *E-mail:* possev-ffm@t-online.de, pg 274

Postreiter-Verlag GmbH (Germany) *Tel:* (030) 8938840 *Fax:* (030) 89388420, pg 274

Potsdamer Verlagbuchhandlung GmbH (Germany) *Tel:* (030) 253738-0 *Fax:* (030) 253738-39, pg 274

Marilyn Potts International Language Consultants (United Kingdom) *Tel:* (0191) 2324895; (0191) 2221775 *Fax:* (0191) 2616426 *E-mail:* 101341.533@compuserve.com *Web Site:* www.marilyn-potts.co.uk, pg 1129

Pournaras Panagiotis (Greece) *Tel:* (0310) 270941 *Fax:* (0310) 228922 *E-mail:* pournarasbooks@the.forthnet.gr, pg 1287

Editions Pourquoi Pas (Switzerland) *Tel:* (022) 7511031, pg 622

Power Publications (Australia) *Tel:* (02) 9351 6904 *Fax:* (02) 9351 7323 *E-mail:* power.publications@arthist.usyd.edu.au *Web Site:* metapix.arts.usyd.edu.au/power/institute/Publications, pg 38

Shelley Power Literary Agency Ltd (France) *Tel:* (01) 42383649 *Fax:* (01) 40407008 *E-mail:* shelley.power@wanadoo.fr, pg 1111

T & AD Poyser Ltd (United Kingdom) *Tel:* (020) 8308 5700 *Fax:* (020) 8308 5702 *E-mail:* cservice@harcourt.com, pg 730

Neri Pozza Editore (Italy) *Tel:* (0444) 320787 *Fax:* (0444) 324613, pg 404

Edizioni Luigi Pozzi SRL (Italy) *Tel:* (06) 8553548 *Fax:* (06) 8554105, pg 404

PPC Editorial y Distribuidora, SA (Spain) *Tel:* (091) 359-2300 *Fax:* (091) 350-5443 *E-mail:* ppcedit@ctv.es, pg 587

PPC Editorial y Distribuidora, SA (Spain) *Tel:* (091) 359-2300 *Fax:* (091) 345-0282, pg 1311

PPP Printers Ltd (New Zealand) *Tel:* (03) 3662727 *Fax:* (03) 3654606, pg 1137, 1158, 1199

Pra Cha Chang & Co Ltd (Thailand), pg 635

Prabhat Prakashan (India) *Tel:* (011) 264676, pg 346

Vydavatepstvo Praca spol sro (Slovakia) *Tel:* (07) 292865; (07) 392890; (07) 392853 *Fax:* (07) 392840; (07) 392853, pg 550

Prace (Czech Republic) *Tel:* (02) 378315; (02) 373507; (02) 377346 *Fax:* (02) 20103376 *E-mail:* prace@terminal.cz, pg 127

Georg Prachner KG (Austria) *Tel:* (01) 512 85 49-0 *Fax:* (01) 512-01-58 *Web Site:* www.indiana.edu, pg 57

Georg Prachner KG (Austria) *Tel:* (0222) 5128549; (0222) 5128540 *Fax:* (0222) 5120158, pg 1275

Pradeepa Publishers (Sri Lanka) *Tel:* (094) 435074; (094) 863261; (071) 735532 *Fax:* (094) 863261, pg 598

Pragma 4 (Czech Republic) *Tel:* (02) 231 58 28; (02) 231 07 76; (02) 231 07 74; (02) 231 65 90 *Fax:* (02) 231 07 76; (02) 231 65 90, pg 127

Agamee Prakashani (Bangladesh) *Tel:* (02) 7111332; (02) 7110021 *Fax:* (02) 9562018; (02) 7123945 *E-mail:* agamee@bdonline.com, pg 62

Prasan Mit (Thailand) *Tel:* (02) 3915287; (02) 3925230, pg 635

Prasenz Verlag der Jesus Bruderschaft eV (Germany) *Tel:* (06438) 81300 *Fax:* (06438) 81310 *Web Site:* www.uni-giessen.de/~gf1002/vdbiol/homepage/jesus.htm, pg 274

Pratibha Pratishthan (India) *Tel:* (011) 3265770, pg 346

Pratiche Editrice (Italy) *Tel:* (02) 29403460 *Fax:* (02) 29513061, pg 404

Wydawnictwo Prawnicze Co (Poland) *Tel:* (022) 496151; (022) 496152; (022) 496153; (022) 494094 *Fax:* (022) 499410 *E-mail:* wp@wp.com.pl, pg 519

Prazske nakladatelstvi Pluto (Czech Republic) *Tel:* (02) 249 301 89; (02) 43 25 05 *Fax:* (02) 249 301 89, pg 127

PRC Publishing Ltd (United Kingdom) *Tel:* (020) 7697 3000 *E-mail:* info@prcpub.com, pg 730

Pre-Textos (Spain) *Tel:* (96) 333 32 26 *Fax:* (96) 395 54 77 *E-mail:* info@pre-textos.com *Web Site:* www.pre-textos.com, pg 587

Precision Publishing Papers Ltd (United Kingdom) *Tel:* (01935) 431800 *Fax:* (01935) 431805, pg 1141

Izdavacko Preduzece Matice Srpske (Yugoslavia) *Tel:* (021) 420 199; (021) 420 837 *Fax:* (021) 27281, pg 765

Ediciones Preescolar SA (Argentina) *Tel:* (011) 581-3182 *Fax:* (011) 581-3182, pg 8

Premop Verlag GmbH (Germany) *Tel:* (089) 562257 *Fax:* (089) 5803214 *E-mail:* premop@aol.com, pg 275

Preney Print & Litho Inc (Canada) *Tel:* 519-966-3412 *Fax:* 519-966-4996 *E-mail:* preney@mnsi.net, pg 1153, 1193

Editorial Prensa Espanola (Spain) *Tel:* (091) 4462616, pg 587

Prensa Medica Latinoamericana (Uruguay) *Tel:* (02) 4092933 *Fax:* (02) 4000916 *E-mail:* prensmed@adinet.com.uy, pg 761

Ediciones Cientificas La Prensa Medica Mexicana SA de CV (Mexico) *Tel:* (05) 5504500 *Fax:* (05) 6589193, pg 466

Prensas Universitarias de Zaragoza (Spain) *Tel:* (034) 976761330 *Fax:* (034) 976761063 *E-mail:* puz@posta.unizar.es *Web Site:* wzar.unizar.es/spub/, pg 587

Prentsmidjan Oddi (Iceland) *Tel:* 5683366 *Fax:* 5676694, pg 328

Prepare Inc (United States) *Tel:* 201-934-8451 *Fax:* 201-934-2992 *E-mail:* csr@emilcomp.it; prepare@optonline.net, pg 1166

Casa Editora Presbiteriana S.C. (Brazil) *Tel:* (011) 270-7099 *Fax:* (011) 279-1255 *E-mail:* cep@cep.org.br *Web Site:* www.cep.org.br, pg 90

Presbyterian Book Depot & Printing Press Ltd (PRESBOOK) (Cameroon) *Tel:* 332114 *Fax:* 332694, pg 1278

Presbyterian Book Depot Ltd (Ghana) *Tel:* (021) 663502; (021) 663124; (021) 662415 *Fax:* (021) 665594 *E-mail:* pcg@africaonline.com.gh, pg 1285

Editorial Presenca (Portugal) *Tel:* (021) 7992200 *Fax:* (021) 7977560 *E-mail:* info@editpresenca.pt *Web Site:* www.editpresenca.pt, pg 528

Presence Africaine Editions (France) *Tel:* (01) 43 54 13 74; (01) 43 54 15 88 *Fax:* (01) 43 25 96 67 *Web Site:* www.letissue.com, pg 180

Editorial Presencia Gitana (Spain) *Tel:* (091) 373 62 07 *Fax:* (091) 373 44 62 *E-mail:* anpregit@teleline.es *Web Site:* www.presenciagitana.org/, pg 587

Preses Nams (Latvia) *Tel:* (02) 465732 *Fax:* (02) 465624, pg 442

President Boekklub (South Africa) *Tel:* (012) 401 0700 *Fax:* (012) 3255498 *E-mail:* lapa@atkv.org.za *Web Site:* www.lapauitgewers.org.za, pg 1231

President Inc (Japan) *Tel:* (03) 32373711 *Fax:* (03) 32373746 *E-mail:* matu-pre@po.iijnet.or.jp, pg 423

Press Agency (Kuwait) *Tel:* 432269; 411495 *Fax:* 411495, pg 441

Press & Publication Administration of the People's Republic of China (China) *Tel:* (010) 5127818 *Fax:* (010) 6512785, pg 1240

Press & Publicity Centre Ltd (United Republic of Tanzania) *Tel:* (051) 127765; (051) 122881; (051) 131078 *Fax:* (051) 113619; (051) 116749, pg 634

The Press & Publishing Engineering Society (Russian Federation) *Tel:* (095) 2906286 *Fax:* (095) 2918506, pg 1257

Press Art (Czech Republic) *Tel:* (048) 29377 *Fax:* (048) 27958, pg 127

Press for Success (Australia) *Tel:* (08) 9221 6166 *Fax:* (08) 9221 6166 *E-mail:* press4@press4success.com.au *Web Site:* www.press4success.com.au, pg 38

Press Mark Media Ltd (Hong Kong) *Tel:* (02) 8822230 *Fax:* (02) 28823949; (02) 28822471 *E-mail:* magazine@todayliving.com, pg 321

Press Photo Publications (Greece) *Tel:* (01) 6429166 *Fax:* (01) 6443618 *E-mail:* photomag@photo.gr *Web Site:* www.photo.gr, pg 1287

The Press (Jamaica) *Tel:* (876) 977-2659 *Fax:* (876) 977-2660 *E-mail:* salex@uwimona.edu.jm *Web Site:* www.uwimona.edu.jm/press, pg 413

Pressa Publishing House (Russian Federation) *Tel:* (095) 2573482 *Fax:* (095) 2505205, pg 541

Presse-Grosso-Bundesverband Deutscher Buch-, Zeitungs-und Zeitschriften-Grossisten eV (Germany) *Tel:* (0221) 9213370 *Fax:* (0221) 92133744 *E-mail:* bvpg@bvpg.de *Web Site:* www.pressegrosso.de, pg 1246

PIAG Presse Informations AG (Germany) *Tel:* (07221) 301 7560 *Fax:* (07221) 301 7570 *E-mail:* office@piag.de; piag.visuell@t-online.de; bestellung@piag.de *Web Site:* www.piag.de; www.pictureexchange.de, pg 275

Presse Verlagsgesellschaft mbH (Germany) *Tel:* (069) 296875 *Fax:* (069) 97460-400 *E-mail:* journal@mmg.de *Web Site:* www.journal-frankfurt.de, pg 275

Presses agronomiques de Gembloux ASBL (Belgium) *Tel:* (081) 62 22 42 *Fax:* (081) 62 22 42 *E-mail:* pressesagro@fsagx.ac.be *Web Site:* www.bib.fsagx.ac.be/presses/, pg 73

Presses de la Cite (France) *Tel:* (01) 44160500 *Fax:* (01) 44160505 *Web Site:* www.pressesdelacite.com, pg 180

Presses de la Renaissance (France) *Tel:* (01) 44 16 05 86 *Fax:* (01) 44 16 05 13 *Web Site:* www.presses-renaissance.com, pg 180

Presses de la Sorbonne Nouvelle/PSN (France) *Tel:* (01) 45874027; (01) 45874168 *Fax:* (01) 45877854; (01) 45874175 *E-mail:* n.carbon@univ-paris3.fr *Web Site:* www.univ-paris3.fr/p.sn, pg 181

Presses de l'Ecole Nationale des Ponts et Chaussees (France) *Tel:* (01) 44582740 *Fax:* (01) 44582744 *Web Site:* www.enpc.fr, pg 181

Les Presses d'Ile-de-France Sarl (France) *Tel:* (01) 44 52 37 37 *Fax:* (01) 42 38 09 87 *E-mail:* scouts@scouts-france.fr *Web Site:* www.scouts-france.fr, pg 181

Les Presses du Management (France) *Tel:* (01) 40 71 11 11 *Fax:* (01) 46 51 45 35, pg 181

Presses Polytechniques et Universitaires Romandes, PPUR (Switzerland) *Tel:* (021) 693 21 30 *Fax:* (021) 693 40 27 *E-mail:* ppur@epfl.ch *Web Site:* www.ppur.org, pg 622

Presses Universitaires de Namur ASBL (Belgium) *Tel:* (081) 72 48 84 *Fax:* (081) 72 49 12 *E-mail:* pun@fundp.ac.be *Web Site:* www.pun.be, pg 73

Presses Universitaires d'Afrique (Cameroon) *Tel:* (023) 22 23 25 *Fax:* (023) 22 23 25, pg 99

Presses Universitaires de Bruxelles ASBL (Belgium) *Tel:* (02) 641 14 46 *Fax:* (02) 647 79 62, pg 73

Presses Universitaires de Caen (France) *Tel:* (02) 31 56 62 20 *Fax:* (02) 31 56 62 25 *Web Site:* www.unicaen.fr, pg 181

Presses Universitaires de France (PUF) (France) *Tel:* (01) 58 10 31 00 *Fax:* (01) 58 10 31 82 *E-mail:* puf.com@puf.com *Web Site:* www.puf.com, pg 181

Presses Universitaires de Grenoble (France) *Tel:* (04) 76 82 56 51; (04) 76 82 56 52 *Fax:* (04) 76 82 78 35 *E-mail:* pug@pug.fr *Web Site:* www.pug.fr, pg 181

Presses Universitaires de Liege (Belgium) *Tel:* (041) 562218, pg 73

Presses Universitaires de Lyon (France) *Tel:* (04) 78 29 39 39 *Fax:* (04) 78 29 39 41 *Web Site:* www.univ-lyon2.fr, pg 181

Presses Universitaires de Nancy (France) *Tel:* (016) 83 96 84 30 *Fax:* (016) 83 96 84 39 *Web Site:* www.univ-nancy2.fr, pg 181

Presses Universitaires de Strasbourg (France) *Tel:* (03) 88 25 97 21 *Fax:* (03) 88 35 65 23 *Web Site:* www.pu-strasbourg.com, pg 181

Presses Universitaires du Septentrion (France) *Tel:* (03) 20 41 66 80 *Fax:* (03) 20 41 66 90 *E-mail:* septentrion@septentrion.com *Web Site:* www.sepentrion.com, pg 181

Presses Universitaires du Zaiire (PUZ) (The Democratic Republic of the Congo) *Tel:* (012) 30652, pg 115

Pressfoto Vydavatelstvi Ceske Tiskove Kancelare (Czech Republic) *Tel:* (02) 727 700 10 *Fax:* (02) 727 700 10, pg 128

Guido Pressler Verlag (Germany) *Tel:* (02429) 1385; (02408) 929692 *Fax:* (02408) 955931 *E-mail:* info@pressler-verlag.com *Web Site:* www.pressler-verlag.com, pg 275

Prestel Verlag (Germany) *Tel:* (089) 38 17 09 0 *Fax:* (089) 33 51 75 *E-mail:* presse@prestel.de *Web Site:* www.prestel.de, pg 275

Prestige Booksellers & Stationers (Kenya) *Tel:* (02) 223515 *Fax:* (02) 2246796 *E-mail:* prest@iconnect.co.ke, pg 1296

Preston Corporation Sdn Bhd (Malaysia) *Tel:* (03) 7563734 *Fax:* (03) 7573607, pg 454

Pretoria Public Library (South Africa) *Tel:* (012) 3088837 *Fax:* (012) 3088873, pg 1498

Helmut Preussler Verlag (Germany) *Tel:* (0911) 95478 18 *Fax:* (0911) 542486 *E-mail:* preussler_verlag@t_online.de, pg 275

Price Publishing (Australia) *Tel:* (02) 9337-1598 *Fax:* (02) 9337-2158 *E-mail:* pricesys@localnet.com.au, pg 39

Mathew Price Ltd (United Kingdom) *Tel:* (01935) 816010 *Fax:* (01935) 816310 *E-mail:* mathewp@mathewprice.com, pg 730

Nelson Price Milburn Ltd (New Zealand) *Tel:* (04) 5687179 *Fax:* (04) 5682115 *E-mail:* npm@xtrq.co.nz, pg 494

Priese GmbH (Germany) *Tel:* (030) 3239089 *Fax:* (030) 3249630, pg 1133, 1154, 1195, 1212, 1221

Priestley Consulting (Australia) *Tel:* (07) 54453968 *Fax:* (07) 54458288 *E-mail:* priestd@squirrel.com.au, pg 39

Prim-Ed Publishing UK Ltd (United Kingdom) *Tel:* (01203) 322860; (0870) 0131208 *Fax:* (01203) 322861; (0870) 0131209 *E-mail:* sales@prim-ed.com *Web Site:* www.prim-ed.com, pg 730

Primary English Teaching Association (Australia) *Tel:* (02) 9565 1277 *Fax:* (02) 9565 1070 *E-mail:* info@peta.edu.au *Web Site:* www.peta.edu.au, pg 39

Edizioni Primavera SRL (Italy) *Tel:* (055) 66791 *Fax:* (055) 6679298, pg 404

Editora Primor Ltda (Brazil) *Tel:* (021) 4744966, pg 90

Primrose Books and Periodicals (Zambia) *Tel:* (02) 210817, pg 1325

Primrose Hill Press Ltd (United Kingdom) *Tel:* (020) 7405 7484 *Fax:* (020) 7405 7459 *E-mail:* info@primrosehillpress.co.uk *Web Site:* www.primrosehillpress.co.uk, pg 730

Principato (Italy) *Tel:* (02) 312025 *Fax:* (02) 33104295 *E-mail:* princi.red@comm2000.it, pg 404

Printafoil Ltd (United Kingdom) *Tel:* (0181) 6403074 *Fax:* (0181) 6402136, pg 1204, 1214

Printcrafters Inc (Canada) *Tel:* 204-633-7117 *Fax:* 204-694-1519 *E-mail:* printcrafters@mb.sympatico.ca, pg 1153, 1193, 1211, 1221

EDITIONS Le Printemps (Mauritius) *Tel:* 6961017 *Fax:* 6867302 *E-mail:* elp@bow.intnet.mu, pg 457

Printer Industria Grafica SA (Spain) *Tel:* (093) 6310123 *Fax:* (093) 6310205; (093) 6310206 *E-mail:* info@printer-spain.com *Web Site:* www.printer-spain.com, pg 1201

Printer Portuguesa Industria Grafica Lda (Portugal) *Tel:* (01) 9216025 *Fax:* (01) 9218363 *E-mail:* lissabon.printerportuguesa@bertelsmann.de, pg 1199

Printing Corp of the Americas Inc (United States) *Tel:* 954-781-8100 *Fax:* 954-781-8421 *E-mail:* pcaprint@bellsouth.net *Web Site:* www.pcaprint.bellsouth.net, pg 1146, 1166, 1208, 1216

Printing Industry Publishing House (China) *Tel:* (010) 8219966 *Fax:* (010) 8214683 *E-mail:* capt@public3.bta.net.cn, pg 108

Printpak (Z) Ltd (Zambia) *Tel:* (01) 611001; (01) 611002; (01) 600113; (01) 612027 *Fax:* (01) 617096, pg 767

Prints India (India) *Tel:* (011) 3268645 *Fax:* (011) 3275542, pg 1290

PrintWest (Canada) *Tel:* 306-525-2304 *Fax:* 306-757-2439 *E-mail:* general@printwest.com *Web Site:* www.printwest.com, pg 1131, 1153, 1211, 1221

Printworld Services Pte Ltd (Singapore) *Tel:* 7442166 *Fax:* 7460845 *E-mail:* printw@mbox2.singnet.com.sg, pg 547

Prion Books Ltd (United Kingdom) *Tel:* (020) 7482 4248 *Fax:* (020) 7482 4203 *E-mail:* books@prion.co.uk *Web Site:* www.prionbooks.com, pg 730

Priroda (Slovakia) *Tel:* (02) 52496335; (02) 55566176 *Fax:* (02) 55566176 *E-mail:* priroda@nextra.sk *Web Site:* www.priroda.sk, pg 550

Prism Press Book Publishers Ltd (United Kingdom) *Tel:* (01258) 817164 *Fax:* (01258) 817635, pg 730

Bokforlaget Prisma (Sweden) *Tel:* (08) 7698900 *Fax:* (08) 7698913 *E-mail:* prisma@prismabok.se *Web Site:* www.prismabok.se, pg 605

Prismi - Editrice Politecnica (Italy) *Tel:* (081) 7612884 *Fax:* (081) 668339, pg 404

Priuli e Verlucca, Editori (Italy) *Tel:* (0125) 239929 *Fax:* (0125) 230085 *E-mail:* priuli.e.verlucca@iol.it, pg 404

Private Libraries Association (PLA) (United Kingdom) *Web Site:* www.the-old-school.demon.co.uk/pla.htm, pg 1267

Privredni Pregled (Yugoslavia) *Tel:* (011) 628477; (011) 620364 *Fax:* (011) 623375; (011) 3281912, pg 765

Pro Juventute Verlag (Switzerland) *Tel:* (01) 2517244 *Fax:* (01) 2522824, pg 622

Pro Media Productions (Suriname) *Tel:* 479355, pg 599

Pro Natur Verlag GmbH (Germany) *Tel:* (069) 9688610 *Fax:* (069) 96886124, pg 275

Editions Pro Schola (Switzerland) *Tel:* (021) 323 66 55 *Fax:* (021) 323 67 77 *E-mail:* benedict@benedict-schools.com *Web Site:* www.benedict-international.com, pg 622

Proa S.A. (Chile) *Tel:* (02) 633 65 34; (02) 633 98 54 *Fax:* (02) 634 02 60 *E-mail:* proa@eutelchile.net, pg 101

Edicions Proa, SA (Spain) *Tel:* (093) 4120030 *Fax:* (093) 3014863 *E-mail:* enciclo.catalan@bcn.servicom.es, pg 588

Procultura SA (Colombia) *Tel:* (01) 2818154 *Fax:* (01) 2815913, pg 113

PRODIG UMR 8586 CNRS-Paris 1,4,7 ephe (France) *Tel:* (01) 44 32 14 81; (01) 42 34 56 21 *Fax:* (01) 43 29 63 83 *E-mail:* prodig@univ-paris1.fr *Web Site:* www.univ-paris1.fr/PRODIG, pg 182

Prodim SPRL (Belgium) *Tel:* (02) 640.59.70 *Fax:* (02) 640.59.91 *E-mail:* prodim.books@prodim *Web Site:* www.prodim.be, pg 73

Productive Publications (Canada) *Tel:* 416-483-0634 *Fax:* 416-322-7434 *Web Site:* www.productivepublications.com, pg 1131, 1193

Professional Book Supplies Ltd (United Kingdom) *Tel:* (01235) 861234 *Fax:* (01235) 861601 *E-mail:* probooks@aol.com, pg 730

Professional Engineering Publishing Ltd (United Kingdom) *Tel:* (01284) 763277 *Fax:* (01284) 718692 (sales & marketing) *E-mail:* orders@pepublishing.com *Web Site:* www.pepublishing.com, pg 730

Professional, Managerial & Healthcare Publications (United Kingdom) *Tel:* (01243) 576444 *Fax:* (01243) 576456 *E-mail:* admin@pmh.uk.com *Web Site:* www.pmh.uk.com, pg 731

Professional Publications (Malaysia) *Tel:* (03) 2325376 *Fax:* (03) 2011928, pg 454

Professional Publishing Co (Hong Kong) *Tel:* 25254623 *Fax:* 28453681, pg 1135

Profile Books Ltd (United Kingdom) *Tel:* (020) 7404 3001 *Fax:* (020) 7404 3003 *E-mail:* info@profilebooks.co.uk *Web Site:* www.profilebooks.co.uk, pg 731

Profile Publishing Ltd (New Zealand) *Tel:* (09) 6308940; (09) 3585455 *Fax:* (09) 3585462 *E-mail:* info@profile.co.nz *Web Site:* www.profile.co.nz, pg 494

Profizdat (Russian Federation) *Tel:* (095) 9245740 *Fax:* (095) 9752329 *E-mail:* iidprof@cityline.ru, pg 541

Progensa (Spain) *Tel:* (0954) 186 200 *Fax:* (0954) 186 111 *E-mail:* progensa@progensa.com *Web Site:* www.progensa.es, pg 588

Editorial Progreso SA de C V (Mexico) *Tel:* (05) 5477304; (05) 5471780; (05) 5411187 *Fax:* (05) 5415342 *E-mail:* editprogresosav@infosel.net.mx, pg 466

Progress Press Co Ltd (Malta) *Tel:* 241464; 241469; 241411; 241412 *Fax:* 241171, pg 456

Progress Publishers (Russian Federation) *Tel:* (095) 2469032 *Fax:* (095) 2302403, pg 541

Progress-Verlag Dr Micolini's Witwe (Austria) *Tel:* (0316) 829508 *Fax:* (0316) 829508, pg 57

Projektion J Buch- und Musikverlag GmbH (Germany) *Tel:* (06443) 680 *Fax:* (06443) 6834 *E-mail:* info@gerth.de *Web Site:* www.gerth.de, pg 275

Prolog Publishing House (Israel) *Tel:* (03) 9022904 *Fax:* (03) 9022906 *Web Site:* www.prolog.co.il, pg 371

De Prom (Netherlands) *Tel:* (035) 5482403 *Fax:* (035) 5418221, pg 483

Promedia Verlagsges mbH (Austria) *Tel:* (01) 405 27 02 *Fax:* (01) 405 71 59 22 *E-mail:* promedia@mediashop.at *Web Site:* www.mediashop.at, pg 57

Promesa, Ediciones (Costa Rica) *Tel:* 253-3759; 225-1511; 283-3033 *Fax:* 225-1286 *E-mail:* edicionespromesa@hotmail.com, pg 116

Ediciones Promesa, SA de CV (Mexico) *Tel:* (05) 5623174 *Fax:* (05) 3938707, pg 466

Prometej Izdatel 'stvo (Russian Federation) *Tel:* (095) 2454495, pg 541

Prometheus (Netherlands) *Tel:* (020) 624 19 34 *Fax:* (020) 622 54 61 *E-mail:* pbo@pbo.nl *Web Site:* www.pbo.nl, pg 483

Prometheus (Netherlands) *Tel:* (020) 6241934 *Fax:* (020) 6225461 *E-mail:* pbo@pbo.nl *Web Site:* www.pbo.nl, pg 483

Promilla and Co (India) *Tel:* (011) 668720 *Fax:* (011) 6448947, pg 346

Promociones de Mercados Turisticos SA de CV (Mexico) *Tel:* (05) 5150925; (05) 5160162 *Fax:* (05) 2725942 *E-mail:* tm@mail.internet.com.mx *Web Site:* www.travelguidemexico.com, pg 466

Editions Promoculture (Luxembourg) *Tel:* 480691 *Fax:* 400950 *E-mail:* promocul@pt.lu *Web Site:* www.promoculture.net, pg 448

Librairie Promoculture (Luxembourg) *Tel:* 480691 *Fax:* 400950 *E-mail:* promocul@pt.lu, pg 1297

Promoedition SA (Switzerland) *Tel:* (022) 8099460 *Fax:* (022) 7811414, pg 622

Promotion Litteraire (France) *Tel:* (01) 45004210 *Fax:* (01) 45001018 *E-mail:* promolit@club-internet.fr, pg 1111

Promotional Reprint Co Ltd (United Kingdom) *Tel:* (020) 7736 5666 *Fax:* (020) 7736 5777, pg 1321

Promotional Publications Int BV (Netherlands) *Tel:* (030) 650650 *Fax:* (030) 620850, pg 483

Prompter Publications (Republic of Korea) *Tel:* (02) 82 2214 1794, pg 439

Pronaos, SA Ediciones (Spain) *Tel:* (091) 4427995 *Fax:* (091) 4203429 *E-mail:* pronaos@teleline.es; jaire@teleline.es, pg 588

PRONI (Public Record Office of Northern Ireland) (United Kingdom) *Tel:* (02890) 251318 *Fax:* (02890) 255999 *E-mail:* proni@nics.gov.uk *Web Site:* www.proni.nics.gov.uk/index.htm, pg 1507

Prontaprint Asia Ltd (Hong Kong) *Tel:* 28657525 *Fax:* 28661064 *E-mail:* postmaster@pronta.com.hk, pg 1135, 1156, 1197, 1212, 1222

Henri Proost & Co, Pvba (Belgium) *Tel:* (014) 40 08 11 *Fax:* (014) 42 87 94 *Web Site:* www.proost.be, pg 73

Propos de Campagne (France) *Tel:* (04) 92 77 03 51 *Fax:* (04) 92 73 08 94 *E-mail:* ProposdeC@aol.com *Web Site:* www.lisez.com/propos/contact.html, pg 182

Propylaeen Verlag, Zweigniederlassung Berlin der Ullstein Buchverlage GmbH (Germany) *Tel:* (0302) 5913500 *Fax:* (030) 25913533, pg 275

ProQuest Information & Learning (United Kingdom) *Tel:* (01223) 215512 *Fax:* (01223) 215514 *E-mail:* marketing@proquest.co.uk *Web Site:* www.proquest.co.uk, pg 731

Proskinio (Greece) *Tel:* (01) 3808348 *Fax:* (01) 3819724, pg 314

Prospect Media Pty Ltd (Australia) *Tel:* (02) 93496077 *Fax:* (02) 94395411 *E-mail:* prospect@prospectmedia.com.au *Web Site:* www.prospectmedia.com.au, pg 39

Prostor, Ltd (Czech Republic) *Tel:* (02) 224826688 *Fax:* (02) 224827722 *E-mail:* prostor@ini.cz *Web Site:* www.prostor-nakladatelstvi.cz, pg 128

Izdatelstvo Prosveshchenie (Russian Federation) *Tel:* (095) 2891405 *Fax:* (095) 2004266, pg 541

Prosveta (Yugoslavia) *Tel:* (011) 642722; (011) 625766; (011) 625760 *Fax:* (011) 627-465, pg 765

Prosveta (Yugoslavia) *Tel:* (011) 642772 (import); (011) 625766 *Fax:* (011) 627-465, pg 1324

Prosveta-Izdavako preduzece (Yugoslavia) *Tel:* (011) 642722; (011) 625766; (011) 625760 *Fax:* (011) 627465, pg 1234

Prosveta Publishers as (Bulgaria) *Tel:* (02) 760651; (02) 9743696; (02) 761182 *Fax:* (02) 764451 *E-mail:* prosveta@intech.bg, pg 97

Editions Prosveta SA (France) *Tel:* (04) 94408241 *Fax:* (04) 94408005 *E-mail:* international@prosvesta.com *Web Site:* www.prosveta.com, pg 182

Prosvetno Delo (The Former Yugoslav Republic of Macedonia) *Tel:* (091) 117255; (091) 118617 *Fax:* (091) 225434; (091) 129402 *E-mail:* prodelo@nic.mpt.com.mk, pg 449

Prosvjeta (Croatia) *Tel:* (01) 4872 477 *Fax:* (01) 434017, pg 120

Prosvjeta (Novinsko-izdavacko i Stamparsko) (Croatia) *Tel:* (043) 245 222; (043) 245 223 *Fax:* (043) 245 220, pg 120

Protestant Publications (Australia) *Tel:* (02) 98684591 *Fax:* (02) 98687953, pg 39

Proton Editora Ltda (Brazil) *Tel:* (011) 2103616; (011) 8147922; (011) 8159708 *Fax:* (011) 8159920, pg 90

Instituto Provincial de Investigaciones y Estudios Toledanos (Spain) *Tel:* (0925) 25 93 00 (ext 367) *Fax:* (0925) 259348 *E-mail:* diputolepu@diputoledo.es, pg 588

Prozoretz Ltd Publishing House (Bulgaria) *Tel:* (02) 765171; (02) 746053 *Fax:* (02) 746053 *E-mail:* prozor@tea.bg, pg 97

Prugg Verlag (Austria) *Tel:* (02682) 2114, pg 57

Przedsiebiorstwo Wydawniczo-Handlowe Wydawnictwo Siedmiorog (Poland) *Tel:* (071) 341-68-71 *Fax:* (071) 341-68-87 *Web Site:* www.siedmiorog.com.pl, pg 519

PSAI Press (Ireland) *Tel:* (01) 7005664 *Web Site:* www.politics.tcd.ie/psai/contact.html, pg 363

M Psaropoulos & Co EE (Greece) *Tel:* (01) 3606808 *Fax:* (01) 3609645, pg 314

Psichogios Publications SA (Greece) *Tel:* (01) 3602535; (01) 3302234 *Fax:* (01) 3640683; (01) 3302098 *E-mail:* psicho@otenet.gr, pg 314

Psicologica Editrice (Italy) *Tel:* (06) 35453558 *Fax:* (06) 35341466 *E-mail:* ontonet@tin.it *Web Site:* www.ontopsicologia.org, pg 404

Bookclub Psyche (Japan) *Tel:* (03) 33290031 *Fax:* (03) 33043822, pg 1230

Psychiatrie-Verlag GmbH (Germany) *Tel:* (0228) 725340 *Fax:* (0228) 7253420 *E-mail:* verlag@psychiatrie.de *Web Site:* www.psychiatrie.de/verlag, pg 275

Psychoanalyticke Nakladatelstvi (Czech Republic) *Tel:* (02) 33340305 *Fax:* (02) 33340305 *E-mail:* georg.phe@worldonline.cz, pg 128

Psychological Corporation Ltd (United Kingdom) *Tel:* (020) 8308 5750 *Fax:* (020) 8308 5702 *E-mail:* tpc@harcourt.com *Web Site:* www.tpc-international.com, pg 731

Psychologie Verlags Union GmbH (Germany) *Tel:* (06201) 60070 *Fax:* (06201) 17464 *E-mail:* info@beltz.de *Web Site:* www.beltz.de, pg 275

Psychosophische Gesellschaft (Switzerland) *Tel:* (071) 591301, pg 622

Psychosozial-Verlag (Germany) *Tel:* (0641) 77819 *Fax:* (0641) 77742 *E-mail:* info@psychosozial-verlag.de; bestellung@psychosozial-verlag.de *Web Site:* www.psychosozial-verlag.de, pg 275

Psykologifoerlaget AB (Sweden) *Tel:* (08) 6810000 *Fax:* (08) 6810002 *E-mail:* info@psykologiforlaget.se *Web Site:* www.psykologiforlaget.se, pg 605

PT Bhakti Baru (Indonesia) *Tel:* (0411) 5192 *Fax:* (0411) 7156, pg 356

PT Pradnya Paramita (Indonesia) *Tel:* (021) 8583369; (021) 8504944 *Fax:* (021) 8583369, pg 357

PT Pradnya Paramita (Indonesia) *Tel:* (021) 8583369 *Fax:* (021) 8583369, pg 1291

PT Pustaka LP3ES Indonesia (Indonesia) *Tel:* (021) 5674211; (021) 5667139; (021) 5667141 *Fax:* (021) 5683785, pg 357

Pt Ravishankar Shukla University Library (India) *Tel:* 23970, pg 1473

PTI - Publicacoes Tecnicas Internacionais Ltda (Brazil) *Tel:* (011) 2596644 *Fax:* (011) 2586990 *E-mail:* gerson@vortex.uol.br, pg 1278

Publi-Fusion (France) *Tel:* (05) 65220303 *Fax:* (05) 65220322, pg 182

Public Lending Right (United Kingdom) *Tel:* (01642) 604699 *Fax:* (01642) 615641 *E-mail:* registrar@plr.uk.com *Web Site:* www.plr.uk.com, pg 1267

Public Lending Right Scheme (Australia) *Tel:* (062) 711650 *Toll Free Tel:* 800 672842 (Australia only) *Fax:* (062) 711651 *E-mail:* plr.mail@dcita.ov.au *Web Site:* www.dcita.gov.au/plr/html, pg 1236

Public Libraries Board (Uganda) *Tel:* (041) 233633 *Fax:* (041) 348625 *E-mail:* library@imul.com, pg 1505

Public Library (Afghanistan), pg 1449

Public Library (Jordan), pg 1479

Public Library of Latakia (Syrian Arab Republic), pg 1502

Public Record Office (United Kingdom) *Tel:* (0208) 3925265 *Fax:* (0208) 3925266 *E-mail:* enquiries@pro.gov.uk *Web Site:* www.pro.gov.uk, pg 1507

Publicaciones Cultural SA de CV (Mexico) *Tel:* (05) 5456860; (05) 5456861; (05) 5456862 *Fax:* (05) 5618155, pg 466

Publicaciones de la Universidad de Alicante (Spain) *Tel:* 965 909 576 *Fax:* 965 909 445 *E-mail:* publicaciones.ventas@ua.es *Web Site:* publicaciones.ua.es/, pg 588

Publicaciones de la Universidad Pontificia Comillas-Madrid (Spain) *Tel:* (091) 734 39 50 *Fax:* (091) 734 45 70 *E-mail:* edit@pub.upco.es *Web Site:* www.upco.es, pg 588

Publicaciones Importantes SA (Mexico) *Tel:* (05) 5101884; (05) 5109489 *Fax:* (05) 5129411, pg 466

Publicaciones Lo Castillo SA (Chile) *Tel:* (02) 235 2606 *Fax:* (02) 235 2007, pg 101

Publicaciones Nuevo Extremo (Chile) *Tel:* (02) 698 1523; (02) 697 2337 *Fax:* (02) 697 2545 *E-mail:* nexxtremo@entelchile.net, pg 101

Publicacoes Dom Quixote Lda (Portugal) *Tel:* (021) 538079 *Fax:* (021) 574595, pg 528

Editora de Publicacoes Medicas Ltda (Brazil) *Tel:* (021) 2654047; (021) 2253516 *Fax:* (021) 2613749, pg 90

Publications & Information Directorate, CSIR (India) *Tel:* (011) 5786301 ext 287; (011) 5786301 ext 288, pg 346

Editions Publications de l'Ecole Moderne Francaise sa (PEMF) (France) *Tel:* (04) 92921757 *Fax:* (04) 92921804, pg 182

Publications de la Fondation Temimi pour la Recherche Scientifique et L'Information (Tunisia) *Tel:* (072) 676 446; (072) 680 110 *Fax:* (072) 676 710 *E-mail:* temimi.fond.@gnet.tn *Web Site:* temimi.org (in Arabic); refer.org/6 (in French), pg 638

Publications de l'Ecole Moderne Francaise (PEMF) (France) *Tel:* (016) 92921757 *Fax:* (016) 92921804, pg 1228

Publications de l'Universite de Rouen (France) *Tel:* (02) 35 14 63 43 *Fax:* (02) 35 14 65 38, pg 182

Publications des Facultes Universitaires Saint Louis (Belgium) *Tel:* (02) 211 78 94 *Fax:* (02) 211 79 97 *E-mail:* mfthoua@fusl.ac.be *Web Site:* www.fusl.ac.be/files/general/publications.html, pg 73

Publications du Palais de Monaco (Monaco) *Tel:* 093 251831, pg 469

Publications (Holdings) Ltd (Hong Kong) *Tel:* (02) 8366088 *Fax:* (02) 8384061; (02) 8730861, pg 321

Publications Orientalistes de France (POF) (France) *Tel:* (04) 71 43 23 78 *Fax:* (04) 71 43 23 78 *E-mail:* sieffert@pofjapon.com *Web Site:* www.pofjapon.com, pg 182

Publik-Forum-Verlagsgesellschaft mbH (Germany) *Tel:* (06171) 70030 *Fax:* (06171) 700340, pg 276

Publishers Marketing Services Pte Ltd (Singapore) *Tel:* 2565166 *Fax:* 2530008, pg 1309

Publishers' and Booksellers' Association of Thailand (Thailand) *Tel:* (02) 5592642 *Fax:* (02) 5592643, pg 1263

Publishers Association (Russian Federation) *Tel:* (095) 2021174 *Fax:* (095) 2023989, pg 1258

The Publishers Association (United Kingdom) *Tel:* (020) 7691 9191 *Fax:* (020) 7691 9199 *E-mail:* mail@publishers.org.uk *Web Site:* www.publishers.org.uk, pg 1267

PUBLISHERS' ASSOCIATION FOR CULTURAL EXCHANGE, PACE, JAPAN — INDUSTRY

Publishers' Association for Cultural Exchange, PACE, Japan (Japan) *Tel:* (03) 32915685 *Fax:* (03) 32333645 *E-mail:* office@pace.or.jp *Web Site:* www.pace.or.jp, pg 1250

Publishers' Association of South Africa (PASA) (South Africa) *Tel:* (021) 7886470 *Fax:* (021) 7886469 *E-mail:* pasa@icon.co.za *Web Site:* www.icon.co.za/~pasa, pg 1258

Publishers' Enterprises Group (PEG) Ltd (Malta) *Tel:* 440083; 448539 *Fax:* 488908 *E-mail:* pegltd@global.net.mt, pg 456

Publishers Group South West (Ireland) (Ireland) *Tel:* (027) 73025 *Fax:* (027) 73131 *E-mail:* 73551.655@compuserve.com, pg 363

Publishers Licensing Society Ltd (United Kingdom) *Tel:* (020) 7829 8486 *Fax:* (020) 7829 8488 *E-mail:* pls@dial.pipex.com *Web Site:* www.pls.org.uk, pg 1267

Publishers United Pvt Ltd (Pakistan) *Tel:* (042) 352238, pg 508

Publishing Center of Belarus State University (Belarus) *Tel:* (0172) 227 18 08 *Fax:* (0172) 226 01 75 *E-mail:* pubcentre@org.bsu.unibee.by, pg 63

Publishing Council of the Academy of Sciences of the Russian Academy of Sciences (Russian Federation) *Tel:* (095) 952905 *Fax:* (095) 2379107, pg 1258

The Publishing House of Shanghai University of Traditional Chinese Medicine (China) *Tel:* (021) 64175039 *Fax:* (021) 64175039, pg 108

The Publishing House of the Lithuanian Writers' Union (Lithuania) *Tel:* (02) 628945; (02) 626154 *Fax:* (02) 619696, pg 446

Publishing Resources Inc (Puerto Rico) *Tel:* (787) 268-8080 *Fax:* (787) 774-5781, pg 531

Publishing Resources Inc (Puerto Rico) *Tel:* (787) 268-8080 *Fax:* (787) 774-5781 *E-mail:* pri@tld.net, pg 1158, 1200, 1222

Publishing Services Suriname (Suriname) *Tel:* 472746; 455792 *Fax:* 410366 *E-mail:* pssmoniz@sr.net *Web Site:* www.parbo.com, pg 599

Publishing Solutions Ltd (New Zealand) *Tel:* (04) 4710717 *Fax:* (04) 4710582 *E-mail:* gen@pubsol.co.nz *Web Site:* www.pubsol.co.nz, pg 494

Publishing Training Centre at BookHouse (United Kingdom) *Tel:* (020) 8874 2718 *Fax:* (020) 8870 8985 *E-mail:* publishing.training@bookhouse.co.uk *Web Site:* www.train4publishing.co.uk, pg 731

Publisud (France) *Tel:* (01) 45 80 78 50 *Fax:* (01) 45 89 94 15, pg 182

Publitec Publications (Lebanon) *Tel:* (01) 495401; (01) 495403 *Fax:* (01) 493330, pg 443

Publitoria Publishers (South Africa) *Tel:* (012) 3290313 *Fax:* (012) 3290306, pg 558

Publitoria Editions (South Africa) *Tel:* (012) 3290313 *Fax:* (012) 3290306, pg 558

Pudeleco/Publicaciones de Legislacion (Ecuador) *Tel:* (02) 543273 *Fax:* (02) 543607, pg 137

Pueblo y Educacion Editorial (PE) (Cuba) *Tel:* (07) 22-1490; (07) 29-4688 *Fax:* (07) 24-0844 *E-mail:* epe@ceniai.inf.cu, pg 121

Ediciones Puerto (Puerto Rico) *Tel:* (787) 7210844 *Fax:* (787) 7250861 *E-mail:* feriapr@caribe.net *Web Site:* www.edicionespuerto.com, pg 531

Puerto Rican PEN Centre (Puerto Rico) *Tel:* (787) 724-0869 *Fax:* (787) 724-2060, pg 1367

Puffin Book Clubs (United Kingdom) *Tel:* (020) 7416 3000 *Fax:* (020) 7416 3099, pg 1233

Editions du Puits Fleuri (France) *Tel:* (01) 64 23 61 46 *Fax:* (01) 64 23 69 42, pg 182

Pulp Master Frank Nowatzki Verlag (Germany) *Tel:* (030) 6868292 *Fax:* (030) 6868292 *E-mail:* master@txt.de, pg 276

Pulso Ediciones, SL (Spain) *Tel:* (093) 5896264 *Fax:* (093) 5895077 *E-mail:* pulso@pulso.com *Web Site:* www.pulso.com, pg 588

Puma Editora Lda (Portugal) *Tel:* (01) 9425394 *Fax:* (01) 9425214, pg 528

Punjab University Library (Pakistan) *Tel:* (042) 868853, pg 1490

Punjab Public Library (Pakistan) *Tel:* (042) 9211649 *Fax:* (042) 9211651 *E-mail:* pplinfo@brain.net.pk *Web Site:* www.brain.net.pk/pplinfo, pg 1490

Punktum AG (Switzerland) *Tel:* (01) 4224540 *Fax:* (01) 4224813, pg 1233

Punktum AG, Buchredaktion und Bildarchiv (Switzerland) *Tel:* (01) 4224540 *Fax:* (01) 4224813, pg 622

Il Punto D Incontro (Italy) *Tel:* (0444) 928793 *Fax:* (0444) 928459 *E-mail:* edpunto@tin.it, pg 404

Punto de Encuentro Ediciones (Uruguay) *Tel:* (02) 405167, pg 761

Pursuit Publishing (New Zealand) *Tel:* (09) 4385725 *Fax:* (09) 4382543, pg 494

Pusat Penelitian Perkebunan Sumbawa (Indonesia) *Tel:* (0711) 312182; (0711) 361793 *Fax:* (0711) 361793, pg 357

Pushtu Toulana, Afghan Academy (Afghanistan) *Tel:* 20350, pg 1

Pustak Mahal (India) *Tel:* (011) 3276539; (011) 3272783; (011) 3272784 *Fax:* (011) 3260518; (011) 2924673 *E-mail:* delaad37@giasd101.vsnl.net.in, pg 346

Pustaka Cipta Sdn Bhd (Malaysia) *Tel:* (03) 2744593 *Fax:* (03) 2749588 *E-mail:* rrapc@pc.jaring.my, pg 454

Pustaka Delta Pelajaran Sdn Bhd (Malaysia) *Tel:* (03) 7570000 *Fax:* (03) 7576688, pg 454

Pustaka Nasional Pte Ltd (Singapore) *Tel:* 7454321; 7454649; 7452417 *Fax:* 7452412, pg 547

Pustaka Sistem Pelajaran Sdn Bhd (Malaysia) *Tel:* (03) 9047558; (03) 9047017; (03) 9047018 *Fax:* (603) 9047573, pg 454

Pustaka Utama Grafiti, PT (Indonesia) *Tel:* (021) 8567502; (021) 8566998 *Fax:* (021) 8582430, pg 357

Verlag Anton Pustet (Austria) *Tel:* (0662) 87350-56 *Fax:* (0662) 87350-58 *E-mail:* buch@verlog-anton-pustet.es, pg 57

Verlag Friedrich Pustet GmbH & Co Kg (Germany) *Tel:* (0941) 9 20 22-0 *Fax:* (0941) 94 86 52 *E-mail:* pustetverlag@donan.de *Web Site:* www.pustetverlag.de, pg 276

Puthigar Ltd (Bangladesh) *Tel:* (02) 231374; (02) 235333; (02) 259867, pg 1275

Verlag Harry Putz (Czech Republic) *Tel:* (048) 515 21 20 *Fax:* (048) 510 32 75 *E-mail:* harrputz@mbox.vol.cz, pg 128

PYC Edition (France) *Tel:* (01) 53 26 48 00 *Fax:* (01) 53 26 48 01 *E-mail:* info@pyc.fr *Web Site:* www.pyc.fr, pg 182

Pyeong-hwa Chulpansa (Republic of Korea) *Tel:* (02) 7343341; (02) 7343343 *Fax:* (02) 7392129, pg 439

Editions Pygmalion - Gerard Watelet (France) *Tel:* (01) 45674077 *Fax:* (01) 47345152 *E-mail:* Pygmalio@easynet.fr, pg 182

The Pythagorean Press (Australia) *Tel:* (02) 3193555 *Fax:* (02) 9314 1760, pg 39

Pyunghwa Dang Printing Co Ltd (Republic of Korea) *Tel:* (02) 7354001 *Fax:* (02) 7345201 *E-mail:* comuser@hitel.kol.co.kr, pg 1158

Pyunghwa Dang Printing Co Ltd (Republic of Korea) *Tel:* (02) 7354001 *Fax:* (02) 7345201 *E-mail:* phdprt@kornet.net, pg 1199

PZWL Wydawnictwo Lekarskie Ltd (Poland) *Tel:* (022) 8312161; (022) 8314281-85 *Fax:* (022) 8310054 *E-mail:* promocja@pzwl.pl *Web Site:* www.pzwl.pl, pg 519

The Q Group Plc (United Kingdom) *Tel:* (020) 7291 1600 *Fax:* (020) 7291 1699 *E-mail:* ppoulter@qgroupplc.com, pg 1141

Qatar National Library (Qatar) *Tel:* 429955 *Fax:* 429976, pg 1494

Qatar University Library (Qatar) *Tel:* 832222; 892406 *Fax:* 83511, pg 1494

Qi Lu Press (China) *Tel:* (0531) 610055-313 *Fax:* (0531) 2906811, pg 108

Qingdao Publishing House (China) *Tel:* (0532) 514611; (0532) 362524 *Fax:* (0532) 515240, pg 108

Qinghua daxue tushuguan (China) *Tel:* (010) 62594591 *Fax:* (010) 6256278, pg 1457

Quaderns Crema SA (Spain) *Tel:* (093) 4144906 *Fax:* (093) 4147107 *E-mail:* qcrema@quadernscrema.com *Web Site:* www.quadernscrema.com, pg 588

Quaid-i-Azam University Department of Biological Sciences (Pakistan) *Tel:* (051) 218911, pg 508

Quaker Home Service (United Kingdom) *Tel:* (020) 7663 1030 *Fax:* (020) 7663 1001 *E-mail:* bookshop@quaker.org.uk *Web Site:* www.quaker.org.uk, pg 731

Quakers Hill Press (Australia) *Tel:* (02) 9626 6112 *Fax:* (02) 6269846 *E-mail:* dayp@mpx.com.au, pg 39

Qualitymark Editora Ltda (Brazil) *Tel:* (021) 3860-8422 *Fax:* (021) 3860-8424 *E-mail:* quality@unisys.com.br *Web Site:* www.qualitymark.com.br/, pg 90

Qualum Publishing (United Kingdom) *Tel:* (020) 7431 7171 *Fax:* (020) 7681 1316 *E-mail:* info@qualum.com *Web Site:* www.qualum.com, pg 731

Quantum Colorgraphics (United States) *Tel:* 873-783-0462 *Fax:* 973-783-0637 *Web Site:* www.quantumcolor.com, pg 1166

Quartet Books Ltd (United Kingdom) *Tel:* (020) 7636 3992 *Fax:* (020) 7637 1866 *E-mail:* quartetbooks@easynet.co.uk, pg 731

Quarto Publishing plc (United Kingdom) *Tel:* (020) 7700 6700 *Fax:* (020) 7700 4191; (020) 7700 0077 *E-mail:* quarto@quarto.com *Web Site:* www.quarto.com, pg 731

Quartz Editions (United Kingdom) *Tel:* (020) 8951 5656 *Fax:* (020) 8381 2588 *E-mail:* quartzeditions@btconnect.com, pg 732

Edizioni Quasar di Severino Tognon SRL (Italy) *Tel:* (06) 84241993 *Fax:* (06) 85833591 *E-mail:* qn@edizioniquasar.it *Web Site:* www.edizioniquasar.it, pg 404

Quatro Elementos Editores (Portugal) *Tel:* (021) 703695, pg 529

Edizioni Quattroventi SNC (Italy) *Tel:* (0722) 2588 *Fax:* (0722) 320998 *E-mail:* quattroventi@info-net.it, pg 404

Queen Anne Press (United Kingdom) *Tel:* (01582) 715866 *Fax:* (01582) 715866 *E-mail:* queenanne@lenqap.demon.co.uk, pg 732

Queen Victoria Museum & Art Gallery Publications (Australia) *Tel:* (03) 6323 3777 *Fax:* (03) 6323 3776 *E-mail:* library@qvmag.tas.gov.au *Web Site:* www.qvmag.tas.gov.au, pg 39

Queensland Art Gallery (Australia) *Tel:* (07) 3840 7333; (07) 3840 7303 *Fax:* (07) 3844 8865; (07) 3840 7350 *E-mail:* gallery@qag.qld.gov.au *Web Site:* www.gag.qld.gov.au, pg 39

Queensway Bookshop and Stores Ltd (Ghana) *Tel:* (021) 62707, pg 1285

Editorial Quehacer Politico SA (Mexico) *Tel:* (05) 5414245 *Fax:* (05) 5384855, pg 466

Queillerie Publishers (South Africa) *Tel:* (021) 4063326 *Fax:* (021) 4063111 *E-mail:* queiller@nbh.naspers.co.za, pg 558

Quell Verlag (Germany) *Tel:* (0711) 601000 *Fax:* (0711) 6010076, pg 276

Quelle Press (Germany) *Tel:* (07664) 7016 *Fax:* (07664) 60979 *E-mail:* qu.pre.frei@lycosmail.com, pg 1112

Quelle und Meyer Verlag GmbH & Co (Germany) *Tel:* (06766) 903140 *Fax:* (06766) 903341 *E-mail:* vertrieb@quelle-meyer.de *Web Site:* www.quelle-meyer.de, pg 276

Quellen-Verlag (Switzerland) *Tel:* (071) 227 47 77 *Fax:* (071) 227 47 58, pg 1313

Quentin Books Ltd (United Kingdom) *Tel:* (01206) 825433 *Fax:* (01206) 822990, pg 732

Em Querido's Uitgeverij BV (Netherlands) *Tel:* (020) 5511262 *Fax:* (020) 6203509, pg 483

Editrice Queriniana (Italy) *Tel:* (030) 2306925 *Fax:* (030) 2306932 *E-mail:* direzione@queriniana.it, pg 404

Querverlag GmbH (Germany) *Tel:* (030) 78 70 23 39; (030) 78702340 *Fax:* (030) 788 49 50 *E-mail:* mail@querverlag.de *Web Site:* www.querverlag.de, pg 276

Quesire (Italy) *Tel:* (06) 3208732 *Fax:* (06) 3208628, pg 404

Quest-Meridien Ltd (United Kingdom) *Tel:* (0802) 470283 *Fax:* (01732) 770620, pg 1121

Quetzal Editores (Portugal) *Tel:* (021) 3426172 *Fax:* (021) 3426173 *E-mail:* quetzal@ip.pt, pg 529

Quetzal-Domingo Cortizo (Argentina) *Tel:* (011) 4641-5639 *E-mail:* profika@ciudad.com.ar, pg 8

Quick Service Books Ltd (Ghana) *Tel:* (021) 224236, pg 308

Quid Juris - Sociedade editora (Portugal) *Tel:* (021) 651946 *Fax:* (021) 3875538 *E-mail:* quidjuris@mail.telepac.pt, pg 529

Quiller Publishing Ltd (United Kingdom) *Tel:* (01939) 261616 *Fax:* (01939) 261606 *E-mail:* info@quillerbooks.com, pg 732

Quimera Editores (Portugal) *Tel:* (021) 8472577 *Fax:* (021) 3431180, pg 529

Quintessence Publishing Co Ltd (United Kingdom) *Tel:* (0181) 9496087 *Fax:* (0181) 3361484 *E-mail:* quintessence@btinternet.com, pg 732

Quintessenz Verlags-GmbH (Germany) *Tel:* (030) 761805 *Fax:* (030) 76180680 *E-mail:* info@quintessenz.de *Web Site:* www.quintessenz.de, pg 276

Quintet Publishing Ltd (United Kingdom) *Tel:* (020) 7700 9000 *Fax:* (020) 7700 5785 *E-mail:* quintet@quarto.com, pg 732

Erik Qvist Bokhandel A/S (Norway) *Tel:* 22440326 *Fax:* 22558889 *E-mail:* qvist.libris@qvist.no, pg 1304

R & R Publications Marketing P/L (Australia) *Tel:* (03) 9381 2199 *Fax:* (03) 9381 2689, pg 39

R Oldenbourg Verlag GmbH (Germany) *Tel:* (089) 45 05 10 *Fax:* (089) 45051333 (Zeitschriften); (089) 4505200 (Schulbuch); (089) 4505333 (Fachbach), pg 276

R P L Books (New Zealand) *Tel:* (09) 4763510 *Fax:* (09) 4763590 *E-mail:* rplbooks@rplbooks.co.nz, pg 495

R V Reise- und Verkehrsverlag GmbH (Germany) *Tel:* (089) 431890; (030) 254098-0 (Berlin) *Fax:* (089) 43189458; (030) 2629115 (Berlin), pg 276

RA-MA, Libreria y Editorial Microinformatica (Spain) *Tel:* (091) 381 03 00 *Fax:* (091) 381 03 72 *E-mail:* editorial@ra-ma.com; info@ra-ma.com *Web Site:* www.ra-ma.com, pg 588

Dr Josef Raabe-Verlags GmbH (Germany) *Tel:* (0711) 629000 *Fax:* (0711) 6290010 *E-mail:* info@raabe.de *Web Site:* www.raabe.de, pg 276

Rabe Verlag AG Zuerich (Switzerland) *Tel:* (01) 2618540 *Fax:* (01) 2618541, pg 622

Raben och Sjoegren Bokfoerlag (Sweden) *Tel:* (08) 7698800 *Fax:* (08) 7698813 *E-mail:* raben-sjogren@raben.se *Web Site:* www.raben.se, pg 605

Raben Verlag von Wittern KG (Germany) *Tel:* (089) 3594879 *Fax:* (089) 3596622, pg 276

Raboni Editora Ltda (Brazil) *Tel:* (019) 32428433 *Fax:* (019) 32428505 *E-mail:* raboni@raboni.com.br *Web Site:* www.raboni.com.br, pg 90

RAC Publishing (United Kingdom) *Tel:* (020) 8686 0088 *Fax:* (020) 8688 2882, pg 732

RACC-62 (Spain) *Tel:* (093) 443 71 00 *Fax:* (093) 443 71 30 *E-mail:* correu@grup62.com *Web Site:* www.grup62.com, pg 588

Editions Racine (Belgium) *Tel:* (02) 646 44 44 *Fax:* (02) 646 55 70 *Web Site:* www.lannoo.be, pg 73

Radcliffe Medical Press Ltd (United Kingdom) *Tel:* (01235) 528820 *Fax:* (01235) 528830 *E-mail:* contact.us@radcliffemed.com *Web Site:* www.radcliffe-oxford.com, pg 732

Wydawnictwa Radia i Telewizji (Poland) *Tel:* (022) 412264, pg 519

Radiant Publishers (India) *Tel:* (011) 6482861 *Fax:* (011) 6479870 *E-mail:* rpblcsind@yahoo.com, pg 347

Radiating Books (Australia) *Tel:* (066) 536280 *Fax:* (066) 514970, pg 39

Radin-Repro I Roto (Croatia) *Tel:* (01) 3863111 *Fax:* (01) 3862673 *E-mail:* radin-repro-i-roto@zg.tel.hr, pg 1132

Izdatelstvo Radio i Svyaz (Russian Federation) *Tel:* (095) 2585351, pg 541

Radius-Verlag GmbH (Germany) *Tel:* (0711) 6076666; (0172) 7126573 *Fax:* (0711) 6075555, pg 276

Radnicka Stampa (Yugoslavia) *Tel:* (011) 3230-927; (011) 3233-038, pg 765

Raduga Publishers (Russian Federation) *Tel:* (095) 2450151 *Fax:* (095) 2416353 *E-mail:* vvm@aoraduga.msk.ru, pg 541

Robert Raeber, Buchhandlung am Schweizerhof (Switzerland) *Tel:* 512371, pg 622

Raethgloben Verlagsgesellschaft mbH (Germany) *Tel:* (0341) 4511212 *Fax:* (0341) 4427537 *E-mail:* raethgloben1917@gmx.de, pg 276

Edition Raetia Srl-GmbH (Italy) *Tel:* (0471) 976904 *Fax:* (0471) 976908 *E-mail:* info@raetia.com, pg 404

Rageot Editeur (France) *Tel:* (01) 45 48 07 31 *Fax:* (01) 42 22 68 01, pg 182

Ragged Bears Ltd (United Kingdom) *Tel:* (01264) 772269 *Fax:* (01264) 772391 *E-mail:* books@ragged-bears.co.uk *Web Site:* www.ragged-bears.co.uk, pg 732

Rahul Publishing House (India) *Tel:* (011) 7212195, pg 347

RALERI (Italy) *Tel:* (06) 3219414 *Fax:* (06) 534732; (06) 321914, pg 405

Rainbow Book Agencies Pty Ltd (Australia) *Tel:* (03) 9481 6611 *Fax:* (03) 9481 2371 *E-mail:* rba@rainbowbooks.com.au *Web Site:* rainbowbooks.com.au, pg 39

Rainbow Grafics Intl - Baronian Books SC (Belgium) *Tel:* (02) 7348114 *Fax:* (02) 7325764, pg 73

Rainbow Graphic & Printing Co Ltd (Hong Kong) *Tel:* 27523423 *Fax:* 28974890 *E-mail:* rgarts@netvigator.com, pg 1156

Raincloud Productions (Australia) *Tel:* (060) 2511765, pg 39

Rainforest Publishing (Australia) *Tel:* (02) 93313004 *Fax:* (02) 93805729 *E-mail:* rod.ritchie@sfine.arts.sa.edu.au, pg 39

Rajasthan Hindi Granth Academy (India) *Tel:* (0141) 61410, pg 347

Rajendra Publishing House Pvt Ltd (India) *Tel:* (022) 6300741; (022) 6300742; (022) 6301930 *Fax:* (022) 6301940; 6322146 *E-mail:* rajendrabook@hotmail.com, pg 347

Rajesh Publications (India) *Tel:* (011) 274550, pg 347

Rajkamal Prakashan Pvt Ltd (India) *Tel:* (011) 3274463 *Fax:* (011) 3278144, pg 347

Rajpal & Sons (India) *Tel:* (011) 223904; (011) 229174 *Fax:* (011) 2967791, pg 347

Rake Verlag GmbH (Germany) *Tel:* (0431) 6611515 *Fax:* (0431) 6611517 *E-mail:* info@rake.de *Web Site:* www.rake.de, pg 277

Rakennusalan Kustantajat Rak (Finland) *Tel:* (09) 5032541 *Fax:* (09) 5032542 *E-mail:* rak@sarmala.pp.fi, pg 144

Rakennustieto Oy - Building Information Ltd (Finland) *Tel:* (09) 5495570 *Fax:* (09) 54955390 *E-mail:* firstname.familyname@rakennustieto.fi *Web Site:* www.rakennustieto.fi, pg 144

Rakla (Bulgaria) *Tel:* (02) 580-569 *E-mail:* grigorit@yahoo.com, pg 97

RAM Editores (Colombia) *Tel:* (01) 2623067, pg 113

Ramakrishna Vedanta Centre (United Kingdom) *Tel:* (0162) 852-6464 *Web Site:* www.ramakrishna.org, pg 732

Dr Mohan Krischke Ramaswamy Edition RE (Germany) *Tel:* (0700) 724 836 638 *Fax:* (0700) 724 836 638 *E-mail:* edition.re@epost.de, pg 277

Ramboro Books Plc (United Kingdom) *Tel:* (020) 7700 7444 *Fax:* (020) 7700 4552 *E-mail:* enquiries@ramboro.co.uk *Web Site:* www.ramborobooks.com, pg 732

Ramboro Books Plc (United Kingdom) *Tel:* (020) 7700 7444 *Fax:* (020) 7700 4552 *E-mail:* enquiries@ramboro.co.uk, pg 1321

Rams Skull Press (Australia) *Tel:* (07) 4093 7474 *Fax:* (07) 4051 4484 *E-mail:* ramskull@tpg.com.au, pg 40

Editions Ramsay (France) *Tel:* (01) 53 10 02 80 *Fax:* (01) 53 10 02 88, pg 182

Ramsay Head Press (United Kingdom) *Tel:* (0131) 662 1915 *Fax:* (0131) 662 1915 *E-mail:* ramsayhead@btinternet.com, pg 732

Randall & Swift Ltd (United Kingdom) *Tel:* (0181) 5591522 *Fax:* (0181) 5591522, pg 1321

Ian Randle Publishers Ltd (Jamaica) *Tel:* (876) 978-0739; (876) 978-0745 *Fax:* (876) 978-1156 *E-mail:* irpl@colis.com *Web Site:* www.colis.com/irp, pg 413

Random House Australia (Australia) *Tel:* (02) 9954 9966 *Fax:* (02) 9954 4562; (02) 9954 9008 *E-mail:* randomhouse@randomhouse.com.au, pg 40

Random House UK Ltd (United Kingdom) *Tel:* (020) 7973 9000 *Fax:* (020) 7233 6125 *E-mail:* enquiries@randomhouse.co.uk *Web Site:* www.randomhouse.co.uk, pg 733

Rankin Publishers (Australia) *Tel:* (07) 3376 9115 *Fax:* (07) 3376 9360 *E-mail:* info@rankin.com.au *Web Site:* www.rankin.com.au, pg 40

Ransom Publishing Ltd (United Kingdom) *Tel:* (01491) 613 711 *Fax:* (01491) 613 733 *E-mail:* ransom@ransompublishing.co.uk *Web Site:* www.ransom.co.uk, pg 733

The Arthur Ransome Society Ltd (TARS) (United Kingdom) *Tel:* (01539) 722464 *E-mail:* tarsinfo@arthur-ransome.org *Web Site:* www.arthur-ransome.org/ar, pg 1371

RAO International Publishing Co (Romania) *Tel:* (01) 2241704; (01) 2241002 *Fax:* (01) 2228059, pg 535

RAO PUBLISHING GROUP INDUSTRY

RAO Publishing Group (Romania) *Tel:* (01) 2241704; (01) 2241002 *Fax:* (01) 2228059 *E-mail:* rao@can.ro *Web Site:* www.rao.inet.ro; www.rao.ro, pg 535

Raphael, Editions (Switzerland) *Tel:* (021) 9215230 *Fax:* (021) 9215237, pg 622

Rapra Technology Ltd (United Kingdom) *Tel:* (01939) 250383 *Fax:* (01939) 251118 *E-mail:* publications@rapra.net *Web Site:* www.rapra.net, pg 733

Rara-lst Editoriale di Bibliofilia e Reprints (Italy) *Tel:* (02) 4983264 *Fax:* (02) 4814676, pg 405

Margi Rastai Publishers (Lithuania) *Tel:* (02) 429526; (02) 427909; (02) 429527; (02) 426705 *Fax:* (02) 426705, pg 446

Rastogi Publications (India) *Tel:* (0121) 24142; (0121) 24688 *Fax:* (0121) 521545, pg 347

F J Ratchford Ltd (United Kingdom) *Tel:* (0161) 4808484 *Fax:* (0161) 4803679, pg 1141

Rationalisierungs-Kuratorium der Deutschen Wirtschaft eV (RKW) (Germany) *Tel:* (0211) 680010 *Fax:* (0211) 68001 68; (0211) 68001 69 *E-mail:* info@rkw-nrw.de *Web Site:* www.rkw-nrw.de, pg 277

Rationalist Press Association (United Kingdom) *Tel:* (020) 7430 1371 *Fax:* (020) 7430 1271 *E-mail:* info@rationalist.org.uk *Web Site:* www.rationalist.org.uk, pg 733

Ratna Book Distributors (Pvt) Ltd (Nepal) *Tel:* (01) 223026 *E-mail:* rpb@wlink.com.np, pg 1300

Walter Rau Verlag GmbH & Co KG (Germany) *Tel:* (0211) 92 80 40 *Fax:* (0211) 28 38 27 *Web Site:* www.rau.de, pg 277

Werner Rau Verlag (Germany) *Tel:* (0711) 687 21 43 *Fax:* (0711) 68 22 47 *E-mail:* info@rau-verlag.de *Web Site:* www.rau-verlag.de, pg 277

Rauhreif Verlag (Switzerland) *Tel:* (061) 8515363, pg 622

Gerhard Rautenberg Druckerei und Verlag GmbH & Co KG (Germany) *Tel:* (0931) 385235 *Fax:* (0931) 385305 *E-mail:* info@verlagshaus.com *Web Site:* www.verlagshaus.com, pg 277

Rav Kook Institute (Israel) *Tel:* (02) 6526231 *Fax:* (02) 6526968, pg 371, 1292

Ravan Press (Pty) Ltd (South Africa) *Tel:* (011) 7897636 *Fax:* (011) 7897653, pg 558

Raven Arts Press (Ireland), pg 363

Ravensburger Buchverlag Otto Maier GmbH (Germany) *Tel:* (0751) 86 0 *Fax:* (0751) 861155; (0751) 861289; (0751) 86 13 11 *E-mail:* buchverlag@ravensburger.de *Web Site:* www.ravensburger.de, pg 277

Ravenstein Verlag GmbH (Germany) *Tel:* (06196) 609630 *Fax:* (06196) 63619 *E-mail:* g.koenig@ravenstein-verlag.de, pg 277

Ravette Publishing Ltd (United Kingdom) *Tel:* (01403) 711443 *Fax:* (01403) 711554 *E-mail:* ravettepub@aol.com, pg 733

Rawlhouse Publishing (Australia) *Tel:* (08) 9321 8951 *Fax:* (08) 9481 1914 *E-mail:* info@rawlhouse.com *Web Site:* www.rawlinsons.com, pg 40

RCS Libri SpA (Italy) *Tel:* (02) 50951 *Fax:* (02) 5065361, pg 405

RCS Rizzoli Libri SpA (Italy) *Tel:* (02) 50951 *Fax:* (02) 5065361, pg 405, 1113

RDC Agencia Literaria (Spain) *Tel:* (091) 3085585 *Fax:* (091) 3085600, pg 1116

Reach Publications (New Zealand) *Tel:* 8176893 *E-mail:* giftedednz@xtra.co.nz, pg 495

Read-a-Book Club (Zambia) *Tel:* (01) 222324; (01) 236629 *Fax:* (01) 225073, pg 1234

Oficyna Wydawnicza Read Me (Poland) *Tel:* (022) 870624 *Fax:* (022) 6771425 *E-mail:* readme@rm.com.pl *Web Site:* www.rm.com.pl, pg 519

Read Well Publishers (South Africa) *Tel:* (0152) 2952193 *Fax:* (0152) 2952194, pg 559

Reader's Digest (Australia) Pty Ltd (Australia) *Tel:* (02) 96906935 *Fax:* (02) 96906390, pg 40

Readers Club of Svoboda (Czech Republic) *Tel:* (02) 24811549; (02) 24225143 *Fax:* (02) 24226026, pg 1227

Reader's Digest AB (Sweden) *Tel:* (08) 6334800 *Fax:* (08) 7528701 *E-mail:* kundtjanst@readersdigest.se *Web Site:* www.readersdigest.se, pg 1232

The Reader's Digest Association Ltd (United Kingdom) *Tel:* (020) 7715 8000 *Fax:* (020) 7715 8181 *Web Site:* www.readersdigest.co.uk, pg 733

Reader's Digest Children's Books (United Kingdom) *Tel:* (01225) 312200 *Fax:* (01225) 460942, pg 733

Reader's Digest SA (Belgium) *Tel:* (02) 5268111 *Fax:* (02) 5268112, pg 73

Reader's Digest Southern Africa (South Africa) *Tel:* (021) 4405145 *Fax:* (021) 4405401 *Web Site:* www.readersdigest.co.za, pg 559

Readers Union (United Kingdom) *Tel:* (020) 7629 8144 *Fax:* (020) 7499 9751, pg 1233

Reading & Language Information Centre (United Kingdom) *Tel:* (0118) 931 8820 *Fax:* (0118) 931 6801 *E-mail:* reading-centre@reading.ac.uk *Web Site:* www.ralic.rdg.ac.uk, pg 733

Readit Books (United Republic of Tanzania) *Tel:* (022) 2184077 *Fax:* (022) 2181077 *E-mail:* readitbooks@yahoo.com, pg 634, 1314

Ready-Ed Publications (Australia) *Tel:* (08) 9349 6111 *Fax:* (08) 9349 7222 *E-mail:* info@readyed.com.au, pg 40

Ready Press (Philippines) *Tel:* (02) 6471163; (02) 6471227 *Fax:* (02) 6471158 *E-mail:* casper@pworld.net.ph, pg 1138

Reaktion Books Ltd (United Kingdom) *Tel:* (020) 7404 9930 *Fax:* (020) 7404 9931 *E-mail:* info@reaktionbooks.co.uk *Web Site:* www.reaktionbooks.co.uk, pg 733

Real Academia Sevillana de Buenas Letras (Spain) *Tel:* (05) 4225200, pg 1368

The Real Estate Institute of Australia (Australia) *Tel:* (02) 6282 4277 *Fax:* (02 6285 2444 *E-mail:* reia@reiaustralia.com.au *Web Site:* www.reiaustralia.com.au, pg 40

Real Ireland Design (Ireland) *Tel:* (01) 2860799 *Fax:* (01) 2829962 *E-mail:* realirel@indigo.ie *Web Site:* www.realireland.ie/mainfrm.html, pg 363

Realisations pour l'Enseignement Multilingue International (REMI) (France) *Tel:* (01) 44 37 00 80 *Fax:* (01) 45 79 06 66, pg 182

Realitatea Casa de Edituri Productie Audio-Video Film (Romania) *Tel:* (01) 6117105; (01) 6517105; (01) 6332468; (01) 6143793 *Fax:* (01) 2105411 *E-mail:* leu@dnt.ro, pg 535

Realizacoes Artis (Portugal) *Tel:* (01) 363796 *Fax:* (01) 9170130, pg 529

Rebel Publishing House Pvt Ltd (India) *Tel:* (0212) 628562 *Fax:* (0212) 624181, pg 347

Rebo Productions BV (Netherlands) *Tel:* (0252) 419105 *Fax:* (0252) 410231, pg 483

Recallmed Oy (Finland) *Tel:* (09) 8797177 *Fax:* (09) 8797088, pg 144

Verlag fuer Recht und Gesellschaft AG (Switzerland) *Tel:* (061) 231775 *Fax:* (061) 7262627 *E-mail:* info@vgr-verlag.com *Web Site:* www.vgr-verlag.ch, pg 622

Verlag Recht und Wirtschaft GmbH (Germany) *Tel:* (06221) 906 0 *Fax:* (06221) 906 259 *E-mail:* verlag@ruw.de *Web Site:* www.ruw-ruw.de, pg 277

Reclam Verlag Leipzig (Germany) *Tel:* (0341) 997170 *Fax:* (0341) 9971730 *E-mail:* info@reclam-leipzig.de *Web Site:* www.reclam.de, pg 277

RECOM Verlag (Switzerland) *Tel:* (061) 253390; (061) 251926; (061) 438760 *Fax:* (061) 2616213, pg 622

Distribuidora Record de Servicos de Imprensa SA (Brazil) *Tel:* (021) 2585-2000 *Fax:* (021) 2585-2085 *E-mail:* record@record.com.br *Web Site:* www.record.com.br, pg 90

Red Bridge International (United Kingdom) *Tel:* (01204) 522254 *Fax:* (01204) 384754 *Web Site:* www.redbridge.co.uk, pg 1214

Red Editorial Iberoamericana Mexico SA de CV (Mexico) *Tel:* (05) 5456860; (05) 5456861 *Fax:* (05) 5619122, pg 466

The Red House Books Ltd (United Kingdom) *Tel:* (01993) 774171; (01993) 771144 *Fax:* (01993) 776813, pg 1234

Red Internacional Del Libro (Chile) *Tel:* (02) 2238100 *Fax:* (02) 2254269 *E-mail:* ril@rileditores.com *Web Site:* www.rileditores.com, pg 101

Red/Studio Redazionale SpA (Italy) *Tel:* (031) 279146 *Fax:* (031) 300135, pg 405

Redcliffe Press Ltd (United Kingdom) *Tel:* (0117) 9737207 *Fax:* (0117) 9238991, pg 734

Rede Das Artes (Boccato Editores Collector's) (Brazil) *Tel:* (011) 246-5556 *Fax:* (011) 246-5556, pg 90

Redhouse Bookstore (Turkey) *Tel:* (01) 5221498 *Fax:* (01) 5190883, pg 1315

Redhouse Press (Turkey) *Tel:* (0212) 5221498 *Fax:* (0212) 5190883, pg 641

Redstone Press (United Kingdom) *Tel:* (020) 7352 1594 *Fax:* (020) 7352 8749 *E-mail:* redstone.press@virgin.net *Web Site:* www.redstonepress.co.uk, pg 734

Redwood Books Ltd (United Kingdom) *Tel:* (01225) 769979 *Fax:* (01225) 769050, pg 1141

Redwood Books Ltd (United Kingdom) *Tel:* (01225) 769979 *Fax:* (01225) 769050 *E-mail:* enquiries@redwood-books.co.uk *Web Site:* www.cpi-group.net, pg 1162

Redwood Books Ltd (United Kingdom) *Tel:* (01225) 769979 *Fax:* (01225) 769050 *E-mail:* enquiries@redwood-books.co.uk, pg 1204, 1214

Reed Business Information (United Kingdom) *Tel:* (01342) 326972 *Fax:* (01342) 335960 *E-mail:* rbi.subscriptions@qss-uk.com (subscription queries) *Web Site:* www.reedbusiness.com, pg 734

Reed Educational & Professional Publishing (United Kingdom) *Tel:* (01865) 311366 *Fax:* (01865) 314641 *E-mail:* reededucational@repp.co.uk *Web Site:* www.repp.com, pg 734

Reed Educational Publishing Australia (Australia) *Tel:* (03) 9245 7188 *Fax:* (03) 9245 7265 *E-mail:* admin@reededucation.com.au; customerservice@reededucation.com.au *Web Site:* www.reededucation.com.au, pg 40

Reed Elsevier Deutschland GmbH (Germany) *Tel:* (089) 898170 *Fax:* (089) 85817-102, pg 277

Reed Elsevier Group plc (United Kingdom) *Tel:* (020) 7222 8420 *Fax:* (020) 7227 5799 *Web Site:* www.reed-elsevier.com, pg 734

Reed Elsevier Nederland BV (Netherlands) *Tel:* (020) 515 9111 *Fax:* (020) 618 0325 *Web Site:* www.elsevier.com, pg 483

Reed Elsevier, South East Asia (Singapore) *Tel:* 6789 9900 *Fax:* 6789 9966, pg 547

Reed Publishing (NZ) Ltd (New Zealand) *Tel:* (09) 480 4950; (09) 480 4988 (customer service) *Fax:* (09) 470 4999; (09) 480 4970 (customer service) *E-mail:* lrobertson@reed.co.nz (customer service) *Web Site:* www.reed.co.nz, pg 495

William Reed Directories (United Kingdom) *Tel:* (01293) 610 400 *Fax:* (01293) 610 322 *E-mail:* directories@william-reed.co.uk *Web Site:* www.william-reed.co.uk, pg 734

References cf (France) *Tel:* (04) 75-27-52-59 *Fax:* (04) 75275259 *E-mail:* refercf@incident.net *Web Site:* www.incident.net/refercf, pg 182

Regalia 6 Publishing House (Bulgaria) *Tel:* (02) 754111 *Fax:* (02) 566573 *E-mail:* vpruu@dir.bg, pg 97

Regenbogen Verlag (Switzerland) *Tel:* (01) 2013676 *Fax:* (01) 2013703, pg 622

Regency House Publishing Ltd (United Kingdom) *Tel:* (01992) 479988 *Fax:* (01992) 479966 *E-mail:* regencyhouse@btinternet.com, pg 734

Regency Press CP Ltd (United Kingdom) *Tel:* (020) 7404 4882 *Fax:* (020) 7404 4885 *E-mail:* info@regency.org *Web Site:* www.regency.org, pg 734

Regency Publications (India) *Tel:* (011) 5712539; (011) 5740038 *Fax:* (011) 5783571 *E-mail:* regency@satyam.net.in, pg 347

Regency Publishing (Australia) *Tel:* (08) 8348 4599 *Fax:* (08) 8348 4400 *E-mail:* julie.fuss@regency.tafe.sa.edu.au *Web Site:* www.tafe.sa-edu.au/institutes/regency/regency-publishing/main.htm, pg 40

REGENSBERG Druck & Verlag GmbH & Co (Germany) *Tel:* (0251) 749800 *Fax:* (0251) 7498040, pg 277

Universitatsbibliothek Regensburg (Germany) *Tel:* (0941) 943390003 *Fax:* (0941) 9433285, pg 1468

Regent Publishing Services (United States) *Tel:* 314-631-7581 *Fax:* 314-638-5113 *E-mail:* regentstl@aol.com, pg 1146, 1166, 1208, 1216, 1225

Editora Regional de Murcia - ERM (Spain) *Tel:* (068) 280246 *Fax:* (068) 298293 *E-mail:* editora.regional@carm.es *Web Site:* www.carm.es, pg 588

Regional ISBN Agency (CARICOM) (Guyana) *Tel:* (02) 69289 *Fax:* (02) 67816; (02) 66091; (02) 57341; (02) 58039 *E-mail:* carisec1@caricom.org; carisec2@caricom.org; carisec3@caricom.og *Web Site:* www.caricom.org, pg 1247

Regional ISBN Centre The ISBN Officer (Fiji) *Tel:* 313900 (ext 2375) *Fax:* 300830 *E-mail:* mamtora_j@usp.ac.fj *Web Site:* www.usp.ac.fj/~library, pg 1242

Verlag fur Regionalgeschichte (Germany) *Tel:* (05209) 6714; (05209) 980266 *Fax:* (05209) 6519; (05209) 980277 *E-mail:* regionalgeschichte@t-online.de *Web Site:* www.regionalgeschichte.de, pg 277

Regione Autonoma della Sardegna - Biblioteca Regionale (Italy) *Tel:* (070) 6065031 *Fax:* (070) 6065002, pg 405

Regura Verlag (Germany) *Tel:* (0711) 2269835 *Fax:* (0711) 2238829 *E-mail:* info@regura.de *Web Site:* www.regura.de, pg 277

Ediciones Rehue Ltda (Chile) *Tel:* (02) 6344653; (02) 6341804 *Fax:* (02) 6351096, pg 101

Reial Academia de Bones Lletres (Spain) *Tel:* (093) 310-2349 *Fax:* (093) 3102349, pg 1368

Konrad Reich Verlag GmbH (Germany) *Tel:* (0381) 693020; (0381) 4922603 *Fax:* (0381) 693021, pg 278

Reich Verlag AG (Switzerland) *Tel:* (041) 4103721 *Fax:* (041) 4103227, pg 622

Dr Ludwig Reichert Verlag (Germany) *Tel:* (0611) 461851 *Fax:* (0611) 468613 *E-mail:* reichert.verlag@t-online.de *Web Site:* www.reichert-verlag.de, pg 278

Reichl Verlag Der Leuchter (Germany) *Tel:* (06741) 1720 *Fax:* (06741) 1749, pg 278

Livraria Cientifica Ernesto Reichmann Ltda (Brazil) *Tel:* (011) 2551342 *Fax:* (011) 2557501 *E-mail:* rrr@lb.com, pg 1278

J R Reid Printing Group Ltd (United Kingdom) *Tel:* (01698) 826000 *Fax:* (01698) 824944 *E-mail:* clindsay@reid-print-group.co.uk *Web Site:* www.reid-print-group.co.uk, pg 1162, 1204

J R Reid Printing Group Ltd (United Kingdom) *Tel:* (01698) 826000 *Fax:* (01698) 824944 *E-mail:* info@reid-print-group.co.uk *Web Site:* www.reid-print-group.co.uk, pg 1215

Reimei-Shobo Co Ltd (Japan) *Tel:* (052) 9623045 *Fax:* (052) 9519065 *E-mail:* reimei@mui.biglobe.ne.jp *Web Site:* wwwl.biz.biglobe.ne.jp/~reimei/, pg 424

Dietrich Reimer Verlag GmbH (Germany) *Tel:* (030) 259 17 1570 *Fax:* (030) 259 17 1577 *E-mail:* vertrieb-kunstverlage@reimer-verlag.de, pg 278

Ernst Reinhardt GmbH & Co KG Verlag (Germany) *Tel:* (089) 17 80 16 0 *Fax:* (089) 17 80 16 30 *E-mail:* contact@reinhardt-verlag.de *Web Site:* www.reinhardt-verlag.de, pg 278

Verlag Friedrich Reinhardt AG (Switzerland) *Tel:* (061) 253390; (061) 438760 *Fax:* (061) 2646488, pg 622

E Reinhold Verlag (Germany) *Tel:* (03447) 311889 *Fax:* (03447) 375611 *E-mail:* erv@querstand.de *Web Site:* www.querstand.de, pg 278

Reinhold Schmidt Verlag (Austria) *Tel:* (02236) 72469 *Fax:* (02236) 73784, pg 57

Reise Know-How (Germany) *Tel:* (06872) 91737 *Fax:* (06872) 91738 *E-mail:* hoff-verlag@reise-know-how *Web Site:* www.reise-know-how.com, pg 278

Reise-Know-How Verlag-Daerr GmbH (Germany) *Tel:* (08065) 9172 *Fax:* (08065) 9173 *E-mail:* rkh.daerr@t-online.de *Web Site:* www.reise-know-how.de, pg 278

Reise Know-How Verlag Dr Hans-R Grundmann GmbH (Germany) *Tel:* (04488) 761994 *Fax:* (04488) 761030 *E-mail:* reisebuch@aol.net, pg 278

Reise Know-How Verlag Peter Rump GmbH (Germany) *Tel:* (0521) 946 490; (0521) 4329186 *Fax:* (0521) 441047 *E-mail:* info@reise-know-how.de *Web Site:* www.reise-know-how.de, pg 278

Reise Know-How Verlag Tondok (Germany) *Tel:* (089) 3514857 *Fax:* (089) 3518485 *E-mail:* rkh@tondok-verlag.de *Web Site:* www.tondok-verlag.de, pg 278

Verlagsgruppe Reise-Know-How (Germany) *Tel:* (521) 946490 *Fax:* (521) 441047 *E-mail:* info@reise-know-how.de *Web Site:* www.reise-know-how.de, pg 278

Peter Meyer Reisefuhrer (Germany) *Tel:* (069) 49 44 49 *Fax:* (069) 44 51 35 *E-mail:* info@PeterMeyerVerlag.de *Web Site:* www.meyer-reisefuehrer.de, pg 278

ReiseHandbuch Stein KG & Outdoor Handbuch Stein KG (Germany) *Tel:* (04671) 93 13 14 *Fax:* (04671) 93 13 15 *E-mail:* outdoor@tng.de *Web Site:* outdoor.tng.de, pg 279

C A Reitzel A/S (Denmark) *Tel:* 33122400 *Fax:* 33140270 *E-mail:* info@careitzel.dk *Web Site:* www.careitzel.dk, pg 134

C A Reitzel A/S (Denmark) *Tel:* 33140451 *Fax:* 33140270, pg 1281

Hans Reitzel Publishers Ltd (Denmark) *Tel:* 33382800 *Fax:* 33382808 *E-mail:* hrf@hansreitzel.dk *Web Site:* www.hansreitzel.dk, pg 134

Rekha Prakashan (India) *Tel:* (011) 3279907; (011) 3279904 *Fax:* (011) 6321783 *E-mail:* rprakashan@satyam.net.in, pg 347

RELATE (United Kingdom) *Tel:* (01788) 573241 *Fax:* (01788) 535007 *Web Site:* www.relate.org.uk, pg 734

Relay Books (Ireland) *Tel:* (010) 6731734 *Fax:* (010) 6731734 *E-mail:* relaybooks@eiscom.net, pg 363

Reliance Publishing House (India) *Tel:* (011) 5852605; (011) 5772768; (011) 5737377 *Fax:* (011) 5786769 *E-mail:* reliance@indiatimes.com, pg 347

Religious Life Review Book Club (Ireland) *Tel:* (01) 8721611 *Fax:* (01) 8731760, pg 1229

Remaja Rosdakarya CV (Indonesia) *Tel:* (022) 5225810 *Fax:* (022) 58226, pg 357

Remzi Kitabevi (Turkey) *Tel:* (0212) 5220583; (0212) 5190981 *Fax:* (0212) 5229055 *E-mail:* post@remzi.com.tr *Web Site:* www.remzi.com.tr, pg 641

La Renaissance du Livre (Belgium) *Tel:* (069) 89.15.55 *Fax:* (069) 89.15.50 *Web Site:* www.larenaissancedulivre.com, pg 73

Gaston Renard Fine & Rare Books (Australia) *Tel:* (39) 4595040 *Fax:* (39) 4596787 *E-mail:* booksaus@ozemail.com.au, pg 1273

Les Editions Albert Rene (France) *Tel:* (01) 45 00 41 41 *Fax:* (01) 40 67 95 12 *E-mail:* rene.cominfo@editions-albert-rene.com *Web Site:* www.editions-albert-rene.com, pg 182

Library of the Renmin University of China (China) *Tel:* (010) 62511371; (010) 62511014 *Fax:* (010) 62515332; (010) 62566374, pg 1457

Rentrop & Straton Verlagsgruppe und Wirtschaftsconsulting (Romania) *Tel:* (01) 6142515 *Fax:* (01) 3112635, pg 535

Verlag Norman Rentrop (Germany) *Tel:* (0228) 36 88 40 *Fax:* (0228) 36 58 75 *E-mail:* tt@rentrop.com; NR@rentrop.com *Web Site:* www.normanrentrop.de, pg 279

Editora Replicacao Lda (Portugal) *Tel:* (021) 3977058 *Fax:* (021) 3969808 *E-mail:* replic@mail.telepac.pt, pg 529

Reporter (Bulgaria) *Tel:* (02) 760834 *Fax:* (02) 718377 *E-mail:* reporter@techno-link.com, pg 97

Representative Church Body Library (Ireland) *Tel:* (01) 4923979 *Fax:* (01) 4924770 *E-mail:* library@ireland.anglican.org *Web Site:* www.ireland.anglican.org/library/library.html, pg 1476

Republicki Zavod za Unapredivanje Vaspitanja i Obrazovanja (Yugoslavia) *Tel:* (011) 659322, pg 765

Res Polona (Poland) *Tel:* (042) 6363634; (042) 6374587; (042) 6374607 *Fax:* (042) 6373010, pg 519

Resch Verlag (Austria) *Tel:* (089) 8 54 65-0 *Fax:* (089) 54 65-11 *E-mail:* info@resch-verlag.com *Web Site:* www.resch-verlag.com, pg 57

Research Centre for Translation (Hong Kong) *Tel:* 26097399 *E-mail:* renditions@cuhk.edu.hk, pg 321

Research Signpost (India) *Tel:* (0471) 452918 *Fax:* (0471) 573051 *E-mail:* ggcom@vsnl.com *Web Site:* www.researchsignpost.com, pg 348

Research Society of Pakistan (Pakistan) *Tel:* (042) 322542, pg 508

Research Studies Press Ltd (RSP) (United Kingdom) *Tel:* (01462) 895060 *Fax:* (01462) 892546 *E-mail:* rsp@rspltd.demon.co.uk *Web Site:* www.research-studies-press.co.uk, pg 734

Researchco Reprints (India) *Tel:* (011) 6781565; (011) 5781566; (011) 5781567 *Fax:* (011) 7276256, pg 348

Editora Resenha Tributaria Ltda (Brazil) *Tel:* (011) 5772822 *Fax:* (011) 5772526, pg 90

Residenz Verlag GmbH (Austria) *Tel:* (0662) 641986; (0662) 641987; (0662) 642571 *Fax:* (0662) 643548 *E-mail:* info@residenzverlag.at *Web Site:* www.residenzverlag.at, pg 58

Resource Books Ltd (New Zealand) *Tel:* (09) 5758030 *Fax:* (09) 5758055 *E-mail:* sales@resourcebooks.co.nz *Web Site:* www.resourcebooks.co.nz, pg 495

Respublica Verlag (Germany) *Tel:* (02241) 62925; (02241) 64039 *Fax:* (02241) 53891, pg 279

Respublika (Russian Federation) *Tel:* (095) 2517956 *Fax:* (095) 2002254, pg 541

Respublikanskij izdatei skij Kabinet (Kazakstan) *Tel:* (03272) 610309 *Fax:* (03272) 631207, pg 430

Retail Entertainment Data Publishing Ltd (United Kingdom) *Tel:* (020) 7566 8216 *Fax:* (020) 7566 8259 (Inquiry); (020) 7566 8316 (Editorial) *E-mail:* info@redpublishing.co.uk *Web Site:* www.redpublishing.co.uk, pg 735

Luis A Retta Libros (Uruguay) *Tel:* (02) 400-0766 *Fax:* (02) 409-0174 *E-mail:* rettalib@chasque.apc.org, pg 761

Editorial Reus SA (Spain) *Tel:* (091) 2213619; (091) 2223054 *Fax:* (091) 5312408, pg 588

Editora Revan Ltda (Brazil) *Tel:* (021) 25027495 *Fax:* (021) 2736873 *E-mail:* editor@revan.com.br *Web Site:* www.revan.com.br, pg 90

Ediciones Luis Revenga (Spain) *Tel:* (091) 2434664 *Fax:* (091) 5434706 *E-mail:* cuadcerv@elr.es *Web Site:* www.eunet.es/InterStand/CuadernoseCervantes, pg 588

Reverdito Edizioni (Italy) *Tel:* (0461) 249995 *Fax:* (0461) 245281, pg 405

Editorial Reverte SA (Spain) *Tel:* (093) 419 33 36; (093) 419 32 76 *Fax:* (093) 419 51 89 *E-mail:* istz0125@tsai.es; prom.reverte@teleline.es *Web Site:* www.ludosoft.net/reverte/present.htm, pg 588

Editorial Reverte Venezolana SA (Venezuela) *Tel:* (02) 5726670; (02) 5724468 *Fax:* (02) 5722598; (02) 5724468; (02) 5726670, pg 763

Review Publishing Co Ltd (Hong Kong) *Tel:* 28382300 *Fax:* 25031526 *Web Site:* www.feer.com, pg 1135

Livraria Editora Revinter Ltda (Brazil) *Tel:* (021) 563-9700 *Fax:* (021) 502-6830 *E-mail:* livraria@revinter.com.br *Web Site:* www.revinter.com.br/, pg 90

Editorial Revista Agustiniana (Spain) *Tel:* (091) 550-5000 *Fax:* (091) 550-5225 *E-mail:* revista@agustiniana.com *Web Site:* www.agustiniana.com, pg 589

Revista Penteados (Portugal) *Tel:* (021) 862963; (021) 8813511 *Fax:* (021) 870972, pg 529

Editions Revue EPS (France) *Tel:* (01) 41 74 82 82 *Fax:* (01) 43 98 37 38 *E-mail:* revue@revue-eps.com *Web Site:* www.revue-eps.com, pg 183

Revue Espaces et Societes (France) *Tel:* (0551) 60 35 70 *Fax:* (0551) 60 49 58 *E-mail:* jjaquin@espacesetsocietes.com *Web Site:* www.espacesetsocietes.com, pg 183

Revue Noire (France) *Tel:* (01) 43 20 92 00 *Fax:* (01) 43 22 92 60 *E-mail:* redaction@revuenoire.com *Web Site:* www.revuenoire.com, pg 183

Rex Book Store Inc (Philippines) *Tel:* (02) 7414956, pg 1306

Rex Bookstores & Publishers (Philippines) *Tel:* (02) 712 4101 (ext 128) *Fax:* (02) 740 2702 *E-mail:* rex@usinc.net, pg 514

Rex Verlag (Switzerland) *Tel:* 514151 *Fax:* 4194711, pg 623

Libreria Universitaria Jose T Reyes (Honduras) *Tel:* 228961 *Fax:* 370575, pg 1287

Reyes Publishing (Philippines) *Tel:* (02) 721827 *Fax:* (02) 7218782 *E-mail:* reyesbub@skyinet.net, pg 1138, 1158

Reyes Publishing, Inc (Philippines) *Tel:* (02) 721-7492; (02) 722-1827; (02) 726-4274; (02) 721-8792 *Fax:* (02) 721-8782 *E-mail:* reyespub@skyinet.net, pg 1306

Borgarbokasafn Reykjavikur (Iceland) *Tel:* 5631717 *Fax:* 5631705 *E-mail:* borgarbokasafn@skyrr.is *Web Site:* www.borgarbokasafn.is, pg 1473

Verlagsgruppe Rhein Main GmbH & Co KG (Germany) *Tel:* (06131) 48-30 *Web Site:* www.main-rheiner.de, pg 279

Rhein-Trio, Edition/Editions du Fou (Switzerland), pg 623

Rheinische Landesbibliothek Koblenz (Germany) *Tel:* (0261) 9150040 *Fax:* (0261) 9150091 *E-mail:* info@rlb.de *Web Site:* www.rlb.de, pg 1468

Verlag Rheinischer Merkur GmbH (Germany) *Tel:* (0228) 88 42 22; (0228) 88 42 25 *Fax:* (0228) 88 41 70 *E-mail:* abo@merkur.de *Web Site:* www.merkur.de, pg 279

RVBG Rheinland-Verlag-und Betriebsgesellschaft des Landschaftsverbandes Rheinland mbH (Germany) *Tel:* (02234) 805 265 *Fax:* (02234) 82503, pg 279

Rheintal Handelsgesellschaft Anstalt (Liechtenstein) *Tel:* (075) 3921882; (01) 8442786 *Fax:* (075) 3923646; (01) 8442806 *E-mail:* vetsch.p@bluewin.ch, pg 445

RHJ Livros Ltda (Brazil) *Tel:* (031) 1334-1566 *Fax:* (031) 332-5823 *E-mail:* rhjbooks@terra.com.br, pg 90

Alice J M Rhodd (Jamaica), pg 413

Rhodes University Library (South Africa) *Tel:* (046) 603-8436 *Fax:* (046) 622-3487 *E-mail:* library@ru.ac.za *Web Site:* www.rhodes.ac.za/library/, pg 1498

Rhodos, International Science & Art Publishers (Denmark) *Tel:* 32543020 *Fax:* 32543022 *E-mail:* rhodos@rhodos.com *Web Site:* www.rhodos.dk, pg 135

Rhombus Verlag (Austria) *Tel:* (01) 526 61 52 *Fax:* (01) 522 87 18, pg 58

Ediciones Rialp SA (Spain) *Tel:* (091) 3260504 *Fax:* (091) 3261321 *E-mail:* ediciones@rialp.com *Web Site:* www.rialp.com/, pg 589

RIBA Publications (United Kingdom) *Tel:* (020) 7251 0791 *Fax:* (020) 7608 2375 *Web Site:* www.ribabookshop.com, pg 735

RIC Publications Pty Ltd (Australia) *Tel:* (09) 9240 1511 *Fax:* (09) 9240 1513 *E-mail:* mail@ricgroup.com.au *Web Site:* www.ricgroup.com.au, pg 40

Biblioteca Riccardiana (Italy) *Tel:* (055) 212586 *Fax:* (055) 211379, pg 1478

Franco Maria Ricci Editore (FMR) (Italy) *Tel:* (02) 414101 *Fax:* (02) 48301488 *E-mail:* ricci@fmrmagazine.it *Web Site:* www.francomariaricci.it, pg 405

Riccardo Ricciardi Editore SpA (Italy) *Tel:* 02 0275421, pg 405

Richardi Helmut Verlag GmbH (Germany) *Tel:* (069) 9708330 *Fax:* (069) 7078400 *E-mail:* kreditwesen@t-online.de, pg 279

The Richmond Publishing Co Ltd (United Kingdom) *Tel:* (01753) 643104 *Fax:* (01753) 646553 *E-mail:* rpc@richmond.co.uk, pg 735, 1321

Richters Bokklubb (Sweden) *Tel:* (040) 380600 *Fax:* (040) 933708, pg 1232

Richters Egmont (Sweden) *Tel:* (040) 380600 *Fax:* (040) 933708, pg 605

Richters Ungdomsbokklubb (Sweden) *Tel:* (040) 380600 *Fax:* (040) 933708, pg 1232

Ricordi Americana SAEC (Argentina) *Tel:* (011) 4373-3405 *Fax:* (011) 4372-3452; (011) 4372 3453 *E-mail:* ricordi@sminter.com.ar, pg 8

G e C Ricordi SpA (Italy) *Tel:* (02) 88812 *Fax:* (02) 88812270, pg 405

RICS Books (United Kingdom) *Tel:* (020) 7222 7000 *Fax:* (020) 7334 3851 *E-mail:* mailorder@rics.org.uk *Web Site:* www.ricsbooks.com, pg 735

RICS Books (United Kingdom) *Tel:* (020) 7222 7000 *Fax:* (0171) 2229430 *E-mail:* rbsbooks@rics.co.uk, pg 1321

Editora Rideel Ltda (Brazil) *Tel:* (011) 6977-8344 *Fax:* (011) 6976-7415 *E-mail:* rideel@virtual-net.com.br *Web Site:* www.rideel.com.br, pg 90

Rights Promotion Distribution Translation (Denmark) *Tel:* 32591556 *Fax:* 32591556, pg 1110

Rigodon-Verlag Norbert Wehr (Germany) *Tel:* (0201) 77 81 11; (0221) 360 21 92 *Fax:* (0201) 77 51 74; (0221) 360 21 92 *E-mail:* Schreibheft@NetCologne.de *Web Site:* www.schreibheft.de, pg 279

Rigsarkivet (Denmark) *Tel:* 33923310 *Fax:* 33153239 *E-mail:* mailbox@ra.sa.dk *Web Site:* www.sa.dk, pg 1461

Rihani Printing and Publishing House (Lebanon), pg 443

Rijksmuseum Library (Netherlands) *Tel:* (020) 6747267 *Fax:* (020) 6747001 *E-mail:* bibliotheek@rijksmuseum.nl *Web Site:* www.rijksmuseum.nl, pg 1486

Bibliotheek der Rijksuniversiteit te Groningen (Netherlands) *Tel:* (050) 3635002 *Fax:* (050) 3634996 *E-mail:* secretarial@ub.rug.nl, pg 1486

Riksarkivet (Norway) *Tel:* 22022600 *Fax:* 22237489 *E-mail:* riksarkivet@riksarkivaren.dep.no *Web Site:* www.riksarkivet.no; www.arkivverket.no, pg 1489

Riksarkivet (Sweden) *Tel:* (08) 7376350 *Fax:* (08) 7376474, pg 1501

Riksbibliotektjenesten (Norway) *Tel:* 23 11 89 00 *Fax:* 23 11 89 01 *E-mail:* rbt@rbt.no, pg 1521

Rimbaud Verlagsgesellschaft mbH (Germany) *Tel:* (0241) 54 25 32; (0241) 9019583 *Fax:* (0241) 514117 *E-mail:* info@rimbaud.de *Web Site:* www.rimbaud.de, pg 279

Rimecu Grupo Editorial (Argentina) *Tel:* (03833) 333136 *Fax:* (03833) 333136, pg 1271

RIMU Publishing Co Ltd (New Zealand) *Tel:* (07) 8555536 *Fax:* (07) 8555536, pg 495

Rinsen Book Co Ltd (Japan) *Tel:* (075) 7816166 *Fax:* (075) 7816168 *E-mail:* rinsen@st.alpha-web.or.jp *Web Site:* www.alpha-web.or.jp/rinsen, pg 424

Edizioni Ripostes (Italy) *Tel:* (089) 336049 *Fax:* (089) 756961, pg 405

Riquelme y Vargas Ediciones SL (Spain) *Tel:* (053) 270066 *Fax:* (053) 270066, pg 589

Rirea Casa Editrice della Rivista Italiana di Ragioneria e di Economia Aziendale (Italy) *Tel:* (06) 8417690 *Fax:* (06) 8845732 *E-mail:* rirea.@infinito.it, pg 405

Riso-Sha (Japan) *Tel:* (047) 3668003 *Fax:* (047) 3607301, pg 424

Rithofundasamband Islands (Iceland) *Tel:* 5683190 *Fax:* 5683192 *E-mail:* rsi@rsi.is *Web Site:* www.rsi.is, pg 1364

Ritter Verlag (Austria) *Tel:* (0463) 42631 *Fax:* (0463) 42631-77 *E-mail:* ritterverlag@magnet.at, pg 58

Ritterbach Verlag GmbH (Germany) *Tel:* (02234) 18 66 0 *Fax:* (02234) 18 66 90 *E-mail:* service@ritterbach.de; coeln.ml@ritterbach.de *Web Site:* www.ritterbach.de, pg 279

Ritzau KG Verlag Zeit und Eisenbahn (Germany) *Tel:* (08196) 252 *Fax:* (08196) 1240 *E-mail:* mail@ritzau.kg.de *Web Site:* www.ritzau-kg.de, pg 279

Editori Riuniti (Italy) *Tel:* (06) 6875453 *Fax:* (06) 6868696, pg 405

River Press (New Zealand) *Tel:* (03) 5738383 *Fax:* (03) 5738383, pg 495

Riverside Agency SAC (Argentina) *Tel:* (011) 957-2336 *Fax:* (011) 956-1985, pg 1271

Riverside Communications (Nigeria) *Tel:* (084) 334042 *Fax:* (084) 334042 *E-mail:* isoun@aol.com; rvsdcom@aol.com, pg 501

Uitgeverij La Riviere (Netherlands) *Tel:* (035) 5486676, pg 483

Yves Riviere Editeur (France) *Tel:* (01) 42747784 *Fax:* (01) 42781265 *E-mail:* yvesrivi@mail.club.internet.fr, pg 183

Rizal Library (Philippines) *Tel:* (02) 426-6001; 5800-5816 (Local) *Fax:* (02) 426-5961 *Web Site:* rizal.lib.admn.edu.ph, pg 1491

Libreria Rizzoli della Rizzoli Editore SpA (Italy) *Tel:* (02) 50951 *Fax:* (02) 5065361, pg 1293

RMIT Publishing (Australia) *Tel:* (03) 9925 8100 *Fax:* (03) 9925 8134 *E-mail:* info@rmitpublishing.com.au *Web Site:* www.rmitpublishing.com.au, pg 41

Road Editions (Greece) *Tel:* (01) 9296535; (01) 9296541 *Fax:* (01) 9296492 *E-mail:* road@enet.gr *Web Site:* www.road.gr, pg 1287

Roadmaster Publishing (United Kingdom) *Tel:* (01634) 862843 *Fax:* (01634) 201555 *E-mail:* roadmasterpublishing@blueyonder.co.uk, pg 735

Editorial Roasa SL (Spain) *Tel:* (058) 0227846 *Fax:* (058) 132530, pg 589

Editions Robert Laffont, Nil, Fixot, Seghers, Julliard (France) *Tel:* (01) 53671400 *Fax:* (01) 53671414 *Web Site:* www.laffont.fr, pg 183

Roberts Rinehart Publishers (Ireland) *Tel:* (01) 497-2399 *Fax:* (01) 497-0927 *E-mail:* books@townhouse.ie, pg 363

Tom Roberts (Pat Roberts) (Australia) *Tel:* (08) 84437578, pg 41

J Robinson & Co (Israel) *Tel:* (03) 5605461; (03) 5601626 *Fax:* (03) 5660439 *E-mail:* rob_book@netvision.net.il, pg 1292

Robson Books (United Kingdom) *Tel:* (020) 7697 3000 *Fax:* (020) 7697 3001 *E-mail:* robson@chrysalisbooks.co.uk *Web Site:* www.batsford.com/robson.htm, pg 735

Laurus Robuffo Edizioni (Italy) *Tel:* (06) 5651492 *Fax:* (06) 5651233, pg 405

Livraria Roca Ltda (Brazil) *Tel:* (011) 221-8609; (011) 221-6814 *Fax:* (011) 3331-8653 *E-mail:* editoraroca@editoraroca.com.br *Web Site:* www.editoraroca.com.br, pg 90

Ediciones Roca, SA (Mexico) *Tel:* (05) 2770744; (05) 2770946 *Fax:* (05) 2714070, pg 466

Ediciones La Rocca (Argentina) *Tel:* (011) 4382-8526 *Fax:* (011) 4384-5774 *Web Site:* www.dtj.com.ar/ediciones_la_rocca.htm, pg 8

Editora Rocco Ltda (Brazil) *Tel:* (021) 507-2000 *Fax:* (021) 507-2244 *E-mail:* rocco@rocco.com.br *Web Site:* www.rocco.com.br, pg 91

Roce (Consultants) Ltd (Uganda) *Tel:* (041) 285630 *Fax:* (041) 259997, pg 642

Editiones Roche (Switzerland) *Tel:* (061) 6883611 *Fax:* (061) 6919391; (061) 6919600, pg 623

Les Editions du Rocher (Monaco) *Tel:* (093) 303341 *Fax:* (093) 507371, pg 469

Rodera-Verlag der Cardun AG (Switzerland) *Tel:* (052) 292442 *Fax:* (052) 292592, pg 623

Rodopi (Netherlands) *Tel:* (020) 6114821 *Fax:* (020) 4472979 *E-mail:* orders-queries@rodopi.nl *Web Site:* www.rodopi.nl, pg 483

Ediciones Joaquin Rodrigo (Spain) *Tel:* (091) 555 2728 *Fax:* (091) 556 4334 *E-mail:* ediciones@joaquin-rodrigo.com *Web Site:* www.joaquin-rodrigo.com, pg 589

Libreria Rodriguez SA, Dto Suscripciones (Argentina) *Tel:* (011) 3263725; (011) 3263826; (011) 3263927, pg 1271

Roehrig Universitaets Verlag Gmbh (Germany) *Tel:* (06894) 8 79 57 *Fax:* (06894) 87 03 30 *E-mail:* info@roehrig-verlag.de *Web Site:* www.roehrig-verlag.de, pg 279

Verlag Roeschnar (Austria) *Tel:* (0463) 740513 *Fax:* (0463) 740817 *E-mail:* roesch@EUnet.at *Web Site:* www.members.EUnet.at/roesch, pg 58

Erich Roeth-Verlag (Germany) *Tel:* (039206) 90103 *Fax:* (039206) 90103, pg 279

Roetzer Druck GmbH & Co KG (Austria) *Tel:* (02682) 62 494 *Fax:* (02682) 65 008 *E-mail:* roetzer@bnet.at *Web Site:* www.buchwirtschaft.at, pg 58

Libreria Editrice Rogate (LER) (Italy) *Tel:* (06) 7023430 *Fax:* (06) 7020767, pg 406

Rogers, Coleridge & White Ltd (United Kingdom) *Tel:* (020) 7221 3717 *Fax:* (020) 7229 9084, pg 1121

Heidi Rogner (Germany) *Tel:* (02429) 2561, pg 279

Rogner und Bernhard GmbH & Co Verlags KG (Germany) *Tel:* (040) 430 2110 *Fax:* (040) 430 2716 *E-mail:* robe@on-line.de *Web Site:* www.zweitausendeins.de, pg 279

Hans R Rohr (Switzerland) *Tel:* (01) 3614846, pg 1313

Hans Rohr Verlag (Switzerland) *Tel:* (01) 3614846 *Fax:* (01) 3639513 *E-mail:* buchhandlung.hans.rohr@dm.krinfo.ch, pg 623

Ediciones ROL SA (Spain) *Tel:* (093) 200 80 33 *Fax:* (093) 200 27 62 *E-mail:* rol@e-rol.es *Web Site:* www.e-rol.es, pg 589

Roli Books Pvt Ltd (India) *Tel:* (011) 6462782; (011) 6442271; (011) 6460886 *Fax:* (011) 6467185 *E-mail:* roli@vsnl.com *Web Site:* rolibooks.com, pg 348

Edicoes Rolim Lda (Portugal) *Tel:* (021) 526375, pg 529

Verlag und Buchversand Wolfgang Roller (Germany) *Tel:* (06103) 71886 *Fax:* (06103) 929501 *E-mail:* greif@12move.de *Web Site:* www.verlag-roller.de, pg 280

Panstwowe Wydawnictwo Rolnicze i Lesne (Poland) *Tel:* (022) 8276338 *Fax:* (022) 8276338, pg 519

Rolnik Publishers (Israel) *Tel:* (03) 6496663 *Fax:* (03) 6478661 *E-mail:* rolknik@attglobal.net *Web Site:* www.rolnik.com; www.bible2000.net, pg 371

Edizioni Universitarie Romane (Italy) *Tel:* (06) 491503 *Fax:* (06) 4453438, pg 406

Romantic Cyprus Publications (Cyprus) *Fax:* (02) 445155, pg 122

Romantic Novelists' Association (United Kingdom) *Tel:* (01827) 714776 (voice & fax) *Web Site:* freespace.virgin.net/marina.oliver/apfrm.htm, pg 1371

Rombach GmbH Druck und Verlagshaus & Co (Germany) *Tel:* (0761) 4500 0 *Fax:* (0761) 4500 2125 *E-mail:* info@buchverlag.rombach.de *Web Site:* www.rombach.de, pg 280

Editions Rombaldi SA (France) *Tel:* (01) 41236500 *Fax:* (01) 46453442, pg 183

Romiosini Verlag (Germany) *Tel:* (0221) 5101288 *Fax:* (0221) 5101288 *E-mail:* romiosini@unisolo.de *Web Site:* www.unisolo.de/pls/romiosini/griechische_literatur, pg 280

George Ronald Publisher Ltd (United Kingdom) *Tel:* (01865) 841515 *E-mail:* sales@grbooks.com *Web Site:* www.grbooks.com, pg 735

Rondeau Giannipiero a Monaco (Monaco) *Tel:* (093) 303075 *Fax:* (093) 257047, pg 469

Rondo Verlag (Switzerland) *Tel:* (055) 953937 *Fax:* (055) 2464293, pg 623

Rooster Books Ltd (United Kingdom) *Tel:* (01763) 242939 *Fax:* (01763) 243332 *E-mail:* rooster@solutions-for-business.co.uk *Web Site:* www.solutions-for-books.co.uk/rooster, pg 735

Roraima Publishers Ltd (Guyana) *Tel:* (02) 273551; (02) 222363; (02) 225057 *Fax:* (02) 262319; (02) 258844 *E-mail:* roraima-distributors@solutions2000.net, pg 317

Mercedes Ros Literary Agency (Spain) *Tel:* (093) 5401353 *Fax:* (093) 5401346 *E-mail:* info@mercedesros.com *Web Site:* www.mercedesros.com, pg 1116

Mercedes Ros Literary Agency (Spain) *Tel:* (093) 540 13 53 *Fax:* (093) 540 13 46 *E-mail:* info@mercedesros.com *Web Site:* www.mercedesros.com, pg 1201

Rosda Jaya Putra (Indonesia) *Tel:* (021) 3904984; (021) 3901692; (021) 3904985 *Fax:* (021) 3901703, pg 357

Rosebud Ediciones (Uruguay) *Tel:* (02) 771773 *Fax:* (02) 771773, pg 761

Archinto Rosellina (Italy) *Tel:* (02) 86460237 *Fax:* (02) 86451955, pg 406

Rosenberg e Sellier SpA (Italy) *Tel:* (011) 8127820 *Fax:* (011) 8127808, pg 1293

Rosenberg e Sellier Editori in Torino (Italy) *Tel:* (011) 8127820; (011) 532150 *Fax:* (011) 8127808, pg 406

Rosendale Press Ltd (United Kingdom) *Tel:* (020) 7834 1123 *Fax:* (020) 7834 1240 *E-mail:* info@rosendale.demon.co.uk, pg 735

Rosenheimer Verlagshaus GmbH & Co KG (Germany) *Tel:* (08031) 2838 0 *Fax:* (08031) 2838 44 *E-mail:* info@rosenheimer.com *Web Site:* www.rosenheimer.com, pg 280

Rosenkilde & Bagger (Denmark) *Tel:* 33157044 *Fax:* 33937007 *E-mail:* r-b@rosenkilde-bagger.dk *Web Site:* www.rosenkilde-bagger.dk, pg 135

Guide Rosenwald (France) *Tel:* (01) 44 30 81 00 *Fax:* (01) 44 30 81 11 *E-mail:* rosenwald@wanadoo.fr *Web Site:* www.rosenwald.com, pg 183

Rosikon Press (Poland) *Tel:* (022) 7226101; (022) 7226102; (022) 7226666 *Fax:* (022) 7226667 *E-mail:* rosikom@ikp.atm.com.pl; office@rosikompress.com *Web Site:* rosikonpress.com, pg 519

Roskilde University Library (Denmark) *Tel:* 46742000 *Fax:* 46743090 *E-mail:* rub@ruc.dk, pg 1461

ROSPO Verlag (Germany) *Tel:* (040) 351603; (040) 351604 *Fax:* (040) 351605 *E-mail:* rospoverlag@t-online.de, pg 280

Louise Ross & Co, Ltd (United Kingdom) *Tel:* (01225) 448786 *Fax:* (01225) 448789, pg 1321

Rossato (Italy) *Tel:* (0455) 411000 *Fax:* (0455) 411550 *E-mail:* grossato@didanet.it, pg 406

Nikolas I Rossi (Greece) *Tel:* (01) 3218572 *Fax:* (01) 3304440, pg 314

Rossiiskaya Nacionalnaya biblioteka (Russian Federation) *Tel:* (0812) 3109850 *Fax:* (0812) 3106148 *E-mail:* mb@glas.apc.org, pg 1495

Gosudarstvennaya publichnaya nauchno-tekhnicheskaya biblioteka Sibirskogo otdeleniya Rossiiskoi Akademii Nauk (Russian Federation) *Tel:* (0382) 661860 (Director); (0382) 661991 *Fax:* (0382) 663365 *E-mail:* root@libr.nsk.su, pg 1495

Rossijskaja Knizhnaya Palata (Russian Federation) *Tel:* (095) 2911278 *Fax:* (095) 2919630 *E-mail:* bookch@postman.tu *Web Site:* www.bookchamber.ru/international, pg 1258

Rossijskoye avtorskoye obshestvo (Russian Federation) *Tel:* (095) 2034991 *Fax:* (095) 2001263 *E-mail:* rao@smtp.cnt.ru, pg 1115

Rossipaul Kommunikation GmbH (Germany) *Tel:* (089) 17 91 06 0 *Fax:* (089) 17 91 06 22 *E-mail:* info@rossipaul.de *Web Site:* www.rossipaul.de, pg 280

Universitaet Rostock Universitaetsbibliothek (Germany) *Tel:* (0381) 4982283 *Fax:* (0381) 4982270 *E-mail:* ub-sekretariat@ub.uni-rostock.de00.de, pg 1468

Rostrum Publishing (Netherlands) *Tel:* (0492) 545268 *Fax:* (0492) 528635, pg 483

Rot-Gelb-Gruen Lehrmittel GmbH & Co Verlagsgesellschaft (Germany) *Tel:* (0531) 809070 *Fax:* (0531) 8090721, pg 280

Rotedic SA (Spain) *Tel:* (091) 8031676 *Fax:* (091) 8038316 *Web Site:* www.rotedic.com, pg 1201

Verlag Roter Morgen (Germany) *Tel:* (0711) 870 2209 *Fax:* (0711) 870 2445 *E-mail:* kpd-roter-morgen@t-online.de, pg 280

Roth et Sauter SA (Switzerland) *Tel:* (021) 8017561 *Fax:* (021) 8023279, pg 623

Rothschild & Bach (Netherlands) *Tel:* (020) 6389329, pg 483

RotoVision SA (United Kingdom) *Tel:* (01273) 716 010 *Fax:* (01273) 727 269 *E-mail:* sales@rotovision.com *Web Site:* www.rotovision.com, pg 735

Rotpunktverlag (Switzerland) *Tel:* (01) 2418434 *Fax:* (01) 2418434 *E-mail:* info@rotpunktverlag.ch *Web Site:* www.rotpunkfverlag.ch, pg 623

Rotten-Verlags AG (Switzerland) *Tel:* (028) 462252, pg 623

Gemeentebibliotheek Rotterdam (Netherlands) *Tel:* (010) 2816100 *Fax:* (010) 2816181, pg 1486

Editions Roudil (France) *Tel:* 01 43544797, pg 183

Editions du Rouergue (France) *Tel:* (05) 65.77.73.70 *Fax:* (05) 65.77.73.71 *E-mail:* info@lerouergue.com *Web Site:* www.lerouergue.com, pg 183

Rough Guides Ltd (United Kingdom) *Tel:* (020) 7556 5000 *Fax:* (020) 7556 5050 *E-mail:* mail@roughguides.co.uk *Web Site:* www.roughguides.com, pg 735

Roularta Books NV (Belgium) *Tel:* (0475) 63 46 23 *E-mail:* info@roularta.be *Web Site:* www.roulartabooks.be, pg 73

Round Hall Sweet & Maxwell (Ireland) *Tel:* (01) 873-0101 *Fax:* (01) 872-0078, pg 363

Roundhouse Publishing Ltd (United Kingdom) *Tel:* (01237) 474 474 *Fax:* (01237) 474 774 *E-mail:* roundhouse.group@ukgateway.net *Web Site:* www.roundhouse.net, pg 736

Roundhouse Publishing Ltd (United Kingdom) *Tel:* (01237) 474474 *Fax:* (01237) 474774 *E-mail:* roundhouse.group@ukgateway.net *Web Site:* www.roundhouse.net, pg 1321

Routledge (United Kingdom) *Tel:* (020) 7583 9855 *Fax:* (020) 7842 2298 *E-mail:* info@routledge.co.uk *Web Site:* www.routledge.com, pg 736

Routledge Curzon (United Kingdom) *Tel:* (020) 7583 9855 *Fax:* (020) 7842 2298 *E-mail:* info@routledge.co.uk *Web Site:* www.routledge.com, pg 736

Antony Rowe Ltd (United Kingdom) *Tel:* (01249) 659705 *Fax:* (01249) 443103, pg 1141

Antony Rowe Ltd (United Kingdom) *Tel:* (0118) 9503911 *Fax:* (0118) 9505776 *E-mail:* 100546.3703@compuserve.com, pg 1162

Antony Rowe Ltd (United Kingdom) *Tel:* (01249) 659705 *Fax:* (01249) 443103 *E-mail:* 100616.40@compuserve.com, pg 1204, 1215

Antony Rowe Ltd (United Kingdom) *Tel:* (0118) 9503911 *Fax:* (0118) 9505776, pg 1224

Rowohlt Berlin Verlag GmbH (Germany) *Tel:* (040) 72 72 0 *Fax:* (040) 72 72 342 *E-mail:* Rowohlt.Berlin@T-online.de *Web Site:* www.rowohlt.de, pg 280

Rowohlt Taschenbuch Verlag GmbH (Germany) *Tel:* (040) 72720 *Fax:* (040) 7272319 *E-mail:* info@rowohlt.de *Web Site:* www.rowohlt.de, pg 280

Rowohlt Verlag GmbH (Germany) *Tel:* (040) 72720 *Fax:* (040) 7272319; (040) 7272213 (Advertising); (040) 7272391 (Production); (040) 7272395 (Press); (040) 7272342 (Sales) *E-mail:* presse@rowohlt.de *Web Site:* www.rowohlt.de, pg 280

Elizabeth Roy Literary Agency (United Kingdom) *Tel:* (01778) 560672 *Fax:* (01778) 560672, pg 1121

Royal Book Co (Pakistan) *Tel:* (021) 5684244; (021) 520628 *Fax:* (021) 5683706, pg 509

Royal Book Co (Pakistan) *Tel:* (021) 5684244; (021) 5670628; (021) 5653418 *Fax:* (021) 5653419 *E-mail:* royalbook@hotmail.com, pg 1305

Royal College of General Practitioners (United Kingdom) *Tel:* (020) 7581 3232 *Fax:* (020) 7225 3047 *E-mail:* info@rcgp.org.uk *Web Site:* www.rcgp.org.uk, pg 736

Royal College of Surgeons in Ireland Library (Ireland) *Tel:* (01) 4022411 *Fax:* (01) 4022457 *E-mail:* library@rcsi.ie *Web Site:* www.rcsi.ie, pg 1476

Royal Dublin Society (Ireland) *Tel:* (01) 6680866 *Fax:* (01) 6604014 *E-mail:* marketing@rds.ie *Web Site:* www.rds.ie, pg 364

Royal Dublin Society Library (Ireland) *Tel:* (01) 6680866; (01) 2407288 *Fax:* (01) 6604014, pg 1476

Royal Institute of International Affairs (United Kingdom) *Tel:* (020) 7957 5700 *Fax:* (020) 7957 5710 *E-mail:* contact@riia.org *Web Site:* www.riia.org, pg 736

Royal Irish Academy (Ireland) *Tel:* (01) 6762570 *Fax:* (01) 6762346 *E-mail:* publications@ria.ie *Web Site:* www.ria.ie, pg 364

Royal Literary Fund (United Kingdom) *Tel:* (020) 7353 7150 *Fax:* (020) 7353 7150, pg 1371

Royal Nepal Academy (Nepal) *Tel:* (01) 221283; (01) 221241 *Fax:* (01) 221175, pg 472

Royal Scientific Society Library (Jordan) *Tel:* (06) 844700 *Fax:* (06) 844806, pg 1479

The Royal Society (United Kingdom) *Tel:* (020) 7839 5561 *Fax:* (020) 7930 2170 *E-mail:* info@royalsoc.ac.uk *Web Site:* www.royalsoc.ac.uk, pg 737

The Royal Society for the Encouragement of Arts, Manufactures & Commerce-RSA (United Kingdom) *Tel:* (020) 7930 5115 *Fax:* (020) 7839 5805, pg 1371

The Royal Society of Chemistry (United Kingdom) *Tel:* (020) 74378656 *Fax:* (020) 74378883 *E-mail:* sales@rsc.org *Web Site:* www.rsc.org, pg 737

Royal Society of Literature of the United Kingdom (United Kingdom) *Tel:* (020) 7845 4676 *Fax:* (020) 7845 4679 *E-mail:* info@rslit.org *Web Site:* www.rslit.org, pg 1371

Royal Society of New South Wales (Australia) *Tel:* (02) 98874448 *Fax:* (02) 9887 4448 *E-mail:* p.williams@uws.edu.au *Web Site:* www.phys.uts.edu.au/rsnsw/intro.html, pg 41

Royal Society of South Africa Library (South Africa) *Tel:* (021) 6502543 *Fax:* (021) 6502726 *E-mail:* roysoc@psipsy.uct.ac.za, pg 1498

Royal Society of Victoria Inc (Australia) *Tel:* (03) 9663 5259 *Fax:* (03) 9663 2301 *E-mail:* sciencevictoria@org.au *Web Site:* www.sciencevictoria.org.au, pg 41

RSVP Publishing Company Ltd (New Zealand) *Tel:* (09) 3723480 *Fax:* (09) 3723480 *E-mail:* rsvppub@iconz.co.nz *Web Site:* www.rsvp-publishing.co.nz, pg 495

Wydawnictwo RTW (Poland) *Tel:* (022) 633-70-10; (022) 39120123 *Fax:* (022) 6486277; (022) 39120123 *E-mail:* rtw@wydawrtw.media.pl *Web Site:* www.wydawrtw.media.pl, pg 520

Josep Ruaix Editor (Spain) *Tel:* (093) 820 81 36 *Web Site:* www.ruaix.com/, pg 589

Ruamsarn (1977) Co Ltd (Thailand) *Tel:* (02) 22216483 *Fax:* (02) 2222036, pg 635

Rubber Research Institute of Malaysia Library (Malaysia) *Tel:* (03) 4567033 *Fax:* (03) 4573512, pg 1483

Rubbettino Editore (Italy) *Tel:* (0968) 662034 *Fax:* (0968) 662055 *E-mail:* commerciale@rubbettino.it *Web Site:* www.rubbettino.it, pg 406

The Rubicon Press (United Kingdom) *Tel:* (01253) 780247 *Fax:* (01253) 780247 *E-mail:* robinrub@aol.com, pg 737

Rubin Mass Ltd (Israel) *Tel:* (02) 627-7863 *Fax:* (02) 627-7864 *E-mail:* rmass@inter.net.il *Web Site:* www.age.co.il/mas, pg 371

Rubin Mass Ltd (Israel) *Tel:* (02) 6277863 *Fax:* (02) 6277864 *E-mail:* rmass@inter.net.il, pg 1292

Libreria Rubinos - 1860 SA (Spain) *Tel:* (091) 4352239 *Fax:* (091) 5753272, pg 1312

Hilary Rubinstein Books (United Kingdom) *Tel:* (020) 7792 4282 *Fax:* (020) 7221 5291 *E-mail:* hrubinstein@beeb.net, pg 1121

Rueda, SL Editorial (Spain) *Tel:* (091) 619 27 79; (091) 619 25 64 *Fax:* (091) 610 28 55 *E-mail:* ed_rueda@infornet.es *Web Site:* www.editorialrueda.es, pg 589

Dieter Ruggeberg Verlagsbuchhandlung (Germany) *Tel:* (0202) 592811 *Fax:* (0202) 592811 *Web Site:* www.vbdr.de, pg 280

Ruegger Verlag (Switzerland) *Tel:* (01) 4912130 *Fax:* (01) 4931176 *E-mail:* info@rueggerverlag.ch *Web Site:* www.rueggerverlag.ch, pg 623

Ruetten & Loening Berlin GmbH (Germany) *Tel:* (030) 283 94 0 *Fax:* (030) 283 94 100 *E-mail:* info@aufbau-verlag.de *Web Site:* www.aufbau-verlag.de, pg 281

Rugginenti Editore (Italy) *Tel:* (02) 89501283 *Fax:* (02) 89531273 *E-mail:* rugginenti@rugginenti.com *Web Site:* www.rugginenti.com, pg 406

Ruh ve Madde Yayinlari ve Saglik Hizmetleri AS (Turkey) *Tel:* (0212) 2431814 *Fax:* (0212) 2520718 *E-mail:* bilyay@bilyay.org.tr *Web Site:* www.ruhvemadde.com, pg 641

Ruhland Verlag Gimblt (Germany) *Tel:* (069) 811768 *Fax:* (069) 811769, pg 281

Verlag an der Ruhr GmbH (Germany) *Tel:* (0208) 4395454 *Fax:* (0208) 4395439 *E-mail:* info@verlagruhr.de *Web Site:* www.verlagruhr.de, pg 281

Rumsby Scientific Publishing (Australia) *Tel:* (02) 98076184 *Fax:* (02) 98076184, pg 41

Runa Press (Ireland) *Tel:* (01) 2801869, pg 364

Rupa & Co (India) *Tel:* (033) 344821; (033) 346305, pg 348

Rupa & Co (India) *Tel:* (033) 344821; (033) 346305 *Fax:* (033) 3277294, pg 1290

Rusconi Libri Srl (Italy) *Tel:* (02) 66191 *Fax:* (02) 66192758 *E-mail:* relazioniesterne@rusconi.it, pg 406

Ruskin Rowe Press (Australia) *Tel:* (02) 9918-8810 *Fax:* (02) 9918-8884, pg 41

The Ruskin Society of London (United Kingdom) *Tel:* (01865) 310987; (01865) 515962 *Fax:* (01865) 240448, pg 1371

Michael Russell Publishing Ltd (United Kingdom) *Tel:* (01953) 887776 *Fax:* (01953) 887762, pg 737

Russian State Historical Archives (Russian Federation) *Tel:* (0812) 311-09-26 *Fax:* (0812) 311-22-52, pg 1495

Russkaya Kniga Izdatelstvo (Publishers) (Russian Federation) *Tel:* (095) 2053377 *Fax:* (095) 2053424, pg 541

Russkij Jazyk (Russian Federation) *Tel:* (095) 9239705 *Fax:* (095) 9288906, pg 541

K Rustem & Bro (Cyprus) *Tel:* (02) 71041; (02) 71418; (02) 52085, pg 1281

The Rutland Press (United Kingdom) *Tel:* (0131) 229 7545 *Fax:* (0131) 228 2188 *Web Site:* www.rias.org.uk/about_the_rutland_press.htm, pg 737

Rux Guru srl (Italy) *Tel:* (075) 5007227 *Fax:* (075) 5051324, pg 1293

Ryland Peters & Small Ltd (United Kingdom) *Tel:* (020) 7436 9090 *Fax:* (020) 7436 9790 *E-mail:* info@rps.co.uk *Web Site:* www.rylandpeters.com, pg 737

John Rylands University Library of Manchester (United Kingdom) *Tel:* (0161) 2753738 (Main Library Bldg); (0161) 8345343 (Deansgate Bldg) *Fax:* (0161) 2737488 (Main Library Bldg); (0161) 8345574 (Deansgate Bldg), pg 1507

Ryosho-Fukyu-Kai Co Ltd (Japan) *Tel:* (03) 38131251 *Fax:* (03) 38116490, pg 424

Simon Rysavy (Czech Republic) *Tel:* (05) 42212052; (05) 42213849; (05) 42219703 *Fax:* (05) 42216633 *E-mail:* info@rysavy.cz *Web Site:* www.itn.cz/rysavy-books, pg 128

Ryvellus Medienagentur Dopfer (Germany) *Tel:* (08801) 12391 *Fax:* (08801) 912323, pg 281

S/A Tiesiskas informacijas cerfus (Latvia) *Tel:* (02) 7220422 *Fax:* (02) 7213854 *E-mail:* mariss@date.lv, pg 442

Livraria Sa da Costa (Portugal) *Tel:* (021) 3460721, pg 1308

Sa da Costa Editora (Portugal) *Tel:* (021) 3460721, pg 529

Edicioes Joao Sa da Costa Lda (Portugal) *Tel:* (021) 8400428; (021) 571118; (021) 563603 *Fax:* (021) 534194, pg 529

Saar Publishing House (Israel) *Tel:* (03) 5445292 *Fax:* (03) 5445293, pg 372

Saara Buddhi Publication (Sri Lanka), pg 598

Saarbrucker Druckerei und Verlag GmbH (SDV) (Germany) *Tel:* (0681) 6650135 *Fax:* (0681) 6650110 *Web Site:* www.sdv-saar.de, pg 281

Saarlaendische Universitaets und Landesbibliothek (Germany) *Tel:* (0681) 3022070 *Fax:* (0681) 3022796 *E-mail:* sulb@sulb.uni-saarland.de *Web Site:* www.sulb.uni-saarland.de, pg 1468

Saatkorn-Verlag GmbH (Germany) *Tel:* (04131) 98 35-02 *Fax:* (04131) 98 35 505 *E-mail:* info@saatkornverlag.de *Web Site:* wwww.saatkorn-verlag.de, pg 281

SAB Schweiz Arbeitsgemeinschaft fuer die Berggebiete (Switzerland) *Tel:* (056) 411079 *Fax:* (056) 413642, pg 623

Sabah State Library (Malaysia) *Tel:* (088) 54333 *Fax:* (088) 233167 *E-mail:* pns@sbh.lib.edu.my, pg 1483

Sabah Kitaplari (Turkey) *Tel:* (0212) 5028572 *Fax:* (0212) 5028346, pg 641

SABDA (India) *Tel:* (0413) 334980; (0413) 223328 *Fax:* (0413) 223328 *E-mail:* sabda@sriaurobindoashram.org *Web Site:* sabda.sriaurobindoashram.org, pg 348

Sabe AG Verlagsinstitut (Switzerland) *Tel:* (01) 2024477 *Fax:* (01) 2021932 *E-mail:* sabeverlag@access.ch, pg 623

Sabe U (Myanmar), pg 1300

Izdatelstvo Sabtchota Sakartvelo (Georgia) *Tel:* (08832) 954201, pg 190

SACEM (Societe des Auteurs Copositeurs et Editeurs de Musique) (France) *Tel:* (01) 47475650 *Fax:* (01) 47451294, pg 1244

Verlag Werner Sachon GmbH & Co (Germany) *Tel:* (08261) 999-0 *Fax:* (08261) 999 391 *E-mail:* info@sachon.de *Web Site:* www.sachon.de, pg 281

Sachse & Heinzelmann Kunst- und Buchhandlung GmbH (Germany) *Tel:* (0511) 360240 *Fax:* (0511) 324167 *E-mail:* info@sachse-heinselmann.de *Web Site:* www.sachse-heinzelmann.de, pg 1284

Sachsenbuch Verlagsgesellschaft Mbh (Germany) *Tel:* (0341) 9602373 *Fax:* (0341) 9784259, pg 281

Sada, Literaturno-Izdatel'skij Centr (Azerbaijan) *Tel:* (012) 927564 *Fax:* (012) 929843, pg 61

Sadan Publishing Ltd (Israel) *Tel:* (03) 6954402 *Fax:* (03) 6953122, pg 372

Sadeepa Bookshop (Sri Lanka) *Tel:* (01) 686114; (01) 694289; (01) 678043 *Fax:* (01) 683813 *E-mail:* sadeepabk@itmin.com *Web Site:* www.neatron-com/sadeepabk, pg 1312

Biblioteca Municipala Mihail Sadoveanu (Romania) *Tel:* (01) 2113625 *Fax:* (01) 2113625, pg 1494

Saechsische Landesbibliothek- Staats- und Universitaetsbibliothek Dresden (Germany) *Tel:* (0351) 4634308 *Fax:* (0351) 4637173 *E-mail:* direktion@slub-dresden.de, pg 1468

Saeculum IO (Romania) *Tel:* (021) 3452827 *Fax:* (021) 3452827; (021) 2228597 *E-mail:* saeculum@tcnet.ro *Web Site:* www.saeculum.ro, pg 535

Saendig Reprint Verlag, Hans-Rainer Wohlwend (Liechtenstein) *Tel:* (0423) 232 36 27 *Fax:* (0423) 232 36 49 *E-mail:* saendig@adon.li *Web Site:* www.saendig.com, pg 445

Saera Shobo (Librairie Ca et La) (Japan) *Tel:* (03) 32684261 *Fax:* (03) 32684262 *Web Site:* www.saela.co.jp, pg 424

Univerzita Pavla Jozefa Safarika (Slovakia) *Tel:* (095) 6222608 *Fax:* (095) 766959 *E-mail:* zahrodd@kosice.upjs.sk, pg 1497

Klub Saffier (South Africa) *Tel:* (011) 6736725 *Fax:* (011) 6736719, pg 1231

Sagano Shoin (Japan) *Tel:* (075) 3917686 *Fax:* (075) 3917321, pg 424

Ratna Sagar Pvt Ltd (India) *Tel:* (011) 7222505; (011) 7216094 *Fax:* (011) 7250787, pg 348

Biblioteca Nazionale Sagarriga Visconti Volpi (Italy) *Tel:* (080) 5212534 *Fax:* (080) 5212667, pg 1478

Sage Publications India Pvt Ltd (India) *Tel:* (011) 6485884; (011) 644 4958; (011) 6453915 *Fax:* (011) 6472426 *E-mail:* sageind@nda.vsnl.net.in, pg 348

Sage Publications Ltd (United Kingdom) *Tel:* (020) 7374 0645; (020) 7330 1234 (book orders hotline) *Fax:* (020) 7374 8741 *E-mail:* info@sagepub.co.uk *Web Site:* www.sagepub.co.uk, pg 737

SAGEP (Italy) *Tel:* (010) 313453 *Fax:* (010) 312621, pg 406

Les Editions du Sagittaire (France) *Tel:* (01) 44392200 *Fax:* (01) 42226418, pg 183

Sahasrara Publications (India) *Tel:* (011) 57-4902, pg 348

Edition Sahel (Senegal) *Tel:* 212164, pg 544

Sahitya Akademi Library (India) *Tel:* (011) 3387064 *Fax:* (011) 3382428, pg 1473

Sahitya Akademi (India) *Tel:* (011) 3386626-629; (011) 3735297; (011) 3364207 (sales) *Fax:* (011) 3382428; (011) 3364207, pg 348

Sahitya Akademi (India) *Tel:* (011) 3387064 *Fax:* (011) 3382428, pg 1364

Sahitya Pravarthaka Co-operative Society Ltd (India) *Tel:* (0481) 4111; (0481) 4112, pg 348

SAIE Editrice SRL (Italy) *Tel:* (011) 871022 *Fax:* (011) 830826, pg 406

Saiensu-Sha Co Ltd (Japan) *Tel:* (03) 54748500 *Fax:* (03) 54748900 *E-mail:* rikei@saiensu.co.jp, pg 424

Saik Wah Press (Pte) Ltd (Singapore) *Tel:* 2928759 *Fax:* 2960638, pg 1138

The Sailor Publishing Co, Ltd (Japan) *Tel:* (03) 38462955 *Fax:* (03) 38460452, pg 424

Sainsbury Publishing Ltd (United Kingdom) *Tel:* (01636) 830499 *Fax:* (01636) 830175, pg 737

Saint Andrew Press (United Kingdom) *Tel:* (0131) 225 5722 *Fax:* (0131) 220 3113 *E-mail:* cofs.standrew@dial.pipex.com *Web Site:* www.churchofscotland.org.uk, pg 737

St Andrew's Biblical Theological College (Russian Federation) *Tel:* (095) 2702200 *Fax:* (095) 2707644 *E-mail:* standrews@standrews.ru *Web Site:* www.standrews.ru, pg 541

Editions Saint Augustin (Switzerland) *Tel:* (024) 486 05 04 *Fax:* (024) 486 05 23 *E-mail:* editions@staugustin.ch, pg 623

Oeuvre St-Augustin (Switzerland) *Tel:* (024) 4860504 *Fax:* (024) 4860523, pg 623

St Clair Press (Australia) *Tel:* (02) 9818 1942 *Fax:* (02) 9418 1923 *E-mail:* stclair@australis.net.au *Web Site:* www.stclairpress.com.au, pg 41

St Clement of Ohrid National & University Library (The Former Yugoslav Republic of Macedonia) *Tel:* (091) 115-177; (091) 115358 *Fax:* (091) 230874 *E-mail:* kliment@nubsk.edu.mk *Web Site:* www.nubsk.edu.mk/; nubsk.nubskedu.mk/, pg 449

S S Saint Cyril & Saint Methodius National Library (Bulgaria) *Tel:* (02) 882811 *Fax:* (02) 435495 *E-mail:* nbkm@bgcict.acad.bg, pg 1456

Verlag St Gabriel (Austria) *Tel:* (02236) 803-225 *Fax:* (02236) 24483 *E-mail:* org.sgww@steyler.at *Web Site:* www.steyler.at, pg 58

St George Books (Australia) *Tel:* (09) 4829051 *Fax:* (09) 4829043, pg 41

St George's Press (United Kingdom) *Tel:* (01273) 473159 *Fax:* (01273) 471918 *E-mail:* sgp17@aol.com *Web Site:* www.eppingforest.co.uk/stgeorgespress, pg 737

Editions Saint-Germain-des-Pres SA (France) *Tel:* (01) 43269724 *Fax:* (01) 43269724, pg 183

St Jerome Publishing (United Kingdom) *Tel:* (0161) 973 9856 *Fax:* (0161) 905 3498 *E-mail:* stjerome@compuserve.com *Web Site:* www.stjerome.co.uk, pg 738

St Joseph Publications (Australia) *Tel:* (02) 99297344 *Fax:* (02) 91303678; (02) 99297994 *E-mail:* sosjelt@internet-australia.com, pg 41

Saint Mary's Publishing Corp (Philippines) *Tel:* (02) 7119730; (02) 7119743 *Fax:* (02) 7350955, pg 515

Saint Michael's Mission (Lesotho), pg 444

Editions Saint-Michel SA (France) *Tel:* (04) 7587-1050 *Fax:* (04) 7587-1061, pg 183

Saint-Paul (The Democratic Republic of the Congo), pg 115

Librairie Saint-Paul (The Democratic Republic of the Congo) *Tel:* 77726, pg 1280

Editions Saint-Paul (Luxembourg) *Tel:* 49931 *Fax:* 4993580, pg 448

Editions Saint-Paul (Switzerland) *Tel:* (026) 4264331 *Fax:* (026) 4264330, pg 623

Editions Saint Paul-Afrique (The Democratic Republic of the Congo) *Tel:* (012) 77726, pg 115

Editions Saint-Paul SA (France) *Tel:* (01) 39 67 16 00 *Fax:* (01) 30 21 41 95, pg 183

St Pauls (Australia) *Tel:* (02) 9746 2288 *Fax:* (02) 9746 1140 *E-mail:* sales@stpauls.com.au *Web Site:* www.stpauls.com.au, pg 41

St Pauls (Republic of Korea) *Tel:* (02) 9861361; (02) 9861364 *Fax:* (02) 984-4622 *E-mail:* miari@paolo.net; felix@paolo.net *Web Site:* www.paolo.net, pg 439

St Paul's Bibliographies Ltd (United Kingdom) *Tel:* (0130) 386 2258 *Fax:* (0130) 386 2660 *E-mail:* stpauls@stpaulsbib.com *Web Site:* www.oakknoll.com/spbib.html, pg 738

Saint Publishing (New Zealand) *Tel:* (09) 623-2510 *Fax:* (09) 623-2890 *E-mail:* info@saintpublish.co.nz, pg 495

Bibliotheque Sainte-Genevieve (France) *Tel:* (01) 44419797 *Fax:* (01) 44419796 *E-mail:* bsg@univ.paris1.fr, pg 1465

Sairaanhoitajien Koulutussaatio (Finland) *Tel:* (09) 5666788 *Fax:* (09) 531504, pg 144

Sajha Prakashan, Co-operative Publishing Organization (Nepal) *Tel:* (01) 521023; (01) 521118, pg 472

The Sakai Agency Inc (Japan) *Tel:* (03) 32951405; (03) 32951406 *Fax:* (03) 32954366 *E-mail:* sakai@sakaiagency.com, pg 1114

Sakkoulas Publications SA (Greece) *Tel:* (010) 3387500 *Fax:* (010) 3390075 *E-mail:* info@sakkoulas.gr *Web Site:* www.sakkoulas.gr, pg 314

Salamander Books Ltd (United Kingdom) *Tel:* (020) 7697 3000 *Fax:* (020) 7700 3572, pg 738

Salamandra Consultoria Editorial SA (Brazil) *Tel:* (021) 2406306 *Fax:* (021) 5331622; (021) 2404775 *E-mail:* salprod@openlink.com.br, pg 91

Adriano Salani Editore srl (Italy) *Tel:* (028) 693 238 *Fax:* (027) 201 8806, pg 406

The Salariya Book Co Ltd (United Kingdom) *Tel:* (01273) 603 306 *Fax:* (01273) 693 857 *E-mail:* salariya@salariya.com *Web Site:* www.salariya.com, pg 738

Saldo Penzugyi Tanacsado es Informatikai Rt (Hungary) *Tel:* (01) 2038213; (01) 2038217, pg 326

Salerno Editrice SRL (Italy) *Tel:* (06) 3608201 *Fax:* (06) 3223132 *E-mail:* salernoeditrice@mclink.it *Web Site:* www.salernoeditrice.it, pg 406

Salesian Press/Don Bosco Sha (Japan) *Tel:* (032) 33517041 *Fax:* (032) 33515430, pg 424

Salesiana Publishers Inc (Philippines) *Tel:* (02) 8161506; (02) 889234 *Fax:* (02) 8939876, pg 515

Edicoes Salesianas (Portugal) *Tel:* (02) 565750 *Fax:* (02) 565800, pg 529

Salmon Publishing (Ireland) *Tel:* (065) 7081941 *Fax:* (065) 7081621 *E-mail:* info@salmonpoetry.com *Web Site:* www.salmonpoetry.com, pg 364

The Saltire Society (United Kingdom) *Tel:* (0131) 556 1836 *Fax:* (0131) 557 1675 *E-mail:* saltire@saltire.org.uk *Web Site:* www.saltire-society.demon.co.uk, pg 738

Salto Publishers (Greece) *Tel:* (031) 262854 *Fax:* (031) 285879 *E-mail:* saltos@spocrk.net.gr, pg 1287

Saltwater Publications (Australia) *Tel:* (03) 5974 1959 *Fax:* (03) 5974 1959, pg 41

Salvat Editores de Mexico (Mexico) *Tel:* (05) 2039343; (05) 2034813 *Fax:* (05) 2506861, pg 466

Salvat Editores SA (Spain) *Tel:* (093) 4301441 *Fax:* (093) 4390579, pg 589

Editorial Miguel A Salvatella SA (Spain) *Tel:* (093) 2189026 *Fax:* (093) 2177437 *E-mail:* editorial@salvatella.com *Web Site:* www.salvatella.com, pg 589

Salvationist Publishing & Supplies Ltd (United Kingdom) *Tel:* (020) 7387 1656 *Fax:* (020) 7383 3420 *E-mail:* addmin@sp-s.co.uk, pg 738

Editions Salvator Sarl (France) *Tel:* (01) 53 10 38 38 *Fax:* (01) 53 10 38 39, pg 183

Salvioni arti grafiche SA (Switzerland) *Tel:* (091) 254141 *Fax:* (091) 261056, pg 623

Salvy Editeur (France) *Tel:* (01) 43257440 *Fax:* (01) 46335621, pg 183

Verlag der Salzburger Druckerei (Austria) *Tel:* (0662) 873507 *Fax:* (0662) 873507, pg 58

Salzburger Kulturvereinigung (Austria) *Tel:* (0662) 845346 *Fax:* (0662) 842665 *E-mail:* kulturvereinigung@salzburg.co.at *Web Site:* www.salzburg.com/kulturvereinigung, pg 58

Eugen Salzer-Verlag GmbH & Co KG (Germany) *Tel:* (07131) 68294 *Fax:* (07131) 171331, pg 281

Sam Woode Ltd (Ghana) *Tel:* (021) 220257 *Fax:* (021) 662210, pg 308

Saman & Madara Publishers (Sri Lanka) *Tel:* (01) 862055 *Fax:* (01) 868071 *E-mail:* prince@eureka.lk, pg 598

Samaya SRL (Italy) *Tel:* (0789) 750039 *Fax:* (0789) 750081, pg 406

Samayawardena Printers Publishers & Booksellers (Sri Lanka) *Tel:* (01) 694682; (01) 687904; (01) 698977; (01) 683525 *Fax:* (01) 698977; (01) 683525 *E-mail:* samaya@applestr.lk, pg 598

Sambandet Forlag (Norway) *Tel:* 55317963 *Fax:* 55310944 *E-mail:* vestlandskes.bokhandel@c2i.net, pg 504

Samdistribution AB (Sweden) *Tel:* (08) 6968000 *Fax:* (08) 6968361, pg 1313

Samfundet De Nio (Sweden) *Tel:* (08) 411 15 42 *Fax:* (08) 21 19 15, pg 1368

Samfundslitteratur (Denmark) *Tel:* 35356366 *Fax:* 35357822 *E-mail:* slforlag@sl.cbs.dk *Web Site:* www.samfundslitteratur.dk, pg 135

Samho Music Publishing Co (Republic of Korea) *Tel:* (02) 5123515 *Fax:* (02) 512-3594 *E-mail:* webmaster@samhomusic.com *Web Site:* www.samhomusic.com, pg 440

Samhwa Publishing Co (Republic of Korea) *Tel:* (02) 7766686 *Fax:* (02) 7732993, pg 440

Samkaleen Prakashan (India) *Tel:* (011) 3523520; (011) 3518197, pg 349

Samkwang Publishing Co (Republic of Korea) *Tel:* (02) 3237275 *Fax:* (02) 3251153, pg 440

Samlerens Bogklub (Denmark) *Tel:* 33128282 *Fax:* 33110323, pg 1228

Samlerens Forlag A/S (Denmark) *Tel:* 33411800 *Fax:* 33411801, pg 135

Verlag fuer Sammler (Austria) *Tel:* (0316) 47 22 30 *Fax:* (0316) 67 39 87 *Web Site:* www.literaturhaus.at/buch/verlagsportraits/sammler.html, pg 58

Samseong Publishing Co Ltd (Republic of Korea) *Tel:* (02) 3470-6852 *Fax:* (02) 7853565, pg 440

Samsom BedrijfsInformatie BV (Netherlands) *Tel:* (0172) 466321 *Fax:* (0172) 435527, pg 483

Samsprak Forlags AB (Sweden) *Tel:* (019) 132445 *Fax:* (019) 187255 *E-mail:* info@samsprak.se *Web Site:* www.samsprak.se, pg 606

Collegio San Bonaventura di Grottaferrata (Italy) *Tel:* (06) 94315318 *Fax:* (06) 9410781, pg 406

San Carlos Publications (Philippines) *Tel:* (032) 70874, pg 515

San Lorenzo (Italy) *Tel:* (0522) 323140 *Fax:* (0522) 323140 *E-mail:* frtt15k1@re.nettuno.it (forte Luciano), pg 406

Editrice San Marco SRL (Italy) *Tel:* (035) 940178 *Fax:* (035) 944385 *E-mail:* sanmarco@ibenet.it, pg 406

Editorial San Martin (Spain) *Tel:* (091) 5483590, pg 589

San Min Book Co Ltd (Taiwan, Province of China) *Tel:* (02) 25006600 *Fax:* (02) 25064000 *E-mail:* sanmin@ms2.hinet.net *Web Site:* www.sanmin.com.tw, pg 631

San Pablo (Argentina) *Tel:* (011) 4953-2421; (011) 4953-2737 *Fax:* (011) 4953-2737 *E-mail:* isanpablo@impsat1.com.ar, pg 8

San Pablo Ediciones (Spain) *Tel:* (091) 7987426; (091) 7987427; (091) 7987375 *Fax:* (091) 7425723 *E-mail:* editorial@sanpablo-ssp.es *Web Site:* www.sanpablo-ssp.es, pg 589

Libreria San Pablo (Chile) *Tel:* (02) 2882026 *Fax:* (02) 6716884, pg 1279

Edizioni San Paolo SRL (Italy) *Tel:* (02) 660751 *Fax:* (02) 66075211 *E-mail:* cb.spe.segreteria@stpauls.it, pg 407

Ediciones San Pio X (Spain) *Tel:* (091) 7262817; (091) 355 2727 *Fax:* (091) 7262817 *E-mail:* espx@planalfa.es, pg 589

Simone Sanchez (French Polynesia) *Tel:* 533260, pg 190

Editions Sand et Tchou SA (France) *Tel:* (01) 44.55.37.50 *Fax:* (01) 40.20.99.74, pg 183

Erik Sandberg (Norway) *Tel:* 22335555 *Fax:* 22413562, pg 504

Sandila Import-Export Handels-GmbH (Germany) *Tel:* (07764) 93970 *Fax:* (07764) 939739 *E-mail:* sandila@t-online.de *Web Site:* www.sandila.de, pg 1284

Sandpiper Books Ltd (United Kingdom) *Tel:* (020) 8767 7421 *Fax:* (020) 8682 0280 *E-mail:* sandpiper@sandpiper.co.uk, pg 1321

Sandpiper Press (Australia) *Tel:* (08) 94810375 *Fax:* (08) 94816547, pg 41

Sandviks Bokforlag (Norway) *Tel:* 51510000 *Fax:* 51526009, pg 505

Lennart Sane Agency AB (Spain) *Tel:* (0952) 834180 *Fax:* (0952) 833196, pg 1116

Lennart Sane Agency AB (Sweden) *Tel:* (0454) 123 56 *Fax:* (0454) 149 20, pg 1116

Sane Toregard Agency (Sweden) *Tel:* (0454) 123 56 *Fax:* (0454) 149 20, pg 1116

Sang Choy International PTE Ltd (Singapore) *Tel:* (065) 6289 0829 *Fax:* (065) 6282 7673 *E-mail:* marketing@sc-international.com.sg, pg 1159

Sang Dad Publishing Company Ltd (Thailand) *Tel:* (02) 5381499; (02) 5387576 *Fax:* (02) 559 2643; (02) 5381499 *E-mail:* sangdad@asianet.co.th, pg 635

Editions Sang de la Terre (France) *Tel:* (01) 42 82 08 16 *Fax:* (01) 48 74 14 88 *E-mail:* editeur@sangdelaterre.com *Web Site:* www.sangdelaterre.com, pg 183

Sang-e-Meel Publications (Pakistan) *Tel:* (042) 7220100; (042) 7228143; (042) 7667970; (042) 7228147 *Fax:* (042) 7245101 *E-mail:* smp@sang-e-meel.com *Web Site:* www.sang-e-meel.com, pg 509

Sangam Books Ltd (United Kingdom) *Tel:* (020) 7377-6399 *Fax:* (020) 7375-1230 *E-mail:* sangambks@aol.com, pg 738

Sangster's Book Stores Ltd (Jamaica) *Tel:* (876) 922-3640 *Fax:* (876) 922-3813, pg 1294

Sangyo-Tosho Publishing Co Ltd (Japan) *Tel:* (03) 32617821 *Fax:* (03) 32392178 *E-mail:* info@san-to.co.jp *Web Site:* www.san-to.co.jp, pg 424

Sankt-Johannis-Druckerei (Germany) *Tel:* (07821) 5810 *Fax:* (07821) 58126, pg 1133

Verlag der Sankt-Johannis-Druckerei C Schweickhardt (Germany) *Tel:* (07821) 5810 *Fax:* (07821) 58126 *E-mail:* johannis-Druck@t-online.de, pg 281

Sankt Otto Verlag GmbH (Germany) *Tel:* (0951) 967120 *Fax:* (0951) 96712235, pg 281

Sankt-Peterburgskogo Gosudarstvennogo Universiteta (Russian Federation) *Tel:* (0812) 2182741 *Fax:* (0812) 2182741, pg 1495

Sankyo Publishing Company Ltd (Japan) *Tel:* (03) 32645711 *Fax:* (03) 32655149, pg 424

Sanra Book Trust (Bulgaria) *Tel:* (02) 721927 *Fax:* (02) 721927, pg 97

Sanseido Bookstore Ltd (Japan) *Tel:* (03) 3896 6332 *Fax:* (03) 5839 0292 *E-mail:* fbook_stock@mail.books-sanseido.co.jp *Web Site:* www.books-sanseido.co.jp, pg 1295

Sanseido Co Ltd (Japan) *Tel:* (03) 32309404 *Fax:* (03) 32309567, pg 424

Sanshusha Publishing Co, Ltd (Japan) *Tel:* (03) 38421711 *Fax:* (03) 38453965 *E-mail:* toshi@sanshusha.co.jp, pg 424

Sansoni Editore (Italy) *Tel:* (02) 50952333 *Fax:* (02) 50952309 *Web Site:* www.sansonieditore.it, pg 407

Sant Jordi Asociados Agencia (Spain) *Tel:* (093) 3091159 *Fax:* (093) 3091160 *E-mail:* santjo@corecta.es, pg 1116

YELLOW PAGES — VERLAG TH SCHAEFER IM VICENTZ VERLAG KG

Libreria Santa Fe (Argentina) *Tel:* (011) 824-5005 *Fax:* (011) 824-7932, pg 1271

Editions du Santal (New Caledonia) *Tel:* (0687) 262533 *Fax:* (0687) 262533 *E-mail:* santal@offratel.nc, pg 488

Graficas Santamaria SA (Spain) *Tel:* (045) 229100 *Fax:* (045) 246393, pg 1139, 1159, 1201

Universidad de Santiago de Compostela (Spain) *Tel:* (0981) 593 500 *Fax:* (0981) 593 963 *E-mail:* spublic@usc.es *Web Site:* www.usc.es/spubl, pg 589

Editorial Santiago Rueda (Argentina) *Tel:* (011) 4611-9174, pg 9

Editorial Santillana (Mexico) *Tel:* (05) 6888966 *Fax:* (05) 6042304, pg 466

Grupo Santillana (Mexico) *Tel:* (05) 6888966 *Fax:* (05) 6042304, pg 466

Editorial Santillana SA (Colombia) *Tel:* (01) 635 12 00; (01) 2189795; (01) 2189935; (01) 2482897; 01 2496350 *Fax:* (01) 236 93 82; (01) 2360311; (01) 2351655; (01) 6351200 *Web Site:* www.santillana.com.co, pg 113

Biblioteca Municipal de Santo Domingo (Dominican Republic), pg 1461

Livraria Santos Editora Comercio e Importacao Ltda (Brazil) *Tel:* (011) 55741200 *Fax:* (011) 55738774 *E-mail:* editorasantos@terra.com.br, pg 91

Editora Santuario (Brazil) *Tel:* (012) 565 2140 *Fax:* (012) 565 2141 *E-mail:* vendas@redemptor.com.br *Web Site:* www.redemptor.com.br, pg 91

Santype International Ltd (United Kingdom) *Tel:* (01722) 334261 *Fax:* (01722) 333171 *E-mail:* post@santype.com *Web Site:* www.santype.com, pg 1163

Sanyo Shuppan Boeki Co Inc (Japan) *Tel:* (03) 36693761, pg 1295

Sanyo Shuppan Boeki Co Inc (Japan) *Tel:* (03) 36693761 *Fax:* (03) 53513028, pg 424

Il Sapere Edizioni (Italy) *Tel:* (089) 254252 *Fax:* (089) 254262 *E-mail:* sapere@elimet.sandera.it, pg 407

Sapere 2000 SRL (Italy) *Tel:* (06) 4465363 *Fax:* (06) 4465363 *E-mail:* sapere2000@flshnet.it, pg 407

Sapes Trust Ltd (Zimbabwe) *Tel:* (04) 726060; (04) 790815 *Fax:* (04) 726060; (04) 732735, pg 769

Paul Sappl, Schulbuch- und Lehrmittelverlag (Austria) *Tel:* (05372) 643 00 *Fax:* (05372) 64 300-17, pg 58

Saqi Books (United Kingdom) *Tel:* (020) 7229 8543; (020) 7221 9347 *Fax:* (020) 7229 7492 *E-mail:* saqibooks@dial.pipex.com *Web Site:* www.saqibooks.com, pg 1322

Saraiva SA, Livreiros Editores (Brazil) *Tel:* (011) 36133000 *Fax:* (011) 36113308 *E-mail:* diretoria.editora@editorasaraiva.com.br *Web Site:* www.editorasaraiva.com.br, pg 91

Saraiva SA, Livreiros Editores (Brazil) *Tel:* (011) 8268422 *Fax:* (011) 8260606, pg 1278

Sarasavi Book Shop Pvt Ltd (Sri Lanka) *Tel:* (01) 852519; (01) 820983; (01) 820230; (074) 304546 *Fax:* (01) 821454; (01) 509503 *E-mail:* sarasavi@slt.lk *Web Site:* www.sarasavibooks.com, pg 1312

Saraswati Publishers & Distributors (India), pg 349

Saray Medikal Yayin Tic Ltd Sti (Turkey) *Tel:* (0232) 3394969; (0232) 3396949 *Fax:* (0232) 3733700 *E-mail:* eozkarahan@novell.cs.eng.dev.edu.tr, pg 641

Fausto Sardini Editrice (Italy) *Tel:* (030) 7750430 *Fax:* (030) 7254348 *E-mail:* sardini@sardini.it, pg 407

M C Sarkar & Sons (P) Ltd (India) *Tel:* (033) 312490, pg 349

Editions Le Sarment (France) *Tel:* (01) 45.49.82.00 *Fax:* (01) 45.48.82.36 *E-mail:* cremond@editions-fayard.fr, pg 184

Saros International Publishers (Nigeria) *Tel:* (084) 331763 *Fax:* (084) 331763, pg 501

Sarpay Beikman Book Club (Myanmar) *Tel:* (01) 83611, pg 1230

Sarpay Beikman Bookshop (Myanmar) *Tel:* (01) 83611; (01) 16611, pg 1300

Sarpay Beikman Board (Myanmar) *Tel:* (01) 83611, pg 471

Sarpay Lawka (Myanmar), pg 1300

Sarvier - Editora de Livros Medicos Ltda (Brazil) *Tel:* (011) 571-3439, pg 91

Sarvodaya Vishva Lekha (Sri Lanka) *Tel:* (01) 714820; (01) 714829; (01) 731601 *Fax:* (01) 738932 *E-mail:* sarvs101@sri.lanka.net, pg 1139

Sasavona Publishers & Booksellers (South Africa) *Tel:* (011) 4032502 *Fax:* (011) 3397274, pg 559

Sassafras Verlag (Germany) *Tel:* (02151) 787770 *Fax:* (02151) 771302, pg 281

Sasta Sahitya Mandal (India) *Tel:* (011) 3310505, pg 349

Sastra Hudaya PT (Indonesia) *Tel:* (021) 3904223, pg 357

Sat Sahitya Prakashan (India) *Tel:* (011) 3276316, pg 349

Sri Satguru Publications (India) *Tel:* (011) 7126497; (011) 7434930 *Fax:* (011) 7227336 *E-mail:* indianbookcentre@v.s.n.l.com, pg 349

Satprakashan Sanchar Kendra (India) *Tel:* 363733; 475744 *Fax:* 475731 *E-mail:* sskin@sancharnet.in *Web Site:* www.educational.vsnl.com/satprakashan, pg 349

Satrap Publishing & Translation (United Kingdom) *Tel:* (020) 8748 9397 *Fax:* (020) 8748 9394 *E-mail:* satrap@btinternet.com, pg 1129

Sattva Kunst Verlag (Germany) *Tel:* (08028) 90 68-0 *Fax:* (08028) 90 68-10; (08028) 90 68-20, pg 281

Oy Satusiivet - Sagovingar AB (Lasten Parhaat Kirjat) (Finland) *Tel:* (09) 6933267 *Fax:* (09) 6944186, pg 1282

Satyr-Verlag Dr Humbel (Switzerland) *Tel:* 01 554620, pg 623

Saudi Publishing and Distribution House (Saudi Arabia) *Tel:* (02) 6424043; (02) 6424255; (02) 6446308 *Fax:* (02) 6432821, pg 543

I H Sauer Verlag GmbH (Germany) *Tel:* (06221) 906-0 *Fax:* (06221) 906 259 *E-mail:* sauerverlag@ruw.de *Web Site:* www.ruw-ruw.de, pg 282

Sauerlaender AG (Switzerland) *Tel:* (064) 268626; (064) 268686 *Fax:* (064) 245780 *E-mail:* verlag@sauerlaendes.ch *Web Site:* www.sauerlaender.ch, pg 623

Verlag Sauerlaender GmbH (Germany) *Tel:* (069) 942118-0 *Fax:* (069) 412099, pg 282

J D Sauerlaender's Verlag (Germany) *Tel:* (069) 555217 *Fax:* (069) 5964344 *E-mail:* j.d.sauerlaenders.verlag@t-online.de, pg 282

W B Saunders & Co Ltd (United Kingdom) *Tel:* (020) 7267 4200 *Fax:* (020) 7485 4752, pg 738

K G Saur Verlag GmbH, A Gale/Thomson Learning Company (Germany) *Tel:* (089) 76902-0 *Fax:* (089) 76902-150 *E-mail:* info@saur.de *Web Site:* www.saur.de, pg 282

Sauramps Medical (France) *Tel:* (04) 67636880 *Fax:* (04) 67525905 *E-mail:* sauramps.medical@livres-medicaux.com *Web Site:* www.livres-medicaux.com, pg 184

Librairie Sauramps Medical (France) *Tel:* (04) 67636880 *Fax:* (04) 67525905 *E-mail:* sauramps.medical@livrelmedicaux.com *Web Site:* www.livrel.medicaux.com, pg 1283

Editions Andre Sauret SA (Monaco) *Tel:* (093) 506794 *Fax:* (093) 307104, pg 469

Savannah Editions SARL (New Caledonia) *Tel:* (0687) 252919 *Fax:* (0687) 282470, pg 488

Savannah Publications (United Kingdom) *Tel:* (020) 8244 4350 *Fax:* (020) 8244 2448 *E-mail:* savpub@dircon.co.uk, pg 738

Savez Inzenjera i Tehnicara Jugoslavije (Yugoslavia) *Tel:* (011) 3243653; (011) 3243652 *Fax:* (011) 3243652 *E-mail:* internet@eunet.yu, pg 765

Savitri Books (United Kingdom) *Tel:* (020) 7436 9932 *Fax:* (020) 7580 6330, pg 738

Savremena Administracija (Yugoslavia) *Tel:* (011) 623-287 *Fax:* (011) 667-277; (011) 623-776, pg 765

Sawan Kirpal Publications (India) *Tel:* (011) 7110757; (011) 7210722 *Fax:* (011) 7210720, pg 349

SAWD Publications (United Kingdom) *Tel:* (01795) 472 262 *Fax:* (01795) 422 633 *E-mail:* wainman@sawd.demon.co.uk *Web Site:* www.sawd.demon.co.uk, pg 738

Tessa Sayle Agency (United Kingdom) *Tel:* (020) 7823 3883 *Fax:* (020) 7823 3363 *E-mail:* info@thesayleagency.co.uk, pg 1121

Sayrols Editorial SA de CV (Mexico) *Tel:* (0525) 147 2300 *Fax:* (0525) 536 4622 *E-mail:* ventas@sayrols.com.mx *Web Site:* www.sayrols.com.mx, pg 466

SB Publications (United Kingdom) *Tel:* (01323) 893498 *Fax:* (01323) 893860 *E-mail:* sales@sbpublications.swinternet.co.uk *Web Site:* www.sbpublications.swinternet.co.uk, pg 738

SBW Publishers (India) *Tel:* (011) 3279603, pg 349

Editions Scaillet, SA (Belgium) *Tel:* (071) 516335 *Fax:* (071) 511795, pg 74

Editions Scala (France) *Tel:* (01) 49 29 42 25 *Fax:* (01) 49 29 99 33 *E-mail:* editions.scala@wanadoo.fr *Web Site:* www.ldj.tm.fr/editeurs/editeurs/scala.htm, pg 184

Scala Group spa (Italy) *Tel:* (055) 623311 *Fax:* (055) 6233280 *E-mail:* scala@scalagroup.com *Web Site:* www.scalagroup.com, pg 407

Scan-Globe A/S (Denmark) *Tel:* 46185400 *Fax:* 46185270 *E-mail:* info@scanglobe.dk *Web Site:* www.scanglobe.dk, pg 135

Scandinavia Publishing House (Denmark) *Tel:* 35 31 03 30 *Fax:* 35 31 03 34 *Web Site:* www.scanpublishing.dk, pg 135

scaneg Verlag (Germany) *Tel:* (089) 759 33 36 *Fax:* (089) 759 39 14 *E-mail:* verlag@scaneg.de *Web Site:* www.scaneg.de, pg 282

Scanvik Books Import ApS (Denmark) *Tel:* 33127766 *Fax:* 33912882 *E-mail:* scanvik@bog.dk, pg 1110

Scanvik Books Import ApS (Denmark) *Tel:* 33127766 *Fax:* 33912882 *E-mail:* scanvik@bog.dk *Web Site:* www.scanvik.dk, pg 1281

Editions du Scarabee (France) *Tel:* (01) 43 26 23 94 *Fax:* (01) 43 26 23 94, pg 184

Lo Scarabeo Srl (Italy) *Tel:* (011) 7716568 *Fax:* (011) 740843, pg 407

Scarthin Books (United Kingdom) *Tel:* (01629) 823272 *Fax:* (01629) 825094 *E-mail:* clare@scarthinbooks.com *Web Site:* www.scarthinbooks.com; www.books.co.uk, pg 738

Scena (Lithuania) *Tel:* (02) 751828; (02) 614145 *Fax:* (02) 610814, pg 446

De Schaar/Geknipt Papier (Belgium) *Tel:* (09) 2255414 *Fax:* (09) 2259724 *E-mail:* geknipt@skynet.be *Web Site:* users.skynet.be, pg 74

Verlag Th Schaefer im Vicentz Verlag KG (Germany) *Tel:* (0511) 9910-012 *Fax:* (0511) 9910-013, pg 282

Schaeffer-Poeschel Verlag fuer Wirtschaft Steuern Recht (Germany) *Tel:* (0711) 2194-0 *Fax:* (0711) 2194-119 *E-mail:* info@schaeffer-poeschel.de *Web Site:* www.schaeffer-poeschel.de, pg 282

Schangrila Verlags und Vertriebs GmbH (Germany) *Tel:* (08343) 581 *Fax:* (08343) 657 *Web Site:* www.schangrila.com, pg 282

Schapen Edition, H W Louis (Germany) *Tel:* (04953) 1360921 *E-mail:* schapen.edition@t-online.de, pg 282

M & H Schaper GmbH & Co KG (Germany) *Tel:* (05181) 8009-0 *Fax:* (05181) 8009-33 *E-mail:* info@shaper-verlag.de *Web Site:* www.schaper-verlag.de, pg 282

F K Schattauer Verlagsgesellschaft mbH (Germany) *Tel:* (0711) 229870 *Fax:* (0711) 2298750 *Web Site:* www.schattauer.de, pg 282

Moritz Schauenburg Verlag (Germany) *Tel:* (07821) 90596-0 *Fax:* (07821) 9059666 *E-mail:* schauenburg_verlag@t-online.de, pg 282

Guillermo Schavelzon (Argentina) *Tel:* (011) 48 13 84 20 *Fax:* (011) 48 13 28 76 *E-mail:* info@schavelzon.com, pg 1109

Scheffler-Verlag (Germany) *Tel:* (02330) 1743 *Fax:* (02330) 2281, pg 282

Scheltema (Netherlands) *Tel:* (020) 5231411 *Fax:* (020) 6227684 *E-mail:* shv@dds.nl *Web Site:* www.scheltema.nl, pg 1301

Schelzky & Jeep, Verlag fuer Reisen und Wissen (Germany) *Tel:* (030) 6939495 *Fax:* (030) 6914697, pg 283

Schena Editore (Italy) *Tel:* (080) 714681 *Fax:* (080) 714690, pg 407

Dr A Schendl GmbH und Co KG (Austria) *Tel:* (01) 484 17 85-0 *Fax:* (01) 484 17 85-15 *E-mail:* info@schendl.at *Web Site:* www.schendl.at, pg 58

Renate Schenk Verlag (Germany) *Tel:* (0341) 2300825 *Fax:* (0341) 2300826 *E-mail:* schenk-verlag@t-online.de *Web Site:* www.schenk-verlag.de, pg 283

Richard Scherpe Verlag GmbH (Germany) *Tel:* (02151) 539-0 *Fax:* (02151) 505390, pg 283

Buchhandlung Scherz AG (Switzerland) *Tel:* (031) 227337 *Fax:* (031) 210375, pg 1313

Scherz Verlag AG (Switzerland) *Tel:* (031) 3277150 *Fax:* (031) 3277171 *E-mail:* scherz@scherzverlag.ch *Web Site:* www.scherzverlag.ch, pg 623

Papierfabrik Scheufelen GmbH & Co KG (Germany) *Tel:* (07026) 66-1 *Fax:* (07026) 66701, pg 1133

Chr Schibsteds Forlag A/S (Norway) *Tel:* 22863000 *Fax:* 22425492, pg 505

Schiffahrts-Verlag (Germany) *Tel:* (040) 79713-02 *Fax:* (040) 79713-324; (040) 79713-208; (040) 79713-214 *E-mail:* r_spieckermann@hansa-online.de, pg 283

Schild-Verlag GmbH (Germany) *Tel:* (089) 8 64 1189 *Fax:* (089) 8 63 2310, pg 283

Schildts Foerlagsaktiebolag (Finland) *Tel:* (00) 8870400 *Fax:* (00) 8043257 *E-mail:* schildts@schildts.fi *Web Site:* www.schildts.fi, pg 144

Verlag der Schillerbuchhandlung Hans Banger OHG (Germany) *Tel:* (0221) 46014-0 *Fax:* (0221) 46014-25; (0221) 46014-26 *E-mail:* banger@banger.de *Web Site:* www.banger.de, pg 283

Schillinger Verlag GmbH (Germany) *Tel:* (0761) 33233 *Fax:* (0762) 39055 *E-mail:* schillingerverlag@t-online.de *Web Site:* schillingerverlag.de, pg 283

Paul Schiltz (Belgium) *Tel:* (087) 553271, pg 74

Karin Schindler (Brazil) *Tel:* (011) 50419177 *Fax:* (011) 2419077, pg 1109

Karin Schindler Representante de Direitos Autorais (Brazil) *Tel:* (011) 241-9177 *Fax:* (011) 241-9077, pg 91

Schirmer/Mosel Verlag GmbH (Germany) *Tel:* (089) 2126700 *Fax:* (089) 338695 *E-mail:* mail@schirmer-mosel.com *Web Site:* www.schirmer-mosel.com, pg 283

Schirner Verlag (Germany) *Tel:* (06151) 29 39 59 *Fax:* (06151) 29 39 87 *E-mail:* schirner.verlag@t-online.de *Web Site:* www.schirner.com, pg 283

Schlaepfer & Co AG (Switzerland) *Tel:* (071) 513131 *Fax:* (071) 525126, pg 624

Schlesinger Institute (Israel) *Tel:* (02) 6555266 *Fax:* (02) 6523295 *E-mail:* medhal@szmc.org.il *Web Site:* www.szmc.org.il, pg 372

Agora Verlag Manfred Schlosser (Germany) *Tel:* (030) 3424824 *Fax:* (030) 8545372 *E-mail:* agora2@gmx.net, pg 283

Thomas Schlueck GmbH (Germany) *Tel:* (05131) 497560 *Fax:* (05131) 497589 *E-mail:* mail@schlueckagent.com, pg 1112

Schmetterling Verlag Jorg Hunger und Paul Sander (Germany) *Tel:* (0711) 62 67 79 *Fax:* (0711) 62 69 92 *E-mail:* info@schmetterling-verlag.de *Web Site:* www.schmetterling-verlag.de, pg 283

Schmid Verlag GmbH (Austria) *Tel:* (0941) 21519 *Fax:* (0941) 28766 *E-mail:* info@schmid-verlag.de *Web Site:* www.schmid-verlag.de, pg 58

Schmid Verlag GmbH (Germany) *Tel:* (0941) 21519; (0941) 26629 *Fax:* (0941) 28766 *Web Site:* www.schmid-verlag.de, pg 283

Verlag Dr Otto Schmidt KG (Germany) *Tel:* (0221) 9 37 38-01 *Fax:* (0221) 9 37 38-09 *E-mail:* info@ottoschmidt.de; verlag@ottoschmidt.de *Web Site:* www.otto-schmidt.de, pg 283

Erich Schmidt Verlag GmbH & Co (Germany) *Tel:* (030) 25 00 85-0 *Fax:* (030) 25 00 85-21 *E-mail:* ESV@esvmedien.de *Web Site:* www.erich-schmidt-verlag.de, pg 283

Erich Schmidt Verlag GmbH & Co (Germany) *Tel:* (030) 25 00 85-0 *Fax:* (030) 25 00 85 11 *E-mail:* vertrieb@esvmedien.de *Web Site:* www.erich-schmidt-verlag.de, pg 284

Verlag Hermann Schmidt Universitatsdruckerei GmbH & Co (Germany) *Tel:* (06131) 506030 *Fax:* (06131) 506080 *E-mail:* info@typografie.de *Web Site:* www.typografie.de, pg 284

Schmidt Periodicals GmbH (Germany) *Tel:* (08064) 221 *Fax:* (08064) 557 *E-mail:* schmidt@backsets.com *Web Site:* www.backsets.com, pg 284

Max Schmidt-Roemhild Verlag (Germany) *Tel:* (0451) 70 31-51 *Fax:* (0451) 70 31-253 *E-mail:* msr-luebeck@t-online.de *Web Site:* www.schmidt-roemhild.de, pg 284

Buchverlag Andrea Schmitz (Germany) *Tel:* (04173) 512612 *Fax:* (04173) 512612 *E-mail:* buchverlag@aol.com, pg 284

Wilhelm Schmitz Verlag (Germany) *Tel:* (06406) 23 24 *Web Site:* www.wilhelm-schmitz-verlag.de, pg 284

Schneekluth Verlag (Germany) *Tel:* (089) 92710 *Fax:* (089) 9271261 *Web Site:* www.schneekluth.de, pg 284

Rudolf Schneider Verlag (Germany) *Tel:* (089) 8113466 *Fax:* (089) 8110619, pg 284

Verlag Schnell und Steiner GmbH (Germany) *Tel:* (0941) 787850 *Fax:* (0941) 7878516 *E-mail:* susvertrieb@t-online.de, pg 284

Schnellmann-Verlag (Switzerland) *Tel:* (055) 2111472; (079) 3175143 *Fax:* (055) 2111477 *Web Site:* www.dictionaries.ch, pg 624

Andreas Schnider Verlags-Atelier (Austria) *Tel:* (0316) 471302 *Fax:* (0316) 4713024, pg 58

Schnitzer GmbH & Co KG (Germany) *Tel:* (07724) 9432-0 *Fax:* (07724) 9432-20 *Web Site:* www.medizin.li, pg 284

Schocken Publishing House Ltd (Israel) *Tel:* (03) 5610130 *Fax:* (03) 5622668 *Web Site:* www.schockem.co.il, pg 372

Schoeffling & Co (Germany) *Tel:* (069) 92 07 87-0 *Fax:* (069) 92 07 87-20 *E-mail:* ida.schoeffling@schoeffling.de *Web Site:* www.schoeffling.de, pg 284

Verlag fuer Schoene Wissenschaften (Switzerland) *Tel:* (061) 723911 *Fax:* (061) 7011417, pg 624

Verlag Hans Schoener GmbH (Germany) *Tel:* (07232) 4007-0 *Fax:* (07232) 4007-99 *E-mail:* info@verlag-schoener.de *Web Site:* www.verlag-schoener.de, pg 284

Ferdinand Schoeningh Verlag GmbH (Germany) *Tel:* (05251) 1275 *Fax:* (05251) 127860; (05251) 127670 *E-mail:* info@schoeningh.de *Web Site:* www.schoeningh.de, pg 284

Schofield & Sims Ltd (United Kingdom) *Tel:* (01484) 607080 *Fax:* (01484) 606815 *E-mail:* post@schofieldandsims.co.uk *Web Site:* www.schofieldandsims.co.uk, pg 739

Editions Musicales de la Schola Cantorum (Switzerland) *Tel:* (025) 652480; (025) 653060, pg 624

Scholastic Australia Pty Ltd (Australia) *Tel:* (02) 4328 3555 *Fax:* (02) 4323 3827 *Web Site:* www.scholastic.com.au, pg 41

Scholastic Ltd (United Kingdom) *Tel:* (01926) 887799; (01926) 813910 (warehouse) *Fax:* (01926) 883331 *E-mail:* scholastic@tens.co.uk *Web Site:* www.scholastic.co.uk, pg 739

Scholastic Publications Ltd (United Kingdom) *Tel:* (01926) 887799 *Fax:* (01926) 883331, pg 1234

Kurt Scholl (Germany) *Tel:* (06221) 707661, pg 1284

Det Schonbergske Forlag (Denmark) *Tel:* 33733585 *Fax:* 33733586 *E-mail:* Schoenberg@nytnordiskforlag.dk *Web Site:* www.nytnordiskforlag.dk, pg 135

School Library Association (United Kingdom) *Tel:* (01793) 791787 *Fax:* (01793) 791786 *E-mail:* info@sla.org.uk *Web Site:* www.sla.org.uk, pg 1525

School of Administration Library (Ghana) *Tel:* (021) 765915 *Fax:* (021) 777024 *E-mail:* soa@ug.gn.apc.org, pg 1470

School of Oriental & African Studies (United Kingdom) *Tel:* (020) 7637 2388 *Fax:* (020) 7436 3844 *E-mail:* md2@soas.ac.uk; aol@soas.ac.uk *Web Site:* www.soas.ac.uk, pg 739

School of Oriental & African Studies Library (United Kingdom) *Tel:* (020) 7323 6109 *Fax:* (020) 7636 2834 *E-mail:* kw@soas.ac.uk, pg 1507

School Supplies Limited (New Zealand) *Tel:* (09) 3023215 *Fax:* (09) 3023209, pg 1302

SchoolPlay Productions Ltd (United Kingdom) *Tel:* (01206) 540111 *Fax:* (01206) 766944 *E-mail:* schoolplay@inglis-house.demon.co.uk *Web Site:* www.schoolplayproductions.co.uk, pg 739

Schott Freres SA (Editeurs de Musique) (Belgium) *Tel:* (02) 5123980 *Fax:* (02) 5142845, pg 74

Schott Musik International GmbH & Co KG (Germany) *Tel:* (06131) 246-0; (06131) 5050 (Auslief) *Fax:* (06131) 2462-11; (06131) 505115 (Auslief) *Web Site:* www.schott-online.com, pg 284

Schrader Verlag Paul Pietsch Verlage GmbH & Co KG (Germany) *Tel:* (0711) 21080-0 *Fax:* (0711) 2360415, pg 285

Verlag Silke Schreiber (Germany) *Tel:* (089) 2710180 *Fax:* (089) 2716957 *E-mail:* metzel@verlagSilkeschreiber.de *Web Site:* www.verlag-silke-schreiber.de, pg 285

Verlag und Schriftenmission der Evangelischen Gesellschaft Wuppertal (Germany) *Tel:* (0202) 278500 *Fax:* (0202) 2785040, pg 285

Schroedel Schulbuchverlag GmbH (Germany) *Tel:* (0511) 8388205 *Fax:* (0511) 8388280 *Web Site:* www.schroedel.de, pg 285

Schubert & Franzke Gesellschaft mbH (Austria) *Tel:* (02742) 78 501-0 *Fax:* (02742) 78 501-15 *E-mail:* office@schubert-franzke.com *Web Site:* www.map2web.cc/schubert-franzke, pg 58

A Schudel & Co AG, Verlag (Switzerland) *Tel:* (061) 671011 *Fax:* (061) 671363 *E-mail:* a.schudel@bluewin.ch, pg 624

Walther-Schuecking-Institut fuer Internationales Recht an der Universitaet Kiel (Germany) *Tel:* (0431) 8802367 *Fax:* (0431) 8801619 *E-mail:* fb.internat-recht@ub.uni-kiel.de, pg 1468

Carl Ed Schuenemann KG (Germany) *Tel:* (0421) 369 03 71 *Fax:* (0421) 369 03 63 *E-mail:* kontakt@kunstverlag.de *Web Site:* www2.schuenemann-verlag.de, pg 285

Schueren Verlag GmbH (Germany) *Tel:* (06421) 6 30 84; (06421) 6 30 85 *Fax:* (06421) 68 11 90 *E-mail:* schueren.verlag@t-online.de *Web Site:* www.schueren-verlag.de, pg 285

Verlag Karl Waldemar Schuetz (Germany) *Tel:* (09561) 80780 *Fax:* (09561) 807820, pg 285

Verlag Schulte und Gerth GmbH & Co KG (Germany) *Tel:* (06443) 680 *Fax:* (06443) 6890, pg 285

Schulthess Polygraphischer Verlag AG (Switzerland) *Tel:* (01) 2519336 *Fax:* (01) 2616394 *E-mail:* schulthess@access.ch *Web Site:* www.schulthess.com, pg 624

Schultz Forlag AB (Sweden) *Tel:* (01) 43298392 *Fax:* (01) 40460821 *Web Site:* www.schultzforlag.com, pg 606

J H Schultz Information A/S (Denmark) *Tel:* 43632300 *Fax:* 43631969 *E-mail:* schultz@schultz.dk *Web Site:* www.schultz.dk, pg 135

Schulz-Kirchner Verlag GmbH (Germany) *Tel:* (06126) 93200 *Fax:* (06126) 9320-50 *E-mail:* info@schulz-kirchner.de *Web Site:* www.schulz-kirchner.de, pg 285

R S Schulz Verlag GmbH (Germany) *Tel:* (08151) 9144-0 *Fax:* (08151) 9144-190 *Web Site:* www.rss.de, pg 285

H O Schulze KG (Germany) *Tel:* (09571) 78026 *Fax:* (09571) 78058 *E-mail:* verkauf@schulze-kg.de *Web Site:* www.schulze-kg.de, pg 285

Theodor Schuster (Germany) *Tel:* (0491) 925900 *Fax:* (0491) 9259059 *E-mail:* buchhandlung-Schuster@t-online.de, pg 285

Schuyt & Co Uitgevers en Importeurs BV (Netherlands) *Tel:* (023) 5325440 *Fax:* (023) 5327017, pg 1301

Heinrich Schwab Verlag (Germany) *Tel:* (0043) 5575-20101 *Fax:* (0043) 5575-4745 *E-mail:* heinrich.schwab@vol.at *Web Site:* www.heinrichschwabverlag.de, pg 285

Schwabe & Co AG (Switzerland) *Tel:* (061) 278 95 65 *Fax:* (061) 272 55 73 *E-mail:* verlag@schwabe.ch *Web Site:* www.schwabe.ch, pg 624

Schwabenverlag Aktiengesellschaft (Germany) *Tel:* (0711) 4406-0 *Fax:* (0711) 4406-177 *E-mail:* buchverlag@schwabenverlag.de, pg 285

Schwaneberger Verlag GmbH (Germany) *Tel:* (089) 3239302 *Fax:* (089) 32393379 *E-mail:* webmaster@michel.de *Web Site:* www.michel.de, pg 286

Otto Schwartz Fachbochhandlung GmbH (Germany) *Tel:* (0551) 50 85 978 *Fax:* (0551) 50 85 983 *E-mail:* Schwartz.Stadt@t-online.de, pg 286

Dr Wolfgang Schwarze Verlag (Germany) *Tel:* (0202) 622005; (0202) 622006 *Fax:* (0202) 63631, pg 286

Verlagsbuero Karl Schwarzer (Austria) *Tel:* (01) 548 31 15-0 *Fax:* (01) 548 31 15-39 *E-mail:* verlagsbuero@schwarzer.at, pg 58

Schweers + Wall GmbH Verlag (Germany) *Tel:* (0241) 87 22 51 *Fax:* (0241) 8 52 06 *E-mail:* schweers-wall@t-online.de *Web Site:* home.t-online.de/home/schweers.wall, pg 286

Schweizer Buchzentrum (Switzerland) *Tel:* (062) 2092525 *Fax:* (062) 2092627, pg 1223

Schweizer Buchzentrum (Switzerland) *Tel:* (062) 476161 *Fax:* (062) 465676, pg 1313

Schweizer Spiegel Verlag Mit (Switzerland) *Tel:* (01) 472195 *Fax:* (01) 7502943, pg 624

Schweizerische Vereinigung fur Dokumentation (Switzerland) *Tel:* (041) 7264505 *Fax:* (041) 7264509, pg 1523

Schweizerische Bibliophilen -Gesellschaft (Switzerland), pg 1368

Schweizerische Landesbibliothek (Bibliotheque nationale suisse) (Switzerland) *Tel:* (031) 3228911 (Secretary); (031) 3228979 (Lending Dept); 3228935 (Information) *Fax:* (031) 3228463 *E-mail:* IZ-Helvetica@slb.admin.ch, pg 1501

Schweizerische Stiftung fuer Alpine Forschungen (Switzerland) *Tel:* (01) 4610147, pg 624

Schweizerischer Buchhaendler- und Verleger-Verband SBVV (Switzerland) *Tel:* (01) 3186430 *Fax:* (01) 3186462 *E-mail:* sbvv@swissbooks.ch *Web Site:* www.swissbooks.ch, pg 1261

Schweizerischer Bund fuer Jugendliteratur (Switzerland) *Tel:* 7413140 *Fax:* 7400159 *E-mail:* sbj@bluewin.ch, pg 1368

Schweizerischer Schriftstellerinnen-und Schriftsteller-Verband (Switzerland) *Tel:* (01) 350 04 60 *Fax:* (01) 350 04 61 *E-mail:* letter@ch-s.ch *Web Site:* www.ch-s.ch, pg 1139

Schweizerischer Schriftstellerinnen-und Schriftsteller-Verband (Switzerland) *Tel:* (01) 3500460 *Fax:* (01) 3500461 *E-mail:* letter@ch-s.ch *Web Site:* www.ch-s.ch, pg 1368

Schweizerischer Verein fuer Schweisstechnik (Switzerland) *Tel:* (061) 233973 *Fax:* (061) 3178480, pg 624

Schweizerisches Wirtschaftsarchiv (Archives Economiques Suisses) (Switzerland) *Tel:* (061) 2673219 *Fax:* (061) 2673208, pg 1501

Schweizerisches Bundesarchiv (Switzerland) *Tel:* (031) 322 89 89 *Fax:* (031) 322 78 23 *E-mail:* bundesarchiv@bar.admin.ch *Web Site:* www.bundesarchiv.ch, pg 1501

Schweizerisches Jugendschriftenwerk, SJW (Switzerland) *Tel:* (01462) 49 40 (ISDN) *Fax:* (01462) 69 13 (ISDN) *E-mail:* office@sjw.ch *Web Site:* www.sjw.ch, pg 624

Verlag Schweizerisches Katholisches Bibelwerk (Switzerland), pg 624

Schwengeler-Verlag (Switzerland) *Tel:* (071) 725666 *Fax:* (071) 725665, pg 624

Sciamed Verlag AG (Switzerland) *Tel:* (061) 231775; (061) 235366 *Fax:* (061) 2722775, pg 624

Salvatore Sciascia Editore (Italy) *Tel:* (0934) 21946 *Fax:* (0934) 551366, pg 407

Science & Technics Publishing House (Viet Nam) *Tel:* (04) 9 424 786; (04) 9 423 172 *Fax:* (04) 8 220 658 *E-mail:* nxbkhkt@hn.vnn.vn *Web Site:* www.nxbkhkt.com.vn, pg 763

Science & Technology Information Institute Department of Science & Technology (Philippines) *Tel:* (02) 8220954, pg 1491

Science Fiction Magazine Club (Thailand) *Tel:* (02) 2330302; (02) 2356931, pg 1233

Science Press (Australia) *Tel:* (02) 5161122 *Fax:* (02) 5501915, pg 41

Science Press (China) *Tel:* (010) 64010642; (010) 64034205 *Fax:* (010) 64010642, pg 108

Science Publications Centre (Republic of Korea) *Tel:* (02) 3254015; (02) 7336719; (02) 3254017 *Fax:* (02) 3335799, pg 1297

Science Reviews Ltd (United Kingdom) *Tel:* (01727) 847322 *Fax:* (01727) 847323 *E-mail:* scilet@scilet.com, pg 739

Scientia Verlag und Antiquariat (Germany) *Tel:* (07361) 41700 *Fax:* (07361) 45620, pg 286

Scientific and Cultural Publications (Islamic Republic of Iran) *Tel:* (021) 685475; (021) 686278, pg 358

Scientific & Technical Information Service (Belgium) *Tel:* (02) 5195640 *Fax:* (02) 5195645 *E-mail:* info@stis.fgov.be *Web Site:* www.stis.fgov.be, pg 1512

Scientific Book Agency (India) *Tel:* (033) 292915; (033) 4642206 *E-mail:* debmalya@giase101.vsnl.net.in, pg 349

Scientific Book Agency (India) *Tel:* (033) 292915; (033) 4642206; (033) 4638273 *E-mail:* psjs@cal3.usnl.net.in, pg 1290

Scientific Documentation Centre (Iraq) *Tel:* (01) 7760023, pg 1475

Scientific Library Voronezh State University (Russian Federation) *Tel:* (0732) 55-35-59 *Fax:* (0732) 78-97-55 *E-mail:* root@lib.vsu.ru *Web Site:* www.lib.vsu.ru, pg 1495

Scientific Library Voronezh State University (Russian Federation) *Tel:* (08632) 654363 *Fax:* (08632) 645335 *E-mail:* root@lib.vsu.ru, pg 1495

Scientific Publishers India (India) *Tel:* (0291) 512712; (0291) 433323 *Fax:* (0291) 512580 *E-mail:* scienti@sancharnet.in, pg 349

Scientific Research Council (Jamaica) *Tel:* (876) 9271771; (876) 9271774 *Fax:* (876) 9271990, pg 413

Edizioni Scientifiche Italiane (Italy) *Tel:* (081) 7645443 *Fax:* (081) 7646477 *E-mail:* info@esispa.com *Web Site:* www.esispa.com, pg 407

Editions Scientifiques et Medicales Elsevier (France) *Tel:* (01) 45589110 *Fax:* (01) 45589425 *Web Site:* www.elsevier.fr, pg 184

Editoriale Scienza (Italy) *Tel:* (040) 364810 *Fax:* (040) 364909 *E-mail:* info@editscienza.it *Web Site:* www.editscienza.it, pg 407

Editora Scipione Ltda (Brazil) *Tel:* (011) 2392255 *Fax:* (011) 2391700 *E-mail:* marketing@scipione.com.br *Web Site:* www.scipione.com.br, pg 91

SciPrint Ltd (Ireland) *Tel:* (061) 472114; (061) 472520 *Fax:* (061) 472021, pg 1157, 1212

Scissors Books (Belgium) *Tel:* (09) 2255414 *Fax:* (09) 2259724 *E-mail:* geknipt@skynet.be, pg 74

SCM Press (United Kingdom) *Tel:* (020) 7359 8033 *Fax:* (020) 7359 0049 *E-mail:* scmpress@btinternet.com *Web Site:* www.scm-canterburypress.co.uk, pg 739

Scorpion Publishers (Russian Federation) *Tel:* (095) 4436991, pg 541

Scottish Affairs (United Kingdom) *Tel:* (0131) 650 2456 *Fax:* (0131) 650 6345 *Web Site:* www.institute-of-governance.org, pg 739

Scottish Book Marketing Group (United Kingdom) *Tel:* (0131) 2286866 *Fax:* (0131) 2283220, pg 1267

Scottish Book Trust (United Kingdom) *Tel:* (0131) 2293663 *Fax:* (0131) 2284293, pg 1267

Scottish Braille Press (United Kingdom) *Tel:* (0131) 6624445 *Fax:* (0131) 6621968 *E-mail:* scot.braille@dial.pipex.com *Web Site:* www.scottish-braille-press.org, pg 739, 1141

Scottish Council for Research in Education (United Kingdom) *Tel:* (0131) 5572944 *Fax:* (0131) 5569454 *E-mail:* scre@scre.ac.uk *Web Site:* www.scre.ac.uk, pg 739

Scottish Cultural Press (United Kingdom) *Tel:* (0131) 660-6366 (editorial); (0131) 660-6414 (editorial); (0131) 660-4666 (orders) *Fax:* (0131) 5555018 *E-mail:* info@scottishbooks.com *Web Site:* www.scottishbooks.com, pg 739

Scottish Library Association (United Kingdom) *Tel:* (01698) 458888 *Fax:* (01698) 458899; (01698) 628159 *E-mail:* sla@slainte.org.uk *Web Site:* www.slainte.org.uk, pg 1525

Scottish Newspaper Publishers' Association (United Kingdom) *Tel:* (0131) 2204353 *Fax:* (0131) 2204344 *E-mail:* info@snpa.org.uk *Web Site:* www.snpa.org.uk, pg 1267

Scottish Office Library & Information Services (United Kingdom) *Tel:* (0131) 2448159 *Fax:* (0131) 2448240, pg 740

Scottish Poetry Library (United Kingdom) *Tel:* (031) 557-2876 *Fax:* (031) 557-8393 *E-mail:* inquiries@spl.org.uk *Web Site:* www.spl.org.uk, pg 1507

Scottish Publishers Association (United Kingdom) *Tel:* (0131) 2286866 *Fax:* (0131) 2283220 *E-mail:* enquiries@scottishbooks.org *Web Site:* www.scottishbooks.org, pg 1267

Scottish Text Society (United Kingdom) *Tel:* (0115) 951 5922 *E-mail:* sts@arts.gla.ac.uk, pg 740

Casa Editrice Mariett Scuola SpA (Italy) *Tel:* (02) 3158711 *Fax:* (02) 3158710, pg 407

Scout Interamericana (Costa Rica) *Tel:* 2292121 *Fax:* 2685332, pg 117

Ediciones Scriba SA (Spain) *Tel:* (093) 215 19 33 *Fax:* (093) 487 37 66, pg 589

Scripta (Greece) *Tel:* (01) 5230382 *Fax:* (01) 5233574, pg 315

SCRIPTA - Distribucion y Servicios Editoriales, SA de CV (Mexico) *Tel:* (05) 5481716 *Fax:* (05) 6161496 *E-mail:* dyse@data.net.mx, pg 467

SCRIPTA - Distribucion y Servicios Editoriales, SA de CV (Mexico) *Tel:* (05) 5481716 *Fax:* (05)5500564, pg 1299

Editions Scriptar SA (Switzerland) *Tel:* (021) 7911065 *Fax:* (021) 7914084 *E-mail:* info@jsh.ch *Web Site:* www.jsh.ch, pg 624

Scriptum (Netherlands) *Tel:* (010) 4271022 *Fax:* (010) 4736625 *E-mail:* info@scriptum.nl *Web Site:* www.scriptum.nl, pg 483

Scripture in Church Book Club (Ireland) *Tel:* (01) 8721611 *Fax:* (01) 8731760, pg 1229

Scripture Union (United Kingdom) *Tel:* (01908) 856000 *Fax:* (01908) 856111 *E-mail:* info@scriptureunion.org.uk *Web Site:* www.scriptureunion.org.uk, pg 740

Editura 'Scrisul Romanesc' (Romania) *Tel:* (051) 113763, pg 536

Scroll Publishers (Australia) *Tel:* (07) 5573-0835 *Fax:* (07) 5529-5155, pg 42

Scuola Vaticana Paleografia - Scuola Vaticana di Paleografia Diplomatica e Archivistica (Holy See (Vatican City State)) *Tel:* (06) 69883595 *Fax:* (06) 69881377, pg 317

SDU Juridische & Fiscale Uitgeverij (Netherlands) *Tel:* (070) 3789860 *Fax:* (070) 3854321, pg 484

SDX (Shenghuo-Dushu-Xinzhi) Joint Publishing Co (China) *Tel:* (010) 555159 *Fax:* (010) 5138378, pg 108

Se-Kwang Music Publishing Co (Republic of Korea) *Tel:* (02) 7140046 *Fax:* (02) 7192191, pg 440

Seagull Press (New Zealand) *Tel:* (03) 3899338, pg 495

Sean Ros Press (Ireland) *Tel:* (051) 428666, pg 364

Seanachas Press (Australia), pg 42

Search Press Ltd (United Kingdom) *Tel:* (01892) 510850 *Fax:* (01892) 515903 *E-mail:* searchpress@searchpress.com *Web Site:* www.searchpress.com, pg 740

Search Press Ltd (United Kingdom) *Tel:* (01892) 510850 *Fax:* (01892) 515903 *E-mail:* searchpress@searchpress.com, pg 1121

Derek Searle Associates (United Kingdom) *Tel:* (01753) 539295 *Fax:* (02753) 551863 *E-mail:* dsapublish@aol.com, pg 1322

Universitas Sebelas Maret (Indonesia) *Tel:* (0271) 46994 (ext 341) *Fax:* (0271) 46655 *E-mail:* due-uns@slo.mega.net.id; pptk-uns@slo.mega.net.id, pg 357

SECAP (Ecuador) *Tel:* (02) 446248 *Fax:* (02) 448644, pg 137

Martin Secker & Warburg (United Kingdom) *Tel:* (020) 7840 8400 *Fax:* (020) 7233 8791 *E-mail:* enquiries@randomhouse.co.uk *Web Site:* www.randomhouse.co.uk, pg 740

Seckin Yayinevi (Turkey) *Tel:* (0312) 4353030 *Fax:* (0312) 4352472 *E-mail:* seckin@seckin.com.tr *Web Site:* www.seckin.com.tr, pg 641

Biblioteca de la Secretaria de Estado de Relaciones Exteriores (Dominican Republic), pg 1461

Secretariado Trinitario (Spain) *Tel:* (0923) 23 56 02 *Fax:* (0923) 23 56 02 *E-mail:* secretrinitario@planalfa.es, pg 590

Secretariat of the Pacific Community Library (New Caledonia) *Tel:* 262000 *Fax:* 263818 *E-mail:* library@spc.int *Web Site:* www.spc.int/library, pg 1487

Seculo XXI Editora e Comercio de Livros (Brazil) *Tel:* (051) 3614459 *Fax:* (051) 3614459 *E-mail:* sewloxxi@poa-online.com.br, pg 91

Sedco Publishing Ltd (Ghana) *Tel:* (021) 221332 *Fax:* (021) 220107 *E-mail:* sedco@africaonline.com.gh, pg 308

Sedit (France) *Tel:* (01) 30852010 *Fax:* (01) 30852038 *E-mail:* costic-sr@costic.asso.fr *Web Site:* www.costic.asso.fr, pg 184

See Australia Guides P/L (Australia) *Tel:* (03) 5962 5723 *Fax:* (03) 5962 4718 *E-mail:* seeaustralia@iprimus.com.au, pg 42

Seghers (France) *Tel:* (01) 53.67.14.00 *Fax:* (01) 53.67.14.14, pg 184

Segment BV (Netherlands) *Tel:* (046) 43894444 *Fax:* (046) 4389401; (046) 4370161 *E-mail:* secretariant@segment.nl *Web Site:* www.segment.nl, pg 484

Edizioni Segno SRL (Italy) *Tel:* (0432) 575179 *Fax:* (0432) 575589 *E-mail:* info@edizionisegno.it *Web Site:* www.edizionisegno.it, pg 407

Segretariato Nazionale Apostolato della Preghiera (Italy) *Tel:* (06) 6976071 *Fax:* (06) 6781063 *E-mail:* adp@adp.it *Web Site:* www.adp.it, pg 407

Nouvelles Editions Seguier (France) *Tel:* (01) 55 42 61 40 *Fax:* (01) 55 42 61 41 *Web Site:* php.atlantica.fr, pg 184

Seibido (Japan) *Tel:* (03) 32912261 *Fax:* (03) 32935490, pg 424

Seibido Shuppan Company Ltd (Japan) *Tel:* (03) 38144351 *Fax:* (03) 38144355 *Web Site:* www.seibidoshuppan.co.jp, pg 424

Seibt Verlag GmbH (Germany) *Tel:* (089) 6 09 03-0 *Fax:* (089) 6 43 17 *E-mail:* info@seibt.com *Web Site:* www.seibt.de, pg 286

Seibu Time Co Ltd (Japan) *Tel:* (03) 52762120 *Fax:* (03) 52762209, pg 425

Seibundo (Japan) *Tel:* (03) 32039201 *Fax:* (03) 32039206, pg 425

Seibundo Shinkosha Publishing Co Ltd (Japan) *Tel:* (03) 33737141 *Fax:* (03) 59995120, pg 425

Seibundo Shuppan (Japan) *Tel:* (06) 2116265 *Fax:* (06) 2116495, pg 425

Seishin Shobo (Japan) *Tel:* (03) 39465666 *Fax:* (03) 39458880, pg 425

Seiwa Shoten Co Ltd (Japan) *Tel:* (03) 33290031 *Fax:* (03) 33043822, pg 425

Seix Barral (Argentina) *Tel:* (011) 382-4043; (011) 382-4045; (011) 381-8285 *Fax:* (011) 383-3793 *E-mail:* planeta@teletel.com.ar *Web Site:* www.seix-barral.es, pg 9

Editorial Seix Barral SA (Spain) *Tel:* (093) 496 7003 *Fax:* (093) 496 7004 *E-mail:* editorial@seix-barral.es *Web Site:* www.seix-barral.es, pg 590

Seizando-Shoten Publishing Co Ltd (Japan) *Tel:* (03) 33575861 *Fax:* (03) 33575867, pg 425

Seizmoloska Opservatorija (The Former Yugoslav Republic of Macedonia) *Tel:* (091) 231953 *Fax:* (091) 114042 *E-mail:* ljupco@iunona.pmf.ukim.edu.mk, pg 449

Sejong Daewang Kinyom Saophoe (Republic of Korea), pg 440

Sekai Bunka Publishing Inc (Japan) *Tel:* (03) 32625111 *Fax:* (03) 32378446, pg 425

Sekreterurbokklubben (Sweden) *Tel:* (08) 6909200 *Fax:* (08) 6909300, pg 1232

Selangor Public Library (Malaysia) *Tel:* (03) 5597667 *Fax:* (03) 5596045 *E-mail:* ppas@sel.lib.edu.my, pg 1483

Select Books Pte Ltd (Singapore) *Tel:* 7321515 *Fax:* 7360855 *E-mail:* info@selectbooks.com.sg *Web Site:* www.selectbooks.com.sg, pg 548

Select Books Pte Ltd (Singapore) *Tel:* 7321515 *Fax:* 7360855 *E-mail:* info@selectbooks.com.sg, pg 1309

Selecta-Catalonia Ed (Spain) *Tel:* (093) 3172331; (093) 3185183 *Fax:* (093) 3024793, pg 590

Selection du Reader's Digest SA (France) *Tel:* (01) 45480426 *Fax:* (01) 46748582, pg 184

Editions Selection J Jacobs SA (France), pg 184

Selector SA de CV (Mexico) *Tel:* (05) 588-7272 *Fax:* (05) 761-5716 *E-mail:* info@selector.com.mx *Web Site:* www.selector.com.mx, pg 467

SELF Syndicate of French Language Authors (France) *Tel:* (01) 46711319 *Fax:* (01) 46707395, pg 1244

Selina Publishers (India) *Tel:* (011) 3280711, pg 349

Selinunte Editora Ltda (Brazil) *Tel:* (011) 2760318, pg 91

Maren Sell (France) *Tel:* (01) 47423833 *Fax:* (01) 47427781 *Web Site:* www.editions-calmann-levy.com, pg 184

Sellerio Editore (Italy) *Tel:* (091) 6259475 *Fax:* (091) 6258802, pg 407

Dr Arthur L Sellier & Co-Walter de Gruyter GmbH & Co KG OHG (Germany) *Tel:* (030) 26005-0 *Fax:* (030) 260 05-251 *Web Site:* www.degruyter.de, pg 286

Sellier Verlag GmbH (Germany) *Tel:* (089) 4705050 *Fax:* (089) 4701081, pg 286

Selwood Printing (United Kingdom) *Tel:* (01444) 236060 *Fax:* (01444) 245043 *E-mail:* systems@selwood.com, pg 1204

SEMAR Publishers SRL (Italy) *Tel:* (06) 6876523 *Fax:* (06) 68308601 *E-mail:* editorial@semarweb.com *Web Site:* semarweb.com, pg 407

Editions Semences Africaines (Cameroon) *Tel:* (023) 224058, pg 99

Bokforlaget Semic AB (Sweden) *Tel:* (08) 7993050 *Fax:* (08) 7993064 *E-mail:* bokforlaget@semic.se *Web Site:* www.semic.se, pg 606

Semic Bokforlaget International AB (Sweden) *Tel:* (08) 7793050 *Fax:* (08) 7993064, pg 606

Semic Junior Press (Netherlands) *Tel:* (035) 6944914 *Fax:* (035) 6944909, pg 484

Seminar on the Acquisition of Latin American Library Materials (SALALM) (United States) *Tel:* 505-277-5102 *Fax:* 505-277-0646, pg 1269

Senate Books Co Ltd (Taiwan, Province of China) *Tel:* (02) 7417576 *Fax:* (02) 7112713 *E-mail:* senatebooks@usa.net, pg 631

Sencor (United States) *Tel:* 212-486-0320 *Fax:* 212-486-0710 *E-mail:* sales@sencor.net *Web Site:* www.sencor.net, pg 1166

Send the Light Ltd (United Kingdom) *Tel:* (01228) 512512 *Fax:* (01228) 514949 *E-mail:* nancy.ursh@stl.org, pg 1322

Editions du Seneve (France) *Tel:* (01) 44 32 05 60 *Fax:* (01) 44 32 05 61, pg 184

Senmon Toshokan Kyogikai (SENTOKYO) (Japan) *Tel:* (03) 3537-8335 *Fax:* (03) 3537-8336 *E-mail:* jsla@jsla.or.jp *Web Site:* www.jsla.or.jp, pg 1519

Senouhy Publishers (Egypt (Arab Republic of Egypt)), pg 139

Sentraldistribusjon ANS (Norway) *Tel:* 22365000 *Fax:* 22365040, pg 1304

Seogwangsa (Republic of Korea) *Tel:* (02) 9246161; (02) 9246165 *Fax:* (02) 9224993, pg 440

Seoul International Publishing House (Republic of Korea) *Tel:* (02) 4698326; (02) 4698327, pg 440

Seoul National University Library (Republic of Korea) *Tel:* (02) 880-5284 *Fax:* (02) 8712972 *E-mail:* joongyo@plaza.snu.ac.kr, pg 1480

Seoul National University Press (Republic of Korea) *Tel:* (02) 8774418 *Fax:* (02) 8884148, pg 440

Sepia (France) *Tel:* (01) 43 97 22 14 *Fax:* (01) 43 97 32 62 *E-mail:* sepia@club-internet.fr, pg 184

Editions de Septembre (France) *Tel:* (01) 53689620 *Fax:* (01) 53689621, pg 184

Serafin (Slovakia) *Tel:* (02) 54432159 *Fax:* (02) 54434342 *E-mail:* vydserafin@gmx.net *Web Site:* www.serafin.sk, pg 550

Ediciones del Serbal SA (Spain) *Tel:* (03) 408 08 34 *Fax:* (03) 408 07 92 *E-mail:* serbal@ed-serbal.es *Web Site:* www.ed-serbal.es, pg 590

Seren (United Kingdom) *Tel:* (01656) 663018 *Fax:* (01656) 649226 *E-mail:* seren@seren.force9.co.uk *Web Site:* www.seren-books.com, pg 740

Serie-pocket-klubben (Sweden) *Tel:* (08) 7993110 *Fax:* (08) 7645764, pg 1232

Serif (United Kingdom) *Tel:* (020) 8981-3990 *Fax:* (020) 8981-3990, pg 740

Serindia Publications (United Kingdom) *Tel:* (020) 8785-6313 *Fax:* (020) 8785-0999 *E-mail:* info@serindia.com *Web Site:* www.serindia.com, pg 740

Le Serpent a Plumes (France) *Tel:* (01) 55 35 95 85 *Fax:* (01) 42 61 17 46 *E-mail:* contact@serpentaplumes.com *Web Site:* www.serpentaplumes.com, pg 184

Serpent's Tail Ltd (United Kingdom) *Tel:* (020) 7354-1949 *Fax:* (020) 7704-6467 *E-mail:* info@serpentstail.com *Web Site:* www.serpentstail.com, pg 740

Servedit (France) *Tel:* (01) 44 41 49 30 *Fax:* (01) 43 25 77 41 *E-mail:* servedit@free.fr, pg 184

Service Central de la Statistique et des Etudes Economiques (STATEC) (Luxembourg) *Tel:* 4781 *Fax:* 464289 *E-mail:* statec.post@statec.etat.lu *Web Site:* www.statec.lu, pg 448

Service Central des Imprimes et des Fournitures de Bureau de l'Etat (Luxembourg) *Tel:* (00352) 498811916; (00352) 498811915 *Fax:* (00352) 400881, pg 448

Service commun de la documentation de l'Universite de Lille III (France) *Tel:* (03) 20417000 *Fax:* (065) 20914650 *E-mail:* scd@univ.lille3.fr, pg 1465

Service de l'Information et des Archives Nationales (Rwanda) *Tel:* 75432, pg 1495

Service des Publications Scientifiques du Museum National d'Histoire Naturelle (France) *Tel:* (01) 40 79 48 38 *Fax:* (01) 40 79 38 58 *E-mail:* diff.pub@mnhn.fr *Web Site:* www.mnhn.fr/publication, pg 184

Service Hydrographique et Oceanographique de la Marine (SHOM) (France) *Tel:* (01) 44 38 41 16 *Web Site:* www.shom.fr, pg 185

Service Technique pour l'Education (France) *Tel:* (01) 45084756, pg 185

Editions Services et Informations pour Etudiants (Morocco) *Tel:* (02) 210163, pg 470

Services for Export & Language (SEL) (United Kingdom) *Tel:* (0161) 7457480 *Fax:* (0161) 2955110 *E-mail:* sel@salford.ac.uk *Web Site:* www.sel-uk.com, pg 1129

Servicio a La Iglesia Catolica AC Edicion y Distribucion de Libros Religiosos (Mexico) *Tel:* (05) 6710269 *Fax:* (05) 5441675, pg 1300

Servicio de Biblioteca (Spain) *Tel:* (04) 6006125 *Fax:* (04) 6006049 *E-mail:* biblioteca.cruces@hcru.osakidetza.net, pg 1499

Servicio de Publicaciones Universidad de Cadiz (Spain) *Tel:* (056) 015268 *Fax:* (056) 220118 *E-mail:* pedro.cervera@uca.es *Web Site:* www.uca.es/serv/publicaciones, pg 590

Servicio de Publicaciones Universidad de Cordoba (Spain) *Tel:* (0957) 21 81 25 *Fax:* (0957) 21 81 96; (057) 218666 (Director) *E-mail:* publicaciones@uco.es; pal1gocag@lucano.uco.es (Director) *Web Site:* www.uco.es/organiza/servicios/publica/presenta.htm, pg 590

Servicio de Publicaciones y Produccion Documental de la Universidad de Las Palmas de Gran Canaria (Spain) *Tel:* (028) 458954; (028) 458952 *Fax:* (028) 458949, pg 590

Servicios Especiales Maciel SA de CV (Mexico) *Tel:* 05 5435533, pg 467

Servicios Especializados y Representacionesen Comercio Exterior SA de CV (Mexico) *Tel:* (05) 7609129; (05) 7605149, pg 1300

Servire BV Uitgevers (Netherlands) *Tel:* (030) 2349211 *Fax:* (030) 2349247 *E-mail:* servire@pi.net, pg 484, 1115

Servitium (Italy) *Tel:* (035) 4398011 *Fax:* (035) 792030 *E-mail:* servitium@spm.it, pg 408

Forlaget Sesam (Denmark) *Tel:* 33305044; 33305522 *Fax:* 33305824 *E-mail:* aschehoug@ash.egmont.com, pg 135

Sesame Publication Co (Hong Kong) *Tel:* (02) 5089920 *Fax:* (02) 5789337 *E-mail:* sesame01@hkstar.com, pg 321

Setberg (Iceland) *Tel:* 5517667; 5529150 *Fax:* 5526640, pg 328

Editions du Seuil (France) *Tel:* (01) 40 46 50 50 *Fax:* (01) 40 46 43 00 *E-mail:* contact@seuil.com *Web Site:* www.seuil.com, pg 185

Seven Hills Publishers (Bulgaria) *Tel:* (032) 262235 *Fax:* (032) 262235, pg 97

Edicoes 70 (Portugal) *Tel:* (021) 8590348 *Fax:* (021) 761736, pg 529

Severn House Publishers Ltd (United Kingdom) *Tel:* (0208) 7703930 *Fax:* (0208) 7703850 *E-mail:* sales@severnhouse.com *Web Site:* www.severnhouse.com, pg 740

Severnside Printers Ltd (United Kingdom) *Tel:* (01684) 594521 *Fax:* (01684) 594344, pg 1163, 1204, 1215

Ediciones Seyer (Spain) *Tel:* (095) 2320887 *Fax:* (095) 2325511, pg 590

Sh Ghulam Ali & Sons (Pvt) Ltd (Pakistan) *Tel:* (042) 7588979; (042) 7501664 *Fax:* (042) 7583611, pg 509

Shaar Zion Library (Israel) *Tel:* 03 6910141, pg 1477

Shaibya Prakashan Bibhag (India) *Tel:* (033) 388268; (033) 2411748, pg 349

Shakai Hoken Shuppan-Sha (Japan) *Tel:* (03) 32919841 *Fax:* (03) 32919847, pg 425

Shakai Shiso-Sha (Japan) *Tel:* (03) 38138101 *Fax:* (03) 38139061, pg 425

Shakespeare Head Press Pty Ltd (Australia) *Tel:* (02) 96485488 *Fax:* (03) 8958181, pg 42

Shakespearean Authorship Trust (United Kingdom) *Tel:* (020) 7242 6995 *Fax:* (020) 7242 6995, pg 1372

Shakti Communications (United Kingdom) *Tel:* (020) 8903 5442 *Fax:* (020) 8903 4684 *E-mail:* shakticom@btinternet.com, pg 741

Shalem Press (Israel) *Tel:* (02) 566-0601 *Fax:* (02) 566-0590 *E-mail:* shalemorder@shalem.org.il *Web Site:* www.shalem.org.il, pg 372

Shandong Education Publishing House (China) *Tel:* (0531) 2050801 *Fax:* (0531) 2061455 *E-mail:* sdjys@jn-public.sd.cninfo.net *Web Site:* www.sjs.com.cn, pg 108

Shandong Fine Arts Publishing House (China) *Tel:* (021) 6911563 *Fax:* (021) 6911563, pg 108

Shandong Friendship Press (China) *Tel:* (0531) 2063686 *Fax:* (0531) 2909354, pg 108

Shandong Literature & Art Publishing House (China) *Tel:* (0531) 610051 (ext 239) *Fax:* (0531) 613584, pg 109

Shandong People's Publishing House (China) *Tel:* (0531) 610051 *Fax:* (0531) 613584, pg 109

Shandong Science & Technology Press (China) *Tel:* (0531) 2065109 *Fax:* (0531) 2023898 *E-mail:* li-yujn@sina.com *Web Site:* www.ikj.com.cn, pg 109

Shandong University Press (China) *Tel:* (027) 642602; (027) 642600 *E-mail:* hustpub@blue.hust.edu.cn, pg 109

Shanghai Academy of Social Sciences Library (China) *Tel:* (021) 2522657, pg 1457

Shanghai Book Co Ltd (Hong Kong) *Tel:* 25486160, pg 321

The Shanghai Book Co (Pte) Ltd (Singapore) *Tel:* 3360144 *Fax:* 3360490 *E-mail:* shanghaibook@pacific.net.sg, pg 548

Shanghai Educational Publishing House (China) *Tel:* (021) 64 37 71 65 *Fax:* (021) 64 33 99 95 *E-mail:* wuyiyang@public2.sta.net.cn, pg 109

Shanghai Fine Arts Publishers (China) *Tel:* (021) 64519016 *Fax:* (021) 64519015, pg 109

Shanghai Foreign Language Education Press (China) *Tel:* (021) 5425300 *Fax:* (021) 5422956 *Web Site:* www.sflep.com, pg 109

Shanghai Science & Technology Publishers (China) *Tel:* (021) 64184881; (021) 64174349 *Fax:* (021) 64730679 *Web Site:* www.sstp.com.cn, pg 109

Shanghai Scientific & Technological Literature Publishing House (China) *Tel:* (020) 4373312; (020) 4370782 *Fax:* (020) 0028621; (020) 4335311, pg 109

Shanghai tushuguan (China) *Tel:* (021) 3273176 *Fax:* (021) 3278493, pg 1457

Sharbain's Bookshop (Jordan) *Tel:* (06) 638709 *Fax:* (06) 699119, pg 1296

Sharda Prakashan (India) *Tel:* (011) 653982, pg 350

David Sharpe (Australia) *Tel:* (03) 93801503, pg 42

Shaw & Sons Ltd (United Kingdom) *Tel:* (01322) 621100 *Fax:* (01322) 550553 *E-mail:* sales@shaws.co.uk *Web Site:* www.shaws.co.uk, pg 741

David Shaw & Associates Ltd (Canada) *Tel:* 416-487-2019 *Fax:* 416-486-1744 *E-mail:* djshaw@simpatico.ca, pg 1153

The Shaw Society (United Kingdom) *Tel:* (020) 86973619 *Fax:* (020) 86973619, pg 1372

Shearwater Associates Ltd (New Zealand) *Tel:* (04) 2399024 *Fax:* (04) 2399024, pg 495

Shearwater Press (Australia) *Tel:* (02) 282 346, pg 42

Shearwater Press Ltd (United Kingdom) *Tel:* (01624) 812114 *Fax:* (01624) 815525, pg 741

Sheck Wah Tong Printing Press (Hong Kong) *Tel:* 25628293 *Fax:* 25655431 *Web Site:* www.sheckwahtong.com, pg 1197

Sheed & Ward Ltd (United Kingdom) *Tel:* (020) 7702 9799 *Fax:* (020) 7702 3583, pg 741

Sheffield Academic Press Ltd (United Kingdom) *Tel:* (0114) 255 4433 *Fax:* (0114) 255 4626 *E-mail:* admin@sheffac.demon.co.uk *Web Site:* www.sheffieldacademicpress.com, pg 741

Sheil Land Associates Ltd Rights Department (United Kingdom) *Tel:* (020) 7405 9351 *Fax:* (020) 7831 2127, pg 1121

Sheil Land Associates Ltd (United Kingdom) *Tel:* (020) 7405 9351 *Fax:* (020) 7831 2127, pg 1121

Caroline Sheldon Literary Agency (United Kingdom) *Tel:* (01983) 760205, pg 1121

Sheldon Press (United Kingdom) *Tel:* (020) 643 0382 *Fax:* (020) 643 0391 *E-mail:* sheldon@spck.org.uk *Web Site:* www.sheldonpress.co.uk, pg 741

Shelfmark Books (United Kingdom) *Tel:* (020) 7226 7767 *Fax:* (020) 7226 7767, pg 741

Shelwing Ltd (United Kingdom) *Tel:* (01303) 850501 *Fax:* (01303) 850162 *E-mail:* info@shelwing.com *Web Site:* www.shelwing.com, pg 1322

Shepheard-Walwyn (Publishers) Ltd (United Kingdom) *Tel:* (020) 7721 7666 *Fax:* (020) 7721 7667 *E-mail:* books@shepheard-walwyn.co.uk *Web Site:* www.shepheard-walwyn.co.uk, pg 741

Frank Shepherd (Australia) *Tel:* (02) 9482 8104, pg 42

Sherbourne Publications (United Kingdom) *Tel:* (01691) 657 853 *Fax:* (01691) 657 853, pg 741

The Sheringa Book Committee (Australia) *Tel:* (086) 878750, pg 42

Sherratt & Hughes (United Kingdom) *Tel:* (01793) 695195, pg 1322

Sherwood Publishing (United Kingdom) *Tel:* (07000) 234683 *Fax:* (07000) 234689 *E-mail:* enquiries@adinternational.com *Web Site:* www.sherwoodpublishing.com, pg 741

R R Sheth & Co (India) *Tel:* (022) 2013441 *Fax:* (079) 5321732 *Web Site:* www.rrsheth.com, pg 350

R R Sheth & Co (India) *Tel:* (079) 5356573, pg 1290

Shibil Publications (Pvt) Ltd (Pakistan) *Tel:* (021) 533414; (021) 539570; (021) 571488, pg 509

Shibundo Co Ltd (Japan) *Tel:* (03) 32682441 *Fax:* (03) 32683550, pg 425

Shiko-Sha Co Ltd (Japan) *Tel:* (03) 34007151 *Fax:* (03) 34007294, pg 425

Shiksha Bharati (India) *Tel:* (011) 386-7791, pg 350

Shimizu-Shoin (Japan) *Tel:* (03) 32605261 *Fax:* (03) 32605270, pg 425

Shin Won Agency Co (Republic of Korea) *Tel:* (02) 3356388; (02) 3356833 *Fax:* (02) 3356389 *E-mail:* main@shinwonagency.co.kr *Web Site:* www.shinwonagency.co.kr, pg 1114

Shincho-Sha Co Ltd (Japan) *Tel:* (03) 32665411 *Fax:* (03) 32665534, pg 425

SHINE-Scottish Health Information Network (United Kingdom) *Tel:* (0131) 6232535 *Fax:* (0131) 3152369 *E-mail:* mdg@ednet.co.uk, pg 1525

Shing Lee Group Publishers (Singapore) *Tel:* 7601388 *Fax:* 7825684, pg 548

Shingakusha Co Ltd (Japan) *Tel:* (075) 5816111 *Fax:* (075) 5929910, pg 425

Shinkenchiku-Sha Co Ltd (Japan) *Tel:* (03) 38117101 *Fax:* (03) 38128229, pg 425

Shinko Tsusho Co Ltd (Japan) *Tel:* (03) 33531751 *Fax:* (03) 33532205, pg 1295

Shinkwang Publishing Co (Republic of Korea) *Tel:* (02) 9255051; (02) 9255053 *Fax:* (02) 9255054, pg 440

Shiraz University (Islamic Republic of Iran) *Tel:* (071) 6260011; (071) 59220 *Fax:* (071) 669225, pg 1475

Shire Publications Ltd (United Kingdom) *Tel:* (01844) 344301 *Fax:* (01844) 347080 *E-mail:* shire@shirebooks.co.uk *Web Site:* www.shirebooks.com, pg 741

Shirikon Publishers (Kenya), pg 433

Shiseido Booksellers Ltd (Japan) *Tel:* (075) 4312345 *Fax:* (075) 4326588 *E-mail:* shiseido@jd5.so-net.ne.jp *Web Site:* www.shiseido-book.co.jp, pg 1295

Shkoder Public Library (Albania), pg 1449

Shoal Bay Press Ltd (New Zealand) *Tel:* (03) 3770370 *Fax:* (03) 3770390 *E-mail:* shoalbay@shoalbay.co.nz, pg 495

Akane Shobo Co Ltd (Japan) *Tel:* (03) 32630641 *Fax:* (03) 32635440, pg 425

Hara Shobo (Japan) *Tel:* (03) 3354 0374 *Fax:* (03) 3226 7950, pg 425

Shobunsha Publications Inc (Japan) *Tel:* (03) 32622141 *Fax:* (03) 3262 2147, pg 426

Shogakukan Inc (Japan) *Tel:* (03) 32305661 *Fax:* (03) 32305840, pg 426

Shogun International Ltd (United Kingdom) *Tel:* (020) 8749 2022 *Fax:* (020) 8740 1086, pg 1322

Mitsumura Suiko Shoin (Japan) *Tel:* (075) 4938244 *Fax:* (075) 4936011, pg 426

Shokabo Publishing Co Ltd (Japan) *Tel:* (03) 32629166 *Fax:* (03) 32629130, pg 426

Shokoku Publishing Co Ltd (Japan) *Tel:* (03) 33593231 *Fax:* (03) 33573961, pg 426

Shorin-Sha Co ltd (Japan) *Tel:* (03) 38154921 *Fax:* (03) 38154923, pg 426

Shortland Publications Ltd (New Zealand) *Tel:* (09) 687128 *Fax:* (09) 6230143, pg 495

SHU Press (United Kingdom) *Tel:* (0114) 225 4702 *Fax:* (0114) 225 4478 *E-mail:* shupress@shu.ac.uk *Web Site:* www.shu.ac.uk, pg 742

Shueisha Inc (Japan) *Tel:* (03) 32306393; (03) 32306320 *Fax:* (03) 32302547, pg 426

Shufu-to-Seikatsu Sha Ltd (Japan) *Tel:* (03) 35635124 *Fax:* (03) 35678793, pg 426

Shufunotomo sha Co Ltd (Japan) *Tel:* (03) 52807555 *Fax:* (03) 52807556 *E-mail:* international@shufunotom.co.jp *Web Site:* www.shufunotom.co.jp, pg 426

Shumawa Book House (Myanmar), pg 1300

Shumawa Publishing House (Myanmar), pg 471

Shunjusha (Japan) *Tel:* (03) 32559611 *Fax:* (03) 32531384, pg 426

Shuppan News Co Ltd (Japan) *Tel:* 03 32622076, pg 426

Oru Shuppan (Japan) *Tel:* (03) 32340971 *Fax:* (03) 32616602, pg 426

Shuter & Shooter (Pty) Ltd (South Africa) *Tel:* (011) 7928363 *Fax:* (011) 7927024, pg 559

Shuter & Shooter (Pty) Ltd (South Africa) *Tel:* (0331) 427419 *Fax:* (0331) 943096, pg 1310

Shuttle Multimedia Inc (Taiwan, Province of China) *Tel:* (02) 5796800 *Fax:* (02) 5796805, pg 631

Shwepyidan Printing & Publishing House (Myanmar), pg 471

Shy Chaur Publishing Co Ltd (Taiwan, Province of China) *Tel:* (02) 22183377 *Fax:* (02) 22183239 *E-mail:* chien218@ms5.hinet.net, pg 631

Shy Mau Publishing Company (Taiwan, Province of China) *Tel:* (02) 22183277 *Fax:* (02) 22183239 *E-mail:* chien218@ms5.hinet.net, pg 631

The Siam Society (Thailand) *Tel:* (02) 6616470 *Fax:* (02) 2583491, pg 1369

Siamantas Publications (Greece) *Tel:* (01) 3627164, pg 315

Sibelius-Akatemian Kirjasto (Finland) *Tel:* (09) 4054539 *Fax:* (09) 4054542 *E-mail:* ikoskimi@siba.fi, pg 1464

Sibi (Bulgaria) *Tel:* (02) 9870141 *Fax:* (02) 9875709 *E-mail:* sibi@sibi.bg, pg 97

SIBS Publishing House Inc (Philippines) *Tel:* (0632) 374-2902 *Fax:* (0632) 372-7301 *E-mail:* sibsbook@info.com.ph *Web Site:* www.sibs.com.ph, pg 515

Wydawnictwo SIC (Poland) *Tel:* (022) 8400753 *Fax:* (022) 8400753 *E-mail:* svc@zigzag.pl; scc@scc.ksiazka.pl; sic@zigzag.pl *Web Site:* www.svc.ksiazka.pl, pg 520

Sicania (Italy) *Tel:* (090) 2936373 *Fax:* (090) 2932641, pg 408

Sichuan Science & Technology Publishing House (China) *Tel:* (028) 664982 *Fax:* (028) 6654063, pg 109

Sichuan University Press (China) *Tel:* (028) 583875-2529, pg 109

Edizioni Librarie Siciliane (Italy) *Tel:* (091) 8570221 *Fax:* (091) 342670, pg 408

Agencia Siciliano de Livros Jornais e Rivistas Ltda (Brazil) *Tel:* (011) 8395500; (011) 8319911 *Fax:* (011) 8328616, pg 91

J Sideris OE Ekdoseis (Greece) *Tel:* (01) 3229638 *Fax:* (01) 3245052, pg 315

Sidgwick & Jackson Ltd (United Kingdom) *Tel:* (020) 7881 8000 *Fax:* (020) 7881 8001, pg 742

Siebenberg-Verlag (Germany) *Tel:* (05695) 1028 *Fax:* (05695) 1027 *E-mail:* fh@huebnerbooks.de *Web Site:* www.huebnerbooks.de, pg 286

Siebert und Engelbert Dessart Verlag GmbH (Germany) *Tel:* (089) 4194020 *Fax:* (089) 4701081, pg 286

Siedler Verlag (Germany) *Tel:* (030) 44 38 45-0 *Fax:* (030) 44384555; (030) 44384546 *E-mail:* bettine.vonborries@bertelsmann.de, pg 286

Siegler & Co Verlag fuer Zeitarchive GmbH (Germany) *Tel:* (02223) 2 10 28 *Fax:* (02223) 2 30 28, pg 286

Siegmund Publishing (Germany) *Tel:* (04) 1656609 *Fax:* (04) 1656011, pg 286

Georg Siemens Verlagsbuchhandlung (Germany) *Tel:* (030) 769904-0 *Fax:* (030) 769904-18 *E-mail:* gsiemensv@t-online.de, pg 286

Sierra Leone Library Board (Sierra Leone) *Tel:* (022) 23848, pg 1496

Sierra Leone Association of Archivists, Librarians and Information Scientists (SLAALIS) (Sierra Leone) *Tel:* 223848, pg 1522

Sierra Leone University Press (Sierra Leone) *Tel:* (022) 27300; (022) 23494; (022) 27399; (022) 27323, pg 544

Sifri Ltd (Israel) *Tel:* (03) 5784679, pg 372

Sifriat Poalim Ltd (Israel) *Tel:* (03) 5183143 *Fax:* (03) 5183191 *E-mail:* akantor@inter.net.il, pg 372

Sifriat Poalim Ltd (Israel) *Tel:* (03) 5183143 *Fax:* (03) 5183191 *E-mail:* akantor@inter.net.il *Web Site:* www.s-poalim.co.il, pg 1292

Siglo XXI Editores de Colombia Ltda (Colombia) *Tel:* (01) 6110787 *Fax:* (01) 6110757, pg 113

Siglo XXI de Espana Editores SA (Spain) *Tel:* (091) 562 37 23; (091) 561 77 48 *Fax:* (091) 561 58 19 *E-mail:* sigloxxi@sigloxxieditores.com *Web Site:* www.sigloxxieditores.com, pg 590

Siglo XXI Editores SA de CV (Mexico) *Tel:* (05) 6587234 *Fax:* (05) 6587999 *E-mail:* sigloxxi@netcorp.net.mx, pg 467

Sigloch Edition Helmut Sigloch GmbH & Co KG (Germany) *Tel:* (07953) 883-138 *Fax:* (07953) 883-130 *E-mail:* edition@sigloch.de *Web Site:* www.sigloch.de, pg 286

Sigma (Greece) *Tel:* (01) 3638941; (01) 3607667 *Fax:* (01) 3638941 *E-mail:* sbooks@otenet.gr *Web Site:* www.sigmabooks.gr, pg 315

Sigma Press (United Kingdom) *Tel:* (01625) 531035 *Fax:* (01625) 536800 *E-mail:* info@sigmapress.co.uk *Web Site:* www.sigmapress.co.uk, pg 742

Edition Sigma e.Kfm (Germany) *Tel:* (030) 623 23 63 *Fax:* (030) 623 93 93 *E-mail:* verlag@edition-sigma.de *Web Site:* www.edition-sigma.de, pg 287

Editorial Sigmar SACI (Argentina) *Tel:* (011) 4381-4474 *Fax:* (011) 4383-5633 *E-mail:* editorial@sigmar.com.ar *Web Site:* www.sigmar.com.ar, pg 9

Editions Du Signal Rene Gaillard (Switzerland) *Tel:* (021) 3290194 *Fax:* (021) 3290194, pg 624

Signament I Comunicacio, SL Signament Edicions (Spain) *Tel:* (093) 4516888 *Fax:* (093) 3234417, pg 590

Editura Signata (Romania) *Tel:* (056) 153081, pg 536

Signes du Monde (France) *Tel:* (06) 12 99 73 37 *Fax:* (0561) 575717, pg 1154, 1194

Signum Verlag GmbH & Co KG (Austria) *Tel:* (01) 40650330 *Fax:* (01) 406503312 *E-mail:* contact.us@signum.at, pg 58

Ediciones Sigueme SA (Spain) *Tel:* (0923) 21 82 03 *Fax:* (0923) 27 05 63 *E-mail:* sigueme@ctv.es, pg 590

Uitgeverij De Sikkel NV (Belgium) *Tel:* (03) 312 86 30 *Fax:* (03) 311 77 39 *E-mail:* info@desikkel.be *Web Site:* www.desikkel.be, pg 74

Sila & Zivot (Bulgaria) *Tel:* (056) 20965 *E-mail:* silajivot@bse.bg, pg 98

Silabo (Portugal) *Tel:* (021) 8130345 *Fax:* (021) 8166719 *E-mail:* silabo@mail.telepac.pt, pg 529, 1138, 1158, 1200, 1222

Silberburg-Verlag Titus Haeussermann GmbH (Germany) *Tel:* (07071) 6885-0 *Fax:* (07071) 6885-20 *E-mail:* info@silberburg.de *Web Site:* www.silberburg.com, pg 287

Die Silberschnur Verlag GmbH (Germany) *Tel:* (02687) 929068 *Fax:* (02687) 929524, pg 287

Silex Ediciones (Spain) *Tel:* (091) 356.69.09 *Fax:* (091) 361.00.75 *E-mail:* silex@silexediciones.com *Web Site:* www.silexediciones.com, pg 590

Silkroad Publishers Agency, Ltd (Thailand) *Tel:* (02) 2584798; (02) 2588266 *Fax:* (02) 6620553 *E-mail:* silkroad@ksc15.th.com, pg 1117

Silkworm Books (Thailand) *Tel:* (053) 4765326 *Fax:* (053) 4765326 *E-mail:* silkworm@pobox.com, pg 635

Silliman University Library (Philippines) *Tel:* (035) 4227208; (035) 4226002 *Fax:* (035) 4227208 *E-mail:* sulib@su.edu.ph *Web Site:* su.edu.ph, pg 1491

Siloe - Kerdore (France) *Tel:* (02) 43532601 *Fax:* (02) 43535601 *E-mail:* siloe-kerdore@wanadoo.fr, pg 185

Silsilah Publication (Philippines) *Tel:* (02) 5663; (02) 5942, pg 515

Silva Artegrafica SRL (Italy) *Tel:* (0521) 804106 *Fax:* (0521) 804406, pg 408

Editions Andre Silvaire Sarl (France) *Tel:* (01) 43.26.72.34 *Fax:* (01) 55.42.16.69, pg 185

Silvana Editoriale SpA (Italy) *Tel:* (02) 6172464 *Fax:* (02) 61836283, pg 408

Silver Link Publishing Ltd (United Kingdom) *Tel:* (01536) 330588 *Fax:* (01536) 330588 *E-mail:* sales@slinkp-p.demon.co.uk *Web Site:* www.nostalgiacollection.com, pg 742

Jeffrey Simmons (United Kingdom) *Tel:* (020) 7235 8852 *Fax:* (020) 7235 9733, pg 1122

Simon & Schuster Australia Pty Ltd (Australia) *Tel:* (02) 9415 9900 *Fax:* (02) 9417 3188, pg 42

Simon & Schuster Ltd (United Kingdom) *Tel:* (020) 7316 1900 *Fax:* (020) 7316 0332 *E-mail:* firstname.surname@simonandschuster.co.uk, pg 742

Gerd Simon & Claudia Magiera, Verlagsbuero (Germany) *Tel:* (089) 21939012 *Fax:* (089) 21939014, pg 287

Simon Stevin NV (Belgium) *Tel:* (02) 5121085; (02) 5138295 *Fax:* (02) 5117015, pg 1276

Samuel Simson Ltd (Israel) *Tel:* (03) 5181604 *Fax:* (03) 5181544 *E-mail:* sefer-lakol@mixam.co.il, pg 372

The Simul Press Inc (Japan) *Tel:* (03) 32262861 *Fax:* (03) 32262860, pg 426

Sin Min Chu Publishing Co (Hong Kong) *Tel:* 33493270 *Fax:* 7658471, pg 322

Sinag-Tala Publishers Inc (Philippines) *Tel:* (02) 8192681 *Fax:* (02) 8192563, pg 515

Sinai Publishing Co (Israel) *Tel:* (03) 5163672 *Fax:* (03) 5176783, pg 372

Sind University Central Library (Pakistan) *Tel:* (0221) 671292 ext 58, pg 1490

Sindhi Adabi Board (Pakistan) *Tel:* (0221) 771276, pg 1367

Sindicato Nacional dos Editores de Livros (SNEL) (Brazil) *Tel:* (021) 2336481 *Fax:* (021) 2538502, pg 1239

Sing Cheong Printing Co Limited (Hong Kong) *Tel:* 25618801 *Fax:* 25659467 *E-mail:* info@singcheong.com.hk, pg 1135, 1197

Singapore Book Publishers' Association (Singapore) *Tel:* (065) 3447801; (065) 4407409 *Fax:* (065) 4470897 *E-mail:* twcsbpa@singnet.com.sg, pg 1258

Singapore University Press Pte Ltd (Singapore) *Tel:* b7761148; b8742382; b8742472; 6874-2382 *Fax:* b7740652 *E-mail:* supbooks@nus.edu.sg *Web Site:* www.nus.edu.sg/sup, pg 548

Single X Publications (Australia) *Tel:* (08) 8363-4272, pg 42

Sinisukk (Estonia) *Tel:* (02) 555748; (02) 65618721 *Fax:* (02) 6561872 *E-mail:* sinisukk@sinisukk.ee, pg 140

Sino Publishing House Ltd (Hong Kong) *Tel:* 28849963; 28973361 *Fax:* 25121154 *E-mail:* sunnyp@hkstar.com, pg 1135, 1197

Sino Publishing House Ltd (Hong Kong) *Tel:* 28849963 *Fax:* 25121154 *E-mail:* sunnyp@hkstar.com, pg 1212, 1222

Editora Sinodal (Brazil) *Tel:* (051) 590-2366 *Fax:* (051) 590-2664 *Web Site:* www.editorasinodal.com.br, pg 91

Editora Sinodal (Brazil) *Tel:* (051) 5926366 *Fax:* (051) 5926543, pg 1278

Sinodalno Izdatelstvo (Bulgaria) *Tel:* (02) 875611; (02) 875237, pg 98

Sinorama Magazine Co (Taiwan, Province of China) *Tel:* (02) 3922256 *Fax:* (02) 3615734, pg 631

Editorial Sintes SA (Spain) *Tel:* (093) 3182838, pg 590

Editorial Sintesis, SA (Spain) *Tel:* (091) 593 20 98 *Fax:* (091) 445 86 96 *E-mail:* sintesis@sintesis.com *Web Site:* www.sintesis.com, pg 590

Sinwel-Buchhandlung Verlag (Switzerland) *Tel:* (031) 425205 *Fax:* (031) 3331376, pg 624

Alex Siokis & Co (Greece) *Tel:* (031) 230257 *Fax:* (031) 281014, pg 315

SIPI (Servizio Italiano Pubblicazioni Internazionali) Srl (Italy) *Tel:* (06) 5920509 *Fax:* (06) 5924819, pg 408

Sir Charles Hayword Lending Library (Bahamas), pg 1452

SIR Publishing (New Zealand) *Tel:* (04) 4727421 *Fax:* (04) 4731841 *E-mail:* sirp@rsnz.govt.nz, pg 495

Siriraj Medical Library (Thailand) *Tel:* (02) 4113112 ext 325 *Fax:* (02) 4128418, pg 1503

Equipo Sirius SA (Spain) *Tel:* (091) 710 73 49 *Fax:* (091) 705 43 04 *E-mail:* sirius@equiposirius.com *Web Site:* www.equiposirius.com, pg 591

R Sirkis Publishers Ltd (Israel) *Tel:* (03) 7510792 *Fax:* (03) 7513750 *E-mail:* sirkispb@inter.net.il, pg 372

Ediciones Siruela SA (Spain) *Tel:* (091) 3555720; (091) 3554605; (091) 3552202 *Fax:* (091) 3552201 *E-mail:* siruela@siruela.com *Web Site:* www.siruela.com, pg 591

Sistema Bibliotecario (Honduras) *Tel:* 322204 *Fax:* 310675, pg 1471

Sistema de Bibliotecas y de Informacion (Argentina) *Tel:* (011) 9511366 *Fax:* (011) 49526557 *E-mail:* postmaster@sisbi.uba.ar, pg 1450

Sistemas Tecnicos de Edicion SA de CV (Mexico) *Tel:* (05) 6559144 *Fax:* (05) 5739412, pg 467

Sistemas Universales, SA (Mexico) *Tel:* (05) 705-4568; (05) 705-5937 *Fax:* (05) 705-3421 *E-mail:* 73661.405@coms, pg 467

Sita-MB (Bulgaria) *Tel:* (092) 872285, pg 98

Sita Publications (India) *Tel:* (022) 5555589 *Fax:* (022) 5561622 *E-mail:* ssrao@bom5.vsnl.net.in, pg 350

6-9 Club (United Kingdom) *Tel:* (01993) 893456 *Fax:* (01993) 6039092, pg 1234

Edicions 62 (Spain) *Tel:* (093) 443 71 00 *Fax:* (093) 443 71 30 *E-mail:* correu@grup62.com *Web Site:* www.grup62.com, pg 591

Edicola-62 (Spain) *Web Site:* www.grup62.com, pg 591

Grup 62 (Spain) *Tel:* (093) 443 71 00 *Fax:* (093) 443 71 30 *E-mail:* correu@grup62.com *Web Site:* www.grup62.com, pg 591

Sjaloom en Wildeboer Publishers (Netherlands) *Tel:* (020) 6206263 *Fax:* (020) 6209253, pg 484

Sjoestrands Foerlag (Sweden) *Tel:* (08) 299932 *Fax:* (08) 984645, pg 606

Skandinavia Verlag (Germany) *Tel:* (030) 8137006 *Fax:* (030) 8141029, pg 1112

SKAT (Swiss Centre for Development Cooperation in Technology & Management) (Switzerland) *Tel:* (071) 2285454 *Fax:* (071) 2285455 *E-mail:* info@skat.ch *Web Site:* www.skat.ch, pg 624

A/S Skattekartoteket (Denmark) *Tel:* 33117874 *Fax:* 33938025 *E-mail:* magnus@cddk.dk, pg 135

Skills Publishing (Australia) *Tel:* (02) 4759 2844 *Fax:* (02) 4759 3721 *E-mail:* aww@skillspublish.com.au *Web Site:* www.skillspublish.com.au, pg 42

Charles Skilton Ltd (United Kingdom) *Tel:* (020) 7351 4995 *Fax:* (020) 7351 4995, pg 742

Editions D'Art Albert Skira SA (Switzerland) *Tel:* (022) 3495533 *Fax:* (022) 3495535, pg 625

Skjaldborg Ltd (Iceland) *Tel:* 5882400; 5531599 *Fax:* 5888994 *E-mail:* skjaldborg@skjaldborg.is, pg 328

Skolebokforlaget A/S (Norway) *Tel:* 22335686 *Fax:* 22335805, pg 505

SKOLSKA KNJIGA

Skolska Knjiga (Croatia) *Tel:* (01) 48 30 511 *Fax:* (01) 48 30 506 *E-mail:* skolska@skolskaknjiga.hr *Web Site:* www.skolskaknjiga.hr, pg 120

Skoob Russell Square (United Kingdom) *Tel:* (020) 7278 8760 *E-mail:* books@skoob.com *Web Site:* www.skoob.com, pg 742

SKT's Boghandel (Denmark) *Tel:* 44686662 *Fax:* 44686660 *E-mail:* skt@sktbooks.dk, pg 1281

Skuggsja bokaforlag (Iceland) *Tel:* 5550045, pg 329

'Slask' Ltd (Poland) *Tel:* (032) 580756; (032) 581913; (032) 585870 *Fax:* (032) 583229 *E-mail:* biuro@slaskwn.com.pl, pg 520

Biblioteka Slaska (Poland) *Tel:* (032) 208 38 75 *Fax:* (032) 208 37 20 *E-mail:* bsl@libra.bs.katowice.pl; bsl@bs.katowice.pl *Web Site:* www.bs.katowice.pl, pg 1492

Slatkine Reprints (Switzerland) *Tel:* (022) 7762551; (022) 3100476 *Fax:* (022) 7763527, pg 625

Slavena (Bulgaria) *Tel:* (052) 602 465 *Fax:* (052) 225 935 *E-mail:* slavena@triada.bg *Web Site:* www.slavena.net, pg 98

Privlacica Slavonska Naklada (Croatia) *Tel:* (032) 332 587; (032) 20716; (032) 331610 *Fax:* (032) 331735, pg 120

Verlag Josef Otto Slezak (Austria) *Tel:* (01) 587 02 59 *Fax:* (01) 587 02 59 *E-mail:* verlag.slezak@aon.at *Web Site:* www.web4you.at/slezak.titel.htm, pg 58

SLG Press (United Kingdom) *Tel:* (01865) 721301 *Fax:* (01865) 790860 *E-mail:* editor@slgpress.co.uk; orders@slgpress.co.uk, pg 742

Slo Viet (Slovakia) *Tel:* (07) 52494886, pg 550

Slon Sociologicke Nakladatelstvi (Czech Republic) *Tel:* (02) 24220979 *Fax:* (02) 24220979-82, pg 128

Slouch Hat Publications (Australia) *Tel:* (03) 5986-6437 *Fax:* (03) 5986-6312 *Web Site:* www.slouch-hat.com.au, pg 42

Slovansky Tatran, Vydavatel 'stro spoi sro (Slovakia) *Tel:* (07) 5335849; (07) 5330141 *Fax:* (07) 5335777, pg 550

Slovart Co Ltd (Slovakia) *Tel:* (07) 230229 *Fax:* (07) 46256, pg 1309

Slovene PEN Centre (Slovenia) *Tel:* (01) 4254847, pg 1368

Slovenska kartografia as (Slovakia) *Tel:* (07) 282001; (07) 286783; (07) 285822; (07) 288215 *Fax:* (07) 286783; (07) 285822; (07) 288215, pg 550

Slovenska matica (Slovenia) *Tel:* (061) 214200; (061) 214227; (061) 1263190 *Fax:* (061) 214200, pg 552

Slovenske pedagogicke nakladateistvo (Slovakia) *Tel:* (07) 55423892 *Fax:* (07) 55571894 *E-mail:* spn@spn.sk, pg 550

Slovensky Spisovatel Ltd as (Slovakia) *Tel:* (07) 399790 *Fax:* (07) 335411, pg 550

SLS Legal Publications (NI) (United Kingdom) *Tel:* (01232) 335224 *Fax:* (01232) 326308 *Web Site:* www.law.qub.ac.uk, pg 742

Sluntse Publishing House (Bulgaria) *Tel:* (02) 9883797 *Fax:* (02) 9871405 *E-mail:* sluntse@dlr.bg, pg 98

Sluzbeni List (Yugoslavia) *Tel:* (011) 651885 *Fax:* (011) 651482, pg 765

Ediciones SM (Spain) *Tel:* (091) 508 49 44 *Fax:* (091) 508 33 66 *E-mail:* comunicacion@grupo-sm.com *Web Site:* www.ediciones-sm.com, pg 591

Small Industry Research Institute (SIRI) (India) *Tel:* (011) 3910805; (011) 3916804; (011) 3971895 *Fax:* (011) 3910805; (011) 3971895 *E-mail:* siri@ndf.vsnl.net.in; siricon@vsnl.com *Web Site:* www.indiaforum.com/siri, pg 350

Smart & Mookerdum (Myanmar), pg 471

SMC Publishing Inc (Taiwan, Province of China) *Tel:* (02) 3620190 *Fax:* (02) 3623834, pg 632

SMD Educational Publishers (Spruyt, Van Mantgem & De Does) (Netherlands) *Tel:* (071) 5797570 *Fax:* (071) 5797571, pg 484

Smeets Illustrated Projects (Netherlands) *Tel:* (04951) 570911 *Fax:* (04950) 46286, pg 484

Smena Publishing House (Slovakia) *Tel:* (07) 491455; (07) 497171, pg 550

Rudolf G Smend (Germany) *Tel:* (0221) 312047 *Fax:* (0221) 9 32 07 18 *E-mail:* smend@smend.de *Web Site:* www.smend.de, pg 287

SMER Diffusion (Morocco) *Tel:* (07) 723725; (07) 725960 *Fax:* (07) 701643, pg 1300

SMG Stiebner Medien gmbh (Germany) *Tel:* (089) 1257378 *Fax:* (089) 162282, pg 287

Smith-Gordon (United Kingdom) *Tel:* (020) 7351-7042 *Fax:* (020) 7351-1250 *E-mail:* publisher@smithgordon.com, pg 743

John Smith & Son (Glasgow) Ltd (United Kingdom) *Tel:* (0141) 2217472 *Fax:* (0141) 2484412, pg 1322

Smith Settle Ltd (United Kingdom) *Tel:* (01943) 467958 *Fax:* (01943) 850057 *E-mail:* sales@smith-settle.co.uk, pg 743

WH Smith PLC (United Kingdom) *Tel:* (020) 7409 3222 *Fax:* (020) 7514 9633 *Web Site:* www.whsmith.co.uk/awards, pg 1322

Smurfit Print (Ireland) *Tel:* (01) 303911 *Fax:* (01) 303287, pg 1136, 1157

Smurfit Print (Ireland) *Tel:* (01) 882 0500 *Web Site:* www.smurfit.ie, pg 1198

Smurfit Print (Ireland) *Tel:* (01) 303911 *Fax:* (01) 303287, pg 1213

Colin Smythe Ltd (United Kingdom) *Tel:* (01753) 886000 *Fax:* (01753) 886469 *E-mail:* sales@colinsmythe.co.uk *Web Site:* www.colinsmythe.co.uk, pg 743

SN-Verlag, Salzburger Nachrichten Verlags GmbH & Co KG (Austria) *Tel:* (0662) 8373-223 *Fax:* (0662) 8373-210 *Web Site:* www.salzburg.com, pg 59

Snayder Verlag Gunter VOB & Jurgen Schroder OHG (Germany) *Tel:* (05251) 760208 *Fax:* (05251) 74398, pg 287

Snoeck-Ducaju en Zoon NV (Belgium) *Tel:* (09) 267.04.11 *Fax:* (09) 267.04.60 *E-mail:* sdz@sdz.be *Web Site:* www.sdz.be, pg 74

Snofugl Forlag (Norway) *Tel:* 72872411 *Fax:* 72871013, pg 505

SNP Pan Pacific Publishing Pte Ltd (Singapore) *Tel:* 261-6288 *Fax:* 261-6088, pg 548

SNP Printing Pte Ltd (Singapore) *Tel:* 7412500 *Fax:* 2854894 *E-mail:* 2028095@syp.com.sg *Web Site:* www.snp.com.sg, pg 1138

SNP Printing Pte Ltd (Singapore) *Tel:* 7412500 *Fax:* 2854894, pg 1159

SNP Printing Pte Ltd (Singapore) *Tel:* 2780881 *Fax:* 2766970; 2782456 *E-mail:* poaylim@snp.com.sg, pg 1200

SNP Printing Pte Ltd (Singapore) *Tel:* 7412500 *Fax:* 2854894 *E-mail:* 2028095@syp.com.sg *Web Site:* www.snp.com.sg, pg 1213

SNP Printing Pte Ltd (Singapore) *Tel:* 7412500 *Fax:* 2854894, pg 1222

SNS Foerlag (Sweden) *Tel:* (08) 4539950 *Fax:* (08) 206206 *E-mail:* bok.info.order@sns.se, pg 606

William Snyder Publishing Associates (United Kingdom) *Tel:* (01865) 513186 *Fax:* (01865) 513186, pg 743

Sober Foerlags AB (Sweden) *Tel:* (08) 789 4958 *Fax:* (08) 204354, pg 606

Sobrindes Linha Grafica E Editora Ltda (Brazil) *Tel:* (061) 2247778; (061) 2247706; (061) 2247756 *Fax:* (061) 2241895 *E-mail:* linhagrafica@conectanet.com.br, pg 91

Sobun-Sha (Japan) *Tel:* (03) 32637101 *Fax:* (03) 32636789 *E-mail:* sobunsha@juno.ocn.ne.jp *Web Site:* www.sobunsha.co.jp, pg 426

Sociaal en Cultureel Planbureau (Netherlands) *Tel:* (070) 3407000 *Fax:* (070) 3407044 *E-mail:* info@scp.ul, pg 484

Social Club Books (Australia) *Tel:* (03) 9473 5555 *Fax:* (03) 9417 5574 *Web Site:* www.scb.com.au, pg 42

Social Science Press (Australia) *Tel:* (02) 4782 2909 *Fax:* (02) 4782 5303 *E-mail:* socsci@ozemail.com.au, pg 42

Social Sciences Library (Viet Nam) *Tel:* (08) 8296744 *Fax:* (08) 223735, pg 1508

Sociedad Biblica Peruana Asociacion Cultural (Peru) *Tel:* (014) 4330232 *Fax:* (014) 4336389 *E-mail:* sbpac01@telemail.telematic.edu.pe, pg 1305

Biblioteca de la Sociedad Cientifica del Paraguay (Paraguay) *Tel:* (021) 24832, pg 1490

Sociedad de Bibliotecarios de Puerto Rico (Puerto Rico) *Tel:* (787) 764-0000 (ext 5204) *Fax:* (787) 763-5685 *E-mail:* vtorres@upracd.upr.clu.edu, pg 1522

Sociedad de Ciencias, Letras y Artes El Museo Canario (Spain) *Tel:* (028) 33 68 00 *Fax:* (028) 33 68 01 *E-mail:* emuseo@ext.step.es, pg 1368

Sociedad Editorial Dominicana SA (Dominican Republic) *Tel:* (809) 6875775; (809) 6889378 *Fax:* (809) 6889378, pg 137

Sociedad General de Autores de la Argentina (Argentina) *Tel:* (011) 8112582, pg 1235

Sociedad General Espanola de Libreria SA - SGEL (Spain) *Tel:* (091) 657 69 00; (091) 657 69 12 *Fax:* (091) 657 69 28; (091) 657 69 19 *Web Site:* www.sgel.es, pg 591

Sociedade Brasileira de Cultura Inglesa - Biblioteca (Brazil) *Tel:* (021) 2870990 ext 303 *Fax:* (021) 2676474, pg 1455

Sociedade Distribuidora de Livros Ltda (Sodilivro) (Brazil) *Tel:* (021) 580-1168; (021) 580-6230 *Fax:* (021) 580-5868, pg 92

Sociedade Portuguesa de Autores (Portugal) *Tel:* (021) 578320 *Fax:* (021) 3530257, pg 1367

Societa Dante Alighieri (Italy) *Tel:* (06) 6873694, pg 1365

Societa Dantesca Italiana (Italy) *Tel:* (055) 287134 *Fax:* (055) 211316 *E-mail:* sdi@leonet.it; sdi.biblio@leonet.it; sdi.biblio2@leonet.it *Web Site:* www.danteonline.it, pg 1365

Societa Editrice Internazionale - SEI (Italy) *Tel:* (011) 52271 *Fax:* (011) 5211320, pg 408

Societa Editrice la Goliardica Pavese SRL (Italy) *Tel:* (0382) 529570 *Fax:* (0382) 423140, pg 408

Societa Napoletana Storia Patria Napoli (Italy) *Tel:* (081) 5510353 *Fax:* (081) 5529238 *E-mail:* snsp@unina.it *Web Site:* www.storia.unina.it/smsp/, pg 408

Societa Stampa Sportiva (Italy) *Tel:* (06) 5817311 *Fax:* (06) 5806526 *E-mail:* segreteria@stampasportiva.com *Web Site:* www.stampasportiva.com, pg 408

Societa Storica Catanese (Italy) *Tel:* (095) 311124, pg 408

Societa Ziaristilor din Romania (Romania) *Tel:* (01) 6171591 *Fax:* (01) 3128266, pg 1257

Societaets-Verlag (Germany) *Tel:* (069) 75010 *Fax:* (069) 75014398, pg 287

Societatea de Stiinte Filologice din Romania (SSF) (Romania) *Tel:* (01) 6151792 *Fax:* (01) 6151792, pg 1367

Societe Africaine d'Edition (Senegal) *Tel:* 217977; 220284, pg 544

La Societe Africaine d'Edition et de Communication (SAEC) (Guinea) *Tel:* 461068 *Fax:* 443291, pg 1247

Societe Belge des Auteurs, Compositeurs et Editeurs (SABAM) (Belgium) *Tel:* (02) 2868211 *Fax:* (02) 2311800 *E-mail:* 101641.2761@compuserve.com, pg 1360

Societe Cherifienne de Distribution et de Presse Sochepress (Morocco) *Tel:* (02) 22400223 *Fax:* (02) 22404032 *E-mail:* infolivre@sochepress.co.ma, pg 1300

Societe de Langue et de Litterature Wallonnes ASBL (Belgium) *Tel:* (086) 344432 *E-mail:* sllw.be@skynet.be *Web Site:* users.skynet.be/sllw, pg 1361

Societe d'Edition d'Afrique Nouvelle (Senegal) *Tel:* (08) 211381; (08) 221580 *Fax:* (08) 223604, pg 544

Societe des Auteurs et Compositeurs Dramatiques (SACD) (France) *Tel:* (01) 40234444 *Fax:* (01) 45267428 *E-mail:* infosacd@sacd.fr, pg 1363

Societe des Editions Grasset et Fasquelle (France) *Tel:* (01) 44392200 *Fax:* (01) 42226418 *E-mail:* editorial@edition-grasset.fr *Web Site:* www.grasset.fr, pg 185

Societe des Editions Privat SA (France) *Tel:* (0534) 31 81 81 *Fax:* (0534) 31 64 44 *E-mail:* editionsprivat@wanadoo.fr, pg 185

Societe des Gens de Lettres de France (France) *Tel:* (01) 53 10 12 00 *Fax:* (01) 53 10 12 12 *E-mail:* sgdlf@wanadoo.fr *Web Site:* www.sgdl.org, pg 1363

Societe des Libraires et Editeurs de la Suisse Romande (SLESR) (Switzerland) *Tel:* (021) 7963300 *Fax:* (021) 7963311 *E-mail:* aself@centrezational.cl, pg 1261

la Societe des Poetes Francais (France) *Tel:* (01) 40469982 *E-mail:* poetesfrancais@aol.com *Web Site:* www.societedespoetesfrancais.asso.fr, pg 1363

Societe d'Etudes Dantesques (France), pg 1363

Societe d'Histoire Litteraire de la France (France) *Tel:* (01) 45872330 *Fax:* (01) 45872330, pg 1363

Societe Ennewrasse Service Librairie et Imprimerie (Morocco) *Tel:* (077) 6413 *Fax:* (077) 6413, pg 470

Societe Francaise des Traducteurs (France) *Tel:* (01) 48784332 *Fax:* (01) 44530114 *E-mail:* sft@sft.fr *Web Site:* www.sft.fr, pg 1125

Societe Internationale des Bibliotheques et des Musees des Arts du Spectacle (SIBMAS) (United Kingdom) *Tel:* (020) 7 943 4720 *Fax:* (020) 7 943 4777 *Web Site:* www.theatrelibrary.org/sibmas/sibmas.html, pg 1267

Societe Mathematique de France - Institut Henri Poincare (France) *Tel:* (01) 44276796 *Fax:* (01) 40469096 *E-mail:* smf@dma.ens.fr *Web Site:* smf.emath.fr, pg 185

Societe Nationale d'Edition et de Diffusion (Tunisia) *Tel:* (01) 255000, pg 1315

Societe Nouveaux Loisirs (France) *Tel:* (01) 49 54 42 00 *Fax:* (01) 45 44 39 45 *Web Site:* www.gallimard.fr, pg 185

Society for Endocrinology (United Kingdom) *Tel:* (01454) 642200 *Fax:* (01454) 642222 *E-mail:* info@endocrinology.org; sales@endocrinology.org *Web Site:* www.endocrinology.org, pg 743

Society for Macedonian Studies (Greece) *Tel:* (031) 268710 *Fax:* (031) 971501 *E-mail:* ems@hyper.gr, pg 315

The Society for Promoting Christian Knowledge (SPCK) (United Kingdom) *Tel:* (020) 7643 0382 *Fax:* (020) 7643 0391 *E-mail:* spck@spck.co.uk; sales@spck.co.uk *Web Site:* www.spck.org.uk, pg 743

Society for the Promotion of African, Asian & Latin American Literature (Germany) *Tel:* (069) 2102247 *Fax:* (069) 2102227 *E-mail:* litprom@book-fair.com *Web Site:* www.litprom.de, pg 1112

Society for the Study of Medieval Languages and Literature (United Kingdom) *Tel:* (01865) 270665 *Fax:* (01865) 270600, pg 1372

Society of Archivists (United Kingdom) *Tel:* (020) 7278 8630 *Fax:* (020) 7278 2107 *E-mail:* societyofarchivists@archives.org.uk *Web Site:* www.archives.org.uk, pg 1525

Society of Arts, Literature and Welfare (Bangladesh), pg 1360

Society of Authors (United Kingdom) *Tel:* (020) 7373 6642 *Fax:* (020) 7373 5768 *E-mail:* info@societyofauthors.org *Web Site:* www.societyofauthors.org, pg 1142, 1267

Society of College, National & University Libraries (SCONUL) (United Kingdom) *Tel:* (020) 7387 0317 *Fax:* (020) 7383 3197, pg 1525

The Society of County Librarians (United Kingdom) *Tel:* (0113) 2478330 *Fax:* (0113) 2478331, pg 1525

Society of Freelance Editors & Proofreaders (United Kingdom) *Tel:* (020) 7403 5141 *Fax:* (020) 7407 1193 *E-mail:* admin@sfep.org.uk *Web Site:* www.sfep.org.uk, pg 1372

Society of Indexers (United Kingdom) *Tel:* (0114) 281 3060 *Fax:* (0114) 281 3061 *E-mail:* admin@socind.demon.co.uk *Web Site:* www.socind.demon.co.uk, pg 1267

The Society of Metaphysicians Ltd (United Kingdom) *Tel:* (01424) 751577 *Fax:* (01424) 722387 *E-mail:* newmeta@btinternet.com; info@metaphysicians.org.uk *Web Site:* www.newmeta.btinternet.co.uk; www.metaphysicians.org.uk; www.metaphysicalresearchgroup.org.uk, pg 743

Society of Women Writers (Australia) *Tel:* (03) 63310267, pg 1236

The Society of Women Writers & Journalists (United Kingdom) *Tel:* (01379) 740550 *Fax:* (01379) 741716 *Web Site:* www.author.co.uk/swwj.html, pg 1372

Edizioni Rosminiane Sodalitas (Italy) *Tel:* (0323) 30091 *Fax:* (0323) 31623 *E-mail:* edizioni@rosmini.it, pg 408

Sodilivros (Portugal) *Tel:* (021) 658902 *Fax:* (021) 3876281, pg 1308

Soederstroem et Co Foerlagsaktiebolag (Finland) *Tel:* (09) 6922010 *Fax:* (09) 6926346; (09) 6822425, pg 144

Soemwit Barwakhan (Thailand) *Tel:* (02) 214541, pg 635

Soez Yayin/Oyunajans (Turkey) *Tel:* (0212) 1668931 *Fax:* (0212) 2454102 *Web Site:* www.oyunajans.com, pg 641

Sofa (Slovakia) *Tel:* (07) 242510 *Fax:* (07) 242510 *E-mail:* sofa@ba.sknet.sk, pg 551

Sofia City & District State Archives (Bulgaria) *Tel:* (02) 9400106 *Fax:* (02) 980 1443, pg 1456

Sofiac (Societe Francaise des Imprimeries Administratives Centrales) (France) *Tel:* (01) 40-64-42-42 *Fax:* (01) 40-64-42-40, pg 185

Sofiiski Universitet Kliment Ohridsky Biblioteka (Bulgaria) *Tel:* (02) 467584; (02) 9443719 *Fax:* (02) 467170 *E-mail:* lsu@libsu.uni-sofia.bg *Web Site:* www.libsu.uni-sofia.bg, pg 1456

Sofiprin (Czech Republic) *Tel:* (02) 291044 *Fax:* (02) 758280, pg 128

Sofradif Editions Philippe Auzou (France) *Tel:* (01) 40.33.84.00 *Fax:* (01) 47.97.20.08, pg 185

Sogang University Press (Republic of Korea) *Tel:* (02) 715-0141; (02) 715-0147 *Fax:* (02) 701-8962, pg 440

Sogensha Publishing Co Ltd (Japan) *Tel:* (06) 62319011 *Fax:* (06) 62333112 *E-mail:* sgse@email.msn.com *Web Site:* www.sogensha.co.jp, pg 426

Sohaksa (Republic of Korea) *Tel:* (02) 7967661 *Fax:* (02) 7968700, pg 440

Verlag SOI (Schweizerisches Ost-Institut) (Switzerland) *Tel:* (031) 431212 *Fax:* (031) 3513801, pg 625

Sojuz na drustvata za makedonski jazik i literatura (The Former Yugoslav Republic of Macedonia), pg 1366

Sokoine University of Agriculture Library (United Republic of Tanzania) *Tel:* (056) 3511 *Fax:* (056) 4088 *E-mail:* sua@hnettan.gn.apc.org, pg 1503

Ediciones Sol del Sur (Uruguay) *Tel:* (02) 621627, pg 761

Soldi-Verlag im Drockzentrum Harburg (Germany) *Tel:* (04181) 29 16 22 *Fax:* (04181) 29 16 23 *Web Site:* www.karismaverlag.de, pg 287

Edizioni del Sole 24 Ore (Italy) *Tel:* (02) 30221 *Fax:* (02) 3022405, pg 408

Editions du Soleil (Haiti) *Tel:* (01) 23147, pg 317

Anna Soler-Pont Literary Agecy (Spain) *Tel:* (093) 201 90 90 *Fax:* (093) 201 90 90 *E-mail:* pontas@intercom.es, pg 591

Solidaridad Publishing House (Philippines) *Tel:* (02) 586581; (02) 591241 *Fax:* (02) 5255038, pg 515

Soline (France) *Tel:* (01) 43 33 74 24 *Fax:* (01) 43 33 67 37 *E-mail:* edsoline@wanadoo.fr *Web Site:* perso.wanadoo.fr/soline, pg 186

Solivros (Portugal) *Tel:* (052) 42385, pg 529

Solum Forlag A/S (Norway) *Tel:* 22500400 *Fax:* 22501453 *E-mail:* solumfor@online.no *Web Site:* www.solumforlag.no, pg 505

Somaiya Publications Pvt Ltd (India) *Tel:* (011) 440030; (011) 3324939; (011) 3324973 *Fax:* (011) 3723351 *Web Site:* www.somaiya.com, pg 350

National Library of Somalia (Somalia) *Tel:* 22758, pg 1497

Michael Somare Library (Papua New Guinea) *Tel:* (0675) 3267280 *Fax:* (0675) 3267187 *E-mail:* 100352.216@compuserve.com, pg 1490

Somawathi Hewavitharana Fund (Sri Lanka) *Tel:* (01) 691335; (01) 695161, pg 598

Somerset Publications (Australia) *Tel:* (07) 3425 1766 *Fax:* (07) 3425 1857 *E-mail:* info@crabbetarabian.com *Web Site:* www.crabbetarabian.com, pg 42

Sommer og Soerensen Forlag ApS (Denmark) *Tel:* 36153615 *Fax:* 36153616, pg 135

Somogy editions d'art (France) *Tel:* (01) 48 05 70 10 *Fax:* (01) 48 05 71 70, pg 186

Edizioni Sonda (Italy) *Tel:* (011) 211442 *Fax:* (011) 2217818, pg 408

Sonnentanz-Verlag Roland Kron (Germany) *Tel:* (0821) 311070 *Fax:* (0821) 158979 *E-mail:* sonnentanz@t-online.de, pg 287

Sonneville Press (Uitgeverij) VTW (Belgium) *Tel:* (050) 321112, pg 74

Johannes Sonntag Verlagsbuchhandlung GmbH (Germany) *Tel:* (0711) 8931-0 *Fax:* (0711) 8931-133 *Web Site:* www.sonntag-verlag.com, pg 287

Sony Magazines Inc (Japan) *Tel:* (03) 32345811 *Fax:* (03) 32346753, pg 426

Sonzogno (Italy) *Tel:* (02) 50951 *Fax:* (02) 5065361, pg 408

Editorial Sopena Argentina SACI e I (Argentina) *Tel:* (011) 4912-2383; (011) 4912-2385; (011) 4912-2386 *Fax:* (011) 4912-2383 *E-mail:* edsopena@elsitio.net, pg 9

Ramon Sopena SA (Spain) *Tel:* (093) 2303809 *Fax:* (093) 3223703, pg 591

Sophia Book Service (Republic of Korea) *Tel:* (02) 362-2036 *Fax:* (02) 362-2036, pg 1297

Educatieve Uitgeverij Sorava (Suriname) *Tel:* 483879, pg 599

Edizioni Sorbona Milano (Italy) *Tel:* (02) 48016464 *Fax:* (02) 48194485, pg 408

Bibliotheque de la Sorbonne (France) *Tel:* (01) 40463027 *Fax:* (01) 40463044 *E-mail:* adminst@biu.sorbonne.fr *Web Site:* www.sorbonne.fr, pg 1465

Publications de la Sorbonne (France) *Tel:* (01) 40 46 28 48 *Fax:* (01) 40 46 28 49 *E-mail:* publisor@univ-paris1.fr, pg 186

Association d'Editions Sorg (France) *Tel:* (01) 48252524 *Fax:* (01) 46052563, pg 186

Soryusha (Japan) *Tel:* (03) 32631471 *Fax:* (03) 32632943, pg 426

Editions SOS (Editions du Secours Catholique) (France) *Tel:* (01) 40354465 *Fax:* (01) 40354273, pg 186

Soshisha Co Ltd (Japan) *Tel:* (03) 34706565 *Fax:* (03) 34702640 *E-mail:* soshisha@magical.egg.or.jp, pg 426

Sota Graphic Arts Co Ltd (Hong Kong) *Tel:* 23427507 *Fax:* 23415426 *E-mail:* sales@goldencup.com.hk, pg 1156, 1197

Editions Louis Soulanges Le Livrer Ouvert (France) *Tel:* (01) 43262538; (01) 43256782, pg 186

Soundbooks (Australia) *Tel:* (03) 98247711 *Fax:* (03) 98247855 *E-mail:* audio@vicnet.com.au *Web Site:* www.soundbooks.com.au, pg 1273

Les Editions de la Source Sarl (France) *Tel:* (01) 45253007, pg 186

Sousa & Almeida Livraria (Portugal) *Tel:* 222050073 *Fax:* 222050073, pg 529

Livraria Sousa e Almeida Lda (Portugal) *Tel:* (02) 22 050 073 *Fax:* (02) 22 050 073 *E-mail:* sousaealmeida@net.sapo.pt, pg 1308

South African Library (South Africa) *Tel:* (021) 246320 *Fax:* (021) 244848 *E-mail:* macmahon@salib.ac.za, pg 1498

South African Booksellers Association (South Africa) *Tel:* (021) 9188616 *Fax:* (021) 9514903 *E-mail:* fnel@naspers.com *Web Site:* sabooksellers.com, pg 1259

South African Extension Unit (United Republic of Tanzania) *Tel:* (051) 37325; (051) 37326 *Fax:* (051) 37325, pg 634

South African Institute of International Affairs (South Africa) *Tel:* (011) 3392021 *Fax:* (011) 3392154 *E-mail:* 160mig@cosmos.wds.ac.za *Web Site:* www.wits.ac.za/saiia.htm, pg 559

South African Institute of Race Relations (South Africa) *Tel:* (011) 4033600 *Fax:* (011) 4033671 *E-mail:* sairr@milkyway.co.za, pg 559

South African Library for the Blind (South Africa) *Tel:* (0461) 27226 *Fax:* (0461) 27650 *E-mail:* blindlib@iafrica.com, pg 1498

South Asia Publications (India) *Tel:* (011) 7241869; (011) 7235539, pg 350

South Asian Publishers Pvt Ltd (India) *Tel:* (011) 276292; (011) 276740 *E-mail:* vchigs@giasdla.vsnl.net.in, pg 350

South China Morning Post Ltd (Hong Kong) *Tel:* 25652435; 25652450; 25622271 *Fax:* 5655380, pg 322

South China Printing Co (1988) Ltd (Hong Kong) *Tel:* 26373611 *Fax:* 26374221, pg 1135

South China University of Science and Technology Press (China) *Tel:* (020) 5516863; (020) 5511311-2802, pg 109

South East Asian Central Banks (SEACEN) Research & Training Centre (Malaysia) *Tel:* (03) 7568622 *Fax:* (03) 7574616 *E-mail:* info@seacen.po.my *Web Site:* www.bnm.gov.my/seacen/index.htm, pg 1483

South Head Press (Australia) *Tel:* (048) 771421, pg 42

South Pacific Association for Commonwealth Literature & Language Studies (SPACLALS) (New Zealand), pg 1255

South Pacific Books Imports Ltd (New Zealand) *Tel:* (09) 3762142 *Fax:* (09) 3762141 *E-mail:* sales@soupacbooks.co.nz *Web Site:* www.soupacbooks.co.nz, pg 1302

University of the South Pacific (Fiji) *Tel:* 313900 *Fax:* 301305 *E-mail:* farkas_g@nsp.ac.fj, pg 141

South Sea Books (New Zealand) *Tel:* (03) 3317630 *E-mail:* southsea@ihug.co.nz *Web Site:* www.abebooks.com/home/southsea, pg 1302

South Sea International Press Ltd (Hong Kong) *Tel:* 28971083 *Fax:* 25581473 *E-mail:* ssiphk@hk.super.net, pg 1135, 1156, 1197

Southeast Asian Ministers of Education Organization Regional Language Centre (SEAMEO RELC) (Thailand) *Tel:* (0662) 3910144 *Fax:* (0662) 3812587, pg 1263

Southeast Asian Regional Branch of the International Council on Archives (SARBICA) (Malaysia) *Tel:* (03) 651 0688 *Fax:* (03) 651 5679 *E-mail:* query@arkib.gov.my *Web Site:* arkib.gov.my/general/inter.html, pg 1252

Southern Book Publishers (Pty) Ltd (South Africa) *Tel:* (011) 3153633 *Fax:* (011) 3153810 *E-mail:* Southern@struik.co.za, pg 559

Southern Cross PR & Press Services (Australia) *Tel:* (02) 6737-5436 *Fax:* (02) 6737-5436, pg 42

Southern Press Ltd (New Zealand) *Tel:* (04) 239-9068 *Fax:* (04) 239-9835, pg 496

Southgate Publishers (United Kingdom) *Tel:* (01363) 776888 *Fax:* (01363) 776889 *E-mail:* info@southgatepublishers.co.uk *Web Site:* www.southgatepublishers.co.uk, pg 743

Southwest China Jiaotong University Press (China) *Tel:* (028) 784160-763 *Fax:* (028) 24377 *E-mail:* swju@swjtu.edu.cn, pg 109

Southwood Press Pty Ltd (Australia) *Tel:* (02) 9560 5100 *Fax:* (02) 9550 0097 *E-mail:* info@southwoodpress.com.au *Web Site:* www.southwoodpress.com.au, pg 1193

Souvenir Press Ltd (United Kingdom) *Tel:* (020) 7580 9307; (020) 7637 5711; (020) 7637 5712; (020) 7637 5713 *Fax:* (020) 7580 5064 *E-mail:* souvenirpress@ukonline.co.uk, pg 743

Sovereign World Ltd (United Kingdom) *Tel:* (01732) 850598 *Fax:* (01732) 851077 *E-mail:* sovereignworldbooks@compuserve.com *Web Site:* www.sovereign-world.org, pg 744

Izdatelstvo Sovetskii Pisatel (Russian Federation) *Tel:* (095) 2025051 *Fax:* (095) 2023200, pg 542

Sovremennik Publishers Too (Russian Federation) *Tel:* (095) 9412992 *Fax:* (095) 9413544, pg 542

SP Interbuk, Russian-Slovenien jv (Russian Federation) *Tel:* (095) 9245081 *Fax:* (095) 2002281; (095) 2302403, pg 542

SPA Books Ltd (United Kingdom) *Tel:* (01438) 225727 *Fax:* (01438) 310104 *E-mail:* strongoakpress@hotmail.com, pg 744

Space Sellers Ltd (Kenya) *Tel:* (02) 555811; (02) 557517; (02) 557863 *Fax:* (02) 557815; (02) 558847 *E-mail:* ssrms@africaonline.co.ke, pg 433

Spacevision Publishing (Australia) *Tel:* (03) 51272398, pg 42

Spala Editora Ltda (Brazil) *Tel:* (021) 542-9995 *Fax:* (021) 542-4738, pg 92

Spaniel Books (Australia) *Tel:* (02) 9360 9985 *Fax:* (02) 9331 4653 *E-mail:* spanielb@matra.com.au, pg 43

Costas Spanos (Greece) *Tel:* (01) 3623917; (01) 3614332 *Fax:* (01) 8953076, pg 315

Specialist Publications (Australia) *Tel:* (02) 97362191 *Fax:* (02) 97362663, pg 43

SpectraComp (United States) *Tel:* 717-697-8600 *Fax:* 717-691-0433 *E-mail:* info@spectracomp.com *Web Site:* www.spectracomp.com, pg 1166

Spectres Familiers (France) *Tel:* (0491) 912645 *Fax:* (0491) 909951, pg 186

Spectrum Books Ltd (Nigeria) *Tel:* (02) 2310058; (02) 2311215; (02) 2312705 *Fax:* (02) 2312705; (02) 2318502 *E-mail:* admin1@spectrumbooksonline.com *Web Site:* www.spectrumbooksonline.com, pg 501

Uitgeverij Het Spectrum BV (Netherlands) *Tel:* (030) 2650650 *Fax:* (030) 2620850 *E-mail:* het@spectrum.nl, pg 484

Spectrum Publications (Australia) *Tel:* (03) 9429 1404 *Fax:* (03) 9428 9407 *E-mail:* spectpub@ozemail.com.au, pg 43

Spectrum Publications (India) *Tel:* (0361) 26381; (0361) 24791 *Fax:* (0361) 544791, pg 350

Spee Buchverlag GmbH (Germany) *Tel:* (0651) 979900; (0651) 9799162; (0651) 9799160 *Fax:* (0651) 9799165, pg 287

Speechmark Publishing Ltd (United Kingdom) *Tel:* (01869) 244644 *Fax:* (01869) 320040 *E-mail:* info@speechmark.net *Web Site:* www.speechmark.net, pg 744

Speedflex Asia Ltd (China) *Tel:* 25422780 *Fax:* 25454026 *E-mail:* info@speedflex.com.hk *Web Site:* www.speedflex.com.hk, pg 1132, 1194

Speedflex Asia Ltd (China) *Tel:* 25422780 *Fax:* 25454026 *E-mail:* info@speedflex.com.hk, pg 1211

Speer -Verlag (Switzerland) *Tel:* (091) 911026 *Fax:* (01) 3424531, pg 625

Spektrum der Wissenschaft Verlagsgesellschaft mbH (Germany) *Tel:* (06221) 91 26 600 *Fax:* (06221) 91 26 751 *E-mail:* marketing@spektrum.com *Web Site:* www.spektrum.de, pg 287

Spektrum Forlagsaktieselskab (Denmark) *Tel:* 33147714 *Fax:* 33147791, pg 135

Spellbound Promotions (Australia) *Tel:* (02) 66542133 *Fax:* (02) 66541258 *E-mail:* Jodiadv@oncs.com.au, pg 43

Spellmount Ltd Publishers (United Kingdom) *Tel:* (01580) 893730 *Fax:* (01580) 893731 *E-mail:* enquiries@spellmount.com *Web Site:* www.spellmount.com, pg 744

Spengler Editeur (France) *Tel:* (01) 49701555 *Fax:* (01) 49701550, pg 186

Sperling e Kupfer Editori SpA (Italy) *Tel:* (02) 217211 *Fax:* (02) 21721277, pg 408

Libreria Internazionale Sperling e Kupfer (Italy) *Tel:* (02) 290341 *Fax:* (02) 6590290, pg 1294

SPES Editorial SL (Spain) *Tel:* (093) 2922666 *Fax:* (093) 2922162, pg 591

Speurwerk Stitching betreffende het Boek (Netherlands) *Tel:* (020) 6254927 *Fax:* (020) 6208871, pg 1255

Sphinx Publishing Co (Egypt (Arab Republic of Egypt)) *Tel:* (02) 392 4616 *Fax:* (02) 391 8802 *E-mail:* sphinx@intouch.com, pg 139

Sphinx Verlag AG (Switzerland) *Tel:* (061) 259292 *Fax:* (061) 2721150, pg 625

Spiegel-Verlag Rudolf Augstein GmbH & Co KG (Germany) *Tel:* (040) 30 07-26 87 *Fax:* (040) 30 07-29 66 *E-mail:* spiegel@spiegel.de, pg 287

Spiess Volker Wissenschaftsverlag GmbH (Germany) *Tel:* (030) 6917073-74 *Fax:* (030) 6914067, pg 287

Spieth-Verlag Verlag fuer Symbolforschung (Germany) *Tel:* (030) 68302041 *Fax:* (030) 683-02042, pg 288

Spinal Publications (New Zealand) *Tel:* (04) 2937020 *Fax:* (04) 2932897, pg 496

Spindulys Printing House (Lithuania) *Tel:* (07) 226243; (07) 225029 *Fax:* (07) 204970, pg 1137

Spindulys Printing House (Lithuania) *Tel:* (07) 226243 *Fax:* (07) 204970, pg 1158, 1199

Spinifex Press (Australia) *Tel:* (03) 9329-6088 *Fax:* (03) 9329-9238 *E-mail:* world@spinifexpress.com.au *Web Site:* www.spinifexpress.com.au, pg 43

Spirali Edizioni (Italy) *Tel:* (02) 8054417 *Fax:* (02) 8692631 *E-mail:* info@spirali.it *Web Site:* www.spirali-vel.com, pg 408

Spiridon-Verlags GmbH (Germany) *Tel:* (0211) 726364 *Fax:* (0211) 786823, pg 288

Spokesman (United Kingdom) *Tel:* (0115) 9708318; (0115) 9784504 *Fax:* (0115) 9420433 *E-mail:* elfeuro@compuserve.com *Web Site:* www.spokesmanbooks.com; www.russfound.org, pg 744

Spoleczny Instytut Wydawniczy Znak (Poland) *Tel:* (012) 4291469; (012) 4219776 *Fax:* (012) 4219814 *E-mail:* rucinska@znak.com.pl, pg 520

Spolok slovenskych spisovatel'ov (Slovakia) *Tel:* (07) 43615, pg 1258

Spon Press (United Kingdom) *Tel:* (020) 7583 9855 *Fax:* (020) 7842 2298 *E-mail:* info@routledge.co.uk *Web Site:* www.sponpress.com, pg 744

Adolf Sponholtz Verlag (Germany) *Tel:* (05151) 200312 *Fax:* (05151) 200319, pg 288

Sport & Hobby Book Club (Greece) *Tel:* (01) 3234217 *Fax:* (01) 3232082 *E-mail:* hcp@photography.gr, pg 1229

Sport Publishing House Ltd (Slovakia) *Tel:* (07) 49249618 *Fax:* (07) 49249586, pg 551

Sportska Knjiga (Yugoslavia) *Tel:* (011) 3220226; (011) 3225361, pg 765

The Sportsman's Press (United Kingdom) *Tel:* (020) 8789 0229 *Fax:* (020) 8789 0229, pg 744

Sportverlag Berlin GmbH SVB (Germany) *Tel:* (030) 2591-3550 *Fax:* (030) 2591-3516 *E-mail:* marketing@sportverlag-berlin.de *Web Site:* www.sportverlag-berlin.de, pg 288

Spotdzielna Anagram (Poland) *Tel:* (022) 6250114, pg 520

Editions Spratbrow (France) *Tel:* (03) 27 33 62 58 *Fax:* (03) 27 45 29 99 *E-mail:* sjbv.cdi@wanadoo.fr, pg 186

Spraymation Inc (United States) *Tel:* 954-484-9700 *Fax:* 954-484-9778 *E-mail:* sales@spraymation.com *Web Site:* www.spraymation.com, pg 1208

Spriditis Publishers (Latvia) *Tel:* (02) 7286516 *Fax:* (02) 7286818, pg 442

Axel Springer Publicaciones (Spain) *Tel:* (091) 514 06 30; (091) 556 00 48 *Fax:* (091) 514 06 30; (091) 556 0324 *E-mail:* info@axelspringer.es *Web Site:* www.axelspringer.es, pg 591

Axel Springer Verlag AG (Germany) *Tel:* (040) 347-00 *Fax:* (040) 345811 *E-mail:* info@asv.de *Web Site:* www.asv.de, pg 288

Editions Springer France (France) *Tel:* (01) 56541313; (01) 56541300 *Fax:* (01) 56541317 *Web Site:* www.springer.de, pg 186

Springer Hungarica Kiado Kft (Hungary) *Tel:* (01) 251-0099, pg 326

Springer-Verlag GmbH & Co KG (Germany) *Tel:* (06221) 487-0 *Fax:* (06221) 487-8366 *E-mail:* orders@springer.de *Web Site:* www.springer.de, pg 288

Springer-Verlag Hong Kong Ltd (Hong Kong) *Tel:* (02) 27239698 *Fax:* (02) 27242366, pg 322

Springer-Verlag Iberica, SA (Spain) *Tel:* (093) 4570227; (093) 4570759 *Fax:* (093) 4571502 *E-mail:* springer.bcn@springer.es, pg 591

Springer-Verlag London Ltd (United Kingdom) *Tel:* (0483) 418800; (01483) 418822 (sales) *Fax:* (01483) 415151; (01483) 415144 *E-mail:* postmaster@svl.co.uk, pg 744

Springer-Verlag Tokyo (Japan) *Tel:* (03) 38120757 *Fax:* (03) 38120719, pg 426

Springer-Verlag Wien (Austria) *Tel:* (01) 3302415 *Fax:* (01) 3302426 *E-mail:* books@springer.at (orders); journals@springer.at (orders) *Web Site:* www.springer.at, pg 59

Springfield Books Ltd (United Kingdom) *Tel:* (01484) 864955 *Fax:* (01484) 865443, pg 1322

SPS Verlaggsservice GmbH (Germany) *Tel:* (0261) 862662 *Fax:* (0261) 8070654, pg 1284

Barbara Spurll Illustration (Canada) *Tel:* 416-594-6594 *E-mail:* bspurll@idirect.ca, pg 1154

Spyropoulos A (Greece) *Tel:* (01) 6712991 *Fax:* (01) 6719622, pg 315

Square Dance Partners Forlag (Denmark) *Tel:* 45 83 99 83, pg 135

Square One Publications (United Kingdom) *Tel:* (01684) 593704 *Fax:* (01684) 594060, pg 744

Square Two Design Inc (United States) *Tel:* 415-437-3888 *Fax:* 415-437-3880 *Web Site:* www.square2.com, pg 1167

Sraka International (Slovenia) *Tel:* (068) 23174 *Fax:* (068) 24094, pg 1309

Arhiv Srbije (Yugoslavia) *Tel:* (011) 3370781 *Fax:* (011) 3370246 *E-mail:* arhvserb@eunet.yu, pg 1509

Srebaren lav (Bulgaria) *Tel:* (02) 752298, pg 98

Y Sreberk (Israel) *Tel:* (03) 6293343 *Fax:* (03) 6299297, pg 372

Sredne-Uralskoye knizhnoye izatelstve (Middle Urals Publishing House) (Russian Federation) *Tel:* (03432) 514162 *Fax:* (03432) 512859, pg 542

Sree Rama Publishers (India) *Tel:* 73128, pg 351

SRHE (United Kingdom) *Tel:* (020) 7637 2766 *Fax:* (020) 7637 2781 *E-mail:* srheoffice@srhe.ac.uk *Web Site:* www.srhe.ac.uk, pg 744

Sri Lanka Library Association (Sri Lanka) *Tel:* (01) 589103 *E-mail:* postmast@slla.ac.lk, pg 1523

Sri Lanka Association of Publishers (Sri Lanka) *Tel:* (01) 695773 *Fax:* (01) 696653 *E-mail:* dayawansajay@hotmail.com, pg 1259

Sri Lanka Jama'ath-e-Islami (Sri Lanka) *Tel:* (01) 687091 *Fax:* (01) 686030, pg 598

Sri Satguru Publications (India) *Tel:* (011) 7126497; (011) 7434930 *Fax:* (011) 7227336 *E-mail:* ibcindia@giasdlo1.vsnl.net.in or ibcindia@ibcindia.com, pg 351

Srinakharinwirot University, Central Library (Thailand) *Tel:* (02) 2584002; (02) 2584003 *Fax:* (02) 2604514 *E-mail:* pimol@psm.swu.ac.th, pg 1503

Srpska Knjizevna Zadruga (Yugoslavia) *Tel:* (011) 3233-545; (011) 3234-977 *Fax:* (011) 626-224, pg 765

Biblioteka Srpske Akademije Nauka i Umetnosti (Yugoslavia) *Tel:* (011) 3342400 *Fax:* (011) 182825; (011) 639120 *E-mail:* admin@bib.sanu.ac.yu *Web Site:* www.sanu.ac.yu, pg 1509

St Pauls Publishing (United Kingdom) *Tel:* (020) 7978 4300 *Fax:* (020) 7978 4370 *E-mail:* editions@stpauls.org.uk *Web Site:* www.stpauls.ie, pg 744

L Staackmann Verlag KG (Germany) *Tel:* (08027) 337 *Fax:* (08027) 816, pg 288

Staatliche Museen Kassel (Germany) *Tel:* (0561) 93 77-7 *Fax:* (0561) 93 77-6 66 *E-mail:* info@museum-kassel.de *Web Site:* www.museum-kassel.de, pg 288

Staats- und Universitaetsbibliothek Hamburg Carl von Ossietzky (Germany) *Tel:* (040) 42838 2233 *Fax:* (040) 42838-3352 *E-mail:* auskunft@sub.uni-hamburg.de *Web Site:* www.sub.uni-hamburg.de, pg 1468

Staats- und Universitatsbibliothek Bremen (Germany) *Tel:* (0421) 2182601 *Fax:* (0421) 2182614 *E-mail:* suub@zfn.uni-bremen.de, pg 1468

Staatsbibliothek zu Berlin - Preussischer Kulturbesitz (Germany) *Tel:* (030) 266-0 *Fax:* (030) 266-1721 *E-mail:* fragen@sbb.spk-berlin.de; webserveradmin@sbb.spk-berlin.de *Web Site:* www.sbb.spk-berlin.de, pg 288

Staatsbibliothek zu Berlin - Preussischer Kulturbesitz (Germany) *Tel:* (030) 266-0 *Fax:* (030) 266-1721; (030) 266-2319 *E-mail:* generaldiv@sbb.spk-berlin.de *Web Site:* staatsbibliothek-berlin.de, pg 1468

Staatsdrukkerij en Uitgeverijbedrijf (Netherlands) *Tel:* (070) 3789860 *Fax:* (070) 3789783, pg 484

Stabenfeldt A/S (Norway) *Tel:* 51845400 *Fax:* 51526217, pg 505

Stacey International (United Kingdom) *Tel:* (020) 7221 7166 *Fax:* (020) 7792 9288 *E-mail:* stacey-inter@btconnect.com *Web Site:* www.thebookplace.com/stacey, pg 745

Stadler Verlagsgesellschaft mbH (Germany) *Tel:* (07531) 898-0 *Fax:* (07531) 898-101 *E-mail:* info@verlag-stadler.de *Web Site:* www.verlag-stadler.de, pg 288

Stadsbibliotheek (Belgium) *Tel:* (03) 2068711 *Fax:* (03) 2068775 *E-mail:* sba@antwerpes.be, pg 1453

Stadt Duisburg - Amt Fuer Statistik, Stadtforschung und Europaangelegenheiten (Germany) *Tel:* (0203) 283 3085 *Fax:* (0203) 288 4404 *E-mail:* amt12@stadt-duisburg.de *Web Site:* uni-duisburg.de/duisburg/statistik.htm, pg 288

Stadt Frankfurt a Main Stadt-und Universitaetsbibliothek (Germany) *Tel:* (069) 21239-381 *Fax:* (069) 21239-062 *E-mail:* ditektion@stub.uni-frankfurt.de, pg 1468

Stadt- und Universitaetsbibliothek (Germany) *Tel:* (069) 21239381 *Fax:* (069) 21239062 *E-mail:* direktion@uni-frankfurt.com, pg 1469

Stadt- und Universitaetsbibliothek (Switzerland) *Tel:* (031) 3203211 *Fax:* (031) 3203299 *E-mail:* info@stub.unibe.ch *Web Site:* www.stub.unibe.ch, pg 1501

Staedte-Verlag, E v Wagner und J Mitterhuber GmbH (Germany) *Tel:* (0711) 576201 *Fax:* (0711) 5762243 *E-mail:* info@staedte-verlag.de *Web Site:* www.staedte-verlag.de, pg 288

Buchhandlung Staeheli AG (Switzerland) *Tel:* (01) 2099111 *Fax:* (01) 2099112 *E-mail:* info@staehelibooks.ch *Web Site:* www.staehelibooks.ch, pg 1313

Staempfli Verlag AG (Switzerland) *Tel:* (031) 3006311 *Fax:* (031) 3006688 *E-mail:* verlag@staempfli.com *Web Site:* www.staempfli.com, pg 625

Stafford Books (Australia) *Tel:* (02) 906 4322 *Fax:* (02) 438 3813, pg 43

Stahlbau Zentrum Schweiz (Switzerland) *Tel:* (01) 261 89 80 *Fax:* (01) 262 09 62 *E-mail:* info@szs.ch *Web Site:* www.szs.ch, pg 625

Verlag Stahleisen GmbH (Germany) *Tel:* (0211) 6707-0 *Fax:* (0211) 6707-555 *E-mail:* stahleisen@stahleisen.de *Web Site:* www.stahleisen.de, pg 289

Stainer & Bell Ltd (United Kingdom) *Tel:* (020) 8343 3303 *Fax:* (020) 8343 3024 *E-mail:* post@stainer.co.uk *Web Site:* www.stainer.co.uk, pg 745

Verlag H Stam GmbH (Germany) *Tel:* (02203) 30290 *Fax:* (02203) 302940, pg 289

Stamford College Publishers/Authors-Publishers (Singapore) *Tel:* 3323639 *Fax:* 3323273 *E-mail:* legaldep@nlb.gov.sq.hdtsdnl@technet.sq, pg 548

Stamford Press Pte Ltd (Singapore) *Tel:* 2947227 *Fax:* 2944396, pg 1138

Stamford Press Pte Ltd (Singapore) *Tel:* 2947227 *Fax:* 2944396 *E-mail:* stamford@singnet.com.sq, pg 1159

STAMFORD PRESS PTE LTD INDUSTRY

Stamford Press Pte Ltd (Singapore) *Tel:* 2947227 *Fax:* 2944396 *E-mail:* stamford@singnet.com.sg, pg 1200

Stampa Alternativa - Nuovi Equilibri (Italy) *Tel:* (0761) 352277 *Fax:* (0761) 352751, pg 409

Standaard Uitgeverij (Belgium) *Tel:* (03) 285 72 00 *Fax:* (03) 285 72 99 *E-mail:* info@standaard.com *Web Site:* www.standaard.com, pg 74

Standard Book Numbering Agency (Argentina) *Tel:* (011) 3819277 *Fax:* (011) 3819253 *E-mail:* postmaster@caarli.org.ar, pg 1235

Standard Book Numbering Agency (Austria) *Tel:* (01) 5121535 *Fax:* (01) 5128482 *E-mail:* isbn@hvb.at *Web Site:* www.buecher.at, pg 1237

Standard Book Numbering Agency (Brunei Darussalam) *Tel:* (02) 382511 *Fax:* (02) 381817, pg 1239

Standard Book Numbering Agency (Chile) *Tel:* (02) 6989519 *Fax:* (02) 6989226; (02) 6874271 *E-mail:* camlibro@reuna.cl, pg 1240

Standard Book Numbering Agency (Colombia) *Tel:* (01) 2886188 *Fax:* (01) 2873320 *E-mail:* camlibro@camlibro.com.co *Web Site:* www.camlibro.com.co, pg 1240

Standard Book Numbering Agency (Costa Rica) *Tel:* (0506) 2331706; (0506) 212479 *Fax:* (0506) 2235510 *E-mail:* elenaalpizar@hotmail.com, pg 1240

Standard Book Numbering Agency (Cyprus) *Tel:* (02) 303180; (02) 676118 *Fax:* (02) 304532 *E-mail:* cypruslibrary@cytanet.com.cy, pg 1241

Standard Book Numbering Agency (Egypt (Arab Republic of Egypt)) *Tel:* (02) 5750856; (02) 5751078; (02) 575886 *Fax:* (02) 775385, pg 1242

Standard Book Numbering Agency (Estonia) *Tel:* (02) 6307372 *Fax:* (02) 6311200 *E-mail:* eraamat@nlib.ee *Web Site:* www.nlib.ee/textid/isbn.html, pg 1242

Standard Book Numbering Agency (Gambia) *Tel:* 228312 *Fax:* 223776 *E-mail:* national.library@ganet.gm, pg 1245

Standard Book Numbering Agency (Ghana) *Tel:* (021) 223526; (021) 228402 *Fax:* (021) 247768 *E-mail:* GeorgePadmore@Africanmail.com *Web Site:* www.ghanacom.gh/Padmore, pg 1247

Standard Book Numbering Agency (Greece) *Tel:* (01) 3608597; (01) 3382549 *Fax:* (01) 3611552; (01) 3608141, pg 1247

Standard Book Numbering Agency (Islamic Republic of Iran) *Tel:* (021) 6414991 *Fax:* (021) 6415360; (021) 6414991 *E-mail:* isbn@ketabnet.org *Web Site:* www.ketabnet.org, pg 1249

Standard Book Numbering Agency (Kenya) *Tel:* (02) 718012; (02) 725859; (02) 725550 *Fax:* (02) 721749 *E-mail:* knls@nbnet.co.ke *Web Site:* www.knls.or.ke, pg 1251

Standard Book Numbering Agency (Latvia) *Tel:* (02) 7212668 *Fax:* (02) 7224587 *E-mail:* anitag@lbi.lnb.lv *Web Site:* www.lnb.lv/eng/centrala.htm, pg 1251

Standard Book Numbering Agency (Lesotho) *Tel:* 340601; 340468 *Fax:* 340000 *Web Site:* www.nul.ls, pg 1251

Standard Book Numbering Agency (The Former Yugoslav Republic of Macedonia) *Tel:* (091) 115358 *Fax:* (091) 226846 *E-mail:* zlata@nubsk.edu.mk *Web Site:* www.nubsk.edu.mk, pg 1252

Standard Book Numbering Agency (Malaysia) *Tel:* (03) 2943488; (03) 2943150; (03) 2943626 *Fax:* (03) 2927502 *E-mail:* isbn@www1.pnm.my *Web Site:* www.pnm.my, pg 1252

Standard Book Numbering Agency (Maldive Islands) *Tel:* 323261; 331627 *Fax:* 321201 *E-mail:* educator@dhivehinet.net.mv *Web Site:* www.thauleem.net, pg 1252

Standard Book Numbering Agency (Malta) *Tel:* 440083; 448539 *Fax:* 488908 *E-mail:* contact@peg.com.mt *Web Site:* www.peg.com.mt, pg 1252

Standard Book Numbering Agency (New Zealand) *Tel:* (04) 474 3074 *Fax:* (04) 474 3161 *E-mail:* isbn@natlib.govt.nz, pg 1255

Standard Book Numbering Agency (Pakistan) *Tel:* (051) 9202544-216; (051) 9202549-216 *Fax:* (051) 9221375, pg 1256

Standard Book Numbering Agency (Papua New Guinea) *Tel:* 256200 *Fax:* 3251331 *E-mail:* ola@datec.com.pg, pg 1256

Standard Book Numbering Agency (Portugal) *Tel:* (021) 8435180 *Fax:* (021) 8489377 *E-mail:* cdb@apel.pt *Web Site:* www.apel.pt, pg 1257

Standard Book Numbering Agency (Puerto Rico) *Tel:* (787) 724-1352 *Fax:* (787) 724-2886 *E-mail:* nisc@caribe.net, pg 1257

Standard Book Numbering Agency (Qatar) *Tel:* 429955 *Fax:* 429976 *E-mail:* qanaly@qatar.net.qa, pg 1257

Standard Book Numbering Agency (Russian Federation) *Tel:* (095) 2034653; (095) 2035608 *Fax:* (095) 2982576; (095) 2889665 *E-mail:* vvc@rkp.msk.su, pg 1258

Standard Book Numbering Agency (Saudi Arabia) *Tel:* (01) 4645197; (01) 4624888 (ext 224) *Fax:* (01) 4645341; (01) 4622707 *E-mail:* isbnic@kfnl.gov.sa, pg 1258

Standard Book Numbering Agency (Singapore) *Tel:* 5467236 *Fax:* 5467286 *E-mail:* legaldep@nlb.gov.sg, pg 1258

Standard Book Numbering Agency (Slovenia) *Tel:* (01) 58 61 333 *Fax:* (01) 58 61 311 *E-mail:* isbn@nuk.uni-lj.si *Web Site:* www.nuk.uni-lj.si/zalozniki/isbn/isbn.html, pg 1258

Standard Book Numbering Agency (Suriname) *Tel:* 472545 *Fax:* 410563 *E-mail:* interf@sr.net, pg 1259

Standard Book Numbering Agency (Taiwan, Province of China) *Tel:* (02) 23619132 (ext 705) *Fax:* (02) 23115330 *E-mail:* isbn@msg.ncl.edu.tw *Web Site:* www.ncl.edu.tw/isbn, pg 1262

Standard Book Numbering Agency (Thailand) *Tel:* (02) 2810263; (02) 6285183 *Fax:* (02) 2815450; (02) 2810263 *E-mail:* suwksir@emisc.moe.go.th; suwaksir@yahoo.com *Web Site:* www.span.com.au/nlt, pg 1263

Standard Book Numbering Agency (Turkey) *Tel:* (0312) 2317962 *Fax:* (0312) 2313564 *E-mail:* kultur@kutuphanelergm.gov.trr *Web Site:* www.kutuphanelergm.gov.tr, pg 1263

Standard Book Numbering Agency (Uruguay) *Tel:* (02) 485030; (02) 496014 *Fax:* (02) 496902, pg 1269

Standard Book Numbering Agency (Venezuela) *Tel:* (02) 938535 *Fax:* (02) 9435718, pg 1269

Standard Book Numbering Agency (Zambia) *Tel:* (01) 292837 (ext 1342) *Fax:* (01) 253952; (01) 250845 *E-mail:* library@unza.zm, pg 1269

Standard Book Numbering Agency (Zimbabwe) *Tel:* (04) 792741 *Fax:* (04) 792398, pg 1270

Standard Book Numbering Agency (Botswana) (Botswana) *Tel:* 352397; 352288 *Fax:* 301149, pg 1238

Standard Book Numbering Agency (ISBN Agency-Sri Lanka) (Sri Lanka) *Tel:* (01) 674387; (01) 685197; (01) 698847 *Fax:* (01) 685201 *E-mail:* natlib@slt.lk *Web Site:* www.slt.lk/nlib, pg 1259

Standard Book Numbering Agency of Iceland (Iceland) *Tel:* 5255643; 5255645 *Fax:* 5255612 *E-mail:* nannab@bok.hi.is, pg 1248

Standard Book Numbering Agency, The National Library of the Philippines (Philippines) *Tel:* (02) 5241011 *Fax:* (02) 5241011 *E-mail:* isbn@nlp.gov.ph *Web Site:* www.nlp.gov.ph, pg 1256

International Standard Buchnummer GmbH (Germany) *Tel:* (069) 1306387 *Fax:* (069) 1306258 *E-mail:* lehr@bhv.de *Web Site:* www.buchandel.de, pg 1246

Standards Association of Australia (Australia) *Tel:* (02) 9634231 *Fax:* (02) 9746 8450, pg 43

Standards Association of Zimbabwe (SAZ) (Zimbabwe) *Tel:* (04) 885511; (04) 885512 *Fax:* (04) 882020 *E-mail:* sazinfo@mweb.co.zw, pg 769

Izdatelstvo Standartov (Russian Federation) *Tel:* (095) 2520348 *Fax:* (095) 2684724, pg 542

Verlag fuer Standesamtswesen GmbH (Germany) *Tel:* (069) 40 58 94 0 *Fax:* (069) 40 58 94 99 *E-mail:* info@vfst.de *Web Site:* www.vfst.de, pg 289

Standing Conference of African Library Schools (SCALS) (Senegal) *Tel:* (08) 250530 *Fax:* (08) 255219, pg 1258

Standing Conference of African University Libraries (SCAUL) (Nigeria) *Tel:* (01) 524968 *Fax:* (01) 822644, pg 1256

Standing Conference on Library Materials on Africa (SCOLMA) (United Kingdom) *Tel:* (20) 7747 6564 *Fax:* (20) 7747 6168 *E-mail:* scolma@hotmail.com, pg 1267

Stanley Editorial (Spain) *Tel:* (0943) 64 04 12 *Fax:* (0943) 64 38 63, pg 591

Stapp Verlag Wolfgang Stapp (Germany) *Tel:* (030) 2622097 *Fax:* (030) 2621990, pg 289

Star Publications (P) Ltd (India) *Tel:* (011) 3268651; (011) 3274874; (011) 3286757 *Fax:* (011) 3273335 *E-mail:* starpub@satyam.net.in *Web Site:* www.starpublic.com, pg 351

Star Publications (P) Ltd (India) *Tel:* (011) 3274874; (011) 3268651; (011) 3261696; (011) 3286757 *Fax:* (011) 3273335; (011) 6427181, pg 1290

Star Publishers' Distributors (India) *Tel:* (011) 3274874; (011) 3268651; (011) 3261696 *Fax:* (011) 3273335; (011) 6481565 *E-mail:* del.starpub@axcess.net.in, pg 1229

C A Starke Verlag (Germany) *Tel:* (06431) 96 15-0 *Fax:* (06431) 96 15 15 *E-mail:* starkeverlag@t-online.de *Web Site:* www.starkeverlag.de, pg 289

Harold Starke Publishers Ltd (United Kingdom) *Tel:* (01379) 388334; (020) 7588 5195 *Fax:* (01379) 388335 *E-mail:* red@eclat.force9.co.uk, pg 745

State Central Library (India) *Tel:* (040) 43107, pg 1474

State Central Library (Democratic People's Republic of Korea) *Tel:* (02) 34066, pg 1480

State Library (South Africa) *Tel:* (012) 218931 *Fax:* (012) 3255984 *E-mail:* hvdwalt@statelib.pwv.gov.za, pg 1498

State Archives (Mongolia) *Tel:* (01) 323100, pg 1485

State Archives of the Russian Federation (Russian Federation) *Tel:* (095) 2458184 *Fax:* (095) 2451287, pg 1495

State Archives Service: Natal Archives Depot (South Africa) *Tel:* (0331) 424712 *Fax:* (0331) 944353, pg 1498

State Book Trading Office (Mongolia) *Tel:* (01) 22312, pg 1300

The State Library of New South Wales (Australia) *Tel:* (02) 92731414 *Fax:* (02) 92731255 *E-mail:* library@sl.nsw.gov.au *Web Site:* www.sl.nsw.gov.au, pg 1450

State Library of NSW Press (Australia) *Tel:* (02) 2301500 *Fax:* (02) 92238807 *Web Site:* www.s/nsw/press, pg 43

State Library of Queensland (Australia) *Tel:* (07) 38407666 *Fax:* (07) 38462421, pg 1450

State Library of South Australia (Australia) *Tel:* (08) 82077200 *Fax:* (08) 82077247 *Web Site:* www.slsa.sa.gov.au, pg 1450

State Library of Tasmania (Australia) *Tel:* (03) 6233 7511 *Fax:* (03) 6231 0927 *E-mail:* state.library@education.tas.gov.au *Web Site:* www.statelibrary.education.tas.gov.au, pg 1450

State Library of Victoria (Australia) *Tel:* (03) 8664 7000 *E-mail:* abirkenbeil@slv.vic.gov.au *Web Site:* www.slv.vic.gov.au, pg 43

State Library of Victoria (Australia) *Tel:* (03) 8664 7000 *Fax:* (03) 96699888; (03) 96699958, pg 1451

State Library of Western Australia (Australia) *Tel:* (08) 9427 3111 *Fax:* (08) 9427 3256 *E-mail:* info@liswa.wa.gov.au *Web Site:* www.liswa.wa.gov.au, pg 1451

State Press (Mongolia), pg 469

State Printing Corp (Sri Lanka) *Tel:* (01) 503694 *Fax:* (01) 503694, pg 598

State Publishing Unit of State Print SA (Australia) *Tel:* (08) 2264677 *Fax:* (08) 2264726, pg 43

State Textbook Publishing House (Albania) *Tel:* (042) 22331 *Fax:* (042) 22331 *E-mail:* apullumbi@tbph.gov.al, pg 1

Statens Information (Danish State Information Service) (Denmark) *Tel:* 33379228 *Fax:* 33379299 *E-mail:* si@si.dk *Web Site:* www.denmark.dk; www.si.dk, pg 135

The Stationery Office (United Kingdom) *Tel:* (020) 7600 5522; (020) 7873 8787 *Fax:* (020) 7873 8200 (orders) *Web Site:* www.tso.co.uk; www.official-documents.co.uk, pg 745

The Stationery Office (United Kingdom) *Tel:* (020) 7600 5522 *Fax:* (020) 7873 8200 (orders) *E-mail:* book.order@theso.co.uk *Web Site:* www.the-stationery-office.co.uk, pg 1122

The Stationery Office (United Kingdom) *Tel:* (020) 7600 5522 *Fax:* (020) 7873 8200 (orders) *Web Site:* www.theso.co.uk, pg 1322

Statiqum Kiado es Nyomda Kft (Hungary) *Tel:* (01) 1803311 *Fax:* (01) 1688635, pg 326

Statistical Service (Ghana) *Tel:* (021) 666512 *Fax:* (021) 667069, pg 1470

Statisticke a evidencni vydavatelstvi tiskopisu (SEVT) (Czech Republic) *Tel:* (02) 855 17 11 *Fax:* (02) 855 34 22 *E-mail:* vydavatel@sevt.cz, pg 128

Statistics Finland Library (Finland) *Tel:* (09) 17342220 *Fax:* (09) 17342279 *E-mail:* kirjasto.tilastokeskus@stat.fi *Web Site:* www.stat/fi/tk/kk/index_en.html, pg 1464

Statistics New Zealand (New Zealand) *Tel:* (04) 4954600 *Fax:* (04) 4729135, pg 496

Statistics Sweden Library (Sweden) *Tel:* (08) 7835066 *Fax:* (08) 7834045 *E-mail:* library@scb.se, pg 1501

Statistisk sentralbyras bibliotek og informasjonssenter (Norway) *Tel:* 21090000; 21094642; 21094643 *Fax:* 21094973; 21094504 *E-mail:* biblioteket@ssb.no *Web Site:* www.ssb.no, pg 1489

Statni technicka knihovna (Czech Republic) *Tel:* (02) 2166 3480 *Fax:* (02) 2222 1340 *E-mail:* techlib@stk.cz *Web Site:* www.stk.cz, pg 1460

Statni Vedecka Knihovna Usti Nad Labem (Czech Republic) *Tel:* (047) 5200045; (047) 5209126; (047) 5200172; (047) 5209669 *Fax:* (047) 5200045 *E-mail:* library@svkul.cz *Web Site:* www.svkul.cz, pg 128

Statsbiblioteket (Denmark) *Tel:* 89462022 *Fax:* 89462220 *E-mail:* sb@statsbiblioteket.dk, pg 1461

Stattbuch Verlag GmbH (Germany) *Tel:* (030) 6913094; (030) 6913095 *Fax:* (030) 6943354, pg 289

Zaklad Wydawnictw Statystycznych (Poland) *Tel:* (022) 6083223; (022) 6083210 *Fax:* (022) 6083867, pg 520

Stauffenburg Verlag Brigitte Narr GmbH (Germany) *Tel:* (07071) 9730-0 *Fax:* (07071) 973030 *Web Site:* www.stauffenburg.de, pg 289

Stedelijk Van Abbemuseum (Netherlands) *Tel:* 040 2387310 *Fax:* 040 2460680 *E-mail:* vanabbe@worldaccess.nl, pg 484

Steidl Verlag (Germany) *Tel:* (0551) 49 60 60 *Fax:* (0551) 49 60 649 *E-mail:* mail@steidl.de *Web Site:* www.steidl.de, pg 289

Steiermaerkische Landesbibliothek (Austria) *Tel:* (0316) 80164600 *Fax:* (0316) 80164633 *E-mail:* post@stlbib.stmk.gv.at *Web Site:* www.stmk.gv.at/verwaltung/stlbib/start.stm, pg 1451

Steiger Verlag (Germany) *Tel:* (0821) 70040 *Fax:* (0821) 7004179, pg 289

Steimatzky Group Ltd (Israel) *Tel:* (03) 5775777 *Fax:* (03) 5794567 *E-mail:* info@steimatzky.co.il *Web Site:* www.ibooks.co.il, pg 372

Steimatzky Group Ltd (Israel) *Tel:* (03) 5775777 *Fax:* (03) 5794567 *E-mail:* info@steimatzky.co.il *Web Site:* www.ibooks.co.il; www.booksholyland.com, pg 1293

Abner Stein (United Kingdom) *Tel:* (020) 7373 0456 *Fax:* (020) 7370 6316 *E-mail:* abnerstein@compuserve.com, pg 1122

Conrad Stein Verlag (Germany) *Tel:* (04671) 93 13 14 *Fax:* (04671) 93 13 15 *E-mail:* outdoor@tng.de *Web Site:* outdoor.tng.de, pg 289

Micheline Steinberg Playwrights' Agent (United Kingdom) *Tel:* (020) 7287 4383 *Fax:* (020) 7794 4011 *E-mail:* steinbergplaywright@freeserve.co.uk, pg 1122

J Steinbrener OHG (Austria) *Tel:* (07712) 2038 *Fax:* (07712) 5161, pg 59

Franz Steiner Verlag Wiesbaden GmbH (Germany) *Tel:* (0711) 2582 0 *Fax:* (0711) 2582 390 *E-mail:* service@steiner-verlag.de *Web Site:* www.steiner-verlag.de, pg 289

Rudolf Steiner Verlag (Switzerland) *Tel:* (061) 7012240 *Fax:* (061) 7012534 *E-mail:* steiner-verlag@magnet.ch, pg 625

Editorial Rudolf Steiner (Spain) *Tel:* (091) 5531481 *Fax:* (091) 5531481 *E-mail:* rudolfsteiner@teleline.es, pg 591

Rudolf Steiner Press (United Kingdom) *Tel:* (01342) 824433 *Fax:* (01342) 826437 *E-mail:* office@rudolfsteinerpress.com *Web Site:* www.rudolfsteinerpress.com, pg 745

Steinhart-Katzir Publishers (Israel) *Tel:* (09) 8854770 *Toll Free Tel:* 800-22-5854 *Fax:* (09) 8854771 *E-mail:* webmaster@haolam.co.il *Web Site:* www.haolam.co.il, pg 372

J F Steinkopf Verlag GmbH (Germany), pg 289

Dr Dietrich Steinkopff Verlag GmbH & Co (Germany) *Tel:* (06151) 82899-0 (bestellungen) *Fax:* (06151) 82899-40 *E-mail:* info.steinkopff@springer.de *Web Site:* www.steinkopff.springer.de, pg 289

Steintor Verlag, Rudolf Juedes (Germany) *Tel:* (05535) 8851 *E-mail:* info@steintor-verlag.de, pg 290

Steinweg-Verlag, Jurgen romHoff (Germany) *Tel:* (0531) 2339197 *Fax:* (0531) 2336649, pg 290

Editorial Stella (Argentina) *Tel:* (011) 4374-0346 *Fax:* (011) 4374-8719 *Web Site:* www.editorialstella.com.ar, pg 9

Gruppo Editoriale Le Stelle SpA (Italy) *Tel:* (02) 55181460 *Fax:* (02) 5400017, pg 409

Steltman Editions (Netherlands) *Tel:* (020) 6228683 *Fax:* (020) 6207588 *E-mail:* steltman@steltman.com, pg 484

Edition Stemmle AG (Switzerland) *Tel:* (01) 7154300 *Fax:* (01) 7154360, pg 625

Verlag Stendel (Germany) *Tel:* (07151) 956603 *Fax:* (07151) 956605 *E-mail:* info@stendel-verlag.de; verlag.stendel@t-online.de *Web Site:* www.verlag-stendel.de, pg 290

Stenlake Publishing (United Kingdom) *Tel:* (01290) 551122 *Fax:* (01290) 551122 *E-mail:* info@stenlake.co.uk *Web Site:* www.stenlake.co.uk, pg 745

Stenstroems Bokfoerlag AB (Sweden) *Tel:* (08) 6637601 *Fax:* (08) 6632201, pg 606

Frank Stenvalls Forlag (Sweden) *Tel:* (040) 127703 *Fax:* (040) 127700 *E-mail:* fstenval@algonet.se, pg 606

Stenvert Systems & Service BV (Netherlands) *Tel:* (036) 5225774 *Fax:* (036) 5226986, pg 484

Stephanus Edition Verlags GmbH (Germany) *Tel:* (07556) 921150 *Fax:* (07556) 921130 *E-mail:* 0755692110@tonline.de, pg 290

Sterling Publishers Pvt Ltd (India) *Tel:* (011) 6313023; (011) 6320118; (011) 6916165; (011) 6916209 *Fax:* (011) 6331241 *Web Site:* www.sterlingpublishers.com, pg 351

Sterling Information Technologies (India) *Tel:* (011) 6313023; (011) 6320118 *Fax:* (011) 6331241, pg 351

Stern-Verlag Janssen & Co (Germany) *Tel:* (0211) 3881-0 *Fax:* (0211) 3881-280 *E-mail:* buchhaus-sternverlag@t-online.de *Web Site:* www.buchsv.de, pg 290

Stern-Verlag Janssen & Co (Germany) *Tel:* (0211) 3881-0 *Fax:* (0211) 3881280 *E-mail:* buchhaus-sternverlag@t-online.de *Web Site:* www.buchsv.de, pg 1285

Sternberg-Verlag bei Ernst Franz (Germany) *Tel:* (07123) 938922 *Fax:* (07123) 938920, pg 290

Ian Stewart Marine Publications (Australia) *Tel:* (08) 9593 1331 *Fax:* (08) 9593 1331, pg 43

Steyler Verlag (Germany) *Tel:* (02157) 120220 *Fax:* (02157) 120222 *E-mail:* steyler.net@t-online.de *Web Site:* www.steyler.de, pg 290

Stichting Arnhemse Openbare en Gelderse Wetenschappelijke Bibliotheek (Netherlands) *Tel:* (026) 3543111 *Fax:* (026) 4458616 *Web Site:* www.biblioarnhem.nl, pg 1486

Stichting Drukwerk in de Marge (Foundation of Marginal Printers) (Netherlands) *Tel:* (020) 6227748 *Fax:* (020) 6227748, pg 1137

Stichting Federatie van Organisaties van Bibliotheek-, Informatie-, Dokumentatiewezen (FOBID) (Netherlands) *Tel:* (070) 3090107 *Fax:* (070) 3090200 *E-mail:* fobid@nblc.nl, pg 1521

Stichting IVIO (Netherlands) *Tel:* (0320) 229900 *Fax:* (0320) 229999 *E-mail:* dir@ivio.nl *Web Site:* www.ivio.nl, pg 484

Stichting Kinderkrant Suriname (Suriname), pg 599

Stichting Kunstboek bvba (Belgium) *Tel:* (050) 312352 *Fax:* (050) 313173, pg 74

Stichting Ons Erfdeel VZW (Belgium) *Tel:* (056) 41 12 01 *Fax:* (056) 41 47 07 *E-mail:* info@onserfdeel.be *Web Site:* www.onserfdeel.be, pg 74

Stichting Wetenschappelijke Informatie (Suriname) *Tel:* 475232 *Fax:* 422195 *E-mail:* swin@sr.net, pg 599

Stiefel GmbH Wandkarten Verlag (Germany) *Tel:* (08456) 924100 *Fax:* (08456) 924134 *E-mail:* stiefel.gmbH@stiefel_eurocart.de *Web Site:* www.stiefel-eurocart.de, pg 290

Stiftsbibliothek (Switzerland) *Tel:* (071) 2273416 *Fax:* (071) 2273418 *E-mail:* stibi@stibi.ch *Web Site:* www.stibi.ch, pg 1501

Stiftung Buchkunst (Germany) *Tel:* (069) 1525-1800 *Fax:* (069) 1525-1805 *E-mail:* buchkunst@dbf.ddb.de *Web Site:* www.stiftung-buchkunst.de, pg 290

Stiftung Lesen (Germany) *Tel:* (06131) 288900 *Fax:* (06131) 230333, pg 1246

Editura Stiintifica (Romania) *Tel:* (01) 2223330, pg 536

Editura Stiintifica si Enciclopedica (Romania) *Tel:* (01) 175168, pg 536

Stil (France) *Tel:* (01) 48 06 28 19 *Fax:* (01) 47 00 41 89, pg 186

Stirling Press (Australia) *Tel:* (08) 327-1166 *Fax:* (08) 327-1166 *E-mail:* stirl@ozemail.com.au, pg 43

STM Publishers Services Pte Ltd (Singapore) *Tel:* 62864998 *Fax:* 62882116 *E-mail:* tonypoh@pacific.net.sg, pg 1309

Stobart Davies Ltd (United Kingdom) *Tel:* (01992) 501518 *Fax:* (01992) 501519 *E-mail:* sales@stobartdavies.com *Web Site:* www.stobart-davies.com, pg 745

Edition Gunter Stoberlein (Germany) *Tel:* (089) 8115289, pg 290

Stochastis (Greece) *Tel:* (01) 3601956 *Fax:* (01) 3610445, pg 315

Editions Stock (France) *Tel:* (01) 42848700 *Fax:* (01) 42848709, pg 186

Verlag Stocker-Schmid AG (Switzerland) *Tel:* (01) 7404444, pg 625

Stockholms Stadsbibliotek (Sweden) *Tel:* (08) 50831100 *Fax:* (08) 50831210, pg 1501

Stockholms Universitetsbibliotek (Sweden) *Tel:* (08) 162000 *Fax:* (08) 152800 *Web Site:* www.sub.su.se, pg 1501

Stoeppel Verlag-Buchvertrieb KG (Germany) *Tel:* (0881) 9224-0 *Fax:* (0881) 2553 *E-mail:* stoeppel@oberland.net *Web Site:* www.stoeppel.de, pg 290

Stofnun Arna Magnussonar a Islandi (Iceland) *Tel:* 5525540 *Fax:* 525-4035 *E-mail:* rosat@rhi.hi.is, pg 329

Stokesby House Publications (United Kingdom) *Tel:* (01493) 750645 *Fax:* (01493) 750146 *E-mail:* stokesbyhouse@btinternet.com, pg 745

Stollfuss Verlag Bonn GmbH & Co KG (Germany) *Tel:* (0228) 7 24-0 *Fax:* (0228) 7 24-92 23; (0228) 7 24-92 95 *Web Site:* www.stollfuss.de, pg 290

Stora Familjebokklubben (Sweden) *Tel:* (08) 6968660 *Fax:* (08) 6968361, pg 1232

Stora Romanklubben (Sweden) *Tel:* (08) 6968660 *Fax:* (08) 6968361, pg 1232

Edizioni di Storia e Letteratura (Italy) *Tel:* (06) 68806556 *Fax:* (06) 68806640 *E-mail:* edi.storialett@tiscalinet.it *Web Site:* www.weeb.it/edistorialett, pg 409

Istituto Storico Italiano per l'Eta Moderna e Contemporanea (Italy) *Tel:* (06) 68806922 *Fax:* (06) 6875127, pg 409

Stott Brothers Ltd (United Kingdom) *Tel:* (01422) 362184 *Fax:* (01422) 353707 *E-mail:* stottbros@aol.com, pg 1204, 1215

Stowarzyszenie Bibliotekarzy Polskich (Poland) *Tel:* (022) 8230270 *Fax:* (022) 8225133, pg 1522

Stowarzyszenie Ksiegarzy Polskich (Poland) *Tel:* (032) 2192393; (022) 256061 *Web Site:* www.bookweb.org/org/1322html, pg 1257

Stowarzyszenie Tlumaczy Polskich (Poland) *Tel:* (02) 6215678; (02) 6212772 *Fax:* (02) 6215678, pg 1127

STP Distributors Pte Ltd (Singapore) *Tel:* 2848844 *Fax:* 2610164; 2854871, pg 1309

Straelener Manuskripte Verlag (Germany) *Tel:* (02834) 6588 *Fax:* (02834) 6588 *Web Site:* www.straelener-manuskripte.de, pg 290

Strandbergs Forlag (Denmark) *Tel:* 45894760 *Fax:* 45894701 *E-mail:* strandberg.publishing@get2net.dk, pg 135

Institut Pro Stredoevropskou Kulturu A Politiku (Czech Republic) *Tel:* (02) 29 51 10 *Fax:* (02) 295 110, pg 128

Stree (India) *Tel:* (033) 4660812 *Fax:* (033) 4644614; (033) 4666677 *E-mail:* stree@cal2.vsnl.net.in, pg 351

Streiffert Forlag AB (Sweden) *Tel:* (08) 6615880 *Fax:* (08) 7830433, pg 606

A J G Strengholt's Boeken, Anno 1928, BV (Netherlands) *Tel:* (035) 6958411 *Fax:* (035) 6946173, pg 484

Strk Publishing House (The Former Yugoslav Republic of Macedonia) *Tel:* (091) 205393, pg 449

Strobel Druck & Verlag - A Strobel GmbH & Co KG (Germany) *Tel:* (02931) 89000 *Fax:* (02931) 890038 *E-mail:* strobel-verlag.enzeigen@t-online.de *Web Site:* www.ikz.de, pg 1133

Stroemberg B&T Forlag AB (Sweden) *Tel:* (08) 6201900 *Fax:* (08) 7399836 *E-mail:* bokforlaget@stromberg.se *Web Site:* www.stromberg.se, pg 606

Stroemfeld Verlag (Germany) *Tel:* (069) 955 226-0 *Fax:* (069) 955 226-22 *E-mail:* info@stroemfeld.de *Web Site:* www.stroemfeld.de, pg 290

Strom-Verlag Luzern (Switzerland) *Tel:* (041) 4408845 *Fax:* (041) 4408844 *E-mail:* pegasus.ebikon@edi.begasoft.ch, pg 625

Stromberg (Sweden) *Tel:* (08) 6201900 *Fax:* (08) 7399836, pg 606

Stroyizdat Publishing House (Russian Federation) *Tel:* (095) 2516967, pg 542

Strubes Forlag og Boghandel ApS (Denmark) *Tel:* 36721750 *Fax:* 36721752, pg 136

Strucmech Publishing (Australia) *Tel:* (03) 95989245 *Fax:* (03) 95989245, pg 43

Struik Publishers (Pty) Ltd (South Africa) *Tel:* (021) 517128; (021) 462-4360 *Fax:* (021) 462-4379, pg 559

The Struik Publishing Group (South Africa) *Tel:* (021) 4624360 *Fax:* (021) 4624379, pg 1310

STS Standard Tabellen und Software Verlag GmbH (Germany) *Tel:* (089) 89517-200 *Fax:* (089) 89517250, pg 291

Studenterboghandelen ved Odense Universitet (Denmark) *Tel:* 66158747 *Fax:* 66158766, pg 1281

Studentlitteratur AB (Sweden) *Tel:* 312000 *Fax:* 305338 *E-mail:* info@studentlitteratur.se *Web Site:* www.studentlitteratur.se, pg 606

Studieforlaget i Goteborg Stiftelsen Kursverksamhetens Forlag (Sweden) *Tel:* (031) 106580 *Fax:* (031) 135359, pg 606

Studien Verlag Gmbh (Austria) *Tel:* (0512) 395045 *Fax:* (0512) 395045-15 *E-mail:* order@studienverlag.at *Web Site:* www.studienverlag.at, pg 59

Studio Bibliografico Adelmo Polla (Italy) *Tel:* (0863) 78522 *Fax:* (0863) 78522, pg 409

Studio Dobre Nalady Spol SRO (Czech Republic) *Tel:* (02) 67910482; (02) 67910486; (02) 67910488, pg 128

Studio Editions Ltd (United Kingdom) *Tel:* (020) 7973 9690 *Fax:* (020) 7233 6057, pg 746

Studio Editoriale Programma (Italy) *Tel:* (049) 8753110 *Fax:* (049) 8755870, pg 409

Edizioni Studio Tesi SRL (Italy) *Tel:* (06) 3201656 *Fax:* (06) 3223540, pg 409

Studio 31 (United States) *Tel:* 772-781-7195 *Fax:* 772-781-6044 *E-mail:* studio31@mindspring.com *Web Site:* www.studio31.com, pg 1167

Libreria Studium SA (Peru) *Tel:* (01) 326278; (01) 275960; (01) 325528 *Fax:* (01) 4325354, pg 511

Libreria Studium SA (Peru) *Tel:* (01) 275960; (01) 326278; (01) 325528 *Fax:* (01) 4325354, pg 1305

Edizioni Studium SpA (Italy) *Tel:* (06) 6865846 *Fax:* (06) 6875456 *E-mail:* edizionistudium@libero.it, pg 409

Sturtz Verlag GmbH (Germany) *Tel:* (0931) 385235 *Fax:* (0931) 385305 *E-mail:* info@verlagshaus.com *Web Site:* www.verlagshaus.com, pg 291

Verlag Styria (Austria) *Tel:* (0316) 8063-7002 *Fax:* (0316) 8063-7034 *E-mail:* verlagstyria@styria.com *Web Site:* www.verlagstyria.com, pg 59

Buchhandlung Styria (Austria) *Tel:* (0316) 80637041 *Fax:* (0316) 80637004, pg 1275

Su Hoc (Historical) Publishing House (Viet Nam), pg 763

Su That (Truth) Publishing House (Viet Nam) *Tel:* (04) 252008, pg 763

Suaver, Javier Presa Suarez (Spain) *Tel:* (086) 439507, pg 591

Sub-Saharan Publishers (Ghana) *Tel:* (021) 233371 *Fax:* (021) 233371 *E-mail:* sub-saharan@ighmail.com, pg 308

Subervie Editions (France) *Tel:* (05) 65 67 20 17 *Fax:* (05) 65 67 36 38 *E-mail:* contact@subervie.com, pg 186

Success Publications Pte Ltd (Singapore) *Tel:* 4431003; 4430512 *Fax:* 4453156, pg 548

SUD (France) *Tel:* (0491) 336068 *Fax:* (0491) 336068, pg 186

Sud Editions (Tunisia) *Tel:* (01) 787626 *Fax:* (01) 792905, pg 638

Editions Sud Ouest (France) *Tel:* (0556) 446821 *Fax:* (0556) 444083 *E-mail:* editions-gso@groupesudouest.com *Web Site:* www.gso.enfrance.com, pg 186

Editorial Sudamericana SA (Argentina) *Tel:* (011) 4300-5400 *Fax:* (011) 4362-7364 *E-mail:* admventas@edsudamericana.com.ar *Web Site:* www.edsudamericana.com.ar, pg 9

The Sudan Bookshop Ltd (Sudan) *Tel:* (011) 74123; (011) 76781, pg 1312

Sudan Literature Centre (Kenya) *Tel:* (02) 564141; (02) 569685; (02) 569688 *Fax:* (02) 564141 *E-mail:* across@maf.or.ke, pg 433

Sudanese Publishers' Association (Sudan) *Tel:* (0249) 11-77820 *Fax:* (0249) 11-77820, pg 1259

Izdatelstvo Sudostroenie (Russian Federation) *Tel:* (0812) 3124479 *Fax:* (0812) 3120821, pg 542

Sueddeutsche Verlagsgesellschaft mbH (Germany) *Tel:* (089) 2183-0 *Fax:* (089) 2183-8315 *E-mail:* verlag@sueddeutsche.de *Web Site:* www.sueddeutsche.de, pg 291

Suedverlag GmbH (Germany) *Tel:* (07531) 9053-0 *Fax:* (07531) 9053-98 *E-mail:* willkommen@uvk.de *Web Site:* www.suedverlag.de, pg 291

Suedwest Verlag GmbH & Co KG (Germany) *Tel:* (089) 5148-0 *Fax:* (089) 5148-2229 *Web Site:* www.suedwest-verlag.de, pg 291

Suedwind - Buchwelt GmbH (Austria) *Tel:* (01) 405 44 34 *E-mail:* buchwelt@suedwind.at *Web Site:* www.suedwind.at, pg 59

Sueleymaniye Kuetuephanesi (Turkey) *Tel:* (0212) 5206460, pg 1504

Sugarco Edizioni SRL (Italy) *Tel:* (0331) 985511 *Fax:* (0331) 985385, pg 409

Suhagsa (Republic of Korea) *Tel:* (02) 584-4642 *Fax:* (02) 521-1458, pg 440

Suhrkamp Verlag (Germany) *Tel:* (069) 75601-0 *Fax:* (069) 75601-522; (069) 75601-314 *Web Site:* www.suhrkamp.de, pg 291

Suin Buch-Verlag (Germany) *Tel:* (06255) 2657 *Fax:* (06255) 2657, pg 291

Suksapan Panit (Business Organization of Teachers Council of Thailand) (Thailand) *Tel:* (02) 811845, pg 635

Suksit Siam Co Ltd (Thailand) *Tel:* (02) 511630, pg 635

Suksit Siam Co Ltd (Thailand) *Fax:* (02) 2511630, pg 1314

Livraria Sulina Editora (Brazil) *Tel:* (051) 228 1966 *Fax:* (051) 228 1966 *E-mail:* sulina@sulina.com.bm, pg 92

Sulina Livraria Editora (Brazil) *Tel:* (0512) 254765; (0512) 250287 *Fax:* (0512) 280734, pg 1278

Sultan Chand & Sons Pvt Ltd (India) *Tel:* 3272532; 3251727 *Fax:* (11) 3254295 *E-mail:* scs@del2.vsnl.in, pg 351

Sultan's Library (Cyprus), pg 1460

Suman Prakashan Pvt Ltd (India) *Tel:* (011) 5710759; (011) 5721750 *Fax:* (011) 5754739, pg 351

Sumatera Utara University Press (Indonesia) *Tel:* (061) 23210 (ext 261), pg 357

Sumathi Book Printing (Pvt) Ltd (Sri Lanka) *Tel:* (01) 330673; (01) 330674; (01) 435225 *Fax:* (01) 449593, pg 1139, 1159

Sumathi Book Printing (Pvt) Ltd (Sri Lanka) *Tel:* (01) 330673; (01) 330674; (01) 435225 *Fax:* (01) 449593 *E-mail:* publish@slt.lk, pg 1201

Summer Institute of Linguistics, Australian Aborigines Branch (Australia) *Tel:* (08) 8922 5700 *Fax:* (08) 8922 5717 *E-mail:* sildarwin@taunet.net.au, pg 43

Summer Institute of Linguistics (Papua New Guinea) *Tel:* (675) 7373544 *Fax:* (675) 7374111, pg 510

Summerson Eastern Publishers Ltd (Hong Kong) *Tel:* 5408123 *Fax:* 5597869, pg 322

Summus Editorial Ltda (Brazil) *Tel:* (011) 38723322 *Fax:* (011) 38727476 *E-mail:* summus@summus.com.br *Web Site:* www.summus.com.br, pg 92

Sun Fung Offset Binding Co Ltd (Hong Kong) *Tel:* 25618109; 25618100 *Fax:* 28110638 *E-mail:* sunfung@sunfung.com.hk *Web Site:* sunfung.com.hk, pg 1197

Sun Mui Press (Hong Kong) *Tel:* 2694 8525 *Fax:* 2697 7976 *E-mail:* auly@chevalier.net, pg 322

Uitgeverij SUN (Netherlands) *Tel:* (024) 3221700 *Fax:* (024) 3235439, pg 484

Sun Ya Publications (HK) Ltd (Hong Kong) *Tel:* (02) 5620161 *Fax:* (02) 5659951, pg 322

Sun Yat-Sen Library (Hong Kong) *Tel:* 23365291, pg 1471

Sunera Publishers (Sri Lanka) *Tel:* 511527, pg 598

Sunflower Books (United Kingdom) *Tel:* (020) 7589 1862 *Fax:* (020) 7589 1862 *E-mail:* mail@sunflowerbooks.co.uk *Web Site:* www.sunflowerbooks.co.uk; www.wwwalking.com, pg 746

Sunny Printing (Hong Kong) Co Ltd (Hong Kong) *Tel:* 25578663 *Fax:* 28898070 *E-mail:* sunnyint@hkstar.com, pg 1197

Sunshine Books International Ltd (New Zealand) *Tel:* (09) 5203049 *Fax:* (09) 5224882 *E-mail:* orders@my-dictionary.com *Web Site:* my-dictionary.com, pg 496

Sunshine Multi Media Ltd, Wendy Pye Ltd (New Zealand) *Tel:* (649) 525-3575 *Fax:* (649) 525-4205 *E-mail:* admin@sunshine.co.nz, pg 496

Sunshine Press Ltd (Hong Kong) *Tel:* 25532386 *Fax:* 28732930 *E-mail:* spl@sunshinepress.com.hk, pg 1136, 1157, 1197

Suomalainen Kirjakauppa Oy (Finland) *Tel:* (00) 852751 *Fax:* (00) 8527888, pg 1282

Suomalainen Tiedeakatemia (Finland) *Tel:* (09) 636800 *Fax:* (09) 660117, pg 1362

Suomalaisen Kirjallisuuden Seura (Finland) *Tel:* (09) 131231 *Fax:* (09) 13123220 *E-mail:* firstname.familyname@finlit.fi, pg 144

Suomalaisen Kirjailuuden Seura (Finland) *Tel:* (09) 131231 *Fax:* (09) 13123220 *E-mail:* sks-kirjasto@helsinki.fi, pg 1362

Suomen Kirjailijaliitto (Finland) *Tel:* (09) 445392; (09) 449752 *Fax:* (09) 492278 *E-mail:* suomen.kirjailijaliitto@cultnet.fi, pg 1242

Suomen Kirjastoseura (Finland) *Tel:* (09) 622 1399; (09) 694 1854 (education); (09) 694 1878 (information); (09) 694 1856 (Kirjastolehi); (09) 694 1858 (Secretary General) *Fax:* (09) 622 1466 *E-mail:* fla@fla.fi, pg 1515

Suomen Kustannusyhdistys (Finland) *Tel:* (09) 22877250 *Fax:* (09) 6121226 *Web Site:* www.skyry.net, pg 1242

Suomen Matkailuliitto ry (The Finish Travel Association) (Finland) *Tel:* (09) 6226280 *Fax:* (09) 654358 *E-mail:* matkailuliitto@matkailuliitto.org *Web Site:* www.tunturioppaat.org, pg 144

Suomen pipliaseura RY (Finland) *Tel:* (09) 625925 *Fax:* (09) 625719 *E-mail:* info@bible.fi, pg 144

Suomen Tieteellinen Kirjastoseura (Finland) *Tel:* (09) 3653148 *Fax:* (09) 3652907 *E-mail:* meri.kuula@arcada.fi, pg 1515

Super Book House (India) *Tel:* (022) 2830446; (022) 2830560 *Fax:* (022) 2834452, pg 1290

Supportive Learning Publications (United Kingdom) *Tel:* (01691) 774778 *Fax:* (01691) 774849 *E-mail:* sales@slpuk.demon.co.uk *Web Site:* www.slpuk.demon.co.uk, pg 746

Supraphon (Czech Republic) *Tel:* (02) 24 94 87 22 *Fax:* (02) 24 94 87 25 *E-mail:* supraphon@bonton.cz *Web Site:* www.supraphon.cz, pg 128

Sur Casa de Estudios del Socialismo (Peru) *Tel:* (01) 423-5431 *Fax:* (01) 423-5431 *E-mail:* casasur@csur.org.pe, pg 511

Suriwong Book Centre, Ltd (Thailand) *Tel:* (053) 281052 *Fax:* (053) 271902 *E-mail:* suriwong@loxinfo.co.th, pg 1314

Suriyaban Bookstore (Thailand) *Tel:* (02) 2347991; (02) 2347992, pg 1314

Suriyaban Publishers (Thailand) *Tel:* (02) 2347991; (02) 2347992, pg 635

Surjeet Publications (India) *Tel:* (011) 2913081; (011) 2923105, pg 351

Ediciones Suromex SA (Mexico) *Tel:* 2770744; 2770946 *Fax:* 2710470 *E-mail:* suromex@mail.internet.com.mx *Web Site:* www.intralector.com/suromex/, pg 467

Surugadai-Shuppan Sha (Japan) *Tel:* (03) 32911676 *Fax:* (03) 32911675, pg 427

Susaeta Ediciones (Colombia) *Tel:* (01) 288 44 22 *Fax:* (01) 288 14 72 *E-mail:* mdsusaet@medellin.impsat.net.co, pg 113

Ediciones Susaeta SA (Spain) *Tel:* (091) 3009110 *Fax:* (091) 3009118 *E-mail:* susaeta@correo.net, pg 592

Sut Phaisan (Thailand) *Tel:* (02) 4682066; (02) 4675066, pg 636

Sutton Publishing Ltd (United Kingdom) *Tel:* (01453) 731114 *Fax:* (01453) 731117 *E-mail:* sales@sutton-publishing.co.uk; editorial@sutton-publishing.co.uk; publishing@sutton-publishing.co.uk *Web Site:* www.suttonpublishing.co.uk, pg 746

Suuri Suomalainen Kirjakerho Oy (Finland) *Tel:* (09) 147 711 *Fax:* (09) 1496 221 *E-mail:* sskk.palaute@kuvalehdet.fi *Web Site:* www.sskk.fi, pg 1228

Suva City Library (Fiji) *Tel:* 313433 *Fax:* 302158, pg 1463

SV-Kauppiaskanava Oy (Finland) *Fax:* (09) 175 426 *E-mail:* kaija.tynkkynen@kesko.fi, pg 144

Bokklubben Svalan (Sweden) *Tel:* (08) 6968660 *Fax:* (08) 6986361, pg 1232

Svato Zapletal (Germany) *Tel:* (040) 4390004; (040) 4300484 *Fax:* (040) 4390004, pg 291

Svaz Antikvaru CR (Czech Republic) *Tel:* (02) 24229205 *Fax:* (02) 262186 *E-mail:* info@meissner.cz *Web Site:* www.meissner.cz, pg 1241

Svaz ceskych knihkupcu a nakladatelu (SCKN) (Czech Republic) *Tel:* (02) 2423 90030150; (02) 90053015; (02) 22513198 *Fax:* (02) 22513198; (02) 90052991 *E-mail:* sckn@mbox.vol.cz *Web Site:* www.sckn.cz, pg 1241

Svaz knihovniku informacnich pracovniku Ceske republiky (SKIP) (Czech Republic) *Tel:* (02) 21663338 *Fax:* (02) 21663175 *Web Site:* www.nkp.cz, pg 1514

Svensk-Norsk Bogimport A/S (Denmark) *Tel:* 33142666 *Fax:* 33143588 *E-mail:* snb@bog.dk *Web Site:* www.snbog.dk, pg 1281

Svenska Forlaggareforeningen (Sweden) *Tel:* (08) 7361940 *Fax:* (08) 7361944 *E-mail:* svf@forlagskansli.se, pg 1259

Svenska alliansmissionens (SAM) foerlage (Sweden) *Tel:* (036) 719870 *Fax:* (036) 719820, pg 606

Svenska Arbetsgivareforeningens forlag (Sweden) *Tel:* (08) 7626000 *Fax:* (08) 7626490, pg 606

Svenska Arkivsamfundet (Sweden) *Tel:* (08) 405100 *Fax:* (08) 6579564 *Web Site:* www.arkivsamfundet.org, pg 1523

Svenska Barnboksinstitutet (Sweden) *Tel:* (08) 54542050 *Fax:* (08) 54542054 *E-mail:* info@sbi.kb.se; biblioteket@sbi.kb.se *Web Site:* www.sbi.kb.se, pg 1501

Svenska Foerlaget liv & ledarskap ab (Sweden) *Tel:* (08) 4122700 *Fax:* (08) 4114121 *E-mail:* kundservice@svenskaforlaget.com, pg 607

Svenska Institutet (Sweden) *Tel:* (08) 789-20-00 *Fax:* (08) 20-72-48 *E-mail:* si@si.se, pg 607

Svenska Litteratursaellskapet i Finland (Finland) *Tel:* (09) 618777 *Fax:* (09) 6187 7377 *E-mail:* sls@mail.sls.fi *Web Site:* www.sls.fi, pg 1362

Svenska Oesterbottens Litteraturfoerening (Finland) *Tel:* (06) 3450286, pg 144

Svenska Oesterbottens Litteraturfoerening (Finland) *Tel:* (06) 3128426 *Fax:* (06) 3242210, pg 1362

Svepomoc (Czech Republic) *Tel:* (02) 24223446; (02) 24223450 *Fax:* (02) 24223439, pg 128

Sveriges Allmaenna Biblioteksfoerening (Sweden) *Tel:* (08) 54513230; (08) 54513230 (SAB office) *Fax:* (08) 54513231 *Web Site:* www.sab.se/, pg 1523

Sveriges Lantbruksuniversitets Bibliotek (Sweden) *Tel:* (018) 671000 *Fax:* (018) 672853 *E-mail:* ultunabiblioteket@bibul.slu.se, pg 1501

Svetovi (Yugoslavia) *Tel:* (021) 28032; (021) 28036 *Fax:* (021) 28036; (021) 28032 *E-mail:* aum.mar@eunet.yu, pg 766

Svetra Publishing House (Bulgaria) *Tel:* (02) 62 27 39; (02) 983 45 41 *Fax:* (02) 234966 *E-mail:* svetlev@cybernet.bg, pg 98

Sveucilisna tiskara doo (Croatia) *Tel:* (01) 4564430; (01) 4564428 *Fax:* (01) 4564427, pg 120

Sviat Publishers (Bulgaria) *Tel:* (02) 892202 *Fax:* (02) 800704; (02) 822851, pg 98

Sviesa Publishers (Lithuania) *Tel:* (037) 341834 *Fax:* (037) 342032 *E-mail:* sviesa@balt.net *Web Site:* www.sviesa.lt, pg 446

Svietimo ir mokslo ministerijos Leidybos centras (Lithuania) *Tel:* (02) 617480; (02) 611060; (02) 616081 *Fax:* (02) 617480 *E-mail:* office@smmlc.elnet.lt, pg 446

Svjetlost (Bosnia and Herzegovina) *Tel:* (071) 200-840, pg 77

Svjetlost (Bosnia and Herzegovina) *Tel:* (071) 443419 *Fax:* (071) 471851, pg 1277

Svoboda Servis GmbH (Czech Republic) *Tel:* (02) 449 132 58 *Fax:* (02) 449 132 58 *E-mail:* svobserv@volny.cz, pg 128

Svojtka & Co (Czech Republic) *Tel:* (02) 71 73 41 43; (02) 71 73 66 10 *Fax:* (02) 72 73 14 13 *E-mail:* svojtka@mbox.vol.cz *Web Site:* www.svojtka.cz, pg 128

Swakopmunder Buchhandlung (Namibia) *Tel:* (0641) 402613; (0641) 2613 *Fax:* (0641) 404183, pg 1300

Swarna Hansa Foundation (Sri Lanka) *Tel:* (01) 712566 *Fax:* (01) 733649, pg 598

Swaziland National Library Service (Swaziland) *Tel:* 42633 *Fax:* 43863, pg 1500

Swaziland Library Association (Swaziland) *Tel:* 43101 *Fax:* 42641, pg 1523

Swaziland College of Technology Library (Swaziland) *Tel:* 42681 *Fax:* 44521, pg 1500

Swedenborg - Verlag (Switzerland) *Tel:* (01) 2515945, pg 625

Swedish-English Literary Translators' Association (SELTA) (United Kingdom) *Tel:* (020) 8641 8176 *Fax:* (020) 8641 8176 *Web Site:* www.swedishbookreview.com, pg 1130

Sweet & Maxwell Ltd (United Kingdom) *Tel:* (020) 7393 7000; (020) 7449 1104 *Fax:* (020) 7449 1144 *E-mail:* info@routledge.co.uk, pg 746

Swets & Zeitlinger Publishers *Tel:* (0252) 435111 *Fax:* (0252) 435447 *E-mail:* orders@swets.nl *Web Site:* www.swets.nl, pg 485

Swindon Book Co Ltd (Hong Kong) *Tel:* 2366 8555 *Fax:* 2739 4975 *E-mail:* swindon@netvigator.com *Web Site:* www.swindonbooks.com, pg 1287

SWP, BV Uitgeverij (Netherlands) *Tel:* (020) 3307200 *Fax:* (020) 3308040 *E-mail:* swp@wxs.nl *Web Site:* www.swpbook.com, pg 485

Syarikat Cultural Supplies Sdn Bhd (Malaysia) *Tel:* (03) 7046628; (03) 7554103; (03) 7915728 *Fax:* (03) 7046629 *E-mail:* malian@po.jaring.my, pg 454

Sybex (France) *Tel:* (01) 55 58 40 00 *Fax:* (01) 49 65 04 10 *E-mail:* contact@sybex.fr *Web Site:* www.sybex.fr, pg 186

Sybex BV (Netherlands) *Tel:* (035) 6027625 *Fax:* (035) 6026556, pg 485

Sybex Verlag GmbH (Germany) *Tel:* (0211) 9739-0 *Fax:* (0211) 9739-199 *E-mail:* verkauf@sybex.de *Web Site:* www.sybex.de, pg 291

Syddansk Universitetsforlag (Denmark) *Tel:* 66 15 79 99 *Fax:* 66 15 81 26 *E-mail:* press@forlag.sdu.dk *Web Site:* www.universitypress.dk, pg 136

Sydney Jary Ltd (United Kingdom) *Tel:* (0117) 974-1640 *Fax:* (0117) 973-7116 *E-mail:* admin@s-jary.co.uk, pg 746

Sydney Studies In English (Australia) *Tel:* (02) 9351 2432 *Fax:* (02) 9351 2434 *Web Site:* www.arts.usyd.edu.au/dep, pg 43

J G Sydys Buchhandlung Ludwig Schubert GesmbH (Austria) *Tel:* (02742) 53189; (02742) 53191 *Fax:* (02742) 5318985 *Web Site:* members.aon.at/schubert, pg 1275

Sygma Publishing (Botswana) *Tel:* 351371 *Fax:* 372531 *E-mail:* sygma@info.bw, pg 77

Syllogos Ekdoton Bibliopolon Athinon (Greece) *Tel:* (01) 3830029; (01) 3303268 *Fax:* (01) 3823222 *E-mail:* seva@otenet.ge, pg 1247

Syndicat des Libraires Universitaires et Techniques (France) *Tel:* (467) 413970 *Fax:* (467) 525905, pg 1244

Syndicat National de la Librairie Ancienne et Moderne (SLAM) (France) *Tel:* (01) 43294638; (01) 43540128 *Fax:* (01) 43254163 *E-mail:* slam@worldnet.fr *Web Site:* www.slam-livre.fr, pg 1244

Syndicat National de l'Edition (France) *Tel:* (01) 4414050 *Fax:* (01) 441 4077, pg 1244

Syndicat National des Auteurs et Compositeurs (France) *Tel:* (01) 42805282 *E-mail:* snac@calva.net *Web Site:* www.snac.fr, pg 1363

Synthesis Verlag (Germany) *Tel:* (0201) 51 01 88 *Fax:* (0201) 51 10 49 *E-mail:* synthesis@synthesis-verlag.com *Web Site:* www.synthesis-verlag.com, pg 291

Systematics Studies Ltd (Trinidad & Tobago) *Tel:* 6453475 *Fax:* 6625654 *E-mail:* dooks@eclacps.undp.org, pg 637

SystemConsult (Czech Republic) *Tel:* (040) 650 1585; (040) 466 501 585 *Fax:* (040) 5165 85; (040) 650 1585 *E-mail:* system.consult@worldonline.cz *Web Site:* www.systemconsult.cz, pg 128

Systex Pty Ltd (Australia) *Tel:* (02) 9944 2668, pg 43

Systhema Verlag GmbH (Germany) *Tel:* (089) 290 88 175 *Fax:* (089) 290 88 160 *E-mail:* info@usm.de *Web Site:* www.systhema.de; www.navigo.de, pg 291

Systime (Denmark) *Tel:* 70 12 11 00 *Fax:* 70 12 11 05 *E-mail:* systime@systime.dk *Web Site:* www.systime.dk, pg 136

Szabad Ter Kiado (Hungary) *Tel:* (01) 1550175; (01) 3755922 *Fax:* (01) 1560998; (01) 3560998, pg 326

Szabvanykiado (Hungary) *Tel:* (01) 1183011; (01) 1183442 *Fax:* (01) 1185125, pg 326

Szarvas Andras Cartographic Agency (Hungary) *Tel:* (01) 363 0672; (01) 221 68 30 *Fax:* (01) 363 0672; (01) 221 68 30 *E-mail:* szarvas.andras@mail.datanet.hu, pg 326

Szazadveg (Hungary) *Tel:* (01) 166-9902; (01) 166-5309; (01) 2010688 *Fax:* (01) 2100384 *E-mail:* stumpf@bsp.mtapti.hu, pg 326

Uniwersytet Szczecinski (Poland) *Tel:* (091) 845338 *Fax:* (09) 845338 *E-mail:* livre.bibl@univ.szczecin.pl, pg 1492

Szepirodalmi Koenyvkiado Kiado (Hungary) *Tel:* (01) 1221285, pg 327

Oficyna Wydawnicza Szkoly Glownej Handlowej w Warszawie Oficyna Wydawnicza SGH (Poland) *Tel:* (022) 494925; (022) 491251 (ext 486) *Fax:* (022) 495312 *E-mail:* wydawn@sgh.waw.pl *Web Site:* www.akson.sgh.waw.pl, pg 520

Magyar Eszperanto Szoevetseg (Hungary) *Tel:* (01) 1564093; (01) 1563659, pg 327

T & E Publishers (Uganda) *Tel:* (041) 542207 *Fax:* (041) 542207, pg 642

Ta Kung Pao (HK) Ltd (Hong Kong) *Tel:* 28363166, pg 322

Edicoes Tabajara (Brazil) *Tel:* (0512) 241073; (0512) 247724, pg 92

Tabansi Press Ltd (Nigeria) *Tel:* (046) 211661, pg 501

Ediciones Tabapress, SA (Spain) *Tel:* (01) 5320876 *Fax:* (01) 5325890 *E-mail:* ediciones.tabapress@tsai.es, pg 592

Tabb House (United Kingdom) *Tel:* (01841) 532316 *Fax:* (01841) 532316 *E-mail:* tabbhouse@connexions.co.uk, pg 746

Les Editions de la Table Ronde (France) *Tel:* (01) 40467070 *Fax:* (01) 40467101, pg 187

Tabletop Press (Australia) *Tel:* (06) 2420995 *Fax:* (06) 2420674, pg 44

Tacor International (France) *Tel:* (01) 39182939 *Fax:* (01) 30824390, pg 187

Tael Ltd (Estonia) *Tel:* (02) 6314162 *Fax:* (02) 6314162 *E-mail:* tael@teleport.ee, pg 140

Tafelberg Publishers Ltd (South Africa) *Tel:* (021) 4241320 *Fax:* (021) 4241320 *E-mail:* tafelberg@tafelberg.com *Web Site:* www.tafelberg.com, pg 560

Tages-Anzeiger (Switzerland) *Tel:* (01) 2484111 *E-mail:* tamedia@tdmedia.ch, pg 625

Tai Yip Co (Hong Kong) *Tel:* (02) 5250496 *Fax:* (02) 8453296, pg 322

Taimeido Publishing Co Ltd (Japan) *Tel:* (03) 32912374 *Fax:* (03) 32912376 *E-mail:* taimell@ibm.net, pg 427

Taipei Yung Chang Printing (Taiwan, Province of China) *Tel:* (02) 5932392 *Fax:* (02) 5932763, pg 1201

Taiwan Branch Library, National Central Library (Taiwan, Province of China) *Tel:* (02) 7718528, pg 1502

Taj Co Ltd (Pakistan) *Tel:* (021) 294221; (021) 295459; (021) 295619, pg 509

Tajak Korok Muzeumok Egyesuelet (Hungary) *Tel:* (01) 2101330 *Fax:* (01) 2101329, pg 327

Takahashi Shoten Co Ltd (Japan) *Tel:* (03) 39434525 *Fax:* (03) 39434288, pg 427

Imprimerie Takariva (Madagascar) *Tel:* 02 23856, pg 450

Take That Ltd (United Kingdom) *Tel:* (01423) 507545 *Fax:* (01423) 526035 *E-mail:* sales@takethat.co.uk *Web Site:* www.takethat.co.uk, pg 746

Talento (Portugal) *Tel:* (021) 7154281 *Fax:* (021) 7154257, pg 529

Talento Publicacoes Editora e Grafica Ltda (Brazil) *Tel:* (011) 8835400 *Fax:* (011) 2823752 *E-mail:* talento@talento.com.br *Web Site:* www.talento.com.br, pg 92

Talentum Konyves es Kereskedo Kft (Hungary) *Tel:* (01) 2057077; (01) 2057138, pg 1287

Editions Tallandier (France) *Tel:* (01) 44 10 10 10 *Fax:* (01) 44 10 10 32, pg 187

Editora Taller (Dominican Republic) *Tel:* (809) 531-7975 *Fax:* (809) 531-7979 *E-mail:* editora.taller@codetel.net.do, pg 137

Talmudic Encyclopedia Publications (Israel) *Tel:* (02) 6423242 *Fax:* (02) 6423919, pg 372

Taltos Kiadasszervezesi Ltd (Hungary) *Tel:* (01) 1213515 *Fax:* (01) 1420676, pg 327

Tamagawa University Press (Japan) *Tel:* (0427) 398935 *Fax:* (0427) 398940 *E-mail:* tup@adm.tamagawa.ac.jp, pg 427

Tamarind Publications (Australia) *Tel:* (02) 467934 *Fax:* (02) 659515 *E-mail:* sigi@hunterlink.net.au, pg 44

Tammi Publishers (Finland) *Tel:* (09) 6937 621 *Fax:* (09) 6937 6266 *E-mail:* firstname.familyname@tammi.net *Web Site:* tammi.net, pg 144

Tampereen Yliopiston Kirjasto (Finland) *Tel:* (03) 2156111 *Fax:* (03) 2157493 *Web Site:* www.uta.fi/~kimiii, pg 1464

Tampereen Kirjakauppa Oy (Finland) *Tel:* (03) 2128380 *Fax:* (03) 2122136 *E-mail:* trekirja@vip.fi *Web Site:* www.tampereenkirjakauppa.fi, pg 1282

Tana Press Ltd & Flora Nwapa Books Ltd (Nigeria) *Tel:* (042) 338857, pg 501

Tandem Press (New Zealand) *Tel:* (09) 480-1452 *Fax:* (09) 480-1455 *E-mail:* customers@tandempress.co.nz *Web Site:* www.tandempress.co.nz, pg 496

Tangens Systemverlag GmbH (Germany) *Tel:* (040) 39901307 *Fax:* (040) 395118, pg 291

Tango Books (United Kingdom) *Tel:* (020) 87461171 *Fax:* (020) 87461170 *E-mail:* sales@tangobooks.co.uk, pg 746

Tanja Howarth Literary Agency (United Kingdom) *Tel:* (020) 7240 5553; (020) 7836 4142 *Fax:* (020) 7379 0969, pg 1122

Tankosha Publishing Co Ltd (Japan) *Tel:* (075) 432 5151 *Fax:* (075) 432 0275 *E-mail:* tankosha@magical.egg.or.jp *Web Site:* tankosha.topica.ne.jp/, pg 427

Tantalum-Niobium International Study Center (Belgium) *Tel:* (02) 6495158 *Fax:* (02) 6496447 *E-mail:* info@tanb.org *Web Site:* www.tanb.org, pg 1238

Tanum Karl Johan A/S (Norway) *Tel:* 22411100 *Fax:* 22333275, pg 1304

Tanzania Library Service (United Republic of Tanzania) *Tel:* (051) 2150048; (051) 150923, pg 1503

Tanzania Library Association (United Republic of Tanzania) *Tel:* (051) 4026121, pg 1524

Tanzania Library Service Director (United Republic of Tanzania) *Tel:* (051) 2150048; (051) 2150049 *E-mail:* tlsb@AfricaOnline.co.tz, pg 1263

Tanzania Library Services Board (United Republic of Tanzania) *Tel:* (051) 110572; (051) 110573 *E-mail:* tlsb@africaonline.co.tz, pg 634

Tanzania Publishing House (United Republic of Tanzania) *Tel:* (051) 32164, pg 634

Taoasis Verlag, Birgit Meyer (Germany) *Tel:* (05261) 2321 *Fax:* (05261) 9383-21 *E-mail:* info@taoasis.de *Web Site:* www.taoasis.de, pg 292

Tapir (Norway) *Tel:* 73593226; 73598422 *Fax:* 73598494; 73598494, pg 1304

Tappeiner (Italy) *Tel:* (0473) 563666 *Fax:* (0473) 563689 *E-mail:* tappeiner@pass.dnet.it, pg 409

Taprobane Ltd (United Kingdom) *Tel:* (020) 8998-3024, pg 746

DB Taraporevala Sons & Co Pvt Ltd (India) *Tel:* (022) 2041433; (022) 2041434, pg 351

Editions Tardy SA (France) *Tel:* (01) 45443834 *Fax:* (01) 42841091, pg 187

Tarea Asociacion de Publicaciones Educativas (Peru) *Tel:* (01) 4242827 *Fax:* (01) 4240997 *E-mail:* postmaster@tarea.org.pe, pg 511

Target Publishers (Edms) Bpk (South Africa) *Tel:* (018) 4627556 *Fax:* (018) 4627557, pg 560

Cartes Taride (France) *Tel:* (01) 433 640 40 *Fax:* (01) 470 727 16, pg 187

Taride Editions (France) *Tel:* (01) 48 78 40 74 *Fax:* (01) 48 78 40 77, pg 187

Tarka Publishing (Australia) *Tel:* (02) 9955 2074 *Fax:* (02) 9925 0664 *E-mail:* howbix@netspace.net.au, pg 44

Tarquin Publications (United Kingdom) *Tel:* (01379) 384 218 *Fax:* (01379) 384 289 *E-mail:* enquiries@tarquin-books.demon.co.uk *Web Site:* www.tarquin-books.demon.co.uk, pg 746

Ediciones Tarraco (Spain) *Tel:* (077) 233813 *Fax:* (077) 233851, pg 592

Tarragon Press (United Kingdom) *Tel:* (01988) 850368 *Fax:* (01988) 850304, pg 746

La Tartaruga Edizioni SAS (Italy) *Tel:* (02) 6555036 *Fax:* (02) 653007, pg 409

Tartu University Library (Estonia) *Tel:* (07) 375 700 (Director); (07) 375 703 (Secretary) *Fax:* (07) 375 701 *E-mail:* library@utlib.ee *Web Site:* www.utlib.ee, pg 1462

TASCHEN GmbH (Germany) *Tel:* (0221) 201 80 0 *Fax:* (0221) 25 49 19 *E-mail:* contact@taschen.com *Web Site:* www.taschen.com, pg 292

Taschen UK Ltd (United Kingdom) *Tel:* (020) 7437 4350 *Fax:* (020) 7437 4360 *E-mail:* contact@tashen.com *Web Site:* www.taschen.com, pg 747

Tassorello, SA (Peru) *Tel:* (01) 4602040; (01) 4600255 *Fax:* (01) 4615714, pg 511

Tassotti Editore (Italy) *Tel:* (0424) 566105 *Fax:* (0424) 566205, pg 409

Est-Samuel Tastet Verlag (Romania) *Tel:* (01) 6386250 *Fax:* (01) 3122012, pg 536

Tate Publishing Ltd (United Kingdom) *Tel:* (020) 7887 8869; (020) 7887 8870; (020) 7887 8871 *Fax:* (020) 7887 8878 *E-mail:* tgpl@tate.org.uk *Web Site:* www.tate.org.uk, pg 747

Tatran Publishing House (Slovakia) *Tel:* (07) 5335849 *Fax:* (07) 5335777, pg 1231

Edition Tau u Tau Type Druck Verlags-und Handels GmbH (Austria) *Tel:* (02625) 32000 *Fax:* (02625) 320003, pg 59

I B Tauris & Co Ltd (United Kingdom) *Tel:* (020) 7243 1225 *Fax:* (020) 7243 1226 *E-mail:* mail@ibtauris.com *Web Site:* www.ibtauris.com, pg 747

Taurus (South Africa) *Tel:* 7860018, pg 560

Taylor Books (New Zealand) *Tel:* (07) 5786024, pg 496

Taylor & Francis Asia Pacific (Singapore) *Tel:* 67415166 *Fax:* 67429356 *E-mail:* info@tandf.com.sg *Web Site:* www.tandf.co.uk, pg 548

Taylor & Francis Group (United Kingdom) *Tel:* (020) 7583 9855 *Fax:* (020) 7842 2298 *E-mail:* info@tandf.co.uk *Web Site:* www.tandf.co.uk; www.taylorandfrancis.com, pg 747

Taylor Graham Publishing (United Kingdom) *Web Site:* www.taylorgraham.com, pg 747

John Taylor Book Ventures (United Kingdom) *Tel:* (01367) 244387 *Fax:* (01367) 244387, pg 747

Taylor Publishing Co (United States) *Tel:* 214-819-8100 *Fax:* 214-630-1852 *E-mail:* web@taylorpub.com *Web Site:* www.taylorpub.com, pg 1146, 1167

Taylor Publishing Co (United States) *Tel:* 214-819-8100 *Fax:* 214-630-1852 *Web Site:* www.taylorpub.com, pg 1208

Taylor Publishing Co (United States) *Tel:* 214-819-8100 *Fax:* 214-630-1852 *E-mail:* web@taylorpub.com *Web Site:* www.taylorpub.com, pg 1217, 1225

TBI Publishers' Distributors (India) *Tel:* (011) 3322314; (011) 0314039 *Fax:* (011) 3325247, pg 1290

TBS-Britannica Co Ltd (Japan) *Tel:* (03) 5436-5721 *Fax:* (03) 54365759, pg 427

Tcherikover Publishers Ltd (Israel) *Tel:* (03) 6870621; (03) 6396099 *Fax:* (03) 6874729, pg 372

Te Reo Publications (New Zealand) *Tel:* (0887) 54887 *E-mail:* jmcveagh@clear.net.nz, pg 496

Te Ropu Kahurangi (New Zealand) *Tel:* (09) 2782731, pg 496

Te Waihora Press (New Zealand) *Tel:* (03) 348-8675 *Fax:* (03) 348-8675, pg 496

Te-Wi Verlag Unternehmensbereich Buch der Ziff Verlag GmbH (Germany) *Tel:* (089) 14312470 *Fax:* (089) 14312469, pg 292

TEA Ediciones SA (Spain) *Tel:* (091) 2705000 *Fax:* (091) 3458608 *E-mail:* madrid@teaediciones.com *Web Site:* www.teaediciones.com, pg 592

TEA Publishers (Estonia) *Tel:* (02) 6459206 *Fax:* (02) 6459208 *E-mail:* tea@tea.ee *Web Site:* www.tea.ee, pg 140

TEA Tascabili degli Editori Associati SpA (Italy) *Tel:* (02) 80206625 *Fax:* (02) 8900844, pg 409

Teachers Book Club (United Kingdom) *Tel:* (01926) 887799 *Fax:* (01926) 883331, pg 1234

Teaterforlaget Drama (Denmark) *Tel:* 33321519 *Fax:* 33329818 *E-mail:* drama@drama.dk *Web Site:* www.drama.dk, pg 136

Tech Publications Pte Ltd (Singapore) *Tel:* 7449113; 7428782 *Fax:* 2991550; 2763622, pg 548

Techbooks (New Zealand) *Tel:* (09) 5240132 *Fax:* (09) 5233769, pg 1302

Technica (Bulgaria) *Tel:* (02) 987 1283 *Fax:* (02) 987 4906, pg 98

Technical University Library (Turkey) *Tel:* (0212) 2763596 *Fax:* (0212) 2761734, pg 1504

Technical Books Ltd (South Africa) *Tel:* (021) 4216540 *Fax:* (021) 4216593 *E-mail:* techbkct@mweb.co.za, pg 1310

Technical Centre for Agricultural & Rural Co-operation (Netherlands) *Tel:* (0317) 467100 *Fax:* (0317) 460067 *E-mail:* cta@cta.nl *Web Site:* www.cta.nl, pg 1255

Library of the Technical Chamber of Greece (Greece) *Tel:* (01) 3254590 *Fax:* (01) 3237525, pg 1471

Technical Chamber of Greece (Greece) *Tel:* (01) 3291601 *Fax:* (01) 3226185 *E-mail:* registry@central.tee.gr, pg 315

Technicka Univerzita (Slovakia) *Tel:* (0855) 635 *Fax:* (0855) 20027, pg 551

Hochschule fur Technik Wirtschaft und Kultur Leipzig (FH) (Germany) *Tel:* (03841) 3076-0 *Fax:* (03841) 3076-6456 *E-mail:* studinf@k.htwk.leipzig.de *Web Site:* www.htwk-leipzig.de, pg 292

Instytut Techniki Budowlanej, Dzial Wydawniczo-Poligraficzny (Poland) *Tel:* (022) 8431471 *Fax:* (022) 8432931, pg 520

Technion - Israel Institute of Technology Libraries (Israel) *Tel:* (04) 292507 (Elyachar Central Library) *Fax:* (04) 8233501, pg 1477

Editions Technip SA (France) *Tel:* (01) 45 78 33 80 *Fax:* (01) 45 75 37 11 *E-mail:* commerce@editionstechnip.com *Web Site:* www.editionstechnip.com, pg 187

Editions Techniques et Scientifiques SPRL (Belgium) *Tel:* (02) 6401040 *Fax:* (02) 6400739, pg 74

Editions Techniques et Scientifiques Francaises (France) *Tel:* (01) 463500 *Fax:* (01) 466100, pg 187

Editions Techniques Specialisees (Tunisia) *Tel:* (01) 262155, pg 638

Universitaetsbibliothek der Technischen Universitaet Wien (Austria) *Tel:* (01) 58801 44051 *Fax:* (01) 5880144099 *E-mail:* info@mail.ub.tuwien.ac.at *Web Site:* www.ub.tuwien.ac.at, pg 1452

Technology Exchange Ltd (Hong Kong) *Tel:* 2602 6300 *Fax:* 2609 1687, pg 322

Technosdar Ltd (Israel) *Tel:* (03) 5607418; (03) 5605951 *Fax:* (03) 5604932 *E-mail:* technos@internet-zahav.net, pg 1136

Technosdar Ltd (Israel) *Tel:* (03) 5607418; (03) 5605951 *Fax:* (03) 5604932, pg 1157

Technosdar Ltd (Israel) *Tel:* (03) 5607418 *Fax:* (03) 5604932 *E-mail:* technos@zahav.net.il, pg 1198

Tecman Bible House (Singapore) *Tel:* 3386764 *Fax:* 3388236 *E-mail:* tecman@tecman.com.sg *Web Site:* www.tecman.com.sg, pg 549

Publicaciones Tecnicas Mediterraneo (Chile) *Tel:* (02) 251 62 57; (02) 233 82 72 *Fax:* (02) 231 06 94 *E-mail:* msalinero@entelchile.net, pg 101

Ediciones Tecnicas Rede, SA (Spain) *Tel:* (093) 4103097 *Fax:* (093) 4392813, pg 592

Tecniche Nuove SpA (Italy) *Tel:* (02) 75701 *Fax:* (02) 7610351 *E-mail:* libri@tecnet.it; vendite-libri@tecnet.it *Web Site:* www.tecnet.it, pg 409

Editores Tecnicos Asociados SA (Spain) *Tel:* (093) 4193336, pg 592

Editorial Tecnologica de Costa Rica (Costa Rica) *Tel:* 552-5333 ext 2297 *Fax:* 552-5354; 551-5348 *E-mail:* editec@itcr.ac.cr *Web Site:* www.itcr.ac.cr, pg 117

Instituto Tecnologico de Galicia, ITG (Spain) *Tel:* (0981) 17 32 06 *Fax:* (0981) 17 32 23 *E-mail:* itg1@itg.es *Web Site:* www.itg.es, pg 592

Editorial Tecnos SA (Spain) *Tel:* (091) 393 88 00; (091) 393 86 86 *Fax:* (091) 742 66 31 *Web Site:* www.tecnos.es, pg 592

Teduca, Tecnicas Educativas, CA (Venezuela) *Tel:* (02) 2355878; (02) 2354395; (02) 2356265 *Fax:* (02) 2397952, pg 763

Teeney Books Ltd (United Kingdom) *Tel:* (01225) 775657 *Fax:* (01225) 775676 *E-mail:* teeneybo@primex.co.uk, pg 747

Editura Tehnica (Romania) *Tel:* (01) 2223321; (01) 2226630 *Fax:* (01) 2223776, pg 536

TEHNICKA KNJIGA

Tehnicka Knjiga (Croatia) *Tel:* (01) 248172 *Fax:* (01) 423611, pg 120

Tehnicka Knjiga (Croatia) *Tel:* (041) 4810818 *Fax:* (041) 481 0821, pg 1280

Tehniska Zalozba Slovenije (Slovenia) *Tel:* (061) 213733 *Fax:* (061) 218246, pg 1310

Otto Teich (Germany) *Tel:* (06151) 824120 *Fax:* (06151) 895656, pg 292

Editorial Teide SA (Spain) *Tel:* (093) 4104507 *Fax:* (093) 3224192 *E-mail:* info@editorialteide.es *Web Site:* www.editorialteide.es, pg 592

Teikoku-Shoin Co Ltd (Japan) *Tel:* (03) 32620834 *Fax:* (03) 32627770 *E-mail:* kenkyu@teikokushoin.co.jp, pg 427

Almerinda Teixeira (Portugal) *Tel:* (01) 2762352, pg 529

Tek Translation International SA (Spain) *Tel:* (091) 4141111 *Fax:* (091) 4144444 *E-mail:* sales@tektrans.com *Web Site:* www.tektrans.com, pg 1127

Tekmirio (Greece) *Tel:* (01) 3637912; (01) 2287548, pg 315

Teknillisen Korkeakoulun Kirjasto (Finland) *Tel:* (00) 4514112 *Fax:* (00) 4514132 *E-mail:* infolib@hut.fi, pg 1464

Tekniska Litteratursaellskapet (Sweden) *Tel:* (08) 6782320 *Fax:* (08) 6782301 *E-mail:* kansliet@tls.se, pg 1523

Teknografiska Institutet AB (Sweden) *Tel:* (08) 834285 *Fax:* (08) 7304131, pg 607

Teknolit Oy (Finland) *Tel:* (014) 3100555 *Fax:* (014) 3100566 *E-mail:* teknolit@teknoli.pp.fi *Web Site:* www.teknolit.fi, pg 144

Teknologisk Forlag (Norway) *Tel:* 22471100 *Fax:* 22471149, pg 505

Tel Aviv Books Ltd (Israel) *Tel:* (03) 6203252 *Fax:* (03) 5257725, pg 372

Tel-Aviv University (Israel) *Tel:* (03) 6424571; (03) 6409200; (03) 6426682 *Fax:* (03) 6422404; (03) 6408355, pg 372

Tel Aviv University Library (Israel) *Tel:* (03) 640-8111 *Fax:* (03) 6409598 *E-mail:* tauinfo@post.tau.ac.il *Web Site:* www.tau.ac.il, pg 1477

Telegraph Books (United Kingdom) *Tel:* (020) 7538 6826 *Fax:* (020) 7538 6064 *Web Site:* www.telegraph.co.uk, pg 748

Editorial Augusto E Pila Telena SL (Spain) *Tel:* (091) 857 28 88; (607) 25 20 82 *Fax:* (091) 857 28 80 *E-mail:* pilatena@arrakis.es, pg 592

Telex-Verlag Jaeger & Waldmann GmbH (Germany) *Tel:* (06151) 33020 *Fax:* (06151) 330250 *E-mail:* jwemail@aol.com *Web Site:* www.jwonline.de, pg 292

Tell Forlag (Norway) *Tel:* 66780918 *Fax:* 66900572 *E-mail:* tell@online.no *Web Site:* www.tell.no, pg 505

Telos Boeken (Netherlands) *Tel:* (020) 5241010 *Fax:* (020) 5241011 *E-mail:* info@buijten.nl, pg 485

Tema Celeste (Italy) *Tel:* (02) 80651754; (02) 80651732 (subscriptions) *Fax:* (02) 80651787 *E-mail:* editorial@temaceleste.com; subscriptions@temaceleste.com *Web Site:* www.temaceleste.com, pg 409

Tema Publishers Ltd (United Republic of Tanzania) *Tel:* (051) 113608 *Fax:* (051) 75422, pg 634

Ediciones Temas de Hoy, SA (Spain) *Tel:* (091) 4230318 *Fax:* (091) 4230309; (091) 5970654 *E-mail:* bnogueras@temasdehoy.es *Web Site:* www.temasdehoy.es, pg 592

Libreria Temis SA (Colombia) *Tel:* (01) 423035; (01) 425581; (01) 2690713; (01) 2693521 *Fax:* (01) 2925801, pg 1280

Edition Temmen (Germany) *Tel:* (0421) 34843-0 *Fax:* (0421) 348094 *E-mail:* info@edition-temmen.de *Web Site:* www.edition-temmen.com, pg 292

Tempo Publishing (M) Sdn Bhd (Malaysia) *Tel:* (03) 7570000 *Fax:* (03) 7576688; (03) 7587001, pg 455

Tempus Editores (Brazil) *Tel:* (01) 4535000 *Fax:* (01) 4426482, pg 92

TEMTO (Bulgaria) *Tel:* (02) 524-924 *E-mail:* temto@sf.icn.bg, pg 98

10/18 (France) *Tel:* (01) 44 16 05 00, pg 187

teNeues Verlag GmbH & Co KG (Germany) *Tel:* (02152) 916-0 *Fax:* (02152) 916-111 *E-mail:* verlag@teneues.de *Web Site:* www.teneues.com, pg 292

Tenri Central Library (Japan) *Tel:* (0743) 631515 *Fax:* (0743) 637728 *E-mail:* info@tcl.gr.jp *Web Site:* www.tcl.gr.jp, pg 1479

Editura Teora (Romania) *Tel:* (01) 6193004 *Fax:* (01) 2103828 *E-mail:* teora@teora.kappa.ro *Web Site:* www.teora.ro, pg 536

Teorema (Portugal) *Tel:* (021) 3129131 *Fax:* (021) 3521480 *E-mail:* editorial.teorema@netc.pt, pg 529

Teorija Verojatnostej i ee Primenenija (Russian Federation) *Tel:* (095) 1352380; (095) 3324410 *Fax:* (095) 1135125 *E-mail:* tvp@caravan.ru, pg 542

Librairie Pierre Tequi et Editions Tequi (France) *Tel:* (02) 43.01.01.81 *Fax:* (02) 43.02.25.52 *E-mail:* pierre.tequi@wanadoo.fr *Web Site:* www.librairietequi.com, pg 187

Terania Rainforest Publishing (Australia) *Tel:* (02) 6688 6204 *Fax:* (02) 6688 6227 *E-mail:* terania@nrg.com.au, pg 44

Tercer Mundo Editores SA (Colombia) *Tel:* (01) 2551539; (01) 2550737; (01) 2556691; (01) 2551695 *Fax:* (01) 2125976 *E-mail:* tmundoed@polcola.com.co, pg 113

Libreria Tercer Mundo (Colombia) *Tel:* (01) 2551539; (01) 2556691 *Fax:* (01) 2125976 *E-mail:* tmundoed@polcola.com.co, pg 1280

Edizioni del Teresianum (Italy) *Tel:* (06) 58540250 *Fax:* (06) 58540300, pg 409

Tern Press (United Kingdom) *Tel:* (01630) 652153, pg 748

Terra Grischuna Verlag Buch-und Zeitschriftenverlag (Switzerland) *Tel:* (081) 2867050 *Fax:* (081) 2867057 *E-mail:* info@terra-grischuna.ch *Web Site:* www.terra-grischuna.ch, pg 625

Terra Publishing Co (Netherlands) *Tel:* (0575) 58 13 10 *Fax:* (0575) 52 52 42 *E-mail:* terra@terraboek.nl *Web Site:* www.terraboek.nl, pg 485

Terra Sancta Arts (Israel) *Tel:* (03) 6499520; (03) 6499525 *Fax:* (03) 6490532, pg 373

Terra-Verlag GmbH (Germany) *Tel:* (07531) 81220 *Fax:* (07531) 812299 *E-mail:* info@terra-verlag.de *Web Site:* www.terra-verlag.de, pg 292

Editorial Sal Terrae (Spain) *Tel:* (0942) 369 198 *Fax:* (0942) 369 201 *E-mail:* salterrae@salterrae.es *Web Site:* www.salterrae.es, pg 592

Editions Pierre Terrail/Finest SA (France) *Tel:* (01) 44 35 59 13 *Web Site:* www.bayardpresse.com/fr/groupe/contacts.asp, pg 187

Terre Vivante (France) *Tel:* (04) 76 34 80 80 *Fax:* (04) 76 34 84 02 *E-mail:* infos@terrevivante.org *Web Site:* www.terrevivante.org, pg 187

Tertiary Press (Australia) *Tel:* (03) 9213 6766 *Fax:* (03) 9213 6806 *Web Site:* www.tertiarypress.com.au, pg 44

Terveystieteiden keskuskirjasto (TERKKO) (Finland) *Tel:* (00) 19126644 *Fax:* (00) 2410385 *E-mail:* terkko-info@helinski.fi, pg 1464

Tesitex, SL (Spain) *Tel:* (0923) 255115 *Fax:* (0923) 258703 *E-mail:* tesitex@tesitex.es *Web Site:* www.tesitex.es, pg 592

INDUSTRY

Tessloff Verlag Ragnar Tessloff GmbH & Co KG (Germany) *Tel:* (0911) 39906-0 *Fax:* (0911) 39906-39 *E-mail:* tessloff@osn.de *Web Site:* www.tessloff.com, pg 292

Nicola Teti e C Editore SRL (Italy) *Tel:* (02) 55015575 *Fax:* (02) 55015595, pg 409

Tetra Verlag Gmbh (Germany) *Tel:* (05402) 8889 *Fax:* (05402) 8811 *E-mail:* info@tetra-verlag.de *Web Site:* www.tetra-verlag.de, pg 292

Tetzlaff Verlag (Germany) *Tel:* (040) 237 14-03 *Fax:* (040) 237 14-233 *Web Site:* www.eurailpress.com, pg 292

B G Teubner GmbH (Germany) *Tel:* (0611) 7878361 *Fax:* (0611) 7878470 *Web Site:* www.gwv-fachverlage.de, pg 292

TEV Leidykla (Lithuania) *Tel:* (02) 729318; (02) 729803 *Fax:* (02) 729804 *E-mail:* tev@omnitel.net; tev@ktl.mii.lt, pg 446

Tevan Kiado Vallalat (Hungary) *Tel:* (066) 23159; (066) 327766, pg 327

Texere Publishing Ltd (United Kingdom) *Tel:* (020) 7204 3644 *Fax:* (020) 7208 6701, pg 748

Editorial Texido Ltda (Chile) *Tel:* (02) 6224652 *Fax:* (02) 6224660, pg 101

edition Text & Kritik im Richard Boorberg Verlag GmbH & Co (Germany) *Tel:* (089) 432929 *Fax:* (089) 433997 *E-mail:* etk.muenchen@t-online.de *Web Site:* etk-muenchen.de, pg 293

Text Book Centre Ltd (Kenya) *Tel:* (02) 330340 *Fax:* (02) 225779, pg 1296

Text Books Malaysia Sdn Bhd (Malaysia) *Tel:* (074) 911181 *Fax:* (074) 911181, pg 455

Text Publishers Ltd Too (Russian Federation) *Tel:* (095) 9169168; (095) 6169411 *Fax:* (095) 9258814 *E-mail:* editor@textpub.msk.ru, pg 542

The Text Publishing Company Pty Ltd (Australia) *Tel:* (03) 9272 4700 *Fax:* (03) 9926 4854 *E-mail:* books@textmedia.au *Web Site:* www.textpublishing.com.au, pg 44

Textile & Art Publications Ltd (United Kingdom) *Tel:* (020) 7499 7979 *Fax:* (020) 7409 2596 *E-mail:* post@textile.art.com *Web Site:* www.textile-art.com, pg 748

Texto Editora (Portugal) *Tel:* (021) 4272200 *Fax:* (021) 4272201 *E-mail:* info@te.pt *Web Site:* www.te.pt, pg 529

Editorial Texto Ltda (Costa Rica) *Tel:* 2316643 *Fax:* 2962429, pg 117

Tf Editores (Spain) *Tel:* (091) 484 1870; (091) 484 1878 *Fax:* (091) 661 3594 *E-mail:* editorial@tfeditores.com *Web Site:* www.tfeditores.com, pg 592

TF Fachverlag Gmbh (Germany) *Tel:* (0711) 2194-0 *Fax:* (0711) 2194-111, pg 293

TF 1 Editions (France) *Tel:* (01) 41413151 *Fax:* (01) 41413153 *Web Site:* www.laffont.fr, pg 187

TFPL (United Kingdom) *Tel:* (020) 7251 5522 *Fax:* (020) 7251 8318 *E-mail:* central@tfpl.com *Web Site:* www.tfpl.com, pg 748

Thai Library Association (Thailand) *Tel:* (02) 2712084, pg 1524

Thai National Documentation Centre (TNDC) (Thailand) *Tel:* (02) 579112130 *Fax:* (02) 5798594, pg 1503

Thai Watana Panich Co, Ltd (Thailand) *Tel:* (02) 6812288 *Fax:* (02) 6819973 *Web Site:* www.twp.co.th, pg 636

Thai Watana Panich Press Co Ltd (Thailand) *Tel:* (02) 2150060 *Fax:* (02) 2152360 *E-mail:* twpp@bkk.loxinfo.co.th, pg 1139

Thalacker Medien GmbH Co KG (Germany) *Tel:* (0531) 38004 0 *Fax:* (0531) 38004 25 *E-mail:* info@thalackermedien.de *Web Site:* www.thalackermedien.de, pg 293

Thales Sociedad Andaluza de Educacion Matematica (Spain) *Tel:* (095) 4623658 *Fax:* (095) 4236378 *E-mail:* thales@cica.es *Web Site:* thales.cica.es, pg 592

Thames & Hudson (France) *Tel:* (01) 42219515 *Fax:* (01) 42213336, pg 187

Thames & Hudson (Australia) Pty Ltd (Australia) *Tel:* (03) 9646 7788 *Fax:* (03) 9646 8790 *E-mail:* thaust@thaust.com.au, pg 44

Thames & Hudson Ltd (United Kingdom) *Tel:* (020) 7845 5000 *Fax:* (020) 7845 5050 *E-mail:* sales@thameshudson.co.uk *Web Site:* www.thamesandhudson.com, pg 748

Thammasat University Libraries (Thailand) *Tel:* (02) 6235176 *Fax:* (02) 6235173 *E-mail:* tulib@alpha.tu.ac.th *Web Site:* 192.150.249.123/, pg 1503

Thanhaeuser Edition (Austria) *Tel:* (07234) 83800 *Fax:* (07234) 83800 *E-mail:* thanhaeuser@otteusheim.at, pg 59

Tharpa Publications (United Kingdom) *Tel:* (01229) 588599 *Fax:* (01229) 483919 *E-mail:* tharpa@tharpa.com *Web Site:* www.tharpa.com, pg 748

Editorial Thassalia, SA (Spain) *Tel:* (093) 211.46.12 *Fax:* (093) 417.91.73, pg 592

Thauros Verlag GmbH (Germany) *Tel:* (08387) 2510 *Fax:* (08387) 3731 *E-mail:* thaurosverlag@t-online.de, pg 293

Editions Theatrales (France) *Tel:* (01) 53102300 *Fax:* (01) 53102301 *E-mail:* info@editionstheatrales.fr *Web Site:* www.theatre-contemporain.net, pg 187

Corry Theegarten-Schlotterer (Germany) *Tel:* (089) 932566 *Fax:* (089) 9303992, pg 1112

Konrad Theiss Verlag GmbH (Germany) *Tel:* (0711) 255 27-0 *Fax:* (0711) 255 27-17 *E-mail:* service@theiss.de *Web Site:* www.theiss.de, pg 293

Theodor (Imprimerie) (Haiti), pg 317

Theologischer Verlag und Buchhandlungen AG (Switzerland) *Tel:* (01) 4617710, pg 625

Theoria SRL Distribuidora y Editora (Argentina) *Tel:* (011) 4381-0131 *Fax:* (011) 4381-0131, pg 9

Theosophical Publishing House (India) *Tel:* (044) 4911338 *Fax:* (044) 4901399; (044) 4902706 *E-mail:* para.vidya@gems.vsnl.net.in, pg 351

Thesen Verlag Vowinckel (Luxembourg) *Tel:* (00352) 748715 *Fax:* (00352) 26740429, pg 448

Theseus - Verlag AG (Switzerland) *Tel:* (01) 9109294 *Fax:* (01) 9108019, pg 625

Thetili Publications (Greece) *Tel:* (01) 3215229, pg 315

Thex Editora e Distribuidora Ltda (Brazil) *Tel:* (021) 252-9338; (021) 221-4458; (021) 221-4079 *Fax:* (021) 252-9338 *E-mail:* thexedit@domain.com.br *Web Site:* www.thexeditora.com.br, pg 92

Druck-und Verlagshans Thiele & Schwarz GmbH (Germany) *Tel:* (0561) 9 59 25-0 *Fax:* (0561) 9 59 25-68 *E-mail:* info@thiele-schwarz.de *Web Site:* www.thiele-schwarz.de, pg 293

Georg Thieme Verlag KG (Germany) *Tel:* (0711) 8931-0 *Fax:* (0711) 8931-298 *E-mail:* kunden.service@thieme.de *Web Site:* www.thieme.de; www.thieme.com, pg 293

BV Uitgeverij en Boekhandel W J Thieme & Cie (Netherlands) *Tel:* (0575) 594911 *Fax:* (0575) 519970, pg 485

ThiemeMeulenhoff (Netherlands) *Tel:* (030) 239 25 55 *Fax:* (030) 239 22 70 *E-mail:* w.de.jager@thiemeulenhoff.nl *Web Site:* www.thiemeulenhoff.nl, pg 485

Thien, Hans-Gunter, u Hanns Wienold (Germany) *Tel:* (0251) 608 60 80 *Fax:* (0251) 608 60 20 *E-mail:* info@dampfboot-verlag.de *Web Site:* www.dampfboot-verlag.de, pg 293

K Thienemanns Verlag (Germany) *Tel:* (0711) 210 55-0 *Fax:* (0711) 210 55 39 *E-mail:* info@thienemann.de *Web Site:* www.theinemann.de, pg 293

James Thin, Bookseller (United Kingdom) *Tel:* (0131) 622 8222 *Fax:* (0131) 557 8149 *E-mail:* enquiries@jthin.co.uk *Web Site:* www.jamesthin.co.uk, pg 1322

Thin Rich Press (Australia) *Tel:* (09) 3644799 *Fax:* (09) 3163338, pg 44

The Third Wave Enterprise Co Ltd (Taiwan, Province of China) *Tel:* (02) 87803636 *Fax:* (02) 87805656, pg 632

34 Literatura S/C Ltda (Brazil) *Tel:* (021) 816-6777 *Fax:* (021) 816-0078, pg 92

Thistle Press (United Kingdom) *Tel:* (01464) 821053 *Fax:* (01464) 821053 *E-mail:* info@oldmilldesign.co.uk, pg 748

Thjodsagao ehf (Iceland) *Tel:* 567-1777 *Fax:* 567-1240 *E-mail:* pbk@centrum.is, pg 329

Verlag Theodor Thoben (Germany) *Tel:* (05431) 3486 *Fax:* (05431) 3584 *E-mail:* info@buecher-thoben.de *Web Site:* www.buecher-thoben.de, pg 293

Thoemmes Press (United Kingdom) *Tel:* (0117) 929 1377 *Fax:* (0117) 922 1918 *E-mail:* info@thoemmes.com *Web Site:* www.thoemmes.com, pg 748

Hans Thoma Verlag GmbH Kunst und Buchverlag (Germany) *Tel:* (0721) 932 750 *Fax:* (0721) 932 7520, pg 294

Alain Thomas Editeur (France) *Tel:* (01) 45 88 28 03 *Fax:* (01) 45 88 49 24 *Web Site:* alainthomasimages.com, pg 188

Thomas Technology Solutions, Inc (United Kingdom) *Tel:* (020) 7559 9810 *Fax:* (020) 7559 9811 *Web Site:* www.thomastechsolutions.com, pg 1163

Thomson Publications (South Africa) *Tel:* (011) 7892144 *Fax:* (011) 7893196, pg 560

Thomson Corporation (Hong Kong) *Tel:* (02) 5335416 *Fax:* (02) 5303588, pg 322

Thomson Learning (Japan) *Tel:* (03) 52825180 *Fax:* (03) 52825181 *E-mail:* yuko@tlj.co.jp *Web Site:* www.tlj.co.jp, pg 427

M & A Thomson Litho Ltd (United Kingdom) *Tel:* (013552) 33081 *Fax:* (013552) 45439, pg 1142

M & A Thomson Litho Ltd (United Kingdom) *Tel:* (013552) 33081 *Fax:* (013552) 45439 *Web Site:* www.plitho.co.uk, pg 1163, 1205, 1215

Thomson Publications Zimbabwe (Pvt) Ltd (Zimbabwe) *Tel:* (04) 736835 *Fax:* (04) 749803 *E-mail:* tpubl@mweb.co.zw, pg 769

Thomson Publishing Services (United Kingdom) *Tel:* (01264) 332424 *Fax:* (01264) 364418, pg 1322

Thornbill Press (Australia) *Tel:* (08) 2705172, pg 44

Caroline Thornton (Australia) *Tel:* (08) 9386 1555 *Fax:* (08) 9389 5162, pg 44

Thornton's of Oxford Ltd (United Kingdom) *Tel:* (01865) 242939 *Fax:* (01865) 204021 *E-mail:* thorntons@booknews.demon.co.uk *Web Site:* www.demon.co.uk/thorntons, pg 1322

D W Thorpe (Australia) *Tel:* (03) 9245 7370 *Fax:* (03) 9245 7395 *E-mail:* yoursay@thorpe.com.au *Web Site:* www.thorpe.com.au, pg 44

Thoth Publishers (Netherlands) *Tel:* (035) 6944144 *Fax:* (035) 6943266 *E-mail:* thoth@euronet.nl, pg 485

3 Dimension World (3-D-World) (Switzerland) *Tel:* (061) 424917, pg 625

Three Sisters Publications Pty Ltd (Australia) *Tel:* (047) 588128, pg 44

3A Corporation (Japan) *Tel:* (03) 32925751 *Fax:* (03) 32925754 *E-mail:* 3ac@mail.at-m.or.jp *Web Site:* www.at-m.or.jpl~3ac, pg 427

Threshold Publishing (Australia) *Fax:* (03) 98534307, pg 44

Thudhammawaddy Press (Myanmar), pg 471

Thueringer Universitaets- und Landesbibliothek Jena (Germany) *Tel:* (03641) 940 000 *Fax:* (03641) 940 002 *E-mail:* thulb@thulb.uni-jena.de, pg 1469

Edi Thule Club (Italy) *Tel:* (091) 323699, pg 1229

J M Thurley (United Kingdom) *Tel:* (0208) 9773176 *Fax:* (0208) 9432678, pg 1122

Edition Thurnhof KEG (Austria) *Tel:* (02982) 3333 *Fax:* (02982) 3333 *Web Site:* www.thurnhof.at, pg 59

Thwe Thauk (Myanmar), pg 1300

Thymari Publications (Greece) *Tel:* (01) 3643015; (01) 3643901 *Fax:* (01) 3636591 *E-mail:* thymari@thymari.gr, pg 315

Edizioni Thyrus SRL (Italy) *Tel:* (0744) 389496 *Fax:* (0744) 388700, pg 409

Tianjin Science & Technology Publishing House (China) *Tel:* (022) 27312755; (022) 700919 *Fax:* (022) 27312755 *E-mail:* tjstp@public.tpt.tj.on, pg 109

Istituto Editoriale Ticinese (IET) SA (Switzerland) *Tel:* (092) 8256622 *Fax:* (092) 251874, pg 626

Tiden Norsk Forlag (Norway) *Tel:* 22007100 *Fax:* 22426458 *E-mail:* trine.lise.linnestad@tiden.no, pg 505

Tiderne Skifter Forlag A/S (Denmark) *Tel:* 33411820 *Fax:* 33411821 *E-mail:* tiderneskifter@tiderneskifter.dk *Web Site:* www.tiderneskifter.dk, pg 136

Tien Wah Press Pte Ltd (Singapore) *Tel:* 64666222 *Fax:* 64693894, pg 1200

Tiessen, Wolfgang, Moderne (Germany) *Tel:* (06102) 53335 *Fax:* (06102) 53335, pg 294

Tietohuollon Neuvottelukunta (Finland) *Tel:* (09) 134171 *Fax:* (09) 1359335, pg 1515

Tietoteos Publishing Co (Finland) *Tel:* (09) 264475 *Fax:* (09) 264575 *E-mail:* jyrki.talvitie@att.inet.fi *Web Site:* www.jkttietoteos.fi, pg 144

Tiger Books International PLC (United Kingdom) *Tel:* (0181) 8925577 *Fax:* (0181) 8916550 *E-mail:* enquires@tigerbooks.co.uk, pg 748

Tiger Books International PLC (United Kingdom) *Tel:* (0181) 8925577 *Fax:* (0181) 8916550, pg 1322

Tihama Bookshops (Saudi Arabia) *Tel:* (02) 6444444 *Fax:* (02) 6519277, pg 1309

Uitgeverij de Tijdstroom BV (Netherlands) *Tel:* (030) 2586900 *Fax:* (030) 2586950, pg 485

Tilburg University Press (Netherlands) *Tel:* (013) 4662909 *Fax:* (013) 4663288 *E-mail:* tup@kub.nl, pg 485

Tilgher-Genova sas (Italy) *Tel:* (010) 839 11 40 *Fax:* (010) 87 06 53 *E-mail:* tilgher@tilgher.it *Web Site:* www.tilgher.it, pg 410

The Tilling Society (United Kingdom) *Fax:* (01424) 813237, pg 1372

Timber Press Inc (United Kingdom) *Tel:* (01954) 232959 *Fax:* (01954) 206040 *E-mail:* timberpressuk@BTInternet.com *Web Site:* www.timberpress.com, pg 749

AB Timbro (Sweden) *Tel:* (08) 58789800 *Fax:* (08) 58789855 *E-mail:* info@timbro.se *Web Site:* www.timbro.se, pg 607

Time-Life Australia Pty Ltd (Australia) *Tel:* (02) 9856 2212 *Toll Free Tel:* 800-251-616 *Fax:* (02) 9856 2255 *Web Site:* www.timelife.com.au, pg 45

Time-Life Internacional de Mexico (Mexico) *Tel:* (05) 5469000, pg 467

Time-Life (UK) (United Kingdom) *Tel:* (020) 7911 8000 *Fax:* (020) 7911 8100 *E-mail:* email@timelife.demon.co.uk *Web Site:* www.twbookmark.com, pg 749

Time Out Group Ltd (United Kingdom) *Tel:* (020) 7813 3000 *Fax:* (020) 7813 6001 *E-mail:* net@timeout.co.uk *Web Site:* www.timeout.com, pg 749

Time-Space Inc (Republic of Korea) *Tel:* (02) 2272-2381 *Fax:* (02) 2632380; (02) 2273 8900 *E-mail:* tspace@timespace.co.kr *Web Site:* www.fotato.com, pg 1114

Time Track (M) Sdn Bhd (Malaysia) *Tel:* (05) 3124329; (05) 3127541 *Fax:* (05) 2630305, pg 455

Time Warner Books UK (United Kingdom) *Tel:* (020) 7911 8000 *Fax:* (020) 7911 8100 *E-mail:* email.uk@timewarnerbooks.co.uk *Web Site:* www.timewarnerbooks.co.uk, pg 749

Times The Bookshop (Singapore) *Tel:* 2848844 *Fax:* 2771186, pg 1309

Times Educational Co Sdn Bhd (Malaysia) *Tel:* (03) 7571766 *Fax:* (03) 7573607, pg 455

Times Graphics (Singapore) *Tel:* 2848844 *Fax:* 2771186, pg 1159

Times Media Pte Ltd (Singapore) *Tel:* 62848844 *Fax:* 62771186 *E-mail:* te@corp.tpl.com.sg *Web Site:* www.timesone.com.sg/te, pg 549

Times Printers Pte Ltd (Singapore) *Tel:* 8623333 *Fax:* 8621313, pg 1138

Times Printers Pte Ltd (Singapore) *Tel:* 8623333 *Fax:* 8621313 *E-mail:* timetppl@singnet.com.sq, pg 1159

Times Printers Pte Ltd (Singapore) *Tel:* 8623333 *Fax:* 8621313 *E-mail:* timetppl@singnet.com.sg, pg 1200, 1213, 1222

Times Publishing Group (United States) *Tel:* 914-366-9888 *Fax:* 914-366-9898 *Web Site:* www.tpl.com.sg, pg 1146, 1167, 1208, 1217, 1225

Times Ringier Ltd (Hong Kong) *Tel:* 2660 2666 *Fax:* 2664 1993 *E-mail:* trhkmktg@timesringier.com.hk, pg 322

Times Store Ltd (Jamaica) *Tel:* (876) 922-4690; (876) 922-4697 *Fax:* (876) 922-4890 *E-mail:* chesrichards@mail.infocham.com, pg 1294

Tintamas Indonesia PT (Indonesia) *Tel:* (021) 3911459; (021) 7393701 *Fax:* (021) 3911459, pg 357

Tipografica Editora Argentina (Argentina) *Tel:* (011) 4373-2581 *Fax:* (011) 4775-2521 *E-mail:* bernardosm@sinectis.com.ar, pg 9

Sociedade Tipografica, SA (Editora Soctip/Livraria Soctip) (Portugal) *Tel:* (021) 543280 *Fax:* (021) 577926, pg 530

Tipress Dienstleistungen fur das Verlagswesen GmbH (Germany) *Tel:* (07634) 591193 *Fax:* (07634) 591192 *E-mail:* tipress@tipress.com *Web Site:* www.tipress.com, pg 294

Tipress Dienstleistungen fur das Verlagswesen GmbH (Germany) *Tel:* (011) 533487 *Fax:* (011) 535283 *E-mail:* tipress@t-online.de, pg 1112

Tir Eolas (Ireland) *Tel:* (091) 637452 *Fax:* (091) 637452 *E-mail:* info@tireolas.com *Web Site:* www.tireolas.com, pg 364

Tirant lo Blanch SL Libreriaa (Spain) *Tel:* (096) 3610048 *Fax:* (096) 3694151 *E-mail:* tlb@tirant.es *Web Site:* www.tirant.es, pg 592

Editions Tiresias Michel Reynaud (France) *Tel:* (01) 42 23 47 27 *Fax:* (01) 42 23 73 27 *E-mail:* firesias@club-internet.fr, pg 188

Tirian Publications (Australia) *Tel:* (02) 9905 0533 *E-mail:* Tirian@bigpond.com, pg 45

Tirion Uitgevers BV (Netherlands) *Tel:* (035) 5486601 *Fax:* (035) 5486615 *E-mail:* tirion-uitgevers@wxs.ul, pg 485

Ramona S Tirona Memorial Library (Philippines) *Tel:* (02) 5268421 (loc 176) *Fax:* (02) 5266935, pg 1491

Tirosh Communication Ltd (Israel) *Tel:* (03) 6044959 *Fax:* (03) 6053840 *E-mail:* hgeffen@netvision.net.il, pg 373

Editrice Tirrenia Stampatori SAS (Italy) *Tel:* (011) 8150826 *Fax:* (011) 8177010, pg 410

Titan Books Ltd (United Kingdom) *Tel:* (020) 7620 0200 *Fax:* (020) 7620 0032 *E-mail:* 101447.2455@compuserve.com, pg 749

Titania-Verlag Ferdinand Schroll (Germany) *Tel:* (0711) 63 81 25 *Fax:* (0711) 63 69 872, pg 294

Titles Old and Rare Books of Oxford (United Kingdom) *Tel:* (01865) 727928 *Fax:* (01865) 727928, pg 1322

Tivenan Publications (Ireland) *Tel:* (069) 62596 *Fax:* (069) 62933 *E-mail:* birth@indigo.ie *Web Site:* www.wellmotion.info, pg 364

TJ International Ltd (United Kingdom) *Tel:* (01841) 532691 *Fax:* (01841) 532862, pg 1142

TJ International Ltd (United Kingdom) *Tel:* (01841) 532691 *Fax:* (01841) 532862 *Web Site:* www.tjinterantional.com, pg 1205

W E J Tjeenk Willink BV (Netherlands) *Tel:* (0570) 647111 *Fax:* (0570) 63740, pg 485

TMS Development International Ltd (United Kingdom) *Tel:* (01904) 641640 *Fax:* (01904) 640076 *E-mail:* enquiry@tmsdi.com *Web Site:* www.tmsdi.com, pg 1224

To Rodakio (Greece) *Tel:* (01) 3221700 *Fax:* (01) 3246008, pg 315

Tobias Associates Inc (United States) *Tel:* 215-322-1500 *Fax:* 215-322-1504 *E-mail:* tobias@densitometer.com *Web Site:* www.densitometer.com, pg 1208, 1225

Tobin Music (United Kingdom) *Tel:* (01279) 726625 *E-mail:* candidatobin@candidatobin.co.uk *Web Site:* www.candidatobin.co.uk, pg 749

Tobler Verlag (Switzerland) *Tel:* (071) 755 6060 *Fax:* (071) 755 1254 *E-mail:* books@tobler-verlag.ch *Web Site:* www.tobler-verlag.ch, pg 626

Todariana Editrice (Italy) *Tel:* (02) 56812953 *Fax:* (02) 55213405 *E-mail:* toeurs@tin.it, pg 410

Today & Tomorrow's Printers & Publishers (India) *Tel:* (011) 5721928; (011) 5727770 *Fax:* (011) 5721928, pg 352

S Toeche-Mittler Verlag GmbH (Germany) *Tel:* (06151) 33665 *Fax:* (06151) 314048 *E-mail:* info@net-library.de *Web Site:* www.net-library.de, pg 294

Tohan Corporation (Japan) *Tel:* (03) 32696111 *Fax:* (03)32668943, pg 1295

Toho Book Store (Japan) *Tel:* (03) 32331005 *Fax:* (03) 32950800, pg 427

Toho Shuppan (Japan) *Tel:* 06 3655421, pg 427

Tohoku University Library (Japan) *Tel:* (0222) 2175933; (0221) 2174844 *Fax:* (0222) 2175949; (0222) 217846 *E-mail:* desk@library.tohoku.ac.jp, pg 1479

Libris Toison d'Or SA (Belgium) *Tel:* (02) 5116400 *Fax:* (02) 5140961, pg 1276

Tokai University Press (Japan) *Tel:* (03) 54780891 *Fax:* (03) 54780870, pg 427

Toker Yayinlari (Turkey) *Tel:* (0212) 5223309, pg 641

Tokuma-Shoten (Japan) *Tel:* (03) 35730111 *Fax:* (03) 35738771, pg 427

Tokyo Kagaku Dozin Co Ltd (Japan) *Tel:* (03) 39465311 *Fax:* (03) 39465316, pg 427

Tokyo Metropolitan Central Library (Japan) *Tel:* (03) 34428451 *Fax:* (03) 34478924 *Web Site:* www.library.metro.tokyo.jp/, pg 1479

Tokyo Publications Service Ltd (Japan) *Tel:* (03) 35619741 *Fax:* (03) 35619743, pg 1295

Tokyo Shoseki Co Ltd (Japan) *Tel:* (03) 53907531 *Fax:* (03) 53907538 *E-mail:* home@tokyo-shoseki.co.jp *Web Site:* www.tokyo-shoseki.co.jp, pg 427

Tokyo Sogensha Co Ltd (Japan) *Tel:* (03) 32688201 *Fax:* (03) 32688230, pg 428

Tokyo Tosho Co Ltd (Japan) *Tel:* (03) 38162561 *Fax:* (03) 38157330, pg 428

Joe-Tolalu & Associates (Nigeria) *Tel:* (01) 4925078, pg 501

Toledo Creative Management (Netherlands) *Tel:* (020) 6226873 *Fax:* (020) 6276720 *E-mail:* agency@toledo-cm.nl, pg 1115

Toleranz Verlag, Nielsen Frederic W (Germany) *Tel:* (0761) 81415, pg 294

The Tolkien Society (United Kingdom) *Tel:* (01242) 529757, pg 1372

Tom Publications (Australia) *Tel:* (09) 4444570, pg 45

Tomar Publishing Ltd (Ireland) *Fax:* (01) 744697, pg 364

Tomo Edizioni srl (Italy) *Tel:* (081) 00920 *Fax:* (081) 00920, pg 410

Tomorrow Publications (Australia) *Tel:* (049) 612115, pg 45

Tomorrow Publishing House (China) *Tel:* (0531) 201 0055 ext 4716, 4622, 4270 *Fax:* (0531) 290 2094 *E-mail:* tomorrow@sd.cei.gov.cn, pg 110

Tomus Verlag GmbH (Germany) *Tel:* (089) 47 07 77-44 *Fax:* (089) 47 07 77-42 *E-mail:* main@tomus.com *Web Site:* www.tomus.de, pg 294

Toneelfonds J Janssens BVBA (Belgium) *Tel:* (03) 366 44 00 *Fax:* (03) 366 45 01 *E-mail:* info@toneelfonds.be *Web Site:* www.toneelfonds.be, pg 74

Toneelfonds J Janssens BVBA (Belgium) *Tel:* (03) 366.44.00 *Fax:* (03) 3664501 *E-mail:* info@toneelfonds.be *Web Site:* www.toneelfonds.be, pg 1109

P J Tonger Musikverlag GmbH & Co (Germany) *Tel:* (0221) 935564-0 *Fax:* (0221) 935564-11 *E-mail:* musikverlag@tonger.de *Web Site:* www.tonger.de, pg 294

Uitgeverij De Toorts (Netherlands) *Tel:* (023) 5532920 *Fax:* (023) 5320635 *E-mail:* uitgeverij@toorts.nl, pg 485

Top Editions (France) *Tel:* (01) 30 14 19 30 *Fax:* (01) 34 60 31 32 *E-mail:* info@casteilla.fr, pg 188

Top Secret Collection Publishers (Russian Federation) *Tel:* (095) 2022011; (095) 2024531 *Fax:* (095) 2913885 *E-mail:* topsec@glasnet.ru, pg 542

Editura Top Suspans (Romania) *Tel:* (01) 6830924; (01) 6103359, pg 536

Topaz Publications (Ireland) *Tel:* (01) 2800460 *Fax:* (01) 2800460, pg 364

Topic Verlag GmbH (Germany) *Tel:* (08131) 97038 *Fax:* (08131) 98404, pg 1133, 1154

Topos Verlag AG (Liechtenstein) *Tel:* 3771111 *Fax:* 3771119 *E-mail:* topos@supra.net *Web Site:* www.topos.li, pg 445

Toppan Co Ltd (Japan) *Tel:* (03) 5418-2535 *Fax:* (03) 5418-2529 *E-mail:* yuri@top.co.jp *Web Site:* www.toppan-pub.topica.ne.jp/, pg 428

Toppan Co Ltd (Japan) *Tel:* (03) 5418-2535 *Fax:* (03) 5418-2529, pg 1295

Toppan Company (S) Pte Ltd (Singapore) *Tel:* 264-0654 *Fax:* 265-8298, pg 1139, 1159, 1200, 1213

Toppan Printing Co America Inc (United States) *Tel:* 212-489-7740; 212-975-9060 *Fax:* 212-246-3067 *Web Site:* www.ta.toppan.com, pg 1146

Toppan Printing Co (HK) Ltd (Hong Kong) *Tel:* 24755666; 25610101 *Fax:* 24740608; 28809970 *E-mail:* mamada@hk.nttdata.net, pg 1157, 1197

Toppan Printing Co (UK) Ltd (United Kingdom) *Tel:* (020) 7828 7292 *Fax:* (020) 7828 5310, pg 1142

Ediciones Toray SA (Spain) *Tel:* (093) 5808124; (093) 6921851 *Fax:* (093) 6921851, pg 593

Torch of Wisdom (Taiwan, Province of China) *Tel:* (02) 7075802 *Fax:* (02) 7085054 *E-mail:* tow@ms2.hinet.net, pg 632

Instituto Torcuato Di Tella (Argentina) *Tel:* (011) 4783-8680 *Fax:* (011) 4783-3061 *E-mail:* postmaster@itdtar.edu.ar *Web Site:* www.aaep.org.ar, pg 9

Gregorio del Toro Editor (Spain) *Tel:* (091) 3080077; (091) 3190139 *Fax:* (091) 3080187, pg 593

Toros Yayinlari Ltd Co (Turkey) *Tel:* (0212) 2444155 *Fax:* (0212) 2452858; (0212) 2444155, pg 641

Ediciones de la Torre (Spain) *Tel:* (091) 692 20 34 *Fax:* (091) 692 20 34 *E-mail:* info@edicionesdelatorre.com *Web Site:* www.edicionesdelatorre.com, pg 593

Torremozas SL Ediciones (Spain) *Tel:* (091) 350 50 27; (091) 359 03 15 *Fax:* (091) 345 85 32, pg 593

Instituto Eduardo Torroja (Spain) *Tel:* (091) 302 04 40 *Fax:* (091) 302 07 00 *E-mail:* director.ietcc@csic.es *Web Site:* www.ietcc.csic.es, pg 593

Tosui Shobo Publishers (Japan) *Tel:* (03) 32616190 *Fax:* (03) 32612234, pg 428

Total Home Entertainment (United Kingdom) *Tel:* (01782) 566566 *Fax:* (01782) 565400 *E-mail:* thenews@the.co.uk, pg 1322

Totalidade Editora Ltda (Brazil) *Tel:* (011) 3064 3688 *Fax:* (011) 3081 9503 *E-mail:* totail@terra.com.br *Web Site:* www.totalidade.com.br, pg 92

Toubis M (Greece) *Tel:* (01) 9923876; (01) 9923806 *Fax:* (01) 9923867 *E-mail:* toubis@otenet.gr, pg 315

Toucan Press (United Kingdom) *Tel:* (01481) 57017, pg 749

Toulon Uitgeverij (Belgium) *Tel:* (059) 800927, pg 74

Editions Tousch (Luxembourg) *Tel:* 452977 *Fax:* 458743, pg 448

Touzimsky & Moravec (Czech Republic) *Tel:* (02) 612 13 631; (02) 612 12 458 *Fax:* (02) 612 12 458, pg 128

Towarzystwo Literackie im Adama Mickiewicza (Poland) *Tel:* (022) 265231 (ext 279), pg 1367

Towarzystwo Naukowe w Toruniu (Poland) *Tel:* (056) 6223941 (ext 8), pg 520

Tower Books (Australia) *Tel:* (02) 9975-5566 *Fax:* (02) 9975-5599 *E-mail:* towerbks@zipworld.com.au, pg 45

Tower Books (Ireland) *Tel:* (021) 872294 (voice & fax), pg 1136

Town House & Country House (Ireland) *Tel:* (01) 4972399 *Fax:* (01) 4970927 *E-mail:* books@townhouse.ie, pg 364

Towy Publishing (United Kingdom) *Tel:* (01267) 236569 *Fax:* (01267) 220444, pg 749

The Toyo Bunko (Japan) *Tel:* (03) 39420121 *Fax:* (03) 39420258 *E-mail:* webmaster@toyo-bunko.or.jp *Web Site:* www.toyo-bunko.or.jp/toyobunko-e, pg 1479

Toyo Keizai Inc (The Oriental Economist) (Japan) *Tel:* (03) 32465469; (03) 32465656 *Fax:* (03) 32704127 *E-mail:* xlk01673@niftyserve.or.jp, pg 428

Wydawnictwo TPPR Wspolpraca (Poland) *Tel:* (022) 200301 (ext 227), pg 520

TR - Verlagsunion GmbH (Germany) *Tel:* (089) 2121 390 *Fax:* (089) 296129; (089) 296357 *E-mail:* vertrieb@tr-verlag.de *Web Site:* www.tr-verlag.de, pg 294

Trachsel - Verlag AG (Switzerland) *Tel:* (33) 6711407 *Fax:* (33) 6712449, pg 626

Tradespools Ltd (United Kingdom) *Tel:* (01373) 461475 *Fax:* (01373) 474112 *E-mail:* sales@tradespools.co.uk *Web Site:* www.tradespools.co.uk, pg 1163

Traditionell Bogenschiessen Verlag Angelika Hornig (Germany) *Tel:* (0621) 68 94 41 *Fax:* (0621) 68 94 42 *E-mail:* info@bogenschiessen.de *Web Site:* www.bogenschiessen.de, pg 294

Trainer International SRL (Italy) *Tel:* (055) 288162 *Fax:* (055) 218951, pg 410

Training Publications Ltd (United Kingdom) *Tel:* (01923) 209800 *Fax:* (01923) 213 144, pg 749

Tranchida (Italy) *Tel:* (02) 66802270 *Fax:* (02) 69003425 *E-mail:* rbuff@abanet.it, pg 410

Trano Printy Fiahyohana Loterana Malagasy (Madagascar) *Tel:* (020) 223340; (020) 24569, pg 1298

Trano Printy Fiangonana Loterana Malagasy (TPFLM)-(Imprimerie Lutherienne) (Madagascar) *Tel:* (020) 223340 *Fax:* (02) 262643 *E-mail:* impluth@dts.mg, pg 450

Trans Tech Publications (Germany) *Tel:* (05323) 96970 *Fax:* (05323) 969796 *E-mail:* ttp@bulkonline.com *Web Site:* www.bulk-online.de, pg 294

Trans Tech Publications SA (Switzerland) *Tel:* (01) 9221022 *Fax:* (01) 9221033 *E-mail:* ttp@ttp.ch *Web Site:* www.ttp.net, pg 626

TransAction Translators Ltd (United Kingdom) *Tel:* (0114) 2661103 *Fax:* (0114) 2670465 *E-mail:* transaction@transaction.co.uk, pg 1130

Transafrica Press (Kenya), pg 433

Transcontinental Printing Book Group (Canada) *Tel:* 514-337-8560 *Fax:* 514-339-2252 *Web Site:* www.transcontinental-gtc.com; www.transcontinental-printing.com, pg 1131, 1154, 1194, 1211, 1221

Transedition ASBL (France) *Tel:* (01) 43211080 *Fax:* (01) 43211079, pg 188

Transedition Ltd (United Kingdom) *Tel:* (01865) 770549 *Fax:* (01865) 712500 *E-mail:* enquiries@transed.co.uk *Web Site:* www.translateabook.com, pg 749

Transeuropa Libri (Italy) *Tel:* (071) 52735 *Fax:* (071) 52610, pg 410

Transeuropeennes/RCE (France) *Tel:* (01) 55 07 88 90 *Fax:* (01) 55 07 97 38 *E-mail:* te.revue@wanadoo.fr *Web Site:* www.transeuropeennes.org, pg 188

Universitatea Transilvania Din Brasov Biblioteca Centrala (Romania) *Tel:* (068) 475348 *Fax:* (068) 475348 *E-mail:* libr@vega.unitbv.ro *Web Site:* www.unitbu.ro/biblio/bib_home.htm, pg 1494

Translators Association (United Kingdom) *Tel:* (020) 7373 6642 *Fax:* (020) 7373 5768 *E-mail:* info@societyofauthors.org *Web Site:* www.societyofauthors.org/translators, pg 1130

Translators Association (United Kingdom) *Tel:* (020) 7373 6642 *Fax:* (020) 7373 5768 *E-mail:* info@societyofauthors.org *Web Site:* www.societyofauthors.org, pg 1372

Translators Guild (Czech Republic) *Tel:* (02) 6911908 ext 30 *Fax:* (02) 3117224, pg 1125

Translegal AG (Switzerland) *Tel:* (033) 221622 *Fax:* (033) 2253933, pg 626

Transpareon Press (Australia) *Tel:* (02) 99874570 *Fax:* (02) 99874570, pg 45

Transport Bookman Publications Ltd (United Kingdom) *Tel:* (020) 8560 2666 *Fax:* (020) 8569 8273, pg 750

Izdatelstvo Transport (Russian Federation) *Tel:* (095) 2625964 *Fax:* (095) 2611322, pg 542

Transportation Publishing House (Democratic People's Republic of Korea), pg 434

Transpress Verlagsgesellschaft mbH (Germany) *Tel:* (0711) 210 80 65 *Fax:* (0711) 210 80 70 *E-mail:* versand@motorbuch.de *Web Site:* www.motorbuch-versand.de, pg 294

Transvaal Provincial Library and Museum Service (South Africa) *Tel:* (012) 3227632 *Fax:* (012) 3227939, pg 1498

Transworld Publishers Ltd (United Kingdom) *Tel:* (020) 8579 2652 *Fax:* (020) 8579 5479, pg 750

Transworld Publishers (NZ) Ltd (New Zealand) *Tel:* (09) 4156210 *Fax:* (09) 4156221, pg 496

Transworld Publishers Pty Ltd (Australia) *Tel:* (02) 96017122 *Fax:* (02) 98211334, pg 45

Transworld Research Network (India) *Tel:* (0471) 452450 *Fax:* (0471) 573051 *E-mail:* ggcom@vsnl.com *Web Site:* www.transworldresearch.com, pg 352

Trauner Verlag (Austria) *Tel:* (0732) 778240; (0732) 778241 *Fax:* (0732) 283516, pg 59

Trautvetter & Fischer Nachf (Germany) *Tel:* (06421) 33309 *Fax:* (06421) 34959 *E-mail:* bestell@trautvetterfischerverlag.de *Web Site:* www.trautvetterfischerverlag.de, pg 294

Trazo Editorial, SL (Spain) *Tel:* (076) 517586 *Fax:* (076) 517464, pg 593

Trea Ediciones, SL (Spain) *Tel:* (098) 5133453 *Fax:* (098) 5131182 *E-mail:* trea@trea.es, pg 593

Institut de Treball Social - Serveis Socials (Spain) *Tel:* (093) 217 26 64 *Fax:* (093) 237 36 34 *E-mail:* intressbar@intress.org *Web Site:* www.intress.org, pg 593

Tree Shade Technical Services (Kenya) *Tel:* (02) 225798; (02) 220712, pg 433

Treehouse Children's Books Ltd (United Kingdom) *Tel:* (01458) 835 757 *Fax:* (01458) 835 758, pg 750

Trees Wolfgang Triangel Verlag (Germany) *Tel:* (0241) 6 99 00 *Fax:* (0241) 6 99 15 *E-mail:* info@triangelverlag.de *Web Site:* www.triangel-verlag.de, pg 294

Treffer-Boekklub (South Africa) *Tel:* (012) 401 0700 *Fax:* (012) 3255498 *E-mail:* lapa@atkv.org.za, pg 1231

Libreria Trejos SA (Costa Rica) *Tel:* 2242411 *Fax:* 2241528, pg 1280

Michael Treloar Antiqvarian Booksellers (Australia) *Tel:* (08) 82231111 *Fax:* (08) 82236599 *E-mail:* treloars@anzaab.com.au, pg 1273

Trentham Books Ltd (United Kingdom) *Tel:* (01782) 745567; (01782) 844699 *Fax:* (01782) 745553 *E-mail:* tb@trentham-books.co.uk *Web Site:* www.trentham-books.co.uk, pg 750

Ediciones Tres Tiempos SRL (Argentina) *Tel:* (011) 4331-8785 *Fax:* (011) 4331-8785, pg 9

Trescher Verlag GmbH (Germany) *Tel:* (030) 2 83 24 96 *Fax:* (030) 2 81 59 94 *Web Site:* www.trescherverlag.de, pg 295

Treves Editions Verein Zur Foerderung der Kuenstlerischen Taetigkeiten (Germany) *Tel:* (0651) 309 010 *Fax:* (0651) 300 699 *E-mail:* mail@treves.de *Web Site:* www.treves.de, pg 295

Casa Editrice Luigi Trevisini (Italy) *Tel:* (02) 5450704 *Fax:* (02) 55195782, pg 410

Publicacoes Trevo Lda (Portugal) *Tel:* (01) 9211461 *Fax:* (01) 9217940, pg 530

Lavinia Trevor (United Kingdom) *Tel:* (020) 8749 8481 *Fax:* (020) 8749 7377, pg 1122

Tri-Graphic Printing (Ottawa) Ltd (Canada) *Tel:* 613-731-7441 *Fax:* 613-731-3741, pg 1132

Tri-Graphic Printing (Ottawa) Ltd (Canada) *Tel:* 613-731-7441 *Fax:* 613-731-3741 *Web Site:* www.tri-graphic.com, pg 1154

Tri-Graphic Printing (Ottawa) Ltd (Canada) *Tel:* 613-731-7441 *Fax:* 613-731-3741, pg 1194

Livraria Triangulo Ltda (Brazil) *Tel:* (011) 2550665; (011) 2310922; (011) 2310362; (011) 2310552 *Fax:* (011) 2310162, pg 1278

Trias-Thieme, Hippokrates Enke (Germany) *Tel:* (0711) 8931-0 *Fax:* (0711) 8931-28 *Web Site:* www.thieme.de, pg 295

Tribhuvan University Central Library (Nepal) *Tel:* (01) 331317 *Fax:* (01) 226964, pg 1486

Editions du Tricorne (Switzerland) *Tel:* (022) 7388366 *Fax:* (022) 7319749 *E-mail:* tricorne@freesurf.ch *Web Site:* tricorne.org, pg 626

Trigon Press (United Kingdom) *Tel:* (0181) 7780534 *Fax:* (0181) 7767525 *E-mail:* trigon@easynet.co.uk, pg 750

Ediciones Trilce (Uruguay) *Tel:* (02) 427722; (02) 427662 *Fax:* (02) 427662 *E-mail:* trilce@adinet.com.uy, pg 761

Editorial Trillas SA de CV (Mexico) *Tel:* (05) 6884233 *Fax:* (05) 6579235, pg 467

Library Association of Trinidad & Tobago (Trinidad & Tobago) *Tel:* (0868) 687 0194, pg 1524

Trinity College Library (United Kingdom) *Tel:* (01223) 338488 *Fax:* (01223) 338532, pg 1507

Trinity College Library Dublin (Ireland) *Tel:* (01) 608 1665 *Fax:* (01) 608 3774 *Web Site:* www.tcd.ie/library, pg 1476

Triom Centro de Estudos Marina e Martin Hawey Editorial e Comercial Ltda (Brazil) *Tel:* (011) 3168-8380 *Fax:* (011) 3845-0966 *E-mail:* info@triom.com.br *Web Site:* www.triom.com.br, pg 92

N M Tripathi Pvt Ltd (India) *Tel:* (022) 2013651; (022) 2050048, pg 352, 1290

Il Tripode Srl (Italy) *Tel:* (081) 7613086 *Fax:* (081) 681267, pg 410

Ediciones Tripode (Venezuela) *Tel:* (02) 2378860; (02) 2378972 *Fax:* (02) 2377697, pg 763

Trito Edicions, SL (Spain) *Tel:* (093) 342 61 75 *Fax:* (093) 302 26 70 *E-mail:* trito@bcn.servicom.es *Web Site:* www.trito.es, pg 593

Editorial Trivium, SA (Spain) *Tel:* (091) 5422388 *Fax:* (091) 5422862, pg 593

Trix Corporation Sdn Bhd (Malaysia) *Tel:* (03) 2532019 *Fax:* (03) 2551068, pg 455

Trizonia (Czech Republic) *Tel:* (02) 6515016 *Fax:* (02) 6515016, pg 128

La Trobe University Bookshop (Australia) *Tel:* (03) 4792969 *Fax:* (03) 470-2011, pg 1273

La Trobe University Press (Australia) *Tel:* (03) 9479 1111 *Fax:* (03) 94702011 *Web Site:* www.latrobe.edu.au/bundoora/contact.html, pg 45

Troika (United Kingdom) *Tel:* (020) 7619 0800 *Fax:* (020) 7619 0801, pg 1323

Editions des Trois Collines Francois Lachenal (Switzerland) *Tel:* (022) 7561309 *Fax:* (022) 7561302, pg 626

Editions Trois Fontaines (France) *Tel:* (04) 74981754 *Fax:* (04) 74981812, pg 188

Troll Books of Australia (Australia) *Tel:* (02) 417 2699 *Fax:* (02) 417 1599, pg 45

Marco Tropea Editore (Italy) *Tel:* (02) 29403460 *Fax:* (02) 29513061 *E-mail:* info@saggiatore.it, pg 410

Tropical Press Sdn Bhd (Malaysia) *Tel:* (03) 22825138; (03) 22825338 *Fax:* (03) 22823526 *E-mail:* feedback@tpress.po.my, pg 455

Tropicana Press (Australia) *Tel:* (02) 9543-7728 *Fax:* (02) 732161344 *E-mail:* infoeis@ozemail.com.au, pg 45

Tropos Zois (Greece) *Tel:* (01) 6840156 *Fax:* (01) 6858851 *Web Site:* www.book.culture.gr/tropos-zois, pg 315

Editorial Troquel SA (Argentina) *Tel:* (011) 4308-3638; (011) 4308-3637 *Fax:* (011) 4941-3110 *E-mail:* troquel@ba.net *Web Site:* www.troquel.com.ar, pg 9

Trotman Publishing (United Kingdom) *Tel:* (020) 8486 1150 *Fax:* (020) 8486 1161 *E-mail:* sales@trotman.demon.co.uk *Web Site:* www.careers-portal.co.uk/trotmanpublishing, pg 750

Trotta SA Editorial (Spain) *Tel:* (091) 5430361 *Fax:* (091) 5431488 *E-mail:* trotta@infornet.es *Web Site:* www.trotta.es, pg 593

John Trotter Books (United Kingdom) *Tel:* (020) 8349 9484 *Fax:* (020) 8346 7430, pg 1323

Trotzdem-Verlags Genossenschaft eG (Germany) *Tel:* (07033) 44273 *Fax:* (07033) 45264 *E-mail:* trotzdemusf@t-online.e *Web Site:* www.txt.de/trotzdem, pg 295

Troubadour Press (Australia) *Tel:* (08) 2704003 *Fax:* (08) 2704003, pg 45

Mario Truant Verlag (Germany) *Tel:* (06131) 961660 *Fax:* (06131) 961670 *E-mail:* viva@truant.com *Web Site:* www.truant.com, pg 295

Trud - Izd kasta (Bulgaria) *Tel:* (02) 9814110 *Fax:* (02) 467565 *E-mail:* kktrud@netel.bg *Web Site:* www.trud.bg, pg 98

Harry S Truman Research Institute for the Advancement for Jerusalem (Israel) *Tel:* (02) 58823000; (02) 58823001; (02) 5882315 *Fax:* (02) 5828076 *E-mail:* mstruman@pluto.mscc.huji.ac.il *Web Site:* atar.mscc.huji.ac.il/~truman, pg 373

Trumpet Publishers (Pvt) Ltd (Sri Lanka) *Tel:* (01) 563598; (01) 573208; (01) 547622 *Fax:* (01) 565778, pg 598

Trung-Tam San Xuat Hoc-Lieu (Viet Nam), pg 763

Tryckeriforlaget AB (Sweden) *Tel:* (08) 7567445 *Fax:* (08) 7560395 *E-mail:* tidkort@tidkort.se, pg 607

Tsileondriaka Edition (Madagascar) *Tel:* (02) 31033; (02) 30659 *Fax:* (02) 31033, pg 450

Tsinghua University Press (China) *Tel:* (010) 62783132 *Fax:* (010) 62770278 *E-mail:* right-tup@mail.tsinghua.edu.cn, pg 110

Tsipika Edition (Madagascar) *Tel:* (02) 24595, pg 450

Tsukiji Shokan Publishing Co (Japan) *Tel:* (03) 35423731 *Fax:* (03) 35415799, pg 428

Tuba Press (United Kingdom) *Tel:* (01285) 760424 *Fax:* (01285) 760766, pg 750

Tuckwell Press Ltd (United Kingdom) *Tel:* (01620) 860 164 *Fax:* (01620) 860 164 *E-mail:* customerservices@tuckwellpress.co.uk *Web Site:* www.tuckwellpress.co.uk, pg 750

Sarospataki Reformatus- Kollegium Tudomanyos Gyuejtemenyei Nagykoenyvtar (Hungary) *Tel:* 4111057, pg 1472

Tudor Australia Press (Australia) *Tel:* (08) 8332-8884, pg 45

Tuduv Verlagsgesellschaft mbH (Germany) *Tel:* (089) 280 90 95 *Fax:* (089) 280 95 28 *E-mail:* vvf-verlag@t-online.de; tuduv@t-online.de *Web Site:* www.tuduv.de, pg 295

Tuebinger Vereinigung fur Volkskunde eV (TVV) (Germany) *Tel:* (07071) 295449; (07071) 2972374 (Orders) *Fax:* (07071) 295330 *E-mail:* info@tvv-verlag.de *Web Site:* www.tvv-verlag.de, pg 295

Tuerdok (Turkish Scientific and Technical Documentation Centre) (Turkey) *Tel:* (0312) 468-53-00; (0312) 4673657 *Fax:* (0312) 4277489, pg 1504

Tuerk Editoerler Dernegi (Turkey) *Tel:* (0212) 5125602 *Fax:* (0212) 5117794, pg 1263

Tuerk Kueuephaneciler Dernegi (Turkey) *Tel:* (0312) 2301325 *Fax:* (0312) 2320453, pg 1524

TUeV-Verlag GmbH (Germany) *Tel:* (0221) 806-3535 *Fax:* (0221) 806-3510 *E-mail:* tuev-verlag@de.tuv.com *Web Site:* www.tuev-verlag.de; www.qm-aktuell.de, pg 295

Tun Razak Library (Malaysia) *Tel:* (05) 508073, pg 1483

Library Tun Seri Lanang, Universiti Kebangsaan Malaysia (Malaysia) *Tel:* (03) 8250001 *Fax:* (03) 8256484 *E-mail:* norsham@pkrisc.cc.ukm.my, pg 1483

Libreria Tuncho Granados G (Guatemala) *Tel:* (02) 24736; (02) 27269; (02) 21181, pg 1287

Societe Tunisienne de Diffusion (Tunisia) *Tel:* (01) 255000; (01) 261799, pg 638

Ediciones Jose Porrua Turanzas SA (Spain) *Tel:* (091) 7021493 *Fax:* (091) 7021538 *E-mail:* info@porrualibros.com *Web Site:* www.porrualibros.com, pg 593

Turinta-Turismo Internacional (Portugal) *Tel:* (01) 4870602 *Fax:* (01) 4872099 *E-mail:* turinta@mail.telepac.pt, pg 530

Turisticka Stampa (Yugoslavia) *Tel:* (011) 750740; (011) 767466 *Fax:* (011) 762236, pg 766

Turkischer Schulbuchverlag Onel Cengiz (Germany) *Tel:* (0221) 5879084; (0221) 5879085 *Fax:* (0221) 488093; (0221) 5879004, pg 295

Cyprus Turkish Public Library (Cyprus) *Tel:* (02) 83257, pg 1460

Turkish Republic - Ministry of Culture (Turkey) *Tel:* (0312) 232 19 66; (0312) 231 54 50 *Fax:* (0312) 231 50 36 *E-mail:* yayimlar@kutuphanelergm.gov.tr *Web Site:* www.kultur.gov.tr, pg 641

Izdatelstvo Turkmenistan (Turkmenistan) *Tel:* (03632) 294275, pg 642

Turm-Verlag Lorber-Verlag Otto Zluhan OHG (Germany) *Tel:* (07142) 940843 *Fax:* (07142) 940844, pg 295

Turnaround Publisher Services (United Kingdom) *Tel:* (020) 8829 3009 *Fax:* (020) 8881 5088 *E-mail:* turnuk@aol.com, pg 1224

Turnaround Publisher Services (United Kingdom) *Tel:* (020) 8829 3009 *Fax:* (020) 8881 5088 *E-mail:* info@turnaround-uk.com *Web Site:* www.turnaround-uk.com, pg 1323

Turnaround Publisher Services Ltd (United Kingdom) *Tel:* (020) 8829 3009 *Fax:* (020) 8881 5088 *E-mail:* sales@turnaround-uk.com, pg 1122

Alexander Turnbull Library (New Zealand) *Tel:* (04) 4743000 *Fax:* (04) 4743063 *E-mail:* atl@natlib.govt.nz, pg 1487

Jane Turnbull (United Kingdom) *Tel:* (020) 8743 9580 *Fax:* (020) 8749 6079 *E-mail:* agents@cwcom.net, pg 1122

Turner Memorial Library (Zimbabwe) *Tel:* (0120) 63412 *Fax:* (0120) 61002, pg 1509

Turner Publicaciones (Spain) *Tel:* (091) 308 33 36 *Fax:* (091) 319 39 30 *Web Site:* www.turnerlibros.com, pg 593

Turpin Distribution Services Ltd (United Kingdom) *Tel:* (01462) 672555 *Fax:* (01462) 480947 *Web Site:* www.turpin-distribution.com; www.turpinbooks.com (online bookshop), pg 1323

Turris (Italy) *Tel:* (0372) 23845 *Fax:* (0372) 413084, pg 410

Tursen, SA (Spain) *Tel:* (091) 3667148 *Fax:* (091) 3653148, pg 593

Turton & Armstrong Publishers Pty Ltd (Australia) *Tel:* (02) 9489-6719 *Fax:* (02) 9489-6719 *E-mail:* turtarm@attglobal.net, pg 45

Turun Yliopiston Kirjasto (Finland) *Tel:* (02) 3336163 *Fax:* (02) 3335050 *E-mail:* annales@utu.fi, pg 1464

Turun Kansallinen Kirjakauppa Oy (Finland) *Tel:* (0921) 2502444 *Fax:* (0921) 2519348, pg 1283

Edition Tusch (Austria) *Tel:* (01) 484 53 30 *Fax:* (01) 484 53 30, pg 59

Tusquets Editores (Spain) *Tel:* (093) 2530400 *Fax:* (093) 4176703; (093) 4188698 (Rights & Editing) *E-mail:* general@tusquets-editores.es *Web Site:* www.tusquets-editores.com, pg 593

Ediciones Tutor SA (Spain) *Tel:* (091) 543 21 72 *Fax:* (091) 549 96 53 *E-mail:* tutor@autovia.com, pg 594

Charles E Tuttle Publishing Co Inc (Japan) *Tel:* (03) 5437 0171 *Fax:* (03) 5437 0755 *E-mail:* tuttle@gol.com, pg 428

Charles E Tuttle Publishing Co Inc (Japan) *Tel:* (03) 5437 0171 *Fax:* (03) 56894927, pg 1295

Tuttle-Mori Agency Inc (Japan) *Tel:* (03) 3230-4081 *Fax:* (03) 3234-5249, pg 1114

Tuum (Estonia) *Tel:* (02) 442272; (02) 6313374 *Fax:* (02) 446832, pg 141

Twente University Press (Netherlands) *Tel:* (053) 4893049 *Fax:* (053) 4892991 *E-mail:* tup@utwente.nl *Web Site:* www.utwente.nl/tupress, pg 485

Twenty-First Century Publishers, Inc (Republic of Korea) *Tel:* (032) 429-9411 *Fax:* (032) 4299418, pg 440

Editions 24 Heures (Switzerland) *Tel:* (021) 349500 *Fax:* (021) 3494224, pg 626

Ediciones 29 - Libros Rio Nuevo (Spain) *Tel:* (093) 675 41 35 *Fax:* (093) 590 04 40 *E-mail:* ediciones29@comunired.com *Web Site:* www.ediciones29.com, pg 594

Twin Guinep Ltd (Jamaica) *Tel:* (876) 944-4624 *Fax:* (876) 944-4324, pg 413

Two-Can Publishing Ltd (United Kingdom) *Tel:* (020) 7224 2440 *Fax:* (020) 7224 7005 *E-mail:* helpline@two-canpublishing.com *Web Site:* www.two-canpublishing.com, pg 750

Editorial Txertoa (Spain) *Tel:* (0943) 45 97 57; (0943) 46 09 41 *Fax:* (0943) 46 09 41 *E-mail:* txertoa@nexo.es, pg 594

Typos (Greece) *Tel:* (01) 3819083; (01) 3819085; (01) 3619083 *Fax:* (01) 3825012, pg 315

Typotex Kft Elektronikus Kiado (Hungary) *Tel:* (01) 2013317 *Fax:* (01) 3163759 *E-mail:* typotex@euroweb.hu *Web Site:* www.vision.euroweb.hu/typotex, pg 327

Tyrolia Verlagsanstalt GmbH (Austria) *Tel:* (0512) 2233-0 *Fax:* (0512) 2233-501 *E-mail:* tyrolia@tyrolia.at *Web Site:* www.tyrolia.at, pg 59

Tyrolia Verlagsanstalt GmbH (Austria) *Tel:* (0512) 2233-0 *Fax:* (0512) 2233-501, pg 1275

Tysk Bogimport ApS (Denmark) *Tel:* 33136016; 33136097 *Fax:* 33142021, pg 1281

Tyto Alba Publishers (Lithuania) *Tel:* (02) 498602 *Fax:* (02) 498602 *E-mail:* tytoalba@taide.lt *Web Site:* www.tytoalba.lt, pg 446

UBS Publishers' Distributors Ltd (United Kingdom) *Tel:* (020) 84508667 *Fax:* (020) 8452 6612 (attn: UBSPD) *E-mail:* ubspd@gobookshopping.com *Web Site:* www.gobookshopping.com, pg 1323

UBS Publishers Distributors Ltd (India) *Tel:* (011) 273601; (011) 3266646 *Fax:* (011) 3276593; (011) 3274261 *E-mail:* ubspddel@del3.vsnl.net.in *Web Site:* www.ubspd.com, pg 352

UBS Publishers' Distributors Pvt Ltd (India) *Tel:* (011) 3273601; (011) 3266645 *Fax:* (011) 3276593; (011) 3274261 *E-mail:* ubspd@ubspd.com *Web Site:* www.gobookshopping.com, pg 1290

Edizioni Ubulibri SAS (Italy) *Tel:* (02) 9404372 *Fax:* (02) 9510265 *E-mail:* ubulibri@libero.it, pg 410

UCA Editores (El Salvador) *Tel:* 234491 *Fax:* 733556, pg 139

Libreria UCA (El Salvador) *Tel:* 240011 (ext 193); 234491 *Fax:* 2731010, pg 1282

UCL Press Ltd (United Kingdom) *Tel:* (020) 7583 9855 *Fax:* (020) 7842 2298 *E-mail:* info@tandf.co.uk *Web Site:* www.tandf.co.uk, pg 751

Universitas Udayana Library (Indonesia) *Tel:* (0361) 71854 ext 151; (0361) 701139 *Fax:* (0361) 71607; (0361) 701907, pg 1474

Verlag Carl Ueberreuter GmbH (Austria) *Tel:* (01) 40 444-0 *Fax:* (01) 40 444-5 *E-mail:* goeller@ueberreuter.at *Web Site:* www.ueberreuter.de, pg 59

Wirtschaftsverlag Carl Ueberreuter (Germany) *Tel:* (069) 58 09 05-0 *Fax:* (069) 58 09 05-10 *E-mail:* info@ueberreuter.de *Web Site:* www.redline-wirtschaft.de, pg 295

Uebersetzergemeinschaft Interessengemeinschaft von Uebersetzerinnen und Uebersetzern literarischer und wissenschaftlicher Werke (Austria) *Tel:* (01) 526204418 *Fax:* (01) 526204430 *E-mail:* ueg@literaturhaus.at *Web Site:* www.translators.at, pg 1125

UGA Editions (Uitgeverij) (Belgium) *Tel:* (056) 363200 *Fax:* (056) 356096 *E-mail:* publ@uga.be *Web Site:* www.uga.be, pg 74

Uganda Library Association (Uganda) *Tel:* (0141) 285001 ext 4, pg 1524

Uganda Bookshop (Uganda) *Tel:* (041) 243756 *Fax:* (041) 245597, pg 1315

Uganda Polytechnic Library at Uganda Technical College (Uganda) *Tel:* (041) 285211 *Fax:* (041) 222643, pg 1505

Uganda Publishers and Booksellers Association (Uganda) *Tel:* (041) 259163; (041) 251112 *Fax:* (041) 251160, pg 1263

Uglan Islenski Kiljuklubburinn (Iceland) *Tel:* 5102525, pg 1229

Evzen Uher, Musikverlag UHER (Czech Republic) *Tel:* (0632) 40376, pg 129

Verlag Dr Alfons Uhl (Germany) *Tel:* (09081) 87248 *Fax:* (09081) 23710, pg 295

Uitgeverij De Garve (Belgium) *Tel:* (050) 400050 *Fax:* (050) 388099 *E-mail:* info@degarve.be *Web Site:* www.degarve.be, pg 75

Uitgevery Scoop Infotex NV (Belgium) *Tel:* (02) 4672495 *Fax:* (02) 4669351 *E-mail:* scoop@infotex.be, pg 75

UK International Standard Book Numbering Agency Ltd (United Kingdom) *Tel:* (01252) 742590 *Fax:* (01252) 742526 *E-mail:* isbn@whitaker.co.uk *Web Site:* www.whitaker.co.uk/isbn.htm, pg 1268

UK Serials Group-UKSG (United Kingdom) *Tel:* (01635) 254292 *Fax:* (01635) 253826 *E-mail:* uksg.admin@dial.pipex.com *Web Site:* www.uksg.org, pg 1142

Ulisse Edition (France) *Tel:* (01) 48 78 40 74 *Fax:* (01) 48 78 40 77, pg 188

Editora Ulisseia Lda (Portugal) *Tel:* (021) 734300; (021) 763467 *Fax:* (021) 56239, pg 530

Ullstein Heyne List GmbH & Co KG (Germany) *Tel:* (089) 5148-0 *Fax:* (089) 5148-2229 *Web Site:* www.ullstein.de, pg 295

Universitat Ulm (Germany) *Tel:* (0731) 502-01 *Fax:* (0731) 5022038, pg 1469

Guenter Albert Ulmer Verlag (Germany) *Tel:* (07464) 98740 *Fax:* (07464) 3054 *E-mail:* info@umlertuningen.de *Web Site:* www.ulmertuningern.de, pg 295

Verlag Eugen Ulmer GmbH & Co (Germany) *Tel:* (0711) 4507-0 *Fax:* (0711) 4507-120; (0711) 4507-185; (0711) 4507-214; (0711) 4507-207 *E-mail:* info@ulmer.de *Web Site:* www.ulmer.de, pg 295

Werner Ulmer & Co (Switzerland) *Tel:* (033) 432220 *Fax:* (033) 434848, pg 626

Ulrich Schiefer bahnVerlag (Germany) *Tel:* (089) 89020999 *Fax:* (089) 89020087, pg 296

Ulrico Hoepli - Libreria Internazionale (Italy) *Tel:* (02) 864871 *Fax:* (02) 8052886, pg 1294

Ulrike Helmer Verlag (Germany) *Tel:* (06174) 93 60 60; (06174) 93 60 61 *Fax:* (06174) 93 60 65; (06174) 93 60 61 *E-mail:* info@ulrike-helmer-verlag.de *Web Site:* www.ulrike-helmer-verlag.de, pg 296

Ulster Historical Foundation (United Kingdom) *Tel:* (02890) 332288 *Fax:* (02890) 239885 *E-mail:* enquiry@uhf.org.uk *Web Site:* www.ancestryireland.com, pg 751

Ultragraphics (Ireland) *Tel:* (01) 4599133 *Fax:* (01) 4512368, pg 1157, 1198

Ultramar Editores SA (Spain) *Tel:* (093) 8410351 *Fax:* (093) 8412334 *E-mail:* ultramar@javajan.com, pg 594

Ulverscroft Large Print Books Ltd (United Kingdom) *Tel:* (0116) 236 4325 *Fax:* (0116) 234 0205 *E-mail:* sales@ulverscroft.co.uk *Web Site:* www.ulverscroft.co.uk, pg 751

Editoriale Umbra SAS di Carnevali e (Italy) *Tel:* (0742) 353174 *Fax:* (0742) 351156 *E-mail:* edit.umbra@cline.it *Web Site:* www.italand.com/eu, pg 410

G Umbreit GmbH & Co KG (Germany) *Tel:* (07142) 5960 *Fax:* (07142) 596199 *E-mail:* edv.bs@umbreit-kg.de, pg 1285

Umea University Library (Sweden) *Tel:* (090) 7865000 *Fax:* (090) 7869626 *E-mail:* www.bibliotekschefen@ub.umu.se *Web Site:* www.ub.umu.se, pg 1501

Umm al Qura University Library (Saudi Arabia) *Tel:* (02) 5564770 *Fax:* (02) 556562, pg 1496

Ummah Press for Translation & Publishing (Egypt (Arab Republic of Egypt)) *Tel:* (03) 378556 *Fax:* (03) 378556, pg 139

Umschau Buchverlag Breidenstein GmbH (Germany) *Tel:* (069) 2600550 *Fax:* (069) 2600559 *E-mail:* umschau-braus@t-online.de, pg 296

Underhallningsbokklubben (Sweden) *Tel:* (08) 6968660 *Fax:* (08) 6968361, pg 1232

Editions Unes (France) *Tel:* (016) 94673158 *Fax:* (016) 94673175, pg 188

Unesco Books and Copyright Division, USBN agency (France) *Tel:* (01) 44412800 *Fax:* (01) 44072033, pg 1245

UNESCO Institute for Education (UIE) (Germany) *Tel:* (040) 4480410 *Fax:* (040) 4107723 *E-mail:* uie@unesco.org *Web Site:* www.unesco.org/education/uie, pg 1246

UNESCO Publishing (France) *Tel:* (01) 45 68 10 00 *Fax:* (01) 45 67 16 90 *Web Site:* www.unesco.org/general/eng/about/address.shtml, pg 188

Unesco Regional Office, Asia & the Pacific (Thailand) *Tel:* (02) 3910577; (02) 3910703; (02) 3910880 *Fax:* (02) 3910866, pg 636

Editora UNESP (Brazil) *Tel:* (011) 3242-7171 *Fax:* (011) 3242-7172 *E-mail:* feu@editora.unesp.br *Web Site:* www.editora.unesp.br, pg 92

Uni-Text Book Co (Malaysia) *Tel:* (03) 7185426, pg 455

Libreria Uniandes (Colombia) *Tel:* (01) 2824066 (ext 2197); (01) 2824066 (ext 2198) *Fax:* (01) 2841890, pg 1280

Uniao dos Escritores Angolanos (UEA) (Angola) *Tel:* (02) 322155, pg 1235

Unichurch Publishing (Australia) *Tel:* (02) 2336399 *Fax:* (02) 9261-5879 *E-mail:* ucb@nsw.uca.org.au, pg 45

Edizioni Unicopli SpA (Italy) *Tel:* (02) 76014680 *Fax:* (02) 76021612, pg 410

Unicorn Books (United Kingdom) *Tel:* (020) 8420 1091 *Fax:* (020) 8428 0125 *Web Site:* www.unicornbooks.co.uk/, pg 751

Unicorn Books Ltd (Hong Kong) *Tel:* 2562-2641; 2561-6151 *Fax:* 2811-1980, pg 322

Unicorn International Printing Co Ltd (Hong Kong) *Tel:* 28980238 *Fax:* 28983812 *E-mail:* unicorn7@netvigator.com, pg 1136, 1197

Unidad Universitaria del Sur (UNISUR) (Colombia) *Tel:* (01) 255 3216; (01) 212 0159; (01) 346 0088 *Fax:* (01) 255 3497 *E-mail:* unisur12@gaitana.interred.net.co, pg 114

Unieboek BV (Netherlands) *Tel:* (030) 6377660 *Fax:* (030) 6377600 *E-mail:* unieboek@worldaccess.nl, pg 485

Uniepers BV (Netherlands) *Tel:* (0294) 285111 *Fax:* (0294) 283013, pg 486

Unigraphics (Pte) Ltd (Sri Lanka) *Tel:* (01) 694538 *Fax:* (01) 693731 *E-mail:* uni.graphics@lanka.ccom.lk, pg 598

UNILINC (Australia) *Tel:* (02) 92831488 *Fax:* (02) 92679247 *E-mail:* rona@unilinc.edu.au *Web Site:* www.unilinc.edu.au, pg 1236

Unimax Macmillan Ltd (Ghana) *Tel:* (021) 227 443; (021) 223 709 *Fax:* (021) 225 215 *E-mail:* info@unimacmillan.com *Web Site:* www.macmillan-africa.com; www.unimacmillan.com, pg 308

Union des Ecrivains Tunisiens (Tunisia) *Tel:* (01) 257591, pg 1369

Union des Libraires de France (ULF) (France) *Tel:* (01) 43298879 *Fax:* (01) 43298879, pg 1245

Ediciones Union (Cuba) *Tel:* (07) 324551; (07) 324252; (07) 324553; (07) 324571 *Fax:* (07) 333158, pg 121

Union Generale d'Editions (France) *Tel:* (01) 44160500 *Fax:* (01) 44160511, pg 188

Union Mundial para la Naturaleza (UICN), Oficina Regional para Mesoamerica (Costa Rica) *Tel:* 356-568; 355-788; 362-733 *Fax:* 409 934 *E-mail:* uicnorma@nicarao.apc.org, pg 117

Union of Translators of Bulgaria, Magazin Panorama (Bulgaria) *Tel:* (02) 655190 *Fax:* (02) 656187, pg 1125

Union of Welsh Publishers & Booksellers (United Kingdom) *Tel:* (1559) 362371 *Fax:* (1559) 363758 *Web Site:* www.wc.org.uk, pg 1268

Union of Writers of the African Peoples (Ghana), pg 1247

Union Press Ltd (Hong Kong) *Tel:* 25673762 *Fax:* 23945084, pg 322

Union-Verlag GmbH (Germany) *Tel:* (089) 4701071 *Fax:* (089) 4701081, pg 296

Unipa A/S (Norway) *Tel:* 55318405 *Fax:* 55324270 *E-mail:* unipa@online.no, pg 1304

Unipress (Italy) *Tel:* (049) 8752542 *Fax:* (049) 8752542, pg 410

Unisa Press (South Africa) *Tel:* (012) 4293549 *Fax:* (012) 4293221 *E-mail:* moolmsj@alpha.unisa.ac.za; kempg@alpha.unisa.ac.za *Web Site:* www.unisa.ac.za/dept/press/index.html, pg 560

Unistad Verspreiding CV (Belgium) *Tel:* (03) 2307725 *Fax:* (03) 2307725, pg 75

Unit Penerbitan Akademik Cancelori~ Universiti Teknologi Malaysia (Malaysia) *Tel:* (07) 576160; (07) 576161; (07) 576162 *Fax:* (07) 5566157, pg 455

Unitas Forlag (Denmark) *Tel:* 36166481 *Fax:* 36160818 *E-mail:* forlag@unitas.dk *Web Site:* www.unitas.dk, pg 136

UNITAS Publishing Co Ltd (Taiwan, Province of China) *Tel:* (02) 27634300 *Fax:* (02) 27567914, pg 632

United Book Distributors (Pty) Ltd (South Africa) *Tel:* 614431, pg 1310

United Book Suppliers (United Kingdom) *Tel:* (01232) 832362 *Fax:* (01232) 848780, pg 1323

United Christian Council Literature Bureau (Sierra Leone) *Tel:* 032462, pg 545

United Nations Library (Switzerland) *Tel:* (022) 9174181 *Fax:* (022) 9170028, pg 1502

United Nations Conference on Trade and Development (UNCTAD) (Switzerland) *Tel:* (022) 9171234; (022) 9071234 *Fax:* (022) 9070057, pg 1261

United Nations Depository Library (Republic of Korea) *Tel:* (02) 3290-1492 *Fax:* (02) 922-4633 *E-mail:* mgc@kulib.korea.ac.kr, pg 1480

United Nations Economic Commission for Africa, ECA (Ethiopia) *Tel:* (01) 517200 *Fax:* (01) 514416, pg 1242

United Nations Economic Commission for Africa Library (Ethiopia) *Tel:* (01) 517200 *Fax:* (01) 514416; (01) 512233 *E-mail:* eca.info@un.org *Web Site:* www.un.org.depts/eca, pg 1463

United Nations Economic Commission for Europe (UNECE) (Switzerland) *Tel:* (022) 917 44 44 *Fax:* (022) 917 05 05 *E-mail:* info.ece@unece.org *Web Site:* www.unece.org, pg 1261

United Nations Educational, Scientific & Cultural Organization (UNESCO) (France) *Tel:* (01) 45 68 1000 *Fax:* 01 45 68 57 39 *Web Site:* www.unesco.org, pg 1245

United Nations Environment Programme (UNEP) (Kenya) *Tel:* (02) 623331 *Fax:* (02) 520711; (02) 623692 *Web Site:* www.unep.org, pg 1251

United Nations Library, Bangkok (Thailand) *Tel:* (02) 2881360 *Fax:* (02) 2881000 *E-mail:* yoo.unescap@un.org; library-escap@un.org, pg 1263

United Nations Publications (United States) *Tel:* 800-983-8302 *Fax:* 212-963-3489 *E-mail:* publications@un.org *Web Site:* www.un.org/pubs/sales.htm, pg 1269

United Nations Research Institute for Social Development (UNRISD) (Switzerland) *Tel:* (022) 917 3020 *Fax:* (022) 917 0650 *E-mail:* info@unrisd.org *Web Site:* www.unrisd.org, pg 1261

United Nations University Press (Japan) *Tel:* (03) 4992811 *Fax:* (03) 34067345, pg 428

United Publishers Services Ltd (Japan) *Tel:* (03) 3291-4541 *Fax:* (03) 3292-8610 *E-mail:* general@ups.co.jp, pg 1295

United States Information Service Library (Sierra Leone) *Tel:* 226481 *Fax:* 225471, pg 1496

United Theological College of the West Indies (Jamaica) *Tel:* (876) 927-2868 *Fax:* (876) 977-0812 *E-mail:* unitheol@cwjamaica.com *Web Site:* www.utcwi.edu.jm, pg 1478

United Writers Publications Ltd (United Kingdom) *Tel:* (01736) 365 954 *Fax:* (01736) 365954 *E-mail:* info@unitedwriters.co.uk, pg 751

Uniting Education (Australia) *Tel:* (03) 9416 4262 *Fax:* (03) 9416 4264 *E-mail:* contact@unitinged.org.au *Web Site:* www.unitinged.org.au, pg 45

Unity Books Lt (New Zealand) *Tel:* (04) 499 4245 *Fax:* (04) 499 4246 *E-mail:* unity.books@clear.net.n2, pg 1302

Unity Press (Australia) *Tel:* (02) 4671342 *Fax:* (02) 9736-2663, pg 46

Unity Publishing & Research Company Ltd (Nigeria) *Tel:* (01) 881504, pg 502

Uniunea Scriitorilor din Romania (Romania) *Tel:* (00) 6507245 *Fax:* (00) 3129634, pg 1257

Editura Univers (Romania) *Tel:* (01) 2226629 *Fax:* (01) 2225652, pg 536

Universal Edition AG (Austria) *Tel:* (01) 337 23-0 *Fax:* (01) 337 23-400 *E-mail:* office@universaledition.com *Web Site:* www.universaledition.com, pg 60

Universal Academy Press, Inc (Japan) *Tel:* (03) 3813 7232 *Fax:* (03) 38135932 *E-mail:* general@uap.co.jp, pg 428

Universal Book Shop (India) *Tel:* (0532) 603012, pg 1290

Universal Book Traders (India) *Tel:* (011) 221966; (011) 741101 *Fax:* (011) 2924152; (011) 7459023, pg 1290

Universal Business Directories, Australia Pty Ltd (Australia) *Tel:* (02) 8881877 *Fax:* (09) 6307505, pg 46

Universal Dalsi (Romania) *Tel:* (01) 4103552; (01) 337 1682 *Fax:* (01) 4121658, pg 536

Libreria Universal (Guatemala) *Tel:* (02) 28484, pg 1287

Universal Postal Union (UPU) (Switzerland) *Tel:* (031) 3503111 *Fax:* (031) 3503110 *E-mail:* info@upu.int *Web Site:* www.upu.int, pg 1262

Universal Press Pty Ltd (Australia) *Tel:* (02) 9857 3700 *Toll Free Tel:* 800 021 987 *Fax:* (02) 9888 9074 *Toll Free Fax:* 800 636 197, pg 46

Universal Publications Agency Press (Republic of Korea) *Tel:* (02) 328175 *Fax:* (02) 328176, pg 440, 1114, 1297

Universidad Autonoma - Biblioteca Universitaria (Spain) *Tel:* (091) 3974399 *Fax:* (091) 3975058 *Web Site:* www.uam.es, pg 1499

Biblioteca de la Universidad Autonoma de Santo Domingo (Dominican Republic), pg 1461

Universidad Autonoma Tomas Frias, Div de Extension Universitaria (Bolivia) *Tel:* (062) 273-28; (062) 273-00 *Fax:* (062) 266-63; (062) 231-96 *E-mail:* rector@rect.nrp.edu.bo *Web Site:* www.unam.mx/udal/afiliacion/frias.htm, pg 76

Universidad Boliviana Tomas Frias, Departmento de Bibliotecas (Bolivia) *Tel:* (062) 27313, pg 1454

Biblioteca de la Universidad Catolica de Valparaiso (Chile) *Tel:* (032) 273261 *Fax:* (032) 273183, pg 1457

Biblioteca de la Universidad Central de Ecuador (Ecuador) *Tel:* (02) 524714, pg 1462

Universidad Central de la Villas, Centro Documentacion e Informacion Cientifica Tecnica (Cuba) *Tel:* (07) 81419, pg 121

Biblioteca General de la Universidad Central de las Villas (Cuba) *Tel:* 81178 *Fax:* 81682; 81608 *E-mail:* ucludri@ucentral.quantum.inf.cu, pg 1459

Biblioteca Central de la Universidad Central de Venezuela (Venezuela) *Tel:* (02) 6628427 *Fax:* (02) 6622486, pg 1508

Universidad Central del Ecuador, Departamento de Publicaciones (Ecuador) *Tel:* (02) 226080 *Fax:* (02) 501207, pg 137

Biblioteca de la Universidad Centroamericana 'Jose Simeon Canas' (El Salvador) *Tel:* 2734400 *Fax:* 2731010 *E-mail:* ucabib.director@bib.uca.edu.sv, pg 1462

Universidad Centroamericana (Nicaragua) *Tel:* (02) 773026 *Fax:* (02) 670106 *E-mail:* ucanic@nicarao.apc.org, pg 1488

Biblioteca de la Universidad Complutense (Spain) *Tel:* (091) 5490256 *Fax:* (091) 3943437, pg 1499

Universidad de Cantabria Biblioteca (Spain) *Tel:* (042) 201180 *Fax:* (042) 201183, pg 1499

Universidad de los Andes, Biblioteca General, Ramon de Zubiria (Colombia) *Tel:* (01) 2866309; (01) 3520466 *Fax:* (01) 2860489; (01) 2841890 *E-mail:* secgral@uniandes.edu.ca, pg 1458

Universidad de los Andes, Consejo de Publicaciones (Venezuela) *Tel:* (074) 402409; (074) 402408 *Fax:* (074) 711955, pg 763

Servicios Bibliotecarios Universidad de los Andes (Serbiula) (Venezuela) *Tel:* (0274) 2402731; (0274) 2402729 *Fax:* (0274) 2402507; (0274) 2402748 *E-mail:* adquisi@serbi.ula.ve *Web Site:* www.serbi.ula.ve, pg 1508

Universidad de Antioquia, Escuela Interamericana de Bibliotecologia, Biblioteca (Colombia) *Tel:* (04) 2105140 *Fax:* (04) 2116939, pg 1458

YELLOW PAGES

Universidad de Antioquia, Division Publicaciones (Colombia) *Tel:* (0574) 210 50 10 *Fax:* (0574) 210 50 12 *E-mail:* direccion@editorialudea.com; comunicaciones@editorialudea.com *Web Site:* www.editorialudea.com, pg 114

Universidad de Buenos Aires, Sistema de Bibliotecas y de Informacion (Argentina) *Tel:* (011) 9511366 *Fax:* (011) 9526557 *E-mail:* postmaster@sisbi.uba.ar, pg 1450

Biblioteca Central de la Universidad de Chile (Chile) *Tel:* (02) 717997, pg 1457

Universidad de Concepcion Direccion de Bibliotecas (Chile) *Tel:* (041) 234985 *Fax:* (041) 244796, pg 1457

Universidad de Costa Rica Sistema de Bibliotecas, Documentacion e Informacion (Costa Rica) *Tel:* 2536152; 2535323 *Fax:* 234809; 2074163; 230452 *E-mail:* mazamora@sibdi.bldt.ucr.ac.cr, pg 1458

Editorial de la Universidad de Costa Rica (Costa Rica) *Tel:* 207-5853 *Fax:* 207-5257 *Web Site:* www.vinv.ucr.ac.cr, pg 117

Biblioteca Central de la Universidad de El Salvador (El Salvador) *Tel:* 2250278 *Fax:* 2250278 *E-mail:* sb@biblio.ues.edu.sv, pg 1462

Universidad de Granada (Spain) *Tel:* (0958) 243932 *Fax:* (0958) 243931, pg 594

Biblioteca General, Universidad de Guayaquil (Ecuador) *Tel:* (04) 282440 *Fax:* (04) 329905, pg 1462

Ediciones de la Universidad de la Frontera (Chile) *Tel:* (045) 325000 *Fax:* (045) 325950, pg 101

Universidad de la Habana, Direccion de Informacion Cientifica y Tecnica (Cuba) *Tel:* (07) 333768 *Fax:* (07) 325774, pg 1459

Universidad de Las Palmas de Gran Canaria, Escuela Universitaria de Informatica (ULPGC) (Spain) *Tel:* (0928) 45-87-19; (0928) 45-87-00 *Fax:* (0928) 45-87-11 *E-mail:* organizacion@sinf.ulpgc.es *Web Site:* www5.ulpgc.es, pg 594

Universidad de Lima-Fondo de Desarollo Editorial (Peru) *Tel:* (01) 4376767 *Fax:* (01) 437-8066; (01) 435-6552 *E-mail:* fondo_ed@lima.edu.pe *Web Site:* www.ulima.edu.pe, pg 512

Universidad de los Andes Editorial (Colombia) *Tel:* (01) 2824066 (ext 2717-2713) *Fax:* (01) 2841890; (01) 2815771, pg 114

Universidad de Malaga (Spain) *Tel:* (095) 213 29 17 *Fax:* (095) 213 29 18 *E-mail:* spicum@uma.es *Web Site:* www.uma.es, pg 594

Universidad de Navarra, Ediciones SA (Spain) *Tel:* (0948) 256850 *Fax:* (0948) 256854 *E-mail:* eunsa@cin.es *Web Site:* www.eunsa.es, pg 594

Universidad de Oviedo Servicio de Publicaciones (Spain) *Tel:* (0985) 210160; (0985) 222428 *Fax:* (0985) 218352 *Web Site:* www.uniovi.es, pg 594

Universidad de Panama, Biblioteca Interamericana Simon Bolivar (Panama) *Tel:* 2636133, pg 1490

Universidad de Puerto Rico-Recinto de Rio Piedras (Puerto Rico) *Tel:* (787) 764-0000; (787) 763-3930 *Fax:* (787) 764-2250, pg 1308

Ediciones Universidad de Salamanca (Spain) *Tel:* (0923) 294598 *Fax:* (0923) 262579 *E-mail:* eus@usal.es *Web Site:* www3.usal.es, pg 594

Biblioteca Central de la Universidad de San Carlos (Guatemala) *Tel:* (02) 767117, pg 1471

Universidad de Sevilla Secretariado de Publicaciones (Spain) *Tel:* (05) 487444; (05) 487442 *Fax:* (095) 487 7443 *Web Site:* publius.cica.es, pg 594

Universidad de Valladolid Secretariado de Publicaciones e Intercambio Editorial (Spain) *Tel:* (0983) 187810 *Fax:* (0983) 187812 *E-mail:* spie@uva.es *Web Site:* www.uva.es, pg 594

Biblioteca Central de la Universidad de Zulia (Venezuela) *Tel:* (061) 515390, pg 1508

Universidad del Pacifico Libreria (Peru) *Tel:* (014) 712277 *Fax:* (01) 2650958 *E-mail:* dri@up.edu.pe, pg 1491

Biblioteca Central, Universidad del Salvador (Argentina) *Tel:* (011) 400422; (011) 3710422 *E-mail:* uds-bibl@salvador.edu.ar, pg 1450

Editorial Universidad SRL (Argentina) *Tel:* (011) 4382-9022; (011) 4382-6850 *Fax:* (011) 4381-2005 *E-mail:* univers@nat.com.ar *Web Site:* www.nat.com.ar/universidad, pg 9

Editorial Universidad Estatal a Distancia (EUNED) (Costa Rica) *Tel:* 234-7954; 253-2121 ext 2440 *Fax:* 234-9138 *E-mail:* editoria@uned.ac.cr *Web Site:* www.uned.ac.cr, pg 117

Biblioteca de la Universidad Iberoamericana (Mexico) *Tel:* (05) 2923508; (05) 2674249 *Fax:* (05) 2923008; (05) 2922838; (05) 2674249; (05) 2674000 (ext 47-05), pg 1485

Biblioteca Central de la Universidad Mayor de San Andres (Bolivia) *Tel:* (02) 25568, pg 1454

Universidad Mayor de San Andres, Editorial Universitaria (Bolivia) *Tel:* (02) 359490 *Fax:* (02) 359491, pg 76

Biblioteca Central de la Universidad Mayor de San Francisco Xavier (Bolivia), pg 1454

Universidad Nacional Autonoma de Mexico (National University of Mexico) (Mexico) *Tel:* (05) 6650584 *Fax:* (05) 5507428 *Web Site:* www.serpientedgsca.unm.mx, pg 467

Universidad Nacional Centro Editorial (Colombia) *Tel:* (01) 2448640, pg 114

Universidad Nacional de Colombia, Biblioteca Central (Colombia) *Tel:* (01) 2691743 *E-mail:* refer@biblioteca.campus.unal.edu.co, pg 1458

Biblioteca Mayor de la Universidad Nacional de Cordoba (Argentina) *Tel:* (351) 4331072 *Fax:* (351) 4331079 *E-mail:* cendoc@sri.hejo.unc.edu.ar *Web Site:* www.bmayor.unc.edu.ar, pg 1450

Biblioteca de la Universidad Nacional de La Plata (Argentina) *Tel:* (021) 25-5004 *Fax:* (021) 255004 *E-mail:* bulap@cespivm2.bitnet, pg 1450

Universidad Nacional del Litoral (Argentina) *Tel:* (042) 571110 *E-mail:* deopint@unl.edu.ar, pg 1450

Editorial Universidad Nacional (EUNA) (Costa Rica) *Tel:* 277-3204; 277-3825 *Fax:* 277-3204 *E-mail:* editoria@una.ac.cr, pg 117

Universidad Nacional Mayor de San Marcos (Peru) *Tel:* (01) 4314629, pg 512

Libreria y Distribuidora de la Universidad Nacional Mayor de San Marcos (Peru) *Tel:* (014) 640560 *Fax:* (014) 640560, pg 1305

Universidad Nacional San Antonio Abad del Cusco (Peru) *Tel:* (084) 222271; (084) 224303, pg 1491

Universidad para la Paz (Costa Rica) *Tel:* 249-1072; 249-1511 ext 20 *Fax:* 249-1929 *E-mail:* upazrena@sol.racsa.co.cr, pg 117

Universidad Pontificia de Salamanca, Biblioteca (Spain) *Tel:* (0923) 277118 *Fax:* (0923) 277118 *E-mail:* bibliotecaio.general@upsa.es *Web Site:* www.upsa.es/biblioteca.html, pg 1499

Universidad Veracruzana Direccion General Editorial y de Publicaciones (Mexico) *Tel:* (029) 28 71316 *Fax:* (029) 28 17 44 35 *E-mail:* direditaspeedy@coacade.uv.mx, pg 468

Universidade de Brasilia, Biblioteca Central (Brazil) *Tel:* (061) 2742412, pg 1455

Editora Universidade de Brasilia (Brazil) *Tel:* (061) 226 6874 *Fax:* (061) 225 5611 *E-mail:* editora@unb.br *Web Site:* www.editora.unb.br, pg 92

Universidade de Luanda Biblioteca (Angola) *Tel:* (02) 30517 *Fax:* (02) 330520, pg 1449

UNIVERSITAETSBIBLIOTHEK LEIPZIG

Editora da Universidade de Sao Paulo (Brazil) *Tel:* (011) 8184160; (011) 8138837 *Fax:* (011) 2116988, pg 93

Sistema Integrado de Bibliotecas da Universidade de Sao Paulo (SIBi) (Brazil) *Tel:* (011) 3031-7448 *Fax:* (011) 3815-2142 *E-mail:* dtsibi@org.usp.br *Web Site:* www.usp.br/sibi, pg 1455

Universidade do Minho (Portugal) *Tel:* (0253) 604150 *Fax:* (0253) 678590 *Web Site:* www.sdum.uminho.pt, pg 1493

Bibliotecas da Universidade Eduardo Mondlane (Mozambique) *Tel:* (01) 425972 *Fax:* (01) 428128, pg 1485

Biblioteca Central da Universidade Federal do Parana (Brazil) *Tel:* (041) 2645545 *Fax:* (041) 2627784, pg 1455

Centro de Ciencias da Saude da Universidade Federal do Rio de Janeiro (Brazil) *Tel:* (021) 2951397 *Fax:* (021) 2952346, pg 1455

Editora Universidade Federal do Rio de Janeiro (Brazil) *Tel:* (021) 2957096 *Fax:* (021) 5423899 *E-mail:* editora@ufrj.br *Web Site:* www.editora.ufrj.br; www.ufrj.br, pg 93

Universidade Federal do Rio Grande do Sul (UFRGS), Biblioteca Central (Brazil) *Tel:* (051) 3163065 *Fax:* (051) 3163984 *E-mail:* biblioteca@bc.ufrgs.br, pg 1455

Universidadede de Macau, Centro de Publicacoes (Macau) *Tel:* 831622; 3974505 (Distribution); 3974430 (University Library) *Fax:* 831694, pg 448

Universita degli Studi di Firenze, Biblioteca di Lettre e Filosofia (Italy) *Tel:* (055) 27571 *Fax:* (055) 243471; (055) 264194, pg 1478

Universita di Roma 'La Sapienza' (Italy) *Tel:* (06) 4456820; (06) 4474021 *Fax:* (06) 4474024 *E-mail:* alessandrina@librari.beniculturali.it *Web Site:* www.alessandrina.librari.beniculturali.it, pg 1478

Oeffentliche Bibliothek der Universitaet Basel (Switzerland) *Tel:* (061) 2673130 *Fax:* (061) 2673103, pg 1502

Universitaet Kaiserslautern (Germany) *Tel:* (0631) 2052241 *Fax:* (0631) 2052355 *E-mail:* unibib@ub.uni-kl.de *Web Site:* www.uni-kl.de/bibliothek, pg 1469

Universitaets - und Landesbibliothek Sachsen-Anhalt (Germany) *Tel:* (0345) 5522001 *Fax:* (0345) 5527140 *E-mail:* direktion@bibliothek.uni-halle.de, pg 1469

Universitaets und Landesbibliothek Muenster (Germany) *Tel:* (0251) 8324022 *Fax:* (0251) 8328398 *E-mail:* ulbmail@uni-muenster.de, pg 1469

Universitaets- und Stadtbibliothek (Germany) *Tel:* (0221) 4702260; (0221) 4702214 *Fax:* (0221) 4705166 *E-mail:* usbsekr@ub.uni-koeln.de; sekretariat@ub.uni-koeln.de *Web Site:* www.nb.nui-koeln.de, pg 1469

Universitaetsbibliothek (Germany) *Tel:* (0761) 2033900 (management); (0761) 2033918 (inquiries) *Fax:* (0761) 2033987 *E-mail:* info@ub.uni-freiburg.de *Web Site:* www.ub.uni-freiburg.de, pg 1469

Universitaetsbibliothek Bamberg (Germany) *Tel:* (0951) 8631503 *Fax:* (0951) 8631565 *E-mail:* unibibliothek.bamberg@unibib.uni-bamberg.de, pg 1469

Universitaetsbibliothek Bochum (Germany) *Tel:* (49234) 3222350; (49234) 3222351 *Fax:* (49234) 3214736 *Web Site:* www.ub.ruhr-uni-bochum.de, pg 1469

Universitaetsbibliothek Erlangen-Nuernberg (Germany) *Tel:* (09131) 85-22151 *Fax:* (09131) 85-29309 *E-mail:* direktion@bib.uni-erlangen.de *Web Site:* www.ub.uni-erlangen.de, pg 1469

Universitaetsbibliothek Heidelberg (Germany) *Tel:* (06221) 542380 *Fax:* (06221) 542623 *E-mail:* ub@ub.uni-heidelberg.de, pg 1469

Universitaetsbibliothek Leipzig (Germany) *Tel:* (0341) 9730500 *Fax:* (0341) 9730599 *E-mail:* ba@ub.uni-leipzig.de, pg 1469

Universitaetsbibliothek Mannheim (Germany) *Tel:* (0621) 181 2941 *Fax:* (0621) 181 2939 *E-mail:* biblubma@bib.uni-mannheim.de *Web Site:* www.bib.uni-mannheim.de, pg 1469

Universitaetsbibliothek Salzburg (Austria) *Tel:* (0662) 842576 *Fax:* (0662) 842576680, pg 1452

Universitaetsbibliothek Tuebingen (Germany) *Tel:* (07071) 2972577 *Fax:* (07071) 293123 *E-mail:* sekretariat@ub.uni-tuebingen.de, pg 1469

Universitaetsbibliothek Wuppertal (Germany) *Tel:* (0202) 439-2690 *Fax:* (0202) 439-2695 *E-mail:* ubwupper@bib.uni-wuppertal.de *Web Site:* www.bib.uni-wuppertal.de, pg 1469

Universitaetsverlag C Winter Heidelberg GmbH (Germany) *Tel:* (06221) 77 02-60 *Fax:* (06221) 77 02-69 *E-mail:* info@winter-hd.de *Web Site:* www.winter-verlag-hd.de, pg 296

Bibliotheek Universitair Centrum (Belgium) *Tel:* (03) 2180788; (03) 2180794 *Fax:* (03) 2180652 *E-mail:* benoni@mare.ruca.ua.ac.be, pg 1453

Bibliotheque Universitaire de Bangui (Central African Republic) *Tel:* 612000, pg 1456

Presses Universitaires de Louvain-UCL (Belgium) *Tel:* (010) 478935 *Fax:* (010) 472531 *Web Site:* www.ucl.ac.ba, pg 75

Editorial Universitaria Centroamericana (EDUCA) (Costa Rica) *Tel:* 2243727; 2258740 *Fax:* 2539141; 2340071 *E-mail:* educacr@sol.racsa.co.cr *Web Site:* www.csuca.ac.cr, pg 117

Editorial Universitaria de America Ltda (Colombia) *Tel:* (01) 2566948; (01) 3201097; (01) 2572679 *Fax:* (01) 3201097; (01) 2480367, pg 114

Livraria e Editora Universitaria de Direito Ltda (Brazil) *Tel:* (011) 605-6374 *Fax:* (011) 3140-0317, pg 93

Editoria Universitaria de la Patagonia (Argentina) *Tel:* (02967) 428834; (02967) 424969 *E-mail:* rcesar@unpbib.edu.ar, pg 9

Editorial Universitaria de la Universidad de El Salvador (El Salvador) *Tel:* 2558826 *Fax:* 254208, pg 139

Editorial Universitaria (Honduras) *Tel:* 312110, pg 318

Editorial Universitaria (Panama) *Tel:* 264-2087 *Fax:* 269-2684, pg 509

Biblioteca Central Universitaria 'Jose Antonio Arze' (Bolivia) *Tel:* (042) 31733 *Fax:* (042) 31691, pg 1454

Editorial Universitaria SA (Chile) *Tel:* (02) 2234555; (02) 2233628 *Fax:* (02) 2099455; (02) 2237982 *E-mail:* achamorrom@hotmail.com *Web Site:* www.universitaria.cl.index.pl, pg 101

Ediciones Universitarias de Valparaiso (Chile) *Tel:* (032) 273087; (02) 6332230 *Fax:* (032) 273429, pg 101

Universitas (France) *Tel:* (01) 45.67.18.38 *Fax:* (01) 45.66.50.70, pg 188

Universitat Autonoma de Barcelona Servei de Biblioteques (Spain) *Tel:* (093) 581 1015 *Fax:* (093) 581 3219, pg 1499

Biblioteca de la Universitat de Barcelona (Spain) *Tel:* (093) 3184266 *Fax:* (093) 3025947 *E-mail:* sbib@org.ub.es, pg 1499

Publicacions de la Universitat de Barcelona (Spain) *Tel:* (093) 403 54 41 *Fax:* (093) 403 54 46 *Web Site:* www.ub.es, pg 594

Universitat de Valencia Servei de Publicacions (Spain) *Tel:* (096) 3864115 *Fax:* (096) 3864067 *E-mail:* publicacions@uv.es *Web Site:* www.uv.es, pg 594

Edicions de la Universitat Politecnica de Catalunya SL (Spain) *Tel:* (093) 4016 883 *Fax:* (093) 4015 885 *E-mail:* edicions-upc@upc.es *Web Site:* www.edicionsupc.es, pg 594

Universitat Wuerzburg (Germany) *Tel:* (931) 8885943 *Fax:* (931) 8885970 *E-mail:* direktion@bibliothek.uni-wuerzburg.de *Web Site:* www.bibliothek.uni-wuerzburg.de, pg 1469

Universitat Zentralbibliothek Zuerich (Switzerland) *Tel:* (01) 2683100 *Fax:* (01) 2683290, pg 1502

Universitatbibliothek (Germany) *Tel:* (0541) 9694320 *Fax:* (0541) 9694482 *E-mail:* aaa@uni-osnabrueck.de *Web Site:* www.uni-osnabrueck.de, pg 1469

Universitatea de Medicina si Farmacie Biblioteca Centrala (Romania) *Tel:* (064) 192629 *Fax:* (064) 190832 *Web Site:* www.bib.umfcluj.ro, pg 1494

Biblioteca Universitatii Politehnica Bucuresti (Romania) *Tel:* (01) 3127044 *Fax:* (01) 3125365, pg 1494

Universitatsbibliothek Augsburg (Germany) *Tel:* (0821) 5985300 *Fax:* (0821) 5985354 *E-mail:* dir@bibliothek.uni-augsburg.de *Web Site:* www.bibliothek.uni-augsburg.de, pg 1469

Der Universitatsverlag Freiburg (Switzerland) *Tel:* (026) 426 43 11 *Fax:* (026) 426 43 00 *E-mail:* eduni@st-paul.ch *Web Site:* www.st-paul.ch/uni-press-FR, pg 626

Universitatsverlag Ulm GmbH (Germany) *Tel:* (0731) 15 28 60 *Fax:* (0731) 15 28 62 *E-mail:* info@uni-verlag-ulm.de *Web Site:* www.uni-verlag-ulm.de, pg 296

Presses de l'Universite du Benin (Togo) *Tel:* 254844 *Fax:* 258784, pg 636

Editions de l'Universite de Bruxelles (Belgium) *Tel:* (02) 650 37 99 *Fax:* (02) 650 37 94 *E-mail:* editions@admin.ulb.ac.be *Web Site:* www.editions-universite-bruxelles.be, pg 75

Universite Catholique de Louvain (Belgium) *Tel:* (010) 478187 *Fax:* (010) 478298 *E-mail:* sceb@sceb.ucl.ac.be *Web Site:* www.bib.ucl.ac.be, pg 1453

Universite Cheikh Anta Diop de Dakar, Bibliotheque Universitaire (Senegal) *Tel:* 825 02 79 *Fax:* 824 23 79, pg 1496

Bibliotheque Centrale, Universite d'Alger (Algeria) *Tel:* (064) 6970, pg 1449

Bibliotheque de l'Universite de Constantine (Algeria) *Tel:* (069) 7385, pg 1449

Universite de la Reunion, Service Commun de la Documentation (Reunion) *Tel:* 938379 *Fax:* 938364, pg 1494

Bibliotheque Centrale de l'Universite de Lubumbashi (The Democratic Republic of the Congo), pg 1458

Bibliotheque de l'Universite de Niamey (Niger) *Tel:* 732713 *Fax:* 733862, pg 1488

Universite de Ouagadougou (Burkina Faso) *Tel:* 307064, pg 1456

Universite de Toulouse-Mirail (France) *Tel:* 50 40 44; 50 40 64 *Fax:* 50 40 50, pg 1465

Universite de Yaounde, Bibliotheque (Cameroon) *Tel:* 220744, pg 1456

Universite de Yaounde Ecole Normale Superieure, Bibliotheque (Cameroon) *Tel:* 220744, pg 1456

Universite d'Oran, Bibliotheque (Algeria) *Tel:* (036) 2788 *Fax:* (038) 8672, pg 1449

Bibliotheque de l'Universite du Benin (Togo) *Tel:* 213027 *Fax:* 218595, pg 1503

Bibliotheque de l'Universite du Burundi (Burundi) *Tel:* (022) 5196; (022) 5446; (022) 2857, pg 1456

Librairie de l'Universite (France) *Tel:* (04) 78379525, pg 1283

Bibliotheque de l'Universite Nationale du Rwanda (Rwanda) *Tel:* 30372, pg 1495

Publications de l'Universite de Pau (France) *Tel:* (05) 59923347 *Fax:* (05) 59923275, pg 188

Bibliotheque de l'Universite Quaraouyine (Morocco), pg 1485

Universiteit Antwerpen Bibliotheek UFSIA (Belgium) *Tel:* (03) 2204996 *Fax:* (03) 2204437 *E-mail:* ludo.simons@ufsia.ac.be *Web Site:* lib.ua.ac.be, pg 1453

Universiteits-Bibliotheek, Universiteit van de Nederlandse Antillen (Netherlands Antilles) *Tel:* (09) 84422 *Fax:* (09) 85465, pg 1487

Universiteitsbibliotheek (Netherlands) *Tel:* (020) 5252301 *Fax:* (020) 5252311 *E-mail:* secr@uba.uva.nl, pg 1487

Universiteitsbibliotheek Leiden (Netherlands) *Tel:* (071) 5272801 *Fax:* (071) 5272836 *E-mail:* secretariaat@library.leidenuniv.nl, pg 1487

Universiteitsbibliotheek Nijmegen (Netherlands) *Tel:* (024) 3612440 *Fax:* (080) 3615944 *E-mail:* secretariaat@ubn.kun.nl, pg 1487

Universiteitsbibliotheek Utrecht (Netherlands) *Tel:* (030) 2538002 *Fax:* (030) 2538398, pg 1487

Universites de Nancy (France) *Tel:* (08) 83370213 *Fax:* (08) 83355790, pg 1465

Universitetsbiblioteket i Bergen (Norway) *Tel:* 55582500 *Fax:* 55589703 *E-mail:* adm@ub.uib.no, pg 1489

Universitetsbiblioteket i Oslo (Norway) *Tel:* 22855050 *Fax:* 22859050 *E-mail:* ubofjernlaan@ub.uio.no, pg 1489

Universitetsbiblioteket i Trondheim (Norway) *Tel:* 73595110 *Fax:* 73595103 *E-mail:* ubit@ub.ntnu.no, pg 1489

Universitetsbogladen (Denmark) *Tel:* 35240444 *E-mail:* uniboghl@mail.teledanmark.dk., pg 1281

Universitetsforlaget (Norway) *Tel:* 22575300 *Fax:* 22575353 *E-mail:* books@scup.no; journals@scup.no *Web Site:* www.scup.no, pg 505

Universiti Putra Malaysia Library (UPM) (Malaysia) *Tel:* (03) 9486101 *Fax:* (03) 9483244 *E-mail:* cans@admin.upm.edu.my, pg 1483

University Library, Universiti Sains Malaysia (Malaysia) *Tel:* (04) 6577888; (04) 6585518 *Fax:* (04) 6571526 *E-mail:* chieflib@notes.usm.my *Web Site:* www.lib.usm.my, pg 1483

Universiti Teknologi Malaysia (Malaysia) *Tel:* (07) 5576160 *Fax:* (07) 5579376 *E-mail:* psz@utm.my, pg 1483

Universities' Central Library (Myanmar) *Tel:* (01) 31144, pg 1486

Universities Administration Office (Myanmar), pg 471

University Library (Afghanistan) *Tel:* 42594, pg 1449

University Publishing Co/Varsity Press & Bookshop (Nigeria) *Tel:* (046) 230013, pg 1115

University Book Shop (Auckland) Ltd (New Zealand) *Tel:* (09) 3771869 *Fax:* (09) 3094278 *E-mail:* ubsauck@ubsbooks.co.nz *Web Site:* www.ubsbooks.co.nz, pg 1302

University Book Shop (Canterbury) Ltd (New Zealand) *Tel:* (03) 488579 *Fax:* (03) 3488851 *Web Site:* www.canterbury.ac.nz, pg 1303

University Book Shop Inc (Papua New Guinea) *Tel:* 267375 *Fax:* 260961, pg 1305

University Book Shop (Otago) Ltd (New Zealand) *Tel:* (03) 4776976 *Fax:* (03) 4776571 *E-mail:* ubs@xtra.co.nz *Web Site:* www.unibooks.co.nz, pg 1303

University Booksellers Association of Nigeria (Nigeria) *Tel:* (052) 200250 (Ugbowo); (052) 200480 (Ekehuan) *Fax:* (052) 241156, pg 1256

University Bookshop (Ghana) *Tel:* (021) 500398 *Fax:* (021) 500774 *E-mail:* bookshop@ug.edu.gh, pg 1247

University Bookshop (Ghana) *Tel:* (021) 500398 *Fax:* (021) 500774 *E-mail:* addae-mensah@ug.gn.ape.org, pg 1285

University Bookshop (Ghana) *Tel:* (051) 60351 *Fax:* (051) 60137 *E-mail:* ustlib@ust.gn.apc.org, pg 1285

University Bookshop (Zambia) *Tel:* (01) 294690; (01) 290319 *Fax:* (01) 253952; (01) 294690, pg 1325

YELLOW PAGES

University Bookshop Ltd (Nigeria) *Tel:* (036) 230290, pg 1303

University Bookshop (Nigeria) Ltd (Nigeria) *Tel:* (02) 400550 (ext 1208); (02) 400550 (ext 1047); (02) 400614 (ext 1244); (02) 400614 (ext 1042), pg 1303

University Bookstore (Liberia) *Tel:* 224671, pg 1297

University Co-operative Bookshop Ltd (Australia) *Tel:* (02) 93259600 *Fax:* (02) 92818390 *E-mail:* info@mail.coop-bookshop.com.au *Web Site:* www.coop-bookshop.com.au, pg 1274

University College Cork, Boole Library (Ireland) *Tel:* (021) 276871 *Fax:* (021) 903119 *E-mail:* library@ucc.ie, pg 1476

University College Dublin Library (Ireland) *Tel:* (01) 716 7694 *Fax:* (01) 283 7667 *E-mail:* library@ucd.ie *Web Site:* www.ucd.ie/library, pg 1476

University of Aberdeen (United Kingdom) *Tel:* (01224) 272579 *Fax:* (01224) 487048 *E-mail:* library@abdn.ac.uk *Web Site:* www.abdn.ac.uk/diss/library, pg 1507

University of Alexandria Library (Egypt (Arab Republic of Egypt)) *Tel:* (03) 5971675 *Fax:* (03) 5960720, pg 1462

University of Asmara Library (Eritrea) *Tel:* (01) 161926; (01) 162553 *Fax:* (01) 162236, pg 1462

University of Auckland Library (New Zealand) *Tel:* (09) 3737999 *Fax:* (09) 3737565 *E-mail:* library@auckland.ac.nz *Web Site:* www2.auckland.ac.nz/lbr/libhome.htm, pg 1488

Central Library of the University of Baghdad (Iraq) *Tel:* (01) 7763091 *Fax:* (01) 7763592, pg 1475

University of Bahrain (Bahrain) *Tel:* 682748 *Fax:* 681465, pg 1452

University of Baluchistan Library (Pakistan) *Tel:* (081) 41770, pg 1490

Central Library of the University of Basrah (Iraq) *Tel:* (040) 417914, pg 1475

The University of Birmingham (United Kingdom) *Tel:* (0121) 414 3344 *Fax:* (0121) 414 3971 *Web Site:* www.general.bham.ac.uk, pg 751

University of Botswana Library (Botswana) *Tel:* 3552295 *Fax:* 356291; 356591, pg 1454

University of Cairo Library (Egypt (Arab Republic of Egypt)) *Tel:* (02) 5729584 *Fax:* (02) 628884, pg 1462

University of Cape Coast Library (Ghana) *Tel:* (042) 24409; (042) 32480 *Fax:* (042) 32485, pg 1470

University of Cape Town Libraries (South Africa) *Tel:* (021) 650-3097 *Fax:* (021) 689-7568, pg 1498

Library of the University of Crete (Greece) *Tel:* (0831) 77900 *Fax:* (0831) 77909, pg 1471

University of Dar es Salaam Library (United Republic of Tanzania) *Tel:* (051) 43241 *Fax:* (051) 43241 *E-mail:* libdirec@udsm.ac.tz, pg 1503

University of Dar Es Salaam Bookshop (United Republic of Tanzania) *Tel:* (022) 2410093; (022) 2410500 (ext 2568) *Fax:* (022) 2410137, pg 1314

University of Dschang Central Library (Cameroon) *Tel:* 45-13-81 *Fax:* 45-23-81, pg 1456

University of Durban-Westville Library (South Africa) *Tel:* (031) 8202640; (031) 2045058 *Fax:* (031) 821873, pg 560

University of Engineering & Technology Central Library (Pakistan) *Tel:* (042) 6829243 *Fax:* (042) 6822566 *E-mail:* central_library@yahoo.com *Web Site:* www.uet.edu.pk, pg 1490

University of Exeter Press (United Kingdom) *Tel:* (01392) 263066 *Fax:* (01392) 263064 *E-mail:* uep@ex.ac.uk *Web Site:* www.ex.ac.uk/uep, pg 751

University of Garyounis Library (Libyan Arab Jamahiriya) *Tel:* (022) 29021, pg 1481

University of Ghana Library (Ghana) *Tel:* (021) 775309; (021) 500014; (021) 302347 *Fax:* (021) 667701 *E-mail:* balme@ug.gn.apc.org, pg 1470

University of Goroka (Papua New Guinea) *Tel:* 7311700 *Fax:* 7322620 *E-mail:* amaras@uog.ac.pg *Web Site:* www.uog.ac.pg, pg 510

University of Haifa Library (Israel) *Tel:* (04) 257753 *Fax:* (04) 342104 *E-mail:* webmaster@lib.haifa.ac.il *Web Site:* www-lib.haifa.ac.il, pg 373

University of Haifa Library (Israel) *Tel:* (04) 257753; (04) 8240289 *Fax:* (04) 342104; (04) 8257753 *E-mail:* sever@lib.haifa.ac.il, pg 1477

University of Hong Kong Libraries (Hong Kong) *Tel:* 2859 7000; 2859 2203 *Fax:* 2859 9420 *E-mail:* libadmin@hkucc.hku.hk *Web Site:* www.hku.hk/lib/, pg 1471

University of Isfahan Library (Islamic Republic of Iran) *Tel:* (031) 71071; (031) 685141 *Fax:* (031) 275145, pg 1475

University of Jordan Library (Jordan) *Tel:* (06) 843555 *Fax:* (06) 832318, pg 1479

University of Jordan Bookshop (Jordan) *Tel:* (06) 843555 (ext 3339) *Fax:* (06) 836446 *E-mail:* admin@ju.edu.jo, pg 1296

University of Kabul Bookstores (Afghanistan) *Tel:* 40341, pg 1271

University of Khartoum Bookshop (Sudan) *Tel:* (011) 80558, pg 1312

University of Khartoum Library (Sudan), pg 1500

University of Lagos Library (Nigeria) *Tel:* (01) 821273 *Fax:* (01) 822644, pg 1489

University of Lagos Bookshop (Nigeria) *Tel:* (01) 820279 *Fax:* (01) 822644, pg 1303

University of Lagos Press (Nigeria) *Tel:* (01) 825048 *Fax:* (01) 825048, pg 502

University of Liberia Libraries (Liberia) *Tel:* 224671, pg 1481

University of London (United Kingdom) *Tel:* (020) 7636 8000 ext 3268 *Fax:* (020) 7636 5874, pg 1323

University of London Careers Service (United Kingdom) *Tel:* (020) 7554 4500 *Fax:* (020) 7383 5678 *E-mail:* careers@lon.ac.uk *Web Site:* www.careers.lon.ac.uk, pg 751

University of London Library (United Kingdom) *Tel:* (020) 7862 8500 *Fax:* (020) 7862 8480 *E-mail:* ull@ull.ac.uk *Web Site:* www.ull.ac.uk, pg 1507

University of Malawi Libraries (Malawi) *Tel:* 524222; 525935 *Fax:* 525225, pg 1482

University of Malawi, Polytechnic Library (Malawi) *Tel:* 670411 *Fax:* 670578, pg 1482

University of Malaya Co-operative Bookshop Ltd (Malaysia) *Tel:* (03) 7565000; (03) 7565425 *Fax:* (03) 7563246; (03) 7554424, pg 1298

University of Malaya, Department of Publications (Malaysia) *Tel:* (03) 79574361 *Fax:* (03) 79574473, pg 455

University of Malta Library (Malta) *Tel:* 333903 *Fax:* 336450, pg 1483

The University of Malta Publications Section (Malta) *Tel:* 343572 *Fax:* 344879, pg 456

University of Malysia Library (Malaysia) *Tel:* (03) 7560022 *Fax:* (03) 7564004, pg 1483

University of Manila Central Library (Philippines) *Tel:* (02) 7413637 *Fax:* (02) 7413640, pg 1491

University of Mauritius Library (Mauritius) *Tel:* 4541041 *Fax:* 4549642, pg 1484

University of Melbourne Library (Australia) *Tel:* (03) 83445382 *Fax:* (03) 83449879, pg 1451

UNIVERSITY OF QUEENSLAND PRESS

Central Library of the University of Mosul (Iraq) *Tel:* (060) 810162 *Fax:* (060) 814765, pg 1475

The University of Nagoya Press (Japan) *Tel:* (052) 7815111 *Fax:* (052) 7802045, pg 428

University of Nairobi Libraries (Kenya) *Tel:* (02) 334244 *Fax:* (02) 336885 *E-mail:* jkml@uonbi.ac.ke *Web Site:* www.uonbi.ac.ke, pg 1480

University of Nairobi Bookshop (Kenya) *Tel:* (02) 334244 *Fax:* (02) 336885, pg 1296

University of Natal Press (South Africa) *Tel:* (0331) 2605226; (0331) 2605225 *Fax:* (0331) 2605599 *E-mail:* books@press.unp.ac/za; moberly@press.unp.ac.za, pg 560

University of New South Wales Library (Australia) *Tel:* (02) 93852615 *Fax:* (02) 93858002 *E-mail:* information@unsw.edu.au *Web Site:* www.library.edu.au, pg 1451

University of New South Wales Press Ltd (Australia) *Tel:* (02) 9664 0900 *Fax:* (02) 9664 5420 *E-mail:* info.press@unsw.edu.au *Web Site:* www.unswpress.com.au, pg 46

University of Newcastle (Australia) *Tel:* (02) 4921 5000 *Web Site:* www.newcastle.edu.au, pg 46

University of Newcastle Upon Tyne (United Kingdom) *Tel:* (0191) 222 6000 *Fax:* (0191) 222 6229 *Web Site:* www.ncl.ac.uk, pg 751

University of Nigeria (Nigeria) *Tel:* (042) 771444 *Fax:* (042) 770644; (042) 771500 *E-mail:* misunn@aol.com, pg 1489

University of Nigeria Bookshop Ltd (Nigeria) *Tel:* (042) 332077; (042) 771911, pg 1303

University of Otago Library (New Zealand) *Tel:* (03) 4791100 *Fax:* (03) 4798947 *E-mail:* office.central@library.otago.ac.nz, pg 1488

University of Otago Press (New Zealand) *Tel:* (03) 479 8807 *Fax:* (03) 479 8385 *E-mail:* university.press@otago.ac.nz *Web Site:* www.otago.ac.nz, pg 496

University of Papua New Guinea Press (Papua New Guinea) *Tel:* 6753260130 *Fax:* 6753260127, pg 510

University of Peradeniya Library (Sri Lanka) *Tel:* (08) 388678; (08) 388301 (ext 2040); (08) 388301 (ext 2042); 386003-04 *Fax:* (08) 388678 *E-mail:* lib@mail.pdn.ac.lk *Web Site:* www.pdn.ac.lk, pg 1500

University of the Philippines Press (Philippines) *Tel:* (02) 992558 *Fax:* (02) 9282558 *E-mail:* press@nicole.upd.edu.ph *Web Site:* www.dilnet.upd.edu.ph.~press, pg 515

University of Port Elizabeth Library (South Africa) *Tel:* (041) 5042281 *Fax:* (041) 5042280 *E-mail:* libref@upe.ac.za, pg 1498

University of Pretoria Academic Information Services (South Africa) *Tel:* (012) 420-2235 *Fax:* (012) 362-5100, pg 1498

University of Puerto Rico, General Library, Mayaguez Campus (Puerto Rico) *Tel:* (787) 832-4040 (ext 2255) *Fax:* (787) 834-3031, pg 1493

University of Puerto Rico, Medical Sciences Campus Library (Puerto Rico) *Tel:* (787) 758-2525 *Fax:* (787) 282-6438, pg 1493

University of Puerto Rico, Library System, Rio Piedras Campus (Puerto Rico) *Tel:* (787) 764-0000 (ext 3296) *Fax:* (787) 764-0270, pg 1493

University of Puerto Rico Press (EDUPR) (Puerto Rico) *Tel:* (787) 758-6932; (787) 758-8345 (sales) *Fax:* (787) 753-9116, pg 531

University of Queensland Library (Australia) *Tel:* (07) 33656209 *Fax:* (07) 33657317, pg 1451

University of Queensland Press (Australia) *Tel:* (07) 3365 2127; (07) 3365 2440 (sales) *Fax:* (07) 3365 7579 *Web Site:* www.uqp.uq.edu.au, pg 46

University of Rajshahi Library (Bangladesh) *Tel:* (0721) 750666 *Fax:* (0721) 750064 *E-mail:* rajuce@citechco.net, pg 1452

The University of Reading (United Kingdom) *Tel:* (0118) 9318770 *Fax:* (0118) 9316636 *E-mail:* library@reading.ac.uk *Web Site:* www.library.rdg.ac.uk, pg 1507

Central Library of the University of Salahaddin (Iraq) *Tel:* 23102, pg 1475

University of San Carlos Library System (Philippines) *Tel:* (032) 220432; (032) 2540432 *Fax:* (032) 54341; (032) 2540432 *E-mail:* direklib@pinya.usc.edu.ph *Web Site:* www.use.edu.ph/administration/library, pg 1491

University of Santo Tomas Library (Philippines) *Tel:* (02) 210081 *Fax:* (02) 7409709 *E-mail:* clib1@ustcc.ust.edu.ph *Web Site:* www.library.ust.edu.ph, pg 1491

University of South Africa Library (South Africa) *Tel:* (012) 4293131 *Fax:* (012) 4292925 *E-mail:* willej@alpha.unisa.ac.za, pg 1498

University of South Australia Library (Australia) *Tel:* (08) 83026611 *Fax:* (08) 83026756 *Web Site:* www.library.unisa.edu.au, pg 1451

University of Southampton (United Kingdom) *Tel:* (01703) 592180 *Fax:* (01703) 593007, pg 1507

University of Stellenbosch Library (South Africa) *Tel:* (021) 959-2911 *Fax:* (021) 959-3627 *E-mail:* jhvi@maties.sun.ac.za, pg 1498

University of Swaziland Library (Swaziland) *Tel:* 84011; 2264 (Manzini) *Fax:* 85276, pg 1500

University of Sydney Library (Australia) *Tel:* (02) 93512990 *Fax:* (02) 93512890, pg 1451

Central Library, University of Tabriz (Islamic Republic of Iran) *Tel:* (041) 344705 *Fax:* (041) 344705, pg 1475

University of Technology, Jamaica (Jamaica) *Tel:* (876) 927-1680; (876) 927-1688 *Fax:* (876) 927-1614 *E-mail:* library@utech.edu.jm *Web Site:* www.utechjamaica.edu.jm, pg 1478

University of Technology, Sydney Library (Australia) *Tel:* (02) 95142000 *Fax:* (02) 95141551, pg 1451

Central Library & Documentation Centre of University of Teheran (Islamic Republic of Iran) *Tel:* (021) 6112503 *Fax:* (021) 6409348, pg 1475

University of Tehran Publications & Printing Organization (Islamic Republic of Iran) *Tel:* (021) 6462622 *Fax:* (021) 6462622 *Web Site:* www.ut.ac.lr, pg 358

University of the East Library (Philippines) *Tel:* (02) 7358544 *Fax:* (02) 7356976 *E-mail:* uel@mozcom.com, pg 1491

University of the Philippines Diliman University Library (Philippines) *Tel:* (02) 926 1877 *Fax:* (02) 92 1876 *E-mail:* salvacion.arlante@up.edu.ph *Web Site:* www.mainlib.upd.edu.ph, pg 1491

University of the South Pacific Library (Fiji) *Tel:* 313900 (ext 2282) *Fax:* 3300830, pg 1463

University of the West Indies Library (Jamaica) (Jamaica) *Tel:* (876) 927-2123 *Fax:* (876) 927-1926 *E-mail:* manlibry@uwimona.edu.jm *Web Site:* www.library.uwimona.edu.jm:1104, pg 1478

University of the West Indies (Trinidad & Tobago) (Trinidad & Tobago) *Tel:* 6622002 *Fax:* 6639684, pg 637

University of the West Indies Library (Barbados) (Barbados) *Tel:* (246) 417-4444 *Fax:* (246) 417-4460, pg 1452

University of the West Indies Library (Trinidad & Tobago) (Trinidad & Tobago) *Tel:* (0868) 662-2002 (ext 2132) *Fax:* (0868) 662-9238 *E-mail:* mainlib@library.uwi.tt, pg 1503

University of the West Indies Press (Jamaica) *Tel:* 9772659; 7024082 *Web Site:* www.uwipress.com, pg 414

University of the West Indies Publishers' Association (Jamaica) *Tel:* (876) 977-2659 *Fax:* (876) 977-2660, pg 1250

University of the Western Cape Library (South Africa) *Tel:* (021) 976161 *Fax:* (021) 576661, pg 1498

University of the Witwatersrand Library (South Africa) *Tel:* (011) 716-2330 *Fax:* (011) 403-1421 *E-mail:* 056heath@libris.wwl.wits.ac.za, pg 1498

Library of the University of Thessaloniki (Greece) *Tel:* (031) 996703 *Fax:* (031) 206138, pg 1471

University of Tokyo Library (Japan) *Tel:* (03) 38122111 *Fax:* (03) 38164208 *E-mail:* kikaku@lib.u-tokyo.ac.jp, pg 1479

University of Tokyo Press (Japan) *Tel:* (03) 38151902 *Fax:* (03) 38126958, pg 428

University of Toronto Press Inc (Canada) *Tel:* 416-667-7767 *Fax:* 416-667-7803 *E-mail:* printing@utpress.utoronto.ca *Web Site:* www.utpress.utoronto.ca, pg 1132, 1154, 1194, 1211

University of Wales Press (United Kingdom) *Tel:* (029) 2049-6899 *Fax:* (029) 2049-6108 *E-mail:* press@press.wales.ac.uk *Web Site:* www.wales.ac.uk/press, pg 751

University of Western Australia Library (Australia) *Tel:* (09) 3802344 *Fax:* (09) 3801012 *E-mail:* liboff@uniwa.uwa.edu.av, pg 1451

University of Western Australia Press (Australia) *Tel:* (08) 9380 3182 *Fax:* (08) 9380 1027 *E-mail:* uwap@cyllene.uwa.edu.au *Web Site:* www.uwapress.uwa.edu.au, pg 46

University of Zambia Press (UNZA Press) (Zambia) *Tel:* (01) 290740; (01) 219624; (01) 252514 *Fax:* (01) 253952, pg 767

University of Zambia Press (UNZA Press) (Zambia) *Tel:* (01) 290740; (01) 290409 *Fax:* (01) 253952, pg 1509

University of Zimbabwe Library (Zimbabwe) *Tel:* (04) 303211 *Fax:* (04) 335383 *E-mail:* mainlib@uzlib.uz.zw *Web Site:* www.uz.ac.zw/library, pg 769

University of Zimbabwe Library (Zimbabwe) *Tel:* (04) 303211 *Fax:* (04) 333407 *E-mail:* mainlib@uzlib.uz.zw, pg 1510

University of Zimbabwe Publications (Zimbabwe) *Tel:* (04) 303211 Ext 1236 *Fax:* (04) 333407; (04) 335249 *E-mail:* uzpub@admin.uz.ac.zn, pg 769

The University Press Ltd (Bangladesh) *Tel:* (02) 9565441; (02) 9565444 *Fax:* (02) 9565443 *E-mail:* upl@bangla.net; upl@bttb.net.bd *Web Site:* www.uplbooks.com, pg 62

University Presses of California, Columbia & Princeton Ltd (United Kingdom) *Tel:* (01243) 842165 *Fax:* (01243) 842167 *E-mail:* webmaster@pupress.princeton.edu *Web Site:* pup.princeton.edu, pg 752

University Publishers & Booksellers (Pty) Ltd (South Africa) *Tel:* (021) 8870337 *Fax:* (021) 8832975, pg 560

University Publishing Co (Nigeria) *Tel:* (046) 230013, pg 502

University Publishing Projects Ltd (Israel) *Tel:* (03) 562-6622 *Fax:* (03) 562-6879 *E-mail:* uppbkshp@upp.co.il *Web Site:* www.upp.co.il/home.htm, pg 373

Editorial Universo SA (Peru) *Tel:* (014) 241639; (014) 233190, pg 512

Universo Editorial SA de CV Edicion de Libros Revistas y Periodicos (Mexico) *Tel:* (048) 21593, pg 468

Editorial Universo SA de CV (Mexico) *Tel:* (05) 5750711 ext 30; (05) 5750711 ext 31, pg 468

Librairie Universsitaire de la Reunion (Reunion) *Tel:* 210758, pg 1308

Univerza v Ljubljani Ekonomska Fakulteta (Slovenia) *Tel:* (061) 1892400 *Fax:* (061) 1892698 *E-mail:* joze.cibej@uni-lj.s1, pg 552

Univerzitet u Beogradu biblioteka 'Svetozar Markovic' (Yugoslavia) *Tel:* (011) 3370509 *Fax:* (011) 3370354, pg 1509

Univerzitna kniznica (Slovakia) *Tel:* (07) 5333247 *Fax:* (07) 5334246, pg 1497

Biblioteka Uniwersytecka we Wroclawiu (Poland) *Tel:* (071) 3463129 *Fax:* (071) 3463166 *E-mail:* infnauk@bu.uni.wroc.pl *Web Site:* www.bu.uni.wroc.pl, pg 1493

Uniwersytet Gdanski (Poland) *Tel:* (058) 5509005; (058) 5511117 *Fax:* (058) 5515221 *E-mail:* bib@bg.univ.gda.pl; info@bg.univ.gda.pl *Web Site:* www.bg.univ.gda.pl/library/, pg 1493

Biblioteka Uniwersytecka w Torruniu (Poland) *Tel:* (056) 654 29 52; (056) 61 14 408 *Fax:* (056) 652 04 19 *E-mail:* umklibr@bu.uni.torun.pl; sekrretariat@bu.uni.torrum.pl *Web Site:* www.bu.uni.torrum.pl/en, pg 1493

Wydawnictwo Uniwersytetu Wroclawskiego SP ZOO (Poland) *Tel:* (071) 3752991; (071) 2752809; (071) 3752773 *Fax:* (071) 3752735 *E-mail:* marketing@wuwr.com.pl *Web Site:* www.wuwr.com.pl, pg 520

UNO-Verlag mbH, Vertriebs und Verlagsgesellschaft (Germany) *Tel:* (0228) 94 90 2-0 *Fax:* (0228) 94 90 2-22 *E-mail:* info@uno-verlag.de *Web Site:* www.uno-verlag.de, pg 296

Unrast Verlag e V (Germany) *Tel:* (0251) 666293 *Fax:* (0251) 666120 *E-mail:* unrast-verlag@gmx.de *Web Site:* www.unrast-verlag.de, pg 296

Editrice Uomini Nuovi (Italy) *Tel:* (0332) 723007 *Fax:* (0332) 723264 *E-mail:* info@eun.ch *Web Site:* www.eun.ch, pg 410

Uplands Books (United Kingdom) *Tel:* (01424) 422306 *Fax:* (01424) 719879 *E-mail:* sales@uplands-books.com, pg 752

UPM-Kymmene Ltd (United Kingdom) *Tel:* (0870) 6000 876 *Fax:* (0870) 6060 876 *Web Site:* www.upm-kymmene.com, pg 1142

Uppsala Universitetsbibliotek (Sweden) *Tel:* (018) 4713900 *Fax:* (018) 4713913, pg 1501

UPS Freight Services (United States) *Tel:* 718-481-4400 *Fax:* 718-528-4191, pg 1225

UPS Translations (United Kingdom) *Tel:* (020) 7837 8300 *Fax:* (020) 7486 3272 *E-mail:* production@upstranslations.com *Web Site:* www.upstranslations.com, pg 1130

Urania Verlag mit Ravensburger Ratgebern (Germany) *Tel:* (030) 28447-112; (030) 28447-113 *Fax:* (030) 28447-123 *E-mail:* urania.ravensburger@dornier-verlage.de *Web Site:* www.urania-ravensburger.de, pg 296

Uranium Verlag Zug (Switzerland) *Tel:* (042) 217744, pg 626

Ediciones Urano, SA (Spain) *Tel:* (093) 2375 564 *Fax:* (093) 4153 796 *E-mail:* atencion@edicionesurano.com *Web Site:* www.edicionesurano.com, pg 595

Urban & Fischer Verlag GmbH & Co KG Niederlassung Jena (Germany) *Tel:* (03641) 62 64 30 *Fax:* (03641) 62 64 21 *E-mail:* journals@urbanfischer.de *Web Site:* www.urbanfischer.de/journals, pg 296

Urban und Fischer Verlag fur Medizin (Germany) *Tel:* (089) 5383-0 *Fax:* (089) 5383-939 *E-mail:* info@urbanfischer.de *Web Site:* www.urban.de; www.urbanfischer.de, pg 296

Urban und Schwarzenberg GmbH (Austria) *Tel:* (01) 4052731 *Fax:* (01) 405272441, pg 60

Urban und Schwarzenberg GmbH (Austria) *Tel:* (01) 4052731, pg 1275

Urbaniana University Press (Italy) *Tel:* (06) 6988 2351; (06) 6988 1745; (06) 6988 2182 *Fax:* (06) 6988 2182 *E-mail:* uupdir@urbaniana.edu; uupamm@urbaniana.edu, pg 410

Urdu Academy Sind (Pakistan) *Tel:* (021) 2631485, pg 509

Urdu Science Board (Pakistan) *Tel:* (042) 5758674, pg 1256

Urim Publications (Israel) *Tel:* (02) 679-7633 *Fax:* (02) 679-7634 *E-mail:* publisher@urimpublications.com *Web Site:* www.urimpublications.com, pg 373

Urmo SA de Ediciones (Spain) *Tel:* (094) 424 53 07 *Fax:* (094) 423 19 84 *E-mail:* urmo@infonegocio.com *Web Site:* www.urmo.com, pg 595

Urozaj (Ukraine) *Tel:* (044) 2451196, pg 643

La Urpila Editores (Uruguay) *Tel:* (02) 9085347, pg 761

Ursa ry (Finland) *Tel:* (09) 684 0400 *Fax:* (09) 6840 4040 *E-mail:* markku.sarimaa@ursa.fi *Web Site:* www.ursa.fi, pg 145

Editia Uruguay (Uruguay) *Tel:* (02) 9159633; (02) 9159759 *Fax:* (02) 9164419 *E-mail:* libros@editia.com, pg 761

Usaha Baru CV (Indonesia) *Tel:* (031) 22128, pg 357

Usborne Publishing Ltd (United Kingdom) *Tel:* (020) 7430 2800 *Fax:* (020) 7430 1562; (020) 7242 0974 *E-mail:* mail@usborne.co.uk *Web Site:* www.usborne.com, pg 752

The Useful Publishing Co (Australia) *Tel:* (09) 370-4577 *Fax:* (09) 370-2540, pg 46

UST Publishing House (Philippines) *Tel:* (02) 731-3522731 *Fax:* (02) 731-3522731, pg 515

Ustav informacii a prognoz skolstva mladeze a telovychovy (Slovakia) *Tel:* (07) 65425166 *Fax:* (07) 65426180, pg 551

Ustredna kniznica Slovenskej akademie vied (Slovakia) *Tel:* (07) 5292 1733 *Fax:* (07) 52921733 *E-mail:* knizhorv@klemens.savba.sk *Web Site:* www.savba.sk/sav/inst/uk/uksav.html, pg 1497

Usus Editora (Portugal) *Tel:* (01) 4535000 *Fax:* (01) 4426482, pg 530

UT Orpheus Edizioni (Italy) *Tel:* (051) 263720 *Fax:* (051) 263720 *E-mail:* mail@utorpheus.com *Web Site:* www.utorpheus.com, pg 411

UTAS-Verlag fur Moderne Lernmethoden Uta Stechl (Germany) *Tel:* (08633) 1450 *Fax:* (08633) 7805, pg 297

UTB fuer Wissenschaft Uni-Taschenbuecher GmbH (Germany) *Tel:* (0711) 7 82 95 55 0 *Fax:* (0711) 7 80 13 76 *E-mail:* utb@utb-stuttgart.de *Web Site:* www.utb.de, pg 297

UTET Periodici Scientifici (Italy) *Tel:* (02) 6241171 *Fax:* (02) 62411720 *E-mail:* utetre@tin.it, pg 411

UTET (Unione Tipografico-Editrice Torinese) (Italy) *Tel:* (011) 65291 *Fax:* (011) 6529240, pg 411

Utusan Publications and Distributors Sdn Bhd (Malaysia) *Tel:* (03) 9856577; (03) 9852645, pg 455

Uudet Kirjat (Finland) *Tel:* (09) 61681 *Fax:* (09) 6168560, pg 1228

UVK Universitatsverlag Konstanz GmbH (Germany) *Tel:* (07531) 90 53 0 *Fax:* (07531) 90 53 98 *E-mail:* willkommen@uvk.de *Web Site:* www.uvk.de, pg 297

UVK Verlagsgesellschaft mbH (Germany) *Tel:* (07531) 90 53 0 *Fax:* (07531) 90 53 98 *E-mail:* willkrommen@uvk.de *Web Site:* www.uvk.de, pg 297

UWI Publishers' Association (Jamaica) *Tel:* (876) 927-1020 *Fax:* (876) 977-2660, pg 414

Izdatelstvo Uzbekistan (Uzbekistan), pg 761

Uzima Press (Kenya) *Tel:* (02) 220239; (02) 216836, pg 433

V S P International Science Publishers (Netherlands) *Tel:* (030) 6925790 *Fax:* (030) 6932081 *E-mail:* vsppub@compuserve.com *Web Site:* www.vsppub.com, pg 486

Edition Va Bene (Austria) *Tel:* (02243) 22 159; (0664) 1616356 (mobile) *Fax:* (02243) 22 159 *E-mail:* edition@vabene.at *Web Site:* www.vabene.at, pg 60

Vacation Work Publications (United Kingdom) *Tel:* (01865) 241978 *Fax:* (01865) 790885 *E-mail:* info@vacationwork.co.uk *Web Site:* www.vacationwork.co.uk, pg 752

Vaccari SRL (Italy) *Tel:* (059) 764106 *Fax:* (059) 760157 *E-mail:* info@vaccari.it *Web Site:* www.vaccari.it, pg 411

Vacher Dod Publishing Ltd (United Kingdom) *Tel:* (020) 7828 7256 *Fax:* (020) 7828 7269 *E-mail:* politics@vacherdod.co.uk *Web Site:* www.vacherdod.co.uk, pg 752

Vaco NV Uitgeversmij (Suriname) *Tel:* 472545 *Fax:* 10563, pg 599

Vadell Hermanos Editores CA (Venezuela) *Tel:* (02) 5723108; (02) 5725243 *Fax:* (02) 5725243, pg 763

Vaga Ltd (Lithuania) *Tel:* (02) 626443; (02) 616002; (02) 613448; (02) 624101 *Fax:* (02) 616902 *E-mail:* vaga@post.omnitel.net, pg 446

La Vague a l'ame (France) *Tel:* 76470784, pg 188

La Vague Verte (France) *Tel:* (03) 22.30.72.50 *Fax:* (03) 22.26.58.73 *E-mail:* edlavagueverte@wanadoo.fr, pg 188

Vaidelote (Latvia) *Tel:* (02) 937943; (02) 2560475 *Fax:* (02) 570828, pg 442

Imprimeur - Editeur Vaillant-Carmanne SA (Belgium) *Tel:* (011) 612452 *Fax:* (011) 612451, pg 75

Les Editions Vaillant-Miroir-Sprint Publications (France) *Tel:* (01) 42819103, pg 188

Vaka-Helgafell (Iceland) *Tel:* 89733 *Fax:* 89733 *E-mail:* vaka@vaka.is, pg 329

Vaka-Helgafell (Iceland) *Tel:* 5503000 *Fax:* 5503033, pg 1288

Vakils Feffer & Simons Ltd (India) *Tel:* (022) 2611221; (022) 2619121 *Fax:* (022) 2614924; (022) 2610432, pg 352

Editura Valahia SRL (Romania) *Tel:* 097 680948, pg 536

Valdonega SRL (Italy) *Tel:* (045) 6020444 *Fax:* (045) 6020334 *E-mail:* valdoneg@valdonega.it, pg 411, 1137

Carlos Valencia Editores (Colombia) *Tel:* (01) 2839040; (01) 3426224; (01) 2114928 *Fax:* (01) 2839235, pg 114

Valeton b v (Netherlands) *Tel:* (020) 6201454 *Fax:* (020) 6279209, pg 1301

Valgus Publishers (Estonia) *Tel:* (02) 6505026 *Fax:* (02) 6505104, pg 141

Vallardi & Assoc (Italy) *Tel:* (02) 6555545 *Fax:* (02) 6555640, pg 411

Vallardi Industrie Grafiche (Italy) *Tel:* (02) 9370284 *Fax:* (02) 93570442, pg 411

Vallentine, Mitchell & Co Ltd (United Kingdom) *Tel:* (020) 8920 2100 *Fax:* (020) 8447 8548 *E-mail:* info@vmbooks.com; vminfo@frankcass.com *Web Site:* www.vmbooks.com; www.frankcass.com/vm, pg 752

Valmartina Editore SRL (Italy) *Tel:* (011) 3158711 *Fax:* (011) 3158710, pg 411

Van Buuren Uitgeverij BV (Netherlands) *Tel:* (03) 0495 548080 *Fax:* (03) 0495 547326 *E-mail:* vanbuuren.uitgeverij@wxs.nl, pg 486

Van Dale Lexicografie BV (Netherlands) *Tel:* (031) 2324711 *Fax:* (031) 2369642 *E-mail:* info@vandale.nl, pg 486

Editions Van de Velde (France) *Tel:* (02) 47 49 43 43 *Fax:* (02) 47 49 43 49 *E-mail:* vandereede.musique@wanadoo.fr *Web Site:* www.yacht-in-books.com, pg 188

Marc Van de Wiele bvba (Belgium) *Tel:* (050) 333805 *Fax:* (050) 346457, pg 75

Dorothea van der Koelen (Germany) *Tel:* (06131) 346 64 *Fax:* (06131) 36 90 76 *E-mail:* dvanderkoelen@xterna-net.de, pg 297

Van Gorcum & Comp BV (Netherlands) *Tel:* (0592) 379555 *Fax:* (0592) 372064 *E-mail:* assen@vgorcum.nl, pg 486

Kelvin Van Hasselt Publishing Services (United Kingdom) *Tel:* (0590) 6 71695; (0590) 6 70004 *Fax:* (0590) 6 71533 *E-mail:* kvhbooks@aol.com, pg 752

Kelvin van Hasselt Publishing Services (United Kingdom) *Tel:* (01590) 671695 *Fax:* (01590) 671533 *E-mail:* kvhbooks@aol.com, pg 1122

Van Lear Associates (United Kingdom) *Tel:* (020) 7610 6165 *Fax:* (020) 7610 6045 *E-mail:* 100700.3266@compuserve.com, pg 1122

The Van Leer Jerusalem Institute (Israel) *Tel:* (02) 5605288; (02) 5605289 *Fax:* (02) 5619293 *E-mail:* values@vanleer.org.il *Web Site:* www.vanleer.org.il/eng, pg 373

Van Molle Publishing (United Kingdom) *Tel:* (01239) 851482 *Fax:* (01239) 851482, pg 752

Uitgeverij G A van Oorschot bv (Netherlands) *Tel:* (020) 6231484 *Fax:* (020) 6254083, pg 486

Van Piere Boeken (Netherlands) *Tel:* (040) 2444045 *Fax:* (040) 2463945 *E-mail:* pierboek@euronet.nl, pg 1301

Van Schaik Bookstore University Bookshop (South Africa) *Tel:* (021) 9188500 *Fax:* (021) 9511670 *E-mail:* vsblv@vanschaik.com *Web Site:* www.vsonline.co.za, pg 1310

Van Schaik Publishers (South Africa) *Tel:* (012) 342-2765 *Fax:* (012) 430-3563 *E-mail:* vanschaik@vanschaiknet.com *Web Site:* www.vanschaiknet.com, pg 560

Uitgeverij Van Walraven BV (Netherlands) *Tel:* (035) 5482411 *Fax:* (035) 5418221, pg 486

Uitgeverij Van Wijnen (Netherlands) *Tel:* (0517) 394588 *Fax:* (0517) 397179, pg 486

Editions Van Wilder (France) *Tel:* (01) 53069212 *Fax:* (01) 53069213, pg 188

Vandenhoeck & Ruprecht (Germany) *Tel:* (0551) 5084-40 *Fax:* (0551) 5084-422 *E-mail:* info@vandenhoeck-ruprecht.de *Web Site:* www.vandenhoeck-ruprecht.de, pg 297

Vander Editions, SA (Belgium) *Tel:* (02) 761 12 12 *Fax:* (02) 761 12 13 *Web Site:* www.adeb.irisnet.be, pg 75

Vandrer mod Lysets Forlag ApS (Denmark) *Tel:* 33157815 *Fax:* 33157815 *Web Site:* www.vandrer-mod-lyset.dk, pg 136

Lok Vangamaya Griha Pvt Ltd (India) *Tel:* (022) 4228222; (022) 4226468, pg 352

Vanguard Books Ltd (Pakistan) *Tel:* (042) 7243779; (042) 7120776; (042) 7120781; (042) 7243783; (042) 7235767 *Fax:* (042) 7245097; (042) 7355197-8 *Web Site:* www.vanguardbooks.com, pg 509

Vani Prakashan (India) *Tel:* (011) 3273167; (011) 2110879; (011) 2286292; (011) 3275710; (011) 225151 *Fax:* (011) 3275710, pg 352

Societa Editrice Vannini (Italy) *Tel:* (030) 313374 *Fax:* (030) 314078, pg 411

Vantage Publishers International Ltd (Nigeria) *Tel:* (022) 415341, pg 502

VAR SKOLA FOERLAG AB

Var Skola Foerlag AB (Sweden) *Tel:* (08) 6623351 *Fax:* (08) 6621843 *E-mail:* var.skola@pi.se, pg 607

Editorial Varazen SA (Mexico) *Tel:* (05) 5146573; (05) 5335274 *Fax:* (05) 2555172, pg 468

D & J Vardikos (Greece) *Tel:* (01) 3631146; (01) 3602150; (01) 3831146 *Fax:* (01) 9564354, pg 315

Fundacao Getulio Vargas (Brazil) *Tel:* (021) 2559 6000 *Fax:* (021) 2553 6372 *Web Site:* www.fgv.br, pg 93

Varlik Yayinlari AS (Turkey) *Tel:* (0212) 5162004; (0212) 5163301; (0212) 5180048; (0212) 4582409 (Direct) *Fax:* (0212) 5162005; (0212) 5162004 (ext 117) *E-mail:* varlik@varlik.com.tr; varlik@isbank.net.tr *Web Site:* www.varlik.com.tr, pg 641

Varsity Book Club (Nigeria) *Tel:* (046) 210013, pg 1230

VAS-Verlag fuer Akademische Schriften, Vas Karl-Heinz Balon (Germany) *Tel:* (069) 77 93 66 *Fax:* (069) 70 73 967 *E-mail:* info@vas.de *Web Site:* www.vas-verlag.de, pg 297

Parlamento Vasco (Spain) *Tel:* (0945) 004 000 *Fax:* (0945) 135 406 *E-mail:* legebiltzarra@parlam.euskadi.net *Web Site:* parlamento.euskadi.net, pg 595

Ladislav Vasicek (Czech Republic), pg 129

Uitgeverij Vassallucci (Netherlands), pg 486

J Vassiliou Bibliopolein (Greece) *Tel:* (01) 3623382; (01) 3623480 *Fax:* (01) 3623580, pg 315

Osuuskunta Vastapaino (Finland) *Tel:* (03) 2146246; (03) 2146245; (03) 2146248 *Fax:* (03) 2146646 *E-mail:* vastapaino@vastapaino.fi, pg 145

Vastu Gyan Publication (India) *Tel:* (011) 3318730, pg 352

Libreria Editrice Vaticana (Holy See (Vatican City State)) *Tel:* (06) 69885003 *Fax:* (06) 69884716, pg 317

Libreria Edtrice Vaticana (Italy) *Tel:* (06) 69885003 *Fax:* (06) 69884716 *E-mail:* lev@publish.va, pg 411

Robert Vaughan Antiquarian Booksellers (United Kingdom) *Tel:* (01789) 205312, pg 1323

Ivan Vazov Publishing House (Bulgaria) *Tel:* (02) 878481; (02) 871572 *Fax:* (02) 878416, pg 98

VCH Verlags-AG (Switzerland) *Tel:* (061) 2710606 *Fax:* (061) 2710618, pg 626

VCL (Netherlands) *Tel:* (038) 3328912 *Fax:* (038) 3327331, pg 1230

VCTA Publishing (Australia) *Tel:* (03) 94199622 *Fax:* (03) 94191205 *E-mail:* vcta@vcta.asn.au *Web Site:* www.vcta.asn.au, pg 46

VdA - Verband deutscher Archivarinnen und Archivare e V (Germany) *Tel:* (03643) 870-235 *Fax:* (03643) 870-164 *E-mail:* info@vda.archiv.net *Web Site:* www.vda.archiv.net, pg 1516

VDE-Verlag GmbH (Germany) *Tel:* (030) 34 80 01 0 *Fax:* (030) 341 70 93 *E-mail:* voss@vde-verlag.de *Web Site:* www.vde-verlag.de, pg 297

Vdf Hochschulverlag AG an der ETH Zurich (Switzerland) *Tel:* (01) 632 42 42 *Fax:* (01) 632 12 32 *E-mail:* verlag@vdf.ethz.ch *Web Site:* www.vdf.ethz.ch, pg 626

VDI-Verlag GmbH (Germany) *Tel:* (0211) 6188 0 *Fax:* (0211) 6188 112 *Web Site:* www.vdi-nachrichten.com, pg 297

Editora Vecchi SA (Brazil) *Tel:* (021) 2444522, pg 93

VEDA (Vydavatel'stvo Slovenskej akademie vied) (Slovakia) *Tel:* (07) 832254; (07) 831172 *Fax:* (07) 835391; (07) 832254, pg 551

Vedecka knihovna V olomouci (Czech Republic) *Tel:* (068) 522 23 75 *Fax:* (068) 522 57 74 *E-mail:* info@vkol.cz *Web Site:* www.vkoe.cz, pg 1460

Veen Bosch & Keuning Uitgevers NV (Netherlands) *Tel:* (030) 2349311 *Fax:* (030) 2300145, pg 486

Veen Bosch & Keuning Uitgevers NV (Netherlands) *Tel:* (030) 2349379 *Fax:* (030) 2300145 *E-mail:* algemeen@veenboschenkeuning.nl, pg 486

Libreria Tecnica Vega (Venezuela) *Tel:* (02) 6221397 *Fax:* (02) 6622092, pg 1324

Vega-Publicacao e Distribuicao de Livros e Revistas, Lda (Portugal) *Tel:* (021) 789414 *Fax:* (021) 786395, pg 530

Ediciones Vega SRL (Venezuela) *Tel:* (02) 6622092; (02) 6621397, pg 763

The Vegetarian Society (United Kingdom) *Tel:* (0161) 925 2000 *Fax:* (0161) 926 9182 *E-mail:* info@vegsoc.org *Web Site:* www.vegsoc.org, pg 752

Veloce Publishing Ltd (United Kingdom) *Tel:* (01305) 260068 *Fax:* (01305) 268864 *E-mail:* info@veloce.co.uk *Web Site:* www.veloce.co.uk; www.velocebooks.com, pg 752

Venezuelan Library & Archives Association (Venezuela) *Tel:* (02) 5721858, pg 1526

Vents d'Ouest (France) *Tel:* (01) 41 46 11 11 *Fax:* (01) 41 46 11 13 *Web Site:* www.glenat.com, pg 189

Ventura Ediciones, SA de CV (Mexico) *Tel:* (05) 5112517; (05) 5530798 *Fax:* (05) 5431173, pg 468

Venture Press Ltd (United Kingdom) *Tel:* (0121) 622 3911 *Fax:* (0121) 622 4860 *E-mail:* info@basw.co.uk *Web Site:* www.basw.co.uk, pg 752

Vera-Reyes Inc (Philippines) *Tel:* (02) 7218792 *Fax:* (02) 7218782, pg 515

Verband der Antiquare Oesterreichs (Austria) *Tel:* (01) 512 15 35 *Fax:* (01) 512 84 82 *E-mail:* sekretariat@hvb.at *Web Site:* www.antiquare.at, pg 1237

Verband der Oesterreichischen Buch-und Presse-Grossisten und der Werbenden Zeitschriftenhaendler (Austria) *Tel:* (01) 5121535 *Fax:* (01) 5128482 *E-mail:* hvb@buecher.at *Web Site:* www.buecher.at, pg 1237

Verband der Schulbuchverlage eV (Germany) *Tel:* (069) 703075 *Fax:* (069) 70790169 *E-mail:* verband-der-schulbuchverlage@t-online.de, pg 1246

Verband der Verlage- und Buchhaendlungen Berlin-Brandenburg eV (Germany) *Tel:* (030) 263918-0 *Fax:* (030) 263918-18, pg 1246

Verband der Verlage und Buchhandlungen in Baden-Wuerttemberg eV (Germany) *Tel:* (0711) 619410 *Fax:* (0711) 6194144 *E-mail:* buchhandelsverband@vvb-bw.de *Web Site:* www.vvb-bw.de, pg 1247

Verband der Verlage und Buchhandlungen in Nordrhein-Westfalen eV (Germany) *Tel:* (0211) 864450 *Fax:* (0211) 324497 *E-mail:* nrw@buchhandel.de *Web Site:* www.buchhandel.de/nrw, pg 1247

Verband der Wissenschaftlichen Gesellschaften Oesterreichs (VWGOe) (Austria) *Tel:* (01) 932166; (01) 934756 *Fax:* (01) 5262054, pg 60

Verband Deutscher Antiquare eV (Germany) *Tel:* (0221) 92548262 *Fax:* (0221) 9257932 *E-mail:* buch@antiquare.de *Web Site:* www.antiquare.de, pg 1247

Verband Deutscher Auskunfts und Verzichnismedien (Germany) *Tel:* (0211) 577995-0 *Fax:* (0211) 577995-44 *E-mail:* info@vdav.org *Web Site:* www.vdav.de, pg 1247

Verband deutschsprachiger Uebersetzer literarischer und wissenschaftlicher Werke eV (VDUe) (Germany) *Tel:* (030) 2829331 *Fax:* (030) 2829331 *E-mail:* kvschweder@aol.com, pg 1126

Verband katholischer Verleger und Buchhaendler eV (Germany) *Tel:* (0228) 2421560 *Fax:* (0228) 2421561 *E-mail:* vkb2000@aol.com, pg 1247

Verband von selbstaendigen Verlagsvertreten Oesterreichs (Austria) *Tel:* (01) 5121535 *Fax:* (01) 5128482 *E-mail:* hvb@buecher.at *Web Site:* www.buecher.at, pg 1237

Verbandsdruckerei AG (Switzerland) *Tel:* (031) 252911, pg 626

INDUSTRY

Verbatim (United Kingdom) *Tel:* (01844) 208474 *Web Site:* www.verbatimbooks.com, pg 752

Verbinum Wydawnictwo Ksiezy Werbistow (Poland) *Tel:* (022) 6107878; (022) 8703286 *Fax:* (022) 6107775, pg 520

Editorial Verbo Divino (Spain) *Tel:* (0948) 556505; (0948) 55 65 11 *Fax:* (0948) 554506 *E-mail:* ventas@verbodivino.es *Web Site:* www.verbodivino.es, pg 595

Editora Verbo Ltda (Brazil) *Tel:* (051) 715-1565 *Fax:* (051) 715-1565 *E-mail:* verbo@virtual-net.com.br *Web Site:* www.editorialverbo.pt, pg 93

Editorial Verbo SA (Portugal) *Tel:* (021) 562131 *Fax:* (021) 3865396; (021) 562139, pg 530

Verbum Foerlag AB (Sweden) *Tel:* (08) 7436500 *Fax:* (08) 6414585 *E-mail:* info@verbum.se *Web Site:* www.verbum.se, pg 607

Verbum Forlag (Norway) *Tel:* 22932700 *Fax:* 22697313, pg 505

Editorial Verbum SL (Spain) *Tel:* (091) 446 88 41 *Fax:* (091) 594 45 59 *E-mail:* verbum@globalnet.es, pg 595

Livraria Verdade e Vida Editora (Portugal) *Tel:* (049) 531417 *Fax:* (049) 531417, pg 530

Editions Verdier (France) *Tel:* (04) 68 24 05 75 *Fax:* (04) 68 24 00 89 *E-mail:* contact@editions_verdier.fr *Web Site:* www.editions-verdier.fr, pg 189

Verein der Benediktiner zu Beuron- Beuroner Kunstverlag (Germany) *Tel:* (07466) 17-228 *Fax:* (07466) 17-209 *E-mail:* kunstverlag@erzabtreibeuron.de *Web Site:* www.erzabtei-beuron.de, pg 297

Verein der Diplom-Bibliothekare an wissenschaftlichen Bibliotheken eV (Germany) *Tel:* (0221) 5747161 *Fax:* (0221) 5747110, pg 1517

Verein Deutscher Bibliothekar eV (Germany) *Tel:* (0251) 8324032 *Fax:* (0251) 8328398, pg 1517

Verein Schweizerischer Archivarinnen und Archivare (Switzerland) *Tel:* (031) 322 89 89; (031) 322 92 85 *Web Site:* www.staluzern.ch/vsa, pg 1523

Vereinigte Fachverlage GmbH (Germany) *Tel:* (06131) 992-01 *Fax:* (06131) 992-100, pg 297

Vereinigung der Buchantiquare und Kupferstichhaendler in der Schweiz (Switzerland) *Tel:* (01) 350-1441 *Fax:* (01) 350-1443 *E-mail:* mail@fluehmann.com *Web Site:* www.vebuku.ch, pg 1262

Vereinigung des katholischen Buchandels der Schweiz (Switzerland) *Tel:* (061) 8210900, pg 1262

Vereinigung Oesterreichischer Bibliothekarinnen und Bibliothekare (VOeB) (Austria) *Tel:* (01) 400084915 *Fax:* (01) 40007219, pg 1512

Vereinte Evangelische Mission, Abt Verlag (Germany) *Tel:* (0202) 89004 134 *Fax:* (0202) 89004 179 *E-mail:* info@vemission.org *Web Site:* www.vemission.org, pg 297

Vereniging van Religieus-Wetenschappelijke Bibliothecarissen (Belgium) *Tel:* (016) 323807 *Fax:* (016) 323862 *E-mail:* etiennedhondt@theo.kuleuven.ac.be *Web Site:* www.theo.kuleuven.ac.be/beth, pg 1512

Javier Vergara Editor SA (Argentina) *Tel:* (011) 4343-7510; (011) 4343-7706 *Fax:* (011) 4334-0173 *E-mail:* ediciones-b-arg@ciudad.com.ar, pg 9

Javier Vergara Editor SA (Spain) *Tel:* (096) 159 05 11 *Fax:* (096) 159 06 97, pg 595

Javier Vergara Editor SA de CV (Mexico) *Tel:* (05) 6053374; (05) 6048283, pg 468

Editions de Vergeures (France) *Tel:* (01) 4543 8260 *Fax:* (01) 4543 8140, pg 189

Varkki Verghese (Luxembourg) *Tel:* 923121 *Fax:* 929076, pg 448

YELLOW PAGES

Buchhandlung Veritas (Austria) *Tel:* (0732) 776451; (0732) 776450 *Fax:* (0732) 776451239, pg 1275

Veritas Co Ltd (Ireland) *Tel:* (01) 8788177 *Fax:* (01) 8786507, pg 364

Veritas Co Ltd (Ireland) *Tel:* (01) 8788177 *Fax:* (01) 8786507 *Web Site:* www.veritas.ie, pg 1292

Veritas Foundation Publication Centre (United Kingdom) *Tel:* (020) 8749 4957; (020) 8749 4965 *Fax:* (020) 8749 4965, pg 752

Veritas Press (Australia) *Fax:* (071) 529256 *E-mail:* copytype@interworx.com.au, pg 46

Verlag Veritas Mediengesellschaft mbH (Austria) *Tel:* (0732) 776451; (0732) 776450 *Fax:* (0732) 776239, pg 60

Verkehrshaus der Schweiz (Switzerland) *Tel:* 314444 *Fax:* 316168, pg 626

Verlag Beltz & Gelberg (Germany) *Tel:* (06201) 60070 *Fax:* (06201) 6007338 *E-mail:* info@beltz.de *Web Site:* www.beltz.de, pg 297

Verlag fur die Frau GmbH (Germany) *Tel:* (0341) 99540 *Fax:* (0341) 9954367 *E-mail:* kuratorium.hdb@t-online.de *Web Site:* www.uni-leipzip.de/leipzig/hdbuches.htm, pg 297

Verlag fur die Rechts- und Anwaltspraxis GmbH & Co (Germany) *Tel:* (0 23 61) 91 42-0 *Fax:* (0 23 61) 91 42-35 *Web Site:* www.zap-verlag.de, pg 298

Verlag fur Schweissen und Verwandte Verfahren (Germany) *Tel:* (0211) 15910 *Fax:* (0211) 1591150 *E-mail:* verlag@dvs-hg.de *Web Site:* www.dvs-verlag.de, pg 298

Verlag Moderne Industrie AG & Co KG (Germany) *Tel:* (089) 54852-02 *Fax:* (089) 54852-8428 *E-mail:* info@mi-verlag.de *Web Site:* www.mi-verlag.de, pg 298

Verlag Anton Schroll & Co (Austria) *Tel:* (01) 5445641-33 *Fax:* (01) 544564166, pg 60

Verlag und Druckkontor Kamp GmbH (Germany) *Tel:* (02 34) 5 16 17-0 *Fax:* (02 34) 5 16 17-18 *E-mail:* verlag@kamp-verlag.de *Web Site:* www.kamp-verlag.de, pg 298

Verlag und Studio fuer Hoerbuchproduktionen (Germany) *Tel:* (06424) 9439-0 *Fax:* (06424) 9439-29 *E-mail:* verlag@hoerbuch.de; info@hoerbuch.de *Web Site:* www.hoerbuch.de; www.hoerbuch.com, pg 298

Verlag Wilhelm Braumuller Universitats-Verlagsbuchhandlung GmbH (Austria) *Tel:* (01) 319 11 59 *Fax:* (01) 310 28 05 *E-mail:* office@braumueller.at *Web Site:* www.braumueller.at, pg 60

Verlagsbuchhandlung AG (Switzerland) *Tel:* (061) 239723, pg 626

Verlagsgruppe Jehle-Rehm GmbH (Germany) *Tel:* (089) 54 8 52-06 *Fax:* (089) 54 8 52-82 30 *E-mail:* verlagsgruppe@jehle-rehm.de *Web Site:* www.jehle-rehm.de, pg 298

Verlegervereinigung Rechtsinformatik eV (Germany) *Tel:* (0221) 943730 *Fax:* (0221) 94373901, pg 1247

Uitgeverij Verloren (Netherlands) *Tel:* (035) 6859856 *Fax:* (035) 6836557 *E-mail:* info@verloren.nl *Web Site:* www.verloren.nl, pg 486

Vernadsky Central Scientific Library of the National Academy of Sciences of Ukraine (Ukraine) *Tel:* (044) 2658104 *Fax:* (044) 2643398, pg 1505

Editions Eliane Vernay (Switzerland) *Tel:* (022) 7350460 *Fax:* (022) 7350460, pg 626

Particip Verold (Iceland) *Tel:* 5688433 *Fax:* 5688142, pg 1229

Veron Editor (Spain) *Tel:* (093) 4781940 *Fax:* (093) 4781908 *E-mail:* veron@veroneditor.com, pg 595

Ediciones Versal SA (Spain) *Tel:* (093) 494 85 90 *Fax:* (093) 419 02 97 *E-mail:* cga.barcelona@cga.es *Web Site:* www.anaya.es, pg 595

Verso (United Kingdom) *Tel:* (020) 7437 3546; (020) 7434 1704; (020) 7439 8194 *Fax:* (020) 7734 0059 *E-mail:* enquiries@verso.co.uk *Web Site:* www.versobooks.com, pg 752

Versus Verlag AG (Switzerland) *Tel:* (01) 2510892 *Fax:* (01) 2626738 *E-mail:* info@versus.ch *Web Site:* www.versus.ch, pg 627

Vertice Ltda (Colombia) *Tel:* (01) 2437113, pg 114

Verulam Publishing Ltd (United Kingdom) *Tel:* (01727) 872770 *Fax:* (01727) 873866 *E-mail:* 100124.2375@compuserve.com; sales@verulampub.demon.co.uk, pg 753

Vervuert Verlagsgesellschaft (Germany) *Tel:* (069) 5974617 *Fax:* (069) 5978743 *E-mail:* info@iberoamericanalibros.com *Web Site:* www.ibero-americana.net, pg 298

Verwertungsgesellschaft Wort (Germany) *Tel:* (089) 514120 *Fax:* (089) 5141258 *Web Site:* www.vgwort.de, pg 1247

Veschi (Italy) *Tel:* (02) 270741 *Fax:* (02) 27074510, pg 411

Veselka Publishers (Ukraine) *Tel:* (044) 2139501 *Fax:* (044) 2133359, pg 643

Editura de Vest (Romania) *Tel:* (056) 191956; (056) 118218 *Fax:* (056) 14212, pg 536

Vestala Verlag (Romania) *Tel:* (01) 3452827 *Fax:* (01) 3452827; (01) 2228597, pg 536

Vesti (Yugoslavia) *Tel:* (031) 21263; (031) 42488; (031) 42203, pg 766

Vett & Viten AS (Norway) *Tel:* 66849040 *Fax:* 66845590 *E-mail:* vv@vettviten.no *Web Site:* www.vettviten.no, pg 505

Verlag Alfred Vetter (Switzerland) *Tel:* (01) 2011184, pg 627

Vexer Verlag (Switzerland) *Tel:* (071) 2778151 *Fax:* (071) 2447987 *E-mail:* vexer@freesurf.ch, pg 627

Vianello Libri (Italy) *Tel:* (0422) 440666 *Fax:* (0422) 440645 *E-mail:* vianello@mail.gpnet.it, pg 411

Vibal Publishing House Inc (VPHI) (Philippines) *Tel:* (02) 993764; (02) 7122722 *Fax:* (02) 7118852, pg 515

Vice Versa Verlag (Germany) *Tel:* (030) 61 60 92 37 *Fax:* (030) 61609238 *E-mail:* viceversa@comp.de, pg 298

Gobierno de Canarias - Viceconsejeria de Cultura y Deportes (Spain) *Tel:* (092) 2474119 *Fax:* (092) 2474165, pg 595

Editorial Vicens-Vives (Spain) *Tel:* (093) 2523700 *Fax:* (093) 2523711 *E-mail:* e@vicensvives.es *Web Site:* www.vicensvives.es, pg 595

Ediciones A Madrid Vicente (Spain) *Tel:* (091) 5336926 *Fax:* (091) 5330286 *E-mail:* amadrid@acta.es *Web Site:* www.amvediciones.com, pg 595

Vicks Lithograph & Printing Corp (United States) *Tel:* 315-736-9344 *Fax:* 315-736-1901, pg 1146, 1208

Ed Victor Ltd (United Kingdom) *Tel:* (020) 7304 4100 *Fax:* (020) 7304 4111, pg 1122

Bibliotheque Victor Schoelcher (Martinique) *Tel:* 04702667 *Fax:* 04724555, pg 1484

Victoria Publishers (Lithuania) *Tel:* (02) 221915; (02) 632632; (02) 221914 *Fax:* (02) 630797, pg 446

Victoria University Press (New Zealand) *Tel:* (04) 4966580 *Fax:* (04) 4711701 *E-mail:* victoria-press@vuw.ac.nz *Web Site:* www.vup.vuw.ac.nz, pg 496

Victorian Arts Centre Trust (Australia) *Tel:* (03) 9281 8000 *Fax:* (03) 9629 2719 *Web Site:* www.artscentre.net.au, pg 46

Victory Offset Prima PT (Indonesia) *Tel:* (021) 460-2742; (021) 460-8968 *Fax:* (021) 460-2740; (021) 4682-0551 *E-mail:* info@victoryoffset.com *Web Site:* www.victoryoffset.com, pg 1136, 1157

Victory Offset Prima PT (Indonesia) *Tel:* (021) 460-8968; (021) 460-2742 *Fax:* (021) 460-2740; (021) 4682-0551 *E-mail:* info@victoryoffset.com *Web Site:* www.victoryoffset.com, pg 1198

Victory Offset Prima PT (Indonesia) *Tel:* (021) 460-2742; (021) 460-8968 *Fax:* (021) 460-2740; (021) 4682-0551 *E-mail:* info@victoryoffset.com *Web Site:* www.victoryoffset.com, pg 1212

Editora Vida Crista Ltda (Brazil) *Tel:* (011) 217-0522 *Fax:* (011) 217-0522 *E-mail:* editora@vidacrista.com.br *Web Site:* www.vidacrista.com.br, pg 93

Videograf II Sp z o o Zaklad Poracy Chronionej (Poland) *Tel:* (03) 2036558; (03) 2036559; (03) 2036560 *Fax:* (03) 2036558; (03) 2036559; (03) 2036560 *E-mail:* videograf@videograf.dnd.com.pl, pg 520

Vidhi (India) *Tel:* (011) 389001, pg 352

Vidura Science Publishers (Sri Lanka) *Tel:* (091) 564713, pg 598

Vidya Puri (India) *Tel:* (0671) 620637; (0671) 617260, pg 352

Vidyarthi Mithram Press (India) *Tel:* (0481) 563281; (0481) 563282; (0481) 564713; (0481) 562616 (after office hours) *Fax:* (0481) 562616, pg 352

Les Editions Vie ouvriere ASBL (Belgium) *Tel:* (02) 5125090 *Fax:* (02) 5145231, pg 75

Vieda (Latvia) *Tel:* (02) 7210943 *Fax:* (02) 7210943, pg 442

Vienna International Centre Library (Austria) *Tel:* (01) 2600 *Fax:* (01) 2600 29584 *E-mail:* vicl@iaea.org, pg 1452

Vier-Tuerme GmbH Benedikt Press (Germany) *Tel:* (09324) 20214 *Fax:* (09324) 20495, pg 1154, 1195

Vier Tuerme GmbH Verlag Klosterbetriebe (Germany) *Tel:* (9324) 20 292 (Verlag); (9324) 20 214 (Druckerei); (9324) 20 213 (Buchhandlung) *Fax:* (9324) 20 495 *E-mail:* info@vier-tuerme.de *Web Site:* www.vier-tuerme.de, pg 298

Friedr Vieweg & Sohn Verlagsgesellschaft mbH (Germany) *Tel:* (0611) 7878361 *Fax:* (0611) 7878470 *Web Site:* www.vieweg.de, pg 298

Editora Vigilia Ltda (Brazil) *Tel:* (031) 3372744; (031) 3372363 *Fax:* (031) 3372834, pg 93

Editions Vigot Freres (France) *Tel:* (01) 4329 5450 *Fax:* (01) 4634 0589, pg 189

Vikas Publishing House Pvt Ltd (India) *Tel:* (011) 4315313; (011) 4315570; (011) 4317857 *Fax:* (011) 4310879, pg 353

Viking (United Kingdom) *Tel:* (020) 7416 3000 *Fax:* (020) 7416 3274, pg 753

Viking Children's Books (United Kingdom) *Tel:* (020) 7416 3000 *Fax:* (020) 7416 3086, pg 753

Viking Sevenseas NZ Ltd (New Zealand) *Tel:* (04) 902-8240 *Fax:* (04) 902-8240 *E-mail:* vikings@paradise.net.nz, pg 496

Viktoria-Verlag Peter Marti (Switzerland) *Tel:* (031) 7911932 *Fax:* (031) 7912564, pg 627

Magyar Tudomanyos Akademia VilagGazdasagi Kutato Intezet (Hungary) *Tel:* (01) 1668433 *Fax:* (01) 1620661, pg 327

Editions Village Mondial (France) *Tel:* (01) 44.32.08.00 *Fax:* (01) 43.25.43.37 *E-mail:* vilmon@easynet.fr *Web Site:* www.village-mondial.com, pg 189

Villamonta Publishing Service Inc (Australia) *Tel:* (03) 5229 6251 *Fax:* (03) 5222 5399 *E-mail:* villapub@ozemail.com.au, pg 47

Biblioteca Daniel Cosio Villegas El Colegio de Mexico AC (Mexico) *Tel:* (055) 5449 3000; (055) 5449 2909; (055) 5449 2936 *Fax:* (055) 5645 0464; (055) 5645 4584 *E-mail:* biblio@colmex.mx *Web Site:* biblio.colmex.mx, pg 1485

Villegas Editores Ltda (Colombia) *Tel:* (01) 6161788 *Fax:* (01) 6160020; (01) 6160073 *E-mail:* villegas@colomsat.net.co; villedi@cable.net *Web Site:* www.villegaseditores.com, pg 114

La Villeguerin (France) *Tel:* (01) 45232132 *Fax:* (01) 47701484, pg 189

Vilnius Art Academy Publishing House (Lithuania) *Tel:* (02) 613004; (02) 613806 *Fax:* (02) 619966 *E-mail:* leidykla@vda.lt, pg 446

Vilnius University Library (Lithuania) *Tel:* (02) 687101 *Fax:* (02) 687104 *E-mail:* mb@mb.vu.lt *Web Site:* www.mb.vu.lt, pg 1482

Editions Vilo SA (France) *Tel:* (01) 45 77 08 05 *Fax:* (01) 45 79 97 15, pg 189

Vinaches Lopez, Luisa (Spain) *Tel:* (01) 3694488 *Fax:* (01) 3694488, pg 595

Curt R Vincentz Verlag (Germany) *Tel:* (05 11) 9910000 *Fax:* (05 11) 9910099 *E-mail:* info@vincentz.de *Web Site:* www.vincentz.de, pg 298

Vinciana Editrice sas (Italy) *Tel:* (02) 4982306 *Fax:* (02) 48003275 *E-mail:* info@vinciana.com *Web Site:* www.vinciana.com, pg 411

Forlaget Vindrose A/S (Denmark) *Tel:* 36153615 *Fax:* 36153616, pg 136

Vine House Distribution Ltd (United Kingdom) *Tel:* (0182) 5723398 *Fax:* (0182) 5724188 *E-mail:* sales@vinehouseuk.co.uk *Web Site:* www.vinehouseuk.co.uk, pg 1323

Vinpress Sdn Bhd (Malaysia) *Tel:* (03) 7173333; (03) 7188877 *Fax:* (03) 7192942, pg 455

Vinten Editor (Uruguay) *Tel:* (02) 2090223 *Fax:* (02) 290223 *E-mail:* dayraq@chasque.apc.org, pg 761

Vipopremo Agencies (Kenya) *Tel:* (02) 227189; (02) 333882, pg 433

Virago Press (United Kingdom) *Tel:* (020) 7911 8000 *Fax:* (020) 7911 8100 *E-mail:* virago.press@timewarnerbooks.co.uk *Web Site:* www.virago.co.uk, pg 753

Viratham (Thailand) *Tel:* (02) 866848, pg 636

Virgin Publishing Ltd (United Kingdom) *Tel:* (020) 7386 3300 *Fax:* (020) 7386 3360 *E-mail:* info@virgin-books.co.uk; info@virgin-pub.co.uk *Web Site:* www.virginbooks.com, pg 753

Virlogeux Francoise-COMEDIT (Martinique) *Tel:* 683985 *Fax:* 683423, pg 456

Visalaandhra Publishing House (India) *Tel:* (040) 4744580 *Fax:* (040) 4735905, pg 1290

Edition Curt Visel (Germany) *Tel:* (08331) 2853 *Fax:* (08331) 490364 *E-mail:* info@editon-curt-visel.de *Web Site:* www.edition-curt-visel.de, pg 298

Vision Srl (Italy) *Tel:* (06) 44292688 *Fax:* (06) 44292688 *E-mail:* Vision.srl@stm.it *Web Site:* www.visionpubl.com, pg 411

Vision Books Pvt Ltd (India) *Tel:* (011) 386-2267; (011) 386-2201 *Fax:* (011) 386-2935 *E-mail:* mail@orientpaperbacks.com, pg 353

Vision Pub Co Ltd (Hong Kong) *Tel:* 26798119 *Fax:* 26798119, pg 322

Vision Publications (Zimbabwe), pg 769

Visor Distribuciones, SA (Spain) *Tel:* (091) 4681248; (091) 4681011; (091) 4681102 *Fax:* (091) 4681098 *E-mail:* editorial@visordis.es *Web Site:* www.visordis.es, pg 596

Visor Libros (Spain) *Tel:* (091) 5492655 *Fax:* (091) 5448695 *E-mail:* visor-libros@visor-libros.com *Web Site:* www.visor-libros.com, pg 596

Vista Computer Services Ltd (United Kingdom) *Tel:* (01923) 820920 *Fax:* (01923) 827713, pg 1142

Vista Point Verlag GmbH (Germany) *Tel:* (0221) 921613-0 *Fax:* (0221) 921613-14 *E-mail:* info@vistapoint.de *Web Site:* www.vista-point.net, pg 299

Vista Productions Ltd (Hong Kong) *Tel:* 25632492; 25623496 *Fax:* 25655803, pg 322

Vista Publications (Australia) *Tel:* (03) 9523 5623 *Fax:* (03) 9523 5623 *E-mail:* vistaof@mbox.com.au, pg 47

S Viswanathan (Printers & Publishers) Pvt Ltd (India) *Tel:* (044) 8265623; (044) 8265633 *Fax:* (044) 8256002 *E-mail:* svprint@md2.vsnl.net.in, pg 353

Vita (Belgium) *Tel:* (09) 3842114 *Fax:* (09) 3842114, pg 75

Vita e Pensiero (Italy) *Tel:* (02) 72342335; (02) 72342259 *Fax:* (02) 72342260 *E-mail:* editvep@mi.unicatt.it *Web Site:* www.vitaepensiero.it, pg 411

La Vita Felice (Italy) *Tel:* (02) 29524600 *Fax:* (02) 29401896, pg 411

Vitagraf (Croatia) *Tel:* (051) 215087; (051) 338489 *Toll Free Tel:* (051) 322880 *Fax:* (051) 212622 *E-mail:* vitagraf@ri.hinet.hr, pg 120

Vital Publications (Australia) *Tel:* (03) 9379-1219 *Fax:* (03) 9379-0015 *E-mail:* vitalpubs@churchesofchrist.org.au; aceditor@ozemail.com.au, pg 47

Vitalis SRO (Czech Republic) *Tel:* (02) 57530732 *Fax:* (02) 57531974 *E-mail:* info@vitalis-verlag.com *Web Site:* vitalis-verlag.com, pg 129

Viva Lithographers Pte Ltd (Singapore) *Tel:* 2721880 *Fax:* 2735425, pg 1139

Vivalda Editori SRL (Italy) *Tel:* (011) 7720444 *Fax:* (011) 7720499 *E-mail:* vivalda@vivalda.com, pg 411

Vivek Prakashan (India) *Tel:* (011) 2529649 *Fax:* (011) 6827347, pg 353

Vivere In SRL (Italy) *Tel:* (080) 065943323 *Fax:* (080) 065943323 *E-mail:* edizionivivierein@tin.it *Web Site:* www.viverein.it, pg 411

Luis Vives (Edelvives) (Spain) *Tel:* (076) 3344890 *Fax:* (076) 3344892, pg 1139, 1201

Luis Vives (Edelvives) (Spain) *Tel:* (091) 3344890; (091) 3344884 *Fax:* (091) 3344892; (091) 3344894, pg 1222

Editions Vivez Soleil SA (Switzerland) *Tel:* (022) 3492092 *Fax:* (022) 3492092, pg 627

Editions Viviane Hamy (France) *Tel:* (01) 53171600 *Fax:* (01) 53171609 *E-mail:* information@viviane-hamy.fr *Web Site:* www.viviane-hamy.fr, pg 189

Viviani Editore srl (Italy) *Tel:* (06) 6872855 *Fax:* (06) 6872856, pg 412

Vivlia Publishers & Booksellers (South Africa) *Tel:* (011) 472-3912 *Fax:* (011) 472-4904 *E-mail:* vivlia@icon.co.ta, pg 560

Vivliothiki Eftychia Galeou (Greece) *Tel:* (01) 6841191 *Fax:* (01) 6825862, pg 315

Vizavi Editions (Mauritius) *Tel:* 2080983 *Fax:* 2113047 *E-mail:* vizavi@intnet.mu, pg 457

Cristina Vizcaino Literary Agency (Spain) *Tel:* (091) 5944992 *Fax:* (091) 5944992 *E-mail:* vizcaino@infornet.es *Web Site:* www.vizcaino.com, pg 1116

Vjesnik dd (Croatia) *Tel:* (01) 3641 543; (01) 3641 453 *Fax:* (01) 3641 486 *E-mail:* hrvatska.tiskara1@zg.tel.hr, pg 1132

VJK Verlag Josef Knecht (Germany) *Tel:* (069) 281767; (069) 281768 *Fax:* (069) 296653, pg 299

Vlaamse Boekverkopersbond (VBB) (Belgium) *Tel:* (03) 2395740; (03) 2308835 *Fax:* (03) 2395740 *E-mail:* vbb@boek.be *Web Site:* www.boek.be, pg 1238

Vlaamse Esperantobond VZW (Belgium) *Tel:* (03) 2343400 *Fax:* (03) 2335433 *E-mail:* esperanto@agoranet.be *Web Site:* bold.belnet.be, pg 75

Vlaamse Uitgevers Vereniging (VUV) (Belgium) *Tel:* (03) 2308923 *Fax:* (03) 2812240 *Web Site:* www.vbvb.be, pg 1238

Vlaamse Vereniging voor Bibliotheek- Archief-en Documentatiewezen (VVBAD) (Belgium) *Tel:* (03) 2814457 *Fax:* (03) 2188077 *E-mail:* vvbad@vvbad.be *Web Site:* www.vvbad.be, pg 1512

Vlassi (Greece) *Tel:* (01) 3812900 *Fax:* (01) 3827557, pg 1287

Vlassis (Greece) *Tel:* (01) 3812900 *Fax:* (01) 3827557, pg 316

Editions VM (France) *Tel:* (01) 49 52 14 53; (01) 49 52 14 00 *Fax:* (01) 49 52 14 41, pg 189

VNU Business Press Group BV (Netherlands) *Tel:* (020) 4875487 *Fax:* (020) 4875700, pg 487

VNU Business Publications (United Kingdom) *Tel:* (020) 7316 9170 *Fax:* (020) 7316 9440 *Web Site:* www.vnu.co.uk, pg 753

VNU Business Publications BV (Netherlands) *Tel:* (020) 4875487 *Fax:* (020) 4875700, pg 487

Vocatio Publishing House (Poland) *Tel:* (022) 648-5450 *Fax:* (022) 648-6382 *E-mail:* vocatio@vocatio.com.pl *Web Site:* www.vocatio.com.pl, pg 520

Voce della Bibbia (Italy) *Tel:* (059) 55 63 03 *Fax:* (059) 57 31 05 *E-mail:* bbbitaly@tin.it *Web Site:* www.vocedellabibbia.org, pg 412

Vodnar (Czech Republic) *Tel:* (02) 51563603 *Fax:* (02) 51563603 *E-mail:* naklvodnar@volny.cz *Web Site:* www.volny.cz/naklvodnar, pg 129

Verlag A Vogel (Switzerland) *Tel:* (071) 335 66 66 *Fax:* (071) 334684 *E-mail:* vavch@access.ch *Web Site:* www.verlag-avogel.ch, pg 627

Vogel Medien GmbH & Co KG (Germany) *Tel:* (0931) 418-2028 *Fax:* (0931) 418-2860 *E-mail:* info@vogel-medien.de *Web Site:* www.vogel-medien.de, pg 299

Voggenreiter-Verlag (Germany) *Tel:* (0228) 93 575-0 *Fax:* (0228) 35 50 53 *E-mail:* info@voggenreiter.de *Web Site:* www.voggenreiter.de, pg 299

Vogt-Schild Ag, Druck und Verlag (Switzerland) *Tel:* (065) 247247 *Fax:* (065) 247244, pg 627

Literarische Agentur Diana Voigt (Austria) *Tel:* (01) 5333191 *Fax:* (01) 5333192 *E-mail:* voigt@literaturagentur.at *Web Site:* www.literaturagentur.at, pg 1109

La Voix du Regard (France) *Tel:* (01) 46.70.88.69 *Fax:* (01) 46.70.88.69 *E-mail:* jnelva@club-internet.fr, pg 189

Vojnoizdavacki i novinski centar (Yugoslavia) *Tel:* (011) 644188 *Fax:* (011) 644042, pg 766

Volk NV, Boekandel het (Belgium) *Tel:* (091) 265 67 20 *Fax:* (091) 225 20 71, pg 75

Volk und Wissen Verlag GmbH & Co (Germany) *Tel:* (030) 201 83-500 *Fax:* (030) 2041846 *E-mail:* mail@vwv.de *Web Site:* www.vwv.de, pg 299

Stichting Volksboekwinkel (Suriname) *Tel:* 472469, pg 599

Verlag Deutsches Volksheimstaettenwerk GmbH (Germany) *Tel:* (0228) 7259930; (0228) 7259931 *Fax:* (0228) 7259919, pg 299

Voltaire Foundation Ltd (United Kingdom) *Tel:* (01865) 284600 *Fax:* (01865) 284610 *E-mail:* email@voltaire.ox.ac.uk *Web Site:* www.voltaire.ox.ac.uk, pg 753

Editorial Voluntad SA (Colombia) *Tel:* (01) 241 04 44 *Fax:* (01) 241 04 39 *E-mail:* secsai@voluntad.com.co *Web Site:* www.voluntad.com.co, pg 114

Volvox Globator (Czech Republic) *Tel:* (02) 242 177 21, pg 129

Verlagsgruppe Georg von Holtzbrinck GmbH (Germany) *Tel:* (0711) 21500 *Fax:* (0711) 2150269 *Web Site:* www.holtzbrink.com, pg 299

Von Kloeden KG (Germany) *Tel:* (030) 887 125 12 *Fax:* (030) 887 125 19 *E-mail:* v.kloeden@t-online.de *Web Site:* www.vonkloeden.de; www.buchkatalog.de/vonkloeden, pg 1285

Dokument und Analyse Verlag Bogislaw von Randow (Germany) *Tel:* (089) 2720100 *Fax:* (089) 2720311, pg 299

von Stengel oHG Verlag (Germany) *Tel:* (040) 2791485 *Fax:* (089) 6099783, pg 299

Verlag Philipp von Zabern (Germany) *Tel:* (06131) 287470 *Fax:* (06131) 223710 *E-mail:* zabern@zabern.de *Web Site:* www.zabern.de, pg 299

Vorarlberger Verlagsanstalt Aktiengesellschaft (Austria) *Tel:* (05572) 2469778 *Fax:* (05572) 24 6 97-78 *E-mail:* office@vva.at *Web Site:* www.vva.at, pg 60

Voronezh State University Publishers (Russian Federation) *Tel:* (0732) 560481, pg 542

VOSA, SL Ediciones (Spain) *Tel:* (091) 7259430 *Fax:* (091) 7259430, pg 596

Votobia sro (Czech Republic) *Tel:* (068) 523 18 90 *Fax:* (068) 522 46 21 *E-mail:* votobia@mbox.vol.cz, pg 129

Votsis Nikos (Greece) *Fax:* (01) 3820646 *E-mail:* mvotsis@otenet.gr, pg 1287

Votum Verlag GmbH (Germany) *Tel:* (0251) 26514-0 *Fax:* (0251) 26514-20 *E-mail:* info@votum-verlag.de *Web Site:* www.votum-verlag.de, pg 299

Vox Verlag und Vertrieb (Romania) *Tel:* (01) 6378584 *Fax:* (01) 6376829, pg 536

Voyenizdat (Russian Federation) *Tel:* (095) 1950154 *Fax:* (095) 1952454, pg 542

Publicaciones Voz de Gracia (Puerto Rico) *Tel:* (787) 784-4366 *Fax:* (787) 261-5401 *E-mail:* vozdegra@caribe.net, pg 531

Vozes Editora Ltda (Brazil) *Tel:* (024) 2375112 *Fax:* (024) 2314676, pg 93

R Vreeland & Co (United Kingdom) *Tel:* (020) 7242 8721 *Fax:* (020) 7379 0801, pg 1130

Vremea Publishers Ltd (Romania) *Tel:* (01) 3358131 *Fax:* (01) 3110219 *E-mail:* vremea@fx.ro, pg 536

H de Vries Boeken (Netherlands) *Tel:* (023) 5319458 *Fax:* (023) 5311680, pg 1301

C De Vries Brouwers BVBA (Belgium) *Tel:* (03) 2374180 *Fax:* (03) 2377001, pg 75

Vrije Universiteit Brussel Universiteitsbibliotheek (Belgium) *Tel:* (02) 6292111 *Fax:* (02) 6292282 *E-mail:* snamenwi@vnet3.uub.ac.be, pg 1453

Librairie Philosophique J Vrin (France) *Tel:* (01) 43 54 03 47 *Fax:* (01) 43 54 48 18 *E-mail:* contact@vrin.fr *Web Site:* www.vrin.fr, pg 189

VS Verlagshaus Stuttgart GmbH (Germany) *Tel:* (0711) 25800 *Fax:* (0711) 2580685 *E-mail:* vstuttgart@aol.com, pg 299

Vysoka skola banska - Technicka Univerzita Ostrava (Czech Republic) *Tel:* (069) 6991278 *Fax:* (069) 6917301, pg 1460

Vserossijskaja gosudarstvennaja biblioteka inostrannoj literatury im M I Rudomino (Russian Federation) *Tel:* (095) 9153621 *Fax:* (095) 9153637 *E-mail:* vgbil@libfl.ru *Web Site:* www.libfl.ru, pg 1495

Vsesoyuznii Molodejnii Knizhnii Centre (Russian Federation) *Tel:* (095) 924 7879, pg 542

Vsesoyuznoe Obyedineniye Vneshtorgizdat (Russian Federation) *Tel:* (095) 2505162 *Fax:* (095) 2539794, pg 542

VSO Books (United Kingdom) *Tel:* (020) 8780 7200 *Fax:* (020) 8780 7300 *E-mail:* vsobooks@vso.org.uk *Web Site:* www.vso.org.uk, pg 1268

VTB-Travel Bookshop (Belgium) *Tel:* (03) 220-33-66 *Fax:* (03) 220-33-84 *E-mail:* boekhandel@vtb.be, pg 1276

VU Boekhandel/Uitgeverij BV (Netherlands) *Tel:* (020) 6444355 *Fax:* (020) 6462719 *E-mail:* vu~uitgevererij@vuboekhandel.ne, pg 487

VUB University Press (Belgium) *Tel:* (02) 6293590 *Fax:* (02) 6292694 *E-mail:* vubpress@vnet3.vub.ac.be *Web Site:* www.vubpress.org, pg 75

Editorial Vuelta, SA de CV (Mexico) *Tel:* (05) 6835633 *Fax:* (05) 6580074, pg 468

Librairie Vuibert (France) *Tel:* (01) 44 08 49 00 *Fax:* (01) 44 08 49 39 *Web Site:* www.vuibert.com, pg 189

Vuk Karadzic (Yugoslavia) *Tel:* (011) 628066; (011) 628043 *Fax:* (011) 623150; (011) 634232, pg 766

Vuk Karadzic (Yugoslavia) *Tel:* (011) 628066; (011) 628043 *Fax:* (011) 623150, pg 1325

Ediciones Vulcano (Spain) *Tel:* (091) 461 44 58; (091) 500 16 49 *Fax:* (091) 461 44 58 *E-mail:* vulcano@vulcanoediciones.com *Web Site:* www.vulcanoediciones.com, pg 596

Vulkan-Verlag GmbH (Germany) *Tel:* (0201) 82002-14 *Fax:* (0201) 82002-34 *Web Site:* www.oldenbourg.de/vulkan-verlag, pg 299

Uitgeverij De Vuurbaak BV (Netherlands) *Tel:* (0342) 411731 *Fax:* (0342) 411631 *E-mail:* vuurbaak@nd.nl *Web Site:* www.vuurbank.nl, pg 487

VVF Verlag V Florentz GmbH (Germany) *Tel:* (089) 285503 *Fax:* (089) 2809528, pg 299

VWB-Verlag fur Wissenschaft & Bildung, Amand Aglaster (Germany) *Tel:* (030) 251 04 15 *Fax:* (030) 251 11 36 *E-mail:* 100615.1565@compuserve.com *Web Site:* www.vwb-verlag.com, pg 300

Vydavatel' Sky odbor (Slovakia) *Tel:* (0842) 31861 *Fax:* (0842) 32993 *E-mail:* vms@esix.matica.sk, pg 551

Vydavatel' Sky odbor (Slovakia) *Tel:* (0842) 31861 *Fax:* (0842) 33188 *E-mail:* snk@matica.sk, pg 1497

Vydavatelstvi Ceskeho Geologickeho Ustavu (Czech Republic) *Tel:* (02) 24002576 *Fax:* (02) 57320438, pg 129

Vydavatelstvo Junior sro Slovart Print (Slovakia) *Tel:* (07) 44872378; (07) 44872379; (07) 44872103 *Fax:* (07) 44872133 *E-mail:* junior@junior.sk, pg 551

Vydavatel'stvo Osveta (Verlag Osveta) (Slovakia) *Tel:* (0842) 33503; (0842) 32921; (0842) 35037 *Fax:* (0842) 35036, pg 551

Vysehrad (Czech Republic) *Tel:* (02) 2326 851; (02) 24 22 17 03 *Fax:* (02) 24 22 17 03 *E-mail:* info@ivysehrad.cz *Web Site:* www.ivysehrad.cz, pg 129

Vysoka Vojenska Skola Letecka (Slovakia) *Tel:* (095) 6512183; (095) 6333851 *Fax:* (095) 333851, pg 551

Izdatelstvo Vysshaya Shkola (Russian Federation) *Tel:* (095) 2000456 *Fax:* (095) 2090350, pg 543

Vyturys Vyturio leidykla, UAB (Lithuania) *Tel:* (02) 613615; (02) 627404; (02) 622542; (02) 629407 *Fax:* (02) 629407; (02) 613615, pg 446

W Ludwig Verlag GmbH (Germany) *Tel:* (089) 51 48 0 *Fax:* (089) 51 48 229 *E-mail:* ludwig-verlag.de@econ-ullstein-list.de *Web Site:* www.ludwig-verlag.de, pg 300

Verlag Die Waage (Switzerland) *Tel:* (01) 7155569; (01) 7241969 *Fax:* (01) 7243127, pg 627

M Waagmeester-Verkuyl (Suriname) *Tel:* 498356, pg 599

Uitgeverij Waanders BV (Netherlands) *Tel:* (038) 4658628 *Fax:* (038) 4655989 *E-mail:* info@waanders.nl *Web Site:* www.waanders.nl, pg 487

Wydawnictwo WAB (Poland) *Tel:* (022) 646 05 10; (022) 646 05 11; (022) 646 01 74; (022) 646 01 75 *Fax:* (022) 646 05 10; (022) 646 05 11; (022) 646 01 74; (022) 646 01 75 *E-mail:* wab@wab.com.pl *Web Site:* www.wab.com.pl, pg 520

Wachholtz Verlag GmbH (Germany) *Tel:* (04321) 906-276 *Fax:* (04321) 906-275 *E-mail:* info@wachholtz.de *Web Site:* www.wachholtz.de, pg 300

Verlag Klaus Wagenbach GmbH (Germany) *Tel:* (030) 23 51 51-0 *Fax:* (030) 2 11 61 40 *E-mail:* mail@wagenbach.de *Web Site:* www.wagenbach.de, pg 300

Friedenauer Presse Katharina Wagenbach-Wolff (Germany) *Tel:* (030) 312 99 23 *Fax:* (030) 312 99 02 *Web Site:* www.friedenauer-press.de, pg 300

Wageningen Pers (Netherlands) *Tel:* (0317) 476515 *Fax:* (0317) 426044 *E-mail:* info@wageningenpers.nl *Web Site:* www.wageningenpers.nl, pg 487

Universitaetsverlag Wagner GmbH (Austria) *Tel:* (0512) 587721 *Fax:* (0512) 582209 *E-mail:* mail@uvw.at, pg 60

Wagner'sche Universitaetsbuchhandlung (Austria) *Tel:* (05222) 22316, pg 1275

AB Wahlstrom & Widstrand (Sweden) *Tel:* (08) 6968480 *Fax:* (08) 6968380 *E-mail:* info@wwd.se *Web Site:* www.wwd.se, pg 607

Wahlstrom & Widstrand (Sweden) *Tel:* (08) 6968480 *Fax:* (08) 6968380, pg 607

B Wahlstroms (Sweden) *Tel:* (08) 6198600 *Fax:* (08) 6189761 *E-mail:* info@wahlstroms.se *Web Site:* www.wahlstroms.se, pg 607

John Waite Ltd (United Kingdom) *Tel:* (1797) 344 177 *Fax:* (1797)) 344 177, pg 754

Wakefield Press Pty Ltd (Australia) *Tel:* (08) 8362 8800 *Fax:* (08) 8362 7592 *E-mail:* info@wakefieldpress.com.au *Web Site:* www.wakefieldpress.com.au, pg 47

Verlag im Waldgut AG (Switzerland) *Tel:* (054) 222344 *Fax:* (054) 7288927, pg 627

Wales Tourist Board (United Kingdom) *Tel:* (029) 2049 9909 *Fax:* (029) 2048 5031, pg 754

Walhalla Fachverlag GmbH & Co KG Praetoria (Germany) *Tel:* (0941) 5684-0 *Fax:* (0941) 5684-111 *E-mail:* walhalla@walhalla.de *Web Site:* www.walhassa.de, pg 300

Walker Books Australia Pty Ltd (Australia) *Tel:* (02) 9517 9577 *Fax:* (02) 9517 9997, pg 47

Walker Books Ltd (United Kingdom) *Tel:* (020) 7793 0909 *Fax:* (020) 7587 1123, pg 754

S Walker Literary Agency (United Kingdom) *Tel:* (01234) 216229, pg 1122

Sally Walker Language Services (United Kingdom) *Tel:* (0117) 9291594 *Fax:* (0117) 9290633 *E-mail:* swls43@aol.com *Web Site:* www.sallywalker.co.uk, pg 1130

Edgar Wallace Society (Netherlands) *Tel:* (045) 5670050 *Fax:* (045) 5670070, pg 1366

Librairie Walter (Togo), pg 1314

Walter Verlag AG (Switzerland) *Tel:* (062) 341188 *Fax:* (062) 321184 *Web Site:* www.walter-verlag.ch, pg 627

Verlag Mag Wanzenbock (Austria) *Tel:* (01) 7148542 *Fax:* (01) 7135814, pg 60

The Warburg Institute (United Kingdom) *Tel:* (020) 7862 8949 *Fax:* (020) 7862 8955 *E-mail:* warburg@sas.ac.uk *Web Site:* www.sas.ac.uk/warburg/, pg 754

Ward Lock Educational Co Ltd (United Kingdom) *Tel:* (01342) 318980 *Fax:* (01342) 410980 *E-mail:* wle@lingkee.com, pg 754

Ward Lock Ltd (United Kingdom) *Tel:* (020) 7420 5555 *Fax:* (020) 7240 7261, pg 754

Peter Ward Book Exports (United Kingdom) *Tel:* (020) 8772 3300 *Fax:* (020) 8772 3309 *E-mail:* pwbookex@dircon.co.uk, pg 1122, 1323

Waren-Erzeungungs-und Handelsgesellschaft GmbH (Austria) Tel: (0662) 88861011 Fax: (0662) 8886202, pg 60

Warna Publishers (Sri Lanka), pg 598

Frederick Warne Publishers Ltd (United Kingdom) Tel: (020) 7010 3000 Fax: (020) 7010 6706, pg 754

Warner Chappell Plays Ltd (United Kingdom) Tel: (020) 8563 5800 Fax: (020) 8563 5801 E-mail: warner.chappell@dial.pipex.com, pg 1122

Uwe Warnke Verlag (Germany) Tel: (030) 29049903 E-mail: warnke@snafu.de, pg 300

Wartburg Verlag GmbH (Germany) Tel: (03643) 24 61-11 Fax: (03643) 24 61-18 E-mail: buch@warbburgverlag.de Web Site: www.glaube-und-heimat.de, pg 300

Waruni Publishers (Sri Lanka) Tel: (08) 24370 Fax: (08) 32343, pg 598

Waseda University Library (Japan) Tel: (03) 32034141 E-mail: intl-ac@mn.naseda.ac.jp, pg 1479

Waseda University Press (Japan) Tel: (03) 32031551 Fax: (03) 32070406 E-mail: kyw03725@nifty.ne.jp Web Site: www.waseda-up.co.jp, pg 428

Ernst Wasmuth Verlag GmbH & Co (Germany) Tel: (07071) 3 36 58; (07071) 3 50 71 Fax: (07071) 3 57 76 E-mail: wasmuth.publish@supra-net.net Web Site: www.wasmuth-verlag.de, pg 300

Water Resources and Electric Power Press (CWPP) (China) Tel: (010) 898031 Fax: (010) 68353010, pg 110

Waterkant-Uitgewers (Edms) Bpk (South Africa) Tel: (021) 215540 Fax: (021) 4191865, pg 560

The Watermark Press (Australia) Tel: (02) 9818 5677 Fax: (02) 9818 5581 E-mail: books@nsw.bigpond.net.au, pg 47

Waterstone & Co Ltd (United Kingdom) Tel: (0181) 7423800 Fax: (0181) 7420215, pg 1323

Waterville Publishing House (Ghana) Tel: (021) 663124; (021) 662415; (021) 665594; (021) 662415, pg 308

Watkiss Automation Ltd (United Kingdom) Tel: (01767) 682177 Fax: (01767) 691769, pg 1142

Watkiss Automation Ltd (United Kingdom) Tel: (01767) 682177 Fax: (01767) 691769 E-mail: info@watkiss.com Web Site: www.watkiss.com, pg 1163, 1205, 1215

Watkiss Automation Ltd (United Kingdom) Tel: (01767) 682177 Fax: (01767) 691769 E-mail: info@watkiss.com, pg 1224

Watson, Little Ltd (United Kingdom) Tel: (020) 7431 0770 Fax: (020) 7431 7225, pg 1122

A P Watt Ltd (United Kingdom) Tel: (020) 7405 6774 Fax: (020) 7831 2154 E-mail: apw@apwatt.co.uk, pg 754

A P Watt Ltd (United Kingdom) Tel: (020) 7405 6774 Fax: (020) 7831 2154 E-mail: apwatt@apwatt.co.uk Web Site: www.apwatt.co.uk, pg 1122

Watthana Phanit (Thailand) Tel: (02) 2217225, pg 636

Watti-Kustannus Oy (Finland) Tel: (09) 1356878 Fax: (09) 1356437, pg 145

Franklin Watts Australia (Australia) Tel: (02) 427-4922 Fax: (02) 418-6935, pg 47

The Watts Publishing Group Ltd (United Kingdom) Tel: (020) 7739 2929 Fax: (020) 7739 2318 E-mail: gm@wattspub.co.uk Web Site: www.wattspub.co.uk, pg 754

Waxmann Verlag GmbH (Germany) Tel: (0251) 26504-0 Fax: (0251) 26504-26 Web Site: www.waxmann.com, pg 300

Wayland Publishers Ltd (Incorporating Macdonald Young Books) (United Kingdom) Tel: (01273) 722561 Fax: (01273) 329314; (01273) 723526, pg 754

WB Verlag (Germany) Tel: (089) 1269900 Fax: (089) 126990-11 E-mail: wb-druck@online-service.de Web Site: www.wb-druck.de, pg 300

WDV Wirtschaftsdienst Gesellschaft fur Medien & Kommunikation mbH & Co OHG (Germany) Tel: (06172) 670-0 Fax: (06172) 670144 Web Site: www.wdv.de, pg 300

Weather Press (Australia) Tel: (03) 9762-1647, pg 47

Weatherbys Allen Ltd (United Kingdom) Tel: (01933) 440077 (ext 351) Fax: (01933) 270300 E-mail: turfnews@weatherbys-group.com, pg 754

Web Printers Sdn Bhd (Malaysia), pg 1199

Webb & Bower (Publishers) Ltd (United Kingdom) Tel: (01803) 835525 Fax: (01803) 835552, pg 755

Webcom Ltd (Canada) Tel: 416-496-1000 Fax: 416-496-1537 E-mail: webcom@webcomlink.com Web Site: www.webcomlink.com, pg 1132, 1194, 1221

Weber SA d'Editions (Switzerland) Tel: (07) 93104541, pg 627

Weber Zucht & Co (Germany) Tel: (0561) 519194; (0561) 515953 Fax: (0561) 5102514 E-mail: wezuco@t-online.de, pg 300

Webster & Associates Pty Ltd (Australia) Tel: (02) 9751466 Fax: (02) 4523493 E-mail: webpub@websterpublishing.com, pg 47

Websters International Publishers Ltd (United Kingdom) Tel: (020) 7940 4700 Fax: (020) 7940 4701 E-mail: info@websters.co.uk Web Site: www.websters.co.uk; www.ozclarke.com, pg 755

Wehr & Wissen Verlagsgesellschaft mbH (Germany) Tel: (0228) 64830 Fax: (0228) 6483109 E-mail: 101336.245@compuserve.com, pg 300

Wei-Chuan Publishing Company Ltd (Taiwan, Province of China) Tel: (02) 5063564 Fax: (02) 5074902, pg 632

A Weichert Verlag GmbH & Co KG (Germany) Tel: (0511) 813068; (0511) 813069 Fax: (0511) 814841, pg 301

Weidler Buchverlag Berlin (Germany) Tel: (030) 394 86 68 Fax: (030) 394 86 98 E-mail: weidler_verlag@yahoo.de Web Site: www.weidler-verlag.de, pg 301

Weidlich Verlag (Germany) Tel: (0931) 385235 Fax: (0931) 385305 E-mail: info@verlagshaus.com Web Site: www.verlagshaus.com, pg 301

Weidmannsche Verlagsbuchhandlung GmbH (Germany) Tel: (05121) 15010 Fax: (05121) 150150 E-mail: info@olms.de Web Site: www.olms.de, pg 301

Fred Weidner & Daughter Printers (United States) Tel: 212-964-8676 Fax: 212-964-8677 E-mail: info@fwdprinters.com Web Site: www.fwdprinters.com, pg 1167, 1208, 1225

Weilburg Verlag (Austria) Tel: (02622) 29538 Fax: (02622) 2953822, pg 60

Weilin & Goeoes Oy (Finland) Tel: (00) 43771 Fax: (00) 4377270 E-mail: firstname.familyname@wgoy.fi, pg 145

Galerie Lucie Weill-Seligmann (France) Tel: (01) 4354 7195 Fax: (01) 4051 8288, pg 189

Verlag W Weinmann (Germany) Tel: (030) 855 48 95 Fax: (030) 8 55 94 64 E-mail: weinmann-verlag.de Web Site: www.weinmann-verlag.de, pg 301

Rupertusbuchhandlung Augustin Weis und Soehne KG (Austria) Tel: (0662) 71661, pg 1275

Dr Otfried Weise Verlag Tabula Smaragdina (Austria) Tel: (01) 804 2974 Fax: (01) 961 8287 E-mail: tabula@smaragdina.at Web Site: smaragdina.at, pg 60

Herbert Weishaupt Verlag (Austria) Tel: (03151) 8487 Fax: (03151) 84874 E-mail: verlag@weishaupt.at Web Site: www.weishaupt.at, pg 60

Weisser Ring, Gemeinnutzige Verlagsgesellschaft mbH (Germany) Tel: (06131) 83 03 51 Fax: (06131) 83 03 45 E-mail: info@weisser_ring.de Web Site: www.weisser-ring.de, pg 301

Weizmann Institute of Science Libraries (Israel) Tel: (08) 9343583 (WIX Central Library); (08) 9343211 (Weizmann Institute) Fax: (08) 9344176 E-mail: rapinsk@wisemail.weizmann.ac.il Web Site: www.weizmann.acie/wis-library/home.htn, pg 1477

Editions Weka (France) Tel: (01) 53 35 16 16; (01) 53 35 17 17 Fax: (01) 53 35 17 01 Web Site: www.weka.fr, pg 189

WEKA Firmengruppe GmbH & Co KG (Germany) Tel: (08233) 23-0 Fax: (08233) 23-7266 E-mail: pr@weka.de Web Site: www.weka.de; www.weka-group.de; www.weka-group.com, pg 301

Weka Informations Schriften Verlag AG (Switzerland) Tel: (01) 4328432 Fax: (01) 4328201, pg 627

Wellcome Library for the History & Understanding of Medicine (United Kingdom) Tel: (020) 7611 8582 Fax: (020) 7611 8369 E-mail: library@wellcome.ac.uk Web Site: library.wellcome.ac.uk, pg 1507

Wellday Ltd (Hong Kong) Tel: 23628489 Fax: 23628564, pg 322

Wellington City Libraries (New Zealand) Tel: (04) 8014040 Fax: (04) 8014047, pg 1488

Wellington Lane Press Pty Ltd (Australia) Tel: (02) 99040962 Fax: (02) 99040962, pg 47

Wellington Orchid Society Publications (New Zealand) Tel: 04 4758765, pg 497

Wellness Australia (Australia) Tel: (08) 9387 5111 Fax: (08) 9383 7323 E-mail: info@workteams.com, pg 47

H G Wells Society (United Kingdom) Web Site: hgwellsusa.50megs.com, pg 1372

Verlag Welsermuehl (Austria) Tel: (07242) 231-0 Fax: (07242) 23118, pg 60

Welsh Library Association (United Kingdom) Tel: (01970) 622174 Fax: (01970) 622190 E-mail: hle@aber.ac.uk, pg 1525

Welsh Academic Press (United Kingdom) Tel: (029) 2056 0343 Fax: (029) 2056 1631 E-mail: post@ashley.drake.com Web Site: www.welsh-academic-press.co.uk, pg 755

Welsh Books Council (United Kingdom) Tel: (01970) 624455 Fax: (01970) 625506 E-mail: castellbrychan@cllc.org.uk Web Site: www.cllc.org.uk; www.gwales.com, pg 1268

Welsh Books Council: Distribution Centre (United Kingdom) Tel: (01970) 624455 Fax: (01970) 625506 E-mail: distribution.centre@cllc.org.uk Web Site: www.gwales.com; www.cllc.org.uk, pg 1323

Verlagsgruppe Weltbild GmbH (Germany) Tel: (0821) 70 04-70 00 Fax: (0821) 70 04-17 90 E-mail: info@weltbild.com Web Site: www.weltbild.com, pg 301

Weltforum Verlag GmbH (Germany) Tel: (0228) 36842430 Fax: (0228) 3682439 E-mail: wfv@internationsafrikaforum.de, pg 301

Weltkunst Verlag GmbH (Germany) Tel: (089) 1269900 Fax: (089) 12699011 E-mail: info@weltkunstverlag.de Web Site: www.weltkunstverlag.de, pg 301

Weltrundschau Verlag AG (Switzerland) Tel: 7615431 Fax: 7614404 E-mail: wrs@bluewin.ch, pg 627

Weltwoche ABC-Verlag (Switzerland) Tel: (01) 2078643; (01) 2078650; (01) 2078756 Fax: (01) 2078680 E-mail: order@baz.ch, pg 627

Verlag Galerie Welz Salzburg (Austria) Tel: (0662) 841771 Fax: (0662) 84177120 E-mail: office@galerie-welz.at Web Site: www.galerie-welz.at, pg 60

Wydawnictwa Przemyslowe WEMA (Poland) Tel: (022) 8275456; (022) 8272117 Fax: (022) 6355779, pg 521

Wennergren-Cappelen A/S (Norway) *Tel:* 23357250 *Fax:* 22337104 *E-mail:* wenca@wenca.no, pg 1304

Wepf & Co AG (Switzerland) *Tel:* (061) 3119576 *Fax:* (061) 3119585 *E-mail:* wepf@dial.eunet.ch, pg 627

Wepf & Co AG (Switzerland) *Tel:* (061) 269 85 15 (Germany) *Fax:* (061) 261 35 97 (Germany) *E-mail:* wepf@dial.eunet.ch *Web Site:* www.wepf.ch, pg 1313

Wer liefert was? GmbH (Germany) *Tel:* (040) 25440 0 *Fax:* (040) 25440 100 *E-mail:* info@wlw.de *Web Site:* www.wlw.de, pg 301

Gideon S Were Press (Kenya) *Tel:* (02) 740819; (072) 716730 (cellular) *E-mail:* gswere@nbnet.co.ke, pg 434

Wereldbibliotheek (Netherlands) *Tel:* (020) 6381899 *Fax:* (020) 6384491 *E-mail:* wereld@euronet.nl, pg 487

Wereldwijd Vzw (Belgium) *Tel:* (02) 513 12 70 *Fax:* (02) 513 12 71 *E-mail:* wereldwijd@wereldwijd.ngonet.be *Web Site:* www.educa.be, pg 75

Werner Druck AG (Switzerland) *Tel:* (061) 2710690 *Fax:* (061) 2710601, pg 627

Werner Shaw Ltd (United Kingdom) *Tel:* (020) 8761 5570 *Fax:* (020) 8761 5570, pg 755

Werner Soederstroem Osakeyhtioe (WSOY) (Finland) *Tel:* (00) 61681 *Fax:* (00) 61683566, pg 145

Werner Soederstroem Osakeyhtioe (WSOY) (Finland) *Tel:* (00) 61681 *Fax:* (90) 61683566, pg 1110

Werner Verlag GmbH & Co KG (Germany) *Tel:* (0211) 3 87 98-0 *Fax:* (0211) 3 87 98-11 *E-mail:* info@werner-verlag.de *Web Site:* www.werner.verlag.de, pg 302

Wespennest - Zeitschrift fuer brauchbare Texte und Bilder (Austria) *Tel:* (043) 1 3326697 *Fax:* (043) 1 3332970 *E-mail:* office@wespennest.at *Web Site:* www.wespennest.at, pg 61

Wessex Translations (United Kingdom) *Tel:* (01794) 512756 *Fax:* (01794) 830145 *E-mail:* sales@wt-languagemanagement.com, pg 1130

West African Book Publishers Ltd (Nigeria) *Tel:* (01) 9007604; (01) 825020; (01) 526616, pg 502

West Country Writers' Association (United Kingdom) *Tel:* (01395) 222749, pg 1372

West-Friesland/Boekproject-ontwikkeling (Netherlands) *Tel:* (0229) 212625 *Fax:* (0229) 216949, pg 487

West Indies Publishing Ltd (Jamaica) *Tel:* (876) 928-9081 *Fax:* (876) 928-5269, pg 414

John West Publications Co Ltd (Nigeria) *Tel:* (01) 932011, pg 502, 1303

West-Pakistan Publishing Co (Pvt) Ltd (Pakistan) *Tel:* (042) 52427, pg 509, 1305

Westdeutscher Verlag GmbH (Germany) *Tel:* (0611) 78780 *Fax:* (0611) 7878470 *Web Site:* www.westdeutschervlg.de, pg 302

Georg Westermann Verlag GmbH (Austria) *Tel:* (01) 7 14 24 74 *Fax:* (01) 7 18 02 81 *E-mail:* westermann@plus.at, pg 61

Westermann Schulbuchverlag GmbH (Germany) *Tel:* (0531) 7 08-0 *Fax:* (0531) 70 82 09 *E-mail:* schulservice@westermann.de *Web Site:* www.westermann.de, pg 302

Uitgeverij Westers (Netherlands) *Tel:* (030) 2931043 *Fax:* (030) 2944586 *E-mail:* boekhandel@westers-utrecht.nl, pg 487

Verlag Westfaelisches Dampfboot (Germany) *Tel:* (0251) 608 60 80 *Fax:* (0251) 608 60 20 *E-mail:* info@dampfboot-verlag.de *Web Site:* www.dampfboot-verlag.de, pg 302

Westholsteinische Verlagsanstalt und Verlagsdruckerei Boyens & Co (Germany) *Tel:* (0481) 6886-151; (0481) 6886-152 *Fax:* (0481) 688467 *E-mail:* buchhandlung@sh-nordsee.de *Web Site:* www.sh-nordsee.de, pg 302

Westminster Abbey Library (United Kingdom) *Tel:* (020) 7222 5152 *Fax:* (020) 7654 4827 *E-mail:* library@westminster-abbey.org, pg 1507

Westview Press (United Kingdom) *Tel:* (01865) 865466 *Fax:* (01865) 862763 *E-mail:* westview@opp.i-way.co.uk *Web Site:* www.westviewpress.com, pg 755

Wettergrens Bokhandel AB (Sweden) *Tel:* (031) 894500 *Fax:* (031) 7062520, pg 1313

Buchverlag der Druckerei Wetzikon AG (Switzerland) *Tel:* (01) 9333111 *Fax:* (01) 9323232, pg 627

Erich Wewel Verlag (Germany) *Tel:* (0906) 73-0 *Fax:* (0906) 73-1 77 *Web Site:* www.klett.de/geschaeftsbereiche/sachhuch_e.html, pg 302

WH Trade Binders Ltd (United Kingdom) *Tel:* (01327) 704911 *Fax:* (01327) 872588 *E-mail:* wh@whtradebinders.demon.co.uk, pg 1205

Wharncliffe Publishing Ltd (United Kingdom) *Tel:* (01226) 734222 *Fax:* (01226) 734438 *E-mail:* sales@pen-and-sword.co.uk, pg 755

A H Wheeler & Co Ltd (India) *Tel:* (011) 3312629; (011) 3318357 *Fax:* (011) 3357798 *E-mail:* wheeler.jeet@axcess.net.in, pg 353

Which? Ltd (United Kingdom) *Tel:* (08453) 010 010 *Fax:* (020) 7770 7485 *E-mail:* books@which.net *Web Site:* www.which.net, pg 755

Whitaker TeleOrdering (United Kingdom) *Tel:* (01252) 742542 *Fax:* (01252) 742543 *E-mail:* help@teleord.co.uk *Web Site:* www.whitaker.co.uk, pg 1323

Whitcoulls Ltd (New Zealand) *Tel:* (09) 3092233 *Fax:* (09) 3095503, pg 1303

White Cockade Publishing (United Kingdom) *Tel:* (01865) 510411 *Fax:* (01865) 463644 *E-mail:* mail@whitecockade.co.uk *Web Site:* www.whitecockade.co.uk, pg 755

White Eagle Publishing Trust (United Kingdom) *Tel:* (01730) 893300 *Fax:* (01730) 892235 *E-mail:* enquiries@whiteagle.org *Web Site:* www.whiteaglelodge.org/books, pg 755

White Lotus Co Ltd (Thailand) *Tel:* (02) 3324915, pg 636, 1314

Whiting & Birch Ltd (United Kingdom) *Tel:* (020) 8244 2421 *Fax:* (020) 8244 2448 *E-mail:* savpub@dircon.co.uk, pg 756

Whittet Books Ltd (United Kingdom) *Tel:* (01449) 781877 *Fax:* (01449) 781898, pg 756

Whittles Publishing (United Kingdom) *Tel:* (01593) 741240 *Fax:* (01593) 741360 *E-mail:* info@whittlespublishing.com *Web Site:* www.whittlespublishing.com, pg 756

Who's Who In Italy SRL (Italy) *Tel:* (02) 66503753 *Fax:* (02) 6105587 *E-mail:* whoswhogc@ibm.net *Web Site:* www.WHOSWHO-SUTTER.COM, pg 412

Who's Who of Southern Africa (South Africa) *Tel:* (011) 8802406 *Fax:* (011) 8802366, pg 560

Whurr Publishers Ltd (United Kingdom) *Tel:* (020) 7359 5979 *Fax:* (020) 7226 5290 *E-mail:* info@whurr.co.uk *Web Site:* www.whurr.co.uk, pg 756

WI Enterprises Ltd (United Kingdom) *Tel:* (020) 7371 9300 *Fax:* (020) 7471 9300 *E-mail:* d.page@nfwi.org.uk *Web Site:* www.womens-institute.co.uk/shop/policies/about.shtml, pg 756

Wichern Verlag (Germany) *Tel:* (030) 28 87 48 10 *Fax:* (030) 28 87 48 12 *E-mail:* info@wichern.de *Web Site:* www.wichern.de, pg 302

Wichern-Verlag GmbH (Germany) *Tel:* (030) 3915075 *Fax:* (030) 3936047 *E-mail:* 101711.1207@compuserve.com, pg 302

Herbert Wichmann Verlag (Germany) *Tel:* (06221) 489395 *Fax:* (06221) 489623 *E-mail:* wichmann@huethig.de *Web Site:* www.huethig.de, pg 302

Widjaya Penerbit (Indonesia) *Tel:* (021) 363446, pg 357

Wiechmann-Verlag Betriebs GmbH (Germany) *Tel:* (08151) 883-0 *Fax:* (08151) 883-48, pg 302

'Wiedza Powszechna' Panstwowe Wydawnictwo (Poland) *Tel:* (022) 8269592 *Fax:* (022) 8269592; (022) 8268594, pg 521

Universitaetsbibliothek Wien (Austria) *Tel:* (01) 427715001 *Fax:* (01) 42779150 *E-mail:* info.ub@univie.ac.at *Web Site:* www.ub.unvie.ac.at, pg 1452

Dinah Wiener Ltd (United Kingdom) *Tel:* (020) 8994 6011 *Fax:* (020) 8994 6044, pg 1122

Wiener Dom-Verlag GmbH (Austria) *Tel:* (01) 512 37 09; (01) 512 77 19 *Fax:* (01) 512 37 09-17 *E-mail:* stephansplatz@dombuchhandlung.at *Web Site:* www.buchwirtschaft.at, pg 61

Wiener Stadt- und Landesarchiv (Austria) *Tel:* (01) 4000; (01) 84808 *Fax:* (01) 4000; (01) 9984819; (01) 1-4000-7238 (international) *E-mail:* post@m08.magwien.gv.at, pg 1452

Wiener Stadt- und Landesbibliothek (Austria) *Tel:* (01) 400084915 *Fax:* (01) 40007219 *E-mail:* post@m09.magwien.gv.et *Web Site:* www.stadtbibliothek.wien.at, pg 1452

Wiese Verlag AG (Switzerland) *Tel:* (061) 661350 *Fax:* (061) 661343 *E-mail:* order@baz.ch, pg 627

Wieser Verlag (Austria) *Tel:* (0463) 37036 *Fax:* (0463) 37635 *E-mail:* office@wieser-verlag.com *Web Site:* www.wieser-verlag.com, pg 61

Verlag Alexander Wild (Switzerland) *Tel:* (031) 224480 *Fax:* (031) 3114470, pg 627

Ediciones Alfred y Cia Wild Ltda (Colombia) *Tel:* (01) 6218000; (01) 2566731 *Fax:* (01) 6114338 *E-mail:* info@galeriaalfredwild.com *Web Site:* www.galeriaalfredwild.com, pg 114

Wild & Woolley Pty Ltd (Australia) *Tel:* (02) 692-0166 *Fax:* (02) 552-4320 *E-mail:* pwoolley@mpx.com.au, pg 47

Wild Goose Publications (United Kingdom) *Tel:* (0141) 332 6292 *Fax:* (0141) 332 1090 *E-mail:* admin@ionabooks.com *Web Site:* www.ionabooks.com, pg 756

Wild Publications (Australia) *Tel:* (03) 9826-8482 *Fax:* (03) 9826-3787 *E-mail:* wild@wild.com.au *Web Site:* www.wild.com.au, pg 47

Wildscape Australia (Australia) *Tel:* (07) 4093 7171 *Fax:* (07) 4093 8897 *Web Site:* www.thunder.com.au, pg 47

Wileman Publications (Australia) *Tel:* (07) 559 0969 *E-mail:* wileman@onthenet.com.au, pg 47

Magazyn Wilenski (Lithuania) *Tel:* (02) 427718; (02) 474007 *Fax:* (02) 474007, pg 447

Wiley Europe Ltd (United Kingdom) *Tel:* (01243) 779777 *Fax:* (01243) 775878 *E-mail:* customer@wiley.co.uk *Web Site:* www.wiley.co.uk, pg 756

John Wiley & Sons (Asia) Pte Ltd (Singapore) *Tel:* 64632400 *Fax:* 64634605; 64634604 *E-mail:* enquiry@wiley.com.sg *Web Site:* www.wiley.co.uk, pg 549

Wiley-VCH Verlag GmbH (Germany) *Tel:* (06201) 606 0 *Fax:* (06201) 606 328 *E-mail:* info@wiley-vch.de *Web Site:* www.wiley-vch.de, pg 302

Wydawnictwo Wilga sp zoo (Poland) *Tel:* (022) 826-08-82; (022) 827-90-11 (ext 282) *Fax:* (022) 826-06-43 *E-mail:* wilga@ternet.pl, pg 521

Bridget Williams Books Ltd (New Zealand) *Tel:* (04) 4738317 *Fax:* (04) 4738417 *E-mail:* bwbooks@ihug.co.nz, pg 497

Jonathan Williams Literary Agency (Ireland) *Tel:* (01) 2803482 *Fax:* (01) 2803482, pg 1112

WJ Williams & Son (Books) Ltd (United Kingdom) *Tel:* (01283) 712948 *Fax:* (01283) 716807 *E-mail:* mail@williams-books.co.uk *Web Site:* www.williams-books.co.uk, pg 1323

Wilmington Business Information Ltd (United Kingdom) *Tel:* (020) 7549 8704 *Fax:* (020) 7490 2979 *Web Site:* www.waterlow.com/signature/, pg 756

Editions Luce Wilquin (Belgium) *Tel:* (019) 69 98 13 *Fax:* (019) 69 98 13 *E-mail:* wilquin.bouquin@skynet.be *Web Site:* www.wilquin.com, pg 75

A S Wilson Inc (Australia) *Tel:* (02) 9528 8977 *Fax:* (02) 5890635, pg 48

Wilson & Horton Publications Ltd (New Zealand) *Tel:* (09) 6388105 *Fax:* (09) 6302140, pg 497

John Wilson Booksales (United Kingdom) *Tel:* (01844) 275927 *Fax:* (01844) 274402 *E-mail:* jw@jwbs.co.uk, pg 1224

Neil Wilson Publishing Ltd (United Kingdom) *Tel:* (0141) 221 1117 *Fax:* (0141) 221 5363 *E-mail:* info@nwp.sol.co.uk *Web Site:* www.nwp.co.uk, pg 757

Philip Wilson Publishers (United Kingdom) *Tel:* (020) 7284 3088 *Fax:* (020) 7284 3099 *E-mail:* pwp@monoclick.co.uk, pg 757

Wimbledon Publishing Company Ltd (United Kingdom) *Tel:* (020) 7401 8855 *Fax:* (020) 7928 9226 *E-mail:* enquiries@wpcpress.com *Web Site:* www.wpcpress.com, pg 757

Windhoek Public Library (Namibia) *Tel:* (061) 224899 *Fax:* (061) 212169, pg 1486

Windhoeker Buchhandlung (Namibia) *Tel:* (061) 225216; (061) 33479 *Fax:* (061) 225011, pg 1300

Windhorse Books (Australia) *Tel:* (02) 9519 8826 *Fax:* (02) 9519 8826 *E-mail:* books@windhorse.com.au *Web Site:* www.windhorse.com.au, pg 48

Windhorse Publications (United Kingdom) *Tel:* (0121) 449 9191 *Fax:* (0121) 449 9191 *E-mail:* windhorse@compuserve.com *Web Site:* www.windhorsepublications.com, pg 757

Windmuehle GmbH Verlag und Vertrieb von Medien (Germany) *Tel:* (040) 86 83 07 *Fax:* (040) 866 31 23 *E-mail:* info@windmuehle-verlag.de *Web Site:* www.windmuehle-verlag.de, pg 303

Windpferd Verlagsgesellschaft mbH (Germany) *Tel:* (08343) 1404 *Fax:* (08343) 1403 *E-mail:* service@windpferd.com *Web Site:* www.windpferd.com, pg 303

The Windrush Press Ltd (United Kingdom) *Tel:* (01608) 658758; (01608) 652012 *Fax:* (01608) 659345 *E-mail:* windrush@windrushpress.com *Web Site:* www.windrushpress.com, pg 757

Windsor Books International (United Kingdom) *Tel:* (01865) 361122 *Fax:* (01865) 361133 *E-mail:* windsorbooks@compuserve.com, pg 757

Windward Publications (Australia) *Tel:* (02) 4464 1977 *Fax:* (02) 4464 1906 *E-mail:* admin@windward.com.au, pg 48

Winetitles (Australia) *Tel:* (08) 8233 4799 *Fax:* (08) 8233 4790 *E-mail:* admin@winetitles.com.au *Web Site:* www.winetitles.com.au, pg 48

Wing King Tong Co Ltd (Printing Factory) (Hong Kong) *Tel:* 24073287 *Fax:* 24074130 *E-mail:* ayan@hk.super.net, pg 1136

Wing King Tong Co Ltd (Printing Factory) (Hong Kong) *Tel:* 24073287 *Fax:* 24074130, pg 1157, 1197, 1212

Rosa Winkel Verlag GmbH (Germany) *Tel:* (030) 85729295 *Fax:* (030) 85729296 *E-mail:* rosawinkel@t-online.de *Web Site:* www.rosawinkel.de, pg 303

Dr Dieter Winkler (Germany) *Tel:* (0234) 9650200 *Fax:* (0234) 9650201 *E-mail:* winkler-verlag.bochum@tonline.de *Web Site:* www.winklerverlag.de, pg 303

Winklers Verlag Gebrueder Grimm (Germany) *Tel:* (06151) 87 68-0 *Fax:* (06151) 87 68-61 *E-mail:* service@winklers.de *Web Site:* www.winklers.de, pg 303

Winter & Co UK Ltd (United Kingdom) *Tel:* (01480) 377177 *Fax:* (01480) 377166 *E-mail:* sales@winteruk.com, pg 1215

Berthold Winter (Germany) *Tel:* (030) 3623530 *Fax:* (030) 3629693, pg 1285

Verlag fuer Wirtschaft & Verwaltung Hubert Wingen GmbH & Co KG (Germany) *Tel:* (0201) 22 25 41; (0201) 22 25 42 *Fax:* (0201) 229660, pg 303

Wisby & Wilkens (Denmark) *Tel:* 7023 4622 *Fax:* 7043 4722 *E-mail:* mail@wisby-wilkens.com *Web Site:* www.wisby-wilkens.com, pg 136

Wisdom Books (United Kingdom) *Tel:* (0208) 553 5020 *Fax:* (0208) 553 5122 *E-mail:* enquiries@wisdombooks.org *Web Site:* www.wisdombooks.org, pg 1323

Wison Verlag GmbH (Germany) *Tel:* (0221) 9440900 *Fax:* (0221) 448911, pg 303

Verlag Wissenschaft und Politik/Helker Pflug (Germany) *Tel:* (221) 219 64 90 *Fax:* (221) 219 64 91 *Web Site:* www/oei.fu-berlin.de, pg 303

Wissenschaftliche Allgemeinbibliothek der Stadt Erfurt (Germany) *Tel:* (0361) 5624876; (0361) 6551590 *Fax:* (0361) 6462071; (0361) 6551599, pg 1469

Wissenschaftliche Buchgesellschaft (Germany) *Tel:* (06151) 33080 *Fax:* (06151) 3308208 *E-mail:* service@wbg-darmstadt.de *Web Site:* www.wbg-darmstadt.de, pg 303

Wissenschaftliche Buchgesellschaft (Germany) *Tel:* (06151) 33080 *Fax:* (06151) 3308208 *E-mail:* service@wbg-darmstadt.de, pg 1228

Wissenschaftliche Verlagsgesellschaft mbH (Germany) *Tel:* (0711) 2582-0 *Fax:* (0711) 2582-290 *E-mail:* service@wissenschaftliche-verlagsgesellschaft.de *Web Site:* www.dav-buchhandlung.de, pg 303

Wissenschaftliche Verlagsgesellschaft mbH (Germany) *Tel:* (0711) 2582-0 *Fax:* (0711) 2582-290, pg 1133

Wissenschaftsrat (Germany) *Tel:* (0221) 3776-0 *Fax:* (0221) 38 84 40 *E-mail:* post@wissenschaftsrat.de *Web Site:* www.wissenschaftsrat.de/wr, pg 303

Wist (Slovakia) *Tel:* (0842) 4289652 *Fax:* (0842) 4289652 *E-mail:* wist@enelux.sk, pg 551

WIT Press (United Kingdom) *Tel:* (023) 8029 3223 *Fax:* (023) 8029 2853 *E-mail:* witpress@witpress.com *Web Site:* www.witpress.com, pg 757

Witherby & Co Ltd (United Kingdom) *Tel:* (020) 7251 5341 *Fax:* (020) 7251 1296 *E-mail:* books@witherbys.co.uk *Web Site:* www.witherbys.com, pg 758, 1323

Witman Publishing Co (HK) Ltd (Hong Kong) *Tel:* (02) 5626279 *Fax:* (02) 5655482 *E-mail:* witmanp@hk.star.com, pg 322

Verlag Claus Wittal (Germany) *Tel:* (0611) 502907 *Fax:* (0611) 503021 *E-mail:* cw@exlibrisart.com *Web Site:* www.exlibrisart.com, pg 303

Friedrich Wittig Verlag GmbH (Germany) *Tel:* (0431) 5197206 *Fax:* (0431) 5197292, pg 303

Verlag Konrad Wittwer GmbH (Germany) *Tel:* (0711) 25 07 0 *Fax:* (0711) 25 07 145 *E-mail:* wittwer@wittwer.de *Web Site:* www.wittwer.de, pg 303

Verlags-und Sortimentsbuchhandlung Konrad Wittwer GmbH (Germany) *Tel:* (0711) 25070 *Fax:* (0711) 2507350, pg 1285

Witwatersrand University Press (South Africa) *Tel:* (011) 4845907 *Fax:* (011) 4845971 *E-mail:* wup@iafrica.com *Web Site:* www.wirs.oc.za/wup.html, pg 560

Wizard Books Pty Ltd (Australia) *Tel:* (03) 53323435 *Fax:* (03) 53311488 *E-mail:* admin@wizardbooks.com.au *Web Site:* www.wizardbooks.com.au, pg 48

The Woburn Press (United Kingdom) *Tel:* (020) 8920 2100 *Fax:* (020) 8447 8548 *E-mail:* info@woburnpress.com *Web Site:* www.frankcass.com/wp, pg 758

Wochenschau Verlag, Dr Kurt Debus GmbH (Germany) *Tel:* (06196) 8 60 65 *Fax:* (06196) 8 60 60 *E-mail:* info@wochenschau-verlag.de *Web Site:* info@wochenschau-verlag.de, pg 304

Die WochenZeitung (Switzerland) *Tel:* (01) 2721500 *Fax:* (01) 2721501 *E-mail:* woz@woz.links.ch, pg 627

Woeli Publishing Services (Ghana) *Tel:* (021) 227182; (021) 229294 *Fax:* (021) 777098; (021) 229294 *E-mail:* woeli@libr.ug.edu.gh; asempa@ghana.com, pg 308

Galerie Esther Woerdehoff (France) *Tel:* (01) 43 2144 83 *Fax:* (01) 43 2145 03 *E-mail:* galerie@falguiere36.org *Web Site:* www.falguiere36.org, pg 189

Edition Woetzel Medizinische und Naturwissenschaftliche Verlags und Vertiebsgesellschaft mbH (Germany) *Tel:* (06103) 3 78 95-50 *Fax:* (06103) 3 78 95-80 *E-mail:* woetzel-buch@t-online.de *Web Site:* www.woetzel.de, pg 304

Gert Wohlfarth GmbH Verlag Fachtechnik & Mercator Verlag, Verlag Puppen & Spielzeug (Germany) *Tel:* (0203) 3 05 27-0 *Fax:* (0203) 3 05 27-820 *E-mail:* info@wohlfarth.de *Web Site:* www.wohlfarth.de, pg 304

Koninklijke Wohrmann Bv (Netherlands) *Tel:* (0575) 582121 *Fax:* (0575) 582128, pg 1199

Forlaget Woldike K/S (Denmark) *Tel:* 33 73 35 85, pg 136

J E Wolfensberger AG (Switzerland) *Tel:* (01) 2857878 *Fax:* (01) 2012054 *E-mail:* wolfsberg@access.ch *Web Site:* www.wolfensberger-ag.ch, pg 628

Wolfgang Arlt u Ute Schiller (Germany) *Tel:* (030) 4622008 *Fax:* (030) 4624936; (030) 4622008, pg 304

Wolfhound Press (Ireland) *Tel:* (01) 6764373 *E-mail:* websales@wolfhound.ie *Web Site:* www.wolfhound.ie; www.drumshee.com, pg 364

Kunstverlag Wolfrum (Austria) *Tel:* (01) 512-41-78 *Fax:* (01) 512-15-57 *Web Site:* www.buchwirtschaft.at, pg 61

Kunstverlag Wolfrum (Austria) *Tel:* (0222) 5125398, pg 1275

Wolf's-Verlag Berlin (Germany) *Tel:* (030) 5675190, pg 304

Wolgang Fietkau (Germany) *Tel:* (033203) 71 105 *Fax:* (033203) 71 109 *E-mail:* fietkau@fietkau.de *Web Site:* www.fietkau.de, pg 304

Wolke Verlags GmbH (Germany) *Tel:* (06192) 7243 *Fax:* (06192) 952939 *E-mail:* wolke-verlag@t-online.de *Web Site:* www.wolke-verlag.de, pg 304

The Wolsey Press (United Kingdom) *Tel:* (01473) 719377 *Fax:* (01473) 272115 *E-mail:* studio@wolseypress.demon.co.uk, pg 1205, 1215

Wolters Kluwer Espana SA (Spain) *Tel:* (091) 6020023 *Fax:* (091) 6020021 *E-mail:* pilarg@wke.es, pg 596

Wolters-Noordhoff B V (Netherlands) *Tel:* (050) 5226888 *Fax:* (050) 5226244 *E-mail:* webmaster@wolters.nl *Web Site:* www.wolters.nl, pg 487

Wolters Plantyn Educatieve Uitgevers (Belgium) *Tel:* (03) 360 03 11 *Fax:* (03) 360 03 30 *E-mail:* klantendienst@woltersplantyn.be *Web Site:* www.woltersplantyn.be, pg 75

Women in Publishing (United Kingdom) *E-mail:* wipub@hotmail.com *Web Site:* www.cyberiacafe.net/wip, pg 1268

Women's Health Advisory Service (Australia) *Tel:* (02) 4655 8855 *Fax:* (02) 4655 8699 *Web Site:* www.whas.com.au, pg 48

The Women's Press Book Club (United Kingdom) *Tel:* (020) 7251 3007 *Fax:* (020) 7608 1938, pg 1234

The Women's Press Ltd (United Kingdom) *Tel:* (020) 7251 3007 *Fax:* (020) 7608 1938 *E-mail:* sales@the-womens-press.com *Web Site:* www.the-womens-press.com, pg 758

Christine Wood Translations (United Kingdom) *Tel:* (015396) 21170 *Fax:* (015396) 21300 *E-mail:* cwtrans@daelnet.co.uk, pg 1130

Woodfield & Stanley Ltd (United Kingdom) *Tel:* (01484) 421467; (01484) 532401 *Fax:* (01484) 510237 *Web Site:* www.woodfield-stanley.co.uk, pg 1324

Woodhead Publishing Ltd (United Kingdom) *Tel:* (01223) 891358 *Fax:* (01223) 893694 *E-mail:* wp@woodhead-publishing.com *Web Site:* www.woodhead-publishing.com, pg 758

Woodlands Publications (Australia) *Tel:* (02) 4950 5100 *Fax:* (02) 4950 5240 *Web Site:* www.woodlandspublications.com, pg 48

Woong Jin Publishing Co Ltd (Republic of Korea) *Tel:* (02) 7427941 *Fax:* (02) 7441904 *E-mail:* wjmap@chollian.dacom.co.kr, pg 440

Woongjin Media Corporation (Republic of Korea) *Tel:* (02) 745-6712 *Fax:* (02) 745-0777 *E-mail:* wjmhky@woongjin.co.kr, pg 440

The Word Factory (United Kingdom) *Tel:* (0115) 921-3263 *Fax:* (0115) 921-5017 *E-mail:* books@thewordfactory.co.uk, pg 1142

Word of Life Press (Republic of Korea) *Tel:* (02) 738-6555 *Fax:* (02) 7393824, pg 440

Words Work (New Zealand) *Tel:* (07) 3482953 *Fax:* (07) 3482953 *E-mail:* wordswrk@clear.net.nz, pg 497

Wordsworth Editions Ltd (United Kingdom) *Tel:* (020) 7706 8822 *Fax:* (020) 7706 8833 *E-mail:* enquiries@wordsworth-editions.com *Web Site:* www.wordsworth-editions.co.uk/distributors.htm, pg 758

Wordwright Publishing (United Kingdom) *Tel:* (020) 7284 0056 *Fax:* (020) 7284 0041 *E-mail:* wordwright@clara.co.uk, pg 758

Workaway Guides (Australia) *Tel:* (02) 9664 4559 *Web Site:* www.workaway.org, pg 48

Working People's Organization Publishing House (Democratic People's Republic of Korea), pg 434

World Affairs Press (China) *Tel:* (010) 5125544 *Fax:* (010) 65265961; (010) 5133181 *E-mail:* wap@bj.col.com.cn, pg 110

World Alliance of Reformed Churches (Switzerland) *Tel:* (022) 7916238; (022) 7916237 *Fax:* (022) 7916505 *E-mail:* warc@warc.ch *Web Site:* www.warc.ch, pg 1262

World Blind Union (WBU) - Union Mondiale des Aveugles (UMA) (Spain) *Tel:* (091) 5713685; (091) 5711236 *Fax:* (091) 5715777 *E-mail:* umc@once.es *Web Site:* www.once.es/wbu, pg 1259

World Book Co Ltd (Taiwan, Province of China) *Tel:* (02) 23113834 *Fax:* (02) 3317963, pg 632

The World Book Co (Pte) Ltd (Singapore) *Tel:* 3382323 *Fax:* 3371186, pg 1309

World Book Publishing (Lebanon) *Tel:* (01) 349370; (01) 743357; (01) 743358 *Fax:* (01) 351226 *E-mail:* wbookpub@inco.com.lb *Web Site:* www.arabook.com, pg 443

World Books Publishing Corporation (China) *Tel:* (010) 4016320 *Fax:* (010) 4016320 *E-mail:* wpc@china.kw.co.cn, pg 110

World Conservation Union (IUCN) (Switzerland) *Tel:* (022) 9990001 *Fax:* (022) 9990002 *E-mail:* mail@hq.iucn.ch, pg 1262

World Council of Churches (WCC Publications) (Switzerland) *Tel:* (022) 7916111 *Toll Free Tel:* 800-523-8211 *Fax:* (022) 7981346 *Web Site:* www.wcc-coe.org, pg 628

World Health Organization (WHO) (Switzerland) *Tel:* (022) 791 2111 *Fax:* (022) 791 3111 *E-mail:* publications@who.int *Web Site:* www.who.int, pg 1262

World Intellectual Property Organization (WIPO) (Switzerland) *Tel:* (022) 3389111 *Fax:* (022) 7335428 *E-mail:* wipo.mail@wpo.int, pg 1262

World Leisure Marketing (United Kingdom) *Tel:* (01332) 573737 *Fax:* (01332) 573399 *E-mail:* office@wlmsales.co.uk *Web Site:* www.maps-guides.com, pg 1324

World Literature Project (Ghana) *Tel:* (022) 2119 *Fax:* (022) 2119, pg 308

World Meteorological Organization (Switzerland) *Tel:* (022) 246400 *Fax:* (022) 7308022, pg 628

World Meteorological Organization (Switzerland) *Tel:* (022) 7308111 *Fax:* (022) 7308022 *E-mail:* pubsales@gateway.wmo.cch, pg 1262

World Microfilms Publications Ltd (United Kingdom) *Tel:* (020) 7266 2202; (0845) 606 0612 *Fax:* (020) 7266 2314 *E-mail:* microworld@ndirect.co.uk *Web Site:* www.microworld.ndirect.co.uk, pg 758

The World of Books Literaturverlag (Germany) *Tel:* (06241) 205352 *Fax:* (06241) 205352 *E-mail:* info@twobl-online.de *Web Site:* www.twobl-online.de, pg 304

World of Information (United Kingdom) *Tel:* (01799) 521150 *Fax:* (01799) 524805 *E-mail:* queries@worldinformation.com *Web Site:* www.worldinformation.com, pg 759

World of Islam Altajir Trust (United Kingdom) *Tel:* (020) 7581 3522 *Fax:* (020) 7584 1977, pg 759

World Publications Printers Pte Ltd (Singapore) *Tel:* 7449888 *Fax:* 8406118 *E-mail:* wphsin@singnet.com.sg *Web Site:* web.singnet.com.sg, pg 1201

World Scientific Publishing Co Pte Ltd (Singapore) *Tel:* 6467-5775 *Fax:* 6467-7667 *E-mail:* wspc@wspc.com.sg, pg 549

The World Society of Victimology eV (Germany) *Tel:* (02161) 186 609 *Fax:* (02161) 186 633 *Web Site:* www.world-society-victimology.de/, pg 304

World Wild Life Films (Pty) Ltd (Switzerland) *Tel:* (01) 4331444 *Fax:* (01) 4331460, pg 628

Worlddidac (Switzerland) *Tel:* (031) 311 76 82; (031) 311 76 83 *Fax:* (031) 312 17 44 *E-mail:* info@worlddidac.org *Web Site:* www.worlddidac.org, pg 1262

Worsley Press (Australia) *Tel:* (03) 5979-1112 *Fax:* (03) 5979-1112 *E-mail:* info@worsleypress.com *Web Site:* www.worsleypress.com, pg 48

Verlag DAS WORT GmbH (Germany) *Tel:* (09391) 504135 *Fax:* (09391) 504133 *E-mail:* info@das-wort.com *Web Site:* www.das-wort.com; www.universal.spirit.cc, pg 304

Wouters Import NV (Belgium) *Tel:* (016) 233481 *Fax:* (016) 398020 *E-mail:* info@import.wouters.be, pg 1276

Wouters Import PVBA (Belgium) *Tel:* (016) 232481 *Fax:* (016) 229841, pg 76

Gordon Wright Publishing Ltd (United Kingdom) *Tel:* (0131) 6671300 *Fax:* (0131) 6671459 *E-mail:* gordonwrightpublisher@compuserve.com; 101370.330@compuserve.com, pg 759

Wrightbooks Pty Ltd (Australia) *Tel:* (03) 9532 7082 *Toll Free Tel:* 800 777 474 *Fax:* (03) 9532 7084 *Toll Free Fax:* 800 802 258 *E-mail:* wbooks@ozemail.com.au *Web Site:* www.wrightbooks.com.au, pg 48

Writers & Scholars International (United Kingdom) *Tel:* (020) 7278 2313 *Fax:* (020) 7278 1878 *E-mail:* indexoncenso@gn.apc.org, pg 1268

Writers' Guild of Great Britain (United Kingdom) *Tel:* (020) 7723 8074 *Fax:* (020) 7706 2413 *E-mail:* admin@writersguild.org.uk *Web Site:* www.writersguild.org.uk, pg 1268

Writers' Publishing House (China) *Tel:* (010) 65004079 *Fax:* (010) 65930761 *E-mail:* wrtspub@public.bta.net.cn *Web Site:* www.zuojiachubanshe.com, pg 110

Writers World (Australia) *Tel:* (075) 552377 *Fax:* (075) 55922001, pg 48

WRS Verlag Wirtschaft, Recht und Steuern GmbH & Co KG (Germany) *Tel:* (089) 89 517-0 *Fax:* (089) 89 517-250 *Web Site:* www.wrs.de, pg 304

WS Bookwell Ltd (Finland) *Tel:* (019) 219 41 *Fax:* (019) 219 4800 *Web Site:* www.wsoy.fi/print/, pg 1132

WS Bookwell Ltd (Finland) *Tel:* (019) 219 41 *Fax:* (019) 219 4800 *E-mail:* pekka.tykkylainen@bookwell.fi *Web Site:* www.bookwell.fi, pg 1194

WS Bookwell Ltd (Finland) *Tel:* (019) 219 41 *Fax:* (019) 219 4800 *Web Site:* www.wsoy.fi/print/, pg 1211

WTO (World Trade Organization) (Switzerland) *Tel:* (022) 7395111 *Fax:* (022) 7395458 *Web Site:* www.wto.org, pg 1262

WTU Todor Kableskov (Bulgaria) *Tel:* (2) 717 104 *Fax:* (2) 706 342 *E-mail:* office@vtu.acad.bg *Web Site:* www.vtu.acad.bg, pg 98

Wu Nan Book Co Ltd (Taiwan, Province of China) *Tel:* (02) 27055066 *Fax:* (02) 27094875 *E-mail:* wunan@wunan.com.tw *Web Site:* www.wunan.com.tw, pg 632

Wuerttembergische Bibliotheksgesellschaft (Germany) *Tel:* (0711) 2124428 *Fax:* (0711) 2124422 *E-mail:* wbg@mailserver.wlb-stutthart.de *Web Site:* www.wlb-stuttgart.de, pg 1517

Wuerttembergische Landesbibliothek (Germany) *Tel:* (0711) 2124424 *Fax:* (0711) 2124422 *E-mail:* direktion@wlb-stuttgart.de *Web Site:* www.wlb-stuttgart.de, pg 1469

Wuhan University Press (China) *Tel:* (027) 812712-427 *Fax:* (027) 712661, pg 110

Das Wunderhorn Verlag GmbH (Germany) *Tel:* (06221) 402428 *Fax:* (06221) 402483 *E-mail:* info@wunderhorn.de *Web Site:* www.wunderhorn.de, pg 304

Wunderlich Verlag (Germany) *Tel:* (040) 72 72 0 *Fax:* (040) 72 72 319 *Web Site:* www.rowohlt.de, pg 304

Fachbuchverlag Armin W Wuth (Germany) *Tel:* (02306) 55686; (02306) 18089 *Fax:* (02306) 55686, pg 304

WUV/Facultas Universitaetsverlag (Austria) *Tel:* (01) 310 53 56 *Fax:* (01) 319 70 50 *E-mail:* verlage@facultas.at *Web Site:* www.wuv-verlag.at, pg 61

Wydawn Na Sprawa' Wydawniczo-Oswiatowa Spotdzielnia Inwalidow (Poland) *Tel:* (022) 6209071 (ext 26) *Fax:* (022) 6209197, pg 521

Wydawnictwa Naukowo-Techniczne (Poland) *Tel:* (022) 8267271 *Fax:* (022) 8268293 *E-mail:* wnt@pol.pl *Web Site:* www.wnt.com.pl, pg 521

Wydawnictwa Szkolne i Pedagogiczne (Polish Educational Publishers-WSiP) (Poland) *Tel:* (022) 8265451; (022) 8265452; (022) 8265453; (022) 8265454; (022) 8265455 *Fax:* (022) 8279280 *E-mail:* wsip@ikp.atm.com.pl; bossrwsip@ikp.atm.com.pl *Web Site:* www.wsip.com.pl, pg 521

Wydawnictwa Uniwersytetu Warszawskiego (Poland) *Tel:* (022) 5531318 *Fax:* (022) 5531318 *E-mail:* wuw@uw.edu.pl, pg 521

Wydawnictwo Baturo (Poland) *Tel:* (33) 8125086 *Fax:* (33) 8140955 *E-mail:* baturo@baturo.com.pl *Web Site:* www.baturo.com.pl, pg 521

Wydawnictwo DiG (Poland) *Tel:* (022) 828-00-96 *Fax:* (022) 828-00-96 *E-mail:* biuro@dig.com.pl *Web Site:* www.dig.com.pl, pg 521

Wyss Verlag AG Bern (Switzerland) *Tel:* (031) 253715; (031) 254425 *Fax:* (031) 3814821; (031) 254821, pg 628

Ediciones Xandro (Spain) *Tel:* (091) 5520261 *Fax:* (091) 5014145, pg 596

Xarait Libros SA (Spain) *Tel:* (091) 534 15 67 *Fax:* (091) 535 08 31, pg 596

Xenos Verlagsgesellschaft mbH (Germany) *Tel:* (040) 538 093-0 *Fax:* (040) 538 60 00; (040) 538 78 63 *E-mail:* xenos.verlag@t-online.de, pg 304

EDICIONS XERAIS DE GALICIA INDUSTRY

Edicions Xerais de Galicia (Spain) *Tel:* (086) 214888 *Fax:* (086) 201366 *E-mail:* xerais@xerais.es *Web Site:* www.xerais.es, pg 596

Xiamen University Library (China) *Tel:* (0592) 2186127 *Fax:* (0592) 2182360 *E-mail:* xiaodh@xmu.edu.cn *Web Site:* library.xmu.edu.cn (Chinese BG), pg 1457

Xiamen International Book Exchange Center (China) *Tel:* (0592) 5061401 *Fax:* (0592) 5061400 *E-mail:* xibc@xpublic.fz.fj.cn, pg 1279

Xiamen University Press (China) *Tel:* (0592) 227128 *E-mail:* chbanshe@jingxian.xmu.edu.cn; xmdx@fjbook.com, pg 110

Xi'an Cartography Publishing House (China) *Tel:* (029) 52831, pg 110

Xinhua Publishing House (China) *Tel:* (010) 63073765; (010) 63073787 *Fax:* (010) 3073880 *E-mail:* nianzh@xinhuanet.com *Web Site:* www.xinhua.2699.com, pg 110

Xunta de Galicia (Spain) *Tel:* (081) 544816 *Fax:* (081) 544887, pg 596

Y Cyfarwyddwr Urdd Gobaith Cymru (United Kingdom) *Tel:* (01970) 613100 *Fax:* (01970) 626120 *E-mail:* urdd@urdd.org *Web Site:* www.urdd.org, pg 759

Y Hoc Publishing House (Viet Nam) *Tel:* (04) 253274, pg 763

Yachdav, United Publishers Co Ltd (Israel) *Tel:* (03) 5614121 *Fax:* (03) 5611996 *E-mail:* maalot@tbpai.co.il, pg 373

Yad Eliahu Kitov (Israel) *Tel:* (02) 6248868 *Fax:* (02) 6248838, pg 373

Yad Izhak Ben-Zvi Press (Israel) *Tel:* (02) 53988888 *Fax:* (02) 5638310 *E-mail:* yadbz@h2.hum.huji.ac.il *Web Site:* ybz.org.il, pg 373

Yad Tabenkin (Israel) *Tel:* (03) 5301217; (03) 5301227; (03) 5344458 *Fax:* (03) 5346376 *E-mail:* yadtab@inter.net.il *Web Site:* www.ic.org/icsa.efal.html, pg 373

Yad Vashem - The Holocaust Martyrs' & Heroes' Remembrance Authority (Israel) *Tel:* (02) 6443400 *Fax:* (02) 6443443 *E-mail:* general.information@yadvashem.org.il *Web Site:* www.yad-vashem.org.il, pg 373

Yakugyo Jiho Sha Company Ltd (Japan) *Tel:* (03) 32657755 *Fax:* (03) 32346573, pg 429

Yakuji Nippo Ltd (Japan) *Tel:* (03) 38622141 *Fax:* (03) 38668408, pg 429

Yale University Press London (United Kingdom) *Tel:* (020) 7431 4422 *Fax:* (020) 7431 3755 *E-mail:* sales@yaleup.co.uk, pg 759

Yama-Kei Publishers Co Ltd (Japan) *Tel:* (03) 3436-4021 *Fax:* (03) 34334057 *E-mail:* info@yamakei.co.jp, pg 429

Yamaguchi Shoten (Japan) *Tel:* (075) 7816121 *Fax:* (075) 7052003, pg 429

Yanagang Publishing (Australia) *Tel:* (03) 9870-3052 *Fax:* (03) 9876-1853 *E-mail:* gallerywithoutwalls@hotmail.com, pg 48

Julio F Yanez, Agencia Literaria S L (Spain) *Tel:* (093) 2007107; (093) 2005443 *Fax:* (093) 2094865 *E-mail:* yanezag@retemail.es, pg 1116

Eric Yang Agency (Republic of Korea) *Tel:* (02) 5923356 *Fax:* (02) 5923359, pg 1114

Yapi-Endustri Merkezi Yayinlari-Yem Yayin (Turkey) *Tel:* (0212) 2193939 *Fax:* (0212) 2256623 *E-mail:* yem-od@yunus.mam.tubitak.gov.tr; kitap@yem.net *Web Site:* www.yem.net, pg 642

Yarmouk University Library (Jordan) *Tel:* (02) 271100 ext 2479 *Fax:* (02) 7271273 *Web Site:* www.yu.edu.jo, pg 1479

Yaron Golan Publishers (Israel) *Tel:* (03) 6992867 *Fax:* (03) 6952664, pg 373

CV Yasaguna (Indonesia) *Tel:* (021) 8290422, pg 357

Roy Yates Books (United Kingdom) *Tel:* (01403) 822299 *Fax:* (01403) 823012, pg 1324

Yavneh Publishing House Ltd (Israel) *Tel:* (03) 6297856 *Fax:* (03) 6293638 *E-mail:* yavneh@attglobal.net *Web Site:* www.dbook.co.il, pg 373

Yavneh Publishing House Ltd (Israel) *Tel:* (03) 6297856 *Fax:* (03) 6293638, pg 1293

Peyo K Yavorov Publishing House (Bulgaria) *Tel:* (02) 875201; (02) 880137; (02) 876765 *Fax:* (02) 875592, pg 98

Yayasan Jaya Baya (Indonesia) *Tel:* (031) 41169, pg 357

Yayasan Kawanku (Indonesia) *Tel:* (021) 583100, pg 357

Yayasan Lontar (Indonesia) *Tel:* (021) 587-904; (021) 574-6880 *Fax:* (021) 573-0353 *E-mail:* lontar@ibm.net *Web Site:* www.lontar.org, pg 357

Yayasan Obor Indonesia (Indonesia) *Tel:* (021) 326978; (021) 324488 *Fax:* (021) 324488 *E-mail:* obor@ub.net.id *Web Site:* www.obor.or.id, pg 357

Kabalci Yayinevi (Turkey) *Tel:* (0212) 5268586; (0212) 5226305 *Fax:* (0212) 5268495, pg 642

Alev Yayinlari (Turkey) *Tel:* (0212) 2921016 *Fax:* (0212) 5168464, pg 642

Yazhou Zhoukan Ltd (Hong Kong) *Tel:* 2515 5111 *Fax:* 2515 2790 *E-mail:* yzzk@mingpao.com, pg 322

YBM/Si-sa (Republic of Korea) *Tel:* (02) 2000-0501 *Fax:* (02) 2265-7573 *E-mail:* suite@ybmsisa.com *Web Site:* www.ybm.co.kr; www.ybmsisa.co.kr, pg 441

Yearim-dang (Republic of Korea) *Tel:* (02) 2493333 *Fax:* (02) 248-7400, pg 441

Yedioth Ahronoth Books (Israel) *Tel:* (03) 6888 466 *Fax:* (03) 5377820 *E-mail:* books@yedioth.co.il *Web Site:* www.yediothsfarim.co.il, pg 373

Yee Wen Publishing Co Ltd (Taiwan, Province of China) *Tel:* (02) 3626012 *Fax:* (02) 3660977 *E-mail:* yeewen@msg.hinet.net, pg 632

Yeha Publishing Co Ltd (Republic of Korea) *Tel:* (02) 5535933; (02) 5535936 *Fax:* (02) 5525149, pg 441

Yeong Mun Copyright Agency (Republic of Korea) *Tel:* (02) 7568944 *Fax:* (02) 7568943, pg 1114

Yetkin Printing & Publishing Co Inc (Turkey) *Tel:* (0312) 4181273; (0312) 2314234, pg 642

Yi Hsien Publishing Co Ltd (Taiwan, Province of China) *Tel:* (02) 22192577 *Fax:* (02) 22198511 *E-mail:* yihsient@ms17.hinet.net, pg 632

Ying Tat Co (Hong Kong) *Tel:* 25645980 *Fax:* 28111280, pg 1136, 1157, 1212

Y L Peretz Publishing Co (Israel) *Tel:* (03) 5281751 *Fax:* (03) 5257983, pg 374

Yliopistopaino/Helsinki University Press (Finland) *Tel:* (09) 70102360 *Fax:* (09) 70102374 *E-mail:* rki@yopaino.helsinki.fi, pg 145

YMCA-Press (France) *Tel:* (01) 4354 7446 *Fax:* (01) 4325 3479, pg 189

Yohan Shuppan (Japan) *Tel:* (03) 32080181 *Fax:* (03) 32042582 *E-mail:* shinsuke@yohan-pub.co.jp, pg 429

Yohan (Western Publications Distribution Agency) (Japan) *Tel:* (03) 3208-0181, pg 1295

Yokendo Ltd (Japan) *Tel:* (03) 38140911 *Fax:* (03) 38122615, pg 429

Zie Yongder Co Ltd (Hong Kong) *Tel:* 29630111, pg 322

Yonsei University Library (Republic of Korea) *Tel:* (02) 3613308 *Fax:* (02) 3936803 *E-mail:* sbchang@bubble.yonsei.ac.kr, pg 1480

Yonsei University Press (Republic of Korea) *Tel:* (02) 3926201 *Fax:* (02) 3931421 *E-mail:* ysup@bubble.yonsei.ac.kr, pg 441

Yorvik Publishing Ltd (Zambia) *Tel:* (02) 311628; (02) 312852; (02) 313707 *Fax:* (02) 311628, pg 767

Yoshioka Shoten (Japan) *Tel:* (075) 7814747 *Fax:* (075) 7019075, pg 429

Anglia Young Books (United Kingdom) *Tel:* (01799) 531192 *Fax:* (01799) 531192 *E-mail:* r.hayes@btinternet.com *Web Site:* www.btinternet.com/~r.hayes, pg 759

Club of Young Readers (Slovakia) *Tel:* (07) 5664512; (07) 5664293 *Fax:* (07) 215714, pg 1231

Youth Cultural Publishing Co (Taiwan, Province of China) *Tel:* (02) 23146001 *Fax:* (02) 3612239 *E-mail:* youth@ms2.hinet.net *Web Site:* www.youth.com.tw, pg 632

Youth Publishing House (China) *Tel:* (010) 4032266-328 *Fax:* (010) 4031803, pg 110

Youval Tal Ltd (Israel) *Tel:* (02) 6248897 *Fax:* (02) 6245434, pg 1136

Yritystieto Oy - Foretagsdata AB (Finland) *Tel:* (00) 648292 *Fax:* (00) 648250, pg 145

Yuan Liou Publishing Co, Ltd (Taiwan, Province of China) *Tel:* (02) 3653707 *Fax:* (02) 3657979; (02) 3658989 *E-mail:* ylib@yuanliou.ylib.com.tw *Web Site:* www.ylib.com.tw, pg 632

Yuce Reklam Yay Dagt AS (Turkey) *Tel:* (01) 5227506 *Fax:* (01) 5163959, pg 642

Yugaku-sha Ltd (Japan) *Tel:* (03) 32333731 *Fax:* (03) 32333730, pg 429

Yuhikaku Publishing Co Ltd (Japan) *Tel:* (03) 32641314 *Fax:* (03) 32628035, pg 429

Yuki Shobo (Japan) *Tel:* (03) 32030151 *Fax:* (03) 32030157, pg 429

Yunatstva (Belarus) *Tel:* (0172) 2333326 *Fax:* (0172) 266616, pg 63

Yunnan Provincial Library (China) *Tel:* (0871) 5298, pg 1457

Yushodo Co Ltd (Japan) *Tel:* (03) 33571411 *Fax:* (03) 33515855; (03) 33571785 *E-mail:* intl@yushodo.co.jp *Web Site:* www.yushodo.co.jp, pg 429

Yushodo Co Ltd (Japan) *Tel:* (075) 4619282 *Fax:* (075) 33515855, pg 1295

Editions Philateliques Yvert et Tellier (France) *Tel:* (03) 22.71.71.71 *Fax:* (03) 22.71.71.89, pg 189

IE Zachariadou OHG (Bucherstube) (Greece) *Tel:* (031) 276334 *Fax:* (031) 229936 *E-mail:* info@lillisbookstore.gr *Web Site:* www.lillisbookstore.gr, pg 1287

S J Zacharopoulos SA Publishing Co (Greece) *Tel:* (01) 3231525 *Fax:* (01) 3243814, pg 316

Zacharopoulos Z & G (Greece) *Tel:* (01) 2111895; (01) 2111897 *Fax:* (01) 2111897, pg 316

Manrique Zago Ediciones SRL (Argentina) *Tel:* (011) 4382-8880; (011) 4382-8881; (011) 4383-2611 *Fax:* (011) 4382-8890 *E-mail:* mzago@lud.com.ar, pg 10

Jorge Zahar Editor (Brazil) *Tel:* (021) 2400226 *Fax:* (021) 2625123 *E-mail:* jze@zahar.com.br *Web Site:* www.zahar.com.br, pg 93

Al Zahiriah (Syrian Arab Republic) *Tel:* (011) 112813, pg 1502

Zakheim Publishing House (Israel) *Tel:* (03) 6130434 *Fax:* (03) 6130443, pg 374

The Zalman Shazar Center (Israel) *Tel:* (02) 5637171 *Fax:* (02) 5662135 *E-mail:* shazar@shazar.org.il *Web Site:* www.shazar.org.il, pg 374

Zalozba Mihelac d o o (Slovenia) *Tel:* (061) 313654 *Fax:* (061) 1331197, pg 552

Zalozba Obzorja d d Maribor (Slovenia) *Tel:* (062) 28971; (062) 125681 *Fax:* (062) 223213, pg 552

Zambia Library Association (Zambia), pg 1526

Zambia Association for Research & Development (Zambia) *Tel:* (01) 222883 *E-mail:* zard@zamnet.zm, pg 767

Zambia Catholic Bookshop (Mission Press) (Zambia) *Tel:* (02) 680456; (02) 680466 *Fax:* (02) 680484 *E-mail:* mpress@zamnet.zm, pg 1325

Zambia Educational Publishing House (Zambia) *Tel:* (01) 229490; (01) 229211 *Fax:* (01) 225073, pg 767

Zambia Library Service (Zambia) *Tel:* (01) 254993 *Fax:* (01) 254993, pg 1509

Zambian Ornithological Society (Zambia), pg 767

Zambon Verlag (Germany) *Tel:* (069) 779223 *Fax:* (069) 773054 *E-mail:* zambon@online.de *Web Site:* www.zambonverlag.de, pg 305

Martha Zamora Edicion de Libros (Mexico) *Tel:* (05) 2940231 *Fax:* (05) 2943856, pg 468

Silvio Zamorani editore (Italy) *Tel:* (011) 8125700 *Fax:* (011) 8126144, pg 412

Zanfi Editori SRL (Italy) *Tel:* (059) 891700 *Fax:* (059) 891701, pg 412

Casa Musicale G Zanibon SRL (Italy) *Tel:* (02) 88811 *Fax:* (02) 88814317, pg 412

Zanichelli Editore SpA (Italy) *Tel:* (051) 293111 *Fax:* (051) 249782 *E-mail:* zanichelli@zanichelli.it, pg 412

Edizioni Zara (Italy) *Tel:* (0521) 489956 *Fax:* (0521) 241750, pg 412

Victor P de Zavalia SA (Argentina) *Tel:* (011) 942-1274; (011) 942-3046 *Fax:* (011) 942-5706, pg 10

Zavod za Izdavanje Udzbenika (Yugoslavia) *Tel:* (021) 23-844; (021) 22-068 *Fax:* (021) 22-062; (021) 623-454, pg 766

Zavod za udzbenike i nastavna sredstva (Yugoslavia) *Tel:* (011) 636-971; (011) 630-317; (011) 639-577 *Fax:* (011) 630-014; (011) 637-429; (011) 637-426, pg 766

Zazusy (Kazakstan) *Tel:* (03272) 422849, pg 430

Zbinden Druck und Verlag AG (Switzerland) *Tel:* (061) 2722104; (061) 2722105 *Fax:* (061) 2726722, pg 628

Zdruzenie Zaloznikov in Knjigotrzcev Slovenije Gospodarska Zbornica Slovenije (Slovenia) *Tel:* (01) 5898277 *Fax:* (01) 5898200; (01) 5898100 *E-mail:* irena.brolez@gzs.si *Web Site:* www.gzs.si, pg 1258

Zebulon Verlag GmbH & Co KG (Germany) *Tel:* (0221) 3405620 *Fax:* (0221) 3405622 *E-mail:* zebulon-koeln@t-online.de, pg 305

Pierre Zech Editeur (France) *Tel:* (01) 44 32 05 60 *Fax:* (01) 44 32 05 61, pg 189

Zed Books Ltd (United Kingdom) *Tel:* (020) 7837 4014; (020) 7837 0384 *Fax:* (020) 7833 3960 *E-mail:* zed@zedbooks.demon.co.uk *Web Site:* zedweb.hypermart.net/zed/contact.htm, pg 759

Zeimukeiri-Kyokai (Japan) *Tel:* (03) 3953 3325 *Fax:* (03) 3565 3391 *E-mail:* postmaster@zeikei.co.jp *Web Site:* www.zeikei.co.jp, pg 429

Zeitgeist Media GmbH (Germany) *Tel:* (0211) 55 62 55 *Fax:* (0211) 57 51 67 *E-mail:* info@zeitgeistmedia.de *Web Site:* www.zeitgeistverlag.de, pg 305

Verlag Zeitschrift fur Naturforschung (Germany) *Tel:* (07071) 31555 *Fax:* (07071) 360571 *E-mail:* znaturforsch.redaktion@t-online.de *Web Site:* www.znaturforsch.com, pg 305

Zeller Verlag GmbH & Co (Germany) *Tel:* (0541) 404590 *Fax:* (0541) 41255 *E-mail:* zeller@zeller.os.eunet.de *Web Site:* www.militaria-biblio.de, pg 305

Zen Now Press (Taiwan, Province of China) *Tel:* (02) 7182727 *Fax:* (02) 7174146, pg 632

Editorial Zendrera Zariquiey, SA (Spain) *Tel:* (093) 280.61.82 *Fax:* (093) 280.61.90 *E-mail:* anazz@wanadoo.es *Web Site:* www.sirpus.com, pg 596

Zenemukiado Vallalat (Hungary) *Tel:* (01) 1176222 *E-mail:* musicpubl@emb.hu, pg 327

Zenkoku Kyodo Shuppan (Japan) *Tel:* (03) 33594811 *Fax:* (03) 33586174, pg 429

Zentral- und Landesbibliothek Berlin (ZLB) (Germany) *Tel:* (030) 902260; (030) 90226-401 *Fax:* (030) 90226-494 *E-mail:* info@zlb.de *Web Site:* www.zlb.de, pg 1469

Zentralantiquariat Leipzig GmbH Buchhandlung (Germany) *Tel:* (0341) 2161717 *Fax:* (0341) 9602819 *E-mail:* info@zvab.com *Web Site:* www.zvab.com, pg 305

Verlag Clemens Zerling (Germany) *Tel:* (030) 6929278 *Fax:* (030) 6929278, pg 305

Uitgeverij 010 (Netherlands) *Tel:* (010) 4333509 *Fax:* (010) 4529825, pg 487

Verlag Andreas Zettner KG (Germany) *Tel:* (0931) 91970 *Fax:* (0931) 960 097, pg 305

Editorial Zeus SRL (Argentina) *Tel:* (0341) 449-5585 *Fax:* (0341) 425-4259 *E-mail:* editorialzeus@citynet.net.ar *Web Site:* www.editorial-zeus.com.ar, pg 10

Klub 707 (South Africa) *Tel:* (011) 6736725 *Fax:* (011) 6736719, pg 1231

Susanna Zevi Agenzia Letteraria (Italy) *Tel:* (02) 6570863; (02) 6570867 *Fax:* (02) 6570915, pg 1113

Zhejiang Education Publishing House (China) *Tel:* (0571) 576944; (0571) 5170300 *Fax:* (0571) 5176944 *E-mail:* cheny@zjcb.com; zjjy@zjcb.com *Web Site:* www.jys.zjcb.com, pg 110

ZheJiang Provincial Library (China) *Tel:* (0571) 773414; (0571) 7046414 *Fax:* (0571) 7046263, pg 1457

Zhejiang University Press (China) *Tel:* (0571) 87984670 *Fax:* (0571) 87952331 *E-mail:* zupress@mail.hz.zj.cn *Web Site:* www.zjupress.com, pg 110

Zhong Hua Book Co (China) *Tel:* (010) 555161; (010) 554504, pg 110

Zhongshan Library of Guangdong Province (China) *Tel:* (020) 330676, pg 1457

Verlag im Ziegelhaus Ulrich Gohl (Germany) *Tel:* (0711) 46 63 63 *Fax:* (0711) 46 13 41 *E-mail:* redaktiousbuero.stuttgart.gohl@n.zgs.de, pg 305

Ziegler Druck- und Verlags-AG, Gemsberg-Verlag, Foto & Schmalfilm-Verlag (Switzerland) *Tel:* (052) 857171 *Fax:* (052) 2133521, pg 628

Ziethen-Panorama Verlag GmbH (Germany) *Tel:* (02253) 6047 *Fax:* (02253) 6746 *E-mail:* mail@ziethen-panoramaverlag.de *Web Site:* www.ziethen-panoramaverlag.de, pg 305

Zig-Zag SA (Chile) *Tel:* (02) 335 7447 *Fax:* (02) 335 7545 *Web Site:* www.zigzag.cl, pg 102

Zilinska Univerzita (Slovakia) *Tel:* (089) 625919; (089) 621247 *Fax:* (089) 620023, pg 551

The Zimbabwe Writers Union (Zimbabwe) *Tel:* (09) 531305, pg 1372

Zimbabwe Library Association (Zimbabwe), pg 1526

Zimbabwe Book Publishers Association (Zimbabwe) *Tel:* (04) 750282 *Fax:* (04) 751202, pg 1270

Zimbabwe Foundation for Education with Production (ZIMFEP) (Zimbabwe) *Tel:* (04) 753991; (04) 771833/4 *Fax:* (04) 749147 *E-mail:* zimfep@africaonline.co.zw, pg 769

Zimbabwe International Book Fair (Zimbabwe) *Tel:* (04) 702104; (04) 702108 *Fax:* (04) 702129 *E-mail:* zibf@samara.co.zw, pg 769

Zimbabwe Publishing House (Pvt) Ltd (Zimbabwe) *Tel:* (04) 497555-8; (04) 497548 *Fax:* (04) 497554 *E-mail:* apg@ld.co.zw, pg 769

Zimbabwe Women Writers (Zimbabwe) *Tel:* (04) 774261 *Fax:* (04) 750282 *E-mail:* zww@telco.co.zw, pg 770

Zimbabwe Women's Bureau (Zimbabwe) *Tel:* (04) 747905; (04) 747809 *Fax:* (04) 747809, pg 770

Zindermans AB (Sweden) *Tel:* (031) 7750400 *Fax:* (031) 120660, pg 607

The Zion Press (Japan) *Tel:* (078) 9757611 *Fax:* (078) 9757373 *E-mail:* greatobe@yo.rim.ur.jp, pg 429

Zip Editora Ltda (Brazil) *Tel:* (021) 2807272, pg 93

Zirkular - Verlag der Dokumentationsstelle fuer neuere oesterreichische Literatur (Austria) *Tel:* (01) 526 20 44-0 *Fax:* (01) 526 20 44-30 *E-mail:* info@literaturhaus.at *Web Site:* www.literaturhaus.at, pg 61

Zmora-Bitan, Publishers Ltd (Israel) *Tel:* (08) 9246565 *Fax:* (08) 9251770 *E-mail:* info@zmora.co.il, pg 374

Znaci Vremena, Institut Za Istrazivanje Biblije (Croatia) *Tel:* (01) 3774 283 *Fax:* (01) 174861, pg 120

Znanje d d (Croatia) *Tel:* (01) 4551500 *Fax:* (01) 4553-652 *E-mail:* znanje@zg.tel.hr, pg 120

Zodiaque (France) *Tel:* (03) 86 33 19 24 *Fax:* (03) 86 33 19 25 *E-mail:* info@editions-zodiaque.fr *Web Site:* www.editions-zodiaque.fr; www.zodiaque.com, pg 190

Zoe Books Ltd (United Kingdom) *Tel:* (01962) 851318 *E-mail:* enquiries@zoebooks.co.uk *Web Site:* www.zoebooks.co.uk, pg 1142

Editions Zoe (Switzerland) *Tel:* (022) 3420578 *Fax:* (022) 3432964, pg 628

Zoe Publishing Pty Ltd (Australia) *Tel:* (07) 55341522 *Fax:* (07) 55341502 *E-mail:* zoemkt@onthenet.com.au, pg 48

ZOI (Greece) *Tel:* (01) 3223560 *Fax:* (01) 3221283, pg 316

Har Zolindakis (Greece) *Tel:* (01) 3216504, pg 316

Zona Ediciones y Publications SA de CV (Mexico) *Tel:* (05) 5547438, pg 468

Zoshindo JukenKenkyusha (Japan) *Tel:* (06) 65321581 *Fax:* (06) 65321588 *E-mail:* zoshindo@mbox.inet-osaka.or.jp *Web Site:* www.zoshindo.co.jp/, pg 429

ZPC Publications (Zambia) *Tel:* (01) 227673; (01) 227674; (01) 227675 *Fax:* (01) 225026, pg 767

ZRD Trust (Zimbabwe) *Tel:* (04) 774775; (04) 744519 *Fax:* (04) 774764, pg 770

Zrinyi Kiado (Hungary) *Tel:* (01) 2100020; (01) 1331170; (01) 3339165 *Fax:* (01) 3142432, pg 327

ZS Verlag Zabert Sandmann GmbH (Germany) *Tel:* (089) 548 25 15-0 *Fax:* (089) 550 18 19 *Web Site:* www.zsverlag.de; www.zabertsandmann.de, pg 305

Paul Zsolnay Verlag GmbH (Austria) *Tel:* (01) 50576610 *Fax:* (01) 505766110 *E-mail:* info@zsolnay.at *Web Site:* www.zsolnay.at, pg 61

Zuid Boekprodukties BV (Netherlands) *Tel:* (0252) 431566 *Fax:* (0252) 431567 *E-mail:* info@rebo-publishers.com *Web Site:* www.rebo-publishers.com, pg 487

Zuid En Noord VZW (Belgium) *Tel:* (011) 34 4991 *Web Site:* www.schrijversnet.nl, pg 76

Zuid-Nederlandse Uitgeverij NV/ Central Uitgeverij (Belgium) *Tel:* (03) 8771464 *Fax:* (03) 8772115, pg 76

Zumpres Publishing Firm (The Former Yugoslav Republic of Macedonia) *Tel:* (091) 163539; (091) 425175 *Fax:* (091) 425176; (091) 429196 *E-mail:* zumpres@yahoo.com, pg 449

Zumstein & Cie (Switzerland) *Tel:* (031) 222215; (031) 222217 *Fax:* (031) 212326 *E-mail:* post_zumstein@briefmarker.ch, pg 628

Zunica (Bulgaria) *Tel:* (02) 551-977, pg 98

ZVAIGZNE ABC PUBLISHERS, LTD

Zvaigzne ABC Publishers, Ltd (Latvia) *Tel:* (02) 372396 *Fax:* (02) 7828431 *E-mail:* zvaigzne@com.latnet.lv, pg 442

Zveza bibliotekarskih drustev Slovenije (ZBDS) Slovenian Library Association (Slovenia) *Tel:* (01) 200 1193 *Fax:* (01) 251 3052 *Web Site:* www.zbds-zveza.si, pg 1523

Zvon (Czech Republic) *Tel:* (02) 20181773 *Fax:* (02) 24315153, pg 129

Zweiburgen-Verlag GmbH (Germany) *Tel:* (06201) 87694-32 *Fax:* (06201) 87694-33, pg 305

Zweimuehlen Verlag GmbH (Germany) *Tel:* (089) 982031 *Fax:* (089) 9827104, pg 305

Zweipunkt Verlag K Kaiser KG (Germany) *Tel:* (06102) 61108 *Fax:* (06102) 63422, pg 305

Zwemmer Holdings Co Ltd (United Kingdom) *Tel:* (020) 7240 4158 *Fax:* (020) 7836 7049 *E-mail:* sales@zwemmer.com *Web Site:* www.zwemmer.com, pg 759

Zwiazek Literatow Polskich (Poland) *Tel:* (022) 826-57-85; (022) 826-08-66 *Fax:* (022) 828-39-20, pg 1257

Instytut Wydawniczy Zwiazkow Zawodowych (Poland) *Tel:* (022) 279011, pg 521

Uitgeverij Zwijsen BV (Netherlands) *Tel:* (013) 5838800 *Fax:* (013) 5838800, pg 487

ZYC Holding Ltd (Hong Kong) *Tel:* 29630111, pg 322

Zyrichidi Bros (Greece) *Tel:* (031) 227915; (031) 266036 *Fax:* (031) 266036, pg 316

Index to Advertisers

C & C Offset Printing Co Ltd..1144, *Bound Insert in Complete Book Manufacturing section*
MapQuest...1123